THE OXFORD ENGLISH
DICTIONARY

SECOND EDITION

THE OXFORD ENGLISH DICTIONARY

First Edited by

JAMES A. H. MURRAY, HENRY BRADLEY, W. A. CRAIGIE
and C. T. ONIONS

COMBINED WITH

A SUPPLEMENT TO THE OXFORD ENGLISH DICTIONARY

Edited by

R. W. BURCHFIELD

AND RESET WITH CORRECTIONS, REVISIONS
AND ADDITIONAL VOCABULARY

THE OXFORD ENGLISH DICTIONARY

SECOND EDITION

Prepared by

J. A. SIMPSON *and* E. S. C. WEINER

VOLUME II

B.B.C.–Chalypsography

CLARENDON PRESS · OXFORD

1989

EB

Oxford University Press, Walton Street, Oxford OX2 6DP
Oxford New York Toronto
Delhi Bombay Calcutta Madras Karachi
Petaling Jaya Singapore Hong Kong Tokyo
Nairobi Dar es Salaam Cape Town
Melbourne Auckland
and associated companies in
Berlin Ibadan

Oxford is a trade mark of Oxford University Press

British Library Cataloguing in Publication Data
Oxford English dictionary.—2nd ed.
1. English language—Dictionaries
I. Simpson, J. A. (John Andrew), 1953-
II. Weiner, Edmund S. C., 1950-
423
ISBN 0-19-861214-1 (vol. II)
ISBN 0-19-861186-2

Library of Congress Cataloging-in-Publication Data
The Oxford English dictionary.—2nd ed.
prepared by J. A. Simpson and E. S. C. Weiner
Bibliography: p.
ISBN 0-19-861214-1 (vol. II)
ISBN 0-19-861186-2 (set)
1. English language—Dictionaries. I. Simpson, J. A.
II. Weiner, E. S. C. III. Oxford University Press.
PE1625.087 1989
423—dc19   88-5330

Data capture by ICC, Fort Washington, Pa.
Text-processing by Oxford University Press
Typesetting by Filmtype Services Ltd., Scarborough, N. Yorks.
Manufactured in the United States of America by
Rand McNally & Company, Taunton, Mass.

KEY TO THE PRONUNCIATION

THE pronunciations given are those in use in the educated speech of southern England (the so-called 'Received Standard'), and the keywords given are to be understood as pronounced in such speech.

I. *Consonants*

b, d, f, k, l, m, n, p, t, v, z *have their usual English values*

g as in *g*o (gəʊ)

h ... *h*o! (həʊ)

r ... *r*un (rʌn), te*rr*ier ('tɛrɪə(r))

(r) ... he*r* (hɜː(r))

s ... *s*ee (siː), suc*c*ess (sək'sɛs)

w ... *w*ear (wɛə(r))

hw... *wh*en (hwɛn)

j ... *y*es (jɛs)

θ as in *th*in (θɪn), ba*th* (bɑːθ)

ð ... *th*en (ðɛn), ba*th*e (beɪð)

ʃ ... *sh*op (ʃɒp), di*sh* (dɪʃ)

tʃ ... *ch*op (tʃɒp), di*tch* (dɪtʃ)

ʒ ... vi*s*ion ('vɪʒən), *d*éjeuner (deʒøne)

dʒ ... *j*u*dg*e (dʒʌdʒ)

ŋ ... si*ng*ing ('sɪŋɪŋ), thi*n*k (θɪŋk)

ŋg ... fi*ng*er ('fɪŋgə(r))

(FOREIGN AND NON-SOUTHERN)

ʎ as in It. serra*gli*o (ser'raʎo)

ɲ ... Fr. cog*n*ac (kɔɲak)

x ... Ger. a*ch* (ax), Sc. lo*ch* (lɒx), Sp. fri*j*oles (fri'xoles)

ç ... Ger. i*ch* (ɪç), Sc. ni*ch*t (nɪçt)

ɣ ... North Ger. sa*g*en ('zaːɣən)

c ... Afrikaans baardmanne*tj*ie ('baːrtmanəci)

ɥ ... Fr. c*ui*sine (kɥizin)

Symbols in parentheses are used to denote elements that may be omitted either by individual speakers or in particular phonetic contexts: e.g. *bottle* ('bɒt(ə)l), *Mercian* ('mɜːʃ(ɪ)ən), *suit* (s(j)uːt), *impromptu* (ɪm'ɒrɒm(p)tjuː), *father* ('fɑːðə(r)).

II. *Vowels and Diphthongs*

SHORT

ɪ as in p*i*t, -n*e*ss (pɪt), (-nɪs)

ɛ ... p*e*t (pɛt), Fr. s*e*pt (sɛt)

æ ... p*a*t (pæt)

ʌ ... p*u*tt (pʌt)

ɒ ... p*o*t (pɒt)

ʊ ... p*u*t (pʊt)

ə ... *a*nother (ə'nʌðə(r))

(ə) ... beat*e*n ('biːt(ə)n)

i ... Fr. s*i* (si)

e ... Fr. b*é*b*é* (bebe)

a ... Fr. m*a*ri (mari)

ɑ ... Fr. b*â*timent (bɑtimɑ̃)

ɔ ... Fr. h*o*mme (ɔm)

o ... Fr. *eau* (o)

ø ... Fr. p*eu* (pø)

œ ... Fr. b*œu*f (bœf)

u ... Fr. d*ou*ce (dus)

ʏ ... G. M*ü*ller ('mʏlər)

y ... Fr. d*u* (dy)

LONG

iː as in b*ea*n (biːn)

ɑː ... b*ar*n (bɑːn)

ɔː ... b*or*n (bɔːn)

uː ... b*oo*n (buːn)

ɜː ... b*ur*n (bɜːn)

eː ... G. Schn*ee* (ʃneː)

ɛː ... Fr. f*ai*re (fɛːr)

aː ... G. T*a*g (taːg)

oː ... G. S*oh*n (zoːn)

øː ... G. G*oe*the ('gøːtə)

œː ... Fr. c*œu*r (kœːr)

yː ... G. gr*ü*n (gryːn)

NASAL

ɛ̃, æ̃ as in Fr. f*in* (fɛ̃, fæ̃)

ɑ̃ ... Fr. fr*anc* (frɑ̃)

ɔ̃ ... Fr. b*on* (bɔ̃)

œ̃ ... Fr. *un* (œ̃)

DIPHTHONGS, etc.

eɪ as in b*ay* (beɪ)

aɪ ... b*uy* (baɪ)

ɔɪ ... b*oy* (bɔɪ)

əʊ ... n*o* (nəʊ)

aʊ ... n*ow* (naʊ)

ɪə ... p*eer* (pɪə(r))

ɛə ... p*air* (pɛə(r))

ʊə ... t*our* (tʊə(r))

ɔə ... b*oar* (bɔə(r))

aɪə as in f*iery* ('faɪərɪ)

aʊə... s*our* ('saʊər)

The incidence of main stress is shown by a superior stress mark (') preceding the stressed syllable, and a secondary stress by an inferior stress mark (,), e.g. *pronunciation* (prə,nʌnsɪ'eɪʃ(ə)n).

For further explanation of the transcription used, see *General Explanations*, Volume I.

LIST OF ABBREVIATIONS, SIGNS, ETC.

Some abbreviations listed here in italics are also in certain cases printed in roman type, and vice versa.

a. (in Etym.)	adoption of, adopted from
a (as a 1850)	ante, 'before', 'not later than'
a.	adjective
abbrev.	abbreviation (of)
abl.	ablative
absol.	absolute, -ly
Abstr.	Abstract(s) (in titles)
acc.	accusative
Acct.	Account (in titles)
A.D.	Anno Domini
ad. (in Etym.)	adaptation of
Add.	Addenda
adj.	adjective
Adv.	Advance, -d, -s (in titles)
adv.	adverb
advb.	adverbial, -ly
Advt.	advertisement
Aeronaut.	(as label) in Aeronautics; (in titles) Aeronautic, -al, -s
AF., AFr.	Anglo-French
Afr.	Africa, -n
Agric.	(as label) in Agriculture; (in titles) Agriculture, -al
Alb.	Albanian
Amer.	American
Amer. Ind.	American Indian
Anat.	(as label) in Anatomy; (in titles) Anatomy, -ical
Anc.	(in titles) Ancient
Anglo-Ind.	Anglo-Indian
Anglo-Ir.	Anglo-Irish
Ann.	Annals
Anthrop., Anthropol.	(as label) in Anthropology; (in titles) Anthropology, -ical
Antiq.	(as label) in Antiquities; (in titles) Antiquity
aphet.	aphetic, aphetized
app.	apparently
Appl.	(in titles) Applied
Applic.	(in titles) Application
appos.	appositive(ly)
Arab.	Arabic
Aram.	Aramaic
Arch.	in Architecture
arch.	archaic
Archæol.	in Archaeology
Archit.	(as label) in Architecture; (in titles) Architecture, -al
Arm.	Armenian
assoc.	association
Astr.	in Astronomy
Astrol.	in Astrology
Astron.	(in titles) Astronomy, -ical
Astronaut.	(in titles) Astronautic, -s
attrib.	attributive, -ly
Austral.	Australian
Autobiogr.	(in titles) Autobiography, -ical
A.V.	Authorized Version
B.C.	Before Christ
B.C.	(in titles occas.) British Columbia
bef.	before
Bibliogr.	(as label) in Bibliography; (in titles) Bibliography, -ical
Biochem.	(as label) in Biochemistry; (in titles) Biochemistry, -ical
Biol.	(as label) in Biology; (in titles) Biology, -ical
Bk.	Book
Bot.	(as label) in Botany; (in titles) Botany, -ical
Bp.	Bishop

Brit.	(in titles) Britain, British
Bulg.	Bulgarian
Bull.	(in titles) Bulletin
c (as c 1700)	circa, 'about'
c. (as 19th c.)	century
Cal.	(in titles) Calendar
Cambr.	(in titles) Cambridge
Canad.	Canadian
Cat.	Catalan
catachr.	catachrestically
Catal.	(in titles) Catalogue
Celt.	Celtic
Cent.	(in titles) Century, Central
Cent. Dict.	Century Dictionary
Cf., cf.	confer, 'compare'
Ch.	Church
Chem.	(as label) in Chemistry; (in titles) Chemistry, -ical
Chr.	(in titles) Christian
Chron.	(in titles) Chronicle
Chronol.	(in titles) Chronology, -ical
Cinemat., Cinematogr.	in Cinematography
Clin.	(in titles) Clinical
cl. L.	classical Latin
cogn. w.	cognate with
Col.	(in titles) Colonel, Colony
Coll.	(in titles) Collection
collect.	collective, -ly
colloq.	colloquial, -ly
comb.	combined, -ing
Comb.	Combinations
Comm.	in Commercial usage
Communic.	in Communications
comp.	compound, composition
Compan.	(in titles) Companion
compar.	comparative
compl.	complement
Compl.	(in titles) Complete
Conc.	(in titles) Concise
Conch.	in Conchology
concr.	concrete, -ly
Conf.	(in titles) Conference
Congr.	(in titles) Congress
conj.	conjunction
cons.	consonant
const.	construction, construed with
contr.	contrast (with)
Contrib.	(in titles) Contribution
Corr.	(in titles) Correspondence
corresp.	corresponding (to)
cpd.	compound
Crit.	(in titles) Criticism, Critical
Cryst.	in Crystallography
Cycl.	(in titles) Cyclopaedia, -ic
Cytol.	(in titles) Cytology, -ical
Da.	Danish
D.A.	Dictionary of Americanisms
D.A.E.	Dictionary of American English
dat.	dative
D.C.	District of Columbia
Deb.	(in titles) Debate, -s
def.	definite, -ition
dem.	demonstrative
deriv.	derivative, -ation
derog.	derogatory
Descr.	(in titles) Description, -tive
Devel.	(in titles) Development, -al
Diagn.	(in titles) Diagnosis, Diagnostic
dial.	dialect, -al

Dict.	Dictionary; spec., the Oxford English Dictionary
dim.	diminutive
Dis.	(in titles) Disease
Diss.	(in titles) Dissertation
D.O.S.T.	Dictionary of the Older Scottish Tongue
Du.	Dutch
E.	East
Eccl.	(as label) in Ecclesiastical usage; (in titles) Ecclesiastical
Ecol.	in Ecology
Econ.	(as label) in Economics; (in titles) Economy, -ics
ed.	edition
E.D.D.	English Dialect Dictionary
Edin.	(in titles) Edinburgh
Educ.	(as label) in Education; (in titles) Education, -al
EE.	Early English
e.g.	exempli gratia, 'for example'
Electr.	(as label) in Electricity; (in titles) Electricity, -ical
Electron.	(in titles) Electronic, -s
Elem.	(in titles) Element, -ary
ellipt.	elliptical, -ly
Embryol.	in Embryology
e.midl.	east midland (dialect)
Encycl.	(in titles) Encyclopaedia, -ic
Eng.	England, English
Engin.	Engineering
Ent.	in Entomology
Entomol.	(in titles) Entomology, -logical
erron.	erroneous, -ly
esp.	especially
Ess.	(in titles) Essay, -s
et al.	et alii, 'and others'
etc.	et cetera
Ethnol.	in Ethnology
etym.	etymology
euphem.	euphemistically
Exam.	(in titles) Examination
exc.	except
Exerc.	(in titles) Exercise
Exper.	(in titles) Experiment, -al
Explor.	(in titles) Exploration
f.	feminine
f. (in Etym.)	formed on
f. (in subordinate entries)	form of
F.	French
fem. (rarely f.)	feminine
fig.	figurative, -ly
Finn.	Finnish
fl.	floruit, 'flourished'
Found.	(in titles) Foundation
Fr.	French
freq.	frequent, -ly
Fris.	Frisian
Fund.	(in titles) Fundamental
Funk or Funk's Stand. Dict.	Funk and Wagnalls Standard Dictionary
G.	German
Gael.	Gaelic
Gaz.	(in titles) Gazette
gen.	genitive
gen.	general, -ly
Geogr.	(as label) in Geography; (in titles) Geography, -ical

Geol.	(as label) in Geology; (in titles) *Geology, -ical*	masc. (*rarely* m.)	masculine	*Palæont.*	(as label) in Palaeontology; (in titles) *Palaeontology, -ical*
Geom.	in Geometry	*Math.*	(as label) in Mathematics; (in titles) *Mathematics, -al*	pa. pple.	passive participle, past participle
Geomorphol.	in Geomorphology	MDu.	Middle Dutch		
Ger.	German	ME.	Middle English	(Partridge),	(quoted from) E. Partridge's *Dictionary of Slang and Unconventional English*
Gloss.	Glossary	*Mech.*	(as label) in Mechanics; (in titles) *Mechanics, -al*		
Gmc.	Germanic				
Godef.	F. Godefroy, *Dictionnaire de l'ancienne langue française*	*Med.*	(as label) in Medicine; (in titles) *Medicine, -ical*		
Goth.	Gothic	med.L.	medieval Latin	pass.	passive, -ly
Govt.	(in titles) *Government*	*Mem.*	(in titles) *Memoir(s)*	pa.t.	past tense
Gr.	Greek	*Metaph.*	in Metaphysics	*Path.*	(as label) in Pathology; (in titles) *Pathology, -ical*
Gram.	(as label) in Grammar; (in titles) *Grammar, -tical*	*Meteorol.*	(as label) in Meteorology; (in titles) *Meteorology, -ical*	perh.	perhaps
				Pers.	Persian
Gt.	Great	MHG	Middle High German	*pers.*	person, -al
		midl.	midland (dialect)	*Petrogr.*	in Petrography
		Mil.	in military usage	*Petrol.*	(as label) in Petrology; (in titles) *Petrology, -ical*
Heb.	Hebrew	*Min.*	(as label) in Mineralogy; (in titles) *Ministry*		
Her.	in Heraldry			(Pettman),	(quoted from) C. Pettman's *Africanderisms*
Herb.	among herbalists	*Mineral.*	(in titles) *Mineralogy, -ical*		
Hind.	Hindustani	MLG	Middle Low German	pf.	perfect
Hist.	(as label) in History; (in titles) *History, -ical*	*Misc.*	(in titles) *Miscellany, -eous*	Pg.	Portuguese
		mod.	modern	*Pharm.*	in Pharmacology
hist.	historical	mod.L	modern Latin	*Philol.*	(as label) in Philology; (in titles) *Philology, -ical*
Histol.	(in titles) *Histology, -ical*	(Morris),	(quoted from) E. E. Morris's *Austral. English*	*Philos.*	(as label) in Philosophy; (in titles) *Philosophy, -ical*
Hort.	in Horticulture				
Househ.	(in titles) *Household*	*Mus.*	(as label) in Music; (in titles) *Music, -al; Museum*	phonet.	phonetic, -ally
Housek.	(in titles) *Housekeeping*			*Photogr.*	(as label) in Photography; (in titles) *Photography, -ical*
		Myst.	(in titles) *Mystery*	phr.	phrase
Ibid.	*Ibidem*, 'in the same book or passage'	*Mythol.*	in Mythology	*Phys.*	Physical; (*rarely*) in Physiology
Icel.	Icelandic				
Ichthyol.	in Ichthyology	N.	North	*Physiol.*	(as label) in Physiology; (in titles) *Physiology, -ical*
id.	*idem*, 'the same'	n.	neuter		
i.e.	*id est*, 'that is'	*N. Amer.*	North America, -n	*Pict.*	(in titles) *Picture, Pictorial*
IE.	Indo-European	*N. & Q.*	*Notes and Queries*	pl., plur.	plural
Illustr.	(in titles) *Illustration, -ted*	*Narr.*	(in titles) *Narrative*	*poet.*	poetic, -al
imit.	imitative	*Nat.*	(in titles) *Natural*	Pol.	Polish
Immunol.	in Immunology	Nat. Hist.	in Natural History	Pol.	(as label) in Politics; (in titles) *Politics, -al*
imp.	imperative	*Naut.*	in nautical language		
impers.	impersonal	N.E.	North East	Pol. Econ.	in Political Economy
impf.	imperfect	*N.E.D.*	*New English Dictionary*, original title of the *Oxford English Dictionary* (first edition)	*Polit.*	(in titles) *Politics, -al*
ind.	indicative			pop.	popular, -ly
indef.	indefinite			*Porc.*	(in titles) *Porcelain*
Industr.	(in titles) *Industry, -ial*			poss.	possessive
inf.	infinitive	*Neurol.*	in Neurology	*Pott.*	(in titles) *Pottery*
infl.	influenced	neut. (*rarely* n.)	neuter	*ppl. a., pple. adj.*	participial adjective
Inorg.	(in titles) *Inorganic*	NF., NFr.	Northern French	pple.	participle
Ins.	(in titles) *Insurance*	No.	Number	Pr.	Provencal
Inst.	(in titles) *Institute, -tion*	nom.	nominative	pr.	present
int.	interjection	north.	northern (dialect)	*Pract.*	(in titles) *Practice, -al*
intr.	intransitive	Norw.	Norwegian	prec.	preceding (word or article)
Introd.	(in titles) *Introduction*	n.q.	no quotations	pred.	predicative
Ir.	Irish	N.T.	New Testament	*pref.*	prefix
irreg.	irregular, -ly	*Nucl.*	Nuclear	pref., Pref.	preface
It.	Italian	*Numism.*	in Numismatics	*prep.*	preposition
		N.W.	North West	*pres.*	present
J., (J.)	(quoted from) Johnson's *Dictionary*	N.Z.	New Zealand	*Princ.*	(in titles) *Principle(s)*
(Jam.)	Jamieson, *Scottish Dict.*	obj.	object	priv.	privative
Jap.	Japanese	obl.	oblique	prob.	probably
joc.	jocular, -ly	*Obs., obs.*	obsolete	*Probl.*	(in titles) *Problem*
Jrnl.	(in titles) *Journal*	*Obstetr.*	(in titles) *Obstetrics*	*Proc.*	(in titles) *Proceedings*
Jun.	(in titles) *Junior*	occas.	occasionally	*pron.*	pronoun
		OE.	Old English (= Anglo-Saxon)	pronunc.	pronunciation
Knowl.	(in titles) *Knowledge*			prop.	properly
		OF., OFr.	Old French	*Pros.*	in Prosody
l.	line	OFris.	Old Frisian	Prov.	Provencal
L.	Latin	OHG	Old High German	pr. pple.	present participle
lang.	language	OIr.	Old Irish	*Psych.*	in Psychology
Lect.	(in titles) *Lecture, -s*	ON.	Old Norse	*Psychol.*	(as label) in Psychology; (in titles) *Psychology, -ical*
Less.	(in titles) *Lesson, -s*	ONF.	Old Northern French		
Let., Lett.	letter, letters	*Ophthalm.*	in Ophthalmology		
LG.	Low German	opp.	opposed (to), the opposite (of)	*Publ.*	(in titles) *Publications*
lit.	literal, -ly				
Lit.	Literary	*Opt.*	in Optics	Q.	(in titles) *Quarterly*
Lith.	Lithuanian	*Org.*	(in titles) *Organic*	quot(s).	quotation(s)
LXX	Septuagint	orig.	origin, -al, -ally	q.v.	*quod vide*, 'which see'
		Ornith.	(as label) in Ornithology; (in titles) *Ornithology, -ical*		
m.	masculine			R.	(in titles) *Royal*
Mag.	(in titles) *Magazine*	OS.	Old Saxon	*Radiol.*	in Radiology
Magn.	(in titles) *Magnetic, -ism*	OSl.	Old (Church) Slavonic	R.C.Ch.	Roman Catholic Church
Mal.	Malay, Malayan	O.T.	Old Testament	*Rec.*	(in titles) *Record*
Man.	(in titles) *Manual*	*Outl.*	(in titles) *Outline*	redupl.	reduplicating
Managem.	(in titles) *Management*	*Oxf.*	(in titles) *Oxford*	*Ref.*	(in titles) *Reference*
Manch.	(in titles) *Manchester*			refash.	refashioned, -ing
Manuf.	in Manufacture, -ing	p.	page	refl.	reflexive
Mar.	(in titles) *Marine*	*Palæogr.*	in Palaeography	*Reg.*	(in titles) *Register*

reg.	regular	str.	strong	*Trop.*	(in titles) *Tropical*	
rel.	related to	*Struct.*	(in titles) *Structure, -al*	Turk.	Turkish	
Reminisc.	(in titles) *Reminiscence(s)*	*Stud.*	(in titles) *Studies*	*Typog., Typogr.*	in Typography	
Rep.	(in titles) *Report(s)*	subj.	subject			
repr.	representative, representing	*subord. cl.*	*subordinate clause*	ult.	ultimately	
Res.	(in titles) *Research*	subseq.	subsequent, -ly	*Univ.*	(in titles) *University*	
Rev.	(in titles) *Review*	subst.	substantively	unkn.	unknown	
rev.	revised	*suff.*	suffix	*U.S.*	United States	
Rhet.	in Rhetoric	superl.	superlative	U.S.S.R.	Union of Soviet Socialist	
Rom.	Roman, -ce, ic	Suppl.	Supplement		Republics	
Rum.	Rumanian	*Surg.*	(as label) in Surgery;	usu.	usually	
Russ.	Russian		(in titles) *Surgery, Surgical*			
		s.v.	*sub voce,* 'under the word'	*v., vb.*	verb	
S.	South	Sw.	Swedish	var(r)., vars.	variant(s) of	
S.Afr.	South Africa, -n	s.w.	south-western (dialect)	*vbl. sb.*	verbal substantive	
sb.	substantive	*Syd. Soc. Lex.*	Sydenham Society, *Lexicon*	*Vertebr.*	(in titles) *Vertebrate(s)*	
sc.	*scilicet,* 'understand' or		*of Medicine & Allied*	*Vet.*	(as label) in Veterinary	
	'supply'		*Sciences*		Science;	
Sc., Scot.	Scottish	syll.	syllable		(in titles) *Veterinary*	
Scand.	(in titles) *Scandinavia, -n*	Syr.	Syrian	*Vet. Sci.*	in Veterinary Science	
Sch.	(in titles) *School*	*Syst.*	(in titles) *System, -atic*	viz.	*videlicet,* 'namely'	
Sc. Nat. Dict.	*Scottish National Dictionary*			*Voy.*	(in titles) *Voyage(s)*	
Scotl.	(in titles) *Scotland*		(in titles) *Taxonomy, -ical*	*v.str.*	strong verb	
Sel.	(in titles) *Selection(s)*	*Taxon.*	(in titles) *Taxonomy, -ical*	*vulg.*	vulgar	
Ser.	Series	*techn.*	technical, -ly	*v.w.*	weak verb	
sing.	singular	*Technol.*	(in titles) *Technology, -ical*			
Sk.	(in titles) *Sketch*	*Telegr.*	in Telegraphy	W.	Welsh; West	
Skr.	Sanskrit	*Teleph.*	in Telephony	wd.	word	
Slav.	Slavonic	(Th.),	(quoted from) Thornton's	Webster	*Webster's (New*	
S.N.D.	*Scottish National Dictionary*		*American Glossary*		*International) Dictionary*	
Soc.	(in titles) *Society*	*Theatr.*	in the Theatre, theatrical	*Westm.*	(in titles) *Westminster*	
Sociol.	(as label) in Sociology;	*Theol.*	(as label) in Theology;	WGmc.	West Germanic	
	(in titles) *Sociology, -ical*		(in titles) *Theology, -ical*	*Wks.*	(in titles) *Works*	
Sp.	Spanish	*Theoret.*	(in titles) *Theoretical*	w.midl.	west midland (dialect)	
Sp.	(in titles) *Speech, -es*	Tokh.	Tokharian	WS.	West Saxon	
sp.	spelling	tr., transl.	translated, translation			
spec.	specifically	*Trans.*	(in titles) *Transaction*	(Y.),	(quoted from) Yule &	
Spec.	(in titles) *Specimen*	*trans.*	transitive		Burnell's *Hobson-Jobson*	
St.	Saint	*transf.*	transferred sense	*Yrs.*	(in titles) *Years*	
Stand.	(in titles) *Standard*	*Trav.*	(in titles) *Travel(s)*			
Stanf.	(quoted from) *Stanford*	*Treas.*	(in titles) *Treasury*	*Zoogeogr.*	in Zoogeography	
	Dictionary of Anglicised	*Treat.*	(in titles) *Treatise*	*Zool.*	(as label) in Zoology;	
	Words & Phrases	*Treatm.*	(in titles) *Treatment*		(in titles) *Zoology, -ical*	
		Trig.	in Trigonometry			

Signs and Other Conventions

Before a word or sense	In the listing of Forms	In the etymologies
† = obsolete	1 = before 1100	* indicates a word or form not actually found,
‖ = not naturalized, alien	2 = 12th c. (1100 to 1200)	but of which the existence is inferred
¶ = catachrestic and erroneous uses	3 = 13th c. (1200 to 1300), etc.	:— = normal development of
	5-7 = 15th to 17th century	
	20 = 20th century	

The printing of a word in SMALL CAPITALS indicates that further information will be found under the word so referred to.

.. indicates an omitted part of a quotation.

-(in a quotation) indicates a hyphen doubtfully present in the original; (in other text) indicates a hyphen inserted only for the sake of a line-break.

PROPRIETARY NAMES

THIS Dictionary includes some words which are or are asserted to be proprietary names or trade marks. Their inclusion does not imply that they have acquired for legal purposes a non-proprietary or general significance nor any other judgement concerning their legal status. In cases where the editorial staff have established in the records of the Patent Offices of the United Kingdom and of the United States that a word is registered as a proprietary name or trade mark this is indicated, but no judgement concerning the legal status of such words is made or implied thereby.

B.B.C. (bi:bi:'si:). Initial letters of *British Broadcasting Corporation*, a public corporation orig. having the monopoly of broadcasting in Gt. Britain, financed by a grant-in-aid from Parliament; established 1927 by royal charter to carry on work previously performed by the British Broadcasting Company; hence **B.B.C. English**, standard English as maintained by B.B.C. announcers; so ***B.B.C. pronunciation***, etc.

1923 *Radio Times* 28 Sept. 12/1 It seems to me that the B.B.C. are mainly catering for the 'listeners' who own expensive sets. **1925** *Punch* 22 Apr. 440/1 The daily wireless programme of the B.B.C. **1926** *Encycl. Brit.* Suppl. I. 454/2 The 'B.B.C.' is constituted as a limited company, the shareholders being wireless manufacturers and traders. **1928** *Times* 13 Jan. 8/5 B.B.C. English. Mr. Lawrence omits from his list of solecisms in pronunciation perpetrated by the B.B.C.'s 'Advisory Committee on Spoken English' the crowning horror. **1932** *Listener* 13 Jan. 45/1 Critics who enjoy making fun of what they are pleased to call 'B.B.C. English' might with profit pay occasional visits to the other side of the Atlantic, in order to hear examples of our language as broadcast where there are no official 'recommendations to announcers'. **1936** W. HOLTBY *South Riding* i. 18 She talked B.B.C. English to her employer .. and Yorkshire dialect to old milkmen. **1938** P. THORESBY JONES *Welsh Border Country* viii. 95 The educated and older local (as opposed to the 'board-school' and B.B.C.) pronunciation of the town's name is *Shrozebury*, not Shroozbury. **1944** *Penguin New Writing* XXII. 47 Her accent was impeccably B.B.C. **1956** A. WILSON *Anglo-Saxon Attitudes* II. ii. 338 B.B.C. officials—programme planners, features-producers, poetry readers.

bdellatomy (dɛ'lætəmɪ). *Med.* [mod. f. Gr. βδέλλα leech + -τομία a cutting.] The name given to the practice of cutting leeches to empty them of blood while they still continue to suck.

1868 *Daily News* 30 July, When the little blood-sucker has taken his fill and is about to release his bite .. a small incision is made in his side that serves as an outlet for the blood, and he goes on sucking .. Bdellatomy is the name given to the practice.

‖**bdellium** ('dɛlɪəm). Forms: 4 **bidellium, bdelyum, bdellyum,** 6 **bedellion,** 6–7 **bdelium,** 6– **bdellium.** [a. L. *bdellium* (Vulgate), ad. Gr. βδέλλιον (according to Dioscorides and Pliny, a plant, and the fragrant gum exuded by it: see senses 1 and 2); used in the Greek versions later then the LXX to translate the Heb. *b'dōlakh*, which Josephus also rendered βδέλλα. The Greek word is evidently of oriental origin, but whether it has any relation either of etymology or sense with the Heb. is uncertain, as is also the meaning and origin of the latter, which the LXX had rendered in Genesis by ἄνθραξ 'carbuncle,' and in Numbers by κρύσταλλος 'crystal': the Rabbins and Bochart explain it as meaning 'pearl, pearls.']

1. The name given to several trees or shrubs of the N.O. *Amyridaceæ*, chiefly of the genus *Balsamodendron*, from which exudes a kind of gum-resin resembling impure myrrh, of pungent taste and agreeable odour, used in medicine and as a perfume.

1398 TREVISA *Barth De P.R.* XVII. xix. (1495) 614 Bidellium is .. a blacke tre moost lyke to the Oliue and the gumme therof is bryght and bytter. **1596** LODGE *Marg. Amer.*, The blacke bdellium [bringeth forth] sweete gumme. **1620** T. PEYTON *Parad.* in Farr's *S.P.* (1848) 178 Where can a man .. Find bdelium, that pleasant tree, to grow. [**1878** H. STANLEY *Dark Cont.* II. xii. 350 Where the myrrh and bdellium shrubs exhaled their fragrance.]

2. The gum-resin thus procured.

1585 LLOYD *Treas. Health* Q v, Afterwarde put .. thervnto .. pouder of Masticke, of Castoreum, bdelii, myrre. **1601** HOLLAND *Pliny* I. 362 The right Bdellium .. being washed and drenched with wine .. is more odoriferous. **1859** R. BURTON *Centr. Afr.* in *Jrnl. R.G.S.* XXIX. 448 The important growths of the interior are frankincense and bdellium.

3. The translation, in the English Bible, of the Hebrew word *b'dōlakh*; see above.

1382 WYCLIF *Gen.* ii. 12 Ther is foundun bdelyum and the stoon onychynus. —— *Num.* xi. 7 Manna forsothe was .. of the colour of bdelli [**1388** of bdellyum, *which is whijt and bryȝt as cristal*]. **1535** COVERDALE *ibid.*, There is founde Bedellion. —— The Manna was .. like Bedellion. **1560** *Genev.* ibid., The Man also was .. the colour of bdelium. **1611** *ibid.*, There is bdellium. —— The colour of Bdelium.

bdellometer (dɛ'lɒmɪtə(r)). [ad. F. *bdellomètre*, f. Gr. βδέλλα leech + μέτρον measure.] A surgical instrument proposed as a substitute for leeches, and fitted to show the amount of blood drawn.

1839 HOOPER *Med. Dict.* 254. **1874** DUNGLISON *Med. Dict.*, *Bdellometer* .. consists of a cupping-glass, to which a scarificator and exhausting syringe are attached.

be (bi:), *v.* [An irregular and defective verb, the full conjugation of which in modern Eng. is effected by a union of the surviving inflexions of three originally distinct and independent verbs, viz. (1) the original Aryan substantive verb with stem *es-*, Skr. *as-*, *'s-*, Gr. 'εσ-, L. *es-*, *'s-*, OTeut. **es-*, *'s-*; (2) the verb with stem *wes-*, Skr. *vas-* to remain, OTeut. *wes-*, Gothic *wis-an* to remain, stay, continue to be, OS., OE., OHG. *wesan*, OFris. *wes-a*, ON. *ver-a*; (3) the stem *beu-* Skr. *bhū-*, *bhaw-*, Gr. φυ-, L. *fu-*, OTeut. **beu-*, *beo-*, OE. *béo-n* to become, come to be. Of the stem *es-*, OE. (like the oldest extant Teutonic) possessed only the present tenses, Indicative and Subjunctive (orig. Optative), all the other parts being supplied from the stem *wes-*, pa. t. *was*, which, though still a distinct and complete vb. in Gothic, was in OE. only supplemental to *es-*, the two constituting the substantive verb *am-was*. *Béon*, *be*, was still in OE. a distinct verb (having all the present, but no past tenses) meaning to 'become, come to be', and thus often serving as a future tense to *am-was*. By the beginning of the 13th c., the Infinitive and Participle, Imperative, and pres. Subjunctive of *am-was*, became successively obsolete, the corresponding parts of *be* taking their place, so that the whole verb *am-was-be* is now commonly called from its infinitive, 'the verb *to be*,' although *be* is no part of the substantive verb originally, but only a later accretion replacing original parts now lost.

In OE. the present Indic. of *am* had two forms of the plural, (1) *sind*, *sindon* (= Goth. and Ger. *sind*, L. *sunt*, Skr. *sánti*) and *earon*, *aron* (= ON. *eru*), the latter confined to the Anglian dialects, where it was used side by side with *sind*, *-un*. Of these, *sind*, *-on* ceased to be used before 1250, its place being taken in southern Eng. by the corresponding inflexions of *be*. We, ye, they *beth*, *ben*, *be*, were the standard forms in southern and midl. Eng. for centuries; and even in the sing., *be*, *beest*, *beth* began to encroach on *am*, *art*, *is*, and are now the regular forms in southern dialect speech. Meanwhile *aron*, *aren*, *arn*, *are*, survived in the north, and gradually spread south, till early in 16th c. *are* made its appearance in standard Eng., where it was regularly used by Tindale. *Be* continued in concurrent use till the end of the century (see Shakspere, and Bible of 1611), and still occurs as a poetic archaism, as well as in certain traditional expressions and familiar quotations of 16th c. origin, as 'the powers that be.' But the regular modern Eng. plural is *are*, which now tends to oust *be* even from the subjunctive. Southern and eastern dialect speech retains *be* both in singular and plural, as 'I be a going,' 'we be ready.']

In treating this important word, the history of the inflexions is first exhibited, and then that of the signification.

A. Inflexions.

I. Inflexions from stem *es-*: partly replaced in ME. by *be*.

1. *Present Indicative.*

* from *es-*, *'s-*.

a. *1 sing.* **am** (æm, əm, (ə)m, m). [= ON. *em*, Gothic *im*, Skr. *ásmi*, Gr. *ἔσμι, εἰμί, L. *sum*: the only Eng. vb. form which retains the old personal suffix *-m* (for *-mi*).] Forms: 1–3 **eom,** 1 *Merc.* **eam,** *North.* **am, amm,** 2–4 **em, eam, æm,** 2– **am** (*Orm.* **amm,** 3–4 **ham,** 4 **ame, emme**), *contr.* 6– **'m** (*I'm*) in verse and familiar prose. In 4–5 *icham* (south and west) was treated as one word, whence later dial. *cham* in 16th c. and recent s.w. dial. *Negative* 1–5 **neom, næm, nam.** (*Northern* **es, is:** see 3rd sing.)

c **885** K. ÆLFRED *Boeth.* xiii. 40 Ic eom ofwundrod. *a* **950** *Durh. Ritual* 10 a, Ic am drihten god ðin. *c* **950** *Lindisf. Gosp.* Matt. xxviii. 20 Ic iuh mið am. *c* **975** *Rushw. G.* ibid., Ic mid eow eam. *c* **1000** *Ags. G.* Matt. xi. 28 Ic eom bilwite. *c* **1160** *Hatton G.* ibid., Ich eom bylewhit. *c* **1175** *Lamb. Hom.* 25 Ic em hal. *c* **1200** *Trin. Coll. Hom.* 256 Ic am þi mon. **1205** LAY. 461 Ich am duc. *Ibid.* 25,943 Ich æm mon [**1250** Ich ham a mon]. *Ibid.* 14,136 Næm ich næuere bute care. *a* **1300** *Cursor M.* 5756 Lord here I ame. *c* **1300** *Beket* 475 So moche wrecche nam y noȝt. **1330** R. BRUNNE *Chron.* 337 Ich emme þat þe bere. **1362** LANGL. *P. Pl.* A. v. 105 'Icham sori' quod Envye, 'I ne am [*v.r.* nam] but seldene oþer.' **1382** WYCLIF *Ex.* iii. 14 Y am that am. *c* **1385** CHAUCER *L.G.W.* Prol. 314 Sir it am I. **1647** COWLEY *Mistr.* lxxvi, No: I'm undone. **1863** GEO. ELIOT *Romola* i, I'm a stranger in Florence.

dial. **1547** BOORDE *Introd. Knowl.* 122 Iche cham a Cornyshe man. **1633** B. JONSON *T. Tub* I. i, 'Cham no man's wife. **1746** *Exmoor Scolding* (1879) 26 Cham a-troubled.

b. *2 sing.* **art** (ɑ:t, ət, (ə)t). [= ON. *est*, after 12th c. *ert*, Goth. *is*, Skr. *ási*, Gr. ἔσσι (ἐσσί, εἶς, εἶ), L. *es*; in Eng., as in later ON., *s* of the stem has become *r*: the final *t* is a pleonastic addition of the 2nd pers. pron., not found in Goth., nor outside Teut.] Forms: 1–2 **eart,** 1 *Merc.* **earð,** *North.* **arð,** 2–3 **ært,** (**eært, æart, hart, ard**), *Orm.* **arrt,** 2–5 **ert,** 2– **art,** capable of contraction, 6– **thou'rt.** *Negative* 1–5 **neart, nert, nart.** *Art-thou* appears 1–2 **eartu, earðu, arðu,** 2–5 **ertu, artu, artow**; in poet. and dial. use, the pron. is now sometimes omitted, as in 'What art doing?' (*Northern* **es, is:** see 3rd sing.)

c **950** *Lindisf. Gosp.* Matt. vi. 9 Fæder user ðu arð *vel* bist in heofnum. *c* **975** *Rushw. G.* ibid., Fæder ure þu þe in heofunum earð. *a* **1000** *Ags. G.* ibid., Fæder ure þu þe eart an heofenum. *c* **1160** *Hatton G.* ibid., Fader ure þu þe ert on heofne. *c* **1175** *Lamb. Hom.* 223 Þu æart dust. *Ibid.* 201 Hwi ertu me so freomede. *a* **1250** *Owl & Night.* 561 Thu art lutel. *c* **1280** *Relig. Songs.* v. 178 Nu thu ard al skere. *a* **1300** *Cursor M.* (Cott.) 14105 In mikel bisenes ert þou, Bise ert þou [*Gött.* bisi es þu] bot mani dede. *c* **1340** *Ibid.* (Fairf.) 12136 Vnneþes artow of vij ȝere. **1340** HAMPOLE *Pr. Consc.* 424 Askes er-tow now. **1382** WYCLIF *2 Sam.* xii. 7 Thou ert thilk man [**1388** Thou art thilke man]. —— *Matt.* vi. 9 Oure fadir that art in heuenes. **1602** DEKKER *Satirom.* 234 Art not famous enough yet, but thou must eate men alive?

c. *3 sing.* **is** (ɪz, (ə)z, (ə)s). [= ON. *es*, after 1200 *er*, Goth., OHG., OS., OFris. *ist*, Skr. *ásti*, Gr. ἔστι, L. *est*: in Eng. as in ON. and Du. the personal suffix *-t* is lost.] Forms: 1– **is;** 1–6 **ys;** *Orm.* **iss;** *North.* 3–5 **es** (**ess, esse, iss, isse**). *Negative* 1–5 **nis, nys.** *Is* still rimed with *miss*, *bliss*, *this*, etc. in 16th c.; it retains the *s* sound in *is't?* and when contracted, after breath mutes as *that's* (ðæts), but = *z* elsewhere, as *he's*, *all's*, *this is* (hi:z, ɔ:lz, 'ðɪsɪz).

c **885** K. ÆLFRED *Oros.* I. i. §13 Hit is eall weste. *c* **1000** *Ags. Gosp.* Matt. xxviii. 6 Nys he her. *c* **1160** *Hatton G.* ibid., Nis he her. *c* **1280** *Sarmun* 38 in *E.E.P.* (1862) 5 Manis lif nis bot a schade, nov he is and nov he nis. *a* **1300** *Cursor M.* (Gött.) 5779 Til ȝou me sendis he þat ess [*Cott.* es, *Fairf.* ys]. *c* **1340** *Ibid.* (Trin.) 13158 Seint Ion þat in prisoun isse. **1340** HAMPOLE *Pr. Consc.* 32 Swa he es, and ay .. sal be. *c* **1386** CHAUCER *Knts. T.* 1267 Ther is [*v.r.* nys] no newe gyse, that is nas old. *c* **1400** MAUNDEV. iii. 19 There nys no Purgatorie. *c* **1450** MYRC 10 Alle ys for defawte of lore. **1483** CAXTON *G. de la Tour* B vij, Is it right or wrong. *c* **1530** REDFORDE *Play Wyt & Sc.* (1848) 3 Ah! syr, what tyme yst? **1635** QUARLES *Embl.* II. xiv. When not himself, he's mad; when most himself, he's worse. **1733** POPE *Ess. Man* I. 286 One truth is clear, Whatever *Is* is RIGHT. **1848** KINGSLEY *Saints' Trag.* II. vii. 100 What's thy name?

¶ In the northern dialect, ME. and mod., *es*, *is*, *ys*, is used for all persons of the sing., and also for the plur., when not immediately joined to the nom. pron., *e.g.* when the subject is a noun or relative; the latter usage is exceedingly frequent in the Shakspere folio of 1623 (though much altered by editors ignorant of its history).

a **1300** *Cursor M.* (Cott.) 5262 Þat þou liuand es! [*Fairf.* On liue þou ys]. *Ibid.* 9727 'Fader,' he said, 'þi sun i es.' *Ibid.* 14105 In mekil besines es þu. *c* **1386** CHAUCER *Reeves T.* 125 (Northern Clerk), I is as ille a millere as are ye [*Lansd.*, I es as il a Melnere as es ye]. *Ibid.* 169 Il hayl! by god, Aleyn, thou is a fonne. **1485** MALORY *Arthur* (1817) II. 391 Here is I. **1570–87** HOLINSHED *Scot. Chron*, II. 50 Giltless persons is condemned. **1574** tr. *Littleton's Tenures* 107 b, Hys heires is in by dyscent. **1578** in *Scot. Poems 16th C.* (1801) II. 133 Our fais that bisie is. **1590** SHAKS. *Com. Err.* III. ii. 20 Ill deeds is doubled with an evil word. **1593** —— *2 Hen. VI*, III. ii. 11 Is all things well? *Ibid.* 303 There's two of you. [*Mod. Sc.* and *north. Eng.* All my hopes is lost. Is your friends coming?]

d. *1–3 plural.*

†*a.* Obs. form from weak stem *'s*: [OE. *sind*, *sindon*. = OS. *sind*, *sindon*, OFris. *send*, OHG. 3 pl. *sint*, *sindun*, Goth. 3 pl. *sind*, Skr. 3 pl. *sánti*, L. *sunt*. The *-on*, *-un*, occurring in WGer. is a second pl. suffix subsequently added.] Forms: 1 **sind, sint, synd, synt, siondon, si(e)ndun, sindon, syndon,** 2 **synde(n, synd, synt,** 2–3 **sende(n,** 3 **sunde(n, sonde(n, seondeþ,** (**seoð**), *Orm.* **sinndenn.** Replaced in south by *be*; in north and at length everywhere by *are*.

β. **are** (ɑ:(r), ə(r), (r)). [= ON. 1 *erum*, 2 *eruð*, 3 *eru*, (:—**erund*), Sw. 1 *äro*, 2 *ären*, 3 *äro*, Da. *ere*; a re-forming of the pl. on the strong stem-form *es-*, analogous to Gr. *ἐσ-μές, ἐσ-τέ, ἔ-ᾱσι (from *ἔσ-αντι), L. *es-tis*, compared with the original type in Skr. *s-más*, *s-thá*, *s-ánti*, L. *s-umus*, *s-unt*, and Gothic *sijum*, *sijuð*, *sind*, OE. *sind* (in α).] Forms: 1 *Merc.* **earun,** *Northumb.* **aron, aro-,** 2–5 *north.* and *n. midl.* **aren,** 2–6 **arn,** 3 *Orm.* **arrn,** (4–5 **arunne**), 4–6 **arne,** 4– **are** (4–6 **ar**); 3–4 *north.* **ern,** 4–5 **ere, er.** (Without pronoun 4– **es, is:** see 3rd sing. above.)

α. *c* **885** K. ÆLFRED *Oros.* I. i. §12 Be norðan him sindon [*later MS.* syndon] Ealdseaxan. *c* **1000** *Ags. Gosp.* Matt. x. 2 Ðis synt [*Lindisf.* sint, *Rushw.* sindun] þæra Apostola naman. *c* **1160** *Hatton G.* ibid., Ðis sende þare apostle namen. *c* **1200** *Moral Ode* 290 in *Trin. Coll. Hom.* 229 Hwu fele senden in helle. *c* **1200** ORMIN 6293 Þa þat sinndenn gode. **1205** LAY. 24763 We sunden twælf cnihtes. *Ibid* 27319 Godd heo seondeð laðe.

β. *a* **950** *Durh. Ritual* 28 Allo ȝie bearno lehtes aro ȝie. *c* **950** *Lindisf. Gosp.* Matt. v. 14 Ȝie aron (*vel* sint) leht middanȝeardes. *c* **1200** *Trin. Coll. Hom.* 73 Swiche ben þe deueles bernes, þe aren cleped ortrowe. *c* **1200** ORMIN 6849 Þa þatt arrn i þine walde. *c* **1250** *Gen. & Ex.* 16 So faȝen so fueles arn. *a* **1300** *Cursor M.* (Cott.) 4847 Elleuen breþer es we [*v.r.* we er, we ar, are we] liuand. *Ibid.* 4878 Yee Ne ern lickli lel men to be. *a* **1300** *E.E. Psalter* xcii. 6 Þine werkes ere þai. *c* **1380** WYCLIF *Sel. Wks.* (1871) III. 169 Bodily werkis arunne more knowen. *c* **1380** *Sir Ferumb.* 2379 Þay aren in grete drede. *c* **1384** CHAUCER *H. Fame* 1008 Al these arne set in heuene [*Caxt.* ar, *Thynne* are]. **1398** TREVISA *Barth. De P.R.* XVIII. xix. (1495) 778 Camelles ben tothlesse aboue as oxen are. **1465** MARG. PASTON in *Lett.* 500 II. 179 They eryn as he left hem .. The place where they ern kept. **1528** MORE *Heresyes* II. Wks. 202/1 Sarasyns, whiche .. arne

of another flocke. **1534** TINDALE *John* x. 30 I and my father are one [WYCLIF ben oon]. **1611** BIBLE *Gen.* xlii. 31 We are true men: we are no spies. We be twelue brethren [*Coverd.* we are; *Genev.*, we be]. **1787** BURNS *Brigs of Ayr*, I'll be a Brig, when ye're a shapeless cairn.

¶ Negative forms colloquial and vulgar, found in dramatists and novels since 17th c. are *ar'n't*, *a'n't* = are not, am not, *e'n't*, *ain't* = am not, is not, are not.

1710 PALMER *Proverbs* 124 The politest atheist can't be sure that their e'nt a God. **1794** SOUTHEY *Wat Tyler* III. ii, You ar'n't to die So easily. **1799** B. THOMPSON *Kotzebue's Stranger* in Mrs. Inchbald *Theat.* I. 17 Sharp lad, a'n't I? **1837** DICKENS *Pickw.* xiii, I an't quite certain. *Ibid.* xxviii, There ain't anything the matter.

** from verb *be*.

e. *1 sing.* †**be** (biː, bɪ). *Obs.* exc. *dial.* [= OS. *bium*, OFris. *bem*, OHG. *pim*, cogn. w. Skr. *bhavāmi*, Gr. **φῦμι*, *φύω*, L. *fui*.] Forms: 1 **bíom, béom**, 1–3 **béo, beon**, 3– **be**, (4–5 **by**, 4–7 **bee**). Like *am*, this had the personal suffix *-m*, which was however dropped already in later OE.

(*a*) as distinct vb. or *future*: I become, come to be, shall be.

c **825** *Vesp. Psalter* cxlvi. 2 Ic singu gode minum swe longe swe ic biom [Lat. *ero*]. *c* **1000** *Ags. Ps.* cxix. 117 Gefultuma me fæste, ðonne béo ic hál. *c* **1200** *Trin. Coll. Hom.* 17 Bispreng me mid edmodnesse louerd þanne be ich clene. **1205** LAY. 28218 Ne beo [**1250** worþe] ich nauere bliðe.

(*b*) as *present*: rare and doubtful in ME., but now the regular form in southern and some midland dialects. The negative *I ben't*, *beant*, *baint* is even more widely used dialectally.

c **1000** *Ags. Gosp.* Matt. xxviii. 20 Ic beo mid eow ealle daȝas [*Lindisf.* am, *Rushw.* eam]. *c* **1160** *Hatton G.* ibid., Ich beo. **1205** LAY. 3945 þa while ich beon on liue. *Ibid.* 11501 þe while þe ich beo [**1250** ham] on liue. **1864** CAPERN *Devon Provinc.* s.v. *Be*, I be going. **1864** TENNYSON *North. Farmer* 3, I beänt a fool.

f. *2 sing.* †**beest, be'st** (biːst, bɪst). *Obs.* exc. *dial.* [= OS. *bist*, OHG. *pis*, *pist*.] Forms: (1 **bis**), 1–3 **bist**, 3 **beost**, 3–4 **'best**, 4 **beste**, 4– **beest** (5 *north.* **bes**), 9 **beest, bist**.

(*a*) as distinct vb., or *future*.

c **1000** *Ags. Gosp.* Luke xxiii. 43 To-dæȝ þu bist mid me on paradiso. *c* **1160** *Hatton G.* ibid., To-daiȝ þu byst. **1205** LAY. 9843 Wið þine sune þu beost iuæid. *c* **1340** *Cursor M.* (Trin.) 2038 þou beste of his blessyng quyt. **1377** LANGL. *P. Pl.* B. v. 598 Bileue so · or þow beest nouȝte ysaued.

(*b*) as *present* = art. Rare in ME., but now widely spread in south. and midl. dialects.

c **950** *Lindisf. Gosp.* Matt. vi. 9 Fæder user ðu arð *vel* bist in heofnum. **1205** LAY. 3053 Al swa muchel þu bist [*v.r.* hart] worþ. **1848** KINGSLEY *Saint's Trag.* II. vii. 100 *Wood cutter*:—Be'est a keeper, man? **1862** BARNES *Rhymes Dorset Dial.* I. 61 Whatever bist about.

g. *3 sing.* **beeth, bes** (biːθ, biːz). *Obs.* exc. *dial.* Forms: 1–3 **bið**, 1 **byð**, 2 **bæð**, 2–3 **beoð**, 3 (**bideð**), **buþ**, 3–5 **beð, beþ, bueð**, 4 **byeþ**, 4–6 **beth(e**. *North.* 4 **betz, beis**, 4–5 **bes(e**, 6 *Sc.* **beis**. *South. dial.* 9 **be**.

(*a*) as distinct vb., or *future*.

c **825** *Vesp. Psalter* ciii. 3 Se milde bið allum unrehtwisnissum ðinum. **1205** LAY. 5763 Anan swa hit beoð auen. *c* **1340** *Cursor M.* (Fairf.) 3762 My hert bese [*Trin.* beþ] neuer broȝt in rest, bi-twix and þis Iacob be slayne. *a* **1400** *Chron. Eng.* 270 in Ritson *M.R.* II. 281 Non ne byth ther nevermore. **1535** STEWART *Cron. Scot.* I. 565 Traist weill..the feild this da beis ouris.

(*b*) as *present*.

c **1175** *Lamb. Hom.* 25 He bið wið-uten feire. *c* **1200** *Moral Ode* 39 in *E.E.P.* (1862) 24 So muchel bet [*v.r.* bið] his mihte. *a* **1300** *Cursor M.* 1175 It beis not sua [*v.r.* bes, beþ]. **1340** *Ayenb.* 54 þe holyist man byeþ..becaȝt. *c* **1386** CHAUCER *Knt's. T.* 1163 Nought beth forgeten the infortune of Mart [*Six-texts* was]. *c* **1460** *Towneley Myst.* 13 It bese the wars for thi sake. **1516–21** BUCKHM. in Ellis *Orig. Lett.* III. I. 217 It bethe matter that I am lothe..to troble you withall. *c* **1570** *Bp. St. Andrews* in *Scot. Poems 16th C.* II. 305 When Plutois palice beis provydit for them. *Mod. East-Anglian* Here he be.

h. *1–3 plural.* **be** (biː, bɪ). [In the other OTeut. langs. only repr. by OHG. *pirumes*, *pirut* (MHG. *birnt*, *bint*).] Forms: α. (type *beoth*, *beth*): 1–3 **béoð** (1 *Northumb.* **bíað, bið-on, bioð-on**, *Merc.* **bioþ, bið-on, beoþ-an**), 1–4 **béo**, 2 **bæð, byð**, 2–3 **bieð, buoð, buð(***ü***)**, 3–4 **bueð, buþ, beoth**, 2–5 **beð, beþ**, 4 **byeþ, beeþ**, 4–5 **beth**, 5– **beeth**, (6–7 *dial.* **beth**).

β. *Midl.* (type *beon*, *ben*, *been*, *be*): 2–4 **beon**, 2 **bienn, bin**, 2–3 **bien**, 2–6 **ben**, 3–4 **buen**, 4–5 **by**, 4–6 **bene**, 4–7 **been(e**, 5 (**byn(ne)**, 5–7 **bin** (*still dial.*), 6–7 **bee**, 4– **be**. *Negative*, *dial.* **ben't, beant**.

γ. *North.* 3 **bes**, 5 **bese**.

(*a*) as *future*.

c **825** *Vesp. Psalter* xcii. 14 Bioð ȝemoniȝfaldade in ældu. *c* **1175** *Cott. Hom.* 239 A domes deiȝ alle godes fend.. abroden bienn. **1205** LAY. 3057 Sone heo bið [hi beoð] ilaȝeð.

(*b*) as *present*.

c **1175** *Cott. Hom.* 219 Her beoð niȝen anglen hapes. *c* **1175** *Lamb. Hom.* 89 La hu ne beað þa..galileisce? *c* **1200** *Trin. Coll. Hom.* 39 þo bin þe gode word of holi boc. **1205** LAY. 4455 Whær beo ȝe mine cnihtes? *c* **1250** *Gen. & Ex.* 107 Watres ben her ðer-under. **1297** R. GLOUC. 368 Hey men, þat in Engelond beþ, Beþ ycome of þe Normans. *a* **1300** *K. Alis.* 4965 Men hy ben. *Ibid.* 6494 Faire wymmen heo buth. *c* **1300** *Beket* 174 To fewe ther beoth. **1307** *Elegy Edw. I.* ix, Our baners that bueth broht to grounde. **1340** *Ayenb.* 1 þise byeþ þe capiteles. *c* **1370** WYCLIF *Wks.* (1880) 33 þei been enemys. *c* **1385** CHAUCER *L.G.W.* 1029 We..Be now disclaundered. **1387** TREVISA *Higden* Rolls Ser. I. 321 þere by gracious tymes. *c* **1420** *Sir Amadace* xlviii, For-sothe thai bynne away. *c* **1460** FORTESCUE *Abs. & Lim. Mon.* (1714) 7 Thes two Princes beth of egall Astate. *Ibid.* 10 Which Lawys ben right good. **1485** CAXTON *Paris & V.* 16 Knyghtes and barons that been here. *a* **1500** *Rob. Hood* (Ritson) I. i. 213 My goodes beth sette and solde. **1534** TINDALE *Rom.* xiii. 1 The powers that be, are ordeyned of God. **1535** COVERDALE *Zech.* i. 19 What be these? **1548** —— *Erasm. Par. Rom.* II. 40 And what thinges bene they? **1557** *K. Arthur* (Copland) *Cont.*, The chapytres that ben conteyned in this present volume. **1582** BENTLEY *Mon. Matrones* ii. 65 They be never offended at anie thing. **1583** STUBBES *Anat. Abus.* II. 2 Surely they are, as all other countries and nations be. **1594** SHAKS. *Rich. III*, IV. iv. 93 Where is thy Husband now? Where be thy Brothers? **1611** BIBLE *2 Kings* vi. 16 They that be with vs are moe than they that be with them. **1669** MILTON *Accedence* Wks. (1847) 461/1 *Ego, tu, sui* be of the first Declension. *a* **1687** PETTY *Pol. Arith.* v. (1691) 87 There be Three distinct Legislative Powers.

¶ Examples of *dial.* and *arch.* retention of *been*, *bin*. *beth* for *be*, and of *be* for *are*.

1576 GASCOIGNE *Philomene* 63 (Arb.) 88 Such as true and stedfast louers bene. *a* **1581** CAMPION *Hist. Irel.* II. vii. (1633) 97 The Irish beene false by kinde. **1584** PEELE *Arraigum. Paris* Prol. 6 Th' unpartial daughters of Necessity Bin aids in her suit. **1586** FERNE *Blaz. Gentrie* 71 You zay zomewhat well vor vs that we beene the most necessary men. **1608** SHAKS. *Per.* II. Prol. 28 To seas, Where when men been, there's seldom ease. **1640** BROME *Antip.* II. ix. 271 We be none of your father, so we beant. **1651** JER. TAYLOR *Holy Dying* iv. §9 (1727) 178 Widows beth slothful, and children beth unkind. **1820** BYRON *Mar. Fal.* v. i. 169 And who be they? **1842** BARNES *Rhymes Dorset Dial.* I. 136 The carpets they do use, Ben't fit to tread..An' chairs an' couches be so neat, You mussen teäke em vor a seat. **1861** THACKERAY *Georges* ii. 114 Where be your painted houris? **1865** SWINBURNE *Queen Busahe* 367 If thou be keen To note things amiss that been. **1879** ESCOTT *England* I. 242 No alarming sound for the powers that be.

i. *Been*, *bin* was erroneously used by 16th c. Sc. writers, in supposed imitation of Chaucer, and by Byron (in supposed imitation of Shaks.) as *singular*.

1513 DOUGLAS *Æneis* I. Pref. 213, I will nocht say all Virgill bene als trew. **1552** LYNDESAY *Monarche* 5768 Gret dule, that day, to Iugis bene. **1556** LAUDER *Tractate* (1864) 65 Nothing..Different..Than bene the purest Creature That euir wes formit of nature. **1823** BYRON *Juan* XIII. xxvi, Also there bin another pious reason For making squares and streets anonymous.

2. *Present Subjunctive.*

* from stem *es-* (in weak form *'s-*).

a. *sing.* †OE. **sie, sí**. [= OFris. *sê*, OS., OHG. *sî*, *sîs*, *sî*, ON. *sê*, *sêr*, *sê*, Goth. *sijau*, *sijais*, *sijai*, Skr. *syām*, *syās*, *syāt*, OL. *siēm*, *siēs*, *siēt*, cl. L. *sīm*, *sīs*, *sīt*. In OE. all 3 persons were levelled under one form, though in ancient times the 1 pers. was distinct *siém*, *sión*.] Forms: 1 (1 pers. **siem, sion**) **síe, sié, sió, sé, siȝ**, 1–2 **sí, sý, sye, syo, seo**.

c **732** BÆDA *Death-song*, Naeniȝ uuiurthit thonc-snotturra than him tharf sie. *c* **1000** *Ags. Gosp.* Matt. xxiv. 3 Hwilc tacn sí þines tocymys. *Ibid.* v. 13 Buton þæt hit sy útaworpen, and sy [*v.r.* sí, siȝ] fram mannum fortreden. *c* **1160** *Hatton G.* ibid., Buton þæt hyt sye ut-aworpen, and syo fram mannen fortredon. *c* **1200** *Trin. Coll. Hom.* 91 Si lof Dauiðes bern, blesced bie he. **1205** LAY. 14893 Alre king si [**1250** beo] he ærmest. *Ibid.* 24759 Hail seo [**1250** beo] þu Arður king!

b. *plural.* †OE. **sien, síe, sín**. [= OS. *sîn*, OFris. *sê*, OHG. *sîmês*, *sît*, *sîn*, ON. *sêm*, *sêt*, *sê*, Goth. *sijaima*, *sijaiþ*, *sijaina*, Skr. *syāma*, *syāta*, *syús*, OL. *siēmus*, *siētis*, *siēnt*, cl. L. *sīmus*, *sītis*, *sīnt*.] Forms: 1 **sien, sín, sýn, síe, sie, sé, sæ**, 2 **syen**, 3 **seon** (**seoð**).

c **950** *Lindisf. Gosp.* Matt. vi. 1 þæt ȝie se ȝeseno. *c* **975** *Rushw. G.* ibid., þæt ȝe sie ȝeseanæ. *c* **1000** *Ags. G.* ibid., þæt ȝe sín ȝeherede. *c* **1160** *Hatton G.* ibid., þæt ȝe syen ȝeherede. **1205** LAY. 13837 Wh[ah]æt cnihtes ȝe seon [**1250** beo].

¶ A present subj. from stem *wes-*, singular *wese*, plural *wesen*, also existed in OE., in poetic use.

c **1000** *Ags. Ps.* cv. 37 Wese swa, wese swa, þurh eall wide ferhð. *Ibid.* lxvii. 5 þa þe wydewum syn wraðe..oþþe steopcildum wesen strange fæderas.

** from verb *be*.

c. *sing.* **be**. Forms: 1 **bío**, 1–3 **béo**, 2 **bo, bie**, 4–5 **bi, by**, 4– **be**, (4–7 **bee**).

a **1000** *Metr. Boeth.* x. 65 Hwæt iow æfre þy bet bío oððe þince. *c* **1200** *Trin. Coll. Hom.* 91 Blesced bie he þe cumeð a godes name. *Ibid.* 107 Be swo it beo. *a* **1250** *Owl & Night.* 566 Thu gredest suich thu bo wod. **1340** *Ayenb.* 219 By hit to þe bodie, by hit to þe zaule. **1377** LANGL. *P. Pl.* B. VI. 207 Be þow went, They wil worche ful ille. **1382** WYCLIF *Gen.* xxvii. 21 Whethir thow be [*v.r.* art] my sone Esau, or noon [**1611** Whether thou bee my very sonne Esau, or not]. *c* **1385** CHAUCER *L.G.W.* 1848 'Be as be may,' quod she. **1582** BENTLEY *Mon. Matrones* ii. 7 If thou be my father. **1611** BIBLE *Jer.* xvii. 5 Cursed be the man that trusteth in man. **1716** ADDISON *Drummer* v. i, Look you if he ben't with my lady. **1830** TENNYSON *Dream Fair Wom.* 251, I am that Rosamond, whom men call fair, If what I was I be. *Mod.* Be he who he may, he has no right here.

(*b*) In the 2nd sing., after *if*, *though*, etc., **beest**, properly an indicative form, was common in 16th and 17th c., and is regularly used by Shakspere.

c **1600** *Rob. Hood* (Ritson) II. ii. 38 Although thou beest in haste. **1606** SHAKS. *Ant. & Cl.* I. v. 59 Bee'st thou sad, or merrie, The violence of either thee becomes. **1667** MILTON *P.L.* I. 84 If thou beest he; But O how fall'n! **1678** CUDWORTH *Intell. Syst.* 462 Whether thou beest a certain Divine Force and Soul.

(*c*) In the 3rd sing., *beis* was formerly used in Sc.

1513 DOUGLAS *Æneis* XII. iv. 70 Bot gif so beis, Mars.. The victory..grantis ws. **1609** SKENE *Reg. Maj.* 79 Gif it beis within borgh. **1641** *Kirkcudbr. War-Comm. Min. Bk.* (1855) 62 Gif neid beis, to assist thame.

d. *plural.* **be**. Forms: 1–3 **beon**, 2–5 **ben**, 2– **be**.

c **1175** *Lamb. Hom.* 73 þeh alle men beon of hore sunnen iclensed. **1205** LAY. 938 þæt we beon iquemed. *c* **1340** *Cursor M.* (Trin.) 14784 But of o þing in were be we. **1362** LANGL. *P. Pl.* A. v. 418 Tyl matynes and masse be do. *c* **1450** *Merlin* x. 150 Loke now that ye be larger. **1611** BIBLE *1 Sam.* xxiii. 21 Blessed be yee of the Lord. **1632** SANDERSON *12 Serm.* 96 If we be of the Spiritualtie. **1728** T. SHERIDAN *Persius* (1739) Ded. 5 Although you be now removed to another Soil. *Mod.* If we be in time, we shall find him at home.

¶ For these the indicative forms have been occasionally substituted since the 15th c., and are now chiefly used after *if*, *though*, *unless*, etc.

1483 CAXTON *G. de la Tour* B vij, Thus oughte euery good woman..to do his commandment, is it right or wrong. **1611** BIBLE *1 John* iv. 1 Try the spirits whether they are of God. **1667** MARVELL *Corr.* II. xxxvi. 81, I can not be wanted though I am missing. *Mod.* I never go unless I am specially invited. Tell me if they are in sight.

II. Inflexions of stem *wes-*; now replaced by *be*.

3. *Present Imperative.*

a. from *wes-*: †OE. **wes**, *pl.* **wesað**. *Obs.* [= OS. *wes*, *wesað*, OFris. *wese*, *wesath*. OHG. *wis*, *wesat*, ON. *ver*, *verið*.] Forms: *sing.* 1 **wes**, (*north.* **wæs**), 2 **wæsse**, 3 **wæs**. *pl.* 1 **wesað, wese(ȝe)**, (*north.* **wosas**), 2 **wese(ȝe)**. (After 1200 only in phrase *wæs hail!* in Layamon. See WASSAIL.)

a **1000** *Andreas* (Gr.) 540 Wes þu ȝebletsod! *c* **1000** *Ags. Ps.* cxiii. 23 Wesað ȝe ȝebletsade. *c* **1000** *Ags. Gosp.* Luke i. 28 Hal wes ðu! *c* **1160** *Hatton G.* ibid., Hal wæsse þu. —— Matt. xxviii. 9 Hale wese ȝe [*Lindisf.* Wosað ȝie hal; *Rushw.* Beoþ hale]. **1205** LAY. 14970 Lauerd king, wæs hail! [**1250** Louerd king, wassail!].

b. from *be*: *sing.* and *pl.* **be** (biː, bɪ). Forms: *sing.* 1–3 **béo**, (2 **ibeo**, 3 **bo, bi**), 4– **be**, (6–7 **bee**). *pl.* 1–3 **béoð, béo(ȝe)**, 3–4 **buð**, 4–5 **beoth, beþ, beth(e**, *north.* 4–5 **bes, beys** (occas. used as sing.), 6 *Sc.* **beis**. *Negative*, *dial.* **beant, baint**, *mod. Sc.* **binna, bynna**.

a **1000** *Satan* 733 (Gr.) Lá! béo nu on yfele. —— *Andreas* 1611 (Gr.) Ne béoþ ȝe tó forhte. *c* **1200** *Trin. Coll. Hom.* 49 Buð admode alse duue. *Ibid.* 256 I-hered ibeo þu swete þing. **1205** LAY. 1499 Hal beo þu Brutus! *Ibid.* 19173 Beoð stille! beoð stille! cnihtes inne halle. *c* **1230** *Ancr. R.* 174 Ne beo ȝe nout Semei, auh beoð Hester. *a* **1250** *Owl & Night.* 262 Bo nu stille, and lat me speke. *a* **1300** *Cursor M.* 10454 Be still, or ga me heiþen fra. *Ibid.* 11161 Bi þou ful traist. *a* **1300** *Havelok* 2246 Bes of him ful glad and blithe. *c* **1320** *Seuyn Sag.* (W.) 3906 Bese meri, & mase gude chere. **1382** WYCLIF *Isa.* i. 16 Be ȝee washen, beth clene [**1388** be ȝe clene]. *c* **1386** CHAUCER *Milleres T.* 392 (Harl.) Beoth [*all 6-texts*, be] merye, for the flood passeth anon. *c* **1400** *Destr. Troy* II. 649 Bes wakond and warly. *c* **1440** LOVE *Bonavent. Mirr.* xxvii. 56 (Sherard MS.), Be þou a man of prayer. **1480** CAXTON *Chron. Eng.* cxcvii. 175 Bethe ware sirs. **1610** SHAKS. *Temp.* I. ii. 38 Obey and be attentiue. **1611** BIBLE *Matt.* vi. 16 When yee fast, bee not as the hypocrites. **1816** SCOTT *Old Mort.* 111 She says to him, Binna cast doun, but gird yoursell up to the great task o' the day. **1839** LONGF. *Ps. of Life*, Be not like dumb driven cattle, Be a hero in the strife!

4. *Present Infinitive.*

a. from *wes-*: †OE. **wes-an**. *Obs.* [= OS., OHG. *wesan*, OFris. *wesa*, ON. *vera*, Goth. *wisan*.] Forms: 1 **wesan**, *north.* **wosa, wossa**. Replaced in 11th c. by *beon*.

a **1000** *Cædmon's Gen.* 283 (Gr.) Ic mæȝ wesan god swá he. *c* **950** *Lindisf. Gosp.* Matt. vi. 8 Nallas ȝe ðonne wosa ȝelic him. [*c* **975** *Rushw. G.*, Ne scule forþon ȝelice beon him.]

b. from *be*: **be** (biː, bɪ). Forms: 1–4 **béon** (1 *north.* **bían**), 2–5 **ben**, 3– **be**; also 2 **bien, boen**, 3–4 **buen**, 4 **byen, bue, by, bi**, 4–6 **bene, been**, 4–7 **bee**.

975 [see prec.]. **1070** *O.E. Chron.* (Parker MS.) Hwi hi ðær beon ne mihton. **1131** *Ibid.* (Laud) an. 1127 þær mihte wel ben abuton twenti. *c* **1175** *Cott. Hom.* 229 Naman ne mai bien ȝehalden. *c* **1200** *Moral Ode* 172 in *Lamb. Hom.* 171 Bliþe mai he þanne buen. *a* **1300** *K. Horn* 446 þat schal beon idone: þu schalt beo dubbed kniȝt. **1280** *Signs bef. Judgem.* 33 in *E.E.P.* (1862) 8 þe first tokning sal be þusse. *a* **1300** *Cursor M.* 1154 þou sal bi halden vile. *c* **1340** *Ibid.* (Trin.) 4601 Suche defaute shal ben of breed, *c* **1380** *Sir Ferumb.* 4137 þay lete it bene. *c* **1386** CHAUCER *Franklin's T.* 36 Love wil nouht buen [*v.r.* been, ben(e, be] constreyned. *c* **1440** *Morte Arth.* (Roxb.) 2 That auntre shall..by spoke of on euery syde. **1485** MALORY *Arthur* (1817) II. 378 Wete ye wel he wold ben here. *Mod.* He bids me be quiet.

c. *Dative Infinitive*: 1 **to béonne**, 2 **to bienne, to boen**, 3–4 **to byenne, to buen, to bue**, 3–5 **to bene**, 4–5 **to ben**, 4– **to be**.

c **1000** *Ags. Gosp.* Luke ii. 49 Me ȝebyrað to beonne [*Lindisf.* to wosanne] on þam ðingum ðe mínes fæder synt. *c* **1175** *Cott. Hom.* 203 To boen moder of swich sune. *Ibid.* 233 [Hit] áh to bienne. ? *a* **1200** *Solomon & Sat.* (1848) 270 Betere were to bue wis. *c* **1300** *Harrow. Hell* 67 Forte buen oure fere. **1340** *Ayenb.* 169 þet wes y-woned to byenne þe ealde manere at rome. **1398** TREVISA *Barth. De P.R.* I. (1495) 6 He knoweth al thynges present and to be. *a* **1440** *Sir Degrev.* 382 He prayd the portere ffor to bene his mesengere. *c* **1440** LOVE *Bonavent. Mirr.* x. 25 (Gibbs MS.), What tyme þey knewen þe chylde sought to bene [*v.r.* ben] slayne. **1602**

SHAKS. *Ham.* III. i. 55 To be, or not to be, that is the Question.

5. *Present Participle.*

a. from stem *wes-*: †OE. **wesende**. *Obs.* [= OS., OFris. *wesand*, OHG. *wesantêr*, ON. *vesandi*, from 12th c. *verandi*, Goth. *wisands*.]

a **1000** *Beowulf* 750 Ic hine cúðe cniht wesende.

b. from *be*: **being** ('biːɪŋ). Forms: 1–4 **béonde**, 4 **beende**, 4–7 *north.* **beand**; 4– **being**, (4 **beoing**, 4–6 **beyng(e**, 6 **bying**, 7 **beinge**, 8 **beeing**).

c **1050** in Wülcker *Voc.* /398 *Existentibus*, wesendum, beondum. *a* **1300** *Cursor M.* (Gött.) 4080 His breder mast in wildrenes beand. *c* **1340** *Ibid.* (Laud) 9428 To Adam being in paradice. *c* **1340** *Ibid.* (Trin.) 15312 In my blisse beonde. **1382** WYCLIF *Rom.* Prol., New causes beende, also questiounes to comen aftir. **1475** CAXTON *Jason* 69 b, None of them beyng in the arke. **1535** COVERDALE *1 Kings* xvi. 4 Who so beynge of him dyeth in the felde. *c* **1538** STARKEY *England* II. i. 159 Some Bying to lytyl, some to grete. **1615** G. SANDYS *Trav.* 115 The buildings now being, are meane and few. *Mod.* For the time being.

III. Parts from stem *wes-* only.

6. *Past Indicative.*

a. *1* and *3 sing.* **was** (wɒz, wəz, wɒs). [= Goth., OHG., OS., OFris. *was*, ON. *var*.] Forms: 1–3 **wæs**, 2–6 **wes**, 3– **was**, (3 **weos**, 4 **wass(e**, **wase**, **wesse**, **wees**, **watz**, 5 **wys**, 6 **wes**). *Negative* 1 **næs**, 3 **neas**, **nes**, 3–5 **nas**, 5 **nasse**. Until 16th or 17th c., *was* rimed with *pass*, etc. In *was 't* = was it, it has still the *s* sound. (For *was* used in the plural, see below **were** ¶).

c **950** *Lindisf. Gosp.* John i. 1 In fruma uæs uord. *c* **1000** *Ags. G.* ibid., On frymðe wæs word. *c* **1160** *Hatton G.* ibid., On anginne ærest wæs word. *c* **1175** *Lamb. Hom.* 17 He wes iboren of ure lefdi. *c* **1200** *Trin. Coll. Hom.* 67 Al mankin, þe was..and nu is. **1205** LAY. 2984 þat þæt wæs þe olde king. *Ibid.* 3466 And ich nas na wurdra, þenne ich nes weldinde. *a* **1300** *Cursor M.* 1074 Wid þe cheke bon of ane asse Men say þat abel slain wasse. *Ibid.* 12695 Sco was wit barn. *c* **1340** *Gaw. & Gr. Knt.* 1 þe assaut watz sesed at Troye. *c* **1420** *Chron. Vilod.* 799 A lytille child ybore þer wys. *c* **1420** *Pallad. on Husb.* IV. 886 Gentiler in kynde never nasse. **1475** CAXTON *Jason* 6 Ther was grete nombre of speeres. **1611** BIBLE *John* i. 1 In the beginning was the Word, and the Word was with God.

¶ Dialectally *were*, *war* occur: hence the negative *warn't*, *wa'n't*, in 18th c. dramatists.

1535 *Bury Wills* (1850) 126 My rynge whych wher my wyffys. **1633** BROME *North. Lass* II. ii, He sed I were a deaft Lasse. **1775** SHERIDAN *Rivals* I. ii. (1883) 85 It wa'n't fit for a Christian to read. **1837** DICKENS *Pickw.* xxxiv, Was one of those voices Pickwick's? Yes, it were, sir. **1865** —— *Mut. Fr.* xii, Warn't I troubled?

b. *2 sing.* **wast** (wɒst, wəst), orig. **were**. [in Goth. *wast*, ON. *vast*, *vart*, OHG., OS. *wâri*, OFris. *wêre*.] Forms: 1 **wǽre**, 2–6 **were**, (3 **wore**), 6–7 **werst**, **wart**, 6– **wert**, **wast**. *North.* 3– **was**. *Negative* 1–3 **nære**, **nere**. The modern analogical *wast* has displaced the etymological *were* (with grammatical ablaut) chiefly under the influence of Tindale and the Bible; the intermediate *wert* (Shakspere's form) prevailed in literature during the 17th and 18th c., and has been used by many 19th century writers.

c **1000** *Ags. Gosp.* John i. 48 þa þu wære [*Rushw.* were] under þam fictréowe. *c* **1300** *Havelok* 684 Cherl, als thou er wore. *a* **1300** *Cursor M.* (Cott.) 6248 Ta þat wand þat þou was wont [*Trin. MS.* þou were] ber in þi hand. **1382** WYCLIF *John* i. 48 Whanne thou were vndir the fyge tree. [**1534** TINDALE, *and all subseq. versions*, When thou wast]. *a* **1520** *Myrr. Our Ladye* 178 Thou O vyrgyn..that were souerayne delyte to god hymselfe..were ioye to aungels. **1611** SHAKS. *Wint. T.* II. i. 174 Thou wer't borne a foole. **1617** HIERON *Wks.* (1628) II. 122 Why did I forget that thou wart an Observer? **1627** HAKEWILL *Apologie* (1630) 83 Thou, who werst a Christian before. **1738** GLOVER *Leonidas* III. 560 Thou, who once wert Lacedæmon's chief. **1748** RICHARDSON *Clarissa* (1811) II. 204 Wert thou bid to come up? **1820** SHELLEY *To Skylark* i, Hail to thee, blithe spirit! Bird thou never wert. **1822** HAZLITT *Table-t.* ser. II. iv. (1869) 91 Thou wert damned. **1875** BROWNING *Aristoph. Apol.* 232 Thou wast less friendly far than thou didst seem.

c. *plural.* **were** (wɛə(r), wɜː(r), wə(r)). [= OFris. *wêran*, OS. *wârun*, OHG. *wârumes*, *wârut*, *wârun*, ON. *vǫ́rum*, *várum*, *váruð*, *váru*, Goth. *wesum*, *wesuþ*, *wesun*.] Forms: 1 **wærun**, 1–2 **wæron**, 2 **wæren**, 2–5 **weren**, 3– **were**; (2 **waren**, 3–4 **weore(n**, **wore(n**, 3–6 **ware**, 4 **warre**, **wair**, **quar**, 4–6 **werne**, **warn**, **wer**, **war**, **wher**, **whar**, 5 **werene**, **werun**, 6 **warren**, **werren**.) Also 4– **was**. *Negative* 1–3 **næron**, **neoren**, **nere**.

(For *were* used in the sing. see above, **was** ¶).

c **1000** *Ags. Gosp.* John i. 24 þá wǽron of sundor-halᵹan. **1160** *Hatton G.* ibid., þá wæren. *c* **1175** *Lamb. Hom.* 15 þas laȝen weren from Moyses. *c* **1200** *Trin. Coll. Hom.* 31 Hie waren swiðe..ofdredde. *Ibid.* 143 Seuen awerȝede gostes ware on hire. *c* **1250** *Gen. & Ex.* 2446 Swilc woren egipte laȝes. *a* **1300** *Havelok* 717 Hise two doutres, that faire wore. *a* **1300** *Cursor M.* (Gött.) 11490 þar iesu and his moder warn [*v.r.* wern, werne]. *c* **1340** *Ibid.* (Trin.) 388 Boþe were [*v.r.* war, ware, wan] made sonne and mone. *c* **1386** CHAUCER *Prol.* 28 And wel we weren esed atte beste. *Ibid.* 41 And eek in what array that they were inne. *c* **1410** LOVE *Bonavent. Mirr.* x. (Gibbs MS.) þei þat werene so noble. **1462** *Paston Lett.* 453 II. 104 Your brother and Debenham were at words. **1557** BARCLAY (Paynell) *Jugurth* 5 b, What tyme ye warre without riches. **1611** BIBLE *Num.* xiii. 33 Wee were in our owne sight as grashoppers, and so we were in their sight.

¶ The plural had formerly also *was*; almost universally so in 16–18th c. with *you* when used as a singular. Still *dial.* in all persons.

c **1340** *Cursor M.* (Trin.) 944 Into þe world þere þei made was. *c* **1430** *Syr Gener.* 5674 Traitoures was him euer loothe. *c* **1460** FORTESCUE *Abs. & Lim. Mon.* 108 When thay came togeders, thay was..occupyyd with their own maters. **1588** SHAKS. *Tit. A.* IV. i. 38 There was more then one..I, more there was. **1671** WILKINS in Grew *Anat. Plants* Pref., You was very happy in the choice of this Subject. **1684** BUNYAN *Pilg.* II. 76, I suppose you was in a dream. **1735** WALPOLE *Corr.* (1820) I. 3 When you was at Eton. **1749** FIELDING *Tom Jones* VI. v, What was you reading when I came in? **1811** MISS AUSTEN *Sense & Sens.* (1870) II. i. 122, I felt sure that you was angry with me. **1837** DICKENS *Pickw.* xxxiii, You was to come to him at six o'clock. *Mod. dial.* They was here.

7. *Past Subjunctive.*

a. *1 and 3 sing.* **were** (wɛə(r), wɜː(r), wə(r)). [= OFris. *wêre*, ON. *væri*, OS. and OHG. *wâri*, Goth. 1 *wesjau*, 3 *wesi*.] Forms: 1–2 **wǽre**, 2– **were**, (2–3 **weore**, 3–4 **wor(e**, 4–5 **ware**, **war**, 6 **weare**.)

c **1175** *Lamb. Hom.* 5 Er þis were. *a* **1250** *Owl & Night.* 1312 ȝif ich were a bisimere. *a* **1300** *Havelok* 1938 Me wore leuere I were lame. *a* **1300** *Cursor M.* 1599 þou he war [*v.r.* were] wrath it was na wrang. *c* **1440** LOVE *Bonavent. Mirr.* x. 25 (Gibbs MS.) As he were a pore man. **1486** *Bk. St. Albans* A iiij, As it ware the mawe of a pegeon. **1529** MORE in *Four C. Eng. Lett.* 12 What way wer best to take. **1788** BURNS Oh, were I on Parnassus' Hill! **1852** MISS YONGE *Cameos* I. vi. 42 By my faith it were treason. **1863** GEO. ELIOT *Romola* x, If I were only a Theocritus. *Mod.* Would I were there!

b. *2 sing.* **wert** (wɛət, wɜːt), formerly **were**. [= OFris. *wêre*, ON. *værir*, OS. and OHG. *wâris*, Goth. *weseis*. The final *-t* in Eng., formerly *-est*, *-st*, is on the analogy of the indic.] Forms: 1–2 **wǽre**, 2–6 **were**; 6–7 **werest**, **werst**; 6– **wert**.

c **1300** *Harrow. Hell* 131 Were thou among men. **1535** COVERDALE *2 Esdras* v. 30 Though thou werest enemye. —— *Ezek.* xxviii. 6 As though thou werst God. **1611** BIBLE *Rev.* iii. 15, I would thou wert cold or hote [WYCLIF, COVERD., CRANMER, *Rhem.* were, *Genev.* werest]. *a* **1796** BURNS Oh, wert thou in the cauld blast.

c. *plural.* **were** (wɛə(r), wɜː(r), wə(r)) with grammatical ablaut. [= OFris. *wêre*, ON. *værim*, *-ið*, *-i*, OS. *wârin*, OHG. *wârîmês*, *-ît*, *-în*, Goth. *weseima*, *-eiþ*, *-eina*.] Forms: 1–2 **wǽren**, 2–4 **weren**, (3 **weoren**, 3–4 **woren**, **waren**), 3– **were**, (3 **weore**, 4 **wore**, **weere**, 4–6 **war(e**, 6 **wer**.)

1205 LAY. 50 Out of þeowedome, freo þat heo weoren [**1250** were]. *a* **1300** *Havelok* 2661 And fouhten so thei woren wode. **1480** *Robt. Devyll* 10 Ye were better lette me a lone. **1571** LYNDESAY *MS. Collect.*, Swownand, lyk as thai war bot life. **1611** BIBLE *John* xv. 19 If ye were of the world, the world would loue his owne [So TINDALE, etc.] **1766** FORDYCE *Serm. Yng. Wom.* II. viii. 4 Were these extinguished, what were this world? **1868** BROWNING *Ring & Bk.* II. 1153 Were they verily the lady's own..she must be the fondest of the frail.

¶ For the singular, the indicative form *was* was common in 17–18th c.; it was even used for the plural by writers who used *was* in the plural indicative.

1684 BUNYAN *Pilg.* II. 77 As if one was awake. **1713** BEVERIDGE *Private Th.* II. (1730) 46 Which certainly would be the greatest Absurdity..was not they God as well as He. **1760** STERNE *Serm. Yorick* viii. (1773) 88 A man, of whom, was you to form a conjecture, etc. **1768** —— *Sent. Journ.* (1778) I. 85 Was I in a desert, I would find out, etc. **1787** G. WHITE *Selborne* v. (1789) 11 The manor of Selborne, was it strictly looked after..would swarm with game.

IV. Parts from *be* only.

8. *Past Participle*: **been** (biːn, bɪn). Forms: *Southern* ? 1–2 **ᵹebéon**, 2–3 **ibeon**, **ibon**, **iben**, **ibi**, 3–4 **ibeo**, **beo**, 3–5 **ibe**, **ybe**, 4 **yben**, **by**, 4–6 **be**. *Northern* ? 2–3 **beon**, 3–7 **ben**, 4 **beyn**, **buen**, 4–7 **bene**, 5–6 **byn(ne**, 6–8 **bin**, 7– **beene**, 5– **been**. Not known in OE., where no pa. pple. of any of these verbs (*am*, *was*, *be*) appears. The common literary form in 14–15th c. was *be*, before the general acceptance of the northern *ben*, *bene*. South-western dialects have still *a-be* = *ibe*. (In U.S. often pronounced *ben*.)

a **1107** *OE. Chron.* (Laud MS.) an. 1096 He heafde ᵹebeon on þes cynges swicdome. *c* **1175** *Lamb. Hom.* 159 Wel longe ich habbe child ibon [*v.r.* iben, ibeo]. *c* **1175** *Cott. Hom.* 239 þus hit hafð ibi and is. *c* **1200** ORMIN 8399 Haffde he beon. *Ibid.* 2311 Hafde ben. **1205** LAY. 8325 þu hafuest ibeon [**1250** beon] ouer-cumen. *c* **1230** *Ancr. R.* 316 Ich habbe ibeon fol. *a* **1300** *Cursor M.* (Cott.) 14638 War yemed haf I ben [*Gött.* bene]. *c* **1300** *Beket* 133 Lute we habbeth to-gadere I-beo. *c* **1300** *Harrow. Hell* 173 So longe we haveth buen herynne. **1375** BARBOUR *Bruce* I. 527 Thai mycht nocht haiff beyn tane. *c* **1375** WYCLIF *Serm.* xliii. Sel. Wks. 1871 II. 346 Trespassours, þat wolden..have be ever wantoun. **1377** LANGL. *P. Pl.* B. XIV. 95 As it neuere had ybe. *c* **1386** CHAUCER *Prol.* 60 At mortal batailles hadde he be [*v.r.* ben, been] fiftene. —— *Merch. T.* 1157 A man that longe hath blynd ybe [*v.r.* ibe, blynde be]. *c* **1400** *Destr. Troy* XII. 8913 þat any dede has be don. *c* **1420** *Sir Amadace* xxxix, A mon that hase alle way bynne kynde. *c* **1450** *Merlin* XV. 239 Where the battle had I-be. **1455** E. CLERE in *Four C. Eng. Lett.* 5 Nor wist not where he had be, whils he had be seke til now. **1483** *Act 1 Rich. III*, i. §1 As..if this Act had not be made. **1526** TINDALE *John* v. 5 Which had bene [**1582** *Rhem.* been] diseased. —— xiv. 9 Haue I bene [**1611** bin] so long tyme with you?. **1575** J. STILL *Gamm. Gurton* v. ii, Had my hens be stolne ehe one. **1579** LYLY *Euphues* (1636) E iij b, Had it not bin better for thee? **1560** JEWEL *Serm. Matt.* ix. 37–8 As if they had byn a flock of sheepe. *c* **1645** HOWELL *Lett.* (1726) 23 Having bin so rocked and shaken at Sea. **1864** TENNYSON *En. Ard.* 420 You have been as God's good angel in our house.

B. Signification and uses.

[The primary sense appears to have been that of branch II below, 'to occupy a place' (i.e. *to sit*, *stand*, *lie*, etc.) in some specified place; thence the more abstract branch I was derived by abstracting the notion of particular place, so as to emphasize that of actual existence, 'to be somewhere, no matter where, to be in the universe, or realm of fact, to have a place among existing things, to exist.' Branch III was derived from II by weakening the idea of actual presence, into the merely intellectual conception of 'having a place' in a class of notions, or 'being identical with' another notion: 'centaurs are imaginary creatures' = 'centaurs have their place in the class of creatures of the imagination.' Branch IV is an obvious extension of III: cf. 'it was annoying to me,' with 'it was annoying me.']

I. *absolutely*: To have or take place in the world of fact, to exist, occur, happen.

1. To have place in the objective universe or realm of fact, to exist; *also*, to exist in life, to live.

c **1000** ÆLFRIC *Exod.* iii 14 Ic eom se þe eom cwæþ he..se ðe ys me sende to eow. *c* **1340** *Cursor M.* (Fairf.) 9732 This world..hast þou made fadir þorogh me to bene. **1548** UDALL *Erasm. Par.* Matt. xxii. 105 They beleue..nothyng to be but that whiche they see. **1587** GOLDING *De Mornay* iii. 26 All things that are, or euer were, or shall hereafter bee. **1611** BIBLE *Gen.* v. 24 Enoch walked with God: and hee was not, for God tooke him. **1698** DRYDEN *Æneid* II. 438 Troy is no more, and Ilium was a Town. **1732** POPE *Ess. Man* I. 109 To Be, contents his natural desire. **1810** SCOTT *Lady of L.* III. i, How are they blotted from the things that be. **1823** BYRON *Juan* IX. xxiv, Tyrants and sycophants have been and are. **1827** CARLYLE *Misc.* (1857) I. 61 God is, nay alone is. **1837** —— *Fr. Rev.* I. i. 6 So much that was not is beginning to be.

b. with *there*. [See THERE, for its use with verbs.]

a **1300** *Cursor M.* 10783 There bene reasons wretyn sere That god wold she spousid were. *c* **1386** CHAUCER *Pers. T.* ¶21 Ther ben thre acciouns of penitence. **1426** AUDELAY *Poems* 16 Ther bene bot feu truly. **1562** J. HEYWOOD *Prov. & Epigr.* (1867) 86 Thers no redempcion. *a* **1586** *Answ. Cartwright* 79 There were of the princes that tooke his parte. **1650** BAXTER *Saints' R.* I. i. (1662) 3 There's few will deny, that God knows. **1711** POPE *Rape Lock* 79 Some nymphs there are, too conscious of their face. *Mod.* There are photographs and photographs.

2. To come into existence, come about, happen, occur, take place, be acted or done.

(*To become*, *come about*, was the OE. and early ME. sense of *béon*, while still a distinct vb., before it became blended with *am*, *was*.)

c **950** *Lindisf. Gosp.* Matt. xxiv. 3 Cueð us, hoenne ðas biðon. *c* **975** *Rushw. G.* ibid., Sæᵹe us hwænne þas beoþ. *c* **1175** *Lamb. Hom.* 177 Hu scal þat bon? *c* **1350** *Will. Palerne* 1930 Manly on þe morwe þat mariage schuld bene. **1530** PALSGR. 421/1 Be as be may, *vaille que vaille*. **1562** J. HEYWOOD *Prov. & Epigr.* (1867) 43 Be as be maie is no bannyng. **1775** SHERIDAN *Rivals* in *Casquet. Lit.* (1877) IV. 37/2 Your husband that shall be. *a* **1804** NELSON in Nicolas *Disp.* II. 457 Marry..speedily, or the to be Mrs. Berry will have very little of your company. *Mod.* When is the wedding to be? The flower-show was last week.

3. To be the case or the fact, *esp.* in the phrases *so be*, *be it that* = if it be the case that, suppose that, and the arch. or dial. ***being***, ***being that*** = it being the case that, seeing that, since. Hence the adverb HOWBEIT.

c **1314** *Guy Warw.* 203 Bi so that he wille kisse me, Euer eft we schul frendes be. *c* **1400** MAUNDEV. v. 40 Beso it be not aȝenst his Lawe. **1547** BRENDE *Let.* in Tytler *Hist. Scot.* (1864) III. 380 If so be he will stand. **1549** LATIMER *Serm. bef. Edw. VI*, vi. I. 178 Be it so, the Corinthians had no such contentions among them. **1611** BIBLE *Job* xix. 4 And be it indeed that I haue erred. **1851** J. HUME *Repent.* iv. Poems 96 So-be the haunting sense of wrong..Were loosen'd from his breast.

1528 T. MORE *Heresyes* III. Wks. 214/2 Beyng though they wer but men. **1597** SHAKS. *2 Hen. IV*, II. i. 199 You loyter heere too long, being you are to take Souldiers vp. **1641** BEST *Farm. Bks.* (1856) 120 They went all for halfe gates, beinge that they coulde not bee discerned. **1641** MILTON *Ch. Discip.* II. Wks. (1851) 61 Being they are Church-men, we may rather suspect, etc. **1659** PEARSON *Creed* To Rdr., Being the Creed comprehendeth the principles of our religion, it must, etc. **1692** LADY RUSSELL *Lett.* 26 May, I believe your newspapers..tell you all, but being there is nothing newer, I would do it too. **1815** SCOTT *Guy M.* ix, With whom he himself had no delight in associating, 'being that he was addicted unto profane and scurrilous jests.'

4. To remain or go on in its existing condition; in the archaic phrase ***let be*** = let alone, leave as it is; leave off, cease; *Sc.* omit, leave out.

1297 R. GLOUC. 153 Uter let al this be. *c* **1380** *Sir Ferumb.* 281 Al ȝour mornyng leteþ now ben. *c* **1386** CHAUCER *Frere's Prol.* 25 Telleth your tale, and let the sompnour be. **1393** LANGL. *P. Pl.* C. v. 174 Let be al ȝoure ianglyng. *c* **1450** *Merlin* i. 16 Let me be, and beth in pes. **1513** DOUGLAS *Æneis* IV. vi. 159 With thi complayntis..Lat be to vex me. *Ibid.* IX. Prol. 25 All lous langage and lychtnes lattand be. **1530** PALSGR. 607/1 Let be this nycenesse, my frende. **1596** SPENSER *F.Q.* II. vii. 18 Lett be thy bitter scorne. **1611** BIBLE *Matt.* xxvii. 49 Let be, let vs see whether Elias will come. **1775** H. BAILLIE *Lett.* I. 51 (JAM.) Morton, Roxburgh, let be Haddington or Stirling, were not of sufficient shoulder. *Ibid.* I. 170 He had never any such resolution, let be plot.

1869 BLACKMORE *Lorna D.* xv. (1872) 89, I thank you; let me be.

b. Here may be included an idiom in which *be* is practically = 'continue, remain,' though the analysis is not clear, and there is apparently confusion of structure.

1601 SHAKS. *All's well* II. i. 94 Ile fit you, And not be all day neither. **1865** CARLYLE *Fredk. Gt.* IV. XII. iv. 151 Town-Officer is some considerable time before he can return [? = It is some considerable time before Town Officer can return. But cf. the following, which have various relations with other senses: **1570** ASCHAM *Scholem.* I. (Arb.) 35, I haue bene longer in describing the nature..of the quicke and hard witte than..the matter doth require. **1600** SHAKS. *A. Y. L.* II. v. 34 He hath bin all this day to looke you. **1628** DIGBY *Voy. Medit.* 1868 7 And they having bin a long time from any port. *Mod.* I was a long while unable to arise; I was [also, it was] a long while before I could rise. You have been rather long about it. Go, but don't be long! Cf. also such phrases as 'We are ten miles, an hour's drive, two hours, from the nearest railway station,' which come under 5.]

II. With adverb or prepositional phrase: stating *where* or *how*, i.e. in what place or state a thing is. [= Sp., Pg. *estar* as distinct from *ser.*]

5. To have or occupy a place (*i.e.* to sit, stand, lie, hang, etc.—the posture not being specified or regarded) *somewhere*, the 'where' being expressed either by an adverb or a preposition with object. Expressing the most general relation of a thing to its place: To have one's personality, substance, or presence, to be present, so as to find oneself, or be to be found (*in*, *at*, or *near* a place, *with* an object, etc.).

a **1000** *Sax. Leechd.* II. 298 On swa hwilcum huse swa he biþ. *c* **1000** *Ags. Gosp.* Matt. xxviii. 20 Ic béo mid eow ealle daᵹas. **1297** R. GLOUC. 374 Hou mony plou lond, & hou mony hyden al so, Were in eueryche ssyre. *c* **1300** *Harrow. Hell* 82 Alle tho that bueth heryne. *c* **1400** MAUNDEV. ii. 10 Some men trowen that half the Cros..be in Cipres. **1465** MARG. PASTON in *Lett.* 505 II. 194 Ryght glad that we err ther a mongs hem. **1674** BREVINT *Saul at Endor* 164 He having bin in his Coffin the greatest part of the night after his death. **1722** DE FOE *Hist. Plague* (1754) 6 Terrible Apprehensions were among the People. **1771** FLETCHER *Check* Wks. 1795 II. 194 You are just where you was. **1821** BYRON *Sardan.* III. i. 401 Again the love-fit's on him. **1861** THACKERAY *Georges* iii. 120 Where be the sentries who used to salute? *Mod.* Your book is here, under the table.

b. Often used with *there*, esp. when the subject is introduced to notice: cf. 'your brother (about whom you ask) is in the garden,' with 'there is a cow (something not previously present to the mind) in the garden.'

[**1475** CAXTON *Jason* 8 b, And were no more on their side but they two only]. **1594** HOOKER *Eccl. Pol.* Pref. i. §2 If there be in you that gracious humility. **1675** EVELYN *Mem.* (1857) II. 103 There was not his equal in the whole world. **1821** BYRON *Sardan.* I. i, There be bright faces in the hall.

6. Idiomatically, in past, now only in perfect and pluperfect tenses, with *to*, and a substantive, or infinitive of purpose: To have been (at the proper place) in order to, or for the purpose of. Cf. Sp. and Pg. *fué* 'I was' in sense of 'I went.'

c **1645** HOWELL *Lett.* (1678) 24, I was yesterday to wait upon Sir Herbert Croft. **1747** LADY SHAFTESB. in *Priv. Lett. Ld. Malmesbury* I. 51, I was to see the new farce. **1760** GOLDSMITH *Cit. W.* (1840) 158, I was this morning to buy silk for a nightcap. *Mod.* Have you been to the Crystal Palace? I had been to see Irving that night.

b. *to be off, be away*: a graphic expression for 'to go at once, take oneself off.'

1826 DISRAELI *Viv. Grey* VI. vi. 352 We had better order our horses and be off. **1873** BLACK *Pr. Thule* xii. 186 The stag..was away like lightning down the bed of the stream. **1884** W. C. SMITH *Kildrost.* 65, I must be off into the woods.

c. *been and* (*gone and*) ——: vulgar or facetious expletive amplification of the pa. pple. of a verb, used to express surprise or annoyance at the act specified.

1836 DICKENS *Pickw.* xxvi, Lauk, Mrs. Bardell,..see what you've been and done! **1847** THACKERAY *Van. Fair* xv, Sir Pitt has been and proposed for to marry Miss Sharp. **1869** W. S. GILBERT *Bab Ballads* 218 The padre said, 'Whatever have you been and gone and done?' **1891** [see GO *v.* 32 c]. **1920** R. MACAULAY *Potterism* II. i. 61 She's been and gone and done it. She's got engaged. **1926** D. L. SAYERS *Clouds of Witness* ii. 48, I say, Helen, old Gerald's been an' gone an' done it this time, what?

7. To sit, stand, remain, etc. in a defined circumstantial position, e.g. *to be in debt, at one's ease*; to have one's existence in a certain state or condition. **a.** with *prep. phrase.*

c **1175** *Lamb. Hom.* 7 ᵹef we beoð under soð scrifte. *c* **1340** *Cursor M.* (Laud MS.) 942 Therfor ye bene in wo and stryfe. *Ibid.* 10446 When þou shuldist be best at ease. *c* **1430** *Syr Gener.* (1865) 41 Al men that on live bene. **1531–2** *Act 23 Hen. VIII*, xvi, One halfe of the price..shalbe to the use of the seysour. **1535** COVERDALE *Zech.* viii. 2, I was in a greate gelousy ouer Sion. **1540** HYRDE *Vives' Instr. Chr. Wom.* (1592) E ij To bee at the lust of the Judge. **1611** BIBLE *Ex.* v. 19 They were in euill case. **1666** MARVELL *Corr.* liv. Wks. 1872–5 II. 191 Proposalls that have bin undir deliberation. **1712** ADDISON *Spect.* No. 369 ¶14 Any one..who will be at the pains of examining it. **1866** KINGSLEY *Herew.* xvii. 214 The battle..is more in my way.

b. with *adverb.*

c **1350** *Will. Palerne* 547 Nay best beþ it nouᵹt so. **1463** *Plumpton Corr.* 8, I trust all shalbe well. **1611** BIBLE *Gen.* xliii. 27 Is your father well? [WYCLIF saaf; COVERD., *Geneva* in good health]. **1807** CRABBE *Par. Reg.* III. 717 Content to be and to be well. **1849** MACAULAY *Hist. Eng.* II. 171 Asking how his Highness was.

8. To belong, pertain, befall: with *dat.* or *to*, = have. Cf. L. *est mihi*, Fr. *c'est à moi.* Now only in exclamations or wishes (where, also, *be* is often omitted), as *Wo is me! Wo be to the transgressor! Success* (be) *to your efforts!*

a **1300** *E.E. Psalter* cxxviii. 2 Wele bes to þe nou. **1382** WYCLIF *Luke* i. 7 A sone was not to hem. *c* **1400** MAUNDEV. 36 The kyngdom of Arabye that was to on of the 3 kynges. **1535** COVERDALE *Ps.* cxxvii. 2 O well is the, happie art thou. **1602** SHAKS. *Haml.* II. ii. 124 Whilst this Machine is to him. **1605** —— *Lear* I. i. 68 To thine and Albanies issues be this perpetuall. **1611** BIBLE *Ecclus.* xxv. 9 Well is him that hath found prudence. —— *Eph.* vi. 23 Peace be to the brethren. —— *Rev.* i. 4 Grace be vnto you, and peace, from him which is.

†**b.** To pertain as a misfortune, to have befallen *to*; to be amiss, be the matter with, ail. *Obs.*

1297 R. GLOUC. 128 Merlyn wat ys the? *a* **1300** *Cursor M.* 4395 Leuedi, quat es at ᵹou? [*v.r.* what is ᵹou? what ayles ᵹou?] *a* **1300** *Floriz & Bl.* 467 [Thei] axede hire what hire were. *a* **1300** *Havelok* 2704 Godrich, wat is þe, þat þou fare þus with me?

III. With adjective, substantive, or adjective phrase; acting as simple copula: stating *of what sort* or *what* a thing is. [= Sp., Pg. *ser*, as distinct from *estar.*]

9. To exist as the subject of some predicate, i.e. to have a place among the things distinguished by a specified quality or name. **a.** with *adj.*

c **1000** *Ags. Gosp.* Matt. xi. 30 Min ᵹeoc is wynsum and min byrðyn ys leoht. *c* **1175** *Lamb. Hom.* 197 Ne beo ich neuer bliðe. *c* **1340** *Cursor M.* (Trin.) 3109 þe folke was gode, þe world was clene. *Ibid.* 12578 Ar he were tuelue ᵹeer olde. **1387** TREVISA *Higden* (1865) I. 9 Now men beþ al sad. *c* **1440** *Morte Arth.* (Roxb.) 74 Wemen are frele. *c* **1440** HYLTON *Scala Perf.* (W. de W. 1494) xx, Ful drye & ful colde arn her hertes. **1534** TINDALE *John* xiii. 11 Ye are not all clene. **1579** LYLY *Euphues* (1636) D viij, Neither haue I bin curious to inquire of his Progenitors. **1611** BIBLE *Ps.* cviii. 30 Then are they glad because they be quiet. **1652** NEEDHAM *Selden's Mare Cl.* 171 Whose name is very frequent in the mouths of men. **1697** DRYDEN *Virg. Georg.* IV. 144 Gaunt are his Sides, and sullen is his Face. **1830** TENNYSON *Mariana*, I am aweary, aweary, I would that I were dead.

b. with *phrase* = *adj.* (closely allied to 7).

a **1200** ORMIN 2455 þu best wiþþ childe. *a* **1300** *Cursor M.* 10303 Fastinge he was in wille to be. *Ibid.* 10572 Anna wit child was of a mai. *c* **1400** *Partonope* 874 Beth of goode comfort. **1592** WEST *Symbol.* I. I. §9 Of which sort bin all naturall Obligations. **1734** tr. *Rollin's Anc. Hist.* (1827) I. III. 260 He was of Memphis. **1748** HARTLEY *Observ. Man* I. i. §1 ¶46 The Instance above noted is most to this Purpose. **1828** SCOTT *F.M. Perth* II. 67 Be of good courage. **1837** NEWMAN *Par. Serm.* I. xxiv. 365 Religion is said to be against nature. **1867** *Times* 18 Nov. 7/2 The advices from Adelaide..are to the 28th September.

c. with *sb.* (used connotatively).

c **950** *Lindisf. Gosp.* Matt. viii. 9 Forðon and ic monn amm under mæht. *c* **1175** *Cott. Hom.* 219 Hi bæ ð alle gastes. *c* **1325** *E.E. Allit. P.* A. 458 Al arn we membrez of Ihesu kryst. *c* **1380** WYCLIF *Sel. Wks.* (1871) III. 442 þese freres bene men of holy Chirche. **1570** ASCHAM *Scholem.* I. (Arb.) 68 You be indeed makers or marrers. **1626** R. BERNARD *Isle of Man* (1627) 155, I haue alwayes bin a free man. **1678** BUNYAN *Pilg.* I. 14 Though I have bin An undeserving rebel. **1817** BYRON *Manfred* II. iv. 133, I feel but what thou art —and what I am. **1850** LYNCH *Theo. Trin.* x. 200 Only by being man can we know man.

d. *colloq.* With idiomatic repetition of the verb in the following clause. (Further examples in Visser *Hist. Syntax* I. 55.) Cf. IT 4 c.

1828 M. MITFORD *Our Village*, III. 202 He's a sad pickle is Sam! **1928** R. MACAULAY *Keeping up Appearances* iv. §1. 35 She's very sympathetic, Daphne is. **1930** BELLOC *Wolsey* iv. 58 It is a rare function, is industry upon this level. **1932** R. KNOX *Broadcast Minds* vii. 156 Yes, he is true to type, is Mr. Heard. **1958** P. GALLICO *Steadfast Man* ii. 43 He was an honest man, was Patrick.

10. with *sb.* To exist as the thing known by a certain name; to be identical with.

c **1000** *Ags. Gosp.* John xix. 21 Ic eom iudea cyning. *c* **1160** *Hatt. G.* ibid., Ich ém iudea kyning. *c* **1340** HAMPOLE *Pr. Consc.* 946 God..es maker of althynge, And of alle creatures þe bygynnynge. *c* **1400** *Gamelyn* 583 Hit ben þe Shirreues men. **1486** *Plumpton Corr.* 49 These bent the tydings that I know. *c* **1530** REDFORDE *Play Wyt & Sc.* (1848) 3 Ah! syr, what tyme of day yst? **1590** SHAKS. *Com. Err.* III. ii. 73 Am I Dromio? Am I your man?. Am I my selfe? **1610** —— *Temp.* I. ii. 434 My selfe am Naples. **1630** WADSWORTH *Sp. Pilgr.* i. 4 'Twas clear it was not gaine was his marke. **1805** FOSTER *Ess.* II. vi. 204 Let thinking be reasoning. **1872** YEATS *Tech. Hist. Comm.* 212 The earth and the atmosphere are the two sources.

11. To be the same in purport as; to signify, amount to, mean.

c **1200** *Trin. Coll. Hom.* 5 Vigilate, þat is beð wakiende. *c* **1220** *Hali Meid.* 3 Him ᵹeme hwat euch word bee sunderliche to seggen. *c* **1230** *Ancr. R.* 58 Best is þe bestliche mon þæt ne þencheð nout of God. **1302** WYCLIF *Gen.* xli. 26 Seuen oxen fayr, and seuen eerys fulle, seuen ᵹeris of plentith ben. **1611** BIBLE *Ibid.*, The seuen good kine are seuen yeares. **1597** BACON *Coulers Good & Evill, Ess.* (Arb.) 153 The burning of that had bin *gradus privationis.* **1884** *Weekly Times* 7 Mar. 4/4 To fall was to die. *Mod.* I'll tell you what it is, you must leave.

12. To amount to (something) of moment or importance, to 'signify' *to* a person; to concern.

a **1300** *Cursor M.* 13383 Quat es þat to me and þe? *Ibid.* 16487 What is that to vs? **1526** TINDALE *Matt.* xxvii. 4 What is that to vs? Se thou to that, **1611** BIBLE *Lam.* i. 12 Is it nothing to you, all ye that passe by? *Mod.* Is it nothing to you, that you have alienated your friends?

13. *ellipt.* To be good for, to be at the expense of, 'stand.' *Obs.* or *dial.*

1749 FIELDING *Tom Jones* VIII. v, The wine being now at an end, the barber pressed very eagerly to be his bottle. *Ibid.* xv. xii, I said I would be my pot too. **1765** GOLDSM. *Strolling Player, Ess.* vi, If I have threepence in my pocket I never refuse to be my three halfpence. *Mod. Colloq.* He was asked to be his share in the expense and refused.

IV. With participles and infinitives, serving as an auxiliary and forming periphrastic tenses.

14. With *past participle*: **a.** in *transitive verbs*, forming the passive voice. (For present pple. passive, see 15 c.)

c **825** *Vesp. Psalter* l. 9 Ðu on-striᵹdes mec mid ysopan ..ðu ðwes mec, & ofer snaw, ic biom ge-whitad [WYCLIF, And I shal ben clensid]. *c* **885** K. ÆLFRED *Boeth.* xiii. 40 Ic eom of wundrod. *c* **1175** *Lamb. Hom.* 59 In þe font we weren eft iboren. *c* **1325** *E.E. Allit. P.* A. 571 Mony ben calle[d]. *c* **1410** LOVE *Bonavent. Mirr.* x. 24 (Gibbs MS.), We shulden not by styred to impacyence. **1606** G. W[OODCOCKE] *Justine* 31 b, Pausanias, being attached for treason, fled. **1637** *Decr. Star Chamb. on Printing* 11 July §2 That no person..print or cause to bee printed. **1674** BREVINT *Saul at Endor* 140 Vows..were never heard to have bin made to any Saint, but to God alone. **1683** *Col. Rec. Pennsylvania* I. 57 Bee it enacted by the Authority aforesaid that yᵉ days of yᵉ week.. shall be called as in Scripture. **1874** HELPS *Soc. Press.* iii. 57 The political aspect of the subject has not been approached.

b. in *intransitive verbs*, forming perfect tenses, in which use it is now largely displaced by *have* after the pattern of transitive verbs: *be* being retained only with *come, go, rise, set, fall, arrive, depart, grow*, and the like, when we express the condition or state now attained, rather than the action of reaching it, as 'the sun is set,' 'our guests are gone,' 'Babylon is fallen,' 'the children are all grown up.'

894 *O.E. Chron.*, Wæs Hæsten þá þǽr cumen mid his herᵹe. *c* **1200** *Trin. Coll Hom.* 173 Alle þe sinfulle þe forð sende farene. *a* **1300** *Cursor M.* 14322 Thre dais es gan. *c* **1350** *Will. Palerne* 1457 þe grete lordes..beþ lenged now here. *c* **1450** *Merlin* x. 165 In euell tyme ben oure enmyes entred. **1523** LD. BERNERS *Froiss.* I. cxxix. 156 They are rested in there batayls. **1556** VERON *Godly Sayings* (1846) 145 Aungels, that bene come down from heaven. **1590** SHAKS. *Com. Err.* v. i. 361 These children, Which accidentally are met together. **1628** HOBBES *Thucyd.* (1822) 62 He gave out they were run away. **1670** G. H. *Hist. Cardinals* I. I. 24 Some there are, who believe that Miracles are not ceas'd. **1671** MILTON *P.R.* II. 140 Therefore I am returned. **1685** *Lond. Gaz.* No. 2069/4 The Dartmouth is Sailed to the Westward. **1773** GOLDSM. *Stoops to Conq.* I. i. (1854) 50 He informs me his son is set out. **1852** MISS YONGE *Cameos* I. ix. 58 His parents were grown old.

15. With the present participle, forming continuous varieties of the tenses. **a.** with *active* signification. In OE. only *wæs* was so used, forming a kind of imperfect; the present was in use by the 13th c. In later times this was confused with a formation upon the vbl. sb., of which see examples under A *prep.*[1] 13; the OE. *he wæs feohtende*, and ME. 'he was a-fighting,' meet in the modern 'he was fighting.'

885 *O.E. Chron.*, Æþelwulf ferde to Rome and þær wæs xii monaþ wuniende. *c* **1175** *Cott. Hom.* 225 Adam þa wes wuniende on þeses life. *a* **1300** *Cursor M.* 15665 Bes [*v.r.* be] wakand ai in orisun. *c* **1400** MAUNDEV. xxiii. 253 Thei trowen..thei schulle be etynge and drynkynge. **1562** J. HEYWOOD *Prov. & Epigr.* (1867) 37 Leat vs be trudgeing. **1576** LAMBARDE *Peramb. Kent*, Some fleeting beene in floodes. **1653** HOLCROFT *Procopius* 29 The Romans being preparing their dinners. **1684** BUNYAN *Pilg.* II. 227 He was talking of thee. **1727** VANBRUGH *Journ. Lond.* I. 1, It's at the Door, they are getting out. **1750** HARRIS *Hermes* (1841) 142 Riseth means, is rising; writeth, is writing. **1774** BURKE *Sp. Amer. Tax.* Wks. II. 401, I hope I am not going into a narrative troublesome to the house. **1863** GEO. ELIOT *Romola* xlv, The bells were still ringing.

b. with passive signification: in such expression as 'the ark was building,' the last word was originally the gerund or verbal substantive, and the full expression was 'the ark was a-building or in building,' of which see instances under A *prep.*[1] 12.

1551 ROBINSON *More's Utop.* (1869) 64 Whyles a commodye of Plautus is playinge. **1557** N. T. (Geneva) *1 Pet.* iii. 20 While the arcke was [**1611** was in] preparing. **1685** R. BURTON *Eng. Emp. Amer.* ii. 28 Strong preparations being making for wars. *Mod.* We stayed there while our house was building.

c. The ambiguity of the construction 'is building' in the two preceding senses has led in modern Eng. to the use in the latter sense of 'is being built,' formed upon the present pple. passive 'being built.'

[**1596** *Of Ghostes and Spirits* 14 The noyse of a leafe being mooved so affrighteth him. **1653** H. MORE *Antid. Ath.* 26 Acting and being acted upon by others. **1754** RICHARDSON *Grandison* III. 46 To sit up late either reading or being read to. **1769** MRS. HARRIS in *Lett. 1st Ld. Malmesbury* (1870) I. 180 There is a good opera of Pugniani's now being acted. **1779** J. HARRIS *Ibid.* I. 410 Sir Guy Carlton was four hours being examined.] **1795** SOUTHEY in C. Southey *Life* I. 249 A fellow..whose grinder is being torn out by the roots. **1797** COLERIDGE in *Biog. Lit.* (1847) II. 317 While my hand was being dressed. **1823** LAMB *Elia, Inconv. being hanged*, A man who is being strangled. **1846** NEWMAN *Ess. Crit. & Hist.* II, 448 At this very moment, souls are being led into the Catholic Church. *a* **1859** DE QUINCEY *Wks.* IV. 7 Not done, not even (according to modern purism) being done. **1873**

HUXLEY *Crit. & Addresses* 247 The corpuscles enter into the eggs while they are being formed.

16. With the dative infinitive, making a future of appointment or arrangement; hence of necessity, obligation, or duty; in which sense *have* is now commonly substituted.

†**a.** with *infinitive active. Obs.*

c **1200** *Trin. Coll. Hom.* 3 Alle þo þe habben ben..and alle þo þe ben to cumen her after. **1382** WYCLIF *Gen.* xiii. 17, I am to [**1388** Y schal] ȝyue it to thee. **1382** —— *Eccles.* ii. 18, I knowe not whether wis or fool he be to ben. **1622** MASSINGER *Virgin Mart.* III. i, A King of Egypt, being to erect The image of Osiris. **1692** LOCKE *Educ.* §167 If a Gentleman be to study any Language, it ought to be that of his own Country. **1703** ROWE *Fair Penit.* Ded., If this be not a receiv'd Maxim, yet I am sure I am to wish it were. **1725** DE FOE *Voy. round World* (1840) 22 Mighty uneasy.. about their being to go back again. **1742** RICHARDSON *Pamela* III. 264, I am to thank you, my dear Miss, for your kind Letter. **1814** SCOTT *Wav.* I. v. 55 Had he been to chuse between any punishment..and the necessity.

†**b.** Hence, ***to be to seek***: to have to seek, to be obliged to seek, to be in want or at a loss. *Obs.*

1601 HOLLAND *Pliny* I. 89 The complete measure of it.. that such as are desirous of knowledge be not to seek in any one thing. **1625** BACON *Usury, Ess.* (Arb.) 544 The Merchant wil be to seeke for Money. **1653** HOLCROFT *Procopius* I. 4 Being to seek his food he would hunt for it. **1654** (12 Sept.) CROMWELL *Sp.* (Carl. 1871) IV. 52 We were exceedingly to seek how to settle things. *a* **1674** CLARENDON *Hist. Reb.* I. v. (1702) 454 They were very much to seek, how the Case of Hull could concern Descents and Purchases. **1832** *Fair of May Fair* III. ii. 278 It was excusable that a man having passed so large a portion of those sixty years in a compting house, could be somewhat to seek in the economy of his social system.

c. with *infinitive passive.*

1581 FULKE in *Confer.* III. (1584) O iiij b, He him selfe being to iudge all men, is to bee iudged of no man. *a* **1674** CLARENDON *Hist. Reb.* I. II. 118 Being to be made Earl of Strafford. **1869** FREEMAN *Norm. Conq.* III. xii. 145 Normandy was to be invaded on each side.

17. The same construction is used in the sense of 'to be proper or fit (to).' **a.** with *infinitive active. arch.* and now commonly expressed by **b.**

c **1175** *Lamb. Hom.* 133 Hit is to witene. *c* **1340** *Cursor M.* (Fairf.) 12861 Wat is to do. **1340** *Ayenb.* 5 þet is to zigge. *c* **1388** in *Wyclif's Sel. Wks.* 1871 III. 468 Hit ys not to gife dymes to a persoun. **1483** CAXTON *G. de la Tour* E v, Suche .. wymmen be to compare to the wyf of Lothe. **1528** PERKINS *Prof. Bk.* i. §36 (1642) 16 Now it is to shew. **1634** *Malory's Arthur* (1816) II. 308 The four..is to understand the four evangelists. *Mod.* Is this house to let? They are not to compare with these.

b. with *infinitive passive.*

1303 R. BRUNNE *Handl. Synne* 1545 Þey beþ to be blamede eft. **1588** J. UDALL *Demonstr. Discip.* (Arb.) 54 If the whole..be to bee obserued vntill the ende. **1679** PENN *Addr. Prot.* II. §2 (1692) 76 Not a Good Samaritan being to be found. **1798** MALTHUS *Popul.* (1817) II. 194 It must be to be depended upon.

18. The past subjunctive *were* with the infinitive makes an emphatically hypothetical condition: cf. the degrees of uncertainty in *If I went, If I should go, If I were to go.*

1596 RALEIGH in *Four C. Eng. Lett.* 37 If I weare..to advize my sealf. *Mod.* If I were to propose, would you accept? Were he to ask me, it would be different.

V. Phraseological combinations.

19. In *I were better* (*best, as good*), the nominative pronoun took catachrestically the place of an earlier dative (*me were better* = it were better to or for me): modern usage substitutes *had better*, after the analogy of *had liefer, rather*, etc. Cf. HAVE, LIEF, RATHER.

(See F. Hall, '*Had Rather*' in *Amer. Jnl. Philol.* II, No. 7. 1881.)

c **1300** *St. Marg.* 180 þe were betere habbe [= it were better for thee to have] bileued atom, þan icome me to fonde. *c* **1430** *Syr Tryam.* 399 Sche wyste not whedur-warde.. Sche was best to goone. *c* **1590** MARLOWE *Jew of M.* IV. iv. 1653, I..told him he were best to send it. **1597** LYLY *Wom. in Moone* III. ii. 185 Sirra, provide the banquet, you are best. **1610** SHAKS. *Temp.* I. ii. 366 Be quicke thou'rt best. **1611** —— *Cymb.* III. ii. 79 Madam, you're best consider. **1612** CHAPMAN *Widdowes' T.* Plays 1873 III. 12 Y'are best take you to your stand. **1647** WARD *Simp. Cobler* 57 They were ..better speake plainer English. **1703** MOXON *Mech. Ex.* 278 You were best to mark the lower Closier in each course.

20. In clauses measuring time: as 'he came here Monday was a week,' i.e. he came here on the Monday a week before Monday last: the phrase became a mere adjective clause, whence arose remarkable constructions, as 'on the evening of Saturday was sennight before the day fixed' = on the evening of the Saturday a week earlier than the Saturday before the day fixed. *Was* is now generally omitted: I was in London Monday (was) three weeks.

[**1449** *Paston Lett.* 68 I. 85 And as God wuld, on Fryday last was, we had a gode wynd.] **1678** *Gunpowder-Treas.* 11 The Evening of the Saturday was Sennight before the appointed time. **1684** BAXTER *Twelve Argts.* Post. M, I have been at no Church since *August* was Twelvemonth. **1691** *Lond. Gaz.* No. 2657/4 Edward Flower..went from his House about last Christmas was 4 years. **1725** *Ibid.* No. 6447/4 About two or three Days after Holy Rood Day last was Twelve Month. **1859** GEO. ELIOT *A. Bede* 343 Did there come no young woman here..Friday was a fortnight?

21. ***to be about to***: see ABOUT A 11, 12.

22. ***what one would be at***: what one aims at; what one means, wishes, or would have.

1705 VANBRUGH *Confeder.* I. i. (1759) II. 13 What wou'd he be at? At her—if she's at leisure. **1749** FIELDING *Tom Jones* (1836) I. I. xi. 51 We cannot always discover what the young lady would be at. **1766** GOLDSM. *Vic. W.* x. (1857) 58 That is very true but not what I would be at. **1848** *Blackw. Mag.* LXIV. 373 What would revolutionising Germany be at?

23. ***to be for***: †**a.** to be ready, prepared, or a match for a person (*obs.*); **b.** to be bound for, to be making for a place; **c.** to be ready to act for, to be on the side of, or in favour of, to advocate; **d.** to be anxious for, to desire, to want (*dial.*).

a. *a* **1622** MIDDLETON, etc. *Old Law* III. ii, My young boys, I shall be for you. **1631** MASSINGER *Beleeve as you list* III. iii, His angrie forhead..No matter—I am for him.

b. **1630** WADSWORTH *Sp. Pilgr.* ii. 6, I was for St. Sebastians, accompanied with one Mr. Pickford. *Mod.* 'Where are you for to-day?'

c. **1636** HEALEY *Epictetus' Man.* 147 Like unto beasts, they are all for the belly. **1692** LOCKE *Toleration* ii. Wks. 1727 II. 289 You cannot be..for a free and impartial Examination. **1799** T. JEFFERSON *Writ.* (1859) IV. 268, I am for free commerce with all nations. **1855** MACAULAY *Hist. Eng.* IV. 511 He was for going straight into the harbour of Brest. **1878** BOSW. SMITH *Carthage* 219 Scipio..was for delay.

24. Many parts of the verb and its tenses are used substantively, adjectively, or adverbially.

a **1679** T. GOODWIN *Wks.* (1864) VIII. 231 How slender these hopes..which these it may bes do afford. **1739** CHESTERF. *Lett.* I. xxxv. 115 May be they were drunk. **1802** G. COLMAN *Br. Grins, Reckoning with Time* iii, List then, old Is-Was-and-To-Be. **1819** BYRON *Venice* ii, The everlasting *to be* which *hath been.* **1837** CARLYLE *Fr. Rev.* II. IV. ii. 189 He goes, as Rabelais did when dying, to seek a great May-be. *Ibid.* III. I. iv. 36 There is a need-be for removing. **1848** CLOUGH *Bothie* III. 159 He to the great might-have-been upsoaring..He to the merest it-was restricting, diminishing. **1852** TUPPER *Prov. Philos.* 173 This would-be god Thinketh to make mind.

be, variant of BEE *sb.*

be, obs. and dial. form of BY *prep.*; see next.

be- *prefix*:—OE. *be-*, weak or stressless form of the prep. and adv. *bí* (*biȝ*), BY. The original Teut. form was, as in Gothic, *bi*, with short vowel, prob. cognate with second syllable of Gr. ἀμφί, L. *ambi*; in OHG. and early OE., when it had the stress, as a separate word, and in composition with a noun, it was lengthened to *bī* (*bî, bí*), while the stressless form, in composition with a vb. or indeclinable word, remained *bi-*; in later OE., as in MHG. and mod.G., the latter was obscured to *be-* (also occasional in OE. as an unaccented form of the preposition): cf. OE. *bí-ȝeng* practice, *bi-gangan, be-gangan*, to practise. In early ME. the etymological *bi-, by-* regularly reappeared in comp. as the stressless form; but in later times *be-* was finally restored. (On the other hand, *be* was used by northern writers as the separate prep., as still in mod. Sc.) In modern use, the unaccented prefix is always *be-*; the accented form *by-* (sometimes spelt *bye-*) occurs in one or two words descended from OE., as *'by-law, 'by-word* (OE. *bí-laȝe, bí-word*), and in modern formations on the adv., as *'by-gone, 'by-name, 'by-play, 'by-road, 'by-stander.*

The original meaning was 'about.' In prepositions and adverbs this is weakened into a general expression of position *at* or *near*, as in *before* (at, near, or towards the front), *behind, below, beneath, benorth, besouth, between, beyond.* With verbs, various senses of 'about' are often distinctly retained, as in *be-bind, be-come* (= come about), *be-delve, be-gird, be-set, be-stir.* In such as *be-daub, be-spatter, be-stir, be-strew*, the notion of 'all about, all round, over,' or 'throughout,' naturally intensifies the sense of the verb; whence, *be-* comes to be more or less a simple *intensive*, as in *be-muddle, be-crowd, be-grudge, be-break*, or specializes or renders figurative, as in *befall* (to fall as an accident), *be-come, be-get, be-gin, be-have, be-hold, be-lieve.* In other words the force of *be-* passes over to an object, and renders an intransitive verb transitive, as in *be-speak* (speak about, for, or to), *be-flow* (flow about), *be-lie, be-moan, be-think, be-wail.* Hence it is used to form transitive vbs. on adjectives and substantives, as in *dim be-dim, fool be-fool, madam be-madam*; also others, in which the sb. stands in an instrumental or other oblique relation, as *be-night* 'to overtake *with* night,' *be-guile, be-witch.* Of these a special section consists of verbs having a privative force, as OE. *belandian, behéafdian*, to deprive of one's land, one's head: cf. *bereave*, and OE. *benim-an* to take away. Finally, *be-* is prefixed with a force combining some of the preceding, to ppl. adjs., as in *be-jewelled, be-daughtered.*

Be- being still in some of its senses (esp. 2, 6, 7 below) a living element, capable of being prefixed wherever the sense requires it, the derivatives into which it enters are practically unlimited in number. The more important, including those that are in any way specialized, or that require separate explanation, are treated in their alphabetical places as Main Words. (In the case of ME. words in *bi-, by-*, all that survived long enough to have BE- appear under this spelling; a few that became obsolete at an early date are left under their only extant form in BI-, BY-.) Those of less importance, infrequent (often single) occurrence, and obvious composition, are arranged under the following groups (in which, however, the senses tend to overlap each other, so as to make the place of some of the words ambiguous):—

1. Forming derivative verbs, with sense of 'around': **a.** all round externally, on all sides, all over the surface, as in BESET, BESMEAR; **b.** from side to side (within a space), to and fro, in all directions, in all ways, in or through all its parts, thoroughly, as in BESTIR, *bejumble.* (Some of these formations appear only in the pa. pple.)

bebang, to bang about; †**bebass**, to kiss all over, cover with kisses; **bebaste** (with a cudgel, or with gravy); †**bebat**, to becudgel; **bebatter, bebite; beblear**, to blear all over; **beblotch**, †**beboss, bebotch, bebrush**; †**becense**, to perfuse with incense; **bechase**, to chase about; **becircle; beclart** *dial.*, to be dirty; **beclasp; becompass**, to compass about; **becramp**; †**becrampoun**, to set (a jewel); **becrimson, becrust**; †**becurry**, to curry one's hide, belabour; **becurse**, to cover with curses; **becut, bedamn, bedamp, bediaper**; †**bedowse**, to souse with water; **bedrape, bedrift, bedrive, be-embroider, befan; befinger**, to finger all over; **befleck**, to cover with flecks; **befreckle, befriz**; †**befrounce**, to frounce or toss about, touzle; †**begarnish, begash, begaud, begirdle**; †**behale**, to drag about; **behammer**, †**behem**; †**behorewe**, to befoul; **bejig**, to jig about; **bejumble**, †**beknit** (OE. *becnyttan*), **belave, belick, bemingle, bemix, bepaste; bepaw**, to befoul as with paws; **bepen**, to pen in; **bepommel**; †**bepounce**, to stud; **beprank**, to prank out or over; **bepuddle** (*e.g.* a spring); **bepurple**; †**bequirtle**, to besprinkle; **berake**, to rake all over; †**beroll**, to roll over; †**beround, bescour, beseam, beshackle**, †**beshield, beshroud**; †**beslab**, to beplaster; **beslash**, †**beslur; beslurry**, to sully all over; **besmother, besmudge** (†**besmouche**); †**besow** (OE. *besáwan*), to sow about; †**besperple**, to bespatter; **bespin**, to spin round, so as to cover; **bespirt**; †**besquatter**, to bespatter with filth; **bestamp**, †**bestroke**, †**beswitch, betinge**, †**beturn, beveil**, †**bewallow** (OE. *bewalwian*), **bewash, bewater, bewhiten, bewreath.** Also BEBAR, BEDELVE, etc., q.v.

1599 PORTER *Angry Wom. Abingd.* (1841) 50 Sheele..*be-bang him with drie bobs and scoffes. **1583** STANYHURST *Æneis* I. (Arb.) 40 Queene Dido shal smacklye *bebasse thee. *Ibid.* III. (Arb.) 79 With larding smearye *bebasted. **1620** ROWLANDS *Nt. Raven* 29 Tom with his cudgell well *bebasts his bones. **1565** CALFHILL *Answ. Treat. Crosse* (1846) 133 To be all to- *bebatted and afterward to be beheaded. **1565** GOLDING *Ovid's Met.* V. (1593) 106 All *be-battred was his head. **1880** WEBB tr. *Goethe's Faust* II. v. 130 Each, from queen to waiting-maid, is Be-devilled and *be-bit! **1609** ARMIN *Ital. Taylor* (1880) 196 Eyes *be-bleard with blindnesse. **1807** SOUTHEY *Lett.* (1856) I. 412 Down comes a proof..*beblotched and bedeviled. **1576** GASCOIGNE *Philomene* (Arb.) 90 A snaffle Bit or brake, *Bebost with gold. **1605** DAVIES *Humours* Wks. (1876) 44 (D.) Petti-botching brokers all *bebotch. **1587** TURBERV. *Trag. T.* (1837) 30 *Bebrusht with bryers her broosed body bled. **1591** G. FLETCHER *Russe Commw.* (1836) 113 Having sprinckled and *besensed the good man and his wife. **1639** AINSWORTH *Annot. Song Sol.* iii. 6 *Becensed with Myrrh. **1574** HELLOWES *Gueuara's Ep.* (1577) 96 In this Courte, none runneth, but they go all *beechased. **1648** EARL WESTMLD. *Otia Sacra* (1879) 128 A grove of Pine *Becircled with Eglantine. **1607** TOPSELL *Serpents* 743 He *beclapseth it with his tail, and giveth it fearful blows. *c* **1230** *Wohunge* in *Cott. Hom.* 279 þat spatel þat swa *biclarted ti leor. **1864** ATKINSON *Whitby Gloss.*, *Beclarted, splashed or bemired. **1480** CAXTON *Chron. Eng.* II. (1520) 10 b/1 An Yle..called Albyon..*becompassed al with the see. **1634** MALORY *Arthur* (1816) II. 257 Him thought there came a man..all *becompassed of stars. **1666** FULLER *Hist. Camb.* (1840) 107 Many whose hands are *becramped with laziness. **1583** STANYHURST *Æneis* IV. (Arb.) 99 With..pure gould neatly *becrampound. **1837** CARLYLE *Fr. Rev.* II. III. VII. vi. 369 Why was the Earth..*becrimsoned with dawn and twilight? **1883** *Century Mag.* XXVII. 47 The lofty hedge is *be-crimsoned with savage roses. *a* **1834** LAMB tr. *Bourne's Ball. Singers* Wks. 633 Two Nymphs..in mud behind, before, From heel to middle leg *becrusted o'er. **1598** R. BERNARD tr. *Terence's Andr.* I. ii. (1629) 16/1, I will all to *becurry thee, or bethwacke thy coate. **1553–87** FOXE *A. & M.* (1596) 247/1 The legat..all to *becurssed the earle of Tholouse, his cities and his people. **1860** READE *Cloister & H.* xlviii. (D.), I was never so *becursed in all my days. **1630** J. TAYLOR (Water P.) *Trav. Twelve P.* Wks. I. 67/2 Me all in

pieces they *becut and quartir'd. **1863** KINGLAKE *Crimea* (1877) VI. vi. 278 This much *be-damned 'Sixth of the Line.' **1870** HAWTHORNE *Eng. Note-Bks* (1879) II. 328 A mist..*be-damped me. **1648** HERRICK *Poems* App. (1869) 457 (D.) Fields *bediaperd with flowers, Presente their shappes. **1576** GOSSON *Spec. Hum.* ii, A bruised barke with billowes all *bedowst. **1865** SWINBURNE *Dolores* 49 We shift and bedeck and *bedrape us. **1837** CARLYLE *Fr. Rev.* (1872) III. III. iii. 109 Poor Orléans..foolishly *bedrifted hither and thither. **1614** RICH *Honest. Age* (1844) 26 Some women goe..to the church..so be-laced and so *bee-imbrodered. **1674** N. FAIRFAX *Bulk & Selv.* Ep. Ded., *Befann'd from next Dogs-day scorchings. **1821** SOUTHEY *Lett.* (1856) III. 233 The dirty and *befingered leaves. **1567** TURBERV. *Ovid's Epist.* 135 b, Why blush you? and why with vermilion taint *Beflecke your cheekes? **1610** G. FLETCHER *Christ's Vict.* II. vii, A grassie hillock..With woodie primroses *befreckell'd. **1772** *Songs Costume* (1849) 249 *Be-friz it, and paste it, and cut it, and curl it. **1581** STUDLEY *Seneca's Herc. Œtæus* 214 b, All her hayre *befrounced, rent and torne. **1647** R. STAPYLTON *Juvenal* 70 What sparagus *begarnishes the dish. **1555** *Fardle Facions* II. ix. 196 [They] all to *begasshe his fore-heade and his nose. **1580** NORTH *Plutarch* (1676) 127 Be-gawded with Chains of Gold and Iewells. **1843** CARLYLE *Past & Pres.* 75 Stately masonries..*begirdle it far and wide. **1574** HELLOWES *Gueuara Ep.* (1584) 310 Also *bee-haileth her by the lockes. **1639** AINSWORTH *Annot. Pentat.* 144 The Hebrew word signifieth stricken ..*behammered. **1598** SYLVESTER *Job Triumph.* i. 688 (D.) Armies of pains..mee round *behem. **1340** *Ayenb.* 237 þe hand þet is uoul and *behorewed. **1821** COMBE (Dr. Syntax) *Wife* v. (D.) When they *bejigg'd it 'neath the steeple. **1565** GOLDING *Ovid. Met.* IV. (R.) Her filthy arms *beknit with snakes about. **1598** SYLVESTER *Du Bartas* II. iii. (1641) 174/1 Me in Thy Bloud *be-lave. *Ibid.* (1608) 1002 The happy plains great Phasis streams *belave. **1559** *Mirr. Mag.* 106 (T.) All his gore *bemingled with this glew. *Ibid., Dk. Clarence* xliii, *Bemixt my swete with bitternes to bad. **1565** GOLDING *Ovid's Met.* IV. (1593) 102 Waves of water ..*Bemixed with the purple bloud. **1684** OTWAY *Atheist* Epil., While Rotten Eggs *bepaw the Scarlet Gown. *c* **1230** *Ancr. R.* 94 Heo beoð her so *bipenned. **1583** STANYHURST *Æneis* I. (Arb.) 32 Thee beams with brazed copper were costlye *bepounced. **1648** HERRICK *Hesper.* (1844) I. 159 A sheep-hook I will send *Beprank'd with ribands. **1642** JER. TAYLOR *Episc.* (1647) 98 While their tradition was cleare.. and not so *bepudled..with the mixture of Hereticks. **1583** STANYHURST *Æneis* I. (Arb.) 37 His sight was youthlye *bepurpled. **1771** *Muse in Miniature* 115 Mossy banks and flower-*bepurpled plains. **1690** *Songs Costume* (1849) 193 Whole quarts the chamber to *bequirtle. **1685** R. BURTON *Eng. Emp. Amer.* ii. 51 Their Guns, with which they so *beraked her from side to side. *c* **1325** *E.E. Allit. P.* B. 959 Al *birolled wyth þe rayn, rostted & brenned. **1642** BRIDGE *Serm. Norf. Volunteers* 9 Are we not *berounded with many enemies? **1837** CARLYLE *Fr. Rev.* II. III. v. iv. 304 France too is *bescoured with a Devil's Pack. **1839** *Blackw. Mag.* XLV. 301 Blue tops..All *beseamed with snow-streaks hoar. **1599** NASHE *Lent. Stuffe* 50 Who this king should bee, *beshackled theyr wits. **1848** H. MILLER *First Impressions of Eng.* xi. (1857) 172 Venerable dwellings, much *beshrouded in ivy and honeysuckle. **1481** CAXTON *Reynard* (1844) 138 They were *byslabbed and byclagged to their eres to in her owen donge. **1581** T. NEWTON *Seneca's Thebais* 44 b, To die this death: or in one part to be *beslashed through. **1635** tr. *Camden's Hist. Eliz.* III. (1688) 291 To *beslurr their Writings with this so impudent a Lie. *c* **1614** DRAYTON *Crt. Fairy* Wks. (1748) 164 All *be-slurried, head and face, On runs he in this wild-goose chase. **1598** FLORIO, *Carbonare*, to besmeare as black as coles, to *besmother. **1600** HAKLUYT *Voy.* (1810) III. 508 Their faces..all *besmouched with cole. *c* **1175** *Lamb. Hom.* 107 þa sunnan þe deouel *bisaweð on us. **1557** *K. Arthur* (W. Copland) VI. viii, The grounde ..was all *besperpled wyth blode. **1865** CARLYLE *Fredk. Gt.* V. XIII. ix. 92 Was a Nation ever so *bespun by gossamer? **1885** SINGLETON *Virgil* I. 171 And on the cattle to *bespirt his bane. **1611** COTGR., *Enfoirir*, to besquirt, *besquatter. **1652** URQUHART *Jewel* Wks. 1834. 256 *Besquatter them on all sides. **1857** *Fraser's Mag.* LVI. 742 That letter..much *bestamped, much stained with travel..is delivered to its owner at Lahore. **1548** HERRICK *Hesp.* Wks. I. 157 *Bestroaking fate the while. **1821** CLARE *Vill. Minstr.* I. 12 *Beting'd with glossy yellow. **1594** CAREW *Tasso* (1881) 110 To their aduises the disdainefull hart, Of this audacious youth, *beturning plies. **1582** STANYHURST *Æneis* II. (Arb.) 55 With darcknesse mightye *beueyled. **1205** LAY. 25989 Al *biwaled [**1250** biwalewed] on axen. **1589** FLEMING *Virg. Georg.* IV. 69 She..all *bewasht the burning Vesta..with pure sweet wine. **1648** HERRICK *St. Distaff's Day, Hesp.* (1859) 451 Let the maides *bewash the men. **1593** BARNES *Parthen.* in Arb. *Garner* V. 363 Why were these cheeks with tears *bewatered? **1812** COMBE (Dr. Syntax) *Picturesque* xix. 71 The cot that's all *bewhiten'd o'er. **1598** *Gorg. Gallery Invent., Louer weryed w. Life*, About mishap that hast thy selfe *bewrethed. *a* **1850** BEDDOES *Song on Water* ii, Heart high-beating, triumph-*bewreathed.

2. Forming intensive verbs, with sense of 'thoroughly (extension of 1), soundly, much, conspicuously, to excess, ridiculously.' (Some of these occur only in the past participle.) †**bebait**, to bait or worry persistently; **bebothered**; †**bebreech**, to breech soundly; **bebusied**, †**becheck**; †**becheke**, to choke, stifle; **bechill** (? nonce-wd.); **beclamour**, **becompliment**, †**becost**, **becovet**, **becrowd**, **becrush**, **becumber**; †**bedare**, to defy; †**bedrown**; **bedrowse**, to make drowsy; **bedrug**, **beduck**; †**bedunch**, to strike against; †**be-earn**, **be-elbow**, †**befavour**, **befilch**; †**beflap**, to clap; **beflout**, **beflustered**, **befraught**; **begall**, to gall, fret, or rub sore; †**beglose**, to deceive; †**begrain**, to dye in the grain, colour permanently; †**begreet**, **begut**, **behallow**, †**behelp**; †**behusband**, to economize to the full; **bekick**, **belade**, †**belash**, **belull**; †**bemar**, to injure seriously; **bemartyr**, **bemaze**, †**bemeet**, **bemuzzle**, **bepaid**, **beparch**, **beparody**; †**bepart**, to divide, share; †**bepiece**, to piece up, patch up; †**bepierce**; †**bepile**, to pile up; †**bepill**, to pillage completely; **bepoetize**; †**bepress**, to oppress; †**bepride**; **bequoted**, quoted to excess; †**beragged**, †**berinse**; **besanctify**, to besaint; **besauce**, **bescent**, **bescorch**; †**bescorn**, to cover with scorn; †**bescourge**, **bescrape**, **beshake**; **beshiver**, to shiver to atoms; **beshod**, †**beshower**, **beshrivel**, †**besinge** (OE. *besengan*); **beslap**, to slap soundly; **besnowball**; †**besob**, to soak; **besoothe**; †**bespend**, to spend, waste; †**besplit**, **besqueeze**, †**bestab**, **bestay**, **besteer**; **bestock**, to stock thoroughly; **bestore**, †**bestrip**, **besuit**, **besweeten**, †**betalk**, †**bethreaten**, †**betire**; †**betrace**, to mark all over, to streak; †**betwattle** (*dial.*), to bewilder; **bewasted**, wasted away; **beweary**, **bewelcome**, **bewidow**, **bewomanize**; †**bewound**, to wound seriously; †**bewreak**, to revenge.

1599 THYNNE *Animadv.* (1865) 61 This syllable [be] is sett before to make yt moore signyficant and of force; as..for 'dewed,' 'bedewed,' etc.

1589 *Almond for P.* 40 It was not for nothing..that he so *bebaited his betters. **1866** *Harvard Memor. Biogr.* I. 263 Seventy miles distant—a long way in this *bebothered state. **1617** COLLINS *Def. Bp. Ely* II. x. 504 As if his wits were *be-breecht. **1603** FLORIO *Montaigne* III. v. (1632) 490 They are not *bebusied about Rhetorike flowers. **1598** SYLVESTER *Du Bartas* II. ii. (1641) 114/1 Brutish Cham..In scornful tearms his Father thus *be-checkt. *c* **1175** *Cott. Hom.* 239 His richtwise deme, þe non ne maie *bechece, non beswice. **1952** AUDEN *Nones* 54 The spreading ache *bechills the rampant glow Of fortune-hunting blood. **1832** WHATELY in *Life* (1866) I. 150 He whined and *beclamoured..but all to no purpose. **1832** tr. *Tour Germ. Prince* IV. v. 195 The chief magistrate..thought fit to *becompliment me by the mission of two of his colleagues. **1513** DOUGLAS *Æneis* x. viii, 135 Na lytill thyng..Hes hym *bycost the frendschip of Ene. **1883** *Gd. Words* 448 The begrudged, *becoveted good of half a lifetime. **1860** TROLLOPE *Framley P.* I. xiv. 281 Barsetshire..is a pleasant, green, tree- *becrowded county. **1607** ROWLANDS *Fam. Hist.* 37 Eskeldart Guy's sword did so *becrush. **1863** G. KEARLEY *Links in Chain* iv. 74 Snails, much despised, bekicked, and *becrushed. **1550** COVERDALE *Spir. Perle* xxi. Wks. 1844 I. 151 Why should any man ..*becumber himself about that thing? **1599** PEELE *David & Beths.* Wks. II. 74 The eagle..emboldened..to *bedare the sun. **1584** HUDSON *Judith* in Sylvester *Du Bartas* (1608) 694 You Tyrant..Who hath *bedround the world with blood. **1877** J. HAWTHORNE *Garth.* II. IV. xxxii. 31 Nor was it the lack of public recognition which had *bedrowsed him. **1874** MOTLEY *Barneveld* II. xi. 19 England and France distracted and *bedrugged. **1596** SPENSER *F.Q.* II. vi. 42 To the flood he came..And deepe himselfe *beducked in the same. **1567** DRANT *Horace' Ars Poet.* B vj, Daunce and *bedunche the grounde with fote. **1602** WARNER *Alb. Eng.* x. liv. 244 Her owne *byearned lot. **1848** H. MILLER *First Impr.* vii. (1857) 119 Sorely *be-elbowed and be-kneed. *a* **1633** MUNDAY *Palm. of Eng.* ii, One of her *befavoured knights. **1566** STUDLEY *Seneca's Agamemn.* (1581) 155 Hercules..left the groue *befilched cleane. **1388** WYCLIF *Lament.* ii. 15 Alle men passynge bi the weie *biflappeden with hondis on thee. **1574** HELLOWES *Gueuara's Ep.* (1577) 232 You had escaped from thence wounded, abhorred, and *beeflowted. **1864** *Morn. Star* 25 June 4 Some panting, blushing, *beflustered honourable member. **1568** T. HOWELL *New Sonn.* (1879) 144 For thou in Barke so well *befraught, hast al our ioyes away. *a* **1656** BP. HALL *Defiance to Snoy* (R.) Pines..*be-gald alone With the deep furrowes of the thunder-stone. **1393** LANGL. *P. Pl.* C. XXI. 383 þou ..*By-glosedest hem and [by]-gyledest hem and my gardyn breke. **1855** SINGLETON *Virgil* I. 204 With full hue of glassy green *Begrained. **1513** DOUGLAS *Æneis* VI. vii. 63 With hartly luif *begrait hir thus in hy. **1648** HERRICK *Poems* App. (1869) 433 (D.) Whose head beefrindged with *behallowed tresses Seemes like Apollo's. **1481** CAXTON *Myrr.* III. xii. 160 A grete philosophre..whiche coude *byhelpe hym. **1640** A. HARSNET *God's Summ.* 388 Bee carefull then to *Be-Husband every moment of thy time. **1862** J. BROWN in *Illustr. Melbourne Post* 26 July, Many generations of starved, *bekicked, and downtrodden forefathers. **1850** BLACKIE *Æschylus* I. 197 Friendly men receive The curse-*beladen wanderer. **1458** *Paston Lett.* 311 I. 422 *Belassch hym, tyl he wyll amend. **1631** BRATHWAIT *Whimzies* 46 To dandle him in the lappe of securitie, and *belull him in his sensuall lethargie. *c* **1400** *Destr. Troy* XXVI. 10701 Paris.. was pricket at his hert, To se his men so *be-mard, & murtherit. **1662** FULLER *Worthies* I. 2 He *bemartyreth such who as yet did survive. **1879** HOWELLS *L. Aroostook* (1883) II. 174 Stanifrid stood *bemazed. **1656** S. H. *Gold. Law* 61 But now the Laicks are a Lay people..till some Moses *be-meet with them. **1857** CARLYLE *Misc.* iv. 86 (D.) The young lion's whelp has to grow up all bestrapped, *bemuzzled. **1838** HAWTHORNE *Amer. Note Bks.* (1871) I. 147 A *bepaid clergyman. **1586** WEBBE *Eng. Poetrie* (1870) 77 Workmen.. with boyling heate so *be-parched. **1828** *Blackw. Mag.* XXIV. 591 It has been bespouted, bequoted, and *beparodied. **1531** ELYOT *Gov.* (1580) 7 Hiero..counsailed him to *beparte his importable labours. **1578** FLORIO *1st Fruites* 50 A language confused, *bepeesed with many tongues. **1839** J. DARLEY in *Beaum. & Fl. Wks.* (1839) I. Introd. 31 Unlike him [i.e. Caesar] *bepierced and bescratched. *a* **1726** VANBRUGH *Journ. Lond.* I. i, Bandboxes ..were so *bepiled up. **1574** HELLOWES *Gueuara's Ep.* (1577) 232 You had escaped from thence wounded, abhorred, and also *beepilled. **1865** *Morn. Star* 20 Nov., The most *bepoetised case of *crim. con.* on record. **1591** in Farr *S.P.* (1845) I. 141 To rescue me *beprest I do thee pray. **1690** E. FOWLER *Serm. Bow-Ch.* 16 Apr. 16 They would..*bepride themselves the more in their own strength. **1822** *Blackw. Mag.* II. 64 Bethumbing and *bequoting their beauties. **1611** COTGR. s.v. *Chipault*, He is all to *be ragged and rent. **1598** SYLVESTER *Du Bartas* (1608) 1013 Princes Whose rage their realms with..bloud *berinses. **1826** SCOTT *Woodst.* v, *Besanctified as you are. *a* **1674** MILTON *Moscovia* Wks. (1738) II. 147 Rare dishes ..*besauc'd with Garlick and Onions. **1863** A. B. GROSART *Small Sins* 40 A..*be-scented, be-ribboned..little fox! **1583** STANYHURST *Æneis* II. (Arb.) 52 Hector..thee Greekish nauye *beskorched. *c* **1386** CHAUCER *Pers. T.* ¶204 Than was he *bescorned, that oonly schulde be honoured. *a* **1300** *Cursor M.* 17771 Bath bi-scurget and bi-spit. **1865** *Athenæum* No. 1951. 375/3 No *bescraped cathedrals. **1664** COTTON *Scarron.* 24 Have you not seen..A water-dog ..*Beshake his shaggy pantaloons? **1556** ABP. PARKER *Psalter* xxxiv. 87 God hateth the proud and them *beshenth. **1648** HERRICK *Noble Numb.* Wks. II. 203 That cloude ..*Beshiver'd into seeds of raine. **1850** CLOUGH *Dipsychus* II. ii. 69 Hexameters..*Beshod with rhyme. *c* **1420** *Pallad. on Husb.* VI. 12 And yf the rayne *beshoure. **1821** COMBE (Dr. Syntax) *Wife* iii. (D.) That *beshrivelled face and mien. **1340** *Ayenb.* 230 þe prive cat *bezengþ ofte his scin. **1858** CARLYLE *Fredk. Gt.* IV. x. I. 488 Philip's Father, son of the *Beslapped. **1611** CHAPMAN *May Day* Plays (1873) II. 360 'Twere a good deed, to..*besnowball him with rotten egges. **1609** HOLLAND *Amm. Marcell.* XXXV. viii. 259 The ground was *besobbed and drenched with the mid-Winter frosts that now thawed. **1614** SYLVESTER *Bethulia's Resc.* vi. 60 The trembling Lady..*besoothes him. **1567** MAPLET *Gr. Forest* 96 Ixion *bespent his seede vpon the Cloude. **1614** CHAPMAN *Odyss.* VIII. 398 All his craft *bespent. *a* **1640** JACKSON *Creed* IX. Wks. VIII. 445 Unless abundance of wit hath *besplitted his understanding. **1600** ROWLANDS *Let. Humours Blood* xxiii. 29 Drinke with his dart hath all *bestabbed mee. *c* **1320** *Sir Tristr.* I. lxii, Tristrem..seyd.. How stormes hem *bistayd. *a* **1618** J. DAVIES *Sonn. Sir T. Erskin* (D.), How blest wert thou that didst thee so *besteere. **1648** HERRICK *Poems* App. (1869) 439 (D.) Lett hym..Soe good a soile *bestocke and till. **1661** HICKERINGILL *Jamaica* 16 *Bestored with all sorts of fruit-bearing Trees. **1340** *Ayenb.* 123 þe holy gost be þise zeue yefþes *bestrepþ þe zeue zennes uram þe herte. **1648** HERRICK *Hesp.* I. 166 Dew..*besweetned in a..violet. **1612** DRAYTON *Poly-olb.* xxviii, The same..*betalk'd on long. **1635** QUARLES *Emb.* III. xi, My rock-bethreaten'd soul. **1594** CAREW *Tasso* (1881) 17 Like rest to gaine in like *betyred plight. *c* **1460** *Towneley Myst.* 288 A goost..lyke hym in blood betraced. **1686** GOAD *Celest. Bodies* III. iv. 507 They are *betwatled in their Understandings. **1844** S. NAYLER *Reynard* 29 Poor Bruin thus was sheer *betwattled. **1593** SHAKS. *Rich. II*, I. iii. 221 My..time- *bewasted light Shall be extinct with age. **1636** HEALEY *Theophrast.* 55 Hee..is all to *bewearied. **1583** STANYHURST *Æneis* III. (Arb.) 81 King Helenus..vs..*bewelcomd. **1787** T. JEFFERSON *Writ.* (1859) II. 127, I shall now feel *bewidowed. **1653** HEMINGS *Fatal Contr.*, O man *be-womaniz'd! **1422–61** *Songs & Carols 15th C.* (1856) 87 Many man..wyste hym wel *bewreke, The hadde wel levere myn hed to-breke.

3. Forming derivative verbs with privative meaning 'off, away,' as in BEDEAL, BENIM, BEREAVE. A very common use of *be-* in OE. and ME., prob. originating in words like BE-SHEAR, 'to cut all round,' whence 'to cut off or away'; but no longer in living use in forming new derivatives.

4. Making verbs transitive, by adding a prepositional relation: primarily 'about,' as in BE-SPEAK, speak about (or for, to), BE-MOAN, moan about (or over); which sense can usually be detected under the various *against, at, for, to, on, upon, over, by*, etc. required by modern idiom: †**bebark**, to bark around or at; †**becack**, to deposit ordure on; **bechatter**, to environ with chattering, etc.; †**bechirm**, to chirm (as birds) around; †**bechirp**, to chirp about; **beclang**, **beclatter**; †**becrave** (OE. *becrafian*), to crave for; **becrawl**, to crawl all over; **becroak**, to croak round or at; †**becry**, to cry at, accuse; **bedin**, to fill with din or noise; **bedribble**, to dribble upon (e.g. as a dog); **bedrivel**; **bedrizzle**; †**bedwell**, to dwell in or around; †**befleet**, to flow round; †**befret**, to fret or gnaw away; **befuddle**, to make stupid with tippling; **begaze**, to gaze at; †**beglide**, to slip away from, escape; †**beglitter**, to irradiate; **begroan**, to groan at; †**begruntle**, to make uneasy; **behoot**, to hoot at; **bejuggle**, to get over by jugglery, to cheat; †**belag**, to make to lag; †**beleap**, to leap on, 'cover'; †**bemew**, †**bemoult**, to mew or moult upon; **bemurmur**, to murmur at or against; †**bemute** (of birds), to mute or drop dung on; **beparse**, to plague with parsing; **bepiss**, to piss on, wet with urine; **bepreach**, to preach at; **bereason**, to reason with, overcome by reasoning; †**bireme**, to cry out upon; **beride** (OE. *berídan*), to ride beside, to override; †**berow**, to row round; †**bescumber**, to scumber on; **beshine** (OE. *bescínan*), to shine on; **beshit(e** (OE. *bescítan*) = *becack* (*Obs.* in polite use, but common in ME. and early mod.E. literature); **beshout**, to shout at, applaud; †**beshriek**, to shriek at; †**besigh**, to sigh for; †**besmell**, to smell out; **besmile**, to smile on; †**bespew**, to spew on; **bestare**, to stare at, to make staring; **bestraddle**, to straddle across, bestride; **bestream**, to stream over; **beswarm**, to swarm over; †**beswelter**; **beswim**, to swim upon; **bethunder**; †**betipple**, to muddle by tippling; **betravel**, to travel over, to overrun with travellers: **bevomit**, to vomit all over; **bewhisper**, to whisper to; **bewhistle**, to whistle round.

1340 *Ayenb.* 66 þe felle dogge þet byt and *beberkþ alle þo þet he may. **1598** FLORIO, *Incacare*, to *becacke. *a* **1618** J. DAVIES *Paper's Compl.* Wks. (1876) 75 (D.), He all my breast becackes. **1875** B. TAYLOR *Faust* I. xxi. 191 If he can't every step *bechatter. *a* **1250** *Owl & Night.* 279 Hi me *bichirmeþ [*v.r.* bichermet] and bigredeth. **1600** T. MORLEY in *Lyric P.* (Percy Soc.) 51 Every bird upon the bush *be-chirps it up so gay. **1875** A. SMITH *Burns' Wks.* (Globe) Introd. 13 A dingy churchyard hemmed by narrow streets—*be-clanged now by innumerable hammers. **1832–53** *Whistle-Binkie* (Sc. Songs) Ser. I. 77 Why sae incessantly deave and *beclatter me, Teasing me mair than a body can bide? *c* **1250** *Gen. & Ex.* 1388 Ðoȝte he, ðis maiden wile ic..*bi-crauen. **1787** BECKFORD *Italy, etc.* II. 19 An oozy beach..*becrawled with worms. **1861** TEMPLE & TREVOR *Tannhäuser* 52 Let..the hoarse chough *becroak the moon! *c* **1440** *Morte Arth.* (Roxb.) 89 Launcelot of treson he *be-cryed. **1880** SWINBURNE *Stud. Song* 192 The darkness by thunders *bedinned. **1620** BP. HALL *Hon. Mar. Clergy* I. §8 Wks. (1628) 747 This whelpe of theirs *commingit cineros*, *bedribbles their ashes. **1653** A. WILSON *Jas. I*, Pref. 4 Why should we *bedribble with our Pens, the Dust that rests there? **1721** BAILEY, Bedrawled, bedrabbled, bedrivelled: cf. BEDRAVEL. **1883** *Harper's Mag.* Jan. 167/1 The *bedrizzled windows of an express train. **1802** W. TAYLOR in Robberds *Mem.* I. 412 Gentry of narrow income used to *bedwell Montreuil. **1817** —— in *Month. Mag.* XLIII. 236 The marble caves ye now bedwell. *a* **1300** *K. Horn* 1396 Strong castel he let sette, Mid see him *biflette. **1598** GREENE *Jas. IV* (1861) 207 A constant heart with burning flames *be-fret. **1802** W. TAYLOR in Robberds *Mem.* I. 411, I could only..*begaze the site of Lord Nelson's misemployment. *c* **1300** in Wright *Lyric P.* xxx. 87 That ded he shal *by-glyde. **1583** STANYHURST *Æneis* I. (Arb.) 30 Shee turned with rose color heaunlye *beglittred. **1837** CARLYLE *Fr. Rev.* II. VI. iii. (D.), [He] shall find himself *begroaned by them. *a* **1670** HACKET *Abp. Williams* I. 131 (D.), The Spaniards were *begruntled with these scruples. **1838** EMERSON *Misc.* 118 It is travestied and depreciated..it is *behooted and behowled. **1680** HICKERINGILL *Meroz* 12 To *bejuggle and beguile the silly Rabble. **1705** —— *Priest-cr.* II. Pref. A iij, Bejuggl'd Mob! you are the Tools, That Priests do work with called Fools. **1851** H. MELVILLE *Moby Dick* III. xlvii. 268 No matter how many..thou may'st have bejuggled and destroyed before. **1721** BAILEY, **Belagged*, left behind. **1513** DOUGLAS *Æneis* VII. iii. 207 Makand his stedis *beleip meris vnknaw. **1630** J. TAYLOR (Water P.) *Wks.* II. 448 So scuruily bescuruide and *bemewde. **1603** FLORIO *Montaigne* III. ix. (1632) 561 Some of Platoes Dialogues: *bemolted with a fantasticall variety. **1837** CARLYLE *Fr. Rev.* III. III. iv. II. 231 Beshouted by the Galleries..*bemurmured by the Right-side. **1875** LOWELL *Poet. Wks.* (1879) 458 She loves yon pine- bemurmured ridge. **1634** A. WARWICK *Spare Min.* (1821) 110 The heron..*bemuting his enemie's feathers to make her flagge-winged. **1880** GRANT WHITE *Every-Day Eng.* 270 Grammar that has so weighed down our poor *beparsed English-speaking people. **1481** CAXTON *Reynard* (Arb.) 6 There he hath *be-pyssed my chyldren where as they laye. **1658** FORD *Witch of Edm.* IV. i, Ready to bepiss themselves with laughing. **1764** T. BRYDGES *Homer Travest.* (1797) II. 16 Ye all bepiss'd yourselves for fear. **1809** W. IRVING *Knickerb.* II. viii. (1849) 130 Our worthy ancestors..never being *be-preached and be-lectured. **1880** *World* 13 Oct. 8 She is alternately be-preached and bepraised by middle-aged spinsterhood. **1826** E. IRVING *Babylon* II. VI. 154 We are *bereasoned out of our faith by the intellectual apostacy of the time. *c* **1200** *Trin. Coll. Hom.* 29 Nu shalt [þu]..*biremen him mid euel wordes. **1690** D'URFEY *Collin's Walk* II. (D.), Those two that there *beride him, And with such graces prance beside him. **1848** in *Proc. Berw. Nat. Club* II. vi. 300 When an insect so beridden is taken up, the mites disperse. **1205** LAY. 20128 He wolde ..æc Bristouwe abuten *birouwen [**1250** birowe]. **1599** MARSTON *Sco. Villanie* III. ix. (1764) 218 This..pedant Mortimers numbers With muck-pit Esculine filth *bescumbers. **1625** B. JONSON *Staple News* V. ii, Did Block bescumber Statute's white suit? **1850** BLACKIE *Æschylus* I. Pref. 23 The large sweeping sun- *beshone tiers of an ancient theatre. *a* **1000** *Ags. Gloss.* in Wr.-Wülcker *Voc.* 507 *Caccabatum*, *besciten. *a* **1300** *K. Alis.* 5485 Bishiten and bydagged foule. *a* **1683** OLDHAM *Wks. & Rem.* 81 Flies which would the Deity beshite. **1727** SWIFT *Acc. E. Curll* Wks. 1755 III. I. 158, I have been frighted, pumped, kicked ..and beshitten. **1828** CARLYLE *Misc.* I. 156 Betrumpeted and *beshouted from end to end of the habitable globe. *a* **1250** *Owl & Night.* 67 Alle ho..the *bi-schricheth and bigredet. *c* **1200** *Trin. Coll. Hom.* 201 þe sinfulle þe his sinnes ..sore *bisicheð. **1803** *Ladies' Diary* 26 Colonial settlements I made, And Spain *be-smelt the prize. **1867** CAYLEY in *Fortn. Rev.* Nov. 590 The levels *besmile thee of ocean. *c* **1600** STOW in *Three 15th c. Chron.* (1880) 162 ᵉ howse was mervelously..*by spewed. *c* **1220** *Leg. Kath.* 309 þe Keiser *bistarede hire wið swiðe steape ehnen. **1780** BECKFORD *Italy, etc.* I. 224 That hobgoblin tapestry which used to bestare the walls of our ancestors. **1807–8** W. IRVING *Salmag.* 12 (D.), The little gentleman who *bestraddles the world in the front of Hutching's Almanack. **1860** PUSEY *Min. Proph.* 488 Shall My dwelling-place..be *bestreamed with rains. **1583** STANYHURST *Æneis* I. (Arb.) 34 Troians with rough seas stormye *besweltred. **1805** W. TAYLOR in *Ann. Rev.* III. 59 Rivers which bridges have yoked, and navigation *beswims. **1581** J. BELL *Haddon's Answ. Osor.* A iiij b, This poysoned Dolldreanche hath *be-typpledd the senses. **1837** CARLYLE *Fr. Rev.* III. III. iv. II. 229 An explosive crater; vomiting fire, *bevomited with fire! **1674** N. FAIRFAX *Bulk & Selv.* To Rdr., Self *be-whispers us, that it stands us all in hand to be forgiven as well as to forgive. **1837** CARLYLE *Fr. Rev.* III. III. vi. (D.), Dumouriez and his Staff..sprawl and plunge for life, *be-whistled with curses and lead.

5. Forming trans. verbs on adjectives and substantives, taken as complements of the predicate, meaning To make: as BEFOUL, to make foul, *orig.* to surround or affect with foulness; BEDIM, to make dim; BEFOOL, to make a fool of; BESOT, to turn into a sot. In modern use, nearly all tinged with ridicule or contempt; cf. to *beknight* with to *knight*. **a.** Formed with adj.: † **bebrave** (1576), to make brave; **bedirty, bedismal, bedumb**; † **befast** (OE. *befæstan*), to fasten; † **begaudy**, † **begay**, † **beglad, begray, begreen, begrim**; † **begrimly**, to begrime; † **beguilty**; † **bepale, bepretty**, † **bered**; **beshag**, to make shaggy; † **beslow**, to retard; **besmooth**, † **besour, bewhite. b.** With sb.: **bebaron**, to make into a baron; **bebishop, beclown**; † **becollier**, to make as black as a collier; **becoward**; † **bedaw** (*a* 1529), to make a 'daw' or fool of; **bedeacon** (1589), **bedoctor**, † **bedolt** (= BESOT), **beduchess, bedunce, befop, beking, beknight; belion**, to make a (society) lion of; **beminstrel; bewhig**, to convert into a whig.

1842 MIALL in *Nonconf.* II. 33 Be-mitred and *be-baroned bishops. **1576** in Collier's *E.E. Pop. Lit.* xvi. 40 Dyvers..gladly would have mee, And being their wyfe would trimly *bebrave me. **1609** ROWLANDS *Crew Gossips* 24 O wretch, O Lob, who would be thus *beclown'd? **1593** NASHE *Lent. Stuffe* (1871) 60 Too foul-mouthed I am, to becollow, or *becollier him, with such chimney-sweeping attributes. **1831** HEIDIGER *Didon.*, A lot of fellows so *becowarded by their stay on shore. *a* **1529** SKELTON *Agst. Garnesche* 182 Ye may well be *bedawyd. **1589** *Hay any Work* 74 The old porter of Paddington, whom John of London *bedeaconed and beminstrelled. **1623** *Accident Blacke Friers* 12 [They] must run from the pure waters of Shiloe, to *bedirty themselves in the filthy puddels of mens traditions. **1803** BRISTED *Pedest. Tour* II. 525 It [a shirt] was ..begrimed and *bedirtied. **1751** *Student* II. 259 Let us see your next number..*bedismalled with broad black lines. **1806** SOUTHEY *Let.* (1856) I. 364 Harry will be *bedoctored in July. **1856** VAUGHAN *Mystics* II. VIII. v. 59 The *be-doctored wiseacres of all the universities of Europe. **1574** HELLOWES *Gueuara's Ep.* (1577) 183 Young men without experience..*bedolted of the thinges of this world. **1804** WOLCOTT (P. Pindar) *Wks.* (1812) V. 180 She's begrac'd and *beduchess'd already. **1615** BP. HALL *Contempl. N.T.* IV. ii, Every soul is more deafened and *bedumbed by increasing corruptions. **1611** COTGR., *Philogrobolizé du cerveau*.. astonied, *bedunced, at his wits end. **1674** N. FAIRFAX *Bulk & Selv.* 43 Motion, which I think is altogether *befasted to Body. **1866** *Reader* 24 Feb. 201/1 The courtier in his new Court suit *be-fopt. **1640** J. GOWER *Ovid's Fast.* 310 Her breasts with glittring gold *begaudy'd were. **1648** J. BEAUMONT *Psyche* iii. §75 (R.), Beauteous things..*Begay the simple fields. *a* **1617** HIERON *Wks.* II. 199 To *beglad your hearts. *a* **1624** BP. M. SMYTH *Serm.* (1632) 234 Age ..*begrayeth our head. **1864** D. MITCHELL *Sev. Stories* 300 Hillsides..*begreened by a thousand irrigating streamlets. **1870** H. MACMILLAN *Bible Teach.* xiii. 267 They..tarnish and *begrim the brightest colours. *c* **1485** *Digby Myst.* (1882) II. 105 Ye were so *be-grymlyd and yt had bene a sowe. **1627** BP. SANDERSON *Serm.* I. 263 Dost..*beguilty thine own conscience with sordid bribery. **1831** GREVILLE *Mem.* (1875) II. xiv. 153 He would do anything to be *be-king'd. **1794** WOLCOTT (P. Pindar) *Celebration* Wks. III. 422 Behold once-Quaker Benjamin *be-knighted. **1808** SCOTT in Lockhart (1839) I. 11 Many worshipful and *be-knighted names. **1837** *New Month. Mag.* LI. 183 Be-scented and *be-lioned petlings! **1640** T. CAREW *Lady to Inconst. Serv.*, Those perjur'd lips of thine, *Bepal'd with blasting sighes. **1872** C. KING *Sierra Nev.* x. 210 What has he done but..belittle and *be-pretty this whole..country? **1604** ROWLANDS *Looke to it* 27 Your head *beshagg'd with nittie lowsie lockes. **1868** HAWTHORNE *Amer. Note-bks.* (1879) IV. 201 All *beshagged with forest. **1645** QUARLES *Sol. Recant.* IV. 20 How art thou clogg'd With dull mortality, *beslow'd..In thine owne frailty! **1615** CHAPMAN *Odyss.* VIII. 495 The Graces..with immortal balms *besmooth her skin. *a* **1660** HAMMOND *Serm.* xv. Wks. 1683 IV. 668 This old leaven that so *besoures all our actions. **1852** JAMES *Peguinillo* I. 154 Five-and-thirty years of peace have so betravelled the world. **1832** SOUTHEY *Q. Rev.* XLVIII. 300 Lord Nugent is lamentably *bewhigged. **1678** *Ripley Reviv'd, Vision*, 12 The Concave of this secret place will be so *bewhited with the fumes.

c. To call, to style, to dub with the title of, etc. Often with a depreciatory or contemptuous force: as **be-blockhead**, † **be-blunderbus, be-brother, be-coward**, † **behypocrite, be-lady, be-ladyship, belout, bemadam, bemistress, bemonster, berascal, be-Roscius, bescoundrel, bevillain.**

1765 TUCKER *Lt. Nat.* I. 476 He so *be-blockheaded and *be-blunderbust me about as was enough to hurry anybody, and throw them off their guard. **1881** PHILLIPPS-WOLLEY *Sport in Crimea* 80 The old gentleman was..much given to kissing and *be-brothering his friends. **1752** FIELDING *Covent Gard. Jrnl.* Wks. (1840) 712 If another hath kicked you, be sure to *becoward him well. **1612** J. DAVIES *Muse's Sacr.* 75 How would'st Thou now *behypocrit man's hart. **1811** E. NARES *Thinks I to Myself* ii. (1816) 38 (D.), How Mrs. Twist did *be-ladyship my poor mother. **1614** B. JONSON *Barth. Fair* v. iii. (D.), They do so all to *bemadam me, I think they think me a very great lady. **1605** CAMDEN *Rem.* 157 He rated and *belowted his Cooke. **1630** J. TAYLOR (Water P.) *Wks.* II. 239/1 Were so *bemadam'd, *bemistrist and Ladified by the beggers. **1692** *Christ Exalted* cxxxix. 105 Not be-heriticking, not *be-monstring Dr. Crisp. **1743** FIELDING *Jon. Wild* II. iii, She beknaved, *berascalled, berogued the unhappy hero. **1596** NASHE *Saffron Walden* V ij, M. Lilly and me, by name he beruffianizd and *berascald. **1774** GOLDSM. *Retal.* 117 While he was *be-Roscius'd and you were be-prais'd! **1885** *Blackw. Mag.* Apr. 543/2 Garrick's generation *be-Rosciused him. **1786** WOLCOTT *To Boswell* Wks. 1794 I. 313 Where surly Sam..Nassau *bescoundrels. *a* **1734** NORTH *Exam.* (1740) 247 (D.), After Mr. S. Atkins had *bevillained the Captain sufficiently.

6. Forming trans. verbs on substantives used in an instrumental relation; the primary idea being; **a.** To surround, cover, or bedaub with, as in BECLOUD, to put clouds about, cover with clouds, BEDEW. Thence, by extension, **b.** To affect with in any way, as in BENIGHT, BEGUILE, BEFRIEND. In both sets there is often an accompanying notion of 'thoroughly, excessively,' as in 2. **c.** An ancient application, no longer in living use, was to express the sense of 'bereave of,' as in BEHEAD, BELIMB, etc., q.v. Cf. 3, above.

a. † **be-ash**, to cover or soil with ashes; † **beblain**, † **bebloom, bebouler, bebutter, becap, becarpet, bechalk, becloak, becobweb, becolour; becoom**, † **becolme**, to smear with coom; **becrime, becurtain**, † **bedot**; † **bedowle**, to cover with dowle or soft hair; **bedust, befetter, befilth, beflannel, beflounce, beflour, beflower, befoam, befringe, befume**, † **beglare, begloom**, † **begum, behorn, behorror, belard**, † **beleaf**, † **beloam**; † **bemail** to cover with mail; **bemantle, bemat, bemeal, bemuck, bepicture, bepimple, beplague, bepowder, berust, bescab, bescarf, bescurf, bescurvy, beslime, besugar, betallow, bethorn, betowel, beulcer, bevenom, bewig**, † **bewimple.**

b. † **beback**, to furnish (a book) with a back; **bebed**, to furnish with a bed; **bebog**, to entangle in a bog, embog; † **bebrine**, to wet with brine; **bebutterfly**, to engross with butterflies; **becivet**, to perfume with civet; **becomma**, to sprinkle with commas; **bedawn, beday**, to overtake with dawn or daylight; † **bedebt**, to indebt; **bedinner**, to treat with a dinner, give a dinner to; † **bedown**, to fill with down; † **befame**, to make famous; † **befancy**, to fill with fancies; **befiddle**, to engross with a fiddle; **befire; befist**, to belabour with the fists; **beflea**, to infest (as) with fleas; † **beflum** (*dial.*), to deceive; † **befrumple**, to crease into frumples or clumsy folds; **befume**, to affect with fumes; † **begall**, to fill with gall, embitter; † **beginger**, to spice with ginger; † **beglew, -glue**, to make game of, befool; **begulf**, to engulf; † **behearse**, to place in a hearse; **behymn, beice, bekerchief; beladle**, to ladle up; **belecture**, to ply with lectures; **beliquor**, to soak with liquor, to alcoholize; † **beman**, to fill with men, to man; **bemissionary**, to pester with missionaries; **bemole**, to mark with moles or dirty spots; **bemoon**, to moon-strike; **bemusk**, to perfume with musk; † **benettle, benightmare, be-ode; bepaper**, to cover or pester with papers; **bephilter**, to treat with a philter; **bephrase**; † **bepistle**, to inflict epistles on; **bequalm**, to affect with qualms; † **berampier**, to surround with a rampart; **berebus**, to inscribe with a rebus; **berubric**, to mark with a rubric or red letter; **besaffron**, to stain or mingle with saffron; **beschoolmaster**, to furnish with schoolmasters; **bescutcheon**, to furnish with an escutcheon; **besentinel**, to surround or guard with sentinels; † **besin**, to stamp with sin, to stigmatize as sinful; **besiren**, to charm with a siren; **beslipper**, to present with slippers; **besnivel, besnuff; besonnet**, to address or celebrate in sonnets; **bespeech; bespy**, to dog with spies; **besquib; bestench, bestink**, to afflict with stench; **bestraw**, to furnish or fill with straw; **betag**, to furnish with a tag; **betask**, to charge with a task; **betocsin, betrumpet; betutor**, to furnish with tutors; **be-urine; beverse**, to celebrate in verse; **beveto**, to put a veto on; **bewall, bewelcome; bewhisker**, to adorn with whiskers; **bewinter**, to overtake or affect with winter; **bewizard**, to influence by a wizard (cf. *bewitch*); **beworm**, to infest with worms; *pass.* to breed worms; **beworship**, to honour with worship.

(Some of these are used only in the passive voice.)

1530 PALSGR. 444/2 You have *beasshed your gloves. **1599** H. BUTTES in *Jas. I Counterbl.* (Arb.) App. 93 The leaues *be-ashed or warmed in imbers and ashes. **1858** *Reeves & Turner's Bk. Catal.* Dec. (No. 278) Folio, newly *bebacked. *a* **1300** *Havelok* 420 He hem ne dede richelike *bebedde. **1605** J. DAVIES *Humours* Wks. (1876) 43 (D.), *Beblaine the bosome of each mistres. **1585** HUNNIS *Handf. Honisuck.* Gen. xl. 8 In the Vyne were Braunches three That al *bebloomed were. **1662** FULLER *Worthies* (1840) I. 458 His feet were fixed in Ireland, where he was not *be-bogg'd. **1862** H. MARRYAT *Sweden* II. 341 The country, though greatly *bebouldered, is wild like fertile Skaane. **1652** BENLOWES *Theoph.* XI. lxviii. 202 Thou peul'st, not repent, but to *bebrine thy woes. **1611** COTGR., *Embeurrer*, to butter or *bebutter. **1759** STERNE *Tr. Shandy* II. iii, The souls of connoisseurs..have the happiness..to get all be-virtued..*be-butterflied, and be-fiddled. **1821** COMBE (Dr. Syntax) *Wife* v. (D.), He thus appear'd..*Becapp'd in due conformity. *a* **1800** CUMBERLAND *Mem.* II. 364 (L.), A floor ..splendidly *bechalked by a capital deseyner. **1805** W. TAYLOR in *Ann. Rev.* III. 46 The distilled perfume of the bookmaker's style, which bemusks and *becivets every London composition. **1598** SYLVESTER *Batt. Ivry* in *Du Bartas* (1608) 1096 Fire and Smoak As with thick clouds, both Armies round *becloak. **1611** COTGR., *Emmantelé* ..*becloked..wrapped as in a cloke. **1788** BURNS *Let.* 9 Sept., Throw my horny fist across my *becobwebbed lyre.

1851 CARLYLE *Sterling* II. iv, Anywhere else in this much *becobwebbed world. **1567** MAPLET *Gr. Forest* 57b, To make black and *becolour the Caruels as it were most browne. **1881** *Academy* 14 May 355 The senseless '*be-commaing' of many Shakespere texts. *a* **1300** *K. Horn* 1064 He makede him a ful chere, And al *bicolmede his swere. **1882** *Pall Mall G.* 18 Apr. 2 A ship's fireman all *becoomed and besmoked. **1844** E. WARBURTON *Cresc. & Cross* xiv. (1859) 144 Every man of any nation, who has so *becrimed himself as to have no country of his own. **1878** H. PHILLIPS *Poems* 71 The heaven with clouds *becurtained. **1827** *Blackw. Mag.* XXI. 783 [He] exclaimed, with visible apprehension of being *bedawned, 'Methinks I smell the morning air.' **1882** G. MACDONALD *Cast. Warl.* III. xxvii. 374 My spirit is the shadow of thy word, Thy candle sun-*bedayed! **1513** DOUGLAS *Æneis* VIII. vii. 20 Albeit that to the childring of Priame King I was *bedettit. **1837** CARLYLE *Fr. Rev.* II. v. x. II. 81 They are harangued, *bedinnered, begifted. **1843** CARLYLE *Past & Pr.* 380 Can he do nothing for his Burns but..lionise him, *bedinner him? **1620** SIR J. DAVIES *Past. W. Brown* What though time yet have not *bedowld thy chin. **1611** COTGR., *Enduvetter*, to *bedowne; to fill..with downe. **1574** HELLOWES *Gueuara's Ep.* (1584) 280 Aristrato..most *befamed the art of phisick. **1567** TURBERV. *Ovid's Ep.* 110b, For everie point I was *Befancide well. **1610** G. FLETCHER *Christ's Vict.* in Farr's *S.P.* (1847) 64 How thou *befanciest the men most wise. **1837** CARLYLE *Fr. Rev.* II. I. x. I. 268 The mute representatives of..*befettered, heavy-laden Nations. **1759** STERNE *Tr. Shandy* II. iii, Be-pictured, be-butterflied, and *befiddled. **1593** NASHE *Christ's T.* (1613) 115 The Buck, hauing *be-filtht himselfe with the female. **1613** F. ROBARTES *Revenue Gosp.* (*title-p.*), A sparke vnseen ..*Befir'd her neast, and burnt vp all her wealth. **1718** MOTTEUX *Quix.* (1733) I. 284 Sancho..rent his Beard ..*befisted his own forgetful Skull. **1859** M. SCOTT *Tom Cringle's Log* xi. 228 Men who..whenever a common cold overtook them..caudled and *beflanneled themselves. **1870** LOWELL *Among my Bks.* (1873) 283 The savages by whom the continent was *beflead rather than inhabited. **1824** MISS MITFORD *Village* Ser. I. (1863) 202 Miss Phœbe..is said to have becurled and *beflounced herself at least two tiers higher on..holidays. **1598** FLORIO, *Farinare*, to *beflowre or *bemeale. **1814** SCOTT *Wav.* lxxi, Then..I *beflumm'd them wi' Colonel Talbot. **1700** DRYDEN *Fables* 106 Froth ..*befoams the Ground. **1611** COTGR. s.v. *Flocquer*, To hang forth loose, to sit bagging, flagging, or *befrumpled, as an ouer-wide garment. **1598** SYLVESTER *Du Bartas* (1608) 809 If such a folly have *befumed your Brain. **1598** GILPIN *Skial.* i, Play the scold..*Begall thy spirit. **1611** COTGR., *Gingembré*, *begingered; seasoned..with Ginger. **1865** DICKENS *Mut. Fr.* III. xvi, The countenance of the *beglared one. **1835** BECKFORD *Recoll.* 46 A square..*begloomed by dark-coloured painted windows. *c* **1430** LYDG. *Minor P.* 115 They went from the game begylyd and *beglued. *a* **1813** A. WILSON *Foresters* Wks. 246 *Begulfed in mire we laboured on. **1730** SWIFT *Lady's Dress.-room*, *Begumm'd, bematter'd, and beslim'd. **1611** COTGR., *Encrasser*, to *begryme..bedawbe with slouenlie filth. **1594** PEELE *Batt. Alcazar* 88 In fatal bed *behearst. **1577** HELLOWES *Gueuara's Ep.* 314 An Oxe..so *behorned. **1630** J. TAYLOR (Water P.) *Wks.* II. 109 She..did *behorne his head. **1857** THACKERAY *White Squall* (D.), The Turkish women..Were frightened and *behorror'd. **1863** *N. Brit. Daily Mail* 13 Oct., *Be-iced in Melville Bay, and presumed to be lost. **1620** SHELTON *Quix.* III. xiii. I. 247 The Curate would not permit 'em to veil and *bekerchief him. **1885** *Spectator* 8 Aug. 1043/1 They were..rather unpleasantly *belarded. **1862** THACKERAY *Four Georges* i. 37 The honest masters of the roast *beladling the dripping. **1631** BRATHWAIT *Whimzies, Ruffian* 83 So *beliquored and belarded, as they have oyle enough to frie themselves. **1611** COTGR., *Enfueiller*, to *beleafe; to stick or set..with leaues. **1598** FLORIO *Smaltare* ..To *belome..to ouercast with mortar or loame. **1594** NASHE *Terrors of Nt.* Gij b, Their armes as it were *bemayled with rich chaynes and bracelets. *c* **1175** *Lamb. Hom.* 23 Þah an castel beo wel *bemoned mid monne. **1620** SHELTON *Quix.* IV. vii. 47 A white long gather'd Stole, so long that it did..*bemantle her from Head to Foot. **1820** COMBE (Dr. Syntax) *Consol.* ii. (D.), The straw-roof'd cot.. With spreading vine *bemantled o'er. **1868** *Morn. Star* 3 Feb., The chaste hall so scrupulously hearthstoned and *bematted. **1623** FAVINE *Theat. Hon.* II. xiii. 208 The idolatry of the Syrians..was planted among the Ægyptians, who *be-mealed the Greeks therewith. **1656** EARL MONM. *Advt. fr. Parnass.* 118 As much *bemealed as those millers who keep there day and night. **1884** in *Pall Mall G.* 31 May 2 Till the end of his days he is *bemissionaried by the society which has made him what he is. **1362** LANGL. *P. Pl.* B. XIV. 4 Children þat wolen *bymolen it many tyme maugre my chekes! **1866** *Lond. Rev.* 23 June 697/2 If you get *be-mooned on a shoemaker's holiday, you had best return home at once. **1530** PALSGR. 306/1 *Bemooked, *breneux*. **1611** COTGR., *Emmusquer*, to *bemuske, or perfume with muske. **1611** COTGR., *Enortier*, To *benettle; to sting..rub ouer, with nettles. **1820** KEATS *St. Agnes* xlii, All his warrior-guests..Were long *be-nightmared. **1814** SOUTHEY *Life & Corr.* (1850) IV. 78 Present copies to the persons *be-oded. **1837** WHITTOCK *Bk. Trades* (1842) 356 His well *be-papered cranium. **1861** M. ARNOLD *Pop. Educ. France* 93 French administration is *bepapered to death. **1690** *Secr. Hist. Chas. II & Jas. II*, 36 The King..had so *bephiltered them with his potions of Aurum potabile, that they passed another act to his heart's desire. **1853** F. HALL *Ledlie's Miscell.* II. 171 Englishmen..are not easily bephrased to death. *a* **1818** MACNEILL *Poems* (1844) 122 The shelving palm-girt beach..*Bepictured o'er. **1648** HERRICK *Hesp.* I. 52 His cheeks *be-pimpled, red and blue. **1860** *All Y. Round* No. 49. 545 Have taken to drinking, and have got blotchy and *bepimpled in consequence. **1589** *Hay any Work* 36 Ile *bepistle you D. Prime, when I am at more leasure. **1870** *Pall Mall G.* 23 Aug. 3 To furnish a concrete and basis for our *beplagued civilization. **1646** G. DANIEL *Poems* Wks. 1878 I. 52 When we are *be-qualm'd, that long imbraces has Made dull Desire. **1582** STANYHURST *Æneis* II. (Arb.) 51 O Troy wals stronglye *berampyerd. **1655** FULLER *Hist. Camb.* (1840) 140 Sir Hugh Ashton..in a tomb..*be-rebussed, according to the ingenuity of that age, with an *ash* growing out of a *tun*. —— *Ch. Hist.* XI. vii. §43 VI. 103 We have *be-rubrick'd each day..with English blood. **1631** BRATHWAIT *Whimzies* 129 His conscience is a Delphian sword..yet annoint him and you *berust him. **1611** COTGR., *Ensafrani*, *besaffroned..seasoned, stained, or coloured with Saffron. —— *Crousteux*, crustie, *bescabbed. **1631** W. SALTONSTALL *Pict. Loq.* (1635) F viij, She is so *bescarf'd that the winde must not breath on her face. **1826** MISS MITFORD *Village* Ser. II. (1863) 327 Miss Reid..*be-scarfed and be-veiled..and all in a flutter of bridal finery. **1810** COLERIDGE *Friend* (1818) III. 224 Young men..expensively *be-schoolmastered, be-tutored, be-lectured, any thing but educated. **1653** URQUHART *Rabelais* V. v, They are thus bescabb'd, *bescurf'd..with Carbuncles, Pashes, and Pockroyals. **1630** J. TAYLOR (Water P.) *Nat. Eng. Poetry* Wks. II. 248/2 So scuruily *bescuruide and bemewde? **1762** CHURCHILL *Ghost* III. 640 A..hearse, *Bescutcheon'd. **1622** H. SYDENHAM *Serm. Sol. Occ.* (1637) 62 Our Apostle *be-sinnes it over and over. **1861** TROLLOPE *Barchester T.* 346 Thus *be-sirened, Mr. Arabin behaved himself very differently from Mr. Slope. **1602** B. JONSON *Poetast.* Prol. (R.), Our fry of writers may *beslime his fame. **1868** HELPS *Realmah* xv. (1876) 416 *Beslimed with disagreeable and injurious talk. **1866** *Reader* 24 Mar. 299 Poor men!..to be be-teapotted and *be-slippered. **1611** COTGR., *Enroupié*, *besniueled, dropping at the nose. **1728** YOUNG *Love Fame* VI. (1757) 147 Unwash'd her hands, and much *besnuff'd her face. **1860** J. KENNEDY *Swallow B.* v. 60 Belles, who had been *besonnetted..for ten years before. **1845** CARLYLE *Cromwell's Lett. & Sp.* (1871) II. 126 Solemnly welcomed, bedinnered, *bespeeched. **1837** —— *Fr. Rev.* III. III. viii. 132 Getting them *bespied. **1813** *Q. Rev.* IX. 107 She was *besquibbed and pasquinaded. **1568** *Like to Like* in Hazl. *Dodsl.* III. 317 To *bestench the place! **1611** COTGR., *Empuantir*, to *bestinke; to fill with stinke. —— *Empaillé*, *bestrawed, filled..furnished with straw. —— *Ensuccrer*, to *besugar; to sweeten..with sugar. *a* **1618** SYLVESTER *Colonies* 356 (D.), Thrace subtle Greece *beswarms. **1762** CHURCHILL *Ghost* III. 640 Bescutcheon'd and *betagged with verse. **1638** FORD *Fancies* i. 2 I will *betallow thy tweezes. **1857** HEAVYSEGE *Saul* (1869) 268 The nymph.. would have *betasked me like a very slave. **1884** G. HAWLEY *Wit, Wisd.* etc. *Richter* 66 The whole..lay prickly and *bethorned before him. **1857** CARLYLE *Fr. Rev.* II. VII. v. 263 It has been *betocsined, bestormed. **1846** H. MILLER *Rambles Geol.* (1858) 399 The *betowelled monkey. **1662** FULLER *Worthies* II. 520 (D.), Satan..having Job in his power..only *be-ulcered him on his skin. **1565** GOLDING *Ovid's Met.* II. (1593) 51 All *be-venimd was his toong. *a* **1764** CHURCHILL *P. Profess.*, When their Ancestors *beversed That glorious Stuart James the first. **1837** CARLYLE *Fr. Rev.* II. v. xii. II. 85 The Priest-Decree, *bevetoed by Majesty. **1250** LAY. 18631 He hadde þare tweie castles *biwalled swiðe faste. **1583** STANYHURST *Æneis* III. (Arb.) 81 King Helenus..vs as his freends freendlye *bewelcomd. **1762** STERNE *Tr. Shandy* V. i. 14 'Twas she who *bewhisker'd St. Bridget. **1820** W. IRVING *Sketch Bk.*, *Xmas Dinner* (D.), Striplings *bewhiskered with burnt cork. **1866** *Lond. Rev.* 9 June 640/1 It drives him to *bewig his bald head. **1393** GOWER *Conf.* II. 360 Where lay *be-wimpled a visage. **1647** COWLEY *Mistr.* (1669) 47 Tears, that *bewinter all my Year. **1652** SPARKE *Prim. Dev.* Pref., The Sun..visiting the *bewintered earth. **1862** H. TAYLOR *St. Clement's Eve* 23 She cannot..Be more *bewizarded than I'm bewitched. **1604** DEKKER *Honest Wh.* in *Dodsley* (1780) X. 253 The body..is gone *be-worm'd. **1787** BECKFORD *Italy, etc.* II. 198 For what purpose they [state pageants] are bedecked and *beworshiped.

7. Forming participial adjectives, which unite the preceding senses, esp. 6 and 2, in the notion of 'covered or furnished with,' usually in a conspicuous, ostentatious, unnecessary, or overdone way. In modern use (e.g. with Carlyle) the force of the *be-* is often merely rhetorical, expressing depreciation, ridicule, or raillery, on the part of the speaker, towards the appendage or ornamentation in question; cf. *booted* and *bebooted*, *gartered begartered*, *wigged bewigged*. Some of these words have no form without *be-*, and closely approach the verbs in 5, e.g. *bedaughtered*, *bepilgrimed* 'overrun with pilgrims.' This is now the most frequent use of *be-*, and the formations of this kind are endless; e.g. ***be-aureoled***, ***bebelted***, ***becloaked***, ***becoroneted***, ***becupolaed***, ***bediamonded***, ***bedragoned***, ***befathered***, ***befezzed***, ***beflogged***, ***beflounced***, ***befrilled***, ***begoggled***, ***bejacketed***, ***bejeaned***, ***bemitred***, ***bemotored***, ***bemuslined***, ***beperiwigged***, ***beribboned***, ***beringleted***, ***beskirted***, ***besleeved***, ***betabbed***, ***betrousered***, ***beturbaned***, ***beuncled***, ***bevillaed***, ***bewinged***. See the quotations.

1923 D. H. LAWRENCE *Birds, Beasts & Flowers* 29 Your.. idealism, Like a *be-aureoled bleached skeleton. **1945** DYLAN THOMAS *Let.* 30 July (1966) 282 Like a be-aureoled bleached skeleton hovering its cage-ribs in the social heaven. **1839** LADY LYTTON *Cheveley* I. v. 105 *Be-balled and *be-chained candelabras. **1854** H. STRICKLAND *Trav. Th.* 18 A besworded..*bebelted official takes all passports. **1831** CARLYLE *Sart. Res.* I. iii, Couriers arrive *bestrapped and *bebooted. **1859** REEVE *Brittany* 138 [A] short-tailed jacket, *bebuttoned and braided throughout. **1884** *Harper's Mag.* Sept. 556/1 Elderly *becapped women. **1883** *Century Mag.* XXVII. 110 [A] country..*becarpeted, and becurtained with grass. **1861** *Sat. Rev.* 18 May 502 The figure of the *becassocked priest spoils all. **1882** MRS. HECKFORD *Lady Trader* 302 Fine-looking Kaffirs, all *be-cat-tailed. **1598** SYLVESTER *Vocation, Du Bartas* (1608) 311 Gawdy plumes of Foes (*be-cedared brave). **1785–95** WOLCOTT (P. Pindar) *Lousiad.* III. Wks. I. 267 *Be-chain'd with all the splendor of Lord May'rs. **1869** *Daily News* 3 July, Genial welcome..to the bewigged and the *bechignoned alike. **1879** MRS. HOUSTON *Wild West* 85 The smiling remonstrance of more than one of his *be-coiffed listeners. **1863** GROSART *Small Sins* 40 It is only a 'small sin,' a smug, be-furred, *be-combed..'little fox!' **1837** CARLYLE *Fr. Rev.* III. v. i. II. 283 Open-Scoundrels rode triumphant, bediademed, *becoronetted, bemitred. **1700** CONGREVE *Way of World* III. xv, Thou art so *becravated, and so beperriwigg'd. **1885** *Times* 28 July 3/1 Very ancient illustrations, crowded with *becrinolined ladies. **1860** READE *Cloister & H.* lv. (D.), My master was at the gate *be-crutched. **1808** W. IRVING *Salmag.* xiv. (1860) 331 The portrait of a young lady dressed in a..gown..be-flowered..and *be-cuffed. **1771** H. WALPOLE *Lett.* III. 375 (D.), The Collisée..is a most gaudy Ranelagh, gilt, painted, and *becupided like an opera. **1883** VERNON LEE in *Mag. Art.* Nov. 3/1 Two rooms..stuccoed, gilded, flowered, *be-cupided. **1861** RUSSELL in *Times* 10 July, A city on a hill..be-steepled, *becupolaed, large-hoteled. **1883** *Century Mag.* XXVII. 110 Is there another country under the sun so *becushioned, becarpeted, and becurtained with grass? **1837** CARLYLE *Fr. Rev.* I. VI. iii. I. 180 Comes this 'Saviour of France,' beshouted, *becymballed by the world. **1830** *Diary of Nun* I. 233 *Bedaughtered dowagers. **1884** *Med. Times* 28 June 875/2 The wan-matrons and *be-dentelured debutantes. **1837** CARLYLE *Fr. Rev.* III. v i. II. 283 Open-Scoundrels rode ..*bediademed, becoronetted, bemitred. **1840** POE *Ulalume, Poems* (1859) 70 Astarte's *bediamonded crescent. **1879** HINGSTON *Austral. Abr.* ix. 101 The garden of China is much *bedotted with mounds of earth. **1925** E. BOWEN in *Lond. Mercury* July 249 Eleanor..followed the *be-dragoned back. **1928** BLUNDEN *Japanese Garland* 22 A wind like fifty winds at once Through the bedragoned kingdom runs. **1960** T. HUGHES *Lupercal* 29 Prehistoric bedragonned times Crawl that darkness with Latin names. **1614** RICH *Honest. Age* (1844) 50 Starcht bands, so *be-edged, and be-laced. **1746** H. WALPOLE *Corr.* (1837) I. 105 Your campaign ..well *be-epitheted would make a pompous work. **1864** *Daily Tel.* 9 Feb., Matrons..*befanned, bejewelled, and speechless. **1839** LADY LYTTON *Cheveley* I. ii. 34 You *be-fathered and *be-uncled young gentlemen. **1885** C. HALL *Amer. Missionary* June 175 Young men [Indians] nude, and painted in parti colors and *befeathered. **1635** QUARLES *Emblems* III. i. (1818) 138 Surveying round her dove-*befeather'd prison. **1761** STERNE *Tr. Shandy* III. xii. 57 Hung round and *befetish'd with the bobs and trinkets of criticism. **1905** *Daily Chron.* 2 June 6/7 The Arab, a *befezzed, well-knit young man. **1932** *Times Lit. Suppl.* 24 Nov. 867/2 The befezzed junior officer. **1832** CARLYLE *Remin.* I. 43 His pale, ghastly, *befilleted head. **1846** LANDOR *Wks.* II. 458 The eagle eye of Buonaparte was *befilmed. **1882** *Standard* 28 Apr. 6 Has the town been *beflagged and decorated. **1843** *Fraser's Mag.* XXVIII. 569 The close bepuckered and *befrilled gowns and collars. **1884** *Cassell's Fam. Mag.* Mar. 216/1 Aprons..befrilled and adorned with lace. **1860** H. MARRYAT *Jutland* I. i. 4 Houses turreted and *begabled..statued, and *befriezed. **1849** MISS MULOCK *Ogilvies* xxix. (1875) 218 The be-laced and *be-furbelowed throng around. **1879** SIR G. SCOTT *Recoll.* ii. 87 [The churches were] *begalleried to the very eyes. **1870** MORRIS *Earthly Par.* II. III. 486 The beasts, sharp horn..and dewlapped neck were well *begarlanded. **1797** W. TAYLOR in *Monthly Mag.* IV. 134 Lordlings all *begarter'd and bestarr'd. **1839** BAILEY *Festus* (1848) 207 Or diamond beetle round *beglobed with light. **1611** COTG., *Engant*é, *begloued. **1903** *Daily Chron.* 30 June 3/7 These *begoggled road demons. **1914** G. B. SHAW *Misalliance* 44 The Passenger, also begoggled, comes in. **1858** *Lond. Rev.* Oct. 112 Bathing machines, with *begowned tenants. **1812** COMBE (Dr. Syntax) *Picturesque* iii. (D.), Thus *behatted, Down on the grass the Doctor squatted. **1742** FIELDING *Miss Lucy in T.* (1762) 179 This..be-curl'd, *behoop'd. **1691** RAY *S. & E. Country Wds.* 89 *Behounc'd; Tricked up and made fine. **1837** C. RIDLEY *Lett.* (1958) 23 We are also **bejacketted* in a very tight fitting style. **1958** *Manch. Guardian* 7 Mar. 8/5 A sulky adolescent and his *be-jeaned girl-friend. **1960** *Bookseller* 28 May 2070/1 The bejeaned and pony-tailed young ladies of my village. **1884** *Pall Mall G.* 7 Oct. 5/1 This awful, befringed, *bekilted, and beflounced dual trouser. **1848** H. MILLER *First Impr.* xi. (1857) 172 Venerable dwellings *belatticed with lead. **1835** BECKFORD *Recoll.* 91 The wildest be-pined, and be-rosemaryed, and *be-lavendered country. **1787** BURNS *Wks.* III. 90 Gie Wealth to some *be-ledger'd Cit. **1854** THACKERAY *Newcomes* II. 58 The steps of a fine *belozenged carriage were let down. **1880** *Blackw. Mag.* Feb. 243 Officers much *be-medalled and much be-crossed. **1878** J. THOMSON *Plenip. Key* 7 Tap your mulls or bejewelled and *beminiatured caskets. **1842** MIALL in *Nonconf.* II. 33 *Be-mitred and be-baroned bishops. **1908** *Westm. Gaz.* 5 June 4/2 The *be-motored and dusty road. **1931** *Times Lit. Suppl.* 12 Feb. 117/4 The boys, hip-flasked and be-motored. **1858** E. JACSON *Harvest Festiv.* 7 A long..*be-mottoed cattle shed. **1882** *Daily News* 10 Oct. 2/4 The becurled and *bemoustachiod tenor. **1850** *Frank Fairlegh* vi. 61 A very pretty girl you would make, too, if you were properly *bemuslined. **1842** H. MILLER *O.R. Sandst.* vii. 155 Its betailed and *bepaddled figure (the Plerichthys). **1849** THOREAU *Week on Concord, Ess.* 331 The stumpy, rocky, forested and *bepastured country. **1614** RICH *Honest. Age* (1844) 26 They are so be-paynted, so *be-periwigd. **1884** E. GOSSE in *Fortn. Rev.* Apr. 534 The rider, the august and *beperiwigged Kurfürst. **1854** H. STRICKLAND *Trav. Th.* 6 A chapel correctly *bepewed à l'Anglaise. **1759** STERNE *Tr. Shandy* II. iii, All be-virtued, *be-pictured, be-butterflied, and be-fiddled. **1857** CARLYLE *Misc.* iv. 168 (D.), There was no literary shrine ever so *bepilgrimed. **1611** COTGR., *Empillier*, *bepillered; set on pillers; made with pillers. **1858** H. MILLER *Rambl. Geol.* 375 Sallied out, *be-plaided and umbrellaed. **1852** JAMES *Pequinillo* I. 154 Five-and-thirty years of peace have so..*be-railroaded..the world. **1831** CARLYLE *Sart. Res.* II. ii, Nut-brown maids and nut-brown men, all clean-washed..and *beribanded. **1863** W. THORNBURY *True as Steel* I. 104 Their *beribboned waists and huge beruffled sleeves. **1951** S. SPENDER *World within World* 5 My father, removing with a flourish his beribboned spectacles. **1954** DYLAN THOMAS *Quite Early one Morning* 16 Autograph albums with a lock of limp and colourless beribboned hair lolling out between the thick black boards. **1614** PURCHAS *Pilgr.* VI. xiv. 647 They found others thus *beringed. **1883** G. MACDONNELL *Chess Life-Pict.* 166 A Frenchman whose be-ringed fingers and be-jewelled scarf betokened a certain amount of pecuniosity. **1880** MRS. PARR *Adam & Eve* vii. 97 A petticoated figure, with a dark *beringleted face. **1862** *Times* 26 Dec., Mr. Anthony Trollope comes to us *berobed and bewigged. **1865** *Reader* 15 Apr. 427/3 Those *berouged, leering, stripped sluts. **1792** *Bot. Mag.* VI. 213 The Stipulae on the stalk..making it look as if *beruffled. **1865** MRS. WHITNEY *Gayworthys* i. (1879) 12 The small, starched, ribboned and beruffled creature. **1848** *Blackw. Mag.* LXIII. 576 Long galleries vainly draperied and *beshawled with all the rich wonders of modern manufacture. **1936** O. NASH *Primrose Path* 165

And all the trim and not so trim ladies who have been betrousered begin thank God once more to be *be-skirted. 1959 Times 16 Nov. 4/1 Even the deployment of the animals, ..high-stepping horses and beskirted chimpanzees, is done with tact and artistic propriety. 1864 Miss Yonge Trial II. 150 Cora tripped in, all *besleeved and smartened. 1837 Carlyle Fr. Rev. II. I. xi. I. 271 Mayor and Curate..also walk *bespaded, and in tricolor sash. 1859 Evening Star 2 Apr. 2/5 These nineteenth century *bestayed women. 1920 Chambers's Jrnl. Sept. 569/1 The whole party indulging in explosive merriment over the quips of the *betabbed gentleman in the centre. 1930 Blunden De Bello Germanico i. 5 We joined the avalanche with which the betabbed encyclopædia was dealing. 1884 A. Putnam Ten Yrs. Police Judge v. 28 The dearly beloved and dearly *betaxed people. 1873 Browning Red Cott. Night-c. 162 Its cobweb-work, *be-tinseled stitchery. 1856 Sat. Rev. 123 Be-cloaked and *be-togaed statesmen. 1611 Cotgr., Entourellé..*betowred; bedecked..with turrets. 1828 Carlyle in Page De Quincy I. xiii. 279 *Betrodden by picturesque tourists. 1934 Webster, *Betrousered. 1936[see be-skirted above]. 1937 Daily Express 3 Mar. 14/2 Betrousered, she hacks in the park at Arundel and once hid when Queen Mary passed by in case her boyish clothes were frowned on. 1865 Pall Mall G. No. 166, 11/2 Fluttering ribbons, *be-tuckered bodices. 1858 De Quincey Autob. Sk. Wks. I. 48 (D.) Bewhiskered and *beturbaned. 1884 Chambers' Jrnl. 4 Oct. 635/2 Never did a *be-uniformed people more thoroughly believe in the dignity of dress. 1866 Alford in Life (1873) 389 Falmouth, with the spruce well *be-vesselled basin. 1866 G. M. Hopkins Let. 30 June (1938) 10 A great fashionable town, and even the country round much *bevillaed. 1784 Wilberforce Life I. 70 Running between two mountains *be-vined. a1849 Poe Cong. Worm, Poems (1859) 87 An angel throng *bewinged. 1869 Palliser Hist. Lace xxii. 268 To keep the ruff erect, *bewired and starched. 1860 Pusey Min. Proph. 342 'Accursed,' or, one might say, 'bewrathed,' lying under the wrath and curse of God.

¶ Examples of the capabilities of be- are seen in be-belzebubbed (= bedevilled), be-blacksmithed, be-cockney'd, to be-documentize (1593), to bedoltify, befrenchify (1603), be-Frenchman'd, be-Germanized, be-lady-loved, belawgiven (Milton) legislated to, be-Legion-of-Honoured, to be-lish-lash to whip soundly, to be-Mary to give us too much of 'Mary,' to be-pamphletize, to be-trash.

1814 Coleridge Let. 16 July, All last Sunday I was thoroughly *be-belzebubbed. 1864 Carlyle Fredk. Gt. IV. 316 Superb betailored running at the ring; *be-blacksmithed running at one another. 1850 W. Irving Salmag. ii. (1860) 39 This poor town..has long been *be-Frenchman'd, *be-cockney'd, be-trash'd. 1593 Nashe Lent. Stuffe in Harl. Misc. VI. 157 (D.), Digests..cited up in the precedents and *bedocumentized most locupleatley. 1698 T. Rymer Short View 146 Never was old deputy Recorder ..so blunder'd and *be-doultefied, as is our Poet. 1603 Florio Montaigne I. lvi. (1632) 173 In a cape-cloake-hood *befrenchifide. 1856 Southey's Lett. (1856) I. Pref. 14 Unnecessary disquisitions, or *be-Germanised excursuses. 1863 Grosart Small Sins 40 Only a 'small sin,' a smug, befurred, be-combed, be-scented, be-ribboned, *be-lady-loved 'little fox!' 1643 Milton Divorce Wks. (1851) Introd. 6 The Almighty..whom they do not deny to have *belawgiv'n his own sacred people with this very allowance. 1860 All Year Round No. 52. 34 The bestarred, beribboned, *be-Legion-of-Honoured..pensioned throng. 1602 in Hazl. Dodsl. IX. 28 He that minds trishtrash..Him will I *be-lish-lash. 1812 G. Colman Br. Grins, Lady of Wreck II. x, The world has been much *be-Maryed of late..we have innumerable sweet little stanzas..ending with 'my Mary.' 1884 Punch 9 Feb. 62 The right to bespatter and *be-pamphletise any particular leader.

beach (biːtʃ), sb. Forms: 6- beach; also 6 bache, bayche, 7 beatch, 7-8 baich(e, 8 beech. [Origin unknown: apparently at first a dialect word, meaning, as it still does in Sussex, Kent, and the adjacent counties, the shingle or pebbles worn by the waves. Thence the transference of the term to the place covered by 'beach,' was easy for those who heard such phrases as ' to lie' or 'walk on the beach,' without knowing the exact significance. The Fr. grève shows precisely the same transference. The spelling shows that the pronunciation in 16-18th c. was (beːtʃ). If OE., the type would be *bǽce. A derivation from ON. bakki 'bank,' which has been proposed (for sense 3), is not admissible phonologically: (cf. BACHE). Another conjecture would derive beach from bleach:—OE. blǽce, f. blác white, with loss of l, of which there is however no evidence.]

1. (Usually collect., formerly occas. with pl.): The loose water-worn pebbles of the sea-shore; shingle.

c1535 Art Suruey 28 The smooth hard beach on the Sea-shoares burnes to a purer white. 1538 Leland Itin. VII. 143 A Banke of baches throwen up by the Se. 1597 Gerard Herbal xxxvi. §16. 249 Rowling pebble stones, which those that dwell neere the sea do call Bayche. 1598 Hakluyt Voy. I. 355 (R.) We haled your barke ouer a barre of beach or peeble stones. 1627 Capt. Smith Seaman's Gram. xii. 57 As many peeble stones or beatch as can there lie. 1721 Perry Daggenh. Beach 116 The Drift or Rolling of the Beach or Shingle along the Shore. 1875 Parish Sussex Dial. (E.D.S.) s.v. Beach, Shingle brought from the sea-coast is always called beach. 1884 Cole Antiq. Hastings 18 All that part between Cambridge Road and the sea is one mass of beach.

†**2.** A ridge or bank of stones or shingle. Obs.

1673 Ray Journ. Low C. 280 The baich or languet of land between the Haven of Messina and the Fretum Siculum. 1692 —— Discourses (1713) 8 Raising up therein a Baich or Bank of Stones as big as Towers.

3. a. The shore of the sea, on which the waves break, the strand; spec. the part of the shore lying between high- and low-water-mark. Also applied to the shore of a lake or large river. In Geol. an ancient sea-margin.

(In early quotations, this sense is often doubtful: it is probably Shakespeare's sense in all the five passages in which he uses beach; though, taken by themselves, 'stand vpon the beach' Merch. V. IV. i. 71, 'the Fishermen, that walk'd vpon the beach' Lear IV. vi. 17, might as well belong to 1.)

1596 Shaks. (see above). 1607 —— Cor. v. iii. 58 The Pibbles on the hungry beach. 1667 Milton P.L. I. 299 On the Beach Of that inflamed sea, He stood. 1756 in Doc. Hist. State N.Y. (1849) I. 478 Upwards of 1000 French and Indians appeared upon the Beech [of Lake Ontario]. 1762 Falconer Shipwr. III. 365 In dreadful form the curving beech appears. 1771 Pennant Tour in Scotl. 201 A little isle, in a small loch in Badenoch, was totally reversed and flung on the beach. 1830 Lyell Princ. Geol. xiii. (1850) 178 These strata passing by the name of 'raised beaches,' occur at moderate elevations on the coast. 1837 Carlyle Fr. Rev. II. I. ii. 13 Like gold-grains in the mud-beach. 1843 N. Boone Jrnl. in L. Pelzer Marches of Dragoons (1917) 189 Captain Boone..commenced his march from the beach of Grand River opposite Fort Gibson. 1880 Geikie Phys. Geog. iii. xvii. 154 The strip of sand, gravel or mud, which is alternately covered and laid bare by the rise and fall of the tidal undulation is called the beach.

b. Naut. The shore, any part of the coastline off which a ship is at anchor; hence **on the beach**, ashore; retired (the beach = land, civilian life); **to take the beach**, to go on shore leave. By extension **on the beach** is used to mean 'beachcombing, unemployed'; also (occas.) penniless, 'broke'.

1903 J. London People of Abyss xi. 127 England is always crowded with sailormen on the beach. 1915 'Bartimeus' Tall Ship iv. 71 The head of the Officer of the Watch appeared... 'Wake up, you Weary Willies. There's a boat to the beach at seven-bells.' 1916 'Ward-room' H.M.S. ii. 29 The captain and the commander had 'taken the beach' for the afternoon. 1923 Daily Mail 15 May 8 Hundreds of the trawlermen to-day find themselves 'on the beach', owing to the distressed condition of the fishing industry. 1925 'Bartimeus' Great Security iii. §2. 181 Hitherto he had been accustomed to view 'the Beach' as an incident in his normal life, an environment that asked nothing of him and gave nothing in return. 1925 Wodehouse Let. 11 Jan. in Perf. Flea (1953) 30 The world is full of poor devils on the brink of being chucked out of jobs and put on the beach. 1935 'G. Orwell' Clergyman's Daughter ii. §1. 99 You on the beach, kid?... On the bum?... What I mean to say, kid—have you got any money? 1938 W. S. Churchill Great Contemporaries 336 The somewhat pathetic appeal of a retired officer mouldering on the beach.

4. Comb., chiefly attrib., as **-bag, -bird, -line, -pea, -pyjamas, -robe, -sand, sandals, shirt, -wear, -wrap.** Also **beach-ball**, a large inflated ball for use at a beach; **beach boy**, a male beach attendant; a play-boy on a beach; **beach buggy** orig. U.S., a low, wide-wheeled motor vehicle designed or adapted for recreational driving on sand: see BUGGY sb. 1 b(c); **beach bum** slang [BUM sb.[4]], an idler or tramp who spends his time on a beach; **beach-comber**,'a long wave rolling in from the ocean' (Bartlett Dict. Amer.); also a settler on the islands of the Pacific, living by pearl-fishery, etc., and often by less reputable means (whence **beach-combing** ppl. adj.); **beach crab**, any crab of a species living on sea-beaches, esp. Ocepoda arenaria; **beach cusp**, a cusp of gravel or sand found at intervals of about 20 to 30 feet on a beach; **beachfront** chiefly U.S., the sea front beside a beach; freq. used attrib. to designate property, etc., located on the sea front or facing a beach; **beach gown**, a bathing-wrap; **beach-grass**, a reedy grass (Arundo arenaria) growing on the sea-shore; **beachhead**, also **beach-head** Mil. [illogically formed after bridge-head], a fortified position of troops landed on a beach; also transf. and fig.; **beach-man**, (a) one who earns his living on the beach; (b) (see quot. a1865); **beach-master**, a superior officer appointed to superintend the disembarkation of troops; **beach-plum** U.S. (see quots.); **beach rest**, a chair-back used for sitting against on the beach; **beach-rock**, a conglomeration of calcareous beach sand cemented by chalk into rock formation, found on coral reefs; **beach-wagon**, a light open wagon, with two or more seats; a station-wagon.

1934 R. Macaulay Going Abroad iv. 40 They gathered up their *beach-bags and went up to the bar. 1940 'N. Blake' Malice in Wonderland I. vi. 73 The combatants were assaulting each other with *beach-balls. 1837 Hawthorne Amer. Note Bks. (1871) I. 187 You are preceded by a flock of twenty or thirty *beach birds. 1939 Time 12 June 87/1 Kilt-style skirt worn over shorts (already fashionable among Florida's rich *beach boys). 1965 'W. Haggard' Hard Sell ii. 20 Penniless Sicilian barons were six a penny among the beach-boys. 1965 N.Z. Listener 17 Dec. 5/2 The Beach Boys are at the front of this wave of frantic surf music. 1961 Webster, *Beach buggy. 1965 Hot Rod Apr. 75 (caption), A duner's delight, this beach buggy will run anywhere 'wheels up' in the toughest terrain. 1969 Daily Tel. 11 Oct. 14 The British public is being given its first chance to see an example of America's newest fun car, the Beachbuggy. 1985 Times 3 Jan. 24/6, 50 blacks stoned people in beach-buggies near Port Alfred on the Natal coast. 1962 Austral. Women's Weekly 24 Oct. (Suppl.) 3/1 *Beach bum, a boy who doesn't work or go to school, just hangs around the beach all day and surfs. 1963 Observer 13 Oct. 15/3 He is the reverse of the popular image of a 'surfie' as a beach bum. 1986 Guardian Weekly 21 Sept. 8 If city ordinances can keep the condominiums away they can certainly handle a few beach bums. 1840 R. H. Dana Bef. Mast (1841) xix. 46/1 In the twinkling of an eye I was transformed from a sailor into a *'beach-comber' and a hide-curer. 1845 E. J. Wakefield Adv. in N.Z. I. xi. 339 Idle, drunken, vagabond..he wanders about without any fixed object, cannot get employed by the whaler or any one else, as it is out of his power to do a day's work; and he is universally known as the 'beach-comber'. 1847 Blackw. Mag. LXI. 757 A daring Yankee beach-comber. 1859 A. S. Thomson Story of N.Z. I. II. iii. 297 The Pakeha Maori must not be confounded with the idlers and beach-combers who loitered about Kororareka. 1880 Athenæum 18 Dec. 809/2 The white scamps who, as 'Beach-combers,' have polluted these Edens and debauched their inhabitants. 1919 W. S. Maugham Moon & Sixpence xlvii. 206 The corpse of a nameless beach-comber would be fished out of the dirty water of the harbour. 1880 J. S. Cooper Coral Lands I. xx. 242 The *beach-combing pioneers of the Pacific. 1909 Webster, *Beach crab. 1900 J. C. Branner in Jrnl. Geol. VIII. 481 (title) The origin of beach *cusps. 1900 Geogr. Jrnl. Dec. 704 The author comes to the conclusion that beach cusps are produced by the interference of two sets of waves of translation on the beach. 1952 F. P. Shepard in Bull. Amer. Assoc. Petrol. Geol. XXXVI. 1909 Following common practice, these relatively small features are being referred to as 'beach cusps'. 1921 N.Y. Times 9 Sept. 15/1 It is calculated that £100,000 was spent by the great *beach front hotels, business places and visitors. 1931 Atlantic City News 7 Aug. 4/2 The beachfront here..and large tracts of land in the most fertile parts of New Jersey..are all part of the Steelman heritage. 1972 Times 7 Aug. (Jamaica Suppl.) p. vi/3 Luxury hotels stand beside their beach-fronts. 1980 Daily Tel. 14 Jan. 1/8 His beachfront residence in Dar es Salaam. 1928 Sunday Dispatch 8 July 16 When getting a bathing suit, don't forget a *beach-gown, which is now worn with a monk's hood, on the shore. 1681 in Rec. of Town (East Hampton, N.Y.) II. 102 Thomas Bee doth..maintaine a sofisient three raile fence one the beach..down so low as any *Beach grass groues. 1852 T. Harris Insects New Eng. 50 note, The advantages to be derived from employing.. beach-grass, in fixing the sands of the shore. 1940 in Amer. Speech (1942) XVII. 122/1 The second theory [of the Germans], to harass communications and airports and *beachheads so effectively that landings could be undertaken. 1941 Time 25 Aug. 22/2 Marines..trained in the terrible job of establishing a beach-head. 1944 Times 24 Jan. 4/3 A substantial beachhead was seized. This beachhead has been widened and deepened. 1949 Koestler Promise & Fulf. xvi. 176 This commonwealth of immigrants would have become a beachhead of European tradition and democracy in the Levant. 1965 C. Walsh in J. Gibb Light on C. S. Lewis 110 The Screwtape Letters established Lewis's beachhead in America. a1865 Smyth Sailor's Word-Bk. (1867) 88 *Beach-man, a person on the coast of Africa who acts as interpreter to shipmasters, and assists them in conducting the trade. 1881 Harper's Mag. LXIII. 494 The beachmen put their shoulders to the stern and gunwhale. 1929 F. Bowen Sea Slang 9 Beach Men, West African surf men and interpreters. 1875 Bedford Sailor's Pocket Bk. vii. 275 The *Beach Master is to take care that..all appliances for disembarking troops..are kept in good order. 1884 Harper's Mag. June 103/2 The *beach pea is found along the North Shore. 1784 in Mem. Amer. Acad. Arts & Sci. (1785) I. 449 The *Beach, or Sea-Side Plumb. 1877 Bartlett Dict. Amer. (ed. 4) 550 Sand-Plum,..a beach-plum. A plum growing on plum-trees whose habitat is sandy beaches. 1928 Vanity Fair Aug. 74 These *beach pyjamas of figured foulard are slipped on over the bathing suit. 1936 M. Laski in Cherwell 7 Mar., They paint their toenails, stroll down the High in beach pyjamas. 1959 New Statesman 13 June 838/2 A lady visitor to an East Coast resort..is discovered dead on the shore..wearing beach-pyjamas at early dawn. 1881 Miss Yonge Rev. Nieces 167, I see the invalid lady creep out with her *beach-rest. 1952 Manch. Guardian Weekly 21 Feb. 5/1 The Admiral Lord Rodney, got up much like Nero in a cool *beachrobe or toga. 1919 R. A. Daly in Carnegie Inst. Year Bk. 192 Cementation of beach sand by calcium carbonate is very common in..tropical seas generally. The product may be called *'beach-rock'. 1940 Geogr. Jrnl. XCV. 30 On tropical beaches the sands, or even coarse shingle, are commonly cemented into a hard rock, called beach-rock or conglomerate, by carbonate of lime precipitated from sea-water. 1934 W. Plomer Invaders xiv. 262 He was wearing only..trousers and *beach sandals. 1966 'A. York' Eliminator iii. 49 She..thrust her feet into gold beach sandals. 1966 G. Lyall Shooting Script viii. 47 There was just one man alone, wearing a vivid *beach shirt. 1868 L. M. Alcott Little Women (1869) II. 35, I shall hire a *beach-wagon. 1935 H. Nicolson Let. 17 July (1966) 209 There was the beach-wagon going down to the village. 1948 Chicago Tribune 9 May 11. 10/4 Use of the parking facilities is restricted to automobiles, beach wagons, and motor cycles. 1928 Men's Wear (U.S.) Oct. 10 (caption) Fantastic *Beach Wear at Juan les Pins. 1952 Vogue June 6 (Advt.), Our gay, new beachwear. 1927 Star 30 May 8/1 Women's *Beach Wraps, made of..coloured towelling.

beach (biːtʃ), v.[1] [f. prec. sb.] trans. To run or haul (a vessel) up on the beach.

1840 Dana Bef. Mast xxvii. 91 We rowed ashore.. beached our boat. 1868 Morris Jason XI. 425 And as the Goddess bade them, there they beached Their sea-beat ship.

beach, -en, obs. forms of BEECH, -EN.

†**beach**, v.[2] Obs. [perh. aphetic f. ABECHE, a. OF. abechier, f. à to + bec BEAK sb.[1]; but cf. also OF. bechier, becher to peck, strike with the beak, also 'to give a beakful.'] trans. To give a beakful to (a young bird); hence spec. in Falconry, to give part of a meal as a whet to appetite.

1575 Turberv. Falconrie 103 Giue hir washte meate and beach [printed beade] hir in the morning.

ˈbeach-ˌcombing, *vbl. sb.* **1.** Living as, or following the occupation of, a beach-comber (see BEACH *sb.* 4); also, the material found by a beach-comber.

a **1865** SMYTH *Sailor's Word-Bk.* (1867) 88 *Beach-combing*, loafing about a port to filch small things. **1910** S. REYNOLDS *Alongshore* IV. xxiii. 257 Our own beachcombings are odds and ends, flotsam and jetsam, to eke out a living. **1918** W. J. LOCKE *Rough Road* iv, An old hand who knew the whole thing backwards, from company promoting to beach combing.

2. *Mining.* Working the sands on a beach for gold, tin, or platinum.

1900 *Coal & Metal Miners' Pocketbk.* (ed. 6) Gloss.

beached (ˈbiːtʃɪd, biːtʃt), *a.* and *pple.* [f. BEACH *sb.* and *v.* + -ED.]

1. Having a beach; *prob.* also, in early use, Covered with 'beach' or shingle. ***beached-up.***

1590 SHAKS. *Mids. N.* II. i. 82 The beached margent of the sea. **1607** —— *Timon* V. i. 219 Timon hath made his euerlasting Mansion Vpon the Beached Verge of the salt Flood. **1889** *Sci.-Gossip* XXV. 162 The fossils..were not in good preservation, owing to the beached-up condition of the formation.

2. Of a ship: Driven or dragged up on the beach.

1871 H. B. FORMAN *Living Poets* 392 Lying in the dark shadow of his beached Argo. *Mod.* The beached fishing-boats at Hastings.

3. *fig.* Laid aside, discarded; unemployed (cf. BEACH *sb.* 3 b).

[**1925** FRASER & GIBBONS *Soldier & Sailor Words* 20 To be beached. To be turned adrift. Put out of employment. (Navy).] **1955** M. MCCARTHY *Charmed Life* (1956) i. 22 All the beached failures and second-raters of the twenties. **1962** J. TUNSTALL *Fishermen* xii. 259 Retired or 'beached' fishermen, as they forlornly call themselves.

beacher (ˈbiːtʃə(r)). [f. BEACH *sb.* + -ER[1].] Used occas. in various (chiefly *slang*) senses (see quots.).

1923 U. L. SILBERRAD *Lett. J. Armiter* ii. 37 She does nothing with a passivity wonderful in a girl of her age, neither looking at her fellow beachers..or playing with the children. **1930** J. R. ELDER *Goldseekers in N.Z.* iv. 155 On this..beach he found..a number of miners who worked.. amid the black-iron sands to be found on the beaches... Many of these 'beachers' or 'surfacers' had prospected the whole southern part. **1946** J. IRVING *Royal Navalese* 28 *Beacher*, a trip ashore, on liberty. **1956** S. HOPE *Diggers' Paradise* xviii. 166 This body-surfing is exclusively an Australian development... It needs..practice if you want to show off..shooting a 'beacher' on your back. The beacher..takes you from deep water right to the shallows.

beaching (ˈbiːtʃɪŋ), *vbl. sb.*[1] [f. BEACH *v.*[1] + -ING[1].] The action of running or hauling a vessel up on the beach. Also *attrib.*, as ***beaching gear***, an appliance for hauling a sea-plane to or from the beach.

1871 *Daily News* 26 Sept., The beaching and wreck of Her Majesty's ship Megæra. **1875** BEDFORD *Sailor's Pocket Bk.* vi. 221 The beaching or landing of a boat. **1936** M. B. GARBER *Mod. Mil. Dict.* 42 *Beaching gear*, an arrangement of wheels to be attached to the hull of a sea-plane to permit landing ashore. **1939** *Meccano Mag.* Aug. 470/3 When the hull was ready it was placed on a specially built 'beaching gear', a 15-ton 8-wheeled cradle of structural steel with a series of air tanks that give it buoyancy in the water.

†**ˈbeaching**, *vbl. sb.*[2] *Obs. Falconry.* [f. BEACH *v.*[2] + -ING[1].] A small meal or 'feed,' given only as a whet to appetite.

1561 DAUS tr. *Bullinger on Apoc.* (1573) 222 Small pittances or beachings to feede them wyth, tyll þe great supper be geeuen them. **1575** TURBERV. *Falconrie* 84 Feede hir with pullets flesh..as much as shall be sufficient for a beaching. **1727–38** CHAMBERS *Cycl.* s.v. *Falcon*, Give her a little beaching of warm meat [*ed.* **1751** a little hot meat].

Beach-la-mar (biːtʃ la mɑː(r)). Also biche-. [Alteration of Pg. *bicho do mar* BÊCHE-DE-MER.] The jargon English used in the Western Pacific.

1911 W. CHURCHILL (*title*) Beach-la-mar. **1912** R. J. FLETCHER *Let.* 10 Sept. in *Isles of Illusion* (1923) 61, I will omit the Biche-la-mar and give you the gist of his story.

beachless (ˈbiːtʃlɪs), *a.* Without beach.

1873 MORRIS *Love is enough* 64 The sea beat for ever 'Gainst..the black rocks, and beachless.

ˈbeachward, -wards, *advs.* [see -WARD, -WARDS.] In the direction of or towards the beach.

1831 *Blackw. Mag.* XXIX. 883 A neap-tide comes flowing beachward. **1895** KIPLING *Seven Seas* (1896) 83 The grandam of my grandam was the Lyre..That the Stealer stooping beachward filled with fire. **1909** *Daily Chron.* 21 Sept. 7/4 He put the dinghey about and ran beachwards.

beachy (ˈbiːtʃɪ), *a.* [f. BEACH *sb.* + -Y[1].] Covered with beach (sense 1); pebbly, shingly.

1597 SHAKS. *2 Hen. IV*, III. i. 50 The beachie Girdle of the Ocean. **1621** G. SANDYS *Ovid's Met.* IV. (1626) 85 Lest the beachy Sands Should hurt the snaky head. **1734** WATTS *Reliq. Juv.* (1789) 213 Smooth pebbles on the beachy shore.

beack, obs. form of BEAK.

beacon (ˈbiːkən), *sb.* Forms: 1 béacen, becen, becun, 2 bæcen, 4 bikene, bekne, 4–5 bekene, beeken, 5–6 beken, -yn, 6 bekin, beakon, 6– beacon, *s.w. dial.* bick'n. [OE. *béacn* (neut.) = OFris. *bácen*, *bécen*, OS. *bôkan*, MDu. *bôkin*, *-en*, OHG. *bouhhan*, MHG. *bouchen*:—OTeut. **baukno(m)*. Not known outside of Teutonic.

(In this and the following words in *bea-* the occasional identity of the OE. and modern spellings is not due to continuity of form, the two being separated by a ME. spelling in *e*, *ee*, which prevailed for more than 3 centuries. Modern *ea* represents not merely OE. *éa* and *ea*, but also many other OE. and OF. vowels, as seen in *bead*, *beadle*, *beak*, *bear*, *beast*. See EA-.)]

†**1.** A sign, a portent. *Obs.*

c **950** *Lindisf. Gosp.* John iv. 48 Buta beceno & soða uundra ȝie ȝesee, ne ȝelefeð ȝie. *c* **1000** *Ags. G.* ibid., Tacna & fore-beacna. *c* **1160** *Hatton G.*, Tacne & fore-bæcne.

†**2.** An ensign, standard. *Obs.*

a **1000** *Beowulf* 5547 Segn éac ȝenom, béacna beorhtost. *c* **1380** WYCLIF *Wks.* (1880) 471 Religioun shal be shewid in sensible signes, as habitis, and bikenes, & hye housis. **1483** *Cath. Angl.* 26/1 A Bekyn or a standard, *statela*.

3. A signal; *spec.* a signal-fire. **a.** A burning cresset raised on a pole, or fixed at the top of a building.

[LAMBARDE *Peramb. Kent* (1826) 64 says he finds it ordained about the eleventh year of Edward III that *beacons* 'should be high standards with their pitchpots.']

a **1859** MACAULAY *Armada*, The beacon blazed upon the roof of Edgcombe's lofty hall. *c* **1870** THORNE *Environs of Lond.* 266 From it [the tower of Monken Hadley Church] projects the ancient iron beacon, one of the last of its kind left.

b. A fire, of wood, pitch, or other material, lighted on an eminence and serving as a signal (of danger, etc.); by a chain of beacons at convenient distances apart, tidings could be rapidly spread over a wide area.

1377 LANGL. *P. Pl.* B. XVII. 262 ȝe brenne, but ȝe blaseth nouȝte, þat is a blynde bekene. **1480** CAXTON *Chron. Eng.* ccvi. 188 That men shold tende the bekenes that the countrey myght be warned. **1533** BELLENDEN *Livy* 348 (JAM.) He tuke thare tentis..and incontinent made ane bekin of reik. **1625** K. LONG tr. *Barclay's Argenis* I. i. 9 Publike trees..which being kindled by the King's command, give notice to the people..and these they call Beacons. **1815** SCOTT *Ld. of Isles* IV. viii, Signal of Ronald's high command, A beacon gleam'd o'er sea and land.

c. = BELISHA BEACON.

4. Hence *gen.* A signal station, watch-tower.

1611 BIBLE *Gen.* xxxi. 49 Therefore was the name of it called..Mizpah [*marg.* that is a beacon or watchtower]. **1772** PENNANT *Tours Scotl.* 104 On the eminencies beacons were established, for alarming the country. **1846** PRESCOTT *Ferd. & Is.* II. xviii. 165 Ascertained by the erection of beacons at suitable distances.

5. a. A conspicuous hill commanding a good view of the surrounding country, on which beacons were (or might be) lighted. Still applied to such hills in various parts of England; *e.g.* Brecon Beacons near Abergavenny, Dunkery Beacon on Exmoor, Culmstock Beacon, Cothelstone Beacon, etc. (On some of these the beacon towers still exist.)

1597 T. BEARD *Theat. Gods Judgm.* 58 He lies upon a beacons side With watchfull eie to circumscribe their traine. **1882** *Athenæum* 26 Aug. 265/3 Nothing can bring up the image of chalk country like the words *combe*, *dean*, *beacon*.

†**b.** A division of a wapentake; probably a district throughout which a beacon could be seen, or which was bound to furnish one. *Obs.*

1641 BEST *Farm Bks.* (1856) 90 There is in everie weapontacke soe many severall divisions or beacons..there is in the weapontacke of Harthill fower beacons, Bainton beacon, Hunsley beacon, etc.

6. a. A lighthouse or other conspicuous object placed upon the coast or at sea, to warn vessels of danger or direct their course.

[*a* **1000** *Beowulf* 6301 Hlæw on hliðe, wæȝ-liðendum wide tó-sýne..beadu-rófes béacn.] **1397** *Act 21 Rich. III*, xviii.§1 Les Beekenes devant le port Moeqes. **1526** *Pilgr. Perf.* (W. de W. 1531) 240 b, The beken lyghted in yͤ nyght, directeth the maryner..to yͤ port entended. **1684** *Lond. Gaz.* No. 1911/4 In the place of the Shore Beacon, there is at present a white Buoy laid. **1837** HAWTHORNE *Amer. Note Bks.* (1871) I. 97 A ledge of rocks, with a beacon upon it. **1850** TENNYSON *In Mem.* xvii, My blessing..Is on the waters day and night, And like a beacon guards thee home.

b. *fig.*

1606 SHAKS. *Tr. & Cr.* II. ii. 16 Modest Doubt is cal'd The Beacon of the wise. **1773** MONBODDO *Lang.* (1774) I. Introd. 3 My errors may be of use, by serving as beacons to direct into the right course men of greater learning. **1840** CARLYLE *Heroes* ii. 82 Great brother-souls, flame-beacons through so many lands and times.

c. *Aeronaut.* A light placed at or in the vicinity of an aerodrome for the guidance of pilots; also *attrib.*

1918 [see *aerial lighthouse* s.v. AERIAL 5]. **1927** V. W. PAGÉ *Mod. Aircraft* (1928) xvii. 700 These beacons are usually mounted on towers of sufficient height so that they will be above obstacles which might obstruct the beam. **1930** *Aircraft Engin.* II. 211 Night Beacons for Night Flying. **1957** *Encycl. Brit.* I. 228/2 Beacon lights, which mark major airways and airports..consist of a searchlight which throws a beam of white light elevated several degrees above the horizontal.

d. A radio transmitter enabling pilots to fix their position or the aerodrome staff to locate, identify, or guide aircraft; also ***marker beacon***, ***radio beacon***, and *attrib.*

1919 *Pop. Sci. Monthly* Oct. 49/2 What is a radio beacon? **1922** Radio-beacon [see RADIOPHARE]. **1929** *Techn. News Bull., Bureau of Standards* Nov. 108 The Bureau has found it necessary to give..attention to marker beacons, for two purposes. One is the adaptation of the marker beacon principle for use..on the airways in connection with the visual beacon system. Another is the provision of marker beacons as auxiliaries..with fog-landing equipment. **1932** F. E. TERMAN *Radio Engineering* xvi. 593 The instant when the received beacon signal goes through zero. **1937** *Jrnl. R. Aeronaut. Soc.* July 591 An analysis of the flight of an aeroplane, when directed by means of a radio beacon. **1962** *Times* 21 Feb. 10/2 Direct communication with the capsule was briefly lost as it reentered the atmosphere because of an ionization process, but beacon signals were received.

7. *Comb.*, chiefly attrib., as ***beacon-bell***, ***-blaze***, ***-grate***, ***-place***, ***-turret***, ***-vessel***; also ***beacon-wise*** adv.

1548 UDALL *Erasm. Par. Luke* xix. 154 Out of the beakon place of the Crosse. **1577** HOLINSHED *Chron.* I. 6/1 He gaue knowledge thereof to his wife, in raising a fire on heigth beaconwise. **1814** SCOTT *Ld. of Isles* I. xxii, By that blithe beacon-light they steer'd. **1820** —— *Monast.* xviii, The glow-worm, which makes a goodly show among the grass of the field, would be of little avail if deposited in a beacon-grate. **1862** MRS. NORTON *Lady La G.* Ded. 30 A voice whose sound Came like a beacon-bell, heard clear above The whirl of violent waters.

beacon (ˈbiːkən), *v.* [f. prec. sb.]

†**1.** *trans.* ***to beacon up***: to raise or kindle as a beacon. *Obs.*

1644 MILTON *Areop.* Wks. 1738 I. 156 We have lookt so long upon the blaze that Zuinglius and Calvin have beacon'd up to us. **1651** BIGGS *New Disp.* Pref. 13 A greater light in Physick then what Galen has beaconed up to us.

2. To light up, as a beacon-fire does.

1803 CAMPBELL *Lochiel's Warn.* (1846) 94 'Tis the fireshower of ruin..that beacons the darkness of Heaven. **1813** SCOTT *Rokeby* V. xxxvii, Where far the mansion of her sires Beaconed the dale with midnight fires.

b. *fig.* To give light and guidance to; to lead.

1835 BROWNING *Paracels.* Wks. I. 37 Some one truth would dimly beacon me..Into assured light. **1856** R. VAUGHAN *Mystics* (1860) I. 11 Whose far glories beacon him ..as he rises step by step.

3. To furnish with beacons; to mark the position of, by beacons or a beacon. Occas. with *off*, *out*.

1821 SHELLEY *Epipsych.* 148 My wisdom..bids me dare Beacon the rocks on which high hearts are wreckt. **1860** *Merc. Mar. Mag.* VII. 174 The..Channel..is as good as buoyed and beaconed by the..Rock and..Reefs. **1883** *Daily News* 12 June 5/2 The Boers have beaconed out a boundary. **1883** *Pall Mall G.* 16 Nov. 2/1 The boundary has never been beaconed off.

4. *intr.* To shine like a beacon.

1821 SHELLEY *Adonais* lv, The soul of Adonais, like a star, Beacons from the abode where the Eternal are. **1864** *N. & Q.* V. 210 Arcturus beaconed from his zenith tower to Cepheus.

beaconage (ˈbiːkənɪdʒ). Also 7 beconage. [f. BEACON *sb.* + -AGE.] **a.** Toll paid for the maintainance of beacons. **b.** A system of beacons.

1607 COWELL *Interpr.*, *Beconage* signifieth money paid for the maintenance of Becons. **1755** MAGENS *Insurances* I. 72 Towage, and Pilotage..Light-money, Beaconage, &c. **1862** *Edin. Rev.* Jan. 183 Our beaconage admits of much improvement.

beaconed (ˈbiːkənd), *ppl. a.* Furnished with, or surmounted by, a beacon.

a **1790** T. WARTON *Ode* x. (T.) The foss that skirts the beaconed hill. **1890** *Harper's Mag.* Sept. 596/2 The beaconed ledges and buoyed reefs..slip helplessly into the Powder Fog. **1931** *Flight* 27 Mar. 275/2 Blind flying..has.. its limit in the event of no beaconed route..being able to give the pilot a chance to unbroken control of his navigation.

Beaconite (ˈbiːkənaɪt). [f. *beacon* in the title of I. Crewdson's *A Beacon to the Society of Friends*, 1835 + -ITE[1].] In the history of the Quakers, one of a party who, following the lead of Isaac Crewdson, held that the current Quaker doctrines were contrary to Scripture and seceded in 1836.

1835 M. HOWITT *Let.* 29 Dec. in *Autobiogr.* (1889) I. vii. 246, I should like to know whether any persons in whom I am interested in Liverpool join the Beaconites. **1836** J. SOUTHALL in *Jrnl. Friends Hist. Soc.* (1920) XVII. 82 The Beaconites preach up charity so exclusively. *Ibid.* 83 A.. man..labouring under disadvantage from Beaconite associations. **1921** R. M. JONES *Later Periods Quakerism* I. ix. 310 The position of the 'Beaconites'—*i.e.* the position of literalism and ultra-orthodoxy.

ˈbeaconless, *a.* *rare*$^{-0}$. [f. as prec. + -LESS.] Without a beacon.

1864 in WEBSTER.

bead (biːd), *sb.* Forms: 1–2 bed, 3–4 beode, 3–7, and (*archaically*) 9 bede, 5 bed, beed, 5–6 bedde, beid, 6–7 beade, 5– bead. [ME. *bede*, pl. *bedes*, *beden*, perh. repr. an OE. **bedu*, **bed* (fem.) = OFris. *bede*, OS. *beda*, MDu. and Du. *bede*, OHG. *beta*, MHG. *bete*, mod.G. *bitte*, Goth. *bida* (str. fem.), f. Goth. *bidjan*, in OE. *biddan* to pray: see BID. But an OE. *bedu* is doubtful, and *bed* occurs only in comb. (*bed-hús*, etc.), the regular OE. word being *ȝebed* (neut.), in ME. IBED, ? *ibede*, pl. *ibeoden*, from which *bede* may have arisen by aphesis in early ME. The name was transferred from 'prayer' to the small

globular bodies used for 'telling beads,' *i.e.* counting prayers said, from which the other senses naturally followed.]

I. Prayer, and connected senses.

†**1. a.** Prayer; *pl.* prayers, devotions. *Obs.*

c885 K. ÆLFRED *Bæda* I. vii. (Bosw.) Ðæt he sceolde ða bedu anescian. c1200 *Trin. Col. Hom.* 193 Þe þridde is bede. *Ibid.* 163 On salmes, and on songes, and on holde bedes. *Ibid.* 201 Alle holie beden ben .. biheue. c1230 *Ancr. R.* 44 Beoð i beoden. c1305 *St. Lucy* 37 in *E.E.P.* (1862) 102 Þer hi leye in hire bedes. 1330 R. BRUNNE *Chron.* 202 Better is holy bede. c1330 *King of Tars* 643 With beodes and with preyere. 1426 AUDELAY *Poems* 15 3if he be besé in his bedus. c1430 *Hymns Virg.* (1867) 6 To þee y make my beed. 1494 FABYAN VI. ccxiii. 229, I hoped to haue ben saued by your bedes & prayers. 1554 *Chron. Grey Friars* (1852) 92 Went unto the crosse, & stode there alle the [sermon] tyme, & whan he came unto the beddes they turnyd unto the precher & knelyd downe.

b. In later usage (after sense 2 became the popular one) there was almost always a reference direct or indirect to the use of the rosary.

?a1550 *Pore helpe* 369 in *E.P.P.* (Hazl.) III. 265 Take you to your beades; All men and women .. That useth so to praye. 1589 NASHE *Almond for P.* 14 b, [He] would haue run a false gallop ouer his beades with anie man in England. 1648 HERRICK *Hesper.* (1869) 70 Be briefe in praying, Few beads are best, when once we goe a maying. 1741 RICHARDSON *Pamela* (1824) I. xxx. 49, I began .. to say the Lord's prayer. None of your beads to me, Pamela, said he; thou art a perfect nun.

c. *to bid a bead*: to offer a prayer; hence ***beads bidding***, the saying of prayers. Also *to say one's beads*.

c1250 *Gen. & Ex.* 2981 Moyses bad is bede. c1330 *Assump. Virg.* 876 To ihesu þei bede a bede. c1380 WYCLIF *Sel. Wks.* 1871 II. 420 Howþei shulen bidde her bedis. 1387 TREVISA *Higden* Rolls Ser. VI. 225 He travailled besiliche in bedes byddynge. 1563 *Homilies* II. *Idolatry* III. (1859) 236 For the which they pray in their beads bidding. 1598 DRAYTON *Heroic. Ep.* iii. 87 The Beades that we will bid, shall be sweet Kisses. [1656 BLOUNT *Glossogr.* s.v., To say our Bedes, is to say our prayers.] 1681 BURNET *Hist. Ref.* II. 55 All the people said their beads in a general silence. 1764 GRAY *Let.* in *Poems* (1775) 381 Bidding his beads for the souls of his benefactors. 1870 MORRIS *Earthly Par.* I. I. 152 To fetch the priest .. To bury her and say her bede.

2. a. A small perforated ball or other body, a series of which (formerly called 'a pair of beads') threaded upon a string, forms the *rosary* or *paternoster*, used for keeping count of the number of prayers said. Hence **b.** *to tell* or *count one's beads*: to say one's prayers. *to pray without one's beads*: to be 'out of one's reckoning.'

1377 LANGL. *P. Pl.* B. xv. 119 A peyre bedes in her hande And a boke vnder hire arme. 1446 *Test. Ebor.* (1855) II. 124 A pare of bedes of corall with gaudes of gete. 1483 *Cath. Angl.* 24/1 A bede, *precula*. 1533 MORE *Answ. Poysoned Bk.* Wks. 1120/1 Away wyth our ladies psalter, and cast the bedes in the fyre. c1550 *Auentur on Weddinsd.* (Bann. MS.) Ane pair of beids about hir throt. 1570 *Act 13 Eliz.* ii. §7 Crosses, Pictures, Beads and such like superstitious Things. 1652 COLLINGES *Caveat for Prof.* (1653) A ij, I no where read, That thy Apostles ever us'd a *Bead*. 1697 *C'tess D'Aunoy's Trav.* (1706) 142 She presented me with a pair of Beads of Paulo d'Aguila, a curious sort of wood. 1732 POPE *Ess. Man* II. 280 Beads and prayerbooks are the toys of age. 1878 B. TAYLOR *Deukalion* II. i. 53 Five hundred have I told upon these beads.

1641 J. JACKSON *Evang. Temper* iii. 188 Telling the panes of glasse, as fast as a Papist doth his Beads. a1659 OSBORN *Machiavel* (1673) 356 In which he prayed without his Beads, being so far out, in the account, as that, etc. 1759 STERNE *Tr. Shandy* I. xl, Cross himself;—tell his beads:—be a good Catholic. 1792 J. BARLOW *Conspir. Kings* 78 He counts his beads, and spends his holy zeal. 1800 COLERIDGE *Christabel* II. ii, The sacristan Five and forty beads must tell. 1883 GILMOUR *Mongols* xvii. 205 Counting beads and making pilgrimages.

3. *Comb.*, chiefly attrib. (mostly archaic, and, when used by modern writers, often spelt *bede*): **bead-child**, a child that prays for the welfare of a benefactor or relative; **bead-folk**, people (often pensioners) who pray for a benefactor; **bead-house** (north. dial. *beadus*, Welsh *Bettws*), originally a house of prayer, *hence* an almshouse, the inmates of which were to pray for the soul of the founder; †**bead-master**, a religious officer who attends to the poor, a deacon; †**bead-song**, song of prayer; **beads-woman**, a woman who prays for a benefactor, an almswoman. Also BEAD-ROLL, BEADSMAN.

?1499 *Plumpton Corr.* 140 Your good son & *beadchild, German Pole. ?1465 *Ibid.* 15 Others your well willers, servants, and *bed folkes. 1849 ROCK *Ch. of Fathers* III. viii. 134 To live and do as *bead-folks should. c1160 *Hatton Gosp.* Matt. xxi. 13 Min hus ys *bed-hus[*Ags. G.* ȝebed-hus]. 1485 *Will* in *Ripon Ch. Acts* 277 The *bedehouse beside the Mawdelayns. 1774 T. WEST *Antiq. Furness* (1805) 180 Lodgyns and *bed-howses for x poor men. 1864 ATKINSON *Whitby Gloss.*, **Beadus* or *Beadhouse*, an almshouse. 1866 NEALE *Seq. & Hymns* 126 They raised full many a *bede-house, but never a bastile. 1579 TOMSON *Calvin's Serm., Tim.* 295/1 The Deacons, that is to say, the *Beade maisters, and such as see to the poore. c1200 ORMIN 1450 Wiþþ fassting, & wiþþ *bedesang. ?1465 *Plumpton Corr.* 14 Your dayly *bedewoman my huswif. 1502 MARG. C'TESS RICHMOND in Ellis *Orig. Lett.* I. 23 I. 48 Your feythfull trewe *bedwoman and humble modyr. 1536 in Strype *Eccl. Mem.* I. i. xxxv. 256 Your poor *bedes women The whole convent of Styxwold. 1629 SHIRLEY *Gratef. Serv.* III. i, My humblest service to his grace: I am his *beads-woman. 1720 *Stow's Surv.* (Strype 1754) I. i. xxvii. 229/1 Ten poor women called *Bedes women, and six poor Clerks. 1864 MISS YONGE *Bk. Gold. Deeds* 194 Asking the Queen to make her a *bedeswoman at Vienna.

II. Extensions of sense 2.

4. a. A small perforated body, spherical or otherwise, of glass, amber, metal, wood, etc., used as an ornament, either strung in a series to form a necklace, bracelet, etc., or sewn upon various fabrics.

c1400 *Destr. of Troy* xv. 7044 Garmentes full gay .. Bright beidis & Brasse broght þai with-all. 1599 HAKLUYT *Voy.* II. II. 32 About their neckes great beades of glasse of diuerse colours. 1647 COWLEY *Mistr., Bargain* ii, The foolish Indian that sells His precious Gold for Beads and Bells. 1753 HANWAY *Trav.* (1762) I. VI. lxxxi. 371 Their old way of reckoning .. is with beads on wires, which they work without pen and ink. 1836 MARRYAT *Japhet* xviii, A long chain of round coral and gold beads.

fig. 1590 SHAKS. *Mids. N.* III. ii. 329 You minimus .. You bead, you acorne. 1870 LOWELL *Study Wind.* 97 Quincy's [life] was strung with seventy active years, each one a rounded bead of usefulness and service.

b. (The *plural* is commonly used in sense of a string of beads for the neck; formerly the *sing.* seems to have been occas. so used.)

c1500 *Mayd Emlyn* in *Poet. Tracts* (1842) 21 And sayth that she lackes Many prety knackes, As bedes and gyrdels gaye. 1596 SHAKS. *Tam. Shr.* IV. iii. 58 With Amber Bracelets, Beades, and all this knau'ry. 1655 H. VAUGHAN *Silex Scint.* I. 77 There's one Sun more strung on my Bead of days. *Mod.* Do they wear beads? She cannot find her beads.

5. In various transf. senses applied to things having some of the characteristics of the prec.

a. A bead-like drop of liquid or of molten metal. *spec.* of sweat, esp. on the face.

1596 SHAKS. *1 Hen. IV*, II. iii. 61 Beds of sweate hath stood vpon thy Brow. 1601 —— *Jul. C.* III. i 284 Seeing those Beads of sorrow stand in thine. 1633 G. HERBERT *Sacrifice* vi. in *Temple* 19 My hearts deare treasure Drops bloud (the onely beads) my words to measure. 1854 SCOFFERN in *Orr's Circ. Sc.* Chem. 507 The bead of impure silver is seen to emit fumes. 1888 A. C. GUNTER *Mr. Potter of Texas* v, [He] wipes the great beads of exhausted toil from his forehead. *Ibid.*, The beads of perspiration.

b. A bubble of foam; *spec.* a bubble in spirits, sparkling wines, etc.; the foam or head upon certain beverages. Cf. *bead-proof* (sense 8 below).

1753 CHAMBERS *Cycl. Supp.*, *Bead* is also used for a little, round, white froth formed on the surface of brandy, or spirit of wine, upon shaking the glass. 1839 BAILEY *Festus* xiv, An eye which outsparkles the beads of the wine. 1863 KINGSLEY *Water-Bab.* vi. 255 Swimming about among the foam-beads below. 1883 *Harper's Mag.* 894/2 There is .. a finer bead on this wine of mirth.

c. A clear nacreous spot on the surface of shells.

1842 JOHNSTON in *Proc. Berw. Nat. Club* II. x. 32 The clear spots or beads of the transverse lines [on a shell] are much larger.

d. The small metal knob which forms the front sight of a gun; *esp.* in the phrase (of U.S. origin) ***to draw a bead upon***: to take aim at. Also *fig.*

1831 AUDUBON *Ornith. Biogr.* I. 294 He raised his piece until the *bead* (that being the name given by the Kentuckians to the *sight*) of the barrel was brought to a line with the spot he intended to hit. 1841 CATLIN *N. Amer. Ind.* (1844) I. x. 77, I made several attempts to get near enough to 'draw a bead' upon one of them. 1844 MARRYAT *Settlers* II. 206 'Now, John,' said Malachi; 'get your bead well on him.' 1875 URE *Dict. Arts* II. 391 The front sight is that known as the bead-sight, which consists of a small steel needle, with a little head upon it like the head of an ordinary pin, enclosed in a steel tube. In aiming with this sight, the eye is directed .. to the bead in the tube. 1919 *Chambers's Jrnl.* June 399/1 I'd got a lovely bead on her with one of my own torpedoes. 1929 G. MITCHELL *Myst. Butcher's Shop* xii. 132 You've got a bead on your man all right.

e. A string of sponges; see quot.

1885 LADY BRASSEY *In Trades* 339 The sponges are strung upon small palmetto strips, three or four to a strip, which is called a 'bead.'

6. a. *Arch.* A small globular ornament, commonly applied in a row like a string of beads. Also in the names of various ornamental designs, as ***bead and butt***, ***flush***, ***reel***, etc. **b.** A narrow moulding having a semicircular section.

1799, etc. Bead and flush [see FLUSH *a.*[1] 5 b]. 1802 *Gentl. Mag.* LXXII. II. 1118 Bead, a globular ornament peculiar to Saxon architecture, carved in the mouldings. 1803 *Phil. Trans.* XCIII. 171 On the edges .. a small regular raised bead or moulding was formed. 1851 RUSKIN *Stones Ven.* (1874) I. xxi. 256, I think *bead* a bad word for a continuous moulding. 1861 PARKER *Goth. Archit.* Gloss. (1874) 320 *Bead*, an ornament resembling a row of beads. 1869 SIR E. REED *Ship Build.* xi. 233 Beads of india-rubber are fitted in the rabbets of the frame. 1904 P. MACQUOID *Hist. Eng. Furniture* vii. 191 The sides are inlaid with the bead and spindle, or husk design so popular at this time. 1909 WEBSTER, Bead and butt, bead and reel. 1937 W. ROSE *Village Carpenter* iv. 42 The outside doors to the ordinary house were made to the still well-known orders of 'bead and butt' or 'bead and flush'. 1955 R. FASTNEDGE *Eng. Furniture Styles* 280 *Bead and reel*, a decorative border found in the form of inlay in the sixteenth and seventeenth centuries.

c. Used of any thickened, rounded edge (cf. *bead rim*).

1962 *Gloss. Terms Glass Ind.* (*B.S.I.*) 27 *Bead*, an enlarged, rounded edge of a glass article, or any raised section extending around the article.

7. ***beads of St. Elline***: certain round roots brought out of Florida (Bullokar 1616). ***St. Martin's beads***: (the sanctuary of St. Martin's-le-Grand, London, was a noted resort of makers of sham jewellery. F. Cohen. in *Archæol.* XVIII. 55, quotes an ordinance of the Star Chamber in 36 Hen. VI. for the regulation of that sanctuary, by which it is declared that 'no workers of counterfeit cheynes, beades, broaches, owches, rings, cups, and spoons silvered, should be suffered therein.') ***Baily's beads***: a phenomenon observed in total eclipses of the sun; see quotations. ***Wilson's*** or ***Lovis's beads***: a series of globular bodies of different densities, formerly used to determine the specific gravity of a spirit into which they were thrown one by one.

1678 BUTLER *Hud.*, *Lady's Answ.* 59 Those false St. Martins Beads. 1867 G. CHAMBERS *Astron.* 175 When the disc of the Moon advancing over that of the Sun has reduced the latter to a thin crescent, it is usually noticed that immediately before the beginning and after the end of complete obscuration, the crescent appears as a band of brilliant points, separated by dark spaces so as to give it the appearance of a string of beads .. These phenomena are generally known as *Baily's beads*, having received their name from the late Mr. Francis Baily, who was the first to describe them in detail. The earliest account of the .. beads is contained in Halley's memoir on the total eclipse of 1715. 1874 S. JOHNSON *Eclipses* 66 An eclipse of the sun A.D 1836, May 15 .. Famous for what is known as 'Baily's beads' noticed by Mr. Baily, at Jedburgh, in Roxburghshire. 1878 NEWCOMB *Pop. Astron.* III. iii. 314 'Baily's beads' .. are caused by the sun shining through the depressions between the lunar mountains.

8. *Comb.*, as ***bead-amber***, ***-berry***, ***-maker***, ***-note***; ***-potato***, ***-string***, ***-work***; ***bead-bonny***, ***-brown***, ***-dark***, ***-eyed***, ***-like*** adj.; also **bead-frame**, a frame containing beads strung upon wires used for teaching numeration, an abacus; **bead lightning** (see quot. 1901); cf. *beaded lightning*; **bead-plane**, a carpenter's plane for running a bead on moulding; **bead-plant**; **bead-proof** *a.* (of alcoholic spirits), such that a crown of bubbles (see 5 b) formed by shaking will stand for some time after on the surface (a fallacious test of strength); also, according to some recent works, of a certain proof, as tested by Wilson's or Lovis's Beads (see 7); **bead rim**, a thickened, rounded rim (cf. 6 c); also *attrib.*; so ***bead-rimmed*** adj.; **bead screen**, beaded screen (see BEADED *ppl. a.* 1 d); **bead-sedge**, the Bur-reed (*Sparganium ramosum*); **bead-snake**, a small American snake (*Elaps fulvus*); **bead-stone**, (*a*) a stone used as a bead, or of which beads are made; (*b*) *Zool.* (see quot. 1896); **bead-tree**, the AZEDARAC; **bead-work**, (*a*) ornamental work with beads; also *attrib.*; so ***bead-worked*** adj.; (*b*) bead moulding (BEAD *sb.* 6). Also BEAD-ROLL.

1611 COTGR., *Ambre de Paternostres*, *Bead-amber; the ordinarie yellow Amber. 1626 BACON *Sylva* §83 Bead-Amber, which is at first is a soft Substance. 1923 D. H. LAWRENCE *Birds, Beasts & Flowers* 107 He squatted and looked at me. With sticking-out, *bead-berry eyes. 1881 G. M. HOPKINS *Poems* (1918) 53 The *beadbonny ash that sits over the burn. 1912 W. DE LA MARE *Listeners* 14 Her small *bead-brown eyes. 1937 —— *This Year:Next Year*, Low head outstretched, and *bead-dark eyes. 1835 F. A. BUTLER *Jrnl.* II. 179 A fat, good tempered, rosy, *bead-eyed, wet-haired, shining-faced looking man accosted me. 1858 CURWEN *Singing for Sch.* Introd. 20 Till the pupil .. is able to perform some of its [arithmetic] simpler operations by the help of the *Bead-Frame or the Box of various Objects. 1901 *Rep. Smithsonian Inst. 1899* 129 *Bead lightning .. is a very beautiful luminous appearance, like a string of beads hung in a cloud. 1876 HUMPHREY *Coin Coll. Man.* xxvi. 400 The minor *bead-like decorations, borders of pearls, &c. 1580 HOLLYBAND *Treas. Fr. Tong*, *Vn paternostrier*, a *beades maker. 1723 *Lond. Gaz.* No. 6172/7 William Dossett .. Beadmaker. 1938 W. DE LA MARE *Memory* 60 *Bead-note of bird where earth and elfland meet. 1858 SIMMONDS *Dict. Trade*, **Bead-plane*, a moulding plane of semicylindrical contour. 1878 R. THOMPSON *Gard. Assist.* 709/2, *Nertera scapanioides* .. Popularly known as the *bead plant, owing to the profusion of golden berries it produces. 1807 VANCOUVER *Agric. Devon* (1813) 455 To produce languid shoots and a number of small *bead potatoes of no value. 1753 CHAMBERS *Cycl. Supp.*, **Bead-proof*, a term used by our distillers. 1936 *Antiquaries Jrnl.* XVI. 270 The *bead rim and the countersunk handle. 1943 R. E. M. WHEELER *Maiden Cas.* III. 204 The rolled or 'bead' rim, which is predominantly characteristic of the 'Wessex hill-fort B' pottery, is in origin a device, not of the potter, but of the metal-worker, who thus gave rigidity to the lip of a vessel of thin metal. 1940 V. G. CHILDE *Prehist. Communities Brit. Isles* xiii. 251 The ceramic industry was industrialized, specialist potters turning out *en masse* *bead-rimmed vases of Continental pattern. 1934 *Amat. Cine World* May 10/1 The most satisfactory type of screen so far evolved .. is that known as the glass, *bead or crystal. 1938 G. H. SEWELL *Amat. Film-Making* vi. 60 The silver and bead screens are an attempt to secure the utmost reflection of light from the projector. 1562 TURNER *Herbal* II. 143 b, It mayе be called *bede sedge or knop sedge. 1863 PRIOR *Plant-n.* 17 Bede-sedge, from its round bead-like burs .. *Sparganium ramosum*. 1736 MORTIMER in *Phil. Trans.* XXXIX. 258 The *Bead-Snake .. commonly found under Ground. 1867 WOOD *Pop. Nat. Hist.* III. 52 One of the brightest and loveliest of Serpents is the Bead Snake of North America. 1677 *Lond. Gaz.* No. 1202/4 Three broad Chains set with *Bead Stones. 1851 D. WILSON *Preh. Ann.* (1863) II. IV. vi.

338 Bone draughtsmen, or bead stones. **1896** *Trans. Victoria Inst.* XXVIII. 206 Bead-stone is also called St. Cuthbert's beads, Fairy beads..and St. Boniface's money. They are the ring-like transverse sections of the so-called Vertical Column of stalked Echinoderms. **1801** W. TAYLOR in *Month. Mag.* XII. 583 The most precious jewel in the long *bead-string of his pedigree. *a* **1872** MAURICE *Friendsh. Bks.* ii. 44 Not even a beadstring to hang the different meanings upon. **1668** WILKINS *Real Char.* II. iv. §7. 115 Clove Tree, *Bede Tree. **1852** TH. ROSS *Humboldt's Trav.* II. xvii. 136 Hedges of bead-trees. **1840** R. DANA *Bef. Mast* xxvi. 85 Indian curiosities..such as bead-work. **1881** *Mechanic* §1597 The mouldings or any bead-work should be painted. **1751** DORRINGTON *Hermit* III. 260 He..makes 24 of those Plaits, which he weaves together, making a flat Piece of *Bead-work. **1919** R. FRY in *Athenæum* 27 June 529/2 As we look at Leech's drawings, or sit in a bead-work chair. **1909** *Daily Chron.* 18 Nov. 4/5 Painted and *bead-worked lampshades. **1920** GALSWORTHY *In Chancery* I. xii, A gilt chair with a bead-worked seat.

bead (biːd), *v.* [f. prec.]

1. *trans.* To furnish, adorn, or work with beads.

1577 [see BEADED]. **1822** BEDDOES *Bride's Trag.* III. iv, Drops enough to bead a thousand such [necklaces.] **1856** MISS YONGE *Daisy Ch.* I. xxii. (1879) 228 Morning dew, which beaded the webs of the spiders.

2. *Arch.* To furnish with a bead or beading.

1851 RUSKIN *Stones Ven.* I. xxii. §13 If we take the plain chamfer..and bead both its edges.

3. *intr.* To form a bead or beads.

1873 BLACKMORE *Cradock N.* viii. (1881) 29 The fescue grass was beading rough with dew. **1884** *Harper's Mag.* Mar. 524/2 Every drop of water beading on the wall becomes a jewel.

4. To string like beads; also *fig.*, and *intr.* const. *out.*

1883 *Harper's Mag.* June 117/1 The houses are beaded along the..stream. **1938** G. GREENE *Brighton Rock* VII. vii. 326 The Brighton lamps beaded out towards Worthing.

5. To aim at (cf. BEAD *sb.* 5 d).

1888 *Eng. Illustr. Mag.* Dec. 214/1 Never fire until you have beaded your man.

beaded (ˈbiːdɪd), *ppl. a.* [f. BEAD + -ED.]

1. a. Worked or ornamented with beads.

1577 HOLINSHED *Chron.* III. 858 A cloake of broched satin..beded from the shoulder to the wast. **1840** HOOD *Up Rhine* 222 The other cap is also embroidered or beaded.

b. Having bead-like protuberances upon the edge.

1697 *Lond. Gaz.* No. 3298/4 One Beaded Salver without Arms. **1870** HOOKER *Stud. Flora* 27 Sisymbrium Trio.. London Rocket..valves beaded. **1870** TYNDALL *Heat* viii. App. 261 A beaded line of great beauty was observed.

c. Furnished with or wearing beads.

1805 SOUTHEY *Madoc in Azt.* xxi. Wks. V. 348 His neck with hearts beaded. **1885** *Pall Mall G.* 13 July 6/2 Monks.. cowled, sandalled, beaded, and picturesque.

d. Applied to a projection screen (see quot. 1959).

1936 *Amat. Cine World* Mar. 552/2 Beaded screens are.. brighter than white and some makes are brighter than silver. **1938** G. H. SEWELL *Amat. Film-Making* vi. 60 There are three types of screen available,..white..silver..beaded. **1959** W. S. SHARPS *Dict. Cinematogr.* 127/2 *Beaded screen*, a beaded projection screen is surfaced with small glass beads and a brilliant image is obtained that is strongly directional towards the projector.

2. a. Formed into or like beads.

1597 SHAKS. *Lover's Compl.* vi, A thousand fauours from a maund she drew, Of amber christall and of bedded Iet. **1820** KEATS *Ode Nightingale* 17 With beaded bubbles winking at the brim. **1872** BLACK *Adv. Phaeton* ii. 15 Portraits..in which the women have all beaded black eyes.

b. Strung out like beads.

1937 WOOLDRIDGE & MORGAN *Physical Basis Geogr.* xxii. 388 Thus a series of fans or deltas may be strung along the 'feeding esker', like beads on a string. To such a form the term 'beaded esker' is applied. **1956** J. C. SWAYNE *Gloss. Geogr. Terms* 22 *Beaded lakes*, strings of long, narrow lakes between sand dunes.

3. Covered with bubbles.

1884 *Harper's Mag.* Sept. 533/2 Beakers of beaded ale.

4. a. *Arch.* Having a bead-moulding.

b. Applied to a thickened, rounded rim, = *bead rim* (see BEAD *sb.* 8).

1917 BULLEID & GRAY *Glastonbury Lake Village* II. xvi. 519 Bowls with beaded rims, a type of pottery belonging to the latter part of the La Tène III period.

5. ***beaded-edge***, defining a kind of pneumatic tyre with bead or thickened edge that fits into the turned-over rim of the wheel; ***beaded lightning***, bead lightning (see BEAD *sb.* 8).

1902 *Windsor Mag.* May (Advt.), Wired or beaded edges optional. **1904** *Westm. Gaz.* 19 Sept. 9/1 The Bartlett beaded-edge—or, as it is more generally known, the Clincher—tyre. **1889** *Morning Post* 29 June 5/7 Photographs of lightning..arranged..according to their form—stream, ..beaded..lightning.

beadel, variant of BEADLE.

beader (ˈbiːdə(r)). [f. BEAD *v.* + -ER[1].] **1.** A tool used in silver chasing to make a bead pattern.

2. a. One who sews beads on fabrics. **b.** One who puts a beading on an article.

1881 *Instr. Census Clerks* (1885) 105 Beader (Coach), Beader (Lace), Beader on Net. **1886** BESANT *Childr. Gibeon* II. iv, She was a beader: she was that clever with her fingers she could do all kinds of things. **1921** *Dict. Occup. Terms* (1927) §254 *Beader*..a press hand who places machine folded body of tin..on block of beading machine and operates lever to form a beaded edge. *Ibid.* 407 *Beader, bead trimmer, bead worker*,..sews beads, by hand, upon a fabric foundation. *Ibid.* 414 *Beader*..applies waxy mixture.. round edge of sole [etc.].

† **ˈbeadful**, *a. Obs.* In 3 beodeful. [f. BEAD *sb.* 1.] Prayerful.

c **1200** *St. Marhar.* 14 Beodefule þohtes þæt ha schulen þenchen.

† **ˈbead-hook.** *Obs.* Also 7 beedhook. [Chiefly in Chapman: can he have formed it from OE. *beadu* battle, war? Cf. OE. *beadu wæpen* weapon of battle, etc.]? A kind of boat hook.

1600 CHAPMAN *Iliad* xv. 356 The Greeks with bead-hooks fought. **1614** —— *Odyss.* IX. 651 A bead-hook then..I snatch'd up. **1631** —— *Cæsar & P.* Plays 1873 III. 180 Yet beare halfe pikes or bead-hookes. **1614** RALEIGH *Hist. World* II. VIII. iii. §18. 474 Corne, Iron, Canuas for Sailes, Axes, Beede-hookes, Hand-milles.

ˈbeadiness. The quality of being beady.

1873 *Spectator* 22 Feb. 239/2 A *bistre* shade around his black eyes which softens away their beadiness.

beading (ˈbiːdɪŋ), *vbl. sb.* [f. BEAD *v.* + -ING[1]].

1. The formation of beads.

1869 *Student's Mag.* 33 A tendency towards beading is very noticeable in the coccoliths I have seen.

2. a. Bead-work, in trimming, etc.

1881 *Daily News* 29 July 3/1 The black silk toilette, with steel beadings.

b. A lace-like edging made of loops; also, an edging with openings through which ribbon, etc., may be run.

1900 *Amer. Mail Order Fashions* in *Americana Review* (1961) 16 Corset Cover..armholes followed with beading and narrow ribbon insertion. **1932** D. C. MINTER *Mod. Needlecraft (caption)* 137 Beading Stitch. **1964** *McCall's Sewing* xiii. 236/1 Beading is a very effective trim but tedious to do.

3. A bead moulding or edge line. *spec.* in *Arch.* and *Joinery*, a bead; also collectively, the beads of a moulding. *attrib.*, as ***beading plane*** = *bead-plane* (see BEAD *sb.* 8).

1858 SIMMONDS *Dict. Trade.* **1873** TRISTRAM *Moab* iv. 67 White chalk and limestone pleasantly relieved by the beading of black lines of flint. **1875** *Carpentry and Join.* 27 The beading planes are made of various widths.

4. A preparation for causing liquor to hang in drops about the glass or bottle when poured out.

beadle (ˈbiːd(ə)l), *sb.* Forms: 1 bydel, 2–4 budel (y), bedele, 3 bidell, 4 bidel, (*Sc.* badal), 5 bydelle, beddell, (betille), 6 beedle, bedyl(l, 6–7 bedelle, bedle, 9 beadel, (*Sc.* beddal); 2–9 bedel, 4–9 bedell, 7– beadle. [Originally OE. *bydel* (= MDu. **bödel*, Du. *beul*, OHG. *butil*, MHG. *bütel*, Ger. *büttel*):—OTeut. **budilo-z*, derivative of *biud-an*, in OE. *béodan*, OHG. *biotan* to offer, present, deliver, announce, command. Some form of the Teutonic was adopted in Romanic: cf. It. *bidello*, Pr., Sp., OF. *bedel*, F. *bédeau*, med.L. *bidellus*, *bedellus*; and in ME. the Fr. form *bedel* gradually superseded the native *bydel*. The ordinary modern spelling is *beadle*, but the archaic forms *beadel*, *bedel*, *bedell*, are in use in specific senses.]

† **1.** One who makes a proclamation (on behalf of another); a herald. *Obs.*

c **1000** ÆLFRIC *Ex.* xxxii. 5 Aaron..het bydelas beodan and þus cweþan. *c* **1200** ORMIN 632 Cristess bidell Sannt Johan. *a* **1300** *Cursor M.* 11006 Sent him forwit his bedele, For-þi sent iesus iohn forwith. *c* **1440** *Gesta Rom.* 15 Whenne the bedell hadde y-makid this proclamacion. **1535** COVERDALE *Dan.* iii. 4 The bedell cried out with all his might. **1644** BULWER *Chirol.* 124 Proclaimed liberty by the Beadle to many of the parts of Greece.

† **b.** The crier or usher of a law-court; a town-crier. *Obs.*

c **1400** *Apol. Loll.* 8 If a bedel, or criare, schewe þe fre graunt of his lord. *c* **1432–50** tr. *Higden* (1865) I. 247 A bydelle, or the crier of the cite ascendede in to a towre..and seyde so mony tymes, 'Calo, calo.' **1691** BLOUNT *Law Dict.*, *Bedel*, a Crier or Messenger of a court.

2. One who delivers the message or executes the mandates of an authority: † **a.** *generally. Obs.*

c **1175** *Lamb. Hom.* 95 þes budeles word. *Ibid.* 117 þe biscop..godes budel is. *c* **1220** *Leg. St. Kath.* 1928 A burhreue..þæt wes þe deoules budel. *c* **1375** WYCLIF *Serm.* Sel. Wks. 1871 II. 100 þei be trewe bedelis to telle it. *c* **1440** *Gesta Rom.* 364 Dethe is the messynger of the hie Emperour ..and..the betille of hym that made hevyn and Erth. *c* **1450** LYDG. *St. Albon* (1534) G j b, As a bedyll to brynge you tydyng. **1513** BRADSHAW *St. Werburge* (1848) 39 This wycked Werebode, the bedyll of Belyall.

† **b.** *spec.* A messenger of justice, a warrant officer; an under-bailiff; a tipstaff. *Obs.*

c **1000** *Ags. Gosp.* Luke xii. 58 þe-læs he þé sylle þam.. bydele, and se bydel þe sende on cwertern. *a* **1300** *Havelok* 266 Schireues he sette, bedels, and greyues..To yemen wilde wodes and pathes Fro wicke men. **1393** LANGL. *P. Pl.* C. III. 60 Budels and bailifs and brokours of chaffare. *c* **1500** *God Speed Plough* 37 Bayllys and bedelles..to doo vs sorowe Inough. **1591** LAMBARDE *Arch.* (1635) 38 Burgesses Serjeants and Beadles have their Courts within every their particular limits. **1628** COKE *On Litt.* 234 b, The oath of a Bedell of a Mannor is, that he shall duly and truly execute all such Attachements and other Proces as shall be directed to him from the Lord or Steward of his Court.

† **c.** An under-officer of the Forest Courts. *Obs.*

1598 MANWOOD *Lawes Forest* xxi. §4 (1615) 206 A Bedle is an officer or seruant of the Forest that doth make all manner of garnishments of the Courts of the Forest, and also all manner of Proclamations as well within the Courts of the Forest as without. **1647** HAWARD *Crown Rev.* 48 Bedle of the Forrest: Fee, £9 2*s.* 6*d.* **1700** TYRRELL *Hist. Eng.* II. 819 No Forester or Bedell..shall make any Ale-shots, or Collect Sheafs of Corn.

3. An apparitor or precursor who walks officially in front of dignitaries, a mace-bearer; **a.** *spec.* in the English universities (at present conventionally spelt *bedel*, *-ell*,) the name of certain officials, formerly of two ranks distinguished as ***esquire bedels*** and ***yeomen bedels***, having various functions as executive officers of the University. Their duties are now chiefly processional: at Oxford there are four, the junior- or sub-bedel being the official attendant of the Vice-chancellor, before whom he bears a silver staff or mace; at Cambridge there are two, called esquire-bedells, both of whom officially walk in front of the Vice-chancellor with maces.

a **1300** *Cursor M.* (Cott.) 12914 Als bedel gais be-for iustis. **1562** *Petition* in Strype *Ann. Ref.* I. I. xxx. 342 The beadles and other officers, belonging to either of the Universities. **1577** HOLINSHED *Chron.* III. 11461 One of the bedels named maister Adams, came weeping to him, & praied him to shift for himselfe. **1641** LAUD *Hist. Chanc. Oxf.* 132 (T.) If the university would bring in some bachelors of Art to be yeomen-bedels..they which thrived well and did good service, might after be preferred to be esquire-bedels. *a* **1763** SHENSTONE *Odes* (1765) 206 When college-students take degrees, And pay the beadle's endless fees. **1797** *Cambr. Univ. Cal.* 143 Esquire Bedells. The Bedells are officers for life, they must be men of learning, and have taken the degree of A.M. **1826–7** *Act 7 & 8 Geo. IV*, lxxv. in *Oxf. & Camb. Enactm.* 144 The Proctors and Bedels for the time being. **1849** MACAULAY *Hist. Eng.* II. 280 The registrar and bedells waited on Francis.

b. The apparitor of a trades guild or company.

1389 *Eng. Gilds* (1870) 35 He [the Alderman] ssal sende forthe þe bedel to alle þe breþeren and þe systeren. **1514** *Ibid.* 144 To be paid yerely..to the beddell of the seid Gilde, Tuppens. **1824** J. JOHNSON *Typogr.* I. 541 He received aid from his Company, and was ultimately appointed their beadle.

4. An inferior parish officer appointed by the vestry to keep order in church, punish petty offenders, and act as the servitor or messenger of the parish generally; a parish constable.

1594 *1st Pt. Contention* (1843) 23 Have you not Beadles in your town? ? *c* **1600** *Distracted Emp.* v. iii. in *Old Pl.* (1884) III. 248 Let the Bedle..with..his owne whypp medle, And lashe theym soundlye. **1712** STEELE *Spect.* No. 509 ¶2 The unlucky boys with toys and balls were whipped away by a beadle. **1818** HAZLITT *Eng. Poets* v. (1870) 128 If Bloomfield is too much of the farmer's boy, Crabbe is too much of the parish beadle. **1845** STEPHEN *Laws Eng.* II. 701 A beadle.. whose business is to attend the vestry, to give notice of its meetings to the parishioners, and execute its orders &c. **1857** TOULM. SMITH *Parish* 55 A printed copy of the notice calling each Vestry, shall be left by the Beadel at every house in the Parish.

b. In Scotland the duties of the beadle or 'church-officer' are more especially connected with attending upon the clergyman; he may be also sexton.

c **1860** RAMSAY *Remin.* i. 6 The beddal and parish oracle. **1884** ROGERS *Soc. Life Scot.* I. v. 163 At Allsa the beadle's fee for the funeral bell was thirteen shillings and fourpence.

† **5.** *fig.* (referring to the punitive functions of the beadle.) *Obs.*

1595 SHAKS. *John* II. i. 189 Her iniurie the Beadle to her sinne. **1650** R. STAPYLTON *Strada's Low-C. Warres* II. 33 Fear, the Beadle of the law, terrified them from the beginning. **1797** GODWIN *Enquirer* I. ix. 84 He is the beadle to chastise their follies.

6. *Comb.*, as ***beadle-office***; ***beadle-watched*** adj.

1876 GEO. ELIOT *Dan. Der.* III. xxxviii., A narrow, beadle-watched portal. **1877** E. THOMAS *Lange's Materialism* (1880) II. 245 The magnificent abstraction.. performed the meanest beadle-offices long enough to excite a universal distrust of philosophy.

beadledom (ˈbiːd(ə)ldəm). [see -DOM.] The embodiment of the characteristics of beadles as a class; stupid officiousness and 'red-tapeism.'

1860 *Temple Bar* I. 80 The defeat of beadledom and vestrydom. **1861** *Blackw. Mag.* 732 [Words] which serve to express the relationship supposed to exist between the higher and lower grades of English society. Flunkeyism, plush, beadledom, lordolatry. **1866** *Reader* 15 Dec. 1006 At present we have too much beadledom on the episcopal bench.

ˈbeadlehood. [see -HOOD.] The state or dignity of a beadle. So **beadleism.**

1838 DICKENS *O. Twist* xvii, Mr. Bumble..was in the full bloom and pride of beadleism. [*Later edd. read* 'beadledom,' and 'beadlehood.' The latter is in the C.D. ed.]

beadlemer (ˈbiːd(ə)lmɛə(r)). [Corruption of F. *bœuf-de-mer* 'the Seale or Sea-calfe' (Cotgr.)] A one-year-old hooded seal.

1859 in WORCESTER.

ˈbeadlery. ? *Obs.* Forms: 7 bedellery, 7–8 bedelarie, -ary. [prob. ad. med.L. *bedellāria*, f.

bedellus: see BEADLE and -ERY, -RY.] The office or jurisdiction of a beadle.

1628 COKE *On Litt.* 234 a, The offices of Steward, Constable, Bedelarie, Bayliwick, or other offices. **1679** BLOUNT *Anc. Tenures* 75 Bedellery is the same to a Bedel, as Bailywic to a Bailiff. **1691** —— *Law Dict., Bedelary.*

beadleship (ˈbiːd(ə)lʃɪp). Also bedel(l)ship. [see -SHIP.] The office of beadle.

1613 SIR H. FINCH *Law* (1636) 106 The grant of a stewardship, Bedleship, Bailiwicke, or other offices. **1691** WOOD *Ath. Oxon.* II. /271 He..was turn'd out of his Beadleship in the year following. **1870** *Daily News* 1 Feb., I should have no objection to the beadleship of any City company which arrays its minion in specially gorgeous attire. **1873** *Ibid.* 22 Sept. 3/5 Cambridge, Sept. 20. The Esquire Bedellship..Mr. Miller resigns the office of Junior Esquire Bedell.

ˈbeadlet. [f. BEAD *sb.* + -LET.] A small or tiny bead, or bead-like drop.

1863 LANCASTER *Præterita* 85 Celandine in wide gold beadlets glared.

beadman: see BEADSMAN.

bead-roll (ˈbiːdrəʊl). Also 6-8 bed-, 6- bede-. [f. BEAD *sb.* + ROLL *sb.*]

†**1.** *orig.* A list of persons to be specially prayed for. *Obs.* or *arch.*

c **1500** FABYAN *Will* in *Chron.* Pref. 6 The soules above written, may be remembred in their parisshe bede rolle by the whole space of a yere after. **1504** in *Bury Wills* (1850) 100 A sangred to be payed for in the bedroule for my soule..by the space of a yeer. **1528** TINDALE *Obed. Chr. Man.* To Rdr., Here a mass-penny, there a trental, yonder dirige-money, and for his bead-roll. **1849** ROCK *Ch. of Fathers* II. vii. 355 Those souls of the dead whose names were written upon the bead-roll just read out.

2. *transf.* A list or string of names; a catalogue; a long line, a pedigree; a long series.

1529 MORE *Supplic. Soules* Wks. 289/1 This he laith to yᵉ onely fault of the cleargie, naming them in his bederolle, bishops, abbottes, etc. **1596** SPENSER *F.Q.* IV. II. 32 Dan Chaucer, well of English undefyled, On fames eternall beadroll worthie to be fyled. **1603** FLORIO *Montaigne* III. viii. (1632) 523 A man..who..doth nothing but molest all men with the impertinent bed-rowle and register of his pedigrees. **1607** HEYWOOD *Wom. Kilde* Wks. 1874 II. 115 Rac'd from the bed-roll of Gentility. **1612** DRAYTON *Poly-olb.* xxii. (1748) 346 Wakefield battle next we in our bedroul bring. **1644** QUARLES *Judgm. & Mercy* 286 The devil presents me with a bead-roll of my offences. **1826** SCOTT in *Lockhart* (1839) VIII. 322 A whole beadroll of cousins. **1868** FREEMAN *Norm. Conq.* (1876) II. viii. 218 The long bead-roll of the worthies of Bec. **1884** SYMONDS *Shaks. Predecess.* v. 191 The whole bede roll of inferior oracles.

3. A string of beads for counting prayers; a rosary.

1598 HAKLUYT I. 115 A certaine string with an hundreth or two hundreth nutshels thereupon, much like to our beadroule. **1816** COLERIDGE *Lay Serm.* 341 Superstition..with its pack of amulets, bead-rolls..fetisches. **1819** WORDSW. *Waggoner* II. 9 Twelve strokes that clock would have been telling..Its bead-roll of midnight. **1866** MRS. STOWE *Lit. Foxes* 22 Let us all make a bead-roll, a holy rosary, of all that is good and agreeable in our position..and charge ourselves to repeat it daily.

†**ˈbead-row.** *Obs.* [see ROW: here perhaps confused with ROLL.] = prec. (sense 2.)

1576 FLEMING tr. *Caius' Dogs* in Arb. *Garner* III. 246 We reckon it [the beaver] not in the beadrow of English Dogs. **1577** tr. *Bullinger's Decades* (1592) 199 A pitifull beadrow of miserable torments. *Ibid.* 263 His Catalog or beadrow of heritikes. **1607** TOPSELL *Four-f. Beasts* 135.

beadsman (ˈbiːdzmən). Forms: 3-4 beodemon, 4-6 bedeman, 4-7 bed-, 6 beid-, bedys-, beids-, 6-7 bead-, 7 beades-, 9 bede-, 6- bedes-, beadsman. [ME. *beodeman*, f. BEAD *sb.*¹ + MAN: with *beadsman* = bead's-man cf. *kinsman*, *craftsman*, *townsman*, etc. The archaic spellings *bedesman*, *bedeman*, are also used as historical forms.]

1. *lit.* A man of prayer; one who prays for the soul or spiritual welfare of another.

c **1230** *Ancr. R.* 356 Beon oðres beodemon. *c* **1425** WYNTOUN *Cron.* IX. xxvii. 99 His Bede-men þai suld be.. And pray for hym. **1538** LATIMER *Serm. & Rem.* (1845) 412 The prior of Worcester, is your orator and beadsman. *c* **1540** *Thrie Priests of Peblis*, Welcum my beidmen, my blesse, and al my beild. **1591** SHAKS. *Two Gent.* I. i. 18 Commend thy grieuance to my holy prayers, For I will be thy beadesman, Valentine. **1647** WARD *Simp. Cobler* (1843) 62 As fervent a Beadsman for your welfare. **1869** FREEMAN *Norm. Conq.* (1876) III. ii. 28 His friend and bedesman, Abbot Eadwine.

2. One paid or endowed to pray for others; a pensioner or almsman charged with the duty of praying for the souls of his benefactors. Hence in later times; **a.** in England: An almsman, an inmate of an almshouse; (so also *beadswoman*: see BEAD *sb.* 3); **b.** in Scotland: A public almsman or licensed beggar (into which position 'the King's Bedesmen' finally sank.)

a **1528** SKELTON *Image Hypocr.* 108 Other smale mynisters, As reders and singers, Bedemen and bellringers. **1593** PEELE *Chron. Edw. I*, 82 He shall have forty pound of yearly fee, And be my beadsman. **1593** SHAKS. *Rich. II*, III. ii. 116 Thy very Beads-men learne to bend their Bowes. **1726** *Lond. Gaz.* No. 6458/5 John Hailes, a Beadsman of the Cathedral Church of Ely.

a. 1524 S. FISH *Supplic. Begg.* 18 Your poore sike lame and sore bedemen. **1582** N. T. (Rhem.) *Acts* x. 21 *marg.*, The praise of our Almsfolkes and beadsmen may do us great good euen after our departure. **1636** DEKKER *Wonder* IV. i. Wks. 1873 IV. 267 To be a Beades-man in your Hospitall. **1862** MRS. WOOD *Channings* i, The decrepit old bedesmen in their black gowns. **1864** ATKINSON *Whitby Gloss.*, *Bedsman* ..now used to denote almspeople in general, and prevalent at Guisborough, as applied to the inmates of the almshouses in that town.

b. 1788 BURNS *Wks.* III. 302 Stranger, go! Heav'n be thy guide! Quoth the Beadsman of Nith-side. **1816** SCOTT *Antiq.* Advt. 6 These Bedesmen are an order of paupers to whom the Kings of Scotland were in the custom of distributing a certain alms..and who were expected in return to pray for the royal welfare and that of the state. *Ibid.* xxxviii, It wadna be creditable for me, that am the king's bedesman, and entitled to beg by word of mouth.

†**3.** A messenger. *Obs.*

1377 LANGL. *P. Pl.* B. III. 41, I shal assoille þe my-selue.. And also be þi bedeman · and bere wel þi message.

†**4.** A petitioner. *arch.*

1600 S. NICHOLSON *Acolastus* (1876) 11 Poore foolish Blinkard, Beads-man vnto Christ, For restitution of long-lacked sight. **1876** BANCROFT *Hist. U.S.* V. xli. 12 Having thus owned the continuing sovereignty of the king, before whom they presented themselves as bedemen.

†**5.** The term by which men used to designate or subscribe themselves in addressing their patrons and superiors, answering to our modern 'humble servant.' (Cf. 'your petitioners will ever pray,' still retained at the end of petitions to Parliament.) *Obs.*

1420 GEORGE & STOKES in Ellis *Orig. Lett.* III. 29 I. 67 We ȝowr seruitours and bede men. **1485** *Plumpton Corr.* 49 Your bedman, Sir Tho. Betanson. **1529** WOLSEY in *Four C. Eng. Lett.* 11 Your dayly bedysman And assuryd friend, T. Carˡⁱˢ Ebor. **1535** BOORDE *Let.* in *Introd. Knowl.* (1870) 53 By þe hond of your saruantt and bedman, Andrew Boord. **1577** HOLINSHED *Chron.* III. 1164/1 Your graces most bounden bedesman and seruant Edmund Boner. **1645** *Let.* in Harrington *Nugæ Ant.* 73 A dailye beadesman for you, and a right obedient subject.

†**ˈbeadsmanry.** *Obs.* [f. prec. + -RY.] The position or place of a beadsman.

1594 NASHE *Unfort. Trav.* 9 His former request to the King to accept his lands, and allow him a beadsmanrie.

beadsteed, obs. form of BEDSTEAD.

beadswoman: see BEAD *sb.* 3.

beadus, north. dial. f. *beadhouse*: see BEAD *sb.* 3.

beady (ˈbiːdɪ), *a.* [f. BEAD *sb.* + -Y¹.]

1. a. Beadlike; (of eyes) small, round and glittering.

1826 DISRAELI *Viv. Grey* I. iv, Small black, beady eyes. **1848** THACKERAY *Van. Fair* xix. (1853) 149 Mrs. Bute's beady eyes. **1879** BLACK *Macleod of D.* I. 170 The ugly brute, with its beady eyes and its black snout.

b. *Comb.*, as **beady-eyed** *a.*

1873 M. F. MAHONY *Chron. Fermors* I. xiii. 249 That beady-eyed,..lanthorn-cheeked little lady. **1897** KIPLING in *Pearson's Mag.* Dec. 615/2 The 600 quick-footed, beady-eyed rank and file. **1904** *Daily Chron.* 15 Sept. 4/4 A beady-eyed inscrutable stare.

2. a. Covered with beads (of liquid, etc.).

1868 GEO. ELIOT *Sp. Gipsy* 243 While he treads painfully with stillest step And beady brow.

b. Of a garment, material, etc.

1892 *Longman's Mag.* May 76 Beady and buttony girls. **1897** *Daily News* 25 June 3/1 Cheap black, sheeny cloth, very beady, much trimmed.

3. Full of bubbles, frothy.

1881 *Harper's Mag.* LXIII. 488 Creamy and beady scum.

beæften, early form of BAFT.

beaf(e, obs. form of BEEF.

beag, beaȝ, early forms of BEE *sb.*², *Obs.*, ring.

1872 E. ROBERTSON *Hist. Ess.* II. i. 39 To swear upon 'the holy beag' was the most solemn oath known.

beagle (ˈbiːg(ə)l). Forms: 5-6 begle, 6 begele, 6- beagle. [Derivation obscure. The F. *bigle* is recognized as borrowed from Eng. The word can scarcely be of OE. origin, because of the hard *g*; in this position the *g* could not have escaped becoming palatalized. Possibly it is from F. *bégueule*, f. *béer* to gape, open wide + *gueule* throat. The OF. *beegueulle*, according to Godefroy, meant a noisy shouting person (*criailleur*); 'open throat,' in this sense, might be an epithet applied to a dog, though there is no evidence that it was so used in Fr.]

1. A small variety of hound, tracking by scent, formerly used in hunting hares, but now superseded by the Harrier, which sometimes takes its name.

?*c* **1475** *Sqr. lowe Degre* 771 With theyr begles in that place, And sevenscore raches at his rechase. **1548** HALL *Chron. Hen. VI*, an. 27 (R.) The Frenchmen stil like good begeles following their prey. **1631** QUARLES *Samson* Wks. (1717) 406 Quick-scented Beagles. **1704** POPE *Windsor For.* I. 121 To plains with well-bred beagles we repair, And trace the mazes of the circling hare. **1862** HUXLEY *Lect. Wrkg. Men* 110 A physiological peculiarity..enables the Beagle to track its prey by the scent.

2. *fig.* One who makes it his business to scent out or hunt down; a spy or informer; a constable, sheriff's officer, bailiff.

1559 *Myrr. Mag.*, *Jack Cade* xix. 2 That restles begle sought and found me out. **1570** B. GOOGE *Pop. Kingd.* II. (1880) 17 Such preetie Begles haue these Bishops..That hunt out Prebendes fatte for them. *a* **1618** RALEIGH *Maxims St.* (1644) 45 To have their Beagles, or listner in every corner..of the Realm. *a* **1640** DAY *Peregr. Schol.* (1881) A brace of beagles in blew. **1837** CARLYLE *Fr. Rev.* III. VII. v. 377 Attorneys and Law-beagles, which hunt ravenous on this Earth.

3. *attrib.*, as in *beagle-chase*, *-dog*, *-hound*.

1552 HULOET, Begle hounde, *catellus*. **1706** *Lond. Gaz.* No. 4223/4 A Beagle-Dog..with..Liver-coloured Spots upon his Ears. **1858** CARLYLE *Fredk. Gt.* I. IV. viii. 471 Hot Beagle-chase, hot Stag-hunt, your chief game deer.

†**beagle-rod.** *Obs. rare*⁻¹. [variant of BAGLE (*-rod*), q.v.] A crosier.

1664 *Flodden F.* ii. 19 And Abots eke as bold as the best For beagle-rods, tooks [? took] bills in hand.

beagling (ˈbiːglɪŋ), *vbl. sb.* [f. BEAGLE *sb.* + -ING¹.] The sport of hunting on foot with beagles. Hence **ˈbeagle** *v. intr.*, to hunt with beagles; **ˈbeagler.**

1824 *Sporting Mag.* XIV. 312/2 There is no prettier sport for youth than rabbit beagling. **1841** C. RIDLEY *Lett.* (1958) 65 Besides the *beaglers*, there was a horseman in white trousers. **1889** *Pall Mall G.* 24 Oct. 7/1, I am in the habit of accompanying my brothers out shooting and beagling. **1896** *Daily News* 20 July 8/2 Coursing—which, with 'beagling' and 'harriers', takes up a large part of the book. **1910** *Humanitarian* Mar. 21/1 Beaglers' manners. **1915** *Oxford Mag.* 5 Mar., He beagled and played cricket. **1923** J. O. PAGET *Beagles & Beagling* i. 15 The sport of beagling is every day becoming more popular.

beak (biːk), *sb.*¹ Forms: 3-6 bec, 4-5 bek, beke, 4-6 beeke, 6 becke (*pl.* bex), 6-7 beake, 7 beack, 7-8 beck, 7- beak. [a. F. *bec* (= It. *becco*, Pr. *bec*, Sp., Pg. *bico*:—late L. *beccus*), of Gaulish origin. Suetonius says (*Vitell.* 18) that Antonius Primus, who was born at Toulouse, had as a boy the nickname of *Beccus*, 'id valet, gallinacei rostrum.' According to Thurneysen, probably related to the Celtic stem *bacc-* 'hook'; but the mod. Celtic words, Irish *bec*, Breton *bek*, *beg*, are 'certainly borrowed' from Eng. and Fr. The original short vowel of Fr. *bec*, ME. *bec*, *bek*, was still retained in *beck* in the 18th c., but the form *beek*, *beak*, with lengthened vowel, occurred in the plural at least, where it evidently originated (*bek-es* being made into *be-kes*, *bē-kes*, *beekes*, *beaks*; cf. *staff*, *staves*) as early as 1400.]

I. Original and allied senses.

1. a. The horny termination of the jaws of a bird, consisting of two pointed mandibles adapted for piercing and for taking firm hold: a bird's bill.

c **1220** *Bestiary* 58 in *O.E. Misc.* 3 Siðen his bec is al to-wrong. **1399** *Pol. Poems* (1859) I. 395 But the nedy nestlingis ..burnisched her beekis, and bent to himwardis. **1486** *Bk. St. Albans* A vj b, Ye shall say this hauke has a large beke or a shortt beke, and call it not bille. *c* **1532** LD. BERNERS *Huon* cxxi. 432 The Gryffon..was redy to dystroye hym with his becke and naylys. *a* **1573** TUSSER *Husb.* (1878) 89 If peacoke and turkey leaue iobbing their bex. **1611** SHAKS. *Cymb.* v. iv. 118 His Royall Bird Prunes the immortall wing, and cloyes his Beake. **1713** C'TESS WINCHELSEA *Misc. Poems* 107 With Vultur's Becks, And Shoulders higher than their Necks. **1831** CARLYLE *Sart. Res.* II. vii. (1838) 187 The Eagle..to attain his new beak, must harshly dash off the old one upon rocks.

b. *birds of a beak* (cf. 'birds of a feather'; see A *a.*² 3).

1607 DEKKER *Knt's Conjur.* (1842) 28 Cut vp one cut vp all; they were birdes all of a beake.

c. *transf.* The long snout of a fish.

1889 in *Cent. Dict.* **1927** *Observer* 24 July 22 A 38-lb. cock-salmon... I was obliged to measure it, and I made it over 50 inches, from tail to beak.

2. The extremities, often horny in structure, of the mandibles of other animals; *e.g.* the turtle, ornithorhynchus, octopus, etc.

1822 BURROWES *Cycl.* s.v. *Sepia*. Their beak is like that of a parrot. **1840** *Penny Cycl.* s.v. *Ornithorhynchus*, The edge of the osseous beak. **1847** CARPENTER *Zool.* §485 Tortoises ..[have] the mouth destitute of teeth, but furnished with a horny beak. **1877** SYMONDS *Renaiss. Italy* vi. 317 An octopus which..shoots its beak into a vital spot.

†**3.** The snout or muzzle of quadrupeds. *Obs.*

1567 MAPLET *Gr. Forest* 85 [The Elephant's] becke is holpen with that snowt that helpeth him euen as our hand doth. **1607** TOPSELL *Four-f. Beasts* 231 The beak or snowt of a Horse, ought not to stand out like a Swines.

4. The elongated head, proboscis, or sucker mouth of certain insects; *e.g.* the weevil, cochineal.

1658 ROWLAND *Mouffet's Theat. Ins.* 1086 The Weevil.. is formed like a small Beetle, it hath a beck proper to it self. **1847** CARPENTER *Zool.* §720 The young larvæ [of the Cochineal]..affix themselves by their sucking-beak. **1866** RYE *Brit. Beetles* xvii. 174 The Rhynchophora..have the head elongated in front into a rostrum or beak.

5. *humorously.* The human nose.

[**1598** FLORIO, *Naso adunco*, a beake-nose.] **1854** THACKERAY *Newcomes* I. 296 The well-known hooked beak of the old Countess. **1865** E. C. CLAYTON *Cruel Fort.* I. 143 A large, fat, greasy woman, with a prominent beak.

II. Transferred and technical senses.

6. A beak-shaped point or projection; a peak.

c **1440** *Partonope* 2100 Wyth the beke yet of his gleve. **1483** in Planché *Brit. Costume* (1834) 212 Two hats of estate ..with the round rolls behind and the beeks before. **1602** CAREW *Cornwall* (J.) Cuddenbeak, from a well advanced promontory, which entitled it beak. **1720** *Stow's Surv.* (Strype 1754) I. III. viii. 691/2 It was ordained..that Beaks of Shin [= shoes] and Boots should not pass the length of two inches. **1855** tr. *Labarte's Arts Mid. Ages* iv. 106 A goose-quill cut to a point..but with a longer beak.

7. The pointed and ornamented projection at the prow of ancient vessels, *esp.* of war galleys, where it was used in piercing and disabling the enemy's vessels; *now* = BEAK-HEAD.

1550 NICOLLS *Thucyd.* 183 (R.) Crushedde and brused in their foore partes with the beckes of the Corynthyans. **1610** SHAKS. *Temp.* I. ii. 197 Now on the Beake, Now in the Waste, the Decke, in every Cabyn, I flam'd amazement. **1738** GLOVER *Leonidas* I. 63 Xerxes' navy with their hostile beaks. **1850** BLACKIE *Æschylus* I. 43 Ship on ship Struck clashing; beak on butting beak was driven.

8. a. In the shells of some univalves: A narrow prolongation of the shell beyond the aperture in the axial line, containing the 'canal.'

b. In those of some bivalves: The projecting apex of each valve, situated directly above the hinge; also called *umbo*.

1851 RICHARDSON *Palæont.* viii. 240 The canal is the elongation of the aperture, in both lips of those shells which have a beak. **1854** WOODWARD *Mollusca* II. 245 The valves of the Conchifera are bound together by an elastic ligament ..The apex is termed the beak, or umbo.

9. *Bot.* A sharp projecting process, or prolonged tip, as in the seeds of Crane's-bill, etc.

[**1578** LYTE *Dodoens* 45 Whose seedes be long and sharpe like to a Hearons beake or byl.] **1820** GALPINE *Brit. Bot.* 67 Siliques linear, smooth, with short beaks. **1870** HOOKER *St. Fl.* 75 Ovary..produced upwards into a styliferous beak.

10. The taper tube of a retort, still, etc.; a spout.

1641 FRENCH *Distill.* v. (1651) 146 Take a Caldron with a ..high cover having a beake or nose. **1827** FARADAY *Chem. Manip.* xx. 542 When the beak of a retort is dipped into such mercury.

†**11.** *pl.* A pair of pincers, a forceps. *Obs.*

1656 RIDGLEY *Pract. Physic* 172 The bone must be cut away either with Beaks or Rasps. *Ibid.* 357 It is taken out with the Fingers, or Bekes, with or without cutting.

12. *technically* in mechanical arts: **a.** in *Printing* (see quot.). **b.** in *Forging* (see BEAK-IRON). **c.** in *Carpentry*, the crooked end of the holdfast of a carpenter's bench. **d.** in *Gas-fitting*, a gas-burner with a circular hole $\frac{1}{28}$ of an inch in diameter. **e.** in *Organ-building*.

1676 MOXON *Print Lett.* 21 The Projecture or Beak of the Stem. *Ibid.* 18 The Beak projects 1 stem on the left hand. **1831** J. HOLLAND *Manuf. Metal* I. 182 The beak or point of his anvil. **1852** SEIDEL *Organ* 82 The mouth-piece.. consists of the block, the beak, the tongue, the spring, the reed.

13. *Farriery*, 'A little horse-shoe, turned up, and fastened in upon the forepart of the hoof. Its use is to keep the shoes fast.' Chambers *Cycl. Supp.*

14. *Arch.* 'A little pendent fillet left on the edge of the larmier, forming a canal behind to prevent the water from running down the lower bed of the cornice.' Gwilt.

1734 in *Builder's Dict.*

III. *Comb.*, chiefly attrib., as ***beak-mouth***, ***-nose*** (see 5), ***-rush***, ***-sedge*** (see quot.); also the adjs. ***beak-bearing***, ***-leaved***, ***-like***, ***-shaped***, ***-sharp***. See also BEAK-HEAD, -IRON.

1830 WITHERING *Bot. Arrangem.* (ed. 7) II. 109 White Beak-rush; *Rhynchospora alba*..[found in] turfy bogs and marshes. **1839-47** TODD *Cycl. Anat. & Phys.* III. 251/2 The beak-bearing mouth of the adult. **1849-52** *Ibid.* IV. 878/2 The dense covering of the beak-like jaws of the Parrot-fishes. **1851** RICHARDSON *Geol.* viii. 232 The dorsal valve is the largest, and..develops a beak-shaped process. **188.** G. M. HOPKINS *Poems* (1918) 52 Only the beak-leaved boughs. **1921** D. H. LAWRENCE *Tortoises* 9 To open your tiny beak-mouth. **1933** W. DE LA MARE *Fleeting* 152 Beak-sharp nose.

†**beak,** *sb.*[2] *Obs. rare*[−1]. [? f. BEAK *v.*[1], or F. *becquer*, in the sense 'to give a stroke with the beak.'] ? A stroke with the beak; a thrust, a poke.

1592 WYRLEY *Armorie* 100 A hardie Britton thinking not to toy Vnto..my seruant gaue a beake.

beak (biːk), *sb.*[3] *slang.* [Derivation unknown. ? from BEAK *sb.*[1]; but in Harman's vocabulary of 'Peddlers' French' in his *Caveat* (1573), *harman beck* is explained as 'the counstable' (*harman* being 'the stocks').]

a. A magistrate or justice of the peace.

[**1573** HARMAN *Caveat* (Shaks. Soc. 1880) 84 The Harman beck, the counstable. *Gipsy Song* in *Shaks. Eng.* (1856) I. viii. 270 The ruffin (devil) cly (take) the nob (head) of the harman beck.] **1799** in *Spirit Pub. Jrnls.* III. 352 Took a gentle walk to the [police] office..paid my respects to Sir William, and the rest of the beaks. *a* **1845** HOOD *Tale Trump.* xxx, Dicky Gossips of birds, That talk with as much good sense and decorum, As many Beaks who belong to the quorum. **1838** DICKENS *O. Twist* (1850) 37/2 Why, a beak's a madgst'rate; and when you walk by a beak's order, it's.. always agoing up, and nivir acoming down agin. **1879** E. WALFORD *Londoniana* I. 233 We hope and trust [they] were brought before the 'beak' and duly punished.

b. *transf.* (*Schoolboys' slang.*) A schoolmaster.

1888 *Pall Mall G.* 9 Feb. 5/1 One of the Eton masters, or 'beaks', if we may be allowed to use a schoolboy phrase. **1916** E. F. BENSON *David Blaize* ix, You can have your crib spread out..and he won't see it. He didn't ought to be a beak at all. **1926** *Spectator* 11 Sept. 383/1 This scholarly Irishman and Eton 'beak'. **1960** BETJEMAN *Summoned by Bells* vii. 69 Comparing bruises, other boys could show Far worse ones that the beaks and prefects made.

beak (biːk), *v.*[1] Forms: 3-5 beke, (4 bike), 6 beake, 7 beck, 7- beak. [a. OF. *beque-r*, *bequier*, f. *bec* BEAK *sb.*[1]; cf. MHG. *becken*, *bicken*.]

1. To strike or seize with the beak, to peck; to push the beak (or snout) into: **a.** *trans.*

c **1230** *Ancr. R.* 118 Ase deð þe pellican..mid hire owune bile bekie hire breoste. **1591** PERCIVALL *Sp. Dict.*, *Hocicar*, to roote as a pigge, to busse, or beake. **1770** LANGHORNE *Plutarch* (1879) I. 513/1 The crows came and beaked it for several days. **1861** MRS. NORTON *Lady La G.* II. 296 Some poor woodland bird, who stays his flight..And beaks the plumage of his glistening wings.

b. *absol.* or *intr.*: occas. *fig.*

c **1230** *Ancr. R.* 84 þe bacbitare..bekeð mid his blake bile o cwike charoines. **1571** FORTESCUE *Forest Hist.* 65 b, Certaine sparrowes..supposing they had been grapes, arrested them to beake thereon. **1780-6** WOLCOTT (P. Pindar) *Odes R. Acad.* Wks. I. 113 Like cocks, for ever at each other beaking.

†**c.** *spec.* in *Falconry*; see quot.

1486 *Bk. St. Albans* C viij, She bekyth when she sewith: that is to say she wypith hir beke.

2. *intr.* To project or stick out with or as a beak; to put or push out the beak; to 'put out the nose,' i.e. to peep out. *rare.*

c **1230** *Ancr. R.* 102 Totilde ancre..þet bekeð euer utward ase untowe brid ine cage. **1547** BOORDE *Introd. Knowl.* 207 On the toppe..is a thyng like a poding bekyng forward.

†**3.** ? To thrust, strike with a pointed weapon.

[In the quotation *biked* may be for *beked*, as *styked* interchanges with *steked*, perh. the original reading here; but it may also be a distinct word. Mätzner compares MHG. *bicken*, and *becken*, 'to pierce, strike through, hack, hew,' ad. F. *piquer*, It. *piccare*.]

c **1300** *K. Alis.* 2337 The thridde, Gildas, faste biked; Ac thorugh the throte he him styked.

4. *trans.* To ram (a vessel). Also *absol.* Hence **'beaking** *vbl. sb.*

1898 KIPLING *Fleet in Being* 55 We could run in and beak 'em while it's thick. I believe in beaking... Oh, he'd beak like a shot, if he saw his chance.

beak, var. form of BEEK *v.* to warm.

beaked (biːkt), *ppl. a.* Also 7 beck'd. [f. BEAK *sb.*[1] + -ED[2].]

1. Furnished with a beak (or peak).

1589 PUTTENHAM *Eng. Poesie* (Arb.) 290 A long beaked doublet hanging downe to his thies. **1611** COTGR. s.v. *Oiseau*, Beaked like a Parrot. **1870** BRYANT *Iliad* I. I. 19, I shall now go home..With my beaked ships.

2. *spec.* **a.** in *Her.* used when the beak or bill of the fowl is of a different tincture from the body.

1572 BOSSEWELL *Armorie* II. 36 b, An Eagle displayed with twoo heades..membred and beaked Gules. **1864** BOUTELL *Hist. Heraldry* xv. §15. 264 Three herons arg..beaked and legged or.

b. in *Bot.* Rostrate: sometimes forming a descriptive epithet of plants, *e.g.* Beaked Parsley.

1841 WITHERING *Bot. Arrangem.* (ed. 5) 143 Common Beaked-parsley. Fruit egg-shaped. **1858** THOREAU *Maine W.* (1882) 119, I saw the aster puniceus and the beaked hazel. **1870** HOOKER *Stud. Flora* 4 Butter-cup..Fruit a head or spike of apiculate or beaked achenes.

c. in *Zool.* Having a beak-like proboscis.

1869 NICHOLSON *Zool.* liv. (1880) 500 Other well-known members of the family [*Batides*] are..the Beaked Rays. **1877** *Encycl. Brit.* VII. 280/2 The *Hyperoodontidæ*, or beaked-whales, are widely distributed in northern, southern, and tropical seas.

3. Resembling a beak, pointed or hooked.

1590 GREENE *Never too late* (1600) 96 His nose..was conquerour like, as beaked as an Eagle. **1637** MILTON *Lycidas* 94 Every gust..That blows from off each beaked promontory. **1863** *Cornh. Mag.* 100 Small, searching eyes, a beaked nose, and white bristly hair.

beaker ('biːkə(r)). Forms: 4 biker, 5 becure, byker, bikyr, 7 beeker, 7- beaker: see also BICKER. [ME. *biker*, ad. ON. *bikarr*; found in other Teutonic langs. (OS. *bikeri*, OHG. *behhâri*, *behhar*, MHG. and mod.G. *becher*:—OTeut. type **bikarjo-(m)*, but not a native Teut. word: considered to be a. L. *bicārium*; but as this is known only in med.L, it is doubtful whether it existed early enough to be the source of the Teutonic. (The Romanic words, It. *bicchiére*, *pécchero*, OF. *pichier*, *pechier*, referred by Diez to the same source, require a Latin type in *biccār-*.) *Bicārium* is referred by Diez to Gr. *βῖκος* 'drinking-bowl,' of which **βικάριον* would be a legitimately formed, though not recorded, diminutive. The original Eng. form is retained in Scotch *bicker*; the mod. form has apparently been assimilated to *beak*.]

1. a. A large drinking vessel with a wide mouth, an open cup or goblet. (Now chiefly in literary use.)

1348 *Acc. Edw. Pr. Wales* in *Promp. Parv.* 35 Magne pecie argenti, vocate Bikers. **1420** *E.E. Wills* (1882) 45 A becure of seluer. *c* **1440** *Promp. Parv.* 35/2 Byker, cuppe (*v.r.* bikyr), *cimbium*. **1600** ROWLANDS *Let. Humours Blood* vi. 75 Fill him his Beaker, he will never flinch, To giue a full quart pot the empty pinch. **1725** POPE *Odyss.* XIV. 117 The prince a silver beaker chose. **1872** FREEMAN *Hist. Ess.* 14 His cupbearer was carrying..a royal beaker full of wine.

b. The contents of a beaker.

1819 SCOTT *Ivanhoe* I. xv. 218 We drink this beaker..to the health of Wilfred of Ivanhoe. **1870** DISRAELI *Lothair* xxx. 146 Stimulated by..beakers of Badminton.

c. *spec.* in *Archæol.* A type of tall wide-mouthed vessel found in the graves of a people who came to Britain from Central Europe in the early Bronze Age; hence *attrib.*, as ***beaker-folk***, ***-maker***, ***people***.

1902 J. ABERCROMBY in *Jrnl. Anthrop. Inst.* XXXII. 374, I propose to substitute for the double-barrelled name 'drinking cup', the compacter term 'beaker'. **1906** *Archaeol. Æliana* II. 147 The Dilstor Park find..also proves the great difficulty of attempting to fix any relevant dates of Bronze Age beakers by a comparison either of their shape or ornamentation. **1916** *Jrnl. Anthrop. Inst.* XLVI. 117 The Borreby, or Beaker-Maker Type... Probably tall and often fair, light eyed, broad headed, short faced. **1922** *Ibid.* LII. 45 The culture is that known in Britain as that of the Beaker-folk. **1932** *Discovery* Aug. 270/1 The Bronze Age in England began roughly about 2,000 B.C. with the arrival of the 'Beaker' people on the east coast—people who used bronze and copper knives and pots of a special type. **1935** *Proc. Prehist. Soc.* I. 83 A solitary beaker from a cist at Barroose, Lonan, and three polished flint discoidal knives from the neighbourhood of Peel, are the only indications of the beaker people on the island. **1963** H. N. SAVORY in Foster & Alcock *Culture & Environment* iii. 26 The barbed and tanged arrowheads which were undoubtedly introduced into south Wales by the 'Beaker Folk'.

2. An open-mouthed glass vessel, with a lip for pouring, used in scientific experiments.

1877 WATTS *Fownes' Chem.* II. 16 The acid containing the ammonia is poured out into a beaker.

beakful ('biːkfʊl). [f. BEAK *sb.*[1] + -FUL.] As much as can be held in a bird's beak.

1794 WOLCOTT (P. Pindar) *Rowl. for Oliver* Wks. II. 365 Got a good handsome beakfull by good pulling. **1884** in *Harper's Mag.* May 927/1 With a beakful of..grass.

beak-head ('biːkhɛd). [f. BEAK *sb.*[1] + HEAD.]

1. *Naval Arch.* **a.** The BEAK or prow of an ancient war-galley. **b.** A small platform at the fore part of the upper deck. **c.** The part of a ship in front of the forecastle, fastened to the stem, and supported by the main knee.

1580 NORTH *Plutarch* (1676) 423 Commanding his Master to turn the beak-head of his galley forward. **1614** RALEIGH *Hist. World* viii, Each of them hung out a burning Cresset vpon two poles, at the Beake-head. **1627** CAPT. SMITH *Seaman's Gram.* ii. 10 The Beak-head is without the ship before the fore-Castle..and of great vse, as well for the grace and countenance of the ship, as a place for men to ease themselues in. *c* **1850** *Rudim. Nav.* (Weale) 95 *Beak head*, the short platform at the fore-part of the upper deck.. placed at the height of the ports from the deck, for the convenience of the chase-guns. **1855** KINGSLEY *Heroes* III. (1868) 105 They..nailed it [the bough] to the beak-head of the ship.

2. *Arch.* An ornament shaped like a bird's beak used in Norman mouldings.

1849 FREEMAN *Archit.* 248 The beak-head is commonly employed to grasp, as it were, one of the heavy roll-mouldings of the style.

3. *attrib.* **beak-head-beam**, **-bulkhead** (see quot.); ***beak-head ornament***, ***moulding*** (cf. sense 2).

1848 RICKMAN *Archit.* Introd. 17 Ornamented with a succession of zigzags and beak-head ornaments. *c* **1850** *Rudim. Nav.* (Weale) 95 Cat-Beam, or Beak-Head Beam.. is the broadest beam in a ship, generally made in two breadths, tabled and bolted together. The foreside is placed far enough forward to receive the heads of the stanchions of the beak-head bulk-head. **1867** SMYTH *Sailor's Word-bk.*, *Beak-head bulkhead*, the old termination aft of the space called *beak-head*, which inclosed the fore part of the ship.

beaking ('biːkɪŋ), *vbl. sb.* [f. BEAK *v.*[1]] The action of striking or seizing with the beak.

1706 PHILLIPS, *Beaking* (a term in Cock-fighting), the fighting of those Birds with their Bills; or their holding with the Bill, and striking with the Heels. **1819** REES *Encycl.*, *Beaking* in Cock-fighting.

beaking ('biːkɪŋ), *ppl. a.* [f. BEAK *v.*[1] + -ING[2].] Forming, projecting like, or furnished with, a beak. ***beaking joint***: that formed by the meeting of several heading-joints in one continuous line; the opposite of ***breaking joint***.

1667 MOXON *Mech. Exerc.* (1703) 150 The ends may all lye in a straight Line, that the straight ends of other Boards laid against them may make the truer Joint, and this they call a Beaking Joint. **1687** HOLME *Armory* II. iii. 48 The Daubil ..of some called a Beaking Glomaine..is a long Apple, having a Beak or Hook, by which it hangs to the stalk.

'beak-iron. Also 9 beck-iron, 9- bick-. [A corruption of BICKERN (= F. *bigorne*, It. *bicornia*, an anvil with two pointed extremities), altered first in form, and then in sense, by popular etymology.] The pike or taper end of a blacksmith's anvil. Also, an anvil with two projecting taper ends.

1667 MOXON *Mech. Exer.* (1703) 3 A Black Smith's Anvil ..is sometimes made with a Pike, or Bickern, or Beak-iron, at one end of it. **1828** SPEARMAN *Brit. Gunner* (ed. 2) 109 Anvil and Bick Iron. **1831** J. HOLLAND *Manuf. Metals* I. 160 The furniture of a blacksmith's shop..comprising..vice,

anvil with bick-iron, etc. *Ibid.* II. 39 A little beaked anvil, called a beck-iron. **1941** *Archit. Rev.* XC. 97/2 The bick iron, a narrow anvil, mounted about 3 feet 6 inches high, is for rounding, boring and cutting the iron hoops.

beakless ('bi:klɪs), *a.* [f. BEAK *sb.*[1] + -LESS.] Having no beak.

1598 SYLVESTER *Du Bartas* II. iv. (1641) 229/2 Hence beakless-Bird; hence winged-Beast, they cride. **1870** *Pall Mall G.* 30 Nov., O dearest, sweetest of beakless singers!

† **'beakment.** *Obs.* or *dial.* Also **beatment.** [perh. f. F. *becquer* to peck + -MENT. Cf. Prof. Skeat's remarks on PECK (the measure).] 'A measure of about a quarter of a peck.' Halliwell.

1673 *Depos. Yrk. Castle* (1861) 194 She gott a beakment of wheat flower. **1863** in Robson *Bards of Tyne* 252 The Farrier's cap Blew off..Into a huckster's shop it went—Now Martin's cap's a tatie beatment.

beaky ('bi:kɪ), *a.* [f. BEAK *sb.*[1] + -Y[1].] **a.** Furnished with or distinguished by a beak.

1718 POPE *Iliad* XIV. 834 The ships, whose beaky prores Lay..on the bending shores. **1867** MISS BROUGHTON *Not wisely* I. 62 Sir Guy Stamer, bald-headed, beaky, ill-natured.

b. *Comb.* **beaky-nosed** *a.*, having a nose shaped like a beak.

1923 R. GRAVES *Feather Bed* 20 A red-haired beaky-nosed burly nun. **1937** C. DAY LEWIS *Starting Point* I. ii. 24 There was another girl, too—a beaky-nosed creature.

† **beal**, *sb.*[1] *Obs.* or *dial.* [Apparently a variant of BOIL *sb.*, which occurs in ME. in the various forms, *byle*, *byil*, *bule*, *buyl*, *buile*, *bile*, *biel*, *bele*, *beel*, the latter apparently the precursor of the 17th c. spelling *beal* (if this does not rather represent the ON. equivalent *beyla*). For the further history, see BOIL.] A pustule or boil.

c **1400** WYCLIF *Lev.* xiii. 18 (MS. D), The skynne in the whiche a beel [*v. r.* bocche] is growun. **1632** SHERWOOD, A beale, *pustule*. **1783** AINSWORTH *Lat. Dict.* (Morell) I. s.v., Full of beals, *pustulosus*.

† **beal(e**, *sb.*[2] Obs. var. PEEL, baker's shovel.

1598 FLORIO, *Impalare*, to put bread into an ouen with a beale. [So s.v. *Impalato*.]

‖ **beal** (be:l, bje:l), *sb.*[3] [Gaelic *béul* mouth.] The mouth of a (highland) river or valley. (Used for the sake of local colouring.)

1818 SCOTT *Leg. Montrose* III. 330 (Jam.) The different passes, precipices, corries, and beals, through which he said the road lay to Inverary.

† **beal**, *v. Obs.* or *dial.* [f. BEAL *sb.*[1]] *intr.* To suppurate, to 'gather.' Still in regular use in Scotland.

1611 COTGR., *Bouër*, to beale, to matter. **1717** *Wodrow Corr.* (1843) II. 244 The remarkable instance of the adulterer, to whom Mr. Peebles said, 'This shall beal out of your breast!' *Mod. Sc.* Take care the sore does not beal.

† **'bealing**, *vbl. sb.* and *ppl. a. Obs.* exc. *dial.* [f. BEAL *v.* + -ING.]

1. *vbl. sb.* Suppuration; a 'gathering'; a boil.

a **1605** MONTGOMERIE *Poems* (1821) 215 Go to—what rek? And gar the bealing brek. **1611** COTGR., *Hypopie*, bealing, or matter growing, or gathering in a crushed eye. **1703** THORESBY *Let.*, *Beiling*, matter mix'd with blood running out of a sore. *Mod. Sc.* To poultice a bealing.

2. *ppl. a.* Suppurating, 'gathering.'

Mod. Sc. To have a bealing hand lanced.

bealk: see BELCH.

be-all ('bi:ɔ:l), *sb. phrase.* That which is or constitutes the whole; the whole being: a Shaksperian phrase in common modern use.

1605 SHAKS. *Macb.* I. vii. 5 That but this blow Might be the be all, and the end all. **1830** GEN. P. THOMPSON *Exerc.* (1842) I. 218 This is the end-all and be-all of the anti-liberals' piety. **1854** E. NEALE *Min. Canon* ii. 30 With whom money was the 'be-all and end-all of existence.'

bealme, obs. variant of BEAM.

be-'altared, *ppl. a.* [f. BE- 7 + ALTAR.] Furnished or filled with altars.

1655 FULLER *Ch. Hist.* VI. vi. §9 III. 471 See how the Church of Saint Paul was be-Altared in that Age.

bealte, early form of BEAUTY *sb.*

bealy(e, obs. form of BELLY.

beam (bi:m), *sb.*[1] Forms: 1 béam, 2 bæm, beam, 3–4 bem, 4–5 beem, 4–6 beme, (5–6 *Sc.* beym(e, beim, 5–6 bealme), 6–7 beame, 6– beam. [Common Teutonic: OE. *béam* 'tree', 'plank,' = OFris. *bâm*, OS. *bâm*, *bôm*, MDu., Du. *boom*, OHG., MHG. *boum*, Ger. *baum* 'tree':—West Ger. **baumo-z*. The East Ger. words, Goth. *bagm-s*, ON. *baðm-r* 'tree,' though supposed to be identical, present phonetic differences of which no explanation has been found, and render somewhat doubtful the original Teutonic form of the word, as also a suggested derivation (which would suit the WGer.) from the vb. root *bû-*, *beu-*, = Gr. *φυ-* (cf. *φῦμα* a growth), Skr. *bhu-*, *bhaw-* to grow (cf. BE). It remains uncertain whether the original sense was 'tree' as a kind of plant, or 'tree' as a wooden stem, stock, or post: OE. had both meanings, but that of (growing) 'tree,' the regular sense in the continental langs., is (exc. in a few compound names) lost in mod.Eng., where the word has received many transferred applications, among which that of *beam of light*, sun-*beam*, is remarkable.]

I. A material beam.

* *of wood* (actually or originally).

† **1.** A tree; only in OE., exc. in the now unanalysed compounds, HORNBEAM, QUICKBEAM, WHITEBEAM or *beam-tree*, names of trees.

826 *Chart. Ecgberht* in *Cod. Dipl.* V. 84 Súðæweardæ oð ðet scírhiltæ on ðonæ gréatan béam. *c* **1000** *Riddles* (Grein) lvi. 7 Ic þæs béames mæʒ éaðe for eorlum æðelu secʒan.

† **2.** The rood-tree or cross. (Cf. 'hanged on a tree,' *Acts* v. 30). ***beam-light***: lighted candles placed before the rood. ***fees of the beam***: perquisites of the unconsumed remnants of such candles.

c **1000** *Crist* (Grein) 1094 He on ðone hálʒan béam ahongen wæs. *c* **1305** in *Leg. Rood* (1871) 146 Cristened we weore in Red rem, Whon his bodi bledde on þe Beem. **1461–83** *Ord. R. Househ.* 49 The Deane of the Chapell hathe all the offerings of wax..with the moderate fees of the beame..wher the tapers be consumed into a shaftmennt. **1529** *Bk. Founders' Comp.* in *N. & Q.* Ser. III. IX. 62 Payd for makyng of viij square tap[rs] for the beme lyght of S[t]. Marg[t]..vs. iiijd. **1720** *Stow's Surv.* (Strype, 1754) I. I. xv. 74/2 The Cross and the Beam beyond the Altar.

3. a. A large piece of squared timber, long in proportion to its breadth and thickness, such as is used in house- or ship-building, where beams form important parts of the structure: originally, the squared timber of a whole tree, but now used without any such restriction. The ordinary current sense: for naval use, see II.

978 *O.E. Chron.*, At Calne..se halʒa Dunstan ana ætstod uppon anum beame. *c* **1000** *Ags. Gosp.* Matt. vii. 3 Þú ne ʒesyhst þone beam on þinum aʒenum eaʒan. *c* **1250** *Gen. & Ex.* 1606 And slep and saȝ, and soðe drem, Fro ðe erðe up til heuene bem A leddre stonden. **1297** R. GLOUC. 288 Þe flor to brac vnder hem..Seyn Dunston by cas..hente hym by a bem, and ysaued was. *c* **1340** *Cursor M.* (Trin.) 8781 Þe beem [*Cotton*, balk] þat most þe werk shulde bynde. **1413** LYDG. *Pylgr. Sowle* IV. iii. (1483) 59 A grete tre was hewen doune for to be made a beme. **1595** SHAKS. *John* IV. iii. 129 A rush will be a beame To hang thee on. **1611** BIBLE *2 Kings* vi. 2 Let vs..take thence euery man a beame, and let vs make vs a place there where we may dwell. **1807** CRABBE *Village* I. 262 Such is that room which one rude beam divides.

b. with special shape or purpose indicated: ***camber-beam***: one with its upper surface curving downward on both sides from the middle. ***collar-beam***: a beam used to join together roof-rafters above the base of the roof, acting either as a tie or a strut. ***dragon-beam***: a short piece of timber lying diagonally with the wall plates at the angles of the roof, for receiving the heel of the hip rafter. ***hammer-beam***: a beam acting as a tie, but not extending across the whole span of the roof. ***tie-beam***: the beam which connects the bottom of a pair of principal rafters, and prevents them from thrusting out the walls.

1734 *Builder's Dict.*, *Dragon Beams* are two strong Braces or Struts..meeting in an Angle upon the Shoulder of the Kingpiece. **1823** P. NICHOLSON *Pract. Build.* 221 Camber-Beams, those beams used in the flats of truncated roofs, and raised in the middle with an obtuse angle, for discharging the rain water towards both sides of the roof. *Ibid.* 222 Dragon-beam, the piece of timber which supports the hip-rafter, and bisects the angle formed by the wall plates. **1845** *Gloss. Gothic Archit.* I. 317 In the Perpendicular style hammer-beam roofs were introduced. *Ibid.* The roof..of Malvern priory had a variety of cross-braces above the tie-beams cut into ornamental featherings.

c. *fig.*, esp. with allusion to the figure of the mote and the beam (*Matt.* vii. 3).

[Cf. *c* **1000** in 3.] **1377** LANGL. *P. Pl.* B. x. 264 Sithen a beem in þine owne ablyndeth þi-selue. *a* **1555** LATIMER *Serm. & Rem.* (1845) 314 Learn from your own beams to make allowance for your neighbour's motes. **1588** SHAKS. *L.L.L.* IV. iii. 162 You found his Moth, the King your Moth did see: But I a Beame doe finde in each of three. **1649** DRUMM. OF HAWTH. *Hist. Jas. IV*, Wks. (1711) 74 Her tears and prayers shook the strongest beams of his resolutions.

4. The wooden roller or cylinder in a loom, on which the warp is wound before weaving; also called ***fore-beam, yarn-beam, yarn-roll.*** The similar roller on which the cloth is wound as it is woven; also called ***back-beam, breast-beam, cloth-beam.***

c **1000** *Supp. Ælfric's Gloss.* in Wülcker *Voc.* /187 *Liciatorium*, webbeam. **1382** WYCLIF 1 *Sam.* xvii. 7 The shaft of his speer was as the beem [COVERDALE, lome] of websters. *c* **1440** *Promp. Parv.* 30/2 Beeme of webstarrys lome, *liciatorium*. **1552** HULOET, Beame of timber wherupon embroderers..do rolle their worke, *iugum*. **1598** SHAKS. *Merry W.* v. i. 23, I feare not Goliah with a Weauers beame. **1675** HOBBES *Odyss.* (1677) 230 So I A beam set up, and then began to weave. **1831** G. PORTER *Silk Manuf.* 215 The beam, or yarn-roll, on which the threads are wound.

5. The great timber of the plough, to which all the other parts of the plough-tail are fixed.

c **1000** ÆLFRIC *Gloss.* in Wülcker *Voc.* /104 *Buris*, sulh-beam. *c* **1450** in *Ibid.* /569 *Burris*, the plowebeme. **1483** *Cath. Angl.* 27/1 A beym of ye plwgh, *buris*. **1592** WARNER *Alb. Eng.* VIII. xlii. (1597) 205 But to the Headland shall our Plough, vnles we breake our Beame. **1787** T. JEFFERSON *Corr.* (1830) 135 The plough here is made with..a beam twelve feet long. **1832** C. HOWARD *Sel. Farms* (L.U.K.) 3 The plough is of a light construction..the length of the beam is six feet six inches.

6. a. The transverse bar from the ends of which the scales of a balance are suspended; the balance itself. Often *fig.* with reference to the scales held by the allegorical figure of justice.

1420 *E.E. Wills* (1882) 46 A beme þat y weye þer-with. **1503** *Act 19 Hen. VII*, vi, Deceivable and untrue Beams and Scales. **1581** LAMBARDE *Eiren.* IV. xix. (1588) 605 Let us holde the beame, and put in balaunce their reasons on either side. **1711** POPE *Rape Lock* v. 73 The doubtful beam long nods from side to side. **1802** REES *Cycl.* s.v. *Balance*, The beam, the principal part of the balance, is a lever of the first kind. **1875** *Encycl. Brit.* (ed. 9) s.v. *Balance*, The beam..is supported on a polished horizontal frame of agate or hard steel.

b. Phrases, ***the common beam, the King's beam*** (*Hist.*); the public standard balance formerly in the custody of the Grocers' Company of London; *fig.* an authorized standard. ***to kick*** or ***strike the beam***: (of one scale of a balance) to be so lightly loaded that it flies up and strikes the beam; to be greatly outweighed; often *fig.*

[**1386** *Records Grocers' Co. Lond.* (facsimile 67), Item paie a Johan Reche pour defendre le pursute dell Bem.] **1448** *MS. Records do.* 147 Weying the same marchaundise at ther owne beeme, and not at the commorn beeme. **1494** FABYAN VII. 341 Than was layde vnto theyr charge, that..they hadde alteryd the kynges beame. *Ibid.* 391 The kynges bealme. **1607** HIERON *Wks.* I. 79 To make the written word (as it were) the standard or the kings beame, by which to try all doctrine. **1647** WARD *Simp. Cobler* 38 A sin..that seemes small in the common beame of the world, may be very great in the scoales of his Sanctuary. **1712** ADDISON *Spect.* No. 463 ¶3 The latter, to shew its comparative Lightness, immediately flew up and kickt the Beam. **1860** G. P. MORRIS *Poems* (ed. 15) 53 Wealth!—a straw within the balance, Opposed to love will strike the beam.

† **7.** The pole or shaft of a chariot. *Obs.*

1600 CHAPMAN *Iliad.* v. 736 The chariot's..beam that look'd before Was massy silver. **1697** DRYDEN *Virg. Æneid* XII. (J.) Juturna..Forc'd from the beam her brother's charioteer.

8. *Tanning.* A block of varying shape upon which hides are fixed to be scraped or shaved.

1875 URE *Dict. Arts* III. 93 The furniture in this department consists of a beam on which the leather is shaved, etc.

** *of other materials.*

† **9.** A large bar of metal; a piece of metal fulfilling the functions of sense 3. *Obs.*

c **885** K. ÆLFRED *Oros.* II. viii. §5 Hiora ærenan beamas..ne mehton from Galliscum fyre forbærnede weorþan. **1387** TREVISA *Higden* Rolls Ser. V. 315 Hormisda lefte in Seynt Peter his chirche a beme [*trabem*] of silver. **1597** HOOKER *Eccl. Pol.* (1841) IV. lxxix. §5 A certain beam of gold about seven hundred and a half in weight. **1613** PURCHAS *Pilgr.* II. vii. 132 A greate beame of gold.

10. The shank or main part of an anchor (Phillips 1706, Johnson, etc.); but according to Admiral Smyth, the stock.

11. In the steam-engine, etc.: A heavy iron lever, having a reciprocating motion on a central axis, one end of which is connected with the piston-rod from which it receives motion, and the other with the crank or wheel-shaft, to which it communicates motion; also called ***working-*** and ***walking-beam.***

1758 FITZGERALD in *Phil. Trans.* L. 727 [In] the fire-engine..it was necessary to contrive some way to make the beam, tho' moving alternately, to turn a wheel constantly round one way. **1851** CARLYLE *Sterling* III. ii. (1872) 175, I saw half the beam of a great steam-engine..cast in about five minutes. **1884** *Harper's Mag.* July 270/1 The walking-beam which drives the side-wheels.

12. The main trunk of a stag's horn which bears the branches or 'antlers.'

1575 TURBERV. *Venerie* 53 When the beame is great, burnished..and not made crooked by the antlyers. **1630** J. TAYLOR (Water P.) *Wks.* I. 93/1 A Buckes hornes are composed of Burre, Beame, etc. **1774** GOLDSM. *Nat. Hist.* I. II. v. (1862) 325 The fourth year that part [of the horn] which bears the antlers is called the beam. **1862** C. COLLYNS *Red Deer* ii, The 'beam,' or main horn, increases in size..as the stag grows older.

† **13.** The part of a cock's leg below the thigh and above the spur. *Obs.*

1614 MARKHAM *Cheap Husb.* (1623) 135 His legs straight, and of a strong beame. [So **1727** in BRADLEY *Fam. Dict.* s.v. *Cock.*]

II. Nautical extensions of senses 1, 3.

† **14.** *poet.* A ship, a bark: perhaps, originally one made of a hollowed trunk. *Obs.*

c **1000** *Riddles* (Grein) xi. 7 Ic of fæðmum cwóm brimes and béames. **1509** BARCLAY *Ship of Fools* (1570) 178 Howe thou thee aventrest in holowe beame To passe the sea.

15. One of the horizontal transverse timbers, stretching from side to side of a ship, supporting the deck, and holding the vessel together. ***on the beams***: cf. *on the beam-ends* (sense 18).

1627 CAPT. SMITH *Seaman's Gram.* ii. 5 The maine beame is euer next the maine mast, where is the ships greatest breadth. **1784** COOK *Voy.* (1790) III. 809 Before we could raise the main tack, the Dolphin was laid upon her beams. **1795** NELSON in Nicolas *Disp.* II. 5 The ships built at Toulon have their sides, beams, decks..from this Island. **1873** *Act 36 & 37 Vict.* lxxxv. §3 The number denoting her registered tonnage shall be cut in on her main beam.

16. a. *Hence*, The greatest breadth of a ship.

1627 CAPT. SMITH *Seaman's Gram.* iii. 15 Suppose a Ship of 300. Tunnes be 29 foot at the Beame. **1781** NELSON in Nicolas *Disp.* I. 43 The Albemarle is not so wide on the gun-deck by four inches, but the same beam. **1875** 'STONEHENGE' *Brit. Sports* II. VIII. i. §3 The shallow hull gave way..to sharp bottoms, less beam, and a great deal of lead.

b. *transf.* The (width of the) hips or buttocks; esp. in colloq. phr. ***broad in the beam.***

1929 H. WALPOLE *Hans Frost* II. vi. 177 He stood watching disgustedly Bigges' broad beam. **1944** MRS. HICKS-BEACH *Annabel & M. Verena* xxiv. 92 A cast-off of Jim's. He's grown too broad in the beam for it. **1960** I. CROSS *Backward Sex* i. 24 'I'm too broad around the beam.' 'What do you mean?..' 'My hips, silly..I've got wide hips.'

17. Hence designating the side of a vessel or sideward direction, *esp.* in technical phrases. ***lee*** or ***weather beam***: the side away from *or* towards the wind. ***on*** or ***upon the*** (***starboard*** or ***larboard***) ***beam***: at some distance on the (right *or* left) side of a ship, at right angles to the keel. ***abaft*** or ***before the beam***: behind *or* before an imaginary line drawn right across the centre of the ship. ***beam sea***: one rolling against the ship's side.

1628 DIGBY *Jrnl.* 83 You gett your chace vpon your beame. **1791** SMEATON *Edystone L.* §159 The wind..was but one point before our beam. **1833** MARRYAT *P. Simple* (1863) 101 Land on the lee beam! **1836** —— *Midsh. Easy* xxx, The other frigate had passed half her length clear of the beam of the Aurora. **1883** FROUDE *Sketches* 67 The wind rose..bringing..a heavy beam sea.

18. beam-ends, the ends of a ship's beams. ***to be,*** or ***be laid, on the beam-ends***: to have them touching the water, so that the vessel lies on its side in imminent danger of capsizing; *fig.* to be quite laid aside, utterly at a loss, hard up.

1773 *Gentl. Mag.* XLIII. 321 The gust laid her upon her beam-ends. **1796** MORSE *Amer. Geog.* I. 517 A number of large river craft..on their beam-ends for want of water. **1830** MARRYAT *King's Own* xxvi, Our first-lieutenant was..on his beam-ends, with the rheumatiz. **1844** DICKENS *Mar. Chuz.* xl. (D.) Tom was thrown upon his beam-ends again for some other solution.

III. An immaterial beam, of light, colour, etc.

19. a. A ray, or 'bundle' of parallel rays, of light emitted from the sun or other luminous body; out-streaming radiance. [Apparently this sense arose in OE. through literal translation from the Lat.; not, however, as often thought, of *radius solis* 'a spoke' of the sun, but of *columna lucis* a 'pillar' or 'column' of light; an expression used more than once by Bæda (e.g. *H.E.* III. xi) to denote a column or stream of light rising from a saint's dead body, which Ælfred renders by *swylce sunne-béam.* Also, in the poetical version of Exodus, the pillars or columns of fire and cloud, are *béamas twégen*; the fiery pillar is *wuldres béam*, column or beam of glory, *byrnende béam*, and in the metrical Psalms, *fýren béam* a fire beam. We may compare the beam- or balk-like appearance of the illuminated dusty atmosphere of a room, and the representations of light from heaven in paintings.]

c **885** in *O.E. Chron.* an. 678 Her ateowede cometa..and scan iii monðas ælce morȝen swilce sunne beam [BÆDA, *excelsam radiantis flammæ quasi columnam.*] *c* **1000** *Ags. Ps.* cv. 34 Het him neode, nihta ȝehwylce, fyrenne beam beforan wisian. **1205** LAY. 17887 Þe leome þa strehte west riht a seouen bæmen [**1250** bemes] wes idiht. *c* **1325** *E.E. Allit. P.* B. 603 Bryȝt blykked þe bem of þe brode heuen. **1375** BARBOUR *Bruce* XI. 190 Armys..blenknyt with the sonnys beyme. *c* **1430** *Hymns Virg.* 208 Þe briȝt beemys blent my siȝt. **1596** SHAKS. *Merch. V.* v. i. 90 How farre that little candell throwes his beames. **1664** POWER *Exp. Philos.* I. 77 So were the Luminous Beams variously transmitted, refracted, or reflected. **1869** TYNDALL in *Fortn. Rev.* 228 But what, in the first instance, is a beam of light? It is a train of innumerable waves, excited in, and propagated through, an almost infinitely attenuated and elastic medium, which fills all space, and which we name the æther.

b. The appearance of rays produced by the sun's shining upon mist through gaps in the clouds.

1846 RUSKIN *Mod. Paint.* (1851) I. II. 3 i. §15. 209 The appearance of beams can only take place in a part of the sky which has clouds between it and the sun.

c. A radiating line of colour.

1705 PETIVER in *Phil. Trans.* XXV. 1953 The other [shells] have red beams, which shoot from the hinge, and are broader at the edges.

d. A directed flow of radiation or particles; freq. *attrib.*

1906 RUTHERFORD in *Phil. Mag.* XI. 168 Radium served as a source of α rays. A narrow beam of rays, after passing through a parallel slit, fell on a photographic plate. **1908** H. GEIGER in *Proc. R. Soc.* A. LXXXI. 174 Scattering is well known in the case of β-particles. A narrow pencil of β-rays emerges after passing through a metal plate as an ill-defined beam. **1933** *Discovery* Aug. 236/2 The new research will be termed 'beam' therapy and will be carried on at the London Radium Institute in Portland Place. **1937** *Ibid.* Nov. 329/2 The mechanical difficulties are obviated by using a beam of electrons for scanning. **1938** R. W. LAWSON tr. *Hevesy & Paneth's Man. Radioactivity* (ed. 2) xxvi. 288 Cockcroft and Walton succeeded in 1932 in the transmutation of light elements, by bombarding them with a beam of fast protons. *Ibid.* 291 The focusing action results in the generation of beams of ions. **1959** *Times* 19 Jan. 8/2 A brain operation in which for the first time a beam of protons was used instead of surgical instruments has been performed at the Werner Institute for Nuclear Chemistry at Uppsala.

20. *transf.* A similar ray of heat.

1860 TYNDALL *Glac.* II. §3. 244 Two beams of heat, from two distinct sources. **1882** *Longm. Mag.* 38 In passing through the liquid layer, a beam of heat encounters the same number of molecules as in passing through the vapour layer.

21. *fig.* Ray, gleam, emanation: †***eye-beam, beam of sight***, a glance.

1579 GOSSON *Sch. Abuse* (Arb.) 33 Basiliskes..poyson as well with the beame of their sighte as with the breath of their mouth. **1587** MARLOWE *Dido* III. i. 708 Lest their gross eye-beams taint my lovers cheeks. **1674** OWEN *Holy Spirit* (1693) 235 A Beam of Truth from the Light of Nature. **1742** COLLINS *Epist.* 56 Bring No beam of comfort to the guilty king. **1818** BYRON *Juan* I. lxi, Her cheek all purple with the beam of youth.

†**22.** *Math.* The radius of a circle, an axial line. (Translating L. *radius*, apparently from the association of *beam* and *ray* of light.) *Obs.*

1570 DEE *Math. Præf.* 19 Beames, or naturall lines. **1589** PUTTENHAM *Eng. Poesie* II. (1811) 81 The beame is a line stretching directly from the circle to the center. **1624** WOTTON *Archit.* in *Reliq. Wotton.* (1672) 52 The Axel-tree, or middle Beam of the Eye.

†**23.** *Arch.* (See quot.) *Obs.*

1664 EVELYN tr. *Freart's Archit.* 130 Raies or Beames, which..are those plain spaces between the Flutings.

24. a. *Radio Communication.* In full ***radio, wireless beam***: radio waves transmitted as a beam, i.e. undispersed, from a special aerial system, part of which acts as a reflector; usu. *attrib.*

[**1899** MARCONI in *Jrnl. Inst. Electrical Engin.* XXVIII. 274 Should it be necessary to direct a beam of rays in one given direction I prefer to use an arrangement similar to a Righi oscillator placed in the focal line of a suitable cylindrical parabolic reflector.] **1924** (July 2) MARCONI in *Jrnl. R. Soc. Arts* 25 July 607/2 The transmission and reception of intelligible signals over a distance of $1\frac{3}{4}$ miles of a beam system employing short waves and reflectors. **1924** *Westm. Gaz.* 24 July, Arrangements had been made for the erection of a beam station in Canada. **1924** *Daily News* 14 Nov. 7/4 Beam wireless. **1925** *Telegr. & Teleph. Jrnl.* Mar. 107/1 Australian papers give the following..information regarding the 'Beam' Radio Stations. **1927** *Daily Mail* 2 Dec. 11/1 Cable Companies and The Beam. **1928** *Morning Post* 23 Mar. 14 Beam-cable fusion [of the Eastern Exchange Cable Company and Marconi Company]... The beam system of telegraphy. **1934** *Nature* 24 Feb. 297/2 One advantage of short-wave transmission in radio communication is that it is possible to concentrate the radiation..in one direction, thus forming a beam of waves. .. A series of vertical aerials..(called a beam array) will act like Hertz's reflector. **1946** *Proc. Inst. Radio Engineers* XXXIV. 335 (*title*) A Current Distribution for Broadside Arrays which Optimizes the Relationship between Beam Width and Side-Lobe Level. **1958** *Engineering* 31 Jan. 157/3 The aerial has been designed to give a sharp beamwidth at high signal strength. At 20 db the horizontal beamwidth extends about 0·65 deg.

b. *Aeronaut.* A directional radio transmission used to guide aircraft or missiles; freq. *attrib.*, as ***beam approach.***

1927 *Sci. Amer.* Jan. 32 Radio along the Airways. Invisible beams guide birdmen in flights between European cities. **1929** *Aviation* 28 Dec. 1277/1 A landing beam transmitter buried flush with the ground in the center of the field. *Ibid.*, After finding the beam the pilot glides down it toward the field. **1933** K. HENNEY *Radio Engin. Handbk.* 537 The diminution of intensity as the airplane drops below the inclined axis is compensated by the increase of intensity due to approaching the beam transmitter. **1941** *Tee Emm* Oct. 8/1 The policy is that Beam Approach training shall be introduced..as equipment becomes available. **1949** A. R. WEYL *Guided Missiles* i. 26 The 'beam-rider' system in which the missile flies along a radar beam. **1958** *Times* 9 Oct. 10/2 It carries a warhead with proximity fuse and a beam guidance system. **1963** *Oxf. Mag.* 9 May 280/2 The Germans with their beam flying provided us with targets that would have been peculiarly favourable to aerial mine defence.

c. ***to be on the beam***, to be on the course indicated by a radio beam; hence *fig.* (*colloq.*) to be on the right track, right, sane. So ***to be off the beam.***

1941 *Amer. Speech* XVI. 238/2 Expressions disparaging a person's mental state..*off his beam* (airplane). **1941** *Daring Detective* Nov. 7/2 'Now we know we're on the beam,' said Brubach. 'Sex maniacs and drinking companions are definitely eliminated.' **1943** HUNT & PRINGLE *Service Slang* 49 *On the beam*, I follow what you are saying. (R.A.F.). **1948** *Observer* 18 Jan. 2/3 Hugh Burden, as Barnaby, was right on the beam from the start. **1949** *Jrnl. Brit. Interplanet. Soc.* VIII. 143 Thus rocket aeroplanes might seem 'off the beam' of true astronautics. **1954** 'N. BLAKE' *Whisper in Gloom* I. iv. 58 Never heard of him. You're off the beam.

IV. *Comb.*, as ***beam-house, -knife, -man*** (sense 8); ***beam-engine, -gudgeon*** (sense 11); ***beam-antler*** (12); ***beam-knee, -plate*** (15); also **beam-action**, the action of a beam-engine; **beam aerial, antenna**, a directional aerial for transmitting a radio beam; **beam-arm**, a crooked timber extending from the side of a beam to the ship's side, in the wake of the hatchway (Adm. Smyth); **beam-bird**, dial. name of the Spotted Flycatcher; **beam-blind** *a.*, uncritical of oneself (cf. sense 3 c); so ***beam-blindness***; **beam-board**, the platform of a steelyard or balance; **beam-centre**, the central pin on which the beam of a steam-engine works; **beam-compass**, an instrument consisting of a wooden or brass beam with sliding sockets, for drawing larger circles than an ordinary pair of compasses can describe; **beam-ends** (see 18); **beam-engine**, a steam engine having a vibrating beam through which the piston effort is transmitted to the crank; **beam-feather** (see quot.); **beam-fish**, ? a shark (see quot.); **beam-like** *a.*, like a beam, of timber or of light; **beam-line**, the line which shows the junction of the upper sides of the successive beams with the ship's sides; **beam-splitter** *Photogr.*, a device consisting of a prismatic arrangement of mirrors (see quots.); so ***beam-splitting*** adj.; **beam-trawl** *v.*, to fish with a trawl-net of which the mouth is kept open by a beam.

1896 *Daily News* 7 Jan. 6/5 The..*beam-action locomotives of that extremely primitive line. **1926** *Gloss. Terms Electr. Engin.* (*B.S.I.*) **Beam Aerial System*, a combination of aerials with their earthing, tuning and reflecting arrangements so disposed as to concentrate the available radiated energy into a beam. **1945** *Electronic Engin.* XVII. 719 Indicating the target by means of a rotating beam aerial. **1935** K. HENNEY *Radio Engin. Handbk.* (ed. 2) 774 The elements of the Walmsley *beam antenna. **1623** COCKERAM s.v. *Pollard*, *Beame antler is the next start growing above the Brow antler. *c* **1850** *Rudim. Nav.* (Weale) 95 *Beam-Arm, or Fork-Beam, a forked piece of timber, nearly of the depth of the beam, scarphed, tabled, and bolted, for additional security to the sides of beams athwart large openings in the decks, as the main hatchway and the mast-rooms. **1766** PENNANT *Zool.* (1768) II. 263 Known in that county [York] by the name of the *beam-bird, because it nestles under the ends of beams in outbuildings, &c. **1879** G. M. HOPKINS *Poems* (1918) 47 What hinders? Are you *beam-blind, yet to a fault In a neighbour deft-handed. **1932** S. C. CARPENTER *Supernat. Relig.* iv. 94 The difference between his [*sc.* our Lord's] moteless eye and the beam-blindness of the Pharisees. **1785** ROY in *Phil. Trans.* LXXV. 402 A *beam-compass, sufficient to take in twenty feet. **1844** H. STEPHENS *Bk. Farm* II. 312 The *beam-engine of 6-horse power. *a* **1877** KNIGHT *Dict. Mech.* 257/1 *Beam-engine*.., an engine with an oscillating beam, to whose respective ends the connecting-rod from the piston and the pitman from the crank are attached. **1486** *Bk. St. Albans* A. viij b, And oon principall feder of thes same is in the myddis ..that is called the *Beme feder of the tayle. **1721** BAILEY, **Beam-feathers* [among falconers], the long feathers of a Hawk's Wing [in mod. dicts.]. **1742** BAILEY, **Beam-fish*, a sea monster like a pike, a dreadful enemy to mankind, seizing like a blood-hound, and never letting go, if he gets fast hold. **1885** *Harper's Mag.* Jan. 274/2 The..tip-cart..makes its appearance..ready to take a load to the *beam-house. **1869** SIR E. REED *Shipbuild.* viii. 145 And the *Beam-knee ends are welded on to the central piece. **1620** QUARLES *Jonah* (1638) 27 The great Leviathan set ope His *beame-like Jawes. **1820** SHELLEY *Sens. Plant* II, The bee and the beamlike ephemeris. **1884** *West. Morn. News* 3 Sept. 2/1 To Tanners.—Wanted, young man as *Beamman. **1614** CHAPMAN *Odyss.* I. 675 And hung them on a *beam-pin near the bed. **1935** *Discovery* July 189/1 Iceland spar..*beam splitter..entirely free from parallax. This system may be employed..to obtain three-colour negatives. **1940** *Chambers's Techn. Dict.* 83/1 *Beam-splitter* or *beam-splitting camera*, a camera for colour photography, in which the beam of light from the object is separated into three components by means of a complicated prism. **1956** A. L. M. SOWERBY *Dict. Photogr.* (ed. 18) 52 *Beamsplitter*, a combination of four mirrors..used either for taking a stereoscopic pair of pictures with an ordinary single-lens camera, or for projecting or viewing a stereo pair so made. **1958** M. L. HALL et al. *Newnes Complete Amat. Photogr.* xxvi. 235 Stereos taken on the same frame by a beam-splitting device. **1658** USSHER *Ann.* vi. 360 The planet of Mercurie..was seen, near to the *beam star in the signe of Libre. **1883** *Fisheries Exhib. Catal.* 3 The rapid growth of *beam-trawling.

†**beam,** *sb.*[2] Only in phr. ***bote of beam***: remedy, improvement, restoration. *Obs.*

[Referred by Mätzner to BEAM *sb.*[1] 2, taking the cross as typical of misfortune and distress. But may not *bote of beam* be = 'repair of timbers,' used proverbially to signify repair or amendment of any kind?]

1330 R. BRUNNE *Chron.* 90 Þer he wist bote of beam, he went þat viage To William þe rede kyng. *Ibid.* 103 For seke is þe kyng, of him is no bote of beem.

beam (biːm), *v.* Forms: 5 beem, beme, 8- beam. [?:—OE. *béamian* (given by Bosworth on Somner's authority), f. BEAM *sb.*[1]]

I. From the 'beam' of light.

†**1.** *trans.* To shed light upon, irradiate, illumine.

c **1430** *Life St. Kath.* 86 (1884) 46 For aungels come from heuene and counforted hir, beeming þat place of derkenesse wyth vnspekable cleernesse.

2. *trans.* To throw out or radiate (beams or rays of light); to emit in rays. Often extended by *forth, out, in.* Also *fig.*

c **1440** *Promp. Parv.* 30/1 Beme lygthte, *radio.* *c* **1690** SOUTH *Serm.* (1843) II. xii. 207 That God beams this light into man's understanding. *a* **1716** SOUTH *Serm.* IV. 9 (R.) God beams in peculiar evidences and discoveries of the truth to such as embrace it in their affections. *c* **1750** SHENSTONE *Love & Hon.* 187 The genial sun..Beams forth ungentle influences. **1785** BURKE *Nab. Arcot's Debts* Wks. 1842 I. 321 What are the sciences they beamed out to enlighten it? **1871** MACDUFF *Mem. Patmos* xviii. 241 That eye which once beamed affection now rayless.

3. a. *intr.* To shine radiantly. *lit.* and *fig.*

1640 S. MARSHALL *Serm.* (1641) 9 No excellencie..like to that which beames out from God in the Covenant of grace. **1820** W. IRVING *Sketch Bk.* I. 52 Her whole countenance beamed with smiles. **1839** BAILEY *Festus* I, Yon sun beams hotliest on The earth when distant most.

b. Of a person: to smile radiantly, broadly, or good-naturedly. Freq. const. *adv.*

1893 *Illustr. Sporting & Dram. News* 11 Mar. 28/2, I.. tried to beam on a friend—albeit, a poor beamer at the best. **1900** E. GLYN *Visits Eliz.* (1906) 14 He..jumped off his horse and beamed—just as if we had parted the best of friends. **1922** H. CRANE *Let.* 7 Aug. (1965) 95, I realize that he insulted me while he was here.. but I shall beam on until all hope of his getting Bill an audience has vanished. **1936** R. A. FREEMAN *Penrose Myst.* I. i. 15 Mr. Polton took the coffee-pot in his.. hands, beamed on it approvingly. **1937** A. J. CRONIN *Citadel* II. ii. 123 He beamed at the watch, for he could contemplate even inanimate objects.. with that bland cordiality which was especially his own.

II. From the 'beam' of timber.

4. To stretch (cloth) over a beam; to use a beam in *Tanning* (see BEAMING *vbl. sb.* 2).

[**1558** *Act. 1 Eliz.* xii. §1 Deceitfull persons.. doe vse to cast the pieces of Cloth ouer a beame.. and doe by sundry deuices racke, stretch, and draw the same.] **1605** in *N. Riding Qr. Sessions Rec.* (1884) I. 9 Did beame ten webbes of lynnen cloth of the length of 20 virgates the piece. **1885** [see BEAMING *vbl. sb.* 2].

5. To roll (yarn or warp) on the beam of a loom.

1864 R. ARNOLD *Cotton Fam.* 34 The yarn, which has now become 'warp,' is then 'beamed.'

6. To shore up or support by a beam.

1538 [see BEAMING *vbl. sb.* 2].

III. *trans.* **7.** To direct (a radio transmission) to a specific area. (Cf. BEAM *sb.*[1] 24.)

1927 *Daily Express* 5 July 3/3 The King's message.. was almost instantaneously 'beamed' to the receiving station at Milnerton, seven miles from Capetown. **1955** *Times* 29 July 3/1 A message announcing the inauguration of 28 new high-power radio transmitters.. was 'beamed' to New York.. and other regions. **1964** *Ibid.* 2 Apr. 20/7 Microwave equipment which will beam large numbers of telephone calls between Bloemfontein.. and East London.

8. *fig.* To direct at, towards.

1956 L. ASHTON in A. Pryce-Jones *New Outline Mod. Knowl.* III. 300 Modern invention is often only a realignment, but for the great artists it is a realignment 'beamed', to use a modern word, on the future. **1959** *Listener* 24 Sept. 469/2 Mr. Khrushchev's tour is beamed —so to speak—at Radio Peking.

beamage (ˈbiːmɪdʒ). [f. BEAM *sb.*[1] + -AGE.] A deduction for loss of weight by evaporation in cooling, made in weighing the dressed carcass of a beast.

1902 in WEBSTER Suppl.

beamed (biːmd), *ppl. a.* [f. BEAM *sb.*[1] or *v.*]

1. Having or furnished with a beam or beams.

a **1711** KEN *Hymnotheo* Poet. Wks. 1721 III. 187 A Chariot.. With Cedar beam'd, and wheel'd with spicy Wreaths. **1865** in *Derby Merc.* 15 Feb., And the waves danced under their beamed bows. **1881** E. POYNTER *Among Hills* I. 162 The low-beamed paper-trellised ceiling.

b. *fig.*; cf. BEAM *sb.*[1] 3 c.

1627 FELTHAM *Resolves* I. viii. Wks. (1677) 12 He that looks upon another with a beamed eye.

2. Of a stag: Having a horn of the fourth year.

1575 TURBERV. *Venerie* 51 Those be verie strong, bearing fayre and high heades well furnished and beamed. **1637** B. JONSON *Sad Sheph.* I. ii. (1641) 121 [The deer] beares a head, Large, and well beam'd. **1810** SCOTT *Lady of L.* I. ii, The antlered monarch of the waste.. Tossed his beamed frontlet to the sky.

3. Arranged on the beam of the loom.

1851 L. GORDON in *Art Jrnl. Illust. Catal.* vii**/1 These bobbins of yarn are then taken to the warping-machine.. to make them into a beamed warp.

4. Having rays or beams of light; radiant.

1480 CAXTON *Chron. Eng.* ccxxiv. 229 A bemed sterre, the whiche clerkes calle stella cometa. **1647** CRASHAW *Poems* 130 Broad-beam'd day's meridian. **1862** BARNES *Rhymes Dorset Dial.* I. 26 When hot-beam'd zuns do strike right down.

beamer (ˈbiːmə(r)). [f. BEAM *sb.*[1] + -ER[1].] **a.** One who works with a beam; *e.g.* one who arranges yarn on the beam of the loom. **b.** One who beams or smiles broadly. **c.** in *Cricket* (see quot. 1961).

1857 DICKENS *Dorrit* II. xxxii. 603 The form of words which that benevolent beamer generally employed ..'everything had been satisfactory to all parties'. **1879** *Temple Bar* LV. 453 You must find some one else to overlook the beamers. **1884** GRAHAM in *U.P. Mag.* July 350, Crofters, beamers, weavers, and traders came forward. **1893** [see BEAM *v.* 3 b]. **1961** F. C. AVIS *Sportsman's Gloss.* 111/2 *Beamer*, a ball aimed high by the bowler, often to the height of the batsman's head. **1962** *Times* 21 Mar. 4/3 Let us not confuse orthodox fast bowling with bouncers and beamers.

beamfill (ˈbiːmˌfɪl), *v.* *Building.* Also 5 bem(e)fell. [f. BEAM *sb.*[1] + FILL *v.*] (See quots.) Hence **ˈbeamˌfilling** *vbl. sb.*

c **1400** in Wülcker *Voc.* 732 *Hec sugrunda*, a bemfellyng. **1469** *Mann. & Househ. Exp.* (1841) 395 My mastyr made a couenaunt wyth Saunsam the tylere, that he schalle pergete, and whighte, and bemefelle all the new byldynge. **1734** *Builders' Dict.*, *Beam filling* in building is plaisterer's work, and is the filling up the vacant space between the raison and the roof. **1842** GWILT *Archit.*, *Beam-filling* is the masonry brought up from the level of the under to the upper sides of the beams. It is also used to denote the filling up of the space from the top of the wall-plate between the rafters to the under side of the slating, board, or other covering.

ˈbeamful, *a.* [f. BEAM *sb.*[1] + -FUL.] Luminous.

a **1631** DRAYTON is cited by HALLIWELL.

beamily (ˈbiːmɪlɪ), *adv.* [f. BEAMY + -LY[2].] In a beamy or beaming manner, radiantly.

a **1821** KEATS *To Byron* (D.), Thou thy griefs dost dress With a bright halo, shining beamily.

beaminess (ˈbiːmɪnɪs). [f. BEAMY + -NESS.] The quality of being beamy; radiance.

1742 RICHARDSON *Pamela* IV. 384 She.. glides along with her paler and fainter Beaminess. **1880** MRS. WHITNEY *Odd or Even* xiii. 107 Its beaminess of red-gold, wavy hair.

beaming (ˈbiːmɪŋ), *vbl. sb.* [f. BEAM *v.*]

1. Emission of beams of light, radiation, radiance.

1398 TREVISA *Barth. De P.R.* VIII. xxviii. (1495) 339 Lyghte is a substaunce beyng in itselfe, and therof comyth bemynge.. of other bodyes. **1660** W. SECKER *Nonsuch Prof.* 14 You do not look for so much splendor from the burnings of a candle as from the beamings of the Sun. **1813** SHELLEY *Q. Mab* II. 36 Whilst suns their mingling beamings darted.

2. The use of a beam: **a.** for shoring up or supporting; **b.** in *Tanning* (see quot. 1885), whence attrib., as in ***beaming-knife***. **c.** The rolling of warp, etc. on a beam. Also *attrib.*

1530 PALSGR. 197/2 Beamyng knyfe for a tanner. **1538** LATIMER *Serm. & Rem.* (1845) 398 Here is much beaming and bolstering, and malefactors do not lack their supporters. **1831** G. PORTER *Silk Manuf.* 220 To roll regularly on the beam.. the different portions of warp threads.. is called beaming. *a* **1877** KNIGHT *Dict. Mech.* 257/2 The beaming-tool *f* is brought in contact with the leather or raised therefrom by means of the eccentric-rods. **1879** *Temple Bar* LV. 453 If you go to the beaming-room. **1885** *Harper's Mag.* Jan. 274/2 'Beaming,' or unhairing, derives its name from an inclined convex wooden form called a 'beam,' on which the hide is spread during the operation.

d. *Comb.*, as ***beaming-tool***; **beaming machine** (*a*) a machine for beaming and working hides; (*b*) a machine for filling the beams of looms with yarn; also called *beaming mill.*

a **1877** KNIGHT *Dict. Mech.* 257/2 Beaming-machine. (Leather.) **1878** *Sci. Amer.* Suppl. 1938 Self-stopping Beaming Machine. *a* **1884** KNIGHT *Dict. Mech.* Suppl. 85/1 *Beaming Machine*, one for filling yarn beams of looms.

beaming (ˈbiːmɪŋ), *ppl. a.* [f. BEAM *v.* + -ING[2].] Radiant, shining, bright; often *fig.*

1667 MILTON *P.L.* III. 625 Of beaming sunnie Raies, a golden tiar Circl'd his Head. **1832** MARRYAT *N. Forster* xxxvii, A beaming eye met his return. **1863** GEO. ELIOT *Romola* I. ii, A broad beaming smile.

ˈbeamingly, *adv.* [f. prec. + -LY[2].] In the manner of beams of light, radiantly.

1662 J. CHANDLER *Van Helmont's Oriat.* 294 Alcali,.. doth disperse its property even thitherto, beamingly onely. **1863** MARY HOWITT *F. Bremer's Greece* I. v. 152 The sky is beamingly bright. **1866** MRS. GASKELL *Wives & Dau.* I. 158 Mrs. Kirkpatrick.. looked beamingly happy.

beamish (ˈbiːmɪʃ), *a.* *arch.* Also 6 beamysshe. [f. BEAM *sb.*[1] + -ISH[1].] Shining brightly, radiant.

1530 PALSGR. 305/2 Beamysshe as the sonne is, *radieux.* **1870** L. CARROLL *Thro' Look.-glass*, Come to my arms, my beamish boy!

beamless (ˈbiːmlɪs). *a.* [f. BEAM *sb.*[1] + -LESS.] Without beams, rayless; occas. *fig.*

1679 DRYDEN *Œdipus* I. i. Wks. 1725 IV. 375 A bald and beamless Fire. **1746-58** HERVEY *Medit.* (1818) 268 At length all her [the moon's] beauty vanishes, and she becomes a beamless orb. **1821** JOANNA BAILLIE *Ld. John* xx, The stony look of his beamless eyes.

beamlet (ˈbiːmlɪt). [f. BEAM *sb.*[1] + -LET.] A little beam or ray of light.

1840 *Culprit Fay* xxxi in N. Willis *Loiter. Trav.* II. ad fin., Her eyes two beamlets from the moon. **1878** H. PHILLIPS *Poems fr. Sp. & Germ.* 63 And all the glittering beamlets Deep in her bosom play.

†**beamling** (ˈbiːmlɪŋ). *Obs.* Also 7 -lin. = prec.

1598 SYLVESTER *Quadr. Pibrac* in *Du Bartas* (1608) 561 What man wee call and count, It is a beamling of Divinity. **1635** BRATHWAIT *Soul's Sole-love*, Graces are divine beamlins. **1659** *Lady Alimony* in Hazl. *Dodsl.* XIV. 305 One beamling to bestow On my obscur'd, once glorious, family.

†**beamsome**, *a.* *Obs.* [f. BEAM *sb.*[1] + -SOME.] Shedding beams, radiant.

1595 B. BARNES in Farr *S.P.* (1845) I. 45 That I by them, as from some beamesome lampe, May find the bright and true direction.

beamster (ˈbiːmstə(r)). [f. BEAM *sb.*[1] 8 + -STER; cf. *teamster*.] The man who works at the beam in a tannery, unhairing the hides.

1885 *Harper's Mag.* Jan. 274/2 The beamsters.. look as if they had taken in a large week's washing.

†**ˈbeamstrid**. *Obs.* In phr. *on beam strid*, app. = astride on a beam.

1575 *App. & Virginia* in Hazl. *Dodsl.* IV. 147 In hazard he was of riding on beamstrid.

ˈbeam-tree. [Improper shortening of *white-beam* (tree), so called from the white under-surface of its leaves, which strikingly characterize it in a wind.] A tree (*Pyrus Aria*) related to the Apple, Pear, and Wild Service, bearing flat corymbs of flowers, succeeded by rich scarlet berries.

1800 SIR J. SMITH *Eng. Flora* (1828) II. 366 *Pyrus Aria*, White Beam-tree, White Wild Pear-tree. **1830** LINDLEY *Nat. Syst. Bot.* 84 The timber of the Beam-tree is invaluable for axletrees. **1879** PRIOR *Plant-n.* 16 Without the *White* prefixed.. *Beam-tree* is a silly pleonasm, a *tree-tree*.

beamy (ˈbiːmɪ), *a.* Forms: 4 bemy, 6-7 beamie, 6- beamy. [f. BEAM *sb.*[1] + -Y[1].]

1. Emitting beams of light, radiant; also *fig.*

1398 TREVISA *Barth. De P.R.* VIII. ii. (1495) 299 Eueryche rounde body and holowe and bryghte in eueryche poynt therof sendith a bemy lyne in to the mydle of that bryghte body. **1582** BENTLEY *Mon. Matrones* 104 The beamie Sun large light doth giue. **1641** MILTON *Animadv.* Wks. (1851) 221 Thy beamy walke through the midst of thy Sanctuary. **1799** SOUTHEY *Love Eleg.* iii. II. 125 The straitening curls of gold so beamy bright. **1813** SHELLEY *Q. Mab* ix. (1853) 49 Bending her beamy eyes in thankfulness.

†**b.** *transf.* Radiated, umbellate. *Obs. rare.*

1562 TURNER *Herbal* II. 79 b, The wilde carot hathe.. a spoky or beamy top lyke vnto dill.

2. Massive as a (weaver's) beam; cf. BEAM *sb.*[1] 4.

1698 DRYDEN *Æneid* XII. 641 The beamy weapon quakes. **1718** POPE *Iliad* III. 180 In single fight to toss the beamy lance. **1809** HEBER *Palestine* 351 Lords of the biting axe and beamy spear. [Cf. 1 Sam. xvii. 7.]

3. Possessing full-grown horns; antlered.

1697 DRYDEN *Virg. Georg.* III. 625 Thou mayst.. beamy Stags in Toils engage. **1735** SOMERVILLE *Chase* III. 407 The Royal Stag.. tosses high his beamy Head.

4. Of a ship: Broad in the beam; cf. BEAM *sb.*[1] 16.

1882 *Century Mag.* XXIV. 671 The speed of beamy vessels. **1883** G. DAVIES *Norfolk Roads & Riv.* vi. 42 The yachts used on Hickling were beamy shallow boats.

bean (biːn), *sb.* Forms: 1-2 béan, 3-6 ben, 4-6 bene, been(e, (*Sc.* and *north.* bein, beyn), 6-7 beane, 6- bean. *Pl.* beans; in 1 béana, 4 bene, benen, 4-6 benes, -ys. [Common Teut.: OE. *béan* (fem.) = OHG. *bôna*, mod.G. *bohne*, MDu. *bone*, Du. *boon*, ON. *baun*:—OTeut. **baunâ* (str. fem.); conjectured by Fick to be for an earlier *babna*, cogn. with L. *faba*, Slav. *bobŭ*, Old Prussian *babo*; but phonetic considerations render this doubtful.]

I. 1. A smooth, kidney-shaped, laterally flattened seed, borne in long pods by a leguminous plant, *Faba vulgaris*.

The garden variety, or *Broad-bean*, is used, in its green state, as a culinary vegetable, esp. in Britain by the poorer classes, as in the proverbial 'beans and bacon'; *Field-* and *Horse-beans*, when ripened to a brownish-black colour, are used as food for horses and cattle, and have also been made into bean-meal, used for coarse bread.

c **1000** *Sax. Leechd.* II. 84 Genim bean mela. *c* **1325** *Coer de L.* 6004 Whete & ooten, pesen and bene. **1377** LANGL. *P. Pl.* B. VI. 184 Lete hem ete.. benes and bren ybaken togideres. *c* **1394** *P. Pl. Crede* 762 A great bolle-full of benen were betere in his wombe. **1475** *Bk. Noblesse* 69 Benys, pesyn, and aveyn for horsmete. **1551** TURNER *Herbal* I. 178 Beanes.. are harde of digestion, and make troblesum dreames. **1620** VENNER *Via Recta* i. 17 Bread made of Beanes is very drie. **1707** *Lond. Gaz.* No. 4357/4 At Ham.. are to be sold, Garden Beans, Gosport-Beans. **1832** *Veg. Subst. Food* 218 In Barbary.. stewed with oil and garlic, beans form.. the principal food of persons of all classes.

2. The cultivated plant that bears this seed; it has fragrant violet-tinted white flowers, whence the often-mentioned 'fragrance of the bean-fields.'

940 *Chart. Eadmund* in *Cod. Dipl.* V. 265 Of þistelleaȝe to beanleaȝe. **1398** TREVISA *Barth. De P.R.* XVII. lxiv, Benes [*ed.* 1495 beenys] bereþ white floures. **1611** COTGR. s.v. *Febve*, In Cuckoe-time when Beanes doe flower. **1728** THOMSON *Spring* (R.) Where the breeze blows from yon extended field Of blossom'd beans. **1837** CARLYLE *Fr. Rev.* II. I. viii. 51 It will grow verily, like the Boy's Bean, in the Fairy-Tale, heaven-high.

3. The plant and seed of the allied genus *Phaseolus*, of which the best-known species are the French, Kidney, or Haricot Bean (*P. vulgaris*), and Scarlet Runner (*P. multiflorus*). The unripe pods of both, and the ripe seeds of the former, are used as culinary vegetables.

(*Navy Bean*: the dried haricot. *Pea Bean*: a small variety of it.)

1548 TURNER *Names of Herbs* (1881) 75 Kydney beanes.. or arber beanes, because they serue to couer an arber for the tyme of Summer. **1562** —— *Herbal* II. 140 b, The vertues of Kidney beanes. The fruyt is sodden wyth the sede, and it is eaten after the maner of a wurt or eatable herbe, as sperage is eaten. **1632** SHERWOOD s.v. *Bean*, French, or Romane Beanes. **1837** CARLYLE *Fr. Rev.* II. v. ix. 302 She who has quietly shelled French-beans for her dinner.

4. Name given to the seeds of other plants, usually from some resemblance in shape to the common bean; e.g. **Queensland** or **Leichhardt's bean**, Australian names for a tall climbing leguminous plant *Entada scandens*, bearing long scimitar-shaped pods, which are used to make match-boxes, snuff-boxes, etc.: the seed is also called *match-box bean* (see MATCH *sb.*[2] 5) and *scimitar-pod* (see SCIMITAR 3); **Egyptian** or **Pythagorean bean**, the seed of the Lotus (*Nelumbium speciosum*); **bean of Molucca**, seed of *Guilandina Bonducella*; **bean of St. Ignatius**, seed of *Strychnos amara*; **Tonka bean**, the perfumed seed of *Dipterix odorata*; so too **coffee-bean**, etc. See also BUCK-, LOCUST-BEAN.

1398 TREVISA *Barth. De P.R.* XVII. lxiv. (1495) 641 Beenys growe in Egypte..wyth a heed as a Popye and therin beenes ben closid: and that heed is red as a Rose. **1484** CAXTON *Curiall* 6 The benes of Pictagoras..gafe better sauour. **1551** TURNER *Herbal* I. 123 The beane of Egipt is..astryngent. **1611** COTGR., *Anacarde*, th' East-Indian fruit called Anacardium, or Beane of Malaca. **1830** LINDLEY *Nat. Syst. Bot.* 215 The St. Ignatius's bean..is prescribed by the native practitioners of India in cholera. *c* **1865** *Circ. Sc.* I. 351/1 The organic acids..of the coffee-beans. **1889** J. H. MAIDEN *Useful Native Plants Australia* 175 *Entada scandens* ..'Queensland Bean'. 'Leichhardt Bean'.

5. a. Any object resembling a bean in shape.

1561 HOLLYBUSH *Hom. Apoth.* 38b, Take the beanes or hinderfallinges of Goates. **1607** TOPSELL *Four-f. Beasts* 215 The dryed beans of a Cutle fish. **1881** RAYMOND *Mining Gloss.*, *Beans* (Newcastle), small coals.

b. The head. *slang* (*orig. U.S.*). **bean ball** *Baseball*, a ball pitched at the batter's head.

c **1905** C. DRYDEN *Champion Athletics* 16 While pitching Mr. Bender places much reliance on the bean ball. **1908** H. GREEN *Maison de Shine* 130 Pop swung on a guy an' come near knockin' his bean offa him. **1910** EVERS & FULLERTON *Touching Second* vi. 92 One of the greatest and most effective balls pitched is the 'bean ball'. 'Bean' is baseball for 'head'. **1912** A. H. LEWIS *Apaches N.Y.* 20 Beat it, before I bump me black-jack off your bean! **1923** R. D. PAINE *Comr. Rolling Ocean* x. 168 If these Dutchmen get nasty, bang their blighted beans together. **1924** WODEHOUSE *Bill the Conqueror* ii. 63 Have I got to clump you one on the side of the bean?

6. Literary and proverbial uses:—

a. in reference to a bean's small value; cf. *straw*.

1297 R. GLOUC. 497 Al nas wurth a bene. *c* **1325** *Poem temp. Edw. II*, xlvii, No rich man..dredeth God The worth of a bean. **1377** LANGL. *P. Pl.* B. III. 141 (Wright), To be corsed in consistorie She counted noght a bene [*v.r.* russhe]. **1413** LYDG. *Pylgr. Sowle* I. xv. (1483) 9 Al my wyt auayleth nought a bene. **1548** HALL *Chron.* (1809) 690 Thei set not by the Frenche Kyng one bene. **1656** HOBBES *Liberty etc.* (1841) 426 But all this will not advantage his cause the black of a bean.

b. in reference to the former use of beans in balloting.

1580 NORTH *Plutarch* (1676) 272 He was one year Mayor, or Provost of Athens..He came to it by drawing of the Bean. **1603** HOLLAND *Plutarch's Mor.* 15 Abstaine from beanes, i.e. Intermeddle not in the affaires of State. **1660** MILTON *Free Commw.* Wks. 1851 438 To convey each Man his bean or ballot into the Box.

c. in reference to the custom of appointing as King of the company on Twelfth-night, the man in whose portion of the cake the bean was found. [Lauder's reference appears to be to this, though he seems to have confounded the 16th c. Eng. *bean* (bɛːn) with his own Sc. *bane* 'bone.']

1556 LAUDER *Tractate* (1864) 29 Thir kyngs þai ar bot kyngs of bane; And schort wyl heir þare tyme be gane. **1592** *Sp. at Sudely* 8 in Nichols *Progr. Q. Eliz.* II, Cut the cake: who hath the beane shall be kinge; and where the peaze is she shall be quene. **1648** HERRICK *Hesper.* 376 (N.) Beane's the king of the sport. **1853** SOYER *Pantroph.* 55 The cake was often full of raisins among which one bean and one pea were introduced.

d. in proverbial expressions.

1562 J. HEYWOOD *Prov. & Epigr.* (1867) 24 Hunger makth hard beanes sweete. *Ibid.* 56 Alwaie the bygger eateth the beane. **1568** *Marr. Wit & Wisd.* 45 (N.) It is not for idlenis that men sowe beanes in the wind [*i.e.* labour in vain]. *a* **1624** BP. M. SMITH *Serm.* (1632) 178 Euery Beane hath his blacke. **1830** GALT *Laurie T.* (1849) II. I. 42 Few men who better knew how many blue beans it takes to make five. **1886** ELWORTHY *W. Somerset Word-Bk.* 51 He knows how many beans make five, is a very common description of a cute, clever fellow. **1898** in M. Beerbohm *Around Theatres* (1924) I. 25 You say you've never heard How many beans make five? It's time you knew a thing or two—You don't know you're alive! **1958** 'A. GILBERT' *Death against Clock* vi. 86 Mr. Crook knew how many beans make five.

e. Slang phrases: ***not to know beans*** (U.S.): not to know something, to be not well informed; ***not to care beans*** (U.S.), not to care at all; ***a hill of beans*** (orig. U.S.): a thing of little value (cf. sense 6 a); ***to spill the beans*** (see SPILL *v.*[1]); ***to be full of beans***: to be full of energy, and in high spirits (cf. BEANY *a.* 1) (see also quot. 1874); ***to give*** (a person) ***beans*** (orig. U.S.): to deal severely with, to punish heavily; so ***to get beans***; ***old bean*** (cf. OLD *a.* 8a), a familiar form of address.

1833 A. GREENE *Life & Adv. D. Duckworth* II. 66 He don't know beans. **1855** *Yale Lit. Mag.* XX. 192 (Th.), Whatever he knows of Euclid and Greek, In Latin he don't know beans. **1857** *Knickerbocker* Feb. XLIX. 138 (Th.), I don't care beans for the railroad. **1863** 'E. KIRKE' *My Southern Friends* v. 80, I..karn't take Preston's note—'taint wuth a hill o' beans. **1901** HARBEN *Westerfelt* 5 He didn't care a hill o' beans fer no gal. **1926** D. H. LAWRENCE *Let.* 4 Jan. (1962) II. 876 Saying my say and seeing other people sup it up doesn't amount to a hill o' beans, as far as I go. **1854** SURTEES *Handley Cross* xxxii. 254 'Ounds, 'osses, and men, are in a glorious state of excitement! Full o' beans and benevolence! **1874** HOTTEN *Slang Dict.* 171 *Full of beans*, arrogant, purseproud. A person whom sudden prosperity has made offensive and conceited, is said to be too 'full of beans'. Originally stable slang. **1875** DISRAELI *Let.* 20 Aug. in *Lett. to Lady Bradford* (1929) I. xvi. 275 The Sultan..was full of beans. **1911** GALSWORTHY *Patrician* I. x, Versatile, 'full of beans'. **1927** J. ELDER *Thomasina Toddy* xxiii. 226 We start off—oh, full of beans—and then we stop. **1835** in *Amer. Speech* (1965) XL. 127, I pose you heard ob de battle New Orleans, Whare Ole Gineral Jackson gib de British Beans. **1892** *Punch* 24 Sept. 133 Bad enough if you 'ave to wolf one, but it fair gives yer beans when 'tis two. **1893** *Pick-me-up* 5 Aug. 302 He would get beans at Bedford. **1900** *Daily News* 5 June 3/4 We started shelling them in the open, and gave them beans. **1914** *Evening News* 29 Sept. 2/2 We can't get them in the open, only on very rare occasions, and when we do, by gum, they don't half get beans! **1917** 'CONTACT' *Airman's Outings* 231 Chorus—'Goodnight, old bean.' **1918** *Blighty Christmas No.* 27 'What made you join the air service?' 'No earthly reason, old bean!' **1920** *Punch* 1 Sept. 168/1 The anxiety of the 'Bewildered Parent' who complains of the child of two and a-half years who addressed her learned parent as 'Old bean'. **1946** WODEHOUSE *Joy in Morning* xvii. 145 He wanted to give me beans, but Florence wouldn't let him. She said 'Father you are not to touch him. It was a pure misunderstanding.' **1955** J. THOMAS *No Banners* xxix. 286, I say, old bean, let's stick together.

f. Formerly, a sovereign or a guinea; now only in phraseological use, a coin, a bit of money (***not a bean***, no money whatever, not a cent). *slang*.

1811 *Lex. Balatr.*, *Bean*, a guinea. **1834** AINSWORTH *Rookwood* III. vi, As yellow as a bean. **1837** *Ibid.* (rev. ed.) xxviii. 245 Offering a *bean* to *half a quid* (in other words, a guinea to a half-guinea). **1885** D. C. MURRAY *Rainbow Gold* v. vi, 'Here's some of the beans,' he continued figuratively, as he drew five sovereigns from the same pocket. **1928** GALSWORTHY *Swan Song* II. iv, They..never saved a bean, having no beans to save. **1928** D. L. SAYERS *Unpleasantness at Bellona Club* iii, None of the Fentimans ever had a bean, as I believe one says nowadays.

II. *Attrib.* and *Comb.*

7. General relations: **a.** objective with agent-noun or vbl. sb., as *bean-setter*, *-setting*; **b.** instrumental, as *bean-election*, *-fed* (1589); **c.** similative, as *bean-ore*, *-shaped*; **d.** attrib. (of the seed), as *bean-bread*, *-broth*, *-corn*, *-diet*, *-flour*, *-meal* (*a* 1000), *-porridge*, *-soup*, *-water*; (of the plant), as *bean-cod* (*a* 1000), *-field*, *-flower*, *-haulm*, *-honey*, *-husk*, *-land* [OE. *bēan-land*], *-plant*, *-plot*, *-pod*, *-rick*, *-row*, *-season*, *-seed* [OE. *bēan-sǣd*], *-stack*, *-stubble*, *-weevil*, *-wood*.

c **1380** WYCLIF *Wks.* (1880) 61 þei myȝtten vnneþe before haue *bene-bred & watir or feble ale. **1701** J. CUNNINGHAM in *Phil. Trans.* XXIII. 1207 *Bean, or Mandarin Broth.. made of the Seed of Sesamum. *c* **1420** *Pallad. on Husb.* IV. 110 Two basketfull of *bene chaf. **1820** T. MITCHELL *Aristoph.* I. 161 One much giv'n To a *bean-diet. **1820** *Edin. Rev.* XXXIV. 303 The folly of the *bean-election. **1589** R. HARVEY *Pl. Perc.* (1860) 34 Forehorse of my *beane-fed Teeme. **1870** MORRIS *Earthly Par.* I. II. 454 Thy soft breezes blow Sweet with the scent of *beanfields far away. **1610** HEALEY *St. Aug. City of God* 164 Brutus..kept her feast..with *beane-flowre, and bacon. *a* **1661** HOLYDAY *Juvenal* (1673) 25 The distilled water of bean-flowers. **1744** W. ELLIS *Mod. Husbandm.* Jan. iv. 46 Keeping the *Bean Land clear of the Thistle. **1960** *Times* 5 July Agric. Suppl. iii/4 The traditional wheat and beanlands—now usually minus the beans—no longer produce the highest yields. *c* **1000** *Sax. Leechd.* II. 84 Genim *Bean mela. **1847** *Gard. Chron.* 144 The fitness of Bean-meal for cheap bread. **1733** W. ELLIS *Chiltern & Vale Farm.* xli. 348 Here is free access even to the minutest part of the Stalk-blossom or *Bean-pod. **1913** D. H. LAWRENCE *Love Poems* 37 You..who fall to earth At last like a bean-pod. **1821** R. B. THOMAS *Farmer's Almanack 1822* 2–6 June, Uncle Jeremy..never turned up his nose at a bowl of *bean-porridge. **1878** B. F. TAYLOR *Between Gates* 286 Two days more would..ripen bean-porridge to the fine perfection of 'nine days old'. **1890** YEATS *Lake Isle of Innisfree* i, Nine bean-rows will I have there, a hive for the honey-bee. **1677** YARRANTON *Engl. Improv.* 18 His Creditors crowd to him as Pigs do..to a *Bean and Peas Rick. **1744** W. ELLIS *Mod. Husbandm.* Jan. iv. 44 They begin..to sow their *Bean Seed in two Forms or Methods. **1934** HALDANE & HUXLEY *Animal Biol.* x. 218 The weights of bean-seeds. **1824** MISS MITFORD *Village* Ser. I. (1863) 25 Troops of stooping *bean-setters. *Ibid.* 26 What work *bean-setting is! **1836–9** TODD *Cycl. Anat. & Phys.* II. 530/2 A kidney or *bean-shaped hole called *foramen ovale*. **1837** J. C. NEAL *Charcoal Sk.* (1838) 98 Hollering oysters and *bean soup has guv' me a splendid voice. **1856** KANE *Arct. Exp.* II. xvi. 169 A stock of concentrated bean-soup was cooked. **1824** MISS MITFORD *Village* Ser. III. (1863) 91 The obstinate bird ran away behind a *bean-stack. **1743** W. ELLIS *Mod. Husbandm.* June iii. 20 To prepare a *Bean Stubble for Turneps. **1833** *Ridgemont Farm Rep.* in *Brit. Husbandry* (1840) III. I. 138. The process of cultivation as thus described on fallow lands, is pursued in the same manner when the wheat has been sown on..a bean-stubble. **1870** in *Mass. Agric. Rep.* I. 370, I sent specimens of the *bean weevil..to Dr. G. A. Horn..who pronounces it to be ..a native species (*B. varicornis* of Leconte). **1959** E. F. LINSSEN *Beetles Brit. Isles* II. 176 (*title*) Phytophaga, Bruchidae—Pea 'Weevils' and Bean 'Weevils'. **1585** JAS. I *Ess. Poesie* 68 Some bucklit on a *benvvod, and some on a bene.

e. in the names of various machines for harvesting field beans and preparing them for use, as *bean-harvester*, *-mill*, *-sheller*, *-thresher*.

1858 SIMMONDS *Dict. Trade*, Bean-mill. *a* **1877** KNIGHT *Dict. Mech.* 257/2 Bean-harvester..Bean-sheller.

8. Special combinations: **bean-bag**, (*a*) a small bag filled with beans, used esp. in children's games; (*b*) orig. *U.S.*, a chair consisting of a large bag partially filled with small plastic or polystyrene 'beads', which moulds itself to the shape of the user; also, **bean-bag chair**; **bean-belly**, a great eater of beans, a nickname of dwellers in Leicestershire; **bean-brush**, the stubble of beans; **bean-butter**, a dish made from unshelled beans; **bean cake**, a material consisting of compressed beans, or some substitute, deprived of oil, used in China as a food and fertilizer; **bean-caper**, English name of the genus *Zygophyllum*, South African plants with fleshy leaves and flowerbuds used as capers; †**bean-cod**, a bean-pod; also applied to a kind of river boat in use in Portugal; **bean-crake**, local name of the Corncrake; **bean curd, paste**, a thick jelly or paste made from beans, eaten in north China and adjacent countries; **bean-dolphin**, the aphis or plant-louse of the bean; **bean-fed** *a. fig.*, living on the best of everything; **bean-fly**, a beautiful insect, of pale purple colour, found on beans; **bean-hull** (*Sc.* **hool**), a bean-pod; **bean metal** *Salt-mining*, marl in the form of granules (cf. *beany metal*, s.v. BEANY *a.* 2); **bean-mouse**, name given to the Long-tailed Field-mouse; **bean oil**, oil expressed from beans in the manufacture of bean cake, used as an illuminant; **bean-pole, -stick**, (**-wood**, *obs.*), one used for beans to twine round, *fig.* a lanky fellow; **bean-shatter**, ? bird-scarer; **bean-shooter** *U.S.*, 'a toy for shooting beans, shot, or other small missiles; a pea-shooter' (*Cent. Dict.* 1889); **bean-shot copper**, that obtained in rounded grains, by pouring it, when melted, into hot water; **bean sprouts** *sb. pl.*, the edible sprouting seeds of any of several varieties of legume (*esp.* the mung bean), used cooked or raw, orig. in Chinese cookery; occas. in *sing.*; **bean-stalk**, the stem of the bean-plant: so called in the fairy-tale of 'Jack and the Beanstalk'; **bean-straw**, the dried stems of the bean-plant; **bean-vine**, common name of *Phaseolus diversifolius*. See also BEAN-FEAST, -GOOSE, -TREE, -TREFOIL.

1871 L. M. ALCOTT *Little Men* xxi. 321 A spirited exhibition of gymnastics..there was some danger of his.. sending his *bean-bags whizzing among the audience. **1895** KIPLING *Day's Work* (1898) xiii. 361 Here are your bean-bags for the Ladies' Competition. **1929** E. BOWEN *Last September* x. 122 At school sports; in a team race, one of those things with bean bags. **1968** *Guardian* 19 Apr. 1/1 The children, all receiving free meals, hurled beanbags at the women serving them. **1969** *Better Homes & Gardens* (U.S.) Nov. 129/3 Bean Bag chair. Upholstered in black Arpel and filled with polystyrene beads. **1975** 'M. COLLINS' *Blue Death* x. 67 She sat cross-legged under her robe on a beanbag, like a child in a big blanket. **1977** *Times* 28 July 9/6 Trevor Baxter's gay Bishop, reclining on a bean-bag while oozing appreciation of Simon and Garfunkel, and executing a sumptuous return to episcopal protocol, is as hilarious as ever. **1986** *N.Y. Times* 28 Aug. C1/4, I remember thinking that one day there would be a New Yorker cartoon in which you walked into an antique store and looked at beanbag chairs and water beds. **1659** E. LEIGH *Eng. Descr.* 114 Leicestershire..yeeldeth great abundance of Peas and Beans..insomuch that there is an old by-word.. Leicestershire *Bean-Belly. **1677** PLOT *Oxfordsh.* 240 Ploughing in the *bean-brush at All-Saints. **1552** HULOET, *Beane butter, *conchis*. **1887** *Encycl. Brit.* XXII. 733/2 *Bean-cake..is also imported in large quantities from New-chwang, Chefoo [etc.]. **1597** GERARD *Herball* II. cccxxxii. 827 Called after the Latine *Beane Caper. *c* **1000** *Ags. Gosp.* Luke xv. 16 His wambe ȝefyllan of þam bean-coddum [*v.r.* bien-coddun; *Lindisf. G.* bean-bælȝum; *Hatton G.* bean-coddan.] **1615** MARKHAM *Eng. Housew.* II. ii. (1668) 52 A good simple Sallet is Camphire, *Bean cods, Sparagus, and Cucumbers. **1769** FALCONER *Dict. Marine* (1789), Bean-cod, a small fishing-vessel..extremely sharp forward, having its stem bent inward above into a great curve. **1909** WEBSTER, *Bean curd. **1967** O. WYND *Walk Softly, Men Praying* vii. 110 The cry of the bean-curd seller. **1889** KIPLING *From Sea to Sea* vi, in *Wks.* (1900) I. 289 The *bean-fed, well-groomed subaltern with the light coat and fox-terrier. **1647** R. STAPYLTON *Juvenal* 259 Give me a *beane-hull. **1818** SCOTT *Hrt. Midl.* xviii, He shall hide himself in a bean-hool if he remains on Scottish ground without my finding him. **1892** *Cornh. Mag.* Sept. 263 A shaft is sunk till the 'flag' or '*bean metal' has been pierced. **1766** PENNANT *Zool.* (1768) I. 103 They are called *bean-mice from the havoke they make among beans when first sown. **1908** *Westm. Gaz.* 15 Oct. 13/2 According to reports from Chefoo,..*Bean-oil is giving place to kerosene. **1904** R. J. FARRER *Garden of Asia* 146 Buns stuffed with the cloying mustiness of *bean-paste. **1798** T. B. HAZARD *Nailer Tom's Diary* 10 May (1930) 210/2, I dug[d] up Dung for to Put on the Garden and gott *Bean and Pee Poles. **1837** HALIBURTON *Clockm.* (1862) 137 Mr. Jehiel, a bean-pole of a lawyer. **1900** E. BRUNCKEN *N. Amer. Forests* 61 Hop poles, bean poles, Christmas trees. **1632** CHAPMAN & SHIRLEY *Ball* IV. i, To fright away crows, and keep the corn, *beanshatter. **1890** *Congress. Rec.* Mar. 1920/1 Some boy, with a *bean-shooter..struck Mr. Benjamin. **1921** *China Med. Jrnl.* XXXV. 428 The mung *bean sprout..has a larger calcium content than the original bean. **1922** *Jrnl. Home Econ.* XIV. 65 The soybean..is the source of a large number of products... The most important are the bean milk, bean curd, bean sauce (soy), bean sprouts, bean oil and bean cake. **1958** *Catal. County Stores* (Taunton) June 16 *Chinese*.. Bean sprouts..a tin 1/7½, 2/4. **1984** M. POLUNIN *New Cookbk.* 18 Mustard and cress and beansprouts have the advantage that they are growing—and maintaining their food value—right up to the moment you eat them. ? *c* **1800** (*title*) The Surprising History of Jack and the *Bean Stalk. **1871** M. COLLINS *Mrq. & Merch.* I. i. 74 Jack's beanstalk was nothing to it. **1823** J. BADCOCK *Dom. Amusem.* 54 Thrust a *bean-stick into the ground. *c* **1386** CHAUCER *Merch. T.* 178 [A] woman thirty yere of age..is but *bene-straw. **1838** HAWTHORNE *Amer. Note Bks.* (1871) I. 127 *Bean-vines running up round the doors.

bean (biːn), *v. slang* (chiefly *U.S.*). [f. prec., sense 5 b.] *trans.* To hit on the head.

1910 *Amer. Mag.* 398/2 He is in extreme danger of being 'beaned', which, in baseball, means hit in the head. **1924**

WODEHOUSE *Bill the Conqueror* v. 93 Why did you not bean him with a shoe before he could make his getaway? **1939** C. MORLEY *Kitty Foyle* xii. 124 She was beaned by a copy of *A Girl of the Limberlost* that fell from the third floor.

beancler, -kler, incorrect f. BEANTLER.

beand, obs. f. of *being*: see BE *v.*

beane, beayne, var. of BAIN *a.*, ready, willing.
a **1400** *Chester Pl.* I. (1843) 50 Lord, to thy byddinge I am beane. *Ibid.* II. (1847) 181 Though I to synne were beayne and bonne.

beane, variant of BENE. *Obs.* a prayer.

beanery ('biːnərɪ). *U.S. slang.* [f. BEAN *sb.* + -ERY.] A cheap restaurant (orig. one where beans were served).
1887 *Grip* (Toronto) 26 Feb. 8/2 Go to, illustrious reader; get thee to a beanery. **1888** *Texas Siftings* 7 Jan. 4/2 In a beanery you get biscuit fresh from the nest, Canada grouse from New Jersey and immigrant waiters. **1894** *San Francisco Midwinter Appeal* 10 Feb. 4/1 Papa Peakers gave a baked bean blowout to..the Press Men at his beanery. **1933** HEMINGWAY *Torrents of Spring* I. v. 50 Inside the door of the beanery Scripps O'Neil looked around him. **1955** E. POUND *Section: Rock-Drill* xci. 74 The american beaneries. **1967** WODEHOUSE *Company for Henry* iv. 66 He used to wander around town trying to find some beanery where they'd have their own specials.

'bean-feast. [f. BEAN *sb.* + FEAST *sb.*]
a. An annual dinner given by employers to their work-people. Also, (*colloq.*) any festive occasion. Hence **bean-feaster**.
1805 *Sporting Mag.* XXVI. 304/2 At a late bean feast, a Gentleman Taylor, celebrated for his liberality, gave a rich treat to his men, at his occasional country residence. It was called a Bean Feast; but, exclusive of the beans, the table literally groaned with bacon [etc.]. **1875** W. T. VINCENT *Warlike Woolwich* 49 The holiday on the second Saturday in July, which is a special and extra holiday, known as 'Bean-feast day', and is usually spent in excursions to some country place and a dinner, at which beans form an indispensable dish. **1882** *Printing Times* 15 Feb. 26/2 A beanfeast dinner served up at a country inn. **1884** *Bath Jrnl.* 26 July 6/1 The annual grant of £20 for their bean feast. **1884** *Cornh. Mag.* Jan. 621 For the delectation of the bold beanfeasters. **1897** *Daily News* 23 Sept. 8/5 A beanfeast party from Woolwich. **1897** [see WAYZGOOSE b].
b. *fig.*
1899 R. WHITEING *No. 5 John St.* xxv. 250 The day was for the Empire-makers... To-night is the bean-feast of the 'hands', of the myriads in collar. **1906** W. J. LOCKE *Beloved Vagabond* iii, He..alluded to 'the regular beanfeast' they would have when they were married. **1922** MRS. A. SIDGWICK *Victorian* xxix, 'Won't life be a beanfeast?' she said. 'We shall enjoy ourselves.'

bean-goose. A species of Goose (*Anser segetum*): see quot. 1766.
1766 PENNANT *Zool.* (1812) II. 234 Called the bean goose, from the likeness of the nail of the bill to a horse bean. **1863** *Spring Lapl.* 14 In Lapland..bean, and white-fronted geese, flock in hundreds.

beanie ('biːnɪ). orig. *U.S.* [cf. BEAN *sb.* 5 b.] A small close-fitting hat worn off the face.
1943 *Mademoiselle* Nov. 196 Matching felt beanie pins. **1944** *Sears Roebuck Midsummer Book* 22 *Beanie*, a clever little dink to perch atop your curls. **1958** *Vogue* Mid-Sept. 58 Back-of-the-head beanies..are a piece of evening prettiness. **1962** M. MCCARTHY *On Contrary* 188 Courageous Mrs. C...wears the same beanies every year regardless of the milliners. **1966** *Punch* 16 Mar. p. xv, Model girls snapping up..tiny beanie hats.

beano ('biːnəʊ). *slang.* orig. Printers' abbreviation of BEAN-FEAST. Later, in gen. use, a festive entertainment frequently ending in rowdyism.
1888 JACOBI *Printers' Vocab.*, *Beano*, a slang abbreviation for 'beanfeast', which is, however, usually termed 'goose' or wayzgoose by compositors. **1897** *N. & Q.* 8th Ser. XII. 175/1, I can remember hearing a street song, some years ago, in which one of the lines ran something to the effect that We don't have a beano every day. **1914** *Evening News* 15 Oct. 4/6, I wish you could hear the men on their first morning in the hospitals... 'Fighting's a beano with this sort of thing for dessert.' **1920** W. J. LOCKE *House of Baltazar* ii, I'll get hold of Dorothy, and you and I and she'll have a little beano at the Carlton. **1924** *Blackw. Mag.* Oct. 494/1 There had been one of those awful last-night-of-leave beanos in town. *a* **1930** D. H. LAWRENCE *Last Poems* (1932) 269 O Pino What a bean-o! When we printed Lady C.! **1967** *Listener* 17 Aug. 205/3 Dear-heart, I fear we will have to make a token appearance at the beano those thrusting young String-Along's are giving tonight.

beant, dial. f. of *be not*: see BE *v.*

beantler, var. BESANTLER, BAY ANTLER.

bean-tree. A name given to several trees bearing podded seeds; esp. the Algarroba or Carob-tree (*Ceratonia siliqua*); also Swedish Bean-tree (*Pyrus intermedia*), Australian Bean-tree (*Castanospermum australe*).
1616 SURFL. & MARKH. *Countr. Farm* 291 Beane-tree, or S. Iohns-bread (bearing a long, flat, and broad fruit, like vnto that of Cassia). **1834** PRINGLE *Afr. Sk.* 22 The bright-blossomed bean-tree shakes Its coral tufts above the brakes.

bean-trefoil. English name of the *Anagyris*, a bushy shrub, bearing axillary racemes of yellow flowers, succeeded by narrow recurved pods. Sometimes applied to the Buckbean (*Menyanthes trifoliata*), and formerly to the Laburnum.
1551 TURNER *Herbal* 28 Anagyris..maye be called in Englishe, benetrifolye: because the leues grow thre together, and the sede is muche lyke a bene. **1607** TOPSELL *Serpents* 773 Leaves of Been-trifoly drunk in Wine. **1725** BRADLEY *Fam. Dict.*, *Bean-Trefoil*, affords many fine yellow Blossoms.

beany ('biːnɪ), *a.* [f. BEAN *sb.* + -Y[1].] **1.** In good condition (? like a bean-fed horse); spirited, fresh. *slang.*
1852 KINGSLEY in *Life* (1877) I. 278 The very incongruity keeps one beany and jolly. **1870** *Daily News* 27 July 5 The horses..looked fresh and beany.
2. In salt-mining: ***beany marl*** or ***metal*** = *bean metal* (BEAN *sb.* 8).
1886 R. HOLLAND *Gloss. Words Chester*, Beany marl. **1892** *Cornh. Mag.* Sept. 258 After a while what is locally termed 'beany metal' is reached.

bear (bɛə(r)), *sb.*[1] Forms: 1 bera, 2–7 bere, (3 beore, ? bore, 4 beeyr, 4–5 beere, 5 barre, beer, 6 *Sc.* beir, 6–7 beare, 7 bare), 7– bear. [OE. *bera* = OHG. *bero*, *pero*, MHG. *ber*, mod.G. *bär*, MDu. *bere*, Du. *beer*:—OTeut. **beron-*. The ON. *björn*:—**bern-oz* seems to be an extended form. Supposed by Fick to be cogn. with L. *ferus* wild, as if '*the* wild beast' of northern nations.]
I. 1. a. A heavily-built, thick-furred plantigrade quadruped, of the genus *Ursus*; belonging to the *Carnivora*, but having teeth partly adapted to a vegetable diet.
The best-known species are the Brown Bear of Europe (*U. arctos*), the White or Polar Bear (*U. maritimus*), the Grizzly Bear (*U. horribilis* or *ferox*) and Black Bear (*U. Americanus*) of North America, and the Syrian Bear (*U. Syriacus*), mentioned in the Bible; there are remains of fossil species, some larger than any now known.
c **1000** ÆLFRIC *On O.T.* in Sweet *Reader* 66 Dauid ..ȝewylde ðone wildan beran. *c* **1200** *Trin. Coll. Hom.* 211 Ech man is efned to þe deore þe he nimeð after geres..sum bere, sum leun. **1398** TREVISA *Barth. De P.R.* XVIII. liii. (1495) 813 Whan beeyrs ben syke they seke amptes and deuoure them. *Ibid.* cxii. 854 The beer can wonderly stye vpon trees. *c* **1420** *Anturs of Arth.* x, Thus were the grehondes a-gast of the gryme bere. **1501** DOUGLAS *Pal. Hon.* III. xxvii, Dauid I saw slay baith lyoun and beir. **1596** SHAKS. *Merch. V.* II. i. 29, I would..Plucke the yong sucking Cubs from the she Beare. **1624** CAPT. SMITH *Virginia* II. 24 Their attire is the skinnes of Beares. **1733** POPE *Horace' Sat.* II. i. 87 Tis a Bear's talent not to kick but hug. **1781** PENNANT *Hist. Quadrup.* II. II. §II. xx. 286 The black bears of America form a very distinct variety. **1860** GOSSE *Rom. Nat. Hist.* 62 The white bear seated on a solitary iceberg in the Polar Sea. *c* **1880** *Cassell's Nat. Hist.* II. 167 The American Black Bear. *Ursus americanus.*
b. in proverbial phrases, referring to the habits of bears, and to the obsolete sport of bear-baiting.
Are you there with your bears? = 'Are you there again, or at it again?' is explained by Joe Miller as the exclamation of a man who, not liking a sermon he had heard on Elisha and the bears, went next Sunday to another church, only to find the same preacher and the same discourse. ***like a bear with a sore head*** and similar phrases: used with reference to bad-tempered behaviour.
1562 J. HEYWOOD *Prov. & Epigr.* (1867) 17 With as good will as a beare goth to the stake. *Ibid.* 54 As handsomly as a beare picketh muscles. **1589** *Pappe w. Hatchet* (1844) 16 Swarmd..like beares to a honie pot. **1601** DENT *Pathw. Heauen* 62 To put his finger into the Lions mouth, and..take the Beare by the tooth. **1602** FULBECKE *1st Pt. Parall.* 28 A man should deuide honie with a Beare. **1736** BAILEY s.v., You dare as well take a Bear by the Tooth, That is, You dare not attempt it. **1742** RICHARDSON *Pamela* III. 335 O ho, Nephew! are you thereabouts with your Bears? **1785** GROSE *Dict. Vulgar T.* s.v. *Grumble*, He grumbled like a bear with a sore ear. **1820** SCOTT *Abbot* xv, 'Marry come up—are you there with your Bears?' muttered the Dragon. **1830** MARRYAT *King's Own* xxvi, As savage as a bear with a sore head. **1831** GEN. THOMPSON *Exerc.* (1842) I. 485 Not fit to carry garbage to a bear. **1858** *Sat. Rev.* 7 Aug. 139 You must not sell the skin till you have shot the bear [cf. II]. **1922** S. J. WEYMAN *Ovington's Bank* v. 49 He's like a bear with a sore head.
c. *fig.* Also *spec.*, Russia.
c **1230** *Ancr. R.* 202 Þe Bore [? bere, beore] of heui Slouhðe haueð þeos hweolpes. *c* **1400** *Apol. Loll.* 58 Þe bere of glotonie romis a bout..for to fille þe wombe. **1591** SPENSER *Ruines Time* 66 What nowe is of th' Assyrian Lyonesse?..What of the Persian Beares outragiousnesse? [**1794** W. B. STEVENS *Jrnl.* 15 Dec. (1965) II. 214 Those Russian Bears after having devoured the Unhappy Poles are..to direct their fell tusks against France.] **1804** M. WILMOT *Let.* 24 July in Londonderry & Hyde *Russ. Jrnls.* (1934) I. 147 Take the two Nations..and trust me the Bears would triumph. **1831** T. CAMPBELL *Wks.* (1907) 220 France turns from her abandoned friends afresh, And soothes the Bear that prowls for patriot flesh. **1853** *Punch* XXIV. 222 We recommend the Bear to hug himself as comfortably as he likes, in his own security, but we would advise him to keep his paws off from Turkey. **1939** W. S. CHURCHILL *Into Battle* (1941) 145 The left paw of the Bear bars Germany from the Black Sea. **1967** *Observer* 15 Jan. 32/8 When he allowed himself to be flown back to Moscow..he was consciously putting his head in the Bear's mouth.
d. A child's toy, esp. TEDDY *bear*.
1907 [see TEDDY]. **1928** A. A. MILNE *House at Pooh Corner* x. 178 In that enchanted place on the top of the Forest a little boy and his Bear will always be playing.
e. *slang* (orig. and chiefly *U.S.*). A policeman; *ellipt.* for SMOKEY BEAR 2. Freq. *attrib.* or in phr.: see also *feed the bears* s.v. FEED *v.* 4 b.
1975 *Atlantic Monthly* May 42/1 There's a four-wheeler coming up fast behind me, might be a Bear wanting to give us some green stamps. **1975** *S9* Oct. 32/2 *Bear's Den*, any police station. **1975** *Washington Post* 16 Nov. (Parade Suppl.) 18/4 All those CB 'bear reports' were actually helping hold speeds down. **1976** *Daily News* (N.Y.) (CB & Sound Suppl.) 11 June 2/1 *Bear Cave*, police station. **1976** *CB Mag.* June 40/3 'The bear's pulling somebody off there at 74,' reported someone else. **1977** *Daily Province* (Victoria, B.C.) 29 Sept. 7/1 The Bear in the Air will be staying up there.
2. *fig.* A rough, unmannerly, or uncouth person. ***to play the bear***: to behave rudely and roughly; const. *with* (colloq.): to play the deuce with, inflict great damage upon (? *obs.*). Also in obs. colloquial sense: see quot. 1832.
1579 TOMSON *Calvin's Serm. Tim.* 473/1 When we haue so turned all order vpsidowne..there is nothing but..playing the beare amongst vs. **1751** CHESTERF. *Lett.* III. cclxii. 202 The French people of learning..are not bears as most of ours are. **1832** *Legends Lond.* II. 247 When I was the youthful Bear—as the disciple of a Private Tutor is called at Oxford. **1854** A. E. BAKER *Gloss. Northampt. Words* I. 38 A market-gardener says, 'A wet Saturday plays the bear with us'; *i.e.* keeps our customers away, and injures our goods. **1855** MACAULAY *Hist. Eng.* III. 51 This great soldier..was no better than a Low Dutch bear. **1888** 'R. BOLDREWOOD' *Robb. under Arms* II. ii. 26 Chaps that have got something on their minds can't stand idleness, it plays the bear with them. **1891** J. M. DIXON *Dict. Idiom. Phr.* s.v., The last storm has played the bear with my crops.
3. *Astr.* Name given to two constellations in the northern hemisphere known respectively as the 'Great Bear,' and 'Lesser Bear.'
1398 TREVISA *Barth. De P.R.* VIII. xxxv, Alwey þoo sterres wyndeþ and turneþ rounde aboute þ at lyne, þat is calde Axis, as a bere aboute þe stake. And þerfore þat cercle is clepid þe more bear. **1551** RECORDE *Cast. Knowl.* (1556) 263 The moste northerly constellation is the lesser Beare..Nigh vnto it is the greater Beare. **1632** MILTON *Penser.* 85 Where I may oft outwatch the Bear. **1868** LOCKYER *Heavens* (ed. 3) 320 Between the Great Bear and Cassiopeia is the Little Bear.
4. In New South Wales, the local name of the *Phaseolarctos*, a Marsupial animal allied to the Phalangers, called by the natives *Koala* or 'Biter.'
1827 [see KOALA]. **1847** CARPENTER *Zool.* §314 By the colonists usually termed the native Bear or Monkey.
5. sea-bear: popular name of a species of seal.
1847 CARPENTER *Zool.* §202 Several species of Seal are known under the names of Sea-Lion, Sea-Bear, etc. **1883** FLOWER in *Glasgow Weekly Her.* 14 July 8/1.
6. A rough mat for wiping boots on; a block covered with shaggy matting, used for scrubbing the decks of vessels.
1795 J. AIKIN *Manchester* 349 The making (by blindfolk) of..white and tarred bears, foot-cloths, etc. **1805** D. JOHNSTON *Serm. for Blind* 20 Rope-bears for cleaning the feet at our doors.
7. a. A machine for punching holes.
1869 SIR E. REED *Ship Build.* xx. 446 The holes which come in the plate-edges are usually punched by a bear.
b. Other technical uses: see quot.
1864 *Reader* No. 85. 203/3 A machine called the bear, which sheltered a number of archers. **1871** *Trans. Amer. Inst. Min. Engineers* I. 112 Metallic iron, not finding heat enough in a lead furnace..congeals in the hearth, and forms what smelters term 'sows,' 'bears,' 'horses.'
II. 8. *Stock Exchange.* A speculator for a fall; *i.e.* one who sells stock for delivery at a future date, in the expectation that meanwhile prices will fall, and he will be able to buy in at a lower rate what he has contracted to deliver at a higher. *Formerly*, The stock so contracted to be delivered, in the phrase 'to buy' or 'sell the bear;' see b.
[As applied to stock thus sold, *bear* appears early in 18th c., and was common at the time of the South Sea Bubble. The term 'bearskin jobber,' then applied to the dealer now called the 'bear,' makes it probable that the original phrase was 'sell the bearskin,' and that it originated in the well-known proverb, 'to sell the bear's skin before one has caught the bear.' The associated BULL appears somewhat later and was perhaps suggested by *bear*.]
a. 1719 *Anat. Change Alley* [in *N. & Q.* 1876 Ser. v. VI. 118 Those who buy Exchange Alley Bargains are styled] buyers of Bear-skins. **1726** DE FOE *Hist. Devil* (1822) 238 Every secret cheat, every bear-skin jobber.
b. 1709 STEELE *Tatler* No. 38 ¶3 Being at that General Mart of Stock-Jobbers called Jonathans..he bought the bear of another officer. *Ibid.* ¶5, I fear the Word Bear is hardly to be understood among the polite People; but I take the meaning to be, That one who ensures a Real Value upon an Imaginary Thing, is said to sell a Bear. **1714** C. JOHNSON *Country Lasses* I. i, Instead of changing honest staple for Gold and Silver, you deal in Bears and Bulls. **1720** POPE *Inscr. Punch Bowl in South-Sea Year* (Globe ed.) 490 Come fill the South Sea goblet full; The gods shall of our stock take care: Europa pleased accepts the bull, And Jove with joy puts off the bear. **1721** CIBBER *Refusal* Wks. 1754 I. 41 (*from end*), And all this out of Change-Alley? Every Shilling, Sir, all out of Stocks, Tuts, Bulls, Rams, Bears, and Bubbles. **1731** BAILEY, *To sell a Bear* [among *Stock-jobbers*], to sell what one hath not.
c. 1744 *Lond. Mag.* 86 These noisy Devotees were false ones, and in Fact were only Bulls and Bears. **1762** *Gentl. Mag.* 18 In contracts for time, he who contracts to sell is called the bear. **1865** *Standard* 23 Feb., The 'bear' party at the Paris Bourse plucked up courage to-day. **1881** *Chicago Times* 30 Apr., The bears made a strong fight against an advance.

III. *Comb.* 9. General relations, chiefly attrib., as *bear-dance*, *-fat*, *-fight*, *-fur*, *-hide*, *-hunt*, *-kin*, *-meat*, *-whelp*; *bear-furred* adj.

c **1230** *Ancr. R.* 202 þes laste bore hweolp is grimmest of alle. *Ibid.* 296 þe deouel is beorekunnes. **1588** SHAKS. *Tit. A.* IV. i. 96 But if you hunt these Beare-whelpes, then beware: The Dam will wake. **1780** W. FLEMING in N. D. Mereness *Trav. Amer. Col.* (1916) 640 Bear fat is preserved sweet and pure. **1803** *Lit. Mag.* (Philadelphia) Oct. 64 A grand bear hunt is proposed on the third Wednesday in October. **1825** SCOTT *Betrothed* (1860) 349 Stretch thyself on the bear-hide, and sleep. **1845** MRS. KIRKLAND *Western Clearings* 125 They were going to have a bear-hunt out there. **1856** KANE *Arct. Exp.* II. 311 Bear-meat, seal, walrus. **1859** MASSON *Milton* I. iv. 113 Dancings, bear-fights, cock-fights, etc. **1920** D. H. LAWRENCE *Lost Girl* i. 11 Winter coats.. flourished their bear-fur cuffs. **1926** E. SITWELL *Elegy on Dead Fashion* 3 Nor walk within vast bear-furred woods.

10. Special combinations: **bear animalcule**, a microscopic animal of the group *Tardigrada*, a water-bear; †**bear-ape**, obsolete name of an American ape (see quot.); **bear-bait** = BEAR-BAITING; **bear-brat**, contemptuous epithet = *bear's cub*; **bear-bug**, variant of BUG-BEAR; †**bear-claw** (= BEAR'S-BREECH); **bear-covering** *vbl. sb.* (see quot. 1930); **bear dance**, a kind of dance practised by American Indians; **bear-dog**, one used in hunting or baiting bears; †**bear-fell**, a bear-skin; **bear-fight** *fig.*, a riotous scuffle; a humorous name for a social gathering; hence as *v. intr.*, to behave rowdily; **bear-garden**, a place originally set apart for the baiting of bears, and used for the exhibition of other rough sports, *fig.* a scene of strife and tumult; **bear-grass** *U.S.*, one of various species of Yucca (esp. *Yucca filamentosa*), or of some similar plants; **bear-hound** (= *bear-dog*); **bear-lead** *v. trans.*, to act as bear-leader or travelling tutor to (a youth); to conduct or lead; hence, to supervise the conduct of, arrange the affairs of; hence *bear-leading* vbl. sb. and ppl. adj.; **bear-leader**, formerly a ludicrous name for a travelling tutor, cf. sense 2 above; also, a captor, custodian; **bear oak** *U.S.*, the black scrub-oak, *Quercus ilicifolia*; **bear-pit**, a sunken enclosure in which bears are kept for exhibition; **bear-play**, rough tumultuous behaviour; **bear('s)-breech**, popular name of the genus *Acanthus*, Brank-ursine; **bear's-ear**, popular name of the AURICULA (sense 3); **bear's-ear sanicle**, herbalists' name of *Cortusa matthioli*; **bear's-garlic**, popular name of *Allium Ursinum* or Ramsons; **bear's-grease**, the fat of the bear, used esp. in medical and cosmetic preparations; **bear's-muck** (see quot.); **Bear State** *U.S.*, the state of Arkansas (occas. also California); **bear-wallow** *U.S.*, a hollow in the ground attributed to the wallowing of bears; **bear-warden** = BEAR-WARD; †**bear-wolf**, a vigorous term of opprobrium; †**bear-worm**, obsolete name of a hairy caterpillar, or 'woolly-bear.'

Also BEAR-BAITING, -BERRY, -FOOT, -SKIN, -WARD.

1889 *Cent. Dict.* s.v. *Arctisca*, *Bear-animalcules. **1607** TOPSELL *Four-f. Beasts* 15 Of the *Bear-Ape Arctopithecus. His belly hangeth very low, his head and face like unto a childs. *c* **1590** in *Chetham Misc.* V, Maigames, rushbearings, *bearebaites. **1583** STANYHURST *Epitaphs* 159 Thee *bearbrat boucher thy corps with villenye mangled. **1562** J. HEYWOOD *Prov. & Epigr.* (1867) 194 They put on blacke scrafs, and go like *beare buggis. **1589** FLEMING *Virg. Eclog.* iii. 8 Compassed about the eares with tender *beare-claw [leaues]. **1929** *Observer* 17 Nov. 4/2 '*Bear-covering'.. and the lowering of the New York discount rate.. were.. partly responsible for this.. partial recovery. **1930** M. CLARK *Home Trade* 271 On the other hand, the bear who does not see prices fall in accordance with his hopes may also have to cut his loss and buy the shares he has already sold when not in possession of them at the best price possible. He enters the market as a buyer and by his buying sends up the price of the securities in which he is dealing. This buying is known as 'bear covering'. **1969** *Daily Tel.* 5 Mar. 4/1 The share-price, helped also by a measure of bear-covering, rose 1s 6d. *a* **1820** in *Western Rev.* II. 161 There are a number of other [Indian] dances, such as the *bear dance, the Turkey dance. **1673** *Lond. Gaz.* No. 763/4 A Blew brinded *Bear Dog of about three quarters old. *c* **1350** *Will. Palerne* 2430 Wiþ hem boþe *bere felles þei bere in here armes. **1855** W. G. SIMMS *Forayers* xxxii. 373 It'll be a *bear fight first, I tell you—tooth and nail! **1861** C. M. YONGE *Stokesley Secret* xiii. 209 'Oh, Papa, may we drink tea with you?'.. 'Yes, to be sure, if you won't make a bear fight.. for your uncle.' **1873** —— *Pillars of House* IV. xlvi. 298, I shall.. come back at dark when the bear fight is over. **1892** *Daily News* 23 Feb. 4/8 Did she bear-fight and play practical jokes on the Lord Admiral? **1900** *Ibid.* 24 Oct. 10/2 A don called Bedmynster used to bearfight in hall. **1596** J. NORDEN *Progr. Pietie* (1847) 177 And go to the.. *bear-gardens.. where they lose their time.. and offend the laws.. of her majesty. **1687** SETTLE *Refl. Dryden's Plays* 33 Our Beargarden Duellers. **1743** WESLEY in *Wks.* 1782 I. 439 One of them having been a prize-fighter at the bear-garden. **1803** BRISTED *Pedest. Tour* II. 543 Squabbles and boxings.. rendering the place more like a bear-garden than a hall of instruction. **1750** T. WALKER *Jrnl.* 12 Apr. in J. S. Johnstone *First Explor. Kentucky* (1898), On the Banks is some *Bear-Grass. **1909** *Cent. Dict.* Suppl., *Bear-grass* 2. a bunch-grass, *Stipa setigera*, ranging from the mountains of California, where it is considered valuable, to Oregon and Texas. **1837** CARLYLE *Fr. Rev.* I. III. i. 80 The Wolfhounds shall fall suppressed, the *Bearhounds, the Falconry. **1891** C. DUNSTAN *Quita* I. i, I do call it hard.. to condemn me to *bear-lead a savage. **1898** *Daily News* 31 Aug. 5/5 It was he who bear-led Admiral Avellane and his officers. *a* **1935** T. E. LAWRENCE *Mint* (1955) III. xi. 188 The Adjutant bear-led poor enduring Dolly down the three interminable lanes of us dressed ham-bones. **1968** *Listener* 21 Mar. 381/1 The Establishment, bear-led by the Hearst Press, had decided that this turbulent man.. must.. go. **1749** H. WALPOLE *Lett. H. Mann* 202 (1834) II. 283 She takes me for his *bear-leader, his travelling governor. **1794** W. GODWIN *Caleb Williams* III. vi. 114 My bear-leaders were considerably surprised with my firmness. **1846** THACKERAY *Snobs of England* in *Punch* 18 Apr. 166/1 They pounced upon the stray nobility, and seized young lords travelling with their bear leaders. **1955** J. MASTERS *Coromandel!* ii. 87 She's picked up dancers and bearleaders and fiddlers and bullies. **1901** 'LINESMAN' *Words Eyewitness* (1902) 289 A guard of honour, and a *bear-leading general officer to see the creature safely and comfortably down to the sea. **1928** *Daily Tel.* 7 Aug. 6/5 There are.. more applicants for what used to be called 'bear-leading' than there are bears to be led. **1810** in *D.A.E.*, Bear oak. **1832** D. J. BROWNE *Sylva Amer.* 263 This diminutive species is known in the Northern and Middle States by the name of *Bear Oak. **1849** MRS. F. L. MORTIMER *Near Home* 297 In the city [*sc.* Berne] there is a *bear pit with three fat lazy living bears. **1862** F. LOCKER *London Lyrics* 66 (*title*) The Bear Pit at the Zoological Gardens. **1883** *Pall Mall G.* 14 June, That the university would not degrade itself in the eyes of the visitors by *bear-play. **1565** GOLDING *Ovid's Met.* XIII. (1593) 315 A traile of flowres of *bearbrich. **1736** BAILEY *Househ. Dict.* 71 Bears breech or Brank Ursine, is an herb of singular use in physick, for.. the gout and cramp. **1597** GERARD *Herball* II. cclxii. 640 There be diuers sorts of Mountaine Cowslips, or *Beares eares. **1671** GREW *Anat. Plants* I. (1682) 31 Sometimes single, as in Beares-Ears. **1611** COTGR., *Ail d'ours*, Ramsons.. *Beares garlicke. **1863** PRIOR *Plant-n.* 17 Bear's-garlick, so called, says Tabernæmontanus, *quia ursi eo delectantur.* *c* **1420** *Pallad. on Husb.* I. 838 And evry tole in *beres grees defoule. **1601** HOLLAND *Pliny* II. 103 Wild Rose leaues reduced into a liniment with Beares grease. **1843** THACKERAY *Irish Sk. Bk.* (1863) 286 A tuft on the chin may be had at a small expense of bear's grease, by persons of a proper age. **1846** CLARKE in *Jrnl. R. Agric. Soc.* VII. II. 517 The 'dead peat,' commonly called '*bear's muck.' **1848** BARTLETT *Dict. Amer.* 392, I once asked a Western man if Arkansas abounded in bears, that it should be designated as the '*Bear State'. **1872** SCHELE DE VERE *Americanisms* 658 Arkansas is called the *Bear State*, though.. the name is pronounced *Bar* State... California enjoys the same title. **1766** in *Amer. Speech* (1940) XV. 155/1 Two White Oaks Saplings by the *Bear Wallow Drains. **1787** *Ibid.*, Standing by two Ironwood trees nigh a bear wallow. **1891** M. E. RYAN *Pagan of Alleghanies* v. 62 He rode.. on through the columns of white-oak, whose feet are caressed by feathers and fern in the long, desolate 'bear-wallow'. **1884** BESANT in *Contemp. Rev.* Mar. 343 The *bear-warden's fiddle. **1545** BRINKLOW *Complaynt* (1874) 89 Turne your chauntries and your obbetes from the profite of these *berewolues whelpes. **1608** TOPSELL *Serpents* 667 These Caterpillers.. by reason of their roughnesse and ruggednesse, some call them *Bear-worms.

bear (bɪə(r)), *sb.*[2] Forms: 1–9 bere, 6 beir, 6–8 beare, beer, 7 bar, 8– bear. [OE. *bere* (masc.):—OTeut. **bariz-* (neut.), found in Gothic in the derivative *barizeins*, adj. 'made of barley.' The thematic *z* of OTeut. was mistaken for the inflexional *z* of the nom. masc., and the noun became masc. in OE. and in ON. *bar-r*: cf. *awe*.]

1. Barley: the original English name, in later times retained only in the north, and esp. in Scotland; hence *spec.* applied to the coarse variety (*Hordeum hexastichon* or *tetrastichon*), with six (or four) rows of grain in its ear, till lately chiefly cultivated in the north; also distinguished as *bear-barley* and *bigg*. ***knocked bear***: pounded barley.

c **950** *Lindisf. Gosp.* John vi. 9 Fife hlafas bero and tuoeȝe fisces. *c* **975** *Rushw. G.* ibid., Fif hlafas of bere. *c* **1000** ÆLFRIC *Gram.* (Z.) 31 *Ordeum*, bere. *a* **1300** *Cursor M.* 13506 Tua fisches and fiue laues o bere. **1340** *Ayenb.* 141 þe asse of þe melle.. ase bleþeliche berþ bere ase huete. *c* **1425** WYNTOUN *Cron.* VII. x. 521 A Boll of Bere for awcht or ten.. sawld wes þen. *c* **1570** *Leg. Bp. S. Andr.* in *Scot. Poems 16th C.* II. 324 To crave there debtis; For kaill, caudle, and knocked beir. **1570** HOLINSHED *Scot. Chron.* (1806) I. 8 Abundance of barleie which the Scots call beir. **1772** PENNANT *Tours Scotl.* (1774) 245 Thatched with the Straw of bear pulled up by the roots. **1799** J. ROBERTSON *Agric. Perth* 152 Bear-barley or big, which consists of four rows in the ear. **1820** SCOTT *Monast.* I The feuars raised tolerable bear.

2. *attrib.*, as in *bear-awns*, *-bannock*, *-bread*, *-corn*, *-flour*, *-meal*; **bear-seed**, the seed or sowing (*obs.*) of bear. See also BEAR-BINE; and cf. BARN, BARTON.

c **950** *Lindisf. Gosp.* Luke iii. 17 Clænseð ber-ern *vel* bere-flor his. *c* **1550** *Description of Pedder Coffeis* (Bann. MS.), And beir bonnokis with thame thay tak. **1587** *Acts Jas. VI* (1814) 447 (JAM.) Thairefter the Sessioun.. to ryse and vacance be for the beirseed during the moneth of Maij. **1591** PERCIVALL *Sp. Dict.*, *Espelta*, beere corne *Spelta, zea.* **1601** HOLLAND *Pliny* I. 559 The Beare corn or bearded Far. *c* **1620** Z. BOYD *Zion's Flowers* (1855) 100 Where pinch'd with want the Bar bread thou shalt eate. **1753** *Scots Mag.* XV. 54/2 Bear-meal 7*d.*

†**bear**, *sb.*[3] *Obs.* [f. BEAR *v.*[1]]

1. = BEARING *vbl. sb.* 2; behaviour.

a **1400** *Chester Pl.* 106, I wotte by this boisters beare That tribute I muste paye.

2. Pressure, thrust.

1674 N. FAIRFAX *Bulk & Selv.* 72 The pent or bear of it beneath vvas nothing at all. *Ibid.* 122 The spring.. may, by its bear or elasticity hitch it forwards.. creeper-like.

bear (bɛə(r), bɪə(r)), *sb.*[4] *Obs.* or *dial.* Forms: 4–6 bere, 5 bare, 5–7 bear(e, 6 beere, ber, 6–7 beier, 7–8 bier, 4– beer. [ME. *bere* cognate w. LG. *büre*, adopted also in modG. as *bühre*. Of obscure origin; Grimm's derivation from OHG. *burjan*, *burren* to raise, is not satisfactory.] A case or covering for a pillow. Usually PILLOW-BERE, q.v.

1369 CHAUCER *Bk. Duchesse* 254 Many a pillow and every bere, Of cloth of Raines to slepe on soft. **1494** *Ord. R. Househ.* 125 Every pillow two bares of raynes For every pillow two beares. **1522** *Bury Wills* (1850) 116, I beqwethe to Fraunces Wrethe.. ij pelows wt the berys. **1641** *Chron. Pret. Snatheuse* in *Jrnl. Statist. Soc.* (1858), 7 linen pillow bears, 8*s.* **1713** *Lond. & Country Brew.* I. (1742) 36 A Bag, like a Pillow-bear. **1850** HOOD *Poems* (1864) 269 Right beautiful the dewy meads appear.. What then,—if I prefer my pillow-beer?

†**bear**, *sb.*[5] *Obs. rare.* Also bere, bier. [Cogn. w. ON. *bára* wave, billow, perh. f. *berja* to strike, dash.] A wave, a billow.

1250 LAY. 1341 He hęþte.. seyles drawe to toppe leten lade þane wind passi ouer bieres [**1205** uðen]. *Ibid.* 28077 þe beares me hire bi-nome. *Ibid.* 28625 A.. sort bot Wandri mid þ[e] beres.

bear, *sb.*[6] *U.S.* Also baire. [Perh. the same as BEAR *sb.*[4], but cf. BAR *sb.*[5]] (See quot. 1775.)

1775 B. ROMANS *Florida* 228 Baires are a kind of tent made of a light coarse cloth, like canvas gauze, called by the French *villemontiers.* **1797** F. BAILY *Jrnl. Tour* (1856) 309 Over the whole [bed] there is a large gauze net (called a *bear*), which is intended as a defence against the mosquitos. **1798** A. ELLICOTT in C. V. Mathews *Life & Lett.* (1908) 158 Our beds are all surrounded with a kind of thin curtains called bears to keep them off when we go to rest. **1895** G. KING *New Orleans* 65 The oarsmen [*c* 1726] made their mosquito *baires* for them.

bear (bɛə(r)), *v.*[1] *str.* Pa. t. bore (bɔə(r)). Pa. pple. borne (bɔən), born (bɔːn). Forms: *Inf.* 1 ber-an, (2 beor-en, bor-en), 2–5 ber-en, 3–6 ber-e, (4 berne, bern), 4–5 ber, 5 beere, *Sc.* 5–6 beir(e, 5–7 beare, (5–8 bare, 6 baire, berie), 6– bear. *Pa. t.* 1–2 bær (*pl.* bǽron), 2–5 ber, bar (*pl.* beren), 4–5 bere, 4–8 bare, (4 beir, beere, baar); 5– bore (*rare* till *c* 1600), 6 boore; *Sc.* 5 bur, 5–6 buir, 6–8 bure; (5 baryd, 7 beared). *Pa. pple.* 1–4 boren, (4–5 borin(e, 5 borun), 4–7 born (*rare*), 5–7 borne (*usual*); also 2–4 iboren, 3–5 ibore, ybore, ibor, (5 ebore), 3–8 bore, (4–5 bor, 6 *arch.* yborne, ybore), 8–9 borne, born differentiated. [Common Teut., and Aryan: OE., OS., OHG. *ber-an*. ON. *ber-a*, Goth. *bair-an*:—OTeut. stem *ber-* = L. *fer-*, Gr. *φερ-*, Skr. *bhar-*. (The compound form, Goth. *ga-bairan*, OHG. *ga-beran*, OS. *gi-beran*, OE. *ȝeberan*, ME. IBERE, is in some of the langs. more usual than the simple verb: cf. MHG. *gebern*, mod.G. *gebären* in sense IV). As the senses of *carry a burden*, and *bring forth fruit* or *offspring*, are both found in the word and its derivatives in the Aryan languages generally, from the earliest period, it is not certain which is the primitive; possibly branch IV preceded I in prehistoric times. In mod.Eng. the originally short vowel of the present has been lengthened by position (*orig.* bɛr, *now* bɛə(r)). The pa. t., in Gothic *bar*, pl. *bêrun*, was regularly in OE. *bær*, *bǽron* (Anglian *béron*); early ME *bar*, *beren*, afterwards by levelling of sing. and pl., in south *ber*, *beren*, *beeren*, in north *bar(e*, *baren*, *bare*, which became the literary form. The later *bore*, assimilated in vowel to the pa. pple., appears in w. midl. texts, about 1400; it was not general till after 1600; the Shaks. folio of 1623 has *bore* and *bare*, but the Bible of 1611 only *bare*. The corresponding Sc. *bure*, *buir* (pointing to earlier *ō*) is found in 15th c. As to the two forms of the pa. pple., *borne*, *born*, see 44 below. The ME. *iboren* may also be referred to the derivative IBERE (see above), which cannot be separated in sense from the simple verb.]

Main senses: I. to carry; II. to sustain; III. to thrust, press; IV. to bring forth.

I. To carry; with its transferred and fig. senses.

1. a. *trans.* To support the weight of (anything) whilst moving it from one place to another; to carry. Now usually restricted in prose to the carrying of something weighty or which requires an effort.

a **1000** *Beowulf* 96 [Hie hina] leton holm beran, ȝeafon on gársecȝ. **1154** *O.E. Chron.* (Laud MS.) an. 1135 Wua sua bare his byrthen. *c* **1200** *Trin. Coll. Hom.* 89 Hie.. beren on here honde blostme. *c* **1250** *Gen. & Ex.* 209 God bar him in-to paradis. *c* **1380** WYCLIF *De Ps. Freris* xxii. Wks. (1880) 307 Boren aboute wiþ windis. *c* **1385** CHAUCER *L.G.W.* 943 On his bak he bar.. Anchises. *c* **1400** MAUNDEV. xvi. 172 Men.. beeren his body in to Mesopatayme.. and aftre he was broughte thidre agen. *c* **1450** *Bk. Curtasye* I. 114 With mete ne bereþy knyfe to mowthe. **1483** *Cath. Angl.* 28 To

bere, *baiulare, portare*. **1588** SHAKS. *L.L.L.* IV. iii. 17 She hath one a' my sonnets already, the Clowne bore it, the foole sent it. *a* **1625** FLETCHER *Eld. Brother* I. ii, Court-admirers..ever echo him that bears the bag. **1704** SWIFT *Batt. Bks.* (1711) 256 The other half was born by the frighted Steed thro the Field. **1740** JOHNSON *Drake* Wks. 1787 IV. 453 Over his head was born a rich canopy. **1816** J. WILSON *City of Plague* I. ii. 138 The wretch who bore them in her womb. **1820** SCOTT *Ivanhoe* viii, He was borne senseless from the lists.

b. *absol.* To carry burdens.

1593 SHAKS. *Rich. II*, V. v. 90 Forgiuenesse, horse: why do I raile on thee, Since thou..Was't borne to beare? **1611** BIBLE *Gen.* xlix. 15 He..bowed his shoulder to beare.

c. To lift, raise, or keep up (a thing) while moving it. *Obs.* or *arch.*

1578 BANISTER *Hist. Man* iv. 62 These two muscles baire the hand vpward. **1677** MOXON *Mech. Exerc.* (1703) 98 When he draws back his Saw, the Work-man bears it lightly off the un-sawn Stuff. *Ibid.* 170 To bear their Work off the Cheeks of the Lathe.

d. *Backgammon*: To remove a piece at the end of a game. Also *absol.*

1562 J. HEYWOOD *Prov. & Epigr.* (1867) 109, I will no more play at tables with thee: When wee come to bearyng, thou begylest mee, In bearyng of thy men. *Ibid.* 110 Eche other caste thou bearest a man to many. **1748** HOYLE *Backgammon* in *Penny Cycl.* III. 240/2 If you bear any number of men, before you entered a man taken up..such men, so borne, must be entered again in your adversary's tables.

†**e.** To take as a companion, take along with one; to carry as a consequence. *Obs.*

1596 SPENSER *F.Q.* I. iv. 2 After that he had faire Una lorne..And false Duessa in her sted had borne. **1607** SHAKS. *Timon* I. i. 131 His honesty rewards him in it selfe, It must not beare my Daughter.

f. *to bear across*: to support (things) going across.

1860 TYNDALL *Glac.* I. §11. 75 Finding a bridge which bore us across the crevasse.

2. a. *fig.* Said in reference to things immaterial, or to ideal carrying.

c **1200** *Trin. Coll. Hom.* 47 We aȝen to beren ure louerd ihesu crist on heorte. *c* **1230** *Ancr. R.* 424 Nouðer of þe wummen ne beren..none idele talen. *a* **1300** *Cursor M.* 2201 Ful fer about men bar his name. *c* **1500** *Merch. & Son* in Halliw. *Nugæ P.* 23 There was not oon man in all thys londe that bare a bettyr brede. **1552** HULOET, Beare tale or tidynges. **1577** HOLINSHED *Chron.* III. 831/2 This pope Leo ..bare but seauen and thirtie yeeres of age. **1725** POPE *Odyss.* XVI. 162 To the Queen with speed dispatchful bear Our safe return. **1768** BLACKSTONE *Comm.* II. 242 The ancestor, during his life, beareth in himself all his heirs. **1805** SOUTHEY *Madoc in Azt.* ii. Wks. V. 213 [He] seem'd to bear at heart Something that rankled there. **1879** MACLEAR *Celts* v. 79 Another..incident, which bears internal evidence of high antiquity.

b. *to bear in mind*: to carry or keep in remembrance.

1538 BALE *God's Promyses* I. in *Dodsley* (1780) I. 12 To beare in mynde..The brute of thy name. **1539** TAVERNER *Erasm. Prov.* 20 Worthy..to be continually borne in mynde. **1852** MᶜCULLOCH *Taxation* II. iv. 199 It should..be borne in mind that this is not a mere agricultural question. **1855** MACAULAY *Hist. Eng.* IV. 313 He promised to bear the subject in mind. **1870** BRYANT *Iliad* I. IV. 106 Bear what I say in mind.

c. *to bear witness, record, testimony*: to testify.

a **1300** *Cursor M.* 6478 Ne ber þou witnes nan bot lele. **1340** HAMPOLE *Pr. Consc.* 585 Als þe buk says and bers witnes. **1526** TINDALE *John* viii. 14 Though I beare recorde [WYCLIF witnessyng, *Rhem.* testimonie] of my selfe, yet my recorde is true. **1611** BIBLE *Ex.* xx. 16 Thou shalt not beare false witnes against thy neighbour. **1671** MILTON *Samson* 1749 [He] to his faithful champion hath in place Bore witness gloriously. **1848** MACAULAY *Hist. Eng.* I. 508 Titles ..against which he had often borne his testimony.

3. With extension, and in phrases; both in lit. and fig. sense.

a. Extended by various advbs., as *about, away, off, out*, etc. Sometimes with specialized sense, as *to bear away*: to carry away as winner; †to carry away in the mind (a thing learned) *obs. to be borne away*: i.e. in opinion by feeling, impulse, etc. †*to bear forth*: to carry out, conduct (a matter); to develop. *to bear off*: to carry off as winner. *to bear out*: to pretend, give out (*obs.*); to extol (*obs.*); to support, back up, corroborate, confirm; to be responsible for (*obs.*). †*to bear over*: to transfer; to carry over, hold over to a later date. *to bear up*: to carry, holding up (a train, etc.).

1823 LAMB *Elia* Ser. II. xxiii. (1865) 396 To bear* about the piteous spectacle of his own self-ruins. **1842** H. E. MANNING *Serm.* (1848) I. 317 The dying body we now bear* about. *c* **1450** *Rob. Hood* (Ritson) I. i. 1132 And he that shoteth alder best The game shall bere* away. **1530** PALSGR. 449/1, I beare* awaye as a well wytted chylde dothe his lesson, *Je apprens*. **1589** PUTTENHAM *Eng. Poesie* 5 Easier to beare* away and be retained in memorie. **1711** *Spect.* No. 548 ¶6 Such tragedies as ended unhappily bore* away the prizes. **1802** MAR. EDGEWORTH *Moral T.* (1816) I. xiv. 114 Borne* away by their prejudices. *c* **1460** *Bk. Quintessence* 11 It berith* forþ þat blood anoon aftir into fleisch. **1631** WEEVER *Anc. Fun. Mon.* 212 This Duke had borne* forth his youth with better respect then Prince Henry his brother had done. **1813** SCOTT *Rokeby* III. xxvi, We are enow to storm the hold, Bear* off the plunder and the dame. **1485** CAXTON *Paris & V.* 10 Somme were that bare* out the beaulte of the syster of the Kyng. **1530** PALSGR. 450/2 This felowe beareth* it out, as he were a great gentylman. **1551** ROBINSON tr. *More's Utop.* 128 He helpeth and beareth* out simple wittes. **1618** BOLTON *Florus* (1636) 153 Thou didst defend thy selfe..against that people which had all the earth to backe, and beare them *out. **1629** GAULE *Pract. The.* 334 Yet he beares* out, As he'd preuent, or pittie the disaster. **1802** MAR. EDGEWORTH *Moral T.* (1816) I. xix. 166 You think, I suppose, that your friends..will bear you* out. **1867** FREEMAN *Norm. Conq.* I. vi. 441 A splendid panegyric which is fully borne* out by his recorded acts. **1382** WYCLIF *Ecclus.* x. 8 Rewme fro folc in to folc is born* ouer. —— *Prov.* xxix. 11 A wis man berth* ouer, and kepith vnto afterward. **1482** *Monk of Evesham* (1869) 40 They ware bore* vppe an hy by the grete vyolente flamys of fier. **1503** HAWES *Examp. Virt.* xiii. 255 Dame grace..bare* vp her trayn.

b. *to bear the bell, coals, the cross, a fagot, the flower, the gree, the palm, the prize, a part, the stroke, the word*: see BELL, COALS, etc. †*to bear low sail*: to demean oneself humbly.

a **1300** *Cursor M.* 12353 þa oþer leonis..wiþ þaire heued þai bare logh saile. **1593** SHAKS. *3 Hen. VI*, V. i. 52, I had rather chop this Hand off at a blow..Then beare so low a sayle, to strike to thee. **1602** CAREW *Cornwall* 135 b, Our Foy gallants, unable to beare a low sayle, in their fresh gale of fortune.

†**c.** *to bear the face, the heart*: to direct, turn, incline it. *Obs.*

c **1300** *Beket* 224 The King also..bar his hurte mest: to do ther Seint Thomas. *c* **1325** *E.E. Allit. P.* A. 67 Towarde a foreste I bere þe face.

d. *to bear (any one) company (fellowship* obs.), *a hand*: to bring, give, lend it. †*to bear one a blow*: to give or 'fetch' him a blow. *Obs.*

a **1300** *Cursor M.* 12568 And quen he suld to metschip ga ..Alle þai felauschip him bare. **1523** LD. BERNERS *Froiss.* I. cxi. 133 We desyre you to bere vs some company of armes. **1591** SHAKS. *Two Gent.* IV. iii. 34, I doe desire thee..To beare me company, and goe with me. **1647** W. BROWNE *Polexander* I. 116 Bajazet..bore him a blow that, in all likelyhood, should have bereft his life. **1749** FIELDING *Tom Jones* VII. vii. (1840) 90 You have promised to bear me company. **1769** FALCONER *Dict. Marine* (1789), *Bear-a-hand*, a phrase of the same import with make haste..quick. **1865** DICKENS *Mut. Fr.* vi. 307 Get him to bear a hand. **1865** CARLYLE *Fredk. Gt.* II. VII. v. 290 This pleasant streamlet.. has borne us company for some time.

†**e.** *to bear (an, a, on) in hand* [= F. *maintenir*, med.L. *manūtenēre*]: to maintain (a statement); maintain or assert to or against (a person); to charge, accuse (*obs. c* 1540); to profess, pretend; to assure, to lead (one) to believe; to delude, abuse with false pretences. †*to bear in hand*: to carry on, manage.

c **1300** *Beket* 909 We wolleth the bere an hond: that thu ert his traitour. *c* **1340** *Cursor M.* 15922 (Trin.) ȝe bere me wrong on honde. *c* **1386** CHAUCER *Man of L.T.* 522 This false knight..Bereth hir an hand that sche hath don this thing. **1461** *Paston Lett.* 396 II. 20 The parson of Snoryng ..beryth hym a hand. *c* **1470** HENRY *Wallace* I. 37 As Con's Cornykle bers on hand. **1513** DOUGLAS *Æneis* VI. xv. 103 The batellis and the weir, Quhilk eftir this he had to beir on hand. **1526** SKELTON *Magnyf.* 357 They bare me in hande . that I was a spye. **1528** MORE *Heresyes* I. Wks. 109/1 To dowte whither Luther himselfe..wrote in dede so euyll as he is borne in hande. **1547** *Homilies* I. *Fear of Death* III. (1859) 103 The love which we bear in hand to bear to him. **1597** DANIEL *Civ. Wars* VI. xxxiii, Devotion..Bears men a Hand on their Credulity. **1599** SHAKS. *Much Ado* IV. i. 305 What, beare her in hand vntill they come to take hands. **1611** —— *Cymb.* v. v. 43 Your daughter, whom she bore in hand to loue. **1625** USSHER *Answ. Jesuit* 4 Not so easie to be discerned, as fooles bee borne in hand they are. *a* **1716** SOUTH (1717) VI. 25 If Popery and Fanaticism are so irreconcilable, as our True Protestants would bear us in hand that they are.

†**f.** *to bear it*: to carry off as a prize, to 'carry' by assault, carry the day. *Obs.*

1604 SHAKS. *Oth.* I. iii. 23 So may he with more facile question beare it? **1612** BACON *Ess.* (Arb.) 216 Some thinke to beare it, by..being peremptorye. *a* **1625** FLETCHER *Mad Lover* II. i. 7 'Tis worth doing..but what doing beares it?

4. *refl. to bear oneself*: to carry, conduct, or deport oneself; behave. acquit oneself. Sometimes (like *behave oneself*) = to conduct oneself properly.

c **1230** *Ancr. R.* 4 Hu me schal beren him wiðuten. **1330** R. BRUNNE *Chron.* 98 þe gode quene gaf him in conseile, To luf his folk bituene..Bere him tille his barons. *c* **1386** CHAUCER *Prol.* 798 Which of yow that bereth him best of alle. *c* **1485** *Digby Myst.* (1882) II. 524 Who-so in pride beryth hym to hye, with myscheff shalbe mekyd. **1530** PALSGR. 450/1, I beare my selfe well. **1593** HOOKER *Eccl. Pol.* II. vii. §10 Wks. 1841 I. 268 Who bear themselves bold upon human authority. ? *c* **1600** *World & Child* in Hazl. *Dodsl.* I. 248 Bear thee prest in every game. **1658** USSHER *Ann.* vi. 163 Clearchus..bearing himself for a Tyrant of Byzantium. **1754** SHERLOCK *Disc.* (1759) I. ix. 257 A Man may bear himself so well in Disguise, as not to be discovered. **1848** MACAULAY *Hist. Eng.* I. 618 The latest generations would know how..he had borne himself.

5. To have as a member or part of the body.

1486 *Bk. St. Albans* E iij, And beerith talow and gris. **1611** SHAKS. *Wint. T.* I. ii. 309 Seruants..that bare eyes To see alike mine Honor, as their Profits. **1808** SCOTT *Marm.* VI. xvi, Eustace, thou bear'st a brain. **1817** BYRON *Manfred* II. iv. 92 Bear what thou borest, The heart and the form.

6. To carry about with or upon one, as material equipment or ornament.

a. To carry about with one, or wear, ensigns of office, weapons of offence or defence. *to bear arms against*: to be engaged in hostilities with.

a **1000** *Beowulf* 432 Secȝas bǽron..beorhte frætwa. *a* **1175** *Lamb. Hom.* 69 Crist..ȝeue us wepne for to beren. *c* **1400** MAUNDEV. vi. 64 Thei beren but o Scheld and o Spere. ? **1568** G. FERRERS in Arb. *Garner* IV. 179 Apt to bear arms. **1609** SKENE *Reg. Maj.* 60 He bure armes, and made weir against the King. **1769** ROBERTSON *Chas. V*, III. XI. 316 An ample..pardon to all who had born arms against him. **1862** STANLEY *Jew. Ch.* (1877) I. v. 94 The staff like that still borne by Arab chiefs.

†**b.** To have upon the body (clothes, ornaments); to wear. *to bear the breech*: to 'wear the breeches.'

c **893** K. ÆLFRED *Oros.* IV. x. §12 [He] bær hæt on his heafde. *c* **1230** *Ancr. R.* 382 Ich wot swulne þet bereð boðe togedere heui brunie and here. *a* **1300** *Cursor M.* 9071 'Tas of'..'mi kinges croun þat i na langer agh to bere.' *c* **1400** *Rom. Rose* 6240 Many..that comyn clothe ay beeren, Yit seyntes neverethelesse they weren. *c* **1500** *Mayd Emlyn* in *Anc. Poet. Tr.* (1842) 20 All women be suche Thoughe the man bere the breche, They wyll be euer checkemate. **1574** HELLOWES *Gueuara's Ep.* (1577) 87 The good or the euil of monasteries lyeth not in yᵉ habite, but in the men that beare it.

c. To display on a heraldic shield; to be entitled to wear or use as coat armour.

a **1450** *Syr Eglam.* 1186 He bare of Aser, a schyp of golde. **1486** *Bk. St. Albans, Her.* A j, Beyng in worthenes aarmes for to bere. **1599** THYNNE *Animadv.* 42 The erle of Kent beareth a wiuer for his Creste and supporters. **1727** BRADLEY *Fam. Dict.* s.v. *Bear*, He that has a Coat of Arms, is said to Bear it in the several Charges or Ordinaries that are in his Escutcheon. **1825** SCOTT *Talism.* (1832) 225 The shield..bore..a serrated and rocky mountain.

7. To carry about with one, to have attached to, or impressed upon one, to own, have: **a.** a feature, external character, look. (= to present.)

a **1300** *Cursor M.* 18823 Bot of his liknes þat he bare. **1393** GOWER *Conf.* I. 339 No life..Which berth visage of mannes kinde. *c* **1550** *Hickscorner* in Hazl. *Dodsl.* I. 171 Outward he beareth a fair face. **1600** HAKLUYT *Voy.* (1810) III. 470 Many Mountaines that beare shewes of Mettals. **1711** STEELE *Spect.* No. 4 ¶8 Falshood..shall hereafter bear a blacker Aspect. **1795** SOUTHEY *Joan of Arc* iv. 28 So firm a front They bear in battle. **1848** MACAULAY *Hist. Eng.* II. 142 Old Cavaliers..who bore the marks of honourable wounds.

b. a name, title, etc.

c **1391** CHAUCER *Astrol.* II. §12. 23 After which planete the day berith his name. **1393** LANGL. *P. Pl.* C. XVII. 203 For bishopes blessed · thei bereþ meny names. **1581** MARBECK *Bk. of Notes* 341 The Epistle which beareth the title to the Hebrues. **1850** PRESCOTT *Mexico* I. 63 Four beautiful girls, bearing the names of the principal goddesses.

c. a reputation, praise, blame, price, value, etc.

c **1425** *Seven Sag.* (P.) 73 The fyfte mayster..That of wisdom bare grete loos. **1588** MUNDAY in Farr's *S.P.* (1845) I. 230 The sweetest face..And highest head.. Beare no more reckoning then the poorest slaue. **1710** *Lond. Gaz.* No. 4658/2 The Blank Tickets bear seven per Cent. Interest. **1816** KIRBY & SP. *Entomol.* (1828) I. 331 It..is exported to India, where it bears a high price. **1845** HOOD *Recipe Civiliz.* Wks. (1871) 298 That which bears the praise of nations. **1866** ROGERS *Agric. & Prices* I. ii. 17 Natural meadow bore a high rental.

8. To wield (power, sway, etc.); to hold (an office). Cf. *office-bearer*.

c **1300** *Beket* 2409, [He] scholde have Ibore the heritage. **1503-4** *Act 19 Hen. VII*, xxvii. §11 No merchaunt..[shall] bere eny voyce ne have eny sayngs in eny Courte. **1534** WHITTINTON *Tullyes Offices* II. (1540) 99 In that yere that I bare roume. **1535** COVERDALE *1 Chron.* xxvii. 6 Sonnes.. which bare rule in the house of their fathers. **1552** LATIMER *Serm.* II. 138 They bear the swing, all things goeth after their minds. **1570** ASCHAM *Scholem.* (1863) 37 To beare some office in the common wealth. **1650** R. STAPYLTON *Strada's Low C. Warres* II. 29 That they should bear all the sway. **1690** *Idiom. Anglo-Lat.* 42 That Office did I bear. **1855** MACAULAY *Hist. Eng.* III. 671 Those great Celtic houses, which..bore rule in Ulster.

9. *fig.* To entertain, harbour, cherish (a feeling).

c **1250** *Gen. & Ex.* 1044 Salt ðu noȝt ðe riȝt-wise weren, Or for hem ðe toðere með beren? *a* **1300** *Cursor M.* 1069 Vntil his broþer nith [*v.r.* ire] he bare. *Ibid.* 12096 Ye ber him right nan au [*v.r.* awe]. **1483** CAXTON *G. de la Tour* F iv b, Obeysshe and bere hym honour. **1512** *Act 4 Hen. VIII*, xix. Pream., The true faythe that hys Highnesse berythe unto Almyghty Gode. **1538** STARKEY *England* iii. (1871) 82 One beryth malyce agayn another. **1570** T. WILSON *Demosthenes* 23 Now that the Thebanes beare us the stomache, that you see they doe. **1598** SHAKS. *Merry W.* IV. vi. 9 The deare loue I beare to faire Anne Page. **1598** GRENEWEY *Tacitus' Ann.* IV. ix. (1622) 103 She beareth the minde to passe the rest of her life with a Gentleman of Rome. **1727** SWIFT *Gulliver* III. ii. 189 The contempt they bear for practical geometry. **1872** BLACK *Adv. Phaeton* xxvi. 356 He bore her no malice.

10. To hold, maintain, possess, or have (a property or attribute, a relation to something else).

a **1300** *Cursor M.* 2682 Circumcising Bers in it-self gret for-biseyng. **1690** LOCKE *Hum. Und.* II. xxix. (1695) 204 Nothing finite bears any proportion to infinite. **1841** MACAULAY *W. Hastings, Ess.* (1851) I. 16 His mind bears a singular analogy to his body. **1857** BUCKLE *Civilis.* I. ix. 576 The relation the nobles bore to the throne. **1863** FAWCETT *Pol. Econ.* II. v. 194 The ratio which population bears to capital.

II. To sustain, support, uphold.

* *To sustain weight or pressure, to endure.*

11. a. *trans.* To sustain, support (a weight or strain).

c **1000** *Ags. Gosp.* Matt. xx. 12 þe bæron byrðena, on þises dæges hætan. *c* **1375** WYCLIF Sel. Wks. I. 66 þei shal bere.. the wiȝte of þe olde lawe. **1399** *Rich. Redeless* I. 41 The braunchis aboue boren grett charge. *c* **1550** *Scot. Poems 16th C.* (1810) II. 160 Our seiknes on thy back thou bure. *a* **1649** DRUMM. OF HAWTH. *Poems* Wks. (1711) 3 Atlas-like it seem'd the heaven they beared. **1793** SMEATON *Edystone L.* §246 Proportionate in every part to the stress it was likely to bear. **1801** STRUTT *Sports & Past.* II. ii. 79 When the ice would bear them. **1849** RUSKIN *Sev. Lamps.* ii. (1855) 34

For the shafts do indeed bear as much as they are ever imagined to bear.

b. *absol.* or *intr.*; *spec.* in *Building*, to stand a strain without intermediate support. Of ice: to support the weight of a person, etc.

1677 MOXON *Mech. Exerc.* (1703) 157 Timber is said to Bear at its whole length, when neither a Brick-wall, or Posts, etc. stand between the ends of it. *Ibid.* 136 Joysts are seldom made to Bear at above ten Foot in length. **1768** WASHINGTON *Diaries* (1925) I. 246 Attempted to go into the Neck on the Ice, but it wd. not bear. **1833** *Chambers's Edin. Jrnl.* XI. 381/2 [He] succeeded in forming a curling rink weeks before the ice would bear in any other quarter. **1917** O. VINEY *Let.* 27 Dec. in E. V. Lucas *Post-Bag Diversions* (1934) 58 We cycled to Hartwell lake.. as we heard that it was bearing.

12. a. *fig.* (of an immaterial burden, charge, cost, responsibility, etc.) Formerly also *bear out.*

1297 R. GLOUC. 379 To bere þeruore a certeyn rente by þe ȝere. *a* **1300** *Cursor M.* 5667 Him þat bare þe wite. **1439** *E.E. Wills* (1882) 125 Certayne annuities borne oute of hem [manors]. **1529** MORE in *Four C. Eng. Lett.* 12 There shall no poore neighbour.. bere no losse. **1598** W. PHILLIPS *Linschoten's Voy.* in Arb. *Garner* III. 403 The Farmers bearing the adventure of the sea. **1606** G. W[ODCOCKE] *Ivstine* 24a, Darius.. promised to beare out the whole charges of those Warres. **1611** BIBLE *Gen.* xiii. 6 The land was not able to beare them, that they might dwell together. **1769** STERNE *Serm. Yorick* v. (1773) 63 It had been.. better for the nation to have bore the expence. **1848** MACAULAY *Hist. Eng.* II. 263 Lewis would bear the charge of supporting two thousand of them [troops].

b. †*to bear the person of*: to sustain the character of, to personate (*obs.*). *to bear a part*: to sustain a part, take part, share *in*.

1605 VERSTEGAN *Dec. Intell.* x. (1634) 320 A vice-roy: that is, he that in the Kings absence supplieth his place and beareth his person. **1651** HOBBES *Leviath.* I. xvi. 80 He that acteth another, is said to beare his Person. *Ibid.* III. xlii. 267 Here wee have the Person of God born now the third time.

13. *trans.* To sustain successfully; *fig.* to stand (a strain, test, examination); to allow or admit of.

1523 FITZHERB. *Husb.* (1882) 60, Lx. mares.. able to beare the horse. **1605** SHAKS. *Lear* v. iii. 26 Thy great imployment Will not beare question. **1627** CAPT. SMITH *Seaman's Gram.* vii. 33 The ship will beare much, that is, carry much Ordnance or goods, or beare much saile. **1697** DRYDEN *Virg.* Ded., No Modern Latin can bear criticism. **1762** FALCONER *Shipwr.* II. 245 The ship no longer can her top-sails bear. **1793** SMEATON *Edystone L.* §137 The cable.. would scarcely have borne to have been heaved up. **1838** MACAULAY in Trevelyan *Life & Lett.* (1876) II. vii. 11 The style will not bear examination. **1849** RUSKIN *Sev. Lamps* i. §15. 25 It is not less the boast of some styles that they can bear ornament.

†**14.** *intr.* (for *refl.*) To hold good; to hold, stand, 'do.' (Cf. also *bring to bear* in 33.) *Obs.*

1710 STEELE *Tatler* No. 199 ¶5 If the Matter bears, I shall not be unjust to his Merit. **1737** WATERLAND *Eucharist* 112 The Argument will not bear in the View before mentioned. **1742** RICHARDSON *Pamela* III. 227 We are going into Personals again, Gentlemen.. And that wont bear.

15. To sustain (anything painful or trying); to suffer, endure, pass through: **a.** without any reference to the manner of bearing.

c **1385** CHAUCER *L.G.W.* 1272 And beryn.. for hire sake Not I not what. *c* **1450** HENRYSON *Mor. Fab.* 71 Three battes hee bure, or hee his feet might find. *c* **1470** HENRY *Wallace* II. 210 In fureous payne, yat ye bur. *c* **1580** *Amadis of Gaule* 273 This great sorow that I beare and suffer. **1718** POPE *Iliad.* I. 270 The wrongs I bear from Atreus son. **1816** J. WILSON *City of Plague* II. ii. 118 A melancholy pleasant to be borne. **1870** MORRIS *Earthly Par.* I. I. 281 That we can bear such things and yet not die.

b. To suffer without succumbing, to sustain without giving way, to endure. Formerly with *away*, *out* (cf. *hold out*, *stand out*).

a **1300** *Cursor M.* 15617 Him.. þat baret for yow bare. **1526** TINDALE *John* xvi. 12, I have yet many thynges to saye vnto you; but ye cannot beare them awaye now. **1547** BALDWIN *Mor. Philos.* vi. iii, Patiently beare the time. **1574** tr. *Marlorat's Apocalips* 17 Blessed is the man that beareth out temptation. **1607** TOPSELL *Four-f. Beasts* 437 The Horses can abide no cold, but the Asses and Mules bear out. **1611** BIBLE *Gen.* iv. 13 My punishment is greater then I can beare. **1697** DRYDEN *Virg. Georg.* III. 542 He who bears in Thrace the bitter Cold. **1755** SMOLLETT *Quix.* (1803) II. 143 With an intrepid heart.. he bears the brunt of their whole artillery. **1796** MRS. GLASSE *Cookery* xiv. 215 Make it as hot as you can bear your finger in it. **1864** *Daily Tel.* 16 May, We can only recommend Alphonse and Theophile.. to grin and bear it; the expression, perchance, savours a little of slang.

c. To endure without opposition or resistance, to tolerate (a thing); also with *inf.* or *subord. cl.*

c **900** *Laws of Ælfred* i. (Bosw.) Ic nelle beran eowre ȝymeleaste. *a* **1300** *Cursor M.* 12991 Na langer Mai i nu þi wicked wordes ber. **1523** LD. BERNERS *Froiss.* I. xxvi. 37 The kyng myght no longer bear by his honour the iniuryes and wronges. **1659** in Burton's *Diary* (1828) IV. 49, I say not but the army will bear, that you sit to levy money. **1704** ROWE *Ulyss.* I. i. 230 My Lords, this Railer is not to be born. **1855** MACAULAY *Hist. Eng.* III. 26 The public would not have borne to see any Papist among the servants of their Majesties.

d. To reconcile oneself to, put up with, tolerate, away with. (Always negatively, interrogatively, or hypothetically: often with infinitive.) Cf. ABEAR.

1710 *Tatler* No. 219 ¶4 There is no reasonable Man can bear him half an Hour. **1802** MAR. EDGEWORTH *Moral T.* (1816) I. xii. 100 [He] could not bear to think of distressing her. **1813** MISS AUSTEN *Pride & Prej.* xv. 62 The man whom she could not bear to speak of. **1865** DICKENS *Mut. Fr.* i. 2 'What hurt can it do you?' 'None, none. But I cannot bear it.' *Mod.* I cannot bear antimacassars!

16. *to bear hard, heavy* or *heavily* (L. *ægre ferre*): to endure with a grudge, take (a thing) ill or amiss, have ill will to, have a resentment against; so *to bear upon the spleen.* *Obs.* exc. *arch.*

c **1400** *Apol. Loll.* Introd. 10 Many beren heuy that freris ben clepid pseudo or ypocritis. **1601** SHAKS. *Jul. C.* II. i. 215 Caius Ligarius doth beare Caesar hard. **1602** *Life T. Cromwell* IV. ii. 112 You bear me hard about the abbey lands. **1629** tr. *Herodian* (1635) 38 Divers, that bore Perennius upon the spleene, for his intolerable haughty and disdainefull carriage. *a* **1674** CLARENDON *Hist. Reb.* I. I. 32 The Ill Success was heavily born, and imputed to ill Conduct. **1874** SWINBURNE *Bothwell* (1882) II. i. 97 It may be you do well to bear me hard.

17. *intr. to bear with*: to put up with, be patient with, make allowance for. (With indirect passive *to be borne with.*)

a **1553** UDALL *Royster D.* IV. vii. (Arb.) 74 The heart of a man Should more honour winne by bearyng with a woman. *a* **1586** *Answ. Cartwright* 72 Ignorance.. is to bee borne with. **1601** SHAKS. *Jul. C.* III. ii. 110 Beare with me, my heart is in the coffin there with Cæsar. **1712** POPE *Spect.* No. 408 ¶7 Little Irregularities are sometimes to be bore with. **1795** SOUTHEY *Joan of Arc* II. 223 He would bid us Bear with our miseries manfully. **1872** FREEMAN *Norm. Conq.* IV. xviii. 113 A foreign King had to be borne with.

** *To support, keep up, maintain.* Usually with *up.*

18. a. *trans.* To hold (*up*) from falling or sinking, to support, keep *up.*

a **1300** *Cursor M.* 537 Hijs fete him bers up fra fall. **1398** TREVISA *Barth. De P.R.* v. liv. (1495) 170 The fote.. beryth vp all the body. **1439** *E.E. Wills* (1882) 117, Ij Greffons to bere hit vppe. **1611** BIBLE *Judges* xvi. 29 The two middle pillars.. on which it was borne vp. **1684** R. WALLER *Nat. Exper.* 50 The Water.. may fill about half the Ball, that the Fishes may move, and bear themselves thereon.

b. *spec.* To hold up a horse's head with a 'bearing rein.' *to bear a rein upon*: to hold in check by this means. Also *fig.*

1603 S. DANIEL *Defence Rhime* (1717) 29 The best Rein, the strongest Hand to make men keep their Way, is, that which their Enemy bears upon them. **1607** TOPSELL *Four-f. Beasts* 284 Let him [a horse with a crick in the neck] be ridden.. by such a one as will bear his head, and make him to bring it in. **1610** HEALEY *St. Aug. City of God* 903 The hand of God bearing a raine upon our condemned soules.

†**19.** *trans.* To uphold (any one in a course of action). *refl.* and *intr.* To exalt or lift up oneself *upon*, to plume oneself, presume. *Obs.*

c **1400** *Apol. Loll.* 64 Maynteynd, & born vp in iuel. **1535** SHAXTON in Strype *Eccl. Mem.* I. II App. lxi. 150 If yee.. bear the Abbot in his evil dealing that he may escape.. see yee thereto. **1565** JEWEL *Def. Apol.* (1611) 227 The truth will be able euermore to beare it selfe. **1603** KNOLLES *Hist. Turkes* (1621) 894 The Spaniards bearing themselves upon their wealth, were too proud. **1635** NAUNTON *Fragm. Reg.* (1870) 17 The Gentleman bearing high on my Lords favor. **1697** POTTER *Antiq. Greece* III. vii. (1715) 67 Families.. bearing themselves much higher on their Original.

20. To sustain, keep up, or keep going (the burden or bass of a song). *arch.*

c **1386** CHAUCER *Prol.* 673 This somnour bar to him a stiff burdoun. **1611** COTGR., *Faire le contre*.. to beare a burden, or sing the plain song wheron another descants. *a* **1656** BP. HALL *Soliloquies* 68 Who hath heard.. the bittern bearing her base in the coldest months? **1813** SCOTT *Rokeby* v. vii, A manly voice.. Bare burthen to the music well.

21. *to bear up*: **a.** (*trans.*) to uphold (a principle); to keep up the spirits of (a person).

1606 BRYSKETT *Civ. Life* 20 Persons to assist my accuser, and beare vp his cause. **1658** (25 Jan.) CROMWELL *Sp.* (Carl.), To bear up our honour at sea. **1852** *Hammers & Ploughshares* iv. 27 What hope have you to bear you up?

†**b.** *refl.* To exalt oneself; cf. 19. *Obs.*

a **1520** *Myrr. Our Ladye* 188 Thou ouercomest them that bere vp themselfe.

c. *intr.* (for *refl.*) To keep up one's courage or spirits; to maintain one's ground (*against* difficulties); not to succumb.

1656 MORE *Antid. Ath.* I. ix. (1712) 26 Bearing up as well as they can. **1668** CHILD *Disc. Trade* (1698) 219 The Portuguese, except they alter their politicks.. can never bear up with us, much less prejudice our Plantations. **1711** ADDISON *Spect.* No. 256 ¶8 To bear up under Scandal and Defamation. **1796** BURKE *Regic. Peace* Wks. 1842 II. 291 Bearing up against those vicissitudes of fortune. **1850** MRS. STOWE *Uncle Tom's C.* iii. 15 'Bear up, now, and good bye; for I'm going.'

*** *To hold up, hold, have upon it.*

22. To uphold, hold up, hold on top or aloft.

c **1380** *Sir Ferumb.* 369 þe nayles three, þat paynede crist wan he was born on þe rode Tree. **1398** TREVISA *Barth De P.R.* XI. i. (1495) 381 Ayre.. beryth the fyre and is boren of the water. **1850** MRS. STOWE *Uncle Tom's C.* xxvii. 252 Eva's little table.. bore on it her favourite vase, with a single white moss rose-bud in it.

23. a. To have written or inscribed upon it. Phr. *to bear date*: to be dated (as specified).

1440, etc. [in *M.E.D.* s.v. *date* n. (2) 2 (a)]. **1446** in *Trevelyan Papers* (1857) 27 Your letters.. beryng date at Westm the xx day of Juyl the xxv yere of your.. regne. **1503-4** *Act 19 Hen. VII*, xxxviii. Preamb., Lettres patentez beryng date at Westminster the xxj day of August. **1660** STANLEY *Hist. Philos.* (1701) 119 A Pillar.. bare this inscription, *Sacred to Diana.* **1712**, **1837** [see DATE *sb.*[2] 1]. **1853** PHILLIPS *Rivers Yorksh.* viii. 195 Coins, bearing the effigy of the Horse. **1864** *Times* 6 Dec., These deeds bear dates from 1573 to about 1660. **1875** *Encycl. Brit.* II. 593/2 Bearing date the 16th April 1871.

b. *passive.* To be entered or registered *in* a list, *on* the books of any establishment, etc.

1758 J. BLAKE *Plan Mar. Syst.* 7 Each man so listed.. shall be borne upon the said ship, in the same class in which he is rated. **1803** NELSON in Nicolas *Disp.* V. 321 A complement of sixty men, including two boys, to be borne on the third class. **1855** MACAULAY *Hist. Eng.* III. 38 Though borne on the English establishment, that regiment.. had been almost exclusively composed of Scotchmen. **1863** COX *Inst. Eng. Govt.* III. viii. 724 All persons borne on the books of Queen's ships in commission.

24. a. *fig.* To have or convey the meaning, to purport (*that*). *arch.*

a **1300** *Cursor M.* 14753 Oure lord hem ȝaf þis vnswere But þei wist not what hit bare. **1589** PUTTENHAM *Eng. Poesie* III. xix. (1811) 167 The Greeks call this figure Anadiplosis, I call him the Redouble as the originall beares. **1663** GERBIER *Counsel* 53 The description of.. the Palace of Solomon bears, that it was made with smooth hard stone. **1746** *Rep. Cond. Sir J. Cope* 116 The Letter bears, that the pretended Prince of Wales came lately on the Coast.

b. To profess, claim, purport (*to be*).

1759 ROBERTSON in H. Campbell *Love-Lett. Mary Q. Scots* (1824) 235 A French translation.. bears to have been printed at Edinburgh by Thomas Waltem, 1572. *a* **1859** L. HUNT *Autobiogr.* iii. (1860) 72 A portrait.. bearing to be the likeness of a certain Erasmus Smith, Esq.

†**25.** *to bear* (a thing) *upon* (one): to allege, charge *upon*, lay to the charge of. [The proper position of this sense is doubtful.]

c **1375** WYCLIF *Antecrist* 133 Crist was.. beten, and skourged, and false borne upon. *c* **1449** PECOCK *Repr.* 363 The seid large endewing Born upon Constantin to be mad to Silvester Pope was neuere doon.

III. *trans.* and *intr.* To push, thrust, press. [This group seems to have arisen in a transference of the sense from *carry* to an action producing the same result (i.e. the moving forward of a body) by a different application of force, that of continuous pressure. This once established, the extension of the idea to pressure of many kinds, both horizontal and vertical, followed. Thus there result senses of *bear* directly contrary to each other, as when a post bears the pressure which is brought to bear upon it, or a man bears up till calamity bears him down.]

* *To push, press.*

26. a. *trans.* To move (a thing) onward by force of pressure; to push, force, drive; cf. 'carry' in same sense.

a **1300** *Cursor M.* 16252 Hu þat þis folk þe beres to þe dede. *c* **1400** *Destr. Troy* IV. 1279 þan pollux.. Bere backeward the batell. *c* **1450** *Merlin* vii. 117 He bar hym ouer the horse croupe. **1652** NEEDHAM tr. *Selden's Mare Cl.* 470 They.. will needs bear all the world before them. **1795** SOUTHEY *Joan of Arc* vi. 397 Borne backward Talbot turns. **1855** MOTLEY *Dutch Rep.* II. ii, (1866) 163 Bearing him off over his horse's tail.

b. *Naut. to bear off.*

1627 CAPT. SMITH *Seaman's Gram.* ix. 44 A ship boord, *beare off* is used to euery thing you would thrust from you.

27. *esp. to bear down*, formerly also *bear over* (whence OVERBORNE): to push to the ground, overwhelm, overthrow, vanquish. Also *fig.*

1398 TREVISA *Barth. De P.R.* IX. xxxi. (1495) 368 Metynge and berynge downe the fende. *c* **1435** *Torr. Portugal* 1171. Hors and man down he bore. **1576** LAMBARDE *Peramb. Kent* (1826) 331 He bare it [a Door] cleane downe before him, and so escaped. **1603** KNOLLES *Hist. Turks* (1621) 132 The Tartars.. bearing downe the world before them. **1633** BP. HALL *Hard Texts* 516 He shall.. beare over and kill those that stood against him. **1680** BURNET *Rochester* (1692) 98 A Doctrine which was born down and persecuted. *a* **1811** LEYDEN *Ld. Soulis*, They bore him down with lances bright. **1840** MACAULAY *Ranke, Ess.* (1854) 550/2 His activity and zeal bore down all opposition.

†**28.** *fig. to bear* (one) *down*: to overthrow in debate; maintain one's point against, insist in opposition to (any one). *Obs.*

1526 TINDALE *Acts* xii. 15 She bare them doune that hit was even so. **1641** MILTON *Prel. Episc.* Wks. (1851) 92 Though hee himselfe.. should beare us downe that there bee three. **1674** N. FAIRFAX *Bulk & Selv.* 87 [He] roundly bears us down, That two such worlds would touch without more ado.

29. a. *intr.* To press (laterally) *on*, to thrust at, to come with force or pressure against. *arch.* Also with *at*, *to* (obs.).

c **1450** *Merlin* vii. 118 Thei bar to hym so harde that Arthur was throwe to the erthe. *Ibid.* viii. 127 And he bar on hym so sore that he threwe the knyght to grounde. **1513** DOUGLAS *Æneis* X. x. 24 The tother.. Buyr at hym mychtely with a lang speyr. **1710** *Lond. Gaz.* No. 4647/3 Two East-India Men.. received Damage by bearing upon one another as they were sailing out of the Harbour.

b. *fig.* To press *hard*(*ly*) or *heav*(*il*)*y* upon, to affect adversely or injuriously. (In mod. use this is prob. often pictured as the downward pressure of a burden: see BEAR)

1699 BENTLEY *Phal.* 272 The next will bear harder upon him. **1713** *Guardian* No. 53 (1756) I. 237, I will not bear hard upon his contrition. **1834** H. MILLER *Scenes & Leg.* xxii. (1857) 322 An open, boisterous winter, that bore heavy on the weak and aged. **1877** TYNDALL in *Daily News* 2 Oct. 2/4 No great mechanical improvement.. is introduced.. that does not bear hardly upon individuals.

30. Transferred to downward pressure, as that of a load: **a.** *trans.* with *down.*

1674 PLAYFORD *Skill Mus.* II. 102 Bearing it [a string of an instrument] hard down with the end of your finger. **1853** FORSTER *Arab. Nts.* (Rtldg.) 327 The branches.. were

almost borne down with the weight of the fruit. **1864** TENNYSON *En. Ard.* 679 The dead weight..bore it down.

b. *intr.* with *down*. Cf. BEARING *vbl. sb.* 8.

1835 TODD *Cycl. Anat.& Phys.* I. 17/2 A woman who 'bears down'..will thus accelerate her delivery.

c. *intr.* with *on*.

1829 SOUTHEY *All for Love* VI. Wks. VII. 186 While she pray'd the load of care Less heavily bore on her heart.

31. *intr.* To exert or transmit mechanical pressure *upon*, *on*, *against* (a point which sustains it); to repose one's weight, to rest *upon*; *also* to press as a spring, to 'thrust' (as an arch against its piers).

1677 MOXON *Mech. Exerc.* (1703) 148 This Post.. bears upon the Floor. **1715** DESAGULIERS *Fires Impr.* 122 Which must bear against the Limbs of the Sector-Pieces. **1854** SCOFFERN in *Orr's Circ. Sc.* Chem. 292 Little collars of leather..bearing against the shoulders of the apparatus.

32. a. To exert a practical effect or influence *on* or *upon*, to tend to affect; to have reference to, relate to, come into practical contact with, touch.

1672 MARVELL *Reh. Transp.* I. 87 Their edge bore alwayes upon J.O. either in broad meanings or in plain terms. **1794** PALEY *Evid.* II. vii. (1817) 187 To point out how the argument bears upon the general question. **1836** *Recoll. House of Lords* viii. 155 His matter..always bears directly on the question before the House. **1869** FREEMAN *Norm. Conq.* (1876) III. xii. 197 How this marriage bears on the history of Maine. **1883** LD. CARLINGFORD in *Echo* 1 Sept. 4/2 A.. collection of artistic objects bearing on industry.

†**b.** To touch *upon*, border close *upon*, lie very near to (in nature or character). *Obs.*

1682 *Lond. Gaz.* No. 1731/4 A..Coat of grey colour'd Cloth bearing upon the blew. **1835** MARRYAT *Jac. Faithf.* xv, He related an accident..which particularly bore upon the marvellous.

33. ***to bring to bear***: to bring into effective operation (*against*, *upon*,etc.); to bring about, to cause to act; to employ, exert. (Cf. also 14.)

1748 RICHARDSON *Clarissa* (1811) VIII. 1 Your cousin.. had with difficulty brought this meeting to bear. **1775** JOHNSON *Lett.* 127 (1788) I. 275, I am still of opinion that we shall bring the Oxford riding-school to bear. **1833** HT. MARTINEAU *Tale Tyne* iii. 64 Whenever legislation is brought to bear directly upon industry. **1853** LYTTON *My Novel* III. iii, Randal now brought his experience and art to bear. **1866** KINGSLEY *Herew.* xxi. 266 Before a bow could be brought to bear. **1871** TYNDALL *Fragm. Sc.* I. vii. 245 No human instrument has been brought to bear upon these stones.

34. Here may also be put the phrases: † ***to bear off***: to resist and cause (a stroke) to rebound, to repel, to ward off, to 'turn' (a shower, etc.). *Obs.* ***to bear in***, pass. ***to be borne in***: to be forced in, impressed with force *upon* (the mind); in which there is also some admixture of notions belonging to I and II.

1542 UDALL *Erasm. Apophth.* 318b, With the sweorde wee laie on, with the bucler wee beare of. **1570** ASCHAM *Scholem.* (1863) 112 A demie bukram cassok..which will neither beare of winde nor wether. **1641** MILTON *Ch. Discip.* I. Wks. (1851) 22 His Helmet, to beare off blowes in battell. **1818** *Q. Rev.* XVIII. 537 It had been born in upon his mind ..that some great man..was to be cut off. **1852** J. H. NEWMAN *Disc. Univ. Educ.* 103 It is borne in upon the many ..as self-evident, that religious men would not thus be jealous.

** *To thrust (through).*

†**35.** *trans.* To thrust, pierce, stab (a person *through* the body, or his body *through*, *with* a spear, etc.) [Cf. the mod. 'to run one through with a rapier' and 'to run a rapier through him.'] Also with other prepositions. *Obs.*

a **1300** *Cursor M.* 7625 Thoru he had his bodi born, If he ne had blenked. *c* **1386** CHAUCER *Knts. T.* 1398 Than pray I the, to morwe with a spere That Arcita me thurgh the herte bere. *c* **1400** *Roland* 689 He brek his sheld, and bar hym to the hert. *c* **1400** *Melayne* 1395 Thurgh the schelde..He was borne with a brande. *c* **1420** *Avow. Arth.* xvi, He bare him inne atte the throte. *c* **1435** *Torr. Portugal* 689 To the hart he baryd hym than. **1470–85** MALORY *Arthur* (1816) II. 440 They met together so furiously, that either bear other through.

*** *To press oneself; move, tend, lie in a given direction.* [An intransitive development of 26.]

36. *intr.* To press, force one's way against resistance; to move with effort, with persistence, or with a distinct bias in some direction. Extended by many advs., as *back*, *away*, *on*, *down*.

1593 SHAKS. *Lucr.* 1417 Here one, being thronged, bears back. **1601** —— *Jul. C.* III. ii. 172 Stand backe; roome, beare backe. **1742** R. BLAIR *Grave* 767 The..bird..claps his.. wings, and bears away. **1754** P. H. *Hiberniad* §2. 14 Let any Stranger..bear away and visit the County of Wicklow. **1810** SCOTT *Lady of L.* II. xvi, Nearer and nearer as they bear. **1842** H. E. MANNING *Serm.* xviii. (1848) I. 272 The stream of this visible world, which bears down in a heavy tide away from God. **1862** TYNDALL *Mountaineer* vi. 47 The queenly orb..clears the mountain, and bears splendidly away. **1872** JENKINSON *Guide Lakes* (1879) 226 On arriving at the top of the crag, bear a little to the right.

37. a. *esp.* in *Nautical* phraseology: To sail in a certain direction; hence, ***to bear away***: to sail away, leave. ***to bear down*** (***upon*** or ***towards***): to sail with the wind (towards). ***to bear off*** : see quot. ***to bear up***: to put the helm 'up' so as to bring the vessel into the direction of the wind. ***to bear up for***, or ***bear with*** (a place): to sail towards.

1605 SHAKS. *Temp.* III. ii. 3 Beare vp, & boord em'. **1611** BIBLE *Acts* xxvii. 15 The ship..could not beare vp into [*Geneva* make way against] the winde. **1627** CAPT. SMITH *Seaman's Gram.* ix. 44 When a ship sailes with a large wind towards the land..we say she beares in with the land..And when she would not come neere the land, but goeth more Roome-way than her course, wee say she beares off. *c* **1630** RISDON *Surv. Devon* §210 (1810) 218 A mark to sailors, who bear with Plymouth haven. **1699** BENTLEY *Phal.* 328 She must not make to the next safe Harbour; but..bear away for the remotest. **1709** *Lond. Gaz.* No. 4521/2 We all bore down to secure what Merchant ships we could. **1712** STEELE *Spect.* No. 428 ¶1 People tost in a troubled Sea, without knowing to what Shore they bear. **1748** ANSON *Voy.* II. xi. 256 We bore down to them, and took them up. **1772–84** COOK *Voy.* (1790) V. 1820 We passed the rocks, and bore up to the southward. **1793** SMEATON *Edystone L.* §98 The wind being now fair for that port, we bore away for it. **1798** *Jrnl.* in Nicolas *Nelson's Disp.* III. 48 Nelson immediately bore up under all sail, for Alexandria. **1812** J. WILSON *Isle of Palms* I. 397 Onwards with the favouring gale..Th' impatient Vessel bore. **1854** H. MILLER *Sch. & Schm.* (1858) 12 They bore out to sea. **1865** PARKMAN *Champlain* i. (1875) 182 The voyagers..bore away for France.

b. *Naut.* and *gen.* ***to bear down upon***: to proceed (esp. with force) towards.

1716 *Lond. Gaz.* No. 5455/3 Our Fleet..bore down upon them..keeping the Wind of them. **1867** BAKER *Nile Tribut.* xiii. 328 A tremendous crashing in the jungle..and continued shouts..assured us that they were bearing down exactly upon our direction. **1878** BOSW. SMITH *Carthage* 15 Both consuls bore down on the left wing of the enemy.

38. To extend or stretch away, to continue to lie in a particular direction, as a coast line, a mountain range, etc.

1601 HOLLAND *Pliny* I. 56 Such an obliquitie and winding might seem to decline and beare out too much vnto one side. *Ibid.* I. 73 From whence proceedeth and beareth forth the necke or cape of Peloponnesus. **1883** *Harper's Mag.* Nov. 822/1 The Battenkill bears southward for twenty miles.

39. Chiefly *Naut.*: To lie off in a certain direction from a given point or place. (Cf. BEARING.)

1594 BLUNDEVIL *Exerc.* VII. xxiv. 682 The Ship-master knowing..how the port..beareth from the place from which he departeth. **1596** SHAKS. *Tam. Shr.* V. i. 10 This is Lucentios house, My fathers beares more toward the market-place. **1668** SMITH *Voy.* in *Misc. Cur.* (1708) III. 59 Then shewed him how Constantinople beared from Candia. **1765** TUCKER *Lt. Nat.* II. 388 You must bring such a hill to bear directly over such a point of the shore. **1835** SIR J. ROSS *N.-W. Pass.* vi. 88 Possession Bay bore due west.

40. a. Of cannon: To lie so as to 'cover,' or be in position for discharging shot effectively (*upon*).

1692 in *Capt. Smith's Seaman's Gram.* I. xvi. 75 *A piece of Ordnance doth come to bear*, that is, lies right with the Mark. **1711** BOURN in *Lond. Gaz.* No. 4906/2, I could not bring a Broadside to bear. *a* **1804** NELSON in Nicolas *Disp.* II. 14 Our after-guns ceased to bear. **1865** CARLYLE *Fredk. Gt.* VIII. XIX. vii. 230 Finck had no artillery to bear on Daun's transit through the Pass.

b. (*casual*). To direct a shot or missile.

1799 G. SMITH *Laboratory* I. 28 You must bear the first fired rocket above the rest.

41. *Painting.* Of colours: ***to bear out***: to 'come out' effectively or with some effect. Cf. *to bring out*, and *to be brought out*. (*rare*.)

1855 J. EDWARDS *Oil Paint.* 28 The colours of pigments 'bear out' with effects differing according to the liquids with which they are combined.

IV. To bring forth, produce, give birth to.

42. To bring forth, produce, yield: **a.** said of plants bearing leaves, flowers, fruit. Also *fig.*

a **1000** *Cædmon's Gen.* 479 (Gr.) Déaþes béam se bær bitres fela. *c* **1000** *Ags. Gosp.* Matt. vii. 17 Ælc gód treow byrð gode wæstmas. **1297** R. GLOUC. 352 To blowe, & suþþe to bere frut. **1398** TREVISA *Barth. De P.R.* XVII. lxi, Trees that beere well fruyte. *c* **1400** *Rom. Rose* 3128 Pulled..Fro the roser that it bere. **1567** DRANT *Horace's Epist.* vii. D iij, Whilst sommer swage, and the figge tree her pryme frute haue Ibore. **1607** SHAKS. *Timon* IV. iii. 422 The Oakes beare Mast, the Briars Scarlet Heps. **1725** BRADLEY *Fam. Dict.* s.v. *Low-worm*, That Turmentle which bears a yellow flower. **1879** MACLEAR *Celts* v. 70 The good seed..sown in early years now bore fruit.

b. said of earth, yielding vegetable productions, and *fig.* animals, gems, metals, etc.

1154 *O.E. Chron.* (Laud MS.) an. 1137 þe erthe ne bær nan corn. **1697** DRYDEN *Virg. Georg.* I. 85 India, black Ebon and white Ivory bears. —— *Eclog.* IV. 29 The sacred ground Shall Weeds..refuse to bear. **1704** ADDISON *Italy* 1 The most uncultivated of 'em bear abundance of sweet Plants.

c. *absol.*

1398 TREVISA *Barth. De P.R.* XVII. lxxxiv. (1495) 654 The lasse Juniperus berith more frute than the more, but eyther beeryth. *c* **1400** *Destr. Troy* II. 412 Bowes for to beire in the bare winttur..she made. *Mod.* A variety of apple that bears well. When does a mulberry tree begin to bear?

43. a. Of female mammalia, and esp. women: To bring forth, produce, give birth to (offspring).

971 *Blickl. Hom.* 13 Heo þone eaþmodon cyning bær. *c* **1200** *Trin. Coll. Hom.* 257 þu bere þine helere. *c* **1250** *Gen. & Ex.* 722 Sarray non childre ne bar. *a* **1300** *Cursor M.* 1051 þe formast barn þat sco him bare. *Ibid.* 11211 Mary beere childe in chastite. *c* **1440** HYLTON *Scala Perf.* (W. de W. 1494) I. xci, My dere chyldern whyche I bere as a woman bereth her chylde. **1559** *Myrr. Mag.*, *Dk. York* xi, Fower goodly boyes in youth my wife she boore. **1611** BIBLE *Lev.* xii. 5 If she beare a maid child. **1855** KINGSLEY *Heroes* I. (1868) 2 Your daughter Danae shall bear a son.

b. *absol.*

1382 WYCLIF *Isa.* liv. 1 Preise, thou bareyne that berst not. **1596** SHAKS. *Tam. Shr.* II. i. 201 Women are made to beare, and so are you. **1611** BIBLE *Gen.* xxx. 9 She had left bearing.

44. The various forms of the pa. pple. had formerly no distinction of sense. In the earlier part of the 17th c., these were *borne* (usual), *born*, *bore* (rare). About 1660, *borne* (the only spelling in Shaksp. folio of 1623) was generally abandoned, and *born* (cf. *torn*, *worn*) retained in all senses, with *bore* as a frequent variant (the latter perhaps not in sense of *nātus*). Dr. Johnson, in his various edd. from 1751 to 1773, says under BEAR, 'part. pass. *bore* or *born*,' and the same is found in other dicts. and grammars of the period. But *c* 1775, a different usage (which some writers or printers had observed as early as 1750) was established: *bore* (common in Addison, Swift, Thomson) was abandoned, *borne* was reinstated, and now used as the ordinary form, and *born* was restricted to a specific sense. Thus, *borne* is now the only pa. pple., active or passive, in senses 1–42 (he has *borne* a burden, the tree has *borne* fruit, the testimony *borne* by him); it is also used in sense 43 in the active always, and in the passive with *by* and name of the mother, that is when it has the literal sense of 'brought forth.' *Born* is used only in sense 43, and there only in the passive, when not followed by *by* and the mother; it has rather a neuter signification = 'come into existence, sprung' without explicit reference to maternal action; hence it is the form used adjectively, and figuratively. Cf. 'She had *borne* several children, the children *borne* to him by this woman, *born* of the Virgin Mary, *born* in a stable, her first-*born* son, a lady *born*, new-*born* zeal, a flower *born* to blush unseen.'

a. In senses 1–42, the following forms appear incidentally under the quotations.

Before **1660**: *boren*, 1380, 1398; *bore*, 1300, 1482, 1567; *born*, 1300, 1375, 1380, 1382, 1400, 1449, 1611; *borne*, 1400, 1439, 1528, 1539, 1586, 1593, 1596, 1611, 1625, 1631.

After **1660**: *born*, 1667, 1674, 1680, 1704, 1740, 1769, 1818 (34); *bore*, 1712, 1751, 1768; *borne*, 1758, 1788, 1793, 1795, 1802, 1803, 1816, 1849, and twenty later.

b. In sense 43; before 1660:

a. *a* **1067** *Chart. Eadw.* in *Cod. Dipl.* IV. 215 Ðat cotlif ðe ic was boren inne bi naman Giðslepe. *c* **1230** *Ancr. R.* 158 Al were he..of barain iboren. *c* **1250** *Gen. & Ex.* 1707 Of rachel iosep was boren. **1297** R. GLOUC. 516 Thei he were a bast ibore. *a* **1300** *Cursor M.* 4966 'Allas!'..þat euer we ware Born. *Ibid.* 10977 Tillþat he be borin. *c* **1300** *Harrow. Hell* 186 That of me Shulde suche a child ybore be. *Ibid.* 198 David..That bore was of thyn ofspring. *c* **1374** CHAUCER *Troylus* II. 94 Never, sethe tyme that she was bor. **1382** WYCLIF *Isa.* xlvi. 3 That ben born [**1388** borun] of my wombe. *c* **1386** CHAUCER *Sir Thopas* 7 I-bore he was in fer contre. *c* **1425** WYNTOUN *Cron.* II. ix. 62 Or Jesus wes of Mary born. *c* **1425** *MS.* Christ was..of Virgin Marie ebore. **1470** HARDING *Chron.* x. iv, His mother dyed..Anone after as he was of hir bore. **1513** DOUGLAS *Æneis* x. Prol. 41 The Fader of nane generat, creat, ne boyr. **1576** GASCOIGNE *Steele Gl.* (Arb.) 61 O Gentle blouds yborne You were not borne alonely for your selues. **1589** WARNER *Alb. Eng.* v. xxviii. (1597) 138 Full deere they were to me vnborne, at birth, and borne, and now. *a* **1593** H. SMITH *Wks.* (1867) II. 65 Leah having borne to Jacob four sons. **1595** SPENSER *Col. Clout* 839 Long before the world he was ybore. **1596** —— *F.Q.* I. xi. 51 That was both borne and bred In hevenly throne. **1611** BIBLE *Gen.* xxi. 7, I haue borne him a sonne in his old age. **1612** BACON *Death, Ess.* (Arb.) 388 It is as naturall to dye, as to be borne. **1614** J. COOKE *Tu Quoque* in *Dodsl.* (1780) VII. 19 A wench that has been bred and born in an alley.

Since 1660:

β. **1676** HOBBES *Iliad* I. 397, I have born you to Short life. **1695** DRYDEN in Macaulay *Ess.* (1854) II. 581/1 Whom I foresee to better fortune born. **1703** ROWE *Ulyss.* I. i. 231 Wherefore art thou born..Thou Tyrant born to be a Nation's Punishment? **1805** H. TOOKE *Purley* II. (1815) 76 *Born*..formerly written *boren*, and on other occasions now written *borne*. *Born* is, *Borne* into life. **1830** CARLYLE *Misc.* (1857) II. 149 She saw..that she, even she, had born [*sic*] a mighty man. **1855** MILMAN *Lat. Chr.* (1864) II. IV. viii. 397 The porphyry chamber in which Irene had borne him—her firstborn son. **1879** FROUDE *Cæsar* xviii. 299 A child which Julia had borne to Pompey.

b. *fig.* **1774** BURKE *Amer. Tax.* Wks. 1842 II. 432 These distinctions, born of our unhappy contest. **1853** KINGSLEY *Hypatia* Pref. 8 The Roman Empire and the Christian Church, born into the world almost at the same moment. **1866** B. TAYLOR *Palm & Pine* 268 What time the morning-star is born. **1875** H. E. MANNING *Mission H. Ghost* i. 21 Living as if they had never been born again.

Phrase-key. To *b* about, 3 a; *b* across, 1 f; *b* against, 31; *b* arms against, 6 a; *b* at, 29; *b* away, 3 a, 15 b, 36, 37; *b* back, 36; *b* in Backgammon, 1 d; *b* a blow, 3 d; *b* the breech, 6 *b*, bring to *b*, 33; *b* children, 43; *b* company, 3 d; *b* the cost, 12; *b* down, 27, 28, 30, 36; *b* down upon, 37; *b* the face, 3 c; *b* fellowship, 3 d; *b* forth, 3 a; *b* fruit, 42; *b* a hand, 3 d; *b* in, 30, 34, 3 e; *b* hard, 16, 29 b; *b* the heart, 3 c; *b* heavily, 16, 29 b; *b* in upon one, 34; *b* it, 3 f; *b* interest, 7 c; *b* low sail, 3 b; *b* in mind, 2 b; *b* a name, 7 b; *b* off, 3 a, 26 b, 34, (*Naut.*) 37; *b* on, 29, 30 c, 31, 32, 36; *b* oneself, 4; *b* oneself upon, 19; *b* out, 3 a, 15 b, 41; *b* over, 3 a; *b* part in, 12 b; *b* person of, 12 b; *b* = produce, 42–3; *b* record, 2 c; *b* a rein, 18 b; *b* on shield, 6 c; *b* upon spleen, 16; *b* strain, 13; *b* sway or swing, 8; *b* testimony, 2 c; *b* through, 35; *b* to, 29; *b* up, 3 a, 18, 21, (*Naut.*) 37; *b* up for, 37; *b* upon, 23 b, 25, 31–3; *b* with, 17, (*Naut.*) 37; *b* witness, 2 c; *b* young, 43.

bear, obs. form of BIER.

bear (bɛə(r)), *v.*² [f. BEAR *sb.*¹]

intr. To act the part of a 'bear' on the Stock Exchange; to speculate for a fall. *trans.* To produce a fall in the price of (any stocks, shares, or commodities liable to speculation); also, to affect (the market) in this way. *transf.* and *fig.* Hence **'bearing** *vbl. sb.*(in quot. *attrib.*)

a **1842** W. MAGINN *Pict. Grave & Gay* (1859) 286 His stories being..lies..I should have been sorry to have bulled or beared in Spanish on the strength of them. **1848** W. ARMSTRONG *Stocks* 19 This is perhaps the grand theatre for bulling and bearing stocks. **1861** *N.Y. Tribune* 29 Nov. (Bartlett), His Lordship is wholly guiltless of the charge which the 'Herald' in its anxiety to bear the market has brought against him. **1869** *Trans. Ill. Agric. Soc.* VII. 431 The strong influences which were used to 'bear' the hog market. **1881** *Chicago Times* 4 June, If we succeed in bulling silver we shall also succeed in bearing gold to the same extent. **1884** *Pall Mall G.* 8 Mar. 5 Mr. Gladstone's speech on Egypt 'beared' Egyptian Stock yesterday. **1887** *Ibid.* 26 Nov. 12 Bulling and Bearing Men's Lives. **1887** *Century Mag.* XXIII. 500 Even the best regulated thermometer will have its vagaries, and there is no protection against it when it does 'bear' the weather. **1897** *Daily News* 26 Apr. 5/4 'Bearing' influences are encouraged, and those whose interest is in forcing down prices are very active in that direction.

bearability (ˌbɛərəˈbɪlɪtɪ). *rare.* [f. BEARABLE *a.* + -ILITY.] **a.** Ability to support the weight of a person, etc. **b.** The quality or state of being bearable.

1926 J. C. LINCOLN *Big Mogul* ii. 21 A boardwalk, some of its boards in the last stages of bearability. **1958** W. T. O'DEA *Soc. Hist. Lighting* 19 Tallow came in various grades, but even the best was near to the minimum standard of bearability.

bearable (ˈbɛərəb(ə)l), *a.* Also 6 bearabil. [f. BEAR *v.*¹ + -ABLE.] **1.** That may be borne; supportable, endurable, tolerable.

c **1550** CHEKE *Matt.* xxiii. 4 Heui burdens and hardlí bearabil. **1763** MRS. F. BROOKE *Lady Mandeville* (1782) II. 34 The most bearable man I have seen. **1788** *Med. Commun.* II. 253 The least motion was scarce bearable. **1854** J. ABBOTT *Napoleon* I. xi. 203 Life becomes bearable for their sakes.

2. Capable of bearing or supporting a weight; esp. of ice that is safe for skating, etc. *rare.*

1895 *Daily News* 11 Feb. 5/4 The Serpentine being covered with bearable ice.

'bearableness. [f. prec. + -NESS.] Capability of being borne.

1850 CLOUGH *Poems & Pr. Rem.* (1869) I. 167.

'bearably, *adv.* Endurably, tolerably.

1846 In WORCESTER from *Westm. Rev.* **1892** *Black & White* 17 Dec. 710/1 The water was bearably cold. **1909** *Daily Chron.* 23 Jan. 4/4 Five out of every ten Americans.. make you shiver when they open their mouths, three speak more or less bearably.

'bearance (ˈbɛərəns). [f. BEAR *v.* + (Romanic suffix) -ANCE. Cf. *abearance*, *forbearance*.]

1. Endurance, patient suffering. *arch.*

1725 BAILEY *Erasm. Colloq.* 577 Their minds are inured to temperance and bearance. **1877** R. D. BLACKMORE *Erema* I. xvi. 190 'You are not what I thought of you,' I cried, being vexed beyond bearance by such words. **1923** D. H. LAWRENCE *Kangaroo* vi. 133 He was glum, silent, tortured by them all a bit beyond bearance.

2. A bearing (in mechanism).

1834 GALLOWAY *Hist. Steam Eng.* 214 Two circular pieces or valves *k*, one of brass and the other of iron, are placed on the bearance. **1851** *Coal-tr. Terms Northumbld. & Durh.* 49 The part of a..coal-tub frame to which the bearances for the wheels are attached.

bearard, obs. f. BEARHERD.

'bear-baiting, *vbl. sb.* [f. BEAR *sb.*¹] The sport of setting dogs to attack a bear chained to a stake; also *fig.*

?*c* **1475** *Hunt. Hare* 232 Sum seyd it was a beyr-beytyng **1586** J. HOOKER *Girald. Irel.* in *Holinsh.* II. 120/2 It was more like a bearebaiting of disordered persons, than a parlement of wise men. **1601** SHAKS. *Twel. N.* II. v. 9 He haunts Wakes, Faires, and Beare-baitings. **1663** BUTLER *Hud.* I. i. 678 An old way of Recreating, Which learned Butchers call Bear-Baiting. **1849** MACAULAY *Hist. Eng.* I. 161 The Puritan hated bearbaiting, not because it gave pain to the bear, but because it gave pleasure to the spectators.

bearberry (ˈbɛəbɛrɪ). [f. BEAR *sb.*¹ + BERRY.] **a.** A procumbent shrub, *Arctostaphylos uva-ursi* (N.O. *Ericaceæ*), the astringent berries of which are a favourite food of grouse; also *A. alpina* (Black Bearberry). **b.** Sometimes applied to the allied Arbutus. †**c.** (erroneously) = BARBERRY.

1625 BACON *Gardens, Ess.* (Arb.) 562 The Standards to be ..Beare-berries but here and there, because of the Smell of their Blossome. **1759** B. STILLINGFL. in *Misc. Tracts* (1762) 205 The bear-berry..an efficacious astringent. **1859** W. COLEMAN *Woodlands* (1862) 97 Common bearberry..Its fair pink blossoms come out in May or June.

bearbine, -bind (ˈbɛəbaɪn). [f. OE. *bęre* BEAR *sb.*² + *bindan* to bind, from winding round and binding the stalks. In an 11th century list of plants, *berwinde* is the gloss for *umbilicum*. Cf. also OE. *wuduwinde*, *wudubind*. WOODBINE.] A popular name applied to two English species of convolvulus, the Lesser Field Convolvulus, and the large white convolvulus of the hedges; also to a species of Polygonum (*P. Convolvulus*), to which it is most appropriate.

[*c* **1000** in Wülcker *Voc.* 300 *Umbilicum*, berwinde.] **1732** DE FOE, etc. *Tour Gt. Brit.* (1748) III. 242 (D.) Small and soft, not unlike the Roots of Asparagus or of Bearbind. **1755** CROKER *Orl. Fur.* xxv. lxix, Entwining bearbind dont more knots unite. **1830** HOOD *Haunted House* I. xxiv, The bearbine with the lilac interlaced.

'bear-cat. [BEAR *sb.*¹] **1.** The panda or red bear-cat (see PANDA¹).

1889 in *Cent. Dict.* **1901** [see PANDA¹].

2. The binturong.

1895 H. N. RIDLEY *Nat. Sci.* VI. 93 The Bear-cat (*Arctictis binturong*), the 'Bintūrong' or 'Menūrong' of the Malays, is generally obtained in Malacca, and is sometimes kept as a pet. **1910** *Encycl. Brit.* III. 952/1 This animal, also called the bear-cat, is allied to the palm-civets. **1934** *Times Educ. Suppl.* 14 Apr. p. iv/3 The binturong, or 'bear-cat', is a native of South-East Asia.

3. *transf.* An aggressive or forceful person; one of great energy or ability. *U.S. slang.*

1916 *Amer. Mag.* Apr. 77/1 The director said he had 'discovered' a bearcat, and engaged Alec at once. **1920** WODEHOUSE *Coming of Bill* I. i. 17 'Were they healthy?' 'Fit as fiddles.' 'And your grandparents?' 'Perfect bear-cats.' **1932** J. T. FARRELL *Young Lonigan* (1936) vii. 147 George was a bearcat at forging handwriting.

beard (bɪəd), *sb.* Forms: 1–3 beard, (3 bærd, beord, burde), 3–6 berd, (4–6 berde), 5–6 beerd(e, 6 (*Sc.* baird, beird), bearde, 6– beard. [Common Teut.: OE. *beard* (:—earlier *bard, *bærd) = MDu. *baert*, Du. *baard*, OHG., mod.G. *bart*, ON. *barðr retained only in comp. as *Langbarðr* (but cogn. with *barð* neuter, 'brim, edge, beak, prow,' whence sense 11 below):—OTeut. *bardo-z (not known in Gothic); cogn. w. OSlav. *barda* beard. Kinship to L. *barba* is, on phonetic grounds, doubtful. As to identity of OE. and mod. spelling see BEACON.]

1. The hair that grows upon the chin, lips, and adjacent parts of an adult man's face; now usually excluding the moustache, or hair of the upper lip.

c **825** *Vesp. Ps.* cxxxiii. 2 Swe swe smiring in heafde ðæt astaȝ in beard Aarones. **1205** LAY. 10753 Ælcne mon..þe hæfde on his chinne bærd [**1250** beord]. *c* **1230** *Wohunge* in *Cott. Hom.* 279 þen mon him for schendlac i þe beard spitted. *c* **1250** *Gen. & Ex.* 3584 Ðo wiste he wel quilc hauen it don, Sene it was here berdes on. *a* **1300** *K. Alis.* 1164 Swithe mury hit is in halle, When the burdes wawen alle! **1382** WYCLIF *Isa.* xiv. 2 Eche berd [**1388** beerd] shal be shaue. **1387** TREVISA *Higden* Rolls Ser. I. 205 Longobardi.. haueþ þe name of her longe berdes. *c* **1449** PECOCK *Repr.* 120 Men leten her berdis growe withoute schering. *a* **1550** *Christis Kirk Gr.* xix, Bludy berkit wes thair beird. **1589** *Pappe w. Hatchet* D, Let me stroake my beard thrice like a Germin, before I speak a wise word. **1716** LADY M. W. MONTAGU *Lett.* vi. I. 20 A decrepit old man, with a beard down to his knees. **1757** BURKE *Abridgm. Eng. Hist.* Wks. X. 184 The Britons..shaved the beard on the chin, that on the upper lip was suffered to remain. **1834** BYRON *Deform. Transf.* I. i Broad brow, and..curly beard.

b. with qualifying epithet, e.g. ***Cads-beard***, ? Cadiz-beard; ***tile-*** or ***cathedral-beard***, one cut square in the shape of a tile.

1590 SHAKS. *Mids. N.* I. ii. 97 Your purple in graine beard, or your French-crowne colour'd beard. **1598** E. GILPIN *Skial.* (1878) 22 His face, Furr'd with Cads-beard. **1837** CARLYLE *Fr. Rev.* VII. vii. I. 325 Who is this..in red-grizzled locks; nay with long tile-beard? **1860** FAIRHOLT *Costume* 229 The soldier wore the spade beard and the stiletto beard.

c. *transf.* or *fig.*

a **1856** LONGF. *Build. Ship* 274 His [the ocean's] beard of snow Heaves with the heaving of his breast.

d. *allusively*, of age, experience, virility; cf. GREYBEARD.

1591 FLORIO *2nd Fruites* 41 A greater beard than mine might be deceaued. *a* **1700** DRYDEN (J.) Some thin remains of chastity appeared Ev'n under Jove, but Jove without a beard. *a* **1704** LOCKE (J.) Would it not be insufferable for a professor to have..a reverend beard overturned by an upstart novelist?

e. Phrases. † ***in spite of*** or ***maugre any one's beard***: in defiance of or direct opposition to his purpose. ***to one's beard***: to one's face, openly. † ***to be, meet,*** or ***run in any one's beard***: to oppose him openly and resolutely, to BEARD. ***to take by the beard***: to attack resolutely (cf. *1 Sam.* xvii. 35). † ***to make a man's beard***: (*lit.*) to dress his beard, (*fig.*) to outwit or delude him. So † ***to make a man's beard without a razor***: (in later sense) to behead him. † ***to put something against a man's beard***: to taunt him with it.

1330 R. BRUNNE *Chron.* 207 þe cuntre sone he fond in his berd redy ran. *c* **1384** CHAUCER *H. Fame* 689 Moo berdys in two oures Withoute Rasour or Sisoures Y-made, then greyndes be of sondes. *c* **1386** —— *Wyf's Prol.* 361 Yit couthe I make his berd, though queynte he be. **1387** TREVISA *Higden* Rolls Ser. II. 325 A morwe a man of Hebrewe putte þat aȝen Moyses berd. *c* **1450** *Rob. Hood* (Ritson) I. i. 361 Thou art euer in my berde, sayd the abbot. *c* **1500** *Lancelot* 3471 If that we met them scharply in the berd. **1525** LD. BERNERS *Froiss.* I. xxiii. 59 If I get you..I shall delyuer you to Joselyn, that shall make your beerdes without any rasoure. **1555** TRAVES *Let.* in Strype *Eccl. Mem.* III. II. App. xxxiii, Yea mawgre the berdis of al hard harts, God wil at length..delyver thee. **1601** DENT *Pathw. Heaven* 80 Yet at last they must (spight of their beards) end where they began. **1785** COWPER *Task* II. 271 Shamed as we have been, to th' very beard. **1809** W. IRVING *Knickerb.* (1861) 21 A gigantic question..which I must needs take by the beard and utterly subdue.

2. The similar hairy tuft or growth on the lower jaw or adjacent parts of the face of other animals; *e.g.* the goat, lion, ibex, seal.

c **1300** *K. Alis.* 6519 A best..y-cleped Cessus..Berd hit hadde long y-waxe. *a* **1300** *Cursor M.* 7509 A bere a lyon baþ I mette..and shoke ham bi þe berde squa. **1480** CAXTON *Chron. Eng.* ccxi. 194 A gote..that shuld haue hornes of siluer and a berde as white as snowe. **1595** SHAKS. *John* II. i. 138 Whose valour plucks dead Lyons by the beard. **1697** DRYDEN *Virg. Georg.* III. 485 The Pastor shears their hoary Beards. *c* **1840** WOOD *Nat. Hist.* I. 670 A Goat..is easily conquered if his beard can only be grasped.

3. *Zool.* **a.** The appendages to the mouth of some fishes. **b.** The rows of gills in certain bivalves, *e.g.* the Oyster. **c.** The byssus or mass of threads by which certain shell-fish (*e.g.* the *Pinna*) attach themselves to rocks, etc. **d.** (See quot. 1802.) **e.** Two small oblong fleshy bodies situated just above the antlia or spiral sucker of moths and butterflies; the corresponding part in some *Diptera*, e.g. the Gnat.

1753 CHAMBERS *Cycl. Supp.*, *Beard* of a muscle..[also of insects]. **1774** GOLDSM. *Nat. Hist.* (1862) II. IV. vi. 367 These threads which are usually termed the beard of the mussel. **1796** MRS. GLASSE *Cookery* xi. 175 Wash the oysters very clean..and take the beards off. **1802** PALEY *Nat. Theol.* xvi. (1817) 140 The play of the rings in an earth-worm..the beards or prickles, with which the annuli are armed. **1838** DICKENS *O. Twist* (1850) 136/2 'A'n't yer fond of oysters?' ..'Here's one with such a beautiful, delicate beard!'

4. *Ornith.* **a.** The cluster of bristles at the base of the beak in some birds, as the Barbet (*Bucco*). **b.** The vane or soft lateral filaments of a feather.

1802 PALEY *Nat. Theol.* xii. (1817) 106 The separate pieces, or laminæ, of which the beard [of a feather] is composed. **1835** *Penny Cycl.* III. 433/2 [In *Bucco*] *Pogonias* ..the beard is very strong. **1836** TODD *Cycl. Anat. & Phys.* I. 350/1 All feathers are composed of..a vane or beard.

5. Applied as specific name of: The freshwater Shrimp, the Hake, and a kind of pigeon.

1611 COTGR., *Petite crevette de rivière*, the Beard, or fresh-water Shrimpe. *a* **1766** PENNANT *Zool.* (1769) III. 158 The lesser hake..is known on the coast of Cornwall by the name of the greater forked beard. **1867** TEGETMEIER *Pigeons* x. 108 In other parts of Germany they have many clean-footed Tumblers of various colours, as Magpies, Helmets, and Beards; but their Beards have only a white beard and flight-feathers, the rest of the body being dark.

6. *Bot.* The awn of grasses; prickles, bristles, or hair-like tufts found on various plants; also quasi-*fig.* in wider application.

1552 HULOET, Beard or eare of corne, *arista.* **1578** LYTE *Dodoens* 456 Rough with many sharp pointed eares or beardes like the eares of Barley. *c* **1600** SHAKS. *Sonn.* xii, Summers green all girded up in sheaves, Borne on the bier with white and bristly beard. **1732** *Acc. Workhouses* 84 Cut off the beards before the wheat is thresh'd. **1813** SIR H. DAVY *Agric. Chem.* (1814) 364 The seeds..like those of the thistle and dandelion, are furnished with beards or wings. **1839** BAILEY *Festus* vii, Sunshine..catching By its soft brown beard, the moss. **1865** BURRITT *Walk Land's End* 106 English downs..yielding a short, crisp beard of herbage.

b. ***old-man's beard***: popular name of the Traveller's Joy (*Clematis Vitalba*).

1821 CLARE *Vill. Minstr.* I. 84 Dig old man's beard from woodland hedge, To twine a summer shade.

†**7.** Obsolete name for the train or tail of a comet when it appeared to precede the nucleus.

1647 H. MORE *Song Soul* II. App. xciv, But for the newfixt starres there's no pretence, Nor beard nor tail to take occasion by. **1713** SWIFT *Eleg. Partridge* Wks. 1755 III. II. 79 No comet with a flaming beard. **1855** T. MILNER *Gallery of Nat.* 108 When the train preceded the nucleus..it was called the beard.

8. *Farriery.* 'That part of a horse's nether jaw whereon the curbe doth rest.' (Cotgr. s.v. *Barbe.*)

1753 CHAMBERS *Cycl. Supp.*, *Beard*, or *under-beard*, called also *chuck*, of a horse, is that part under the lower mandible or the outside, and above the chin, which bears the curb of the bridle. **1792** OSBALDISTON *Brit. Sportsm.* 49 Beard of a horse, should neither be too high raised, nor too flat, so that the curb may rest in its right place. [In mod. dicts.]

9. a. The barb of an arrow, fish-hook, etc. *Obs.* **b.** Hence, The hook at the end of a knitting-needle in a knitting-machine, which holds the yarn.

1611 MARKHAM *Countr. Content.* I. x. 56 Cut out and raise up the beard, which you shall make..according to the bigness of the hook. **1712** *Phil. Trans.* XXVII. 444 The Beard or Hooks thereof [of the Harping Iron] did penetrate. **1713** DERHAM *Phys. Theol.* IV. xv. 257 The Common Heron hath..a long sharp Bill to strike their Prey..with sharp hooked Beards standing backward, to hold their Prey fast when struck. **1753** HANWAY *Trav.* (1762) I. III. xxxvii. 171 Who wore in their caps the beard of an arrow. **1793** SMEATON *Edystone L.* §42 *note*, Jag or bearded bolts..have a beard raised upon their angles, somewhat like that of a fish-hook.

10. (See quot.)

1871 E. PEACOCK *R. Skirlaugh* II. 166 Cattle, which had at these points to be kept out by a stout 'beard' of thorns stuck in the ground. **1878** HALLIWELL, *Beard-hedge*, the bushes which are stuck into the bank of a new-made hedge, to protect the fresh-planted thorns.

11. In mechanical arts: **a.** in *Ship building*, The angular fore-part of the rudder; the corresponding bevel of the stern-post. **b.** in *Carpentry*, The sharp edge of a board. **c.** in *Organ-building* (see quot.) **d.** A spring-piece at the back of a lock to prevent the parts from rattling.

1691 T. H[ALE] *Acc. New Invent.* 82 To sheath the.. Beard of the Rudder with Lead. **1852** SEIDEL *Organ* 79 Some organ-builders provide the height on both sides with what they call a beard. **1876** HILES *Catech. Organ* iv. (1878) 27 Flue-pipes have also occasionally a beard, which is a cross piece fastened on just below the under-lip.

e. *Printing.* (*a*) That part of the type above and below the face, which allows for ascending and descending letters, and prevents their meeting those in the lines above or below. (*b*) The horizontal bases and tops added to the letters.

1823 J. BADCOCK *Dom. Amusem.* 144 A moveable square of wood, which rises nearly as high as the beard of the letter. **1824** J. JOHNSON *Typogr.* II. 521 He examines if the beards of the letter print at the feet of the pages. **1860** *Bookseller* 26 Oct. 574 [In] the Franklin type.. there are no sharp beards to the letters, and the outline is consequently distinct.

12. 'The coarser parts of a joint of meat. The bad portions of a fleece of wool.' Halliwell.

13. The brim or margin of a vessel. [Directly from ON. *barð*.] *Obs.* or *dial.*, but possibly the origin of some of the prec. specific uses.

1398 TREVISA *Barth. De P.R.* XVII. liii, Þe wyne wol flete oute ouer þe berdes [**1535** brynke]. *c* **1440** *Promp. Parv.* 32 Berde, or brynke of a wesselle, or other like, *margo*

14. *Comb.*, chiefly attrib., as ***beard-brush***, ***-hook***, ***-stubble***; also **beard-grass**, the genus of grasses *Polypogon*; † **beard-grave** *a.*, having the gravity of a bearded face; **beard-moss**, a British lichen (*Usnea barbata*); **beard-tree**, the Hazel.

1630 B. JONSON *New Inn* I. i, He'll tell you what is Latin for a looking-glass, A *beard-brush. **1841** *Withering's Brit. Plants* (Macgillivray) 73 Annual *Beard-grass.. grows in moist pastures. **1599** MARSTON *Sc. Villanie* III. x. 222 Tut, tut, a toy.. Cryes *beard-graue Dromus. **1799** G. SMITH *Laborat.* II. 266 The *Beard Hook, by some anglers is preferred before any other in winter trolling. **1837** CARLYLE *Fr. Rev.* III. v. iii. 268 Plenteous.. *beard-stubble, of a tile-colour.

beard (bɪəd), *v.* Forms: 5 berde, 6 berd, 7 bearde, beard. [f. prec. sb.]

† **1.** *intr.* To become bearded, get a beard. *Obs.* as used of men.

1483 *Cath. Angl.* 28/1 To berde, *puberare*. **1552** HULOET, Berden, or begyn to haue a berd, *pubeo*. **1672** SIR T. BROWNE *Let. Friend* (1881) §11. 135 Lewis, King of Hungary.. was said.. to have bearded at fifteen.

2. a. *trans.* To cut or strip off the beard of (*e.g.* oysters). † **b.** To clip off the defective parts of (a fleece). **c.** To chip or plane away the edge of (timber) to a required shape.

1429 *Act 8 Hen. VI*, xxii, No stranger shall cause to be forced, clacked or bearded any manner of woolles to carry them out of the realm. **1855** *Househ. Cookery, Carving* 104 We think it unnecessary to beard the oyster. **1863** WYNTER *Subtle Brains, etc.* 275 Another machine rebated and bearded the keel. **1867** [see BEARDING 4].

3. To oppose openly and resolutely, with daring or with effrontery; to set at defiance, thwart, affront. Esp. in fig. phr. ***to beard the lion in his den*** or ***lair***. [Partly from the idea of taking a lion by the beard, partly from the use of *beard* as = face; see BEARD *sb.* 1 e.]

1525 *St. Papers Hen. VIII*, VI. 454 If they [Frenchmen] be kept shorte, and berdyd, their stomakkis will soone wax more mylde. **1596** SHAKS. *1 Hen. VI*, IV. i. 12 No man so potent breathes vpon the ground, But I will Beard him. **1682** *Addr. Lancaster* in *Lond. Gaz.* No. 1727/5 A Proceeding that Beards the Regal Power, Outfaces the Law, etc. **1749** SMOLLETT *Regicide* II. vii. (1777) 39 Sooner would'st thou beard The lion in his rage. **1808** [see LION *sb.* 2 a]. **1820** SCOTT *Monast.* xvii, Shall that English silkworm presume to beard me in my father's house? **1882** W. S. GILBERT *Iolanthe* 11, Beard the lion in his lair—None but the brave deserve the fair. **1894** R. D. BLACKMORE *Perlycross* II. iv. 68 Nothing less would satisfy her than to beard—if the metaphor applies to ladies—the lion in the den, the arch-accuser, in the very court of judgment.

4. To furnish with a beard.

[*c* **1380** see BEARDED 4]. **1791** E. DARWIN *Bot. Gard.* I. 33 Beard the bright cylinder with golden wire. **1824** J. JOHNSON *Typogr.* II. iii. 21 Short letters.. all which will admit of being bearded above and below their face.

5. To brush or rub with the beard.

1859 *Autobiog. Beggar Boy* 56 Some of the young men were romping with the girls and bearding their rosy faces.

bearded (ˈbɪədɪd), *ppl. a.* [f. BEARD *sb.* or *v.*]

1. Of man and animals: Having a beard; *spec.* in names of animals, as Bearded Collies, Bearded Eagle, and Bearded Tit, Titmouse, or Pinnock.

1530 PALSGR. 306/1 Berded, *barbu*. **1600** SHAKS. *A.Y.L.* II. vii. 150 A Soldier, Full of strange oaths, and bearded like the Pard. **1802** BINGLEY *Anim. Biog.* (1813) II. 39 The Bearded Eagle, or Lammer-Geyer. **1868** MISS BRADDON *Run to Earth* I. i. 9 Black-bearded, foreign-looking seamen. **1879** BROWNING *Ivan Ivanov.* 39 Each bearded mouth. **1880** H. DALZIEL *Brit. Dogs* II. i. 208 In the west of Scotland there is a rough-faced and very shaggy-coated dog called the bearded colley, differing mainly from the true colley in being rough-faced, rather heavier built, altogether less elegant, and with a shaggier and harsher coat. **1928** F. T. BARTON *Kennel Encycl.* 91 *The Bearded Collie.*—In certain parts of Scotland there is a type of sheep-dog or collie which has a beard, or profusion of hair on the muzzle.

2. Of plants, seeds, etc.: Furnished with bristles or hairy tufts, awned; as in ***bearded wheat***.

1578 LYTE *Dodoens* 461 His long bearded eares doth much resemble Barley. **1667** MILTON *P.L.* IV. 983 Her bearded Grove of ears. **1772–84** COOK *Voy.* (1790) I. 196 The ground being covered with grass, the seeds of which were sharp and bearded. **1842** TENNYSON *L. of Shalott* I. iv, Only reapers, reaping early, In among the bearded barley.

3. *transf.* in gen. sense: Covered with beard-like tufts or appendages.

1847 LONGF. *Evang.* Prel. 2 The hemlocks, Bearded with moss. **1870** TYNDALL *Heat* ii. §29. 33 The pipe from which the air issued became bearded with icicles.

4. Of a comet, meteor, etc.: Having a train or tail; cf. BEARD *sb.* 7. *arch.* or *poet.*

c **1380** WYCLIF *De Pseudo-freris* v. Wks. (1880) 308 þe sterre herid or beerdid erriþ fro heuene in his mouyng and bitokeneþ pestilence. *a* **1638** RANDOLPH *Muses' Look.-Gl.* II. ii. (1640) 22 Let fooles gaze At bearded starres. **1783** W. F. MARTYN *Geog. Mag.* I. Introd. 21 Comets.. are vulgarly distinguished into three kinds, bearded, tailed, and hairy. **1842** TENNYSON *L. of Shalott* III. iii, Some bearded meteor, trailing light Moves over still Shalott.

5. a. Barbed or jagged like an arrow or fish-hook.

1613 M. RIDLEY *Magn. Bodies* 28 The bearded end of the [compass] needle doth onely offer itself. **1659** GAUDEN *Tears Ch.* 105 Reputation is the bearded hook, which holds most men faster than conscience. **1753** DOUGLASS *Brit. Settl. N. Amer.* 262 The best Iron Bars break fibrous and bearded. **1793**[see BEARD *sb.* 9]. **1813** H. & J. SMITH *Rej. Addr.* 48 Rest there awhile, my bearded lance.

b. Of type: Furnished with a BEARD *sb.* 11 e.

beardedness (ˈbɪədɪdnɪs). [f. BEARDED *ppl. a.* + -NESS.] Bearded condition.

1888 *Times* 18 Aug. 9/1 The beardedness of the chief. **1917** W. J. LOCKE *Red Planet* xii, Their composite paunchiness, beardedness, scragginess,.. impressed me unfavourably.

bearder (ˈbɪədə(r)). [f. BEARD *v.* + -ER[1].] One who beards.

1605 CAMDEN *Rem.* (1657) 41 To air, to beard.. and their derivations, ayring, ayred, bearder, bearding, bearded.

beardie (ˈbɪədɪ). Also **beardy**. [f. BEARD *sb.* + -IE = -Y[4].] **1. a.** Also **beardie-loach**. A name given, chiefly in Scotland, to a small fish, the Loach (*Cobitis barbatula*), from the 'beards' or bristles on its gills.

1828 *Blackw. Mag.* Sept. 274 In mute.. hope of some time or other catching a minnow or beardie. **1859** YARRELL *Brit. Fishes* (ed. 3) I. 448 The habits of the Beardie in confinement.

b. The bearded collie. Cf. BEARDED *ppl. a.* 1.

1907 R. LEIGHTON et al. *New Bk. Dog* 102/2 Peeblesshire is regarded as the true home of the Beardie. **1931** A. CROXTON SMITH *About our Dogs* xviii. 269 The hero of Alfred Ollivant's 'Owd Bob' is said to have been a 'beardie'. **1945** BAKER *Austral. Lang.* iii. 73 The *beardy* or *bearded collie* is a type of sheep dog with long hair that resembles the hair of a Skye terrier.

2. a. (A nickname for) a bearded man. *colloq.* Also as *adj.*: bearded.

[**1808** SCOTT in Lockhart *Life* (1837) I. i. 3 My father's grandfather was Walter Scott, well known in Tiviotdale by the surname of *Beardie*... *Beardie*.. derived his cognomen from a venerable beard, which he wore unblemished by razor or scissors.] **1941** BAKER *Dict. Austral. Slang* 9 *Beardy*, a person with a beard or with long hair. **1959** I. & P. OPIE *Lore & Lang. Schoolchildren* iii. 54 Someone with a beard has 'Beardie!' or 'Fungus face!' shouted after him. **1960** *Spectator* 22 Apr. 569 There were more than forty thousand of us—weirdies and beardies, colonels and conchies, Communists and Liberals. **1961** *Observer* 28 May 1/5 The beardy weirdies with their querulous bleatings.

b. A local Australian nickname applied to a body of Southcotians, followers of John Wroe, who called themselves Christian Israelites.

1875 *Melbourne Spectator* 21 Aug. 190/1 The Beardies or Christian Israelites of Ballarat. **1905** *Daily Chron.* 8 Mar. 4/7 There is only one founder of a religion buried in Australia—John Wroe, who started the 'Christian Israelites', nicknamed the 'Beardies', since they never cut their hair. **1961** W. H. G. ARMYTAGE *Heavens Below* III. viii. 275[John] Wroe.. let his beard grow (his followers were known as the beardies).

ˈbearding, *vbl. sb.* [f. BEARD *v.* + -ING[1].]

† **1.** The action of cutting off the beard, *e.g.* the inferior parts of a fleece. Cf. BEARD *v.* 2. *Obs.*

1483 *Act 1 Rich. III*, viii. §4 That the same Wolle be as it is shorn.. without any sortyng, berdyng, clakkyng.

2. Open, resolute opposition; insolent defiance.

1577 HOLINSHED *Chron.* II. 36/2 Leaue lieng for varlets, berding for ruffians, facing for crakers. **1864** *Linnet's Trial* I. III. i. 310 Would you do the bearding for us?

3. Beard-like growth; also *transf.*

1607 TOPSELL *Four-f. Beasts* 9 They have.. bearding about the lips like a Dragon. **1865** CARLYLE *Fredk. Gt.* IV. XII. x. 219 A Plain of silent snow, with sparse bearding of bushes.

4. *Shipbuilding* and *Carpentry*. The bevelling of a piece of timber or plank to any required angle; *concr.* = BEARD *sb.* 11 a; also *attrib.*, as in ***bearding-line***.

1833 RICHARDSON *Merc. Mar. Arch.* 26 Cutting down and bearding lines are not introduced. *c* **1850** *Rudim. Nav.* (Weale) 144 The bearding-piece, which forms the fore-part [of the rudder] is of elm. **1867** SMYTH *Sailor's Wd.-bk.*, *Bearding line*, a curved line made by bearding the dead-wood to the shape of the ship's body.

beardless (ˈbɪədlɪs), *a.* [f. BEARD *sb.* + -LESS.] Having no beard; hence *fig.* youthful, immature.

c **1325** *E.E. Allit. P.* B. 789 Bolde burnez wer þay boþe with berdles chynnez. **1480** CAXTON *Trevisa's Descr. Brit.* 50 Ther come xv. yong berdles men clothed like wymmen. **1595** SHAKS. *John* v. i. 69 Shall a beardlesse boy, A cockred-silken wanton, braue our fields? **1621** QUARLES *Esther* (1638) 112 Rash, and beardlesse Counsell. **1712** *Spect.* No. 527 ¶2 A beardless stripling. **1825** SYD. SMITH *Wks.* 1867 II. 72 Is beardless youth to show no respect for the decisions of mature age?

b. *Bot.* Without beard or awn.

1861 MISS PRATT *Flower. Pl.* VI. 127 Common Rye-grass, Red Darnel, or Beardless Darnel. **1870** HOOKER *Stud. Flora* 97 Milk-vetch, style filiform, beardless.

ˈbeardlessness. [f. prec. + -NESS.] Beardless condition; absence of beard.

1861 G. MOORE *Lost Tribes* 137 Baldness and beardlessness were signs of mourning among the Hebrews. **1880** MISS BIRD *Japan* I. 55 The beardlessness of the ordinary Japanese.

ˈbeardlet. A tiny beard or awn, like that of some grasses. Also, a small beard on a man's face. Hence **ˈbeardleted**.

1909 in *Cent. Dict.* Suppl. **1928** *Daily Express* 21 July 15/2 The beardlet adorning the under-lip of Lord Bertie of Thame. **1930** H. BELLOC *Richelieu* v. 73 The military moustache and beardlet of that pointed face.

† **ˈbeardling.** *Obs.* [f. BEARD *sb.* + -LING.] One who wears a beard; a layman.

1622 MABBE *Aleman's Guzman d'Alf.* II. 261 Leauing out neither beardling nor shaueling, high nor low.

beardom (ˈbɛədəm). [f. BEAR *sb.*[1] + -DOM.] Bearish quality or personality.

1842 MRS. BROWNING *Grk. Chr. Poets* 191 Johnson was Dryden's critical bear, a rough bear, and with points of noble beardom.

beardy (ˈbɪədɪ), *a.* [f. BEARD + -Y[1].] Bearded.

1598 SYLVESTER *Du Bartas* I. iii. (1641) 26/2 Beard-less Apollo's beardy son. **1855** CARLYLE *Prinzenraub* 102 George the Rich, called also the *Barbatus*, Beardy.

beare, obs. f. BEER, BERE, BIER and BIRR.

bearer (ˈbɛərə(r)). Forms; 4 berere, 4–6 -er, 5 -are, -our, berrer, 5–6 berar, 6 bearor, 6– bearer. [f. BEAR *v.*[1] + -ER[1].]

I. He who or that which carries or brings.

1. One who carries or conveys; a carrier, a porter. **a.** *generally.*

1382 WYCLIF *Isa.* xlvi. 2 Oure chargis with heuy berthene .. to-brosyd ben.. thei myȝten not sauen the berere. **1483** *Cath. Angl.* 29 A berer, *baiulus*. **1547** *Act 1 Edw. VI*, iii. §9 The.. nurse, or other the bearer about of the childe. **1611** BIBLE *2 Chron.* ii. 18 To be bearers of burdens. **1727** SWIFT *Gulliver* II. iv. 131 To crowd about the sedan.. to make the bearers stop. **1870** MORRIS *Earthly Par.* III. IV. 239 Fleeces .. In their own bearer's blood were dyed. **1870** NICHOLSON *Zool.* (1880) 235 The scolex [a tapeworm] apparently leads an independent life in water, and its intermediary bearer (supposed by some to be a fish..) is at present unknown.

b. of a non-material burden.

c **1425** WYNTOUN *Cron.* VIII. x. 94 He wes chosyn þare Of þis charge to be berare. **1483** *Cath. Angl.* 29 A berer of wytnes, *testis*. **1526** *Pilgr. Perf.* (W. de W. 1531) 67 b, Lucifer, that is to say, the lyght berer.

c. One who helps to carry a corpse to the grave, or who holds the pall in a funeral procession.

1633 P. FLETCHER *Elisa* II. xli, Six mournfull bearers, the sad hearse attending. **1789** MRS. PIOZZI *Journ. France* II. 291 A burial.. not one.. bearer being dressed in black. **1859** CAPERN *Ball. & Songs* 179 The tramp of the bearers and horses Beats out the death-march on the air.

d. In India: (*a*) A palanquin carrier; (*b*) A domestic servant who has charge of his master's clothes, furniture, and (often) his ready money. [Wilson conjectured this latter name to be a corruption of Bengali *behārā*; but the domestic 'bearer' was simply the headman of a set of palanquin bearers when the latter were universally used.]

1766 J. GROSE *Voy. E. Ind.* I. 153 (Y.) The poles which.. are carried by six, but most commonly by four bearers. **1811** MRS. SHERWOOD *Henry & Bearer* 3 A bearer, who.. had taken care of Henry from the day that he was born. *Note.* A servant, whose work is to carry a palanquin; but who is frequently employed to take care of children. *c* **1813** —— *Ayah & Lady* vii. 39 The bearers had nothing to do but to carry their Lady to church. **1880** G. A. MACKAY *21 Days in Ind.* (1882) 92 The Ayah and Bearer sit with Baby in the verandah.

e. In comb. with various sbs., as ***cup-***, ***palanquin-***, ***pall-***, ***shield-***, ***standard-bearer***.

c **1500** *Cocke Lorelles B.* 10 Tankarde berers.. and spere planers. **1611** BIBLE *Nehem.* i. 11 For I was the kings cup-bearer [COVERDALE, butler]. **1824** MACAULAY *Ivry*, And should my standard-bearer fall, as fall full well he may. **1832** MARRYAT *N. Forster* xxxviii, A double set of palanquin-bearers. **1862** F. GRIFFITHS *Artill. Man.* (ed. 9) 40 Pall-bearers on each side of the corpse.

f. ***bearer company***, ***corps***, a medical division for military field service.

1878 (*title*) Stretcher-Bearers and Bearer-Companies. Manual of Exercises for, Horse Guards. **1899** *Daily News* 27 Nov. 5/3 More assistance will be necessary, both in skilled attention to wounded, and in carrying them from the field. This is provided for by 'bearer companies'. **1901** *Empire Rev.* I. 432 The work of the bearer company is intermittent, having to collect the sick and wounded after a fight, and to bring them to the field hospital. **1902** *Encycl. Brit.* XXV. 352/1 The bearer company.. is composed of three officers, thirteen non-commissioned officers, and forty-eight privates of the Royal Army Medical Corps, with a detachment of the Army Service Corps for transport duties. **1909** WEBSTER, Bearer corps.

2. One who brings a letter, a verbal message, tidings, rumours, etc.

a **1300** *Cursor M.* 3226 Apon his kne he did him suere þat he suld be lel errand berer. **1462** J. PASTON in *Lett.* 442 II. 92 The berour here of can enfourme you. **1566** KNOX *Hist. Ref.* Wks. 1846 I. 268 The rest of our myndis this faythfull berare will schaw you at lenth. **1695** PEPYS *Diary* VI. 182 In behalf of this young man, the bearer. **1850** MRS. STOWE *Uncle Tom's C.* xxix. 271 An order.. to give the bearer fifteen lashes. **1855** MACAULAY *Hist. Eng.* III. 589 Others.. trafficked in the secrets of which they were the bearers.

3. a. The actual holder or presenter of a cheque, draft, or other order to pay money.

1683 *Lond. Gaz.* No. 1862/8 A Note.. for Ninety nine Pounds.. paid to Edward Callender or Bearer. **1809** R. LANGFORD *Introd. Trade* 12 A Promissory Note payable to *Bearer*, need not be endorsed. **1832** MARRYAT *N. Forster* xxix, Fill up a cheque for five hundred pounds, self or bearer.

b. ***bearer security***, an unregistered security the title to which is vested in its possessor and is transferred by simple delivery. So ***bearer bond, stock, warrant***.

1897 *Westm. Gaz.* 5 Aug. 6/3 These bearer-warrants are, we venture to imagine, part of the £140,000 in fully-paid shares. **1906** *Ibid.* 12 July 9/2 All kinds of bearer securities. **1911** *Encycl. Brit.* XXV. 933/2 It has been found necessary to convert a part of the stocks into bearer bonds or shares. **1964** *Financial Times* 10 Feb. 10/7 Holders of Bearer Stock, to obtain this dividend, must deposit Coupon No. 251.

4. *Her.* One who bears heraldic arms.

¶ The sense of 'supporters,' copied in mod. dictionaries from Johnson, (who inserted it from BAILEY's folio of 1731), is apparently only a traditional dictionary error: see quot. 1885.

1610 GWILLIM *Heraldry* §3 x. (1660) 144. **1787** PORNY *Heraldry* 19 *note*, Such [tinctures] as should be used for marks of disgrace in the Bearers. **1885** G. E. COCKAYNE (Norroy King of Arms) in *letter*: We never use the word 'bearers' for 'supporters': the 'bearers' of the arms of Howard are the Duke of Norfolk, Earl of Carlisle, etc., themselves, not the supporters used by these noblemen.

5. The possessor of any personal endowment or quality; the holder of rank or office; hence ***office-bearer***, etc.

1597 SHAKS. *2 Hen. IV*, IV. v. 29 O Maiestie! When thou do'st pinch thy Bearer. **1606** —— *Tr. & Cr.* III. iii. 104 The beautie that is borne here in the face, The bearer knowes not. **1818** SCOTT *Hrt. Midl.* xvi, 'That's speaking to the purpose'.. said the office-bearer.

6. That in, or by means of, which anything is carried; *e.g.* a bier.

1847 HALLIWELL *s.v.*, In Kent the bier is sometimes called a bearer. **1862** F. GRIFFITHS *Artill. Man.* (ed. 9) 116 Nos. 8 and 9 bring up hot shot on a bearer. **1883** *Daily News* 27 July 2/1 For carrying this.. bearer poles of very ingenious design have been devised.

II. He who or that which supports or sustains.

†7. One who supports or sustains a weight, or who holds up what would fall; an upholder. *Obs.*

1483 CAXTON *Gold. Leg.*, A susteynour and a berar up of the church. **1555** BP. FERRAR in Strype *Eccl. Mem.* III. II. App. xlvii, The bolsterors and bearors of the promoters. **1655** FULLER *Ch. Hist.* v. 333, Many have reported, that I have been a bearer of such as have maintained evil opinions.

†8. One who sustains or joins in sustaining a charge or responsibility. *Obs.*

1641 BEST *Farm. Bks.* (1856) 89 The richest and ablest men in everie towne are.. subsidymen, and the poorer.. onely bearers with them. *a* **1663** SANDERSON *Wks.* (1854) I. 185 (D.) As men use to do in common payments and taxes, we plead hard to have bearers and partners that may go a share with us. *a* **1737** STRYPE *Eccl. Mem.* I. I. xxviii. 202 A bearer with them.. in printing of their books.

9. a. *Mechanics.* Anything used as a support or stay.

1677 MOXON *Mech. Exerc.* (1703) 157 Bearer, a Post or Brick-wall that is Trimmed up between the two ends of a piece of Timber, to shorten its Bearing. **1823** P. NICHOLSON *Pract. Build.* 219 Bearer—any thing used by way of support to another. **1861** SMILES *Engineers* II. 183 To check the effect of the bearers or strutts of the ribs.

b. *spec.* Applied to various mechanical contrivances for sustaining or taking off pressure: *e.g.* in *Printing*, to a kind of 'packing' used to lessen the pressure upon the types in certain places.

1846 *Print. Appar. Amateurs* 30 The introduction of 'bearers' which serve to reduce the pressure upon the types, or rather to bear off a part of the pressure. **1881** C. EDWARDS *Organs* 57 The bearers are strips of wood fixed between the sliders, which.. support the weight of the upper boards, pipes, &c. **1884** F. BRITTEN *Watch & Clockm.* 32 [A] Bearer .. [is] a piece of metal soldered to the 'middle' of a watch case as a support for the joint.

10. *dial.* (See quot.)

1871 E. PEACOCK *R. Skirlaugh* II. 89 Where in one of the drains a sunken floor of wood, called a bearer, was deposited for.. making a safe watering place for the cattle.

III. 11. She who, or that which, brings forth or produces; *spec.* a fruit-yielding tree.

1413 LYDG. *Pylgr. Sowle* IV. vii. (1483) 61, I maye wel be cleped only the Appeltree and berer of this Appel. **1719** LOUDON & WISE *Compl. Gard.* 76 The Tree is a great Bearer. **1872** H. MACMILLAN *True Vine* v. 190 The celebrated vine of Hampton Court is a most productive bearer.

IV. 12. *Geom.* A space of any sort which is the locus of a collection of geometrical objects of any sort; e.g. a straight line is the *bearer* of the set of all points on it.

1909 in *Cent. Dict.* Suppl.

'bearess. *nonce-wd.* A she-bear.

1840 HOOD *Kilmansegg* lxxv, Snips and snaps, As if from a Tigress or Bearess.

†**'bear-gear.** *Obs.*; = *bearing gear* (see BEARING 17). Hence, ***to be*** or ***draw in the bear gears.***

bearȝ, obs. form of BARROW *sb.*[2] a swine.

†**'bearherd.** *Obs.* Also 6–7 **beare-heard, bearhard, bearard, berard, berrord.** [f. BEAR *sb.*[1] + HERD. Shakspere's *Bearard*, etc., are assigned to this, rather than to BEAR-WARD, to which some editors refer them, chiefly because he elsewhere uses *bear-heard*, and not *bear-ward*: cf. *shepherd*, formerly also *shepard, sheppard.*] The keeper of a bear, who leads him about for exhibition.

1589 R. HARVEY *Pl. Perc.* (1860) 14 Nor a bear-heard.. to put his staffe in the mouth of the beare, or pull off these dogs? **1593** SHAKS. *2 Hen. VI*, v. i. 149 Wee'l bate thy Bears to death, And manacle the Berard in their Chaines. —— *Ibid.* 210 Despight the Bearard, that protects the Beare. **1597** —— *2 Hen. IV*, I. ii. 191 True valor is turn'd Beare-heard. **1599** —— *Much Ado* II. i. 43 Take sixepence in earnest of the Berrord, and leade his Apes into Hell. **1655** GOUGE *Comm. Hebrews* i. 13 Bearhards that have their Bears at command. **1860** KENNEDY *Swallow-B.* 14 It gave me over to the great bear-herd.

bearing ('bɛərɪŋ), *vbl. sb.* [f. BEAR *v.*[1] + -ING[1].]

I. from BEAR *v.*[1] I.

1. a. The action of carrying or conveying. In *Backgammon*, see BEAR *v.* 1 d.

c **1384** WYCLIF *De Eccl.* Sel. Wks. III. 347 In þe olde lawe weren preestis and dekenes myche chargid in beryng of þe tabernacle. *c* **1485** *Digby Myst.* (1882) II. 645 In a beryng baskett or a lepe.. I shall me conuay [over wall]. **1598** BARRET *Theor. Warres* Pref. 3 Your yong yeares haue scarse arriued yet to the bearing of Armes. **1645** DURYE *Israel's Call* 27 To serve him in the bearing of his vessels. **1675** COTTON *Compl. Gamester* xxvi. (1680) 111 When you come to bearing, have a care of making when you need not.

b. things immaterial, *e.g.* the bringing forward of testimony.

1393 LANGL. *P. Pl.* C. XVII. 360 Brawelynge and bacbytynge and beryng of false wittnesse. *Mod.* 'The continual bearing of a grudge.'

2. a. The carrying of oneself (with reference to the manner); carriage, deportment; behaviour, demeanour.

c **1250** *Gen. & Ex.* 2178 Bi ȝure bering men mai it sen. *c* **1374** CHAUCER *Troylus* I. 181 Symple of beryng [*v.r.* attire] and deboner of chere. **1495** *Act 11 Hen. VII*, ix. §2 To be of goode beryng ayenst the King. **1599** SHAKS. *Much Ado* II. i. 166 That is Claudio, I know him by his bearing. **1814** SCOTT *Ld. of Isles* IV. xxii, The bearing of that stranger Lord. **1873** BLACK *Pr. Thule* vi. 79 The.. courtesy of his bearing towards women.

b. Behaviour in battle, etc., achievement.

1387 TREVISA *Higden* (1865) I. 3 Greet berynge and dedes of oure forme fadres.

3. *Her.* That which is borne upon an escutcheon; a single charge or device.

1562 LEIGH *Armorie* (1597) 120 b, And vpon the valence of that studie, were Scocheons of vnperfite bearing. **1614** SELDEN *Titles Hon.* Pref., When the Prince ennobled any, he vsually gaue him the particular of his Bearing in Blazon. **1790** BOSWELL *Johnson* II. 35 Armorial Bearings.. Johnson said.. were as ancient as the siege of Thebes. **1858** BUCKLE *Civilis.* (1869) II. ii. 112 In the twelfth century armorial bearings were invented.

II. from BEAR *v.*[1] II.

†4. Upholding, supporting; maintenance. *Obs.*

1548 HALL *Chron.* (1809) 600 Indicted of riottes and maintenaunce of bearynges of divers misdoers within the countie. **1552** LATIMER *Serm. Lord's Pr.* iii. II. 34 In the place of justice, there I have seen bearing and bolstering.

5. Sustaining, supporting, endurance.

1526 *Pilgr. Perf.* (W. de W. 1531) 45 In suffrynge or beryng aduersitees and troubles. **1640** SANDERSON *Serm.* II. 174 Our bearing with their infirmities. **1815** T. JEFFERSON *Corr.* (1830) 263 Considering the government of England as totally without morality, and insolent beyond bearing.

6. A material support; a supporting surface; supporting power.

a **1300** *K. Alis.* 484 A goshauk with gret flyght Setlith on his beryng. **1677** MOXON *Mech. Exerc.* (1703) 148 This Post .. bears upon the Floor, to make its Bearing the stronger. **1732** POPE *Ess. Man* I. 29 But of this frame the bearings, and the ties. **1793** SMEATON *Edystone L.* §274 Each floor.. lying upon the horizontal bearings furnished by these ledges. **1876** *Handbk. Sc. App. S. Kens.* 5 A greater number of bearings is required to prevent the mirror from becoming strained by its own weight.

7. *Carpentry.* The length of a beam between two supports, span; the distance between the cutting-edge of a tool and the rest in which it is held.

1677 MOXON *Mech. Exerc.* (1703) 136 This short Bearing .. renders the whole Floor firm enough for all common Occupation. *Ibid.* 186 Its edge cutting at a greater Bearing from the Rest.. it is then more subject to tremble. **1823** P. NICHOLSON *Pract. Build.* 219 *Bearing*, the distance in which a beam or rafter is suspended in the clear.

III. from BEAR *v.*[1] III.

8. A thrusting, pressing, or straining in any direction; thrust, pressure.

1591 PERCIVALL *Sp. Dict.*, *Salidizo*.. the bearing out of a wall, *Proiecta.* **1753** CHAMBERS *Cycl. Supp.* s.v., Bearing of an arch, or vault, denotes the efforts which the stones make to burst open the piers. **1784** *Med. Commun.* II. 7 Such a bearing down, as made her fearful of a miscarriage. **1797** M. BAILLIE *Morb. Anat.* (1807) 415 An inversion of the vagina is attended with a sense of bearing down.

9. Tendency to exert influence, practical relation or reference to other things; aspect.

1785 BURKE *Nab. Arcot's Debts* Wks. IV. 201 Having had .. a just sense of their true bearings and relations. **1804** T. JEFFERSON *Corr.* (1830) 18 In its unfortunate bearings on my private friendships. **1828** SOUTHEY *Ess.* (1832) II. 243 The subject.. was thoroughly examined in all its bearings. **1867** A. BARRY *Sir C. Barry* vi. 177 The legal bearings of the case.

†10. A taking effect; operation, effective result.

1723 WODROW *Corr.* (1843) III. 89 Whether I shall ever be able to bring anything of this to a bearing, I know not.

†11. Spring, elasticity. *Obs.* Cf. BEAR *sb.*[3]

1674 N. FAIRFAX *Bulk & Selv.* 118 Slower motions are made up of starts and bearings, or springsomness. *Ibid.* 119 A pend or earnest strift fromwards, which we call springsomness or bearing.

12. *Mech.* (generally in *pl.*) Those parts of a machine which bear the friction; the block or supports on which a shaft or axle turns, and also the part of the shaft or axle resting upon these supports. [This combines II and III of the vb.]

1791 *Specif. Patent* No. 1794 Water wheels to be made and fixed upon bearings. **1793** WOLLASTON in *Phil. Trans.* LXXXIII. 137 A better bearing, and much less likely to wear the pivots. **1861** SMILES *Engineers* II. 139 The shafts and axles were of iron, and the bearings of brass. **1881** *Print. Trades Jrnl.* XXXI. 38 Heated bearings in machinery may be relieved.. by the use of graphite as a lubricator.

13. a. The direction in which any point lies from a point of reference, esp. as measured in degrees from one of the quarters of the compass; also, the direction of an arriving radio wave or radar echo determined by a direction-finding system. In *pl.* the relative positions of surrounding objects. ***to take one's bearings***: to determine one's position with regard to surrounding objects; also *fig.*

1635 N. CARPENTER *Geog. Del.* I. vii. 171 Great errours not only in the situation of diuers places, but also in the bearing of places one to the other. **1711** F. FULLER *Med. Gymn.* 29 When they [jockeys] design to take the Bearings of a Running Horse. **1750** SMEATON in *Phil. Trans.* 5 July, To make the compass useful in taking.. the bearing of head-lands, ships and other objects. **1805** FLINDERS in *Phil. Trans.* XCV. 189 On the first bearings the ship's head was six points on one side of the meridian. **1858** in *Merc. Mar. Mag.* V. 229 All Bearings herein given are Magnetic. **1875** BEDFORD *Sailor's Pocket Bk.* I. (ed. 2) 41 The difference between the sun's true bearing and its compass bearing. **1907** *Electr. Engin.* II. 775/2 The bearings of quite a number of wireless telegraph stations in the Channel have been determined. **1920** *Discovery* May 131/2 By means of the direction-finding apparatus a bearing to the source from which the wireless waves are coming may be obtained. **1942** *Electronic Engin.* XV. 9 Long wave pulse transmitter.. to enable bearings on the aircraft to be obtained on the ground. **1950** *Gloss. Terms Radar (B.S.I.)* 7 *Automatic range, bearing* .., the automatic determination of range, bearing.. by a mechanism actuated by the echo. **1952** F. J. WYLIE *Use of Radar at Sea* viii. 121 Taking a radar bearing of the side of a prominent land feature.

b. *Mus.* (see quot.)

1835 *Penny Cycl.* XXV. 356/2 The parts [of a piano, etc.] which are first tuned by the fifths, and from which all the others are tuned by octaves, are called *bearings*.

14. a. The direction of any line on the earth's surface in relation to a meridian.

1802 PLAYFAIR *Illustr. Hutton. The.* 229 Vertical strata, having the same bearing with respect to the meridian. **1881** RAYMOND *Mining Gloss.*, *Bearing*.. the direction of a horizontal line, drawn in the middle plane of a vein or stratum not horizontal.

b. *fig.* Tendency, natural leaning, bent.

1862 TROLLOPE *Orley F.* xv. 121 In the publicity of such sympathy there was something that suited the bearings of Miss Furnival's mind.

c. ***line of bearing***: the direction in which a thing lies or moves.

1839 URE *Dict. Arts* 967 When the line of dip, and consequently the line of bearing which is at right angles to it, are unknown, they are sought for by making three bores. **1920** *Discovery* Nov. 330/1 Collingwood signalled to some of his ships to spread out.., the result being a partial resemblance to what is called a line of bearing.

†15. *Mus.* The variation allowed from the true pitch of a note, in tuning an instrument upon the method of unequal temperament. *Obs.*

1698 WALLIS in *Phil. Trans.* XX. 256 Pipes at equal Intervals do not give the just desired Harmony, without somewhat of Bearing.

16. *Naut.* 'The widest part of a vessel below the plank-shear. The line of flotation which is formed by the water upon her sides when she sits upright with her provisions, stores, and

ballast, on board in proper trim.' Smyth *Sailor's Wd.-bk.*

1627 CAPT. SMITH *Seaman's Gram.* ii. 3 There doth begin the compasse and bearing of the ship. **1835** MARRYAT *Pirate* iii, The wind howled, and..the vessel was pressed down to her bearings by its force.

17. *Comb.* and *attrib.* in prec. senses: as, ***bearing-chair***, ***-point***, ***shaft***, ***-surface***; † **bearing-back**, a pedlar's staff for carrying his pack; † **bearing-cloth**, a child's christening-robe; **bearing-door**, (*Coal-mining*), one of the main doors in a pit for regulating the ventilation; † **bearing-gear**, the gear or apparatus (usually a twisted withe passed through the collar so as to form a loop) by which, in old times, a pair of horses supported the ends of the swingle-tree of a plough, or of the cross-bar from which the pole of a wagon was suspended; † **bearing-leap**, a carrying-basket; see BEAR-LEAP; **bearing metal**, metal having antifrictional properties, used for bearings (sense 12); **bearing pile** (see PILE *sb.*[1] 3 b).

1544 ASCHAM *Toxoph.* (1654) 115 They be good ynough for bearynge gere. **1570** *Bury Wills* (1850) 156, I beqwethe to my dawghter Jone Kenam one berynge sheet. **1598** GREENWEY *Tacitus' Ann.* XIV. ii. (1622) 200 Agrippina.. caused her-selfe to be carried to Baias in a bearing-chaire. **1601** HOLLAND *Pliny* II. 341 If a child be lapped in a mantle or bearing-cloth made of an asse skin, it shall not be affrighted at any thing. **1607** TOPSELL *Four-f. Beasts* (1673) 437 A bearing back or colt staffe, as we say in English, whereupon poor men carry their burdens. **1611** SHAKS. *Wint. T.* III. iii. 119 Looke thee, a bearing-cloath for a Squires childe. **1616** SURFL. & MARKH. *Countr. Farm* 533 When they [horses] draw two and two together in the beare-geares..then there is needfull the plow clevise..the harnesse, the collars, the round withs or bearing geares. **1851** *Coal-tr. Terms Northumbld. & Durh.* 24 A bearing or main door, is a door which forces the air through an entire district. **1856** KANE *Arct. Exp.* I. xxix. 402 Passed the chain cable under the keel at four bearing-points. **1893** T. E. THORPE *Dict. Appl. Chem.* III. 1052/1 Part of the tin in gun metal and in bearing metal is frequently replaced by zinc. **1905** *Engineering Mag.* XXIX. 592/1 A paper was presented by Professor Melvin Price, upon the microstructure and frictional characteristics in bearing metals. **1906** *Westm. Gaz.* 23 Aug. 10/1 The foundations of each pier are formed by 145 bearing-piles. **1923** GLAZEBROOK *Dict. Appl. Physics* V. II. 233/1 The antimony-tin alloys are rarely used by themselves, but form the basis of bearing metals.

IV. from BEAR *v.*[1] IV.

18. a. The action of bringing forth (offspring); birth. Also in comb. ***child-bearing***.

a **1300** *Cursor M.* 11079 All mad þai mirth at his bering. *c* **1400** *Epiph.* (Turnb. 1843) 908 As women..When thei ben in berung of chylde. **1611** BIBLE *1 Tim.* ii. 15 Notwithstanding she shall be saued in child-bearing.

b. *attrib.*, as in ***bearing-pain***, ***-place***, ***-throe***, ***-time***.

1587 GOLDING *De Mornay* xxi. 323 Wouldst thou haue Children? It is hee that openeth and shutteth the bearing place. **1597** DANIEL *Civ. Wares* VI. cv, To stay beyond the bearing-time, so long. **1787** *Med. Commun.* II. 227 The throes which the women call bearing pains.

19. The action of producing leaves, flowers, and *esp.* fruit; yielding, production.

1583 PLAT *Jewell ho.* (1594) 5 He did greatly backward the tree in his bearing. **1709** STANHOPE *Paraphr.* IV. 255 Bearing will be required from every Branch. **1861** DELAMER *Kitch. Gard.* 160 Wall-trees..come into early bearing.

20. That which is produced; fruit, a crop.

1838 WORDSW. *Sonn.* II. xix, Rich mellow bearings, that for thanks shall call.

21. Those external parts of animals which are concerned in parturition. *Obs.* or *dial.*

1674 *Lond. Gaz.* No. 911/4 A Bright bay Mare..lately Stackt behind under her Bearing. **1779** *Phil. Trans.* LXIX. 285 The teats and the external female parts, called by farmers the bearing.

bearing (ˈbɛərɪŋ), *ppl. a.*[1] [f. BEAR *v.*[1].]

1. That bears, carries, supports, endures, drives, presses, pierces, stands out, etc. (See various meanings of the vb.)

c **1500** *Rob. Hood* (Ritson) II. xii. 131 Clifton with a bearing arrow, Hee clave the willow wand. **1551** ROBINSON tr. *More's Utop.* 158 Drawing and bearinge beastes. **1642** HOWELL *For. Trav.* (1869) 61 Large and bearing streames. **1674** N. FAIRFAX *Bulk & Selv.* 122 Lockt up in a bearing or pressing posture. **1677** MOXON *Mech. Exerc.* (1703) 69 Plane both the Bearing sides thinner. **1702** PENN in *Pa. Hist. Soc. Mem.* IX. 162 Be as bearing as you can with hasty and fretful tempers. **1850** LEITCH tr. *Müller's Anc. Art* § 275. 305 The architectural members..are divided into bearing, borne, and intermediate. Among the bearing the column is the form naturally suggested.

†**2.** Of food: Sustaining, substantial. *Obs.*

c **1618** FLETCHER *Wom. Pleased* I. ii, A good bearing dinner. **1633** MASSINGER *New Way, etc.* v. i, Bearing dishes.

3. In *comb.*, as: ***burden-***, ***interest-bearing***; **bearing-rein**, a short fixed rein which passes from the bit to the saddle, intended to keep the horse's head up and its neck arched; *fig.* a check or restraint upon movements.

1620 QUARLES *Jonah* (1638) 43 The burden-bearing Camell. **1794** W. FELTON *Carriages* (1801) II. 138 The bearing rein is what prevents the horse from holding his head down. **1839** SYD. SMITH *Wks.* 1859 I. Pref. 8 Lord Grey had not then taken off the bearing-rein from the English people. **1866** CRUMP *Banking* xi. 245 Having an interest-bearing reserve. **1882** *Macm. Mag.* XLV. 464 When horses are unnecessarily restrained by bearing-reins.

4. Bringing forth, producing (offspring, fruit, etc.). Often as second element in a compound, as ***berry-***, ***fruit-***, ***spectre-bearing***.

1398 TREVISA *Barth. De P.R.* XVII. cxvii. (1495) 682 Thycke settyng of knottes is token of a good vyne and berynge. **1672** PETTY *Pol. Anat.* (1691) 53 A Cow continues Milch and bearing, from 3 or 4 years old to 12. **1831** CARLYLE *Sart. Res.* II. vi, The Future is wholly a Stygian Darkness, spectre-bearing. **1858** W. ELLIS *Vis. Madagascar* viii. 225 The fruit-bearing olive.

5. Fertile, productive. Also of years, etc.

c **1420** *Pallad. on Husb.* I. 28 Eke se thi lande Be bering, and commodiously stande. **1742** ELLIS *Timber-Tree* (ed. 3) II. xxi. 130 The second [kind of cherry]..may be enjoyed at so cheap a Rate, in a bearing Year, as a Penny a Pound. **1860** *Trans. Mich. Agric. Soc.* X. 614 Of fruits, although it was not a 'bearing year', the exhibition was very fine. **1882** S. MACADAM *Manitoba Soil*, Soils of a good bearing quality.

'bearing, *ppl. a.*[2] [f. BEAR *v.*[2] + -ING[2].] Acting as a 'bear' in Stock Exchange transactions.

1884 *Pall Mall G.* 7 Aug. 5/1 The shrewd men who are so ..anxious to put money in the pockets of the bulling or bearing public.

bearish (ˈbɛərɪʃ), *a.* [f. BEAR *sb.*[1] + -ISH[1].]

1. Bear-like, esp. in manner or temper; rough, rude, and uncouth; growling, surly.

1744 HARRIS *Three Treat. Wks.* (1841) 99 We call men, by way of reproach, sheepish, bearish, etc. **1800** COLERIDGE *Piccolom.* V. iv, Forgive me too my bearish ways, old father. **1863** SARAH TYTLER in *Gd. Words* 705 As unmannerly and bearish as two gentlemen..could contrive to be.

2. *Stock Exchange.* Belonging or tending to a fall in the price of stocks.

1881 *Chicago Times* 30 Apr., The movement was bearish, and prices all around averaged a trifle lower. **1884** *Manch. Exam.* 8 Sept. 8/3 Bearish news from the oilfields brought down prices.

Hence **bearishly** *adv.*

'bearishness. [f. prec. + -NESS.] Bearish quality; rough unmannerliness; surliness.

1861 COLLIER *Hist. Eng. Lit.* 162 He never lost a certain bearishness of temper. **1884** *Church Union* (*N.Y.*) 15 Nov. 8 Private boorishness and domestic bearishness.

† **'bearleap, -lep(e.** In 4–5 berlep(e, bere lepe, 7 beer-lip. [f. ME. *ber-en* to BEAR + LEAP basket.] A carrying basket.

1325-40 HAMPOLE *Psalm* lxxx. 6 His hend seruyd in ber-lepe, *v.r.* bere lepe [*in cophino*]. that is a vessel in the whilke the iwes bare mortere in egipt. *c* **1375** WYCLIF *Serm.* Sel. Wks. I. 17 þei gedriden seven berlepis of relief þat was left [WYCLIF *Mark* viii. 8 *has* lepis, leepis]. **1677** PLOT *Oxfordsh.* 256 They draw a Cubb or Beerlip..up the middle of the mow or stack, and through the hole, that this leaves, the heat will ascend, and so prevent mow-burning.

Cf. also the following: *c* **1440** *Medulla Gramm.*, *Sporta*, a berynge lep. **1440** *Prom. Parv.*, Barlylepe, to kepe yn corne, *Cumera* [**1499** Pynson's ed. *has here* Barlep; *also elsewhere* Beringe lepe *Canistra*]. **1500** *Ortus Vocab.*, *Sporta*, a bere lepe or basket. *c* **1485** *Digby Myst.* (1882) II. 645 In a beryng baskett or a lepe.

† **'bearless**, *a. Obs. rare*—[1]. [f. BEAR *v.*[1] IV + -LESS.] Barren.

1611 SPEED *Theat. Gt. Brit.* xiv. (1614) 27/1 Barkeshire.. from a naked and bearelesse Oke-tree, whereunto the people usually resorted..to conferre for the State.

'bear-like, *a.* and *adv.* [f. BEAR *sb.*[1] + LIKE.] Like, or after the manner of, a bear; rough, rude.

1605 SHAKS. *Macb.* v. vii. 2, I cannot flye, But Beare-like I must fight the course. **1663** GERBIER *Counsel* D iij a, Some of them Bear-like-whelps (by licking and smoothing) have gotten some fashionable like shape. **1823** SCOTT in *Lockhart* (1839) VII. 174, I was rather a Bear-like nurse for such a lamb-like charge.

bearn, obs. form of BAIRN, and of BURN, *v.*

Béarnaise (beɪɑːˈneɪz, ‖bearnɛz). [Fr., fem. of *béarnais* of Béarn, a region of south-western France.] ***Béarnaise sauce***, also in Fr. form *sauce béarnaise*, a rich white sauce flavoured with tarragon.

1877 E. S. DALLAS *Kettner's Book of Table* 58 Béarnaise Sauce is made with yolks of egg and ounces of butter in equal numbers. **1885** MAJOR L— *Pytchley Bk. Refined Cookery* ii. 112 *Béarnaise*... This sauce should be the substance of and resemble Mayonnaise Sauce. **1906** I. BEETON *Househ. Managem.* x. 220 Bearnaise Sauce. **1926** RADCLYFFE HALL *Adam's Breed* II. vi. §6. 202 Get that Sauce Béarnaise remade, and be quick! **1936** WODEHOUSE *Young Men in Spats* ix. 238 You wouldn't know a martyred proletariat if they brought it to you on a skewer with Béarnaise sauce.

bear's-foot. *Herb.* [f. BEAR *sb.*[1]]

1. Popular name of various species of Hellebore, *esp.* of the Black Hellebore (*H. fœtidus*), a handsome plant with spreading panicles of globular flowers, their sepals green edged with pink.

1551 TURNER *Herbal* 126 Thys herbe whyche they call chrystes wurtz and we berefoot. **1629** J. PARKINSON *Parad. in Sole* lxxxi. 344 There are three sorts of blacke Hellebor or Beares foote. **1697** DRYDEN *Virg. Georg.* IV. 185 The late Narcissus, and the winding Trail Of Bears-foot. **1863** PRIOR *Plant-n.* 17 Bear's-foot, from its digitate leaf.

2. Also applied loosely to Bear's-breech or Acanthus, to Lady's Mantle, and to Monkshood.

1552 HULOET, Bere fote herbe, *Acantha.* **1563** SHUTE *Archit.* B j b, An herbe called Acanthus, in frenche Branck-ursine, or bearefote with vs.

bearship (ˈbɛəʃɪp). [f. BEAR *sb.*[1] + -SHIP.] The personality of a bear. (Humorous.)

1800 SOUTHEY *Lett.* (1856) I. 90 If you were a dancing bear, and I had a string tied to the ring in your bearship's nose.

bearskin (ˈbɛəskɪn). [f. BEAR *sb.*[1]]

1. The skin of a bear used as a wrap or garment.

1823 BYRON *Juan* x. xxvi, In this gay clime of bear-skins black and furry. **1835** SIR J. ROSS *N.-W. Pass.* xli. 547 Natives came..bringing..a bearskin and some clothing. **1855** KINGSLEY *Heroes* II. 205 Wrapt in a bearskin cloak.

b. *fig.* in reference to the torture of Christians by baiting them in bearskins.

1677 GALE *Crt. Gentiles* III. 123 The Pelagian Iesuites oppose the Dominicans in this point under the Bears skin of being Calvinists. **1711** SHAFTESB. *Charac.* (1737) I. 29 If they had chosen to bring our primitive founders upon the stage in a pleasanter way than that of bear-skins and pitch-barrels.

2. The tall furry cap worn by the Guards in the British Army.

[**1848** THACKERAY *Van. Fair* xxiv, Ensign Spooney..tried on a new bearskin cap, under which he looked savage beyond his years.] **1863** KINGLAKE *Crimea* II. 338 The towering bearskins which mark a battalion of the English Guards.

3. A shaggy kind of woollen cloth used for overcoats.

4. See BEAR *sb.*[1] 8. ***bearskin jobber***, early name of the 'bear' on the Stock Exchange.

bearskinned (ˈbɛəskɪnd), *a.* [f. BEARSKIN + -ED[2].] Wearing a bearskin.

1694 T. ROGERS *Loyal & Impartial Satyrist* 14 When Bearskin'd Men in Floating Castles land. **1909** *Daily Chron.* 1 Oct. 4/6 The bearskinned heroes. **1966** *Listener* 17 Nov. 715/3 The bearskinned guards who stand outside the doors of the palace.

bearward (ˈbɛəwɔːd) Also 4 **bereward**, 5 **barreward**, 5–6 **berward(e** (see BEARHERD). [f. BEAR *sb.*[1] + WARD.]

1. The keeper of a bear, who leads it about for public exhibition of its tricks, etc.; also *fig.*

1399 *Pol. Poems* (1859) I. 364 A bereward fond a rag. **1463** *Mann. & Househ. Exp.* 156, I toke to the lord Stanley is berward..vjs. viijd. **1550** BALE *Eng. Votaries* II. 118 They played with those worldly rulers..as the bearwardes do with their apes and their beares. **1644** EVELYN *Mem.* (1857) I. 95 [They] command them, as our bearwards do the bears, with a ring through the nose. **1826** SCOTT *Woodst.* ix, The army is your bear now, and old Noll is your bearward.

†**2.** The constellation Bootes, or its chief star Arcturus, from its position in reference to *Ursa Major*.

1483 *Cath. Angl.* 23/1 Barrewarde, *arctophilax.* **1577** B. GOOGE *Heresbach's Husb.* (1586) 39 b, The rising of the star called the Berward. **1883** LIDDELL & SCOTT *Grk. Lex.* s.v. Ἄρκτος, The star just behind is called Ἀρκτοῦρος, Ἀρκτοφύλαξ, the Bear-ward, or Βοώτης, the Waggoner.

† **'bearwort.** *Herb. Obs.* [f. BEAR *sb.*[1] + WORT.] The herb *Meum Athamanticum*.

1597 in GERARD. **1863** in PRIOR *Plant-n.*

beasantlier, obs. form of BESANTLER.

beasaunte, obs. form of BEZANT.

bease, obs. form of BAIZE.

be-ash, etc.: see BE- *pref.*

beasom, obs. f. BESOM, and BISEN, *Obs.* blind.

beast (biːst), *sb.* Forms: 3–6 **beste**, **best**, **beest(e**, 4–6 *Sc.* **beist**, 6–7 **beaste**, (6 **bieste**, 7 **beise**), 6– **beast**. (*Pl. dial.* **beas(e**, **beeas(e**, **beass.**) [a. OF. *beste*:—L. *bestia*. The earliest use of the word was to translate L. *animal*, in which it took the place of OE. *deór*, just as it was, in this sense, subseq. replaced by *animal* itself.]

I. *Literal senses.*

1. A living being, an animal. (Used to translate Gr. ζῷον, or L. *animal*, esp. in versions of the Bible. Now restricted in literary use as in sense 2; but still widely applied in dialect and colloquial use, including e.g. newts, insects, centipedes.)

†**a.** In early times, explicitly including man. *Obs.*

b. In later times, applied to the lower animals, as distinct from man.

c **1220** *Hali Meid.* 25 Beastes þat dumbe neb habbeð. *a* **1300** *Cursor M.* 6039 Þan sent drightin a litel beist [locust]. *Ibid.* 700 Þe nedder..was mast wis of ani best. **1493** *Festivall* (1515) 3 b, All the fysshes and beestes in the see. **1535** COVERDALE *Ecclus.* xi. 3 The Bey is but a small beast amonge the foules, yet is hir frute exceadinge swete. **1611** BIBLE *Rev.* iv. 6 Foure beastes full of eyes before and behinde. **1658** ROWLAND *Mouffet's Theat. Ins.* 931 Nor know I the little Beast [Hornet] it self. **1771** *Phil. Trans.* LXI. 240 Monoculi, some of which had their ovaria full of eggs, and others of little live beasts. **1827** MOORE *Periwink. & Soc.* Wks. (1862) 529 Of all the beasts that ever were born, Your Locust most delights in corn. **1875** BUCKLAND

Log-Bk. 91 These Cod, poor Beasts. *Mod. dial.* There's a little beast crawling up your back!

a. *c* **1374** CHAUCER *Boeth.* I. vi. 27 Axest not me quod I. wheþir þat [man] be a resonable best mortel. **1387** TREVISA *Higden* Rolls Ser. III. 367 Al þing þat haþ lif and felynge is i-cleped a beste. **1547** BOORDE *Brev. Health* clxxxii, A man or a woman, which be resonable beastes.

b. **1610** SHAKS. *Temp.* II. ii. 34 There would this Monster make a man: any strange beast there, makes a man. **1780** HARRIS *Philol. Enq.* (1841) 538 To render the nature of man odious, and the nature of beasts amiable.

c. The animal nature (in man).

1667 *Decay Chr. Piety* ix. §9. 302 Those advantages which may..exalt the man, and depress the beast in us. **1850** TENNYSON *In Mem.* cxviii. 27 Move upward, working out the beast, And let the ape and tiger die. **1895** W. D. HOWELLS *My Literary Passions* xvi. 110 The base of the mind is bestial, and so far the beast in us has insisted upon having its full say. **1948** J. THURBER (*title*) The Beast in Me and Other Animals.

2. a. A quadruped (or animal popularly regarded as such), as distinguished from birds, reptiles, fishes, insects, etc., as well as from man. (Now the ordinary literary use.)

c **1230** *Ancr. R.* 416 ȝe..ne schulen habben no best, bute kat one. *c* **1360** *Deus Caritas* in *E.E.P.* (1862) 127 Lord þou madest . boþe foul and best. **1393** GOWER *Conf.* III. 74 As lion is the king of bestes. **1526** *Pilgr. Perf.* (W. de W. 1531) 151 In the sixth daye..all beestes were create. **1559** *Mirr. Mag., Dk. Clarence* xxviii, Compare them vnto birdes and beastes. **1611** BIBLE *1 Kings* iv. 33 Hee spake also of beasts, and of foule, and of creeping things, and of fishes. **1691** RAY *Creation* (1722) 21 Animate bodies are divided into four great genera or orders: Beasts, Birds, Fishes, and Insects. **1849** MARRYAT *Valerie* vi, Like the bat, they are neither bird nor beast.

b. *spec.* An animal of the chase; fourfooted game.

1297 R. GLOUC. 375 Þe nywe forest..he..astored yt wel myd bestys. *c* **1420** *Avow. Arth.* xvii, Sethun brittuns he the best, As venesun in forest. **1539** *Act 31 Hen. VIII*, v. A chase..for..feeding of beastes of venery. **1592** WARNER *Alb. Eng.* VII. xxxvii. (1597) 180 They feede Mongst Beasts of chace. **1697** DRYDEN *Virg. Georg.* I. 211 Then Toils for Beasts, and Lime for Birds were found. **1751** CHAMBERS *Cycl.* s.v., Beasts of Chase, in our statute-books are five; the buck, doe, fox, martin, and roe. Beasts of the forest are, the hart, hind, hare, boar, and wolf. Beasts and fowls of the warren are, the hare, coney, pheasant, and partridge.

c. ***wild beast***: an animal not domesticated, formerly esp. a beast of the chase, now esp. a ferocious animal from a foreign land; = L. *fera*, Gr. *θηρίον*.

1297 R. GLOUC. 376 Men ne dorste..wylde best nyme noȝt, Hare ne wylde swyn. **1393** LANGL. *P. Pl.* C. XVIII. 28 And woneden in wildernesse · among wilde bestes. **1590** SHAKS. *Mids. N.* II. i. 228 Ile..leaue thee to the mercy of wilde beasts. **1591** SPENSER *Daphn.* xviii, And of the race, that all wild beastes do feare. **1697** DRYDEN *Virg. Georg.* iv. 758 Whom ev'n the savage Beasts had spar'd, they kill'd. **1833** MARRYAT *P. Simple* ix, To see the wild beasts fed at Mr. Polito's menagerie.

3. A domesticated animal owned and used by man, as part of his farm 'stock' or cattle [F. *bestiaux*, *bétail*]; at first including sheep, goats, etc., but **a.** gradually more or less restricted to the bovine kind; and now chiefly applied by farmers, graziers, etc. to fatting cattle. (In this sense there is also a collective plural *beast*.)

c **1230** *Ancr. R.* 58 ȝif eni unwrie put were, and best feolle þer inne. *a* **1300** *Cursor M.* 6137 Ta your beistes wit yow bun. *c* **1450** *Merlin* 3 This riche man hadde grete plente of bestes and of othir richesse. **1514** BARCLAY *Cyt. & Uplondyshm.* (1847) Introd. 9 Sometime the wolfe our beastes doth devour. **1704** BAILY *Dict. Rustic.* s.v. *Common*, Which Common must be taken with Beasts commonable, as Horses, Oxen, Kine, and Sheep. **1882** ROSSETTI *Ball. & Sonn.* 87 I am Berold the butcher's son, Who slays the beasts in Rouen Town.

a. **1523** FITZHERB. *Husb.* (1534) G ij, Beastes alone, nor horses alone, nor shepe alone..wyll not eate a pasture euen. **1641** HINDE *J. Bruen* xxix. 90 There was spent in his house a fat Beise, and a half, within the space of three dayes. **1720** *Lond. Gaz.* No. 5880/5 Robert Watson, late of Uttoxeter.. Dealer in Beasts. **1807** J. STAGG *Poems* 63 To th' fells they druive beath bease and sweyne. **1863** ATKINSON *Whitby Gloss.*, *Beast*, an..animal of the Ox kind—The plural..is *beeas* or *beas*; applied to Cows or farting-stock collectively. **1865** *Daily Tel.* 22 Aug. 6/5 One half..is devoted to 'beasts'; the other half to sheep, pigs, and calves, none of which creatures are 'beasts' according to the natural history of the Caledonian-road. **1884** *W. Sussex Gaz.* 25 Sept. (*Advt.*) The Live Stock comprises the valuable herd of Sussex Beast, including cows, heifers, bulls and steers.

b. An animal used in riding, driving, etc., as the horse and ass; a 'beast of burden,' a 'yoke beast,' a draught animal. [In some parts of England, *beast* in the sing. means spec. 'horse,' while the pl. *beasts*, *beastës*, *beass* means 'oxen.']

a **1300** *Cursor M.* 14963 Þar sal yee find an ass beist. **1388** WYCLIF *Luke* x. 34 And leid hym on his beest [**1382** hors], and ledde in to an ostrie. **1523** FITZHERB. *Surv.* xi. (1539) 26 His werke bestis to his plough. **1529** FRITH *Ep. Chr. Reader* Wks. (1829) 462 His Son..was made our beast, bearing our sins upon his own back. **1611** BIBLE *Luke* x. 34 And bound vp his wounds, powring in oile and wine, and set him on his owne beast. **1803** WELLINGTON in Gurw. *Disp.* II. 199 Coolies and bullocks and every animal that can be procured of the description of a beast of burthen. **1816** SCOTT *Antiq.* xxv, There sall nane o' my gear gang on your beast's back. **1848** MACAULAY *Hist. Eng.* I. 374 Travellers..compelled to alight and lead their beasts.

II. *fig.* and *transf.*

4. a. A human being under the sway of animal propensities.

c **1400** *Rom. Rose* 5065 No such beeste [a harlot] To be loved is not worthy. **1598** SHAKS. *Merry W.* V. v. 5 O powerfull Loue, that in some respects makes a Beast a Man: in som other, a Man a beast. **1647** SANDERSON *Serm.* II. 215 All histories afford us strange examples..of voluptuous beasts. **1709** STEELE *Tatler* No. 2 ¶2 Till Morn' sends stagg'ring Home a Drunken Beast. **1845** HOOD *Open Quest.* xv, Better..spend a leisure hour amongst the brutes, Than make a beast of his own self on Sunday.

b. ***the beast with two backs***, a man and woman in the act of copulation. (Cf. Rabelais's *faire la bête à deux dos.*)

1604 SHAKES. *Oth.* I. i. 117 Your Daughter and the Moore are making the Beast with two backs. *a* **1693** *Urquhart's Rabelais* I. iii. 18 These two did often times do the two backed beast together. **1785** GROSE *Dict. Vulgar T.*, *Beast with two backs*, a man and woman in the act of copulation. **1921** A. HUXLEY *Crome Yellow* x. 94 There they were, Anne and Gombauld, moving together as though they were a single supple creature. The beast with two backs. **1922** JOYCE *Ulysses* 546 The beast that has two backs at midnight. **1950** AUDEN *Enchafèd Flood* (1951) iii. 115 It is possible to attach too much importance..to the sexual symbolism of the Whale as being at once the *vagina dentata* and the Beast with two backs or the parents-in-bed.

5. a. 'A brutal, savage man; a man acting in any manner unworthy of a reasonable creature.' J. In earlier usage, often connoting stupidity or folly (cf. Fr. *bête*); in modern phraseology opprobriously employed to express disgust or merely aversion. Now freq. in weaker sense.

c **1210** *Leg. Kath.* 2067 Hwet medschipe makeð þe, þu bittre balefule beast! **1393** GOWER *Conf.* I. 202 O beste of helle, in what guise Hast thou deserved for to deie. **1594** R. CAREW *Huarte's Exam. Wits* (1616) He that goes a beast to Rome, returns a beast againe. **1603** SHAKS. *Meas. for M.* III. i. 137 Oh you beast, Oh faithlesse Coward, oh dishonest wretch. **1723** MCWARD *Earn. Contend.* 151 (Jam.) Putting the Beast upon ourselves, for having been so base. **1772** NICHOLLS in *Gray's Corr.* (1843) 170 It is this moment only that I have received nine letters..from that cursed beast Belloni's Abbé. **1841** WARREN *Ten Thous. Year* I. v, Mr. Sharpey..is coming down from dinner, directly, the beast! **1875** MISS BROUGHTON *Nancy* ii. 12 (1875) 'You beast' cried I, in good nervous English, turning sharply round. **1899** KIPLING *Stalky & Co.* 49 He's an awfully sensitive beast. **1923** D. L. SAYERS *Whose Body?* i. 13 I'll..try and console the poor little beast.

b. *fig.* Applied to things; also in colloq. phr. ***a beast of a*** ...: an abominable or disgusting..., a beastly....

1862 S. HALE *Lett.* (1919) 13 One thing shall I rejoice at, — my own bed,—for this husk thing we sleep on is a beast. **1878** W. S. GILBERT *Pinafore* I, It's a beast of a name. **1891** H. C. BUNNER *Zadoc Pine* 196 I've got to stay and finish my grind. It's a beast. **1898** *Westm. Gaz.* 4 May 2/2 I've had a beast of a time.

†**6.** Applied to the devil (the 'old serpent' or 'dragon') and evil spirits. *Obs.*

c **1220** *St. Marher.* 11 Hu ha..þæt bittre best makede to bersten. *a* **1300** *Cursor M.* 12954 Bot herdili he [þe warlau] yode him nerr, Qua herd euer best sua bald. *c* **1305** *Miracle St. Jas.* 57 in *E.E.P.* 59 Þu liþere best oure leuedi seide.

7. ***the Beast*** (*fig.*): Antichrist, or the Antichristian power. (From the Apocalypse of St. John.) Phr. ***the mark of the beast***: see MARK *sb.*[1] 11 c.

1382 WYCLIF *Rev.* xiii. 18 He that hath vndirstonding, acounte the noumbre of the beest. **1382** [see MARK *sb.*[1] 11 c]. **1526** *Pilgr. Perf.* (W. de W. 1531) 37 Wonders whiche that beest the Antechryst (as Saynt Paule sayth) shall shewe. **1577** HOLINSHED *Chron.* III. 1265/2 They..which suffer death vnder the beast, for confession of Christs religion. **1649** OWEN *Serm.* Wks. 1851 VIII. 235 God will bring the followers after the beast to destruction. **1833** M. EDGEWORTH *Thoughts on Bores* in *Tales & Novels* XVII. 327 Lord Chesterfield set the mark of the beast, as he called it, on certain vulgarisms in pronunciation. **1847** J. BATES *Seventh Day Sabbath* (ed. 2) 59 Is it not clear that the first day of the week for the Sabbath or holy day is a mark of the beast. **1847** E. G. WHITE in J. White *Word to 'Little Flock'* 19 All we were required to do, was to give up God's Sabbath, and keep the Pope's, and then we should have the mark of the Beast. **1849** CUMMING *God in Hist.* (1851) 115 In 1807 the ten kings or horns (Britain excepted..) joined in desolating 'the Beast.' **1874** [see MARK *sb.*[1] 11 c]. *c* **1875** CALVERLEY *Fly-leaves*, Leave the number of the beast to puzzle Doctor Cumming? **1888** E. G. WHITE *Great Controversy* xxv. 449 They will thereby accept the sign of allegiance to Rome—'the mark of the beast'. **1891** KIPLING *Life's Handicap* 208 (*title*) The mark of the beast. **1954** A. S. C. ROSS in *Neuphilologische Mitteilungen* LV. 22 At the beginning of the century many slang phrases were used to designate non-gentlemen e.g...*showing* (or similar introduction) *the mark of the beast*.

III. In *Card-playing.* [orig. *beste* as in 17th c. French, then englished as *beaste*, *beast*, pronounced (beːst), a pronunciation still retained by some who spell it *baste*, *bast*; but more usually spelt and pronounced as in the other senses. Mod.F. *bête*.]

8. a. An obsolete game at cards, resembling the modern *Nap*.

b. A penalty at this game; also at Ombre and Quadrille.

[The name *Ombre* is derived from Sp. *Hombre* man. At Ombre, the one who undertakes the game has to beat each of the other two; if he fails, he is said to be beasted, and pays forfeit to the pool; hence it has been suggested that having failed to maintain himself as *Hombre* or *man*, he becomes *beast*. In the earlier quotations it occurs only with Ombre.]

1668 R. LESTRANGE *Vis. Quev.* (1708) 97 Spend whole Nights at Beste or Ombre with my Lady Pen-Tweezel. **1674** COTTON *Compl. Gamester* (1725) 97 Beast..called by the French, La Bett. **1678** BUTLER *Hud.* III. I. 1007 These at Beste and L'Ombre woe And play for loue and money too. **1734** R. SEYMOUR *Compl. Gamester* (1739) 22 The Beaste is made whenever he who undertakes the game (that is to say the Ombre) does not win. *Ibid.* 23 Whoever Renounces several times in a Deal suffers a Beaste for every Renounce. *Ibid.* All the Beastes that are made in one Deal, must be together upon the Board and be played for the next. **1727–51** CHAMBERS *Cycl.* s.v. *Ombre*, The oversights and irregularities committed in the course of the game, are called beastes. [See also BASTE *sb.*[1]]

IV. *Comb.* **a.** objective gen. with verbal sb. or agent-noun, as ***beast-baiting***, ***-subduer***; **b.** similative, as ***beast-blindness***; **c.** attrib., as ***beast-body***, ***-dance***, ***-epic*** (cf. G. *tier-epos*), ***-fable***, ***-fight***, ***-figure***, ***-hide***, ***-kind***, ***-market***, ***-oblation***, ***-poetry***, ***-saga***, ***-tale***. Also **beast-fly**, the gad-fly; **beast-gates** (*north. dial.*), pastures where beasts may go; **beastman** *local*, a cattleman.

1606 HOLLAND *Sueton.* 262 Wardens..who were to exhibite..*Beastbaitings and stage playes. **1802** SOUTHEY *Thalaba* x. xxxiii, Live With such *beast-blindness in the present joy. **1884** TENNYSON *Becket* 93 This *beast-body That God has plunged my soul in. **1900** J. C. LAWSON in *Ann. Brit. Sch. Athens* VI. 125 A *beast-dance in Scyros. **1889** J. JACOBS *Fables of Aesop* I. 159 The so-called *Beast-Epic of Reynard the Fox. **1908** *Publ. Mod. Lang. Assoc. Amer.* XXIII. 497 There was the distinctively medieval set of [animal] stories, told because of their own intrinsic power of affording amusement, to which is generally given the name 'beast epic'. Of this..set of beast tales..which is so well represented in the branches of the French *Roman de Renard*, English offers few specimens. **1924** *Ibid.* XXXIX. 764 Chaucer's readers were educated to expect satirical hits and some more than didactic pieces of allegory in their beast epic and beast fable. **1932** E. WEEKLEY *Words & Names* ix. 121 The beast-epic obviously belongs to very primitive races. **1865** TYLOR *Early Hist. Man.* i. 10 Stories known as *Beast Fables. **1933** E. K. CHAMBERS *Eng. Folk-Play* 215, I am inclined to think that there must have been an early variant of the *ludus*, in which a single *beast-figure was alone represented. **1658** ROWLAND *Mouffet's Theat. Ins.* 935 This *Beast-fly is in Latine called *Asilum*. **1566** *Richmond Wills* (1853) 185 The *beast gates..uppon the more and in the feild onely except. **1601** HOLLAND *Pliny* I. 507 When the haires of *beast-hides haue bin soked therewith. **1616** SURFL. & MARKH. *Countr. Farm*, At the end of all these *Beast-houses..you shall appoint a Dog-house. **1311** in *N. & Q.* (1963) July 250/2 *Bestemon. **1899** *Yorkshire Post* 26 Dec., Wanted, beastman,..on farm, near Hull. **1921** *Dict. Occupational Terms* (1927) §22, *Cattleman*, beastman, byreman. **1634** BRERETON *Trav.* (1844) 52 A charter for a *beast-market. **1885** *Weekly Times* 2 Oct. 18/4 Trade today in the beast-market has been almost at a standstill. **1888** J. JACOBS *Fables of Bidpai* p. xxxix, Benfey..claims a Western (Greek) origin for *beast-tales in which animals act 'as sich'. **1951** DICKINS & WILSON *Early M.E. Texts* 62 The comparative lack of beast tales in ME is particularly surprising when contrasted with their popularity abroad.

beast (biːst), *v.* [f. prec. sb.] See also BASTE *v.*[4]

†**1.** *trans.* To make a beast of, treat as a beast.

1646 S. BOLTON *Arraignm. Err.* 151 And having thus beasted men, they [Papists] say to them..'You are..in no way able to judge of Questions of truth.'

2. *passive.* In the game of Ombre: To fail to win the game (said of the Ombre), or to incur a forfeit for breaking the rules.

1653 URQUHART *Rabelais* I. v, We will not be beasted at this bout, for I have got one trick. **1712** ARBUTHNOT *John Bull* in *Swift's Wks.* 1824 VI. 163 Lewis Baboon attempted to play a game solo in clubs, and was beasted. **1768** *Acad. of Play* 83 He who looks at the cards that remain in the Stock is beasted. **1811** E. NARES *Thinks I* II. 136 Not being able to save her from being beasted.

[**beast**, *v.* 'To hunt for beasts,' which modern dictionaries have inserted each from its predecessor, is a figment founded on a grotesque misreading of Spenser's *Amoretti* Epigr. ii.:

With that [i.e. Dian's dart] Love wounded my Loves hart,
But Diane [wounded] beasts with Cupids dart.]

beastal, obs. form of BESTIAL.

beastdom (ˈbiːstdəm). *rare.* [f. BEAST *sb.* + -DOM.] The condition of a beast; beasthood.

c **1872** ADDIS-*Elizab. Echoes* (1879) 57 Sorrow..had freed the woman-soul from that foul den of crusting beastdom.

†**beasten** (ˈbiːstən), *a. Obs.* In 4 besten(e, 5 bestyn. [? f. BEAST *sb.* + -EN[1]; but *bestene* may be gen. pl. of *beste*, BEAST.] Of beasts.

c **1325** *E.E. Allit. P.* B. 1446 Wyth besten blod busily anoynted. **1387** TREVISA *Higden* Rolls Ser. II. 181 Oistres and schelle fische, that beeth..lowest in bestene kynde. *a* **1400** *Octauian* 478 That bestyn kyng.

beasthood (ˈbiːsthʊd). [f. BEAST *sb.* + -HOOD.] The rank, condition, or nature of beasts.

1837 CARLYLE *Fr. Rev.* III. I. vii. 61 Many a Circe Island, with temporary..conversion into beasthood and hoghood. **1851** MAYHEW *Lond. Labour* I. 25 Instinct with all the elements of manhood and beasthood. **1868** BROWNING *Ring & Bk.* VIII. 510 Beasts..Do credit to their beasthood.

beastial, -iary, -iarian, obs. ff. BESTIAL, etc.

beastie (ˈbiːstɪ). [f. BEAST + -IE = -Y[6].] A little animal; an endearing form of BEAST. Also applied jocularly to insects. (orig. *Scotch.*)

1785 BURNS *To Mouse*, Wee, sleekit, cowrin', tim'rous beastie. **1852** C. M. YONGE *Two Guardians* vii. 118 Having the little beastie down to show the company. **1864** D.

THOMPSON *Daydreams* 229 Dogs..are religious beasties: but idolaters. **1880** LADY BARKER in *Macm. Mag.* 388 The sheep..are compact little beasties. **1952** *Arena* (N.Z.) XXXI. 14 But the leaving open of all doors and windows.. often lets in innumerable small beasties. **1955** E. POUND *Classic Anthol.* III. 181 Beasties on wing Time's dart shall touch presently.

beastily ('biːstɪlɪ), *adv.* [f. as if from *beasty* adj. + -LY²: on analogy of *hastily*, *lustily*, etc.] After the manner of a beast; bestially.

a **1823** SHELLEY *Scenes fr. Faust* 702 To live more beastily than any beast.

beastings, var. form of BEESTINGS.

'beastish, *a.* Now *rare*. Also 5 best-, 6 beestysshe. [f. BEAST *sb.* + -ISH¹.] Partaking of the nature of a beast; = BEASTLY (in various senses).

1398 TREVISA *Barth. De P.R.* III. i. (1495) 48 Bestysshe men and symple. **1502** *Ord. Crysten Men* (W. de W.) I. iii. 24 Beestysshe, deuyllysshe and worldly..be they. **1643** MILTON *Divorce* Wks. 1738 I. 182 Else it [marriage] would be but a kind of animal or beastish meeting. **1664** *Flodden F.* III. 32 Your beastish acts. **1923** A. HUXLEY *On Margin* 206 Human beings..he takes as he finds, noble and beastish, but ..decent.

†**'beastishness.** *Obs.* Also 6 bestysshnesse. [f. prec. + -NESS.] The condition of being 'beastish,' brutishness.

1530 PALSGR. 197/2 Bestysshnesse, *besterie*. *c* **1561** VERON *Free-will* 32 a, The beastishnesse of these bragging marchauntes of the cleargy.

†**'beastlihead.** *Obs.* 6–7; also **beastlyhead, -lihed.** = BEASTHOOD, BEASTLINESS.

1579 SPENSER *Sheph. Cal.* May 265 Sicke, sicke, alas, a little lack of dead, But I be relieued by your beastlyhead. **1616** *W. Browne's Past.* (R.) Peregall to nymphes of old, From which their beastlihed now freely start.

†**'beastlihood.** *Obs.* = prec.

1612 CHAPMAN *Widow's T.* in *Dodsley* (1780) VI. 162 Manhood! quoth you? Nay, beastlyhood I might say.

'beastlike, *a.* and *adv.* [f. BEAST *sb.* + LIKE.]

A. *adj.* Like a beast in nature, or in habits.

1526 *Pilgr. Perf.* (W. de W. 1531) 117 b, We be all carnall and beestlyke. **1588** SHAKS. *Tit. A.* v. iii. 199 Her life was Beast-like and deuoid of pitty. **1601** BP. BARLOW *Defence* 148 Those beastlike passions..which rage within us. **1868** TENNYSON *Lucr.* 228 Why should I, beastlike as I find myself, Not manlike end myself?

B. as *adv.*

1604 E. G[RIMSTON] *D' Acosta's Hist. Indies* VII. ii. 497 They lived..beastlike, without any pollicie.

beastliness ('biːstlɪnɪs). [f. BEASTLY + -NESS.] Beastly quality; resemblance to a beast in various points, *e.g.* unintelligence, rudeness, brutality, cowardice, gluttony, drunkenness, filthiness; bestiality.

1370 *Lay-Folk's Mass-Bk.* App. III. 122 Alle beestelynesse of synne. *c* **1440** *Promp. Parv.* 33 Bestylynesse [**1499** bestlynesse], *bestialitas*. **1526** *Pilgr. Perf.* (W. de W. 1531) 110 Beestlynesse or rude maner. **1580** NORTH *Plutarch* (1676) 769 By their beastliness..they had like to haue made all the Army fly. *a* **1618** RALEIGH *To Son* ix. in *Rem.* (1661) 102 A Drunkard will never shake off the delight of beastlinesse. **1751** H. WALPOLE *Lett. H. Mann* (1834) II. 388 Whithed..had forgiven all his elder brother's beastliness. **1854** DUFF in *Life* xxi. (1881) 342 Such drunkenness, such beastliness, such unblushing shamelessness.

b. *concr.* = 'beastly stuff.'

1834 L. HUNT *Lond. Jrnl.* No. 8. 58 The ale too!..not the beastliness of these days.

beastling ('biːstlɪŋ). [f. BEAST *sb.* + -LING.] A little beast or animal.

1872 MISS BRADDON *Bitter End* vii. 51 Tender young beastlings of the squirrel tribe.

beastlings, var. form of BEESTINGS.

beastly ('biːstlɪ), *a.* Forms: 3 best-, beaste-, beastlich, 4 besteli, bestely, bestly, 4–6 bestely, beestly, 6 beastlye, 6–7 -lie, 6– beastly. [f. BEAST + -LY¹.]

†**1.** Of the nature of living creatures (including man); animal, natural, 'carnal.' *Obs.*

1382 WYCLIF *1 Cor.* xv. 44 It is sowun a beestly [**1388** beestli] body, it schal ryse a spiritual body. **1526** *Pilgr. Perf.* (W. de W. 1531) 95 The beestly man can not perceyue those thynges yᵗ be godly.

2. Of or pertaining to the lower animals (as opposed to man); merely animal, bestial. *arch.*

1393 GOWER *Conf.* I. 144 And wailend in his [Nebuchadnezzar's] bestly steven. **1571** DIGGES *Pantom.* Pref. A iv, Wherein..the nature of man surmounteth beastly kinde. **1608** *Gt. Frost* in Arb. *Garner* I. 89 Charge of feeding so many beastly mouths. **1615** BEDWELL *Arab. Trudg.*, See more of this beastly fable, at the 14 Chapter. **1657–83** EVELYN *Hist. Relig.* (1850) I. 143 To be appeased by bloody and beastly sacrifices. **1873** RUSKIN *Fors Clav.* xxv. 27 The 'breeding' of a man is what he gets from the Centaur Chiron; the 'beastly' part of him in a good sense.

†**3.** Resembling a beast in unintelligence; brutish, irrational, without thought. *Obs.*

c **1230** *Ancr. R.* 58 Þe bestliche mon þæt ne þencheð nout of God. **1542** RECORDE *Gr. Arts* (1640) Pref., To bring the people from beastly rage to manly reason. **1563** *Homilies* II. *Idolatry* III. (1859) 236 More beastly than the Ass. **1598** DRAYTON *Heroic. Ep.* xxii. 150 When it doth passe by beastly ignorance. *a* **1703** BURKITT *On N.T.* Matt. xxii. 33 The beastly opinion of the mortality of the soul.

4. a. Resembling a beast in conduct, or in obeying the animal instincts.

c **1220** *Hali Meid.* 9 Þat beasteliche gederinge, þat schomelese somming. *c* **1449** PECOCK *Repr.* IV. vii. 463 To bacbite in this wise..is a beestly gouernaunce. **1567** *Trial Treas.* in Hazl. *Dodsl.* III. 264 The beastly desires of inordinate lust. **1604** ROWLANDS *Looke to it* 33 Thou filthy fellow of a beastly life. **1709** SWIFT *Adv. Relig.* Wks. 1755 II. I. 105 The beastly vice of drinking to excess. **1885** *Pall Mall G.* 29 May 4 They are frankly and cynically beastly.

†**b.** Inhuman, brutally cruel. *Obs.*

1558 KNOX *First Blast* (Arb.) 52 Open testimonie of her and their beastlie crueltie. **1587** TURBERV. *Trag. T.* (1837) 71 That blooddie beastlie king.

†**c.** Unmanly, cowardly. *Obs.*

1584 T. HUDSON *Judith* in Sylvester *Du Bartas* (1608) 752 Some brave in words, are beastly of their hands.

5. Unfit for human use or enjoyment; abominable; disgusting, or offensive, especially from dirtiness: applied, by those who use strong language, to anything that offends their tastes. Also with weakened emphasis, as a mere expletive.

1603 SHAKS. *Meas. for M.* II. i. 229 In the beastliest sence, you are Pompey the great. **1611** DEKKER *Roar. Girle* Wks. 1873 III. 159 I thought 'twould bee a beastly iourney. **1763** MRS. HARRIS in *Ld. Malmesbury's Lett.* I. 93 We had a beastly walk through the Borough. **1798** LD. CLARE in *Ld. Auckland's Corr.* (1862) III. 395 The pamphlet..is full of beastly blunders committed in the printing-office. **1830** DISRAELI *Home Lett.* (1885) 3 The steam packet is a beastly conveyance. **1878** MISS BROUGHTON *Cometh up as Flower* xiv. 150 That beastly hole, London. **1883** *American* VI. 245 This beastly English weather, you know. **1888** A. C. GUNTER *Mr. Potter* xxiii, I..came to tell her that story of her father's flying to escape arrest is all beastly rot. **1961** B. E. FERGUSSON *Watery Maze* xi. 278 The second major item was of equally beastly complexity.

6. *Comb.* †**beastlywise**, in a beastly manner.

c **1440** *Promp. Parv.* 33 Bestylywyse, *bestialiter*.

beastly, *adv.* Forms: 4 bestly, 6 -lie, (beasly), beastlie, -lye, 6– beastly. [f. BEAST *sb.* + -LY².] After the manner or likeness of a beast.

†**1.** In a beastly manner, like a beast. *Obs.*

c **1400** *Apol. Loll.* 58 Onclen suyn, fyling oþer, lyfing bestly, are sett in þe kirk. **1513** MORE *Rich. III* (1641) 459 Hee would bite and chew beasly his nether lip. **1514** BARCLAY *Cyt. & Uplondyshm.* (1847) Introd. 51 Some jangle when they be beastly fed. **1562** BULLEYN *Bk. Sicke Men* 77 b, Wastyng their wealthe..foolishely, and moste beastly. **1596** SHAKS. *Tam. Shr.* IV. ii. 35 Fie on her, see how beastly she doth court him. **1652** GAULE *Magastrom.* 371 Bellantius..was most beastly murdered.

2. As adjunct to an adj.: Brutishly, brutally, abominably, offensively. (In society slang, often merely = Exceedingly.)

1561 T. NORTON *Calvin's Inst.* I. 25 So beastly folish are men. *Ibid.* 23 b, They are to much beastly witted. **1803** BRISTED *Pedest. Tour* I. 298 He..comes home every morning about two or three o'clock quite beastly drunk. **1844** DICKENS *Lett.* I. 130, I was so beastly dirty when I got to this house. [**1865** *Daily Tel.* 24 Oct. 5/3 He was in good health..looked almost 'beastly well,' as I once heard it described.]

beastship ('biːst-ʃɪp). *rare.* [f. BEAST *sb.* + -SHIP.] The position of a beast.

1875 BROWNING *Aristoph. Apol.* 153 Shamed to brutebeastship by comparison!

beat (biːt), *v.*¹ *str.* & *wk.* Pa. t. beat (biːt). Pa. pple. beaten ('biːt(ə)n), beat. Forms: *Inf.* 1–2 béat-an, 2–3 beat-en, 3–5 bet-en, 4 beet-e(n, 4–6 bete, 5 beite, 5–6 bette, 5–7 beate, 7– beat. *Pa. t.* 1–4 béot, 3 biet, 3–7 bet, 4–6 bett, bete, 4 but, 4–7 bette, 5 bote, 6– beat, 7 *Sc.* bet; also 3–6 beted, beated. *Pa. pple.* 1–2 béaten, 3 bætenn, i-bet, i-beaten, 4 y-bete, i-bete, 4–6 beten, 4–7 bett(e, 5–6 bete, 5–7 bet, 6 betten, beate, y-bet, 7 beated, 6–9 beat, 5– beaten. [Com. Teut.; OE. *béatan*, str. vb., identical with ON. *bauta*, OHG. *bôzan*, MHG. *bôzen*:—OTeut. **baut-an*, not found in Gothic. The OE. pa. t. *béot* (repr. earlier reduplicated **bebôt*, **baibaut*), duly became in ME. *bēt*, *bete* (with close *ē*, as distinct from the open e or *ę* of the present); its mod. form would be *beet*, but this became obs. in 16th c. The actual pa. t. *beat* is prob. shortened from the ME. weak form *beted*, in 16th c. *beated*. The pa. pple. *beat*, still occasional for *beaten* in all senses, but chiefly used in sense 10, and in phrases like 'dead-beat' belonging to that sense, may also be from *beated*, but comes naturally enough from ME. *bet*, shortened from *bete*, *beten*, found already in 13th c., and having the open e of the present.]

I. The simple action: to strike repeatedly.

1. a. *trans.* To strike with repeated blows. *to beat the breast*: i.e. in sign of sorrow.

c **1000** *Ags. Ps.* lx. 1 Nu me caru beateð heard æt heortan. **1362** LANGL. *P. Pl.* A. v. 227 Bet þi- self on þe Breste. **1398** TREVISA *Barth. De P.R.* XVII. lii. (1495) 634 The tree ebenus tornyth in to stoon if it is longe beten. **1594** SHAKS. *Rich. III*, II. ii. 3 Why do weepe so oft? And beate your Brest? **1751** JOHNSON *Rambl.* No. 98 ¶ 13 At what hour they may beat the door of an acquaintance. **1798** COLERIDGE *Anc. Mar.* I. xi, The Wedding-Guest he beat his breast, Yet he cannot choose but hear. **1799** G. SMITH *Laborat.* I. 405 Then wring it out and beat it. **1850** TENNYSON *In Mem.* lxvi. 13 He plays with threads . he beats his chair.

b. With extension, expressing the result of the process: *to beat to powder*, *beat black and blue*, etc.

1598 SHAKS. *Merry W.* IV. v. 115 Mistris *Ford* (good heart) is beaten blacke and blew. **1755** SMOLLETT *Quix.* (1803) 215 My poor father, whom two wicked men are now beating to a jelly. **1807** MILNER *Martyrs* I. §2. 49 He was..beat to death with cudgels.

c. *to beat the air*, *the wind*, (*the water* obs.): to fight to no purpose or against no opposition; in reference to 1 Cor. ix. 26. Sometimes referring to the ordeal by battle, when one of the parties made default, in which case the other is said to have gained his cause by dealing so many blows upon the air.

c **1375** WYCLIF *Serm.* Sel. Wks. 1871 II. 258 Not as betinge þe eir. **1579** TOMSON *Calvin Serm. Tim.* 988/2 As we say in a common prouerbe, to beate the water, Saint Paule saith to beate the ayre. **1611** BIBLE *1 Cor.* ix. 26 So fight I, not as one that beateth the ayre. **1815** *Encycl. Brit.* (ed. 5) III. 488/2 If either of the combatants did not appear in the field..the other was to beat the wind, or to make so many flourishes with his weapon. **1884** FROUDE *Carlyle* II. xviii. 49 He cared little about contemporary politics, which he regarded as beating the wind.

2. a. *intr.* To strike or deliver repeated blows (*on*, *at* anything); †to knock (*at* a door). *to beat away* or *on*: to go on beating.

c **1230** *Ancr. R.* 18 Beateð on ower breoste. *c* **1385** CHAUCER *L.G.W.* 863 Betynge with his helis on the grounde. *c* **1435** *Torr. Portugal* 1515 On the dragon fast he bett. *c* **1450** *Gologras & Gaw.* liv. (1839) 158 Thai bet on sa bryimly, thai ..Bristis birneis with brandis. **1535** STEWART *Cron. Scot.* II. 576 Thir bernis bald ilkone on vther bet. **1605** SHAKS. *Lear* I. iv. 293 O Lear, Lear, Lear! Beate at this gate, that let thy Folly in. **1611** BIBLE *Judg.* xix. 22 Certaine sonnes of Belial..beat at the doore.

b. Said of hares and rabbits in rutting-time.

1610 GWILLIM *Heraldry* III. xiv. (1660) 166 You shall say a Hare and Conie Beateth or Tappeth. **1650** FULLER *Pisgah* III. ix. 338 Here the bellowing Harts are said to harbour.. beating Hares to forme. **1721** in BAILEY.

3. a. *trans.* Said of the action of the feet upon the ground in walking or running; hence, *to beat the streets*: to walk up and down. *to beat a path* or *track*: to tread it hard or bare by frequent passage; *hence*, to open up or prepare a way. Often *fig.*

a **1000** *Beowulf* 4522 Se mearh burhstede béateð. *c* **1375** WYCLIF *Wks.* (1880) 166 Bete stretis vp & doun & synge & pleie as mynystrelis. **1587** TURBERV. *Trag. T.* (1837) 249 And as enamored wightes are wont, He gan the streetes to beate. **1590** NASHE in *Greene's Arcadia* Pref. (1616) 8 Master Gascoigne..who first beate the path to that perfection. **1596** SPENSER *F.Q.* I. i. 11 That path they take that beaten seemed most bare. **1637** W. AUSTIN in Spurgeon *Treas. David* I. 235 Jesus Christ..who hath beaten the way for us. **1693** W. FREKE *Sel. Ess.* 18 Our Ancestors haue beat the Track before us. **1718** POPE *Iliad* II. 184 Their trampling feet Beat the loose sands. **1742** YOUNG *Nt. Th.* ix. 521 The paths she trod; Various, extensive, beaten but by few. **1875** CHR. ROSSETTI *Goblin Market* 193 This beaten way thou beatest, I fear is Hell's own track.

b. *to beat one's way*: to travel, or make one's way, *spec.* by illicit means. *U.S.*

1883 G. W. PECK *Peck's Sun* (Milwaukee) 16 June 1/2 He started home, beating his way on the trains. **1891** C. ROBERTS *Adrift Amer.* 53 To beat one's way, or to beat the conductor or the railroad, are equivalent phrases for travelling in the cars without paying any fare. *Ibid.* 195 There was nothing for it but to start out and beat my way there. **1904** *N.Y. Tribune* 8 May 10 [They should] stop trying to 'beat their way' by stealing a right of way that belongs to other people. **1926** J. BLACK *You can't Win* vi. 75 'Traveling?' he asked... 'Beating it.'

c. *to beat it*: to go away, to 'clear out'. orig. *U.S.*

1906 H. GREEN *Actors' Boarding House* 108, I told 'em to beat it. **1908** A. RUHL *Other Americans* ii. 10 He'll be beatin' it for Paris pretty soon where the rest of 'em all went. **1917** MATHEWSON *Sec. Base Sloan* xiv. 193 You get your boss to let you off for that long, beat it over to Harrisville tomorrow night. *Ibid.* xxi. 283 Beat it! Get out of here. **1926** LEACOCK *Winnowed Wisd.* 79 'To your posts, all of you!' she cried, 'Beat it,' she honked. **1928** C. F. S. GAMBLE *North Sea Air Station* xii. 170 We were all awakened at 1.30 a.m., and told to beat it to the air station. **1930** P. WYNDHAM LEWIS *Apes of God* XII. vi. 469 That's enough! Don't waste my time but beat it... Get to hell out of this! **1951** 'J. WYNDHAM' *Day of Triffids* ii. 38 Fedor had not waited once the plane was down. He had switched off the lights, and beat it.

4. a. To strike (a man or beast) with blows of the hand or any weapon so as to give pain; to inflict blows on, to thrash; to punish by beating.

971 *Blickl. Hom.* 23 Hie hine..mid heora fystum béotan. *c* **1175** *Lamb. Hom.* 121 Summe..hine on þet neb mid heore hondan stercliche beoten. *c* **1220** *St. Marher.* 5 Beateð hire bare bodi wið bittre besmen. *c* **1280** *Fall & Pass.* 61 in *E.E.P.* (1862) 14 He was ibund to a tre . an ibet wiþ scurges kene. *a* **1300** *Cursor M.* 15827 Wit þair bastons bete þai him. **1483** CAXTON *G. de la Tour* L vi b, [She]..may wel bete herself with her owne staf. **1501** *Plumpton Corr.* 157 All ther servant[s] beated me one after another. *c* **1532** LD. BERNERS *Huon* 433 The Gryffen bet hym merueylusly with her beke, wyngis, and talouns. **1556** *Chron. Grey Friars* (1852) 78 And then was..bettyn at the same pyller. **1557** *Primer* C iij, Thy heavenly sonne..was cruellye bette and scourged. **1609** BIBLE (Douay) *Num.* xxii. 27 Who being angrie, bette her sides with a staffe. *a* **1618** RALEIGH *Rem.* (1664) 5 Beaten with their own rods. **1712** ARBUTHNOT *John Bull* (1755) 47

They were beat..and turned out of doors. **1856** RUSKIN *King Gold. Riv.* i. (ed. 3) 8 My brothers would beat me to death, Sir.

†**b.** *intr.* To exchange blows, fight. (Fr. *se battre.*)

1586 WARNER *Alb. Eng.* IV. xxi. (1597) 106 They spur their Horses, breake their Speares, and beat at Barriars long.

†**5. a.** *trans.* To strike with heavy blows or discharges of missiles; to batter, bombard. *Obs.* See also 17, 36, 37.

c **1400** *Destr. Troy* XXXII. 12664 þe buernes on þe bonk bet hym with stonys. *c* **1600** SHAKS. *Sonn.* LXII, Beated and chopt with tand antiquitie. **1603** KNOLLES *Hist. Turks* (1621) 702 Upon this hill, Rogendorff to beat the Castle.. planted his batterie. **1664** *Floddan F.* III. 22 With Bombard shot the walls he bet.

†**b.** *intr. Obs.*

c **1400** *Destr. Troy* XXIV. 9669 Beiton þurgh basnettes with the brem egge. **1633** STAFFORD *Pac. Hib.* xvii. (1821) 392 And caused the Artillery to beate upon that place.

6. a. *trans.* Of water, waves, wind, weather, the sun's rays, and other physical agents: To dash against, impinge on, strike violently, assail. (*poetical.*) Cf. *weather-beaten.*

a **1000** *Riddles* (Grein) iii. 6 Stréamas staðu béatað. **1579** SPENSER *Sheph. Cal.* Aug. 47 The Sunnebeame so sore doth vs beate. **1664** *Floddan F.* III. 25 Weary men with weather bet. **1697** DRYDEN *Virg. Eclog.* IX. 59 Let the wild Surges vainly beat the Shoar. **1814** WORDSW. *White Doe* VII. 10 Some island which the wild waves beat. **1830** TENNYSON *To J.S.* i, The wind that beats the mountain.

b. *intr.* with *on, upon, against*; also *absol.*

c **885** K. ÆLFRED *Boeth. Metr.* vi. 15 Sǽ..on staðu béateþ. *a* **1300** *Cursor M.* 1844 þe wawis bett on euer-ilk a side. **1513** DOUGLAS *Æneis* VIII. viii. 161 The fyreflaucht beting from the lyft on far. **1530** PALSGR. 452/2 The rayne bette..in my face. **1611** BIBLE *Mark* iv. 37 The waues beat into the ship. —— *Jonah* iv. 8 The Sunne beat vpon the head of Ionah. **1759** B. MARTIN *Nat. Hist. Eng.* I. 53 Bristol Channel beats upon it on the North. **1795** SOUTHEY *Joan of Arc.* I. 352 We heard the rain beat hard. **1859** TENNYSON *Idylls* Ded. 26 That fierce light which beats upon a throne.

†**c.** (said of a river): To meet, join. *Obs.*

1577 HARRISON *Descr. Brit.* in *Holinshed* xii. 55 Two rilles ..joining in Wadeleie parke they beat upon the Test, not verie far from Nurseling.

7. *trans.* Said of the impact of sounds. *arch.* or *Obs.*

1382 WYCLIF *Ecclus.* xliii. 18 The vois of his thunder schal beten the erthe. **1581** MARBECK *Bk. of Notes* 1020 Not so much as the wordes or voices are heard, onely the sound beateth the eares. **1597** SHAKS. *2 Hen. IV*, I. iii. 92 With what loud applause Did'st thou beate heauen with blessing Bullingbrooke? **1677** GILPIN *Dæmonol.* (1867) 136 Yet are their ears so beaten with the objection of sects and schisms.

†**8. a.** *trans.* To labour or 'hammer' at (a subject), to thresh out; to debate, discuss; reason about, argue. *Obs.*

1470 SIR J. PASTON in *Lett.* 637 II. 393, I have betyn the mater ffor yow, your onknowleche, as I tolde hyr. **1542** BECON *Pathw. Prayer* Wks. (1843) 145 When he hath once thoroughly debated and beaten with himself his own misery. **1546** *St. Papers Hen. VIII*, XI. 197 Prayed him, in the beatinge of the matur with the Quene, to consyder and waye all partes. **1636** HEALEY *Epictetus' Man.* 160 Beate this discourse of mine over and over untill you have gotten the habite thereof. **1659** *Instruct. Oratory* 2 Diligently beating and examining..whatever may have relation to your subject.

†**9.** *intr.* To insist with iteration *on* or *upon. Obs.*

1579 TOMSON *Calvin Serm. Tim.* 374/2 When we beate vpon these promises to purpose. **1593** HOOKER *Eccl. Pol.* II. iv. §3 Their earnestness, who beat more and more upon these last alleged words. **1612** T. TAYLOR *Comm. Titus* iii. 1 Often to inculcate and beat vpon this point. **1633** SANDERSON *Serm.* II. 29 The holy Apostles..beat so much ..upon the argument of Christian subjection.

10. a. *trans.* To overcome, to conquer in battle, or (in mod. use) in any other contest, *at* doing anything; to show oneself superior to, to surpass, excel. Phr. ***to beat all, anything, everything***, etc., has been common in the U.S. since the second quarter of the 19th cent. (A natural extension of 4: cf. similar use of *thrash, drub, lick*, etc. The earlier examples show the transition. In the colloquial ***to beat one hollow, to sticks, to ribands***, etc., there is a play upon other senses of *beat.*)

[*c* **1460** FORTESCUE *Abs. & Lim. Mon.* (1714) 23 The Scotts and the Pyctes, so bette and oppressyd this Lond. **1480** CAXTON *Chron. Eng.* lxii. 46 The whyte dragon strongly fought with the reed dragon and bote hym euel and hym ouercome.] **1611** BIBLE *2 Kings* xiii. 25 Three times did Ioash beat [**1382** WYCLIF smoot; COVERD. did smyte] him, and recouered the cities of Israel. **1634** *Malory's Arthur* (1816) I. 424 They came home all five well beaten. **1664** PEPYS *Diary* 22 Dec., I hear fully the news of our being beaten to dirt at Guinny by De Ruyter. **1704** *Hymn to Vict.* lxvi. 12 Never was braver Army better Beat. **1711** STEELE *Spect.* No. 180 ¶ 13 He had beat the Romans in a pitched battle. **1778** BURKE *Corr.* (1844) II. 213 We were beat about the light-house. *c* **1800** SOUTHEY *Devil's Walk* xxii, This Scotch phenomenon, I trow, Beats Alexander hollow. **1802** MAR. EDGEWORTH *Moral T.* (1816) I. xi. 92 Favourite had been beat..by Sawney. **1812** T. JEFFERSON *Writ.* (1830) IV. 177 How many children have you? You beat me, I expect, in that count. **1818** MOORE *Fudge Fam. Paris* iii, The old Café Hardy..Beats the field at a *dejeuner à la fourchette.* **1822** BYRON *Juan* VII. xlii, Few are slow In thinking that their enemy is beat (Or *beaten*, if *you* insist on grammar). **1827** HALLAM *Const. Hist.* (1876) II. xii. 440 The ministers were constantly beaten in the house of lords. **1839** C. BRONTË *Let.* in Mrs. Gaskell *Life of C. B.* (1857) I. 199 Well! thought I, I have heard of love at first sight, but this beats all! **1847** BARHAM *Ingol. Leg.* (1877) 55 Many ladies..were beat all to sticks by the lovely Odille. **1863** DICKENS in *All Year Round* (Christmas No.) 7/2 'Well!' I says, 'if this don't beat everything!' **1871** WHYTE-MELVILLE *Kate Cov.* I, I rode a race against Bob Dashwood..and beat him all to ribands. **1872** FREEMAN *Gen. Sketch* xiv. §11 (1874) 295 He first beat the Danes, and then the Russians. **1879** LOWELL *Poet. Wks.* 418 And there's where I shall beat them hollow.

b. *spec.* in *Cricket.* (See quots.)

1867 G. H. SELKIRK *Guide Cricket Ground* ii. 22 The striker is said to be beat when he receives a ball so good that he is unable to play it properly and without a mistake. **1891** GRACE *Cricket* ix. 246 Try to have sufficient command of the ball so that if it beat the batsman it will hit the wicket. **1925** *Times* 27 Aug. 6/1 Douglas..beat the bat once or twice with balls that broke back and kept low.

c. Of a difficulty: To master (a person), to defy all his efforts to conquer it. Also, to baffle, perplex. Phrases ***to beat the band, rap***: see the sbs.

c **1810** in Smiles *Engineers* (1862) III. 51 The engineers hereabouts are all bet; and if you really succeed in accomplishing what they cannot do, etc. **1882** J. PAYN *Cash Only* II. 316 'This beats me altogether,' mused the lawyer. **1930** W. DE LA MARE *On the Edge* 135 Why you should have taken so much trouble about it simply beats me.

d. *absol.* To gain the victory.

1770 J. LOVE *Cricket* 24 Jove, and all-compelling Fate, In their high Will determin'd Kent should beat. **1876** HARDY *Ethelberta* Sequel II. 309 She threatened to run away from him..and being the woman, of course she was sure to beat in the long run. *a* **1887** *Mod.* Which side beat?

e. To get the better of (one) by trickery; to cheat or defraud. *U.S.*

1873 *Newton* (Kansas) *Kansan* 1 May 2/2 Johnson..left.. for the east, after having beat several creditors. **1886** *Century Mag.* Feb. 513/2 How do I know you ain't tryin to beat me? **1888** *Daily Inter-Ocean* 23 Mar. (Farmer), Two boys..were each fined twenty-five dollars... They have been beating boarding-houses all over the West Side. **1891** [see 3 b above]. **1904** *Columbus Even. Dispatch* 29 June 4 The ..people who try to beat the street car conductors out of their fare.

f. To get ahead of; so, ***to beat*** (one) ***to it***: to anticipate in doing something. orig. *U.S.*

1847 E. BRONTË *Wuthering Heights* II. xvii. 327 She would gladly have gathered it [*sc.* a letter] up..but Hareton beat her; he seized, and put it in his waistcoat. **1898** H. S. CANFIELD *Maid of Frontier* i. 21 He's watching the rangers, ..and will probably try to beat them there. **1904** *McClure's Mag.* Mar. 556/2 'They simply beat us to it,' complained Barrett, as we rode south. **1937** M. ALLINGHAM *Dancers in Mourning* xvi. 203 Poor old Chloe! I never thought she'd beat me to it.

g. Slang phr. ***to have*** (a person) ***beat***: to be sure of his defeat; hence *gen.* to have got the better of; to baffle.

1916 'BOYD CABLE' *Action Front* 30 Why..you can't make your hands do what your tongue says 'as me beat. **1945** *Coast to Coast 1944* 103 Well, he's got me beat.

h. Slang phr. ***can you beat it?***: an expression of surprise or amazement.

1917 WODEHOUSE *Uneasy Money* vii. 79 They pay me money for that!..Can you beat it? **1926** *S.P.E. Tract* XXIV. 121 *Can you beat it?* can you imagine anything worse than that? **1951** H. HASTINGS *Seagulls over Sorrento* III. iii, Oh, boy, can you beat it! Fourteen days leave... And we thought it was gonna be thirty days' cells.

†**11.** *trans.* To strike *together* the eyelids (= BAT), or the teeth; also *intr.* either of a person, or his teeth (= chatter). *Obs.*

c **1360** WYCLIF *De Dot. Eccl.* 96 [Then] shal antecrist grenne..& bete to gedre wiþ hise teeþ. *a* **1450** *Knt. de la Tour* (1868) 16 Ever beting her eyelyddes togedre. **1597** R. JOHNSON *Sev. Champ.* I. xvi. (1867) 127 Who, at the first sight of St. George, beat his teeth so mightily together, that they rang like the stroke of an anvil. **1617** GREENE *Alcida* Wks. (Gros.) IX. 17 My teeth for cold beating in my head.

12. *trans.* To flap (the wings) with force so that they beat the air or the sides; also *intr.* (*absol.*)

c **1386** CHAUCER *Frankl. T.* 38 The god of loue anon Beteth hise wynges and farewel he is gon. **1596** SHAKS. *Tam. Shr.* IV. i. 199 These Kites, That bait and beate, and will not be obedient. **1640** W. HODGSON *Div. Cosmogr.* 101 The Eagle..beating her wings on high. *a* **1700** DRYDEN (J.) Thrice have I beat the wing and rid with night About the world.

13. *intr.* Of the heart: To strike against the breast; *hence*, to throb, palpitate, pulsate. (Said also of the pulse, etc. and *fig.* of passions.)

c **1200** *Trin. Coll. Hom.* 169 And sore sihte, and his heorte biet. *c* **1384** CHAUCER *H. Fame* 570 And felte eke, that my hert bete. **1526** *Pilgr. Perf.* (W. de W. 1531) 119 We may fele our pulses bete quikly. **1530** PALSGR. 452/2 Fele howe my vaynes beate. **1663** PEPYS *Diary* 19 Oct., Her pulse beats fast. **1664** POWER *Exp. Philos.* I. 37 We have observ'd her [a Black Snail's] Heart to beat fairly for a quarter of an hour after her dissection. **1697** DRYDEN *Virg. Georg.* IV. 299 Such Rage of Honey in their Bosom beats. **1785** MRS. A. ADAMS *Lett.* (1848) 260 How the pulse of the ministry beats, time will unfold. **1837** *Penny Mag.* VI. 212 My heart beat with such transports of joy. **1845** LONGFELLOW *Belfrey Bruges* v, I heard a heart of iron beating in the ancient tower. *c* **1863** JEAN INGELOW *Four Bridg.* Wks. (1874) 242 Beat high, beat low, wild heart so deeply stirred.

14. *intr.* Hence, applied to other pulsating actions and their sounds. **a.** Said of a watch, etc. **b.** *Music.* To sound in pulsations; said of the undulating sound produced by two notes of slightly differing pitch sounding at the same time; see BEAT *sb.*[1] 8. **c.** *trans.* ***to beat seconds***, etc. See 33.

1614 MARKHAM *Cheap Husb.* II. iv. 152 Whose voyce (if you lay your eare to the Hiue) you shall distinguish..louder and greater, and beating with a more solemne measure. **1737** M. GREEN *Poems* (1796) 71 There let the serious death-watch beat. **1801** COOPER in *Phil. Trans.* XCI. 442 The trial with the watch was again resorted to; and she could hear it beat. **1819** REES *Encycl.* s.v. *Beats*, And like the human pulse in a fever, the more dissonant are the sounds, the quicker they beat. **1883** SIR E. BECKETT *Clocks, &c.* 295 In a pocket lever watch the balance generally beats in 2-9ths of a second. **1962** A. NISBETT *Technique Sound Studio* 242 If two tones which are within about fifteen cycles per second of each other are played together the combined signal is heard to pulsate or beat at the difference frequency.

II. Of the action and its effects: to do something by repeated striking.

* *To affect the place of by beating.*

15. a. *trans.* To force or impel (a thing) by striking, hammering, etc. With the direction expressed, as ***to beat down, out of***, or ***into*** (a position or thing).

1607 SHAKS. *Timon* III. vi. 123 He gaue me a Iewell th' other day, and now hee has beate it out of my hat. **1660** BOYLE *Seraph. Love* §16 (1700) 95 When we beat the Dust out of a Suit. **1719** DE FOE *Crusoe* (Rtldg.) 18/2 The blow.. beat the breath, as it were, quite out of my body. **1793** SMEATON *Edystone L.* §238 The stone..was then lowered.. and beat down with a heavy wooden maul.

b. fig. ***to beat*** (a thing) ***into one's head, mind***, etc.

1533 MORE *Answ. Poyson. Bk.* Wks. 1099/2 In suche effectuall wise inculked it, and as who should say, bette into theyr heades. **1556** VERON *Godly Sayings* (1846) 18 They must beat into yᵉ heartes of the people..studye of concord and true innocencie. **1571** ASCHAM *Scholem.* (1863) 29 Fond scholemasters, by feare, do beate into them the hatred of learning. **1612** BRINSLEY *Lud. Lit.* 74 You may beat the Latine into their heads. **1848** L. HUNT *Jar Honey* Pref. 15 The classics were beaten into their heads at school.

16. To drive by blows (a person, etc.) *away, off, from, to, into, out of* (a place or thing). In ***beat out of the field***, there is perhaps some mixture of sense with 10.

c **1325** *E.E. Allit. P.* C. 248 A wyld walterande whal..þat watz beten fro þe abyme. *c* **1384** CHAUCER *H. Fame* 1150 They were..not awey with stormes bete. **1570** ASCHAM *Scholem.* (1815) 205 In beating, and driving away the best natures from learning. **1603** SHAKS. *Meas. for M.* II. i. 262, I shall beat you to your Trent. **1611** —— *Wint. T.* I. ii. 33 He's beat from his best ward. **1603** KNOLLES *Hist. Turks* (1621) 132 Seeing the..Sultan..beaten out of his kingdome by the Tartar. **1738** WESLEY *Wks.* (1872) I. 91, I was beat out of this retreat too. **1885** N. POCOCK in *Book Lore* 28 July, Their version of the Psalms was ignominiously beaten out of the field.

17. To break, crush, smash, or overthrow by hard knocks; to batter. Cf. 5.

1570 T. WILSON *Demosthenes* 68 Which places he hath so cruelly overthroune and bet to the ground. **1603** KNOLLES *Hist. Turks* (1621) 265 Part of the wals we have beaten even with the ground. **1611** BIBLE *Micah* iv. 13 Thou shalt beat in pieces many people. **1798** NELSON in Nicolas *Disp.* III. 2 The man who may have his Ship beat to pieces.

†**18.** ***to beat the price, the market, the bargain***: to endeavour to bring down the price, to chaffer for the lowest terms; to cheapen; = ABATE, or BATE. Now only in ***beat down***: see 36 d.

1592 GREENE *Art Conny Catch.* II. 6 Hee bet the price of him, bargained, and bought him. **1630** LORD *Banians* 84 The broaker that beateth the price with him that selleth. **1632** QUARLES *Div. Fanc.* I. lxix. (1660) 29 How loth was righteous Abraham to cease, To Beat the price of lustful Sodoms peace! **1640** W. HABINGTON *Hist. Edw. IV*, 135 To beate the bargaine of peace to a lower rate. **1655** GURNALL *Chr. in Arm.* xviii. §3 (1669) 76 How low did Abraham beat the Market for Sodoms preservation? **1667** PEPYS *Diary* (1879) IV. 467 With a little beating the bargain, we came to a perfect agreement. **1785** C. BURNEY in *Parr's Wks.* VII. 398, I have been beating the market for them.

19. a. *Naut.* (*intr.*) To strive against contrary winds or currents at sea; to make way in any direction against the wind. ***to beat about***: to tack against the wind. [Cf. nautical use of Icel. *beita* to bait: some conjecture that *beat* here represents a lost **bait.*]

1677 YARRANTON *Engl. Improv.* I We must lye beating at Sea while the Dutch are at Anchor. **1687** RANDOLPH *Archipel.* 99 An English ship called the President..had been beating (i.e. striving against the wind) above 6 weeks in the channel. **1748** ANSON *Voy.* I. x. 102 The time of our beating round Cape Horn. **1765** TUCKER *Lt. Nat.* II. 552 Those who still beat about in the boisterous seas of life. **1819** *Merc. Mar. Mag.* (1860) VII. 291 They could not beat to the anchorage. **1837** HAWTHORNE *Amer. Note-bks.* (1871) I. 75 The hull of a small schooner came beating down towards us. **1839** MARRYAT *Phant. Ship* ix, They beat against light and baffling winds. **1840** R. DANA *Bef. Mast* i. 1 We..hove up our anchor, and began beating down the bay. *Ibid.* xxiii. 69 The wind drew ahead, and we had to beat up the coast. **1841** TYTLER *Hist. Scot.* (1864) III. 57 The transports..should beat in as near as possible to the shore. **1853** KANE *Grinnell Exp.* xlvii. (1856) 431 Beating hard to windward. **1858** *Merc. Mar. Mag.* V. 123 A ship has no chance to beat off.

b. *esp.* ***to beat up*** against the wind.

1720 *Lond. Gaz.* No. 5827/1 He beat up to Windward. **1784** KING *Voy.* (1790) V. 1712 We remained several days beating up, but in vain, to regain our former birth. *a* **1848** MARRYAT *Pirate* xiii, From Carthagena, probably, beating up.

c. *trans.* said of the ship beating the sea.

1718 POPE *Iliad* xx. 82 The toss'd navies beat the heaving main. **1758** J. BLAKE *Plan Mar. Syst.* 58 Others beat the Channel with great danger, rather than put into a port.

d. *trans.* said of the mariners beating the ship up or to windward.

1839 *Sat. Mag.* 18 May 192/1 We might continue to beat the ship up. *Ibid.* 192/2 We..kept beating the ship to windward.

20. *Venery.* (*intr.*) **a.** To run hither and thither in attempting to escape. **b.** To take to the water, and go up the stream; also *trans.* ***to beat the stream, a brook***, etc.

c 1470 *Hors, Shepe, & G.* (1822) 31 A herte, yf he be chasid, he wil desire to haue a ryuer. As sone as he taketh the Riuer, he soileth..yf he take agayn the streme he beteth or els he bekeṫh. 1575 TURBERV. *Venerie* 241 The Otter..is sayde to beate the Streame. 1727–51 CHAMBERS *Cycl.* s.v. *Hunting*, The buck will beat a brook, but seldom a great river, as the hart. 1815 *Encycl. Brit.* (ed. 5) III. 489/1 *Beating*, with hunters, a term used of a stag, which runs first one way and then another. It is then said to beat up and down.

** *To affect the state or condition of by beating.*

21. *trans.* To work metal or other malleable material by frequent striking; to hammer. †**a.** To inlay metal, to enchase, or emboss (*obs.*). **b.** To shape by beating, to forge, to flatten or expand superficially by beating; also with *out*. †**c.** To coin (money). Also *fig.*

c 1386 CHAUCER *Knts. T.* 121 His pynoun Of gold..in which ther was i-bete The Minatour. 1430 LYDG. *Chron. Troy* I. ix, His armes..Branded or bete vpon his coote armure. 1483 *Churchw. Accts. St. Mary H. Lond.* (Nichols 1797) 96 For betyng and steynynge of the same pinons, 6*d.* 1611 BIBLE *Isa.* ii. 4 They shall beate [1382 WYCLIF bete togidere, 1388 welle togider] their swords into plow-shares. 1614 RALEIGH *Hist. World* II. VIII. vi. §1. 611 Prerogatiues belonging to a Monarch..To beat Monie. 1640 HODGSON *Div. Cosmogr.* 71 Beating out chains and nets.. so thin that the eye could not see them. 1751 CHAMBERS *Cycl.* s.v. *Gold Leaf*, An ounce may be beaten into sixteen hundred leaves each three inches square. 1815 *Encycl. Brit.* (ed. 5) III. 487/2 To forge and hammer; in which sense smiths and farriers say, to beat iron. 1821 CRAIG *Lect. Drawing* vii. 372 An anvil, a hammer..to beat out and repair any part of the work that may seem to be ill done. 1884 CHURCH *Bacon* ix. 220 He..beat out his thoughts into shape in talking.

d. To become by being beaten out.

1873 BROWNING *Red Cott. Night-c.* 219 One particle of ore beats out such leaf!

22. To make into a powder, or paste, by repeated blows; to pound, pulverize. Generally with a complemental word or phrase.

c 1420 *Pallad. on Husb.* XI. 414 Bete all this smal, and sarce it smothe atte alle. 1535 COVERDALE *Num.* xi. 7 The people ..gathered it..and beate it in mortars. 1616 SURFL. & MARKH. *Countr. Farm* 235 Sowen with fine sand well bet. *a* 1618 W. BRADSHAW in Spurgeon *Treas. David* Ps. xc. 3 Thou beatest him to dust again. 1772–84 COOK *Voy.* (1790) V. 1772 The bark of the pine-tree, beat into a mass resembling hemp. 1815 *Encycl. Brit.* (ed. 5) III. 487/2 We say, to beat drugs, to beat pepper, to beat spices; that is to say, to pulverize them. 1871 RUSKIN *Fors Clav.* III. 2 Pick the meat clean off and beat it in a marble mortar.

23. To mix (liquids) by beating with a stick or other instrument; to make into a batter; to switch or whip (an egg, etc.). Also with *up*.

1486 *Bk. St. Albans* C vj a, Take yolkys of egges rawe and whan they be wele beton to geder. 1541 R. COPLAND *Guydon's Formul.* U iij, The whytes of egges, and oyle of roses bet togyther. 1664 *Crt. & Kitch. J. Cromwell* 104 Take twenty Eggs, beat them in a dish with some salt. 1793 SMEATON *Edystone L.* §237 The mortar..was prepared for use by being beat in a very strong wooden bucket. *c* 1813 W. PYBUS *Ladies' Rec. Bk.* 26 Beat well up together equal quantities of honey and common water. 1882 MRS. REEVE *Cookery & Housek.* 320 Take three or more eggs..beat yolks and whites separately.

24. *techn.*, expressing various operations in the arts; as in *Printing*, to ink the forms with beaters; in *Bookbinding*, *Paper-making*, *Flax-dressing*, etc.

1753 CHAMBERS *Cycl. Supp.* s.v., *Beating* flax or hemp is an operation in the dressing of these matters, contrived to render them more soft and pliant. *Beating* among book-binders denotes the knocking a book in quires on a block with a hammer, after folding, and before binding or stitching. *Beating* in the paper-works, signifies the beating of paper on a stone with a heavy hammer with a large, smooth head, and short handle, in order to render it more smooth, and uniform, and fit for writing. 1824 J. JOHNSON *Typogr.* II. 524 All pressmen do not beat alike. *Ibid.* The great art in beating is to preserve uniformity of colour.

25. To strike so as to cause appendages to come off. ***to beat a carpet***, so as to rid it of dust. ***to beat a tree***, so as to cause its fruit to fall.

1611 BIBLE *Deut.* xxiv. 20 When thou beatest thine olive trees, thou shalt not go over the boughs again. 1872 RUSKIN *Fors Clav.* II. 16 From a distance it sounds just like beating carpets.

26. a. To strike (water, bushes, or cover of any kind) in order to rouse or drive game; to scour or range over (a wood, etc.) in hunting. ***to beat the bush*** is also *fig.* as in c.

a 1400 *Cov. Myst.* 119 Many a man doth bete the bow, Another man hath the brydde. 1486 *Bk. St. Albans* D j a, Cast yowre sparehawke in to a tre and beete the bushes. 1526 *Pilgr. Perf.* (W. de W. 1531) 141 Whiche..hath.. betten the busshe that you may catche the byrde. 1655 GURNALL *Chr. in Arm.* 19 viii. §1 (1669) 502/2 How shall we get them to come into it? Truly, never, except we first beat the River. *a* 1667 WITHER *I loved a Lass*, 'Twas I that beat the bush, The birds to others flew. 1707 *Refl. Ridicule* (1717) II. 183 [They] can only beat the Bush, and never tend to the Head of the Business. 1741 *Compl. Fam. Piece* II. i. 289 The Huntsman..must..beat the Outside of the Springs or Thickets. 1772 GOLDSM. *Stoops to Conq.* I, Beating the thicket for a hare. 1814 SCOTT *Wav.* Pref. App. (1842) 30 The cover being now thoroughly beat by the attendants. 1872 BAKER *Nile Tribut.* xvii. 290, I took a few men to beat the jungle.

fig. 1732 POPE *Ess. Man* I. 9 Together let us beat this ample field. 1790 R. CUMBERLAND *West Indian* II. 21 He.. has been beating the town over to raise a little money. 1861 SALA *Tw. round Clock* One A.M. ¶5 When the shadowy hero of the 'Virginians' was beating the town with my Lords Castlewood and March.

b. *intr.* or *absol.* Also *fig.* esp. with ***about***. ***to beat over the old ground***: to discuss topics already treated of.

1709 STEELE *Tatler* No. 73 ¶8 Some [dogs] beat for the Game, some hunt it. 1711 BUDGELL *Spect.* No. 116 ¶5 We came upon a large Heath, and the Sportsmen began to beat. 1828 LANDOR *Imag. Conv.* (1846) 470 The light dog beats over most ground. 1865 *Times* 2 Jan., They both saw a man beating towards the place where the net was fixed. 1878 H. SMART *Play or Pay* vii. 149 What do you expect us to do —beat, or carry cartridges?

fig. 1713 *Guardian* (1756) I. 312 Beasts of prey, who walk our streets in broad day-light, beating about from coffee-house to coffee-house. *Ibid.* II. 83, I am always beating about in my thoughts for something that may turn to the benefit of my dear country. 1738 POPE *Epil. Sat.* II. 102 To find an honest man I beat about. 1792 MARY WOLLSTONECR. *Rights Wom.* v. 225, I do not mean to allude to all the writers who have written on the subject of female manners: it would, in fact, be only beating over the old ground.

c. ***to beat about the bush***: *lit.*, as in 12; *fig.* To engage in preliminary operations, *esp.* to approach a matter in a cautious or roundabout way.

1572 GASCOIGNE *Wks.* (1587) 71 He bet about the bush, whyles other caught the birds. 1687 T. BROWN in *Dk. Buckhm.'s Wks.* (1705) II. 115 He..often beat about the Bush, to start a Convert in him. 1798 MAR. EDGEWORTH *Pract. Educ.* (1822) I. 268 This ludicrous and perverse method of beating about the bush. 1834 PRINGLE *Afr. Sk.* vii. 259 After some hours spent in beating about the bush. 1884 *Punch* 29 Nov. 256/2 Obliged to be off: Excuse me.. But no good beating about the bush.

27. *fig.* With ***up*** in many constructions, as ***to beat up for recruits***, ***to beat up the town for recruits***, ***to beat up recruits***, and *ellipt.* ***to beat up***.

1696 BROOKHOUSE *Temple Open.* 21 Beating up for Voluntiers, by a New Predication. 1711 ADDISON *Spect.* No. 261 ¶1 A Captain of Dragoons..beating up for Recruits in those Parts. 1758 J. RAY *Rebellion* 151 They also endeavour'd to levy Men here, and beat up publickly for that Purpose. 1794 SOUTHEY *Bot. Bay Eclog.* ii. Wks. II. 78 A sergeant to the fair recruiting came..to beat up for game. 1809 W. IRVING *Knickerb.* III. v. (1849) 171 He tarried..to beat up recruits for his colony. 1824 TREVELYAN in *Life Macaulay* (1876) I. iii. 146 Macaulay beat up the Inns of Court for recruits. 1879 LOWELL *Poet. Wks.* 418 If a poet Beat up for themes, his verse will show it. 1885 *Manch. Exam.* 8 July 5/3 Any effort to beat up pecuniary help outside the ranks.

28. ***to beat up the quarters of***: to arouse, disturb; *colloq.* to visit unceremoniously.

1670 COTTON *Espernon* I. I. 3 Now beating up one quarter, now alarming another. *Ibid.* I. II. 63 An opportunity to beat up a Quarter of twelve hundred Light Horse. 1741 RICHARDSON *Pamela* II. 179 To..travel round the Country, and beat up their Friends Quarters all the Way. 1761 HUME *Hist. Eng.* II. xxix. 151 His quarters were every moment beaten up by the activity of the French Generals. 1823 LAMB *Elia* Ser. I. xv. (1865) 119 To beat up the quarters of some of our less known relations.

29. a. ***to beat the brains, head***, etc.: to think persistently and laboriously. Cf. CUDGEL *v.*

1579 TOMSON *Calvin Serm. Tim.* 457/2 Yet do the Papistes, but beate the water, when they stand & beate their heads only about ceremonies. *a* 1593 MARLOWE *Massacre Paris* I. i, Guise..beats his brains to catch us in his trap. 1677 YARRANTON *Engl. Improv.* 108, I have beat my Noddle a good while, considering of the reasons. 1686 W. DE BRITAINE *Hum. Prud.* §1 Never..Beat your Brain about the Proportion between the Cylinder and the Sphere.

†**b.** *intr.* predicated of the brain, etc. *Obs.*

1602 SHAKS. *Ham.* III. i. 182 This..matter in his heart; Whereon his Brains still beating, puts him thus From fashion of himselfe. 1639 FULLER *Holy War* II. xliv. (1840) 111 A lawyer's brains will beat to purpose when his own preferment is the fee.

30. a. ***to beat a drum***, etc.: to strike it so as to produce rhythmical sound. (Formerly with *up*.)

1603 KNOLLES *Hist. Turks* D. (1621) 1381 Beating up his drummes in every quarter. 1647 MAY *Hist. Parl.* II. v. 92 Drums were beat up in London..for Souldiers to be sent to Hull. 1697 DRYDEN *Virg. Georg.* II. 789 E'er hollow Drums were beat. 1832 HONE *Year Bk.* 1294 Beating a drum, and blowing the hautboy.

b. ***to beat an air, a tattoo, a signal***, and hence ellipt., ***a charge, a parley, a retreat***, etc. on the drum. Also fig. ***to beat a retreat***: to retreat.

1706 *Lond. Gaz.* No. 4221/2 The Enemy beat a Parley. 1765 FALCONER *Demag.* 409 He bids enraged sedition beat the charge. 1841 THACKERAY *Ballads, Chron. Drum* I. 21 At midnight I beat the tattoo. 1855 MACAULAY *Hist. Eng.* III. 680 A parley was beaten. 1861 HUGHES *Tom Brown Oxf.* III. iv. 74 With the help of his pipe [he] debated with himself the question of beating a retreat.

c. *intr.* and *absol.*

1841 THACKERAY *Chron. Drum* 1879 Wks. XXI. 6 He.. will never more beat on the drum. 1860 *All Y. Round* 403 The captain ordered the drummer..to beat to quarters.

d. Phr. ***to beat it out***: in Jazz (see quots.). Cf. BEAT *sb.*[1] 4.

1945 L. SHELLY *Hepcats Jive Talk Dict.* 21 *Beat it out*, play it hot. 1947 *The Beat* July–Aug. 10/2 *Beat it out*, play 'hot' music with plenty of rhythm in the background. 1948 *Penguin Music Mag.* V. Feb. 64 In the style of a couple of rhythm boys beating it out.

31. (Predicated of a drum or other instrument itself): **a.** *intr.* = To be beaten, to sound when beaten.

1656 *Rec. New Haven Col.* (1858) 603 The second Drum hath left beating. 1723 DE FOE *Mem. Cavalier* (1840) 137, I was glad to hear the drums beat for soldiers. 1758 J. RAY *Rebellion* 147 The Drums beat to Arms. 1808 CAMPBELL *Hohenlinden*, But Linden saw another sight When the drums beat at dead of night. 1822 SCOTT *Nigel* xxi, Every brass basin betwixt the Bar and Paul's beating before you. 1851 LONGF. *Wks.* (Rtldg.) 57 And the muffled drum should beat To the tread of mournful feet. 1871 L. MORRIS *Songs Two W.* 167 The mad chimes were beating like surf in the air. 1882 ROSSETTI *White Ship* in *Ball. & Sonn.* 85 High do the bells of Rouen beat.

b. *trans.* with the sound or signal as obj.: To express by its sound when beaten.

1636 MASSINGER *Bashfl. Lov.* IV. iii, Nor fife nor drum beat up a charge. 1672 T. VENN *Mil. & Mar. Discipl.* xxii. b 169 Before the Drum beates a march. 1822 SCOTT *Nigel* xxi, With all the brass basins of the ward beating the march to Bridewell before me. 1841 THACKERAY *Chron. Drum* II. 4 My drum beat its loudest of tunes. 1848 MACAULAY *Hist. Eng.* II. 535 Before him the drums beat Lillibullero. *Ibid.* xvii. (1871) 289 The drums of Limerick beat a parley.

c. *intr.* predicated of the signal, etc. = To be beaten, to be expressed by beating.

1816 C. JAMES *Mil. Dict.* (ed. 4) 178 The Réveillé always beats at break of day. 1848 THACKERAY *Van. Fair* II. v. 55 Wake me about half an hour before the assembly beats.

32. ***to beat time***: to mark musical time by beating a drum, by tapping with the hands, feet, a stick, etc., by striking the air with a baton; also *fig.* to keep time with.

1697 DRYDEN *Virg. Georg.* III. 301 With Pride to prance; And (rightly manag'd) equal Time to beat. 1709 ADDISON *Tatler* No. 157 ¶2 The Part rather of one who beats the Time, than of a Performer. 1807 ROBINSON *Archæol. Græca* V. xxiii. 535 The leaders of choruses beat time sometimes with the hand, and sometimes with the foot. 1842 TENNYSON *Miller's Dau.* 67 A love-song I had somewhere read..Beat time to nothing in my head. 1847 LONGF. *Ev.* (1851) 172 And anon with his wooden shoes beat time to the music.

33. There is often a combination of the notions of the beating of the heart, the pulse, or chronometer (senses 13, 14) with that of the beating of a drum, the beating of time, etc.

1602 SHAKS. *Ham.* I. i. 39 The Bell then beating one. *a* 1656 BP. KING *Poems & Ps.* (1843) 38 My Pulse, like a soft Drum, Beats my approch. 1704 STEELE *Lying Lover* I. i. (1732) 23 To all, my Heart and every Pulse beat time. 1769 MASKELYNE in *Phil. Trans.* LIX. 279 A pendulum clock beating half seconds. 1792 MARY WOLLSTONECR. *Rights Wom.* vii. 278 The heart made to beat time to humanity, rather than to throb with love. 1812 WOODHOUSE *Astron.* viii. 53 The seconds which it [a clock] beats. 1839 LONGF. *Ps. Life* iv, Our hearts..like muffled drums are beating Funeral marches to the grave.

III. With adverbs, and in phrases.

* *With adverbs.*

34. beat about: see 26 b. **beat away**: see 2 and 16.

35. beat back: **a.** To force back by beating (cf. 15); **b.** To drive back by force, to repel, repulse; **c.** To cause to rebound (cf. 16).

1593 HOOKER *Eccl. Pol.* III. xi. §21 That our pride..be controlled, and our disputes beaten back. 1621 MOLLE *Camerar. Liv. Libr.* I. vii. 23 The souldiers..knew not how to doe to beat backe the enemy. *a* 1656 BP. HALL *Occas. Medit.* (1851) 28 We beat back the flame; not with a purpose to suppress it, but to raise it higher. 1715 DESAGULIERS *Fires Impr.* 7 By Reflection when they are beaten back from Bodies, against which they strike. 1855 MACAULAY *Hist. Eng.* IV. 588 On the eighth a gallant sally of French dragoons was gallantly beaten back.

36. beat down: **a.** To force or drive downward by beating or hammering (cf. 15); **b.** To batter or break down by heavy blows, to demolish, knock down (cf. 17); **c.** *fig.* To overthrow (an institution, opinion, etc.); **d.** To force down (a price) by haggling (cf. 18). With these cf. ABATE. **e.** *intr.* To come down with violence, like rain blown by the wind, the sun's rays, etc. (cf. 6); **f.** (see 19); **g.** To reduce by beating (cf. 22).

a 1400 *Destr. Troy* XXIX. 11931 The knightes..brentyn and betyn doun all the big houses. 1547 *Homilies* I. *Salvation* (1859) 30 This doctrine..beateth down the vain glory of man. 1552 *Bk. Com. Prayer, Litany*, And finallye to beate downe Satan under our feete. 1586 WARNER *Alb. Eng.* II. xii. (1597) 53 Fighting to beate downe the Gates. 1602 FULBECKE *Pandects* 28 Democracie hath beene bette doune, and Monarchie established. 1603 KNOLLES *Hist. Turks* (1621) 63 The enemy with great slaughter still beaten downe. 1667 PEPYS *Diary* (1877) V. 87 To alter my office by beating down the wall and making me a fayre window there. 1793 BENTHAM *Wks.* (1843) IV. 413 Thus monopoly will beat down prices. 1849 MACAULAY *Hist. Eng.* xvii. (1871) II. 280 One whole side of the castle had been beaten down. *c* 1850 *Rudim. Nav.* (Weale) 107 For the purpose of keeping the sea from beating down. 1860 GEO. ELIOT in Cross *Life* (1885) II. xi. 273 The fields that were so sadly beaten down a little while ago are now standing in fine yellow shocks. 1860 TYNDALL *Glac.* I. §16. 113 The sun..beat down upon us with intense force.

37. beat in: **a.** To knock or force in by beating (cf. 15); **b.** To drive in by force (cf. 16); **c.** To smash or break in by blows, to batter in (cf. 17); **d.** To inculcate (cf. 15 b); **e.** (see 19).

1561 DAUS tr. *Bullinger on Apoc.* (1573) 260b, Thys should the Monkes and Fryers haue beaten in and set forth. **1589** WARNER *Alb. Eng.* VI. xxix. (1597) 143 Scots but brag, and he did beate them in. **1874** BOUTELL *Arms & Arm.* vi. 91 An axe-blow..would even beat in a shield.

38. beat off: **a.** To drive away from by blows, attacks, volleys (cf. 16, 17); **b.** (see 19).

1650 R. STAPLYTON *Strada's Low C. Warres* VII. 41 When the Enemye..attacques the Towne, it cannot beat them off. **1764** HARMER *Observ.* XIV. i. 37 No rain fell in the day-time, to beat off the workmen.

c. beat on: (see 2.)

39. beat out: **a.** To trace out a path by treading it first, to lead the way (cf. 3); **b.** To knock or force or shape out by beating (cf. 15); **c.** To drive out by force or fighting (cf. 16); **d.** To hammer out into a bulge, to extend by hammering (see 21); **e.** To thresh (corn); **f.** To work out or get to the bottom of (a matter, laboriously), to 'hammer' out; **g.** (in *U.S.*) To overpower completely, to exhaust; **h.** To measure out by beats (cf. 33).

1577 tr. *Bullinger's Decades* 293 To beate out the causes of these calamities. **1603** SHAKS. *Meas. for M.* IV. iii. 58 They shall beat out my braines with billets. **1606** G. W[OODCOCKE] *Hist. Ivstine* 14a, Themystocles..began to beat out what they intended. **1611** BIBLE *Ruth* ii. 17 So she gleaned in the field vntill euen, and beat out [**1388** WYCLIF beet with a ȝerde, and schook out; COVERD. shaked out] that she had gleaned. **1612** BRINSLEY *Lud. Lit.* xxi. (1627) 244 The..labours of others, which beat out the..sense of every word and phrase. **1667** MILTON *P.L.* XI. 446 A stone That beat out life. **1667** SIR R. MORAY in *Lauderd. Papers* (1885) II. 42 Wee beat out the bottom of the matter. **1672** BP. LLOYD *Fun. Serm. Bp. Wilkins* 39 Sometimes beating out new untravell'd ways, sometimes repairing those that had been beaten already. **1775** FIELDING *Miser* v. iv, Lovegold.. I'll beat out your brains. **1780** G. CLINTON in Sparks *Corr. Amer. Rev.* (1853) III. 132 They were so beat out with fatigue. **1850** TENNYSON *In Mem.* I. II. iv, The clock Beats out the little lives of men.

i. *U.S. colloq.* To defraud (a person or institution) *of* money, etc. by deception, blackmail, or other dishonest means (cf. 10d).

1851 *Oquawka* (Illinois) *Spectator* 5 Feb. 1/7 He then went to Cincinnati where he *beat* another man out of $12. **1904** [see sense 10d above]. **1929** W. FAULKNER *Sound & Fury* 255, I reckon you'll know now that you cant beat me out of a job. **1944** E. M. KAHN *Cable Car Days* 82 One never attempted to 'beat' the conductor out of his fare.

j. *N. Amer. colloq.* To get ahead of or prevail over (another), *esp.* in competition; to anticipate, improve upon (cf. 10a).

1893 *Outing* May 155/2 The act of starting consisted in beating out the pistol. **1903** A. D. MCFAUL *Ike Glidden* xxii. 190 Since I have driven him I've become satisfied that he can beat out any horse in the State. **1970** *Globe & Mail* (Toronto) 28 Sept. 22/4 Revson..easily beat out Ferrari's Jim Adams for third place. **1985** *Sci. Amer.* June 112/3 This arrangement gives an overhang approximately 1.1679 times a domino's long dimension, barely beating out the previous arrangement.

40. beat together: (see 23.) **beat up**: **a.** To tread up by much trampling (cf. 3); **b.** To make way against the wind or tide (see 19b); **c.** To bring a soft or semi-fluid mass to equal consistency by beating (see 23); **d.** (see 30, 31b); **e.** ***to beat up for*** recruits, etc. (see 27); ***to beat up quarters*** (see 28).

1882 *Daily Tel.* 24 June, At the commencement of play the wicket was moderately good, but it was beaten up considerably during the latter half of the Australian innings. *Mod.* 'We had an egg beaten up and biscuits.'

f. To knock about savagely, to thrash. orig. *U.S.* Cf. BEATING *vbl. sb.* 1b.

1907 'O. HENRY' *Trimmed Lamp* (1916) 157, I wouldn't have a man..that didn't beat me up at least once a week. **1912** MULFORD & CLAY *Buck Peters* i. 24, I found that I'd beat up a couple of policemen when I was drunk. **1928** E. WALLACE *Flying Squad* i. 14, I don't say they intended killing him, but they certainly beat him up. **1938** E. AMBLER *Cause for Alarm* ix. 155 'Is he drunk?'.. 'No—beaten up.' **1939** *War Illustr.* 21 Oct. 190 We heard the police in the room next door beating up another prisoner. **1958** *Times Lit. Suppl.* 8 Aug. 450/2 Mr. Szabo was captured by the AVO and beaten up.

g. ***to beat it up***: = to 'whoop it up' (see WHOOP *v.* 1e). *slang.*

1933 *Times Lit. Suppl.* 19 Oct. 713/2 James, the son, grows up, 'beats it up' a little in Paris, and finally gets a job in Malaya. **1958** *Daily Tel.* 1 July 11/1 What sort of noise did the neighbours complain about? Did the Purdoms and their friends beat it up a little in the evenings?

h. *Aeronaut. slang.* (See quots.)

1940 *Bulletins from Britain* 11 Dec. 3 in *Amer. Speech* (1941) XVI. 76/1 *To beat up*, to dive on to a friendly flying field as practice, a gesture of triumph or sheer joie-de-vivre. **1942** T. RATTIGAN *Flare Path* I, I put the old Wimpey into a dive and beat him up—you know, pulled out only a few feet above his head and stooged round him.

** In the phrases:

41. ***to beat the bounds***: to trace out the boundaries of a parish, striking certain points with rods, etc., by way of a sensible sign patent to witnesses. ***to beat goose***, or (Naut.) ***the booby***: to strike the hands under the armpits to warm them. † ***to beat the hoof***, ***beat it on the hoof***: to go on foot (*obs.*). ***to beat the knave out of doors***, name of an obsolete game of cards.

1570 B. GOOGE *Popish Kingd.* IV. (1880) 53 (*margin*) Procession weeke. Bounds are beaten. **1687** T. BROWN *Saints in Up.* Wks. 1730 I. 78 We beat the hoof as pilgrims. **1691** WOOD *Ath. Oxon.* II. /412 They all beated it on the hoof..to London. **1816** SINGER *Hist. Cards* 260 A childish pastime with cards played..under the title of 'Beat the Knave out of doors.' **1879** SALA in *Daily Tel.* 21 July, You and your mates were provided with long willow wands with which, at appointed spots, to beat the bounds. **1883** *Times* 15 Mar. 9/6 The common labourers at outdoor work were 'beating goose' to drive the blood from their fingers.

42. *Horsemanship.* Technical phrases: ***to beat a curvet, the dust, upon a walk, upon the hand***, etc. (See quot.)

1607 MARKHAM *Caval.* I. (1617) 16 To manage, to beat a coruet and such like. **1753** CHAMBERS *Cycl. Supp.* s.v. *Beat*, A horse is said to beat the dust, when at each stroke or motion, he does not take in ground or way enough with his fore-legs..He beats the dust at curvets, when he does them too precipitantly, and too low..He beats upon a walk, when he walks too short, and thus rids but little ground, whether it be in streight lines, rounds or passings. *Ibid.*, *Chack* in the Manege is taken in the same sense, as beat upon the hand; it is applied to a horse, when his head is not steady, but he tosses up his nose and shakes it all of a sudden, to avoid the subjection of the bridle.

43. Phrases treated under senses 1–33:

To beat about the bush (see 26c), *the air* (1c), *a bargain* (18), *black and blue* (1b), *one's brains* (29), *the breast* (1), *a brook* (20), *the bush* (26), *a carpet* (25), *a charge* (30b), *a door* (1), *a drum* (30), *the ears* (7), *one's head* (29), *hollow* (10), *the market* (18), *money* (21), *out of the field* (16), *a parley* (30b), *a path* (3), *the price* (18), *a retreat* (30b), *seconds* (33), *the ship* (19d), *small* (22), *the stream* (20), *the streets* (3), *time* (32), *to arms* (30), *to ribbons*, *to sticks* (10), *a track* (3), *a tree* (25), *up quarters* (28), *the water* (1c, 26), *the wind* (1c), *the wings* (12).

beat (biːt, beɪt). *v.*[2] [Either the direct derivative, or immediate source, of BEAT *sb.*[3], q.v.

(Marshall in 1796 (Eng. Dial. Soc. B. VI. p. 70) seems to identify this with BEAT *v.*[1]; others have tried to identify it with BEET *v.* (ME. *béten*), either in the sense of *improving* the soil, or of *kindling*, or feeding fire, which seems phonetically inadmissible, even if the sense were more probable.)]

To slice off the rough sod from uncultivated or fallow ground, with a beat-ax or breast-plough, in order to burn it, for the purpose at once of destroying it, and of converting it into manure for the land. Hence BEATING *vbl. sb.*; and the compound **beating-ax** = BEAT-AX (under BEAT *sb.*[3]).

1534 FITZHERB. *Husb.* §8 They must go beate theyr landes with mattockes as they do in many places of Cornewayle, and in som places of Deuonshyre. **1602** CAREW *Cornwall* 19b About May, they cut vp all the grasse of that ground which must newly be broken, into Turfes, which they call Beating. **1796** MARSHALL *Econ. W. Eng.* I. 324 Performed with a *Beating-axe*—namely, a large adze—some five or six inches wide, and ten or twelve inches long; crooked and somewhat hollow or dishing... This operation is termed *hand-beating*. **1808** *Monthly Mag.* Dec. 422 *To beet ground*: to pare off the turf in order to burn it (Cornwall and Devon).

beat (biːt), *sb.*[1] [f. BEAT *v.*]

1. a. A stroke or blow in beating.

c **1615** FLETCHER *Valent.* II. iii, For thus we get but years and beets. **1687** DRYDEN *Hind & P.* I. 253 The Smith Divine, as with a careless beat, Struck out the mute creation at a heat. **1805** SOUTHEY *Madoc in Azt.* xxiii, Instrument of touch, Or beat, or breath.

b. *Ballet.* = BATTEMENT.

1913 C. D'ALBERT *Dancing* 6 Ailes de Pigeon... These two beats are performed with both feet off the floor. **1931** C. W. BEAUMONT *Dict. Techn. Terms Classical Ballet* 14 The noun *entrechat* is qualified..according to the number of crossings required; in this calculation the beats by each foot are included. **1950** *Ballet Ann.* IV. 69 An admirable facility for the execution of beats. **1952** KERSLEY & SINCLAIR *Dict. Ballet Terms* 17 *Beats*, the dancer executes a beat in the course of a jumping step when he strikes both calves sharply together so that they rebound. The legs are then ready to beat again, to change places before beating again, or to continue the movement.

2. *Fencing.* A particular blow struck upon the adversary's sword or foil.

1753 CHAMBERS *Cycl. Supp.* s.v., There are two kinds of beats; the first performed with the foible of a man's sword on the foible of his adversary's..The second..is performed with the fort of a man's sword on the foible of his adversary's ..with a jerk or dry beat. **1833** *Regul. Instr. Cavalry* I. 153 The smarter the beat is given, the more effectual they will be as 'Guards' and 'Parries.'

3. A stroke upon a drum, the striking of a drum with the sound produced; the signal given thereby; also in ***drum-beat***. Sometimes *fig.*

1672 T. VENN *Mil. & Mar. Discipl.* I. iv. 45 There are these several Beates [of the Drum] to be taken notice of as military signs. **1687** DRYDEN *St. Cecilia's Day* iii, The double double double beat Of the thundering drum. **1791** PAINE *Rights M.* 44 By the beat of drum a proclamation was made. **1816** C. JAMES *Mil. Dict.* (ed. 4) 178/2 The Church Call;..a beat to summon the soldiers of a regiment, or garrison, to church. **1848** MACAULAY *Hist. Eng.* xvii. (1871) II. 284 Every man should be under arms without beat of drum. *c* **1850** LONGF. *My lost Youth*, The drum-beat repeated o'er and o'er.

4. 'The movement of the hand or baton, by which the rhythm of a piece of music is indicated, and by which a conductor ensures perfect agreement in tempo and accent on the part of the orchestra or chorus; also, by analogy, the different divisions of a bar or measure with respect to their relative accent.' Grove *Dict. Mus.* (1880). Also *spec.*, the strongly-marked rhythm of jazz and popular music.

1911 *Encycl. Brit.* XXIII. 279/1 Simple time is that in which the normal subdivision of its beats is by two, whether the number of the beats themselves is duple or triple. Compound time is that in which the beats are regularly divided by three. **1933** S. MOUGIN in *Hot News* (1935) June 16/1 Swing..is the balance found between the strong beat and the weak beat or beats in any bar. **1939** W. HOBSON *Amer. Jazz Music* iii. 49 To make this matter of beat and rhythm, so far as jazz is concerned, somewhat clearer for the layman, it may be pointed out that often in a jazz performance the only instruments playing regularly *on the beat* are, say, the bass drum and string bass; the rest are playing rhythms variously suspended around the beat. **1954** L. ARMSTRONG in *Grove's Dict. Mus.* IV. 600/2 Anything played with beat and soul is jazz. **1958** B. ULANOV *Hist. Jazz in Amer.* xxv. 349 *Beat*, jazz time; more meaningful to jazz musicians as an honorific description of rhythmic skill ('he gets a fine beat') than as a description of an underlying 2/4 or 4/4..or any other time. **1959** *Punch* 19 Aug. 60/2 Miss A likes it [*sc.* a pop record]. Oh, yes, it's got that beat and will sell. **1964** *Daily Tel.* 20 Feb. 22/6 Who dares to say that the cult of the beat groups by the young for the young is not vastly superior to the flood of pulp literature and horror comics pumped out for them by their commercially minded elders? **1967** *Crescendo* Dec. 33/3 The strange sounds emanating from an upstairs room revealed just who the Jazz Messengers were—yes, a beat group!

5. Any measured sequence of strokes or blows, or the sound thereby produced; the march of measured sound or of verse. Also ***beat-rhythm*** (see quot.).

1795 SOUTHEY *Vis. Maid Orleans* iii. 37 The regular beat Of evening death-watch. *a* **1822** SHELLEY *Cloud*, The beat of her aëry feet, Which only the angels hear. **1848** MRS. GASKELL *M. Barton* 66/2 The measured beat of the waters against the sides of the boat. **1851** LONGF. *Village Blacksm.*, You can hear him swing his heavy sledge With measured beat and slow. *c* **1873–4** G. M. HOPKINS *Note-books* (1937) 235 We have said that rhythm may be accentual or quantitative, that is go by beat or by time... The Saturnian ..must have been chanted, as the beats often disagree with the word-accents. This beat-rhythm allows of development as much as time-rhythm. **1885** *Contemp. Rev.* Apr. 555 Though it scarcely can be said to indicate the beat of the iamb.

6. The rhythmical throbbing of the heart or pulses; sometimes in comb., as ***pulse-beat***.

1755 JOHNSON *Dict.* s.v., The beat of a pulse. **1836** TODD *Cycl. Anat. & Phys.* I. 674/1 The flow from a vein is accelerated after each beat of the heart. **1877** O. W. HOLMES *Fam. Record* Poems (1884) 319 In every pulse-beat of their loyal sons. **1877** M. FOSTER *Phys.* I. iv. 97 Regarded as a pump its (i.e. the Heart's) effects are determined by the frequency of the beats, by the force of each beat, by the character of each beat.

7. a. In a clock or watch: The stroke of a pallet of the pendulum or balance on a tooth of the scape wheel; the sound thus produced; also the regular succession of such strokes. Hence ***beat-pin***. Phr. ***in*** or ***out of beat***, ***off the beat***: making a regular or irregular succession of strokes.

1706 PHILLIPS, *Beats* in a watch or clock. **1819** REES *Cycl.* s.v. *Beat*, The interval between two successive beats, in a clock or watch. **1828** ARNOTT *Physics* I. 90 In storm and in calm its [the chronometer's] steady beat went on. **1860** B. DENISON *Clocks, Watches, & Bells* (ed. 4) 101 The proper way to try whether a clock is in beat is to let the pendulum swing only just far enough for the escape, and then you will easily hear if the beats are unequal. **1874** BECKETT *Ibid.* (ed. 6) 73 When a clock with any kind of anchor escapement.. sounds 'out of beat', it wants either one side lifting or the crutch bending. **1883** SIR E. BECKETT *Clocks, etc.* 131 In very large clocks the pallet tails are too thick to bend for adjustment of the beat, and these eccentric beat pins are used. **1884** F. BRITTEN *Watch & Clockm.* 32 Beat Pins [are] small screws to adjust the position of the crutch with relation to the pendulum. **1889** HASLUCK *Clock Jobber's Handybk.* v. 94 Put on the pendulum, and set the clock 'in beat'. The meaning of 'in beat' is, that the escape takes place at equal distances each side of the pendulum's centre of gravity... When 'in beat' the tick sounds regular, and nearly equal, differences of the drop making it slightly uneven.

b. *fig.*

1865 J. H. NEWMAN *Gerontius* ii. 14 How still it is! I hear no more the busy beat of time.

8. a. A throbbing or undulating effect taking place in rapid succession when two notes not quite of the same pitch are sounded together; the combined note alternates rapidly between the minimum of sound produced by the mutual interference of their vibrations, and the full effect produced by the coincidence of their vibrations.

a **1733** NORTH *Lives* I. 247 How it [the organ at Exeter] is tuned, whether by measure or the beats, we were not informed. **1819** REES *Cycl.* s.v. *Beat*, The beats of two dissonant organ pipes, resemble the beating of the pulse to the touch. **1834** MRS. SOMERVILLE *Connex. Phys. Sc.* x. vi. (1849) 154.

b. *Radio.* The periodic variation of amplitude produced by the combination of oscillations of different frequencies. Also *attrib.*

1918 W. H. ECCLES *Wireless Telegr.* Gloss., *Beats* occur when two oscillations of differing frequencies occur simultaneously in the same system. The gradual change of phase difference causes the amplitudes to be opposed at one instant, and to concur at a later instant, with all the intermediate stages in the interval; the time between two successive oppositions, *i.e.* between two instants of minimum resultant amplitude, is called the time of a beat. The beat frequency is therefore equal to the difference between the frequencies of the two oscillations. *Ibid.*, *Beat Reception* (or Interference Reception) is the process of making high-frequency oscillations received by an antenna audibly evident by combining with them other oscillations of suitably different frequency. **1921** L. B. TURNER *Wireless*

Telegr. 74 During a signal, the two oscillations are combined, with the interference or beat effect familiar in acoustics when two musical tones of slightly different pitch are mingled. **1942** *Electronic Engin.* XV. 120 It is often necessary to retune the oscillator after a short while to obtain the correct beat frequency.

9. *Music.* 'The name given in English to a melodic grace or ornament, but with considerable uncertainty as to which particular ornament it denotes, the word having been variously applied by different writers.' Grove *Dict. Mus.* (1880).

1803 REES *Cycl.* s.v., Beat in music is a grace.

10. a. The round or course habitually traversed by a watchman, sentinel, or constable on duty. [It is uncertain to which sense of BEAT *v.* this is to be referred: cf. prob. to 3, but cf. 26 b, 41.]

1721 *New-Eng. Courant* 2–9 Oct. 2/2 The several Clerks of the Train-Bands made a strict Enquiry at all the Houses within their respective Beats. **1825** HOOD *Ode Graham* xxxvii, I hear the watchmen on their beats, Hawking the hour about the streets. **1840** *Penny Cycl.* XVIII. 335 Every part of the metropolis is divided into beats. *c* **1860** THACKERAY *Ball. Policem.* (1879) 251, I paced upon my beat With steady step and slow.

b. A course habitually traversed by any one; sometimes *fig.*, esp. in phrase, ***out of one's beat***: not in one's sphere or department.

1786 W. COWPER *Let.* 1 May (1904) III. 27 The Chesters, the Throckmortons, the Wrightes, are all of them good-natured agreeable people, and I rejoice, for your sake, that they lie all within your beat. **1836** GEN. P. THOMPSON *Lett. Represent.* 153 A highwayman could never get more than the value of his beat. **1836** DICKENS *Sk. Boz* i. 31 The costermongers repaired to their ordinary 'beats' in the suburbs. **1839** CARLYLE *Chartism* iv. (1858) 21 Europe, Asia, Africa, and America lay somewhere out of their beat. **1854** MRS. GASKELL *Let.* 27 Oct. (1966) 318 She [*sc.* Florence Nightingale] said, 'The prostitutes come in perpetually—poor creatures staggering off their beat!' **1862** *Sat. Rev.* 15 Mar. 295 Ask him why anything is so and so, and you have got out of his beat. **1872** 'MARK TWAIN' *Roughing It* vi. 28 His [*sc.* superintendent of a stage company's] beat or jurisdiction..was called a 'division'. **1937** N. MARSH *Vintage Murder* xxii. 245, I am very busy—consulting-room hours in town, and a wide country beat. **1965** *New Statesman* 7 May 715/2 The world is James Cameron's beat; he has visited every country but three covering the great events of our time, from the Allied victory in Germany to Vietnam, for press and television.

c. *U.S.* (See quot. 1857.)

[**1736** in *Smithtown Rec.* (N.Y., 1898) 229 The place called the Horse beat.] **1834** AUDUBON *Ornith. Biog.* II. 433 When we went to look for the other [moose]..we found that he had ..gone to the 'beat'. **1857** *Harper's Mag.* Nov. 819/1 The bear goes to and from his den..by certain paths called 'beats'... A bear will use the same 'beat' for years.

d. 'In Alabama and Mississippi, the principal subdivision of a county; a voting-precinct' (*Cent. Dict.* 1889).

1860 J. F. H. CLAIBORNE *Sam. Dale* x. 166 Governor Holmes appointed me..commissioner to take the census and organize beats or precincts. **1893** *Congress. Rec.* Feb. 2298/1 The evidence shows that his tickets were brought to the polls by friends of Turpin, and peddled there by them. This is shown to have been the case at Steep Creek beat,.. at Hopewell beat, in Loundes County. **1896** *Ibid.* Mar. 2788/1 Testimony was taken to show that fraud was committed in certain beats,—the River beat, Union, and one or two others.

e. The stretch of country assigned to a musterer (of sheep or cattle). *Austral.* and *N.Z.*

1873 J. E. TINNE *Wonderland of Antipodes* 38 As they complete each flock, it is turned over to a shepherd, who would drive it off with the aid of his dogs to a beat; possibly ten or twenty miles distant. **1941** BAKER *Dict. Austral. Slang* 9 *Beat*, the area patrolled by a sheep or cattle musterer. **1953** B. STRONACH *Musterer on Molesworth* ii. 13 Boy ..hunted them all [*sc.* the sheep] on to the next man's beat. **1958** J. PASCOE *N.Z. Sheep-Station* 22 Getting the sheep off the mountain is more difficult. Usually one man and his dogs will climb well above the sheep to what is known as the 'top beat'... The man half way down the slopes has what is called the 'middle beat'.

11. A tract over which a sportsman ranges in pursuit of game.

1875 'STONEHENGE' *Brit. Sports* I. I. i. §1 The frauds..are enough to make him cautious before engaging a beat. **1884** *Weekly Times* 29 Aug. 14/4 On the first day's beat he saw one brace of barren birds.

12. In sailing: One of the transverse courses in beating to windward.

1880 *Daily Tel.* 7 Sept., Anxious moments follow next on the beat to windward.

13. ***beat-up of quarters***: assault, reconnaissance.

1870 *Daily News* 18 Oct., The beat-up of the enemy's quarters..took place after all.

14. The action or an act of beating in order to rouse game.

1876 A. A. A. KINLOCH *Large Game Shooting* II. i. 2 The howdah elephants on which the sportsmen are mounted are distributed at intervals along the line, and as the beat progresses, some commotion may be observed as various species of game are roused. **1897** *Encycl. Sport* I. 84/2 The Sloth Bear..except when driven out in the course of a beat ..will not be observed during the day.

15. *U.S.* (chiefly *dial.*). **a.** That which surpasses, excels, or outdoes (something). Only in phr. ***to see,*** or ***hear, the beat*** (***of***).

c **1827** R. M. BIRD *News of Night* in E. H. O'Neill *Cowled Lover* (1941) 147 Did you ever see the beat o' that? **1833** S. SMITH *Major Downing* 129, I never see the beat of it. **1847** *Great Kalamazoo Hunt* (Philad.) 100 (Th.), You don't tell me so! Did I ever hear the beat o' that! **1878** H. B. STOWE *Poganuc P.* x. 86 That Bill is saassy enough to physic a hornbug. I never see the beat of him. **1888** 'C. E. CRADDOCK' *Broomsedge Cove* v. 80 Waal, sir, eatin' supper by a tallow dip—who ever hearn the beat! **1907** 'O. HENRY' *Trimmed Lamp* (1916) 209 Count Fernando Mazzini was his name. I never saw the beat of him for elegance.

b. ***to get a beat on***: (see quot.).

1888 FARMER *Americanisms* s.v., *To get a beat on* is to get the advantage of... As used by thieves and their associates, *to get a beat on one*..also implies that the point has been scored by underhand, secret, or unlawful means.

c. A success scored against rivals by a reporter or newspaper; an item of news secured and published in advance of competitors.

1873 *Harper's Mag.* July 231/1 One of these 'enterprising' individuals secured his first 'beat' by riding in..on a horse not his own, and taking news of the disaster to Philadelphia by rail, before an injunction was laid on the transmission of the truth. **1887** *Detroit Tribune* 27 June 3/2 They finally succeeded, and cheered lustily as the Ocean King steamed for New York with a big 'beat' for the Times. The office was safely reached, and the 'beat' appeared that morning. **1905** E. WALLACE *Four Just Men* i, The obedient reporter went forth. He returned in an hour in that state of mysterious agitation peculiar to the reporter who has got a 'beat'. **1940** GRAVES & HODGE *Long Week-end* xvii. 283 The newspapers paid well for 'beats', as 'scoops' were now called. **1969** S. GREENLEE *Spook who sat by Door* xvii. 152, I have a beat for you... That is the right word, beat? They stopped using scoop in the movies in the thirties.

16. [f. BEAT *ppl. a.*] An idle, worthless, or shiftless fellow. (Cf. DEAD-BEAT *sb.*[2]) *U.S.*

1865 *Canteen Songster* (1868) 26 Before 'this cruel war' broke out, he was what's termed 'a beat'. **1887** J. D. BILLINGS *Hard Tack & Coffee* 95 (Th.), The original idea of a beat was that of a lazy man or a shirk who would by hook or by crook get rid of all military or fatigue duty that he could. **1887** *Harper's Mag.* Dec. 107/1 The inevitable squad of 'beats' with bleary eyes and wolfish faces infesting the doorways of the saloons. **1903** *Boston Herald* 19 Aug., He would not loan money to policemen or firemen, stating that they were the biggest beats in the country.

beat (biːt, *dial.* beːt), *sb.*[2] Forms: 5 bete, 6 beit, 7 bayt, 8 bait, 8– beat, 9 beet. [Of uncertain form and etymology; the 15th c. *bete* and 18th c. frequent *bait*, point to *beat* as the 16th c. and normal modern form, *bait* being only a phonetic variant at a time when the pronunciation was still (beɪt) as in *great*, and *beet* being a modern phonetic spelling since the pronunc. became (biːt) as in *meat, meet.* Possibly from the vb. *beat*, in sense of a 'beating,' or quantity to be beaten at once; see BEAT *v.*[1] 24, and cf. *stack*, etc.] A bundle of flax or hemp made up ready for steeping.

c **1450** HENRYSON *Mor. Fab.* 60 The Lint ryped, the Churle pulled the Lyne, Ripled the bolles, and in beites it set; It steeped in the burne, and dryed syne, And with ane beittel knocked it and bet, Syne swyngled it well, and hekled in the flet. *a* **1500** *Cath. Angl.* 30 *note*, A bete as of hempe or lyne, *fascis.* **1616** SURFL. & MARKH. *Countr. Farm* 567 Hempe..bound vp in bundles, which they do call bayts. **1725** BRADLEY *Fam. Dict.* s.v. *Hemp*, Laying Bait upon Baits till all be laid in, and so that the Water covers 'em all over. **1744** D. FLINT *Raising Flax* ix. 11 The lint is..tied up in large but manageable Beats or Sheaves. **1839** STONEHOUSE *Axholme* 29 Flax..a week after midsummer, is pulled and bound in sheaves or beats. **1847** *Jrnl. R. Agric. Soc.* VIII. II. 453 The flax..must be tied up in small sheaves or beets.

beat (biːt, beɪt), *sb.*[3] Forms: also 7 baite, 7–9 bait, 8–9 bate. [Of doubtful phonetic form, and unknown origin. The modern Devonsh. pronunciation is (beɪt) variously spelt *bait, bate, beat.* Although *bait* occurs constantly in Gervaise Markham, *beat(e* was the spelling of the vb. with Fitzherbert in 1534, Carew in 1602, and of the sb. with Worlidge in 1681, and is apparently the proper form. The vb. is found nearly a century before the sb., and may thus be its immediate source, but on general grounds, the converse is more likely.

The suggestion that *beat* is another form of PEAT, is incompatible with the history of the latter, q.v. The ON. *beit* 'pasturage,' *beiti* 'pasture,' also 'heath, ling,' would barely do for the sense, and phonetically would give *bait*, not *beat.* See BEAT *v.*[2]]

The rough sod of moorland (with its heath, gorse, etc.), or the matted growth of fallow land, which is sliced or pared off, and burned (at once to get rid of it and to make manure), when the land is about to be ploughed. See Eng. Dial. Soc. B. vi. p. 70. ***to beat-burn***, also BURN-BEAT: to treat land in this way. ***to lie to beat***: to lie fallow till covered with a matted growth of grass and weeds which may be thus pared off and burned.

1620 MARKHAM *Farewell to Husb.* (1649) 22 After you have thus burnt your baite and plowed up your ground. —— *Ibid.* II. xxi. (1668) 115 To break up Pease-earth, which is to lye to bait. **1796** MARSHALL *Econ. W. Eng.* I. 323 *Beat*, the roots and soil subjected to the operation of 'burning beat.' **1830** MRS. BRAY *Fitz of F.* xvi. (1884) 137 The burning of bate, as it is called; a mode of manuring land, known elsewhere by the name of *denshiring.* **1864** CAPERN *Devon Provincialism, Beat* or *Bate*, the spine of old fallow lands. **1885** F. T. ELWORTHY (in letter) A field is described as 'all to a beat' when it has become matted with weeds, especially couch-grass or twitch.

Comb. **beat-ax** (in Devonsh. *dial.* bidax, bidix), the ax or adze with which the beat is pared off in hand-beating: see BEATING-AX under BEAT *v.*[2]; **beat-borough, beat-hill**, one of the heaps in which the beat is collected and burned; **beat-field**, a field in which the beat is being burned.

1602 R. CAREW *Survey of Cornwall* 19 b A little before plowing time, they scatter abroad those Beat-boroughs.. upon the ground. **1813** C. VANCOUVER *Agriculture of Devon* 92 It is utterly impossible, at a distance, to distinguish a village from a beatfield. **1885** F. T. ELWORTHY (letter) The operation is performed with a *bidiks* (beat-ax), or more commonly with a breast-plough called a *spader.*

beat, *sb.*[4]: see BEAT GENERATION.

beat (biːt), *ppl. a.* For forms see BEAT *v.*[1] **1.** Shortened form of BEATEN, often used as *pple.*; as *adj.* chiefly in the sense: Overcome by hard work or difficulty; common in the expression ***dead-beat.*** **a.** literally. *Obs.*, *arch.*, or *dial.*

c **1400** *Rowland & Ot.* 417 A Sercle of golde That bett was wonder newe. *c* **1440** *Bone Flor.* 182 Hur clothys wyth bestes and byrdes wer bete All abowte. **1589** WARNER *Alb. Eng.* v. xxiii. (1579) 113 The storm-beate English ship. **1793** SMEATON *Edystone L.* §239 A proper quantity of the beat mortar was liquefied. *c* **1817** HOGG *Tales & Sk.* IV. 13 A little bowl of beat potatoes and some milk.

b. figuratively *in current use.* Also ***beat out, up***, worn out, exhausted; ***dead beat***: see DEAD BEAT *ppl. a.*; ***beat generation***: see as separate entry.

1758 in *Essex Inst. Hist. Coll.* (Salem, Mass.) XVIII. 92 Some was very much beat out by their march from Northampton. **1832** MOORE *Jerome on E.* II. Wks. (1862) 558 Till fairly beat the saint gave o'er. **1833** S. SMITH *Major Downing* 127 At last he got so beat out he couldn't only wrinkle his forehead and wink. **1868** DICKENS *Lett.* (1880) II. 334, I was again dead beat at the end. **1879** HOWELLS *L. Aroostook* (1882) I. 20 'Is the young lady ill?' 'No..a little beat out, that's all.' **1914** *Daily Express* 2 Sept. 3/1 We were all beat up after four days of the hardest soldiering you ever dreamt of. **1945** L. SHELLY *Hepcats Jive Talk Dict.* 7 *Beat*, worn out. **1954** P. FRANKAU *Wreath for Enemy* III. iv. 191, I was too beat and hazy to take anything in. **1956** J. HEARNE *Stranger at Gate* xii. 92 'You look beat up.'.. 'I couldn't look as beat up as I feel.'

2. ***beat elbow, hand, knee***: injuries incident to miners caused by the jarring and friction of the pick. Cf. *miner's elbow* s.v. MINER 6 b.

1905 *Daily Chron.* 17 Mar. 5/6 Judge Greenwell decided that 'beat hand' could not be classed as an accident... He found similarly in a claim with respect to 'beat knee'. **1907** *Ibid.* 17 May 5/5 'Beat hand', 'beat knee', and 'beat elbow'. **1935** A. J. CRONIN *Stars look Down* III. xii. 588 He worked with this committee on nystagmus, beat knee and the incidence of silicosis in non-metalliferous mines.

'beatable, *a.* That can be beaten.

1611 COTGR., *Batable*, beatable; batterable. **1892** *Atlantic Monthly* Mar. 331 A more beatable child than Samuel Taylor it would be hard to find.

beatch, obs. variant of BEACH.

ˌbea'tee. [see -EE.] One who is beaten: correlative to *beater.*

1860 L. HARCOURT *Diaries G. Rose* I. 184 You are the beater, I am only the beatee. **1876** R. BLACK tr. *Guizot's Hist. Fr.* V. lv. 262 Put the beatee in the Bastille to tranquillize the beater.

'beatemest, *a. U.S. dial.* Also **-omest.** [app. f. *beat 'em* + -EST *superl. suffix.*] Most excellent or splendid.

1831 *Boston Evening Transcript* 9 Aug. 2/3 Beatemest feller with a gun ever you seed. **1838** B. DRAKE *Tales* 30 Your the beatomest shakes I ever seed. **1851** S. JUDD *Margaret* (ed. 2) III. 245 Take it by and large fifty head a season, and she is the beatomest.

beaten ('biːt(ə)n), *ppl. a.* For forms see BEAT *v.*[1] Used adjectivally in many of the senses of the verb.

1. Struck with repeated blows.

1599 SANDYS *Europæ Spec.* (1632) 124 On whom..so many..beaten breasts, and lift uppe eyes attended. **1633** P. FLETCHER *Elisa* II. l, Sleep beaten breast; no blows shall now molest thee. **1859** BARNES *Rhymes Dorset Dial.* II. 4 Wi' drubbens of a beaten drum.

2. Struck or pressed by frequent feet; trodden; worn hard, bare, or plain by repeated passage. Often in *fig.* expressions.

1477 NORTON *Ord. Alch.* in Ashm. Introd. 3 A Booke of secrets given by God; to men Elect, a Beaten-Trod. **1583** BABINGTON *Commandm.* 97 Had wee any feeling left within our sides, and our heartes were not altogether so hard trampled and beaten as they are. **1642** CARPENTER *Experience* II. vi. 221 Our beaten, customary, and daily practice. **1748** ANSON *Voy.* II. xii. 263 They had marched.. about ten miles in a beaten road. **1751** JOHNSON *Rambl.* No. 86 ¶3 The imitator treads a beaten walk. **1860** TYNDALL *Glac.* I. §9. 64 We were far from the beaten track. **1865** M. ARNOLD *Ess. Crit.* viii. (1875) 318 Subjects out of the beaten line of the reading and thought of their day.

†**3.** Well-worn, trite. *Obs.*

a **1543** FENNER *Def. Ministers* (1587) 98 These also are knowen and beaten sentences alleadged by Bishop Iewell. **1642** R. CARPENTER *Experience* IV. ix. 159 If God had talked to them..in a worne and beaten phrase. **1712** ADDISON *Spect.* No. 289 ¶6 One of the most ancient and most beaten Morals. **1756** J. WARTON *Ess. Pope* (1782) I. iii. 102 This Essay..on a beaten subject.

†**4.** Of persons: Inured *to* (anything), experienced. *Obs.*

a **1593** H. Smith *Serm.* (1866) I. 220 Rehoboam's sage and beaten counsellors. **1603** Knolles *Hist. Turks* K (1621) 870 An armie..most strong and puissant, old beaten souldiors almost throughout it. **1611** Cotgr., *Fauls rompu*, a subtill fellow, one that hath bin much beaten to the world. *a* **1639** S. Ward *Serm.* (1862) 117 (D.) A beaten politician of our times. *c* **1700** *Gentl. Instruc.* (1782) 522 (D.) A man beaten to the trade may wrangle..better.

5. Worked by hammering, as metal.

a. Hammered into thin foil or leaf; shaped by the hammer, as repoussé work.

c **1300** in Wright *Lyric P.* ix. 35 Hire gurdel of bete gold is al. **1483** *Cath. Angl.* 30 Betyn gold, *braccea.* **1611** Bible *Numb.* viii. 4 Vnto the flowres thereof was beaten worke. **1659** in Rushw. *Hist. Coll.* I. 169 The Earls of Carstile and Holland, Ambassadors, were both clad in Beaten-Silver. **1760** Mrs. Delaney *Autobiog.* (1861) III. 591 Fine ladies in beaten silver, and glittering with jewels. **1879** C. Hibbs in *Cassell's Techn. Educ.* IV. 263/1 It resembles, therefore, beaten or repoussé work.

b. Hence, because the purest gold is the most malleable: Fine, of pure quality; also *fig.*

1535 Coverdale *1 Kings* x. 16 Two hundreth speares of beaten golde. **1670** Eachard *Cont. Clergy* 103 Sincere and pure beaten virtue, like the gold of the first age.

†**c.** Overlaid, inlaid, embossed, damascened *with* gold or other precious material; embroidered. *Obs.*

a **1300** *K. Alis.* 1518 An ymage was therynne, Y-beten al with gold fyne. *c* **1340** *Gaw. & Gr. Knt.* 78 Enbrawded & beten wyth þe best gemmes. *c* **1400** *Roland* 287 Baners beten with gold. **1470** Harding *Chron.* cxcv. ii, The lordes..wᵗ penouns proudly bette. **1611** L. Barrey *Ram Alley* III. in *Dodsley* (1780) V. 452 [Clad] In beaten velvet. **1641** Baker *Chron.* (1679) 236/1 A red fiery Dragon, beaten upon white and green Sarcenet.

6. Pounded small; whipped up to uniform consistency.

1535 Coverdale *1 Kings* v. 11 Twentye quarters of beaten oyle. **1667** Boyle *Orig. Formes & Qual.* 15 Beaten Glasse is commonly reckoned among Poisons. **1769** Mrs. Raffald *Eng. Housekpr.* (1778) 295 Season it with beaten mace.

7. Conquered, defeated.

1562 J. Heywood *Prov. & Epigr.* (1867) 95 One of the beaten syde, Ran home. **1855** Macaulay *Hist. Eng.* IV. 94 The beaten army had now lost all the appearance of an army.

8. Overcome by hard work, exhausted. ***dead-beaten***: exhausted as if to death. Cf. beat *ppl. a.*

1681 Temple *Mem.* III. Wks. 1731 I. 331 Use of an old beaten Horse. **1854** *Blackw. Mag.* Apr. 459/2 At the next post-house the unhappy animals [post-horses] are left dead beaten. **1878** H. Smart *Play or Pay* v. 89 There is little object in going on with a beaten horse.

9. Systematically scoured for game.

1883 *Pall Mall G.* 1 Oct. 2/1 A pheasant..from a beaten cover.

10. With prec. sb. in instrumental relation, as ***weather-beaten, wave-beaten***, etc. See beat *v.*^{1} 6.

1579 E. K. in *Spenser's Sheph. Cal.* Jan. *Argt.*, His..winter beaten flocke. **1596** Drayton *Bar. Wars* Ded. 1 Anchor of my poore Tempest-beaten State. **1620** Quarles *Jonah* (1638) 27 The weather-beaten Ship. **1873** Black *Pr. Thule* 1 A desolate waste of rain-beaten sea.

11. With adv., as ***beaten down***, dejected, subdued.

1876 Geo. Eliot *Dan. Der.* II. xxvii. 176 The beaten-down consciousness.

12. Special Combs.: **beaten biscuit** *U.S.*, a small hard biscuit, the dough for which is thoroughly beaten and frequently folded; **beaten zone**, the area of ground struck by gun-fire; also *transf.*

1876 M. F. Henderson *Pract. Cooking* 69 Little machines ..for the purpose of making beaten biscuit. **1902** G. C. Eggleston *Dorothy South* 312 Slipping a surreptitious beaten biscuit into his pocket. **1918** E. S. Farrow *Dict. Mil. Terms* 67 Beaten Zone. **1962** *Times* 10 Oct. 13/7 Sticks are infinitely more efficient than stones for knocking down conkers: their 'beaten zone', as it were, is greater.

'beatenest, *a. U.S. dial.* Also beatin'est, -enes'. [f. beaten *ppl. a.* or *beating* pres. pple. of beat *v.*^{1} + -est *superl. suffix.*] Most excellent or splendid; most unusual.

1860 *Harper's Mag.* 135 A countryman..attracted by the white slab..exclaimed, 'Well, if this ain't the beatenest town I ever saw!' **1874** E. Eggleston *Circuit Rider* 147, I reckon I am the beatin'est man to ax questions in this neck of timber. **1884** 'Mark Twain' *Huck. Finn* xiii. 114 It's the beatenest thing I ever struck. **1889** *Harper's Mag.* Dec. 120/1 Thet thar rock house o' his'n,..I 'low it's the beatenes' house in creation. **1909** 'E. C. Hall' *Aunt Jane of Kentucky* ii. 33 Of the preachers that ever I heard, he certainly is the beatenest.

beater ('biːtə(r)). [f. beat *v.*^{1} + -er^1.] He who, or that which, beats. (In various senses of the vb.)

1. a. A person who beats; one who strikes repeated blows, a striker; a punisher; one who 'beats' or walks the streets (*obs.*); one who beats metals, e.g. a ***gold-beater***; one who beats a drum, etc.

1483 *Cath. Angl.* 30 A beter, *verberator..baculator.* **1509** Barclay *Shyp of Folys* (1570) 116 Of night watchers and beters of the stretes, playing by night on instrumentes. **1571** Ascham *Scholem.* (1863) 11 Even the wisest of your great beaters, do as oft punishe nature, as they do correcte faultes. **1647** R. Stapylton *Juvenal* 45 He must the hand that bastinades him kisse; And give his beater thanks with all his heart.

b. A man employed in rousing and driving game.

1825 Ford *Handbk. Spain* i. 105 The intelligence with which these Spanish beaters track and recover a wounded deer. **1859** Tennent *Ceylon* II. viii. iv. 350 The beaters address themselves to drive in the elephants.

c. In comb., as ***beater up***.

1711 E. Ward *Vulg. Brit.* viii. 87 Who were beholders Of these the Beaters up for Soldiers.

2. a. An instrument or contrivance for beating; generally, an implement for beating flat or pounding; but used in many specific technical senses (see quots.).

1611 Cotgr., *Eschandole*..Thatchers Beater. *Ibid.*, *Rabat* ..a beater, the staffe wherwith Plaisterers beat their morter. **1632** Sherwood s.v. *Ball*, A Printer's ball, Pompet, or beater. **1727** Bradley *Fam. Dict.* s.v. *Building*, The mortar must be well beaten with a beater. **1828** Steuart *Planter's G.* 303 Wooden Beater, made in the fashion of the beater used by paviers. **1851** *Coal-tr. Terms. Northumbld. & Durh.*, *Beater*, an iron rod, used for stemming or tamping a hole, preparatory to blasting. **1879** *Cassell's Techn. Educ.* IV. 210/1 The beater [in cotton-spinning]..is composed of two, and sometimes three iron bars or blades. **1883** *Gd. Words* July 442/1 Pounding it [rice] in a wooden or stone mortar with hard wooden beaters. **1883** *Blackw. Mag.* Aug. 234 All armed with one or two long switches of birch called technically 'beaters' or 'trees.'

b. *Paper-manuf.* A pulping machine. Also *attrib.* and *Comb.*, as ***beater plate, roll***; **beater-man**, the operative who has charge of a pulping machine or beating-engine.

1825 J. Nicholson *Operat. Mechanic* 368 (Paper manufacture) The only difference between the washing-engine and the beater is that the teeth of the latter are finer. **1880** J. Dunbar *Pract. Papermaker* 44 Two chests should be used, the beaterman emptying into the one, and the machine-man working from the other. *Ibid.* 71 The beater roll and plate should..be in good order.

3. A person or thing that beats or excels others. *U.S. colloq.*

1845 S. Judd *Margaret* II. v. 283 Take it by and large.. and she is the beater of all. **1886** *Harper's Mag.* Sept. 580/2 I've heerd news that beats the beater! *Ibid.* Nov. 835/1 Well, for getting sunthin outer northing, she's a beater!

beat generation. [Etym. disputed; the evidence suggests that it is f. beat *ppl. a.* 1 b, perh. infl. by beat *sb.*^{1} 4, but the coiner of the expression, J. Kerouac (1922–69), connected *beat* with beat(itude (see quot. 1958^1).] An expression applied at first to a group of young people, predominantly writers, artists, and their adherents, in San Francisco, later to similar groups elsewhere, adopting unconventional dress, manners, habits, etc., as a means of self-expression and social protest.

1952 J. C. Holmes in *N.Y. Times* 16 Nov., Mag. 10/2 It was the face of a Beat Generation... It was John Kerouac.. who..several years ago..said 'You know, this is really a *beat* generation'. The origins of the word beat are obscure, but the meaning is only too clear to most Americans. More than the feeling of weariness, it implies the feeling of having been used, of being raw. It involves a sort of nakedness of mind. **1955** 'Jean-Louis' [= J. Kerouac] in *New World Writing* 10 Jazz of the Beat Generation... Here we were dealing with the pit and prune juice of poor beat life itself and the pathos of people in the Godawful streets. **1958** J. C. Holmes in *Esquire* Feb. 35/2 'The Beat Generation,' he [*sc.* J. Kerouac] said, 'is basically a religious generation.' And later, in another interview, Kerouac amplified '..Beat means beatitude, not beat up.' **1958** *Sunday Times* 25 May 6/4 'Where go? What do? What for?..' That is the cry and philosophy of the beat generation, if a philosophy can be distilled from bewilderment, aimlessness and apathy. **1958** *Observer* 14 Sept. 4/5 The 'beat generation' is beginning to acquire the same kind of dubious place in American culture as the Young Angries in Britain. **1963** *New Statesman* 8 Feb. 202/3 The Beat Generation have come and gone, making a lot of noise but little real impact.

Hence **beat** *sb.*^{4}, **beatnik** ('biːtnɪk) [*-nik* arbitrarily after sput)nik, infl. by Yiddish *-nik*], **'beatster**^{2}, one of the beat generation, one who leads a 'beat' life (cf. beat *sb.*^{1} 16, from which *beat* in the present sense cannot be entirely dissociated); **beat** *attrib.*, or as *adj.*, **'beatniky** *a.*, of, or characteristic of, the beat generation or of a beatnik; **'beatness**, such a state.

1955 [see above]. **1958** *Daily Express* 23 July 4/2 This [*sc.* San Francisco] is the home and the haunt of America's Beat generation and these are the Beatniks—or new barbarians. **1958** J. Kerouac *On the Road* ix. 87 The beat countermen and dishgirls who made no bones about their beatness. **1958** *New Statesman* 6 Sept. 294/3 The 'beats' reached literary respectability in Jack Kerouac's *On the Road.* **1959** *Encounter* June 42 Portrait of the Beatnik... The Beatnik in his bold rebellion against American Bourgeois Values. *Ibid.* July 56/2 'Beat Zen' followers take dope or alcohol to reach a giggly state of ecstasy. **1959** *New Statesman* 6 June 795/1 The post-Presley teenage beatsters. **1959** *Guardian* 14 Oct. 7/3 He calls a flat a 'pad' (Beatnik language). **1964** *Listener* 5 Nov. 709/1 Suddenly everybody was slightly beatniky. **1965** *Spectator* 22 Jan. 98/2 One of the first changes he noticed was that the beats, instead of writing poems, were making films. **1966** *English Studies* XLVII. 154 In the mid-twentieth century the typical Bohemian has become the beatnik poet or pseudo-philosopher.

beath (biːð), *v. Obs.* exc. *dial.* Forms: 1 beði-an, 1–5 bethe, 6– beath. [OE. *bęðian* to foment:—OTeut. **baþian*; a parallel form to OE. *baðian* (:—**baþôn*) to bathe, preserving the original notion of *heat*: see bath.]

1. To foment, bathe with warm liquid.

c **1000** *Sax. Leechd.* I. 72 Beða ðá éaʒan. *c* **1250** *Gen. & Ex.* 2447 First .ix. niȝt ðe liches beðen, And smeren.

2. To heat unseasoned wood for the purpose of straightening it.

1496 *Bk. St. Albans, Fysshyng* 8 Ye shall kytte..a fayr staffe..and bethe hym in a hote ouyn. **1580** Tusser *Husb.* (1878) 62 Yokes, forks, and such other, let bailie spie out.. And after at leasure let this be his hier, to beath them. **1653** W. Lauson *Secr. Angling* in Arb. *Garner* I. 192 Beath them a little..all in a furnace. (Still in dialectal use. Also, 'Meat improperly roasted is said in the Midland Counties to be *beathed.*' Hal.)

'beathing, *vbl. sb. Obs.* or *dial.* [OE. *bęðing*, f. *bęðian* (see beath *v.*) + -ing^1.] Fomentation; the heating of wood in order to render it flexible.

c **1000** *Sax. Leechd.* II. 36 Wiþ pocce on eaʒum, ʒenim wad..wyl on meolce..& wyrc beþinge. **1591** Percivall *Sp. Dict.*, *Borne*, the bending of a staffe or timber by beathing in the fire, *lentatio. Ibid.*, *Bornear*, to bend timber by beathing in the fire, *lentare.*

beatific (biːə'tɪfɪk), *a.* Also 7–8 -ick. [ad. L. *beātific-us*, f. *beāt-us* blessed (pa. pple. of *beāre* to bless) + *-ficus* making: see -fic. Cf. F. *béatifique.*] Making blessed; imparting supreme happiness or blessedness.

1649 Lovelace *Poems* 47 Such a beatific Face. **1746** Hervey *Medit.* (1818) 169 Where the Lamb that was slain, manifests his beatific presence. **1880** L. Morris *Ode of Life* 120 A beatific peace greater than tongue can tell.

b. ***beatific vision***: a sight of the glories of heaven; *esp.* that first granted to a disembodied spirit.

1639 Rouse *Heav. Univ.* Advt. (1702) 4 The Beatifick Vision of the Supream Good hereafter. **1704** Nelson *Fest. & Fasts* xxviii. (1739) 361 Martyrs..upon their Death.. were immediately admitted to the Beatifick Vision. **1869** Freeman *Norm. Conq.* (1876) III. xi. 30 A soul which.. angels had already borne to the beatific vision.

bea'tifical, *a.* [f. as prec. + -al^1.] = prec.

1610 G. Fletcher *Christ's Vict.* in Farr *S.P.* (1848) 73 In midst of this citie celestiall, Lightned th' Idea Beatificall. **1681** Glanvill *Sadducismus* II. (1726) 453 To talk trivially of beatifical enjoyments.

b.

1605 Bell *Motives Rom. Faith* 95 That so the faithfull may..be made partakers of the vision beatificall. **1702** *Bruyn's Voy. Levant* xii. 55 A Beatifical Vision of God.

c. *absol.* quasi-*sb.*

a **1711** Ken *Hymnotheo* Poet. Wks. 1721 III. 320 In God all Beatificals conspire.

bea'tifically. *adv.* [f. as prec. + -ly^2.] In a beatific manner; in a way that blesses; *catachr.* with supreme felicity.

1627 Hakewill *Apol.* 495 (R.) Beatifically to behold the face of God..is a blessednes..no way incident vnto the creature beneath man. **1667** H. More *Div. Dial.* II. xviii. (1713) 148 And enjoy them there more fully and beatifically. **1869** *Daily News* 12 June, Gleaming beatifically with a proud confidence in himself as a work of art.

bea'tificate, *v.* ? *Obs. rare.* [f. L. *beātificāt-* ppl. stem of *beātificāre* to make happy or blessed.] = beatify; cf. also beatification 2.

a **1636** E. Dacres *Machiavel's Disc. Livy* II. 267 The ancient Religion did not beatificate, but onely men fraught with worldly glory. **1655** Fuller *Ch. Hist.* x. ii. §55 V. 363 It seemed good..to his Holinesse not to canonize Garnet.. but only to beatificate him.

beatification (biːˌætɪfɪ'keɪʃən). Also 6 beatyfycacyon. [a. F. *béatification*, n. of action and state f. L. *beātificāt-*; see prec.]

1. The action of rendering, or condition of being rendered, supremely happy or blessed.

1502 *Ord. Crysten Men* (W. de W. 1506) II. xviii. 133 Yᵉ blyssed trynyte promytteth for to gyue unto us eternall beatyfycacyon. *a* **1631** Donne *Serm.* xii. 120 All the Beatification and Glorification of our bodies consists in this. **1824** *Blackw. Mag.* XVI. 5 That picture which Horace has given us of human beatification. **1865** Neale *Hymns Parad.* 66 What the beatification Of the spirits round the Throne?

2. *R.C. Ch.* An act of the Pope, by which he declares that a deceased member of the Church is in the enjoyment of heavenly bliss, and grants to certain persons the privilege of paying a particular form of worship or reverence to him.

This ceremony is the first step towards canonization, which confers the full honours of a saint, and makes worship of him incumbent on the whole Church.

1626 L. Owen *Spec. Jesuit.* (1629) 32 You may see, how the..Beatification and Canonization of this wicked.. Ignatius did..fore-shew some great disaster. **1781** J. Moore *View Soc. It.* (1790) I. xlii. 454, I have been witness to the beatification of a saint. **1864** *Daily Tel.* 6 May, To hear his Holiness read a couple of decrees—one of beatification, the other of canonisation. *Mod.* The beatification of Joan of Arc.

b. *transf.* with allusion to the halo of a saint.

1794 G. Adams *Nat. & Exp. Philos.* IV. xlvi. 289 This experiment [with silvered leather on the head] has been called the diadem of beatification.

beatified (biː'ætɪfaɪd), *ppl. a.* [f. next + -ed.]

1. Made supremely happy or blest.

1575 Laneham *Let.* (1871) 32 They vaunted their play waz neuer so dignified, nor euer any players afore as beatified. **1690** Norris *Beatitudes* (1694) I. 231 Angels and

beatify'd Spirits. **1848** Mrs. Jameson *Sacr. & Leg. Art* (1850) 315 They are beatified children, not winged angels. **1860** Pusey *Min. Proph.* 562 The..glorious body of the beatified.

2. *R.C. Ch.* Declared to be in the enjoyment of heavenly bliss; see prec. 2.

1650 R. Stapylton *Strada's Low-C. Warres* VII. 43 The already beatified Didacus. *a* **1837** Miss Knight *Autobiog.* II. 312 The feast of a beatified saint is not observed by the church in general, but only by his own order. **1852** Mrs. Jameson *Leg. Madonna* (1857) 92 The beatified members of these orders.

beatify (biːˈætɪfaɪ), *v.*; also 7 -fie. [a. F. *béatifier*, ad. L. *beātificāre* to make happy.]

1. *trans.* To make supremely happy or blessed.

1535 *Trevisa's Barth. De P.R.* III. iii, The sowle departed from the body is..beatified..with angels. **1860** Pusey *Min. Proph.* 119 He can beatify, because He is Bliss.

2. To pronounce or declare supremely blessed.

a **1677** Barrow *Wks.* 1686 III. 161 The common conceits and phrases which so beatify wealth.

3. *R.C. Ch.* To pronounce (a person) to be in enjoyment of heavenly bliss: see beatification 2.

1629 Wadsworth *Sp. Pilgr.* 79, I examined the cause why the Pope should beatifie Garnet. **1704** Addison *Italy* (1733) 225 Who has been beatify'd tho' never Sainted. **1865** Pusey *Tr. Eng. Ch.* 101 One who has since been beatified.

be'atiˌfying, *vbl. sb.* [f. prec. + -ing¹.] The action of making supremely blest; beatification.

c **1630** Jackson *Creed* VI. xiii. Wks. V. 139 God's glory must..appear..in the beatifying of the elect.

be'atiˌfying, *ppl. a.* [f. as prec. + -ing².] Making supremely happy or blest.

a **1682** Sir T. Browne (J.) The fullest good..the most beatifying of all others. **1822** K. Digby *Broadst. Hon.* (1848) I. 183 Oh! the sublime..and already beatifying philosophy of Christians! **1869** Ld. Lytton *Orval* 45 Image of all beatifying beauty.

beatilia, beatilla, -illes; see battalia pie.

beating (ˈbiːtɪŋ), *vbl. sb.* [f. beat *v.*¹ + -ing¹.]

1. a. The infliction of repeated blows; *spec.* the action of inflicting blows in punishment; the dashing of waves against the shore; the whipping up of a fluid; the flapping of wings; rousing of game, exercising the brain, etc.

c **1230** *Ancr. R.* 366 Seið Isaye..ure beatunge ueol upon him. *c* **1374** Chaucer *H. Fame* 1034 Betynge of the see..ayen the roches holowe. *c* **1440** Lonelich *Grail.* lv. 297 He herd abowtes hym a wondir thinge: betyng of bryddes wynges in fere. **1526** *Pilgr. Perf.* (W. de W. 1531) 114 b, Remember his scourgynges, buffettes & beatynges. **1606** G. W[oodcocke] *Hist. Ivstine* 5 b, Darius..bestowed much beating..in his troubled pate. **1656** H. More *Antid. Ath.* II. iii. 82 The couragious beating of the Drum. **1860** Pusey *Min. Proph.* 460 The restless beating of the barren, bitter sea. **1879** *Photogr.* in *Cassell's Techn. Educ.* III. 207 Upon the perfect beating of the albumen the success of the operation mainly depends.

b. with *adv.*, as ***beating down, beating off, beating-up*** (cf. beat *v.*¹ 40 f.), etc.

1530 Palsgr. 198/1 Beatyng downe of any buyldynge, *demolition.* **1803** Nelson in Nicolas *Disp.* (1845) V. 227 This beating off the Tunisians will have a very good effect. **1915** A. Conan Doyle *Valley of Fear* II. vii. 629 I've a mind to send a couple of the boys round before evening to give him a beating up and see what they can get from him. **1939** G. Greene *Confid. Agent* I. ii. 70 If they began with a beating-up, their next attempt was likely to be drastic. **1947** *Penguin New Writing* XXX. 127 The director seems determined to equal in savagery the beatings-up in *The Glass Key.*

2. In various technical uses: see beat *v.*¹ 24.

1687 T. Brown *Saints in Uproar* Wks. 1730 I. 80 A fortnight's beating of hemp. **1824** J. Johnson *Typogr.* II. 525 After the form has been lately washed..the letter will not take the ink without several beatings. **1875** Ure *Dict. Arts* II. 415 As in hand-scutching, the operation consists of two processes: first the bruising of the stems; and secondly, the beating away of the woody parts from the fibre. *Ibid.* II. 728 Four principal operations constitute the art of gold-beating. 1 The casting of the gold ingots..4 The beating.

3. A defeat in any contest.

1883 *American* VI. 245 Our American rifle-team has had its beating, but not a bad beating.

4. *Naut.* Sailing against the wind.

1883 *Contemp. Rev.* Aug. 231 Of all the modes of progression invented by man, beating to windward in a sailing vessel is morally the most beautiful.

5. A pulsating or throbbing movement, like that of the heart, of a watch or clock, of two notes not in unison.

1601 Shaks. *Twel. N.* II. iv. 97 The beating of so strong a passion As loue doth giue my heart. **1798** Southey *St. Patrick's Purg.* xxiii, In short quick beatings toil'd his heart. **1801** *Phil. Trans.* XCI. 442 Whether she really heard the beating of the watch. **1872** Huxley *Phys.* ii. 42 Beating of the heart..is the result of the striking of the apex of the heart against the pericardium.

6. *Comb.*, as ***beating-board***; **beating-dog**, a dog trained to put up game; **beating-engine**, a machine (*a*) for preparing the materials used in the manufacture of paper, strawboard, millboard, etc.; (*b*) for opening, beating, and cleaning cotton in cotton-manufacture; **beating-net**, a kind of fishing-net; **beating-order**, a certificate given to a recruiting sergeant; † **beating-stock**, a jocular title given to one who is subjected to beating.

1552 Huloet, Beatynge stocke, *subiculum flagri.* **1669** Worlidge *Syst. Agric.* (1681) 248 You may go into the Fens, Marshes, or places with a Spaniel, or other Beating-dog. **1679** Plot *Staffordsh.* (1686) 123 Then they bring it [potter's clay] to their beating board, where with a long Spatula they beat it till it be well mix't. **1721** *Lond. Gaz.* No. 5947/4 Has a Beating-Order about him, was lately a Serjeant and employed in Recruiting. **1825** J. Nicholson *Operat. Mechanic* 368 (Paper-manufacture) The beating-engines..are seldom provided with these waste-pipes. **1846** Dodd *Brit. Manuf.* VI. 21 The rags are..conveyed to the washing-engine,..then let off into the beating-engine. **1880** J. Dunbar *Pract. Papermaker* 61 Alum intended for the beating-engine should be perfectly pure. **1883** *Fisheries Exhib. Catal.* 125 Beating net..used by fishermen in the freshwater..It is a trammel or armoured net.

'beating, *ppl. a.* [f. beat *v.*¹ + -ing².]

1. That strikes successive blows.

1718 Pope *Iliad* II. 383 Seiz'd by the beating wing.

2. Of wind, rain, etc.: That strikes violently, or batters; driving.

1702 Rowe *Tamerl.* IV. i. 1576 To bear the beating Storm That roars around me. **1885** *Cornh. Mag.* July 74 Chinese hat, suitable in case of beating rain or fierce sun.

3. Palpitating, throbbing.

1702 Rowe *Tamerl.* III. i. 1039 My beating Heart Bounds with exulting motion. **1805** Wordsw. *Prel.* II. (1850) 34 Feverish with weary joints and beating minds. **1810** Southey *Kehama* XVII. ix, To meet with beating heart. **1850** Mrs. Browning *Poems* I. 301 The fever and the beating pain.

† **be'ation.** *Obs. rare*⁻¹. [n. of action f. L. *beāt-* ppl. stem of *beāre* to bless.] Blessing.

1652 Benlowes *Theoph.* VI. lxxxvi, Præcelling Seraphs shew Gods ardor still:..Beations Thrones instill.

beatitude (biːˈætɪtjuːd). Also 5 beatitud, 5–6 beatytude. [a. F. *béatitude* (15th c. in Littré), ad. L. *beātitūdo* blessedness, f. *beāt-us* blessed: see -tude.]

1. a. Supreme blessedness or happiness.

1491 Caxton *Vitas Patr.* (W. de W.) I. xliv. (1495) 75 a/2 How by abstynence..myghte be goten the souerayne beatytude or blessydnesse. *a* **1555** Bradford *Wks.* 397 There shall be joy..and all kind of beatitude. **1643** Prynne *Power Parl.* I. 48 Knowing better..what conduced to the beatitude of the Empire. **1667** Milton *P.L.* III. 62 The Sanctities of Heaven..from his sight receiv'd Beatitude past utterance. **1794** Coleridge *Relig. Musings* Wks. I. 105 Such strange beatitudes Seize on my young anticipating heart. **1875** Ruskin *Lect. Art* i. 5 The consummate beatitude of being rich.

b. An honorific title (rendering Gr. μακαριότης) applied esp. to ecclesiastics of the Eastern Church of patriarchal rank.

1658 J. Burbury tr. *Gualdo Priorato's Hist. Christina Q. Swedland* 127 When his Beatitude had declared four extraordinary Nuntii, to receive her on the confines of the Ecclesiastical State. **1751** Chambers *Cycl.* s.v. *Holyness*, S. Gregory compliments some of his cotemporary bishops with, your beatitude, and your holyness. **1925** *Glasgow Herald* 7 Sept. 11 His Beatitude the Lord Photios, Patriarch and Pope of Alexandria.

2. A declaration or ascription of special blessedness; *esp.* (in *pl.*) those pronounced by Christ in the Sermon on the Mount.

1526 *Pilgr. Perf.* (1531) 43 b, The viii beatitudes that..spryngeth of grace and the other vertues. **1588** A. King *Canisius' Catech.* 186 These quhilk S. Ambrose callis our Lords beatitudes. **1777** Fletcher *Reconcil.* Wks. 1795 IV. 319 Bent upon the inheriting the seventh beatitude. **1877** Farrar *Thy Youth* i. 10 The priceless beatitude of the pure in heart.

3. = beatification 2.

1847 Disraeli *Tancred* (1871) I. v. 30 The saint was scarcely canonised, before his claims to beatitude were impugned. **1865** Bushnell *Vicar. Sacr.* v. (1868) 116 Candidates for beatitude.

fig. **1837** Carlyle *Fr. Rev.* I. II. viii. 69 Burnt by the commmon hangman..perhaps the last notable Book that had such fire-beatitude.

beatitudinous (biːˌætɪˈtjuːdɪnəs), *a. rare.* [f. L. *beātitūdin-* stem of *beātitūdo* blessedness + -ous.] Characteristic of blessedness or happiness.

1926 D. H. Lawrence *Plumed Serpent* xiv. 229 Her childish..slightly imbecile face would take on a black, arch, beatitudinous look.

† **'beatizing,** *ppl. a. Obs.* [In form a pr. pple. of *beatize*, f. L. *beāt-us* blessed + -ize.] Beatifying, blessing.

1652 Benlowes *Theoph.* XIII. xxxiii, All beatizing sweets.

Beatle (ˈbiːt(ə)l). [f. 'The Beatles', the name of a group of pop singers from Liverpool.] Applied *attrib.* to the hair-style or other characteristics of 'The Beatles' or of their imitators. Also, **Beatle'mania** [-mania], addiction to the Beatles and their characteristics; the frenzied behaviour of their admirers. Hence other nonce-formations (see quots.).

1963 *The Beatles* 3 Their unique hair-styles have forced hair-dressers to follow the Beatle cut—for girls as well as boys. **1963** *Daily Tel.* 1 Nov. 15/6 Beatle fans hold up premier's car. **1963** *Times* 27 Dec. 4/6 The social phenomenon of Beatlemania, which finds expression in handbags, balloons and other articles bearing the likeness of the loved ones, or in the hysterical screaming of young girls whenever the Beatle Quartet performs in public. **1964** *Daily Tel.* 10 Feb. 1/3 Outside, hundreds of squealing Beatlemaniacs carried such signs as 'We love you—never leave us'. *Ibid.* 20 Feb. 22/7 The first export consignment of Beatle wallpaper will be flown from Manchester to Canada to-day. **1964** *Daily Mail* 11 Feb. 6/8, I hope someone explains to the Americans that we wear our Beatle wigs and bowlers on separate occasions. **1968** *Courier-Mail* (Brisbane) 22 June 3/3 Of the Beatles he [*sc.* Maharishi Yogi] said: '..They weren't prepared to end their beatledom for meditation.'

beatless (ˈbiːtlɪs), *a.* [f. beat *sb.*¹ + -less.] Destitute of beats, not beating.

1849 Rock *Ch. of Fathers* III. viii. 85 That heart is now cold and beatless.

beatling, obs. form of beetling.

beatment, dial. form of beakment.

beatnik: see beat generation.

ˌbea'tor. *nonce-wd.* [see -or.] = beater.

1719 Ozell *Misson's Trav. Eng.* 304 If he is the Beator, the Beatee must pay the money about which they quarrell'd.

Beatrician (biːəˈtrɪʃən), *a.* [f. name of *Beatrice*, character in Dante's *Vita Nuova* and *Divina Commedia*, + -ian.] Of, pertaining to, or resembling (Dante's vision of) Beatrice; of or concerning a revelatory or transcendental vision, experience, etc.

1943 C. Williams *Figure of Beatrice* 123 The Beatrician moment is a moment of revelation and communicated conversion by means of a girl. **1948** C. S. Lewis in C. Williams *Arthurian Torso* II. iii. 116 The Beatrician experience may be defined as the recovery (in respect to one human being) of that vision of reality which would have been common to all men in respect to all things if Man had never fallen. **1958** *Times* 8 Nov. 7/3 Moments of Beatrician vision are experienced by a great many people when they first fall in love.

beatster¹ (ˈbiːtstə(r)). *local.* Also **beetster.** [f. beet *v.* 1 + -ster.] A mender or mounter of fishing-nets. (Sense of 1575 quot. uncertain.)

1575 *Aldeburgh Rec.* in *N. & Q.* (1920) VII. 226/2 To iiii^or^ poore foulks for carienge yᵉ beetster to hir buryall..viiiᵈ. **1641** S. Smith *Herring-Busse Trade* 4 For the Tanning and Beetsters work. **1808** *Norfolk Tour* (ed. 6) 43 This fishery gives bread..to about 2,000 fishermen, and 4,000 braiders, beetsters, towers, rivers, ferry-men [etc.]. **1858** *N. & Q.* V. 116/1 Modern terms, such as one..hears among the fishermen of this coast [e.g. *Beatsters*, i.e. net menders (females)]. **1866** J. G. Nall *Great Yarmouth & Lowestoft* 292 In a long loft adjoining that of the ransackers, is the work-room of the *beetsters*, women and girls engaged in *betting* or mending up the nets. **1920** *N. & Q.* VII. 267/2 A notice-board at Lowestoft..'2 Beatsters wanted'. **1921** *Dict. Occup. Terms* (1927) §398 *Beatster, beetster*; fishing net mender, net mender, net repairer,..sometimes also a net mounter. **1932** *Daily Mail* 22 Sept. 4/6 Beatsters on the drift nets—stabbing their needles through a myriad meshes with rhythm.

beatster²: see beat generation.

beat-up, *sb.* and *a. slang.* Chiefly *U.S.* [cf. beat *v.*¹ 40 f, i.] **a.** *sb.* (See quot. 1940.) **b.** *adj.* Worn out, shabby, showing signs of over-use.

1940 N. Monks *Squadrons Up!* i. 14 Comes back over the 'drome, above the heads..twenty feet off the ground... The boys call this a 'beat-up'. **1946** *Amer. Speech* XXI. 251 *Beat up*, an adjectival phrase of all work meaning damaged, worn-out or of unimpressive appearance. **1951** J. D. Salinger *Catcher in Rye* ii. 11 He showed us this old beat-up Navajo blanket. **1953** W. R. Burnett *Vanity Row* xviii. 135 The girl was sitting once more in the beat-up leather chair.

Beatus (beɪˈɑːtəs). [L.] Esp. in ***Beatus page***: the page of a psalter containing the initial B of Psalm 1 (Beatus vir...), which was frequently decorated in medieval manuscripts, often with elaborate designs.

[**1892** J. H. Middleton *Illum. MSS. Classical & Mediaeval Times* p. viii, The first letter B of the beginning of the Psalms (*Beatus vir* etc.) is in this and some other illuminated *Psalters*..of such size and elaboration that it occupies most of the first page.] **1911** J. A. Herbert *Illum. MSS.* x. 180 The *Beatus vir* page is of an unusual and amusing type. The 'B', made of narrow entwined ribbons on a gold field, forms a small and rather insignificant foundation; but round about it..are eight gold medallions containing delightful figures of animal musicians. **1926** E. G. Millar *Eng. Illum. MSS. X to XIII Cent.* 91 David harping, and Beatus page; the medallions at bottom and top of the stem of the B contain respectively David slaying Goliath, and bringing Goliath's head to Saul. **1954** M. Rickert *Painting in Brit.: Middle Ages* iv. 80 The identification of the Edmund artist with the illuminator of the Albani *Beatus* initial seems to be confirmed by a comparison..with the very lively single combat scene above the B on the same *Beatus* page of the Psalter. *Ibid.* 98 A full-page *Beatus* and eight large initials to the psalms.

beaty (ˈbiːtɪ), *a.* [f. beat *sb.*¹ 4 + -y¹.] (Of jazz, etc.) full of 'beat', swinging.

1956 S. Traill *Play that Music* vi. 60 Drumming..reached an altogether higher standard of crisp beaty playing. **1960** *Melody Maker* 31 Dec. 6/3 Dean sings with the requisite fervour to a beaty accompaniment. **1963** *Today* 30 Nov. 18/4 Ringo ad-libs a beaty blues.

beau (bəʊ), *a.* and *sb.* Forms: 4– beau 4 bieu, 4–5 beu, 6 beaw; also in comb. 5 baw-, be-, bew-; see beausire. [a. late OF. *beau, biau*, earlier *bel, beal, bial*:—L. *bellus* fine, pretty. The adj., in ME.

quite naturalized and pronounced as in *beauty*, *Beaulieu* (bjuːlɪ), has been long obs.: the sb. has been reintroduced from mod.Fr., whence its pronunciation.]

†**A.** *adj.* **1.** Fair, beautiful. *Obs.*

c **1325** *E.E. Allit. P.* A. 197 Al blysnande whyt watz hir beau uiys. **1399** LANGL. *Rich. Redeless* III. 1 Now leue we þis beu brid.

2. Used in affection, friendship, or politeness, in addressing relations, friends, etc. (usually with their French titles): equal to the English 'fair' (fair sir), 'good' (good people), 'dear' (dear sir). With some words it entered into more or less permanent combination: see BEAUPERE, BEAUSIRE, and BEL-.

c **1300** *Beket* 1903 Beau frere, quath Seint Thomas, that ne mai ich do noȝt. *c* **1314** *Guy Warw.* 4 Bieus amis, molt gramerci! **1513** DOUGLAS *Epilogue* to *Eneid*, Lo, this is all, bew schirris haue gude day!

B. *sb.* Pl. **beaux, beaus** (bəʊz).

1. A man who gives particular, or excessive, attention to dress, mien, and social etiquette; an exquisite, a fop, a dandy.

1687 T. BROWN *Lib. Consc.* in *Dk. Buckhm's Wks.* 1705 II. 128 You're a perfect Woman, nothing but a Beau will please you! **1700** DRYDEN *Cock & Fox* 624 What will not beaux attempt to please the fair? **1738** BIRCH *Life of Milton* in *Wks.* I. 20 Young Sparks of his Acquaintance.. the Beaus of those Days. **1824** W. IRVING *T. Trav.* I. 341 The painted beau with.. long, flimsy, sky-blue coat.

2. The attendant or suitor of a lady; a lover, sweetheart.

?**1720** *Mountford's Elegy* in *Collect. Poems* 43 No Lady henceforth can be safe with her Beau. *a* **1777** GOLDSM. *Doubl. Transform.* 87 Her country beaux and city cousins, Lovers no more, flew off by dozens. *a* **1845** HOOD *Number One* I It's very hard.. that every Miss But me has got a Beau. **1875** B. TAYLOR *Faust* I. x. 130 If not a husband, then a beau for you!

3. *attrib.*, †**beau-catcher**, a kiss-curl. *Obs.*

1818 *Publ. Ledger* 18 Apr. 3/2 A girl.. twisting her hair into rings, which they term 'beau-catchers'. **1857** M. J. HOLMES *Meadow-Brook* ii, Arranging just in front of her ears two spit curls, sometimes called 'beau catchers'. **1909** WARE *Passing Eng.* 23/1 *Beau-catcher*, a flat hook-shaped curl, after the Spanish manner, gummed on each temple, and made of the short temple hair, spelt sometimes *bow-catcher*... Now obsolete on this side of the Pyrenees.

beau, *v.* [f. prec. sb.] *trans.* To act the beau to, to attend or escort (a lady).

1843 *Commissioner* 411 Chevalier, you shall beau the young lady. **1878** WINGFIELD *Lady Grizel* I. viii. 151 His Grace.. is to beau your ladyship to Ranelagh.

†**beaubelet.** *Obs. rare*⁻¹. [a. OF. *baubelet, beubelet*, dim. of *baubel* child's plaything, toy, trinket, BAUBLE.] A small toy, trinket, plaything.

c **1205** *Ancr. R.* 388 He.. sende hire beaubelet(z) [*v.r.* beau-, beawbelez] boðe ueole and feire.

Beauclerk (ˈbəʊklɑːk). Now *Hist.* Also 6 -clark, 7 -clark, 9 -clerc. [a. F. *beau* fine + *clerc*:—L. *clēricus* 'clergyman,' hence 'scholar,' as opposed to the uneducated laity: see CLERK.] A learned man, a scholar. (Given as a surname to Henry I.)

c **1367** *Eulog. Hist.* (1863) III. v. ci. 40 Henricus cognomento Beauclerk. **1586** WEBBE *Eng. Poetrie* (Arb.) 31 Henry the first King of that name in England.. was named by his surname Beaucleark. **1641** J. JACKSON *True Evang. T.* iii. 206 Erasmus and Ferus, two Beauclerks. **1856** KNIGHT *Pop. Hist. Eng.* I. xvi. 218 The brutal Rufus, or the crafty Beau Clerc.

†ˈ**beaudoy.** *Obs. rare.* Some worsted material.

1759 B. MARTIN *Nat. Hist. Eng.* II. 279 Worsted Goods, as Beaudoys, Camblets, Shalloons, etc.

†ˈ**beauetry.** *Obs.* [f. BEAU, in jocular imitation of *coquetry*.] Dandyism; dandy outfit.

1702 *Eng. Theophrast.* 53 When all the rest of his Beauetry is rightly adjusted. **1709** STEELE *Tatler* No. 29 ¶2 One may easily distinguish the Man that is affected with Beauetry.

beaufet, beaufin: see BUFFET, BIFFIN.

†ˈ**beaufort.** *Obs.* A material used for flags.

1712 *Lond. Gaz.* No. 5051/3 Three Pence half Peny per Yard for Beaufort of 11 Inches broad.

Beaufort scale (ˈbəʊfət). *Meteorol.* [Devised by Admiral Sir Francis *Beaufort* (1774–1857).] A series of numbers from 0 to 12 assigned by Captain (later Admiral Sir Francis) Beaufort to indicate the strength of the wind from a calm, force 0, to a hurricane, force 12.

The Beaufort numbers and their limits of velocity have varied in different countries since the scale was devised *c* 1805. The specification of the Beaufort scale adopted now by the Meteorological Office allows for 17 Beaufort numbers ranging in velocity from 0–0·2 metres per second (0) to 56·1–61·2 metres per second (17).

1858 [see STORM *sb.* 1 b]. **1906** *Beaufort Scale of Wind-Force* (Rep. Meteorol. Office) 5 Assume first that the velocity of motion of the air is the ultimate measurement to which the numbers of the Beaufort scale shall be referred. **1933** *Jane's Fighting Ships* 22 *Trials*.. 151,000 S.H.P. = 32·07 kts. (run in bad weather, wind force 6 Beaufort scale). **1961** *Times* 5 Aug. 3/1 South-westerly winds between force 5 and force 6 on the Beaufort scale meant rigorous yachting conditions.

‖**beau garçon** (bo garsɔ̃). Also 7 -garzon. [F.] A handsome fellow; an exquisite, a fop.

c **1665** VILLIERS (Dk. Buckhm.) *Adv. Painter* Wks. 1705 II. 81 Povey the Wit, and R—— the Beau-garzon. **1815** SCOTT *Guy M.* xlix, 'And then,' said the old *beau garçon*.

‖**beau geste** (bo ʒɛst). [Fr., = fine gesture.] A display of magnanimity.

1920 *John O'London's Weekly* 21 Feb. 562/1 The *beau geste* is less a physical than a mental and literary revelation. **1922** *Westm. Gaz.* 9 Dec., I think Germany can pay,.. and Italy is too poor to make the *beau geste* of abandoning her claims. **1925** W. DEEPING *Sorrell & Son* xv. §3 He gave in. .. He was not going to quarrel with a *beau geste*.

beaugle, obs. form of BUGLE.

Beau-gregory (bəʊˈgrɛgərɪ). Also **Beau Gregory, Beau Gregoire** (bəʊgrɪˈgwɑː(r)). [Etym. unknown.] A brightly coloured fish (*Eupomacentrus leucostictus*) of the family *Pomacentridæ*, found in Florida and the West Indies; the cockeye pilot.

1847 R. H. SCHOMBURGK *Hist. Barbados* III. 674 Pomacentrus leucostictus, *Müll. et Tr.* nov. spec... Black Pilot. Beau Gregory... In the younger specimens the white dots are much more distinct, and this may have induced the fishermen to give them the name of Beau Gregory; the full-grown specimen is called Black Pilot. **1929** C. M. BREDER *Field Bk. Marine Fishes* 199 Beau-gregory occurs in the West Indies north to Florida. **1930** D. S. JORDAN et al. *Check List of Fishes of N. & Middle Amer.* 413 Cockeye pilot; Beau Gregoire; Black pilot. West Indies to Snapper Banks, West Florida. **1933** BEEBE & TEE-VAN *Shore Fishes of Bermuda* 191 Yellow Belly; Beau Gregory.

beau-ideal (ˌbəʊaɪˈdiːəl). [a. F. *beau idéal* the ideal Beautiful, 'the Beautiful' as an abstract conception; *beau* being the sb., and *idéal* the adj. But in Eng., where the adj. usually precedes the sb., there has been a tendency to take *ideal* as the sb. part, whence the current usage; cf. IDEAL.]

†**1.** The ideal Beautiful; the Beautiful, or beauty, in its ideal perfection. *Obs.*

1801 MAR. EDGEWORTH *Belinda* xix. (D.) The image which they have in their own minds of the beau ideal is cast upon the first objects they afterwards behold.

2. The highest conceived or conceivable type of beauty or excellence of any kind; that in which one's 'ideal' is realized, the perfect type or model.

1820 IRVING *Sketch-Bk., John Bull* (D.) Wonderfully captivated with the *beau idéal* which they have formed of John Bull. **1827** *Gent. Mag.* XCVII. II. 516 The *beau ideal* of manly beauty. **1854** H. MILLER *Sch. & Schm.* xxii. 231 The Highlanders came to regard him as the very beau-ideal of a minister.

ˌ**beauiˈdealize,** *v. nonce-wd.* [f. prec.] To form a beau ideal, or charming conception, of.

a **1839** L. LANDON in *Blanchard's Life* (1841) I. 60 (D.) I shall spare you the flowers I have gathered, the trees I have seen, leaving you to beauidealize them for yourself.

beauish (ˈbəʊɪʃ), *v.* [f. BEAU *sb.* + -ISH¹.] After the manner of a beau; foppish, dandified.

1699 BENTLEY *Phal.* 395 Some common and obvious Thought, dress'd and curl'd in the Beauish way. **1858** LYTTON *What will he do* VIII. ix, Those beauish brigands.

beauism (ˈbəʊɪz(ə)m). [f. as prec. + -ISM.] The characteristic practice of a beau.

1844 *Blackw. Mag.* LV. 769 The flame of beauism was expiring. **1844** TUPPER *Crock of G.* xviii. 151 The extremest mode of rustic beauism.

Beaujolais (ˈbəʊʒəleɪ). [Name of a former district of France.] The name given to several light Burgundies, both red and white, produced in the Beaujolais district.

1863 T. G. SHAW *Wine* viii. 258 All common cheap French red wines seem now to have got the name of Beaujolais, as white have that of Chablis. **1879** STEVENSON *Trav. Cevennes* 33, I uncorked my bottle of Beaujolais, and asked the host to join me. **1960** *Farmer & Stockbreeder* 22 Mar. Suppl. 6/2 The next stew is a party dish and is best made with topside of beef and a respectable wine like Beaujolais.

beaulte, -tye, obs. forms of BEAUTY *sb.*

Beaumé: see BAUMÉ.

‖**beau-monde** (bomɔ̃d, bəʊˈmɒnd). [a. F. *beau monde*, i.e. fine world.] The fashionable world, 'society.'

1714 POPE *Rape Lock* v. 133 This the beau monde shall from the Mall survey. **1756** NUGENT *Gr. Tour.* I. 116 The *beau-monde* used to go in masquerade about the streets. **1823** BYRON *Juan* XIV. xx, Of the beau monde a part potential.

beaumontage (bəʊmɒnˈteɪg). Also **-montague.** [? f. name of Élie de *Beaumont* (1798–1874), French geologist.] A composition (of various mixtures) used by cabinet-makers, pattern-makers, and iron-founders for the concealment of cracks and holes in wood or metal work. Also *fig.* (see quot. 1895).

1886 ELWORTHY *W. Somerset Word-bk.*, Boman teg. **1888** *Chambers's Encycl.* II. 3 Beaumontague is a composition.. which is used to fill up cracks in an iron casting. **1895** BREWER *Dict. Phrase & Fable, Beaumontague* (pronounced *bo-mon-taig*), bad work, especially ill-fitting carpenter's work; literary padding; paste and scissors literature. **1899** HASLUCK *Wood Finishing* ix. 67 Beaumontage.. is generally called 'stopping-out wax'.

Beaune (bəʊn). [The name of a town in the department of Côte d'Or, France.] A red wine of Burgundy, produced in the district around Beaune.

1818 MOORE *Fudge Fam. Paris* iii. 51 Some glasses of *Beaune*. **1841** THACKERAY *Mem. Gormandising* Misc. Essays, &c. (1885) 386 Always drink red wine with beef-steaks.. good Beaune, say. **1863** T. G. SHAW *Wine* viii. 255 Beaune, 1858, first growth, high flavour, much body, fine. **1875** *Ure's Dict. Arts* III. 1143 Haute-Burgogne.. produces the most famous wines in Burgundy... Here grow the renowned *Volnay, Pomard, Beaune, Nuits*. **1958** A. L. SIMON *Dict. Wines* 27/2 *Beaune*.. Among the many fine red wines of the vineyards of Beaune, some of the better known are: Grèves, Fèves, Clos des Mouches [etc.].

†ˈ**beauˈpere.** *Obs.* Forms: 4–6 bewpere, beaupere, 4–7 beaupeere, 5 beawpere, bepyr, bewpyr, 6 bewpeer, 7 beawpeer. [f. OF. *beau* fine, good + *père* father, or, in sense 2, *per, peer* (mod. *pair*) equal, PEER. See BEAU. In OF., *beau père* was politely used in addressing every one whom one called 'father'; i.e. one's own father, a 'father' in the church, a god-father, a step-father, a father-in-law, an elderly man occupying a fatherly position in one's regard; about the 16th or 17th c., this use of *beau* became obsolete, and *beau-père* was retained as a distinctive term for 'father-in-law' and 'step-father' as distinct from a real father. In English the use appears to have been much more limited. See also BEL.]

1. A term of courtesy for 'father,' used esp. to or of a spiritual or ecclesiastical 'Father.'

c **1300** *Beket* 1299 The Bischop of Cicestre gon arise: Beau pere, he seide to the Pope. *c* **1375** WYCLIF *Serm.* Sel. Wks. 1871 II. 380 Summe children þus maad freris ben worse þan her bewperis. *c* **1450** *Pol. Poems* (1859) II. 229 Bridelle, you, bysshoppe.. And biddeth yowre beawperes se to the same. **1599** *Broughton's Lett.* v. 17 The holy fathers of the Church, the reuerend Beaupeeres of diuine knowledge.

2. Good fellow, fellow, companion, compeer.

1377 LANGL. *P. Pl.* B. XVIII. 229 Boke hiȝte þat beupere, a bolde man of speche. **1572** *Schole-house Wom.* 774 in Hazl. *E.P.P* IV. 135 In her lap sleeping she clipt of his hear, Betraied her Lord and her bewpeer. **1610** G. FLETCHER *Christ's Vict.* in Farr *S.P.* (1848) 74 There The saints with their beawpeers whole worlds outweare.

†ˈ**beaupers, bewpers.** *Obs.* Also 6 bowpres. [Deriv. unknown: it has been referred to *Beaupreau*, a town of France with manufactures of linen and woollen.] A fabric, apparently linen; used for flags.

1592 *Wills & Inv. N.C.* II. (1860) 211 Lawne cufes 3s.,peace of bowpres 16s. **1660** *Act 12 Chas. II*, iv. Sched., Beaupers the piece *jl. vs.* **1664** PEPYS *Diary* (1879) III. 56 Among the Linnen Wholesale Drapers.. to see what can be done with them for the supplying our want of Bewpers for flaggs. *Ibid.* 16 June, Supplying us with bewpers from Norwich. **1720** *Stow's Surv.* (1754) II. v. xviii. 382/2 Bolters and Bewpers the dozen pieces 1*d.*

beauˈpleader. *Law.* [a. AF. *beul pleder* = F. *beau plaider* 'fair or correct pleading'; cf. *fair copy*.] The amendment of a defective plea; a writ lying against those who levied a fine for amendment of plea.

[**1267** *Act 52 Hen. III*, xi, *transl.*, No fines shall be taken for Beaupleader. **1292** BRITTON I. xxi. §4 Ceux qi pernent fins pur coungé de beul pleder (*transl.* Those who take fines for leave of beau pleader).] **1700** TYRRELL *Hist. Eng.* II. 1112 That no Fines be taken for *Beaupleader*, or fair Pleading.

beau-pot (ˈbəʊpɒt). [f. F. *beau* beautiful + *pot* POT: possibly, in its origin, a mistaken spelling of BOUGH-POT q.v.] A large ornamental vase for cut flowers.

1761 GARRICK & COLMAN *Cland. Marr.* II. Wks. 1798 III. 27 A bunch of flowers as big as the cook or the nurse carry to town.. for a beaupot. **1867** MISS MULOCH *Two Marr.* II. 80 Flowers to replenish the beau-pot in the grate.

‖**beau rôle** (bo rol). [Fr., = fine rôle.] A fine acting part; the leading part; also *transf.*

1887 *Athenæum* 29 Oct. 561/3 Each assumed the moral government of the world without appealing to any revelation. This assumption, of course, gives the *beau rôle* to a prophet. **1927** in D. MCCARTHY *Drama* (1940) 102 In Ibsen the woman nearly always has the *beau rôle*. **1938** *Times Lit. Suppl.* 10 Sept. 581/4 The *beau rôle* at Fontenoy was that of the Irish Brigade. **1939** A. TOYNBEE *Study of Hist.* IV. 221 The beau rôle of 'the prisoner of the Vatican'.

‖**beau sabreur** (bo saˈbrœːr). [Fr., lit. 'handsome (or fine) swordsman'; cf. SABREUR.] A sobriquet for Joachim Murat (1767–1815), a famous French cavalry officer, brother-in-law of Napoleon I; hence used *transf.*: a fine soldier, a handsome or dashing adventurer.

1834 *Baboo & Other Tales Descr. Soc. India* I. vii. 113 Handsome, gallant, and young, he held the place that Murat did in the armies of Italy, and might have been called our 'beau sabreur'. Although, like Murat, without many pretensions to genius, his soldierly qualities invested him with a kind of romance. **1865** 'OUIDA' *Strathmore* I. i. 9 The Beau Sabreur, as he had been nicknamed, à la Murat, was

soft as silk in the hands of a beauty. **1888** *Athenæum* 5 May 573/1 [His] long fair hair, bound in braids about his head, after the fashion of his people (a fashion revived by the *beaux sabreurs* of Napoleon's time). **1919** G. B. SHAW *Playlets of War* 234 We women admire..the heroic warrior, the *beau sabreur*. **1947** WODEHOUSE *Full Moon* i. 14 The latter's sister ..considered that *beau sabreur* and man about town a blot on the escutcheon of a proud family.

beauship ('bəʊʃɪp). [f. BEAU + -SHIP.] The position or personality of a beau; cf. *lordship*.
1696 CONGREVE *J. Dryden's Husb. Cuckold* Prol., You laugh not..At what his beauship says, but what he wears.

† **beausire.** *Obs.* Forms: 4 beau sir(e, 5 **bawshere, besher, bewsher(e, 6 beaw schirre, bew schyre, bew schirre.** See also BELSIRE. [a. F. *beau* fair, *sire* sir, lord. In OF. *bel sire, beau sire* was a general form of respectful address: see BEAU, BEAUPERE.] Fair sir, a form of address.
c **1300** *Beket* 768 Beau sire..thu spext as a fol. *c* **1340** *Gaw. & Gr. Knt.* 1222 'Nay, for soþe, beau sir,' sayd þat swete. *c* **1400** *Destr. Troy* v. 1863 Beusher, who so euer þou be..Me meruellis of þi momlyng. *c* **1460** *Towneley Myst.* 66 Be stylle, beshers. *Ibid.* 69 Welcom, bawshere. *Ibid.* 241 Thou shalle abak, bewshere. **1513** DOUGLAS *Æneis* IX. Prol. 79 Sa faris with me bew schirris.

beaut (bjuːt). *Chiefly U.S., Austral.* and *N.Z. slang.* Also (now rare) bute. [Abbrev. of BEAUTY *sb.* 5.] A beautiful or outstanding person or thing. Also *attrib.*, passing into *adj.*
1866 'F. KIRKLAND' *Bk. Anecdotes* 178 Hopeful is not a beauty..and though some of the rustic wits call him 'Beaut', he is well aware that they intend it for irony. **1896** ADE *Artie* i. 5 They was beauts too. **1903** CLAPIN *Dict. Amer.*, Bute. **1909** T. H. THOMPSON *Ballads about Business* 79 Well, I guess she ain't a bute. **1910** O. JOHNSON *Varmint* i. 16 The tin one was easier, but it's a beaut. *Ibid.* v. 67 Some of the fellows have perfect beauts. **1929** W. SMYTH *Girl from Mason Creek* xv. 161 We didn't quite git th'hang of things first go off, but now I reckon it will be a 'beaut'. **1934** T. WOOD *Cobbers* v. 68 The last of the big sticks in this sector, and a real beaut. **1936** WODEHOUSE *Laughing Gas* xiii. 139, I seemed to be getting a lot of steam behind the punch... I got those two bozoes a couple of beauts! **1944** *Coast to Coast* 98 'We're a pair of beauts,' he said with the semblance of a grin. **1952** *Arena* (N.Z.) XXXII. 5, I scratched her a beaut. **1952** J. CLEARY *Sundowners* i. 6 Ain't that a beaut farm? **1957** 'N. SHUTE' *On Beach* ii. 71 It's been a beaut evening. **1968** K. WEATHERLY *Roo Shooter* 22 The bushie grabbed a plate and headed for the camp oven. 'You beaut,' he said. 'Coffee 'll do.'

‖ **beauté du diable** (bote dy djabl). [Fr., lit. 'devil's beauty'.] Superficial attractiveness; captivating charm.
[**1825** H. WILSON *Memoirs* III. 8 She possessed, what the French term, la beauté du diable, namely, youth, and a particularly youthful appearance.] **1863** *Fraser's Mag.* Mar. 309/1 The increasing number of barristers who find themselves unable to resist the *beauté du diable* of the fair daughters and sisters of the proscribed race [*sc.* attorneys]. **1870** R. BROUGHTON *Red as Rose* I. viii. 157 Hers is essentially *beauté du diable*..one of those little faces that have been at the bottom of half the mischiefs the world has seen. **1936** E. BOWEN in Verschoyle *Eng. Novelists* 104 Henry Crawford is more energetic, dashing and unscrupulous. He has a certain *beauté du diable*. **1967** H. MCCLOY *Further Side of Fear* iii. 41 He studied both photographs. 'They can't mean ugly as sin! They must mean *beauté du diable*.'

beauteous ('bjuːtɪəs), *a.* Forms: 5 **bewtyose,** 5–6 **beauteuous,** 6 **beuteus, bewtyous,** 7 **beuteous, bewtious,** 6–8 **beautious,** 6– **beauteous.** [f. *beaute*, BEAUTY *sb.* + -OUS. Cf. *plenteous.*]
Distinguished by beauty, exceedingly fair in appearance or elegant in form, pleasing to the sight, beautiful. (*Literary* and chiefly *poetical.*)
c **1440** *York Myst.* xlvi. 175 As bewteous braunche for to bere. **1480** CAXTON *Descr. Brit.* 6 England is beauteuous.. flour of londes all aboute. **1596** SHAKS. *Tam. Shr.* I. ii. 86 A wife With wealth enough, and yong and beautious. **1667** MILTON *P.L.* IV. 697 Each beauteous flour. **1711** STEELE *Spect.* No. 144 ¶1 There is something irresistible in a beauteous Form. *c* **1805** WORDSW. *Sonn.* I. xxx. Wks. III. 32 It is a beauteous evening, calm and free. **1855** BROWNING *In Balcony* in *Men & Wom.* II. 105 The dearest, richest, beauteousest and best Of women.

'beauteously, *adv.* [f. prec. + -LY[2].] In a beauteous manner; beautifully.
1471 RIPLEY *Compl. Alch.* III. in Ashm. (1652) 141 Wyth Flowers dyscoloryd bewtyosely to syght. **1650** JER. TAYLOR *Holy Living* ii. §1 (1727) 54 Look upon pleasures not upon that side..where they look beauteously. **1807** WORDSW. *Sonn.* v. Wks. 1840 III. 208 The ruddy crest of Mars Amid his fellows beauteously revealed.

'beauteousness. [f. as prec. + -NESS.] The quality of being beauteous; beauty.
1855 SINGLETON *Virgil* II. 419 Whose brilliance not as yet hath passed away, Nor yet its beauteousness. **1882** J. PARKER *Apost. Life* I. 137 Its ineffable beauteousness.

beautician (bjuː'tɪʃən). orig. *U.S.* [f. BEAUTY + -ICIAN.] One who runs a beauty parlour; a beauty specialist.
1924 *Cleveland Teleph. Directory* (Mencken, Suppl. I, 572), Very efficient beauticians. **1926** *Glasgow Herald* 12 June 8 The immense growth of 'beauty parlors' in the United States has added to the American language the word 'beautician'. **1934** *Southport Visiter* 8 Dec. (Advt.), J. H... beautician..modern hairdressing..rejuvenating facials. **1948** M. SHARP *Foolish Gentlewoman* xviii. 190 'I'm going to be a Beautician.'..'They get good money..and it's nice work.' **1959** *Observer* 15 Mar. 14/4 Most of the beautician's clients form the habit early. Others drop in late in life as a result of some personal crisis.

beautied ('bjuːtɪd), *ppl. a.* [f. BEAUTY *v.* and *sb.* + -ED.]
1. Endowed with beauty, beautified. See BEAUTY *v.*
2. (in *comb.*) Having beauty.
1614 CHAPMAN *Odyss.* XI. 374 A daughter that surpass'd Rare-beautied Pero.

beautification (ˌbjuːtɪfɪ'keɪʃən). [f. BEAUTIFY; see -FICATION, and cf. *amplify, -fication*, etc.] The action of beautifying; embellishment, adornment.
a **1640** JACKSON *Creed* XI. xvi. Wks. X. 313 Unuseful beautifications. **1798** MAVOR *Brit. Tourist* V. 35 The church is antique, but its venerable beauties have been spoiled by offensive and injudicious beautifications. **1881** G. MACDONALD *M. Marston* II. xiii. 213 To minister to the comfort or beautification of her cousin.

beautified ('bjuːtɪfaɪd), *ppl. a.* [f. BEAUTIFY + -ED.] Made beautiful; adorned, embellished.
1580 SIDNEY *Arcadia* (1622) 305 Thou art gone to a beautified heauen. **1602** SHAKS. *Ham.* II. ii. 110 To the Celestiall, and my soules Idoll, the most beautified Ophelia. **1684** BUNYAN *Pilgr.* II. 99 How green this Valley is, also how beautified with Lillies. **1870** HAWTHORNE *Eng. Note-bks.* (1879) I. 102 It is the ideal of a goose,—a goose beautified and beatified.

beautifier ('bjuːtɪfaɪə(r)). [f. as prec. + -ER[1].] He who, or that which, makes beautiful.
1612 R. SHELDON *Serm. St. Martins* 50 God the Dignifier, the Sanctifier, and Beautifier of the Sacrifice. **1712** tr. *Pomet's Hist. Drugs* 14 Pomatums, and other external Beautifiers. **1758** *Month. Rev.* 161 Narses, the repairer and beautifier of it [a bridge]. **1849** MISS MULOCH *Ogilvies* x. (1875) 81 There is no beautifier like happiness.

beautiful ('bjuːtɪfʊl), *a.* (and *sb.*) Forms: 6 **beaute-, beuti-, beuty-, bewti-, bewtyfull, beuty-, butyful,** 6–7 **beauti-, beautyfull,** 6– **beautiful.** [f. BEAUTY *sb.* + -FUL. Occas. compared with *-er, -est*, usually with *more, most.*] **A.** *adj.* Full of beauty, possessing the qualities which constitute beauty.
1. Excelling in grace of form, charm of colouring, and other qualities which delight the eye, and call forth admiration: **a.** of the human face or figure.
1526 *Pilgr. Perf.* (W. de W. 1531) 3 Whose swete visage was moost beautefull. **1642** FULLER *Holy & Prof. St.* v. ii. 362 Lewis, Prince of Tarentum, one of the beautifullest men in the world. **1716–8** LADY MONTAGUE *Lett.* I. xiii. 46 The only beautiful young woman I have seen. *a* **1842** TENNYSON *Ode to Mem.* 39 Spirit-thrilling eyes so keen and beautiful.
b. of other objects.
1526 TINDALE *Matt.* xxiii. 27 Paynted tombes, which appere beautyfull outwardes. **1611** BIBLE *Ps.* xlviii. 2 Beautifull for situation, the ioy of the whole earth is mount Sion. **1788** *Lond. Mag.* 64 One of the beautifullest of the whole parrot kind. **1860** TYNDALL *Glac.* I. §12. 90 Below us was the beautiful valley of Chamouni.
c. Used for emphasis or ironically, after the noun it qualifies.
The expression *the House Beautiful* is taken from Bunyan's *Pilgrim's Progress*, where Beautiful is to be regarded as a proper name.
1857 C. M. YONGE *Dynevor Terrace* II. xx. 306 'I must look in at the House Beautiful,' said Louis. **1880** W. ROBINSON (*title*) God's Acre Beautiful or the Cemeteries of the Future. **1883** O. WILDE *Lett.* (1962) 151 (*lecture-title*) The House Beautiful. **1899** W. ROBINSON *Eng. Flower Garden* (ed. 7) 181 The Summer Garden Beautiful. *Ibid.* 378 The Orchard Beautiful. **1904** KIPLING *Traffics & Discoveries* 357 The front of the House Beautiful. **1917** *Ladies' Home Jrnl.* Feb. 78/4 Send two cent stamp for 'The Body Beautiful' and trial plan today. **1929** *Melody Maker* Feb. 128 (Advt.), The new song-sensation by the writer of 'Charmaine'. 'Anita'. 'The waltz beautiful.' **1941** L. MACNEICE *Poetry of W. B. Yeats* iv. 82 Pater's doctrine of the Body Beautiful.
2. a. Affording keen pleasure to the senses generally, especially that of hearing; delightful. In modern colloquial use the word is often applied to anything that a person likes very much, *e.g.* 'beautiful pears,' 'she makes beautiful soup,' 'a beautiful ride.' (Sometimes difficult to distinguish from 3.)
1868 HAWTHORNE *Amer. Note-bks.* (1879) II. 202 It had been the beautifullest of weather all day. *a* **1887** *Mod.* Beethoven's most beautiful sonata. **1899** KIPLING *Stalky & Co.* 60 Everybody paid in full—beautiful feelin'.
b. ***beautiful people*** orig. *U.S.* (occas. written with capital initials), (*a*) 'flower' people, hippies; (*b*) wealthy, fashionable people; the 'smart set'.
1964 *Vogue* 15 Feb. 49 What the beautiful people are doing to keep fit. **1966** MRS. L. B. JOHNSON *White House Diary* 23 Jan. (1970) 356 'The Beautiful People' are all heading for Acapulco and in the list of the beautiful people was Lynda Bird's name. **1967** *Spectator* 4 Aug. 131/1 Far from being one of the Beautiful People, I was in an ugly frame of mind. **1970** *Ladies Home Jrnl.* Sept. 81/1 Cleveland Amory..feels that the Beautiful People and the Jet Set are being threatened by current economics. **1986** *Photography* Nov. 61/1 The socialites..take Olympus cameras among people who are not photographers—the beautiful people.
3. Impressing with charm the intellectual or moral sense, through inherent fitness or grace, or exact adaptation to a purpose; *hence* sometimes applied to things that, in other aspects, are even repulsive, as 'a beautiful operation in surgery.'
1587 GOLDING *De Mornay* vi. 77 The vnderstanding is beautifull, and the most beautifull of all. **1650** B. *Discollimin.* 19 The Providences of God are wonderfull and beautifull. **1739** HUME *Hum. Nat.* II. ii. Wks. 1874 I. 337 Another argument..which seems to me very strong and beautiful. **1819** J. Q. ADAMS in Davies *Metr. Syst.* 148 The theory of this nomenclature is perfectly simple and beautiful. **1824** *Sporting Mag.* XIV. 165/2 Spring made some beautiful stops, left and right [in boxing]. **1876** HAMERTON *Intell. Life* VIII. i. 275 A beautiful patience, and resignation. **1929** M. DE LA ROCHE *Whiteoaks* xvi. 226 I'll never forget how beautiful you were to me. **1967** *N. Y. Times* (Internat. Ed.) 11–12 Feb. 9/2 The beautiful part of it..is that the trade is across the board, not limited to certain big sectors. **1967** *Boston Sunday Herald Mag.* 30 Apr. 32/3 'We had one guy,' he said, 'he was so beautiful. A jazz musician who also wrote children's books.' **1968** *Crescendo* June 12/2 Maynard was a great leader... He was beautiful for the whole spirit of the band.
4. Relating to the beautiful; æsthetic. *rare.*
1814 W. TAYLOR *Month. Rev.* 155 Lady Russell's letters have rather a moral and political than a beautiful value.
5. *Comb.*, as ***beautiful-browed, -minded.***
a **1830** TENNYSON *Œnone* 69 Beautiful-browed Œnone, my own soul. **1865** MASSON *Rec. Brit. Philos.* 43 A beautiful-minded Berkeley.
B. *absol.* quasi-*sb.*
1. = Beautiful one.
1535 COVERDALE *Song Sol.* ii. 10 My loue, my doue, my beutyfull. **1819** BYRON *Juan* IV. lviii, Where late he trod, her beautiful, her own.
2. That which is beautiful. ***the beautiful***: the name given to the general notion which the mind forms of the assemblage of qualities which constitute beauty.
1756 BURKE *Subl. & B.* IV. §22. 299 We may here call sweetness the beautiful of the taste. **1856** MRS. BROWNING *Aur. Leigh* II. 97 So you judge! Because I love the beautiful I must Love pleasure chiefly. **1861** in *Macm. Mag.* June 126 The Beautiful in nature is the unmarred result of God's first creative or forming will; and the beautiful in art is the result of an unmistaken working of man in accordance with the beautiful in nature.

'beautifully, *adv.* [f. prec. + -LY[2].] In a beautiful manner, with beauty; charmingly, delightfully, admirably.
1548 HALL *Chron. Hen. VI*, an. 14 (R.) The bright sunne that..shone in Fraunce feaire and beautifully. **1576** LAMBARDE *Peramb. Kent* (1826) 223 He brought Plantes.. and furnished this ground with them beautifully. *c* **1730** PRIOR *Hen. & Emma* 323 Fine by degrees and beautifully less. **1820** SCOTT *Abbot* xix, A short but beautifully-wrought sword. **1841** MARRYAT *Poacher* xxiv, She could read and write beautifully. **1856** KANE *Arct. Expl.* I. xxxi. 421 The atmosphere was beautifully clear.

'beautifulness. [f. as prec. + -NESS.] The quality of being beautiful, beauty, loveliness; *concr.* in *pl.* things in which this quality is embodied.
1526 *Pilgr. Perf.* (W. de W. 1531) 63 Beautefulnesse of nature. **1625** tr. *Camden's Hist. Eliz.* I. (1635) 67 Queene Elizabeth..at Oxford..being much delighted with the.. beautifulnesse of the Colledges. **1849** ROBERTSON *Serm.* Ser. I. xiii. 192 The beautifulness of obedience is perceived. **1870** HAWTHORNE *Eng. Note-bks.* (1879) II. 15 The house..is filled with..ingenious..beautifulnesses.

beautify ('bjuːtɪfaɪ), *v.* Forms: 6 **beuti-, beuty-, bewtifie, beaute-, bewti-, bewtyfy, beauti-, beauty-, bewtyfye,** 6–7 **beautifie,** 6–8 **-yfy,** 6– **beautify.** [f. BEAUTY *sb.* + -FY.]
1. *trans.* To render beauteous or beautiful; to make fair or lovely; to adorn, embellish, decorate.
1526 *Pilgr. Perf.* (W. de W. 1531) 83 Virginite ioyned with mekenes..beautefyeth all vertues. **1576** LD. BURGHLEY in Thynne *Animadv.* (1875) App. 114 Whome princely garter, with his azurd hue, dothe bewtyfye. **1604** HIERON *Wks.* I. (1625) 678 To beautifie the house of God. **1697** COLLIER *Ess. Mor. Subj.* I. (1709) 69 Whose mind is..beautified with all sorts of useful Knowledge. **1703** MAUNDRELL *Journ. Jerus.* (1721) 136 It is..beautified all round with exquisite Sculpture. **1860** MAURY *Phys. Geog. Sea* x. §488 No coral islands to beautify its landscapes.
2. *refl.* and *intr.* To grow beautiful. *intr.* To make oneself beautiful.
1593 SHAKS. *Lucr.* 404 Each in her sleep themselves so beautify. **1711** ADDISON *Spect.* No. 111 ¶8 It must be a Prospect pleasing to God himself, to see his Creation for ever beautifying in his Eyes, and drawing nearer to him. **1902** H. JAMES *Wings of Dove* v. xiv. 224 How tremendously Susie must be beautifying!
¶ *catachr.* for BEATIFY, q.v.
1626 L. OWEN *Spec. Jesuit.* (1629) 31 Ignatius..was afterwards Beautified by Pope Paul. **1703** MAUNDRELL *Journ. Jerus.* (1721) 64 That beautifying vision of God.

'beautifying, *vbl. sb.* [f. prec. + -ING[1].] The action or process of making beautiful; adornment, embellishment; *pl.* things that beautify.
1532 THYNNE in *Animadv.* (1875) Introd. 24 The beautifyeing..of thenglysh tonge. **1665** *P. della Valle's Trav. E. India* 78 The buildings..are rather plain, and almost all without beautifyings. **1798** SOUTHEY *Eng. Eclog.*

i. Wks. III. 3, I can remember.. The beautifying of this mansion here.

ˈbeautifying, *ppl. a.* [f. as prec. + -ING².] That beautifies or makes beautiful.

1687 H. MORE *Death's Vis.* viii. 88 Amidst the Streams Of Beautifying Beams. **1702** *Lond. Gaz.* No. 3856/4 A most excellent Beautifying Water, called the Pearl Cosmetick.

beautiless (ˈbjuːtɪlɪs), *a.* [f. BEAUTY *sb.* + -LESS.] Void of beauty.

c **1600** *Lyrics for Lutenists* (Collier) 20 (*title*) Beauty when beautiless. **1669** BUNYAN *Holy Citie* 155 A forlorn beautiless World. *c* **1835** JAMES *De L'Orme* xlv. 301 A withered, formless, beautiless thing.

†**ˈbeautitude, bewtitude.** *Obs.* Apparently for BEATITUDE, perh. confused with *beauty*.

a **1400** *Chester Pl.* I. 8 My beames be all bewtitude. **1660** STANLEY *Hist. Philos.* (1701) 334/1 God is an Immortal being, rational, perfect, or intellectual in Beautitude.

beauty (ˈbjuːtɪ), *sb.* Forms: 3 bealte, buute, 3–4 beute, 4 beuaute, bewtee, 4–5 bewte, 4–6 beaute, 5 beaultye, bewete, boutte, 5–6 beaulte, 6 beaulty, beawtye, bewtie, -tye, 6–7 beautie, 7 beuty, 6- beauty. [ME. *bealte, beute*, a. OF. *bealte, beaute, biaute*, earlier *beltet*, mod. *beauté*, (cogn. with Pr. *beltat, beutat*, Sp. *beldad*, It. *beltà*):—late L. **bellitātem*, f. *bellus* beautiful: see -TY.]

I. *abstractly.*

(**1756** BURKE *Subl. & B.* III. xii. (1808) 235 Beauty is, for the greater part, some quality in bodies acting mechanically upon the human mind by the intervention of the senses. **1784** J. BARRY *Lect. Art* ii. (1848) 103 According to the definitions generally given, Beauty consists of unity and gradual variety; or unity, variety, and harmony.. Our rule for judging of the mode and degree of this combination of variety and unity seems to be no other than that of its fitness and conformity to the designation of each species. **1827** HARE *Guesses* (1859) 77 Beauty is perfection unmodified by a predominating expression.)

1. Such combined perfection of form and charm of colouring as affords keen pleasure to the sense of sight: **a.** in the human face or figure.

c **1275** in Wright *Lyric P.* xvi. 53 Heo is cristal of clannesse, Ant baner of bealte. *c* **1325** *E.E. Allit. P.* A. 764 He ȝef me myȝt & als bewte. *c* **1350** *Will. Palerne* 4074 A worschipful lady, þat burde was of beuaute briȝtest in erþe. *c* **1485** *E.E. Misc.* (Warton) 10 Alle owre pryd, owre jollytte and fayre boutte. **1485** CAXTON *Chas. Gt.* 240 Samblant to ..Absalon in beaulte! **1592** SHAKS. *Rom. & Jul.* v. iii. 94 Beauties ensigne yet Is Crymson in thy lips. **1651** HOBBES *Leviath.* III. xxxiv. 212 A Man, or Child of never so great beauty. **1711** POPE *Rape Lock* II. 28 Fair tresses man's imperial race insnare, And beauty draws us with a single hair. **1847** TENNYSON *Princ.* II. 20 There sat.. All beauty compass'd in a female form, The Princess.

b. of other objects.

1340 HAMPOLE *Pr. Consc.* 7857 þare es bryghtnes and bewte Of alle thing þat men salle þare se. **1413** LYDG. *Pylgr. Sowle* IV. xxviii. (1483) 74 The wonderful beaute of creatures. *c* **1532** LD. BERNERS *Huon* (1883) 412 The rychesse and beaulty of that chaumbre can not be dyscryuyd. **1752** JOHNSON *Rambl.* No. 192 ⁋5 Describing the beauty of his brother's seat. **1818** KEATS *Endym.* I. 1 A thing of beauty is a joy for ever; Its loveliness increases: it will never Pass into nothingness.

2. That quality or combination of qualities which affords keen pleasure to other senses (*e.g.* that of hearing), or which charms the intellectual or moral faculties, through inherent grace, or fitness to a desired end; cf. BEAUTIFUL *a.* 3.

c **1300** *Cursor M.* 14115 Of all thing scho [Mary] tok till ane, widvten quam es buute [*v.r.* beute] nane. *c* **1449** PECOCK *Repr.* 255 To speke and write the wordis in sum gaynes and bewte. **1599** THYNNE *Animadv.* (1875) 56 The dialecte of oure tonge, whiche withe beawtye vsethe suche transmutacione. **1677** GALE *Crt. Gentiles* II. IV. 17 Beautie is defined by Plato the Fulgor, *i.e.* Lustre of Good. **1860** EMERSON *Cond. Life* viii. 168 We ascribe beauty to that which is simple; which has no superfluous parts; which exactly answers its end. **1876** HAMERTON *Intell. Life* II. ii. 62 The beauty and solidity of the moral constitution. **1876** GREEN *Short Hist.* viii. §10 (1882) 584 The large but ordered beauty of form which he [Milton] had drunk in from the literature of Greece and Rome.

†**3.** The prevailing fashion or standard of the beautiful. *Obs.*

a **1667** JER. TAYLOR (in Webster) She stained her hair yellow, which was then the beauty.

4. The abstract quality (*esp.* in sense 1 a) personified.

1667 MILTON *P.L.* VII. 533 The charm of Beauties powerful glance. **1730** THOMSON *Autumn* 209 Thoughtless of beauty, she was beauty's self. *a* **1842** TENNYSON *Gard. Dau.* 57 Such a lord is Love, And Beauty such a mistress of the world.

II. *concretely.*

5. a. A beautiful person or thing; *esp.* a beautiful woman. (Often used ironically). Also applied colloquially to an exceptionally good specimen of something (as a ball in cricket, a blow, etc.); cf. BEAUT.

1483 CAXTON *Gold. Leg.* 273/2, I haue loued the ouer late, thou beaulte. **1596** SHAKS. *Merch. V.* III. ii. 99 The beautious scarfe Vailing an Indian beautie. **1711** ADDISON *Spect.* No. 37 ⁋4 Leonora was formerly a celebrated Beauty, and is still a very lovely Woman. **1753** HOGARTH *Anal. Beauty* i. 14 When a vessel sails well, the sailors always call her a beauty. **1826** DISRAELI *Viv. Grey* v. vi. (1868) 173 He was to be introduced to some of the most fashionable beauties. **1832** CARLETON *Traits Irish Peasant* 380 Faith, you're a beauty, Elisha. **1882** *Australians in England 1882* 46 Spofforth was bowled by a 'beauty' from Mycroft. **1897** I. SCOTT *How I stole 10,000 Sheep in Austral.* iii. 11 Our own dogs.. turned out to be 'beauties'. **1899** J. BELL *Shadow of Bush* viii. 46, I saw a beauty of a two-bladed knife at Buncombe's store. **1923** J. MANDER *Strange Attraction* vi. 71, I had a beauty of a little boat. **1924** WODEHOUSE *Bill the Conqueror* viii. 147 She.. swung her right and plugged Slingsby a perfect beauty in the eye.

b. *collectively*, The beautiful women, etc.

1611 BIBLE *2 Sam.* i. 19 The beauty of Israel is slaine vpon thy high places. **1613** SHAKS. *Hen. VIII*, I. iii. 55 There will be The Beauty of this Kingdome. **1816** BYRON *Ch. Har.* III. xxi, Belgium's capital had gather'd then Her Beauty and her Chivalry.

c. In various collectors' names of butterflies and moths.

1766 M. HARRIS *Aurelian: Nat. Hist. Moths & Butterflies* 19 The Brindled Beauty.. prettily diamonded on the Back with black, and spotted with yellow. **1832** J. RENNIE *Consp. Butterfl. & M.* 104 The Oak Beauty (*Biston prodromarius*, Leach). The Brindled Beauty (*Biston hirtarius*, Leach). **1847** [see CAMBERWELL BEAUTY]. **1921** *Conquest* Sept. 495/3 The Pale Brindled Beauty (*Phigalia pilosaria*).. has a particularly handsome black form.

6. a. A beautiful feature or trait; an embellishment, ornament, grace, charm.

1563 SHUTE *Archit.* D iij a, The which is a beautie vnto the whole Coronix. **1611** BIBLE *Ps.* cx. 3 In the beauties of holinesse. **1711** POPE *Rape Lock* IV. 170 These, in two sable ringlets taught to break, Once gave new beauties to the snowy neck. **1712** ADDISON *Spec.* 291 ⁋7 To discover the concealed Beauties of a Writer. **1849** MACAULAY *Hist. Eng.* II. 630 The one beauty of the resolution is its inconsistency. **1860** TYNDALL *Glac.* I. §1. 1 Guided by a friend who knew the country, I became acquainted with its chief beauties.

b. *pl.* In the titles of collections of the beautiful or choice passages of a writer or speaker, or examples of art.

1737 (*title*) The Beauties of the English Stage, consisting of all the celebrated passages, soliloquies, similies, descriptions and other poetical beauties in the English plays, *etc.* **1752** W. DODD (*title*) The Beauties of Shakespear, regularly selected from each play. **1767** (*title*) The Beauties of English Poesy. Selected by Oliver Goldsmith. **1786** (*title*) The beauties of the British Senate, taken from the debates of the Lords and Commons. **1860** *Athenæum* 31 Mar. 442/1 It might have been fancied that the days of 'Beauties', 'Gems', 'Anthologies' were over. **1865** (*title*) Beauties of Poetry and Art.

7. Colloq. phrases, as †*it was great beauty* (obs.): it was a fine sight. *that's the beauty of it*: i.e. the feature or phase that affords special pleasure and satisfaction.

1523 LD. BERNERS *Froiss.* I. xli. 57 It was a great beauty to beholde the baners and standerdes wauyng. *Ibid.* cxliv. 172 Hit was great beautie to beholde their puyssant array. **1754** RICHARDSON *Grandison* III. xviii. 159 That's the beauty of it; to offend and make up at pleasure.

8. *beauty of wildness*: see quot.

1611 GWILLIM *Heraldry* III. xiv. (1660) 174 Foresters and Hunters do call this yearly mewing of their heads, the beauty of their wildnesse: not the Mewing of their Horns.

III. *Comb.* **a.** poet., as ***beauty-bow, -crest, -in-the-ghost; beauty-beaming, -blooming, -blushing, -breathing, -bright, -clad, -drunken, -waning.*** **b.** Also **beauty-bloom**, beautiful tint or colour; **beauty contest**, a competition of women for a prize or distinction awarded to the most beautiful; **beauty culture** chiefly *U.S.*, use of cosmetics, etc., to improve a person's appearance; hence ***beauty culturist***; also ***beauty doctor, specialist***; †**beauty-man** *Obs.*, a handsome fellow, a dandy, a lady's man; **beauty-manner**, the bearing of a 'beauty'; †**beauty-mock**, an imitation of beauty; **beauty parlour** orig. *U.S.*, an establishment in which the trade of a beauty specialist is carried on; **beauty-proof** *a*, proof against the influence of beauty; **beauty queen** orig. *U.S.*, name given to the winner of a beauty contest; **beauty salon** = *beauty parlour*; cf. SALON 4; **beauty shop** *U.S.* = *beauty parlour*; **beauty show** = *beauty contest*; **beauty-sleep**, the sleep secured before midnight; **beauty treatment**, the use of cosmetics, etc., in order to improve personal beauty; **beauty-wash**, a liquid employed to preserve or heighten beauty, a cosmetic.

a. **1594** SHAKS. *Rich. III*, III. vii. 185 A Beautie-waining and distressed Widow. **1595** CHAPMAN *Banq. Sence* (1639) 23 This Beauty-clad naked lady. **1597** DRAYTON *Mortimer.* 13 This beauty-blushing orient of his rise. **1727** THOMSON *Summer*, All the varied hues Their beauty-beaming parent can disclose. **1813** BYRON *Genevra* 10 When from his beauty-breathing pencil born.. The Magdalen of Guido saw the morn. **1818** KEATS *Endym.* i. 363 To nightly call Vesper, the beauty-crest of summer weather. *a* **1889** G. M. HOPKINS *Poems* (1918) 83 Rough-Robin or five-lipped campion clear For a beauty-bow to his hat. *a* **1889** *Ibid.* (1918) 56 Beauty-in-the-ghost, deliver it, early now, long before death Give beauty back. **1928** YEATS *Tower* 62 The Great Mother, mourning for her daughter And beauty-drunken by the water.

b. **1853** KINGSLEY *Hypatia* xxv. 318 Young Apollo, with the *beauty-bloom upon his chin! **1899** A. M. BINSTEAD *Gal's Gossip* v. 77 Just the sort of woman who could apparently hold her own either in a *beauty contest, a political debate, or a scrape. **1933** J. B. PRIESTLEY *Wonder Hero* iv. 129 She had won a beauty contest, and was probably easily the prettiest girl staying in the hotel. **1909** *Harper's Bazaar* Feb. 172 (*title*) Modern *beauty culture. **1911** W. A. WOODBURY (*title*) Beauty Culture: A Practical Handbook on the Care of the Person. **1928** *Punch* 5 Sept. 280/1 Valuable information which is afforded about domestic economy, feminine attire, cookery, beauty-culture. **1933** *Times Lit. Suppl.* 29 June 448/4 A small American town, whose main interests are bridge, poker, 'beauty-culture' and gossip. **1911** W. A. WOODBURY *Beauty Cult.* 14 The successful *beauty culturist must, above all, be modest, tactful, and discreet. **1919** *Honey Pot* I. iii. 40 Dr. Caissarate, that wonderful beauty culturist. **1905** E. WHARTON *House of Mirth* II. ix. 430 A strange throng of hangers-on—manicures, *beauty-doctors, hair-dressers. **1921** *Dict. Occup. Terms* (1927) §920 Beauty specialist, beauty doctor. **1837** LYTTON *Ernest Maltrav.* I. II. ii. 181 The *Beauty-man is, nine times out of ten, little more than the oracle of his aunts, and the '*sitch* a love' of the housemaids. **1860** *Temple Bar Mag.* I. 68 A beauty-man, who rides and dances well. **1888** F. HUME *Mystery of Hansom Cab* xix. 130 A clergyman.. preached a sermon to prove that good looks and crime were closely connected, and that both Judas Iscariot and Nero were beauty-men. **1598** SYLVESTER *Du Bartas* II. iv. IV. Argt. (1641) 227 Achabs Stock, With his proud Queen (a painted *Beauty-mock). **1908** *Harper's Weekly* 24 Oct. 22/1 The *'beauty parlors' of a large department store. There are a number of booths divided off by wooden partitions. **1932** *Daily Express* 20 Sept. 5/5, I have decided to go into a beauty parlour when I grow up. **1938** E. BOWEN *Death of Heart* II. iv. 244 She was the receptionist in Southstone's biggest beauty parlour. **1753** RICHARDSON *Grandison* (1781) III. xiv. 105, I am *Beauty-proof. **1922** *N.Y. Times* 5 Sept. 19/6 The winning beauty will be heralded as America's *'Beauty Queen'. **1933** J. B. PRIESTLEY *Wonder Hero* iii. 86 The girl who's just won the *Morning Pictorial*'s beauty competition.. the Beauty Queen. **1960** *Guardian* 11 June 7/4 Seventeen national beauty queens compete for the title 'Miss Europe'. **1922** *Amer. Hairdresser* Sept. 114/1 A. Simonson on September 5 opened new *beauty salons at 54 West 57th street. **1954** J. L. MORSE *Unicorn Bk. 1953* 18/2 Beauty salons had special prices. **1982** *Amer. Speech* LVII. 187 No doubt many of the businesses listed in the 'Yellow Pages' under *Beauty Salon* are actually incorporated. **1901** *Current Lit.* Apr. 446/1 The Oldest *Beauty-Shop. **1939** A. HUXLEY *After many a Summer* I. i. 6 Next door to the beauty shoppe was a Western Union office. **1948** MENCKEN *Amer. Lang.* Suppl. I. 573 *Beauty-parlor* began to appear before World War I, and soon afterward it was displaced by *beauty-shop*. Sometimes the latter is spelled *beauty-shoppe*, or even *beauté-shoppe*. **1969** B. KNOX *Tallyman* vii. 132 Janey Milton.. on her way to have her hair set at a local beauty shop. **1896** C. S. *Leaves from Diary in Lower Bengal* v. 74 The idea occurred to him to have a *Beauty Show of our servants.. the prize to be given to the ugliest. **1907** G. B. SHAW *Let.* 7 Sept. (1941) 37 You would make me a curtain-raiser for a beauty show. **1857** KINGSLEY *Two Y. Ago* II. xv. 148 A medical man, who may be called up at any moment, must make sure of his '*beauty-sleep.' **1907** M. E. BRADDON *Dead Love has Chains* vii. 148 She must have *beauty-specialists, massage, electricity. **1938** N. MARSH *Death in White Tie* xxix. 305 Mrs. Halcut-Hackett.. looking like a beauty-specialist's mistake. **1928** B. BUSHBY (*title*) Postal Tuition Course of *Beauty Treatment. **1934** R. MACAULAY *Going Abroad* xxxiii. 282 Beauty treatment is never cheap. **1709** STEELE *Tatler* No. 34 ⁋2 The only true Cosmetick or *Beauty-Wash in the World.

ˈbeauty, *v. arch.*; also 4–5 **bewtye, bewte**, 6 **beautye**. [f. prec. sb.] *trans.* To render beautiful; to beautify, adorn, deck.

1398 TREVISA *Barth. De P.R.* XVII. lxxiii. (1495) 647 Floures.. defoyleth not the yerde: but bewtyeth it. **1525** LD. BERNERS *Froiss.* II. xlii. 131 The Pecocke sayd, he is gretly beautyed by reason of my fethers. **1602** SHAKS. *Ham.* III. i. 51 The Harlots Cheeke beautied with plaist'ring Art. **1855** SINGLETON *Virgil* I. 201 The altars of the gods in wreathed festoons Are beautied.

beautydom (ˈbjuːtɪdəm). The estate or rank of a 'beauty' or of beautiful women.

1881 *World* 28 Dec., The system of professional beautydom.

beautyhood (ˈbjuːtɪhʊd). Also **beautihood.** [f. BEAUTY *sb.* + -HOOD.] A woman's 'reign' as a beauty; society of beauties, also beauties collectively.

1889 M. E. MARTIN *Common Clay* III. xv. 240 The short season of her beautihood in London. **1889** H. F. WOOD *Englishman Rue Caïn* xvi, Initiation into the Fashionable Beauty-hood.

ˈbeautyship. The personality of a 'beauty.' Used sportively in address; cf. *ladyship*.

1839 BAILEY *Festus* 56/2 If your beautyship would condescend To teach us what true melody might be.

ˈbeauty-spot. [f. BEAUTY *sb.* + SPOT.]

1. A spot or patch placed upon the face by ladies in the method of adornment formerly fashionable: originally intended to heighten by contrast the charm of some neighbouring feature; *fig.* a foil.

1657 REEVE *God's Plea* 123 The setting of every hair.. the placing of every beauty-spot. **1705** HICKERINGILL *Priest-cr.* I. (1721) 45 Their Black Patches, which in former Times have been taken for Beauty-Spots. *a* **1711** GREW (J.) The filthiness of swine makes them the beauty-spot of the animal creation. **1864** H. SPENCER *Illust. Univ. Progr.* 90 From painted faces to beauty-spots.

2. *gen.* A feature or place of special beauty.

1682 BUNYAN *Holy War* 110 If righteousness be such a beauty-spot in thine eyes. **1879** CHR. ROSSETTI *Seek & Find* 91 Hill-streams and waterfalls rank among the beauty-spots of this beautiful world.

Beauvais (bəʊ'veɪ). The name of a town in northern France, used *attrib.* to designate things manufactured there, as ***Beauvais tapestry***.

1885 L. J. DAVIS tr. *Müntz's Short Hist. Tapestry* xiv. 335 (*caption*) Louis XV. Fauteuil, covered in Beauvais tapestry. **1899** R. GLAZIER *Man. Hist. Ornament* 118 There are some fine Gobelin and Beauvais tapestries in Windsor Castle. **1961** *Connoisseur* Dec. p. xxxviii, A fine Louis XV Beauvais tapestry.

‖**beaux arts** (bozar). Also **beaux-arts.** [Fr. *beaux-arts.*] The fine arts. Also used *ellipt.* for the *École des Beaux-Arts* in Paris; freq. *attrib.*, of the standards of architecture and art maintained by the École in France in the nineteenth century and early part of the twentieth century and imitated elsewhere, characterized by the influence of older styles and a reliance on decorative and period design.

1821 M. WILMOT *Jrnl.* 26 Oct. (1935) 134 Went to the top of the tower to see the view of all Venice... Next the Academy of beaux arts. **1833** J. S. MILL *Let.* 5 Sept. in *Wks.* (1963) XII. 177 The beaux-arts (what beaux-arts!) which had been the glory of the *siècle de Louis 14*. **1854** THOREAU *Walden* 52 So are made the *belles-lettres* and the *beaux-arts* and their professors. **1924** *Arts & Decoration* July 10/1 The French or Beaux Arts method of developing the finished drawing, or 'project' on a competition is followed by the Institute [*sc.* Beaux-Arts Institute of Design, N.Y.]. **1931** tr. *Willy & Colette's Claudine in Paris* xi. 17 He's at the Beaux Arts and he's going to be a great artist. **1945** *Encycl. Brit.* II. 273/1 The largest school of architecture in England is that of the Architectural Association and the next largest that of Liverpool university. Both these schools show definite tendencies away from the *Beaux Arts* influence and towards contemporary architecture, period design having been dropped almost entirely. **1956** K. CLARK *Nude* ix. 351 The classic nude with its exhausted *beaux-arts* associations. **1961** *Listener* 10 Aug. 201/2 He [*sc.* the architect] has failed to make proper use of technology, and is perpetuating *beaux arts* attitudes to design. **1967** E. WYMARK *As Good as Gold* xv. 219, I left the Beaux Arts and went back to New York.

beauxite, var. BAUXITE.

‖**beaux yeux** (bozjø). [Fr., = fine eyes.] Beautiful eyes; attractive beauty; admiring glances, favour.

[**1825** H. WILSON *Memoirs* I. 110, I tried this method of making a little whig of myself, pour les beaux yeux de mi Lord Ponsonby.] **1828** LYTTON *Pelham* I. xxii. 182 He will scratch out the lady's *beaux yeux*. **1850** THACKERAY *Pendennis* I. xxvii. 262 The poor fellow is mad for your *beaux yeux*, I believe. **1908** MRS. H. WARD *Diana Mallory* II. xii. 252 Oliver condemn himself to the simple life.. for the sake of the *beaux yeux* of Diana Mallory! **1931** *Times Lit. Suppl.* 5 Mar. 165/1 The *beaux yeux* of Victor Emmanuel and Cavour were being expensively purchased at the price of thousands of French lives.

beaver ('biːvə(r)), *sb.*[1] Forms: 1 beofor, befor, (byfor, befer), 2–7 beuer, 4–8 bever, 5 bevere, -yr, 6 beauer, 7 beavor, 6– beaver. [One of the animal names common to the Aryan family: OE. *beofor*, earlier *befor* (= *bevor*), identical with LG. and Du. *bever*, OHG. *bibar*, mod.G. *biber*:—OTeut. **bebru-z*; cogn. w. Lith. *bebru-s*, Boh. *bobr*, OSlav. *bebru-*, L. *fiber*, 'beaver'; also with Skr. *babhrús* 'brown,' and as sb. 'great ichneumon':—OAryan **bhebhrú-s*, reduplicated deriv. of *bhru-* brown, with sense of 'brown' or 'red-brown,' and 'brown water-animal.']

1. a. An amphibious rodent, distinguished by its broad, oval, horizontally-flattened, scaly tail, palmated hind feet, coat of soft fur, and hard incisor teeth with which it cuts down trees; remarkable for its skill in constructing huts of mud and wood for its habitation, and dams for preserving its supply of water.

c **1000** ÆLFRIC *Gram.* (Zup.) 27 *Fiber*, befor, beofor. *c* **1200** *Moral Ode* 362 in *Lamb. Hom.* 181 Ne scal þer beo fou ne grei.. ne beuer ne sabeline. **1387** TREVISA *Higden* Rolls Ser. VI. 205 Beverlay.. the place or lake of bevers. *c* **1460** J. RUSSELL *Bk. Nurture* in *Babees Bk.* (1868) 153 To peson or frumenty take þe tayle of þe bevere. **1591** SPENSER *M. Hubberd* 1124 Monstrous beasts.. Bred of two kindes, as Griffons, Minotaures.. Beavers, and Centaures. *a* **1667** COWLEY *Love's Riddle* I. i, His lips.. Softer than Bevers Skins. **1776** ADAM SMITH *W.N.* I. I. vi. 49 One beaver should exchange for or be worth two deer. **1855** LONGF. *Hiaw.* III. 153 How the beavers built their lodges.

b. ***bank beaver***, a beaver living in a burrow apart from the colony. *N. Amer.*

1903 *Outing* (U.S.) Mar. 669/1 You find the bank beaver mostly on lakes, or large rivers, which they are unable to dam. **1953** *Canadian Geogr. Jrnl.* Sept. 88/2 All along the river we came upon bank beaver.

c. *coll.* Beavers. Chiefly *U.S.*

a **1649** J. WINTHROP *Jrnl.* (1908) I. 61 A sagamore.. offered to give them yearly eighty skins of beaver. **1770** WASHINGTON *Diaries* I. 441 Then Bever catch it in there way up. **1778** J. KING *Jrnl.* Sept. in Cook *Jrnls.* (1967) III. II. 1439 Their jackets were principally of Deer Skins, edg'd with the Skin of other Animals, as Wolves, foxes, beaver &c. **1789** MORSE *Amer. Geogr.* 198 In this country are.. beaver, otters, sables. **1840** C. F. HOFFMAN *Greyslaer* I. v. 60, I had gone clean up to Racket Lake.. hoping to get a few beaver. **1890** L. C. D'OYLE *Notches* 66, I knew that beaver were plentiful.

d. Phr. ***to work like a beaver***: to work hard. orig. *U.S.*

1741 in H. M. Brooks *Days of Spinning-Wheel* (1886) II. 31 To be sold.., the very best negro woman in this town, who.. will work like a beaver. **1877** RAYMOND *Mines* 225 Mr. Baldwin.. has worked like a beaver since he assumed the management of the mine. **1915** *Lit. Digest* 21 Aug. 347/2 Every one knows what 'working like a beaver' means.

e. ***Beaver***, a member of the youngest section of the Scout movement, consisting of groups (Colonies) for six- (*Canad.* five-) to seven-year old boys affiliated to the Scout Association and sponsored by local Scout Groups; also attrib. as ***Beaver Colony***. orig. *Canad.*

1975 *Canad. Leader Mag.* Jan. 8/1 On September 23, 1971 .. the first Beaver colony was started in St. Cuthbert's Anglican Church, Winnipeg... Fifteen thousand Beavers later, on November 15, 1974, Beavers-Canada was adopted as a regular section program of Boy Scouts of Canada. **1977** *Globe & Mail* (Toronto) 23 July Suppl. 7/3 There are now 35,000 Beavers in Canada and the membership crisis is over. **1978** *Tower Times* (Kingston, Ont.) 22 Mar. 5/1 The Beaver Colony know already that they will need at least five new leaders. **1983** J. DEFT *Beaver Leader's Handbk.* 7 In 1982 The Scout Association gave general approval for the formation of Beaver Colonies within existing Scout Groups. .. The purpose of a Beaver Colony is thus to provide enjoyable and worthwhile activities for boys of six- and seven-years-old. *Ibid.*, Beavers are not Members of The Scout Association. *Ibid.* 8 Beaver Leaders.. are full Members of the Scout Group which sponsors the Colony. **1985** *Oxford Times* 11 Jan. 4/5 Beaver leader Mrs Val Wells .. launched the 12-strong colony in July last year. *Ibid.* 4/6 The beaver colony is an organization for boys before they join cubs.

2. a. The fur of the beaver.

c **1394** *P. Pl. Crede* 295 A cote haþ he furred, Wiþ foyns.. oþer fyn beuer. **1532-3** *Act 24 Hen. VIII*, xiii, Any maner of furre, other then.. otter and beuer. **1613** WITHER *Epithal.* in *Juvenilia* (1633) 363 A hat of Bever. **1739** GRAY in Mason *Life* (ed. 2) 62 With muffs, hoods, and masks of bever. **1837** MARRYAT *Dog-Fiend* x, He pulled off some beaver from his hat to staunch the blood.

fig. **1598** SYLVESTER *Du Bartas* I. iii. (1641) 30/1 Green Carpets, thrumd with mossie Bever, Fringing the round Skirts of his winding River.

b. *attrib.*, esp. in ***beaver hat, bonnet***: see next.

c **1386** CHAUCER *Prol.* 272 On his hed a Flaundrish bever hat. **1583** STUBBES *Anat. Abus.* (1877) 50 *note*, Bever hattes, of xx., xxx., or xl shillinges price. **1740** SWIFT *Will* Wks. 1745 VIII. 383 The second best beaver hat I shall die possessed of. **1844** DICKENS *Mar. Chuz.* v, Farmers' wives in beaver bonnets and red cloaks. **1862** G. BORROW *Wild Wales* I. i. 7 He made his appearance very respectably dressed, in a beaver hat, blue surtout [etc.]. **1928** D. BYRNE *Destiny Bay* iii. 236 There comes an old fellow in a beaver hat.

c. A shade of brown resembling that of the fur of a beaver; more explicitly ***beaver-brown***; also ***beaver-coloured, -hued*** adjs.

13.. *Gaw. & Gr. Knt.* 845 Brode, bryȝt, watȝ his berde, and al beuer-hwed. **1888** *Cassell's Family Mag.* Apr. 313/1 Many new colourings.. Beaver is such a becoming tone. **1895** *Ibid.* Feb. 234/1 A picture hat.. of beaver brown velvet. **1895** *Windsor Mag.* I. 340/2 The cloak is in beaver-coloured velvet. **1914** *Scotsman* 26 Oct. 12/2 The shades are Steel, Oxford and Parson Grey, Mole, Beaver, Fawn.

3. a. A hat made of beaver's fur, or some imitation of it; formerly worn by both sexes, but chiefly by men.

1528 ROY *Sat.*, To exalte the thre folde crowne Of anti-christ hys bever. **1642** H. MORE *Song of Soul* I. ii. xxxviii, A Yongster gent With bever cock't. **1661** PEPYS *Diary* 27 June, Mr. Holden sent me a bever, which cost me 4*£.* 5*s.* **1766** [ANSTEY] *Bath Guide* xi. 97 To preside at her Balls in a Cream-colour'd Beaver. **1810** CRABBE *Borough* iv. Wks. 1834 III. 80 The simple Friend.. in drab and beaver. **1885** *Cornh. Mag.* June 649 His crumpled beaver—there might be some difficulty in lighting on a beaver nowaday except in a museum.

b. *in beaver* (Univ. slang). In a tall hat (and the costume which accompanies it) instead of cap and gown; in non-academical costume.

1840 *New Monthly Mag.* LIX. 271 He.. went out of college in what the members of the United Service call *mufti*, but members of the University *beaver*, which means, not in his academics—his cap and gown.

4. A felted cloth, used for overcoats, etc.

1756 *Gentl. Mag.* XXVI. 618 Their carpets and bevers.. retain the electrical virtue, and prevent its spreading to the floor. **1810** J. T. in *Risdon's Surv. Devon* Introd. 25 Coatings, beavers.. found a market.

5. A particular kind of glove.

1816 MISS AUSTEN *Emma* (1870) II. vi. 169 Well tied parcels of 'Men's Beavers' and 'York Tan.' [**1836** DICKENS *Sk. Boz* (1850) 131/2 In a black coat.. gaiters, and brown beaver gloves.]

6. *Comb.*, chiefly attrib., as ***beaver-fur***, ***-intellect***, ***-kind***, ***-pond***, ***-skin***, ***-wool***(= fur); ***beaver-like*** adj. Also **beaver-board**, a trade-mark (U.S.) for a kind of wood-fibre building board; **beaver cloth** (cf. sense 4); **beaver-dam**, a dam made by beavers; **beaver-eater** (see quot. 1771); **beaver finish**, a finish giving a resemblance to beaver fur; hence, a finish in which the fibres are all laid in one direction; so ***beaver-finished*** adj.; **beaver lamb**, lambskin cut and dyed to resemble beaver fur; also *attrib.*; **beaver-poison** *U.S.*, the water-hemlock, *Cicuta sp.*; **beaver-rat**, the musquash or MUSKRAT; **beaver-root** *N. Amer.*, a pond-lily, *Nymphæa odorata*; **beaver-stones**, the two small sacs in the groin of the beaver, from which the substance 'castor' is obtained; **beaver-tail**, the tail of a beaver; also *transf.*; **beaver-tree**, *Magnolia virginiana*, the sweet or white bay of the U.S.; **beaver-wood**, (*a*) the hackberry tree of the U.S., *Celtis occidentalis*; (*b*) the beaver-tree; the wood of this tree.

1909 *Sat. Even. Post* 20 Feb. 35/1 [Advt. Beaver Manuf. Co., Buffalo, N.Y.], *Beaver Board.. Takes Place of Both Lath and Plaster. **1933** D. L. SAYERS *Murder must Advertise* viii. 145 The thinness of the beaverboard partition between Mr. Hankin's room and Mr. Copley's. **1948** 'N. SHUTE' *No Highway* i. 7 A shabby little room of glass and beaverboard. **1858** SIMMONDS *Dict. Trade*, **Beaver-cloths*, a species of felted woollens made in America. **1904** GOODCHILD & TWENEY *Technol. & Sci. Dict.* 46/2 *Beaver Cloth*, a thick woollen fabric covered with fibre or nap. The best qualities are made in the West of England; medium and lower qualities in the heavy woollen districts of Yorkshire. **1968** IRONSIDE *Fashion Alphabet* 213 *Beaver cloth*, a heavily-napped overcoating resembling the beaver fur. **1725** *Lond. Gaz.* No. 6383/4 Ann Messenger,.. *Beaver-Cutter. **1638** in *Amer. Speech* (1940) XV. 155/1 Upon the branches of a swamp runing North west up into the woods from the head of the said Vlyes Creeke out of a *Bever dam. **1676** T. GLOVER in *Phil. Trans.* XI. 626 The Bevers.. gnaw down trees, wherewith they make.. Bever-damms. **1703** in *Cal. Virginia St. Papers* I. 83 To three white oakes, by the East side of the Tuckahoe Bever Dam. **1903** S. E. WHITE *Forest* xvi. 231 He knows the beaver-dams, how many animals each harbors. **1931** W. CATHER *Shadows on Rock* (1932) II. i. 46 A group of little boys played just below, building 'beaver-dams' in the gutter to catch the overflow. **1968** *Globe & Mail* (Toronto) 3 Feb. 43/2 (Advt.), Large trout stream 15 acres flooded by beaver dam. **1771** PENNANT *Syn. Quadrup.* 197 Wolverene.. in America is called the *Beaver-Eater. **1791** J. LONG *Voy. & Trav. Indian Interpreter* 41 The country everywhere abounds with wild animals, particularly bears.. beaver eaters, [etc.]. **1804-5** LEWIS & CLARK *Jrnls.* (1905) VI. ii. 107 Carkajous, wolverine or Beaver Eaters.. or Links. **1904** GOODCHILD & TWENEY *Technol. & Sci. Dict.* 46/2 *Beaver Finish. **1909** R. BEAUMONT *Finishing Textile Fabrics* 11 The lateral surfaces of the fibres mainly resist the friction in the *beaver-finished cloth. **1855** WOOD *Anim. Life* 421 The *beaver-fur will work its way completely through the felt. **1850** CARLYLE *Latter-d. Pamph.* iv. 2 The intellect of the Nineteenth Century.. is itself a mechanical or *beaver-intellect. **1735** SOMERVILLE *Chase* IV. 379 This subtle Spoiler of the *Beaver kind. **1939** *Fur Times* 12 May 2/3 *Beaver lamb is shown in swaggers and short jackets. *Ibid.* 25 Aug. 8/1 Beaver lamb coats.. are now offered at eleven-and-a-half guineas. **1953** *Economist* 9 May 346/2 Thanks to the postwar prices of woollen (cloth) coats, 'beaver lamb' coats have provided the English fur manufacturers with a mass market. **1960** A. BURGESS *Right to Answer* ix, Alice in her beaver lamb. **1875** HELPS *Anim. & Mast.* iii. 59 Words of wisdom, of *beaver-like sagacity. **1857** A. GRAY *First Less. Bot.* 157 Spotted cowbane. Musquash-root. *Beaver-poison... The root is a deadly poison. **1884** *Cassell's Fam. Mag.* Apr. 272/2 The *'beaver-rat' is another singular animal. **1832** W. D. WILLIAMSON *Hist. Maine* I. 126 Of the Lily tribe, we have several species .. such as the yellow water-lily, or dog-lily, or *beaver-root. **1856** W. E. CORMACK *Narr. Journey Newfoundland* (1874) 27 They also subsist on the large roots of the white waterlilly .. called by the Indians beaver-root. **1761** *Brit. Mag.* 7 Jan. II. 52 This day 10,000 *beaver skins.. were entered from Quebec. **1697** DRYDEN *Virgil* (1806) I. 207 Pontus sends her *beaver-stones from far. *a* **1811** J. J. HENRY *Campaign against Quebec* (1812) 23 They returned two fresh *beaver tails, which when boiled, renewed ideas. **1909** WARE *Passing Eng.* 23/2 *Beaver-tail* (Mid.-class, 1860). A feminine mode of wearing the back-hair, turned up loose in a fine thread net .. which fell well on to the shoulders... Obviously from the shape of the netted hair [compared] to a beaver's flat and comparatively shapeless tail. **1937** *Discovery* Sept. 259/2 The last coach [of the L.N.E.R. 'Coronation' streamlined train] now has a streamlined 'beaver' tail, and is an observation car. **1960** *Aeroplane* XCVIII. 521/2 Major assembly has begun on the first AW 660 for the R.A.F. This version has a 100,000-lb. gross weight, 'beaver-tail' rear doors, and no nose doors. **1756** P. KALM *Resa till N. Amer.* II. 324 *Magnolia*,.. *Beawer-Tree. **1866** LINDLEY & MOORE *Treas. Bot.* s.v. *Magnolia, Magnolia glauca*.. is also known by the name of Beaver-tree, because the root is eaten by beavers. **1901** C. T. MOHR *Plant Life Ala.* 505 White Bay. Sweet Bay. Beaver Tree... The bark is used medicinally. **1810** F. MICHAUX *Hist. des Arbres* I. 33 Small magnolia.. ou *Beaver wood. **1813** H. MUHLENBERG *Cat. Plantarum* 95 Beaver wood [or] hoop ash. **1880** *Encycl. Brit.* XI. 360/1 [The hackberry tree] is also known under the name of 'beaver-wood', and 'nettle tree'. **1780** COXE *Russ. Disc.* 114 One side set close with *beaver-wool like velvet.

beaver ('biːvə(r)), *sb.*[2] *Obs.* exc. *Hist.* Forms: 5 baviere, 6 bauour, -er, 6–7 beuer, 7 bauier, beauer, beavoir, 8–9 bever, 9 beavor, 6– beaver. [ME. *baviere*, a. OF. *bavière*, orig. a child's bib, f. *bave* saliva; cf. It. *baviera*, Sp. *babera*.]

1. 'The lower portion of the face-guard of a helmet, when worn with a visor; but occasionally serving the purposes of both.'

'In 14th c. applied to the moveable face-guard of the basinet, otherwise called *viziere*, *ventaile*, or *aventaile*. In the early part of 15th c. the beaver appears formed of overlapping plates, which can be raised or depressed to any degree desired by the wearer. In the 16th c. it again became confounded with the visor, and could be pushed up entirely over the top of the helmet, and drawn down at pleasure.' (Planché.)

1481-90 HOWARD *Househ. Bks.* 274 A peir brigandines ....ij. bavieres [and] iij. peire ganteletz. **1557** *K. Arthur* (Copland) VI. ix, Syr Launcelot.. gate hym by the bauour of hys helmet. **1600** FAIRFAX *Tasso* II. xlviii, The Virgin gan her Beavoir vale. **1602** SHAKS. *Ham.* I. ii. 230 Then saw you not his face? O yes, my Lord, he wore his Beaver vp. **1765** H. WALPOLE *Otranto* iii. (1798) 51 Two knights in complete armour, their beavers down. **1820** SCOTT *Ivanhoe* viii, The conqueror called for a bowl of wine, and opening the beaver, or lower part of his helmet.. quaffed it. **1876** PLANCHÉ *Cycl. Costume* I. 39 One of the earliest examples of a movable

beaver is seen in the effigy of Thomas, Duke of Clarence, slain 1421.

b. *fig.*

1838 SOUTHEY *Doctor* Wks. V. 148, I will maintain.. as publicly (only that my bever must be closed). **1845** R. HAMILTON *Pop. Educ.* iii. 49 Why should the Author suppress this anecdote now that his beaver is up?

2. *Comb.*, as **beaver-sight**, eye-hole of a helmet.

a **1843** SOUTHEY *G. Hermiguez* I. Wks. 1853 VI. 163 Through the bever-sight his eye Glared fierce and red.

beaver, *sb.*[3] (ˈbiːvə(r)) *slang.* [Etym. uncertain.] **1.** (*a*) A beard; (*b*) a bearded person; (*c*) a game, in which points are scored in various ways by 'spotting' beards.

In the U.S., *beaver* (prob. BEAVER[1]) is recorded in the sense 'a person' (not necessarily one with a beard): 1850–66 examples in D.A.

1910 F. RICHARDSON *Whiskers & Soda* 211 He provided a list of celebrated clean-shaven men and also of celebrated beavers, as bearded men are technically termed. **1922** J. KETTELWELL *Beaver* 58 The outlines of the game itself are so simple.. that the question of rules scarcely arises. A bearded man is a Beaver, claim him, crying aloud, as musically as possible, 'Beaver, fifteen love'—or appropriately to the score. If both players cry aloud simultaneously it is a 'no ball'. **1922** *New Statesman* 12 Aug. 511/1 This amazing game of Beaver.. is played.. by two persons, and the points are scored as in tennis. Whichever of the two first cries 'Beaver!' as a beard heaves into sight, scores. **1922** *Westm. Gaz.* 12 Oct. 6/5 He was a beaver of a pronounced type, wore horn-rimmed spectacles, and two huge opal rings. **1927** W. E. COLLINSON *Contemp. Eng.* 63 About three years ago a fashion was started among men of wearing beards. These were greeted with the cry: Beaver!, a term now often applied to the beard itself [o]n 'a beaver'. **1936** WODEHOUSE *Laughing Gas* xxiv. 255, I had fallen among a band of criminals who were not wilful beavers, but had merely assumed the fungus for purposes of disguise. **1959** I. & P. OPIE *Lore & Lang. Schoolchildren* iii. 54 The cry 'Beaver!' is a thing of the past.

2. a. The female genitals or the pubic area in general; also *attrib.*, denoting films, literature, etc., in which nude females are portrayed; *split beaver*: see SPLIT *ppl. a.* 3 a. Chiefly *U.S.*

1927 *Immortalia* 166 She took off her clothes From her head to her toes, And a voice at the keyhole yelled, 'Beaver!' **1939** JOYCE *Finnegans Wake* 537 Thou, Frick's Flame, Uden Sulfer, who strikest only on the marryd bokks, enquick me if so be I did cophetuise milady's maid! In spect of her beavers she is a womanly and sacret. **1969** *Films & Filming* Aug. 25/2 The Supreme Court ruling that pubic hair wasn't obscene.. led directly to a crop of self-styled 'beaver movies'. **1976** *Listener* 12 Feb. 180/1 Like the beaver mags (Kurt Vonnegut's word for the glossies that concentrate on the female pudenda), television has only a limited number of shots with which to titillate the viewer. **1978** J. IRVING *World according to Garp* xiii. 241 Pictures of naked women... If you could see the sex parts, which were sometimes partially hidden by the hair, that was a beaver. **1981** M. GEE *Dying, in Other Words* 101 He hadn't been very intelligent.. showing him the skin flick picture of Moira... It was probably too dirty, they can't use beaver shots, although she was cracked up her beaver, Macbeth felt it briefly.

b. Hence, a girl or woman, *esp.* one who is sexually attractive. *U.S.*

1968–70 *Current Slang* (Univ. S. Dakota) III–IV. 8 *Beaver*, a girl.—College males, Kansas. **1976** LIEBERMAN & RHODES *Compl. CB Handbk.* vi. 121 'Beaver', meaning a girl, was taken from a phrase used to describe pornographic films. **1977** *Rolling Stone* 13 Jan. 42/2, 10–4, Beaver [CB talk for a female], we're all going down to Plains tomorrow after Jimmy Carter wins.

ˈbeaver, *v.* **1.** *local.* [cf. E.D.D. *beaver* sb.[2] (Lincs.), a term applied to fine woad.] (See quots.)

1799 A. YOUNG *Gen. View Agric. County Lincoln* vii. 155 Without these attentions the woad will not *beaver* well, a term descriptive of the fineness of the capillary filaments into which it draws out when broken between the finger and thumb. **1805** R. W. DICKSON *Pract. Agric.* II. xi. 771 When this attention is neglected, the woad will not, on being broken between the finger and thumb, draw out into fine hair-like filaments, or, in the language of the manufacturer, *beaver* well. **1942** J. M. DOWSETT *Romance of England's Forests* viii. 210 This powder was spread on the floor, moistened with water and allowed to 'couch' (ferment), a process which required very considerable care if the material was to 'beaver' well.

2. [f. BEAVER[1].] Const. *away*: to work like a beaver.

1946 *Time* 22 Apr. 49 He found time to dash off five other books while beavering away at his vast *History*. **1966** M. R. D. FOOT *SOE in France* p. xxi, The gaullists beavered away at their own plans, irrespective of the prospects of putting them into action. **1967** *Spectator* 15 Dec. 740/2 The Germans beaver away at their scheme for 'entry by stages'.

beaver, variant of BEVER.

beavered (ˈbiːvəd), *ppl. a.* Also 7 **bevered**. [f. BEAVER + -ED[2].]

a. Of a helmet: Furnished with a beaver. **b.** Covered with or wearing a beaver (hat).

1610 GWILLIM *Heraldry* IV. xiv. 342 The Helmets.. sometimes close Bevered. **1742** POPE *Dunc.* IV. 141 His beaver'd brow a birchen garland wears. **1797** WOLCOTT (P. Pindar) *Out at Last* Wks. 1812 III. 499 To grace the beaver'd brows of Christian Kings.

c. [f. BEAVER[3] + -ED[2].] Bearded.

1928 *Sunday Express* 6 May 2/3 My beavered friend became more lugubrious than ever.

Beaverette (biːvəˈrɛt). [f. BEAVER *sb.*[1] + -ETTE.] An imitation beaver fur; also, cloth with a beaver finish (see BEAVER[1] 6).

1922 *Daily Mail* 12 Dec. 1 Pelt in superb quality pulled Beaverette. **1923** *Ibid.* 16 Jan. 1 Beaverette stoles. *Ibid.* 29 Jan. 1 Rubber on strong Beaverette cloth.

beaverish (ˈbiːvərɪʃ), *a.* [f. BEAVER *sb.*[1] + -ISH[1].] Like a beaver in nature or habit; merely instinctive.

1850 CARLYLE *Latter-d. Pamph.* iv. 3 All intellect.. will tend to become beaverish. **1858** —— *Fredk. Gt.* I. IV. viii. 473 Irrational man-mountains, of the beaverish or beaverish-vulpine sort.

ˈbeaverism. The condition of a beaver; a beaverish quality or trait.

1850 CARLYLE *Latter-d. Pamph.* v. 17 He will contract himself into beaverism. *Ibid.* 37 Beaverisms, astucities, and sensualisms.

ˈbeaverkin. A little beaver (hat).

1867 CARLYLE *Remin.* (1881) II. 98 Dainty little cap, perhaps little beaverkin.

beaverteen (ˈbiːvəˌtiːn). [f. BEAVER *sb.*[1]; after *velvet-een*.] A cotton twilled cloth, in which the warp is drawn up into loops, forming a pile, which is left uncut, whereas in velvet it is cut.

1827 *Hull Advert.* 7 Dec. 2/2 Fustians, Beaverteens, Moleskins, and Velveteens. **1872** *Echo* 27 Sept., Velveteens striped with beaverteen.. make a very lady-like petticoat.

beavery (ˈbiːvərɪ). [f. BEAVER *sb.*[1] + RY; cf. *grocery*.] A place in which beavers live or are kept.

1877 *Daily News* 26 Dec. 7/3 Lord Bute's beavers have bred in their beavery. **1882** F. BUCKLAND *Notes & Jottings* 281 By the curator of the beavery.

beaw, beawper, etc.: see BEAU, BEAUPERE, etc.

bea-wailing, -waymenting: see BAA *sb.*

†**beayell.** *Obs. rare.* [Early form of BESAIEL, q.v.; cf. *beantler, bisantler, bayantler*.] A grandfather's father, a great grandfather.

c **1400** *Destr. Troy* 13474 His beayell aboue on þe burne syde, On his modur halfe.

beazar, -er, -il, obs. ff. BEZOAR, BEZEL.

beazler, obs. f. BEZZLER, *Obs.*, drunkard, sot.

beb, obs. or Sc. form of BIB *v.*

beback, bebait, bebang, etc.: see BE- *pref.*

†**bebally**, *a.* *Her. Obs. rare.* [Etymol. unknown.] Said of a shield: = *party per pale*, i.e. divided into two parts by a vertical line.

1486 *Bk. St. Albans, Her.* B iij b, Bebally is calde in armys whan a cotearmure is calde endentyde of ij dyuerse colowris in the length. **1586** FERNE *Blaz. Gentrie* 205 Blazons called Bebally, Lentally, and Fessely. *Ibid.* 208 Bebally indented.

†**bebar** (bɪˈbɑː(r)), *v. Obs.*; in 3 bibarre, 6–7 bebarre. [f. BE- 1 + BAR *v.*] *trans.* To bar about; to debar.

a **1230** *Ancr. R.* 170 Uor ȝe beoð mid Iesu Criste bitund ase ine sepulcre & bibarred. **1581** T. HOWELL *Deuises* (1879) 230 Though eyes bebarred be, From that fayre sight. **1649** BP. HALL *Cases Consc.* 236 Neither doth the want.. bebarre any man from.. fruition of these earthly inheritances.

bebark, bebass, bebaste, bebat, bebatter, etc.: see BE- *pref.*

bebathe (bɪˈbeɪð), *v.*; 1–6. [OE. *bebaðian*, f. BE- 2 + *baðian* to BATHE.] *trans.* To bathe completely; suffuse.

a **1000** *Phœnix* (Grein) 107 Se æðela fuȝel hine bibaðaþ in ðam burnan. *c* **1575** GASCOIGNE *Fruites Warre* (1831) 210 Thine owne head bebathed with enmies teares.

bebauch, *v. Obs.* = DEBAUCH. (Cf. *bebar*.)

1607 R. C. *World of Wonders* 258.

†**beˈbay**, *v. Obs. rare.* [f. BE- + BAY *sb.*[2] or [3].] *trans.* To bay about, embay, hem in, surround.

1506 GUYLFORDE *Pilgr.* (1851) 62 We were so bebayed that we had no remedy but to trust to our ancre holde. **1583** STANYHURST *Æneis* III. (Arb.) 76 Uoyded of al coast sight, with wild flouds roundly bebayed.

‖**bébé** (bebe). [F. *bébé*, ad. Eng. BABY; used attrib. in technical senses.] (See quot.)

1883 MRS. LEACH *Dressm. Pocket Dict.*, *Bébé bodice*, a round-waisted bodice with sash. **1884** *West. Daily Press* 11 Apr. 7/6 Loops of narrow bébé ribbon.

†**bebeast** (bɪˈbiːst), *v. Obs.* [f. BE- 6 + BEAST.] **1.** *trans.* To make a beast of.

1640 BP. REYNOLDS *Passions* xl. 527 [He] hath.. bebeasted himselfe by setting his Desires onely on Transitory and Perishable goods. **1713** BEVERIDGE *Priv. Th.* (1730) 127 To.. be-beast themselves by drinking to Excess.

2. To treat as a beast; to call 'beast.'

1659 EADES *Christ's Exalt.* 16 They will.. bebeast themselves, for their carlesness. —— *Wisd. Justif.* 72 They will condemn themselves, and befoole and bebeast themselves.

bebed, bebelted, etc.: see BE- *pref.*

‖**bebeeru, bibiru** (bɪˈbɪəruː). Also beebeeru, bibiri. [native name in Guiana.] The Greenheart Tree of Guiana (*Nectandra Rodiæi* or *leucantha*). **beˈbeeria, bebeerine** (bɪˈbɪəraɪn), also beber- bibir-, an alkaloid resembling quinine, yielded by the bark and seeds of this tree.

1851 *Art Jrnl. Illustr. Catal., Sci. Exhib.* IV. xv*/1 Quinine, beberine, morphine. **1875** WOOD *Therap.* 56 Bebeeria.. as a substitute for quinia in malarial diseases.

bebite, beblain, beblear, etc.: see BE- *pref.*

†**beˈblast**, *v. Obs.*; also *pa. pple.* [f. BE- 2 + BLAST *v.*] *trans.* To blast completely, wither up.

1558 PHAËR *Æneid* II. E iv b, Me the father of Gods.. Beblasted with his lightning wynd. *c* **1575** GASCOIGNE *Fruites Warre* (1831) 211 Are both thine eyes beblast? **1595** HUNNIS *Joseph* 17 Beblasted with the Easterne wind.

beˈbleed, *v. Obs.* or *arch.* [f. BE- + BLEED *v.*] To cover, or stain with blood, make bloody.

a **1230** *Ancr. R.* 118 Bledinde mon [*v.r.* a mon bibled] is grislich. *c* **1380** *Sir Ferumb.* 1380 Sche caste hure eȝe on Olyuer: & saw him al be-bled. **1485** CAXTON *Chas. Gt.* 77 The place was alle bybled of the blood. **1600** FAIRFAX *Tasso* XIX. ciii. 357 Where lay a warriour murdred new, That all bebled the ground. **1866** KINGSLEY *Herew.* xlii, He is all wounded and be-bled.

bebless (bɪˈblɛs), *v.* [f. BE- 2 + BLESS.] *trans.* To bless amply or profusely. Hence **beblest** *ppl. a.*

1598 SYLVESTER *Job. Triumph.*, *Du Bartas* (1608) 933 If his Loynes beblest not me from harm. **1610** BP. HALL *Apol. Brownists* 141 *note*, The vilest miscreants.. are beblest by her. **1799** W. TAYLOR in *Month. Mag.* VII. 139 A becross'd, beblest, Besprinkled bag of holy sackcloth.

†**beˈblind**, *v. Obs.* [f. BE- 2 + BLIND.] *trans.* To make completely blind. Also as *pa. pple.*

1575 GASCOIGNE *Flowers* Wks. (1587) 105 Courage quailes where love beblinds the sense. **1580** NORTH *Plutarch, Romulus*, In fervent flames of beastly love beblynde.

beblister (bɪˈblɪstə(r)), *v.* [f. BE- 1 + BLISTER.] *trans.* To blister badly, cover with blisters.

1575 TURBERV. *Venerie* 33 Running through the hard.. stonie grounde they.. beblister their feete. **1611** COTGR., *Vessié*.. beblistered, or full of blisters. **1802** SOUTHEY *Lett.* (1856) I. 201 How Bella's knee is be-blistered.

beblockhead, bebloom, beblotch, see BE-.

beblood (bɪˈblʌd), *v.* [f. BE- 5 + BLOOD.] *trans.* To smear or stain with blood; = BEBLEED.

1580 NORTH *Plutarch* (1676) 26 Whose foreheads they touch with the knife bebloouded with the bloud of the Goats. **1623** LISLE *Ælfric on O. & N.T.* 8 There lay in a dish a joynt of a finger all beblouded. **1859** SINGLETON *Virgil* II. 398 And, dying.. bebloods the shattered darts.

†**beˈbloody**, *v. Obs.* Forms: 3 biblod(e)ge, 4 biblodke, 7 bebloudy. [f. BE- 2 + BLOODY *v.*:—OE. *blódeȝian, blódȝian*, f. *blodiȝ* bloody; but the earlier forms point to an OE. **blódcian* on type of ON. vbs in *-ka*.] *trans.* To make bloody.

c **1210** *Leg. Kath.* 203 Of þat balefule blod al biblodked. *c* **1220** *St. Marher.* 3 Wið þe luðere.. þat beoð al blodi biblodeget mid sunne. **1580** NORTH *Plutarch* (1676) 727 Antonius.. did shew them his Gown all bebloodied. **1647** W. BROWNE *Polexander* II. 336 To bebloudy the Chronicle of their owne times.

†**beblot** (bɪˈblɒt), *v. Obs.* Also 4 biblotte, 6 (*pa. pple.*) beblot. [f. BE- 2 + BLOT.] *trans.* To blot all over; also *fig.*

c **1374** CHAUCER *Troylus* II. 982 Biblotte it with thy teris. **1575** GASCOIGNE *Flowers* Wks. (1587) 114 A roll of Sable, black and foule beblot. **1580** NORTH *Plutarch* (1676) 72 Any wrong, Which might beblot the glory of my name.

beblubbered (bɪˈblʌbəd), *ppl. a.* Also 6 bebloubered, beblubred. [f. BE- + BLUBBER *v.*] Disfigured by blubbering; befouled with tears; also (*obs.*) with blood.

1583 STANYHURST *Æneis* I. (Arb.) 25 With tears Venus heauye beblubbered Prest foorth in presence. **1596** COLSE *Penelope* (1880) 182 Beblubred all with bloud, Antinous lieth under bord. **1661** USSHER *Power Princes* II. (1683) 198 Covered with dust, and beblubbered with tears. **1873** MISS BROUGHTON *Nancy* II. 33 What does it matter what colour my eyelids are?.. or how be-blubbered my cheeks?

†**beˈblur**, *v. Obs.* [f. BE- 1 + BLUR *v.*] *trans.* To blur all over.

1598 FLORIO, *Pattacchiare*, to besmeare.. to beblurre. *a* **1644** QUARLES *Hymn to God, Div. Poems* (1717) 56 Be-blur thy Book with tears.

bebod, variant form of BIBOD, command.

bebog, bebooted, beboss, bebotch, bebother, beboulder, etc.: see BE- *pref.*

bebop (ˈbiːbɒp). orig. *U.S.* Also rebop, and abbrev. BOP *sb.*[2]. [App. imitative (see quot. 1955).] A development of jazz, begun in the U.S. at the end of the 1939–45 war, characterized by complex harmony, dissonant chords and highly syncopated rhythm. Also

attrib. Hence **'bebopper**, a performer or supporter of bebop.

P. Tamony in *Jazz* (1959) II. 114-19 cites instances of *bebop, rebop, bop*, etc., as onomatopœic or nonsense syllables, from jazz recordings of 1928 on: e.g. McKinney's Cotton Pickers, *Four or Five Times* (1928), Bop-do-de-de-do-do.. Bebop one, bebop two, bebop three.

1945 *Down Beat* 1 Aug. 8/2 (*title of gramophone record*) Dizzy Gillespie. Salted Peanuts/Be-Bop. *Ibid.* 1 Sept. 3/3 Much controversy has arisen of late over the claims of altoist Charlie Parker and trumpeter Dizzy Gillespie to the origination of their fantastic and exciting 're-bop' style. **1946** *Melody Maker* 31 Aug. 5/4 Whenever Be-Boppers and the others got together, trouble was..the outcome. *Ibid.* 19 Oct. 5/2 The music isn't rebop stuff. *Ibid.* 26 Oct. 3/1 The re-bop (or, if you prefer it, be-bop: they're using both names for it in America) is clearly evident. **1948** *Life* 11 Oct. 139/2 Boppers go gaga over such bebop classics as *OO Bop Sha Bam.* **1950** E. Hyams *From Waste Land* 203 A kind of bebop or boogy-woogy. **1955** L. Feather *Encycl. Jazz* (1956) 27 As musicians gathered outside the clubs along Fifty-Second Street to discuss the music of Charlie Parker..or of Dizzy Gillespie.., they would use an onomatopoetic expression to describe a typical phrase played by these musicians: 'rebop' or 'bebop' they would say. Eventually the word became shortened and 'bop' was accepted as the name for the new branch of jazz. **1959** J. Cary *Captive & Free* xiv. 71 He was all for the teenager, except the Teddy boys and the bebop parties. **1966** *Crescendo* Jan. 3/1 The young aspiring beboppers..were trying to play the new thing.

bebove, *prep.*, above: see BIBUVEN.

bebrave, bebreach, bebrine, bebrother, bebrush, etc.: see BE- *pref.*

† **be'broyde**, *v. Obs. rare.* [f. BE- 1 + *-broyde*; cf. EMBROYDE.] *trans.* To embroider about.

1583 Stanyhurst *Æneis* III. (Arb.) 85 Andromachee.. Presented vestures of gould most ritchlye bebroyded.

† **bebump**, *v. Obs.*; 7-8. [f. BE- 2 + BUMP.] *trans.* To bump thoroughly, to belabour.

1653 Urquhart *Rabelais* IV. xiii, You have..bethwack'd, belamm'd, and bebump'd the catchpole. **1718** Motteux *Quix.* (1733) I. 266 You bebump'd your Poll against the Point of a Rock.

‖ **bebung** ('beɪbʊŋ). *Mus.* [G., lit. 'trembling'.] A pulsating or trembling effect given to a sustained note, a tremolo; *spec.* such an effect produced on the clavichord.

1879 Grove *Dict. Mus.* I. 160/1 *Bebung*, a certain pulsation or trembling effect given to a sustained note in either vocal or instrumental music, for the sake of expression. **1885** *Encycl. Brit.* XIX. 67/1 The clavichord was obedient to a peculiarity of touch possible on no other keyboard instrument... It is the 'Bebung'..gained by a repeated movement of the fleshy end of the finger while the key was still held down.

† **be'bury**, *v. Obs.* Forms: 1 bebyriȝan, 2 bebyri, 3 biburi-en, -burye, -buriȝe. [OE. f. BE- 2 + *byriȝan* to BURY.] To entomb, bury.

c **1000** Ælfric *Gen.* xlix. 31 Þær wæs Isaac bebirȝed. *c* **1175** *Cott. Hom.* 229 Tweȝen ȝelefde men him arwrðlice bebyriddon. **1297** R. Glouc. 166 Hii let hym beburye.

bebusy, bebutter, bebutterfly, see BE- *pref.*

bec, obs. form of BEAK.

becafica, -fico, variants of BECCAFICO.

becall (bɪ'kɔːl), *v.*; also 3-5 bi-, by-, -cal, -kalle. [f. BE- 4, 2 + CALL *v.* There was app. no connexion between the early and modern uses.]

† **1.** *trans.* To accuse *of*. *Obs.*

c **1250** *Gen. & Ex.* 2314 Ðis sonde hem ouertakeð raðe, And bi-calleð of harme and scaðe. *c* **1440** *Morte Arth.* (1819) 48 Syr Mador loudeste spake The quene of treson to by-calle.

† **2.** To call upon, call forth, challenge. *Obs.*

c **1325** *E.E. Allit. P.* A 912 Neuer-þe-lese cler I you by-calle If ȝe con se hyt to be done. *c* **1420** *Anturs of Arth.* xxxii, Here I the be-calle, For to fynde me a freke to feȝte on my fille. ? *a* **1500** *Eger & Grine* 693 He becalled any cristen Knight, or any 5 that with him wold fight.

† **3.** To call, summon. *Obs.*

c **1325** *E.E. Allit. P.* A. 1162 When I schulde start inþe strem astraye, Out of þat caste I watz by-calt.

4. To call names, miscall.

1683 *Case Consc. Symbolizing w. Ch. Rome* 12 The Devil ..is conjured as before, and most wofully becalled. **1825** Cobbett *Rur. Rides* 407 Not to becall the King of Spain is looked upon as a proof of want of 'liberality.'

becalm (bɪ'kɑːm), *v.* [f. BE- 2 + CALM *v.*]

1. *trans.* To make calm or still; to calm, quiet; *fig.* to assuage, mitigate, soothe, tranquillize.

1613 Bp. Hall *Holy Panegyr.* 77 He..hath becalmed the world, and shut the iron gates of warre. *a* **1649** Drumm. of Hawth. *Poems* Wks. (1711) 38 Thou becalm'st Mind's easeless anguish. **1718** Pope *Odyss.* IV. 515 What power becalms the innavigable seas? **1873** W. Mayo *Never Again* xxxii. 417 Thy medic touch becalms my throbbing brow.

2. *Naut.* To shelter from, or deprive (a ship) of, wind; usually in pass. *to be becalmed*: to lie motionless for want of wind.

1595 Maynarde *Drake's Voy.* (1849) 8 Being becalmed under the lee of the land. **1627** Capt. Smith *Seaman's Gram.* xiii. 62 To martiall..those squadrons..a good berth or distance from each other, that they becalme not one another. **1704** in *Lond. Gaz.* No. 4033/1 The Charles Gally ..being becalmed, was attacked. **1855** Macaulay *Hist. Eng.* IV. 1 The fleet was becalmed off the Godwin Sands.

b. *fig.*

1559 *Mirr. Mag.* 196 (R.) I and mine becalm'd from hatred's blast. **1672** Dryden *Conq. Granada* I. v. i. 88 'Twas Life becalm'd, without a gentle Breath.

becalmed (bɪ'kɑːmd), *ppl. a.* [f. BECALM *v.* + -ED.] **a.** Calmed, quieted, stilled. **b.** Motionless for want of wind.

a **1667** Cowley *Solit.* Wks. 1710 II. 693 They're like a becalmed Ship. *a* **1674** Clarendon *Hist. Reb.* III. xv. 491 The silence..of a becalm'd Conscience. *a* **1700** Dryden (J.) The moon shone clear on the becalmed flood.

be'calming, *vbl. sb.* [f. as prec. + -ING[1].] The act of calming, assuaging, tranquillizing.

1625 Donne *Serm.* 26 For the becalming of tempestuous humours.

be'calming, *ppl. a.* [f. as prec. + -ING[2].] Calming, tranquillizing, soothing.

1827 Moore *Epicur.* xi. (1839) 101 The becalming influence of the hour.

becap, becarpet, becassocked, etc.: see BE-.

becarve (bɪ'kɑːv), *v.* [OE. *beceorfan*, f. BE- 3 + *ceorfan* to CARVE.]

† **1.** *trans.* To cut off. *Obs.* (Cf. *behead.*)

a **1000** *Beowulf* 3185 And hine þá héafde becearf. *a* **1230** *Ancr. R.* 362 Loðlease meidenes þe..hefdes bikoruen.

† **2.** To cut up, open up (land). *Obs.*

1388 Wyclif *Isa.* xxviii. 24 Whether he that erith..schal be kerue [**1382** forth cutten] and purge his londe?

3. To cut in pieces, carve.

1863 Alcock *Capit. Tycoon* I. 272 The chance of being becarved by two-sworded samourai in pursuit of their game.

† **be'cast**, *v. Obs.* [f. BE- 4 + CAST *v.*]

1. *trans.* To cover or surround, by casting something about.

c **1300** *St. Brandan* 92 Hi leten hem diȝte a gret schip, and above hit al bi-caste With bole huden. *c* **1500** *Egyncourte* 272 in *E.P.P.* (Hazl.) II. 104 The frenchemen our kynge about becaste With batayles stronge on euery side.

2. *intr.* To cast about, plan, plot.

1563 *Myrr. Mag., Rich. III*, xiv, Becast them to kyl by smothering in theyr bed.

† **be'catch**, *v. Obs.* Also bi-, by-; for forms see CATCH. [f. BE- 2 + CATCH *v.*]

1. *trans.* To lay hold of, seize upon.

c **1200** *Trin. Coll. Hom.* 35 Þe wilde deor þe þis oref waneð, and wile bicachen it..and wile mid strengðe binimen.

2. To take by craft; to beguile, cheat, deceive.

c **1200** Ormin 11628 Ȝiff þe Laferrd haffde þær þatt wise makedd lafess..þa wære he þær bikæchedd. **1340** *Ayenb.* 125 Prudence lokeþ þane scele, þet hi ne bi becaȝt. *c* **1460** *How Wif taught Doughter* 174 in Hazl. *E.P.P.* 192 What man that the wedde schalle, than is he nought bycaught.

because (bɪ'kɔːz, -'kɒz), *adv.* and *conj.* Forms: 4-7 bi-, bycause, 4-6 by cause, (6 be cause), 4- because; *dial.* 'cause. [f. BY *prep.* + CAUSE *sb.* Orig. a phrase, consisting of prep. and subst.; after which the cause or purpose was expressed by a subst. governed by *of*, a dative infinitive, or a subord. clause introduced by *that* or *why*. See also *cause why*, s.v. CAUSE. Such subord. clauses fell into two classes, one expressing cause or reason, the other purpose. In the former *that* was at length omitted, leaving *because* only. The same was often done from 15th to 17th c. with the latter class, but modern usage here drops *because* and uses *that* alone. There was an equivalent *for cause* (see CAUSE *sb.*); hence, perhaps the former use of *for because*, in nearly all the constructions.]

A. *adv.*

1. Followed by *that* or *why*: For the reason *that*. (Formerly *for* was sometimes prefixed.) *arch.* Also ***because why*** used interrogatively, = 'why?' (cf. *cause why?* s.v. CAUSE *sb.* 3 c); chiefly *dial.*

c **1305** *Deo Gratias* 37 in *E.E.P.* (1862) 125 Þou hast herd al my deuyse, Bi cause whi, hit is clerkes wise. *c* **1386** Chaucer *Frankl. T.* 233 By cause that he was hire Neighebour. *c* **1400** Maundev. xv. 162 For because that Saturne is of so late sterynge. *c* **1486** *Bk. St. Albans* D iij b, Theis be not enlured..by cause that thay be so ponderowse. **1541** Copland *Galyen's Terap.* 2 B iv b, For bycause that the sayde indication is nat taken of the same cause, it is euydent, etc. **1611** Bible *John* vii. 39 The Holy Ghost was not yet giuen; because that Iesus was not yet glorified. **1821** Byron *Heav. & Earth* iii. 442, I abhor death, because that thou must die. **1887** Parish & Shaw *Dict. Kentish Dial.* 10 *Because why*, why? wherefore? A very common controversy amongst boys:—'No it ain't'—'Cos why?'—'Cos it ain't.' **1921** D. H. Lawrence *Sea & Sardinia* i. 12 The painters try to paint her [*sc.* Etna]..in vain. Because why? **1937** D. L. Sayers *Busman's Honeymoon* xiv. 253 It's a cur'ous thing you askin' about that there sun-dial, because why? The very man wot sold vicar the chimbley-pot, 'e wos found dead in his own 'ouse only yesterday. **1961** S. Chaplin *Day of Sardine* viii. 164, I know a lot of people that rant on about their religion and it doesn't do any good. Because why? Because they're trying to convince themselves, maybe?

2. Followed by *of* and subst.: **a.** By reason *of*, on account *of*. (*For* formerly sometimes prefixed.)

1356 Wyclif *Last Age Ch.* (1840) 31 Þe synnes bi cause of whiche suche persecucioun schal be in Goddis Chirche. **1393** Gower *Conf.* II. 169 His wife, because of this, Goddesse of corn cleped is. *a* **1400** *Cov. Myst.* 31 My husbond is lost because of me. **1578** Timme *Calvin on Gen.* 173 Man ought to have excelled all other Creatures, for because of the mind wherewith he was indued. **1717** Lady M. W. Montagu *Lett.* xxxvi. I. 133 It is a particular art to load them [camels], because of the bunch on their backs. **1816** J. Wilson *City of Plague* I. i. 331, I cling to thee with a more desperate love Because of thy ingratitude.

† **b.** For the sake *of*, for the purpose *of*. *Obs.*

1480 Caxton *Trevisa's Descr. Brit.* 15 Elidurus was logged atte cite Alcluid by cause of solace and hunting. **1523** Ld. Berners *Froiss.* I. cxxv. 150 The kynge made none assaut, bycause of the sparynge of his people.

† **c.** For the sake *of* not; for fear of.

1470-85 Malory *Arthur* (1817) II. 452 By cause of brekynge of myn avowe, I pray yow all lede me thyder.

† **3.** Followed by *to* with inf. = In order *to*. *Obs.*

1523 Ld. Berners *Froiss.* I. ccxxxix. 346 Bycause to gyue ensample to his subgettes..he caused the..erle of Auser to be putte in prison. **1546** Langley *Pol. Verg. De Invent.* I. xv. 28 a, Arithmetike was imagyned by the Phenicians, because to vtter theyr Merchaundyse.

B. *conj.* [from A 1.]

1. For the reason that; inasmuch as, since. (*For* formerly sometimes prefixed.)

c **1386** Chaucer *Frankl. Prol.* 8 By cause I am a burel man ..Haue me excused of my rude speche. **1477** *Paston Lett.* 794 III. 186 Putt hym away by cause he is daungerous. **1509** Hawes *Past. Pleas.* 147 For bicause I was in her presence, I toke acquaintaunce of her excellence. **1526** Tindale *John* xvi. 4 These thinges sayde I not..be cause [**1534** because] I was present with you. **1578** Lyte *Dodoens* 10 Names..giuen to this plante, bycause it is very good. **1607** Topsell *Serpents* 789 They are much deceived..for because the Stellion hath a rustie colour. **1616** Sir R. Dudley in *Fortesc. Papers* 17 Nor am I so vaine..bycause I am not worth so much. **1771** *Junius Lett.* xlviii. 253 Their will must be obeyed; not because it is lawful and reasonable, but because it is their will. **1857** Buckle *Civiliz.* I. x. 616 We wonder because we are ignorant and we fear because we are weak.

† **2.** With the purpose that, to the end that, in order that, so that, that. *Obs.* (Common *dial.*)

1485 Caxton *Paris & V.*, Told to hys fader..by cause he shold..doo that which he wold requyre hym. **1526** Tindale *Matt.* xii. 10 They axed him..because [*other versions* 'that'] they might acuse hym. **1621** Burton *Anat. Mel.* III. ii. IV. i. (1651) 525 Anointing the doors and hinges with oyl, because they should not creak. **1656** H. More *Antid. Ath.* II. ix. (1712) 67 The reason why Birds are Oviparous is because there might be more plenty of them.

¶ Used *substantively*.

1736 Bailey s.v., 'Because' is a Woman's Reason. **1875** A. Swinbourne *Pict. Logic* 162 Our 'whys' and our 'becauses' are obliged to stop.

C. Used elliptically in answer to a question, implying that a fuller reply is being withheld for some reason.

1871 'L. Carroll' *Through Looking-Glass* vi, in *Wks.* (1939) 200 The little fishes of the sea, They sent an answer back to me. The little fishes' answer was 'We cannot do it, Sir, because—.' **1924** 'W. Fabian' *Sailors' Wives* vi. 84 'Mustn't we? Why not?' 'Oh, Warren! Because.' She might have been the fifteen-year-old child again. **1967** C. Fremlin *Prisoner's Base* vii. 48 'Why *do* you go out with him, Helen?' 'Because.' Helen didn't mean to be cheeky. **1968** M. Carroll *Dead Trouble* x. 175 'Why didn't you leave the bottle?' 'Because!' I said shortly. I wasn't going to explain my feelings on the matter.

‖,**becca'bunga.** *Bot.* [med.L, f. Ger. *bachbunge*, f. *bach* brook + *bunge*:—OHG. *bungo* 'bulb, swelling' (Grimm).] A plant growing on the water's edge; the BROOKLIME (*Veronica beccabunga*).

1706 Phillips, *Becabunga*, the Herb Sea-purslain, or Brooklime. **1778** *Phil. Trans.* LXVIII. 673 Antiscorbutic plants, such as cochlearia,..becca bunga.

‖ **beccaccia** (bɛk'kattʃa). [It.] A woodcock.

1855 Browning *Pict. Flor.* in *Men & Wom.* II. 47 Fine as the beak of a young beccaccia.

‖ **beccafico** (bɛkka'fiko). Forms: 7-9 beccafigo, 7 becchafigge, 8-9 beccafica, 8 beccifigo, 9 becafico, -ca, beccafigue, 7- beccafico. [It.; lit. 'fig-pecker,' f. *beccare* to peck + *fico* fig.] A name given in Italy to small migratory birds of the genus Sylvia, much esteemed as dainties in the autumn, when they have fattened on figs and grapes: they are identified with the British Pettychaps and Blackcaps.

1621 Burton in Lamb *Cur. Fragm.* (1823) 574 Beccaficos which men in Sussex eat. **1708** W. King *Cookery* (1807) 81 Quails, beccafigoes, ortolans, were sent To grace the levee of a gen'ral's tent. **1732** Pope *Hor. Sat.* II. ii. 39 Children sacred held a Martin's nest, Till Becca-ficos sold so dev'lish dear. **1817** Byron *Beppo* xliii, I also like to dine on becaficas. **1835** E. Jesse *Gleanings Nat. Hist.* Ser. III. 77 The Beccafico annually visits the fig orchard near that place [Worthing]. **1861** Miss Beaufort *Egypt. Sepul.* I. vii. 144 Delicious little beccafigues, of which a hundred may be shot in one tree.

† **'becco.** *Obs.* [a. It. *becco* goat.] A cuckold.

1604 Marston *Malcontent* IV. 20 Duke, thou art a becco, a cornuto. *P.* How? *M.* Thou art a cuckold. **1623** Massinger *Bondman* II. iii, They'll all make Sufficient beccos, and with their brow-antlers Bear up the cap of maintenance.

becense, bechained, bechalk, etc.: see BE-.

bechamel (‖ beʃamɛl, ˌbeɪʃə'mɛl). *Cookery.* Also 8 bishemel. [Named after the inventor, the

Marquis de Béchamel, steward of Louis XIV.] A kind of fine white sauce thickened with cream.
1796 MRS. GLASSE *Cookery* v. 44 Have ready a bishemel. **1835** BECKFORD *Recoll.* 95 The sautés and bechamels [were] beyond praise.

bechance (bɪˈtʃɑːns, -æ-), *v.* [f. BE- + CHANCE *v.*]
1. *intr.* To happen, fall out, chance.
1527 KNIGHT in Pocock *Rec. Ref.* I. xxviii. 58 It may bechance that the king..may be right well content. *a* **1555** RIDLEY *Wks.* 376 Ye do know what hath bechanced unto my brother. **1591** SHAKS. *Two Gent.* I. i. 61 All happinesse bechance to thee in Millaine. **1814** CARY *Dante's Inf.* IV. 143 My words fall short of what bechanced.
2. (with dative object.) To befall (a person).
1530 TINDALE *Exp. & Notes* (1849) 329 Let whatsoever rebuke bechance my brother. **1593** SHAKS. *Lucr.* cxl, Let there bechance him pitiful mischances.

† **beˈchance**, *adv.* prop. *phrase. Obs.* [f. BY *prep.* + CHANCE *sb.*] By chance.
1548 GRAFTON *Hen. VIII*, an. 14 (R.) At the last battayle ..we bechaunce lost our soueraigne lorde. *c* **1570** *Scot. Poems 16th C.* II. 334 Were not bechance he had a man.

becharm (bɪˈtʃɑːm), *v.* [f. BE- + CHARM.] *trans.* To charm, to fascinate; to hold by a charm or spell. Hence **becharming** *ppl. a.*
1340 *Ayenb.* 60 Hy becharmeþ zuo moche þane man þet he ylefþ ham. **1616** BEAUM. & FL. *Laws of Candy* v. i. (R.) My reason long Hath been becharm'd. **1638** FORD *Fancies* IV. i, The paradise of my becharming thoughts. **1883** *Harper's Mag.* Dec. 36/1 The forest where Merlin was becharmed.

bechase, bechatter, becheck, etc.: see BE-.

beche. [Etymol. uncertain: cf. F. *bêche* mattock.] (See quot.)
1851 *Coal-tr. Terms, Northumbld. & Durh.* 8 *Beche* (called by the workmen *Bitch*), an instrument..used in boring, for the purpose of extricating the bottom portion of a broken set of bore-rods from a bore-hole.

beche, obs. form of BEECH.

‖ **bêche-de-mer** (bɛʃ də mɛr). [Fr., altered from *biche de mer*, a. Pg. *bicho do mar*, lit. sea-worm.] A marine animal, an echinoderm (*Holothuria edulis*), called also Trepang, Sea-cucumber, Sea-slug, eaten as a luxury by the Chinese. Hence a vb. *to bêche-de-mer*. **b.** = BEACH-LA-MAR.
1814 FLINDERS *Voy. Terra Austr.* in *Penny Cycl.* XII. 270/2 The *beche-de-mer*, or sea-cucumber, which we had first seen on the reefs of the east coast. **1847** CARPENTER *Zool.* §1023 Those who go *bêche-de-mer-ing*, as the employment is commonly termed. **1849** W. T. POWER *Sketches in N.Z.* xxiii. 216 The *bêche-de-mer* and shark-fins, both of which..are valuable articles of trade with China. **1884** [see SEA-SLUG 1]. **1911** J. LONDON *Cruise of Snark* xvi, Bêche de mer English was the product of conditions and circumstances. **1947** I. L. IDRIESS *Isles of Despair* xxxviii. 251 The venturesome crews had found a rich patch of bêche-de-mer. **1951** *Amer. Speech* XXVI. 25 The pidgin of Hawaii differs markedly from the pidgin English..of the China coast, the pidgin of Melanesia, and the bêche-de-mer of the western Pacific.

bechic (ˈbɛkɪk, ˈbiːkɪk), *a.* and *sb. Med.*; also 7–8 becchick, bechick. [ad. F. *béchique*, ad. L. *bēchicus*, a. Gr. βηχικός, f. βήξ cough.]
A. *adj.* Tending to cure or relieve a cough.
1678 SALMON *Pharm. Lond.* VI. ii. 813 Bechick [preparations], such as are good against Coughs, Colds, Asthma's.
B. *sb.* A cough medicine.
1661 LOVELL *Hist. Anim. & Min.* 359 The cough's.. cured by..bechicks. **1684** tr. *Bonet's Merc. Compit.* XVII. 595 The Lungs smoothed and moistned with Becchicks.

† **ˈbechical,** *a. Obs.* = prec. adj.
1657 TOMLINSON *Renou's Disp.* 86 Bechical confections. **1771** J. S. *Le Dran's Observ. Surg.* (ed. 4) 107 Bechical Medicines..to facilitate the Expectoration.

bechignoned, bechirm, bechirp, etc.: see BE-.

Bechuana (bɛtʃʊˈɑːnə, also bɛkjʊˈɑːnə). Pl. **Bechuana, -anas** (-z). Also **Bechwana,** and other variants. A member of a negroid people inhabiting the country between the Orange and Zambezi rivers in Southern Africa, speaking Tswana (formerly called *Sechuana*), a Bantu language. Also *attrib.*
1804 J. BARROW *Trav. S. Afr.* II. ii. 114 The city *Leetakoo*, the capital of a tribe of Kaffers called *Booshooanas*, situate at the distance of sixteen days' journey beyond the Orange River, in the direction of north-east from the Cape. **1822** W. J. BURCHELL *Trav.* I. 581 *Bichuána*; or the country of the Bichuana (Bitjuána) nations. **1826** R. MOFFATT (*title*) A Bechuana Catechism. **1850** J. W. APPLEYARD *Kafir Language* 31 The terms Bechuana (a variation of Bachuana) and Sechuana, are different forms of the same verbal root, the former referring to people, and the latter to language... By the Hottentot tribes, the Bechuanas are called *Briqua*, the goat-people. **1875** *Encycl. Brit.* III. 478/1 The Bechwana are divided into numerous tribes. **1936** *Discovery* June 172/1 The Southern Bantu comprise the Shona peoples, the Xulu-Xosa.., the Suto-Chawana (Bechwana, Basuto, etc.), and the Herero-Ovambo. **1964** E. HUXLEY *Back Street New Worlds* xiii. 125 A group of Bechuana girls pitchforked by air..into a big London hospital.

beck (bɛk), *sb.*[1] Forms: 3 becc, 5–6 bek, 6–7 becke, 7 beke, 5– beck. [a. ON. *bekk-r* (Du. *bæk*, Sw. *bäck*), brook, rivulet:—OTeut. **bakki-z* masc.; cognate with **baki-z*, whence OE. *bęce* masc., OS. *bęki*, MDu. *bēke*, Du. *beek* fem., and OHG. *bah*, mod.G. *bach* masc., also fem. provincially. Gothic preserves no form of this word, which is also unknown beyond Teutonic.]
1. A brook or stream: the ordinary name in those parts of England from Lincolnshire to Cumberland which were occupied by the Danes and Norwegians; hence, often used *spec.* in literature to connote a brook with stony bed, or rugged course, such as are those of the north country.
a **1300** *Cursor M.* (Gött.) 8946 Made a brig, Ouer a littel becc [*Cott.* burn, *Trin.* ryuere] to lig. *c* **1440** *Promp. Parv.* 29 Bek watyr, rendylle, *riuulus, torrens.* **1481** in *Ripon Ch. Acts* 341 Markington beck. **1538** LELAND *Itin.* I. 70 There cummith a very little Bek thorough the Toun of Northalverton..communely callid Sunnebek. **1610** HOLLAND *Camden's Brit.* I. 722 Wandering beckes [*printed* beakes] and violent swift brookes. **1630** SANDERSON *Serm.* II. 276 Shallowest becks run with the greatest noise. **1691** RAY *N. Countr. Wds.* 131 A Beck, a Rivulet or small Brook. **1795** SOUTHEY *Joan of Arc* I. 235, I have laid me down..and watch'd The beck roll glittering to the noon-tide sun. **1872** BLACK *Adv. Phaeton* xxvii. 369 Each gorge and valley has its beck.
2. The valley-bottom through which a beck flows: cf. BACHE.
1641 BEST *Farm. Books* (1856) 28 Keepe them [sheep] togeather in some well fenced place, as the Bricke close..the Newe Intacke in the towne becke.

beck (bɛk), *sb.*[2] Forms: 4–6 bek, 5 beke, 5–7 becke, 6 bekke, 4– beck. [f. BECK *v.*]
1. A mute signal or significant gesture, especially one indicating assent or notifying a command; *e.g.* a nod, a motion of the hand or fore-finger, etc.
1382 WYCLIF *Job* xxvi. 11 The pileris of heuene..quaken at his bek. **1398** TREVISA *Barth. De P.R.* XVIII. xlviii. (1495) 809 Thyse ben acounted tonglesse: and vse signes and beckes in stede of spekynge. **1486** *Bk. St. Albans* D j. **1502** ARNOLD *Chron.* (1811) 161 They w^t a bek on thinge wyl afferme, and the same streit wyl denye. **1598** YONG *Diana* 162 Giuing a becke with his head to his Shepherdesse in token of thanks. **1635** QUARLES *Embl.* I. xiii. (1718) 54 If pleasure beckon with her balmy hand, Her beck's a strong command. **1728** DE FOE *Syst. Magick* I. vii. 204 With a beck of the head or hand, as we beckon to servants. **1862** TRENCH *Mirac.* xxxii. 452 Armies of heaven..whom a beck from Him would bring forth.
2. Hence, The slightest indication of will or command, and *transf.* absolute order or control; *esp.* in phrases ***to have at one's beck, to hang upon the beck of, to be at the beck and call of.***
a **1470** TIPTOFT *Cæsar* iii. (1530) 4 It should be ready at a beck. **1587** *Myrr. Mag., G. Cordila* xxv, I had the Britaynes at what becke I wou'd. **1635** PAGITT *Christianogr.* 117 Bound to your Holinesse, and wholly hanging upon your becke. **1642** ROGERS *Naaman* 229 His conversion brought the whole Towne into order under Gods becke. **1750** JOHNSON *Rambl.* No. 74 ⁋7 He..expects to find the world rolling at his beck. **1875** MCLAREN *Serm.* 65 Christ's love is not at the beck and call of our fluctuating affections.
3. A gesture expressive of salutation or respect; an inclination of the head; an obeisance, a bow, a curtsey, a nod. Chiefly *Sc.*
c **1375** WYCLIF *Antecrist* 149 Ne wiþ beckus, ne wiþ dugardes, as ypocritis usen. *c* **1440** *Promp. Parv.* 29 Bek, or lowte, *conquiniscio.* *c* **1450** HENRYSON *Mor. Fab.* 24 Welcome..(Quod hee) with many bing and many becke. **1538** BALE *Thre Lawes* 1470 As good is a becke, as is a dewe vow garde. **1557** SURREY in *Tottell's Misc.* (Arb.) 218 With a beck full low he bowed at her feete. *c* **1633** MILTON *L'Allegro* 28 Nods and Becks and wreathed Smiles. **1724** RAMSAY *Tea-t. Misc.* (1733) II. 138 She right courteously Return'd a beck. *c* **1817** HOGG *Tales & Sk.* III. 267 Ellen came into the parlour with a beck as quick and as low as that made by the water ouzel. **1863** GEO. ELIOT *Romola* (1880) I. I. vi. 84 He retreated with a bow to Romola and a beck to Tito.

beck (bɛk), *sb.*[3] *dial.* [In OE. *becca*; cf. Pr. *beca* hook, perh. from Celtic root *bacc-*; cf. Ir. *bacc*, *bac* (masc.) 'hook, crook.'] An agricultural implement with two hooks, for dressing turnips, hops, etc.; a kind of mattock.
c **1000** ÆLFRIC *Gloss.* in Wülcker *Voc.* /106 *Ligo*, becca. **1875** PARISH *Sussex Dial.*, *Beck*, a mattock. **1884** *West Sussex Gaz.* 25 Sept. Turnip cutters, fold bars, becks.

beck (bɛk), *sb.*[4] [? corruption of BACK *sb.*[2]; but cf. Du. *bekken*, G. *becken*, basin.] A large shallow vessel or tub, used in brewing, dyeing, etc.
1828 *Hull Rockingham* 14 June 84/2 Three large guile tubs, several mash tubs and under becks.

beck (bɛk), *v.* Forms: 3–7 becke, 4–6 bekke, bek, 6 beake, (7 *Sc.* baik), 5– beck. [shortened form of BECKON *v.* (in ME. *becni-en, bekn-en, beken-en*), the *-en* of the stem *beken-* being apparently taken as the infinitive ending, whence an assumed stem *bek-*; the Promp. Parv. has both *bekn-yn* and *bek-yn* 'annuto'; cf. *open, ope,* etc.]
1. *intr.* To make a mute signal, or significant gesture, as by nodding, shaking the fore-finger, etc.
a **1300** *E.E. Psalter* xxxiv. 19 Whilk þat hates me wilfulli, And beckes with þair eghen lesli. *c* **1386** CHAUCER *Manc. T.* 346 Spek nat, but with thyn heed thou bekke. *c* **1460** *Towneley M.* 319. **1548** HALL *Chron.* (1809) 703 At the whiche wise menne becked and lyht men laughed, thynkyng great foly in his high presumpcion. **1625** K. LONG *Barclay's Argenis* I. ix. 22 Secretly becking and winking on the Maids, she bade them speake softlier. **1884** WOOLNER *Silenus*, Our sweetest hopes That ever beck with smiles of welcoming.
b. *trans.* To express by a beck.
1821 CLARE *Vill. Minstr.* II. 72 While turning nods beck thanks for kindness done.
2. *trans.* (obj. *orig.* dative.) To make a mute signal to (a person, *to* approach); to beckon.
1486 *Bk. St. Albans* A j b, With yowre hande or with yowre tabur styke, becke yowre hawke to come to you. **1595** SHAKS. *John* III. iii. 13 When gold and siluer becks me to come on. **1629** GAULE *Pract. The.* 305 Hee [Christ] bowes his Head; as though hee would becke us towards him. **1839** BAILEY *Festus* (1848) 40/2 The star Which beams and becks the spirit from afar.
3. *intr.* To make a sign of recognition, respect, or obeisance; to nod, make a slight bow; to curtsey. (Chiefly in Sc. writers.)
1535 STEWART *Cron. Scot.* II. 575 And call him schir, bekkand with bayth his kneis. **1571** T. FORTESCUE *Forest* Pref., Verses, Beake, then, and bowe thee lowe. **1686** G. STUART *Joco-Ser. Disc.* 50 She laighly baiking made her honour. **1712** ARBUTHNOT *John Bull* (1755) 51, I mun stand becking and binging. **1877** H. PAGE *De Quincey* I. viii. 156 Two philosophers becking and bowing to each other.

beck, -ed, -er, obs. forms of BEAK, -ED, -ER.

ˈbecker, becket. *dial.* Sea-bream, braize.
1602 CAREW *Cornwall* 320 Of flat [fish there are] Brets, Turbets..Becket, Haddock, &c. **1880** T. COUCH *E. Cornw. Gloss.*, *Becker*, a species of bream, *Sparus pagrus.*

† **ˈbecket,** *sb.*[1] *Obs. rare.* (See quot.)
1352–98 [in Rogers *Agric. & Prices* (1866) I. xxii. 580 We find purchases of silk on behalf of the warden of Merton. These purchases are called 'beckets' or 'begens.' Three begens or beckets were equal in quantity and price to the amount ordinarily used for lining the summer robes of a great person.]

becket (ˈbɛkɪt), *sb.*[2] *Naut.* [Etymology unknown. Du. *bogt*, *bocht* 'bend' of rope, has been suggested. Falconer *Dict. Marine*, thought it 'probably a corruption of *bracket*.']
A simple contrivance, usually a loop of rope with a knot on one end and eye at the other, but also a large hook, or a wooden bracket, used for confining loose ropes, tackle, ropes, oars, spars, etc. in a convenient place, and also for holding or securing the tacks and sheets of sails, and for similar purposes.
1769 FALCONER *Dict. Marine* (1789), Beckets are either large hooks, or short pieces of rope, with a knot on one end and an eye in the other, or formed like a circular wreath; or they are wooden brackets. **1830** MARRYAT *King's Own* xxx, A pistol stuck..in a becket at the side of the boat. *c* **1860** H. STUART *Seaman's Catech.* 45 Bunt beckets are sewn on the after part of the sail.

becket (ˈbɛkɪt), *v.* [f. prec. sb.] *trans.* To fasten or secure by beckets; to furnish with beckets.
1823 F. COOPER *Pioneer* xv. (1869) 66/2, I larnt..how a top-gallant-sail was to be becketted. **1853** KANE *Grinnell Exp.* xxxiii. (1856) 295 Preserved meat boxes..ready strapped and becketed (*nautice* for trunk-handled).

becking (ˈbɛkɪŋ), *vbl. sb.* [f. BECK *v.* + -ING[1].] The action of BECK *v.*: **a.** Significant gesture. **b.** Nodding, bowing, obeisance, curtsey.
1542 UDALL *Erasm. Apoph.* 91 a, Excepte thei make much doukyng, stoopyng, beckyng. **1569** J. SA[NFORD] *Agrippa's Van. Artes* 124 Birdes flewe to him at his beckinge. **1583** STANYHURST *Æneis* II. (Arb.) 63 With menacing becking.

beckiron, obs. form of BEAK-IRON.

beckite: see BEEKITE.

beckon (ˈbɛk(ə)n), *v.* Forms: 1 bíecn-, bécn-, bícn-, býcn-ian, béacn-an, 2–4 becn(i)-en, 3 bæcni-en, 4–5 beken, biken, 5 bekn-yn (? bekyn, beccyn), 6–8 becken, 7 becon, 5– beckon. [OE. *bíecnan*:—OTeut. **bauknjan*, f. *baukno-*, in OE. *béacn* sign, BEACON; cogn. w. OS. *bôknian*, OHG. *bouhhanjan, bouhnen.* Also OE. *béacnian*, a later formation on the sb.: cf. ON. *bákna*, and BEACON *v.*]
1. *intr.* To make a mute signal or significant gesture with the head, hand, finger, etc.; now *esp.* in order to bid a person approach.
c **950** *Lindisf. Gosp.* Luke i. 22 He wæs becnende ðæm. *c* **1000** *Ags. G.* ibid., He wæs bicniende him. *c* **1160** *Hatton G.* ibid., He wæs beacniende heom. *c* **1200** ORMIN 223 Comm he siþþenn út All dumb..And toc to becnenn till þe follc. **1388** WYCLIF *Ps.* xxxiv. 19 Aduersaries..haten me with out cause, and bikenen with iȝen. *c* **1440** *Promp. Parv.* 29 Beknyn, *annuto.* **1530** PALSGR. 444/2, I becken with the heed to gyve one warnynge of a thynge. **1675** HOBBES *Odyss.* (1677) 259 Then to his son with's eye he beckoned. **1719** DE FOE *Crusoe* I. 241, I beckon'd with my Hand to him, to come

back. **1834** HT. MARTINEAU *Demerara* vii. 89 He was about to beckon to his companion.

†**b.** To act as a beacon. *Obs. rare.*

c **1400** *Destr. Troy* XIV. 6037 Brode firis & brem beccyn in þe ost, That yche freike in the fild his felow might know.

2. *trans.* (the object orig. *dat.*; see sense 1): To make a mute signal or significant gesture of head or hand to (a person), as commanding his attention or action, and esp. his approach; hence, to summon or bid approach by such a gesture.

[*c* **1000** *Ags. G.* Luke v. 7 Hiȝ bicnodon hyra ȝeferan. *c* **1160** *Hatton G.* ibid., Hyo becneden heore ȝe-feren.] *c* **1400** *Destr. Troy* VII. 3112 And ho..beckonet hym boldly ..his place to Remeve. *c* **1440** *Generydes* II. 3827 With hir kerche she bekenyd hym aside. **1604** SHAKS. *Oth.* IV. i. 134 Iago becons me: now he begins the story. **1712** STEELE *Spect.* No. 498 ¶ 3 A lively young fellow..beckoned a coach. **1732** SWIFT *Lett.* 58 Wks. 1761 VIII. 133 You may becken a blackguard-boy under a gate. **1816** J. WILSON *City of Plague* I. iv. 138 He beckon'd me to ascend a cart.

†**b.** To summon by a signal of any kind. *Obs.*

1205 LAY. 21938 He lette blæwen bemen and þa Scottes bæcnien [**1250** bannien].

†**3.** *intr.* To nod; to bow. *Obs.* Cf. BECK *v.* 3.

1578 LYTE *Dodoens* 330 The flowers hang uppon tender stalkes, nodding or beckning downewardes.

beckon (ˈbɛk(ə)n), *sb.* [f. prec. vb.: of late formation.] A significant gesture of head, hand, etc., *esp.* one indicating assent or command.

a **1718** PENN *Tracts* Wks. 1726 I. 623 Æshilus makes a sincere Beckon to a matter, a firm Oath. **1817** W. TAYLOR in *Month. Mag.* XLIII. 237 Their beckon intimates no ambush nigh. **1875** B. TAYLOR *Faust* II. III. 204 Strong men obedient stand waiting his every beckon.

ˈbeckoning, *vbl. sb.* [f. as prec. + -ING[1].] The action of the vb. BECKON; = preceding.

c **1380** *Sir Ferumb.* 3577 þe frensche þanne..made a bekenynge to Richard, To take ys way forþ riȝte. **1382** WYCLIF *Gen.* xliii. 6 At his bikenyng [**1388** wille] whete cornes weren solde to the peplis. *c* **1450** *Bk. Curtasye* 249 in *Babees Bk.* (1868) 306 Bekenyng, fynguryng non thou use. **1562** J. HEYWOOD *Prov. & Epigr.* (1867) 61 Before I was wedded..I made recknyng, To make my wyfe boow at euery becknyng. **1828** CARLYLE *Misc.* (1857) I. 113 Incited by capricious beckonings.

ˈbeckoning, *ppl. a.* [-ING[2].] Making mute signs of assent, invitation, etc.; signalling.

1637 MILTON *Comus* 205 A thousand fantasies..Of calling shapes, and beckoning shadows dire. **1852** TUPPER *Proverb. Philos.* 270 Many lovers..follow her beckoning finger.

beclad, pa. pple. of BECLOTHE.

beclag, variant of BECLOG.

†**beˈclam,** *v. Obs.* or *dial.* [f. BE- + CLAM.] *trans.* To beclog with anything clammy or sticky.

1674 N. FAIRFAX *Bulk & Selv.* 77 Angels..being no wayes beclam'd with body as to ubiety or whereness. **1864** ATKINSON *Whitby Gloss.*, *Beclamed*, splashed or bemired.

beclamour, beclang, beclart, beclatter, becloak, etc.: see BE- *pref.*

†**beˈclap,** *v. Obs.* In 4-5 by-, 5-6 beclappe. [f. BE- + CLAP.] To catch or lay hold of suddenly.

c **1386** CHAUCER *2nd Nonnes T.* 9 He..continuelly us wayteth to byclappe. **1530** PALSGR. 445/1, I beclappe or be trappe, or take in a snare.

beclaw (bɪˈklɔː), *v.* [f. BE- 4 + CLAW.] *trans.* To scratch or tear all over with claws or nails.

1603 HOLLAND *Plutarch's Mor.* 1231 Crœsus..caught one of the nobles..and within a fullers mill all to beclawed and mangled him. **1609** ROWLANDS *Knaue of C.* 6 And with her Nailes be clawd Them cruelly.

†**beˈclepe,** *v. Obs.* For forms see CLEPE *v.* [OE. *becleop-, -cliep-, -clepian,* f. BE- 4 + *cleopian, clypian* to call, cry, CLEPE.]

1. *trans.* To complain against; to indict, accuse.

c **1030** *Cnut's Sec. Laws* §28 I. 392 (Bosw.) Ælcere spæce, ðe he ǽr beclyped wæs. *c* **1200** *Trin. Coll. Hom.* 173 Here owen sinnes hem biclepieð. *c* **1300** *Beket* 365 That of man-slaȝt was Bi-cliped.

2. To call upon, address, accost; with *compl.* to address as, call, name.

c **1220** *Hali Meid.* 33 ȝif þu ert feir & wið glad chere bi-clepest alle feire. *a* **1300** *Cursor M.* 15323 Me yur maister yee bi-clepe, And yur lauerd yee call.

3. To summon to a higher court; *absol.* to appeal.

1297 R. GLOUC. 473 Bote the erche bissope's court to riȝte him wolde bringe, That he solde fram him bi clupe biuore the Kinge. *c* **1300** *Beket* 1016 You bischops ich biclipie: to the Court of Rome also.

b. To appeal against, object to, disapprove.

c **1320** *Cast. Love* 498 We be-clepeþ þe dom for-þi.

beclip (bɪˈklɪp), *v.*[1] *arch.* For forms see CLIP. [OE. *beclyppan,* f. BE- 1 + *clyppan* to clasp, embrace; see CLIP *v.*]

†**1.** *trans.* To fold in the arms, embrace, clasp. *Obs.*

c **1000** *Ags. Gosp.* Mark ix. 36 þa nam he anne cnapan..he hine beclypte. *c* **1220** *Ureison* in *Cott. Hom.* 201 Hire leoue child for to bi-cluppen. **1297** R. GLOUC. 469 Hii custe hom & bi clupte. **1393** GOWER *Conf.* II. 95 Whan I may her hond beclippe. **1474** CAXTON *Chesse* 16 Her right arme shal beclyppe me. **1643** HORN & ROBOTHAM *Gate Lang. Unl.* xx. §229 Hugging, beclipping, and embracing her foster-child. **1669** J. WORLIDGE *Syst. Agric.* (1681) 113 A Pear-tree..as much as three Men, from hand to hand, could beclip.

2. To wrap round, enclose, encircle, surround.

c **1000** *Ags. Ps.* cxix. 61 Me fyrenfulra fæcne rapas..oft beclyptan. *c* **1330** *Arth. & Merl.* 6109 Of Sarraȝins gret threng..hem biclepten in that place. **1387** TREVISA *Higden* Rolls Ser. I. 59 Occean byclippeþ al þe erþe aboute as a garlond. **1494** FABYAN VI. cxlviii. 134 The Wandalis.. approchid the cytie..and it enuyroned, or beclypped with a stronge siege. **1541** R. COPLAND *Guydon's Quest. Chirurg.* F iij 2 b, The muscles and cordes..beclyppeth all the ioynt of the bone called vlna. **1602** WARNER *Alb. Eng.* XIII. lxxviii. (1612) 323 Yeat Sea the Earth, the Aier them both, the skie be-cleaps them all. **1855** SINGLETON *Virgil* II. 121 The flood ..beclips, and whirls The booming rocks.

†**3.** To include, comprise, comprehend, contain.

c **1230** *Hali Meid.* 19 þe hehscipe of þe mede þat tis ilke lut wordes bicluppen abuten. **1393** GOWER *Conf.* II. 194 He wolde embrace All that this wide world beclippeth.

†**4.** To lay hold of, seize upon, grip; to catch, overtake. *lit.* and *fig. Obs.*

c **1380** WYCLIF *Wks.* (1880) 462 þe pope will beclippe worldly worchip. **1382** —— *Isa.* v. 29 He shal..holden the prei, and biclippen, and ther shal not be that delyuere out. **1491** CAXTON *Vitas Patr.* (W. de W. 1495) II. 180 b/1 He toke his waye..but was beclypped of the nyghte. **1493** *Festivall* (1515) 17 b, A grete blacke toode..had beclypped his faders herte. **1557** TUSSER *Husb.* (1878) 224 Get euer before hande..least winter beclip thee.

†**b.** To curdle (milk). *Obs.* Cf. *catch.*

c **1400** MAUNDEV. 52 Take also a drope of Bawme, and put it in to a Dissche..with Mylk of a Goot; and ȝif it be naturelle Bawme, anon it wole take and beclippe the Mylk.

beclip (bɪˈklɪp), *v.*[2] [f. BE- 1 + CLIP *v.*] *trans.* To clip about, crop.

1794 MARTYN *Rousseau's Bot.* xvi. 207 Alaternus, formerly so shorn and beclipped in hedges.

†**beˈclipping,** *vbl. sb.* [f. BECLIP *v.*[1]] Embrace.

1340 *Ayenb.* 96 þet word is worþ ase moche ase a beclepping of love. *c* **1420** WYCLIF *Gen.* xlvi. 29 (MS. C.). *c* **1449** PECOCK *Repr.* II. xx. 271 An handling or a biclipping.

beclog (bɪˈklɒg), *v.*; also 4 biclag, 5 byclag. [f. BE- + CLOG.] *trans.* To encumber with a sticky substance; hence **beclogged** *ppl. a.*

c **1340** *Auent. Sir Gawayne* ix, Al biclagged in clay. **1481** CAXTON *Reynard* (Arb.) 98 They were byslabbed and byclagged to their eres. **1578** *Gorgious Gallery Inuent.*, Thy loving mate, Whom thou hast left beclogged now, in most unhappy state. **1628** EARLE *Microcosm.* x. 23 A miry way, where the spirits are beclog'd. **1866** J. ROSE *Virgil* 125 At eve returning, thighs beclogged with thyme.

†**beˈclose,** *v. Obs.* Forms: 1 beclýs-an, 2-3 biclus-en, 4, 7 beclose. [Orig. OE. *beclýsan,* f. BE- 1 + *clýsan*: see CLUSE; subseq. changed to CLOSE after Fr.] *trans.* To shut up or in; to enclose, imprison. Hence **beˈclosing** *vbl. sb.*

c **1000** *Ags. Gosp.* Luke iii. 20 He be-clysde iohannem on cwearterne. **1205** LAY. 15023 Sculden þer swiðe faste biclusen heom in ane castle. *a* **1230** *Ancr. R.* 108 þu uorsoke þene world i þine biclusinge. *c* **1325** *Cœur de L.* 5185 Richard seygh..That the Sarezynes hoost beclosyd is. **1677** GILPIN *Dæmonol.* (1867) 166 Beclosed in the mi[l]dhead of God.

beclothe (bɪˈkləʊð), *v.* Pa. t. and pple. beclothed, beclad. [f. BE- 1 + CLOTHE.] *trans.* To clothe about, cover with clothes.

1509 HAWES *Past. Pleas.* XLII. iii, Thy beaute..becladde with cloth of pleasaunce. **1640** FULLER *Joseph's Coat* (1867) 213 The night, with mourning weeds, the world beclad. **1775** R. CHANDLER *Trav. Greece* (1825) II. 153 Enwrapped and beclothed in such a manner, it is impossible to discern whether they are young or old. **1821** CLARE *Vill. Minstr. etc.* I. 106 Brown heaths be-clothed in furze.

becloud (bɪˈklaʊd), *v.* Also 7 -clowd. [f. BE- 6 + CLOUD.]

1. *trans.* To cover or obscure with clouds (of vapour, smoke, etc.); to make misty or murky.

1598 SYLVESTER *Du Bartas* (1608) 359 With a sable cloud Of horned locusts doth the sun becloud. **1636** R. GRIFFIN in *Ann. Dubrensia* (1877) 52 These..beclowd the azure skies. **1854** WOODWARD *Mollusca* (1856) 15 The cuttle-fish escapes by..beclouding the water with an inky discharge.

2. *fig.* To make obscure; to darken, to hide.

1619 DONNE *Serm.* Wks. 1839 VI. 20 Howsoever the Understanding be Beclouded. **1782** PRIESTLEY *Nat. & Rev. Relig.* II. 161 Beclouding and puzzling the business. **1876** GEO. ELIOT *Dan. Der.* II. xix. 7 These fine words with which we fumigate and becloud unpleasant facts.

beˈclouded, *ppl. a.* [f. prec. + -ED.] Covered or beset with clouds; made obscure, or gloomy.

1581 SIDNEY *Astr. & Stella* (T.) Woe Painted in my beclouded stormy face. **1875** HELPS *Organiz. Daily L.* 138 Houses are constructed after the same pattern..for cloudless and beclouded districts.

beclout (bɪˈklaʊt), *v.*; also 3 biclute. [f. BE- + CLOUT.] *trans.* To cover with a clout or cloth; to dress up; chiefly *fig.*

a **1230** *Ancr. R.* 316 þis nis nout naked schrift..biclute þu hit nowiht. **1873** T. COOPER *Parad. Martyrs* (1877) 299 The mimesters who beclout themselves anew with rags of Rome.

†**beˈclumpse,** *v. Obs.* [f. BE- 2 + CLUM(P)SE *v.*; cf. *clumper, clumsy.*] *trans.* To benumb.

1611 COTGR., *Glacer*..to benumme, beclumpse. **1653** URQUHART *Rabelais* III. xxxi, Certain Drugs..do..benumb mortifie and beclumpse with cold the prolific Semence.

becn-ian, -en, obs. form of BECKON.

becobweb, becollier, becolme, becolour, becombed, becomma, becompass, etc.: see BE-.

become (bɪˈkʌm), *v.* Pa. t. **became**; Pa. pple. **become.** Forms as in COME: also in 16-17th c. *pa. t.* and *pa. pple.* often **becomed,** esp. in senses 5-8: see next word. Prefix in ME. also **bi-, by-.** [Common Teut.: OE. *becuman* to arrive, attain, happen, corresponding to OHG. *biqueman,* mod.G. *bekommen,* Du. *bekomen,* Goth. *biquiman,* f. *bi-* BE- 1 + *quiman,* in OE. *cuman,* to COME. With the development of senses 5, 6, cf. Fr. *devenir*; with that of 7 cf. L. *convenire,* Gr. προσήκειν.]

I. To come, come about.

†**1.** *intr.* To come (to a place), to arrive; passing in later use into 'betake oneself, go.' *Obs.*

c **885** K. ÆLFRED *Oros.* IV. viii. §3 Hannibal to þam lande becom. *c* **1175** *Lamb. Hom.* 129 Hwer bicomen heo þa? *c* **1250** *Gen. & Ex.* 1744 To ðe munt galaad he bi-cam. *c* **1340** *Cursor M.* 13748. **1475** CAXTON *Jason* 92 b, Where may I become for to haue good conceyll. **1533** BELLENDEN *Livy* v. (1822) 450 Thay war becumin oure the said montanis. **1535** COVERDALE *Prov.* xvii. 8 Where so euer he becometh he prospereth. **1554** MOUNTAIN in Strype *Eccl. Mem.* III. I. xxiv. 198 Knew not where to become that night. **1625** BACON *Ess.* xlv. (Arb.) 551 Houses so full of Glasse, that one cannot tell, where to become, to be out of the Sunne. **1737** WHISTON *Josephus' Antiq.* VIII. iii. §2 That they might become into one through another.

†**b.** *where became it, is it become,* etc. (= 'where went it, has it gone') are now expressed by *what became of it, has become of it*: see 4.

1205 LAY. 21913 Wær scullen we bicumen? *a* **1300** *Cursor M.* 8998 Quar be-com al his in-sight? *c* **1380** WYCLIF *Wicket* 13 Where then becommeth your ministrations? *c* **1400** *Ywaine & Gaw.* 1652 No man wist whor he bycome. **1483** CAXTON *G. de la Tour* xvi. 22 He asked his wiff wher the ele was become. **1528** MORE *Heresyes* IV. Wks. 1557, 274/1 Where were become al good ordre among men. **1628** WITHER *Brit. Rememb.* 24 Why should the wicked..say, Where is their God become? **1636** *Ariana* 130 Where is become of this honour and this vertue?

†**2.** *transf.* To come, in reference to time or state. *Obs.*, or (with infinitive) *arch.*

Beowulf 2 31 Syþþan niht becom. *c* **888** K. ÆLFRED *Boeth.* xxxix. §11 Oft becymþ se ánweald þisse worulde to swiþe godum monnum. *a* **1230** *Juliana* 21 Ich schal bliðe bicumen to endelese blissen. **1483** CAXTON *Gold. Leg.* 431/1 Thenne the sayd Saynt..became to al maner perfeccion of lyf. **1513-75** *Diurn. Occur.* (1833) 75 The said arch-bischope.. become in the Quenis will. **1542** UDALL *Erasm. Apoph.* 112 b, Why Diogenes first became to bee a philosopher. **1618** BOLTON *Florus* IV. ii. 265 The whole World was now become to be held by three Princes. **1730** A. GORDON *Maffei's Amphith.* 345 The Senatorian Order..became to have Seats in the Amphitheatre. **1806** SYD. SMITH *Elem. Mor. Philos.* (1850) 369 It becomes to be loved on its own account.

†**b.** To come, in reference to origin. *Obs.*

a **1300** *Cursor M.* 9354 His moder..was be-comen al o þair kin. *Ibid.* 10936 þis zachari..Becummen was o leui sede. **1606** G. W[ODCOCKE] *Hist. Justine* 137 a, A country.. wherof became the Ryuer so called.

†**3.** To come about, come to pass, happen; to fall to one's lot, befall. **a.** with *dative* or *to. Obs.*

c **888** K. ÆLFRED *Boeth.* xxxix §9 Swa hit hwilum gewyrþ þæt þæm godum becymþ anfeald yfel. *c* **1250** *Gen. & Ex.* 2227 Wel michel sorȝe is me bicumen. **1556** LAUDER *Tractate* (1864) 1 And quhat sall becum to Kyngis that contynewis in Iniquitie. **1655** JENNINGS *Elise* 147 What became this woman, when she heard this news?

†**b.** without construction; often impersonally.

c **1210** *Leg. Kath.* 1563 Bicom [to] þat te king maxence moste fearen. *c* **1250** *Gen. & Ex.* 1577 Quad esau, grot sal bi-cumen. **1483** CAXTON *G. de la Tour* F ij, It becam ones that the good man made semblaunt to goo oute. **1530** PALSGR. 445/2 It becometh, it happeneth, it chaunseth.

4. *become of* (after 'what') was used formerly in sense of 'come out of, result from,' but has also taken the place of 'where is it become,' etc., in 1 b., in reference to the later locality, position, or fate of a person or thing.

1535 COVERDALE *Ex.* xxxii. 1 We can not tell what is become [**1382** WYCLIF, what is befallyn; **1388** what befelde] of this man Moses. **1601** SHAKS. *Twel. N.* II. ii. 37 What will become of this?.. My state is desperate. **1611** BIBLE *Gen.* xxxvii. 20 We shall see what will become of his dreames. **1663** BUTLER *Hud.* I. iii. 263 Nor do I know what is become Of him more than the Pope. **1707** FREIND *Peterboro's Cond. Sp.* 211 It is no Matter what becomes of the Town. **1790** PALEY *Horæ Paul., Rom.* ii. 18 [St. Paul] is telling what was become of his companions. **1862** H. SPENCER *First Princ.* II. v. §56 (1875) 183 What becomes of this element at either extreme of the oscillation?

II. To come to be. (Closely related to sense 2.)

5. To come to be (something or in some state).

†**a.** with *to, into. Obs.*

c **1175** *Lamb. Hom.* 215 To lure hit bi-kumeð of hwuche half so hit falleð. *a* **1250** *Prov. Alfred* 383 in *O.E. Misc.* 126 Werldes welþe schulle bi-cumen to nouhte. *c* **1305** *St. Kenelm* 129 in *E.E.P.* (1862) 51 To a litel foȝel he bicom.

1483 CAXTON *G. de la Tour* A i, The..myrthe was soone falle doune and..become in to grete trystesse. **1657** HOWELL *Londinop.* 51 The rest of the ground is become into smal tenements. **1683** EVELYN *Hist. Relig.* (1850) II. 28 The Church of God, being now become, from a private family.. to a great and numerous nation.

b. with *subst.* or *adj. complement.*

c **1175** *Lamb. Hom.* 47 þa bicom his licome swiðe feble. *c* **1200** *Trin. Coll. Hom.* 21 And þus bicam ure lafdi mid childe. *c* **1350** *Will. Palerne* 881 He cast al his colour and bicom pale. **1398** TREVISA *Barth. De P.R.* v. lxii. (1495) 178 Goddis sone bycame man and dwellyd among vs. **1483** CAXTON *Gold. Leg.* 135/4 So wyse a man is such a fole becomen. **1549** *Compl. Scot.* 2 The vniuersal pepil ar be cum distitute of iustice. **1611** BIBLE *Gen.* xix. 26 His wife looked backe..she became a pillar of salt. **1625** BACON *Ess.* (Arb.) 479 Their Boughs were becommen too great. **1717** LADY M. W. MONTAGUE *Lett.* II. xlvi. 30 The asmack, or Turkish veil, is become..agreeable to me. **1774** CHESTERF. *Lett.* I. 11 Unfortunately for her, she became in love with him. **1810** HENRY *Elem. Chem.* (1840) II. 699 When..more largely diluted with water, it becomes hot. **1848** MACAULAY *Hist. Eng.* I. 4 When first they became known to the Tyrian mariners. **1876** GREEN *Short Hist.* vi. §4. 298 Florence.. became the home of an intellectual Revival.

6. To come into being or existence.

1598 SYLVESTER *Du Bartas* I. i. (1641) 1/2 In the instant when Time first became. **1876** HAMERTON *Intell. Life* II. ii. 56 The powers given us by Nature are little more than a power to become.

III. To agree or accord with; suit, befit, grace.

7. *trans.* To accord with, agree with, be suitable to; to befit (object orig. *dative*).

a **1230** *Juliana* 7 He wes freo boren, and hem walde bicumen a freo boren burde. **1564** BAULDWIN *Mor. Philos.* (Palfr.) i. 51 They should doe such things as becommed their shape. **1596** SHAKS. *Merch. V.* v. 57 Soft stilnes and the night Become the tutches of sweet harmonie. **1611** BIBLE *Heb.* vii. 26 Such an high Priest became vs. —— *Prov.* xvii. 7 Excellent speech becommeth not a foole. **1723** DE FOE *Col. Jack* (1840) 171 A book would become his hands better than a hoe. *a* **1778** *Anecd. W. Pitt* (1792) III. 29 A tone of modesty..would become them better. **1810** WORDSW. *Sonn. Liberty* II. xxv, A garland..Becomes not one whose father is a slave. **1844** DISRAELI *Coningsby* II. ii. 62 He had that public spirit which became his station.

8. *impers.* (now usually with *it*).

†**a.** (*absol.*, with *to*, *for*, or *clause.*) To be congruous, appropriate, fitting. *Obs.*, replaced by 'it is becoming.'

c **1175** *Lamb. Hom.* 45 Nu bi-comeð hit..to uwilchen cristene monne..to haliȝen þenne dei. **1297** R. GLOUC. 36 Doþ hem alle wel an horse, as a kyng bi comeþ to. **1393** LANGL. *P. Pl.* C. IV. 266 Hyt by-cometh for a kyng..To ȝeve men mede. **1535** COVERDALE *2 Macc.* xii. 14 Speakynge soch wordes as it becommeth not. **1589** PUTTENHAM *Eng. Poesie* (Arb.) 25 It became that the high mysteries of the gods should be reuealed and taught. **1591** SHAKS. *1 Hen. VI*, v. iii. 17 Set this Diamond safe..as it becomes.

b. with *object.* (orig. *dative*) To befit; to be proper to or for.

a **1230** *Juliana* 55 Wel bisemeð þe to beon and bikimeð [*v.r.* bicumeð] to beo streon of a swuch strunde. *c* **1300** *Beket* 1179 Uvele Bicom him to gon afote. **1480** CAXTON *Chron. Eng.* ccxliv. 295 To play with tenys balles become hym better. **1541** BARNES *Wks.* (1573) 192 It had becommed them a great deale better, to haue punished their seruant. **1577** HOLINSHED *Chron.* III. 1140/1 We haue begun, as becommed vs. **1644** *Direct. Publ. Worship* 17 Gravely, as becommeth the word of God. **1661** MARVELL *Corr.* xxviii. Wks. 1872–5 II. 66 There are nakednesses which it becomes us to cover. **1788** PRIESTLEY *Lect. Hist.* v. xxxvi. 276 It becomes men..to make provision for rectifying their mistakes. **1826** SCOTT in *Lockhart* (1839) VIII. 230, I thought it became me to make public how far I was concerned. **1869** FREEMAN *Norm. Conq.* III. xii. 95 He was fonder of hunting than became an Archbishop.

9. Hence, To look well (on or with), to set out.

†**a.** *absol.* To look well (i.e. in its place); to be comely or becoming. *Obs.*

c **1300** *Beket* 2351 Wel bicom the brighte gold, upon the rede blod.

b. Said, *esp.* of an accessory, property, attribute, quality, or action, suiting or gracing its owner or subject. At first with an adv. (*well*, etc.), but afterwards also without one.

c **1314** *Guy Warw.* 4 The kirtel bicom him swithe wel. *c* **1400** A. DAVY *Dreams* 11 A Coroune of gold Bicom hym wel. **1589** PUTTENHAM *Eng. Poesie* (Arb.) 297 Nothing in the world could worse haue becomen them. **1605** SHAKS. *Macb.* I. iv. 7 Nothing in his Life became him, Like the leauing it. **1642** FULLER *Holy & Prof. St.* IV. i. 240 Bluntnesse of speech hath becom'd some, and made them more acceptable. **1716** ADDISON *Drummer* II. i, Her Widow's weeds became her. **1824** COLERIDGE *Aids Refl.* 53 So anxious to have their dress become them.

c. Of a person: To grace or adorn his surroundings, place, or position, to occupy or wear with fitting grace.

1596 SHAKS. *Tam. Shr.* II. 260 Did euer Dian so become a Groue As Kate this chamber? **1610** —— *Temp.* III. ii. 112 She will become thy bed. *a* **1674** CLARENDON *Hist. Reb.* II. VI. 162 Which place he became well. **1713** STEELE *Guardian* No. 21 ¶7 A graceful man..who became the dignity of his function.

d. Hence, To look well in (a dress, etc.).

1660 MARVELL *Corr.* iii. Wks. 1872–5 II. 19 The youth of your own town..become their arms much better than any soldiers. **1750** JOHNSON *Rambl.* No. 75 ¶9 The splendour which I became so well. **1874** HELPS *Soc. Press.* i. 23 She with her dark hair did most become that yellow gown.

†**be'comed**, *ppl. a. Obs. rare*⁻¹. [f. BECOME (sense 8) + -ED[1].] Befitting, becoming.

¶*Became* in Spenser *F.Q.* I. x. 66, may perh. be equal to *becomed*: but it may also, of course, be the pa. t. of the vb.

1592 SHAKS. *Rom. & Jul.* IV. ii. 26, I..gaue him what becomed Loue I might.

†**be'comely**, *a.* and *adv. Obs.* Forms: 2–3 bicumelic, -lich; *adv.* bicumeliche. [f. BECOME + -LY.] **A.** *adj.* Becoming, fitting, acceptable.

c **1175** *Lamb. Hom.* 129 Him þuhte bicumelic þet we weren ..alesede. *c* **1200** *Trin. Coll. Hom.* 127 Swo þat he was bicumelich to his wuninge.

B. *adv.* Becomingly, properly.

c **1200** *Trin. Coll. Hom.* 9 We gon å dai bicumeliche.

†**be'comeness.** *Obs. rare*⁻¹. [f. *become* pa. pple. + -NESS.] = BECOMINGNESS.

1656 DU GARD *Gate Lat. Unl.* §673. 287 You may bee adorned..with bashfulness..becomness, faithfulness.

becoming (bɪˈkʌmɪŋ), *vbl. sb.* [f. BECOME *v.*]

1. The action of befitting or gracing; that which befits or graces. *rare.*

c **1600** SHAKS. *Sonn.* 150 Whence hast thou this becomming of things ill. **1606** —— *Ant. & Cl.* I. iii. 96 My becommings kill me, when they do not Eye well to you.

2. A coming to be, a passing into a state.

1853 ROBERTSON *Serm.* Ser. III. xi. 139 Everything else is in a state of becoming, God is in a state of Being. **1860** PUSEY *Min. Proph.* 613 Our life is a 'becoming' rather than a simple 'being.'

be'coming, *ppl. a.* [f. as prec. + -ING[2].]

1. Befitting, suitable, having graceful fitness.

1565 *Sc. Metr. Ps.* cxxxiii. 1 How good a thing it is and how becoming well. **1588** SHAKS. *L.L.L.* II. i. 67 Within the limits of becoming mirth. **1686** W. DE BRITAINE *Hum. Prud.* §4. 19 Let your Behaviour, like your Garment, be..fit and becoming. **1713** *Guardian* No. 1 ¶1 Coming up to town in a very becoming periwig. **1833** HT. MARTINEAU *Cinn. & Pearls* i. 4 He spoke with becoming indifference of all meaner accomplishments.

2. *the becoming*: **a.** that which is befitting or proper; decorum.

1842 *Realities of Life* 207 Some of whom..study the becoming in their own persons. **1848** MACAULAY *Hist. Eng.* II. 540 Selfcommand and a fine sense of the becoming.

b. that which is coming into existence.

1856 FERRIER *Inst. Metaph.* XVII. xvii. 349 The usual synonym for this was the Becoming (τὸ γιγνόμενον), that is, inchoate existence.

be'comingly, *adv.* [f. prec. + -LY.] In a becoming manner; befittingly; with graceful fitness.

1624 HEYWOOD *Gunaik.* III. 131 Her nose somewhat (but most becomminglie) hooked. **1694** KETTLEWELL *Comp. Persecuted* 145 To act..in all things, wisely and becomingly. **1884** BLACK *Jud. Shaks.* xiii, She was becomingly dressed.

becomingness (bɪˈkʌmɪŋnɪs). [f. as prec. + -NESS.] The quality of being becoming; fitness, suitability; graceful propriety or fitness.

1657 W. DILLINGHAM in *Sir F. Vere's Comm.* Pref. A iv, The becomingness of the stile did much affect me. **1690** NORRIS *Beatitudes* (1692) 214 A kind of Congruity or Becomingness on God's part so to do. **1866** FELTON *Anc. & Mod. Greece* I. i. 283 A propriety and becomingness of demeanour. **1876** MISS YONGE *Womankind* xv. 116 Taking questions of complexion and becomingness into account.

†**be'comse**, *v. Obs. rare*⁻¹. [f. BE- + COMSE, syncopated for *commence.*] To begin, commence.

c **1350** *Will. Palerne* 2523 þe kolieres bi-komsed to karpe kenely i-fere.

becon, -age, obs. f. BECKON, BEACON, -AGE.

becoom, becost, becovet, becoward: see BE-.

†**be'cover**, *v. Obs.* [f. BE- + COVER *v.*] *trans.*

1. To recover.

c **1325** *E.E. Allit. P.* B. 1327 þat he ful clanly bi-cuv-er his carp bi þe laste.

2. To cover over.

c **1325** *Coer de L.* 3925 Alle becoveryd wer feeldes and pleynes With knyghtes. **1594** CAREW *Tasso* (1881) 63 That great one seene with blacke becouered so.

Becquerel (ˈbɛkrəl). [The name of a French physicist, Antoine Henri *Becquerel* (1852–1908).] **1.** Used *attrib.* in *Becquerel('s) rays*, formerly a general term for the radiation from radioactive substances.

1896 S. P. THOMPSON in *Phil. Mag.* July 105 While agreeing with the Röntgen rays in the property of penetrating aluminium [etc.], the Becquerel rays differ in the circumstance that they can be refracted and polarized. **1897** —— *Light Visible & Invis.* 279 Becquerel's rays possess ..the property of diselectrifying charged bodies. **1898** *Physical Rev.* Apr. 239 Becquerel rays, or uranium rays, as Becquerel himself called them. **1931** *Discovery* July 212/2 When X-rays and the Becquerel rays from uranium were discovered it was demonstrated that these rays could make air into a conductor.

2. (Written **becquerel.**) The SI unit of radioactivity, equal to one disintegration per second (superseding the curie, equal to $3{\cdot}7 \times 10^{10}$ becquerels). Symbol Bq.

1975 *Physics Bull.* Mar. 105/1 The CIPM will recommend to the CGPM that the SI unit of activity should be given the name 'becquerel', symbol Bq. **1976** *Sci. Amer.* Mar. 60A/2 Among the SI's derived units with special names are those for..radioactivity (the becquerel, or spontaneous nuclear transitions per second) and absorbed dose of radiation (the gray, or joules per kilogram). **1986** *Times* 7 May 7 The Agriculture Minister insisted that his official figures for iodine radiation in milk showed levels up to 60 becquerels a litre, 'miles below' the safe limit of 1,000.

becram, becrampoun, becrave, becrawl, becrime, becrimson, becripple, becroak, becrowd, becrush, becrust, becry, etc.: see BE-.

becripple (bɪˈkrɪp(ə)l), *v.* [f. BE- 2 or 5 + CRIPPLE.] To make lame, to cripple.

1660 H. MORE *Myst. Godl.* VI. xix. 277 Those who you do bedwarfe and becripple with your poisonous medicines. **1755** BP. WARBURTON *Lett.* (ed. Parr 1809) 180 Bringing himself down to a lame becrippled world.

becross (bɪˈkrɒs, -ɔː-), *v.* [f. BE- + CROSS.] *trans.* To mark with the sign of the cross; to surround or decorate with crosses. Hence **becrossed** *ppl. a.*

1565 CALFHILL *Answ. Treat. Crosse* (1846) 79 Your spiritual fathers, all to becrossed about their beds. **1581** in *Confer.* IV. (1584) Z iij, *Campion* becrossed himselfe on the forehead. **1799** W. TAYLOR *Month. Mag.* VII. 139 A becross'd, beblest..bag of holy sackcloth. **1880** *Blackw. Mag.* Feb. 243 Officers much be-medalled and much be-crossed.

becrown (bɪˈkraʊn), *v.* [f. BE- 2 + CROWN *v.*] To crown.

1583 STANYHURST *Aeneis* III. (Arb.) 87 Father Anchises a goold boul massye becrowning. **1800** W. TAYLOR *Month. Mag.* VIII. 806 The cool And shadowy forest, which becrowns the isle. **1850** LYNCH *Theo. Trin.* viii. 145 Gabriel, perhaps..dispports himself..becrowned with roses.

becudgel (bɪˈkʌdʒəl), *v.* [f. BE- + CUDGEL *v.*] To cudgel soundly.

1591 G. FLETCHER *Russe Commw.* (1836) 67 You shall see ..their shinnes thus becudgelled and bebasted every morning. **1881** A. DUFFIELD *Quix.* 34 To think I will return to mine [home] until I have becudgelled Don Quixote, is vain.

becuffed, becumber, becurry, becurse, becurtain, becushioned, becut, etc.: see BE- *pref.*

becuiba (bɪˈkwiːbə). Also bicuiba. [Pg. *bicuíba*, f. Tupi *bicuiba*, *bicuhyba.*] A Brazilian timber tree, *Virola bicuhyba*; used *attrib.* in **becuiba nut**, the fruit of an aromatic Brazilian tree (*Myristica bicuhyba*) of the nutmeg family; **becuiba tallow** or **fat**, a balsamic product of the becuiba nut.

1842 DUNGLISON *Dict. Med. Sci.* (ed. 3) *s.v.* Ibicuiba 371/2 *Becuiba*, or *Becuiba nux*, a species of nut from Brazil, the emulsive kernel of which is ranked amongst balsamic remedies. **1884** *Encycl. Brit.* XVII. 744/2 Becuiba tallow. [Source] *Myristica Becuhyba.* [Principal use] medicine; candles. **1889** *Cent. Dict.*, Becuiba-nut. **1934** WEBSTER, *Becuiba*, a Brazilian timber tree (*Virola becuhyba*), family Myristicaceae. **1955** *Nomencl. Commerc. Timbers (B.S.I.)* 88 Bicuiba.

becum, -in, -cummen, obs. ff. BECOME *v.*

becure, obs. var. of BEAKER.

becurl (bɪˈkɜːl), *v.* [f. BE- + CURL *v.*] To cover or deck out with curls. Hence **becurled** *ppl. a.*

1614 SYLVESTER *Bethulia's Rescue* v. 201 Judith..Becurles her Tresses. **1624** MILTON *Paraph. Ps.* cxiv, To hide his frost-becurled head. **1824** MISS MITFORD *Village* Ser. I. (1863) 202 Miss Phœbe..is said to have becurled..herself at least two tiers higher. **1860** A. WINDSOR *Ethica* vii. 352 Questions..discussed by becurled young declaimers.

becwethe, obs. form of BEQUEATH.

bed (bɛd), *sb.* Forms: (1–2 bed(d), 3 bæd, 3–6 bedd, 5–7 bedde, (4 bidd, 3–7 bede, 6 beed), 3– bed. [Com. Teut.: OE. *będd*, *będ*, neut., OS. *bed*, MDu. *bedde*, *bed*, *bet*, Du. *bed*, OHG. *betti*, MHG. *bette*, *bet*, mod.G. *bett*, Goth. *badi* (gen. *badjis*):—OTeut. **badjo-*(*m*) neut.; cf. ON. *beðr*, masc.:—OTeut. **badjo-z*. Referred by Franck with some probability to Aryan **bhodh-*, whence L. *fod(i-* to dig, as if orig. 'a dug out place,' a 'lair' of beasts or men: but this primitive notion had quite disappeared in Teutonic, in which the word had only the two senses 'sleeping-place of men' and 'garden-bed': it is uncertain whether the latter came independently from the root idea of 'dig,' or whether it was a transference from a bed for sleeping, with reference to its shape or purpose.]

I. The sleeping-place of men or animals.

1. a. A permanent structure or arrangement for sleeping on, or for the sake of rest. In some form or other it constitutes a regular article of household furniture in civilized life, as well as part of the equipment of an army or expedition. It consists for the most part of a sack or mattress of sufficient size, stuffed with something soft or springy, raised generally upon a 'bed-stead' or

support, and covered with sheets, blankets, etc., for the purpose of warmth. The name is given both to the whole structure in its most elaborate form, and, as in 'feather-bed,' to the stuffed sack or mattress which constitutes its essential part. (A person is said to be *in bed*, when undressed and covered with the bedclothes.)

c **995** *Will* in *Cod. Dipl.* VI. 132 Án bedreaf eal ðæt tó ánum bedde gebyreð. *c* **1000** *Ags. Gosp.* John v. 8 Aris: nim þin bed [*c* **1160** *Hatton G.* bedd] and ga. **1205** LAY. 6701 þe king læi in his bædde [**1250** bedde]. *a* **1300** *Cursor M.* 12392 He suld him mak a treen bedd [*Fairf. MS.* a bed of tree]. *c* **1300** *St. Brandan* 125 Beddes ther were al ȝare y-maked. **1382** WYCLIF *Mark* ii. 9 Ryse, take thi bed and walke. *c* **1400** *Destr. Troy* XXIX. 11933 Buernes in hor bednes britnet all naked. **1424** *E.E. Wills* (1882) 57, I wul þat ilk of my said childre haue a bed, þat is to say, couerlide, tapite, blankettis, too peyre schetes, matras, and canvas. **1480** CAXTON *Chron. Eng.* ccxlii. 277 He was in his bed and a slepe on a fethyr bedde. **1562** HEYWOOD *Prov. & Epigr.* (1867) 16 In house to kepe housholde, whan folks wyll needis wed, Mo thyngs belong, than foure bare legs in a bed. **1611** BIBLE *1 Sam.* xix. 15 Bring him vp to me in the bedde. **1648** JENKYN *Blind Guide* iv. 115 Sollid matter lodgeth in his great booke of words, as a childe of two days old in the great bed of Ware. **1716** LADY M. W. MONTAGUE *Lett.* I. xv. 51, I carried my own bed with me. **1761** STERNE *Tr. Shandy* II. xxix. 142 An old..chair..stood at the bed's head. **1851** TENNYSON *May Queen* iii. 23 Sit beside my bed, mother.

b. Often used somewhat elliptically for the use of a bed for the night, the condition or position of being in bed, sleeping in bed, the time for sleeping, etc. Cf. also the phrases under 6.

1474 *Ord. R. Househ.* 28 Make him joyouse and merry towardes his bedde. **1666** PEPYS *Diary* 12 Aug., We began both to be angry, and so continued till bed. **1769** WESLEY *Jrnl.* 19 Apr., Archdeacon C——e..desired I would take a bed with him. **1845** FORD *Handbk. Spain* §1. 20 The traveller should immediately on arriving secure his bed. **1874** BLACKIE *Self-Cult.* 50 Let a man walk for an hour before bed. **1879** M. PATTISON *Milton* 151 Bed, with its warmth and recumbent posture, he found favourable to composition.

c. ***bed and board***: entertainment with lodging and food. Of a wife: full connubial relations, as wife and mistress of the household.

c **1403** *York Manual* (1881) Pref. 16 Here I take þe N. to be my wedded wyfe, to hald and to haue at bed and at borde, for fayrer for layther, for better for wers..till ded us depart. **1596** SPENSER *F.Q.* III. x. 51 She [should be] receivd againe to bed and bord. **1756** C. LUCAS *Ess. Waters* III. 17 There is no city..better supplied for dress, carriage, bed and board. **1823** GALT *Entail* II. xv. 135 What..was due for bed and board. **1868** BROWNING *Ring & Bk.* II. 1287 Pompilia sought divorce from bed and board.

d. *fig.* The 'sleeping-place' attributed to things personified; that on which persons figuratively 'repose.'

a **1600** in *1001 Gems of Song* (1883) 3 The merrie horne wakes up the morne To leave his idle bed. **1817** JAS. MILL *Brit. India* II. IV. viii. 285 The treaty with Hyder was the bed on which the resentments of the Directors sought to repose. **1861** GEO. ELIOT *Silas M.* 74 The money..'ull be a bad bed to lie down on at the last.

e. *spec.* = *hospital bed* s.v. HOSPITAL *sb.* 6; also with qualifying adj.; cf. *pay-bed* s.v. PAY- 1 d.

1881 *Encycl. Brit.* XII. 307/2 In New York there is a large amount of hospital accommodation—about 6000 beds, or about 1 in 1500 of the population. **1914** *Surg., Gynecol. & Obstetr.* XIX. 114 (*title*) Demonstration of a universal extension apparatus applied to a surgical bed. **1930** A. FLEXNER *Universities* 88 Certain professors in medicine..have a few beds at one hospital or another. **1943**, etc. [see *orthopædic bed* s.v. ORTHOPÆDIC, -PEDIC *a.*]. **1969** *Times* 14 Aug. 2/2 Twenty beds have been closed at the 52-bed post-operative Courtaulds Hospital. **1985** *New Statesman* 27 Sept. 5/1 Every day since 1 October last year they have picketed the 700 bed hospital.

f. Chiefly used as an advertising term: bedroom.

1926 R. MACAULAY *Crewe Train* II. ix. 172 How many bed and recep.? **1939** [see BATH *sb.*[1] 12]. **1961** WODEHOUSE *Ice in Bedroom* xxii. 177 A joyous suburban villa equipped with main drainage,..four bed, two sit and the usual domestic offices.

g. ***bed and breakfast***: (*a*) the provision of a bed for a night and breakfast the following morning: an arrangement offered by hotels, boarding houses, etc.; also *attrib.*

1910 *Bradshaw's Railway Guide* Apr. 1125/1 Residential Hotel... Bed and breakfast from 4/-. **1930** *Morning Post* 17 June 18/5 (Advt.), Married couple for bed and breakfast house; Kitchen Man and House-Parlourmaid. **1936** J. L. HODSON *Our Two Englands* x. 174 It is true that I have seen the signs 'Bed, breakfast and garage'—a new form which the historian should make a note of. **1967** *Listener* 10 Aug. 178/1, I had previously booked bed and breakfast somewhere in Bloomsbury.

(*b*) *spec.* in financial contexts, used *attrib.* to designate a transaction in which shares are sold late in the day and bought back early the next morning so as to gain a tax advantage. Hence as *v. trans.*, to sell and rebuy (shares) in this way; ***bed-and-breakfasting*** vbl. sb.

1974 *Observer* 17 Feb. 15/4 Bed and breakfast operations ..allow investors to establish a gains tax loss yet effectively remain in the same shares on which losses have accumulated... Bed and breakfasting has become more and more popular over the years. **1980** *Daily Tel.* 29 Mar. 24/5 Investment trust shareholders who are sitting on large gains or have some disposals in mind..are well advised to sell or 'bed-and-breakfast' their shares before April 5. **1982** *Observer* 18 Apr. 18/5 Confusion still reigns with investors over the demise of bed and breakfast operations. **1984** *Daily Tel.* 31 Mar. 19/4 We will do a bed and breakfast transaction, but we don't encourage it. **1986** *Times* 8 Mar. 27/1 The Bed & Breakfasting ploy of selling the shares late one day and buying back early the next is cheaper than a normal Stock Exchange transaction.

2. *transf.* **a.** As the place of conjugal union; *hence* matrimonial rights and duties.

c **1200** ORMIN 2447 Hu..þatt I maȝȝ ben wiþþ childe I min maȝȝþhad, i clene bedd. *c* **1305** *St. Edmund Conf.* 106 in *E.E.P.* (1862) 73 Hire cloþes he dude of anon: as hit is lawe of bedde. **1382** WYCLIF *Gen.* xlix. 4 Thow has defoulid the bedde of hym. **1611** SHAKS. *Cymb.* III. iv. 42 False to his Bed? **1611** BIBLE *Hebr.* xiii. 4 Mariage is honorable in all, and the bed vndefiled. **1697** DRYDEN *Virg. Eclog.* IV. 78 No God shall crown the Board, nor Goddess bless the Bed. **1711** STEELE *Spect.* No. 51 ¶7 He betrays the Honour and Bed of his Neighbour.

b. As the place of procreation and child-birth; *hence* parental union, parentage; also birth, progeny.

c **1430** LYDG. *Bochas* II. xxii. (1554) 58 a, Socrates..Of ful lowe bed..was discended. *a* **1674** CLARENDON *Hist. Reb.* I. I. 9 George, the eldest son of this second bed. **1807** CRABBE *Par. Reg.* I. 485 And hoped, when wed, For loves fair favours, and a fruitful bed. **1832** SIR E. BRYDGES *Geneva* III. 104 A younger brother..One of a numerous bed.

3. *gen.* A sleeping-place generally; any extemporized resting-place for the night.

a **1300** *Cursor M.* 902 In cald sal euer be þi bedde. *c* **1440** *Gesta Rom.* i. 4 Encresing of his peyne in þe bed of hell. **1590** SHAKS. *Mids. N.* II. ii. 39 Finde you out a bed, For I vpon this banke will rest my head. **1598** —— *Merry W.* III. i. 20 There will we make our Beds of Roses. **1877** BRYANT *Odyss.* v. 579 Ulysses heaped a bed Of leaves.

4. *fig.* The grave: usually with some qualification, as *narrow bed*, or contextual indication.

a **1300** *Cursor M.* 6962 Iosep banis..þai haue graued in erþe bed. **1535** COVERDALE *Job* xvii. 13 The graue is my house, and I must make my bed in the darcke [WYCLIF In dercnessis I beddede my bed]. **1611** SHAKS. *Cymb.* IV. iv. 52 If in your Country warres you chance to dye, That is my Bed to. **1793** BURNS *Scots wha hae*, Welcome to your gory bed, Or to victorie. **1817** WOLFE *Burial Sir J. Moore* v. 1 As we hollowed his narrow bed.

5. The resting-place of an animal, *esp.* one strewed or made up for a domestic beast.

1697 DRYDEN *Virg. Georg.* III. 813 The Water-Snake..lyes poyson'd in his Bed. **1726** THOMSON *Winter* 831 He makes his bed beneath th' inclement drift. **1831** YOUATT *Horse* vi. (1872) 126 The bed of the horse, viz. wheat and oat straw. **1853** 'STONEHENGE' *Greyhound* 242 Clean straw..for her [a greyhound] to make her bed on.

6. Phrases and locutions belonging to prec. senses:

a. Qualified by an adj. or attributive sb., as ***bridal bed, nuptial bed***, the bed in which a newly-married pair sleep; ***narrow bed***, the grave; ***wedlock bed*** = MARRIAGE-BED, q.v.

1667 MILTON *P.L.* IV. 710 With flow'rs..Espoused Eve deck'd first her nuptial bed. **1796** SCOTT *Will. & Helen* xli, To-night I ride, with my young bride, To deck our bridal bed. **1819** —— *Noble Moringer* i, In wedlock bed he lay. **1854** *Househ. Words* VIII. 427 There is another bed to come —the grave..Poetry names it the 'narrow bed.'

b. Qualified by prep. phrase, as *bed of death* = DEATH-BED, also used as synonymous with next; ***bed of dust***, the grave; ***bed of down, flowers, roses***, (*fig.*) a delightful resting-place, a comfortable or easy position; ***bed of honour, honour's bed***, (*spec.*) the grave of a soldier who has died on the field of battle; ***bed of pleasure***; ***bed of sickness*** (cf. SICK-BED) that upon which a person lies during illness; ***bed of state***, a superb and finely decorated bed for show, or for laying out the corpse of a distinguished person (see STATE-BED).

1549–59 *Bk. Com. Prayer, Visit. Sick*, Look down..upon this child now lying upon the bed of sickness. **1604** SHAKS. *Oth.* I. iii. 232 Custome..Hath made the flinty..Coach of Warre My thrice-driuen bed of downe. **1648** HERRICK *Hesper., Connub. Flor.*, Go then discreetly to the bed of pleasure. *Ibid. To Mrs. Eliz. Herrick*, Thy bed of roses. **1663** BUTLER *Hud.* I. iii. 147 If he that in the field is slain Be in the bed of honour lain. **1676** C. JEAFFRESON in *Young Squire* (1877) Those [English] behaved themselves gallantly, and were most of them layd in the bed of honour. **1713** *Lond. Gaz.* 5099/1 The Corps of the late King is expos'd in a Bed of State. **1735** POPE *Prol. Sat.* 408 Smooth the bed of death. **1747** *Gent. Mag.* XVII. 326 In that Bed of Dust, I leave him to repose till a General Resurrection. **1764** GOLDSM. *Trav.* 86 These rocks by custom turn to beds of down. **1777** ROBERTSON *Hist. Amer.* v. Wks. (1831) 890/1 Am I now reposing on a bed of flowers? **1806** LD. CASTLEREAGH 3 Apr. in *Cobbett's Parl. Debates* (1806) VI. 707 The present administration may be considered as on a Bed of Roses. **1834** MARY HOWITT *Sk. Nat. Hist.* (1851) 105 That soldiers die upon honour's bed! **1838** T. JACKSON *E. Meth. Preachers* (1846) I. 377 My death-bed is a bed of roses.

c. Verbal phrases: ***to bring to bed, a-bed***, formerly = put to bed; now generally passive, to be delivered of a child; also *fig.* (see also ABED); ***to die in one's bed***: to die at home or of 'natural causes,' as opposed to violent death in war, persecution, etc.; ***to go to bed***: (*a*) to go to lie down to sleep; (*b*) *fig.* (of a newspaper, journal, etc.), to go to press (cf. sense 11), start printing; also, ***to see, put*** (a paper) ***to bed***; (*c*) *colloq.*, to have sexual intercourse (*with*), have a sexual relationship (*with* someone); †***to have one's bed***: to give birth to a child, 'lie in'; ***to keep one's bed***: to remain in bed through sickness or other cause; ***to leave one's bed***: to recover from sickness; ***to make a bed***: to put a bed in order after it has been used; ***to lie*** or ***sleep in the bed one has made*** (fig. extension of prec.): to accept the natural fruits or results of one's own conduct; ***to make up a bed***: to prepare sleeping accommodation not previously available; ***to take a bed, to bed*** = 'bring to bed' (see above); also *fig.*; ***to take to one's bed***: to become confined to bed through sickness or infirmity.

c **1320** *Seuyn Sages* (W.) 525 An even late, the emperowr Was browt to bedde with honour. *c* **1530** LD. BERNERS *Arth. Lyt. Bryt.* (1814) 540 Florence was brought a bed, and had a fayre sonne. **1649** LD. HERBERT *Hen. VIII*, 66 The Queene ..being brought to bed of a daughter. **1685** *Gracian's Courtier's Orac.* 161 There are some artificial men, that..are brought to bed of mistakes. **1742** JARVIS *Quix.* I. I. vi, The knights eat, sleep, and die in their beds. **1205** LAY. 711 A þeon time..þonne men gað to bedde. **1377** LANGL. *P. Pl.* B. Prol. 43 In glotonye, god it wote gon hij to bedde. **1601** SHAKS. *Twel. N.* II. iii. 7 To go to bed after midnight, is to goe to bed betimes. **1859** SALA *Tw. round Clock* 35 For the 'Times'—the mighty 'Times'—has 'gone to bed'. **1933** M. LUTYENS *Forthcoming Marriages* 197 He nearly always had to stay on at the office till after midnight when the paper 'went to bed'. **1945** A. HUXLEY *Time must have Stop* iv. 46 How much less awful the man would be..if only he sometimes lost his temper,..or went to bed with his secretary. **1962** J. WAIN *Strike Father Dead* vi. 264 'If you go to bed with a man, he won't marry you,' she used to say. 'Every girl knows that.' **1963** A. HERON *Towards Quaker View of Sex* v. 44 A young doctor..may think it all right to propose 'going to bed' to a nurse he has only just met. **1848** MRS. GASKELL *M. Barton* (1882) 1 My Mary expects to have her bed in three weeks. **1534** TINDALE *Acts* ix. 33 A certayne man whych had kepte hys bed viii. yere. *c* **1590** MARLOWE *Faust.* (2nd vers.) 981 All this day the sluggard keeps his bed. **1828** SCOTT *F.M. Perth* xvi, To speak plainly, she keeps her bed. **1742** JARVIS *Quix.* I. I. vii, Two days after, when Don Quixote left his bed. **1598** SHAKS. *Merry W.* I. iv. 102, I wash, ring, brew..make the beds, and doe all my selfe. **1745** SWIFT *Direct. Servants* Wks. 1756 VII. 404 Your master's bed is made..lock the chamber door. **1832** HONE *Year Bk.* 1301 He would not allow his bed to be made oftener than once a-week. **1883** FLOR. NIGHTINGALE in *Quain's Dict. Med.* s.v. *Nursing*, A true nurse always knows how to make a bed, and always makes it herself. **1753** HANWAY *Trav.* I. III. xxxi. 136 They might sleep in the bed which they had made. **1878** LADY BARKER *Bedr. & Boudoir* iii. 42 This could be removed at night, and the bed made up in the usual way. **1951** M. DICKENS *My Turn to make Tea* iii. 31 We went to press, or, as we liked to say in our nonchalant Fleet Street jargon, we put the paper to bed. **1899** *Daily News* 30 Sept. 6/1 Night by night he remained at the office till the last, seeing the paper to bed (to use the old-fashioned phrase), and examining the first copies printed. **1883** *Harper's Mag.* Dec. 135 By-and-by he took to his bed.

d. Prepositional phrases: *in, to, out of bed.*

1382 WYCLIF *Luke* xi. 7 My children ben with me in bed. **1742** JARVIS *Quix.* I. I. vii, They found him already out of bed. **1761** CHURCHILL *Night*, Poems (1769) I. 78 'Till vain Prosperity retires to bed. **1790** MRS. ADAMS *Lett.* (1848) 349 She has not been out of bed since. **1875** JOWETT *Plato* (ed. 2) I. 129 Prodicus was still in bed.

7. ***bed of justice*** (Fr. *lit de justice*): a bed adorned in a particular way in the French king's bedchamber, where he gave receptions; *spec.* the throne of the king in the Parliament of Paris; also, a sitting of this parliament at which the king was present. As the king sometimes convened the parliament to enforce the registration of his own decrees, the term came to be chiefly or exclusively applied to sessions held for this purpose.

1753 CHAMBERS *Cycl. Suppl.*, *Bed of justice*..is only held on affairs relating to the state. **1787** T. JEFFERSON *Writ.* II. (1859) 251 The King has been obliged to hold a bed of justice, to enforce the registering of new taxes. **1837** CARLYLE *Fr. Rev.* I. III. iv. 102 On the morrow, this Parlement..declares all that was done on the prior day to be null, and the Bed of Justice as good as a futility. **1875** STUBBS *Const. Hist.* II. xv. 265 The..bed of justice, in which the king..solemnly attested the decisions..put in form by parliament.

II. The flat base or surface on which anything rests.

8. A level or smooth piece of ground in a garden, usually somewhat raised, for the better cultivation of the plants with which it is filled; also used to include the plants themselves which grow in it.

c **1000** *Sax. Leechd.* I. 96 Ðeos wyrt..bið cenned..on wyrtbeddum. *Ibid.* 98 Ðeos wyrt..bið cenned..on hreod-beddon. **1475** *Bk. Noblesse* 70 The gardyns..rengid withe beddis bering..divers herbis. **1535** COVERDALE *Song Sol.* v. 13 His chekes are like a garden bedd. **1632** MILTON *Allegro*, Beds of violets blue. **1690** LOCKE *Hum. Und.* II. xxix. (1695) 198 If I believed, that Sempronia digged Titus out of the Parsley-Bed, as they use to tell Children, and thereby became his Mother. **1727** SWIFT *Country Post* Wks. 1755 III. I. 175 Not a turnip or carrot can lie safe in their beds. **1847** TENNYSON *Princess* ii. 416 The long hall glitter'd like a bed of flowers.

fig. **1647** WARD *Simp. Cobbler* 22 The bed of Truth is green all the yeare long.

9. The bottom of a lake or sea, or of the channel of a river or stream.

a **1586** SIDNEY in *Sel. Poetry* (Parker Soc.) I. 67 On sea's discovered bed. **1610** SHAKS. *Temp.* v. i. 151, I wish My selfe were mudded in that oozie bed. *c* **1645** HOWELL *Lett.* IV. xix, Rivers..have still the same beds. **1779** *Phil. Trans.*

LXIX. 609 While the volume of water in the bed of a river increases. **1814** SCOTT *Ld. of Isles* III. xii, A wild stream.. Came crawling down its bed of rock. **1830** LYELL *Princ. Geol.* I. 85 Donati explored the bed of the Adriatic.

10. An extended base upon which anything rests firmly or securely, or in which it is embedded; a basis, a matrix.

1633 T. STAFFORD *Pac. Hib.* xvi. (1821) 175 Ready to make a bed for the placing of the powder. **1676** GREW *Luctation* ii. §2 Bolus's are the Beds, or as it were, the *Materia prima*, both of opacous Stones, and Metals. **1803** WELLINGTON *Mem.* in Gurw. *Disp.* I. 487 A bed for the boat ought to be fixed on each axle tree. **1839** HOOPER *Med. Dict.* (ed. 7) 1218 Shock.. sufficient to shoot off an ovulum from its bed. **1859** TODD *Cycl. Anat. & Phys.* V. 477/1 In the dog and cat the bed of the claw is laminated as in man.

11. A level surface on which anything rests, *e.g.* the level surface in a printing press on which the form of type is laid; the flat surface of a billiard-table, which is covered with green cloth; etc.

1846 *Print. Appar. Amateur* 10 The press.. consists of two stout blocks of mahogany; the lower piece called the bed .. the upper piece called the platten, which closes upon the bed.

12. In various technical uses (from 10 and 11): **a.** *Gunnery.* The portion of a gun-carriage upon which the gun rests; formerly *spec.* a movable block of wood laid under the breech to give the general elevation, quoins being driven between it and the gun.

b. *Arch.* and *Building.* The surface of a stone or brick which is embedded in the mortar; the under side of a slate.

c. *Mech.* Any foundation, framework, or support, which furnishes a solid or unyielding surface upon which to rest a superstructure, or execute a piece of work.

d. *Carpentry.* A support or rest, *e.g.* for a ship on the stocks, for the lodging of a bowsprit, etc.

e. *Railway-making.* The layer of broken stone, gravel, clay, etc., upon which the rails are laid.

f. The body of a cart or wagon. *dial.* and *U.S.*

a. 1598 BARRET *Theor. Warres* v. iii. 135 Certaine cariages, or beds for the Artillery. **1694** LUTTRELL *Brief Rel.* (1857) III. 387 The new mortars.. are laid in beds of brasse. **1811** WELLINGTON in Gurw. *Disp.* VII. 569 Have the carriages of the 24 pounders, as well as the mortar beds and howitzer carriages.. put in a state to be fit for service. **1816** C. JAMES *Mil. Dict.* s.v., Sea-Mortar-beds are.. made of solid timber .. having a hole in the center to receive the pintle or strong iron bolt, about which the bed turns. **1862** F. GRIFFITHS *Artill. Man.* (ed. 9) 127 A 13-inch mortar, and its bed, require each a waggon.

b. 1677 MOXON *Mech. Exerc.* (1703) 245 The bed of the Brick, (viz. that side which lies in the Morter). **1816** C. JAMES *Mil. Dict.* (ed. 4) s.v. *Bed of Stone*, The joint of the bed is the mortar between two stones placed over each other. **1823** P. NICHOLSON *Pract. Build.* 384 Bed of a Brick.—The horizontal surface as disposed in a wall. **1842** GWILT *Archit.* (1876) 655 The bed of a slate is its under side. *Ibid.* 1194 In general language the beds.. are the surfaces where the stones or bricks meet.

c, d. 1793 SMEATON *Edystone L.* §201 It is beat by iron-headed Stampers upon an iron bed. **1823** P. NICHOLSON *Pract. Build.* 242 [In a Plane] the bed.. is the aperture in the stock, upon which the iron is laid, and secured by the wedge. The angle of the bed.. is generally from 42 to 45 degrees. **1831** J. HOLLAND *Manuf. Metal* I. 198 Cut the nails out with a bed and punch. **1881** *Mechanic* §581 A good working lathe with strong wooden standards and wooden 3 ft. bed. *c* **1860** H. STUART *Seaman's Catech.* 74 Where it rests on the stem is the bed.

f. *c* **1700** KENNETT *B.M. MS. Lansdowne 1033*, Bedd of a cart, the body of it. **1851** MAYHEW *London Lab.* I. 26/2 Other commodities are laid in the bed of the cart. **1854** A. E. BAKER *Gloss. Northampt. Words, Bed...* 3. The body of a cart or waggon. **1873** J. H. BEADLE *Undevel. West* xxiv. 491 In this [bayou] we encountered dangerous whirls and jump-offs, the wagon often plunging in up to the bed. **1904** W. H. SMITH *Promoters* xviii. 270 Some of these beds will hold more than a hundred bushels. **1952** S. CLOETE *Curve & Tusk* (1953) i. 21 The hen stood near the truck because when they cleaned its bed, bits of meat often fell out on the ground.

III. A layer or bed-like mass.

13. a. A layer, a stratum; a horizontal course.

1616 SURFL. & MARKH. *Countr. Farm* 407 Lay them orderly in a vessel, hauing in the bottome of it a bed of Sauorie.. laying a bed of Sauorie, and a bed of Cherries. **1672** T. VENN *Compl. Gunner* xxxi. 51 Two foot high of Earth, bed upon bed, unto eleven foot high. **1725** POPE *Odyss.* IX. 449 The stake now glow'd beneath the burning bed. **1783** AINSWORTH *Lat. Dict.* (Morell) I, A bed of Sand, &c. *stratum*. **1833** TENNYSON *Poems* 84 Clusters and beds of worlds, and bee-like swarms Of suns. **1875** URE *Dict. Arts* II. 373 The filter-beds.. are large square beds of sand and gravel.

b. *Geol.* A layer or stratum of some thickness.

1684 RAY *Philos. Lett.* (1718) 166 That Bed of Sand and Cockle Shells found in sinking a well. **1793** SMEATON *Edystone L.* §106 The bed or stratum of freestone worked here. **1863** RAMSAY *Phys. Geol. Gt. Brit.* (1878) 254 In the Bembridge beds there has also been found the Anoplotheroid mammal. **1874** LYELL *Elem. Geol.* xxi. 355 The lowest 'bed' of the Lias. **1878** HUXLEY *Physiogr.* 28 The pervious substance being thus enclosed between two impervious beds, one forming its floor and the other its roof.

14. a. A layer of small animals, especially reptiles, congregated thickly in some particular spot. Cf. *nest* in a similar sense.

1608 SHAKS. *Per.* IV. ii. 155 Thunder shall not so awake the beds of eels. **1666** J. H. *Treat. Gt. Antidote* 10 This Medicene breaks the bed of Worms. **1692** R. LESTRANGE *Fables* 209 (1708) I. 228 Apt to run.. into a Bed of Scorpions. **1731** BAILEY, *Bed of Snakes*, a knot of young ones.

b. *esp.* A layer of shell-fish covering a tract of the bottom of the sea.

1688 R. HOLME *Armory* II. xiv 325 A Bed of Oysters, Muscles, and Cockles. **1865** PARKMAN *Huguenots* ix. (1875) 152 The channel was a bed of oysters. **1879** *Cassell's Techn. Educ.* IV. 97/1 The spat.. drifted.. from the natural beds.

IV. Various transferred uses.

15. A division of the ground in the game of 'hopscotch,' also called locally the game of 'beds.'

1801 STRUTT *Sports & Past.* IV. iv. 339 A parallelogram.. divided into compartments, which were called beds.

†**16.** The placenta or after-birth. *Obs.*

1611 COTGR., *Arguelette*, their bed, or after birth.. is more grosse.

17. The 'silver side' of a round of beef.

1864 *Derby Mercury* Dec., Good beef (beds and rounds taken off at the joints).

V. *Comb.* and *Attrib.*

18. General relations: **a.** attrib., as ***bed-apparel, -blanket, -board, -bolster, -bottom, -candle, -cap, -carriage, -case, -clothing, -curtain, -damask, -flea, -foot, -frame, -furniture, †-glee, -hangings, -head, -hour, -house, †-joiner, -knob, -mat, -mate, -pal, -place, -quilt, -rite (-right), -rug, †-sabbath,*** (a sabbath in bed), ***-sheet, -stand, -steps, -stuff, -tester, -thane***; **b.** objective gen. with verbal sb. or pple., as ***bed-bound, †-presser; -making, †-spreading.***

1822 BYRON *Werner* I. i. 264 Madame Idenstein.. shall furnish forth the *bed-apparel. **1701** *Lond. Gaz.* No. 3696/4 Fine Flannel *Bed-Blankets. **1530** PALSGR. 197/1 *Bedde borde, *sponde*. **1684** I. MATHER *Remark. Provid.* v. 104 When the man was.. a bed, his bed-board did rise out of its place. *a* **1000** ÆLFRIC *Gloss.* in Wr.-Wülcker *Voc.* 124 *Plumacius*, *bedbolster. **1922** *Daily Mail* 30 Nov. 14 It is often, however, a problem to know what to choose that will most amuse the girl or boy who is *bed-bound. **1961** *Guardian* 30 June 8/3 Another bed-bound reader edits the religious page. **1850** THACKERAY *Pendennis* II. xv. 146 Martha from Fairoaks appeared with a *bed-candle. **1858** TROLLOPE *Dr. Thorne* I. xi. 240 The doctor, taking his bed-candle.. left the room. **1864** MRS. GASKELL *French Life* i, in *Fraser's Mag.* Apr. 438/1 When we return from our party.. we.. light our own particular bed-candles at the dim little lamp. **1820** *Missouri Intell.* 18 Apr. 4/1 Bed Caps. **1921** W. DE LA MARE *Crossings* 39 In a high frilled *bed-cap, swaying balloon-like skirts. **1869** TROLLOPE *He knew he was Right* II. xcv. 354 We got a *bed-carriage [on a train] for him at Dover. **1889** F. E. GRETTON *Memory's Harkback* iv. 65 He never walked again, but was drawn about lying at full length in a sort of bed-carriage. **1557** *Lanc. & Chesh. Wills* 71, I bequethe all my harnes and all the *bedcasis, etc. **1852** H. B. STOWE *Uncle Tom's Cabin* xxxii, A tattered blanket.. formed his only *bed-clothing. **1774** *Phil. Trans.* LXV. 274 We have seen.. *bed-fleas.. swarming at the mouths of these holes. **1483** *Cath. Angl.* 24 A *Bedfute, *fultrum*. **1670** COTTON *Espernon* III. xii. 647 He had.. a Crucifix fastned to his Beds-feet. **1865** SWINBURNE *Poems & Ball.*, *Xmas Carol* 46 The bedstead shall be gold two spans, The bedfoot silver fine. **1815** SCOTT *Guy M.* xliv, Iron *bedframes and straw mattresses. **1861** MRS. BEETON *Bk. Househ. Managem.* 993 The *bed-furniture requires changing. **1583** STANYHURST *Æneis* IV. (Arb.) 91 Had not I such daliaunce, such pipling *bed-gle renounced. **1566** *Eng. Ch. Furnit.* (1866) 100 Fyve banner clothes.. and he haith made *bedd hengings therof. **1864** *Chambers's Jrnl.* 8 Oct. 642 Hair like the fringe to bed-hangings. **1579** FULKE *Confut. Sanders* 649 He worshipped toward the *bedshead. **1853** KANE *Grinnell Exp.* v. (1856) 35 The temptation to avoid a regular *bed-hour was sometimes irresistible. **1881** DU CHAILLU *Land Midnt. Sun* II. 276 A larder and a separate *bed-house. **1725** *Lond. Gaz.* No. 6385/4 Richard Bedersley.. *Bed-Joyner. **1927** W. DE LA MARE *Stuff & Nonsense* 74 A visage, with eyes like brass *bed-knobs. **1931** J. MOCKFORD *Khama* xxxi. 222 The women-folk follow after, balancing *bed-mats and food-baskets on their heads. **1583** STANYHURST *Æneis* III. (Arb.) 75 With iealosie kindled Orestes For los of his *bed-mate. **1850** BLACKIE *Æschylus* I. 157 He was thy bed-mate living, Be then his comrade, dead. **1922** JOYCE *Ulysses* 40 Papa's little *bedpal. Lump of love. **1566** T. NUCE *Seneca's Octavia* (1581) 177 Fasten Poppie sure in our *bed-place. **1833** MARRYAT *P. Simple* (1863) 362 Retired to my standing bed-place in the cabin. **1598** SHAKS. *1 Hen. IV*, II. iv. 268 This sanguine Coward, this *Bed-presser. **1601** CORNWALLYES *Ess.* (1632) xviii, Fame never knew a perpetuall Bedpresser. **1765** in E. Singleton *Social N.Y.* (1902) 334 Knoting for *Bed Quilts or Toilets. **1803** MRS. E. BOWNE *Let.* 8 July (1888) 164 One poor bed quilt is all I have towards housekeeping. *a* **1847** MRS. SHERWOOD *Lady of Manor* vi. 193 A patch-work bedquilt. **1610** SHAKS. *Temp.* IV. i. 96 No *bed-right shall be paid Till Hymens Torch be lighted. **1647** in *Probate Rec. (Essex Co., Mass.)* (1916) I. 78 An old Straw bed and Creadle Rugg with an old *Bed Rugg. **1850** *Knickerbocker* XXXVI. 73 Open the door and the gentle breeze from without will waft aside the blue woollen 'bed-rug'. **1684** P. HENRY *Diaries & Lett.* (1882) 323, Feb. 23, a *Bed-Sabbath, few such, cup'd and blister'd. **1481–90** *Howard Househ. Bks.* 274, Iiij. peir schitz for my Lord, [and] ij. *bedschitz. *a* **1930** D. H. LAWRENCE *Last Poems* (1932) 217 Who is it smooths the bed-sheets? **1610** HEALEY *City of God* 132 The Sybils bookes directed the first *Bed-spreading to last eight dayes. **1833** LOUDON *Encycl. Archit.* §2135 A set of *bed-steps, with two of the steps arranged as cupboards. **1535** COVERDALE *2 Sam.* xvii. 28 And Barsillai.. broughte *bed-stuffe, tapestrie worke. **1704** *Lond. Gaz.* No. 4068/4 Old Serge *Bed-Testers. **1843** CARLYLE *Misc.* (1857) IV. 269 For bed-tester is the canopy of everlasting blue. **1922** JOYCE *Ulysses* 379 Truest *bedthanes they twain are, for Horne holding wariest ward.

19. Special combinations: †**bed-ale** (see quot.); †**bed-bere**, a pillow-case; **bed-bolster, -bolt**, in *Gunnery* (see quots.); **bed-book**, a book suitable for reading in bed; **bed-bottle**, a bottle for urination for the use of male patients in bed; also, a bottle for heating a bed; †**bed-broker**, a pander, pimp; **bed-card**, a card fixed at the head of a hospital patient's bed, giving a statement of the 'case'; **bed-chair**, a chair for the sick, with a movable back, to support them while sitting up in bed; **bed-coach**, a coach with sleeping accommodation; †**bed-company; bed-cord**, a cord for stretching the sacking of a bed; **bed-cover**, (*a*) a covering or case for a feather- or flock-bed, etc.; (*b*) a bed-quilt (Webster 1828); **bed-eel** (see quot.); †**bed-evil**, illness that confines to bed; †**bed-game**; †**bed-gang, -gate**, going to bed; †**bed-geld** (see quot.); **bed-irons**, the iron framework for a bed (cf. *fire-irons*); **bed-jacket**, a short jacket worn by women sitting up in bed; **bed-joint**, (*a*) a split or parting in a rock parallel to the surface of the earth; (*b*) *Building*, a horizontal joint (cf. sense 12 b); **bed-key**, an iron tool for screwing and unscrewing the nuts and bolts of a bedstead; **bed-lift**, a canvas stretched by a wooden frame, with an aperture in the centre for defæcation, upon which a patient may be raised (*Syd. Soc. Lex.*); **bed-litter**, straw, etc. to make up a bed; **bedlock** *noncewd.* = WEDLOCK; †**bed-loft** (transl. of L. *pulvinar*), a couch made of cushions, upon which images of the gods were placed at festivals; †**bed-match**, marriage, wedlock; **bed-moulding** (*arch.*), 'the mouldings under a projection, as the corona of a cornice' (Gwilt); **bed-piece** (*Mech.*), the foundation or support of any mechanical structure; **bed-plane** *Geol.*, the junction between two layers or strata; **bed-plate** = *bed-piece* above; **bed-rest**, (*a*) a support for a person in bed; (*b*) confinement of a sick person to bed; **bedroll**, †(*a*) a list of women to sleep with *Obs.*; (*b*) *U.S.* and *N.Z.* bedding rolled into a bundle for carrying; **bed-sack**, 'a sack made to hold (army) bedclothes for convenience of carrying them' (D.A.E.); **bed-screw**, a screw used for holding together the posts and beams of a wooden bedstead; also, a powerful machine for lifting heavy bodies, often used in launching vessels; †**bed-seller** (see quot.); **bed-settee**, a settee that can be converted into a bed; **bed-sick**, sick and in bed; †**bed-sister**, the mistress of a married man in relation to his lawful wife; **bed-sock**, a sock worn in bed; **bed-sore**, a soreness of the skin produced by long lying in bed; **bed-stone**, a large heavy stone used as the foundation and support of girders, etc. in building; also, the lower stone in an oil-mill, on which the runners roll; **bed-string** (= *bed-cord*); †**bed-swerver**, one unfaithful to the marriage-bed; **bed table**, a small table or tray usually with a ledge at the back and sides, adapted for placing on or over the bed of an invalid person; **bed-vow**, promise of fidelity to the marriage-bed; **bed-warmer**, a device for warming a bed; **bed-way** in *Geol.* (see quot.); **bed-ways** *adv.*, in the direction of the beds or strata; **bed-wetting** *vbl. sb.*, incontinence of urine while in bed; hence ***bed-wet*** v., ***bed-wetter***; **bed-winch, -wrench**, an instrument for tightening up or loosening the screws of bedsteads; †**bedwoman**, a woman confined to bed; †**bed-work**, work that is or can be done in bed or without toil, easy work; **bed-worthy** *a. colloq.*, sexually attractive; hence ***bed-worthiness.***

1880 *W. Cornw. Gloss.* (E.D.S.), **Bed-ale*, groaning ale; ale brewed for a christening. **1420** *E.E. Wills* (1882) 41 That Anneys Tukkysworthe have þe beste *bedbere. **1769** FALCONER *Dict. Marine* (1789) C c iv, On the fore-part of the bed a piece of timber is placed transversely, upon which rests the belly of the mortar.. This piece is called the *bed-bolster. *Ibid.* I iv, The *bed-bolt, upon which the bed rests to support the breech of the cannon. **1906** A. BENNETT *Whom God hath Joined* i. 49 'Dip into it anywhere. It's a *bed-book.'.. Both Lawrence and Mark had read in bed every night of their lives. **1928** *Publishers' Weekly* 9 June 2373 'Cranford' was one of the favorite bed-books of the late A. C. Benson. **1907** N. MUNRO *Daft Days* i. 1 The burgh town turned on its pillows, drew up its feet from the *bed-bottles, last night hot, now turned to chilly stone. **1950** 'G. ORWELL' *Shooting an Elephant* 21 The bedbottles and the grim bedpan. **1592** DANIEL *Compl. Rosamond* (1717) 58 And fly.. these *Bed-Brokers unclean. **1885** *Standard* 4 Aug. 3/7 A *bed-card bearing on the case had been taken away. **1685** BP. BURNET *Trav. France* iii. (1752) 96 His was a huge *bed-coach, all the outside black veluet. *a* **1555** LATIMER *Serm. & Rem.* (1845) 101 The lawful *bed-company that is between married folks. *a* **1625** FLETCHER *Nt. Walker* v. i, With the *bed-cord he may pass for a porter. **1720** GAY *Poems* (1745) II. 59 Beneath the frighted guest The bed-cords trembled. **1874** J. W. LONG *Wild-Fowl Shooting* 107 All you need to

carry besides your ordinary bed-clothes is a common bed-cord. **1886** *Harper's Mag.* June 58/2 Traces are made of hickory or papaw, as also are bed-cords. **1828** WEBSTER, *Rug*,..in America, I believe,..is applied only to a *bed cover for ordinary beds, and to a covering before a fire-place. **1837** *United Service Jrnl.* June 107 Those bed-covers which our grandmamas were delighted to cobble together. **1967** E. SHORT *Embroidery & Fabric Collage* iii. 67 Three of the most popular forms of embroidery for bed-covers, namely quilting, patchwork and candlewick. **1769** PENNANT *Zool.* III. 112 A variety of small eel..that is found in clusters in the bottom of the river, and is called the *Bed-eel. **1609** SKENE *Reg. Maj.* 107 Na defaulte nor essonzie of law, bot gif it be *mal de lit*, that is *bed evill. **1602** WARNER *Alb. Eng.* XI. lxi. (1612) 268 But deified swore he him her *bed-game sweets might taste. *a* **1300** *E.E. Psalter* lv. 2 Dreried I am in mi *bed-gange. *c* **1440** *Morte Arth.* (Roxb.) 1030 Thre balefulle birdez..That byddez his *bedgatt. **1483** *Cath. Angl.* 25 Bedgate, *conticinium, concubium.* **1844** R. HART *Antiq. Norfolk* xxiv. 79 *Bedgeld was the fine paid to the lord on the marriage of his vassal. **1863** *Cornh. Mag.* Mar. 446 The *bed-irons are turned up. **1914** MILLICENT, DUCHESS OF SUTHERLAND *Six Weeks at War* ii. 21 Our nurses cut out red flannel *bed-jackets and tried to take photographs. **1919** H. WALPOLE *Secret City* III. xii. 405 An old quilted bed-jacket of a purple green colour. **1747** HOOSON *Miner's Dict.* L iij b, In some..Veins..the *Bed-joynts themselves will often carry it a little aside. **1876** *Encycl. Brit.* IV. 305/2 The *joints*, or bed-joints, are the surfaces separating the voussoirs. **1861** WYNTER *Soc. Bees* 343 Winding up some moaning machinery with a *bed-key. *c* **1425** in Wright *Voc.* 199 *Hoc stratum*, *bed-lytter. **1922** JOYCE *Ulysses* 483 Born out of *bedlock hereditary epilepsy is present, the consequence of unbridled lust. **1606** HOLLAND *Sueton.* 60 *marg.*, The *bedloft wher the sacred Images of the Gods were devoutly bestowed. **1583** STANYHURST *Æneis* IV. (Arb.) 96 Juno, the chaplain, Seams vp the *bedmatch. **1703** *Chatsworth Build. Accts.* in *Jrnl. Derbysh. Archæol. Soc.* III. 39 The lower member of the *bedmolding of the cornice. **1727–51** CHAMBERS *Cycl.* s.v., A bed-moulding usually consists of these four members, an O-G, a list, a large boultine, and another list under the coronet. **1895** DANA *Man. Geol.* (ed. 4) 111 *Bed-plane faults are still another kind in which the plane of displacement is that between two layers or strata. **1850** *Ann. Rep. Commissioner Patents 1849* (U.S.) 211 This is combined with the *bed plate for guiding and keeping the edge of the tire true. **1850** N. KINGSLEY *Diary* (1914) 107 Putting in timbers to set the bed-plates to the Engines. **1959** *Times* 19 Nov. 14/6 That there winch'd lift straight out of its bedplate. **1964** *McCall's Sewing* v. 69/2 Close the bed plate. **1968** *Gloss. Terms Offset Lithogr. Printing (B.S.I.)* 36 *Bed plate*, the component upon which is mounted the main structure of a printing machine. **1872** GEO. ELIOT *Middlem.* II. xiv. 233 His uncle..propped up comfortably on a *bed-rest. **1899** R. WHITEING *No. 5 John St.* xvii. 172 This spring lowers the bed-rest, so as he can sit up an' read. **1950** *New Engl. Jrnl. Med.* CCXLIII. 486 Bed rest has long been the *sine qua non* in the treatment of myocardial infarction. **1958** *Times* 15 Oct. 19/2 So effective is the modern treatment of pulmonary tuberculosis that the traditional sanatorium treatment..with its prolonged bed-rest..is seldom necessary. *a* **1652** R. BROME *Madd Couple Well Matcht* III. i, But why me up in your *bedroll George? **1910** S. E. WHITE *Rules of Game* vi. 203 Thus instead of his 'turkey'—or duffle-bag—he speaks of his 'bed-roll', and by that term means not only his sleeping equipment but often all his worldly goods. **1916** H. KEPHART *Camping & Woodcr.* II. 136 A bed roll made with flaps and sides and ends is best for this purpose. **1950** G. WILSON *Brave Company* 20, I can distinguish the long vermouth stain above Hope's bedroll. **1958** *Landfall* XII. 115 When he had spread out his bedroll, the little man came out of his cell. **1661** in *Probate Rec. (Essex Co., Mass.)* (1916) I. 323 A *bead sacke,..a cheste. **1861** *Revised Regulations U.S. Army* 169 Bed-sacks are provided for troops in garrison. **1757** in *Phil. Trans.* L. 289 There were set up, under the wales..of the ship..nine pair of *bed-screws. **1832** BABBAGE *Econ. Manuf.* xvii. 153 Bed-screws, 6 inches long. **1553** *Lanc. Wills* (1857) I. 91 Y^e courtens and hangings bed-stocke and *beddseller of ye same. **1933** *Discovery* July 219/1 There is a demand for less and smaller furniture..and for the dual-purpose piece—the table-bookcase, table-stool, even *bed-settee, which converts the living room into a bedroom for the unexpected guest. **1958** *House & Garden* Feb. 21 (Advt.), Here at last is a bed-settee... To convert the settee into a bed the back is simply swung down. **1961** *B.S.I. News* Nov. 20/2 Bed-settee mattresses. *c* **1550** SIR J. BALFOUR *Practicks* (1754) 361 If it be provin..that he is *bed-seik and may not travel. **1611** BARKSTED *Hirem* (1876) 81 Like to a man Rich and full cram'd..Yet lyes bed-sicke. **1297** R. GLOUC. 27 Astrilde hire *bedsuster (hire lordes concubine). **1870** L. M. ALCOTT *Old-Fashioned Girl* iii. 43 She began to knit a pretty pair of white *bed-socks..for her mother. **1914** W. OWEN *Let.* 1 Jan. (1967) 225 And only one bed-sock. **1934** L. A. G. STRONG *Corporal Tune* 266 Continuing to read even while she pulled great clumsy bedsocks up his shrunken legs. **1861** FLOR. NIGHTINGALE *Nursing* 57 Where there is any danger of *bed-sores a blanket should never be placed under the patient. **1878** T. BRYANT *Pract. Surg.* I. 34 In theory bed-sores should never occur. **1723** S. MORLAND *Spec. Lat. Dict.* 6 Nor have they the least mention of *Bed-stone in the English. **1862** *Report E. Midl. R'way Co.* 26, Pier No. 14..has the bedstones for the girders set. **1848** THACKERAY *Van. Fair* v. (1853) 31 They cut his *bed-strings. **1611** SHAKS. *Wint. T.* II. i. 93 Shee's A *Bed-swaruer. **1811** *London Cabinet-Makers Book of Prices* 314 A *Bed-Table. All solid.—Two feet five inches long. **1853** MRS. GASKELL *Cranford* xi. 208 Lady Glenmire..rummaged up all Mrs. Jamieson's medicine glasses, and spoons, and bed-tables. **1894** *Daily News* 28 June 6/3 In white enamelled wood are some bed tables... They are for resting on the knees while sitting up in bed. **1948** L. A. G. STRONG *Trevannion* 167 Mrs. Bracegirdle drew up a rosewood bed-table, which fitted right across the bed, and slid her tray upon it. **1600** SHAKS. *Sonn.* clii, Thy *bed-vow broake and new faith torne. **1922** JOYCE *Ulysses* 200 But she, the giglot wanton, did not break a bedvow. **1931** *Kansas City Star* 2 Sept., One electric *bed warmer. **1933** W. DE LA MARE *Lord Fish* 101 A ship's compass, a brass cannon, a bed-warmer,..—such curios as that. **1881** RAYMOND *Mining Gloss.*, **Bed-way*, an appearance of stratification, or parallel marking in granite. **1883** *Stonemason* Jan., The blocks..are usually sawn through bedways about two feet from the top. **1952** S. SPENDER *Learning Laughter* viii. 112 The children don't only suck their thumbs. They also *bed-wet. **1938** *Time* 16 May 72/3 *Bed-Wetters Belled. **1940** MRS. ST. L. STRACHEY *Borrowed Children* v. 69 As the younger evacuee was a bed-wetter..the billet-mother said she could not keep the younger. **1969** *New Scientist* 16 Jan. 148/3 Mousepie, still made in country districts for bed-wetters. **1890** J. MCGREGOR-ROBERTSON *Househ. Physic.* xv. 463 **Bed-wetting*..is due very often to the presence of some irritant in the bowels. **1940** HARRISSON & MADGE *War begins at Home* xii. 310 Bed-wetting was one of the main faults found with evacuee children. **1848** DICKENS *Dombey* lix. 592 The men with the carpet-caps gather up their screw-drivers and *bed-winches into bags. **1568** R. BERTIE in Lady Bertie *Loyal Ho.* (1845) 42 Though she continue a *bedwoman and not a footwoman. **1606** SHAKS. *Tr. & Cr.* I. iii. 203 They call this *Bed-worke, Mapp'ry, Closset-Warre. **1959** T. GIRTIN *Unnatural Break* xxi. 72 Certificate of *Bedworthiness, eh? **1936** A. HUXLEY *Eyeless in Gaza* liv. 608 In fact, thoroughly *bed-worthy. Or at least he looks it. Because one never really knows till one's tried, does one? **1954** J. B. PRIESTLEY *Magicians* ii. 38 Bed-worthy luscious blonde. **1844** *Regul. & Ord. Army* 235 See that the different parts of the bedsteads are properly screwed together, (for which purpose a *bed-wrench is to be hung in every room).

bed, *v.* Pa. t. and pple. bedded. Forms: 1 beddian, 2–3 beddi-en, 3 beddy, 2–5 bedd-e(n, 4–7 bedde, 6– bed. [OE. *beddian* f. *bed(d)*, BED.]

I. Connected with a bed for sleeping.

†**1.** *intr.* To spread or prepare a bed. Const. *dat.*; also with *cognate object. Obs.*

a **1000** in Thorpe's *Laws* II. 282 (Bosw.) Féde þearfan, and beddiȝe him. *a* **1000** *Sax. Leechd.* III. 140 Bedde hys bed myd mór-secȝe. **1382** WYCLIF *Job* xvii. 13 In dercnessis I beddede my bed.

2. a. *trans.* To lay in bed, put to bed; to furnish (a person) with a bed.

c **1200** ORMIN 2712 To wasshenn hem, to warrmenn hemm, To beddenn hemm & frofrenn. **1382** WYCLIF *1 Sam.* ix. 25 He beddide Saul in the solere, and he slepte. **1394** *P. Pl. Crede* 772 þey schulden nouȝt..bedden swiche broþels in so brode schetes. **1646** W. PRICE *Mans Delinq.* 20 It will not leave us, if we welcom and bed and board it. **1863** B. TAYLOR *Poet's Jrnl.* (1866) 35 Beds me in its balmy green. **1866** G. MACDONALD *Ann. Q. Neighb.* vii. (1878) 120 No end of work..to get them all bedded for the night.

b. *spec.* To put (a couple) to bed together.

a **1300** *Havelok* 1235 He sholen bedden hire and the. *a* **1639** W. WHATELEY *Prototypes* II. xxxi. (1640) 118 To see a stranger bedded with him instead of his owne Spouse. **1680** *Lond. Gaz.* No. 1494/4 The Dauphin and the Dauphiness were Bedded. *a* **1743** *Ld. Hervey's Mem.* Introd., Sure Venus had never seen bedded So lovely a beau and a belle.

3. To take (a wife) to bed. *arch.*

1548 HALL *Chron. Hen. VIII* (R.) She was both wedded and bedded with his brother Prince Arthur. **1596** SHAKS. *Tam. Shr.* I. i. 149 That would thoroughly woe her, wed her, and bed her, and ridde the house of her. **1653** HOLCROFT *Procopius* IV. 140 Askt him why he would neglect his Vow, and bed another Woman. **1740** L. CLARKE *Hist. Bible* I. i. 63 Jacob..then married and bedded Rachel.

4. Also with *down.* **a.** *intr.* To go to bed; to retire for the night.

1635 HEYWOOD *London's Sinus Salut.* 289 Rise earlie, and bed late. **1822** HOOD *Lycus* (1871) 61 The cave where I bedded. **1906** E. DYSON *Fact'ry 'Ands* ix. 117 Ther Firm and its missus was preparin' t'bed down. **1914** B. M. BOWER *Flying U Ranch* 7 Throw out your war-bag and make yourself to home, Mig-u-ell; some of the boys'll show you where to bed down. **1944** G. NETHERWOOD *Desert Squadron* 115 Being forced to spend the night in the desert there was nothing else to do but 'bed-down'.

b. *spec.* Said of a couple sleeping together.

c **1315** SHOREHAM 76 Ʒef thon thother profreth, Wyth any other to beddy. **1583** STANYHURST *Æneis* III. (Arb.) 79 Andromachee dooth bed with a countrye man husband. **1668** EVELYN *Mem.* (1857) II. 37 Sir Samuel Tuke, Bart., and the lady he had married this day, came and bedded at night at my house. **1740** H. CAREY *Sally in our Alley* vii, O then we'll wed, and then we'll bed, But not in our Alley. **1763** C. JOHNSTON *Reverie* II. 6 No man can bear to bed with such an ugly, filthy brute. **1938** N. MARSH *Artists in Crime* ix. 120 She meant to come back and bed down with Garcia..you know—to spend the night with him.

c. Of cattle: to be bedded *down* for the night. *U.S.*

1903 A. ADAMS *Log Cowboy* viii. 110 Not a hoof would bed down. **1920** MULFORD *J. Nelson* xxvi. 267 After..the great herd had bedded down.

†**5.** *fig.* To lodge, find a resting-place. *Obs.*

c **1175** *Lamb Hom.* 185 Eorþliche lou and heouenliche ne maȝen..beddin in a breoste. *a* **1220** *Hali Meid.* 43 Ne muhen ha nanes weis bedden in a breoste.

6. *trans.* To put (animals) to rest for the night; to provide with 'bedding' or litter for sleeping purposes. Also with *up*, *down.*

c **1480** *King & H.* 166, *E.P.P.* (1864) 20 Hys stede into the house he lede, With litter son he gan hym bed. *a* **1791** WESLEY *Wks.* (1872) VIII. 318 See..that your horse be rubbed, fed, and bedded. **1856** OLMSTED *Slave States* 380 They were obliged to bed their horses with pine leaves. **1859** *Art Taming Horses* xi. 188 My Lord, the horses are bedded up. **1863** *Cornh. Mag.* Mar. 448 Bedding down the horses and making them snug for the night.

7. *intr.* Of an animal; To make its lair; the specific term used of the roe.

c **1470** *Hors, Shepe, & G.* (1822) 33 A roo is bedded. **1610** GWILLIM *Heraldry* III. xiv. (1660) 166 You shall say that a Roe Beddeth. **1819** REES *Cycl.* s.v. *Bedding*, A roe is said to bed; a hart to harbour.

8. *trans.* To furnish (a room) with a bed. *rare.*

1758 MRS. CALDERWOOD *Jrnl.* (1884) 44 The captain has the cabin bedded at his expense.

II. Connected with a garden bed, a layer, base.

9. *trans.* To plant in or as in a garden bed; to plant deeply. *to bed out*: to plant out in a bed or beds.

1671 GREW *Anat. Plants* (1682) 28 Trunk-Roots newly bedded. *a* **1750** MORTIMER (J.) Mould to bed your quick in. *Mod.* May is rather too early to bed out your geraniums.

10. a. To sink or bury in a matrix of any kind, to cover up or fix firmly in any substance; to EMBED.

1586 HOOKER *Girald. Irel.* in *Holinsh.* II. 4/1 A place where the ships lie bedded. **1692** RAY *Disc.* II. iv. (1732) 200 The Minerals wherein they are bedded. **1803** *Phil. Trans.* XCIII. 142 Bedded and fixed firmly in a brass socket. **1874** MRS. WOOD *Mast. Greylands* xxvii. 320 The bullet..must have bedded itself in the wall.

fig. **1862** TRENCH *Mirac.* xxviii. 385 Testimonies..which ..not lying on the surface of Scripture, are bedded deeply in it.

b. *intr.* To rest *on*, to lie *on* for support. Also with *down.*

1875 URE *Dict. Arts* III. 692 The rail, therefore, beds throughout on the ballast. **1892** STEVENSON & OSBOURNE *Wrecker* xiii. 213 When she [*sc.* a boat] first struck and before she bedded down, seven or eight hours' work would have got this hooker off.

11. *Building. trans.* To lay (bricks or stones) in position in cement or mortar.

1685 BOYLE *Effects of Motion* viii. 104 Stones..taken out of the cement wherein they were bedded. **1823** P. NICHOLSON *Pract. Build.* 398 Both plain and pan tiles are commonly bedded in mortar.

fig. **1831** CARLYLE *Sart. Res.* I. viii. 62 Words well bedded also in good Logic-mortar.

12. *Masonry.* To dress the face or 'bed' of a stone (cf. BED *sb.* 12 b.).

1793 SMEATON *Edystone L.* §169 Each size and species of stone were to be worked..to a given parallel thickness..and ..when so bedded..to be cut..to the true figure.

13. To spread, strew, or cover with a bed or layer of anything. Cf. *to carpet.*

1859 KINGSLEY *Misc.* II. 299 Those dells bedded with dark velvet green fern.

fig. **1839** BAILEY *Festus* (1848) v, It is fear which beds the far to-come with fire.

14. To lay in a bed or layer; e.g. to lay (oysters) in beds prepared for their reception.

1721 *Phil. Trans.* XXXI. 250 The Bottom of its Channel ..all bedded with good Oysters. **1861** HULME tr. *Moquin-Tandon* II. III. 169 The Oysters are placed in large reservoirs ..this is called 'Bedding the Oysters.'

15. *intr.* To form a compact layer.

1615 MARKHAM *Eng. Housew.* II. v, By reason of the softnesse thereof it beddeth closer. **1641** BEST *Farm. Bks.* 144 The wette strawe coucheth better, and beddes closer. **1787** BEST *Angling* (ed. 2) 168 Hairs bed well when they twist kindly.

16. *to bed up*: to lie up in beds or strata *against.*

1782 WITHERING in *Phil. Trans.* LXXII. 329 The limestone rocks..bed up against it, and the coal comes up to the surface against the lime-stone.

17. *refl.* and *intr.* Of eels (see quots.).

1653 WALTON *Angler* 190 Many of them [eels] together bed themselves, and live without feeding upon anything. **1746** R. GRIFFITHS *Ess. Jurisdict. Thames* 194 [Eels] get into the soft Earth or Mud..and bed themselves. **1883** G. C. DAVIES *Norfolk Broads* xxxi. 213 Big and little [eels], start on this singular voyage,..and 'bed' themselves. **1902** CORNISH *Naturalist Thames* 216 In winter the eels 'bed', *i.e.* bury themselves in the mud.

bedabble (bɪˈdæb(ə)l), *v.* [f. BE- 1 + DABBLE.] *trans.* To wet with dirty liquid, or in such a way as to make untidy or dirty. Hence **bedabbled** *ppl. a.*

1590 SHAKS. *Mids. N.* III. ii. 443 Bedabbled with the dew, and torne with briars, I can no further crawle. **1644** *Vind. Featley* Pref. 1 Pens bedabbled in the Gall of bitternesse. **1811** SCOTT *Don Roderick* xxxi, Idols of gold..Bedabbled all with blood. **1862** *Luck Ladysmede* II. 78 Whose stained and bedabbled head and face made him appear more of a sufferer than he really was.

bedad (bɪˈdæd), *int. Irish.* [= *By dad*, or *by God* (cf. *begad*).] An asseveration.

1710 SWIFT *Lett.* (1768) III. 25 Only because it is Tuesday, a Monday bedad. **1848** THACKERAY *Van. Fair* II. ix. 39 'Bedad it's him,' said Mrs. O'Dowd. **1871** J. YOUNG *Mem. C.M. Young* 324, Standing where, bedad, I'm standing now.

†**beˈdaff**, *v. Obs.* [f. BE- 5 + DAFF *sb.*] *trans.* To befool, make a fool of, make foolish. Hence **bedaft** *ppl. a.*, foolish, stupid.

c **1386** CHAUCER *Clerkes T.* 1135 Beth not bedaffed for your innocence. **1572** GASCOIGNE *Flowers* Wks. (1587) 67 Bartholmew hys wits had so bedaft, That all seemed good. **1580** NORTH *Plutarch* 105 When you come ysore [eye-sore] in all your factes Then are you blynde, dull witted and bedaft.

†**beˈdag**, *v. Obs.* [f. BE- 2 + DAG *v.*] To bemire the bottom of (dress).

a **1300** *K. Alis.* 5485 Alisaunder cometh upon his mule, Bishiten and bydagged foule. **1530** PALSGR. 445/2, I bedagge, I araye a garment aboute the skyrtes with myre.

†**beˈdaggle**, *v. Obs.* [f. BE- + DAGGLE. A kind of frequentative to BEDAG.] = prec.

1580 HOLLYBAND *Treas. Fr. Tong*, *Crotté*, bedagled. **1583** STANYHURST *Æneis* II. (Arb.) 40 With dust al powdred, with filthood dustie bedagled. **1660** PEPYS *Diary* 5 July, I saw the King..go forth in the rain..and it bedaggled many a fine suit of clothes. **1755** in JOHNSON; in mod. Dicts.

bedaghe, var. of BEDAW, *v. Obs.*

bedamn, bedamp, etc.: see BE- *pref.*

bedangled (bɪˈdæŋg(ə)ld), *ppl. a.* [f. BE- 1 + DANGLE.] Beset with things dangling about one.
1601 WEEVER *Mirr. Mart.* E ij b, Direct my course To the dew-bedangled Oceanitides. **1732** SWIFT *Corr.* Wks. 1841 II. 691 Worthless bishops, all bedangled with their illiterate relations and flatterers.

bedare, bedaughtered, etc.: see BE- *pref.*

bedark (bɪˈdɑːk), *v.*; also 4 **bederk**. [f. BE- 1 + DARK *v.*] *trans.* To involve in darkness.
1393 GOWER *Conf.* I. 81 Whan the blacke winter night.. Bederked hath the water stronde. **1855** SINGLETON *Virgil* I. 297 Every mist which.. bedarks thee round, I'll take away.

bedarken (bɪˈdɑːk(ə)n), *v.* [f. BE- 1 + DARKEN.] *trans.* To involve in darkness. Also *fig.*
1596 FITZ-GEFFREY *Sir F. Drake* (1881) 24 Boughes bedarkning all the daie. **1834** SIR H. TAYLOR *Artevelde* II. III. ii, Guilt bedarkens and confounds the mind of man.
Hence **beˈdarkened, beˈdarkening** *ppl. a.*
1809 SOUTHEY *Ess.* (1832) II. 282 It is still the same bedarkened and bedarkening superstition. **1833** H. COLERIDGE *Poems* I. 54 Sweet snatches of delight That visit our bedarken'd day. **1847** SIR H. TAYLOR *Eve of Conq.* 36 If thou cast reproachful looks On sports bedarkening custom erst allowed.

bedash (bɪˈdæʃ), *v.* [f. BE- 1 + DASH *v.*] *trans.* **a.** To dash against, dash about. **b.** To injure or spoil by dashing (as the wind or rain dashes flowers). **c.** To cover with dashes of colour or adornment.
1564 GOLDING *Justine* 90 (R.) Bedect with skarlet and bedashte with golde. **1594** SHAKS. *Rich. III*, I. ii. 164 Like Trees bedash'd with raine. **1609** HOLLAND *Amm. Marcel.* 196 It bedasheth on that side Cyzicum and Dindyma. **1621** QUARLES *Esther* in *Div. Poems* (1717) 46 His comfort is bedasht and done. **1640** J. GOWER *Ovid's Fest.* II. 25 The battred billows all bedash the Shippe. **1850** BLACKIE *Æschylus* I. 131 Purple gouts bedash The guilty ground.

bedaub (bɪˈdɔːb), *v.* [f. BE- 1 + DAUB *v.*]
1. *trans.* To daub over with anything that sticks, to plaster.
1558 PHAËR *Æneid* II. (R.) But now in dust his beard bedawb'd [is]. **1683** LORRAIN *Muret's Rites Fun.* 5 They all bedawbed their faces with mire and dirt. **1763** J. BROWN *Poetry & Mus.* §6. 119 Thespis and his Company bedaubed their Faces with the Lees of Wine. **1860** GOSSE *Rom. Nat. Hist.* 24 And with a painter's brush [he] had bedaubed the trunks of several large trees.
b. *fig.* To bespatter with abuse, to vilify.
1553–87 FOXE *A. & M.* (1596) 532/1 Your dirtie pen.. hath not so bedaubed and bespotted me..but I hope to spunge it out. **1662** PEPYS *Diary* 30 Oct., He prepares to bedaube him. **1705** OTWAY *Orphan* Prol. 18 The names of Honest Men bedawb'd.
2. To ornament clumsily or vulgarly; to bedizen.
1581 J. BELL *Haddon's Answ. Osor.* 309 They bedawbe their Temples on every side, with pictures, and Poppettes. **1716** LADY M. W. MONTAGU *Lett.* xxii. I. 67 The emperor and empress have two of these little monsters..all bedaubed with diamonds. **1862** THACKERAY *Four Georges* i. (1862) 63 Are now embroidered and bedaubed.
b. *fig.* To load with rhetorical devices, with praise, etc.; to belaud to excess.
1581 J. BELL *Haddon's Answ. Osor.* 493 Untymely applications, wherewith his discourse is altogether bedawbedd. **1672** MARVELL *Reh. Transp.* I. 23 Set off, and bedawb'd with Rhetorick. **1790** BOSWELL *Johnson* III. 57 *note*, That I..should have..bedawbed him, as the worthy gentleman has bedawbed Scotland?
beˈdaubed, -ing *ppl. a.*, **bedaubing** *vbl. sb.*
1624 QUARLES *Sion's Sonn.* (1717) 416 A newer fashion.. Than eye bedawbing tears, and printed lamentation. **1788** BURNS *Lett.* 40 Those bedaubing paragraphs with which he is eternally larding the lean characters of certain great men. **1863** MISS WHATELY *Ragged L. Egypt* xii. 105 Disgust at the bedaubed face of the little one.

bedauer, -aver, obs. dial. f. *bed-ifere*, BEDFERE, bed-fellow.

†**beˈdaw**, *v. Obs. rare*; also 4–5 **bedaghe**. [f. BE- 4 + DAW *v.*] *trans.* To dawn upon. Cf. BEDAWN, BEDAY in BE- *pref.*
1393 GOWER *Conf.* II. 193 There is no day which hem bedaweth. *c* **1400** *Destr. Troy* III. 758 Hit is best þat we buske & of bede rise, Lest þe day us be-daghe.

bedaˈwee, -wi, -wy, *pl.* **bedaˈween, -win**, forms of BEDOUIN, -S.

bedaze (bɪˈdeɪz), *v.* Also 7 **bedeaze** (*Sc.*). [f. BE- 2 + DAZE.] Emphatic form of DAZE. Hence **bedazed** *ppl. a.*, Dazed, stupefied; besotted.
a **1605** MONTGOMERIE *Poems* (1821) 173 Quhais frostie head..Bedeazit evry vane. **1870** *Daily News* 10 June, The baby-acrobat may fall, bedazed and stunned. **1882** E. PLUMPTRE *Eccles.* (*Camb. Bible for Sch.*) 167 The besotted and bedazed spiritual pride which St. Paul paints by the participle 'puffed up.'

bedazement (bɪˈdeɪzmənt). [f. BEDAZE *v.* + -MENT.] Bedazed condition.
1887 M. ARNOLD *Ess. Crit.* (1888) Ser. II. ix. 311 This bedazement with the infinite. **1903** *Westm. Gaz.* 30 June 7/2 The Unionist Party is being caught in the Protectionist toils before it can recover from its bedazement. **1918** A. T. QUILLER-COUCH *Foe-Farrell* x. 175 He followed me..in mere bedazement, speechless.

bedazzle (bɪˈdæz(ə)l), *v.*; also 6–7 **bedazle**. [f. BE- 2 + DAZZLE.] Intensive form of DAZZLE; to dazzle thoroughly, confuse by dazzling.
1596 SHAKS. *Tam. Shr.* IV. v. 46 That haue bin so bedazled with the sunne. **1870** HAWTHORNE *Eng. Note-bks.* (1879) II. 291 They bedazzle one another with cross lights.

beˈdazzled, *ppl. a.* [f. prec. + -ED¹.] Dazzled so as to be confused.
1805 SCOTT *Last. Minstr.* VI. xxv, Full through the guests' bedazzled band Resistless flashed the levin brand. **1837** CARLYLE *Fr. Rev.* II. III. II. i. Poor bedazzled mortals.

beˈdazzlement. [f. as prec. + -MENT.] The fact of being bedazzled; the action of bedazzling.
1806 KNOX & JEBB *Corr.* I. 295 To the bepuzzlement of the ignorant, and the bedazzlement of the superficial. **1877** *V. Hugo's Miserables* II. lxxix, All the other historians suffer with a certain bedazzlement in which they grope about.

beˈdazzling, *ppl. a.* [f. as prec. + -ING².] Dazzling so as to confuse. Hence **bedazzlingly** *adv.*
1852 D. MOIR II. 73 When are swept aside The court's bedazzling pageantry and pride.

bed-bug. [BED *sb.*] = BUG *sb.*² 2 a.
Freq. in U.S., on account of the use of *bug* in the general sense of 'insect'.
1809 *Farmer's Almanack* (Boston) July 1 Ladies, for mercy's sake, see about the bed bugs. **1813** BINGLEY *Anim. Biog.* III. 181 The Bed Bug is a nauseous and troublesome inhabitant of most of the houses in large towns. **1861** MAYHEW *Lond. Lab.* III. 35/1 The bed-bug is not the only one of its congeners which preys upon man. **1909** *Cent. Dict.* Suppl., *Bedbug-hunter*, a reduviid bug,..which inhabits houses, where it preys upon bedbugs. **1964** M. HYNES *Med. Bacteriol.* (ed. 8) xxx. 462 Bed-bugs live in hiding places such as the crevices of furniture and behind pictures, from which they emerge at night to suck blood.

bedchamber (ˈbɛd,tʃeɪmbə(r)). Also 4 **cha(u)mbre**. [f. BED *sb.* + CHAMBER. Cf. MHG. *bettekammere.*]
A chamber or room intended for holding a bed; *arch.* and displaced in common use by *bedroom*, exc. in reference to the royal bedchamber, as in *gentleman, groom, lord*, or *lady* of the *bedchamber*.
1362 LANGL. *P. Pl.* A. v. 136 Þe Beste in þe Bed-chaumbre lay bi þe wowe. **1611** SHAKS. *Cymb.* II. iv. 66 Her Bedchamber..was hang'd With Tapistry of Silke and silver. **1685** *Lond. Gaz.* No. 2028/2 Then the Lord Churchill Gentleman of the Bedchamber, followed by Two Grooms of the Bed-Chamber. **1702** *Ibid.* No. 3862/1 The Ladies of the Bed-chamber, Maids of Honour, and other Ladies. **1776** GIBBON *Decl. & F.* I. 70 Those menial offices, which, in the household and bedchamber of a limited monarch, are so eagerly solicited by the proudest nobles. **1789** LD. AUCKLAND *Corr.* (1861) II. 188 We are obliged to have all the six children in our bedchamber to-night. **1849** MACAULAY *Hist. Eng.* I. 248 Letting us know how the parlours and bed-chambers of our ancestors looked.
b. *attrib.*, as **bed-chamber candle, plot, -man.**
1643 PRYNNE *Sov. Power Parl.* III. 89 Nor [must] his Bedchamber-men attire him, for feare of high Treason. **1671** F. PHILIPPS *Reg. Necess.* 46 All the Chamberlains or Bed-chamber-men. **1833** MACAULAY *War Success.*, *Ess.* (1854) I. 259/1 The great party..was undermined by bedchamber-women at St. James's. **1854** THACKERAY *Newcomes* I. 32 A bed-chamber candle. **1880** DISRAELI *Endym.* lviii, The famous Bed-Chamber Plot..which terminated in the return of the Whigs to office.

bed-clothes (ˈbɛd-kləʊðz), *sb. pl.* (The sing. bedcloth is obs.) [f. BED *sb.* + CLOTHES.] The sheets and blankets with which a bed is covered.
1387 TREVISA *Higden* Rolls Ser. VI. 87 A burþen of bed-cloþes. *c* **1440** *Promp. Parv.* 27 Bedclothe, or a rayment for a bed. **1601** SHAKS. *All's Well* IV. iii. 287 In his sleepe he does little harme, saue to his bed-cloathes about him. **1818** BYRON *Juan* I. cxl, To fling the bed-clothes in a heap.

beddable (ˈbɛdəb(ə)l), *a.* [f. BED + -ABLE.] That may be taken to bed; sexually attractive.
1941 *Sat. Rev. Lit.* 29 Nov. 13 Byron only tolerated brains in women who were too old to be beddable. **1952** E. GRIERSON *Reputation for Song* xxi. 172 Favours granted him ..by ladies just as succulently beddable. **1957** W. CAMP *Prospects of Love* II. iii, There must be something about her ..which screams that she's beddable. A girl doesn't have to be pretty to be sexy.

†**bedde.** *Obs.* [short form of *ibedde*, OE. *ȝebedda*: cf. OFris. *bedda*, MHG. *bette.*] A bedfellow.
c **1250** *Owl & Night.* 1498 Ȝif aht man is hire bedde.

bedded (ˈbɛdɪd), *ppl. a.* [f. BED *v.* + -ED¹.]
1. Put to bed, having gone to bed; lying in bed.
1393 LANGL. *P. Pl.* C. XVIII. 197 Vuel-cloþed.. Baddeliche beddyd. **1625** BOYS in Spurgeon *Treas. Dav.* Ps. xlv. 9 Spiritually the wedded and bedded wife to the king of glory. **1773** J. ROBERTSON *Poems* 292 All silent was the bedded house. **1839** HALIBURTON *Lett. Bag. Gt. W.* i. 4 Bedded all day..Rose in the Evening. **1855** LONGF. *Hiaw.* III. 76 Bedded soft in moss and rushes.
2. Lying at rest in their lair, or bed; cf. BED *v.* 14.
1653 WALTON *Angler* 185 Let coarse bold hands, from slimy nest, The bedded fish in banks outwrest.
3. Growing in a bed.
1818 KEATS *Endym.* I. 239 Dost sit and hearken The dreary melody of bedded reeds?
4. Deeply or firmly fixed; embedded.
1641 D. CAWDREY *Three Serm.* The spawne and seed of corruption which lies bedded in our hearts. **1813** SCOTT *Rokeby* II. xv, Yon earth-bedded jetting stone.
5. Laid or strewn in a smooth layer.
1602 SHAKS. *Ham.* III. iv. 121 Your bedded haire Start up, and stand an end. **1795** SOUTHEY *Joan of Arc* iii. 443 Light-edged shadows on the bedded sand.
6. Existing in beds or layers; stratified in beds.
1830 LYELL *Princ. Geol.* (1833) III. 65 A similar compact variety of the limestone occurs..often very thick bedded. **1858** GEIKIE *Hist. Boulder* xii. 247 The bedded or contemporaneous trap-rocks.
7. In *comb.* Having a bed.
1831 CARLYLE *Sart. Res.* II. ix, Not sufficiently honoured, nourished, soft-bedded. **1862** BARNES *Rhymes Dorset Dial.* II. 100 Above the gravel-bedded rill.

beddel(l, obs. or dial. form of BEADLE, BEDREL.

bedder¹ (ˈbɛdə(r)). Also 8 **beder**. [f. BED *v.* or *sb.* + -ER¹. With sense 2, cf. *hedger, potter*; with 3, cf. *header, drawer.*]
1. One who puts to bed; one who litters cattle.
c **1612** FLETCHER *Thierry* I. 450 All your guilded knaves, brokers, and bedders.
†**2.** A bed-maker, an upholsterer. *Obs.* or *dial.*
1803 S. PEGGE *Anecd. Eng. Lang.* 273 Upholsterer, Called ..in some parts of the kingdom..a bedder.
3. The lower stone in an oil-mill; the bed-stone.
1611 COTGR., *Gisant d'vn moulin*, the Bed, Bedder, or under-millstone. **1706** PHILLIPS, *Bedder, bedetter*, the neither-stone of an Oil-mill. **1755** in JOHNSON: and in mod Dicts.
4. A plant adapted for being grown in a flower bed; a 'bedding-out plant.'
1862 *Times* 10 Apr., Plants..possessing the properties required in bedders, that is..adapted to form masses of uniform colour. **1882** *Garden* 21 Jan. 34/1 It will be a new sensation..to grow bedders on rockwork.
5. (See quot.)
1879 C. HIBBS *Jewellery* in *Cassell's Techn. Educ.* IV. 309/1 It was the custom formerly to lay a heavy block of iron, called a 'bedder,' on the two metals and strike upon it with sledge hammers until..the contact was complete.

bedder² (ˈbɛdə(r)). [See -ER¹.] One who goes to bed. In collocations **early, late (go-to-) bedder.**
1908 *Daily Chron.* 27 Oct. 6/7 The late-go-to-bedder and the early riser. **1921** *Glasgow Herald* 19 May 6 Our forefathers were 'earlier bedders' and risers than the present artificial age. **1961** Y. OLSSON *Syntax Eng. Verb* vi. 125 He's a late bedder and a later riser.

bedder³ (ˈbɛdə(r)). *slang.* [See -ER⁶.] A bedroom.
1897 *Westm. Gaz.* 2 Feb. 1/3 She'd want to come up to my bedder and give me Somebody's beastly food for infants. **1908** D. COKE *House Prefect* xvii. 219 He's been nabbed, and shut up in his bedder.

bedding (ˈbɛdɪŋ), *vbl. sb.* [f. BED + -ING¹.]
I. Connected with BED *sb.*
1. a. A collective name for the articles which compose a bed, esp. the mattress, feather-bed, or other article lain upon, and the bed-clothes.
a **1000** *Lamb. Psalter* vi. 7 (Bosw.), Mid minum tearum mine beddinge ic beþwea. *a* **1000** *Ags. Gloss.* in Wr.-Wülcker *Voc.* 187 *Mataxa*, uel *corductum*, uel *stramentum*, stræl, uel bedding. **1303** R. BRUNNE *Handl. S.* 3432 Ȝyf þou delyte þe yn ryche beddyng. **1388** WYCLIF *2 Sam.* xvii. 28 Brouȝten to hym beddyngis and tapitis. **1486** *Act 3 Hen. VII*, ix, Things that be good..for Houshold..Brass, Pewter, Bedding. **1566** *Wills & Inv. N.C.* (1835) 254 All bedding as feather-bedds, mattrasses wᵗʰ all that pertenithe thervnto. **1610** B. JONSON *Alch.* v. i, He hath sold my hangings, and my beddings! **1700** DRYDEN *Pal. & Arc.* II. 159 Bedding and clothes I will this night provide. **1815** *Encycl. Brit.* III. 503/2 In the Highlands heath..is very generally used as bedding. **1861** F. NIGHTINGALE *Nursing* 50 Whenever you can, hang up the whole of the bedding to air for a few hours.
b. A supply of bed-clothes for one bed.
1620 R. SETON in *Rep. Eglinton Papers* No. 128 (1885) 45 Your lordship most also send tuo bedding of clothes. **1724** RAMSAY *Tea-t. Misc.* (ed. 9) I. 28 With an auld bedden o' claiths Was left me by my mither.
c. Anything used to sleep on or in; sleeping accommodation. *arch.* or *Obs.*
1393 LANGL. *P. Pl.* C. XVII. 74 He goþ to a cold beddyng. **1463** *Mann. & Househ. Exp.* 225 He schalle have mete, and drynke, and beddynge. *a* **1550** *Peblis to Play* xiv, Gilbert in ane guttar glayde; He gat na better beddin. **1596** SPENSER *State Irel.* (1809) I. 161 The ground..which useth to be his bedding. **1675** HOBBES *Odyss.* (1677) 31 So rude or poor, As not good bedding for a friend t' afford.
d. Litter for horses and cattle.
1697 DRYDEN *Virg. Georg.* III. 465 Spread with Straw, the bedding of thy Fold. **1840** J. STEWART *Stable Econ.* 137 Some people give the horse no bedding, or almost none.
2. A bottom layer or foundation, in or on which anything rests, or may be firmly fixed.
1611 MARKHAM *Countr. Content.* II. ii. (1688) 161 Straws which do belong to the bedding of the [malt-] kiln. **1677** EVELYN *Mem.* (1857) II. 119 The bedding being soft mud it is safe for shipping. **1787** BEST *Angling* Gloss., *Bedding.* the body of an artificial-fly. **1881** *Ev. Man his own Mechanic* III. §1696 A bedding of putty must be carefully laid round that part..against which the glass is to be placed.
†**3.** *Building.* The upper and lower surfaces of stones when worked for building. See BED 12 b.
1401 *Contr. Durham Dorm.* in *Gloss. Gothic Archit.* (1845) I. 52 Et erit le beddyng cujuslibet achiler ponendi in isto opere longitudinis unius pedis de assyse.

4. Arrangement of rocks, etc. in beds or layers; stratification or any similar structure.

1860 TYNDALL *Glac.* I. §11. 75 Walls, across which the lines of annual bedding were drawn. **1862** ANSTED *Channel Isl.* II. x. 264 Veins..at right angles to the apparent cleavage or bedding. **1878** LAWRENCE tr. *Cotta's Rocks Class.* 97 The word 'Bedding' is used..in speaking of all rocks, whether stratified or not. It is taken as the equivalent of the German 'Lagerung.' **1878** HUXLEY *Physiogr.* 238 Running along the planes of stratification or bedding.

II. Connected with BED *v.*

5. A putting to bed; *esp.* of a bride.

1589 PUTTENHAM *Eng. Poesie* I. xxvi. (1811) 41 Epithalamies..ballades at the bedding of the bride. **1622** MASSINGER, etc. *Old Law* v. i, Case up thy maidenhead: no priest, no bedding. **1822** SCOTT *Nigel* xxxvii, A circumstantial description of the wedding, bedding, and throwing the stocking.

6. The process of planting flowers in beds; also called *bedding out.*

1862 *Cott. Gardener* 3 June 182 The week has been taken up chiefly with bedding. **1885** *Garden* 4 June 521 There has been no time for bedding out.

III. *Attrib.* and *comb.*, as ***bedding ballad***, ***-plant***, ***bedding-out plant***; also **bedding fault** *Geol.*, a fault parallel to a bedding-plane; **bedding-ground** *U.S.* = BED-GROUND; **bedding-moulding** = BED-MOULDING; **bedding-plane** = *bed-plane* (BED *sb.* 19); **bedding-plate** = *bed-plate* (BED *sb.* 19); **bedding-roll**, a roll of bedding (sense 1); **bedding-stone** (see quot.).

1589 PUTTENHAM *Eng. Poesie* (Arb.) 68 Epithalamie or *bedding ballad of the ancient times. **1909** *Cent. Dict.* Suppl., *Bedding fault. **1961** J. CHALLINOR *Dict. Geol.* 21/1 *Bedding-fault*, the result of bedding-plane slip. **1884** W. SHEPHERD *Prairie Exper.* 199 For the *bedding-ground a bare open spot..away from damp. **1920** J. M. HUNTER *Trail Drivers of Texas* 215 It looked like a 'round up' when turning them off of the bedding ground. **1664** EVELYN *Freart's Archit.* 136 Modilions..supply the part of the *bedding-moulding as our Workmen style the Ovolo in this place. **1865** *Cornh. Mag.* May 587 To put down some *bedding-out plants. **1897** *Q. Jrnl. Geol. Soc. Index I–L* 33/2 *Bedding-planes comp. w. cleavage-planes in N. Wales. **1908** *Daily Chron.* 15 Dec. 1/5 Originally..horizontal, the bedding plane now dips gently to the south. **1920** L. V. PIRSSON *Physical Geol.* (ed. 2) 271 The two layers will be separated by a distinct juncture plane..; this is stratification, and the juncture plane is called a bedding plane. **1856** *Gard. Chron.* 55 Many of the *bedding-plants were either dead or in a dying state. **1879** *Man. Artill. Exerc.* 255 The racer is secured to the *bedding-plate by steel bolts with wrought-iron nuts. **1901** KIPLING *Kim* vii. 179 His new bullock-trunk..and *bedding-roll lay in the empty sleeping-room. **1963** *Times* 5 Mar. 12/7 His bedding-roll in one hand. **1823** P. NICHOLSON *Pract. Build.* 384 *Bedding Stone.—A straight piece of marble used to try the rubbed side of a brick. **1862** ANSTED *Channel Isl.* IV. xxi. 495 The scarlet *bedding varieties often live for many years in the open ground.

beddred, obs. form of BEDRID.

beddy ('bɛdɪ), *a.* [f. BED *sb.* + -Y[1].] Of stone: having natural cleavages, with liability to split.

1709 T. ROBINSON *Nat. Hist. Westmld. & Cumbld.* xiv. 79 Under this white Metal, comes in a beddy Free-stone, which is always of a grey Colour. **1829** S. GLOVER *Hist. Derby* I. 88 The freestones,..often called building stone ..(in distinction from beddy stone, flags or paviers). **1888** BARING-GOULD *R. Cable* xlii, He may discover, when he's half cut it [*sc.* granite], that it's beddy (liable to split). **1892** HESLOP *Northumb. Words*, 'Beddy freestone' is thus distinguished from a compact, granular deposit.

beddy-byes ('bɛdɪ,baɪz). Also **-bye**. [f. BED *sb.* + -Y[6] + BYE(-BYE[1].] A nursery and facetious term for 'bed' or 'sleep' (BYE-BYE[1]).

1906 E. DYSON *Fact'ry 'Ands* xvii. 234 Booser M'Gunn.. went ter beddy-bye. **1926** P. GIBBS *Young Anarchy* x. 59 Come on, little one. Bedibyes. **1930** WODEHOUSE *Very Good, Jeeves!* vii. 181 And then off to beddy-bye. **1946** 'S. RUSSELL' *To Bed with Grand Music* iv. 62 Mrs. Chalmers rolled up her knitting and said she supposed it was time for beddy-byes.

bede, *sb.*[1] ME. form of BEAD *sb.*, often used in mod.Eng. in the now archaic sense of 'prayer.' So **bedehouse**, **bedesman**, **bedeswoman**.

†**bede**, *sb.*[2] *Obs. rare*[−1]. [? f. ME. *beden, beoden*, OE. *béodan* to command (cf. Ger. *gebiet*): if not a sense of prec.] Command, bidding.

c **1175** *Lamb. Hom.* 7 ȝef we haldeþ his beode. **1330** R. BRUNNE *Chron.* 335 Þei bed þe same bede. *c* **1430** *Hymns Virg.* (1867) 49 Þoruȝ pride ȝe offendid my fadris bede.

bede (biːd), *sb.*[3] 'A miner's pickaxe.' Raymond *Mining Gloss.*

bedeacon, **bedebt**, etc.: see BE- *pref.*

bedead (bɪ'dɛd), *v.* ? *Obs.* [f. BE- 2 + DEAD *v.*] *trans.* To deaden. Only found in pples. **be'deaded**, deadened; **be'deading**, deadening.

1656 H. MORE *Enthus. Tri.* §28. 27 His body so deeply overwhelmed and bedeaded with sleep. —— *Antid. Ath.* III. xvi. (1712) 141 A dark bedeading Melancholy. **1681** HALLYWELL *Melampr.* (T.) Bedeaded and stupified as to their morals. **1736** in BAILEY; and in mod. Dicts.

†**be'deaf**, *v. Obs.* [f. BE- + DEAF.] To deafen.

1620 QUARLES *Jonah* (1638) 26 Bedeafing him with what he knows and heares.

bedeafen (bɪ'dɛf(ə)n), *v.* [f. BE- 2 + DEAFEN *v.*] Intensive of DEAFEN. Found only in pa. pple.

1631 QUARLES *Samson* in Farr *S.P.* (1848) 126 Did wake His father's sleep-bedeafned eares. **1808** SCOTT *Marm.* IV. xvi, Bedeafen'd with the jangling knell.

†**be'deal**, *v. Obs.* Forms: 1 **bedǽlan**, 3 **bidælen**, 2–3 **bidelen**. [f. BE- 3 + OE. *dǽlan*, to part, DEAL.] *trans.* To deprive, bereave, free *of*.

c **1000** ÆLFRIC *Gen.* xxvii. 45 Hwi sceal ic beon bedæled ægðer minra sunena. *c* **1200** ORMIN 4676 Loc nu ȝiff þatt tu narrt..wittes bidæledd. **1205** LAY. 17364 Seouen þusend þer leien liues bidæled. *a* **1275** *Prov. Alfred* in *O.E. Misc.* 134 Gif þu i þin helde best welþes bi-delid.

bedeck (bɪ'dɛk), *v.* [f. BE- 1 + DECK.] *trans.* To deck about, to cover with ornament, to adorn.

a **1566** R. EDWARDS in Ellis II. (R.) May bedecks each branch with green. **1628** tr. *Camden's Hist. Eliz.* II. 251 That part of the Heaven..was bedecked with but few Stars. **1720** GAY *Poems* (1745) II. 18 Three gold rings her skilful hand bedeck. **1850** BLACKIE *Æschylus* II. 173 Spear-pierced trophies, Argive harnesses, Bedeck their holy halls. *fig.* **1559** *Mirr. Mag.* 187 (R.) So that I was bedeckt with double praise.

Hence **be'decked** *ppl. a.*, **be'decking** *ppl. a.* and *vbl. sb.*

1671 MILTON *Samson* 712 But who is this?.. That, so bedecked, ornate, and gay, Comes this way sailing. **1588** SHAKS. *L.L.L.* II. i. 79 Bedecking ornaments of praise. **1612** W. PARKES *Curtaine-Dr.* (1876) 54 The wife in her faire ornaments and bedeckings.

bedee, variant of BEDET, *obs.* 'a soldier's boy.'

bedeguar ('bɛdɪgə(r)). Also **-gar**, **-gaur**, **-guar**, [a. F. *bédeguar, bédegar*, ad. ult. Pers. (and Arab.) *bādāwar, -ard*, lit. 'wind-brought,' according to the *Burhani Kati* 'a thorny bush with a white flower, resembling the thistle.' Thence sense 1. Later writers seem to have fancifully attributed to the word a derivation from Pers. *bād* wind, breath + Arab. *ward* 'rose,' and applied it to something growing on the rose. Gerard of Cremona, in his *Synonymy* (1481) explains *bedegar* both ways, by 'spina alba vel odor rosæ' (Devic).]

†**1.** A white spiny or thorny plant, perh. originally an *Echinops*, but taken by western herbalists for the Milk Thistle (*Silybum Marianum*).

1578 LYTE *Dodoens* 525 This Thistell is called..of the Arabian Physitiones, Bedeguar: in Englishe, Our Ladies Thistell. **1601** HOLLAND *Pliny* II. 92 Our chaplet makers vse the floures also of Bedegnar or white Thistle.

2. A moss-like excrescence on rose-bushes: it is a kind of gall produced by the puncture of a small insect *Cynips rosæ*.

1578 LYTE *Dodoens* 655 The spongious bawle..uppon the wilde Rose..is called of som Apothecaries Bedegar; but wrongfully. **1695** W. WESTMACOTT *Script. Herb.* 30 These Briars yield an Excrescence..called, tho' falsly, Bedegaur or Bedegnar. **1872** OLIVER *Elem. Bot.* II. 171 Rose Bedeguars or 'Robin Redbreast's Pincushions', are frequent upon the Dog Rose. **1883** *Pall Mall G.* 3 Sept. 2/1 The hedgerows.. beautiful with clematis, and scarlet and yellow foliage, with hip and haw, and the bedeguar of the rose.

bede house, earlier form of BEAD-HOUSE.

bedel, **bedell**, archaic forms of BEADLE, officially retained in the Universities of Oxford and Cambridge. So **bedelry**, etc.

bedelary, **bedellarie**, var. of BEADLERY.

†**be'delve**, *v. Obs.* Forms: *Inf.* 1 **bedelfan**, 3–4 **bydelve**, 4–5 **bi-**, **bedelue** (**-ve**). *Pa. pple.* 1 **bedolfen**, 3 **bydeolve(n**, 4 **by-**, **bedolve(n**, 6 **bedolvyne**, *Sc.* **bedelvyn**. [OE. *bedelf-an*, f. BE- + *delf-an* to DELVE.]

1. *trans.* To dig round or about.

c **1000** *Ags. Gosp.* Luke xiii. 8 Oþ ic hine bedelfe. *a* **1500** *E.E. Misc.* 68 The tre schal be bedolvyne abowte.

2. To bury.

a **1000** *Dream of Rood* 75 Bedealf us man on deopan seaðe. *c* **1374** CHAUCER *Boeth.* v. i. 151 And fond þere a gobet of golde by-doluen. *c* **1440** LONELICH *Grail* li. 14 And him.. putten there-inne, and him bedelven. **1513** DOUGLAS *Æneis* x. ix. 49 Quharin bedelvyn lyis a gret talent.

bedeman, obs. form of BEADSMAN.

†**be'dene**, *adv. Obs.* exc. *dial.* Forms: 3–6 **bidene**, 4 **biden**, **bedeine**, 4–6 **by-**, **bedene**, **bedeyne**, 5 **bydeene**, **beedene**, **beden**, 6 **bedyn**, 8–9 **bedeen**. [ME. *bidene*, a word of constant occurrence in northern ME. verse, but of uncertain origin; its senses run partly parallel with those of ANON, but it is often used without any appreciable force, as a rime word, or to fill up the measure. Its latter part is almost certainly the early ME. adv. *æne, ene*, OE. *ǽne* 'once, at once, in one, together' (cf. the ME. phrases *at ene* at once, *for ene* for once, and see ENE): but the *bid-* is difficult of explanation.

Marsh and Mätzner compared Du. *bijdien*, MDu. *bidên, bidien*, LG. *bidên* 'by that, thereby, beside that,' which must be discarded; Stratmann compared LG. *binêne* (? for *bî êne*), and suggested that *bidene* might be for *bi ene*, but offered no explanation of the *-d-*. Prof. Zupitza (note to *Guy of Warwick*, 15th c. version, l. 2408) suggests a corruption of **mid ene*, comparing MHG. *mitein, mit eine*, 'together, *unà*.' This completely suits the sense; also, the change of initial *m* to *b*, though unusual, is not unexampled; cf. esp. MHG. *bitalle* for *mit alle* 'wholly, entirely.' But there are historical difficulties in the non-appearance of **mid ǽne* in OE., or of *mid ēne, bidene*, in early southern ME., where alone *mid* was retained; in the rise and use of *bidene* in the north, where *mid* was not retained in ME; and in the fact that the Old Northumbrian had not *mid*, but *mið*, so that the Anglian form would have been *mið ēne*. These difficulties are only partially removed, if, for *mid*, we start from the more northern *with*. In the *Old Usages of Winchester* (*E.E. Guilds*), we see *wiþ-inne, wiþ-owte*, transformed into *by-þinne, by-powte*, through assimilation to *by*; similarly **wið ene*, **wiþ ene*, might be changed into **bi-ðene*, **by-þene*; but the change of the latter into *bi-dene*, would still remain to be explained.]

1. In one body or company, together. ***all bedene***: all together; altogether, completely. Cf. ANON 1.

c **1200** ORMIN 4793 He [Job] forrlæs his streon Onn an daȝȝ all bidene, Tenn menn. *a* **1300** *Cursor M.* 1553 Manes sinne..corrupt all þis world bidene. **1340** HAMPOLE *Pr. Consc.* 8044 A vesselle dypped alle bidene In water. **1450** MYRC *Par. Pr.* 1870 And also halowet alle by-dene. **1522** *World & Child* in Hazl. *Dodsl.* I. 268 All this company that is gathered here bi-dene.

2. Sometimes perhaps: Straight on, continuously, right through so as to include the whole quantity or number; one after another. Cf. ANON 3.

a **1300** *Cursor M.* 1457 Enos son liued al biden Nine hundret yeir and fiue, i wene. *Ibid.* 11560 To sle the childryn alle by-dene [*v.r.* be-, bidene] Wyth-ynne the toun of bedlem. **1375** BARBOUR *Bruce* v. 144 [He] sperit tithandis of the queyn, And of his frendis all bedeyn. *c* **1400** *Destr. Troy* XXIX. 12092 He besit hym..Fele dayes bedene, or he þat dere fonde. *c* **1420** *Pallad. on Husb.* I. 184 To till a felde man must have diligence, And balk it not; but eree it up bydene. ? *c* **1475** *Sqr. Lowe Degree* 272 Take thy leve of kinge and quene, And so to all the courte bydene.

3. Straightway, at once, forthwith, immediately. Cf. ANON 4.

a **1300** *E.E. Psalter* l. 4 Nou mare me wasche of min ivel bi-dene. *c* **1460** *Launfal* 907 in Ritson *Met. Rom.* I. 209 The kyng answerede bedene, Well come, ye maydenes schene. **1513** G. DOUGLAS *Æneis* I. ii. 33 Warp all thair bodyis in the deip bedene. **1786** *Har'st Rig* in *Pop. Sc. Poems* 49 The master is set sair, And vows bedeen that he will share His staff amang them. **1791** A. WILSON *Laurel Disput.* Wks. (1846) 124 A saxpence too, to let me in bedeen.

4. Sometimes perhaps: In a little while, by and by, 'anon.' Cf. ANON 5.

1330 R. BRUNNE *Chron.* 149 And Richard oste bidene at Marsille left alle þo. **1470** HARDING *Chron.* ccxv, To Caleice so he came and home bee dene. *a* **1550** *Christis Kirke Gr.* xxii, Fresch men cam in and hail'd the dulis, And dang them doun in dailis Bedene. **1830** HOGG in *Blackw. Mag.* XXVIII. 738 Read on our Bibles, pray bedeen.

5. As an expletive, or without appreciable force.

c **1350** *Med. MS. Archæol.* XXX. 351 And stampe alle togedir bedene And wryngis thorow a cloth clene. **1375** BARBOUR *Bruce* XV. 108 Fra develling came schippis xv Chargit with armyt men bedeyne [*v.r.* bedene, bedeene]. *c* **1420** *Anturs Arth.* liii, Bothe the king and the quene, And other duȝti bi-dene. **1810** TANNAHILL *Poems* (1846) 139 Ye'll baith come owre on Friday bedeen, And join us.

beder, obs. form of BEDDER[1].

bederal, variant of BEDRAL, beadle.

bedered(e obs. form of BEDRID.

bederepe, **bederpe**, variants of BEDRIP.

bederk, obs. form of BEDARK.

bede-roll, obs. form of BEAD-ROLL.

†**bedet**. *Obs.* Also 7 **bedee**. [ad. F. *bidet* little baggage horse.] A horseman's or soldier's boy employed to carry his baggage.

1633 AMES *Fresh Suit agst. Cerem.* II. 452 Not stragling Souldiers..but Souldiers boyes or Bedees. **1660** HEXHAM, *Een Ruyters jongen*, a Horse-man's boy, or a Bedet.

bedevil (bɪ'dɛv(ə)l), *v.*; also 6 **beedivel**. [f. BE- 5, 6 + DEVIL.]

1. To treat diabolically, with diabolical violence, ribaldry, or abuse.

1768 STERNE *Sent. Journ.* (1775) I. 34 He had been..bedevil'd..at every stage he had come at. **1809** BYRON *Eng. Bards & Sc. Rev.* (ed. 2) Postscr., My poor..Muse..they have..so be-deviled with their..ribaldry.

2. To 'possess' with, or as with, a devil.

1831 CARLYLE *Sart. Res.* III. iii, One age, he is hagridden, bewitched; the next, priestridden, befooled; in all ages, bedevilled. **1862** THACKERAY *Four Georges* i. 45 People who have to deal with her are charmed, and fascinated, and bedeviled.

3. To drive frantic, to bewilder with worry; to torment, worry, 'bother.'

1823 T. MOORE *Fables, Holy Alliance* Fab. 2. 107. 549 Satires at the Court they levelled..That soon, in short, they quite bedevilled Their Majesties and Royal Highnesses. **1878** P. BAYNE *Pur. Rev.* vi. 230 He did so dazzle and bewilder and bedevil the poor man.

4. To 'play the devil with'; to transform mischievously or bewilderingly, to corrupt, spoil, confound, or muddle.

1800 *Edin. Rev.* IX. 108 A room and furniture 'bedeviled' by taste. **1826** Disraeli *Viv. Grey* vi. i. 273 So bedevil a bottle of Geisenheim..you wouldn't know it from the greenest Tokay. **1844** —— *Coningsby* iv. v. 129 The country attorneys..had so bedevilled the registration. **1851** Kingsley *Yeast* ix. 186 To bedevil, by the light of those very already dimmed eyes, the objects around.

5. To bring into the condition of a devil.

1862 J. Brown *Horae Subs.* 219[Art] cannot regenerate, neither can it..bedevil mankind.

6. To call devil, stigmatize as a devil.

be'devilled, -iled, *ppl. a.* [f. prec. + -ed.]

1. Possessed with, or as with, a devil.

1574 Hellowes *Gueuara's Ep.* (1577) 310 He commeth from abroade so furious..and so beediveld, that none may abide him. **1668** R. Lestrange *Vis. Quev.* (1708) 2 You are to say, this is a Devil Catchpol'd, and not a Catchpole bedevil'd. **1785–95** Wolcott (P. Pindar) *Lousiad* Wks. iv. I. 296 No sheep, like sheep be-devill'd, ran about. **1879** R. Stevenson *Trav. Cevennes* 180 Those who took to the hills ..had all gloomy and bedevilled thoughts.

2. Driven frantic, as if by satanic agency; worried, 'bothered.'

1828 Southey *Lett.* (1856) IV. 92 This be-duped and bedevil'd nation. **1852** Hawthorne *Blithed. Rom.* II. iii. 61 Bedevilled with one grief or another.

3. Mischievously or bewilderingly transformed, utterly confused, or muddled.

1755 Smollett *Quix.* (1803) I. 47 The unintelligible and bedeviled discourses of his author. **1809** Windham *Let.* in *Speeches* (1812) I. 114 The whole is so bedevilled, that there is no restoring things to their original state.

4. *Cookery.* Grilled or broiled, with the addition of hot spice; = devilled.

1814 Southey in *Q. Rev.* XII. 223 The gizzard was..sent from the table to be broiled and seasoned, and..returned thus bedevilled. **1862** *Sat. Rev.* 13 Sept. 309 Whitebait simple and whitebait bedevilled.

bedevilment (bɪ'dɛv(ə)lmənt). [f. as prec. + -ment.]

1. Possession by an evil spirit.

1861 A. Clington *Fr. O'Donnel* 25 Whatever bedevilment seized me, I let some of it [opium] spill into his punch. **1878** P. Robinson *My Ind. Gard.* 18 Are not these unequivocal signs of bedevilment?

2. Maddening or bewildering trouble.

1844 Dickens *Lett.* (1880) I. 132 The greater chance of no such bedevilment happening to me. **1882** Rossetti in Hall Caine *Recoll.* 273 Bedevilments thicken: the Garden is ploughed up.

3. Maddening confusion or disorder.

1843 *Blackw. Mag.* LIII. 361 The confusion and bedevilment was ten times worse. **1852** Dickens *Bleak Ho.* viii. (D.) The lawyers have twisted it into such a state of bedevilment. **1861** Sala *Tw. round Clock* 87 What a chaos of cash debtor, contra creditor..brokerage, agio, tare and tret, dock warrants, and general commercial be-devilment!

bedew (bɪ'dju:), *v.* Forms: 4–5 **bydewe**, 4–7 **bedeaw**, 5– **bedew**. [f. be- + dew; cf. MHG. *betouwen*, MLG. *bedauwen*.]

1. *passive.* To be wetted with dew; hence *active*, To cover with dew-like moisture.

1398 Trevisa *Barth. De P.R.* xiv. ii. (1495) 468 Yf good londe is bydewed..it fattyth. **1665–6** *Phil. Trans.* I. 257 The outside of the Metalline Vessel will be bedew'd (if I may so speak) with..Drops of Water. **1706** Addison *Rosamond* ii. vi, In the dreadful pains of death, When the cold damp bedews your brow. **1830** Herschel *Stud. Nat. Phil.* ii. vi. (1851) 159 The moisture which bedews a cold metal or stone when we breathe upon it.

2. *transf.* To wet or moisten gently or by drops; also, *poet.* or *rhet.*, to perfuse with moisture.

c **1374** Chaucer *Boeth.* iv. vii. 144 þe fletyng reyne bydeweþ þe wynter. **1491** Caxton *Vitas Patr.* (1495) 140 The ryver of Nyle that bedewyth and watreth the londe. **1578** Lyte *Dodoens* 53 As though it were bedewed..with honie. **1593** Shaks. *Rich. II*, iii. iii. 99 Bedew Her Pastors Grasse with faithfull English Blood. **1596** Spenser *F.Q.* i. xii. 16. *a* **1674** Milton in Birch *Milton's Wks.* (1738) I. 43 That Herod had well bedew'd himself with Wine. **1746** Smollett *Tears Scot.* 43 While the warm blood bedews my veins. **1864** H. Ainsworth *Tower Lond.* 363 Tears bedewed her cheeks.

3. *fig.* To perfuse with any influence figured as like dew in its operation.

1340 *Ayenb.* 94 þe virtues þet þe Holy Gost bedeaweþ myd his grace. **1483** Caxton *Gold. Leg.* 301/4, I shalle arrouse and bydewe her body with so ardaunt desyre. **1639** Rouse *Heav. Univ.* iv. 33 When the soul is inwardly bedewed..by the Spirit. **1860** Pusey *Min. Proph.* 336 So did the Apostles bedew the souls of believers with the word of godliness.

bedewed (bɪ'dju:d), *ppl. a.* [f. prec. + -ed¹.] Moistened with or as with dew.

1530 Palsgr. 445/2 In Aprill it is a pleasant syght to se the yonge herbes bedewed. **1646** Crashaw *Steps to Temp.* 59 His sweat-bedewed bed. **1876** G. Chambers *Astron.* 736 Its transfer into warm air will probably lead to its becoming bedewed.

be'dewer. One who or that which bedews.

1611 Cotgr., *Arroseur*, a bedeawer, a besprinkler.

be'dewing, *vbl. sb.* [f. as prec. + -ing¹.] A wetting with or as with dew.

1580 Hollyband *Treas. Fr. Tong*, *Aspersion & Arrousement*, besprinckling or bedewing. **1674** N. Fairfax *Bulk & Selv.* 128 The bedewings of the raughty mold soaking in between its crevices.

be'dewing, *ppl. a.* [f. as prec. + -ing².] That bedews or moistens like dew.

1611 Cotgr., *Rosillant*, dewie, bedewing, dew-dropping. *a* **1834** Coleridge, All-bedewing prayer.

† **be'dewment.** *Obs. rare.* [f. bedew + -ment.] = bedewing *vbl. sb.* (*fig.*) Cf. bedew 3.

a **1679** T. Goodwin *Wks.* (1861) II. 452 Those refreshing bedewments which the Holy Ghost vouchsafeth.

† **be'dewy,** *a.* *rare*⁻¹. [Irregularly formed by assoc. w. bedew and dewy.] = dewy.

1607 A. Brewer *Lingua* v. xvi, Night from her bedewy wings Drops Sleepie silence.

'bedfast, *a. north. dial.* and *Sc.* [f. bed *sb.* + fast *a.* Cf. OE. *legerbedde fest* buried; and MDu. *beddevass* bedfast.] Confined to bed.

a **1639** Spottiswood *Hist. Ch. Scot.* vi. (1677) 341 Farnherst lying bedfast at the time in Aberdene. **1796** Burns *Lett.* (Globe ed.) 564, I have been ailing, sometimes bedfast. **1863** Mrs. Gaskell *Sylvia's L.* I. 30 My old woman is bed-fast.

bedfellow ('bɛd,fɛləʊ). For forms see bed and fellow.

1. One who shares a bed with another; also *fig.*

1478 Sir J. Paston *Lett.* III. 235 [He] hathe entryd the maner of Scolton uppon your bedffelawe Conyerse. **1571** Ascham *Scholem.* (1863) 96 John Whitneye, a yong jentleman, was my bedfeloe. **1610** Shaks. *Temp.* ii. ii. 42 Misery acquaints a man with strange bedfellowes. **1711** Addison *Spect.* No. 90 ¶7 My Bed-fellows left me about an Hour before Day. **1834** J. Wilson *Noct. Ambr.* xxxv. Wks. 1864 IV. 102 *Tickler.* I request to have Fang for my bed fellow.

† **2.** *spec.* A husband or wife; a concubine. *Obs.*

1490 *Plumpton Corr.* 89 My simple bedfelow, your bedewoman and servant..recomendeth hir unto your mastership. **1564** P. Moore *Hope Health* Ep. Ded. 9 Vnto your worship, and to my good Ladie your bedfellowe. **1579** Fulke *Ref. Rastel* 725 Haue not some Popish Priestes such seruants and bedfellowes also? **1684** *Contempl. State Man* i. vi. (1699) 61 Altho' she had a great Dowry, none would covet such a Bed-fellow.

bed-fellowship ('bɛd,fɛləʃɪp). [f. prec. + -ship.] The condition of being bed-fellows.

1611 Tourneur *Ath. Trag.* i. i, Her husbands bedfellowship. **1854** H. Miller *Sch. & Schm.* (1858) 186 The strange bed-fellowship which our recent misery had made.

† **bed-fere, bed-ifere.** *Obs.* Forms: 3–4 **bed-yver(e**, 4–5 **bed-ifere, bedde-fere**, 4–6 **bed-fere**, 6 *s.w. dial.* **bed-aver**, 7 **bed-phe(e)re**. [cf. bed + ifere, and fere:—OE. *ȝefera* companion, fellow. The longer form *bed-ifere* was retained in s.w. dial., where it appeared in 16th c. as *bed-aver*; *bed-fere* was the literary form till 17th c.]

c **1300** in Wright's *Lyric P.* xv. 49 Lyare wes mi latymer, Sleuthe ant slep mi bedyuer [*printed* bedyner]. **1393** Gower *Conf.* II. 229 Unto his bed[i]fere, Deidamy he hath by night. *Ibid.* III. 65 He shal be your beddefere. **1547** Boorde *Introd. Knowl.* 122 Wyl your bedauer, gosse, come home at the next tyde?..My bedauer wyl to London, to try the law. **1609** B. Jonson *Sil. Woman* ii. v, Her that I mean to choose for my bedphere. **1614** Chapman *Odyss.* iii. 542 His bed-fere was Pisistratus. **1656** Blount *Glossogr.*, *Bedpheere* (Sax.) a Bed-fellow.

Bedford ('bɛdfəd). ***Bedford cord***, a woven fabric with prominent cords running in the direction of the warp. Hence in *pl.*, trousers made of Bedford cord. Also ***Bedfords*** ellipt.

1862 *Catal. Internat. Exhib., Brit.* II. No. 4152 Woollen cords, Bedford cords, and velveteens. **1912** *Encycl. Brit.* III. 278/1 *Bedford cord*, a cheaper variety of piqué in which the stripes run the length of the piece. **1914** W. S. Murphy *Mod. Drapery* IV. 20 *Bedford cord*, a kind of ribbed cotton fabric, woven with heavy warp, which composes the main face of the cloth, the weft floating at the back of the structure. **1954** W. Faulkner *Fable* (1955) 33 In the Bedford cords of a British officer. *Ibid.* 83 Official slacks in place of pink Bedfords and long boots. **1966** 'E. Peters' *Piper on Mountain* viii. 136 He had on Bedford cords and a tweed jacket.

Bedfordshire ('bɛdfədʃə(r)). Name of an English county; humorously put for *bed.*

1665 Cotton *Poet. Wks.* (1765) 76 Each one departs to Bedfordshire, And Pillows all securely snort on. *c* **1706** Swift *Polite Conv.* iii. (D.), Faith, I'm for Bedfordshire. [*a* **1845** Hood *Kilmansegg* (D.), There was the bed, so soft, so vast, Quite a field of Bedfordshire clover.]

'bedful. [f. bed *sb.* + -ful]. As much or as many as would fill a bed. (Half humorous.)

1621 Burton *Anat. Mel.* iii. iii. i. i. (1651) 599, I have an old grim sire to my husband..a bedfull of bones.

bedgown ('bɛdgaʊn). [see gown.]

1. A woman's night-gown or 'night-dress.'

1756 Toldervy *Hist. 2 Orphans* I. xiii. 120 No night-cap .., fetid bed-gown, or greasy sack, were appendages to the bodies of these agreeable women. **1762** Sterne *Tr. Shandy* V. vii. 43 Her bed-gowns, and..under-petticoats. *c* **1860** Whittier *Sisters* iii, Annie rose up in her bed-gown white.

2. A kind of jacket worn by women of the working class in the north.

c **1806** D. Wordsworth *Tour Scotl.* in *Jrnls.* (1941) I. 257 The maid-servant..was..dressed in a white bed-gown. *a* **1823** —— *Second Tour Scotl.* in *Ibid.* II. 341 Pity the dress of the young at harvest work is so slovenly. Loose Bed-gowns mostly of white calico. **1827** Scott in *Lockhart* (1839) IX. 168 The women had no other dress than a bed-gown and petticoat. **1863** Kingsley *Water Bab.* 52 The nicest old woman that ever was seen, in her red petticoat and short dimity bedgown.

Hence **bedgowny** *a. colloq.*

1885 *Pall Mall G.* 30 Apr. 6/1 Sloppy, bed-gowny, *décollettée* dresses.

bed-ground. *U.S.* [bed *sb.* or *v.*] Ground on which cattle are bedded for the night.

1880 *Scribner's Monthly* Mar. 770/2 There the cattle are huddled together or 'rounded up' in as small a compass as possible, called 'the bed-ground', and the herders stand guard over them..until morning comes. **1920** Mulford *J. Nelson* xxvi. 267 The bed ground was well chosen and the night promised to be a good one. **1921** —— *Bar-20 Three* xvii. 220 The best bed-ground on the ranch.

'bed-'head. [see head.]

† **1.** The part of a bed on which the head rests; a pillow or bolster. *Obs.*

1483 *Cath. Angl.* 25 Bedhede, *cubitale.*

2. The upper end of a bed.

c **1386** Chaucer *C.T. Prol.* 293 For hym was leuere haue at his bed hede [*v.r.* beddes hede] Twenty bookes clad in blak or rede. **1883** Sir F. Pollock in *Fortn. Rev.* i Oct. 536 A Book..such as every one would like to have at his bed-head.

bediademed, -diamonded, -diaper: see be-.

† **be'didder,** *v. Obs.* Forms: 1 **bedidri-an**, 3 **bididdr-en**. [OE. *bedidrian*, f. be- + *dydrian*, *dyderian* to deceive.] To deceive, delude.

c **1000** Ælfric *Gen.* xliv. 15 Wendon ȝe þat ȝe mihton bedidrian minne ȝelican. *c* **1200** Ormin 19137 Te defell haffde hemm all Bididdredd.

bedight (bɪ'daɪt), *v. arch. Pa. t.* **bedight.** *Pa. pple.* **bedight, -ed.** [f. be- + dight.] *trans.* To equip, furnish, apparel, array, bedeck. (Now only poetical.)

c **1400** in *Pol. Rel. & L. Poems* (1866) 23 Wat is he þis þat comet so briht Wit blodi cloþes al be-diht? **1559** *Mirr. Mag.* 270 (R.) A troope of men..in armes bedight. **1598** Sylvester *Du Bartas* (1608) 462 A garland..The royal bridegrooms radiant brows bedights. **1621** Quarles *Esther* (1717) 8 Jonah straight arose, himself bedight With fit accoutrements for hasty flight. **1642** Milton *Apol. Smect.* Wks. (1851) 269 Whose outward garment hath bin injur'd and ill bedighted. **1674** N. Fairfax *Bulk & Selv.* 129 She not only bedights them with many springs. **1856** Longf. *Elected Knt.* viii, Three modest maidens have me bedight.

Hence **bedight** *ppl. a.*

a **1440** *Sire Degrev.* 144 Lothlych by-dyght. **1598** Yong *Diana* 428 Thy fieldes bedight with Daffodillies. *a* **1849** Poe *Eldorado* i, Gaily bedight, a gallant knight. **1863** C. M. Smith *Dead Lock* 296 Lilian..With gems and gold bedight.

† **be'dighting,** *vbl. sb. Obs.* [f. prec. + -ing¹.] Outfit, furnishing: hence, property, attribute.

1674 N. Fairfax *Bulk & Selv.* 108 Having pared off from body all its parts, we have also bereaved it of all those bedightings or affections that belong to it.

† **be'dilt,** *pa. pple. Obs. rare.* [f. be- + dill, ON. *dylja* to conceal, hide.] Hidden, covered.

1660 T. Hall *Funebria Fl.* ad fin., In bowers May-sprigs gaily built With flowers and garlands all bedilt.

bedim (bɪ'dɪm), *v.*; also 6–7 **bedym, -dymn.** [f. be- + dim.] *trans.* To make dim, cover with dimness, becloud.

1583 Stanyhurst *Æneis* iii. (Arb.) 84 Soomtyme owt it bolcketh from bulck clowds grimly bedimmed. **1610** Shaks. *Temp.* v. i. 41, I haue bedymn'd The Noone-tide Sun. **1878** Huxley *Physiogr.* 75 The surface [is] soon bedimmed on exposure to the atmosphere.

b. *esp.* the eyesight.

1811 Byron *Curse Minerva* 86 Celestial tears bedimm'd her large blue eye. **1850** Blackie *Æschylus* II. 24 A tearful cloud My woeful sight bedims.

c. *fig.* the mind, mental vision, memory, etc.

[**1566** Gascoigne *Jocasta* Wks. (1587) 85 Those raging storms of wrath That so bedym the eyes of thine intent.] **1816** J. Wilson *City of Plague* ii. iv. 179 Nor can the shadow of this passing world Bedim thy holy spirit. **1817** Coleridge *Biog. Lit.* 93 The detestable maxims..of the late French despotism had already bedimmed the public recollections of democratic phrensy. **1849** Hare *Par. Serm.* II. 169 Fear so troubles and bedims and confounds the mind.

bedimmed (bɪ'dɪmd), *ppl. a.* [f. prec. + -ed¹.] Obscured in brightness or clearness.

1790 Cowper *Odyss.* i. 459 The palace dark be-dimm'd. **1831** Carlyle *Misc.* (1857) II. 305 An ancient, bedimmed, half obliterated woodcut. **1858** Hawthorne *Fr. & It. Jrnls.* II. 177 The backgrounds still retain a bedimmed splendor of gilding.

bedimming (bɪ'dɪmɪŋ), *ppl. a.* [f. as prec. + -ing².] That bedims or obscures.

1810 Coleridge *Friend* (1865) 57 Vain halos and bedimming vapours. **1849** Wordsw. *Sonn.* Wks. III. 66 A dragon's eye that feels the stress Of a bedimming sleep.

bedimple (bɪ'dɪmp(ə)l), *v.* [f. be- + dimple.] *trans.* To cover or mark over with dimples.

1718 Motteux *Quix.* (1733) II. 276 The whitest Pebbles bedimple its smooth surface. **1821** Clare *Vill. Minstr.* I. 30 The shower-bedimpled sandy lanes.

bedin, bedinner, etc.: see be- *pref.*

be'dip (bɪ'dɪp), *v.* [OE. *bedyppan*, f. BE- + *dyppan* to DIP. *Obs.* after 12th c., but formed anew *c* 1600.] *trans.* To dip, immerse, treat to a dipping.

c **1000** ÆLFRIC *Gen.* xxxvii. 31 Hiȝ.. bedypton his tunecan on ðam blode. *c* **1000** *Ags. Gosp.* Matt. xxvi. 23 Se þe bedypð [*c* **1160** *Hatton* bedepð] on disce mid me his hand. **1598** SYLVESTER *Du Bartas* (1608) 993 Her.. hands in snow bedipt. **1820** COMBE (Dr. Syntax) *Consol.* II. (D.), The warrior's spear bedipp'd in blood. *a* **1845** HOOD *Storm Hastings* i, Crowds of idlers willing or unwilling To be bedipped.

† **bedirt** (bɪ'dɜːt), *v. Obs.* Also 7 **bedurt.** [f. BE- + DIRT.] *trans.* To cover or defile with dirt; *fig.* 'to throw dirt at,' to vilify.

1622 MABBE tr. *Aleman's Guzman d' Alf.* II. 56 My Master knew I was all bedurted. **1673** PENN *Life* Wks. 1782 I. 39 An Independent and an Anabaptist.. have lately bedirted us in three discourses. **1684** *Contempl. State of Man* I. ix. (1699) 98 Be dirted and defiled with abominable.. crimes.

Hence **bedirted, bedirten** (*Sc.*) *ppl. a.*

1528 A. DALABER *Narr.* in Froude *Hist. Eng.* (1856) II. 56 All bedirted as I was. *a* **1550** *Peebles to Play* (1862) 10 She.. all bedirten drew him out. **1721** STRYPE *Eccl. Mem.* I. I. xxii. 160 A long gown.. all bedirted like, and sloven.

† **be'dirter.** *Obs.* A thrower of dirt; a vilifier.

1747 T. STORY *Life* 64 The Stoners and Bedirters among his Hearers.

bedirty, bedismal, etc.: see BE- *pref.*

bedizen (bɪ'daɪz(ə)n, -'dɪz(ə)n), *v.*; also **bedizzen.** [f. BE- + DIZEN. All English orthoepists have (aɪ); Webster has the alternative (ɪ).] *trans.* To dress out, especially in a vulgar or gaudy fashion.

1661 K. W. *Conf. Charac.* (1860) 81 These petty ladies.. are bedizned in sable sacks, or.. in white sarcenet wallats. **1755** JOHNSON, *Bedizen*, to dress out: a low word. *a* **1779** LANGHORNE *County Just.* (R.) Ye cits, that sore bedizen Nature's face. **1825** SCOTT *Talism.* (1854) 267 You have bedizened me in green, a colour he detests.

b. *fig.*

a **1788** HEADLEY *Parod. Gray's El.* (T.) The name bedizen'd by the pedant muse. **1806** *Edin. Rev.* VIII. 268 The quotations.. with which Mr. Lemaistre has thought fit to bedizzen his pages. **1820** W. IRVING *Sketch Bk.* II. 130 Bedizened out into a burlesque imitation of an antique masque.

bedizened (bɪ'daɪz(ə)nd, -'dɪznd), *ppl. a.* [f. prec. + -ED[1].] Dressed up with vulgar finery.

1707 FARQUHAR *Beaux' Strat.* III. i. 23, I took him for a Captain, he's so bedizen'd with Lace. **1860** MOTLEY *Netherl.* (1868) I. ii. 37 Bedizened dresses. **1867** SMILES *Huguenots Fr.* xix. (1880) 349 A poor bedizened creature.. was led through.. Paris in the character of the Goddess of Reason.

be'dizening, *vbl. sb.* Dressing out.

1863 HOLLAND *Lett. Joneses* xiv. 206 In your devotion to dressing and bedizening of your persons.

be'dizenment. The process, result, or material of bedizening; vulgar or gaudy attire.

1837 CARLYLE *Fr. Rev.* III. IV. iv. 227 They sit there.. with oak-branches, tricolor bedizenment. **1859** KINGSLEY *Misc.* I. 48 Even if there were no bedizenment of jewels.

bedlam ('bɛdləm). Forms: 1–3 **betleem,** 3 **beþþleæm,** 3–6 **beth(e)leem,** 4 **bedleem,** 4–8 **bethlem,** 6– **-lehem,** 3–7 **bedlem,** 5 **bedelem,** 6 **bedleme,** 6–7 **-lame,** 6– **bedlam.** [ME. *Bedlem* = *Bethlem, Bethlehem*; applied to the Hospital of St. Mary of Bethlehem, in London, founded as a priory in 1247, with the special duty of receiving and entertaining the bishop of St. Mary of Bethlehem, and the canons, etc. of this, the mother church, as often as they might come to England. In 1330 it is mentioned as 'an hospital,' and in 1402 as a hospital for lunatics (Timbs); in 1346 it was received under the protection of the city of London, and on the Dissolution of the Monasteries, it was granted to the mayor and citizens, and in 1547 incorporated as a royal foundation for the reception of lunatics. Thence the modern sense, of which instances appear early in 16th c.]

† **1.** The town of Bethlehem in Judea. *Obs.*

971 *Blickl. Hom.* 93 þa he on Betleem wæs acenned. *c* **1200** *Trin. Coll. Hom.* 31 And tealde þe herdes þe wakeden ouer here oref biside þe burch belleem [? betleem]. *c* **1200** ORMIN 3360 He borenn iss I Daviþþ kingess chesstre, þat iss ȝehatenn Beþþleæm. *a* **1300** *Cursor M.* 11234 þat blisful birþ in bethleem [*Gött.* betheleem, *Laud a* **1400** bedlem]. **1382** WYCLIF *Luke* ii, A cite of Dauith that is cleped Bedleem. *c* **1440** *Lay-Folks Mass-Bk.* C. 109 Ihesu, þat was in bedlem borne. **1616** *Pasquil & Kath.* v. 206 M. Mamon is in a Citie of Iurie, called Bethlem, alias, plaine Bedlame.

2. The Hospital of St. Mary of Bethlehem, used as an asylum for the reception and cure of mentally deranged persons; originally situated in Bishopsgate, in 1676 rebuilt near London Wall, and in 1815 transferred to Lambeth. ***Jack*** or ***Tom o' Bedlam***: a madman.

1528 TINDALE *Obed. Chr. Man* (1848) 184 For they.. do things which they of Bedlam may see that they are but madness. **1562** J. HEYWOOD *Prov. & Epigr.* (1867) 107 Lyke Iacke of Bedlem in and out whipping. **1589** *Pappe w. Hatchet* (1844) 34 Could sute them in no place but in Bedlam and Bridewell. **1593** SHAKS. *2 Hen. VI*, v. i. 131 To Bedlem with him! Is the man growne mad? **1605** —— *Lear* I. ii. 148 With a sighe like Tom o' Bedlam. **1678** EVELYN *Mem.* (1857) II. 126, I went to see new Bedlam Hospital.. most sweetly placed in Moorfields, since the dreadful fire. **1866** G. MACDONALD *Ann. Q. Neighb.* xi. (1878) 223 There was I.. in as strait a jacket as ever poor wretch in Bedlam.

3. By extension: A lunatic asylum, a madhouse.

1663 *Aron-bimnucha* 32 The Bedlam.. the skrews.. are the best instances of our kindness. **1699** POMFRET *Love triumph. Reason* 170 'Twas both an hospital and bedlam too. **1702** C. MATHER *Magn. Christi* VII. iv. (1852) 525 A Bethlehem seems to have been fitter for them than a gallows. *a* **1743** LD. HERVEY *Beauties Eng.* (1804) I. 106 Those virgins act a wiser part Who hospitals and bedlams would explore.

b. *abstr.* Madness, lunacy. Also *interjectionally.*

1598 MARSTON *Pygmal.* III. 149 Bedlame, Frenzie, Madnes, Lunacie, I challenge all your moody Empery. *a* **1645** HABINGTON *Fine Y. Folly* v, Bedlam! this is pretty sport.

4. *fig.* A scene of mad confusion or uproar.

a **1667** COWLEY *Cromwell* Wks. 1710 II. 627 Thou dost.. A Babel, and a Bedlam grow. **1713** *Guardian* No. 132 (1756) II. 194 Our house is a sort of Bedlam, and nothing in order. **1850** CARLYLE *Latter-d. Pamph.* viii. (1872) 276 That all this was a Donnybrook Bedlam.

† **5.** An inmate of Bethlehem Hospital, London, or of a lunatic asylum, or one fit for such a place, a madman; *spec.* one of the discharged, but often only half-cured, patients of the former, who were licensed to beg, wearing as a badge a tin plate on their left hand or arm; called also ***bedlam-beggars, bedlamers, bedlamites.*** Obs.

1522 SKELTON *Why not to Courte* Wks. II. 653 Such a madde bedleme For to rewle this reame. **1541** BARNES *Wks.* (1573) 294/2 A scorge to tame those bedlames with. **1545** COVERDALE *Abridgm. Erasm. Enchir.* iii. Wks. 1844 I. 500 The world judgeth us to be fools.. and to be mad bedlames. **1594** T. B. *La Primaud. Fr. Acad.* II. 169 The veriest bedlems that can be. **1611** COTGR. s.v. *Affamé*, A hungry Boore is halfe a bedlam. **1626** L. OWEN *Spec. Jesuit.* (1629) 37 The Duke imagining him to bee a foole, or a bedlem.. let him goe. **1678** BUNYAN *Pilgr.* I. 123 Some [said] they were Bedlams. **1701** SWIFT *Mrs. Harris' Petit.* Wks. 1755 III. II. 61 She roar'd like a Bedlam.

6. *attrib.*, at length *adj.* Of, belonging to, or fit for Bedlam or a mad-house; mad, foolish.

a **1535** MORE *Wks.* (1557) 16 The rauing of bethlem people. **1575** TURBERV. *Falconrie* 254 Falcons.. when they bee impatient and bedlam in the mewe. **1599** SHAKS. *Hen. V*, v. i. 20 Ha, art thou bedlam? **1642** MILTON *Apol. Smect.* Wks. (1851) 275 But this which followes is plaine bedlam stuffe. **1788** COWPER *Table-T.* 609 Anacreon, Horace, play'd.. This Bedlam part.

7. *Comb.*: sbs., as ***Bedlam beggar*** (cf. BEDLAM 5), ***-house, -man***; adjs., as ***bedlam-mad, -ripe, -witted.***

1525 TINDALE *N.T.* Prol., Who ys.. so bedlem madde to affyrm that good is the naturall cause of yuell? **1533** MORE *Answ. Poyson. Bk.* Wks. (1557) 1036/2 More bedelem rype then thys booke is. **1556** J. HEYWOOD *Spider & F.* lxxxiv. 28 Beetill blind, and bedlem mad. **1572** R. H. tr. *Lavaterus' Ghostes* (1596) 13 Bedleme houses where madde and frantike men are kept. **1605** SHAKS. *Lear* II. iii. 14 The country giues me proofe, and president Of Bedlam beggers. **1646** G. DANIEL *Poems* Wks. 1878 I. 60 All Bedlam-witted, walke in Bedlem wise. **1658** USSHER *Ann.* vi. (1688) 106 Like a bedlam-man. **1837** CARLYLE *Fr. Rev.* III. VI. vii. 346 Hardly audible amid the Bedlam-storm.

† **'bedlamer**[1]. *Obs.* [f. BEDLAM + -ER[1].] A lunatic; *spec.* a Bedlam-beggar.

c **1675** W. BLUNDELL *Crogsby Rec.* 137 A gentleman who passed as a Bedlamer. *a* **1733** NORTH *Lives* I. 287 This country was then much troubled with Bedlamers.

bedlamer[2] ('bɛdləmə(r)). [? ad. F. *bête de la mer* sea-beast.] A seal-hunters' name for a hooded seal of one year old and a harp-seal of two years old.

1773 G. CARTWRIGHT *Jrnl.* 15 Nov. (1792) I. 284 He saw a shoal of bedlamers before his door one day last week. **1895** *Outing* (U.S.) XXVII. 22/1 The harp seals.. post a sentinel, usually a bedlamer or two-year-old harp, on one of the highest pinnacles of the floe. *Ibid.* 23/2 The 'Sculp'.. of the harp and bedlamer will average one hundred and fifty pounds.

'bedlamism. A word or thing characteristic of Bedlam; a trait of madness.

1843 CARLYLE *Past & Pr.* 288 Nothing but a noisy bedlamism in your mouth. **1865** —— *Fredk. Gt.* VI. XV. xi. 80 A strict place, moreover; its very bedlamisms flowing by law.

bedlamite ('bɛdləmaɪt), *sb.* and *a.* [f. as prec. + -ITE.] **A.** *sb.* An inmate of Bedlam or of a lunatic asylum; a madman or lunatic.

1621 BURTON *Anat. Mel.* II. iv. I. v, Such raging bedlamites, as are tied in chains. **1691** WOOD *Ath. Oxon.* II. 489 More fit.. to be read by Bedlamites than pretenders to vertue and modesty. **1751** SMOLLETT *Per. Pic.* (1779) III. lxxxi. 168 Lord B—— raved like a bedlamite. **1822** BYRON *Juan* VI. xxxiv, Like.. bedlamites broke loose.

B. *attrib.* or *adj.* Lunatic, mad.

1815 SCOTT *Guy M.* liii, 'The devil take the bedlamite old woman!' *a* **1852** MOORE *Three Doctors* v, Dr. Slop, upon subjects divine, Such bedlamite slaver lets drop.

bedlamitish ('bɛdləmaɪtɪʃ), *a.* [f. prec. + -ISH[1].] Like a bedlamite; mad; foolish.

1824 *Blackw. Mag.* XVI. 179 None.. was so Bedlamitish, as to fancy that he himself was personally aggrieved.

'bedlamlike, *a.* and *adv.* Like a madman.

A. *adj.* Mad-looking.

1618 M. BARET *Horsemanship* I. 58 That will.. make him [the horse] more bedlam-like.

B. *adv.* After the manner of a madman.

1576 NEWTON tr. *Lemnie's Complex.* (1633) 68 Many being angred.. will Bedlam-like run upon their enemies with minds enraged. **1581** —— *Seneca's Thebais* 41 Agaue (bedlemlike) raunged up and downe the woode With systers hers.

† **'bedlamly,** *adv. Obs.* [f. BEDLAM *a.* + -LY[2].] Like a madman, insanely.

1553–87 FOXE *A. & M.* (1596) 996/1 To speake as undiscreetlie and bedlemly, as ye doe.

† **bedlar, -lawer,** *a.* (and *sb.*) *Obs.* exc. *dial.* [ME. *bedlawere*, f. BED + ? ON. *lag* lying: cf. MHG. *betteliger, -ic*, G. *bettläger, -ig*, in same sense.] Bed-ridden; a person confined to bed.

c **1440** *Promp. Parv.* 28 Bedlawyr, *decumbens.* **1447** BOKENHAM *Seyntys* (1835) 288 Seke wummen.. wych bedlaure dede lye. **1468** *Medulla Gram.*, *Clinicus*, a bedlawere. **1474** *Act. Audit.* 36 (JAM.) Johne of Kerss wes seke and bedlare. **1868** G. MACDONALD *Seaboard Par.* I. x. 146 Patients, who considered themselves *bedlars*.. bedridden.

b. *Comb.* † ***bedlawerman.***

1419 in *Promp. Parv.* 28 Item lego cuilibet pauperum vocatorum bedlawermen.. iiij *d.*

bedlar, local variant of BEDRAL, beadle.

bedle, obs. form of BEADLE.

† **bedle,** *Obs.* BDELLIUM; cf. L. *bedella.*

1591 PERCIVALL *Sp. Dict.*, *Bedel*, a bedle stone, *Bethillus.*

'bedless, *a.* [f. BED *sb.* + -LESS.] Without a bed, unprovided with a bed.

1707 J. STEVENS tr. *Quevedo's Com. Wks.* 430, I am careless and bedless. **1864** SALA *Daily Tel.* 13 Oct., Bedless and supperless wanderers. **1870** R. ANDERSON *Missions Amer. Bd.* IV. xlii. 413 The people seem to be almost bedless.

Hence, **'bedlessness.**

1861 SALA *Tw. round Clock* 7 Were it winter, our bedlessness would be indefensible.

'bed-linen. [f. BED *sb.* + LINEN.] Bed-clothes, esp. sheets and pillow-cases, originally of linen.

1815 SCOTT *Guy M.* xliv, She proceeded.. to arrange the stipulated bed-linen.

Bedlington ('bɛdlɪŋtən). [Named after *Bedlington* in Northumberland.] In full ***Bedlington terrier***: a short-haired terrier characterized by a narrow head, short body, and longish legs.

[**1867** *Field* 3 Aug. 102/1 In the dog show a local breed of terriers was distinguished by a separate class. They are named after the town of Bedlington.] *Ibid.* 102/2 (*heading*) Prize List.. Bedlington Terriers. **1869** *Ibid.* 27 Mar. 265/3 In 1825 she [*sc.* 'Coates's Phoebe'] was mated with Anderson's Piper, and the fruit of this union was the Bedlington terrier.. The model Bedlington should be rather long and small in the jaw, but withal muscular. **1875** in V. Shaw *Illustr. Bk. Dog* (1881) xix. 144 The Bedlington Terrier should be broad in the nostril, with a flesh-coloured nose. **1881** *Ibid.* 143 The support of the public at large has not hitherto extended much beyond affording prizes for Bedlingtons.

'bed-ˌmaker. [f. BED *sb.* + MAKER.]

1. One who constructs beds.

c **1500** *Cocke Lorelles B.* (1843) 9 Bedmakers, fedbed makers, and wyre drawers; Founders.. and broche makers.

2. One who arranges beds for use again, after they have been slept in; the official name in the English universities for old women or men who make the beds and sweep the rooms in college.

1465 *Mann. & Househ. Exp.* 184 Iteme.. the bede-maker a pelow. **1552** HULOET, Bedde maker, *Lectisterniator.* **1678** *Yng. Mans Call.* 107 His health.. is his best bed-maker, that makes his bed so easie to rest on. **1691** *Case of Exeter Coll.* 18 For fear she should.. lose her place of Bed-maker. **1716** CIBBER *Love Makes Man* I. i. 21 He never spoke six Words to any Woman in his Life, but his Bed-maker. **1789** MRS. PIOZZI *Journ. France* II. 118 A person not unlike an Oxford or Cambridge bed-maker. **1825** BENTHAM *Ration. Rew.* 337 The barbers, cooks, bed-makers, errand-boys, and other unlettered retainers to the university, are sworn in English to the observance of these Latin statutes.

So **bed-making.**

1670 EACHARD *Cont. Clergy* 16 To prevent sizars over heating their brains: bedmaking, chamber-sweeping, and water-fetching, were doubtless great preservatives. **1691** *Case of Exeter Coll.* 19 Her Employ of Bed-making in Exeter Colledge. **1883** *Glasgow Wkly. Her.* 21 Apr. 8/4 Ladies' Baking, Cooking and Bedmaking Aprons. **1885** *Oxf. Student's Handbk.* 235 In addition, £7 a year for bedmaking.

bedman, obs. variant of BEADSMAN.

† **be'do,** *v. Obs.* In 1–3 **bedón, bidón.** [OE. *bedón*, f. BE- + *dón* to put, Do. With sense 2, cf. Ger. *bethun, bemachen.*]

1. *trans.* To put to, to shut.

c **1000** *Ags. Ps.* cxlvii. 2 þæt þu þine doru mihtest bedón.

2. To befoul, defile with ordure.

c **1230** *Ancr. R.* 130 þus wende Saul into hole uort te bidon þene stude. *Ibid.* 216 Habbeð þeos þet fuluste mester..þet so bidoð ham suluen.

3. To adorn, ornament, garnish.

? *a* **1500** in Furniv. *Percy Fol.* II. 305 A kirtle and a mantle ..with branches and ringes full richely bedone. *a* **1765** '*Ld. Thomas & Fair Annet*' xx, in Child *Ballads* III. (1885) 183 The belt that was about her waist Was a' wi' pearls bedone.

bedoctor, bedolt, bedot, etc.: see BE- *pref.*

bedog (bɪˈdɒg), *v.* [f. BE- + DOG *sb.* and *v.*]

1. *trans.* To call 'dog.'

1794 WOLCOTT (P. Pindar) *Rowl. for Oliver* Wks. II. 260 Be-dogging this poor singer, that be-bitching.

2. To follow about like a dog, to dog.

1858 TRELAWNY *Rec. Shelley, Byron, etc.* ii. (1878) 57 Envy, malice, and hatred bedogged his steps.

Hence **beˈdogged** *ppl. a.*, Become like a dog.

1672 COTTON *Scarron* II. (1692) 43 She had told her dear bedogged.

†**beˈdote,** *v. Obs.* [f. BE- 3 + DOTE.] *trans.* To cause to dote, make silly, befool.

c **1385** CHAUCER *L.G.W.* 1547 Ffor to be-dote this queen was here assent. **1449** PECOCK *Repr.* 145 Salomon..fonned and bidotid with his wijfis, made ydolis false goddis. **1583** GOLDING *Calvin on Deut.* clxxxiii. 1139 So bedoted that they could not come to the knowledge of their sinnes.

†**bedoubt,** *v. Obs.* Also 5 pa. pple. bedoute. [f. BE- 2 + DOUBT *v.* Cf. F. *redouter.*] To dread.

1470 HARDYNG *Chron.* cli, Aboue all men he was there moste bedoute.

Bedouin (ˈbɛduːiːn, now usu. -ɪn), *sb.* (and *a.*) Forms: 4 *pl.* bedoynes, 7 *pl.* baduini, *sing.* bedwin, 8 bedonian, bedouia, bedoween, 8- bedouin (9 beduin). Also *β.* 9 *sing.* bedawy, -awee, *pl.* bedawin, -een. [a. F. *bedouin*, 12th c. OF. *li bedowin* (pl.), 13th c. *beduins, beduyn* (sing.), a. Arab. *badāwīn*, or *badawīn*, pl. of *badāwīy* or *badawīy* a dweller in the desert, f. *badw* desert. First known to Europeans in Crusading times. The plural, being of most frequent use, was adapted in med.L. as *beduīni, bedewīni*, It. *beduini, baduini*, whence a sing. L. *beduīnus*, It. *beduino*, F. *beduin*, etc., with the Arab. pl. ending *-īn* retained: cf. *assassin*, also *cherubin, seraphin, rabbin.* In English apparently forgotten after Crusading times till the 17th c. The mod. spelling is French: travellers acquainted with Arabic often substitute the forms in *β.*] An Arab of the desert.

c **1400** MAUNDEV. v. 35, I duelled with him as soudyour in his werres..aȝen the Bedoynes. **1603** R. JOHNSON *Kingd. & Commonw.* 171 Parte of the Arabians..live in the fields and mountaines, and are termed Baduini. **1635** PAGITT *Christianogr.* I. ii. (1636) 71 A few Christians remaining, called Bedwins. **1767** RUSSEL in *Phil. Trans.* LVIII. 144 The Bedouins at this place. **1788** GIBBON *Decl. & F.* (1802) IX. 223 The same life is uniformly pursued by..the modern Bedoweens. **1796** MORSE *Amer. Geog.* II. 609 The Bedonians, or wandering Arabs. **1847** KINGLAKE *Eöthen* 180, I was now amongst the true Bedouins.

β. **1865** *Fam. Treas. Sund. Read.* VII. 442 The tent of the modern Bedawy. **1870** R. ANDERSON *Missions Amer. Bd.* III. iii. 45 The wild Bedawin..were worse than the Greeks.

b. *transf.* One who leads a Bedouin-like life elsewhere; a gipsy. (Cf. *City Arab.*)

1863 *Times* 2 May, Where were all the dingy bedouins of England who travel through to this great gathering?

2. *attrib.* or as *adj.*

1844 *Mem. Babylonian P'cess.* 82, I had seen several Bedouin girls. **1861** SALA *Tw. round Clock* 45 Half-starved Bedouin children, mostly Irish.

ˈBedouinism. The Bedouin life or system.

1865 *Sat. Rev.* 5 Aug. 176 It is against this ideal Bedouinism that Mr. Palgrave is chiefly vehement.

†**beˈdove, beˈdoven,** *pa. pple. Obs.* Forms: 1 bedofen, 6 *Sc.* bedoif, bedowyn, -ovin. [:—OE. *bedofen*, pa. pple. of *bedúfan* to submerge, f. BE- + *dúfan* to dive, sink.] Immersed, plunged.

a **1000** ÆLFRIC *Hom.* II. 472 Bedofen on deoppre nytennysse. **1513** DOUGLAS *Æneis* v. vi. 125 All his membris in mude and dung bedoif. *Ibid.* VII. Prol. 60 Bedovin in donkis deyp was every syk.

†**beˈdow(e,** *v. Sc. Obs.* [perh. f. BE- + DOWIE, sad, or its root DOLE, sorrow.] *trans.* ? To sadden.

1513 DOUGLAS *Æneis* XIII. i. 42 The gret syte Thar breistis had bedowit and to smyte.

bedowle, bedown, bedowse, etc.: see BE-.

beˈdown, *prep. rare*⁻¹. [f. BE- + DOWN, on some mistaken analogy.] = DOWN, ADOWN.

? *a* **1800** in Aytoun's *Ballads Scot.* (1858) II. 369 Bedown the bents of Banquo brae My lane I wandered.

bed-pan (ˈbɛd,pæn). [cf. MDu. *beddepanne*: see PAN.]

1. A pan for warming beds; a warming-pan.

1585 J. HIGGINS *Junius' Nomencl., Batillus cubicularius*.. un eschauffoir de lit, a bed pan, or warming pan. **1597** GERARD *Herbal* (1633) 1066 A little bag with some..Baysalt, and made hot vpon a bed-pan. **1699** GARTH *Dispens.* 72 Each Combatant his Adversary mauls With batter'd Bedpans.

2. A chamber utensil constructed for use in bed.

1678 in *Rec. New Castle Del. Court* (Penn.) (1904) 361 Two Earthen bed Pans. **1711** in *Essex Inst. Hist. Coll.* IV. 187/1 A bed pan and stool pan. **1805** *Med. Jrnl.* XIV. 254 The urine has continued to flow involuntarily, but a few spoons full have been occasionally voided into the bed pan. **1883** FLOR. NIGHTINGALE in Quain's *Dict. Med.* 1046 Bedpans should have Carbolic powder in them lavishly.

bed-post (ˈbɛd,pəʊst). [see POST.] A post of a bed, one of the upright supports of the framework of a bed. Also in phr. ***the twinkling of a bedpost***: cf. BEDSTAFF; ***between you and me and the bed-post***: in all confidence or secrecy.

1598 MARSTON *Pygmal.* iii. 149 The antique Bed-post. **1815** SCOTT *Guy M.* xliv, One of the bed-posts of a sort of tent-bed. **1830** MRS. ROYALL *Lett. fr. Alabama* 136 Between you and I and the bed post, I begin to think it all a plot of the priests. **1832** [see POST *sb.*[1] 1 c]. **1871** M. COLLINS *Mrq. & Merch.* III. iii. 78 In the twinkling of a bed-post Is each savoury platter clear. **1882** BLACKMORE *Christowell* xiii, Between you and me and the bed-post, Short—as the old ladies say—I don't want Jack to have her.

bedrabble (bɪˈdræb(ə)l), *v.* Chiefly in ppl. adj. bedrabbled. [f. BE- 2 + DRABBLE.] *trans.* To make wet and dirty with rain and mud.

c **1440** *Promp. Parv.* 28 Be-drabylyd or drabelyde, *paludosus.* **1850** KINGSLEY *Alt. Locke* xi, Jacket and leather gaiters, sufficiently bedrabbled with mud. **1879** *Scribn. Mag.* July 334 The bedrabbled snows of March shrank away.

Hence **beˈdrabbling** *vbl. sb.*

1884 *Harper's Mag.* Sept. 623/2 With no disfigurement of scorching or bedrabbling.

bedraden, obs. form of BEDRID.

bedraggle (bɪˈdræg(ə)l), *v.* [f. BE- + DRAGGLE.] **a.** To wet (dress, skirts, or the like) so that they drag, or hang limp and clinging with moisture. **b.** 'To soil clothes by suffering them, in walking, to reach the dirt.' Johnson. (Rare in the active till modern times.)

1727 SWIFT *Past. Dial.* Wks. 1755 IV. I. 78 Poor Patty Blount, no more be seen Bedraggled in my walks so green. **1857** MRS. BROWNING *Aur. Leigh* 9 The very sky Bedraggled with the desolating salt. **1871** *Daily News* 24 Aug., The rain has fallen..bedraggling the flags and banners.

Hence, **bedraggled** *ppl. a.*, **bedragglement.**

1727 [see prec.] **1824** W. IRVING *T. Trav.* I. 36 Such pale, careworn faces, such bedraggled dresses. **1852** HAWTHORNE *Tanglew. T.* 105 All in a terribly bedraggled condition. **1882** *Standard* 7 June 3/1 Elaborate costumes..much the worse, not for wear, but for..bedragglement.

bedral, bederal (ˈbɛd(ə)rəl). *Sc.* Also bethral, -el, betheral, -el. [App. a corruption of BEADLE: the ending may be due to form-assoc.]

A church officer in Scotland with duties akin to, but not identical with, those of the English beadle, often combining those of clerk, sexton, and bell-ringer.

1815 SCOTT *Guy M.* lv, Put in auld Elspeth, the bedral's widow—the like o' them's used wi' graves and ghaists, and thae things. **1823** BYRON *Juan* x. lxxiii, Black Edward's helm, and Becket's bloody stone, Were pointed out as usual by the bedral. **1834** M. SCOTT *Cruise Midge* (1863) 211 The Dominie was sitting..opposite the auld Betherel.

bedrape, etc.: see BE- *pref.*

†**beˈdravel,** *v. Obs.* Also 8 bedrawl. [f. BE- + DRAVEL.] *trans.* To cover with drivel or saliva.

1377 LANGL. *P. Pl.* B. v. 194 þanne com couetyise..His berde was bidraueled. [**1721** BAILEY, *Bedrawled*, bedrabbled, bedrivelled.]

†**beˈdread,** *ppl. a. Obs. rare.* Dreaded.

c **1485** *Digby Myst.* (1882) I. 64, I am most be-dred with my bronde bright.

bedread, -red(e, -reed, obs. ff. BEDRID.

beˈdreint, obs. f. *bedrenched*: see BEDRENCH.

†**ˈbedrel,** *a.* (and *sb.*) *Obs. rare.* Also 6 beddrell, bedral, 7 bedrell, 9 *Sc.* beddel. [? Corrupted from *bedred*, BEDRID, or from BEDLAR.]

A. *adj.* = BEDRIDDEN.

1513 DOUGLAS *Æneis* XII. vii. 32 Quhilk as beddrell [*v.r.* bedrel] lay Befor hys zet. **1603** FLORIO *Montaigne* I. xix. (1632) 32 There is no man so crazed, bedrell, or decrepit.

B. as *sb.* A bedridden person.

a **1572** KNOX *Hist. Ref.* 109 (JAM.) The Blind, Crooked, Bedralis, Widowis, Orphelingis. **1815** CHALMERS *Let.* in *Life* (1851) II. 13 Is the beddel got better? **1845** *Statist. Acc. Scot.*, Kincard. XI. 249 The poor were of three classes, viz. beddels, those who were confined by infirmity, etc.

bedrench (bɪˈdrɛnʃ), *v. Pa. t.* and *pa. pple.* bedrenched; also 4-6 bedreint, 6 bedrent. [f. BE- + DRENCH.] Intensive of DRENCH; to soak.

c **1450** *Crt. of Love* 577 Lady Venus..Receive our billes with teres al bedreint. **1563** SACKVILLE *Mirr. Mag., Induct.* xxi, And showers..all bedrent the place. **1593** SHAKS. *Rich. II*, III. iii. 46 Such Crimson Tempest should bedrench.. king Richard's land. **1656** SANDERSON *Serm.* (1689) 362 Their heads..bedrencht..with Ointments. **1812** W. TENNANT *Anster F.* II. lviii, They..bedrench their blood with wine.

bedress (bɪˈdrɛs), *v.* [f. BE- + DRESS.] *trans.* To dress up. Hence **bedressed** (bɪˈdrɛst), *ppl. a.*

1821 COMBE (Dr. Syntax) *Wife* v. (D.) The bride..had bedress'd Her upright form in all her best. **1863** G. CALVERT *Gentlem.* i. 8 Let no bedressed, bescented passer curl his lip.

†**beˈdrib,** *v. Obs.* [cf. DRIB.]

1681 OTWAY *Soldier's Fort.* IV. i, A swinging drubbing to bedrib him.

bedribble, bedrift, etc.: see BE- *pref.*

bedrid (ˈbɛdrɪd), *a.*, orig. *sb.* Forms: 1-2 bedreda (-rida), 4 bederede, 4-5 bedrede, 4-8 bedred, 5 -ered, beedered, 6 beddred, bedread, -reed, -ridde, 7 beddered, -ridde, 6- bedrid. [OE. *bedreda, -rida*, f. *bed* bed + *rida* rider, f. *rídan* to ride. LG. has, in same sense, *bedderede, -redig*; the dulling of the atonic vowel in OE. is frequent in forms like *misleca*, for *mislíca*, etc.]

1. Confined to bed through sickness or infirmity. The usual prose form is now BEDRIDDEN.

c **1000** Thorpe's *Hom.* II. 422 (Bosw.) Ðær læʒ be ðám weʒe án bedreda. *Ibid.* I. 472 Drihten cwæþ to sumum bedridan. **1340** HAMPOLE *Pr. Consc.* 6198 Seke I was, and bedred lay. *c* **1430** *How Gd. Wife taught Dau.* 19 in *Babees Bk.* (1868) 37 þe poore & þe beedered, loke þou not loþe. **1535** *Act 27 Hen. VIII*, xxv, All leprouse and pore beddred creatures. **1565** JEWELL *Repl. Harding* (1611) 393 Lying Bed-read many yeeres for sicknesse of Body. **1588** SHAKS. *L.L.L.* I. i. 139 To her decrepit, sicke, and bed-rid Father. *a* **1626** BP. ANDREWES *Serm.* xix. (1661) 430 *Clinici Christiani*, beddered Christians. **1765** WESLEY in *Wks.* (1872) III. 207 He is..now quite bed-rid. **1815** SOUTHEY *Roderick* I. 141 Bed-rid infirmity alone was left behind.

2. *fig.* Worn out, decrepit, impotent.

1621 QUARLES *Argalus & P.* (1678) 73 Whose richly furnish'd Table would invite A bedrid stomack to an appetite. **1641** MILTON *Animadv.* Wks. (1851) 217 What an over-worne and bedrid Argument is this. **1822** HAZLITT *Table-t.* I. vi. 130 In danger of being bed-rid in his faculties. **1837** CARLYLE *Fr. Rev.* I. I. III. vii. 75 Orthodoxy, bedrid as she seemed.

bedridden (ˈbɛd,rɪd(ə)n), *a.* (*sb.*) Forms: 4 bedreden, -redden, -raden, 5 bedredene, -redyn, -ryden, 8- bedridden. [f. BEDRID, the *-en* being added on the analogy of ppl. adjs.]

A. *adj.* = BEDRID 1.

1340 HAMPOLE *Pr. Consc.* 808 When he is seke, and bedreden lys. **1393** LANGL. *P. Pl.* C. VIII. 108 A bedreden womman. *c* **1440** *Gesta Rom.* lxxxv. 459 He laye bedredene vij. yere. **1711** F. FULLER *Med. Gymn.* 28 A kind of bedridden Creature. **1796** MORSE *Amer. Geog.* II. 25 The bedridden may hear divine service in their beds. **1856** R. VAUGHAN *Mystics* (1860) I. 239 He tells a bedridden man to climb the mountains.

fig. **1816** COLERIDGE *Lay Serm.* 319 Truths..considered as so true as to lose all the powers of truth, and lie bedridden in the dormitory of the soul.

†**B.** as *sb.* A bedridden person. *Obs. rare.*

1429 *Wills & Inv. N.C.* (1835) 78 Euery hows of almouse ordeynet for bedrydens.

ˈbed,riddenness. Also 7 bedridnesse. [f. BEDRID, -DEN + -NESS.] Bedridden condition.

1630 DONNE *Serm.* 245 Bind me..in the Corde of Decrepitnesse and Bedridnesse. **1871** HAWTHORNE *Sept. Felton* (1879) 49 My old grandmother laments her bedriddenness.

†**ˈbedrip.** *Obs.* Also bedrepe, (bederpe), bederepe, -rape, bedripe, bidrip(e, -repe. [OE. *bed-ríp*, f. *bed-* prayer, request (see BEAD) + *ríp* reaping, harvest: lit. 'reaping by request'; called also *bén-ríp*, f. *bén* prayer. Retained as a technical term in charters, etc., and variously corrupted: seems to have become obs. in 15th c.]

A service which some tenants had to perform to their lord, viz. at his request or bidding to reap his corn at harvest-time. The days thus employed were sometimes called *boon-days.*

1226 10 *Hen. III. Rot.* 8 (Blount) Debent venire in autumpno ad precariam quæ vocatur *a le bederepe.* **1417** *E. E. Wills* (1882) 27 My poure tenauntes..that haueth yȝeue to me Capouns & bederpes, and Plouwys. **1670** BLOUNT *Law Dict.* Bederepe, Bidrepe is a service, which some Tenants were anciently bound to perform, viz. To reap their Landlord's Corn at Harvest.

bedrit, -ite, obs. Sc. form of BEDIRT *v.*

†**beˈdrive,** *v. Obs.* [f. BE- + DRIVE: in Caxton, directly after Flem. *bedryven*, or G. *betreiben.*] **a.** *trans.* To drive about; **b.** To commit, perpetrate, do; **c.** *intr.* To have to do *with.*

c **1205** LAY. 6206 Sæ-werie men mid wedere bi-driuene. **1481** CAXTON *Reynard* (Arb.) 78 Ony that wolde bedryue ony thyng ayenst you. *Ibid.* 114 No man dar..but preyse alle that they bedryue. *Ibid.* 27 Also I have bydryuen with dame erswynde his wyf.

bedrivel, bedrizzle: see BE- *pref.*

bed-rock. *Geol.* (orig. *U.S.*) The solid rock underlying alluvial and other superficial formations; also *fig.* bottom, lowest level.

1850 N. KINGSLEY *Diary* (1914) 154 We are in for seeing the bed rock all along the bottom. **1872** SCHELE DE VERE *Americanisms* 171 The miner..hopes to reach bed-rock,

where gold is found in quantities. **1873** G. A. LAWRENCE *Silverland* 181 The material invariably waxes greatly richer as the 'bed-rock' is neared. **1879** *Encycl. Brit.* X. 745/1 In alluvial deposits the richest ground is usually found in contact with the bed rock.

fig. **1869** S. BOWLES *Our New West* v. 99 We came down to 'bed-rock' as the miners say, i.e. an extra flannel shirt and a pocket-comb. **1881** *Chicago Times* 11 June, The transactions..having been based on bed-rock prices. **1883** *Century* 581 The family is about down to bedrock. **1884** NYE *Baled Hay* 65 Whenever the dead-beat poet strikes bedrock. **1900** 'O. HENRY' *Roads of Destiny* iii. 52 From general topics the conversation concentrated to the bed-rock of grim personalities. **1912** J. S. HUXLEY *Individ. in Animal Kingdom* vi. 151 We have come down to the bed-rock questions of biology.

bedroom (ˈbɛdruːm). [see ROOM.]

1. Room in bed, sleeping room or space. *rare.*

1590 SHAKS. *Mids. N.* II. ii. 51 Then by your side, no bedroome me deny.

2. A room used or intended to contain a bed or beds; a sleeping apartment. (Now in common use instead of the earlier BED-CHAMBER.)

1616 SURFL. & MARKH. *Countr. Farm* 16 On the other side of the Kitchin shall be the Farmers Bed-roome. **1792** *Munchausen's Trav.* iii. 9 The windows of my bed-room. *a* **1859** MACAULAY *Hist. Eng.* V. 73 The gentlemen of the retinue..were..thrust into a single bedroom.

3. a. *attrib.* and *Comb.*

1813 SOUTHEY *Life Nelson* I. i. 7 He was lowered down at night from the bed-room window by some sheets. **1816** SCOTT *Antiq.* I. ix. 208 The Antiquary took up a bedroom candlestick of massive silver and antique form. **1834** DICKENS *Sk. Boz* (1836) ser. I. I. 211 Plated bedroom candle-sticks. **1905** F. H. BURNETT *Little Princess* viii. 120 She shuffled across the attic in her bedroom slippers. **1928** J. CARY *Castle Corner* 455 He had a full inventory of the marriage chamber, including the bedroom china, decorated with primroses. **1967** E. SHORT *Embroidery & Fabric Collage* iii. 80 For bedroom cushions finer fabrics and technique could be used.

b. In extended use, usu. implying sexual relationship; sexy.

[**1915** E. POUND in *Lett. J. Joyce* (1966) II. 366 Bed rooms scenes where the audience can be tittivated, eroticised.] **1924** M. ARLEN *Green Hat* iv. 112, I thought the editor might take objection to certain passages, as there is some strong bedroom stuff in it. **1947** AUDEN *Age of Anxiety* (1948) ii. 41 Here a dean sits Making bedroom eyes at a beef steak. **1953** *Time* 6 July 72/1 It has also been described as a bedroom farce set in a living room. **1959** M. CHAMBERLAIN *Dear Friends & Darling Romans* (1960) iv. 41 Italians are bedroom-eyed gigolos. **1967** J. POTTER *Foul Play* i. 11 George's wife had blue bedroom eyes.

Hence **ˈbedroomed** *a.*, having a bedroom; **ˈbedroomy** *a. colloq.*, characteristic of a bedroom.

1865 *Pall Mall G.* 20 Apr. 3 Eight and nine people were found in the single bedroomed houses. **1866** HOWELLS *Venetian Life* vii. 90 A bed-roomy smell.

bedrop (bɪˈdrɒp), *v.* Pa. pple. **bedropped, bedropt.** [f. BE- 4 + DROP.]

1. *trans.* To drop upon, cover or wet with drops.

1393 GOWER *Conf.* III. 254 As men sene the dew bedroppe The leves and the floures eke. **1667** MILTON *P.L.* x. 527 The Soil Bedropt with blood of Gorgon. **1829** WORDSW. *Liberty* Wks. V. 102 Life's book for Thee may lie unclosed, till age Shall with a thankful tear bedrop its latest page.

2. *pa. pple.* Sprinkled as with drops.

1658 ROWLAND *Mouffet's Theat. Ins.* 965 The..body yellow, bedropt with black from the neck to the tail. **1858** *Blackw. Mag.* 482 Lomond and Awe bedropt with woody isles.

b. *fig.* Strewn, interspersed.

1377 LANGL. *P. Pl.* B. XIII. 321 It was bidropped with wratthe and wikked wille. **1855** GILFILLAN *Dryden* Introd. 20 A tale..bedropt with the most flagrant falsehoods.

bedrown, bedrowse, bedrug, etc.: see BE-.

bedryden, obs. form of BEDRIDDEN.

bedside (ˈbɛdˌsaɪd). [Coalesced from *bed's side* in prep. phrases like 'by the beddes side' = beside the bed; thus not a true compound.] **a.** Place or position by a bed: used in various phrases, to signify proximity to, companionship with, or attendance on, one confined to bed.

c **1374** CHAUCER *Parl. Foules* 99 Right at my beddis side. *c* **1435** *Torr. Portugal* 1364 The damyselle..Set hym on her bed-syde. *c* **1440** *Gesta Rom.* i. 3 My wif..wolle hyde his body by hire beddys syde. **1628** EARLE *Microcosm.* 11 A meer dull Physician; His practice is some business at bed-sides. **1713** SWIFT *Fr. J. Denny* Wks. 1755 III. I. 145 Snatched up a peruke-block that stood by the bedside. **1752** MRS. LENNOX *Fem. Quix.* I. III. viii. 176 Never-ceasing attendance at the bed-side of her sick father. **1840** THIRLWALL *Greece* VII. lv. 94 He instantly hurried to his friend's bedside.

b. *attrib.*, as *bedside book, literature*; **bedside manner**, the deportment of a medical man towards his patient.

1837 DICKENS *Pickw.* xxxviii. 416 A female servant came out..to shake some bed-side carpets. **1860** F. NIGHTINGALE *Notes on Nursing* viii. 46 If a patient can turn on his side, he will eat more comfortably from a bed-side table. **1869** PRENTISS *Stepping Heavenward* (1870) xxv. 237 He was her 'pet-doctor', he had such 'sweet, bed-side manners'. **1879** C. M. YONGE *Magnum Bonum* II. xxvii. 570 Poor Janet found the thing in the back of the bedside table-drawer. **1884** *Punch* 15 Mar. 121 *Lady Visitor.* 'Oh that's your Doctor, is it? What sort of a doctor is he?' *Lady Resident.* 'Oh well, I don't know much about his ability; but he's got a very good bedside manner!' **1907** *Brit. Med. Jrnl.* 28 Dec. 1845/1 The ordinary notion is that a good bedside manner consists of suavity carried to the verge of civility. **1920** *Cornh. Mag.* July 63 Bedside Books. *Ibid.* 64 Bedside literature. **1949** D. SMITH *I capture Castle* I. ii. 12, I keep my bedside candlestick on a battered tin trunk.

bed-sitting-room. [f. the sbs.] A room serving both as a bedroom and as a sitting-room. Also (orig. *University slang*), **bed-sitter**, whence abbrev. **bed-sit, bedsit.**

1892 ZANGWILL *Childr. Ghetto* I. xvi. 29 The bed-sitting-room which they rented was turned into a salon of reception. **1905** G. B. SHAW *Passion, Poison & Petrifaction* in *H. Furniss's Annual* 11/1 In a bed-sitting room in a fashionable quarter of London. **1927** W. E. COLLINSON *Contemp. Eng.* 89 The problem of house-hunting brought with it various technical terms or rather revived interest in them viz...bed-sitter (bedroom and living-room combined). **1933** C. DAY LEWIS *Magnetic Mountain* 12 Then book your bed-sitter at the station hotel. **1933** *Archit. Rev.* LXXIV. 23/1 No one who has seen this will be content with the unhandiness and drab squalor of the usual bed-sitting-room method of living. **1938** N. MARSH *Artists in Crime* xv. 225 I'm going to spend the..morning in a chorus lady's bed-sit. in Chelsea. **1957** *Oxford Mag.* 293 But pressure for admissions does mean that some freshmen sit disconsolate in a 'bedsit' far down the Iffley Road. **1959** *House & Garden* July 44/1 When the children are older, their play space and bedrooms will be planned as two large bed-sitting-rooms. **1967** *Spectator* 14 July 53/2 Permanent homes are no longer necessities and a bed-sit mentality has taken over.

Hence **bed-sitter-land**, an area of a town, etc., in which such rooms are commonly found for rent; the world of rented accommodation in bed-sitting-rooms.

1968 D. E. ALLEN *British Tastes* ii. 48 The eight boroughs in the inner western districts [of London] that constitute 'bed-sitterland'. **1970** *Guardian* 3 June 7/3 The upshot..of the shifting vote, especially the shifting young votes in bedsitter-land. **1980** M. A. DOODY in Michaels & Ricks *State of Lang.* 121 The addition of the last phrase is irresistibly comic, reminiscent of bed-sitter-land. **1986** *Options* Apr. 178/3 Serious boys..whose modern elegiac sound seems to..echo the bedsitter land once evoked by Cat Stevens.

bedspread (ˈbɛdsprɛd). orig. *U.S.* [f. BED *sb.* + SPREAD *sb.* 8a; cf. Du. *bed(de)sprei.*] A light coverlet for a bed, usually removed when the bed is occupied.

1845 W. T. PORTER *Big Bear Arkansas* 30, I made a bedspread of his skin. **1848** BARTLETT *Dict. Amer.*, *Bed-spread*, in the interior parts of the country, the common name for a *bed*-quilt, or coverlet. **1887** *Queen* 29 Oct. 558/1 For bedspread and chair-seats in your pink room. **1914** *Evening News* 15 Oct. 7/6 You will have a pretty, light, and warm bedspread at a cost of 1s. 7½d. **1926** *British Weekly* 24 June 250/5 Silk bedspreads in rich colourings, with shot effects.

†**bedstaff** (ˈbɛdstɑːf, -æ-). *Obs.* Pl. **-staffs, staves.** [see STAFF.] A staff or stick used in some way about a bed. Formerly well-known as a ready weapon: hence, probably, the phrase ***in the twinkling of a bedstaff***: cf. 'the twinkling of an eye.'

a. Dr. Johnson explains it as: 'A wooden pin stuck anciently on sides of the bed-stead to hold the cloaths from slipping on either side.' (For this, no authority is given, and no corroborative evidence has been found.) **b.** The stout sticks or staves laid (loose) across the bed-stocks in old wooden bedsteads, to support the bedding (the precursors of the modern 'laths'), are in Scotland called *bed-rungs* (*rung* = staff, cudgel), and in some parts of England *bed-sticks*: they often served as improvised weapons. **c.** When a bed is fixed in a recess, a stick or staff is used to help in making it, and sometimes called a *bed-stick*. (The 'bed-staves' in quot. 1626, six to each bed, were, of course, b.)

1576 BAKER *Gesner's Jewel of Health* 147/1 Starring it well about with a short bedde staffe. **1626** *Alleyn's Will* (N.) All the furniture in the twelve poor schollars chamber, that is to say, six bedsteads, sixe mattresses, six feather beds..three dozen of bedstaves, and six pewter chamber potts. *a* **1652** BROME *City Wit* IV. iii, Say there is no virtue in cudgels and bedstaves. **1711** F. FULLER *Med. Gymn.* 42 Beating his bare Hip with a Bedstaff. **1845** BARHAM *Ingol. Leg.* (1862) 183 In her hand she grasped the bedstaff, a weapon of mickle might.

1660 *Charac. Italy* 78 In the twinkling of a Bedstaff he disrobed himself..and was just skipping into Bed. **1676** SHADWELL *Virtuoso* I. i, I'll do it instantly, in the twinkling of a Bed-staff.

bedstead (ˈbɛdstɛd). [see STEAD.] Strictly, the place occupied by a bed; but long ago transferred to the wooden or metal stand on which a bed is raised; the framework of a bed.

c **1440** *Promp. Parv.* 28 Bedstede, *stratum.* **1530** PALSGR. 197/1 Bedde stede, *chalit.* **1535** COVERDALE *Song Sol.* iii. 7 Aboute Salomons bedsteade there stonde LX. valeaunt men. **1611** BIBLE *Deut.* iii. 11 Behold, his bedsted was a bedsted of yron. **1621** G. SANDYS *Ovid's Met.* VIII. (1626) 167 A homely bed-steed made of willow. **1713** SWIFT *Fr. J. Denny* Wks. 1755 III. I. 145 We bound our lunatick..down to the bedsted. **1872** YEATS *Techn. Hist. Comm.* 352 Celebrated for its bedsteads of cast iron.

ˈbedstock. [see STOCK.] Earlier name of a BEDSTEAD, or rather of its front and back parts, between which the cross staves or rungs were laid; still used in the north.

1483 *Cath. Angl.* 25 Bedstoke. *sponda, fultrum.* **1534** *Eng. Ch. Furniture* (1866) 189 A peire of bedstockes & an olde presse. **1599** HARSNET *Agst. Darell* 181 His toe rapping on the Ende of the Bedstocke. **1624** *Invent.* in *Archæol.* (1884) XLVIII. I. 139 A bed stockes, a matteresse, a boulster. **1822** BEWICK *Mem.*, *note* 43 Trunks of two old trees..answer the ..purpose of bed-stocks. **1864** ATKINSON *Whitby Gloss.*, *Bedstocks*, the frame of the bedstead for the sacking on which the mattress and bed rest.

bedstraw (ˈbɛdstrɔː). [see STRAW.]

†**1.** The straw which (covered by a sheet) formerly constituted the bedding in an ordinary bed, and which still serves in rural districts instead of a palliasse, or under-bed. *Obs.* (See also STRAW.)

c **1386** CHAUCER *Merch. T.* 539 O perilous fyr that in the bedstraw bredeth. **1388** WYCLIF *Ps.* vi. 7 Y schal moiste my bedstre [**1382** bedding] with my teeris. **1483** *Cath. Angl.* 25 Bedstrey, *stratum, stratorium.* **1578** LYTE *Dodoens* 402 Ferne put into the bedstrowe, drieth away the stinking punayses. **1626** BACON *Sylva* §696 The Chamber and Bedstraw, kept close, and not Aired. *a* **1637** DEKKER *Witch Edm.* IV. ii. Wks. 1873 IV. 413 More fire i' th' Bed-straw?

2. Name applied to a genus of plants (*Galium*, N.O. *Rubiaceæ*) containing many species, with slender ascending stems, whorled or cruciate leaves, and small clustered flowers. One of these (*G. verum*) has long borne the legendary name of *Our Lady's Bedstraw* (cf. the similarly allusive *Our Lady's Garters, Mantle, Slippers, Smock*, etc., etc.); whence recent writers have somewhat irrationally taken 'Bedstraw' as an English book-name for the whole genus making 'Our Lady's B.' a species.

1527 ANDREW *Brunswyke's Distyll. Waters* O iv, Our lady bedstrawe, *serpillum* in latyn. **1543** TRAHERON *Vigo's Chirurg.* v. v. 169 b, Decoction of the herbe called our ladyes bedstrawe. **1597** GERARD *Herbal* II. ccccIxix. 1126 There be divers sorts of the herbes called Ladies Bedstraw or Cheese renning. **1784** TWAMLEY *Dairying* 119 The Runnet Plant.. English Names, are yellow ladies bedstraw or Cheese renning, or petty muguet. **1820** SOWERBY *Eng. Bot.* s.v., Rough Marsh Bed straw. **1854** S. THOMSON *Wild Fl.* I. 68 In the bedstraws..we count four stamens.

bedtick (ˈbɛdtɪk). Also 6 **-tyke.** [see TICK.] A large flat quadrangular bag or case, into which feathers, hair, straw, chaff, or other substances are put to form a bed.

1569 *Wills & Inv. N.C.* (1835) 303 Item one fether bedtyke xij*d.* **1658** ROWLAND *Mouffet's Theat. Ins.* 916 The use of wax..for bed-ticks that the feathers fly not out. **1861** *Morn. Post* 27 Nov., Found under a mattress and bed-tick.

Hence **ˈbedˌticking**, bedticks collectively, or the material of which they are made; also *attrib.*

1705 *Overseers' Acc. Holy Cross, Canterb.*, Pd. for mouing Rich. Silks Goods and for a bedtickin, 00. 02. 01. **1884** *Harper's Mag.* July 304/1 The bed-ticking bag.

bedtime (ˈbɛdtaɪm). [see TIME.] **a.** The hour or time for going to bed. *fig.* = 'hour of death.'

a **1250** *Owl & Night.* 324 Ich singe an eve..And soththe won hit is bed-time. **1590** SHAKS. *Mids. N.* v. i. 34 What dances shall we haue..Between our after supper, and bedtime? **1743** WESLEY *Jrnl.* (1749) 62 The Lord's prayer, which they were made say at rising and bed-time. **1837** DICKENS *Pickwick* xxxvii. 406 Master opens it, and reads the label, 'Draught to be taken at bedtime'.

fig. **1870** ALFORD in *Life* (1873) 457, I only hope the Master's work may be got done by bedtime.

b. *attrib.* **bedtime story**, a story told (to a child) at bedtime; also *fig.*

1894 S. FISKE *Jack's Partner* iv. §iii. 80 Rose had suggested this partnership to John during a bed-time conference. **1899** (*title*, Blackie & Son) Bedtime Stories, a picture-book for little folk. **1926** A. HUXLEY *Jesting Pilate* III. 254 Racing results and bed-time stories. **1940** A. HOCKING *Wicked Flee* viii. 173 If we come to the conclusion that it's all just a bedtime story, you're left to assume that Lavinia is unhinged.

Bedu (ˈbɛduː), *sb.* and *a.* [Arab. *badw* desert, Bedouins, *badawī* Bedouin: see BEDOUIN.] (Of or pertaining to) a Bedouin.

1912 T. E. LAWRENCE *Home Lett.* (1954) 188 Egypt is not to be ranked with Syria for a moment: you have only to think of fellahin—and ours are Bedu. **1917** —— *Lett.* (1938) 234 The Bedu had their own food with them in their saddle bags. **1940** F. STARK *Winter in Arabia* iii. 15 We..took with us a bedu wounded in the foot by stones. **1959** *Listener* 19 Nov. 893/2 The vanishing life of his Bedu friends.

bedub (bɪˈdʌb), *v.* [f. BE- 2 + DUB.] *trans.*

†**a.** To adorn. *Obs.* **b.** To denominate.

1657 TOMLINSON *Renou's Disp.* Pref., You live in a city.. bedubbed and adorned with..blessings. **1884** *Times* 25 Feb. 4 We poor Army tutors who undertake to teach, by first unteaching, such specimens..are bedubbed crammers.

beduck, bedumb, bedunch, etc.: see BE- *pref.*

beduin, variant of BEDOUIN.

bedull (bɪˈdʌl), *v.* [f. BE- + DULL *v.*] To make dull. Hence **bedulling** *ppl. a.*

a **1617** HIERON *Wks.* (1620) II. 380 Time..bedulleth the tendernes of his [man's] conscience. **1836** *Blackw. Mag.* XL. 724 A mist bedulls mine eyes. **1656** TRAPP *Comm. 1 Thess.* v. 17 A lazy, customary, bedulling strain.

bedung (bɪˈdʌŋ), *v.* [f. BE- + DUNG.] *trans.* To treat with dung or manure; to befoul with dung; also *fig.*

1639 HORN & ROBOTHAM *Gate Lang. Unl.* xiv. §157 What he [the thrush] bedungeth, that sprouteth forth to misselen, whence comes bird-lime. **1650** BP. HALL *Cases Consc.* 83

Leaving all but his head, to bedung that earth, which had lately shaken at his terrour. **1679** Puller *Moder. Ch. Eng.* (1843) 300 Soundly bedunged with calumny and filth.

bedusk (bɪˈdʌsk), *v.* [f. BE- 6 + DUSK.] *trans.* To shroud in gloom, as of twilight.

1566 Drant *Wail. Jerim.* K iij, Howe hath the Lord.. beduskde his daughter dere, Tsyon. *a* **1670** Hacket *Cent. Serm.* (1675) 455 Some dark cloud bedusks all wordly glory.

bedust (bɪˈdʌst), *v.* [f. BE- 6 + DUST.] *trans.* To cover with dust. Hence **beˈdusted** *ppl. a.*

1530 Palsgr. 445/2 You have bedusted your shoes. *a* **1679** T. Goodwin *Wks.* (1863) VII. 278 They suffer their hearts and lives to lie bedusted. **1832–53** *Whistle-Binkie* (Sc. Songs) Ser. II. 51 Lang Miller Geordie, wi' meal a' bedusted.

bedward, -wards (ˈbɛdwəd, -z), *adv.* [f. BED *sb.* + -WARD(S: orig. *to bedward.*]

1. Towards bed, in the direction of bed.

c **1530** J. Rhodes *Bk. Nurture* in *Babees Bk.* (1868) 69 When your mayster intendeth to bedward. **1667** Milton *P.L.* IV. 352 Others on the grass Coucht..Or Bedward ruminating. **1820** Scott *Monast.* xiv, The signal to move bedward. **1834** Lamb *Wks.* (1852) 181 When the dark night comes and they are creeping bedwards.

†**2.** Towards bedtime; just before going to bed.

c **1430** *Diatorie* in *Babees Bk.* (1868) 56 Use fier bi þe morewe, & to bedward at eue. *c* **1515** Barclay *Eglog.* iii. (1570) B vj/1, I dranke to bedwarde (as is my common gise). **1615** Markham *Eng. Housew.* II. i. (1668) 47 Drink of it at night to bedward. *a* **1661** Fuller in *H. Smith's Wks.* (1867) I. 20 These sermons have been used as a handmaid to prayer bedward in some families. **1669** W. Simpson *Hydrol. Chym.* 355 That may be done over night, last to bed-ward.

bedwarf (bɪˈdwɔːf). [f. BE- 2 + DWARF.] Intensive of DWARF *v.* Hence **beˈdwarfed** *ppl. a.*

1633 Donne *Poems* (1650) 207 'Tis shrinking..hath thus, In minde and body both bedwarfed us. **1664** H. More *Myst. Iniq.* 334 Some big Mastiff or bedwarfed Nag. **1678** Norris *Misc.* (1699) 283 Self-esteem..bedwarfs all our Excellencies.

†**bedwele(n**, *v. Obs.* Also biˈdweolien, beˈduelen. [f. BE- + DWELL *v.*², OE. *dwęllan, dwęlian.*] *trans.* To mislead, lead into error.

c **1205** *Ancr. R.* 128 Te valse ancre..weneð forte gilen God, ase heo bidweolieð simple men. *c* **1210** *Leg. Kath.* 1257 Euch an biheold oðer as heo bidweolet weren. *a* **1300** *Cursor M.* 19526 He cuth mak þe men be dueld.

bedwell, etc.: see BE- *pref.*

bedwoman, obs. form of BEADWOMAN.

†**beˈdwynge**, *v. Obs.* Pa. pple. **bydwongen.** [Only in Caxton: prob. a. Flem. *bedwing-en.*] *trans.* To constrain, to restrain.

1480 Caxton *Ovid's Met.* XII. iii, I oughte well thenne bedwynge myn herte. **1481** —— *Reynard* (Arb.) 37 They had none lorde ne were not bydwongen.

bedye (bɪˈdaɪ). [f. BE- + DYE.] Intensive of DYE *v.* Chiefly in pa. pple.

1513 Douglas *Æneis* I. iv. 31 Thair lithis and lymmis be salt watter bedyit. **1596** Spenser *F.Q.* I. xi. 7 Bryton fieldes with Sarazin blood bedyde. **1866** J. Rose *Virgil* 50 With cheeks..Bedyed with sanguine berry-juice.

bedysman, obs. form of BEADSMAN.

bed-yuer(e (mispr. *bedyner*), var. of *bed-ifere*, BED-FERE, *Obs.* bed-fellow.

bee¹ (biː). Forms: 1–3 béo, 3–9 bee (5 by, 5–6 be, 6 bey). *Pl.* bees: also 1–2 beon, 3–7 been, 4 bene, bein, 6 beene. [Com. Teut.: OE. *béo* = OHG. *bîa* (G. dial. *beie*), MLG. *bîe*, LG. *bigge*, MDu. *bie*, Du. *bij*, all fem.; ON. *bý* (? neut.):—OTeut. **bîon-* or *bîon*; beside which there is OHG. *bini* neut., MHG. *bine, bin*, fem., mod.G. *biene*:—OTeut. **bini*; all going back to root *bi-*, perh. = Aryan *bhi-* 'to fear,' in the sense of 'quivering,' or its development 'buzzing, humming.']

1. a. A well-known insect, or rather genus of insects, of the Hymenopterous order, living in societies composed of one queen, or perfect female, a small number of males or 'drones,' and an indefinite number of undeveloped females or 'neuters' (which are the workers), all having four wings; they produce wax, and collect honey, which they store up for food in the winter.

a **1000** *Ags. Ps.* cxvii. 12 þá hí me ymbsealdon samod.. swá béon. *a* **1100** *Ags. Gloss.* in Wülcker *Voc.* 318 *Apis*, beo. *c* **1275** *Pains of Hell* in *O.E. Misc.* 148 þickure hi hongeþ þer ouer-al þan don been in wynterstal. *a* **1300** *Cursor M.* 7113 In leon muth he fand, was slain, A bike o bees [*v.r.* bes] þar-in be-bredd. **1382** Wyclif *Deut.* i. 44 As been [**1388** bees] ben wont to be pursued. *c* **1430** Lydg. *Bochas* I. xix. (1554) 35 b, A swarm of been entred on his head. **1481–90** *Howard Househ. Bks.* (1844) 207 Paid..to Jodge for a heve for beys iiij. *d.* **1535** Coverdale *Ecclus.* xi. 2 The Bey is but a small beast amonge the foules, yet is her frute exceadinge swete. **1538** Starkey *England* II. i. 153 Delytyng in idulnes as a drowne Be doth. **1609** C. Butler *Fem. Mon.* (1634) 139 Whoso keep well Sheep and Been, Sleep or wake, their thrift comes in. **1697** Dryden *Georg.* IV. 801 A buzzing noise of Bees his Ears alarms. **1855** Longf. *Hiaw.* XXII. 11 Passed the bees, the honey-makers.

b. Often used as the type of busy workers.

1535 Stewart *Cron. Scot.* II. 445 Now ar tha maid als bissie as ane be. **1580** Baret *Alv.* To Rdr., A great volume which (for the apt similitude betweene the good Scholers and diligent Bees) I called then their *Aluearie*, for a memorial by whom it was made. **1655** Fuller *Ch. Hist.* IX. vii. §24 V. 137 The Popish Clergy..were as busie as Bees, newly ready to swarme. *c* **1720** Watts *Div. Songs*, How doth the little busy bee Improve each shining hour! **1807** Crabbe *Par. Reg.* III. 150 Busy and careful, like that working bee.

c. A model or image of this insect.

1816 J. Scott *Vis. Paris* 239 The remains found in the tomb of Childeric, were chiefly gold bees, from which Buonaparte took the hint of covering his mantle..with representations of that insect.

d. One of the southern constellations, so figured.

2. Applied to a large group of allied insects, chiefly with a distinguishing epithet, e.g. Humble Bee, Mason Bee, Carpenter Bee, etc.; in scientific use, including all insects of the *Melliferous* or honey-gathering division of the *Aculeate* (or sting-bearing) *Hymenoptera*, and comprising two families, the Social Bees or *Apidae*, and Solitary Bees or *Andrænidæ*.

c **1000** *Sax. Leechd.* II. 308 Feld beon huniȝ meng to somne. **1532** More *Confut. Tindale* Wks. (1557) 502/1 Till either some blind bettle, or some holy humble bee come flye in at their mouthes. **1802** Bingley *Anim. Biog.* (1813) III. 275 The Garden Bee. **1847** Carpenter *Zool.* §697 Of the solitary bees,..there are many curious varieties; some of which go under the names of Mason, Carpenter, and Upholsterer Bees, from the materials on which they respectively work. **1861** Hulme tr. *Moquin-Tandon* II. v. ii. 279 The Humble Bees are larger than the Bees.

3. *fig.* **a.** A sweet writer. **b.** A busy worker.

1753 Chambers *Cycl. Supp.* s.v. *Bee*, Xenophon is called the Attic bee. **1791–1824** Disraeli *Cur. Lit.* (1866) 319/2 A complete collection of classical works, all the bees of antiquity..may be hived in a single glass case.

c. 'A lump of a yeast (*Saccharomyces pyriformis*) intermittently rising and releasing bubbles in brew;—usually in *pl.*' (Webster 1934). So **bee wine** (see quot. 1960).

1923 *Harmsworth's Househ. Encycl.* I. 312/2 Bee wine is a modern name for the fermented drink produced by what was known as the ginger beer plant. *Ibid.*, In its dry, inert condition the bee is a shapeless mass of gelatinous material. **1938** R. Graves *Count Belisarius* x. 206 The Massagetic Huns carried with them what is called a 'bee', a sort of yeast that they put into mare's milk to make it ferment. **1960** A. E. Bender *Dict. Nutrition* 16/1 *Bee wine*, wine produced by the usual alcoholic fermentation of sugar, but using yeast in the form of a clump of yeast and lactic bacteria. The clump rises and falls with bubbles of carbon dioxide produced, hence the 'bee'.

4. In allusion to the social character of the insect (originally in U.S.): A meeting of neighbours to unite their labours for the benefit of one of their number; e.g. as is done still in some parts, when the farmers unite to get in each other's harvests in succession; usually preceded by a word defining the purpose of the meeting, as ***apple-bee, husking-bee, quilting-bee, raising-bee***, etc. *Hence*, with extended sense: A gathering or meeting for some object; esp. ***spelling-bee***, a party assembled to compete in the spelling of words. ***lynching bee***: see LYNCHING *vbl. sb.*

1769 *Boston Gaz.* 16 Oct. (Th.), Last Thursday about twenty young Ladies met at the house of Mr. L. on purpose for a Spinning Match; (or what is called in the Country a Bee). **1809** W. Irving *Knickerb.* Wks. I. 238 Now were instituted quilting bees and husking bees and other rural assemblages. **1830** Galt *Laurie T.* (1849) III. v. 98, I made a bee; that is, I collected as many of the most expert and able-bodied of the settlers to assist at the raising. **1864** Miss Yonge *Trial* II. 281 She is gone out with Cousin Deborah to an apple bee. **1876** Lubbock *Educ.* in *Contemp. Rev.* June 91 He may be invincible at a spelling bee. **1884** *Harper's Mag.* Sept. 510/2 This execution,..in Idaho phrase was a 'hanging-bee.'

5. a. To have ***bees in the head*** or ***the brains, a bee in one's bonnet***: *i.e.* a fantasy, an eccentric whim, a craze on some point, a 'screw loose.' (Cf. *maggot*, and F. *grille.*)

1513 Douglas *Æneis* VIII, Prol. 120 Quhat bern be thou in bed with heid full of beis? *a* **1553** Udall *Roister D.* (Arb.) 29 Who so hath suche bees as your maister in hys head. **1657** Colvil *Whigs Supplic.* (1751) 74 Which comes from brains which have a bee. **1724** Ramsay *Tea-t. Misc.* (ed. 9) II. 119 But thy wild bees I canna please. **1845** De Quincey *Coleridge & Opium* Wks. XII. 91 John Hunter, notwithstanding he had a bee in his bonnet, was really a great man.

b. ***bee's knee***: (*a*) a type of something small or insignificant; (*b*) *pl.* (*slang*, orig. *U.S.*), the acme of excellence; 'the cat's whiskers'; ***to put the bee on*** (*slang*, chiefly *U.S.*): (*a*) to quash, put an end to; to beat; (*b*) to ask for a loan from, to borrow money from (cf. STING *v.*¹ 2 e).

1797 Mrs. Townley Ward *Let.* 27 June in *N. & Q.* (1896) X. 260 It cannot be as big as a bee's knee. **1870** G. M. Hopkins *Jrnl.* (1937) 133 Br. Yates gave me the following Irish expressions... *As weak as a bee's knee.* **1894** G. F. Northall *Folk-phrases* 7 As big as a bee's knee. **1923** H. C. Witwer *Fighting Blood* iii. 101 You're the bee's knees, for a fact! **1936** H. L. Mencken *Amer. Lang.* (ed. 4) 561 *The flea's eyebrows, the bee's knees* and *the canary's tusks* will be recalled. **1958** *Times* 15 Aug. 9/4 Lord Montgomery..holds that to label anything the 'cat's whiskers' is to confer on it the highest honour, and the 'bee's knees' is not far behind it as a compliment.

1918 H. C. Witwer *Baseball to Boches* 131 It's always open season for Americans over here. They sure know how to put the bee on you too. **1923** L. J. Vance *Baroque* xxvii. 264 I've heard a heap of fairy tales in my time..but this puts the bee on the lot. **1927** Wodehouse in *Sunday Express* 23 Oct. 9 The old boy..got the idea that I was off my rocker, and put the bee on the proceedings. **1929** *Amer. Speech* IV. 338 'To put the bee on', means to beg. **1931** G. Irwin *Amer. Tramp & Underworld Slang* 25 To say 'I put the bee on him' usually means that the donor has been 'stung', when he gives up the loan, since seldom is it repaid. **1936** J. Curtis *Gilt Kid* v. 47 If a bloke had come up and put the bee on him all the handout would have been..a lousy tanner.

c. ***bees and honey***: rhyming slang for 'money'.

1892 *Answers* 10 Sept. 276/1 'Bees and honey'..for 'money'. **1935** 'L. Luard' *Conq. Seas* iii. 47 A skipper's life ain't all bees and honey. **1944** *Amer. Speech* XIX. 191/1. **1960** J. Ashford *Counsel for Defence* v. 65 D'you reckon we'd waste good bees and honey on a slump like you for nothing.

6. *Comb.* and *Attrib.* General relations: **a.** attrib., as ***bee-book, -comb, -garden, -grub, -house, -mouth, -palace, -sting, -swarm, -woman, -yard; bee-winged*** adj. **b.** objective with vbl. sb. or agent-noun, as ***bee-culture, -farming, -fumigator, -herd, -hunt, -hunter, -hunting, -keeper, -keeping, -owner, -shepherd, -ward***; instrumental, as ***bee-beset, -infested, -studded, -thronged***.

1870 Morris *Earthly Par.* III. IV. 383 The *bee-beset ripe-seeded grass. **1870** Lowell *Among my Bks.* Ser. I. (1873) 84 The teaching of the latest *bee-book. **1882** *Harper's Mag.* Dec. 63/1 *Bee-culture is an important industry. **1908** Wodehouse & Westbrook *Globe by Way Book* 124 Lord Sangazure has tired already of his latest hobby, *bee-farming. **1609** *Gd. Speed to Virginia* 13 The maister of the *bee-garden..reapeth a greater gaine by his waxe and honie. *a* **1750** Mortimer (J.) A convenient..place ..for your apiary or bee-garden. **1672** *Phil. Trans.* VII. 5060 The *Bee-grubbs actually feed on Mites. **1483** *Cath. Angl.* 26 *Beehyrd, *apiaster.* **1861** Pearson *Early & Mid. Ages Eng.* 201 It was preferable to be tenant of a holding rather than a swine-herd or bee-herd. **1675** *Lond. Gaz.* No. 987/4 A new Invention for the Improvement of Bees, by certain *Bee-houses and Colonies. **1851** *Gard. Chron.* 755 A very convenient bee-house. **1835** W. Irving *Tour on Prairies* ix. 61 (*heading*) A *bee hunt. **1837** —— *Capt. Bonneville* I. ii. 52 These frontier settlers..prepare for a bee hunt. **1776** *Phil. Trans.* LXVII. 44 The *bee-hunters never fail to leave a small portion for their conductor. **1954** J. R. R. Tolkien *Two Towers* 67 Bear bee-hunter, boar the fighter. **1824** W. N. Blane *Excursion U.S.* 239 It is a favourite amusement..to go *bee-hunting. *a* **1882** Emerson *Fragm. Nature* in *Poems* (1904) 343 *Bee-infested quince or plum. **1950** D. Gascoyne *Vagrant* 61 A loud Bee-Infested Lion-skin. **1817** Kirby & Spence *Entomol.* II. xx. 211 It is a saying of *bee-keepers in Holland, that [etc.]. **1937** *Discovery* June 191/2 The most enthusiastic bee-keepers. **1839** *Sat. Mag.* 23 Feb. 69 The Economy of *Bee-Keeping. *a* **1821** Keats *Melancholy* 24 Pleasure..Turning to poison while the *bee-mouth sips. **1845** *Gard. Chron.* (1845) 171 Grove's American *bee-palace is similar to the collateral hive. **1689** P. Henry *Diaries & Lett.* (1882) 346 Your Mother hath been afflicted this night with a *Bee-sting. **1881** Wilde *Burden of Itys* in *Poems* 68 Brown *bee-studded orchids. **1910** Kipling *Rewards & Fairies* p. x, Winter's *bee-thronged ivy-bloom. *c* **1500** *Cocke Lorelles B.* 10 Mole sekers, and ratte takers; *Bewardes. **1883** Green *Conq. Eng.* 330 The bee-ward received his dues from the store of honey. **1923** E. Sitwell *Bucolic Comedies* 40 The *bee-wing'd warm afternoon. **1833** Ht. Martineau *Br. Creek* iii. 52 The *bee-women laughed in anticipation of their sport. *c* **1420** *Pallad. on Husb.* I. 1009 The *Bee-yerd be not ferre, but faire asyde Gladsum, secrete, and hoote. **1577** B. Googe *Heresbach's Husb.* (1586) 179 About the Beeyard, and neare to the hives, set flowers.

7. Special comb.: **bee-bike** (*Sc.*), a wild bee's nest; **bee-bird**, the Spotted Fly-catcher, also a humming-bird; **bee-bonneted** *a.*, having a bee in his bonnet, somewhat crazed; **bee-cell**, one of the hexagonal cells of the comb; **bee-cuckoo**, an African bird (*Cuculus Indicator*), also called 'Honey-guide,' which indicates the nests of wild bees; **bee-driving**, the driving of bees into an empty hive; **bee-feeder**, a contrivance for feeding bees within the hive; **bee-fertilized** *a.*, (of flowers) having their pollen conveyed to the stigma by the agency of bees; **bee-flower**, a flower loved, visited, or fertilized by bees, *spec.* the Wall-flower; also, a flower resembling a bee, the Bee Orchis; **bee-fly**, a two-winged fly resembling a bee, esp. certain of the *Bombylidæ* and *Syrphidæ*; **bee-fold**, an enclosure for hives; **bee-glue**, the glue-like substance with which bees fill up crevices, and fix the combs to the hives, propolis; **bee-gum**, a term in parts of U.S. for a bee-hive (orig. a hollow gum tree or log housing a swarm of bees); **bee-hawk**, a bird of prey (*Pernis apivora*), also called Honey Buzzard; also a clear-wing hawk-moth (*Sesia fuciformis*), something resembling a wild bee; also ***bee-hawk-moth***; **bee-head**, a crazy pate; *hence* **bee-headed**; **bee-larkspur** (see quot.); **bee-like** *a.*, resembling a bee; **bee-line**, a straight line between two points on the earth's surface, such as a bee was supposed instinctively to take in returning to its hive; **bee-loud** *a.*,

resonant with the hum of bees; **bee-louse**, an insect of the family Braulidæ, parasitic on bees, esp. *Braula cœca*; **bee-maggot**, the larva of a bee; **bee-man**, a bee-keeper; **bee-master**, a keeper of bees, an apiarian; so **bee-mistress**; **bee-moth** *U.S.*, *Galleria mellonella*: = *wax-moth* (see WAX *sb.*[1] 13); **bee-nettle**, species of Dead-nettle much visited by bees; **bee-orchis**, a plant (*Ophrys apifera*) noted for the resemblance of part of its flower to a bee; **bee-range** *U.S.*, a row of beehives; **bee-skep (-scap)**, a straw bee-hive; **bee-smoker**, a bee-keeper's apparatus for driving smoke into a hive to stupefy the bees while the honeycomb is being removed; †**bee-stall**, a bee-hive; **bee-tree** orig.*U.S.*, a tree in which bees have hived; **bee-wine**, nectar of a flower. See also BEE-BREAD, -EATER, -HIVE, BEES-WAX, -WING.

1837 R. NICOLL *Poems* (1843) 95 Nae apples he pu'ed now, nae *bee-bikes he knowed. **1789** G. WHITE *Selborne* ix. (1853) 181 These vast migrations, consist not only of hirundines, but of *bee-birds. **1850** BROWNING *Xmas Eve & Easter D.* 240 The bee-bird and the aloe-flower! **1856** MRS. BROWNING *Aur. Leigh* i. 1097 Whom men judge hardly as *bee-bonneted, because he holds, etc. **1868** WOOD *Homes without H.* xxiii. 427 The primary object of the *bee-cell is to serve as a storehouse and a nursery. **1786** tr. *Sparrman's Voy.* II. 186 The *bee-cuckow (*Cuculus Indicator*)..deserves to have more particular notice. **1802** BINGLEY *Anim. Biog.* (1813) II. 125 The Bee Cuckoo, in its external appearance, does not much differ from the common sparrow. **1884** *Pall Mall G.* 12 July 10/2 A sum of money which will enable them to give demonstrations of *bee-driving. **1881** F. DARWIN in *Nature* XXIII. 334 The spread of the *bee-fertilised ancestors. **1852** T. HARRIS *Insects New Eng.* 484 The *bee-flies..often hover..over the early flowers, sucking out the honey thereof. **1609** C. BUTLER *Fem. Mon.* (1623) ii. E iij, The vnequall leuelling of the ground, in a great *Bee-fold is best. **1940** C. DAY LEWIS tr. *Virgil's Georgics* IV. 82 Shoo the drones—that work-shy gang—away from the bee-folds. **1598** FLORIO, *Propoli*, that which Bees make at the entrance of the hiues to keepe out cold, called *Beeglue. **1658** ROWLAND *Mouffet's Theat. Ins.* 907 Wax, Bee-bread, Bee-glew, Rosin, etc. **1817** M. L. WEEMS *Lett.* (1929) III. 215 To be run..round & round the circumference of a *Bee-Gum. **1859** BARTLETT *Dict. Amer.* (ed. 2), *Bee-gum*, in the South and West, a term originally applied to a species of the gum-tree from which bee-hives were made; and now to beehives made of any kind of boards. **1884** *Cent. Mag.* Jan. 442/2 The bees were for the most part rudely hived in cross sections of the gum-tree..whence..a bee-hive of any kind is often called a bee-gum. **1837** MAC GILLIVRAY *Hist. Brit. Birds* III. 259 *Bee-Hawk is of rare occurrence in any part of Britain. **1857** STAINTON *Brit. Butterfl. & Moths* I. 99 *Sesia fuciformis*, Broad-bordered Bee-Hawk. **1815** KIRBY & SPENCE *Entomol.* I. vi. 207 The *bee-hawk-moth (*Sesia apiformis*, F.)..feeds upon the poplar. **1657** COLVIL *Whigs Supplic.* (1751) 135 Ye sectaries, quoth he, have *bee-heads. **1879** JAMIESON s.v., Ye needna mind him, he's a *bee-headit bodie. **1846** MRS. LOUDON *Ladies' Comp. Fl. Gard.* 37 The *Bee Larkspurs..their petals are folded up in the centre of the flower, so as to resemble a bee or a blue-bottle-fly. **1657** *S. Purchas' Pol. Flying-Ins.* Pref. Verses, To the Learned Author of this *Bee-like laborious Treatise. **1823** BYRON *Juan* XI. viii, That bee-like, bubbling, busy hum Of cities. **1830** *Massachusetts Spy* 24 Nov. (Th.), The squirrel took a *bee line, and reached the ground six feet ahead. *a* **1849** POE *Gold-Beetle, Tales* I. 44 A bee-line, or, in other words, a straight line, drawn..to a distance of fifty feet. **1870** EMERSON *Soc. & Solit.* x. 219 Men, who, almost as soon as they are born, take a bee-line to the rack of the inquisitor. **1882** J. HAWTHORNE *Fort. Fool* I. viii, This disreputable clergyman would make a bee-line for Castlemere. **1890** YEATS *Lake Isle of Innisfree* i, [I will] live alone in the *bee-loud glade. **1840** J. & M. LOUDON tr. *Köllar's Treat. Insects* I. 74 A bee infested with a *bee-louse, endeavours..to get rid of such an unwished-for guest. **1875** J. HUNTER *Man. Bee-keeping* xxx. 198 On the Continent of Europe a small insect known as the Bee-louse, *Braula Cœca*, often infects the Bees. **1679** PLOT *Staffordsh.* (1686) 221 Of the corruption of which *bee-maggots..are bred. **1861** *Trans. Ill. Agric. Soc.* IV. 82 Our best *bee men. **1928** *Daily Tel.* 11 May 19/5 Uncontrolled swarming..is not permitted by the experienced modern beeman. **1658** ROWLAND *Mouffet's Theat. Ins.* 902 The *Bee-masters with clapping of their hands, and with the sound of the brasse. **1866** ROGERS *Agric. & Prices* I. xviii. 399 The bee-master was apparently as rare as he is at present. **1859** *Edin. Rev.* CIX. 301 The *bee-mistresses..gain a living by their honey in many rural districts. **1829** *Massachusetts Spy* 27 May (Th.), Instinct teaches the *bee-moth to secrete herself, during the day, in the corners of the hive. **1838** H. COLMAN *Rep. Agric. Mass.* 71 The bee moth is to be guarded against by making the crevices of the hive tight with putty or glue. **1862** T. W. HARRIS *Insects Injur. Veget.* 489 The group called Crambidæ, or Crambians, among which the bee-moth or wax-moth is to be placed. **1597** GERARD *Herbal* I. ci. §1. 163 *Bees Orchis or Satyrion. **1857** HUGHES *Tom Brown* i, Not one in twenty of you knows where to find the ..bee-orchis..on the down. **1845** S. JUDD *Margaret* III. 402 In the garden is a large *Bee-range. *a* **1640** DAY *Parl. Bees* (1881) 44 And set fier of all there *Beeskepps. **1822** *Steam-Boat* 83 (JAM.) My head was bizzing like a bee-scap. **1897** *Westm. Gaz.* 7 Aug. 8/1 A *bee-smoker filled with tobacco and brown paper. **1572** BOSSEWELL *Armorie* III. 18 b, The weasel..is..a destroyer of *Beestals, and eateth up their honey. **1782** ST. J. DE CRÈVECŒUR *Lett.* 37 If we find ..what is called a *bee-tree, we must mark it. **1834** BRACKENRIDGE *Recoll.* xii. 129 A harmless fellow, who followed hunting bee trees on the mountains for a living. **1849** W. IRVING *Crayon Misc.* 49 Honey, the spoils of a plundered bee-tree. **1818** KEATS *Endymion* IV. Honeysuckles full of clear *bee-wine.

bee[2] (biː). Forms: 1–2 **béah**, 3 **beȝ**, **beie**, **beh**, **behȝ**, 3–4 **beȝe**, 4 **beygh**, **byȝe**, **bie**, **beeȝ**, 5 **beghe**, **be**, **bey**, 4–5 **by(e**, 4–9 **bee**. [Com. Teut.: OE. *béaȝ*, *béah* = ON. *baugr*, OHG. *bouc*:—OTeut. **baugo-z* ring, f. pret. stem of the vb. **bug-*, *baug-*, to bow, bend (intr.). The modern form in south would prob. have been *by*, or *bigh* (cf. *high*, *nigh*): *bee* is the northern type.]

†**1.** A ring or torque of metal, usually meant for the arm or neck; but in one case at least used of a finger-ring. *Obs.*

c **1009** ÆLFRIC *Gen.* xxxviii. 18 þinne hring & þine béah and þinne stæf. *a* **1100** in Wr.-Wülcker *Voc.* 313 *Armilla*, beah. *c* **1175** *Lamb. Hom.* 193 þu ham ȝiuest..beies and gold ringes. **1205** LAY. 24520 Enne beh of rede gold. *Ibid.* 21640 Behȝes [**1250** beȝes] of golde. *c* **1300** *K. Alis.* 1572 Riche beyghes, besans, and pans. *c* **1325** *E.E. Allit. P.* A. 466 On arme oþer fynger, þaȝ þou ber byȝe. **1377** LANGL. *P. Pl.* B. Prol. 161 Beren biȝes [*v.r.* beiȝes, behes, byes, beȝes] ful briȝte abouten here nekkes. **1382** WYCLIF *Prov.* i. 9 A beȝe [**1388** bie] to thi necke. **1387** TREVISA *Higden* Rolls Ser. III. 331 A bye is *torques* in Latyn. *c* **1440** *Morte Arth.* (Roxb.) 84 Pomelles bryghte as goldis beghe. *Ibid.* 102 W[t] many a besaunte, broche, and be. **1483** *Cath. Angl.* 24 A Bee, *armilla, brachiale.* **1487** *Paston Lett.* III. 464 A bee with a grete pearl. *c* **1490** *Howard Househ. Bks.* 394 Item, for beyes, roppe, and streyneres xj*d.* **1552** HULOET, Bee or collar of gold or syluer, *torques.*

2. Nautical: ***bees***, ***bee-blocks***, ***bee-seating***; see quot.

c **1860** H. STUART *Seaman's Catech.* 74 At the outer end, and on each side of the bowsprit, inside the cap, bees and bee blocks are bolted, for the topmast stays to reeve through. *Ibid.* Where it rests on the stem is the bed, and the remainder the beeseating. **1867** SMYTH *Sailor's Word-bk.*, *Bee*, a ring or hoop of metal..*Bee-blocks*, pieces of hard wood, bolted to the outer end of the bowsprit, to reeve the fore mast stays through.

bee[3]. The name of the letter B, used for 'bloody' (see BLOODY A. 10 and B. 2); so ***bee aitch***, bloody hell; ***bee eff***, bloody fool. *slang.*

1926 GALSWORTHY *Silver Spoon* I. iii. 21 This is a bee map... Quite the bee-est map I ever saw. *Ibid.* III. ii. 230 It's a bee nuisance. *Ibid.* 231 We have the best goods..and we must bee well deliver them. **1928** —— *Swan Song* I. vii, Mr. Blythe's continual remark: 'What the bee aitch are they all about?' **1960** M. CECIL *Something in Common* i. 22 'Your mother's relations,' he muttered, 'bee effs, every one of 'em.'

be-east (biːˈiːst), *prep.*, orig. *advb. phr.* In 1 **be éastan**. [OE. *be éastan* 'on the east,' (*be* 'by, about,' *éastan* 'from the east,' f. *éast* 'east'); used *advb.*, and also with following dative. In later times only in Sc.] East of.

894 *O.E. Chron.* Of ælcre byriȝ be eastan Pendredan . ȝe be westan Seal wuda ȝe be eastan. **1559–66** in *Misc. Wodrow Soc.* (1844) 78 Twoe mile be-east the said towne. **1819** *Blackw. Mag.* V. 637 Lodge them be-east the town.

Beeb (biːb). Repr. a colloq. contraction of B.B.C. (the British Broadcasting Corporation). Freq. with *the.*

1967 (*private communication from M. Laski*) Beeb. My daughter, who works in the B.B.C., always calls it so. **1971** *Guardian* 26 Mar. 15/1 Anything the Beeb does..which can be called political means somebody can get 'the right of reply'. **1971** *It* 2–16 June 19/3, I doubt that this album will receive any airplay 'cos the lyrics might offend the grey minds up at the beeb. **1976** *Star* (Sheffield) 29 Oct. 2/5 BBC2..9.30 *A world of music*: Surely worth a plum Beeb-1 spot as it's John Denver and Friends. **1980** B. W. ALDISS *Life in West* xii. 254 In the sixties,..it was fashionable for everyone to be radical,..whether they worked for Apple or the Beeb. **1985** *Times* 11 Feb. 15/5 The licence fee the 'Beeb' is asking for is a shade less than the 18p a day for a popular newspaper.

‖**beebee** (ˈbiːbiː). [a. Urdū, *bībī* lady, from Pers., orig. Eastern Turki *bībī* 'lady, lawful wife.'] Hindustani name for a lady. (Now superseded in application to European ladies by 'Mem-sāhib,' but applied to Englishwomen of lower rank, to a (native) mistress, etc.)

1816 'QUIZ' *Grand Master* XI. 34 Its oppressive beams had made Buff'los and beebees seek the shade. *a* **1847** MRS. SHERWOOD *Lady of Manor* V. xxix. 96 Being the burree beebee [chief lady] of the night, I moved for an adjournment.

ˈ**bee-ˌbread.** Forms: 1 **béa-**, **béo-**, **bí-bread**, 2 **bei-**; 7– **bee-bread**. [f. BEE + BREAD: cf. MHG. *bîe brôt*, G. *bienen brot*. The modern word is probably a new combination, not historically related to the OE., which had also a different sense.]

†**1.** *orig.* In OE. as in the other Teutonic languages: Honey-comb with the honey in it. *Obs.*

c **825** *Vesp. Psalter* cxviii. 103 Hu swoete..ofer huniȝ & biabread. *a* **1000** *Boeth. Metr.* xii. 17 þynceþ..huniȝes bí-bread healfe þý swetre. *c* **1000** *Ags. Gosp.* Luke xxiv. 42 Dǽl ȝebrǽddes fisces and béobréad [*Hatton* bei-brad].

2. Pollen, or a compound of honey and pollen, consumed by the nurse-bees.

1657 S. PURCHAS *Pol. Flying Ins.* I. xv. 95 [Bees] gather as often Bee-bread as honey. **1750** *Phil. Trans.* XLVI. 538 A Bee loading the Farina, Bee-Bread, or crude Wax, upon its Legs. **1815** R. HUISH *Treat. Bees* xi. (1817) 147 The crude wax, which is called..in English Bee-bread. **1816** KIRBY & SP. *Entomol.* xi. (1828) I. 376 Little or no honey is collected until an ample store of bee-bread has been laid up for food. **1868** WOOD *Homes without H.* xxiii. 436 Bee-bread..is a compound of honey and the pollen of flowers.

fig. **1870** LOWELL *Among my Bks.* Ser. I. (1873) 66 He had ..been feeding on the bee-bread of Shakespeare.

3. Applied locally to certain plants yielding nectar: viz. the White Clover, and Borage. (Britten and Holland.)

beech (biːtʃ). Forms: 1 **bóece**, **béce**, 3–6 **beche**, 3 **bech**, 6 **beetch**, 6–7 **beeche**, 6–9 **beech**. [OE. *bóece*, *béce*, cogn. with MLG. *bōke*, *bȫke*, mod.LG. *baike*, weak fem. (:—OTeut. **bōkjōn-*), a derivative form from OTeut. **bōkā-*, str. fem., whence also ON. *bók*, OE. *bóc*, OHG. *buohha*, MHG. *buoche*, G. *buche*, MDu. *boeke* (Du. *beuk*, Flem. *boek*), 'beech.' OTeut. **bokā-* was cogn. w. L. *fāgus* 'beech,' and Gr. *φᾱγός*, *φηγός* 'esculent oak'; meaning originally 'tree with eatable fruit', from root found in Gr. *φαγεῖν* to eat. The more primitive Eng. *bóc* is not found after the 12th c. exc. in BUCK-MAST, BUCK-WHEAT, and their abbreviation BUCK.]

1. a. A well-known forest tree indigenous to Europe and Western Asia, having fine thin smooth bark, and glossy oval leaves; its boughs and foliage form a dense mass, and it bears triquetrous nuts (called *mast*) placed in pairs in a rough or prickly involucre. It has several ornamental varieties distinguished by the colour or shape of the leaves, as the Purple, Copper, and Fern-leaved Beech.

b. The genus *Fagus*. N.O. *Corylaceæ*, including the Common Beech (*F. sylvatica*) and other species.

a **800** *Epinal Gl.*, *Fagus*, boecae, *Corpus Gl.*, boece (Sweet, *O.E.T.* 61, 62). [*a* **1000** Wr.-Wülcker *Voc.* 137 *Fagus*, boc.] *Ibid.* 402 *Fagus*, bece. [*a* **1200** *Ibid.* 545 *Fagus*, boctreow.] *a* **1300** W. DE BIBLESW. in Wright *Voc.* 171 *Quyr enclowé à foust de fou* (of bech). *a* **1300** *K. Alis.* 5242 Beches, birches of the fairest. **1340** *Ayenb.* 23 þe greate beches ine wodes. *c* **1440** *Promp. Parv.* 27 Beche tre, *fagus.* **1577** B. GOOGE *Heresbach's Husb.* (1586) 101 b, The next among the Mast trees is the Beech. **1600** FAIRFAX *Tasso* VII. xix. (R.) Engrau'd in barke of beeche and baies. **1704** POPE *Summer* 13 Ye shady beeches, and ye cooling streams. **1727** THOMSON *Summer* 1362 The spreading beech, that o'er the stream Incumbent hung. **1845** DARWIN *Voy. Nat.* xiii. (1852) 281, I was also pleased to see, at an elevation of little less than 1000 feet, our old friend the southern beech.

c. The wood of this tree. Often *attrib.*, as in ***beech-coal*** (i.e. charcoal), ***beech bedstead***, etc.

1607 *Lingua* IV. i. in Hazl. *Dodsl.* IX. 411 How shall I devise to blow the fire of beech coals? **1730** SOUTHALL *Bugs* 34 Also Beach-Bedsteds, for all such afford them much Harbour and Food. **1823** P. NICHOLSON *Pract. Build.* 259 Beech, a wood which, from its hardness, closeness, and strength..holds a prominent place.

2. Applied with or without distinguishing epithet to various other trees more or less resembling the beech of Europe; in Australia, *Tectona australis* (a kind of Teak); in New South Wales, *Monotoca elliptica* (an Epicrad); in Jamaica, *Exostemma caribæum* (a Cinchonad). **blue beech** (U.S.), an American species of Hornbeam (*Carpinus Americana*); †**Dutch beech**, old name in England of the Abele (*Populus alba*); **horn**, **horse**, or **hurst beech**, dial. names of the HORNBEAM; **sea-side beech**, the 'Beech' of Jamaica (see above); **water beech**, the same as *Blue Beech*; **white beech**, dial. name of the HORNBEAM.

3. *Comb.*, chiefly *attrib.*, as ***beech-apple***, ***-bole***, ***-gall***, ***-leaf***, ***-nut***, ***-root***, ***-timber***, ***-tree***, ***-wood***; ***beech-green*** adj.

c **1450** in Wright *Voc.* 228 *Hec fagus*, a bech-tre. **1551** TURNER *Herbal* (1568) 12 The sede is thre square like bucke wheat or beach aples. **1586** WEBBE *Eng. Poetrie* (Arb.) 71 Tyterus happily thou liest tumbling vnder a beetchtree. **1681** GREW *Musæum* III. §1. ii. 269 A Stone..which looks like a piece of Beech-wood. **1712** *Lond. Gaz.* No. 4964/1 The Assize of Billet, made..of Beech-wood. **1739** E. SMITH *Compl. Housew.* (ed. 9) 316 A quarter of a spoonful of oil of beech-nuts. *Ibid.* 317 The beech-nut-oil. **1814** SOUTHEY *Roderick* vii, And from his head the ashes fell, like snow Shaken from some dry beech-leaves. **1831** CARLYLE *Sart. Res.* II. ii, The little Kuhbach gushing kindly by, among beech-rows. **1851** *Gard. Chron.* 740 A disease which is making great ravages amongst our Beech trees. *Ibid.* 550 The beech-timber of the Chiltern Hills is harder and heavier. *c* **1865** LETHEBY in *Circ. Sc.* I. 106/1 Oils are.. extracted from the beech-nut, weld seed, etc. **1908** R. SOUTH *Moths* II. 184 The Beech-Green Carpet (*Amoebe olivata*). **1909** L. HUXLEY in *Westm. Gaz.* 22 Jan. 2/3 The silver beechboles burn to gold. **1916** D. H. LAWRENCE *Amores* 109 The woods where the beech-green spurts Like a storm of emerald snow.

4. Special comb.: **beech disease** (see quots.); **beech-drops**, a North American plant, *Epiphēgus*, N.O. *Orobanchaceæ*, parasitic upon the roots of the beech; **beech-fern**, common name of *Polypodium Phegopteris*; **beech-finch**, local name of the Chaffinch; **beech marten**, see MARTEN; **beech-mast**, the fruit of the beech; **beech-oil**, oil extracted from beech-mast; **beech-owl**, local name of the Tawny Owl; **beech-weevil** (see quot.); **beech-wheat** = BUCKWHEAT; **beech-wood sugar** (see quots.).

1905 *Daily Chron.* 3 July 9/1 *Beech disease (*cryptococcus fagi*) is widely distributed throughout England. **1815** DRAKE *Cincinnati* ii. 86 *Beech drops. **1876** CHAMBERS *Cycl.*, *Cancer Root*, or Beech-drops..a parasitic plant. **1816** STEPHENS in *Shaw's Gen. Zool.* IX. II. 444 It [the Chaffinch] is called by various names in this country, such as..Flax-finch, *Beech-finch, [etc.]. **1841** FENNELL *Nat. Hist. Quadr.* 106 The Beech Marten is the *Martes foina* of modern zoologists..Besides *Beech Marten, it is called Stone Marten. **1577** B. GOOGE *Heresbach's Husb.* (1586) 31 The graine..three-corned, not unlike the *Beechemast both in colour and forme. **1876** DIGBY *Real Prop.* i. §1. 17 Feeding swine on the acorns and beechmast. **1716** *Lond. Gaz.* No. 5468/4 Fine *Beech Oil cold drawn. **1882** *Garden* 25 Mar. 198/2 The *Beech weevil..feeds on the leaves of Beech trees. **1913** DORLAND *Med. Dict.* (ed. 7) 919/1 **Beechwood sugar*, xylose.

beech, obs. variant of BEACH.

beechen ('biːtʃən), *a. arch.* and *poet.* In 1 bécen, 4–5 bechen, 7 beachen. [OE. *bécen*:—*bóecen*:—OTeut. **bōkīno-z* (cogn. w. L. *fāginus*, Gr. *φήγινος*), f. *bôkâ-* beech: see prec. and -EN¹.]

1. Of, pertaining to, or derived from the beech.

c **1000** ÆLFRIC *Gloss.* in Wülcker *Voc.* 137 *Faginus*, bécen. *c* **1000** *Sax. Leechd.* I. 182 þær heo on becenan treowes wyrttruman ȝewexen sy. *c* **1386** CHAUCER *Chan. Yem. Prol.* & *T.* 607 This false chanoun Out of his bosom took a bechen cole. **1622** PEACHAM *Compl. Gentl.* II. ii. (1634) 110 By his beechen garland is signified the great plenty of beech-trees which grow about Fasterona. **1697** DRYDEN *Virg. Eclog.* i. 1 Beneath the Shade which Beechen Boughs diffuse. **1773** G. WHITE *Selborne* xxxix. (1788) 117 Before our beechen woods were so much destroyed. **1878** B. TAYLOR *Deukalion* III. i, Under yonder beechen shade.

2. Made of the wood of the beech.

1663 COWLEY *Verses & Ess.* (1669) 87 Canst look upon thy Beechen Bowl, and Dish. **1741** RICHARDSON *Pamela* (1824) I. xxix. 46 As hard as a beechen trencher. **1822** WORDSW. *Eccl. Sonn.* I. xxii, A beechen bowl, A maple dish, my furniture should be. **1870** BRYANT *Homer* I. v. 176 The beechen axle groaned beneath the weight.

¶ Now superseded in common use by BEECH *attrib.*

beechy ('biːtʃɪ), *a.* [f. BEECH + -Y.] Of, characterized by, or abounding in, beeches.

1612 DRAYTON *Poly-olb.* xix. (1748) 333 Vast beechy banks. **1647–9** G. DANIEL *Poems* Wks. II. 130 Titirus sitting vnder Beechie Shade. **1830** DISRAELI *Home Lett.* ii. 6 Our beloved and beechy Bucks.

beed, beedered, obs. ff. BEAD, BED, BEDRID.

be-edged, etc.: see BE- *pref.*

beedle, obs. variant of BEADLE.

beedom ('biːdəm). *rare.* The realm of bees.

1868 G. MACDONALD *Seaboard Par.* I. xi. 158 As if he were the beadle of all bee-dom, and overgrown in consequence.

'bee-,eater. A genus of birds (*Merops*) which devour bees and flies, one species of which (*M. apiaster*) is an occasional visitant to England. Many of the species are brilliantly coloured.

1668 CHARLETON *Onomast.* 87 *Merops*..Apiaster, the Bee-eater. **1768** CROKER, etc. *Compl. Dict.* II, *Merops*, the bee-eater..a very beautiful bird, somewhat larger than the common king-fisher. **1877** A. B. EDWARDS *Up Nile* xxii. 684 The bee-eaters flash like live emeralds across our path. **1896** H. A. BRYDEN *Tales S. Afr.* vi. 129 Gem-like bee-eaters flashed among the reeds. **1955** BANNERMAN *Birds Brit. Isles* IV. 43 The European bee-eater and the blue-cheeked bee-eater, which has once wandered to Britain,..have overlapping migration routes in Egypt, Syria and Persia.

beef (biːf), *sb.* Forms: 3–4 boef, beef, 4 bouf, 5 befe, byffe, beoff, buif, 5–6 beff, 6 beafe, biefe, beffe, 6–7 beefe, 7 (bœufe), bief, beife, 7– beef. Plural: beeves; also 5 beoffes, buefs, beuys, 5–7 beues, beves, 6 beafes, beffes, bevis, beoves, 6–7 beefes, bieves, beeffes, 9 (in U.S.) beefs. [a. OF. *boef* (= mod.F. *bœuf*):—L. *bov-em*, acc. of *bos* ox, cogn. with Gr. *βοῦς*, Skr. *go-*, Eng. cow.]

1. The flesh of an ox, bull, or cow, used as food. Often preceded by words indicating the exact part of the animal, e.g. *sirloin*, *ribs of beef*, etc. *sea-beef*: beef pickled for use at sea.

a **1300** *K. Alis.* 5248 To mete was greithed beef and motoun. *c* **1350** *Will. Palerne* 1849 Fair bouf wel sode. *c* **1386** CHAUCER *Merch. T.* 176 Bet than olde boef is tendre vel. *c* **1420** *Liber Cocorum* (1862) 27 Fresshe brothe of the befe. *c* **1440** *Promp. Parv.* 28 Byffe, flesche [*v.r.* beff]. **1533** ELYOT *Cast. Helthe* II. i. (1541) 16 b, Biefe is better digested than a chykens legge. **1552** HULOET, Beafe, *bubula.* **1596** SHAKS. *Tam. Shr.* IV. iii. 23 What say you to a peece of Beefe and Mustard? **1607** DEKKER *Knts. Conjur.* (1842) 34 More stale then sea-beefe. **1653** WALTON *Angler* 191 Powdered Bief is a most excellent bait to catch an Eele. **1662** PEPYS *Diary* 29 May, We had cakes, and powdered beef, and ale. **1712** ADDISON *Spect.* No. 269 ⁋8, I have always a Piece of cold Beef and a Mince-Pye upon the Table. **1818** COBBET *Pol. Reg.* V./302 They dine..upon good roast-beef and port. **1876** WHYTE-MELVILLE *Katerfelto* xx. 228 'What can we have for supper?' 'Aitch-bone of beef, my lord.'

2. *transf.* **a.** Applied to other kinds of flesh or food.

1661 LOVELL *Hist. Anim. & Min.* 233 Ling..is counted the beefe of the Sea. **1868** LOSSING *Hudson* 145 The Sturgeon..are sold in such quantities in Albany, that they have been called, in derision, 'Albany beef.'

b. *mod. colloq.* = 'Flesh' (of men). Also, strength, muscular power; effort. Cf. BEEF *v.* 2, BEEFY.

1851 MELVILLE *Moby Dick* II. xxxix. 261 Oh, *do* pile on the beef... Oh! my lads, *do* spring. **1862** *Cork Examiner* 28 Mar., Chelmsford stood higher in the leg, and showed less beef about him. **1863** *Cornh. Mag.*, Feb. *Life Man of War*, Useful at the heavy hauling of braces, etc.—Where plenty of 'beef' is required. **1968** R. M. PATTERSON *Finlay's River* 25 We on the other hand, were paddling our canoe and putting all the beef we could behind it.

c. Slang phr. ***beef to the heel(s)***: of a person: massive, bulky, brawny.

1867 R. BROUGHTON *Cometh Up* I. xviii. 294 Dolly was not a fine person, as they say, at all; not *beef to the heels*, by any means. **1922** JOYCE *Ulysses* 65 We did great biz yesterday. Fair day and all the beef to the heels were in. *Ibid.* 366 Transparent stockings, stretched to breaking point. Not like ..the one in Grafton street. White. Wow! Beef to the heel. **1958** A. WALL *Queen's English* xxxi. 110 'Beef' and 'beefy' are not complimentary terms, and 'beef to the heels' is even less so.

3. An ox; any animal of the ox kind; *esp.* a fattened beast, or its carcase. **a.** Usually in *pl. arch.* or *techn.*

c **1320** *Seuyn Sag.* (W.) 1095 Hit mote bothe drink and ete ..Beues flesch, and drink the broht. **1475** *Bk. Noblesse* 68 Grete providence of vitaille of cornys, of larde, and beoffes. **1485** CAXTON *Chas. Gt.* 107 Grete oxen and buefs slayn. **1523** BERNERS *Froiss.* I. cccxciii. 675 Mo than xx. thousande beastes, swyne, beufes, kene, and moutons. **1596** SHAKS. *Merch. Ven.* I. iii. 168 As flesh of Muttons, Beefes, or Goates. **1611** BIBLE *Lev.* xxii. 21 A free will offring in beeues or sheepe. **1669** WORLIDGE *Syst. Agric.* (1681) 170 Our Beves yield much Butter, Cheese..and Meat. *a* **1674** CLARENDON *Hist. Reb.* II. VII. 323 One half in Money, and the other half in good Beefs. **1780** T. JEFFERSON *Corr.* Wks. 1859 I. 252 To collect beeves in our southern counties. **1861** MAY *Const. Hist.* (1863) I. iv. 192 The supply of beeves and grain for his household. **1884** in *Glasgow Her.* 5 Jan. 5/2 All the beefs that are ready for shipping.

b. Also in *sing.* (Now chiefly *U.S.*)

1583 STUBBES *Anat. Abus.* II. 26 Whereas they pay a certeine price for a fat beefe. **1601** HOLLAND *Pliny* II. 420 If either a bœufe or mutton be rubbed with salt. **1609** BIBLE (Douay) *Deut.* xiv. 5 The pygargue, the wilde beefe, the cameloparde. **1668** WILKINS *Real Char.* II. v. §5. 164 Either to a Beef, or a Sheep, or a Wolf. **1758** in *Essex Inst. Hist. Coll.* (1881) XVIII. 93 Six men..put under Guard on suspicion of killing a young Beef and 2 Calves. **1775** JOHNSON *West. Isl.* Wks. X. 456 When a beef was killed for the house. **1844** MRS. HOUSTON *Yacht Voy. Texas* II. 180 The cook went on shore and 'shot a beef.' **1878** *Southern Hist. Soc. Papers* VI. 212 Behind these came a beef, driven by soldiers... The beef was immediately shot at and butchered. **1904** J. H. CLAIBORNE *Seventy-five Yrs. Old Virginia* 289 A beef..was driven up and shot.

fig. **1596** SHAKS. *1 Hen. IV*, III. iii. 199 O, my sweet Beefe I must still be good Angell to thee.

c. *collect.* Cattle. *U.S.*

c **1706** *Voy. Maryland* in *Amer. Hist. Rev.* (1907) XII. 329 They have fatt Beefe and fatt Porke Comes home to their Doores without giving 'em any Corne. **1840** J. BUEL *Farmer's Compan.* (ed. 2) 318/2 The fattening of beef. **1907** S. E. WHITE *Arizona Nights* ii. 30 We was just gettin' back from drivin' some beef up to the troops.

4. A protest, (ground for) complaint, grievance. *slang* (orig. *U.S.*). Cf. BEEF *v.* 4.

1899 ADE *Fables in Slang* (1900) 80 He made a Horrible Beef because he couldn't get Loaf Sugar for his Coffee. **1931** D. RUNYON *Guys & Dolls* (1932) iv. 79 To round himself up with his ever-loving wife in case of a beef from her over keeping the baby out in the night air. **1945** *Daily Express* 22 May 2/6 The beef is, Why should every battle we fight have to be a 'Battle of Britain'? **1946** WODEHOUSE *Money in Bank* xii. 95 What's your beef about taking ninety per? **1949** [see *beefcake* below].

5. *Attrib.* and in *comb.*, as ***beef animal, -boat, -bone, -cattle, -collops, -fat, -flick, -house, -market, -merchant, -net, -pot, -shop, -steer, -suet***; ***beef-boiler, -eating, -grower, -making, -roaster***; ***beef-faced*** adj.

1838 H. COLMAN *Rep. Agric. Mass.* 73 They agree to pay 32 cents. for the offal of every *beef animal there slaughtered. **1837** MARRYAT *Dog-Fiend* xii, He jumped into the *beef boat to go on board of the cutter. **1611** COTGR., *Archimarmitonerastique*..or Arch-frequenter of the Cloyster beefe-pot, or *beefe-boyler. **1758** J. S. *Le Dran's Observ. Surg.* (1771) 279 It seemed to be the Scale of a *Beef-Bone. **1820** SCOTT *Abbot* xix, Such bare beef-bones, such a shouldering at the buttery-hatch. **1758** T. WALKER *Let.* 14 Aug. in *Amer. Antiq. Soc. Proc.* (1932) XLI. 130 Five Hundred *Beef Cattle are to set off tomorrow. **1899** *Scribner's Mag.* XXV. 116/2 We passed a herd of fine beef cattle on their way to Santiago. **1815** SCOTT *Guy M.* xliv, A plate of *beef-collops. **1838** DICKENS *O. Twist.* (1850) 68/1, I know a friend who has a *beef-faced boy. **1836** TODD *Cycl. Anat. & Phys.* II. 233/1 The *elain* of *beef fat is colourless. **1462** *Test. Ebor.* (1855) II. 261 Iiij. bakon-fliks, ij. *beffe-fliks. **1880** *Victorian Rev.* 2 Feb. 670 For the American *beef-grower to fatten their beef cattle. **1807** J. BERESFORD *Miseries* II. xix. 211 Taking your dinner from an a-la-mode *beef-house. **1881** *Gentl. Mag.* Jan. 67 They [wild cattle] are ..illbred, and averse to *beef-making. **1480** *Robt. Devyll* 38 Robert toke a quycke catte..And threwe her quycke into the *beefe potte. **1703** *Art's Improv.* I. 14 As big as an ordinary Beef-Pot. **1880** *Victorian Rev.* 2 Feb. 665 The production of cheap *beef steers. **1853** *Q. Rev.* Mar. 397 An equal quantity of melted *beef-suet.

6. Special comb.: † **beef-brained** *ppl. a.*, thick-headed, stupid; † **beef-brewis, -broth**, broth made from beef; **beefburger** ('biːfbɜːgə(r)) [BURGER], a hamburger, (orig. *U.S.*); **beefcake** ('biːfkeɪk) (*slang*, orig. *U.S.*) [humorous, after CHEESECAKE], (a display of) sturdy masculine physique; **beef chit** *Naut. slang*, a menu; **beef-dairy** *a.*, applied to a cross between beef and dairy cattle; **beef essence** (see quot. 1890); **beef-extract**, an extract of the soluble fibrin of beef; **beef-fed** *a.*, fed on beef; esp. as an epithet for a typical Englishman; **beef-ham**, beef cured in the same fashion as a ham, by salting, smoking, etc.; **beef-head**, a thick-head, a block-head; **beef-headed** *a.*, = *beef-brained*; **beef-measles**, a parasitic disease, which sometimes attacks cattle; **beef stroganof(f)** (see STROGANOFF); **beef-tapeworm**, *Tænia mediocancellata*; **beef-tea**, the juice of beef extracted by prolonged simmering in a very little water, used as a nutritious food for invalids; **beef trip** *Naval slang*, (*a*) a routine trip in the ship's boat assigned to bring the meat ration from the shore; (*b*) an escort of food ships in convoy in the 1914–18 war; **beef-witted** *a.* (= *beef-brained*); hence **beef-wittedness**. See also BEEFEATER, BEEF-STEAK, BEEF-WOOD.

1627 FELTHAM *Resolves* I. x. (1647) 28 A *beefe-brain'd fellow that hath only impudence enough to shew himself a foole. **1820** SCOTT *Abbot* xiv, The monks..are merriest.. when they sup *beef-brewis for lenten-kail. **1703** *Art's Improv.* I. 26 Supply it with the Fat of Powder'd *Beef-broth. **1940** in *Amer. Speech* XV. 452/1 Hamburgers are out, *beefburgers are in! **1959** *Observer* 8 Nov. 3/5 We can expect the kind of hamburger proliferation that exists in America, with beefburgers, eggburgers, [etc.]. **1949** in *Amer. Speech* (1954) XXIX. 282 Alan Ladd has a beef—about '*beefcake', the new Hollywood trend toward exposing the male chest. **1954** *Sunday Pictorial* 18 Apr. 15/1, I learned that beefcake was bunk because one of my jobs in the circus was lacing the strongman's shoes. **1963** *Guardian* 29 June 5/4 The other poster..shows Albert Finney in a beefcake pose with his shirt slit to the navel. **1911** 'GUNS' et al. *Middle Watch Musings* 54 The Commander (having failed to arouse the Wardroom Waiters from their lethargy; sitting for five minutes without being offered the *beef chit). **1962** *John o'London's* 14 June 571/1 The beef chit, or [wardroom] menu. **1960** *Farmer & Stockbreeder* 16 Feb. 15/1 *Beef-dairy crosses include crosses between beef breeds and Friesians or Dairy Shorthorns. **1853** DUNGLISON *Dict. Med. Sci.* (ed. 9) 130/1 *Beef essence. **1890** BILLINGS *Med. Dict.*, *Beef essence*, cooked juice of beef, prepared by introducing lean beef in small pieces into a bottle, and subjecting it to heat of a boiling water-bath for an hour. **1890** W. JAMES *Princ. Psychol.* II. xxiii. 380 The stimulating effects of tobacco, smoke, alcohol, *beef-extract (which is innutritious), etc. etc., may be partly due to a dynamogenic action of this sort **1903** KIPLING *Five Nations* 78 And *beef-fed zealots threaten in To Buddha and Kamakura. **1903** A. MCNEILL *Egreg. English* viii. 79 A beef-fed army and a beef-fed navy are what Englishmen believe they get for their money. **1934** E. H. W. MEYERSTEIN *Let.* 3 Apr. (1959) 159 Of course you (i.e. beef-fed materialistic Englishman (woman)) can argue. **1815** SCOTT *Guy M.* xxiv, A huge piece of cold *beef-ham. **1775** LD. CAVENDISH in *Burke's Corr.* (1844) II. 86 The petition..should be framed so as to..draw off some of the *beef-heads who are disposed against it. **1828** MRS. ROYALL *Black Book* II. 114 Such a great *beef-headed fellow as you editor of a paper. **1900** E. TERRY *Let.* 28 Jan. (1931) 372 The war—and the disgrace of it (beef-headed Buller's doings). **1884** *Health Exhib. Catal.* 20/1 Drawings of..*Beef Measles and the *Beef-tapeworm. **1783** *Med. Commun.* I. 140 She was ordered *beef-tea. **1861** FLOR. NIGHTINGALE *Nursing* 52 A small quantity of beef tea added to other articles of food makes them more nourishing. **1870** LOWELL *Study Wind.* 91 He gives us the very beef-tea of history, nourishing and even palatable enough. **1919** 'TAFFRAIL' *H.M.S. Anonymous* vii. §2. 139 We called it the '*Beef trip' because in some remote fashion it reminded us of our midshipman days, when, in charge of the 'blood boat' we left our ships..to bring off from the shore the fresh meat which would..be served out to the ship's company. *Ibid.* 142 In spite of all precautions on our part the German flotillas from Zeebrugge..might altogether have put a stop to the 'beef trip' carried on under their very noses. *Ibid.* §3. 152 The 'beef trip' was over. Yet another consignment of margarine and Dutch cheeses had been brought into the United Kingdom. **1925** FRASER & GIBBONS *Soldier & Sailor Words* 21 *On the beef trip*, a Navy term in the War, used of the vessels carrying meat to the Grand Fleet at Scapa. **1606** SHAKS. *Tr. & Cr.* II. i. 14 Thou mungrel *beefe-witted Lord. **1863** *Reader* 22 Aug., This British bull-neckedness, this British *beef-wittedness.

beef, *v.* [f. prec.] **1.** *trans.* To apply raw beef to (a bruise).

1870 T. SIMMONS *Oakdale Gr.* 124 [It] will show up in blue and yellow relief..unless they beef it.

2. a. To put more muscle into, to drive harder. *U.S.* (College slang.)

1860 *Yale Lit. Mag.* XXVI. 83 (Th.), The first boat in is the winner of the race, so round they turn, and 'beef her' for the home stretch.

b. *slang.* To strengthen; to add vigour, power, or importance to. Const. *up* (occas. *out*). Hence ***beefed-up*** (or *-out*), ppl. a. Cf. BEEF *sb.* 2 b.

1941 A. O. POLLARD *Bombers over Reich* xi. 155 When the Fortresses reach Britain from the United States certain alterations are made; the larger guns are..'beefed up' so as to give them a rate of fire of 900 rounds a minute. **1944** *Time* 24 Jan. 22/3 The Eighth [Air Force] proved that it had beefed up its reserves. **1958** *Observer* 2 Feb. 1/2 This main stage—the 'beefed-up' Redstone—uses a secret formula 'exotic' fuel. **1960** *Times* 21 Jan. 13/6 Economic planners.. may be tempted to beef-up a project to make it ambitious enough to qualify for large-scale aid. **1963** *Language* XXXIX. 242 A new generation was fed the nonsense of Marr, only partially beefed out with surreptitious teachings. **1966** *New Scientist* 10 Mar. 618/1 The Defense Department has spent £50 billion building and beefing up the non-nuclear elements of the armed forces.

3. To slaughter (an ox, etc.) for beef. Also *transf.*, to knock down. *U.S. slang.*

1869 *Harper's Mag.* Jan. 159/1 They [*sc.* the buffalo] were to be beefed and sent East or put into cattle-cars, and killed after they had arrived in the Eastern cities. **1916** B. M. Bower *Phantom Herd* xvi. 268, I calc'late I'd better beef another critter. **1926** J. Black *You can't Win* xiii. 185 When one of them got peeved..some hard-fisted miner beefed him like an ox. **1934** A. Hyder *Black-Girl, White-Lady* xxi. 309 'Yo'kills niggers?' 'Like flies,' Charley assured her. 'You want me to beef a few for you?'

4. *intr.* To complain, grumble, protest. *slang* (orig. *U.S.*). Hence '**beefing** *vbl. sb.*

1888 *N.Y. World* 13 May (Farmer), He'll beef an' kick like a steer an' let on he won't never wear 'em. **1889** *The Road* (Denver) 28 Dec. 4/3 He will be coming down town again soon on crutches, 'beefing' about cancer of the stomach. **1922** S. Lewis *Babbitt* v. 60 Course I wouldn't beef about it to the fellows at the Roughnecks' Table there. **1930** Wodehouse *Very Good, Jeeves!* iii. 74 You have beefed about Miss Wickham. **1931** E. Linklater *Juan in America* ii. xvii. 182 'So I'm a slave, am I? Like hell I am!' 'Stop beefing,' said Spider. **1939** J. B. Priestley *Let People Sing* viii. 210 Too much arguin' an' beefin', majority an' minority nonsense, talkin' shop stuff. **1957** H. Croome *Forgotten Plan* xi. 138 Stop beefing, Frank. You'll be seeing her again soon enough.

† **beef-eat**, *v. nonce-wd.* (Cf. next word.)

1671 Crowne *Juliana* iv. 44 Sirrah, I could find in my heart to beef-eat you.

'**beef,eater.** [f. beef + eater; cf. OE. *hláf-æ̂ta*, lit. 'loaf-eater,' a menial servant.

(The conjecture that sense 2 may have had some different origin, e.g. from *buffet* 'sideboard,' is historically baseless. No such form of the word as **buffetier* exists; and *beaufet*, which has been cited as a phonetic link between *buffet* and *beefeater*, is merely an 18th c. bad spelling, not so old as *beef-eater*.)]

1. An eater of beef; *contemptuously*, a well-fed menial. (Properly with hyphen, *beef-eater*.)

1610 *Histrio-m.* iii. 99 Awake yee drowsie drones That long have suckt the honney from my hives: Begone yee greedy beefe-eaters y'are best. *a* **1628** F. Greville *Sidney* (1652) 109 We conquered France, more by such factions and ambitious assistances than by any odds of our Bows, or Beef-eaters, as the French were then scornfully pleas'd to terme us. **1854** Badham *Halieut.* 516 Amongst immortal gluttons, Hercules (βουφάγος) the beef-eater was chief.

2. a. Popular appellation of the Yeomen of the Guard, in the household of the Sovereign of Great Britain, instituted at the accession of Henry VII in 1485; also of the Warders of the Tower of London, who were named Yeomen Extraordinary of the Guard in the reign of Edward VI, and wear the same antique uniform as the 'Beefeaters of the Guard.'

1671 Crowne *Juliana* iv. 44 The Beef-eaters o' the Guard. *Ibid.* You Beef-eater, you saucy cur. **1736** Fielding *Pasquin* ii. i, Is not there a sort of employment, sir, called —beef eating? If your lordship please to make me a beef-eater. **1779** Sheridan *Critic* iii. i. (1883) 175 Enter *Beef-eater*, with his halbert. **1848** Macaulay *Hist. Eng.* I. 293 Without some better protection than that of the trainbands and beefeaters. **1864** H. Spencer *Illustr. Univ. Progr.* 63 The Beefeaters at the Tower wear the costume of Henry VIIth's body-guard.

b. A style of hat worn by women, resembling that worn by a Yeoman of the Guard. Also *attrib.*

1785 Betsy Sheridan *Jrnl.* 5 July (1960) ii. 59 Hats tied under the chin, beefeaters etc are not worn by fashionable people. **1895** *Daily News* 3 Sept. 6/3 The black straw sailor hat, with Beefeater crown. **1909** *Westm. Gaz.* 4 Jan. 5/2 A style of hat which was a favourite with us a year or two ago —viz., a velvet beefeater—has been brought in again.

3. *Ornith.* A genus of African birds (*Buphaga*), called also Ox-peckers, allied to the Starling family, which live chiefly on parasitic larvæ hatched under the skin of cattle.

1836 *Penny Cycl.* VI. 22 The Beef-eater..or *Pique-bœuf* ..digs and squeezes out with his forceps of a beak the larva that lies festering under the tough hide of the quadruped.

beefer ('biːfə(r)). [f. beef *sb.* + -er^1.] An animal bred for beef.

1660 May *Accompl. Cook* 113 Take the blood of the beefer when it is warm, put in some salt, and then strain it. **1809** T. Batchelor *Anal. Eng. Lang.* v. 127 A beefer; a familiar name for a calf. **1938** J. Moses *Nine Miles from Gundigai* 17 Milkers, too, very fine, And beefers off the Considine.

beefiness ('biːfinɪs). [f. beefy *a.* + -ness.] Beefy quality; *transf.* fleshy development.

1859 Smiles *Self-Help* 160 It is..the one pull more of the oar that proves the beefiness of the fellow, as Oxford men say. **1882** Annie Thomas *Allerton T.* III. ix. 164, I like to have my animal..dressed in such a way that its original beefiness or muttoniness is completely concealed.

'**beefing, beefin.** *dial.* [f. beef + -ing.] An ox for slaughter.

1466 *Paston Lett.* 549 II. 269 All the velys, lambes, beefins. **1847** Halliwell, *Beefing*, a bullock fit for slaughter. (Suffolk dialect.)

beefing, var. of biffin, a kind of apple.

beefish ('biːfɪʃ), *a.* [f. beef *sb.* + -ish^1.] **a.** Beefy (with favourable implication). **b.** = *beef-fed* (beef *sb.* 6).

1882 G. M. Hopkins *Let.* 3 Apr. (1935) 143, I hope..you are now..well; strong, vigorous, lusty, beefish. **1887** *Andover Rev.* VII. 32 This degeneracy has turned him into that 'beefish, porterish', bellowing sort of a John Bull.

'**bee-flower.**

1. A flower resembling a bee; the Bee Orchis.

1626 Bacon *Sylva* §609 The Figure maketh the Fable; For so we see, there be Bee-Flowers, etc. **1749** Mrs. Delany *Autobiog.* (1861) II. 531 Could Mrs. Viney send the Duchess a root or two of the bee-flower?

2. A flower visited or fertilized by bees.

1615 Lawson *Orch. & Gard.* iii. vi. (1668) 12 Wall flowers, commonly called Bee-flowers, or Winter Gilly-Flowers. **1879** Lubbock *Sci. Lect.* ii. 32 Bee-flowers (if I may coin such an expression) have generally bright clear colors.

beef-steak ('biːfsteɪk). **a.** A steak or thick slice of beef, cut from the hind-quarters of the animal, suitable for grilling or frying.

1711 [see **b.**] **1715** *Spect.* No. 639 (1734) IX. 13 He tossed his Hat into the Frying-pan, and made a Beef-stake of it. **1783** Johnson in *Boswell* III. 449 Let you and I, Sir, go together and eat a Beef-steak in Grub-Street. **1849** Dickens *Dav. Copp.* xviii. 162, I am taken home..have beef-steaks put to my eyes.

b. *attrib.*, as in ***beef-steak pie, pudding***; **Beef-steak Club**, a celebrated society founded by Lord Peterborough; the members wore a gridiron upon their buttons; **beef-steak fungus**, a fungus, *Fistulina hepatica*, somewhat resembling a beef-steak in appearance; also ***beef-steak mushroom***.

1711 Addison *Spect.* No. 9 ¶8 The Beef-steak and October Clubs are neither of them averse to eating and drinking. **1841** Marryat *Poacher* x, She was carving a beefsteak-pie. **1851** Mayhew *Lond. L.* I. 359 A good beef-steak supper. **1886** J. Stevenson *Brit. Fungi* II. 183 Fistula ..F. hepatica..Edible and nourishing, but rather coarse, and not a very pleasant flavour. Known as the beef-steak fungus. Slices exactly like beef-steak. **1895** W. H. Gibson *Our Edible Toadstools & Mushrooms* 213 The *beefsteak* mushroom—*Fistulina hepatica*... Its upper surface was dark meaty red or liver colored. **1953** J. Ramsbottom *Mushrooms & Toadstools* xix. 231 *Fistulina hepatica*, the Beef-Steak Fungus, looking somewhat like an ox-tongue with a glutinous upper surface, yellow tubes and streaky flesh exuding a red juice.

Hence **Beefsteaker**, a member of the Beefsteak Club.

1883 *Cornh. Mag.* (article) *Beefsteakers.*

beef-wood ('biːfwʊd). [f. beef *sb.* + wood.]

1. The timber of an Australian tree (*Casuarina*), so called from its red colour; the tree has long, pendent, jointed, thread-like branches, without leaves, but with small sheaths at the joints.

1836 *Penny Cycl.* VI. 358 The timber of some species [*Casuarina*] forms the beefwood of the New South Wales colonists. **1880** Silver *Handbk. Australia* 275 The beef-wood..and tulipwood take a high polish.

2. Applied to various other trees, e.g. in N.S. Wales to *Stenocarpus salignus*; in Queensland to *Banksia compar* (both N.O. *Proteaceæ*); in Jamaica to evergreen shrubs or low trees of the genus *Ardisia* (N.O. *Myrsinaceæ*).

1756 P. Browne *Jamaica* 201 This tree is commonly called by the name of Beef-wood..from the fleshy colour of the interior bark. **1819** *Blackw. Mag.* IV. 654 Well wooded with..the Beefwood.

beefy ('biːfɪ), *a.* [f. beef *sb.* + -y^1.] **a.** Abounding in beef; resembling beef; fleshy; obese; stolid or brawny.

1743 H. Walpole *Let.* 20 Aug. (1903) I. 373, I here every day see men, who are mountains of roast beef... I have an Aunt..who..is as beefy as her neighbours. **1853** Kane *Grinnell Exp.* xvii. (1856) 129 One day he [the bear] is quite beefy and bearable. **1859** Smiles *Self-Help* 291 This dunce had a dull energy and a sort of beefy tenacity of purpose. **1860** *All Y. Round* No. 66. 367 There are no beefy boys at these schools. **1862** Calverley *Verses & Tr.* 48 The beefy market-place. **1865** *Slang Dict.*, *Beefy*, unduly thick or fat, commonly said of women's ancles. **1876** Miss Braddon *J. Haggard's D.* x. 134 Added the farmer in his beefy voice. **1889** *Cent. Dict.*, *Beefy*..2. Brawny; muscular; hardy. **1890** Kipling *Barrack-r. Ballads* (1892) 52 Beefy face an' grubby 'and—Law! wot do they understand?

b. *Schoolboys' slang.* Good, clever, fair, attractive.

1903 Wodehouse *Prefect's Uncle* xv. 213, I doubled across to bring off a beefy c-and-b. **1905** H. A. Vachell *Hill* i. 15 Comparing these [*sc.* other rooms] with his own apartment, John said shyly—'It's not very beefy.' 'Beefy? You smell of a private school.'

beega(h, varr. bigha.

beegum, variant of begum.

beehive ('biːˌhaɪv). [f. bee *sb.*^{1} + -hive *sb.*]

1. a. A receptacle used as a home for bees; usually made of thick straw work in the shape of a dome; but there are modern contrivances made of many materials, and adapted to special purposes.

c **1325** *Coer de L.* 2885 And commaunded hys men, belyve To bryng up many a bee-hyve. **1483** *Cath. Angl.* 26 Be-hyve, *apiarium.* **1593** Shaks. *2 Hen. VI*, iv. i. 109 Drones sucke not Eagles blood, but rob Bee-hiues. **1855** Macaulay *Hist. Eng.* III. 611 The farmhouse peeping from among beehives and apple-blossoms.

b. *fig.* A place swarming with busy people; a 'hive of industry'. (Cf. hive *sb.* 3.)

1616 R. Carpenter *Larum Love* 33 A profitable and behoouefull member in the Bee-hiue of Christs Church. **1725** *New-Eng. Courant* 8 Mar. 1 If we could..make that Building a Bee-Hive of Business. **1940** *Manch. Guardian Weekly* 15 Mar. 216 He works in a great hospital now, a beehive of a place—swarming with people. **1949** Koestler *Promise & Fulf.* iii. iv. 324 The bustling bee-hive activity of the whole country.

c. A hat shaped like a beehive. Cf. *beehive-hat* below (sense 3).

1909 *Westm. Gaz.* 2 Mar. 5/2 A useful hat..is one of the new shape, which some milliners are calling the 'Beehive'. **1937** N. Coward *Present Indic.* i. xix. 66 Gertie Millar in *Our Miss Gibbs*, wearing a beehive.

d. A high beehive-shaped hair-style.

1960 *Guardian* 22 July 7/2 Three East Berlin peroxide girls whose beehives tower over provocative curves. *Ibid.* 26 Aug. 6/4 Exaggerated beehive hair-styles. **1962** *New Statesman* 18 May 708/2 Rube, neck stiff so as not to shake her beehive, stares sultry round the packed pub.

2. Name of a nebula in the constellation Cancer.

1869 Dunkin *Midn. Sky* 136 A small nebulous-looking object in the crab's body, is known by the name of the Præsepe, or the Beehive.

3. *Comb.* and *attrib.*, chiefly in sense of 'shaped like a bee-hive,' as in ***beehive-basket, -chair*** (i.e. with a top like a bee-hive), ***beehive-hat, -hut, -oven***; also ***beehive-like, beehive-shaped***, adjs. **beehive coke**, coke produced in a beehive oven; **beehive tomb**, a dome-shaped tomb of the Mycenæan age in Greece, cut in a hillside.

1816 Southey *Essays* (1832) I. 181 His place in the chimney-corner, or the *bee-hive chair. **1909** Webster, *Beehive coke. **1914** J. S. S. Brame *Fuel* vi. 97 It is found that the lower portions of beehive coke are more dense than the upper. **1909** *Daily Chron.* 22 Feb. 7/5 The latest *beehive hat. **1961** *Guardian* 19 Jan. 9/7 Worn with a.. beehive hat. **1863** Lubbock *Preh. Times* ii. (1878) 56 From these we pass naturally to the *beehive houses. **1884** J. Colborne *Hicks Pasha* 84 The..*beehive huts of the narrow street. **1881** Raymond *Mining Gloss.*, **Beehive oven*, an oven for the manufacture of coke, shaped like the old-fashioned beehive. **1858** W. Ellis *Vis. Madagascar* ix. 235 Low, *beehive-shaped huts. **1887** Mahaffy *Rambles Greece* xv. (ed. 3) 417 A race..who constructed great *beehive tombs. **1957** Childe *Dawn Europ. Civ.* (ed. 6) v. 80 These [*sc.* chieftains] celebrated their elevation by erecting stately beehive tombs or tholoi.

'**beehive**, *v. rare.* [f. prec.] *intr.* To cluster like bees in a hive. (U.S.A.)

1883 *N.E. Jrnl. Educ.* XVII. 325 The girls bee-hive together to discuss mysteries.

'**beehived**, *a.* [f. beehive *sb.* + -ed^2.] Made or shaped like a beehive.

1885 *Contemp. Rev.* May 742 Beehived cells..for churches occur abundantly at Innismurry.

bee-hivy, *a. nonce-wd.* Beehive-like.

1864 Lady D. Gordon in *Vac. Tourists*, Bamboo canes close together across the rafters, and bound together between each with transverse bamboo—a pretty beehivey effect.

† '**beeishness.** *Obs.* *rare*$^{-1}$. [f. bee; after *waspish, waspishness.*] The quality of being like bees: used by Penn in his answer to the divines, who had termed the Friends 'wasps.'

1674 Penn *Rebuke Divines* 12 Doth this flow from the Beeishness of your Nature?

beek, *sb. Sc.* [f. beek *v.*^{1}] A warming or basking in the heat, a bask.

1725 Ramsay *Wks.* 1848 II. 133 Glaud by his morning ingle takes a beek. **1788** Picken *Poems* 88 (Jam.) Life's just a wee bit Sunny beek, That bright, and brighter waxes.

beek (biːk), *v.*^{1} Now only *Sc.* or *north. dial.* Forms: 3–6 **beke**, 5–6 **beyke**, 6 *Sc.* **beik**, 6–7 **beak**, 6– **beek**. [Chiefly northern: of uncertain origin. The analogy in form and sense of *bake, beek*, to *bathe, beathe*, suggests possible connexion with *bake*. An OTeut. **bôkian* f. *bôk*, pa. t. of *bakan* would have given an OE. **bóecen, bécen*, and ME. *beke, beek*; but no trace of the older forms is found. Another suggestion would refer *beke* to the stem of *bæwen* to foment (in Ormin) with suffixal *k*: cf., in same sense, dial. G. *bächeln, bächern*, which Grimm refers to *bähen* to foment.]

1. *trans.* and *refl.* To suffuse with genial warmth; to expose (oneself, one's limbs, etc.) to the pleasurable warmth of sun, fire, etc.

c **1230** [see beeking *ppl. a.*^{2}] **1375** Barbour *Bruce* xix. 552 Ane ynglish man, that lay bekand Hym by a fyre. *c* **1400** *Bone Flor.* 99 A gode fyre..To beyke hys boones by. **1553** Brende *Q. Curtius* ii. 11 Diogenes..was beking of himself in yᵉ sunne. **1627** H. Burton *Bait. Pope's Bull* 26 The foolish fish, which beaking hir selfe neere the banke, suffereth the fisher to tickle..her. *a* **1774** Fergusson *Cauler Oysters* Poems (1845) 8 How aften at that ingle cheek Did I my frosty fingers beek. (In modern Scotch.)

b. To season (wood) by exposure to heat.

1483 *Cathol. Angl.* 26 To beke wandes, *explorare.* **1523** Fitzherb. *Husb.* §24 A good husbande hath his forkes and rakes made redye in the winter before..and beyked..and than they wyll be harde, styffe and drye. **1641** Best *Farm. Bks.* (1856) 122 After that we have cutte our wilfes and saughs..wee sette our foreman and another to beaking of them.

2. *intr.* To expose oneself to, or disport in, pleasurable warmth; to bask.

c **1400** *Ywaine & Gaw.* 1459 That Knyght es nothing to set by That..ligges bekeand in his bed. *?a* **1568** *Wife Auchterm.* in *Bannatyne Poems* 215 (JAM.) He saw the wif.. sittand at ane fyre, beikand bawld. **1730** RAMSAY *Gent. Sheph.* Wks. II. 95 She and her cat sit beeking in her yard. *a* **1801** MACNEILL *Poet. Wks.* (1844) 54 To sport on fancy's flowery brink, And beek a wee in love's warm blink.

† **beek,** *v.*[2] *Obs.* A term of the chase: see quot.

c **1470** *Hors Shepe & G.* (1822) 31 A herte, yf he be chasid, he wil desire to haue a ryuer..yf he take agayn the streme, he beteth or els he beeketh.

beeke, beeker, obs. f. BEAK, BEAKER.

'beeking, *vbl. sb. Obs.* exc. *Sc.* [f. BEEK *v.*[1] + -ING[1].] Exposure to genial warmth or heat.

1523 FITZHERB. *Husb.* §24 All the beykyng and driynge that can be had. **1623** COCKERAM, *Aprication*, a beaking in the Sunne.

'beeking, beaking, *ppl. a. Obs.* exc. *Sc.* [f. as prec. + -ING[2].] That gives genial warmth.

c **1230** *Wohunge* in *Cott. Hom.* 269 Al þat pinende pik ne walde ham þunche bote a softe bekinde bað. *a* **1652** BROME *Queene's Exch.* II. ii. Wks. III. 480 Our Masters grudge to give us wood Enough to make a beaking Bonfire.

beekite ('bi:kaɪt). *Min.* Also **beckite** ('bɛkaɪt). [f. the name of Henry *Beeke*, dean of Bristol (d. 1837): see -ITE[1].] (See quots.)

[**1847** A. DUFRÉNOY *Traité de Minéralogie* III. 750 *Beckite*, petites masses concrétionnées, à structure botrioïde, d'un gris rougeâtre, d'un gris sale, qui rayent le verre.] **1856** W. PENGELLY in *Rep. Brit. Assoc. Advancem. Sci.* (Trans.) 74 The most interesting things found in the red Triassic conglomerates of Torbay are the Beekites, so named from the late Dr. Beeke, Dean of Bristol, by whom, it is believed, they were first noticed. *Ibid.*, The interior of the Beekite is calcareous. **1896** A. H. CHESTER *Dict. Min.* 29 *Beekite*,..a chalcedonic pseudomorph after corals or shells, often called beckite. The specimens are locally known as beekites, the name probably being used prior to the reference given [i.e. 1847, cited above]. **1950** *New Biol.* VIII. 85 Replacement by silica may also start from various centres on the shells of molluscs, producing an imperfect crystallization in rings (known as beekite structure).

beel, obs. form of BEAL; see also BOIL *sb.*

be-elbow, be-embroider, etc.: see BE- *pref.*

beeld(e, -yng, obs. forms of BIELD, BUILDING.

† **beele**[1]. *Obs.* [Prob. a variant of *bill (not actually found in this sense, but cf. BILLET) a. F. *bille* 'a young stocke of a tree to graft on' (Cotgr.); cf. 12th c. med.L. *billa, billus* 'branch, trunk of a tree.'] ? The crossbar of the yoke.

1616 SURFL. & MARKH. *Countr. Farm* 650 The young plants are good to make beeles for Yoakes.

† **beele**[2]. *Obs.* or *dial.* [app. a variant form of BILL. But cf. MHG. *bîl, bîhel*, mod.Ger. *beil* ax.] A pick-ax with both ends sharp, used to pick out the ore from the rocks.

1671 *Phil. Trans.* VI. 2104 The Instruments commonly used in Mines..are; (1.) A Beele or Cornish Tubber of 8*l.* or 10*l.* weight, sharped at both ends. **1753** CHAMBERS *Cycl. Supp.*, *Beele*, an instrument used by the workmen to break and pick out the ore from the rocks in which it lies.

[Not in modern Cornish Gloss. of E.D. Soc.; but *W. Corn. Gl.* has '*Beal* a bird's bill.']

Hence **beele-man.**

1671 *Phil. Trans.* VI. 2104 The Beele-men rip the Deads and Ore. **1753** CHAMBERS *Cycl. Supp.* s.v. *Beele*, The miners, who dig up the ore in the mines, are, from the use of this instrument called beele-men..In Cornwall..they allow two shovellers to three beele-men.

beele, obs. or dial. f. BILL 'a beak.'

beely obs. form of BELIE.

Beelzebub (bi:'ɛlzɪbʌb). Also 4 **Belsebub**, 4–6 **Belsabub, -bbe**, 1–9 **Belzebub**. [a. L. *Beëlzebūb*, used in the Vulgate to render both the Gr. βεελζεβούβ of the received text of the N.T. (for which early MSS. have βεελζεβούλ), and the Heb. *baʿal-z'būb* 'fly-lord,' mentioned in 2 Kings i. 2, as 'the god of Ekron,' which Aquila had also reproduced in Gr. as βεελζεβούβ, though the LXX rendered it βάαλ μυῖαν. The relation between the Heb. and Gr. words is not settled. The earlier Eng. translations, and the Douay, followed the Vulgate in identifying them in form, but the Geneva Bible of 1560, followed by the 'Authorized' of 1611, represent the O.T. word more exactly as *Baal-zebub*. From the N.T. designation of Beelzebub as 'prince of demons,' the word became at an early period one of the popular names of the Devil. Milton used it as the name of one of the fallen angels.] The Devil; a devil; also *transf.*

c **950** *Lindisf. Gosp.* Matt. xii. 24 In Belzebub ðone aldormenn diobla. *c* **975** *Rushw. G.* ibid., Belzebub þæt is aldor deofla. *c* **1000** *Ags. G.* ibid., þurh Belzebub deofla ealdre. *c* **1175** *Lamb. Hom.* 55 Loke weo us wið him misdon þurh beelzebubes swikedom. **1377** LANGL. *P. Pl.* B. II. 130 A bastarde y-bore Of Belsabubbes kynne. **1562** J. HEYWOOD *Prov. & Epigr.* (1867) 51 Ye be a baby of Belsabubs bowre. **1601** SHAKS. *Twel. N.* V. i. 291 He holds Belzebub at the staues end as well as a man in his case may do. **1759** LAW *Lett. Import. Subj.* 193 To crucify the Christ of God, as a beelzebub and blasphemer. **1816** KIRBY & SP. *Entomol.* (1843) I. 124 This fly is truly a beelzebub and perhaps..the prototype of the Philistine idol worshipped under that name and in the form of a fly. **1848** MACAULAY *Hist. Eng.* I. xiii, His old troopers, the Satans and Beelzebubs who had shared his crimes (i.e. of Claverhouse).

Be,elze'bubian, *a. rare*; only in form **Bel-**. [f. prec. + -IAN.] Devilish.

1867 FITZGERALD 75 *Brooke St.* I. 239 There'll be the most infernal Belzebubian row.

beem, obs. form of BEAM.

been, *pa. pple.* of BE *v.* Also, obs. form of *be*, pres. infin., and pres. indic. plural.

been, obs. plural of BEE *sb.*[1] var. of BEIN *a.*

been, beenge, var. f. of BEHEN, BEN, BINGE *v.*

beënt ('bi:ənt), *a. Metaph.* [f. BE *v.* + L. suffix -ENT.] That is or exists; existing (in the most abstract sense); also used substantively. (Introduced to represent Germ. *seiend*, as expressing *pure being* in the Hegelian sense.)

1865 J. H. STIRLING *Secrets of Hegel* I. 321 Something, however, is already a definite Beënt. —— 362 Quality distinguished as beënt is Reality. **1885** R. ADAMSON in *Mind* Oct. 575 The changing, variable, transitory, and relatively non-beënt, world of finite fact.

been-to ('bi:ntu:). Also **bintu**. [f. BEEN *pa. pple.* + TO *prep.*] A term used in Africa and Asia for a person who has been to England, usu. for education. Also *attrib.*

1960 M. LAURENCE *This Side Jordan* iv. 82 Who did he think he was, a 'been-to' man, educated abroad, like Victor? *Ibid.* xiv. 251 She was obviously a 'been-to', probably trained in England. **1961** *Time* 3 Nov. 65/1 An educated modern African..sometimes calls himself a Bintu, meaning 'been to' Oxford or Cambridge.

beep (bi:p), *sb.* [Imitative.] The sound made by a horn on a motor car or other vehicle; a short high-pitched sound such as is emitted by an echo-sounder, a radar device, etc. Also *attrib.* So **beep-beep**, such a (reduplicated) sound; also concr., a horn.

1929 E. WILSON *I thought of Daisy* v. 299 Did you ever hear them talk about auto-horns?..There's a *toot-toot*, and a *beep-beep*. **1937** N. MARSH *Vintage Murder* xxii. 250 This horn is called a 'beep-beep'. **1951** A. C. CLARKE *Sands of Mars* iv. 45 The carrier wave..now modulated into an endless string of 'beep-beep-beeps'. **1952** [see BEEPER]. **1956** J. POTTS *Diehard* vii. 109 The ritual beep-beep of his horn. ..Two brief, muted beeps. **1957** *Economist* 2 Nov. 399/1 A four-stage research rocket..sent back beeps. **1962** A. NISBETT *Technique Sound Studio* vii. 131 Time signal pips or 'beep' tones: the very words 'pip' and 'beep' suggest the effect I mean.

beep (bi:p), *v.* [Imitative; cf. prec.] **a.** *trans.* To sound (a horn); to make (something) emit a short high-pitched sound; to indicate by sounding beeps. **b.** *intr.* To emit beeps. Hence **beeped, 'beeping,** *ppl. adjs.*

1936 O. NASH *Primrose Path* 101 Beep the horn and howl the klaxon For Hebrew, Latin and Anglo-Saxon; Howling klaxon, beeping horn. **1953** POHL & KORNBLUTH *Space Merch.* (1955) xiii. 140 He went pale, but beeped his alarm, and went down in a tangle of fists and boots. **1958** *New Scientist* 16 Oct. 1060/1 The first Russian moon rose beeping into the sky a year ago. **1962** *Flight Internat.* LXXXI. 299/1 An Aero Commander was fitted with Lear L-5B autopilot (modified for close pitch control, decrabbing and 'beeped' pitch trim).

beeper ('bi:pə(r)). [f. BEEP *v.* + -ER[1].] A device that emits beeps (see also quot. 1946); also *attrib.*

1946 *Sun* (Baltimore) 7 Aug. 1/3 Planes called 'Beepers'. *Ibid.*, Mother planes were piloted by Capt. Ragner Carlson. .. Radio operators of the drone-controlled planes, or 'beepers', were Capt. John Evans, [etc.]. **1952** A. C. CLARKE *Islands in Sky* iv. 72 A Beeper..is a tiny radar set..used to locate objects that have drifted away from the Station... When its beam hits anything you hear a series of 'Beeps'. **1957** *Time* 2 Sept. 32/2 Drowning out racy epithets with an electronic beeper signal.

beer (bɪə(r)), *sb.*[1] Forms: 1–3 **béor (bear)**, 3–4 **ber**, 4 **bor**, 5–7 **bere, beere**, 6 **bier**, *Sc.* **beir**, 6–7 **bear(e**, 6– **beer**. [Common WGer.: OE. *béor* = OHG. *bior*, MHG. and mod.G. *bier*, MLG. *bêr*, MDu. and Du. *bier*, all neut.; cf. also ON. *bjor-r* masc. Etymology uncertain.

The OTeut. form might be **beuro-(m)*, f. **beuwo-* barley (whence ON. *bygg*: see BIGG); Kögel, taking the same derivation, has suggested as the Gothic form **biggwis*:—OTeut. **beuwiz-*; Sievers points out that one of the other forms of the neuter suffix *-os, -es, -s*, viz. **beuwoz-*, or rather **beuwz-* would better account for the WGer. forms. Others (see Kluge) have thought of a connexion with *brew* (taking *beuro-* as for **breuro-*). Franck's suggestion of an Aryan **bhur-* 'to ferment' seems unwarranted, there being no known Aryan roots in *-ur*.]

I. 1. a. An alcoholic liquor obtained by the fermentation of malt (or other saccharine substance), flavoured with hops or other aromatic bitters. Formerly distinguished from *ale* by being hopped; but now the generic name of malt liquor, including ale and porter, though sometimes restricted and used in contradistinction to ale. The word occurs in OE., but its use is rare, except in poetry, and it seems to have become common only in the 16th c. as the name of hopped malt liquor. Not in Chaucer or *Piers Ploughman*. See further under ALE.

c **1000** *Ags. Gosp.* Luke i. 15 He ne drincð win ne béor [*Lindisf.* and *Rushw.* bear]. *c* **1205** LAY. 8124 Weoren þa bernes iscængte mid beore. *a* **1250** *Owl & Night.* 1009 Hi nabbeth noth win ne bor. *c* **1340** *Gaw. & Gr. Knt.* 128 Good ber and bryȝt wyn boþe. *c* **1440** *Promp. Parv.* 31 Bere, a drynke, *hummuli potus, aut cervisia hummulina.* **1502** ARNOLD *Chron.* (1811) 247, X. quarters malte, ij quarters wheet, ij quartersootes, xl. ll' weight of hoppys. To make lx. barellis of sengyll beer. *a* **1529** SKELTON *El. Rummyng* in *Harl. Misc.* I. 415 (D.) The Dutchman's strong beere Was not hopt over heere. **1535** STEWART *Cron. Scot.* II. 583 With Marche aill and also doubill beir. **1542** BOORDE *Dyetary* x. 256 Bere is made of malte, of hoppes, and water: it is a naturall drynke for a Dutche man. And nowe of late dayes it is moche vsed in Englande to the detryment of many Englysshe men. **1570** LEVINS *Manip.* 84 Bere, *potus lupinatus.* **1574** R. SCOT *Hop Gard.* (1578) 6 If the controuersie be betwixt Beere and Ale, which of them two shall have yᵉ place of preheminence? **1578** LYTE *Dodoens* 17 In barrels of Bier. **1597** SHAKS. *2 Hen. IV*, II. ii. 7 Doth it not show vildely in me, to desire small Beer? **1620** VENNER *Via Recta* ii. 36 Ale by reason of the grossenesse of the substance of it..is more nourishing then Beere. **1641** BAKER *Chron.* (1696) 298 Turkeys, carps, hops, piccadel, and beer, Came into England all in one year. *c* **1645** HOWELL *Lett.* II. liv, Since Beer hath *hopp'd* in among us, Ale is thought to be much adulterated. **1872** YEATS *Techn. Hist. Comm.* 119 A beer was made by the Germans..from oats and wheat. **1883** PROF. GARDNER in *Glasg. Wkly. Her.* 1 Sept. 8/1 The present proper definition of beer may be as follows:—'A saccharine fluid flavoured with hops, or other aromatic bitters, which has been rendered alcoholic by fermentation.'

b. buttered beer: see ALE 4. **small beer**: weak beer; hence *fig.* trifling matters, small things, as in the colloquial phrase ***to think no small beer of oneself***; ***to be in beer***: to be under the effects of beer, to be more or less intoxicated; ***on the beer***: on a bout of drinking (cf. *on the booze* s.v. BOOZE *sb.* 2 b); ***beer and skittles***: see SKITTLE *sb.* 1 b.

1532 MORE *Confut. Tindale* Wks. 423/1, I stande in so great peryll of chokyng with lucre, as Tindal standeth in daunger of choking with the bones of buttred beere. **1604** SHAKS. *Oth.* II. i. 161 To suckle fooles, and chronicle small Beere. **1631** J. ROUS *Diary* (1856) 66 Warren (that was in beere)..urged the maide to ride behinde him. **1712** ADDISON *Spect.* No. 269 ¶8, I allow a double Quantity of Malt to my small Beer. **1840** DE QUINCEY *Style* Wks. XI. 174 Should express her self-esteem by the popular phrase, that she did not 'think small beer of herself.' **1880** *Academy* 25 Sept. 219 Two such chroniclers of small beer as Boswell and Erskine. **1887** F. T. HAVERGAL *Herefordshire Words* 6/2 When a man is in a fuddled state it is said that 'he is on the beer'. **1959** *Listener* 4 June 980/2 A riotous evening on the beer.

2. Applied to fermented liquors of various kinds, or flavoured by various ingredients, as ***nettle beer, spruce beer, tar beer, treacle beer***, GINGER BEER.

a **1100** *Ags. Gloss.* in Wülcker *Voc.* 329 *Ydromellum vel mulsum*, beor. **1656** RIDGLEY *Pract. Physic* 102 The beer of the decoction of Camomill flowers is miraculous. **1850** T. SMITH *Terebinth. Med.* 61 Beverage, pale ale, dandelion beer, spruce beer.

II. *Comb.* and *Attrib.*

3. General relations: **a.** objective gen. with vbl. sb. or agent-noun, as ***beer-bibber, -bibbing, -brewer, -brewing, -buttering, -carrier, -drinker, -drinking, -monger, -seller, -soaking***; ***beer-swilling*** ppl. a. and vbl. sb. **b.** instrumental with pa. pple., as ***beer-bemuddled***; **c.** attrib. (of, made of or with, beer), as ***beer-broth, -posset, -soup, -stain, -yeast***; **d.** attrib. (of, for, or connected with the manufacture, sale, or use of beer), as, ***beer-barrel, -bottle, -cellar, -gallon, -mat, -shop, -vat.***

a. 1840 DICKENS *Barn. Rudge* xiii, To be looked upon as a common pipe-smoker, *beer-bibber. **1465** *Mann. & Househ. Exp.* 201 My mastyr payd to Clayson *berebrewer of Herewyche, for iiij. barelles of bere..vj. viij.*d.* **1565** JEWELL *Def. Apol.* (1611) 295 This Thomas Beckets Father was a Iew, and a Béere-Brewer of London. **1766** ENTICK *London* IV. 179 The drink is supplied by two beer-brewers. *a* **1628** F. GREVILLE *Sidney* (1652) 24 The Burgesses of that *beer-brewing town [Delft]. **1598** MARSTON *Pygmal.* ii. 147 From Belgia what? but their deep bezeling, Their boote-carouse, and their *Beere-buttering. **1664** KILLIGREW *Parson's Wed.* I. iii, By the way of a country-gentleman and a *beer-drinker. **1839** CARLYLE *Chartism* iii. 121 A bounty on unthrift..and *beer-drinking. **1622** MALYNES *Anc. Law-Merch.* 321 *Beere-mongers, Inne-keepers and Tapsters. **1849** T. MARTIN *Ballads* 165 In *beer-swilling Copenhagen I have drunk your Danesman blind. **1908** *Westm. Gaz.* 28 Sept. 3/2 Beer-swilling in Hyde Park on a Sunday afternoon was not..one of the regular sights of London.

b. 1851 KINGSLEY *Yeast* xiii. 238 Afraid of the jealousy of some *beer-bemuddled swain.

c. 1648 HERRICK *Hesper.* II. 176 He Must not vary, From *beer-broth at all. **1842** MRS. GORE *Fascin.* 109 Having eaten a slice of cold venison, with a basin of *beer-posset. **1857** ELIZA ACTON *Eng. Bread-Bk.* II. §3. 121 For two pounds of flour half an ounce..of *beer-yeast is used.

d. 1602 SHAKS. *Ham.* V. i. 235 Why of that Lome might they not stopp a *Beere barrel? **1773** GOLDSM. *Stoops to Conq.* IV, Unless you'd have the poor devil soused in a beer-

barrel. **1839** C. Sinclair *Holiday House* i. 13 If I want to draw a cork out of a *beer bottle. **1968** B. K. Martin *Editor* xi. 237 Many of the men..wore chains round their necks made of the tops of beer-bottles. **1865** Baring-Gould *Werewolves* v. 54 They burst into the *beer-cellars. **1661** S. Partridge *Double Sc. Proport.* 68 To know how many Ale or *Beer-gallons are in it, divide 24839, 56 the content in inches. **1939** C. Day Lewis *Child of Misf.* iii. v. 323 The *beer-mats on the mantlepiece (what odd things for her to have brought out of Germany). **1848** Kingsley *Saint's Trag.* i. ii. 44 Poor men give them [priests] Their power at the Church and take it back at the *beer-shop. **1837** Carlyle *Fr. Rev.* II. vi. vi. 356 Thou laggard sonorous *Beer-vat [Santerre]..is it time now to palter?

4. Special combinations: †**beer-bombard**, a large can or vessel for holding beer; **beer-boy** = pot-boy; **beer-cellar**, (*a*) an underground room for storing beer; (*b*) a beer-shop in a cellar or basement; **beer-chiller**, a funnel-shaped pot made of tin, used to warm, or 'take off the chill' of beer over the fire; **beer-cooler**, a large shallow vat for cooling beer; **beer-corn**, grain used for brewing; **beer drink** *S. Afr.*, a native gathering for the purpose of drinking Kaffir beer; **beer-engine**, a machine for drawing or pumping up beer from the casks to the bar; **beer-faucet**, a machine for injecting air into flat beer to make it foam; **beer-float**, a hydrometer for ascertaining the density of beer-wash; **beer-fountain** (= *beer-engine*); **beer-garden**, a garden attached to an inn for the consumption of beer; **beer-glass**, a glass holding half a pint; a tumbler; **beer-hall** *S. Afr.*, a public hall where Kaffir beer is sold to non-whites; **beer-heading**, a mixture intended to revive flat beer; †**beer-horse**, a brewer's horse; **beer-house**, a house licensed for the sale of beer, but not of spirits; **beer-machine** (= *beer-engine*); **beer money**, an allowance of money to servants, instead of beer; also gen., a small amount of money earned or allowed; **beer-off** *slang*, an off-licence; **beer-parlor, -parlour** [cf. parlour 3] *Canadian*, a room in a hotel or tavern where beer is served; **beer-pot**, now a pewter vessel holding a quart or a pint, formerly probably made of wooden staves, and hooped; **beer-pull**, the handle of a beer-engine; **beer-pump** (= *beer-engine*); **beer-tray**, a tray fitted with two upright ends, and an upright division from one to the other, so as to hold two rows of beer pots; **beer-up**, a drinking-bout or -party; **beer-vinegar**, vinegar made from beer (cf. beeregar).

1840 Dickens *Old C. Shop* xxxiv. 285 A *beer-boy happened to pass. **1908** *Westm. Gaz.* 5 Feb. 12/1 His silk hat ..had been ruined by the beer-boy spilling a pint of ale into it. *a* **1652** Brome *Jov. Crew* i. 362 We have unloaden the Bread-basket, the Beef-kettle, and the *Beer-Bumbards. **1732** *S. Carolina Gaz.* 28/2 At the *Beer Cellar, over against Mr. Elliot's Bridge. **1817** J. K. Paulding *Lett. from South* II. 57 Diving into stews and beer-cellars. **1820** *Sporting Mag.* VI. 225/1 The coffee-houses and beer-cellars of the *Palais-Royal* [in Paris] teem indiscriminately with both sexes. **1865** [see sense 3 d]. **1952** A. Bullock *Hitler* i. 43 He [*sc.* Hitler] spent much time in cafés and beer-cellars, devouring the newspapers and arguing about politics. **1836** Dickens *Sk. Boz* (1850) 145/2 Until..the little *beer-chiller on the fire, had started into life. **1594** Plat *Jewell-ho.* i. 15 A due proportion between the mault and other *beer-corn. **1895** Scully *Kafir Stories* 182 Lukwazi rode..from *beer-drink to beer-drink, and he was drunk most of his days. **1899** W. H. Brown *On S. Afr. Frontier* xv. 213 When the bride reaches her new home the event is celebrated with a big dance and a 'beer drink'. **1959** *Rand Daily Mail* 21 Jan. 9/6 Police investigating housebreaking on a farm stumbled on an illicit beer-drink and arrested 14 Africans. **1823** J. Badcock *Dom. Amusem.* 78 Pliable composition tube, employed by the makers of *beer engines. **1863** Trollope in *Tales of all Countries* (ser. 2) 302 They all passed their evenings together in the *beer-garden. **1884** *Harper's Mag.* Jan. 299/1 The bowling-ally is..an adjunct of what is known as a beer garden. **1594** Plat *Jewell-ho.* iii. 36 The aptest glasses..were streight upright ones, like to our single *beere glasses. **1707** *Lond. Gaz.* No. 4391/3 A Silver cup.. the Form of a Beer-Glass. **1900** *Statute Law of S. Rhodesia 1899* II. 90 '*Beer Hall Licenses' may be issued to brewers of beer manufactured in Southern Rhodesia for the sale of such beer by retail. **1942** *Cape Times* 24 Dec. 7 The shebeeners of large townships naturally press for the abolition of municipal beer-halls. **1958** N. Gordimer *World of Strangers* xiii. 193 The people..read of strikes, of beer-hall riots. **1562** J. Heywood *Prov. & Epigr.* (1867) 178 The butler and the *beere horse both be like one They drawe beere both. **1494** Fabyan vii. 658 The Kentysshemen.. robbyd and spoyled the Flemynges, and all the *bere-howses. **1864** *Derby Merc.* 7 Dec., A beer-house keeper.. had been convicted of selling beer during the prohibited hours on Sunday. **1827** J. Wight *More Mornings at Bow St.* 24 Recommending him to spend his **beer-money* at home instead of abroad. **1845** Disraeli *Sybil* (1863) 90 There is beer-money allowed,..and that makes nearly a shilling per week additional. **1961** A. Miller *Misfits* xi. 125 There's hardly beer money in it for six, Gay. **1965** G. Melly *Owning-Up* iv. 38 We, poor fools, made nothing but a little beer money. **1939** *Nottingham Jrnl.* 15 Mar. 4/4 Children and *beer-offs. **1958** A. Sillitoe *Sat. Night & Sun. Morning* vii. 98 Bill..had called at the beer-off by the street-end. **1925** in E. Tuck *Brief Hist. Pouce Coupe Village, B.C.* 14 *Beer parlour was opened in Pouce Coupe. **1935** *Calgary Typogr. News* 26 Apr. 3/1 There is a growing agitation, both in Calgary and Edmonton, against the segregation of women customers of the beer parlors of these two cities in separate rooms. **1937** I. Baird *John* xix. 226 He took Albert and Red ..to the beer parlour and stood them a bottle apiece. **1968** *Globe & Mail* (Toronto) 11 July 5/2 The prostitutes..who hang around the beer parlors are having poor pickings. **1562** J. Heywood *Prov. & Epigr.* (1867) 42 She was made lyke a *beere pot, or a barell. **1864** Dickens *Mut. Fr.* i. vi. 46 Polite *beer-pulls that made low bows. **1627** Capt. Smith *Seaman's Gram.* ii. 9 A *beare Pumpe. **1863** Smiles *Indust. Biogr.* 191 Another popular machine of his is the beer-pump, patented in 1797. **1862** Mayhew *Crim. Prisons* 183 *Beer-trays—such as the London pot-boys use for the conveyance of the mid-day porter. **1919** W. H. Downing *Digger Dialects* 10 **Beer-up*, a drunken orgy. **1941** K. Tennant *Battlers* xxviii. 314 'If he's on a real proper beer-up,' the Stray whispered, 'he may go on for days.' **1945** E. Taylor *At Mrs. Lippincote's* x. 89 Does you good to have a bit of a beer-up now and then. **1672** Davenant *Ballad* Wks. (1673) 339 Sack which like *Beer-Vinegar looks.

†**beer** ('biːə(r)), *sb.*[2] *Obs. rare.* Also 4 **beere**. [f. be *v.* + -er[1].] One who is or exists; sometimes *spec.* the Self-existent, the great *I Am*.

1382 Wyclif *Ecclus.* xix. 28 Ther is a beere stille [**1388** a stille man]. **1587** Golding *De Mornay* iii. (1617) 29 He calleth God..the Beer—that is to say; Hee who only is or hath beeing. **1602** Warner *Alb. Eng.* xvii. lxxviii, The Beer, Cause Divine in all, all Godheads Essence.

beer, *sb.*[3] *Weaving.* Also 9 **bier**. [The same word as bier 'a means of carrying,' cf. the synonym porter used in Scotland.] The name given to a (variable) number of ends (interlaced with a cord or cords), into which a warp is divided in the process of warping, in order to facilitate the opening and dividing of the warp, after sizing, while being wound on the beam; it also facilitates the subsequent process of weaving.

1712 J. Beaumont *Math. Sleaing Tables* 40 Every weaver should be obliged to run a coarse coloured thread through every forty threads in the breadth of the cloth to mark the beers or scores. **1819** Peddie *Linen Weaver's Assist.* 178 In Manchester and Bolton..these biers contain 19, but more frequently 20 splits, or what is termed there dents. **1860** White *Weaving* 277 The hundred splits..is nominally divided into five equal portions for the sake of calculation, called porters in Scotland and beers in England. **1880** T. R. Ashenhurst *Use & Abuse of Arithmetic* in *Textile Calculations* 5 Beers are variable quantities according to the custom of the district.

‖**beer**, *sb.*[4] *Obs. rare.* [Du.] A mole or pier.

1629 *S'hertogenbosh* 13 The water..was stayed with two stone beeres on the Bulworkes, next to the boome.

beer (bɪə(r)), *v.* [f. beer *sb.*[1]] *intr.* To drink or indulge in beer. (*colloq.* and *humorous.*)

1780-6 Wolcott (P. Pindar) *Odes R. Acad.* Wks. 1794 I. 105 He surely had been brandying it, or beering. **1824** Miss Mitford *Village* Ser. ii. (1863) 242 A cart and a waggon watering (it would be more correct, perhaps, to say *beering*) at the Rose.

beer, Obs. f. bear *v.* and *sb.*[2], bier, and birr force, impetus.

beerage ('bɪərɪdʒ). *slang.* [blend of beer *sb.*[1] and peerage.] Brewers collectively, esp. those who are made into peers; the beer industry; also, the British peerage (viewed as containing a large number of brewers).

1891 *Pall Mall Gaz.* 14 Dec. 1/3 The peerage is becoming the beerage. **1901** *Westm. Gaz.* 17 May 6/2 The following members of the Upper House are interested in Public House property... Another link..between the peerage and the beerage. **1958** *Observer* 14 Dec. 15/2 Mrs. Dot, the elegant, brewing millionairess—a figure of some social significance in 1908 when the capture of society by the beerage was not yet consolidated.

beerd(e, ME. form of beard.

beeregar ('bɪərɪgə(r)). ? *Obs.* Also **berhegor**, 6 **beereager, bear-, beareger**, 7 **beeregre**. [f. beer *sb.*[1] + *egre*, eager = F. *aigre* sour; after *vinegar*, *alegar*.] Sour beer; vinegar formed by the acetous fermentation of beer.

a **1500** *Manners & Househ. Exp. of Eng.* 456 The master of the schepe hathe..vij. galones berhegor. **1586** Bright *Melanch.* vi. 29 Of sauces those that be sharpe, as veriuyce aliger, or beareger, vinegar. **1592-3** *Act 35 Eliz.* xi. §3 To carrie any Wyne Caske out of this Realme with any Beere or Beereager. **1720** *Stow's Survey* (Strype, 1754) II. v. xv. 324/1 The Flemings bought great quantities..of Beeregre for the cooling of their Ordinance. **1882** Rogers *Hist. of Agric. Prices* IV. 618 Aleager and bereager..are malt vinegar.

‖**beerenauslese** ('beːrəˌnaʊsleːzə). Also with capital initial. Pl. **-lesen**. [Ger., f. *Beeren-*, comb. form of *Beere* berry, grape + auslese.] Sweet white wine made (esp. in Germany) from selected individual grapes picked later than the general harvest (an official category of German wine); a wine of this category.

1926 P. M. Shand *Bk. Wine* vi. 185 In cases where the wine is a selected one—that is, made from grapes carefully chosen for their over-ripeness—the inscription should terminate with the word *Auslese*, *Goldbeerenauslese*, *Beerenauslese*...[etc.]. **1951** R. Postgate *Plain Man's Guide to Wine* vi. 98 *Beerenauslese* means that the grapes for the wine were specially selected. **1963** [see trockenbeerenauslese]. **1980** M. Broadbent *Gt. Vintage Wine Bk.* 301/1 *Beerenauslese* wines are always sweet, like Sauternes.

beerhood ('bɪəhʊd). *rare*[−1]. [f. beer *sb.*[1] + -hood, after *manhood*, etc. Cf. OE. *ȝebeorscipe* 'beership.'] A beer-drinking class or set.

1865 E. Burritt *Walk Land's End* 103 All his old beerhood fraternity warned him against such a resolution.

'**beeriness.** [f. beery + -ness.] *colloq.* Beery quality or condition.

1877 F. Hall *Eng. Adj. in -able* 158 Our distant forefathers who..divided their energy pretty impartially between bloodshed and beeriness. **1921** W. De Morgan *Old Man's Youth* xxiii. 202 A negligible quantity of beeriness.

beerish ('bɪərɪʃ), *a.* [f. beer *sb.*[1] + -ish.] Having the nature or properties of beer; beery.

1694 Westmacott *Script. Herb.* 16 Beerish drink keeps the stomach clean.

'**beerishly**, *adv.* [f. prec. + -ly[2].] In beerish or beery fashion.

1865 *Spectator* 2 Sept. 980/1 Nothing better than beerishly and boorishly jolly.

beerless ('bɪəlɪs), *a.* [f. beer *sb.*[1] + -less.] Without or unprovided with beer.

1846 R. Ford *Gather. Spain* xv. 169 This..tealess, beerless, beefless land. **1909** *Daily Chron.* 24 June 4/4 A beerless public-house, where sugary non-alcoholic beverages are sold. **1970** *Daily Tel.* 19 Oct. 15/8 Some villages..are left beerless.

beer-lip, var. form of bear-leap, *Obs.* a basket.

beerne, obs. form of bairn.

beerocracy (bɪə'rɒkrəsɪ). [f. beer *sb.*[1] + -(o)cracy; one of the numerous burlesques upon *aristocracy*.] A ludicrous or polemical name for: The brewing and beer-selling interest.

1881 *World* 19 Jan. 10/2 The startling mixture of peerage and beerocracy..was absent this time.

Beer stone (bɪə stəʊn). (Also with lower-case initial letter.) A kind of limestone used in building, obtained from Beer Head in Devonshire, England.

1871 *Q. Jrnl. Geol. Soc.* XXVII. 98 Cliff west of Beer Head... An old quarry in the high cliff above the western end of the great landslip is in what I take to be the 'Beer stone'. **1894** *Daily News* 16 Mar. 5/2 A handsome building of white brick and beer-stone. **1910** *Encycl. Brit.* V. 806/2 The more important building stones are 'Beer stone', from Beer Head in Devonshire [etc.].

beery ('bɪərɪ), *a.* [f. as prec, + -y[1].] Belonging to, or abounding in beer; characterized or influenced by beer; beer-like.

1848 Thackeray *Van. Fair* lxvi. 600 Idlers, playing cards or dominoes on the sloppy, beery tables. **1854** J. R. Planché *Once Upon Time* ii. ii. 37, I'm not jolly—even when I'm beery. **1861** Geo. Eliot *Silas M.* 67 [The kindness] was often of a beery and bungling sort. **1870** Lowell *Among my Bks.* Ser. i. (1873) 15 The 'first sprightly running' of Dryden's vintage was..a little muddy, if not beery. *Mod.* An election of the old beery sort.

bees-antler: see bes-antler.

beesom(e, obs. form of besom.

beest, obs. or dial. 2nd sing. pres. of be *v.*

beest(e, obs. form of beast, and best.

beest (biːst). [Common Teut., or at least WGer.: OE. *béost* = OHG. *biost*, MHG., mod.G. *biest* (masc.), MDu. and mod.Du. *biest* (fem.), MLG. *best*, North Fris. *bjast*, *bjüst*, all in same sense. Of unknown derivation, not found beyond Teutonic.] The first milk drawn from a mammal, especially a cow, after parturition.

c **1000** Ælfric *Gloss.* in Wr.-Wülck. 14/36 *Colostrum* beost. —— *ibid.* 210/17 *Colostrum*, i.e. *lac novum*, beost *uel* obestum. **1611** Cotgr., *Beton*, Beest, the first milke a female giues after the birth of her young one. **1611** [see next]. **1688** R. Holme *Armory* ii. ix. 173 Beest, the first Milk after Calving. **1796** Mrs. Glasse *Cookery* xxi. 520 Pour your hot beest upon it.

beestie: see bheesty.

1922 *Blackw. Mag.* Sept. 408/2 A beestie..splashed a little water from his mussack on his upturned face.

beesting, obs. variant of buisting.

beestings ('biːstɪŋz). Forms: 1 **býsting**, 5 **bestynge**, 6 **biestings**, 7 **beestins, beestning, beestlings**, 7-8 **beestings**, 7-9 **beastlings, -ges**, 8- **beastings**, 9 *dial.* **beastin, biznings, beslings**. [OE. **bíesting*, *býsting*, as if f. a vb. **biestan* 'to yield beest,' f. *béost*: see beest. Now usually in pl. form, which however is sometimes construed as a (collective) sing.]

1. = beest.

c **1000** Ælfric in Wright *Voc.* 28 *Colustrum*, býsting, þicce meolc. **1483** *Cath. Angl.* 30 A bestynge, *colustrum.* **1574** Newton *Health Mag.* 32 The thicke and curdie Milke ..commonly called Biestings, is very dangerous. **1611** Cotgr., *Colostre*, the first milke, tearmed beest, or beestings. **1625** B. Jonson *Pans' Annivers.* ad fin., Both the beesting of our Goates, and Kine. **1641** Best *Farm. Bks.* (1856) 11 An ewe is say'd to give beastlings three or fower

dayes. **1697** DRYDEN *Virgil* (1806) II. 14 Who fill'd the pail with beestings of the cow. **1757** LISLE *Husb.* 353 Roman writers on husbandry forbid the colastra or beestings to be given to the calf. *Mod. Northampt. Dial.*, We shall have some biznings tomorrow for a custard. **1844** H. STEPHENS *Bk. Farm* II. 458 The first milk that comes from the cow after calving is of a thick consistence and yellow colour, and is called biestings. **1847** W. C. L. MARTIN *Ox* 173/2 Some farmers refuse the first milk or *beastings* to the calf, ignorant that it is a purgative expressly intended by nature for this purpose. **1950** *N.Z. Jrnl. Agric.* July 4/2 The [cow's] first milk known as colostrum or 'beestings' contains substances which increase a calf's resistance to scours.

attrib. **1881** TENNYSON *North. Cobbler* xx, A beslings-puddin' an' Adam's wine.

†**2.** A disease caused by imbibing beastings. L. *colostratio. Obs.*

1607 TOPSELL *Four-f. Beasts* 18 It breedeth in their mouthes the Colostracion or Beestings.

bees-wax ('biːz,wæks). [f. BEE[1] + WAX.] The wax secreted by bees as the material of their combs, and used for various purposes in the arts.

1676 MOXON *Print Lett.* 12 You may rub your Stone over with a little Bees Wax. **1753** HANWAY *Trav.* (1762) I. VII. lxxxviii. 406 They also export beeswax annually to near one thousand schippounds. **1876** HARLEY *Mat. Med.* 793 Bees Wax is secreted by glands on the ventral scales of the bee, whence they collect it.

'beeswax, *v.* [f. prec.] *trans.* To rub or polish with bees-wax. Hence **'beeswaxed** *ppl. a.*, and **'beeswaxing** *vbl. sb.*

1836 DICKENS *Sk. Boz* ii. (1879) 7 The table-covers are never taken off except when the leaves are turpentined and bees-waxed. **1873** MISS BRADDON *Str. & Pilgr.* I. ix. 103 A .. Turkey carpet covered the centre of the floor—a mere island in an ocean of bees-waxed oak. **1876** —— *J. Haggard's Dau.* III. 62 The dusting and beeswaxing were duly done.

beeswing ('biːzwɪŋ). Also **bee's wing, bee's-wing, bees'-wing, bees-wing.** [f. BEE + WING, from its appearance.] The second crust, consisting of shining filmy scales of tartar, formed in port and some other wines after long keeping; so called from its appearance; *ellipt.*, old wine showing beeswing. Hence **'bees-winged** *a.*, so old as to show beeswing.

1860 GEN. P. THOMPSON *Audi Alt.* III. cxiv. 44 His richer or more showy neighbour .. is curious in 'bee's wing.' **1864** TENNYSON *Aylmer's F.* 405 Fetched His richest beeswing from a binn reserved. **1880** BROWNING *Dram. Idyls* II. Clive 47 Too much bee's-wing floats my figure? **1873** F. HALL *Mod. Eng.* 32 His port is not presentable, unless bees'-winged.

beet (biːt). Forms: 1 béte, 4–6 bete, 5–7 beete, 6– beet. [OE. *béte*, ad. L. *bēta*, whence also OHG. *bieza* (8th c.), MHG. *bieze*, MLG. and MDu. *bête*, etc. The plant was of early cultivation, and the name was adopted from Latin into the Teutonic languages, but though common in OE., no further mention of it occurs before *c* 1400.]

1. A plant or genus of plants (N.O. *Chenopodiaceæ*), having, in cultivation, a succulent root much used for food, and also for yielding sugar. There are two species, the Common or Red Beet (*Beta vulgaris*), found wild on the British coasts, and cultivated in several varieties, both as an esculent, and as an ornamental foliage plant, and the White Beet (*B. cicla*), chiefly used in the production of sugar. Formerly almost always spoken of in plural 'beets,' like *beans, pease, greens*, etc. Now usu. in *sing.* form, but the *pl.* form is still current in the U.S.

c **1000** *Sax. Leechd.* II. 226 þás wyrta sindon .. éaðbeȝeatra, béte and mealwe. **1398** TREVISA *Barth. De P.R.* XVII. xxii. (1495) 616 Men may graffe on a bete stocke as men doon on a Caustocke. *a* **1400** *Cov. Myst.* 22 Erbys and gresse, both beetes and brake. *c* **1440** *Promp. Parv*, 34 Betys herbe, *beta*. **1551** TURNER *Herbal.* (1568) F iij a, There are twoo kyndes of Betes, the white bete whyche is called sicula, and blake betes. **1616** SURFL. & MARKH. *Countr. Farm* 173 If you would make choyce of faire beets, chuse rather the white than either the blacke or red. **1712** tr. *Pomet's Hist. Drugs* 47 Leaves, like those of the Beet or Winter-green. **1732** ARBUTHNOT *Rules of Diet* i. 249 Beets, emollient, nutritive, and relaxing. *a* **1772** BORLASE in C. Johns *Week at Lizard* (1848) 185 One year nothing will grow but mallows, and the next nothing but beets. **1844** H. STEPHENS *Bk. Farm* III. 1038 The beets should always be small, evenly sized, straight and even. **1870** H. MACMILLAN *Bible Teach.* v. 100 The wild beet and cabbage still grow on our sea-shores. **1883** *Rep. Indian Affairs* 17 (D.A.E.), They will raise about 100 bushels of beets. **1917** *U.S. Dept. Agric. Yearbk.* 405 The development of desirable strains of beets.

2. *Comb.* and *Attrib.*, as **beet leaves, -sugar; beet-grower, -growing**; BEET-ROOT. † **beet-raves** [a. F. *bette-rave* 'beet,' lit. 'beet-turnip'], the small red beet.

1719 LOUDON & WISE *Compl. Gard.* 197 Beet-raves, or Beet-Radishes, that is, Red Beets, produce roots for Sallads. **1736** BAILEY *Housh. Dict.* s.v. *Beets*, Beet-raves are made use of to colour wine. **1769** MRS. RAFFALD *Eng. Housekpr.* (1778) 131 Leave on the bacon and beet leaves. **1833** R. PHILLIPS *Fam. Cycl.* 230 The French .. still persevere in manufacturing beet-sugar. **1837** HT. MARTINEAU *Soc. in Amer.* II. 55 The interest excited by this subject of beet-growing is very strong.

beet, bete (biːt), *v. Obs.* exc. *dial.* Forms: 1 bóetan, bétan, 2–5 beten, 3–5 bete, 5–6 beete, 6– *Sc.* beit, 8– beet; (3 betten, 5 beton, bet, beethe, beytt). *Pa. t.* bet: 1 bétte, 2–5 bette, 4 bett, bet (bete, beit). *Pa. pple.* bet; 1 béted, 1–5 bet, 3–5 ibet, bett (4 bete, bette). [Common Teut.: OE *bóetan, bétan*, to make good, make better, amend = Goth. *bôtjan*, OS. *bôtjan*, MDu. *boeten*, MLG. *bôten*, OHG. *buozzen*, MHG. *büezzen*, G. *büszen*:—OTeut. **bôtjan* to advantage, profit, be of use to, a derivative vb. from *bôtâ-* good, profit, advantage, in OE. *bôt*, BOOT, q.v. Now only Sc. and north. dial.; it became obs. in literary Eng. before 1500, while still spelt *bete.*]

I. To make good, amend, make amends for.

1. *trans.* To make good or better; to mend or repair (things damaged), mend or heal (wounds, sickness), improve (land). Still *dial.*

c **975** *Rushw. Gosp.* Matt. iv. 21 þonan ȝesæȝh oþre tweȝen ȝebroþer .. boetende heora nett [WYCLIF, makynge aȝein or beetynge her nettis]. *c* **1000** *Sax. Leechd.* I. 398 Hu ðu meaht ðine æceras betan. *Ibid.* 116 Ðonne bið hit [the wound] sona ȝebet. *c* **1200** *Trin. Coll. Hom.* 215 Mineȝeð þat ane niwe cloðes, oðer elde bete. *c* **1386** CHAUCER *Reves T.* 7 Pipen he koude, and fisshe, and nettes beete. **1572** *Scot. Poems 16th C.* II. 247 The prouerb is, of palice, kirk, and brig, Better in tyme to beit, nor efter to big. **1808** JAMIESON *Sc. Dict.* (Provb.) Daily wearing neids yearly beiting. [**1873** EARLE *Philol* §82 The fishermen of Yarmouth have sometimes astonished the learned .. by talking of beating their nets (so it sounds) when they mean mending them.]

†**2.** To bring into better state, put right, correct, amend, reform (faults, evil ways, etc.); to make good (misdeeds): **a.** those of others.

c **950** *Lindisf. Gosp.* Matt. xviii. 15 Gif ðec ȝeheres, boetend ðu bist broðeres ðines. *a* **1000** ÆLFRIC *Deut.* i. 17 Ic hit bete. *c* **1175** *Lamb. Hom.* (1867) 113 ȝif he hit [uuel] betan mei. *a* **1300** *Cursor M.* 9790 No patriarck ne ȝeit prophete, Miht be sent adames sine to bete. *c* **1300** *Harrow. Hell* 229 That thou woldest come to bete The sunnes that Adam thohte suete.

†**b.** To amend, make good (one's own faults); *hence*, to repent of, make amends for, expiate, atone for (one's sin). The usual word in early ME.; afterwards superseded by AMEND. *Obs.*

c **897** K. ÆLFRED *Gregory's Past.* 220 Ealle scylda þe wið god beoð unȝebetta. *c* **1200** *Trin. Coll. Hom* 169 Bute his sunnes him ben ere forgieuene · oðer bette. *a* **1250** *Moral Ode* 121 in *E.E.P.* (1862) 29 Hi mihten here sunne beten. *Ibid.* 138 And gunnen here gultes beten, & betere lif leden, *c* **1300** *Beket* 2417 And wende to the holi lond: here synnes forto bete. *c* **1325** *Metr. Hom.* (1862) 10 [Jon the Baptist] .. taht the folk thair sine to bete.

†**c.** *absol.* To amend, repent, *Obs.*

c **1200** *Trin. Coll. Hom.* 223 For þi he [is] wis þe bit and biȝiet and bet bifore dome. *a* **1250** *Owl & Night.* 863 Vorthi he mot .. Mid teres an mid woþe bete.

3. To relieve *hunger, thirst*, or any form of want; to supply *wants, needs* (Sc. *misters*). Hence subst. in comb. *beet-need, beet-mister. Sc.* and *north.*

a **1300** *Cursor M.* 3279 Sco þat sal bete me my thrist. **1362** LANGL. *P. Pl.* A. VII. 224 No mon [schal] beete his hunger. **1513** DOUGLAS *Æneis* I. viii. 105 Grantit eik leif wod to hew, and tak Tymmer to beit ayris [= oars] and wther mysteris. **1816** SCOTT *Tales Landl.* IV. 252 (JAM.) She enlarged on the advantage of saving old clothes to be what she called beetmasters to the new. **1823** *Blackw. Mag.* 314 (JAM.) If twa or three hunder pounds can beet a mister for you in a strait, ye sanna want it. **1875** *Lancash. Gloss.* (E.D.S.) *Beet-need*, a help that may be had at will.

†**b.** To relieve, help, aid, assist (a person in need or trouble), to supply the wants of. *Obs.*

a **1300** *Cursor M.* 9592 And þi pite þat es sa suete Aght þi prisun [= prisoner] o bandes bete. *c* **1325** *E.E. Allit. P.* A. 756 My makelez lambe þat al may bete. *c* **1440** *Gesta Rom.* 86 Reson betith him so ofte tyme as he stondith ayens þe Synner. *c* **1450** HENRYSON *Mor. Fab.* 51 Who shall mee beete? who shall my bands breck? *c* **1470** HENRY *Wallace* II. 18 With stuff of houshald strestely he thaim bett.

†**c.** esp.: *to bete one's bale* (see BALE *sb.*[1] 6); also *to bete one of one's bale* (cf. sense 2). *Obs.*

a **1300** *Cursor M.* 105 Til all oure bale ai for to bete. *Ibid.* 14415 þar he .. o mani bale þam bete. *c* **1440** *Epiph.* (Turnb. 1843) 223 That was the angell to beton is bale. *c* **1460** *Launfal* 971 Sche myghte me of my balys bete. **1513** DOUGLAS *Æneis* XII. Prol. 233 To beyt [*v.r.* bete] thar amouris of thar nychtis baill.

II. To beet a fire.

[The development of this (the chief extant) sense, the antiquity of which is shown, not merely by the OS. *fýr bétan*, but by its existence in the other Teutonic languages (cf. Du. *vuur boeten*, LG. *für böten*, etc.), is somewhat obscure, from the fact that in the earliest instances it appears to mean, not 'to *mend* a fire,' but as in modern Dutch, 'to *make, kindle, put on* a fire.' Perhaps this is to be explained by the primitive conditions (which prevailed more or less till the days of phosphorus matches), according to which fire was not generated anew each time it was required, but was usually propagated by a 'glede' from an existing fire, often carried and kept alive for days (cf. Genesis xxii. 6), which was surrounded with combustibles, and 'beeted' into a blaze, when a fire was required.]

4. To make, kindle, put on (a fire). Now *dial.*

c **885** K. ÆLFRED *Oros.* VI. xxxii, Ða het he betan þærinne micel fýr. *c* **1325** *Seuen Sag.* (W.) 2122 The clerkes .. bet a fir strong and sterk. *c* **1325** *E.E. Allit. P.* B. 1012 When bryȝt brennande brondez ar bet þer an-vnder. *c* **1386** CHAUCER *Knts. T.* 1434 Tuo fyres on the auter gan sche beete. **1430** *Chev. Assigne* 157 The goldesmyȝth gooth & beetheth hym a fyre. *a* **1500** *Sir Aldingar* 53 in Furniv. *Percy Folio* I. 168 And fayre fyer there shalbe bett. **1513** DOUGLAS *Æneis* VII. Prol. 127 Bad beit the fyire, and the candill alycht. **1875** *Lancash. Gloss.* (E.D.S.) s.v. *Beet*, Tha mun get up an' beet t' fire to-morn.

5. To mend, make up, keep up, add fuel to, feed (a fire). Still in *Sc.* See also BOTE, FIRE-BOTE.

1205 LAY. 25977 His fur he beten agon. *c* **1325** *E.E. Allit. P.* B. 627 Quyl I fete sum quat fatþou þe fyr bete. *c* **1386** CHAUCER *2nd Nonnes T.* 581 In a bath thay gonne hir faste schetten, And nyght and day greet fuyr they under betten. **1810** TANNAHILL *Poems* (1846) 48 The wither'd twigs to beet her fire. **1826** J. WILSON *Noct. Ambr.* Wks. 1855 I. 262 A fire, that they keep beetin wi' planks and spars o' the puir man o' war. **1857** J. SCHOLES *Jaunt to See Q.* 14 (Lanc. Gloss.) Then aw beetud fire, un rattl't fire-potter ogen't back o'th grate.

b. *fig.*

1784 BURNS *Epist. Davie* viii, It heats me, it beets me And sets me a' on flame! **1787** —— Wks. III. 179 Or noble Elgin beets the heav'n-ward flame.

beet, variant of BEAT, bundle of flax.

† **'beeter.** *Obs. rare*⁻¹. [f. BEET *v.* + -ER[1].]

1578 COOPER *Lat. Dict.*, *Cereosus*, a beeter or little waxe candle.

beeth, obs. south. pres. indic. pl. of BE *v.*

Beethovenian (,beɪthəʊ'viːnɪən), *a.* and *sb.* [-IAN.] **A.** *adj.* Of or pertaining to the German composer Ludwig van *Beethoven* (1770–1827), his music and theories of musical composition. **B.** *sb.* An admirer or adherent of Beethoven; an interpreter of his works.

1894 G. B. SHAW in *World* 2 May 26/1 The Beethovenian music. **1947** A. EINSTEIN *Music in Romantic Era* ix. 90 Schubert .. enlarged this ensemble along Beethovenian lines. **1947** C. GRAY *Contingencies* vi. 130 Many devout Beethovenians regard the last movement of the Ninth as the summit of the later master's achievement. **1958** *Times* 10 Nov. 14/4 Miss Eleanor Fine .. is an unstylish Bach pianist, and a capable but dull Beethovenian.

Also **Beethove'nesque** *a.*, resembling the style of Beethoven; **'Beethovenish** *a.*, = BEETHOVENIAN *a.*; **'Beethovenized** *ppl. a.*, made to resemble the style of Beethoven.

1879 GROVE *Dict. Music* I. 201/2 Some will find it hard to place the Quartet in F minor, which Mendelssohn thought the most *Beethovenish* of all Beethoven's works, in anything but the third style. **1927** G. B. SHAW *Pen Portraits & Reviews* (1932) 35 Jazz, by the way, is the old dance band Beethovenized. **1935** D. F. TOVEY *Ess. Mus. Anal.* 86 The accompaniment of a very Beethovenish rhythm. **1955** R. BLESH *Shining Trumpets* (ed. 3) v. 108 The harmonic changes, simple, rugged, and Beethovenesque.

† **beeting,** *vbl. sb. Obs.* [f. BEET *v.* + -ING[1].] The action of making good; mending, repair; making (a fire), kindling.

1517 *Churchw. Acc., Heybridge, Essex* (Nichols 1797), 168 Half of betynge lyght ageynst the feste of the Natyvyte of oure Blessed Lady. **1594** *Act Jas. VI.* (1814) IV. 80 (JAM.) The beiting and reparatioun of thair wallis, streittis, havynnis and portis. *a* **1615** *Brieue Cron. Erlis of Ross.* (1850) 20 The miln decayed in default of beiting and holding up of the same. **1808** [see BEET *v.* 1.]

beetle ('biːt(ə)l), *sb.*[1] Forms: 1 bíetel, bítel, býtel, 3 bettle, 4 bytylle, 4–6 betel, 5 betylle, bittill, 5–6 betell(e, 6 betill, -yll, betle, beetel(le, 7 boytle, 8–9 *dial.* beatle, bittle, 6– beetle. [OE. *bíetel*, in Anglian **bétel*, 'beating implement,' :—OTeut. **bautilo-z*, f. *bautan*, in OE. *béatan*, 'to beat' + *-*il, -el, -l*, -LE, suffix denoting an instrument; cogn. w. MHG. *bôzel* cudgel, LG. *betel, bötel* 'a mall' (*Bremisches Wb.* I. 126). The variant forms in *i* and *e* in middle and mod.Eng. are due to the late WSax. *bítel, býtel*, and Anglian *bétel* respectively; of the latter the mod. *beetle* is the regular representative. Those like *bittle* show the ordinary shortening of a long vowel before two consonants: thus, the OE. genitive *bítles*, and plur. *bítlas*, would naturally give *bittles* in ME. The identification of the form with those of BEETLE *sb.*[2] has led to confusion in their fig. senses: see sense 2.]

1. An implement consisting of a heavy weight or 'head,' usually of wood, with a handle or stock, used for driving wedges or pegs, ramming down paving stones, or for crushing, bruising, beating, flattening, or smoothing, in various industrial and domestic operations, and having various shapes according to the purpose for which it is used; a mall. *three-man beetle*: one that requires three men to lift it, used in ramming paving-stones, etc.

c **897** K. ÆLFRED *Gregory's Past.* xxxvi. 253 Nán monn ne ȝehíerde ne axe hlem ne bietles [*Cotton* bítles] sweȝ. *a* **1000** *Judith* iv. 21 Séo wífman ȝeslóh mid ánum býtle. *a* **1225** *Ancr. R.* 188 Þer ȝe schulen iseon bunsen ham mit tes deofles bettles. *a* **1400** Wright's *Lat. Stories* 29 (Mätz.) Wyht suylc a betel be he smyten. *c* **1400** in Wright *Voc.* 180 *Mallus*, bytylle. **1413** LYDG. *Pylgr. Sowle* III. x. (1483) 56 Somme were brayned with betels and somme beten with staues. *c* **1440** *Promp. Parv.* 34 Betylle, *malleus, malleolus. c* **1450** HOLLAND *Houlat*, He could wark wundaris Mak..A lang spere of a bittill. **1530** PALSGR. 198/1 Betyll to bete clothes with, *battoyr.* **1577** B. GOOGE *Heresbach's Husb.* (1586) 39 Then the bundels [of flax]..are beaten with betelles. **1589** *Pappe w. Hatchet* (1844) 7 Make your tongue the wedge, and your head the beetle. **1597** SHAKS. *2 Hen. IV*, I. ii. 255 If I do, fillop me with a three-man-Beetle. *a* **1626** FLETCHER *Wom. Prize* II. vi, Have I lived thus long to be knockt o' th' head With half a washing beetle? **1639** FULLER *Holy War* III. xxiv. (1840) 162 To cleaue a tree with a beetle without a wedge. **1791** HAMILTON *Berthollet's Dyeing* I. I. II. i. 132 In the fulling mill..it is beaten with large beetles in a trough of water. **1822** SCOTT *Pirate* I. 128 (JAM.), Out of an honest house, or shame fa' me, but I'll take the bittle to you! **1845** DE QUINCEY *Wks.* XII. 73 *note*, A beetle is that heavy sort of pestle with which paviours drive home the paving-stones ..sometimes..fitted up by three handles..for the use of three men.

b. *fig.*

1562 FOXE *A. & M.* I. 265/1 [King Henry the Second].. the Mall and Beetle of the Church. **1581** J. BELL *Haddon's Answ. Osor.* 278 An..argument such as all yᵉ Heretiques wedges with all their Beatelles and malles can not beate abroad. *c* **1626** *Dick of Devon* IV. i. in *Old Pl.* (1883) II. 61 Now the Beetle of my head beates it into my memory. **1674** FLATMAN *To Austin* 41 The Beetles of our Rhimes shall drive full fast in The wedges of your worth.

c. Phrase. ***between the beetle and the block.***

[**1541** *Act 33 Hen. VIII*, xii. §18 The serieant..shal bring to the said place of execucion a blocke with a betill, a staple, and cordes to binde the saide hande.] **1589** R. HARVEY *Pl. Perc.*, Thou must come to Knokham faire, and what betweene the block and the beetle, be thumpd like a stock-fish. **1613** HAYWARD *Norm. Kings* 274 Earle William being thus set, as it were, betweene the beetle and the blocke, was nothing deiected.

2. Used as the type of heavy dullness or stupidity. The phrase ***deaf,*** or ***dumb as a beetle***, probably belongs here; but cf. BEETLE *sb.*[2] 3.

1520 WHITTINTON *Vulg.* (1527) 2 Tendre wyttes..be made as dull as a betell. **1566** KNOX *Hist. Ref.* Wks. (1846) I. 164 That dolt had not a worde to say for him self, but was as doume as a bitle in that mater. **1642** ROGERS *Naaman* 4 Our faculty to understand is still left..we are not meere blockes and beetles. **1867** *N. & Q.* Ser. III. XI. 106/2 'As deaf as a beetle' no doubt refers to this wooden instrument.

3. *Comb.*, as ***beetle-fish, -man, -stock*** (i.e. handle); ***beetle-beaten*** adj.; also as contemptuous epithets (from sense 2), ***beetle-brain, -head*** (cf. *block head*), whence ***beetle-headed*** adj.; also **beetle-head**, the 'monkey' of a pile-driving engine.

1654 GAYTON *Fest. Notes* III. ii. 76 As if she had been *beetle-beaten to be laid in a pastry. *a* **1604** CHURCHYARD in Nichols *Progr. Q. Eliz.* III. 239 *Beetle-braines cannot conceive things right. **1783** AINSWORTH *Lat. Dict.* (Morell) I, The *beetle fish, *cantharus piscis.* **1577** BRETON in *Heliconia* I. 7 Because that *Beetle-heads doo serve for such instructions fit. **1617** COLLINS *Def. Bp. Ely* I. i. 54 The more to condemne the blindnesse of this *beetle-head. **1656** EARL MONM. *Advt. fr. Parnass.* 425 Had returned some brains into the *beetle-heads of those Frenchmen. **1553-87** FOXE *A & M.* (1596) 1171/2 Learne, learne, yee *beetel headed Asses. **1596** SHAKS. *Tam. Shr.* IV. i. 161 A horson *beetle-headed flap-ear'd knaue. **1870** *Daily News* 30 Nov., To persuade the conscientious but *beetle-headed monarch. **1587** FLEMING *Cont. Holinshed* III. 1544/2 The ..*beetlemen..who serued to beat or driue the fleech to the sides of the wals. **1591** SPENSER *M. Hubberd* 507 To crouche to please, to be a *beetle stock Of thy great Masters will. **1816** C. JAMES *Mil. Dict.*, *Beetlestock, the stock or handle of a beetle.

beetle ('biːt(ə)l), *sb.*[2] Forms: 1 bitula, bitela, ? betel; 5 bityl, bytylle; betylle, 6 betel, -ell, -yll, betle, bettil, -le; bitle, bytell, bittil, byttil, -el, -ell; 6- beetle. [OE. *bitula, bitela* (the sense of which is established by the glosses quoted) is app. a sb. formed on an adj. **bitul, bitol*, biting, *mordax* (in early ME. BITEL, q.v.), f. *bitan* to BITE; cf. the gloss '*mordiculus*' (little biter), which occurs in a list *De Nominibus Insectorum* in Wülcker *Voc.* 122. As in similar OE. derivatives the *i* was certainly short; thence the ME. *bityl*, 16th c. *bittil*, and mod. dial. *bittle*. The form *betlas*, pointing to a nom. *betel*, has not been etymologically explained, but it may, if genuine, be the source of ME. *betylle*, 16th c. *betel*, mod. *beetle*, though the latter may also be from the normal *bitela*, with the vowel lengthened, as in *evil* from OE. *yfel*, *weevil* from OE. *wifel* (OHG. *wibil*), Sc. *meikle* from OE. *mycil*, dial. *leetle* from *little*, etc. The later forms are confused with those of BEETLE *sb.*[1], whence also confusion in their fig. use: see sense 3.]

1. The class name for insects of the coleopterous order, having the upper pair of wings converted into hard sheaths or wing-cases (elytra) that close over the back, and protect the lower or true wings, which most species are able to use in flight.

a **800** *Epinal, Erfurt & Corpus Glosses* (Sweet *O.E.T.* 44, 45) *Blattis, blatis*, bitulum. *a* **1000** *Harl. Gl.* in Wülcker *Voc.* 196 *Blattis*, bitelum. *c* **1000** ÆLFRIC *Voc.* (*ibid.*) 122 *Mordiculus*, bitela. [Also *c* **1050** *ibid.* 448; and 456 *Nigro colore*, þa blacan betlas]. *c* **1440** *Promp. Parv.* 37 Bytylle worme [*v.r.* bityl wyrme], *buboscus. c* **1450** in Wright *Voc.* 255 *Hic carembes*, a betylle. **1552** HULOET, Bettil or byttil vermine, *scarabæus.* **1570** LEVINS *Manip.* 124 A bittil, flee, *scarabeus.* **1581** J. BELL *Haddon's Answ. Osor.* 308 An other compareth a Byttell with an Egle. **1603** SHAKS. *Meas. for M.* III. i. 79 The poore Beetle that we treade vpon. **1653** WALTON *Angler* 54 A Bob which..in time will be a Beetle. **1765** TUCKER *Lt. Nat.* I. 640 The beetle, whose characteristic is stupidity and unwieldiness of limbs, beats himself down against a tree, or overturns himself in crawling, and lies sprawling upon his back. **1852** T. HARRIS *Insects New Eng.* 20 Beetles are biting-insects, and are provided with two pairs of jaws moving sidewise.

2. a. In popular use applied especially to those of black colour, and comparatively large size; hence many coleopterous insects of different appearance, as the glow-worm, lady-birds, death-ticks, etc. are usually excluded, and other insects included under the name; among the latter are the **black-beetle** or COCKROACH (q.v.), which is not a beetle.

c **1050** [see 1.] **1530** PALSGR. 198/1 Bettle, a blacke flye. **1552** HULOET, Byttel, flye with a blacke huske. **1590** SHAKS. *Mids. N.* II. ii. 22 Beetles blacke approach not neere. **1864** *Realm* 16 Mar. 8 Tosser is thrust into a cupboard among the blackbeetles. **1878** BLACK *Green Past.* xvi. 132 They were at all events human beings..not black-beetles.

b. A dice game having as its object the drawing or assembly of a beetle-shaped figure. So ***beetle drive*** (after *whist drive*).

1936 B. STANLEY *Games for Party* 124 (Advt.), Have you played the Beetle Game?.. Simple rules..allow for the game to be played either in pairs..or arranged as a Beetle Drive. **1959** *Guardian* 23 Dec. 4/5 Parents play whist and 'beetle' madly throughout the winter. **1960** *Ibid.* 10 Nov. 6/7 A more civilised Britain..will not be built on a foundation of beetle drives and bingo.

c. Also **Beetle.** [Cf. G. *Käfer* in same sense.] An affectionate name for the original small Volkswagen saloon car (and for subsequent developments of this model), characterized by a compact rounded design.

A proprietary term in the U.S.

[**1946** G. WILKINS in *Motor* 8 May 290/3 The German K.d.F. or Volkswagen..represents the interim type produced in the change-over from war to peace production. It has the civilian saloon body on the military chassis with the higher ground clearance, and it looks rather like a beetle on stilts.] **1958** *Amer. Mercury* Nov. 87/2 While the American firms nevertheless continue to increase the size and horsepower of their automobiles, it will be interesting to watch the progress of this wonderful little beetle from Wolfsburg. **1960** *Motor* 3 Aug. 20/1 The 1961 version is still the familiar 'beetle'. **1969** A. LURIE *Real People* 97 They won't have to go in Gerry's dumb old beetle that's probably going to break down anyhow. **1971** *Country Life* 9 Dec. 1674/1 The Volkswagen Beetle, is it now unashamedly termed even by the makers, is a car to defy comparison... Look at any Beetle on the road and often only the registration gives its age away. **1972** *Official Gaz.* (U.S. Patent Office) 16 May 179/2 Volkswagenwerk Aktiengesellschaft, Wolfsburg, Germany. Filed Nov. 4, 1970... *Beetle*... For Automobiles [etc.]. **1976** *Road & Track* 49 You must remember though, that Healeys are not Beetles or Impalas. **1980** R. FRY *VW Beetle* vi. 160 John Baber played a major part in publicising the name. Whenever he was spotted..by local children they would all shout, 'Here comes Baber in his Beetle'.

3. Taken as a type of blindness: see quot. 1747. (*as dumb, as deaf as a beetle*, see BEETLE *sb.*[1] 2.)

1548 UDALL, etc. *Erasm. Par. Mark* i. 5 Jerusalem..albeit she were in very dede as blynde as a betell. **1579** TOMSON *Calvin's Serm. Tim.* 471/2 Wee cease not to bee bruite beasts, as blinde as betles. **1747** BAKER in *Phil. Trans.* XLIV. 581 They frequently dash themselves against People's Faces with great Violence, and by their so doing occasioned the common Proverb, *As blind as a Beetle.*

4. a. Hence *fig.* An intellectually blind person.

1579 TOMSON *Calvin's Serm. Tim.* 931/2 They that had charge to guyde other, were poore blinde betels themselues. **1692** WASHINGTON tr. *Milton's Def. Pop.* v. (1851) 132 They ..confute such a Beetle as you are. **1765** TUCKER *Lt. Nat.* I. 475 A blockhead, yea a numskull, not to say a beetle.

†**b.** *attrib.* or as *adj.* **blind-beetledness** *sb.*, the quality of being mentally blind as a beetle. Cf. also *beetle-head* in BEETLE *sb.*[1] 3.

1566 STAPLETON *Ret. Untr. Jewell* iii. 91 With such Betle arguments as you make. *Ibid.* iv. 184 Peuish absurditie or blinde bettle ignorance. **1649** LIGHTFOOT *Battle Wasp's Nest.* Wks. (1825) I. 389 If you must shame anybody for blind beetledness, it must be Mr. Heming.

5. *Comb.*, as ***beetle-blind, -droning, -eyed, -grub, -like***; **beetle-back**, a back shaped like the wings of a beetle; so ***beetle-backed*** adj.; **beetle-crusher, -squasher** *slang*, a boot or foot, esp. a big one; an infantry soldier (Farmer *Slang*); so **beetle-crushing** *a.*, wearing big boots; belonging to the infantry; **beetle-stone** = SEPTARIUM 2; † **beetle-wig** (*obs.*), an ear-wig.

1933 J. E. LIBERTY *Pract. Tailoring* vii. 113 **Beetle back.* This is an extended back, with rounded corners. The bottom edge of the back being longer than the lines of the edge on the foreparts. **1958** *Vogue* Sept. 103 Falling loose at the back and following the line of the spine in a just discernible beetle-back curve. **1959** S. GIBBONS *Pink Front Door* vii. 87 What a thrilling two-piece..that's the first *beetle-backed jacket I've seen actually *on* anyone. **1962** *Times* 10 Apr. 6/5 A little beetle-backed 1,200 c.c. car. **1556** J. HEYWOOD *Spider & F.* xix. Thou nor no flie is so *beetle-blinde. **1617** COLLINS *Def. Bp. Ely* To Rdr. 14 Hee was starke beetle-blind at broad noone day. **1860** HOTTEN *Slang Dict.* (ed. 2) 94 **Beetle-crushers*, or *squashers*, large flat feet. **1869** 'WAT BRADWOOD' *The O.V.H.* xxi, The infliction which the beetle-crusher of a recent arrival had just inflicted on his pet corn. **1870** R. BROUGHTON *Red as Rose* xxxv, What howible boots! Whoever could have had the atwocity to fwame such beetle-cwushers? **1897** *Punch* 30 Oct. 195/1 If you need a meal, you can boil your beetle-crushers. **1958** 'A. GILBERT' *Death agst. Clock* 155 He looked down..at his own enormous beetle-crushers in bright tan Oxfords. **1871** G. A. LAWRENCE *Anteros* xiv, The possibility..of exchange into a sedate, *beetle-crushing corps. **1917** MASEFIELD *Lollingdon Downs* 31 This *beetle-droning downland. **1594** T. B. *La Primaud. Fr. Acad.* II. To Rdr., These *beetle-eyed atheists may as well be deprived of their bodily eyes. **1843** *Ainsworth's Mag.* III. 563 On stealthily raising his eyes.., he descried a toothless beetle-eyed antique. **1884** *Littel's Living Age* 688 To get *beetle-grubs out of the ground. **1908** *Westm. Gaz.* 22 Aug. 16/3 A great *beetle-like shape. **1859** PAGE *Handbk. Geol. Terms* s.v. *Septarium*, Such..nodules.. when split up..exhibit very curiously marked sections; hence the names **beetle-stones, turtle-stones.* **1595** *Widowes Treas.* C ii b, A medicine for to get the *Beetelwigges out of a mans eare.

beetle ('biːt(ə)l), ? *a.* In beetle brows, beetle-browed. Forms; 4 bitel, bytel(l, 5 betyl, bittil, 6 beetell, -ill, -yll, 7 betle, bittle, 6- beetle. [Found first in the comb. *beetle-browed* (1362); much later (1532), *beetle* is treated as a separate word in *beetle brow(s*; whence a derived verb to BEETLE (see next) formed by Shakspere.

(As the 14-15th c. form had *bitel-, bytel-*, it has been proposed to identify it with BITEL *a.* 'biting, cutting like a sharp-edged tool,' used by Ormin and Layamon, which is phonetically possible: but, beside the hardly satisfactory sense, there is the difficulty that *bitel* appears to have been obsolete for 160 years when the first example of *bitel-browed* occurs. It is more likely that the word here is one of the two sbs. BEETLE, both extant in 14th c., and both having the form *bitel*. The choice depends largely upon the exact meaning originally attached to 'beetle-browed,' which was a reproachful epithet, and appears to have referred to the shaggy prominence of the eye-brows. (*Brow* in ME. was always = eyebrow, not = forehead.) It is probable therefore (as suggested by Dr. F. Chance) that the comparison is to the short tufted antennæ of some species of beetles, projecting at right angles to the head, which may have been called 'eyebrows' in Eng. as well as in Fr.; for in French the expression *sourcils de hanneton* 'cockchafers' eyebrows' is the name given to a species of fringe made in imitation of the *antennæ* of these insects.)]

1. beetle-browed: 'Having prominent brows,' Johnson; 'having black and long eyebrows,' Bailey (1782); with earlier authorities 'Having shaggy, bushy, or prominent eye-brows'; see esp. quots. 1400, 1591. Dr. Johnson's explanation probably owes something to the sense attached to BEETLE *v.*[1] Almost always reproachful, and sometimes in 17th c. simply = lowering, scowling, sullen, surly. Cf. *supercilious* f. L. *supercilium* 'eyebrow.'

1362 LANGL. *P. Pl.* A. v. 109 He was bitel-brouwed with twei blered eiȝen [*v.r.* He was bitel-browid & babirlipped, *also* biter-, bitter-browid. B. v. 190 bitelbrowed and baberliped also, With two blered eyghen, as a blynde hagge; *v.r.* bytter browid. C. VII. 198 bytelbrowed; *v.r.* bitturbrowed.] *c* **1400** *Destr. Troy* VIII. 3824 Grete ene and gray, with a grym loke..Bytell browet was the buerne, þat aboue met. *c* **1450** *York Myst., Cutlers* Q iij b, Say bittilbrowed bribour! **1562** J. HEYWOOD *Prov. & Epigr.* (1867) 42 A crooked hooked nose, beetyll browde. **1591** PERCIVALL *Sp. Dict., Cejunto*, beetle browed, *toruus* [**1623** *Cejunto*, that hath bushy eie-browes, beetle-browed, or the haire of the eye-browes meeting]. **1591** HARINGTON *Orl. Fur.* XLIII, cxxviii. (1634) 368 All blablipt, beetle-browd, and bottle-nozed. **1611** COTGR., Beetle-browed, *sourcilleux.—Sourcilleux*, having very great eye brows, frowning, or looking sowrely; surlie or proud of countenance. *c* **1645** HOWELL *Lett.* (1650) I. 355 A beetle-browed sullen face. **1755** SMOLLETT *Quix.* (1803) I. 126 Beetlebrow'd, flat-nosed, blind of one eye. **1840** BARHAM *Ingol. Leg.* 231 A beetle-browed hag With a knife and a bag.

b. *fig.* or *transf.*

1651 J. C[LEVELAND] 30 The Sun wears Midnight, day is beetle-brow'd. **1837** HAWTHORNE *Twice-told T.* (1851) II. xii. 174 One of those..wooden houses..with a beetle-browed second story projecting over the foundation. **1865** *Cornh. Mag.* XI. 157 Jealous loopholes or beetle-browed machicolations.

2. beetle (qualifying *brows*).

1532 MORE *Confut. Tindale* Wks. (1557) 398/1 Tindall.. so long pryed vpon them with bitle browes and his britle spectacles of pride and malice. **1562** J. HEYWOOD *Prov. & Epigr.* (1867) 115, I rather would a husband wed With a beetill brow, than with a beetell hed. **1596** SPENSER *F.Q.* II. ix. 52 Bent hollow beetle browes. **1600** FAIRFAX *Tasso* X. xxii. 182 His beetle browes the Turke amazed bent. **1713** *Lond. Gaz.* No. 5157/4 Lost..a..Nag..very stout grown, a bittle Brow. **1837** CARLYLE *Fr. Rev.* (1857) I. I. IV. iv. 108 Through whose shaggy beetle brows..there look[s]..fire of genius.

b. Of the brow or ridge of a mountain, as projecting, or perhaps as tree-clad. Cf. L. *supercilium* 'eyebrow,' also 'brow or ridge of a mountain.'

1580 SIDNEY *Arcadia* (1622) 35 A pleasant valley of either side of which high hills lifted vp their beetle-browis, as if they would ouer looke the pleasantnesse of their vnder prospect. **1601** WEEVER *Myrr. Mart.* E vij, Tree-garnisht Cambriaes loftie mountaines Did ouer-shade me with their beetle browes.

¶ (Confused with BEETLE *sb.*[1])

1553-87 FOXE *A. & M.* III. 140 Then my Lord said 'Thou art an ignorant Beetle-brow.'

beetle (ˈbiːt(ə)l), *v.*¹ [f. BEETLE *a.* 2b. Apparently used as a nonce-word by Shakspere, from whom it has been taken by later writers.]

1. *intr.* To 'lift up beetle brows' (Sidney), look with beetle brows, scowl; taken by modern writers as simply 'to project, overhang'; but probably used by Shakspere with some reference to eyebrows.

1602 SHAKS. *Ham.* I. iv. 71 The dreadfull summit of the Cliffe, That beetles o'er his base into the Sea. **1798** J. HUCKS *Poems* 82 The bleak cliffs shaggy steep, That beetles o'er the hoarse resounding deep. **1814** SCOTT *Lady of L.* II. xxxi, The verge which beetled o'er The ocean. **1824** W. IRVING *T. Trav.* II. 107 The rocks often beetled over the road.

2. *fig.* To hang threateningly.

1859 MERIVALE *Rom. Emp.* (1865) VII. lvi. 87 This double invasion..was..beetling on the summits of the Alps. **1870** EMERSON *Soc. & Solit.* iv. 75 The justice of states, which we could well enough see beetling over his head.

beetle (ˈbiːt(ə)l), *v.*²; also (*Sc.*) bittle. [f. BEETLE *sb.*¹] *trans.* To beat with a beetle, in order to thresh, crush, or flatten; also, *techn.*, to emboss fabrics by pressure from figured rollers.

1608 in *N. Riding Qr. Sessions Rec.* (1884) I. 136 Betling ..& stretchinge three webbes of lynnen cloth, etc. **1706** MARY LEADBEATER in *Leadb. Papers* I. 52 The bleach green for the clothes, the large stone to beetle them on. **1745** tr. *Columella's Husb.* XII. xix, Raw Spanish broom, that is, which has not been beetled. **1815** SCOTT *Guy M.* xxiv, Bleached on the bonny white gowans, and bittled by Nelly and hersell. **1863** SMILES *Industr. Biog.* 270 Patents for.. weaving, beetling, and mangling fabrics of various sorts.

beetle (ˈbiːt(ə)l), *v.*³ *colloq.* [f. BEETLE *sb.*²] *intr.* To fly off; to go, make one's way, move (like a beetle); freq. with *off*, *away*, etc.

1919 W. H. DOWNING *Digger Dialects* 11 *Beetle about*, fly aimlessly (of an aeroplane). **1920** W. NOBLE *With Bristol Fighter* i. 20 We were on our side of the line, and the Huns had beetled away eastwards. **1923** WODEHOUSE *Good Morning, Bill!* I. 19 'What are you doing about two weeks from now?'..'Nothing in particular. Just beetling around.' *Ibid.* II. 104 Did he specify that you were to come beetling in at midnight? **1925** FRASER & GIBBONS *Soldier & Sailor Words* 21 To *beetle-off*: Air Force slang. To fly straight. To go off direct, as a beetle flies; *e.g.*, 'I just beetled off home.' **1943** P. BRENNAN et al. *Spitfires over Malta* i. 31, I beetled about the mess and the bastions. **1948** C. DAY LEWIS *Otterbury Incident* vi. 74 E. Sidebotham beetled up the ladder to examine the window-sill. **1952** N. COWARD *Rel. Values* I. ii. 29 There was..a terrible scene..and Freda beetled off to America.

beetle, obs. form of BETEL.

ˈbeetled, *a.* = BEETLE *a.* 2.

1509 HAWES *Past. Pleas.* xxix. ii. 135 His head was greate, beteled was his browes. **1832** LYTTON *Eugene A.* IV. ix, The frowning and beetled ruins of the shattered castle.

beetledness: see BEETLE *sb.*² 4b.

beetler (ˈbiːtlə(r)). [f. BEETLE *v.*² + -ER¹.] One who beetles (cloth, etc.).

1885 *Manch. Guard.* 16 May 1 (*Advt.*) To Bleachers, Dyers, Finishers, Beetlers, etc.

beetling (ˈbiːtlɪŋ), *vbl. sb.* [f. as prec. + -ING¹.] Beating with a beetle; embossing fabrics with a *beetling-machine*.

1859 *Edin. Rev.* CIX. 302 The care of the crop..the steeping, beetling, and dressing. **1859** SMILES *Self-Help* 33 The beetling and mangling of textile fabrics.

ˈbeetling, *ppl. a.* [f. BEETLE *v.*¹ + -ING².] Projecting, overhanging.

1728 THOMSON *Spring*, The hawk High in the beetling cliff his aery builds. **1809** W. IRVING *Knickerb.* (1861) 197 From the beetling brow of some precipice. **1840** DICKENS *Barn. Rudge* xxxvi, His beetling brow almost obscured his eyes.

beet-root (ˈbiːtruːt). The root of the beet; also *attrib.*, as in ***beetroot sugar***. **ˈbeetrooty** *a. colloq.*, of the nature or appearance of beet-root.

1579 LANGHAM *Gard. Health* (1633) 66 Strake a little salt on a Beete roote, and put it into the fundament. **1834** HT. MARTINEAU *Hist. Peace* (1877) III. v. xi. 405 The beet-root sugar of France supplied one-third of the national consumption. **1842** DICKENS *Amer. Notes* (1850) 109/1 Those who fancy slices of beet-root. **1859** *All Y. Round* No. 35. 198 The smallest boy, with the whitest face, the most beetrooty nose..ever seen.

beeve (biːv). [sing. form derived from *beeves*, pl. of BEEF *sb.*] An ox; = BEEF *sb.* 3.

1847 WHITTIER *Drovers* 61 Each stately beeve bespeaks the hand That fed him unrepining. **1899** *Daily News* 4 Dec. 8/3 Herefords are a noble type in all the points that are expected in the modern beeve.

beeveedee, var. B.V.D.

beeves (biːvz). Pl. of BEEF (q.v.); now usually poetic for 'oxen, cattle.'

beezel, variant of BEZZLE.

beezer (ˈbiːzə(r)). [Origin obscure.] **1.** [App. orig. Sc.] A smart fellow (quot. 1914); a person, a 'chap'. See *Sc. Nat. Dict.*

1914 J. L. WAUGH *Cracks wi' Robbie Doo* ix. 110 Weel dune, Robin Hood; dash it, man, but you're a beeser. **1935** 'N. BLAKE' *Question of Proof* viii. 156 He's not a bad sort of beezer at all, if he wasn't such an absolute ass. **1963** 'G. CARR' *Lewker in Norway* ii. 30 Get this beezer outa my sight, someone!

2. (Perhaps a different word.) Nose. *slang.*

1915 C. E. VAN LOAN in C. Grayson *New Stories for Men* (1941) 550 Perhaps it should be explained that, in the patois of the [boxing] profession..the nose becomes a beezer. **1920** ADE *Hand-made Fables* i. 12 One brilliant Man about Town, with a Beezer that never could have been coloured by the use of Malted Milk. **1932** WODEHOUSE *Hot Water* vi. 112 Back home..a cop..don't hardly even notice it if you sock him on the beezer. **1960** —— *Jeeves in Offing* v. 52 It is virtually impossible to write a novel of suspense without getting a certain amount of ink on the beezer.

befall (bɪˈfɔːl), *v.*; also 2–5 bi-, by-, 2–4 be-, bivalle, 6– befal. Pa. t. befell (2– -fel). Pa. pple. befallen. Variant forms generally as in FALL. [OE. *bef(e)all-an* f. BE- 2 + *f(e)allan* to fall; = OS., OHG. *bifallan*, mod.G. *befallen*.]

†**1.** *intr.* To fall. (Chiefly *fig.*) *Obs.*

c **897** K. ÆLFRED *Past. Ca.* xl. (Bosw.), Hie oft befeallað on micel yfel. *c* **1000** *Ags. Gosp.* Matt. x. 29 An of ðam ne befylþ on eorþan. *c* **1160** *Hatton G.* ibid., Ne befalð on eorðen. *c* **1200** *Trin. Coll. Hom.* 73 Þe sinfulle man beoð bifallen on depe sinne. **1470** HARDING *Chron.* Pref. 2 Iff that he were in suche a jupertee Of werre by falle. **1649** SELDEN *Laws Eng.* I. lxvii. (1739) 177 Many mens cases befel not directly within the Letter of the Law.

2. To fall *to* as one's share or right; to pertain, belong; be fitting. Also *impers. arch.*

c **1175** *Lamb. Hom.* 161 Mest al þet ich habbe idon bi-fealt to child-hade. *c* **1305** *St. Lucy* 170 in *E.E.P.* (1862) 106 Þe reisouns were alle iseid þat bifulle þerto. **1393** LANGL. *P. Pl.* C. II. 48 '*Reddite Caesari*,' seide god, 'þat to cesar by-falleþ.' *c* **1460** *Towneley Myst.* 209 Sirs, a kyng he hym cals, Therfor a crowne hym befals. **1649** SELDEN *Laws Eng.* I. xiii. (1739) 23 It now befals to touch upon the manner of the Government of the Church. **1850** NEALE *Med. Hymns* 197 Giving to the dearer ones What to each befalleth.

†**3.** To fall to (as an inheritance). *Obs.*

a **1617** BAYNE *On Eph.* (1658) 131 Goodly Lands, which in likelihood will befal him. **1704** *Lond. Gaz.* No. 4049/4 He is desired to return..he having an Estate befallen him.

4. To fall out in the course of events, to happen, occur: **a.** *simply. arch.*

a **1300** *Sarmun* 57 in *E.E.P.* (1862) 7 Þe mest ioi þat mai befalle. *c* **1420** *Anturs Arth.* lv, This ferli be-felle in Ingulwud forest. **1513** DOUGLAS *Æneis* IX. i. 48, I sal persew, and follow quhat befaw. **1610** HEALEY *St. August. City of God* 126 The Eclipse which befell at our Saviours death was quite against the regular course of the stars. **1765** TUCKER *Lt. Nat.* I. 372 There are seldom any events befalling.. which concern no more than a single person. **1855** THACKERAY *Newcomes* xx, Ethel's birthday befel in the Spring.

b. with indirect obj. (dative). The most frequent modern use.

1297 R. GLOUC. 556 Ac after þulke time..Lute god cas him biuel. **1477** EARL RIVERS (Caxton) *Dictes* 91 They knowe not what good may befall them thereby. **1597** HOOKER *Eccl. Pol.* v. xxxix. §4 Wks. 1841 I. 553 Heavy accidents which befall men in this..life. **1611** BIBLE *Gen.* xlii. 4 Lest peraduenture mischiefe befall him. **1709** STEELE *Tatler* No. 128 ¶6 The most deplorable misfortune that possibly can befal a Woman. **1858** J. MARTINEAU *Stud. Chr.* 90 The disaster which then befell the human race.

c. with *to*, *unto*, or *upon*. *arch.*

a **1225** *Ancr. R.* 344 Swuche openliche sunnen þet to alle men biualleð. **1583** GOLDING *Calvin on Deut.* xvii. 97 If this befell to Moses. **1667** MILTON *P.L.* VII. 43 What befell in Heaven To those Apostates. **1814** CARY *Dante's Inf.* XXIII. 5 What fate unto the mouse and frog befel.

d. *impers.*, or with subject *it* representing a clause.

c **1175** *Cott. Hom.* 231 Þa be-fel hit swa þat hym a þance befell. **1250** LAY. 27135 Luþer him bifalle was. *c* **1386** CHAUCER *Prol.* 18 Byfel that, in that sesoun on a day, In Southwerk at the Tabbard as I lay, etc. **1393** LANGL. *P. Pl.* C. I. 7 On Maluerne hulles Me byfel for to slepe. **1483** CAXTON *G. de la Tour* D vi, As in like wise bifelle to Eue that touchid of the fruyt. **1590** SHAKS. *Com. Err.* v. i. 208 So befall my soule, As this is false. **1667** MILTON *P.L.* IX. 1185 Thus it shall befall Him who..Lets her Will rule. **1857** KINGSLEY *Two Y. Ago* (1877) 54 And so it befell that they often quarrelled and wrangled.

†**e.** In phrases: ***Fair befall, foul befall.*** Obs.

1377 LANGL. *P. Pl.* B. v. 59 Þat feire hem bifalle þat suweth my sermon. *c* **1460** *Towneley Myst.* 33 Fayre myght the befalle. *a* **1550** *J. Bow & Person* 67 in Hazl. *E.P.P.* IV. 9 Then myght he laye him, so fowle befalde. **1588** SHAKS. *L.L.L.* II. i. 124 Now faire befall your maske.

†**5.** To fall in one's way, happen to be, turn up, occur. *Obs.*

1591 SPENSER *Virgil's Gnat.* ix, To feede abroad, where pasture best befalls.

†**6. a.** with *compl.* To become as it were by chance, to grow. *Obs.*

1592 WYRLEY *Armorie* 146 Passing darke it was befaln.

†**b.** To become *of*. *Obs.*

1470–85 MALORY *Arthur* (1816) II. 125 Needs must I revenge my lord, and so will I whatsoever befal of me. *a* **1520** *Myrr. Our Ladye* 320 Thoughe they be roten or brente, or what euer befalle of them. **1590** SHAKS. *Com. Err.* I. i. 124 To dilate What haue befalne of them and they till now.

†**7.** ? To surround. *Obs. rare.*

1205 LAY. 25736 Uppen ane hulle Mid sae ulode bi uallen [**1250** mid see flode bifalle].

†**beˈfall**, *sb. Obs.*; also befalle, byfalle. [f. prec.] A case, circumstance, incident, accident.

1491 CAXTON *Vitas Patr.* (W. de W. 1495) 150 Or he had tolde al his befall. *Ibid.* I. cxx. 141 b, He sholde enquyre ferder of the trouth of the befall.

befalling (bɪˈfɔːlɪŋ), *vbl. sb.*; also bifallynge. [f. BEFALL *v.* + -ING¹.] Happening, occurrence; *concr.* occurrence, chance, event.

c **1374** CHAUCER *Troylus* IV. 990 It bihoveth, that the bifallynge Of thynges..Be necessarie. **1388** WYCLIF *Wisd.* viii. 8 The bifallyngis of tymes and of worldus. **1839** FR. KEMBLE *Rec. Later Life* I. 218 These and other befallings may serve for talking matter.

†**befalling**, *ppl. a. Obs.* [f. as prec. + -ING².] Appertaining, appropriate, fitting.

1542 UDALL *Erasm. Apoph.* 215 a, Bountie and largesse is befallyng for kynges.

befan, befast, befavour, befathered: see BE-.

†**beˈfate**, *v. Obs.* Only in pa. pple. befated. [f. BE- + FATE *sb.* (or ? *v.*)] Fatally possessed, infatuated (by his destiny). Cf. Sc. FEY.

a **1659** OSBORN *Essex's Death* Wks. (1673) 668 If he had not been befated with a strong Opinion of success.

befe, beff(e, obs. forms of BEEF.

befeather (bɪˈfɛðə(r)), *v.* [f. BE- 6 + FEATHER *sb.*] *trans.* To deck with feathers. Hence **befeathered** *ppl. a.*

1611 COTGR., *Emplumer*..befeather..to dresse with feathers. **1635** QUARLES *Emblems* III. i. 33 (D.) Her dove-befeathered prison. *c* **1850** tr. *V. Hugo's Hunchback* I i. 1 Some bedizened and befeathered embassy.

befetter, etc.: see BE- *pref.*

†**beff**, *sb. Sc. Obs.* [Cf. BEFT *v.*, and BAFF *sb.*] A blow, buffet.

1768 BEATTIE in *Ross' Helenore* vi, With beffs and flegs, Bumbaz'd and dizzie.

beff *v.*: see BEFT.

†**beˈfie**, *v. Obs. rare*⁻¹. ? To defy; or to say *fie!* to.

1589 *Hay any Work* 48 Ile befie em that will say so of me.

†**beˈfight**, *v. Obs.* [f. BE- 4 + OE. *feohtan*, ME. *fight*: cf. MHG. *bevehten*. The OE. and ME. uses seem to be unconnected.]

1. *trans.* To deprive of by fighting. Only in OE.

c **1000** *Riddles* iv. 32 Feore bifohten.

2. To fight against, do battle with.

1474 CAXTON *Chesse* 87 To-fore or he dyd doo assaylle hit or befight hit. *a* **1547** EARL SURREY *Æneid* II. 532 As wrastling windes..Befight themselves.

Hence **beˈfighting** *vbl. sb.*

1489 CAXTON *Faytes of A.* II. xiv. 116 In fayttes of befyghtyngis and sawtynges of cytees.

befilch, befilth, befinger, etc.: see BE- *pref.*

†**befile**, *v. Obs.* Forms: *Inf.* 1 be-, bifylan, 3 bifulen(*ü*), 4 bifilen, (*Kentish*) bevelen, 6 befyle, befile. [OE. *befýlan*, f. BE- 1 + *fýlan* to FILE (:—OTeut. **fûljan*, f. *fúl*, FOUL). Afterwards superseded by BEFOUL.] *trans.* To make foul or dirty; to defile. Hence †**befiling** *vbl. sb.*

c **1000** *Sax. Leechd.* III. 208 Handa him befylde ȝesihð weorca unrihta ȝetacnað. *a* **1225** *Ancr. R.* 272 Uorte bifulen hire mid þouhte of olde sunnen. **1340** *Ayenb.* 40 Maystres of gyle and of contak and of be-uelynge. **1530** PALSGR. 445/2 You have befyled your hosen with duste and you have befouled your cappe with asshes. **1532** MORE *Confut. Tindale* Wks. (1557) 685/1 Then shall ye see..thys fayre egle byrde foule befile hys nest.

†**beˈfind**, *v. Obs.* [ME., f. BE- 2 + OE. *findan* to FIND; cf. OHG. *bifindan*.]

1. *trans.* To find, discover.

c **1200** *Trin. Coll. Hom.* 47 Hire ferede was bifunden alse hie frend hedde. **1413** LYDG. *Pylgr. Sowle* v. iii. (1483) 93 The fyrst that was byfound with this vertu.

2. To invent, contrive.

1297 R. GLOUC. 267 Þeruor he byuonde þat þer were hondredes in eche contreye. *Ibid.* He byuond vorst a queintyse aȝen þe Deneys to anstond.

3. In *passive*, 'To be found' = to be. Cf. Ger. *sich befinden*, F. *se trouver*.

c **1200** ORMIN 129 Forr ȝho wass swa bifunndenn wiþ þatt ȝho ne mihhte tæmenn. *c* **1230** *Hali Meid.* 31 Ne beon ha neauer swa wið fulðe bifunden.

befit (bɪˈfɪt), *v.* [f. BE- 2 + FIT *v.*]

1. *trans.* To be suited to, or fit for; to agree with, be in harmony with; to become.

c **1460** FORTESCUE *Abs. & Lim. Mon.* (1714) 49 That befittith the Kyngs Liberalite. **1598** BARRET *Theor. Warres* IV. i. 93 He ought..to haue a certaine naturall instinct befitting this office. **1610** SHAKS. *Temp.* II. i. 289 They'l tell the clocke to any businesse that We say befits the houre. **1667** MILTON *P.L.* x. 868 Thou Serpent! that name best Befits thee with him leagu'd. **1748** RICHARDSON *Clarissa* (1811) IV. xii. 70 Let me know, whether she wants anything that befits her case. **1843** PRESCOTT *Mexico* (1850) I. 137 The various duties befitting his princely station.

2. Of moral fitness: To be proper to, or incumbent upon, as a duty or task; to be right for.

1602 SHAKS. *Ham.* I. ii. 2 It us befitted To beare our hearts in greefe. **1647** COWLEY *Mistr.* i. (1669) 21 She came for that, which more befits all Wives, The art of Giving, not of Saving Lives. **1875** B. TAYLOR *Faust* II. iii. II. 141 At home, be wise as it befits thee there.

†3. To fit out *with*. *Obs.*
1598 BARRET *Theor. Warres* v. ii. 143 A..horse..befitted with a saddle, bridle, etc. **1759** STERNE *Tr. Shandy* I. x, He had..befitted him with just such a bridle and saddle.

befitting (bɪˈfɪtɪŋ), *ppl. a.* [f. prec. + -ING².] Fitting, suitable, becoming, due.
1564 HARRINGTON *To Isa. Markham* 8 The lipps [speake] befitting wordes moste kynde. **1875** E. WHITE *Life in Christ* 215 This must be done with a befitting sense of awe.

beˈfittingly, *adv.* [f. prec. + -LY².] In a befitting manner, suitably, becomingly.
1638 EARL PEMBROKE in *Verney Papers* 205 A curassier..befittingly horsed. **1821** BYRON *Sardan.* v. i. 347 They are to deem that I reject their terms, And act befittingly.

†**beˈfittingness.** *Obs.* [f. as prec. + -NESS.] The quality of being fitting; appropriateness.
1647 W. BROWNE *Polexander* II. 9 To discerne what the befittingnesse of her condition permitted.

†**beˈflake**, *v. Obs. rare.* [f. BE- 6 + FLAKE.] To take off an external layer, to skin in thin flakes.
1649 BLITHE *Eng. Improv. Impr.* (1652) 234 So to pare off the husk that it [madder] may be..beflaked or flayed that it may all go one way.

beflannel, beflap, befleck, befleet: see BE-.

beflatter (bɪˈflætə(r)), *v.* [f. BE- 2 + FLATTER.] Intensive of FLATTER.
1340 *Ayenb.* 60 (Roxb.), Huanne hi yzeþ þet he oþer hy þet hi wylleþ beulatery [*v.r.* beuly] habbeþ wel yzed. **1828** SOUTHEY in *Q. Rev.* XXXVIII. 590 Looking to see how far we might be..beflattered and befooled into a departure, etc.

†**beˈflay**, *v. Obs.* [OE. *befléan*, f. BE- 1 + *fléan* to FLAY.] *trans.* To flay, strip.
a **1000** in Wülcker *Voc.* 218 *Deglobere, spoliare*, beflean. **1340** *Ayenb.* 38 Kueade lordes..þet beulaȝeþ þe poure men. *Ibid.* 218 Þo þet be-uleaþ þe poure uolk. **1393** GOWER *Conf.* III. 183 Out of his skin he was beflain All quick.

†**beˈflee**, *v. Obs.* [OE. *befléon*, f. BE- 4 + *fléon* (pa. t. *fléah fluȝon*, pa. pple. *floȝen*) to FLEE, q.v. for forms.] *trans.* To flee from, flee, avoid, shun.
c **1000** *Ags. Ps.* lxi. 6 Ne mæȝ ic hine ahwær befleon. *c* **1315** SHOREHAM 36 And the ferste hys that he by-fle Chypeans of sennes rote.

beflounce, beflour, beflout, befluster: see BE-.

†**beˈflow**, *v. Obs.* [OE. *beflowan* f. BE- 1 + *flówan* to FLOW, q.v. for forms.] **a.** To flow by, about, or around. **b.** To flow all over, overflow.
a **1000** *Wife's Lament* 49 Wine weriȝmod, wætre beflowen. *c* **1250** LAY. 25738 An oþer hulle was þar heh, þe séé hine bifloȝede [**1205** bifledde] swiþe neh. **1387** TREVISA *Higden* (1865) I. 133 After þat he [Nilus] haþ so biflowe and i-watred þe lond..þe water falleþ into þe chanel aȝe.

beflower (bɪˈflaʊə(r)), *v.* [f. BE- 6 + FLOWER *sb.*] *trans.* To cover or deck with, or as with, flowers.
1594 CAREW *Tasso* (1881) 53 She trimmes her selfe and golden hed Beflowres with Roses culd in Paradize. **1628** HOBBES *Thucyd.* (1822) 99 Their bodies..reddish livid and beflowerd with little pimples. **1795** WOLCOTT (P. Pindar) *Pindar.* Wks. 1812 IV. 188 Damask well beflower'd with blue.

†**beˈfly**, *v. Obs.* [OE. *befléoȝan* f. BE- 4 + *fléoȝan* to FLY, q.v. for forms. (Not separated in ME. from BEFLEE, the pa. tenses being identical.)] *trans.* **a.** To fly about. **b.** To fly from, shun, escape.
a **890** K. ÆLFRED *Bæda* III. x, Þa spearcan befluȝon þæs huses hrof. *c* **1175** *Lamb. Hom.* 169 Wið þet þe mihte helle pine bi-flien and bi-sunien. **1340** *Ayenb.* 77 Þe greate filosofes þet þise guodes beuloȝe.
Hence, **beˈflying** *vbl. sb.*, shunning, avoiding.
1340 *Ayenb.* 121 Be þe beuliynge of kueade.

befoam (bɪˈfəʊm), *v.* [f. BE- 6 + FOAM *sb.*] *trans.* To cover with foam.
a **1618** SYLVESTER *Handy-Cr.* Wks. 463 Th' angry Steed..Befoams the path. **1697** DRYDEN *Ovid's Met.* viii. (R.) And part he [the boar] churns and part befoams the ground. **1863** BARNES *Poems Dorset Dial.* 50 The clear brook that did slide..befoam'd white as snow.

befog (bɪˈfɒg), *v.* [f. BE- 6 + FOG *sb.*] *trans.* To envelope in fog; *fig.* to obscure, confuse.
1603 HARSNET *Pop. Impost.* 134 What time that popish mist had befogged the eyes of our poore people. **1850** W. IRVING *Goldsmith* 249 The wine and wassail..befogged his senses. **1879** *Cornh. Mag.* Dec. 695 He befogs the whole matter wih a cloud of abuse.
Hence, **befogged** *ppl. a.*
1601 DENT *Pathw. Heauen* 254 You are altogether befogd and benighted in this question. **1868** G. MACDONALD *R. Falconer* II. 13 The pale, faintly befogged moon overhead. **1882** *Standard* 6 Oct. 2/1 A benighted or befogged wayfarer.

†**beˈfold**, *v. Obs.* [OE. *befaldan, -fealdan*, f. BE- 1 + *f(e)aldan* (pa. t. *feold*, pa. pple. *f(e)alden*) to FOLD.] *trans.* To fold up, wrap up, envelope.
a **1000** ÆLFRIC *Gen.* xxvii. 16 And befeold his handa mid þæra tyccena fellum. **1340** *Ayenb.* 8 Zuich wreþe long yhyealde and byuealde ine herte. *c* **1400** *Le Freine* 172 Therin she leyed the childe, for cold, In the pel as it was bifold.

†**beˈfong**, *v. Obs.* Forms: 1-3 befón, 3 bifon, -von; 1-3 be-, bifeng. *Pa. pple.* 1-3 be-, bifongen, 3 biuonge. [OE. *befón:—*befa(n)han* (pa. pple. *befangen*), f. BE- about + **fanhan, fón* to seize, grasp. Corresp. to mod.G. *befangen*, OHG. *pifâhan*, MHG. *bevân* to comprehend.]
1. *trans.* To lay hold on, seize, grasp, catch.
a **1000** *Cædmon's Gen.* 374 (Gr.) Habbaþ me helle clommas fæste befangen. *c* **1160** *Hatton Gosp.* Matt. xxii. 15 Hyo wolden þanne Hælend on his sprace befon. **1250** LAY. 830 Þer Brutus bifenge: al þat him bifore was.
2. *intr.* To take hold *on*, begin or commence *upon*. (Cf. Ger. *anfangen*.)
c **1200** *Trin. Coll. Hom.* 143 Þo þe hadden here sinnes forleten and bet, oðer þar-on biuonge.
3. *trans.* To encompass, enclose, comprehend.
971 *Blickl. Hom.* 5 God Fæder Sunu, þone ne maȝon befón heofon and eorþe. **1205** LAY. 24748 Mid æne bende of golde: ælc hafde his hæfd biuonge. *a* **1225** *Ancr. R.* 76 Þe Louerd, þat al þe world ne muhte nout biuon.

befool (bɪˈfuːl), *v.* in 4-5 befole. [f. BE- 5 + FOOL *sb.*]
1. *trans.* To make a fool of; to dupe, delude.
1393 GOWER *Conf.* III. 236 Many wise Befoled have hem self er this. **1622** HEYLIN *Cosmogr.* III. (1682) 220 Befooling him with as glorious Titles. **1673** H. STUBBE *Furth. Vind. Dutch War* App. 81 The old Rumpers were befoold by Cromwel. **1765** WESLEY *Wks.* (1872) XII. 323 Be temperate in speaking: else Satan will befool you. **1831** CARLYLE *Sart. Res.* II. iii. 260 One age he is hagridden, bewitched; the next, priestridden, befooled.
2. To treat as a fool, call 'fool.'
1612 W. SCLATER *Sick Souls Salve* 33 That rash censuring and befooling others. *a* **1617** HIERON *Wks.* II. 166 Who is hee, whom Salomon doth so often be-foole in his Prouerbs? **1684** BUNYAN *Pilgr.* II. 180 They..befooled themselves for setting a Foot out of Doors in that Path. **1864** TENNYSON *Aylmer's F.* 590 Being much befool'd and idioted By the rough amity of the other.
3. To squander foolishly, 'fool away.' *rare.*
1861 SMILES *Engineers* I. 468 In this way Sir Thomas seems to have befooled his estate, and it shortly after became the property of the Alsager family.
Hence, **beˈfooled, beˈfooling** *ppl. a.*; **beˈfooling** *vbl. sb.*; **beˈfoolment** *sb.*
1677 GILPIN *Dæmonol.* (1867) 197 Either of these ways Satan makes use of for the befooling of men. **1681** BAXTER *Search Schism.* iii. 44 A transitory befooling dream. **1842** MIALL *Nonconf.* II. 8 Ah! we are a befooled people. **1881** *Pall Mall G.* 14 May 11/2 For the general befoolment of those easy souls.

†**beˈforce**, *v. Obs. rare.* [f. BE- 2 + FORCE *v.*]
1. *trans.* To force, ravish.
c **1375** ? BARBOUR *St. Theodera* 556 Þe monk Theoderus..me beforsit be his slycht.
2. ? To impose by force, to enforce.
1532 *Dice Play* (1850) 33 If there be broad laws beforced aforehand.

before (bɪˈfɔə(r)), *adv.*, *prep.*, and *conj.* Forms: 1 bi-, beforan, 2-4 bi-, beforen, 4- before. (Also 3 biuore(n, biforenn, byuore, biforr; 4-5 bi-, byforne, bifor(e, 4-6 byfore, 4-7 beforn(e, 5 befoore, 5-6 *Sc.* befoir, beforrow, 7 *arch.* beforen, biforn, 8 *arch.* beforne.) [OE. *beforan* (cogn. w. OS. *biforan*, OHG. *bifora*, MHG. *bevor*, also *bevorne, bevorn*), f. *bi-*, BE- by, about + *foran* adv.:—OTeut. **forana* from the front, advb. derivative of *fora*, FOR. Cf. also FORE, AFORE, ATFORE, TOFORE. Primarily an adverb; its relation to a sb. was expressed by putting the latter in the dative, 'in front *as to* a thing,' whence it passed into a preposition (cf. B 2, quot. 971). Elision of a relative particle has given it also the force of an adverbial conjunction *e.g.* in 'think before (that) you speak.']
A. *adv.* **I.** Of sequence in space.
1. Of motion: Ahead, in advance, in front.
a **1000** *Beowulf* 2829 He feara sum beforan gengde wisra monna. *c* **1175** *Lamb. Hom.* 41 Mihhal eode biforen and Poul com efter. *c* **1350** *Will. Palerne* 3193 And bifore went william and afterward þe quene. **1375** BARBOUR *Bruce* x. 245 Thai that war went furth beforn. *c* **1430** *Chev. Assigne* 322 Euur feraunce by-forne & þat other aftur. **1590** SHAKS. *Mids. N.* v. i. 397, I am sent with broome before, To sweep the dust behinde the door. **1610** HOLLAND *Camden's Brit.* I. 3 Nor Twins, the horned Bull of Crete, untimely go beforn. **1740** JOHNSON *Sir F. Drake* Wks. IV. 403 Advertised by two Symerons, whom he sent before. **1859** TENNYSON *Enid* 863 Not at my side. I charge thee ride before, Ever a good way on before.
2. Of position or direction: In front, in or on the anterior or fore side.
a **1300** *Cursor M.* 16637 Þai hailsed him be-for, bihind. **1413** LYDG. *Pylgr. Sowle* IV. xxxviii. 64 Full of eyen byfore and behynd. **1420** *E. E. Wills* (1882) 53 A habirgoun of Mylen, opyn be-for. **1523** LD. BERNERS *Froiss.* I. cliii. 183 Bare a starre on his bonet and on his mantell before. **1596** SHAKS. *Tam. Shr.* III. ii. 56 His horse..neere leg'd before. **1605** —— *Macb.* v. viii. 46 Had he his hurts before? **1635** PAGITT *Christianogr.* I. ii. (1636) 77 His upper garment..buttoned before. **1722** *Lond. Gaz.* No. 6088/3 Has lost a Tooth before. **1855** OWEN *Teeth* 302 Counting the molars from before backwards.
fig. **1821** SHELLEY *Skylark*, We look before and after, And pine for what is not.
†**3.** Before the face of men; openly. *Obs.*

c **1000** *Andreas* 1212 (Bosw.), Wundor on eorþan he beforan cyþde. *c* **1175** *Lamb. Hom.* 41 Þe þet spekeð faire biforen and false bihinden.
†**4.** In a position of pre-eminence or superiority *to*. *Obs.*
1377 LANGL. *P. Pl.* B. xx. 23 For is no vertue by fer · to *spiritus temperancie* [*C. text reads* by-fore to, to-fore, by ȝer, by fer, be ver, so fair as]. **1382** WYCLIF *Gen.* i. 26 Bifore be he [man] to the fishis of the see.
II. Of sequence in time or order.
5. a. In time previous or anterior to a time in question, previous to that or to this, earlier, sooner; *hence* beforehand; already, heretofore, in the past. Often with adverbs or advb. phrases of time, as *long before*, *three years before*, *the week before*, etc.
a **1225** *Ancr. R.* 240 Vor þi, mine leoue sustren, beoð biuoren iwarre. **1258** *Procl. Hen. III*, Alse hit is biforen iseid. **1297** R. GLOUC. 443 Roberd..les þat lyf Aboute þre ȝer byoure. *a* **1300** *Cursor M.* 8523 Dauid..spak..O cristes birth sua lang be-forn. **1340** *Ayenb.* 260 Ase ich habbe beuore yzed. **1477** EARL RIVERS (Caxton) *Dictes* 2 Whyche book I had neuer seen before. **1512** *Act 4 Hen. VIII*, xi, Everything..byfore rehersed. **1513** BRADSHAW *St. Werburge* (1848) 38 As our mother sayd to the byforne. *c* **1560** A. SCOTT *Counsale Wanton W.*, Ye trest to find thame trew That nevir wes beforrow. **1579** SPENSER *Sheph. Cal.* May 104 For ought may happen that hath bene beforne. *c* **1600** SHAKS. *Sonn.* xl, What hast thou then more then thou hadst before? **1610** —— *Temp.* III. ii. 2 When the But is out we will drinke water . not a drop before. **1766** GOLDSM. *Vic. W.* ix. (1806) 44 The conversation at this time was more reserved than before. **1798** COLERIDGE *Anc. Mar.* v. II. 47 The Mariners all return'd to work As silent as beforne. **1848** MACAULAY *Hist.* I. 153 Charles the First, eighteen years before, withdrew from his capital.
†**b.** In Scotch, *of before* = of aforetime, formerly.
c **1505** DUNBAR *Gold. Targe* xxiv, Scho semyt lustiar of chere..Than of before. **1513-75** *Diurn. Occurr.* (1833) 109 Sho past a lytill of befoir to vesie hir sone.
c. Used in contrast with *after* in various locutions to designate a set of two contrasting pictures, cartoons, etc., esp. illustrating the efficacy of a remedy, product, etc., alleged to produce a remarkable change for the better. Hence allusively.
1768 W. HOGARTH in *Trusler's Hogarth Moralized* (Index), A List of Prints published by Mr. Hogarth... Before and After. **1846** *Punch* XI. 243/1 (*captions*) Before. After. *Ibid.*, Here are two portraits, both of myself: the one before, the other after the cold Brandy-and-Water Cure. **1853** *Ibid.* XXV. 45 (*title of cartoon representing a difference of opinion between cabman and fare*) Before and after. **1889** *Puck* 3 July 307/1 I'm working a 'before and after' racket for a hair-renewer advertisement. **1902** *Little Folks* II. 432/1 Those restaurants which advertise by means of looking-glasses labelled 'before' and 'after'. As you go in you behold yourself very thin..as you go out..fat and well-satisfied. **1938** N. MARSH *Artists in Crime* iii. 24 You're not doing a 'before and after', like a strip advertisement.
B. *prep.* **I.** Of sequence in space.
1. a. Of motion: In advance of, ahead of.
c **1000** ÆLFRIC *Ex.* xiii. 21 And Drihten fór beforan him and swutelode him þone weȝ. *c* **1175** *Lamb. Hom.* 5 Al þe hebreisce folc þe eode efter him and biuoren him. **1388** WYCLIF *Ex.* xiii. 21 Forsothe the Lord ȝede bifore hem to schewe the weie. **1436** *Test. Ebor.* II. (1855) 75 Pore men berand..torches before my cors. **1526** *Pilgr. Perf.* (W. de W. 1531) 4 Theyr gyde..to go before them, and conducte or leade them. **1611** BIBLE *Josh.* viii. 10 And Ioshua..went vp; he, and the Elders of Israel, before the people to Ai. **1843** MACAULAY *Armada* 20 Behind him march the halbardiers; before him sound the drums.
b. Driven in front of, hurried on by; e.g. in the phrase *before the wind*: said of a ship sailing directly with the wind; also *fig.*
1598 W. PHILLIP *Linschoten's Trav.* in Arb. *Garner* III. 23 We got before the wind to the Cape of Good Hope. **1697** DRYDEN *Virg. Georg.* III. 822 Tisiphone..Before her drives Diseases and Affright. **1726** THOMSON *Winter* 171 Before the breath Of full exerted Heaven they wing their course. **1769** FALCONER *Dict. Marine* (1789) *Arriver*, to bear away before the wind. **1853** KINGSLEY *Hypatia* xviii, He had been only the leaf before the wind. **1865** DICKENS *Mut. Fr.* i, Kept the boat in that direction going before the tide. *Mod.* A man who carries everything before him.
c. *Hence*, with distinct causal force.
1535 COVERDALE *1 Sam.* viii. 33 Smytten before their enemies. **1590** SHAKS. *Mids. N.* III. ii. 423 Thou runst before me. **1593** —— *2 Hen. VI*, IV. ii. 37 Our enemies shall falle before us. **1599** —— *Hen. V*, III. Cho. 34 Downe goes all before them. **1850** MRS. BROWNING *Poems* I. 4 Recoil before that sorrow, if not this sword.
2. a. Of position or direction: In front of.
[**971** *Blickl. Hom.* 15 [He] ȝehyrde myccle meniȝo him beforan feran.] *a* **1200** *Moral Ode* 44 in *E.E.P.* (1862) 25 He is buuen vs & bi-neþen . biforen & bi-hinde. *c* **1250** *Gen. & Ex.* 2272 Al ðo briðere..fellen bi-forn ðat louerd-is fot. *c* **1340** *Cursor M.* 15023 (Trin.) Biforn her kyng childre cast braunches broken of bowȝe. *c* **1386** CHAUCER *Knts. T.* 776 He caryed al this harneys him byforn. *c* **1450** *Merlin* xv. 237 He dide after-mete chiualries be-fore the castell. **1593** HOOKER *Eccl Pol.* II. iv. §5 Wks. 1841 I. 240 When many meats are set before me. **1652** NEEDHAM tr. *Selden's Mare Cl.* 96 Wee decree that every Man possess his Vestibula or Seas lying before his lands. **1766** GOLDSM. *Vic. W.* viii. (1806) 42 On the grass-plot before our door. **1871** BLACK *Dau. Heth* xviii, Peering over the edge of the rock before him.
fig. **1848** MACAULAY *Hist. Eng.* I. 84 Great statesmen who looked far behind them and far before them.
b. In front of, at the beginning of (a writing).
1535 JOYE *Apol. Tindale* 19 Tindals incharitable pistle set before hys newe Testament.

c. ***before the face*** or ***eyes***: = 3.

c **1175** *Lamb. Hom.* 111 þine welan forrotiað biforan þine ehȝan. **1611** BIBLE *Ps.* xxxi. 22, I am cut off from before thine eies. **1711** ADDISON *Spect.* No. 12 ¶2 The Mistress.. scolds at the Servants as heartily before my Face as behind my Back. **1832** TENNYSON *Talking Oak* 3 Once more before my face I see the moulder'd Abbey-walls.

d. ***before the mast***: a phrase said of the common sailors, who are berthed in the forecastle in front of the fore-mast.

1627 CAPT. SMITH *Seaman's Gram.* ix. 39 The Boatswaine, and all the Yonkers or common Sailers vnder his command is to be before the Mast. **1840** R. DANA (*title*) Two years before the mast.

3. a. In front of so as to be in the sight of; under the actual notice or cognizance of; in presence of.

c **1000** ÆLFRIC *Ex.* xi. 10 [Hi] worhton ealle þa wundru.. beforan Faraone. *c* **1175** *Lamb. Hom.* 53 þe speket alse feire biforen heore euencristene. *a* **1300** *Cursor M.* 13137 Bifor þis king in his palis, His broþer doghter.. Com.. for to bale. *c* **1450** HENRYSON *Tale of Dog* 22 This summond is made befoir witnes. **1526** *Pilgr. Perf.* (W. de W. 1531) 156b, Though the kynge were before hym in his robes of golde, he wolde lytell regarde his royalte. **1601** F. GODWIN *Bps. Eng.* 398 Preaching at Sittingborne before a great auditory. **1611** BIBLE *John* xii. 37 Though he had done.. miracles before them. **1883** GILMOUR *Mongols* xvii. 209 Those who will confess Him before their countrymen.

b. *spec.* Said in reference to a tribunal, of the persons or matters of which it has cognizance.

c **1000** *Ags. Gosp.* Matt. xxvii. 11 Ða stod se Hælend beforan þam deman. *c* **1200** ORMIN 6901 Wreȝedd Biforr þe Romanisshe king. **1512** *Act 4 Hen. VIII*, x, Any office or offices found before Eschetour or Eschetours. **1601** F. GODWIN *Bps. Eng.* 451 Both of them being.. before the Pope, they fell.. into by matters and articling one against another. **1712** STEELE *Spect.* No. 270 ¶1 As ill an Action as any that comes before the Magistrate. **1838** ARNOLD *Hist. Rome* (1848) I. 17 The appeal was tried before all the Romans. **1883** *Law Rep.* xi. *Q. Bench Div.* 595 The proceedings before the police court.

c. with the added idea of deference toward.

1816 J. WILSON *City of Plague* I. i. 30 No knee.. hath bent before its altar. **1848** MACAULAY *Hist. Eng.* I. 146 The military power now humbled itself before the civil power.

4. In the (mental) view of; in the opinion, regard, or consideration of. *arch.*

c **1000** ÆLFRIC *Ex.* iii. 21 Ic sylle þison folce ȝife beforan þam Egiptiscean folce. *c* **1000** *Ags. Gosp.* Luke xv. 22 Fæder ic syngude on heofon & beforan ðe. *c* **1175** *Lamb. Hom.* 15 Eour eyþer suneȝað biforan drihten. *c* **1200** ORMIN 117 Teȝȝ wærenn biforenn God Rihhtwise menn. **1583** STUBBES *Anat. Abus.* II. 14 Though this be not theft before the world, nor punishable by penall lawes. **1611** BIBLE *Gen.* xliii. 14 God Almightie giue you mercie before the man.

5. a. Open to the knowledge of, displayed to or brought under the conscious knowledge or attention of. *Hence*, as an asseveration, ***before God!*** = As God knows, by God.

[*c* **1000** *Ags. Gosp.* Luke xii. 28 Swa hwylc swa me andet beforan mannum, þone mannes sunu andet beforan godes englum. *c* **1160** *Hatton G.* ibid., Beforen mannen.. beforen godes ængles.] **1393** LANGL. *P. Pl.* C. XVI. 139 By-for perpetuel pees · ich shal preoue þat ich seide, And a-vowe by-for God. **1599** SHAKS. *Hen. V*, V. ii. 149 Before God, Kate, I cannot looke greenely. **1711** ADDISON *Spect.* No. 9 ¶4 That of the Georges, which used to meet at the sign of the George.. and swear 'Before George.' **1712** STEELE *ibid.* No. 284 ¶6, I shall therefore with your Leave lay before you the whole Matter. **1815** *Scribbleomania* 234 The subject having been so recently before the public in all the diurnal prints. **1857** BUCKLE *Civilis.* I. xii. 671 The accusations brought against these great men are before the world.

b. Claiming the attention of.

a **1711** KEN *Div. Love* Wks. (1838) 217 That which now lies before you is to shew, how your abrenunciation is preparatory to the love of God. **1857** BUCKLE *Civilis.* I. i. 19 The problem immediately before us, is to ascertain the method.

6. In front of one in the course of action or of life; in prospect. **a.** Awaiting the coming action of, at the disposal of, open to. ***to have a penny before him***: i.e. in hand for future needs, remaining over (now *dial.*).

[*c* **1000** ÆLFRIC *Gen.* xx. 15 Land liþ ætforan eow.] **1382** WYCLIF *Gen.* xx. 15 The lond is bifore ȝow; where euer it shal plese to thee, dwel. *c* **1420** *Sir Amadace* xxix, In gud tyme were he borne, That hade a peny him bi-forne. **1535** COVERDALE *Gen.* xx. 15 Beholde, my londe stondeth open before the [**1611** is before thee], dwell where it liketh the. **1667** MILTON *P.L.* XII. 646 The World was all before them, where to choose, Their place of rest. **1882** HUGHES *Life D. Macmillan* ii. 10 He had the world before him.

b. Ahead or in front of (one) in the future; awaiting.

1807 CRABBE *Par. Reg.* II. 386 Their graves before them and their griefs behind. **1831** CARLYLE *Sart. Res.* III. v, The golden age.. which a blind tradition has hitherto placed in the Past, is Before us.

II. Of time.

7. Preceding in order of time; anterior to.

c **1000** *Ags. Gosp.* John i. 15 Se þe to cummene is æfter me wæs geworden beforan me. *c* **1200** *Trin. Col. Hom.* 219 þe laste man is sib þe formeste, þe was biforn us. *a* **1300** *E.E. Psalter* lxxvii. 5 Our fadres us bifore. **1480** CAXTON *Chron. Eng.* lvi. 40 They mowe lyuen as hyr auncestres dyde byforne hem. **1678** CUDWORTH *Intell. Syst.* I. i. §28. 35 All the other ancient Physiologers that were before Anaxagoras. **1819** BYRON *Juan* I. v, Brave men were living before Agamemnon. **1870** TROLLOPE *Phineas F.* 401 It is so easy to be a lord if your father is one before you.

8. Previous to, or earlier than (a point of time, date, or event).

c **1200** ORMIN 177 He shall newenn cumenn forþ Biforenn Cristess come. *a* **1300** *Cursor M.* 4236 Es noght his murning may a-mend I trou bi-fore his liues ende. *Ibid.* 5064, I saghe þe neuer be-for þis day. **1485** *Act 1 Hen. VII*, x.§1 Byfore the fest of Ester than next ensuyng. **1506** *Bury Wills* (1850) 108, I anulle and revoke all the villes mad by for this date. **1603** SHAKS. *Meas. for M.* IV. iv. 10 And why should wee proclaime it in an howre before his entring? **1712** STEELE *Spect.* No. 493 ¶4 He wondered I was not dead before now. **1779** JOHNSON *Dryden* Wks. VII. 182 It was written before the Conquest of Granada. **1832** HT. MARTINEAU *Life in Wilds* iii. 39 Would be back before dark. **1848** MACAULAY *Hist.* I. 561 Thirty-five years before this time.

9. †**a.** Previous to a past space of time, before the beginning of. *Obs.* In mod. usage *before three months* is replaced by *three months before*. Cf. A 5.

c **1340** *Cursor M.* 10675 (Laud), Hyt was by-fore many a day commoundid in the olde lay.

b. Previous to the expiration of a future space of time.

1865 TROLLOPE *Belton Est.* xxvii. 326 This grief, I hope, may be cured some day before long. *Mod.* I hope to be there before another year.

III. Of rank.

10. In precedence of, superior to; in advance of in development.

c **1230** *Hali Meid.* 19 Se schene biforen alle oðre. *a* **1300** in Wright *Pop. Sc.* 367 Al that a man hath bifore a best. **1526** *Pilgr. Perf.* (W. de W. 1531) 8b, The philosophers that trusted in theyr owne connynge.. that they had before other. **1676** HOBBES *Iliad* I. 266 Atrides is before you in command. **1755** JOHNSON s.v. *Before*, He is before his competitors both in right and power. **1848** MACAULAY *Hist. Eng.* I. 413 The nation which was so far before its neighbours in science.

11. In preference to; rather than.

c **1230** *Hali Meid.* 23 He menskeð ham se muchel biforen alle þe oðre. *c* **1380** WYCLIF *Sel. Wks.* (1871) III. 83 þow schalt not haue bifore me alyen Goddis. **1450** Q. MARGARET in *Four C. Eng. Lett.* 8 To do you worship by wey of mariage, bifore all creatures lyvyng. **1611** BIBLE *2 Sam.* vi. 21 The Lord, which chose me before thy father, & before all his house. **1653** WALTON *Angler* i. 16 Action is.. to be preferr'd before Contemplation. **1742** YOUNG *Nt. Th.* (1751) 243 Why then is health preferr'd before disease? *a* **1884** *Mod.* They would die before yielding. **1897** C. GARNETT tr. *Turgenev's Torrents of Spring* xliv. 240 Then Gemma.. wished him before everything peace and a tranquil spirit. **1911** D. H. LAWRENCE *White Peacock* II. ii. 231, I was a good animal before everything, and I've got some children.

12. In comparison with, in respect to.

1711 ADDISON *Spect.* No. 98 ¶1 The Women were of such an enormous Stature, that we appeared as Grashoppers before them. **1832** TENNYSON *St. Agnes* ii, So shows my soul before the Lamb, My spirit before Thee.

C. *Conj.* or *conjunctive adv.*

1. Of time: Previous to the time when.

a. *orig.* with *that*: now *arch.*

c **1200** ORMIN 964 Biforenn þatt te Laferrd Crist Wass borenn her to manne. *a* **1300** *Cursor M.* 10603 Beforn þat sco was of hir moder born. **1382** WYCLIF *John* viii. 58 Bifore that Abraham was maad, I am. **1542** UDALL *Erasm. Apoph.* 280a, Neither did he repaire vnto Sylla before that he had.. vanquyshed diuerse capitaines of enemies. **1611** BIBLE *John* i. 48 Before that Philip called thee.. I saw thee.

b. without *that*.

c **1325** *E.E. Allit. P.* A. 529 On oure byfore þe sonne go doun. *c* **1400** MAUNDEV. 18, 2000 ȝeer before oure Lord was born. **1503–4** *Act 19 Hen. VII*, xxxvi. Pream., Sir William .. lay both at Surgery and fesyk.. by the space of ij yeres.. byfore he was able to ride. **1588** A. KING *Canisius' Catech.* 76 The day befoir he sufferit. **1658** USSHER *Ann.* 405 Seleucus was dead before he came. **1711** ADDISON *Spect.* No. 1 ¶2, I threw away my Rattle before I was two Months old. **1816** J. WILSON *City of Plague* I. ii. 90 Ay, she intends to look before she leaps.

†**c.** Formerly also with *ere* (*than*), *or*. *Obs.*

1297 R. GLOUC. 40 Fyf hundred ȝer.. bifore Er þan oure Lord.. on erþe was ybore. **1340** HAMPOLE *Pr. Consc.* 9 Before ar anythyng was wroght. *c* **1400** MAUNDEV. 83 Before or thei resceyve hem thei knelen doun.

2. Of preference: Sooner than, rather than.

1596 SHAKS. *Merch. V.* III. ii. 303 Treble that, Before a friend.. Shall lose a haire. *Mod.* I will die before I submit.

D. Used as *adj.* and *sb.*

1. quasi-*adj.* = Anterior; previous.

1382 WYCLIF *1 Esdras* ix. 1 Risende up Esdras fro the beforn porche of the temple. *c* **1400** *Test. Love* I. (1560) 279 I rehearse thy before deed. **1599** SHAKS. *Hen. V*, IV. i. 179 Men are punisht for before breach of the Kings Lawes.

2. quasi-*sb.*

1850 TENNYSON *In Mem.* xxvi. 3 Oh, if indeed that eye foresee Or see (in Him is no before) In more of life true life no more. **1897** *Daily News* 6 Mar. 6/1 One who has witnessed the before and after of the abolition of pain.

E. *Comb.*

1. a. In combination with participles where the hyphen has merely a syntactical value, showing that *before* is an adverbial qualification of the following pple., with sense of 'previously, formerly'; as ***before-created***, ***-going***, ***-mentioned***, ***-named***, ***-noticed***, ***-recited***, ***-told***, ***-written***, BEFORE-SAID.

1786 BURKE *W. Hastings* Wks. XII. 360 The pernicious consequences of his *before-created unwarrantable, and illegal arrangements. **1606** HIERON *Wks.* I. 44 Let vs remember the *before-deliuered matter. **1382** WYCLIF *Rom.* iii. 25 Remiscioun of *bifore goynge synnes. **1677** HALE *Prim. Orig. Man.* I. iv. 99 Somewhat which hath been before said touching the Question *before-going. **1593** HOOKER *Eccl. Pol.* III. xi. §9 Wks. 1841 I. 331 Till the time *before-mentioned was expired. **1671** F. PHILIPPS *Reg. Necess.* 534 By the *beforemention'd Opinions of Sir Christopher Wray. **1815** *Encycl. Brit.* V. 781/1 The queen.. takes all the steps of the *before-mentioned pieces. **1467** *Bury Wills* (1850) 48 The ferme of the seide londys, medews, and pasture *bee-for-namyd. *a* **1626** BACON *New Atl.* in *Sylva* (1658) 12 All the Nations *beforenamed. **1864** *Times* 13 Oct., A dry chapter on the *before-named science. **1807** VANCOUVER *Agric. Devon* (1813) 127 The mattock, *before-noticed, is used to grub up.. the surface. **1786** BURKE *W. Hastings* Wks. XII. 399 In consequence of all the *before-recited intrigues. **1697** *Snake in Grass* (ed. 2) 288 Like Fox's Apology *beforetold. **1825** BENTHAM *Ration. Rew.* 123 A new and *before-unknown splendour. **1382** WYCLIF *2 Chron.* xxx. 5 As in the lawe it is *befornwriten.

b. The prep. in comb. with a sb., used *attrib.*

1865 C. M. YONGE *Clever Woman of Family* II. xiii. 248, I have just lighted on poor little Rosie's before-breakfast composition. **1898** *Daily News* 28 Sept. 5/1 The 'before luncheon' rehearsal. **1902** M. BARNES-GRUNDY *Thames Camp* 83 These before-breakfast expeditions. **1919** WODEHOUSE *Damsel in Distress* iv, A fellow with the appearance of a before using advertisement of an anti-fat medicine. **1926** D. H. LAWRENCE *Glad Ghosts* 64 The tender before-dawn freshness of a new understanding. **1966** 'W. COOPER' *Memoirs of New Man* III. ii. 214 We were going upstairs to have our before-dinner drink in the library. **1968** D. TORR *Treason Line* 24 He had had his first before-breakfast swim of the year.

c. The prep. in comb. with a sb., as ***before-life***.

1927 D. H. LAWRENCE *Morn. Mex.* 154 They were the lords of shadow, the intermediate twilight, the place of after-life and before-life.

†**2.** In many obsolete compound verbs and vbl. sbs. etc., esp. in Wyclif, representing L. *præ-* and *ante-*, some of which have mod. representatives with FORE-: as **before-bar**, to preclude, foreclose; **before-casting**, forecasting, pre-calculation; **before-come**, to prevent; **before-cut**; **before-gird**; **before-goer**, a predecessor; **before-graithe**, to prepare, make ready beforehand; **before-had**, held previously; **before-know**; **before-passing**, excelling; **before-ripe**, premature; **before-runner**; **before-say**, to predict, foretell; **before-sayer**, **-speaker**, a prophet; **before-see**; **before-set**, to promote, set over; **before-show**; **before-sing**; **before-stretch**, to extend forth; **before-take**, to anticipate; **before-taste**; **before-tell**; **before-walling**, *antemurale*, outer defence; **before-warn**; **before-weave**, to fringe, hem in, *prætexere*; **before-witting**, foreknowledge.

c **1449** PECOCK *Repr.* v. i. 477 What euer religioun lettith and *biforbarrith. *Ibid.* v. i. 478 Alle.. letten and *bifore-barren, ȝhe and forbeden, thilk religioun to be doon & usid. **1388** WYCLIF *Ex.* xxi. 14 If ony man sleeth his nieȝbore bi *beforecastyng. **1382** —— *2 Macc.* xiv. 31 As he knewȝ hym strongly *byforecummen of the man. —— *Dan.* iv. 11 *Bifore-kitte ȝe the braunchis therof. —— *Ps.* xvii. 33 God that *befor-girte me with vertue. —— *Gal.* i. 17 Nether I cam to Ierusalem to my *bifore goeris apostlis. *c* **1388** in *Wyclif's Sel. Wks.* 1871 III. 476 He þat is *biforegoar be he as a servant. **1382** WYCLIF *Ps.* lxxxviii. 5 In to withoute ende I shal *beforgreithe thi seed. *Ibid.* 15 Riȝtwisnesse and dom *beforgreithing of thi sete. —— *Gen.* xl. 13 Pharao shal restore thee to the *biforehad gree. **1388** —— *Gen.* xv. 13 God *biforeknew also the things to comynge. **1382** —— *2 Pet.* i. 16 The vertu and prescience, or *bifore knowing. —— *Ecclus.* xxxiii. 23 In alle thi werkes *beforn passende be thou [**1388** be thou souereyn]. **1388** —— *Num.* xiii. 21 The *before rijp grapes. **1382** —— *Ex.* xxxiii. 2 Y shal sende an aungel, thi *before renner. —— *Isa.* xlviii. 5, I *beforn-seide to thee fro thanne, er thei camen I shewede to thee. —— *Deut.* viii. 19 Loo! now y *before seye to thee, that vtterly thow schalt perishe. **1388** —— *Eccles.* iv. 13 That cannot *bifore se in to tyme to comynge, **1382** —— *Ecclus.* xvii. 14 Into eche folc of kinde he *beforn sette a gouernour. *c* **1440** *Promp. Parv.* 28 *Before sette, *prefixus*. **1382** WYCLIF *Gen.* xli. 11 A sweuen *biforeshewynge of thingis that ben to comun. **1388** —— *Ps.* cxlvi. 7 *Bifore synge ȝe to the Lord. —— *Ex.* xv. 21 With the whiche she beforesonge. *c* **1400** —— *Ex.* vii. 1 (MS. B), Profete, that is, interpretour other *biforspekere. **1382** —— *Ps.* xxxv. 11 *Beforstrecche thi mercy to men. ——*Ps.* lxxviii. 8 Soone shul *beforetaken vs thi mercies. **1526** *Pilgr. Perf.* (W. de W. 1531) 150 A *before tastynge of the ioye and glory of heuen. **1382** WYCLIF *Ps.* xlix. 6 Heuenes shulen his riȝtwisnes *beforetelle. —— *Isa.* xxvi. 1 The wal and the *biforwalling. —— *Wisd.* xviii. 19 The viseouns.. these thingus *bifornwarneden. —— *Job* xxxvi. 28 The cloudis.. that *beforeweuen alle thingus theraboue. *c* **1400** *Test. Love* III. (1560) 298 In the chapitre of Gods *befornewetting.. all these matters apertely may be founden.

beforehand (bɪˈfɔəhænd), *adv.* (and *a.*) Also 3–4 **biforen hond**(**e**, 4–6 **before hand**(**e**, 4 **bi-**, **by-**, **be-forhand**, **biforand**. [Originally two words, *before hand*, also *before the hand*, perhaps from the idea of one working *before the hand* of another, and so in anticipation of his action. But cf. L. *præ manu*, *manibus*, 'at hand, in readiness, in hand,' used in ME. as = 'beforehand.']

A. *adv.* **1.** In anticipation of something so as to be ready for it; in advance.

a **1225** *Ancr. R.* 212 Heo beoð þe lesse te menen, þet heo biuoren hond leorneð hore meister to makien grimme chere. **1534** TINDALE *2 Cor.* ix. 5 To come before honde [WYCLIF bifor] vnto you for to prepare youre good blessynge. **1551** RECORDE *Pathw. Knowl.* Pref., He.. was so skylfull in Astronomie, and coulde tell before hande of Eclipses. **1611** BIBLE *Mark* xiii. 11 Take no thought before hand what ye shall speake. **1710** STEELE *Tatler* No. 86 ¶1, I thought it proper to acquaint you before-hand.. that you might not be surpriz'd therewith. **1875** B. TAYLOR *Faust* I. iv. 78 Prepare beforehand for your part.

b. *spec.* in reference to payment in advance.

1393 LANGL. *P. Pl.* C. IV. 301 [Ich halde hym ouer-hardy oþer elles nouht trewe, þat *pre manibus* ys payed.] *c* **1450** HENRYSON *Tale of Dog* 88 Ane soume I payit haif befoir the hand. **1552** HULOET, Before handes, *præ manibus.* **1583** STUBBES *Anat. Abus.* II. 32 To pay a yeere or two yeeres rent before hande. **1755** SMOLLETT *Quix.* (1803) IV. 129 He demanded two ducats for the job, and they paid him beforehand. *Mod. maxim.* There are two bad payers—he that pays beforehand, and he that never pays at all.

c. ***to be beforehand with***: to anticipate, to be earlier than; to outstrip or forestall in action. (In this and the next, often used *adjectively*.)

1595 SHAKS. *John* V. vii. 111 Let vs pay the time but needfull woe, Since it hath beene before hand with our greefes. *a* **1619** DANIEL *Coll. Hist. Eng.* 30 Then was he before-hand with Pope Alexander..promising likewise to hold it..of the Apostolique Sea. **1701** W. WOOTTON *Hist. Rome* i. 203 If you are not before-hand with them, you will perish. **1863** MRS. C. CLARKE *Shaks. Char.* ix. 222 Like Napoleon, he knew the value of being beforehand with an enemy.

d. ***to be beforehand, to be beforehand with the world, to have something beforehand***: to have more than sufficient to meet present demands; to have money in hand for future contingencies; to have the balance on the right side. So ***to bring, get beforehand.*** All *arch.*

1526 *Pilgr. Perf.* (W. de W. 1531) 133 He wyll..labour diligently to brynge hym selfe beforehande agayn, & to recouer his losse. **1591** G. FLETCHER *Russe Commw.* (1857) 13 [They] regard not to lay up anything, or to haue it before hand. *c* **1645** HOWELL *Lett.* (1650) III. 9 Hee is the happy man who can square his mind to his means..he who is before hand with the world. **1651** FEATLY in *Fuller's Abel Rediv.* (1867) II. 228 He brought the college much beforehand, which before..was very much impoverished. **1712** STEELE *Spect.* No. 450 ¶3 Having little or nothing beforehand, and living from Hand to Mouth. **1771** FRANKLIN *Autobiog.* Wks. 1840 I. 59, I now began to think of getting a little beforehand. *c* **1812** MISS AUSTEN *Sense & Sens.* (1849) 25, I shall see how much I am beforehand with the world in the spring.

†**2.** Before this or that, previously. *Obs.*

a **1300** *Cursor M.* 3393 His sede suld multipli, als godd him had biforand hiht. *Ibid.* 6512 He tok him tablis of þe lay. As ȝe herd me bifor-hand say. **1382** WYCLIF *Gen.* xxviii. 19 The cyte Bethel, that biforn hoond was clepid Luza. **1413** LYDG. *Pylgr. Sowle* IV. i. (1483) 58 This appel was hanged vpon this drye tree whiche that grewe before hand vpon this grene florisshynge tree. *a* **1520** *Myrr. Our Ladye* 186 As I haue sayde ofte before hande.

†**B.** as *adj.* Ready, prepared. *Obs. rare.*

a **1704** LESTRANGE (J.), What is a man's contending with insuperable difficulties but the rolling of Sisyphus's stone up the hill, which is soon beforehand to return upon him again?

be'foreness. *rare.* [f. BEFORE + -NESS: cf. *aforeness.*] Priority, anteriority, pre-existence.

1625 GILL *Sacr. Philos.* I. 57 In the infinitie of being.. therefore there can bee no beforenesse nor afternesse. **1908** 'MRS. WILLETT' *Let.* 9 Oct. in *Proc. Soc. Psychical Res.* (1935) XLIII. 49 The words seemed to form in my brain before the pen set them down, just before, as if tripping on the written word—a sort of hair's-breadth beforeness.

be'foresaid, *ppl. a.* [See BEFORE E 1.] Mentioned, or treated of before or already. Now *arch.* or *Obs.*, its place being taken by AFORESAID.

a **1225** *Ancr. R.* 42 Ðeos biuore seide psalmes. *c* **1391** CHAUCER *Astrol.* 58 Eche of þe poyntis be-fornseyd. **1480** *Bury Wills* (1850) 55 The highe auter of the chirche of oure lady befornseyde. **1574** tr. *Littleton's Tenures* 79 b, In witnesse whereof, yᵉ parties beforesaid interchaungeably haue put to their seales. **1766** in Entick's *London* IV. 319 That you cause to be proclaimed the beforesaid fair.

be'foretime, *adv.* [f. BEFORE- + TIME, i.e. 'the time that was before': cf. *aforetime.*] In former time, formerly, previously.

a **1300** *Cursor M.* 2110 Affrick..þat bifor time was cald libye. *c* **1440** *Promp. Parv.* 28 Beforetyme, *ante, antea.* **1611** BIBLE *1 Sam.* ix. 9 He that is now called a Prophet, was beforetime called a Seer. **1865** SWINBURNE *Ball. Burdens* 36 And no more as the thing beforetime seen.

¶ Sometimes two words = Time preceding.

c **1450** *Knt. de la Tour* cxiii. 153 The bifore tyme they had be maried. **1614** CHAPMAN *Odyss.* VI. 392 Having touch'd no meat A long before time.

†**be'foretimes,** *adv. Obs.* [f. prec. + genitival *-s*: cf. *aforetimes.*]

a **1555** LATIMER *Serm. & Rem.* (1845) 192 Saints, that departed in faith out of this world beforetimes. **1647** W. BROWNE *Polexander* II. 83 In all appearance, he was the same man he had been before times.

beforn(e, obs. form of BEFORE.

beforrow, obs. Sc. f. BEFORE [cf. *morn, morrow.*]

be'fortune, *v. rare.* [f. BE- + FORTUNE *v.*, after *bechance, befall.*] *intr.* and *with dative obj.* To befall, happen, chance.

1591 SHAKS. *Two Gent.* IV. iii. 41 As much, I wish all good befortune you. **1855** SINGLETON *Virgil* II. 51 Whatever shall befortune, every hap Is by endurance to be overcome.

befoul (bɪ'faʊl), *v.* [f. BE- 5 + FOUL: a later formation, which ran parallel to BEFILE in ME., and at length displaced it.] *trans.* To make foul, cover with filth or dirt; often of moral filth; *esp.* in the proverbial ***to befoul one's own nest.***

c **1320** *Cast. Love* 1147 Al was his face bi-foulet wᵗ spot. *c* **1430** *Syr Gener.* 4610 The last he fond Darel Al be-fouled in the grauel. **1526** SKELTON *Magnyf.* 885, I befoule his pate. **1726** AMHERST *Terræ Fil.* v. 22 'Tis an ill bird which befouls his own nest. **1844** MACAULAY *Chatham, Ess.*, Fox had stumbled in the mire, and had not only been defeated but befouled.

Hence **be'fouler, be'foulment.**

1842 LD. JEFFREY in *Napier's Corr.* (1879) 388 A befouler of his own nest. **1862** F. HALL *Hind. Philos. Syst.* 272 The ignorant..think the blueness of the sky to be the befoulment of ether.

befraught, befreckle, befret, etc.: see BE- *pref.*

be'freeze, *v.* [f. BE- 1 + FREEZE *v.*] *trans.* To freeze up or over; to freeze intensely.

c **1200** ORMIN 13854 All iss itt uss bifrorenn. **1393** GOWER *Conf.* I. 220 Danubie..Whiche alle befrose thanne stood. **1623** BINGHAM *Xenophon* 69 Scorching and befreezing the limbes of the Souldiers.

befriend (bɪ'frɛnd), *v.* [f. BE- 2 + FRIEND *v.*]

1. *trans.* To act as a friend to, to help, favour; to assist, promote, further.

1559 *Mirr. Mag.* 613 (R.), That..you may befriend My wretched soule with quicke dispatch in death. **1607** SHAKS. *Timon* III. ii. 64 Will you befriend mee so farre as to vse mine owne words to him? **1709** POPE *Ess. Crit.* 474 Be thou the first true merit to befriend. **1752** YOUNG *Brothers* II. i, Wait an occasion that befriends your wishes. **1867** (29 June) BRIGHT *Amer., Sp.* 147 Persons..who befriended the negro in his bondage.

2. *spec.* of a Samaritan (sense c): to (set out to) give the companionship and support of a friend to (a client), esp. in a lay capacity; also *absol.* and *transf.* in other areas of social work.

1962 [implied at BEFRIENDING *vbl. sb.*]. **1965** E. C. VARAH *Samaritans* 34 Continuation Classes are able to go much more deeply into the big question of how to befriend. **1978** [see SAMARITAN *sb.* c]. **1983** *Brit. Med. Jrnl.* 12 Nov. 1436/2 Samaritan volunteers are..supremely ordinary people... Our only aim is to befriend and support the suicidal or despairing people who contact us.

Hence **befriender, befriending** *vbl. sb.* and *ppl. a.*; **befriendment;** also **befrien'dee,**

1681 C. COTTON *Poet. Wks.* (1765) 321 At the very first befriending Knock. **1856** LONGF. *Childr. Lord's Supper* 226 Hope, the befriending, does what she can. **1856** E. BOND *Russia 16th C.* 108 As the befriender of her subjects. **1962** *Lancet* 24 Nov. 1103/1 Some 60%..will go forward to the next stage of observation duty..under the charge of a senior Samaritan, answering the telephone, doing simple befriending perhaps, and car duties. **1965** E. C. VARAH *Samaritans* 24 From that moment (early in 1954) the original concept of a non-medical (but still professional) counselling service was abandoned, and its place was taken by the concept of a *befriending* service by lay volunteers. *Ibid.* 25, I could not have done what that befriender did. **1977** *Gay News* 24 Mar. 18/4 A marriage..cannot be re-routed by one evening's conversation with a befriender. **1977** *New Yorker* 8 Aug. 12/3 A befriending doctor tells Stroszek that he doesn't know how to look after himself. **1978** *Intercom* Mar. 2/3 Potential befrienders often go along to a club or day centre as part of their preparation and sometimes meet potential 'befriendees' there. **1983** *Brit. Med. Jrnl.* 12 Nov. 1436/2 Helping our callers to seek necessary medical advice is..a regular part of Samaritan befriending.

befringe (bɪ'frɪndʒ), *v.* [f. BE- 1 + FRINGE *v.*] *trans.* To border, furnish, or adorn with (or as with) a fringe. Hence, **be'fringed** *ppl. a.*

1611 COTGR., *Enfranger*, to befringe; to edge, or set with fringe. **1639** FULLER *Holy War* 78 Befringed with gold. **1737** POPE *Horace Ep.* II. i. 419 Let my dirty leaves..Befringe the rails of Bedlam and Soho. **1848** H. MILLER *First Impr.* xiv. (1857) 239 A placid stream, broadly befringed with sedges. **1884** *Manch. Exam.* 10 Dec. 3/7 Christmas cards..of the gorgeous befringed upholstered sort.

befriz, befrounce, befrumple, etc.: see BE- *pref.*

befrogged (bɪ'frɒgd), *a.* [f. BE- 7 + FROGGED *ppl. a.*] Decorated with frogging. So **be'frogging** *vbl. sb.*

1843 *Blackw. Mag.* LIV. 65 The betasseling, the befrogging, the flaunting attempts at 'costuming'. **1895** A. M. STODDART *J. S. Blackie* (ed. 3) I. ix. 205 A lustrous gown, befrogged and ample. **1958** E. HYAMS *Taking it Easy* 292 A crimson flannel dressing-gown heavily befrogged.

befroy, beffroy, obs. forms of BELFRY.

beft, *v. Obs. north. dial.* found only in *pa. t.* and *pa. pple.* [It is uncertain whether the present tense would be *beff*, of same origin as BAFF *sb.*¹, or *beft*:—Old Northumb. **beafta* or **beaftia* (for **behaftian*, f. BE- + OE. *haftian* to clap, strike with the flat of the hand). The late sb. BEFF may be merely for *baff*, or a wrong formation on *beft.*]

1. *intr.* To strike, give blows. *rare.*

[*c* **950** *Lindisf.* Matt. xi. 17 We mið hondum beafton.] *c* **1505** DUNBAR *Daunce* 40 Sum vpoun vdir with brandis beft.

2. *trans.* To beat, buffet, slap.

a **1300** *Cursor M.* 2264 Als þai had sare þar fra ben beft. *Ibid.* 15831 Wit bastons þai him beft ful grimli to þe grund. *c* **1375** ? BARBOUR *St. Johannes* 421 He rafe his clathis & befte his face. *c* **1505** DUNBAR *Fenȝeit Friar* x, [They] Beft him with buffets quhill he bled. **1513** DOUGLAS *Æneis* II. xi. 78 The wroth of the goddis has doun beft The cietie of Troye.

befuddle, befume, etc.: see BE- *pref.*

befuddle (bɪ'fʌd(ə)l), *v.* [f. BE- 4.] To make stupid with tippling; also, to confuse, to stupefy. Hence **be'fuddlement,** intoxication; confusion, stupefaction.

1887 in *N.E.D.* s.v. BE- 4. **1905** *Academy* 11 Feb. 132/2, I am not aiming at a general befuddlement..when I call it [*sc.* matter]..an expression of a relation. **1922** *Public Opinion* 11 Aug. 135/2 Freedom from the befuddlement of drink. **1926** *Contemp. Rev.* July 40 Their propaganda has befuddled public opinion. **1945** A. J. P. TAYLOR *Course German Hist.* 7 The only ones to escape from complete befuddlement are the Marxists.

befur (bɪ'fɜː(r)), *v.* [f. BE- + FUR *v.* and *sb.*] Chiefly in *pa. pple.*

†**1.** To fur over, encrust. *Obs.*

1581 T. NEWTON *Seneca's Thebais* 49 b, What rauenous Harpye Burd..all with filth, and dirty dung befurde.

2. To cover or deck out with furs.

1470–85 MALORY *Arthur* I. xvii, And Merlyn was so disguysed that kynge Arthur knewe hym not for he was al be furred in black shepe skynnes and a grete payre of bootes. **1842** *Fraser's Mag.* XXVI. 362 A..middle-aged man, bespectacled and befurred. **1859** HELPS *Friends in C.* Ser. II. II. ix. 199 Those clattering, befurred..gentry called soldiers. **1864** *Daily Tel.* 12 Mar., Our grotesquely befurred Aldermanic body.

befyle, var. of BEFILE *v. Obs.* to befoul.

beg (bɛg), *v.* Forms: 3 beggen, 4–7 begge, 4–6 begg, 6 (*Sc.*) bayg, 5– beg. [Of uncertain origin: see note below.]

1. To ask alms or by way of alms.

a. *trans.* To ask (bread, money, etc.) in alms or as a charitable gift; to procure (one's living) by begging.

a **1225** *Ancr. R.* 356 Scheome ich telle uorte..beggen ase on harlot..his liuenеð. **1377** LANGL. *P. Pl.* B. VI. 195 Blynde and bedreden..þat seten to begge silver. *c* **1440** *Promp. Parv.* 28/2 Beggyn bodely fode. *c* **1500** *Bk. Mayd Emlyn* xxvii. in *Poet. Tracts* (Percy Soc.) 28 Longe or she were dede, She wente to begge her brede. **1611** BIBLE *Ps.* xxxvii. 25 Yet haue I not seene the righteous forsaken, nor his seede begging bread. **1805** SCOTT *Last Minst.* 24 He begged his bread from door to door.

b. *intr.* To ask alms; *esp.* to ask alms habitually, to live by asking alms. Const. *absol.*; *of, from,* formerly *at,* a person; *for* alms.

[*c* **897** K. ÆLFRED *Gregory's Past.* 284 Hit is swiðe wel be ðæm ȝecweden ðæt he eft bedeciȝe on sumera, & him mon ðonne noht ne selle.] *a* **1300** *Cursor M.* 4708 Þai war sa fele þat begand [*v.r.* beggand] yode. **1382** WYCLIF *John* ix. 8 He that sat and beggide. **1386** CHAUCER *Sompn. T.* 4 Ther wente a lymytour aboute To preche and eek to begge. *a* **1450** *York Myst., Barbers* 8 What riche man gose from dore to dore To begge at hym þat has right noght. **1530** PALSGR. 446/1 I begge for the guylde of saynt Anthonye. **1562** J. HEYWOOD *Prov. & Epigr.* (1867) 138 Thou begst at wrong doore, and so hast begd longe. **1601** SHAKS. *Per.* I. iv. 41 Those palates..Would now be glad of bread, and beg for it. **1602** WARNER *Alb. Eng.* IX. xlvii. (1612) 218 Fring'd and ymbroidred Petticoats now begge [i.e. are worn by beggars]. *a* **1617** HIERON *Wks.* II. 392 We haue an ordinary saying ..'They which begge must not choose.' **1718** LADY M. W. MONTAGUE *Lett.* II. liv. 80 While the post-horses are changed, the whole town comes out to beg. **1856** FROUDE *Hist. Eng.* I. i. 74 Licences to beg were at that time granted.

2. *transf.* To ask as a favour or act of grace; *hence* to ask humbly, earnestly, supplicatingly; to crave, entreat. (With many const.: cf. ASK.)

a. *trans.* Const. *of, from* (formerly *at*). Also in colloq. phr. ***to beg, borrow, or steal.***

The early instances are closely connected with sense 1.

[**1340** HAMPOLE *Pr. Consc.* 3219 Þai may nathyng begg ne borowe, To help þam, þat þai war out broght [of purgatory]. *c* **1386** [see INDIGENCE 2 a]. **1399** LANGL. *Rich. Redeless* III. 149 Beggith and borwith of burgeis in tounes Ffurris of ffoyne, and oþer felle-ware.]

1526 *Pilgr. Perf.* (W. de W. 1531), The miserable nature of man..beggeth and craueth of god socour and relefe. **1534** TINDALE *Matt.* xxvii. 58 Ioseph..went to Pilate and begged the body of Iesus. **1590** SHAKS. *Mids. N.* I. i. 41, I beg the ancient priuiledge of Athens. **1605** *Bk. Com. Prayer, Gunpowd. Tr.*, All which we humbly beg for the sake of our blessed Lord and Saviour. **1667** PEPYS *Diary* (1879) IV. 239 All the world will believe, that we do go to beg a peace. **1711** STEELE *Spect.* No. 168 ¶11, I beg the Favour of you..to send us Word. **1746** H. WALPOLE *Corr.* 12 June, I have three favours to beg of you. **1752** MRS. LENNOX *Fem. Quix.* I. II. ix. 116 She refused to give him a glorious scarf which she wore, though he begged it on his knees.

1760 STERNE *Tr. Shandy* III. xxxviii. 177 He has taken in, Sir, the whole subject..begging, borrowing, and stealing, as he went along. **1794** F. BURNEY *Let.* 22 Mar. (1905) V. 240 He has been drawing a plan for it, which I intend to beg, borrow, or steal (all one), to give you some idea how seriously he studies. **1840** CARLYLE *Heroes* iii. 141 The Florentines begged back his [Dante's] body..the Ravenna people would not give it. **1859** *Macmillan's Mag.* Dec. 118/1 Not because they want to beg, borrow, or steal thoughts which are not theirs.

b. *absol.* or *intr.*; with same const.

1588 SHAKS. *L.L.L.* v. ii. 207 How I would make him fawne, and begge, and seeke. **1609** SKENE *Reg. Maj., Stat. Robt. II*, 48 Na Schiref..sall dar or presume to begge..fra the inhabitants of the cuntrie. **1718** POPE *Iliad* I. 19 Apollo's awful ensigns grace his hands: By these he begs. **1845** HOOD *Last Man* xxxvii, In vain My desperate fancy begs.

c. To beg *for* a thing.

1576 FLEMING tr. *Caius' Dogs* in Topsell *Four-f. Beasts* (1673) 139 Dogs..are taught..to beg for their meat. **1588** SHAKS. *Tit. A.* I. i. 455 Kneele in the streetes, and beg for grace in vaine. **1649** BP. REYNOLDS *Hosea* iii. 11, I must.. begge for pardon. **1876** GREEN *Short Hist.* iv. §3 (1882) 177 Single-handed [he] forced him to beg for mercy.

d. To beg *to do* a thing, or *that* a thing may be.

1576 THYNNE in *Animadv.* (1875) Introd. p. lvi, I most humbly..do submytt my cause and my selfe, begginge, uppon the knees of my harte, to come before your Lordship. **1591** SHAKS. *1 Hen. VI*, IV. i. 72, I should haue begg'd I might haue bene employd. **1605** —— *Lear* II. iv. 157 On my knees I begge, That you'll vouchsafe me Rayment, Bed, and Food. **1654** EARL ORRERY *Parthenissa* (1676) 679, I passionately beg'd to wait upon him. **1767** WILKES *Corr.* (1805) III. 197, I shall very soon beg to call the public attention to some points of national importance. **1855** MACAULAY *Hist. Eng.* III. 613 Shrewsbury begged that..he might be appointed.

†**e.** To beg *of* a person *for* a thing. *Obs.*

1590 SHAKS. *Mids. N.* III. ii. 108 If she be by, Beg of her for remedy.

f. To beg *of* (formerly *at*) a person *to do* a thing, or *that* a thing may be.

1604 SHAKS. *Oth.* V. ii. 229 He begg'd of me to steale 't. **1665** EVELYN *Mem.* (1857) III. 174 Our prisoners..beg at us, as a mercy, to knock them on the head. **1769** *Junius Lett.* xxi. 99, I must beg of you to print a few lines in explanation. **1799** SOUTHEY *Eng. Eclog.* vii. Wks. III. 35 [He] would come ..and beg of me To tell him stories of his ancestors. **1842** TENNYSON *Dora* 121, I will beg of him to take thee back.

g. *trans.* To beg a person *to do* a thing.

1675 LOCKE *Let. Person of Qual.* Wks. 1794 IX. 207 He begged me to consider..whether in such a case, etc. **1711** ADDISON *Spect.* No. 117 ¶5, I begged my friend Sir Roger to go with me. **1778** H. BOWMAN *Trav.* 266, I begged him to explain himself. **1876** GREEN *Short Hist.* iii. §5 (1882) 142 The king..begged him to write the story of the day's proceedings.

h. *Card-playing.* In All Fours (*U.S.* Seven-up), to ask for a point, or three additional cards and a new trump (said of the elder hand).

1793 *Sporting Mag.* II. 160/1 The Duke of York and Lord Barrymore were playing the game of All Fours... The Duke ..overlooked his cards, and..begged one, which was granted, though he held the ace, deuce, and jack of trumps. **1800** HOYLE & JONES *Hoyle's Games Improved* 308 The Game of All-Fours... If the eldest [hand] don't like his cards, he may, for once in a hand, say, *I beg*, when the dealer must either give a point or three more cards to each..player. **1897** R. F. FOSTER *Complete Hoyle* 289 If the eldest hand is not satisfied, he says: I beg; and the dealer, after examining his own hand, has the option of giving him a point or running the cards. *Ibid.* 290 Begging is resorted to by a player who holds no trumps.

i. Said of a dog trained to sit up and hold up its fore paws when told to beg.

1816 *Sporting Mag.* XLVIII. 23/2 He began to teach me [*sc.* a puppy] to beg, and to fetch and carry. **1837** JAS. PRIOR *Life Goldsmith* II. 33 Teaching a favourite dog to sit upright upon its haunches, or as is commonly said, to beg. **1854** J. G. WOOD *Anim. Life* 98 Four cats..had taught themselves the art of begging like a dog... They waited until they saw the dog sit up in the begging position, and immediately assumed the same attitude. **1884** *Century Mag.* Dec. 198/2 To squat back and raise his front legs from the ground, much in the position of a 'begging' poodle. **1927** E. V. LUCAS *More I see of Men* iv. 32 He begs even when there is no meal in progress.

3. a. In ***beg pardon, excuse, leave***, etc.: beside the strict sense as in 2, the whole expression is often merely a courteous or apologetic mode of asking what is expected, or even of taking as a matter of course.

1600 SHAKS. *A.Y.L.* III. v. 6 Falls not the axe vpon the humbled neck, But first begs pardon. **1602** —— *Ham.* IV. vii. 45 To-morrow shall I begge leaue to see your Kingly Eyes. **1711** ADDISON *Spect.* No. 74 ¶2, I must however beg Leave to dissent from so great an Authority. *Ibid.* ¶15, I shall only beg Pardon for such a Profusion of Latin Quotations. **1734** WATTS *Reliq. Juv.* (1789) 270 In the business of Transubstantiation, he begs your excuse. **1754** CHATHAM *Lett. Nephew* iv. 22 There is likewise a particular attention required to contradict with good manners; such as, begging pardon, begging leave to doubt, and such like phrases. **1802** MAR. EDGEWORTH *Moral T.* (1816) I. iii. 17 You begged my pardon. *Mod.* I beg your pardon; I did not quite catch what you said. I have received your letter, and beg leave to say in reply...

b. ellipt. for ***beg leave***.

1767 WILKES *Corr.* (1805) III. 197, I shall very soon beg to call the public attention to some points of national importance. **1898** *Westm. Gaz.* 29 Oct. 7/3 You say, 'I beg to take exception', which, of course, is not English at all. You mean, 'I beg (leave) to take exception'.

c. Also *ellipt.* in epistolary formulas of goodwill: to desire to send, to offer.

1755 H. WALPOLE *Let.* 7 Jan. (1903) III. 277 He would.. beg his compliments to Miss Montagu. **1816** A. CONSTABLE *Let.* 9 July in *J. Constable's Corr.* (1962) 137, I am glad to hear so good an account of Miss B's health, I beg best regards. **1836** DICKENS *Let.* 27 Feb. (1965) I. 134 Begging my best remembrances to Mrs. Thomson. **1839** —— *Let.* ? Apr. (1965) I. 546 Begging my best compliments at home.

†**4.** In Anglo-French and probably also in English '*begger* to beg' was used euphemistically in sense of 'exact as a benevolence.'

1292 BRITTON I. xxii. §11 Et de ceux qi coillent garbes en Aust, agneus et purceus, et issi vount begaunt, et les fount norir en lour baillies al grevaunce del people. *Ibid.* §15 Touz nos autres, qe gentz de religioum et autres gentz grevent.. par begger [*v.r.* beguigner] merrym ou fustz ou autre chose a eus.

5. †**a.** ***to beg a person***: to petition the Court of Wards (established by Hen. VIII, and suppressed under Chas. II) for the custody of a minor, an heiress, or an idiot, as feudal superior or as having interest in the matter; hence also fig. ***to beg*** (any one) ***for a fool*** or ***idiot***: to take him for, set him down as, a fool. *Obs.*

1584 D. FENNER *Def. Ministers* (1587) 51 Then would you haue proued vs asses, not begged vs for innocents. **1589** *Hay any Work* 71 It is time to begg the for a swagg. **1596** HARINGTON *Met. Ajax* 46 He proued a wiser man by much, then he that begged him. **1604** T. WRIGHT *Passions* III. i. 81 He may be begd for an ideot. **1636** DAVENANT *Wits* in *Dodsley* VIII. 509 (N.), I fear you will be begg'd at court, unless you come off thus. **1639** J. MAYNE *City Match* II. vi, And that a great man Did mean to beg you for—his daughter. **1696** STILLINGFL. *12 Serm.* ii. 59 That we may not therefore seem to beg all wicked men for fools. **1736** HERVEY *Mem.* II. 143 Moyle either deserved to be..begged for a fool, or hanged for a knave.

b. ***to beg off*** (trans., and intr. for refl.): to obtain by entreaty the release of (any one), or of oneself, from a penalty, or liability.

1741 RICHARDSON *Pamela* II. 292 What, said she, is the Creature begging me off from Insult? *a* **1884** *Mod.* He promised at first to go with us, but he has since begged off. **1854** E. RUSKIN *Let.* 28 Feb. in M. Lutyens *Millais & Ruskins* (1967) 145 What does John do but..say that he wishes to beg off to dine with his Father and Mother. **1966** *Amer. Speech* XLI. 174 He begged off because he had just moved from his librarianship at Kassel.

6. To take for granted without warrant; *esp.* in ***to beg the question***: to take for granted the matter in dispute, to assume without proof.

1581 W. CLARKE in *Confer.* IV. (1584) F fiij, I say this is still to begge the question. **1687** SETTLE *Refl. Dryden* 13 Here hee's at his old way of Begging the meaning. **1680** BURNET *Rochester* (1692) 82 This was to assert or beg the thing in Question. **1788** REID *Aristotle's Log.* v. §3. 118 Begging the question is when the thing to be proved is assumed in the premises. **1852** ROGERS *Ecl. Faith* 251 Many say it is begging the point in dispute. **1870** BOWEN *Logic* ix. 294 The vulgar equivalent for *petitio principii* is begging the question.

7. To make (one's way) begging.

1840 DICKENS *Old C. Shop* xliv, To-morrow we will beg our way to some quiet part of the country.

[The notion that *beg* had to do with the *bag* carried by a beggar, as if he were a 'bagger,' finds no etymological corroboration. The Flemish *beggen* appealed to by Littré under *Beguin* has no existence (Cosijn). Mr. H. Sweet has suggested that ME. *beggen* might be worn down from the rare OE. *bedecian* 'to beg,' found once (in *Past. Care*), and obscurely connected with Gothic *bidagwa* 'beggar,' f. *bidjan* 'to ask, beg.' This has much to recommend it; but the phonetic connexion of *beggen* and *bedecian* is by no means established, and there is the serious historical difficulty that no connecting links are to be found, there being no trace of the word in any form between K. Ælfred's *bedecian* before 900 and the regular use of the modern *beg* and *beggar* in the 13th c. Perhaps the most likely derivation is from the OF. *begart, begard*, and *begar*, med.L. *begardus* = BEGHARD, or its synonym *beguin*, BEGUIN, and deriv. vb. *beguigner, beguiner* 'to act the beguin.' It is known that the *Beghards* or *Beguins* were, or soon became, a lay mendicant order, and that in the 13th c. mendicants calling themselves, or called, by these names, swarmed over Western Europe, 'laici, qui sub prætextis cujusdam religionis fictæ Begardos se appellant.. qui extra religionem approbatam validam mendicantes discurrunt' (Council of Treves 1310). It is notable that in one of the two passages where Britton has Anglo-French *begger* to beg (see 4 above), the reading of two 14th c. MSS. is *beguigner*, showing that this was at any rate identical in sense with 'beg.' So also we find in Sym. de Hesdin *a* 1380 (Godef.), 'il n'y eust pas tant de begars et de begardes qui mengassent leur pain en oiseuse' (there would not have been so many begards, male and female, to eat their bread in idleness), which strongly suggests the Eng. *beggar*. About this time the words *beggare* and *beggen* arose in English: the exact process of their formation, and their actual relation to each other can only be conjectured: possibly *begg-en* was shortened from *beguin-er*, possibly it was taken from *begg-are*, and this directly from OF. *begar* above. The *-are* of the Ancren Riwle proves nothing, being the regular agent ending, as seen in *bacbitare, demare, reuare*, etc.]

†**beg**, *sb.*[1] *Obs.* Also 7 becg. [a. Osmanli *beg* 'prince, governor,' now pronounced as *bey*: see BEY, and cf. BEGUM.] A bey. Now only used as part of Eastern names. ***beg beg*** = BEGLERBEG.

1686 *Lond. Gaz.* No. 2198/3 The Grand Visier had sent a Becg..to desire a treaty. **1687** *Ibid.* No. 2285/2 The Beg Beg that commanded there..yielded at Discretion. **1818** JAS. MILL *Brit. India* (1848) II. 254 Togrul Beg..offered himself as a leader and bond of union to the Turks.

beglic, -lik, -luc, province of a bey, BEYLIC.

1614 SELDEN *Titles Hon.* 377 Beg is Lord..and *Begluc* is the Dignitie of the [Beg].

beg, *sb.*[2] [f. BEG *v.*] **a.** An act of begging.

1814 J. MAYNE *Jrnl.* 13 Sept. (1909) iii. 60 This was an invocation to some saint for a prosperous beg. **1912** GAMBIER-PARRY *Alleg. of Land* iv. 134 Letters simply mean begs, bothers, and bills. **1920** *Punch* 30 June 508/1 Agenda and minutes and constituents' grievances, and charitable appeals and ordinary begs.

b. *spec.* in All Fours (*U.S.* Seven-up) (see BEG *v.* 2 h).

1897 R. F. FOSTER *Complete Hoyle* 289 (*Seven-up*) No second beg is allowed, but when only two play, if either player is dissatisfied with the new trump he may propose to bunch the cards.

†**be'gab**, *v. Obs.* [f. BE- 2 + GAB *v.* to impose upon.] *trans.* To delude, impose upon.

1297 R. GLOUC. 458 Ichot ynam noȝt bygabbed. *c* **1375** ? BARBOUR *St. Clemens* 704 And wend [þat] he begabbit had bene Be wesch-crafte.

begad (bɪ'gæd), *int.* Not in polite use. [Altered form of *by God*; cf. *bedad, begar.*] An exclamation, used to give weight to a statement.

1742 FIELDING *J. Andrews* (L.) 'Begad, madam' answered he, 'tis the very same I met.' **1848** THACKERAY *Van. Fair* II. iv. 39 Only one, begad, in the World.

†**Begadores**, *sb. pl. Obs. rare*[−1]. The same as BEGHARDS or BEGUINS.

1586 T. ROGERS *39 Art.* (1607) 101 We stand therefore.. Against the Begadores in Almaine.

†**be'gair**, *v. Sc. Obs.* [app. ad. F. *bigarre-r*: see BEGARY; but perhaps associated with GAIR 'stripe, streak.'] *trans.* To diversify or variegate, as with stripes or streaks. Hence **be'gaired** *ppl. a.*

1552 LYNDESAY *Monarche* 5868 For cowlis blak, gray, nor begaird, ȝe sall, that day, get no rewaird. *a* **1609** A. HUME *Summer's Day*, Begaired..With sprainges of scarlet hue.

begall, begarnish, begash, etc.: see BE- *pref.*

†**be'gallow**, *v. Obs.* [f. BE- 2 + GALLOW *v.* to terrify; cf. OE. *agælwan, agǽlwan* to stupefy, throw into consternation.] *trans.* To frighten or terrify.

c **1320** *Sir Beves* in Ellis *Spec.* (1811) II. 171 That horse was swift as any swalowe, No man might that horse begallowe. [*MS. Cantab. Ff.* ii. 38. f. 124 (Halliw.) Ther myȝt no hors hym begalowe.]

began (bɪ'gæn), pa. t. of BEGIN.

begane, *obs. Sc.* form of BEGONE.

be'gar, *int.* Not in polite use = BEGAD.

[**1598** SHAKS. *Merry W.* I. iv. 123 By gar, I vill kill de Iack-Priest.] **1759** P. WHITEHEAD in Evans *O. Ball.* (1784) II. xxviii. 164 Begar we can beat them in heels.

†**be'gary**, *v. Sc. Obs.* [ad. F. *bigarrer* to diversify with contrasting colours: cf. *begair.*] *trans.* To variegate with colours, whether by way of adornment or of disfigurement.

1501 DOUGLAS *Pal. Hon.* I. xlvi, Velvot robbis maid with the grand assise, Dames, Satyne, begaryit mony wise. **1538** LYNDSAY *Syde Taillis* 35 The dust fleis hiest in the air, And all thar faces does begarie. *a* **1560** ROLLAND *Crt. Venus* I. 120 Barrit braid Begaryt all with sindrie silkis hew. **1657** COLVIL *Whigs Supplic.* (1751) 62 Some Whally's bible did begarie, By letting flee at it Canarie.

†**be'gary, begairie**, *sb. Sc. Obs.*; usually in *pl.* [f. BEGARY *v.*, or directly ad. F. *bigarré* pa. pple.] Ornamental facings of different colour or fabric worn on dress. (Jamieson.)

1575 *Declar. Gen. Assembly* in Calderwood's *Hist. Kirk* (1842) III. 354 All kind of broidering..all begaris of velvet, in goune, hose or coat. **1581** *Act James VI*, cxiii, Ony begairies, frenyies, pasments or broderie of gold, silver or silk.

begass(e, variant of BAGASSE.

1839 URE *Dict. Arts* 1195 Liquor which is speedily absorbed by the spongy begass. *Ibid.* 1197 The begass..is tied up in bundles, and..is finally stored in the begass-house. **1867** F. STEWART *Sorghum* 54 This property of the dried begasse suggests the propriety of using it for thatching. **1887** *Harper's Mag.* Feb. 336 An old begass chimney against the sky.

begat, arch. pa. t. of BEGET.

begaud, begaudy, begay, begaze: see BE-.

bège, var. BEIGE.

†**be'geck**, *v. Obs.* or *Sc.*; also **-gaik, -geik.** [f. BE- + GECK *v.*] To befool, to gull; to jilt.

a **1513** DUNBAR *Tua Mariit Wemen* 452 With gret engyne to begaik [*v.r.* beiaip] ther ielyus husbandis. **1768** ROSS *Helenore* 85 (JAM.) Ye'd better want him than he sud begeck you.

†**be'geck**, *sb. Obs.* or *Sc.* Also 8 **begeek.** [f. BEGECK *v.*] A cheating disappointment.

c **1600** *Rob. Hood* (Ritson) 79 And give them a begeck. *c* **1774** C. KEITH *Farmer's Ha'* in Chambers' *Pop. Sc. Poems* (1862) 32 He meets wi' a great begeek Frae empty binks.

begele, obs. form of BEAGLE.

begem (bɪ'dʒɛm), *v.* [f. BE- + GEM *sb.*] *trans.* To set about or stud with gems; also *transf.* Hence **be'gemmed** *ppl. a.* (also *absol.*).

1749 L. PILKINGTON *Mem.* I. 151 With glittering Glow-worms begemming each Tree. **1800** T. MOORE *Anacreon* l. 16 Flowers begemmed with tears of wine. **1852** D. MOIR *Daisy* v, Stars are the Daisies that begem The blue fields of the sky. **1916** BLUNDEN *Harbingers* 60 The lopped tree.. begems its leafits in a year. **1927** W. DE LA MARE *Told Again* 101 The three twigs of the trees—the silver and the gold and the begemmed.

†**begenild.** *Obs. rare.* Also **Begeneld, -el, -yld.** [App. f. BEGUIN + -ILD a female suffix: see BEGGILD. But in one passage the name seems to be applied to a male, and in the other it is doubtful.] A beggar; ? properly, a beggar woman.

1393 LANGL. *P. Pl.* C. x. 154 With a bagge at hus bak, a begeneldes [*v.r.* begenildys] wyse. *Ibid.* XI. 263 A begeneldes [*v.r.* begenyldis] douhter, that no curtesye can.

begess, obs. Sc. f. *by guess*: see GUESS.

beget (bɪˈgɛt), *v.* Pa. t. beˈgot, *arch.* beˈgat. Pa. pple. beˈgotten, formerly bi-, begeten, -get, begot. Forms as in GET. [Comm. Teut.: OE. *beȝit-an* = Goth. *bi-gitan*, f. *bi-* BE- + *gitan* to get. The normal form, from OE. *beȝitan*, would have been *be-yet*; for the substitution of *be-get*, see GET.]

†**1.** *trans.* To get, to acquire (usually by effort).

a **1000** *Beowulf* 2297 Fin eft beȝeat sweord. **1154** *O.E. Chron.* an. 1137 [He] wæs wæl underfangen fram þe pape, and begæt þare priuilegies. *c* **1200** ORMIN 13986 þærþurrh bigatt he þær att Crist þurrh himm to wurrþenn borrȝhenn. *a* **1225** *Ancr. R.* 196 Heo biȝited þe blisfule kempene crune. *a* **1300** *Cursor M.* 4913 Ne haue we wit vs trussed noght, Bot ..of our lele bi-geten [*v.r.* begityn] thing. **1393** GOWER *Conf.* I. 82 Whan he weneth most beȝete, Than is he shape most to lese. **1602** SHAKS. *Ham.* III. ii. 8 You must acquire and beget a Temperance that may giue it Smoothnesse.

2. To procreate, to generate: usually said of the father, but sometimes of both parents.

1205 LAY. 15792 þus wes Mærlin biȝeten and iboren of his moder. *c* **1300** *Beket* 119 Bituene hem biȝute was The gode child of wham we speketh. **1460** CAPGRAVE *Chron.* 15 The Sones of God..comouned with the Douteris of men..and thei begotin geauntis. **1611** BIBLE *Prov.* xvii. 21 He that begetteth a foole, doth it to his sorrow. **1711** STEELE *Spect.* No. 2 ¶5 He has good Blood in his Veins; Tom Mirabell begot him. **1788** J. POWELL *Devises* (1827) II. 205 Without having any children issue lawfully begotten or to be begotten. **1875** JOWETT *Plato* (ed. 2) I. 226 What could he have been thinking of when he begat such wise sons?

b. Const. *on*, *upon*, or *upon the body of*.

1297 R. GLOUC. 516 Sire Morisse of Berkeleye wedded.. Is doȝter, and biȝet on hire the kniȝt Sir Tomas. *c* **1386** CHAUCER *Melib.* ¶1 Melibeus..bigat vp on his wyf..a doghter. **1509–10** *Act 1 Hen. VIII*, xix. Pream, The heires males whiche he shulde begett on the body of the said Elizabeth. **1641** HINDE *J. Bruen* xxx. 92 [Wakes] are begotten of Sathan, upon the body of that Whore of Rome. **1742** YOUNG *Nt. Th.* IX. 447 Num'rous is the race Of blackest ills..Begot by madness on fair liberty.

†**c.** = GET (with child). *Obs.*

c **1450** *Knt. de la Tour* 6 That other knight..begate her with childe. **1603** SHAKS. *Meas. for M.* v. i. 517 There's one Whom he begot with childe. **1611** CORYAT *Crudities* 101 For shee reported that shee was begotten with child by a certaine Dragon.

3. *Theol.* Applied to the relationship of the Father to the Son in the Trinity; also to the spiritual relationship of God to man in regeneration.

1388 WYCLIF *1 Peter* i. 3 Which begat [**1382** gendride, **1611** hath begotten] vs aȝen in to lyuyng hope. **1534** TINDALE *1 John* v. 1 Every one that loveth him which begat [WYCLIF gendred, **1611** begate], loveth him also which was begotten [W. borun] of him. **1549** *Bk. Com. Pr.*, *Athanas. Cr.*, The Son is of the Father alone: not made, nor created, but begotten. **1587** GOLDING *De Mornay* vi. 71 God.. begate the Sonne or Word equall to himselfe.

4. *fig.* and *transf.* To call into being, give rise to; to produce, occasion.

1581 LAMBARDE *Eiren.* II. ii. (1588) 124 The doing thereof doth also beget a forfeiture of the Recognusance that is made. **1588** SHAKS. *L.L.L.* II. i. 69 His eye begets occasion for his wit. **1675** TRAHERNE *Chr. Ethics* vi. 71 Fire begets water by melting ice. **1691** RAY *Creation* II. (1704) 335 How can all these things..but beget Wonder? **1845** MIALL *Nonconf.* V. 133 One falsehood usually begets a necessity for a dozen others.

†**beˈget**, *sb. Obs.* Forms: 2–3 biȝeate, biȝæte, 2–4 biȝete, 4–5 beȝete, biyete, beyete, 4 byyate, beȝeitt, biyett, bigeet, ? bygate, ? bigete; 4–5 bigate, 5 begete. [ME. f. BEGET *v.*; cf. OE. *ǫndȝit*, *-ȝet*, f. *ǫnȝitan*.]

1. The action of acquiring; acquisition, gaining; acquisition, gain, profit, advantage.

c **1175** *Lamb. Hom.* 23 Iblesced beo þet þus went lure to biȝeate. *a* **1225** *Ancr. R.* 166 þe þridde reisun of þe worldes fluhte is þe biȝeate of heouene. **1393** GOWER *Conf.* Prol. I. 14 For pompe and for beȝete.

b. *concr.* The thing acquired; acquisition, acquirement, gain, proceeds; spoils of war.

c **1200** *Trin. Coll. Hom.* 37 þe fule man..of unrihte biȝete ofte filleð [his wombe]. *a* **1225** *Ancr. R.* 160 He biȝet þeos þreo biȝeaten. *c* **1250** *Gen. & Ex.* 895 Habram gaf him ðe tiȝðe del Of alle is biȝete. *c* **1430** *Syr Gener.* 4810 Al to smal is oure begete.

2. Procreation, generation; begetting.

c **1330** *Arth. & Merl.* 1437 Al he teld ther the king Of his bigete, of his bereing.

b. *concr.* That which is begotten, progeny.

c **1315** SHOREHAM 68 And eke hem that hym hebbeth so, And alle hare bi-ȝete. *a* **1400** *Octouian* 848 He was som gentylmannes beyete.

†**beˈgetel**, *a. Obs.* [f. BEGET *v.* + *-el*, -LE, repr. an OE. **beȝitol*.] Advantageous, profitable.

c **1250** *Gen. & Ex.* 1992 Wið putifar..He maden swiðe biȝetel forward.

begettal (bɪˈgɛtəl). *rare.* [f. BEGET *v.* + -AL[1], cf. *committal*.] Begetting.

1873 C. M. DAVIES *Unorth. London* 247 They believe in his preternatural begettal by the Holy Spirit.

begetter (bɪˈgɛtə(r)). Also 5 begetare, 6 begettor. [f. BEGET *v.* + -ER[1].]

1. One who begets; a procreator.

c **1440** *Promp. Parv.* 28/2 Begetare, as a fathyr, *genitor*. Begetare, as mothere, *genitrix*. **1587** FENNER *Def. Ministers* (1587) 126 The begettor of this base-borne childe. **1616** CHAPMAN *Musæus* 200 Blest was thy great begetter; blest was she Whome womb did bear thee. **1875** G. SMITH *Assyr. Discov.* 321 Esarhaddon, king of Assyria,..my begetter.

2. *fig.* and *transf.* The agent that originates, produces, or occasions.

1587 GOLDING *De Mornay* iii. 28 The onely one God..the Begetter of the Soules of the other Gods. **1606** SHAKS. *Sonnets* (*Inscr.*) To the onlie begetter of these insuing sonnets. **1637** BASTWICK *Litany* III. 11 The word of God is both the begetter of faith, and the increaser of it. **1884** *Pall Mall G.* 2 Aug. 4/2 Dr. Alfred Wright, the ostensible begetter of these very light and graphic sketches.

beˈgetting, *vbl. sb.* [f. as prec. + -ING[1].] The action or process of generating or producing; generation; *also*, the result of the action, progeny.

c **1300** *K. Alis.* 6866 Er thou weore in thy bygetyng. **1398** TREVISA *Barth. De P.R.* VI. xiv. (1495) 198 A fader is heed and welle of bygetynge and gendringe. **1611** TOURNEUR *Ath. Trag.* IV. ii. 104 Tush! they onely father bastards That father other men's begettings. **1765** TUCKER *Lt. Nat.* II. 469 Begotten, not of bloods, nor of the will of the flesh, nor of the will of man, but of God. Here is a variety of begettings.

beˈgetting, *ppl. a.* [f. BEGET *v.* + -ING[2].] Producing, creative; chiefly in comb., as ***spring-begetting***, ***life-begetting***, etc.

1597 DRAYTON *Mortimer.* 42 Like Promethian life-begetting flame. **1848** KINGSLEY *Saint's Trag.* II. x. 126 Marriage is the life-long miracle, The self-begetting wonder.

beggable (ˈbɛgəb(ə)l), *a.* [f. BEG *v.* + -ABLE.] Capable of being begged, or obtained by begging.

a **1680** BUTLER *Rem.* (1759) II. 88 Things that are disposed of or not beggable.

beggar (ˈbɛgə(r)), *sb.* Forms: 3 beggare, 4–5 beggere, 4–7 begger, 4– beggar. [See BEG *v.* The spelling in *-ar* has been occasional from 14th c., but the usual form in 15–17th c., as an ordinary agent-noun from BEG, was *begger*: see 3].

1. a. One who asks alms, especially habitually; one who lives by so doing.

a **1225** *Ancr. R.* 168 Hit is beggares [*v.r.* beggilde] rihte uorte beren bagge on bac. *a* **1300** *K. Horn* 1133 þu wenest I beo a beggere. **1382** WYCLIF *Deut.* xv. 4 Nedi and begger there shal not be amongȝow. *c* **1400** *Destr. Troy* xxxv. 13549 And now me bus, as a beggar, my bred for to thigge. **1480** CAXTON *Chron. Eng.* ccxxxvii. 262 Beggers that were knowe openly for nedy poure beggers. *c* **1538** STARKEY *England* iii. 91 The multytude of Beggarys in our cuntrey. **1610** SHAKS. *Temp.* II. ii. 34 They will not giue a doit to relieue a lame Begger. **1611** BIBLE *Luke* xvi. 20 A certaine begger named Lazarus. **1673** RAY *Journ. Low C.* 423 Near the door..an incredible number of Beggers. **1797** GODWIN *Enquirer* II. iii. 187 Those who pursue the trade of a common beggar. **1857** KINGSLEY *Misc.* II. 326 The beggars became a regular fourth-estate.

b. ***sturdy beggar***: an able-bodied man begging without cause, and often with violence.

c **1538** STARKEY *England* 176 Thys grete nombur of sturdy beggarys therby schold utturly be taken away. **1597** *Act 39 Eliz.* iv. §1 For the suppressing of rogues, vagabonds and sturdy beggers. **1711** STEELE *Spect.* No. 48 ¶5 The Heroes appear only like sturdy Beggars. **1860** R. VAUGHAN *Mystics* (ed. 2) I. 143 There are some sturdy beggars who wander about the country availing themselves of the name of Beghard to lead an idle life.

c. In many proverbial expressions.

1539 TAVERNER *Erasm. Prov.* (1552) 9 One begger byddeth wo that another by the dore shuld go. *Ibid.* 39 A beggars scryp is never fylled. **1562** J. HEYWOOD *Prov. & Epigr.* (1867) 23 Beggers should be no choosers. *Ibid.* 38 The begger maie syng before the theefe. *Ibid.* 171, I know him as well as the begger knowth his bag. **1581** RICH *Farew. Mil. Prof.*, She sware by no beggers she would be so revenged. **1594** *2nd Pt. Contention* (1843) 132 Beggers mounted run their horse to death. **1613** *Uncasing Machiavil's Instr. Sonne* 7 Proue the prouerbe often tolde, 'A carelesse Courtier yong, a Begger olde.' **1617** MORYSON *Itin.* III. II. i. 61 Who know the way as well as a begger knowes his dish. **1682** BUNYAN *Holy War* 260 When Cerberus and Mr. Profane met, they were presently as great as beggars. **1690** W. WALKER *Idiom. Anglo-Lat.* 46 Sue a beggar and catch a louse. **1706** SWIFT *Polite Conv.* i. (D.) Know him? Ay Madam, as well as a beggar knows his dish. **1809** COBBETT *Pol. Reg.* XV. xii. 429 Our own old saying: 'Set a beggar on horse-back, and he'll ride to the devil.'

2. *transf.* One in indigent circumstances.

1340 *Ayenb.* 36 Vor hire time-zettinge hi destrueþ and makeþ beggeres þe knyȝtes. **1535** COVERDALE *Ecclus.* xxxvii. 30 Some man..can geue.. prudent councell..and contynueth a begger. *c* **1550** CHEKE *Matt.* v. 3 Happí be yᵉ beggars in sprijt. **1596** SHAKS. *Merch. V.* III. i. 48 A begger that was vsd to come so smug vpon the Mart. **1621** BURTON *Anat. Mel.* I. ii. III. xv. (1651) 128 Origanus assigns the same cause why Mercurialists are so poor, and most part beggers.

†**3.** One who begs a favour; one who entreats, a suppliant. *Obs.* (The regular mod. form of this and 4 would be *begger*, as 'a begger for mercy.')

1589 PUTTENHAM *Eng. Poesie* III. xxiv. (1811) 247 He had spent much and was an ill beggar: the king aunswered..If he be ashamed to begge, we are ashamed to giue. **1601** SHAKS. *All's Well* I. iii. 22 Wilt thou needes be a begger? *Clo.* I doe beg your good will in this case.

†**4.** One who begs the question. *Obs.*

1579 FULKE *Heskins's Parl.* 130 O shamelesse begger, that craueth no lesse then the whole controuersie to be giuen him! *a* **1694** TILLOTSON (J.) These shameful beggars of principles..assume..to be men of reason.

5. Applied to a mendicant friar or to a Beghard.

c **1384** WYCLIF *De Eccl.* Sel. Wks. III. 359 Newe sectis or ordris, boþe possessioneris & beggeris shulden ceese bi Cristis lawe. *c* **1400** *Rom. Rose* 7258 But beggers [Fr. *Beguins*] with these hodes wide, With sleight and pale faces lene.

6. As a term of contempt: **a.** = Mean or low fellow.

a **1300** *Cursor M.* 13662 'Herd yee þis lurdan,' coth þai, 'þat beggar þat in sin was goten?' *c* **1460** *Towneley Myst.* 70 If siche a beggere shold My kyngdom thus reyf me. **1869** MISS BROUGHTON *Not Wisely* 121 A sulky ill-conditioned sort of beggar.

b. Used familiarly or playfully. (Cf. *baggage*, *dog*, *rogue*, etc.)

1833 MARRYAT *P. Simple* xxxiii, Sir John left Sir W. Parker..to watch the Spanish beggars. **1857** HUGHES *Tom Brown* I, You're uncommon good-hearted little beggars. **1873** BLACK *Pr. Thule* xvii. 267 The cheekiest young beggar I have the pleasure to know.

c. In *cards*, applied to the small cards 2 to 10.

d. A person who is remarkably adept at or keen on a particular pursuit, subject, etc. Const. *for* or with *inf. colloq.*

1859 *Chambers's Jrnl.* 29 Jan. 77/1 He was..what Mr. Leech's miner denominated the conciliating curate, 'a beggar to argue', a stiffish one to tackle upon any mortal subject. **1949** PARTRIDGE *Dict. Slang* (ed. 3) 987/2 *A beggar for work*, a constant hard worker: coll.: late C. 19–20.

7. *Comb.* (in which *beggar* approaches in use to an adj.) General relations: **a.** appositive, as ***beggar-beard***, ***-body***, ***-boy***, ***-brat***, ***-child***, ***-clan***, ***-girl***, ***-king***, ***-maid***, ***-man***, ***-wife***, ***-woman***; **b.** *attrib.* (of or befitting a beggar, beggarly), as ***beggar-fear***, ***-pride***, ***-sport***, ***-whine***; **c.** ***beggar-wise*** adv.; ***beggar-patched*** adj.

1955 J. R. R. TOLKIEN *Return of King* 354 Here's your fee, *beggar-beard. **1765** TUCKER *Lt. Nat.* II. 126 Above the dirty *beggar boys in the street. *a* **1631** DRAYTON *Wks.* I. 244 (JOD.) Those *beggar brats wrapped in our rich perfumes. **1938** L. MACNEICE *Earth Compels* 54 The shapes of mist like hooded *beggar-children. *a* **1821** KEATS *The Poet*, Poorest of the *beggar-clan. **1593** SHAKS. *Rich. II*, I. i. 189 Or with pale *beggar-feare impeach my hight. **1863** E. CLAYTON *Queens of Song* II. 172 She heard a *beggar-girl sing beneath the window of her hotel. **1938** YEATS *New Poems* 32 Some boast of *beggar-kings. **1592** SHAKS. *Rom. & Jul.* II. i. 14 When King Cophetua lou'd the *begger Maid. **1605** —— *Lear* IV. i. 32 Is it a *Beggar-man? *Oldm.* Madman, and beggar too. **1882** R. STEVENSON in *Longm. Mag.* I. 74 That wooden crowd of kings and genies, sorcerers and beggarmen. **1658** A. FOX tr. *Wurtz' Surg.* I. iv. 15 A *Beggar-patch'd coat of severall sorts of old rags. **1764** GOLDSM. *Trav.* 277 Here *beggar pride defrauds her daily cheer. **1652** BROME *Jov. Crew* v. Wks. 1873 III. 451 The Gentleman..that would have made *Beggar-sport with us. **1820** KEATS *Isabella* xvii, Paled in and vineyarded from *beggar-spies. **1796** SCOTT *Wild Huntsm.* xxvii, To stop my sport Vain were thy cant and *beggar whine. **1623** J. PENKERTON *Handf. Hon.* IV. i, Wealth despise Which they that doat vpon, liue *beggar-wise. **1530** PALSGR. 197/1 *Beggar woman, *belistresse*. **1594** *1st Pt. Contention* (1843) 53 One of them was stolne away by a begger-woman. **1859** TENNYSON *Enid* 1528 This silken rag, this beggar-woman's weed.

8. Special combinations: †**beggars' bolts**, stones; †**beggar-brach**, a female beggar (see BRACH, a female hound); **beggar's brown** (*colloq.*), Scotch snuff; †**beggar's-bush**, a bush under which a beggar finds shelter (name of 'a tree near Huntingdon, formerly a noted rendezvous for beggars'—Brewer), *fig.* beggary, ruin; **beggar's buttons**, the heads of the burdock; †**beggar-charge**, allowance to a steward for the relief of beggars; **beggar's-haven**, a beggar's shelter, beggary; **beggars'-lice**, the plant called Clivers, also (in U.S.) applied to certain boraginaceous plants, whose prickly fruit or seeds stick to the clothes; †**beggar-niggler**, one who toys with a beggar-woman; †**beggar's plush**? cotton velvet, or ? corduroy; †**beggar-staff**, the staff of a beggar, *fig.* beggary; **beggar's tape**; **beggar-tick** (in U.S.), a name for the plant *Bidens frondosa*; †**beggar's velvet**, see **beggar's plush**; also quot.; **beggar-weed** (see quot.).

1584 HUDSON *Judith* in Sylvester's *Du Bartas* (1608) 698 A pack of country clowns..that them to battail bownes With *beggers bolts and levers. *a* **1652** BROME *Jov. Crew* III. Wks. 1873 III. 401 A brace of the handsomest *Beggar-braches that ever grac'd a Ditch or a Hedge-side. **1879** JAMIESON *Sc. Dict.*, *'Beggar's brown*..light brown snuff which is made of the stem of tobacco. **1592** GREENE *Upst. Courtier* (1871) 6 Walking home by *Beggars Bush for a penance. *a* **1640** DAY *Peregr. Schol.* (1881) 75 Notwithstanding..Industry..he was forct to take a napp at *Beggars Bushe. **1677** YARRANTON *Eng. Improv.* 99 We are almost at *Beggars-bush, and we cannot tell how to help our selves. *a* **1652** BROME *Jov. Crew* II. Wks. 1873 III. 382 Here's five and twenty pounds for this Quarters *Beggar-charge. **1532** *Dice Play* (1850) 22 He must needs sink, and gather the wind into *beggars haven. **1880** *New Virginians* I. 133 Look at the weeds..cockle-burrs, Spanish needles, *beggars'-lice. *a* **1652** BROME *Jov. Crew* II. Wks. 1873 III. 392 Do we look like *beggar-nigglers? **1688** *Lond. Gaz.* No. 2379/4 A Person..in a dark grey Cloth Coat..Breeches of *Beggars Plush. ? **1506** *Plumpton Corr.* 199 We are brought to *begger staffe. **1864** ATKINSON *Whitby Gloss.*, *Beggarstaff*, 'They brought him to *beggarstaff.' **1796** GLASSE *Cookery* xviii. 289 Tie it very tight with *beggar's

tape. **1854** Thoreau *Walden, Ess.* 202 It was over-run with Roman worm-wood and *beggar-ticks, which last stuck to my clothes. **1711** *Lond. Gaz.* No. 4888/3 A green *Beggars Velvet Frock with Metal Buttons. **1847** Halliwell, **Beggar's velvet*, the light particles of down shaken from a feather-bed, and left by a sluttish housemaid to collect under it. **1878** Britten *Plant-n.* I. 33 **Beggar-weed*, a name applied to several plants by farmers, either because they denote poverty of soil, or because they are such noxious weeds as to beggar the land. **1884** *Times* 15 Apr. 8 The '*beggar weed' (unknown in England)..stands 6 feet high all over the fields.

beggar ('bɛgə(r)), *v.* 6–7 **begger.** [f. prec. sb.]
1. *trans.* **a.** To make a beggar of, exhaust the means of, reduce to beggary; to impoverish.
1528 Roy *Sat.* 845 Oure master shalbe beggered Of all his ryche possession. **1592** Greene *Upst. Courtier* in *Harl. Misc.* (Malh.) II. 232 These lawiers..beggering their clients..purchase to themselues whole lordships. **1594** Shaks. *Rich. III*, I. iv. 145 [Conscience] beggars any man that keepes it. **1650** Fuller *Pisgah* IV. i. 5 Excess will begger wealth it-self. **1709** Steele *Tatler* No. 25 ¶8 He would beggar him by the exorbitant Bills which came from Oxford. **1864** Bright *Distrib. Land, Sp.* (1876) 455 The Cornlaw..beggared hundreds and thousands of the people.
b. *fig.*
1642 Fuller *Holy & Prof. St.* II. iv. 61 Beggering the Opponent to maintain such a fruitful generation of absurdities. **1679** Plot *Staffordsh.* (1686) 152 It sometimes beggers it [the ground] for ever after. **1735** Bolingbr. *Parties* 19 (T.) To beggar them out of their sturdiness.
2. To exhaust the resources of, go beyond, outdo; as in *to beggar description, compare*, etc.
1606 Shaks. *Ant. & Cl.* II. ii. 203 For her owne person It beggerd all discription. **1789** Mrs. Piozzi *Journ. France* I. 363 A place which beggars all description. **1815** *Scribbleomania* 15 Hunger's a sauce, sir, that beggars compare. **1825** Cobbett *Rur. Rides* 297 It beggars one's feelings to attempt to find words whereby to express them.
3. *Comb.* **beggar-my-neighbour**: a simple game at cards often played by children. Also *fig.*
1734 *Poor Robin's Almanack* C6 The Lawyers play at beggar my Neighbour. **1777** Brand *Pop. Antiq.* (1849) II. 396 *Birkie*, a childish game at cards: in England..called Beggar-my-neighbour. **1843** Southey *Doctor* cxlii. (D.) I cannot call to mind anything which is estimated so much below its deserts as the game of Beggar-my-neighbour. **1874** Helps *Soc. Press.* xxiv. 355, I believe he would throw some spirit and some hope into 'Beggar my Neighbour.' **1930** *Times Educ. Suppl.* 20 Dec. 511/2 The..argument..that the scale for Middlesex should be nearer to that for London..was merely playing 'beggar-my-neighbour'. **1958** *Spectator* 1 Aug. 174/3 The continuous concentration on national selfishnesses and beggar-my-neighbour is distasteful.

beggardom ('bɛgədəm). [see -DOM.] The beggar's profession; the mendicant fraternity.
1882 *Athenæum* 23 Dec. 842/3 The kindly hospitality of the farmers on whose charity beggardom mainly throve. **1884** C. Dickens *Dict. Lond.* 36/1 London beggardom is a close corporation.

beggared ('bɛgəd), *ppl. a.* [f. BEGGAR *v.* + -ED[1].] Reduced to destitution; impoverished.
1599 Shaks. *Hen. V*, IV. ii. 43 Bigge Mars seemes banqu'-rout in their begger'd Hoast. **1790** Burke *Fr. Rev.* Wk. V. 88 The discredited paper securities of impoverished fraud, and beggared rapine, held out as a currency for the support of an empire. **1857** Buckle *Civiliz.* I. xi. 653 A rapacious government, and a beggared exchequer.
fig. *c* **1600** Shaks. *Sonn.* lxvii, Beggerd of blood to blush through liuely vaines. **1742** Young *Nt. Th.* iv. 425 Their beggar'd blaze wants lustre for my lay.

'beggarer. [f. as prec. + -ER[1].] One who beggars or impoverishes.
1630 Brathwait *Eng. Gentl.* (1641) 161 Enrichers of their retinue, but beggerers of their posterity. *a* **1640** Day *Parl. Bees* x. 65 The poore fryes beggerer and rich Bees betrayer.

'beggaress. *nonce-wd.* A female beggar.
1863 Miss Power *Arab. Days & N.* 19 The blind beggars and beggaresses, who kiss the hem of your garment.

beggarhood ('bɛgəhʊd). [f. BEGGAR *sb.* + -HOOD.] The condition of a beggar; *concr.* people in this condition.
1843 Thackeray *Irish Sk. Bk.* Wks. 1879 XVIII. 50 Benedictions delivered gratis from the beggarhood of the city. **1883** *Sunday Mag.* Aug. 487/2 A happy combination of the gentility and beggarhood of Seville.

'beggaring, *vbl. sb.* [f. BEGGAR *v.* + -ING[1].] Reduction to beggary. (Now gerundial.)
a **1536** Tindale *Wks.* 375 (R.) Vnto the vtter beggering of our selues. **1609** *Man in Moone* (1849) 8 His childrens beggering, if he be a father. **1674** Brevint *Saul at Endor* 235 For fear of beggering themselves.

'beggaring, *ppl. a.* [f. BEGGAR *v.* + -ING[2].] That beggars or brings to beggary, ruinous.
1883 *Edinb. Rev.* Oct. 308 A hundred ducats raised..at beggaring interest.

†'beggarish, *a. Obs.* = BEGGARLY.
1530 Palsgr. 305/2 Beggerishe, *blistreux.*

'beggarism. [f. as prec. + -ISM.] Practice characteristic of a beggar; professional beggary; beggarliness; extreme poverty.
1636 R. James *Iter Lanc.* (1845) Introd. 85 He must leave his humility and the beggarism of a set speech. **1818** Lyell *Life, etc.* I. iv. 106 A man who rose..from beggarism to enormous affluence. **1865** *Times* 4 Feb. 5/4 A good many instances of this sturdy beggarism.

beggar-like, *a.* Like a beggar; mean, poor.
1586 T. B. *La Primaud. Fr. Acad.* 717 Not a souldiour so beggerlike, but will have his foure lackeis. **1851** H. Melville *Whale* xix. 104 The beggar-like stranger.

beggarliness ('bɛgəlɪnɪs). [f. BEGGARLY + -NESS.] Beggarly quality or condition.
1542 Udall *Erasm. Apoph.* 97 b, His slouenrie and beggerlynesse of liuyng. **1650** T. Goodwin *Wks.* (1862) IV. 227 The beggarliness of these rudiments. **1804** Southey in *Ann. Rev.* II. 67 Poverty of imagination..beggarliness of language. **1816** J. Scott *Vis. Paris* 148 An apparent beggarliness as to real comforts.

beggarly ('bɛgəlɪ), *a.* Also 6 **bedgarly**, 6–7 **beggerly.** [f. BEGGAR + -LY[1].]
1. In the condition of a beggar, indigent; befitting a beggar, mean, poverty-stricken.
1545 Joye *Exp. Dan.* vii. (R.) Poore beggerly fryers. **1596** Shaks. *Tam. Shr.* IV. i. 140 The rest were ragged, old, and beggerly. **1704** Pope *Lett.* (1736) V. 2 No beggar is so poor but he can keep a cur, and no author is so beggarly but he can keep a critic. **1848** Macaulay *Hist. Eng.* I. 330 As children multiplied..the household..became more and more beggarly.
2. *fig.* Intellectually poor, destitute of meaning or intrinsic value.
1526 Tindale *Gal.* iv. 9 Weake and bedgarly [**1611** beggerly] cerimones. *a* **1674** Clarendon *Hist. Reb.* III. xv. 491 Weak and beggarly Arguments. **1883** *Edin. Daily Rev.* 6 June 2/7 That most crude and beggarly conception of reform.
3. Displaying the spirit of a beggar; mean, sordid.
1577 Northbrooke *Dicing* (1843) 140 The beggerly and greedy desire. **1580** Sidney *Arcadia* III. 319 Thou art the beggerliest dastardly villain. **1600** Shaks. *A.Y.L.* II. v. 29 He renders me the beggerly thankes. **1640** Bp. Hall *Episc.* II. xix. 197 A very poor and beggarly evasion. **1870** Emerson *Soc. & Solit.* viii. 170 Lapsing into a beggarly habit.
4. *Comb.*, as *beggarly-looking*.
1818 Scott *Rob Roy* xxxi, A forked, uncased, bald-pated, beggarly-looking scare-crow.

'beggarly, *adv.* [f. as prec. + -LY[2].] After the manner of a beggar or of one who begs; **a.** indigently, meanly; **b.** suppliantly, entreatingly.
c **1400** *Rom. Rose* 223 And both bihynde & eke biforne Clouted was she beggarly. **1551** Robinson tr. *More's Utopia* (1869) 67 The resydewe lyve myserablye, wretchedlye, and beggerlye. **1633** Donne *Poems* (1650) 122 But he is worst, who (beggerly) doth chaw Others wits fruits. **1850** Mrs. Browning *Poems* I. 58 Eve, who beggarly entreats your love.

†'beggarty. *Sc. Obs.* [f. BEGGAR, after *poverty*, etc.] = BEGGARY.
c **1505** Dunbar *Discretioun* iv, To serve and leif in beggartie. *c* **1540** Lyndesay *Pedder Coffeis* 5 Knavis..That wait of nocht but beggartie.

beggary ('bɛgərɪ). Forms: 4 **beggeri, begry(e,** 4–6 **beggerye,** 4–7 **-erie,** 6 **-arie,** 6–7 **-ery,** 6– **beggary.** [f. BEGGAR + -Y[3].]
1. The state or condition of a beggar; extreme poverty. Also *fig.*
1377 Langl. *P. Pl.* B. VII. 88 The boke banneth beggarie [*v.r.* beggerie, beggerye]. **1581** Marbeck *Bk. of Notes* 7 Adulterie bringeth a man to..beggerie, and vtter destruction. **1611** Shaks. *Cymb.* V. v. 10 One that promist nought But beggery, and poore lookes. **1681** Baxter *Apol. Nonconf. Min.* 58 [They] drank themselves into beggery. **1724** Swift *Drapier's Lett.* Wks. 1755 V. II. 58 This coin..will reduce the kingdom to beggary. **1841** Borrow *Zincali* I. 242 Passing their days in beggary and nakedness.
†2. The action or habit of begging; the beggar's trade, mendicancy. *Obs.*
1608 Dekker *Belman Lond.* Wks. 1885 III. 88 An Oration in praise of Beggerie, and of those that professe the Trade. **1649** Jer. Taylor *Gt. Exemp.* II. x. 139 We must be carefull that our charity do not minister to idlenesse and the love of beggery. **1650** B. *Discollim.* 19 Witnesse the dayly Beggaries, and nightly Robberies throughout the Land. **1764** Burn *Poor Laws* 176 Beggary is become an art or mystery, to which children are brought up from their cradles.
3. *concr.* The profession or class of beggars; a place where beggars live.
1615 Chapman *Odyss.* XVIII. 147 Not presume to be Lord of the guests or the beggary. **1816** J. Wilson *City of Plague* I. i. 195 Scoffing thus At the white head of hunger'd beggary? *a* **1834** Lamb *Sir J. Dunstan* Misc. Wks. (1871) 391 A burial alive in the fetid beggaries of Bethnal.
†4. Beggarliness; contemptible meanness. *Obs.*
1611 Shaks. *Cymb.* I. vi. 117 Not I..pronounce The Beggery of his change. **1629** Ford *Lover's Mel.* I. ii. (1811) 132 So do thy knavery and desperate beggary.
†5. Beggarly stuff, rubbish; 'beggarly elements.' *Obs.*
1538 Bale *Thre Lawes* 1674 Of yow God doth axe no soch vayne beggerye. **1553–87** Foxe *A. & M.* III. 319 Your Ceremonies in the Church be beggary and poyson. **1641** Milton *Ch. Discip.* Wks. 1738 I. 1 The Jewish beggery of old cast Rudiments. **1644** J. Fary *God's Severity* (1645) 9 The briars and beggery that growes about it.
†6. Begging of the question. *Obs.*
a **1603** T. Cartwright *Confut. Rhem. N.T.* (1618) 448 Where..you conclude authoritie to forgiue temporall punishment, your beggary is too shamelesse.

†'beggary, *a. Obs.* [f. BEGGAR *sb.* + -Y[1].] Beggarly, poor; mean, contemptible.
1542 Udall *Erasm. Apoph.* 116 a, Suche beggery wretches as had nothyng to leese. *Ibid.* 266 b, He passed by a beggerie litle toune. **1544** Ascham *Toxoph.* (Arb.) 83 A Booke..wherin he..settes out much rifraffe..baggage and beggery ware. **1641** J. Johnson *Acad. Love* 84 [They] blow a beggery echo into the eares of their auditors.

begged (bɛgd), *ppl. a.* [f. BEG *v.* + -ED[1].]
1. Obtained or sustained by begging.
1570–87 Holinshed *Scot. Chron.* (1806) II. 121 To lead a bare and begged life. **1641** Smectymnuus *Vind. Answ.* 30 What the Bishop of Salisbury saith in his begged suffrage.
2. *begged fool.* see BEG *v.* 5.
1693 W. Robertson *Phraseol. Gen.* 621 Beg'd fools, *insigniter stulti, qui gemmas vitro, aurum plumbo permutarent.*

†'begged, -eth. *Obs.* [Only in phrase *a-begged, -eth*; f. BEG *v.* Prof. Skeat takes the original form as *beggeth*, formed in imitation of 'a hunteth' (used by Robt. Glouc. in 'to wende an honteth'), from OE. *huntað* sb. 'hunting,' the ending *-eth* being extended in ME. to other verbs, and confused in form with the pa. pple. See other instances in Skeat's ed. of Chaucer's *Man of Law's T.* 146.] In phrase *to go a-begged*: to go a begging.
c **1386** Chaucer *Frankl. T.* 852 To goon a begged in my kirtle bare. **1393** Langl. *P. Pl.* C. IX. 137 Folk that gon a-begged [*v.r.* abegged, a-beggyd, abeggeþ, beggen].

†'beggild. *Obs. rare*$^{-1}$. [f. *begg-en* to BEG + -ILD, termination forming female names; cf. *cheapild* female bargainer, *fostrild* foster-mother; also *begenild.*] ? A female beggar.
a **1225** *Ancr. R.* 168 Hit is beggilde [*v.r.* beggares] rihte uorte beren bagge on bac.

begging ('bɛgɪŋ), *vbl. sb.* [f. BEG *v.* + -ING[1].]
1. The action or habit of asking earnestly; *spec.* of asking alms.
c **1380** Wyclif *Wks.* (1880) 128 Summe by bygging and some by ȝifte. *c* **1410** Love *Bonavent. Mirr.* xii. (Gibbs MS.) 30 For beggynge wytoute forthe, bote þere be a meke herte wyt in forthe, is lytyll werth as to perfeccioune. **1602** *Return fr. Parnass.* IV. ii. (Arb.) 55 There is a statute come out against begging. **1706** tr. *Dupin's Eccl. Hist. 16th C.* II. IV. xviii. 267 Those pressing and indecent Beggings of Alms. **1837** Hare *Guesses* (1859) 152 To no kind of begging are people so averse, as to begging pardon; that is when there is any serious ground for doing so.
2. *to go* (or *have been*) *a begging*: **a.** to go about begging. (Cf. BEGGED.)
1535 Coverdale *Prov.* xx. 4 Therfore shal he go abegginge and haue nothinge. **1641** Milton *Ch. Discip.* Wks. 1738 I. 17 Where they have been a begging for it. **1825** *Bro. Jonathan* III. 221, I dared not go a-begging of those that knew me.
b. *fig.* (said of situations, offices, in need of men to fill them; things offered for sale and finding no purchaser; and the like.)
a **1593** H. Smith *Wks.* 1867 II. 218 Sin might go a-begging for want of service. **1597** Howson *Serm.* 24 Dec. 34 Benefices went a begging as Ministers doe nowe. **1873** Dixon *Two Queens* I. III. i. 117 Land almost went a-begging. **1878** H. Smart *Play or Pay* viii. 160 I'll not believe a good horse goes begging in the Coverly country.
3. *begging of the question*: a taking for granted of the thing to be proved.
1579 Fulke *Heskins' Parl.* 153 Alas, this is such a poore begginge of that in question. **1644** Jessop *Angel of Ephesus* 19 An usuall fallacie, a shamefull begging of the question. **1847** L. Hunt *Men, Women, & Bks.* I. iv. 87 Reasonings of this description..are but so many beggings of the question.
4. *Attrib.* and *comb.*, as *begging-bowl, -box, -expedition, -letter, -letter-writer*; **begging Thursday**, ? Maundy Thursday; **begging-wise** *adv.*, by way of begging, in begging fashion. .
1546 *Plumpton Corr.* 250 Tomorrow begging Thursday, I must of force ride to Tankerslay. **1645** Rutherford *Tryal Faith* (1845) 87 All that faith hath, is by way of receiving and begging-wise. **1651** C. Cartwright *Cert. Relig.* II. 3 The Author..rid upon a long stick, or in begging shooes, as he did when he was a Friar. **1668** Dryden *Evening's Love* (1671) III. i. 32, I must be fain to take up their Questions in a cleft-Cane, or a Begging-box, as they do Charity in Prisons. **1818** Scott *Ht. Midl.* li, They..entered the Krames, and passed the begging-box. **1846** *Times* 12 Feb. 6/6 (*heading*) Begging-letter writers. **1849** C. Brontë *Shirley* III. xiv. 299 He sent out begging-letters far and wide. **1852** Dickens *Bleak Ho.* xii. 117 He was a begging-letter writer. **1867** *Times* 7 Oct., The Begging Letter Writer has talents which it is impossible not to admire. **1868** Freeman *Norm. Conq.* (1876) II. App. 545 This was not the last begging expedition of Gervinus to our shore. **1871** Ruskin *Fors Clav.* I. i. 4 My desk is full of begging letters. **1894** Kipling *2nd Jungle Bk.* (1895) 35 Let the begging-bowl be placed outside the shrine.

begging ('bɛgɪŋ), *ppl. a.* [f. BEG *v.* + -ING[2].] That begs, mendicant; *spec.* in *begging friar.*
1583 *Exec. for Treason* (1675) 32 Forced to go up and down in the streets..like a begging Fryer. **1591** Spenser *M. Hubberd* 198 A ciuile begging sect. **1725** Pope *Odyss.* XVII. 657 With the begging kind Shame suits but ill. **1766** Entick *London* IV. 80 An order of begging friars.

beggingly ('bɛgɪŋlɪ), *adv.* [f. prec. + -LY[2].] In the manner of one who begs.
1598 Florio, *Implorare*..to crave beggingly. **1824** Miss Mitford *Village* Ser. I. (1863) 51 Even my bonnet—how beggingly she looks at that. **1857** Dickens in Forster *Life* 319, I don't mean to do it beggingly.

† ˈ**beggingness.** *Obs.* [f. as prec. + -NESS.] The condition of a beggar, indigence, beggary.

1382 WYCLIF *Prov.* xxiv. 34 Beggingnesse [**1388** beggerie] as a man armyd. *c* **1384** —— *Sel. Wks.* (1871) III. 371 Gif not to me beggyng or beggyngnesse.

Beghard (ˈbɛgəd). [ad. med.L. *beghardus, begardus, beggardus, begehardus, begihardus* (see Du Cange); cf. F. *béguard*, OF. *bégard, -art*, Flemish *beggaert*, MHG. *beghart, begehard*, either directly from the same word as BEGUINE (i.e. the surname *Bègue*), or at a later date from *béguine* itself, with the masc. ending *-ard, -hard*, here pejorative; see -ARD. OF. had also a masc. *béguin*, in which the pejorative sense was absent; and a fem. *bégarde* formed on *bégard*, with its reproachful force.

This word has been the subject of much etymological conjecture. An extraordinary error, which appears even in Littré, refers it to an alleged Flemish *beggen* 'to beg,' which never existed. (On the contrary, OF. *begard* may be the source of the English *beggar* and *beg*; see these words.) It has been by some referred directly to the adj. *bègue* 'stammering' as if it meant originally 'stammerer,' and has been 'derived' in various other ways. But its origination in the name of *Lambert Bègue* is 'now established beyond all dispute' (Prof. Cosijn).]

A name given to the members of certain lay brotherhoods which arose in the Low Countries early in the 13th c., subsequent to, and in imitation of, the female BEGUIN. 'They took no vow, and were allowed to leave the company when they liked.' The name is said soon to have been adopted by many who were simply idle mendicants: see BEGGAR. From the 14th c. they were denounced by Popes and Councils, and persecuted by the Inquisition. In the 17th c. such of them as still survived were absorbed in the Tertiarii of the Franciscans. (The name was sometimes thrown abusively at other 'heretics,' as the Albigenses and Waldenses.)

1656 H. MORE *Enthus. Triumph.* 23 That religious sect of the *Beguardi*. **1764** MACLAINE *Mosheim's Eccl. Hist.* (1844) I. 333/2 *note*, The denominations Beghards and Beguines were given to above thirty sects or orders, which differed widely from each other in their opinions, their discipline, and manner of living. **1782** PRIESTLY *Corrupt. Chr.* I. I. 7 The early reformers from popery got the name of Beghards. **1829** SOUTHEY *Sir T. More* II. 329 Both Beghards and Beguines, throughout Germany, very generally became Lutherans. **1863** J. LUDLOW in *Gd. Words* July 497/2 So complete was the change, that the very name of *béghard*.. surviving in our *beggar*, has come to designate clamorous pauperism.

† **be-ˈghost,** *v. Obs.* [f. BE- 5, 6 + GHOST *sb.* Cf. *bespirit*.] *trans.* **1.** To make a ghost of; to teach (one) how to play the ghost. **2.** To endow with a spirit or soul. Hence † **beghosted** *ppl. a.*

1620 ROWLANDS *Nt. Raven* 29 Let me alone.. I will be-ghost him. **1674** N. FAIRFAX *Bulk & Selv.* 182 That the same body.. the same Man with body beghosted, rises.

be-ˈgift, *v.* [f. BE- 6 + GIFT *sb.*] *trans.* † **1.** To entrust. *Obs.* **2.** To present with gifts.

a **1400** *Octouian* 675 Thefe, where haste thou my oxen done, That y the be-gyfte? *c* **1590** in Hazl. *E.P.P.* IV. 196 The friendes that were together met, Be-gyfted them richely. **1837** CARLYLE *Fr. Rev.* (1857) II. II. v. x. 81 They are harangued, bedinnered, begifted, the very Court.. contributing something.

begild (bɪˈgɪld), *v.*; also 7 beguild. [f. BE- + GILD.] *trans.* To cover with, or as with, gold.

1600 FAIRFAX *Tasso* XVIII. xv. 318 Begilding (with the radiant beames she threw) His helme. **1630** J. TAYLOR (Water P.) *Wks.* II. 47/1 To waste as muche to polish and be-guild As would a charitable Almes-house build. **1648** EARL WESTMORLD. *Otia Sacra* (1879) 38 We may with Eloquence Beguild our Speech.

Hence **beˈgilded, beˈgilt** *ppl. a.*

1594 CAREW *Tasso* (1881) 60 Her beguil[d]ed lockes.. betainted red, As gold growes ruddie. *a* **1637** B. JONSON *Underwoods* (L.) Begilt white sleeves. **1831** CARLYLE *Sart. Res.* I. iv, Any Drawing room.. were it never so begilt.

begile, obs. form of BEGUILE.

begin (bɪˈgɪn), *v.*¹ Pa. t. began (bɪˈgæn). Pa. pple. begun (bɪˈgʌn). Forms: 1 bi-, beginnan, 2-4 biginnen, 3-4 biginne, 3-7 beginne, 3- begin. (Also 3 bigunen, 4 bigine, -gyn(e, bygyn(ne, 4-6 begyn(ne.) *Pa. t. sing.* 1- began, 1-5 bigan. (Also 2-5 bigon, 3-5 bygan, 4 bigane, 4-5 bygon(ne, 4-6 begann(e, begon(ne, 6-9 begun.) *plur.* 1 bi-, begunnon, 2-4 -gunnen, 3-4 bigun(ne, 4-6 begunne, 4-9 begun; 4-5 bi-, begann(e, 4- began. (Also 3-4 bygun(ne, -gonne, 6 -gane.) *Sc.* 4-7 begouth, 6 -gould, -guld, 6-8 -goud, 7-9 -gude. *Pa. pple.* 1-4 bi-, begunnen, 3-5 bigun(ne, 4-7 begunne, 4- begun. (Also 4-5 bygun(ne, begonnen, bygonne, 4-6 begonne, begunnyn, 6-7 begon, 7 begone, 7- *occ.* began.) [Of common WGer. or ? OTeut. formation: OE. *bi-, be-ginnan* is identical with OS. and OHG. *bi-ginnan*, MHG., mod.G., Du. *be-ginnen*, MDu. *beghinnen*; f. *bi-*, BE- about + **ginnan*, an original Teutonic vb., of which however only compounds have come down to us, including (beside the preceding) Goth. *du-ginnan* to begin, OE. *on-ginnan, a-ginnan*, to begin, OHG. *in-ginnan*, MHG. *en-ginnen*. The latter (OHG. and MHG.) had the senses 'to cut open, open up, begin, undertake'; hence it is inferred that the root sense of **ginnan* was 'to open, open up,' and that it was cogn. w. ON. *gína*, OE. *gínan* 'to gape, yawn,' from a stem **gi-*, appearing also in OSlav. *zij-ati*, L. *hi-āre* 'to gape, open':—Aryan **ghi-*. '*Gi-nn-an* might originally be a form of the *nu-* class, in which, as in *ri-nn-an, skī-n-an*, and other verbs, the formative of the present was carried over into the other tenses' (Sievers). The transition of sense from 'open up' to 'begin,' is a frequent one: cf. F. *entamer*, Eng. ATTAME; also Ger. *eröffnen* and Eng. 'open' a speech, 'open' fire, 'open up' negotiations; also the parallel use of 'close, close up, conclude, shut up,' in sense of 'to end.' *Beginnan* was very rare in OE., where the ordinary word was *onginnan*: see ONGIN, AGIN, and the aphetic GIN, GAN. As in other verbs having grammatical vowel change in the pa. t., there was an early tendency to level the forms of the 1-3 sing. *began*, and of the 2 sing. *begunne*, pl. *begunnon*, which has resulted in the establishment of *began* as the standard form; but an alternative from the old plural *begun* has also come down to the present day. The rare pa. pple. *began* shows form-levelling in another direction. The Sc. forms *begouth, begoud*, seem due to some form-association with *couth, could*, probably through the aphetic form *gan*, which became in Sc. *can*, and was thus identical in form with *can* 'to be able.']

1. *intr.* To open operations upon or in reference *to* (any action), to set oneself effectively *to do* (something), to be at the point of first contact with; to enter upon, take the first step, do the first or starting part; to commence, to start. An abstract notion, which is reached in various languages through the concrete notions of opening, broaching (F. *entamer*), going into or entering upon (L. *inīre*), rousing oneself to, attacking (L. *adorīri*), setting oneself to (F. *se mettre*), seizing hold of, or taking in hand (G. *anfangen*), rousing oneself from inaction into activity (*start*).

a. with dative inf. with *to* (formerly often *for to*; occasionally with the inf. without *to*).

c **1000** ÆLFRIC *Gen.* ix. 20 Noe þa began to wircenne þæt land. *c* **1175** *Lamb. Hom.* 77 Nu bi-gon paul to wepen. *c* **1250** *Gen. & Ex.* 188 Ðan ðat he singen bi-gan. *a* **1300** *Cursor M.* 3565 His heued bigines for to scak. *Ibid.* 5942 Ful yern on godd bi-gun [*v.r.* beganne] þai call. *c* **1374** CHAUCER *Boeth.* II. iii. 37 þou bygunne raþer to ben leef and deere þan forto ben a neyȝbour. **1375** BARBOUR *Bruce* IX. 183 Thair hertis all begouth to fale. *c* **1420** *Avow. Arth.* xxx, The day be-ganne to daw. **1526** *Pilgr. Perf.* (W. de W. 1531) 1 b, Therupon I begon.. to wryte in latyn. *a* **1572** KNOX *Hist. Ref.* Wks. 1846 I. 389 Thay begould to requyre that Messe sould be sett up agane. **1581** SAVILE *Tacitus' Hist.* (1622) 198 The troopes of the horsemen beganne for to flee. **1611** BIBLE *Gen.* iv. 26 Then began men to call vpon the Name of the Lord. **1646** ROW *Hist. Kirk* (1842) 245 Many.. ill-principled ministers begouth to acknowledge them. **1647** W. BROWNE *Polexander* I. 183 The faire Gardeneresse then began speake. **1793** SMEATON *Edystone L.* §323 The storm.. begun at the south-east. *a* **1813** A. WILSON *Hogmenae* Wks. 295 Auld Saunders begoud for to wink. **1819** BYRON *Juan* II. clxvii, He begun To hear new words, and to repeat them. **1821** T. H. SCOTT in *Parr's Wks.* (1828) VII. 242 They have already began to export fine wool. **1826** J. WILSON *Noct. Ambr.* Wks. 1855 I. 238 Day-life begude to roar again. **1870** H. MACMILLAN *Bible Teach.* x. 208 We began to die the moment we began to live.

¶ When the following verb is transitive, e.g. 'they have begun to cleanse it,' the passive has been variously 'it has been begun-to-cleanse,' 'it has been begun to be cleansed,' 'it has begun to be cleansed'; the last is the form now used.

c **1200** *Trin. Coll. Hom.* 99 þe is of sinne clensed oðer bigunne to clensende. *c* **1400** MAUNDEV. v. 40 When the gret Tour of Babel was begonnen to be made. *a* **1657** SIR J. BALFOUR *Ann. Scotl.* (1825) II. 72 Wedinsday, the 18 of Nouember, a blazinge star begude to be seine in the southe.

b. *absol.* To start or take the first step in any matter in question, or in action generally.

c **1200** *Trin. Coll. Hom.* 85 Ðu bigunne betere þenne þu ende. *c* **1380** WYCLIF *Wks.* (1880) 78 Charite schuld bigyne at hemself. **1458** *MS.* in *Dom. Archit.* III. 41 The kynge bad hem begynne apon Goddes blissing. **1535** STEWART *Cron. Scot.* III. 314 With als grit anger that tyme as tha culd, Tha left the mater war than tha beguld. **1591** SHAKS. *Two Gent.* II. iv. 32, I know it wel sir, you alwaies end ere you begin. **1612** DEKKER *If not good* Wks. 1873 I. 276 Well to begin, and not to end were base. *a* **1762** LADY M. W. MONTAGUE *Lett.* lxxx. 132, I do not know how to begin.

c. *spec.* To begin a speech, to start speaking, to speak.

1563 *Mirr. Mag.* Induct. xix, My spirits returnd, and then I thus begonne:.. **1667** MILTON *P.L.* I. 83 To whom th' Arch-Enemy.. Breaking the horrid silence, thus began:.. **1725** POPE *Odyss.* IV. 82 Soft-whispering thus to Nestor's son.. young Ithacus begun:..

d. Const. *to begin at* (formerly ***from***): to start from a point. *to begin with* (formerly *at, from, by*): to start with an action or thing affected; to begin *by* doing something. ***to begin with***, (***withal*** obs.), advb. phr.: At the outset, as the first thing to be considered.

c **1325** *E.E. Allit. P.* A. 546 Bygyn at þe laste þat standez lowe, Tyl to þe fyrste þat þou at-teny. *c* **1380** WYCLIF *Tres Tract.* 24 Bigynne we at the freris, the whiche he brouȝte laste inne. **1382** —— *Luke* xxiii. 5 Bigynnyng fro Galilee til hidur [TINDALE, at Galile even to this place; *Rhemish*, from Galilee euen hither; **1611** from Galilee to this place]. **1531** TINDALE *Expos. & Notes* (1849) 220 And, to begin withal, they said *Confiteor*. **1536** R. BEERLEY in *Four C. Eng. Lett.* 35 Sume cum to mattens, begenynge at the mydes, and sume when yt ys allmost done. **1562** FOXE *A. & M.* I. 452/2 First, beginning with that godly man.. the Author of the Book. *a* **1563** BALE *K. Johan* (1837) 47 Fyrst to begyne with, we shall interdyte the lond. **1611** BIBLE *Matt.* xx. 8 Beginning from the last vnto the first [WYCLIF, to; *Geneva*, at the laste til [to] the firste]. **1631** GOUGE *God's Arrows* iii. §2. 182, I will begin with the Assaulter, who is.. said to be Amalek. **1697** DRYDEN *Alexander's Feast* ii, The song began from Jove. **1739** CHESTERF. *Lett.* I. xxxix. 124 The Spaniards began their conquests.. by the islands of St. Domingo and Cuba. **1774** —— *Ibid.* 2, I am told, Sir, you are preparing to travel, and that you begin by Holland. **1819** BYRON *Juan* I. vii, My way is to begin with the beginning. **1843** CARLYLE *Past & Present* 324 The noble Priest was always a noble *Aristos*, to begin with. **1860** MILL *Repr. Govt.* 278 It is obvious, to begin with, that all business purely local.. should devolve upon the local authorities.

e. Usu. with preceding negative: To make any (or the least) approach to, to come anywhere near. *colloq.* (orig. *U.S.*).

1833 *Niles' Reg.* XLIV. 348/1 The one in Bleecker street.. cost ten thousand dollars, and that does not begin to be as expensive as this. **1865** *Congress. Globe* Feb. 664/1 New York does not begin to have sixty-nine thousand square miles. **1888** *Harper's Mag.* Sept. 545/2 He got Bret to take her picture,.. and he said it didn't begin to do her justice. **1907** HOWELLS *Through Eye of Needle* 43 Often there's a.. dinner that you couldn't begin to get for the same price anywhere. **1915** W. RALEIGH *Let.* 30 Mar. (1926) II. 420, I can't *begin* to tell about America. **1957** R. W. ZANDVOORT *Handbook Eng. Gram.* I. ii. 27, I felt I did not begin to understand her. (*footnote*) American, but spreading in England. **1963** *Listener* 24 Jan. 168/2 The *Aeneid* is not an Augusteid, because Augustus could not begin to embody Virgil's feelings. **1968** *Observer* 22 Dec. 8/5 Dollar for dollar, man in space does not begin to be cost-effective.

f. To compare in any degree *with. U.S.*

1862 O. W. NORTON *Army Lett.* (1903) 47 There is no other man whom I would be so much pleased to have taken as.. Floyd. Jeff Davis wouldn't begin. **1877** 'MARK TWAIN' in *Atlantic* Nov. 590 There ain't a book that begins with it. **1897** —— *Following Equator* xxxviii. 347 Indeed, our working-women cannot begin with her as a road-decoration.

2. a. *trans.* (in same sense) with a *vbl. sb.*, or other noun expressing action; also *ellipt.* with any sb. treated as a piece of work, as *to begin (writing) a letter, to begin (reading) a book*.

c **1175** *Lamb. Hom.* 93 þet weorc wes bigunnen on-ȝen godes iwillan. *a* **1300** *Cursor M.* 266 Now þis prolouge wil we blin, In crist nam our bok begin. **1307** *Elegy Edw. I*, viii, Bringe to ende that thou hast by-gonne. **1433** CAXTON *G. de la Tour* E vj b, He began werre to his neyghbours and to his Barons. **1513** DOUGLAS *Æneis* v. ii. 36 This sacrifice quhilk I begunnyn haif. **1699** BENTLEY *Phal.* ii. 62 They begun their Reigns at the same time. **1722** *Lond. Gaz.* No. 6051/1 His Royal Highness began the Ball with the Princess. **1751** CHATHAM *Lett. Nephew* ii. 6, I rejoice to hear you have begun Homer's Iliad. **1835** CRABBE *Par. Reg.* I. 276 With evil omen, we that year begin.

b. *intr.* To begin *on* or *upon*: To set to work upon, begin to deal with.

1808 SOUTHEY *Life* (1850) III. 163, I will not begin upon it till I come to a stop in Kehama.

3. *trans.* To start (anything) on its career, to give origin to, bring into existence, create; to be the first to do or practise. Of works, practices, or institutions, lasting through time.

c **1175** *Lamb. Hom.* 59 Alle þe scafte þe he bi-gon. *c* **1250** *Gen. & Ex.* 447 Ðis Lamech was þe firme man ðe bigamie first bigan. *c* **1385** CHAUCER *L.G.W.* 1007 Dido.. This noble toun of Cartage hath bygunne. **1704** POPE *Windsor For.* 61 Proud Nimrod first the savage chace began. **1846** GROTE *Greece* I. xviii. II. 14 Archelaus.. alleged to have first begun the dynasty of the Temenid Kings.

4. *intr.* To enter upon its career, come into existence, take its rise, originate; to arise, start.

a. in reference to time.

c **1250** *Gen. & Ex.* 236 Here first name ðor bigan. *a* **1300** *Cursor M.* 5342 þar lijs adam, þe formast man, And eue of quam we all bigann. **1393** GOWER *Conf.* I. 26 And than a newe [world] shal beginne. **1513** MORE *Rich. III.* (1641) 235 If the world would have begunne as I would have wished. **1598** SYLVESTER *Du Bartas* I. i. (1641) 2/1 Eternally before this World begun. **1602** FULBECKE *1st Pt. Parall.* 28 All perfection, goodnes, and iustice beginneth at him. **1611** BIBLE *Num.* xvi. 46 There is wrath gone out from the Lord; the plague is begun. **1875** BRYCE *Holy Rom. Emp.* (ed. 5) Sup. 405 The greatness of the Prussian monarchy begins with Frederick II. **1883** H. DRUMMOND *Nat. Law in Spir. W.* 386 All life begins at the Amœboid stage.

b. of order in a list or series, place in a book, etc.

a **1225** *St. Marher.* 1 Her beginneð þe liflade and te passiun of seinte Margarete. **1382** WYCLIF *Matt.* ad fin., Here endith the gospel of Matheu and bigynneth the prolog of Mark. **1485** CAXTON *Chas. Gt.* 3 Here begynnen the chapytres and tytles of this book folowing. *Mod.* A new

story begins in the present number. The paragraph begins about the middle of the page.

c. in reference to space.

a **1300** *Cursor M.* 1035 þis flummes four þat þar biginnes, thoru out all oþer contres rinnes. **1517** TORKINGTON *Pilgrimage* (1884) 23 At this Jaffe begynnyth the holy londe. *Mod.* The pine-forests begin at an elevation of two thousand feet.

5. Phrases. † *to begin the board, dais*, etc.: to sit at the head of the table. † *to begin a toast*: to propose a toast. † *to begin to a person*: to pledge, toast that person. *to begin the world*: to start in life. *to begin upon a person* (colloq.): to attack or assail a person.

c **1386** CHAUCER *Prol.* 52 Ful ofte tyme he hadde the bord bygonne Aboven alle naciouns in Pruce. *c* **1430** *Syr Tryam.* 1636 Quene Margaret began the deyse. **1493** *Festivall* (W. de W. 1515) 85 b, That they sholde bere them to hym that began the table [at Cana]. **1628** EARLE *Microcosm.* lxxvi. 157 That is kind o'er his beer, and protests he loves you, And begins to you again. **1633** BP. HALL *Hard Texts* 36 Can yee drinke of that bitter cup wherein I shall begin to you? **1715** BURNET *Own Time* II. 117 At Sancroft's consecration dinner, he began a health, to the confusion of all that were not for a war with France. *c* **1825** MRS. SHERWOOD *Houlston Tr.* II. xxxii. 4 All the company began upon her, and bade her mind her own affairs. **1833** HT. MARTINEAU *Br. Farm* iv. 53 Do you know..with how much land Mr. Malton began the world?

† **begin** (bɪˈdʒɪn), *v.*[2] *Obs.* Forms: 3- bygynne, 4 bigin, bigyn, biginn(e, begyn, begin. [f. BE- + GIN, a trap.] *trans.* To entrap, ensnare.

c **1250** *O.E. Misc.* 79 Ure wyþerwine þat þencheþ vs to bigynne. *a* **1300** *Cursor M.* 3880 Allas for sinn, qua wend he wald þus me biginn.

† **beˈgin**, *sb. Obs. rare*[-1]. [f. BEGIN *v.*[1]] Beginning.

1596 SPENSER *F.Q.* III. iii. 21 Let no whit thee dismay The hard beginne that meetes thee in the dore.

begin, begink, obs. f. BEGUIN, BIGGIN, BEGUNK.

beginger, etc.: see BE- *pref.*

beginner (bɪˈgɪnə(r)). [f. BEGIN *v.*[1] + -ER[1].]

1. One who begins; an originator, founder.

c **1325** *E.E. Allit. P.* A. 436 Blessed bygynner of vch a grace. **1480** CAXTON *Chron. Eng.* cxxxvii. 117 Of the whiche abbay he was begynner and foundour. **1547** BAULDWIN *Mor. Philos.* (Palfr. 1564) x. v, The most gracious and mighty beginner is God, which in the beginning created the world. **1592** SHAKS. *Rom. & Jul.* III. i. 146 Where are the vile beginners of this Fray? **1790** BURKE *Fr. Rev.* Wks. V. 49 All the beginners of dynasties. **1863** (16 June) BRIGHT *Amer., Sp.* 130 The South, which was the beginner of the war.

2. *spec.* **a.** One beginning to learn; a novice, a tyro.

1470-85 MALORY *Arthur* II. xlv. (1634) 367 But young beginners. **1526** *Pilgr. Perf.* (W. de W. 1531) 156 b, Suche that be vnlerned in religyon..as nouyces or yonge begynners. **1601** HOLLAND *Pliny* VIII. xlviii. (R.) New beginners (namely, young souldiours, barristers, and fresh brides). **1780** SIR J. REYNOLDS *Disc.* vii. (R.) The very enumeration of its kinds is enough to frighten a beginner. **1807** BYRON *Granta* xx, A band of raw beginners. **1875** JOWETT *Plato* (ed. 2) I. 139 For the use of the young beginner.

b. Phr. *beginner's luck*: the good luck supposed to attend a novice at betting, games, etc.

1897 KIPLING *Capt. Courageous* iii. 55 'Beginner's luck,' said Dan...'He's all of a hundred [*sc.* pounds, in weight].' **1902** A. BENNETT *Anna of Five Towns* x. 227 'You have covered yourself with glory.'..'How?' 'By not being ill.' 'That's always the beginner's luck.' **1966** J. POTTS *Footsteps on Stairs* ix. 115 Beginner's luck. It went smooth as silk all the way.

† **3.** He who or that which goes or comes first, or takes the lead. *Obs.*

c **1613** ROWLANDS *More Knaues* 35 Being set to dinner, A legge of mutton was the first beginner. Next he deuoured vp a loyne of veale.

4. *Arch.* The lower part of a mullion worked on the stone forming the sill.

1886 WILLIS & CLARK *Cambridge* II. 514 The mullions of the four-light window..do not correspond with the 'beginners' on the sill.

beginning (bɪˈgɪnɪŋ), *vbl. sb.* Also bi-, bygyn(n)yng; 2-3 -unge. [f. BEGIN *v.*[1] + -ING[1].]

1. The action or process of entering upon existence or upon action, or of bringing into existence; commencing, origination.

a **1225** *Leg. Kath.* 289 As euch þing hefde beginnunge of his godlec. *a* **1300** *Cursor M.* 838 Þar þai biginning gan to tak. *c* **1400** MAUNDEV. 316 Withouten begynnynge and withouten endynge. **1570** BILLINGSLEY *Euclid* I. def. iii. 2 A line hath his beginning from a point. **1579** FENTON *Guicciard.* (1618) 288 Maximilian then being come to Trent, to giue beginning to the warre. **1635** SWAN *Spec. M.* (1670) 17 The world..was not for everlasting, but took beginning. **1883** FROUDE *Short Stud.* IV. II. i. 171 The beginning of change, like the beginning of strife, is like the letting out of water.

b. viewed as a definite fact belonging to anything extended in time or space.

a **1225** *Ancr. R.* 18 Et te biginnunge of þe Venite. *c* **1530** R. HILLES *Comm.-pl. Bk.* (1858) 140 All thyngs hath a begynyng. **1539** TAVERNER *Erasm. Prov.* 9 The beginnynge is halfe the hole. **1562** J. HEYWOOD *Prov. & Epigr.* (1867) 21 Of a good begynnyng cometh a good end. **1590** SHAKS. *Mids. N.* v. i. 111 That is the true beginning of our end. **1780** J. HARRIS *Philol. Enq.* (1841) 421 A beginning is that, which nothing necessarily precedes, but which something naturally follows. **1836** GEN. P. THOMPSON *Exerc.* (1842) IV. 99 As was shrewdly intimated, in respect of the question of Primogeniture this is only 'the beginning of the end.'

2. The point of time at which anything begins; *absol.* the time when the universe began to be.

c **1175** *Lamb. Hom.* 81 Þis bitacneð þe world þet wes from biginnegge. **1388** WYCLIF *Gen.* i. 1 In the bigynnyng God made of nouȝt heuene and erthe. **1535** COVERDALE *Hab.* i. 12 Thou o Lorde..art from the begynnynge. **1611** BIBLE *1 John* ii. 13 Yee haue knowen him that is from the beginning. **1875** BRYCE *Holy Rom. Emp.* vi. (ed. 5) 77 Germany proclaims the era of A.D. 843 the beginning of her national existence.

3. That in which anything has its rise, or in which its origin is embodied; origin, source, fount.

c **1200** *Trin. Coll. Hom.* 73 Þe shame þe þe man haueð of his sinne..is þe biginnigge of fremfulle sinbote. *a* **1225** *Ancr. R.* 54 Biginnunge & rote of þis ilke reouðe. **1486** *Bk. St. Albans, Her.* A j b, Adam the begynnyng of man kynde. **1611** BIBLE *Col.* i. 18 The head of the body, the Church: who is the beginning, the first borne from the dead. **1831** CARLYLE *Sart. Res.* II. i. (1838) 101 Thy true..Beginning and Father is in Heaven.

† **b.** A first cause, first principle. *Obs.*

1587 GOLDING *De Mornay* vi. 63 The Magies held three beginnings, whom..they called Oromaces, Mitris, and Ariminis, (that is to say) God, Minde, and Soule.

c. *concr.* The head or chief extremity.

1483 *Cath. Angl.* 26 Begynnynge, *caput.* **1578** BANISTER *Hist. Man* IV. 62 The second Muscle begynneth at the same Tubercle..with a sharpe begynnyng.

4. The earliest or first part of any space of time, of a book, a journey, etc.

1297 R. GLOUC. 399 In þe bygynnynge of Jule þys batayle was ydo. *c* **1380** WYCLIF *Wks.* (1880) 385 As Lyncolnyence saiþ in þe bygynnynge of his dictis. **1473** WARKW. *Chron.* 11 In the begynnynge of the moneth of Octobre. **1549** *Bk. Com. Pr., 3rd Collect Grace*, Who hast safely brought us to the beginning of this day. **1611** BIBLE *Num.* x. 10 In the beginnings of your monethes, ye shall blow with the trumpets ouer your burnt offerings. **1743** J. MORRIS *Serm.* ii. 35 He explains himself in the begining of this chapter.

5. The initial or rudimentary stage; the earliest proceedings. Often in *plur.*

c **1200** *Trin. Coll. Hom.* 83 Þerfore wurð here ende werse þene here biginninge. **1340** *Ayenb.* 72 Þane dyaþ þet is to þe guoden begynnynge of liue. **1548** COVERDALE *Erasm. Par. Gal.* 14 Vnder the grosse beginnynges of this worlde. **1611** BIBLE *Job* viii. 7 Though thy beginning was small, yet thy latter end should greatly increase. **1690** W. WALKER *Idiom. Ang.-Lat.* Pref. i, A considerable encrease to my beginnings. **1776** ADAM SMITH *W.N.* I. I. x. 132 Great fortunes acquired from small beginnings. **1790** BURKE *Fr. Rev.* Wks. V. 39 The beginnings of confusion with us in England. **1876** GREEN *Short Hist.* ix. §1. (1882) 597 The beginnings of physical science were more slow and timid there.

† **6.** An undertaking. *Obs.*

1481 CAXTON *Myrr.* III. xxiv. 192 In alle begynnynges and in all operacions the name of god ought to be called.

beˈginning, *ppl. a.* [f. BEGIN *v.*[1] + -ING[2].]

1. a. That comes into existence or begins its course; incipient, commencing.

1576 GRINDAL *Custom & Ver.* Wks. (1843) 72 The primitive and beginning church. **1650** JER. TAYLOR *Holy Living* (1727) 201 He helpt my slow and beginning endeavours. **1775** DE LOLME *Eng. Constit.* II. xvii. 293 He peaceably weathered the beginning storm. **1829** S. TURNER *Mod. Hist. Eng.* III. II. xviii. 540 [She] waited for her parliament to be the beginning innovators.

b. *spec.* Of a course of study, book, student, etc.: preceding others in a series; elementary. *N. Amer.*

1923 E. M. ROBERTS *(title)* The beginning telegrapher. **1928** ALMACK & LANG *(title)* The beginning teacher. **1962** W. S. AVIS et al. *(title)* Dictionary of Canadian English. The Beginning Dictionary. **1962** S. E. MARTIN in Householder & Saporta *Problems in Lexicography* 153 In a sense, the beginning student needs something very similar. **1964** *Amer. Speech* XXXIX. 51 It is intended as a textbook for a beginning course.

2. Coming first or in front; leading the way.

1609 DOULAND *Ornith. Microl.* 40 Euery Beginning Note without a tayle, if the second Note ascend, is a Breefe.

Hence † **beginningly**, *Obs.* in 4 **begynandly**, initially, at the beginning.

a **1340** HAMPOLE *Psalter* cxviii. 152 Bigynandly . that was fra bigynynge of mannys kynd . i . knew that thou hight the kyngdome of heuen till thi lufers.

beˈginningless, *a.* [f. BEGINNING *vbl. sb.* + -LESS.] Without beginning; uncreate. Hence **beˈginninglessness.**

1587 GOLDING *De Mornay* ix. 119 And that time should be beginning lesse, what els is it to say, than that time is not time. **1602** J. DAVIES *Mirum in M.* (1875) 16 All wise, all good, all great, beginninglesse. **1674** N. FAIRFAX *Bulk & Selv.* 158 A beginningless, endless now. **1832** CARLYLE in Froude *Life* II. xii. 271 All speculation is beginningless and endless. **1865** GINSBURG *Kabbalah, Proc. L'pool. Lit. & Phil. Soc.* XIX. 299 On the beginninglessness of the first and necessary first Emanation.

begird (bɪˈgɜːd), *v.* Pa. t. and pple. **begirt.** [OE. *begyrdan* (= OHG. *bigurten*) f. *bi-*, BE- 1 + *gyrdan*:—OTeut. **gurdjan* to GIRD.]

1. *trans.* To gird about or around; chiefly used of fastening a girdle or belt round the body, or of fastening on a sword by means of a belt. Also *fig.*

c **1000** *Ags. Ps.* xvii. 37 Þu me begyrdest mid mæȝenum. *c* **1315** SHOREHAM 51 Hym with a touwayle schete Ihesus.. by-gerte. **1583** STANYHURST *Æneis* I. (Arb.) 28 My deere sisters with quiuer closelye begyrded. **1768** BEATTIE *Minstr.* II. xxxv, Breasts begirt with steel! **1860** ADLER *Fauriel's Prov. Poetry* xv. 399 Begirding the young warrior with the sword.

2. To encircle, encompass, enclose, *with.*

c **890** K. ÆLFRED *Bæda* I. v, He þæt ealond begyrde and ȝefæstnade mid dice. *a* **1225** *Ancr. R.* 378 Ȝunge mipen me bigurt mid þornes. **1622** HEYLIN *Cosmogr.* II. (1682) 114 A Demi-Island begirt with rocks. **1667** MILTON *P.L.* I. 581 Vthers Son Begirt with British and Armoric Knights. **1814** CARY *Dante's Inf.* XVIII. 11 Where..many a foss Begirds some stately castle. **1846** LONGF. *Occult. Orion* 33 Begirt with many a blazing star.

fig. **1633** G. HERBERT *Sinne* in *Temple* 37 Lord, with what care hast thou begirt us round! **1876** MISS SIDGWICK *Live & let Live* 62 With what blessings has..Providence begirt labor!

† **3.** *spec.* To beset in hostile array, to besiege. *Obs.* as a *spec.* use.

1587 GREENE *Arcad.* (1616) 62 Melicertus begirt the Castle with a siege. **1618** BOLTON *Florus* II. xvi. 139 Now the City it selfe was begirt with a siege. **1643** [ANGIER] *Lanc. Vall. Achor* 32 Lancaster called aloud for relief, having been begirt twenty dayes. **1791** COWPER *Iliad* II. 885 The Epean host had round Begirt the city.

beˈgirding, *vbl. sb.* [f. prec. + -ING[1].] The action of girding about or enclosing.

1641 C. BURGES in Spurgeon *Treas. Dav.* Ps. lxxvi. 10 The begirding or binding of it in on every side.

beˈgirding, *ppl. a.* [f. as prec. + -ING[2].] That begirds or encloses all round.

1877 WRAXELL *Hugo's Miserables* V. xviii. 11 The masonry of the begirding drain.

begirdle (bɪˈgɜːd(ə)l), *v.* [f. BE- 1 + GIRDLE.] *trans.* To encompass or bind like a girdle or belt.

1837 CARYLE *Fr. Rev.* III. VII. iii. 368 Like a ring of lightening, they..begirdle her from shore to shore. **1850** —— *Latter-d. Pamph.* viii. (1872) 285 Restless gnawing ennui..begirdles every human life so guided.

Hence, **beˈgirdled** *ppl. a.*

1813 SCOTT *Rokeby* II. i, Rock-begirdled Gilmanscar.

begirt (bɪˈgɜːt), *v.*; also 7 **begirth.** [f. BE- 1 + GIRT *v.*, a late secondary form of GIRD, taken apparently from the pa. pple. *girt*, or perhaps from *girt*, obs. f. of GIRTH *sb.*] *trans.* To surround, encompass, enclose. (It has not the literal sense of *begird.*)

1608 HIERON *Wks.* I. 747 Begirt vs with Thy fauour. **1658** USSHER *Ann.* 530 He had begirthed the place with a triple wall. **1720** STRYPE *Stow's Surv.* II. VI. 87 The Parish of St. Martin's..begirteth it on all Parts. **1862** DANA *Elem. Geol.* 733 The lofty mountains and volcanoes which begirt it.

Hence **beˈgirt, beˈgirting** *ppl. a.*, **beˈgirting** *vbl. sb.*

1645 MILTON *Tetrach.* Wks. (1851) 233 With a begirting mischief. **1660** H. MORE *Myst. Godl.* V. xvi. 198 The begirting of the holy City by numerous armies of Gog and Magog. **1790** COWPER *Iliad* II. 681 Sea-begirt Ægina.

beglad, beglare, etc.: see BE- *pref.*

beglamour (bɪˈglæmə(r)), *v.* [f. BE- 6 + GLAMOUR *sb.*] *trans.* To invest with glamour; = GLAMORIZE *v.*; also, to deceive or impress with glamour. So **beˈglamour(iz)ed, beˈglamouring** *ppl. adjs.*

1840 *Fraser's Mag.* XXI. 8 A new Pactolus..seemed to the beglamoured eyes of the prosperity-men to have overflowed the land. **1926** *Chambers's Jrnl.* July 437/2 He's beglamoured her—she worships courage—and he's a brave man. **1932** F. R. LEAVIS *New Bearings* i. 16 The appropriate metaphor would suggest something not only beglamoured, but also ritualistic and religiose. **1948** A. WAUGH *Unclouded Summer* xii. 231 It had been a bondage, yes, but a beglamoured bondage. *Ibid.* xiv. 246 It was the very fact that they had not been equal that had so beglamoured him. **1953** H. P. COLLINS in *Ess. in Crit.* Jan. 61 The passion, the Protestant fury, the beglamouring naturalism of Charlotte Brontë. **1958** *Times Lit. Suppl.* 21 Feb. 101/2 The city is beglamourized.

begle, obs. form of BEAGLE.

‖ **beglerbeg** (ˈbɛgləbɛg). Also 6 bellerbey, 6-9 beglerbey, 7 beglarbeg. [a. Turk. *beglerbeg* bey of beys; cf. BEG (of which *begler* is plural).] The governor of a province of the Ottoman empire, in rank next to the grand vizier.

Hence **begler-beglic, -lik, -luc**, the district over which a beglerbeg rules, the dignity or office of a beglerbeg. Also **beglerbegship.**

1594 T. B. *La Primaud. Fr. Acad.* 631 Neither doth any other sit there but the twelve bellerbeis. **1602** CAREW *Cornwall* 126 a, A Turkish Beglerbey of Greece. **1603** KNOLLES *Hist. Turkes* (1621) 945 It is now one of the Turkes proud Beglerbegships. **1614** SELDEN *Titles Hon.* 377 *Begler-Beg* is *Lord of Lords*, that is one which hath vnder his gouernment diuers Begs of lesser Prouinces. And *Beglue* is the Dignitie of the one, *Beglarbegluc* of the other. **1624** MASSINGER *Renegado* III. iv, What places of credit are there? .. There's your beglerbeg. **1813** C. HOBHOUSE *Journey* 162 Reckoned the eighth under the Beglerbey of Romania.

'beglic(k, variant of BEYLIC.

beglide, beglitter, beglose, etc.: see BE- *pref.*

begloom, (bɪˈgluːm), *v.* [f. BE- + GLOOM.] To render gloomy, to overshadow with gloom.

1799 CORRY *Sat. Lond.* (1803) 197 Sometimes.. melancholy begloomed his mind. **1835** BECKFORD *Recoll.* 46 The refectory..begloomed by dark-coloured painted

windows. **1855** SINGLETON *Virgil* II. 369 Sirius..doth arise, And with disastrous light beglooms the sky.

†**be'glue**, *v. Obs.* Also 7 beglew. [f. BE- 2 + GLUE *v.*] *trans.* To fix with glue, or by gluing.
1658 ROWLAND *Mouffet's Theat. Ins.* 1067 The Spider either new weaves them, or else beglewes them anew. **1664** POWER *Exp. Philos.* I. 5 She can..be-glew herself to the plain she walks on.

b. ? To ensnare, delude, cheat. (But there may be some error in the quotation; or is it = *illusi* from *glewen* to play?)
c **1430** LYDGATE *Min. Poems* 115 Thus they went from the game, begylyd and beglued.

begnaw (bɪ'nɔː), *v.* Pa. pple. 6 begnawn. [OE. *begnaȝan*, f. BE- 1 + *gnaȝan* to GNAW.] *trans.* To gnaw at; to corrode; to nibble.
a **1000** *Martyrol.* 9 Jul. (Bosw.). **1555** PHAËR *Æneid* III. G ij b, The pray..begnawn ful fowle they leaue. **1594** SHAKS. *Rich. III*, I. iii. 222 The Worme of Conscience still begnaw thy Soule. **1880** WEBB tr. *Goethe's Faust* I. iii. 87 Commands thee [i.e. a rat]..yonder threshold spell begnaw.

†**be'go**, *v. Obs.* exc. in *pa. pple.* Pa. pple. begone. Forms: 1 begán, 3 bigan, 4 begon, bigo. *Pa. t.* 1 beéode, 3 bieode, 4 byȝede, 4–5 bywent. *Pa. pple.* 1 begán, 2 bigan, 3 bigon, 4 bego(n, -goo, bigo, -gon(nen, -gone, -goo(n, bygo(n, -gone, -goo(n, *Sc.* begane, 5 begoon, bygone, *Sc.* bigane, 5–6 begon, 6 *Sc.* bygane, 4– begone. [Comm. Teut.: OE. *begán*, Goth. *bigaggan*, OS. *bigangan*, OHG. *bigân*, MHG. *begân*, *-gên*, mod.G. *begehen*, Du. *begaan*; f. *bi-*, BE- about + *gangan*, *gân* to Go.]

†**1.** *trans.* To go about, occupy, inhabit; to work, cultivate. (L. *colere*.) *Obs.*
c **890** ÆLFRED *Bæda* I. xxvi. (Bosw.) Mid ðy Romane ða ȝyt Breotone be-eodan. *c* **1000** ÆLFRIC *Gram.* (Zup.) 24 *Agricola*, se ðe æcer begæð. *c* **1000** *Sax. Leechd.* I. 94 þeos wyrt..wihst on beȝanum landum. **1393** GOWER *Conf.* I. 152 The erthe it is, whiche evermo With mannes labour is bego.

†**2.** To go round; to compass, encompass. *Obs.*
c **1000** ÆLFRIC *Job* i. 7 Ic ferde ȝeond ðas eorþan and hi be-eode. **1205** LAY. 11200 Al þat þe sæ bigæð. **1387** TREVISA *Higden* I. 311 [Crete] is bygoo wiþ þe see of Gres.

†**3.** To go about hostilely, beset, overrun (in hostile sense). Also *fig.*; cf. 8. *Obs.*
a **855** *O.E. Chron.* an. 775 He..þone bur utan beeode. *c* **1175** *Lamb. Hom.* 149 þet isich..his emcristene.. mid sicnesse bigan. *c* **1380** *Sir Ferumb.* 3429 Al þe contre..ful by-gon wyþ enymys. *c* **1400** *Warres of Jewes* in Warton *Hist. Poetry* (1840) II. 106 Whippes..bywent his white sides. **1602** WARNER *Alb. Eng.* Epit. (1612) 363 Bremcia, and Daira ..were begone seuerally within three yeares..vnder two Saxons named Ida and Ella.

†**4.** To get round with craft, to talk over. *Obs.*
1362 LANGL. *P. Pl.* A. II. 24 Gyle haþ bigon hire so heo grauntеþ al his wille. *c* **1380** *Sir Ferumb.* 2013 Many ys þe manlich man : þat þorw womman ys by-go. **1387** TREVISA *Higden* VI. 213 þe queene byȝede here housbonde.

†**5.** To surround, environ, furnish. *Obs.*
1393 GOWER *Conf.* II. 227 He was wel begone With faire doughters manyone.

†**6.** To dress; to clothe, attire, deck, adorn. *Obs.*
a **1225** *Leg. Kath.* 1614 þe engles..smireden hire wunden, and bieoden swa þe bruchen of hire bodi. *c* **1325** *Coer de L.* 5661 Hymself was rychely begoo, From the crest unto the too. **1393** GOWER *Conf.* II. 45 The sadels were..With perle and gold so well begone. *Ibid.* 228 His moder to him tolde [the cause] That she him hadde so begone. *c* **1420** *Pallad. on Husb.* I. 630 All golde begoon his tail. **1513** DOUGLAS *Æneis* VI. i. 28 The..hous of brycht Appollo gold bygane.

†**7.** *passive.* To be permeated, tainted, infected.
1205 LAY. 19773 þa wes þa welle anan al mid attre bigon. *c* **1430** *Syr Gener.* 4195 The ground was al begoon with bloode.

8. To beset as an environment or affecting influence, good or evil; to affect as one's environment does. Now only in pa. pple. in *woe-begone* 'affected by an environment of woe,' and the like. (The original phrase was 'him was wo begone,' i.e. to him woe had closed round; but already in Chaucer we find the later construction in 'He was wo begone'; *need-begone* is in Barbour.)
c **1300** *Vox & Wolf* 53 Go wei, quod the kok, wo the bi-go! *c* **1314** *Guy Warw.* 120 Yuel ous worth than bigo. *c* **1375** ? BARBOUR *St. Alexis* 92 Al þat he saw ned-begane. *c* **1386** CHAUCER *Man of Lawes T.* 820 Wo was this wrecched womman tho bigoon. —— *Wife's Prol.* 606, I was..riche and yonge and wel begon. —— *Miller's T.* 472 Absolon that is for loue alwey so wo bigon. *a* **1400** *Sir Perc.* 349 The lady was never more sore bygone. *c* **1440** LONELICH *Grail* xlviii. 373 Elles ben we ful evele be-gon. *c* **1450** *Sir Gowther* 435 Ful wel was him by gone. **1593** T. WATSON *Sonn.* (Arb.) 197 My hart doth whisper I am woe begone me. **1794** W. BLAKE *Songs Exper., Little Girl Found*, Tired and woe-begone. **1825** WATERTON *Wand. S. Amer.* 310 It appears sad and woe-begone.

begob (bɪ'gɒb), *int.* Also begobs. = BEGORRA.
1889 *St. James's Gaz.* 1 Aug. 7/1 It's Irish, begobs! **1892** BARLOW *Irish Idylls* ii. 34 No begob; I'll just be keepin' the feel of it in me hand for this night. **1907** G. B. SHAW *John Bull's Other Island* IV, Begob, it just tore the town in two. **1958** BETJEMAN *Coll. Poems* 70 The feast is spread out, and begob! what a sight.

†**be'god**, *v. Obs. rare.* [f. BE- 5 + GOD.] *trans.* To make a god of, to deify.
a **1576** GRINDAL *Fruitful Dial.* Wks. (1843) 48 Caused men to kneel and crouch down and all-to be-god him. **1656** H. MORE *Enthus. Tri.* Wks. (1712) 27 Tho' they have so deify'd, or (as they phrase it) begodded themselves.
Hence **be'godded** *ppl. a.*
1660 H. MORE *Myst. Godl.* VI. xviii. 273 This begodded Mock-Prophet. *a* **1716** SOUTH *Serm.* xix. (1843) II. 329 Setting up..begodded tutelar saints.

begone (bɪ'gɒn), *ppl. a.*: see BEGO *v.* 8.

begone (bɪ'gɒn), *v.*; also 7 begon. [Really two words *be gone* (cf. *be off*), long used without analysis in the imperative as expressing a single notion, and so written as one word; recent writers have extended this, without any good reason, to the infinitive. But cf. the similar *beware*.]
a. *c* **1370** *Robt. Cicyle* 52 He stode, And callyd the portar, 'Gad'lyng, begone!' **1610** *Histrio-m.* III. 99 Begone yee greedy beefe-eaters. *a* **1719** ADDISON (J.) Begone! the goddess cries with stern disdain. **1853** *Arab. Nts.* (Rtldg.) 89 Begone, and remember I am impatient for your return.
b. [**1660** JER. TAYLOR *Worthy Commun.* i. 61 He bad him be gon and fly from his Fathers wrath.] **1816** J. WILSON *City of Plague* I. i. 265 Let us begone, the day is wearing fast. **1865** CARLYLE *Fredk. Gt.* (1873) II. 135 Kaiser's Ambassador..is angrily ordered to begone.
¶ Used for the word or command 'Begone!'
1820 SCOTT *Abbot* xi, My Lady made me brook the 'Begone.'
¶ Formerly sometimes for *be* (= *been*) *gone*.
1440 J. SHIRLEY *Dethe K. James* (1818) 17 The Kyng.. denyd that they had all begone [been gone].

begonia (bɪ'gəʊnɪə). [Named by Plumier after Michel Begon, a French promoter of botany, 1638–1710.] A genus of succulent under-shrubs and herbaceous plants, mostly of tropical nativity, having flowers without petals but with coloured perianths, and often richly-coloured foliage, for the sake of which many species are cultivated as ornamental plants. Said by Loudon to have been introduced into Great Britain from Jamaica in 1777, but little cultivated before 1840.
1751 CHAMBERS *Cycl. Supp.* s.v. The great purple *begonia* with auriculated leaves. **1881** MISS BRADDON *Asph.* I. 304 All the tribe of begonias, and house-leeks, newly bedded out. **1883** *Pall Mall G.* 7 Sept. 4/1 The well-known Begonias and Fuchsias; which have..withstood the late storms better than any of their rarer rivals.

†**be'gore**, *v. Obs.*; also 6–7 begoar. [f. BE- 6 + GORE.] *trans.* To besmear with gore. Hence **be'gored** *ppl. a.*
c **1500** *Cocke Lorelles B.* (1843) 2 A bocher..All be gored in reed blode. **1573** TWYNE *Æneid* x. G gj, The corps he liftes, begoaring all with blood. **1614** SYLVESTER *Bethulia's Resc.* VI 156 The Sword Which had so oft the groaning Earth begor'd. **1683** TRYON *Way to Health* 445 To think of putting those be-gored Gobbits into our Mouthes.

begorra (bɪ'gɒrə), *int.* Also begarra, begorrah. Anglo-Irish alteration of the expletive *by God* (see GOD *sb.* 13); cf. BEGAR, and dial. *begor(z.*
Rarely heard in current speech.
1839 CARLETON *Fardorougha* xvi, Begarra, Captain dear, it seems that good people is scarce. **1843** LEVER *J. Hinton* ii, 'Begorra, you're in it', was the answer. **1856** —— *Martins of Cro' M.* x, Be gorra! when a man would give four hundred for a bull, there's no saying what he'd stop at. **1895** J. BARLOW *Strangers at Lisconnel* i, Fine company they'd be for anybody begorrah.

begotten (bɪ'gɒt(ə)n), *ppl. a.*; also 4 bigetun, 5 bygoten, 5–6 begot(e. [pa. pple. of BEGET *v.*]
†**1.** Gotten. (With *right-*, etc. prefixed.) *Obs.*
c **1200** ORMIN 1645 Rihhtbiȝetenn ahhte. **1523** FITZHERB. *Husb.* (1525) 63 A glad gyuer..of true begotten goodes.
2. Procreated. (Usually with *only-*, *first-*.)
1382 WYCLIF *John* iii. 16 His oon bigetun sone. **1480** CAXTON *Chron. Eng.* ccxxvi. 232 Edward his first bygoten sonne. **1587** GOLDING *De Mornay* vi. 66 [Plato] calleth him the begotten Sonne of the Good. **1597** HOOKER *Eccl. Pol.* v. xlviii. §5 The only begotten Son of God. **1602** WARNER *Alb. Eng.* x. lix. 261 [Ammon] his Issue first-begot.
b. *absol.*
1382 WYCLIF *John* i. 14 The glorie as of the oon bigetun of the fadir. **1611** BIBLE *Rev.* i. 5 The first begotten of the dead. **1685** BAXTER *Paraphr. N.T.* Matt. i. 8 With the Hebrews called the Son or Begotten.

beg-'pardon, *sb. Austral.* and *N.Z. colloq.* [f. phr. *to beg pardon*: see BEG *v.* 3 and PARDON *sb.*[1] 6.] An expression of apology.
1906 E. DYSON *Fact'ry 'Ands* xv. 198 'Twas quick business down below here, 'n' no beg-pardons with Bunyip. **1916** J. B. COOPER *Coo-oo-ee* i. 11 Then without a 'beg pardon', off she goes again. **1965** F. SARGESON *Memoirs of Peon* vi. 187 Tony, after a maternally-directed beg pardon.. rapped out a command. **1967** *Sunday Mail Mag.* (Brisbane) 8 Jan. 6/2 There were no beg-pardons about Mrs. Hodges (or Debbie, as she insisted I call her). **1969** *Sun-Herald* (Sydney) 13 July 45/7 Rucking was heavy and there were no 'beg pardons' as each pack used its weight.

begrace (bɪ'greɪs), *v.* [f. BE- 5 c + GRACE.] To address as 'your grace.'
c **1530** MORE *De quat. Nouiss.* Wks. 86/1 They knele and.. at euerye word barehed bigrace him. **1586** J. HOOKER *Girald. Irel.* in *Holinsh.* II. 86/2 You are begraced and belorded, and crouched & kneeled vnto. **1802** WOLCOTT (P. Pindar) *Gt. Cry & Lit. Wool* Wks. 1812 V. 180 She's begraced and beduchess'd already.

begrain, begray, begreen, begreet: see BE-.

†**be'grave**, *v. Obs.* Forms: 1 be-, bigrafan, 4–6 bi-, by-, be-grave, (*Sc.* begraif). *Pa. t.* 5 begrove. *Pa. pple.* 6 begraven. [Comm. Teut.: OE. *bi-*, *begrafan*, cogn. w. OHG. *bigraban*, to bury, Goth. *bigraban* to dig a ditch round, mod.G. *begraben*; f. BE- + *graban*, in OE. *grafan* to dig.]
1. *trans.* To bury (a corpse, treasure, etc.).
a **1000** *Elene* (Gr.) 835 Roda ætsomne greote begrafene. *c* **1330** *Arth. & Merl.* 98 At Winchester..that king bigrauen wes. **1393** GOWER *Conf.* II. 197 They..have Her gold under the erth begrave. *c* **1450** LONELICH *Grail* li. 122 They him begroven as he desired him-selve. **1528** ROY *Rede & be nott wrothe* (Arb.) 45 His dedde coors rychly to begraue.
2. To engrave; to ornament with graved work.
c **1325** *Coer de L.* 62 Every nayl with gold begrave. **1393** GOWER *Conf.* I. 127 With great slighte Of werkmanship it was begrave.

begrease (bɪ'griːs), *v.* [f. BE- 1 + GREASE *v.*] *trans.* To besmear with grease.
1565 CALFHILL *Answ. Treat. Crosse* (1846) 175 The marrowbones of their matter; wherewith they did so begrease themselves. *a* **1641** BP. MOUNTAGU *Acts & Mon.* 426 They..held him polluted who had been so begreased. **1783** AINSWORTH *Lat. Dict.* (Morell) I, To begrease the fat sow in the tail..*locupletem donis cumulare*.

†**begrede**, *v. Obs.* Forms: 3–4 bigreden, -graden, 5 begreden. [ME., f. BE- + GREDEN, OE. *grǽdan* to cry.]
1. To cry about, to weep for.
c **1300** *K. Alis.* 5175 The gentil men Bigradden, and wepden her ken.
2. To cry out against; to upbraid, reproach, accuse.
c **1200** *Trin. Coll. Hom.* 69 And shameliche hem bigredeð. and fule shendeð. *c* **1320** *Seu. Sages* (W.) 1518 Lohtliche driuen & bigrad Ase a thef. *c* **1440** *Morte Arth.* (Roxb.) 57 Launcelot of tresson they be gredde.

†**be'grey**, *prep. Obs. rare*$^{-1}$. [? Corruption of F. *bon gré*; or f. BE- = *by* + *gre*, GREE 'liking,' a. F. *gré*. But the sense is doubtful, and it may be for *malgré*.]
1614 J. DAVIES *Eclog.* Wks. 1876–8 II. 20 And wrap hem in thy loue begrey their wils.

begrim, begrimly, begroan, etc.: see BE- *pref.*

begrime (bɪ'graɪm), *v.* [f. BE- 6 + GRIME.] *trans.* To blacken or soil with grime, or dirt which sinks into the surface, and discolours it.
a **1553** UDALL *Roister D.* (Arb.) 48 All to begrime you with worshyp. **1603** HOLLAND *Plutarch* 215 (R.) Enjoyning men to begrime and bewray themselves with dirt. **1853** SIR J. HERSCHEL *Pop. Lect. Sc.* i. §21 (1873) 15 In your eyes, in your mouth, begriming every pore.
Hence **be'grimed** *ppl. a.* **be'grimer** *sb.*
1604 SHAKS. *Oth.* III. iii. 387 My name that was as fresh As Dians Visage, is now begrim'd and blacke As mine own face. **1611** COTGR., *Patrouilleur*, a smeecher, begrimer, besmearer. **1865** *Sat. Rev.* 8 July 48/1 The blackened and begrimed people who had worked so hard.

†**be'gripe**, *v. Obs.* Forms: 1 begrípan, 2–3 bi-, begripen, 4 bigrype(n, 4–7 begripe. [Comm. WGer.: OE. *begrípan*, f. BE- + *grípan* to GRIPE = OHG. *begrîfan*, mod.G. *begreifen*, Du. *begrijpen*.]
1. *trans.* To catch hold of, apprehend; to seize and hold fast. Also *fig.*
c **1175** *Cott. Hom.* 237 Al se middennard was mid senne begripe. *c* **1220** *Bestiary* 516 in *O.E. Misc.* 16 Ðe grete maiȝ he noȝt bigripen. *c* **1340** *Gaw. & Gr. Knt.* 214 þe stele of a stif staf þe sturne hit bi-grypte. **1470–85** MALORY *Arthur* (1816) II. 295 This sword..shall never no man begripe.
2. To take in, contain, hold, comprehend.
1393 GOWER *Conf.* III. 102 Asie, Aufrique, Europe..Begripeth all this erthe round. *c* **1420** *Pallad. on Husb.* II. 278 Let stand as feel as may thi land begripe.
3. To take to task, reprehend.
a **1000** *Ags. Gloss. to Psalm* xv. 7. *c* **1200** ORMIN 19857 Sannt Johan haffde þe king Bigripenn off hiss sinne.

†**be'griple**, *v. Obs.* [Cf. GRIP, GRAPPLE.]
1607 TOPSELL *Four-f. Beasts* 178 The Crow with his talons so be-gripling the Foxes mouth that he could not bark.

begrown (bɪ'grəʊn), *ppl. a.*; also 3–4 bi-, begrowe, 6 begrowen. [f. BE- 1 + GROWN *ppl. a.*] Grown over *with*, covered with a growth.
a **1250** *Owl & Night.* 27 Mid ivi al bi-growe. **1393** GOWER *Conf.* II. 358 Of Timolus which was begrowe With vines. **1558** PHAËR *Æneid* VII. T iij, Ouer all begrowen with snakes. **1812** W. TAYLOR in *Month. Mag.* XXXIV. 210 Land begrown with trees.

begrudge (bɪ'grʌdʒ), *v.*; also 4 bi-, bygrucche(n, bygroch, 7–8 begrutch. [f. BE- + GRUDGE, ME. *grucchen* to murmur.] To grumble at, show dissatisfaction with; *esp.* to envy (one) the possession of; to give reluctantly, to be reluctant.
a. *trans.*, and with *inf. obj.*

1362 LANGL. *P. Pl.* A. VII. 62 And make him murie with þe Corn · hose hit euere bigrucceþ. **1642** FULLER *Holy & Prof. St.* II. xix. 125 Our Souldier..begrutcheth not to get to his side a probability of victory by the certainty of his own death. **1658** A. FOX *Wurtz' Surg.* II. xxv. 149 Begrudge not your labour you bestow. **1702** C. MATHER *Magn. Chr.* III. III. (1852) 551 To begrutch the cost of a school. **1711** SHAFTESB. *Charac.* III. 290 They will..begrudg the pains of attending. **1861** *National Rev.* Oct. 413 They did begrudge to pay the smart. **1862** TROLLOPE *Orley F.* xiii. 91 He had begrudged her nothing.

b. *intr. rare. Obs.*

1690 PENN *Rise & Progr. Quakers* (1834) 69 And not begrudge at one anothers increase.

Hence **be'grudged** *ppl. a.*

1840 R. DANA *Bef. Mast* xxxi. 117 Our common beverage—'water bewitched, and tea begrudged.'

begrudgingly (bɪ'grʌdʒɪŋlɪ), *adv.* [f. *begrudging* ppl. adj. + -LY[2].] In a grudging manner or spirit.

1853 *Fraser's Mag.* XLVIII. 159, I looked begrudgingly on them as they occupied the whole pool. **1878** HARDY *Ret. Native* VI. iv, The original owners..cackled begrudgingly at sight of such a quantity of their old clothes. **1890** *Illustr. Lond. News* 29 Nov. 686/1 It was a narrow little way begrudgingly left between these sullen hedges. **1968** *Listener* 11 July 44/1 Begrudgingly, the situation was accepted.

begruntle, etc.: see BE- *pref.*

begrutten (bɪ'grʌt(ə)n), *ppl. a. Sc.* [f. BE- 4 + *grutten*, pa. pple. of GREET *v.* to weep.] Marred or swollen in face with much weeping.

1805 A. SCOTT *Poems* 85 (JAM.) A hopeless maid of fifty years Begrutten sair, and blurr'd wi' tears. **1820** SCOTT *Monast.* viii, Poor things..they are sae begrutten.

begry, obs. form of BEGGARY.

†**'begster.** *Obs.* Also 4 beggestere. [f. BEG *v.* + -STER: cf. *trickster*.] A beggar (*fem.* and *pejorative*).

1386 CHAUCER *Prol.* 242 He knew the Tauernes wel in al the toun Bet than alaȝar or a beggestere. **1549** CHALONER *Erasm. Moriæ Enc.* N j a, Pestryng men every where..not a little to the hyndrance of other begsters.

†**be'guard**, *v. Obs.* Also 6 begard. [f. BE- 6 + GUARD *sb.*] *trans.* To adorn or furnish with 'guards' or facings, generally of lace or embroidery. Hence **be'guarded** *ppl. a.*

1605 J. DAVIES *Humours* 43 (D.) My too strait-laced all beguarded girles. **1640** FULLER *Joseph's Coat* (1867) 51 To seek with our own inventions to beguard that which God will have plain.

†**'beguel.** *Obs.* [ad. Du. *beugel* 'iron hoop or ring, bow, cramp iron,' f. *buigen* to bow. A Du. or Flemish term used in connexion with hops.]

1737 MILLER *Gard. Dict.* s.v. *Lupulus*, The Beguels of the Steddle where the Fire is kept.

be'guess, *adv. Sc.* Also 6–7 beges, begess. [f. *be* = BY *prep.* + GUESS.] By guess, at a venture.

c **1500** SCOTT in *Evergr.* I. 113 (JAM.) And hits begess. **1597** MONTGOMERIE *Cherry & Slae* xciii, A tentless Merchand..bying geir begess. **1724** RAMSAY *Tea-t. Misc.* (1733) I. 28 Twa pistals charg'd beguess.

beguild, obs. form of BEGILD.

beguile (bɪ'gaɪl), *v.* Forms: 3–4 bigile(n, 4 bygille, 4–5 bigyle, bygile, 4–6 begile, 4–7 begyle, 5 bygyle, -ile, 4– beguile. [f. BE- 2 + GUILE *v.*, cognate with WILE. The development of senses 3, 4, 5, is analogous to that of AMUSE, q.v.]

1. *trans.* To entangle or over-reach with guile; to delude, deceive, cheat.

a **1225** *Ancr. R.* 270 Non so wis ne so war..þet nis bigiled oðer hwules. *a* **1300** *Cursor M.* 716 And thoght hou he mith man bigile [*v.r.* bi-will]. *c* **1386** CHAUCER *Canon-Yem. Prol. & T.* 832 Lo thus byiaped and bigiled [*v.r.* bygiled, begiled, bygyled] was he. *c* **1450** *Merlin* 9 The feende myght neuer be-gyle her. **1552** LATIMER *Serm. Lincoln* ii. 73 Esau wept when Jacob begyled him. **1653** WALTON *Angler* 170 That you may..beguile this crafty fish. **1663** COWLEY *Verses & Ess.* (1669) 20 The foolish Lights which Travailers beguile. **1821** JOANNA BAILLIE *Met. Leg., Lady G. B.* ii, Are not my eyes beguiled? **1858** LONGF. *M. Standish* VIII. 81 Into an ambush beguiled, cut off with the whole of his forces.

b. *absol.*

c **1305** *St. James* 39 in *E.E.P.* 59 Leue to bigyli & bitraye also In eche quyntise þat mai. **1382** WYCLIF *Isa.* xxviii. 22 And now wileth not bigilen [**1388** nyle ȝe scorne; COVERD., make no mockes]. —— *Job* xl. 24 Whether thou shalt begile to hym as to a bird. **1602** WARNER *Alb. Eng.* x. liv. 242 For it a Nature was in Stukelie to begile.

2. To deprive *of* by fraud, to cheat out *of*.

a **1300** *Cursor M.* 8632 Qui has þu me bigiled [*Cott.* bisuiken] sua Of mi child þat mi-selue bar? **1394** *P. Pl. Crede* 51 Wymmen..begileth hem of her good wiþ glaueryngе wordes. **1593** HOOKER *Eccl. Pol.* III. i. §12 Wks. 1841 I. 285 Infants are beguiled of their right. **1611** BIBLE *Col.* ii. 18 Let no man beguile you of your reward. **1771** MACKENZIE *Man Feel.* xxxiv. (1803) 62 'I fear..sleep has beguiled me of my time.' **1826** SCOTT *Woodst.* xxxviii, Time is beguiling man of his strength.

†**3.** To cheat (hopes, expectations, aims, or a person in them); to disappoint, to foil. *Obs.*

1483 CAXTON *Cato* C vi, He is begyled for he findeth nothyng. **1576** BAKER *Gesner's Jewell Health* 201 a, This drinck rightly ministred never fayleth nor beguyleth the Phisition. **1591** SHAKS. *Two Gent.* v. iv. 37 Thou hast beguil'd my hopes. **1596** SPENSER *F.Q.* I. xi. 25 The knight was wroth to see his stroke beguil'd. *a* **1670** SPALDING *Troub. Chas. I*, (1792) I. 165 (JAM.) Still looking for the coming of his soldiers, but he was beguiled.

4. To win the attention or interest of (any one) by wiling means; to charm, divert, amuse; to wile (one) on, or into any course.

[*a* **1225** *Ancr. R.* 330 Edmodnesse eadiliche bigileð ure Louerd..& biȝit of his gode.] **1593** SHAKS. *Lucr.* 1404 It beguil'd attention, charm'd the sight. **1829** I. TAYLOR *Enthus.* vii. 177 Fertile in devices for beguiling mankind into virtue. **1872** JENKINSON *Guide Eng. Lakes* (1879) 198 The charms of this stream will beguile the tourist and diminish the toil of the ascent.

5. To divert attention in some pleasant way from (anything painful, or irksome); to elude the disagreeable sensation of, and so to cause to pass insensibly or pleasantly; to charm away, wile away.

1588 SHAKS. *Tit. A.* IV. i. 35 Take choyse of all my Library, And so beguile thy sorrow. **1601** —— *Twel. N.* III. iii. 41, I will bespeake our dyet, Whiles you beguile the time. **1718** POPE *Iliad* II. 788 Pleasing conference beguiles the day. **1764** GOLDSM. *Trav.* 152 By sports like these are all their cares beguil'd. **1802** SOUTHEY *Thalaba* IV, With various talk beguiling the long way. **1820** W. IRVING *Sketch Bk.* I. 177 Took a book to beguile the tedious hours.

beguile (bɪ'gaɪl), *sb. Sc.* [f. prec.] Deception.

1637 RUTHERFORD *Lett.* 176 (1862) I. 417, I will die in that sweet beguile. *a* **1709** W. GUTHRIE *Serm.* 20 (JAM.) Yond man has given himself a great beguile. **1768** ROSS *Helenore* 70 (JAM.), I gets the beguile. Nae thing I finds.

beguiled (bɪ'gaɪld), *ppl. a.* [f. BEGUILE *v.* + -ED.] **a.** Concealed or disguised by guile. **b.** Deluded, deceived by guile; self-deluded, mistaken.

1534 LD. BERNERS *Gold. Bk. M. Aurel.* (1546) B iv, I thinke I am not begyled in the histories. **1561** JR. HEYWOOD *Seneca's Herc. Furens* (1581) 3 b, He his begiled hookes doth bayte. **1876** GEO. ELIOT *Dan. Der.* III. xxxvii. 103 The beguiled mortal.

be'guileful, *a.* [f. BEGUILE *sb.* or *v.* + -FUL: cf. *assistful*.] Guileful, deceiving, deceptive.

1530 PALSGR. 305/2 Begylefull, disfaythfull, *cautelleux*. [**1613** R. C. *Table Alph.*, *Infallible*, vndeceiueable, vnbeguilefull.]

beguilement (bɪ'gaɪlmənt). [f. BEGUILE *v.* + -MENT.] The action or process of beguiling; also, its agencies and resulting condition or state.

1805 FOSTER *Ess.* I. ii. 24 The same beguilement in favour of ourselves. **1842** MRS. BROWNING *Grk. Chr. Poets* (1863) 69 From my heart in its beguilement. **1862** THORNBURY *Turner* I. 339 The aërial witchery and beguilement of such an hour. **1881** J. HAWTHORNE *Fort. Fool* I. iii.

beguiler (bɪ'gaɪlə(r)). [f. as prec. + -ER[1].] One that beguiles or deludes; a deceiver.

1382 WYCLIF *Job* xii. 16 The begilere [**1388** hym that disseyueth] and hym that is begiled. *a* **1450** *Knt. de la Tour* (1868) 175 Deceyuours or begylers of the ladyes and damoysels. **1526** TINDALE *Jude* i. 18 That there shulde be begylers in the last tyme. **1623** WOODROEPHE *Fr. & Eng. Gr.* 476 To-day a beguiler, to-morrow beguiled. *Mod.* A beguiler of the unwary.

beguiling (bɪ'gaɪlɪŋ), *vbl. sb.* [f. as prec. + -ING[1].] The action of the vb. BEGUILE: deluding, delusion, deception; beguilement.

c **1400** *Test. Love* II. (1560) 283/2 The false disceivable conjectments of mans beguilings. **1490** CAXTON *Eneydos* xv. 54 The perfytte begylynge that Juno had founde soo soone. **1594** CAREW *Huarte's Exam. Wits* ix. (1596) 125 Beguilings (saith Plato) neuer befall in things vnlike and very different. **1625** *Modell of Wit* 68 To preserue you from any such beguiling.

be'guiling, *ppl. a.* [f. as prec. + -ING[2].] That beguiles; deluding; charming, wiling away.

1593 SHAKS. *Ven. & Ad.* 24 Such time-beguiling sport. **1646** CRASHAW *Steps to Temple* 63 Some smiling But beguiling Spheres of sweet and sugar'd lies. **1814** WORDSW. *White Doe* IV. 106 The sense Of that beguiling influence.

be'guilingly, *adv.* [f. prec. + -LY[2].] In a beguiling or deceiving manner; illusively.

1847 in CRAIG.

†**be'guilous**, *a. Obs. rare*[−1]. = BEGUILEFUL.

1483 *Cath. Angl.* 26/1 *Begylows*, vbi false.

†**be'guilty**, *v. Obs. rare.* [f. BE- 5 + GUILTY.] *trans.* To render guilty.

a **1653** BP. SANDERSON *Serm.* 275 (T.), [Thou] dost at once beguilty thine own conscience with sordid bribery.

†**be'guily**, in expression *wily beguily*: see WILY.

‖**béguin** (begæ̃). [colloq. Fr.] An infatuation; a fancy.

1919 W. S. MAUGHAM *Moon & Sixpence* li. 223 It appears that she has a *béguin* for you... She's willing if you are. **1930** *Times Lit. Suppl.* 30 Oct. 886/2 Lady Bettine herself conceives a *béguin* for Arden. **1942** E. WAUGH *Put out More Flags* i. 34 Cedric Lyne..used to tell himself..that a béguin like that could not possibly last.

Beguinage ('begi,naʒ, 'bɛgɪnɪdʒ). [f. BEGUINE + -AGE.] An establishment of, or house for, beguines; often giving a name to a part of a town in the Low Countries.

1815 SOUTHEY in C. Southey *Life & Corr.* IV. 127. **1819** —— in *Q. Rev.* XXII. 94 The house at Little Gidding bore no resemblance whatever to a beguinage. **1854** H. STRICKLAND *Trav. Th.* 26 Went to the Beguinage. Nunnery of nuns who are not nuns; that is, who vow no vows, and may go away and marry whenever they like.

Beguine (be'gin, 'bɛgɪn). Forms: 5 bygyn, begyne, 6 begine, -ghine, -gyn, biggayne, 7 beguin, beggin, 6– beguine. [a. F. *béguine* (13th c. in Littré), in med.L. *beguīna*, *begīna*, *beghīna* (Du Cange), an appellative derived from the surname of Lambert Bègue or *le Bègue* ('the Stammerer'), a priest of Liège, in the 12th c., the founder of the order.

(Cf. the annal of 1180, quoted in Du Cange: 'God stirred up the spirit of a certain holy priest, a man of religion, who was called Lambert le Bègue (because he was a stammerer) of St. Christopher [in Liège], from whose surname women and girls who propose to live chastly, are called *Beguines*, because he was the first to arise and preach to them by his word and example the reward of chastity.' The cap *béguin* derives its name from them, and not *vice versâ*.)]

A name for the members of certain lay sisterhoods which began in the Low Countries in the 12th century, who devoted themselves to a religious life, but did not bind themselves by strict vows, and might leave their societies for marriage. They were protected by Pope John XXII, when he persecuted the male Beguins or Beghards, and are still represented by small communities existing in the Netherlands, with an organization somewhat similar to some Anglican sisterhoods.

1483 CAXTON *Gold. Leg.* 431/1 Almoses to y[e] blynde begynes, doughters of god. **1552** BALE *Apol.* 20 Not to vysite..wydowes in their trouble, but wanton wenches, beghines, nunnes and vowesses. **1595** *World of Wond.* (1608) 184 Young wanton wenches, and beguins, nuns, and naughty packs. **1599** THYNNE *Animadv.* 37 But this woorde 'Begyn' sholde in his owne nature rightlye haue ben expounded, 'supersticious or hipocriticall wemenne.' **1629** *S'hertogenbosh* 37 The Beggins..did make cushions for the Souldiers. **1765** STERNE *Tr. Shandy* (1802) VIII. xx. 162 She was a young Beguine..they can quit their cloister if they choose to marry. *a* **1843** SOUTHEY *Poet's Pilgr.* Proem. xvi, Behold the black Beguine, the Sister grey. **1851** KINGSLEY *Yeast* ix. 182 To write at once to the Superior of the Béguines.

attrib. **1850** THACKERAY *Pendennis* lvi, The Béguine convents which they visited.

beguine[2] (bɪ'gi:n). [Amer. Fr., f. Fr. *béguin* (see BÉGUIN).]

A kind of popular dance, orig. associated with Martinique; also applied to a kind of syncopated dance rhythm.

1935 COLE PORTER (*song title*) Begin the Beguine. **1939** W. HOBSON *Amer. Jazz Music* 53 Jazz rhythms have been partly affected by West Indian rhythms, such as the rhumba, beguine, etc. **1950** J. VEDEY *Band Leaders* xviii. 131 The 'Beguine' from Mexico..has an essentially Afro-Spanish flavour. **1961** A. BERKMAN *Singers' Gloss. Show Bus.* 8 *Beguine*, a rhythm used to give a certain amount of 'lift' to a sustained melody by doubling up the rhythmic beats... In the Beguine the rhythm instruments repeat the same rhythmic pattern over and over, without variation.

begulf, begum, begut, etc.: see BE- *pref.*

†**be'gull**, *v. Obs.* [f. BE- 2 or 5 + GULL.] *trans.* To make a gull of; to gull, impose upon.

1605 BRETON *Olde Man's Less.* (1876) 13 Trauailers are giuen..to begull the worlde with gudgins. **1620** SHELTON *Quix.* IV. xxi. II. 252 You are..begull'ed and made a Fool.

‖**begum** ('bi:gəm). Also 7 beggoon, begun, 9 beegum, begaum. [Urdū (Pers.) *begam*, ad. Eastern Turkish *bigim* princess, fem. of *big*, *bik* prince (in Osmanli BEG, BEY).] A queen, princess, or lady of high rank in Hindustan.

1634 SIR T. HERBERT *Trav.* (1677) 99 Queen, *Begun.* **1786** BURKE *Art. W. Hastings* Wks. XI. 381 Prayer was made not to dishonour the Begum (a princess of great rank, whose husband had been killed in the battle). **1841** MACAULAY *W. Hastings, Ess.* III. 431 Jewels torn from Indian Begums.

begun (bɪ'gʌn), *ppl. a.* Also 6 begon, began. [f. BEGIN *v.*] That has begun, or has been begun.

1483 *Cath. Angl.* 26 Begunne, *exorsus*, *jnceptus*, *jnitus.* **1597** J. PAYNE *Royal Exch.* 33 That begon roote not beinge norrished..yt becomes weaker. *a* **1610** BABINGTON *Wks.* 9 A steadfast heart to effect a good begun is a great vertue. **1847** BUSHNELL *Chr. Nurt.* II. iv. (1861) 309 To be recognized in a begun relationship.

begunk (bɪ'gʌŋk), *v. Sc.* [Cf. BEGECK.] *trans.* To delude, play a deceiving trick on, 'take in.'

1821 *Blackw. Mag.* Jan. 426 (JAM.) Is there a lad, whose father is unkind..Whose sweetheart has begunked him?

be'gunk, *sb. Sc.* Also 8 begink. [f. prec.] A befooling or deluding trick, a piece of deception.

1725 RAMSAY *Gentle Sheph.* II. i. 30 Ane ca'd Monk Has play'd the Rumple a right slee begunk. **1790** MORISON *Poems* 137 (JAM.) Our sex are shy..they think, Wha yields o'er soon fu' aft gets the begink. **1814** SCOTT *Waverley* III. 354 If I have na gien Inch-Grabbit and Jamie Howie a bonnie begunk, they ken themselves.

begyle, obs. form of BEGUILE.

begyn, begyrd, obs. forms of BEGIN, BEGIRD.

† **be'hack**, *v. Obs.* [f. BE- 1 + HACK *v.*] *trans.* To hack about.

1565 CALFHILL *Answ. Treat. Crosse* (1846) 3 The blade itself is all to behacked. **1631** *Celestina* XII. 143 My sword like a saw, all to behack't and hew'd.

behale, behallow, behammer, etc.: see BE-.

behalf (bɪ'hɑːf). Forms: 4 **bihelue, bihalf,** 4–5 **bi-, byhalve,** 4–6 **behalve,** 4–7 **behalfe,** 6 **behave,** 5– **behalf.** *Pl.* 6–7 **behalfes, behalfs.** [Used only in the phrases *on, in behalf (of), in, on (his,* etc.) *behalf*, which arose about 1300, by the blending of the two earlier constructions *on his halve* and *bihalve him*, both meaning 'by or on his side': see HALF. By the mixture of these in the construction *on his bihalve*, BIHALVE, previously a preposition, and originally a phrase, *be healfe* 'by (the) side,' became treated, so far as construction goes, as a sb., and had even a plural *behalfes, behalfs* in 16–17th c. The final *-e* of ME. was the dative ending. In modern use, construed either with a possessive pronoun (in my behalf), a possessive case (in the king's behalf), or with *of* (in behalf of the starving population); the choice being determined by considerations of euphony and perspicuity. Formerly *of* was sometimes omitted.]

I. 1. *on behalf of*: † **a.** (*lit.*) On the side of. *Obs.*

1502 ARNOLD *Chron.* (1811) 29 Other Sherefs on this behalfe trente.

† **b.** (*fig.*) On (one's own) part or side. *Obs.*

c **1386** CHAUCER *Melib.* ¶831 Tellynge hem on youre bihalue [*v.r.* behalue, bihalfe, behalf] þat if they wole trete of pees..that they shape hem..to comen vnto vs. **1538** STARKEY *England* 11 They Turkys wyl surely say on theyr behalfe that theyr lyfe ys most natural and polytyke..the Sarasyn contrary, apon hys behalfe, wyl defend hys pollycy.

c. On the part of (another), in the name of, as the agent or representative of, on account of, for, instead of. (With the notion of official agency.)

1303 R. BRUNNE *Handl. Synne* 9066 On Goddes behalve y ȝow forbede þat ȝe no lenger do swych dede. *c* **1374** CHAUCER *Troylus* II. 1409 Spek thow thiself also to Troylus On my bihalve [*v.r.* behalfe]. **1485** CAXTON *Paris & V.* (1868) 80 So say ye to hym on my behalve. **1535** COVERDALE *1 Sam.* xxv. 6 Salute him frendly on my behalfe. **1768** BLACKSTONE *Comm.* I. 429 Things which a servant may do on behalf of his master..proceed upon this principle, that the master is answerable for the act of his servant, if done by his command, either expressly given, or implied. **1883** SIR J. MATTHEW *Law Rep.* XI. *Q. Bench Div.* 592 An application was made on behalf of the prosecutor for a remand.

† **d.** As concerns, with regard to, in the matter of. Also, *on this behalf*, etc. *Obs.* Cf. 2 c.

1581 J. BELL *Haddon's Answ. Osor.* 431 Your utter destruction, which..is much to be feared on your behalfes. **1611** BIBLE *Ex.* xxvii. 21 It shall be a statute for euer..on the behalfe of [COVERD. among] the children of Israel. **1623** LISLE *Test. Antiq.* Introd., The common taught doctrine of the Church of England on this behalfe. **1674** N. FAIRFAX *Bulk and Selv.* 164 Why could not God as well make the world everlasting *a parte ante*, on the behalf of formerness, as he did the soul of man *a parte post*, on the behalf of latterness?

¶ In recent use we often find *on behalf* in the sense of *in behalf* 2 b, to the loss of an important distinction.

1791 COWPER *Iliad* IV. 63, I will not interpose on their behalf. **1851** DIXON *W. Penn* xx. (1872) 174 A petition on behalf of Sydney was sent to the House of Commons. **1852** MISS YONGE *Cameos* II. xxxvii. 287 They interfered on his behalf. **1862** TRENCH *Mirac.* xxxii. 448 This gracious work wrought on behalf of one who was in arms against his life.

2. *in behalf of*: † **a.** In the name of. *Obs.* Cf. 1 c.

c **1320** *Seuyn Sag.* (W.) 324 The seven wise thai grette In th'emperours bihelue. *c* **1400** *Apol. Loll.* 38 We forbede him in almiȝti Goddis behalue..þe entre of þe kirk. **1523** LD. BERNERS *Froiss.* I. cviii. 130 Ther is no persone in his behalfe, that wyll stoppe you of your way. **1606** SHAKS. *Tr. & Cr.* v. iii. 22 And rob in the behalfe of charitie.

b. In the interest of, as a friend or defender of, for the benefit of. (With the notion of interposition: 'speak in my behalf' = in my interest, say a good word for me, intercede for me.)

1598 SHAKS. *Merry W.* I. iv. 168 Let mee haue thy voice in my behalfe. **1711** STEELE *Spect.* No. 51 ¶2 There is a great deal to be said in Behalf of an Author. **1719** W. WOOD *Surv. Trade* 28 Speaking in Behalf the Trading Interest. **1749** FIELDING *Tom Jones* VII. xiv, She should immediately have interposed in his behalf. **1848** MACAULAY *Hist.* I. 620 Imploring the Queen Dowager..to intercede in his behalf.

c. *in this* or *that behalf*: in respect of, in regard to, in reference to this or that; in this or that matter, or aspect of the matter. *arch.* Cf. 1 d.

1458 EARL SALISBURY in *Paston Lett.* I. 421 The said diseas which hath right fervently and sore holden me in many diversez bihalvez. **1489** CAXTON *Faytes A.* I. xv. 40 Takyng of gode kepe vpon hys peple in this byhalue. **1534** WHITTINTON *Tullyes Offices* I. (1540) 10 In this behalfe we be bounde to folowe nature as a gyde. **1598** GREENWEY *Tacitus' Ann.* III. iii. (1622) 65 Not hoping to find him cruell in his behalfe..but rather fauorable. **1621** *Bk. Discip. Ch. Scot.* 84 To assist and fortifie the godly proceedings of the Kirk in all behalfes. **1658** A. FOX *Wurtz' Surg.* II. v. 60 More could be said in that behalf, but..[it] would be too great a labour. **1772** *Junius Lett.* lxviii. 338 Our statute in law, in this behalf..is directed by the same spirit.

II. Obsolete phrases.

† **3.** *of his behalf*: of or from his side or part; on his part. Cf. 1 a. *Obs.*

c **1450** *Merlin* xv. 241 The londe that cometh of youre behalue ne may I not lese. ? *c* **1500** *Virgilius* in Thomas *E.E. Rom.* II. 24 This Nemus had a knyght of his moders behalfe. **1551** ROBINSON tr. *More's Utop.* 155 The loue and honoure whiche of theire behalfe is dewe to God.

† **4.** *to* or *for the behalf of*: to the interest or advantage of, for the behoof of. Cf. 2. *Obs.*

1562 COOPER *Answ. Priv. Masse* (1850) 56 Ye never affirmed mass to be private, but to pertain to the behalf of all states and sorts of men. **1566** *Wills & Inv. N.C.* (1835) 255 For the behave of my wif and children. **1576** LAMBARDE *Peramb. Kent* (1862) 295 Some others seised some of the Kings owne Castles to the behalfe of the Empresse.

† **be'hang**, *v. Obs.* For forms see HANG *v.* [OE. *behón* (= OS. *bihâhan*; cf. mod.G. *behängen*), f. BE- about + *hón* (:—*hanhan*) to HANG. *Obs.* since 17th c. exc. in *pa. pple.* BEHUNG.] To hang (a thing) about *with* (bells, hangings, drapery, etc.).

c **897** K. ÆLFRED *Past.* xv. (Sw. 92) Se sacerd sceolde bion mid bellum behangen. *c* **1200** *Trin. Coll. Hom.* 89 þat burh folc..bihengen it mid palmes. *c* **1300** *K. Alis.* 758 He dude his temple al by-honge With bawdekyn, brod and longe. **1393** GOWER *Conf.* II. 384 With great richesse he him behongeth. **1597** R. JOHNSON *Sev. Champ.* I. x. 65 Winter..behung the trees wit crystal icicles. **1648** HERRICK *Poems* (1869) I. 13 And with rich clusters..her temples I behung.

† **be'hanged**, *ppl. a. Obs.* Forms: 2–3 **bihenged,** 3–4 **be-, bihonged,** 5–7 **behanged.** [f. prec. + -ED.] Hung about, draped, hung.

c **1200** ORMIN 951 þatt tall Iudisskenn preost wass swa Bihenngedd all wiþþ belless. *c* **1330** *Arth. & Merl.* 3549 Eueri strete Was behonged..With mani pal and riche cloth. **1553–87** FOXE *A. & M.* (1596) 114/2 A faire palace richlie behanged. **1601** HOLLAND *Pliny* I. 255 Our dames and gentlewomen must haue their eares behanged with them.

† **be'hap**, *v. Obs.* [f. BE- 2 + HAP *v.*] To befall, happen. Const. with *dative obj.*

c **1450** LONELICH *Grail* xiii. 26 What so behapped him in oni chaunce. *Ibid.* lv. 417 It behappede that kyng Lambors And this kyng Varlans..assembled were. *a* **1450** *Knt. de la Tour* vi. 9 And this behapped her. **1714** GAY *Sheph. Week, Thursd.* 125 Behap what will.

† **be'happen**, *v. Obs.* [f. BE- 2 + HAPPEN.] To befall, happen. Const. with *dative obj.*, or *to, unto*.

1515 *Scot. Field* 97 in Furniv. *Percy Folio* I. 217 Care him be-happen! **1596** SPENSER *F.Q.* v. xi. 52 That is the greatest shame..Which unto any knight behappen may. **1631** WEEVER *Anc. Fun. Mon.* 201 Many remarkable occurrences behappened this Martyr.

Behari, var. BIHARI *a.*

behate, early form of BEHOTE *sb.*, BEHIGHT *v.*

† **be'hate**, *ppl. a. Obs.* Also 4 **by-.** [f. BE- 2 + HATE.] To hold in hatred, to hate greatly, detest.

c **1340** *Cursor M.* 11962 (Laud MS.) Why he makyth vs for his maners by-hatid [*v.r.* be hated] þus. *c* **1374** CHAUCER *Boeth.* III. iv. 75 Al was he byhated of all folk. **1474** CAXTON *Chesse* 89 He was sore behated. **1577** HOLINSHED *Chron.* II. 34/1 Through false informations wrongfullie behated.

behave (bɪ'heɪv), *v.* Pa. t. **behaved** (in 6 **behad.**) [Formed, app. in 15th c., from BE- 2 + HAVE *v.*, in order to express a qualified sense of *have*, particularly in the reflexive 'to have or bear oneself (in a specified way),' which answers exactly to mod.G. *sich behaben.* (OE. had *behabban* = OHG. *bihabên*, f. BE- about + *habban* to hold, HAVE, in senses 'encompass, contain, detain'; but there was no historical connexion between that and the 15th c. *behave.*)]

1. *refl.* To bear, comport, or conduct oneself; to act: **a.** with *adv.* or qualifying phrase, expressing the manner. (Formerly a dignified expression, applied e.g. to the bearing, deportment, and public conduct of persons of distinction; in 17–18th c. commonly used of the way in which soldiers acquit themselves in battle; but now chiefly expressing observance of propriety in personal conduct, and usually as in b. The intr. sense 3, preserves the earlier use.)

c **1440** *Bone Flor.* 1567 To lerne hur to behave hur among men. **1474** CAXTON *Chesse* 74 Ony man that wylle truly behaue hym self. *a* **1520** *Myrr. Our Ladye* 241 Yet in all her trybulacions she behad her so paciently. **1533** BELLENDEN *Livy* I. (1822) 15 The mair princely that he behad him in his dignite riall. **1611** BIBLE *1 Chron.* xix. 13 Let vs behaue our selues valiantly for our people. **1665** MANLEY *Grotius' Low-C. Warres* 303 The Sea-men..would be ready to mutiny for their Pay, and threaten to behave themselves as Enemies. **1711** STEELE *Spect.* No. 2 ¶4 He was some Years a Captain, and behaved himself with great Galantry in several Engagements. **1715** in *Lond. Gaz.* No. 5390/2 The Clans behave themselves with great Insolence. **1733** PENDARVES in *Swift's Lett.* (1768) IV. 39 Let me know if I have behaved myself right. **1823** SCOTT *F.M. Perth* III. 303 The Chief had behaved himself with the most determined courage.

b. Without qualification: To conduct oneself well, or (in modern use) with propriety. Now chiefly said of children or young people, who might possibly *misbehave* themselves.

1691 LUTTRELL *Brief Rel.* (1857) II. 209 The French King hath given large gratuities to Mr. Vauban and other officers that behaved themselves before Mons. *Mod. colloq.* If you cannot behave yourself, you had better stay at home. *Mod. Sc. maxim*, 'Behave yourself before folk.'

c. *transf.* of things: To comport itself in any relation, to act (*towards* other things).

1541 R. COPLAND *Galyen's Terap.* 2 Bjb, Euery thyng that behaueth it wel and is accordyng to nature. **1650** FULLER *Pisgah* I. xi. 36 If these three Provinces be.. compared together, they behave themselves as followeth. **1674** N. FAIRFAX *Bulk & Selv.* 54 How the Worlds vastness behaves it self towards Gods Immensity.

† **2.** *trans.* To handle, manage, wield, conduct, regulate (in some specified way). *Obs.*

1526 SKELTON *Magnyf.* 1366 Without crafte nothynge is well behavyd. **1557** NORTH *Gueuara's Dial. Pr.* (1585) 277 These pinchpenies do behave their persons so evil, etc. **1596** SPENSER *F.Q.* II. iii. 40 Who his limbs with labours and his mind Behaues with cares, cannot so easie mis. **1607** SHAKS. *Timon* III. v. 22 With such sober and vnnoted passion He did behaue [*printed* behooue] his anger.

3. *intr.*: in same senses as 1 a and b (which it now to a great extent replaces).

1719 YOUNG *Revenge* I. i, As you behave, Your father's kindness stabs me to the heart. **1812** LD. CATHCART in *Examiner* 12 Oct. 649/1 Those who were engaged behaved well. **1855** MACAULAY *Hist. Eng.* III. 678 He behaved like a man of sense and spirit. **1866** KINGSLEY *Herew.* vii. 129 She behaved not over wisely or well. **1872** RUSKIN *Eagle's N.* §161 You must very..thoroughly know how to behave.

b. *to behave towards* or *to*: to conduct oneself in regard *to*, act, deal with, treat (in any way).

1754 CHATHAM *Lett. Nephew* iv. 24 As to your manner of behaving towards these unhappy young gentlemen. **1875** JOWETT *Plato* (ed. 2) I. 51 Did you ever behave ill to your father or your mother? *Mod.* They have behaved very handsomely to you.

c. *transf.* of things.

1854 SCOFFERN in *Orr's Circ. Sc.* Chem. 463 It combines violently with water, behaving like the bichloride of tin. **1871** B. STEWART *Heat* §38 Glass will also behave in a very different manner according as it is annealed or unannealed.

† **be'have**, *sb. Obs.* [f. prec.] = BEHAVIOUR.

1615 CHAPMAN *Odyss.* XXII. 545 Only there were twelve that gave Themselves to impudence and light behave.

behaved (bɪ'heɪvd), *ppl. a.* [pa. pple. of BEHAVE: cf. *learned, well-read*, etc.] Conducted, mannered; usually with qualifying adv., as ***well-behaved, ill-behaved.***

1602 SHAKS. *Ham.* III. i. 35 And gather by him, as he is behaued, If't be th' affliction of his loue or no. **1713** *Guardian* No. 6 ¶4 Their servants well behaved. **1837** CARLYLE *Fr. Rev.* I. IV. iv. 167 The brown-locked, light-behaved, fire-hearted Demoiselle. **1858** W. ELLIS *Vis. Madagascar* iv. 89 Well-behaved scholars.

behaving (bɪ'heɪvɪŋ), *vbl. sb.* [f. BEHAVE *v.* + -ING[1].] Conduct, behaviour.

c **1450** *Merlin* 49 And I will also that ye tweyn prively in counseile knowe my condicions and my behavynge. **1482** *Monk of Evesham* (Arb.) 47 Wyth an enarrabulle gestur and behauing of gladnes. **1495** *Act 2 Hen. VII*, ii. § 5 To take suertie of the kepers of ale houses of their gode behavyng. **1523** LD. BERNERS *Froiss.* I. xiv. 14 All his vsages, and euyll behauyngis. **1817** FRERE *K. Arthur* I. x, For fine behaving King Arthur's Court has never had its match.

behaviour (bɪ'heɪvjə(r)), *sb.* Forms: 5–6 **behauour(e,** 6–7 **behauiour(e, -ior,** 6 **behauer, -eour(e, behauyour,** 7 **behauor, behavier,** ? 6– **behaviour.** [f. BEHAVE *v.*, by form-analogy with HAVOUR, *havyoure*, common 15–16th c. forms of the word which was orig. AVER *sb.* (q.v.), *aveyr*, also in 15th c. *avoir*; really OF. *aveir, avoir*, in sense of 'having, possession,' but naturally affiliated in Eng. to the native verb *have*, and spelt *haver, havour, haviour*, etc. Hence, by analogy, *have*: *havour, -iour*: *behave*: *behavour, -iour.* The formation might be confirmed by the (apparently) parallel *demeanour*, from *demean* (oneself). For the *-iour* see HAVOUR.]

1. a. Manner of conducting oneself in the external relations of life; demeanour, deportment, bearing, manners.

1490 CAXTON *Eneydos* xxxi. 120 For hys honneste behauoure [he] began to be taken with his loue. **1530** BALE *Thre Lawes* 53 In clennes of lyfe and in a gentyll behauer. **1601** SHAKS. *Twel. N.* III. iv. 202 The behauiour of the yong Gentleman, giues him out to be of good capacity, and breeding. **1754** CHATHAM *Lett. Nephew* v. 32 Behaviour is of infinite advantage or prejudice to a man. **1797** GODWIN *Enquirer* I. xiii. 111 Their behaviour is forced and artificial. **1862** H. SPENCER *First Princ.* II. i. §36 Special directions for behaviour in the nursery, at table, or on the exchange. **1875** JOWETT *Plato* (ed. 2) IV. 226 His courage is shown by his behaviour in the battle.

b. Also in *pl.*

1538 BALE *Comedy* in *Harl. Misc.* (Malh.) I. 211 Your fastynges, longe prayers, with other holy behauers. **1601** SHAKS. *Jul. C.* I. ii. 42 Which giue some soyle (perhaps) to my Behauiours. **1678** CUDWORTH *Intell. Syst.* I. iv. §19. 366 To observe the actions, manners and Behaviours of men. *a* **1763** 'GEO. PSALMANAZAR' *Mem.* (1764) 186, I could see.. thro' all his artifices and different behaviours. **1959** *Camb. Rev.* 7 Mar. 405/1 We must surely accept that the pattern of associated behaviours first noticed by Weber was one of the most brilliantly successful suggestions in the whole history of intellectual endeavour.

†**c.** The bearing of the character of another; personification, 'person.' *Obs.*

1595 SHAKS. *John* I. i. 3 Thus speakes the King of France, In my behauiour, to the Maiesty..of England heere.

†**d.** 'External appearance with respect to grace.' Johnson. *Obs.*

a **1586** SIDNEY (J.) He marked, in Dora's dancing, good grace and handsome behaviour. **1639** FULLER *Holy War* I. vi. (1840) 8 [Mahometanism] having neither real substance in her doctrine, nor winning behavior in her ceremonies to allure professors.

e. *absol.* Good manners, elegant deportment.

1591 LAMBARDE *Arch.* (1635) 91 A man of behaviour and countenance. **1701** DE FOE *True Born Eng.* Wks. (1841) 24 Strong aversion to Behaviour. **1711** ADDISON *Spect.* No. 119 ¶1 By Manners I do not mean Morals, but Behaviour and Good-breeding.

2. Conduct, general practice, course of life; course of action *towards* or *to* others, treatment of others.

1515 BARCLAY *Cyt. & Uplondyshm.* (1847) 70 All people of good behavour By rightwise battayle, justice and equitie. **1535** COVERDALE *1 Macc.* xiv. 35 His godly behauoure, and faithfulnesse which he kepte vnto them. **1584** POWEL *Lloyd's Cambria* 88 By his rich gifts and princely Behauior. **1641** J. JACKSON *True Evang. Temp.* II. 124 The blamelesse behaviour of the Christians. **1719** YOUNG *Revenge* I. i, This severe behaviour Has, to my comfort, made it sweet to die. **1768** BLACKSTONE *Comm.* IV. 251 Recognizances, for the peace, and for the good behaviour. **1858** FROUDE *Hist. Eng.* IV. xviii. 36 Henry's early behaviour to James.

3. Phrase. *to be* (or *stand*) *on* or *upon one's behaviour*, or *one's good behaviour*: to be placed on a trial of conduct or deportment, to be in a situation in which a failure in conduct will have untoward consequences; hence, to behave one's best.

1538 STARKEY *England* 196 And much bettur hyt were that they schuld stond apon theyr behavyour. **1698** NORRIS *Pract. Disc.* IV. 261 Man..is now upon his Behaviour in order to a Better World. **1689** SHERLOCK *Death* i. §1 (1731) 20 Adam..was but upon his good Behaviour, was but a Probationer for Immortality. **1779** BURKE in Boswell *Johnson* III. 172, I should be obliged to be so much upon my good behaviour. *Mod.* Tell the children to be on their best behaviour.

†**4.** Handling, management, disposition *of* (anything); bearing (*of* body). *Obs.*

1549 COVERDALE *Erasm. Par. 1 Peter* 8 Welfavourednes of beautie, and behaviour of apparel. **1563** *Homilies* II. *Fasting* (1859) 281 Both with words and behavour of body to shew themselves weary of this life. **1589** PUTTENHAM *Eng. Poesie* (Arb.) 262 Your misplacing and preposterous placing is not all one in behaviour of language.

5. *transf.* The manner in which a thing acts under specified conditions or circumstances, or in relation to other things.

1674 N. FAIRFAX *Bulk & Selv.* 82 All local habitude or behaviour must be between two things or more, in a place so or so. **1866** ARGYLL *Reign Law* ii. 67 In Chemistry the behaviour of different substances towards each other, in respect to combination and affinity. **1878** HUXLEY *Physiogr.* 135 To watch..the behaviour of the water which drains off a flat coast of mud. **1882** *Daily Tel.* 4 May, The behaviour of the vessel during her maiden voyage across the Atlantic.

6. *attrib.* and *Comb.*, esp. in *Psychol.*, as *behaviour-cycle, data, -study, -system, -trend*; **behaviour pattern**, a set or series of acts regarded as a unified whole; **behaviour segment**, a part of a behaviour pattern; **behaviour therapy**, a method of treating neurotic disorders (see quots.).

1921 B. RUSSELL *Anal. Mind* iii. 65 A '*behaviour-cycle' is a series of voluntary or reflex movements of an animal, tending to cause a certain result, and continuing until that result is caused, unless they are interrupted by death, accident, or some new behaviour-cycle. **1913** J. B. WATSON in *Psychol. Rev.* XX. 158 On this assumption, *behavior data (including under this term everything which goes under the name of comparative psychology) have no value *per se.* **1926** *Psychol. Rev.* XXXIII. 51 Is this modification of activity the result of environmentally conditioned learning or of the maturing of certain innate *behavior patterns or 'instincts'? **1929** B. RUSSELL *Marriage & Morals* ii. 19 Where human beings are concerned we do not have the precise behaviour-patterns which are to be found among other animals. **1956** *Evolution* X. 421 (*title*) A gene mutation which changes a behavior pattern. **1960** *20th Cent.* Apr. 372 As far as behaviour patterns are concerned, I feel..a greater affinity with the working-class Briton than with the middle-class man. **1934** H. C. WARREN *Dict. Psychol.* 31/1 *Behavior segment. **1936** J. KANTOR *Objective Psychol. Gram.* vi. 74 B..now becomes speaker. His speaking behaviour constitutes his second linguistic behaviour segment, his first being his audient response. **1953** N. TINBERGEN *Herring Gull's World* vii. 64 A man who does not have the patience simply to sit and watch for hours, days,.. is not the type of man to undertake a *behaviour-study. **1927** G. A. DE LAGUNA *Speech* vi. 132 The *behavior-system of one species differs from that of another. **1938** A. N. WHITEHEAD *Modes of Thought* i. 20 There is no one behaviour-system belonging to the essential character of the universe, as the universal moral ideal. **1958** A. R. RADCLIFFE-BROWN *Method in Social Anthrop.* I. iv. 103 Psychology is here taken to mean the study of the mental or psychic systems—if you will, the behaviour systems—of organisms. **1959** H. J. EYSENCK in *Jrnl. Mental Sci.* CV. 66, I have called these methods [of treatment] '*behaviour therapy' to contrast them with methods of psychotherapy. .. Psychoanalysts show a preoccupation with psychological methods involving mainly *speech*, while behaviour therapy concentrates on actual *behaviour* as most likely to lead to the extinction of the unadaptive conditioned responses. **1961** *Guardian* 12 May 6/6 This new approach, which owes much to J. B. Watson,..and to J. Wolpe, the well-known South African psychologist, has been christened Behaviour Therapy... Behaviour therapy..tries to understand neurotic symptoms..in terms of..experimentally established facts of human and animal behaviour. **1949** G. RYLE *Concept of Mind* iv. 110 To explain an action as done from a certain motive is..to subsume it under a ..*behaviour-trend.

behavioural (bɪˈheɪvjərəl), *a.* [f. BEHAVIOUR + -AL.] Concerned with, or forming part of, behaviour. Hence **be'haviourally** *adv.*

a **1927** E. B. TITCHENER *Systematic Psychol.* (1929) iii. 263 All biological facts, we propose to say, are 'behavioural'. **1936** J. KANTOR *Objective Psychol. Gram.* xv. 213 Vocabulary phenomena.., though remote from things,.. operate behaviourally in a definite adjustmental manner. **1946** C. W. MORRIS *Signs, Lang. & Behavior* i. 4 A behavioral theory of signs. *Ibid.* i. 21 Vagueness shows itself behaviorally in an uncertain and hesitant response to an object to which the organism has been directed by a sign. **1956** *Camb. Rev.* LXXVII. 301 Some contrasting of C and I behavioural and linguistic patterns is possible. **1958** *New Statesman* 6 Sept. 300/2 The so-called 'behavioural sciences'..—sociology, social psychology, social anthropology—have been much pushed by the foundations.

†**be'havioured**, *a. Obs.* [f. BEHAVIOUR *sb.* + -ED².] Conducted, mannered, behaved.

1589 PUTTENHAM *Eng. Poesie* (Arb.) 157 Men ciuill and graciously behauoured and bred. **1591** HARINGTON *Orl. Fur.* XLII. lxv, A well behavioured knight. **1624** CAPT. SMITH *Virginia* IV. 123 They haue seene many English Ladies worse faured, proportioned and behauiored.

behaviourism (bɪˈheɪvjərɪz(ə)m). *Psychol.* [f. BEHAVIOUR + -ISM.] A theory and method of psychological investigation based on the study and analysis of behaviour. Hence **be'haviourist**, one who practises this method; also *attrib.*; **behaviou'ristic** *a.*, of or belonging to the behaviourists; characterized by behaviourism; also *gen.*, pertaining or relating to behaviour; **behaviou'ristically** *adv.*; **behaviou'ristics** *sb. pl.*, the study of the responses of organisms to their environment.

1913 J. B. WATSON in *Psychol. Rev.* XX. 158 Psychology as the behaviorist views it is a purely objective experimental branch of natural science. Its theoretical goal is the prediction and control of behavior. *Ibid.* 166, I feel that *behaviorism* is the only consistent and logical functionalism. **1914** E. G. TITCHENER in *Proc. Amer. Philos. Soc.* LIII. 3 Most of the essential problems with which psychology as an introspective science now concerns itself are open to behaviorist treatment. *Ibid.* 13 The facts of psychology..are also to be carried, by way of behavioristic substitution, to the bodily periphery. **1916** *Boston Even. Transcript* 26 July 116 A behavioristic psychology. **1920** A. N. WHITEHEAD *Concept of Nature* ix. 185 Our attitude towards nature is purely 'behaviouristic'. **1921** *Edin. Rev.* Apr. 351 Psychologists are divided into several camps, one of which, the American 'Behaviourists', cares very little for the social aspects of the subject. **1922** *Times Lit. Suppl.* 20 July 478/4 The determinist is logically driven to 'behaviourism'. **1924** J. B. WATSON in *Psyche* July 11 Behavioristic psychology. **1933** *Mind* XLII. 381 The Communist studies religion, as a social phenomenon, *behaviouristically*. **1936** E. E. EVANS-PRITCHARD *Ess. Soc. Anthrop.* (1962) viii. 196 We treat them [*sc.* the ideas] behaviouristically as ritual responses and do not attempt to create for them an ideology that will explain them by seeming to cause them. **1940** BRYANT & AIKEN *Psychol. of English* i. 5 The English language and grammar are the products of the group thinking of billions of people whose minds have worked psychologically rather than logically; and the fruit..is a system which reflects behavioristic patterns rather than formal regularity. **1941** O. NEURATH in *Proc. Arist. Soc.* XLI. 128 There is a trend to build up a Lingua Franca..which would enable us to pass from the theory of behaviour ('behaviouristics') to geology, biology and mechanics without any alteration of the type of our expressions. **1945** *Mind* LIV. 193 Scientific psychology is either behaviouristic or physiological. **1953** J. B. CARROLL *Stud. Lang.* iii. 107 The kind of analysis suggested by Miller and Frick (1949) in their paper on what they call 'statistical behavioristics'. Statistical behavioristics is the theory of stochastic processes applied to the study of sequences of responses. **1960** *Times* 5 Feb. 3/6 The third difficulty was that some mosquitoes were developing what is technically known as behaviouristic resistance to insecticides. What this means is that, after entering a house and feeding on the occupants, they escaped to outdoor resting places, thus avoiding the lethal effects of the insecticide sprayed on the walls of the house.

behead (bɪˈhɛd), *v.* Forms: 1 **behéafdi-an**, 2 **behæfdien**, 2–3 **bihaued-en**, 3 **biheafdin**, **bihafdi**, 3–4 **bihefden**, 4 **biheueden**, 4–5 **behevede(n**, **bi-**, **byhede(n**, **-heede**, 4–6 **behede**, **-heede**, 5–6 **be-**, **byhedde**, 6 **beheadde**, 6– **behead**. [OE. *behéafdi-an*, f. BE- 3 (with privative force) + *héafod* HEAD; cf. MHG. *behoubeten* in same sense, mod.G. *enthaupten*.]

1. *trans.* To deprive (a man or animal) of the head, to decapitate; to kill by cutting off the head.

c **1000** *Ags. Gosp.* Matt. xiv. 10 He asende þa and beheafdode Iohannem. *c* **1160** *Hatton G.* ibid., behæfdede. **1205** LAY. 26296 þat heo us wulle bihafdi. *a* **1225** *Juliana* 40 To bihefden [*v.r.* beheafdin] pawel. **1382** WYCLIF *Matt.* xiv. 10 He sente, and bihedide [*v.r.* byheuedede] Joon in the prisoun. *c* **1450** LONELICH *Grail* xlvii. 155 Beheveded on aftyr anothir. **1474** CAXTON *Chesse* 36 Other said that they shold be beheded. **1513** MORE *Rich. III.* Wks. 54/1 To bee byhedded at Pountfreit. **1593** SHAKS. *2 Hen. VI*, IV. vii. 102 Take him away and behead him. **1781** GIBBON *Decl. & F.* II. xlvi. 719 A great number of the captives were beheaded. **1873** H. SPENCER *Stud. Sociol.* vii. 156 We beheaded 2000 fellahs, throwing their headless corpses into the Nile.

fig. **1594** HOOKER *Eccl. Pol.* IV. xiv. §7 To repair the decays thereof by beheading superstition. **1726** M. HENRY *Wks.* II. 370 It adds to our grief to see a family beheaded.

2. Of things: To deprive of the top or foremost part. *rare.*

1579 FULKE *Heskins' Parl.* 271 Maister Heskins beheadeth the sentence. **1796** MARSHALL *Garden.* §20 (1813) 400 Graffs of last year, cut to a few eyes, behead as at 98. *Mod.* Beheaded and curtailed words.

beheadal (bɪˈhɛdəl). [f. prec. + -AL² 5, which see. Apparently in no Dict. hitherto.] Beheading, execution by decapitation.

1859 WINGFIELD *Tour Dalmatia* 6 The drums announcing Mary's beheadal. **1881** BESANT & RICE *Whittington* ii. 54 The beheadal of Sheriff Richard Lions. **1882–3** SCHAFF in *Herzog's Encycl. Rel. Knowl.* II. 1191 The reason for the beheadal was jealousy at John's preponderant influence with the people.

beheading (bɪˈhɛdɪŋ), *vbl. sb.* [f. BEHEAD *v.* + -ING¹.] The action of cutting off the head; *spec.* of execution by decapitation.

a **1225** *Ancr. R.* 184 Nolde me tellen him alre monne dusiȝest, þet forsoke..ane nelde prikunge, uor ane bihefdunge. **1541** R. COPLAND *Guydon's Quest. Cyrurg.*, Whan he had a deade body by beheadyng or other wyse. **1585** THYNNE in *Animadv.* Introd. 75 The duke of Buckinghams beheadding. **1586–7** *Churchw. Acc. St. Margaret's, Westm.*, (Nichols 1797) 21 Paid for ringing at the beheading of the Queen of Scotts. **1615** HIERON *Wks.* I. 664 That story, which reports his beheading at Rome. **1732** LEDIARD *Sethos* II. VII. 54 The easiest and shortest of all deaths, beheading. **1863** THACKERAY in *Cornh. Mag.* Jan., Battles and victories, treasons, kings, and beheadings.

fig. **1641** MILTON *Ch. Govt.* v. (1851) 115 For if the type of Priest be not taken away, then neither of the high Priest, it were a strange beheading.

be'heading, *ppl. a.* [f. as prec. + -ING².] That severs the head or decapitates.

1845 BROWNING *Soul's Trag.* I, The beheading axe!

be'hear, *v. Obs.* (Pseudo-archaic.) To hear.

a **1600** *R. Hood & Guy Gisborne* 187 That beheard the sheriffe of Nottingham. *a* **1700** *Childe Waters* in Evans *O. Ball.* II. xxxv. 214 And that beheard his mother deare.

behearse, behelp, behem, etc.: see BE- *pref.*

beheast, obs. form of BEHEST.

†**be'heaven**. *v. Obs.* [f. BE- 6 + HEAVEN.] *trans.* To endow with celestial bliss, to beatify.

1601 W. PARRY *Sherley's Trav.* (1863) 4 Such a man.. woulde be beheavened with the joy. **1609** J. DAVIES *Holy Roode* Wks. 1876 I. 7 O faire Jerusalem..Yet wast beheau'nd through blessèd Bethelem.

behecht, -heet, -height, obs. var. of BEHIGHT.

behefe, variant of BIHEVE.

beheft, for BEHAVED.

a **1637** B. JONSON *Underwoods* (1692) Wks. 587 But he was wiser, and well beheft, For this is all that he hath left.

†**behele**, *v. Obs.* Also bihele. [OE. *behelian*, f. BE- + *helian* to cover: see HELE.] To conceal, cover, envelop. *lit.* and *fig.*

c **1000** ÆLFRIC *Gen.* vii. 19 Wurdon ta behelede ealle ta hehstan duna. *c* **1275** in *O.E. Misc.* 91 Al þes world is biheled myd heþene-hode. *c* **1325** *Coer de L.* 5586 As snowgh lygges on the mountaynes, Behelyd were hylles and playnes, With hawberk bryghte and helmes clere.

†**behem**, *v. Obs.* Forms: 3 **bihemmen**, 6–7 **behemm.** [f. BE- 1 + HEM.] *trans.* To hem round. *lit.* and *fig.*

a **1250** *Owl & Night.* 672 He mot bihemmen and bilegge. **1567** MAPLET *Gr. Forest* 44 Those I call coates which are as it were on both their sides behemmed and parted. **1598** SYLVESTER *Du Bartas* (1608) 993 Her musky mouth..a swelling welt of Corall round behemms.

behemoth (bɪˈhiːməθ, -ɔːθ). Forms: 4–5 **bemoth**, **behemot**, 6– **behemoth.** [Heb. *b'hēmōth*, used in Job xl. 15. In form the word is the plural of *b'hēmāh* 'beast,' and might be interpreted 'great or monstrous beast' (*plural of dignity*). But most moderns take it as really an Egyptian word *p-ehe-mau*, which would mean 'water-ox,' assimilated in Hebrew mouths to a Hebrew form.] An animal mentioned in the book of Job; probably the hippopotamus; but also used in modern literature as a general expression for one of the largest and strongest animals. Cf. LEVIATHAN.

1382 WYCLIF *Job* xl. 10 Lo! bemoth [**1388** behemot, **1611** behemoth] that I made with thee. **1430** LYDG. *Chron. Troy* II. xvii, Whom the Hebrues..call Bemoth that doth in latin playne expresse A beast rude full of cursednesse. **1667** MILTON *P.L.* VII. 471 Behemoth biggest born of earth. **1727** THOMSON *Summer* 710 The flood disparts: behold! in plaited mail, Behemoth rears his head. **1818** KEATS *Endym.* III. 134 Skeletons of man, Of beast, behemoth, and leviathan. **1820** SHELLEY *Prometh. Unb.* IV. i. 310 The might Of earth-convulsing behemoth. **1857** EMERSON *Poems* 306 Be swift their feet as antelopes, And as behemoth strong.

fig. **1592** G. HARVEY *Pierces Super.*, Will soone finde the huge Behemoth of conceit to be the sprat of a pickle herring. **1850** MRS. STOWE *Uncle Tom's C.* xv. 140 He's a perfect behemoth.

behemothian (bɪhiːˈməʊθɪən), *a.* Chiefly *poet.* [f. BEHEMOTH + -IAN.] Monstrously large; of or belonging to a large animal.

1910 W. DE LA MARE *Three Mulla-Mulgars* iii. 47 A behemothian bull-Elephanto. **1911** H. S. HARRISON *Queed* i. 3 Down the street came a girl and a dog, rather a small girl, and quite a behemothian dog. **1946** H. READ *Coll. Poems* 145 Faced by the behemothian jaws.

‖**behen** (ˈbiːhɛn). Also **behn, beën, ben.** [a. med.L. *behen* (found in other mod. langs.), app. corruption of Arab. *bahman, behmen,* a kind of root, also a dog-rose.]

1. A name which the old herbalists had received apparently from Arabic sources, without knowing to what plant it belonged, and which different authors consequently tried to identify with many different plants. In England it was chiefly affixed to the Bladder Campion ('White Behen'), and Sea Lavender ('Red Behen').

1578 LYTE *Dodoens* III. xxii, Called..of herboristes at this day Behen, or Beën album. **1682** GREW *Anat. Seeds* i. §7 The Seed also of Ben or spatling Poppey is somewhat like a Kidney. **1769** SIR J. HILL *Fam. Herbal* (1812) 33 Red Behen, a wild plant about our sea coasts..also called by some sea lavender. **1721** BAILEY, *Behen, Behn,* the root of Valerian, either red or white. **1783** —— *Behen, Behn,* there is the white and red; the first is likewise called..Bladder Campion; the other is also called..Sea Lavender.

2. = BEN.

behenetic, behenic: see BENIC.

beheouen, obs. form of BEHOVE *v.*

†**beˈheretic,** *v. Obs.* [f. BE- 5 + HERETIC.] *trans.* To call, stigmatize, or treat as a heretic.

1539 TAVERNER *Gard. Wysdome* II. 16 b, Some, we beheretike, we call Lutheranes, and all that naught is. **1656** S. H. *Gold. Law* 13 Would you that Prelacy and Priesthood should ..be-heretick and sect you?

behest (bɪˈhɛst), *sb.* Forms: 1 **behǽs,** 2-3 **bihese, biheaste,** 2-6 **bi-, byheste,** 3-6 **beheste,** 4-5 **be-, bi-, byheest(e,** 4-6 **bi-, byhest,** 6-7 **beheast,** 4- **behest.** [OE. *behǽs* fem. (acc. *behǽse*) was the regular repr. of OTeut. **bihait-ti-,* abst. sb. f. *bihait-an,* in OE. *behátan* to BEHIGHT (see Sievers, *Ags. Gr.* §232); thence, early ME. *bihese,* soon altered to *bihes-te,* by form analogy with words in *-te,* OE. *-t.* For full phonetic history see HEST. The OE. *bihǽs,* like the vb. *bihátan,* occurs only in the sense of 'promise, vow,' but in ME. *biheste* acquired the sense of the simple *hǽs,* HEST, f. *hátan* 'to command'; see HIGHT. Cf. the equivalent BEHOTE, OE. *behát* neut., with its ME. variants BEHETE, BEHIGHT.]

†**1.** A vow, promise. Very common in the phr. ***land of behest***: land of promise. *Obs.*

a **1200** *Trin. Coll. Hom.* 61 But [we] lesten ure bihese. **1205** LAY. 1263 He bi-heihte hire biheste. *c* **1230** *Hali Meid.* 39 Ich habbe ihalden mine biheaste þruppe. *c* **1300** *St. Brandan* 76 Bifore the ȝates of Paradys in the Lond of Biheste. *c* **1386** CHAUCER *Frankl. Prol.* 26 Breken his biheste. **1388** WYCLIF *Heb.* xi. 9 Bi feith he dwelte in the loond of biheest. **1496** *Dives & Paup.* (W. de W.) IV. xxvi. 193 Why is this commaundement gyuen with a byhest of helthe. **1562** FOXE *A. & M.* I. 454/1 He behight to him and to his Heirs the Land of behest. **1587** TURBERV. *Trag. T.* (1837) 89 She made a large behest, Of gold that she would franklike give. **1634** *Malory's Arthur* (1816) I. Prol. 13 Duke Joshua, which brought the children of Israel into the land of beheast.

2. A command, injunction, bidding.

c **1175** *Lamb. Hom.* 33 Þu scoldest halden cristes biheste. **1388** WYCLIF *Ecclus.* xxiv. 33 Moises comaundide a lawe in the comaundementis of riȝtfulnessis..and biheestis to Israel. **1528** MORE *Heresyes* I. Wks. 157/2 That thei should kepe his byhestes. **1591** SPENSER *Ruines Time* 73 To fall before her feete at her beheast. **1667** MILTON *P.L.* VIII. 238 Us he [God] sends upon his high behests. **1857** BUCKLE *Civilis.* iii. 140 We see the subtlest..of all forces..obeying even the most capricious behests of the human mind.

†**beˈhest,** *v. Obs.* Also 2 **bihaste,** 6 **beheast;** *pa. pple.* 6 **behest.** [f. prec. sb.] *trans.* (or with *subord. cl.*) To vow, promise.

c **1175** *Lamb. Hom.* 185 Þu..bihastest us wiþ þon þet we neomen hit heouenliche blissen. *c* **1430** LYDG. *Bochas* II. xii. (1554) 51 God hath behested to Dauid and his lyne..In Jerusalem how they shal succede. *c* **1440** *Promp. Parv.* 29. **1477** MARG. PASTON in *Lett.* 809 III. 215 The gyrdyl that my fadyr be hestyt me. **1519** HORMAN *Vulg.* 3 b, I haue behest a pygge to saynt Anthony. **1548** UDALL, etc. *Erasm. Par. Luke* xiii. 3 Thou haddest euen vowed and beheasted thy selfe to utter ruine. **1566** GASCOIGNE *Jocasta* Wks. (1587) 92 As much as late I did behest to thee.

†**beˈhesting,** *vbl. sb. Obs. rare*⁻¹. [f. prec. + -ING¹.] Bidding, command.

1583 STANYHURST *Æneis* IV. (Arb.) 115 We rely toe thyn hautye behestings.

behet, obs. pa. t. of BEHIGHT

†**beˈhete,** *sb. Obs.* [f. *behete,* one of the forms of BEHIGHT, *v.*: cf. the earlier BEHOTE, and parallel BEHIGHT *sb.*] A promise, a vow.

c **1460** *Towneley Myst.* 159 Thise prophetys..That have knowyng of his behetys. **1470** HARDING *Chron.* cxl. xi, Traytour he was, and false of his behete.

behete, variant of BEHIGHT *v.* to promise.

†**beˈheter, beheeter.** *Obs.* [f. *behete* = BEHIGHT *v.* + -ER: cf. BEHIGHTER.] A promiser.

1382 WYCLIF *2 Macc.* x. 28 Hauynge the Lord biheeter [*v.r.* beheteré] of victorie. —— *Heb.* vii. 22 Jhesu is maad biheter of the betere testament.

†**beˈheting,** *vbl. sb. Obs.* [f. as prec. + -ING¹: cf. BEHOTING.] Promise, promising.

1303 R. BRUNNE *Handl. Synne* 11220 x, Ȝe shende hyt [wedlock] wyþ ȝoure fals behetyng. **1400** in *Pol. Rel. & L. Poems* (1866) 242 A fals by-hety[n]g.

†**beˈhew,** *v. Obs.* Pa. pple. **behewen, behewe.** [f. BE- 1 + HEW *v.* Cf. OE. *behéawan* to hew off.] *trans.* To hew about, to carve.

c **1314** *Guy Warw.* 125 Stonis..Bihewe quarre for the nonis. *c* **1384** CHAUCER *H. Fame* 1306 It was all with [*v.r.* of] gold behewe.

†**beˈhide,** *v. Obs.* Forms: 1 **behýdan,** 2 **behuden.** [OE. *behýdan*; f. BE- + *hýdan* to HIDE.] *trans.* To hide away, conceal.

c **1000** *Ags. Gosp.* Matt. xxv. 25 Ic..behydde [*c* **1160** *Hatton* behedde] þin pund on eorðan. *c* **1175** *Lamb. Hom.* 109 þe bihut his gold hord on heouene riche. *a* **1225** *Ancr. R.* 100 Hit is bilepped & bihud.

†**beˈhie,** *v. Obs.* In 4 **bihyȝe,** 5 **byhye.** [f. BE- + HIE *v.*] *refl.* To hie oneself, make haste.

c **1340** *Cursor M.* 5087 Bihyȝe ȝou swiþe hoom to go. *c* **1425** *Seven Sag.* (P.) 952 The bore byhyde hym thydyr faste.

†**beˈhight,** *v. Obs.* For forms see below. [An OTeut. compound vb.: OE. *bi-, behátan* = OHG. *biheizan,* Goth. *biháitan* (in derivatives), f. *bi-,* BE- + OE. *hátan* = Goth. *háitan* to call, pa. t. *haiháit,* (= *heháit*), pa. pple. *haitans.* The reduplicated pa. t. appeared in OE. as *heht* (:—**ˈhehat*:—**heˈhât*:—*heˈhait*), contr. *hét* (pl. *héton*). As there was no other Eng. vb. exactly parallel, the isolated inflexion of *hátan* and *behátan* was in ME. subjected to a remarkable series of changes, resulting finally in the loss of the original present stem, and the substitution of that of the past as a new present, with weak inflexions. 1. The OE. original forms of the pres. *beháte,* and pa. pple. *beháten,* gave regularly the ME. *behote* and *behoten* (to *c* 1525). The OE. pa. t. *behét* gave ME. *behet* (*-heet, -hete*), found after 1400; *beheht* gave *bi-heyght, -height,* more usually *behiȝt, -hight* (*-hyht, -hyght,* and in 15th c. *-hite*). But in the course of the 14th c., the normal forms, *behote, behet -height -hight, behoten,* began to be disturbed under the influence of levelling, and of various assumed analogies. 2. Thus, the Present took the vowel of the then archaic past, and became *behete, -heete,* frequent in Wyclif, Chaucer, and Lydgate. The Past was occasionally assimilated to the pple. as *behotte, behote*; but far more frequently the pple. was assimilated to the pa. t., first as *behet, -hete,* then as *beheyght, behight,* in 16th c. also *behite.* The Past *behight* was then made weak, as *be-hight-e* (3 syllables; cf. forms like *mighte, lighte*); and finally *behight* (*behite*) was taken as present, and the pa. t. and pple. duly became in 16th c. *behighted* (*behited*); cf. *lighted* for earlier *lighte.* Rare forms of the pa. t. were *c* 1400 *behit* (cf. *lit* = *lighted*), and in 16th c. *behoted,* formed on the original present *behote.* See further under the simple HIGHT *v.* Towards the end of the 16th c. *behight* became obsolete, but was kept up by the Spenserian archaists, who often misunderstood its meaning, and employed it in mistaken senses.]

A. Illustration of Forms.

1. *Present.* α. 1-3 **beháte;** 3-4 **bi-,** 3-6 **behote.**

a **1000** ÆLFRIC *Deut.* xxiii. 21 Ðonne ðu behat behætst. *c* **1175** *Lamb. Hom.* 161 Moni mon bihateð wel þe hit forȝeteð sone. *a* **1225** *Ancr. R.* 8 Ȝe ne schulen nout bihoten hit, auh ..doð hit as þauh ȝe hefden hit bihoten. **1340** *Ayenb.* 65 Ȝuyche men þet..behoteþ þing þet hi nele naȝt healde. *c* **1400** *Gamelyn* 378 ffor to holden myn a-vow as I the byhoote. *a* **1520** *Myrr. Our Ladye* 61 He behoteth that..there shall be encresed peace and accorde. [**1591** LAMBARDE *Arch.* 141 That the Lord of Bedford..nor other of the Councell shall behote any favour.]

β. 4-6 **behete, beheete.**

c **1340** *Cursor M.* 6872 So dud prince & als prophete As god dud to him bihete [*v.r.* hete, hette]. *c* **1388** WYCLIF *Wisd.* ii. 13 He biheetith [**1382** behoteth] that he hath the kunnyng of God. *c* **1386** CHAUCER *Chan. Yem. Prol. & T.* 154 Neuere heere after wol I with hym meete..I yow biheete [*v.r.* be-, by-, -hete]. *a* **1400** *Chester Pl.* 31, I thee behette. *c* **1420** *Chron. Vilod.* 1014 Depe dampnacyon God byhetuth alle þo. *c* **1530** HANLEY in Prynne *Sov. Power Parl.* II. (1643) 67 The King shall answer, I grant and behete.

γ. 4-5 **behyte,** 6 **behyȝt, -height, -hite,** *Sc.* **hecht,** 6-7 **-hight.**

c **1400** *Apol. Loll.* 11 If þe pope..behiȝt ani swilk þingis. *Ibid.* 69 Wan þe prest..behytiþ suelk an absolucoun. **1513** DOUGLAS *Æneis* I. vi. 94, I ȝou behecht [*v.r.* hecht]. **1548** HALL *Chron.* (1809) 136 Promisyng and behightyng by the faith of his body. **1581** MARBECK *Bk. Notes* 458 It bringeth and beheighteth good thinges. **1610** BARROUGH *Meth. Physick* I. xxviii. (1639) 45 [They] often behight and determine to kill themselves.

2. *Past t.* α. 1-4 **behét,** 2 **-heot,** 4 **-heet, -hete, -hett.**

c **1000** ÆLFRIC *Deut.* v. 2 Drihten God behet us wed. *a* **1100** *O.E. Chron.* an. 1036 Ælc man yfel him behet. *c* **1175** *Lamb. Hom.* 71 Swa he þurh þe witeȝa bihet. *a* **1225** *Ancr. R.* 176 Salue ich bihet to techen ou. *c* **1300** *Harrow. Hell* 199 Do me as thou bihete. *c* **1400** *Gamelyn* 783 He him beheet That he wolde be redy whan the justice seet. *c* **1430** *Hymns Virg.* 98 He..þat biheet me riȝt.

β. 1 **beheht,** 3-5 **-heyght(e,** 5-6 **-height;** 4 **-hyȝt,** 4-6 **-hight,** 5 **-hite,** 5-6 **-hyght,** 6 *Sc.* **-hicht.**

c **1300** *K. Alis.* 3925 A byheste, That Darie byheyghte. *c* **1320** R. BRUNNE *Medit.* 1027 As þou me behyȝte. *c* **1386** CHAUCER *Knts. T.* 1614 Myn owen knight Schal have his lady, as thou him bihight. *c* **1440** *Gesta Rom.* 122 Vertuys, þe whiche he be-hite in baptyme. *c* **1500** *Lancelot* 1481 The lond, the wich he them byhicht. **1527** *Caxton's Trevisa's Higden* I. lviii. 53 b, Scottes sente yᵉ Pyctes..and behyght them helpe. **1569** TURBERV. *Poems,* Your comely hewe behight me hope.

γ. 4-5 **be-, bi-, byhiȝte, -hyȝte, -higte,** 5-6 **-hyghte, -highte.** After final *e* became mute, this was of course identified with β.

c **1374** CHAUCER *Troylus* v. 1204 He niste what he juggen of it myghte, Syn she hath broken that she hym byhighte. **1382** WYCLIF *Matt.* xiv. 7 He byhiȝte for to ȝeue to hir. *c* **1449** PECOCK *Repr.* 404 Wole not performe what he so be-hiȝte. *a* **1520** *Myrr. Our Ladye* 309 Iesu hathe sente the holy goste that he behyghte.

δ. 4-5 **behit.**

c **1400** *Apol. Loll.* 10 Crist..behit vs heuenly kyndom.

ε. 5 **behotte,** 5-6 **behote.**

c **1425** *Three Kings Cologne* (1885) 9 And [þei] byhotten ȝiftes to þe kepers. **1493** *Festivall* (W. de W. 1515) 115 Thou behote me a chylde, and now is the mother deed.

ζ. 6 **behoted.**

1520 *Caxton's Chron. Eng.* II. 15/2 Those that me other wise behoted [ed. **1480** Tho that me other wyse behyghten].

η. 6 **behighted, -hited, -heighted.**

1562 FOXE *A. & M.* I. 456/2 For so thou behited us sometime. **1587** GOLDING *De Mornay* xxix. 452 Let vs see what time they behighted for his comming.

3. *Pa. pple.* α. 1-3 **beháten,** 2-6 **-hoten,** 3-6 **-hote.**

c **1175** *Cott. Hom.* 225 Swa swa him aér be-haten wes. *c* **1314** *Guy Warw.* 104 Bihoten Ich it haue a maiden of priis. *c* **1400** *Beryn* 2528 Delyvir me of sorowe, as yee be-hote have. *a* **1520** *Myrr. Our Ladye* 267 He hathe behote..to gyue a hundereth folde. **1562** FOXE *A. & M.* I. 454/2 It was byhoten by Jeremiah. **1579** SPENSER *Sheph. Cal.* Dec. 54 But better mought they haue behote him Hate.

β. 4 **behet,** 5 **-hete.**

a **1400** *Cursor M.* 3010 (Trin.) 8 Hir son..þat was longe bihet toforn. *Ibid.* 13137 This childe was by-hete [*v.r.* bihett] many a yere Ar he were sent. *c* **1460** *Towneley Myst.* 31 As thou me behete hase.

γ. 4 **byheght,** 4-5 **bihyȝt, -hyght, -hiȝt, -hight, behiȝt, -hyȝt, -hyt;** 4-6 **behight, -hyght, -hite.**

c **1325** *E.E. Allit. P.* C. 29 Þe happes alle aȝt þat vus bihyȝt weren. *c* **1380** WYCLIF *Sel. Wks.* III. 429 God haves byheght hom. **1388** —— *Ecclus.* viii. 16 If thou hast bihiȝt. **1447** BOKENHAM *Seyntys* Introd. 6 Aftyr I had behyht the ryng. **1510** LOVE *Bonavent. Mirr.* xviii. E v, The mede of theym is behyght for to come. **1553-87** FOXE *A. & M.* I. 541/1 To wakers God has behite the Crown of Life. **1596** SPENSER *F.Q.* I. x. 50 The keys are to thy hand behight.

δ. 6 **behited, -highted, -heighted.**

1574 tr. *Marlorat's Apocalips* 37 He hath behyghted vs euerlasting life. **1577** *St. Aug. Manuell* 26 The light that God hath behighted them. **1606** WARNER *Alb. Eng.* ci. 399 His knights had all behited them fulfild.

B. Signification.

I. Proper senses. **1.** To vow, to promise.

a. *trans.* (with *dative* of the person.)

a **1000** ÆLFRIC *Gen.* xxxviii. 17 Oð þæt þu me sende þæt þu me behætst. *c* **1300** *Beket* 1010 The King bihet hem gret honur. **1369** CHAUCER *Bk. Duchesse* 631 The trayteresse false and full of gyle, That al behoteth, and nothing halt. *a* **1420** OCCLEVE *De Reg. Princ.* 2337 A kyng ought..No thyng bihete but yf he it perfourme. **1556** ABP. PARKER *Psalter* cxvi. 16, I now will paye, My vowes that I behight. **1621** BP. MOUNTAGU *Diatribae* 506, I behight thee the Tenth of all my gettings.

b. with *inf.* or *subord. cl.*

c **1205** LAY. 18396 Godde we scullen bihaten ure sunnen to beten. *c* **1340** *Cursor M.* 5431 (Trin.), I bihete þe riȝt hit shal be done. *c* **1450** *Knt. de la Tour* (1868) 92 The payens behight her..that she shulde haue a gret somme of moneye. **1480** CAXTON *Chron. Eng.* ccxxi. 211 He..behiȝt hym for to done his message. **1496** *Dives & Paup.* (W. de W.) I. xl. 81 He that behoteth to come ayen. **1610** BARROUGH *Meth. Physick* I. xxviii. (1639) 45 [The melancholious] desire death, and do very often behight and determine to kill themselves.

2. *trans.* To encourage expectation, to hold out hope of (life, recovery, etc.).

c **1420** *Chron. Vilod.* 788 He had..þe fevere quarteyne, þat no mon þat sye hurre by-hette hurr þe lyff. *a* **1552** LELAND *Brit. Coll.* I. 231 This William..was wounded so sore that no man beheight him life. **1571** GOLDING *Calvin on Ps.* ix. 14 He behighteth himselfe saufty even in the mouth of death.

3. *trans.* To assure (one) of the truth of a statement; to warrant. (Cf. mod. *I promise you.*)

c **1386** CHAUCER *Wife's Prol.* 1034 Litel whil it last, I you biheete. *c* **1430** *Syr. Tryam.* 18 He had a quene.. Trewe as stele, y yow be-hett. **1513** DOUGLAS *Æneis* I. vi. 94 Dido heyrat comouit, I ȝou behecht..followschip redy made.

II. Improper uses by the archaists of the 16th and 17th cc., when the word was becoming obsolete; cf. the simple *hight*, also *behest*.

4. *trans.* To grant, deliver.

1596 SPENSER *F.Q.* I. x. 50 The keys are to thy hand behight By wise Fidelia.

5. To command, bid, ordain.

c **1591** SPENSER *Muiopotmos* 241 It fortuned (as heavens had behight) That, etc. **1596** —— *F.Q.* VI. ii. 39 He..with her marched forth, as she did him behight.

6. To call, to name.

1579 SPENSER *Sheph. Cal.* Apr. 120 They bene all Ladyes of the lake behight. *Ibid.* Dec. 54 Love they him called..But better mought they have behote him Hate. **1599** NASHE *Lent. Stuffe* (1871) 72 Which..are behighted the trees of the sun and moon. **1652** ASHMOLE *Theat. Chem.* I. 129 After Philosophy I you behyte.

7. To bespeak, invoke.

1615 T. ADAMS *Lycanthr.* Ep. Ded. 3, I behight you in my prayers, a happy progresse in grace.

† **be'hight,** *sb. Obs.* Forms: 5 **behiȝt,** 6 **-hight,** *Sc.* **behicht, -hecht.** [f. prec. vb.: cf. the parallel BEHETE, BEHOTE.] A promise.

c **1400** *Apol. Loll.* 57 After His blessing and silk behiȝt. *c* **1505** DUNBAR *None may Assure* xii, Quhais fals behechtis as wind hym wavis. **1533** BELLENDEN *Livy* II. (1822) 130, I wil nocht dissave the Tarquinis..with vane behichtis. *a* **1547** EARL SURREY *Psalm* lxxiii. 25 [Not] In other succour..But only thine, whom I have found in thy behight so just.

† **be'highted,** *ppl. a. Obs.* Promised.

1571 GOLDING *Calvin on Ps.* xi. 2 This behyghted kingdome. **1589** WARNER *Alb. Eng.* Prose Add. (1612) 332 His Troians disanker from Thrace in quest of the behighted Italie.

† **be'highter.** *Obs. rare.* A promiser.

c **1400** *Apol. Loll.* 105 Þei are largist bihiȝtars, and scarsist geuars.

behind (bɪ'haɪnd), *adv., prep.* (*sb.*) Forms: 1 **behindan,** (*Northumb.* **bihianda**), 2–3 **bihinden,** 3 (*Orm.*) **-hinndenn,** 2–4 **-hinde,** 3–4 **byhynde,** 4 **bi-, by-hynden, bi-henden, -hynde, -hind, beheinde,** 4–6 **behynde,** 5–7 **behinde,** 4– **behind.** [OE. *bi-, behindan*, identical w. OS. *bihindan*, f. *bi-*, BE- + *hindan*, OHG. *hintana*, mod.G. *hinten*, Gothic *hindana* adv., 'from behind,' 'behind,' f. root *hind-* in HINDER, HINDMOST, with advb. suffix *-ana*, orig. meaning direction *from*: the notion of position is given by BE-. *Behind* is used both absolutely (as adv.), and with an object (as prep.), the latter originating in an OE. dative of reference, *behindan him* 'in the rear *as to him*'; in Gothic *hindana* took a genitive, *hindana Iaurdanaus* 'from the back *of* the Jordan.' In its sense-development the word is one, though for practical purposes the adverbial and prepositional construction are here treated separately.]

A. *adv.* I. *In relation to an object in motion.*

1. In a place whence those to whom the reference is made have departed; remaining after the others have gone. Esp. used with *leave* (*let* obs.), *remain, stay, abide.* **a.** *lit.*

c **900** *O.E. Chron.* an. 894 Ða Deniscan sæton þær be hindan. *a* **1000** *Boeth. Metr.* xxiv. 29 Þu..þone hehstan heofon behindan lætest. *Ibid.* xxvi. 23 He let him behindan hyrnde ciolas. *c* **1305** *St. Swithin* 99 in *E.E.P.* (1862) 46 Ne lef þu noȝt bihynde. *c* **1450** *Rob. Hood* (Ritson) I. i. 46 We shall abide behynde. *c* **1500** *Merch. & Son* in Halliw. *Nugæ Poet.* 26 Here ys a fytt of thys matere; the bettur ys behynde. **1697** DRYDEN *Virg. Georg.* III. 306 He..leaves the Scythian Arrow far behind. **1766** GOLDSM. *Vic. W.* iii. (1806) 13 Too generous to attempt leaving us behind. **1782** COWPER *J. Gilpin* 60 Betty screaming came downstairs, 'The wine is left behind!' **1874** STUBBS *Const. Hist.* (1875) I. 64 Even the slaves were not left behind.

b. *fig.* In the position, condition, or state which a person or thing has left: *e.g.* in existence after one's death.

c **1400** *St. Alexius* 20 Richesse he lete al Bihynde. ? **1595** *Babes in Wd.* (Ritson) 16 They died And left two babes behind. *a* **1631** DONNE *Poems* (1650) 15 To leave this world behinde, is death. **1652** CULPEPPER *Eng. Physic* 68 Gross humours Winter hath left behinde. **1764** GOLDSM. *Trav.* 132 All evils..That opulence departed leaves behind. **1829** SOUTHEY *Sir T. More* II. 138 When they were advanced from a private station, they left behind them the leisure. **1878** HUXLEY *Physiogr.* 73 The salt is left entirely behind, and nothing but pure water evaporated.

c. In the time which one has lived beyond, in the past.

[**1382** WYCLIF *Phil.* iii. 13 Forȝetinge..tho thingis that ben bihyndis.] **1526** TINDALE *ibid.*, I forget that which is behynde. *c* **1600** SHAKS. *Sonn.* l, My grief lies onward and my joy behind. **1850** TENNYSON *In Mem.* lxxvii, As in the winters left behind, Again our ancient games had place.

†**2.** After one has left (a company), in one's absence. *Obs.*, and now expressed by 'behind one's back': see B 9.

a **1000** *Bi manna Lease* (Gr.) 4 Eorl oðerne..mid teonwordum tæleð behindan, spreceð fagere beforan. *c* **1175** *Lamb. Hom.* 143 Þe þet spekeð faire biforen and false bihinden. **1413** LYDG. *Pylgr. Sowle* III. iii. (1483) 51 Ye have shewed them in presence good chere..but behynde ye have ben fals traytours.

3. **a.** In the rear of anything moving; following, in the train; not so far forward. *to come behind*: to follow, come after. *to fall behind*: to fall into the rear through not going so fast or 'keeping up.'

[*c* **950** *Lindisf. Gosp.* Mark v. 27 [Wif] cwom in ðreat bihianda.] **1393** LANGL. *P. Pl.* C. IV. 37 Ther connynge clerkus shulleþ clocke by-hynde. **1562** J. HEYWOOD *Prov. & Epigr.* (1867) 72 The further ye go, the further behynde. *c* **1575** J. STILL *Gamm. Gurton* v. in *Dodsley* (1780) II. 77 As proude come behinde, as anie goes before. **1697** DRYDEN *Virg. Georg.* III. 708 Late to lag behind, with truant pace. **1857** MARY HOWITT *Web-Spinner*, I am wearied with a long day's chase, My friends are far behind. **1858** C. PATMORE *Angel in Ho.* XII. iii, Her laughing sisters lagg'd behind.

†**b.** of following in time: Later. *those that come behind*: posterity. *Obs.*

c **1600** *Rob. Hood* (Ritson) I. v. 420 Least his fame should be buried clean From those that came behind. **1628** HOBBES *Thucyd.* (1822) 40 Men..are many times to fall first to action, the which ought to come behind.

4. *fig.* (from 1) In reserve, kept back, not yet brought forward or mentioned; still to come.

1250 LAY. 18012 He hadde bihinde ehtetene þousend. **1526** *Pilgr. Perf.* (W. de W. 1531) 6 b, Smoke, the more it encreaseth, the lesse is behynde. **1542** UDALL *Erasm. Apoph.* 276 b, There is but a veraye litle litle tyme of my life behinde. **1603** SHAKS. *Meas. for M.* v. 545 Wee'll show What's yet behinde. **1630** WADSWORTH *Sp. Pilgr.* v. 46 He..told what was behinde of his former discourse. **1687** T. BROWN *Saints in Upr.* Wks. 1730 I. 73 The oddest and most comical scene is still behind. **1750** JOHNSON *Rambl.* No. 67 ¶2 The expectation of some new possession, or of some enjoyment yet behind. **1818** MACAULAY in Trevelyan *Life* I. ii. 96 But stronger evidence is behind.

5. *fig.* (from 3.) **a.** Of progress, advancement, or attainment; *hence*, of rank, order, subordination.

c **1200** *Trin. Coll. Hom.* 213 Þenne man bipecheð oðer · he him makeð to ben bihinden of þat he weneð to ben biforen. *c* **1300** *Cursor M.* 6073 Qua for pouert ys be-hinde. **1526** TINDALE *1 Cor.* i. 7 So that ye are behynde [WYCLIF fail, **1611** come behinde] in no gyfte. **1586** WARNER *Alb. Eng.* III. xviii. 83 You..shall see Yourselues to come behind in Armes. **1788** MISS BURNEY *Diary, etc.* (1842) IV. 42 Mrs. Montagu, who was behind with no one in kind speeches. **1817** JAS. MILL *Brit. India* II. v. iv. 462 The opponents were not behind in violence.

b. In reference to the fulfilment of an obligation, *esp.* of paying money due: In arrear. Const. *with* money unpaid, or the person to whom it is due; *in* fulfilling an obligation.

c **1375** WYCLIF *Serm.* Sel. Wks. II. 252 So many men in þis world ben byhynde of dette of love. **1454** *E.E. Wills* (1882) 133 His wages beyng be-hynde. **1493** *Festivall* (W. de W. 1515) 20 Ye that be behynde [in making shrift]..come and shryve you. **1512** *Act 4 Hen. VIII*, xi, If the seid annuell rentes..be behynde. **1596** DANETT *Comines' Hist. Fr.* (1614) 239 Maximilian was behind with them for certaine moneths pay. **1614** R. TAILOR *Hog hath lost Pearl* I. i. in *Dodsley* (1780) VI. 381, I am behind with my landlord a year. **1697** *C'tess. D'Aunoy's Trav.* (1706) 86 A man of good quality..much behind in the world. **1765** *Act 5 Geo. II*, xvii. §3 in *Oxf. & Camb. Enact.* 75 In case the rent or rents..shall be behind or unpaid. **1885** *Manch. Exam.* 21 July 5/2 If the tenant falls behind with his instalments.

6. **a.** After due time; late or slow in coming forward. *Obs.* exc. *Sc.*

c **1330** *Assumpt. Virg.* 808 Euer art þou bi-hynde, Whare hast þou so longe bene? **1414** BRAMPTON *Penit. Ps.* lxv. 25 Lete noȝt thi mercy be behynde. **1727** WALKER *Life Peden* 38 (JAM.) He was never behind with any that put their trust in him. **1787** BEATTIE *Scotticisms* 14, I fear I shall be behind, i.e. not arrive in time.—Late, too late.

b. Of a watch or clock: Slow.

1787 BEATTIE *Scotticisms* 15 My watch is behind, before: slow, fast, are better.

II. *In relation to objects at rest.*

7. **a.** On the back side, at the back; in the rear of anything stationary having a recognized front.

c **1220** *Sawles Warde* in *Cott. Hom.* 251 Speoweð ham eft ut biuoren ant bihinden. *c* **1305** *Judas Iscar.* 83 in *E.E.P.* 109 He smot him wiþ a ston bihynde in þe pate. *c* **1400** *Destr. Troy* XXIII. 9540 He was brochit þurgh the body with a big speire, þat a trunchyn of þe tre tut out behynd. *a* **1540** *Pilgrim's T.* 66 in *Thynne's Animadv.* 79 In myn eyr behynd I herde a bussinge. **1601** SHAKS. *Jul. C.* v. i. 43 Caska, like a curre, behinde Strooke Cæsar on the necke. **1713** STEELE *Englishm.* No. 1. 5 The Servants behind..were unable to contain from laughing. **1795** SOUTHEY *Joan of Arc* IV. 388 From behind a voice was heard. **1831** R. KNOX *Cloquet's Anat.* 152 A..smooth surface, concave from behind forwards. **1837** MARRYAT *Dog-Fiend* viii, She had..a back-door into the street behind.

†**b.** *fig.* At one's back, supporting, backing up.

1630 WADSWORTH *Sp. Pilgr.* vii. 71 The remainder of the regiment..[was] giuen to Sir Iames Creeton, there being behind Captain Lucy..with diuerse other..Captaines.

c. At the back or on the farther side of some object, so as to be hidden. Chiefly *fig.*

a **1887** *Mod.* That seems fair enough, but is there anything behind?

d. *ellipt.* for *behind the scenes* (see sense B. 6 c).

1824 J. DECASTRO *Memoirs* 8 To visit the theatre whenever he was so disposed, either in front or behind. **1856** DICKENS *Dorrit* I. xx. 283 But the idea, Amy, of *you* coming behind! I never did! **1885** G. B. SHAW in *Works* (1932) VI. 202, I am going to take a peep behind: that is, if non-performers may be admitted. **1926** R. MACAULAY *Crewe Train* II. ii. 64 Leonard's fate will be settled by the time the curtain goes up. He's gone behind, poor Leonard.

8. Towards the rear, backwards. (With *look* or equivalent verbs.)

c **1340** *Ayenb.* 130 Yzyþ aboue and beneþe, and beuore and behynde. **1382** WYCLIF *Judg.* xx. 40 Beniamyn biholdynge bihynde..turnede the face. **1604** SHAKS. *Oth.* II. i. 158 She that could..See suitors following, and not looke behind. **1692** E. WALKER *Epictetus' Mor.* (1737) xii, Run, Nor look behind. **1697** DRYDEN *Virg. Georg.* IV. 708 Th' unwary Lover cast his Eyes behind. **1799** WORDSW. *Lucy Gray* xvi, O'er rough and smooth she trips along, And never looks behind. **1867** ALFORD *Hymn 'Forward,'* Seek the things before us, Not a look behind.

9. To the back, into the rear. †*to put behind* (obs.): to put into the rear, out of sight, into the background, or into a subordinate position.

c **1380** WYCLIF *3 Treat.* i. 61 Shrift to God is put bihynde ..but privey shrift newe foundun is autorisid as nedeful to soulis heele. *c* **1400** *Apol. Loll.* 90 Put not His bidding be hynd. *c* **1430** LYDG. *Bochas* I. iii. (1544) 6 a, The pride of Nembroth there was put behind. *c* **1450** *Rob. Hood* (Ritson) I. 1072, I dyd holpe a pore yeman, With wronge was put behynde. *a* **1887** *Mod.* Go behind and look for it.

B. *prep.* I. *With the object in motion.*

1. **a.** In a place left by (one who has gone on). Usually with *leave, remain, stay,* expressed or understood.

c **1200** ORMIN 8913 He wass þa bihinndenn hemm bilefedd att te temmple. *a* **1300** *Cursor M.* 15879 Lafte þei not bihynden hem þe fals feloun Iudas. **1526** *Pilgr. Perf.* (W. de W. 1531) 143 To leue our beest behynde vs. **1613** SHAKS. *Hen. VIII*, IV. ii. 84 Leaue me heere in wretchednesse, behinde ye. **1874** FARRAR *Christ* I. 477 Leaving behind him those Phœnician shrines. *a* **1887** *Mod.* She has resolved to stay behind me for a few days.

b. *fig.* In a condition or state left by (one); in existence, in life, in the world after one is 'gone.'

1601 SHAKS. *Twel. N.* II. i. 20 He left behind him myself and a sister. *a* **1694** TILLOTSON (J.) Piety and virtue are not only delightful for the present, but they leave peace and contentment behind them. **1759** JOHNSON *Rasselas* xxx. Wks. (1825) I. 263 The old Egyptians have left behind them monuments of industry. **1867** FREEMAN *Norm. Conq.* I. vi. (1876) 420 The last King who left behind him a name for just and mild government.

c. *fig.* In time left by (one); in time past.

1832 TENNYSON *Locksley H.* 13 When the centuries behind me like a fruitful land reposed.

†**2.** After the departure of (a person); in the absence of. *Obs.* (Now, *behind his back*: see 9.)

c **1300** *Beket* 1374 To deme a man bihynden him theu wost hit nere no lawe. **1340** *Ayenb.* 10 Þo þet misziggeþ guode men behinde ham. **1470–85** MALORY *Arthur* (1816) I. 357 Many speak more behind him than they will say to his face.

3. **a.** In the rear of (one moving); following, after.

c **1385** CHAUCER *L.G.W.* 185 By-hynde this god..I saw comynge of ladyis nynetene. **1610** SHAKS. *Temp.* IV. i. 11 She will outstrip all praise And make it halt, behinde her. **1697** DRYDEN *Virg. Georg.* IV. 700 And close behind him follow'd she. **1742** YOUNG *Nt. Th.* I. 171 Joy behind joy, in endless perspective! **1808** SCOTT *Marm.* I. vii, Behind him rode two gallant squires.

b. with reference to any kind of progress, attainment, or position or order attained: Inferior to.

1526 TINDALE *2 Cor.* xi. 5, I suppose that I was not behynde the chefe apostles. **1593** HOOKER *Eccl. Pol.* I. vi. §2 Wks. 1841 I. 164 Beasts, though otherwise behind men, may ..in actions of sense and fancy go beyond them. **1625** BURGES *Pers. Tithes* 24 The practise of such as are behind him in estate. **1823** LAMB *Elia* Ser. I. xv. (1865) 121 She is in some things behind her years. **1848** MACAULAY *Hist. Eng.* I. 68 They were some centuries behind their neighbours in knowledge.

c. To be *behind the times*: see TIME *sb.* 5 a. Also *attrib.*

1905 *Daily Chron.* 14 Feb. 6/3 A slow-going, old-fashioned, behind-the-times country.

4. Later than, after (the set time), i.e. after the set time has passed. In 'behind time' there is an expression of blame not present in 'after time.'

1600 SHAKS. *A.Y.L.* IV. i. 195 If you..come one minute behind your hour. **1632** RUTHERFORD *Lett.* 26 (1862) I. 98 We be but half-hungered of Christ here, and many a time dine behind noon. **1853** C. BRONTË *Villette* 180 'Ten minutes behind his time,' said she.

II. *With the object at rest.*

5. **a.** In the space lying to the rear of, on the back side of (a person, or object that has a front and back). *behind fortifications*, etc.: inside of, so as to be defended by them.

c **1175** *Lamb. Hom.* 165 He is buuen us and beneþen, biforen and bihinden. *a* **1225** *Juliana* 73 Bihinden hare schuldren. *c* **1300** *K. Alis.* 2013 Y wol..faste bynde, His honden his rug byhynde. *c* **1320** *Seuyn Sag.* (W.) 553 He hadde, bihinden his paleys, A fair gardin. **1611** BIBLE *Ex.* xiv. 19 The pillar of the cloud..stood behinde them. **1760** JOHNSON *Idler* No. 95 ¶6 They wondered how a youth of spirit could spend the prime of life behind a counter. **1766** GOLDSM. *Vic. W.* xxii. (1806) 132 Next morning I took my daughter behind me, and set out on my return home. **1849** KINGSLEY *Pr. Idylls* (1875) 295 The gentleman from Lloyd's with the pen behind his ear.

b. *fig.* At the back of (any one) as a support; backing (one) up.

1882 *Pall Mall G.* 24 June 1 The great arbitragists who have behind them the wealthy financial houses in London.

6. **a.** On the farther side of (an object) from the spectator or point of reference; beyond.

c **1325** *E.E. Allit. P.* B. 653 þe burde byhynde þe dor for busmar laȝed. *a* **1400** *Chester Pl.* 209 Alas! that I were awaie Ferre behynde France! **1653** HOLCROFT *Procopius* IV. 120 All behinde the end of the Euxine is Lazica. **1697** DRYDEN *Virg. Georg.* III. 330 Behind the Mountain, or beyond the Flood. **1820** KEATS *St. Agnes* xi, He stood hid..Behind a broad hall-pillar. **1832** HT. MARTINEAU *Life in Wilds* i. 3 The mountains behind the Cape of Good Hope.

b. *fig.* At the back of, hidden by, on the side remote from our observation.

1866 J. MARTINEAU *Ess.* I. 198 Behind every phenomenon we must assume a power.

c. ***behind the scenes***: in the rear of the scenery of a theatre; *hence*, behind what is publicly displayed, out of sight, in private. Also *attrib.* and ***behind-scene***. See also SCENE 7.

1711 ADDISON *Spect.* No. 44 ¶5 Murders and Executions are always transacted behind the Scenes in the French Theatre. **1779** HORNE *Disc.* (1799) IV. vii. 169 In the Scripture-histories we are as it were admitted behind the scenes. **1841** E. FITZGERALD *Let.* 16 Jan. (1889) I. 64 And go right through it [*sc.* a picture] into some behind-scene world on the other side. **1856** FROUDE *Hist. Eng.* I. 316 There lay, ..behind the scenes a whole drama of contention and bitterness. **1933** *Essays & Studies* XVIII. 156 They [*sc.* 'stream of consciousness' novels] have..a strong behind-the-scenes interest. **1961** *John o'London's* 5 Oct. 374/2 His political novel tells the story of the behind-the-scenes struggle for power. **1968** J. W. WAINWRIGHT *Web of Silence* 100 It hit the headlines..but it didn't help the behind-scene manœuvring.

7. Backwards from (oneself), towards what lies in the rear of. (With *look* and equivalent verbs.)

c **1374** CHAUCER *Boeth.* III. xii. 108 Yif he loke byhynden hym. **1382** WYCLIF *Gen.* xix. 26 The wijf of hym [Lot], biholdynge bihynde her. **1611** BIBLE *Judg.* xx. 40 The Benjamites looked behind them. **1750** JOHNSON *Rambler* No. 6 ¶13 Venturing to look behind him. **1860** TYNDALL *Glaciers* I. §14. 94 The prospect..behind us..grew worse.

8. a. Into the space lying to the rear of, to the back or farther side of.

1250 LAY. 26057 Arthur..storte bi-hinde an treo. *c* **1385** CHAUCER *L.G.W.* 643 By-hyndyn the mast begynnyth he to fle. **1611** BIBLE *Matt.* xxvi. 23 Get thee behind mee, Satan. —— *2 Kings* ix. 19 Turne thee behinde me. *Mod.* The mouse ran behind the sidebord. The sun has sunk behind the mountains.

b. *fig.* Out of attention or consideration.

1866 MOTLEY *Dutch Rep.* v. i. 673 The plan of Don John ..I put entirely behind me.

c. ***to go behind***: to press an enquiry into what does not appear on the surface of (any matter), or is not avowed.

1884 M. WHITE in *Law Times Rep.* LII. 548/2 The rate.. was valid and good on the face of it, and the justices were not entitled to go behind it and inquire whether there was a concurrent rate.

III. *Phrase.*

9. ***behind*** (***one's***) ***back*** has been used as a more emphatic expression for *behind* (*one*), in all senses; but now spec. in sense 2, in which ***behind-backs*** also occurs in Scotch.

c **1325** *E.E. Allit. P.* B. 980 þe balleful burde..Bluschеd byhynden her bak. **1382** WYCLIF *Gen.* xxii. 13 Abraham.. sawe bihynd his bak a wether among the thornes. **1470-85** MALORY *Arthur* (1816) I. 307 To say of me wrong or shame behind my back. **1611** BIBLE *Ex.* xxiii. 35 Thou hast forgotten me, and cast me behinde thy backe [**1388** WYCLIF, behynde thi bodi]. **1645** RUTHERFORD *Tryal & Tri. Faith* (1845) 78 The Father and the Son are speaking of thee behind backs. **1711** STEELE *Spect.* No. 109 ¶5 Sir Andrew Freeport has said behind my Back, that, etc. **1782** BP. NEWTON *Wks.* II. xxii. 460 The flatterer will..trumpet forth your praises behind your back. *c* **1817** HOGG *Tales & Sk.* IV. 14 Tibby was sitting behind backs enjoying the meal. **1864** *Linnet's Trial* I. III. i. 303, I should be very sorry not to defend people behind their backs.

C. as *sb.*

1. (*colloq.* and *vulgar*): The back side or rear part (of the person or of a garment); the posteriors.

1786 *Lounger* No. 54. 17 Two young Ladies..with new Hats on their heads, new Bosoms, and new Behinds in a band-box. *a* **1830** GEORGE IV in *Sat. Rev.* (1862) 8 Feb., Go and do my bidding—tell him he lies, and kick his behind in my name! **1833** MARRYAT *P. Simple* (1863) 49 That I might not have the front of my trowsers torn as well as the behind. **1926** D. H. LAWRENCE *Let.* 19 Jan. (1932) 647 Lucky I'm not a professional behind-kicker. **1928** G. B. SHAW *Intell. Woman's Guide* lxxiv. 362 You can say 'If I catch you doing that again I will..smack your behind'.

2. a. *Australian National Football.* A scoring kick that earns one point (see quot. 1968). Also *attrib.*

1888 *Pall Mall G.* 23 July 6/2 The visitors won by five goals and ten behinds to four goals and eight behinds. **1890** *Melbourne Punch* 14 Aug. 107/2 South Melbourne 3 goals 10 behinds. **1968** EAGLESON & MCKIE *Terminology Austral. Nat. Football* I. 14 A behind is scored when the ball, after being kicked, is touched by or touches any player before passing through the goal posts; or when it touches a goal post; or when it passes immediately above a goal post or between a goal post and a behind post; or when it is kicked or knocked through the goal posts by one of the defending players. *Ibid.* 15 *Behind line*, the line between the goal and behind posts. *Ibid., Behind post*, a post seven yards to the side of a goal post, and not as tall as the goal post.

b. (See quots.)

1898 *Encycl. Sport* II. 143 (Eton football) Each side consists of the 'bully', outsides, and behinds, but all except the behinds are commonly spoken of as 'the bully'. *Ibid.*, The 'behinds' are 'short' and 'long behind' and 'goals'.

D. *Comb.* †**behind-back(s**, see 9 above; **behind-forth** (*obs.*), from behind forward; **behind-rider**, a rear guard; **behind-sight** *nonce-wd.* (as contrast to *foresight*), backward view, retrospection.

1398 TREVISA *Barth. De P.R.* XVIII. lxvii. (1495) 823 [The leoperde] reseth on hym behyndeforth wyth bytyng and wyth clawes. **1471** *Hist. Arriv. Edw. IV* (1838) 14 A good bande of speres and archars his behynd-rydars. **1884** *Pall Mall G.* 8 Feb. 1/1 If our foresight were as good as our 'behindsight,' many disasters would never happen.

behinder (bɪ'haɪndə(r)). [f. BEHIND *adv.* + -ER[1].] An operative in certain trades, as a tinplate worker whose work lies behind the rolling-mill, and the man who works at the back of a welding-furnace in a tube mill.

1881 *Instr. Census Clerks* (1885) 105 Behinder. Tin Plate Worker. **1906** *Westm. Gaz.* 10 June 2/1 Behinders [tinplate millmen].

behindhand (bɪ'haɪndhænd), *adv.* (and *a.*) Also 6-7 **behind the hand.** [f. BEHIND *prep.* + HAND, probably on the analogy of *beforehand*. Properly an adverb, but in common use as complement of the predicate, in 'to be behindhand,' where the distinction of adverb and adjective breaks down: hence sometimes attributively.]

1. In arrear as to the discharge of one's liabilities, in a state of insolvency, in debt. (Const. *with.*)

1530 PALSGR. 423/2, I am behynde the hande as a man is that is fallen in pouerty. **1535** LATIMER *Serm. & Rem.* (1845) 367 He can tell you of more as far behindhand as he. **1542** UDALL *Apoph. Erasm.* 319 b, Sore behynde hande in debte. **1618** WOTTON in *Reliq. Wotton.* (1685) 258 He was Poor and somewhat behind hand. **1647** W. BROWNE *Polexander* I. 134, I finde my selfe behindehand with him more than I am able to pay him. **1704** SWIFT *T. Tub* §2 (1709) 48 Having run something behind-hand with the world. **1752** JOHNSON *Rambl.* No. 191 ¶1 A cold which has..put me seventeen visits behind-hand.

b. In the position of a creditor, entitled to money which is in arrear.

1666 PEPYS *Diary* 19 Dec., Many..are ready to starve, they being five years behind-hand for their wages.

2. Behind time, late, too late, 'after the event'; out of date, behind the times.

1549 *Compl. Scot.* 115 This vryting is cum ouer lait and behynd the hand. **1645** W. LITHGOW *Siege Newcastle* (1820) 31 Scottish-men are aye wise behinde the hand. **1711** ADDISON *Spect.* No. 129 ¶5 A Justice of Peace's Lady, who was at least ten years behindhand in her Dress. **1837** CARLYLE *Fr. Rev.* I. I. v. ii. 131 Folly is that wisdom which is wise only behindhand. **1875** BROWNING *Aristoph. Apol.* 302 Am I perhaps behindhand? come too late?

3. In a state of backwardness, less advanced than others (*in*); ill provided or prepared (*with*).

1542 UDALL *Apoph. Erasm.* 169 a, Leauyng me behynd hande in bountifulnesse. **1601** R. JOHNSON *Kingd. & Commw.* 84 Unfurnished of warre provision..being exceedingly behind hand. **1701** W. WOTTON *Hist. Rome* 285 Severus was not behind-hand in anything that had been customary. **1768** STERNE *Sent. Journ.* (1778) I. 140 Not to be behind-hand in politeness. **1845** DISRAELI *Sybil* (1863) 59 Ah! you were abroad at the time, and so you are behindhand. **1851** HAWTHORNE *Snow Image* (1879) 223 A whole class who were behindhand with their lessons.

b. In an incomplete state, unfinished.

1853 ROBERTSON *Serm.* Ser. II. vii. 101 Was there.. something behindhand of Christ's sufferings remaining uncompleted?

4. *attrib.* Backward, tardy, hanging back.

1611 SHAKS. *Wint. T.* v. i. 151 Interpreters Of my behind-hand slacknesse.

†**5.** quasi-*sb.* The state of being behind. *Obs.*

1580 SIDNEY *Arcadia* II. (1613) 123 Hee..invaded Thessalia, and brought Dorilaus to some behind-hand of fortune. **1611** COTGR., *Perdre pied*, to..be driuen to a behind-hand.

†**be'hinds**, *adv. Obs. rare.* [f. BEHIND with advb. genitive *-es*, *-s*, for earlier *-en.*] = BEHIND.

1382 WYCLIF [see BEHIND A 1 c].

†**be'hindward**, *adv. Obs.* [f. as prec. + -WARD.] In the direction that is behind.

c **1440** HYLTON *Scala Perf.* (W. de W. 1494) xiii. Bj, That I myght forgete all thynges the whyche ben behyndwarde.

behite, obs. form of BEHIGHT *v.*

†**be'hither**, *adv.* and *prep. Obs.* [f. BE- + HITHER, cf. *behind, before, besides, beyond*, etc. (A useful word, worth reviving.)]

A. *prep.* **1.** On this side of. (L. *cis, citra.*)

1521 ABP. WARHAM in Ellis *Orig. Lett.* Ser. III. I. 241 Yt shuld engendre grete obloquy and sclandre to the Universitie, bothe behyther the See and beyonde. **1589** PUTTENHAM *Eng. Poesie* (Arb.) 257 The Italian..calleth the Frenchman..and all other breed behither their mountaines Appennines, *Tramontani.* **1679** EVELYN *Diary* (1827) III. 14, I called at my cousin Evelyn's who has a very pretty seat in the forest, 2 miles behither Cliefden. **1711** J. GREENWOOD *Eng. Gram.* 82 The Parlour lies behither, or on this Side the Kitchin.

2. Short of, barring, save.

1633 G. HERBERT *H. Baptism* in *Temple* 36 Let me be soft and supple to thy will..to others, mild, Behither ill. **1671** OLEY *Herbert's C. Parson* Pref. A ij b (N.), I have not any one thing, behither vice, that hath occasioned so much contempt of the clergie.

B. *adv.* On this side, on the nearer side.

1650 ELDERFIELD *Tythes* 280 Of what is behither..I need say nothing.

Behmenism, -ist, var. forms of BŒHMENISM, BŒHMENIST.

behof(e, obs. f. of BEHOOF and BEHOOVE.

behoft(e: see BIHOFTHE.

behold (bɪ'həʊld), *v.* Pa. t. **beheld.** Pa. pple. **beheld**, *arch.* **beholden.** Chief forms: *Inf.* 1-2 biheald-an, 2 -helden, 2-5 -hald-e(n, 3-5 -holde(n, 6- behold. *Ind. pres. 3rd sing.* 2 bihalt. *Pa. t.* 1-4 beheold, -hield, -held, -huld, -heild, -heeld, 5- beheld, (4 beholded). *Pa. pple.* 4 bihalden, 4- beholden, 4-5 beholde, 7- beheld, (4 behelded, beholdyd, 4-6 -ed). For other forms see HOLD. [OE. *bihaldan* (WSax. *behealdan*), identical w. OS. *bihaldan*, OFris. *bihalda*, OHG. *bihaltan*, mod.G. *behalten*, Du. *behouden*, f. *bi-* BE- 2 + *haldan, healdan* to HOLD. The application to watching, looking, is confined to English.]

I. To hold by, keep, observe, regard, look.

†**1.** *trans.* To hold by, keep hold of, retain. *Obs.*

a **1000** *Cædmon's Gen.* 366 (Gr.) Ðæt Adam sceal..minne stronglican stol behealdan. *c* **1380** WYCLIF *Serm.* Sel. Wks. I. 384 Men that biholden [*MS.* E holden] bileve of Crist. **1525** LD. BERNERS *Froiss.* II. lxiv. [lxix] 222 Euery man behelde the same oppynyon.

b. *intr.* (for *refl.*) To hold, keep *to.*

a **1300** *Cursor M.* 9483 To quas seruis straitly he bi-held.

†**2.** *trans.* To hold by some tie of duty or obligation, to retain as a client or person in duty bound. Found only in the pa. pple. BEHOLDEN, q.v.

†**3. a.** *intr.* To hold on *by*, appertain or belong *to*. **b.** *trans.* To pertain, relate or belong to, to concern. *Obs.*

a **1067** *Chart. Eadweard* in *Cod. Dipl.* IV. 214 God eów ȝehealde and alle ðe ðat beholde intó ðáre hálaȝen stowe. *c* **1175** *Lamb. Hom.* 65 þe pater noster bihalt me noht, bute ic þis habbe in mi þoht. *a* **1250** *Moral Ode* 156 in *E.E.P.* (1862) 31 Al hit hanged and bihalt bi þisse twam worde. *c* **1449** PECOCK *Repr.* I. ix. 45 Ech of hem [gouernauncis] whiche biholden the making..of the said sacramentis.

†**4.** *trans.* To hold or contain by way of purport or signification, to signify, mean. *Obs.*

c **1200** ORMIN 13408 We muȝhenn sen whatt itt bihallt. *a* **1225** *St. Marher.* 7 Whet bihalt,..þat tu ne buhest to me?

†**5.** *trans.* To hold in regard, keep, observe (commands, appointed days, etc.). *Obs.*

971 *Blickl. Hom.* 11 Symle bliþe mode Godes beboda utan we behealdan. **1387** TREVISA *Higden* (1865) I. 243 þe Romaynes..byhelde þilke dayes and wrouȝt nouȝt þilke dayes.

†**6. a.** *trans.* To regard (with the mind), have regard to, attend to, consider. **b.** *intr.* To give attention or regard, have regard *unto, to. Obs.*

c **825** *Vesp.* Ps. lx. 1 Bihald to ȝebede minum. *a* **1000** *Ags. Ps.* lx. 1 Beheald min ȝebed. *a* **1300** *E.E. Psalter* lxi. 1 Unto mi bede bihald þou. *c* **1300** *Beket* 760 Al this (ho so riȝt bihalth) thu gynnest forth to drawe. **1382** WYCLIF *Gen.* iv. 5 The Lord bihelde to Abel and to his ȝiftis. ? *a* **1400** *Cato Major.* II. xxv, Ende and biginnynge of þe werk Boþe þou hem bi-holde.

7. *trans.* **a.** To hold or keep in view, to watch; to regard or contemplate with the eyes; to look upon, look at (implying active voluntary exercise of the faculty of vision). *arch.* This has passed imperceptibly into the resulting passive sensation: **b.** To receive the impression of (anything) through the eyes, to see: the ordinary current sense. (It is not easy to show the beginning of sense b, as nearly all the early instances have some suggestion of the former: the earlier quotations under b. must therefore be treated as merely introductory.)

a. 971 *Blickl. Hom.* 11 Englas hie ȝeorne beheoldan. *a* **1200** *Trin. Hom.* 29 þe wimman bihalt hire sheawere and cumeð hire shadewe þaronne. *c* **1250** *Owl & N.* 1323 On ape mai a boc bi-halde, An leves wenden. *a* **1300** *Cursor M.* 290 Behald þe sune and þou mai se. *c* **1450** *Merlin* xiv. 225 The maiden hym be-heilde moche, and he her. **1523** LD. BERNERS *Froiss.* (1812) I. 423 They brought him to the princis..who behelde hym right fersly and felly. **1530** PALSGR. 447/1 To se an olde ryddylled queene to beholde herselfe in a glasse. **1605** BACON *Adv. Learn.* I. §2 (1873) 1 Beholding you not with the inquisitive eye of presumption. **1667** MILTON *P.L.* IX. 1080 How shall I behold the face Henceforth of God or Angel, earst with joy And rapture so oft beheld? **1676** HOBBES *Iliad* 291 And when enough beholden them he had. **1718** POPE *Iliad* I. 553 From far Behold the field.

b. *c* **1175** *Lamb. Hom.* 177 He muwen ben of-drad þe hine sculleð bi-helde. *a* **1225** *Ancr. R.* 106 He biheold hu his deore deciples fluen alle vrom him. **1382** WYCLIF *Gen.* xxiv. 64 Rebecca, Isaac biholdyd, descendide of the camel. **1483** *Cath. Angl.* 26/1 To behalde: *asspicere casu.* **1565** STAPLETON *Fortresse* 56 And such as haue not heard haue yet beholded. **1596** SHAKS. *Tam. Shr.* II. i. 11, I neuer yet beheld that speciall face, Which I could fancie. **1697** DRYDEN *Virg. Georg.* iii. 711 On Winter Seas we fewer Storms behold. **1850** MRS. BROWNING *Poems* I. 90 These are stars beholden By your eyes in Eden. **1860** TYNDALL *Glac.* I. §16. 109 Anything more exquisite I had never beheld.

†**8.** *intr.* To look. Const. with various adverbs and prepositions. *Obs.* (exc. as absolute use of 7.)

c **1175** *Lamb. Hom.* 133 Bihald he seide up to heouene. *c* **1200** *Trin. Coll. Hom.* 153 Bi-hold up to heuene and tel þe

sterres. *c* **1325** *E.E. Allit. P.* A. 809 Hys face..þat watz so fayr on to byholde. *c* **1386** CHAUCER *Frankl. T.* 135 Thanne wolde she..pitously in to the see biholde. **1393** LANGL. *P. Pl.* C. I. 14 Esteward ich byhulde· after þe sonne. **1491** CAXTON *Vitas Patr.* (W. de W. 1495) II. 210 b/2 The holy fader..beholdynge upon hym. **1509** BARCLAY *Ship of Fooles* (1570) ¶¶ vj, Beholde vnto the shore. **1601** SHAKS. *Jul. C.* V. iii. 33 Come downe, behold no more. **1634** *Malory's Arthur* (1816) II. 95 They took their horses, and beheld about them. **1795** SOUTHEY *Joan of Arc* VI. 277 The Maiden's host beheld.

†**9. a.** *intr.* To look or face (as a building) *against* or *to* (a direction). **b.** *trans.* To face. *Obs.*

1382 WYCLIF *Song Sol.* vii. 4 The tour of Liban that beholdith aȝen Damasch. *c* **1449** PECOCK *Repr.* III. i. 280 At the see that biholdith to the west. **1593** FALE *Dialling* 8 Let the arke behold the South. **1634** SIR T. HERBERT *Trav.* 209 The Land is high..chiefly where it beholds the Sea. **1677** MOXON *Mech. Exerc.* (1703) 310 The South Erect..whose Plane..directly beholds the South.

†**10.** *trans.* To look upon, view, consider *as* (something); to consider or hold in a certain capacity.

1642 ROGERS *Naaman* 344 To behold himselfe the true bread and..water of life. **1650** FULLER *Pisgah* III. i, It is beheld in Scripture as most solemn and of highest importance. **1662** —— *Worthies* (1840) II. 223 Though beans be generally beheld but as horse and hog-grain. *Ibid.* 551 He is beheld one of the first merchants.

†**II.** Senses apparently derived from HOLD at a later period. Only in Sc. *Obs.* (Some of these are doubtful.)

†**11.** *intr.* To 'hold,' stop, wait.

a **1670** SPALDING *Troub. Chas. I*, I. 143 (JAM.) They beheld but keeped still the fields. **1768** ROSS *Helenore* 21 (JAM.) 'That's true,' quo' she, 'but we'll behad a wee.'

†**b.** *trans.* 'To await.' Jam.

1639 *Act Chas. I*, Addit. (1814) V. 665 (JAM.) To behold the treattie with the commissioneris. *a* **1662** BAILLIE *Lett.* (1775) I. 24 (JAM.) To behold the event of that meeting.

†**12.** *trans.* 'To connive at, take no notice of.' Jam.

a **1670** SPALDING *Troub. Chas. I*, I. 154 (JAM.) To understand if his lordship would behold them, or if he would raise forces against them.

†**13.** 'To permit.' Jam.

a **1670** SPALDING *Troub. Chas. I*, I. 117 (JAM.) They.. desired him out of love..that he would be pleased to behold them to go on, otherwise they were making such preparations that they would come and might not be resisted.

behold (bɪˈhəʊld), *int.* The imperative of the preceding verb, used to call attention; = LO *int.*

[*c* **1440** *York Myst.* xx. 193 Be-halde howe he alleggis oure lawe.] **1535** COVERDALE *Mal.* iii. 1 Beholde, I will send my messaunger. **1590** SHAKS. *Mids. N.* I. i. 147 Behold, The iawes of darknesse do deuoure it vp. *a* **1764** LLOYD *Dial.* Wks. II. 2 Behold! to yours and my surprize, These trifles to a volume rise. **1831** CARLYLE *Sart. Res.* III. viii, Fortunatus ..when he..wished himself Anywhere, behold he was There.

†**beˈholdable,** *a. Obs.* In 5 bi-. [f. BEHOLD *v.* + -ABLE.] That admits of being contemplated.

c **1449** PECOCK *Repr.* I. vii. 37 A lawe..doable and not oonli knoweable and biholdeable. *Ibid.* II. i. 134 Ech..is a treuthe considerable, or speculable, or biholdable oonli.

beholden (bɪˈhəʊld(ə)n), *ppl. a.*; also 4 **bihalden, biholde,** 5–6 **behold(e,** 5 **byholden, -halden, behoulden,** 9 (*dial.*) **behauden, behadden, behodden.** [Originally pa. pple. of BEHOLD *v.*; but senses 1 and 2 are not actually found in other parts of the vb., though 'hold or retain under obligation' was a natural enough sense of *behold.* See also BEHOLDING *ppl. a.*]

1. Attached, or obliged (*to* a person); under personal obligation for favours or services.

c **1340** *Gaw. & Gr. Knt.* 1547, I am hyȝly bihalden, & euer-more wylle Be seruaunt to your-seluen. *Ibid.* 1841, I am derely to yow biholde. **1414** BRAMPTON *Penit. Ps.* li. 20 Manye, that were to me beholde. **1489** CAXTON *Faytes of A.* III. x. 188 The more beholden is the lorde unto hym. **1592** tr. *Junius on Rev.* xiii. 1 The beast is beholden for all unto the Dragon. **1656** BRAMHALL *Replic.* vii. 283, I am much beholden to him for easing me of the labour of replying. **1741** RICHARDSON *Pamela* (1824) I. xxvii. 41 Besides I don't love to be beholden. **1816** SCOTT *Old Mort.* 49 'And wad keep ye in bread without being behadden to ony ane.' **1873** F. HALL *Mod. English* 101 How deeply we are beholden to the happy daring of translators, for the amplitude and variety of our diction.

†**2.** Under moral obligation, in duty bound (*to do* something). *Obs.*

a **1450** *Knt. de la Tour* (1868) 108 Eueriche fader and moder is be holde to praie for her children. *c* **1485** *Digby Myst.* (1882) III. 1814 To worchep Iesu þey ar be-hold. **1502** *Ord. Crysten Men* I. vii. (1506) 82 He is bounde and beholde for to byleue that who so trespasseth..is in deedlye synne.

†**3.** Regarded, considered. *Obs.*

a **1520** *Myrr. Our Ladye* 310 The thynge byholden ys to say, the beholdynge of the causes.

†**beholdenness:** see BEHOLDINGNESS.

[Richardson's pretended quotation of *beholdenness* from Sir P. Sidney is a double error, reprehensibly copied by subsequent dictionaries: the quotation is from R. Beling (1628), and the word is *beholdingnesse,* q.v.]

beholder (bɪˈhəʊldə(r)). Also 4 bi-, by- beholdar, -ere. [f. BEHOLD *v.* + -ER¹.] One who beholds, a watcher, looker on, spectator.

c **1374** CHAUCER *Boeth.* v. vi. 178 God byholder and forwiter of alle þinges. *c* **1400** *Apol. Loll.* 32, I haue sett þe a beholdar to þe hows of Israel. **1526** *Pilgr. Perf.* (W. de W. 1531) 203 Beynge the very seers & beholders of his magesty. **1535** COVERDALE *Esther* xv. 2 God, which is the beholder & Sauioure of all thinges. **1600** SHAKS. *A. Y. L.* I. ii. 139 All the beholders take his part with weeping. **1660** FULLER *Mixt Contemp.* (1841) 242 The multitude of actors and beholders at the mustering in Hyde Park. **1712** BUDGELL *Spect.* No. 404 ¶6 If Cælia would be silent, her Beholders would adore her. **1875** JOWETT *Plato* (ed. 2) I. 492 A sight to gladden the beholder's eye.

beholding (bɪˈhəʊldɪŋ), *vbl. sb.*; also 3 **bihaldung, biholdung,** 4 **by-, behaldyng.** [f. BEHOLD *v.* + -ING¹.]

1. The action of looking at; contemplation, sight.

a **1225** *St. Marher.* 14 Wið luueliche lates, wið steape bihaldunge eiðer on oðer. **1382** WYCLIF *2 Chron.* xxv. 21 Thei ȝeuen to hem silf beholdingis either to other. **1483** CAXTON *G. de la Tour* D v, The fourthe foly of Eue was the foolyssh beholdynge. **1605** SHAKS. *Lear* III. vii. 10 The reuenges..are not fit for your beholding. **1702** ROWE *Tamerl* I. i. 321 My Eyes first own'd thee..the Joy of their Beholding.

†**2.** Mental contemplation; consideration. *Obs.*

a **1520** *Myrr. Our Ladye* 310 The beholdynge of the causes. **1540** COVERDALE *Pref. Fruitful Less.* Wks. 1844 I. 206 Sweet contemplation and beholding of God's almightiness.

†**3.** Regard, reference. *Obs.*

c **1449** PECOCK *Repr.* I. iii. 17 Thouȝ no biholding therto were maad into Holi Scripture.

4. The thing beheld: †**a.** An image, a spectre. *Obs.* **b.** A vision. *arch.*

c **1440** *Gesta Rom.* 240 She shalle loke in the glas, & hir owne beholdyng shalle bowe & passe to hir ayene. **1824** COLERIDGE *Aids Refl.* (1848) I. 322 Shadows and imperfect beholdings and vivid fragments of things distinctly seen. **1826** E. IRVING *Babylon* I. III. 161 Twice..doth the Prophet mention this part of his beholding.

¶ The sense 'Obligation,' the only one recognized by Dr. Johnson, assigned by him on the strength of a quotation from Carew, is a mere blunder, mechanically perpetuated by subsequent dictionaries: Carew's word is *beholdingnes,* q.v.

beˈholding, *ppl. a.* [f. as prec. + -ING². Sense 1 evidently originated in an error for BEHOLDEN, either through confusion of the endings (cf. esp. the 15th c. spelling *-yne* for *-en*), or, more probably, after *beholden* was shortened to *beholde, behold,* and its grammatical character obscured; the general acceptance of 'beholding' may have been due to a notion that it meant 'looking (*e.g.* with respect, or dependence),' or to association with the idea of 'holding of' or 'from' a feudal superior. (It was exceedingly common in the 17th c., for which no fewer than 97 instances have been sent in by our readers.)]

†**1.** Under obligation, obliged, indebted, BEHOLDEN; in late use often: Dependent. *Obs.*

[*a* **1450** *Knt. de la Tour* viii. 11 Doughter, ye are moche beholde to serue God.] **1483** CAXTON *ibid.* C viij b, Dame ye ben moche beholdynge to god. **1551–6** ROBINSON tr. *More's Utop.* 36, I was muche bounde and beholdynge to the righte reuerende father. **1598** SHAKS. *Merry W.* I. i. 283 A Iustice of peace sometime may be beholding to his friend, for a Man. **1662** H. MORE *Antid. Ath.* I. vi. (1712) 19 We have some Ideas that we are not beholding to our Senses for. *a* **1704** T. BROWN *Eng. Sat.* Wks. 1730 I. 25 Posterity has been very little beholding to the ancient Greeks for satire. **1719** D'URFEY *Pills* (1872) I. 67 And he for their..bread, Beholding to his wife.

†**2.** ? That holds fast the eyes; engaging, attractive. *Obs. rare*⁻¹.

1580 SIDNEY *Arcadia* (1598) I. 50 When he saw me..my beautie was no more beholding to him then my harmony.

3. Looking on, gazing.

1593 SHAKS. *Lucr.* 1590 Which when her sad-beholding husband saw, Amazedly in her sad face he stares.

†**beˈholdingness.** *Obs.* [f. prec. + -NESS.] The condition of being beholden to any one; obligation, indebtedness; (in late use) dependence.

1580 SIDNEY *Arcadia* III. 253 All other meanes, that might either establish a beholdingnes, or at least awake a kindnesse. **1602** CAREW *Cornwall* 60 b, My love to vertue, and not any particular beholdingnes, hath expressed this my testimony. **1628** R[ICHARD] B[ELING] *Sidney's Arcadia* VI. (1628–38) 492 Leonatus the yong king of Pontus (who had bin there to acknowledge his beholdingnesse to them). **1658** SLINGSBY *Diary* (1836) 200 That servile condition.. beholdingness or dependance on the elder [brother].

beˈhoney, *v.* [f. BE- 6 + HONEY.] To smear or sweeten with honey, or *fig.* with honied words.

1611 COTGR., *Emmieller,* to behonie, to sweeten, dresse.. with honie. **1845** *Whitehall* xix. 120 This behoneying and larding of women with high-seasoned compliments.

behoof (bɪˈhuːf). Forms: (1–2 bi-, behóf,) 3–5 (*dative*) **bihoue,** 4–5 **bihove,** 4–6 **behoue,** 4–7 **behove,** 6–7 **behoove,** 6–8 **behoofe,** 6– **behoof.** (Also 4–5 **bihufe,** 4–6 **byhove, behuf,** 5 **byhoff, beofe,** 5–6 **behofe, -houfe,** 6 *Sc.* **behowe, -hufe, -huif,** 7 **behoolfe.**) [OE. **bihóf* 'utility,' occurring in the deriv. *bihóf-líc* useful, necessary; = OFris. *bihof*, Du. *behoef*, MHG. *bihuof*, mod.G. *behuf*, of same meaning; f. **bihóf*, pa. t. of Orig. Teut. **bihafjan*, MHG. *beheben* 'to take, hold, receive,' f. *bi-*, BE- + *hafjan*, OE. *hębban*, pa. t. *hóf*, 'to HEAVE, raise,' orig. 'to take up, take,' cogn. w. L. *cap(i)ĕre*. The original sense seems to have been either, 'taking in, reception, acquisition,' whence 'gain, advantage,' or 'taking away, taking to oneself, taking the use of,' whence 'use.' See also the synonyms BIHEVE, BIHOFTHE.]

1. Use, benefit, advantage. Chiefly in *to, for, on,* (formerly *into, till*) (*the*) *behoof of.* (*In, on behoof of,* are due to confusion with *behalf.*) *pl.* rare.

c **1205** LAY. 1050 Ʒe ʒeorneð.. mine leoue dohter to swa laðe mannes bihoue [**1250** bihofe]. **1340** HAMPOLE *Pr. Consc.* 70 He ordaynd, for mans byhufe, Heven and herth. **1375** BARBOUR *Bruce* XV. 517 [Douglas] held no thing till his behuf. **1393** GOWER *Conf.* I. 15 Upon the hond to were a sho ..Accordeth nought to the behove Of resonable mannes use. **1482** MARG. PASTON in *Lett.* 861 III. 286, I bequeth an C marc..to the use and byhoff of the seid William Paston. **1483** CAXTON *Cato* E ij b, Alle thynges shal come to your behoufe in habundaunce. **1491** *Act 7 Hen. VII*, xx, Londes ..which be..to his use or behove had. *c* **1530** MORE *De quat. Noviss.* Wks. 93 For whose vse and behoofe thei kepe it. **1532** HERVET *Xenophon's Househ.* (1768) 28 Delyuered it vnto you to kepe for bothe our behoues. **1549** OLDE *Erasm. Par. 1 Tim.* iii. 1 [A bishop is] one that careth for yᵉ commodities and behoufes of others. **1553** T. WILSON *Rhet.* 7 In behove of the publique weal. **1611** BIBLE *Pref.* 5 For the behoofe and edifying of the vnlearned. **1625** MILTON *Death Fair Inf.* vii, Which careful Jove in nature's true behoof Took up. **1667** —— *P.L.* II. 982 No mean recompence it brings To your behoof. **1768** BLACKSTONE *Comm.* II. 365 To the use and behoof of A and his heirs. **1769** ROBERTSON *Chas. V*, III. VII. 35 Taking towns for his own behoof. **1855** MOTLEY *Dutch Rep.* (1861) I. 31 Fines are imposed for the behoof of the count. **1857** MISS WINKWORTH *Tauler's Life & Serm.* 386 They devote all their prayers..to their own behoof. [**1868** F. PAGET *Lucretia* 207 The parlour had been turned into a bedroom on my behoof.]

†**2.** ? What it behoves one to do; obligation, duty. *Obs. rare.*

1594 SOUTHWELL *M. Magd. Fun. Teares* 161 It considereth behoofe more than benefit, and what in duty it should, not what indeed it can.

†**3.** ? A gift for behoof of the recipient, a 'benefit' or benefaction, a gratuity, a 'tip.' *Obs. rare.*

1596 SPENSER *State Irel.* 529 No offices should be sold for money..nor no behoves taken for captaincies of counties.

behooped, behoot, etc.; see BE- *pref.*

behoove, variant of BEHOVE *v.*

behorewe, behorn, behorror, etc.: see BE- *pref.*

†**beˈhote,** *sb. Obs.* [OE. *behát*, f. *behátan* to promise: cf. BEHETE, BEHIGHT *sb.*] A promise.

c **1000** *Ags. Gosp.* Luke xxiv. 49 Ic sende on eow mines fæder behat. *c* **1175** *Cott. Hom.* 225 Ic wille settan mi wed.. to þisan behate. *a* **1300** *E.E. Psalter* cxv. 14 Mi be-hotes yhelde sal I Bifore alle his folke.

behote, earlier and better form of BEHIGHT *v.*

†**beˈhoten,** *ppl. a. Obs.* [f. prec.] Promised.

c **1200** *Trin. Coll. Hom.* 185 Ðat is þat bihotene lond.

†**beˈhoting,** *vbl. sb.* Also bi-, by-. [f. as prec. + -ING¹: cf. BEHIGHTING.] Promising, promise.

c **1300** *K. Alis.* 4000 Thou, for mede, or byhotyng, Stal byhynde on oure kyng Him to slen. **1340** *Ayenb.* 40 Be yefþes, oþer be behotinges. **1496** *Dives & Paup.* (W. de W.) II. xv. 125 Auowe is byhotynge of some good thynge made to god with avysement.

behoufe, obs. form of BEHOOF.

behounced, etc.: see BE- *pref.*

†**beˈhovable,** *a. Obs.* [f. BEHOVE *v.* + -ABLE.] Useful, profitable, advantageous; incumbent.

c **1460** J. RUSSELL *Bk. Nurture* in *Babees Bk.* (1868) 172 þerfore stuffe of household is behoveable. **1482** *Monk of Evesham* (Arb.) 49 Y toke hem, and to behouable vsus ful treuly y spende hem. **1553–87** FOXE *A. & M.* (1596) 1021/1 Gamaliel did see better what was behooueable. **1596** BELL *Surv. Popery* II. II. viii. 172 It was as well behoouable to haue the wiues confirmed, as the husbandes.

†**beˈhovably,** *adv. Obs.* [f. prec. + -LY².] Usefully, profitably, advantageously, advisably.

1512 *Act 4 Hen. VIII*, xix. §6 To do all that..shall seme behoveably and necessarye.

behove, behoove (bɪˈhuːv, -ˈhəʊv), *v.* Forms: 1 **behófian,** 2–3 **bihouen,** (3 **-hofen, -heouen, bioue, behafe),** 3–5 **bi-, byhoue,** (4 **behowe, byhufe, behowue, behowf),** 4–6 **behuif,** 4–7 **behoue,** (5 **behofe),** 6 **behooue,** (**bihoove, behoofe, behuf, behof),** 6– **behoove,** 5 – **behove.** *Pa. t.* **behoved,** (4 **byhod).** For contracted impersonal forms, see BUS. [OE. *bi-*, *behófian* (corresp. to

MLG. *behoven*, MDu. and Du. *behoeven*), f. *bihóf sb.*: see BEHOOF. Lit. 'to be of behoof or use.' Historically, it rimes with *move*, *prove*, but being now mainly a literary word, it is generally made to rime with *rove*, *grove*, by those who know it only in books. Cf. *prove*, *proof*: *behove*, *behoof*. The spelling with *-oo-* is now restricted to the United States.]

†**1.** *trans.* To have use for or need of, to require; to be in want of. (Object orig. *genitive*.) *Obs.*

c **890** K. ÆLFRED *Bæda* IV. v, Mycel wund behófaþ mycles læcedomes. *c* **1000** *Sax. Leechd.* III. 440 Þeah þa scearp þanclan witan..þisse engliscan ȝeþeodnesse ne behofien. *c* **1175** *Lamb. Hom.* 63 Swa bi-haueð þe saule fode. **1483** CAXTON *Gold. Leg.* 281/2 Somme sekenes in the legge whiche behoueth a medycyne. **1523** LD. BERNERS *Froiss.* (1812) I. 626 One of the most strongest townes of the worlde; for it behoveth mo than ii. C. M. men to besiege it rounde. *a* **1670** HACKET *Abp. Williams* I. 39 (D.) He had all those endowments..which are behoved in a scholar.

†**2.** To be physically of use, needful, or necessary *to*; (only in 3 *pers.*). *Obs.* Object orig. *dative*.

1154 *O.E. Chron.* (Laud MS.) an. 1137 §6 Al þat heom behoued. *c* **1175** *Lamb. Hom.* 65 He us ȝeue..þet us bihoueð ulche dei. *c* **1230** *Hali Meid.* 27 Me beheoueð his help. **1297** R. GLOUC. 177 Ech [erne] ys in a roche hym sulf..Vor hem byhoueþ muche mete. *c* **1350** *Will. Palerne* 2349 Alle harneys þat be hoves to werre. **1489** CAXTON *Faytes of A.* II. xxxi. 142 Gonnes and the pouldre that behoueth therto. *c* **1530** MORE *De quat. Noviss.* Wks. 90 Labour..to geate that thee and thyne behoueth. **1667** MILTON *P.L.* II. 942 Behoves him now both Oare and Saile.

3. a. To be morally needful or requisite *to*; to be incumbent, proper, or due.

c **1175** *Lamb. Hom.* 109 Þan alden bihouað duȝende þewas. **1387** TREVISA *Higden* (1865) I. 67 Ouþer vnderstondynge bihoueþ of þe ryueres of Paradys, þan auctours writeþ. **1538** BALE *Thre Lawes* 873 Those are perswaded all thynges them to behoue. **1572** FORREST *Theophilus* 358, I will informe him what doth behove in þis case. **1684** *Contempl. State Man* II. vi. (1699) 190 They informed him of the King's Testament and what behoved him. **1860** TRENCH *Serm. Westm. Ab.* xiv. 158 If this behoves in the time of a great joy, it behoves still more in the time of a great sorrow.

b. To befit, be due *to*; to belong, pertain, suit.

1470–85 MALORY *Arthur* (1816) II. 221 This shield beboveth to no man but unto sir Galahad. **1485** CAXTON *Paris & V.* 67 Now see I wel that now me byhoueth noo hoope ne truste. **1502** *Ord. Crysten Men* (W. de W.) I. vii. 56 It behoueth unto all the moost grete clerkes. **1577** HARRISON *Descr. Eng.* II. xx. (1877) 87 We wold haue them in reuerence as to their case behooveth. **1814** SCOTT *Ld. Isles* VI. ix, With honour, as behoved To page the monarch dearly loved. **1881** ROSSETTI *Ball. & Sonn.* 119 To such bright cheer and courtesy That name might best behove.

4. quasi-*impers.* (the subject being a clause). In early ME. without *it*, which is now ordinarily used. **a.** with the thing incumbent expressed by an infinitive, and with personal object: It is incumbent upon or necessary for (a person) *to do* (something).

c **1200** ORMIN 16706 Bihofeþþ..þe mannes sune onn erþe To wurrþen hofenn upp. *c* **1325** *E.E. Allit. P.* A. 927 A gret cite..Yow byhod haue. **1382** WYCLIF *2 Sam.* iv. 10 To whom it hadde bihouid [**1388** it bihofte] me to ȝeue mede. **1485** CAXTON *Chas. Gt.* 103 Vs behoueth fyrst to passe. **1591** SPENSER *Virgil's Gnat* lix, She..observ'd th' appointed way, as her behooved. **1611** BIBLE *Heb.* ii. 17 In all things it behooued him to bee made like vnto his brethren. **1649** MILTON *Eikon.* iii. Wks. (1851) 355 Wherefore did he goe at all, it behooving him to know there were two Statutes that declar'd he ought first, etc. **1756** C. LUCAS *Ess. Waters* III. 341 It behooves the more weakly..to be more cautious. **1792** BURKE *Corr.* (1844) IV. 33 It greatly behoved government to keep its temper. **1820** W. IRVING *Sketch Bk.* II. 354 It behoved him to keep on good terms with his pupils. **1855** H. REED *Lect. Eng. Lit.* i. (1878) 28 What books does it behoove me to know? **1952** M. MCCARTHY *Groves of Academe* (1953) iii. 40 It behooved him to tread warily with Domna. **1955** *Sci. Amer.* Aug. 71/1 It behooves us to know as much as possible about this problem.

b. without pers. obj.: It is proper or due. *arch.*

a **1240** *Wohunge* in *Cott. Hom.* 275 Bihoues þurh þi grace ȝapliche to wite me. **1340** HAMPOLE *Pr. Consc.* 945 God war worthy mare to be lufed þan any creature, and swa byhufed. **1563** SHUTE *Archit.* D iiij b, Now it behoueth to make mention of an other order. **1633** G. HERBERT *Agonie* in *Temple* 29 Two..things, The which to measure it doth more behove. **1876** SWINBURNE *Erecth.* 1452 Yet no pause behoves it make.

c. the thing incumbent expressed by a clause. *arch.*

c **950** *Lindisf. Gosp.* Matt. xviii. 6 Behofas [*c* **975** *Rushw.* beþearfeþ] him þæt he ȝehongiȝa coern-stan. *Ibid.* John xviii. 14 Behofað þætte an monn sie dead fore ðæm folce. *c* **1200** ORMIN 17966 Itt bihofeþþ wel þatt he nu forrþwarrd waxe. *a* **1240** *Sawles Warde* 247. **1375** BARBOUR *Bruce* VI. 114 And than behufit, he chesit him ane Of thir twa. *c* **1440** *Gesta Rom.* 403 It behouys that the blynde bere the halte. **1533** TINDALE *Lord's Supper* 31 It behoveth, that the son of man must die. **1547** *Homilies* I. *Read. Script.* II. (1859) 15 It behooveth not, that such..should set aside reading. **1647** W. BROWNE *Polexander* I. 126 It behooves, likewise, that you give some roome and place to those that speake to you. **1860** ADLER *Fauriel's Prov. Poetry* xvii. 389 It well behooves that every faithful friend..should dread to disclose..his passion.

†**d.** the thing incumbent elliptically omitted. *Obs.*

c **1175** *Lamb. Hom.* 75 He nis nawiht alse leful alse him bi-houede. **1502** ARNOLD *Chron.* (1811) 207 The sacramentis freely to make and bere to whom it behougthe. **1644** MILTON *Areop.* (Arb.) 54 If he be of such worth as behoovs him.

5. a. Used, owing to confusion between the accusative and nominative (see first two quots.), as a personal verb: To be under obligation (*to do*); = must needs, ought, have. Of northern origin, and since 1500 only Scotch.

[*c* **1340** HAMPOLE *Prose Tr.* (1866) 5 Þe nam of Ihesu es helefull and nedys by-houys be lufed of all. *c* **1386** CHAUCER *Pers. T.* ¶557 A servaunt of God bihoveth nought to chide.] *c* **1400** *Apol. Loll.* 31 Swelk men be howuen tak hede. **1475** CAXTON *Jason* 76 The..craft that he behoueth to obserue and kepe. **1549** *Compl. Scot.* xv. 131 We behufit fyrst to reueil it. **1637** GILLESPIE *Eng. Pop. Cerem.* II. ix. 52 He behooved to offend the Iewes. **1759** ROBERTSON *Hist. Scot.* II. VIII. 45 They behoved to esteem them traitors. **1832** SIR W. HAMILTON *Disc.* (1853) 101 He behoved..clearly to determine the value of the principal terms.

†**b.** To owe. *Obs.*

1496 *Dives & Paup.* iv. 24/2 He that moche hath byhoueth moche. And he that hath lesse byhoueth lesse.

¶ error for BEHOTE.

1470–85 MALORY *Arthur* I. xxxix. 72 'Then I behove you,' said Balin, 'part of his blood to heal your son withal.' **1502** ARNOLD *Chron.* 296 Promyttynge and behofynge by the fayth of his body, worde of his princehode, and kyngis sonne.

†**behove, byhoue**, ? *a.* or *pa. pple. Obs.* [f. BEHOVE *v.*] In want. Cf. BIHEVE.

1413 LYDG. *Pylgr. Sowle* I. xv. (1483) 13, I that am poure and hugely byhoue, Of help I pray yow of almysdede.

behove, obs. form of BEHOOF.

be'hoveful, -'hooveful, *a. arch.* Forms: 4–5 behof-, 5 byhoof-, behoe-, behowe-, behuf-, 5–6 beho-, 5–7 behofe-, 5 behoue-, 6–7 behov-, behoof-, behoofe-, behooue-, 7 behoov-, 6–9 behoove-, 5– behoveful. [f. BEHOOF *sb.* + -FUL. (Extremely common from 1400 to 1700; but used since only by archaists.)] Useful, of use; advantageous, expedient; needful, necessary, due.

1382 WYCLIF *Ps.* cxliv. 15 Thou ȝyuest the mete of hem in the behofful time. [**1388** in couenable tyme]. **1432** *Paston Lett.* 18. I. 32 Not behovefull nor expedient to be aboute the king. **1485** CAXTON *Chas. Gt.* 145 It is not behoeful to put hym so to deth. **1533** MORE *Answ. Poyson. Bk.* Wks. 1124/2 How necessary..for mans redempcion, that is to witte so behofull therto, that without it we shoulde not haue bene saued. **1570** DEE *Math. Pref.* 40 It is behofefull for an Architect to haue the Knowledge of Painting. **1589** *Marprel. Epit.* 40 Behooful to the honor of god, and the good of common welth. *a* **1674** CLARENDON *Surv. Leviath.* (1676) 159 His friendship was the more behoovfull and necessary to the King. **1736** in Arb. *Garner* II. 528 [They] thought it more behoveful for themselves and their Religion. **1865** CARLYLE *Fredk. Gt.* V. XIII. i. 8 For a Nation, as for a man, it is very behoveful to be honest.

†**be'hovefully**, *adv. Obs.* [f. prec. + -LY.] Usefully, profitably, duly; necessarily.

1443 HEN. VI in Ellis *Orig. Lett.* III. 34 I. 80 Vndir the whiche the seid pees shall mowe behouefully be treted to a good conclusion. *c* **1449** PECOCK *Repr.* 47 [They] techen ful clereli and bihouefulli the treuthis. **1594** HOOKER *Eccl. Pol.* III. (1617) 112 Most behoouefully spoken. *a* **1603** T. CARTWRIGHT *Confut. Rhem. N.T.* (1618) 630 It must behouefully be now remembred.

†**be'hovefulness.** *Obs.* [f. as prec. + -NESS.] The quality of being behoveful; usefulness, use.

1592 WYRLEY *Armorie* 141 Declaring how for their behoofulnes It was. **1607** HIERON *Wks.* I. 260 The Apostle, knowing the behoouefulnesse of it.

†**be'hovely**, *a. Obs.* exc. *arch.* [OE. *behóflíc*, f. *behóf* BEHOOF + *-líc*: see -LY[1].] Of use; useful, profitable; needful, necessary. Const. *to*, orig. *dat.*

c **950** *Lindisf. Gosp.* Mark xi. 3 [The ass] Drihtne behoflic is. *c* **1250** *Gen. & Ex.* 4108 Alswilc als hem bi-hu[f]lik bee. **1330** R. BRUNNE *Chron.* Pref. 190 If it be a behouely þing at nede. *c* **1386** CHAUCER *Pers. T.* ¶312 Now it is bihovely thing to telle whiche been dedly synnes. **1393** GOWER *Conf.* II. 186 All was behovely to the man. **1942** T. S. ELIOT *Little Gidding* iii. 13 Sin is Behovely, but All shall be well.

†**be'hovely**, *adv. Obs.* [f. as prec. + -LY[2]: OE. **behóflíce*.] Usefully, needfully, necessarily.

c **1430** *Life St. Kath.* (Gibbs MS.) 90 Syth þou behouely sturest my counsayl.

be'hoven, *ppl. a.* [f. BEHOVE *v.* 5: on wrong analogy.] Under obligation, beholden.

1880 *Mehalah* I. ii. 26, I will in nothing be behoven to the man I abhor.

†**be'hovesome**, *a. Obs.* In 4 behouesum, behofsam. [f. BEHOOF + -SOME.] Useful, of service.

c **1330** *Arth. & Merl.* 2803 Pray to Crist..A king ous sende that bihouesum be To the right ogains the wrong. **1340** *Ayenb.* 99 He is þe vayreste and mest behofsam.

be'hoving, *ppl. a. arch.* [f. BEHOVE *v.* + -ING[2].] That behoves; of use, needful, appropriate, incumbent.

c **1175** *Lamb. Hom.* 109 Hwet is elde bihoui[n]ge. **1572** FORREST *Theophilus* 966 As speciallye ys mee behovinge. **1573** TUSSER *Husb.* (1878) 8 Things to plough behoouing. **1614** RALEIGH *Hist. World* II. IV. vii. §2. 252 Very vnpleasing, though greatly behoouing to their Estate. **1850** MRS. BROWNING *Poems* II. 399 Unless you can dream that his faith is fast, Through behoving and unbehoving.

†**be'hovingly**, *adv. Obs.* [f. prec. + -LY[2].] As it behoves one; usefully, appropriately.

1556 J. HEYWOOD *Spider & F.* lxxxviii. 56 Things that I shall moue, Which, to your behofe, behouinglie behoue.

behowl (bɪˈhaʊl), *v.* [f. BE- 4 + HOWL *v.*; first suggested by Warburton, 1746, as an emendation of *behold* in the passage from *Mids. N. Dream.*] *trans.* (and *refl.*) To howl at; to bewail with howls.

1590 SHAKS. *Mids. N.* v. 379 Now the hungry Lyons rores, And the Wolfe beholds [behowls] the Moone. **1838** EMERSON *Misc.* 118 It is travestied and depreciated..behooted and behowled. **1853** KINGSLEY *Hypatia* I. xiii. 287 Behowling your fate like Achilles on the shores of Styx. **1859** — *Misc.* I. 35 No wonder, poor fellow, if he behowls himself lustily..to Cecil.

behuf, obs. form of BEHOOF.

behung (bɪˈhʌŋ), *ppl. a.* Forms: 1–3 be-, bihonge(n, 3 bihangen, 4 byhong, 7– behung. [See BEHANG.] Hung about; draped *with* (hangings, etc.).

c **897** K. ÆLFRED *Gregory's Past.* xv. §4 Ðæs sacerdes hrægl..mid bellum behongen. *c* **1205** LAY. 3637 Hallen bihongen [**1250** bihonge] mid pellen. *c* **1300** *K. Alis.* 201 Al theo cite was by-hong Of riche baudekyns. **1622** HEYLIN *Cosmogr.* III. (1682) 192 Their noses..behung with Jewels. **1858** CARLYLE *Fredk. Gt.* II. VI. iii. 163 A Serene Highness ..of polite turn, behung with titles.

behusband, behymn, behypocrite, beice, etc.: see BE- *pref.*

bei(en, var. of BEY *v. Obs.* to bend.

beidellite (baɪˈdɛlaɪt). *Min.* [f. *Beidell* (see def.) + -ITE[1].] A clay mineral from Beidell, Colorado.

1925 LARSEN & WHERRY in *Jrnl. Washington Acad. Sci.* XV. 465 Beidellite, a new mineral name..we now propose ..from the locality of the first occurrence described in detail, Beidell, Colorado..$Al_2O_3.3SiO_2.XH_2O$. **1932** E. S. DANA *Textbk. Mineral.* v. vii. 682 Beidellite, $Al_2O_3.3SiO_2.4H_2O$. Probably orthorhombic..*Iron-beidellite* is a variety with considerable amount of Fe_2O_3. **1955** BROWN & DEY *India's Min. Wealth* (ed. 3) xiii. 532 Beidellite, anauxite and others, in which the proportion of water varies and the ratio of the silica to the alumina changes. **1963** D. W. & E. E. HUMPHRIES tr. *Termier's Erosion & Sedimentation* vi. 135 More often..the clay formed is beidellite (Al, Mg)$_4$ (Si Al)$_8$ $O_{12}(OH)_{20}$ which is closely related to montmorillonite.

beidman, beidsman, obs. ff. BEADSMAN.

†**'beienlich**, *a. Obs.* [? f. *beien*, *pa. pple.* of BEY, to bend + *-lich*, -LIKE[1]: but cf. BAIN-LY.] Humble, submissive.

c **1205** LAY. 4930 Þa answerede Brennes mid beienliche worden.

beife, obs. form of BEEF.

beige (beɪʒ), *sb.* and *a.* Also formerly **bège**. [a. F. *beige* adj.] **A.** *sb.* **1.** A fine woollen fabric used as a dress-material, originally left in its natural colour but later dyed in various colours. Also ***beige cloth***.

1858 SIMMONDS *Dict. Trade*, *Beige*, a French coarse cloth. **1879** *Cassell's Fam. Mag.* Sept. 634/2 The young lady..is in bège and silk. *Ibid.* Nov. 755/1 Her skirt is of silk and beige cloth. **1882** CAULFEILD & SAWARD *Dict. Needlework* s.v. *Beige* or *Bège*, Beige is made of undyed wool, is an extremely soft textile, graceful in draping, and employed for morning and out-door wear... There is a description of this textile, called snowflake beige, of a neutral ground.

2. A shade of colour like that of undyed and unbleached wool; yellowish-grey. Also ***beige colour***, whence ***beige-coloured*** adj.

1879 *Cassell's Fam. Mag.* Mar. 249/1 Beige shades go with moss-green. *Ibid.* 250/2 The hat..is of bège-coloured plush. **1896** *Daily News* 9 May 8/6 The colour of grass lawn is technically known as beige. **1899** *Ibid.* 19 Aug. 7/4 Beige is the coolest possible colour.

B. *adj.* Of wool or woollen and other fabrics, etc.: of a natural yellowish-grey colour.

1879 [implied in 2 above]. **1899** *Daily News* 20 Mar. 8/7 The creamy lace..will be deep enough in tint to be beige. **1926** *British Weekly* 24 June 250/5 The dress of beige lace is very much liked just now.

beigel, var. BAGEL.

[**1892** ZANGWILL *Childr. Ghetto* I. iii. 96 Moses..treating his children to some *Beuglich*, or circular twisted rolls.] **1919** *Century Mag.* July 381/2 The bread-rings called beigel. **1959** *Times* 8 Dec. 15/4 Six taxi drivers on night duty went to an East End bakery to buy bread rolls known as beigels. **1967** L. DEIGHTON *London Dossier* 135 An old woman selling *beigels*.

beigh, obs. form of BEE *sb.*[2] ring, and BEY *v. Obs.* to bow.

beignet (bɛɲɛ). *Cookery.* [Fr.] A fritter.

1835 IRVING *Tour Prairies* xxxiii. 306 We..supped heartily upon stewed buffalo meat,..beignets, or fritters of flour fried in bear's lard. **1892** T. F. GARRETT *Encycl. Cookery* I. 132/1, II. 34/2. **1901** *Daily Chron.* 7 Sept. 8/4 Cheese beignets.

beik, Sc. form of BEEK *v.* to warm, and BIKE.

Beilby ('beɪlbɪ). [Surname of Sir George Thomas *Beilby* (1850–1924), Scottish industrial chemist.] **Beilby layer** *Metallurgy* (see quot. 1958).

1930 N. K. ADAM *Phys. & Chem. Surfaces* vi. 172 The mechanical processes of grinding always result in the formation of a certain amount of the amorphous 'Beilby' layer which is obtained by polishing. **1937** *Ann. Reg. 1936* 63 Electron diffraction examination of engine cylinders showed that a substantial Beilby layer is formed by the 'running in' process. **1958** A. D. MERRIMAN *Dict. Metallurgy* 16/2 *Beilby Layer.* Beilby's experiments led him to conclude that the action of polishing a metal surface caused the surface layer to flow like a liquid and then to solidify without recrystallisation, forming an amorphous layer.

beild, variant of BIELD, *sb.* and *v.*

beim, obs. form of BEAM.

bein (biːn), *a.* and *adv. Obs.* except *dial.* Forms: 2–7 **bene,** 5–6 **beene,** (*Sc.*) **beyne, beine,** 8–9 **bien, bein,** 9 **been.** [Of unknown derivation: the spellings *bein, bien,* are merely modern Sc. ways of writing *been,* the regular repr. of ME. *bene*; the latter rimed with words in *ē,* from OE. *é* or *eo,* but no OE. **bén,* **béne,* **beon* is found or etymologically accounted for.

The phonetic history shows that the word cannot be connected with ON. *beinn,* to which, in its fig. sense of 'hospitable,' some have plausibly referred it; that word duly survives in north. Eng. as BAIN. Others have turned to the L. *bene* or Fr. *bien* well; but it is not intelligible how either of these could have been adopted in Eng. as an adjective, which appears to have been the earlier use of *bene.*]

A. *adj.*

†**1.** Pleasant, genial, kindly; 'nice.' (L. *amœnus, almus, benignus.*) *Obs.*

a **1200** *Moral Ode* 170 in *E.E.P.* (1862) 32 Læte we þe brode stret, & þe wei bene. *c* **1325** *E.E. Allit. P.* A. 110 Bonkez bene of beryl bryȝt. *Ibid.* C. 418 þy bounte of debonerte & þy bene grace. *c* **1340** *Gaw. & Gr. Knt.* 2475 Gaweyn on blonk ful bene To the kynges burȝ buskez bolde. *c* **1450** HENRYSON *Mor. Fab.* 45 On sleepe I fell among the Bewes beene. **1513** DOUGLAS *Æneis* VI. x. 108 In soft bene medois by clere strandis..Our habitatioun is. *Ibid.* VI. v. 36 Into sum benar realm and warm countre. *Ibid.* IX. xi. 41 Besyde the bene river Athesys.

2. Comfortable, comfortably furnished.

1533 BELLENDEN *Livy* (1822) 401 Somer fowlis, quhilkis flies, als sone as hervist cummis, to sum bene hous or secrete hollis. *a* **1560** ROLLAND *Crt. Venus* II. 130 Thair riche array, and thair habillement..So bene, so big, and so Auripotent. **1725** A. RAMSAY *Gentle Sheph.* I. i, Were your bien rooms as thinly stock'd as mine. *a* **1805** MACNEILL *Poems* (1844) 110 A bein house to bide in, a chaise for to ride in. **1816** SCOTT *Antiq.* xlv, 'This is a gey bein place, and it's a comfort to hae sic a corner to sit in.' **1837** NICOLL *Poems* (1843) 141 To make our bien but-house his chaumer.

3. a. Of persons: Comfortable, well-to-do, well off.

a **1548** *Thrie Priests Peblis* (1603) 78 Syne in ane Hal..He harbourit al his Burgessis rich and bene. **1603** *Philotus,* He wantis na jewels, claith, nor waith, Bot is baith big & beine. **1784** BURNS *Wks.* III. 155 The great folk..that live sae bien an' snug. **1816** SCOTT *Old Mort.* 58 'If we're no sae bein and comfortable as we were up yonder, yet life's life ony gate.' **1830** GALT *Lawrie T.* IV. i. (1849) 14 A mother-looking personage, not unlike a bein Scotch wife.

b. Of a horse: Well fed, lazy.

1847 MRS. GASKELL *Sexton's Hero* in *Howitt's Jrnl.* II. 151/1 The old mare..was a deal beener than she was in the morning.

¶**4.** In thieves' cant [perh. distinct from the prec., and immediately from L. *bene* or F. *bien*]: Good. **bene bowse**: good drink; hence **bene-bowsie** *a.*

1567 HARMAN *Caveat* (1869) 59 Sell it out right, for bene bowse at their bowsing ken. **1609** DEKKER *Lant. & Candle-Lt.* Wks. 1885 III. 198 Cut benar whiddes [= speake better words]. **1621** B. JONSON *Gipsies Metam.*, You must be ben-bowsy, And sleepy and drowsy. **1622** FLETCHER *Beggar's Bush* III. iii, I crown thy nab with a gage of bene-bowse. **1652** BROME *Jov. Crew.* II. Wks. 1873 III. 388 For all this bene Cribbing and Peck let us then Bowse a health to the Gentry Cofe of the Ken. *Ibid.* 391 This is Bien Bowse, this is Bien Bowse, Too little is my Skew. **1834** *New Dict. Canting Crew, Bene cove,* a good fellow.

B. *adv.* Pleasantly, genially, kindly.

c **1400** *Anturs Arth.* vi, A lefe sale, Of box and of barbere byggyt ful bene. *Ibid.* xxix, Beten with besandus, and bocult ful bene. **1513** DOUGLAS *Æneis* XIII. ix. 76 And full beyne [*ed.* **1553** bene] Tawcht thame to grub the wynis.

†**bein** (biːn), *v. Obs.* [f. prec.] To make 'bein'; to furnish bounteously, to fill. (L. *locupletare.*)

c **1450** HENRYSON *Mor. Fab.* 55 Haruest heat, when Ceres that goddesse Her barnes beined hes with aboundance.

be-in ('biːɪn), *sb.* [f. BE *v.* + IN *adv.* after *teach-in,* etc.] A public gathering of hippies.

1967 *Daily Tel.* 23 Mar. 18/8 Thousands of people with painted faces and chests and love on their minds pranced through New York's Central Park yesterday to celebrate Easter Sunday with a 'be-in'. **1967** *Nova* Oct. 115/1 Activities at be-ins have included chanting Hindu prayers, carrying crosses, ringing bells, striking gongs, uttering the word 'banana', staring into space, examining other people's beaded necklaces.

beine = both: see BO.

being ('biːɪŋ), *vbl. sb.* Forms: 3–6 **beinge,** 4–6 **beyng(e,** 5 **beenge, beying(e, byinge,** 6–7 **beeing,** 5– **being.** [f. BE *v.* + -ING[1].]

1. a. Existence, the fact of belonging to the universe of things material or immaterial.

c **1325** *E.E. Allit. P.* A. 446 þe court of þe kyndom of god alyue, Hatz a property in hyt self beyng. **1340** *Ayenb.* 103 Þet ne ziggeþ propreliche þe zoþe of þe byinge of God. **1413** LYDG. *Pylgr. Sowle* IV. xxviii. (1483) 74 The seed..wherof they taken their beynge. **1506** *Ord. Crysten Men.* (W. de W.) I. vi. 50, I byleue in the holy chyrche catholyke..the beynge of all sayntes. **1534** TINDALE *Acts* xvii. 28 In him we lyve, move & have oure beynge. **1647** MAY *Hist. Parl.* II. ii. 22 To subvert the very Rights and Beeings of Parliament. **1667** MILTON *P.L.* II. 441 With utter loss of being Threatens him. **1712** ADDISON *Spect.* No. 381 ¶4 The great Author of our being. **1734** POPE *Ess. Man* iv. 1 Oh happiness! our being's end and aim. **1750** JOHNSON *Rambl.* No. 72 ¶2 Good humour..is the balm of being. **1868** FREEMAN *Norm. Conq.* (1876) II. App. 610 The house had no corporate being.

b. *in being*: existing, extant, alive.

1676 ALLEN *Addr. Non-Conf.* 48 The Church in being before, had thereby a new Illumination. **1702** ADDISON *Chr. Relig.* (1727) 278 Had he quoted a record not in being, or made a false statement. **1788** J. POWELL *Devises* (1827) II. 91 A legacy, to a person in being at the time the will is made.

c. Life, physical existence.

1596 SHAKS. *Tam. Shr.* I. i. 10 Pisa..Gaue me my being. **1662** STILLINGFLEET *Orig. Sacræ* III. ii. §10 That a power infinite should raise an Insect into Being. **1676** DRYDEN *Aureng-z.* III. i. 1476 Our Prophet's care Commands the Beings ev'n of Brutes to spare. **1713** *Guardian* No. 1 ¶2 In all the occurrences of a various being. **1754** SHERLOCK *Disc.* (1759) I. II. 76 To call Men from the Graue into Being. **1766** C. BEATTY *Two Months Tour* (1768) 92 In this pleasurable manner they spent their beings. **1812** J. WILSON *Isle of Palms* II. 155 Hopeless woe the spring of being feeds.

†**d.** Occurrence, happening. *Obs.*

1624 CAPT. SMITH *Virginia* (1629) 180 *margin,* A strange being of Rauens.

2. a. Existence in some relation of place or condition.

1526 TINDALE *Luke* ix. 33 Master, it is goode beinge here for us. **1535** COVERDALE *ibid.*, Master here is good beynge for vs. *a* **1617** HIERON *Wks.* I. 3 Entrance in at the gate presupposeth a beeing without the gate. **1682** BURNET *Rights Princes* iii. 81 What he has acquired during his being a Bishop. **1692** RAY *Disc.* II. v. (1732) 208 The Being of Wolves and Foxes..anciently in this Island. *Mod.* After being at home for some time. Through being so tired.

†**b.** Condition. *Obs.*

c **1300** *K. Alis.* 224 Heo asked his beinge, an hast. *c* **1440** LONELICH *Grail* xlii. 232 Now have I ȝow told al in fere Of owre beenge & of owre manere. **1548** THOMAS *Ital. Gram., Freschezza,* lustinesse or fresh beyng.

†**c.** Position, standing (in the world). *Obs.*

1627 FELTHAM *Resolves* I. lxxvi. (1677) 116 Whosoever comes to place from a mean being, had need haue..Virtue. **1685** EVELYN *Mem.* (1857) II. 246 Colonel Norton, who though now in being..was formerly a very fierce commander in the first rebellion. **1712** STEELE *Spect.* No. 544 ¶2 Such..as want help towards getting into some being in the world. **1818** COBBETT *Resid. U.S.* (1822) 349 He has not kept house; he has had no being in any neighbourhood.

†**d.** Livelihood, living, subsistence. *Obs.*

1579 SPENSER *Sheph. Cal.* Sept. 33 No being for those, that truly mene, But for such as of guile maken gayne. **1667** *Decay Chr. Piety* viii. §44. 292 A bare being was all could be expected. **1722** STEELE *Consc. Lovers* III. i. (1755) 46 It will be nothing for them to give us a little Being of our own, some small Tenement, out of their large Possessions. **1731** MEDLEY *Kolben's Cape G. Hope* II. 45 Several others..had likewise very good Beings there.

3. a. Existence viewed as a property possessed by anything; substance, constitution, nature.

1340 HAMPOLE *Pr. Consc.* 17 Als God in a [= one] substance and beyng With outen any bygynnyng. **1398** TREVISA *Barth. De P.R.* II. ii. (1495) 28 The comparyson bitwene a poynte and a lyne in beynge. **1581** FULKE in *Confer.* III. (1584) Y, The proper substance of Christes body remaineth not, but a generall being thereof. **1659** J. ARROWSMITH *Armilla Catech.* IV. iii. §3. 187 Our very being is none of ours. **1855** PRESCOTT *Philip II,* I. II. v. 192 The Romish faith may be said to have entered into the being of the Spaniard. **1860** HAWTHORNE *Marble Faun* xiii. (1883) 147 Nature has made women especially prone to throw their whole being into what is technically called love.

b. Essential substance, essence.

1530 PALSGR. 197/1 Beyng, *essence.* **1656** H. MORE *Antid. Ath.* I. iii. (1662) 13, I define God therefore an Essence or Being fully and absolutely perfect. **1860** EMERSON *Cond. Life* 187 We are one day to deal with real being—essences with essences.

4. a. That which exists or is conceived as existing; in philosophical language, the widest term applicable to all objects of sense or thought, material or immaterial.

a **1628** F. GREVILLE *Cœlia, Sonn.* vii. 46 No being was secure. **1690** LOCKE *Hum. Und.* III. v. §5 Species of Actions which were only the Creatures of their own Understandings; Beings that had no other existence, but in their own Minds. *a* **1704** —— *Posth. Wks.* (1706) 86 A word may be made use of, as if it stood for some real Being. **1714** FORTESCUE-ALAND *Fortescue's Abs. & Lim. Mon.* 6 In the Nature of Ideas, Legal Beings, as I may call them, are as capable of Demonstration, as Mathematical ones. **1843** MILL *Logic* I. iii. §2. 62 *Being* is..applied impartially to matter and to mind..A Being is that which excites feelings, and which possesses attributes.

b. Applied with various qualifications, e.g. 'the Supreme Being,' to God.

c **1600** J. DAVIES in Farr's *S.P.* I. 244 He that was, and is, and cannot fade, This Beeing infinite. **1688** CUDWORTH *Immut. Mor.* IV. iv. (1731) 250 There is a God, or an Omnipotent and Omniscient Being. **1712** ADDISON *Spect.* No. 381 ¶8 Atheism, by which I mean a disbelief of a Supreme Being. **1761** STERNE *Tr. Shandy* III. xlix, That kind Being, who is a friend to the friendless, shall recompence thee for this. **1875** SCRIVENER *Lect. Grk. Test.* 6 That the Supreme Being should have thus far interfered with the course of his providential arrangements.

c. A human being, a person. (Sometimes contemptuous; sometimes idealistic.)

1751 JOHNSON *Rambl.* No. 141 ¶6 A wit..a species of beings only heard of at the university. **1802** MAR. EDGEWORTH *Moral T.* (1816) I. xii. 100 This mean, incorrigible being said to himself. **1816** J. WILSON *City of Plague* I. iii. 33 There I saw A white-robed Being on her knees. **1852** MISS YONGE *Cameos* II. xxix. 307 The veiled girlish being on whom Henry had set his vehement heart.

d. Phrases in *Philos.*, formed mainly to translate the corresponding Ger. and Fr. expressions, as **being-for-(it)self,** conscious being; being as actuality; **being-in-(it)self,** being that lacks conscious awareness; being as mere potentiality; **being-itself,** pure being, regarded as infinite and uncharacterizable; **being-with,** human existence, regarded as membership of the community of persons.

1854 FERRIER *Inst. Metaph.* 525 Our alleged ignorance of 'Being in itself'. **1865** J. H. STIRLING *Secret of Hegel* II. III. 8 *Being-for-self* is the literal rendering of *Fürsichseyn*; which, indeed, cannot be translated otherwise. **1874** G. S. MORRIS tr. *F. Ueberweg's Hist. Philos.* II. III. 241 The Idea runs through a series of stages, from its abstract being-out-of-self in space and time to the being-in-self of individuality in the animal organism, their succession depending on the progressive realization of the tendency to being-for-self, or to subjectivity. **1892** E. S. HALDANE tr. *Hegel's Lect. Hist. Philos.* I. 20 Two different states must be distinguished. The first is what is known as capacity, power, what I call being-in-itself..; the second principle is that of being-for-itself, actuality. *Ibid.* 24 Being-in-self and being-for-self are the moments present in action. **1892** W. WALLACE tr. *Hegel's Logic* vii. 179 The readiest instance of Being-for-self is found in the 'I'. We know ourselves as existents. **1945** *Mind* LIV. 177 Since the subject realises itself as a subject, it has being-for-itself and therefore also possesses being-in-itself. **1956** F. COPLESTON *Contemp. Philos.* xi. 180 Being-in-the-world is being-with (*Mitsein*). **1957** *Sc. Jrnl. Theol.* X. 236 Being-itself, for Tillich, is the only non-symbolic or literal definition of God. **1962** R. G. OLSON *Existentialism* ii. 38 In Satre's system the noumenal world..is named 'being-in-itself' or sometimes simply 'the in-itself'. **1963** *Times Lit. Suppl.* 24 May 376/5 A certain..complacency..seems..to pervade this world of mutual 'being-with'.

being ('biːɪŋ), *ppl. a.* [f. BE *v.* + -ING[2].]

1. Existing, present; *esp.* in phr. ***the time being.***

1458 *Test Ebor.* (1855) II. 225 The covent of the priore.. for the tyme beyng, and thair successours. **1523** LD. BERNERS *Froiss.* I. ccxii. 257 The kynges of Englande for the tyme beynge. **1788** J. POWELL *Devises* (1827) II. 341 Where there is a gift to the elder son in terms which would carry it to the eldest for the time being.

2. *absol.* = It being the case that, seeing, since. See BE *v.* B. I.3.

beingless ('biːɪŋlɪs), *a.* [f. BEING *sb.* + -LESS.] That has no being, non-existent.

1840 GALT *Demon Dest.* III. 22 We are but things like thee All beingless—the substance of idea. **1864** C. KING *Gnostics* 38 When first the Father, the Inconceivable, Beingless, Sexless, began to be in labour.

beingness ('biːɪŋnɪs). [f. as prec. + -NESS.] The quality of existing, entity, actuality.

1662 J. CHANDLER *Van Helmont's Oriat.* 29 The Entity or Beingness of vertue and operation. **1897** J. H. STIRLING *Secret of Hegel* (ed. 2) 374 One gets a vivid glance of the direct beingness which immediacy amounts to. **1933** *Mind* XLII. 319 It may be possible to isolate certain aspects of the Aristotelian doctrine of 'beingness' or essence which have an obvious affinity with the ideas connoted by the word 'substance'. **1957** J. F. HORNER *Summary of Scientology* 57 The term, 'Thetan', refers to the single unit of beingness which each person is.

be-inked (bɪ'ɪŋkt), *ppl. a.* [f. BE- + INK.] Smeared or stained over with ink.

1853 C. BRONTË *Villette* xxxv. (D.), A sorry paletot much be-inked, and no little adust.

beinly ('biːnlɪ), *adv. Sc.* Also 5 **beenlie.** [f. BEIN + -LY[2].] Pleasantly, comfortably, cosily.

c **1450** HENRYSON *Mor. Fab.* 14 Her den..Full beenlie stuffed both butte and ben Of Beines and Nuttes. **1572** *Scot. Poems 16th C.* II. 249 Ȝon carle..dois beinly dwell. **1790** A. WILSON *Discons. Wren* Wks. 97 Fu' cleanly and beinly We lined it [our nest] a' wi' down.

beinness ('biːnnɪs). *Sc.* Also **bienness.** [f. BEIN + -NESS.] Comfort, well-to-do condition.

1874 BLACK *Pr. Thule* 20 There was a prevailing air of comfort and bienness about the people.

beir, beire, Sc. f. BEAR, BEER, BERE, BIER, BIRR; obs. pa. t. BEAR *v.*; also = of both: see BOTH.

beiram, variant spelling of BAIRAM.

beird, obs. Sc. form of BEARD.

beis, obs. f. BEAST-S; see also BE *v.* A. I.**

beisa (ˈbaɪsə). [Native name.] An African antelope, *Oryx gazella beisa*.

1850 *Proc. Zool. Soc.* XVIII. 134 Oryx Beisa. The Bëisa. Horns straight; throat without any bunch of hairs; black face-streaks separate... Inhabits Abyssinia. **1902** *Encycl. Brit.* XXV. 454/2 Widely different..is the African group of *Hippotraginæ*... Among these are..the straight-horned gemsbok and beisa (*Oryx*). **1921** *Edin. Rev.* July 105 Others ..are driving ostriches, gemsbok, and beisa antelopes. **1969** *Times* 30 Jan. p. iii/2 The proposed park will contain no unique mammals, but harbours large herds of Beisa oryx.

†ˈ**beisance.** In 6–7 **baysance, beysaunce, bezaunce.** Aphetic f. OBEISANCE, ABAISANCE.

1556 HUGGARD *Display. Protest.* 85 (D.) To make beysaunce to the magistrates. **1604** A. SCOLOKER *Daiphantus* (1880) 11 Her lowly bezaunce doth regreat With her chast silence. *c* **1650** in Furniv. *Percy Folio* I. 159 When the[y] came it Lamwell by, baysance the[y] made certainly.

beisand, obs. form of BEZANT.

beist, obs. form of BEAST, BEST.

†**beisum,** *a. Obs.* [f. *beien*, BEY, to bend + *-sum*, -SOME: cf. *buxom*.] Pliable, flexible, docile.

a **1225** *Leg. Kath.* 1805 þeo þat..buhsume and beisume haldeð his heastes.

beit(e, obs. form of BEET *v.*, BEAT.

beizle, obs. form of BEZZLE *v.*

Beja (ˈbɛdʒə). Also **Bedja.** A nomadic people of Hamitic extraction living between the Nile and the Red Sea; the Cushitic language of this people. Also *attrib.*

1819 J. L. BURCKHARDT *Trav. Nubia* 503 In battle the Bedja pursue each other with their camels. *Ibid.* 526 People were found among the Djidda inhabitants who spoke Bedja. **1884** *Encycl. Brit.* XVII. 611/2 The Hamitic Beja. **1955** *Times* 8 July 7/2 The Beja is the tribe immortalized by Kipling under the name of Fuzzy Wuzzies after they had broken or nearly broken a British square at the battle of Tamai in 1884. **1961** *Listener* 16 Nov. 797/1 The Beja people of the Red Sea coast.

bejab(b)ers (bɪˈdʒeɪbəz, -ˈæ-), *int.* Also **be (by) jappers**, etc. [Corruption of *by Jesus*.] A *dial.* (esp. Irish) expletive.

In quot. 1962 used as a nonce-verb.

1821 D. HAGGART *Life* 118 By jappers, we were tould he was the boy. **1866** MAYNE REID *Headless Horseman* v. 30 'Be japers!' he exclaimed. **1890** HUME NISBET *Bail Up!* xxxviii. 265 A head wind, be jabbers! **1892** —— *Bush-ranger's Sweetheart* xx. 152 Arrah, be jabbers! but that's the foinest song I have listened to since I left Ould Oirland. **1895** J. BARLOW *Strangers at Lisconnel* iv. 58 Bejabers, you've got it now. **1939** *Times Lit. Suppl.* 25 Nov. 668/1 A Londoner who speaks nothing but cockney feels it [*sc.* the sentence] ought to be rounded off with 'bejabers'. **1962** *Listener* 9 Aug. 214/2 To live as an Irishman in England is to be forced to play a part. To begorra, to bejaper, and to be always after having a drink.

†**beˈjade,** *v. Obs.* [f. BE- + JADE *v.*]

1. *trans.* To weary, tire out.

1620 MELTON *Astrolog.* 14 He had so bejaded and tyred mine eares. **1641** MILTON *Animadv.* Wks. (1851) 240 Spare your selfe, lest you bejade the good galloway, your owne opiniaster wit.

2. To make a jade of.

1705 HICKERINGILL *Priest-cr.* II. vi. 61 Some Women.. are Skitish, and will not suffer themselves tamely to be Rid and Bejaded by ne're a Priest of them all.

Hence **beˈjaded** *ppl. a.*

1687 *Elegy* in *Cleveland's Wks.* 284 Jogg still as things bejaded ride in black. **1694** SOUTH *12 Serm.* II. 197 A tired, languishing, and be-jaded Devotion.

bejan (ˈbiːdʒən). Forms: 7 **bajon,** 7–9 **bajan,** 9 **bejaune, bejeant, bejan, bigent.** [a. F. *béjaune* novice, freshman (f. *bec jaune* 'yellow beak,' in allusion to young birds. See Littré, s.v. *Bec*, *Béjaune*); cf. Ger. *gelbschnabel*.] A freshman at the Scotch universities, where the term was adopted from the University of Paris. (Now obsolete at Edinburgh.) Also *attrib.*

[**1611** COTGR., *Bejaune*, a novice..or yong beginner in, a Trade, or Art. *Payer son bejaune*, to pay his welcome; a fee exacted by schollers, of such as are newly admitted into their societie.] **1642** BAILLIE *Lett.* 10 May 794 There will be near 60 Bajons already. *c* **1670** T. CRAUFURD *Hist. Univ. Edin.* 63 (JAM.) No Bajans convened all that year. **1708** J. CHAMBERLAYNE *St. Gt. Brit.* II. III. x (1743) 441 The first year the students [at Edinburgh] who are called Bajans, are taught only Greek. **1814** W. TENNANT *Anster Fair* ii, Up from their mouldy books..had sprung Bigent and Magistrand to try the game. **1864** BURTON *Scot. Abr.* I. v. 270. **1868** G. MACDONALD *R. Falconer* II. 65 His grandmother yielded, and Robert was straightway a Bejan or Yellow-beak. **1884** SIR A. GRANT *Story Univ. Edin.* I. iii. 144.

†**beˈjape,** *v. Obs.* [f. BE- 2 + JAPE *v.*] *trans.* To play a trick on; to trick or befool.

1377 LANGL. *P. Pl.* B. XVIII. 290 God wil nouȝt be bigiled ..ne bi-iaped. *c* **1386** CHAUCER *Knts. T.* 727 And hast by-japed here the duke Theseus. *a* **1420** OCCLEVE *De Reg. Princ.* 112 The smert of thought..hath..so me by-japed. *a* **1500** *Piers of F.* 168 in Hazl. *E.P.P.* II. 8 An olde fowle..May cawse many othyr to be bejaped.

bejel (ˈbeɪdʒəl, ˈbɛ-). [Arab.] (See quot. 1961.)

1928 E. H. HUDSON in *U.S. Nav. Med. Bull.* XXVI. 818 The Bedouins have a disease which they call bejel. The practitioners of medicine..refer to this disease without hesitation as syphilis... Bejel is usually contracted in childhood, and apparent recovery follows quickly. **1945** *Lancet* 21 Apr. 505/2 Why..is syphilis spread venereally, while yaws and bejel are spread either by contact or by various insects feeding on the infected discharging sores? **1961** *Brit. Med. Dict.* 184/1 *Bejel*, a non-venereal form of syphilis which is endemic among the Arabs (particularly the children) of the valleys along the Middle Euphrates. The infecting organism is morphologically indistinguishable from *Treponema pallidum*.

beˈjesuit. [f. BE- 5 + JESUIT.] To initiate in Jesuitism; to work upon by, or subject to, Jesuits.

1644 MILTON *Areop.* (Arb.) 76 Who hath so bejesuited us that we should, etc.? **1680** HICKERINGILL *Meroz* 12 Both are Bejesuited and Breath nothing but Blood and Ruin. **1865** CARLYLE *Fredk. Gt.* IX. xx. ii. 24 The..garrison..had been well bejesuited during those seven weeks.

bejesus (bɪˈdʒiːzəs), *int.* Also (esp. Anglo-Irish) **bejasus** (-ˈdʒeɪzəs). An alteration of the oath *by Jesus*. Also as *sb.* in phr. ***to beat the bejesus out of***, to give a good hiding to.

1908 *Dialect Notes* III. 290 *Bejazus*, interj., a mild expletive: often used in the phrase 'Faith and bejasus!' **1934** A. WOOLLCOTT *While Rome Burns* 258 My partner..will.. beat the be-Jesus out of you. **1949** 'J. TEY' *Brat Farrar* xv. 136, I know men who'd beat the bejasus out of you for that. **1956** J. DICKSON CARR *P. Butler for Defence* iv. 38 'Oh, bejasus!' roared the Irishman. **1960** *Guardian* 28 Feb. 8/3 She would put her fingers in her ears and scream: 'Bejasus, will ye stop it?'

bejewel (bɪˈdʒ(j)uːɪl), *v.* [f. BE- 6 + JEWEL *sb.*] *trans.* To deck or adorn with or as with jewels; to spangle. Also *fig.*

1557 NORTH *Gueuara's Diall Pr.* (1582) 387b, The gorgeous courtyer, bedeckt with gold, be buttoned, & be iewelled. **1647** R. STAPYLTON *Juvenal* 21 Those priests.. Bejewel all their necks. **1877** BROWNING *La Saisiaz* 588 Laughter so bejewels Learning.

Hence **beˈjewelled** *ppl. a.*

1848 *Fraser's Mag.* XXXVII. 404 Bearing in his hand a bejewelled club. **1876** GEO. ELIOT *Dan. Der.* I. i. 2 The white bejewelled fingers of an English countess. **1922** C. E. MONTAGUE *Disenchantment* xii. 168 Now the men would be rising..with smoking breath and bejewelled eyebrows.

bejig, bejuggle, bejumble, etc.: see BE- *pref.*

bejuco (beɪˈhuːkəʊ). [Sp.] A liana, esp. the vine *Hippocratea scandens* of tropical America.

1848 WHITTIER *Slaves of Martinique* 19 As the serpent-like bejuco winds his spiral fold on fold Round the tall and stately ceiba, till it withers in its hold.

bek(e, obs. form of BEAK, BECK, BEEK.

†**beˈken,** *v. Obs.* Forms: 3–4 **bi-, bykennen,** 4 **biken(ne,** 4–5 **beken.** [f. BE- + KEN.]

1. *trans.* To make known, to declare, to show.

a **1300** *Havelok* 1268 Kinges sone, and kinges eyr That bikenneth that croiz so fayr.

2. To deliver.

a **1300** *Cursor M.* 7242 Till his foos sco him be-kend. **1330** R. BRUNNE *Chron.* 332 A wif þei him bikenne. ?*a* **1400** *Morte Arth.* 2355 They..Bekende theme the caryage, kystis and oþer.

3. To commend or commit to the care of.

c **1350** *Will. Palerne* 5423, I bikenne ȝou to Crist þat on Croyce was peyned. *a* **1400** *Relig. Pieces fr. Thornton MS.* (1867) 90 His modir in keping to þe he bekende. ?*a* **1400** *Morte Arth.* 482 Sir Cadore..to Crist þeme be-kennyde. *c* **1420** *Sir Amadace* xxxii, Cryst of hevon, Y yo beken!

¶ See also BIKENN.

†ˈ**beken, bekin,** *sb. Obs.* [Identical in spelling with 16th c. forms of BEACON, but nothing appears to be known of the word beyond what is contained in the quotations.]

1538 ELYOT *Dict.*, *Cinclidæ* are bayes or parclosis made aboute the places of judgement, where men not being sutars, may stande, beholde, and here what is done and spoken amonge the juges and pledours. Such a lyke thing is at Westmynster Hall about the common place, and is called the bekens. **1577** HOLINSHED *Chron.* III. 934/1 The kings of armes..stood in their place, which was in the bekins at the kings bench.

beken, obs. form of BEACON, BECKON.

†**beˈkend,** *ppl. a. Sc. Obs.* [f. BEKEN *v.* + -ED[1].] Known.

1513 DOUGLAS *Æneis* IV. xii. 12 Sone as scho beheld..the bed bekend. *Ibid.* II. xii. (xi.) 94 For throw the secrete stretis fast I rane Before the laif, as weil bekend mane.

†**beˈkenning,** *vbl. sb. Obs.* [f. as prec. + -ING[1].] Knowledge, acquaintance.

c **1380** WYCLIF *Serm.* Sel. Wks. II. 79 þei tellen more bi þer owne bekenyng..þan þei don bi Goddis heestis.

beker, -kir, obs. forms of BICKER.

bekerchief, bekick, beking, etc.: see BE- *pref.*

bekeryn, obs. form of BICKER.

beking, obs. form of BEAKING.

bekiss (bɪˈkɪs), *v.* [f. BE- + KISS *v.*] *trans.* To kiss to excess, to cover with kisses. Hence **bekissed** (bɪˈkɪst), *ppl. a.*

1587 TURBERV. *Trag. T.* (1837) 195 Shee all bekist the face. **1677** MRS. BEHN *Rover* III. i. (1716) 119 To hug, and all to bekiss me. **1862** TROLLOPE *Orley F.* xiv, In such cases one cannot but pity her who is bekissed. **1809** W. IRVING *Knickerb.* (1861) 237 The most thoroughly be-kissed community in all Christendom.

bekke, -nynge, obs. ff. BECK, BECKONING.

bekko (ˈbɛkəʊ). [Jap.] Tortoise-shell.

1889 REIN *Industries Japan* 421 Bekkô, tortoise-shell, comes principally from *Chelonia imbricata*, L., the genuine loggerhead turtle.

beknave (bɪˈneɪv), *v.* [f. BE- 5 + KNAVE *sb.*] *trans.* To treat as a knave, to call 'knave.'

c **1525** SKELTON *Agst. Garnesche* 9 So currysly to be-knave me in the kynges place. **1539** TAVERNER *Gard. Wysed.* II. 16a, Some we call Pharisees, we be knave, we defye as naughtye papistes. *c* **1720** POPE *Gentle Sheph.* (Globe) 475 May satire ne'er befool ye, or beknave ye. **1876** GREEN *Short Hist.* vii. §1 Beknaved by the King.

beknit, beknight, etc.: see BE- *pref.*

beknotted (bɪˈnɒtɪd), *ppl. a.* [f. BE- 2 + KNOT *v.*] Tied into or covered with knots. Hence **beˈknottedness.**

1882 *Nature* XXV. 595 The difficulty of measuring beknottedness electromagnetically.

†**beˈknow,** *v. Obs.* For forms see KNOW. [f. BE- 2 + KNOW.] *trans.*

1. To become acquainted with, to recognize.

c **1300** *Relig. Songs* i. 31 Mon, hwi nultu the bi-cnowe? **1314** *Guy Warw.* (Abbotsf.) 106 The Soudan him biknewe anon. **1393** GOWER III. 357 So fit it wel, that thou beknowe Thy feble estate. **1475** CAXTON *Jason* 48 In no wyse I wold not ben beknowen. **1560** PHAËR *Æneid* Cc ij b, The lords beknew that god. [See BEKNOWN.]

2. To admit one's knowledge of; to acknowledge, confess.

c **1325** *Coer de L.* 1700 That he thynkes he wyl beknawe. **1340** *Ayenb.* 69 [Hi] hare folyes ne beknaweþ. *c* **1386** CHAUCER *Pers. T.* ⁋96 To destroye him that wolde not by-knowe his synnes. *c* **1440** *Morte Arth.* (Roxb.) 31 She moste there by know the dede. **1580** HOLLYBAND *Treas. Fr. Tong*, *Confesser*, to confesse, to beknowe.

3. To acknowledge or recognize (a person) in some capacity or relation; *e.g.* to confess Christ.

c **1315** SHOREHAM 15 To biknowe Cristes name. **1377** LANGL. *P. Pl.* B. XVIII. 24 þat cryst be nouȝt biknowe here for *consummatus deus*.

4. ***to be beknown***: to be aware or conscious *of* anything; *hence*, to avow, confess. Used like 'to be ACKNOWN,' but rarer.

a **1300** *Cursor M.* 1905 þan was noe wel be-knauin þat þe flode it was wit-drauin. *c* **1374** CHAUCER *Boeth.* III. x. 90, I am byknowen and confesse..þat god is ryȝt worþi abouen alle þinges. **1413** LYDG. *Pilgr. Sowle* I. xv. 11, I am byknowe that I haue done amys. *c* **1500** *Lancelot* 1627 Qwho that is of an of thir byknow. **1523** LD. BERNERS *Froiss.* (1812) I. 694 If they aske the any thyng of me, be not be knowen that I am in the toune.

†**beknowing,** *vbl. sb. Obs.* [f. prec. + -ING[1].] Knowledge.

1340 *Ayenb.* 126 Hi ne hedden naȝt riȝte byleue..ne zoþe beknawynge.

†**beˈknowledge,** *v. Obs.* [f. BE- 2 + KNOWLEDGE *v.* Cf. *acknowledge*.] *trans.* To acknowledge. Hence **beˈknowledging** *vbl. sb.* (4 **beknaulechinge**): Acknowledgement, confession.

1340 *Ayenb.* 32 Beknaulechinge of mouþe, boȝsamnesse in dede.

beknown (bɪˈnəʊn), *ppl. a. arch.* [See BEKNOW.] Known, acquainted, familiar.

1429 *Pol. Poems* (1859) II. 147 A Marschalle full woorthyly beknowe. **1513** DOUGLAS *Æneis* VII. ii. 17 On bankis weilbiknaw. **1589** PUTTENHAM *Eng. Poesie* (Arb.) 241 Let our figure enjoy his best beknowen name. *a* **1618** SYLVESTER *Job Triumph.* I. 486 Nor of his place is any more beknown. **1865** DICKENS *Mut. Fr.* xii, The seaman was beknown to me.

bekuyde, obs. form of BEQUEATH *sb.*

bekyn(e, obs. form of BEACON and BECKON.

bekyre, obs. form of BICKER.

‖**bel,** *a.* and *formative.* Forms: 4–5 **bele,** 7 **bell.** [a. F. *bel, belle* 'beautiful, fair, fine':—L. *bell-um, -am*. Naturalized in ME.; but after 1600 consciously French.]

†**A.** *adj.* Fair, fine, beautiful. *Obs.*

c **1314** *Guy Warw.* 68 Bele ost, Y bidde say thou me What may al this erning be. *c* **1384** CHAUCER *H. Fame* 1796 Bele Isawde Ne coude hem noght of loue werne. *c* **1475** *Babees Bk.* (1868) 3 A Bele Babees, herkne now to my lore! [**1605** CHAPMAN *All Fooles* Plays (1873) I. 136 With a Bell regard aduant mine eye.] **1678** MRS. BEHN *Pat. Fancy* II. 253 If you are not the most *Bell Person I ever saw [? A pun on the name *Isabella*].

B. Used as a formative prefix in *belfader*, *belsire*, *beldame*, *belmoder*, grandfather, grandmother. The explanation of this use, which seems to be entirely English and unknown to French, is not clear; but it answers to the Eng. use of *good* in *goodsire* (*gudscher*, *gutcher*), *gooddame* (*gudame*), '*godson* or *gosson* filiolus,' and '*goddowter* filiola,' in *Promp. Parv.*, which is again partly paralleled by the mod.F.

bon-papa, *bonne-maman*, grandpapa, grandmamma. The French and English use of *grand*, in *grandpère* grandfather, grandsire, *grand'mère* grandmother, grandame, is capable of more obvious explanation; while the tendency to allow analogy to prevail over sense appears in the Eng. *grandson* as compared with F. *petit-fils*. Still further analogies in the parallel use of *beau*, *belle*, and *good* (though to express a different relationship) are presented by the F. *beau-père* father-in-law, *belle-mère* mother-in-law, *beau-frère* brother-in-law, etc., for which the north. Eng. and Sc. forms are *good-father*, *good-mother*, *good-brother*, *good-sister*, etc.

bel (bɛl), *sb. Electr. Communic.* [f. name of A. G. *Bell* (1847–1922), inventor of the telephone.] A unit, equivalent to ten decibels (see DECIBEL), used in the comparison of two levels of power in an electrical communication circuit. (Non-technical sense in quot. 1958.)

The *bel* as a unit of power level is defined logarithmically as $N = \log_{10}(P_1/P_2)$, where N designates the number of bels and P_1 and P_2 the two amounts of power.

1929 W. H. MARTIN in *Bell System Techn. Jrnl.* VIII. 2 It was further suggested that the naperian unit be called the 'neper' and that the fundamental decimal unit be called the 'bel', these names being derived from..Napier..and Alexander Graham Bell. **1930** *Gloss. Terms Electr. Engin.* (*B.S.I.*) 13 The bel is a unit used in the comparison of the magnitudes of powers, voltages or currents at two different points in a network of lines or apparatus. **1937** *Nature* 11 Sept. 447/1 The unit adopted..is the *bel*, which is a ratio signifying a 10-fold increase in intensity, power or energy. Two bels signify a 100-fold increase, three bels a 1000-fold increase, and so on. **1958** K. AMIS *I like it Here* vi. 70 Relaying a girls' choir at a volume of a couple of bels.

bel: see BAEL; also obs. variant of BELL.

be'laborous, *a. nonce-wd.* [f. next + -OUS.] Given to belabouring or thrashing.

1860 *All Y. Round* No. 52. 47 Coleridge, who had many a thrashing..from the belaborous Doctor..at the Blue-coat School.

belabour (bɪ'leɪbər), *v.* [f. BE- 4 + LABOUR.]

†**1.** *trans.* To labour at, work at; to exert one's strength or ability upon, to ply. *Obs.*

1604 DEKKER *Honest Wh.* Wks. 1873 II. 73 Husbands, whom they would belabour by all means possible to keepe em in their right wits. *a* **1631** DRAYTON *Nymphal* 8 (R.) Let the nimble hand belabour The whistling pipe. **1686** BARROW *Serm.* III. 205 If the earth is belaboured with culture.

2. To thrash or buffet with all one's might.

1600 ABP. ABBOT *Jonah* 529 The tempest which belaboured him. **1609** ROWLANDS *Doct. Merrie-m.* 9 His Maister tooke a Cudgell, And belabour'd him withall. **1724** SWIFT *Misc.* (1735) V. 60 He saw Virago Nell belabour, With Dick's own Staff his peaceful Neighbour. **1876** SMILES *Sc. Natur.* i. 6 They were belaboured with every kind of weapon.

b. *fig.* To assail with words.

1596 NASHE *Saffron Walden* 108 With..complements hee belaboured him till his eares tingled. **1779** COWPER *Lett.* 31 Oct., [He] has belaboured that great poet's character with the most industrious cruelty. **1832** AUSTIN *Jurispr.* (1879) I. vi. 323 Nonsense wherewith the haters of improvement would belabour the audacious innovators.

†**bel-accoil, -accoyle.** *Obs.* [a. OF. *bel* (*biel*, *beal*) *acoil* fair welcome: cf. ACCOIL.] Kindly greeting, welcome.

c **1400** *Rom. Rose* 2984 Bialacoil forsothe he hight, Sone he was to Curtesie. **1596** SPENSER *F.Q.* IV. vi. 25 Glaucè..her salewd with seemely bel-accoyle.

belace (bɪ'leɪs), *v.*[1] [f. BE- + LACE *v.* and *sb.*]

1. *trans.* To border or adorn with lace. Usually in ppl. a. BELACED.

1648 JOS. BEAUMONT *Psyche* II. 48 How to belace and fringe soft love.

†**2.** To streak, stripe. *Obs.*

1648 EARL WESTMORLD. *Otia Sacra* (1879) 88 The Crimson streaks belace the Damaskt West.

†**3.** To beat with stripes. *Obs.*

1736 BAILEY, *Belace*, the same as to belabour. **1857** in Wright.

be'lace, *v.*[2] '*Sea Term.* To fasten; as to belace a rope.' Johnson. [This is found only in Dictionaries. It appeared first in Bailey's folio, 1730, was retained by Dr. Johnson (who used a copy of that as the basis of his own work), and from him it has been perpetuated by later dictionaries. In Bailey it appears to be merely a mistake for BELAGE, q.v. Bailey's 8vo of 1721 (like the earlier dictionaries of Phillips and Kersey) has '*Belage*, also *Belay* (*Sea Term*), to fasten any running Rope when it is haled, that it cannot run forth again.' This the folio of 1730 splits up into '*Belace* (*Sea Term*), to fasten any Rope,' and '*Belay*, to fasten any running Rope, so that when it is haled it cannot run out again.' Thence Johnson's *Belace* and *Belay*. But the 8vo editions of Bailey retained the original entry and took no notice of *Belace*, till after the appearance of Johnson's Dictionary, when the editor of the edition of 1783 added the fictitious *Belace* from Johnson, while retaining Bailey's original *Belage* or *Belay*.]

belaced (bɪ'leɪst), *ppl. a.* [f. BELACE *v.*[1] + -ED[1].] Bordered or adorned with lace.

1648 JOS. BEAUMONT *Psyche* XVI. x. (N.) In thy bravest And most belaced servitude. **1879** MRS. OLIPHANT *Reign Geo. II*, II. 78 His 'long lean' form bepowdered, belaced, bescented.

†**be'lack**, *v. Obs.* [f. BE- 2 + LACK *v.* to depreciate.] *trans.* To depreciate, find fault with.

a **1555** LATIMER *Serm. & Rem.* (1845) 329 As for my preaching itself..my lord of London cannot rightfully belack it, nor justly reprove it.

belade, -ladle, belady, -ship: see BE-.

†**be'lag**, *v. Obs.* [f. BE- 2 + LAG *v.*] ? To clog with wet mud. (Cf. *beclag*, also *water-logged*.)

a **1300** W. DE BIBLESW. in Wright Voc. 173 *Cy vent un garsoun esclaté*, bilagged wit swirting. *c* **1440** *Promp. Parv.* 29 Be-laggyd, *madidatus* [**1499** *paludosus*]. [**1721** BAILEY *Belagged* left behind].

†**be'lage**, *v. Naut. Obs.* [Either ME. *belegge*, obs. form of BELAY, or, what is not improbable, ad. Du. *beleggen*, in same sense. (It is also possible that it may have originated as a misprint or misreading of *belaye*. See also BELACE *v.*[2])]

1678 PHILLIPS, *Belage* in Navigation is to fasten any running Rope when it is haled, that it cannot run forth again. [So in ed. **1696**: *Belay* in nautical sense not given in either; but ed. **1706** has *Belay* or *Belage*, explained as in **1678**]. **1692** in *Capt. Smith's Seaman's Gram.* I. xvi. 75 *To Belage*, to make fast any running Rope. **1707** in KERSEY. **1721** BAILEY *Belage, Belay* (*Sea Term*) [expl. as in PHILLIPS].

belah ('biːlə). Also belar, †beela, beal. [Aboriginal name.] The Australian name for various trees, chiefly of the genus *Casuarina*; also the wood of these trees.

1862 H. C. KENDALL *Poems, Kooroora* 14 A voice in the beela grows wild in its wail. **1868** J. A. B. *Meta* 19 Blazing fire of beal. **1873** RANKEN *Dom. Australia* vi. 110 These scrubs..sometimes crown the watersheds as 'belar'. **1911** C. E. W. BEAN '*Dreadnought' of Darling* xix. 188 Mulga trees, and belar. **1933** *Bulletin* (Sydney) 20 Sept. 28/2 The casuarinas—she-oak, silky oak, belar, forest oak and creek or river oak—are all valuable for foilage, timber and bark. **1936** F. CLUNE *Roaming round Darling* xiv. 118 Plenty of timber: wilga, box, cypress, pine, and belah. **1944** F. D. DAVISON in *Coast to Coast 1943* 228 The line of wallaby snares in the belah scrub at the back of his selection.

belakin, variant of *byrlakin*: by our Ladykin.

†**belam**, *v. Obs.* or *dial.* Also 6 belamb, 7 belamme. [f. BE- + LAM *v.*] *trans.* To thrash.

1595 *Witts, Fittes, & F.* 146 His father mainly belamb'd him for the fact. **1611** COTGR., *Coutonner*, to cudgell, thwacke, baste, belamme. **1653** URQUHART *Rabelais* III. xxxvi. III. 53, I shall bang, belam thee, and claw thee well for thy labour.

†**bela'mour**. *Obs.* Also bellamour(e. [f. F. *bel* fair + *amour* love.]

1. A loved one of either sex; lady love, fair lady.

1596 SPENSER *F.Q.* II. vi. 16 She decks her bounteous boure, With silken curtens..to shrowd her sumptuous belamoure. **1603** J. DAVIES *Microcosm.* 92 His wisdome's pow'r Did choose me for his chiefest Bellamoure.

2. Love; a glance or look of love.

1610 G. FLETCHER *Christ's Vict.* xlvii, Those eyes from whence are shed Infinite belamours.

3. Applied to some unidentified flower.

1595 SPENSER *Sonn.* lxiii, Her snowy browes lyke budded Bellamoures.

†**'belamy.** *Obs.* Forms: 3–4 belami, 3–6 belamy, 4 bele amys, 7 bellamy. [a. F. *bel ami* (nom. sing. *amis*) fair friend.] Fair friend, good friend (esp. as a form of address).

a **1225** *Ancr. R.* 306 O, belami, þis þu dudest. *c* **1325** *Coer de L.* 3253, I suffre, sere, bele amys. *c* **1400** *Ywaine & Gaw.* 278 What ertow, belamy? *c* **1460** *Towneley Myst.* 127 Welcom be thou, belamy! **1596** SPENSER *F.Q.* II. vii. 52 To the fayre Critias, his dearest belamy! **1689** BAXTER *Cain & Abel Malig.* Wks. 1830 X. 493 True Protestants (such as the pseudo-bellamy in Philanax Anglicus hatefully calleth Protestants off sincerity).

belandre, obs. form of BILANDER.

†**belap** (bɪ'læp), *v. Obs.* [f. BE- 1 + LAP.] *trans.* To lap about, clasp, enfold, envelop; to environ, surround. Chiefly in pa. pple. **be'lapped.**

c **1200** ORMIN 14267 All Bilokenn & bilappedd Inn all þatt boc. *a* **1225** *Ancr. R.* 100 Hit is bilepped & bihud. ? *c* **1330** *Amis & Amil.* 1014 He seighe Sir Amis..Bilapped among his fon. **1494** *Dives & Paup.* (W. de W.) IV. xxiii. 189/2 Her good angell..belapped her with so grete lyght that ther myght no man loke upon her. *a* **1529** SKELTON *Col. Cloute* 312 In purple & paule belapped. **1562** A. SCOT *Poems*, This belappit body here.

belard, belash, belatticed, etc.: see BE- *pref.*

†**be'last**, *ppl. a. Obs.* [? f. OE. *behlæstan* to load; cf. Ger. *belasten*.] Burdened, charged, bound.

1441 in *Archæol.* XVII. 214 (Halliw.) James Skidmore is belast and wt holden toward the seid Sir James for an hole yeer. **1470** HARDING *Chron.* ccxxi, The duke of Brytain then was his manne, For fee belaste without rebellion. *c* **1572** GASCOIGNE *Fruites Warre* (1831) 215 At euery porte it was.. belast, That I..might not go out.

belate (bɪ'leɪt), *v.* [f. BE- 5 + LATE *a.*] *trans.* To make late, detain beyond the usual time, delay.

1642 H. MORE *Song of Soul* I. I. xxxi, Night..quick to work the fate Of murd'red travellers, when they themselves belate. **1669** PENN *No Cross* Wks. 1726 I. 273 Wilt thou then for such a World, be-late thyself, over-stay the Time of thy salvation? **1805** SOUTHEY *Madoc in W.* x. Wks. V. 79 A little while to old remembrance given Will not belate us.

belated (bɪ'leɪtɪd), *ppl. a.* [f. prec. + -ED[1].]

1. Overtaken by lateness of the night; *hence*, overtaken by darkness, benighted.

1618 ROWLANDS *Sacr. Memorie* 24 We are belated, and the time farre spent. **1667** MILTON *P.L.* I. 783 Faerie Elves Whose midnight Revels..some belated Peasant sees. **1789** G. WHITE *Selborne* (1853) 4 Belated shepherd swains See the cowl'd spectre.

2. Detained beyond the usual time, coming or staying too late; out of date, behind date.

1670 MILTON *Hist. Eng.* Wks. 1738 II. 38 Authors..in time not much belated, some of equal age. **1785** BURKE *Nab. Arcot's Debts* Wks. 1842 I. 327 Who contested this belated account? **1857** LD. DUFFERIN *Lett. High Lat.* (1867) 70 Our belated baggage-train. **1877** MRS. OLIPHANT *Makers Flor.* iii. (1877) 52 Information..got but slowly..to the ears of the belated ambassador.

belatedly (bɪ'leɪtɪdlɪ), *adv.* [f. BELATED *ppl. a.* + -LY[2].] In a belated manner.

1896 *Westm. Gaz.* 21 Sept. 3/3 A fact..which her allies.. appear now somewhat belatedly to recognise. **1910** H. G. WELLS *Hist. Mr. Polly* ix. 240 He came belatedly in. **1917** CHESTERTON *Short Hist. Eng.* 219 Gladstone..rather belatedly realized that the freedom he loved in Greece and Italy had its rights nearer home. **1950** *Engineering* 2 June 625/1 A reversal of the trend..is now belatedly in evidence.

be'latedness. [f. BELATED *ppl. a.* + -NESS.] The quality or state of being belated.

1631 MILTON *Wks.* (1738) I. 4, I..do take notice of a certaine Belatedness ine me. **1922** *Glasgow Herald* 12 Oct. 9 Considerable comment is being aroused by the long delay .., but this belatedness is, I understand, unavoidable.

belaud (bɪ'lɔːd), *v.* [f. BE- 2 + LAUD.] *trans.* To load with praise.

a **1849** POE *Wks.* (1864) III. 139 Was belauded by the universal American press. **1882** FARRAR *Early Chr.* I. 14 Suicide..which many Stoics belauded.

Hence **be'lauded** *ppl. a.*

1857 HUGHES *Tom Brown* I. iii. (1871) 61 Abused and much belauded institutions. **1866** *Sat. Rev.* 25 Aug. 236/2 The belauded administration of the Duke of Somerset.

be'lauder. [f. prec.] One who belauds.

1884 J. W. EBSWORTH *Roxb. Bal.* V. 203 The erudite belauder of Ignoramus Juries.

†**be'lave**, *v. Obs.* Also 3 by-. [f. BE- + LAVE *v.*] *trans.* To lave about, wash all over; to lave its banks as a river.

a **1300** *O.E. Misc.* 140 þu stode Naked and bylaued myd blode. **1598** SYLVESTER *Du Bartas* II. iii. (1641) 174/1 Me in thy Bloud belaue. *Ibid.* (1608) 1002 The happy plains great Phasis streams belaue.

belawgive (Milton): see BE- 7¶.

belay (bɪ'leɪ), *v.* Forms: 1 belecgan, 3–4 bi-, belegge(n, 6– belay. *Pa. t.* 1 beleȝde, belede, 3 bilæde, 4 -laide, 6 belaied, 7 -laid, (*Naut.*) 7– -layed. *Pa. pple.* 1 beleȝd, beléd, 3 bileȝȝd, 4 bi-, beleyd, -leid, 6 -layd, 6–7 -laied, 7 -laid, (*Naut.*) 7– -layed. [OE. *bi-*, *belęcgan*:—OTeut. **bilagjan*, in OHG. *bileckan*, *bilegen*, mod.G. *belegen*, Du. *beleggen*; f. *bi-*, BE- + *lagjan*, in OE. *lęcgan* to LAY. Prof. Skeat suggests that the nautical use may have been taken from Du. *beleggen*: cf. BELAGE.]

†**1.** *trans.* To lay (a thing) about *with* other objects (*i.e.* by putting them about or around it); to surround, environ, invest, enclose, etc. *with*. *Obs.*

†**a.** *lit.*

a **1000** *Andreas* (Grein) 1562 We..ellþeódiȝne.. clommum beleȝdon vitebendum! *c* **1205** LAY. 14223 [With a strip of hide] A-buten he bilæde muche del of londe. *a* **1300** *Cursor M.* 5739 Him þouȝte brennynge a tre As hit wiþ loue al were bileyde.

†**b.** *fig.*

c **893** K. ÆLFRED *Oros.* III. viii. §3 Papirus wæs mid Romanum swylces domes beled. **1606** J. REYNOLDS *Dolarnys Prim.* 69 With many fauours, still thou didst belay mee.

†**c.** *esp.* To set about *with* (ornamentation), to lay *with* (a margin of gold, etc.). Cf. OVERLAY.

c **1200** ORMIN 8167 All þe bære wass bileȝȝd Wiþþ bærne gold. **1577** DEE *Relat. Spir.* I. (1659) 206 His robes all belayed with lace of gold. **1596** SPENSER *F.Q.* VI. ii. 5 A wood-mans iacket..Of Lincolne greene, belayd with silver lace.

†**2.** *spec.* **a.** To beset with armed men; to besiege, invest, beleaguer. *Obs.*

c **1320** *Sir Beves* 3189 Themperur theroute us wille belegge. **1595** SPENSER *Sonn.* xiv, Those small forts which ye were wont belay. **1610** HOLLAND *Camden's Brit.* (1637) 281 It was by King Stephen belaied once or twise with

sieges. **1648** G. Sandys *Paraphr. Div. Poems, Deo Opt. Max.*, When Arabian Theeves belaid us round.

†**b.** To beset or line (a way or passage) with armed men so as to intercept an enemy; or *with* anything for the use of those who pass. *Obs.*

1603 Knolles *Hist. Turkes* (1621) 945 Simon..had so belayed that strait, as that the Turkes could not..passe the same. **1611** Speed *Hist. Gt. Brit.* vi. xlv. 156 Constantine..hasted from Rome, hauing belaid al the way with Posthorses for the purpose. *a* **1639** Spottiswood *Hist. Ch. Scot.* ii. (1677) 44 Frederick..having belayed the ways made the Bishops..prisoners. **1698** Dryden *Æneid* ix. 515 The speedy Horse all passages belay.

†**c.** To waylay, lie in wait for (a person). *Obs.*

1470–85 Malory *Arthur* (1816) I. 273 All kings and knights of king Arthur's part belayed him, and waited for him. **1603** Knolles *Hist. Turkes* (1621) 717 He was by certain Spaniards..belaid upon the river Padus. **1760** Sterne *Tr. Shandy* (1802) I. xviii. 70 Other cases of danger, which belay us in getting into the world.

†**d.** *fig.* To forestall, make preparations for. *Obs.*

1598 Bacon *Sacr. Medit.* v. *Ess.* (Arb.) 109 They who..haue entred into a confidence that they had belayed all euents.

†**3.** To invest (words) with a sense or meaning.

†**a.** To explain or expound (in some way). *Obs.*

c **1175** *Lamb. Hom.* 67 þet we seggeð and þus þa wordes we bi-leggeð. *a* **1250** *Owl & Night.* 903 3et ich þe wile an oþer segge 3if þu hit const a riht bilegge.

†**b.** To gloze (so as to conceal meaning). *Obs.*

a **1250** *Owl & Night.* 672 He most bi-hemmen and bi-legge. *Ibid.* 837 Alle thine wordes thu bileist, That hit thincth soth al that thu seist.

†**c.** ? To illustrate by evidence or action. *Obs.*

c **1175** *Lamb. Hom.* 65 Gif we þos bode þus bileggeð.

†**4.** (Predicated of the thing which lies around): To encircle, clasp or coil round (*about*). *Obs.*

c **1340** *Cursor M.* 1336 (Trin.) þis tre..A nedder hit had aboute bileide. *c* **1320** R. Brunne *Medit.* 274 Sorwe 3oure hertes haþ alle be leyd. [**1836** Landor *Lett. Conserv.* 86 Under the slightest whipping that ever belayed the shoulders of malefactor.]

5. a. *Naut.* To coil a running rope round a cleat, belaying pin, or kevel, so as to fasten or secure it; to fasten by so putting it round. Said especially of one of the small ropes, used for working the sails. Also in *Mountaineering*. Hence **be'layed** *ppl. a.*

1549 *Compl. Scot.* vi. 41 Mak fast and belay. **1627** Capt. Smith *Seaman's Gram.* ix. 42 To belay, is to make fast the ropes in their proper places. *Ibid.* ix. 38 Bits..are..placed abaft the Manger..to belay the Cable thereto. **1706** Phillips, *Belay* or *Belage* [see belage]..Belay the Sheat, or Tack, i.e. fasten it to the Kennel, etc. **1762** Falconer *Shipwr.* ii. 83 Taught aft the sheet they tally and belay. **1840** R. Dana *Bef. Mast.* xxiii, The weather cross-jack braces and the lee main braces are each belayed together upon two pins. **1910** J. M. Archer-Thomson *Climbing in Ogwen District* viii. 79 After belaying the rope to a bollard on the right, the second man can assist the leader to start. **1957** Clark & Pyatt *Mountaineering in Brit.* ix. 160 Belayed by the third man, the second steadies the leader's foot. **1957** R. G. Collomb *Dict. Mountaineering* 28 *Belay*, to tie oneself, as a stationary member of a roped party, to a firm rock projection ..or to a piton, etc...in order to secure oneself and to afford a safeguard to the moving climber.

b. *transf.* To make fast, tie, secure.

1751 Smollett *Per. Pick.* (1779) IV. lxxxvi. 23 Pipes had found it very difficult to keep him [Peregrine] fast belayed. **1802** W. Giffard *Juvenal* ii. 84 The distaff, to a block belay'd. **1849** Curzon *Visits Monast.* 376 The bridle, which was safely belayed to the pack-saddle.

c. *Sailor's slang.*

1796 Dibdin *Poor Jack* ii, My timbers! what lingo he'd coil and belay. **1866** G. Macdonald *Ann Q. Neighb.* xxxi. (1878) 536 Belay there, and hearken. **1867** Adm. Smyth *Sailor's Word-bk.* 94 *Belay there*, stop! that is enough! *Belay that yarn*, we have had enough of it!

†**6.** *intr.* To lay *about one* (sc. blows). *Obs. rare.*

1598 Yong *Diana* 109 They belaied about them, passing actiue and nimble in lending blowes.

†**7.** ? To lay down: but see allay *v.*[1] 14. *Obs.*

1562 Turner *Bathes* 5 Youre wyne must be cleare and well belayd, accordinge vnto..the streingth and wekenes of the wyne.

belay (bɪ'leɪ), *sb. Mountaineering.* [f. belay *v.*] A turn or fastening of a rope by belaying (see belay *v.* 5). Also *attrib.* and *Comb.*

1908 *Westm. Gaz.* 12 June 5/1 A special knowledge of knots and roping method and belays might be their [*sc.* mountaineers'] only salvation. **1920** G. Winthrop Young *Mountain Craft* v. 226 A very common position upon steep rock..is to turn face inward, and pass the rope round some belay-point from one hand to the other. **1957** Clark & Pyatt *Mountaineering in Brit.* xiii. 212 The use of the shoulder belay, and the technique that went with it, became standardised.

be'laying, *vbl. sb.* [f. belay *v.* + -ing[1].]

†**1.** A lying in wait. *Obs.*

1677 Feltham *Disc. Eccles.* ii. 11, 346 Experienc'd in the belayings, the ingrossings, the circumventions of Merchandizing.

2. *Naut.* The coiling of running ropes round pins, etc.; chiefly *attrib.*, as in ***belaying-cleat, -pin.*** Also in *Mountaineering*.

1836 Marryat *Pirate* iii, Ropes..neatly secured to copper belaying-pins. **1862** F. Griffiths *Artil. Man.* 133 The belaying cleats on the bow beam. **1903** *Climbers' Club Jrnl.* VI. 5 So excellent was the anchorage afforded by this colossal belaying-pin that [etc.]. **1920** G. Winthrop Young *Mountain Craft* v. 220 A direct belaying-point which only leaves a short run-out.

bel canto (bɛl 'kæntəʊ). [It., = fine song.] Singing characterized by full, rich, and broad tone.

1894 G. du Maurier *Trilby* I. i. 46 It was lost, the *bel canto*—but I found it. **1908** *Daily Chron.* 9 May 4/4 In New York musical critics complain that audiences do not want Wagner,..and that the public flocks to the Italian bel canto. **1920** *Glasgow Herald* 14 May 8 For pure bel canto the English blackbird is hard to beat. **1938** *Oxf. Compan. Music* 85 *Bel canto*..This comprehensive term covers the vocal qualities of the great singers of the seventeenth and eighteenth centuries—the palmy days of Italian singing.

belch (bɛltʃ, bɛlʃ), *v.* Forms: 5–6 belke, 5–7 belche, 6 balche, bealche, 6–8 belk, 7 bealke, 9 *dial.* belk, 6– belch. [OE. *bealcian, bælcian*: cf. Du. *balken* to bray, shout. See belk.]

1. *intr.* To void wind noisily from the stomach through the mouth, to eructate. (Now *vulgar.*)

a **1000** *Be Manna Mode* (Gr.) 28 Breodað he and bælceð. *c* **1460** *Towneley Myst.* 314 To belke thai begyn and spew that is irke. **1483** *Cath. Angl.* 27 Belche [*v.r.* Belke or Bolke], *ructare.* **1530** Palsgr. 447/2 Harke howe the churle belcheth. **1574** Hellowes *Gueuara's Ep.* (1577) 185 The olde..glutton..shall belk much and sleepe little. **1623** Cockeram, *Parbreake*, to bealke. **1727** Bradley *Fam. Dict.* s.v. *Belch*, If an Asthmatical Person comes to belch, it is a good Sign. **1860** J. Wolff *Trav. & Adv.* I. xi. 341 They sit ..and belch, because, they say, that they are filled with the mystical wine of truth. **1864** Atkinson *Whitby Gloss.*, *Belk*, to belch.

2. *trans.* To ejaculate, to give vent to; to vent with vehemence or violence (words, feelings). In early use, translating L. *ēructāre*, and having no offensive meaning; but in later use confined, by association with other senses, to the utterance of things foul or offensive, or to furious vociferation compared to the action of a volcano or cannon.

a **1000** *Ags. Ps.* (Spelm.) xix. 2 Dæʒ ðam dæʒe bealceþ word. *c* **1500** Wyclif *Ps.* xlv. 2 (MS. X.) Myn herte hath teld ethir belkid [**1382** bowide] out a good word. **1581** Marbeck *Bk. of Notes* 637 As the rich glutton..belked out these glorious words. **1583** Stanyhurst *Aeneis* ii. (Arb.) 67, I belcht owt blasphemye bawling. **1594** Carew *Tasso* (1881) 73 His fell griefe, as some begoared Bull, Roaring and sighing out he belkes at full. **1612** T. Taylor *Comm. Titus* i. 16 (1619) 323 And openly belch out blasphemies against God. **1692** Washington tr. *Milton's Def. Pop.* Wks. 1738 I. 509 Belching out the same slanders. **1791** Wolcott (P. Pindar) *Magpie & Rob.* Wks. 1812 II. 473 Belching wisdom in one's face. **1856** Capern *Poems* (ed. 2) 176 The war-fiend shrieks and belches out his fury.

3. *trans.* To emit (wind, fumes, etc.) by belching. Also *fig.*

1561 Norton *Calvin's Inst.* iii. 195 What spirit do they belche out? **1607** Walkington *Opt. Glasse* 37 He breathing belketh out such sulphure aires. **1611** Shaks. *Cymb.* iii. v. 137 The bitterness of it I now belch from my heart. **1634** A. Warwick *Spare Min.* (1637) 113 What more..noisome smells can a new opened sepulcher belch out? **1641** Milton *Ch. Discip.* i. Wks. (1851) 12 Belching the soure crudities of yesterdayes Poperie. **1648** G. Daniel *Eclog.* iii. 207 Noe morning penitence Belches the folly of my last offence.

4. *trans.* To vomit. †**a.** *lit. Obs.*

1558 Phaër *Æneid.* iii. (R.) Belching raw gobbets from his maw. **1587** Turberv. *Trag. T.* (1837) 256 The venomd worme Had bealchd his poyson out. **1718** Pope *Iliad* xvi. 200 Their black jaws belch the gore. **1783** Blair *Rhet.* (1812) I. iv. 83 Belching up its bowels with a groan.

b. *fig.*

1610 Shaks. *Temp.* iii. iii. 56 Destiny..the neuer surfeited Sea, Hath caus'd to belch vp you! **1648** *Hunting of Fox* 36 Deadly Poyson, belch'd up by a Consistorian Schismatick.

5. *trans.* To eject, throw out. †**a.** *gen. Obs.*

1668 Culpepper & Cole *Barthol. Anat.* i. xvi. 40 Which vessel some will have to belch out acid blood.

b. *esp.* Said of the eruptive emission of fire and smoke by volcanoes; *hence* of cannons, etc.

1580 H. Gifford *Gilloflowers* (1875) 125 Aetna hill doth belke forth flakes of fire. **1667** Milton *P.L.* i. 671 A Hill.. whose griesly top Belch'd fire and rowling smoak. *a* **1733** North *Lives* (1826) II. 339 Strombolo..belched out fire and smoke in a most terrible sort. **1865** Parkman *Huguenots* iii. (1875) 34 Rebel batteries belched their vain thunder. **1874** Holland *Mistr. Manse* xv. 200 The cloud of menace belched its brand.

c. *absol.*

1837 Carlyle *Fr. Rev.* I. i. vii. vii. 208 Rusty firelocks belch after him.

†**6.** *intr.* To rise in eructation; to heave like a confined fluid or gas seeking to escape. *Obs.*

1576 Lambarde *Peramb. Kent* (1826) 420 Envious rancour so boiled in the brest, that it not onely belched, but also brake foorth immediately.

†**7.** *intr.* To gush out; to flow in gulps. *Obs.*

1581 Marbeck *Bk. of Notes* 218 Their plenteous wine presses, and their full sellers, belking from this vnto that. **1587** Fleming *Cont. Holinshed.* III. 1351/1 The blood still belched out into the basen.

belch (bɛltʃ, bɛlʃ), *sb.* [f. prec. vb.]

1. An eructation.

1570 Levins *Manip.* 58 A Belche, *ructus.* **1574** Hellowes *Gueuara's Ep.* (1577) 132 The sight thereof moueth belkes, and makes the stomach wamble. **1580** Hollyband *Treas. Fr. Tong*, *Vne route*, a belch. **1763** Churchill *P. Professor*, Salute the royal babe in Welsh, And send forth gutturals like a belch.

2. *fig.* Said of the sea, hell, a volcano, cannon.

1513 Douglas *Æneis* vii. vi. 110 Pluto eik..Reputtis that bismyng belch haitfull to se. **1642** H. More *Song of Soul* ii. iii. iv. xxii, O belch of hell! O horrid blasphemy! **1837** Carlyle *Fr. Rev.* II. ii. vi. vii. 118 And at every new belch, the women..shout.

b. A slang name for poor beer: see quot. 1796.

1706 E. Ward *Hud. Rediv.* I. vii. 18 A little House, Where Porters do their Belch carouse. **1712** Henley *Spect.* No. 396 ¶2 Owing to the use of brown juggs, muddy belch, etc. **1796** Grose *Class. Dict.*, *Belch*, all sorts of beer: that liquor being apt to cause eructation. **1858** A. Mayhew *Paved w. Gold* iii. iii. 265 Whilst my mates are drinking the 'belch.'

'belcher[1]. [f. belch *v.*] One who belches.

1598 Florio, *Rottatore*, a belcher, a spuer, a rasper. **1699** Coles, Belcher, *ructator.*

belcher[2] ('bɛlʃə(r)). A neckerchief with blue ground, and large white spots having a dark blue spot or eye in the centre, named after a celebrated pugilist called *Jim Belcher*; sometimes applied to any particoloured handkerchief worn round the neck.

1805 *Sporting Mag.* XXVII. 126/1 Their opponents were decked in the yellow stripe [handkerchief], which has acquired the appellation of the Belcher. **1809** *Monthly Pantheon* XIV. 546/1 If there be any of them who will spar with each other, let them wear the appropriate *Belcher handkerchief*. **1812** *Examiner* 21 Sept. 607/1 The traverser.. tied a Belcher handkerchief round his neck. **1825** T. Lister *Granby* xxxix. (1836) 261 Instead of the Belcher he has a loose black handkerchief round his neck. **1846** Lytton *Lucretia* (1853) 154 The lower part of which [a face] was enveloped in an immense 'belcher.' **1862** Burton *Bk. Hunter* i. 31 The fragments of a parti-coloured belcher handkerchief.

belching ('bɛltʃɪŋ, bɛlʃ-), *vbl. sb.* Also 6–7 belking. [f. belch *v.* + -ing[1].] The action of voiding wind from the stomach through the mouth; eructation; *also*, the utterance of foul or violent language; the eruptive action of volcanoes.

1528 Paynell *Salerne Regim.* Biij, Sower belchynges. **1576** Newton *Lemnies' Complex.* 233 Subject to belking and sowre vomiting. **1655** Gurnall *Chr. in Arm.* xviii. 231/2 Rather the belching of a Devil, than the voice of a saint. **1859** Todd *Cycl. Anat. & Phys.* V. 316/1 Simple eructation or belching.

'belching, *ppl. a.* Also 6 belking, bealking. [f. as prec. + -ing[2].] That belches, eructates, etc. (Cf. the various meanings of the vb.)

1581 Studley *Seneca's Hippolitus* 71 The belking Seas yell out. **1585** Lloyd *Treas. Health* I v, A weake bealkyng stomake. **1601** R. Yarrington *Two Traj.* iv. vi. in Bullen *O. Pl.* IV, That belching voice, that harsh night-raven sound. *a* **1700** Dryden (J.) His crest..On which with belching flames Chimæra burn'd. **1833** Ht. Martineau *Tale of Tyne* iii. 45 To face the belching cannon.

belcony, obs. form of balcony.

beld(e, obs. ff. of bald, bield, bold, build.

beldam, -dame ('bɛldəm). Forms: 5–9 beldame, 7 belldame, 5– beldam. [Not a direct adoption of the F. *belle dame* 'fair lady,' but formed upon *dam*, earlier *dame*, in its Eng. sense of 'mother,' with *bel-* employed to express relationship, as in *belsire, belfader*: see bel B. For the transference to a more remote ancestor see also belsire; for the extension to old woman, etc., cf. *gaffer, gammer, goody, grandame, granny.*]

†**1.** A father or mother's mother, a grandmother. Also *fig. Obs.*

c **1440** *Promp. Parv.* 29 Beldam [*v.r.* beldame], faders and moders modyr, bothe. **1483** *Cath. Angl.* 27 Beldame, *auia.* *c* **1483** Caxton *Bk. Trav.* in *Promp. Parv.* 29 note, Recommaunde me to your bel-fadre, and to your bel dame, *à vostre tayon et à vostre taye.* **1530** Palsgr. 179/2 Beldame, *meregrant.* *c* **1550** Paynell tr. *Vives' Duty Husb.* (T.) The mother, the beldame, the aunt, the sister, the cosyn. **1593** Shaks. *Lucr.* 953 To shew the beldame daughters of her daughter. **1613** Drayton *Polyolb.* vi. (T.) The beldam and the girl, the grandsire and the boy. **1628** Milton *Vac. Exerc.* 46 When beldam Nature in her cradle was

†**b.** A great-grandmother, or still more remote ancestress; by Plot used for a woman who has lived to see five generations of female descendants.

1679 Plot *Staffordsh.* (1686) 322 She lived to be a Beldam, that is to see the sixt generation. **1863** Chambers *Bk. of Days* I. 306 At the same rate she might have been beldam at sixty six.

2. An aged woman, a matron of advanced years. (In 16th c. used in addressing nurses.)

1580 Gifford *Gilloflowers* (1875) 98 And thus..This aged beldam speakes. **1596** Spenser *F.Q.* iii. ii. 43 [To 'her aged nourse'] 'Beldame, your words doe worke me litle ease.' **1598** Drayton *Heroic. Ep.* xix. 15 Here is no Beldam Nurse, to powt nor lowre. **1709** Steele *Tatler* No. 83 ¶2, I am neither Childish-young, nor Beldam-old. **1752** Foote *Taste* i. i, This superannuated Beldame gapes for Flattery. **1768** Beattie *Minstr.* i. xliii, Her legend when the Beldame 'gan impart. **1821** Byron *Sardan.* i. ii. (1868) 352 That blood-loving beldame, My martial grandam. **1856** Longf. *Blind Girl* i. 122 The beldame, wrinkled and gray takes the young bride by the hand.

3. *esp.* with depreciative sense: A loathsome old woman, a hag; a witch; a furious raging woman (without the notion of age), a virago.

a **1586** SIDNEY *Arcadia* (1613) 10 A beldame..accused for a witch. **1608** R. JOHNSON *Sev. Champions* 212 Come all you witches, beldames, and Fortunetellers. *a* **1641** BP. MOUNTAGU *Acts & Mon.* (1642) 177 Tarquinius taking her to be some frantick Beldame. **1706** ADDISON *Rosamond* I. iii, Fly from my passion, Baldame, fly! **1822** SCOTT *Nigel* xxxv, That accursed beldam whom she caused to work upon me. **1857** F. LOCKER *Lond. Lyrics* (1862) 100 The beldams shriek, the caldron bubbles.

'beldamship. [f. prec.: after *ladyship*.]

1633 SHIRLEY *Yng. Admiral* IV. i, I beseech your learned beldamship to accept it. **1636** DAVENANT *Wits* in *Dodsley* (1780) VIII. 512 We'll make her costive beldamship Come off.

belders, var. of BILDERS, *Obs.*, a plant-name.

bele, obs. f. BEAL: see also BOIL *sb.*

†**be'lead**, *v. Obs.* [OE. *belǽdan*, f. BE- *pref.* 2 + *lǽdan* to LEAD.]

1. *trans.* To lead away, lead astray.

a **1000** *Benedict. Rule* (Schr.) 27 Ðu belæddest us on grin. **1340** *Alex. & Dind.* 906 So be ȝe, ludus, by-lad · and lawles also. ?*a* **1500** *Pore Helpe* 285 in Hazl. *E.P.P.* III. 262 We maye go to bed, Blyndefylde and beled.

2. *fig.* To conduct, lead, use, treat.

c **1275** *Passion Our Lord* 278 in *O.E. Misc.* 45 He iseyh hw ihesu crist wes vuele biled. *a* **1300** *Cursor M.* 17049 Whenne þou þi son say so biled. **1485** CAXTON *Trevisa's Higden* IV. x. (1527) 159 He was..harde cruelly beladde.

beleaf, beleap, etc.: see BE- *pref.*

beleaguer (bɪ'liːgə(r)), *v.* Also 6 **belegar**, 7 **-guer, beleager, -gre**, 8 **-gure**. [a. Du. *belegeren*, f. *be-* + *leger* camp; cf. mod.G. *belagern*: see LEAGUER.]

1. To surround (a town, etc.) with troops so as to prevent ingress and egress, to invest, besiege.

1590 SIR J. SMYTHE *Weapons* 4 These..haue so affected the Wallons, Flemings, and base Almanes discipline, that.. they will not..affoord to say that such a towne is besieged, but that it is belegard. **1598** BARRET *Theor. Warres* V. iii. 134 Antwerpe,..then by him beleaguered. **1648** EVELYN *Mem.* (1857) III. 26 The castle of Dover, which some say is beleagured. **1846** PRESCOTT *Ferd. & Is.* I. ix. 392 He reflected that the Castilians would soon be beleaguered. **1856** LONGF. *Beleag. City* vii, That an army of phantoms vast and wan, Beleaguer the human soul.

2. *transf.* To surround, beset (generally with some idea of hostility or annoyance). Cf. BESIEGE.

1589 NASHE *Almond for P.* 5 a, A whole hoast of Pasquils ..will so beleaguer your paper walles. **1614** LODGE *Seneca* 4 Beleager him on euery side by thy bountie. **1741** RICHARDSON *Pamela* (1824) I. iv. 239 The girl is.. beleaguering, as you significantly express it, a worthy gentleman. **1822** W. IRVING *Braceb. Hall* xxvii. 253 It [the house] has been beleaguered by gipsy women.

†**beleaguer**, *sb. Obs.* = BELEAGUERER.

1611 SPEED *Hist. Gt. Brit.* IX. iii. 31 His men sallied out.. in the face of their beleaguers. **1611** COTGR., *Assiegeur*, a besieger, a beleaguer. [ed. 1632 beleaguerer.]

beleaguered (bɪ'liːgəd), *ppl. a.* [f. BELEAGUER *v.* + -ED[1].] Besieged, invested, beset.

1644 MILTON *Areop.* (Arb.) 69 In defence of beleagured truth. **1647** SPRIGG *Angl. Rediv.* IV. vii. (1854) 281 To know themselves a beleagured enemy. **1762** FALCONER *Shipwr.* III. 165 Beleaguer'd Troy. **1852** THACKERAY *Esmond* III. x. (1876) 416 The poor beleaguered garrison. **1862** GOULBURN *Pers. Relig.* III. viii, The key of a beleaguered position.

beleaguerer (bɪ'liːgərə(r)). [f. as prec. + -ER[1].] One who beleaguers: a besieger.

1628 EARLE *Microcosm.* lxxvii. 159 He is a sore beleaguerer of chambers. **1817** COLERIDGE *Zapolya* II. Wks. IV. 232 A wall, that wards off the beleaguerer.

beleaguering (bɪ'liːgərɪŋ), *vbl. sb.* [f. as prec. + -ING[1].] The act of besieging; investment.

1601 R. JOHNSON *Kingd. & Commw.* 29 The beleaguerings of Harlem. **1869** FREEMAN *Norm. Conq.* (1876) III. xii. 187 The actual beleaguering of Rome.

beleaguering (bɪ'liːgərɪŋ), *ppl. a.* [f. as prec. + -ING[2].] That beleaguers; besieging, investing.

1753 *Scots Mag.* XV. 76/2 Beleag'ring foes. **1870** *Even. Standard* 28 Oct., Break through the beleaguering lines.

beleaguerment (bɪ'liːgəmənt). [f. as prec. + -MENT.] The fact of beleaguering; siege, blockade.

1826 E. IRVING *Babylon* I. III. 186 Two beleaguerments of the capital. **1870** MORRIS *Earthly Par.* II. III. 5 In the last month of Troy's beleaguerment.

†**be'leave, -eve**, *v. Obs.* Forms: 1 belǽfan, 2 bilæfen, -læuen, -leauen, 2-4 bi-, beleue(n, (4 bi-, bylaue), 4-5 beleve, bleve, blewy(n, (5 byleve), 6 beleaue. *Pa. t.* 1-2 be-, bilǽfde, -leafde, 2-3 -lefde, 3 -leaued(e, -lefte, 3-4 -leued(e, -left(e, -lafte, blefede, 4 blefte, 4-7 beleft(e. *Pa. pple.* 1 belǽfed, 2-4 bi-, beleued, 3 (-lefued), -leved, -left, 4 bleft, 4-5 byleft, -lefft, -laft. [OE. *belǽfan*:—OTeut. and Goth. *bilaibjan*, f. *bi-*, BE- + *laibjan*, in OE. *lǽfan* to LEAVE, a casual deriv. of OTeut. **lîban* to remain, which appeared in Eng. in BELIVE. Thus originally and properly transitive; but very early substituted for the intrans. *belīve*. In 14th c. often syncopated to *bleve(n*, esp. in Kentish; cf. mod.G. *bleiben*, Du. *blijven*.]

I. *transitive.*

1. To let or cause to remain behind, to go away without taking with one, to abandon.

c **1175** *Lamb. Hom.* 79 Ho hine bilefde liggen half quic. *c* **1200** ORMIN 8913 He wass þa behinndenn hemm Bilefedd att te temmple. *c* **1205** LAY. 18648 þe eorl..bilefde his wif in Tintaieol. **1297** R. GLOUC. 421 Hys fader..ladde hym.. into Normandye, & byleuede hym þere. *c* **1330** *Assump. Virg.* 759 Thei leide þe bodi in a stone, And bileft alle in þat stede. ?*a* **1400** *Morte Arth.* 2380 The cors of Kayone..at Came es belevefede. **1513** DOUGLAS *Æneis* X. xi. 166 Men.. Quham..to myschewus deyd beleft haue I. **1627** MAY *Lucan* VIII. (T.) Wondering at fortune's turns, and scarce is he Beleft, relating his own misery.

b. To leave (something) behind *to*; to leave at death; to leave in the possession or power of.

c **1200** *Trin. Coll. Hom.* 183 Hie bileueð uncuðe men þe aihte. **1387** TREVISA *Higden* Rolls Ser. VI. 367 þe kyngdom [they] byleft to Colwlufus. *c* **1410** LOVE *Bonavent. Mirr.* vi. (Gibbs MS.) Lord to þe is bylafte [**1530** belefte] þe pore peple. **1557** *K. Arthur* (Copland) VII. i, The two men.. belefte him to Syr Kay.

2. To allow to remain over; to leave out of count or process: to pass over, let go, omit.

c **1205** LAY. 29363 Ælcne bilefued mon he lette bilimien. **1297** R. GLOUC. 173 He ne beleuede no3t on. *c* **1450** *Merlin* xvii. 276 And v C men that were hym be-lefte of the bataile.

3. To go away from (a person or place); to depart from, forsake, quit, abandon.

c **1205** LAY. 8569 Lundene we mote bilæuen. *a* **1225** *Ancr. R.* 110 And fluen alle vrom him & bilefden him ase vreomede. *c* **1400** *Destr. Troy* XXXV. 13456 A buyldyng..was of long tyme beleft, & no lede there.

b. *fig.* To turn from, forsake.

c **1175** *Lamb. Hom.* 81 He scal his sunne uor-saken and bileuen. *a* **1225** *Ancr. R.* 394 Heo wule..bileauen þene deouel. *a* **1300** *Cursor M.* 9053, I haf bi-left mi lauerd lau. *c* **1400** *Ywaine & Gaw.* 35 Trowth and luf es al bylaft.

c. To leave off, cease give up, abandon (action).

c **1175** *Lamb. Hom.* 93 Bileafden heo heore timbrunge. *c* **1380** *Sir Ferumb.* 3344 Het hem þe assaut be-leue. *c* **1400** *Solomon's Bk. Wisd.* 82 Ne bileue þou nou3th to trauaile.

4. To let go (from one's hold).

a **1225** *Ancr. R.* 232 Hwon two bereð one burðene, & te oðer bileaueð hit.

II. *intr.* [taking place of BELIVE: = Ger. *bleiben*.]

5. To remain over, survive, be left in existence.

a **1000** *Psalms* (Spelm.) cv[i]. 10 An of him ne belæfde [Vulg. *non remansit*]. **1297** R. GLOUC. 372 þer ne byleuede no3t..þat nas to grounde ybro3t. *c* **1350** *MS.* in *Archæol.* XXX. 352 Of y[e] ewyll xal no thynge blewyn. *c* **1435** *Torr. Portugal* 359 Had byn the gyant belevand, They had not partyd soo.

b. To remain behind in a place.

c **1250** *Gen. & Ex.* 3114 La! god it wot, sal ðe[r]-of bi-leuen non fot. **1340** *Ayenb.* 190 Yrobbed..zuo þet him na3t ne blefte. *c* **1380** *Sir Ferumb.* 1595 þe hedes on þe tre by-lafte. *a* **1400** *Octouian* 1540 The Soudan..Bleft yn Fraunce, Cytes to brenne. **1480** CAXTON *Chron. Eng.* lxi. 45, I beleft allone in my chambre.

c. To remain in a condition or state, to continue.

c **1200** *Trin. Coll. Hom.* 87 þe children weren clensed of sinnen and þus bilefden. *c* **1250** *Gen. & Ex.* 671 Babel, ðat tur, bilef unmad. *a* **1300** *Cursor M.* 7662 þer mani man fell vnder scheild, Bot with dauid be-left þe feild. **1340** *Ayenb.* 12 þe mayde Marie blefte eure mayde. *c* **1430** *Syr Gener.* 5737 Here speres beleft hole booth.

6. To remain for the time being (in a place); to stay, abide, continue, dwell *with* (a person).

c **1175** *Lamb. Hom.* 149 3e moten..him, foleȝe and mid him bileue. *c* **1205** LAY. 19777 Ne dursten heo þer bilæfen. *c* **1250** *Gen. & Ex.* 800 Abram..and sarray bileften bi-twen betel and ay. **1340** *Ayenb.* 245 Mid Him uor to bleve. *c* **1425** *Seven Sag.* (P.) 48 Gyf he schal byleve with me.

7. *to be beleft* was often used in the sense of 'To remain, to be'; also 'to be become of.'

c **1340** *Cursor M.* 7736 (Trin.) His coupe his spere where mai hit be..Where be þei now bileued. *Ibid.* 18558 He wrou3te bi wicche-craft And wiþ þe deuel was bilaft. *c* **1440** *Bone Flor.* 733 He ys beleft wyth Syr Garcy Ageyn you.

†**be'leaving**, *vbl. sb. Obs.* [f. prec. + -ING[1].]

1. Remaining, tarrying, abiding, abode.

c **1330** *Arthur & Merl.* 8611 Withouten bileueing ani more, Thai went. **1340** *Ayenb.* 72 þer hy habbeþ hyre bleuinge.

2. Remaining steadfast, endurance, perseverance.

1340 *Ayenb.* 232 þet zixte leaf is bleuinge, þet is stedeuest wyl to loki þet me heþ behote god.

3. That which is left, a leaving.

c **1440** *Promp. Parv.* 39 Blevynge, or releve, or relefe, *reliquia vel reliquiæ*. *Ibid.* 428 Releef, or brocaly of mete (or blevynge), *fragmentum*. **1592** GREENE *Disputat.* 17 Hee had nothing for his pence, but the waste beleauings of others beastly labours.

belecture, beledgered, etc.: see BE- *pref.*

†**belee**, *v. Obs. rare*⁻¹. [f. BE- 6 + LEE *sb.*] *trans.* To get (a ship) into such a position that the wind is intercepted from her; also *fig.*

1604 SHAKS. *Oth.* I. i. 30, I..must be be-leed and calm'd.

beleeve, obs. form of BELIEF, BELIEVE.

†**'belef, -if.** *Obs.* [a. OF. *à belif, beslif* (:—late L. type **bis-līquus* = *oblīquus*; cf. F. *beslong*, med.L. *beslongus* = L. *oblongus*). Cf. EMBELIFE.] In advb. phr. ***a belef***: obliquely, aslant; scarf-wise.

c **1340** *Gaw. & Gr. Knt.* 2486 þe blykkande belt he bere þeraboute, A belef as a bauderyk. *Ibid.* 2517 Vche burne.. a bauderyk schulde haue, A bende a belef hym aboute.

beleft(e, pa. t. of BELEAVE *v. Obs.*

belemnite ('bɛlɪmnaɪt). *Palæont.* [f. mod.L. *belemnītes* (formerly used in Eng.), f. Gr. βέλεμν-ον a dart + -ITE (cf. AMMONITE): so named in allusion to the popular notions mentioned below.]

a. A fossil common in rocks of the Secondary formation; a straight, smooth, cylindrical object, a few inches long, convexly tapering to a sharp point, formerly known, from its shape and supposed origin, as *thunder-bolt, thunder-stone, elf-bolt*, but now recognized as the internal bone of an animal allied to the cuttle-fish. **b.** The extinct animal to which this belonged.

1646 SIR T. BROWNE *Pseud. Ep.* 53 The figures are regular in many other stones, as in the Belemnites. **1677** PLOT *Oxfordsh.* 41 Meeting by the way with a bed of Belemnites, or (as they call them) Thunder-bolts. **1698** T. MOLYNEUX in *Nat. Hist. Irel.* (1726) 160 One plain homogeneous body, without any mixture of Cochlite, Belemnite,..or such like extraneous matter. **1833** LYELL *Princ. Geol.* III. 325 The belemnite, one of the cephalopodes not found in any tertiary formation.

belemnitic (bɛlɪm'nɪtɪk), *a.* [f. prec. + -IC.] Of, pertaining to, or characterized by belemnites.

1847 ANSTED *Anc. World* viii. 148 Preserved in connexion with the belemnitic shell. **1878** tr. *Cotta's Rocks* 376 Belemnitic strata (of the oldest deposits of the Jurassic period).

†**be'leper**, *v. Obs.* [f. BE- *pref.* 5 + LEPER.] *trans.* To afflict with, or as with, leprosy. Hence **be'lepered** *ppl. a.*

c **1623** FLETCHER *Laws Candy* V. i. 66 Beleapred with the Curse Of foule ingratitude. **1633** FORD *'Tis Pity* IV. iii. (1839) 41 Thy lust beleper'd body. **1649** MILTON *Eikon.* xiv. Wks. (1851) 449 Impuritie and Church revenue rushing in, corrupted and beleper'd all the Clergie.

beleric, variant of BELLERIC.

‖**bel-esprit** (bɛlɛspri). Pl. **beaux esprits** (bozɛspri). [Fr.; = 'fine mind, wit, wittiness'; hence 'a man of culture and talent.']

1. A clever genius, a brilliant wit.

1638 CHILLINGW. *Relig. Prot.* I. Pref. §8 Which I feare is a great scandall to many *Beaux Esprits* among you. **1721** AMHERST *Terræ Fil.* xxv. 129 The finest geniuses and beaux esprits of the university. **1801** MAR. EDGEWORTH *Belinda* I. iii. 44 The world thought me a beauty and a bel esprit. **1813** —— *Patron.* I. xiv. 228 One could hand her verses about, and get her forward in the bel-esprit line.

2. Wit, wittiness. (Hardly in Eng. use.)

1806 M. EDGEWORTH *Leonora* II. lxv. 107 In these times a woman has no choice at a certain period but politics, or bel esprit. **1860** ADLER *Fauriel's Prov. Poetry* xviii. 401 The mannered subtilties of a vitiated taste and of bel-esprit.

belet(t, obs. form of BILLET.

†**belette.** *Obs.* [a. OF. *belette* in same sense, f. *bel* beautiful.] A jewel, an ornament.

1522 in *Bury Wills* (1850) 116, I beqwethe to my dowghter the steynyd clothes..and a golde corse with belettes harnes lesse.

beletter (bɪ'lɛtə(r)), *v.* [f. BE- *pref.* 6 + LETTER.]

†**1.** *trans.* To serve with letters, to write to. *Obs.*

1655 FULLER *Hist. Camb.* (1840) 179 The University-Orator..be-lettered all the lords of the privy-council.

2. *nonce-wd.* To decorate with letters (such as F.R.S., Ph.D., etc.) appended to one's name.

1883 *Athenæum* 19 May 638/3 The mania prevalent among people of more ambition than performance for belettering themselves.

†**be'leve.** *nonce-wd. Obs.* = LEAVE.

1575 J. STILL *Gamm. Gurton* III. iii. 15 Mine owne goods I will have, and aske the no beleve.

beleve, var. BELEAVE *v.*; obs. f. BELIEF, -LIEVE.

belew, -yng, obs. form of BELLOW, -ING.

†**be'lewe**, *v. Obs.* [OE. *belǽwian* f. BE- 2 + *lǽwian* to betray.] *trans.* To betray.

c **1000** *Ags. Gosp.* Matt. xxvi. 15-16 And ic hyne belæwe [*Hatton*, beleawiȝe] eow..He hyne wolde belæwan. *c* **1175** *Lamb. Hom.* 229 Hu hé Christ heom belēwen michte.

†**'belfather.** *Obs.* Also 5 **-fader**. [f. BEL + FATHER: cf. *beldame, belsire*.] Grandfather.

c **1440** *Promp. Parv.* 30 Belsyre or belfather, faders or moders fader, *avus*. **1483** CAXTON *Gold. Leg.* 414/1 Here lyeth henry the sone of henry the fader henry the belfader henry the olde belfader.

belfried ('bɛlfrɪd), *ppl. a.* [f. BELFRY + -ED[2].] Having a belfry.

1841 LADY F. HASTINGS *Poems* 150 The belfried tower. **1860** MRS. GASKELL *C. Brontë* 4 Parsonage, Church, and Belfried school-house.

belfry ('bɛlfrɪ). Forms: (2–3 berefreid, berfreit), 4 berfrey, -fray, -froiss, 5 barfray, 5–7 belfray(e, 6 belfroy, bellfray, -froy, belfrie, -fre, 6–7 belfery, 6– belfrey, belfry, (7 belfore, befroy, beffroy, 8 bellfry.) [ME. *berfrey, -ay* a. OF. *berfrei, -ai, -ay* (also *berfroi*, later *belfrei, belfroi, befroi*, mod. *beffroi*), pointing to a late L. type *berefrēdus*, from *bere'frīdus*, adopted f. Teutonic **bergfrid*; in MHG. *bercvrit, -frit, berchfrit, berfrit* (also *berhfride*), MDu. *bergfert, -frede*, in sense 1 below. The subsequent change of the first *r* to *l* by dissimilation from following *r* (as in *armarium, almarium, almerie; peregrinum, pelegrin, pilgrim; parafredus, palefrei, palfrey*) is common in later med.L.; it is rare, and exceptional in Fr. (where the normal form dropped the *r*, *befroi, beffroi*); in Eng. *belfray* did not appear bef. 15th c., being probably at first a literary imitation of med.Lat.; its acceptance was doubtless due to popular association with BELL, and the particular application which was in consequence given to the word. The meaning has passed from a 'pent-house' a 'movable-tower' used by besiegers and besieged, to 'a tower to protect watchmen, a watch-tower, beacon-tower, alarm-bell tower, bell-tower, place where a bell is hung.' The sense of 'pent-house' or 'shelter-shed' is retained dialectally in Lincolnshire and Notts.

The etymology of Ger. *bergfrid, bercvrit*, presents some difficulties; but it is generally agreed that the latter part is a form of OHG. *fridu*, OTeut. *friþu-z*, 'peace, security, shelter, place of shelter or safety' (cf. the range of meaning of OE. *friðu, frið*, ME. FRITH), the final vowel being dropped as in proper names, *Gottfrid, Sigfrid*, etc.; and that the former part is the stem of *berg-en* to protect, defend; the whole meaning 'protecting' or 'defensive place of shelter,' an obvious description of a pent-house fitted to ward off missiles from those to whom it gave shelter during siege operations. (The possibility that *berg-* here means 'mountain' seems precluded by the sense: but see the discussion of the word by Dr. Chance in N. & Q. VI. xii. 284, 412, etc.). For the form taken by *bergfrid* in Romanic, and thus in Eng., cf. the adoption of OHG. *fridu* in late L. as *fridus, frēdus* 'peace, protection,' the proper names from G. *-frid, Gottefridus, Godefrey, Galfridus, Geoffrey*, and the sb. AFFRAY, OF. *esfrei*, mod. *effroi*, parallel to *berfrei, beffroi*. MedL. had the forms *berefridus, berfredus, bil-, bal-, belfredus, berte-, balte-, bati-, buti-fredus*, with the latter of which cf. the It. *battifredo*, assimilated by popular etymology with *battere* to beat (the tocsin), to strike (as a clock).]

†**1.** A wooden tower, usually movable, used in the middle ages in besieging fortifications. Probably, in its simplest form, it was a mere shed or pent-house, intended to shelter the besiegers while operating against a fortification; but in its developed form it was constructed with many offensive appurtenances, so as to make it a formidable engine of attack. See the quotation from Ld. Berners. *Obs.*

[WILL. OF MALMESB. IV. 141 (in Du Cange), Turris non magna in modum aedificiorum facta (Berefreid [*other MSS.* berfreit] appellant), quod fastigium murorum æquaret. SIMEON DURH. an. 1123 Ligneam turrim quam Berfreit vocant, erexit.] *c* **1300** *K. Alis.* 2777 Alisaundre.. Fast asailed heore wallis, Myd berfreyes, with alle gyn. *c* **1325** *E.E. Allit. P.* B 1187 At vch brugge a berfray on basteles wyse, þat seuen syþe vch a day asayled þe ȝates. **1375** BARBOUR *Bruce* x. 708 Alexander.. Lap fra a berfrois on the wall. *c* **1430** *Syr. Gener.* 7811 He purveid for maygnelles and belfrayes, And othre ordinaunce. **1483** *Cath. Angl.* 21. **1523** LD. BERNERS *Froiss.* I. cix. 131 Two belfroys of great tymbre, with iii. stages, euery belfroy on four great whelys, and the sydes towardes the towne, were covered with cure boly [F. *cuir bouilli*] to defende them fro fyre and fro shotte; and into euery stage, ther weren poynted C. archers. **1530** PALSGR. 197 Bellfray, *beavfroy*.

2. A shed used as a shelter for cattle or for the protection of carts and agricultural implements, or produce. Still in local use: 'a shed made of wood and sticks, furze, or straw.' (E. Peacock *Gloss. of Manley & Corringham, Lincoln.*)

1553 *Court-Roll of Manor of Scotter, Lincoln* 9 Octr., R.R. amovit omnia ligna sua super le belfrey et jacent in communi via. **1590** Invent J. Nevil in *Midl. Co. Hist. Collector* II. 29 Item the belfrey with other wood, xx[s]. **1873** in PEACOCK *Gloss M. & C.* 21 The belfrey.. was ruinous, and liable to fall upon the passers-by.

†**3.** A tower for the protection of a watchman, a watch-tower; a beacon-tower, alarm-bell tower. (A sense perhaps not used in England, though common in France.) *Obs.*

1612 FOXE *A. & M.* (1684) III. 899 Being now come nigh to the Befroy (which is a watchtower standing before the City-Hall where the Clock is). *c* **1645** HOWELL *Lett.* (1650) I. 461 A beacon or watch-tower is called *beffroy*, whereas the true word is *l'effroy*.

4. a. A bell-tower; generally attached to a church or other building, but sometimes standing separate.

c **1440** *Promp. Parv.* 30 Bellfray, *campanarium*. **1494** FABYAN VII. 330 The scolars.. put the legatte in such feere, that he, for his sauegarde, toke the belfray of Osney, and there helde hym. **1556** *Chron. Grey Friars* (1852) 73 The grett belfery that stode in Powlles church-yerde. **1674** tr. *Scheffer's Lapland* viii. 26 Adjoining to their churches they have belfrys, and houses for the use of Priests. **1849** FREEMAN *Archit.* 177 The introduction of steeples or belfries. **1861** N. WOODS *Pr. Wales in Canada* 347 A little glass lantern, like a belfry.

b. The room or storey of the church tower in which the bells are hung.

1549 THOMAS *Hist. Italie* 74 Saincte Markes steeple is.. so well built, that withinfoorth an horse maie be ledde vp vnto the bellfroy. **1601** SHAKS. *Per.* II. i. 41 If I had been the sexton, I would have been that day in the belfrey. **1714** GAY *What d'ye call it* Prel. 3 Fetch the Leathern Bucket that hangs in the Bellfry. **1823** P. NICHOLSON *Pract. Build.* 571 The part above the belfrey, which contains the clock-work, is of an octagonal form.

†**c.** That part of the floor of the church under the tower, where the ringers stand to ring the bells, sometimes parted from the main body of the church by a curtain; this was the seat of the poor, and sometimes used as a schoolroom. *Obs.*

1549 LATIMER *Serm. bef. Edw. VI.* (Arb.) 125 Yea, a poor woman in the belfre hath as good authoritie to offer vp thys sacrifyce, as hath the byshop in his pontificalibus. **1588** FRAUNCE *Lawiers Log.* Ded. ¶iv. b, They may plague poore boyes with false Latine in a belfraye. *a* **1617** HIERON *Wks.* II. 75 The gentleman that sitteth in the quire, as well as the poore that is ranged in the belfry. **1637** BASTWICK *Litany* II. 17 In the Font or before, or other part of the Church. **1659** GAUDEN *Tears Ch.* 253 (D.) Teaching school in a belfry.

d. (See quot.)

1753 CHAMBERS *Cycl. Supp.*, *Belfry* is more particularly used for the timber-work, which sustains the bells in a steeple: or that wooden structure to which the bells in church-steeples are fastened.

e. The head. See also BAT *sb.*[1] 1 b. *slang.*

1907 N. MUNRO *Daft Days* xxxii. 267 When they've got cobwebs in their little brilliantined belfries, I'm full of the songs of spring. **1907**, **1911**, etc. [see BAT *sb.*[1] 1 b]. **1911** H. S. HARRISON *Queed* vii. 84 Something loose in his belfry.

5. *Naut.* 'An ornamental framing, made of stanchions, at the after-beams of the forecastle, with a covering, under which the ship's bell is hung.' Weale's *Rudim. Navigation.*

1769 FALCONER *Dict. Marine* (1789), *Ecusson*,..a.. scutcheon upon the stern, forecastle, or belfry. **1776** *Phil. Trans.* LXVII. 88 The electrical matter darted from the mast to the belfry.

6. *attrib.*, as in ***belfry-key, -stage, -tower, -window***.

1870 F. WILSON *Ch. Lindisf.* 169 The belfry stage has semi-circular headed couplets. **1874** PARKER *Illustr. Goth. Archit.* I. vi. 202 Magdalen College.. tower was originally intended to stand alone as a campanile, or belfry-tower. **1879** SIR G. SCOTT *Lect. Archit.* II. 38 The belfry-windows are often of two lights. **1883** *St. James's Gaz.* 30 Nov. 5/1 [The churchwardens] have also the custody of the belfry-keys.

†**bel'gard**. *Obs.* [ad. It. *bel guardo* 'lovely look.']

A kind or loving look.

1590 SPENSER *F.Q.* II. iii. 25 Upon her eyelids many graces sate.. Working belgardes and amorous retrate. **1593** BARNES *Parthenophil & P.* in Arb. *Garner* V. 385 To bandy with belguards in interchange. **1610** G. FLETCHER *Christ's Vict.* I. xlvi, They move To earth their amourous belgards from above.

Belgic ('bɛldʒɪk), *a.* and *sb.* [f. L. *Belgicus*, *Belgæ*, + -IC.]

A. *adj.* **a.** Of or pertaining to the Belgæ (see BELGIUM).

1589 A. FLEMING tr. *Virgil's Georg.* III. 43 And he shall better beare and draw *Belgic* coches with His gentle soft or tender necke. **1740** STUKELEY *Stonehenge* xi. 47 It seems not improbable, that the Wansdike was made, when this Belgic kingdom was at its height. **1743** —— *Abury* vii. 28 The great belgic rampart, the Wansdike, licks all the southern horizon. **1835** *Penny Cycl.* IV. 177/2 The whole southern coast from Suffolk to Devonshire was occupied by Belgic tribes. **1947** J. & C. HAWKES *Prehist. Britain* vi. 121 The Belgæ.. had overflowed into south-eastern Britain, and had made the lands they had settled provinces of Belgic culture.

b. Of or pertaining to the Netherlands.

1618 *Barnevelt's Apol.* F b, That difficult, bloudy and chargeable Belgicke Warre. **1764** GOLDSM. *Trav.* 313 Their Belgic sires of old!

B. *sb.* A Low German.

1608 TOPSELL *Serpents* 647 Called.. of the Belgics 'Besonder Strael,' of the Spaniards 'Zangane.'

Hence **'Belgicized** *ppl. a.* (esp. of pottery), made Belgic in form, appearance, etc. So **,Belgici'zation**.

1941 *Oxoniensia* VI. 87 Belgicized pottery.. dating just before or just after the Roman conquest. **1942** *Ibid.* VII. 59 Sherds from a quarry on Akeman Street... The cordoned forms indicate fairly recent Belgicisation, but may prove to be survivals into the post-conquest period.

Belgium ('bɛldʒɪəm). **a.** Latin name of the territory occupied by the Belgæ, stretching from the Marne and Seine to the Rhine; **b.** subsequently used loosely as an appellation for Low Germany or the Netherlands; **c.** in 1830 adopted as title of the new kingdom established by the separation of the provinces watered by the Meuse and Scheldt from the kingdom of the Netherlands. **Belgia** = prec. b. **Belgian** ('bɛldʒɪən), *a.*, of or pertaining to Belgium; as *sb.* †(*a*) one of the ancient Belgæ of southern England; †(*b*) a Low German; (*c*) a native of modern Belgium; (*d*) a kind of canary. †**'Belgies** *sb. pl.* = BELGIAN *sb.* (*b*).

1602 WARNER *Alb. Eng.* x. lxi. 267 By Embassies Spayne often mou'd to doe the *Belgies right. **1623** COCKERAM II, *Netherland*, *Belgian. *Ibid.* III, **Belgeans*, People of the low Countries, Somerset-shire, Wiltshire and Hampshire. **1629** HEYLIN, *Microcosm*... Germany is divided into the higher and the lower; the latter is called Belgium. **1631** CHAPMAN *Cæsar & P.* Plays (1873) III. 128 Britaine, *Belgia, France & Germanie. **1709** *Lond. Gaz.* No. 4584/4 A neat and large Map of Modern *Belgium, or Lower Germany. **1835** MARRYAT *Olla Podr.* vi, *Belgian flags, of yellow, red, and black. **1865** *Derby Merc.* 25 Jan., The crested *Belgians.. had five entries.

Belgravia (bɛl'greɪvɪə). [f. *Belgrave* Square, named after Belgrave, a town in Leicestershire + -IA.] A fashionable residential district in London, south of Knightsbridge. Hence **Bel'gravian** *a.*, pertaining to, or characteristic of, Belgravia; as *sb.*, a resident of Belgravia.

1848 THACKERAY *Van. F.* li, Ask the Reverend Mr. Thurifer if Belgravia is not a sounding brass, and Tyburnia a tinkling cymbal. *Ibid.*, Her [*sc.* Semele's] myth ought to be taken to heart amongst.. the Belgravians. **1849** —— *Pendennis* I. xxxvii. 358 The most elderly Belgravian Venus, or inveterate Mayfair Jezebel. **1850** C. KINGSLEY *Alton Locke* I. ii. 34 Shriek not in your Belgravian saloons. **1851** KNIGHT *Cycl. Lond.* 758 Architecture.. in the Belgravian style. *a* **1852** MAYHEW *Lond. Labour* (1861) II. 395/2 The patrician squares of what has been called Belgravia and Tyburnia. **1864** M. ARNOLD *Let.* 10 May (1895) I. 232, I just get here, within reach of the Belgravian paradise. **1882** *Encycl. Brit.* XIV. 851/1 The fashionable Belgravia was built about 1825. **1891** *Athenæum* 27 June 824/2 That ineffable Belgravian, Lady Galbraith. *Ibid.*, The De Moleyns are excellent conventional Belgravians.

beli, obs. sing. f. of BELLY and BELLOWS.

Belial ('bi:lɪəl). Also 6 **Belyall**. [a. Heb. *b'li-yaʿal*, f. *b'li* not, without + *yaʿal* use, profit; hence lit. 'worthlessness,' and 'destruction'; but in later use and in the N.T. treated as a proper name = ὁ πονηρός, the evil one, Satan. In the Eng. transl. it is retained untranslated in the phrase 'sons of Belial' and the like, as it is generally also in the Vulgate, though in *1 Kings* xxi. 13 it is rendered *filii diaboli*, as in mediæval use.]

1. The spirit of evil personified; used from early times as a name for the Devil or one of the fiends, and by Milton as the name of one of the fallen angels. Also *attrib.*

c **1225** *Juliana* 38 Ich am þe deouel belial, deoflene wurest, ant mest is awariet. *Ibid.* 16 ȝe beliales budeles. **1377** LANGL. *P. Pl.* B. XVIII. 319 And with þat breth helle brake with Beliales barres. *c* **1384** WYCLIF *De Eccl.* Sel. Wks. III. 339 Christ comouneþ not wiþ Belial. **1572** FORREST *Theoph.* 416 This Belyall bill written with his bloode. **1663** *Bk. Com. Prayer, Chas. Mart.*, In permitting cruel men, sons of Belial, (as on this day) to imbrue their hands in the blood of thine Anointed. **1667** MILTON *P.L.* I. 490 Belial came last, then whom a Spirit more lewd Fell not from Heaven. **1822** SCOTT *Monast.* xxxiv, A scoffer, a debauched person, and, in brief, a man of Belial. **1879** FARRAR *St. Paul* II. 108 *note*, Belial is not originally a proper name.. this is why there was no worship of Belial.

Hence **Beli'alic** *a.*, **'Belialist**.

1631 BP. WEBBE *Quietn.* (1657) 145 The most unquiet Belialist in his parish. **1656** TRAPP *Comm. Matt.* xi. 29 Christians must not be yokeless.. Belialists. **1822** *Blackw. Mag.* XI. 464 Belialic qualities I could not have expected to find in him.

belibel (bɪ'laɪb(ə)l), *v.* [f. BE- 4 + LIBEL *v.*] *trans.* To assail with libels; to traduce, slander, calumniate. Hence **be'libelled** *ppl. a.*

a **1626** BRETON *Packet Lett.* II. xvi, Belibelling the wicked, abusing the honest, or pleasing the foolish. **1683** CAVE *Ecclesiastici* 493 To be thus traduced and.. be-libelled in publick Sermons. **1881** *Athenæum* 13 Aug. 209/3 Sir John Fastolf, the much be-libelled original of Falstaff.

belick, belish-lash, etc.: see BE- *pref.*

†**belie** (bɪ'laɪ), *v.*[1] *Obs.* Forms: 1 beliċȝan, 2–3 biliggen, 5 ? belye. *Pa. t.* 1 belæȝ, 2–3 bilæi, -lai, 3–5 bi-, by-, be-lay(e. *Pa. pple.* 1 beleȝen, 3–4 bi-, by-, beleyn, -layn(e, -lay(e, 7 beely'd. [OE. *bi-, be-licȝan* = OHG. *biligan, hilikan*, MHG. *biligen*, Ger. *beliegen*, f. *bi-*, BE- about + *ligan*, in OE. *licȝan* to LIE.]

1. *trans.* To lie around, encompass.

a **1000** *Cædmon's Gen.* (Grein) 229 Sio ea Ethiopia land beliȝeð uton. **1430** LYDG. *Chron. Troy* III. xxiv, Dimmed with skyes foule.. with tempest all be-layne. **1627** MAY *Lucan* III. (1631) 219 From Pholoe Beely'd with Centaures.

2. *spec.* To lie with an army round, to beleaguer.

a **1000** ÆLFRIC *Joshua* vii. 9 Hi beliċȝaþ us mid fyrde. *c* **1200** *Trin. Coll. Hom.* 51 þe king.. bilai þe burh ierusalem. *c* **1330** *Arth. & Merl.* 5378 He was belayn in that cite. *c* **1380** *Sir Ferumb.* 4483 Now haþ þe A[meral] by-leyn hem þer.

3. To lie with (carnally).

c **1325** *Cœur de L.* 1119 Hys daughtyr that was bylayn. *c* **1460** *Towneley Myst.* 328, I slew my fader, and syn bylay my moder.

4. *intr.* To lie near; to pertain or belong *to*; *impers.* it is pertinent or proper.

c **1200** *Trin. Coll. Hom.* 15 þe six werkes of þesternesse þe biliȝe to nihte. *Ibid.* 61 þe habbeð þo sinnes don þe bi-liggeð to here shrifte. **1387** TREVISA *Higden* (1865) I. 147 þerto [to Cappadocia] be-lyeþ Cilicia. *a* **1400** *Old Usages Winchester* in T. Smith *Eng. Gilds* (1870) 350 Also twey coroners by-lyth that ther be in Wynchestre. **1522** *World & Child* in Hazl. *Dodsl.* I. 258 Covet..no good that him be-lith.

belie (bɪˈlaɪ), *v.*[2] Forms: 1 beléoȝan, 2-3 -leoȝen, 4-7 belye, 6-8 -ly, 6 -belie. *Pa. t.* 1 beléaȝ, 6- belied. *Pa. pple.* 1 beloȝen, 3-4 belowen, 6- belied. [OE. *beléoȝan* = OFris. *biliuga*, OHG. *biliugan* to lie about, f. *bi-*, BE- + OE. *léoȝan* = Gothic *liugan* to LIE, tell lies. Originally, like the simple LIE, a strong vb., but rare exc. in present in ME.] Always *trans.*

†**1.** To deceive by lying. *Obs.*

a **1000** *Gregory's Dial.* (Bosw.) I. 14 Beloȝen beon, *falli.*

2. To tell lies about; *esp.* to calumniate by false statements.

a **1225** *Ancr. R.* 68 þe treowe is misleued, and te sakelease ofte bilowen, uor wone of witnesse. **1377** LANGL. *P. Pl.* B. II. 22 She hath..ylakked my lemman, and bilowen hire to lordes. *Ibid.* v. 414, I haue leuere..lesynges to laughe at and belye my neighbore. **1481** CAXTON *Reynard* (Arb.) 96 He belyeth me falsely. **1581** J. BELL *Haddon's Answ. Osor.* 490 Wherein you doe unhonestlye slaunder him and belye him, without cause. **1667** PEPYS *Diary* (1879) IV. 396 Saying that he had belied him to our King. **1762** HUME *Hist. Eng.* (1806) IV. lxiv. 762 It was rendered criminal to belie the subjects of the king. **1876** HOLLAND *Sev. Oaks* xv. 213, I think she is shamefully belied.

†**b.** ***to belie the truth.*** *Obs.*

1377 LANGL. *P. Pl.* B. x. 22 þei lede lordes with lesynges and bilyeth treuthe. **1635** AUSTIN *Medit.* 123 The Judge of Heaven is judg'd; the Truth be-lide.

†**3.** To assert or allege falsely, or with a lie.

1561 DAUS. tr. *Bullinger on Apoc.* (1573) 123 He belyed hymselfe to be the Prophet of God. **1581** J. BELL *Haddon's Answ. Osor.* 110b, Whiche..is most falsely belyed upon him. **1659** MILTON *Hirelings* Wks. 1738 I. 570 To belye divine Authority, to make the name of Christ accessory to Violence.

4. To give a false representation or account of, to misrepresent; to present in a false character.

1601 CORNWALLYES *Ess.* xxii, It is a strange thing how men bely themselves: every one speaks well, and meanes noughtily. **1649** MILTON *Eikon.* 143 He a declar'd Papist, If his own letter to the Pope belye him not. **1709** LADY M. W. MONTAGUE *Lett.* lxiv. II. 106, I know not..how much my face may belie my heart. **1814** BYRON *Lara* I. xxi, His brow belied him if his soul was sad. **1851** KINGSLEY *Yeast* xv. You are an Englishman..unless your physiognomy belies you. *absol.* **1871** R. ELLIS *Catullus* x. 16 They grow quantities, if report belies not.

†**b.** To disguise (a person or thing) so as to make it appear something else. *Obs.*

1711 POPE *Temple F.* 154 His hornèd head bely'd the Libian God. *a* **1725** —— *Odyss.* IV. 618 A boar's obscener shape the god belies. **1810** CROMEK *Nithsd. & Galloway Song* App. (1880) 225 To belie the form of God in the unholy semblance of cats.

†**c.** To assume falsely the character of; to counterfeit. *Obs. rare.*

a **1700** DRYDEN (J.) Durst, with horses hoofs that beat the ground, And martial brass, belie the thunder's sound.

†**5.** To give the lie to, call false, contradict as a lie or a liar; to reject as false, deny the truth of.

1577 HOLINSHED *Chron.* III. 1158/1 This that I haue said, I will stand vnto, for I will neuer beelie my selfe. **1611** BIBLE *Jer.* v. 12 They haue belyed the Lord, and said; It is not he. **1626** T. H. tr. *Caussin's Holy Crt.* 21, I will not be-lye the law of my Maister. **1649** *Alcoran* 45 If they bely thee, know, they belyed the Prophets that were before thee.

6. To call (a thing) false practically, to treat it as false by speaking or acting at variance with it; to be false or faithless to.

1698 NORRIS *Pract. Disc.* IV. 27 If a Man..does not appear to bely his Discourse by his Practice. **1790** BURKE *Fr. Rev.* 356 Who in his last acts does not wish to belye the tenour of his life. **1810** SHELLEY *Q. Mab* 22 Those who dare belie Their human nature. **1868** G. DUFF *Pol. Surv.* 196 Her life as a nation will not belie her great gifts as a country. **1868** FREEMAN *Norm. Conq.* (1876) II. viii. 207 But..he grossly belied his faith.

7. To show to be false, prove false or mistaken; to falsify (expectations, etc.).

1685 tr. *Gracian's Courtier's Orac.* 7 It is the victory of an able man to correct, or at least bely the censure. **1781** COWPER *Retirem.* 714 Novels..Belie their name, and offer nothing new. **1833** HT. MARTINEAU *Tale of Tyne* iii. 53 There was..a quaver of the voice which belied what he said. **1857** BUCKLE *Civiliz.* vi. 296 The subsequent actions of Arthur did not belie his supernatural origin.

†**8.** ? To fill with lies. *Obs. rare.*

1611 SHAKS. *Cymb.* III. iv. 38 'Tis Slander..whose breath Rides on the posting windes, and doth belye All corners of the World.

belied (bɪˈlaɪd), *ppl. a.* [f. prec. + -ED[1].] Calumniated, falsified, proved false.

1610 G. FLETCHER *Christ's Vict.* in Farr *S.P.* 59 A painted face, belied with vermeyl store. **1848** KINGSLEY *Saint's Trag.* Proem 28 Fathers, long belied, and long forsaken. **1853** MAURICE *Proph. & Kings* xix. 339 But the words lived on, established, not belied, by that apparent confutation.

belied, obs. form of BELLIED.

belief (bɪˈliːf). Forms: 2 bileafe, 2-3 -leaue, 2-5 -leue, 5 -leve, 4-6 beleue, -ve, 5-6 -leeve, 6-7 -leefe, 7 -liefe, 7- belief. (Also 5 bileeve, byleyue, belyefe, 5-6 byleue, -ve, 6 b'leue, 6-7 *Sc.* beleif.) [Early ME. *bileafe, -leaue, -leue,* f. *bi-*, BE- + *leafe*:—OE. (Northumb.) *léafa*, shortened from *ȝe-léafa* 'belief,' a common WGer. abstract sb. (= OS. *gilôbo*, MDu. *gelôve*, Du. *geloof*, OHG. *giloubo*, MHG. *geloube*, Ger. *glaube*):—OTeut. type **galaubon-* (but not found in Gothic, which had the cogn. *galaubeins* fem.); f. *galaub-* 'dear, esteemed, valued, valuable'; see BELIEVE. The orig. *ȝeléafa*, *ileafe*, ILEVE, and its short form *léafa*, *leafe*, LEVE, survived till the 13th c., when the present compound, which had appeared already in the 12th c., superseded both. The *be-*, which is not a natural prefix of nouns, was prefixed on the analogy of the vb. (where it is naturally an intensive), so that *believe*, *belief*, go together, as the earlier *ȝelíefan*, *ȝeléafa*, and *líefan*, *léafa*, did. The vowel of the sb. (*éa*) and vb. (WSax. *íe*, Anglian *é*) were originally different; but the distinction was lost in ME. On the other hand the final consonants were differentiated in 16th c. the sb. changing from *beleeve* to *beleefe*, apparently by form-analogy with pairs like *grieve grief*, *prove proof*. The normal mod.Eng. would have been *beleave* or *beleeve*.]

1. The mental action, condition, or habit, of trusting to or confiding in a person or thing; trust, dependence, reliance, confidence, faith. Const. *in* (*to*, *of* obs.) a person.

(*Belief* was the earlier word for what is now commonly called *faith*. The latter originally meant in Eng. (as in OFrench) 'loyalty to a person to whom one is bound by promise or duty, or to one's promise or duty itself,' as in 'to keep faith, to break faith,' and the derivatives *faithful*, *faithless*, in which there is no reference to 'belief'; i.e. 'faith' was = fidelity, fealty. But the word *faith* being, through OF. *fei, feith*, the etymological representative of the L. *fides*, it began in the 14th c. to be used to translate the latter, and in course of time almost superseded 'belief,' esp. in theological language, leaving 'belief' in great measure to the merely intellectual process or state in sense 2. Thus 'belief in God' no longer means as much as 'faith in God' (cf. quot. 1814 in 2). See BELIEVE 1, and 1 b.)

c **1175** *Lamb. Hom.* 101 Cristene men ne sculen heore bileafe bisettan on þere weor[l]dliche eahte. *c* **1375** WYCLIF *Serm.* Sel. Wks. I. 59 Affie þe, douȝter, þi bileve haþ made þee saif. *c* **1386** CHAUCER *2nd Nonnes. T.* 63 And though that I, unworthy sone of Eve, Be synful, yet accepte my bileve. *c* **1400** *Melayne* 438 What myghte es in a rotyn tree þat ȝoure byleue es in. *c* **1450** *Merlin* 50 It is grete merveile that ye haue so grete bileve to this man. **1508** FISHER *Wks.* 271 A stedfast byleue of God. **1535** COVERDALE *Tob.* ii, We..loke for the life, which God shal geue vnto them, that neuer turne their beleue from him. **1626** BACON *Sylva* §327 We knew a Dutch-man, that had wrought himself into the beleif of a great Person by undertaking that he could make Gold. **1837** CARLYLE *Fr. Rev.* I. IV. iv. 183 Belief in high-plumed hats of a feudal cut; in heraldic scutcheons; in the divine right of Kings. **1859** TENNYSON *Elaine* 961 Beyond mine old belief in womanhood.

b. *absol.* Trust in God; the Christian virtue of faith. *arch.* or *Obs.*

c **1375** WYCLIF *Serm.* Sel. Wks. I. 21 Neither wiþ figis of bileve, ne wiþ grapis of devocioun. *c* **1400** *Apol. Loll.* Introd. 6 It is sooth that bileue is grounde of alle vertues. *c* **1400** *Destr. Troy* x. 4287 ffor lacke of beleue þai light into errour, and fellen vnto fals goddes. **1578** Q. ELIZAB. in Farr *S.P.* (1845) I. 1 Who shall therefor from Syon geue That helthe whych hangeth on our b'leue? **1593** HOOKER *Eccl. Pol.* III. i. §5 The Church hath from the apostles..received belief. **1840** CARLYLE *Heroes* vi. 320 That war of the Puritans..the war of Belief against Unbelief.

†**c.** ***out of belief***: unbelieving, outside the pale of the faith. *Obs.*

1493 *Festivall* (W. de W. 1515) 60 The Jewe that was out of beleve.

2. Mental acceptance of a proposition, statement, or fact, as true, on the ground of authority or evidence; assent of the mind to a statement, or to the truth of a fact beyond observation, on the testimony of another, or to a fact or truth on the evidence of consciousness; the mental condition involved in this assent. Constr. *of* a statement, or (*obs.*) a speaker; *that* ...; *belief in* (a thing); persuasion of its existence.

1533 FRITH *Bk. agst. Rastell* (1829) 236 That I would bring the people in belief that repentance of a man helpeth not for the remission of his sin. **1580** SIDNEY *Arcadia* III. (1590) 385 My onely defence shal be beleefe of nothing. **1680** MORDEN *Geog. Rect.* (1685) 254 There is no belief of men that were always accounted Lyers. **1790** BOSWELL *Johnson* 100 We talked of belief in ghosts. **1814** WORDSW. *Excursion* IV. Wks. VII. 161 One in whom persuasion and belief Had ripened into faith. **1843** MILL *Logic* I. i. §2 The simplest act of belief supposes, and has something to do with, two objects. **1849** ABP. THOMSON *Laws Th.* §118 (1860) 240 The amount of belief we have in our judgment has been called its Modality, as being the mode in which we hold it for truth. **1872** CALDERWOOD *Handbk. Mor. Philos.* (1874) 248 Belief is the assent of the mind to a truth, while the reality so acknowledged is not matter of observation. *Mod.* His statements are unworthy of belief.

3. The thing believed; the proposition or set of propositions held true; in early usage, *esp.* the doctrines believed by the professors of a religious system, a religion. In modern use often simply = opinion, persuasion.

a **1225** *St. Marher.* 4 Ant heide his hethene godes..ant lei to his luthere bileaue. *a* **1340** HAMPOLE *Pr. Consc.* 4335 And turne þam til a fals belyefe. *c* **1380** *Sir Ferumb.* 829 Til he wer cristned..& y-broȝt to þe riȝt beleue. **1393** GOWER *Conf.* II. 152 The beleves, that tho were. *c* **1400** MAUNDEV. x. 121 Thei holden the Beleeve amonges us. **1530** RASTELL *Bk. Purgat.* II. iv, Of thys beleve, that the soule shall never dye. **1535** COVERDALE *Esther* viii. 17 Many of the people in the londe became of the Iewes beleue. **1714** LADY M. W. MONTAGUE *Lett.* lxxxvi. II. 141 It is my belief you will not be at all the richer. **1836** HOR. SMITH *Tin Trump.* (1876) 56 Throughout the world belief depends chiefly upon localities, and the accidents of birth. **1877** E. CONDER *Bas. Faith* i. 8 The belief that there is no God is as definite a creed as the belief in one God or in many gods.

b. The term is applied by some philosophers to the primary or ultimate principles of knowledge received on the evidence of consciousness; intuition, natural judgement.

1838 SIR W. HAMILTON in *Reid's Wks.* 743/1 *note*, The primary truths of fact, and the primary truths of intelligence (the contingent and necessary truths of Reid) form two very distinct classes of the original beliefs or intuitions of consciousness. **1877** CONDER *Basis of Faith* iv. 157 Primary judgments (as that every change must have a cause) are often called beliefs, though 'intuitions' would be a better term.

4. A formal statement of doctrines believed, a creed. ***the Belief***: the 'Apostles' Creed.' *arch.*

c **1175** *Lamb. Hom.* 73 Buten heo cunnen heore bileue. þet is . pater noster . and credo. **1377** LANGL. *P. Pl.* B. v. 7, I..sat softly adown and seide my bileue. *c* **1550** *How Plowm. lerned Pater-Noster* 54 in Hazl. *E.P.P.* 211, I mervayll ryght gretly, That thy byleve was never taught the. **1637** HEYWOOD *Dialogues* i. 101 Some sung, and some did say Haile Virgin: others, their Beleefe. **1712** PRIDEAUX *Direct. Ch.-Wardens* (ed. 4) 11 Kneeling at the Prayers, Standing at the Belief. **1840** MARRYAT *Olla Podr.* (Rtldg.) 331, I said..the Belief.

†**5.** Confident anticipation, expectation. *Obs.*

1513 DOUGLAS *Æneis* x. ix. 44 That gude beleif quhilk thou has eyk Of Ascanyvs vprysyng to estait. **1535** STEWART *Cron. Scot.* II. 235 In the feild sa mony als war slane, Without beleif to gif battell agane.

†**beliefful** (bɪˈliːfful), *a. arch.* or *Obs.* Forms: 2-3 bileaful, bileffull, 6 beliefull. [f. prec. + -FUL.] Full of faith, believing.

c **1175** *Lamb. Hom.* 73 þet heo sculen beon bileffulle. *c* **1200** *Trin. Coll. Hom.* 25 þe rihtwise and þe bileafule. **1548** UDALL, etc. *Erasm. Par. Luke* i. (R.) A minde beliefull and readie to obeie.

beˈlieffulness. *arch.* [f. prec. + -NESS.] The quality of being full of belief or faith.

1548 UDALL, etc. *Erasm. Par. Luke* iv. 24 Y[e] godly beliefulnesse of the heathen. **1853** CLOUGH *Poems & Pr. Rem.* I. 213 And there is a hopefulness and a belieffulness, so to say, on your side.

beliefless (bɪˈliːflɪs), *a.* [f. BELIEF + -LESS.] Without belief or faith.

1612 SYLVESTER *Henrie Gt.* Wks. 512 (D.) Heav'n's Embassage to Belief-less Soules. **1849** CLOUGH *Relig. Poems* xiii. 81 We are most hopeless, who had once most hope, And most beliefless, that had most believed.

belier (bɪˈlaɪə(r)). [f. BELIE *v.*[2] + -ER[1].] One who belies.

1547 COVERDALE *Old Faith* Prol. Wks. 1844 I 8 Blasphemers, backbiters, beliers of good men. **1605** B. JONSON *Volpone* II. ii. (1616) 467 Belyers Of great-mens fauors. **1824** COLERIDGE *Aids Refl.* (1848) I. 89 Foul-mouthed beliers of the Christian faith and history.

believability (bɪˌliːvəˈbɪlɪtɪ). [f. next: see -BILITY.] Capability of being believed, credibility.

1865 MILL *Logic* (ed.6) I. 305.

believable (bɪˈliːvəb(ə)l), *a.* [f. BELIEVE *v.* + -ABLE.] Capable of being believed; credible.

1382 WYCLIF *Ps.* xcii[i]. 5 Thi witnessingis ben maad beleevable ful myche. **1548** GESTE *Pr. Masse* 86 Ryght true and belevable. **1611** COTGR., *Credible*, beleeuable; to be credited or beleeued. **1859** TENNYSON *Vivien* 610 And that he sinn'd, is not believable.

beˈlievableness. [f. prec. + -NESS.] The quality of being believable; credibility.

a **1679** T. GOODWIN *Wks.* IV. I. 88 The credibility and believableness, as I call it, of those promises. —— Wks. 1864 VIII. 116 Gives a subsistence to the object of faith that doth put into it..a being of believableness.

believe (bɪˈliːv), *v.* Forms: 2-3 bileuen, 4-5 bileue, -leve, -leeve, 4-6 beleue, -leve, 6-7 -leeve, 6- believe. (Also, 3 biliuen, byleuen, 4-5 byleeue, 4-6 byleue, -leve, 7 -leeue, -leive.) *Pa. t.* and *pple.* believed, *occas.* in 6-7 beleft (still *dial.*). [Early ME. *bileven*, f. *bi-*, BE- + *leven*:—OE., Anglian *léfan*, short. f. *ȝeléfan*, WSax. *ȝelíefan*, *ȝelýfan*, a Common Teut. vb. (in OS. *gilôbian*, Du. *gelooven*, OHG. *gilouben*, MHG. *gelouben*, *glöuben*, mod.G. *glauben* (earlier *glouben*, Gothic *galaubjan*):—OTeut. **galaubian* to believe, probably, 'to hold estimable, valuable, pleasing, or satisfactory, to be satisfied with,' f. *galaub-* 'dear, pleasing'; cf. Goth. *liuban*, *lauf*, *lubum*, *lubans*, Teut. root **lub-*, Aryan *lubh-*, to hold dear, to like, whence also LOVE, LIEF. The original *ȝeléfan*, *ileven*, ILEVE, survived to the

14th c., and the shortened LEVE to the 15th; the present compound, which eventually superseded both, appears in the 12th. The historical form is *beleeve*. *Believe* is an erroneous spelling of the 17th c., prob. after *relieve* (from Fr.). Cf. BELIEF.]

I. *intr.*

1. To have confidence or faith *in* (a person), and consequently to rely upon, trust to. Const. *in*, and (in theological language) *on* (*an* obs.); formerly with *into*, *unto*, *of* (rare). *On hine ʒelýfan* to believe *in* or *on* him, was common in OE. No difference can be detected between the use of 'believe *in*' and 'believe *on*,' in the 16th c. versions of the Scriptures, except that the latter was more frequent; it is now used chiefly (but not exclusively) of 'saving faith.'

a. To believe in *a person* (also in Scripture in, or on, *his name*). [Cf. late L. *credere in aliquem*.]

c **1200** *Trin. Coll. Hom.* 23 Ich bileue on þe holie gost. *Ibid.* 19 To bileuen in god. *c* **1205** LAY. 13966 Woden ure lauerd, þe we on bi-liueð. **1340** *Ayenb.* 12 Ich beleue ine God. *c* **1380** WYCLIF *Wicket* (1828) 16 Into whome ye nowe not seynge bileue. **1382** —— *John* i. 12 To hem that bileueven in his name [so **1388**, *Geneva*, *Rhem.*; but TIND. CRANM., **1611** To them that beleeue on his name]. *Ibid.* viii. 30 Many men bileueden in to him [**1388** in hym; TIND., CRANM., *Geneva*, **1611** on him; *Rhem.* in him]. *Ibid.* xiv. 1 ȝe bileuen in to God, and bileue ȝe in to me [**1388**, TIND., CRANM., *Geneva*, *Rhem.*, **1611** in God..in me]. **1549** *Bk. Com. Prayer* Q vj, I Beleue in God the father almightie, maker of heauen and yearth. **1649** BP. REYNOLDS *Hosea* iii. 7 All that should beleeve on him unto eternall life. **1860** PUSEY *Min. Proph.* 279 To believe God is to believe what God says, to be true. To believe in or on God, expresses not belief only, but that belief resting in God, trusting itself and all its concerns with Him.

b. To believe in *a thing*, e.g. the truth of a statement or doctrine; also in mod. usage, in the genuineness, virtue, or efficacy of a principle, institution, or practice.

c **1250** LAY. 13890 ȝoure bi-leue þat ȝeo an bi-lefeþ. **1569** J. ROGERS *Gl. Godly Love* 181 We repent and beleeve in the promise of God in Christ. **1865** MOZLEY *Mirac.* vii. 139 In this sense St. Paul, if I may use the expression, believes in human nature; he thinks it capable of rising to great heights even in this life. *a* **1887** *Mod.* To believe in universal suffrage, free education, vegetarianism, the college system; *colloq.* To believe in public schools, in the roast beef of Old England, in bicycles, the telephone, gas, etc. **1948** G. VIDAL *City & Pillar* (1949) I. v. §2. 117 Sullivan believed in exercise.

c. Formerly with *of* = *on*, *in*.

c **1532** LD. BERNERS *Huon* (1883) 464 They were al content to leue theyr law and to byleue of Iesu chryst. **1630** PAGITT *Christianogr.* I. iii. (1636) 160 They do not well beleeve of the primacy of the Bishop of Rome.

d. *absol.* To exercise faith.

1377 LANGL. *P. Pl.* B. v. 598 All þe wallis ben of witte.. Boterased with bileue-so-or-þow-beest-nouȝte-ysaved. **1562** J. HEYWOOD *Prov. & Epigr.* (1867) 74 Beleue well, and haue well, men say. **1611** BIBLE *Mark* v. 36 Be not afraid, onely beleeue. **1627** SANDERSON *12 Serm.* (1637) 252 Who so forward as they to repent, and beleeue, and reforme their liues. **1633** DONNE *Poems* (1650) 7, I can love..Her who beleeves, and her who tries. **1870** M. CONWAY *Earthw. Pilgr.* xiv. 178 The man who really believes follows that which he believes, fearless of consequences.

e. *absol.* To think. Cf. 7.

1749 FIELDING *Tom Jones* II. vii. (1840) 160/2, I will not believe so meanly of you.

†**2.** To give credence *to* (a person, or his statement); to trust (from L. *credere alicui*). *Obs.* Replaced by 5, 6.

1382 WYCLIF *1 John* iv. 1 Nyl ȝee bileue to eche spirit. —— *John* x. 37 If I do not the workis of my fadir nyle ȝe bileue to me [so **1388**; TINDALE and *later versions*, believe me not]. *c* **1430** *Life St. Kath.* xviii. (Gibbs MS.) 71 At þe lest byleueth to ȝoure owne goddes [*diis saltem vestris credite*]. **1530** LOVE *Bonavent. Mirr.* (W. de W.) iii, Mary through mekenes byleuynge to the aungell Gabryell. **1647** W. BROWNE *Polexander* I. 67 Beleeve lesse to your courage then judgement.

3. *ellipt.* To believe *in* (a person or thing), i.e. in its actual existence or occurrence.

1716 LADY M. W. MONTAGUE *Lett.* ix. I. 29, I find that I have..a strong disposition to believe in miracles. **1877** SPARROW *Serm.* xxii. 290 No civilized..nation appears.. which did not believe in a God. *Mod.* To believe in ghosts, in the sea-serpent, in Romulus and Remus.

†**4.** To trust, expect, think *to do* (something). *Obs.* Cf. BELIEF 5.

c **1400** *Destr. Troy* XXVII. 10919 Priam was proude, & prestly beleuyt For to couer of care thurgh hir kyd helpe. *c* **1550** *Scot. Poems 16th C.* II. 109 Beleuand for to bring vs to despair. **1560** WHITEHORNE *Arte of Warre* (1573) 107 b, There shall never bee founde any good mason whiche will beleeve to bee able to make a faire image of a peece of Marbell ill hewed.

II. *trans.*

5. To give credence to (a person in making statements, etc.). Object orig. *dat.*: cf. 2. Phrases. ***I believe you***, an expression of emphatic agreement; ***believe (you) me***, phr. strengthening an assertion.

1393 GOWER *Conf.* I. 13 But if Gregoire be beleved, As it is in the bokes write. *c* **1450** *Merlin* 3 Sholde he be bileved of moche peple. **1590** SHAKS. *Com. Err.* v. i. 306 You are now bound to beleeue him. **1611** BIBLE *Ex.* xix. 9 That the people may..beleeue thee for euer. **1627** MAY *Lucan* VIII. 20 And scarse is he Beleft, relating his owne misery. **1646** CRASHAW *Delights of Muses* 130 The modest front of this small floore, Beleeve mee, Reader can say more Then many a braver Marble can. *a* **1674** CLARENDON *Hist. Reb.* I. I. 4 A man..who deserves to be believed. **1743** FIELDING *J. Wild* III. iii. 208 Believe me, Lad, the Tongue of a Viper is less hurtful than that of a Slanderer. **1790** WALPOLE *Let.* 11 Dec. (1944) XI. 158 Believe me it is not for my own sake that I desire this. **1820** MOORE *Irish Melodies* 51 Believe me, if all those endearing young charms..Were to change by to-morrow [etc.]. **1832** DICKENS *Let.* 4 Feb. (1965) I. 3 Believe me Yours Truly Charles Dickens. **1834** —— *Sk. Boz* (1836) ser. I. I. 175 'Were you not a little surprised?' 'I b'lieve you!' **1859** TENNYSON *Enid* 1592, I do believe yourself against yourself. **1910** KIPLING *Rewards & Fairies* 233 'The tides run something furious here.' 'I believe you,' said the Archbishop. **1918** C. SANDBURG *Cornhuskers* 30 Pike's Peak is a big old stone, believe me. **1926** *S.P.E. Tract* XXIV. 119 Believe *me* (sometimes expanded to 'believe you me')—take my word for it. **1943** 'E. M. DELAFIELD' *Late & Soon* iv. 63 Believe you me, that's no hardship. *Ibid.* ix. 123 Believe you me, in all the years, and all the adventures I've deliberately sought out..it's never been like this. **1951** L. MACNEICE tr. *Goethe's Faust* II. iv. p. 256 No, you shall win it, believe you me. It's you to-day are C. in C. **1967** 'O. MILLS' *Death enters Lists* v. 47 *Someone's* making a good thing out of the contracts, believe you me.

6. a. To give credence to, to accept (a statement) as true [cf. L. *credere aliquid*]. Also in colloq. phrases strengthening an assertion, as ***believe it or not, would you believe it?*** (see WILL *v.*[1] 43), ***you'd better believe*** (see BETTER *a.* 4 b).

c **1315** SHOREHAM 7 He that bilefeth hit nauȝt. **1340** *Ayenb.* 151 Huanne me belefþ..al þet God made, zayþ, and hat. *c* **1380** WYCLIF *Wicket* (1828) 6 They make us beleue a false law. **1528** MORE *Heresyes* I. Wks. 133/1 Ye be so cyrcumspect that ye will nothing beleue without good sufficient & full profe. **1549** *Bk. Com. Prayer, Athan. Cr.*, This is the Catholike faithe: whiche excepte a man beleue faithfully, he cannot be saued. **1627** MAY *Lucan* VI. 262 Aulus beleft These fained words of his. **1649** BP. REYNOLDS *Hosea* ii. 71 Our faith to beleeve Gods promises. **1667** MILTON *P.L.* x. 42 Believing lies Against his Maker. **1741** WATTS *Improv. Mind* II. iii. 264 Men cannot believe what they will. **1776** H. MORE *Let.* (1925) 33 Would you believe it? In the midst of all the pomps and vanities of this wicked town, I have taken it into my head to study like a dragon. **1855** H. REED *Lect. Eng. Hist.* ii. 67 It is..as irrational to believe too little, as to believe too much. **1860** TYNDALL *Glac.* I. §24. 171 The Guide Chef evidently did not believe a word of it. **1860** TROLLOPE *Framley P.* II. ii. 35 Now, would you believe it? I have used up three lifts of notepaper already. **1929** R. L. RIPLEY (*title*) Believe it or not! **1931** L. STEFFENS *Autobiogr.* III. xxxvi. 617 But the only individual he ever exposed was Martin Lomasy, who, believe it or not, was one of the best men I met in Boston. **1968** *Sunday Express* 8 Dec. 8/1 Having died for a minute and a half I suppose I am one of those believe-it-or-not Ripley characters.

†**b.** To accept (a thing) as authentic. *Obs.*

1721 STRYPE *Eccl. Mem.* II. I. xv. 118 That these pensions should presently be sent to the hands of the auditors..with strait commandment to believe the same patents immediately.

7. With clause or equivalent inf. phrase: To hold it as true *that*..., to be of opinion, think.

1297 R. GLOUC. 229 þe heþene Englysse men..Byleuede, þat in heuene Godes hii were bo. **1393** GOWER *Conf.* I. 273 To make us full beleve That he was verray Goddes sone. **1513** BRADSHAW *St. Werburge* (1848) 32 Who byleveth her chast. **1603** SHAKS. *Meas. for M.* III. ii. 27, I beleeue I know the cause. **1667** MILTON *P.L.* I. 144 Our Conqu'ror whom I now Of force believe Almighty. **1719** DE FOE *Crusoe* (1858) 312 He believed there were more wolves a coming. **1853** H. ROGERS *Ecl. Faith* 326 He believes..that 'probability is the guide of life.' **1862** H. SPENCER *First Princ.* II. iv. §52 (1875) 172 If men did not believe this in the strict sense of the word..they still believed that they believed it. **1875** JOWETT *Plato* (ed. 2) I. 151 Some one—Critias, I believe—went on to say.

†**8.** To hold as true the existence of. *Obs.* (Now expressed by 3.)

1481 CAXTON *Reynard* (Arb.) 119 Ther ben many thynges in the world whiche ben byleued though they were neuer seen. **1708** SWIFT *Sentim. Ch. Eng. Man* Wks. 1755 II. I. 57 Whoever professeth himself a member of the Church of England, ought to believe a God. **1732** BERKELEY *Alciphr.* v. §2 Shall we believe a God?

III. ***to make believe***: to pretend. Subst. ***make-believe***: a pretence; see MAKE.

believed (bɪˈliːvd), *ppl. a.* [f. prec. + -ED[1].] Credited, held for true.

1615 W. HULL *Mirr. Maiestie* 21 He is now a beleeued trueth, not yet a seene trueth. **1874** SULLY *Sensation & Int.* 87 The believed reality.

believer (bɪˈliːvə(r)). [f. as prec. + -ER[1].] One who believes. **a.** One who has faith in the doctrines of religion; *esp.* a Christian, Christian disciple.

1549 *Bk. Com. Prayer, Te Deum*, Thou diddest open the kyngdome of heauen to all beleuers. **1611** BIBLE *1 Tim.* iv. 12 Be thou an example of the beleeuers. **1704** NELSON *Fest. & Fasts* xxv. (1739) 319 They who first embraced the Faith were styled Disciples or Believers. **1779** J. NEWTON *Hymn*, How sweet the name of Jesus sounds In a believer's ear.

b. *gen.* One who believes *in*, (or *of*) anything.

a **1600** HOOKER (J.) Discipline began to enter into conflict with Churches which, in extremity, had been believers of it. **1724** SWIFT *Drapier's Lett.* Wks. 1755 V. II. 126, I could get but few believers, when I attempted to justify you. **1876** GREEN *Short. Hist.* viii. §2. 470 James was a fanatical believer in the rights and power of his crown.

beˈlieving, *vbl. sb.* [f. as prec. + -ING[1].] The having faith; confidence, trust; the accepting of a statement as true.

1523 LD. BERNERS *Froiss.* I. cccxlvi. 548 The beleuyng thus of the frenche kyng vpon Clement. **1633** P. FLETCHER *Purple Isl.* III. xxxi, Thy little fault was but too much beleeving. **1796** PEGGE *Anonym.* (1809) 448 Seeing is believing: this old saying is taken to task by those who write upon Faith. **1825** SOUTHEY *Paraguay* IV. 21 How at believing aught should these delay?

beˈlieving, *ppl. a.* [f. as prec. + -ING[2].] That believes, or has faith.

c **1440** *Three Kings Col.* (1885) 2 þes III kynges, þat of myscreauntys were þe first bileuyng men. **1593** SHAKS. *2 Hen. VI*, II. i. 66 God be prays'd, that to beleeuing Soules Giues Light in Darknesse. **1762** GOLDSM. *Nash* 76 Poor, believing girls deceived by such professions. **1875** M. PATTISON *Casaubon* 252 A scandal and stumbling-block to believing calvinists.

beˈlievingly, *adv.* [f. prec. + -LY[2].] In a believing manner, with belief.

1643 CARYL *Sacr. Covt.* 36 Walke believingly. **1824** COLERIDGE *Aids Refl.* (1848) I. 273 Do they believingly suppose a spiritual regenerative power..accompanying the sprinkling of a few drops of water on an infant's face? **1854** JAMES *Ticonder.* III. 173 She gazed at him believingly.

belif(e, obs. form of BELIVE.

beˈlight, *v.*[1] *Obs.* or *dial.* In 3 bilihten, 5 by lyght. [f. BE- + LIGHT.] Hence **beˈlighted** *ppl. a.*

1. *trans.* To light up, illuminate.

c **1200** *Trin. Coll. Hom.* 31 Godes brihtnesse bilihte hem. **1575** LANEHAM *Let.* (1871) 48 Euery room so..well belighted. **1863** BARNES *Rhymes Dorset Dial.* II. 43 Moon-belighted boughs.

2. *intr.* ? To shine up, to dawn.

c **1440** *Morte Arth.* (Roxb.) 55 We shalle hym haue withouten wene To morow or any day by lyght.

†**beˈlike**, *v.*[1] *Obs.* In 3 bilike, 5 belyke. [? f. BE- 5 + LIKE *a.*]

1. *trans.* To make like, to simulate.

a **1250** *Owl & Night.* 839 All thine wordes beth isliked, And so bisemed and biliked, That alle tho that hi avoth Hi weneth that thu segge soth.

2. *trans.* To be like, to resemble.

1481 CAXTON *Reynard* (Arb.) 25 Reynkin my yongest sone, belyketh me so wel, I hope he shal folowe my stappes.

†**belike**, *v.*[2] *Obs.* [f. BE- 2 + LIKE *v.*]

1. *impers.* To be pleasing to, to please.

1764 T. BRYDGES *Homer Travest.* (1797) II. 207 Let him, since it belikes him well, Stay where he is.

2. *trans.* To like, to be pleased with.

1557 NORTH *Gueuara's Diall Pr.* (1582) 403 a, Those that are beloued and belyked of prynces. **1567** TURBERV. *Ovid's Epist.* 144 b, Such things as I in thee should have belikte.

Hence **beˈliked** *ppl. a.*

1557 NORTH *Gueuara's Diall Pr.* (1582) 406 a, Therfore let not the beliked think, if he dare beleeue mee, etc.

belike (bɪˈlaɪk), *adv.* Also 6 belyke, bylyke, -like, 7 bee-like. [? f. *be* = BY *prep.* + LIKE *a.* or *sb.*; ? 'By what is likely, by what seems.']

A. *adv.* To appearance, likely, in all likelihood, probably; not unlikely, perhaps, possibly.

a **1533** FRITH *Purgatory* (1829) 121 Belike this man hath drunk of a merry cup. **1579** FULKE *Heskins' Parl.* 73 By like all their ceremonies bee not so auncient. **1691** WOOD *Ath. Oxon* I. 157 In 1572, and belike before, he had a Chamber. **1741** RICHARDSON *Pamela* I. 238 All these three, belike, went together. **1800** WORDSW. *Pet Lamb*, Things that I know not of belike to thee are dear. **1873** BROWNING *Red Cott. Night-c.* 268 Caterpillar-like..Become the Painted Peacock, or belike The Brimstone-wing.

†**B.** *adj.* Like, likely (*to do* something). *Obs.*

1550 LEVER *Serm.* 30 For they seme belyke to do moste good wyth the ryches. **1805** SOUTHEY *Madoc in W.* IV. Wks. V. 35 They saw..our food belike to fail.

†**beˈlikely**, *adv. Obs.* Also 6 belikly. [f. prec. + -LY[2]; after *likely*.] = prec.

a **1552** LD. SOMERSET in Foxe *A. & M.* 730 b, Images be great letters..and belikly they are so likly to be red amis, that God himself..did forbid them. *a* **1656** BP. HALL *Rem. Wks.* (1660) 9 [He] having belikely heard some better words of me.

†**beˈlim**, *v. Obs.* Forms: 3–4 bilimien, -limen, -lymen, lymme. [f. BE- 6 c. + OE. *lim*, LIMB: cf. *behead*.] *trans.* To cut off a limb or the limbs, to dismember, mutilate; to disfigure.

c **1205** LAY. 29353 Ælcne bileafued mon He lette bi-limien. *c* **1300** *Beket* 560 Bote ther man schal beo bylymed: other to dethe ido. *c* **1330** *Arth. & Merl.* 5775 The Knighte ..Mani ther slough in litel stounde And bilimeden. *a* **1528** SKELTON *Bowge of Courte* 289 His face was belymmed, as byes had him stounge. [Or can this be *belimn*?]

†**beˈlime**, *v. Obs.* or *arch.* [f. BE- 6 + LIME *sb.*]

1. *trans.* To cover as with bird-lime.

1555 *Fardle Facions* Pref. 12 When he..had with all kinde of wickednes belimed yᵉ world. *a* **1656** BP. HALL *Wks.* (1661) II. 301 Ye whose foul hands are belimed with bribery.

2. To entangle as with bird-lime; to ensnare.

1601 DENT *Pathw. Heauen* 83 This world..is very bird-lime, which doth so belime our affectiones, that they cannot ascend vpward. **1651** HOBBES *Leviath.* I. iv. 15 As a bird in lime-twiggs; the more he struggles, the more belimed. *a* **1674** CLARENDON *Surv. Leviath.* (1676) 289 Where he

found it necessary for his own purpose, sometimes to perplex and belime his Readers.

¶ Used for Ger. *leimen* to glue.

1875 B. TAYLOR *Faust* I. vi. 105 Oh be then so good With sweat and with blood The crown to belime!

†**be'limp**, *v. Obs.* Pa. t. belamp. [OE. *belimpan*, f. BE- 2 + *limpan* to happen: see LIMP *v.*[1]]

1. *intr.* To happen, occur, befall (with *dat.* = to).

a **1000** *Beowulf* 4928 þa him sio sar belamp. **1154** *O.E. Chron.* (Laud MS.) an. 1137 §7 Wat belamp on Stephnes kinges time. *a* **1250** *Prov. Ælfred* 486 in *O.E. Misc.* 132 Ef it so bilimpit.

2. To pertain, belong *to*, to befit; also *impers.*

c **888** K. ÆLFRED *Boeth.* xxxviii. §2 Hit belimpþ ȝenoȝ wel to þære spræce. *c* **1175** *Lamb. Hom.* 51 þet scrift þe þer to bilimpeð. *c* **1200** *Trin. Coll. Hom.* 258 Hit bilimpeð forte speke. *c* **1270** in *O.E. Misc.* 146 To Westsexene lawe bilympeþ ix. schiren.

belion, beliquor, etc.: see BE- *pref.*

†**be'lirt**, *v. Obs.* [OE. *belyrtan*; f. BE- 2 + **lyrtan* cogn. w. MHG. *lürzen* 'to deceive,' pointing to a WGer. **lurtjan*, of uncertain derivation; related perh. to MHG. *lerz, lurz* 'left, lefthand,' or perh. to ON. *lortr* ' filth, ordure'; cf. also the Romanic words treated by Diez under *lordo*.] *trans.* To deceive, cheat, befool.

c **950** *Lindisf.* Matt. ii. 16 Ða Herodes.. bisuicen *vel* bilyrtet wæs from dryum. *c* **1220** *Bestiary* 403 in *O.E. Misc.* 13 Forto bilirten fuȝeles. *c* **1250** *Gen. & Ex.* 316 Ic, and eue hise wif, sulen adam bilirten of hise lif. *c* **1400** *Destr. Troy* III. 715 þat such a lady belirt with þi lechur dedes.

belise, obs. form of BELLOWS.

Belisha beacon (bɪ'li:ʃə 'bi:kən). [f. surname of Leslie Hore-*Belisha*, Minister of Transport 1931–7 + BEACON *sb.*] A post about seven feet high surmounted by a flashing amber-coloured globe and erected on the pavement at officially recognized pedestrian crossings of the highway. Also **Belisha**. Hence ***Belisha crossing***.

1934 *Punch* 21 Nov. 583/1 One of the clever people who have been going about stealing and even shooting the Belisha Beacon globes—(1) 'as a protest against their futility'; (2) 'because they slow down the traffic'. *Ibid.* 5 Dec. 617 (*caption*) Why not be in the movement, Sir, and 'ave a Belisha? **1936** *N. & Q.* CLXXI. 355/1 With a view to learning what people in general called these crossings, I asked two intelligent young working-women. One said 'Belisha crossing', the other 'pedestrian crossing'. **1942** *Motor Driving Made Easy* (Autocar) (ed. 7) ix. 121 Once he [*sc.* the pedestrian] has left the pavement at a Belisha beacon, motor and other traffic must yield to him. **1958** L. BLIGHT *Love & Idleness* iii. 29 The yellow belishas going on and off at the zebra crossings.

belitter (bɪ'lɪtə(r)), *v.*[1] [f. BE- 6 + LITTER[1].]

†**1.** *trans.* To strew with litter (for the floor). *Obs.*

1660 FULLER *Mixt Contemp.* (1841) 255 Contented with a house belittered with straw.

2. To bestrew with rubbish or things in disorder.

1678 *Quack's Acad.* in *Harl. Misc.* II. 33 (D.) A chamber ..belittered with urinals or empty gally-pots.

†**be'litter**, *v.*[2] *Obs. rare.* [f. BE- + LITTER[2].] To bring forth a litter, to have young; to litter.

c **1325** *Gloss* in *Rel. Ant.* II. 78 Be-litter, *enfaunter.*

belittle (bɪ'lɪt(ə)l), *v.* [f. BE- + LITTLE *a.* The word appears to have originated in U.S.; whence in recent English use in sense 3.]

1. *trans.* To diminish in size, make small.

1782 JEFFERSON *Notes Virginia* (1787) 107 So far the Count de Buffon has carried this new theory of the tendency of nature to belittle her productions on this side the Atlantic. **1796** MORSE *Amer. Geog.* I. 230 On this side of the Atlantic there is a tendency in nature to belittle her productions. **1866** *N.Y. Herald* Jan., His occupation is not absolutely gone; but the end of the war has belittled it sadly.

2. To cause to appear small; to dwarf.

1850 MISS COOPER *Rur. Hours* I. 127 The hills.. belittle the sheet of water. **1862** B. TAYLOR *Home & Abr.* Ser. II. i. 22 A tower.. not so tall as to belittle the main building.

3. To depreciate, decry the importance of.

1797 *Independent Chron.* (U.S.) 30 Mar., [He] is.. an honorable man,.. let the writers.. endeavour to belittle him as much as they please. **1837** HALIBURTON *Clockm.* Ser. I. xxii. 226 When.. they began to raise my dander, by belittleing the Yankees. **1843** —— *Attaché* II. xviii. 39, I won't stay here and see you belittle Uncle Sam, for nothin'. **1862** TROLLOPE *N. Amer.* II. 25 Washington was a great man, and I believe a good man. I, at any rate, will not belittle him. **1870** GRANT WHITE *Words & Uses* (1881) 219 Time.. spent by each party in belittling and reviling the candidates of its opponents. **1881** *Pall Mall G.* 10 Dec. 20/2 The *Times* in 1809 belittled the victory of Talavera.

Hence **be'littling** *ppl. a.* and *vbl. sb.*, **be'littlement**.

1859 *Hills of Shatemuc* 175, I never heard such a belittling character of the profession. **1882** *Pop. Sc. Monthly* XX. 370 A systematic belittlement of the essential.. in the story. **1884** FAIRBAIRN in *Contemp. Rev.* Mar. 377 The belittling burden of an exhausted yet authoritative past.

belittler (bɪ'lɪt(ə)lə(r)). [f. BELITTLE *v.* + -ER[1].] One who belittles or depreciates.

1887 *Daily News* 27 Jan. 6/3 The belittlers more than half confirm the story they would be delighted to contradict. **1898** *Pop. Sci. Monthly* LIII. 396 His belittlers emphasize Gerarde's ignorance of the classic writers on botany. **1920** *Contemp. Rev.* Aug. 171, I protest against all the patriotic belittlers of their own nations.

†**be'live, bilive, blive**, *v. Obs.* Forms: 1 belífan (5 bleve). *Pa. t.* 1 beláf, *pl.* belifon, 3 bilæf, -leaf, -lef, 5 bleef. *Pa. pple.* 1 belifen, 5 blyven. [OE. *bi-, belífan*:—OTeut. **bilîban* 'to remain over,' in Goth. *beleiban*, OHG. *bilîban*, MHG. *bilîben, blîben*, OS. *bilibian*, OFris. *bilîva, blîva*, mod.G. *bleiben*, MDu. **belîven, blîven*, Du. *blijven*; f. *bi-*, BE- + OTeut. **lîban* 'to remain, be left.' Already in OTeut., the simple *lîban* appears to have been superseded by its compound *bilîban*, which takes its place in all the languages; and in most the prefix was at length syncopated to *b-* so as to make the compound look like a simple verb. In Ger. and Du., *bleiben, blijven*, remain verbs of great importance, but in Eng. *belīve* was at an early period confused with, and in 13th c. superseded by, its transitive derivative *beleve*, BELEAVE, which finally was discarded also; so that the simple LEAVE now remains as the only cognate of Ger. *bleiben*. In the 15th c., when *beleve* had been reduced to *bleve*, Caxton used the pa. t. *bleef*, and pa. pple. *blyven*, app. from Flemish, but no one followed him.]

1. *intr.* To remain.

c **1000** ÆLFRIC *Exod.* xxiii. 18 Ne se rysel ne belifþ oþ morȝen. *c* **1200** ORMIN 2391 3ho bilæf wiþþ hire frend. *c* **1250** *Gen. & Ex.* 2776 Ðe grene leaf.. ðoȝ grene and hol bi-leaf. *Ibid.* 1801 He bi-lef ðor on ðe niȝt. **1297** R. GLOUC. 288 þat he ssolde alyȝte, and byleue myd[h]yre al day. **1475** CAXTON *Jason* 17 b, Ther bleef no moo but tweyne. **1483** —— *Gold. Leg.* 67/2 Ther shold not haue blyuen unto nabal ..one pyssyng ayenst a walle. *Ibid.* 383/2 There bleueth no more but I.

2. *trans.* (confused with BELEAVE.) To leave.

c **1250** *Gen. & Ex.* 3066 And ðat [h]ail ða bileaf sal al ben numen.

belive (bɪ'laɪv), *adv. Obs.* exc. *dial.* Forms: 3 bi-life(s, -liues, -leue, -liue, 3–6 biliue, 3–5 bliue, 4 belif, bileve, 4–5 by lyve, blyue, blyve, 4–6 beliue, 4–7 blive, 5 belyff(e, beeliue, blif, blyf, bleyve, 5–6 belyve, -life, 5–8 belyfe, 6 byliue, 9 *Sc.* belyve, 4– belive. [Orig. two words, in ME. *bi life, be life, be live*, f. *be, bi*, BY *prep.*, and *life, live*, dat. of *līf*, LIFE; lit. 'with life, or liveliness'; cf. QUICK, and Fr. *vif*, and mod. *look alive!* For forms cf. ALIVE.]

1. With speed, with haste, quickly, eagerly. (Still *Sc.*)

c **1200** ORMIN 17943 He fulltneþþ nu bilife. *c* **1205** LAY. 26504 Æuere þe eorles arnde biliues. ——4545 Brennes flæh bliue. **1297** R. GLOUC. 50 þo Romaynes flowe bi lyue. *c* **1300** *Alisaunder* 1492 He wendith out of londe blive. **1375** BARBOUR *Bruce* x. 238 Thai that war within the wayn Lap out belif. *c* **1400** *Roland* 52 They herd hym blif. *c* **1420** *Chron. Vilod.* 626 Also blyve as he myȝt.. go. *c* **1460** *Frere & Boye* 210 in Ritson *Anc. Pop. P.* 43 He ranne fast and blyue. *c* **1570** THYNNE *Pride & Lowl.* (1841) 63 They al tooke hold belyve. **1613** W. BROWNE *Sheph. Pipe* Wks. (1772) 25 This noise he heard, and blive he to her ran. **1836** J. MAYNE *Siller Gun* in Chambers' *Pop. Scot. P.* (1862) 140 His father gar'd them flee for fear, And skulk belyve.

†**b.** *as blive*: as quickly as possible, immediately; = AS-SOON, AS-TITE; Fr. *aussitôt*. *Obs.*

1413 LYDG. *Pylgr. Sowle* IV. xx. (1483) 66 Slee me here as blyue. *c* **1450** LONELICH *Grail* (Roxb.) II. 391 On hym scholde I ben venged as blyve.

†**2.** At once, immediately, directly. *Obs.*

c **1220** *St. Marher.* 3 Olibrius.. beth bringen hire biuoren him bliue. *a* **1300** *Cursor M.* 5021 Fottes me ruben biliue. *c* **1325** *E.E. Allit. P.* A. 625 As sone as þay arn borne, bylyue In þe water of baptem þay dyssente. *c* **1400** *Roland* 167 It is best I busk me blif. *a* **1547** SURREY *Aeneid* II. 293 To bring the horse to Pallas' temple blive. **1563** SACKVILLE *Dk. Buckhm.* ii, Mark well my fall, which I shall show belive.

†**b.** Of order or position: Immediately, directly. *Obs.*

c **1400** *Destr. Troy* VI. 2226, I am Eldest and heire after hym belyue. *c* **1420** *Pallad. on Husb.* I. 250 Lande.. acclyned blyve uppon the sonne.

3. This passes insensibly into: Before long, soon; 'by-and-by,' 'anon.' (Still *Sc.*)

1616 BULLOKAR, *Belive*, by and by, anon. **1637** B. JONSON *Sad Sheph.* II. ii. (1641) 142 Twentie swarme of Bees, Whilke (all the Summer) hum about the hive, And bring me Waxe, and Honey in by live. **1785** BURNS *Cotter's Sat. Nt.* iv, Belyve, the elder bairns come drapping in. **1816** SCOTT *Old Mort.* 295 'Nearly a mile off'.. 'We'll be there belive.'

¶ Like *bedene*, sometimes merely expletive, or for the sake of a rime.

†**4.** as *adj.* Eager; glad (perhaps by confusion for *blithe*). *Obs.*

a **1400** *Cov. Myst.* (1841) 13 Than Pylat is besy and ryth blyff, And prayth that Cryst he xuld not quelle. *c* **1430** *Syr Gener.* 3105 Oon told hir he was yet on liue, And she was therof ful bliue. **1651** *Ordinary* v. iv. in Hazl. *Dodsley* XII. 311 This buss is a blive guerdon.

†**be'lived**, *ppl. a. Obs. rare.* [f. BE- + -LIVE *v.*] In *evil-belived*: evil-living, of ill life.

1557 *K. Arthur* (Copland) IV. vii, He is so euyl belyued and hated that there is no knyght that wyll fyght for hym.

†**be'lively**, *adv. Obs. rare*[−1]. Also **blively**. [f. BELIVE *adv.* + -LY[2].] Quickly, at once.

c **1400** *Test. Love* III. 296/1, I will answere thee blively.

†**belives**, *adv. Obs. rare*, a variant of BELIVE q.v. [with *s* of advb. genitive.]

Belizean (bɛ'li:zɪən), *sb.* and *a.* Also **Belizan, Belizian**. [f. *Belize*, the official name since 1973 of the country formerly known as British Honduras, + -AN.] **A.** *sb.* A native or inhabitant of the independent country of Belize in Central America. **B.** *adj.* Of, pertaining to, or characteristic of Belize or the Belizeans.

1959 *Belize Times* 1 Jan. 2/1 Most Belizeans look to the New Year with hope. **1964** *Economist* 12 Sept. 1014/1 The last thing most Belizans want is to become Guatemalans. **1968** *Ibid.* 30 Mar. 37/1 Mr. George Price.. and his party are pursuing what they call 'the Belizean way to independence'. .. The thesis is that the 'Belizeans' inherited the Guatemalan dispute through no fault of their own. **1971** *Jamaican Weekly Gleaner* 17 Nov. 12/5 Jamaican manufacturers were eager to work with Belizians in any kind of industrial venture. **1974** *Caribbean Contact* Aug. 21/4 The resolution on Belize recognised 'the continuing aspirations of the Belizean people for freedom from colonialism'. **1980** *New Statesman* 26 Sept. 15/1 Tate & Lyle entered the Belizean sugar industry in 1963. **1985** T. PARKER *Soldier, Soldier* XI. 131 The Belizians are apprehensive about Guatemala coming in.

†**belk**, *v.* Obs. and dial. form of BELCH; used in various senses, esp. in that of: To boil, to heave like a boiling fluid, to throb.

1648 JOS. BEAUMONT *Psyche* II. cxlvi, My guilt is hot, And belks and boils. *a* **1656** BP. HALL *Soliloq.* 61 The sting of some heinous sin, which lies belking within us.

Hence **'belking** *vbl. sb.* and *ppl. a.* (applied to the gout).

1640 BP. HALL *Chr. Moder.* 24/2 Thy belking gouts, thy scalding fevers, thy galling ulcers. **1650** —— *Balm Gil.* 290 What aches of the bones, what belking of the Joynts? *a* **1656** —— *Serm.* xx. Wks. V. 279 Girds of the colic, or belking pains of the gout.

bell (bɛl), *sb.*[1] Forms: 1–7 belle, (4 bill), 4–7 bel, 6– bell. [A common LG. word: OE. *belle* wk. fem. = MDu. and MLG. *belle*, Du. *bel* (in Icel. *bjalla* from OE.), not occurring in other Teutonic languages; perhaps from same root as BELL *v.*[4] to make a loud noise, roar. The history of the transferred sense 4 is not quite certain.]

I. Properly.

1. A hollow body of cast metal, formed to ring, or emit a clear musical sound, by the sonorous vibration of its entire circumference, when struck by a clapper, hammer, or other appliance. The typical form, found in all large bells (and indicated by the expression *bell-shaped*), is that of an inverted deep cup with a recurving brim, which is struck by a 'clapper' or 'tongue,' usually suspended from the centre of the interior.

Other forms, used only in small bells, are a section of a hollow sphere, struck by a hammer impelled by a spring as in the bell of a house-clock, a table bell, etc., and a hollow sphere containing an unattached or freely suspended solid metal ball which answers the purpose of the tongue.

Bells of the regular form vary greatly in size and weight.

a. The larger kinds are used for giving signals of various import (time, danger, etc.) to the inhabitants of a town or district, and especially in connexion with public worship (cf. CHIME); the smaller kinds are used for similar purposes in a house (e.g. *door-bell, dinner-bell, electric-bell*). **b.** Small bells are frequently used for decoration, e.g. on a horse's trappings, a falcon's leg, the cap of a fool or jester, etc.

a. *a* **1000** *Chart. Leofric* in *Cod. Dipl.* IV. 275 He hæfð ðiderynn ȝedon.. vii. uphangene bella. *c* **1200** *Trin. Coll. Hom.* 215 Boc oðer belle, calch oðer messe-ref. **1297** R. GLOUC. 509 Me rong bellen, & vaste the ropes drou. *c* **1425** *Seven Sag.* (P.) 2285 Quod the emperour, 'By Goddis belle, Of that cas thou most me telle.' **1538** BALE *Thre Lawes* 1197 In bedes and in belles, not vsed of the turkes. **1602** *Return fr. Parnass.* II. vi. (Arb.) 33 Then goe to his meate when the Bell rings. **1692** BP. ELY *Answ. Touchstone* 72 A man.. to whom the Bell clinks just as he thinks. **1782** COWPER *A. Selkirk* iv, The sound of the church-going bell. *a* **1815** in G. Rose *Diaries* (1860) II. 438 He put out his hand to pull the bell. **1835** MARRYAT *Olla Podr.* x, He's running.. to answer the bell.

b. *c* **1200** ORMIN 950 Tatt Iudisskenn preost wass.. Bihenngedd all wiþþ belless. **1382** WYCLIF *Judg.* viii. 21 The ournementis, and billis [**1388** bellis] with the whiche the neckis of kyngis chamels ben wonyd to be anourned. **1486** *Bk. St. Albans* D iij, The bellis that yowre hawke shall wheer, looke.. that thay be not to heuy. **1600** SHAKS. *A.Y.L.* III. iii. 81 As the Oxe hath his bow.. and the Falcon her bels. **1611** BIBLE *Zech.* xiv. 20 Vpon the bels of the horses, Holines Vnto the Lord. **1742** JARVIS *Quix.* I. III. xxiii. (1885) 134, I will not have a dog with a bell. **1855** TENNYSON *Maud* I. VI. vii, Often a man's own angry pride Is cap and bells for a fool.

2. With various words prefixed to describe its shape, material, etc., or define its use, as ALARM-

BELL, *bridle-bell, church-bell, clock-bell, curfew-bell, dinner-bell, door-bell, hand-bell, marriage-bell, night-bell, sheep-bell, town-bell*; and esp. in eccles. use, as ***bearing-bell, houseling-bell, lich-bell, sacring-bell, sanctus-*** or ***saunce-bell***; **death-bell, passing-bell**, a bell tolled to announce a death.

a **1508** KENNEDY *Flyting w. Dunbar* 506 Ane benefice quha wald gyue sic ane beste, Bot gif it war to gyngill Iudas bellis! **1548** PATTEN *Exp. Scotl.* in Arb. *Garner* III. 71 Pardon beads, Saint Anthony's bells, Tauthrie laces. **1552-3** *Inv. Ch. Goods Staffordsh.* (has *passim*), Bearing-bell, clock-bell, hand-bell, houseling-bell, lyche-bell, sacring-bell, sanctus-bell, visiting-bell. **1592** SHAKS. *Rom. & Jul.* IV. iv. 4 The curphew Bell hath rung. *c* **1620** Z. BOYD *Zion's Flowers* (1855) 36 Thou a passing bell, 'Gainst their transgressions did so loudly knell. **1816** BYRON *Ch. Har.* III. xxi, And all went merry as a marriage bell. **1818** SCOTT *Hrt. Midl.* xxvii, Every word fell on Butler's ear like the knell of a death-bell. **1842** TENNYSON *Lady of Shal.* III. ii, The bridle bells rang merrily. **1861** *Romance Dull L.* xlviii. 358 Listening to the idly busy sound of sheep-bells. **1863** LONGF. *Falc. Federigo* 110 A passing bell Tolled from the tower.

3. *spec.* **a.** A bell rung to tell the hours; the bell of a clock; whence the obs. phrases ***of, on, at the bell*** = o'clock.

1422 *MS. at Hatfield Ho.*, In the morowe tide bitwene vj and vij of the belle died Kyng Charles. *c* **1447** *Eng. Chron.* App. 117 Appon iij on the belle at aftrenone. **1448** SHILLINGFORD *Lett.* (1871) 61 On tuysday..at iij. atte belle afternone. **1523** LD. BERNERS *Froiss.* I. ccxxxii. 322 This batayle endured fro ix. of ye bell, tyll it was past hye none. **1590** SHAKS. *Com. Err.* I. ii. 45 The clocke hath strucken twelue vpon the bell. **1742** YOUNG *Nt. Th.* I. 55 The bell strikes one. **1848** THACKERAY *Van. Fair* III. vi 81 As the shrill-toned bell of the black marble study-clock began to chime nine.

b. *Naut.* The bell which is struck on shipboard, every half hour, to indicate by the number of strokes the number of half-hours of the watch which have elapsed; a period of half-an-hour thus indicated. (See quots.).

1836 MARRYAT *Midsh. Easy* ix, It struck seven bells, and he accompanied Mr. Jolliffe on deck. **1840** R. DANA *Bef. Mast* iv. 8 At seven bells in the morning all hands were called aft. **1867** SMYTH *Sailor's Wd-bk.* 94 We say it is two bells, three bells, etc., meaning there are two or three half-hours past. The watch of four hours is eight bells.

II. Transferred to bell-shaped objects.

4. A corolla shaped like a bell; hence in the name of various flowering plants, esp. of the genus *Campanula*, e.g. BLUE-BELL, CANTERBURY BELLS, HAREBELL; ***dead men's bells*** (dialectal name of the Foxglove), HEATHER-BELL, etc.

1610 SHAKS. *Temp.* v. i. 90 In a Cowslips bell, I lie. **1637** MILTON *Lycidas* 135 Bid them hither cast Their bells and flowerets. **1742** R. BLAIR *Grave* 254 Dew-drops on the bells of flowers. **1847** DE QUINCEY *Joan of Arc* Wks. III. 209 Flower nor bud, bell nor blossom would ever bloom for her.

5. Frequently applied to vessels bell-shaped, as a bell-glass, diving-bell, etc.

1641 FRENCH *Distill.* iii. (1651) 68 The Bell must hang at such a distance from the other vessell. **1693** EVELYN *De la Quint. Compl. Gard.* Gloss., *Bells*, are large Glasses made in the form of Bells, to clap over tender Plants or such as are to be forced. *c* **1715** HALLEY in *Sat. Mag.* 20 Apr. (1839) 147/1 The..cavity of the [diving] bell was kept..free from water.

6. Any object or portion of an object shaped like a bell; esp. in various technical uses:

a. *Arch.* 'The naked vase or corbeille of the Corinthian or Composite capitals, round which the foliage and volutes are arranged.' Gwilt.

1848 RICKMAN *Archit.* 33 The bell is set round with two rows of leaves, eight in each row. **1851** RUSKIN *Stones Ven.* I. ix. 102 The sloping stone is called the Bell of the capital.

b. The everted orifice of a trumpet or other wind instrument.

1806 BUSBY *Dict. Mus.* (ed. 2), *Bell of a Horn*, the large, open part of the instrument, from which the sound immediately issues. **1856** MRS. C. CLARKE *Berlioz' Instrum.* 130 The narrower the opening left in the bell [of a horn], the ..rougher the note. **1926** WHITEMAN & MCBRIDE *Jazz* ix. 201 The players [of cornets] got that effect by inverting glass tumblers over the bells of the instruments. **1966** *Crescendo* Oct. 22/3 Sitting only three feet from the..bell of Jimmy Heath's tenor [saxophone].

c. The body of a helmet.

1874 BOUTELL *Arms & Arm.* iii. 55 The other variety.. has the bell of a more conical form. *Ibid.* v. 77 The figures ..on the sides of the bell of the head-piece.

d. *Mech.* (See quots. 1881, 1893.)

1881 RAYMOND *Mining Gloss.*, *Bell and hopper*..an iron hopper with a large central opening, which is closed by a cone or bell, pulled up into it from below. **1893** *Funk's Stand. Dict.*, *Bell*, the movable cap at the top of a modern blast-furnace, which is lifted to put in the charge of ore, etc. **1930** *Engineering* 2 May 589/1, 10 per cent of the total gas made was lost owing to the use of single bells on the blast-furnaces. **1944** *Gloss. Terms Gas Industry* (*B.S.I.*) 26 *Bell*, the hollow cylinder closed at its upper end which forms the gas container.

e. (See quot.) Cf. *bell-tent* in 12.

1858 BEVERIDGE *Hist. India* III. IX. i. 559 The bells, or small huts, where the native arms..were deposited.

III. Phrases.

7. a. ***to bear the bell***: to take the first place, to have foremost rank or position, to be the best. ***to bear*** or ***carry away the bell***: to carry off the prize. The former phrase refers to the bell worn by the leading cow or sheep (cf. BELL-WETHER) of a drove or flock; the latter, perhaps, to a golden or silver bell sometimes given as the prize in races and other contests; but the two have been confused.

c **1374** CHAUCER *Troylus* III. 149 And, let se which of yow shal bere the belle To speke of love aright? *c* **1460** *Towneley Myst.* 88 Of alle the foles I can telle..Ye thre bere the belle. **1470** HARDING *Chron.* lxxxi. xi, At the last the Brytons bare the bell, And had the felde and all the victorye. **1594** BARNFIELD *Aff. Sheph.* II. xxxix, For pure white the Lilly beares the Bell. **1594** CAREW *Huarte's Exam. Wits* xiii. (1596) 215 Iulius Cæsar..bare away the bell (in respect of fortunatenesse) from all other captains of the world. **1621** BURTON *Anat. Mel.* To Rdr. 49 True merchants, they carry away the bell from all other nations. **1713** *Lond. & Countr. Brew.* IV. (1743) 295 A very heady Malt Liquor, which.. carries the Bell, by having the Name of the best Drink far and near. **1773** *Pennant's Tour N. Wales*, A little golden bell was the reward of victory in 1607 at the races near York, whence came the proverb for success of any kind, to bear the bell. **1817** BYRON *Beppo* x, Venice the bell from every city bore.

†**b.** Similarly, ***to deserve*** or ***lose the bell, to give the bell***. *Obs.*

1600 FAIRFAX *Tasso* XVII. lxix, When in single fight he lost the bell. *a* **1619** FOTHERBY *Atheom.* I. iv. §4 (1622) 25 The follie of the Romanes doth well deserue the Bell. **1686** AGLIONBY *Paint. Illustr.* 278 Which gave him the Bell above all Modern Artists.

c. ***to ring the bell*** (colloq.): to carry off the prize; to be the best of a lot: in allusion to the ringing of the bell attached to a strength-testing machine.

1900 J. M. BARRIE *Tommy & Grizel* viii. 102 It was a shot that rang the bell. **1928** *Publishers' Weekly* 26 May 2094 This [book] liberally illustrated, with a great jacket, rings the bell.

d. ***to ring a bell*** (colloq.): to awaken the memory, to set one remembering.

[**1934** A. HUXLEY *Beyond Mexique Bay* 51 Why should the Local Pavlov have chosen to ring just those particular bells which happen to be rung?] **1939** N. MONSARRAT *This is Schoolroom* II. xi. 239 The things we talked about meant nothing to them: they rang no bell. **1945** M. AGATE *Madame Sarah* xii. 171 They would be quick to recognize a great performance, but would it 'ring a bell' with them, I wonder? **1945** M. ALLINGHAM *Coroner's Pidgin* xxiii. 203 That's where I saw the name, then... It rang only a very faint bell. **1957** P. FRANKAU *Bridge* 64 'Do you remember..the stage-hands who built the set?' 'That rings a bell.'

e. ***to give*** (someone) ***a bell***, to call (someone) by telephone, to ring up. Cf. TINKLE *sb.* d. *colloq.*

1982 *Brit. Jrnl. Photogr.* 23 July 785/2 'An audition.'..'I understand... I'll set it up and give you a bell.' **1985** *Music Week* 2 Feb. (Advt. section) 4 Give them a Bell on 402 3105. **1986** G. F. NEWMAN *Set Thief* v. 58, I was going to give you a bell. But I thought it best to give the phone a miss.

8. ***by bell and book, book and bell*** (*i.e.* those used in the service of the mass): a frequent asseveration in the Middle Ages. ***to curse by bell, book, and candle***: referring to a form of excommunication which closed with the words, 'Doe to the book, quench the candle, ring the bell!' Also used as summarizing the resources of the hierarchy against heretics, or the terrors of excommunication; and humorously, to indicate the accessories of a religious ceremony.

a **1300** *Cursor M.* 17110 Curced in kirc þan sal þai be wid candil, boke, and bell. *c* **1400** *Ywaine & Gaw.* 3023 So bus the do, by bel and boke. *c* **1420** *Anters Arth.* iii, That borne was in Burgoyne, be boke and by belle. **1595** SHAKS. *John* III. iii. 12 Bell, Booke, & Candle, shall not driue me back, When gold and siluer becks me to come on! **1611** BARREY *Ram Alley* in Dodsley *O. Pl.* V. 447, I have a priest will mumble up a marriage, Without bell, book, or candle. **1680** *Spir. Popery* 45 The Field-Preachers damned this Bond with Bell, Book, and Candle. **1828** SCOTT *F.M. Perth* I. 155 Hold thy hand, on pain of bell, book, and candle.

9. With allusion to the fable of the mice (or rats) who proposed to hang a bell round the cat's neck, so as to be warned of its approach. See also ***bell the cat*** in BELL *v.*[5]

1377 LANGL. *P. Pl.* B. Prol. 168 Bugge a belle of brasse.. And hangen it vp-on þe cattes hals; þanne here we mowen Where he ritt or rest. *a* **1529** SKELTON *Col. Cloute* 164 Loth to hang the bell aboute the cattes necke. **1562** J. HEYWOOD *Prov. & Epigr.* (1867) 32, I will hang the bell about the cats necke. **1627** E. F. *Hist. Edw. II.* (1680) 14 Wishing some one would shew undaunted valour, to tye the Bell about the Cat's neck.

10. ***as sound*** or ***as clear as a bell***; see SOUND *a.*, CLEAR *a.*

IV. *Comb.* and *Attrib.*

11. General relations: **a.** simple attrib., as ***bell-canopy, -chamber, -chime, -clapper, -cot, -cote, -end*** (see 6 b), ***-loft, -steeple, -toll, -tower***; **b.** objective, as ***bell-baptism, -bearer, -caster, -casting, -hallower, -maker***; **c.** similative and parasynthetic, as ***bell-barrow*** [BARROW *sb.*[1] 3], ***-beaker*** [BEAKER 1 c], ***-button, -cup, -lamp, -mouth, -net, -shape***; ***bell-bored, -crowned, -fashioned, -hooded, -mouthed, -nosed, -shaped***; **d.** instrumental with pa. pple., as ***bell-hung***. Also ***bell-like*** adj.

1872 ELLACOMBE *Bells of Ch.* v. 78 The ceremony of *bell baptism exceeds in splendour and minutiæ the baptism of Christians. [**1743** STUKELY *Abury* ix. 41 Barrows with ditches round them. These are..generally of an elegantly turn'd bell-form.] **1812** R. COLT HOARE *Anc. Hist. S. Wilts.* 21 **Bell Barrow*. This, from the elegance of its form, seems to have been a refinement on the Bowl Barrow: they abound in the neighbourhood of Stonehenge. **1928** CRAWFORD & KEILLER *Wessex from Air* iv. 13 Some *Bell-barrows* certainly belong to the very beginning of the period... The name is, of course, derived from the form. The mound is high, and is usually separated from the surrounding ditch by a narrow shelf or berm of natural soil. **1902** *Jrnl. Anthrop. Inst.* XXXII. 390 The different class of beaker..is often called the '*Bell-beaker', from its caliciform or bell-shaped form. **1925** V. G. CHILDE *Dawn Europ. Civilization* xix. 293 In Bavaria and Thuringia as elsewhere, the bell-beaker folk had used metal. **1967** *Antiquaries Jrnl.* XLVII. 182 Crichel Down in Dorset..where one sherd of rusticated ware was found associated with small sherds of the Bell-Beaker class. **1607** TOPSELL *Four-f. Beasts* 189 Neither have Goats a Captain or *Bell-bearer like unto Sheep. **1775** ADAIR *Amer. Ind.* 7 The beaus..choose *bell-buttons, to give a greater sound. **1851** H. MELVILLE *Whale* vi. 36 He orders bell-buttons to his waistcoats. **1628** in Earwaker *E. Cheshire* I. 107 *note*, Going to enquire for the *bellcaster. **1872** ELLACOMBE *Bells of Ch.* i. 3, I describe the modern process of *bell casting. **1848** RICKMAN *Archit.* 153 Sound-holes.. are not used in the *bell-chamber. **1819** SHELLEY *Peter Bell* VI, Like a crazed *bell-chime, out of tune. **1498** *Church-w. Acc. St. Dunstan's, Canterb.*, For makyng of new *belclappers..xiijs. iiij*d.* **1677** MOXON *Mech. Exerc.* (1703) 14 Large Bell-clappers..and all thick strong Bars, etc. **1859** TURNER *Dom. Archit.* III. II. vii. 338 A *bell-cot projecting from the face of the wall. **1877** L. JEWITT *Half-hrs. Eng. Antiq.* 175 The Sanctus Bell..hung in a small *bell-cote at the apex of the gable. **1823** J. DODDRIDGE *Dial. Backwoodsman & Dandy* in *Logan* (1868), Your *bell crowned hat. **1854** J. STEPHENS *Centr. Amer.* (1854) 18 A bell-crowned straw hat. **1910** J. FARNOL *Broad Highway* I. xvi. 86 It's precious lucky for you as you are a-wearin' that there bell-crowned 'at! *a* **1849** MANGAN *Poems* (1859) 308 From gloomy iron *bell-cups they drank the Saxon wine. **1874** CHAPPELL *Hist. Music* I. ix. 267 The *bell-ends of certain pipes. **1698** J. PETIVER in *Phil. Trans.* XX. 315 A large *Bell-fashioned cinereous Calyx. **1549** LATIMER *Serm. bef. Edw. VI* (Arb.) 135 Preachers, not *Belhalowers. **1883** *Harper's Mag.* Jan. 208/1 The smoke..escaped up a big *bell-hooded flue. **1870** MORRIS *Earthly Par.* II. III. 145 The *bell-hung bridle-rein. **1836** DICKENS *Sk. Boz*, The *bell-lamp in the passage. **1769** SIR J. HILL *Fam. Herbal* (1789) 307 The flowers are..of a *bell-like shape. **1865** BOYLE *Dyaks Borneo* 56 Sending forth his clear bell-like challenge. **1764** in *Phil. Trans.* LIV. 213 In the *bell-loft at St. Bride's. *c* **1400** *Destr. Troy* v. 1589 *Belmakers, bokebynders, brasiers fyn. **1483** *Cath. Angl.* 27 A Belle maker, *campanarius*. **1837** MARRYAT *Dog-Fiend* ii, The *bell-mouth of his speaking trumpet. **1896** *Daily News* 29 May 6/7 The huge brass bellmouth apparatus fixed on the prompt side of the opera proscenium is an electrophone. **1930** *Engineering* 4 Apr. 436/1 The lining at both extremities of the cutout ends, including the bell-mouth. **1958** J. S. SCOTT *Dict. Civ. Engin.* 22 *Bellmouth overflow*, an overflow from a reservoir through a tower built up from the bed to the overflow level. **1967** *Jane's Surface Skimmer Systems 1967–68* 106/1 There is a dam for solid water separation and four right angle turns before the air reaches the engine bellmouths. **1797** J. CURR *Coal Viewer* 47 For the common engine..[cylinders] must be *bell-mouthed ¼ of an inch on each side. **1823** BYRON *Juan* XIII. lxxii, His bell-mouth'd goblet makes me feel quite..Dutch with thirst. **1946** *Nature* 2 Nov. 635/2 A bell-mouthed estuary. **1856** MRS. BROWNING *Aur. Leigh* 9 The very sky Dropping its *bell-net down upon the sea. **1881** GREENER *Gun* 6 The barrel is ..*bell-nosed upon the outside. **1874** BOUTELL *Arms & Arm.* iii. 55 One is a helm of a deep *bell shape. **1757** *Phil. Trans.* L. 65 Campaniform or *bell-shaped flowers. **1879** A. BENNETT in *Academy* 32 The open bell-shaped mouth of the corolla. **1847** LD. LINDSAY *Chr. Art* I. 22 The round towers of Ireland..are *bell-steeples. **1861** T. PEACOCK *Gryll Gr.* 308 On the dreary midnight air Rolled the deep *bell toll. **1614** SPEED *Theat. Gt. Brit.* xxxiv. 67 Whose steeple or *bell-tower being both beautiful and high. **1879** SIR G. SCOTT *Lect. Archit.* I. 258 The bell-tower..becomes the culminating ornament of the whole exterior.

e. *poet.*

1879 G. M. HOPKINS *Poems* (1918) 41 Cuckoo-echoing, bell-swarmèd, lark-charmèd. **1888** —— *Poems* (1918) 89 Bellbright bodies huddling out. **1889** YEATS *Wand. Oisin* III. 38, I gazed on the bell-branch, sleep's forebear. **1919** W. DE LA MARE *Flora* 33 On the mirroring sands Bell-shrill the oyster-catchers. **1935** W. EMPSON *Poems* 24 Drowned under flounces and bell-calm of trees. **1945** W. DE LA MARE *Burning-glass* 75 Its secret bell-clear song.

12. Special combinations: **bell-animalcules, -animals**, English name for the *Vorticellidæ*, infusorial animalcules having a bell- or wine-glass-shaped body on a long flexible stalk; **bell-binder**, the large Wild Convolvulus or Bindweed; **bell-bit**, 'the bit of a bridle made in the form of a bell' (Halliw.); **bell-boat**, a boat with a bell freely suspended on it so as to ring as the vessel is moved by the waves, and thus give notice of danger; so **bell-buoy**, a buoy with a bell; **bell-bottomed** *a.*, of trousers, having a considerable increase in width from below the knee to the bottom of the leg, giving a bell-shaped appearance; also, of an individual, esp. of a class accustomed to wear such trousers; **bell-bottoms** *sb. pl.*, bell-bottomed trousers; **bell-bridle**, a bridle hung or adorned with bells; **bell captain** *U.S.*, one who supervises a group of bell-boys; **bell cord**, a cord to be pulled in order to ring a bell, spec. in a passenger vehicle; †**bell-course**, a race for a bell; **bell-crank**, a crank or species of lever adapted to communicate motion from one bell-wire to another lying at right angles to it; also *attrib.*; **bell-crater** *Gr. Antiq.*, a bell-shaped bowl (see CRATER *sb.* 1); †**bell-dream**, the sound or music of a bell; **bell-faced** (of a hammer), having the striking surface convex or rounded; **bell-gable**,

a gable or turret in which bells are hung; **bell-girdle**, a girdle or belt hung or adorned with bells; **bell-handle**, the handle by which a bell-rope or bell-wire is pulled; **bell-hanger**, one whose business it is to put up bells, bell-wires, etc.; hence **bell-hanging**; **bell-harp** (see quot.); **bell-heather**, the cross-leaved heath, *Erica tetralix* (Jam.); **bell-hop, -hopper** *U.S.* and *Canada*, a hotel page-boy (cf. BELL-BOY 2); **bell-horn**, a horn which gives a bell-like tone; **bell-horse**, a horse wearing a bell or bells, *esp.* a horse adorned with bells, flowers, ribbons, etc. to celebrate the advent of May; the leading horse of a pack-train; hence **bell-horse-day**, the first of May; **bell-jar**, a bell-shaped glass jar used in chemical and physical laboratories; **bell-less** *a.*, destitute of a bell; **bell-mare**, in herding mules on the prairies, a mare which wears a bell and acts as leader to the troop, etc.; † **bell-melter**, a bell-founder, a founder; **bell-moth**, a group of moths of the family *Tortricidæ*, named from their outline when at rest; **bell-mouth** *v. trans.*, to furnish with a bell-mouth; **bell-pepper**, a species of Capsicum (*C. grossum*), so called from the shape of the fruit; **bell-polype** (= *bell-animalcule*); **bell-pull**, a cord or handle attached to a bell-wire, by pulling which the bell is rung; **bell-punch** (see quot. *a* 1884); **bell-push**, the button that is pushed to ring an electric bell; also, a table bell to be rung in this way; **bell-rheometer**, a bell-shaped instrument for measuring the strength of an electric current; **bell-roof**, a roof shaped like a bell; **bell-rose**, the daffodil (Somerset); **bell-shade**, a bell-shaped light-shade; **bell-sheep** *Austral.* (see quot.); **bell-signal**, a signal transmitted by the bell-telegraph; so ***bell-signalling*** (both *disused*); **bell-skirt**, a bell-shaped skirt of a garment; **bell-sleeve**, a long sleeve flared at the lower edge; **bell-stone**, the part of a column which lies between the shaft and the abacus (cf. 6 a); **bell strap** = *bell cord* (Funk, 1893); **bell-string** = BELL-ROPE; **bell-team**, a team of horses adorned with bells; **bell-telegraph**, an instrument in which two bells are used to transmit a message, one indicating (by its tone) the movement of the needle to the right, the other, to the left (*disused*); **bell-tent**, a tent resembling a bell in shape; **bell-top** (see quot.); **bell-topper**, a 'topper', or top-hat, esp. one of old-fashioned type with a bell-shaped crown; **bell-trap**, a stench-trap resembling a bell in shape; **bell-tubing**, tubing through which a bell-wire is passed in order to protect it; † **bell-vessel**, a diving-bell; **bell-ware** (see quot.); **bell-waver** *v. Sc.*, 'to fluctuate, to be inconstant; applied to the mind' (Jam.); **bell-weight**, a weight shaped somewhat like a bell; **bell-wheel**, the wheel to which an ordinary church-bell is attached, and by which it is swung; **bell-wire**, the wire by which a bell-pull is connected with the bell; † **bell-yetter**, a bell-founder (lit. 'bell-pourer').

See also BELL-BIRD, -FLOWER, -FOUNDER, -GLASS, -HOUSE, -MAN, -METAL, -RAGS, -RINGER, -ROPE, -WETHER, -WORT.

1875 *Med. Trainer & Gaz.* 8 May 495/1 A species of *Amphileptus* has been observed to swallow—or rather envelope—a stalked *bell-animalcule (*Vorticella*). **1959** J. CLEGG *Freshwater Life* (ed. 2) v. 100 The Bell Animalcules, as the various species of *Vorticella* are popularly called, are found in dense masses at times. **1617** MARKHAM *Caval.* II. 58 That bytt which we call the.. Campanell or *Bell bytt. **1858** in *Merc. Mar. Mag.* V. 253 A *Bell Boat has been placed just outside the bar. **1626** CAPT. SMITH *Accid. Yng. Seamen* 32 To know wether she be.. taper or *belbored. **1891** *Argus* 5 Dec. 13/2 (Morris), The *bell-bottomed ballottee. **1904** *Daily Chron.* 6 June 4/5 The crews were not less smart in.. blue jackets and white bell-bottomed ducks. **1955** 'NEVIL SHUTE' *Requiem for Wren* 83 A naval cutter manned by two Wrens in jerseys and bell-bottomed trousers. **1898** J. D. BRAYSHAW *Slum Silhouettes* 220 They 'ad a crease right dahn 'em, an' *bell bottoms. **1929** *Daily News* 10 Apr. 7/3 An official [of the Admiralty] said: '.. Bell-bottoms are the Navy. Abolish them and you abolish the Navy.' **1838** E. FLAGG *Far West* in R. G. Thwaites *Early Western Trav.* (1908) XXVI. 52 The hated clang of the *bell-boy [*sic*] was soon after heard.. throughout the cabins. **1884** Bell-buoy [see BUOY *sb.* 1]. *a* **1910** 'O. HENRY' *Trimmed Lamp* (1916) 60 A pale-faced, fat man huskily enveloped him with a raised, red fist, and the voice of a bell buoy. **1836** MARRYAT *Midsh. Easy* (1863) 143 Two fine mules with *bell bridles. **1926** *Sat. Rev. Lit.* 20 Nov. 315 His experienced demeanor among hotel porters and ticket agents and.. *Bell Captains. **1944** *Reader's Digest* Mar. 108 The coruscating bell captain commands an army of bell-boys. **1843** *Knickerbocker* XXI. 332 He found no *bell-cord to pull. **1875** *Chicago Tribune* 2 July 8/1 When a half-drunken man has hold of the bell-cord instead of the strap to steady himself by. **1617** MARKHAM *Caval.* I. 12, I haue seene them vsed at our English *Bell-courses. **1884** F. BRITTEN *Watch & Clockm.* 32 *Bell Crank Lever.. a lever whose two arms form a right angle. **1921** *Brit. Mus. Return* 61 *Bell-crater, late red-figure style. **1939** PENDLEBURY *Archaeol. Crete* vi. 309 The bell-kraters are deeper and less swelling. *c* **1200** ORMIN 922 þe *belledræm bitacneþþ ȝuw.. dræm þatt ȝuw birrþ herenn. **1845** *Gloss. Goth. Arch.* I. 54 In small churches and chapels that have no towers, there is very frequently a *bell-gable or turret at the west end in which the bells are hung. **1831** CARLYLE *Sart. Res.* I. v. 39 Whether he.. tower up in high headgear, from amid peaks, spangles and *bell-girdles. **1765** TUCKER *Lt. Nat.* I. 387 A *bell-handle hanging by your chimney side. **1540** in W. H. Turner *Select. Records of Oxford* (1880) 160 John Payne, *bellehanger. **1789** BETSY SHERIDAN *Jrnl.* (1960) 180, I have scribbled thus far in the midst of the noise of Bell-hangers who are rectifying all negligence of our predecessors. **1791** in *Harper's Mag.* Mar. 1885. 534/2 P[d] a bell hanger on a/c 5*s.* **1851** W. IRVING in *Life* IV. 71 Plumbers and bellhangers [are] to attack the vitals of the house. **1798** W. HUTTON *Autobiog.* 17 One of them played upon the *bell-harp. **1815** *Encycl. Brit.* (ed. 5) X. 277/1 *Bell-Harp*, a musical instrument of the string kind, thus called from the common players on it swinging it about, as a bell on its basis. **1910** ADE *I knew him When* 14 He is not a *bell hop—the boys used to dress like that. **1919** D. L. CADY *Rhymes Vermont Rural Life* (1923) 99 The traveler saw no bellhops hop. **1925** A. LOOS *Gentlemen prefer Blondes* (1926) 83 The boy friend of ours who is the bell hop, waked me up at ten o'clock. **1900** ADE *More Fables* 5 When he got back to his Room the *Bell-Hopper came round and asked him if he cared to Sit in a Quiet Game. **1622** FLETCHER *Beggars' B.* III. iv, Rouse ye the lofty stag, and with my *bell-horn Ring him a knell. **1775** ADAIR *Amer. Ind.* 337 But they [*sc.* the Choctaw Indians].. stole one of the *bell horses. **1891** *Harper's Mag.* Nov. 890/1 The pack trains consisted of a 'bell-horse' and boy, and six horses following. **1878** HUXLEY *Physiogr.* 77 These bubbles may be.. collected in the *bell-jar. **1667** WATERHOUSE *Fire Lond.* 87 The tops of Steeples *Belless. **1859** MARCY *Prairie Trav.* iv. 101 A *bell-mare, to which the mules soon become so attached that they will follow her wherever she goes. **1604** *Supplic. Masse-priests* §10 *note*, Popes, Monkes, or Friars, the originall *belmelters of Poperie. **1841** E. NEWMAN *Hist. Insects* IV. ii. 214 *Bell-moths.. with filiform antennæ. **1880** *Encycl. Brit.* XII. 463/2 It is often desirable to *bell-mouth the ends of pipes. **1707** SLOANE *Jamaica* I. 241 **Bell Pepper*. The fruit is large .. somewhat shaped like a bell. **1832** *Veg. Subst. Food* 314 The Bell Pepper.. a biennial.. native of India. **1832** MISS MITFORD *Village* Ser. III. (1863) 496 The *bell-pull was within reach: but she had an aversion to ringing the bell. **1846** LYTTON *Lucretia* (1853) 185 Beside the door.. a row of some ten or twelve bell-pulls. **1865** *Cornh. Mag.* XI. 167 A pair of large tassels with loops of cord-like bell-pulls. **1877** BARTLETT *Dict. Amer.* 253 *Gong-Punch*, an instrument used by conductors [etc.].. a *bell-punch. *a* **1884** KNIGHT *Dict. Mech.* Suppl., *Bell Punch*, a hand-punch, for perforating a ticket or trip slip. It secures the piece punched out, and rings a bell; in some instruments it also registers the fares collected. **1894** *Westm. Gaz.* 26 Sept. 2/2 Thanks to the bell-punch, the number of passengers carried can now be estimated with tolerable accuracy. **1884** D. P. HEAP *Report Internat. Exhib. Electricity, Paris 1881* 26 This little battery .. is contained in the ordinary *bell-push. **1887** *Cassell's Fam. Mag.* 703/2 An indicating disc, which by its vibrations tells the bell push.. of the person who has rung up. **1921** *Blackw. Mag.* June 739/2 Pressing the bell-push to call the steward. **1876** GWILT *Archit.* 1195 *Bell Roof.. is often called an ogee roof, from its form. **1890** W. J. GORDON *Foundry* 140 At one chair here some large *bell-shades for lamps are being made. **1900** LAWSON *On Track* (1945) xvi. 99 He times himself to get so many sheep out of the pen *before* the bell goes [for breakfast or dinner], and *one more* —the '*bell-sheep'— as it is ringing. **1905** *Westm. Gaz.* 19 Apr. 8/1 He announced the fact.. by sending to him the block telegraph *bell-signal 'Vehicles running away on right line'. **1905** *Daily Chron.* 16 Nov. 7/3 Bell-signalling between torpedo craft and submarines in night-time. *a* **1910** 'O. HENRY' *Strictly Business* xx, The latest thing in suitings with side vents and *bell skirt. **1940** W. EMPSON *Gathering Storm* 35 One swing of the bell skirt. **1892** *Daily News* 26 Oct. 2/1 The '*bell' sleeves are turned back with white silk. **1960** C. W. CUNNINGTON et al. *Dict. Eng. Costume* 15/1 *Bell sleeve*, second half 19th c. Close-fitting to mid-forearm and there expanding into a bell-shaped opening. **1522-4** *Church-w. Acc. St. Dunstan's, Canterb.*, For mendyng of the *bellstoke viij*d.* **1851** RUSKIN *Stones Ven.* I. ix. §vi, [The] treatment of the capital depends simply on the manner in which this *bell stone is prepared. **1922** JOYCE *Ulysses* 219 The conductor pulled the *bellstrap. **1464** in *Ripon Ch. Acts* 222 Le *bell strynges *sunt defectiva*. **1824** MISS MITFORD *Village* Ser. I. (1863) 199 Walking.. by the side of his *bell-team. *a* **1877** KNIGHT *Dict. Mech.*, **Bell-telegraph*,.. invented by Sir Charles Bright. **1785** ROY in *Phil. Trans.* LXXV. 393 One of the pyramidal *bell-tents.. being placed at the station. *c* **1850** *Rudim. Navig.* (Weale) 96 **Bell-top*, a term applied to the top of a quarter-gallery when the upper stool is hollowed away. **1858** W. KELLY *Life in Victoria* I. xvi. 268 *Bell-topper was the derisive name given by diggers to [an] old style hat, supposed to indicate the dandy swell. *Ibid.*, Merchants ventured to the Chamber of Commerce in the regular British 'bell-topper', some of the nattier going the length of sporting kid gloves. **1871** *Fav. Reciter* (Simpkin) 6 A bell-topper hat. **1888** B. L. FARJEON *Miser Farebrother* II. i. 3 On his head the shiniest of belltoppers. **1936** I. L. IDRIESS *Cattle King* xxxi. 274 Sitting next to him was a 'swell' whose belltopper Kidman was quietly admiring. **1876** GWILT *Archit.* §2218 b, The usual iron *bell trap, as supplied to a sink. **1881** *Mechanic* §1540. 692 It is usual.. to provide for the passage of the bell wires from floor to floor by inserting *bell-tubing in the walls. **1816** *Chron.* in *Ann. Reg.* 93/1 The *bell-vessel was.. lowered with Fisher and two other men.. in 33 feet of water. **1812** *Agric. Surv. Caithn.* 182 (Jam.) *Bell-ware.. is the kelp weed along the Scottish shores. **1820** SCOTT *Monast.* vii, 'I doubt me his wits have gone a *bell-wavering.' **1743** *Phil. Trans.* XLII. 552 Pound *Bell-Weights, and the single Pound flat Weight. **1529** *Church-w. Acc. St. Dunstan's, Canterb.*, For mendyng of the *belwhele, x*d.* **1759** *Phil. Trans.* LI. 288 The *Bell-wire, coming from the parlour below. **1865** N. ARNOTT *Elem. Physics* II. 445 Bell-wires too slack in summer, may be of the proper length in winter. *c* **1440** *Promp. Parv.* 30 *Bellȝetare, *campanarius*. **1881** J. BRISCOE *Nottinghamsh.* 118 The bellyetters trade has now found its way.. into the hands of a few great firms.

bell, *sb.*[2] [Belongs to BELL *v.*[2] The actual history is uncertain. (It may be only a fig. use of BELL *sb.*[1], from its shape.)] The strobile, cone, or catkin, containing the female flowers of the hop.

1594 PLAT *Jewell-ho.* I. 43 His hops are more kindly, and the bels of them much larger. **1727** BRADLEY *Fam. Dict.* s.v. *Hop*, About August the Hop will begin to be in the Bell or Button.

bell, *sb.*[3] [Etymology obscure: identical in meaning with Mod.Du. *bel*, which, with the accompanying MDu. vb. *bellen* 'to bubble up,' is considered by Franck to have arisen out of MDu. *bulle* (ad. L. *bulla* bubble in water) under the influence of *wellen* to well or boil up; but in presence of the existence of the vb. and sb. in Eng. this seems doubtful.] A bubble formed in a liquid. (The ordinary word for 'bubble' in modern Scotch, whence occasional in English literature.)

1483 *Cath. Angl.* 27/1 A belle in þe water, *bulla*. **1530** PALSGR. 197/2 Bell of snevyll at ones nose, *rovpie*. **1533** ELYOT *Cast. Helth* (1541) 88 Sometyme belles or bobles. **1576** WOOLTON *Chr. Manual* 109 Mans life flieth away.. as the bells which bubble up in the water. **1743** DAVIDSON *Æneid* VII. 203 In Frisky Bells the Liquors dance. **1815** SCOTT *Guy M.* xxvi, The twinkling of a fin, the rising of an air-bell. **1872** BLACK *Adv. Phaeton* vi. 75 Bells of air in a champagne glass.

bell, *sb.*[4] [f. BELL *v.*[4]] The cry of a stag or buck at rutting time.

[The first quot. is possibly the verb.]

1510 *Inscr. Wharncliffe Lodge, Sheffield*, For his plesor to here the Hartes bel. **1862** C. COLLYNS *Chase Red Deer* iii, What I had heard was the 'bell' of the stag. **1865** BOYLE *Dyaks Borneo* 56 Few people in England know the melody of a wild buck's bell.

† **bell** (bɛl), *v.*[1] *Obs. Pa. pple.* bollen. [Of doubtful origin; apparently repr. OE. *belȝan*, pa. pple. *bolȝen* to swell, be proud or angry = OHG. *belgan* to swell; the total loss of the guttural presents difficulties, but occurs also in ME. *boln-e(n*, a. ON. *bolgna*, Da. *bolne* to swell. Cf. also BOLLED.]

intr. To swell up (like a boil).

a **1225** *Ancr. R.* 282 Auh heorte to-bollen and to-swollen, and ihouen on heih ase hul. A bleddre ibollen ful of winde. *c* **1320** *Sir Beves* 2655 His flesch gan ranclen and te belle. **1664** in Pepys *Diary* (1876) III. 96 [*Charm against a thorn*] Jesus.. Was pricked both with nail and thorn; It neither wealed, nor belled, rankled, nor boned. *Ibid.* [*Another*] And he was pricked with a thorn; And it did neither bell, nor swell.

b. *fig.* To be puffed up or proud.

1382 WYCLIF *2 Tim.* iii. 4 Men schulen be.. bollun with proude thouȝtis. *c* **1450** *Compl. Lover's Life* 101 Hyt wolde aswage Bollyn hertes.

bell, *v.*[2] [Cf. BELL *sb.*[2], from which the vb. is prob. formed.] *intr.* Of hops: To be, begin to be, in bell.

1574 R. SCOT *Hop Gard.* (1578) 33 At Saint Margarets daye Hoppes blowe, and at Lammas they bell. **1669** W[ORLIDGE] *Syst. Agric.* (1681) 150 *marg.*, When Hops Blow, Bell, and Ripen. **1753** CHAMBERS *Cycl. Supp.* s.v. *Belling*, Hops blow towards the end of July, and bell the latter end of August. **1819** REES *Cycl.*, *Belling* of hops, denotes their opening and expanding to their customary shape.

bell, *v.*[3] *Obs.* exc. *dial.* [This goes with BELL *sb.*[3], being identical with MDu. *bellen* to bubble up, as the sb. is with mod.Du. *bel* bubble.] *intr.* To bubble.

1598 FLORIO, *Vena di fontana*.. the belling or rising vp of water out of a spring. **1822** HOGG *Perils Man* II. 44 (JAM.) The blood bells through.

bell (bɛl), *v.*[4] Also 5 belle, 6 bel, beale, 9 *dial.* beal. [OE. *bellan* str. vb., to roar, bark, bellow = OHG. *bellan*, mod.G. *bellen* to bark; cf. ON. *belja* to bellow. Cf. BELLOW.]

1. *intr.* To bellow, roar, make a loud noise.

a **1000** *Riddles* xli. 106 (Gr.) Amasted swin, bearȝ bellende on boc-wuda. *a* **1300** W. DE BIBLESWORTH in *Promp. Parv.* 30 *note*, *Tor torreye*.. bole belleth. *c* **1350** *Will. Palerne* 1891 þe werwolf.. went to him evene bellyng as a bole. *c* **1384** CHAUCER *H. Fame* 1803 He gan to blasen out a soun, As loude as belleth winde in Hell. *c* **1440** *Promp. Parv.* 30 Bellyn, or lowyn, as nette, *mugio*. **1570** LEVINS *Manip.* 207 To Beale, *boare*. **1589** *Gold. Mirr.* (1851) 3 Which rored and beld, in th' eares of some. **1872** BROWNING *Fifine* lxxv. 27 You acted part so well, went all fours upon earth.. brayed, belled.

2. *spec.* of the voice of deer in rutting time.

1486 *Bk. St. Albans* E v a, Iche Roobucke certayne bellis by kynde. **1610** GWILLIM *Heraldry* III. xiv. (1660) 166 You shall say, a Roe Belleth. **1774** GOLDSM. *Nat. Hist.* (1862) I. II. v. 324 When the stag cries, he is said to bell. **1808** SCOTT *Marm.* IV. xv, The wild buck bells from ferny brake. **1875** 'STONEHENGE' *Brit. Sports* I. I. x. §8. 133 We start them [the hinds], and they go on belling.

3. *trans.* To utter loudly, to bellow forth.

1596 SPENSER *Astroph.* Eclog. 21 Their leaders bell their bleating tunes In doleful sound. **1868** BROWNING *Ring & Book* VIII. 1400 Bell us forth deep the authoritative bay.

bell, *v.*[5] [f. BELL *sb.*[1]]

1. *trans.* To furnish with a bell. ***to bell the cat***: to hang a bell round the cat's neck, according to

the Fable (see BELL *sb.*[1] 9), and *esp.* **a.** to perform personally this hazardous feat, to undertake a perilous part or be the ring-leader in any movement.

In the latter use, there is immediate reference to the story or legend, related by Lindsay of Pitscottie, that when certain of the Scottish barons formed a secret conspiracy to put down the obnoxious favourites of James III. in 1482, a moment of grave suspense followed the inquiry 'Who would undertake to enter the royal presence and seize the victims?' which was terminated by the exclamation of Archibald Douglas, Earl of Angus, 'I will bell the cat,' whence his historical appellation of 'Archibald Bell-the-cat.'

1762 J. MAN *Buchanan's Hist. Scot.* XII. §41. 349 *note*, Earl Archbald hearing the parable answered sadly, I shall bell the cat, meaning Cochrane, the great and terrible minion. **1791** D'ISRAELI *Cur. Lit.* (1858) 169/2 He would be glad to see who would bell the cat, alluding to the fable. **1840** ARNOLD *Life & Corr.* (1844) II. ix. 186, I was willing to bell the cat, hoping that some who were able might take up what I had begun. **1861** HUGHES *Tom Brown Oxf.* I. xii. 232 As nobody was afraid of him, there was no difficulty in finding the man to bell the cat.

b. To venture to grapple or contend *with* (a dangerous opponent). *Sc.*

1721 WODROW *Hist. Ch. Scot.* II. 384 (JAM.) How little justice.. poor simple country people, who could not bell the cat with them, had to look for. **1825** SCOTT *Betrothed* Introd. (1876) 19 It has fallen on me, as we Scotsmen say, to bell-the-cat with you.

2. a. *trans.* To cause to swell or bulge out.

1870 *Eng. Mech.* 11 Feb. 535/2 He must bell them [tubes] out a little.

b. *intr.* with *out.* To spread *out* like the mouth of a bell. So ***belled-out*** ppl. a.

1922 *Blackw. Mag.* June 731/2 The skirt belled out like an inverted campanula bloom. **1959** *New Scientist* 11 June 1291/1 Shafts can be dug, 'belled out' at the base to get a larger load bearing area. *Ibid.* 1291/2 A concrete cylinder with a 'belled out' foot.

3. (*nonce-wd.*)

1863 DICKENS *Mrs. Lirriper's Lodgings* i. They [servant girls] get bell'd off their legs [i.e. 'run off their legs' in answering bells].

† **be'llacity.** *Obs.*—[0] [f. L. *bellāc-em* (*bellax*), f. *bell-um* war; see -ACITY.] 'Warlikeness.' Blount *Glossogr.* 1656.

‖ **belladonna** (ˌbɛlə'dɒnə). [mod.L.; a. It. *bella donna*, lit. 'fair lady,' name given in Italy to the plant, on uncertain grounds.

(The usual statement, current since the time of Ray and Tournefort, is given in quot. 1757; a different account is in quot. 1851. A well-known property of the juice is to enlarge the pupil of the eye.)]

I. 1. *Bot.* The specific name of the Deadly Nightshade or Dwale (*Atropa Belladonna*), occasionally used as English.

1597 GERARD *Herbal* II. lvi. (1633) 341 In English, Dwale, or sleeping nightshade: the Venetians and Italians call it *Belladona.* **1757** PULTNEY in *Phil. Trans.* L. 62 Bella-donna is the name, which the Italians, and particularly the Venetians, apply to this plant; and Mr. Ray observes, that it is so called because the Italian ladies make a cosmetic from the juice. **1851** E. HAMILTON *Flora Homœop.* iii. 64 Belladonna, because it was employed by Leucota, a famous poisoner of Italy, to destroy the beautiful women. **1876** HARLEY *Mat. Med.* 488 Belladonna is cultivated for medicinal use at Hitchin.

2. *Med.* The name, in the pharmacopœia, of the leaves and root of this plant, and of the drug thence prepared, the active principle of which is the alkaloid *atropine.*

1788 *Edinb. New Dispens.* II. (1791) 145 The belladonna taken internally has been highly recommended in cancer. **1866** *Treas. Bot.* 109 Belladonna is said by homœopathists to act as a preventative of scarlet fever. **1875** H. WOOD *Therap.* (1879) 250 Belladonna is not a hypnotic.

3. *attrib.*

1856 *Med. Times & Gaz.* XIII. 513 Case of poisoning from the application of belladonna plaster to the skin. **1869** G. LAWSON *Dis. Eye* iv. 126 A fold of lint.. kept moist with .. the belladonna lotion. **1885** *Buck's Handbk. Med. Sci.* I. 486/2 The clinical history of a case of belladonna poisoning. *Ibid.*, The patient.. had eaten.. about thirty belladonna berries. **1890** BILLINGS *Med. Dict.*, Belladonna-leaves... B. plaster. **1896** *Daily News* 10 Sept. 2/6 Belladonna poisoning. *Ibid.*, The belladonna liniment. **1968** *Times* 3 Dec. 10/8 Drugs of the belladonna group.

II. belladonna lily, *Amaryllis Belladonna*, a native of the Cape of Good Hope.

1734 MILLER *Gard. Cal.* 140 The roots of the Guernsey and Belladonna Lillies. **1862** ANSTED *Channel Isl.* IV. xxi. 499 The belladonna is a yet more handsome lily. **1866** T. MOORE in *Treas. Bot.* 48 The name Belladonna Lily was given.. from the charmingly blended red and white of the perianth, resembling the complexion of a beautiful woman.

bellamy, variant of BELAMY, fair friend.

bellan(e, obs. var. BALEEN (sense 3), whalebone.

1513 DOUGLAS *Æneis* v. vii. 73 Erix was wont.. In that hard bellane his brawnis to embrace.

† **bellandine.** *Obs. rare*—[1]. (See quot.)

1721 C. KING *Brit. Merch.* II. 218 Importation of Bellandine, or white Turkey Silk, and of Sherbassee of Persia.

† **'bellaries**, *sb. pl. Obs.* [ad. L. *bellāria* viands of the dessert.] (See quot.)

1623 COCKERAM II, Banquetting Dishes, *Bellaries.*

bellarmine ('bɛləmiːn). *Obs.* exc. *Hist.* A large glazed drinking-jug with capacious belly and narrow neck, originally designed, by the Protestant party in the Netherlands, as a burlesque likeness of their great opponent, Cardinal Bellarmine. (See Chambers *Bk. of Days* I. 371.)

1719 D'URFEY *Pills* (1872) VI. 201 With Jugs, Mugs, and Pitchers, and Bellarmines of State. **1783** AINSWORTH *Lat. Dict.* (Morell) v, *Amphithetum*, a great cup or jug.. a rummer, a bellarmine. **1861** *Our Eng. Home* 170 The capacious bellarmine was filled to the brim with foaming ale.

† **'bellatory**, *a. Obs. rare.* [ad. L. *bellātōrius*, f. *bellātor* warrior: see -ORY.] Warlike, of war.

1657 TOMLINSON *Renou's Disp.* 429 Their bellatory arms were not of steel but brass.

† **'bellatrice.** *Obs.*—[0] [a. F. *bellatrice*, ad. L. *bellātrīc-em* (*bellātrix*), fem. of *bellātor* warrior: see -RICE.] 'A warrioress, a woman well skill'd in war, a Virago.' Blount *Glossogr.* 1656.

† **'bellaview.** *Obs. rare*—[1]. [for F. *belle vue.*] Fine view or outlook.

1611 BOYS *Expos. Gosp.* (1630) 345 This text is as it were the bellaview of the whole Chapter, in which a Christian may behold al sufficient fortifications against.. assaults.

bell-bird ('bɛlbɜːd). [f. BELL *sb.*[1] + BIRD *sb.*] A name given to two distinct birds, the *Procnias carunculata* or Campanero of Brazil, and the *Myzantha melanophrys* of Australia, both remarkable for their clear ringing notes. Also used as the name of various birds with a clear ringing call.

1802 BARRINGTON *Hist. New S. Wales* viii. 284 The cry of the bell-bird seems to be unknown here. **1825** WATERTON *Wand. S. Amer.* 117 The celebrated Campanero of the Spaniards, called.. bell-bird by the English. **1828** WORDSWORTH *On Power of Sound* ii, Toll from thy loftiest perch, lone bell-bird, toll. **1845** E. J. WAKEFIELD *Adv. N. Zealand* I. 23 The melodious chimes of the bell-bird were especially distinct. *a* **1848** BP. STANLEY *Fam. Hist. Birds* iv. (1854) 60 The Bell-Bird's note was borne upon the wind. **1865** *Ibis* I. 90 The Costa-Rican Bell-bird (Chasmorhynchus tricarunculatus). **1868** WOOD *Homes without H.* xxv. 470 To this group [the Honey-eaters] belong many.. species, such as that which produces a sound like the tinkling of a bell and is in consequence called the Bell-bird. **1882** W. L. BULLER *Man. Birds N.Z.* 11 Anthornis melanura .. Bell-bird. Mocker. Kori-mako. Makomako. **1887** *Ibid.* (ed. 2) I. 92 Anthornis Melanocephala. (Chatham-Island Bell-Bird.) **1903** *Westm. Gaz.* 28 Oct. 12/2 The Banded Bell-Bird.. (*Cotinga cincta*). **1966** G. M. DURRELL *Two in Bush* i. 45 A Bellbird.. entertained us with a concert of wonderful, flute-like notes, wild, liquid and beautiful.

bell-boy. [BELL *sb.*[1] I.] **1.** A boy who rings a bell.

1851 MELVILLE *Moby Dick* I. xxxix. 274 Eight bells there! d'ye hear, bell-boy? *Ibid.* III. xxxix. 227 'Who art thou, boy?' 'Bell-boy, sir; ship's-crier. Ding, dong, ding!'

2. A hotel page-boy. *U.S.*

1861 G. F. BERKELEY *Eng. Sportsman* 366 'What are you, then, young fellow?' 'I'm bell-boy.' **1897** KIPLING *Capt. Courageous* ix. 196 Hotel piazzas where the ingenuous young of the wealthy play with or revile the bell-boys. **1932** E. WILSON *Devil take Hindmost* xxiii. 245 Glimpses as a bellboy of the luxurious life of the hotel.

belldars, obs. f. BILDERS, name of a plant.

belle (bɛl), *a.* and *sb.* [a. mod.F. (17th c.) *belle*, OF. *bele*:—L. *bella*, fem. of *bellus* beautiful, fair: see BEAU, BEL.]

A. *adj.* † **1.** Pretty, handsome. *Obs.* as Eng.

1668 PEPYS *Diary* 16 May, I did kiss her maid, who is so mighty belle.

2. In certain French phrases, which have been used in Eng., as ***belle assemblée*** brilliant assembly or gathering; ***belle dame*** fair lady, belle; ***belle laide***, an attractively ugly woman; ***belle passion*** the tender passion, love; also BELLES-LETTRES, q.v.

1698 CONGREVE *Way of W.* Epil. (1866) 287 Whole belles assemblées of coquettes and beaux. **1711** SHAFTESB. *Charac.* (1737) III. 31 The gallant sentiments, the elegant fancys, the belle-passions. **1716** LADY M. W. MONTAGUE *Lett.* xi. I. 40 In what a delicate manner the belles passions are managed in this country. **1767** H. BROOKE *Fool of Q.* (1859) I. 375 (D.) Should we see the value of a German prince's ransom gorgeously attiring each of our belle-dames? **1908** W. S. MAUGHAM *Magician* ii. 19 She was one of those plain women whose plainness does not matter. A gallant Frenchman had.. called her a *belle laide.* **1946** 'J. TEY' *Miss Pym Disposes* xiv. 152 A woman with the makings of a *belle laide.* **1956** L. E. JONES *Edwardian Youth* i. 6 Conscious of the physical failings of that fascinating *belle-laide.*

B. *sb.* A handsome woman, *esp.* one who dresses so as to set off her personal charms; the reigning 'beauty' of a place; a fair lady, a fair one.

1622 FLETCHER *Beggar's B.* IV. iv, Vandunke's daughter, The dainty black-ey'd belle. **1712** POPE *Rape Lock* II. 16 Might hide her faults, if Belles had faults to hide. **1712** ARBUTHNOT *John Bull* (1755) 42 Fantastical old belles, that dress themselves like girls of fifteen. **1779** JOHNSON *Lett.* 220 (1788) II. 79 My Master.. courts the belles, and shakes Brightelmston. **1860** O. MEREDITH *Lucile* 56 The belle of all Paris last winter; last spring The belle of all Baden.

belle, obs. form of BELL; also in comb.

belled (bɛld), *ppl. a.* [f. BELL *sb.* or *v.* + -ED.]

1. Furnished with a bell or bells. Often in comb., as ***double-belled.***

1833 HT. MARTINEAU *Manch. Strike* vii. 81 His belled cap. **1865** RUSKIN *Sesame* 4 To ring with confidence the visitors' bell at double-belled doors.

2. Bell-flowered. Often in comb., as ***blue-belled.***

a **1850** BEDDOES *Alpine Spir. Song* i, Where the gentians blue-belled blow. **1856** RUSKIN *King Gold. Riv.* v. 51 Soft belled gentians, more blue than the sky. **1869** —— *Q. of Air* §83 The belled group, of the hyacinth and convallaria.

belled, obs. var. of BELD, BALD.

1568 *Wills & Inv. N.C.* (1860) 297 A little belled meare and a fole.

Belleek (bɛ'liːk). The name of a town in Fermanagh, Ireland, used *attrib.* or *absol.* to designate a kind of pottery produced there (see quot. 1960).

1869 *Arts Jrnl.* May 149 (*title*) The Belleek Pottery. *Ibid.* 151/1 Neither of these glazes.. can compare with the beauty of Belleek ware... The most welcome of the patrons of Belleek is the Prince of Wales. **1935** *Discovery* July 205/2 Thin section of Belleek china showing layer of crystals found between body and glaze. **1960** H. HAYWARD *Antique Coll.* 29/1 *Belleek*, a light, fragile feldspathic porcelain cast in moulds, with lustrous pearly glaze.

bellementte, var. BILIMENT, *Obs.*, ornament.

belleric, beleric (bɪ'lɛrɪk), *a.* and *sb.* [a. F. *bellėric*, more correctly *belliric*, ad. (ultimately) Arab. *balīlaj*, f. Pers. *balīlah.*] The astringent fruit of *Terminalia Bellerica*, also called Bastard Myrobalan, imported from India for the use of calico-printers, and used for the production of a permanent black.

1757 PARSONS in *Phil. Trans.* L. 403 Distinguished.. by its round figure; and called the belleric Myrobalan. **1808** COLEBROOKE *Dict. Sanscr.* 90 Beleric Myrobalan. **1858** R. HOGG *Veg. K.* 635 The Belleric is.. the size of a nutmeg and very astringent.

‖ **belles-lettres** (ˌbɛl 'lɛtr), *sb. pl.* Also 8 -letters, belle-lettre. [Fr.; lit. 'fine letters, *i.e.* literary studies,' parallel to *beaux arts* the 'fine arts'; embracing, according to Littré, grammar, rhetoric, and poetry.] Elegant or polite literature or literary studies. A vaguely-used term, formerly taken sometimes in the wide sense of 'the humanities,' *literæ humaniores*; sometimes in the exact sense in which we now use 'literature'; in the latter use it has come down to the present time, but it is now generally applied (when used at all) to the lighter branches of literature or the æsthetics of literary study.

1710 SWIFT *Tatler* No. 230 ¶2 The Traders in History and Politicks, and the Belles Lettres. **1747** *Scheme Equip. Men of War* 23 Civil or Military Law, or any other Part of the Belles Letters. **1801** FINLAYSON *H. Blair*, To endow a Professorship of Rhetoric and Belles Lettres in the University of Edinburgh. **1848** L. HUNT *Town* iii. 138 A strong union has always existed between the law and the belles-lettres. **1855** H. REED *Lect. Eng. Lit.* i. (1878) 34 That vapid, half naturalized term 'belles-lettres,' which has had some currency as a substitute for the term 'literature.'

bellet, obs. variant of BILLET *sb.*[2]

belleter ('bɛlɪtə(r)). *Hist.* [= *bell-yetter* (BELL *sb.*[1] 12).] A bell-founder.

1891 *Athenæum* 12 Sept. 360/2 On the tenor at Great Bradley we recognize the time-honoured name of a belleter whom Mr. Stahlschmidt.. restored to renown. **1898** *Ibid.* 16 July 103 The Van den Ghens, of Louvain and Malines, were belleters of renown.

belletrist, -lettrist (bɛl'lɛtrɪst). Also 9 belles-lettreist. [f. BELLES-LETTRES *sb.pl.* + -IST.] One devoted to belles-lettres. *attrib.* or as *adj.* = BELLETRISTIC *a.*

1816 GILCHRIST *Philos. Etym.* 193 The great Quintilian, or any of his worthy disciples the French *Belles-lettreists.* **1858** DE QUINCEY *Whiggism* Wks. VI. 130 As an orator, an essayist, or, generally, as a bellettrist. **1889** J. M. ROBERTSON *Ess. Crit. Method* 40 The belletrist essays of Mr. Lowell have had a wide public. **1894** J. DAVIDSON *Ballads & Songs* 38 Heed not bellethrist [*sic*] jargon. **1923** J. M. MURRY *Pencillings* 108 No amount of sedulous apery or word-mosaic will make a writer of the dilettante bellelettrist.

Hence **be'lletrism**, the study or composition of belles-lettres.

1938 *Scrutiny* VII. 208 Her university.. could only be a breeding-ground for boudoir scholarship.. and belletrism. **1961** *Essays in Crit.* XI. 196 Some of the assumptions he has innocently taken over from stock Victorian-romantic theory .. serve only for effusions of belletrism such as this.

belletristic (bɛlə'trɪstɪk). *a.* [f. prec. + -IC.] Of or pertaining to belles-lettres.

1821 COLERIDGE in *Blackw. Mag.* X. 254, I wish I could find a more familiar word than *æsthetic*, for works of taste and criticism. It is, however, in all respects better, and of more reputable origin, than *belletristic.* **1864** *Reader* 2 Apr. 427/2 To start from the first of April the *Grand Journal*, as a belletristic weekly. **1866** M. ARNOLD in *Cornh. Mag.* XIII. 290 An unlearned belletristic trifler like me. **1868** PATTISON *Academ. Org.* §5. 293 We have risen above the mere belletristic treatment of classical literature.

So **belle'tristical** († **belles-le'ttristical**) *a.*, **belle'tristically** *adv.*

1799 W. TAYLOR in Robberds' *Mem.* I. 259 His belles-lettristical pedantry. **1840** *Fraser's Mag.* XXI. 199 No historical, biographical, geographical, or *belle lettristical* book..would now have much chance. **1894** *Westm. Gaz.* 25 June 3/1 He trifles bellettristically around ghosts,..and the relation of ghosts to religion.

bellewe, -ewing, obs. ff. BELLOW, -ING.

bell-flower ('bɛlflaʊə(r)). [f. BELL *sb.*[1] + FLOWER.] The common name of the various species of flowering plants of the genus *Campanula*, distinguished by their handsome bell-shaped blossoms.

1578 LYTE *Dodoens* 172 In English they be called Belfloures, and of some Canterbury Belles. **1741** *Compl. Fam.-Piece* II. iii. 374 Nettle-leav'd Bell-flowers. **1855** BROWNING *Toccata* Wks. VI. 55 On her neck the small face buoyant, like a bell-flower on its bed. **1882** J. HARDY in *Proc. Berw. Nat. Club* IX. 430 The giant bell-flower (*Campanula latifolia*) grows near the footpath.

bell-founder ('bɛlˌfaʊndə(r)). [f. BELL *sb.*[1] + FOUNDER.] A founder, caster, or maker of bells. **bell-founding**, the art or process of founding or casting bells. **bell-foundry**, a place where bells are cast.

1530 PALSGR. 197/2 Bell founder, *fondevr de cloches*. **1643** HORN & ROB. *Gate Lang. Unl.* x, Of bell-metal Bell-founders cast bells. **1856** tr. *Berlioz' Instrument.* 225 Bell-founders can all manufacture these small cymbals. **1872** ELLACOMBE *Bells of Ch.* 216 A masterpiece of bellfounding.

bell-glass ('bɛlˌglɑːs, -æ-). [f. BELL *sb.*[1] + GLASS.] A bell-shaped glass vessel or cover, used chiefly for the protection of plants.

1682 WHELER *Journ. Greece* II. 193 A large square Room ..covered with a Cuppalo, thorough which the Light is let by Bell-glasses. **1737** MILLER *Gard. Dict.* s.v. *Lupulus*, When they..put Bell-glasses over their Cauliflowers. **1809** ALLEN & PEPYS in *Phil. Trans.* XCIX. 413 We placed a Guinea pig upon it, with the bell-glass over him. **1851** GLENNY *Handbk. Fl.-gard.* 36 Cuttings may be planted.. and covered by a bell-glass.

'bellhouse. *arch.* and *dial.* Also 1 bell-hús, 4 belhows, 5 belhowse, bellehowse, 5–7 belhouse. [f. BELL *sb.*[1] + HOUSE.] A tower or other erection for containing a bell or set of bells; a belfry; *properly* used of a detached structure, but also applied to the belfry of a church, etc.

a **1000** Thorpe's *Laws* I. 190 (Bosw.) Gif ceorl hæfde fif hida agenes landes, cirican and cycenan, bell-hus. *a* **1100** *Gloss.* in Wr-Wülcker *Voc.* 327 *Cloccarium, uel lucar*, Belhus *c* **1425** *Ibid.* 648 *Hoc campanare*, A[e] belhowse. **1483** *Cath. Angl.* 27/1 Belhouse, *campanile*. **1598** HAKLUYT *Voy.* I. 126 A Church and a Kitchin, a Belhouse, and a gate. **1766** ENTICK *London* IV. 223 The bell-house stood on the said ground. **1855** *Whitby Gloss.*, *Bell-house*, the tower of a church, the belfry.

† **'bellibone.** *Obs. rare.* [? corruption of F. *belle bonne* or *belle et bonne* fair and good; if not a humorous perversion of BONNIBEL, q.v.] A fair maid, a bonny lass.

1579 SPENSER *Sheph. Cal.* Aug. 61, I saw the bouncing Bellibone. *Ibid.* Apr. 92 *Gloss.*, A bellibone, or a Bonibell, homely spoken for a fair mayde, or Bonilasse. **1586** WEBBE *Eng. Poetrie* 83 With a bellibone trym for to be loaden.

† **'bellic,** *a. Obs.* [a. F. *bellique*, ad. L. *bellicus*, f. *bellum* war.] Of war; warlike.

1627 FELTHAM *Resolves* II. lii. (1677) 262 The bellic [*other edd.* bellique] Cæsar. **1680** PELLING *Good Old Way* 128 (L.) His machines and bellick instruments.

† **'bellical,** *a. Obs.* [f. as prec. + -AL[1].] Pertaining to war, warlike.

1513 DOUGLAS *Æneis* VII. xi. 54 Itale Now birnis into fury bellicale. **1572** BOSSEWELL *Armorie* II. 97 Two maces bellicall. **1602** FULBECKE *1st Pt. Parall.* 20 Some [tenures are] both domesticall & bellicall, as grand sergeancy.

† **'belliche,** *adv. Obs. rare*[−1]. [f. BEL *a.* + *-liche* = -LY[2].] Beautifully.

1394 *P. Pl. Crede* 344 Wiþ arches on eueriche half and belliche y-corven.

bellicose (ˌbɛlɪ'kəʊs), *a.* [ad. L. *bellicōs-us*: see -OSE.] Inclined to war or fighting; warlike.

1432–50 tr. *Higden* (1865) I. 321 Germanye, the peple of whom was..bellicose. **1535** STEWART *Cron. Scot.* (1858) I. 134 Our godis aboue..In Albione hes plantit..The perfite pepill, bald and bellicois. **1706** MAULE *Hist. Picts* in *Misc. Scot.* I. 32 The bellicose Romans. **1880** KINGLAKE *Crimea* VI. iii. 13 Their bellicose names were deceptive.

ˌ**belli'cosely,** *adv.* [f. prec. + -LY[2].] In a bellicose or warlike manner or direction.

1882 O'DONOVAN *Merv* I. xxiv. 415 Bellicosely inclined.

bellicosity (bɛlɪ'kɒsɪtɪ). Warlike inclination.

1884 *Manch. Exam.* 9 July 5/1 There is no suggestion of bellicosity in these utterances.

† **'bellicous,** *a. Obs.* Also 7– quous. [a. F. *belliqueux*, ad. L *bellicōsus*.] = BELLICOSE.

1536 *Exhort. Northe* in Furniv. *Ballads* I. 304 Cheiff bellicous champions. *a* **1577** SIR T. SMITH *Commw. Eng.* 106 Bellicous nations. **1628** DIGBY *Voy. Medit.* (1868) 65 The Greekes of the countrie..would soone become a belliquous [*printed* belliguous] nation.

bellied ('bɛlɪd), *ppl. a.* Forms: 5 balyd, 6 belied, 6–7 bellyed, 7 belly'd, belli'd, 6– bellied. [f. BELLY *v.* or *sb.* + -ED.]

1. Having a belly. Often in *comb.*, e.g. *big-* or *great-bellied*, having a big belly, corpulent; *hence*, pregnant. See also GOR-, POT-, SHADBELLIED.

? *c* **1475** *Hunt. Hare* 187 Sym, that was balyd lyke a cow. *c* **1520** ANDREWE *Noble Lyfe* in *Babees Bk.* (1868) 237 Scilla ..is belied like a beste, & tayled lyke a dolphin. **1567** *Triall Treas.* (1850) 14 The great bellied loute. **1650** J. GREGORY *Learned Traits* 98 When the great belli'd woman's time is com. **1697** DRYDEN *Virg. Georg.* III. 126 The Colt..Sharp headed, Barrel belly'd, broadly back'd. **1803** BRISTED *Pedest. Tour* II. 687 The big-bellied hostess.

b. Big-bellied, corpulent; *fig.* inflated.

1532 FRITH *Mirror* (1829) 272 Bellied monks, canons, and priests. *a* **1564** BECON *Fl. Godly Pr.* in *Prayers, etc.* (1844) 39 The dreams of the bellied hypocrites. *a* **1813** A. WILSON *Insult. Pedlar* Poet. Wks. (1846) 199 A bellied gent. steps owre the run.

2. *transf.* Made large and full, rounded; bulging; blown or puffed out.

a **1593** H. SMITH *Serm.* (1622) 207 It becomes them well ..to wear bellied doublets. **1649** BLITHE *Eng. Improv. Impr.* (1653) 70 The neather part of the bit a little bellied or square. **1678** *Lond. Gaz.* No. 7332/4 A bellied porringer. **1747** FRANKLIN *Wks.* (1840) 192 A vinegar-cruet, or some such bellied bottle. **1878** B. TAYLOR *Deukalion* III. vi. 130, I see a glorious barque With bellied canvass.

bellies, pl. of BELLY; also obs. f. BELLOWS.

† **be'lliferous,** *a. Obs.* [f. L. *bellifer*, f. *bellum* war + *-fer*, -bringing.] 'That bringeth war.' Bailey.

† **'bellify,** *v. Obs. rare*[−1]. [f. L. *bell-us* beautiful + -FY.] *trans.* To embellish, beautify. Hence **'bellifying** *ppl. a.*

1540 RAYNALD *Birth Man* IV. vi. (1634) 197 Embellishing or bellifying Medicines..to remove certaine blemishes.

† **be'lligerate,** *v. Obs.*[−0] [f. L. *belligerāt-* ppl. stem of *belligerāre* to wage war, f. *belliger*: see BELLIGEROUS.] 'To make war.' Cockeram 1623; whence in Bailey, etc.

† **beˌllige'ration.** *Obs.*[−0] [formed as prec.] 'Waging, or making war.' Bullokar 1676.

belligerence (bɛ'lɪdʒərəns). [f. BELLIGERENT *a.*: see -ENCE.] The carrying on of hostilities; also = BELLIGERENCY.

1814 W. TAYLOR in Robberds' *Mem.* II. 422 From your belligerence I seek refuge in his pacific philanthropy. **1882** *Punch* 9 Sept. 102 The thought of belligerence made him feel faint.

be'lligerency. Also -ancy. [f. as prec.: see -ENCY.] The position or status of a belligerent.

1863 *Boston Commw.* 11 Sept., The absurdity and wrong of conceding Ocean Belligerancy to a pretended Power. **1864** *Times* 22 Dec., To concede to Russia the rights of naval belligerency. **1877** MORLEY *Crit. Misc.* Ser. II. 392 Macaulay..steeps us in an atmosphere of belligerency.

belligerent (bɛ'lɪdʒərənt), *a.* and *sb.* Also 6–8 -gerant. [The earlier *belligerant* (cf. F. *belligérant*) was ad. L. *belligerānt-em*, pr. pple. of *belligerāre* to wage war: see BELLIGERATE, -OUS. The current spelling, if due to imitation of L. *gerentem*, is etymologically erroneous, since the word is not derived from *gerĕre*; but cf. *magnificent*.]

A. *adj.*

1. Waging or carrying on regular recognized war; actually engaged in hostilities; formerly also said of warlike engines, and the like.

1577 DEE *Relat. Spir.* I. (1659) 171 Four..belligerant Castles, out of the which sounded Trumpets thrice. **1765** TUCKER *Lt. Nat.* II. 408 Religion and reason are so far from being belligerent powers..that they join in alliance. *a* **1773** CHESTERF. (T.) The belligerent and contracting parties. **1775** JOHNSON, *Belligerant*, waging war. *Dict.* [i.e. from some dictionary.] **1846** PRESCOTT *Ferd. & Is.* I. iv. 213 A truce of six months between the belligerent parties.

2. *fig.* or *transf.* to other hostilities.

1809 W. IRVING *Knickerb.* (1861) 117 He assumed a most belligerent look. **1812** *Examiner* 11 May 290/2 The belligerent journalists..are unanimously for the military. **1850** THACKERAY *Pendennis* xlvi (1884) 458 Costigan called for a 'waither' with such a belligerent voice.

3. *attrib.* from the sb.: Of or pertaining to belligerents.

1865 (13 Mar.) BRIGHT *Canada, Sp.* (1876) 68 The acknowledgment of the belligerent rights of the South. **1881** J. WESTLAKE in *Academy* 15 Jan. 41/2 Controversies.. concerning the capture of private belligerent property at sea.

B. *sb.* **1.** A nation, party, or person waging regular war (recognized by the law of nations).

1811 *Hist. Eur.* in *Ann. Reg.* 75/2 The common rules between civilized belligerents. **1839** HALLAM *Hist. Lit.* II. II. iv. §86 War itself..even for the advantage of the belligerents, had its rules. **1864** *Times* 22 Dec., Deprived the blockaded Power of its rights as a maritime belligerent.

2. *fig.* or *transf.* to other hostile agents.

1839 DICKENS *Nich. Nick.* ii, A loud shout attracted the attention of even the belligerents [*i.e.* policemen]. **1849** MACAULAY *Hist. Eng.* xviii, Out of Parliament..the belligerents were by no means scrupulous about the means which they employed.

be'lligerently, *adv.* [f. prec. adj. + -LY[2].] In a belligerent manner or way; in a warlike way.

1837 *New Month. Mag.* L. 291 They feel belligerently inclined. **1881** *Standard* 18 Apr. 4/6 The whole Eastern Question..actively and belligerently reopened.

† **be'lligerous,** *a. Obs. rare.* [f. L. *belliger* war-waging, f. *bellum* war + *-ger*, -carrying on.] Waging war; belligerent.

1731 BAILEY, *Belligerous*, making or waging war. **1755** in JOHNSON. **1784** J. BARRY *Lect. Art* i. (1848) 66 The public energies, seldom belligerous, were generally directed to objects of public utility.

belling ('bɛlɪŋ), *vbl. sb.*[1] [f. BELL *v.*[4] + -ING[1].]

† **1.** The roaring of animals; bellowing. *Obs.*

c **1440** *Promp. Parv.* 30 Bellynge, of [? or] rorynge of bestys (*v.r.* bellinge of nete), *mugitus*.

2. *spec.* The cry of deer in the rutting season; hence *ellipt.* the season itself. Occas. *attrib.*

1513 DOUGLAS *Æneis* IV. Prol. 68 The meik hartis in belling oft ar found Mak feirs bargane. *c* **1560** A. SCOTT *Adv. Wanton Wowaris*, As bukkis in belling tyme. **1858** LYTTON *What will he do?* v. iv (D.) A melancholy belling note like the belling itself of a melancholy hart.

† **3.** Crying, roaring of human beings. *Obs.*

1583 STANYHURST *Æneis* II. (Arb.) 68 With mournful belling I namde expreslye Creüsa.

belling, *vbl. sb.*, in sense of BELL *v.*[1–3, 5]: see these.

belling ('bɛlɪŋ), *ppl. a.* [f. BELL *v.*[4] + -ING[2].]

† **1.** *gen.* Roaring, bellowing. *Obs.*

1583 STANYHURST *Æneis* III. (Arb.) 92 Loud the lowbye brayed with belling monsterus eccho. *Ibid.* IV. 120 With belling skrichcrye she roareth.

2. *spec.* Uttering the cry of deer in rutting-time.

1650 FULLER *Pisgah* III. ix. 338 Here..the belling Roes [are said] to bed.

bellipotent (bɛ'lɪpətənt), *a.* [ad. L. *bellipotent-em*, f. *bell-um* war + *potent-em* powerful.] Mighty or powerful in war. (*Obs.* in serious use.)

1635 HEYWOOD *Lond. Sinus Salut.* Wks. IV. 294 Bellipotent Mars is from his spheare come downe. **1656** BLOUNT *Glossogr.*, *Bellipotent*, mighty in wars, puissant at arms. **1825** *Blackw. Mag.* XVII. 62 General W.—a 'bellipotent' officer, who sent in a bill to Congress, for sugar plums.

† **'bellish,** *v. Obs.* Forms: 5 bels(c)h-yn, belch-yn. [Either shortened from EMBELLISH, or adopted from rare OF. *belir*, *bellir*, *bellissant* (used in same sense as *embellir*), f. *bel* beautiful.] = EMBELLISH. Hence **'bellishing** (in 15th c. belshynge) *vbl. sb.*; cf. next.

c **1440** *Promp. Parv.* 30 Belschyd, or made fayre [**1499** belched], *venustus*. Belchyn or make fayre, *decoro*, *venusto*. Belshynge, *venustacio*.

† **'bellishment.** *Obs.* [prob. a. OF. *belissement*: see prec.]

1611 SPEED *Hist. Gt. Brit.* v. vi. (1632) 42 Some other bellishments they had.

† **'bellitude.** *Obs.*[−0]. [ad. L. *bellitūdo*, f. *bell-us* fine, pretty: see -TUDE.] Beauty, fairness.

1623 in COCKERAM.

'bell-kite. *Sc.* and *north. dial.* In 5 beld cytt. [f. *beld*, *bell*, northern forms of BALD + *cytt*, *kite*, here a corruption of COOT.] The northern form of BALD-COOT. Also *fig.* as term of contempt.

c **1450** HOLLAND *Houlate* iii. 1 Busardis and Beld cyttes. **1876** *Mid-Yorksh. Gloss.* s.v. *Bellkite*, The usual application of this term is in the way of good-humoured reproach, 'Thou little bellkite, get out o' t' road.'

bellman ('bɛlmən). Also 4–7 belman. [f. BELL *sb.*[1] + MAN.]

1. A man who rings a bell; *esp.* a man employed to go round the streets of a town and make public announcements, to which he attracts attention by ringing a bell; a town-crier.

(Formerly a bellman announced deaths, and called on the faithful to pray for the souls of the departed; a bellman also acted as night-watchman, and called the hours).

1391 *Test. Ebor.* (1836) I. 163 Le belman portand' campanam per villam..ij.*d.* **1463** *Bury Wills* (1850) 17 Item I wele the ij bellemen haue ij. gownys. **1577** HOLINSHED *Chron.* III. 1209/1 Certaine houses in Cornehill, being.. cried by a belman. **1648** HERRICK *Hesper.* (1869) 221, I heare the cock, The bell-man of the night. **1659–60** PEPYS *Diary* 16 June, I staid up till the bell-man came by..and cried, 'Past one of the clock, and a cold, frosty, windy morning.' **1858** DICKENS *Lett.* (1880) II. 80 There is a bellman announcing something.

† **2.** He who 'bears the bell'; the best or most excellent. *Obs. rare.*

1617 MARKHAM *Caval.* v. 55 Repaire to the Stable of great Princes, where commonly are the bell-men of this Art.

Hence **'bellmanship**, the office of bellman.

1839 *Blackw. Mag.* XLVI. 386 The election of John Tapps to the bellmanship of Buzzleton.

'bell-ˌmetal.
The substance of which bells are made; an alloy of copper and tin, the tin being in larger proportion than in ordinary bronze.

The proportions of the constituents vary within the limits of 3¼ and 4 of copper to 1 of tin: the former is suited for large bells, the latter for small house-bells.

1541 *Act 33 Hen. VIII*, vii. §1 No person..should.. conuey anie brasse..laten, bell metall, gun metall..into.. partes beyonde the sea. **1522-3** *Inv. Ch. Goods Staffs.* 24 A bokett of belmettel. **1613** SIR H. FINCH *Law* (1636) 235 A licence to carrie Bell-mettall out of the Realme. **1812** SIR H. DAVY *Chem. Philos.* 420 Copper alloyed with from 1/12 to 1/5 of tin forms the different species of bronze and bell-metal.

b. *attrib.* Made of or resembling this alloy. Also *fig.* applied to a loud ringing voice.

1780 *Chron.* in *Ann. Reg.* 225/2 By eating mushrooms stewed in a bell-metal saucepan. **1816** SOUTHEY in *Q. Rev.* XVI. 271 Any blockhead with a brazen face and a bell-metal voice. **1837** DANA *Min.* (1880) 68 [Stannite] frequently has the appearance of bronze or bell metal, and hence the name *bell-metal ore*.

bellomancy, obs. var. BELOMANCY.

† **'bellomy.** *Sc. Obs.* [Derivation uncertain.] A blustering or audacious man.

1535 STEWART *Cron. Scot.* II. 666 Ane bellomy that busteous wes and bald. *Ibid.* 621 Of thir tratouris..Ane bellomye wes callit Makdouald.

bellon ('bɛlən). A term for lead-colic.

1794 E. DARWIN *Zoon.* (1801) II. 114 In the bellon, or colica Saturnina, the patients are said to bite their own flesh. **1819** REES *Encycl.*, *Bellon* or *Belland*, a distemper very common in Derbyshire..where they smelt lead ore.

Bellona (bɛ'ləʊnə). [L. *Bellōna*, the goddess of war, f. *bellum* war.] Proper name of the Roman goddess of war; *transf.* a spirited woman of commanding presence. **Be'llonian** *a.*, warlike.

1605 SHAKS. *Macb.* I. ii. 54 Bellona's Bridegroom, lapt in proofe. **1667** MILTON *P.L.* II. 922 Bellona storms, With all her battering Engines. **1711** E. WARD *Quix.* I. 64 His Steel Belonian Bright-Cap. **1820** SCOTT *Abbot* xxxi, Her features ..inflamed and resembling those of a Bellona. **1859** G. MEREDITH *R. Feverel* xxxvii. (1885) 346 He had recognized his superb Bellona in the lady by the garden window.

2. Name of one of the asteroids.

belloot, belote (bə'luːt, bə'ləʊt). [ad. Sp. *bellota* acorn.] The edible acorn of a species of oak (*Quercus Ballota*), in Barbary, Spain, and Portugal. **bellote oak**: the tree which bears it.

1866 *Treas. Bot.* 951/1 The acorns of *Q. Ballota*, and of its variety *Q. Gramuntia*, are eaten..under the name of Belotes. **1878** HOOKER & BALL *Marocco* 268 The belloot oak ..which is spread through North Africa and Spain.

† **bellosious,** *a.* *Obs. rare*⁻¹. [erroneously f. L. *bellōsus* warlike.] Warlike.

1586 WARNER *Alb. Eng.* lxxxvi (1606) 354 These two bellosious people cleer'd no sooner forren swords.

bellougina: see BELUGA.

bellow ('bɛləʊ), *v.* Forms: 4 belwe, bellewe, 4-5 below, 6 bellue, 6- bellow. [Of uncertain etymology. The equation of ME. *belwen* with the rare OE. *bylȝian* suggests that the latter is late WSax. for **bielȝian*, Anglian **belȝian*; but the origin of this is not evident, unless it be a parallel formation to the synonymous *bellan*, BELL *v.*[4], say from OTeut. **balligôjan*: cf. OE. *a-dilȝian*, OS. *dîligôn*, OTeut. **dîligôjan*, parallel to **dîlôjan*, in OHG. *tîligôn* and *tîlôn* to destroy.]

1. *prop.* To roar as a bull, or as a cow when excited. (Ordinarily, a cow *lows*.)

c **1000** *Martyrol.* 17 Jan. (Cockayne *Shrine* 52) Hwilum þa deofol hine swungon..hwilum hi hine bylȝedon on swa fearras gan ðuton eall swa wulfas. *c* **1305** *Leg. Rood* 145 Beestes gan belwe in eueri binne. **1377** LANGL. *P. Pl.* B. XI. 333 Þere ne was cow..þat wolde belwe after boles. **1388** WYCLIF *Jer.* l. 11 And lowiden either bellewiden, as bolis. **1580** NORTH *Plutarch* 358 (R.) Like wild beasts bellowing and roaring. **1611** SHAKS. *Wint. T.* IV. iv. 28 Iupiter Became a Bull, and bellow'd. **1784** BURNS *Lett.* x. Wks. (Globe) 302 A cow bellowing at the crib without food. **1868** *Once a Week* No. 5. 99 The first bull advances bellowing fiercely.

b. *trans.*

1868 *Once a Week* No. 5. 99 A young bull bellows a challenge.

2. Applied to the roaring of other animals; used formerly in sense of BELL *v.*[4] 2.

1486 *Bk. St. Albans* E v, An hert belowys. **1575** TURBERV. *Venerie* 238 An harte belloweth. **1596** SHAKS. *Merch. V.* v. i. 73 Youthful and vnhandled Colts..bellowing and neighing loud. **1602** —— *Ham.* III. ii. 264 The croaking Rauen doth bellow for Reuenge. **1738-51** CHAMBERS *Cycl.* s.v. *Hunting.* The terms for their noise at rutting time..A hart *belleth*; a buck *growns* or *troats*; a roe *bellows*. **1766** *Vacation* in Dodsley *Coll. Poems* III. 153 The master stag.. Bellows loud with savage roar. **1875** B. TAYLOR *Faust* iii. I. 51 Poodle..Cease to bark and bellow.

3. Of human beings: To cry in a loud and deep voice; to shout, vociferate, roar (*depreciative* or *humorous*); also (*seriously*) to roar from pain.

1602 SHAKS. *Ham.* III. ii. 36 There bee Players..that.. haue so strutted and bellowed. **1649** MILTON *Eikon.* Wks. (1738) I. 43 Not fit for that liberty which they cried out and bellowed for. **1709** STEELE *Tatler* No. 54 ¶3 He is accustom'd to roar and bellow so terribly loud in the Responses. **1718** POPE *Iliad* v. 1053 Mars bellows with the pain. **1824** W. IRVING *T. Trav.* II. 234 Like a bully bellowing for more drink.

b. *trans.* To utter (words or cries) in a loud and deep voice; frequently with *out*, *forth*.

1581 NOWELL & DAY in *Confer.* I. (1584) Diiij b, Beelzebub bellowed out most horrible blasphemies. **1603** KNOLLES *Hist. Turkes* (1621) 663 Bellowing out certaine superstitious charms. **1771** SMOLLETT *Humph. Cl.* (1815) 143 Noisy rustics bellowing 'Green pease' under my window. **1881** MISS YONGE *Lads & L. Langley* i. 41 Some used to bellow or screech out any familiar hymn in an irreverent way.

c. *to bellow off*: to drive off by shouting, to shout down.

1837 CARLYLE *Fr. Rev.* II. III. III. ix. 249 Fain would Reporter Rabaut speak his..last-words; but he is bellowed off.

4. Of thunder, cannon, wind, the sea, and other inanimate agents: To make a loud hollow noise; to roar.

1384 CHAUCER *House F.* (Fairf.) 1803 A soun As lowde as beloweth [*v.r.* belwith, bellyth, belleth] wynde in helle. **1596** SPENSER *F.Q.* I. vii. 7 A dreadfull sownd, Which through the wood loud bellowing did rebownd. **1653** HOLCROFT *Procopius* 36 Mount Vesuvius bellowed. **1727** THOMSON *Summer* 1168 Thule bellows through her utmost isles. *c* **1800** WORDSW. *Sonn. Liberty* xii, And Ocean [should] bellow from his rocky shore. **1866** B. TAYLOR *Soldier & Pard* 27 Our cannon bellowed round.

b. With *obj.*: To give forth, emit, utter, or proclaim with loud noise.

1706 WATTS *Horæ Lyr.* II. I. 236 Till the hollow brazen clouds Had bellow'd..Loud thunder. **1852** TENNYSON *Wellington* 66 His captain's-ear has heard them boom, Bellowing victory, bellowing doom. **1858** HAWTHORNE *Fr. & It. Jrnls.* I. 141 A large cannon-ball..rolling down.. bellowing forth long thunderous echoes.

'bellow, *sb.* [f. prec. vb.]

1. The roar of a bull, or similar cry of other animals.

1779 HUNTER in *Phil. Trans.* LXIX. 286 The bellow of the free martin is similar to that of an ox. **1870** LUBBOCK *Orig. Civilis.* ix (1875) 408.

2. *transf.* of human beings: A loud deep cry or roar.

a **1835** HOGG *Tales* (1837) III. 37 As loud as he could roar ..never letting one bellow abide another. **1859** G. MEREDITH *R. Feverel* xxi (1885) 151 He heard a bellow for help.

3. The loud deep roar of cannon, thunder, a storm, and other inanimate agents.

1826 DISRAELI *Viv. Grey* VII. viii. 430 The bellow of the martial drum. **1856** FROUDE *Hist. Eng.* (1858) II. VII. 229 Mere idle sounds, like the bellow of unshotted cannon.

bellow(e, obs. form of BILLOW.

bellowed ('bɛləʊd), *ppl. a.* [f. prec. + -ED.] Uttered with a loud roar.

1806 J. BERESFORD *Miseries Hum. Life* I. vi. 130 Your bellowed intreaties that he would stop. **1859** R. BURTON *Centr. Afr.* in *Jrnl. R.G.S.* XXIX. 323 The frequent recurrence of bellowed exclamations.

bellower ('bɛləʊə(r)). [f. as prec. + -ER[1].] He who or that which bellows.

a **1634** CHAPMAN *Hymn Hermes* (1818) 56 Full fifty of the violent bellowers. **1796** GROSE *Dict. Vulgar T.*, *Bellower*, the town crier. *a* **1848** MARRYAT *R. Reefer* xli, We had the report from the said brass bellowers. **1840** MACAULAY in *Leis. Ho.* (1881) 477/1 The steady bellowers of the Opposition had been howling from six o'clock.

bellowing ('bɛləʊɪŋ), *vbl. sb.* Also 4 bellewing, 5 belewyng. [f. as prec. + -ING[1].]

a. The roaring of a bull, or similar noise of other animals. **b.** Loud and continued vociferation of human beings, especially when inarticulate; noisy outcry. **c.** Roaring of cannon, thunder, the sea, etc.

1393 GOWER *Conf.* III. 203 It shulde seme..A bellewing in a mannes ere. *c* **1450** LONELICH *Grail* xliii. 172 As thowh it hadde ben a develes belewyng. **1552** HULOET, Bellowyng or rorynge of neate, *mugitus*. **1580** NORTH *Plutarch* 358 (R.) The bellowing of such a multitude of beastly people. **1610** SHAKS. *Temp.* II. i. 311 We heard a hollow burst of bellowing Like Buls, or rather Lyons. *c* **1620** Z. BOYD *Zion's Flowers* (1855) 11 Wee heare no thing but bellowing of the wind. **1774** GOLDSM. *Nat. Hist.* (1824) I. 56 [They] believe the bellowings of Hecla are nothing else but the cries of the damned. **1852** HAWTHORNE *Grandf. Chair* II. iii. (1879) 86 What a bellowing the urchins make!

'bellowing, *ppl. a.* [f. as prec. + -ING[2].] That bellows or roars: see the vb.

1618 BOLTON *Florus* III. viii. 195 They raised a bellowing cry, like so many beasts, and fled to shore. **1635** SWAN *Spec. M.* v. §2 (1643) 173 Blustering Boreas..is a bellowing wind. *c* **1746** HERVEY *Medit. & Contempl.* (1818) 165 Signals of distress are heard from the bellowing deep. **1847** LONGF. *Ev.* I. v, Bellowing herds of buffaloes rush to the river.

bellows ('bɛləʊz, 'bɛləs), *sb.* Forms: *α. sing.* 1 **-bælȝ, belȝ, beliȝ, bylȝ, byliȝ,** 3 **beli,** 3-4 **bely,** ? **buly;** *pl.* 3-4 **belies, bulies,** 5 **belyes, belise, belice,** 6 **bales, bellies, bellyis.** *β. sing.* 4 **belw, belu, below,** 5-6 **bel(l)owe;** *pl.* 4 **belwes, bellows,** 5 **belwis, -wys, -owys,** 6 **belowse,** 5-7 **bellowes,** 7- **bellows,** (*double pl.* 7 **bellowses,** still *dial.*). [Now used only in plural: the sing. was still in use in 15th c., and still later in compounds. The OE. name for 'bellows' was *blǽstbęl(i)ȝ*, *blǽst-bęl(i)ȝ* 'blast-bag, blowing-bag' (= ON. *blástr-belgr*, Sw. *blåsbälg*, Da. *blæsebælg*, mod.G. *blasebalg*); but already in the 11th c. the simple *bęlȝ*, *bylȝ*, *byliȝ* 'bag' occurs in this sense in the glossaries. (So also mod.Sw. *bälg*, and Da. *bælger* pl. = 'bellows.') Thence the ME. *beli*, *bely*, *buly* (*ü*), really the same word as BELLY, under which see the remoter etymology. In the sense 'bellows,' *bely* was still used in the sing. by Chaucer, but after 1400 we find this only with the sense 'belly,' though the pl. *belies*, *bellies* retained the sense 'bellows' late in the 16th c. in literature, and *bellis*, *bellice*, is still common in the dialects. But in Wyclif we find another form, *belu*, *belw*, in 15th c. *bellowe* (apparently of northern or north. midl. origin), of which the plur. *belwes*, *belowes*, *bellows* became established in 16th c. as the literary form, *bellies* being thenceforth used only as the plur. of 'belly' in the modern sense. In later times *bellows* has often been construed as a sing., 'a bellows,' and occasionally has even received a second plural inflexion, *bellowses*, which is common in the dialects; cf. 'a gallows,' and obs. or dial. pl. *gallowses*. Hence also the pronunciation ('bɛləs), the only one known to orthoepists early in the present century, which has however of late largely given place to ('bɛləʊz).

The evidence at present available does not settle whether *belu*, *belw*, came down from a non-palatalized form of OE. *bęlȝ*, or from the plural inflexions *bęlȝa*, *bęlȝum*, while *beli* represented the sing. forms *bęliȝ*, *bęlȝe* (cf. ME. sing. *dai*, *dei*, pl. *dawes*:—OE. *dæȝ*, *daȝas*); or, finally, whether it was a northern Eng. adoption of ON. *belgr*: for each of these hypotheses something may be said. *Bellows* is app. not cognate with L. *follis*: see BALL *sb.*[1] and BELLY.]

1. An instrument or machine constructed to furnish a strong blast of air. In its simplest form, it consists essentially of a combination of bag and box, formed of an upper and lower board joined by flexible leather sides, enclosing a cavity capable of expansion and contraction, and furnished with a valve opening inwards, through which air enters and fills the expanded cavity, and with a tube or nozzle, through which the air is forced out in a stream when the machine is compressed. It has many modifications of form and structure according to its purpose; and the name is sometimes applied to the 'blower' of a blast-furnace.

a. An instrument or machine of this kind used to blow a fire; it may be portable, as the common hand-bellows, or fixed, as a smith's bellows. Often, with reference to the two halves or handles, called a ***pair of bellows***, rarely, as sing., ***a bellows***.

α. *a* **800** *Epinal & Erf. Gl.* (Sweet *O.E.T.* 64) *Follis*, blestbælȝ, *Corpus Gl.* blæsbælȝ. *a* **1000** in Wülcker *Voc.* 241 *Folliginis*, belȝum; *follis*, blædbylȝum. —— 272 *Follis*, blæstbelȝ. *a* **1100** —— 336 *Follis*, byliȝ. —— 517 *Follibus*, bylȝum. *a* **1225** *Ancr. R.* 296 Þe deouel..mucheleð his beli bles. *Ibid.* 284 No fur in his smiððe—ne belies. *a* **1300** W. DE BIBLESW. in Wright *Voc.* 171 *Le foufou*, the bely. *c* **1300** *St. Brandan* 467 Tho hurden hi of bulies gret blowinge there. *c* **1400** *Leg. Rood* (1871) 85 Scho blew þe belise ferly fast. *a* **1440** *Isumbras* 410 A smethymane..blewe thaire belyes bloo. **1523** FITZHERB. *Surv.* 9 b, The whele gothe by drifte of water to blowe the bales. *a* **1600** *Purgatory* in *Ever-Green* (1761) II. 246 Thocht thay..blaw Ay quhill thair Bellyis ryve.

β. **1388** WYCLIF *Jer.* vi. 29 The belu [*v.r.* belw, bely] failide, leed is waastid in the fier. **1398** *Test. Ebor.* (1836) I. 250 Unum par de melioribus belowes. *c* **1440** *Promp. Parv.* 30 Belowe [ed. Pynson 1499, belows], *follis*. **1463** *Bury Wills* (1850) 23 A peyre tongys, and a peyre belwys. **1483** *Cath. Angl.* 27 A Bellowe [*v.r.* belowys or belice], *follis*. *a* **1568** COVERDALE *Hope Faithf.* xxvii. 189 The Lords breath, which is..as a belowes. **1570** LEVINS *Manip.* 180 A Belowe, *follis*. **1611** BIBLE *Jer.* vi. 29 The bellowes are burnt, the lead is consumed of the fire. **1660** BOYLE *New Exp. Phys.-Mech.* x. 74 The blasts of a pair of Bellows. **1676** HOBBES *Iliad* XVIII. 427 Twenty Bellowses in all he had. *a* **1700** DRYDEN (J.) Thou..like a bellows, swell'st thy face. **1715** DESAGULIERS *Fires Impr.* 137 The Bellows..blows so much the stronger. *Ibid.* 139 A pair of Bellows that blow constantly. **1791** COWPER *Iliad* XVIII. 585 Full twenty bellows working all at once. **1796** SOUTHEY *Lett. Spain & Port.* (1799) 199 The people make use of a hollow cane instead of a bellows. **1821** CLARE *Vill. Minstr.* II. 26 Taking the bellows up the fire to blow. **1870** BRYANT *Iliad* II. XVIII. 200 From twenty bellows came Their breath into the furnaces.

b. A similar contrivance for supplying air to a wind-instrument, as an organ, harmonium, or concertina. (In large organs the bellows are usually blown by hydraulic power.)

1542 *Rec. St. Michaels, Stortf.* (1882) 43 For ij schepe-kynnes to amend wᵗ all the bellis for the orgons, vijd. **1566** *Church-w. Acc. St. Dunstan's, Canterb.*, One payer of orgens lackeng iij pypes, also thear lacketh the pesyes of led belongen to the belowes. **1697** DRYDEN *Alexander's F.* 156 Ere heaving bellows learned to blow, While organs yet were mute. **1795** MASON *Ch. Music.* I. 37 Twelve pair of Bellows, rang'd in stated row, Are joined above, and fourteen more below. **1855** HOPKINS & RIMBAULT *Organ* II. (1877) 9 There are two kinds of bellows to be met with in church organs.. diagonal and horizontal bellows.

2. *fig.* Applied to that which blows up or fans the fire of passion, discord, etc.

c **1386** CHAUCER *Pers. T.* ¶277 The deueles bely..bloweth in man þe fire of fleshly concupiscence. **1576** LAMBARDE *Peramb. Kent* (1826) 427 By mediation of the Frenche King, a very Bellowse of this fire. **1600** *Cherrie & Slae* in *Ever-Green* (1761) II. 110 By Luve his Bellies blawin. **1608** SHAKS. *Per.* I. ii. 39 (1878), Flattery is the bellows blows up sin. **1665** BOYLE *Occas. Refl.* I. iv. (1675) 24 As Bellows to blow or rekindle Devotion. **1820** KEATS *Hyperion* II. 176 My voice is not a bellows unto ire.

3. *fig.* Applied to the lungs.

bellows to mend, said of a broken-winded horse; also *transf.*

1615 LATHAM *Falconry* (1633) 115 The lungs doe draw a breath..When these bellowes doe decay, then health from both doth fade away. **1631** DONNE *Elegy* in Farr's *S.P.* (1848) 21 We, to live, our bellows wear, and breath. **1711** *Vind. Sacheverell* 91 He..would be insufferably noisy in Company, if his Bellows would hold. **1829** P. EGAN *Boxiana* 2nd Ser. II. 133 It was completely 'bellows to mend!' with poor Davy. **1854** 'C. BEDE' *Further Adv. Verdant Green* iv. 31 To one gentleman he would pleasantly observe, as he tapped him on the chest, 'Bellows to mend for you, my buck!' **1875** WHITNEY *Life Lang.* iv. 59 The lungs are, as it were, the bellows of the organ. **1888** F. W. J. HENNING *Recoll. Prize Ring* 156 As the two were sent up it was a case of 'bellows to mend', especially with Grant. **1923** J. M. MURRY *Pencillings* 248 Johnny Keats always did have bellows to mend.

4. The expansible portion of a photographer's camera.

1884 *Jrnl. Phot. Alman.* 115 Attached to BB [the wooden frame of the camera] is a bellows stretching back some six inches when open. *Ibid.* 116 The back bellows acts as a focussing-cloth.

5. ***hydrostatic bellows***: see HYDROSTATIC.

6. *Comb.* chiefly *attrib.*, as ***bellows action***, ***-blast***, ***-board***, ***-pedal***, ***-sound***, ***-spring***; also **bellows-blower**, the person who works or blows the bellows; hence, *fig.* a fanner, inciter of strife, etc.; also, an unskilled assistant whose part is merely mechanical like that of the blower of an organ; **bellows-engine**, an engine that works bellows; **bellows-fever** (see quot.); **bellows-fish** (so called from its general shape: see quot.); **bellows-like** *a.*, resembling or acting like bellows; **bellows-maker**; **bellows-mender**; **bellows-nail**, a very small nail used in the construction of bellows; **bellows pocket** (see quot. 1960); **bellows press**, a small hand printing-press formerly used; **bellows-tail** (see quot.); **bellows-treader**, one who works bellows with his feet by treadles.

1881 C. EDWARDS *Organs* 44 The *bellows action..resembles an ordinary pump action. **1674** PETTY *Disc. bef. R. Soc.* 104 The Strength of such *Bellows-blast. **1658** LENNARD tr. *Charron's Wisd.* II. iii. §16 (1670) 250 The Player or Organist may in every point exercise his Art, without the *bellows-blower. ? **1849** SOUTHEY *Comm.-pl. Bk.* II. 191 The trumpeters and drummers and bellows-blowers of rebellion were conformable Episcopalians. **1865** *Times* 2 Feb., The prelates play the new organ; the lay members are the mere bellows-blowers. **1831** J. HOLLAND *Manuf. Metal* I. 162 The length and leverage..of the *bellows boards. **1831** CARLYLE *Sart. Res.* II. viii, Its *bellows-engines (in these Churches), thou still seest. **1852** SEIDEL *Organ* 133 *Bellows fever, that is, the trembling or faultering of the wards, is a great defect. **1684** *Phil. Trans.* XXIX. 479 The *Scolopax* or *Trombetta*, call'd by our Seamen the *Bellows or Trumpet-Fish. **1836** *Penny Cycl.* VI. 422/1 *Centriscus Scolopax*..known in Cornwall by the name of the bellows-fish. **1715** DESAGULIERS *Fires Impr.* 140 They..may be had at several *Bellows-makers. **1590** SHAKS. *Mids. N.* IV. i. 210 Flute the *bellowes-mender. **1765** GOLDSM. *Ess.* i, Mr. Bellows-mender hoped Mr. Curry-comb-maker had not caught cold. **1730** SAVERY in *Phil. Trans.* XXXVI. 296 Nails of several Sizes, from the smallest Sort of *Bellows-Nails to the largest Sort of Rafter-Nails. **1922** JOYCE *Ulysses* 435 Mrs. Breen in man's frieze overcoat with loose *bellows pockets. **1960** C. W. CUNNINGTON et al. *Dict. Eng. Costume* 14/2 *Bellows pocket*, late 19th c. A patch-pocket with side folds capable of expanding or lying flat, like a bellows. Common in Norfolk jackets from 1890 on. **1846** *Print. Appar. Amateurs* 5 A small and old instrument known amongst printers as the *Bellows Press. **1834** FORBES *Dis. Chest* 517 Most commonly the *bellows sound is..confined within the limits of the artery or ventricle. **1852** SEIDEL *Organ* 39 This ledge is called the *bellows-spring. *Ibid.* 38 The upper-board has on its end..a prolongation..called the *bellows tail. **1876** HILES *Catech. Organ* viii. (1878) 53 In many Continental Organs the inflation of the bellows is by treadles instead of handles, and hence the name '*bellows-treader.'

† **ˈbellows**, *v. Obs. rare.* [f. prec.]

To blow (with bellows). *to bellows up*: to gather *up* (wind).

1605 TIMME *Quersit.* II. vii. 137 The fire..which he had spread abroad, and winded or bellowsed, in vaine. **1648** *Persecutio Undecim* 9 The kindle-coale that the Faction bellowsed to that flame that must consume, etc. **1748** RICHARDSON *Clarissa* (1811) V. 318 She pouted out her blubber-lips, as if to bellows up wind.

† **bellrags.** *Herb. Obs.* A water plant, identified by Britten with *Nasturtium amphibium*.

1548 TURNER *Names of Herbes* D viij b, Lauer or Sion, is called of some Bellragges, of other some yealowe water-cresses. **1578** LYTE *Dodoens* 611 Turner and Cooper do call it [Water Parsely]..Yellow water cresses, and Bell ragges. **1611** COTGR., *Persil aigrun*, Wild Parseley..Bellrags.

bell-ringer (ˈbɛlˌrɪŋə(r)). [f. BELL *sb.*[1]] One whose business it is to ring a church or town bell at stated times or on stated occasions.

1543 BALE *Yet a Course* 24 Parysh clarkes and bellryngers. **1682** N. O. tr. *Boileau's Lutrin* iv. 133 Who should come in, but Girard the Bell-ringer? **1841** DICKENS *Barn. Rudge* 3/2 The parish clerk and bellringer of Chigwell.

So **bell-ringing** *vbl. sb.* and *ppl. a.*

c **1315** SHOREHAM 8 Holi thynges, As hali water..Liȝt, and bel-ryngynges. **1408** *E.E. Wills* (1882) 15 Wyth Belle Ryngyng..and Masse of requiem. **1883** *Daily News* 30 July 5/8 Bellringing showy equipages conducted by postillions and drawn by four strong horses.

bell-rope (ˈbɛlrəʊp). [f. as prec.]

The rope by which a bell is rung, *i.e.* either those in a belfry, or those which hang from the bell-levers in a room or chamber.

1638 FORD *Fancies* III. ii. 163 Why hang thy looks like bell ropes? **1781** COWPER *Truth* 82 Girt with a bell-rope that the pope has blessed. **1871** *Mad. Simple's Invest.* iii. in *Casquet Lit.* (1877) I. 311/1 He pulled a bell-rope which hung at his bed's head. **1883** *St. James' Gaz.* 30 Nov. 5/1 It has been decided that the bell-ropes are the legal property of the churchwardens.

bellswagger, -syre, var. BELSWAGGER, -SIRE.

bell-tongue: see BILTONG.

bellue, obs. form of BELLOW.

† **ˈbelluine**, *a. Obs.* Also 7 **beluin**. [ad. L. *belluīn-us*, f. *bellua* beast: see -INE.] Pertaining to or characteristic of beasts; brutal.

1618 MYNSHUL *Ess. Prison* 35 Barbarous cruelty is a Belluine quality. **1702** C. MATHER *Magn. Chr.* VII. vi. (1852) 575 The dying beast, with belluine rage, got such hold on his head. a **1731** ATTERBURY (J.) At this rate the animal and belluine life would be the best.

bellum (ˈbɛləm). Also **bellam**, etc. [a. Pers. *balam*; cf. *balaum* s.v. *Baloon* in Yule *Hobson-Jobson*.] A small boat or canoe used in ports along the shores of the Persian Gulf.

1901 *Wide World Mag.* VI. 464/1 Queenie was landed easily enough in a *bellum*. **1916** V. HORSLEY *Let.* 18 May in S. Paget *Life* (1919) 319 The whole real traffic of the place is done..by 'bellums': these are exactly like dugouts. **1916** T. E. LAWRENCE *Home Lett.* (1954) 319 The native boats give a character to Basra... You..shop or pay your calls in a 'Bellam'. A bellam is a sort of gondola, thirty or forty feet long, about four feet wide, and shallow. Two men work them, either by sculls, or by poling along with a light bamboo... The bellam is the passenger boat. **1919** *Chambers's Jrnl.* Jan. 23/2 The *bellem*..is a down-river boat peculiar to the city of pale-pink Persian roses—Basra.

bell-wether (ˈbɛlˌwɛðə(r)). Forms: 5 **belleweder, belwedyr**, 5–7 **-weather**, 6– **-weder, -wedder, -weadder**, 6–8 **bellweather**, 5– **bel-wether**, 6– **bellwether**. [f. BELL *sb.*[1] + WETHER.]

1. The leading sheep of a flock, on whose neck a bell is hung.

c **1440** *Promp. Parv.* 30/1 Belwedyr, shepe, *titurus*. **1549** *Compl. Scot.* vi. 66 The bel veddir for blythtnes bleyttit rycht fast. **1591** SPENSER *M. Hubberd* 296 To follow after their Belwether. **1718** MOTTEUX *Quix.* (1733) I. 237 He that steals a Bell-weather, shall be discover'd by the Bell. **1847** LEWES *Hist. Philos.* (1867) II. 254 Men are for the most part like sheep, who always follow the bell-wether.

2. *fig.* A chief or leader. (Mostly *contemptuous.*)

c **1430** LYDG. *Bochas* (1554) 224 a, I was cleped in my countrey The belweather. **1577** HOLINSHED *Chron.* II. 40/2 Thomas being the ring-leader of the one sect, and Scotus the belweadder of the other. **1687** T. BROWN *Saints in Upr.* Wks. 1730 I. 73 The principal bell-weathers of this mutiny. **1794** SOUTHEY *Wat Tyler* III. i. Wks. II. 50 You bell-wether of the mob. **1848** LOWELL *Biglow P.* i, 'Taint afollerin' your bell-wethers Will excuse ye in His sight.

3. *fig.* **a.** A clamorous person, one ready to give mouth. **b.** (Used *opprobriously*.)

c **1460** *Towneley Myst.* 86 Go now, belleweder. **1598** SHAKS. *Merry W.* III. v. 111 To be detected with a iealious rotten Bell-weather. **1620** SHELTON *Quix.* IV. xiii. 109 She made me weep, that am no Bell-weather. **1847** HALLIWELL, *Bell-wedder*, a fretful child. *North.*

Hence **bell-wethering**, the fact of leading and being led 'like sheep.' **bell-wetherishness**, tendency to follow one who takes the lead.

1882 *Spectator* 25 Mar. 388 But for the bell-wethering, there could have been no crinoline at all. *Ibid.* 387 The gregariousness, and bell-wetherishness of the English people, who must all do the same thing at once.

bellwort (ˈbɛlwɜːt). [f. BELL *sb.*[1] + WORT.] A general name in English botany for the plants of the N.O. *Campanulaceæ*, of which the type is the Campanula or Bellflower. Also, in U.S., a name for the genus *Uvularia*.

1785 *Memoirs Amer. Acad. Arts & Sci.* I. 434 *Uvularia*,.. Bellwort, sweet-smelling Solomon's Seal. **1845** A. WOOD *Class-bk. Bot.* 396 Uvularia..1. *U. Sessilifolia*..Bell-wort. Wild Oats. 2. *U. perfoliata*..Perfoliate Bell-wort. **1884** *Garden. Illustr.* 8 Nov. 426/2 A garden of Bell Worts..only would be very interesting.

belly (ˈbɛlɪ), *sb.* Forms: 3–4 **bali**, 4 **baly(e**, 4–5 **bale**, 4–6 **bely**, (5 **bylly**), 6 **bally, bealy(e, bellye**, 6–7 **bellie**, 5– **belly**. [ME. *bali*, *bely*:—OE. *bæliȝ*, *bęliȝ*, earlier *bælȝ*, *bęlȝ* 'bag, skin, envelope, hull (of beans and peas),' identical with ON. *belgr* 'skin, bag,' OHG. *balg*, MDu. *balch*, Goth. *balgs* 'bag, sack':—OTeut. **balgi-z* 'bag,' lit. 'inflated or swollen thing,' f. *belgan*, pa. t. *balg*, 'to be inflated, swell up.' The same word of which the plural appears as BELLOWS. The sense 'belly' did not exist in OE., and has not been developed in the cognate langs. Evidence is wanting to show whether it came directly from the sense of a material 'bag,' or whether the meaning 'body' (as the shell or husk of the soul) intervened: cf. senses 2 and 3. The history of the differentiation of *belly* and *bellows* is complicated. The various dialectal forms of the OE. word were WSax. *bięlȝ*, later *bylȝ*, *byliȝ*, Kentish and ESax. *bęlȝ*, *bęliȝ*, Anglian *bælȝ*, *bæliȝ*; these gave the early ME. *buli* (*ü*), *beli*, *bali*, respectively. Of these *beli*, *bely* occurs in sense both of 'bellows' and 'belly'; *bali* only as = 'belly'; *buli*(*es*) only as = 'bellows.' Hence it may be inferred that the sense 'body, belly' arose first in dialect where the form was *bali*, *baly*, and that this form passed with this sense into other dialects, which could thus discriminate *bali* 'belly,' from *beli*, *buli*, 'bellows.' Meanwhile the north. dial. obtained the distinction in another way, viz. by the establishment of *belw* in sense of 'bellows': thus the *Promp. Parv.* has Bely *venter*, Below *follis*. Finally the pl. *belwes*, *belowes* was generally adopted in that sense, and *beli*, *bely* became the literary form for the part of the body. *Bally* still occurs dialectally, e.g. in Lancashire and Shropshire.]

I. Original sense, in OE.

† **1.** A bag, skin-bag, purse, pod, husk. Freq. in comb. as ***béan bælȝ*** 'bean-pod,' ***blást-bælȝ*** BELLOWS q.v., ***met-bæl(i)ȝ*** 'meat-bag, scrip,' ***winbel(i)ȝ*** 'wine-skin, leather bottle.' Only in OE.

c **950** *Lindisf. Gosp.* Luke xv. 16 And wilnade ȝefylle womb his of bean-bælȝum. —— *ibid.* xxii. 35 Ic sende iuih buta seame and met-bæliȝ. c **975** *Rushw. G.* ibid., Butu seome and metbælȝe. —— Matt. ix. 17 Ne menn ȝeotaþ win niowe in win belȝas alde, elles to berstеþ þa belȝas..and þa belȝas to lore weorðaþ. **971** *Blickl. Hom.* 31 þa nam he fif stanas on his herdebelig. c **1050** *Gloss.* in Wr.-Wülcker *Voc.* 360 *Bulga*, bælȝe oððe bylȝe.

II. Of the body of man and animals.

† **2.** The body (? as the shell or integument of the soul. Cf. Ger. *madensack* 'worm-sack,' the body). *Obs.*

c **1275** *Sinners Beware* 199 in *O.E. Misc.* 78 Hwenne bali me byndeþ And bryngeþ hine on eorþe. c **1275** *Death* 83 in *O.E. Misc.* 172 þenne saið þe sawle..Awai þu wrecche fole bali (*l.* 83 baly), Nu þu list on bere. *Ibid.* 137 Li awariede bali [*later vers.* bodi], that neauer thu ne arise.

3. a. That part of the human body which lies between the breast and the thighs, and contains the bowels; the abdomen. (The ordinary mod. sense.)

1340 HAMPOLE *Pr. Consc.* 679 þe brest with þe bely. c **1380** WYCLIF *Pseudo-Freris* Wks. (1880) 315 To breede hem grete balyes. c **1440** *Promp. Parv.* 30 Bely, *venter*, *alvus*, *uterus*. ? c **1475** *Hunt. Hare* 187 Won hit hym on the bale with a mall. **1600** SHAKS. *A.Y.L.* II. vii. 154 The Iustice in faire round belly, with good Capon lin'd. **1803** BRISTED *Pedest. Tour* II. 643 A secret retained four and twenty hours would have burst his belly. **1834** MARRYAT *P. Simple* xxi, We must creep to the ramparts on our bellies. **1843** *Watson's Pract. Physic* II. 342 Organs..in the cavity of the belly. *fig.* **1677** GILPIN *Dæmonol.* (1867) 254 [To] go over the belly of their scruple to the performance of their action.

b. The part of a garment covering the belly.

1599 B. JONSON *Ev. Man out of Hum.* III. i, Such a sleeve, such a shirt, belly and all. **1601** CORNWALLYES *Ess.* II. xxviii, Our Taylors gave us a little belly to our doublets.

4. a. The under part of the body of animals.

c **1440** *Anc. Cookery* in *Househ. Ord.* (1790) 451 Take pykes, and undo hom on the bale, and wash hom clene. **1535** COVERDALE *Gen.* iii. 14 Vpon thy bely [WYCLIF, breest] shalt thou go & earth shalt thou eate. **1667** MILTON *P.L.* x. 514 A monstrous Serpent on his Belly prone. **1711** *Lond. Gaz.* No. 4792/4 Two Geldings, the one black..carrying a small Belly. **1862** JOHNS *Brit. Birds* (1879) 419 The Common Curlew..belly white, with longitudinal dusky spots.

b. As a joint of meat.

1883 *Enquire Within* (ed. 67) §1044 A belly of pork is excellent in this way.

c. In full ***belly-wool***. The wool from a sheep's belly, of inferior quality to the main fleece. *Austral.* and *N.Z.*

1851 F. A. WELD *Hints to Sheep-farmers in N.Z.* 10 Their mothers do not lose the belly wool, as they would do by lambing in spring. **1900** LAWSON *Over Sliprails* 32, I had just slipped a light ragged fleece into the belly-wool and 'bits' basket. **1911** E. M. CLOWES *On the Wallaby* iv. 101 Clipping the belly-wool. **1933** L. G. D. ACLAND in *Press* (N.Z.) 9 Sept. 15/7 *Belly*..(2) the wool off a sheep's belly, pressed and sold as 'bellies'. **1956** G. BOWEN *Wool Away!* (ed. 2) vii. 94 A bale of bulk ewe bellies can be depreciated a grade because of the inclusion of a few wethers' bellies from which urine stains have not been removed.

d. Applied to the under part of the fuselage of an aeroplane. Hence ***belly-landing***, a crash-landing of an aeroplane on its belly without use of the undercarriage; also (as a back-formation)

belly-land v.; ***belly tank***, a reserve fuel tank carried in the 'belly' of an aeroplane.

1917 'CONTACT' *Airman's Outings* 50 They saw an enemy plane turn over, show a white, gleaming belly, and drop in zigzags. **1939** *Flight* 19 Oct. 314/1 A bellylanding can be made without personal damage in almost any reasonable terrain. **1940** R. HARTLEY *Aeronaut. Dict.* 16 Belly Tank. **1942** *Aircraft of Fighting Powers* III. 66/1 The S-OO fighters could pursue them over long distances due to their long range of 1,600 miles when fitted with the external stream-lined belly tank. **1943** T. D. GORDON *Coastal Command at War* x. 94 The Hudsons..went down to sea-level, to guard themselves from a belly attack. **1944** *Sun* (Baltimore) 10 June 2/3 Johnson bellylanded his plane safely near the spot where he had seen Allied troops from the air. **1958** *Times* 15 Oct. 16/6 A Jordanian Air Force pilot.. climbed without a scratch..from a Vampire jet aircraft yesterday after a 'belly-landing' at nearly 200 m.p.h.

5. a. That part of the body which receives food; the stomach with its adjuncts.

1362 LANGL. *P. Pl.* A. Prol. 41 Heor Bagges and heore Balies weren [bratful] I-crommet. *c* **1375** WYCLIF *Epist. Dom.* xii. Sel. Wks. II. 257 þer owene bely þat þei feden as þer God. **1394** *P. Pl. Crede* 1521 With the bandes of bakun His baly for to fillen. *c* **1485** *Digby Myst.* (1882) III. 1156 Ye have so fellyd yower bylly with growell. **1526** TINDALE *Luke* xv. 16 He wold fayne have filled his bely [WYCLIF, wombe] with the coddes that the swyne ate. **1554–9** *Songs & Ball. Q. Mary* v. (1860) 13 Glade when the may fyll up thear ballys with bennys. **1562** J. HEYWOOD *Prov. & Epigr.* (1867) 45 Whan the bealy is full, the bones wold be at rest. **1629** FORD *Lover's Melanch.* II. ii, Get some warm porridge in your belly. **1712** ARBUTHNOT *John Bull* (1755) 16 He that sows.. upon marble, will have many a hungry belly before harvest. **1857** Bohn's *Handbk. Prov.* 70 The belly is not filled with fair words.

b. Hence, Put for the body in its capacity for food: opposed to *back*, as the recipient of clothing. *Also*, the appetite for food.

1555 *Fardle Facions* I. vi. 102 They sitte them downe together, and eate by the bealy. **1653** WALTON *Angler* 144 It is a hard thing to perswade the belly, because it hath no ears. **1719** W. WOOD *Surv. Trade* 312 The Labourers or Manufacturers that..wrought for the Backs and Bellies of other People. **1726** AMHERST *Terræ Fil.* 62 The best way.. is to pinch their bellies. **1763** JOHNSON in *Boswell* (1831) I. 479 He who does not mind his belly, will hardly mind any thing else. **1845** FORD *Handbk. Spain* i. 30 The way to many an honest heart lies through the belly.

c. The body in its capacity for indulgence of appetite; gluttony.

1526 TINDALE *Phil.* iii. 19 Whose God is their bely [WYCLIF, the wombe]. *c* **1538** STARKEY *England* II. ii. 171 Drunkerys, gyuen to the bely and pleasure therof. **1561** DAUS tr. *Bullinger on Apoc.* (1573) 37 b, Beastly bondslaues of the bealy. **1837** A. COMBE *Princ. Physiol.* iv. (ed. 6) 120 Let it not be supposed that I wish to make a god of the belly.

†**d.** A glutton. *Obs.*

1526 TINDALE *Tit.* i. 12 Evyll beastes, and slowe belies [WYCLIF, of slowe wombe]. **1577** tr. *Bullinger's Decades* (1592) 1114 Tributes..by wicked Princes bestowed vpon flatterers and bellies. **1655** MOUFFET *Health's Impr.* (1746) 133 They called the Eaters of it Savages and Bellies.

6. The bowels.

c **1340** *Gaw. & Gr. Knt.* 1330 þen brek þay þe bale, þe balez out token. **1553** BRENDE *Q. Curtius* Ff ij He felt a payne in his bealye. **1607** TOPSELL *Four-f. Beasts* (1673) 92 Good against all pains in the small guts, for it dryeth and stayeth the belly. **1671** J. WEBSTER *Metallogr.* xii. 186 It doth not loose the belly, or purge.

7. The womb, the uterus.

c **1440** *Promp. Parv.* 30/1 Bely, *uterus*. **1549–50** *Plumpton Corr.* 254 As yet my wife hath not laid her belly. **1596** SHAKS. *Merch. V.* III. v. 41, I shall answer that better than you can the getting vp of the Negroes belly; the Moore is with childe by you. **1602** WARNER *Alb. Engl.* IX. xlvii. 222 My belly did not blab, so I was still a Mayde. **1607** TOPSELL *Four-f. Beasts* (1673) 472 While they smell and taste of their dams belly. **1728** GAY *Begg. Op.* I. (1772) 75 Why, she may plead her belly at worst. **1853** 'STONEHENGE' *Greyhound* 178 'Flirt' ran second for the same cup with 'War Eagle' in her belly.

8. The internal cavity of the body; the 'inside.'

1491 CAXTON *Four Sons* (1885) 173 He braste the herte in hys bely. **1535** COVERDALE *Jonah* ii. 1 So was Ionas in the bely [WYCLIF, wombe] of the fysh, thre dayes and thre nightes. **1625** tr. *Gonsalvio's Sp. Inquis.* 43 Neither hath he any mans heart in his belly, that can without teares reade or heare these things. **1629** R. BERNARD *Terence's Andr.* I. i. 12/1 It made my heart cold in my belly. *c* **1645** HOWELL *Lett.* (1650) I. 472 Some shallow-pated puritan..will..cry me up to have a Pope in my belly.

9. The interior, the inside; *esp.* of things having a hollow cavity within, but also of other things material and immaterial.

1535 COVERDALE *Jonah* ii. 2 Out of the bely [WYCLIF, wombe] off hell I cried. **1658** USSHER *Ann.* v. 78 Out of Scythia, went over the belly of all Asia, till he came into Egypt. **1664** BUTLER *Hud.* II. III. 164 Speak i' th' Nun at London's Belly? **1697** POTTER *Antiq. Greece* III. xiv. (1715) 123 Ships of Burden..having large and capacious Bellies. **1832** AUSTIN *Jurispr.* (1879) II. xlvi. 801 They treat of *obligationes*..as it were in the belly of the opposite class, or that of *dominia*. **1884** FROUDE *Carlyle* II. xix. 65 A..candle lighted in the belly of a dark dead past.

†**10.** An internal cavity. *Obs.*

1594 T. B. *La Primaud. Fr. Acad.* II. 148 There are hollowe places [of the braine], called 'little bellies.' *Ibid.* 220 Wee divided..the internall parts of the frame..of man into three bellies.

11. 'The part of anything that swells out into a larger capacity' (Johnson); the bulging part *e.g.* of a pot or bottle; a suddenly widened part of a vein of ore; the central portion of a muscle, etc.

1591 SPENSER *Bellay's Vis.* IX, Leaning on the belly of a pot. **1615** CROOKE *Body of Man* 759 [This muscle] was called Digastricus because it hath two Venters or Bellies. **1625** BACON *Delays, Ess.* (Arb.) 525 The Handle of the Bottle, first to be received, and after the Belly. **1674** GREW *Anat. Plants* I. vii. §12 Against the Belly of the Bean. **1710** LONDON & WISE *Compl. Gard.* IV. (1719) 62 A handsome Pear..its Belly round. **1747** HOOSON *Miners' Dict.* s.v., Such Bellys prove oftentimes very well filled with Ore. **1799** KIRWAN *Geol. Ess.* 416 Sulphurated Iron occurs in strata in bellies and in veins. **1835–6** TODD *Cycl. Anat. & Phys.* I. 711/1 The belly of the shell comprises the greatest part of the exterior surface. **1845** TODD & BOWMAN *Phys. Anat.* I. 176 Muscles which have a bulging centre or belly.

12. A concave or hollow surface; a concavity formed in a surface, *e.g.* of a sail.

1607 TOPSELL *Four-f. Beasts* (1673) 443 Citherns or Lutes, upon whose bellies the Musitians played their Musick. *a* **1626** BACON (J.) An Irish harp hath the concave or belly, not along the strings, but at the end of the strings. **1701** *Phil. Trans.* XXIII. 1277 They wholly laid aside the Tortoise shell, and the sonorous part or Belly of the Lyre, was made of..different Figures. **1840** R. DANA *Bef. Mast* v. 12 To fall from aloft and be caught in the belly of a sail.

13. The front, inner, or lower surface of anything, as opposed to the *back*; *e.g.* the front bulging surface of a violin, the inside of curved timber, the angle formed by the meeting of the two lower sides of a burin or graver, the convex under edge of the tumbler of a lock, etc.

c **1790** IMISON *Sch. Art* II. 44 Great pains is required to whet the graver nicely, particularly the belly of it. **1843** *Penny Cycl.* XXVI. 346/1 The back [of the violin] is worked out much in the same proportion as the belly. *c* **1850** *Rudim. Nav.* (Weale) 96 *Belly*, the inside or hollow part of compass or curved timber, the outside of which is called the *Back*. **1867** TYNDALL *Sound* iii. 90 The two feet of the bridge rest upon the most yielding portion of the belly of the violin. **1884** F. BRITTEN *Watch & Clockm.* 143 The teeth of the wheel in passing just clear the belly of the pallets.

14. In various technical uses derived from the preceding: e.g. in *Coach-building*, the wooden casing of the axle-tree; in *Leather trade*, the belly hide of an ox or other beast (cf. BEND, BACK); in *Saddlery*, a piece of leather fastened to the back of the cantle, and sometimes forming a point of attachment for valise-straps; the sound-board of a piano. Also *attrib.*, as ***belly-bar***, ***-bridge***; **bellyman**, the workman who makes and fits the 'belly'.

1845 G. DODD *Brit. Manuf.* IV. 155 The 'bellyman' or 'sounding-board maker'. **1880** *Daily News* 10 Nov. 3/8 Leather..There is a short supply..of..light English.. bellies. **1905** HASLUCK *Pianos* 21 Prick through the belly about every 2 in. with a small bradawl; this will help in putting on the belly bridges. **1905** *Sci. Amer.* Suppl. 6 May 24536 The sound-board..barred beneath with batons.. technically 'belly-bars', which strengthen the belly. **1910** *Daily Chron.* 19 Jan. 12/7 Pianos. Bellyman and marker-off contractor wanted.

III. *Comb.* and *Attrib.*

15. *attrib.* (often = *adj.*) Pertaining to the belly: **a.** *lit.* Ventral, abdominal, as in ***belly-fin***, ***-part***, ***-place***, ***-worm***.

1594 BLUNDEVIL *Exerc.* IV. xix. 473 The lower belly-part of the former fish. **1607** TOPSELL *Four-f. Beasts* (1673) 156 His tender belly-parts. **1748** tr. *Vegetius' Distemp. Horses* 93 Proper for destroying Maw- or Belly-worms. **1774** GOLDSM. *Nat. Hist.* (1862) 294 The ventral, or belly fins, are either wholly wanting, as in the eel, etc. **1869** BLACKMORE *Lorna D.* iii. 17 'Us must crawl on our belly-places.'

†**b.** Pertaining to the supply of food, to bodily nourishment or appetite, as in ***belly-care***, ***-joy***, ***-matter***. *Obs.*

1377 LANGL. *P. Pl.* B. VII. 118 I shall cessen of my sowyng ..Ne about my bely ioye so bisi be na-more. *c* **1530** MORE *De quat. Noviss.* Wks. 101 Preferring their belly ioy before all the ioyes of heauen. **1549** COVERDALE *Erasm. Par. 1 Cor.* 2 The Lordes souper..was no bealy matter. *a* **1564** BECON *Fortr. Faithful* Wks. (1844) 602 This belly-care..is a great temptation to man..when he seeth all things so dear.

†**c.** *Theol.* Pertaining to the service of the flesh; fleshly, carnal: as in ***belly-doctrine***, ***-ease***, ***-wisdom***.

1528 TINDALE *Obed. Chr. Man* To Rdr. Wks. I. 138 Our fleshly wit, our worldly understanding, and belly-wisdom. **1528** ROY *Satire* (1845) A belly beast engendred amonge the ..papystical secte. **1645** MILTON *Tetrach.* Wks. (1851) 146 Deluded through belly-doctrines into a devout slavery. **1711** SHAFTESB. *Charac.* (1737) I. 283 Apt to construe every divine saying in a belly-sense.

16. a. objective with vbl. sb. or pr. pple., as ***belly-worshipper***, ***-worshipping***. **b.** locative and adverbial, as ***belly-beaten***, ***-devout***, ***-fed***, ***-gulled***, ***-laden***, ***-naked***, ***-pinched***, ***-proud***, ***-sprung***; also ***belly-like*** adj.

1642 ROGERS *Naaman* 219 Children..backe and *belly-beaten. **1599** SANDYS *Europæ Spec.* (1632) 140 The *belly-devout Friers. **1574** B. GOOGE *Lett.* in *N. & Q.* III. III. 181 The *bellyfedd mynysters that came over, att..a miserabell hard dyett. **1640** BROME *Sparagus Gard.* v. xiii. 221, I have been..backe-guld and *belly-guld. **1727** BRADLEY *Fam. Dict.* s.v. *Badger*, The other lays Earth on his Belly, and so ..draws the *Belly-laden Badger out of the Hole. **1847–9** TODD *Cycl. Anat. & Phys.* IV. 486/2 The posterior *belly-like part of the cell. **1525** *Basyn* 168 in Hazl. *E.P.P.* III. 51 Upstert the wench..And ran to hir maistrys all *baly naked. **1611** COTGR., *Tout fin mere nu*, all discouered..starke *bellie naked. **1605** SHAKS. *Lear* III. i. 13 The lion and the *belly-pinched wolf. **1675** *Three Inhumane Murth.* 2 Growing *Belly-proud, and Prodigal. **1607** *Lingua* IV. i. in Hazl. *Dodsl.* IX. 412 *Belly-sprung invention.

17. Special combinations: **belly-bound** *a.*, constipated, costive; **belly-brace**, a cross-brace passing beneath the steam-boiler of a locomotive; **belly-button** *colloq.*, the navel (Bartlett, 1877); †**belly-cheat** (*slang*), something for the belly, food; also, an apron; **belly-critic**, a connoisseur of good living; †**belly-cup**, ? a cup with a swelling body; **belly-dance**, an erotic oriental dance performed by women, involving abdominal contortions; hence ***belly-dancing*** vbl. sb.; ***belly-dancer***; †**belly-doublet**, a doublet covering the belly; **belly-flop** *colloq.*, (of troops) a sudden drop to the ground to avoid enemy fire; (of a swimmer) a dive that brings one's body flat on the water (also ***belly-flopper***); hence as *v.*, and *transf.*; **belly-fretting**, 'a great Pain in the Belly of a Horse; also the Wounding, or Galling of that Part with Fore-girths' (Phillips 1706); †**belly-friend**, a parasite; **belly-grinding**, pain in the bowels, colic; **belly-gut**, a slothful glutton; **belly-guy** (*Naut.*), 'a tackle applied half-way up sheers, or long spars that require support in the middle' (Adm. Smyth); **belly-helve** (see quot.); **belly-laugh** *colloq.*, a deep, unrestrained laugh; **belly-metal**, food, BELLY-TIMBER; †**belly-mountained** *a.*, having a large prominent belly; †**belly-paunch**, (*fig.*) a great eater, a glutton; **belly-pinched** *a.*, pinched with hunger; **belly-roll**, a roller with a central bulge, adapted to roll land between ridges or in hollows; **belly-sacrifice**, ? a sacrifice to the belly; **belly-shot** *a.*, a disease of cattle (see quot.); †**belly-slave**, one devoted to eating and drinking, a glutton; **belly-stay** (*Naut.*), a stay 'used half-mast down when a mast requires support' (Adm. Smyth); †**belly-swain**, ? a glutton; †**belly-sweep** *v.*, to sweep (the ground) with the belly; **belly-thrawe** (*Sc.*), pain in the belly, colic; **belly-vengeance** (*dial.*), sour ale, cider, wine, etc. Also BELLY-ACHE, BELLY-GOD, BELLY-TIMBER, etc., q.v.

1607 TOPSELL *Four-f Beasts* 302 Of Costiveness, or *Belly-bound, when a Horse is bound in the belly, and cannot dung. **1934** KIPLING in *Strand Mag.* Apr. 350/1 Why waste time fighting atomies who do not come up to your *belly-button? **1946** J. B. PRIESTLEY *Bright Day* iii. 66 If you'd ever gone to school with your belly-button knockin' against your backbone. **1609** DEKKER *Lanth. & Candle Lt.* Wks. 1885 III. 196 A Smelling cheate, signifies a Nose:..A *Belly chete, an Apron. **1622** FETCHER *Begg. Bush* II. i, Each man shall eat his own stol'n eggs,..ay, and possess What he can purchase, back or belly-cheats, To his own prop. *a* **1711** KEN *Urania* Wks. 1721 IV. 468 The *Belly-Criticks study how to eat. **1673** *Lond. Gaz.* No. 764/4 Several Canns, Bouls, *Belly-Cups, Spoons. **1899** MORROW *Bohem. Paris* iv. 95 The *danse du ventre* (literally, *belly-dance) is of Turkish origin. **1943** KOESTLER *Arrival & Departure* 54 The loud-speakers blared a hot belly-dance with drums and castanets. **1931** C. BEATON in *Wandering Years* (1961) 217 The wow of the evening was Carmen, the *belly-dancer. **1957** R. CAMPBELL *Portugal* ix. 192 The *lundum*..was a highly sensual song accompanied by much belly-dancing. **1588** SHAKS. *L.L.L.* III. i. 19 Your armes crost on your thin *bellie doublet. **1925** FRASER & GIBBONS *Soldier & Sailor Words* 21 **Belly flopping*, a term for the sectional rushes of troops in an attack in which the men advance in a crouching posture. **1931** BROPHY & PARTRIDGE *Songs & Slang 1914–18* (ed. 3) 282 In France, whenever one heard a shell coming uncomfortably close, one *belly-flopped* or *did a belly-flop*. **1937** 'R. HYDE' *Wednesday's Children* ii. 49 'It hurt,' she added.. 'So I didn't do any more worshipful belly-flops.' **1945** PARTRIDGE *Dict. R.A.F. Slang* 15 *Belly-flop*, a landing effected with the wheels unlowered. **1953** R. LEHMANN *Echoing Grove* 238 The nasty expectation of a belly-flop:.. the water has become so huge. **1916** E. F. BENSON *David Blaize* iv. 81 A loud, flat smack was heard as he fell into the water. And Ferrers said to Mullins: 'I say, can your pater take *belly-floppers?' **1941** *Lancet* 12 July 31/2 Perhaps the nearest experience that many of us may have had to blast-concussion is the flat dive—the 'belly-flopper' of our schooldays. **1960** BETJEMAN *Summoned by Bells* v. 50 The belly-floppers from the punt. **1579** LANGHAM *Gard. Health* (1633) 529 [For] *Belly grinding, bake a cake of Rye flower ..and apply it as hot as may be suffered. **1540** MORYSINE tr. *Vives' Introd. Wisd.* D viij, Suche as be skoffers, smell feastes..*bely guts. **1733** BAILEY *Erasm. Colloq.* (1877) 346 (D.), Thou wouldst not have a belly-gut for thy servant, but rather one brisk and agile. **1881** RAYMOND *Mining Gloss.*, **Belly-helve*, a forge-hammer, lifted by a cam..midway between the fulcrum and the head. **1921** S. H. ADAMS *Success* III. iv. 397 'I'm after the laugh that starts down here.' He laid hand upon his rotund waistcoat. '*The belly-laugh.' **1931** E. LINKLATER *Juan in Amer.* v. ii. 376 He laughed, deep belly-laughs. **1957** R. HOGGART *Uses of Literacy* vii. 191 Sensationalism..is as much without a belly-laugh as it is without bowels of compassion. **1590** *Plain Perc.* A iij, Old wringers..that fell out at their *belly-mettall. **1654** GATAKER *Disc. Apol.* 65 A man of puf-past, like that fat *bellie-mountaind Bishop. **1553–87** FOXE *A. & M.* (1596) 28/2 Heliogabalus that monsterous *belli-paunch. **1725** BRADLEY *Fam. Dict.* s.v. *Ridge*, It is harrow'd right up and down, and roll'd with a *Belly-Roll that passes between the Ridges. **1555** *Fardle Facions* II. ix. 200 Acquaintaunce and kindesfolke, assembled together, make a *bealie sacrifice of hym [*i.e.* devour him]. **1688** J. CLAYTON in *Phil. Trans.* XVII. 986 Their Guts [*i.e.* of cattle] shrink up, and they become *Belly-shot. **1562** *Homilies* II. *Agst. Gluttony* (1859) 300 These beastly *belly-slaves..continually day and night, give themselves wholly to bibbing and banqueting. *a* **1587** CAMPION *Hist. Irel.* II. i. (1633) 67 Proud, *belly-swaines fed with extortion and bribery. **1638** G. DANIEL *Eclog.* v. 146 Some *belly-sweep the Earth, and some have wings To cut the purer Ayre. **1595** DUNCAN *Append. Etymol.* (E.D.S.),

Tormen, the *bellie-thrawe. **1826** *Blackw. Mag.* XIX. 631 A diet of outlandish soups and *belly-vengeance.

belly (ˈbɛlɪ), *v.* [f. prec. sb.]

1. *trans.* To cause to swell out.

1606 SHAKS. *Tr. & Cr.* II. ii. 74 Your breath with full consent bellied his sailes. **1790** COLERIDGE *Happiness* Poems I. 33 Fortune's gale Shall belly out each prosperous sail. **1848** LOWELL *Biglow P.* Poet. Wks. (1879) 179/1 But could see the fair west wind belly the homeward sail.

2. *intr.* To bulge out, swell out.

1624 SAUNDERSON *12 Serm.* (1637) 172 The Morter getting wet dissolveth, and the wals belly-out. **1718** POPE *Iliad* I. 626 The milk-white canvass bellying as they [the gales] blow. **1775** M. GUTHRIE in G. Colman *Posth. Lett.* (1820) 119 An earthen pot that Bellys towards the top. **1883** SPURGEON in *Chr. Her.* 277/1 Her white sails bellying to the wind.

†**3.** *intr.* To become corpulent or stout. *Obs.*

1641 BEST *Farm. Bks.* (1856) 73 Your hogges will beginne to belly againe. **1679** SHADWELL *True Widow* I. Wks. 1720 III. 120, I begin to belly, I think, very much. **1772** BURKE *Corr.* (1844) I. 381 We..flatter ourselves that, while we creep on the ground, we belly into melons.

4. *trans.* To remove the wool on the belly of (a sheep) before shearing. *Australia.*

1909 in WEBSTER.

belly-ache (ˈbɛlɪeɪk), *sb.* [f. BELLY *sb.* + ACHE, which see for forms.]

a. 'The colic or pain in the bowels.' Johnson. **bellyache (-bush, -weed)**, names given to the *Jatropha gossypifolia*; **belly-ache-root** = ANGELICA.

1552 HULOET, Disceased with bealye ache, or freatynge in the bealye. **1750** G. HUGHES *Barbados* 152 The Belly-Ach. The roots of this shrub are..white, penetrating deep into the earth. **1775** ADAIR *Amer. Ind.* 412 Angelica, or belly-ach-root is one of their physical greens. **1804** SOUTHEY *Lett.* (1856) I. 268 A supper so hearty, That it gave him a sad belly-ache. **1967** A. WILSON *No Laughing Matter* II. 76 Don't blame me if you all get the bellyache.

b. [f. next.] A querulous complaint.

1930 W. R. BURNETT *Iron Man* I. i. 9 'Now start your belly-ache,' said Regan. 'To hear you talk you'd think you really did some training.'

ˈbelly-ache, *v. slang.* orig. *U.S.* [f. BELLY-ACHE *sb.*] *intr.* To complain querulously or unreasonably; to whine, grizzle. Hence **belly-aching** *vbl. sb.* and *ppl. a.*; **belly-acher**, one who so complains.

1888 FARMER *Americanisms* 50/2 Employés *bellyache* at being overworked, or when they fancy themselves underfed. A vulgarism. **1923** U. L. SILBERRAD *Lett. J. Armiter* vi. 132 Not a bad sort of woman, except that she's always belly-aching about money. **1930** S. HENRY *Conquering Amer. Plains* xvii. 221 These voluble doubters were commonly called old croakers, backbiters, 'belly-achers'. **1931** E. LINKLATER *Juan in Amer.* IV. i. 272 Another of these belly-aching German war books. Who started the War, anyway? **1933** E. CALDWELL *God's Little Acre* i. 8, I reckon there's enough to complain about these days if a fellow wants to belly-ache some. **1934** 'G. ORWELL' *Burmese Days* xv. 230 Other people..will listen to their belly-achings with sympathy. *Ibid.* xv. 232 It was an impertinence to go belly-aching on and on about myself. **1958** *Listener* 13 Nov. 791/2 The subordinate who argued about orders was always 'a bellyacher'. **1959** *Times* 22 July 5/4 The 'belly-aching' was over the pay cut, not the principle of negotiation.

ˈbelly-band. [f. BELLY *sb.* + BAND.]

1. The band which passes round the belly of a horse in harness, to check the play of the shafts.

1523 FITZHERB. *Husb.* §5 A cart-sadel, bakbandes, and belybandes. **1837** MARRYAT *Olla Podr.* xxxvi, The shaft horse neither felt his saddle nor his belly-band.

2. *Naut.* 'A slip of canvas stitched across a sail to strengthen the parts most liable to pressure.' Smyth *Sailor's Word-bk.* See BAND *sb.*[2] 6.

1860 H. STUART *Seaman's Catech.* 45 The reef bands and belly bands stretch from leech to leech.

3. The piece of string on the face of a kite to which the ball of twine is attached.

4. A wide belt, such as a cholera-belt or (*slang*) corset.

1888 KIPLING *Soldiers Three* (1889) 54 He ran forward.. an' swung a Paythan clear off his feet by the belly-band av the brute. **1922** JOYCE *Ulysses* 231 She was well primed with a good load of Delahunt's port under her bellyband. **1925** FRASER & GIBBONS *Soldier & Sailor Words* 21 *Belly band*, the flannel cholera belt issued to the troops.

ˈbelly-blind. *Sc.* [The meaning and origin of *belly* here is uncertain: it may possibly = *billie* 'fellow, comrade.' *Belly Blind* or more commonly *Billie Blin'* is the name of 'a serviceable household demon of a decidedly benignant disposition' in several Scottish ballads: see Child *Eng. and Sc. Pop. Ballads* I. 67, where the name is discussed and compared with Du. *belewitte*, Ger. *bilwisz*, and other Teutonic words of kindred use. But the connexion between these and the sense of *belly-blind* below is not obvious.] A blind-folded person; esp. in the game of Blindman's Buff; hence used as a name for that game, also (as in first quot.) for 'Hide and Seek.'

c **1450** HENRYSON *Mor. Fab.* 77 Thou playes belly blind, Wee seeke all night, but nothing can wee finde. *c* **1510** *Adv. Luvairs*, Sum led is lyk the belly-blind With luve.

†**ˈbelly-cheer,** *sb. Obs.* [f. BELLY *sb.* + CHEER, which see for forms.]

1. The gratification of the belly; feasting, gluttony; luxurious eating.

1549 OLDE *Erasm. Par. Eph.* Prol., Onely for pelfe, bely-cheare, ease and lucre. **1580** LUPTON *Siquila* 56 That gave himself to nothing but to drincking, bybbing, and bellycheare. **1606** HOLLAND *Sueton* 235 Given most of all to excessive bellie-cheere [*luxuriæ*]. **1650** S. CLARKE *Eccl. Hist.* 245.

2. *concr.* Food, viands.

1579 FULKE *Refut. Rastel* 712 Prophane banquets of bellie cheare. **1611** COTGR., *Carrelure de ventre*, meat, belly timber, belly cheere. *a* **1619** FOTHERBY *Atheom.* I. xi. §4 Wine, and Belli-cheere. **1699** COLES, Belly-cheer, *cibaria.*

†**ˈbelly-cheer,** *v. Obs.* [f. prec. sb.] *intr.* To feast luxuriously.

1549 UDALL, etc., *Erasm. Par. Eph.* Prol. (R.) Riotous bankettyng, potte-companyoning, and belychearynge. **1648** MILTON *Tenure Kings* 41 A pack of Clergie men..to belly cheare in their presumptuous Sion, or to promote designes.

ˈbelly-flaught, *a. Sc.* [f. BELLY *sb.* + FLAUGHT, 'in full flight' (Jam.).]

1. Headlong; precipitate.

c **1375** ? BARBOUR *St. Barthol.* 316 And bely-flawcht flede alsone. **1712-58** A. RAMSAY *Poems* (1844) 78 The bauld guid-wife..Came *bellyflaught. **1805** NICOLL *Poems* I. 31 (JAM.) Beath flew bellie-flaught I' the pool.

2. *to flay belly-flaught*: i.e. by pulling the skin off entire over the head.

a **1550** *Priests of Peblis* 25 (JAM.) Thus fla they al the puir men belly flaught. **1774** MONRO *Descr. Hebr.* 47 (JAM.) Quhen they slay their sheepe, they flay them belly flaught.

belly-ful (ˈbɛlɪfʊl). [f. BELLY *sb.* + -FUL.]

1. As much as the belly will contain; a sufficiency of food.

1573 TUSSER *Husb.* (1878) 101 No spoone meat, no bellifull, labourers thinke. **1595** SPENSER *Epithal.* 251 Poure not by cups, but by the bellyfull. **1755** SMOLLETT *Quix.* (1803) IV. 158, I never once had my belly-full, even of dry bread. **1881** J. HAWTHORNE *Fort. Fool* I. xxiii, What I need now is a bellyful of venison and acorn-bread.

2. A sufficiency; quite as much (*of* anything) as one wants or cares to take. (Now rather *coarse.*)

1535 COVERDALE *Ezek.* xxvi. 2, I haue destroyed my bely full. **1583** GOLDING *Calv. on Deut.* ci. 684 Let him thunder his belly full. **1687** A. LOVELL *Bergerac's Com. Hist.* II. 42 The Spectators, having had their Belly-fulls of Laughing. **1705** HICKERINGILL *Priest-cr.* II. vi. 61 Take your Bellyfulls of Sermons. **1852** THACKERAY *Esmond* III. v. (1876) 357 The nation had had its bellyful of fighting.

belly-god (ˈbɛlɪˌgɒd). [f. as prec. + GOD.]

1. One who makes a god of his belly; a glutton.

c **1540** *Compl. Rodk. Mors* xxii. F iv b, A sort of bellygods and ydle stoute and strong lorrels. **1620** VENNER *Via Recta* vi. 102 Mixt sauces..which of ingurgitating belly-gods are greatly esteemed. **1683** TRYON *Way to Health* 395 Many of our English Belly-Gods suppose Flesh to be most mighty in its operation. **1818** SCOTT *Rob Roy* xxviii, 'To see thae English belly-gods!'

attrib. *c* **1570** *Bp. St. Andrew's* in *Scot. Poems* II. 307 Fals Pharisianis, Bellie god bischopis. **1634-46** ROW *Hist. Kirk* (1842) 344 Bellie-god bishops hes little will of that work.

2. A god presiding over the appetites.

a **1619** FOTHERBY *Atheom.* I. xi. §4 (1622) 117 These three Belly-gods; Bacchus, Ceres, Venus.

bellying (ˈbɛlɪɪŋ), *vbl. sb.* [f. BELLY *v.* + -ING[1].] A swelling or bulging out.

1662 HOBBES *Seven Prob.* Wks. 1845 VII. 45 The bellying of the sail. **1753** FRANKLIN *Wks.* (1840) 299 They will comply better with the bellying of the glass.

ˈbellying, *ppl. a.* [f. as prec. + -ING[2].] Swelling, bulging out.

a **1700** DRYDEN *Iliad* I. Wks. (1700) 213 The bellying Canvass strutted with the Gale. **1822** W. IRVING *Braceb. Hall* (1845) 325 As if the bellying clouds were torn open by the mountain tops.

fig. **1830** *Fraser's Mag.* I. 133 His fame, buoyant and bellying as it is.

bellyis, obs. form of BELLOWS.

†**ˈbelly-piece.** *Obs.* [f. BELLY *sb.* + PIECE.]

1. The flesh covering the belly; the peritoneum.

1591 PERCIVALL *Sp. Dict.*, *Ijada*, the small ribs, the collike, the belly peece of a fish. **1633** P. FLETCHER *Purple Isl.* II. *note*, The muscles of the belly-peece, or the inner rimme of the belly. *a* **1659** CLEVELAND *Pet. Poem* 31 My Belly-pieces are so fat, they will If toasted, serve for Belly-pieces still.

2. The part of the dress covering the belly; an apron.

1689 SHADWELL *Bury Fair* II i, My fat Host's Belly-pieces.

3. The piece forming the belly of a violin, etc.

1609 DOULAND *Ornithop. Microl.* 22 Let it be couered with a belly peece well smoothed..like the belly of a lute.

4. A concubine.

1632 RANDOLPH *Jealous Lovers* Wks. (1668) 37 Blush not, belly-piece.

ˈbellyship. *nonce-wd.* In 7 belliship. [See -SHIP.] The personality of the belly; cf. *lordship.* (*Humorous.*)

1600 ROWLANDS *Let. Humours Blood* vii. 84 His belliship containes th' insatiate gutte.

belly-swagger: see BELSWAGGER.

†**beˈllyter.** *Obs. rare*[−1]. [a. F. *bélître*, *belistre* beggar, vagabond; of unknown origin: see Diez, Littré, Scheler.] A beggar.

a **1528** SKELTON *Image Hypocr.* 386 Oh ye kynde of vypers Ye beestly bellyters.

ˈbelly-ˌtimber. *Obs.* exc. *dial.* [f. BELLY *sb.* + TIMBER.] Food, provisions. (Formerly in serious use, as still in dialects (cf. TIMBER); but since the time of Butler tending to be ludicrous.)

1607 *Mis. Enforced Marr.* III. in Hazl. *Dodsl.* IX. 519 We had some belly timber at your table. **1625** PURCHAS *Pilgrims* II. 1643 They make Florentines, and verie good belly-timber. **1663** BUTLER *Hud.* I. I. 331 Belly-Timber above Ground Or under was not to be found. **1753** SMOLLETT *Ct. Fathom* (1784) 63/2 Here is no solid belly-timber in this country. [**1820** SCOTT *Monast.* (1830) I. 222 The ample provision they have made for their own belly-timber.] **1855** *Whitby Gloss.*, *Belly-timber*, food.

belman, obs. form of BELLMAN.

belmontin, -ine (ˈbɛlmɒntiːn), *sb.* [f. the 'Belmont Works' at Vauxhall.] 'A fatty substance prepared from Burmese naphtha.' Watts *Dict. Chem.* I. 538. Also used *attrib.*

1870 *Eng. Mech.* 11 Mar. 626/1 It requires no stronger light than that afforded by a..belmontine lamp.

beloam *v.*: see BE- *pref.*

†**beˈlock,** *v. Obs. rare*[−1]. [f. BE- *pref.* 2 + LOCK *v.* (Cf. BELOUKE).] Intensive of LOCK.

1603 SHAKS. *Meas. for M.* v. 210 This is the hand, which with a vowd contract Was fast belockt in thine.

belocke, beloke(n, var. of BELOUKE *v. Obs.*

beloid (ˈbiːlɔɪd), *a.* [f. Gr. βέλος arrow, dart + -OID.] Arrow-shaped; spec. in *Craniometry*, having a broad occiput and narrow frontal region.

1901 G. SERGI *Mediterranean Race* v. 110 These six photographs present one [skull] of beloid shape.

belomancy (ˈbɛləʊmænsɪ). Also 8 bell-. [f. Gr. βέλος a dart + μαντεία divination: see -MANCY.] Divination by means of arrows.

1646 SIR T. BROWNE *Pseud. Ep.* 272 A like way of Belomancy or Divination by Arrowes hath beene in request with Scythians, Alanes, Germans. **1883** *Sat. Rev.* 841/2 These..divining arrows or rods or the knotched [*sic*] sticks of belomancy.

‖**belone** (ˈbɛləʊniː). [L. *belone*, a. Gr. βελόνη a needle.] Generic name of the GAR-FISH.

†**beˈlong,** *a. Obs. rare.* In 3 bilong. [Early ME., answering in form and meaning to OS. *bilang*, MDu. *belangh*, *belanc* adj.; f. *bi-*, BE- *pref.* + LONG *a.*[2], app. shortened form of OE. *ȝe-lang*, ME. *y-long*, *i-long*, ALONG *a.*[1] As in other words (cf. BELIEF), the *ȝe-* may have been dropped already in OE.; Ormin has 'lang o Crisstes helpe.' The primary notion was apparently 'equally long, corresponding in length,' whence 'running alongside of, parallel to, going along with, accompanying as a property or attribute'; cf. BELONG *v.*, also BILENGE *a.*] Pertaining, belonging, or appropriate; 'along of.' Const. *on.*

c **1250** *Gen. & Ex.* 2058 Tel me ðin drem, mi broðer her ..ðe reching wurð on god bi-long.

belong (bɪˈlɒŋ), *v.* Forms: 4 bi-, 4–5 bylong, 4– belong; *north.* and *Sc.* belang. [ME. *bi-*, *belongen* appears to be an intensive (with BE- *pref.*) of the simple *longen*, common in the same sense from 13th c.: see LONG *v.*[2] OHG. has, in same sense, *bilangên*, MDu. *belanghen*, mod.G. and Du. *belangen*, also a sb. *belang* 'concern, interest, importance'; but no trace of such forms is found in OE. For the sense, cf. the prec. adj.]

1. a. *intr.* To go along with, or accompany, as an adjunct, function, or duty; to be the proper accompaniment, to be appropriate, to pertain *to.*

1340 *Ayenb.* 176 Þe ulessliche [þoȝtes] belongeþ to lost an to wylninges. **1377** LANGL. *P. Pl.* B. Prol. 110 For in loue and letterure þe eleccioun bilongeth. *c* **1386** CHAUCER *Merch. T.* 215 Suffisaunt To doon al that a man bilongeth unto. **1486** *Bk. St. Alban's* D iij b, Theys haukes belong to an Emproure. **1580** SIDNEY *Arcadia* (1613) 209 To learne the good what trauailes do belong. **1599** SHAKS. *Much Ado* III. iii. 40 Wee know what belongs to a Watch. **1611** BIBLE *Dan.* ix. 9 To the Lord our God belong mercies and forgiuenesses. **1667** MILTON *P.L.* VI. 807 Of this cursed crew The punishment to other hand belongs. **1712** ADDISON *Spect.* No. 397 ¶3 Grief has a natural Eloquence belonging to it. **1861** GEO. ELIOT in Cross *Life* (1885) II. xi. 322 He..works with all the zest that belongs to fresh ideas.

b. *impers.*, or with subject *it* repr. a clause.

1413 LYDG. *Pylgr. Sowle* I. xii, Neuer ne left he..his burdon, as it bylongeth to a good pylgrym. *c* **1450** *Merlin* xv. 239 He was wele horsed as to soche a man be-longeth. **1588** A. KING *Canisius' Catech.* 188 To rakin thame al in this place it belanges nat to our purpose. **1667** MILTON *P.L.* III. 111 They therefore, as to right belongd, So were created. **1821** KEATS *Isabel* xlix, Here..it doth not well belong To speak.

2. To pertain, concern, refer. or relate *to. arch.*

1340 *Ayenb.* 12 Þe oþer article [of the Creed] belongeþ to þe zone. **1549** COVERDALE *Erasm. Par. 1 Cor.* i. 24 Nor

belongen these my woordes onelye to you, but generally to all nacions. **1593** HOOKER *Eccl. Pol.* II. viii. §4 Whatsoever belongeth unto the highest perfection of man. **1611** SHAKS. *Cymb.* v. v. 147 All that belongs to this. **1611** BIBLE *1 Cor.* vii. 22 He that is unmarried careth for the things that belong to the Lord.

3. a. To be the property or rightful possession of. Const. *to*; occas. with *indirect obj.*

1393 LANGL. *P. Pl. C.* II. 43 Telle ȝe me now to wham þat tresour by-longeþ. **1508** FISHER *Wks.* I. (1876) 290 The Blessyd Martha was a woman of noble blode, to whom by enheritaunce belonged the castel of bethany. *a* **1692** ASHMOLE *Antiq. Berks* (1723) II. 424 The Hundred of Wargrave did for many Ages belong to the Bishops of Winchester. **1764** BRYDGES *Homer Travest.* (1797) I. 128 Thy buxom wench.. Belongs a better man than thee. **1835** *Penny Cycl.* XIV. 365/2 Rushen Abbey belonged to the Cistercian order. **1852** MᶜCULLOCH *Comm. Dict.* 1105 Property belonging to another state.

b. To be a property or attribute of.

1662 STILLINGFL. *Orig. Sacræ* III. ii. §18 It must have equall motion in all its particles, if motion doth belong to it. *a* **1704** LOCKE *Wks.* (1706) 191 This way of containing all things can by no means belong to God. **1855** BAIN *Senses & Int.* II. ii. §14 (1864) 204 The accompaniment of activity belongs to every one of the senses. **1885** J. MARTINEAU *Ethical The.* I. 275 The innumerable 'attributes' which must belong to an infinite nature.

4. a. To be connected with in various relations; to form a part or appendage of; *e.g.* to be a member of a family, society, or nation, to be an adherent or dependent of, to be a native or inhabitant of a place; to be a dependency, adjunct, or appendage of something; to be one of a generation or time. Also const. *to*, †*unto*.

1393 GOWER *Conf.* I. 121 Þe nimphes of the welles, And other.. Unto the wodes belongende. **1485** CAXTON *Paris & V.* Prol., I belong to the parish of Saint Pierre. **1535** COVERDALE *Esther* viii. 1 Hester tolde how that he belonged vnto her. **1601** SHAKS. *Twel. N.* v. i. 9 Belong you to the Lady Oliuia, friends? **1613** —— *Hen. VIII*, v. iv. 3 Good M. Porter, I belong to th' Larder. **1711** ADDISON *Spect.* No. 121 ¶1 The great Yard that belongs to my Friend's Country-House. **1856** *Sat. Rev.* II. 189 Mr. Pierce belongs to New Hampshire. **1875** MACDONELL in *Macm. Mag.* XXXII. 545 His finest figures belong to [an early] period in American history. **1883** M. CRAWFORD *Mr. Isaacs* iv. 71 To what confession do you yourself belong? **1884** H. DRUMMOND *Nat. Law in Spir. W.* 112 Those who belong to the rank and file of life need this warning most. **1922** D. H. LAWRENCE *England* (1924) 232 He was still in the choir of Morley Chapel—not very regular. He belonged just because he had a tenor voice, and enjoyed singing.

b. With an adv. or advb. phr. (esp. *here*, *where* = to this or these, to which), also with various preps. or without const.: to be related or connected; to have a certain connection indicated or implied in the context; to fit a certain environment, group, etc. orig. *U.S.*

1822 COOPER *Spy* xxvi, I have never known whether he belonged above or below. **1861** O. W. HOLMES *Elsie Venner* xxvii, You belong with the last [set], and got accidentally shuffled in with the others. **1867** A. WILSON *St. Elmo* x, To replace it in the glass box where it belongs. **1889** WALT WHITMAN in *Century Mag.* (1911) 11 Jan. 256/2 He was not a closet man, belonged out-of-doors. **1897** *N.E.D.* s.v. *Fit v.*[1] 2 The first examples given under.. 3 may belong here. **1924** A. D. SEDGWICK *Little French Girl* I. x, I saw you took to each other. I saw you belonged with each other. *Ibid.* II. xiv, From the first moment I saw her I felt that she belonged. **1936** WODEHOUSE *Laughing Gas* iii. 31, I looked as if I belonged in Whipsnade. **1942** M. MCCARTHY *Company she Keeps* (1943) v. 164 It was the Moscow trials that made him know, for the first time, that he did not really 'belong'. **1949** *Scrutiny* XVI. 9 This remark of Eliot's.. suggests that Byron doesn't quite 'belong'. **1960** *Guardian* 4 Mar. 8/7 People also feel they want to belong and matter.

c. With inf.: to be accustomed, ought; to seem, intend. *U.S. dial.*

1901–7 in H. WENTWORTH *Amer. Dial. Dict.* (1944) 53/1 John Henry belongs to folla afteh Sayrah. **1935** A. C. BAUGH *Hist. Eng. Lang.* xi. 453 The expression reported from South Dakota, 'I got up at six o'clock this morning although I don't *belong to* get up until seven.' **1938** M. K. RAWLINGS *Yearling* iv. 29 You belong to figger.. a man.. cain't out-run a bear, but he's a sorry hunter if he cain't out-study him. *Ibid.* 35 When it back-fired, that belongs to mean the mainspring's got weak.

†**be'longer.** *Obs. rare.* [f. prec. + -ER[1].] He who or that which belongs; an attribute.

1674 N. FAIRFAX *Bulk & Selv.* 12 The two first.. things that the mind is likest to fasten on, as the main belongers to the world. *Ibid.* 112 That one belonger of unthroughfareness.

belonging (bɪˈlɒŋɪŋ), *vbl. sb.* [f. as prec. + -ING[1]. Perhaps the pl. *belongings* was orig. taken from the pr. pple., in sense of 'things belonging.']

I. Usually in *pl.* only.

1. Circumstances connected with a person or thing; relations with another person or thing.

1603 SHAKS. *Meas. for M.* I. i. 30 Thy selfe and thy belongings Are not thine owne so proper. **1867** FURNIVALL *Percy Folio* Pref. 5 Such information.. as he would wish.. in order to understand the belongings of it. **1873** BROWNING *Red Cott. Night-c.* 220 All my belongings, what is summed in life, I have submitted wholly.. to your rule.

2. Possessions, goods, effects.

1817 B'NESS BUNSEN in Hare *Life* I. v. 117 [They] did the honors of their belongings with ease. **1857** RUSKIN *Pol. Econ. Art* Add. §8 Jewels, liveries, and other such common belongings of wealthy people. **1871** A. HOPE *Schoolboy Fr.* (1875) 158 Rushing about collecting their belongings.

3. Persons related in any way; relatives.

1852 DICKENS *Bleak H.* II. 103, I have been trouble enough to my belongings in my day. **1866** *Sat. Rev.* 24 Feb. 224/2 The rich uncle whose mission is to bring prosperity to his belongings.

4. A thing connected with, forming a part, appendage, or accessory of another.

1863 D. MITCHELL *Farm Edgew.* 196 When I have shown some curious city visitor all these belongings of the farm. **1868** LOCKYER *Heavens* (ed. 3) 26 These are the 'Sun-spots,' real movable belongings of the surface of the Sun. **1883** *Harper's Mag.* Mar. 533/2 She had shown us the rest of the château with a sense of being a belonging of the place.

II. 5. The fact of appertaining, relationship. *Esp.* a person's membership in, and acceptance by, a group or society (cf. BELONG *v.* 4 b).

1879 WHITNEY *Skr. Gram.* 275 There remain, as cases of doubtful belonging, etc. **1934** W. PLOMER *Invaders* ii. §4. 43 He had little sense of belonging, of being necessary to the world he lived in. **1958** H. REILLY *Ding Dong Bell* (1959) i. 16 What the child needs is a settled home, a feeling of permanence, security, of *belonging*.

6. *Comb.* *belonging-together(ness)* (cf. BELONGINGNESS 2).

1890 W. JAMES *Princ. Psychol.* I. x. 337 It seems as if our description of the belonging-together of the various selves, as a belonging-together which is merely *represented*, in a later pulse of thought, had knocked the bottom out of the matter. *Ibid.* II. xxviii. 671 *Any* really inward belonging-together of the sequent terms, if discovered, would be accepted as what the word cause was meant to stand for. **1938** *Mind* XLVII. 380 From the outset our perceptual world is a continuum organised into 'belonging-togethernesses'. **1939** *Ibid.* XLVIII. 247 This *belonging together* is the basis of 'Gestalt' psychology.

be'longing, *ppl. a.* [f. as prec. + -ING[2].] Proper, appropriate; appertaining, accompanying.

1648 MILTON *Tenure of Kings* (1650) 45 In hands better able and more belonging to manage them. **1869** RUSKIN *Q. of Air* §141 Sanctifying noble thought with separately distinguished loveliness of belonging sound.

be'longingness. [f. BELONGING *vbl. sb.* + -NESS.] †**1.** The state of having the properties appropriate to something. *Obs.*

1656 BLOUNT *Glossogr.*, *Radicality*, the belongingness of a thing to a root. *Ibid.*, *Seminality*.. a belongingness to seed.

2. [Cf. G. *zugehörigkeit.*] The state or condition of belonging.

1931 E. L. THORNDIKE *Human Learning* ii. 23 With only a fourth as many repetitions the greater belongingness results in.. nearly twice as many correct responses. **1938** E. LEEN *Why the Cross?* ix. 355 By the holocaust man signified to God his utter 'belongingness' to Him. **1951** D. RIESMAN in A. W. Loos *Relig. Faith & World Culture* 69 We must skeptically question the demands for greater social participation and belongingness among the group-minded. **1957** W. H. WHYTE *Organization Man* 7 A belief in 'belongingness' as the ultimate need of the individual.

belonite (ˈbɛlənaɪt). *Min.* [f. L. *belonē*, Gr. βελόν-η needle + -ITE.] A mineral variety occurring in microscopic needle-shaped crystals.

1879 RUTLEY *Stud. Rocks* xi. 190 The augite and hornblende exist.. as minute acicular bodies and spicular forms ('belonites'). **1880** DANA *Min.* 805 The belonite may be a feldspar.

†**be'look,** *v. Obs.* Forms: 2 beloc-en, 3 bilok-en(n, -in. [ME., f. BE- *pref.* 1 + *lokien*, OE. *lócian* to LOOK. Cf. senses of BEHOLD, BESEE.]

1. *intr.* To look.

c **1175** *Cott. Hom.* 233 To neowelnesse þe under eorðe is be-locest. *a* **1225** *Ancr. R.* 132 Heo mot wel.. bilokin [*v.r.* biholden] on euch half.

2. *trans.* To look at, consider. Also *absol.*

c **1200** *Trin. Coll. Hom.* 77 Nu hit is god time to beloken þe sicnesse of þe sowle. *a* **1400** *Octouian* 1046 Of many a knyght he was beloked.

3. *refl.* To look about one, cast one's eyes about.

a **1225** *Ancr. R.* 132 [He] bilokeð him euer ȝeorneliche al abuten. *c* **1220** *Bestiary* 529 in *O.E. Misc.* 17 Ðe sipes ðat arn on se fordriuen.. biloken hem and sen ðis fis.

belord (bɪˈlɔːd), *v.* [f. BE- 5 + LORD *sb.*]

1. *trans.* To call 'lord,' address as 'my lord.'

1586 J. HOOKER *Girald. Irel.* in *Holinsh.* II. 86/2 You are begraced and belorded, and crouched and kneeled unto. **1883** SALA in *Illustr. Lond. News* 7 July, An American never fails to belord Francis of Verulam.

2. To act the lord over.

Belorussian (bɛləʊˈrʌʃən), *a.* and *sb.* Also **Byelorussian** (bjɛləʊ-). [f. Russ. *Belorussiya* Belorussia, f. *belo-* white + RUSSIA + -AN.] **A.** *adj.* Of or pertaining to Belorussia, one of the constituent republics of the Soviet Union, its people or its language. **B.** *sb.* = *White Russian* (see WHITE *a.* 11 e).

[**1911** *Encycl. Brit.* XXIII. 884/2 The White Russians (the Byelorusses).] **1944** G. VERNADSKY *Hist. Russia* i. 3 The Polish influence to which the Ukrainians and Byelo-Russians had been subjected for several centuries. *Ibid.* xvi. 319 Other Socialist Soviet republics were founded—the White Russian (Byelo-Russian) [etc.]. **1948** J. TOWSTER *Polit. Power in U.S.S.R.* iv. 90 The Ukrainian and Belorussian Republics. **1949** *Amer. Slavic & East Europ. Rev.* VIII. 205 The Belorussians 'borrowed' many important characteristics.. from the Slavs. **1950** *Ibid.* IX. 140 The absence of special contributions to.. Byelorussian literature is an unfortunate omission. **1956** *Archivum Linguisticum* VIII. II. 174 The same problem exists in.. Belorussian. **1958** *Economist* 1 Nov. 424/2 General Uborevich, commander of the Byelorussian district.

belote (bəˈlɒt). Also belotte. [a. F. *belote*, f. the name of F. *Belot*, a Frenchman who perfected the game.] A game of cards resembling pinocle, played with a 32-card pack.

1941 KOESTLER *Scum of Earth* 7 Soldiers—grumbling, drinking red wine, playing belotte, and bored. **1944** W. S. MAUGHAM *Razor's Edge* iii. 93 There were men with sweaty faces round tables playing belote with loud shouts. **1959** *Sunday Times* 1 Mar. 4/2 Belote, or 'Klabrias', as it is named in Germany.. is certainly the best and wittiest card game... In France it has become the most popular national card game, as in Switzerland.

belote, var. of BELLOOT.

†**be'louke,** *v. Obs.* Forms: 1 belúc-an, 2–3 biluk-en, 4 belouke, (belok). *Pa. t.* 1–3 be'léac, 3 bilek, -leck, -loc. *Pa. pple.* 1–2 belocen, 2–4 beloken, 3–4 biloken, -luken, biloke, 5 belocke. [OE. *bi-*, *be-lúcan* (corr. to OS. *bilûcan*, OHG. *bilûhhan*, MHG. *belûchen*), f. *bi-*, BE- about + *lúcan*, in Goth. *lūkan*, to shut, close.]

1. *trans.* To close, to shut (a door, etc.).

971 *Blickl. Hom.* 9 Heofonrices duru.. belocen standeþ. He þone halȝan ham beléac. *c* **1000** *Ags. Gosp.* Matt. xxv. 10 Seo duru wæs belocyn. *c* **1160** *Hatton G.*, Beloken.

2. To shut (a person, etc.) *in* or *out.*

c **897** K. ÆLFRED *Past.* 399 On sumere lytelre byriȝ belocene. *c* **1175** *Cott. Hom.* 225 God be-léac hi binnan þan arce. *a* **1250** *Owl & Night.* 1079 He hire bi-lek in one bure. *c* **1320** *Sir Beves* 3024 Belok hem thar oute for love o me. **1430** LYDG. *Chron. Troy* III. xxiii How ye may suffre the great harmes kene.. Duryng the syege in this towne beloke.

3. To enclose, encompass.

c **825** *Vesp. Ps.* xxx. 9 [xxxi. 8] Ne biluce me in honda feondes. *c* **1200** ORMIN 12126 þatt Æst, and West, and Suþ, and Norrþ þiss middellærd bilukenn. *a* **1300** *E.E. Psalter* xxx[i]. 8 Ne þou me belouked in hend of fa. *c* **1314** *Guy Warw.* 229 A strong cite biloken with walle.

4. To include *in* an expression.

c **1200** ORMIN 11495 Cristess lare.. bilokenn iss I tene bode-wordess. **1340** *Ayenb.* 99 He beloukþ ine ssorte wordes al þet we may wylny of herte.

belout: see BE- *pref.*

belove (bɪˈlʌv), *v.* Forms: 2–3 biluuien, biluuen, bilouen, 3 bileouen, bilufen, 4–5 bi-, bylove, 6 beloue, *Sc.* beluve, 5– belove. [ME. *biluven*, *-loven*, f. *bi-*, BE- 2 + *luven*, *loven* to LOVE. Cf. mod.G. *belieben* and Du. *believen*, both usually impersonal.]

†**1.** *intr.* To please, be pleasing (to a person).

c **1205** LAY. 989 ȝif hit eow bilouеð.. fare we from þisse londe. *a* **1225** *Juliana* 24 ȝef me sua biluuede hit were sone. *a* **1240** *Sawles Warde* in *Cott. Hom.* 259 Wel us biluueð hit.

†**2.** *trans.* To be pleased with, approve, like. *Obs.*

c **1205** LAY. 1013 Alle hit bi-lueeden. *Ibid.* 19121 Al þat leodliche folc bilufde þesne ilke ræd.

3. To love. Now only in *passive.* Const. *with* (obs.), *of* (arch., poet.), *by.*

1377 LANGL. *P. Pl.* B. III. 211 Mede maketh hym bi-loued. **1481** CAXTON *Reynard* (Arb.) 118 The money is better byloued than God. **1535** STEWART *Cron. Scot.* II. 521 Quhilk with the king all tyme wes best belude. **1590** SHAKS. *Mids. N.* I. i. 104, I am belou'd of beauteous Hermia. **1604** T. WRIGHT *Passions* v. §4. 212 Those persons cannot but bee accounted hard hearted.. who belove not them of whom they are loved. **1623** WODROEPHE *Marrow Fr. Tongue* 322, I would wear it about my neck for a certain testimony that I belove it much. **1818** BYRON *Mazeppa* vii, I loved, and was beloved again. **1825** SOUTHEY *Paraguay* ii. 10 Beloving and beloved she grew, a happy child. **1871** R. ELLIS *Catullus* viii. 5 By me belov'd as maiden is belov'd no more.

†**be'love,** *sb. Obs. rare*[—1]. [f. prec.: cf. LOVE *sb.*[1]] = BELOVED *sb.*

1546 BALE *Eng. Votaries* I. (1550) 48 Only Lieba and Tecla ij Englysh nonnes his best beloues.

beloved (bɪˈlʌvɪd, -ˈlʌvd), *ppl. a.* and *sb.* Also 4 by-luffede, 5 bylouyd, 6–7 beloued. [f. as prec. + -ED[1].]

A. *ppl. adj.* Loved. (Often *well-*, *best-*, *first-*, etc.)

1398 TREVISA *Barth. De P.R.* XII. xiii. (1495) 423 Gnattes ben beste bylouyd meete to swalowes. *c* **1485** *Digby Myst.* (1882) II. 510 Welbelouyd frendes. **1535** COVERDALE *Song 3 Childr.* 11 For thy beloued Abrahams sake. **1552** *Bk. Com. Prayer*, Dearly beloved brethren, the Scripture moveth us in sundry places. **1591** SHAKS. *Two Gent.* II. ii. 57 How happily he liues, how well belou'd. **1647** W. BROWNE *Polexander* II. 143 The fairest and best belovedst daughter of the Emperour. **1817** COLERIDGE *Sibyl. Leaves* (1862) 243 'Twas even thine, beloved woman mild! **1855** MACAULAY *Hist. Eng.* IV. 1 Impatient to be once more in his beloved country.

B. *sb.* (ellipt. use of adj.: cf. *dear.*) One who is beloved, a loved one.

1526 TINDALE *1 John* iii. 2 Derely beloved, now are we the sonnes of God. **1589** WARNER *Alb. Eng,* VI. xxxi. 155 The Louer and Beloued are not tyed to one Law. **1611** BIBLE *Song* v. 9 What is thy beloued more then another beloued? **1748** G. WHITE *MS. Serm.*, 'Tis the nature of Love to extend itself to all things belonging to it's Beloved. **1850** MRS. BROWNING *Consolation*, There are left behind Living Beloveds. **1872** SPURGEON *Treas. Dav.* Ps. lxxi. 24 Others talk of their beloveds, and they shall be made to hear of mine.

† **belovedly** (bɪˈlʌvɪdlɪ), *adv. Obs. rare.* [f. prec. + -LY².] So as to be beloved.

1667 WATERHOUSE *Fire Lond.* 186 My Worthy.. Father, who hath lived long, creditably and belovedly in it.

† **beˈlover.** *Obs. rare*⁻¹. In 5 bylouer. [f. BELOVE *v.* + -ER¹.] A lover.

1491 CAXTON *Vitas Patr.* II. (1495) 196 a/2 Wymmen that utter swetly theyr wordes for to gete loue of theyr bylouers.

† **beˈloving,** *vbl. sb. Obs. rare.* [f. as prec. + -ING¹.] Liking, pleasure.

1589 WARNER *Alb. Eng.* v. xxix. 145 No bettring but as your belouing is.

† **beˈloving,** *ppl. a. Obs.* [-ING².] Loving.

1606 SHAKS. *Ant. & Cl.* I. ii. 22 You shall be more belouing then beloued.

below (bɪˈləʊ), *adv.* and *prep.* Forms: 4 bilooghe, 6 by lowe, beloe, belowe, 6– below. [f. BE *prep.* + LOW *a.* (in ME. *loȝ, loogh*). Very rare in ME., and only as an adverb; it began apparently as a variant of the earlier *a-lowe*, A-LOW, the parallel form to *an-high* (now *on high*); the synonymous pair, *a-low be-low*, were analogous to *a-fore be-fore*, etc. *Below* was not a common word till the 16th c., towards the end of which the prepositional use (not found with *a-low*) arose, and is frequent in Shakspere. *Below* and *beneath* constitute together the opposite of *above*. As to their use, and relations to *under*, see BENEATH B.]

A. (without object expressed.) *adv.*

1. a. *gen.* In a low position relatively to another place; in or to a lower position, lower down. Phr. ***below there!*** a warning addressed to persons to beware of a descending object.

c **1325** *E.E. Allit. P.* B. 116, & syþen on lenþe bi-looghe ledez inogh. **1567** TURBERV. in Chalmers *Eng. Poets* II. 616/2 It makes the Oke to overlooke the slender shrubs bylow. **1626** BACON *Sylva* (J.) To men standing below on the ground, those that be on the top of Paul's seem much less than they are. **1697** DRYDEN *Virg. Georg.* III. 373 The Waters..belching from below, Black Sands, as from a forceful Engine throw. **1700** —— *Pal. & Arc.* I. 218 Then look'd below, and from the Castle's height Beheld a.. pleasing sight. **1766** GOLDSM. *Vic. W.* xxiii. (1806) 137 The child..leaped from her arms into the flood below. **1842** TENNYSON *Fatima* iv, From below Sweet gales, as from deep gardens, blow. **1896** *Bow Bells* 6 Mar. 264/2 One man was tying a paint-pot to the rung of the ladder, the cord slipped, down came the pot, the man singing out 'Below there!'

b. Lower on a written sheet or page; *hence*, later in a book or writing; at the foot of the page.

1694 SALMON *Iatrica* I. v. 292/1 He may use the pills below described. **1784** R. BURROW *Comp. Ladies Diary* 35 Read what's below. **1807** F. WRANGHAM *Serm. Transl. Script.* 38 The passages alluded to below have been quoted almost to satiety. **1863** A. HORWOOD *Yearbks. 30 & 31 Edw. I.* Pref. 29 The forms subjoined in the note below.

2. In a lower position relatively to some place of permanent reference: **a.** Under heaven; on earth. Often prec. by *here. arch.* or *poet.*

1574 A. L. *Calvin's Foure Serm.* i, God faileth not to send down certain beames hether by lowe to lighten us. **1680** BUTLER *Elephant in Moon* 284 That Elephant may differ so From those upon the Earth below. **1764** GOLDSM. *Trav.* 63 Where to find that happiest spot below. **1766** —— *Hermit* viii, Man wants but little here below, Nor wants that little long. **1821** KEATS *Lamia* 280 Finer spirits cannot breathe below In human climes. **1832** *Athenæum* 377 The merry stream floweth For all below.

b. Under the earth; in Hades, in hell.

1610 SHAKS. *Temp.* IV. i. 31 Or Phœbus Steeds are foundered Or Night kept chain'd below. *a* **1740** TICKELL (J.) Prosp'rous traitors gnash their teeth below. **1813** HOGG *Queen's Wake*, Macgregor would dive to the mansions below! *a* **1843** SOUTHEY *Inchc. Rock* xvii. 4 As if with the Inchcape Bell, The fiends below were ringing his knell. **1847** BARHAM *Ingol. Leg.* (1869) 191 They say she is now leading apes, and mends Bachelors' small clothes below.

c. On a lower floor, down-stairs, 'below-stairs'; under the deck, in or into the cabin or hold of a ship.

1598 SHAKS. *Merry W.* II. ii. 150 There's one Master Broome below would faine speake with you. *c* **1600** *Rob. Hood* (Ritson) II. xvi. 90 Fell down on the ship hatch And under the hatches there below. **1712** ADDISON *Spect.* No. 269 ¶1 A man below desired to speak with me. **1840** R. DANA *Bef. Mast* xxiii. 68 It being the turn of our watch to go below. **1859** G. MEREDITH *R. Feverel* xxii. (1885) 155 This Adonis of the lower household was a mighty man below.

3. Lower down a slope, valley, or course of a river; nearer to the sea. *U.S.*

1645 in *Springfield Rec.* (1898) I. 164 The Brooke in the longe meddow..and the Brooke a little below on the other side. **1810** JEFFERSON *Corr.* (1830) 151 She expected..a British fleet from below. **1817** in *Essex Inst. Hist. Coll.* VIII. 238 Mr. Lefavour of Salem, who was living below, had come up here on business. **1845** SIMMS *Wigwam & Cabin* Ser. I. 16 There's ne'er a house either above or below for a matter of fifteen miles.

4. *fig.* In a lower rank, grade, or station.

1606 SHAKS. *Tr. & Cr.* I. iii. 130 The Generall's disdain'd By him one step below. **1882** *Times* 15 Mar. 9/3 It was impossible for Alexander II to resist the pressure from below in 1877. **1884** SIR W. BRETT *Law Rep.* XIV. *Q. Bench* 798 The view which the judgment of the Court below upholds.

5. = below zero (see B. 6 a).

1795 E. P. SIMCOE *Diary* 12 Jan. (1911) 265 Thermometer 10 degrees below. **1896** W. D. HOWELLS *Impressions* 9 The frosts of ten and twenty below. **1904** M. E. WALLER *Wood-Carver* ii. 82 [It was] twenty-seven below this morning. **1968** *Globe & Mail* (Toronto) 17 Feb. 1/6 The predicted high [temperature] for Elliot Lake today is 5 below; the low tonight 20 below.

B. (with obj.) *prep.*

1. a. Lower than, at a less elevation than.

c **1575** TURBERV. *All Things as used* (R.) Bylowe the lampe of Phœbus light. **1607** SHAKS. *Timon* IV. iii. 2 O blessed breeding Sun..below thy Sisters Orbe Infect the ayre. **1677** MOXON *Mech. Exerc.* (1703) 33 The Screw-plate will, after it gets a little below the Tapering, go no farther. **1805** SCOTT *Last Minstr.* IV. xvii. 8 He never counted him a man Would strike below the knee. **1849** MRS. SOMERVILLE *Phys. Geog.* II. xxiv. 136 Immediately below the snow-line. **1855** MOTLEY *Dutch Rep.* (1876) I. 1 A district lying partly below the level of the ocean. **1863** C. ST. JOHN *Nat. Hist. Moray* i. 2 The bird is looking in all directions below her for any enemy.

b. *below-stairs* (now usually *down-stairs*): at the foot of the staircase, on or to the floor below, *esp.* the ground-floor; *hence*, in or into the kitchen or servants' hall.

1599 SHAKS. *Much Ado* v. ii. 10 Why shall I alwaies keepe below staires? **1667** E. CHAMBERLAYNE *St. Gt. Brit.* I. (1684) 153 The Cofferer..is to pay the Wages to the King's Servants above and below stairs. **1749** FITZCOTTON *Iliad* I. Pref. 14 Leaving the young people below-stairs, to divert themselves. **1840** DICKENS *Old C. Shop* viii, Kit's mother, poor woman, is waiting at the grate below stairs. **1850** MRS. STOWE *Uncle Tom's C.* xvi. 144 St. Clare will have high life below stairs.

c. Of position in a writing or on a printed page.

1743 J. BARCLAY *Educ.* 85 Below the simple verbs are translated into English all the useful rules. **1858** W. HOLDSWORTH *Law of Wills* 13 No signature will give effect to any disposition or direction which is inserted below or after it in point of place.

d. *fig.* Too low for the influence of, too low to be affected by.

1848 MACAULAY *Hist. Eng.* I. 168 It is possible to be below flattery as well as above it. One who trusts nobody will not trust sycophants.

2. a. Lower on a slope than; farther down a valley or stream than: hence ***below-bridge*** = lower than London (or other) Bridge; nearer the bottom, or what is considered the bottom, of a room than, as ***below the gangway*** in the British House of Commons.

1603 SHAKS. *Meas. for M.* IV. iii. 103 At the consecrated Fount, A League below the Citie. **1691** T. H[ALE] *Acc. New Invent.* C, Below bridge, where the great Scene of Navigation lyes. **1871** RUSKIN *Fors Clav.* II. xiv. 11 Below the village, the valley opens..into a broad flat meadow. **1878** HUXLEY *Physiogr.* i. 2 The water sweeps down below bridge in the direction of Greenwich. **1885** *Weekly Times* 8 May 15/4 Below the gangway sat a strong Radical party.

b. Of time: Later than, after. *rare.*

a **1790** T. WARTON (L.) The most eminent scholars.. before and even below the twelfth century, were educated in our religious houses.

3. Deeper than. Also *fig.*

1849 MRS. SOMERVILLE *Phys. Geog.* II. xxiv. 129 The ground is perpetually frozen at a very small depth below the surface. **1872** *Mem. Agnes E. Jones* vi. 387 This call was followed by one or two more, but we did not get below the surface. **1884** G. SYMONS *Brit. Rainf.* 21 That water is usually about 3 ft. below the surface of the ground. **1885** SIR W. THOMSON in *Nature* XXXI. 409 The necessity for study below the surface seems to have been earliest recognised in anatomy.

4. Directly beneath; under the covering or canopy of; underneath. More strictly expressed by *under, beneath.*

1605 SHAKS. *Lear* v. iii. 137 To the discent and dust below thy foote. **1697** DRYDEN *Virg. Georg.* IV. 472 From her Mossy Bow'r below the Ground. **1719** WATTS *Ps.* cxvii, From all that dwell below the skies. **1816** J. WILSON *City of Plague* I. iii. 21 Sitting on this stone, And thinking who it was who lay below it. **1831** CARLYLE *Sart. Res.* I. iii, Books lay on tables and below tables. **1850** TENNYSON *In Mem.* XII. i, Some dolorous message knit below The wild pulsation of her wings.

5. Under the influence of; = BENEATH 4. *rare.*

1813 BYRON *Ch. Har.* I. xlvii, His vineyard..Blasted below the dim hot breath of war.

6. Of position in a graduated scale, *e.g.* that of a barometer: *hence* **a.** Lower, in amount, weight, strength, value, price, degree of any quality, than.

1721 PERRY *Daggenh. Breach* 30 Having made it sure that no Man else would go below [underbid] him. **1788** PRIESTLEY *Lect. Hist.* v. liii. 416 In this case, the exchange is said to be below par at London. **1840** E. TURNER *Elem. Chem.* (ed. 7) II. 445 In this state it..fuses below redness. **1848** MILL *Pol. Econ.* II. v. iii. § 5. 377 Incomes below a certain amount should be altogether untaxed. **1849** MRS. SOMERVILLE *Phys. Geog.* II. xxiv. 124 The cold has been 120° below Zero. **1884** MRS. H. WOOD *White Witch* II. viii. 190 He threw himself into the seat beside her, and said below his breath, etc. **1884** G. SYMONS *Brit. Rainf.* 84 The rainfall of this month..is considerably below the average. *Mod.* Throughout England the barometer stood below 29.

b. *fig.* Lower in rank, dignity, or station than.

1601 SHAKS. *All's Well* II. ii. 32 From below your Duke to beneath your Constable. **1668** DRYDEN *Maiden Q.* I. iii, I love below myself, a Subject. **1711** STEELE *Spect.* No. 49 ¶7 He..gives his Orders..to the Servants below him. **1751** JORTIN *Serm.* (1771) II. iv. 73 Unless he is sunk below a beast. **1823** LAMB *Elia* Ser. II. ii. (1865) 248 No woman dresses below herself from caprice. **1849** MACAULAY *Hist. Eng.* II. 227 A man far below them in station. **1885** J. MARTINEAU *Ethical The.* I. 275 What he treats as *Substance* relatively to phenomenal nature below it, he regards as *Attribute* relatively to a prior infinite nature above it.

c. Lower, in quality or excellence, or in some particular quality, than; inferior to.

1711 FELTON (T.) His idylliums of Theocritus are as much below his Manilius, as the fields are below the stars. **1766** GOLDSM. *Vic. W.* viii. (1806) 34 The finest strokes.. are much below those in the Acis and Galatea of Ovid. **1839** BAILEY *Festus* viii, So far is the lightest heart below True happiness. **1847** MACAULAY *Let.* in Trevelyan *Life* (1876) II. xi. 232 How far my performance is below excellence. **1871** HAWEIS *Mus. & Mor.* (1874) 505 We place England and France below Germany.

7. Unworthy of, unbefitting, lowering to. More usually expressed by BENEATH.

1637 BRIDGMAN in Prynne's *Prelate's Tyrr.* (1641) 223 It is much below me to be an Informer. **1709** STEELE *Tatler* No. 23 ¶2 It was below a Gentlewoman to wrangle. **1712** —— *ibid.* No. 522 ¶2 A man..of birth and estate below no woman to accept. **1743** J. BARCLAY *Educ.* 36 Such things some may reckon below attention. **1827** HALLAM *Const. Hist.* (1842) I. 139 A compiler..who thinks no fact below his regard. **1883** PROCTOR in *Knowledge* 10 Aug. 94/1 Too far below contempt to be worth castigating.

8. *Comb.* **below-ground,** (*a*) *adj.*, that is below the ground; (*b*) *sb.*, a place or places below the ground; **below-the-belt** *a.*, unfair, underhand (see BELT *sb.*¹ 1 d).

1941 L. A. G. STRONG *Bay* viii. 183 The soft pressure, the below-the-belt, if-you-love-me stuff that women employ so readily. **1960** *Farmer & Stockbreeder* (Suppl.) 16 Feb. 35/1 A below-ground, outside concrete tank. **1960** E. BOWEN *Time in Rome* iv. 118 From Rome's below-ground I must not omit the Catacombs.

† **below,** *v. Obs. rare.* [f. BE- 1 + LOW *v.*] To make low or lowly, to humble.

1377 LANGL. *P. Pl.* B. VI. 230 If þow wil[t]..biloue [*v.r.* bilow, bylowe] þe amonges low men · so shaltow lacche grace.

below, -es, -ys, obs. forms of BELLOW-S.

‖ **bel paese** (bɛl paˈeze). [Italian proprietary term, f. It. *bel* beautiful + *paese* country, region.] A rich, white, creamy cheese of mild flavour originally made in Italy.

1935 O. BURDETT *Bk. Cheese* iv. 54 Bel Paese, another round, flat, spongy cheese, is also a shade less mild than Port Salut. **1948** W. S. MAUGHAM *Here & There* ii. 25 The maid brought us *bel paese* cheese and a plate of figs. **1951** 'M. INNES' *Operation Pax* III. iii. 91, I have been able to buy some *salami*—and a *bel-paese* too.

belschyd, -shynge, pa. pple. and vbl. sb. of BELLISH *v. Obs.*

Belsen (ˈbɛlsən). The name of a concentration camp in Germany in the war of 1939–45, applied hyperbolically to any very unpleasant place. Also *attrib.* and *Comb.*

1948 PARTRIDGE *Dict. Forces' Slang* 14 *Belsen.* Most army camps sooner or later acquired, with or without justification, the name of this most notorious of Nazi concentration camps. **1953** L. A. G. STRONG *Hill of Howth* ix. 194 It was a Belsen urge, a blast from the pit. **1956** 'M. INNES' *Appleby plays Chicken* I. i. 16 My public school was a regular old Belsen. **1959** *News Chron.* 12 Dec. 7/1 Allegations about 'hoodlum warders' with 'Belsen-type mentalities' at Exeter prison.

Belshazzar, see BALTHAZAR.

† **ˈbelsire.** *Obs.* Also 4–6 bel(l)syre, 5 beelesire, 6 belsier. [f. BEL + SIRE: cf. *beldame, belfader.* The components are the same as in *beausire*, with which, however, this has no connexion, being of Eng. formation.] A grandfather; an ancestor.

1377 LANGL. *P. Pl.* B. IX. 142 Here abouȝte þe barne þe belsyres gultes. **1483** *Cath. Angl.* 27/1 Bellsyre, *auus.* **1494** FABYAN VII. ccxxvii. 256 The sone here lyeth with also the fader, The belsyre, for & yᵉ great graundfader. **1530** PALSGR. 197/2 Belsyre, *grant pere.* **1573** TWYNE *Æneid* XII. Mm iij, Antique names of noble Belsiers old. **1612** DRAYTON *Poly-olb.* xiv. 233 When he his long descent shall from his Belsires bring. *a* **1631** WEEVER *Anc. Fun. Mon.* 615 The great Belsire, the Grandsire, Sire, and Sonne Lie here interred vnder this Grauestone.

† **ˈbelˌswagger.** *Obs.* Also bell-, belly-. [Perhaps a contr. of *belly-swagger* (as in Ash) 'one who *swags* or *sways* his belly.'] A swaggering gallant or bully; a whoremonger, pimp.

1592 GREENE *Def. Coney-catch.* (1859) 47 [Nothing] can draw them from the love of the Poligamoi or bel-swaggers of the country. **1680** DRYDEN *Kind Kpr.* IV. i. Wks. IV. 337 Fifty Guineas! Dost thou think I'll sell my self?..thou impudent Belswagger. **1721** BAILEY, *Bellswagger*, a swaggering Fellow, a hectoring Blade, a Bully. **1775** ASH *Belly-swagger*, a bully, a hectoring fellow. *Belswagger*, a whore-master.

belt (bɛlt), *sb.*¹ Also 5–7 belte. [Common Teut.: OE. *bęlt*, cogn. with OHG. *balz* (? masc.), prob.:—OTeut. **baltjo-z*, ad. L. *balteus* girdle. ON. has *balti* (neut.), perh. ad. L. *balteum*, common in med.L.]

1. a. A broadish, flat strip of leather or similar material, used to gird or encircle the person, confine some part of the dress, and to support various articles of use or ornament. Often described by the part of the body encircled (as

waist-belt, shoulder-belt), or the article supported (as ***sword-belt, cartridge-belt***).

a **1000** *Harl. Gloss.* in Wr.-Wülcker *Voc.* 192 *Baltheum, cingulum, uel* belt. *a* **1100** *Cott. Gl.* ibid. 359 *Balteum* gyrdel, oððe belt. **1375** BARBOUR *Bruce* x. 175 And ber Ane hatchat, that wer scharp to scher Undre hys belt. *c* **1386** CHAUCER *Reeve's T.* 9 And by his belt he baar a long panade. **1597** SHAKS. *2 Hen. IV*, I. ii. 159 He that buckles him in my belt. **1676** ETHEREDGE *Man of Mode* III. i. (1684) 31 Get your right leg firm on the ground, adjust your Belt. **1715** *Lond. Gaz.* No. 5376/3 A Cartouch Pouch, with a Shoulder belt, a Sword with a Waist-belt. **1874** BOUTELL *Arms & Arm.* ii. 24 The sword..hung from a belt that passed over the shoulder.

b. *esp.* one worn as a mark of rank or distinction e.g. in *Boxing* and *Wrestling*. In *Judo*: see BLACK BELT 3.

c **1340** *Gaw. & Gr. Knt.* 162 Boþe þe barres of his belt & oþer blyþe stones. **1673** CAVE *Prim. Chr.* i. v. 110 An officer ..threw away his belt, rather than obey that impious command. **1812** 'ONE OF THE FANCY' *Boxiana* 422 We understand that an emblematical Belt has been some time preparing for the Champion, but not yet presented to him. **1822** *Sporting Mag.* X. 106/2 Cribb was decorated with the *belt*, in the front of which are a couple of silver fists, and on each side are two large circles of silver plate, with inscriptions engraved on them. **1850** THACKERAY *Pendennis* xlv, They fight each other for the champion's belt and two hundred pounds a side. **1872** R. D. BLACKMORE *Maid of Sker* II. xxvii. 10 He had held the belt seven years..for wrestling, as well as for bruising. **1889** E. B. MICHELL *Boxing & Sparring* (Badm. Libr.) i. 125 The belt—the emblem of modern championship in the P.R.

c. *fig.*

1483 *Cath. Angl.* 27/1 A belte of lechery, *cestus*. *a* **1500** *Songs Costume* (1849) 60 Hir belt suld be of benignitie About her middill meit. **1605** SHAKS. *Macb.* v. ii. 17 He cannot buckle his distemper'd cause Within the belt of Rule.

d. ***to hit*** (or ***strike***) ***below the belt*** (from the language of pugilists) is used *fig.* for 'to act unfairly in any contest'.

1889 E. B. MICHELL *Boxing & Sparring* (Badm. Libr.) i. 125 The rule against hitting below the belt. **1890** FARMER *Slang* I. 175/1 To strike a man *below the belt*..is akin with 'To stab a man in the back'. **1891** *Chambers's Encycl.* VIII. 485/2 No man might be struck below the belt—the belt in practice being a handkerchief tied tightly round the waist. **1891** [see HITTING *vbl. sb.*]. **1903** *Punch* 1 July 453 Call this *Fair* Trade, hitting me below the Belt?

e. ***to tighten*** (etc.) one's ***belt***: to stave off hunger, to bear the pangs of hunger philosophically. Also *fig.*

[**1841** LEVER *C. O'Malley* xx, 'Perhaps not' lisped Melville, tightening his belt; 'but it's devilish convivial.'] **1887** KIPLING *Life's Handicap* (1891) 290, I also was once starved, and tightened my belt on the sharp belly-pinch. **1907** MULFORD *Bar-20* v. 46 They's three things that's good for famine... Yu can pull in your belt, yu can drink, an' yu can eat. **1927** *Observer* 24 Apr. 15/3 A travelling troupe who quoted Corneille while tightening their belts.

f. Colloq. phr. ***under one's belt***, in one's stomach. Also *fig.*

1839 *Spirit of Times* 21 Dec. 498/3 Away we went, each bearing, under his belt, his full share of the antifogmatical.. compound. **1938** CRAIGIE & HULBERT *Dict. Amer. Eng.* I. 193/2 *Belt*, v... To put under one's belt; to swallow. **1954** *Manch. Guardian Weekly* 12 Aug. 12 His wife had 135,000 miles driving in the States under her belt..but was still failed. **1954** WODEHOUSE in *Encounter* Oct. 19/1 Just as you have got Hamlet and Macbeth under your belt. **1962** J. WAIN *Strike Father Dead* v. 216 He wanted me to get plenty of Latin and Greek under the belt so that I could be like him.

g. One used to support the figure; a suspender-belt; a corset.

1880 *Draper's Jrnl.* 24 June p. iii (Advt.), Important to ladies. The new model figure belts. *Ibid.*, Our special ladies supporting belts are strongly recommended..for giving great support both before and after accouchement. **1932** R. LEHMANN *Invit. Waltz* I. ix. 98 Etty wears..just her belt and knickers. **1952** C. W. CUNNINGTON *Eng. Women's Clothes* vii. 238 Slim-fitting knickers to replace panties and belt. **1961** *Housewife* Apr. 114/2 Dainty bra..matching belt with adjustable suspenders.

2. *transf.* A broadish strip or stripe of any kind, or a continuous series of objects, encircling or girdling something: **a.** *gen.*

1753 CHAMBERS *Cycl. Supp.*, s.v., The denomination *belt* is also applied to a sort of bandage in use among surgeons. **1788** J. C. SMYTH in *Med. Commun.* II. 184 The Zona, or Belt..seems to partake of the nature of a herpes. **1857** EMERSON *Poems* 163 A belt of mirrors round a taper's flame. **1875** FORTNUM *Maiolica* v. 49 The body is decorated with two belts of grotesques.

b. *esp.* of the physical features of a landscape.

1810 SOUTHEY *Kehama* XXI. iii, A level belt of ice which bound..The waters of the sleeping Ocean round. **1834** *Brit. Husb.* I. 473 To plant a belt of Scotch firs around the inside of the circular drain. **1850** PRESCOTT *Peru* II. 216 The American hunter, who endeavours to surround himself with a belt of wasted land, when overtaken by a conflagration.

c. *spec.* in *Astr.*

1664 *Phil. Trans.* I. 3 He hath remarked in the Belts of Jupiter the shaddows of his satellites. **1787** BONNYCASTLE *Astron.* iii. 44 The body of Jupiter is surrounded by several parallel faint substances called Belts. **1830** TENNYSON *Poems* 113 The burning belts, the mighty rings, The murmurous planets' rolling choir.

3. *Mech.* **a.** A broad flat strap of leather, india-rubber, etc. passing round two wheels or shafts, and communicating motion from one to the other.

1795 *Specif. Patent* No. 2034 The wood roller..has its motion by a pulley and belt. **1885** *Engineer* 15 May (*Advt.*), Main Driving Belts..to transmit any required H.P.

b. In a machine gun, a length of woven fabric or of metal plates pinned together, fitted with cartridges and revolving on the feed-block.

1902 *Encycl. Brit.* XXX. 403/1 Figs. 7 and 8 show the feed-block and method of packing the cartridge belts. The greatest number usually carried in a belt is 250. *Ibid.* 406/1 A belt of cartridges..has been placed on the feed-wheel. **1914** *Scotsman* 26 Sept. 5/6 The belt of the gun [*sc.* a Maxim] was still charged.

c. An assembly-belt or conveyor. Also *transf.* orig. *U.S.*

1908, 1909 [see *belt conveyor*]. **1936** B. & S. SPEWACK *Boy meets Girl* I. 13 We are dealing here with a factory that manufactures entertainment in approved sizes; that puts the seven arts right on the belt. **1937** U. SINCLAIR *Flivver King* (1938) lxxiv. 194 I'd rather take my chance on the belt. **1938** *Reader's Digest* Jan. 123/2 Automobiles leaving the belt as finished products.

4. A broadish flexible strap. (The idea of encircling or girdling here begins to disappear.)

1672 T. VENN *Mil. & Mar. Discip.* iii. 8 He is to have a good Harquebuz, hanging on a belt into a swivel. **1753** DOUGLASS *Brit. Settlem. N. Amer.* 219 Our Indians formerly accounted by single Wampum, by Strings of Wampum, and by Belts of Wampum, in the same manner as the English account by the Denominations of Pence, Shillings, and Pounds. **1885** *Nature* XXXI. 415 The cartridges [of a self-loading gun] are placed in a belt formed of two bands of tape, before they are placed in the box, and one end of this belt is placed in the gun.

5. a. A broad band or stripe characteristically distinguished from the surface it crosses; a tract or district long in proportion to its breadth. Also, a zone or district, usu. with defining term denoting the principal product or characteristic. Cf. *Bible belt*, BLACK BELT 1, GREEN BELT. orig. *U.S.*

1808 WILFORD *Sacr. Isles* in *Asiat. Res.* VIII. 264 A range or belt about forty degrees broad, across the old continent. **1852** CONYBEARE & H. *St. Paul* (1862) I. vi. 159 Three belts of vegetation are successively passed through in ascending from the coast. **1869** *Overland Monthly* III. 12 Between the short-staple [cotton] belt and the rice and long-staple belt of the coast. **1871** R. SOMERS *Southern States* xxxvii. 263 The 'Cotton Belt' of the Southern States. **1875**, etc. [see BLACK BELT 1]. **1877** H. SPOFFORD *Pilot's Wife* in *Casquet Lit.* IV. 13/2 Bert's boat might have been beyond its [the storm's] belt. **1879** TOURGEE *Fool's Err.* xlvi. 353 You have just come through the infected belt [of yellow fever]. **1891** *Harper's Mag.* Aug. 446/2 A fierce storm swept over the whole gold belt. **1903** A. B. HART *Actual Govt.* 116 Illinois is divided into a wheat belt, a corn belt, and the city of Chicago. **1960** *Spectator* 29 July 173 The Copper Belt is necessary to Southern Rhodesia. **1960** *Observer* 25 Dec. 7/6 A stately great drag headed for the stockbrokers' belt. **1968** D. E. ALLEN *Brit. Tastes* ii. 43 Affluent couples..on the coast who leapfrog the dormitory belt altogether. **1968** C. FORSYTE *Murder with Minarets* iii. 11 One could live abroad and still be only on the tattered fringes of the servant belt.

b. *Geog.* ***Great*** and ***Little Belts***, two channels between the Cattegat and the Baltic.

1753 CHAMBERS *Cycl. Supp.* s.v., The belts belong to the King of Denmark.

c. *Arch.* 'A course of stones projecting from the naked, either moulded, plain, or fluted.' Gwilt.

d. *Naval Arch.* A series of thick iron plates running along the water-line in armoured vessels.

1885 *Pall Mall G.* 21 Jan. 1/1 Naval officers will feel profoundly uncomfortable in taking an ironclad without a complete belt into action. **1885** *Times* 10 Apr. 3 A short armoured belt..extending over less than half the length of the ship.

¶ ***belt of pater-nosters*** or ***of Our Fathers***:

In the Acts of the Council of Celchyth, an. 816 (Haddan & Stubbs *Councils & Eccl. Doc.* III. 584), occurs the passage 'et xxx diebus canonicis horis expleto synaxeos æt VII beltidum, Paternoster pro eo cantetur,' of which the latter part 'at the seven bell-hours let the Paternoster be sung for him,' has given rise to one of the most grotesque blunders on record. The OE. words *æt* VII *beltidum*, 'at the seven bell-hours,' a gloss on '*canonicis horis*' preceding, were taken by Spelman as Latin, and construed with the following word as a 'paternoster of seven belts,' which he explained as a *rosary*. Du Cange repeated the explanation, though questioning the existence of the rosary at that date. Johnson the Nonjuror (*Eccl. Laws* 1720) elaborately described 'belts' set with studs serving the purpose of a rosary. Scott (Suppl. to Chambers, 1753) suggested as a better rendering, 'a paternoster to be repeated seven times.' In all these there was an attempt to construe the passage, but in later 'explanations' the grammatical construction has been dismissed, and 'VII beltidum, paternoster' transmuted into 'seven belts of paternosters,' as in the following curious specimens of modern mythology:

1844 LINGARD *Anglo-Sax. Ch.* (1858) II. ix. 62 The frequent repetition of the Lord's Prayer, technically called a belt of Pater-nosters. *Note.* A belt of Pater-nosters appears to correspond with a string of beads of later times..It is probable that the belt contained fifty Pater-nosters. **1849** ROCK *Ch. of Fathers* III. viii. 8 Seven belts of Our Fathers had to be said for the deceased.

6. *Comb.* and *Attrib.*: **a.** objective with vbl. sb. or pple., as ***belt-cutter, -maker, -splicing, -stretcher, -tightener***; **b.** attrib., as ***belt-armour, -clasp, -coupling***. Also **belt conveyor** (see quot. 1909) = *conveyor belt*; **belt-driven** *a.* (*Mech.*), driven by means of a flexible endless belt; hence **belt drive**, driving mechanism of this type; **belt-driving** *vbl. sb.*; **belt-knife**, (*a*) a knife carried in a belt for use as a weapon, hunting-knife, etc.; (*b*) *U.S.*, a revolving knife on the bandsaw principle, used in splitting hides or skins; **belt-lacing**, thongs for lacing together the ends of machine belts; **belt line** (*U.S.*), a railway, tram-line, or road that makes a complete circuit of a city; also *attrib.*; so ***belt tram***; † **belt-money**, ? a gratuity to soldiers; **belt-pipe**, a steam-pipe surrounding the cylinder of a steam-engine; **belt-punch**, an instrument for punching holes in belts; **belt-saw** (= *band-saw*; see BAND *sb.*[2] III); **belt-shifter**, a contrivance for shifting a belt from pulley to pulley; **belt-speeder**, a contrivance consisting of two cone-pulleys carrying a belt, by which varying rates of motion are transmitted; † **belt-stead, -stid**, the place of the belt, the waist; **belt-tightening** *vbl. sb.*, (*a*) the tightening of a belt; (*b*) *fig.* (the introduction of) rigorous economies (cf. sense 1 e above); also *attrib.*; **belt-wise** *adv.*, in the manner of a belt.

1885 *Pall Mall G.* 14 Jan. 11/1 Ships stripped of their *belt armour. **1908** *Engineering Mag.* Dec. 440 The original *belt conveyor consisted of a very wide belt running on straight idlers and carrying a small amount of material distributed along the middle. **1909** *Cent. Dict.* Suppl. s.v. *conveyer*, A *belt-conveyer* employs a broad endless belt of leather, rubber, or similar fabric, running over stationary rollers placed at equal distances apart. When in operation a stream of light material, such as grain, can be fed to the belt and be transported at high speed in large quantities. **1930** *Engineering* 13 June 783/1 (*heading*) Portable Belt Conveyor. **1906** *Motor Cycles & how to manage Them* (ed. 10) 89 Types of *Belt Drive. **1907** *Daily Chron.* 17 Oct. 8/2 A motor cycle ..with belt drive. **1934** *Discovery* Nov. 324/2 Two-stroke petrol engine, connected by belt-drive to a 200 watt alternator. **1893** *Jrnl. Soc. Arts* 5 May 622/1 Seventeen dynamos, all *belt-driven. **1906** *Westm. Gaz.* 26 Mar. 10/2 The old belt-driven Benz [motor car] of a prehistoric past. **1908** *Ibid.* 30 Jan. 4/1 A belt-driven fan. **1892** NASMITH *Students' Cotton Spinning* Index 428 *Belt Driving. **1902** H. STURMEY in A. C. Harmsworth *Motors* x. 186 Belt driving is quite silent in running. *Ibid.* 195 Belt-driving cars have usually two belts running on pulleys of different sizes. **1856** KANE *Arct. Exp.* II. xv 159 The *belt-ice at their foot was old and undisturbed. **1840** C. F. HOFFMAN *Greyslaer* I. 234 The hand of the Mohawk clutched the *belt-knife..half drawn from its sheath. **1895** *Daily News* 21 Mar. 5/7 That they had not..so much as a belt knife. **1909** H. G. BENNETT *Manuf. Leather* 279 There are three types of splitting machine, the 'union', the vibrating knife, and the band-knife (or belt-knife) machine. **1894** *Cent. Mag.* Dec. 290 De *Belt Line stables ain't no Hoffman House. **1900** *Engineering Mag.* XIX. 698 The belt-line railway, running largely in cuttings and underground. **1903** *N.Y. Times* 24 Oct. 2 George B. McClellan and Edward M. Grout were scheduled for a belt line tour of speechmaking. **1922** *Daily Ardmoreite* (Ardmore, Okla.) 6 Jan. 6/5 A belt line of gravel highway is now under construction around the city of Ardmore. **1966** *Economist* 26 Mar. 1234/1 Circumferential 'belt lines' around cities could be built more quickly than radial routes leading into their older centres. **1483** *Cath. Angl.* 27/1 A *belte maker, *zonarius*. **1679** *Trial Wakeman* 44 Mr. Cott, a Beltmaker in the New Exchange. **1648** *Petit. Eastern Ass.* 18 Is not *Belt-money the dispendium of our possessions? *c* **1400** *Destr. Troy* XIV. 5940 Slit hym down sleghly thurghe the slote euyn, Bode at the *belt stid, and the buerne deghit. **1879** *Daily News* 6 Nov. 5/3 They were armoured on the *belt system, their thickest plates being confined to the neighbourhood of the water-line. **1910** *Installation News* IV. 50/2 Shifting the motor along the slide rails for *belt tightening purposes. **1961** *Atlantic Monthly* Jan. 13/2 Belt tightening is not just a phrase but must become a reality. **1979** *Dædalus* Spring 121 Instead of this belt-tightening strategy, these countries [*sc.* non-oil developing countries] have in fact maintained important levels of imports and of economic activity. **1983** *Listener* 19 May 4/1 A further round of belt-tightening will be required, through additional cuts in public spending. **1894** J. DALE *Round the World* 333 The *belt tram took us round the city, 8 miles. **1667** E. CHAMBERLAYNE *St. Gt. Brit.* I. III. iv. (1743) 173 They wear a scarlet Ribbon *belt-wise.

† **belt**, *sb.*[2] *Obs.* [Prob. distinct from prec., but nothing is known of its derivation.] An axe.

a **1300** W. DE BIBLESW. in Wright's *Voc.* 163 The belte, *le coing*. **1499** *Promp. Parv.* (Pynson), Belt or ax, *securis*. *c* **1500** *Carpenter's T.* in Halliw. *Nugæ P.* 13 'Wherefore,' seyd the belte, 'With grete strokes I schalle hym pelte.'

belt, *sb.*[3] ? *Obs.* (See BELT *v.* 5 and *ppl. a.*)

c **1640** J. SMYTH *Lives Berkeleys* (1883) I. 156 What money was yearly made by sale of the locks belts and tags of the sheep. **1741** *Compl. Fam. Piece* III. 494 Of the Tag or Belt in Sheep. **1753** in CHAMBERS *Cycl. Supp.*; and in later. Dicts.

belt, *sb.*[4] *colloq.* [f. BELT *v.* (sense 4).] A heavy blow or stroke.

1899 SOMERVILLE & 'ROSS' *Exper. Irish R.M.* 217 Will I give him [*sc.* a horse] a couple o' belts, your Honour? **1911** MASEFIELD *Everl. Mercy* 33 I'd like to hit the world a belt. **1927** *Glasgow Herald* 26 Aug. 11 [He] took three mighty belts at the ball. **1934** in *Sc. Nat. Dict.*, He gave the man a belt on the jaw. **1953** L. A. G. STRONG *Hill of Howth* 68 He'd give Moo a belt in the puss.

belt (bɛlt), *v.* Pa. pple. 6 belt. [f. BELT *sb.*[1]]

1. a. *trans.* and *refl.* To gird with a belt; to engirdle; *spec.* to invest with a distinctive belt, *e.g.* of knighthood.

a **1300** *Cursor M.* 15285 Wid a tuel he belted his sides. *Ibid.* 3365 Sco belted hir bettur on hir wede. *Ibid.* 6087 Yee be alle belted, wit staf in hand. *c* **1425** WYNTOUN *Cron.* IX. xix. 51 Þe Lord Schire Davy de Lyndesay Wes Erle maid.. and he beltit swa. *c* **1570** *Bp. St. Andrew's* in *Scot. Poems 16th C.* II. 327 A cott of kelt, Weill beltit in ane lethrone belt. **1813** SCOTT *Rokeby* III. xxx, Allen-a-Dale was ne'er belted a knight.

fig. **1536** BELLENDEN *Cron. Scot.* (1821) I. 238 Belt you thairfore, lusty gallandis, with manheid and wisdome. **1552** ABP. HAMILTON *Catech.* 267 Belt our loynyeis with verite.

b. *refl.* To gird oneself *with* a weapon.

c **1425** WYNTOUN *Cron.* VII. viii. 444 Beltyd wyth his Swerd alsua. **1513** DOUGLAS *Æneis* IV. v. 159 Belt he was with a swerd of mettall brycht. **1820** SCOTT *Abbot* iii, There ne'er was gentleman but who belted him with the brand.

c. *trans.* To fasten on with a belt, gird on (a weapon, shield, etc.).

1513 DOUGLAS *Æneis* II. x. (ix.) 9 A swerd, but help, about him beltis he. *a* **1560** ROLLAND *Crt. Venus* I. 163 Ane sword was belt about his [loins]. **1583** STANYHURST *Æneis* II. (Arb.) 60 Bootelesse morglay to his sydes hee belted. **1782** PENNANT *Journ. Chester* (R.) An enormous shield..is belted to his body. **1822** SCOTT *Nigel* xi, A trustier old Trojan never belted a broadsword by a loop of leather.

2. *transf.* To surround with a circle or zone of any kind; to engirdle; to mark with an encircling band. *spec.* to girdle (a tree) by stripping off the bark (*U.S.*).

1536 BELLENDEN *Cron. Scot.* I. 117 Thay wer belttit about on every side with enimes. **1812** H. MARSHALL *Hist. Kentucky* 14 These improvements..consisted principally in ..belting the larger trees. **1814** WORDSW. *Wh. Doe* IV. 205 They belt him round with hearts undaunted. **1832** HT. MARTINEAU *Each & All* vi. 72 The trees belted the churchyard. **1837** W. IRVING *Capt. Bonneville* (1849) 225 He [the beaver] makes incisions round them [trees], or, in technical phrase, belts them with his teeth. **1853** P. P. KENNEDY *Blackwater Chron.* xiv. 216 One man,..in a hundred days, would belt or deaden one hundred acres.

3. To mark with bands or stripes of colour, etc.

1782 T. WARTON *Hist. Kiddington* 67 (R.) Ramperts.. belting the hills far and wide with white. **1868** LOCKYER *Elem. Astron.* cccv, Moments in which the meteors belted the sky like the meridians on a terrestrial globe.

4. a. To thrash with a belt. Cf. *to strap.*

1649 in ROGERS *Soc. Life Scotl.* II. 217 Comitted to Alexander Cuming to see him belted be his mother. *a* **1700** in Somers *Tracts* (1811) V. 460, I wad she were wele belted with a bridle. **1818** HOGG *Brownie* II. 162 (Jam.), 'I wish he had beltit your shoulders.' **1867** SMYTH *Sailor's Wd.-bk.*, *Belt*, to beat with a colt or rope's end.

b. Various slang uses: (*a*) To hit; to attack; (*b*) *to belt* (*the bottle*), to drink heavily; (*c*) to sing, play, or speak with great vigour (const. *out*).

1838 J. C. NEAL *Charcoal Sketches* 46 He intends to belt me, does he? Take a stick —. **1884** 'MARK TWAIN' *Huck. Finn* 21 They [*sc.* genies] don't think nothing of..belting a Sunday-School superintendent over the head. **1909** WARE *Passing Eng.* 25/2 There comes that old maid; belt her. **1912** GALSWORTHY *Pigeon* II. 55 Megan'll get his mates to belt him. **1957** I. CROSS *God Boy* (1958) xviii. 152 It [*sc.* a dog] cut right across the road..and was belted by a wool truck. **1931** RUNYON *Guys & Dolls* (1932) ii. 43 Jack takes to belting the old grape right freely to get his zing back. **1960** *Observer* 18 Sept. 19/2 He is given to belting the bottle. **1953** *Sat. Rev. Lit.* 12 Dec. 55/1 Standing there..belting out the sophisticated sweetness of Porter's 'Get Out of Town'. **1959** J. STEINBECK *Once there was War* xix, One of the finest jazz combos I ever heard was belting out pure ecstasy.

5. (See quots.: app. To shear off a belt of wool.)

1523 FITZHERB. *Husb.* §41 To belte shepe. Yf any shepe raye or be fyled with dounge about the tayle, take a payre of sheres, and clyppe it awaye, etc. **1688** HOLME *Armory* II. ix. 176 Belting of sheep, is the dressing of them from filth. **1842** C. JOHNSON *Farmer's Encycl.* I. 196 To belt, in some districts signifies to shear the buttocks and tails of sheep.

6. *trans.* To connect with a machine-driven belt. Also *absol.*

1902 J. S. THOMPSON *Mech. Linotype* (1908) xxiv. 169 The size of the pulley on the motor to which it is belted will decrease the speed. *Ibid.* 172 To drive the machine by belting directly to the intermediate shaft.

7. *intr.* To hurry, to rush. *slang* (orig. *dial.* and *U.S.*).

1890 J. D. ROBERTSON *Gloss. Dial. Gloucester*, *Belt v.* to racket or bustle about. **1894** *Outing* (U.S.) XXIV. 57/2, I belted along as fast as the waders and treacherous footing would allow. **1942** *We speak from Air* vii. 24 A picture of two Me. 109's belting down on your tail from out of the sun. **1949** D. M. DAVIN *Roads from Home* III. iii. 227 Looked like the one that raced us on the way up this morning... He's belting it out by the look of him. **1958** K. AMIS *I like it Here* 179 Getting up as she often did to..switch off the immersion heater, belting downstairs to let that sod of a dog in. **1962** *New Statesman* 18 May 710/1 Cor, we used to belt along that road.

8. Slang phr. *to belt up*: to be quiet, 'shut up'. Usu. as *imp.*

1949 PARTRIDGE *Dict. Slang* (ed. 3) Add., *Belt up*: Shut up!: R.A.F.: since ca. 1937. **1958** *News Chron.* 22 May, Belt up is just another way of saying be quiet. **1959** M. PUGH *Chancer* v. 57 Why don't you belt up?.. Go and boil your can. **1969** *Listener* 30 Jan. 147/3 May we hope that Hamilton will do a service to art by belting up and going back to school?

belt, *ppl. a.* [? short for *belted*, f. prec.; sense 5. Cf. BELT *sb.*[3]] (See quot.)

1614 MARKHAM *Cheap Husb.* III. xvii. (1668) 91 A sheep is said to be Tag'd or Belt, when by a continual squirt running out of his ordure he berayeth his tail, in such wise, that through the heat of the dung it scaldeth, and breedeth the scab therein. [So in **1741** *Compl. Fam. Piece* III. 494.]

Beltane ('bɛltən). [Adopted in Lowland Scotch from Gaelic *bealltainn*, *bealtuinn* (in Irish *bealtaine*, Manx *boaltinn*, *boaldyn*) the Celtic name of the first of May, the beginning of summer.

OIr. forms are *beltene* (in a text), *belltaine*, *beltine* in Cormac's Glossary (9th to 12th c.). The first is prob. the earliest quotable form of the word, of which the original meaning seems to have been unknown even to the glossarist, since he makes a desperate guess at it by transposing *bel-tine* or *bil-tene* into *tene-bil*, and explaining *bil* as '*Bil* from *Bial*, i.e. an idol god,' evidently meaning the Bel, or Baal, of the Old Testament: so that *bel-tene* became 'fire of Bel,' or (?) 'Baal.' Dr. Whitley Stokes has shown that the latter part of the word is not *teine* 'fire,' since this is a *-t* stem (OIr. *tene*, *tened*), while *Beltene* is a feminine *-ya* stem. Whether it can be a parallel derivative of the same root, or whether, as is more likely, the notion that *-taine* was = *teine* 'fire' is due merely to 'popular etymology' cannot be determined. (The ancient Gaels kindled bonfires not only on Beltane, but also on Lammas and Hallowmas.) The rubbish about *Baal*, *Bel*, *Belus*, imported into the word from the Old Testament and classical antiquity, is outside the scope of scientific etymology.]

1. The first day of May (reckoned since 1752 according to Old Style); Old May-day. The quarter-days anciently in Scotland were Hallowmas, Candlemas, Beltane, and Lammas. ***Beltane day*** (Gael. *la bealltainn*) appears sometimes to have been identified with the nearest Church Feast, the Invention of the Cross (May 3rd), and the name seems even to have been applied to Whit-sunday (May 15th), when this took its place as term day.

1424 *Acts Jas. I*, (1597) §19 And the nest be funden in the Trees at Beltane the trees sall be foirfaulted to the King. **1536** BELLENDEN *Cron. Scot.* XVII. ii. (JAM.) On Beltane day, in the yeir nixt followyng, callit the Inventioun of the haly Croce. *a* **1550** *Peblis to Play* i. 1 At Beltane, quhen ilk bodie bownis To Peblis to the Play. **1716** MARTIN *West. Isles Scotl.* 240 In the Highlands, the first day of May is still called *La Baaltine*—corruptly *Beltan-day*. **1721** KELLY *Sc. Proverbs* 376 (JAM.) You have skill of man and beast, you was born between the Beltans; i.e. the first and eighth of May. *a* **1835** MOTHERWELL *Jeanie Morrison* 5 The fire that's blawn on Beltane e'en May weel be black gin Yule. **1862** Hislop's *Prov. Scotl.* 8 A gowk at Yule'll no be bright at Beltane. **1876** GRANT *Burgh Sch. Scotl.* II. xiii. 469 The old quarterly terms for paying the School fees were Lammas, Hallowmas, Candlemas and Beltane.

‖**2.** Name of an ancient Celtic anniversary celebration on May-day, in connexion with which great bonfires were kindled on the hills.

This use of the word appears in English much later than the preceding, and only as an alien term applied to the Celtic custom; it may be the original use in Celtic. Cormac's Glossary explains *belltaine* as 'two fires which the Druids used to make, and they used to bring the cattle [as a safe-guard] against the diseases of each year to those fires.' Also under *Bil*, 'a fire was kindled in his name at the beginning of summer always, and cattle were driven between the two fires.' Various accounts of Beltane observances lingering in the Highlands and Islands of Scotland, are to be found in 18th c. writers, and esp. in the old *Statistical Accts. of Scotland* 1794–99. A large number of these are collected in Jamieson.

1772 PENNANT *Tours Scotl.* (1774) 42 The superstition of the Bel-tein was kept up. *Ibid.* (JAM.) On the first of May the herdsmen of every village hold their *Bel-tein* or rural sacrifice. *c* **1795** *Statist. Acc. Scotl.* V. 84 (Logierait, Perthsh.), On the first of May, Old Style, a festival called Beltan is annually held here. **1807** BYRON *Oscar of Alva* lv. For him thy beltane yet may burn.

b. *attrib.*, as in ***Beltane fire***, ***games***, etc.

1801 SCOTT *Glenfinlas*, How blazed Lord Ronald's beltane tree. **1810** —— *Lady of L.* II. xv, When at Beltane game, Thou ledst the dance with Malcolm Græme. **1814** —— *Ld. Isles* I. viii, The shepherd lights his beltane fire. **1883** *Harper's Mag.* Feb. 331 The time when the Beltane fires were lit near this well on Midsummer-eve.

belted ('bɛltɪd), *ppl. a.* [f. BELT *v.*, *sb.*[1]]

1. Wearing, or girded with, a belt; *spec.* as describing the distinctive cincture of an earl or knight (cf. BELT *sb.*[1] 1 b); fastened on by means of a belt.

1483 *Cath. Angl.* 27/1 Beltyd, *zonatus, cinctus*. *c* **1565** R. LINDSAY *Cron. Scotl.* 17 (JAM.) This Willame was the sixt belted earle of the hous of Douglas. **1795** BURNS '*A Man's a Man*', A prince can mak a belted knight. **1805** SCOTT *Last Minstr.* I. iv, With belted sword and spur on heel. **1820** —— *Abbot* ii. Were he himself the son of a belted earl.

2. Furnished with a belt or belts of any kind; marked by belts or bands of distinctive colour, etc. ***belted cattle***: black cattle of Dutch origin with a broad band of white round the middle.

1785 COWPER *Tiroc.* 633 The moons of Jove and Saturn's belted ball. **1844** MARRYAT *Settl. Canada* ix. 67 The belted kingfisher darted up and down. **1884** *Pall Mall G.* 8 Dec. 5/1 Belted cruisers of the *Mersey* type.

'belter. *Sc.* and *north.* [Cf. BELT *sb.*[1], BELT *v.* 4.] A heavy blow or series of blows; ? a pelting.

1823 GALT *Entail* II. xvii. 160 I'll stand ahint a dike, and gie them a belter wi' stones. *Mod. Lancash. dial.* Hoo then fot me another belter reet across th' een.

'beltful. [f. BELT *sb.*[1] + -FUL.] As many cartridges, etc., as are contained in a belt.

1916 'BOYD CABLE' *Action Front* 131 The first [anti-aircraft] gun opened with a trial beltful.

belting ('bɛltɪŋ), *vbl. sb.* [f. BELT *v.*, *sb.*[1]]

1. a. The action of the vb. BELT.

b. Beating, thrashing.

1854 A. E. BAKER *Gloss. Northampt. Words* s.v. *Belt*, 'He got a good belting.' **1896** A. MORRISON *Child of Jago* 33 The belting was bad..very bad. **1907** *Westm. Gaz.* 16 Aug. 5/2 He is a very bad boy... After a 'belting' he seems worse.

2. *concr.* Belts collectively, or material for making them; also, a belt.

1567 *Wills & Inv. N.C.* (1835) 277 To my sister Margrett my best deny, my long belting best crooks. **1571** *ibid.* 362, ij doss' ½ of crewle beltinge iijs. **1855** *Engineer* 15 May (*Advt.*) Single and Double Leather Belting. **1876** *Daily News* 3 Nov. 4/4, I rode into a belting of wood. **1884** A. DANIELL *Princ. Phys.* 162 Belting.—There is a very interesting and familiar case in which friction serves as a means for the transmission of energy—that is, transmission by machine-belting. **1898** *Westm. Gaz.* 14 Jan. 9/3 Men mounted the belting of the ship. **1910** *Ibid.* 11 Jan. 5/2 The snapping of some of the steel belting. **1964** *McCall's Sewing* xii. 225/1 Commercial belting gives the most professional looking belt and never loses its shape.

'belting, *ppl. a.* [f. BELT *v.* + -ING[2].] Girdling, encircling, surrounding.

1857 EMERSON *Poems* 178 From nodding pole and belting zone. **1871** G. MACDONALD *Bk. Dreams* in *Wks. Fancy & Imag.* 120 The belting trees.

beltless ('bɛltlɪs), *a.* [f. BELT *sb.*[1] + -LESS.] Without a belt.

1884 *Pall Mall G.* 5 June 11/1 Beltless trousers. **1884** GILMOUR *Mongols* 276 The common word for 'woman' in Mongolia is 'beltless.'

beltong, variant of BILTONG.

belu, obs. sing of BELLOWS.

†**belue.** *Obs. rare.* [a. OF. *belue*, *bellue*, ad. L. *belua*, *bellua* great beast.] A great beast, a monster; *spec.* a sea-monster, a whale.

1474 CAXTON *Chesse* 113 To be lyke vnto belues of the see. **1483** —— *Gold. Leg.* 122/1 That he..shold be deuoured in the see of belues and grete fysshes. **1572** BOSSEWELL *Armorie* II. 65 A Belve.. Thys is a great fishe in the Sea, and is called Belua. He casteth out water at hys iowes with vapoure of good smell.

‖**beluga** (bɪ'luːgə). Also 6 bellougina. [In sense 1, a. Russ. *bělūga*; in sense 2, a. Russ. *bělūχa*; both f. *bělo-*, white + *-uga*, *-uχa*, augmentative formatives. Fletcher's word is evidently the Russ. deriv. *bielūzhina* flesh of the beluga.]

1. A species of fish: the Great or Hausen Sturgeon (*Acipenser huso*), found in the Caspian and Black Seas, and their tributary rivers.

1591 G. FLETCHER *Russe Commw.* (1857) 12 Of ickary or cavery, a great quantitie is made upon the..Volgha out of the fish called bellougina. **1772** JACKSON *Isinglass* in *Phil. Trans.* LXIII. 7 The Beluga yields the greatest quantity. **1869** NICHOLSON *Zool.* (1880) 493 The various species of sturgeon attain a great size, one—the Beluga—often measuring 12 or 15 feet in length.

2. The white Whale (*Delphinapterus leucas*), an animal of the Dolphin family, found in herds in the Northern Seas, and in the estuaries of rivers.

1817 in BURROWES *Cycl.* **1847** CARPENTER *Zool.* §211 The Beluga or White Whale..rarely visits our own coasts. **1884** *Pall Mall G.* 25 July 11/2 In the placid..waters of the fjords ..one meets with..shoals of the beluga, or white whale.

beluin, obs. form of BELLUINE.

†**belus eye.** *Obs.* [transl. of L. *Beli oculus* (Pliny); see quot.] A precious stone, Eye Onyx.

1601 HOLLAND *Pliny* II. 625 The stone called Belus eie is white, and hath within it a black apple, the mids wherof a man shall see to glitter like gold: this stone for the singular beautie that it hath, is dedicated to Belus the most sacred god of the Assyrians.

belute (bɪ'l(j)uːt), *v.* [f. BE- + LUTE ad. L. *lutum* mud.] **a.** *trans.* To cover with mud or dirt. **b.** To coat with lute or cement of any kind.

1760 STERNE *Tr. Shandy* (1802) II. ix. 172 Never was a Dr. Slop so beluted, and so transubstantiated. **1837** *New Month. Mag.* XLIX. 524 Bird-lime, with which it belutes its eyes till they are sealed up.

belvedere (bɛlvɪ'dɪə(r)). Also 9–8 **belvidere**. [a. It. *belvedere* 'a faire sight, a place of a faire prospect,' f. *bel*, *bello*, beautiful + *vedere* (inf. mood used subst.) a view, sight. The It. word was adopted in Fr. as early as 16th c. as *belveder*, *belvédère*, whence perhaps the Eng. pronunciation.]

1. *Arch.* A raised turret or lantern on the top of a house, or a summer-house erected on an eminence in a garden or pleasure-ground, for the purpose of viewing the surrounding scene.

1596 BELL *Surv. Popery* III. ii. 213 Walking in his garden, or looking about him in his Bel-videre. **1623** WEBSTER *Devil's Law Case* I. i, They build their palaces and belvederes With musical water-works. **1755** HERVEY *Dial.* in Southey *Comm.-pl. Bk.* Ser. I. (1850) I. 314 Over this recess, so pleasingly horrid..arose an open and airy belvidere. **1834** *Penny Cycl.* II. 165/1 Apollo Belvedere, a celebrated statue of Apollo..placed by him [Pope Julius II] in the Belvidere of the Vatican, whence it derives its present name. **1873** BROWNING *Red Cott. Night-c.* 148 What means this Belvedere? This Tower, stuck like a fool's-cap on the roof?

2. *Hort.* A plant, *Kochia scoparia* (N.O. *Chenopodiaceæ*), cultivated as an ornamental garden plant. Also called *Summer Cypress*, and *Broom Toad-flax*.

1597 GERARD *Herbal* III. clxv. (1633) 556 This Belvidere, or Scoparia is the Osyris described by Dioscorides. **1725** BRADLEY *Fam. Dict.*, *Belvedere*. **1797** C. MARSHALL *Garden.* (1805) 326 Belvidere, annual, summer or mock cypress.

belw(e, **belwys**, obs. ff. BELLOW, BELLOWS.

belwedder, -wether, obs. ff. BELLWETHER.

bely, obs. form of BELIE *v.*, BELLY, BELLOWS.

bely-; for words formerly so spelt, see BELI-.

belying (bɪˈlaɪɪŋ), *vbl. sb.* [f. BELIE *v.*[1] + -ING[1].]
1. Giving of the lie; denial.
1587 GOLDING *De Mornay* xi. 150 If the denying that there is any God be a belying of a mans owne sences. **1611** FLORIO, *Dimentita*, a belying.
2. Telling lies of any one, calumniation.
1632 SHERWOOD, A belying, *calumnie*. **1875** SWINBURNE *Ess. & Stud.* Pref. 10 The right of backbiting and belying.

belzaar, obs. form of BEZOAR.

Belzebub, variant of BEELZEBUB.

bem, beme, obs. forms of BEAM.

‖**bema** (ˈbiːmə). [a. Gr. βῆμα, lit. 'a step' (f. βα-γο); hence, a raised place to speak from, the tribune, or rostrum; whence, the apse or chancel of a basilica, in which sense it first appears in Eng.]
1. *Eccles. Antiq.* 'The altar part or sanctuary in the ancient churches' (Chambers); the chancel.
1683 T. SMITH *Observ. Constantinop.* in *Misc. Cur.* (1708) III. 46, I observed but one step from the Body of the Church to the Bema or place where the Altar formerly stood. **1753** CHAMBERS *Cycl. Supp.*, *Bema* made the third, or innermost part of the church, answering to the chancel among us. **1861** A. B. HOPE *Eng. Cathedr. 19th C.*, At Torcello the episcopal cathedra is raised aloft in the bema or apse.
2. *Grecian Antiq.* The platform or tribune from which an Athenian orator addressed the assembly.
1820 T. MITCHELL *Aristoph.* I. 225 The most worthless of those who mount the bema. **1864** LEWES *Aristotle* 9 For sixty years Pericles had ceased to thunder from the bema.

bemad (bɪˈmæd), *v.* [f. BE- 2 + MAD *v.*] *trans.* To make mad, to madden. Hence **be'madded, be'madding** *ppl. a.*
1605 SHAKS. *Lear* III. i. 38 Unnatural and bemadding sorrow. **1655** FULLER *Ch. Hist.* IV. §5 II. 319 His practical Tenents..did enrage and bemadd his adversaries. **1850** BLACKIE *Æsch.* II. 189 O god-detested! god-bemadded race!

bemadam, bemail, beman, etc.: see BE- *pref.*

be-maddening, *ppl. a.* Intensive of MADDENING.
1850 CLOUGH *Dipsychus* II. iv. 13 These be-maddening discords of the mind.

bemaim (bɪˈmeɪm), *v.* [f. BE- 2 + MAIM *v.*] Intensive of MAIM.
1605 STOW *Ann.* 673 Spoiled of their goods, bemaimed and slaine. **1881** DUFFIELD *Quix.* II. 422 Envious fate.. Struck down Cervantes and bemaimed his hand.

bemangle (bɪˈmæŋg(ə)l), *v.* [f. BE- 2 + MANGLE *v.*] *trans.* To cut about, hack, mangle. Hence **be'mangled** *ppl. a.*
1553–87 FOXE *A. & M.* (1596) 71/1 [He was] so scotched and bemangled with the shards of sharpe and cutting shels. **1601** R. YARINGTON *Two Traj.* I. i. in Bullen *O. Pl.* IV, So foule a deede, Thus to bemangle a distressed youth. **1648** JOS. BEAUMONT *Psyche* IX. lxiv. (J.) Those bemangled limbs.

bemantle, bemar, bemartyr, bemat: see BE-.

†**be'mark,** *v. Obs. rare*[−1]. [f. BE- 2 + MARK *v.*] *trans.* ? To mark with the sign of the cross, to cross oneself; = med.L. *signare*.
1544 LATIMER *Lett. fr. Bocardo* Wks. 1845 II. 441 Because they worship not, nor kneel not down [neither bemark not] as others do, but sit still in their pews.

†**be'martelled,** *ppl. a. Obs.* [f. BE- 2 + MARTEL *v.* to hammer, beat.] ? Hammered, beaten.
1598 T. BASTARD *Chrestoleros* (1880) 60 Steru'de mutton, beefe with foote bemartelled, And skinn and bones.

bemask (bɪˈmɑːsk, -æ-), *v.* [f. BE- 2 + MASK *v.*] *trans.* To mask, to cover or conceal with a mask. Hence **be'masked** *ppl. a.*
1579 TOMSON *Calvin's Serm. Tim.* 409/2 The Popish Bishops..doe so bemaske them selues, as though they should play the part in a play. **1620** SHELTON *Quix.* I. IV. i. (T.) Which have thus bemasked your singular beauty under so unworthy an array. *Ibid.* I. ix. (R.) The bemasked gentleman.

bemaster (bɪˈmɑːstə(r), -æ-), *v.* [f. BE- 2 + MASTER *v.*] *trans.* To master (*emphatic*).
1875 B. TAYLOR *Faust* II. iii. II. 106 One must with modern thought the thing bemaster. **1880** MISS BROUGHTON *Sec. Thoughts* II. III. i. 105 Gawky, romping, but thoroughly be-mastered Jane.

bematist (ˈbiːmətɪst). [ad. Gr. βηματιστής, f. βηματίζειν to measure by paces, f. βῆμα pace, step.] An official road-measurer or surveyor in the time of Alexander the Great and the Ptolemies.
1875 *Encycl. Brit.* II. 748/2 The bematists or surveyors of Alexander and the Ptolemies. **1886** SHELDON tr. *Flaubert's Salammbô* x. 242 The bematists of Euergates, who measured the heaven by calculating the number of their paces.

bemaul (bɪˈmɔːl), *v.* [f. BE- 2 + MAUL *v.*] *trans.* To maul thoroughly.
1620 SHELTON *Quix.* IV. xxii. 179 (R.) So the poor soul [Sancho] was sore bruised and bemauled. **1761** STERNE *Tr. Shandy* (1802) IV. xxvii. 120 To snatch the cudgels..to bemaul Yorick to some purpose. **1846** HAWTHORNE *Mosses* I. vi. 155 Bemauled as the poor fellow had been.

bemazed (bɪˈmeɪzd), *ppl. a.* [f. BE- 2 + MAZE *v.*] Stupefied, bewildered. (Cf. AMAZE *v.*)
a **1225** *Ancr. R.* 270 Isboset on Ebrewish is 'bimased mon' on Englisch. *a* **1400** *Chester Pl.* II. 93 And lefte us lyinge.. Al bemased in a soune. **1783** COWPER *Task* v. 848 Intellects bemaz'd in endless doubts. **1879** HOWELLS *L. Aroostook* xxvi. 311 Staniford stood bemazed, though he knew enough to take the hand she yielded him.

Bembo (ˈbɛmbəʊ). *Typogr.* The name given to a type face cut in 1929 by the Monotype Corporation after that used by Aldus Manutius (see ALDINE) in his edition of *De Ætna*, a tract by the Italian cardinal and scholar Pietro Bembo (1470–1547).
1930 *Fleuron* VII. 178 The consummate distribution of the shading over the finely proportioned skeleton gives the new Bembo a singular 'presence' on the page. **1935** BERRY & JOHNSON *Catal. Specimens Printing Types* l, The extension of the ascenders makes the 12-point size [of Perpetua] look 'small' in comparison with the 12 point of Fournier, Baskerville, and the Aldine Bembo. **1945** O. SIMON *Introd. Typogr.* iii. 12 The roman lower-case letters of Scotch and Baskerville, for instance, are wide and generous, whilst, at the other extreme, Fournier and Bembo occupy considerably less width.

†**beme,** *sb. Obs.* Forms: 1 býme, béme, 2–5 beme, (3, 6 beame, 5 beeme); *pl.* 1–3 beman, 2–4 -en, 3–6 -es, 5 -ys. [OE. *béme*, WSax. *bíeme*, later *býme*, pointing to OTeut. *baumjôn-, of unknown etymology.] A trumpet.
a **800** *Corpus Gloss.* in Wr.-Wülcker *Voc.* 15 *Concha*, beme. *c* **897** K. ÆLFRED *Past.* 244 Biemena dæʒ & ʒedynes ofer ealla truma ceastra. *c* **1000** *Ags. Gosp.* Matt. vi. 2 Ne blawe may byman [*Rushw.* beman, *c* **1160** *Hatt. G.* beman] beforan þe. *c* **1205** LAY. 5107 Bemen þer bleowen. *c* **1250** *Gen. & Ex.* 3521 Ðat dredful beames blast. *a* **1340** HAMPOLE *Pr. Consc.* 4676 Þe beme þat blaw sal on domsday. *c* **1460** *Towneley Myst.* 53 At hys commyng shalle bemys blaw. *c* **1500** *Death* in Halliw. *Nugæ P.* 40 When bemes shalle blawe rewly one rawe.
b. *fig.* (in allusion to *Matt.* vi. 2) ? Noise, parade.
c **1440** *Arthur* 108 Seyeþ a Pater noster wythout any Beeme.

†**beme,** *v. Obs.* Forms: 1 *bémian, býmian, 3–6 bemen. [f. prec. sb.]
1. *intr.* To blow on a trumpet.
c **1000** ÆLFRIC *Gloss.* in Wr.-Wülcker *Voc.* 190 *Salpizo vel buccino*, ic byme. *c* **1000** *Lamb. Ps.* lxxx[i]. 4 (Bosw.) Bymiaþ oððe hlyriaþ on niwum monþe mid byman.
2. *transf.* **a.** *intr.* To make a loud din or noise.
b. *trans.* To trumpet or din (a thing).
a **1225** *Ancr. R.* 430 And ʒe..þet ower beoden bemen & dreamen wel ine Drihtenes earen. **1513** DOUGLAS *Æneis* v. iii. 90 Quhill the meikle hillis Bemys agane hit with the brute so schill is. *Ibid.* v. vii. 40.
3. *trans.* To summon with a trumpet.
c **1450** *Gaw. & Gologras* iii. 8 The folk..That bemyt war be the lord.

†**be'mean,** *v.*[1] *Obs.* Forms: 3–4 bimene, 3 bemene, 4–5 bymene, 5 bemeyne, 6 beemene. [f. *bi-*, BE- 2 + MEAN *v.*, OE. *mǽnan*; cf. OHG. *bimeinan*, MHG. *bemeinen*, with same senses.]
1. *trans.* To mean, signify, import.
a **1300** *Havelok* 1259 Wat may this bimene. *c* **1340** *Cursor M.* (Fairf.) 10853 Her by-thoght What this gretyng myght be-mene. *c* **1440** *Gesta Rom.* i. 4 Þan most a prelate honge the wif—what bymenyth that? **1502** ARNOLD *Chron.* (1811) 265 Yf a man aske hem [the Sarasyns] what Paradyse beemeneth, they sayn it is a place of delytis.
2. To signify or communicate to (a person). *rare.*
c **1340** *Cursor M.* (Trin.) 15495 Petur him bymened & seide þis resoun, þou shal bitrayed be lord to nyʒt.

†**be'mean,** *v.*[2] *Obs. rare.* [f. BE- *pref.* 5, or perh. two words, BE *v.* + *mene*, MEAN, 'intermediate, a mediator.'] *intr.* To mediate, intercede.
1459 MARG. PASTON in *Lett.* (1872) I. 438 He desyryd Alblaster to bemene to yow for hym. *a* **1520** *Myrr. Our Ladye* 232 Pray for the people, by meane for the clerge.

bemean (bɪˈmiːn), *v.*[3] [f. BE- *pref.* 5 + MEAN *a.*] *trans.* To render mean or base, to lower in dignity, abase. (In first quot. for *demean* = 'behave.')
1651 GATAKER *Ridley* in Fuller *Abel. Rediv.* 193 How he bemeaned himselfe, shall hereafter be related. **1688** ROKEBY *Diary* (1858) 29 Foolish frothy things, that bemean it [my memory] before the Lord. **1742** JARVIS *Quix.* II. III. xx. (D.), I renounce my gentility..and bemean myself to the lowness of the offender. **1866** READE *G. Gaunt* II. 92 Oh, husband, how can you so bemean yourself?

bemean, *v.*[4], **bemene;** see BEMOAN.

†**be'meet,** *v. Obs.* [f. BE- *pref.* 2 + MEET *v.*] **a.** *trans.* To meet with. **b.** *intr.* To meet *with*.
1605 SHAKS. *Lear* V. i. 20 Our very loving sister, well bemet. **1656** S. H. *Gold. Law* 61 The Laicks are a Lay people..till some Moses be-meet with them.

†**'bemer.** *Obs.* Forms: 1 beamere, bemere, bymere, 2–3 bemare. [f. BEME *v.* or *sb.* + -ER[1].] A trumpeter.
c **950** *Lindisf. Gosp.* Matt. ix. 23 And ʒesæh beameres [*Rushw.* piperas, *Ags.* hwistleras] mænende. *c* **1000** ÆLFRIC *Gloss.* in Wr.-Wülcker *Voc.* 190 Býmere, *salpista*. *a* **1225** *Ancr. R.* 210 Þe prude beoð his bemares.

†**be'mercy,** *v. Obs.* [f. BE- *pref.* 6 + MERCY *sb.*] *trans.* To treat with mercy, show mercy to.
1640 T. GOODWIN *Justif. Faith* I. iii. ii, I was bemercied (if we may so speak), endowed with mercy, encompassed with mercy. **1660** T. WATSON in Spurgeon *Treas. Dav.* Ps. xxxii. 1 The Greek signifies, 'I was be-mercied.'

†**be'mete,** *v. Obs.* [OE. *bemetan*, f. BE- *pref.* 2 + *metan* to METE; but in Shaks. prob. an independent re-formation.] *trans.* To measure.
c **893** K. ÆLFRED *Oros.* III. ix. §7 Hie..hie selfe sipþan wið Alexander to nohte ne bemætan. **1596** SHAKS. *Tam. Shr.* IV. iii. 113, I shall so be-mete thee with thy yard.

bemfelling, obs. form of BEAMFILLING.

†**'beming,** *vbl. sb. Obs.* [f. BEME *v.* + -ING[1].] Trumpeting; *transf.* noisy buzzing.
1513 DOUGLAS *Æneis* VII. ii. 88 A gret flycht of beis.. Wyth loud bemyng gan alycht.

bemingle, etc.: see BE- *pref.*

bemire (bɪˈmaɪə(r)), *v.* [f. BE- *pref.* 6 + MIRE *sb.*] Hence **be'mired** *ppl. a.*, **be'miring** *vbl. sb.*
1. *trans.* To cover or befoul with mire.
c **1532** MORE *Answ. Frith* Wks. 833/2 If only they that are alredy bymired, were..myred on more and more. **1727** SWIFT *Gulliver* II. v. 144, I was filthily bemired. **1837** HAWTHORNE *Twice-told T.* (1851) II. xvi. 237 His shoes were bemired, as if he had been travelling on foot.
b. *fig.* **1587** GOLDING *De Mornay* Pref. 1 Bemiring it [reason] in the filthy and beastly pleasures of the world. **1601** CORNWALLYES *Ess.* x. (1632), Good safe care to keep herself from bemiring. **1870** SPURGEON *Treas. Dav.* Ps. xvii. 3 The purest innocence will be bemired by malice.
2. To plunge or roll in the mire; in *pass.* to sink in the mire, be bogged. *lit.* and *fig.*
1574 HELLOWES *Gueuara's Ep.* (1577) 354 If we sinke not to the bottome, at the leaste we remaine all bemyred. **1654** TRAPP *Comm. Ps.* xl. 2. II. 690 As a bemired beast he was in a perishing condition. **1771** WESLEY *Wks.* (1872) VI. 36 Doubt..bemires the soul. **1883** *Century* 377 Bemired in the deeply rutted roads.

be'mirror, *v.* [f. BE- 2 + MIRROR *v.*] To image or show as in a mirror. Hence, **bemirrorment**.
a **1849** POE *Quacks of Helicon* Wks. 1864 IV. 412 The wofully over-done be-mirrorment of that man-of-straw.

bemissionary, bemitred, bemix: see BE-.

bemist (bɪˈmɪst), *v.* [f. BE- *pref.* 6 + MIST *sb.*]
1. *trans.* To overtake with, or involve in mist; *fig.* to confuse the senses of, bepuzzle, bewilder.
1609 HOLLAND *Amm. Marcell* Annot. D ij b, The Greekes ..were bemisted and overcast with darknesse. **1627** FELTHAM *Resolves* II. iv. Wks. (1677) 166 How can that Judg walk right, that is bemisted in his way? **1677** GALE *Crt. Gentiles* II. III. Pref., God bemisted the degenerate mindes of those proud Sophistes. **1864** *Sat. Rev.* 278/2 Many a mountain climber..has been benighted or bemisted.
2. To cover or obscure (a thing) with, or as with, mist; to becloud, dim.
1598 E. GILPIN *Skial.* (1878) 36 He is the deuill, Brightly accoustred to bemist his euill. **1630** T. WESTCOTE *Devon.* (1845) 453 Antiquities are often bemisted, and leave their surveyor perplexed. **1720** WELTON *Suff. Son of God* II. xxii. 595 The more sublime..his Doctrine was, the more they strove to darken and Be-mist it.

bemoan (bɪˈməʊn), *v.* Forms: 1 bi-, -bemǽnan, 3 bimen-en, 4–5 bi-, bymene, 4–6 bemene, 5 bimeane; 6 beemone, bemoane, 6–7 bemone, 7– bemoan. [OE. *bi-*, *bemǽnan*, f. *bi-*, BE- + *mǽnan* to moan; the regular modern repr. of this would have been *bemean*: for the substitution of the existing form, see MOAN.]
1. *trans.* To moan for; to lament, weep for.
c **1000** ÆLFRIC *Deut.* xxxiv. 8 Þa heofungdaʒas wæron þa ʒefyllede þe hiʒ Moisen bemændon. *c* **1175** *Lamb. Hom.* 13 Þenne wille ʒe..sunne bimenen. *c* **1250** *Gen. & Ex.* 4150 .xxx. daiʒes wep israel for his dead and bi-ment it wel. *c* **1380** *Sir Ferumb.* 4225 Ys trewe baronye be-mend him sore. **1430** LYDG. *Chron. Troy* IV. xxx, They playne and the death bimeane Of worthy Hector. **1563** *Myrr. Mag., Induct.* xvii. 2 Luckeles lot for to bemone. **1653** WALTON *Angler* i. 17 The children of Israel..bemoaning the ruines of Sion. *a* **1732** GAY *Poems* (1745) I. 97 Her piteous tale the winds in sighs bemoan. **1840** DICKENS *Barn. Rudge* lix, She bemoaned her miseries in the sweetest voice.
2. *refl.* To lament or bewail one's lot.
c **1220** *Bestiary* 798 in *O.E. Misc.* 25 Bimene us, we hauen don wrong. *c* **1314** *Guy Warw.* 5 He gan to wepe.. And biment him wel reweliche. **1413** LYDG. *Pylgr. Sowle* IV. xx. (1483) 67 See how my sone..Bymeneth hym in herte chere and voys. **1625** BACON *Envy, Ess.* (Arb.) 514 Politique persons..are euer bemoaning themselues, what a Life they lead. **1855** MACAULAY *Hist. Eng.* III. 486 Tillotson bemoaned himself with unfeigned..sorrow to Lady Russell.
3. *intr.* or with *subord. cl.* To lament, grieve.
c **1305** *St. Edm. Conf.* 426 in *E.E.P.* 82 Hi bimende & ofþoʒte sore: þat hi hiʒede þider so faste. **1460** in *Pol. Rel. & L. Poems* (1866) 157 Yf thow owght morne, I shall bemene. **1655** FULLER *Ch. Hist.* I. ii. §5 We rather bemoan she lost it so soon. **1833** LAMB *Elia* (1860) 238, I do not know whether I ought to bemoan or rejoice that my old friend is departed.

†**4.** *trans.* with cogn. obj.: To utter with moans.

1393 GOWER *Conf.* I. 346 His firste pleinte to bemene Unto the citee of Athene He goth him forth.

5. To express pity for, condole with.

c **1300** *Beket* 983 Therfore we ne bymeneth the noȝt: for thu noldest beo awar bifore. *c* **1305** *St. Kenelm* 236 in *E.E.P.* (1862) 54 He nere noȝt to bymene þeȝ his larder were neȝ ido. **1611** BIBLE *Job* xlii. 11 They bemoned him, and comforted him ouer all the euill..brought vpon him.

†**be'moanable,** *a. Obs.*—⁰ [f. prec. + -ABLE.] Deplorable, lamentable.

1611 COTGR., *Regretable*, bemonable, bewailable.

bemoaning (bɪ'məʊnɪŋ), *vbl. sb.* Also 3 bimening. [f. as prec. + -ING¹.] Lamentation, wailing, grief loudly expressed.

c **1250** *Gen. & Ex.* 2484 He ðer abiden, And bi-mening for iacob deden. *c* **1300** *K. Alis.* 534 The kyng..Wolde..make bymenyng Of his wyves misdoyng. **1592** GREENE *Poems* 41 Send forth winter in her rusty weed To wail my bemoanings. **1705** STANHOPE *Paraphr.* III. 434 The Samaritane..did not express his Pity in idle and unprofitable Bemoanings. **1870** SPURGEON *Treas. Dav.* Ps. xxv. 7 Sincere penitents..are constrained to use many bemoanings.

be'moaning, *ppl. a.* [f. as prec. + -ING².] Lamenting, miserably plaintive. Hence **be'moaningly** *adv.*

1639 FULLER *Holy War* II. vii. (1840) 57 Sending his bemoaning letters to Boemund prince of Antioch. **1655** —— *Hist. Camb.* (1840) 173 A bemoaning letter to king Henry. **1647** J. MAYNE *Serm.* (1647) 38 You, Sir, who have..thus bemoaningly pitied our divisions.

†**be'moat,** *v. Obs.* [f. BE- 6 + MOAT *sb.*] To surround with, or as with, a moat; to flood.

1598 SYLVESTER *Du Bartas* I. vii. (1641) 59/1 A silver Brook..A goodly Garden it be-moateth round. **1686** W. DE BRITAINE *Hum. Prud.* ix. 43 When I have heard that my Friend was dead, I have bemoated my Eyes with Tears.

bemock (bɪ'mɒk), *v.* [f. BE- *pref.* 2 + MOCK *v.*] *trans.* To mock at, flout; to delude mockingly. Hence **be'mocked** *ppl. a.*

1607 SHAKS. *Cor.* I. i. 261 He will not spare to gird the Gods—Bemocke the modest Moone. **1610** —— *Temp.* III. iii. 63 Or with bemockt-at-Stabs Kill the still closing waters. **1798** COLERIDGE *Anc. Mar.* IV xi, Her [the moon's] beams bemock'd the sultry main. **1870** MORRIS *Earthly Par.* II. III. 427 Why was I then bemocked with days of bliss?

†**be'moil,** *v. Obs.* [f. BE- *pref.* 1 + MOIL *v.*] *trans.* 'To encumber with dirt and mire: to bemire' (Johnson).

1596 SHAKS. *Tam. Shr.* IV. i. 77 How her horse fel..in how miery a place, how she was bemoil'd. **1636** HEALEY *Theophrast.* 93 When hee..riding upon a borrowed horse..falling all-to-bemoiles himself.

†**be'moist,** *v. Obs.* [f. BE- 5 + MOIST *a.*] = next.

1567 DRANT *Horace' Epist.* I. ii. C v, What iuse first bemoysts a shel, the shel..wil reteyne the tast. **1587** TURBERV. *Trag. T.* (1837) 193 Which made her to bemoyst her face And bosome all with teares.

bemoisten (bɪ'mɔɪs(ə)n), *v.* [f. BE- *pref.* 1, 2 + MOISTEN *v.*] Hence **be'moistened** *ppl. a.*

1. *trans.* To make moist.

1590 LODGE *Euphues' Gold. Leg.* in Halliw. *Shaks.* VI. 20 First time shall stay his stayless race..And snow bemoysten Julies face. **1820** COMBE (Dr. Syntax) *Consol.* vi. (D.) Wiping her bemoisten'd eye.

2. *intr.* To become moist. *rare.*

1821 CLARE *Vill. Minstr.* I. 57 With tears the while bemoist'ning in his eye.

†**bemol.** *Obs.* Also 5 bemole, 7 beemol. [a. Fr. *Bemol* (med.L. *B mollis*) 'softened B.' In the harmonic system of Guido of Arezzo, which divided the scale into hexachords beginning from every G, C, and F, it was found necessary in the hexachord which started on F to introduce an additional note a semitone lower than B, which note was called *B mollis*, or *Bemol*; this was written in the old literal notation as a rounded *b*, a sign afterwards corrupted into ♭: see B II. 1.]

1. Name given to B♭, when that note was first introduced into the scale.

a **1327** *Rel. Ant.* I. 292 Thu holdest nowt a note..in riht ton..Thu bitist a-sonder bequarre, for bemol i the blame. **1387** TREVISA *Higden* Rolls Ser. I. 355 [In their harp-playing they] bygynneþ from bemol [L. *a B molli incipiunt*]. *a* **1529** SKELTON *P. Sparow* 530 Synge the verse, Libera me, In de, la, soll, re, Softly bemole For my sparowes soule.

2. By extension: **a.** A flat.

1609 DOULAND *Ornithop. Microl.* 6 Of Voyces, some are called b Mols, Naturals, Sharps. **1656** [see 2 b].

b. A semitone.

1626 BACON *Sylva* §104 There be intervenient in the Rise of Eight (in Tones) two Beemolls, or Half-notes. *Ibid.* §105 There fall out to be two Beemols between the Vnison and the Diapason. [**1656** BLOUNT *Glossogr.*, *Beemol* (Fr.), the flat key in musick. *Bacon.*]

bemole, bemoon, bemoult, etc.: see BE- *pref.*

bemong: see BIMONG.

bemonster (bɪ'mɒnstə(r)), *v.* [f. BE- 5 + MONSTER.] *trans.*

1. To make monstrous or hideous; to deform.

1605 SHAKS. *Lear* IV. ii. 63 Be-monster not thy feature. **1608** MACHIN *Dumb Knt.* III. i, Ile rather wed a sootie blackamore, Then her that hath bemonstered my pure soule.

2. To regard, treat as, or 'call' a monster.

1692 *Christ Exalted* §139 Yet he writes..like a Gentleman, not be-heriticking, not be-monstring Dr. Crisp. **1880** SWINBURNE *Birthd. Ode* 421 A man by men bemonstered.

†**be'mourn,** *v. Obs.* [OE. *be-*, *bimurnan*, f. *bi-*, BE- 2 + *murnan* to MOURN.]

1. *trans.* To mourn over, lament, bewail.

a **1000** *Crist* (Grein) 176 Hwæt bemurnest þu? *c* **1200** *Trin. Coll. Hom.* 111 þe makeð him his sinnes swiðe bimurnen. **1382** WYCLIF *Luke* xxiii. 27 Wymmen that weileden, and bymoornyden him. **1622** MABBE *Aleman's Guzman de Alf.* II. 249 Bemourne the miseries wherein you are.

2. *intr.* To mourn, lament.

c **1400** *Destr. Troy* VII. 3279 þus [ho] bemournet full mekull & no meite toke.

bemouth (bɪ'maʊð), *v.* [f. BE- 2 + MOUTH *v.*] *trans.* To mouth the praises of (a person); to talk grandiloquently, to declaim.

a **1843** SOUTHEY *Nondescr.* i, They heard the illustrious furbelow'd Heroically in Popean rhyme Tee-ti-tum'd, in Miltonic blank bemouth'd. **1882** F. HARRISON *Crisis in Egypt* 6 The peace and good name of a great people are not to be bemouthed away by diplomatic brag.

†**be'mow,** *v. Obs.* [f. BE- + MOW *sb.* a grimace.] *trans.* To mock, mock at, *lit.* with grimaces.

1388 WYCLIF *2 Chron.* xxx. 10 Thei scorniden and bimowiden hem. *c* **1400** *Apol. Loll.* 81, I schal..bymowe ȝow wen þis schal cum to ȝow þat ȝe dred.

bemud (bɪ'mʌd), *v.* [f. BE- 6 + MUD.] Hence **be'mudded** *ppl. a.*, **be'mudding** *vbl. sb.*

1. *trans.* To cover, bespatter, or befoul with mud.

1580 HOLLYBAND *Treas. Fr. Tong*, *Embouër*, to bedirt, or bemud one. **1611** COTGR., *Enfangement*, a bedurtying, bemyring, bemudding. **1659** ARROWSMITH *Armilla Catech.* I. iv. §5 Elephants..are wont, before they drink, to bemud the water. **1832** *Fraser's Mag.* VI. 251 He often rides in swampy ways..and bemuds his friends.

2. *fig.* To confuse, muddle.

1599 NASHE *Lent. Stuffe* (1871) 35 And so troubledly bemudded with grief and care..my purer intellectual powers. **1790** COLERIDGE *Devonsh. Roads* Poems I. 14 Dull sounds the Bard's bemudded lyre. **1863** CHAMBERS *Bk. of Days* 124 Satan..first tried by bemudding his thoughts, to divert him from the design of becoming a monk.

bemuddle (bɪ'mʌd(ə)l), *v.* [f. BE- 2, 6 + MUDDLE.] *trans.* To confuse or muddle completely. Hence **be'muddled** *ppl. a.*, **be'muddlement.**

1862 *Sat. Rev.* XIII. 619/1 Novel readers who..bemuddle their brains in the reading-room day after day. **1883** A. WATSON in *Mag. Art* 486/1 A wild, bemuddled dream. **1884** *Pall Mall G.* 13 May 1/2 In such a state of bemuddlement and confusion.

bemuffle (bɪ'mʌf(ə)l), *v.* [f. BE- 1 + MUFFLE *v.*] To muffle up; often *fig.* Hence **be'muffled** *ppl. a.*

1583 STANYHURST *Æneis* IV. (Arb.) 111 The earth with the shaads of night was darcklye bemuffled. **1611** COTGR., *Emmouflé*..bemuffled, wrapped, or lapped close within (warme) clothes. **1760** STERNE *Serm. Yorick.* III. 225 So bemuffled with the externals of religion, that he has not a hand to spare for a worldly purpose!

bemulce, for DEMULCE, to soothe or soften.

1531 ELYOT *Gov.* (1580) 64 Wherwith Saturne was eftsones bemulced and appaysed. [*The original ed. has* demulced.]

bemurmur, bemusk, bemute, bemuzzle, etc.: see BE- *pref.*

bemuse (bɪ'mju:z), *v.* [f. BE- 2 + MUSE *v.*: cf. *amuse.*] *trans.* To make utterly confused or muddled, as with intoxicating liquor; to put into a stupid stare, to stupefy. Hence **be'mused,** **be'musing** *ppl. a.*

1735 POPE *Prol. Sat.* 15 A parson much be-mus'd in beer. **1771** J. FOOT *Penseroso* IV. 196 [With] fairy tales bemused the shepherd lies. **1847** H. MILLER *First Impr.* xix. (1861) 265 The bad metaphysics with which they bemuse themselves. **1880** MCCARTHY *Own Times* xxx. III. 2 A Prussian was regarded in England as a dull beer-bemused creature.

¶ *humorously*, To devote entirely to the Muses.

1705 POPE *Let. H. Cromwell* Wks. 1735 I. 15 When those incorrigible things, Poets, are once irrecoverably Be-mus'd.

bemusedly (bɪ'mju:zɪdlɪ), *adv.* [f. BEMUSED *ppl. a.* + -LY².] In a bemused or bewildered manner or condition.

1896 A. MORRISON *Child of Jago* 141 'Lor,' she said bemusedly. **1921** A. S. M. HUTCHINSON *If Winter Comes* III. ii. §1 He spoke bemusedly. No need for caution that he could see.

bemusement (bɪ'mju:zmənt). [f. BEMUSE *v.* + -MENT.] Bemused condition.

1907 GALSWORTHY *Country House* I. viii, The devilry, mockery, admiration, bemusement, had gone out of his face. **1921** A. S. M. HUTCHINSON *If Winter Comes* II. iv. §9 She threw away the bemusement in which she had sat.

bemy, obs. form of BEAMY.

ben (bɛn), *adv.*, *prep.*, *a.*, *sb.*¹ *Sc.* and *north. dial.* Forms: 4 bene, 5- ben. [Appears first in 14th c. There is no cognate in Scand. languages; so that it must be a dial. variant of ME. *binne*, BIN 'within':—OE. *binnan*, cogn. w. Du., Ger. *binnen.*]

A. *adv.* Within, towards the inner part; *esp.* in or into an inner part of the house relatively, in or into the inner part absolutely; into the parlour, etc. from the kitchen; in the parlour or chamber.

The words *but* and *ben* have special reference to the structure of dwelling houses formerly prevalent in the north, in which there was only one outer door, so that it was usual to enter through the kitchen into the parlour, and through the latter to an inner chamber, bedroom, or the like. In reference to the kitchen, the two latter rooms are *ben* and *far-ben* respectively; they constitute the *ben-end* of the house: in reference to the parlour, the kitchen is *but*, or *but the house*, or the *but end*. These phrases are retained even in more modern houses, where the parlour has a separate entrance: 'go but' = 'go into the kitchen'; 'come ben' = come into the parlour, etc. Also apartments on opposite sides of a passage are said to be *but and ben* with each other, though neither is farther out or farther in than the other: *come ben, go but* are then used of either. Their occupants are said to live *but and ben* with each other.

c **1425** WYNTOUN *Cron.* VII. x. 39 Hyr cors þai tuk wp, & bare ben. **1535** STEWART *Cron. Scot.* III. 271 Intumulat..Ben in the queir. **1686** G. STUART *Joco-ser. Disc.* 35 When doors stand open, dogs come ben. **1816** SCOTT *Antiq.* xv, Baby [= Barbara], bring ben the tea-water..and we'll steek the shop, and cry ben..and take a hand at the cartes. **1865** J. GROVES in Harland *Lanc. Lyrics* 128 Come ben, an' shelter frae the storm.

b. Phrases: ***but and ben***: in the outer and inner apartment, in both (or all) parts of the house. ***to live but and ben with***: see above. ***far ben***: far within, in the innermost chamber; *fig.* admitted beyond the ante-room, or to special intimacy or favour, 'far in.' ***o'er far ben***: too intimate.

c **1375** ? BARBOUR *St. Barthol.* 22 þe tempil..Wes fillit ful, but & bene. *c* **1536** LYNDESAY *Compl. Bagsche* 137, I was anis als far ben as ȝe ar, And had in Court als greit credence. **1632** RUTHERFORD *Lett.* 20 (1862) I. 83 Ye are..far ben in the palace of our Lord. **1786** BURNS *Holy Fair* xviii, Now butt an' ben the change-house fills. **1814** SCOTT *Wav.* xlviii, I admit I could not be so far ben as you lads.

c. ***there-ben***, corrupt. ***the-ben*** [cf. *there-out*], also ***ben-by*** (arch.): inside; = G. *darinnen.*

c **1575** ROLLAND *Seuin Seages* Prol., For to bring but its ill thats not there ben. **1650** *Vind. Hammond's Addr.* 22 note, That cannot be brought But, that is not the Ben. **1768** ROSS *Helenore* 33 (JAM.) Your bed s' be made the-ben. *a* **1774** FERGUSSON *Election*, *Poems* (1845) 40 The coat ben-by, I' the kist-nook..Is brought ance mair thereout.

B. *prep.* In or into the inner part of (a house).

1684 R. LAW *Memorials* Pref. (1818) 60 (JAM.) Ye..bad the father and mother go ben the house a whylle. **1810** TANNAHILL *Cragie Lee*, *Poems* (1846) 132 Far ben thy dark green planting's shade. **1827** J. WILSON *Noct. Ambr.* Wks. 1855 I. 354 When ye gaed ben the house.

C. *adj.* Inner, interior: as in ***ben end***, ***ben room***. Compared ***benner***, ***benmost***.

1774 FERGUSSON *Poems* (1789) II. 44 (JAM.) The benmost part o' my kist nook. **1785** *Poems in Buchan Dial.* 34 (JAM.) Their benner pantries. **1818** HOGG *Brownie* II. 18 (JAM.), I was a free man i' my ain ben-end. **1820** SCOTT *Abbot* xxviii, A door leading into the ben or inner chamber of the cottage.

D. *sb.* (Elliptical use of the adj.) The inner room.

1791–9 *Statist. Acc. Scotl.* XV. 339 The rent of a room and kitchen, or what..is stiled a but and a ben, gives at least two pounds sterling. **1807** SIR J. CARR *Caledon. Sk.* 405 (JAM.) A tolerable hut is divided into three parts—a butt..a benn..and a byar, where the cattle are housed. *Mod. Sc.* 'Their house is a long low thatched cottage consisting of a *but*, a *ben*, and a *far-ben*.'

‖**ben** (bɛn), *sb.*² Also 8 bin. [Gael. *beann*:—OCelt. **benno-*, **bendo-*, 'peak, horn, conical point.'] A mountain-peak. Used with the names of Scottish mountains; *e.g.* Ben Nevis, Ben Lomond.

1788 R. GALLOWAY *Poems* 75 (JAM.) From Lomond bin to Pentland know. **1813** HOGG *Queen's W.* 355 Ben—is a Highland term and denotes a mountain of a pyramidal form, which stands unconnected with others. **1819** —— *Jacob. Relics* II. 421 (JAM.) Sweet was..the river that flow'd from the Ben. **1884** *Manch. Exam.* 13 Sept. 5/3 Lowlanders and Irishmen who never climbed a ben.

ben (bɛn), *sb.*³ Also 6 benn, 7 behen. [a. Arab. *bān*, 'the ben-tree' (Lane). The form *behen* is due to confusion with another word.] The winged seed of the Horse-radish tree (*Moringa pterygosperma*); also called ***ben-nut.***

1559 MORWYNG *Evonym.* 239 The fruites of Ben..are found about Gonna plenteously. **1601** HOLLAND *Pliny* I. 374 The Egyptian Ben is more oleous and fat. **1769** SIR J. HILL *Fam. Herbal* (1812) 33 Ben-Nut-Tree..an Arabian tree. **1783** AINSWORTH *Lat. Dict.* (Morell) II, *Myrobalanum*..myrobalan, Ben, or a fruit of Ægypt, about the bigness of a filberd. **1866** *Treas. Bot.* 756 The seeds of..the Horse-radish tree are winged, and are called Ben-nuts.

b. ***oil of ben***: oil obtained from the ben-nut.

1594 PLAT *Jewell-h.* II. 16 The oile of Benn..is made of the Italian nuts. **1736** BAILEY *Househ. Dict.* 268 The oil of Ben has no smell of it self, but will readily receive any smell

that you would impart to it. **1875** Ure *Dict. Arts* I. 337 Oil of ben..is much used by watchmakers.

ben, obs. form of BEHEN, the plant.

ben, obs. pres. indic., subj. pl., and inf. of BE *v.*

benab ('bɛnæb). Also **benaboo**. [Arawak *(u)bannabuhu*.] In Guyana, a shelter made of a framework of poles, covered with branches and leaves.

1867 W. T. Veness *El Dorado* 141 'Buck Houses', or models of the huts of the Indians of British Guiana, containing in miniature all the articles usually found in Indian 'benaboos'. **1875** —— *Mission Life Brit. Guiana* ii. 21 They [*sc.* the Indians] have no burying ground, the grave is always made in the benab occupied by him during his lifetime. **1899** Rodway *Guiana Wilds* 251 The benab was the property of the Mission, and had been put up for the accommodation of visitors. **1922** *Blackw. Mag.* July 10/1 There are Indian benabs, close by in the forest. **1959** P. Capon *Amongst those Missing* 159 Women sat outside the benabs, suckling babies and grinding cassava.

†**be'name**, *v. Obs.* (*arch.* in pa. pple.) Forms of pa. t. and pple. 6 **benamed**, **bynempt**, 6–9 **benempt** (9 **benempted**). [OE. *benęmnan*, f. BE- + *nęmnan* to NAME; cf. MHG., mod.G. *benennen*, Sw. *benämna*, to name. With *benempt* cf. *inempned* from *name* in *Ancren Riwle*, Trevisa, etc.]

†**1.** *trans.* To declare or utter solemnly or on oath; to promise with an oath. *Obs.*

c **1000** *Ags. Ps.* lxxxix. 3 Ic Dauide..on áð-sware ær benemde, þæt ic, etc. *c* **1315** *Poem temp. Edw. II* in *Pol. Songs* 327 Thouh the bishop hit wite, that hit bename kouth, He may wid a litel silver stoppen his mouth. **1579** Spenser *Sheph. Cal. Nov.*, Kid or cosset, which I thee bynempt. **1615** Crooke *Body of Man* 249 Iphis her vow benempt a Maide, But turned boy her vow she paide.

†**2.** To name, mention by name. *Obs. rare.*

1579 Spenser *Sheph. Cal.* July 214 What is Algrin, he that is so oft bynempt?

3. With *compl.*: To name, call, style, describe as.

1580 Sidney *Arcadia* III. 391 Hee a Courtier was benamed. **1748** Thomson *Cast. of Indol.* II. xxxii, A fiery-footed boy, Benempt Dispatch. **1814** Scott *Wav.* xxx, The master smith, benempt, as his sign intimated, John Mucklewrath. **1832** *Blackw. Mag.* XXXII. 257 A Virgin, benempted Prudence Smith.

benatura (bɛna'tuːra). [app. alteration of BÉNITIER on some wrong analogy.] A holy-water stoup, bénitier.

1873 J. Maclean *Hist. Trigg Minor* I. 508 On the eastern side of the south door is a fine Benatura,..well carved. **1891** *Athenæum* 28 Mar. 412/3 Dr. Fryer..reported the discovery of the site of an ancient Benatura in the south porch of St. Mary Redcliffe.

Bence-Jones ('bɛns 'dʒəʊnz). The name of Henry *Bence-Jones* (1813–1873), English physician, applied *attrib.* to a protein found esp. in the urine in the disease myelomatosis, and characterized by precipitation on moderate heating followed by re-solution at higher temperatures.

1902 Anders & Boston in *Trans. Coll. Physicians* (Philad.) XXIV. 175 Bence-Jones Albumosuria... In 1847 Henry Bence-Jones presented the first recorded instance before the Royal Society of London. *Ibid.* 192 The urine contained Bence-Jones albumose and albumin. **1961** *Lancet* 5 Aug. 291/2 Bence Jones protein which behaves classically in the heat test.

bench (bɛnʃ), *sb.* Forms: 1 benc(e, 3–6 benche, (*Orm.* bennche), 4– **bench**. For Sc. and northern forms, see BENK, BINK. [Comm. Teut.: OE. *bęnc* = ON. **benkr* (Sw. *bänk*, Da. *bænk*, Icel. *bekkr*), OS., MHG., MDu. *banc*, OHG. *banch*, mod.G., Du. *bank*:—OTeut. **banki-z* 'bench': cf. BANK *sb.*[1], [2], which are originally the same word as this, introduced into English at a later time through Romanic. In sense 2, *bench* translates L. *bancum*, AF. *baunc*, *baunk*.]

1. a. A long seat, with or without a back, usually of wood, but also of stone, etc. 'Distinguished from a *stool* by its greater length.' J.

a **1000** *Beowulf* 659 Buȝon þa to bence. *c* **1200** Ormin 14087 He wollde sittenn þær, To drinnkenn þære on bennche. **1393** Langl. *P. Pl.* C. I. 200 To cracchen ous [rats]..þouh we crepe vnder benches. *c* **1440** *Promp. Parv.* 30 Benche, *scamnum*. **1535** Coverdale *Esther* i. 6 The benches were of golde and siluer. **1611** Bible *Ezek.* xxvii. 6 Thy benches of Yuorie. **1712** Steele *Spect.* No. 509 ¶3 The benches around are so filthy, that no one can sit down. **1870** F. Wilson *Ch. Lindisf.* 69 The nave is now seated with two rows of low-backed benches.

b. A seat or thwart in a boat.

1552 Huloet, Benches in a barge, bote, or shyppe, *juga*. **1791** Cowper *Odyss.* xv. 666 Each obedient, to his bench repaired. **1867** Smyth *Sailor's Word-bk.*, Benches of Boats.

c. *Baseball*, *Football*, etc. A seat provided for the members of a team who are waiting to bat, play, etc. *N. Amer.*

1912 C. Mathewson *Pitching in Pinch* 93 The *bench*! To many fans..this is a long, hooded structure from which the next batter emerges and where the players sit while their club is at bat. **1916** *Spalding's Baseball Guide* 316 All players and substitutes of the side at bat must be seated on their team's bench, except the batsman, base-runners and such as are legally assigned to coach base-runners. **1967** *Boston Globe* 5 Apr. 51/1 For the first play-off game..Auerbach sat next to the Boston bench. **1968** *Globe & Mail* (Toronto) 15 Jan. 19/2 The Boston team then became involved in a fight with some fans behind its bench. *Ibid.* 13 Feb. 28/4 Davis seldom went to his bench and his players appeared very tired in the final quarter.

2. a. The seat where the judges sit in court; the judge's seat, or seat of justice; hence, the office or dignity of a judge, as in 'to be raised to the bench.'

c **1275** Mapes *Body & Soul* 305 Theiȝ alle the men nouȝ. under mone to demen weren sette on benche. **1597** Shaks. *2 Hen. IV*, v. ii. 86 To plucke down Iustice from your awefull Bench. **1663** Butler *Hud.* I. I. 23 Great on the Bench, Great in the Saddle. **1848** Macaulay *Hist. Eng.* I. 450 These qualifications he carried..from the bar to the bench. *Ibid.* 662 On the bench sate three judges who had been with Jeffreys.

b. *Hence*, the place where justice is administered: orig. applied to ***The* (*Court of*) *Common Bench***, or (later) ***Common Pleas*** at Westminster, Anglo Fr. *le baunc*, L. *bancum*; also ***The* (*Court of*) *King's*** or ***Queen's Bench***, in which originally the sovereign presided, and which followed him in his movements. (These now form divisions of the High Court of Judicature.)

1292 Britton I. xxvii. §13 Brefs pledables par devaunt nos Justices du baunc a Westmouster [before our Justices of the Bench at Westminster]. *Ibid.* —— §14 Si soint ajournez en baunc en presence des parties [they shall be adjourned into the Bench]. *Ibid.* —— xxii. §18 Des clers..del un baunc et del autre, et des clers del Escheker [the clerks..of the one Bench and the other]. **1297** R. Glouc. 570 Biuore þe iustises atte benche. **1330** [See BENK.] **1362** Langl. *P. Pl.* A. Prol. 95 To ben Clerkes of þe Kynges Benche. **1474** Caxton *Chesse* 79 The courtes of the chaunserye, kynges bench, comyn place. **1628** Coke *On Litt.* 71 b, Called the Kings Bench.. because Kings in former times haue often personally set there. **1768** Blackstone *Comm.* III. 41 The court of king's bench..is the supreme court of common law in the kingdom. **1809** Tomlins *Law Dict.* s.v. *King's Bench*, During the reign of a Queen, it is called the Queen's Bench; and in Cromwell's time, it was stiled the Upper Bench. **1835** *Penny Cycl.* III. 376/1 Of the modern Court of Common Pleas..the judges..retain the technical title of 'Justices of the Bench at Westminster' to the present day.

c. Any court of justice; a tribunal.

1589 *Pasquil's Ret.* B ij, The Courtes, Benches, Sessions, that are helde..in her Maiesties name. **1660** Milton *Free Commw.* Wks. (1851) 451 Monarchs..will have all the Benches of Judicature annex'd to the Throne. **1863** Kingsley *Water-Bab.* iv. 149 The other two [days] he went to the bench and the board of guardians.

d. The judges or magistrates collectively, or the judge or magistrate sitting in the seat of justice.

1592 Greene *Art Conny Catch.* 10 The bench, that neuer heard this name before, smiled. **1677** Marvell *Corr.* 296 II. 355 Sir, Your's and the Bench's most humble servant. *a* **1716** Blackall *Wks.* I. 318 He had been asked some questions by the Bench. **1753** Pringle in *Scots Mag.* XV. 42/1 The bench consisted of six persons. **1837** Disraeli *Venetia* I. xvi, Now, prisoner, the bench is ready to hear your confession.

3. a. A seat where a number of persons sit side by side in some official capacity; *e.g.* those in the British Houses of Parliament (originally simple wooden benches), that occupied by the Aldermen in a Council Chamber, etc.

[**1607** Shaks. *Timon* IV. i. 5 Slaues and Fooles Plucke the graue wrinkled Senate from the Bench.] **1742** Shenstone *Schoolmistr.* xxviii, A little bench of heedless bishops And there a chancellor in embryo. **1771** Smollett *Humph. Cl.* (1815) 132 Every individual that now filled the bench of bishops in the house of Lords. **1812** *Examiner* 4 May 280/1 (Parliament. Rep.), Loud cheering from the Treasury bench. **1849** Ht. Martineau *Hist. Eng.* I. 15 The cross-benches of neutrality in the House of Commons. **1883** May *Law of Parl.* 16 The spiritual and temporal lords..sit apart, on separate benches. **1885** *Manch. Exam.* 24 July 6/1 The comparative bareness of..the Whig benches on the left of the Speaker's chair.

Hence, **b.** The dignity of occupying such a seat, as 'to be raised to the episcopal bench,' i.e. the Bishop's bench in the House of Lords, 'to aspire to the civic bench,' i.e. to be an Alderman, etc. **c.** Applied collectively to the persons who occupy, or have a right to occupy, such a seat.

[**1494** Fabyan VII. 665 By a consent of the benche [of aldermen], and of the comyn counsayll.] **1600** Chapman *Iliad* VI. 513 Those loving vows to living Jove he used And all the other bench of gods. **1801** Bp. Lincoln in G. Rose *Diaries* (1860) I. 359 It has..excited no small alarm amongst some of our bench. **1853** Bright *India, Sp.* (1876) 2, I do not allude to the whole of the Treasury bench. **1860** Forster *Gr. Remonstr.* 196 The conflict with the Right Reverend Bench which ended in their committal to the Tower.

4. An article of furniture similar in form to the long seat (sense 1): †**a.** a footstool; **b.** the rough strong table at which carpenters and other mechanics work; **c.** a banker's counter.

c **1386** Chaucer *Pers. T.* ¶515 Ne schal ye not swere..by the eorthe, for it is the benche of his feet. **1727** Chambers *Cycl.* s.v. *Foundery*, Two workmen..have a table or bench in common. **1755** Johnson *Dict.* s.v. *Bankrupt*, When any became insolvent his..bench was broke. **1881** *Mechanic* I. viii §466 A carpenter's bench may be either fixed or moveable. **1885** Hesba Stretton in *Good Words* XIV. 27/2, I have begun to work a little now at the bench.

5. *Hence*, A collection of dogs as exhibited at a show on benches or platforms; hence *attrib.*

1883 *Chamb. Jrnl.* 305 The 'bench' and field properties of a greyhound.

6. = BANK *sb.*[1] I.

c **1450** *Why not Nun* 114 in *E.E.P.* (1862) 141 Vn-to a benche of camomylle My wofulle hede I dyd inclyne. **1551** Robinson tr. *More's Utop.* 30 Vpon a bench couered with greene torves we satte. **1652** Ashmole *Theat. Chem.* 215 Benches coverid with new Turves grene.

7. a. Any conformation of earth, stone, etc., which has a raised and flat surface: *e.g.* the coping of a wall (? *obs.*); a level ledge or set-back in the slope of masonry or earthwork; in *U.S.* a level tract between a river and neighbouring hills; a horizontal division or layer of a coal-seam, cut by itself. Hence ***bench-land***.

1730 A. Gordon *Maffei's Amph.* 399 The Bench or Out-jutting, which is above the highest Ridge of the Building. **1793** Smeaton *Edystone L.* §111 Its slope..being formed into a sort of steps, or benches. **1811** *Deb. Congress* (1853) 2116 Towards the left flank this bench of high land widened considerably. **1857** W. Chandless *Visit Salt Lake* II. x. 326 Bench-land fifty or hundred feet above the water-level. **1862** R. Mayne *Brit. Columbia* 108 These flats or benches.. are found generally at the bends of the river. **1873** J. H. Beadle *Undevel. West* xxiv. 481 We turn south-west, rising by successive 'benches' to a vast barren table land. **1881** Raymond *Mining Gloss.* s.v. *Bench*, One bench or layer [of coal] being cut before the adjacent one. **1920** Mulford *J. Nelson* xii. 129 Right on them benches on th' east end of th' mountain.

b. *Geol.* A natural terrace marking the outcrop of a harder seam or stratum.

1884 *Science* 13 June 729/1 On this rest argillaceous, splendent, siliceous talc schists..; and on these, three benches of conglomerates, tuffs, and argillaceous schists and lime-stones. **1898** *Westm. Gaz.* 20 May 9/1 The same feature will doubtless exist as each bench is worked.

c. The ledge or floor upon which the retorts stand in a retort-house; also, a set of retorts; also, the complete furnace or oven containing a set of retorts.

1841 *Civil Eng. & Archit. Jrnl.* IV. 100/2 The works are laid out in eight distinct sections of ten 'benches', or thirty retorts each. **1920** *Conquest* May 320/3 In a large retort-house the settings are built in benches containing as many as 150 'through' retorts.

8. *Law.* See FREE-BENCH.

9. *Comb.*, chiefly *attrib.*, as ***bench-cloth***, ***-tied*** (sense 1), ***bench-business***, ***-mute*** (sense 2), ***bench-cheek***, ***-drill***, ***-jaw*** or ***-vice*** (4 b). Also **bench-babbler** = BENCH-WHISTLER; **bench-clamp**, a kind of vice with sliding side used to force together the parts, *e.g.* of a window-frame; **bench-coal** (see 7); **bench-end**, the end of a seat in a church, freq. ornamented (see POPPY-HEAD 2); **bench-hammer**, a finisher's or blacksmith's hammer; **bench-holdfast**, an iron hook, sliding in a socket, by which a plank may be gripped; †**bench-hole**, a privy; **bench-hook**, (*a*) = *bench-holdfast*; (*b*) (see quot. 1888); **bench-key**, a particular key used by a watchmaker for winding watches upon which he is employed; **bench-man**, an operative who works at a bench, in various trades, as a joiner; also, a cabinet-maker who assists at bench-work, a labourer who works at a coke bench; **bench-plane**, a joiner's plane for working on a flat surface; **bench-reel**, a spinning reel on the pirn of which sailmakers wind their yarn; **bench-room**, sitting accommodation; **bench-root** *Agric.*, 'an abnormal root development due to the presence of tough seed coats; the roots are often twisted together or badly formed' (Webster *Addenda* 1918); **bench-screw** (see quot.); **bench-shears**, shears used by copper- and zinc-workers; **bench-show** (see 5); **bench-stop**, **-strip**, a strip of wood or metal fixed on a carpenter's bench to rest his work against; **bench-table**, a low stone seat on the inside of walls, or round the bases of pillars, in churches, cloisters, etc.; **bench test**, a test of a motor engine carried out in a workshop before fitting it to a motor body; also *transf.*, preliminary testing of equipment, software, etc.; hence as *v. trans.*, to run a series of tests on (an engine or other equipment), usu. before its public use; **bench-testing** *vbl. sb.*; **bench warmer** *U.S. slang*, a person who sits idle on a bench, *esp.* a substitute in a sports team; also, any idle or ineffectual person; **bench-warrant**, one issued by a judge, as opposed to a *justice's* or *magistrate's warrant*; **bench-winder** = *bench-key*. See also BENCH-MARK, -WHISTLER.

1549 Bale in *Cheke's Hurt Sedit.* (1641) Pref., These chimney-Preachers, and *bench-Bablers. **1850** J. Smith *Rep. Sanit. Condition Hull* 17 Forming *bench-beds for the vessels. **1647** Fuller *Good Th. Worse T.* (1841) 103 As if he made a session or *bench-business thereof. **1881** *Mechanic* §505 Pins running through the bench leg and *bench cheek respectively. **1552** Huloet, *Benchclothe, or carpet cloth. **1712** *Phil. Trans.* XXVII. 541 Coal, called *Bench-Coal.

1898 A. JESSOPP in *19th Cent.* Jan. 56 We get a payment entered for the carving of the *bench-ends in a little church, 500 years ago. **1960** *Times* 12 Aug. 12/7 This church..is full of interest, with exceptionally attractive poppyhead benchends. **1555** *Fardle Facions* 19 Whiche dreamed not their knowledge in the *benchehole at home. **1606** SHAKS. *Ant. & Cl.* IV. vii. 9 Wee'l beat 'em into Bench-holes. *a* **1656** HALL *Rem. Wks.* (1660) 231 The stoutest Atheist turnes pale, and is ready to creep into a bench-hole. **1823** P. NICHOLSON *Pract. Build.* 236 The *bench-hook is to keep the wood steady. **1888** J. G. HORNER *Dict. Mech. Engin.* 28 *Bench hook*, a stop for sawing light work on the bench without damaging the bench itself. It is a block of wood about 12 in. long, furnished with a projecting stop at each end placed on opposite faces of a central web. One face of the web being laid on the bench, the lower stop is pressed against the bench edge, while the upper one takes the thrust of the wood which is being cut by the saw. **1901** *Daily Chron.* 7 May 10/6 Boot trade.—Good *benchman wanted for repairs. **1961** *Oxford Mail* 5 Oct. 2/2 Benchman required ..footwear. **1635** BRATHWAIT *Arcad. Pr.* ii. 13 Thou..sitt'st *Bench-mute with thy decayed braines. **1601** HOLLAND *Pliny* II. 358 Sufficient bed and *bench-room to rest and repose. **1823** P. NICHOLSON *Pract. Build.* 237 The *bench-screw is used to fasten boards between the cheeks, in order to plane their edges. **1874** *Forest & Stream* 29 Oct. 182/1 The first regular *bench show of dogs. **1887** *Harper's Mag.* May 934/1 The American bench shows furnish an opportunity to most readers to see the best mastiffs in the country. **1881** *Mechanic* §464 An ordinary carpenter's bench ..with a bench vice and *bench stop. **1849** FREEMAN *Archit.* 197 A *bench table along the east wall. **1909** *Westm. Gaz.* 6 Apr. 4/2 Their..38 h.p. motors which recently underwent a 132 hours' continuous running *bench test at Coventry. **1959** *Time* 19 Jan. 54/3 By 1922 he was bench-testing in secrecy the world's first liquid-fueled rocket. **1971** *Daily Tel.* 16 July 7 (Advt.), Thomas Mann benchtests the famous 6-cylinder XK engine. **1984** *Which Micro?* Dec. 98 (Advt.), Comparisons, bench tests, reviews and answers to all your questions. **1973** *Inst. Environm. Sci. Proc.* XIX. 24/2 One of the ATS-F spacecraft heat pipes was discovered to have a thin wall, and upon *bench testing (protected), ruptured. **1985** *Which Computer?* Apr. 5/1 When you think of computer 'benchtesting' you probably imagine tens of computer experts performing exhaustive hands-on studies under what amount to laboratory conditions. **1820** T. MITCHELL *Aristoph.* I. 33 My poor *bench-tied countrymen. **1892** *N.Y. Sporting Times* 9 Jan., The days for '*bench warmers' with salaries are also past. **1978** *Washington Post* 31 May B11/3 Rivera..is a barely competent bench warmer. Her technical skills are evident .., but an ascetic stance makes her music..dull. **1986** *Los Angeles Times* 19 Oct. III. 2/3 He thought about leaving after the 1984 season, his third straight year as a bench-warmer. **1696** LUTTRELL *Brief Rel.* IV. 108 A *bench warrant was issued. **1878** J. H. BEADLE *Western Wilds* xxxii. 514 Another called for the immediate arrest of Brigham on a bench warrant before he could fly the country. **1883** *Wharton's Law-Lexicon* (ed. 7) 92/1 *Bench warrant*, an attachment issued by order of a criminal court against an individual..a warrant signed by a judge, or two justices of the peace, to apprehend a prisoner charged with an offence. **1959** JOWITT *Dict. Eng. Law* I. 225 *Bench warrant*, a warrant issued by a court of record, *sedente curia*, for the arrest of a person against whom an indictment for treason, felony or misdemeanour has been found.., if such person does not appear to answer the indictment or articles. **1884** F. BRITTEN *Watch & Clockm.* 293 *Bench Winder..[is] a key used for winding watches by a watch maker.

bench (bɛnʃ), *v.* [f. prec. sb.]

1. *trans.* To furnish with benches.

c **1385** CHAUCER *L.G.W.* 98 I-benchede newe with turvis. **1615** G. SANDYS *Trav.* 130 This entry [of the pyramid] was ..benched on each side. **1729** SAVAGE *Wanderer* v. v, There, bench'd with turf, an oak our seat extends. **1847** TENNYSON *Princess* ii. 348 Stately theatres Bench'd crescent-wise.

†**2.** To bank up, bank back. *Obs. rare.*

1587 FLEMING *Cont. Holinshed* III. 1547/1 Yf there were anie issue or draining of water vnder the wals..they benched it, digging a trench at the foot of that part of the wall, and filling the same with earth.

3. a. *trans.* To seat on a bench. **b.** *refl.* and *intr.* To seat oneself, or take a seat, upon a bench.

1605 SHAKS. *Lear* III. vi. 40 Thou his yoke-fellow of equity, Bench by his side. **1611** —— *Wint. T.* I. ii. 314 His Cup-bearer, whom I from meaner forme Haue Bench'd, and rear'd to Worship. **1624** HEYWOOD *Captives* IV. iii. in Bullen *O. Pl.* IV, The fryar..Hath lyke a surly Justyce bensht himself. **1816** W. TAYLOR in *Month. Mag.* XLI. 331 They..bench their weary joints.

c. *trans.* To put (a dog) on a show-bench for exhibition; to exhibit at a dog-show.

1891 *Times* 28 Oct. 11/5 Almost every breed of spaniel is benched. **1898** *Standard* 1 Dec. 2/6 Possibly the soundest coloured Chow ever benched. **1924** *Westm. Gaz.* 22 Oct., Among those benched at the Toy Dog Show..will be black-and-tan miniature dogs.

4. *intr. to bench in*: to recede in terraced levels.

1737 L. CLARKE *Hist. Bible* VII. (1740) 409 The whole ascent to it was, by the benching in, drawn in a sloping line from the bottom to the top. *Ibid.*, Calling it a Pyramid, because of its..benching in at every Tower.

5. *trans. N. Amer.* In Baseball, Football, etc., to remove a player from a game or prevent him from taking part in it. Cf. BENCH *sb.* 1 c.

1917 MATHEWSON *Sec. Base Sloan* xvi. 224 Some of you stuffed sausages will be benched mighty quick if you don't wake up. **1947** *Harper's Mag.* June 560/2, I should have benched him long ago, he got only nineteen hits all season. **1967** *Boston Herald* 8 May 16/5 Second baseman Woody Woodward, benched because he was in a hitting slump, returned to Atlanta's starting lineup Sunday.

benched (bɛnʃt), *ppl. a.* [f. prec. + -ED.] **a.** Furnished with benches. **b.** Seated on a bench.

1394 *P. Pl. Crede* 205 An halle Wiþ brode bordes aboute y-benched wel clene. **1636** HEYWOOD *Loves Mistr.* v. i. Wks. 1874 V. 148 Minos bench'd. **1873** MISS BROUGHTON *Nancy* III. 72, I sit benched among the old women.

bencher (ˈbɛnʃə(r)). [f. BENCH *sb.* + -ER[1].]

1. One who sits on a bench (or thwart); one who frequents the benches of a tavern.

1534 LD. BERNERS *Gold. Bk. M. Aurel.* (1546) D d viij, If the pyllers bee of syluer, and benches of golde, and though the benchers be kynges. **1598** B. JONSON *Ev. Man in Hum.* IV. i, O, the benchers phrase: *pauca verba.* **1858** HAWTHORNE *Fr. & It. Jrnls.* II. 286 The benchers joke with the women passing by. **1860** HUGHES *Tom Brown Oxf.* xiii, Old companions, θρανῖται, benchers (of the gallant eight-oar).

2. One who officially sits on a bench; a magistrate, judge, assessor, senator, member of the Sanhedrim, alderman, etc. *arch.*

1571 *Damon & P.* in Hazl. *Dodsl.* IV. 17 Of parasites and sycophants you are a grave bencher. **1607** SHAKS. *Cor.* II. i. 91 A necessary Bencher in the Capitoll. **1612** BP. HALL *Contempl. N.T.* IV. xxx, The grave benchers of Ierusalem.. Rabbies of Israel. *a* **1693** ASHMOLE *Antiq. Berks* (1723) III. 58 Ten of them Aldermen or chief Benchers.

3. *spec.* One of the senior members of the Inns of Court, who form for each Inn a self-elective body, managing its affairs, and possessing the privilege of 'calling to the bar.'

1582 *Act 5 Eliz.* i. §5 As well Utter-Barresters as Benchers. **1691** WOOD *Ath. Oxon.* II. 311 He was made successively Barrester, utter Barrester, Bencher and Reader. **1711** ADDISON *Spect.* No. 21 ¶4 Benchers of the several Inns of Court, who seem to be Dignitaries of the Law. **1855** MACAULAY *Hist. Eng.* IV. 774 The benchers of the Inner Temple could bear the scandal..no longer.

'benchership. [f. prec. + -SHIP.] The position or dignity of a bencher in an Inn of Court.

1823 LAMB *Elia, Benchers Inner Temple*, They were co-evals, and had nothing but that and their benchership in common. **1865** *Pall Mall G.* 29 Sept. 6/2 A benchership of Gray's-inn has become vacant.

benching (ˈbɛnʃɪŋ), *vbl. sb.* [f. BENCH + -ING[1].] **a.** The action of the vb. BENCH. **b.** ***benching up***: working on the top of coal (Raymond *Mining Gloss.* 1881). **c.** *concr.* A provision or range of benches or seats.

1398 TREVISA *Barth. De P.R.* XIX. cxxix. 938 *Diuerticulum* is a benchynge besyde the waye. **1866** HOWELLS *Venet. Life* xx. 335 The benching that passes round the shop.

bench-legged, *a. U.S.* [BENCH *sb.* 1.] Having the fore-legs wide apart.

1866 C. H. SMITH *Bill Arp* 159 Dodds says,..he'd have his soul transmigrated to a bench-leg'd fice [*sc.* dog]. **1889** *Harper's Mag.* Aug. 485/2 Selling his little bench-legged mule to a travelling showman. **1903** A. ADAMS *Log Cowboy* xii. 79 The Indians' little bench-legged ponies were no match for them. *Ibid.* xv. 100 A long bench-legged black dog with a Dutch name.

benchlet (ˈbɛnʃlɪt). [f. BENCH *sb.* + -LET.] A little bench, a stool.

1865 CARLYLE *Fredk. Gt.* X. xxi. vii, Three little benchlets or stools..stood before him. **1884** A. PUTNAM *Police Judge* xvi. 165 The petit judge might sit on his benchlet.

'bench-mark. a. A surveyor's mark cut in some durable material, as a rock, wall, gate-pillar, face of a building, etc., to indicate the starting, closing, or any suitable intermediate, point in a line of levels for the determination of altitudes over the face of a country. It consists of a series of wedge-shaped incisures, in the form of the 'broad-arrow' with a horizontal bar through its apex, thus ⊼. When the spot is below sea-level, as in mining surveys, the mark is inverted.

[The horizontal bar is the essential part, the broad arrow being added (originally by the Ordnance Survey) as an identification. In taking a reading, an angle-iron 7 is held with its upper extremity inserted in the horizontal bar, so as to form a temporary bracket or *bench* for the support of the levelling-staff, which can thus be placed on absolutely the same base on any subsequent occasion. Hence the name.]

1842 FRANCIS *Dict. Arts, Bench marks*, in surveying, fixed points left on a line of survey for reference at a future time, consisting of cuts in trees, pegs driven into the ground, etc. **1883** G. SYMONS *Brit. Rainf.* 134 A series of levels has been taken from the gauge to an Ordnance bench mark.

b. *transf.* and *fig.* A point of reference; a criterion, touchstone.

1884 *Science* IV. 202/1 These star-places..are the reference-points and bench-marks of the universe. **1957** R. K. MERTON *Student-Physician* III. 195 Standards represent 'benchmarks' with which students compare their ability and performance. **1963** *Economist* 18 May 663/2 Foreign firms have failed to get..orders unless they have offered a price advantage of at least 50 per cent. This is the 'bench-mark'.

bench-table. *Hist.* [f. BENCH *sb.* + TABLE *sb.* 8 c.] An official body of benchers of the Inner Temple: see quot. 1896.

1673 *Cal. Inner Temple Rec.* (1901) III. 92 Ordered at the bench table that Kenricke Eyton..and Ralph Sumner..do by the beginning of Michaelmas term next write a court hand. **1692** W. SHERLOCK (*title*) A Sermon Preached at the Temple-Church, May 29. 1692. And Printed at the Desire of the Bench-Table of the Honourable Society of the Inner-Temple. **1896** *Cal. Inner Temple Rec.* I. Introd. p. xxxiii, The officers of the house..met together frequently..at what was and is known as the Bench Table, when orders were made for the governance of the Inn.

†**'bench-,whistler.** *Obs.* One who sits idly whistling on a bench: a term of reproach.

1542 BOORDE *Dyetary* viii. 245 Fye on the, benche-whystler, wylt thou sterte away nowe? **1607** CHAPMAN *All Fooles* Plays (1873) I. 137 Y'are but bench-whistlers now a dayes to them that were in our times. **1618** HORNBY *Sco. Drunk.* (1859) 17 He that will not drinke off his whole scowre Is a bench-whistler.

bend (bɛnd), *sb.*[1] Forms: 1– bend; also 3 biend, 4 beend. [Com. Teut., OE. *bęnd* str. fem. (pl. *bęnda*) = OS. *bendi*, OFris. *bende*, MDu. *bende*, Goth. *bandi*:—OTeut. **bandjâ-*, f. *band-*, stem of *bindan* to BIND; also in OE. str. masc. (pl. *bęndas*). This is the original English word, now superseded, exc. in nautical use, by the cognate BAND *sb.*[1], BOND, from ON., the senses of which ran in ME. alongside of those of *bend*, so as to make it appear only another phonetic variant of those. The OE. pl. *benda* remained in ME. as *bende* in collective sense of 'bonds, imprisonment.']

†**1.** Anything with which one's body or limbs are bound; a band, bond, or fetter. *pl. collective*, Bonds, fetters, confinement, imprisonment. *Obs.*

c **890** K. ÆLFRED *Bæda* IV. xxii. (Bosw.) Þa benda sumes ʒehæftes. *c* **1000** *Ags. Ps.* cvi[i]. 13 Heora bendas towearp. *c* **1000** *Ags. Gosp.* Matt. xi. 2 Ða Johannes on bendum [*Hatton* benden] ʒehyrde Christes weoruc. *c* **1175** *Moral Ode* 180 in *Lamb. Hom.* 171 For lesen hi of bende. *Ibid.* 289 In þo loþe biende [*Trin. MS.* in þe loðe bende]. *c* **1205** LAY. 18459 þe king heom lette binden mid irene bænde [**1250** bendes]. *c* **1300** *Beket* 15 Oft in feteres and in othe[r] bende. *c* **1400** *Gamelyn* 457 To brynge me out of bendes. *Ibid.* 837 Gamelyn leet unfetere his brother out of beende.

†**b.** *fig.* The 'fetters' or 'shackles' of habit, etc.; custody, keeping; = BAND *sb.*[1] 8.

971 *Blickl. Hom.* 9 þa wæs ʒesended þæt goldhord..on þone bend þæs clænan innoðes. *c* **1200** *Trin. Coll. Hom.* 63 Ac þat..unbindeð þe bendes of wiðerfulnesse.

†**c.** A moral or spiritual bond or restraint; the bands or bonds of matrimony. = BAND *sb.*[1] 9.

a **1250** *Owl & Night.* 1426 Thurh chirche bende. *Ibid.* 1470 Thah spusing bendes thuncheth sore. **1340** *Ayenb.* 48 þet ne habbeþ nenne bend ne of wodewehod ne of spoushod.

†**d.** 'Confinement' at child-birth: 'Our Lady's Bands': see BAND *sb.*[1] 1 c.

1297 R. GLOUC. 379 ȝyf God me wole grace sende Vorto make my chyrche gon, & bringe me of þys bende. *c* **1330** *King of Tars* 539 By the fourti wikes ende, Heo was delyvered out of beende, Thorw help of Marie mylde.

†**2.** A clamp or band (of iron, etc.) for strengthening a box, etc.; a connecting piece by which the parts of anything are bound together; = BAND *sb.*[1] 4, 5. *Obs.*

a **1225** *Ancr. R.* 382 Ibunden mid iren..and mid brode þicke bendes. **1523** FITZHERB. *Husb.* §4 Somme plowes haue a bende of yron. **1596** SPENSER *F.Q.* II. vii. 30 Huge great yron chests, and coffers strong, All bard with double bends.

3. *Naut.* A knot, used to unite one rope to another, or to something else; there are various kinds, as the ***cable bend, carrick bend, fisherman's bend***, etc. (The only extant sense.)

1769 FALCONER *Dict. Marine* (1789) *Bend*, the knot by which one rope is fastened to another. **1819** REES *Cycl.* s.v. *Bends*, For a carrick bend, lay the end of a rope, or hawser, across its standing part. **1829** GEN. P. THOMPSON *Exerc.* (1842) I. 114 Taking a bend on the bight of the rope. **1833** MARRYAT *P. Simple* xiv, He taught me a fisherman's bend, which he pronounced to be the king of all knots.

†**4.** *Comb.* **bend-ful** (*obs.*), a bandful, a bundle.

? *a* **1480** *Kyng & Hermit* 169 in Hazl. *E.P.P.* 20 The frere he had bot barly stro, Two thake bendsfull without mo.

bend (bɛnd), *sb.*[2] Forms: 1 bend, 5–6 bende. [Apparently originally English, as a sense of the prec. word: see the early quotations. But afterwards naturally identified with OF. *bende* (mod.Fr. *bande*): see BAND *sb.*[2]; whence the later sense-development. Now used only in the Heraldic and technical senses 3, 4 (if 4 really belongs here).

The OF. *bende, bande*, corresponds to med.L. *binda, benda*, Lombard *benda*, It. *benda, banda*, Sp. and Pg. *venda* and *banda*; pointing to a Romanic adoption of OHG. *bindâ*, 'band, fillet, tie, sash,' and also of Gothic *bandi* or other equivalent of OE. *bend*, with similar sense.]

†**1.** A thin flat strip adapted to bind round.

†**a.** A riband, fillet, strap, band, used for ornament or as part of a dress; a sash, swaddling-band, hat-band, bandage; = BAND *sb.*[2] 1–5. *Obs.* or ? *dial.*

c **1000** ÆLFRIC *Gloss.* in Wr-Wülcker *Voc.* 152 *Diadema*, bend aȝimmed and ʒesmiðed. *Ibid. Nimbus*, mid golde ʒesiwud bend. *c* **1205** LAY. 24747 And mid æne bende of golde ælc hafde his hæfd biuonge. *c* **1340** *Gaw. & Gr. Knt.* 2517 Vche burne..a bauderyk schulde haue, A bende a belef hym aboute, of a bryȝt grene. *c* **1450** *Crt. of Love* 810 A bend of golde and silke. **1463** in *Bury Wills* (1850) 41 My bende for an hat of blak sylk and silvir. Item to John Coote my bende of whit boon with smale bedys of grene. **1491** CAXTON *Vitas Patr.* (W. de W.) I. xlviii. (1495) 93* b/1 A lytyll bende, to swadle a lytyll chylde beynge in his cradle. **1513** DOUGLAS *Æneis* II. iii. (ii.) 138 About my heid ane gairland or a bend. **1552** HULOET, Bende, fillet or kerchiefe. *amiculum.* **1601** HOLLAND *Pliny* II. 365 Bast dogs haire down to a bend or piece of cloth, and fasten the same close to the said forehead. **1790** GROSE *Prov. Gloss.*, *Bend*, a

border of a woman's cap; *north.* **1791-9** *Statist. Acc. Scot.* XI. 173 (JAM.) The [Archery] prize [at Kilwinning], from 1488 to 1688, was a sash, or as it was called, a benn..a piece of Taffeta or Persian, of different colours, chiefly red, green, white, and blue.

†**b.** *Anat.* A band, a ligament. *Obs.*

1398 TREVISA *Barth. De P.R.* v. v, The þridde curtel foloweþ, þat hat 'cerotica' [*sclerotica*], þat..defendeþ all þe oþer from þe hardnesse of þe bon, and is as it were þe bende [*ligamentum*] of þe ye.

†**c.** A scroll or riband in decorative work. ? *Obs.*

c **1535** in Gutch *Coll. Cur.* I. 206 And for 246 bends or poses..set up in the same windows. **1743** A. MILNE in Wade *Melrose Ab.* (1861) 33 On the East of this Window there is a Niche, having a monk for the supporter of the statue, holding a Bend with each Hand about his Breast. [**1861** WADE *ibid.* 314 A venerable monk, bearing a band or scroll.]

†**2.** A 'stripe' inflicted by a lash or rod. *Obs. rare.* (Also in form *band*, belonging to BAND *sb.*[2] after sense 8.)

c **1400** *Ywaine & Gaw.* 2394 He bar a scourge with cordes ten..Efter ilka band brast out the blode. *a* **1550** *Peebles to Play*, Quoth he, 'Thy back sall bear ane bend'; 'In faith,' quoth she, 'we meit not.'

3. *Her.* An ordinary formed by two parallel lines drawn from the dexter chief to the sinister base of the shield, containing the fifth part of the field in breadth, or the third if charged. (See quot. 1872.) ***bend sinister***: a similar ordinary drawn in the opposite direction: one of the marks of bastardy. Cf. BATON *sb.* ***in bend***: placed bendwise. ***parted per bend***: divided bendwise.

c **1430** *Syr Gener.* 3924 Armes he bereth riche and clene, With bendes of gold wel besene. **1480** CAXTON *Chron. Eng.* cxciv. 170 Euery bataylle had cote armures of grene clothe and therof the ryght quarter was yelowe with whyte bendes, wherfor that parlement was callyd the parlement of the whyte bende. **1572** BOSSEWELL *Armorie* II. 33 b, Thei are called Bendes. **1598** DRAYTON *Heroic. Ep.* xxi. 95 That Lyon plac'd in our bright Silver bend. **1622** PEACHAM *Compl. Gentl.* i. (1634) 9 Some [bare] their Fathers whole Coate..in bend dexter. *Ibid.*, Yet it is the custome with vs, and in France, to allow them for Noble, by giving them sometimes their Fathers proper Coate, with a Bend sinister. **1662** FULLER *Worthies* I. 48 A Bend is esteemed the best Ordinarie, being a Belt born in its true posture athwart. **1688** R. HOLME *Armory* I. 74 Parted per Bend Sinister. **1816** SCOTT *Antiq.* xii, The bend of bastardy upon the shield yonder. **1872** RUSKIN *Eagle's N.* §235 The Bend..represents the sword-belt.

4. A shape or size in which ox- or cow-hides are tanned into leather, forming half of a 'butt.'

A 'butt' is the entire hide of the back and flanks reduced to a rough rectangle, by what is technically called 'rounding,' i.e. cutting off the surrounding thinner parts (the hide of the head and shoulders, and of the belly and shanks on each side of the 'butt'). When this is cut in two by a line down the middle of the back, before tanning (as is mostly done in Scotland and the north of England), each half is called a 'bend.' Butts and bends contain the thickest and strongest hide, the qualities of which are further developed by special processes in tanning, so as to make the stoutest leather. Hence:

b. bend-leather (orig. *northern*): the leather of a 'bend,' i.e. the thickest and stoutest kind of leather (from the back and flanks), used for soles of boots and shoes; sole-leather.

1600 HEYWOOD *1 K. Edw.* Wks. 1874 I. 40, I had rather than a bend of leather Shee and I might smouch together. **1865** *Times* 29 Apr., An average amount of business has been done in leather during the month. Foreign heavy butts and bends have been in only moderate demand.

b. **1581** LAMBARDE *Eiren.* IV. 164 If any tanner have raised with any mixture any hide to bee converted to backes, bend-leather, clowting-leather. **1709** BLAIR in *Phil. Trans.* XXVII. 76 Of Substance not unlike to English Bend or Sole-Leather. **1811** SCOTT in *Lockhart* (1839) III. 344 Sir ..can you say anything clever about bend leather? **1880** *Blackw. Mag.* Feb. 254 But Jem was a tough one and never knew pains In his vulcanite bowels and bend-leather brains.

†**bend**, *sb.*[3] *Obs.* Forms: 5-6 **bende**, 6-7 **bend.** [Late 15th c. *bende*, a. F. *bende*, another (? earlier) form of F. *bande* (corresp. to It., Sp., Pg. *banda*) 'an organized company of men,' a BAND. Both forms, *bende* and *bande*, appear to have been introduced from Fr. by Caxton (see BAND *sb.*[3]); but *bende* was by far the more frequent form till late in the 16th c., being always used by Ld. Berners, Sir T. More, Grafton, etc., though *band(e*, alone appears in the versions of the Bible (Tindale and Coverdale have *bonde* in *John* xviii. 3, where the later versions have *bande*; but the word is not frequent in any form before the Geneva version of 1557). *Bend* is rare after 1600; the Shaks. folio of 1623 has always *band.* The sense of 'faction, party,' is assigned also by Cotgrave to F. *bande*, and by Minsheu to Sp. *banda.*]

An organized company of men; = BAND *sb.*[3]; a party, a faction; a gang.

1475 CAXTON *Jason* 78 Upon them that they founde not of their bende. **1509** FISHER *Fun. Serm. C'tess Richmond* (1708) 15 Yf ony faccyons or bendes were made secretly amongst her hede Officers. **1539** TONSTALL *Serm. Palm Sund.* (1823) 33 Cornelius the Centuryon, capytayne of the Italyons bende. **1544** STALBRIDGE *Epist.* 24 A bende of bolde braggers. **1552** HULOET, Bende of men, commonly of ten souldiers, *manipulus.* **1579** SPENSER *Sheph. Cal.* May 32 A fresh bend Of louely Nymphs. **1600** HOLLAND *Livy* XXIII. 473 The bend and faction of the Cossanes..kept him downe. **1611** SPEED *Hist. Gt. Brit.* IX. xviii. 15 The Duke of Gloucester..and other Lords, the chiefe of his bend

bend (bɛnd), *sb.*[4] [A late derivative of BEND *v.*, appearing in the 16th c.]

I. Related to BEND *v.* II.

1. The action of the verb BEND; bending, incurvation; bent condition, flexure, curvature.

1597 *Way to Thrift* 62 Too mickle bend will breake thy bow When the game is alder best. *c* **1790** IMISON *Sch. Arts* I. 112 When the strong spring C is set on bend against the opposite ends of the pins. *c* **1806** A. MACKINTOSH *Driffield Angler* 229 The effect of the proper degree of bend. **1816** BYRON *Ch. Har.* III. cii, The gush of springs..the bend Of stirring branches. **1858** HAWTHORNE *Fr. & It. Jrnls.* I. 236 A wave just on the bend, and about to break over.

2. a. A bending of the body; a bow. *Obs.* except with defining words, as an instance of sense 1.

(Cf. the slang phrase *Grecian Bend*, denoting a certain bending forward of the body in walking, affected by some women *c* 1872-80.)

1529 LYNDESAY *Complaint* 181 With bendis and beckis For wantones. *a* **1550** *Christis Kirk Gr.* vi, Platefute he bobit up with bendis, For Mald he made requiest. [*Mod.* With a quick bend of the body, a slight bend of the knee, etc.]

b. ***the bends***: the acute attacks of pain in muscles and joints suffered on over-rapid reduction of the surrounding air pressure, chiefly by workers in compressed air who are decompressed too quickly, with consequent liberation of dissolved nitrogen from the body tissues. Also, more loosely, the whole disease (also called *caisson-disease*) produced by decompression.

1894 *Westm. Gaz.* 16 Oct. 3/2 The pressure..is quite enough to give the men a dose of the 'bend' [*sic*] as it is called. **1902** *Idler* July 485 That..terrible air-pressure disease known as the 'bends'. **1913** PEMBREY & RITCHIE *Gen. Path.* 494 These pains [in Caisson disease] pass off in a few hours, and are known to the workmen as 'bends', apparently because of the flexed positions which they induce. **1962** *Listener* 29 Mar. 562/1 Nitrogen narcosis must not be confused with decompression sickness, commonly known as the bends.

†**3.** Inclination of the eye in any direction, glance. *Obs. rare.*

1601 SHAKS. *Jul. C.* I. ii. 123 That same eye whose bend doth awe the world.

4. Turn of mind, inclination, bent. *Obs.* except with defining words, as an instance of sense 1.

1591 in *Harl. Misc.* (1809) II. 211 For the more forcible attraction of these vnnaturall people (being weake of vnderstanding) to this their bend, these seedemen of treason bring certain bulles from the Pope. **1610** FLETCHER *Faithf. Sheph.* (T.) Farewel, poor swain: thou art not for my bend. *c* **1815** FUSELI *Lect. Art* vii. (1848) 491 The prevalent bend of the reigning taste.

5. *concr.* **a.** A thing of bent shape; the bent part of anything, e.g. of a river, a road; a curve or crook.

c **1600** *Rob. Hood* (Ritson) II. xi. 17 A herd of deer was in the bend All feeding before his face. **1727** CHAMBERS *Cycl.* s.v. *Flying*, The bony part, or bend of the wing into which the feathers are inserted. **1803** SOUTHEY *Eng. Eclog.* ix A long parade..Round yonder bend it reaches A furlong further. **1879** FROUDE *Cæsar* xix. 319 At a bend of the river four miles below Paris. **1883** *Century Mag.* 378 The perfection of fishhooks in shank, bend, barb and point.

b. The curve of a gun-stock, shaped to fit the arm of the person for whose use it is made.

1859 'STONEHENGE' *Shot-gun & Sporting Rifle* IV. i. 229 In addition to the adaptation in length and bend of the stock, it is also..bent sideways. **1892** W. W. GREENER *Breech-Loader* 73 The distance from A to heel, and from B to comb. This is the bend.

c. A curved drain-pipe.

a **1884** KNIGHT *Dict. Mech.* Suppl., *Bend*, a flexed pipe, changing the direction. **1908** *Animal Managem.* 53 Any change of direction being made by curved pipes or 'bends'.

d. In a carding machine, the semicircular frame which carries the brackets in which the rollers are borne; also, in a carding machine of the revolving flat type, the curved surface which sustains the chain of flats.

1882 *Spon's Encycl. Industr. Arts* V. 2073 As the periphery passes round to the cylinder, the teeth are then in the act of ascending (the bend being thus in the opposite direction), and presenting facilities for being stripped of the wool they have acquired. **1890** NASMITH *Mod. Cotton Spinn. Mach.* 64 The phrase 'bend' should only be applied to that portion of the mechanism upon which the flats actually travel. **1892** —— *Students' Cotton Spinning* 101 The whole of the rollers are borne in brackets fixed to a semicircular frame bolted on the lower frame P, and known as the 'bend', the brackets having open bearings formed at their heads.

6. *Naut.* **a.** *pl.* 'The crooked timbers which make the ribs or sides of a ship' (J.); the wales.

1626 CAPT. SMITH *Accid. Yng. Seamen* 11 The Orlope, the ports, the bend, the bowe. **1627** —— *Seaman's Gram.* ii. 6 From bend to bend, or waile to waile, which are the outmost timbers on the ship sides, and are the chiefe strength of her sides, to which the foot-hookes, beames, and knees are bolted, and are called the first, second, and third Bend. **1725** SLOANE *Jamaica* II. 344 A signal of distress from a plank being started on her bend, on the forepart of the ship. **1803** NELSON in Nicolas *Disp.* (1845) V. 127 She is to be caulked, her bends blacked and painted.

b. 'The chock of the bowsprit.' Smyth *Sailor's Word.-bk.*

†**7.** See quots. (Perhaps belongs here.)

1847-78 HALLIWELL, *Bend*, a semicircular piece of iron used as part of a horse's harness to hold up the chains when ploughing. **1881** EVANS *Leicester Wds.* (E. Dial. Soc.) 103 *Bend*, a piece of bent plate-iron which went over the back of the last horse at plough. Now (1848) disused.

II. Probably related to BEND *v.* V.

†**8.** 'A spring, a leap, a bound.' Jamieson. *Sc. Obs.* [Cf. BEND *v.* 22.]

1513 DOUGLAS *Æneis* V. vi. 58 Befoir thaim all furth bowtis with a bend Nisus a far way. **1550** LYNDESAY *Sqr. Meldrum* 519 Quhairon [a steed] he lap, and tuik his speir..And bowtit fordward with ane bend.

9. A long draught, 'a pull of liquor.' Jamieson. Only in *Sc.* [Cf. BEND *v.* 23.]

1725 RAMSAY *Gentle Sheph.* in Poems (1844) 31 Come, gie's the other bend, We drink their healths, what ever way it end.

10. a. Phrases. ***on the bend***: by means that are not straightforward, 'crookedly'; ***to go on the*** (or ***a***) ***bend***: to go 'on the spree'; also ***to have a bend***; cf. BENDER 5 b. *slang.*

1863 JEAFFRESON *Live it Down* xxviii, I'll order my executor to buy my coffin off the square. He shall get it on the bend, somehow or other. **1879** KIDSTON in *Proc. Gen. Assembly Free Church Scotl.* 62 'Going on the spree' or 'having a bend'. **1887** F. FRANCIS Jr. *Saddle & Mocassin* 84 They do say as he was 'customed to go on a scoop—on a bend, occasionally, as it were. **1891** KIPLING *City Dreadf. Nt.* 71 The gallant apprentice may be a wild youth with an earnest desire to go occasionally 'upon the bend'. **1891** —— *Life's Handicap* 60, I went on the bend with a intimate friend. **1936** L. A. G. STRONG *Last Enemy* I. x. 152 Been on the bend, 'aven't you?

b. ***above one's bend***: beyond one's powers. *U.S.*

1835 CROCKETT *Tour down East* 44, I shall not attempt to describe the curiosities here [*sc.* at Peale's Museum]; it is above my bend. **1848** J. F. COOPER *Oak Open.* (De Vere), It would be above my bend to attempt telling you all we saw among the Redskins. **1872** SCHELE DE VERE *Americanisms* 577 *Above one's bend* means, above one's power of bending all his strength to a certain purpose.

c. ***round the bend***: crazy, insane. *colloq.*

1929 F. C. BOWEN *Sea Slang* 114 *Round the bend*, an old naval term for anybody who is mad. **1951** 'N. SHUTE' *Round the Bend* xi. 361 People are saying that I've been out in the East too long, and I've gone round the bend. **1955** J. I. M. STEWART *Guardians* vii. 78 Right round the bend..I mean ..as mad as a hatter.

bend (bɛnd), *v.* Forms: *Pa. t.* 1-3 **bende**, 4-6 **bend**, 4-5 **bente**, 3- **bent**, 6- **bended.** *Pa. pple.* 1 **bended**, 4-5 **y-**, **i-**, **ye-bent**, 4-6 **bente**, 6 **y-**, **i-bente**, **bende**, 4- **bended**, **bent.** [OE. *bęndan*, prob. identical with ON. *benda* 'to join, strain, strive, bend.' (The rare MHG. *benden* 'to fetter' is perhaps of independent formation.) OTeut. **bandjan*, f. *bandjâ-* 'string, band,' in OE. *bęnd.* In OE. used only in the senses 'to restrain with a bond, fetter, confine,' and 'to bend a bow,' orig. 'to hold in restraint or confine with the string.' From the latter by transference of the word to the bowed or curved condition of a bent bow, came the now main sense of 'to bow, curve, or crook.' Cf. the partly parallel history of F. *bander*, OF. *bender* (= Pr. and It. *bendare*, *bandare*, Sp. and Pg. *vendar*, *bandar*).]

Gen. sign. I. To fasten or constrain with a 'bend' or bond; to confine, fetter. *spec.* To constrain a bow with the string (hence, to wind up a cross-bow, cock a pistol); to fasten ropes, sails to the yards, horses to a vehicle. Hence arise two lines of development; II. To bow or curve, deflect, inflect, bow oneself, stoop, submit, yield; III. To direct or level a weapon, to aim, bring to bear, bring one's force or energies to bear. By blending of these; IV. To direct or turn one's steps, oneself, one's mind, eyes, ears, in any specified direction.

I. To bind, to constrain, to make fast.

†**1.** *trans.* To put in bonds, to fetter. *Obs.*

1036 *O.E. Chron.* (MS. C.) Sume hi man bende.

2. *spec.* **a.** To constrain or bring into tension by a string (a bow, an arbalest, a catapult, etc.) Formerly also ***bend up***; = L. *tendere.* In later times associated with the curved shape into which the bow is brought; = L. *flectere.* (Hence branch II.)

c **1000** *Ags. Ps.* vii. 13 He bende his boȝan, se is nu ȝearo to sceotanne. **1297** R. GLOUC. 377 So styf man he was in harmes, in Ssoldren, & in lende, þat vnneþe eny man myȝte hys bowe bende. *Ibid.* 536 Arblastes sone & ginnes withoute me bende. **1375** BARBOUR *Bruce* XVII. 682 The Engynour than deliuerly Gert bend the gyne in full gret hy. *a* **1400** *Octovian* 1495 And they withoute gynnes bente, And greet stones to hem sente. *c* **1400** *Destr. Troy* XXIII. 9475 Paris bend vp his bow with his big arme. *c* **1440** *Promp. Parv.* 30 Bende bowys, *tendo.* *c* **1500** *Rob. Hood* (Ritson) I. i. 1266 Sone there were good bowes ibent. **1599** GREENE *George a G.* (1861) 264 Bend up your bows, and see your strings be tight. **1697** DRYDEN *Virg. Georg.* II. 774 The Groom his Fellow-Groom at Buts defies; And bends his Bow, and levels with his Eyes. **1870** BRYANT *Homer* I. II. 71 Philoctetes, A warrior skilled to bend the bow.

†**b.** Transferred to the harquebus, pistol, etc. when these took the place of the bow and arbalest; perhaps, as Littré suggests in regard to

the similar use of Fr. *bander*, with special reference to the old form of lock which had to be wound up like a clock: To cock. *Obs.* (Hence branch III.)

1633 T. STAFFORD *Pac. Hib.* vi. (1821) 82 The Pistoll bent, both heart and hand, ready to doe the deed.

c. *fig.*

1611 BIBLE *Jer.* ix. 3 And they bend their tongue like their bow for lies.

3. *fig.* To strain, brace, tighten, wind up, bring into tension (like a strung bow or wound up harquebus). *refl.* To strain every nerve, brace or wind oneself up, nerve oneself; = Fr. *se bander*. *Obs.* or *arch.* Also ***bend up***: cf. 2.

c **1380** *Sir Ferumb.* 545 Wiþ þat þe Sarsyn þat was þor: wax wroþ on his herte & bente hym brymly as a bor. *a* **1529** SKELTON *Agst. Garnesche* 41 Boldly bend you to batell, and buske yourself to save. *c* **1565** R. LINDSAY *Chron. Scot.* (1814) 79 Nothing effeired of this disadvantage, bot rather bendit up, and kindled thereat, [he] rushed forward upon Craigiewallace. **1599** SHAKS. *Hen. V*, III. i. 16 Now set the Teeth..Hold hard the Breath, and bend vp euery Spirit To his full height. **1605** —— *Macb.* I. vii. 79, I am settled, and bend up Each corporal agent to this terrible feat. **1816** SCOTT *Old Mort.* vii, Her whole mind apparently bent up to the solemn interview.

4. *Naut.* To tie, fasten on, make fast (cf. BEND *sb.*[1] 3): e.g. ***to bend a rope. to bend the cable***: to fasten it to the ring of the anchor. ***to bend a sail***: 'to extend or make it fast to its proper yard or stay' (Adm. Smyth).

1399 *Rich. Redeless* IV. 72 They bente on a bonet, and bare a topte saile Affor the wynde ffresshely, to make a good ffare. *c* **1440** *Morte Arth.* (Roxb.) 34 A clothe that ouer the bote was bente Sir Gawayne lyfte vp and wente in bayne. **1626** CAPT. SMITH *Accid. Yng. Seamen* 16 Bend your cables to your Anchors. **1793** SMEATON *Edystone L.* §262 We concluded..to bend our sails (which had indeed been all unbent and stowed down in the hold for the summer) and try to gain Plymouth Sound. **1833** MARRYAT *P. Simple* xv, He desired Mr. Falcon to get new sails up and bend them. **1867** SMYTH *Sailor's Wd.-Bk.*, *Bending the Cable*, the operation of clinching, or tying the cable to the ring of its anchor. *Ibid. Bending* ropes is to join them together with a bowline knot, and then make their own ends fast upon themselves.

†**5.** To harness the horses to (a cart or other vehicle); to yoke. *Obs.* (Cf. Ger. and Du. *spannen* to stretch, to bend a bow, to yoke a vehicle. See also BIND in this sense.)

1513 DOUGLAS *Æneis* XII. v. 169 Sum brydillis stedis, and cartis vp dyd bend. **1535** COVERDALE *Gen.* xlvi. 29 Then Joseph bended his charett fast [Vulgate *juncto curru*; WYCLIF, Joseph ioyned his chare; **1611** made ready], and wente vp to mete Israel his father.

II. To bring into the shape or direction of a bent bow. **Of the shape of a thing.*

6. *trans.* **a.** To put or bring into the shape of a bow; to arch. *Obs.* exc. as a specific sense of 7.

c **1320** *Cast. Loue* 743 For heuene-bouwe is abouten i-bent, Wiþ alle þe hewes þat him beþ i-sent. **1382** WYCLIF *Isa.* li. 13 The Lord thi shapere, that bente heuenes, and foundide the erthe. **1483** *Cath. Angl.* 27/1 To bend, *arcuare.* **1655** VAUGHAN *Silex Scint.* (1858) 50 Who gave the clouds so brave a bow, Who bent the spheres. [**1839** BAILEY *Festus* x, Who bendst the Heavens before thee like a bow.]

b. ***to bend the brows***: (*orig.*) to arch the eyebrows; (*later*) to wrinkle or knit the brow; to frown, scowl. Cf. BENT.

a **1300** in Wright *Lyric P.* 34 (Mätz.) Heo hath browes bend an heh. *c* **1340** *Gaw. & Gr. Knt.* 305 He..Bende his bresed broȝez. **1387** TREVISA *Higden* (1865) I. 9 (Mätz.) Now men..wolde..whette her tunges and bende hire browes. **1530** PALSGR. 448/2 Thou bendest thy browes upon me as thou woldest eate me. **1559** *Myrr. Mag., Dk. Suffolk* xvii, Fortune can both bend and smothe her browe. **1631** GOUGE *God's Arrows* I. §41. 66 Passion will soone manifest it selfe..by bending his browes. **1774** BLACKLOCK *Graham* I. xx, In vain that rage which bends thy brow. [Cf. **1593** SHAKS. *Rich. II*, II. i. 170 Or bend one wrinckle on my Soueraigne's face.]

7. a. To constrain (anything straight) into any kind of arched or angular shape; to stretch out of the straight; to bow, curve, crook, inflect. Usually said of things linear, but also of surfaces, to dint. 'Bend' is not said of flaccid things, such as cotton, cloth, paper, which are 'folded'; but only of such as possess some rigidity, as a card, wood, metal, gristle; or of rigid things having joints, as the arm or backbone. Now the main sense.

1393 GOWER *Conf.* II. 247 On knees down bent. **1415** *Pol. Poems* (1859) II. 125 His basonet to his brayn was bent. *c* **1435** *Torr. Port.* 2590 No man..That myght make Torent to bowe, Ne his bak to bend. **1584** LYLY *Campaspe* v. i, To bend his body every way, and his mind no way. **1593** SHAKS. *Rich. II*, v. iii. 98 *Aum.* Vnto my mothers prayres, I bend my knee. *Yorke.* Against them both, my true ioynts bended be. **1597** GERARD *Herbal* III. xlii. (1633) 1357 Branches..so easie to be bent or bowed, that hereof they make Hoops. **1667** MILTON *P.L.* I. 616 Their doubled ranks they bend From wing to wing, and half enclose him round. **1751** DESAGULIERS *Fires Impr.* 19 A Tube..bended in the manner of a Syphon. *a* **1776** J. FERGUSON *Astron.* (1803) 111 Take about seven feet of strong wire, and bend it into a circular form. **1813** BYRON *Giaour* 68 He who hath bent him o'er the dead. **1836** DICKENS *Sk. Boz* iv. (C.D. ed.) 39 His form is bent by age.

b. To apply the same kind of action to alter curvature in any way, e.g. to straighten what is crooked.

1616 R. C. *Times' Whistle* (1871) 125 The tree growing crooked, if you'l have it mended, Whilst that it is a twigg it must be bended. **1674** PETTY *Disc. bef. R. Soc.* 2, I haue therefore, to streighten this crooked stick, bent it..the quite contrary way.

c. To make (a thing fixed at one end) curve over for the time from the erect position.

1681 CHETHAM *Angler's Vade-m.* i. §9 The Yew, though much bended, will quickly return to its former standing. **1692** R. LESTRANGE *Fables* 215 (1708) I. 233 The Oak was stubborn and chose rather to Break than to Bend. **1832** A. CUNNINGHAM *Song* 'A Wet Sheet', A wind that follows fast ..And bends the gallant mast. **1885** *Truth* 28 May 848/2 The poplars are bent by the rising wind.

8. *intr.* **a.** To assume or receive a curved form, or a shape in which one part is inclined at an angle to the other.

1398 TREVISA *Barth. De P.R.* VI. iv. (1495) 191 For tendernes the lymmes of the chylde maye..bowe and bende and take dyuers shapes. **1577** GASCOIGNE in Farr's *S.P.* (1845) I. 37 The Rainbowe bending in the skie, Bedeckte with sundrye hewes. **1815** *Encycl. Brit.* (ed. 5) VIII. 436 Their knees..bend so, that they are apt to trip and stumble. **1816** J. WILSON *City of Plague* I. i. 30 No knee This day.. hath bent before its altar.

b. To curve over from the erect position. (Usually said of things that recover their position when the bending force is withdrawn.)

c **1374** CHAUCER *Troylus* II. 1378 Thogh she bende, yet she stont a-rote. *a* **1593** H. SMITH *Wks.* (1867) II. 90 A house bending to fall. **1697** DRYDEN *Virg. Georg.* III. 311 The waving Harvest bends beneath his Blast. **1751** JOHNSON *Rambl.* No. 144 ¶8 The trees that bend to the tempest erect themselves again when its force is past. **1753** HERVEY *Medit.* II. 33 The knotty Oaks bend before the Blast.

9. *spec.* **a.** Of persons: To bend the body, to stoop; to assume a bent or stooping posture. ***to bend over*** (prep.), i.e. with attention. ***to bend over*** (adv.): to put oneself into position to receive a beating; also as *v. trans.* ***to bend over backwards***: see BACKWARDS *adv.* A.

c **1374** CHAUCER *Anel. & Arc.* 186 Hir daunger made him boothe bowe and beende. **1599** SHAKS. *Much Ado* v. i. 39, I vvould bend vnder anie heauie vvaight. **1667** MILTON *P.L.* IV. 462 A Shape within the watry gleam appeerd, Bending to look on me. **1727** SWIFT *Gulliver* II. viii. 174 One of the servants opening the door, I bent down to go in. **1831** CARLYLE *Sart. Res.* I. xi, The sooty smith bends over his anvil. **1850** LYTTON *My Novel* VI. vi, He bent down and kissed her cheek. **1889** in BARRÈRE & LELAND *Dict. Slang* I. 107/2, Bend over. **1946** B. MARSHALL *George Brown's Schooldays* ii. 6 They make you bend over again and the second time they often draw blood. *Ibid.* vii. 36 'Bend him over,' the Bruiser order[ed]. He took a great run and smote the tight little bottom mightily. **1948** C. DAY LEWIS *Otterb. Incident* iii. 24 He doesn't offer to bend over when one of *us* is going to be beaten. **1960** BETJEMAN *Summoned by Bells* v. 49 Bravely I answered, 'Please, sir, it was me.' 'All right. Bend over.'

b. To stoop down as from a height.

1839 SIR R. GRANT *Hymn* 'Saviour, when in dust to Thee' i, Bending from Thy throne on high, Hear our solemn Litany! **1853** MAURICE *Theol. Ess.* vi. 108 We want to see absolute Goodness and Truth. We want to know whether they can bend to meet us.

c. *esp.* To bend the body in submission or reverence; to bow (*unto, to, before, towards*).

a **1586** SYDNEY in Farr's *Sel. P.* I. 63 The desert-dwellers at his beck shall bend. **1611** BIBLE *Isa.* lx. 14 The sonnes also of them that afflicted thee, shall come bending vnto thee. **1648** MILTON *Psalm* lxxxi. 62 Who hate the Lord should then be fain To bow to him and bend. **1667** —— *P.L.* II. 477 Towards him they bend. **1763** CHURCHILL *Poems* I. 72 Here let me bend, great Dryden, at thy shrine. **1813** SCOTT *Rokeby* IV. xxx, Their chief to Wilfrid bended low. **1850** ROBERTSON *Serm.* Ser. II. ii. (1864) 24 Science bending before the Child, becoming childlike.

d. ***to catch*** (a person) ***bending***: to catch (someone) at a disadvantage. *colloq.*

1910 WODEHOUSE *Psmith in City* xviii. 163 If any tactless person were to publish those..speeches..our revered chief would be more or less caught bending..as regards his chances of getting in as Unionist candidate at Kenningford. **1938** —— *Code of Woosters* iv. 97 You'll get the poor bird unfrocked... It's something they do to parsons when they catch them bending. **1967** A. WILSON *No Laughing Matter* II. 139 He then goes off singing, 'My word, if I catch you bending, my word, if I catch you bending.'

10. *fig.* To submit, to bow; to yield, give way *to*; to prove pliant, tractable, or subservient.

? *a* **1400** *Cursor M.* 1584 (Fairfax MS.) He wende þat alle sulde til his wil bende. **1644** QUARLES *Judgm. & Mercy* 146 Whose leaden souls are taught by stupid reason to stand bent at every wrong. **1723** SHEFFIELD (Dk. Buckhm.) *Wks.* 1753 I. 9 Under this law both kings and kingdoms bend. **1763** J. BROWN *Poetry & Mus.* §12. 207 Well attested Facts are stubborn Things, and will not bend to general Affirmations. **1823** J. BADCOCK *Dom. Amusem.* 92 If any excessive paroxysms do not immediately bend before it. **1841** MACAULAY *Let.* in Trevelyan *Life* (1876) II. ix. 108 All considerations as to dignity of style ought to bend to his consideration.

11. *trans.* To cause (a person, the temper, spirit, mind, or will) to bow, stoop, incline, or relent.

1538 STARKEY *England* 24 Bend your selfe to that to the wych you are borne. **1583** STANYHURST *Aeneis* II. (Arb.) 65 Yf that prayer annye the bendeth. **1652** L. S. *People's Lib.* i. 2 Seeing he will not be bended by reason. **1848** MACAULAY *Hist. Eng.* II. 331 The spirit of the rustic gentry was not to be bent. **1872** FREEMAN *Norm. Conq.* (1876) IV. xviii. 156 The sight in no way bent the hearts of the men of Exeter. **1877** MRS. OLIPHANT *Makers Flor.* xv. 367 To ask pardon, no doubt a hard thing to bend his mind to.

12. a. ***to bend the head*** or ***face***: to lower it or direct it downwards, by bending the neck; to bow the head.

a **1652** J. SMITH *Sel. Disc.* i. 6 With their faces bended downwards. **1697** DRYDEN *Virg. Georg.* IV. 740 Trees bent their Heads to hear him. *c* **1720** S. WESLEY *Hymn of Eupolis* 102 Bend your heads, in homage bend. **1860** TYNDALL *Glac.* I. §3. 29 He took my hand and, silently bending down his head, kissed it.

b. *intr.* (for *refl.*) Predicated of the head.

1872 GEO. ELIOT in Cross *Life* III. 169 The sight of the dull faces bending round the gaming tables. **1875** MISS THACKERAY *Miss Angel* xxi. 195 The heads bend in long line.

** *Of the direction in which a thing lies.*

13. *trans.* To turn away from the straight line (without reference to the curve imparted); to incline in any direction; to deflect, turn.

1513 DOUGLAS *Æneis* IX. vi. 23 The cartis stand with lymowris bendyt strek. **1563** HYLL *Arte Garden.* (1593) 155 [They] will in the next morrow, bee turned or bended another way. **1661** LOVELL *Hist. Anim. & Min.* Introd., The foremost longest [legges] are bended forewards; but those that leap..are bended backward. **1877** PROCTOR *Spectroscope* i. 11 The ray is again bent from the perpendicular.

fig. **1882** PEBODY *Eng. Jrnlism.* xvi. 123 He used generally to bend conversation in such way as to avoid coming into dispute with his companions.

14. *intr.* **a.** To have a direction away from the straight line, to incline in any direction, to trend.

1572 MASCAL *Govt. Cattle* (1627) 255 His groyne and snout short, and beinding backeward. **1600** HAKLUYT *Voy.* (1810) III. 216 The Island..bending from him full West. **1601** HOLLAND *Pliny* I. 117 That mountaine of the one side bendeth downe toward Euxinus. **1609** BIBLE (Douay) *1 Sam.* xx. 41 David rose out of his place which did bend to the South. **1730** A. GORDON *Maffei's Amphith.* 267 Spikes.. which stretched forward into the Arena, and..bended towards it. **1858** LONGF. *Discov. North Cape* xviii, And now the land..Bent southward suddenly.

†**b.** *fig.* To tend. *Obs.*

1579 TOMSON *Calvin's Serm. Tim.* 641/1 These three bend (as it were) to one, to wit, the riche men must do good, and part with their goodes to other, and giue willingly.

15. *trans.* (*fig.*) To turn aside or pervert from the right purpose or use; to twist, wrest. *spec.* in mod. *slang*: to use for 'crooked' or wrongful purposes; to steal; to 'throw' (a contest, etc.).

a **1555** LATIMER *Serm. & Rem.* (1845) 332 Forasmuch as I have heard, *Ecce vobiscum sum*..bended to corroborate the same. **1562** COOPER *Answ. Def. Truth* (1850) 91 Their successors, by little and little, bent the same name unto the action and celebration of the Sacrament.

1864 O. W. NORTON *Army Lett.* (1903) 242 Perhaps you think it bending the Sabbath to build while I should be at church. **1930** *Amer. Mercury* XXI. 454/2 We bend a boat to hist the hooch. **1958** *Observer* 30 Nov. 13/8 There are honest landladies in districts like Victoria who let a flat to someone they think is an ordinary girl, who then proceeds to 'bend' it: uses it for prostitution. **1960** *Sunday Express* 16 Oct. 1/7 Watford players shared £110 given to them by the Brighton players to 'bend' a home and away game with them.

†**16. a.** *trans.* To incline, dispose in mind; mostly in *pass.* to be inclined or disposed *to, towards*; to be prone, liable, ready; to be addicted, given. *Obs.*

1538 STARKEY *England* 78 Thys idulnes and vanyte, to the wych the most parte of our pepul ys much gyven and bent. **1579** E. K. in Spenser's *Sheph. Cal.* Apr. 5 *Gloss.*, Aprill.. is most bent to showres. **1607** TOPSELL *Serpents* 72 There is not one of them so ill bent, so malapertly sawcy, and impudently shamelesse. **1708** SWIFT *Sacr. Test* Wks. 1755 II. I. 124, I am hugely bent to believe, that whenever you concern yourselves in our affairs, it is certainly for our good. **1749** FIELDING *Tom Jones* VII. xi, Seemed bent to extenuate.

†**b.** *intr.* To incline, lean, in mind or conduct.

1567 *Triall Treas.* (1850) 16 He that bendeth to folowe his own inclination. **1577** HOLINSHED *Chron.* III. 1029/2 Although Ket bent to all vngratiousnes.

III. To direct, aim (as a bow bent for shooting).

Cf. Jer. li. 3 Against him that bendeth let the archer bend his bow.

†**17. a.** *trans.* To direct, turn, aim, level, bring to bear (cannon, forces, etc.) *against, upon, at. Obs.*

1530 PALSGR. 448/1 They bended agaynst the castell ten courtaultes and fyftene serpentynes. **1577** HOLINSHED *Chron.* III. 1095/2 They bent their ordinance against the gate. **1595** SHAKS. *John* II. i. 37 Our cannon shall be bent Against the browes of this resisting towne. **1649** CROMWELL in Carlyle *Lett.* cvii. (1871) II. 163 They bent their guns at the frigate. **1801** SCOTT *Cadyow Castle* xxxv, With hackbut bent, my secret stand Dark as the purposed deed I chose.

†**b.** To aim, couch, direct (a spear or sword).

1591 SPENSER *Virg. Gnat.* lii, Each doth against the others bodie bend His cursed steele. **1596** —— *F.Q.* I. iii. 34 So bent his speare and spurd his horse with yron heele. **1594** SHAKS. *Rich. III*, I. ii. 95 Thy murd'rous Faulchion..The which thou once didd'st bend against her brest.

†**c.** *fig.* To direct (hostile action or words) *against, on,* (prayers) to heaven, etc. *Obs.*

1577 HANMER *Anc. Eccl. Hist.* (1619) 96 The persecution ..was so vehemently bent against him. **1605** SHAKS. *Lear* II. i. 48 The Gods 'Gainst Paricides did all the thunder bend. **1653** CROMWELL *Lett. & Sp.* (Carl.) III. 219, I shall rather bend my prayers for you. **1681** E. SCLATER *Serm. Putney* 12 All their Subtlety and Polity must be bent against them.

†**d.** *intr.* (for *refl.*) *Obs.*

a **1636** MILTON *Arcades* 6 This, this is she To whom our vows and wishes bend.

18. a. *trans.* To direct, apply, or bring to bear strenuously (one's mind, energies, etc.) *on, upon.*

c **1510** MORE *Picus* Wks. (1557) 30 A very louer beleueth in his mynde, On whom so euer he hath his heart Ibente, That in that person menne maye nothing finde, But honorable. **1577** HARRISON *England* II. iii. (1877) 79 If they bend their minds to the knowledge of the same. **1605** BACON *Adv. Learn.* I. v. §10 The scope..whereunto they bend their endeavours. **1796** BURKE *Regic. Peace* Wks. 1842 II. 313 They bent..their designs and efforts to revive the old French party. **1876** GREEN *Short Hist.* ii. §8 (1882) 102 A sovereign who bent the whole force of his mind to hold together an Empire.

b. *refl.* To direct or apply *oneself. rare.*

1591 LOK in Farr's *S.P.* (1845) I. 140 Whilst in the garden of this earthly soile Myself to solace and to bath I bend. **1593** BILSON *Govt. Christ's Ch.* 362 Many Bishops bent themselves to alter the Emperours minde. **1669** BUNYAN *Holy Citie* 56 If any shall..bend themselves to disappoint the designs of the Eternal God. **1850** THACKERAY *Pendennis* lxxi, To the completion of which he bent himself with all his might.

c. *intr.* (for *refl.*)

1697 DRYDEN *Virg. Georg.* iii. 285 If to the Warlike Steed thy Studies bend, Or for the Prize in Chariots to contend. **1856** KANE *Arct. Exp.* II. xxvi. 258 Bending to our oars as the water opened [we] reached the shore.

19. *to be bent*: to be intent, determined, resolved. Const. *on* or *upon* (*to, for,* obs.) an object or action; also (arch.) *to do* (something).

c **1400** *Cov. Myst.* (1841) 3 Now be we bent In this pagent the trewthe to telle. **1561** T. NORTON *Calvin's Inst.* I. 66 To bring him to be more hedefully bent to make amendes. **1626** BACON *New Atl.* 15 And was only bent to make his Kingdom and People happy. **1762** GOLDSM. *Cit. W.* vi. (1837) 26 The youth seems obstinately bent on finding you out. *a* **1859** DE QUINCEY *Wks.* XIII. 49 He is..bent upon confusing us; and I am bent upon preventing him. **1868** MORRIS *Earthly Par.* II. (1870) 173 Like my fathers, bent to gather fame. **1868** FREEMAN *Norm. Conq.* (1876) II. vii. 158 A project on which the King was fully bent.

IV. Figurative uses in which 'direct, aim,' and 'bow, deflect, turn,' are combined.

20. a. *intr.* To direct oneself, proceed, turn. *arch.*

1399 LANGL. *Rich. Redeless* III. 76 þei..burnisched her beekis, and bent to-him-wardis And ffolowid him ffersly. *c* **1460** *Towneley Myst.* 303 (Mätz.) To hir buxumly I red that we bende. **1601** SHAKS. *All's Well* III. ii. 57 Thence we came: And..Thither we bend againe. **1698** DRYDEN *Æneid* VI. 438 Why to the Shore the thronging people bent. **1713** ADDISON *Cato* III. ii. 124 But see! My brother Marcus bends this way! **1813** BYRON *Corsair* I. xvii, He..Down to the cabin with Gonsalvo bends.

b. *trans.* To direct or turn (one's steps, course, way, etc.).

1579 GOSSON *Sch. Abuse* (Arb.) 19 Hee knewe not which way to bende his pace. **1583** STANYHURST *Æneis* I. (Arb.) 24 Oure course tward Italye bending. **1667** MILTON *P.L.* III. 573 Thither his course he bends Through the calm Firmament. **1718** POPE *Iliad* II. 64 To the fleet Atrides bends his way. **1821** JOANNA BAILLIE *Wallace* xxii, And to the wild woods bent his speed. **1883** M. CRAWFORD *Mr. Isaacs* xii. 268 Thither we all three bent our steps.

c. *trans.* To direct (anything led, driven, or carried). *arch.*

1583 STANYHURST *Æneis* II. (Arb.) 47 To Troy ward when first you bended a nauye. **1594** SHAKS. *Rich. III*, IV. v. 14 Many other of great name and worth: And towards London do they bend their power. **1746** COLLINS *Ode to Peace*, To Britain bent his iron Car.

21. *trans.* To direct, turn, or incline (the eyes, or ears), in the direction of anything seen or heard.

1581 J. BELL *Haddon's Answ. Osor.* 314 b, The pearcyng light of the Sunne..doth blinde the sight, if the eyes be over much bente thereunto. **1586** *Let. Earle Leycester* 31, I neuer..bent my eares to credite a tale that first was tolde mee. **1648** MILTON *Psalm* lxxxviii. 8 And to my cries..Thine ear with favor bend. *a* **1795** SOUTHEY *Joan of Arc* IV. 62 Every eye on her was bent. **1833** HT. MARTINEAU *Manch. Strike* iv. 54 His eyes bent on the ground in deep thought.

V. Senses of doubtful origin.

†**22.** *intr.* 'To spring, to bound.' *Sc. Obs.* [Perh. related to 3, or 17.]

c **1530** LYNDESAY is referred to by Jamieson.

23. 'To drink hard; a cant term' (Jamieson). [Perh. 'to pull, strain' in reference to pulling or straining a bow (cf. 3); or 'to ply, apply oneself to' (cf. 18).] *trans.* and *intr.*

a **1758** A. RAMSAY *Poems* (1800) I. 215 (JAM.) Braw tippony..Which we with greed Bended, as fast as she could brew. *Ibid.* ii. 73 (JAM.) To bend wi' ye, and spend wi' ye, An evening, and gaffaw. [**1860** RAMSAY *Remin.* Ser. I. (ed. 7) 47 Bend weel to the Madeira at dinner, for here ye'll get little o't after. Cf. 18 b.]

bendable ('bɛndəb(ə)l), *a.* [f. prec. + -ABLE.] Capable of being bent; flexible.

1611 COTGR., *Ployable*, pliable, bowable, bendable. **1642** R. CARPENTER *Experience* III. 47 The chiefe acts of nature in the soule are, of themselves, inclinable and bendable to Grace. **1755** in JOHNSON and in mod. Dicts.

Ben Day (bɛn deɪ). *U.S.* Applied *attrib.* to a process in photo-engraving developed by Benjamin Day (1838–1916), a New York printer. (See quot. 1949.)

1912 F. WEITENKAMPF *Amer. Graphic Art* 217 The 'Ben Day' process of quick mechanical production of tints by 'rapid shading mediums' has also been a time-saver. **1949** *Manual of Style* (Chicago Univ. Press) 245 *Ben Day Process*, an engraving process for producing a variety of shaded tints by the use of gelatin films, particularly in connection with line (zinc) etchings.

†'**bended**, *a. Obs.* [f. BEND *sb.*[2]] Striped or banded; in *Her.* having a bend or bends; = BENDY *a.*.

c **1400** MAUNDEV. 276 Five saphires bended with gold. *c* **1430** *Syr Gener.* 4538 Hou he with the bended sheld Smote the othre thurgh the bodie. **1572** BOSSEWELL *Armorie* II. 85 b, One greate difference betwene Armes Bended, and these Armes..For in Armes Bendee the colours contained in the shielde are equally diuided.

bended ('bɛndɪd), *ppl. a.* The original pa. pple. of BEND *v.*, superseded in ME. by *bend, bent,* but used again, from 14th c. onwards, as a longer form of BENT (q.v. for the sense); it is now semi-archaic, and used chiefly in ***on bended knees***, etc.

1398 TREVISA *Barth. De P.R.* XVIII. iii. (1495) 749 The hornes of a ramme ben crokyd and bended as a rounde shell. **1599** SHAKS. *Hen. V*, v. Chor. 18 His bruised Helmet, and his bended Sword. **1660** BLOUNT *Boscobel* 55 And now on my bended knees, let me joyfully congratulate His restored Majesty. *c* **1790** IMISON *Sch. Arts* I. 73 Fix the bended glass-pipe C air-tight into the bottle D. **1810** SCOTT *Lady of L.* v. ix, Bonnets and spears and bended bows. **1837** SIR F. PALGRAVE *Merch. & Friar* iv. (1844) 176 'Gracious Sovereign,' replied the Chancellor, dropping off the Woolsack upon his bended knees.

†'**bendel.** *Obs.* [a. OF. *bendel, bandel,* dim. of *bende, bande*: cf. BANDEAU, BANDEL. (It is only accidentally that this coincides in form and sense with mod.G. *bendel* a fillet, OHG. *bendil, bentil, pentil,* and ON. *bendill* a small cord.)]

1. A little band or scarf; a fillet, a ribbon.

1483 CAXTON *Gold. Leg.* 244/1 She wyped it..with a bendel of sylke. **1537** *Act Hen. VIII* in Planché *Brit. Cost.* (1834) 365 Or use or weare any shirt, smock, kurchar, bendel, ankerchour, mocket or linen cappe, etc.

2. *Her.* A little bend; = BENDLET.

c **1325** *Coer de L.* 2964 And off asur a fayr bendel. **1486** *Bk. St. Albans, Her.* E j b, Littill bendys..be calde bendyllys to the differans of grete bendys.

bender ('bɛndə(r)). [f. BEND *v.* + -ER[1].] He who or that which bends.

1. An instrument for bending; a pair of pliers.

1496 *Bk. St. Albans, Fysshynge* 14 For makynge your hokis..a bender, a payr of longe and smalle tongys. **1598** FLORIO, *Piegatoie*, a paire of benders that goldsmithes vse, called bowing pincers or plyers. **1833** RENNIE *Alph. Angling* 69 The artist, of [fish-hooks] requires a hammer, a knife, a pair of pincers..a bender.

†**2.** A mechanical contrivance for bending, 'drawing up,' or setting cross-bows. *Obs.*

1684 R. WALLER *Nat. Exper.* 146 Cros-bows that are bent with a Bender.

3. One who bends.

1596 SPENSER *F.Q.* I. i. 9 The eugh, obedient to the benders will. **1833** MEDWIN in *Fraser's Mag.* VII. 18 He..leads on the benders of the bow.

4. †**a.** A flexor muscle. *Obs.*

1615 CROOKE *Body of Man* 791 This muscle with the second and third benders of the thumb. **1668** CULPEPPER & COLE *Barthol. Anat.* IV. viii. 165 Two Benders of the Cubit.

b. A leg or knee. *slang* (orig. *U.S.*).

1849 LONGF. *Kavanagh* xii, Young ladies are not allowed to cross their benders in school. **1925** A. S. M. HUTCHINSON *One Increasing Purpose* III. xi, They say family prayers there with the servants every night, all down on their benders.

5. †**a.** *Sc.* A hard drinker. *Obs.* (Cf. BEND *v.* 23.)

1728 RAMSAY *Poems* (1848) III. 162 Now lend your lugs, ye benders fine, Wha ken the benefit of wine. **1810** TANNAHILL *Poems* (1846) 53 Or benders, blest your wizzens weetin'.

b. A bout of drinking; a riotous party. *slang* (orig. *U.S.*).

1846 D. CORCORAN *Pickings from Portfolio* 62, I was on an almighty big bender last night..and the way we *did* walk into the highly concentrated hard cider. **1887** J. HATTON *Old Ho. Sandwich* I. II. iv. 82 The boss of Drummond's Gulch may be said to have begun his 'bender', as a bout of drunken dissipation was called in these regions. **1929** K. S. PRICHARD *Coonardoo* 7 And I've warned Paddy Hanson to look after Hughie if Sam does get on a bender. **1933** *Bulletin* (Sydney) 14 June 11/4 Being on a strenuous bender, he had forgotten to sign a cheque. **1951** WODEHOUSE *Old Reliable* iv. 64 Where's the harm in an occasional bender? Boys will be boys.

6. *slang.* A sixpence. (? Because it bends easily.)

1836 DICKENS *Sk. Boz* (1850) 68/2 'Niver mind the loss of two bob and a bender!' **1837** —— *Pickw.* xlii. (D.) 'Will you take three bob?' 'And a bender,' suggested the clerical gentleman. **1855** THACKERAY *Newcomes* xi, 'A half-crown, Honeyman? By cock and pye it is not worth a bender.'

7. A big or good specimen of its kind; a 'whopper', 'corker' (*s.w. dial.*).

1842 DANIEL *Bride of Scio* 190 (E.D.D.), Ma vice [= fist] es wat I kal a bendur. **1891** CHOPE *Dial. Hartland* s.v., 'A proper bender, an' no mistake!' **1895** KIPLING *Day's Work* (1898) 180 By Jove, it's a bender of a night.

bending ('bɛndɪŋ), *vbl. sb.*[1] [f. BEND *v.*]

†**1.** Drawing tight with a string, tension. *Obs.*

c **1440** *Promp. Parv.* 30 Bendynge of bowys, or oþer lyke, *tencio*.

2. a. Curving, crooking, flexure; bowing, inclination, deflection.

1398 TREVISA *Barth. De P.R.* VIII. xxx. (1495) 342 And yf the sonne beme..metyth wyth a body that puttyth and smytyth the lyghte ayenwarde, suche a smytynge and puttynge is callyd bendynge of the beme. **1593** SHAKS. *Rich. II*, III. iii. 73 Thus long haue we stood To watch the fearefull bending of thy knee. **1651** JER. TAYLOR *Course Serm.* I. ix. 117 Rent in sunder with trees returning from their violent bendings. **1662** GERBIER *Princ.* 19 To prevent the sinking and bending of their Walls. **1712** BUDGELL *Spect.* No. 277 ¶17 The various Leanings and Bendings of the Head. **1823** LAMB *Elia* Ser. I. i, That gentle bending of the body forwards.

fig. **1615** W. HULL *Mirr. Maiestie* 47 Prayer is a deuout bending of the minde to God.

b. *spec.* The curvature of a beam. So ***bending moment***, the moment tending to produce curvature in a beam; ***bending stress***, the stress that causes curvature in a bar, beam, etc.

1858 Bending moment [see MOMENT *sb.* 8 b]. **1876** *Encycl. Brit.* IV. 290/1 The moment of this couple must be equal to the moment of the couple tending to bend the beam at this section, or to what is called the bending moment. **1887** *Ibid.* XXII. 604/1 The strain produced by bending stress in a bar or beam. **1888** *Lockwood's Dict. Terms Mech. Engin.*, *Bending*, or *Flexure*, the curvature of a beam about its axis or central plane. **1961** C. C. T. BAKER *Dict. Math.* 29 The bending moment at any section of a beam is the couple which one part of a beam exerts on the other part at that section.

3. The place or part where such curving occurs; a curve, angle, corner; a bend; the spring of an arch or vault.

1523 FITZHERB. *Husb.* §95 A selander is in the bendynge of the legge behynde. **1665** MANLEY *Grotius' Low-C. Wars* 626 Not far from Harwarden are the bendings of the River. **1737** WHISTON *Josephus' Hist.* v. iv. §2 The wall..having its bending above the fountain.

4. *Naut.* The fastening with a 'bend' or knot.

1627 CAPT. SMITH *Seaman's Gram.* vii. 30 To tie two ropes or cables together is called bending. **1829** MARRYAT *F. Mildmay* v, The bending of the cable escaped my memory.

†**5.** The contrivance for drawing up a cross-bow; = BENDER 2. *Obs.*

1530 PALSGR. 197/2 Bendyng for a crosbowe, *bendage*.

6. (See quot.)

1816 C. JAMES *Mil. Dict.* 51/1 Bendings, in military and sea matters, are ropes, wood, &c. bent for several purposes.

7. The action or process of shaping wood, iron, or other material by pressure instead of by cutting or casting. Chiefly *attrib.* and *Comb.*: ***bending machine, rolls***; **bending cradle** (see quot. 1874); **bending form**, a kind of bench anvil used in bending steam, gas, and water pipes; **bending slab**, an iron floor upon which ships' frames are bent.

1874 THEARLE *Naval Archit.* 132 The 'bending cradle' is composed of a pair of stout iron vertical frames, between the bars of which transverse beams of iron, bent to the necessary curvature, are secured. *a* **1884** KNIGHT *Dict. Mech.* Suppl. 97/2 A French bending machine, for cart and wagon tires. **1888** *Lockwood's Dict. Terms Mech. Engin.*, *Bending Rolls*, heavy rollers of cast iron or steel set in strong standards, and used either for the straightening of crooked plates or for bending them into arcs of circles or into complete cylinders. *Ibid.*, *Straightening machine*,..a machine in which channel, angle, and bar iron are straightened or bent, in boiler and smiths' shops, by squeezing... Since it will bend as well as straighten it is also called a bending machine. **1890** W. J. GORDON *Foundry* 60 The 'bending-slab'—a pavement of square masses of iron,..large enough to take any frame required in the ship to be built.

8. *Horsemanship.* (See quot. 1891.)

1891 J. M. BROWN *Polo* 323 The 'bending' course is a capital institution, of which I believe the Earl of Harrington was the originator about eight years ago. Two lines of sticks should be set up 20 yards apart and parallel to each other. The sticks should be about 7 feet high and 8 yards apart... Then begin by cantering your pony up one side and down the other zigzagging between the posts. *Ibid.*, I may here remark that this 'bending' competition is the most invaluable practical test of a really good polo pony. **1900** *Daily News* 16 Mar. 3/4 The bending competition, in which the considerations of pace, precision, riding, and 'make' [of a pony] are joined in equal importance. **1922** *Times* 20 June 7/2 Both [polo ponies] being particularly handy at turning and bending.

†'**bending**, *vbl. sb.*[2] *Obs.* [? f. BEND *sb.*[2] + -ING[1].] Decoration with 'bends' or stripes.

c **1386** CHAUCER *Pers. T.* ¶343 Swandyng, palyng or bendyng, and semblable wast of cloth in vanite.

'**bending**, *ppl. a.* [f. BEND *v.* + -ING[2].] That bends (in various senses of the vb.); curving, curved, inclined, bowing; flexible, pliable, supple.

1567 MAPLET *Gr. Forest* 109 With hir bending bodie. **1571** NORTON & SACKV. *Gorboduc* I. i. (1847) 104 Their yet greene bending wittes. **1605** SHAKS. *Lear* IV. i. 76 A Cliffe, whose high and bending head Lookes fearfully on the confined Deepe. **1697** DRYDEN *Virg. Eclog.* x. 103 Bending Osiers into Baskets weav'd. —— *Georg.* III. 512 Some bending Valley. **1715** POPE *Iliad* IV. 555 To shape the circle of the bending wheel. **1810** SOUTHEY *Kehama* xv. xi, Behold her go..Along the bending sand.

'**bendingly**, *adv.* [f. prec. + -LY[2].] In a curving direction or attitude, obliquely.

1658 ROWLAND *Mouffet's Theat. Ins.* 1051 [Scorpions] which have seven or nine joints on their tails, are the most curst: many have but six, it strikes athwart and bendingly. **1839** *New Monthly Mag.* LV. 128 'Parson, say grace!' Millingham bendingly murmured three words.

bendlet ('bɛndlɪt). *Her.* Also 6 bendelet. [prob. f. earlier BENDEL + -ET[1] dim. But OF. had also *bendelette*, in *Bk. of St. Albans* transl. *bendil* (see BENDEL, also BANDLET, BANDELET).] A smaller bend, containing a sixth part of the field.

1572 BOSSEWELL *Armorie* 12 Bendelet. **1605** CAMDEN *Rem.* (1637) 224 Roger Clifford..for the bendelet tooke a fesse Geules. **1864** BOUTELL *Heraldry Hist. & Pop.* xiv. 155 They appear..to have cotised their own silver bend with the two bendlets.

†'**bendly**, *adv. Obs.* [f. BEND *sb.*[1], [2] + -LY[2].]

1. *Her.* Bend-wise.

1486 *Bk. St. Albans. Her.* D viij a, Ther be forsothe certan armys bendli barrit..for ij colouris are iunyt together in euery barre bendly.

2. (See quot.)

1552 HULOET, Bendly, or by bendes or handful.

†'**bendroll.** *Obs. Sc.* A variant of BANDEROL(E: here perhaps used in the sense of 'the strap of a musket,' one of the senses of F. *banderole*.

1598 *Sc. Acts, Jas. VI*, IV. 169/1 Or ells ane muscat, with forcat, bendrole, and heidpece. **1599** *Ibid.* —— 191/1 Or ellis ane muscat, with heid peice, foirchet, and band roll.

'**bendsome**, *a.* [f. BEND *v.* + -SOME.] Flexible.

1861 BARNES in *Macm. Mag.* June 134 Some softer or more brittle or bendsome substance.

'**bendwise** ('bɛndwaɪz), *adv. Her.* Also 7 -**waies**, 8- -**ways**. [f. BEND *sb.*[2] + -WISE.] In the position occupied by a bend on a shield; in the direction of a bend, diagonally.

1610 GUILLIM *Heraldry* II. vi. 63 Hee beareth Azure, a Pile waued, issuing out of the Dexter corner of the Escocheon Bendwaies, Or. **1727** CHAMBERS *Cycl.*, *Bendy*.. An escutcheon divided bend-wise. **1864** BOUTELL *Heraldry Hist. & Pop.* xviii. 289 Standards were also generally divided bend-wise into compartments by Motto-bands.

†'**bendwith.** *Herb. Obs.* [probably f. BEND *sb.*[1] + WITH: perh. another form of BINDWITH. The word in *Promp. Parv.* suggests the Sw. *benved* 'bone-wood,' expl. as 'dogberry, wild cornel,' and Icel. *beinviðir* a willow (*Salix arbuscula* Vigf.), the meaning of which is 'bone-withy.'] The name of a shrub of which the twigs are used to tie up fagots, etc. Identified by Bradley with the Way-faring Tree or Wild Guelder Rose.

c **1440** *Promp. Parv.* 31 Benwyttre [**1499** benewith tre]. **1727** BRADLEY *Fam. Dict.*, *Bendwith*, in Latin, Viburnum.. they make use of its Branches to tie Faggots with. **1783** AINSWORTH *Lat. Dict.* (Morell) I, Bendwith, *viburnum*.

bendy ('bɛndɪ), *a. Her.* [ad OF. *bendé*, mod.F. *bandé*: see BEND *sb.*[2]] Of a shield: Divided diagonally into an even number (usually six) of equal divisions, coloured alternately. **bendy-wavy**: when the bends or bendlets have wavy margins.

1486 *Bk. St. Albans, Her.* D viij a, He bereth barri bendy, of gowles and golde. **1610** GWILLIM *Displ. Heraldry* v. iii. (1660) 370 He beareth Bendy-wavie of six Argent and Azure. **1727** BRADLEY *Fam. Dict.*, *Bendy*, a Term in Blazonry for an Escutcheon being divided Bendways into an even Number of Partitions; but if they are odd, the Field must first be named, and then the Number of the Bends. **1766** PORNY *Heraldry* (1787) 69 When the Shield is filled with six Bendlets of metal and colour, it is called Bendy; but if the number is either more or less than six, they are to be blazoned by the name of Bendlets and their number specified. **1864** BOUTELL *Heraldry* viii. 36.

bendy ('bɛndɪ), *sb.* Also **bendee, bendi, bindy, banda.** [Hind. (Hindi) *bhindī.*] The plant *Hibiscus* (or *Abelmoschus*) *esculentus*, also the fruit of this plant. Also *attrib.* = OKRO.

1812 M. GRAHAM *Jrnl. Resid. India* 24 The *bendy*, called in the West Indies *okree*, is a pretty plant, resembling a dwarf holyhock. **1813** JAS. FORBES *Oriental Mem.* I. 32 The banda (hibiscus esculentus, Linn.) is a nutritious oriental vegetable. **1866** LINDLEY & MOORE *Treas. Bot.* 1135/1 *Tetrameles*... This tree is the Jungle-bendy of India, and the Weenong of Java. **1927** *Blackw. Mag.* Nov. 678/2 Flanking the western slopes..were the dense bendi scrubs.

bendy-tree. (See quot.)

1886 YULE & BURNELL *Hobson-Jobson*, *Bendy-tree*, this, according to Sir G. Birdwood, is the *Thespesia populnea*.

†**bene.** *Obs.* Forms: 1 bén, 2-4 bene, (6 ? beane). [OE. *bœn*, *bén*, cogn. with ON. *bón*, *bœn* (Sw., Da. *bön*):—OTeut. **bôni-z*; perh. from root *ba-* 'cry': see BAN.]

a. Prayer, petition, boon; *esp.* prayer to God.

c **1000** *Ags. Gosp.* Luke i. 13 þin bén ys ȝehyred. **1160** *Hatton G.* ibid., þin bene is ȝe-herd. *c* **1175** *Lamb. Hom.* 67 Hu maȝen heo bidden eni bene. *c* **1250** *Gen. & Ex.* 2511 Ðat mine bene ne be for-loren, wið ȝu ben mine bones boren. *a* **1300** *K. Horn* 508 Grante me a bene. **1340** *Ayenb.* 211 Mj bene bi ydiȝt beuore þe. [**1594** NASHE *Unfort. Trav.* 86 Then was the maid in my grandames beanes. **1807** WORDSW. *Force of Prayer* i, What is good for a bootless bene?]

b. *Comb.* **bene-day**, ? rogation-day (cf. OE. *béntíd*); **bene-tiðe, -tuðe** *sb.*, success in prayer; *adj.* (OE. *béntíðe, -týðe*) successful in prayer; **bene-rip** = BEDRIP.

c **1200** *Trin. Coll. Hom.* 27 We muȝen mid one worde þese þrie þing bidden, and ben bene tiðe. *Ibid.* 201 To ure drihten . þat he..ȝife us bene tuðe. **1499** *Promp. Parv.* 30/2 Beneday, *precare*.

bene, obs. f. BEAN *sb.*, BEEN, BEN; obs. infin. and 3 pl. of BE *v.*, and variant of BEIN.

beneaped (bɪ'ni:pt), *ppl. a. Naut.* [f. BE- *pref.* 7 + NEAP.] **a.** Of a ship: Left aground by the neap tide, and so lying beyond the reach of high water, until the tide flows higher.

1692 in *Capt. Smith's Seaman's Gram.* I. xvi. 80 A Ship is beneaped..when the water does not flow high enough to bring [it] off the ground, or out of a Dock, or over a Bar. **1868** *Exeter & Plymouth Gaz.* 13 Mar., The ship was beneaped. **1884** F. POLLOCK in *Eng. Illus. Mag.* Dec. 156 These [trawlers] are now and again 'beneaped' at low tides.

b. *fig.*

1913 T. HARDY *Places* in *Coll. Poems* (1930) 332 One there is..To whom to-day is beneaped and stale.

beneath (bɪ'ni:θ), *adv.* and *prep.* Forms: 1 **beniþan, -neoðan, -nyðan,** 2-3 **bi-neoðen, -neoþen, -neðen, noþen,** (*Orm.*) **-neþenn,** 3 **bi-neoðe, -neoþe, -neðe,** 3-4 **bi-neþe(n,** 4 **-nethen, by-neþen, -neathe, be-nyþe,** 4-5 **by-nethen, -neþe, beneþe,** 4-6 **bynethe,** 5 **byneithe, bineth,** 5-6 **by-, beneth(e,** 5- **beneath;** 8- **'neath.** [OE. *bi-niðan*, *be-neoðan*, f. *bi-* BE- + *niðan*, *neoðan* 'below, down,' orig. 'from below,' earlier *neoðane*, *neoðone*, = OS. *nithana*, OHG. *nidana*, MHG. *niden(e*, mod.G. *nieden*, f. OTeut. *niþar* 'lower, farther down, down': see NETHER + advb. ending *-ana*, originally expressing motion 'from.' The *be-* gave or emphasized the notion of 'where,' excluding that of 'whence' pertaining to the simple *niðan*. The modern *'neath* is abbreviated from *beneath*. Originally an adverb, but already in OE. construed with dative (of reference), as a prep.]

A. *adv.*

1. *gen.* In a low position relatively to some other place; in a lower position; low or lower down; downward; = BELOW *adv.* 1.

c **1205** LAY. 25610 Ofte wes þe drake buuen: And eft seoððen bineoþen. *a* **1225** *Ancr. R.* 390 Brod ase scheld buuen..and neruh bineoðen. *c* **1305** *St. Kenelm* 127 in *E.E.P.* (1862) 51 On of his beste freond..In þe grounde stod byneþe. *c* **1400** *Destr. Troy* XIII. 5529 A mon fro þe myddell vp, And fro the nauyll by-neithe, vne an abill horse. **1413** LYDG. *Pylgr. Sowle* IV. xxxiv. (1483) 82 As well of tho that ben bynethen as tho that ben aboue. **1602** SHAKS. *Ham.* I. iv. 78 And hears it [the sea] roar beneath. **1605** —— *Lear* IV. vi. 128 To the Girdle do the Gods inherit, beneath is all the Fiends. **1795** SOUTHEY *Joan of Arc* III. 298 Pure water in a font beneath reflects The many-colour'd rays.

†**b.** Lower on a written or printed page; = BELOW *adv.* 1 b. *Obs.*

854 *Chart. Æthelwulf* in *Cod. Dipl.* V. 106 Ðara naman her beneoðan awritene standað. **1668** CULPEPPER & COLE *Barthol. Anat.* I. xxvii. 64 Of which see other Anatomists.. and my father Bartholinus beneath.

2. With reference to certain understood points:

†**a.** Beneath the skies; in the world, on the earth. *Obs.* or *arch.*; expressed by BELOW *adv.* 2 a.

c **1250** *Gen. & Ex.* 9 Ðan sal him almightin luuen Her bineðen and..abuuen. **1340** HAMPOLE *Pr. Consc.* 5055 We synful..bynethe on þe erthe. **1382** WYCLIF *Ex.* xx. 4 In heuene aboue, and..in erthe benethe [so in **1611**]. *c* **1460** *Towneley Myst.* 183 Say youre prayers here by nethe. **1526** TINDALE *John* viii. 23 Ye are from beneth; I am from above. [**1875** BROWNING *Aristoph. Apol.* 106 Our world beneath Shows..grimly gross.]

b. Beneath the earth; in Hades, in hell.

1340 HAMPOLE *Pr. Consc.* 5408 Helle bynethen..Sal þan be open. **1611** BIBLE *Isa.* xiv. 9 Hell from beneath is mooued for thee. *a* **1736** YALDEN (J.) The dread abyss beneath, Hell's horrid mansions.

3. Directly below; underneath.

c **1250** *Gen. & Ex.* 4082 Hise hore bi-neðe and him abuuen. *a* **1300** *Cursor M.* 1681 þu sal bi-neþ en on þe side Mak a dor wit mesur wide. **1517** TORKINGTON *Pilgr.* (1884) 43 Whiche Ryft..appereth by nethe. **1596** SHAKS. *Merch. V.* IV. i. 186 It droppeth as the gentle rain from heaven Upon the place beneath. **1697** DRYDEN *Virg. Georg.* III. 43 High o'er the Gate..The Crowd shall Cæsar's Indian War behold; The Nile shall flow beneath. **1873** BROWNING *Red Cott. Night-c.* 1639 Shaggy eyebrows elevate With twinkling apprehension in each orb Beneath.

b. Under some covering or surface, underneath; underground, under the earth.

1297 R. GLOUC. 131 Lat delue vnder þe fundement, & þou schalt bineþe fynde A waterpol. **1388** WYCLIF *Job* xviii. 16 The rootis of hym be maad drie bynethe. *c* **1400** *Destr. Troy* v. 1609 The water..clensit by ocurse all þe clene Cite Of filth and of feum, throughe fletyng by nethe. **1611** BIBLE *Jer.* xxxi. 37 If..the foundations of the earth [can be] searched out beneath. **1697** DRYDEN *Virg. Georg.* III. 466 Spread with Straw, the bedding of thy Fold; With Fern beneath.

4. Lower down on a slope, or in the course of a river. *rare.* Now BELOW *adv.* 3.

1393 GOWER *Conf.* II. 161 On the mount of Parasie..And eke beneth in the valey. **1650** FULLER *Pisgah* II. 62 The stopping of the waters [of Jordan] above must necessarily command their defection beneath.

5. Down or lower in fortune, station, dignity, rank, or quality. *arch.*

c **1000** ÆLFRIC *Deut.* xxviii. 13 þu bist æfre bufan and na beniþan. *c* **1205** LAY. 9839 ȝif mi cun clembeð & bineoðen þe ibringeð. **1297** R. GLOUC. 258 An batayle at Elendone hii smyte..þe Kyng Bernulf was þere byneþe, & bynome al ys bost. *c* **1400** *Apol. Loll.* 53 þe pope, cardinalis, bischopis, & oþer prelats be neþe, are disciplis of anticrist. **1535** COVERDALE *Deut.* xxviii. 13 Thou shalt be aboue onely, and not benethe [WYCLIF, vndur; **1611** beneath]. **1606** SHAKS. *Tr. & Cr.* I. iii. 131 That next [is disdain'd] by him beneath.

B. (with object expressed) *prep.*

The prepositional use of *beneath* seems originally to have been introduced to express the general notion of 'lower than,' as distinguished from the specific sense of UNDER. But in process of time *beneath* was so largely used for *under*, that BELOW was laid hold of to express the more general idea. In ordinary spoken English, *under* and *below* now cover the whole field (*below* tending naturally to overlap the territory of *under*), leaving *beneath* more or less as a literary and slightly archaic equivalent of both (in some senses), but especially of *under*. The only senses in which *beneath* is preferred are 7 ('beneath contempt'), and fig. uses of 4 (e.g. 'to fall beneath the assaults of temptation').

†**1.** *gen.* In a position down from or lower than. *Obs.* or *arch.* Now expressed by BELOW *prep.* 1. †*beneath stair*: = below stairs.

a **900** *Pol. Laws Ælfred* §63 in Thorpe I. 96 Gif se sconca biþ þyrel beneoðan cnéowe. *c* **1205** LAY. 14985 Heo bar bineoðen his tite ane guldene ampulle. *c* **1305** *St. Edm. Conf.* 164 in *E.E.P.* (1862) 75 He was byneþe his brech igurd faste ynouȝ. *c* **1391** CHAUCER *Astrol.* II. §25 By-nethe the Orisonte. **1605** SHAKS. *Lear* IV. vi. 27 For all beneath the Moone would I not leape upright. **1631** T. POWELL *Tom All Trades* 168 The chiefest hand in preferring to any office beneath stayer.

2. Directly down from, overhung or surmounted by; under, underneath.

a **1200** *Moral Ode* in *Lamb. Hom.* 87 He is buuen us and binoþen . biforen and bihinden. *a* **1225** *Ancr. R.* 304 Bineoðen us..þe wide þreote of helle. *a* **1520** *Myrr. Our Ladye* 119 Aboue vs, bynethe vs. **1611** SHAKS. *Wint. T.* I. ii. 180 You'le be found, Be you beneath the Sky. **1697** DRYDEN *Virg. Georg.* II. 737 Lands that lye beneath another Sun. **1770** GOLDSM. *Des. Vill.* 13 The hawthorn bush, with seats beneath the shade. **1821** KEATS *Isabel* i, They could not, sure, beneath the same roof sleep. **1832** TENNYSON *Audley Crt.* 78 We..saunter'd home beneath a moon..In crescent.

b. At the base or foot of (a wall, cliff, etc.).

1387 TREVISA *Higden* (1865) I. 209 Hercules, Italus his sone, bulde a citee..by neþe þe Capitol. **1535** COVERDALE *Ex.* xxxii. 19 [He] brake them beneth [WYCLIF, at the rotes of] the mount. **1808** SCOTT *Marm.* I. iii, Beneath the sable palisade..His bugle horn he blew. **1870** R. ANDERSON *Missions Amer. Bd.* II. viii. 61 In a frail canoe beneath a tall cliff overhanging the sea.

3. Immediately under, in contact with the under side of; covered by; under, underneath.

1611 BIBLE *Deut.* v. 8 The waters beneath the earth. **1697** DRYDEN *Virg. Georg.* IV. 60 In Chambers of their own, beneath the Ground. **1718** POPE *Iliad* I. 651 One hand she placed Beneath his beard. *a* **1744** —— *Epitaph Rowe* 3 Beneath a rude and nameless stone he lies. **1726** DYER *Grongar H.* 22 So oft I have..Sat..With my hand beneath my head. **1831** R. KNOX *Cloquet's Anat.* 309 The axilla is the angle or cavity that lies beneath the junction of the arm with the shoulder. **1816** J. WILSON *City of Plague* I. i. 275 The brown red grass Rustling beneath your feet. **1854** MRS. JAMESON *Bk. of Th.* (1877) 34 No wise man kicks the ladder from beneath him.

b. Hence: Farther from (the surface); covered or concealed by; inside of, behind. More commonly UNDER.

1727 THOMSON *Summer* 753 Thou art no Ruffian, who beneath the mask Of social commerce comest to rob their wealth. **1863** E. NEALE *Anal. Th. & Nat.* 192 Beneath the movement of self-assertion appears the repose of self-government. **1871** HAWEIS *Mus. & Mor.* (1874) 7 The Musician's art lies beneath the surface. **1882** STANLEY *Chr. Instit.* viii. 156 A woollen vest, which sometimes had beneath it another fitting close to the skin.

4. 'Under, as overborne or overwhelmed by some pressure' (J.); often *fig.* subject to, under subjection to, under the influence, action, or control of.

1297 R. GLOUC. 491 There he broȝte al binethe hom that were is fon. **1605** SHAKS. *Macb.* IV. iii. 39 Our Country sinkes beneath the yoake. **1660** STANLEY *Hist. Philos.* (1701) 216/2 The comprehension made by the Senses..omits nothing that can fall beneath it. **1719** YOUNG *Busiris* I. i. (1757) 10 Elephants..Bending beneath a weight of luxury. **1792** *Munchausen's Trav.*, Thou shalt instant perish 'neath my potent arm. **1795** SOUTHEY *Joan of Arc* IV. 402 Thou shouldst set forth Beneath another's guidance. **1800** BLOOMFIELD *Farmer's B.*, *Spring* 221 Brisk goes the work beneath each busy hand. **1885** W. C. SMITH *Kildrostan* 43 The carved work mouldered fast 'Neath the suns, and the frosts.

†**5.** Lower on a slope, in a valley, etc., than; = BELOW *prep.* 2. *Obs.*

1551 TURNER *Herbal* (1568) 53, I went by the Rhene side iiij miles beneth Bingen. **1667** MILTON *P.L.* I. 355 Her barbarous sons..spread Beneath Gibraltar to the Lybian sands. **1691** T. H[ALE] *Acc. New Invent.* 68 Obstructions in all Navigable Rivers beneath the first Bridges. **1704** HEARNE *Duct. Hist.* I. 430 A Quarter of a Mile beneath the Village.. is the fallen Ruines of the Tower of Babel.

6. *fig.* Lower in the scale of being, station, rank, excellence, or dignity. Now commonly BELOW.

a **1000** *Metr. Boeth.* xx. 444 Hio biþ swiðe fior hire selfre beneoðan. *c* **1200** ORMIN 10729 To settenn þe Bineþenn þine lahȝhre. *c* **1374** CHAUCER *Boeth.* II. v. 49 It is brouȝt byneþen all bestes. *c* **1375** WYCLIF *Serm.* Sel. Wks. 1869 I. 15 Creatures bineþe men. **1611** SHAKS. *Cymb.* IV. i. 11 Not beneath him in Fortunes. **1667** MILTON *P.L.* I. 115 That were an ignominy..beneath This downfall. **1711** ADDISON *Spect.* No. 162 ¶4 Beings above and beneath us have probably no Opinions at all. **1849** MACAULAY *Hist. Eng.* I. 421 Beneath them lay a large class which could not subsist without some aid from the parish.

7. Unbefitting the dignity of; unworthy of, unbeseeming, undeserving of; lowering to.

c 888 K. ÆLFRED *Boeth.* xxxvi. §5 Nis nán wuht benyðan him [*i.e.* beneath his notice]. *c* 1380 WYCLIF *Pseudo-Fr.* vi. (1880) 310 Talis byneþe bileeue. 1601 SHAKS. *Twel. N.* v. i. 332 So farre beneath your soft and tender breeding. 1712 STEELE *Spect.* No. 53 ¶10 We do not esteem it beneath us to return you our Royal thanks. 1767 FORDYCE *Serm. Yng. Wom.* I. vi. 227 No woman..ought to think it beneath her to be an œconomist. 1871 HAWEIS *Mus. & Mor.* 499 Beneath the attention of serious critics. 1883 *Times* 23 Oct. 9 Thinking nothing beneath the notice of a man of business.

b. Lower than (any standard of quantity or quality). Better expressed by BELOW.

1849 RUSKIN *Sev. Lamps* i. §10 We are none of us so good architects as to be able to work habitually beneath our strength. 1850 McCOSH *Div. Govt.* II. i. (1874) 135 The copies ever fall beneath the original.

†**C.** quasi-*adj. Obs. rare.*

1607 SHAKS. *Timon* I. i. 43 A man Whom this beneath world doth embrace.

D. *Comb.* †**beneath-forth**, out from beneath; beneath. *Obs.*

1398 TREVISA *Barth. De P.R.* VII. xlvii. (1495) 259 A stronge colde in the mouthe of the stomak..is cause of out puttynge bineth forthe. *c* 1410 LOVE *Bonavent. Mirr.* xxvi. 56 Thyng þat longeth to þe worlde..here byneth forthe. *c* 1467 *Ord. Worcester* in *E.E. Gilds* 373 In one of the Chambers benethforth.

†**benecarlo, -icarlo.** *Obs.* (See quot. 1851)

1734 T. SHERIDAN in *Swift's Wks.* 1841 II. 724 You drink benicarlo wine, I drink right French margose. 1851 H. MAYO *Philos. Living* i. 66 Benecarlo is a coarse-flavoured astringent Spanish wine.

†**be'necking,** *ppl. a. Obs. rare*$^{-1}$. [f. BE- *pref.* 6 + NECK.] Bowing the neck, cringing.

1705 *Ess. Govt.* 68 Oliver's..benecking ministers pleaded obedience to the supreme power for the time being.

benedicence. *rare.* [f. L. *benedic-us* (in adv. *benedicē*), or *benedīcĕre*, f. *bene* well + *-dicus* speaking, *dīcĕre* to speak; see -ENCE.] Kindliness in speech.

1881 MONIER WILLIAMS in *19th Cent.* IX. 168 His benevolence, his benedicence (if I may coin a new word), and his beneficence.

‖**benedicite** (bɛnɪ'daɪsɪtiː), *int.* and *sb.* Also 4-5 **bendicite, benste.** [L.; 2nd pl. imper. of *benedīcĕre* 'to praise, commend,' later 'to bless, wish well to,' f. *bene* well + *dīcĕre* to speak, say. In early use shortened to *bendicite, benste.*]

A. *interj.*

1. as expressing a wish: Bless you!

1377 LANGL. *P. Pl.* B. v. 397 He bygan benedicite with a bolke. 1393 GOWER *Conf.* I. 48 Benedicite, My sone..Thou shalt be shrive of bothe two. 1603 SHAKS. *Meas. for M.* II. iii. 39 Grace goe with you, Benedicite.

2. as expressing astonishment or remonstrance: Bless us! Good gracious!

c 1374 CHAUCER *Troylus* I. 780 What? liveth not thy lady, benedicite? *c* 1386 —— *Freres T.* 156 A! quod the somnour, benedicite! what ye say. *c* 1420 *Sir Amadace* 647 Sir Amadas seyd Benedicite! Sir, leyt such wordes bee.

B. *sb.*

1. Invocation of a blessing on oneself or others.

1610 G. FLETCHER *Christ's Vict.* in Farr *S.P.* (1848) 55 And all the way he went he ever blest With benedicities. 1808 SCOTT *Marm.* II. ii, One eyed the..swelling sail, With many a benedicite. 1823 —— *Quentin D.* ii, The friar answered his reverend greeting with a paternal benedicite.

2. *esp.* The blessing asked at table. (The earliest sense in English.)

a 1225 *Ancr. R.* 44 Bitweone mete, hwo se drinken wule, sigge benedicite: potum nostrum filius Dei benedicat. 1725 tr. *Dupin's Eccl. Hist.* I. v. 208 The first [prayer] at the Beginning of the Repast..what we call Benedicite. 1842 MRS. GORE *Fascin.* 109 We may repent having laughed at the benedicite last night at supper!

†**3.** A blessing, deliverance from evil. *Obs.*

a 1300 *Dame Siriz* 193 Bendicite be herinne! *c* 1314 *Guy Warw.* 206 Gaf him swiche bendicite That he brak his nek ato. *c* 1460 *Towneley Myst.* 85 Benste, benste, be us emang.

4. The canticle in the Book of Common Prayer, known also as 'The Song of the Three Children.'

c 1661 *Papers on Alter. Prayer-bk.* 3 You will not allow the omission of the Benedicite.

benedict ('bɛnɪdɪkt), *a.* and *sb.* Also 6-9 **benedick.** [ad. L. *benedictus* blessed; see prec.]

†**A.** *adj.* Blessed, benign, salutary; *spec.* in *Med.* mildly laxative. *Obs.*

1576 BAKER *Gesner's Jewell of Health* 209a, The Oyle Benedict or Oyle of Tyle stones. 1626 BACON *Sylva* §19 Rhubarb and other Medicines that are benedict. 1657 J. GOODWIN *Triers Tried* 4 That the two Commissions specified be..benedict to the interest of the Gospel. *a* 1693 SANCROFT *Serm.* 110 (T.) If the more benign and benedict medicines will not work.

†**b.** *priest benedict*: = BENET, exorcist. *Obs.*

1660 R. COKE *Power & Subj.* 160 No Priest, whether consecrate at [? or] Benedict shall forsake his Church.

B. *sb.*

1. A newly married man; *esp.* an apparently confirmed bachelor who marries. [From the character of that name in Shaks. *Much Ado about Nothing.*]

[1599 SHAKS. *Much Ado* v. iv. 100 How dost thou Benedicke the married man?] 1821 SCOTT in *Lockhart* (1839) VI. 313 Wish the veteran joy of his entrance into the band of Benedicts. 1843 *Life in West* (L.) He is no longer a benedick, but a quiet married man.

†**2.** 'A good saying, an honest report.' Blount *Glossogr.* 1656.

†**bene'dicted,** *ppl. a. Obs.*$^{-0}$ [f. L. *benedict-us* (see prec.) + -ED.] 'Blessed.' Cockeram 1623.

Benedictine (bɛnɪ'dɪktɪn), *a.* and *sb.* [a. F. *bénédictin*, f. L. *benedictus*; see -INE.]

A. *adj.* Of or belonging to St. Benedict or the religious order founded by him.

1630 WADSWORTH *Sp. Pilgr.* vi. 49 [He] had a Benedictine Monke to his Tutor. 1861 A. B. HOPE *Eng. Cathedr. 19th C.* 265 The chapter-house of Westminster, a Benedictine abbey before the Reformation.

B. *sb.* **1.** One of the order of monks, also known, from the colour of their dress, as 'Black Monks,' founded by St. Benedict about the year 529.

1602 W. WATSON *Decacordon* 185 Sequestred..as.. Augustines from Benedictines. 1721 *Lond. Gaz.* No. 5954/2 Dom Thierry, a Benedictine, is banished the Kingdom. 1866 GEO. ELIOT *F. Holt* (1868) 40 When the black Benedictines ceased to pray and chant in this church.

2. A kind of liqueur.

1882 J. HAWTHORNE *Fort. Fool* I. xviii, It smelt rather like Benedictine, but..it was difficult to be certain about these liqueurs.

Benedictiness (bɛnɪ'dɪktɪnɪs). [f. BENEDICTINE + -ESS.] A nun of the Benedictine order.

1872 J. MORRIS *Condit. Cath. under Jas. I* (ed. 2) p. ccvii, Father Gerard..took one [image] to Ghent, which he gave to the English Benedictinesses there. 1909 *Dublin Rev.* Jan. 61 We have Benedictinesses at East Bergholt [etc.].

Bene'dictinism. [f. BENEDICTINE *a.* and *sb.* + -ISM.] The system of the Benedictines.

1826 SOUTHEY *Vind. Eccl. Angl.* 40 That Benedictinism, and Franciscanism,..with their respective..superstitions, are no part of the Roman Catholic system. 1884 *Athenæum* 23 Aug. 235/3 The history of Benedictinism in England requires reconsideration.

benediction (bɛnɪ'dɪkʃən). Also 5 **-dyctyon,** 5-6 **-diccion.** [ad. L. *benedictiōn-em*, n. of action f. *benedict-*; see BENEDICT and -TION. Cf. F. *bénédiction* (16th c. in Littré, replacing the regular *beneiçon, beneisson*, whence Eng. BENISON).]

1. The utterance of a blessing; solemn invocation of blessedness upon a person; devout expression of a wish for the happiness, prosperity, or success of a person or enterprise: **a.** *gen.*

1432-50 tr. *Higden* (1865) I. 377 He openethe the durre with a benediccion, makenge the durre sure after hym. 1485 CAXTON *Paris & V.* (1868) 51 Gyue to me your benedyctyon. 1552 HULOET, Benediction, *benedictio.* 1605 SHAKS. *Lear* IV. vii. 58 Hold your hand in benediction o're me. 1752 JOHNSON *Rambl.* No. 204 ¶2 Thy path perfumed by the breath of benediction. 1860 FROUDE *Hist. Eng.* V. 329 Amidst the benedictions of tens of thousands of people.

b. as officially pronounced by an ecclesiastical functionary; *spec.* the ceremony of consecration of an abbot.

1638 *Penit. Conf.* xi. (1657) 306 The Priest is to marry him and to give the Benediction. 1679 *Season. Adv. Protest.* 11 This Catholick Religion, and Holy Cause sanctified by the Popes Benediction. 1726 AYLIFFE *Parergon* (J.) What consecration is to a bishop, that benediction is to an abbot. 1781 GIBBON *Decl. & F.* II. xlv. 671 Their choice was sanctified by the benediction of the patriarch. 1802 FOSBROOKE *Brit. Monachism* (1843) 86 Between the election and benediction the Abbot used the Prior's chamber.

c. as pronounced by the officiating minister at the conclusion of divine worship.

1549 *Bk. Com. Prayer, Ord. Deacons* (Rubr.), After the last Collect, and immediately before the benediction, shall be said these collects. 1622 SPARROW *Bk. Com. Prayer* (1843) 266 A most excellent and pious benediction of the priest concludes all. 1856 LONGF. *Day is Done* ix, Such songs..come like the benediction That follows after prayer.

d. as an expression of thanks; *spec.* as 'grace' before or after meals.

1671 MILTON *P. R.* III. 127 Of whom what could he less expect Than glory and benediction—that is, thanks. 1753 CHAMBERS *Cycl. Supp.*, *Benediction* is still applied to the act of saying grace before or after meals. 1806 WORDSW. *Ode Immort.* 135 The thought of our past years in me doth breed Perpetual benediction. 1818 LAMB *Elia, Grace bef. Meat*, The form, then, of the benediction before eating has its beauty at a poor man's table.

e. as a service in the Roman Catholic Church.

1812 P. GAUDOLPHY *Liturgy Com. Prayers* (1815) 227 An act of adoration and thanksgiving in honour of the Blessed Sacrament of the Altar, commonly called Benediction. 1853 FABER *All for Jesus* 6 Even in the churches during Mass or Benediction, they are hard at work. 1884 ADDIS & ARNOLD *Cath. Dict.*, *Benediction of the Blessed Sacrament*, a rite which has now become very common in the Catholic Church.

2. Blessing carried into practical effect, blessedness; kindly favour, grace.

1483 CAXTON *Cato* Ej, That we may haue his glorye and benediccion at the end of our dayes. 1526 *Pilgr. Perf.* (W. de W. 1531) 69 We shall neuer be parteners..of the benediccyon of the whiche the sone of god spake. 1611 SHAKS. *Wint. T.* IV. iv. 614 As if my Trinkets had beene hallowed, and brought a benediction to the buyer. 1702 *Eng. Theophrast.* 73 The inward joy of contemplating the Benedictions of another World. 1872 RUSKIN *Fors Clav.* II. xviii. 5 Has had at least some measure of Christian Benediction.

benedictional (bɛnɪ'dɪkʃənəl), *sb.* [ad. med.L. *benedictiōnālis* (sc. *liber*), i.e. book of benedictions; cf. *hymnal*, etc.] A book containing the forms of episcopal benedictions formerly in use.

1844 LINGARD *Anglo-Sax. Ch.* I. vii. (1858) 271 *note*, The Benedictional of St. Ethelwold. 1849 ROCK *Ch. of Fathers* IV. ii. 37 The head deacon..gave the benedictional to the bishop. 1879 J. SIMMONS in *Lay Folks Mass Bk.* 351 *note*, The new words..were rendered in the vulgar tongue, as ..*sang-boc* (psalter), *bletsing-boc* (benedictional).

benedictional (bɛnɪ'dɪkʃənəl), *a.* [f. BENEDICTION + -AL.] Of or pertaining to the pronouncing of a benediction.

1902 *Encycl. Brit.* XXVII. 238/2 Small benedictional crosses belong to each altar, and processional crosses are common [in the Coptic Church].

benedictionally (bɛnɪ'dɪkʃənəlɪ), *adv.* [f. prec. + -LY².] In or by way of benediction.

1911 W. DE MORGAN *Likely Story* 208 The old lady.. kissed her benedictionally.

bene'dictionary. [f. BENEDICTION + -ARY; cf. *antiphonary*.] = BENEDICTIONAL *sb.*

1780 DODSLEY *O. Pl.* II. 57 *note*, Not the least mention.. in the benedictionary of Bishop Athelwold.

benedictive (bɛnɪ'dɪktɪv), *a.* [f. L. *benedict-* ppl. stem of *benedīcere* to bless + -IVE.]

1. Characterized by blessing; tending to bless.

1660 GAUDEN *Mem. Bp. Brownrig* 201 (L.) His paternal prayers and benedictive comprecations. *c* 1746 HERVEY *Medit.* (1818) Introd. 2 That the high and lofty One.. should there manifest an extraordinary degree of his benedictive presence.

2. *Gram.* A form of the Optative Mood in the Sanskrit verb, also called the 'precative,' the use of which is to express wish or desire.

1841 H. H. WILSON *Skr. Gram.* (1847) 114 The benedictive or optative mood is considered as a modification of the potential. 1879 WHITNEY *Skr. Gram.* §533 The aorist has also an optative, of somewhat peculiar inflection, usually called the precative (or benedictive).

Hence **benedictively** *adv.* With the force of the benedictive mood.

†**bene'dictor.** [Agent-noun on L. type, f. *benedīcere*: see prec.] A eulogist, a well-wisher. *Obs.*

a 1633 T. ADAMS *Wks.* (1861-2) I. 179 (D.) Ministers have ..many benedictors, few benefactors.

bene'dictory, *a.* [ad. med.L. *benedictōri-us*: see BENEDICT and -ORY.] Of or pertaining to the utterance of benediction.

1710 C. WHEATLEY *Illustr. Bk. Com. Prayer* iii. §26 That benedictory prayer of St. Paul. 1860 ELLICOTT *Life our Lord* viii. 400 With words of holy and benedictory greeting. 1863 GEO. ELIOT *Romola* I. xiv, With hands outstretched in a benedictory attitude.

‖**Bene'dictus.** [L.; pa. pple. of *benedīcere* to bless: see above.]

1. The fifth movement in the service of the Mass, beginning with the words 'Benedictus qui venit'; (the name is given both to the words of the service, and to their musical setting).

1880 GROVE *Dict. Music* II. 233/1 After the Elevation.. the Choir begin the *Benedictus*, in soft low tones.

2. The hymn of Zacharias (Luke i. 68), used as a canticle in the morning service of the Church of England.

1552 *Bk. Com. Prayer, Matins* (Rubr.), And after the Second Lesson shall be used and said, *Benedictus*, in English, as followeth. 1641 S. MARSHALL *Peace-Off. God* 33 Uttering a Benedictus or Te Deum laudamus.

bene'dight, *ppl. a. Obs.* or *arch.* Also **-diht.** [ad. L. *benedictus*: see prec. Cf. MHG. *gebenediget*, mod.G. *benedeiet.*] Blessed.

a 1300 *Cursor M.* 18705 Bot þa men sal be benedight Sal trou in me wit-vten sight. *c* 1460 *Towneley Myst.* 91 For ferde we be fryght a crosse let us kest, Cryst crosse, benedyght. *a* 188. LONGFELLOW *Sonn. Mrs. Longf.*, Nor can in books be read The legend of a life more benedight.

bene esse: see ESSE 2 b.

†**benefact,** *sb. Obs.*$^{-0}$. [ad. L. *benefactum*: see BENEFIT.] 'A good deed or benefit.' Blount *Glossogr.* 1656.

benefact ('bɛnɪfækt), *v.* [Back-formation f. BENEFACTOR.] *trans.* To help or endow as a benefactor.

[1594 O. B. *Questions* 3 Whose benefacting..extended chieflie to their supposed children and Paramoures.] 1898 E. W. B. NICHOLSON in *Westm. Gaz.* 10 June 2/3 Mr. Gladstone..offered to try to get one of the richest men in the world to benefact us. 1923 *Chambers's Jrnl.* Aug. 507/2 He did not want to benefact Hamborne in any kind of way.

benefaction (bɛnɪ'fækʃən). [ad. L. *benefactiōn-em*, n. of action f. *benefacĕre*: see BENEFIT.]

1. A doing good, beneficence, kindly or generous action; a benefit or blessing.

a **1662** HEYLIN *Laud* (1668) 245 Marks of his Benefaction we find none, in places of his Breeding. **1728** NEWTON *Chronol. Amended* 15 For which Benefaction she [Ceres] was Deified after death. **1875** E. WHITE *Life in Christ* (1878) 442 What it [divine goodness] will do in the way of positive benefaction.

2. *esp.* The bestowal of money for a charitable purpose; a grant, gift, bounty, endowment.

1674 *Scheffer's Lapland* viii. 28 Retaining to the crown the superintendency of the benefaction. **1779** JOHNSON *Milton* in *L.P.* (1816) 132 This was the greatest benefaction that Paradise Lost ever procured the author's descendants. **1855** PRESCOTT *Philip II*, iv. (1857) 58 She was liberal in her benefactions to convents and colleges.

beneˈfaction, *v. rare.* [f. prec. sb.] To endow with a benefaction. Cf. prec. 2.

1822 DRAKARD *Hist. Stamford* in Nichols *Progr. Q. Eliz.* I. 199* It [the Friary at Stamford] was..further benefactioned by King Edward the Third.

benefactive (bɛnɪˈfæktɪv), *a.* (and *sb.*) [ad. L. *benefact-us* capable of giving + -IVE.] Used of an affix or verbal aspect, esp. in various American Indian languages, to indicate that a benefit is conferred on someone. Also as *sb.*, a benefactive form or set of forms.

1943 W. L. WONDERLEY *Notes on Zoque Gram.* 92 The suffix *-hay-*..at times does not parallel indirect or benefactive uses in other languages. **1946** E. A. NIDA *Morphology* viii. 160 (*caption*) Benefactive indirective. **1947** *Internat. Jrnl. Amer. Linguistics* XIII. 28/2 The benefactive suffix -y is suffixed to themes containing stems ending in a vowel or in w. **1964** E. A. NIDA *Toward Sci. Transl.* ix. 200 Voice specifies the relationship between the participants and the event indicated in the verb; e.g...benefactive (*worked for him*). **1965** *Amer. Speech* XL. 116 In combining Zoque *-hay-*, a benefactive morpheme, with *-pa*, a present-tense morpheme, one should get only *-hapya*.

benefactor (bɛnɪˈfæktə(r)). Also 5 -our. [a. L. *benefactor*, f. *benefacĕre*: see BENEFIT.]

1. One who renders aid or kindly service to others, a friendly helper; one who advances the interests of a cause or institution, a patron.

1532 TINDALE *Expos. & Notes* (1849) 71 It is not inough for thee to loue thy benefactors only. **1605** BACON *Adv. Learn.* I. vii. §5 There was not a greater admirer of learning or benefactor of learning. **1769** *Junius, Lett.* xxxv. 159 They ..have transferred their gratitude from their parents to their benefactors. **1848** MACAULAY *Hist. Eng.* I. 362 The greatest of all the benefactors of his city.

2. *esp.* One who makes a benefaction to a charitable or religious institution; one who makes a bequest or endowment.

1494 FABYAN VII. 480 Quene Philyp..the which was a great benefactour vnto the Chanons of Seynt Stephans Chapell at Westmynster. **1626** BACON *New Atl.* (1650) 33 These we call Dowry-men or Benefactors. **1752** JOHNSON *Rambl.* No. 197 ¶9, I was..inquiring the age of my future benefactors or considering how I should employ their legacies. **1851** LONGF. *Gold. Leg.* 132 Whose tomb is that, Which bears the brass escutcheon? A benefactor's.

3. With reference to the etymology: a well-doer.

1603 SHAKS. *Meas. for M.* II. i. 50 Well: What Benefactors are they? Are they not Malefactors? **1870** J. CAMERON *Phases of Th.* 160 Books are to us according as we deal with them—malefactors or benefactors.

beneˈfactorate, *v. nonce-wd.* [f. prec. + -ATE.] To act the benefactor to; to benefaction.

1769 H. WALPOLE *Corr.* (1837) II. 432 A plan for the East window of his Cathedral which he intends to benefactorate with painted glass.

beneˈfactorship. [f. as prec. + -SHIP.] The office or action of a benefactor.

1652 BROME *Jov. Crew* II. Wks. 1873 III. 377 His great Benefactorship among the Beggars. **1691** T. H[ALES] *Acc. New Invent.* 41 His Benefactorship to his Countrey in the doing it at his own charge.

benefactory (bɛnɪˈfæktərɪ), *a.* [ad. med.L. *benefactōri-us*, f. *benefactōr-em* BENEFACTOR: see -ORY.] Of or pertaining to a benefactor; conferring a benefit; beneficial.

1744 J. LEWIS *Life Pecocke* 150 Saying of special prayers for people by name, as..benefactory. **1884** THORLEY *Farmers' Alm.* 42 The great benefactory result from continually strewing handfuls of salt on hay..has long been known.

benefactress (bɛnɪˈfæktrɪs). [f. BENEFACTOR + -ESS.] A female benefactor.

1711 SWIFT *Vind. Dk. Marlborough* Wks. 1814 V. 397 While his gracious benefactress is contented to take up her residence in an old patched-up palace. **1781** GIBBON *Decl. & F.* III. xlviii. 32 They basely conspired against their benefactress. **1834** LAMB *Elia, Oxford in Vac.*, And pay a devoir to some Founder, or noble or Royal Benefactress.

†**beneˈfactrice.** *Obs. rare*$^{-1}$. [f. as prec., after F. *bienfaitrice*.] = prec.

1711 SHAFTESB. *Charac.* (1737) I. 331 The pure grace and favour of the benefactrice.

beneˈfactrix. [f. BENEFACTOR, after Lat. analogy: see -TRIX.] = prec.

1615 J. DAY *Festivals* xi. 301 The Widowes that wept so much for the Death of Dorcas their Benefactrix. **1713** *Lond. Gaz.* No. 5124/4 The great Benefactrix unto the Nations of the Earth. **1775** CHALLONER in E. H. Burton *Life* (1909) II. xxviii. 116 God reward the good Lady, our benefactrix. **1907** W. DE MORGAN *Alice-for-Short* xxxii, The expedient of merging her personality in that of an imagined benefactrix.

†**beneˈfacture.** *Obs.* [f. L. *benefact-* ppl. stem of *benefacĕre* + -URE; as if ad. L. **benefactūra*.] Beneficence, benefaction.

a **1656** BP. HALL *Soliloquies* Wks. VIII. 256 All these dispositions are but inclosures: give me the open champain of a general and illimited benefacture. **1777** DYCHE & PARDON, *Benefacture*, a kind, friendly, good-natured deed, a charitable gift or donation.

†**benefeter, -our.** *Obs. rare.* [a. OF. *bienfetor*, mod. *bienfaiteur*: cf. also *benefet*, early form of BENEFIT.] = BENEFACTOR.

c **1449** PECOCK *Repr.* III. ix. 333 The ȝeuer or benefeter. *Ibid.* 511 Summe of Cristen neighboris as ben grete to him Benefetouris he ouȝte love in Affect and Effect.

benefic (bɪˈnɛfɪk), *a.* Also 7 -ick, -ique. [ad. L. *benefic-us*, f. *bene* well + *-fic-us* doing: see -FIC.]

1. *Astrol.* Of good or favourable influence.

1600 B. JONSON *Cynthia's Rev.* V. i. 36 The fourth is the kind, and truly benefique Eucolos. **1618** GOAD *Celest. Bodies* II. ii. 162 Our Venus is reckoned moist and therefore Benefique. **1884** *Zadkiel's Alm.* 40 The Moon forms benefic aspects with the primary planets.

2. *gen.* Beneficent, kindly, benign.

1641 MILTON *Animadv.* Wks. (1851) 219 He being..of free power to turne his benefick and fatherly regard to what Region or Kingdome he pleases. **1873** BROWNING *Red Cott. Night-c.* 951 Is there not the Church To intercede and bring benefic truce At outset? **1876** EMERSON *Ess.* Ser. II. vi. 149 As if that terrific or benefic force did not find us then also, and fashion cities.

beˈnefical, *a.* ? *Obs.* [f. prec. + -AL^1.] = prec.

1647 LILLY *Chr. Astrol.* clv. 643 Some very beneficall prohibition of the Fortunes intervenes. **1652** GAULE *Magastrom.* 92 Whether all such astronomicall demonstrations..be any reall proofes of beneficall and maleficall influences.

benefice (ˈbɛnɪfɪs), *sb.* Forms: 4 benyfice, -iss, benefise, benfice, 4–5 benefys, 5 -fyce (bonfice), 6 benyfyce (bunfyce), 7 beni-, 4- benefice. [a. OF. *benefice*, ad. L. *beneficium*, f. *bene* well + *-ficium* a doing: cf. BENEFIC.]

†**1.** A good deed, kindness, favour; a grace or 'indulgence.' *Obs.*

1340 HAMPOLE *Pr. Consc.* 5582 Agayne þam sal Crist allege..And reherce his benefices, mare and les. *c* **1380** WYCLIF *Sel. Wks.* III. 200 þanke þei God for al his mercyes and benefices. *c* **1400** *Apol. Loll.* 11 Alle þat persewen for swilke indulgens, or benefices, or oþer graces. **1549** *Compl. Scot.* 20 Them that ar ingrate of the benefecis of gode. **1677** GALE *Crt. Gentiles* III. 109 He can incline them..to performe his benefices or to inflict his punishments.

†**2.** Favourable influence or operation; advantage, favour, protection, benefit. *Obs.* exc. *Hist.*

1424 *Paston Lett.* 4 I. 14 He schuld no benefice take by noon proteccion. *c* **1440** *Gesta Rom.* xlix. 174 The knyȝt seide to the iuge, 'My lorde, I aske the benefice of [the law].' **1685** BAXTER *Paraph. Peter* ii. 3 Their business is to sell Souls to the Devil for their own worldly Benefice. **1875** POSTE tr. *Gaius* I. Introd. 24 Justinian's benefice of inventory,..was another fundamental change in hereditary succession.

b. *benefice of clergy*: see BENEFIT 3 c.

1489 *Act 4 Hen. VII*, xiii, Euery persone..whiche ones hath bene admitted to the benefice of his clergie.

†**3.** Beneficial property or action (as of natural agents or causes). *Obs.*

1387 TREVISA *Higden* (1865) I. 415 Many benefices of kynde Beeþ now i-hidde fro manis mynde. *c* **1420** *Pallad. on Husb.* II. 365 The bonfice of sonne and wynde wol harde Hem sure ynough. *a* **1520** *Myrr. Our Ladye* 210 Theyr fruytes..shall..the more parfytly wax rype of the benefyce of the hete. **1652** GAULE *Magastrom.* 77 Made to consist by the stars, and to thrive, or dwindle away, according to the benefice, or malefice, of their influences?

†**4.** A gift; gratuity. *Obs.*

c **1380** WYCLIF *Confession* Wks. (1880) 331 Who shuld take ony benyfiss of þe puple. *c* **1440** *Gesta Rom.* 349 Myghty men..have resceived benefice, after her wille.

5. Land granted in feudal tenure, a fief. (Only in modern legal and historical writers, as transl. L. *beneficium*.)

[**1681** NEVILE *Plato Rediv.* 87 If these *Beneficia* had not afterwards been made Hereditary.] **1753** CHAMBERS *Cycl. Supp.*, *Benefice* was an estate in land, at first granted for life only..In after times, as these tenures became perpetual and hereditary, they left their name of *beneficia* to the livings of the clergy. **1861** MAINE *Anc. Law* vii. (1876) 229 Benefices ..were grants of Roman provincial land to be holden by the beneficiary on condition of military service. **1867** FREEMAN *Norm. Conq.* (1876) I. iii. 92 Rewarding their followers with grants of land, in short with benefices or fiefs. **1876** DIGBY *Real Prop.* i. §2. 38.

6. *esp.* An ecclesiastical living.

1340 *Ayenb.* 42 Þe prouendres and þe parosses oþer oþre benefices of holy cherche. **1393** LANGL. *P. Pl.* C. IV. 33 And bigge ȝow benefices pluralitie to haue. **1480** CAXTON *Chron. Eng.* IV. (1520) 32 b, That no bysshop sholde be receyved into his benefyce but with the popes letters. **1592** SHAKS. *Rom. & Jul.* I. iv. 81 Then he dreames of another benefice. **1691** WOOD *Ath. Oxon.* II. /554 He had a small benifice in Norfolk conferr'd on him, but could not pass the Triers. **1756** BLACKSTONE *Comm.* I. II. xviii. 220 In case a benefice becomes void by death. **1855** PRESCOTT *Philip II*, II. iii. 229 A tract which he published against plurality of benefices.

7. *Comb.* and *attrib.*, as *benefice farm*, *-monger*; also **beneficeless** *adj.*, destitute of a benefice.

1583 STUBBES *Anat. Abus.* II. 76, I aduise al benefice mongers, that haue mo charges than one, to take heede to themselues. *a* **1654** SELDEN *Mirr. Antichr.* 190 (R.) That competency of means which our beneficeless precisians prate of. **1882** *Pall Mall G.* 14 July 4/2 There are the contadini who work the benefice farm.

benefice (ˈbɛnɪfɪs), *v.* Also 4–5 benefise, beny-, 6 benifice. [f. prec. sb. Cf. OF. *beneficier*.] *trans.* To endow or invest with a benefice or church living.

c **1383** WYCLIF *Sel. Wks.* III. 330 A worldly clerk..is preised and benefised among grete men. **1393** LANGL. *P. Pl.* C. IV. 186 Hue blesseþ [MS. F (*a* **1500**) benefiseth] þese byshopys. **1494** FABYAN VII. 400 Certayne aliauntes, whiche were rychely benyficed in Englande. **1608** T. JAMES *Life Wickliffe* K iv, He had sometimes before beene..beneficed in Oxford. **1826** SOUTHEY in *Q. Rev.* XXXIV. 338 The many eminent men who have been beneficed in that cathedral.

Hence **ˈbeneficed** *ppl. a.* holding a benefice.

c **1425** WYNTOUN *Cron.* IX. xxvii. 385 Benefist Men and Chanownis..Of þat kyrk. **1561** T. NORTON *Calvin's Inst.* IV. 28 b, The secular Priestes: which are partly beneficed men, that is to saye, haue benefices whereupon to liue. **1704** *Lond. Gaz.* No. 4034/1 The humble Address of the..Beneficed Clergy. **1850** LYTTON *My Novel* V. x. 250 Your father was such a respectable man—beneficed clergyman!

beneficence (bɪˈnɛfɪsəns). Also 6 -fycence. [a. F. *bénéficence*, ad. L. *beneficentia*, f. *benefic-us*: perh. directly f. the L.]

1. Doing good, the manifestation of benevolence or kindly feeling, active kindness.

1531 ELYOT *Gov.* II. x. (1883) II. 112 Beneficence can by no menes be vicious and retaine still his name. **1548** UDALL *Erasm. Par. Mark* v. 24 (R.) Like as the lodestone draweth vnto it yron, so dothe the benefycence and well doing allure all men vnto her. **1651** HOBBES *Govt. & Soc.* iii. §8. 42 By this meanes all beneficence..would be taken from among men. **1790** BURKE *Fr. Rev.* 87 It is an institution of beneficence; and law itself is only beneficence acting by a rule. **1853** LYTTON *My Novel* VIII. viii, What does intellectual power.. stripped of beneficence, most resemble?

2. *concr.* A benefaction, a beneficent gift, deed, or work.

1654 EVELYN *Mem.* (1857) I. 320 The market-place is.. remarkable for old Hobson the pleasant carrier's beneficence of a fountain. **1851** CARLYLE *Sterling* II. i. (1872) 87 Sterling now..zealously forwarded schools and beneficences. **1858** HAWTHORNE *Fr. & It. Jrnls.* II. 197 Distributed their beneficence in the shape of some handfuls of copper.

†**beˈneficency.** *Obs.* [ad. L. *beneficentia*: see prec. and -ENCY.] The quality of being beneficent; beneficence.

1576 WOOLTON *Chr. Manual* 70 The sixth [commandment] commandeth justice and judgment.. beneficency and innocency. **1662** FULLER *Worthies* (1840) III. 310 Queen's College in Oxford, owing the glazing of many windows therein to his beneficency. **1682** SIR T. BROWNE *Chr. Mor.* (1716) 105 Such tempers..make beneficency cool unto acts of obligation.

beneficent (bɪˈnɛfɪsənt), *a.* Also 7 benificent. [f. L. **beneficent-*, whence *beneficenti-or*, compar. of *beneficus*, and *beneficentia*: see prec. Cf. *magnificent*.] Doing good, performing kind deeds, characterized by beneficence. (*Beneficial* was previously used in this sense.) **a.** of persons.

1616 BULLOKAR, *Beneficent*, liberall, louing. *a* **1677** BARROW *Wks.* (1683) 173 A most wise, most powerfull, most beneficent authour. **1725** POPE *Odyss.* IV. 917 Gentle of speech, beneficent of mind. **1879** LEFEVRE *Philos.* i. 20 Confucius is still revered as a beneficent genius.

b. of things.

1677 HALE *Prim. Orig. Man.* 5 Objects, the knowledge whereof is..very beneficent to Mankind. **1772** PENNANT *Tours Scotl.* (1774) 38 That beneficent luminary the Sun. **1855** MACAULAY *Hist. Eng.* IV. 530 That disease, over which science has since achieved a succession of glorious and beneficent victories. **1871** R. W. DALE *Commandm.* iv. 103 The Sabbath was a singularly beneficent institution.

beneficential (bɪˌnɛfɪˈsɛnʃəl), *a.* [f. L. *beneficentia*: see prec. + -AL^1.] Of or pertaining to beneficence; concerned with what is most beneficial to mankind.

1869 J. MORLEY in *Fortn. Rev.* May 533 The beneficential moralist esteems this a particularly virtuous type, because it is particularly conducive to the greatest happiness of the greatest number. *Ibid.* 538 The central principle of the utilitarian or beneficential ethics.

beˈneficently, *adv.* [f. BENEFICENT *a.* + -LY^2.] In a beneficent manner; with beneficence.

a **1717** PARNELL *Q. Anne's Peace* (R.) All mortals once beneficently great. **1797** HOLCROFT *Stolberg's Trav.* III. lxxx. (ed. 2) 246 Airs beneficently tepid. **1852** HAWTHORNE *Wonder-bk., Mirac. Pitcher*, A spot on which Heaven had smiled so beneficently. **1875** FARRAR *Silence & V.* ii. 33 Pain comes..to warn us beneficently of our danger.

†**ˈbeneficer.** *Obs.* [f. BENEFICE *sb.* + -ER^1.] One who holds a benefice.

1621 R. BOLTON *Act 36 Hen. VI* in *Stat. Ireland* 26 All maner Beneficers within the said land,..shall keepe residence continually in their proper persons in the said land.

‖**beneficiaire** (benefisjɛr). [a. F. *bénéficiaire*, f. *bénéfice* benefit.] A player who is taking a benefit (BENEFIT *sb.* 4 a).

1840 *Fistiana* 49 Some dozens of noblemen and persons of high rank, whose liberal contributions.. added greatly to the receipts of the *beneficiare*. **1843** *Bell's Life* 27 Aug. 3/6 The *beneficiaire* was, no doubt, rather unnerved by the applause. **1862** *Sporting Mag.* XL. 11 A *bénéficiaire* very often cannot prevent that. **1905** *Daily Chron.* 13 July 3/5 Fifty baskets of flowers.. were brought on the stage and surrounded the beneficiaire. **1927** *Daily Tel.* 23 Aug. 5/3 Sandham's Benefit Match... The beneficiaire was not destined to do well.

beneficial (bɛnɪˈfɪʃəl), *a.* and *sb.* Also 6 **benyfycyal(l, bunfycyal, beneficiall.** [a. F. *bénéficial*, ad. L. *beneficiāl-em*, f. *beneficium*: see -AL[1].]

A. *adj.* †**1.** = BENEFICENT. *Obs.*

1526 *Pilgr. Perf.* (W. de W. 1531) 244 Whome.. thou hast founde moost.. redy helper, and moost beneficiall lorde. **1551** ROBINSON tr. *More's Utop.* 129 Other to whome they haue bene beneficiale they call their frendes. **1593** BILSON *Govt. Christ's Ch.* 301 You are so liberall and beneficiall. **1658** A. FOX *Wurtz' Surg.* I. ii. 3 We ought to be beneficial to our neighbours.

2. Of benefit; advantageous, serviceable, profitable.

1494 FABYAN *Hen. III*, an. 1262 (R.) To deuise suche thynges as might be benyfycyall for the cytie. **1593** HOOKER *Eccl. Pol.* I. ii. §4 Not that anything is made to be beneficial unto Him. **1604** SHAKS. *Oth.* II. ii. 7 Besides these beneficiall Newes, it is the Celebration of his Nuptiall. *a* **1674** CLARENDON *Hist. Reb.* I. I. 76 He was so entirely devoted to what would be Beneficial to the King. **1732** ARBUTHNOT *Rules of Diet* 346 Diluents with nitrous Salts are beneficial. **1876** GREEN *Short Hist.* ii. 83 No measures could have been more beneficial to the kingdom at large.

†**b.** Profitable in a pecuniary sense, lucrative.

1526 TINDALE *Acts* xix. 19 Not a litell beneficiall vnto the craftes men. **1647** R. STAPYLTON *Juvenal* 48 Officers, that make use of their authority to monopolise all beneficiall places and good bargaines. **1830** GALT *Lawrie T.* (1849) II. iii. 50 Finding me a beneficial customer.

3. *Law.* †**a.** Of or pertaining to a benefice; having a benefice, beneficed. *Obs.*

1592 *Act James VI*, (1814) 573 (JAM.) The occasion thairof is the directioun of lettrez of horning in beneficiall materis generallie. **1660** R. COKE *Power & Subj.* 230 Any person.. not being beneficiall, or having any spirituall promotion. *a* **1859** HALLAM (in Ogilvie), An engagement was tendered to all civil officers and beneficial clergy.

b. Of or pertaining to the usufruct of property; enjoying the usufruct.

1844 J. WILLIAMS *Real Prop. Law* (1877) 162 He is the beneficial owner of the property. **1863** KEBLE *Bp. Wilson* v. 168 Such a formal surrender as should secure.. the lord's beneficial interest in them. **1868** ROGERS *Pol. Econ.* ix. 87 The beneficial lessees of the various monastic corporations.

B. *sb.* ? A letter presenting to a benefice; a presentation. (Johnson says 'A benefice.')

1591 SPENSER *M. Hubberd* 486 How to a Benefice he might aspire. 'Marie, there (said the Priest) is arte indeed.. For that the ground-worke is, and end of all, How to obtain a Beneficiall.

beneˈficially, *adv.* [f. prec. + -LY[2].] In a beneficial manner.

†**1.** Beneficently, liberally, bountifully. *Obs.*

1530–1 *Act 22 Hen. VIII*, xv, His said free pardon.. shall be.. taken.. most beneficially.. to all.. his sayed subiectes. **1609** R. CAWDRAY in Spurgeon *Treas. Dav.* Ps. xix. 1–4 As the sun with his light beneficially comforteth all the world. **1611** COTGR., *Liberalement*, bountifully; beneficially, with an open hand.

2. Advantageously, profitably, helpfully.

1531 *Act 23 Hen. VIII*, x. §3 This estatute shalbe alweys expounded as beneficially as may be to the destruccion and utter avoyding of such use, intentes and purposes. *c* **1771** MASON in Johnson *Gray* Wks. (1787) IV. 300 To others, at least innocently employed; to himself, certainly beneficially. **1878** SEELEY *Stein* III. 529 France.. has influenced it [the Greek cause] at once benevolently and beneficially.

3. *Law.* In the way of a beneficial owner or interest. Cf. BENEFICIAL A. 3.

1788 J. POWELL *Devises* (1827) II. 249 The person beneficially entitled for life. **1875** POSTE *Gaius* III. (ed. 2) 430 Both the agent and the principal are beneficially interested. **1885** *Law Times Rep.* LII. 650/1 The various persons beneficially entitled under W. Plowright's will.

beneˈficialness. [f. as prec. + -NESS.]

†**1.** Beneficent character, beneficence. *Obs.*

1528 ROY *Sat.* (Arb.) 35 They reputed vs for haulfe goddes and more, thorowe the masses beneficialnes. *a* **1568** COVERDALE *Spir. Perle* xxiv. 240 If God of his naturall loue, beneficialnesse and free liberalitie geueth here.. health, strength, richesse. **1691** NORRIS *Pract. Disc.* 115 The goodness and beneficialness of the Divine Nature.

2. Beneficial quality, usefulness, profitableness.

1587 GOLDING *De Mornay* xi. 157 Shouldest thou not rather commend the beneficialnesse thereof [the Sea]? **1677** HALE *Prim. Orig. Man.* 5 They do not commend their knowledge to us upon the account of their usefulness and beneficialness. **1739** BURKITT *On N.T.* Matt. iv. 24 *note*, A life of universal serviceableness and beneficialness to Mankind. **1862** RUSKIN *Unto this Last* 46 The beneficialness of the inequality depends, first, on the methods by which it is accomplished.

beneficiary (bɛnɪˈfɪʃ(ɪ)ərɪ), *a.* and *sb.* [ad. L. *beneficiārius*: cf. F. *bénéficiaire* and see -ARY.]

A. *adj.*

1. Holding, held as, or pertaining to the holding of, a benefice: *spec.* to the holding of land by feudal tenure; feudatory.

a **1626** BACON (J.), To be made a feudatory or beneficiary king of England, under the seignory in chief of the pope. *a* **1641** SPELMAN *Feudes & Tenures* xxv. (R.) Beneficiary services.. done by the middling or lesser Thanes to the King and the greater Thanes. **1682** BURNET *Rights Princes* vi. 218 Not so ancient as their Beneficiary Tenures. **1768** BLACKSTONE *Comm.* II. 51 As if they had received their lands from his bounty.. as pure, proper, beneficiary feudatories. **1818** HALLAM *Mid. Ages* (1872) I. 147 Alodial lands are commonly opposed to beneficiary or feudal.

2. Of a kind by which one benefits or profits. *rare.*

1836 J. GILBERT *Chr. Atonem.* viii. (1852) 244 His justice.. is not to be considered as the prosecutor of a beneficiary claim, but as an exactor from himself.

B. *sb.*

1. The holder of a feudal 'benefice'; a feudatory.

1611 SPEED *Hist. Gt. Brit.* IX. vii. 138 Wee (being their Beneficiaries or Free-holders for such Countries as wee held in France). **1654** LESTRANGE *King Chas. I*, 121 He demanded from the Prince.. that he.. should repute himself as his Beneficiary and Vassal. **1754** ERSKINE *Princ. Sc. Law* (1809) 199 The legislature, looking upon vassals as proprietors, and not merely as beneficiaries. **1818** HALLAM *Mid. Ages* (1872) I. 131 The great beneficiaries, the most wealthy and potent families in Neustria or France.

2. The holder of an ecclesiastical living.

1641 MILTON *Animadv.* Wks. 1738 I. 77 Your Beneficiaries the Priests. **1726** AYLIFFE *Parerg.* 112 If it [a benefice] be annex'd to another Benefice, the Beneficiary is obliged to serve the Parish Church in his own proper Person. **1846** PRESCOTT *Ferd. & Is.* I. Introd. 39 The subordinate beneficiaries of his Church.

3. One who receives benefits or favours; a debtor to another's bounty.

1662 W. SCLATER *Exp. 2 Thess.* (1627) Ep. Ded. 3, I rest, your thankfull, and most obseruant Beneficiary. **1663** BAXTER *Div. Life* 14 We are his Children as he is our Father; or his obliged Beneficiaries as he is our Benefactor. **1856** OLMSTED *Slave States* 606 Another young man, who looked like a beneficiary of the Education Society. **1858** HOLLAND *Titcomb's Lett.* vii. 65 Content to be a beneficiary of society —to receive favors and confer none.

beneficiate (bɛnɪˈfɪʃɪeɪt), *v. Mining.* [f. Sp. *beneficiar* to benefit, to derive profit from a mine, + -ATE[3].] *trans.* To reduce (ores). Hence **beneˈficiating** *ppl. a.*, **beneficiˈation**, the reduction of ores.

1871 *Trans. Amer. Inst. Mining Eng.* I. 92 Such works as beneficiate ores directly in the mining districts. **1883** W. BISHOP *Old Mexico* v. xviii. 238 His ancient beneficiating hacienda of Regla. **1881** RAYMOND *Mining Gloss.*, *Beneficiation*, usually means the reduction of ores.

†**beneficie.** *Obs. rare*⁻¹. [ad. L. *benefici-um* BENEFICE.] Benefit, benign influence, favour.

c **1449** PECOCK *Repr.* 200 Graunte to this peple of Crist the Beneficie of the Crosse.

[**beneficience, -ficiency, -ficient**, erroneous forms of BENEFICENCE, -FICENCY, -FICENT, found passim as misprints in various books or editions, whence the last two have been accepted by Todd, and uncritically copied by subsequent compilers.]

†**beneˈficious**, *a. Obs.* [f. L. *benefici-um* + -OUS: cf. *officious*.] = BENEFICENT.

1535 FISHER *Wks.* 377 So liberall and beneficious. **1610** HOLLAND *Camden's Brit.* 362 (D.) The Beauchamps.. acknowledge Haber de Burgo.. beneficious to them.

benefit (ˈbɛnɪfɪt), *sb.* Forms: 4 **benfet, bynfet, benfait,** (*pl.* **benfes**), 4–5 **benefet(e, benfeet, beenfete, bienfait, -fet(e,** 5 **benefayte, benfeyte, bienfette, -faytte,** 6 **benifit(e, benyfyt, bunfyte, benefact, -faict,** 7 **benefit(t)e, -fict,** 7– **benefit.** [ME. *benfet*, a. AFr. *benfet*, = Central Fr. *bienfait*:—L. *benefactum* good deed, kind action, *lit.* (a thing) well done, f. *bene facĕre* to do well. In 15–16th c. the first syllable was assimilated to the L.; the later change of the second syllable to *fit* seems merely phonetic.]

†**1.** A thing well done; a good or noble deed.

1377 LANGL. *P. Pl.* B. v. 621 Þe boldnesse of þi bienfetes maketh þe blynde þanne. **1393** GOWER *Conf.* III. 187 Of every bienfait the merite The god him self it woll aquite. **1480** CAXTON *Ovid's Met.* XIV. xi, Alle.. that hade seen hys bienfayttes, wer mevyd wyth grace toward hym. **1811** LANDOR *Ct. Julian* Wks. 1846 II. 523 Man's only relics are his benefits.

2. a. A kind deed, a kindness; a favour, gift. *arch.*

1377 LANGL. *P. Pl.* B. v. 436 ȝif any man doth me a benfait [*v.r.* benfeet, bienfait, -fet, C bynfet]. *c* **1430** *Life St. Katharine* (1884) 27 Þe sonne and þe mone.. whos benefettys alle deedly creatures vse. *c* **1449** PECOCK *Repr.* 161 Rememoratyf syignes of God and of his Benefetis. **1526** TINDALE *Acts* xiv. 17 In that he shewed his benefaictes. **1557** N. T. (Geneva) *Philemon* 14 That thy benefit shuld not be as it were of necessitie, but willingly. **1611** *ibid.* [as prec.]. **1600** SHAKS. *A.Y.L.* I. ii. 37 Her [Fortune's] benefits are mightily misplaced. **1628** HOBBES *Thucyd.* (1822) 63 For the men which thou hast saved.. thy benefit is laid up in our house indelibly registerd.

†**b.** *by* (occas. *through*) *the benefit of*: by or through the kindness or favour of; by the agency or help of, by means of (a person or thing). *Obs.*

1538 STARKEY *England* 14 By the bunfyte and powar of nature. **1578** BANISTER *Hist. Man* IV. 51 By the benefitte of the third Muscle the shoulder blade is lifted vp. **1590** SHAKS. *Com. Err.* I. i. 91 By the benefit of his wished light The seas waxt calme. **1609** SKENE *Reg. Maj.* 23 He sall be made frie be the Kings benefite and decreit. **1709** STEELE *Tatler* No. 181 ¶1 By the Benefit of Nature.. Length of Time.. blots out the Violence of Afflictions.

c. A benefaction (in somewhat of a legal sense).

1591 SHAKS. *1 Hen. VI*, V. iv. 152 Accept the Title thou vsurp'st, Of benefit proceeding from our King, And not of any challenge of Desert. **1594** —— *Rich. III*, III. vii. 196 Take to your Royall selfe this proferr'd benefit of Dignitie.

3. a. Advantage, profit, good. (The ordinary sense.) ***for the benefit of***: for the advantage of, on behalf of. †***to take benefit of*** (a thing): to take advantage of, avail oneself of. ***benefit of the doubt***: see DOUBT *sb.*[1] 1 b.

[**1393** GOWER *Conf.* I. 304 Whan Jupiter this harm hath sein Another bienfait there ayein He yaf. **1483** CAXTON *Gold. Leg.* 362/2 We receyue dayly many bienfaites of this cyte.] **1512** *Act 4 Hen. VIII*, ii. § 2 He to have non avauntage or benefette of the matter alleged by hym. **1576** LAMBARDE *Peramb. Kent* (1826) 209 If you minded to haue benefit by the Roode of Grace. **1651** HOBBES *Leviath.* II. xxviii. 162 If the harm inflicted be lesse than the benefit. **1752** JOHNSON *Rambl.* No. 199 ¶2 Having long laboured for the benefit of mankind. **1789** BELSHAM *Ess.* ix. I. 173 Government is an institution for the benefit of the people governed. **1875** JOWETT *Plato* (ed. 2) I. 28, I have an impression that temperance is a benefit and a good.

b. A natural advantage or 'gift.'

1600 SHAKS. *A.Y.L.* IV. i. 34 Disable all the benefits of your owne Countrie. **1613** —— *Hen. VIII*, I. ii. 115 When these so Noble benefits shall proue Not well dispos'd.

c. *Law.* The advantage of belonging to a privileged order which was exempted from the jurisdiction or sentence of the ordinary courts of law; the exemption itself: in the phrases ***benefit of clergy***, ***benefit of peerage***; see CLERGY, PEERAGE.

1488–9 *Act 4 Hen. VII*, xiii. (*title*), An act to take awaye the benefytt of Clergye from certayne persons. **1718** HICKES & NELSON *J. Kettlewell* II. §56. 175 To this they Pleaded the Benefit of their Peerage. **1827** HALLAM *Const. Hist.* (1876) I. ii. 58 In 1513 the benefit of clergy was entirely taken away from murderers and highway robbers.

d. Pecuniary advantage, profit, gain.

1592 *No-body & Some-b.* (1878) 336 The grand benefit you get by dice, Deceitfull Cards, and other cozening games. **1612** DAVIES *Discov. why Irel.* (1787) 29 Why the King received no benefit of his land of Ireland. **1712** STEELE *Spect.* No. 310 ¶2 My Estate is seven hundred Pounds a Year, besides the Benefit of Tin-Mines. **1885** *Law Times Rep.* LII. 706/1 The secretary transferred the benefit of his contract as to three of the lots to other persons.

4. Hence in special senses: **a.** A theatrical performance the receipts from which are given to a particular actor, the playwright, or some other person connected with the theatre. (First granted to Mrs. Barry 16th Jan. 1687. *Hist. Stage* (1792) 29.) Hence, any entertainment or display the receipts from which are given to a particular player or company; also, the proceeds from such an entertainment.

[Cf. **1629** SIR H. HERBERT in Malone *Eng. Stage* (1821) III. 177 The benefitt of the winters day from the kinges company.. upon the play of 'The Moor of Venice,' comes, this 22 of Nov. 1629, unto 9*l.* 16*s.* 0*d.*] **1709** STEELE *Tatler* No. 1 ¶6 Acted for the Benefit of Mr. Betterton. **1721** SWIFT *Epil. to Play* Wks. 1755 III. II. 181 Actors, who at best are hardly savers, Will give a night of benefit to weavers? **1798** *Times* 3 Oct. *Advt.*, Royal Circus. For the Benefit of Mr. Simpson. **1802** *Sporting Mag.* XXI. 17/1 The grand display of pugilistic dexterity, advertised by Belcher, for his benefit, at Sadler's Wells. *Ibid.* 17/2 Spectators at Mr. Belcher's benefit. [**1846** *Spirit of Times* (N.Y.) 18 Apr. 91/2 A disposition prevails to give him a sort of 'benefit' as an offset to the late loss he sustained by fire.] **1850** THACKERAY *Pendennis* vi, She was going to have a benefit and appear as Ophelia. **1854** *Lillywhite's Guide to Cricketers* 85 Those noblemen, gentlemen, and clubs.. who were kind enough to honour him with a 'donation' towards his benefit. **1890** CONAN DOYLE *Sign of Four* v. 74 Don't you remember the amateur who fought three rounds with you.. on the night of your benefit four years back?

†**b.** A prize in a lottery; a winning ticket. *Obs.*

1694 LUTTRELL *Brief Rel.* (1857) III. 384 Yesterday 72 benefits were drawn in the million lottery. **1694** *Lond. Gaz.* No. 2968/2 That Benefit does belong to the Person that shall produce a Ticket of the same Number. **1710** STEELE *Tatler* No. 202 ¶5 After their Number is drawn, whether it was a Blank or Benefit. **1711** *Lond. Gaz.* No. 4903/4 The number'd Tickets entitled to Benefits in the Lottery. **1715** *Ibid.* No. 5326/3 The Tickets called Benefits [carry] an interest at the Rate of 4*l.* per Cent. per Ann.

†**c.** An ecclesiastical living, benefice, endowment. *Obs.*

1554 in Strype *Eccl. Mem.* III. II. App. xvi. 40 Whether he doth bestow yearly the fift part of his benefit. **1719** D'URFEY *Pills* (1872) IV. 86 Your Benefits you'll keep, whilst another feeds the Sheep.

d. That which a person is entitled to in the way of pecuniary assistance, medical or other attendance, pension, and the like, under the National Insurance Act of 1911 and similar subsequent Acts, or as a member of a benefit (or friendly) society; more explicitly ***maternity, medical, sick(ness benefit.***

1875 *Act 38 & 39 Vict.* c. 60 §24 (8), Provided as follows as respects friendly societies: (*a*) No special resolution..is valid..without the written consent of every person for the time being receiving or entitled to any relief..or other benefit from the funds of the society. **1891** [see SICKNESS 6]. **1895** *Daily News* 7 June 2/3 Contributions..providing for confinement benefit. **1901** B. S. ROWNTREE *Poverty* 362 In addition to the sick benefit there is a funeral benefit of £10. **1911** *Act 1 & 2 Geo. V*, c. 55 §8 Payment in the case of the confinement of the wife..of an insured person..of a sum of thirty shillings (in this Act called 'maternity benefit'). *Ibid.*, In the case of insured persons who have attained the age of seventy, the right to sickness benefit and disablement benefit shall cease. *Ibid.* §10 His right to medical benefit, sanatorium benefit, and maternity benefit shall be suspended. **1927** CARR-SAUNDERS & JONES *Soc. Struct. Eng. & Wales* 150 The applicant may at the discretion of the Ministry of Labour receive 'extended' benefit for the remainder of the benefit year. **1958** *Listener* 23 Oct. 634/1 Unemployment and sickness benefit were put on a new basis [in 1946].

5. *Comb.* and *attrib.* (only in senses 4 and 5), as ***benefit-bill, -concert, -day, match, -night, -play, -social***; also **benefit-club, -society**, an association whose members, by the regular payment of small sums, are entitled to pecuniary help in time of age or sickness; also *fig.*; **benefit-ticket**, (*a*) a winning ticket at a lottery (cf. 5 b.); (*b*) a ticket for a benefit (sense 4 a).

1755 MRS. C. CHARKE *Life* 56 To inform all my Acquaintance, that I was the Person so set down in Mrs. Thurmond's *Benefit-Bills. **1844** J. COWELL *Thirty Yrs. Among Players* (1845) I. ix. 23 For so he used to designate himself in his benefit-bills. **1812** *Examiner* 11 May 291/1 The *benefit club..forms something of a provision against adversity. **1817** COLERIDGE *Poems* 111 One Benefit-Club for mutual flattery. **1759** JOHNSON in *Boswell* I. 342 Mrs. Ogle ..hopes by a *benefit concert to set herself free from a few debts. **1712** STEELE *Spect.* No. 288 ¶3 The *Benefit Days of my Plays and Operas. **1871** *Baily's Mag.* June 169 The great compliment of a *benefit match at Lord's has been granted to Willsher by the Committee of the M.C.C. **1748** SMOLLETT *Rod. Rand.* (1812) I. 439 My play..could not have been ready until the end of March, when the *benefit nights came on. **1824–9** LANDOR *Imag. Conv.* (1846) I. 254 Their opera-girls vie in benefit-nights. **1740** CIBBER *Apol.* (1756) I. 120 The indulgence of having an annual *benefit-play. **1929** *Collier's* 12 Jan. 10/2 He met her at a church *benefit-social the very same day he arrived at Bellwood. **1801** H. MORE *Let.* in J. Aitken *Eng. Lett. XIX cent.* (1946) 52, I have instituted..friendly *benefit societies for poor women, which have proved a great relief to the sick and lying-in. **1837** DICKENS in *Sk. Boz* 2nd Ser. 322 There is not a parlour, or club-room, or benefit society..without its red-faced man. **1845** DISRAELI *Sybil* (Rtldg.) 293 The Benefit Societies..have money in the banks that would maintain the whole working classes..for six weeks. **1694** LUTTRELL *Brief. Rel.* (1857) III. 382 Yesterday the million lottery drew 66 *benefit tickets. **1746** GARRICK *Corresp.* (1831) I. 41 A terrible 'Row' ensued, between the few who paid ready money, and those who brought in his benefit-tickets. **1859** SALA *Tw. round Clock* (1861) 257 Solicitations for engagements, cards, bills, and applications for benefit tickets.

benefit ('bɛnɪfɪt), *v.* Pa. t. and pple. **benefited.** [f. prec. sb.]

1. *trans.* To do good to, to be of advantage or profit to; to improve, help forward.

1549 CHEKE *Hurt Sedit.* (R.), Ye be not so muche worthie as to be benefited in anye kinde. **1611** SHAKS. *Wint. T.* IV. iv. 514 What course I mean to hold, Shall nothing benefit your knowledge. *a* **1613** OVERBURY *Worthy Comm.* Wks. (1865) 107 If ever a man will benefit himselfe upon his foe, then is the time, when they have lost force. **1792** BURKE *Let. Dundas* Wks. IX. 283 The cause of humanity would be far more benefited by the continuance of the trade. **1879** LUBBOCK *Addr. Pol. & Educ.* i. 8 A system of duties which injures our interests without benefiting those of the colonies.

2. *intr.* (for *refl.*) To receive benefit, to get advantage; to profit.

1613 SHAKS. *Hen. VIII*, I. ii. 80 Malicious censurers, which euer, As rau'nous Fishes, doe a Vessell follow That is new trim'd; but benefit no further Then vainly longing. **1644** MILTON *Educ.* Wks. (1847) 98/2 To tell you therefore what I have benefited herein. **1884** *National Rev.* July 720 One who has never directly or indirectly benefited a single shilling by any humble efforts he may have put forth.

'benefited, *ppl. a.* [f. prec. + -ED.]

1. That has received benefit or profit.

1837 HT. MARTINEAU *Society in Amer.* II. 102 Repayment from the benefited parties being secured.

†**2.** Carrying a 'benefit' (in a lottery). *Obs.*

1693 LUTTRELL *Brief Rel.* (1857) 160 The other 22,500£ he devides into 250 benefitted lotts or tickets.

benefiter ('bɛnɪfɪtə(r)). [f. as prec. + -ER¹.] He who confers, or (more usually) derives, benefit.

1883 *St. James's Gaz.* 15 June, The only benefitter is the ship-owner.

'benefiting, *vbl. sb.* [f. as prec. + -ING¹.] The conferring or deriving of benefit.

1594 T. B. *La Primaud Fr. Acad.* II. 301 Mercie is often taken in the holy Scriptures for..good will, benefiting, friendship. *Mod.* He returned without benefiting by the change.

†**be'negro,** *v.* ? *Obs.* [f. BE- *pref.* 6 + NEGRO.] *trans.* To make Negro; to make of the colour of a negro; to blacken, darken.

1646 SIR T. BROWNE *Pseud. Ep.* 330 If we derive the curse on Cham..we shall Benegroe a greater part of the earth than ever was, or so conceived. **1650** CHARLETON *Paradoxes* 19 No reason..why that particular place..should be benegroed and torrified. **1658** HEWYT *Serm.* 109 (T.), Benegroed in more than Cimmerian..darkness.

beneit, obs. form of BENNET *sb.*¹

Benelux ('bɛnɪlʌks). [f. *Be*lgium, *Ne*therlands, *Lux*embourg.] The customs union of Belgium, the Netherlands, and Luxembourg formed in October 1947. Also *attrib.*

1947 *Foreign Affairs* July 692 The Secretariat prepared a common tariff for the 'Benelux Union'. **1947** *Spectator* 10 Oct. 454/1 Success would make 'Benelux'..the third trading power in the world. **1960** *New Statesman* 26 Mar. 434/3 This means that British exports will be discriminated against, especially in the German and Benelux countries.

†**be'neme,** *v. Obs.* Forms: 1 **benǽman, -néman,** 3–5 **bineme(n,** 4–6 **byneme.** [OE. *bi-, benǽman*, on OTeut. type **binamjan*, deriv. of *binemen*, pa. t. *benam*. The ME. *beneme* may however be merely a variant of BENIM, with which it coincides in use.] *trans.* **a.** To deprive (with *gen.*). **b.** To deprive (a person) of (a thing), to take away (a thing) from (a person). **c.** To take away.

c **893** K. ÆLFRED *Oros.* I. x. §4 Ne mehte hie þæs londes benæman. *c* **1205** LAY. 13155 þou..þat binemest vs houre broþer. *c* **1325** *Coer de L.* 1403. **1387** TREVISA *Higden* (1865) I. 73 ȝif Paradys were so hiȝe, somtyme it schulde byneme þe liȝt, and make þe clips of þe mone. **1481** *Reynard* (1844) 144 Thenne shal ye byneme hym his syght. **1562** FOXE *A. & M.* I. 455/2 He bynemeth Christ his Worship.

†**bene-merent,** *a. Obs. rare*⁻⁰. [f. L. *bene* well + *merent-em*, pres. pple. of *merēre* to deserve.] 'That deserves well.' Blount *Glossogr.* 1656.

benempt, obs. pa. t. and pa. pple. of BENAME.

†**beneplacit.** *Obs. rare.* Also **-placity.** [ad. late L. *beneplacit-um* (see Vulgate *Eph.* i. 9) good pleasure, f. *bene* well + *placitum* pleased, pa. pple. of *placēre* to please, as adj. 'pleasing, acceptable.' (In the two unauthorized edd. of *Religio Med.* of 1642, *beneplacity*; which Blount inserted in his *Glossogr.*)] Good pleasure, gracious purpose.

1643 SIR T. BROWNE *Relig. Med.* 130 The cause of my salvation, which was the mercy and beneplacit [edd. **1642** beneplacity] of God. **1656** BLOUNT *Gloss.*, *Beneplacity*, that which pleaseth well, good liking. **1658** PHILLIPS, Beneplacitie.

†**beneplacit,** *a. Obs. rare.* [ad. L. *beneplacitus* well-pleased; see prec.] Pleased, satisfied.

1678 GALE *Crt. Gentiles* III. 18 God's Beneplacite wil, commonly stiled his wil of good pleasure..is that whereby he decrees, effects, or permits al events & effects.

†**,bene-'placiture.** *Obs. rare*⁻¹. [f. as prec. + -URE.] = BENEPLACIT *sb.*

1662 GLANVIL *Lux Orient.* iv. (1682) 28 Hath he by his holy penmen told us that either of the other ways was more sutable to his beneplaciture?

[**beneship.** In 16th c. 'Peddelars' Frenche' (Harman's *Caveat* 83–86) = 'very good.' Apparently the source of Bailey's '*Beenship*, worship, goodness.']

beneson, obs. form of BENISON.

benet ('bɛnət), *sb.* Forms: 5 **benett, benott,** 5–6 **benette,** 4– **benet.** [a. OF. *beneit* (mod.F. *bénit*):—L. *benedict-us* blessed: see BENEDICT.] The third of the four lesser orders in the Roman Catholic Church, one of whose functions was the exorcizing of evil spirits.

c **1383** WYCLIF *Sel. Wks.* (1871) III. 285 Of..crowning of benetis renneþ þe same extorsion. **1480** CAXTON *Chron. Eng.* IV. (1520) 38/2 He ordeyned that he that was worthy sholde ascende gree by gree to his ordre, fyrst benet, than colet, subdeacon, deacon, and than preest. **1509** *Ortus Voc.* in *Promp. Parv.* 30 *Exorcista*, id est adjurator vel increpator, a benette or a conjurer. **1553–87** FOXE *A. & M.* III. 125 The lowest Vesture, which they had only in taking Benet and Collet. **1846** C. MAITLAND *Ch. Catacombs* 194 It is related of Huss the Martyr, that..he was degraded from all his orders ..and the offices of exorcist, sexton, and benet.

benet (bɪ'nɛt), *v.* [f. BE- 6 + NET *v.* or *sb.*] *trans.* **a.** To cover as with a net. **b.** To catch in a net, ensnare, entangle; usually *fig.*

1602 SHAKS. *Ham.* V. ii. 29 Being thus benetted round with Villaines. **1614** SYLVESTER *Bethulia's Resc.* IV. 60 Her Robe, Sky-colour'd Silk, with curious Caul Of golden Twist, benetted over all. **1860** T. MARTIN *Horace* 188 The gaudier charms Of a girl that's both wealthy and wanton benet him.

benet, variant of BENNET.

benettle, etc.: see BE- *pref.*

†**beneurous,** *a. Obs.* Also **bien-, benewrous.** [a. OF. *beneureus* (mod.F. *bienheureux*).] Happy, blessed. So †**be'newred** [ad. OF. *beneuré*; see -ED.] = prec. †**be'newrely** *adv.* [cf. OF. *beneure(e)ment*], happily. **be'neurte** [a. OF. *beneureté*], happiness, blessedness. (Only in Caxton.)

1483 CAXTON *Cato* F ij b, The beneurous or happy. —— *Golden Leg.* 428/3 He took the righte benewrous reste of deth. *Ibid.* 426/1 Fylled with benewred auncyente of dayes. *Ibid.* 428/2 He comyng benewrelye unto his laste dayes. **1480** —— *Ovid's Met.* XIII. ix, Benewrte & honour laste her not longe.

Beneventan (bɛnɪ'vɛntən), *a.* Also (formerly) **Beneventine.** [It. *beneventano*, f. med.L. *Beneventanus*, f. *Beneventum* Benevento, province of Italy + -AN.] Of or pertaining to a medieval script principally of southern Italy.

1882 *Catal. Add. MSS. Brit. Mus. 1876–81* 70 [Exultet Roll]..written in Italy in Lombardic or Beneventine characters of the twelfth century. **1912** E. M. THOMPSON *Introd. Gr. & Lat. Palaeogr.* xvi. 348 Although the title of Lombardic is applied as a general term to the writing of Italy in the early middle ages, that title might be more properly restricted to its particular developement in the south, to which the titles [*sic*] of Beneventan is also given. **1914** E. A. LOEW *Beneventan Script* ii. 22 The peculiar script which grew up and flourished within the ancient duchy of Benevento..we shall consistently call..Beneventan. **1959** *Chambers's Encycl.* X. 358/1 It is known by its mediaeval name of Beneventan script (*littera Beneventana*; the term 'Lombardic' by which it was known until quite recently should be avoided).

benevolence (bɪ'nɛvələns). Forms: (5 **bienueullance**), 5–6 **beneuolens, beniuolence, benyuolence, -ens,** 4– **benevolence,** (4–7 **beneu-**). [a. OF. *benivolence*, ad. L. *benevolentia* well-wishing, f. *benevolent-em*: see BENEVOLENT. This OF. form was a learned or semi-popular adaptation of the Lat. word; its genuine F. descendant being *bienvoillance*, later *-veuillance* (whence Caxton's *bienveullance*), now corruptly *bienveillance*. In Eng. *benivolence* was further latinized as *benevolence* at an early period (if this was not directly from L.]

1. Disposition to do good, desire to promote the happiness of others, kindness, generosity, charitable feeling (as a general state or disposition towards mankind at large).

c **1384** CHAUCER *Mother of G.* 10 Sauer of vs by thy beneuolence. **1423** JAMES I. *King's Q.* xcix, Hye Quene of Lufe! sterre of beneuolence. **1481** CAXTON *Myrr.* III. xii. 159 Of the fader..he [Plato] sayde the power and puissaunce, of the sone, the sappyence, and of the holy gost the bienueullaunce. **1552** LYNDESAY *Tragedy* 125 With supporte of sum Lordis beneuolens. **1605** THYNNE *Animadv.* App. (1865) 111 By the..support of your Majesties benevolence and liberality. **1726** BUTLER *Serm. Hum. Nat.* i. Wks. 1874 II. 6 If there be any affection in human nature, the object and end of wᶜʰ is the good of another, this is itself benevolence, or the love of another. **1781** GIBBON *Decl. & F.* III. l. 142 Benevolence is the foundation of justice. **1876** MOZLEY *Univ. Serm.* ix. 192 The poor and dependent..exercise our active benevolence.

†**2. a.** Favourable feeling or disposition, as an emotion manifested towards another; affection; goodwill (towards a particular person or on a particular occasion). ***to do one's benevolence***: to lend one's friendly offices. *Obs.*

1423 JAMES I. *King's Q.* cviii, Though I geve the beneuolence, It standis noght ȝit in myn aduertence. *c* **1430** LYDG. *Bochas* Tab. Contents (1554) Bij, Roboam..loste the benevolence of his people. **1526** TINDALE *1 Cor.* vii. 3 Let the man geve vnto the wyfe due benevolence. **1598** SHAKS. *Merry W.* I. i. 32, I..will be glad to do my beneuolence. **1645** USSHER *Body Div.* (1647) 284 When due benevolence is not yielded, although there be aptness there-unto. **1817** JAS. MILL *Brit. Ind.* II. IV. ii. 70 His dislike of application and control prevented his acquiring the benevolence of his superiors.

b. ***love of benevolence***: see LOVE *sb.*¹ 2.

3. *concr.* An expression of goodwill, an act of kindness; a gift or grant of money; a contribution for the support of the poor.

c **1425** WYNTOUN *Cron.* VII. vii. 157 Recoveryd þe benevolens Wyth trawayle. **1583** STUBBES *Anat. Abus.* II. 101 To make collections for the poore, to gather beneuolences, and contributions of euerie one that was disposed to give. **1622** LEY in *Fortescue Papers* 175 What Benevolence we would willingly bestow towardes the Palatinate. **1650** FULLER *Pisgah* 400 Convenient for such as went up to sacrifice, to cast in their benevolence. **1766** ENTICK *London* IV. 58 Towards the charge whereof the companies gave great benevolences. **1868** MILMAN *St. Paul's* xi. 282 The City of London gave first a great benevolence.

4. *Eng. Hist.* A forced loan or contribution levied, without legal authority, by the kings of England on their subjects. First so called in 1473 when astutely asked by Edward IV., as a token of goodwill towards his rule. Sometimes loosely applied to similar impositions elsewhere.

1483 *Act 1 Rich. III*, ii. §1 A newe imposicion named a benevolence. **1494** FABYAN vii. 664 He rode about the more parte of the lande, and vsed the people in suche fayre maner, that he reysed therby notable summes of money, the whiche way of the leuyinge of this money was after named a benyuolence. *c* **1534** *Pol. Verg. Eng. Hist.* II. 161 Perchance very many gave that benevolence with evil will. **1644** LD. DIGBY in Rushworth *Hist. Coll.* III. (1692) I. 31 The granting of Subsidies, and that under so preposterous a name as of a Benevolence, for that which is a malevolence indeed. **1661** PEPYS *Diary* 31 Aug., The Benevolence proves ..an occasion of so much discontent every where, that it had better it had never been set up. **1775** CHATHAM in *Parlt.*,

The spirit which now resists your taxation in America is the same which formerly opposed loans, benevolences, and ship-money in England. **1875** STUBBS *Const. Hist.* III. xviii. 213. **1882** FARRAR *Early Chr.* I. 56 Resentment was kept alive by the benevolences and imposts which Nero now demanded.

† **beˈnevolency.** *Obs.* [ad. L. *benevolentia*: see prec. and -ENCY.] The quality of being benevolent; also *concr.* a gift of money, a 'benevolence.'

1540 RAYNALD *Birth Man* (1634) Prol. 7 The benevolencie and willing fauour of all. **1698** NORRIS *Pract. Disc.* IV. 340 They retrench their Expenses, and withdraw their wonted Benevolencies. **1766** *Hist. Europe* in *Ann. Reg.* 38/1 The body of the Clergy, till very late taxed themselves and granted to the King benevolencies.

benevolent (bɪˈnɛvələnt), *a.* Also 5 benvolent, 5–6 benyuolente, 6 beneuolent. [a. OF. *benivolent, benvolent*, ad. L. *bene volent-em*, f. *bene* well + *volent-em* wishing, willing, pr. pple. of *velle* to will, wish: see BENEVOLENCE.]

1. Of the general frame or habit of mind: Desirous of the good of others, of a kindly disposition, charitable, generous.

1482 *Monk of Evesham* (Arb.) 75 Redy and benyuolente to alle men whilys he leuyd. **1548** UDALL, etc. *Erasm. Par. N.T.* Pref. 5 Our beneuolent loue and affeccion. **1725** POPE *Odyss.* III. 456 Beloued old man! benevolent as wise. **1781** J. MOORE *View Soc. It.* (1790) I. xxxix. 424 The mild precepts of a benevolent religion. **1848** MACAULAY *Hist. Eng.* I. 406 A small body of sages had turned away with benevolent disdain from the conflict.

b. *transf.* of things: Kindly, fostering.

1677 HALE *Prim. Orig. Man.* 306 The benevolent Heat of the Sun hath a great influence thereupon.

2. With the literal force of the Latin *bene volens*: Well-wishing, well-disposed *to, unto* (another).

1502 ARNOLD *Chron.* (1811) 161 A thinge..for the which wee shal [be] more ben volent unto thy Holynesse. **1509** HAWES *Past. Pleas.* XX. v, She [Sapience] is to man ryght benyvolent. **1667** MILTON *P.L.* VIII. 65 Raphael now.. Benevolent and facil thus repli'd.

†**3.** quasi-*sb.* = BENEVOLENCE 3. *Obs.* (? error.)

a **1639** SPOTTISWOOD *Hist. Ch. Scot.* VII. (1677) 541 The Noblemen..made offer to give a benevolent according to their abilities.

beˈnevolently, *adv.* [f. prec. + -LY[2].] In a benevolent manner; with benevolence.

1532 ELYOT in *Gov.* (1883) 77 It pleasid you so benevolently to remembre me. **1543–4** *Act 35 Hen. VIII*, xii, His subiectes..most willyngly and beneuolently..do remit..the same summes of money. **1779** SHERIDAN *Critic* I. ii. (1883) 156 A debt benevolently contracted to serve a friend. **1879** *Sat. Rev.* 5 July 21 He was benevolently engaged in making catches [at cricket].

beˈnevolentness. *rare*[−0]. [f. BENEVOLENT + -NESS.] = BENEVOLENCE.

1736 in BAILEY. Hence in Johnson, and mod. Dicts.

† **beˈnevoler.** *Obs. rare*[−1]. A well-wisher.

1486 *Paston Lett.* 889 III. 327 Her benevolers willith hir to continue hir sute.

benevolist (bɪˈnɛvəlɪst). [f. L. *benevol-us* (see prec.) + -IST.] A professor of benevolence. Cf. prec.

1825 (*title*) School for Patriots and Benevolists. **1863** *Scotsman* 14 Aug., To be experimented upon..by contending sets of sectarians and 'benevolists.'

† **beˈnevolous,** *a. Obs.* Also 5–6 benivolous, -us, benyvolouse. [f. as prec. + -OUS.]

1. Well-wishing, kindly, friendly, benevolent.

1470 HARDING *Chron.* xxxi. iv, Amendyng all their faultes and errours, With all their hertes full beneuolous. **1513** BRADSHAW *St. Werburge* 213 Vnclose thy succours, and be beniuolous. **1536** BELLENDEN *Cron. Scot.* (1821) I. 247 Maximus..schew him sa benivolus to the pepil. **1645** J. G[OODWIN] *Innoc. & Truth Tri.* To Rdr., A man of no benevolous or friendly comportance. *a* **1670** HACKET *Abp. Williams* I. (1693) 66 Such as knew not the wherefore were the more benevolous to the Arch-Bishop's misfortune.

2. *Astrol.* Of the planets, etc.: Of favourable influence, auspicious.

1642 SIR T. BROWNE *Relig. Med.* 43 The benevolous Aspects of my Nativity. **1652** GAULE *Magastrom.* 86 Planets amicall, benevolous, auspicious.

benewith, variant of BENDWITH.

benewrous, etc., variant of BENEUROUS, etc.

benfait, -fet, -feet, obs. forms of BENEFIT *sb.*

beng, variant of BHANG.

Bengal (bɛŋˈgɔːl). In 7 bengall. [Name of a province of Hindustan (in Marco Polo, 1298, as *Bangala*; in Vasco de Gama, 1498, as *Bemgala*; in Ovington, 1690, as *Bengala*; Col. Yule).]

1. Applied to piece goods (apparently of different kinds) exported from Bengal to England in the 17th c.: cf. Bengal Stripes in 2.

c **1680** POLEXFEN *Coll. Poems* 205 Their Persian Silks, Bengalls, Printed and Painted Callicoes..are used for Beds, Hanging of Rooms. **1696** LUTTRELL *Brief Rel.* (1857) IV. 147 A bill to be brought in to forbid the wearing of wrought silks brought from Persia and East India, with bengalls, callicoes, etc. **1696** *Merchant's Ware-ho.* 30 There is two sorts, strip'd and plain, by the Buyers called Bengalls..they are very fine stripes, but are of no great use or service. **1701** *Lond. Gaz.* No. 3740/3 All Wrought Silks, Bengalls, and Stuffs mixed with Silk. **1755** JOHNSON *Bengal*, a sort of thin slight stuff, made of silk and hair, for women's apparel. **1855** MACAULAY *Hist. Eng.* IV. 141 The importation of silks and of Bengals, as shawls were then called, was pronounced to be a curse to the country.

2. *Comb.* and *attrib.*, as **Bengal fire, flash** = *Bengal light*; **Bengal isinglass** = AGAR-AGAR; **Bengal light,** a kind of firework producing a steady and vivid blue-coloured light, used for signals; also *fig.* (see also quot. 1899); **Bengal quince,** the fruit of *Ægle Marmelos*, belonging to the orange family; **Bengal root** (see quot.); **Bengal silk; Bengal stripes,** striped ginghams, originally brought from Bengal, afterwards manufactured at Paisley, etc.; **Bengal tiger,** the tiger proper, so called from its abundance in lower Bengal.

1941 J. CARY *House Childr.* xliv. 191 If you have a sea battle, Harry, we must get you a *Bengal fire—it's the finest thing in the world for a ship blowing up after a battle. **1946** KOESTLER *Thieves in Night* 68 In the reddish *Bengal flashes which accompanied the detonations the silhouette of the barbed wire emerged. **1863** *Bengal isinglass [see AGAR-AGAR]. **1791** *Aris's Gazette* (Birmingham) 5 Sept. 3/5 A *Bengola Light. **1818** in *Pall Mall Gaz.* (1885) 5 Nov. 4/2 Superior Fireworks... A Bengal light. **1852** GEO. ELIOT *Lett.* (1954) II. 54 Froude is good—writes very judiciously and pleasantly, except that at the end he brings on Bengal lights and goes off in a Carlylian flourish. *c* **1865** J. WYLDE in *Circ. Sc.* I. 381/1 Used for the manufacture of Bengal lights. **1899** *Connorton's Tobacco Brand Directory U.S.* 550 Bengal Lights (cigarettes and cheroots). **1866** *Treas. Bot.* 953 *Bengal Quince, *Ægle Marmelos*. *Ibid.* 135 *Bengal Root, an old name for the roots of the Yellow Zedoary. **1711** *Lond. Gaz.* No. 4850/3, 15 Pound of Single E *Bengal Silk. **1875** URE *Dict. Arts* I. 336 *Bengal stripes, Ginghams; a kind of cotton cloth woven with coloured stripes, so called from the cottons which we formerly imported from Bengal.

Bengalese (bɛŋgɔːˈliːz), *a.* and *sb.* [f. BENGAL + -ESE.] = BENGALI *a.* and *sb.*

1778 HALHED *Gram. Bengal Lang.* p. xxi, The native Bengalese. **1872** CALVERLEY *Fly Leaves* (1903) 91 A patient of Skey's, Who is prone to catch chills, like all old Bengalese.

Bengali, Bengalee (bɛŋˈgɔːliː), *a.* and *sb.* [a. native *Bangālī*.] **A.** *adj.* Of or belonging to Bengal. **B.** *sb.* A native of Bengal; the language of Bengal, one of the Aryan vernaculars of India. So the obs. **Benˈgalan, Benˈgalian** *a.* and *sb.*; **Benˈgalic** *a.*

1613 PURCHAS *Pilgr.* I. v. v. 404 The Bengalans have a tradition or fable amongst them. **1768** *Phil. Trans.* LVIII. 130 Having met with a Bengalian doctor. **1801** H. LEBEDEFF *Gram. Ind. Dial.* Introd. 3 My Sircar..introduced me to a Bengallic School Master. **1848** THACKERAY *Van. Fair* lix, That gentleman would not let the Bengalee rest until he had executed his promise. **1858** W. ELLIS *Visits Madagascar* iii. 54 Bengalee or Chinese merchants. **1862** D. FORBES (*title*), Bengali Grammar.

‖ **bengaline** (ˈbɛŋgəliːn). [mod.F.; so called from similarity to the fabric mentioned under BENGAL 1.] A new (French) name for poplin, a mixed fabric of silk and worsted.

1884 *Pall Mall G.* 20 Sept. 4/1 *Autumn Fashions*, Bengaline (a superior substitute for Irish poplin).

benge, variant of BINGE *v. Obs.* to bow.

† **benger(e, byngger.** *Obs.* A corn-bin.

c **1440** *Promp. Parv.* 31 Bengere of corne [**1499** bengge], *techa* [= *theca*]. *Ibid.*, Bengere of a mylle [**1499** bengge], *ferricapsia*.

bengewine, bengwine, obs. ff. BENZOIN.

benic (ˈbɛnɪk), *a. Chem.* Also **behenic.** [f. BEN + -IC.] Obtained from oil of ben.

1873 WATTS *Fownes' Chem.* 695 Benic or Behenic Acid is a white crystalline fat. **1879** —— *Dict. Chem.*, *Benic acid*, This name has been applied to two different fatty acids.. benostearic acid, and..benomargaric acid.

† **ˈbenight,** *adv. Obs.* By night, ere night.

1642 GEN. PRESTON in Carte's *Coll.* (1735) 120, I will not trouble your Lordship with more benight.

benight (bɪˈnaɪt), *v.* [f. BE- 6 + NIGHT.]

1. *trans.* **a.** *pass.* To be overtaken by the darkness of night (before reaching a place of shelter).

1560 DAUS *Sleidane's Comm.* 326 The Emperour..was benighted and rode at Ancker. **1598** HAKLUYT *Voy.* I. 112 When we lay in the fields or were benighted before we came to oure iourneis end. **1678** BUNYAN *Pilgr.* I. (1862) 43, I am like to be benighted, for the day is almost spent. **1748** RICHARDSON *Clarissa* (1811) I. xxvii. 190 A gentleman.. would rather be benighted, than put up at his house. **1839** DE QUINCEY *Recoll. Lakes* Wks. 1862 II. 172 The tourists were benighted in a forest.

b. *active.* To involve in the darkness of night; *refl.* to hide oneself in the night. *rare. arch.*

1654 GAYTON *Fest. Notes* II. vi. 59 She straightway dight Her robes, & did herselfe benight. *a* **1691** BOYLE (J.) Those bright stars that did adorn our hemisphere, as those dark shades that did benight it, vanish. **1839** BAILEY *Festus* (1848) vi, Benighting even night with its grim limbs.

2. To involve in darkness, to darken, to cloud. Also *fig.*, of the effect of sorrow, disappointment, etc., upon one's face, prospects, or life.

a **1631** DONNE *Select.* (1840) 3 As the sun does not set to any nation..God..does not set to thy soul, though he benight it with an affliction. **1651** DAVENANT *Gondibert* III. v. xvi, Now jealousie no more benights her face. **1699** GARTH *Dispens.* (J.) The clouds look heavy and benight the sky. *Ibid.* (1706) 36 Smoth'ring Fogs of Smoke benight the Fire.

b. To involve in intellectual or moral darkness, in the 'night' of error or superstition.

1610 HEALEY *St. Aug. City of God* 414 Nor is the creature ever be nighted but when the love of the Creator forsakes him. **1692** E. WALKER *Epictetus' Mor.* lxiii. Whose Reason's Light Is clouded o'er, whom Error doth benight. **1712** HENLEY *Spect.* No. 396 §2 These Portraitures benight the faculties. **1831** J. WILSON *Unimore* vi. 281 What men..call Religion, now benighting half the earth.

3. To blind, to dazzle; to deprive of vision.

1621 G. SANDYS *Ovid's Met.* II. (1626) 26 Pale sudden feare..in so great a light, be-nights his eyes. **1651** J. C[LEVELAND] *Poems* 32 This Cabinet, whose aspect would benight Critick spectators with redundant light. **1652** BENLOWES *Theoph.* III. lvi. 44 O're-fulgent Beams daz'd Eyes benight.

benighted (bɪˈnaɪtɪd), *ppl. a.* [f. prec. + -ED[1].]

1. Overtaken by the darkness of the night; affected by the night (*obs.*).

1575 in Farr's *Sel. P.* (1845) II. 516 And so are all my lockes Bedecked..With these benighted drops. **1810** SCOTT *Lady of L.* I. xxi, He told of his benighted road. **1815** —— *Guy M.* xlviii, Some benighted fisherman, he thought.

2. *fig.* Involved in intellectual or moral darkness.

1634 MILTON *Comus* 384 He that hides a dark soul and foul thoughts, Benighted walks under the mid-day sun. **1856** MRS. BROWNING *Aur. Leigh* IV. 339 You poets are benighted in this age. **1863** KINGLAKE *Crimea* (1877) I. iii. 51 He was a benighted Moslem.

†**b.** Involved in obscurity. *Obs.*

1647 WARD *Simp. Cobler* 19 Seekers, looking for new Nuntio's from Christ, to assoile these benighted questions.

Hence **beˈnightedness.**

1865 *Pall Mall. G.* 5 July 1/2 Respectable old Russell Whigs, on whom charges of moral corruption operate much more powerfully than charges of intellectual benightedness.

beˈnighten (bɪˈnaɪt(ə)n), *v. rare.* [f. BENIGHT, app. after *enlight-en*: see -EN.] *trans.* To benight. Hence **beˈnightening** *vbl. sb.*

1844 *Blackw. Mag.* LVI. 787 A mere priestly delusion to enslave and benighten mankind. **1860** PUSEY *Min. Proph.* 193 Moral benightening which seems to cast the shadow of death over the soul.

benighter (bɪˈnaɪtə(r)). [f. BENIGHT + -ER[1].] One who keeps others in darkness.

1818 MOORE *Fudge Fam. Paris* vi. 208, I, from my soul, profess To hate all bigots and benighters.

beˈnighting, *vbl. sb.* [f. BENIGHT + -ING[1].] The fact of being benighted or overtaken by night away from shelter.

a **1639** W. WHATELEY *Prototypes* II. xxvi. (1640) 90 To meet with such kinde of accidents, as benighting. **1819** L. HUNT *Indicator*, No. 8 (1822) I. 60 Spenser..seems to have taken the idea of a benighting from Apollonius.

beˈnighting, *ppl. a.* [f. as prec. + -ING[2].] That benights or involves in darkness.

1649 DRYDEN *Death Ld. Hastings* 50 That veil which shrouds Our day-spring in so sad benighting clouds.

benightmare, etc.: see BE- *pref.*

beˈnightment. [f. as prec. + -MENT.] The state or condition of being involved in physical, intellectual, or moral darkness.

1651 BIGGS *New Disp.* §162 Confesses their benightment to the black paths of ignorance and error. **1850** ALISON *Hist. Europe.* xcvi. §99 The benightment of superstition.

benign (bɪˈnaɪn), *a.* Forms: 4–6 benygn(e, -yngne, -yng(e, -ing, 4–7 benigne, -ingne, 7– benign. [a. OF. *benigne, benin*:—L. *benignus* 'kindly,' prob. for *benigenus*, f. *bene* well + *-genus* born, of kind. Cf. *malignus, prīvignus*; for the sense L. *gentīlis*, F. *gentil*, Eng. *gentle*; also, Eng. *kind, kindly*, L. *generōsus*, Gr. γενναῖος.]

1. Of a kind disposition, gracious, kindly.

c **1320** R. BRUNNE *Medit.* 1103 ȝe weten weyl how benygne my dere sone was. *c* **1380** WYCLIF *Wks.* (1880) 353 Charity is benyngne. **1422** in Ellis *Orig. Lett.* II. 30 I. 96 That it please your..Grace of your benigne pitee and grace, to releve and refresh your said pouere Oratour. *c* **1550** *Scot. Poems 16th C.* II. 130 Hee is fair, sober and bening, Sweet, meek, and gentle in all thing. *a* **1619** FOTHERBY *Atheom.* II. xiv. § 4 It's he alone, euen he, the God beningne, That vs instructs, in euery blessed thing. **1850** MRS. BROWNING *Dr. Exile* Poems I. 7 As well As the benignest angel of you all.

†**b.** Gentle, meek, humble. *Obs.*

1377 LANGL. *P. Pl.* B. XVI. 7 Þe blosmes beth boxome speche and benygne lokynge. *c* **1386** CHAUCER *Clerkes T.* 287 Thise arn the wordes that the markis sayde To this benigne, verray, feithful mayde. *c* **1440** *Gesta Rom.* xci. 419 All men and women..that are lowe, ande meke, ande benigne.

2. Exhibiting or manifesting kindly feeling in look, gesture, or action; bland, gentle, mild.

c **1374** CHAUCER *Troylus* III. 1753 Benyng he was to eche in general. **1493** *Petronylla* (Pynson) 5 Benygne of porte, humble of face and chere. **1542** HEN. VIII. *Decl.* 193 We.. gaue..benigne and gentyl audience to suche Ambassadours, as repayred hither. **1663** BUTLER *Hud.* I. III. 880 Benigne &

not blustrous Against a vanquisht Foe. **1777** WATSON *Philip II* (1793) II. XIII. 114 Requesens indeed had a more benign and placid countenance than Alva. **1871** BLACKIE *Four Phases* i. 58 That when a thief takes your cloak you should thank him, like a benign Quaker, for his kindness.

3. *transf.* Of things: Favourable, kind, fortunate, salutary, propitious; *esp.* in *Astrol.* opposed to *malign, malignant*, etc.

a **1619** DONNE *Biathan.* 32 Those reasons which are most Benigne..ought to have the best acceptation. **1667** WATERHOUSE *Fire Lond.* 34 By concurrence of circumstances, benign to, and corresponding with a vastative event. **1667** MILTON *P.L.* XII. 538 So shall the World goe on, To good malignant, to bad men benigne. *a* **1674** CLARENDON *Hist. Reb.* III. XII. 262 The Government of these benign Stars was very short. **1743** FIELDING *J. Wild* III. x, His affairs began to wear a more benign aspect. **1853** C. BRONTË *Villette* xvi. 169 On whose birth benign planets have certainly smiled.

4. Of weather, soil, climate, etc.: Mild, salubrious, genial, kindly.

c **1386** CHAUCER *Sqrs. T.* 44 ffful lusty was the weder and benigne. **1503** DUNBAR *Thistle & Rose* 32 Thy air it is nocht holsum nor benyng. **1665** G. HAVERS *P. Della Valle's Trav. E. Ind.* 86 The Air becomes more healthful, sweet, and more benigne both to sound and infirm. **1772** PENNANT *Tours Scot.* (1774) 306 He sows his seed, and sees it flourish beneath a benign sun. **1868** G. DUFF *Pol. Surv.* 209 The climate is benign, even in low marshy neighbourhoods.

5. *Med.* †**a.** Of medicines: Gentle or mild in operation. Of food: Easily digested. *Obs.*

1651 tr. *Bacon's Life & Death* 23 Celsus adviseth Interchanging, and Alternation of the Diet, but still with an Inclination to the more Benigne. **1652** FRENCH *Yorksh. Spa* vi. 64 More benigne purgatives. **1733** CHEYNE *Eng. Malady* II. ix. §3 (1734) 208 Aromatick Medicines..increase their benign, and..hinder their destructive Effects. *a* **1735** ARBUTHNOT(J.) These salts are of a benign mild nature.

b. Of diseases: Of a mild type; not malignant.

1743 tr. *Heister's Surg.* 207 There is little or no difference between them [certain virulent tumours] and the benign sort. **1876** tr. *Wagner's Gen. Pathol.* 13 Benign Diseases are those in which the appreciable group of phenomena indicates a surely favorable issue. **1878** T. BRYANT *Pract. Surg.* I. 549 Benign tumours are of slow growth.

6. quasi-*adv.* = BENIGNLY.

1535 STEWART *Cron. Scot.* II. 374 Beseikand thame rycht hartlie and benyng, For to ressaue than as thair prince and king This Alpynus. *a* **1725** POPE *Odyss.* XIII. 63 His words well weigh'd, the general voice approved Benign.

benignancy (bɪˈnɪgnənsɪ). [f. BENIGN-ANT: see -ANCY.] Benignant quality or manner.

1876 GEO. ELIOT *Dan. Der.* IV. lxx. 364 M's eyes..dwelt on the scene with the cherishing benignancy of a spirit. **1881** *Blackw. Mag.* CXXIX. 186 Abraham regarded him with an expression of imperturbable benignancy.

benignant (bɪˈnɪgnənt), *a.* [A recent formation on BENIGN, or L. *benignus*, after *malignant*, which is of much earlier standing, and has a Latin prototype. Not in Johnson; nor in Bailey 1800, though freely used by Burke and Boswell in 1791.]

1. Cherishing or exhibiting kindly feeling towards inferiors or dependants; gracious, benevolent (with some suggestion of condescension or patronage).

a **1782** *Maiden's Wish* in Ritson *Coll. Eng. Songs* I. iv. 20 (T.) Defend my heart, benignant Power. **1791** BURKE *Let. Memb. Nat. Assembly* Wks. VI. 45 The king..was..the very reverse of your benignant sovereign. **1859** GEO. ELIOT *A. Bede* 2 His glance, instead of being keen, is confiding and benignant. **1875** BROWNING *Aristoph. Apol.* 119 Theirs would be To prove benignantest of playfellows.

2. *transf.* **a.** Of things: Exerting a good or kindly influence; favourable, beneficial, salutary.

1790 BOSWELL *Johnson* IV. 314 (T.) As if its [Christianity's] influence on the mind were not benignant. **1798** SOUTHEY *Sonn.* xiii. Wks. II. 96 For like a God thou [O Sun] art, and on thy way Of glory sheddest with benignant ray, Beauty, and life, and joyance from above. **1844** *Mem. Babylonian P'cess* II. 183 Our destiny is settled in this world by the benignant or malignant character of our natal star.

b. Of a disease: not malignant or recurrent; = BENIGN *a.* 5 b.

1897 [see SIPHONED *a.* 2]. **1932** *Discovery* Dec. 376/2 Similar rays..are given out..by cancerous growths, but not by so-called 'benignant' growths.

beˈnignantly, *adv.* [f. prec. + -LY².] With kindly manner or intent, graciously.

1790 BOSWELL *Johnson* II. 240 (JOD.) Dr. Johnson smiled benignantly at this. **1814** SOUTHEY *Roderick* xiv, Benignantly, With voice and look and gesture, did the Prince..Respond. **1831** CARLYLE *Misc.* (1857) II. 219 Friends, who were in life so benignantly united.

†**beˈnignate**, *a. Obs. rare*⁻¹. [f. L. *benign-us* + -ATE: cf. next.] A by-form of BENIGN.

1533 BELLENDEN *Livy* III. (1822) 254 Na benignate nor swete contenance semit be his proude havingis.

†**beˈnigned**, *a. Obs. rare.* [f. L. *benign-us* or F. or Eng. *benign(e* + -ED.] A by-form of BENIGN.

1470 HARDING *Chron.* cxiv. vi, And Athilstane at the daye assigned Made hym redy the battaill to haue smitten Again Colbrond, armed with hart benyngned.

benignity (bɪˈnɪgnɪtɪ). Forms: 4–6 benyngnite, -yte, -ete, benignite(e, -yte(e, benygnite(e, -yte, -ete, 5–7 benignitie, -itye, 7– benignity. [ME. *benignete*, a. OF. *benignité*, ad. L. *benignitāt-em*; see -ITY.]

1. Kindly feeling and its manifestation; kindness of disposition, or of manner. (Now attributed to superiors or those who are venerable.)

c **1374** CHAUCER *Troylus* II. 483 O God..Thow be my sheld, for thy benignite. **1382** WYCLIF *Ps.* li[i]. 5 Thou looued ist malice ouer benygnete; wickidnesse mor than to speke equite. ?*c* **1480** *Ragman Roll* 64 in Hazl. *E.P.P.* 72 But paciently your benygnyte Taketh all in gre. **1531** ELYOT *Gov.* II. viii, Beneuolence, beneficence, and liberalitie, which maketh up the said principall vertue called benignitie or gentilnes. **1659** HAMMOND *On Ps.* li. 1 Out of the riches of thy benignity. **1737** WHISTON *Josephus' Antiq.* VII. iii. §3 A peculiar benignity and affection which he had to the King. **1844** THIRLWALL *Greece* VIII. lxvi. 383 It [the senate] received him with the most gracious benignity. **1865** CARLYLE *Fredk. Gt.* X. XXI. ix. 180 Such a fatherly benignity of look.

b. *concr.* A manifestation of kindness, a kindly or generous deed; a kindness, a favour bestowed.

c **1534** tr. *Pol. Verg. Eng. Hist.* Pref. 6 The receiuer of that so liberall benignitye. **1590** SWINBURN *Testaments* 78 Many great and ample grants and benignities. *a* **1711** KEN *Preparat.* Poet. Wks. 1721 IV. 74 The Benignities which shine, From Love divine. **1865** BUSHNELL *Vicar. Sacr.* III. vi. 337 They look to see it [the gospel] operate by mere benignities.

2. Of things: **a.** (*Astrol.*) of a planet; **b.** of weather, climate; **c.** of medicine, disease. *arch.* See BENIGN.

a. 1665 GLANVILL *Sceps. Sci.* xx. 130 That planet receives the dusky light we discern in its Sextile Aspect, from the Earth's benignity. **1722** POPE *Let.* Wks. 1737 VI. 87 A star that..is all benignity, all gentle and beneficial influence. **b.** *a* **1640** JACKSON *Creed* XII. xiii. Wks. XII. 98 No benignity of native soil..can quicken..them. **1778** ROBERTSON *Hist. Amer.* II. VII. 333 The fertility of the soil corresponds with the benignity of the climate. **1814** WORDSW. *Excursion* IV. 430 That benignity..that warms The mole.

c. 1605 TIMME *Quersit.* I. xvi. 80 The mercurials doe exceede the antimonials in benignitie and sweetnesse. **1684** tr. *Bonet's Merc. Compit.* XIX. 765 The Humours are reduced to benignity. **1880** *Syd. Soc. Lex., Benignity*, a term applied in recognition of the mildness and favourable progress of a disease; and also to a tumour which is not cancerous or malignant.

benignly (bɪˈnaɪnlɪ), *adv.* [f. BENIGN + -LY².]

1. In a benign manner; kindly, graciously.

c **1380** WYCLIF *Wks.* (1880) 44 þe mynystris owe to resceyue hem benygnely and bi charite. **1528** MORE *Heresyes* III. Wks. 213/1 The gretest prelate in this realme..dismissed him very benygnely. **1862** LYTTON *Str. Story* I. 129 Mrs. Ashleigh looked at me benignly.

†**2.** Meekly, gently, humbly. *Obs.*

c **1386** CHAUCER *Pers. T.* ¶35 Penitence destreyneth a man to accepte benygnely euery peyne that hym is enioyned. **1393** LANGL. *P. Pl.* C. XV. 57 Yf men wolde hit [mercy] aske Buxumliche and benygneliche. **1557** PAYNELL *Barclaye's Jugurthe* 7 He answered benygnely for the tyme.

3. Of things: Genially, favourably, auspiciously.

a **1687** WALLER (J.) Yet they [eyes] so benignly shine. **1752** YOUNG *Brothers* I. i. (1757) II. 202 Benignly bright, as stars to mariners. **1871** R. ELLIS *Catullus* xlvi. 2 Zephyrus, health benignly breathing.

beˈnignness. [f. as prec. + -NESS.] The quality of being benign.

1731 in BAILEY vol. II.

†**beˈnim**, *v. Obs.* Chief forms: *Inf.* 1 beniman, 2–4 binime(n, 4–5 bynymen, 6 benymme, (bynemme) *Pa. t.* 1 benam, 1–5 binam, 2–4 binom, 4–5 by-, benam(e, -naam, -nom. *Pa. pple.* 1 benumen, 2–3 binume(n, 3–5 bi-, benome, -nomin, -nummen, (5 byname, 6 binomed). [A common Teut. compd. vb.: OE. *bi-, be-niman* = OHG. *bineman*, MHG. *benemen*, mod.G. *benehmen*, Du. *benemen*, Goth. *biniman*, f. *bi-*, BE- + *niman*, OTeut. **neman* to take: see NIM *v.*¹. Little used after 1500; exc. in pa. pple. *benumen, benum*, now BENUMB, BENUMBED. See also BENEME.]

1. *trans.* To take away generally.

a **1000** *Metr. Boeth.* 271 þa ær se swearta storm benumen hæfde leafa ʒehwelces. *c* **1200** *Trin. Coll. Hom.* 143 þis woreld hwile ʒifð wunne . and hwile hit eft binimð. **1297** R. GLOUC. 375 Vor he..by nome her lond. **1436** *Pol. Poems* (1859) II. 159 Allas! oure reule halteth, hit is benome. **1486** *Bk. St. Albans* B ij b, Hit shall benymme hir grece.

b. with *dat.* of possessor (= from).

a **1000** *Cædmon's Gen.* (Gr.) 362 He us hæfþ heofonrice benumen. *c* **1250** *Gen. & Ex.* 772 Sone him was sarrai binumen. **1382** WYCLIF *Ecclus.* xxviii. 19 And shal bynyme them ther trauailes [**1388** hath priued hem of her trauelis]. *c* **1430** *Hymns Virg.* (1867) 92 þis word..binam me al my list. **1493** *Festivall* (W. de W. 1515) 170b, Thou benymest the aungelles in heven their Joye. [**1560** *Chaucer's Boeth.* (ed. Speght) 204/1 (ed. 1868 II. iv. 43) Ne Fortune may not benemme [**1374** by-nyme] it thee. *Ibid.* 208/1 (ed. 1868 III. iii. 70) Money, that hath been binomed [**1374** bynomen] hem.]

c. *from* a possessor.

c **1250** *Gen. & Ex.* 1764 [I]c was for-dred ðe miʒte timen, fro me ðine doutres bi-nimen. *c* **1386** CHAUCER *Pers. T.* ¶486 It bynymeth fro man his witte. **1494** FABYAN III. lx. 39 Offa King of Mercia..by name & toke from them that dignyte.

2. *trans.* To rob, deprive, bereave. Const. orig. *gen.*, later *of* (? *at, from*).

c **890** K. ÆLFRED *Bæda* III. vii. (Bosw.) He hine his rîces benam. *c* **1205** LAY. 8798 þat he me nolde ut driuen, binimen me æt þan liue. *c* **1230** *Hali Meid.* 35 þe care aʒain þi pinunge þrahen binimeð þe nihtes slepes. *c* **1460** J. RUSSELL *Bk. Nurture* in *Babees Bk.* (1868) 140 þese may benym þy souerayne from many nyghtis restis. **1480** CAXTON *Chron. Eng.* VII. 93/1 To benymme Edwarde of his ryght.

b. Without const.: To rob; to spoil, ravish.

c **1250** *Gen. & Ex.* 1706 Lia bar last dowter dinam, Sichem, siðen, hire ille bi-nam. **1340** *Ayenb.* 23 Ydelblisse benimþ god and stelþ þet his is. *Ibid.* 39 þise greate prela[te]s þat benimeþ and robbeþ hire onderlinges. **1480** CAXTON *Chron. Eng.* xcvi. 76 Euer he that was strengest bynome hym that was feblyst.

†**beˈnimming**, *vbl. sb. Obs.* [f. prec. + -ING¹.] The taking away.

a **1400** in *Reliq. Ant.* II. 52 Pley of the fleysh is not covenable, but to the bynymmynge of the spiritus heretage.

Benin (bəˈniːn). Also Beˈni, Bini (bɪˈniː). (A member of) a Negro people of southern Nigeria, noted for their production of fine bronzes and carved ivories. Also *attrib.* or as *adj.* So **Beniˈnese** *sb. pl.*

1875 *Encycl. Brit.* III. 573/1 The Beninese weave their cotton into a fine kind of muslin. **1893** *Geogr. Jrnl.* I. 127 The Benin people, the regular inhabitants of the vast Benin kingdom..are somewhat superior to the neighbouring coast tribes. **1897** R. H. S. BACON *Benin City of Blood* i. 14 One of the Jijus of the Beni is never to cross water. **1902** *Encycl. Brit.* XXXI. 115/1 *Niger-Benue Groups*—Benin; Ibo; [etc.]. **1903** H. L. ROTH *Great Benin* i. 3 The Jekri had a most profound fear of the Binis' knowledge and use of poisons. **1925** A. HUXLEY *Along Road* III. 191 A statuette that was sixth-century Greek, subtly mingled with Benin. **1963** *Times* 12 Feb. 12/4 The same purchaser gave £750 for a cast bronze head of a Benin chieftain, about A.D. 1800.

bening(ne, obs. form of BENIGN.

benioin, -ione, -ioyn: obs. forms of BENZOIN.

benish (bɪˈniːʃ). Also 8 **beniche**, 9 **beneesh.** [Turkish *biniş* (properly = riding-habit), f. *binmek* to mount a horse.] An outer garment of cloth with very full sleeves.

1797 *Encycl. Brit.* VI. 403/2 [The Mamlouks] have an outer covering called the *beniche*, which is the cloak or robe of ceremony... Thus when the beniche and other accoutrements are on, the whole body appears like a long sack. **1836** LANE *Mod. Egypt.* I. 34 A *beneesh*, of *benish*; which is a robe of cloth, with long sleeves. **1840** J. B. FRASER *Koordistan* II. 404 The furred *kuirks* and flowing *benishes* of former days.

benison (ˈbɛnɪsən). Forms: 3 **beneysun**, 3–4 **benesun, -nis(s)un, -niscon, -un**, 3–5 **beneson**, 4 **benisone, -sune, benesoun, -isoun, -ysoun, -yssoun**, 4–5 **benyson**, 5 **beneyson, benzown**, 5–6 **benysone**, 6 **bennysoun, benizon**, 8–9 *Sc.* **bennison**, 4– **benison.** [ME. *beneysun*, etc., a. OF. *beneiçun, -çon, -sson, son, -zon*:—L. *benedictiōn-em*. Dr. Johnson says, 'not now (1755) used, unless ludicrously.' But it is now common as a poetic or quaint form of *benediction*.]

1. Blessing, beatitude. **a.** That blessing which God gives; a giving of blessedness.

a **1300** *Cursor M.* 3345 On morn wit godds beniscon Was mai rebecca lede o ton. *Ibid.* 264 [He] sal haue pardon And part of cristes benison. **1394** *P. Pl. Crede* 654 Alle þat persecution in pure lijf suffren, þei han þe benison of god blissed in erþe. **1605** SHAKS. *Lear* IV. vi. 228 The bountie, and the benizon of Heauen To boot, and boot. **1632** BROME *North. Lasse* II. iv. Wks. 1873 III. 33 Now Gods benison light o'ye for it. **1642** JER. TAYLOR *Episc.* (1647) Pref., The most glorious issues of Divine Benison upon this Kingdome.

b. That which any one receives; beatitude.

a **1400** *Relig. Pieces fr. Thornton MS.* (1867) 29 þairs es þe joye of heuene, ffor þat es þe benysone of þe pure. **1724** RAMSAY *Tea-t. Misc.* (1733) II. 170 There is nae bennison like mine, I have amaist nae care. **1851** MRS. BROWNING *Casa Guidi Wind.* II, Her patriot Dead have benison.

2. The pronouncing or invocation of a blessing; benediction. **a.** *gen.* = BENEDICTION 1. In early usage *esp.* that of a father; approaching 1 a.

a **1300** *Cursor M.* 5356 Quen he was til his ending bun I had his brad beniscun. *Ibid.* 5461 His suns blessed he on rau, He gaue ilkan seir benissun. *c* **1320** *Seuyn Sag.* (W.) 3485 Tharfore, son, for my benzown, Tel vs al now that resown. **1382** WYCLIF *Gen.* xxxii. 12 Y drede lest he brynge on me malysoun for benysoun. **1568** *Jacob & Esau* IV. i. in Hazl. *Dodsl.* II. 230 Kill him some venison, Which brought and dressed, he is to have his benison. **1649** JER. TAYLOR *Gt. Exempl.* III. xiv. 27. **1767** FAWKES *Theocritus* xvii. (R.) Twelve noble virgins..pleas'd the vocal benison to shower. **1815** SOUTHEY *Roderick* III. 72 Short interchange of benison As each to other gentle travellers give. **1828** SCOTT *F.M. Perth* xv, I have slept sound under such a benison.

†**b.** *ecclesiastical*; = BENEDICTION 1 b. *Obs.*

a **1340** HAMPOLE *Pr. Consc.* 3405 Benyssoun of bisshope of his digníté; And benyssoun of prest, þat gyyen es Namly, in þe end of þe mes. **1387** TREVISA *Higden* Rolls Ser. VI. 411 Noþer he was..i-hiʒt wiþ sacrynge and benesouns. **1513** BRADSHAW *St. Werburge* (1848) 90 They toke lycence and had the popes benesoun.

fig. (*ironical*) **1592** GREENE *Upst. Courtier*, Bending his staffe as if he meant..to bestow his benison.

†**c.** Grace before meat; = BENEDICTION 1 d. *Obs.*

a **1300** *Havelok* 1723 Thanne [he] were set, and bord leyd, And the beneysun was seyd.

†**3.** Disposition to bless; graciousness, grace, benignity. *Obs.*

c **1450** *Lay-Folks Mass-Bk*, F. 352, I pray him of his benisoun.. Sey a pater-noster for the writere.

‖**bénitier** (benitje). [Fr., f. *bénit(e* blessed + *-ier* -ER² 2.] A vessel to contain holy water.

1853 C. BRONTË *Villette* I. xiv. 255 In the presence of *bénitier*, candle, and crucifix. **1858** SIMMONDS *Dict. Trade, Benitier*, a holy-water pot or vessel, sometimes a large shell, used in Catholic countries. **1907** *Connoisseur* 1 Oct. 4/6 For benitiers—especially of the domestic type—Flanders will safely bear the palm. **1908** B. HARRADEN *Interplay* II. i, A photographic series of bénitiers and drinking horns. **1923** *Blackw. Mag.* Aug. 156/2 Marie took it to the church and dipped it into the bénitier.

benitoite (bɛˈniːtəʊaɪt). *Min.* [f. San *Benito* County, California, where found: see -ITE¹.] A sapphire-blue crystallized barium titano-silicate.

1907 G. D. LOUDERBACK in *Bull. Dept. Geol. Univ. Calif.* V. 149 It is a new mineral species, it has been called benitoite, as it occurs near the head waters of the San Benito River in San Benito County. **1912** *Brit. Museum Return* 196 Benitoite crystals. **1965** PHILLIPS & WILLIAMS *Inorg. Chem.* I. xiv. 541 This ion occurs in benitoite $BaTiSi_3O_9$.

benivolence, -ous, obs. ff. BENEVOLENCE, etc.

benj, variant of BHANG.

benjamin¹ (ˈbɛndʒəmɪn). Also 6–7 **beniamin**. [Corruption of *benjoin*, earlier form of BENZOIN, assimilated to the proper name Benjamin.]

1. Gum benzoin.

1580 HOLLYBAND *Treas. Fr. Tong, Du Benjoin*, Beniamin. **1599** HAKLUYT *Voy.* II. I. 260 The marchandise which be in Pegu, are.. muske, beniamim or franckincense, etc. **1648** HERRICK *Hesper.* (1869) 139 Leave a name as sweet As Benjamin and Storax when they meet. **1744** MRS. DELANY *Autobiog.* (1861) II. 270 Seeds and tincture of benjamin. **1799** W. TAYLOR in *Month. Rev.* XXVIII. 570 Terms so inexpressive or improper as Benjamin for Benjoin.. will disappear by simple exposure. **1851–9** HOOKER in *Adm. Man. Sci. Enq.* 425 Benzoin or Gum Benjamin.

2. Benjamin tree: a name applied to three trees: **a.** *Styrax Benzoin*, the tree from which benzoin is obtained; a native of Sumatra, Borneo, etc.; **b.** the *Benzoin odoriferum* or *Lindera Benzoin*, a North American shrub, which has an aromatic stimulant tonic bark, and berries yielding an oil of similar properties; called also *Benjamin-bush* and in U.S. *Benjamin*; **c.** sometimes applied to *Ficus Benjamina* (*Treas. Bot.* 135).

1640 PARKINSON *Theat. Bot.* 1572 The fruite of this Benjamin-tree. **1693** *Phil. Trans.* XVII. 619 The Benjamin-Tree.. from the Continent of Virginia. **1777** MILLER *ibid.* LXVIII. 169 Camphire and Benjamin trees are in this Country in great abundance. **1789** ABERCROMBIE *Pract. Gard.* (1823) 321 *Laurus*, Laurel; comprehending the Benjamin-Tree and Sassafras. **1812** REES *Cycl.* s.v. *Laurus*, The true Benjamin-tree or Gum Benzoin is a species of Styrax. **1867** GRAY *Bot. N.U. States* 423 *Lindera Benzoin*, Spice Bush, Benjamin Bush.

benjamin² (ˈbɛndʒəmɪn). [according to Brewer from the name of a tailor.] An overcoat of a particular shape formerly worn by men. (Still in slang or humorous use.)

1810 *Sporting Mag.* Dec. 127/1 One article was an *upper benjamin*, eight guineas. **1812** [see JARVEY *sb.* 1]. **1817** T. PEACOCK *Nightm. Abbey* 159 His heart is seen to beat through his upper benjamin. **1837** LOCKHART *Scott* (1839) V. 59 A vastly scientific and rather grave professor in a smooth drab benjamin. **1841** *Punch* I. 98. **1865** *Pall Mall Gaz.* 7 Mar. 3/2 [quoting East-end slang].

ˈ**Benjamin**³. The name of the patriarch Jacob's youngest son. Hence *allusively*, the youngest (and, consequently, favourite) son of a family; also *transf.*; ***Benjamin's mess*** or ***portion***: the largest share (with allusion to Gen. xliii. 34).

1840 G. A. LUNDIE *Jrnl.* May in M. Duncan *Missionary Life in Samoa* (1846) xvii. 109 Our share was ten live pigs, (a truly Benjamin's portion). **1852** H. W. GREVILLE *Leaves fr. Diary* (1883) 417 Another person was chaffing Lady Colchester.. upon the Government being designated 'Benjamin's Mess' [with allusion to Benjamin Disraeli]. **1913** A. R. HOPE *Half and Half Tragedy* 219 The new uncle being my granny's Benjamin. **1925** W. DEEPING *Sorrell & Son* xviii. §1 Kit was his Benjamin of pupils.

Benjamite (ˈbɛndʒəmaɪt). [see prec. and -ITE¹.] A descendant of Benjamin. Also as *adj.*, used allusively (see prec.).

1611 BIBLE *Judges* iii. 15 Ehud the son of Gera, a Benjamite. **1625** T. GODWIN *Moses & Aaron* I. x. 46 S. Paul was a Beniamite. **1857** DUFFERIN *Lett. High Lat.* 61 The dinner was excellent, and.. we were helped in Benjamite proportions. **1867** C. M. YONGE *Pupils St. John* ii. 12 That Cilician Benjamite, at home called by his Jewish name of Saul.

benjarry, obs. form of BRINJARRY.

benjoin, earlier form of BENZOIN.

†**benk.** *Obs.* Northern form of BENCH. (Now BINK.) Hence **benked** *ppl. a.*, **benking** *vbl. sb.*

c **1200** ORMIN 15231 Wiþþ þrinne bennkess bennkedd. *Ibid.* 15232 For þær wass an bennkinng lah. **1330** R. BRUNNE *Chron.* 281 His benk he did þer crie: shireues, balifes he ches. *c* **1340** *Cursor M.* (Fairf.) 5058 And on benke sete ham by. *c* **1440** *York. Myst.* xxvi. 189, I schall buske to the benke Where baneres are bright.

ˈ**benmost**, *a. Sc.* [f. BEN *adv.* and *a.* + -MOST.] Superlative of BEN, q.v.; innermost.

benn, var. of BEN *sb.*³, the Horse-radish tree.

benne (ˈbɛnɪ). Also **bene, beni, benni, benny.** [ad. Mende (Sierra Leone) *bene.*] Sesame, the plant *Sesamum indicum.* Chiefly *attrib.*, as ***benne-oil, -seed.***

1769 in *Early Proc. Amer. Philos. Soc.* (1884) 44 On cutting & gathering the Bene seed. **1775** ROMANS *Florida* 130 The negroes use it as food either raw, toasted, or boiled in their soups and are very fond of it; they call it *Benni.* **1853** MAYNE *Expos. Lex.*, Benne oil. **1874** FLÜCKIGER & HANBURY *Pharmacogr.* 425 Oleum Sesami. Sesamé Oil, Gingeli,.. Tii or Teel Oil, Benné Oil. **1885** *Buck's Handbk. Med. Sci.* I. 487/1 The Benné plant is a native of Africa, and probably also of Asia. *Ibid.* 487/2 The leaves of Benné are very mild and mucilaginous. **1887** MOLONEY *Forestry W. Afr.* 50 Beni-seed (*Sesamum indicum*). **1941** *N. & Q.* CLXXXI. 204/2 Some ten years or so ago, Sierra Leone began to include benniseed among its exports. **1960** *Times* 29 Sept. (Nigeria No.) x/6 Benniseed and soya beans are grown.

bennet¹ (ˈbɛnət). Also 5 **benet, bennett.** [ME. *herbe beneit*, prob. a. OF. *herbe beneite* (in mod.F. *benoîte*), transl. L. *herba benedicta* 'blessed herb,' in It. *erba benedetta*, Ger. *benedicte*, also *benedictenkraut, benedictenwurz.* Of *herba benedicta* Platearius is quoted in the *Ortus Sanitatis* of 1486, as saying 'Where the root is in the house the devil can do nothing, and flies from it; wherefore it is blessed above all other herbs.' (Prior.) To what plant these virtues were originally ascribed, and how the name was eventually attached to *Geum urbanum*, cannot be determined: see Prior.]

In Herb Bennet, name of a species of Avens, *Geum urbanum* (N.O. *Rosaceæ*), a common European wayside plant with yellow flower. The name was vaguely or inaccurately applied by early herbalists, being given also to the Hemlock and, according to Prior, to the Wild Valerian.

c **1460** J. RUSSELL *Bk. Nurture* in *Babees Bk.* (1868) 184 Herbe benet, bresewort, & smallache. **1578** LYTE *Dodoens* 133 The leaues of.. Auens, or Herbe Bennet, are rough. **1653** URQUHART *Rabelais* III. xxxi, The Fervency of Lust is abated by certain Drugs, Plants, Herbs, and Roots.. Mandrake, Bennet, Keckbuglosse. **1883** *Longm. Mag.* July 308 The roadside herb-bennet or common avens is yellow, like cinquefoil.

ˈ**bennet**². An earlier form of BENT, still commonly retained in the south of England, in the sense of 'grass-stalk,' 'old stalk of grass.' ***way bennet***: the Wild Barley-grass (*Hordeum murinum*). See BENT *sb.*¹ Also in comb.

1669 WORLIDGE *Syst. Agric.* (1681) 177 Only feeding of them [Pigeons].. about Midsummer before Pease be ripe, which time they usually call Benting-time, because then necessity inforceth them to feed on the Bents or seed of Bennet-grass. **1862** BARNES *Rhymes Dorset Dial.* II. 85 Wither'd bennet-stems. *Ibid.* Ser. III. 73 Above the bennet-bearing land. **1880** JEFFERIES *Hodge & M.* I. 135 The lowly convolvulus grew thickly among the tall dusty bennets.

†ˈ**bennet**³. *Obs.* A fish of the African seas.

1731 MEDLEY *Kolben's Cape G. Hope* II. 187 In the sea about the Cape there is plenty of the fish call'd Bennets. **1772–84** COOK *Voy.* (1790) I. 322 The Bennet is near three feet long.. the eyes and tail are red, the fins yellow, and the scales purple with gold streaks.

benneting, obs. form of BENTING.

Bennettitales (ˌbɛnətɪˈteɪliːz). *Palæobotany.* [mod.L. (A. Engler 1897, in *Engler & Prantl's Natürl. Pflanzenfam.* Nachtrag to Parts II–IV. 5), f. next + *-ales* pl. of *-alis* Lat. suffix (see -AL).] A class of gymnospermous fossil plants found chiefly in Mesozoic rocks. Hence ˌ**Bennettiˈtalean** *a.*, of or belonging to the Bennettitales.

1907 *Jrnl. Linnean Soc.* XXXVIII. 52 Engler.. adopts the derivative Bennettitales. **1910** A. C. SEWARD *Fossil Plants* II. xxii. 396 The microsporophylls of the Mesozoic Bennettitales produced their spores in sporangial compartments. **1917** *Ibid.* III. xxxvi. 366 The term Bennettitales is used by Engler, Nathorst, and several other authors as a class-designation for a large number of Mesozoic Cycads agreeing in their.. morphological characters with the Lower Cretaceous stems on which Carruthers founded the genus Bennettites. *Ibid.* 386 The memoir by Carruthers.. contains the first account of the morphological features of Bennettitalean flowers based on petrified material.

Bennettites (ˌbɛnəˈtaɪtiːz). *Palæobotany.* [mod.L., f. surname of John Joseph *Bennett* (1801–1876), English botanist, + *-ites* (see -ITE¹).] A genus of gymnospermous fossil plants having seeds borne on long stalks.

1871 W. CARRUTHERS in *Trans. Linnean Soc.* XXVI. 695 To this genus I have given the name *Bennettites*, after my distinguished colleague. **1911** *Encycl. Brit.* XX. 546/1 The best preserved specimens of the true *Bennettites* type.. are from the Lower Greensand and Wealden of England, and from Upper Mesozoic strata in North America, Italy and France. *Ibid.* 547/1 It is clear that *Bennettites* differed in many essential respects from the few modern survivors of the Cycadophyta.

benniseed: see BENNE.

bennison, -ysoun, obs. forms of BENISON.

Bennite (ˈbɛnaɪt), *a.* and *sb. Pol.* [f. the name of Tony (Anthony Wedgwood) *Benn* (see below) + -ITE¹.] **A.** *adj.* Of or pertaining to the Labour politician Tony Benn (b. 1925); supporting Mr. Benn, the left-wing policies associated with him, or such policies in general. **B.** *sb.* A supporter of (the policies of) Mr. Benn, or of policies considered to be towards the left wing of Labour Party thinking.

1975 *Economist* 5 Apr. 30/3 The Bennite charge is unfounded. Most advisers share the broad outlook of the ministers to whom they are attached. **1976** *Ibid.* 11 Sept. 18/3 His views are mainstream Labour, but he is a Bennite on industrial policy. **1981** *Guardian Weekly* 3 May 5/3 The Bennite candidacy has split the Left. *Ibid.*, The Bennites are continuing to gain ground. **1984** *Economist* 2 June 41/2 Parity with Britain prevents local measures to clear markets, or even (for Bennites) to protect them. **1984** *Financial Times* 27 July I. 3/4 A new industrial and business policy which is highly interventionist, and, in some places, positively Bennite.

benny¹ (ˈbɛnɪ). *U.S. slang.* [app. shortening of BENJAMIN²; cf. -Y⁶.] A sack coat; an overcoat.

1903 R. L. MCCARDELL *Conversations of Chorus Girl* 29 He had on one of them dust-proof Bennys that delegates to Granger conventions wear. **1914** JACKSON & HELLYER *Vocab. Criminal Slang* 17 *Benny.* General usage. A sack coat; derived from Benjamin, some say the biblical character, while others say the New York manufacturer of men's garments. **1931** 'DEAN STIFF' *Milk & Honey Route* xiii. 145 The benny, or overcoat, he should have for at least four months in winter. **1945** L. SHELLY *Hepcats Jive Talk Dict.* 7/2 *Benny*, an overcoat. **1955** D. W. MAURER in *Publ. Amer. Dial. Soc.* XXIV. 126 An overcoat of full size and weight is called a *benny.*

benny² (ˈbɛnɪ). orig. *U.S.* Slang abbrev. of BENZEDRINE.

1955 *Amer. Speech* XXX. 89. **1956** S. LONGSTREET *Real Jazz* xviii. 146 Of course, you can take bennies (Benzedrine).. but they make me too nervous. **1957** J. KEROUAC *On Road* (1958) I. i. 6 You've got to stick to it with the energy of a benny addict. **1967** A. DIMENT *Dolly Dolly Spy* i. 11 The benny was starting to wear out and I was hot, thirsty and exhausted.

beno (ˈbiːnəʊ). [Pseudo-phonetic repr. of Sp. *vino* wine, with bilabial *v.*] In the Philippine Islands: = AGUARDIENTE. Also *Comb.*

1903 *Med. Record* 4 Apr. 547 The vile whiskey and 'beno' selling dens.

†**beˈnoint**, *v. Obs. rare*⁻¹. [f. BE- 1 + NOINT, aphetic form of ANOINT.] = ANOINT.

1594 *2nd Rep. Faustus* in Thoms *E.E. Pr. Rom.* (1858) III. 356 He had all benointed the walls with holy water.

†**benoom**, *v. Obs.* Mistaken form of BENIM.

1563 SACKVILLE *Buckingham's Compl.* xv, His body gored whiche he of liefe benooms.

benorth (bɪˈnɔːθ), *adv.* and *prep.* Also **bynorth.** [OE. *be northan*, f. BE- prep. and pref. + *norþan* adv. from the north; cf. *beforan, behindan.*]

†**A.** *adv.* To the north. *Obs.*

1087 *O.E. Chron.*, Se b[isceop] of Dunholme dyde to hearme þæt he mihte ofer ealle be norðan. **1535** STEWART *Cron. Scot.* II. 437 And ȝe in peice to bruik the laue benorth.

B. *prep.* North of. Now only *Sc.*

1387 TREVISA *Descr. Brit.* (Caxton) 12 Tetbury that is thre myle bynorth Malmesbury. *c* **1425** WYNTOUN *Cron.* VIII. i. 18 Wardanys be-north þe scottis se. **1533** *Act 25 Hen. VIII*, iv, Anie place.. benorth the riuer of Humbre. **1676** ROW *Suppl. Blair's Autobiog.* x. (1848) 206 Athol and other engagers be-north Tay. **1854** *Blackw. Mag.* LXXV. 337 Be-north the Forth.

†**beˈnote**, *v.*¹ *Obs.* [OE. *benotian* f. BE- 2 + *notian*, ME. NOTE, to use.] *trans.* To use, make use of.

a **1100** *O.E. Chron.* (MS. Cott. Tiber. A. vi) an. 894 Hie hæfdan heora mete benotodne. **1340** *Ayenb.* 90 Vor þet he his benoteþ naȝt ariȝt.

benote (bɪˈnəʊt), *v.*² [f. BE- 6 + NOTE *sb.*] *trans.* To annotate, to make notes upon.

1767 WILKES *Corr.* (1805) III. 115 He proceeded to make very fair extracts, and afterwards to be-note them in the foulest manner. **1837** WHITTOCK *Bk. Trades* (1842) 244 A work which the facetious Charles Cotton benoted and travestied with poetic scraps.

†**be-ˈnothing**, *v. Obs. rare.* [f. BE- 5 + NOTHING.] *trans.* To reduce to nothing, annihilate.

1674 N. FAIRFAX *Bulk & Selv.* To Rdr., I had both lost and benothing'd myself. *Ibid.* 36 Suppose this [world] to be benothing'd, and.. another to be made.

benott, obs. form of BENET *sb.* exorcist.

†**be'notte**, *v. Obs. rare*⁻¹. [f. BE- 2 + NOTTE *v.* to cut round, lop, crop.] *trans.* To crop close.
1594 *2nd Rep. Faustus* in Thoms *E.E. Pr. Rom.* (1858) III. 386 These benotted him round upon his head and beard, which is the foulest reproach and disgrace that can be offered unto the Turk.

benow, dial. f. *by now*, by this time.

'**bensel**, *sb. Sc.* and *north. dial.* Also **bensell**, **-sall**, **-sail**, **-sil**, **bent-sail**. [a. ON. *benzla* (or *benzl* Vigf.) bending, bent, tension, f. *benda* to bend (a bow). The spelling *bent-sail* is merely conjectural. With quot. 1659 cf. Icel. *taka boga af benzlum* to take a bow out of bensel.] Bending, tension, spring (of mental faculties); strong bent or determination; impetus (of a body in motion).
1513 DOUGLAS *Æneis* VIII. xii. 37 Ourweltit wyth the bensell of the ayris [=oars]. **1659** DURHAM *Scandal* 79 (JAM.) Men weary..for our spirits are soon out of bensall. *a***1662** R. BAILLIE *Lett.* (1775) II. 306 (JAM.), I found the bent-sail of the spirits of some so much on the engagement. **1734** A. WELWOOD *Glimpse Glory* ix. 192 Surely, if you be partakers of his [God's] nature, you cannot but bend to him with a strong Bensil. **1807** STAGG *Poems* (*Cumberl. dial.*) 61 A hangrell gang Com with a bensil owr the sea.

'**bensel**, *v. dial.* Also **bansel**. [prob. f. prec., in sense of 'impetus.'] *trans.* To drive, knock (*about*); to bang, beat.
1674 RAY *N.C. Wds.* 6 *Bensel*, to bang or beat. **1824** *Craven Dial.* i. 8 Warmed her jerkin wi' a sound switching, an bensill'd her purely. *Northampton & Staffordsh. dial.*, The child never rests: it is always being banselled about for something.

benshi, -shie, variant of BANSHEE.

Bensonian (bɛn'səʊnɪən), *a.* and *sb.* [f. the name of Sir F. R. *Benson* (1858–1939), actor-manager: see -IAN.] **A.** *adj.* Of or belonging to Sir F. R. Benson or his Shakespearian company. **B.** *sb.* A member of this company.
1901 M. BEERBOHM *Around Theatres* in *Wks.* (1924) VIII. 237 Last year, when the Bensonians were figuring in the Lyceum Theatre. *Ibid.*, The removal of the Bensonian venue from the Lyceum to the Comedy is a welcome change. **1917** W. OWEN *Let.* 30 July (1967) 479 She is an old Bensonian, like her husband, who played Shylock. *Ibid.* 15 Aug. 484 My first make up was done with the real Bensonian touch. **1927** *Daily Express* 2 Sept. 3/5 Sir Frank Benson, who has produced Shakespeare for more than forty years, and has trained famous actors and actresses by the dozen, all of whom still proudly call them selves 'Old Bensonians' will be joined by Gerald Lawrence in the management of a company known as 'The Bensonians'. **1928** *Daily Tel.* 19 July 21/1 The cast will include..Harcourt Williams, the Bensonian actor. **1958** *Times* 31 Oct. 3/6 By degrees the Bensonians became the nursery of the English stage.

benste, obs. form of BENEDICITE.

benswine, obs. form of BENZOIN.

†**bensy**, *v. Obs. rare.* [The form suggests OE. *bénsian* to make prayer, to pray; perh. confused in form and sense with OF. *beneïss-*, lengthened stem of *beneïr* to bless, consecrate, hallow.] *trans.* To sanctify, hallow, purify.
*c***1315** SHOREHAM 50 That hy ham scholde clensy..And myd water bensy.

bent (bɛnt), *sb.*¹ Also **bennet**. [A word of difficult history. In the sense of 'stiff-grass' or 'grass-stalk' (in which alone the variant *bennet* occurs), it appears to be the representative of OE. *beonet-*, found as a frequent element in proper names, as *Beonet-léah* Bentley (see Index to *Cod. Dipl. ævi Saxon.*). These names do not show the meaning; but *beonet*:—earlier **binut* (with *eo* as *u*- umlaut of *i*), in OS. *binet* (Schade), is phonetically identical with OHG. *binuz*, MHG. *binez*, *binz* (str. masc.), mod.G. *binse* 'rush, reed, stout grass growing in wet places':—WGer. **binut*, of unknown etymology. But distinct instances of this sense are not found before the 15th c., while the sense of 'grassy field or surface' is common in northern writers from the earliest appearance of northern literature. Whether this is the same word is uncertain: it is possible enough that the pl. *bents* was used for a place where 'bents' grew (cf. local names like *Totley Bents* near Sheffield) and that this led to the use of the sing. *bent* as 'open grassy place.' They are here united provisionally.]

I. 1. A name given to grass of a reedy or rush-like habit, or which has persistent stiff or rigid stems; also to various grass-like reeds, rushes, sedges, and other plants.
Britten and Holland *Plant-n.* give a long list of grasses and other plants, to which the name, either simply or with attribute, is locally applied: by the seashore it very generally means the Sea Reed Grass, *Psamma or Ammophila arenaria*, but also *Carex arenaria*, *Elymus arenaria*, *Triticum junceum*, according to locality; on northern moorlands often *Juncus squarrosus*, but also *Nardus stricta*, etc.; in some pastoral and hay districts *Cynosurus cristatus* ('Hendon Bent'), *Agrostis vulgaris*; in other localities, *Phalaris arundinacea*, *Scirpas lacustris*, or other marsh-grasses, bulrushes, reeds, or sedges: in Chester and Wiltshire, the name is even given to the common heath and ling, perhaps because they grow on bents: cf. 'heath.'

a. *sing.* 'bent'; *plural* 'bents.'
*c***1425** in Wr.-Wülcker, *Voc.* 644 *Hoc gramen*, a bent. **1547** BOORDE *Brev. Health* ccxcix. 98 b, Use no olde Ryshes nor Bentes in the house. **1601** HOLLAND *Pliny* II. 216 Rushes or bents. **1625** BACON *Gardens, Ess.* (Arb.) 558 The dust of a Bent. **1783** COWPER *Task* v. 22 The bents, And coarser grass, upspearing o'er the rest. **1834** MUDIE *Brit. Birds* (1841) I. 293 The nest is formed of bents, or other plants growing near the sea. *a***1847** MRS. SHERWOOD *Visit Grandpapa* 21 His foot caught in a bent, and he fell. **1864** SIR F. PALGRAVE *Norm. & Eng.* IV. 61 The bents and sedges where the ox could not feed were excluded from the ox gang. [cf. sense 5.]

b. *collectively*. Cf. *grass*.
1570 LEVINS *Manip.* 66 Bent, smal rushes, *iuncus*. **1580** NORTH *Plutarch* (1676) 366 He..couered him with a great deal of Reed and Bent. **1778** LIGHTFOOT *Fl. Scot.* I. 107 *Arundo arenaria*, Sea Reed-Grass, *Anglis*. Bent, *Scotis*. Muran, *Gaulis*. **1791** NEWTE *Tour Eng. & Scot.* 152 It had been the custom to pull up the bent, a long spiry grass, near the shore. **1795** BURKE *Th. on Scarcity* Wks. VII. 406 The rye-grass, or coarse bent, suffered more than the clover. **1848** W. GARDINER *Flora Forfar.* 194 It [*Ammophila arundina*] is termed Bent, and..is valuable in binding the loose sand. **1882** *Proc. Berw. Nat. Club* IX. iii. 463 There is a considerable ascent over ground rough with bent (*Nardus stricta*).

†**c.** in *pl.* A bundle of reed-grass. *Obs.*
1597 GERARD *Herbal* I. iii. (1633) 6, I take this last to be the grasse with which we in London do usually adorn our chimneys..: and we commonly call the bundle of it handsomely made up for our use by the name of Bents.

2. The stiff flower-stalk of grasses. (In this sense *bennet* prevails in the southern counties.)
1577 B. GOOGE *Heresbach's Husb.* (1586) 45 The time of cutting of it [grass] is when the Bent beginneth to fade and waxe stiffe, and before it wither. **1601** HOLLAND *Pliny* II. 273 It hath certain little husks or cods hanging by small bents. **1752** LISLE *Husb.* 308 The grass will not grow afresh, unless the dying bennetes be cut off. (*Gloss.*) *Bennets, bents*, Spiry grass running to seed. **1881** JEFFERIES *Wood Magic* I Then he drew forth a bennet from its sheath.

b. 'Applied usually to the old stalks of various grasses.' Britten and Holland.
1827 KEBLE *Chr. Y.* 20 Sund. Trin. ii, Through withered bents. **1848** KINGSLEY *Saint's Trag.* II. vii. 7 Mow the dry bents down. **1866** *Treas. Bot.* 135 *Bents*, a common country name for the dried stalks or culms of various grasses occurring in pastures.

c. The stalks and seeding heads of two species of Plantain (*Plantago major* and *lanceolata*); in East Yorkshire, the dry stalks of *Hypochæris radicata*. Britten and Holland.
1612 CHAPMAN *Widows T.* in *Dodsley* VI. 192 As a mower sweeps off the heads of bents. **1655** MOUFFET & BENNET *Health's Impr.* (1746) 173 [Birds] that feed upon good Corn, Bents, or wholesome Seeds.

3. In English Botany, the name of the genus *Agrostis*. More fully ***bent-grass***: see III.
1796 MORSE *Amer. Geog.* I. 186 Many species of Bent (*Agrostis*), particularly the Rhode Island Bent (*Agrostis interrupta*). **1838** LOUDON *Encycl. Plants* s.v. *Agrostis*, *A. vulgaris*..is the most common and earliest of the bents.

4. star or **stool bent**, *Juncus squarrosus*, *Psamma arenaria*; **sweet bent**, *Luzula campestris*; **way bent**, *Hordeum murinum*; **white**, or **wire bent**, *Nardus stricta*.
1597 GERARD *Herball* (1633) 73 Wilde barley, called.. after old English writers, Way Bennet. **1620** MARKHAM *Farew. Husb.* II. xix. (1668) 103 These mats should rather be made of dry white bents, then of flags and bulrush.

II. 5. A place covered with grass, as opposed to a wood; a bare field, a grassy plain, unenclosed pasture-land, a heath. Of northern origin. In ME. the stock poetic word for 'the field' (of battle), L. *campus*, due partly at least to its alliteration with *battle*, *bicker*, *bide*, *brush*, *busk*, *bleed*, *bold*, *bale*, etc. Used by some modern poets.
*c***1325** *E.E. Allit. P.* B. 1675 As best, byte on þe bent of braken & erbes. *c***1360** *Song of Merci* in *E.E.P.* (1862) 118 Lyouns raumpyng vppon bente. *c***1400** *Destr. Troy* IV. 1192 Bothe batels on bent brusshet to-gedur. **1420** *Siege Rouen* in *Archæol.* XXI. 51 Buschys, brerys, and bowys they brent, They made hyt bare as evyr was bent. *a***1500** *Chevy Chase* 11 Bomen byckarte vppone the bent with ther browd Aros cleare. **1535** STEWART *Cron. Scot.* (1858) I. 152 Thre litill battellis buskit on the bent. *a***1552** LELAND *Brit. Coll.* I. 232 They mette at a bent by Bourne at a bridge ende a litle from Ludlow. **1552** LYNDESAY *Dreme* 919 We saw a boustius berne cum ouir ye bent. **1664** *Floddan F.* ix. 84 [Three lords] Upon the bent did breathlesse bide. **1808** SCOTT *Marm.* IX. xxv, Since Marmion saw that martial scene Upon the bent so brown. **1858** KINGSLEY *Ode N.E. Wind* 32 On by holt and headland, Over heath and bent.

b. ***to flee, go, take to the bent***: to escape to the moors or the open country, e.g. to avoid danger, creditors, etc.
*c***1450** HENRYSON *Lyon & Mous* xxxv, And he start up annone, And thankit them; syn to the Bent is gane. **1725** RAMSAY *Gentle Sheph.* I. ii, Wi' gloomin' brow, the laird seeks in his rent; It's no to gie; your merchant's to the bent. **1818** SCOTT *Rob Roy* II. 259 Take the bent, Mr. Rashleigh. Make ae pair o' legs worth twa pair o' hands.

6. ? A hill-side, rising ground, slope, brae. (Perhaps because these were the localities naturally left in permanent pasture; but the sense is doubtful. Only in southern writers. (Cf. next word.)
*c***1386** CHAUCER *Knts. T.* 1123 And downward on an hil under a bent, Ther stood the tempul of Marz armypotent. ? *c***1475** *Sqr. lowe Degree* 65 in Hazl. *E.P.P.* II. 25 In to that arber wolde he go, And vnder a bente he layde hym lowe. **1600** FAIRFAX *Tasso* XX. ix. 365 To the left wing, spred vnderneath the bent Of the steepe hill. **1870** MORRIS *Earthly Par.* I. I. 320 Worn out, he fell beneath a woody bent. **1876** —— *Sigurd* I. 19 They came to the topmost of a certain grassy bent.

III. *Comb.* chiefly *attrib.*, as ***bent-mat, -rope, -stalk***. Also **bent-grass** = BENT (sense 1), esp. in Eng. Bot. the genus *Agrostis*; **bent-land**, land covered with stiff grass, reeds, etc.; **bent-star** [ON. *störr*, gen. *starar*, Sw. *starr* 'bent-grass, carex'], the Sea Bent or Sea Reed Grass (*Psamma arenaria*): cf. sense 4.
1778 LIGHTFOOT *Fl. Scot.* I. 93 *Agrostis canina*, Brown *Bent-grass. **1854** H. MILLER *Sch. & Schm.* (1858) 458 Tufts of the *bent-grass (*Arundo arenaria*, common here, as in all sandy wastes). **1884** *Weekly Times* 19 Sept. 5/2 Planting *bent grass along the sea-shore to check the drifting by the Sands. **1883** *Birmingh. Weekly Post* 1/5 A 'Golf Club' which..wields its clubs on the sandy *bentlands near Bawdsey Ferry, close by. **1615** MARKHAM *Eng. Housew.* II. vii. (1668) 163 *Bent Mats, where one bent or straw is laid by another, and so woven together with a good strong pack-thread. **1821** CLARE *Vill. Minstr.* II. 144 Slender *bent-stalks topt with feathery down. **1822** J. PLATTS *Bk. Curios.* 523 Known to the Highlanders by the name of muran, and to the English by that of *bent-star.

bent (bɛnt), *sb.*² Also 6 **bente**. [f. BEND *v.*; probably on analogy of words from L. or Fr.: cf. *descend, descent, extend, extent*; F. *pendre, pente, rendre, rente*. There appears to be no sufficient analogy for its formation from the past pple.]

1. A curved position or form; curvature, bending degree of curvature. Also *fig.* (Now *rare*.)
1541 ELYOT *Image Govt.* (1549) 100 For the Theatre was a place made in the fourme of a bowe, that hath a great bente. **1610** GUILLIM *Heraldry* II. v. 49, I find the Bend drawne somewhat Archwise or after the resemblance of the Bent of a Bow. **1755** BORLASE in *Phil. Trans.* XLIX. 375, I attribute it to..the bent of the western land. **1860** *Heads & Hats* 20 With trifling modification of brim and bent and height of crown, we retain the thing [hat] in all its offensive characteristics!

†**2.** A curved part, a bend, a crook. *Obs.*
1572 MASCAL *Govt. Cattle* (1627) 271 Hard vnto the bent of the staple. **1607** TOPSELL *Four-f. Beasts* 313 Overthwart the bent of the [horse's] knee. **1653** WALTON *Angler* 111 Make these fast at the bent of the hook.

†**3.** A piece bent into a curve; a bow. *Obs.*
1521 *Will Pylbarowgh* (Somerset Ho.), Gown whiche I ware every daye with a bent of velvett to the skyrte. **1588** W. AVERELL *Combat Contrar.* B, Their bents of Whale bone to beare out their bummes. **1607** MIDDLETON *Michaelm. Term* I. ii. Wires and tires, bents and bums, felts and falls. **1677** PLOT *Oxfordsh.* 84 Clay thus pretily dispersed in the form of a bent.

†**4.** Flexure, bending, crooking. *Obs.*
1567 *Triall Treas.* (1850), It is I that doe guyde the bent of your bowe. **1590** GREENE *Arcad.* (1616) 57 With reuerence and lowly bent of knee. **1642** ROGERS *Naaman* To Rdr. §2 Rather then she will come to the bent of Gods bow.

†**5.** Inclination, bowing, stooping, nodding. *Obs.*
1584 T. LODGE *Forb. & Prisc.* 22 b, With..a seemely bent, as requiting his curtesie. **1596** CHAPMAN *Iliad* II. 95 To vow, and bind it with the bent Of his high forehead. **1713** C'TESS WINCHELSEA *Misc. Poems* 231 In vain the shrubs, with lowly bent, Sought their Destruction to prevent.

6. a. The condition of being deflected, inclined, or turned in some direction; a turn, twist, inclination; direction given by bending; cast (of the eye), etc. Usually *fig.*
1534 MORE *Comf. agst. Trib.* II. Wks. 1206/1 For a little coumfort, is bent ynough therto for them. *a***1600** HOOKER (J.) The wilful bent of their obstinate hearts against it. **1601** SHAKS. *Jul. C.* II. i. 210, I can giue his humour the true bent. **1611** —— *Cymb.* I. i. 13 They weare their faces to the bent Of the Kings lookes. **1664** J. NALTON in Spurgeon *Treas. Dav.* Ps. lxxvii. 10 The bent of it [a magnet] will be toward the North Pole. *a***1700** DRYDEN (J.) My reason took the bent of thy command. *a***1704** LOCKE (J.) The exercising the understanding..teacheth the mind suppleness, to apply itself more dexterously to bents and turns of the matter, in all its researches. **1713** STEELE *Guardian* No. 15 ¶1 To cross the bent of a young lady's genius. **1820** W. IRVING *Sketch Bk.* I. 328 To follow the bent of her own taste. **1875** JOWETT *Plato* (ed. 2) II. 281 To counteract wholly the bent of natural character.

b. *esp.* Mental inclination or tendency; disposition; propensity, bias. The usual modern sense.
1586 J. HOOKER *Girald. Irel.* in *Holinsh.* II. 155/1 He saw the bent and disposition of the earle. **1605** BACON *Adv. Learn.* I. iv. §2 The whole inclination and bent of those times. **1692** SOUTH 12 *Serm.* (1697) I. 429 Bents, and Propensities, and Inclinations, will not do the Business. **1762** H. WALPOLE *Vertue's Anecd. Paint.* (1786) III. 83 He knew he did not like to be a carpenter, but had not discovered his own bent. **1840** ARNOLD in *Life & Corr.* (1844) II. ix. 200 If your bent seems to be to the work of a Missionary.

c. †Phrase. ***to bring any one to***, or ***have him at, one's bent***. *Obs.*
1575 TURBERV. *Venerie* 136 Such toyles and toyes as hunters use to bring me to their bents. **1658** BRAMHALL *Consecr. Bps.* iii. 59 That by this meanes they should..bring

the Queene to their bent. **1660** BONDE *Scut. Reg.* 286 They would have had the King buckled to their bent.

d. Tendency of motion, course, 'set' of a current.

1648 MILTON *Tenure Kings* 39 The whole bent of their actions was against the King. **1817** WORDSW. *Lament Mary Q. Scots*, A sister Queen, against the bent Of law and holiest sympathy, Detains me. **1855** M. ARNOLD *Sonn. Cruikshank*, Man can control To pain, to death, the bent of his own days.

†**7.** That towards which an action, etc. is directed; aim, purpose, intention. *Obs.*

1579 SPENSER *Sheph. Cal.* Ded., For, not marking the compasse of his bent, he will iudge of the length of his cast. **1594** CAREW *Huarte's Exam. Wits* x. (1596) 141 The Oratour ..it behooueth..to vse rules..to the end the hearers may not smell out his fetch and bent. **1798** MALTHUS *Popul.* (1817) III. 297 The principal bent of this work.

†**8.** Force with which a bow bent or a spring wound up tends to spring back; *hence*, impetus, concentrated energy. F. *élan*. *Obs.*

1581 J. BELL *Haddon's Answ. Osor.* 454 He rusheth upon Haddon with all the bent of his Eloquence. **1690** NORRIS *Beatitudes* I. 107 Such a Desire as carries in it the full bent and stress of the Soul. **1742** YOUNG *Nt. Th.* VIII. 796 False joys, indeed, are born from want of thought; From thought's full bent, and energy, the true.

9. Extent to which a bow may be bent or a spring wound up, degree of tension; *hence* degree of endurance, capacity for taking in or receiving; limit of capacity, etc. Now only in the Shaksperian phrase: ***to the top of one's bent***, or the like.

1594 DRAYTON *Idea* 596 Beyond the bent of his unknowing Sight. **1602** SHAKS. *Ham.* III. ii. 401 They foole me to the top of my bent. **1641** MILTON *Reform.* I. Wks. (1851) 1 Suffering to the lowest bent of weaknesse in the Flesh, and presently triumphing to the highest pitch of glory in the Spirit. **1871** SMILES *Charac.* vi. (1876) 178 He flattered French vanity to the top of its bent. **1875** JOWETT *Plato* (ed. 2) II. 238 When you have allowed me to add μηχανή (contrivance) to τέχνη (art) I shall be at the top of my bent.

10. Technical uses, of various origin. *Building, Carpentry*, etc.: a section of a framework or framed building. (orig. *U.S.*).

1674 COTTON in Singer *Hist. Cards* 343 First, for cutting be sure of a good putt-card, they use the bent, the slick, and the breef; the bent is a card bended in play which you cut. **1815** *Niles' Reg.* IX. 200/2 On each of them [*sc.* the floats] were raised two bents or frames. *Ibid.*, This made sixteen bents, on which the grand and enormous structure was raised. **1824** T. HOGG *Carnation* 23 Veins of rust or oxyde of iron..in soil..[are] called by farmers, till or fox bent. *a* **1877** KNIGHT *Dict. Mech.*, *Bent*, one section of the frame of a building, which is put together on the ground..and then raised. **1881** GREENER *Gun* 245 A very old smooth file, worn almost to a burnisher, is used to finish the bents and bearings of the lock. *Ibid.* 263 The sear may then be lifted off, if the tumbler is not in bent. **1898** *Engineering Mag.* XVI. 91 The cradle is composed of forty-three inverted bents, twelve feet apart. **1952** *Archit. Rev.* CXI. 179 At the top of the boom may be seen the steel cables, attached to the [timber] bent.

¶ *Bent* of a hill occurs too early to belong to this word, but it was perhaps afterwards confused with it. See BENT *sb.*[1] 6.

bent (bɛnt), *ppl. a.* Also 6 bend(e [f. BEND *v.*]

1. a. Constrained into a curve, as a strung bow; curved, crooked, deflected from the straight line.

c **1374** CHAUCER *Troylus* III. 575 The Bente Mone with her hornys pale. **1483** *Cath. Angl.* 28 Bent as a bowe, *extensus*. **1523** FITZHERB. *Husb.* §3 A bende pece of yren. **1656** tr. *Hobbes' Elem. Philos.* (1839) 478 The particles of the bended body, whilst it is held bent. **1831** R. KNOX *Cloquet's Anat.* 141 The two bones..constitute a bent and horizontal lever. **1879** FARRAR *St. Paul* (1883) 402 That bent and weary Jew.

b. ***bent brow***: an arched eyebrow (*obs*); a wrinkled or knit brow.

c **1380** *Sir Ferumb.* 1074 A wel schape man was hee, With Browes bente & ȝen stoute. *c* **1400** *Rom. Rose* 861 Bent were hir browis two, Hir yen greye, & glad also. *a* **1641** STRAFFORD *Lett.* I. 179 This bent and ill-favoured brow of mine. **1853** LYTTON *My Novel* II. vii, The sad gaze of the Parson, the bent brow of the Squire.

c. Forming part of the name of various modifications of tools or apparatus which have the blade, or other part bent to adapt them to special purposes: as ***bent-gauge***, ***-gouge***, ***-graver***, ***-rasp***, which have a bent or curved blade; **bent-lever**, a lever of the first kind, whose arms form an angle with each other, as a bell-crank lever; **bent-lever balance**, a balance having a short bent arm bearing a scale, and a long weighted arm the leverage of which increases as it ascends, ending in an index pointing to divisions in a graduated arc.

d. In the names of articles, work, etc., in which the materials are bent to shape, as **bent iron work**, the making of ornamental ironwork as a home occupation, by bending strips of iron to form the various parts of the design; also, the ornamental ironwork thus made; **bent-panel**, one that is bent to shape instead of framed; in quot. *attrib.*

1858 SIMMONDS *Dict. Trade*, *Bent-timber Manufacturer*, a shaper of timber by steam and pressure. **1902** P. N. HASLUCK *(title)* Bent Iron Work. **1909** *Stratford-on-Avon Herald* 7 May 4/3 For sale, excellent Bent-panel dog cart.

†**2.** Braced, nerved, or wound up for action; couched for a spring; levelled or aimed as a weapon. †***sharp-bent***: sharp-set, hungry. *Obs.*

c **1330** *Arth. & Merl.* 1486 To dragouns ther layen y-bent. *c* **1500** *Rob. Hood* (Ritson) I. ii. 57 Robin howt with a swerd bent, A bokeler en hes honde [therto]. **1633** P. FLETCHER *Purple Isl.* II. v, Stood at the Castlesgate, now ready bent To sally out. **1675** WYCHERLEY *Country Wife* v. (1735) 95 Ceremony and Expectation are unsufferable to those that are sharp bent; people always eat with the best stomach at an ordinary.

†**3.** Determined, resolute, devoted, inclined, set.

1548 UDALL, etc. *Erasm. Par. Matt.* xxvi. 116 With bent myndes had conspired the death. **1571** ASCHAM *Scholem.* (1863) 87 The bent enemie against God and good order. **1645** RUTHERFORD *Tryal & Tri. Faith* (1845) 66 With a bent affection. **1655** MRQ. WORC. *Cent. Inv.* 2nd. Ded. ad. fin., My Lords and Gentlemen, Your most passionately-bent Fellow-Subject. **1740** L. CLARKE *Hist. Bible* I. IX. 579 Being bent to have his revenge on the inhabitants of Ptolemais.

4. Directed in a course, on one's way, bound.

1697 DRYDEN *Virg. Georg.* I. 296 Nor must the Ploughman less observe the Skies..Than Saylors homeward bent.

5. *fig.* (cf. CROOKED *a.* 3). In various slang uses: **a.** Dishonest, 'crooked', criminal. Also as *sb.* orig. *U.S.* **b.** Illegal; stolen. *orig. U.S.* **c.** Of things: out of order, spoiled. Of persons: eccentric, perverted; *spec.* homosexual (also as *sb.*). (In quot. 1958 'faithless'.)

a. 1914 JACKSON & HELLYER *Vocab. Criminal Slang* 17 *Bent*, crooked; larcenous. Example: His kisser shows that he's bent. **1948** *Sunday Pictorial* 29 Aug. 6/5 A 'bent screw' ..a crooked warder who is prepared to traffic with a prisoner. **1958** *Times* 14 Feb. 3/5 What made the witness think the two officers were offering a bribe? Mitchell replied, 'I had known for years that certain members of the Brighton police force were what we call bent.' *Ibid.*, There were plenty of ways in which bents could help. **1963** *Ibid.* 2 Feb. 9/6 Successful crime preventing does not make criminals give up; they simply change their methods, or as Mr. Brown said: 'They stay bent but alter their tactics.'

b. 1930 E. H. LAVINE *Third Degree* (1931) iv. 39 For having sold a stolen or *bent* car to a complainant. **1955** P. WILDEBLOOD *Against Law* 151 He had got a short sentence for receiving stolen goods, which he swore he had not known to be 'bent'.

c. *c.* **1930** BROPHY & PARTRIDGE *Songs & Slang 1914–18* (ed. 2) 210 *Bent*, spoiled, ruined, e.g. 'a good man bent' or even 'good tea bent'. **1942** BERREY & VAN DEN BARK *Amer. Thes. Slang* §143/4 *Eccentric*. Balmy, bats, bent, [etc.]. *Ibid.* §152/5 *Insane*; *crazy*... bent. **1956** I. ASIMOV 9 *Tomorrows* (1963) iii. 87 He's gone crazy... He was always a little bent. Now he's broken. **1957** RAWNSLEY & WRIGHT *Night Fighter* v. 75 Whenever a set became unserviceable in the air the code word used to notify ground control was to say that the weapon was 'bent'. **1957** A. WILSON *Bit off Map* 29 'I shouldn't think you did know any Teddy boys, but if you did, I know what they'd call you—a f— bent, see.'..Mr. Fleet..reddened with fury; his reputation as a womaniser was known to everyone. **1958** F. NORMAN *Bang to Rights* III. 72 My bird's gone bent... She went case with some geezer now she's liveing [*sic*] with him. **1959** C. MACINNES *Absolute Beginners* 64 No one..cares..if you're boy, or girl, or bent, or versatile, or what you are. **1960** F. RAPHAEL *Limits of Love* I. v. 70 'Great thing about gay people...' 'Gay?' Tessa said. 'Bent, queer, you know. Homosexual.'

†'**benter.** *Obs.* Short for DEBENTURE.

1571 EDWARDS *Damon & P.* in Hazl. *Dodsl.* IV. 77 These benters, I trow, shall anon get me more. *Ibid.* (1744) I. 281 (D.) My pouche, my benters, and all is gone.

benthal ('bɛnθəl). [f. Gr. βένθος the depth of the sea + -AL[1].] Of or pertaining to ocean-depths exceeding 1000 fathoms.

1881 *Nature* No. 588. 324 [They] occur in great abundance in the benthal or deepest zone.

Benthamism ('bɛnθəmɪz(ə)m). [see -ISM.] The philosophical system of Jeremy Bentham, an eminent English jurist and writer on law and ethics, 1748–1832, who taught that the aim or end of life is happiness, identified by him with pleasure, and that the highest morality is the pursuit of the greatest happiness of the greatest number. So **Ben'thamic** *a.*, of or according to Bentham (for this Carlyle has the contemptuous **Bentha'mee**). '**Benthamite** *sb.*, an adherent of the Benthamic philosophy; *a.* = prec. '**Benthamry**, a contemptuous appellation for 'Benthamism.'

1826 *Times* 8 Nov. 2/6 The Ghost of Miltiades came at night, And he stood by the bed of the Benthamite. **1829** J. STERLING *Let.* in *Ess. & Tales* (1848) I. p. xxix, It was the first help I had in getting out of the slough of Benthamism. **1829** MILL in *Autobiogr.* (1924) App. 301 Those who are ignorant enough to fancy that there is a Benthamite sect. *Ibid.*, What are vulgarly considered to be the Benthamite doctrines. **1832** —— *Let.* 22 Oct. in *Wks.* XII. (1963) 128 You know our Benthamic Utilitarians. **1840** CARLYLE *Heroes* v. 271 Benthamism is an eyeless Heroism. **1865** M. ARNOLD *Ess. Crit.* (1875) Pref. 11 The British nation..has finally anchored itself..on Benthamism. *a* **1866** J. GROTE *Exam. Util. Philos.* xv. 227 Benthamic utilitarianism. *Ibid.* xvi. 247 Benthamic despotism. **1840** CARLYLE *Heroes* ii. 119 Benthamee utility, virtue by Profit and Loss. *a* **1852** MOORE *Ghost of Miltiades* 54 A parting kick to the Benthamite. **1882** *Athenæum* 15 Apr. 468/1 The too confident optimism of the Benthamites. *Ibid.* 28 Jan. 117/3 Summarizing and co-ordinating the work of the Benthamite circles. **1855** *Ess. Intuit. Morals* 149 *note*, Public Eudaimonism, however, as I have described it, is not Benthamry.

benthos ('bɛnθɒs). *Biol.* [a. Gr. βένθος depth of the sea.] Haeckel's name for the flora and fauna at or near the bottom of the sea. So ***abyssal benthos***, plants and animals of the deep sea; ***littoral benthos***, those of the sea near the coast. Hence '**benthic, ben'thoal, ben'thonic** *adjs.*

1891 G. W. FIELD tr. *Haeckel's Planktonic Studies* in *Rep. U.S. Fish. Comm.* XVII. 582 The abyssal benthos. **1895** *Nat. Sci.* July 29 The greatest part of the..discoveries.. concerns the Benthos. **1897** T. J. PARKER & HASWELL *Zool.* II. 600 Others [*sc.* marine animals]..are either permanently fixed, like Zoophytes and Stalked Crinoids, or move by creeping over the sea-bottom, like Starfishes, Holothurians, Chætopods, etc.; such forms constitute the *Benthos*, or 'bottom-fauna'. **1902** *Encycl. Brit.* XXXIII. 933 Each of the three benthic groups is well characterized by a special fauna. **1905** *Q. Jrnl. Geol. Soc.* LXI. Proc. p. lxxiv, The benthoal organisms existing in tracts where the physical conditions.. vary rapidly, are limited as to their horizontal range by the distribution of those conditions which determine their station. **1909** WEBSTER, Benthonic. **1913** J. MURRAY *Ocean* viii. 160 Pelagic larvæ of benthonic animals are abundant near shore in shallow water, but become less numerous farther out to sea. **1921** *Discovery* Oct. 265/1 Marine organisms can be roughly divided into..the *plankton* or drifters, the *nekton* or swimmers, and the *benthos* or fixed organisms. **1923** W. A. HERDMAN *Founders Oceanogr.* 327 The demersion upon which hordes of benthonic animals can browse. **1942** H. U. SVERDRUP *Oceans* viii. 276 The benthic division may be subdivided into..the *littoral* and the *deep-sea systems*... [This] is divided into an upper (*archibenthic*) and a lower (*abyssalbenthic*) zone. **1956** *Nature* 25 Feb. 375/1 The animals were only about 5 mm. long, and as lancelets are benthic forms it is most unlikely that the scattering layer consisted of this species. **1959** A. HARDY *Fish & Fisheries* v. 94 All these other forms of life, referred to collectively as the *benthos*..are vitally important to the fish either as their prey or as voracious competitors for limited supplies of food.

'**Bentinck.** [f. name of the inventor, Captain Bentinck.]

1. *pl.* Triangular courses, now superseded by storm stay-sails; also used in U.S. as try-sails.

2. Bentinck-boom; a boom which stretches the foot of the fore-sail in many small square-rigged merchantmen; particularly used by whalers among the ice, with a reefed foresail, to see clearly ahead. **Bentinck shrouds**: shrouds extending from the weather-futtock staves to the opposite lee-channels: not now used. Smyth *Sailor's Word-bk.* 1867.

'**bentiness.** [f. BENTY + -NESS.] The condition of being covered with bent.

benting ('bɛntɪŋ), *vbl. sb.* [f. BENT *sb.*[1] + -ING[1]: cf. *nutting*, *bird-nesting*.]

1. The going after bents [see BENT *sb.*[1] 2c]. ***benting-*** (***benneting-***) ***time***: the time when pigeons, etc., are reduced to feed on bents; also *transf.*

1672 RAY *Coll. Prov.* (1678) 49 The pigeon never knoweth wo, But when she doth a benting go. **1687** DRYDEN *Hind & P.* III. 1283 Bare benting times, and moulting Months may come. **1725** BRADLEY *Fam. Dict.* s.v. *Pigeon*, Be sure to feed them in hard Weather, and in Benting-time. **1752** LISLE *Husb.* 320 Midsummer is the oxen and cow-cattle's bennetting-time.

2. = BENT *sb.*[1] 2c; the seeding stalks of the plantain (herb).

1807 VANCOUVER *Agric. Devon* (1813) 357 They live upon the seeds of weeds and bentings. **1824** FORSYTH *Fruit Trees* ix. 237, I generally cover them with bentings.

†'**bently,** *adv. Obs.* In a bent manner: **a.** like a bow; **b.** determinedly, with set purpose.

1552 HULOET, Bentlye lyke a bowe, *arcuatim*. **1645** RUTHERFORD *Tryal & Tri. Faith* (1845) 58 The malice of the devil..worketh as intently & bently as he can.

bentonite ('bɛntənaɪt). *Min.* [f. *Benton* (see below) + -ITE[1].] A clay found in the Fort Benton strata of the Cretaceous of Wyoming. Also, any of several clayey deposits containing montmorillonite which have various practical applications (see quots.).

1898 W. C. KNIGHT in *Engineering & Mining Jrnl.* 22 Oct. 491/1 In a recent article..the writer described briefly a new variety of clay found in Wyoming and suggested the name Taylorite... It has since been learned that the name Taylorite is preoccupied; consequently the clay will hereafter be known as Bentonite. **1939** *Jrnl. R. Aeronaut. Soc.* XLIII. 647 Highly diluted water dispersions of natural bentonite have proved very suitable for such work [*sc.* detection of turbulence of a liquid by means of polarization]. **1943** *Electronic Engin.* XV. 322 X-ray analysis has..made possible the gaining of valuable knowledge of the crystals forming the extremely plastic and interesting substance 'bentonite'. **1956** *New Biol.* XXI. 20 Another method of attacking this difficult problem [*sc.* haze formation in beer] is by the adsorption of the undesirable material on to an inert material such as bentonite. **1959** *New Scientist* 2 July 21/2 The manufacture of British bentonites used in foundry moulding sands, paints, oil-well drilling muds and other things. **1964** R. F. FICCHI *Electr. Interference* viii. 159 The anodes were placed in a 8-in. diameter well..then back-filled with bentonite.

‖**ben trovato** (bɛn tro'vato), *adj. phr.* [It., = well found.] Of a story, etc.: appropriate; happily invented if untrue.

Se non è vero, è molto ben trovato 'if it is not true, it is a happy invention' was app. a common saying in the 16th cent. It is found, for example, in Giordano Bruno (1585).

[**1771** SMOLLETT *Humph. Cl.* II. 1 Your fable of the monkey and the pig, is what the Italians call *ben trovata*.] **1883** W. PATER *Let.* 22 July (1970) 78 The title of your proposed volume is I think ben trovato. **1884** *N. & Q.* 29 Mar. 244/2 It must be admitted that all this has a *ben trovato* character about it. **1886** HAVELOCK ELLIS in Landor *Imag. Conv.* Introd. p. xv, A story told of him by the Italians round Fiesole, where he lived for many years, is at least *ben trovato*. **1952** R. M. HARE *Lang. Morals* 53 We might say that to tell a story about someone, which every one knows is *ben trovato*, is not *lying*. **1966** *Punch* 16 Nov. 726/1 Who..are *we* and *they* can be illustrated by a story, true or *ben trovato*, told of Rose Macaulay.

bent-sail, obs. variant of BENSEL.

benturong, var. BINTURONG.

'bent-'wood. Also **bentwood.** [f. BENT *ppl. a.* + WOOD.]

1. Wood curved by machinery, used for making furniture. Chiefly *attrib.*

1862 *Illustr. Times* 15 Nov. 473/1 Messrs. Thouet Brothers 'Bent-Wood' Furniture at the Great Exhibition. The manufactory of these bent-wood chairs and couches is in the Carpathian Mountains, between Hungary and Moravia, in the district of Koritchan. **1884** *Health Exhib. Catal.* 90/1 Austrian Bentwood Furniture. **1933** *Archit. Rev.* LXXIV. 77 A typical example of bent-wood chairs for children. **1959** *House & Garden* Sept. 71/2 Chair in foreground, bentwood upholstered in black leather.

2. *north dial.* Ivy. [prob. for *bendwood*, i.e. *bindwood*: cf. BEND *sb.*[1]]

benty ('bɛntɪ), *a.* [f. BENT *sb.*[1] + -Y[1].]

1. a. Of the nature of a rush or grass-stalk. **b.** Of or pertaining to bent or bent-grass.

1597 GERARD *Herball* I. iii. §1. 4 Slender bentie stalks. **1807** HEADRICK *Arran* 124 The benty grasses, which grow on the sea beach. **1841** LD. COCKBURN *Jrnl.* I. 305 The gray benty colour of the always drenched pasture.

2. Covered with bent or bent-grasses.

a **1700** in Maidment's *Scot. Ball* (1868) II. 197 As he came down by Merriemass, And in by the benty line. **1834** *Brit. Husb.* xii. 292 Coarse benty sward. **1876** BLACKIE *Songs of Relig.* 137 Above the benty golfing ground.

†**be'numb,** *ppl. a. Obs.* Forms: 5 be-, bynomen, benome, 6 **benombe.** [Orig. *benomen*, OE. *benumen*, pa. pple. of *beniman* 'to deprive,' in phrase 'to be benome(n the power of one's hands, etc.,' in which sense the simple word was subseq. used elliptically. After giving origin to the vb. BENUMB (see next), its place was taken by the pa. pple. *benumbed*. See also BENIM.]

[**1393** GOWER *Conf.* III. 2 Altogether he is benome The power both of hand and fete.] *a* **1400** *Cursor M.* 22829 (Tr.) Wemmed..on foot or honde,..crupel, croked, or bynomen. **1474** CAXTON *Chesse* 104 Peple lese her membris and become half benomen. **1483** —— *Gold. Leg.* 85/3 Theyr armes were bynomen and of no power. **1530** PALSGR. 306/1 Benombe of ones lymbes, *perclus*. *Ibid.* 448/2 He is now benomme of his lymmes.

benumb (bɪ'nʌm), *v.* Forms: ? 5–6 **benome**, 6 **benomme**, 6–8 **benum**, **-numm(e**, 7–8 **benumn**, 6– **benumb.** [A verb of late origination, f. prec.; cf. for sense *to lame*, etc., for formation *to astound*. *Benumb* is a bad spelling of *benum*, after *dumb*, *limb*, etc.]

1. *trans.* To make (any part of the body) insensible, torpid, or powerless; *occas.* to stupefy or stun, as by a blow or shock; but now mostly used of the effects of cold.

1530 PALSGR. 448/2, I benomme, I make lame or take awaye the use of ones lymmes. **1579** SPENSER *Sheph. Cal.* Aug. 4 Or hath the Crampe thy ioynts benomd with ache? **1580** NORTH *Plutarch* (1676) 348 The tile..brake his neck-bone asunder..wherewith he was so suddenly benummed, that he lost his sight with the blow. *a* **1623** SIR J. BEAUMONT *Ode Blessed Trin.*, No cold shall thee benumme, Nor darknesse taint thy sight. **1651** HOBBES *Leviath.* I. ii. 6 The Organs of Sense being now benummed. **1706** ADDISON *Rosamond* II. vi. Wks. 1726 I. 122 The sleep of death benumbs all o'er My fainting limbs. **1861** SWINHOES *N. China Camp.* 370 The excessive cold benumbs all kinds of game.

2. To render (the mental powers, the will, or the feelings) senseless or inert; to stupefy, deaden.

c **1485** *Digby Myst.* (1882) II. 374 It rauysshid hym, and his spirites did be-nome. **1563** *Myrr. for Mag.*, *Somerset* ix, Did ever madnes man so much benomme. **1580** SIDNEY *Arcadia* (1622) 107 Mopsa was benummed with joy when the Princesse gaue it her. **1665** GLANVILL *Sceps. Sci.* xxiv. 147 There are few but find some Companies benumn and cramp them. **1781** GIBBON *Decl. & F.* III. liii. 303 A lethargy of servitude had benumbed the minds of the Greeks. **1818** BYRON *Ch. Har.* IV. xix, Some feelings Time can not benumb.

absol. **1667** MILTON *P.L.* II. 73 If the sleepy drench Of that forgetful Lake benumme not still.

3. *fig.* To paralyze.

1789 T. JEFFERSON *Wks.* (1859) II. 589 The accident in England has benumbed her mediation between the Swedes and Danes. **1825** —— *Autobiog.* I. 78 To benumb the action of the Federal government.

benumbed (bɪ'nʌmd), *ppl. a.* [pa. pple. of prec. vb., taking the place of the earlier *benomen*, *benome*, pa. pple. of *benim*: see BENUMB *ppl. a.*] Rendered torpid or numb; deprived of strength or the power of motion by a chilling influence. *lit.* and *transf.* as in BENUMB *v.* 1 and 2.

1547 BOORDE *Brev. Health* cclxxi. 90 b, The one legge and the one arme is benomed or astouned. **1624** CAPT. SMITH *Virginia* III. ii. 46 They chafed his benummed limbs. **1691** NORRIS *Pract. Disc.* 174 The torpid and benumm'd World. **1704** J. TRAPP *Abra-Mule* II. i. 440 To melt the most benumn'd of Hearts. **1861** GEO. ELIOT *Silas M.* 12 Silas Marner's benumbed faith. **1870** HAWTHORNE *Eng. Note-Bks.* (1879) II. 34 Our benumbed bodies.

be'numbedness. [f. prec. + -NESS.] The state of being benumbed; numbness; torpor.

1566 DRANT *Horace Sat.* I. iii. G vj b, The boye through chille benummednesse his ague worse shall gette. **1662** J. CHANDLER *Van Helmont's Oriat.* 58 The deep or profound benummednesses of the Schooles, and the drowsie distemper of the auntients. **1701** T. FULLER *Pharmacop.* (1710) 57 A Cephalic Decoction..for prevention of..Benummedness. **1731** BAILEY II, *Benummedness*, a being benummed.

benumbing (bɪ'nʌmɪŋ), *vbl. sb.* [f. BENUMB *v.*] A rendering torpid or inactive, benumbment.

1552 HULOET, *Benumming* or taken, which is a sycknes that..taketh awaye the sinnowes. *a* **1569** KYNGESMILL *Confl. with Satan* (1578) 45 Because of his great delight hee taketh in sinne, the Apostle compareth it to benomming. **1671** SALMON *Syn. Med.* I. lii. 126 Catalepsis..is a sudden detention or benumning both of Mind and Body.

be'numbing, *ppl. a.* [f. as prec. + -ING[2].] That benumbs or renders torpid; paralyzing.

1628 LAYTON *Sion's Plea* 2 One benumming bruise of judgment. **1630** J. TAYLOR (Water P.) *Wks.* III. 37. §2 The benumming frigiditie of Greenland. **1774** *Phil. Trans.* LXV. 109 The benumbing effect of that fish. **1879** M. ARNOLD *Democracy*, *Mixed Ess.* 11 To be profoundly insignificant has..a depressing and benumbing effect on the character.

be'numbment. [f. as prec. + -MENT.] The action of benumbing; the fact or condition of being benumbed; torpor.

1816 KIRBY & SP. *Entomol.* (1843) II. 357 At first a partial benumbment takes place. **1851** BUNSEN in *Macready's Remin.* II. 388 After one century of bloody internal wars and another of benumbment.

benvenue, variant of BIENVENUE.

benvolent, obs. form of BENEVOLENT.

'benward, *adv. Sc.* Also **benwart.** Inward, towards the interior (of a house).

c **1475** *Rauf Coilȝear* 131 Than benwart thay yeid, quhair brandis was bricht.

benweed ('bɛnwiːd). *Herb.* [Possibly for *bendweed* (cf. BENDWITH): but the variants *bun-*, *bin-*, *bindweed*, leave the etymology uncertain.]

A popular name in Scotland and north of Ireland of the Ragweed (*Senecio Jacobæa*). Also BUNWEED.

1822 GALT *Entail* III. 115 (JAM.) Switching away the heads of the thistles and benweeds in his path.

benwyt-tre, var. of BENEWITH (tree).

benyfet, obs. form of BENEFIT.

benyng, benyson, obs. f. BENIGN, BENISON.

benyvolent, -ous, obs. ff. BENEVOLENT, etc.

benzaldehyde (bɛn'zældɪhaɪd). *Chem.* Also formerly **benz-aldehyd.** [ad. G. *benzaldehyd*, f. BENZO- + ALDEHYDE.] A colourless liquid aldehyde, C_6H_5CHO, having the odour of bitter almonds and used in the manufacture of perfumes, dyes, etc.

1866 W. ODLING *Animal Chem.* 117 Some tolerably simple well-characterised substance—such..as benz-aldehyd, or essential oil of bitter almonds. **1882** [see BENZO-]. **1920** *Lancet* 18 Sept. 615/2 He also found that the anæsthetic action which he had shown to be marked for benzyl alcohol is exhibited in a high degree by benzaldehyde. **1962** *Ibid.* 1 Dec. 1168/1 Some substances such as benzaldehyde and camphor excite trigeminal afferents as well as olfactory afferents in the nasal passages.

benzedrine ('bɛnzɪdriːn). [Proprietary term, f. BENZO- + *-edrine* as in EPHEDRINE.] A preparation of amphetamine. Also *ellipt.*, a dose of benzedrine in tablet form.

1933 *Lancet* 16 Dec. 1383/1 A new drug has recently been introduced into rhinology under the name of benzedrine. It is a synthetically prepared compound, the carbonate of benzyl-methyl-carbinamine, which is described as a racemic mixture of bases having the formula $C_6H_5CH_2.CH.NH_2.CH_3$. **1935** *Trade Marks Jrnl.* 22 May 634/1 *Benzedrine*, a medicated preparation consisting of benzyl-methyl-carbinamine, oil of lavender and menthol..Smith, Kline & French..Laboratories..Pennsylvania. **1938** *Times* 22 June 17/4 The victims [of hay-fever]..fumble for the benzedrine. **1938**, **1939** [see AMPHETAMINE]. **1956** J. HEARNE *Stranger at Gate* v. 38 He went in and bought a benzedrine inhaler: the sort one uses for colds. **1958** *Listener* 3 July 15/2 They..swallow a benzedrine.

benzene ('bɛnziːn). *Chem.* [f. BENZ-OIC (acid) + -ENE, q.v. The name originally given by Mitscherlich in 1833 was *benzin* or *benzine*, for which Liebig in 1834 substituted BENZOL. See BENZINE.]

1. An aromatic hydrocarbon, C_6H_6, the first or simplest member of the *benzene series*, C_nH_{2n-6}; a thin, colourless, strongly refracting fluid, volatile and highly inflammable, formed by distilling benzoic acid with lime, and found in 1849 in the more volatile parts of coal-tar; it dissolves fats, resins, gutta-percha, etc. whence it is used for removing grease-spots and cleaning gloves, as well as for illuminating purposes. (See BENZOLINE.)

1872 WATTS *Dict. Chem.* I. 541 *Benzene* or *Benzol* (Hydride of phenyl)..The most abundant source of benzene is coal tar. **1878** KINGZETT *Anim. Chem.* 29 Benzene ..is capable of yielding hundreds of different substances.

2. Entering into the name of substitution-products, as ***chloro-benzene***, ***nitro-benzene*** $C_6H_5NO_2$.

3. *Attrib.* and *Comb.*, as **benzene hexachloride**, a compound, the gamma isomer of which is used as an insecticide, = GAMMEXANE; abbrev. *B.H.C.*; **benzene ring** (*Chem.*), a name for the ring-like arrangement of the six carbon atoms in the formula of the benzene molecule, by which the phenomena of its combinations are explained.

1877 WATTS *Fownes' Chem.* II. 419 In the homologues of benzene, the six carbon-atoms belonging to the benzene itself are said to form the *benzene-ring*, *benzene-nucleus*, or principal chain, while the groups, CH_3 etc., joined on to these carbon-atoms, are called *lateral chains*. **1884** *Jrnl. Chem. Soc.* XLVI. 887 Determination of the vapour-density of the new isomeride of benzene hexachloride..shows that its formula is $C_6H_6Cl_6$. **1945** *Times* 9 Mar. 2/5 Gammexane ..is the gamma isomer of benzene hexachloride. **1952** *Oxf. Jun. Encycl.* VI. 248 BHC (*benzene hexa-chloride*) can penetrate the insect's skin.

benzenoid ('bɛnziːnɔɪd), *a.* [f. BENZENE + -OID.] Derived from, related to, or pertaining to benzene.

1887 *Standard* 16 Sept. 3/3 Transition from tars of the paraffinoid to those of the benzenoid or ordinary gas tar varieties. **1900** *Rep. Brit. Assoc. Advancem. Sci.* 166 Like hexamethylene, tetrahydrobenzene shows no selective absorption. The examination of these two substances thus confirms the conclusion previously reached, that the banded spectrum is shown only by substances which possess the true benzenoid structure. **1964** N. G. CLARK *Mod. Org. Chem.* ii. 20 The first group is generally known by its original name 'aromatic', although the alternative 'benzenoid' is more accurate, for it comprises derivatives of the hydrocarbon benzene. **1967** *Times Rev. Industry* July 66/3 The very big benzenoid chemical market of America.

benzine ('bɛnziːn). *Chem.* Also **-in. a.** The name originally given to BENZENE. **b.** An inflammable liquid (petroleum ether) prepared by purifying, deodorizing, and distilling natural petroleum, and used as a solvent; it is a mixture of hydrocarbons of the paraffin series.

1835 *Penny Cycl.* IV. 255 M. Mitscherlich obtained a fluid ..to which the name of benzine is given. **1853** MAYNE *Expos. Lex.*, Benzin. **1864** *Q. Jrnl. Science* I. 523 Benzine has come largely into use to supply the place of turpentine. **1865** *Med. & Surg. Reporter* (Philad.) XIII. 188/1 In the vicinity of refineries, where this gas exists..Benzine gas is known to be very inflammable, highly volatile, and to permeate almost all substances. **1879** MISS BRADDON *Clov. Foot* xxi. 174 It is like the blood-stain on Lady Macbeth's hand. All the benzine in the world won't take it out. **1885** *Buck's Handbk. Med. Sci.* I. 487/2 Benzin is not used in medicine, but is useful to the pharmacist for its solvent powers over fats, resins, volatile oils, and other bodies. **1887** J. W. RICHARDS *Aluminium* 236 Mourey..recommends the employment of benzine in the melting of all the noble metals. **1895** *Bloxam's Chem.* (ed. 8) 515 Benzine (sp. gr. 0·74), a solvent which must not be confounded with benzene, the coal-tar product. **1908** *Chemist & Druggist* 25 July 144/2 Benzine..in U.S. means always petroleum benzin, while benzole is the name for the coal-tar product C_6H_6. **1912** G. MARTIN *Ind. Chem.*, *Org.* 8 Coal-Tar Naphtha, Benzene or Benzol, C_6H_6, is quite a different product from benzine or petroleum naphtha, being obtained by distilling coal-tar. **1928** *Observer* 26 Aug. 6/4 Another fuel..called Steiger-Brennstoff..contains no benzin or benzol at all.

c. *Comb.* **benzine-collas** (see quot.).

1864 *Pop. Science Rev.* III. 432 About 1850 impure benzol was sold..under the name of benzine-collas for cleaning gloves, tissues.

benzo-, before a vowel **benz-**. *Chem.* [f. BENZOIC.] A formative of the names of substances belonging to, or derived from, the benzene series.

'benzamide, C_7H_7NO, the amide of benzoic acid, a crystalline substance; **benzhydrol**, a camphor obtained from oil of cassia, or one of its constituents. **'benzidine**, an organic alkali, $C_{12}H_{12}N_2$, deposited in crystals by the reduction of azobenzene. **'benzil, -ile**, a yellowish crystalline substance, $C_{14}H_{10}O_2$, formed by the action of oxidizing agents on benzoin; hence **'benzilam, 'benzilim**

(*benzilimide*), products of the action of ammonia on benzil. **ben'zilic acid**, $C_{14}H_{12}O_3$; a salt of which is a **'benzilate**. **'benzoate**, a salt of benzoic acid; hence, **'benzoated** *a.* **benzocaine** ('bɛnzəʊkeɪn) [-*caine*, after COCAINE], a white crystalline powder, ethyl para-amino-benzoate, used mainly as a local anæsthetic. **ben'zoicin**, an artificial fat obtained by the action of benzoic acid on glycerin. **'benzone**, the ketone of benzoic acid (diphenyl ketone), a crystalline substance. **benzo'nitrile**, cyanide of phenyl, C_7H_5N, a clear, colourless oil, smelling like bitter almonds. **benzophenone** (= *benzone*). **benzoyl** ('bɛnzəʊɪl), the hypothetical radical, C_7H_5O, of benzoic acid and its kindred compounds; hence, **benzo'ylic** *a.* **benzpyrene** (ˌbɛnz'paɪəriːn) [PYRENE[2]], a carcinogenic hydrocarbon found in coal-tar, etc. **'benzyl**, the hypothetical radical, $C_6H_5.CH_2$, contained in *benzyl alcohol* and many other substances; hence, **ben'zylic** *a.* **'benzylaˌmine**, $N.C_7H_7.H_2$, an aromatic base metameric with toluidine, a colourless liquid. **'benzylene**, a hypothetical diatomic radical, C_7H_6, found in chlorobenzyl; hence, **benzy'lenic** *a.* Also in innumerable combinations as ***benz-hydramide***; ***benzo-acetic***, ***-carbolic***, ***glycolic***, ***-lactic***, ***-tartaric***, etc.

1882 *Boston Jrnl. Chem.* Feb. 13/2 It is a by-product in the manufacture of benzaldehyde, benzoic acid, and benzoic ethers. **1850** DAUBENY *Atom. The.* viii. 244 *Benzamide* was regarded as a compound of a body called amidogen (H_2N).. with the radical of benzoic acid. **1877** WATTS *Fownes' Chem.* 815 Hippuric Acid, or Benzamidacetic Acid, is produced by the action of benzoyl chloride on the zinc salt of amidacetic acid. *Ibid.* 825 Benzilic Acid is produced by the action of alcoholic potash on benzoin. **1878** *Jrnl. Chem. Soc.* XXXIV. 668 This glyoxal derivative of benzidine differs from the preceding compounds. **1916** CROSS & BEVAN *Paper-Making* (ed. 4) ix. 261 Benzidine is para-diamino-diphenyl, composed of two benzene rings joined together, each containing the amino radical NH_2. **1946** *Nature* 30 Nov. 791/2 Such soil extracts gave a strong blue coloration with benzidine. **1966** G. P. ELLIS *Mod. Textbk. Org. Chem.* xiv. 366 Benzidine (4, 4'-diaminodiphenyl).. is obtained by an interesting isomerization (the benzidine rearrangement) of hydrazobenzene.. when it is heated with an acid. **1967** KARCH & BUBER *Offset Processes* vii. 268 Benzidine yellows also are very strong, but not as fast to light as the Hansa yellows, but are more transparent. **1806** DAVY in *Phil. Trans.* XCVII. 18 Benzoate of ammonia, and alum were used. **1810** HENRY *Elem. Chem.* (1826) II. 237 The compounds, which this [benzoic] acid forms with alkaline and earthy bases, called benzoates. **1876** GROSS *Dis. Bladder* 274 Benzoated zinc ointment. **1922** *Chem. Abstr.* 1487 Benzocaine.. was formerly made in Germany and sold under the name 'anesthesine'. The Council on Pharmacy and Chemistry of the Am. Med. Assoc. adopted the newer name. **1959** *Sunday Graphic* 25 Jan. 4 (Advt.), De Witt's Antibiotic Throat Lozenges also employ benzocaine, the swift pain-killer. **1927** A. W. STEWART *Rec. Adv. Org. Chem.* (ed. 5) I. vi. 123 The polyketide derivatives yield members of the pyrone, benzopyrone, benzpyrene, pyridine, and isoquinolone series. **1951** M. J. D. WHITE in G. H. Bourne *Cytology* (ed. 2) v. 221, 1, 2, 5, 6-dibenzanthracene and benzpyrene.. have been shown to produce chromosome rearrangements in *Drosophila*. **1865** MANSFIELD *Salts* 399 Two of the atoms of Carbon in the Benzylic molecule. **1869** ROSCOE *Elem. Chem.* 407 This is termed the Benzyl series. **1920** *Lancet* 4 Sept. 512/1 A man.. complained of persistent hiccough... He was given a 20 per cent. solution of benzyl benzoate. **1932** *Times* 1 Nov. (Brit. Industries no.) p. xxiv/4 A recent development in the plastics industry involves the use of esters and derivatives of cellulose or wood fibre, such as benzyl cellulose. **1947** ARNSTEIN & COOK in *Brit. Jrnl. Exper. Path.* XXVIII. 94 The present paper records.. experiments leading to the final identification of the major constituent of the material as penicillin-II (penicillin-G or benzylpenicillin). **1951** YARSLEY & KITCHEN in H. M. Langton *Synth. Resins* (ed. 3) ii. 107 Benzyl cellulose.. is thermoplastic and can be heated up to 180° C without fear of decomposition.

benzodiazepine (bɛnzəʊdaɪ'æzəpiːn). *Chem.* and *Pharm.* [f. BENZO- + DI-[2] + AZO- + *-epine*, suffix denoting a seven-membered ring containing nitrogen, (f. H)EP(TA- + -INE[5]).] Any compound whose molecule contains a benzene ring fused to a seven-membered ring containing two nitrogen atoms; *spec.* any of a group of such compounds used as hypnotics and anxiolytics and sometimes causing psychological dependence.

1934 *Chem. Abstr.* XXVIII. 8031 C_6-C_5N_2 Benzodiazepine. **1960** *Jrnl. Pharmacol. & Exper. Therap.* CXXIX. 163/1 Methaminodiazepoxide HCl (Librium HCl) is a psychosedative drug of a new chemical type... Methaminodiazepoxide.. is 7-chloro-2-methylamino-5-phenyl-3H-1,4-benzodiazepine 4-oxide hydrochloride. **1961** *Current Therapeutic Res.* III. 424 Valium is a new psychotherapeutic agent in the 1,4-benzodiazepine class. **1968** *Chem. Rev.* LXVIII. 748/1 The 1,4-benzodiazepines form the most extensively explored group in this series, largely owing to the discovery of their interesting biological activity, which has led to the introduction of four drugs... The 1,5-benzodiazepines have been thoroughly studied during a period of several decades, largely because of their relatively easy synthesis. **1976** *Lancet* 30 Oct. 936/2 Barbiturates or benzodiazepines were given to ensure sleep during the preceding night. **1984** A. SMITH *Mind* IV. xiv. 265 Over sixty million prescriptions for benzodiazepines are filled in annually.

benzoic (bɛn'zəʊɪk), *a. Chem.* [f. BENZO-IN + -IC. (The first of the chemical terms so formed.)] Of or derived from benzoin; as ***benzoic acid***, $C_7H_6O_2$ (= $C_6H_5.CO.OH$), a monobasic acid of the Aromatic series, existing in large quantity in gum benzoin, from which it was at first prepared.

1791 HAMILTON *Berthollet's Dyeing* I. I. I. v. 85 Benzoic acid, or salt of benzoin. **1819** J. CHILDREN *Chem. Anal.* 274 Benzoic acid, formed from gum benzoin, is solid, white, and slightly ductile.. it crystallizes in long white opaque prisms, with a satiny lustre. **1830** LINDLEY *Nat. Syst. Bot.* 303 The fragrance of some grasses.. depends, according to Vögel, upon the presence of Benzoic acid.

benzoin ('bɛnzəʊɪn, -zɔɪn). Forms: 6 **belzoin, benjoin, bengwin, bengewyne**, 6-7 **-wine**, 7 **bengwine, benzwine, benswine, benioyn, benjoine, benjouin, benzoine, benzion, bezoin**, 7-8 **benione**, 6- **benzoin**. [In 16th c. *benjoin*, a. F. *benjoin* (also *benjaoy*, quoted by Devic from Déterville *Dict. Hist. Nat.* 1816), repr. Sp. *benjui*, *benjuy* (Barbosa 1516), Pg. *beijoim* (Vasco da Gama 1498), It. *benzoi* (Venetian records, 1461), for **lo-benzoi*, **lo-benjuy*, a. Arab. *lubān jāwī* 'frankincense of Jāwā' (Sumatra), by which name benzoin is called by Ibn Batuta *c*1350 (ed. Paris IV. 228). The *lo-* appears to have been dropped in Romanic, as if it were the article. The word was naturally much corrupted in European langs.; later It. forms are *belgivino*, *belzuino*, mod.L. 1584 *belzuinum*, whence occas. Eng. *belzoin*. In Eng., *benjoin* was soon corrupted to BENJAMIN, which still survives as a synonym. *Benzoin*, which is farther from the original, and appears to owe its *z* to the It., began to prevail *c*1650. From *benzoin*, was formed *a*1800 the chemical term *benzoic* (acid), whence at a later period *benzin*(*e*, *benzol*, and the numerous names of the *benzene* series.]

1. A dry and brittle resinous substance, with a fragrant odour and slightly aromatic taste, obtained from the *Styrax benzoin*, a tree of Sumatra, Java, etc. It is used in the preparation of benzoic acid, in medicine, and extensively in perfumery. For scientific distinction it is now termed ***gum benzoin***. Also called by popular corruption BENJAMIN.

1558 WARDE *Alexis' Secr.* (1568) 3 a, An unce of Bengewine. **1562** TURNER *Herbal* II. 30 b, Belzoin or Benzoin is the rosin of a tree. **1601** HOLLAND *Pliny* I. 480 The herbe.. (which beareth the gum Benjoine) grew there first. **1616** BULLOKAR, *Benzwine*, a sweet smelling gumme. **1616** SURFL. & MARKH. *Countr. Farm* 484 Your hard gums, such as is frankincense, benjouin.. and waxe. **1653** WALTON *Angler* (Arb.) 42 There is an herb *Benione*, which.. makes him (the Otter) to avoid that place. **1658** ROWLAND *Mouffet's Theat. Ins.* 1000 *Asa dulcis*, Wine and Honey, or Benzoin dissolved in warm water. **1671** GREW *Anat. Plants* I. 17 Benzoine, by Distillation [yieldeth] Oyl; by Vstion, white Flowers. **1834** J. GRIFFIN *Chem. Recr.* 117 Gum benzoin (or benjamin) is a prime constituent of fumigating pastiles. **1875** JEVONS *Money* vii. 28 Cubes of benzoin, gum or beeswax.. are other peculiar forms of currency.

2. *Bot.* Name of a genus of *Lauraceæ*, of which the Benjamin-tree of North America is the chief species. Also called ***benzoin laurel***.

1866 *Treas. Bot.* 135 Benzoin, a genus of Lauraceæ, inhabiting.. North America. **1875** LOUDON *Abridgm. Arboretum* 685 The Benzoin Laurel, or Benjamin Tree.

3. *Chem.* Bitter-almond-oil camphor: one of the constituents of gum-benzoin, also frequently contained in crude bitter-almond oil, whence it is obtained as a by-product, when the oil is purified by lime and ferrous chloride; it is a ketone, $C_{14}H_{12}O_2$, of the di-phenyl group, and crystallizes in shining prisms.

1863 WATTS *Dict. Chem.* I. 559. **1880** *Syd. Soc. Lex.* s.v., Gum Benzoin.. contains benzoic acid, benzoin, and resin.

'benzoinate, *v.* [f. prec. + -ATE[3].] *trans.* To impregnate with benzoin. Hence **'benzoinated**.

1861 HULME *Moquin-Tandon* II. III. 187 Benzoinated fat.

benzol, benzole ('bɛnzɒl, -zəʊl). [f. BENZ-OIC + the ending of ALCOHOL. The spelling -OLE, is prob. intended to refer to L. *oleum* oil.]

1. *Chem.* (Benzol) The name given by Liebig in 1834 to what had at first been called *benzine*; generally used in chemistry till recent times, when it has been largely superseded by Hofmann's name BENZENE. (Less correctly spelt *benzole.*)

1838 THOMSON *Chem. Org. Bodies* 609 Mitscherlich.. has given the name of benzin, altered by Liebig to benzol. **1869** ROSCOE *Elem. Chem.* 408 Benzol (or Benzene).. can be prepared from its elements by synthesis. **1875** URE *Dict. Arts* I. 337 Benzole is excessively inflammable, and its vapour mixed with air is explosive.

2. In comb., as ***amido-benzol*** (= aniline), ***nitro-benzol***: see BENZENE.

1869 ROSCOE *Elem. Chem.* 409 In contact with reducing agents, nitro-benzol undergoes reduction to aniline. *Ibid.*, *Aniline*.. is benzol in which one atom of hydrogen is replaced by the monad group NH_2, and it is therefore properly called Amido-benzol. **1875** URE *Dict. Arts* I. 338 Nitro-benzole.. odour greatly resembling bitter almonds.

3. *Min.* (Benzole) Dana's name for native benzene or benzol, as a species of his *benzole group* of mineral 'oils' of the general formula C_nH_{2n-6}; it has been detected in Rangoon tar.

benzoline ('bɛnzəliːn, -lɪn). [f. BENZOL + -INE = derivative.]

1. *Chem.* An earlier name for AMARINE, $C_{21}H_{18}N_2$, isomeric with hydrobenzamide.

2. A commercial name for impure benzene, and often for other volatile inflammable liquid hydrocarbons, esp. for coal-tar naphtha, of which benzene is a chief constituent, and which is used for removing grease-spots, cleaning gloves, etc. Also, less correctly, for a light hydrocarbon obtained by the fractional distillation of crude petroleum, and used to burn in lamps.

1874 (On the 2nd Oct. a barge carrying gunpowder and 'benzoline' along the Regent's Canal in London was blown up by the accidental ignition of the vapour of the benzoline, causing much destruction in the neighbourhood). **1875** URE *Dict. Arts* I. 338 Its power of dissolving greasy matters, has caused it [benzole] to become an article of commerce under the name of *benzoline*.

3. *attrib.* (in sense 2), as in ***benzoline lamp*** (introduced about 1864).

benzown, -wine, obs. ff. BENISON, BENZOIN.

beo-, in OE. usually became in later times BE-, BEE-; but the earlier spelling lingered in Early ME., especially in the following forms:

beo, obs. f. of BEE *sb.*[1], and of pres. indic, subj., imper. and infin. of BE *v.*

†**beod.** *Obs.* Also 2 bied. [OE. *béod* = OS. *biod*, *bied*, OHG. *biot*, *biet*, ON. *biodr*, Goth. *biuds*:—OTeut. *biudo-z* table, f. *biud-an* to offer.] A table.

c **1000** *Ags. Gosp.* Matt. xv. 27 Of þam crumum þe of hyra hlaforda beodum feallað. *c* **1200** *Trin. Coll. Hom.* 228 Þan he sat at his biede [*Jesus MS.* borde; *Egerton MS.* beode].

be-ode, etc.: see BE- *pref.*

beode, -mon, early f. BEDE, BEAD *sb.*, BEADSMAN.

beoden, obs. form of BID *v.*

beofe, obs. form of BEHOOF.

beoff, beoves, obs. sing. and pl. form of BEEF.

beon, beonde, early f. *ben*, *been*, *being*: see BE *v.*

beord, obs. variant of BEARD.

beoren, obs. infin. form of BEAR *v.*[1]

beorn, early form of BERNE, *Obs.*, man.

†**beot**, *sb. Obs.* [OE. *béot*, contr. from earlier **bíhát* 'promise,' the original noun-form, corresponding to the vb. *bi-*, *be-'hátan*: see BE-, BY-. For the contraction cf. *héold* (:—*'he-hald*), *béo*, etc. A shifting of the stress from *'bíhát* to *bi-'hát*, on analogy of the vb., gave the late OE *be'hát*, whence ME. BEHOTE, which is thus a doublet of *béot.*] A promise, vow, threat, boast.

a **1000** Cædmon's *Genesis* (Gr.) 70 Wæs him gylp forod, beot forborsten. *c* **1205** LAY. 23680 His beot [so **1250**] imaked hafde bi-foren al his duȝeðe. *Ibid.* 24929 Þat Romanisce leoden sunden swa ræie and heore beot [**1250** þret] makieð.

†**beote(n**, *v. Obs.*[−1] [OE. *béotian* f. prec.] To boast, threaten.

a **1000** *Juliana* (Gr.) 137 Hildewoman, þe þu hæstlice man-fremmende to me beotast. *c* **1205** LAY. 20522 Heo beoteden swiðe.. þat heo wolden igræten Cheldric.

beoth, obs. pl. pres. indic. and imper. of BE *v.*

Beothuk ('beɪəθʊk), *sb.* and *a.* Also †**Bœothic**, **Boethic**; **Beothuck**. [ad. Beothuk *beathook*, recorded as their self-designation in 1819 by Rev. John Leigh (see J. Hewson, *Beothuk Vocabularies*, 1978, pp. 35, 44).]

A. *sb.* **1.** (A member of) an Indian people of Newfoundland, said to be extinct by 1827.

1828 J. MCGREGOR *Hist. Maritime Colonies Brit. Amer.* xvi. 206 The natives, now dwindled to a few families of Micmacs, Mountaineers and Boethics (Red Indians) are not included. **1842** R. H. BONNYCASTLE *Newfoundland in 1842* II. xiv. 266 The bark of the spruce pine.. was taken off, it being one of the customs of the Bœothics to use the inner bark as food. **1914** F. G. SPECK *Beothuk & Micmac* 15 The fame of the Beothuk seems to have reached regions quite distant from Newfoundland in Indian times. **1915** J. P. HOWLEY *Beothucks* 25 The poor Beothuck, armed only with his bow and arrow and spear, was no match for the fisherman with his deadly fire-arms. **1921** *Contemp. Rev.* Feb. 188 Our settlers in Newfoundland were killing out the harmless Beothuks. **1932** D. JENNESS *Indians of Canada* xviii. 266 The Beothuk attempted to retaliate, but, armed only with bows and arrows, they could not withstand the combined attacks of white and Micmac, and the last known

survivor died in captivity at St. Johns in 1829. **1968** J. M. MURRAY *Newfoundland Jrnl. Aaron Thomas* x. 135 For the next sixty years succeeding governors tried to establish friendly relations between the settlers and the Beothucks. **1973** *Islander* (Victoria, B.C.) 2 Dec. 14/1 The Beothuk, whose home was Newfoundland, are thought to be the first North American Indians to encounter the white man. Indeed, it is said that their use of red ochre on their bodies is what prompted the term, Red Indian.

2. The language of this people, perh. of Algonquian affiliation.

1856 R. G. LATHAM in *Trans. Philol. Soc.* 58 The Bethuck is the native language of Newfoundland. **1886** A. S. GATSCHET in *Proc. Amer. Philos. Soc.* XXIII. 411 There is no *f* in Beothuk. **1979** I. GODDARD in Campbell & Mithun *Languages Native Amer.* 107 The only conclusion possible is that the comparisons between Beothuk and Algonquian are not yet on firm ground. **1982** *Canad. Jrnl. Linguistics* XXVII. II. 175 If Beothuk is not Algonquian, what is it? It bears no greater resemblance to Eskimo or Iroquoian than it does to Algonquian, yet to say that it is an isolate just ignores the problem.

B. *adj.* Of, pertaining to, or designating the Beothuks or their language.

1842 R. H. BONNYCASTLE *Newfoundland in 1842* II. xiv. 264 In 1827, a society was formed in St. John's, called the Bœothic Society for the Civilization of the Native Savages. **1856** R. G. LATHAM in *Trans. Philol. Soc.* 58 The collation of a Bethuck vocabulary enabled me to state that..it was Algonkin rather than aught else. **1885** A. S. GATSCHET in *Proc. Amer. Philos. Soc.* XXII. 411 We possess but few notices conveying graphic sketches of the appearance and daily life of the Beothuk Indians. **1932** D. JENNESS *Indians of Canada* vii. 86 When the Beothuk Indians of Newfoundland moved out to the coast during the summer months they preferred to camp in small, sheltered bays that had freshwater streams at their heads and gravel or sandy beaches that offered good landing-places for the birch-bark canoes. **1968** J. M. MURRAY *Newfoundland Jrnl. Aaron Thomas* x. 131 This description of Northern Newfoundland Indians almost certainly refers to Esquimos and not to the Beothuck Indians. **1971** E. R. SEARY *Place Names Avalon Peninsula of Newfoundland* ii. 19 Perhaps only three Beothuck names are to be found in the whole island. **1972** *Evening Telegram* (St. John's, Newfoundland) 23 June 8/6 Volunteers have been working for over two years to gather artifacts on Beothuck and Dorset Eskimo cultures.

beoust, beowust, variants of BEWIST *Obs.*

bepaddle, bepaid, etc.: see BE- *pref.*

bepaint (bɪˈpeɪnt). [f. BE- 1 + PAINT *v.*] *trans.* To paint over, cover, or smear with paint or paintings; to paint obtrusively; to colour, tinge.

c **1555** HARPSFIELD *Divorce of Hen. VIII* (1878) 282 The walls all bepainted..with places of holy Scripture. **1567** MAPLET *Gr. Forest* 12 b, Black, yet bepainted with other colours. **1592** SHAKS. *Rom. & Jul.* II. ii. 86 Else would a maiden blush bepaint my cheeke. **1647** BP. CORBET *Poems* (1807) 14 Their colledges were new be-painted. **1831** CARLYLE *Sart. Res.* I. vii, Buff-belts, complicated chains.. have been bepainted in Modern Romance.

Hence **beˈpainted** *ppl. a.*

1592 SHAKS. *Ven. & Ad.* 901 Whose frothy mouth, bepainted all with red. **1858** CARLYLE *Fredk. Gt.* II. VI. vi. 96 A bepainted, beribanded, insulting Playactor Majesty.

bepale, bepaper, beparch, beparody, beparse, bepart, bepaste, bepaw, etc.: see BE-.

bepat (bɪˈpæt), *v.* [f. BE- 2 + PAT *v.*] *trans.* To pat frequently; to strike, beat.

1676 ETHEREDGE *Man of Mode* II. i. (1684) 15 He calls me Rogue, tells me he can't abide me; And does so bepat me. *a* **1841** MISS BAILLIE *Eng. Minstr., Kitten,* Thy clutching feet bepat the ground.

bepatched (bɪˈpætʃt), *ppl. a.* [f. BE- + PATCH *v.*] **1.** Mended with patches; wearing patched clothes.

1605 STOW *Ann.* 1291 Their habit was Russet, all bepatched. **1846** *Sir R. de Coverley* II. 186 You ragged vagabond..you bepatched and bespattered knave.

2. Wearing 'patches' on the face as an ornament.

1719 OZELL *Misson's Trav. Eng.* 214 (D.) In England, young, old, handsome, ugly, all are bepatch'd till they are bedrid. **1865** *Publ. Opinion* 4 Mar. 237/1 When Cleopatra appeared bepatched in a farthingale, and Alexander wore his helmet over a full-bottomed wig.

bepearl (bɪpɜːrl), *v.* [f. BE- 6 + PEARL.] To cover or set with or as with pearls. Hence **bepearled** *ppl. a.*

1640 CAREW *Poems* Wks. (1824) 134 This Primrose all bepearl'd with dew. **1863** GEO. ELIOT *Romola* II. vi, The brilliant tints of the embroidered and bepearled canopy.

bepelt (bɪˈpɛlt), *v.* [f. BE- 1 + PELT *v.*] *trans.* To pelt soundly; to assail with missiles.

1622 MABBE *Aleman's Guzman d' Alf.* I. 94 They shrewdly be-pelted their Pates. **1630** J. TAYLOR (Water P.) *Wks.* II. 145 [They] Bepelted me with Lome, with Stones, and Laths. **1832** *Fraser's Mag.* V. 756 The Duke..was hissed and bepelted. **1852** HAWTHORNE *Wonder-Bk.* (1879) 117 The children..bepelted him with snowballs.

bepen, beperiwigged, bepewed, etc.: see BE-.

bepepper (bɪˈpɛpə(r)). [f. BE- 1 + PEPPER *v.*] *trans.* To pelt with shot, sand, etc.; or with blows thickly falling.

1613 ROWLANDS *Four Knaves* (1843) 52 He is be-peper'd over head and eares. **1760** STERNE *Tr. Shandy* (1802) VIII. v. 112 Grinding the faces of the impotent,—bepeppering their noses.

† **beˈpeps,** *v. Obs. rare*⁻¹. [f. BE- 2 + PEPS *v. dial.* to throw at, pelt.] *trans.* To pepper.

1622 MABBE *Aleman's Guzman d' Alf.* I. 233 They [the Mosquitos] did so be-peps him.

bepester (bɪˈpɛstə(r)), *v.* [f. BE- 2 + PESTER *v.*¹] *trans.* To pester greatly, plague, vex, harass.

1600 ABP. ABBOT *Exp. Jonah* 13 When Valens the Emperor with his Arrian opinions, had bee-pestered much of the world. **1885** *Academy* 19 Sept. 188 Since Locke has bepestered the human mind with his unspeakably valuable chapter upon 'words.'

bephilter, bephrase, bepicture, bepiece, bepierce, bepile, bepilgrimed, bepill, bepillared, bepimple, etc.: see BE- *pref.*

bepinch (bɪˈpɪnʃ), *v.* [f. BE- 1 + PINCH *v.*] *trans.* To pinch or bruise all over.

1600 CHAPMAN *Iliad* xxiii. (J.) In their sides, arms, shoulders, all bepincht, Ran thick the weals. **1612** ROWLANDS *More Knaues Yet* 40 Bepinch a lazie queane. **1742** JARVIS *Quix.* II. III. xvii, Sad and sorely bepinched.

† **bepink** (bɪˈpɪŋk), *v. Obs.* [f. BE- 1 + PINK *v.*] *trans.* To cut in small scollops; to work in eyelet-holes; to pierce with small holes.

1567 MAPLET *Gr. Forest* 39 b, Crowfoote..His leafe is cut about or bepinked. **1615** ROWLANDS *Melanch. Knt.* 11 With poniard point his doublet Ile bepinke.

bepiss, bepistle, etc.: see BE- *pref.*

† **beˈpitch,** *v. Obs.* [f. BE- 6 + PITCH *sb.*] *trans.* To cover or stain with pitch; also *fig.* Hence **beˈpitched** *ppl. a.*, **beˈpitching** *vbl. sb.*

1547 *Life 70 Abps. Canterb.* To Rdr. E vij b, Who liued in those pitchie tymes, and was not bepitched? **1611** COTGR., *Poixement,* a pitching, or bepitching. *Poissard,* pitchie, bepitched. *a* **1618** SYLVESTER *Ark* 479 When th' air with midnight shal your noon be-pitch.

bepity (bɪˈpɪtɪ), *v.* [f. BE- 2 + PITY *v.*] *trans.* To pity exceedingly.

1587 TURBERV. *Trag. T.* (1837) 61 But divers moe, that there about did dwell, Bepitied those that loving hearts did beare. **1749** FIELDING *Tom Jones* x. ix, Mercy on him, poor heart! I bepitied him, so I did.

beplague, beplaided, etc.: see BE- *pref.*

beplaster (bɪˈplɑːstə(r), -æ-), *v.* Also 7–8 beplaister. [f. BE- 1 + PLASTER *v.*] *trans.* To plaster over or about; to cover or smear thickly.

1611 COTGR., *Emplastré..* plaistered, beplaistered; couered with a plaister. **1753** SMOLLETT *Ct. Fathom* (1784) 63/2 We Englishmen don't beplaister our doublets with gold and silver. **1812** H. & J. SMITH *Rej. Addr., Drury L. Hustings* iii, Some old harridans who beplaster their cheeks. **1865** *Sat. Rev.* 5 Aug. 169 To plaster his friends with praise in order that he in turn may be similarly beplastered.

Hence **beˈplastered** *ppl. a.*, **beˈplastering.**

1598 FLORIO, *Pastegli..* plaisters or beplaistrings. **1862** MISS YONGE *C'tess Kate* vii. (1880), They hurried her along as fast as their beplastered garments would let her move.

† **beˈplotmele,** *adv. Obs.* [f. *be-* = BY + PLOT patch + MEAL, OE. *mǣl* time: cf. *piece-meal.*] Part by part, one portion after another.

c **1440** *Promp. Parv.* 31 Beplotmele, *particulariter.*

beplumed (bɪˈpluːmd), *ppl. a.* [f. BE- 7 + PLUME *sb.*] Furnished or adorned with feathers.

1582 STANYHURST *Æneis* I. (Arb.) 27 Hee flitters with wynges ful fledgye beplumed. **1768** STERNE *Sent. Journ.* (1775) I. 56 Be-plumed with each gay feather of the east. **1860** MISS YONGE *Stokesley Secr.* ix. (1880) 260 It was the first time Christabel had seen Ida out of her beplumed hat.

bepoetize, bepounce, etc.: see BE- *pref.*

bepommel (bɪˈpʌm(ə)l), *v.* [f. BE- 2 + POMMEL *v.*] *trans.* To pommel soundly, drub; also *fig.*

1553–87 FOXE *A. & M.* (1596) 152/2 He [Hildebrand].. there all to bepomild pope Alexander with his fists. **1609** ROWLANDS *Crew Kind Gossips* 9, I..got him downe, and with my very fist I did bepommell him. **1858** THACKERAY *Virgin.* xlix. (1878) 388, Still bepommeled and stoned by irreproachable ladies of the straightest sect of the Pharisees.

bepowder (bɪˈpaʊdə(r)), *v.* [f. BE- 1 + POWDER *v.*] *trans.* To powder over.

1583 STANYHURST *Æneis* IV. (Arb.) 100 Thee chase is ensued with passadge dustye bepowdred. **1760** STERNE *Tr. Shandy* 243 Bepowdering their wigs,—bepeppering their noses. **1879** G. MACDONALD *P. Faber* I. xvii. 227 The ashes of life's volcano are falling; they bepowder my hair.

Hence **beˈpowdered** *ppl. a.*

1742 FIELDING *Lucy in Town* Wks. 1784 III. 439 And is this bepowder'd, becurl'd, behoop'd madwoman my daughter? **1829** SOUTHEY *Epist. A. Cunningham,* Armorial bearings and bepowdered pates!

bepraise (bɪˈpreɪz), *v.* [f. BE- 2 + PRAISE *v.*] *trans.* To laud or praise greatly or to excess.

1774 GOLDSMITH *Retal.* 118 How did Grub-street re-echo the shouts that you raised When he was be-Roscius'd and you were bepraised. **1824** BENTHAM *Fallacies* Wks. 1843 II. 399 The same man who bepraises you when dead.

Hence **beˈpraised** *ppl. a.*; **beˈpraisement; beˈpraiser.**

1843 MIALL *Nonconf.* III. 457 Contented, submissive and bepraised agriculturalists. **1831** *Fraser's Mag.* III. 113 The ..puffing bepraisement of the Court Journal. —— II. 78 Ruin would fall not only upon the head of the pseudo-poet, but his shivering bepraisers.

beprank, bepreach, bepress, bepretty, bepride: see BE- *pref.*

bepray, *v.* = PRAY. (Of doubtful use.)

1588 SHAKS. *L.L.L.* v. ii. 702 (Qᵒ 1), I bepray you, let me borrow my arms again. [*Qᵒ 2 and Folios,* pray.]

beprose (bɪˈprəʊz), *v.* [f. BE- 5 + PROSE *sb.*] *trans.* **a.** To turn into prose. **b.** To discuss in prose, to 'prose' about.

1739 MALLET *Verbal Crit.* (R.) To blast all beauty and beprose all rhyme. **1880** SWINBURNE *Study Shaks.* ii. (ed. 2) 151 More plentifully beprosed than ever Rosalind was berhymed.

bepuddle, bepurple, etc.: see BE- *pref.*

bepuff (bɪˈpʌf), *v.* [f. BE- 2 + PUFF *v.*] *trans.* **a.** To puff or blow out, to swell. **b.** *fig.* To puff up, praise greatly. Hence **beˈpuffed** *ppl. a.*

1843 CARLYLE *Past & Pr.* 392 Doggeries never so diplomaed, bepuffed, gas-lighted. *a* **1849** POE Wks. 1864 IV. 303 Altering my countenance..from its bepuffed and distorted appearance. **1860** DICKENS *Uncomm. Trav.* ix. (D.) Even the Lord Mayor—not a Fiction conventionally bepuffed on one day in the year by illustrious friends.

† **beˈpurfurate,** *ppl. a. Obs.* [? for *bepurpurate,* f. L. *purpur* (cf. Gr. πορφύρεος) purple.] Purpled, rosy-tinged, rosy-coloured.

1584 LODGE *Forb. & Prisc.* 30 a, Her daintie nose of ivorie faire and sheene Bepurfurate with ruddie roses beene.

bepuzzle (bɪˈpʌz(ə)l), *v. rare.* [f. BE- 2 + PUZZLE *v.*] *trans.* To puzzle greatly.

1599 NASHE *Lent. Stuffe* 6 A matter that egregiously bepuzled and entranced my apprehension.

Hence **beˈpuzzlement,** perplexing, perplexity.

1806 KNOX & JEBB *Corr.* I. 295 To the bepuzzlement of the ignorant, and the bedazzlement of the superficial. **1885** *Daily News* 21 Feb. 5/6 Stewart..used to express to me his bepuzzlement as to what could be the object of the campaign.

bepuzzled (bɪˈpʌz(ə)ld), *ppl. a.* [f. BEPUZZLE *v.* + -ED¹.] Utterly puzzled.

1826 *Examiner* 647/2 The bepuzzled scribblers. **1888** *Westm. Rev.* July 2 The bepuzzled claimant for a vote. **1909** J. LONDON *Let.* 2 Aug. (1966) 282, I..gave eminent satisfaction to the be-puzzled inquirers.

bepyr, var. of BEAUPERE, *Obs.*

beqhweytt, obs. form of BEQUEATH.

be-qualify (bɪˈkwɒlɪfaɪ), *v. rare*⁻¹. [f. BE- 2 + QUALIFY *v.*] *trans.* To ascribe qualities to, to celebrate the qualities of.

1600 B. JONSON *Cynthia's Rev.* IV. iii. 12 How hee doe's all to bequalifie her!..as if there were not others in place as.. polite as shee.

bequalm, etc.: see BE- *pref.*

† **bequarre.** *Obs.* [a. OF. *béquarre,* mod. F. *bécarre* (= Lat. *B quadratum*): see BEMOL.] *Mus.* Old name for the note B♮. See B II. 1.

a **1350** *Song* in *Rel. Ant.* I. 292 Thu bitist a-sonder bequarre, for bemol i the blame. **1806** CALCOTT *Mus. Gram.* v. 57 *note,* The French call the Natural *Bequarre.*

† **beˈquarrel,** *v. Obs.* [f. BE- 4 + QUARREL *v.*] *trans.* To quarrel with, find fault with, abuse.

1624 F. WHITE *Repl. Fisher* 165 Pontificians bequarrel vs in this argument. **1637** H. SYDENHAM *Serm. Sol. Occ.* 14 Afterwards bequarrell'd by Sabellius the Hereticke..as being the author of Innovation.

† **beˈquash,** *v. Obs. rare*⁻¹. [f. BE- 2 + QUASH *v.*] *intr.* To shake or fall in pieces, to be shattered.

1377 LANGL. *P. Pl.* B. XVIII. 246 The erthe..Quaked as quykke þinge, and al biquasht[e] þe roche [**1393** C. XXI. 64 The erthe quook and quashte as hit quyke were].

bequeath (bɪˈkwiːð), *v.* Forms: 1 bi-, becweðan, 2–5 bi-, byqueðen, -þe(n, -the(n, 4–6 bequethe, 4–5 -qweth(e, 6 -queath(e, (5 -quete, -wheth(e, -wete, -qwithe, -quaythe, and innumerable illiterate spellings in wills). *Pa. t.* 6- bequeathed; in 1 becwæð, 2 -quað, 2–3 -queð, 2–4 -queþ, 3 -quaad, 5 -quath(e, -quaythed. *Pa. pple.* 6- bequeathed; in 1 becweden, 3 -queðe(n, 5 -quethe(n, -quette, -witt, -quothen, -quethed. [OE. *bi-, becweðan,* f. BE- 4 + *cweðan* to say: see QUETHE and QUOTH. An ancient word, the retention of which is due to the traditional language of wills. Originally, like its radical *cweðan,* a strong vb.; but having only weak inflexion since 1500. In north. dial. written in 15th c. *bewhethe,* and variously perverted as *-whete, -weth, -withe, -wite, -wit, -quite, -quit,* which show the groping of popular etymology after some known verb to which the derivative might be referred.]

I. To say, utter, declare.

† **1.** *trans.* To say, utter, express in words. *Obs.*

c **1000** *Ags. Ps.* lxxxviii. 44 [-ix. 51] þæt þinum criste becweþað swiðe. *c* **1000** *Andreas* (Gr.) 418 Gif þu þegn sie.. wuldor cyninges, swa þu worde becwist.

†**b.** Of language: To express, signify, mean.

c **1175** *Lamb. Hom.* 75 Ic ou wile seggen word efter word and þermide hwat þet word bi-queþ. *Ibid.* 133 Hwet þeo saȝe bicweðe. *c* **1200** *Trin. Coll. Hom.* 17 Alle cunne ower crede ..þeih ȝe alle nuten hwat hit biqueðe.

†**2.** ? To speak about in sorrow, to bewail. *Obs.* (Or is this error for *bigreden*, or *bigreithen*?)

c **1250** *Gen. & Ex.* 2448 De liches beðen, And smeren, and winden, and bi-queðen.

II. To 'say (a thing) away'; to give or part with by formal declaration.

†**3.** To assign, ordain, appoint, allot, give as an attribute (a thing *to* a person, etc.). *Obs.*

c **1250** *Gen. & Ex.* 117 God bi-quuad watres here stede. **1674** N. FAIRFAX *Bulk & Selv.* 79 Yet these belongers to body are helpful enough, wherewith to set forth the nature of the things to which we bequeath them.

4. To make a formal assignation of (property of which one is possessed) *to* any one, †**a.** so as to pass to him at once: To transfer, hand over, make over, assign, deliver. *Obs.*

c **1305** *Edmund Conf.* 132 in *E.E.P.* (1862) 74 þis catel þat ich biqueþe þis dede forto do. **1480** CAXTON *Chron. Eng.* xciv. 74 He had the reame..sauf he byquath and yafe it to his broder. **1595** SHAKS. *John* I. i. 149 Wilt thou..Bequeath thy land to him, and follow me? **1611** —— *Wint. T.* v. iii. 102 Bequeath to Death your numnesse.

b. so as to pass to the recipient after one's death: To 'leave' by will. (The only surviving sense, for which it is the proper term.)

1066 *Chart. Eadweard* in *Cod. Dipl.* IV. 191 Swa full fre and swa forð swa he it sainte Petre bequað. *c* **1200** *Trin. Coll. Hom.* 183 Gief þe quike haueð aihte þe were þe dedes ærrure þe he him biqueð. *c* **1393** CHAUCER *Gentilesse* 17 There may noman..Beqweythe his heyre his vertuous noblesse. **1418** *E. E. Wills* (1882) 25 My godys..I be-quethe to Ione my wyfe. *c* **1440** *Promp. Parv.* 31. **1440** *Test. Ebor.* II. (1855) 134 A speciall wille..in wheche I have bequothen and sette diverse thyngys to certenn persouns. **1443** *Ibid.* 106, I gyffe and bewhete..xl *s.* *c* **1440** *Gesta Rom.* (1879) 23 He bequathe to his dowter all his Empire. **1530** PALSGR. 448/2 My grant mother byquaythed me a hundred pounde. **1601** SHAKS. *Jul. C.* III. ii. 141 Bequeathing it as a rich Legacie Vnto their issue. **1782** PRIESTLEY *Corrupt. Chr.* II. vi. 28 Sums of money were..bequeathed to the priests. **1876** GREEN *Short Hist.* ii. §6 (1882) 85 William had bequeathed Normandy to his eldest son, Robert.

c. *fig.* To transmit (to posterity), to 'leave.'

1614 RALEIGH *Hist. World* II. 415 Jacob in his blessing prophetically bequeathed it. **1752** JOHNSON *Rambl.* No. 205 ¶13 This narrative he has bequeathed to future generations. **1875** SCRIVENER *Lect. Grk. Test.* 11 Antiquity has bequeathed to us nothing else that can be compared with them.

†**5.** To commit *to*, *unto* (any one) with recommendation to his acceptance or care; to commend, entrust. Also *fig. Obs.* or *arch.*

c **1225** *Rel. Ant.* I. 235 Louerd Godd, in hondes tine I biqueðe soule mine. **1436** *Test. Ebor.* II. (1855) 75, I bewitt my saule to Gode Allmighty. **1591** SPENSER *Virg. Gnat* 633 Them therefore as bequeathing to the winde, I now depart. **1596** DRAYTON *Legends* iii. 16 Let Me to Thee, my sad Complaints bequeathe. **1700** DRYDEN *Pythag. Philos.* 57 *Fables* (1721) 301 The judges to the common urn bequeath Their votes. **1718** POPE *Iliad* VII. 399 We to flames our slaughtered friends bequeath.

†**6.** *gen.* To deliver, bestow, give, yield, furnish.

c **1440** *Gesta Rom.* (1879) 25 To whom god hath ȝevin and bequeþon..paradise. **1608** *Pennyless Parl.* in *Harl. Misc.* (Malh.) III. 72 A niggards purse shall scarce bequeath his master a good dinner. **1674** N. FAIRFAX *Bulk & Selv.* 122 That which bequeaths it this slow pace.

†**7.** *refl.* To commit oneself, give oneself up, devote oneself. *Obs.* or *arch.*

1555 PHAËR *Æneid* III. —iv, This fleete at last..I see..I did myself bequeth thereto to flee. **1652** EVELYN *State of France* Misc. (1805) 85 Gentlemen..who generally so bequeath themselves to this service. **1829** K. DIGBY *Broadst. Hon.* I. 166 Orpheus..bequeaths himself to a solitary life in the deserts.

†**be'queath**, *sb. Obs.* Forms: 3 **byquide**, 4 **bekuyde**, **-quide**, 5 **beqweth**, 6 **bequede**, **bequeth**, 7 **bequeath**. [ME. *byquide*:—OE. *bícwide*, '*biȝcwide*, quotable only in sense of 'byword, proverb' (cf. BEQUEATH *v.* 1), f. *bi-*, emphatic form of *bi-*, BE- *pref.* + *cwide* a sentence, a saying, cogn. w. OS. *quidi*, OHG. *chwiti*:—OTeut. **qidi-z*, f. *qiþan* (OS. *quethan*, *queðan*, OE. *cweðan*) to say; pa. pple. (with grammatical consonant-change) OE. *cweden*. In later times, gradually assimilated in form to the vb. BEQUEATH.]

1. Byword, proverb. (Only in OE.)

c **1000** ÆLFRIC *Deut.* xxviii. 37 Ge forwurðaþ þurh biȝspell and biȝcwidas.

2. Bequest, testament, will.

1297 R. GLOUC. 384 Gret folc he sende also Fram Normandye to worry, & hys fader byquide vndo. **1340** *Ayenb.* 38 Kueade exequitours of bekuydes. **1490** *Church-w. Acc. St. Dunstan's, Canterb.*, Rec. the full of the beqweth of Mother Belser xxxiijs. iiijd. **1527** *Lanc. & Chesh. Wills* (1854) 35 All the foresaid gyftes and bequedes. **1642** *Fragm. Reg.* in *Select. Harl. Misc.* (1793) 185 They may express more affection to one in the abundance of bequeaths.

b. *fig.*

1340 *Ayenb.* 112 He hit ous let: at his [Christ's] yleaue nymynge and at his laste bequide. *a* **1617** BAYNE *On Eph.* 11 Peace is that golden bequeath which Christ did leave us.

bequeathable (bɪˈkwiːðəb(ə)l), *a.* [f. BEQUEATH *v.* + -ABLE.] Capable of being bequeathed.

1655 FULLER *Ch. Hist.* IX. IV. 398 Bequeathable..like goods and Chattells. **1875** POSTE *Gaius* II. 287 Legacies bequeathable to legatees who were capable of taking.

bequeathal (bɪˈkwiːðəl). [f. as prec. + -AL[2].] The action of bequeathing.

1642 *Act Harvard Coll.* in Shurtleff *Records Mass. Bay* II. 30 All gifts, legacies, bequeathalls, revenues, lands, and donations. **1861** PEARSON *Early & Mid. Ages Eng.* 186 The bequeathal of folc-land would require a guarantee from the state.

bequeathed (bɪˈkwiːðd), *ppl. a.* [f. as prec. + -ED[1].] Left by will; *fig.* handed down, transmitted to posterity.

1618 BOLTON *Florus* III. xv. 220 The late bequeathed kingdome of Attalus. **1679** *Establ. Test.* 21 Capable of taming this bequeathed Fierceness.

bequeather (bɪˈkwiːðə(r)). [f. as prec. + -ER[1].] One who bequeaths, a testator.

1502 ARNOLD *Chron.* (1811) 274 Ageyn the wyll of the yeuar or byquyether. **1638** FEATLY *Strict. Lyndom.* II. 121 The disposer and bequeather of the land. **1883** L. CAMPBELL *Sp. at St. Andrews* 1 Nov., The munificent donors and bequeathers of large sums to the university.

be'queathing, *vbl. sb.* [f. as prec. + -ING[1].] The action of leaving by will; *fig.* handing down to posterity; also *concr.* a legacy, bequest.

1674 N. FAIRFAX *Bulk & Selv.* 131 The bequeathing of that hord of sprightfulness. **1768** BLACKSTONE *Comm.* II. 491 The power of bequeathing. **1855** BROWNING *Saul Men & Wom.* II. 123 His rents, the successive bequeathings of ages untold.

be'queathment. [f. as prec. + -MENT.] The action of bequeathing; usually *concr.* a bequest.

1607 W. SCLATER *Fun. Serm.* (1629) Pref. If such vertues were capable of bequeathment. *a* **1634** RANDOLPH *Amyntas* III. ii. 32 Nymph take this Whistle..'Tis Amaryllis last bequeathment to you. **1871** SMILES *Charac.* i. (1876) 24 Among the most cherished bequeathments from the past.

bequeaue, -queue, obs. phonetic corruptions of BEQUEATH.

bequest (bɪˈkwɛst). Also 3-4 **biqueste**, 4 **byquyste**, 5 **bicquest**, **byqueste**, 6 **bequeste**, 5- **bequest**. [ME. *biquyste*, *biqueste*, prob. for an earlier **bícwis*, *bí-cwiss(e*, f. *bí-*, accented form of *bi-*, BE- + *cwis*, *cwiss(e* 'saying':—OTeut. **qissi-z*:—**qiþ-ti-z*, f. *qiþan* to say (cf. Sievers *Ags. Gram.* §232). *Bequest* thus represents a type *'*biqissi-z* answering to the vb. **bi'qiþan*, BEQUEATH. The later change is parallel to that of BEHEST (q.v.), and the accentuation is assimilated to that of the verb.]

1. The act of bequeathing; transference or bestowal by will, or by a similar procedure.

c **1300** R. BRUNNE *Chron.* 86 Of ȝour fader biqueste dome þan salle ȝe se. **1393** LANGL. *P. Pl.* C. IX. 94 For-thi ich wolle, er ich wende · do wryten my by-quyste. *c* **1600** SHAKS. *Sonn.* iv, Natures bequest gives nothing, but doth lend. **1848** MILL *Pol. Econ.* I. 259 Bequest in a primitive state of society, was seldom recognized. **1876** FREEMAN *Norm. Conq.* V. xxiv. 388 When he made his bequest, if bequest we are to call it, in favour of Rufus.

2. *concr.* That which is bequeathed; a legacy.

1496 in Blades *Caxton* 162 Itm in bokes called legendes, of the bequest of William Caxton, xiijd. **1553** T. WILSON *Rhet.* 246 Al bequestes and goodes of suche his frendes as dyed intestate. **1618** BOLTON *Florus* II. xx. 156 The estate of kings, and the riches of whole Realmes comming to them as bequests, and Legacies. **1790** BURKE *Fr. Rev.* Wks. V. 437 Let us imitate their caution, if we wish to deserve fortune, or to retain their bequests.

†**be'quest**, *v. Obs.* Also 5 **bi-**, **by-**. *Pa. pple.* **bequested**, **bequest**. [f. prec. sb.]

trans. To give as a bequest, to bequeath.

1394 *P. Pl. Crede* 69 Her money may biquest, and testament maken. **1479** *Bury Wills* (1850) 54 A cloos.. byfor byquestyd to Thomas my sone. **1480** *Ibid.* 55, I byqwest to the ffryerez of Clare xxs. **1526** *Pilgr. Perf.* (W. de W. 1531) 299 b, Testament of peace..gyuen and bequest to thy disciples. **1795** *Haunted Castle* II. 74 He broke open the papers of Du Pin..bequesting him all his estates.

†**be'questing**, *vbl. sb. Obs.* Bequeathing.

1572 *Richmond. Wills* (1853) 235 In witnesse of the bequesting of a bull of the said Adam Kirkbie.

bequirtle, bequote, etc.: see BE- *pref.*

†**be'quit**, *v. Obs. rare*[−1]. [? f. BE- 2 + QUIT.] *refl.* To acquit oneself.

1577 STANYHURST *Descr. Irel.* in *Holinshed* VI. Ep. Ded., My fast friend..did learnedlie bequit himselfe in the penning of certeine breefe notes concerning that countrie.

beqwete, -qweth(e, -qweythe, -qwithe, obs. forms of BEQUEATH.

ber (bɛə(r)). Also **bher**, **bir**. [Hindi.] The Chinese date or jujube (genus *Zizyphus*). Also *attrib.*, as *ber-fruit*, *-tree*.

1860 in H. F. C. CLEGHORN *Forests & Gardens S. India* (1861) 60 The bér tree (*Zizyphus jujuba*) is approved for saddletrees. **1861** —— *Ibid.* 244 The wild bèr tree, common almost everywhere. *Ibid.* 281 The Ber-fruit tree..is used for native sandals. **1874** STEWART & BRANDIS *Forest Flora India* 87 All Bĕr trees of North and Central India. **1886** YULE & BURNELL *Hobson-Jobson*, Bear-tree, Bair, &c. **1887** MOLONEY *Forestry W. Afr.* 299 Jujube or Ber Tree. **1895** MRS. CROKER *Village Tales* (1896) 22 The sahibs shall sit above in the old bher tree. **1908** *New Reformer* I. 414 The *Zezyphus Jujuba*, the Bir universally known in India. **1924** *Blackw. Mag.* Oct. 478/1 Thickets of *ber* and acacias. **1925** *Ibid.* Jan. 66/2 These [bears] had fallen out to-night over their supper of *ber*-fruit. **1969** *Hindu* 28 July 6/5 The most striking thing about cuscuta is that it is notoriously partial to ber.

ber, obs. and dial form of BIRR force, impetus, BEAR, BIER.

beraft, obs. form of BEREFT; see BEREAVE *v.*

beragged, berailroaded, etc.: see BE- *pref.*

beraid, -raied, pa. t. and pa. pple. of BERAY.

†**be'rain**, *v. Obs.* Forms: 3 **birein**, 4-5 **be-**, **bi-**, **byrein**, **-reyn**, 5 **berayn**, **byrayn(e**, 6 **berain(e**. [f. BE- 4 + RAIN; cf. OHG. *bireganôn*, mod.G. *beregnen*, in same sense.]

1. *trans.* To rain upon. (Chiefly in pa. pple.)

a **1225** *Ancr. R.* 344 Cloðes unseouwed ! bireined oðer unwaschen. **1388** WYCLIF *Ezek.* xxii. 24 A lond vncleene and not bireyned. **1398** TREVISA *Barth. De P.R.* XIV. i, Yf good londe is bidewid or bireynid it fatteþ and amendeþ. [**1582** BATMAN *Barth. De P.R.* XIV. xlvi. 210 Also downes be more bedewed and berained than vallies.]

2. a. To besprinkle as with rain; to wet, bedew.

c **1374** CHAUCER *Troylus* IV. 1144 After that he long had.. with his teris salt hire breest byreyned. *a* **1547** SURREY *Pris. in Windsor* 42 The tears berain my cheeks of deadly hew. **1567** TURBERV. in Chalmers' *Eng. Poets* II. 641/1 Teares.. beraine my brest.

b. To sprinkle or pour (a liquid) in drops.

c **1420** *Pallad. on Husb.* I. 952 Byrayne aboute uppon thi wortes this.

berake, berampier, etc.: see BE- *pref.*

berande, obs. north. form of BEARING *ppl. a.* Also *subst.* Bearer, carrier.

c **1460** *Towneley Myst.* 82 Prowde men and hyghe berand. **1483** *Cath. Angl.* 28 Berande, *baiulus.*

berapt *ppl. a.* [f. BE- + RAPT, or for *beraft* = BEREFT.]

1581 STUDLEY *Seneca's Agamemn.* 153 b, Me berapt of sence, with prickes of fury fresh yee fill.

berar(e, obs. form of BEARER.

†**berard**, *Obs. rare*[−1]. A viper.

c **1475** in Wr.-Wülcker *Voc.* 766 *Hec vispera*, a berard.

berard, obs. f. BEARHERD.

berate (bɪˈreɪt), *v.* [f. BE- 2 + RATE *v.* This word appears to have become rare in the 19th c. in England, but remained in common use in U.S., whence we have many 19th c. instances.]

trans. To rate or chide vehemently; to scold.

1548 UDALL, etc. *Erasm. Par. Mark* xv. (R.) So is the veritie of the gospell berated and laughed to skorne of the miscreantes. **1572** tr. *Lavaterus' Ghostes* (1596) 158 They all berated him for occupying his head about questions nothing appertaining unto him. **1601** HOLLAND *Pliny* II. 162 Antony ..fell into a furious fit of choler, and all to berated.. Toranius. **1855** MOTLEY *Dutch Rep.* VI. i. (1866) 779 Never was unlucky prince more soundly berated by his superiors. **1864** E. SARGENT *Peculiar* III. 290 An ancient virago..was berating a butcher. **1871** MEREDITH *H. Richmond* liii, What! You think he was not punished enough when he was berated and torn to shreds in your presence? **1881** *Boston Lit. World* 22 Oct. 365/2 Berating Puritanism in his diary. **1893** *Times* 1 Feb. 9/5 The famous allocution in which he [*sc.* Sir James Mathew] berated Lord Clanricarde before a single witness had been heard. **1952** M. LASKI *Village* xvii. 238 She perceived that Miss Evadne was not antagonistic, had not sent for her to berate her. **1965** *Times Lit. Suppl.* 23 Sept. 834/1 'She is..an assiduous toady, and a petty thief.' Further to berate her or the book would be supererogatory.

†**be'rattle**, *v. Obs. rare.* Also 7 **beratle**. [f. BE- 4 + RATTLE *v.*] *trans.* To rattle away upon; to fill with rattling noise or din; also, to rattle away at, assail with din.

1553 T. WILSON *Rhet.* 180 (R.) He did all berattle him. **1602** SHAKS. *Ham.* II. ii. 358 An ayrie of Children, little Yases, that crye out on the top of question; and are most tyrannically clap't for't; these..so beratled the common Stages..that many wearing Rapiers, are affraide of Goose-quils.

be'ray, *v. Obs.* or *arch.* Forms: 6 **beraye**, (**berey**), 6-7 **beray**, 7-9 *erroneously* **bewray**. *Pa. t.* and *pa. pple.*: 6-7 **beraid**, **-raied**, **-rayed**. [f. BE- 2 + RAY *v.* (aphetic form of ARRAY: cf. for the sense ARRAY *v.* 10). Generally mis-spelt by modern writers through erroneous confusion with BEWRAY.] Hence **berayed** *ppl. a.*

1. *trans.* To disfigure, dirty, defile, befoul (with dirt, filth, ordure).

1530 PALSGR. 449/1 You have berayed your gowne with myer. **1570** HOLINSHED *Scot. Chron.* (1806) I. 296 The King was slaine..and the bed all beraied with bloud. **1678** N. WANLEY *Wonders* v. ii. §28. 470/1 When he was Baptized, he berayed the Font. **1670** RAY *Prov.* (T.) It is an ill bird that berays its own nest. **1701** DE FOE *True-born Englishm.* Pref. 1, I am tax'd with Bewraying my own Nest. **1863** SALA *Capt. Dangerous* I. vii. 190 His Countenance and his Raiment were all smirched and bewrayed with dabs and patches of what seemed soot.

b. *refl.* and *intr.*

1561 AWDELAY *Frat. Vacab.* 13 This knave berayeth many tymes in the corners of his maisters chamber. **1611** COTGR. s.v. *Arc*, To be beshitten; to beray himselfe. **1649** R. HODGES *Plain. Direct.* 27 The childe did bewray, that hee would beray himself.

2. *fig.* To befoul, stain, disfigure; to asperse, to cover with abuse.

1576 GASCOIGNE *Steele Gl.* (Arb.) 56 Wherein I see a quicke capacitye Berayde with blots of light Inconstancie. **1602** *Return fr. Parnass.* IV. v. (Arb.) 58 Our fellow Shakespeare hath giuen him a purge that made him beray his credit. **1863** SALA *Capt. Dangerous* I. x. 287 [She] did so bemaul and bewray Madam Macphilader with her tongue.

†**be'rayer.** *Obs.* Also 7 (*erron.*) be-wrayer. [f. prec. + -ER[1].] One who berays or defiles.

1699 COLES, Bewrayer (defiler), *concacator*.

berayn, obs. form of BERAIN.

†**'berber**[1]. *Sc. Obs.* [a. OF. *berbère* 'barberry,' in med.L. *berberis*, which is also used as the botanical name of the genus.] = BARBERRY.

From *Berberis* (stem *berberid-*) also; **'berberal** *a. Bot.*, of or related to the Barberry, or genus *Berberis*; applied by Lindley to the 'alliance' including the N.O. *Berberidaceæ*. **'berberid,** any member of the natural order to which the barberry belongs. **berberi'daceous,** belonging to the N.O. *Berberidaceæ*, of which the barberry is the type. **berbe'rideous,** belonging to the tribe *Berberideæ* which includes the barberry. **ber'beria, 'berberine,** a yellow bitter principle, obtained from the barberry and other plants.

c **1440** *Gaw. & Gologr.* (JAM.) Of box and of berber, bigged ful bene. **1878** MISS BRADDON *Open Verd.* xxv. 176 The shining leaves of bay and berberis. **1866** *Treas. Bot.* 136 Lindley includes the order in his Berberal Alliance. **1847** LINDLEY *Veg. Kingd.* (ed. 2) 421 Anonads are connected with Berberids through *Bocagea*. **1852** TH. ROSS *Humboldt's Trav.* II. xviii. 171 It was perhaps a tree of the berberideous family. **1876** HARLEY *Mat. Med.* 725 Berberia is an alkaloid found abundantly in the common barberry. *Ibid.* 778 Contains a considerable amount of berberine. **1880** *Syd. Soc. Lex.*, *Berberin* is..given as a bitter tonic in dyspepsia.

Berber[2] ('bɜːbə(r)). [For derivation see BARBARY.]

A. *sb.* A name given by the Arabs to the aboriginal people west and south of Egypt; applied by modern ethnologists to any member of the great North African stock to which belong the aboriginal races of Barbary and the Tuwariks of the Sahara.

1842 PRICHARD *Nat. Hist. Man* 261 In the Northern parts of Atlas, these people are called Berbers. **1883** CUST *Mod. Lang. Africa* I. 98 Strictly speaking a Moor must be a native of Mauritania, and a Berber, and the term could not be applied with propriety to an Arab.

B. *adj.* Of or pertaining to the Berbers or their language; applied (often *absol.*) to one of the three great subdivisions of the Hamitic group, called also *Lybian* and *Amazirg*, containing, according to Cust, nine North African languages.

1854 LATHAM in *Orr's Circ. Sc.* Org. Nat. I. 367 The Amazirg tongues are often called Berber. **1883** CUST *Mod. Lang. Africa* I. 104 The Berber Family of Languages is one of striking unity.

berberia, same as BERIBERI, a disease.

berberine[1]. **berberine tree,** an African tree, *Xylopia polycarpa*, which yields a yellow dye containing berberine.

1861 BENTLEY *Man. Bot.* 440 The Berberine or Yellow-dye tree of Soudan.

Berberine[2] (bɜːbə'riːn). [prop. pl. used as sing., f. BERBER + Arab. pl. suffix *-in* (cf. *fellaheen*, pl. of FELLAH).] A Berber. Also *attrib.* Also **'Berberin** *pl.*, Berbers; **Berbe'ree, Berberi,** a Berber; **'berberize** *v. trans.*, to impart a Berber character to; **'berberized** *ppl. a.*

1852 B. ST. JOHN *Village Life in Egypt* II. i. 9 Berberi race, black and well-featured. *Ibid.* iii. 30 In the neighbourhood of Essouan..is a curious race of people..distinct from the Berberis, although confounded with them by many travellers. **1875** *Encycl. Brit.* I. 260/2 The Barâbra or Berberines are a people well known in Egypt. **1900** CONAN DOYLE *Green Flag* 270 In front rode the three Berberee body-servants upon donkeys. **1906** *Daily Chron.* 22 Sept. 2/7 The municipality of Alexandria are now endeavouring to induce the surplus Berberin, &c., to return to their own country, on the upper reaches of the Nile. **1914** *Eng. Hist. Rev.* Oct. 786 Many Arabs..had settled down [in Tunisia, Algeria, and Morocco] and become in part Berberized. **1928** *Blackw. Mag.* Mar. 406/1 This..was given to me..by a grateful Berberine. **1930** C. G. SELIGMAN *Races of Afr.* vi. 137 It is always difficult to decide whether any particular people..are to be regarded as arabized Berbers or as berberized Arabs. **1938** *Times Lit. Suppl.* 8 Oct. 645/2 A lady's maid who managed Berberine servants with grim efficiency.

berberry, -bery, variants of BARBERRY.

Berbice (bə'biːs). The name of a river and a county in Guyana, applied to a type of long chair (see quots.).

1951 E. MITTELHOLZER *Shadows Move* II. ii. 172 An easy chair provided with long projecting arms for resting one's outstretched legs (a Berbice chair, he had heard it called). **1959** 'A. GLYN' *I can take it All* xiii. 241 Berbice chairs—the ones with long wooden extensions in the arms for you to hitch your legs over.

‖**berceau** (bɛrso). [Fr., 'arbour, bower'; lit. 'cradle'.] An arbour, bower; a shaded or foliage-covered walk. Also *attrib.*

1699 M. LISTER *Journ. to Paris* 209 The small leaved Horne-Beam; which serves for Arcades, Berceaus. **1771** PENNANT *Tour Scotl. 1769* 77 The Berceau walk [at Taymouth] is very magnificent, composed of great trees, forming a fine gothic arch. *a* **1794** E. GIBBON *Memoirs* in *Misc. Wks.* (1796) I. 182, I took several turns in a *berceau*, or covered walk of acacias. *a* **1828** D. WORDSWORTH *Tour Cont.* in *Jrnls.* (1941) II. 61 The country richer than ever—Berceaus of vines—yards and courts roofed with vines. **1828** —— *Tour Isle of Man* (1941) 415 He had contrived to bury his house among trees and..to make the approach to it (a long berceau) as dark as a dungeon alley. **1853** C. BRONTË *Villette* I. viii. 142 Under the vast and vine-draped berceau madame would take her seat on summer afternoons. **1960** M. SHARP *Something Light* viii. 72 No head-high *berceaux* of Gloire de Dijon roses.

berceau'nette. [A tradesman's perversion of BASSINET or *bassinette*, whereby that word is ignorantly referred to the F. *berceau* 'cradle,' with which it has no connexion. *Berceaunette* is, of course, an impossible form in Fr., and is a patent modern instance of pseudo-etymological spelling.]

1885 *Bazaar* 30 Mar. 1250/3 Berceaunette carriage, nearly new, must be sold. *Ibid.* Splendid berceaunette perambulator, one of the handsomest carriages ever made.

†**'bercel.** *Obs. rare.* Also 5 berseel, bersell, byrselle. [a. OF. *bersel*, also *bersail, -eil*, in same sense; cf. *berser*: see next.] An archer's butt.

c **1440** *Promp. Parv.* 32 Bercel [**1499** berseel], *meta*. *Ibid.* 56 But, or bercel or byrselle [**1499** bersell], *meta*.

†**'bercelet.** *Obs.* Forms: 4 barselette, -slett, 4–5 barslet, bercelett, -selette, -slet, 5 breslet, 5–7 bercelett. [Corruption of OF. *berseret* hunting-dog, dim. of *bersier* huntsman (in med.L. *bersārius*), f. *berser, bercer* (in med.L. *bersāre*) to hunt, esp. with the bow, orig. to shoot with the bow. Thence also Ger. *berschen* to shoot game, It. *bersaglio* an archer's butt, whence *bersagliere* archer, sharp-shooter, rifleman.] A hunting dog, a hound.

c **1340** *Alexander* 786 (Dublin MS.) Was neuer barslett in band more buxum to hys lord. *c* **1400** *Destr. Troy* VI. 2196 Ger hom bowe as a berslet & þi blithe seche. *c* **1420** *Anturs of Arth.* iii, Wyth bow, and wyth berselette Vndurneth the boes. *c* **1420** *Avow. Arth.* vii, He [the boar] brittunt bercelettis bold. **1679** PLOT *Staffordsh.* 444 Every day for his servant and his bercelett..twelve pence.

‖**berceuse** (bɛːrsøːz). *Mus.* [Fr., f. *bercer* to rock + fem. agent-suffix *-euse*.] A cradle-song, lullaby; an instrumental piece with a lulling rhythm.

1876 STAINER & BARRETT *Dict. Mus. Terms* 58/1 *Berceuse*, a cradle song. **1879** GROVE *Dict. Mus.* I. 229/2 His [*sc.* Schumann's] 'Schlummerlied' is a berceuse in all but name. **1889** G. B. SHAW in *Star* 13 Dec. 2/4 Composes fantasias, berceuses, serenades, etc., with great facility. **1931** E. DANNREUTHER *Oxf. Hist. Mus.* (ed. 2) VI. xi. 257 In the Barcarolle, the Berceuse, and the Ballades..Chopin discovered a form of expression peculiar to himself.

bercke, berd(e, obs. ff. BARK *v*, BEARD, BIRD *sb.*

berdache (bə'dæʃ). Also **berdash.** [ad. F. *bardache*: see BARDASH.] Among N. American Indians: a transvestite (see esp. quot. 1955).

1806 A. HENRY *Jrnl.* 21 July in E. Coues *New Light Hist. Greater Northwest* (1897) I. 348 The Mandanes..often prefer a young man to a woman. They have many berdashes amongst them, who make it their business to satisfy such beastly passions. **1843** H. S. LLOYD tr. *Maximilian's Trav. N. Amer.* xxv. 351 Among all the North American Indian nations there are men dressed and treated like women, called, by the Canadians, Bardaches. **1906** R. G. THWAITES *Early Western Trav.* XXIII. 284 The berdash was noted by most early travellers among Western Indians. **1912** *Anthrop. Pap. Amer. Mus. Nat. Hist.* IX. 226 Berdaches naturally associate with girls and pretend to have sweethearts among men. **1949** M. MEAD *Male & Female* vi. 129 Among many American Indian tribes the *berdache*, the man who dressed and lived as a woman, was a recognized social institution. **1955** ANGELINO & SHEDD in *Amer. Anthropologist* LVIII. 125 In view of the data we propose that berdache be characterized as an individual of a definite physiological sex (male or female) who assumes the role and status of the opposite sex, and who is viewed by the community..as having assumed the role and status of the opposite sex.

berdash, variant form of BURDASH.

berdyd, obs. form of BEARDED *ppl. a.*

†**bere,** *sb. Obs.* Also 3 beare, 4 ber, 5 beyr, 6 (*Sc.*) beir. [ME. *beare, bere*, apparently short for *ibere* 'clamour, outcry'; the earlier text of Layamon has always *ibere*, the latter only *beare*. In form, *ibere* is:—OE. *ȝebǣre* 'bearing, behaviour, gesture,' = OS. *gibâri*, MDu. *gebaar*, MHG. *gebære*, in same sense, f. *beran* to bear. The history of the change of meaning is not evident; but it appears also in OFris. *bǣre* 'strepitus, clamour' (Mätzner), where also the prefix *ge-* has been dropped; the MDu. *gebaar* also meant 'noise, strepitus,' as well as 'behaviour.' In later times the word is only Sc., whence the spelling *beir*: the mod. Eng. would have been normally *bear*.]

Clamour, outcry, shouting, roaring; the noise of voices of men or animals.

[*a* **800** *O.E. Chron.* an. 755 On ðæs wifes ȝebærum [*Laud MS.* ȝe bæron] onfundon ðæs cyninges ðegnas ða unstilnesse.] *c* **1205** LAY. 25828 Wanliche iberen [**1250** reuliche beares]. *Ibid.* —— 28162 Me mihte iheren Brutten iberen [Bruttune beare]. *c* **1330** *Florice & Bl.* 457 Asked what here were That hi makede so loude bere. *c* **1400** *Rowland & Ot.* 183 3elde thi suerde to mee, & late be alle this bere. **1460** *Towneley Myst.* 249 Abyde withe alle thi boste and beyr. **1549** *Compl. Scot.* vi. 38 Foulis..ande..beystis..maid grite beir.

†**bere,** *v. Obs.* Also 3 ibere. [ME. *beren*, short for *iberen* (see 1st quot.):—OE. *ȝebǣran* to bear oneself, behave = OS. *gibârjan*, OHG. **gabarjan*, MHG. *gebâren, gebæren*, f. BERE *sb.*, which see for change of sense.] *intr.* To cry, roar. Hence **'berand** *ppl. a.*

c **1225** *Juliana* 53 He..iberde [*v.r.* berde] as þe ful wiht. *a* **1300** *E.E. Psalter* xxxii[i]. 3 Well singes to him in berand steven. *c* **1400** *Leg. Rood* (1871) 140 Beerynge as a beore-whelp. *c* **1470** HENRY *Wallace* VII. 157 The peple beryt lyk wyld bestis. *a* **1550** *Christis Kirke Gr.* xxii, Quhyn thay had berit lyk baitit bullis.

bere, obs. f. BEAR, BEER, BIER, BIRR, BOAR.

bereager, variant of BEEREGAR.

bereall, obs. form of BURIAL.

bereason, etc.: see BE- *pref.*

bereave (bɪ'riːv), *v.* Pa. t. and pa. pple. bereaved; pa. pple. also bereft. Forms: 1 beréafian, 2–3 biræuien, 2–6 bireve, 3 bireave(n, 3–4 birefe(n, 4–6 byreve, bereve, 5 berefe, bereffe, byreeve, 6 bereeve, (berive, byryve), 6–7 berieve, 7 bereauve, 6– bereave. *Pa. t.*, 1 bereafode, 2–3 bereafde, beræfde, 2–4 biræuede, bireuede, 4 birefte, 4–5 byrafte, 4–6 beraft(e, berefte, 5 berafft, berefte, 5– bereft, 6– bereaved. *Pa. pple.* 6– bereaved, bereft. Early forms corres. to pa. t.; also 6–7 bereiven, 6–9 bereaven. [Com. Teut.: OE. *bi-, beréafian* = OFris. *birâv(i)a*, OS. *birôbôn*, (MDu. *beroven*, Du. *berooven*), OHG. *biroubôn*, (MHG. *berouben*, mod.G. *berauben*), Goth. *biraubôn*:—OTeut. **biraubôjan*, f. *bi-*, BE- + **raubôjan*, in OE. *réafian* to plunder, spoil, rob; see REAVE *v.*]

1. *trans.* To deprive, rob, strip, dispossess (a person, etc., *of* a possession; the latter orig. expressed by the genitive). Since *c*1650 mostly of immaterial possessions, *life, hope*, etc., except in reference to the loss of relatives by death. (In the former case *bereft*, in the latter *bereaved*, is more usual in the pa. t. and pa. pple.)

c **888** K. ÆLFRED *Boeth.* v. §3 Heo hit ne mæg his ȝewittes bereafian. *c* **1205** LAY. 2896 Þus wes þas kineriche · of heora kinge biræued [**1250** bireued]. *c* **1400** *Rom. Rose* 6671 Lest they berafte..Folk of her catel or of her thing. **1529** MORE *Conf. agst. Trib.* II. Wks. 1183/2 He hadde..byreued hym of hys rest. **1577** HARRISON *England* II. xx. 330 Beereving some fruits of their kernels. **1596** SHAKS. *Merch. V.* III. ii. 177 Madam, you have bereft me of all words. **1622** HEYLIN *Cosmogr.* I. (1682) 104 They bereaved the women..of the hair of their heads. *a* **1649** DRUMM. OF HAWTH. *Poems* Wks. (1711) 17 That angel's face hath me of rest bereaven. **1756** C. LUCAS *Ess. Waters* II. 106 It is there bereft of all its volatile parts. **1833** H. COLERIDGE *Poems* I. 143 Ere thy birth, of sire bereaven. **1841** D'ISRAELI *Amen. Lit.* (1867) 222 The accident which had bereaved the father of his child.

†**b.** with *at* for *of*. *Obs.*

c **1205** LAY. 30311 Ic hine biræuien wulle · at his baren liue [**1250** bireaue..of his bare liue].

c. with double object (to bereave *any one a possession*), the former probably at first dative. In the passive the impersonal object was originally the subject, but in 17th c. either object might be so used. *arch.*

c **1200** *Trin. Coll. Hom.* 33 Hie him bireueden alle hise riche weden. *c* **1200** ORMIN 2832 Himm wass hiss spæche..all biræfedd. *c* **1386** CHAUCER *Knts. T.* 503 His sleep, his mete, his drynk is him byraft. **1530** ELYOT *Gov.* I. xii, Enuy had..bireft hym his lyfe. **1557** *K. Arth.* (Copland) I. vii, Many landes that were bereued lordes, knyghtes, ladyes and gentylmen. **1593** SHAKS. *2 Hen. VI*, III. i. 85 All your Interest in those Territories Is utterly bereft you. **1667** MILTON *P.L.* x. 918 Bereaue me not..thy gentle looks, thy aid. **1806** SCOTT *Wandering Willie*, All joy was bereft me the day that you left me.

2. To rob, plunder, despoil (a possessor); to deprive of anything valued; to leave destitute, orphaned, or widowed. See also BEREAVED.

c **1175** *Lamb. Hom.* 79 Ho him bireueden and ho him ferwundeden. *c* **1430** *Hymns Virg.* (1867) 124, I was ofte berevyd. **1611** SPEED *Hist. Gt. Brit.* IX. xiv. (1632) 763 The King bereauing enemies, to enrich his friends. **1867** G. MACDONALD *Poems* 10, I cry to thee with all my might Because I am bereft.

†**3.** To snatch away (a possession); to remove or take away by violence. *Obs.*

c **1320** *Cast. Loue* 1349 Þe meste strengþe he al bi-reuede. *c* **1386** CHAUCER *Sompn. T.* 403 Who so wold us fro the world byreve.. He wolde byreve out of this world the sonne. **1571** NORTON & SACKV. *Gorboduc* IV. i. (1847) 132 Whome no mishap..could haue bereued hence. *c* **1600** *Death Jane Seymour* in Evans *O. Ball.* (1784) II. viii. 57 He from this joy was soon bereav'n. *a* **1617** BAYNE *On Eph.* (1658) 13 When the blessings of this life are bereaved. *a* **1622** WITHER *Brit. Rememb.* 170 Have..(Like Iezabell) oppressed and bereav'n The poore mans portion. **1718** POPE *Iliad* XX. 549 Thy life, Echechus! next the sword bereaves.

†**b.** Const. *from* a possessor. *Obs.*

c **1440** *Partonope* 3267 This craft Ye haue clene from me beraft. *c* **1530** LD. BERNERS *Arth. Lyt. Bryt.* (1814) 109 Fro the thyrde [knight] he berafte his sholder with the arme. **1593** SHAKS. *Lucr.* 835 From me by strong assault it is bereft. **1606** G. W[OODCOCKE] *Hist. Iustine* 119a, They wold bereaue kingdomes from these kings in despight of them.

bereaved (bɪˈriːvd), *ppl. a.* [f. prec. + -ED.] Deprived or robbed; taken away by force; *spec.* deprived by death of a near relative, or of one connected by some endearing tie.

?*a* **1200** Notes to LAY. III. 447 Kenelm kine-bearn, Liþ under þorne, Heafode bireavod. **1605** SHAKS. *Lear* IV. iv. 8 What can man's wisedome In the restoring his bereaued sense? **1828** SCOTT *F.M. Perth* III. 333 The distraction of a bereaved father. **1858** J. MARTINEAU *Stud. Chr.* 194 Who.. bids bereaved affection weep no more.

bereavement (bɪˈriːvmənt). [f. as prec. + -MENT.] The fact or state of being bereaved or deprived of anything; *spec.* as in prec.

1731 BAILEY II, *Bereavement*, a deprivation or being bereav'd or depriv'd of anything. **1827** HOR. SMITH *Tor Hill* (L.) He bore his bereavement with stoical fortitude. **1858** J. MARTINEAU *Stud. Chr.* 197 Total bereavement and utter death of joy. **1866** ALGER *Solit. Nat. & Man* II. 40 Bereavement, in its essence, is always the loss of some object accustomed to draw forth the soothing or cheering reactions of the soul.

bereaven (bɪˈriːv(ə)n), *ppl. a. arch.* Also 7 bereiven. [On partial analogy of strong vbs.] By-form of BEREAVED, occasional in the poets.

a **1619** DANIEL *Ode* in Arb. *Garner* III. 620 My field, of flowers quite bereaven. **1848** LYTTON *Harold* i, As shepherd to thy bereaven flock.

bereaver (bɪˈriːvə(r)). [f. as prec. + -ER¹.] One who bereaves.

1592 WYRLEY *Armorie* 151 Ah filching death..Bereauer of my sole deliueraunce. **1614** RALEIGH *Hist. World* II. 411 The bereaver being Lord of many. **1624** W. HALL *Man's Gt. Enemy* in Farr's *S.P.* (1848) 199 Of soule and bodie's good hee's a bereauer.

beˈreaving, *vbl. sb.* Also 6 byryvinge. [f. BEREAVE + -ING¹.] The action of the vb. BEREAVE in various senses. Now only gerundial.

1529 MORE *Comf. agst. Trib.* III. Wks. 1232/2 The byryuinge from vs of our wretched worldlye goodes. *c* **1630** DRUMM. OF HAWTH. *Hist. Jas. III*, Wks. (1711) 45 After this violent bereaving him of his wife. **1648** MILTON *Tenure Kings* Wks. 1738 I. 315 The oppressing and bereaving of Religion and their Liberty. *Mod.* By bereaving him of his only son.

beˈreaving, *ppl. a.* That bereaves.

1621 QUARLES *Esther* (1638) 102 This sense-bereaving Song. *Mod.* The bereaving hand of death.

†**bere-bag.** ME. form of *bear-bag*, whether in sense of 'barley-bag' or of 'bag-bearer' (cf. *turn-key*); applied opprobriously to the Scotch.

1352 MINOT *Poems* ii. 17 Bere-bag with thi boste, thi biging es bare. *Ibid.* i. 41 He brought meni bere-bag With bow redy bent.

berebus, bered, etc.: see BE- *pref.*

†**berede,** *v. Obs.* Forms: 3 birǣde(n, -reade(n, 3–5 bi-, byrede(n, 4–6 berede. [f. BE- 2 + *rede*, READ, to advise.]

trans. To advise, inform, counsel; to plan.

a **1225** *Leg. Kath.* 1235 Þe witti Wealdent..bireadde [*v.r.* biradde] hit swa swiðe wel. *c* **1315** SHOREHAM *Poems* 7 Bote he thorwe hys sacrament Ous thos bi-redde. *c* **1330** *Florice & Bl.* 435 Ne were thai nought aright birede. *c* **1350** *Lyric P.* 41 Anon he was byrad To werk.

b. *refl.* To advise or bethink oneself, deliberate.

c **1205** LAY. 31072 Ich me biræden [**1250** bireaden] wolde of swulchere neode. *c* **1314** *Guy Warw.* 118 Therof thou most birede the. **1530** PALSGR. 449/2, I wyll berede me first, and then you shall have your answere.

bereft (bɪˈrɛft), *ppl. a.* [f. BEREAVE.]

1. Forcibly deprived, robbed, having lost the possession or use *of*; void *of*.

1586 BRIGHT *Melanch.* xvii. 105 Man transported with passion is utterly bereft of advisement. **1596** SHAKS. *Tam. Shr.* v. ii. 143 A woman mou'd, is like a fountaine troubled ..thicke, bereft of beautie. **1699** POMFRET *Love triumph. over Reason* 194 Not quite bereft Of sense, tho' very small remains were left. **1858** J. MARTINEAU *Stud. Chr.* 108 A pinched and anxious mind bereft of power.

†**2.** Taken away, removed, quite gone. *Obs.*

1531 ELYOT *Gov.* III. xxiii. Deade or birefte from the minde.

3. Deprived of a near relation, BEREAVED. *rare.*

1828 SCOTT *F.M. Perth*, The helpless and bereft father.

†**beˈreft,** *v. Obs. rare.* [f. prec.] By-form of BEREAVE: to deprive.

1557 RECORDE *Whetst.* A iij, To berefte the realme of some singulare commoditie. **1564** HAWARD *Eutropius* To Rdr. 6 That Tully should..bereft yᵉ Grecians of theyr exactnesse in all sciences.

berein, -reyn, obs. forms of BERAIN *v.*

berel, bereel, obs. forms of BERYL.

berelepe, variant of BEARLEAP, *Obs.*, a basket.

berend (bɪˈrɛnd), *v.* [f. BE- 2 + REND *v.*] *trans.* To rend or tear badly. Hence **beˈrent** *ppl. a.*

1582 BRETON *Dolor. Disc.* in *Heliconia* I. 119 Who all berent, dooth chaunge among the breares. **1596** W. SMITH *Chloris* (1877) 9 Then red with ire, her tresses she berent. **1608** R. JOHNSON *Sev. Champions* 66 With limbes and members all to berent and torne.

berene, variant of BERNE, *Obs.*, man of valour.

bereness, variant of BURINESS. *Obs.*

berengelite (bɪˈrɛŋgəlaɪt). *Min.* A variety of asphalt from St. Juan de Berengela in Peru.

Berenice's hair (bɛrəˈnaɪsɪz hɛə(r)). [f. Berenice, name of the wife of Ptolemy Euergetes, king of Egypt, *c* 248 B.C., whose hair, vowed by her to Venus, was said to have been stolen from the temple of the goddess, and afterwards taken to heaven and placed in a constellation.] The name of a small northern constellation of indistinct stars situated near the tail of Leo; formerly of the southern star Canopus.

1601 HOLLAND *Pliny* I. 34 Neither hath Italy a sight of Canopus, named also Berenices haire. **1714** POPE *Rape Lock* v. 129 Not Berenice's locks first rose so bright, The heav'ns bespangling with dishevell'd light. **1868** LOCKYER *Heavens* (ed. 3) 372 In Berenice's Hair most of the stars are visible to the naked eye.

berere, obs. form of BEARER.

beres, impers. variant of BIR, *v. Obs.* to behove.

beresite (ˈbɛrɪsaɪt). *Min.* See quot. 1879.

1849 MURCHISON *Siluria* xix. 454 The shaft traverses a mass called 'beresite.' **1879** WATTS *Dict. Chem.* I. 580 Beresite is a fine-grained granite..occurring at Beresowsk in the Ural.

beret, berret (‖bɛrɛ, ˈbɛrɪt; now usu. bɛreɪ). [Fr.; ad. Béarnese *berreto* = Catal. *baret*, Pr. *birret*:—late L. *birretum* cap: see BIRETTA.]

a. A round flat woollen cap worn by the Basque peasantry; also, a clerical biretta, and a cap named from it.

1850 MRS. JAMESON *Leg. Monast. Ord.* (1863) 211 The four-cornered cap or beret, worn by the Augustine canons. **1862** H. MARRYAT *Yr. in Sweden* II. 334 With plumed beret and costume of the time. **1864** *Mag. for Young* 47 Dressed in the usual blouse and berret of the peasants. **1883** *Harper's Mag.* 684/2 His crimson *beret* with its cock's feather.

b. A cap resembling the Basque béret, worn by men and women, esp. for casual or holiday wear; also, such a cap forming part of many British service and other uniforms.

1827 *Lady's Mag.* Feb. 117/2 Berets of black velvet, decorated with gold lace,..are much in request at evening parties. *Ibid.* June 343/2 Beret-hats are more in request than the beret-turbans, at the opera. **1832** F. KEMBLE *Jrnl.* (1835) I. 68 Saw a woman riding to-day; but she has gotten a black velvet beret upon her head.—Only think of a beret on horse-back! **1894** G. DU MAURIER *Trilby* I. i. 18 He..wore a red *béret* and a large velveteen cloak. **1901** *Daily Chron.* 3 Aug. 10/3 The beret so specially becoming to a young face. *Ibid.* 7 Sept. 8/3 The beret shape is always modish on the moors. **1909** *Ibid.* 18 Jan. 7/5 A beret of sable. **1948** A. BARON *From City* 38 The corporals rose and pulled their berets from under their shoulder-straps. **1960** O. LANCASTER in *Daily Express* 21 Jan. 1/3 Isn't it strange the way a beret always seems to *do* something to generals?

†**berewick.** *Obs.* exc. *Hist.* [OE. *bęrewíc*, in Ingulphus 1030–1109 *berewike*; in Domesday Bk. *bereuuicus, -uuica, -uuichus, -uuicha*; f. OE. *bęre* barley + *wíc* dwelling, habitation, village, place.] A demesne farm; = BARTON (in sense 3).

[**1060** *Chart. Edw. Conf.* in Thorpe's *Diplom Angl.* (1865) 382 Hoc est Uppwude cum Ravelega berewico suo.] **1809** BAWDWEN tr. *Domesday Bk.* 10 To this manor belong 11 berewicks. **1863** *Cornhill Mag., Domesday Bk.* Oct. 609 A hamlet or member of a manor was often called a Berwick (literally, corn-farm).

berey, obs. form of BERAY.

berfrai, -fray, -frey, obs. forms of BELFRY.

berg¹ (bɜːg). [from ICEBERG, a. Ger. *eisberg* = ice-mountain.] Short for *iceberg*: A (floating) mountain or mass of ice; (only used when ice is mentioned or understood in the context).

1823 BYRON *Island* IV. iv, Steep, harsh, and slippery as a berg of ice. **1830** LYELL *Princ. Geol.* (1875) I. I. vi. 106 Ice-drifted fragments which have been dropped in deep water by melting bergs. **1847** TENNYSON *Princess* IV. 53 Glittering bergs of ice. **1878** HUXLEY *Physiogr.* 163 The finer detritus which the berg carries.

b. *Comb.*, as **berg-field**, an expanse of ice covered with bergs.

1856 KANE *Arct. Exp.* I. xxiii. 284 On quitting the berg-field, they saw two dovekies in a crack.

berg² (bɜːg). *S. Afr.* [Afrikaans, f. Du., = OE. *beorg*, etc., BARROW *sb.*¹] A mountain.

1840 B. SHAW *Mem. S. Afr.* i. 27 To Cape Town school —o'er *bergs* and *knowes*, They sent the tawney-coloured boy. **1865** T. LEASK *S. Afr. Diary* 12 June (1954) 2 The wind was blowing down the berg, almost cutting us thro'. **1902** DE WET *Three Years' War* 25 As there was no water to be obtained nearer than a mile from the berg, we suffered greatly from thirst. **1929** D. REITZ *Commando* xiii. 121 Having left..for Waterval-onder below the berg.

b. *attrib.*, as *berg-top*; **berg adder**, a South African adder, *Bitis atropos*, found chiefly on high ground and the hillsides; **berg cypress**, a mountain shrub, *Widdringtonia cupressoides*, found growing from Cape Town to Natal; **Berg Damara**, see DAMARA; **berg wind**, a hot, arid wind coming from the mountains, prevalent in several coastal districts of the Cape Province and Natal at various times of the year.

1818 LATROBE *Jrnl.* (1905) v. 89 A wood-keeper..had lately lost his life by the bite of a Berg-adder. **1912** FITZSIMONS *Snakes S. Afr.* 243 The Berg adder is as venomous as the Puff Adder. **1905** *Westm. Gaz.* 9 Oct. 10/1 Patches of berg cypress..afford splendid cover for that magnificent antelope the eland. **1953** *Cape Times* 4 July 3/1 Berg-top rescue ends in romance. **1905** *Nature* 2 Nov. 19/2 Remarkable winds, locally called 'Berg winds', blew from the plateau. **1959** *Cape Times* 27 June 9/3 Berg winds blow in different months in different areas. In winter they are most frequent along the west and south coasts extending to beyond Knysna.

berg, obs. form of BARROW *sb.*¹

ˈBergamask. Also 6 Bergomask, 7 Burgomaske. [ad. It. *Bergamasco* of Bergamo.]

†**1.** *Bergomask dance*: a rustic dance, framed in imitation of the people of Bergamo (a province in the state of Venice), ridiculed as clownish in their manners and dialect. Nares.

1590 SHAKS. *Mids. N.* v. 360 Will it please you..to heare a Bergomask dance..Come, your Burgomaske.

2. A native or inhabitant of Bergamo.

1602 MARSTON *Ant. & Mellida* I. Introd., A wealthie mountbanking burgomasco's heire of Venice. **1821** BYRON *Doge of Ven.* IV. ii. 295 'Tis a certain Bertram..*Doge.* Bertram, the Bergamask.

ˈBergamasque, *a.* [Fr., f. It. *Bergamasco*: see BERGAMASK.] Of or pertaining to the province or city of Bergamo in northern Italy; *spec.* pertaining to or characteristic of a school of painting originating in Bergamo.

1879 *Encycl. Brit.* VIII. 214/1 The lower Alps feed large herds of cows, the upper are let to Bergamasque shepherds, who travel thither every summer with their flocks. **1938** *Burlington Mag.* LXXII. 33/2 Other paintings of the Bergamasque school. **1939** *Ibid.* LXXV. 141/2 His particular Bergamasque variant of Giorgionesque sentiment. **1959** J. CHAPIN tr. *Giovannetti's We have Pope* i. 8 The Bergamasque shrines of our Lady.

bergamot¹ (ˈbɜːgəmɒt). Also 7–8 burg-, bourgamot, 8 burgemott. [App. from *Bergamo*, the Italian town.]

I. 1. A tree of the orange and lemon kind (*Citrus Bergamia*); from the rind of the fruit a fragrant oil is prepared, called Essence of Bergamot. Also *attrib.*, as in **bergamot-orange, -tree.**

1696 *Lond. Gaz.* No. 3196/4 A parcel of Orange and Burgamot Trees. **1712** tr. *Pomet's Hist. Drugs* I. 150 That which bears the Name of the Cedre or Bourgamot. **1876** HARLEY *Mat. Med.* 696 The Bergamot..is regarded by Gallecio as a hybrid between the orange and lemon.

2. The essence extracted from the fruit.

1766 ANSTEY *Bath Guide* iii. 67 Bring thy Essence Pot, Amber, Musk, and Bergamot. **1829** THACKERAY *Bk. Snobs* Wks. IX. 380 The worthy dealer in bergamot. **1850** —— *Pendennis* xiv. (1884) 123 A delightful odour of musk and bergamot was shaken through the house.

†**3.** Snuff scented with bergamot. Also *attrib.*

1706 *Songs Costume* (1849) 201 A wig that's full, An empty skull, A box of burgamot. **1715** *Lond. Gaz.* No. 5394/4 Fine Portugal..Burgemott, and Orangere Snuffs. **1716** CIBBER *Love makes Man* IV. iv. 66, I first introduc'd myself with a single Pinch of Bergamot. **1785** COWPER *Task* II. 452 The better hand, more busy, gives the nose Its bergamot.

4. A kind of mint (*Mentha citrata*) from which is obtained an oil, the odour of which resembles essence of bergamot. **Wild Bergamot** (in U.S.), *Monarda fistulosa*. Applied in Britain most commonly to *Monarda didyma*.

1843 J. TORREY *N.Y. Nat. Hist. Surv.: Flora* II. 59 *Monarda Fistulosa*..Horse Mint. Wild Bergamot. **1858** HOGG *Veg. Kingd.* 575 Bergamot Mint (*M. citrata*) has an odour of citron or lemon. **1866** *Treas. Bot.* I. 137 Bergamot, *Mentha citrata* or *odorata*. **1958** *Popular Gardening* 15 Feb.

34 All the charm of an old-world garden is fast locked in the heart of the Bergamot, botanically Monarda didyma.

II. 5. A woven fabric or tapestry composed of a mixture of flock and hair, said to have been first produced at Bergamo in Italy.

1882 BECK *Draper's Dict.* 19 Bergamot, a common tapestry, made of ox and goats' hair with cotton or hemp.

bergamot² ('bɜːgəmɒt). Also 7 **bargamot, bergamy, -amote, -ume, burgamet, -my,** 7–8 **burgamot.** [a. F. *bergamotte*, ad. It. *bergamotta*, app. a popular perversion of Turkish *beg-armūdi* 'prince's pear, Bergamot'; cf. the German name *Fürstenbirne*.] A fine kind of pear. Also *attrib.*

1616 SURFL. & MARKH. *Countr. Farm* 417 The best.. perrie is made of.. Bargamot. **1677** GREW *Anat. Plants* IV. III. ii. §1 A Burgamy, or other soft and sweet Pear. *c* **1680** *Crys of London* in *Bagford Ball.* I. 115 Do you want any damsons or Bergume Pare? **1697** DRYDEN *Virg. Georg.* II. 127 Bergamotes and pounder Pears. **1824** MISS MITFORD *Village* Ser. I. (1863) 48 A pelting shower of stony bergamots. **1868** LONGF. *Falc. Federigo* 210 The juicy bergamot.

Bergan ('bɜːgən). Also **Bergan(s), Bergen** and with small initial. [Manufacturer's name.] A proprietary name for a type of rucksack supported on a frame; *loosely*, any rucksack.

1923 *Official Gaz.* (U.S. Patent Office) 19 June 516/2 Sverre Young, Christiania, Norway... Bergan... Claims use since 1911. **1935** *Encycl. Sports* 514/1 The great advantage of the frame type, which is known, from its original model, as the 'Bergans' type, is that the weight is supported off the back. **1940** W. S. GILKISON *Peaks, Packs & Mountain Tracks* 37 Eighty pounds of cargo stowed inside a Bergan pack. **1965** A. BLACKSHAW *Mountaineering* iii. 104 Frames are usually 15 ins. (for women) and 17 ins. (for men). Lightweight versions (e.g. the Bergen) can be used for a day in the hills. **1980** *Globe & Laurel* July/Aug. 213/2 C/Sgt Millerchip (39) picked up several 'Brownie points' by repeatedly carrying Nurse Julie Chapman's (22) bergen. **1983** MCGOWAN & HANDS *Don't cry for Me* iv. 81 The Marines.. carried their 'bergans' or back-packs. **1985** *Survival Weaponry* Dec. 51/2, I carried this one in my bergan. **1986** *Official Gaz.* (U.S. Patent Office) 3 June TM65/2 F. E. Dahl & Co. A/S, Drammen, Norway.. Bergans of Norway.. for rucksacks and fabric pack-type infant carrier.

bergan, -gayne, obs. forms of BARGAIN *sb.*

ˌ**ber'gander.** *Ornith. Obs.* or ? *dial.* Forms: 7 **burgander, brigander,** 7–8 **birgander,** 8 **bergender,** 6– **bargander, bergander.** [Of uncertain derivation: perh. f. ME. *berȝ* shelter, burrow (see BERRY *sb.*²; and cf. *bergh, berghman, berman, barman*) + GANDER: cf. the synonyms *burrow-duck*, Da. *grav-gaas.* The word has however a curious resemblance to the North Fris. name *barg-aand* (Borkum), Du. *berg-eend*, G. *bergente* 'mountain-duck,' the analysis of which is of course altogether different.] An old name (apparently still lingering on the Northumbrian coast) of the Sheldrake, *Tadorna vulpanser* (Leach), a bird related to the duck and goose, which inhabits the seashore and breeds in rabbit-holes or burrows, whence also called by some authors *burrow-duck.*

1544 TURNER *Avium Hist.* 23 Nostrates [i.e. Northumbrians] hodie bergandrum nominant (*margin*, A bergander). **1570** LEVINS *Manip.* 79 Bargander, *vulpancer.* **1572** BOSSEWELL *Armorie* III. 20 The Bergander is a byrde of the kinde of Geese, somewhat longer, and bigger then a Ducke. **1601** HOLLAND *Pliny* I. 281 Of the Geese kind are the Birganders named Chelanopeces. **1611** COTGR., *Cravant*, the small Goose, or Goose-like fowle, tearmed, a Brigander. *a* **1682** SIR T. BROWNE *Wks.* (Bohn) III. 509 Burganders.. common in Norfolk, as abounding in vast and capacious warrens. **1753** CHAMBERS *Cycl. Supp.*, *Bergander*, a name by which some have called the shell-drake or burrough-duck. **1783** AINSWORTH *Lat. Dict.* (Morell) I, Bergender (fowl), *Vulpanser.* —— A birgander (bird), *Vulpanser.* **1879** JOHNS *Brit. Birds* 608 Bargander, the Sheldrake.

bergantine: see BRIGANTINE.

1555 EDEN *Decades W. Ind.* (Arb.) 108 Twoo smaule shyppes commenly cauled bergantines or brygantynes.

bergell, -ill: see BERGLE.

Bergenia (bɜː'giːnɪə). *Bot.* [mod.L. (N. J. Necker 1790, *Elem. Bot.* II. 108), f. the name of K. A. von *Bergen* (1704–60), German physician and botanist, + -IA¹.] A genus of perennial herbs of the family Saxifragaceæ, having large, thick leaves and usually pink, red, or purple flowers; also (with lower-case initial), a plant of this genus.

1838 C. S. RAFINESQUE *Sylva Telluriana* 102 Bergenia was Necker's name for G. Cuphea. **1886** *Encycl. Brit.* XXI. 350/2 The Bergenias or Megaseas with their large fleshy leaves and copious panicles of rosy or pink flowers. **1962** *Amateur Gardening* 17 Mar. 4/2 Bergenias.. are useful.. the fat stems packed with purplish pink flowers often appearing in late February or early March.

† '**berger.** *Obs. rare*⁻¹. [? a. F. *bergère* a négligé style of dressing the hair: see Littré.] 'A name given to a curl of hair as worn by ladies, *temp.* Chas. II.' (Planché); 'a plain small Lock (*a la Shepherdesse*) turn'd up with a Puff.' *Fop Dict.* 1690.

1690 EVELYN *Mundus Mul.* 6 Nor Cruches she, nor Confidents, Nor Passagers, nor Bergers wants.

‖ **bergère** (bɛːrʒɛːr). Also 8 **bergier, burgair, burjair,** etc. [Fr., lit. 'shepherdess'.] **1.** A large easy chair of a style fashionable in the eighteenth century (see quot. 1952); also, a kind of couch.

1762 INCE & MAYHEW *Univ. Syst. Houshold Furn.* Pl. lx, Burjairs. *Ibid.* 8/1 Two Designs of Birjairs, or half Couches. **1773** in E. SINGLETON *Social N.Y.* (1902) 83 All sorts of.. settees, couches, burgairs. **1784–87** in J. GLOAG *Short Dict. Furnit.* (1952) 141 A large and handsome mahogany bergier, stuffed back in green morocco. **1803** T. SHERATON *Cabinet Dict.* 19 Arm-chair, No. 5, is a bergere, having a caned back and arms. Sometimes the seats are caned, having loose cushions. **1814** M. EDGEWORTH *Patronage* I. v. 145 Miss Hauton seated herself.. upon a *bergère.* **1934** H. NICOLSON *Curzon: Last Phase* 299 There were palms in the room upon high white stands, and bergère chairs, and little round tables with glass ashtrays. **1942** N. MARSH *Death & Dancing Footman* ii. 27 The armchairs and the bergère [*sic*] sofas. **1942** J. CARY *To be a Pilgrim* cxlvi. 324 The armchair, a tattered bergère in white and gilt. **1952** J. GLOAG *Short Dict. Furnit.* 141 *Bergère*, an armchair with canework sides, back, and seat, with a loose cushion on the seat, or an upholstered seat.

2. *bergère hat*, a large straw hat.

1873 *Young Englishwoman* July 339/1 Bergère hat with gauze veil. **1905** *Daily Chron.* 13 Feb. 8/1 A pretty bergère hat made of fine straw.

bergeret, etymol. sp. of BARGERET, *Obs.*, pastoral.

‖ **bergerette** (bɛəʒə'rɛt, French bɛrʒərɛt). *Mus.* [Fr., see BARGERET.] = BARGERET.

[**1876** STAINER & BARRETT *Dict. Mus. Terms* 50/2 *Barginet, berginet, bargaret,* or *bergeret.* Shepherd's songs, to accompany dances. Songs relating to pastoral matters.] **1924** E. SITWELL *Sleeping Beauty* xxi. 79 A florid bergerette. **1959** *Times* 15 Sept. 14/3 There were occasional glimpses of the old finesse: in the bogus *bergerette*, for example.

Berger rhythm ('bɜːgə(r)). [f. name of Hans *Berger* (d. 1944), German neurologist.] = *alpha rhythm* (ALPHA 3 f).

1934 ADRIAN & MATTHEWS in *Brain* Dec. 355 (*heading*) The Berger rhythm: potential changes from the occipital lobes in man. *Ibid.* 356 Since the effect is so characteristic we shall refer to it in future as the Berger rhythm. **1936** [see ALPHA 3 f]. **1938** *Jrnl. Neurol. & Psychiatry* I. 366 Berger's first papers described two electrical rhythms. The first, which he called 'alpha waves' and which was referred to five years later by Adrian and his collaborators as the 'Berger rhythm', consists of an almost sinusoidal discharge with a frequency of about 10 per second and with a potential varying irregularly from zero to about 100 microvolts. **1941** [see ALPHA 3 f].

‖ **bergfall** ('bɛrçfal, 'bɜːgfɔːl). [Ger. *bergfall* fall of a mountain.] The ruinous fall of a mountain peak or crag, an avalanche of stones.

1856 RUSKIN *Mod. Paint.* IV. v. xiv. §5. 180 Terrific and fantastic forms of precipice; not altogether without danger, as has been fearfully demonstrated by many a 'bergfall' among the limestone groups of the Alps. **1862** *Peaks, Passes, & Glac.* II. x. 202 It is the wildest scene of desolation I ever saw; the celebrated bergfall of the Diablerets cannot at all compare with it.

† **bergh, berȝe, berwe,** *v. Obs.* Forms: 1 **beorȝan,** 2–4 **berȝe(n.** Also 2–3 **bereȝen, bireȝen, bureȝen** (*ü*), **buruwen,** *Orm.* **berrȝhenn,** 3 **berwen.** *Pa. t.* 1 **bearȝ,** 2–3 **barȝ,** 3 **barw.** *Pa. pple.* 1 **borȝen,** 2–4 **borȝen,** 3 *Orm.* **borrȝhenn, boreȝen, iboreuwen, iboruwen, iborhen.** [Common Teut.: OE. *beorȝan* (:—*bergan*) = OS. (*gi*)*bergan* (MDu. *berghen*, Du. *bergen*), OHG. *bergan* (MHG. and mod.G. *bergen*), ON. *bjarga*, Goth. *bairgan*:—OTeut. **berg-an* to protect, shelter, to shut in for protection or preservation.] To give shelter; to protect, preserve; to deliver, save. (Orig. with *dat.*, which was afterwards treated as *direct obj.*).

a **1000** *Andreas* (Grein) 1540 Weras.. woldon feore beorȝan. *c* **1000** *Ags. Psalter* xvi[i]. 8 Beorh me, swa swa man byrhð þam æplum on his eaȝum. *c* **1175** *Lamb. Hom.* 39 Þenne bureȝest þu here saule.. from þan ufele deaðe. *c* **1200** *Trin. Coll. Hom.* 61 Min red is þat we berȝen us wið ech of þese þre duntes. *c* **1200** ORMIN 4394 Þu ne mihht nohht borrȝhenn ben. *a* **1225** *Ancr. R.* 162 Tu schal beon iboruwen. *c* **1250** *Gen. & Ex.* 1330 Oc angel.. barȝ ðe child fro ðe dead. *a* **1300** *Havelok* 697 Betere us is.. to fle, And berwen bothen ure liues. *Ibid.* 2022 God self barw him wel. **1340** *Ayenb.* 251 He þet him wille berȝe.

¶ The weak pa. t. and pa. pple. *beryhed*, so frequent in the Northern Psalter, are ascribed by Mätzner to a distinct vb. *beryhien, berȝien*, which he compares with ON. *byrgja* (= Eng. *bury*), but this appears to be very doubtful: ON. *bjarga* has itself weak inflexions from an early period in Norway (Vigf.).

a **1300** *E.E. Psalter* xliii. [iv]. 4 Ne þar arme beryhed þam ai. *Ibid.* xxxii[i]. 17 Swikel hors.. of his might noght beryhed es.

† **bergh,** *sb. Obs.* [OE. *beorȝ, beorh* 'protection, shelter,' only in compounds as *scúr-beorȝ*; f. the verb.] Protection, shelter. Hence '**berghless** *a.*, shelterless, unprotected.

[*c* **1000** *Ags. Ps.* xlv[i]. 1 Dryhten ys ure ȝebeorh.] *c* **1250** *Gen. & Ex.* 926 Ðin berȝ and tin werȝer ic ham. *Ibid.* 3048 Al ðat it fond Berȝles, it sloȝe in ðat lond.

bergh, obs. form of BARROW *sb.*¹ a hill.

berghaan ('bɛrxhɑːn). *S. Afr.* [Afrikaans, f. BERG² + *haan* COCK.] A South African eagle, esp. the bateleur eagle, *Terathopius ecaudatus.*

1867 E. L. LAYARD *Birds S. Afr.* 11 *Aquila Verreauxii*.. *Dassie Vanger* and *Berghaan* of Colonists... It is called '*Dassie Vanger*' (coney-eater) and '*Berghaan*' (mountain-cock) by the colonists, from feeding principally on the coney, or rock-rabbit (*Hyrax capensis*). **1889** H. A. BRYDEN *Kloof & Karroo* 273 Suddenly.. comes.. a great black mountain eagle. We know him at once for a berghaan. **1893** NEWTON *Dict. Birds*, *Berghaan* (Mountain-cock), the name given to some of the larger Eagles, and especially to the beautiful *Helotarsus ecaudatus*.. by the Dutch colonists in South Africa. **1910** J. BUCHAN *Prester John* viii, A brace of white *berghaan* circled far up in the blue.

berȝe, obs. form of BERGH, BERRY, BARROW.

† '**bergher.** *Obs.* In 4 **berȝere, beryher.** [f. BERGH *v.* + -ER¹.] A protector, deliverer, saviour.

a **1300** *E.E. Psalter* lxi[i]. 7 He es mi God and my beryher al. [**1598** TATE in Gutch *Coll. Cur.* I. 5 I have David's Psalms in very old Metre, and, in the 25th Psalm, *Bericher* is used for a Saviour.]

berghman, -master, -mote: see BERMAN, BARMASTER, -MOOT.

† '**bergier.** *Obs. rare*⁻¹. [a. F. *berger* peasant, shepherd.] A peasant, a woodman.

1480 CAXTON *Ovid's Met.* XI. xi, And for the prouffyte.. the bergier norysshed hym wel and diligently.

bergle ('bɜːg(ə)l). Also **bergell, -gill.** [Perh. the same word as BERGYLT: Jamieson refers it to ON. *berg* rock.] The name of a rock-fish, the Wrasse, in Orkney.

1805 G. BARRY *Orkney Isl.* 389 (JAM.) The Wrasse.. has here got the name of *bergle.* **1795** *Statist. Acc. Scot.* XIV. 314 Fish.. called in this country milds, bergills.

bergmannite ('bɜːgmənaɪt). *Min.* [f. Bergmann (name of a mineralogist) + -ITE.] A variety of Natrolite, white or red in colour, occurring massive, or in prisms, in southern Norway.

1811 PINKERTON *Petral.* I. 291 The most celebrated rock of this denomination is the Grison, or Bergmanite. **1880** DANA *Min.* 427 Crocalite.. is a red zeolite, identical with the bergmannite of Laurvig.

Bergomask: see BERGAMASK.

bergschrund ('bɛkʃrʊnt). *Phys. Geogr.* [G., f. *berg* (see BARROW *sb.*¹) + *schrund* cleft, crevice.] A crevasse or series of crevasses often found near the head of a mountain glacier.

1843 J. D. FORBES *Trav. through Alps* 298, I perceived an enormous *Berg-schrund*, or well defined crevass, which separated the higher summits from the glacier steep. **1860** J. TYNDALL *Glaciers of Alps* I. xiv. 98 This slope was intersected by a so-called Bergschrund, the lower portion of the slope being torn away from its upper portion to form a crevasse. **1871** [see FRINGE *sb.* 2 a]. **1957** J. MASTERS *Mountain Peak* 99 There was the usual bergschrund between the snow and the warmer rock of the gendarme.

Bergsonian (bɜːg'səʊnɪən), *a.* and *sb.* [f. the name *Bergson* (see below) + -IAN.] **A.** *adj.* Of, pertaining to, or characteristic of the French philosopher, Henri Bergson (1859–1941). **B.** *sb.* A follower or adherent of Bergson. So **Bergsonism** ('bɜːgsənɪz(ə)m), the philosophical doctrine of Bergson.

1909 W. JAMES *Plural. Univ.* v. 215, I must.. give some preliminary account of the bergsonian philosophy. *Ibid.* vi. 266 They are now Bergsonians.. and possess the principal thoughts of the master all at once. *Ibid.* vii. 277 Philosophy, you will say, doesn't lie flat on its belly in the middle of experience, in the very thick of its sand and gravel, as this Bergsonism does. **1920** H. BEGBIE *Wm. Booth* I. 146 Bergsonism has here a most admirable example of its thesis. **1944** G. B. SHAW *Everybody's Political What's What* viii. 62 When will the royalist lie down with the republican.. the Bergsonian with the Darwinian? **1955** D. DAVIE *Artic. Energy* i. 6 Much modern criticism is Bergsonian, perhaps without knowing it.

bergy ('bɜːgɪ), *a.* [f. BERG¹ + -Y¹.] **a.** Abounding in icebergs; of the nature of an iceberg.

1856 KANE *Arct. Exp.* I. iii. 32 The bergs which infest this region, and which have earned for it.. the title of the 'Bergy Hole.' **1876** DAVIS *Polaris Exp.* xi. 266 A considerable bergy mass of ice.

b. spec. *bergy bit*: a large piece of ice that has broken away from an iceberg (see also quot. 1958).

1935 *Geogr. Jrnl.* LXXXVI. 301 The channel carrying ice-floes and bergy bits. **1958** *New Scientist* 10 July 358/3 As it weathers away, a berg becomes known as a 'bergy bit' (when about the size of a small house).

bergylt, berguylt ('bɜːgɪlt). [Jamieson refers it to ON. *berg* rock; cf. BERGLE.]

1. The name of a fish, the Black Goby, in Shetland, and elsewhere.

1809 EDMONSTONE *Zetl.* II. 310 (JAM.) Black Goby.. is called *berguylt* in Zetland.

2. The Norwegian haddock or Sea Perch (*Sebastes Norvegicus*), an arctic fish, found occasionally on the coasts of Scotland.

1838 *Proc. Berw. Nat. Club* I. 170 *Scorpæna norvegica*, Cuvier Sea Perch, Penn. The Bergylt, Yarrell. **1883** *Morn. Post* 20 June 6/5 Central Fish Market: A large supply of fish .. bergylt, 4*d.* per lb.

berhegor, variant of BEEREGAR, *Obs.*

berhom, obs. form of BARGHAM.

berhyme: see BERIME.

berial, -alle, obs. forms of BERYL, BURIAL.

‖**'beri'beri.** *Med.* Also (all *obs.*) beriberia, beriberii, beribery, berri berri. [A Sinhalese word, f. *beri* weakness; the reduplication being intensive.] An acute disease generally presenting dropsical symptoms, with paralytic weakness and numbness of the legs, prevalent in many parts of India.

1703 tr. *Nieuhoff's Voy.* in A. & J. Churchill *Voy.* (1704) II. 340/2 They [*sc.* the shrubs] have a peculiar Virtue.. to cure the Indian Gout or Barrenness, called Beribery. **1769** tr. *Bontius's Acc. Diseases of East Indies* i. 1, The inhabitants of the East Indies are much afflicted with a troublesome disorder which they call the Beriberii (a word signifying a sheep). The disease has, probably, received this denomination on account that those who are seized with it.. exhibit to the fancy a representation of the gait of that animal. **1832** H. S. FLEMING in *Fort St. George Gaz.* 12 May 1 On the disease called 'Beriberi'. **1879** KHORZ *Princ. Med.* 84 In beriberi there is scurvy from the first. **1884** YULE *Anglo-Ind. Gloss.* s.v., In 1879 the total number of beri-beri patients.. amounted to 9873.

†**bericorn.** *Obs.* Prob. = *bere-corn* barleycorn, or the variety called bigg: see BEAR *sb.*[2]

1284–1355 in Rogers *Agric. & Pr.* II. 173–7. See also I. 222.

berid, variant of BERRIED *ppl. a.*

be'ride (bɪ'raɪd), *v.* Also 3 biride(n. [OE. *berīdan* f. BE- + *rīdan* to RIDE.]

†**1.** *trans.* To ride around; to beset with horsemen. *Obs.*

a **1000** Thorpe's *Laws* I. 90 (Bosw.) Ðæt he his ʒefan beride. *c* **1205** LAY. 10739 Bruttes þa burȝen gunnen biriden [*c* **1250** bi-ride].

2. To ride by the side of (*obs.*); to ride upon, infest.

1690 D'URFEY *Collin's Walk* II. (D.) Those two that there beride him, And with such graces prance beside him. **1848** in *Proc. Berw. Nat. Club.* II. vi. 300 When an insect so beridden is taken up, the mites disperse.

berie, obs. form of BURGH, BURY.

beriel(le, berien, obs. forms of BURIAL, BURY.

berig, obs. form of BOROUGH.

beriglia, berilla, obs. forms of BARILLA.

beriing, beril, obs. forms of BURYING, BERYL.

†**beri'mancorn.** *Obs.* [Prob. f. *bere*, BEAR, *sb.*[2] barley, *mang* mixture, and *corn*; cf. BERICORN.] A mixed crop of barley and some other grain.

1359 in Rogers *Agric. & Prices* II. 177. See also I. 222.

berime, berhyme (bɪ'raɪm), *v.* [f. BE- 4 and 6 + RIME.]

1. *trans.* To compose rimes about, to celebrate in rime; often, to lampoon.

1589 *Almond for Parrat* 42 Another while hee would all to berime Doctour Perne.. and make a by word of his bald pate. **1600** SHAKS. *A.Y.L.* III. ii. 186, I was neuer so berim'd since Pythagoras time that I was an Irish Rat. **1790** WOLCOTT (P. Pindar) *Adv. Future Laureat* Wks. 1812 II. 333 Rush loyal to berhyme a King and Queen. **1824** W. IRVING *T. Trav.* I. 260 Some glowing lines, in which I berhymed the little lady.

2. To compose in rime, put into rime.

1801 W. TAYLOR in Robberds *Mem.* I. 382 The ladies cannot endure the metre of 'Thallaba'.. Berime it, and they will bepraise it.

†**be'rine**, *v. Obs. rare.* [f. BE- 1 + RINE:—OE. *hrīnan* to touch; cf. AT-RINE.] *trans.* and *intr.* To touch; fall upon, fall.

a **1300** *K. Horn* 11 Fairer ne mihte non beo born Ne no rein upon birine Ne sunne upon bischine. —— *Harl. MS.* For reyne ne myhte byryne.. Feyrore child þen he was.

bering(e, obs. form of BEARING, BURYING.

beringed, beringleted, berinse, etc.: see BE-.

†**be'risp**, *v. Obs.* [a. Fl. *berispen*, in same sense.] To censure, reprove. (Only in Caxton).

1481 CAXTON *Reynard* (1844) 136, I can not telle it so wel, but that he shal beryspe me.

berk (bɜːk). *slang.* Also birk, burk(e. [Abbrev. of *Berkeley* (or *Berkshire*) *Hunt*, rhyming slang for *cunt.*] A fool.

1936 J. CURTIS *Gilt Kid* vi. 66 'The berk.' Jealousy and savage contempt blended in the Gilt Kid's tone. **1938** W. GREENWOOD *Only Mugs Work* vii. 49 'Stick the burke in a taxi,' he said. **1954** 'N. BLAKE' *Whisper in Gloom* II. xiv. 197 'Don't be a little berk,' he said, as Foxy showed signs of recalcitrance. **1959** J. OSBORNE *Paul Slickey* I. iv, The Tories were burglars, berks and bloodlusters. **1960** H. PINTER *Dumb Waiter* in *Birthday Party & other Plays* 141 You mutt... You birk! **1963** *Sunday Express* 10 Mar. 22/5 All my mates thought I was a burk to try to break away: now they know they were the burks.

†**berk**, *v. Obs.* [Variant of BARK *v.*[2] 4.] *trans.* To clot, make matted. Hence BERKIT *ppl. a.*

a **1550** *Christis Kirke Gr.* xx, Bludy berkit wes thair berd. **1641** H. BEST *Farm. Bks.* (1856) 11 Theire excrementes which berke togeather theire tayles and hinder partes.

berk- in various words: see BARK-.

Berkefeld ('bɜːkfɛld, -ɛlt). Also (erron.) Berkefield. The name of W. *Berkefeld* (1836–1897), German mine-owner, used to designate a bacterial filter containing diatomaceous earth.

1894 *Brit. Med. Jrnl.* 29 Dec. 1489/2 We must conclude that the Berkefeld filters may afford an efficient safeguard against the passage of disease germs. *Ibid.* 1488/2 The Berkefeld Filter Company Ltd. **1902** *Encycl. Brit.* XXXIII. 790/1 The Berkefield filter, constructed of baked infusorial earth. **1946** *Nature* 17 Aug. 217/2 Preparing from the eggs Berkefeld filtrates. **1951** R. J. LUDFORD in G. H. Bourne *Cytology* (ed. 2) ix. 402 A filterable tumour.. yields by Berkefeld-filtration a cell-free filtrate.

Berkeleian (bɜː'kliːən), *a.* and *sb.* [f. name of *Berkeley*, Bishop of Cloyne (died 1753), a celebrated philosopher who denied the objective or independent existence of the material world.]

A. *adj.* Of or originating with Berkeley. **B.** *sb.* A follower or disciple of Berkeley. Hence **Berke'leianism, 'Berkeleyism**, the philosophical opinions held by Berkeley and his followers.

1860 MANSEL *Prolegom. Log.* v. 145 Taking the Berkleian theory in its whole extent. **1878** J. FISKE in *N. Amer. Rev.* CXXVI. 32 Materialists, as a rule, have not mastered the Berkeleian psychology. **1804** *Edin. Rev.* IX. 158 The reasoning of the Berkeleians. **1830** MACKINTOSH *Progr. Eth. Philos.* §6 (1862) 269 His adoption of Berkeleianism is a proof of an unprejudiced and acute mind. **1864** J. H. NEWMAN *Apol.* 78 The connexion of this philosophy of religion with what is sometimes called 'Berkeleyism' has been mentioned. **1881** *Athenæum* 30 July 137/1 Whether the mind will not at last be driven into actual Berkeleyism.

Berkeley Hunt ('bɑːkliː hʌnt). [The name of a celebrated hunt in Gloucestershire.] Rhyming slang for CUNT (usu. in sense 2, 'a fool'). Also *ellipt.* as **Berkeley**. Cf. the abbrev. BERK.

1937 PARTRIDGE *Dict. Slang* 48/1 *Berkeley*, the *pudendum muliebre*: C. 20. Abbr. *Berkeley Hunt.* **1937** Sir Berkeley [see SIR *sb.* 1 b]. **1940** A. BRACEY *Flower on Loyalty* I. iii. 49 Lane's face cleared. 'Tell us, chum.' 'And spoil the nice surprise! Not bloody likely!' 'You always was a berkeley,' said Lane cheerfully. 'Well, I can wait.' **1960** J. FRANKLYN *Dict. Rhyming Slang* 38/2 *Berkeley hunt.* This is an accidental formation serving as an alternative for [*Berkshire hunt*]. **1977** *Custom Car* Nov. 67/3 Berkeley hunt: *fica* (fee-ka).

berkelium (bə'kiːlɪəm, 'bɜːklɪəm). *Chem.* [mod.L., f. *Berkeley*, California, where the element was first made + -IUM.] A metallic radioactive transuranic element not occurring in nature but made artificially; symbol Bk; atomic number 97.

1950 S. G. THOMPSON et al. in *Physical Rev.* LXXVII. 838/2 It is suggested that element 97 be given the name berkelium (symbol Bk), after the city of Berkeley. **1951** J. R. PARTINGTON *Gen. & Inorg. Chem.* (ed. 2) xxvi. 760 Berkelium.. and californium.. are formed by bombarding americium and curium, respectively, with high-energy helium ions.

Berkshire ('bɑːkʃə(r)). **1.** Name of an English county, applied to a famous breed of pig.

1811 R. HENDERSON *Treat. Breeding Swine* i. 13 The Berkshire pig, is generally allowed to be a good kind. **1814** —— *Ibid.* (ed. 2) ii. 29, I would give the preference to the Cheshire, or rather the Berkshire hog. **1831** LOUDON *Encycl. Agric.* (ed. 2) III. 1069 The old Irish breed are a long-legged .. unprofitable sort of swine; but when they have been crossed with the Berkshire, they are considerably improved. **1842** D. LOW *Dom. Anim. Brit. Isl.* I. 17 The true Berkshires are of the larger races of Swine, though they fall short in size of some of the older breeds. *Ibid.*, The Berkshire breed has .. been crossed and recrossed with the Chinese. **1855** MORTON *Cycl. Agric.* II. 941/2 The Berkshire breed of pigs has probably been the best known, and had in the highest estimation of any of our British breeds. **1953** A. JOBSON *Household Crafts* vi. 65 Almost every county in England has produced its own breed of pigs, and we have.. Berkshire, Essex Black, [etc.].

2. Berkshire Hunt *Rhyming slang* = BERKELEY HUNT.

1960 J. FRANKLYN *Dict. Rhyming Slang* 38/2 *Berkshire Hunt*... This is not an objective, anatomical term, neither does it imply coitus. It connects with that extension of meaning of the unprintable, *a fool*, or a person whom one does not like.

†**berkyne.** *Obs.* Also berekyn. [perh. *berekyn*, i.e. *beer-kind*, any kind of beer.]

1436 *Pol. Poems* (1859) II. 169 That twoo Fflemmynges togedere Wol undertake.. Or they rise onys, to drinke a barelle fulle of gode berkyne [*v.r.* bere, berekyn].

berlady, berlaken: see BYRLADY, BYRLAKIN.

berlaw, -man, obs. form of BYRLAW, -MAN.

berlepe, variant of BEARLEAP, carrying basket.

c **1330** HAMPOLE *Ps.* lxxx[i]. 6 Berlepe [*v.r.* bere lepe].. that is a vessel in the whilke the iwes bare mortere in egipt.

berley ('bɜːlɪ). *Austral.* Also **burley**. [Of unknown origin.] Ground-bait.

1874 E. S. HILL in J. E. Tenison-Woods *Fish & Fisheries of N.S.W.* (1882) iii. 75 The bait should be crabs. It is usual to wrench legs and shell off the back, and cast them out for berley. **1896** *Badminton Mag.* Aug. 201 Sometimes adding bait chopped small to serve for what Australian fishermen call Berley.

b. (See quots.)

1941 BAKER *Dict. Austral. Slang* 15 *Burley*, humbug, nonsense. **1943** *Ibid.* (ed. 3) 9 *Berley*, nonsense, humbug; e.g. 'a bit of berley'.

berley, -lik, obs. forms of BARLEY.

Berlin ('bɜːlɪn, bɜː'lɪn). [The name of the capital of Prussia, used *attrib.*, and transferred to things that come or were supposed to come thence.]

1. An old-fashioned four-wheeled covered carriage, with a seat behind covered with a hood. [Also *Berline* from Fr.; so in Ger. Introduced by an officer of the Elector of Brandenburg, *c* 1670.]

1694 EARL OF PERTH *Let.* 17 June (1845) 30 A woman with a maid following her came to the Berline side (this is a kind of traveling coach used here). **1717** LADY MONTAGU *Let.* 29 May (1763) 110 The meadows being full of all sorts of garden flowers, and sweet herbs, my berlin perfumed the air as it pressed them. **1731** SWIFT *Answ. Simile* Wks. 1755 IV. I. 222 Jealous Juno ever snarling, Is drawn by peacocks in her berlin. **1746** CHESTERF. *Lett.* I. cxiii. 307 Your distresses in your journey.. and your broken Berline. **1850** ALISON *Hist. Europe* II. vi. §79. 75 They entered a berline which was ready harnessed by M. de Fersen's care.

2. Short for 'Berlin wool.'

1881 *Girls Own Paper* II. 420/3 Any of the Scotch fingering yarns are too thin, but double Berlin.. will do.

3. Short for 'Berlin Glove': A knitted glove (of Berlin wool).

1836 DICKENS *Sk. Boz, Tuggses at Ramsgate*, A fat man in black tights, and cloudy Berlins. *Ibid. Astley's*, The dirty white Berlin Gloves.

4. *Attrib.* or *Comb.*, as **Berlin black**, a black varnish used for coating the better kinds of ironware; **Berlin blue** = PRUSSIAN BLUE, or the finest kind of it; **Berlin castings**, ornamental objects imported from Prussia, of **Berlin iron**, a very fusible quality of iron, smelted from bog-ore, containing much phosphorus, and suitable for casting figures and delicate articles, which are often lacquered or bronzed; **Berlin pattern**, a pattern in Berlin work; **Berlin spirit** (see quot. 1878); **Berlin ware**, an earthenware of a quality which resists the action of most chemical re-agents; **Berlin warehouse**, a shop or repository for Berlin wool and similar fancy wares; **Berlin wool**, a fine dyed wool used for knitting, tapestry, and the like; **Berlin work**, fancy work in Berlin wool, worsted embroidery.

1795 R. KIRWAN *Elem. Min.* (ed. 2) I. 491 The Berlin blue, so I call the Prussian blue of the shops, is not pure Prussiated iron, but a mixture of this with embryon alum. **1829** R. C. SANDS *Writings* (1834) II. 163 Her girdle was fastened in front with a massive shining clasp of Berlin ware. **1841** LADY WILTON *Art of Needlework* xxv. 397 The style of modern embroidery, now so fashionable, from the Berlin patterns, dates from the commencement of the present century. *Ibid.* 398 The 'Berlin wools'... These yarns, however, are only dyed in Berlin, being manufactured at Gotha. **1845** G. DODD *Brit. Manuf.* IV. iv. 110 The 'Berlin' patterns now so well known. *c* **1845** C. BRONTË *Professor* (1857) I. xvii. 285 You can work with Berlin wools. **1853** E. M. SEWELL *Exper. of Life* xiii. 131 The.. footstool, worked in the homely period between mediæval tapestry and modern Berlin patterns. **1854** *Encycl. Brit.* IV. 667/2 Its [*sc.* Berlin's] principal branches of industry.. are porcelain, silks .. Berlin iron, &c. **1854** C. M. YONGE *Castle Builders* vi. 78 Their purse netting and Berlin work. **1862** —— *Countess Kate* iii. 52 She had a bunch of flowers in Berlin wool which she was supposed to be grounding. **1863** G. M. HOPKINS *Note-Bks.* (1937) 8 She abominated the Berlin wool shop. **1878** *Chambers's Encycl.* II. 52/2 *Berlin spirit*, a coarse whisky made chiefly from beetroot, potatoes, &c.

berlin, -ling, var. of BIRLING, a galley.

1815 SCOTT *Guy M.* v, The Highlanders, that came here in their berlings.

‖**ber'lina, -ino.** *Obs.* [It. in same sense.]

[**1598–1611** FLORIO, *Berlina, Berlino* [Italian], a pillerie; Also a cucking-stool, heretofore called a tombrell.] **1605** B. JONSON *Volpone* v. xii, To mount (a Paper Pinned on thy Breast) to the *Berlino*. [**1824** BARETTI *Ital. Dict.*, *Berlina*, pillory.]

Berliner (bɜːˈlɪnə(r)). [a. G. *Berliner*, f. BERLIN + -ER[1].] A native or inhabitant of Berlin, Germany.

1859 L. WRAXALL tr. *Robert-Houdin's Mem.* II. vi. 172 The reception I obtained from the Berliner will ever remain one of my pleasantest reminiscences. **1959** *Times* 18 Feb. 14/4 It would be a mistake to assume that only east Berliners trade in the west. **1963** V. NABOKOV *Gift* i. 35 The perpetual fetters that chain a Berliner to the door lock.

†ˈ**berling.** *Obs.* [ME. f *bere*, BEAR *sb.*[1] + -LING: cf. ME. *derling*, now *darling* little dear. A modern *bearling* formed afresh from *bear* is of course possible.] A little bear, a bear's cub.

1399 LANGL. *Rich. Redeles* III. 96 Tho' all the berlingis brast out at ones.

Berliozian (bɛəlɪəˈʊzɪən), *a.* and *sb.* [f. the name of *Berlioz* (see below) + -IAN.] **A.** *adj.* Of, pertaining to, resembling, or characteristic of Hector Berlioz (1803–1869), French composer, or his music. **B.** *sb.* An admirer of Berlioz; an interpreter of his work.

1910 *Westm. Gaz.* 9 Mar. 4/2 Robert Houdin—whose Berliozian portrait adorns this volume. **1936** *Scrutiny* Dec. 270 That extraordinarily subtle and flexible organism the Berliozian melody. **1951** J. BARZUN *Berlioz* II. 303 The Berliozians could do little. **1961** *Times* 7 June 17/1 Mr. Davis, a perceptive Berliozian. **1962** *Ibid.* 18 Apr. 7/5 This is scored, with Berliozian grandeur, for 90 percussion instruments.

berm (bɜːm). Also 8–9 berme, 9 birm. [a. F. *berme*, a. MDu. and Ger. *berme*, in mod.Du. *berm*, in same sense; prob. cognate w. ON. *barmr* brim, edge, border of a river, the sea, etc.]

1. a. A narrow space or ledge; *esp.* in *Fortif.* a space of ground, from 3 to 8 feet wide, sometimes left between the ditch and the base of the parapet.

1729 SHELVOCKE *Artillery* IV. 197 Round which shall be formed a Berm or Ledge, for the conveniently ranging of certain Paper Tubes or Cases. **1775** R. MONTGOMERY in Sparks *Corr. Amer. Rev.* (1853) I. 470 By the time we arrived there, the fraise around the berme would be destroyed, the rampart in a ruinous state. **1816** C. JAMES *Mil. Dict.* (ed. 4) 248/2 Berm..is to prevent the earth from rolling into the ditch, and serves likewise to pass and repass. As it is in some degree advantageous to the enemy, in getting footing, most of the modern engineers reject it. **1850** ALISON *Hist. Europe* X. lxviii. §49. 335 The ladders..enabled them to reach an intermediate ledge or berm.

b. *spec.* in *Geol.* (See quots.)

1931 F. BASCOM in *Science* LXXIV. 172/1 The word *berm* ..should be used to distinguish those terraces which originate from the interruption of an erosion cycle with rejuvenation of a stream in the mature stage of its development. **1942** C. A. COTTON *Geomorphology* (ed. 3) xviii. 242 The term 'berm' has been introduced for any remnant of a surface developed to full maturity in a cycle that has since been interrupted. Though it has been said to be a kind of 'terrace', a berm may include more than the valley floor which becomes a true river terrace. **1942** O. D. VON ENGELN *Geomorphology* xii. 221 Such a remnantal flat, which has a surface slope downstream, may be called a strath or sometimes, together with the valley shoulder, a berm.

2. berm-bank, the bank of a canal opposite the towing-path. [? Actually used only in U.S.A.]

1854 *N. & Q.* Ser. I. X. 12/2 [A writer from Philadelphia] The bank of a canal opposite to the towing-path is called the birm-bank. **1877** *Engineer* 3 Aug. 89/1 To lay a rail upon the berme bank (the bank opposite the towing path).

3. A ledge or flat of land bordering either bank of the Nile and inundated when the river overflows.

1891 *Daily News* 31 Oct. 6/4 To raise the Nile at the apex of the Delta to a level sufficient to flood the islands and berms of the two branches in the Delta. **1900** *Westm. Gaz.* 10 July 2/2 The water level in the winter was some fifty centimètres below the general level of the berm.

†**berm(e,** *v. Obs.* [ME. *berm-en*, f. *berme*, BARM *sb.*[2] An earlier form of BARM *v.*]

trans. To work out, as barm: to purge out.

c **1315** SHOREHAM *Poems* 15 Ine the foreheved the crouche a set Felthe of fendes to bermi. *c* **1440** *Promp. Parv.* 32 Bermyn or spurgyn as ale, *spumo.*

berm(e, obs. form of BARM.

†ˈ**berman**[1]. *Obs.* [OE. *bærman*, f. *bær* BIER, *beran* to bear + MAN.] A bearer, carrier, or porter.

c **1000** ÆLFRIC *Josh.* iii. 15 Þa bærmenn ȝesetton heora fottest. *c* **1205** LAY. 3317 We habbet bermen & birles inowe. *a* **1300** *Havelok* 876 Þe bermen let he alle ligge, And bar þe mete to þe castel. *Ibid.* 885 Bermen, bermen, hider swiþe!

†ˈ**berman**[2]. *Obs. rare.* [f. *berghman*, cf. Ger. *bergmann* miner; see BARMASTER.] A miner.

1677 PLOT *Oxfordsh.* 59 Without the advice of ancient and experienced Bermen.

†ˈ**bermother.** *Obs.* [f. BEAR *v.* (OE. *beran*, ME. *bere*) + MOTHER: possibly after Ger. *gebärmutter*, in same sense.] The womb or uterus.

1527 ANDREW *Brunswyke's Distyll. Waters* N v, Water of nettles..is good for the bermoder [*v.r.* ber mother] whan she pussheth upwarde.

Bermuda (bəˈmuːdə, -ˈmjuːdə). The name of a group of islands in the N. Atlantic; *hence* a variety of cigar, or rolled tobacco. **Bermuda(s cedar,** a species of juniper, *Juniperus bermudiana*; **Bermuda grass,** name in U.S. of *Cynodon Dactylon*, a kind of grass growing on a sandy seashore; **Bermuda lily,** a lily of the variety *Lilium longiflorum eximium*, also known as *Lilium harrisii*, originally obtained from Bermuda; **Bermuda rig** = BERMUDIAN *rig*; **Bermuda shorts,** knee-length shorts; also *ellipt.* as ***Bermudas***; **Bermuda Triangle**: see TRIANGLE *sb.* 2 a.

c **1640** [SHIRLEY] *Capt. Underwit* IV. ii. in *O. Pl.* (1883) II. 381 Will you take Tobacco in the Roll? here is a whole shiplading of Bermudas. **1808** H. MUHLENBERG *Let.* 5 July in Rowland *Life W. Dunbar* (1930) 199 The *Bermuda grass* is..the same with Cumberland grass. **1879** *New Orleans Paper*, An inquiry comes to us about Bermuda-grass. *Ibid.* Bermuda is emphatically a Southern grass..adapted to a hot climate. **1906** F. LYNDE *Quickening* 11 The dooryard with its thick turf of uncut Bermuda grass. **1899** G. JEKYLL *Wood & Garden* ix. 106 The Bermuda Lilies (*Harrisi*) are intergrouped with *L. speciosum*. **1911** *Sutton's Amateur's Guide in Hort.* 195 *Lilium Harrisii* (Bermuda Lily). A large and elegant pure white Lily, adapted for forcing or growing in pots. **1853** R. KIPPING *Mast-making & Rigging* ii. 5 Brig Forward, Common, and Bermuda Rig. **1928** *Daily Mail* 9 Aug. 19/7 Most sailing men agree that the Bermuda rig is preferable for smaller boats. **1756** P. BROWNE *Civil & Nat. Hist. Jamaica* (1789) II. 362 Juniperus 1... The Bermudas Cedar. **1794** [see CEDAR 3]. **1829** LOUDON *Encycl. Plants* 848 *Juniperus bermudiana*, Bermudas Cedar. **1876** *Encycl. Brit.* V. 286 The Bermuda cedar..used in joinery and in the manufacture of pencils. **1953** R. CHANDLER *Long Good-Bye* iii. 17 Loafing around one of the swimming pools in Bermuda shorts. **1961** *Times* 11 July 12/6 No right-thinking suburbanite would be seen on his lawn without wearing Bermudas.

Bermudan (bəˈmjuːdən), *a.* [f. BERMUDA + -AN.] = BERMUDIAN *a.*

1895 *Outing* (U.S.) XXVII. 240/2 The oval top of the Bermudan ocean peak. **1923** *Public Opinion* 24 Aug. 180/2 Her lofty Bermudan main-sail. **1928** *Daily Express* 20 July 10/2 The Astra and Cambria..carry the Bermudan-rig—a high tapering sail like the wing of a gigantic bird.

Bermudian (bəˈmjuːdɪən), *a.* and *sb.* [f. BERMUDA + -IAN.] **A.** *adj.* Of or pertaining to the Bermudas or their inhabitants. **Bermudian rig,** a rig for a yacht, carrying a high tapering sail, called a ***Bermudian mainsail.*** So ***Bermudian-rigged*** adj., fitted with a rig and sail of this kind. **B.** *sb.* An inhabitant of the Bermudas; a Bermudian ship; a Bermudian-rigged ship.

1777 J. ADAMS *Let.* in *Mass. Hist. Soc. Coll.* (1917) LXXII. 313 Many french Vessells have arrived there, some Bermudians, and some of their own. **1803** A. ELLICOTT *Jrnl.* x. 287 Bermudian mulberry, (callicarpa americana). **1821** G. GLEIG *Campaigns Brit. Army* vi. 73 You may perhaps consider me as too severe upon the Bermudians. **1895** *Boy's Own Paper* XVII. 429/3 One of the Manchester boats being a schooner and another a Bermudian. **1915** C. P. LUCAS *Brit. Emp.* 163 The little Bermudian Assembly is..the oldest Parliamentary institution in the British Empire outside the United Kingdom. **1926** *Glasgow Herald* 20 Aug. 9 She is Bermudian rigged. **1926** *Blackw. Mag.* Nov. 698/1 By implicitly obeying the Bermudian, we escaped this danger. **1928** *Observer* 15 Apr. 29/5 The 12-metre yachts..with a Bermudian rig of moderate area, can be sailed efficiently with four paid hands. **1928** *Daily Tel.* 1 May 16/6 The Cambria will be Bermudian rigged, carrying a Bermudian mainsail. **1933** *Amer. Speech* VIII. 3/1 Bermudians would be justified in taking pride in their speech. **1953** 'N. SHUTE' *In Wet* 92 She's a Bermudian cutter, five and a half ton.

bern(e, obs. form of BAIRN, BARN, BURN.

bernacle, -icle, bernag, -nak(e, variant and early forms of BARNACLE.

bernard, variant of BARNARD.

Bernardine (ˈbɜːnədɪn), *a.* Of or pertaining to St. Bernard (abbot of Clairvaux in 1115), or to the monastic order bearing his name. *sb.* A monk of this order; a Cistercian.

1676 BULLOKAR, *Bernardines*, a certain Order of Monks, so called from their first Founder. **1792** A. YOUNG *Trav. France* 41 Pass a convent of Bernardine monks. **1797** HOLCROFT *Stolberg's Trav.* II. xlvi. (ed. 2) 110 One of these temples..is..become the church of the Bernardines. **1864** *Gentl. Mag.* CXXXIV. II. 25 The Bernardine reform soon spread to this country.

†**berne.** *Obs.* Forms: 1 biorn, 1–3 beorn, 3–6 bern(e, burn(e. Also 3 bearn, 3–4 bieren, 4 beern(e, berene, biern(e, byern(e, buirn, buyrn(e, beurn, bourne, borne, 4–5 beryn, buern(e, barn(e, 5 byrne, birn(e, buirn(e. [OE. *beorn*, earlier *biorn* (:—**bern*) 'warrior, hero, man of valour,' hence 'man' pre-eminently, *vir*, ἀνήρ; a word exclusively poetical; of disputed origin. The ME. forms were very varied; the most common midland type in 14th c. was *burn(e*; after 1400 the word was retained chiefly in the north, where it was a favourite term of alliterative poetry; in the form *berne* it survived in Scotch till after 1550. In some of its spellings it was occasionally confounded with forms of BAIRN, and BARON; with the latter it was often actually interchanged: see quots. 1205, 1300.

Phonetically, OE. *beorn* 'man of valour' answers exactly to ON. *bjǫrn*, gen. *bjarnar*, 'bear'(:—OTeut. *bernu-z*, the Celtic representative of which Prof. Rhys sees in the Gaulish proper name *Brennus*); but the ON. word has never the sense of 'warrior,' while the OE. has never that of 'bear.' To this, however, a striking analogy is offered by the case of OE. *eofor*, ON. *jǫfurr* (:—OTeut. *eburo-z* = L. *aper*), which has in Old English only the sense of 'wild boar,' in ON. only that of 'warrior, hero.' The use of the name of a fierce animal as a fig. appellation for 'warrior, brave,' seems very natural, and the fact that OE. *beorn* belonged only to the language of poetry and is never found in prose, suggests that it was a word of which the literal sense was lost, and only a figurative one traditionally retained. Nevertheless some eminent Teutonic scholars doubt the identification. Some have considered the word to be an early variant of *bearn*, BAIRN, or at least a cognate derivative of *beran* to BEAR. Mr. H. Bradley has suggested the possibility of connecting it with the British root of *Beornice* Bernicia, Welsh *bryneich*, and of Welsh *brenhin* king; but the nature of the connexion is not apparent.]

A warrior, a hero, a man of valour; in later use, simply one of the many poetic words for 'man.'

Beowulf 5111 Biorn under beorȝe bordrand onswaf. **937** *Batt. Brunanburh* in *O.E. Chron.*, Gelpan ne þorfte beorn blanden-feax. *c* **1205** LAY. 16923 Æuerælche eorle & æuerælche beorne [**1250** euch eorl and barun]. *a* **1300** *Cursor M.* 7 Brut, þat bern [*v.r.* berne, baroun] bald of hand, þe first conquerour of Ingland. *a* **1300** *E.E. Psalter* cxxxix. [xl] 2 Fra ivel man; Fra wike bieren outake me on-an. *c* **1325** *E.E. Allit. P.* A. 616 Where wystez þou euer any bourne abate. *Ibid.* B. 80 Boþe burnez & burdez, þe better and þe wers. *Ibid.* C. 302 Ay sykerly he herde þe bygge borne on his bak. *Ibid.* C. 340 He brakez vp þe buyrne, as bede hym oure lorde. *c* **1350** *Will. Palerne* 1708 Þer as burnes were busy bestes to hulde. **1377** LANGL. *P. Pl.* B. XI. 353 So heighe þere noither buirn [*v.r.* burn, barne, barn] ne beste may her briddes rechen. ? *a* **1400** *Morte Arth.* 1391 Than a ryche mane of Rome relyede to his byerns. *c* **1400** *Destr. Troy* VII. 2887 Ffairest be ferre of his fre buernes. *c* **1400** *Roland* 2237 He bad no bern be so bold upon mold. *c* **1400** *Rowland & Ot.* 1416 Thay brittenede many a beryn. *c* **1420** *Anturs of Arth.* x, Then this byrne braydet owte a brand, and the body bidus. *Ibid.* xiv, Quen birdus and birnys ar besy the aboute. *c* **1465** *Chevy Chase* lviii, A bolder barne was never born. *c* **1470** HENRY *Wallace* IV. 310 A squire come, and with him bernys four. **1515** *Scot. Field* 400 in *Chetham Misc.* II, There was never burne borne, that day bare him better. **1528** LYNDESAY *Dreme* 919 We saw a boustius berne cum ouir ye bent.

†ˈ**berner.** *Obs.* [a. OF. *berner* (*bernier*, *brenier*) feeder of hounds, huntsman, f. *bran* bran; cf. *brenerie* duty to provide bran to feed the hounds of the feudal lord; also med.L. *bernarius*, (explained by Hearne as keeper of a *berne* or 'bear').'] An attendant in charge of a pack of hounds.

a **1425** *Master of Game* (*MS. Bodl.* 546) Every man..saf the berners on foote and the chacechyens..sholde stonden afront..with roddes. **1601** F. TATE *Househ. Ord. Edw. II*, §57 (1876) 45, Fiftene buck houndes and one berner. The residew of the doges and the other berner shal be at the kinges costes.

Bernese (bɜːˈniːz), *a.* and *sb.* [f. *Bern(e)* (see below) + -ESE.] **A.** *adj.* Of or pertaining to Bern (or Berne), a city and canton of Switzerland, or its inhabitants. **B.** *sb.* A native or inhabitant of Bern(e); also *collect.* as *pl.*; also, one of a Swiss breed of large, long-coated, black dogs (in full ***Bernese mountain dog***).

1806 W. GUTHRIE *New Geogr. Gram.* (ed. 20) 533 The defeat of the Bernese was followed by the submission of nearly the whole of Switzerland. **1816** BYRON *Let.* 30 Sept. (1830) II. 13, I have lately been over all the Bernese Alps and their lakes. **1822** L. SIMOND *Switzerland* I. 218, I never saw such a proud looking set of men as the Bernese peasantry. **1863** *Miss Jemima's Swiss Jrnl.* 3 July (1963) ii. 49 Stuffed bears, suspended by some patriotic Bernese under the eaves of his chalet. **1904** J. M. STONE *Reform. & Renaiss.* viii. 315 If the Bernese gained a footing in Geneva. *Ibid.*, The Bernese army smashed all the statues of saints. **1935** *Hutchinson's Dog Encycl.* III. 1800/1 The Bernese Mountain Dog..is now generally considered the best-looking of all Mountain Dogs. **1936** *Dog World Ann.* 62 Swiss Mountain Dogs... The Bernese, from the Canton of Berne..is the only one with a long coat. **1939** *S.P.E. Tract* LII. 83 We speak of the Bernese Oberland.

†ˈ**bernet.** *Obs. Law.* In 1 bærnet, -nytte, 1–3 bernet. [OE. *bærnet*, f. *bærnan* to burn.] Burning, combustion; *hence*, the crime of arson. Retained as a technical archaism in the Laws of Henry I, whence in 17th c. law dictionaries.

c **1000** ÆLFRIC *Gen.* xxii. 9 He wudu ȝeloȝode.. to his sunu bærnytte. *c* **1000** *Cnut's Sec. Laws* §65 Husbryce and bærnet..is botleas. *c* **1150** *Leg. Hen. Primi* c. 1281 (Schmidt 444) Quaedam non possunt emendari, quae sunt: husbreche et bernet. [In COWELL and other Law Dicts, as an obs. term.]

†ˈ**bernete.** *Obs.* [ad. L. *vernetum* (through mediæval form *bernetum*).] ? Fallow ground ploughed in spring.

c **1420** *Pallad. on Husb.* IV. 48 Bernetes that beth made in Janyveer Goode tyme it is forto repete hem heer.

Bernician (bəˈnɪʃ(ɪ)ən), *sb.* and *a.* [f. med.L. *Bernicia* (cf. OE. *Beornice* inhabitants of Bernicia) + -AN.] **A.** *sb.* A native or inhabitant of Bernicia, an Anglian kingdom founded in the 6th cent. A.D., extending from the Tyne to the

Forth and eventually united with Deira to form Northumbria. **B.** *adj.* Of or pertaining to Bernicia or its inhabitants; spec. *Geol.*, designating the carboniferous limestone rocks of Northumberland and its borders.

1819 J. LINGARD *Hist. Engl.* I. ii. 89 The Bernicians submitted cheerfully to the good fortune of the son of Ælla. **1856** S. P. WOODWARD *Man. Mollusca* III. iii. 409 *(heading)* Geological table..Bernician. **1878** G. A. LEBOUR *Geol. Northumberland* i. 2 Lower carboniferous... Bernician series. *Ibid.* viii. 32 The Bernician Rocks... The series consists essentially of numerous beds of limestone. **1907** H. M. CHADWICK *Orig. Eng. Nation* vii. 182 These persons again were nearly related to the ancestors of the Bernician royal family. **1932** G. SHELDON *Transit. Roman Britain* viii. 134 A member of the Bernician royal house and a pretender to the throne. *Ibid.* 144 The ever-smouldering feud between Bernician and Deiran.

Bernkasteler (ˈbɜːnkɑːstlə(r), -æ-). [Ger.] Any of a group of Moselle wines produced in the villages of Bernkastel and Cues, of which the best known is ***Bernkasteler Doctor***.

[**1875** H. VIZETELLY *Wines of World* 51 Graach, Zeltinger, and the Berncastle wine, known locally as 'the doctor', all three of such excellent quality as to secure a couple of medals to their exhibitors.] **1891** in C. Ray *Compleat Imbiber* (1967) IX. 122 Moselle... Berncastler Doctor. **1920** G. SAINTSBURY *Notes on Cellar-Bk.* vi. 85 Nor did I ever much affect the loudly-trumpeted Berncastler Doktor. **1967** A. LICHINE *Encycl. Wines & Spirits* 365/1 Some Bernkastelers, and especially Bernkasteler Doctor, have a slight smoky under-taste.

†**Bernois(e.** *Obs.* [Fr.] = BERNESE *sb.*

1687 I. SPON *Hist. Geneva* II. 86 The Bernoises.. banished the Roman Catholick Religion from their City. **1761** G. KEATE *Short Acc. Geneva* 53 The Bernois coming to the Assistance of Geneva, drove away the Troops of the Duke and Bishop. **1832** W. LIDDIARD *Three Months' Tour* 88, I have already had more than one application from different Bernois, looking out..to get fares on their return to Berne.

bernoo, bernous, variants of BURNOUS.

Bernoulli (bəˈnuːlɪ). The name of a Swiss family which in the 17th and 18th centuries contained several eminent mathematicians and scientists, applied to various principles, theorems, etc., formulated by them (see quots.). Hence **Berˈnoullian** *a.*

B.'s formula and ***B.'s theorem*** in hydrodynamics were proposed by Daniel Bernoulli (1700–1782); ***B.'s numbers*** and ***B.'s theorem*** in statistics were proposed by Jacob (also known as James) Bernoulli (1654–1705).

1749 J. STIRLING *Differential Method* 94 The first series is not extended to those cases in which the first ordinate touches the curve, nor does Bernoulli's series extend to those cases wherein the last ordinate touches the curve. **1842** A. DE MORGAN *Diff. & Integr. Calculus* xiii. 247 The values of U, U′, &c. are called the numbers of Bernoulli; and though they do not follow a visibly regular law, yet the connexion between them is simple. *Ibid.* 248 The development of tan x by Bernoulli's numbers. **1865** I. TODHUNTER *Math. Theory Probability* vii. 71 In the fourth part of the *Ars Conjectandi* is the enunciation and investigation of what we now call *Bernoulli's theorem. Ibid.* xi. 226 Let x denote the age expressed in years; let ξ denote the number who survive at that age out of a given number who were born; let s denote the number of these survivors who have not had the small-pox... Daniel Bernoulli's formula then gives the value of s. **1875** *Encycl. Brit.* I. 114/1 The basis of Bernoulli's [*sic*] Theory of Pipes. **1876** *Messenger Math.* VI. 49 Bernoullian and Eulerian numbers. **1888** *Encycl. Brit.* XXIII. 14/1 Bernoullian numbers. **1920** L. BAIRSTOW *Appl. Aerodynamics* vi. 281 The simple form of Bernoulli's equation developed in the chapter on fluid motion may be applied separately to the two parts of streamlines which are separated by the actuator disc. **1922** GLAZEBROOK *Dict. Appl. Physics* I. 26/2 *Bernoulli's theorem.* Along any stream line in a liquid subject only to gravity $p + g\rho z + \frac{1}{2}\rho v^2$ = constant, p being the pressure at a point at a depth z below the plane of reference, ρ the density, and v the velocity. **1937** *Mind* XLVI. 488 The least rigid of these suggested conditions is that the series must be 'Bernoullian'.

bernston, obs. form of BRIMSTONE.

berob (bɪˈrɒb), *v.* [f. BE- 2 + ROB.] To rob.

1340 *Ayenb.* 39 Robberes..þet berobbeþ þe pilgrimes. *c* **1515** BARCLAY *Egloge* i. (1570) A ij/4 He hath small reason that hath a hood more fine And would for malice berob thee here of thine. **1596** SPENSER *F.Q.* I. viii. 42 That of your selfe ye thus berobbed arre. **1855** SINGLETON *Virgil* II. 82 After ..Achilles him Berobbed of life.

‖**Beroe** (ˈbɛrəʊiː). *Zool.* [a. L. *Beroë*, Gr. βερόη, name of a daughter of the mythical Oceanus.] A genus of small, gelatinous, marine animals classed by Huxley among the Cœlenterata; they swim freely in the sea, and are phosphorescent at night.

1769 *Phil. Trans.* LIX. 144 The beroe is a marine animal found on our coasts. **1835** KIRBY *Hab. & Inst. Anim.* I. vi. 198 [The gelatines] as well as the beroe, are said to form part of the food of the whale. **1883** *Harper's Mag.* Jan. 181/2 The beroes are perhaps the most familiar.

†**beˈrogue,** *v. Obs.* [f. BE- 5 c + ROGUE.] *trans.* To call (one) a rogue, to abuse.

1673 CLEVELAND *Wks.* (1687) 236 Kick a poor Lacquey, and berogue the Cook. **1682** *2nd Plea Nonconf.* 45 To hear a zealous Ignorant be-rogue and damn the House-Preachers. *a* **1733** NORTH *Exam.* I. ii. ¶ 155. 117 After these Intrigues, who wonders that Hayns..should be so berogued.

beroll, be-Roscius, berouged, beround, berow, etc.: see BE- *pref.*

beronnen, -yn, pa. pple. of BERUN *v. Obs.*

berour, obs. form of BEARER.

berowe, variant of BERWE, *Obs.*, a grove.

berrage, obs. form of BEVERAGE.

berral, berrer, obs. ff. BERYL, BEARER.

berret, berretta, obs. ff. BERET, BIRETTA.

berrghe, berrȝhe, variants of BERGH, *Obs.*

†**ˈberrhless.** *Obs.* [:—OE. **berȝels* (cf. *recless*:—*récels*), f. *berȝen*: see BERGH *v.*] Salvation.

c **1200** ORMIN 7028 þatt nittenn eche lifess bræd Till þeȝȝre sawle berrhless.

berrie. *Obs.* Also berie. [App. related to OE. *beru, berwes,* ME. BERWE grove, mod. *Bere* in *Beere Regis*, etc.; but Harrington's form is not phonetically explicable.] See quot.

1591 HARRINGTON *Ariosto* XLI. lvii, The cell..had..Upon the western side a grove or berrie [*ed.* **1634** berie; *Ital.* bosco].

berried (ˈbɛrɪd), *a.* [f. BERRY *sb.* + -ED².]

1. Having or bearing berries.

1794 GISBORNE *Walks Forest* (1796) 112 While the keen thrush the berried twig invades. **1860** RUSKIN *Mod. Paint.* V. VI. x. 99 The berried shrubs. **1871** M. COLLINS *Mrq. & Merch.* II. ii. 42 Red-berried holly.

2. Formed as or consisting of a berry; baccate.

1824 *Blackw. Mag.* XV. 169 Bushes hung with berried fruits. **1830** LINDLEY *Nat. Syst. Bot.* 130 Fruit either berried or membranous. **1851** BALFOUR *Bot.* §550 Baccate or berried is applied to all pulpy fruits.

3. Bearing eggs; 'in berry.' Cf. BERRY *sb.*¹ 3.

1868 *Macm. Mag. Nov.* 18 Lobster-sauce..improved by 'berried hens,' that is by female lobsters full of eggs.

†**ˈberried,** *ppl. a. Obs.* Forms: 4 **beryd, berid,** 6 **beryed, -ied, buried, (barrowid).** [f. BERRY *v.*¹ + -ED¹.] Beaten; threshed; trodden, beaten as a path.

1382 WYCLIF *Num.* xx. 19 Bi the beryd [**1388** comynli usid] weye we shulen goon. —— *Jer.* xviii. 15 Thei go bi them in a weye not berid [**1388** not trodun]. **1557** *Wills & Inv. N.C.* I. 158 In beryed corn in the barne viijd. **1569** *Richmond. Wills* (1853) 218 Haver barrowid and unbarrowed. **1570** *Wills & Inv. N.C.* I. 341 Otes buried eight lode . xxs.—in vnberied whete xiiij thraves . xxs.

†**ˈberrier.** *Obs.* [f. BERRY *v.* + -ER¹.] A thresher; a barnman.

1573 *Wills & Inv. N.C.* 399 Iij plewmen, j berryer, & j hird. **1721** BAILEY *Berrier*, a Thresher (Country Word).

berrord, obs. form of BEARHERD.

berrugate (bɛrʊˈgeɪt). [f. Sp. *verruga* wart. Cf. VERRUGA.] A fish, *Verrugato pacificus*, found on the Pacific coast of Central America, used as a food.

1898 JORDAN & EVERMANN *Fishes N. & Mid. Amer.* III. 2858 Abundant at Panama, where it is known as *Berrugate.*

berry (ˈbɛrɪ), *sb.*¹ Forms: 1 **beriae, berie, beriȝe, berȝe,** 2–6 **berie,** 3–6 **bery(e,** (4 **burie**), 6–7 **berrie,** 6– **berry.** [Found, with some variety of form, in all the Teutonic langs.: with OE. *berie* wk. fem., cf. ON. *ber* (Da. *bær*, Sw. *bär*), OS. *beri* (in *wînberi*), MDu. *bêre*, OHG. *beri* str. neut., MHG. *ber* and *bere* neut. and fem., mod.Ger. *beere* fem. These point to an OGer. **bazjo-m*, as a byform of **basjo-m*, whence Goth *basi* neut. (in *weinabasi* 'grape'). The *s* type is also preserved in MDu. *beze*, mod.Du. *bes*, also MDu. and mod.Du. *bezie* fem. The fem. forms Du. *bēzie* and OE. *berie* answer to an OTeut. extended form **basjôn-*, **bazjôn-*. The ulterior history is uncertain: **bazjo-* has been conjecturally referred to **bazo-z* BARE (q.v.), as if a bare or uncovered fruit, also to the root represented by Skr. *bhas-* to eat.]

1. a. Any small globular, or ovate juicy fruit, not having a stone; in OE. chiefly applied to the grape; in mod. popular use, embracing the gooseberry, raspberry, bilberry, and their congeners, as well as the strawberry, mulberry, fruit of the elder, rowan-tree, cornel, honeysuckle, buckthorn, privet, holly, mistletoe, ivy, yew, crowberry, barberry, bearberry, potato, nightshade, bryony, laurel, mezereon, and many exotic shrubs; also sometimes the bird-cherry or 'hag-berry' (which is a stone-fruit), the haw, and hip of the rose; *spec.* in Scotland and north of England, it means the gooseberry.

c **1000** ÆLFRIC *Deut.* xxiii. 24 Gif tu gange binnan þines freondes wineard, et þæra berȝena. *c* **1000** *Sax. Leechd.* III. 114 Nym winberian þe beoþ acende æfter oþre beriȝian. *a* **1225** *Ancr. R.* 276 Breres bereð rosen & berien. *c* **1250** *Gen. & Ex.* 2062 [A win-tre] blomede, and siðen bar ðe beries ripe. *c* **1386** CHAUCER *Prol.* 207 His palfrey was as broune as is a bery. **1387** TREVISA *Higden* Rolls Ser. IV. 121 þe juse of grapes and of buries [*mori*]. **1470–85** MALORY *Arthur* XVI. x. (Globe) 385 A strong black horse, blacker than a bery. *a* **1500** *Songs & Carols 15th C.* 85 Ivy berith berys black. **1590** SHAKS. *Mid. N.* III. ii. 211 Two louely berries molded on one stem. **1667** MILTON *P.L.* v. 307 For dinner savourie fruits..Berrie or Grape. **1793** SOUTHEY *Lyric Poems* II. 149 The cluster'd berries bright Amid the holly's gay green leaves. **1842** TENNYSON *Œnone* 100 Garlanding the gnarled boughs With bunch and berry and flower. **1883** *Birmingh. Weekly Post* 11 Aug. 4/7 Last year the heaviest berry shown scaled 31 dwt.

b. *loosely.* A coffee 'bean.'

1712 POPE *Rape Lock* III. 106 The berries crackle, and the mill turns round.

c. *slang* (*U.S.*). A dollar; also (in *U.K.*), a pound. Usu. in *pl.* Hence ***the berries***: an excellent person or thing; 'the cat's whiskers'.

1918 H. C. WITWER *From Baseball to Boches* IV. ii. 147 When..I go back to baseball, I can drag down six thousand berries a year. **1920** 'B. L. STANDISH' *Man on First* 127 It don't take the shine off your little performance. You were there with the berries. **1922** S. LEWIS *Babbitt* vii. 103 A fellow that..pulls down fifteen thousand berries a year! **1925** H. FOSTER *Trop. Tramp Tourists* 300 You think you're the berries, don't you? Well, you might have been once, but you're a flat-tire these days! **1926** *S.P.E. Tract* XXIV. 120 *That's the berries*, that's just right. **1934** *Humorist* 26 May 482/1 An attachment worth ten thousand berries in the open market. **1936** J. DOS PASSOS *Big Money* 43 He had what was left of the three hundred berries Hedwig coughed up. **1943** WYNDHAM LEWIS *Let.* 9 Nov. (1963) 369 No intelligent book *could* get accepted by a N.Y. publisher, except perhaps a little publisher, who would give you a maximum of a thousand berries.

2. *Bot.* A many-seeded inferior pulpy fruit, the seeds of which are, when mature, scattered through the pulp; called also *bacca.* In this sense, many of the fruits popularly so called, are not berries: the grape, gooseberry and currants, the bilberry, mistletoe berry, and potato fruit, are true berries; but, botanically, the name also includes the cucumber, gourd, and even the orange and lemon.

1809 SIR J. SMITH *Bot.* 284 The simple many-seeded berries of the Vine, Gooseberry, &c. The Orange and Lemon are true Berries, with a thick coat. **1880** GRAY *Bot. Text-bk.* vii. §2. 299 The Berry..comprises all simple fruits in which the pericarp is fleshy throughout.

3. One of the eggs in the roe of a fish; also, the eggs of a lobster. A hen lobster carrying her eggs is said to be ***in berry*** or *berried.*

1768 TRAVIS in *Penny Cycl.* II. 513/2 Hen lobsters are found in berry at all times of the year. **1876** *Fam. Herald* 9 Dec. 95/1 A large specimen [of lobster] will yield from five to eight ounces of 'berry.'

4. *Comb.* and *attrib.*, as ***berry-bush, -pie, -tree; berry-bearing, -brown, -like, -shaped*** adjs.; **berry alder, berry-bearing alder,** a shrub (*Rhamnus frangula*) = Alder Buckthorn; **berry-button,** a berry-shaped button; **berry wax,** wax obtained from the wax-berry (*Myrica* spp.), used for making candles and polishing floors (cf. *bayberry-wax* in quot. 1769 s.v. BAYBERRY 2).

1863 PRIOR *Plant-n.* 20 *Berry-alder, a buckthorn.. distinguished from them [the alders] by bearing berries. **1742** W. ELLIS *Timber-tree* II. xxiv. 140 A bacciferous, or *berry-bearing, Tree or Shrub. **1785** COWPER *Task* v. 82 Berry-bearing thorns That feed the thrush. **1796** W. H. MARSHALL *Planting* II. 313 Frangula, or Berry-bearing Alder. **1933** *Jrnl. R. Hort. Soc.* LVIII. 400 *Wilsonii* with leaves as large as *Marnockii*, but dull green and spiny, also berry-bearing. **1611** *Art Venerie* 96 He seemed fayre tweene blacke and *berrie brounde. **1820** SCOTT *Abbot* xvi, The Friars of Fail drank *berry-brown ale. **1818** —— *Rob Roy* vi, 'Pleased wi' the freedom o' the *berry-bushes.' **1702** *Lond Gaz.* No. 3783/4 A..Stuff Wastcoat with black and red *Berry-Buttons. **1864** *Monthly Even. Readings* May 161 *Berry-like galls are formed on the peduncles. **1836–9** TODD *Cycl. Anat. & Phys.* II 485/2 *Berry-shaped corpuscles seem to be appended. **1398** TREVISA *Barth. De P.R.* XVII. c. (1495) 666 The fruyte of the wilde *bery tree. **1897** EDMONDS & MARLOTH *Elem. Bot. S. Afr.* xvii. 169 The genus *Myrica*, of which *M. cordifolia* and others supply the *berry-wax. **1913** R. MARLOTH *Flora S. Afr.* I. 133 The layer of wax on the berries of some species [of *Myrica*] is so considerable that it is technically exploited. The farmers boil the berries with water, strain the hot mixture and allow the melted wax to solidify. The *berry wax* (myrica wax) is of a pale greenish colour and considerably harder than beeswax.

ˈberry, *sb.*² *Obs.* exc. *dial.* [f. OE. *beorȝ* hill: a variant of BARROW *sb.*¹ (While the nom. gave ME. *beruh, berw, barw, barow*, the dat. *beorȝe*, with palatalized *ȝ*, gave *berȝe, beryhe, berye.*)] A mound, hillock, or barrow.

1205 LAY. 12311 Vnder ane berhȝe. **1393** LANGL. *P. Pl.* B. v. 589 Thanne shaltow blenche at a berghe. *a* **1553** UDALL *Royster D.* II. iii. 36 Heigh derie derie, Trill on the berie. *c* **1563** *Thersytes* in *Four O. Plays* (1848) 79 We shall make merye and synge tyrle on the berye. **1613** W. BROWNE *Brit. Past.* I. ii. (1772) I. 56 Piping on thine oaten reede Upon this little berry (some ycleep A hillocke). **1807** VANCOUVER *Agric. Devon* (1813) 195 Removing the potatoes to the caves, heaps..ricks, or berrys (for by all such terms they are known in this country).

¶ It is doubtful whether the quotation belongs to this or to BERRY *sb.*³.

a **1700** DRYDEN *Ovid's Art Love* I. 103 The theatres are berries for the fair, Like ants on molehills thither they repair.

† **'berry**, *sb.*³ *Obs.* Forms: 5 bery, 6 beery, 6–7 berrie, berry. [See BURROW.]

1. A (rabbit's) burrow. Hence, the spec. name for a company of rabbits.

1486 *Bk. St. Albans* F vi, A Bery of Conyis. **1519** HORMAN *Vulg.* 283 b, I haue nede of a feret, to let into this beery to styrt out the conies. **1585** *Mod. Curiosities Art & Nat.*, To make rabbets come out of their berries without a ferret. **1613** PURCHAS *Pilgr.* IX. vii. 862 It [the penguin]..feeds on fish and grass and harbors in berries. **1685** R. BURTON *Eng. Emp. Amer.* xiii. 165 Musk-Rats who live in holes and Berries like Rabbits.

2. *transf.* An excavation; a mine in besieging.

1598 SYLVESTER *Du Bartas* (1608) 514 Till one strict berrie, till one winding cave, Become the fight-field of two armies.

† **'berry**, *sb.*⁴ *Obs.* [Cf. BIRR: perh. f. BERRY *v.*¹; or, since found only in Florio and Cotgrave, an erroneous form.] A gust or blast (of wind).

1598 FLORIO, *Biffera*..a whirlewind, a gust or berry of wind. **1611** —— *Folata di uento*..a gaile or berrie of winde. **1611** COTGR., *Tourbillon de vent*..a gust, flaw, berrie of wind.

'berry, *v.*¹ *Obs.* exc. *dial.* Also bery, bury. [ME. *berien*, *bery*, ad. ON. *berja* to strike, beat, thresh = OHG. *berjan*, MHG. *berren*, *beren*, *bern*; repr. in OE. only by pa. pple. *ȝebered*. Cogn. w. L. *ferīre* to strike.]

1. *trans.* To beat, thrash.

a **1225** *Ancr. R.* 188 Þer ȝe schulen iseon bunsen [*v.r.* berien] ham mit tes deofles bettles. **1808** JAMIESON, *Berry*, to beat; as to berry a bairn, to beat a child.

2. To thresh (corn, etc.). See BERRIED *ppl. a.*

1483 *Cath. Angl.* 29 Bery..*vbi* to thresche. **1641** BEST *Farm. Bks.* (1856) 142 Thrashers that bury by quarter-tale. **1691** RAY *N. Country Wds.*, *Berry*, to thresh, i.e. to beat out the berry or grain of the corn. **1808** JAMIESON, *Berry*, to thrash corn, *Roxb.*, *Dumfr.*

3. To beat (a path, etc.). See BERRIED *ppl. a.*

berry ('bɛrɪ), *v.*² [f. BERRY *sb.*¹; cf. to APPLE.]

1. *intr.* To come into berry; to fill or swell.

1865 E. BURRITT *Walk Land's End* 402 The wheat, oats and barley..were now berrying full and plump. **1873** BLACKMORE *Cradock N.* xxx. (1883) 167 The late bees were buzzing around him though the linden had berried.

2. To go a berrying, i.e. gathering berries.

a **1871** MISS SEDGWICK in *Life & Lett.* 44, I went with herds of school-girls nutting and berrying.

berry, obs. form of BURY.

† **berry-block**. *Obs.* ? A beating of the block, a missing of the thing intended.

1603 *Philotus* clv, Haue I not maid a berrie block, That hes for Jennie maryit Jock?

† **'berrying**, *vbl. sb.*¹ *Obs.* In 7 burying. [f. BERRY *v.*¹ + -ING¹.] The threshing (of corn).

1641 BEST *Farm. Bks.* (1856) 132 For Buryinge of Corne.

Hence **berrying stead**, a threshing-floor. BAILEY 1721.

'berrying, *vbl. sb.*² [f. BERRY *v.*² + -ING¹.] A gathering of berries. Also *attrib.*

1884 *Lisbon (Dakota) Star* 25 July, On a berrying and picnic excursion.

berryless ('bɛrɪlɪs), *a.* [f. BERRY *sb.*¹ + -LESS.] Without producing berries; not berried or furnished with berries.

1887 *Sat. Rev.* 30 Apr. 624 The female plant..berryless, may be said to have suffered a grass-widowhood of some eighty years. **1924** *Glasgow Herald* 3 Jan. 6 Berryless holly. **1942** H. J. MASSINGHAM *Field Fellowship* xii. 110 A bleached and berryless powder with the courtesy title of flour.

bers, *v. impers.*, var. form from BIR to behove.

‖ **bersagliere** (ˌbersaʎ'ʎɛre). Usu. in pl. **bersaglieri** (-i). [It., f. *bersaglio* target, mark.] A rifleman or sharpshooter in the Italian army.

1862 CROWN PRINCESS OF PRUSSIA *Let.* 8 Nov. in R. Fulford *Dearest Mama* (1968) 129 As one is not safe from Banditti—General La Marmora gave us an escort of Bersaglieri and Gendarmes. **1875** *Encycl. Brit.* II. 612/2 The Italian army consists of 80 regiments of the line, 10 of *bersaglieri* (riflemen), [etc.]. **1883** *Daily News* 7 Sept. 3/1 The same war cry would resound from a battalion of dark-plumed Bersaglieri as they dashed up a bank at their peculiar pace. **1929** HEMINGWAY *Farewell to Arms* viii. 47 The drivers..wearing red fezzes..were bersaglieri.

b. *attrib.* and *Comb.* **bersaglieri hat**, a hat with a dark plume of cock's feathers, as worn by the bersaglieri.

1875 *Encycl. Brit.* II. 613/1, 4 *bersaglieri* battalions. **1946** KOESTLER *Thieves in Night* 10 About half of them wore.. Bersaglieri hats which made their faces look even more adolescent.

† **berse**. *Obs.* [a. OF. *berche*, (also *barce*, Cotgr.) in same sense. Cf. *berser* to shoot.] A small species of ordnance, formerly often used at sea. = BASE *sb.*⁶

1549 *Compl. Scot.* vi. 41 Mak reddy ȝour cannons..bersis, doggis, double bersis.

berseel, berselet: see BERCEL, -ET.

berserk, -er ('bɜːsɜːk, -ə(r); as adj., also pronounced bə'sɜːk, bə'zɜːk). Also **berserkar, -ir**; bersark. Cf. BARESARK. [Icel. *berserkr*, acc. *berserk*, pl. *-ir*, of disputed etymology; Vigfusson and Fritzner show that it was probably = 'bear-sark,' 'bear-coat.'] A wild Norse warrior of great strength and ferocious courage, who fought on the battle-field with a frenzied fury known as the 'berserker rage'; often a lawless bravo or freebooter. Also *fig.* and *attrib.* Now usu. as *adj.*, frenzied, furiously or madly violent; esp. in phr. ***to go berserk***.

1822 SCOTT *Pirate* Note B, The berserkars were so called from fighting without armour. **1837** EMERSON *Misc.* 85 Out of terrible Druids and Berserkers, come at last Alfred and Shakspeare. **1839** CARLYLE *Chartism* (1858) 19 Let no man awaken it, this same Berserkir rage! **1851** KINGSLEY *Yeast* i. 16 Yelling, like Berserk fiends, among the frowning tombstones. **1861** PEARSON *Early & Mid. Ages Eng.* 430 Mere brotherhood in arms..did not distinguish the civilized man from the berserkar. **1867** H. KINGSLEY *Silcote* I. xii. 136 With her kindly, uncontrollable vivacity, in the brisk winter air she became more 'berserk' as she went on. **1879** E. GOSSE *Lit. N. Europe* 166 He was a dangerous old literary bersark to the last. **1887** E. C. DAWSON *Bp. Hannington* v. 57 He..was filled with a Berserk rage and thirst for retribution. **1908** KIPLING *Diversity of Creatures* (1917) 264 You went Berserk. I've read all about it in *Hypatia*..you'll probably be liable to fits of it all your life. **1940** *Chicago Daily Tribune* 20 Nov. 10/3 America goes berserk. *Ibid.*, The recent addition of the word 'berserk', as a synonym for crackpot behaviour, to the slang of the young and untutored... American stenographers..are telling one another not to be 'berserk'. **1944** 'P. QUENTIN' *Puzzle for Puppets* xvii. 121 Edwina [*sc.* an elephant], had gone berserk. **1961** G. SMITH *Business of Loving* iii. 124 Hammond converted and Shallerton came back as if berserk. *Ibid.* 132, I think Ken Heppel will go berserk. **1962** P. BRICKHILL *Deadline* xviii. 213, I went berserk, kicking his head again and again. *Ibid.* 214 In that berserk mood I think I could have bent an iron bar. **1964** J. SYMONS *End of S. Grundy* I. i. 27 If you have chaps like old Sol going berserk, it's enough to break up any party.

berserkly (bɜː'sɜːklɪ), *adv.* [f. BERSERK + -LY².] In a berserk manner; madly.

1963 *Economist* 28 Dec. 1318/2 It is berserkly dangerous. **1967** 'C. FRANKLIN' *Death in East* ii. 27 The headlamps illuminated a tree which seemed to be leaping berserkly towards her.

berskin, obs. form of BEARSKIN.

c **1350** *Will. Palerne* 1735 In þat oþer bere-skyn be-wrapped william þanne. **1386** CHAUCER *Knts. T.* (Lansd. MS.) 1284 He hadde a berskinne cole-blake for olde [*Corpus* berskynne, *other MSS.* beres skyn].

berstel, obs. form of BRISTLE.

berst-en, obs. form of BURST and BREST.

† **bersuell**. *Mil. Obs.* [a. OF. *berçuel*, *bersuel*, in same sense.] A disposition of fighting-men in a triangular phalanx with the apex towards the enemy. (Called also in OF. *coing*, i.e. wedge.)

1489 CAXTON *Faytes of A.* I. xxiv. 74 In a manere of a tryangle that men called at that bersuell.

berte, variant of BIRT, *Obs.* a fish.

bertes, Sc. var. BRETASCE, -ACHE; cf. BARTIZAN.

berth (bɜːθ), *sb.* Also 6–7 byrth, 6–9 birth. [A nautical term of uncertain origin: found first in end of 16th c. Most probably a derivative of BEAR *v.* in some of its senses: see esp. sense 37, quot. 1627, which suggests that *berth* is = 'bearing off, room-way made by bearing-off'; cf. also *bear off* in 26 b. The early spellings *byrth*, *birth*, coincide with those of BIRTH '*bearing* of offspring, bringing forth,' but it is very doubtful whether the nautical use can go back to a time when that word had the general sense 'bearing'; it looks more like a new formation on *bear*, without reference to the existing *birth*.

(Of other derivations suggested, an OE. **beorȝþ*, **beorhþ* 'protection, defence, shelter' (see BARTH), and Icel. *byrði* 'the board, i.e. side of a ship' (see BERTH *v.*²), do not well account for the original sense 'sea-room.' The sense is perhaps better explained by supposing *berth* to be a transposition of north. dial. *breith* = *breadth*; but of this historical evidence is entirely wanting.)]

1. *Naut.* 'Convenient sea-room, or a fit distance for ships under sail to keep clear, so as not to fall foul on one another' (Bailey 1730), or run upon the shore, rocks, etc. Now, chiefly in phrases, ***to give a good, clear,*** or (usually since 1800) ***wide berth to, keep a wide berth of***: to keep well away from, steer quite clear of. Also *transf.* and *fig.*

1622 R. HAWKINS *Voy. S. Sea* (1847) 117 There lyeth a poynt of the shore a good byrth off, which is dangerous. **1626** CAPT. SMITH *Accid. Yng. Seamen* 24 Watch bee vigilant to keepe your berth to windward. **1627** —— *Seaman's Gram.* xiii. 60 Run a good berth ahead of him. **1740** WOODROOFE in Hanway *Trav.* (1762) I. 274 It is necessary to give the..bank a good birth. **1793** SMEATON *Edystone L.* 193 Giving the Lighthouse a clear birth of 50 fathoms to the southward. **1829** SCOTT *Demonol.* x. 383 Giving the apparent phantom what seamen call a wide berth. **1854** THACKERAY *Newcomes* II. 150, I recommend you to keep a wide berth of me, sir. **1870** MORRIS *Earthly Par.* I. I. 17 To keep the open sea And give to warring lands a full wide berth.

2. *Naut.* 'Convenient sea-room for a ship that rides at anchor' (Philips 1706); 'sufficient space wherein a ship may swing round at the length of her moorings' (Falconer).

1658 PHILLIPS, *Berth*, convenient room at Sea to moor a Ship in. **1692** *Capt. Smith's Seaman's Gram.* I. xvi. 75 *A Birth*, a convenient space to moor a Ship in. **1696** [PHILLIPS has both *Berth* as in **1658** and *Birth* as in Smith.] **1721** BAILEY, *Birth* and *Berth* [as above]. **1769–89** FALCONER *Dict. Marine*, *Evitee*, a birth [expl. as above]. **1781** *Westm. Mag.* IX. 327 Perceiving neither the Isis nor Diana making any signs to follow, though both of them lay in clear births for so doing [cf. *clear berth* in 1]. **1854** G. B. RICHARDSON *Univ. Code* v. (ed. 12) 423 You have given our ship a foul berth, or brought up in our hawse. **1858** in *Merc. Mar. Mag.* V. 226 The ship..may..choose her anchorage by giving either shore a berth of a couple of cables' length.

3. Hence, 'A convenient place to moor a ship in' (Phillips); the place where a ship lies when at anchor or at a wharf.

1706 PHILLIPS, *Birth* and *Berth* [see above]. **1731** BAILEY, *Birth* and *Berth* [as in Phillips]. **1754** FIELDING *Voy. Lisbon*, Before we could come to our former anchoring place, or berth, as the captain called it. **1793** SMEATON *Edystone L.* § 266 We let go an anchor and warped the buss to her proper birth. **1801** NELSON in Nicolas *Disp.* (1845) IV. 366 That the squadron may be anchored in a good berth. **1879** CASTLE *Law of Rating* 75 Certain berths for the use of steamers.

4. a. *Naut.* 'A proper place on board a ship for a mess to put their chests, etc.' (Phillips); whence, 'The room or apartment where any number of the officers, or ship's company, mess and reside' (Smyth, *Sailor's Word-bk.*).

1706 PHILLIPS s.v. *Birth*, Also the proper Place a-board for a Mess to put their chests, etc., is call'd *the Birth of that Mess.* **1748** SMOLLETT *Rod Rand.* xxiv. (Rtldg.) 63 When he had shown me their berth (as he called it) I was filled with astonishment and horror. **1836** MARRYAT *Midsh. Easy* x. 30 The first day in which he had entered the midshipmen's berth, and was made acquainted with his messmates.

b. *fig.* (*Naut.*) Proper place (for a thing).

1732 DE FOE, etc. *Tour Gt. Brit.* (1769) I. 147 For the squaring and cutting out of every Piece, and placing it in its proper Byrth (so they call it) in the Ship that is in Building. **1758** J. BLAKE *Mar. Syst.* 6 A hammock..shall be delivered him, and a birth assigned to hang it in.

c. *transf.* An allotted or assigned place in a barracks; a 'place' allotted in a coach or conveyance.

c **1813** MRS. SHERWOOD *Stories Ch. Catech.* xiv. 115 Fanny Bell's berth was in one corner of the barracks. *Ibid.* 116 Kitty Spence was in her berth, playing at cards with her husband and two other men. **1816** SCOTT *Antiq.* i, The first comer hastens to secure the best berth in the coach.

5. a. *Naut.* A situation or office on board a ship, or (in sailors' phrase) elsewhere.

1720 DE FOE *Capt. Singleton* x. (Bohn) 130 Going to Barbadoes to get a birth, as the sailors call it. **1755** MAGENS *Insurances* II. 115 When Sailors..are discharged in Foreign Parts, and do not meet with another Birth there. **1840** R. DANA *Bef. Mast* xxii. 65, I wished..to qualify myself for an officer's berth. *Ibid.* xxviii. 97 He left us to take the berth of second mate on board the Ayacucho. **1876** C. GEIKIE *Life in Woods* x. 177 He hoped to get a good berth on one of the small lake steamers.

b. *transf.* A situation, a place, an appointment. (Usually a 'good' or 'comfortable' one.)

1778 MISS BURNEY *Evelina* xvi. (1784) 103 You have a good warm birth here. **1781** MRS. DELANY *Corr.* (1860) III. 51, I think I could find out a berth (the sea-phrase) for a chaplain. **1788** T. JEFFERSON *Corr.* (1830) 412 Both will prefer their present births. **1850** MRS. STOWE *Uncle Tom* iv. 26 I'll do the very best I can in gettin' Tom a good berth.

6. a. *Naut.* A sleeping-place in a ship; a long box or shelf on the side of the cabin for sleeping.

1796 T. JEFFERSON *Corr.* (1830) 339 Better pleased with sound sleep and a warmer birth below it. **1809** BYRON *Lines to Hodgson* iii, Passengers their berths are clapt in. **1842** T. MARTIN in *Fraser's Mag.* Dec., Just in time to secure the only sleeping-berth in the..steam-packet.

b. A sleeping-place of the same kind in a railway carriage or elsewhere.

1806 Z. M. PIKE *Acc. Exped. Mississippi* (1810) 81 We returned to the chief's lodge, and found a birth provided for each of us. **1838** *Amer. Railroad Jrnl.* VII. 328 If you travel in the night you go to rest in a pleasant berth. **1885** *Harper's Mag.* Apr. 698/2 The traveller..goes to sleep in his Pullman berth. **1885** *Weekly Times* 2 Oct. 14/2 In the kitchens..are a couple of berths reached by a ladder. **1967** *Gloss. Caravan Terms (B.S.I.)* 3 A caravan with two double beds, or one double and two singles, is a four-berth caravan. **1968** *Globe & Mail* (Toronto) 17 Feb. 33 (Advt.), First Class all-inclusive fare, including lower berth and all meals.

7. *Comb.* **berth-boards**, ? the partitions dividing berths in a ship; **berth-deck**, the deck on which the passengers' berths are arranged; **berth and space** (see quot.).

1833 RICHARDSON *Merc. Mar. Arch.* 7 The distance from the moulding edge of one floor to the moulding edge of the next floor is called the birth and space, and is the room occupied by two timbers, the floor, and the first futtock. **1853** KANE *Grinnell Exp.* xxvi. (1856) 213 This condensation is now very troublesome, sweating over the roof and berth-boards. **1856** OLMSTED *Slave States* 550 Scattering the passengers on the berth deck.

berth (bɜːθ), *v.*¹ Also 6 byrth, 7 birth. [f. prec. sb.]

1. a. *trans.* To moor or place (a ship) in a suitable position. Also *refl.* of the ship or sailors.

1667 PEPYS *Diary* 30 June, The 'Henery'..berthed himself so well as no pilot could ever have done better. **1673** *Camden Soc. Misc.* (1881) 27 We..anchored againe, and

birth'd our selves in our anchoring posture agreed on. **1871** *Daily News* 30 June, There was no dry dock..where the monster ship could be berthed and cleaned.

b. *intr.* (for *refl.*) said of the ship.

1868 MACGREGOR *Voyage Alone* 57 The Rob Roy glided past the pier and smoothly berthed upon a great mud bank.

2. a. *trans.* To allot a berth or sleeping-place to (a person), to furnish with a berth. Usually in *passive.*

1845 STOCQUELER *Handbk. Brit. India* (1854) 81 A general cabin, where two others are berthed. **1869** *Daily News* 12 June, The lower deck, where the officers and crew are berthed. **1876** DAVIS *Polaris Exp.* v. 122 Joe and Hans, with their families, were brought down and berthed below.

b. *intr.* To occupy a berth or berths.

1886 STEVENSON *Kidnapped* vii. 61 The round-house, where he berthed and served. **1902** *Westm. Gaz.* 13 Sept. 6/2 The accommodation is very simple, consisting of berthing in two tiers in the women's ward, and feeding and living in a separate saloon.

3. To provide with a situation or 'place.'

1865 LESLIE & TAYLOR *Sir J. Reynolds* II. viii. 365 Comfortably berthed in the City Chamberlainship. **1885** *Manch. Exam.* 14 Nov. 5/1 All four are berthed; not a man of the Fourth Party is left out.

berth, *v.*² Also 6 byrth. [perh. f. Icel. *byrði* board or side of a ship.] To board, cover or make up with boards. (Chiefly in Ship-building.) Hence **berthed** *ppl. a.* boarded. See BERTHING².

1574 R. SCOT *Hop Gard.* (1578) 52 The chynkes creuises, and open ioyntes of your Loftes being not close byrthed, will deuoure the seedes of them. **1627** CAPT. SMITH *Seaman's Gram.* ii. 5 When you haue berthed or brought her vp to the planks. *c* **1850** *Rudim. Navig.* (Weale) 96 To berth up. A term generally used for working up a topside or bulkhead with board or thin plank.

berth(e, obs. form of BIRTH.

bertha¹, **berthe** ('bɜːθə, bɜːθ). [a. F. *berthe*, englished as *bertha*, from the proper name, F. *Berthe*, Eng. *Bertha*.] A deep falling collar, usually of lace, attached to the top of a low-necked dress, and running all round the shoulders.

1842 C. RIDLEY *Let.* in Ridley *Cecilia* (1958) ix. 109, I shall be very glad..of the bugle flowers and bertha and rosettes. **1842** *Illustr. Lond. News* 24 Dec. 525/1 The berthe had a double row of point d'Argentan. *a* **1856** ALB. SMITH *Sketches of Day* Ser. I. III. i, She dresses by the fashion books, believing berthe and birth to be words of equal worth in the world. **1869** *Athenæum* 18 Dec. 826 A Bertha of ancient point lace. **1881** MISS BRADDON *Asphodel* xix. 208 Neat laced berthas fitting close to modestly-covered shoulders.

Bertha² ('bɜːθə). [Named after Frau *Bertha* Krupp von Bohlen und Halbach, owner of the Krupp steel works in Germany from 1903 to 1943.] Soldiers' name for a German gun or mortar of large bore, used in the war of 1914–18; freq. *Big Bertha.*

1914 *Scotsman* 30 Oct. 9/6 This mortar of 42 centimeters was made at the Krupp works, and for this reason the Germans have baptised it '*Bertha—die fleissige*' (Bertha, the Zealous), Bertha being the name of Madame Krupp von Bohlen. *Ibid.*, 'Bertha' is not the delicate plaything that it has sometimes been represented to be, and the maximum of 150 shells that they say can be fired from the gun is below the truth. **1918** *Sphere* 20 July 48/2 Big Bertha spoke for the first time on March 23, and at the sound of her voice Paris was intensely surprised. **1958** HAYWARD & HARARI tr. *Pasternak's Dr. Zhivago* I. iv. 111 That's a Bertha, a German sixteen-inch.

berthage ('bɜːθɪdʒ). [f. BERTH *v.*¹ + -AGE.]

a. Accommodation for mooring vessels, harbourage.

1881 *Daily News* 25 Jan. 5/8 The new sea wall..provides berthage for as many as thirty vessels at once.

b. The dues payable for mooring a vessel.

1893 in *Funk's Stand. Dict.*

berthen, obs. form of BURDEN *sb.*

berther ('bɜːθə(r)). [f. BERTH *v.*¹ + -ER¹.]

1867 SMYTH *Sailor's Wrd.-Bk.*, *Berther*, he who assigns places for the respective hammocks to hang in.

berthierite ('bɜːθɪəraɪt). *Min.* [Named 1827 after *Berthier*, a French naturalist.] A sulphide of antimony and iron, occurring native in elongated masses or prisms; also called Haidingerite.

berthing ('bɜːθɪŋ), *vbl. sb.*¹ [f. BERTH *v.*¹]

1. a. The action of mooring or placing a ship in a berth or harbour.

1800 COLQUHOUN *Comm. Thames* x. 287 Jurisdiction..respecting the birthing or placing of Vessels.

b. The occupation of a berth or mooring position; also, mooring position.

1891 *Daily News* 15 July 5/8 There being a high wind from the north north-east..the berthing was very uncomfortable for the..launches. **1906** *Westm. Gaz.* 9 July 4/2 Berthing accommodation will be provided for about 300 boats. **1908** *Ibid.* 26 May 9/1 The..Railway Company's boats..have changed their berthing from North Wall to Carlisle Pier. **1909** *Daily Chron.* 6 Dec. 6/7 They..came up practically to the berthing which the Ellan Vannin used to occupy.

2. The arrangement of berths or the provision of sleeping accommodation; accommodation in berths.

1863 LUCE *Seamanship* (ed. 2) xvi. 297 Berthing requires the earliest attention, and the operation may be facilitated by having a plan of the decks. *a* **1871** C. F. HALL *Polar Exp.* (1876) 123 The special object of these [changes] was the economy of fuel, and the berthing of the whole crew below deck.

'berthing, *vbl. sb.*² [f. BERTH *v.*² + -ING¹.] The upright planking of the sides and various partitions of a ship; *esp.* the planking outside above the sheer-stroke, the bulwark.

1706 PHILLIPS, *Birthing*, a Term us'd at Sea, when the Ship's sides are rais'd, or brought up. *c* **1850** *Rudim. Navig.* (Weale) 107 It is the berthing or hood round the ladder-way. **1869** SIR E. REED *Ship Build.* xii. 240 A plate-rail is fitted upon the top of the frames, and supports the hammock berthing. **1883** *Pall Mall G.* 20 Nov. 7/2 An able seaman..fell from the maintopmast rigging, and pitched on the berthing of the ship's side.

berthinsek, variant of BURDENSAK.

Berthon ('bɜːθɒn). The name of the Revd. Edward Lyon *Berthon* (1813–1899), used *attrib.* to designate a small collapsible boat invented by him. (Freq. with lower-case initial.)

1878 G. S. NARES *Voy. to Polar Sea* I. i. 20 The light canvas Berthon boats, available for one or two persons, proved of great service. **1898** W. A. BEAUCLERK in W. A. Morgan '*House' on Sport* 444 A berthon canoe..is very useful for cripples [*sc.* birds] when they get into shallow water. **1901** *Boy's Own Paper* 19 Oct. 48/2 A small Berthon dinghy that you can carry on board is much better.

‖**Bertillon** (bɛrtijɔ̃). [See next.] ***Bertillon system*** = BERTILLONAGE. So ***Bertillon measurement.***

1896 W. A. MCCORN in *Amer. Jrnl. Insanity* LIII. 47 (*title*) Degeneration in criminals as shown by the Bertillon system of measurement and photographs. *Ibid.* 50 The Bertillon system does not take account of the facial angle. **1902** *Encycl. Brit.* XXV. 468/1 Previously to the introduction of the Bertillon system the means relied upon were (1) the memory of warders [etc.]. **1928** G. B. SHAW *Crude Criminology* in *Doctors' Delusions* (1932) 246 We were assured that the Bertillon measurements were infallible until the fingerprint method was substituted.

‖**bertillonage** (bɛrtijɔ'naʒ). [Fr., f. the name of the inventor (see below).] The system of identification of criminals by anthropometric measurements, finger-prints, etc., invented by Alphonse *Bertillon* (1853–1914), French criminologist.

1892 F. GALTON *Finger Prints* 156, 562 prisoners who gave false names in the year 1890 were recognised by *Bertillonage.* **1892** *Athenæum* 24 Dec. 893/3 An interesting part of the work is the criticism of Bertillonage. **1901** E. R. HENRY *Finger Prints* (ed. 2) 63 The system suggested by Mr. Galton..fails to deal as effectively as Bertillonage with primary classification. **1920** *Discovery* Apr. 124/1 Extended examples are given of the possibilities of variation curves, variation 'steps', and 'gradation curves'; the combination of such data, constituting a quantitative diagnosis of a species, is defined as 'Bertillonage'.

bertin, -yn, Sc. var. of BRITTEN *v. Obs.*

bertisene, obs. form of BARTIZAN.

†**'bertram.** *Herb.* Also **bartram.** [a. Ger. *bertram, berchtram*, corruption of L. *pyrethrum*, Gr. πύρεθρον, f. πῦρ fire.] Obsolete name of the *Anacyclus Pyrethrum*, or Pellitory of Spain.

1578 LYTE *Dodoens* 342 Of bastard Pelitory or Bartram..In French *Pyrethre*, or *Pied d' Alexandre*: in high Douch *Bertram.* **1640** PARKINSON *Theat. Bot.* 858 Bertram is Pellitory of Spaine. **1783** AINSWORTH *Lat. Dict.* (Morell), Bartram, *pyrethrum.* **1863** PRIOR *Plant-n.* 20 *Bertram*, a corruption of L. *pyrethrum.*

bertrandite ('bɜːtrəndaɪt). *Min.* [a. F. *Bertrandite* (A. Damour 1883, in *Bull. Soc. Min.* VI. 254), after E. *Bertrand*, who first described it: see -ITE¹.] Hydrous silicate of beryllium.

1887 DANA *Man. Min. & Petrog.* (ed. 4) 275 Bertrandite is related to phenacite in composition. **1911** *Encycl. Brit.* VII. 578/2 Examples of other substances belonging to this [*sc.* pyramidal] class are..Bertrandite ($H_2Be_4Si_2O_9$). **1914** *Parl. Papers* LXXI. 414 Twinned crystals of felspar from Portugal and of bertrandite from Cornwall have been measured and described.

[**bertying,** error for BERTHING: see BERTH *v.*²

1678 PHILLIPS, *Bertying* a Ship, the raising up of the Ship's sides. So in BAILEY.]

berubric, beruffled, berust, etc.: see BE- *pref.*

be'ruffia,nize, *v.* [f. BE- + RUFFIANIZE.] *trans.* To call or stigmatize as a ruffian.

1596 NASHE *Saffron Wald.* v. ii, M. Lilly and me, by name he beruffianizd and berascald.

†**be'run,** *v. Obs.* For forms see RUN *v.* [Com. Teut.: OE. *berinnan*, = OHG. and Goth. *birinnan*, f. *bi-*, BE- 4 + *rinnan*, to RUN.]

1. *trans.* To run or flow about, or over the surface of; *esp.* in passive phr. ***berun with tears, with blood; bloody berunnen.***

a **1000** *Crist* (Gr.) 1176 Beam..blodiȝum tearum birunnen. *a* **1300** *K. Horn* 654 Heo sat on þe sunne, Wiþ tieres al birunne. *c* **1400** *Destr. Troy* XXII. 9052 Mony buernes on þe bent blody beronen! **1460** *Pol. Rel. & L. Poems* (1866) 246 To-ward caluery Al be-ronne with red blod. **1513** DOUGLAS *Æneis* VIII. iv. 31 Heidis..wyth vissage blayknit, blude byrun, and bla. *c* **1515** *Scot. ffeilde* 31 in Furniv. *Percy Folio* I. 213 Till all his bright armour: was all bloudye beronen.

2. To run round about, encompass.

c **1205** LAY. 1233 þat lond is biurnon mid þære sæ. *Ibid.* 26064 Arður..þat treo bieorn [**1250** biorne] abute. **1513** DOUGLAS *Æneis* V. v. 13 Ane mantill..With purpour selvage writhin mony fold, And all byrunnyn and lowpit lustely. *fig.* *a* **1300** *Cursor M.* 8351 Wit eild i am be-runnun nou.

berward, obs. form of BEARWARD.

†**'berwe.** *Obs.* Also 5 berowe. [OE. *bearu* (infl. *bearwes*) grove. (The mod. repr. would be *berrow*. The nom. *bearu*, ME. *bere*, survives in *Bere, Beere, Bear*, as a place-name).] A grove, a shady place.

c **890** K. ÆLFRED *Bæda* v. ii. (Bosw.) Wic mid bearuwe ymbsealde. *c* **1440** *Promp. Parv.* 33 Berwe or schadewe [**1499** berowe or shadowe], *umbraculum, umbra.*

berwham, early form of BARGHAM.

a **1300** W. DE BIBLESW. in Wright *Voc.* 168 Coleres de quyr, beru-hames. *c* **1440** *Promp. Parv.* 33 Berwham, horsys colere [**1499** beruham for hors].

berwick: see BEREWICK.

bery, beryal, -lle, -el, obs. ff. BURY, BURIAL.

berycoid ('bɛrɪkɔɪd), *a.* and *sb. Ichthyol.* [f. mod.L. *Berycoidei*, f. *Beryc-, Beryx*, generic name: see -OID.] **A.** *adj.* Belonging to the group Berycoidei. **B.** *sb.* A fish of this group.

1880 GÜNTHER *Fishes* 420 Fossil Berycoids show a still greater diversity of form than living. *Ibid.*, Berycoid fishes have a wide horizontal range. **1887** *Athenæum* 9 July 58/3 The genus had hitherto been erroneously associated with the percoids and berycoids. **1955** E. A. LECHNER in *Proc. U.S. Nat. Mus.* CV. (*title*) Populations of the Berycoid Fish Family Polymixiidae.

beryd, variant of BERRIED *ppl. a. Obs.*

beryl ('bɛrɪl). Forms: 3–4, 6– beryl; 4, 7–9 beril; also 4–6 beryll, 4–5 -ylle, 5 -ille, -ile, -yle, -al, -el, -ell, birell, 5–6 berall, birrall, byral, byrrall, 5–7 berill, byrall(e, 6 berral, birall, 8 berryl; *Sc.* 5–6 berial, -iall, -yall, 6 bureall. [a. OF. *beryl, beril*:—L. *bēryllus*, a. Gr. βήρυλλος, prob. a foreign word; identified by Weber with Skr. *vaidūrya*. Cf. also Arab. and Pers. *ballūr* crystal. In med.L. *berillus* was applied also to crystal, and to an eyeglass or spectacles, whence MHG. *berille*, mod.G. *brille* spectacles: cf. branch II.]

A. *sb.* **I.** *literal.*

1. a. A transparent precious stone of a pale-green colour passing into light-blue, yellow, and white; distinguished only by colour from the more precious emerald. When of pale bluish green it is called an *aquamarine*; its yellow or yellowish varieties are the chrysoberyl, and, perhaps, the chrysoprase, and chrysolite of the ancients. (The name is used in early literature without scientific precision: it is also doubtful if the 'beryl' of the Old Testament is correctly identified.)

c **1305** *Land of Cokayne* 92 Beril, onix, topasiune. **1382** WYCLIF *Rev.* xxi. 20 The eiȝthe . berillus. **1398** TREVISA *Barth. De P.R.* XVI. xx. (1495) 559 Beryll is a stone of Ynde lyke in grene colour to Smaragde. **1459** *Test. Ebor.* (1855) II. 229 Duos lapides de byrral. **1488** *Invent.* in Tytler *Hist. Scot.* (1864) II. 391 A ruby, a diamant, twa uther ringis, a berial. *Ibid.* A berial hingand at it. **1529** MORE *Comf. agst. Trib.* I. Wks. 137/1 Some white safyre or byrall. **1601** HOLLAND *Pliny* II. 613 Many are of opinion, that Berils are of the same nature that the Emeraud. **1811** PINKERTON *Petral.* I. 41 No one has supposed that berils are produced by fire. **1817** R. JAMESON *Char. Min.* 107 The hexahedral prism occurs in beryl. **1861** C. KING *Ant. Gems* (1866) 38 The Beryl is of little value at our present day.

b. In this sense ***beryl-stone*** was often used.

c **1380** WYCLIF *Sel. Wks.* III. 102 Take a berille-ston and holde it in a cleer sonne. *c* **1475** *Gloss.* in Wright *Voc.* 256, *Hic berellus*, a berelle ston. **1611** BIBLE *Ezek.* x. 9 The appearance of the wheeles was as the colour of a Berill stone. **1881** ROSSETTI *Rose Mary* I. ii, You've read the stars in the Beryl-stone.

†**c.** *fig.* Applied in admiration to a woman; cf. *gem, jewel, pearl. Obs.*

c **1440** *York Myst.* xxv. 505 Hayll! rose ruddy! hayll birrall clere. *c* **1485** *Digby Myst.* (1882) III. 958 Now godamercy, berel brytest of bewte! *c* **1535** LYNDESAY *Satyre* 132 Fair ladye Sensualitie, The beriall of all bewtie, And portratour preclair.

2. *Min.* A mineral species including not only the beryl of the lapidary in all its sub-varieties, but also the emerald, a variety of the beryl, distinguished by the presence of oxide of chromium, to which it owes the deep rich colour, named from it emerald-green. Beryl is a silicate of aluminium and glucinum, and occurs only crystalline, usually in hexagonal prisms.

1837 DANA *Min.* (1868) 246 Beryls of gigantic dimensions have been found in the United States..one beryl from

Grafton weighs 2,900 lbs. **1863** WATTS *Dict. Chem.* I. 582 Beryls are found in various parts of the world: the finest emeralds come from Peru.

II. *transferred.*

†**3. a.** A fine description of crystal or glass, used for vases, caskets, etc., and for glazing windows.

c **1384** CHAUCER *H. Fame* 1288 And oft I mused longe while Upon these walles of berile. *c* **1430** LYDG. in *Dom. Archit.* III. 121 The worke of wyndowe & eke fenestrall Wrouȝte of beryle. **1528** *MS. List Jewelry*, Another coffer of byrall, standing upon lyons. **1530** PALSGR. 197/2 Berall, fyne glasse, *beril*. **1538** LATIMER *Serm. & Rem.* (1845) 412 In plate, my new years gifts doth my need with glass and byrral. **1577** HARRISON *England* II. xii. (1877) 237 The houses were often glased with Berill. *a* **1625** BOYS *Wks.* (1630) 429 The cunning Lapidarie, who sels a Byrall for a Diamond.

b. Used as the type of clearness, as 'crystal' now is. (Some may have meant the gem.)

c **1300** in Wright *Lyric P.* v. 25 A burde in a bour ase beryl so bryht. *c* **1450** *Compl. Lover's L.* 37 Water clere as birell or cristall. **1549** *Compl. Scotl.* vi. 37 Ane fresche reueir as cleir as berial.

†**4.** A mirror: more fully called a ***beryl-glass.***

1540 *Lanc. Wills* (1857) II. 151 A byrrall glasse wt a cover. **1576** GASCOIGNE *Steele Gl.* (Arb.) 54 The days are past.. That Berral glas.. Might serve to shew aseemely favord face.

5. The colour of beryl (pale sea-green).

1834 R. MUDIE *Feath. Tribes Brit.* (1841) I. 3 It.. blends its beryl with the subdued sapphire of the horizon sky.

B. *attrib.* and hence as *adj.*

1. a. *attrib.* Of beryl; composed of or furnished with a beryl; also *formerly*, Of crystal.

1594 BLUNDEVIL *Exerc.* III. I. viii. 289 Cleere and transparant like fine Birall Glasse. **1658** SIR T. BROWNE *Hydriot.* ii. 23 The Gemme or Berill Ring upon the finger of Cynthia. **1810** *Edin. Rev.* XVII. 120 The apatit accompanies berilemerald.

b. *Comb.*, as ***beryl-blue, -covered*** adjs.

1881 W. D. HAY *300 Years Hence* vii. 141 The great basin of beryl-blue water. **1871** G. M. HOPKINS *Poems* (1930) 144 Long reefs of violets In beryl-covered fens so dim.

2. *adj.* †**a.** Clear as crystal, crystal-like (*obs.*).

b. Beryl-like in colour, clear pale green.

c **1496** DUNBAR *Gold. Terge* 23 The rosis yong.. War powderit brycht with hevinly beriall droppis. **1501** DOUGLAS *Pal. Hon.* Prol. 53 The beriall stremis rynning men micht heir. **1545** JOYE *On Dan.* xii. GG vij, The swete clere and byral dewe droppes of the morninge. **1857** EMERSON *Poems* 178 He smote the lake to feed his eye With the beryl beam of the broken wave.

beryllia (bəˈrɪlɪə). *Chem.* [f. BERYLLIUM; cf. *magnesia, magnesium.*] The oxide of beryllium or glucinum, otherwise called GLUCINA.

1873 WATTS *Fownes' Chem.* 375 An ignited mixture of beryllia and charcoal.

berylline (ˈbɛrɪlaɪn), *a.* [f. BERYL + -INE[1].] Beryl-like, beryl-coloured.

1847 in CRAIG. **1876** T. HARDY *Hand Ethelb.* II. xxxiii. 47 A berylline and opalized variegation of ripples.

beryllium (bəˈrɪlɪəm). *Chem.* [f. BERYL + -IUM.] A synonym for the metal GLUCINUM; so called as entering into the composition of the beryl.

1863 WATTS *Dict. Chem.*, *Glucinum* (Glycium, Beryllium). **1873** —— *Fownes' Chem.* 375 Beryllium forms but one class of compounds. *Ibid.* 375 Beryllium Chloride is formed by heating the Metal in chlorine or hydrochloric acid gas **1955** *Sci. News Let.* 16 Apr. 249/1 There is one other sort of beryllium, isotope 10, with a half life of 2,500,000 years, that it is expected will be found to be cosmic-ray produced. **1958** *Chambers's Techn. Dict.* 960/1 *Beryllium*, used in nuclear reactors, as it reflects neutrons. **1961** *Times* 11 July 7/2 It is expected that beryllium-clad fuel elements, more resistant to corrosion, will be developed.

berylloid (ˈbɛrɪlɔɪd). *Crystallog.* [f. L. *beryllus*, a. Gr. βήρυλλος beryl + -OID.] A geometrical solid consisting of two twelve-sided pyramids put base to base, as in the beryl.

beryllonite (bəˈrɪlənaɪt). *Min.* [f. BERYLL(IUM + *-on*, mod.L. form of Gr. *-ον* + -ITE[1].] A phosphate of beryllium and sodium, $NaBePO_4$.

1888 E. S. DANA in *Amer. Jrnl. Sci. & Arts* XXXVI. 291, I would suggest the name *Beryllonite*, in allusion to the fact that it contains the rare element beryllium. **1896** A. H. CHESTER *Dict. Min.* 30 *Beryllonite*, so named because it contains the rare element beryllium. An anhydrous phosphate of glucinum (beryllium) and sodium, occurring in transparent, colorless, orthorhombic crystals. **1957** *Encycl. Brit.* III. 469/2 *Beryllonite*, a mineral phosphate of beryllium and sodium.. found.. at Stoneham and Newry [Maine].

beryn, variant of BERNE and BAIRN.

beryn, beryng: see BEAR *v.*

berynes, var. of BURINESS, *Obs.*, burial.

berzelianite (bəˈziːlɪənaɪt). *Min.* [f. name of *Berzelius*, the celebrated chemist and mineralogist.] A native selenide of copper, silver-white with metallic lustre. With same etymology: **berzeliite** (bəˈziːlɪaɪt), an anhydrous arsenate of lime and magnesia, called also magnesian pharmacolite, and Kühnite. **ˈberzeline**, an obsolete name of Berzelianite; also a white variety of Haüynite. **ˈberzelite**, a native di-chloride of lead, called by Dana MENDIPITE.

bes-, representing OF. *bes-*:—L. *bis* 'twice, at two times, in two ways, doubly'; in Romanic, also, with the sense of 'secondarily, in an inferior way'; whence, with pejorative force, 'improperly, unsymmetrically, not right or straight, awry, aslant.' Found in Eng. as *bes-*, *be-*, *bez-*, in *besage, besagew, besaiel, besantler, bestourn*; *beayel, beantler, belif, bevue*; *bezantler*.

bes(e, obs. pres. indic. and imper. of BE *v.*

besaar, obs. form of BEZOAR.

besaffron, etc.: see BE- *pref.*

†**ˈbesage.** *Obs.* [a. F. *besace*, ad. Sp. *bisaza* or It. *bisaccia*:—L. *bisaccia*, pl. of *bisaccium* a double bag, saddle-bags, f. *bis* twice + *saccus* bag, sack.] A pair of saddle-bags, carried by a pack-horse. Hence in comb. ***besage-horse, -man.***

1526 *Ord. R. Househ.* 204 The number of all the Kings Horses, &c... Pack horses.. Sompters & Besage horses. *Ibid.* 201 The six sumpter men and one Besage man.

†**ˈbesague, -agew.** *Obs.* [a. F. *besaiguë* 'double axe or bill,' f. OF. *bes*:—L. *bis* twice + *aigu* sharp; L. type *bis-acūta*.] A double-edged axe.

c **1430** LYDG. *Chron. Troy* III. xxii, Thereon sette were besaguys also. *c* **1440** *Partonope* 1936 On eche shulder of steele a besagew.

†**beˈsaiel, besaile.** *Obs.* exc. *Law*. Forms: 4–5 beayell, 5 bysayeul, -sale, 6 besayle, 6–7 besaile, 7 besayel, (8 besail, 9 besael). [a. OF. *besayel*, *besaiol* (mod.F. *bisaïeul*), f. *bes*:—L. *bis* twice + *ayel, aiol, aieul* grandfather (see AIEL). The earlier Eng. form was *beayel* from AFr.]

A grandfather's father, a great-grandfather.

c **1400** *Destr. Troy* 13474 His beayell aboue on þe burne syde, On his modur halfe. **1480** CAXTON *Ovid's Met.* XIII. ii, Jupiter, the god of goddes, is my bysayeul. **1586** FERNE *Blaz. Gentrie* 102 There is Besaile, Graundsire, father. [**1762** RUFFHEAD *Act 32 Hen. VIII*, ii. §2 *note*, The Tresail, that is, the Father of the Besail, or Great Grandfather.]

b. *Law.* ***writ of besaile*** (see quot.).

1598 KITCHIN *Courts Leet* (1675) 424 In a Writ of Besayle he shall not have the View. **1641** *Termes de la Ley* 40 Besaile is a writ that lies for the heire, where his great grandfather was seised the day that he died, or died seised of Land in fee-simple, & a stranger enters the day of the death of the great grandfather, or abates after his death, the heire shall have this writ against such a disseisor or abator. [**1865** NICHOLS *Britton* II. 59 Such kindred.. shall have their remedy by our writs of Cosinage, of Ael, Aele, Besael, and Besaele.]

†**beˈsail,** *v. Obs. rare.* In 5 besale. [f. BE- 1 + SAIL *v.*, aphet. f. ASSAIL.] *trans.* To assail, attack.

1460 *Pol. Rel. & L. Poems* (1866) 103 þai me besale both strange & styfe.

besain, obs. form of BESEEN.

beˈsaint (bɪˈseɪnt). [f. BE- 5 + SAINT.] *trans.* To make a saint of, canonize.

a **1603** T. CARTWRIGHT *Confut. Rhem. N.T.* (1618) 658 Thomas Aquinas, whom they haue besainted unto the ninth degree. **1646** J. HALL *Poems* I. 3 [If you] besaint Old Jesabel for shewing how to paint. **1680** *Refl. Libel on Curse-ye-Meroz* 35 Another sort of People would have almost canoniz'd and besainted the Preacher.

beˈsainted, *ppl. a.* [f. prec. + -ED.]

1. Canonized, credited with sanctity.

1615 CORBET *Poems* (1807) 14 Their colledges were new be-painted, Their founders eke were new be-sainted. **1711** E. WARD *Vulg. Brit.* I. 9 Most were of some Faults attainted, Whether bedevil'd or besainted.

2. Peopled with or haunted by saints.

1865 E. BURRITT *Walk Land's E.* 299 Popular traditions in this most profusely be-sainted and be-spirited county.

besan, -sand(e, -saunt(e, obs. ff. BEZANT.

besanctify, besauce, -scab, -scarf: see BE-.

bes-antler, var. of BEZ-ANTLER.

besar, obs. form of BEZOAR.

†**beˈsay,** *v. Obs.* [OE. *besęcgan*, f. BE- 2 + *sęcgan* to SAY; cf. OHG. *bisagen*, mod.G. *besagen*.]

1. *trans.* To defend. (Only in OE.)

2. To declare, speak about.

c **1200** *Moral Ode* 112 in *Lamb. Hom.* 167 þe ðe lest wat biseið ofte mest. *c* **1200** *Trin. Coll. Hom.* 173 Elch sinne þare him seluen biseið, bute hit be here forȝieue.

bescatter (bɪˈskætə(r)), *v.* [f. BE- 1 + SCATTER.] *trans.* **a.** To besprinkle, strew *with*. **b.** To sprinkle, scatter about.

1640 FULLER *Joseph's Coat, David's Rep.* (1867) 219 It with moans bescattered the skies. **1659** —— *App. Inj. Innoc.* (1840) 327 The Animadvertor hath bescattered his [comment] every where with verses. **1855** SINGLETON *Virgil* III. 500 The nimble hoof bescatters dews of blood.

Hence **bescattered** *ppl. a.*

1574 HELLOWES *Gueuara's Ep.* (1577) 192 Although I goe bescattered and wandering in this Courte. **1883** STEVENSON *Silverado Sq.* 120 The battlemented pine-bescattered ridges.

bescent, beschoolmaster, bescorch, bescorn, bescoundrel. etc.: see BE- *pref.*

†**beˈscramble,** *v. Obs. rare*[−1]. [f. BE- + SCRAMBLE *v.*] *trans.* To scratch, tear.

1598 SYLVESTER *Du Bartas* II. i. IV. 104 The ragged Bramble With thousand scratches doth their skin bescramble.

bescratch (bɪˈskrætʃ), *v.* [f. BE- + SCRATCH *v.*] *trans.* To cover with scratches, to scratch all over.

1555 *Fardle Facions* I. vi. 98 He that hath this disease.. all to beskratcheth his bodie. **1628** WITHER *Brit. Rememb.* VI. 312 Our pleasant Fig trees, are bescratcht and dropt. **1839** DARLEY in *Beaum. & Fletcher's Wks.* (1839) I. Introd. 31 Bepierced and bescratched.

bescrawl (bɪˈskrɔːl), *v.* Also 7 bescraul(l. [f. BE- 1 + SCRAWL *v.*] *trans.* To scrawl or scribble over, to cover with scrawling.

1641 MILTON *Ch. Govt.* i. Wks. (1851) 99 These wretched projectors of ours that bescraull their Pamflets every day with new formes of government for our Church. **1802** SOUTHEY *Lett.* (1856) I. 194 Bescrawling this paper.

Hence **beˈscrawled** *ppl. a.*

1880 MRS. READE *Brown Hand & White* I. ii. 60 Freely-bescrawled sheets of foolscap.

bescreen (bɪˈskriːn), *v.* [f. BE- 1 + SCREEN *v.*] *trans.* To hide from sight, to screen; to cover with shade, overshadow, darken.

1592 SHAKS. *Rom. & Jul.* II. ii. 52 What man art thou, that thus bescreen'd [*Q*[o]. I. beskrind] in night So stumblest on my counsell. **1657** TOMLINSON *Renou's Disp.* Pref., Ignorance beskreens the soul. **1855** SINGLETON *Virgil* I. 48 Which you bescreens With broken shade.

bescribble (bɪˈskrɪb(ə)l), *v.* [f. BE- 2 and 4 + SCRIBBLE *v.*] Hence **beˈscribbled** *ppl. a.*

1. *trans.* To write in a scrawling hand, to scribble.

1583 STANYHURST *Æneid* III. (Arb.) 84 Her prophecyes in greene leaues nicelye bescribled. **1840** T. HOOK *Fitzherb.* III. xvii. 333 The superscription was so bescribbled that even Miss Bartley's sidelong glance could decipher nothing.

2. To scribble about; to scribble on. Also *fig.*

1643 MILTON *Divorce* II. xii. Wks. (1851) 93 That power ..[he] hath improperly usurpt into his Court-leet, and bescribbl'd with a thousand trifling impertinencies. **1808** W. IRVING *Salmag.* ii. (1860) 36 He be-scribbled more paper than would serve the theatre for snow-storms a whole season.

bescumber, bescurf, bescurvy, bescutcheon, etc.: see BE- *pref.*

beˈsee, *v. Obs.* or *arch.* [Common. Teut.: OE. *biséon, beséon* = OS., OHG. *bisehan*, Goth. *bisaihwan*:—OTeut. **bisehwan*, f. *bi*, BE- + **sehwan*, in OE. *séon* to SEE, which see for forms.]

I. †**1.** *intr.* To look about, to look (in any direction); to see. *Obs.*

c **1000** ÆLFRIC *Gen.* xviii. 2 Abraham beseah upp and ȝeseah þri weras standende. *c* **1200** *Moral Ode* 19 in *O.E. Misc.* 58 Ne may ich bi-seo me bi-fore for smoke. *a* **1225** *St. Marher.* 6 Heo biseh up on heh. *a* **1240** *Sawles Warde* in *Lamb. Hom.* 253 To.. biseon on hare grimfule.. nebbes.

b. *fig.* To look *to*, give heed to, attend *to*.

c **1200** *Trin. Coll. Hom.* 125 He bise to us and giue us.. mihte him to understonde. *a* **1240** *Ureisun* in *Lamb. Hom.* 195 Ilch mon þet to þe bisihð þu ȝiuest milce and ore.

†**2.** *refl.* To look about oneself, look round. *Obs.*

c **1000** ÆLFRIC *Gen.* xxiv. 63 þa he hine beseah þa ȝeseah he olfendas þyder weard. *c* **1000** *Ags. Gosp.* Mark ix. 8 Sona ða hi besawon hi.

b. *fig.* To look to oneself, take heed to oneself, consider.

a **1225** *Ancr. R.* 132 Heo mot wel biseon hire, & biholden hire ilchere half. *c* **1230** *Hali Meid.* 33 Bisih þe seli meiden. **1297** R. GLOUC. 505 The king ne ssolde king leng be, Then holi Thorsdai at non, bote he wolde him bet bise. **1382** WYCLIF *Matt.* xxvii. 5 What to vs? bise thee. **1388** —— *Acts* xviii. 15 Bisee ȝou silf. **1413** LYDG. *Pylgr. Sowle* I. xxi. (1859) 22 That I myght haue leyser to bysene my self.

†**3.** *trans.* To look at, look to, behold; to see. *Obs.*

c **1000** *Ags. Psalter* lxxix. [lxxx.] 14 Gehweorf nu.. and beseoh wingeard þisne. *c* **1175** *Cott. Hom.* 231 Gief he fend wére. me sceolden.. stiarne hine besié. and binde him. *c* **1250** *Gen. & Ex.* 2141 [He] bad him al his lond bisen. **1413** LYDG. *Pylgr. Sowle* II. xlv. (1859) 52 Al these pilgrims ne wylle not.. euery daye besene their owne self in a good myrrour.

b. *fig.* To regard, attend to, give heed to.

a **1225** *Juliana* 57 Vnseli mon, bisih þe hei godd. **1297** R. GLOUC. 456 þre þynges he mot bysee atte bygynnyng. *a* **1300** *E.E. Psalter* v. 2 Myne wordes, Laverd, with eres by-se.

†**4.** To see to, provide for, attend to; *hence*, to deal with, treat, use (*well* or *ill*). *Obs.*

c **1300** *K. Alis.* 4605 Foundelynges weore they two, That heore lord by-sayen so. **1393** LANGL. *P. Pl.* C. XXIII. 201 Lo, hou elde þe hore hap me byseye. *c* **1425** *Seven Sag.* (P.) 507 Euele thai gonnen him bisen. *c* **1500** *Prymer* in Maskell *Mon. Rit.* II. 45 *note*, Thus thei biseien foule, oure lord king of grace. **1596** SPENSER *F.Q.*, *Mutab.* i. 11 Ah! gentle Mole, such ioyance hath thee well beseene.

†5. To provide, arrange, ordain, determine. *Obs.*

c **1250** *Gen. & Ex.* 1411 Quan god haueð it so bi-sen, Alse he sendet, als it sal ben. *Ibid.* 1313 God sal bisen, Quor of ðe ofrende sal ben. **1297** R. GLOUC. 422 Þe Sonday he was ycrouned..as hys conseyl bysay. *c* **1305** *St. Swithin* 103 in *E.E.P.* (1862) 46 Þat oure louerd hit haþ biseȝe þat mie bodi schal beo ido In churche in an heȝe stede.

II. Later uses of the pa. pple. **beseen**, with qualifying adv. or phrase. Two notions here come in: 1. Seen, as in 'well-beseen' = seen to look well; 2. Provided, as in 'beseen of such power.'

†6. Seen, viewed; having an appearance, looking. ***well-beseen***: good looking, well favoured. *Obs.*

c **1374** CHAUCER *Troylus* I. 167 Meny a fressh lady, and maydyn bryght, Full wele byseyn. *a* **1450** *Knt. de la Tour* (1868) 51 The squier come from a uiage that he hadde ben atte, fresshe and iolyly beseen. **1542** UDALL *Erasm. Apoph.* 283 Hymself should ryde in a chairette moste goodly beseen. [**1678** PHILLIPS, App., *Besey* (old word), of good aspect.]

7. Appearing in respect of dress, etc.; dressed, apparelled, appointed; furnished. *Obs.* or *arch.*

c **1450** *Floure & Leafe* 169 More richly beseene, by many fold She was..in every maner thing. *c* **1500** DUNBAR *Thistle & Rose* 45 Full hestely besene, In serk and mantill after her I went. **1530** PALSGR. 423, I am besene, I am well or yvell apareylled. **1533** in Arb. *Garner* II. 47 Well beseen in velvet. **1629** HOLLAND *Cyrvpædia* (1632) 15 Himselfe also in person, all royally beseene, was present.

8. Appearing as to accomplishments; furnished; informed, versed, read, accomplished. *arch.*

1393 GOWER *Conf.* I. 341 How that her kinges be besein Of suche a power. *c* **1565** R. LINDSAY *Chron. Scotl.* (1728) 12 Prudent men, well beseen in histories both old and new. **1581** J. BELL *Haddon's Answ. Osor.* 509 Rhetoricke wherein he is well beseene. **1591** SPENSER *Tears Muses* 180, I late was wont to..maske in mirth with Graces well beseene. **1870** MORRIS *Earthly Par.* I. I. 380 Each seemed a glorious queen, With all that wondrous daintiness beseen.

9. Of things, in senses analogous to 6, 7. *arch.*

c **1386** CHAUCER *Clerkes T.* 909 Thogh thyn array be badde, and yuel biseye. **1430** LYDG. *Story Thebes* 33 To a chamber she led him..Ful wel beseine. *a* **1440** *Sire Degrev.* 1686 [The]re gay gownus of grene [We]re ful schamely besene. **1603** HOLLAND *Plutarch's Mor.* 224 Set in meddow greene With pleasant flowers all faire beseene. *a* **1850** WORDSW. *Cuckoo & Night.* lvii, Under a maple that is well beseen.

†b. Hence **best beseen**: best attire. *Obs.*

1602 CAREW *Cornwall* (1723) 137 b, The Curate in his best beseene, solemnly receued him at the Churchyard stile.

beseech (bɪˈsiːtʃ), *v.* Pa. t. and pa. pple. **besought** (bɪˈsɔːt). Forms: *Inf.* 2 **bisec-en**, 2–5 **bisechen, bysech-e(n**, 3–6 **beseche** (3 **-secchen**, 4 **bezeche, bicheche**, 5 **bysuche**), 6–7 **beseeche**, 6– **beseech**. Also *north.* and *n. midl.* 2–4 **biseke**, 4–5 **be-, by-**, (4 **bezeke**, 5 **besike, beseyk**, 5–6 *Sc.* **beseik**, 6 **bezeik**), 6–7 **beseek(e**. *Pa. t.* 3 **bisohte**, 3–4 **-soȝte, -souhte, -souȝte**, 4 **bi-, bysought, -sowght, besoght**, 5 **-sougt**, 5–6 **-soughte**, 5–9 *Sc.* **besocht**, 6– **besought**; also 6– **beseeched** (now regarded as incorrect). [f. *bi-*, BE- 2 + ME. *secen, sechen, seken* to SEEK. In contrast to the simple vb., in which the northern *seek* has displaced the southern *seech*, in the compound *beseech* has become the standard form.]

†1. *trans.* To seek after, search for, try to get. *Obs.*

c **1200** *Trin. Coll. Hom.* 121 Ure drihten..lokede gif here ani understoden oðer bi-sohten him. *c* **1300** *Cursor M.* 5357 Gött., Mi broþer esau me bi-soght [*C.* soght, *T.* bisouȝt, F. be-soȝt] To dyserit me, if þat he moght. *c* **1374** CHAUCER *Boeth.* 159 Þilk clernesse þat nis nat approched no raþer or þat men by-seken it.

†b. To seek to know. *Obs.*

c **1250** *Gen. & Ex.* 3236 He bi-soȝte godes wil.

2. To beg earnestly for, entreat (a thing).

c **1175** *Lamb. Hom.* 135 Euric neodi ðe heo biseceð. *c* **1200** *Trin. Coll. Hom.* 157 Ech nedi þe hit bisekeð. *c* **1205** LAY. 3494 Nu ich mot bisecchen [**1250** bisechе] þat þing þat ich ær forhowede. **1393** LANGL. *P. Pl.* C. II. 167 Myldeliche with mouthe mercy he by-souhte. *c* **1400** *Destr. Troy* XXIX. 12138 Þis holly with hert here I beseke! **1590** SHAKS. *Mids. N.* III. i. 183, I beseech your worship's pardon. **1612** DEKKER, etc. *If not Good Play* Wks. 1873 I. 318, O I beseeke Thy attention to this Reuerend sub-Prior. **1641** MILTON *Ch. Discip.* II. Wks. (1851) 59 It hath beene more and more propounded, desir'd, and beseech't. **1803** MISS PORTER *Thaddeus* ii. (1831) 19 His majesty..beseeched permission to rest for a moment. **1885** RUSKIN *Præterita* iii. 105, I besought leave to pat him [a dog].

b. with *subord. cl.* or *infin.* as obj.

c **1205** LAY. 17043 Faire he bisecheð þat þu him to buȝe. *c* **1325** *E.E. Allit. P.* C. 375 Þay..dymly bisoȝten, þat þat penaunce plesed him. **1489** CAXTON *Faytes of A.* IV. ii. 232, I..beseke that hyt may be enteryned and kepte to me. **1622** MABBE *Aleman's Guzman d'Alf.* I. 97 Both which besought to be baptized. **1667** MILTON *P.L.* XII. 236 They beseech That Moses might report to them his will.

†c. Const. *of* (a person). *Obs.*

? *a* **1400** *Morte Arth.* 305 [He] of hyme besekys To ansuere þe alyenes wyth austerene wordes. **1563** *Mirr. Mag.* Induct. xliv. 7 And to be yong againe of Joue [he would] beseke.

3. To supplicate, entreat, implore (a person).

c **1175** *Lamb. Hom.* 23 He hine wile biseche mid gode heorte. *a* **1300** *Cursor M.* 15807 If i mi fader wald beseke, I moght..Haf tuelue thusand legions. *c* **1350** *Will. Palerne* 1258 Lette me nouȝt lese þe liif ȝut lord, y þe bi cheche. *c* **1460** in *Pol. Rel. & L. Poems* (1866) 253 Leue lord I þee byseke. **1591** SHAKS. *Two Gent.* II. iv. 100 Mistris, I beseech you Confirme his welcome. **1597** —— *2 Hen. IV*, II. iv. 175, I beseeke you now, aggrauate your Choler. **1611** BIBLE *Ex.* xxxiii. 18, I beseech thee, shew me thy glory. **1875** JOWETT *Plato* (ed. 2) I. 196 Tell me, I beseech you, what that noble study is?

†b. a person a thing. (Perhaps the person was originally a dative.) *Obs.*

c **1205** LAY. 21543 Iþencheð what Ardur..at Baðen us bisohte. *c* **1250** *Gen. & Ex.* 3600 For to bi-seken god merci. **1340** *Ayenb.* 98 Yef we hym bezechiþ þing þet ous is guod. **1588** SHAKS. *L.L.L.* II. i. 197, I beseech you a word.

c. a person *that*, etc.

a **1240** *Ureisun* 161 in *Lamb. Hom.* 199 Ich þe bi-seche ..þet þu þine blescinge..ȝiue me. *c* **1386** CHAUCER *Melib.* ¶270, I biseke yow..that ye wol nat wilfully replie agayn my resouns. *c* **1470** HENRY *Wallace* II. 317 Scho..thaim besocht ..scho micht thine with him fayr. **1536** WRIOTHESLEY *Chron.* (1875) I. 40, I beseche God that I may be an example to you all. **1590** SHAKS. *Mids. N.* I. i. 62, I beseech your Grace that I may know The worst. **1742** JARVIS *Quix.* I. II. x, Beseeching God..that he would be pleased to give him the victory.

d. a person *to do* a thing.

c **1400** *Destr. Troy* XXI. 8452 Ho..besechis the souerain.. Hir lord for to let. **1552** *Bk. Com. Prayer* Morn. Pr., I pray and beseech you..to accompany me. *c* **1620** A. HUME *Brit. Tong.* (1865) 3 Beseeking your grace to accep my mint, and pardon my miss. **1647** WARD *Simp. Cobler* 78 Be.. beseeched, not to slight good ministers. **1709** *Tatler* No. 42 ¶2 A Poor Man once a Judge besought, To judge aright his Cause. **1835** BECKFORD *Recoll.* 183, I beseeched him..to remain quiet. **1844** BROUGHAM *Brit. Const.* xvi. (1862) 243 He besought the King to refuse his consent.

†e. a person *of* a thing. *Obs.*

a **1300** *Cursor M.* 3258 Þus he bisoght god of his grace. *c* **1386** CHAUCER *Knts. T.* 60 (Lansd. MS.), We beseke ȝowe of socoure and of mercye. *c* **1440** LONELICH *Grail* xlvi. 51 Of baptesme I the beseke. **1604** SHAKS. *Oth.* III. iii. 212, I humbly do beseech you of your pardon.

f. a person *for* a thing.

a **1300** *Cursor M.* 20655 And þat þou wil bisek [*v.r.* be-seke, bisече] me fore..It sal be als tu it wille. *c* **1440** *York Myst.* xxvi. 126 All samme for þe same we beseke ȝou. **1594** MARLOWE *Dido* I. i. 60 She humbly did beseech him for our bane. **1859** THACKERAY *Virgin.* (1876) 539 The wretch.. besought him for mercy.

4. *intr.* To make supplication or earnest request; to ask. *arch.*

a **1225** *Ancr. R.* 230 Þeo deoflen..bisouhten & seiden.. mitte nos in porcos. *a* **1300** *E.E. Psalter* lxiii[iv]. 1 Here, God, mi bede, when I biseke swa. **1340** *Ayenb.* 194 Hit behoueþ ham bidde and bezeche beuore er hi wylleþ aȝt do. *c* **1449** PECOCK *Repr.* Prol. 1 Vndirnyme thou, biseche thou, and blame thou, in all pacience. **1552** *Bk. Com. Prayer* Consecr. Bps., That he, preaching thy Word, may..be earnest to reprove, beseech, and rebuke. **1655** tr. *Milton's 2nd Def. Pop.* 223 Well, I beseech, who are you?

b. Const. *to* or *unto* a person (obs.); *of* (obs.) or *for* a thing.

a **1300** *E.E. Psalter* xxix. [xxx.] 9 To þe..crie I sal, And to mi God biseke. **1330** R. BRUNNE *Chron.* 158 To Ihesus scho bisouht. **1393** GOWER *Conf.* II. 172 The Grekes to hem beseke. **1377–99** in Hallam *Mid. Ages* (1872) III. 90 The comune of youre lond bysechyn vnto youre riȝt riȝtwesnesse. **1647** W. BROWNE *Polex.* II. 298, I prayed, and with teares besought for an end of our contestations. **1805** SOUTHEY *Madoc in W.* v, We now besought for food.

†5. To bring (a person) *into* (a certain state of mind) by entreaty. *Obs.* (Cf. *to argue* into.)

a **1718** PENN *Life* Wks. 1726 I. 173, I rather chuse to beseech People into that Commendable Disposition.

†**be'seech**, *sb. Obs. rare.* [f. prec.] Beseeching, entreaty, petition.

1606 SHAKS. *Tr. & Cr.* I. ii. 319 Atchievement, is command; ungain'd, beseech. *a* **1625** BEAUM. & FL. *Bloody Bro.* (T.), The suit that Edith urges With such submiss beseeches.

be'seeched *ppl. a.* See BESEECH *v.*

1646 MAYNE *Serm.* (1647) 16 An equality between the beseecher and the beseeched.

beseecher (bɪˈsiːtʃə(r)). Also 4–6 **besecher**. [f. BESEECH *v.* + -ER[1].]

1. One who beseeches; a suppliant, a petitioner.

1382 WYCLIF *Zeph.* iii. 10 Fro thennis my bisecheris.. shuln brynge a ȝift to me. **1508** FISHER *Wks.* I. 253 Shewe hymselfe yrefull ayenst his subgecte and besecher. *c* **1600** SHAKS. *Sonn.* cxxxv, Let no vnkinde, no faire beseechers kill. **1751** SMOLLETT *Per. Pic.* (1779) I. vi. 43 He terrified the poor beseecher into immediate silence.

2. *spec.* A petitioner to the king or his courts.

c **1400** *Petit. Ld. Vesey* in Whitaker *Hist. Craven* (1812) 251 Yor said besecher standeth gretely chargeably to the execucon of..the last wille of, etc. **1448** SHILLINGFORD *Lett.* (1871) 130 Iugges betwene the seid Bisshop..and your seid besechers. **1488–9** *Act 4 Hen. VII*, xxii, Youre besechers shall ever pray, etc. **1523** *Act 14 & 15 Hen. VIII*, vi, It shalbe leful to your said besecher.

beseeching (bɪˈsiːtʃɪŋ), *vbl. sb.* [f. as prec.]

1. Earnest entreaty, intercession, supplication.

c **1300** in Wright's *Lyric P.* xxxiv. 95 Heo mai don us god, thurh hire bysechynge. **1480** CAXTON *Chron. Eng.* ccxii. 198 At the prayer and besechyng of his lieges. **1872** HOLLAND *Marb. Proph.* 29 With a look of wild beseeching.

2. An earnest request, entreaty, prayer.

a **1300** *E.E. Psalter* xvi[i]. 1 Bihald whit mi bisekinge es. **1340** *Ayenb.* 98 Þe bezechinge þet he ous made..þet wes þet pater noster. **1480** CAXTON *Chron. Eng.* ccxxxii. 251 Continuel besechynges of many noble man. **1659** MILTON *Rupt. Commw.* Wks. (1851) 403 By publick Addresses, and brotherly beseechings. **1882** W. S. BLUNT *Sonn. Proteus, Vanitas Van.*, O glorious sighs, Sublime beseechings.

†b. A plea, petition. *Obs.*

1340 *Ayenb.* 39 Ualse playneres þet makeþ ualse bezechinges.

be'seeching, *ppl. a.* [f. as prec. + -ING[2].] That beseeches; entreating, appealing, suppliant.

1704 J. TRAPP *Abra-Mulé* Prol. 3 With beseeching Hands. **1753** SMOLLETT *Ct. Fathom* (1784) 173/1 In an humble and beseeching strain. **1868** HOLME LEE *B. Godfrey* xvii. 100 Emmot cast a beseeching look.

be'seechingly, *adv.* [f. as prec. + -LY[2].] In a beseeching manner; imploringly.

1830 MARRYAT *King's Own* lix, 'Don't talk so loud!'..said the hag, beseechingly. **1881** J. HAWTHORNE *Fort. Fool* I. xiii, Her childish face looked up at him beseechingly.

be'seechingness (bɪˈsiːtʃɪŋnɪs). [f. as prec. + -NESS.] The quality of being beseeching.

1863 GEO. ELIOT *Romola* xlviii, The husband's determination to mastery, which lay deep below all blandness and beseechingness.

beseechment (bɪˈsiːtʃmənt). [f. BESEECH *v.* + -MENT.] Beseeching, supplication.

a **1679** T. GOODWIN *Wks.* (1863) VI. 118 Which beseechment denotes..their gracious condescension. **1880** MISS BROUGHTON *Sec. Th.* II. III. viii. 253 Casting a glance of abject beseechment at his niece.

†**be'seeing**, *vbl. sb. Obs.* In 4 **bezyinge**. [f. BESEE *v.*] Circumspection, consideration.

1340 *Ayenb.* 184 Greate beþenchinge, þet is, grat bezyinge.

be'seek, *v. nonce-wd.* [f. BE- 4 + SEEK *v.* (cf. BESEECH 1).] *trans.* To seek or search about.

1880 L. WALLACE *Ben-Hur* I. ix. (1884) 46 These people have all besought the town, and they report its accommodations all engaged.

beseek(e, obs. form of BESEECH.

beseem (bɪˈsiːm), *v.* Also 3–6 **bi-, by-**. For forms see SEEM *v.* [f. BE- 2 + SEEM *v.*]

†1. *intr.* To seem, appear, look. (Almost always in 3rd pers.) *Obs.*

a **1225** *Ancr. R.* 148 Moiseses hond..bisemede oðe spitelvuel. **1330** R. BRUNNE *Chron.* Prol. 152 He telles..Alle þer lymmes how þai besemed. **1470–85** MALORY (1816) I. 191 Sir, thou besemest well. **1586** WEBBE *Eng. Poetrie* (Arb.) 82 She sittes..in a goodly scarlett brauely beseeming. **1779** MASON *Eng. Gard.* XIV. (R.) His manly form, His virtues..beseem'd no sentiment to wake Warmer than gratitude.

b. *impers.* with *dat. obj.* or *to*.

c **1400** *Destr. Troy* VII. 2886 Paris was pure faire..full stithe hym besemyt. **1470–85** MALORY *Arthur* (1816) I. 361 Him beseemeth well of person, and of countenance, that he shall prove a good man. **1598** SYLVESTER *Du Bartas* I. i. (1641) 2/1 To deep Wisdome and Omnipotence, Nought worse beseems, then sloth and negligence.

2. To suit in appearance; to become, befit, be in accordance with the appearance or character of. With *dative obj.* (rarely *to*).

a. *orig.* with *well*, *ill*, or other qualification: *lit.* To appear or look well, etc., for a person to wear, to have, to do, etc.

a **1225** *Juliana* 55 Wel bisemeð þe..to beo streon of a swuch strunde. *c* **1325** *E.E. Allit. P.* A. 309 A poynt of sorquydryȝe þat vche god mon may euel byseme. **1393** GOWER I. 110 As though it shulde him well beseme That he all other men can deme. **1398** TREVISA *Barth. De P.R.* VI. vi. (1495) 193 Semely clothynge bysemyth to them well that ben chaste damoysels. **1590** MARLOWE *Edw. II*, I. i. ad fin., A prison may best beseem his holiness. *a* **1674** CLARENDON *Hist. Reb.* II. VI. 137 A duty well beseeming the Preachers of the Gospel. **1843** LYTTON *Last Bar.* ii. 41 It would ill beseem you, so young and so comely, to go further.

b. *Hence*, without qualification, in the sense of 'well beseem.'

1388 WYCLIF *Prov.* xvii. 7 Wordis wel set togidere bisemen not a fool. *a* **1520** *Myrr. Our Ladye* 126 Euerlastynge holynesse bysemyth lorde thy howse. **1593** SHAKS. *Lucr.* 277 Sad pause and deep regard beseem the sage. **1639** FULLER *Holy War* III. xi. (1840) 134 Being more prodigal of his person than beseemed a general. **1729** T. COOKE *Tales* 45 Her Mind beseem'd her Angel's Face. **1837** HAWTHORNE *Twice-told T.* (1851) II. i. 12, I have already laughed more than beseems my cloth. **1884** BROWNING *Ferishtah* (ed. 3) 61 Man acts as man must; God, as God beseems.

3. *absol.* To be seemly, to be becoming or fitting, to be meet: *orig.* with qualification as in 2.

c **1340** *Cursor M.* 8734 (Trin.) Say me what wol best biseme. **1382** WYCLIF *Rom.* i. 28 Tho thingis that acoorden not, *or bysemen not*. **1388** —— *Hebr.* vii. 26 It bisemyde that sich a man were a bischop to us. *c* **1449** PECOCK *Repr.* 552 The receyuers wolden expende thilk good..not other wise than it bisemed. **1596** SPENSER *F.Q.* I. viii. 32 His reverend haires..The knight much honord, as beseemed well. **1671** MILTON *P.R.* II. 331 To treat thee as beseems. **1871** PALGRAVE *Lyr. Poems* 44 Silence beseemeth most.

†**be'seemed**, *ppl. a. Obs.* [f. prec. + -ED[1].] Having an appearance (of such a kind), appearing, looking; = BESEEN; esp. in *well-beseemed*. (Cf. also *well-behaved*, *well-spoken*.)

a **1250** *Owl & Night.* 842 Þine wordes beoþ..so bisemed and biliked. *c* **1430** *Syr. Tryam.* 720 Ther was no prynce.. That was so semely undur schylde, Nor bettur besemyd a

knyght. *a* **1440** *Ipomydon* 353 Ther was non..So wele besemyd, doughty of hand.

beseeming (bɪˈsiːmɪŋ), *vbl. sb.* [f. as prec.]

†**1.** Appearance, look. *Obs.*

1611 SHAKS. *Cymb.* v. v. 409, I am, sir, The Souldier that did company these three In poore beseeming.

2. Becoming appearance, becomingness, fitness.

c **1440** *Promp. Parv.* 27 Besemynge, or comelynesse, *decencia.* **1552** HULOET, Beseamynge, *condecentia.* **1580** BARET *Alv.* B 557 A Beseeming or comelinesse, *condecentia.*

beˈseeming, *ppl. a.* [f. as prec. + -ING².] That beseems (in senses 2, 3); becoming, befitting, seemly, comely.

1526 *Pilgr. Perf.* (W. de W. 1531) 201 Moche besemyng it was..that we sholde haue suche a bysshop. **1592** SHAKS. *Rom. & Jul.* I. i. 100 Cast by their Graue beseeming Ornaments. **1594** HOOKER *Eccl. Pol.* I. (1632) 65 Those things which men..know to be beseeming or unbeseeming. **1641** MILTON *Animadv.* Wks. (1851) 236 Contented with a moderate and beseeming allowance. **1821** SCOTT *Kenilw.* xvi, Tressilian..made a low and beseeming reverence.

beseeming, besemyng, for *by seeming,* seemingly: see SEEMING.

beˈseemingly, *adv.* [f. prec. + -LY².] In a beseeming manner; befittingly.

1611 COTGR., *Decentement,* decently, comelily, handsomely, gracefully, beseemingly. **1674** N. FAIRFAX *Bulk & Selv.* Ep. Ded., To love knowingly and beseemingly. **1866** J. H. NEWMAN *Gerontius* v. 40 The Angels, as beseemingly To spirit-kind was given, At once were tried and perfected.

beˈseemingness. [f. as prec. + -NESS.] Beseeming quality; fitness, becomingness.

1656 J. FERGUSSON *On Coloss.* 142 [It] doth not import a dignity or worth in our walking, to recompence the Lord, but onely a beseemingnesse. **1840** BROWNING *Sordello* I. 282 Till two or three amassed Mankind's beseemingnesses.

beseemly (bɪˈsiːmlɪ), *a. rare.* [Irregularly formed on BESEEM *v.*, after *seemly.*] Seemly, becoming, befitting. Hence **beseemliness.**

1647 W. BROWNE *Polex.* II. 292 Preferring false beseemlinesse before loyall affection! **1742** SHENSTONE *Schoolm.* xxiv. 209 To their seats they hye..And in beseemly order sitten there. **1849** ROCK *Ch. of Fathers* III. ix. 264 An architectural feature..as beautiful as it was beseemly.

besege, etc., obs. form of BESIEGE, etc.

†**beˈsekandlik,** *a. Obs. north.* [f. *besekand,* north. form of BESEECHING *pr. pple.* + *-lik,* -LIKE.] Able to be besought, propitious.

a **1300** *E.E. Psalter* cxxxiv. 14 He sal..in his hine besekand-lik be [*v.r.* besoght sal he be] with-al.

beseke, etc., obs. form of BESEECH, etc.

besem, obs. form of BESOM.

†**beˈsench,** *v. Obs.* Forms: 1 besencan, 2-3 besencen, (*Orm.*) bisennkenn, bisenchen. *Pa. t.* 2-3 bisencte, -seinte. [OE. *besęncan* wk. vb., f. BE- 2 + *sęncan*:—OTeut. *sanqjan,* causal of *sinqan* to SINK.] *trans.* To cause to sink, submerge, plunge down, overwhelm.

971 *Blickl. Hom.* 33 Se þe mihte þone costiȝend instepes on helle grund besencean. *c* **1000** *Ags. Gosp.* Matt. xviii. 6 Besenced [*Rushw.* besenked] on sæs grund. *c* **1175** *Lamb. Hom.* 87 God bisencte þa þe pharaon: and al his genge. *Ibid.* 107 Hi bisencheð us on helle. *c* **1200** ORMIN 19689 þatt mihhte hemm alle..Inn helle wel bisennkenn. *a* **1225** *Ancr. R.* 334 [He] biseinte [*v.r.* bisencte] Sodome & Gomorre.

†**beˈsend,** *v. Obs.* [f. BE- 4 + SEND *v.*] *trans.* To send to, to send (a message) to.

1297 R. GLOUC. 491 Erl Jon, is brother, bisende him al so, & bisouȝte is grace of that he adde misdo. **1330** R. BRUNNE *Chron.* 309 For chance þat him bitidde, þe kyng þus þam bisent, I praie ȝow in þis nede, to help me with ȝour oste.

besenes, obs. form of BUSINESS.

besense, obs. f. BECENSE: (see BE- *pref.* I.)

besert, obs. variant of BEZOAR.

†**beˈserve,** *v. Obs.* [f. BE- 2 + SERVE *v.*] *trans.* To serve diligently.

a **1300** *Cursor M.* 23053 Did þair bodis in prisun And suonken þam bath dai and night For to beserue vr lauerd.

besestano, -tein, obs. variant of BEZESTEEN.

beset (bɪˈsɛt), *v.* Pa. t. and pa. pple. beset. Also 1-6 bi-, by-. For forms see SET. [Com. Teut.: OE. *bi-, besęttan* = OHG. *bisezzan* (MHG. and mod.G. *besetzen*), OS. *bisettjan* (MDu. *besetten,* Du. *bezetten*), Goth. (and OTeut.) *bisatjan,* f. *bi-,* BE- about + *satjan* (OE. *sęttan*) to SET, causal of *sitjan* to SIT. *Beset* is thus the causal to BESIT.]

I. To set about, surround. All *trans.*

1. To set (a thing) about *with* accessories or appendages of any kind; to surround with things set in their places. Now only in pa. pple.

a **1000** *Beowulf* 2910 Swa hine fyrn-dagum worhte wæpna smið wundrum teode besette swin-licum. *c* **1200** ORMIN 8169 Itt wass eȝȝwhær bisett Wiþþ deorewurþe staness. **1388** WYCLIF *Ecclus.* xxviii. 28 Bisette thin eeris with thornes. *a* **1529** SKELTON *Vox Pop.* Wks. 1843 II. 404 His tabell..With platt besett inowe. **1563** PILKINGTON *Serm.* Wks. (1842) 657 Many of the university..beset the walls of the Church and Church-porch on both sides with verses. **1598** BARCKLEY *Felic. Man* III. (1603) 253, I made orchards and gardens, and beset them with all kinde of trees. **1607** TOPSELL *Four-f. Beasts* 557 They take a..young man, whom they dress in the apparel of a woman, besetting him with divers odoriferous flowers and spices. **1760** J. LEE *Introd. Bot.* (1776) 196 The Disk is beset with Points that are sharp and stiff. **1834** DE QUINCEY *Cæsars* Wks. X. 231 A diadem or tiara beset with pearls.

†**b.** *more vaguely*: To surround, encircle, cover round *with. Obs.*

1580 LYLY *Euphues* (1636) I ij b, His face did shine as it were beset with the Sun-beames. **1593** NASHE *Christ's T.* Wks. 1883-4 IV. 207 Euen as Angels are painted..besette with Sunne-beames so beset they theyr fore-heads..with glorious borrowed gleamy bushes. **1727** BRADLEY *Fam. Dict.* s.v. *Distilling,* It's necessary you should beset it [a Retort], even to the very End of the Beak, with a Sort of Stuff made of Potters Earth.

2. To set or station themselves round, to surround with hostile intent.

a. To set upon or assail on all sides (a person).

a **1225** *Meid. Maregr.* xvii, Ðes houndes habbet me biset. *a* **1300** *Cursor M.* 15783 þei bigon to awake And him faste aboute biset. *c* **1380** WYCLIF *Sel. Wks.* III. 143 Monkynde in þo stat of innocense when he..was not bysett wiþ enmyes. *c* **1440** *York Myst.* xliv. 55 þe Jewes besettis vs in ilke aside. **1526** *Pilgr. Perf.* (W. de W. 1531) 19 b, Than he is a strypplynge, all beset aboute with ennemyes. **1601** SHAKS. *Twel. N.* v. i. 88, I..Drew to defend him, when he was beset. **1718** POPE *Iliad* XVII. 148 The lioness..beset by men and hounds. **1873** SYMONDS *Grk. Poets* vii. 194 The Erinnyes, whose business it is to beset the house of the evil-doer.

b. To invest, or surround (a place); to besiege. (Not now said of a regular army besieging a town).

a **1225** *Ancr. R.* 300 þe buruh..þet he heueden biset. **1297** R. GLOUC. 387 þuderward he heyde vaste, And þer castel bysette. *a* **1300** *Cursor M.* 7056 In his tyme was troy biset. *c* **1380** *Sir Ferumb.* 3539 For þe Amyral..had be-set þe brigge aboute With strengþe and with gynne. *c* **1520** *Adam Bel* 47 in Hazl. *E.P.P.* II. 141 Thys place hath ben besette for you. **1624** CAPT. SMITH *Virginia* III. ix. 79 Salvages, well armed, had inuironed the house, and beset the fields. **1740** L. CLARKE *Hist. Bible* VI. 341 They went and beset the town by night. **1871** FREEMAN *Norm. Conq.* (1876) IV. xviii. 107 The partizans of Oswulf beset the house where Copsige was.

c. To occupy (a road, gate, or passage), *esp.* so as to prevent any one from passing.

a **1300** *Cursor M.* 15012 Wiþ harpe & pipe..þe weye þei him bisette. **1580** BARET *Alv.* B 559 All the wayes were beset with garrisons of enemies. **1635** N. R. tr. *Camden's Hist. Eliz.* I. 75 Morton in the meane time beset all passages of access. **1753** *Life J. Frith* (1829) 76 Sir Thomas More..persecuted him both by land and sea, besetting all the ways, havens, and ports. **1852** MᶜCULLOCH *Taxation* Introd. 28 The mob, which beset all the avenues to the House of Commons.

†**d.** To circumvent, entrap, catch. *Obs.*

1616 SURFL. & MARKH. *Countr. Farm* 37 Hee shall make readie his Nets to catch Birds, and to beset the Hares.

3. *fig.* To encompass, surround, assail, possess detrimentally: **a.** said of temptations, dangers, difficulties, obstacles, evil influences.

a **1000** *Andreas* (Gr.) 1257 þa se halȝa wæs..earoþancum beseted. *c* **1200** ORMIN 12954 O mannkinn þatt wass all bisett Wiþþ siness þessterrnesse. *a* **1450** *Knt. de la Tour* (1868) 58 Whanne that two vices be sette one euelle delite, gladly they bringe her maister into temptacion. **1611** BIBLE *Heb.* xii. 1 Let vs lay aside..the sinne which doth so easily beset vs. **1712** ADDISON *Spect.* No. 441 ¶ 1 [Man] is beset with Dangers on all sides. **1741** RICHARDSON *Pamela* I. 73 A poor Maiden, that is hard beset. **1848** MACAULAY *Hist. Eng.* I. 240 The difficulties by which the government was beset. **1874** HELPS *Soc. Press.* ii. 18 The hopelessness which gradually besets all people in a great town like London.

b. of the difficulties, perils, obstacles which beset an action, work, or course.

1800 CURRIE *Life Burns* (1800) I. Ded. 21 The task was beset with considerable difficulties. **1869** FREEMAN *Norm. Conq.* (1876) III. xii. 254 The tale is beset with contradictions. **1878** HUXLEY *Physiogr.* 138 The difficulties that beset such an explanation.

c. of actual enemies forming schemes against one's life or property. *rare.*

1682 LUTTRELL *Brief Rel.* (1857) I. 202 Our lives and estates are besett here.

†**d.** *pass.* To be possessed (with devils). *Obs.*

1483 CAXTON *Gold. Leg.* 176/1 The deuyls that Saynt Germayn had dryuen out of suche bodyes as were biseten. *Ibid.* 196/3 Men that were wood and byset with deuyls.

4. *gen.* To close round; to surround, hem in. (Often with some allusion to senses 2 and 3, as in 'to be beset by ice.')

c **1534** tr. *Pol. Verg. Eng. Hist.* (1846) I. 57 The towne..being on all sides beesett with wooddes and fenns. **1642** ROGERS *Naaman* 345 Foggy clouds which doe beset the cleare sky. **1738** WESLEY *Ps.* cxxxix. iv, Within thy circling Arms I lie Beset on every side. **1853** KANE *Grinnell Exp.* x. (1856) 73 We are now again fast, completely 'beset.' **1870** HAWTHORNE *Eng. Note-Bks.* (1879) II. 243 The mountains which beset it round.

II. To set (in fig. sense), to bestow. All *trans.*

†**5.** To set or place (one's mind, affections, faith, trust, love) *on* or *upon* (any one); = SET *v.*¹ *Obs.*

c **1175** *Lamb. Hom.* 101 Cristene men ne sculen heore bileafe bisettan on þere weor(l)dliche eahte. *c* **1386** CHAUCER *Pers. T.* ¶ 532 Thay ben accursed..that on such filthe bisetten here bileeve. *c* **1440** *Generydes* 5021, I do very right, Though I besette my loue on suche a knyght. *c* **1449** PECOCK *Repr.* 295 His over great trust which..he bisettid upon hem. **1627** BP. HALL *Metaphr. Ps.* iv, Offer the truest sacrifice Of broken hearts, on God besetting Your only trust.

†**6.** To employ, expend, spend (one's words, wit, money, time, pains, study). *Obs.* Cf. *bestow.*

a **1240** *Sawles Warde* in *Lamb. Hom.* 249 Warschipe þat best con bisetten hire wordes ant ec hire werkes. *a* **1300** *Dame Siriz* 274 Neren never penes beter biset. **1340** *Ayenb.* 214 Me ssel alneway wel do and wel besette þane time ine guode workes. *c* **1386** CHAUCER *C.T.* Prol. 279 This worthi man ful wel his witte bisette. *c* **1449** PECOCK *Repr.* II. ix. 195 Forto bisette so mich labour and coste aboute ymagis. *c* **1560** in Hazl. *E.P.P.* I. 207 Here ys thy penyworth of ware; Yf thou thynke hyt not wele besett, Gyf hyt another.

†**7.** To bestow, apportion, allot, transfer; *spec.* to bestow or give in marriage. *Obs.*

c **1230** *Hali Meid.* 9 The poure [wummon] þat beoð wacliche iȝeouen and biset uuele. *c* **1325** *Chron. Eng.* 492 in Ritson's *Met. Rom.* II. 290 Thilke he delede on threo, Wel he bisette theo. **1480** CAXTON *Chron. Eng.* cxii, Orgarus thought his doughter shold wel be maryed, and wel beset upon hym. **1494** FABYAN I. iv. 11 He beset or apoynted to hym the Countre of Walys. **1599** BP. HALL *Sat.* IV. iii. 69 The beare his feirce-nesse to his brood besets.

†**8.** To set in order; arrange; ordain. *Obs.*

1413 *E.E. Wills* (1882) 19, I, Richard ȝonge, Brewer of London, be-set my testament in thys maner. **1494** FABYAN VI. clxxx. 178 Than this noble prynce Edward, after thise thinges, be set hym in an ordre. *c* **1500** *Blowbol's Test.* in Halliw. *Nugæ P.* 3 Withoute tarying ye make your Testament, And by good avice alle thing well besett.

III. To become, suit. Cf. Sc. *set,* Fr. *seoir.*

†**9.** To become, look well on, befit, set off. *Obs.*

1567 DRANT *Horace De Arte P.* A iiij, Sad wordes beset a sorye face; thretynge, the visage grim. **1598** R. POLLOCK *On 1 Thess.* (1616) 258 (JAM.) If thou be the childe of God, doe as besets thy estate—sleep not, but wake.

†**b.** *intr.* To go well or accord *with. Obs.*

1599 BP. HALL *Sat.* I. vi. 13 How handsomely besets Dull spondees with the English dactilets.

besetment (bɪˈsɛtmənt). [f. prec. + -MENT.]

1. The fact of besetting; *concr.* that by which one is beset; *esp.* a besetting sin, weakness, or influence.

1830 S. WARREN *Diary Physic.* (1838) II. vi. 231 To her other dreadful besetments, Mrs. Dudleigh now added the odious and vulgar vice of—intoxication! **1858** GEN. P. THOMPSON *Audi Alt. P.* I. xliv. 173 They yield to their peculiar besetments. **1867** W. PENGELLY *Trans. Devon Assoc.* II. 36 Amongst the besetments of the cultivators..is that of trusting to negative evidence.

2. A condition of being hemmed in by persistent obstacles, *e.g.* that of a ship enclosed in ice.

1853 KANE *Grinnell Exp.* xi. (1856) 84 My journal must give its own picture of this season of 'besetment.' **1861** *Life W. Scoresby* v. 91 A laughable incident occurred during the besetment.

3. A condition of being beset by enemies.

1872 SPURGEON *Treas. Dav.* Ps. lix. 16 David's besetment by Saul's bloodhounds.

besetter (bɪˈsɛtə(r)). [f. as prec. + -ER¹.] One who or that which besets.

1820 COLERIDGE in *Blackw. Mag.* VII. 630 There is one class of literary besetters who..are highly amusing to all but the unlucky patient himself.

beˈsetting, *vbl. sb.* [f. as prec. + -ING¹.] The action of surrounding with hostile intent.

1549 CHEKE *Hurt Sedit.* (1641) 27 The besetting of one house to robbe it.

beˈsetting, *ppl. a.* [f. as prec. + -ING².] That besets; esp. in the expression *besetting sin,* and the like, in allusion to *Heb.* xii. 1.

1795 SOUTHEY *Joan of Arc* II. 69 Retaining still..their old besetting sin. **1860** TRENCH *Serm. Westm. Ab.* xiii. 144 We have every one of us besetting sins..sins, that is, which more easily get advantage over us than others. **1868** M. PATTISON *Academ. Org.* §5. 210 The besetting danger of endowments—mental stagnation and apathy.

†**beˈsew,** *v. Obs.* For forms see SEW. [OE. *besíwian,* f. BE- 1 + *síwian* to SEW.] *trans.* To sew about, sew up. Hence **beˈsewed** *ppl. a.*

a **800** *Epinal Gl.* 699 (Sweet, *O.E.T.* 80) *Opere plumario* bisiuuidi uuerci [*Corpus Gl.* 1450 bisiudi werci]. *a* **1100** *Gloss.* in Wr.-Wülcker *Voc.* 459 Besiwed feðerȝeweorc. *c* **1350** *Will. Palerne* 1688 Miȝt we by coyntise com bi too skynnes of þe breme beres, and bisowe ȝou þerinne. *Ibid.* 3117 We be so sotiliche besewed in þise hides. **1393** GOWER *Conf.* III. 312 The dede body was besewed In cloth of gold and laid therinne. **1599** A. M. *Gabelhouer's Bk. Physic* 185/2 The besowede two little bandes.

besey, beseyge: see BESEE, BESIEGE.

beshackle, etc.: see BE- *pref.*

beshade (bɪˈʃeɪd), *v.* [OE. *besceadian,* f. BE- 1 + *sceadian* to SHADE.] To envelop in shade, overshadow. Hence **beˈshaded** *ppl. a.*

a **1000** *Salomon & Sat.* (Gr.) 339 For hwam besceadeð heo muntas and moras? **1393** GOWER III. 111 The highe tre the ground beshadeth. **1423** JAS. I. *Kingis Q.* xxxii, So thik the bewis and the leues grene Beschadit all the aleyes that there were. *a* **1606** SYLVESTER *Magnif.* 975. **1621** QUARLES *Argalus & P.* III. Wks. 1881 III. 273/1 She wore A Crowne of burnisht Gold, beshaded o're With Foggs and rory mist. **1827** CARLYLE *Germ. Rom.* III. 274. **1862** BARNES *Rhymes Dorset Dial.* II. 125 Bezide the hill's besheäded head.

beshadow (bɪˈʃædəʊ), *v.* For forms see SHADOW. [ME. *bishadewen*, prob. OE. **besceadwian*; cf. OHG. *biscatawên*, MHG. *beschatewen*, Du. *beschaduwen*; f. *bi-*, BE- 1 + OTeut. (Goth.) *skadwjan*, in OE. *sceadwian*, to SHADOW.] *trans.* To cast a shadow upon, to shade, overshadow; also *fig.* Hence **beˈshadowed** *ppl. a.*

a **1300** *Cursor M.* 10885 And goddes owne vertu now Shal þe bishadewe for monnes prow. *c* **1320** *Seuyn Sag.* (W.) 586. **1496** *Dives & Paup.* (W. de W.) IV. v. 166/1 The croppe.. bysshadoweth the rote for the hete of the sonne. **1558** PHAER *Æneid* IX. Cciij, Their heads to heauen they lift.. Beshadowyng broad the bows. **1883** *Century Mag.* XXVII. 47 All is so profoundly beshadowed by huge trees.

beshag, beshake, beshawled; see BE- *pref.*

beshame (bɪˈʃeɪm), *v.* [f. BE- 4 + SHAME *sb.*] To cover with shame, put to shame.

1556 ABP. PARKER *Psalter* xxxviii. [ix]. 109 Beshame me not. **1832** THIRLWALL in *Philol. Mus.* I. 490 Controversy is the element of the learned person who has undertaken to beshame and chastise me.

beshan, native name of Balm of Mecca: see BALM *sb.* 10.

beˈshear, *v.* For forms see SHEAR *v.* [WGer.: OE. *bescieran* = OHG. *bisceran* (MHG. *beschern*, Ger. and Du. *bescheren*), f. *bi-*, BE- 1, 3 + *sceran* to SHEAR.] *trans.* To shear or shave all round; *hence*, to shear, shave, or cut clean off.

[Still possible: at least in pa. pple. *beshorn*.]

c **893** K. ÆLFRED *Oros.* IV. xi. § 1 Hie eal hiera heafod bescearen. *c* **1000** ÆLFRIC *Judg.* xvi. 17 Ic næs næfre geefsod ne næfre bescoren. *a* **1300** *Cursor M.* 12231, I caitif al nu am bi-scorn [*Gött.* bischorn].

† **beˈshed**, *v. Obs.* Also bisched. [ME. f. BE- 2 + SHED *v.*] *trans.*

1. To perfuse, drench, moisten, wet (*with*).

1382 WYCLIF *1 Kings* xviii. 28 To the tyme that thei weren alle beshed with blood. **1388** —— *Isa.* lv. 10 As reyn and snow.. fillith the erthe, and bischedith it. —— *Esther* xv. 8.

2. To shed (blood).

1474 CAXTON *Chesse* III. iii. (1860) 7 Or he had do beshedde [? be shedde] ony blood he wepte.

† **beˈshend**, *v. Obs. rare*⁻¹. [f. BE- 2 + SHEND *v.*] *trans.* To ruin.

a **1300** *Cursor M.* 14838 Allas! nu has he ȝu bischent.

besher, variant of BEAUSIRE, ancestor. *Obs.*

beshet, obs. form of BESHUT *v.*

beshield, etc.: see BE- *pref.*

beshine (bɪˈʃaɪn), *v.* For forms see SHINE. [Com. Teut.: OE. *bi-*, *bescinan* = OFris. *bischîna*, OS., OHG. *biscînan* (MHG. *beschînen*, mod.G. *bescheinen*), Du. *beschijnen*, Goth. *biskeinan*:—OTeut. **biskînan*; f. *bi-*, BE- 1 + *skînan*, in OE. *scínan*, to SHINE.] Hence **beshone** *ppl. a.*

1. *trans.* To shine about or upon; to light up, illumine. Obs. bef. 1600, but used anew by Carlyle.

a **1000** *Riddles* (Gr.) lxxii. 17 þonne mec heaðosiȝel scir bescineð. *c* **1200** ORMIN 18851, And heffness lihht bishineþþ all Mannkinne þessterrnesse. *a* **1300** in Wright *Pop. Treat. Sc.* 132 As an appel the urthe is round, so that evere mo Half the urthe the sonne bi-schyneth, hou so hit evere go. **1387** TREVISA *Higden* (Rolls Ser.) VI. 293 Alcuinus byschoon þat lond wiþ liȝt of his lore. **1534** LD. BERNERS *Gold. Bk. M. Aurel.* (1546) Q b, Whan the sonne is sette, it beshyneth not the world. **1831** CARLYLE *Misc.* (1857) II. 270 The world —beshone by the young light of Love. **1850** BLACKIE *Æschylus* I. Pref. 23 The sun-beshone tiers of an ancient theatre.

†**2.** *intr.* with *upon*. *Obs.*

a **1300** *K. Horn* 12 Fairer ne miste no beo born, Ne no rein upon birine Ne sunne upon bischine.

†**3.** *trans.* To fall or light upon. *Obs. rare.*

1574 HELLOWES *Gueuara's Ep.* (1584) 275 Every time, that with the cold my stomach beginneth to belke, presently I say, a shame beshine Doctor Melgar.

† **beˈshining**, *vbl. sb. Obs.* [f. prec. + -ING¹.] Illumination, lighting up; ? effulgence. (See quot.)

1398 TREVISA *Barth De P.R.* VIII. xlii, [*Lumen differt a luce, sicut species a genere*] Byschinynge and lyȝt ben diuerse, as species and gendir, for euery bischinynge is lyȝte, but not aȝenwarde euery lyȝte is bischinynge. *Ibid.* VIII. xxviii. 340 One bishynynge comyth nat in to the substaunce of a nother though it seme to the syghte that they ben joyned.

beshiver, beshod, beshout, beshower: see BE- *pref.*

beshrew (bɪˈʃruː), *v. arch.* Forms: 4 be-, byschrewe, bishrewe, (6 bescro), 6–7 beshrow(e, 4–7 beshrewe, 5– beshrew. [f. BE- 2 + SHREW *v.*]

†**1.** *trans.* To make wicked or evil; to deprave, pervert, corrupt. *Obs.*

c **1325** *Poem temp. Edw. II.* 45 þis world is al beshrewed. **1382** WYCLIF *Prov.* x. 9 Who forsothe beshrewith [**1388** makith schrewid; *Vulg.* depravat] his weies, shal be maad opene. —— *1 Kings* xi. 4 The herte of hym is beshrewid bi wymmen. **1393** GOWER *Conf.* I. 63 His herte is all beshrewed. **1556** ABP. PARKER *Psalter* lvi. 161 What flesh can do, though all beshrowd, I feare no whit at all.

†**2.** To treat evilly, use ill, abuse. *Obs.*

c **1430** LYDG. *Min. Poems* 115 Thus they went from the game begylyd and beglued Nether on other wyst hom they went beshrewyd.

†**3.** To invoke evil upon, to wish (one) all that is bad, to invoke a curse on; to curse, objurgate, or blame greatly, as the cause of misfortune. *Obs.*

1377 LANGL. *P. Pl.* B. IV. 168 A schireues clerke byschrewed al þe route. *c* **1386** CHAUCER *Wife's Prol.* 844 Now elles, frere, I bishrewe thy face. Quod this Somonour, and I bishrewe me But if I telle tales two or thre Of freres. *c* **1485** *Digby Myst.* (1882) II. 88 Hye the faster, I beshrew thi skynne. **1533** MORE *Debell. Salem* Wks. 948/2, I durste well in the same worde (Some saye) beshrewe hym, and beshrowe hym agayne. **1642** FULLER *Holy & Prof. St.* IV. ix. 280 He hath just cause to beshrew his fingers. **1682** N. O. *Boileau's Lutrin* II. 106 Trembling she lay, and in her heart beshrewed him.

b. Now only in imprecatory expressions (*beshrew me, thee*, etc.): 'Evil befall, mischief take, devil take, curse, hang!'; also, with weakened force, 'plague on,' and often humorous or playful. *arch.* [Perhaps not imperative, but an elliptical form like *(I) thank you! (I) pray! (I) prithee!*]

1566 T. STAPLETON *Ret. Untr. Jewell* iii. 63 Then beshrowe the lyar. **1599** SHAKS. *Much Ado* v. i. 55 Marry beshrew my hand, If it should giue your age such cause of feare. **1604** —— *Oth.* IV. iii. 78 Beshrew me, if I would do such a wrong For the whole world. **1768** STERNE *Sent. Journ.* (1775) 85 Beshrew the sombre pencil! said I. **1828** SCOTT *F.M. Perth* ii, Beshrew me if thou passest this door with dry lips. **1856** BRYANT *Strange Lady* iii, Be-shrew my erring bow!

† **beˈshrewing.** *Obs.* [f. prec.] Used by Purvey to translate *refrenantem* of the Vulgate. ? Turning awry.

1388 WYCLIF *Isa.* ix. 14 And the Lord schal leese fro Israel the heed and the tail, crokynge and bischrewynge, [**1382** shrewende] *ether refreynynge*, in o dai.

beshriek, beshrivel, beshroud, etc.: see BE-.

† **beˈshromp**, *v. Obs. rare*⁻¹. ? = BESHREW 3.

1547 BOORDE *Introd. Knowl.* 207 When they be angry, lyke bees they do swarme; I beshromp them, they have don me much harme.

† **beˈshut**, *v. Obs.* For forms see SHUT. [ME. *be-*, *bishet*, *-shut*, f. *bi-*, BE- 1 + SHUT *v.*]

1. *trans.* To shut in, enclose, surround; to shut up, confine, imprison.

a **1300** *K. Alis.* 5765 Hy founden many lake and pett With trowes and thornes byshett. **1393** LANGL. *P. Pl.* C. XXII. 167 In an hous al by-shutt and here dore barred. **1470** HARDING *Chron.* cxlii. iv, A lady of greate beautee she was hold Beshet in pryson in paynes strong.

b. *fig.* To include, comprise.

1340 *Ayenb.* 97 Ine þise zeue wordes byeþ besset.. as þe summe of þe newe laȝe.

2. To shut out, exclude.

c **1330** *Amis & Amil.* 1907 And that brought him to that state Stode bischet, withouten the gate.

† **beˈsibbing**, *ppl. a. Obs. rare.* [f. BE- + SIB *a.* of kin, *sb.* affinity; cf. *resembling*.] Used by Warner for: Resembling, having a likeness to.

1602 WARNER *Alb. Eng.* x. lv. 246 Her selfe meane while, false-Paradiz'd, besybbing Æsops croe.. did end her song in woe. **1606** —— xvi. ciii. 405 Such bastard Courtnals serue but Turns, besibbing Coyns of brasse.

beside (bɪˈsaɪd), *adv.* and *prep.* Forms: 3–4 bisiden, 3–5 bi-side, -syde, byside, 4 bisid, -syd, -seid, (bezide), 4–5 besiden, bysyde, 4–6 bisyde(n, besyde, 5 byside(n, 4– beside. [ME. *bi siden*, *bisiden*:—OE. *be sídan*, i.e. *be* by, *sídan* (dat. sing.) side. Found in OE. only as two words, but by 1200 used as an adverb and preposition. Cf. the similar history of BIHALVE, which in early times was a synonym of this.]

A. *adv.*

1. By the side, by one's side. †**a.** *lit. Obs.*

c **1205** LAY. 12281 Bisiden heo gunnen heongen cniues swiðe longe. *c* **1386** CHAUCER *Frankl. T.* 513 To Britaigne tooke they the righte way Aurelius and this Magicien bisyde. *c* **1430** *Syr Tryam.* 545 Some on horsys and some besyde. **1590** A. MUNDAY *Eng. Romayne Life* in *Harl. Misc.* v. (1811) 156 Kirbie, quaking when he felt the cart goe away, looked styll how neere the end of it was, till he was quite beside.

†**b.** Side by side in rank, on a level. *Obs. rare.*

1340 *Ayenb.* 125 Hi yelt.. loue to ham þet byeþ bezide, grace to ham þet byeþ beneþe.

c. Hard by, close, near. *arch.* †Rarely of time (see quot. 1380). *Obs.* (Mostly an elliptical use of the *prep.*, or with *here-*, *there-*, in place of object.)

1297 R. GLOUC. 558 þo sei he þer biside.. þe erles baner of Gloucetre. *c* **1314** *Guy Warw.* 56 An abbay That was bisiden on the way. *c* **1380** WYCLIF *Sel. Wks.* III. 44 [Vulg. *Juxta est dies perdicionis*] Bisyde is þe day of perdicioun.. Biside, þat is, neer is þe day [**1611** *Deut.* xxxii. 35 at hand]. **1517** TORKINGTON *Pilgr.* (1884) 20 A lityll ther be syd stondyth an old Churche. **1798** COLERIDGE *Anc. Mar.* IV. x, The moving moon went up the sky.. and a star or two beside. **1805** SOUTHEY *Madoc in Azt.* xvi, Mervyn beside, Hangs over his dear mistress silently.

2. In addition, over and above; = BESIDES 2 (by which this is now usually expressed).

1297 R. GLOUC. 92 Of þe lond of France, and of oþer londes bi syde. **1393** GOWER *Conf.* I. 30 Hem nedeth.. Of straunge londes helpe beside. **1477** EARL RIVERS (Caxton) *Dictes* 144 The goode dedis that thou shalt do besyde. **1591** SHAKS. *1 Hen. VI*, IV. i. 25 My selfe, and diuers Gentlemen beside. **1692** E. WALKER *Epictetus' Mor.* xx, Now if the same Behaviour be your Guide, In all the actions of your life beside. **1766** GOLDSM. *Vic. W.* xxiv. (1806) 143 We can marry her to another.. and what is more, she may keep her lover beside. **1825** CARLYLE *Schiller* I. (1845) 11 It was by stealth if he read or wrote any thing beside.

b. As an additional consideration; moreover; = BESIDES A. 2b (by which now usually expressed).

1592 GREENE *Art Conny Catch.* III. 8 The Maide.. was not a little ioyfull to see him: beside, shee seemed proud that her kinsman was so neat a youth. **1663** BUTLER *Hud.* I. i. 127 Beside he was a shrewd philosopher. **1871** BROWNING *Balaustion* (1881) 148 Beside, when he found speech, you guess the speech.

3. Otherwise, else; = BESIDES 3 (by which this is now usually expressed).

1588 SHAKS. *L.L.L.* I. i. 40 And one day in the week to touch no food, And but one meal on euery day beside. **1649** MILTON *Eikon* Pref. C, Rebels.. to God in all thir actions beside. **1734** POPE *Ess. Man* IV. 243 To all beside as much an empty shade. **1816** J. WILSON *City of Plague* II. i. 146 We talk'd Of thee and none beside. **1843** E. JONES *Sens. & Event* 57 And these forgetting, all beside In life will darken.

†**4.** On or to one side, apart. *Obs.* (Now ASIDE.)

a **1375** *Cursor M.* 3622 (Trin.), She went bi syde & hir biþouȝt. **1375** BARBOUR *Bruce* XI. 344 The toythir bataills suld be gangand Bisid on sid, a litill space. *c* **1400** *Apol. Loll.* 56 Peter tok him be side, & be gan to blam him. *c* **1485** *Digby Myst.* (1882) II. 191 Goo thou.. In-to the Cyte a lytyll be-syde. **1551** ROBINSON tr. *More's Utop.* 152 Whiles yᵉ armies be fighting together in open feld, they a litle beside not farre of knele upon their knees.

†**b.** *esp.* with *set, put, leave*, etc. (See ASIDE 4).

1414 BRAMPTON *Penit. Ps.* lxxxvi. 33 Lust and lykyng I sette be syde. **1436** *Pol. Poems* (1859) II. 187 Yeue us grace alle sloughte to leue bysyde. **1548** UDALL, etc. *Erasm. Par. Matt.* i. 21 He set his elder brother besyde. *a* **1604** HANMER *Chron. Irel.* 17 In the end the two sonnes were put beside.

†**5.** Toward the side, sidewise. *Obs.* (= ASIDE 7).

c **1400** *Destr. Troy* 1221 Lamydon at the laste lokit besyde.

†**6.** By the side so as to miss, by, past. ***to go beside***: to pass on one side, to miss. *Obs.*

c **1430** *Stans Puer* 60 in *Babees Bk.* (1868) 31 Fille not þi spoon lest in þe cariage It scheede bi side, it were not commendable. **1526** *Pilgr. Perf.* (W. de W. 1531) 35 b, And where it purposeth to go ouer the brydge, it gothe besyde, and falleth into the dyche. **1592** SHAKS. *Ven. & Ad.* 981 Yet sometimes falls an orient drop beside Which her cheek melts.

B. *prep.*

1. *lit.* By the side of; *hence*, close to, hard by.

a. *strictly.* By the side of a person, animal, or thing that has a recognized side. (The more definite *by the side of*, *by his*, *her*, etc. *side*, is now often used instead, as being more distinct from b.)

c **1205** LAY. 21408 þer fæht Baldulf bisiden his broðer. *a* **1300** *Cursor M.* 3873 Bisid lya al night he lai. *Ibid.* 1787 þe leon suam beside þe hert. **1493** *Festivall* (W. de W. 1515) 10 Thenne falleth his sede besyde the waye. **1526** *Pilgr. Perf.* (W. de W. 1531) 155 The thefe that honge on the crosse besyde our lorde. **1611** BIBLE *Ps.* xxiii. 2 He leadeth mee beside the still waters. **1712** STEELE *Spect.* No. 460 ¶7 The boy who stood beside her. **1727** THOMSON *Summer* 11 Beside the brink Of haunted stream. **1766** GOLDSM. *Vic. W.* xxi. (1806) 125 We sate beside his kitchen fire. **1816** J. WILSON *City of Plague* I. i. 319 Let me sit down beside you.

b. Less exactly: Close to, near any part of, by.

a **1300** *Cursor M.* 8207 And did be siden þaim laumpis liht. *c* **1320** *Seuyn Sag.* (W.) 3315 That castell That the se ran fast byside. *c* **1375** WYCLIF *Wks.* (1880) 189 She saat bisiden cristis feet. *c* **1430** *How Good Wife, etc.* 172 in *Babees Bk.* (1868) 41 Please weel þi neiȝboris þat dwelle þee biside. **1611** BIBLE *Song. Sol.* i. 8 Feede thy kiddes beside the shepheards tents. *c* **1680** BEVERIDGE *Serm.* (1729) II. 299 It doth not fall upon him but beside him. **1884** L. KEITH *Venetia's Lov.* II. 11 You'll come beside us in the drawing room.

†**c.** Formerly with names of towns, etc., where we now use *by*, *near*. *Obs.*

c **1200** *Trin. Coll. Hom.* 31 þe herdes wakeden ouer here oref biside þe burch belleem. **1297** R. GLOUC. 558 To a toun biside Wircetre, þat Kemeseie ihote is. **1382** WYCLIF *Gen.* xiii. 18 Abram.. dwellide biside the valey of Mambre. **1418** *E.E. Wills* (1882) 32 Seint Gyles beside Holbourne. **1523** LD. BERNERS *Froiss.* I. xiv. 14 At the palaice of Westminster, beside London. **1581** MARBECK *Bk. of Notes* 556 He.. was buried a little beside the same Citie.

d. *fig.* (*a*) Side by side with in rank, on a level with. (*b*) By the side of for comparison, compared with.

1513 DOUGLAS *Æneis* I. Prol. 365 Besyde Latyne our langage is imperfite. **1843** RUSKIN *Mod. Paint.* (1851) I. Pref. 20 Gainsborough's power of colour.. is capable of taking rank beside that of Rubens.

2. In addition to, over and above, as well as; = BESIDES B. 2 (by which now usually expressed).

1340 HAMPOLE *Pr. Consc.* 3697 Bot speciel prayers with gude entente, þat es made besyde þe sacramente. *c* **1380** WYCLIF *Sel. Wks.* III. 435 For þise sixe kyndenessis bysyde goostliche suffragies. **1558** BP. WATSON *Sev. Sacr.* xxx. 191 The priest.. beside his praiers, doth minister the outwarde sacrament of Aneiling. **1611** BIBLE *Lev.* xxiii. 38 Beside the Sabbaths of the Lord, and beside your gifts. **1774** SIR J. REYNOLDS *Disc.* vi. (1876) 396 Beside his master Andrea

Sacchi, he imitated Rafaelle. **1832** J. C. Hare in *Philol. Museum* I. 59 Beside the planets usually seen, there are other stars. **1879** Lewes *Study Psychol.* 70 Other men beside ourselves.

†**b.** with *obj. clause*; = besides B. 2 b. *Obs.*

1651 *Life Father P. Sarpi* (1676) 87 The Pope, beside that he is the head of Religion, is also a Prince.

3. Other than, else than; = besides B. 3 (by which this is now usually expressed).

c **1400** *Apol. Loll.* 43 If he haue ani þing bi syd þe Lord, þe Lord schal not be his part. **1526** *Pilgr. Perf.* (W. de W. 1531) 238 b, In yᵉ whiche commaundement is prohybyte..all other maner of lechery, besyde the acte of matrimony. **1621** Bp. Mountagu *Diatribae* 422 No man beside Festus, in that fragment, doth tell us, etc. **1710** Shaftesb. *Charac.* I. §3 (1737) I. 65 None can understand the Speculation beside those who have the Practise. **1827** Bp. Heber *Hymn*, Only Thou art holy, there is none beside Thee, Perfect in power, in love, and purity.

†**4.** Outside of, out of, away from. *Obs.*

†**a.** By the side of so as to pass without contact, by the outside of, past, by. ***to go beside*** (L. *præterīre*): to pass by, pass over, miss. ***to look beside***: to overlook, fail to see, miss. *Obs.*

c **1375** Wyclif *Serm.* Sel. Wks. I. 15 Þei tristen on riȝt of mannis lawe, and gone ofte beside þe soþe. **1382** —— *Prov.* xix. 11 The glorie of hym is to go beside wicke thingys [**1388** to passe ouere wickid thingis]. **1627** Bp. Hall *Epist.* iv. iii. 341 Let vs but open our eyes, we cannot looke beside a lesson. **1629** Gaule *Holy Madn.* 95 Oh, doe him not the wrong to looke beside him, for if you see him not, hee comes by to no purpose.

†**b.** Of position: Outside of, out of, away from.

c **1400** *Apol. Loll.* 1 To reduce me in to þe riȝt wey, if I haue gon biside þe wey in ani þing. **1555** in Strype *Eccl. Mem.* III. ii. App. xlvii. 143 Beside and without the compasse of the same Articles. **1663** Butler *Hud.* i. i. 502 As of Vagabonds we say That they are ne'er beside their way.

†**c.** Of removal, deprivation: Out of, away from; *esp.* with *put*, *set*, *pluck*, etc. *Obs.*

1548 Udall, etc. *Erasm. Par., Matt.* ii. 25 Least he should be set beside the kingdome whiche he..held. **1551** Robinson tr. *More's Utop.* 133 If they by couyne or gile be wiped beside their goodes. **1553–87** Foxe *A. & M.* II. 384 He put the new Pope Alexander beside the cushion and was made pope himself. **1570–87** Holinshed *Scot. Chron.* (1806) II. 60 One of them taking displeasure with his father ..stepped to him and plucking her [a falcon] beside his fist wrong her neck. **1660** Stanley *Hist. Philos.* (1701) 2/1 Neleus Son of Cordrus being put beside the Kingdom of Athens by his younger Brother Medon.

5. *fig.* senses from 4.

a. Out of a mental state or condition, as ***beside one's patience***, ***one's gravity***, ***one's wits***; now only in ***beside oneself***: out of one's wits, out of one's senses; cf. F. *hors de soi*, Ger. *ausser sich*.

1490 Caxton *Eneydos* xxvii. 98 Mad and beside herself. **1526** Frith *Disp. Purgat.* 175 The man was almost beside himself, and then was he sent to Oxford. **1596** Shaks. *1 Hen. IV*, iii. i. 179 Enough to put him quite beside his patience. **1611** Bible *Acts* xxvi. 24 Festus saide with a lowd voyce, Paul, thou art beside [*Tindale* besides] thy selfe, much learning doeth make thee mad. **1716** Lady M. W. Montague *Lett.* I. vi. 20 This question almost put him beside his gravity. **1827** Hood *Hero & Leand.* cvii, Like an enchanted maid beside her wits. **1884** Q. Victoria *More Leaves* 399, I felt quite beside myself for joy and gratitude.

b. Away from, wide of (a mark); apart from, not embraced within (a plan, purpose, question).

1533 More *Debell. Salem* Wks. 1021/2 He speketh al beside the purpose. **1573** G. Harvey *Letter-bk.* (1884) 51, I take it, M. Proctor was beside his book. **1691** Ray *Creation* i. (1704) 64 Because it is beside my Scope. **1853** Robertson *Serm.* Ser. iii. xiii. 158 The distinction..is an altogether false one and beside the question. **1856** Froude *Hist. Eng.* (1858) I. iii. 285 The point on which the battle was being fought lay beside the real issue. **1883** *Manch. Guard.* 22 Oct. 5/3 Really this question is beside the mark.

†**c.** Beyond the range or compass of (L. *præter*); utterly apart from; *hence* sometimes approaching the sense 'contrary to.' *Obs.*

1526 *Pilgr. Perf.* (W. de W. 1531) 14 b, No persone may receyue..the counseyles of the holy goost, excepte he haue besyde nature a spirituall eare. **1548** Geste *Pr. Masse* 98 It is institute besyde Gods wrytten wordes and so contrarie to the same. *a* **1619** Fotherby *Atheom.* ii. viii. §2 (1622) 281 Vertues are begotten in vs, neither by nature, nor beside nature. *c* **1688** South *Serm.* (1715) 462 A Lye is properly an outward Signification of something contrary to, or, at least, beside the inward Sense of the Mind. *a* **1758** J. Edwards in N. Worcester *Atoning Sacr.* (1830) 140 Old men seldom have any advantage from new discoveries, because these are beside a way of thinking which they have been long used to. **1773** Johnson *Lett.* (1788) I. lxxiii. 106 At Durham, beside all expectation, I met an old friend.

†**C.** *Comb.* **be'side-forth, besides-forth** *adv.*, moreover, further; **beside-sitter**, one who sits beside, an assessor; **be'sideward**, ? outside, hard by, in the vicinity. *Obs.*

1377 Langl. *P. Pl.* B. xvii. 22 Judas Macabeus, ȝe and sexty þousande bisyde forth · þat ben nouȝt seyen here. **1548** Udall, etc. *Erasm. Par. Luke* i. 17 And yet was besides-forth an ungodly and a wicked person. **1340** *Ayenb.* 40 Þe kueade bezidezitteres, þet yeueþ þe kueade redes to þe demeres. **1460** *Pol. Rel. & L. Poems* (1866) 116 To men þat in þe cyte dwelle; And men þat dwellen be-sydwarde.

besides (bɪˈsaɪdz), *adv.* and *prep.* Forms: 3–4 bisides, 4 bi-, bysidis, bysydes, 5–6 besydes, -is, 5– besides. [f. beside + *s* of the advb. genitive, here probably a northern substitute for the southern *-en* of *bisiden*. This has been used in all the senses of beside, but is now used, in prose, only in senses 2, 3, for which it is the proper word.]

A. *adv.*

†**1.** By the side; close by, near; = beside A. 1.

c **1205** Lay. 5181 Brennes [wende] bisides mid his folke of Burguine. *c* **1340** *Gaw. & Gr. Knt.* 76 Smal sendal bisides, a selure hir ouer. *c* **1440** *Gesta Rom.* 114 Heer besydes is a foreste. *c* **1450** Lonelich *Grail* xliv. 388 Iosephs in that Castel not ne was, but at anothir besides in that plas.

2. In addition, over and above, as well.

1564 Haward *Eutropius* vi. 52 He deprived him of a portion of his kingdom, and assessed hym to pay a great summe of mony besides. **1611** Bible *Gen.* xix. 12 And the men said vnto Lot, Hast thou here any besides? **1821** Keats *Isabel* liv, It drew Nurture besides, and life, from human fears. **1863** Mary Howitt *F. Bremer's Greece* II. xvi. 149 There are, besides, many marble slabs with long Greek inscriptions.

b. Introducing a further consideration: As an additional or further matter, moreover, further.

1596 Shaks. *Merch. V.* ii. i. 15 Besides, the lottrie of my destenie Bars me the right of voluntarie choosing. **1682** Norris *Hierocles* 8 Besides, God is not at all Honour'd by the most costly oblations. **1774** Burke *Amer. Tax.* Wks. II. 384 Besides, they were indemnified for it. **1858** Bright *Reform, Sp.* (1876) 282 There is, besides, this great significant fact. *Mod.* It is rather too late to go out; besides, I am tired.

3. Other than mentioned, otherwise, else.

1596 Shaks. *1 Hen. IV*, iii. i. 185 Which..leaves behinde a stayne Upon the beautie of all parts besides. *a* **1694** Tillotson *Serm.* I. i. (R.) An ignorant man, whatever he may know besides. *a* **1704** Locke (J.) Robbers, who break with all the world besides, must keep faith among themselves. **1768** Blackstone *Comm.* I. 4 Knowledge in which the gentlemen of England have been more remarkably deficient than those of all Europe besides.

†**4.** = beside A. 6. *Obs.* (Now aside.)

1611 Beaum. & Fl. *Maid's Trag.* v. (1679) 19 The blows thou mak'st at me are quite besides. **1650** Bulwer *Anthropomet.* xi. (1653) 184 They never faile, or cast it besides. **1660** Stanley *Hist. Philos.* (1701) 152/2 He was so thoughtful, that going to put Incense into a Censer, he put it besides.

B. *prep.*

†**1.** = beside B. 1. *Obs.*

c **1200** *Trin. Coll. Hom.* 31 Ða com on angel of heuene to hem, and stod bisides hem. *a* **1300** *Cursor M.* 16878 In a ȝard bisides þe tune. **1382** Wyclif *Matt.* xiii. 1 Jhesus..sat bisides the sæ. **1480** Caxton *Trevisa's Descr. Eng.* 6 At Stonhenge besides Salesbury. **1542** Udall *Erasm. Apoph.* 316 b, I would..make you roome here besides me, but that I sitte in so narrowe a roome myself. **1605** Stow *Ann.* 372 King Edward kept his Christmasse at Kenington besides Lambeth. **1677** Moxon *Mech. Exerc.* (1703) 208 Hold.. your Right Hand close besides your Left Hand.

2. Over and above, in addition to, as well as. (This and the next are the ordinary current senses.)

1535 Joye *Apol. Tindale* 24 Besydis thys condempnacion of me by hearsaye. **1552** Huloet, Besydes that, *præterea*. **1557** N. T. (Geneva) *Luke* xvi. 26 Besydes all this, betwene you and us there is a great gulfe set. [So **1611**.] *c* **1680** Beveridge *Serm.* (1729) I. 484 Besides that..they have some part of his word solemnly read. **1783** Ld. Hailes *Anc. Chr. Ch.* ii. 50 St. Paul..became acquainted with many Christians besides his converts. **1875** Bryce *Holy Rom. Emp.* vii. (ed. 5) 112 The Emperor, besides the sword.. receives a ring as the symbol of his faith.

b. with *obj. clause.*

1579 E. K. in *Spenser's Sheph. Cal.* Mar. *Gloss.*, Besides the..affection..tormenteth the mynde. **1586** Cogan *Haven Health* (1636) 97 Besides that this water cooleth all the inward parts, it doth greatly helpe the stone. **1860** Mill *Repr. Govt.* (1865) 59/2 The representatives of the majority, besides that they would themselves be improved in quality ..would no longer have the whole field to themselves.

3. Other than, else than: in negative and interrogative (formerly sometimes in affirmative) sentences, capable of being rendered by 'except, excluding.'

c **1375** Wyclif *Wks.* (1880) 393 No man may putt an-oþer ground bysidis þat þat is putt [So **1382** N. T. *1 Cor.* iii. 11; **1388** outtakun; Tind., Coverd., *Genev.*, **1611**, then; *Rhem.* beside.] *c* **1534** tr. *Pol. Verg. Eng. Hist.* I. 22 England is well stored with all kinde of beeastes, besides asses, mules, cammels, and elephants. **1651** Hobbes *Leviath.* ii. xxii. 116 Not the act of the Body, nor of any other Member thereof besides himselfe. *a* **1716** South *12 Serm.* (1717) IV. 37 The Jews..for ever unsainting all the world besides themselves. **1711** Addison *Spect.* No. 110 ⁋1 No living Creature ever walks in it besides the Chaplain. **1758** Jortin *Erasm.* I. 266 In the opinion of every one besides himself. *Mod.* Have you nothing to tell us besides what we have already heard?

†**4.** = beside B. 4. **a.** Past, by. *Obs.*

1634 Preston *New Covt.* 62 Careful that none of this water run besides the mill. **1639** Fuller *Holy War* v. ii. (1647) 232 King Philip missed of his expectation, and the morsel fell besides his mouth. **1660** Stanley *Hist. Philos.* (1701) 468/2 [He] proposed sophisms to the disputants, slipping besides the sense. **1680** *Observ. on 'Curse Ye Meroz'* 5 No sooner did they perceive the waters begin to run besides their Mill..but they turned *Cat in Pan*, and cursed as fast the contrary way.

†**b.** Opposition: Out of, away from, off. *Obs.*

1537 Tindale *Exp. 1 John* Wks. II. 183 Thou mayest well, besides Christ, know him [God] as a tyrant. **1607** Topsell *Serpents* 769 Ælianus was a little besides the way, when he set down *macrous* for *microus*. **1641** *Vind. Smectymnuus* §7. 90 He tels us we are besides the Cushion.

†**c.** Of removal: Out of, away from, off. ***to put besides***: to put out of, do out of, deprive of.

1551 Robinson tr. *More's Utop.* 41 The husbandmen.. by coueyne and fraude..be put besydes it. **1577** Holinshed *Chron.* I. 173/1 The Englishmen..desirous..to shake off the yoke of Danish thraldome besides their necks and shoulders. **1605** Bacon *Adv. Learn.* ii. xiv. §5 (1873) 159 Doth not only put a man besides his answer. **1654** Ussher *Ann.* v. 88 That no God was able to put him besides his Kingdom. **1702** *Eng. Theophrast.* 47 An extravagant love.. puts the Philosopher besides his Latin.

5. *fig.* (from 4.) = beside B. 5.

†**a.** Out of any mental state; hence ***besides oneself***: see beside B. 5 a. *Obs.*

1526 Tindale *Acts* xxvi. 24 Paul, thou arte besides thy selfe. **1535** Joye *Apol. Tindale* 36, I am suer Tindale is not so farre besydis his comon sencis. **1611** Bible *2 Cor.* v. 13 Whether wee bee besides our selues..or whether we bee sober. **1690** Locke *Hum. Und.* ii. xxvii. (1695) 186 Our way of speaking in English, when we say such an one is not himself, or is besides himself..as if..the self same Person was no longer in that Man.

†**b.** = beside B. 5 b. *Obs.*

1581 R. Goade in *Confer.* ii. (1584) I iiij b, You fall to discoursing cleane besides the purpose. **1651** Lilly & Ashmole *Autobiogr.* (1774) 172 Its besides my task to write the life of the late King. **1699** Bentley *Phal.* 219 Though it be quite besides the subject.

†**c.** Beyond; = beside B. 5 c. *Obs.*

1564 *Brief Exam.* **b, Nothyng muste be brought into the Churche, besides or contrary to Scripture. **1577** Vautroullier *Luther's Ep. Gal.* 8 This thou doest besides thine office; keepe thy selfe within thy bounds. *Ibid.* 36 If it teach any thing besides or against Gods word. **1661** Bramhall *Just. Vind.* vii. 196 The Pope can do nothing in France..either against the Canons or besides the Canons. **1668** Culpepper & Cole *Barthol. Anat.* iv. i. 159 Tis besides nature. **1692** Locke *Toleration* iii. iv. Wks. 1727 II. 355 A model so wholly new, and besides all experience.

besie, obs. form of busy.

besiege (bɪˈsiːdʒ), *v.* Forms: 3–6 bysege, 4 biseche, 4–5 be-, bisege, 5 biseige, 7 besiedge, -sige, 5– besiege. [ME. *bi-*, *by-*, *besege(n*, f. be- 1 + *sege(n*, aphetic f. *asege(n*, assiege.]

1. *trans.* To sit down before (a town, castle, etc.) with armed forces in order to capture it; to lay siege to, beleaguer, invest.

1297 R. Glouc. 387 Þys ost wende þuderward..And byseged þen castel syx wouke wel vaste. *a* **1300** *Cursor M.* 9211 Twelve moneþ he biseged hit. *c* **1380** *Sir Ferumb.* 4275 Þyn barons..þat so buþ be-seged on þat tour. **1382** Wyclif *Isa.* xxi. 2 Steeȝh vp, Elam, and bisege [*v.r.* biseche] Medeba. *c* **1440** *Gesta Rom.* 9 A certeyn Cite..was biseigyd with..enemeys of þe Emperoure. **1595** Shaks. *John* ii. i. 489 This Cittie now by vs besiedg'd. **1611** Bible *1 Sam.* xxiii. 8 Saul called all the people together..to besiege Dauid, and his men. **1671** Milton *P.R.* iii. 339 Agrican with all his northern powers Besieg'd Albracca. **1844** Thirlwall *Greece* VII. lx. 67 Antigonus besieged the city for ten months.

b. *fig.* and *transf.*

c **1600** Shaks. *Sonn.* ii, When forty winters shall besiege thy brow. **1601** —— *All's Well* ii. i. 10 The mallady That doth my life besiege. **1608** Armin *Nest Ninn.* 31 Having wrung off her neck, begins to besiedge that good morsel.

2. *transf.* To crowd round like a besieging army; to block up, hem in.

1686 *Gentl. Recr.* i. 101 A Planet is besieged, when he is between the Bodies of the two..Malevolents, Saturn and Mars. **1717** Pope *Elegy Unfort. Lady* 38 Frequent hearses shall besiege your gates. **1789** Jefferson *Corr.* (1830) 20 The people have besieged the doors of the bakers.

3. *fig.* To assail with importunate addresses or prayers.

1712 Steele *Spect.* No. 534 ⁋5 There is one gentleman who besieges me as close as the French did Bouchain. **1737** Pope *Hor. Ep.* i. vii. 29 Fools with compliments besiege ye. **1850** Alison *Hist. Europe* VIII. l. §45 The ministers were besieged with innumerable applications for every office. **1867** Parkman *Jesuits N. Amer.* xix. (1875) 293 Pious souls ..who daily and nightly besieged Heaven with supplications.

†**be'siege**, *sb. Obs.* Also 6 beseyge, 7 beseige. [f. prec. vb.] Besieging, siege.

1552 Huloet, Besiege laier, *obsessor*. **1599** Hakluyt *Voy.* II. 15 The besiege of Sagitta. **1611** Speed *Hist. Gt. Brit.* ix. xxiv. (1632) 1191 The besiege of Inis-Kellen. **1664** *Floddan F.* iii. 22 Your saults and hard besiege.

besieged (bɪˈsiːdʒd), *ppl. a.* [f. prec. vb. + -ed¹.]

1. Invested or surrounded by hostile forces.

c **1440** *Promp. Parv.* 27 Besegyde, *obsessus*. **1603** in *Shaks. C. Praise* 57 Of Helens rape and Troyes besieged Towne. **1795** Southey *Joan of Arc* vi. 158 Our foes Haply may.. quit in peace Besieged Orleans.

b. *absol.* The people besieged.

1603 Knolles *Hist. Turkes* (1638) 320 Offering vnto the besieged..easie conditions of peace. **1863** Stanley *Jew. Ch.* xi. 239 The besieged and the besiegers alike were taken by surprise.

2. *transf.* Beset by an importunate crowd.

1866 Crump *Banking* ii. 55 The funds..were instantly returned to the besieged bank.

besiegement (bɪˈsiːdʒmənt). Also 7 besiedg-. [f. as prec. + -ment.] The action of besieging or state of being besieged; also *fig.*

1564 Golding *Justine* 31 (R.) Setting before their eies besiegement, hungar, and the arrogant enemy. **1577** *Test. 12 Patriarchs* (1604) 75 The Lord shall bring upon you famine, and..wrathful besiegement. *a* **1679** T. Goodwin *Wks.* (1865) X. 481 An unheard-of way of besiegement.

besieger (bɪˈsiːdʒə(r)). [f. as prec. + -er¹.] One who besieges.

1580 Baret *Alv.* B 570 A besieger, *obsessor*. **1594** T. B. *La Primaud. Fr. Acad.* 313 Demetrius, surnamed the Besieger. **1633** H. Cogan *Pinto's Trav.* liii. (1663) 209 Permission for the Besieged to converse with the Besiegers. **1709** Steele

Tatler No. 18 ¶6 The Besiegers were quiet in their Trenches. **1860** FROUDE *Hist. Eng.* V. 80 The advanced works of the besiegers were..close to the town.

be'sieging (bɪ'siːdʒɪŋ), *vbl. sb.* Also 4 bi-, 5 besegynge. [f. as prec. + -ING[1].] The action of laying siege to (a place); the condition of being besieged.

1382 WYCLIF *Ezek.* iv. 2 Thou shalt ordeyne aȝens it a bisegynge. **1388** —— *Jer.* x. 17 Thou that dwellist in bisegyng. **1560** WHITEHORNE *Art Warre* (1588) 93 b, The defending and besieging of townes. **1611** BIBLE *Ecclus.* l. 4 He..fortified the citie against besieging. **1801** STRUTT *Sports & Past.* II. ii. 66 Chiefly used in besieging of cities.

be'sieging, *ppl. a.* [f. as prec. + -ING[2].] That besieges; employed in a siege.

1813 *Examiner* 17 May 307/2 The besieging corps before Dantzick. **1820** KEATS *St. Agnes* xl, The arras..Flutter'd in the besieging wind's uproar. **1863** HOLLAND *Lett. Joneses* xv, A will as patient..as that which a besieging army needs.

be'siegingly, *adv. rare.* [f. prec. + -LY[2].] Urgently, importunately.

1822 DE QUINCEY *Confess.* Wks. I. 270 Any particular death..haunts my mind more obstinately and besiegingly, in that season.

besigh (bɪ'saɪ), *v.* [f. BE- 4 + SIGH *v.*] To sigh over.

c **1200** *Trin. Coll. Hom.* 201 þe sinfulle þe his sinnes..sore bisicheð. **1827** CARLYLE *Germ. Romance* I. 46 Besighing his past madness.

†**be'sight.** *Obs. rare.* In 3 besiȝte, 4 besiht. [ME. *besiȝte*, f. BESEE *v.*, and *siȝte*, SIGHT.] Consideration, determination, ordinance.

1258 *Proclam. Hen. III*, The besiȝte of than to foren iseide redesmen. *c* **1320** *Cast. Loue* 311 A þral..þorw be-siht of riht dom To strong prison was i-don.

besil(e, obs. form of BEZZLE.

besilver (bɪ'sɪlvə(r)), *v.* [f. BE- 1 + SILVER *v.*] *trans.* To silver over, to cover or line with silver; also *fig.* Hence **be'silvered** *ppl. a.*

1610 G. FLETCHER *Christ's Vict.* in Farr's *S.P.* (1847) 61 Many streams his banks besilvered. **1800** W. TAYLOR in Robberds *Mem.* I. 330 Yet how well he amalgamates and besilvers all! **1825** *Blackw. Mag.* XVIII. 436 The moon-besilver'd casements guided us. **1864** R. BARTON *Dahome* II. 33 Wives and Amazons, copiously besilvered.

besin, besinge, besiren: see BE- *pref.*

besing (bɪ'sɪŋ), *v.* [f. BE- 4 + SING *v.*] *trans.* **a.** To sing (into some state). **b.** To sing about (a person, etc.); to celebrate in song; to sing to. Hence **besung** (bɪ'sʌŋ), *ppl. a.*

1566 DRANT *Horace Sat.* x. E iv b, If the plaintife Poet shoulde besing his muses horce. **1828** CARLYLE *Misc.* (1857) I. 239 Let him worship and besing the idols of the time. **1860** DICKENS *Uncomm. Trav.* iii, In the Charter which has been so much besung. **1865** CARLYLE *Fredk. Gt.* IV. XII. i. 119 The Mountain part..besung by rushing torrents.

†**be'sink,** *v. Obs.* Forms: 1 besincan, 2-3 bisinken; *Pa. t.* -sank; *Pa. pple.* -sunken. [OE. *besincan* str. vb., f. BE- 2 + *sincan* to SINK.]

1. *intr.* To sink, fall down through any substance.

c **893** K. ÆLFRED *Oros.* III. xi. 10 Sio burȝ besanc on eorþan. *c* **1230** *Hali Meid.* 33 Hwase lið ileinen deope bisunken.

2. *trans.* To submerge. For BESENCH.

c **1200** *Trin. Coll. Hom.* 177 þe storm bisinkeð þe ship.

†**besire,** a bad form for DESIRE.

1589 *Marprel. Epit.* C, Ile besire them to leaue this order, or els they are like to heare of it..And ile besire you.

†**be'sit,** *v. Obs.* Also 4-5 bisit. [OE. *besittan* to sit about, besiege f. BE- 1 + *sittan* to SIT. The primary verb, of which BESET is the causal.]

1. *trans.* To encamp about, besiege.

a **1100** *O.E. Chron.* (Laud MS.) an. 1087 Se cyng..let besittan þone castel. **1154** *Ibid.* an. 1135 Te king it besæt.

2. To sit upon; to lie heavy upon; to weigh upon.

1362 LANGL. *P. Pl.* A. II. 110 Hit schal bisitten oure soules sore atte laste. **1377** *Ibid.* B. x. 361 It shal bisitten vs ful soure, þe siluer þat we kepen.

3. To sit properly upon (as a dress): to fit, suit, become. Cf. F. *seoir*.

c **1449** PECOCK *Repr.* I. xiv. 73 This..bisittith not his wisdom. *c* **1471** FORTESCUE *Wks.* (1869) 463 Yt besatt not his magnifycence to have done otherwise. **1603** HOLLAND *Plutarch's Mor.* 227 Affections for to change it well besits. **1614** C. B. *Ghost Rich. III*, Yeelding thoughts besit the basest slaves.

†**beskyfte,** *v. Obs. rare*$^{-1}$. [f. BE- 3 + ME. *skyfte*: see SHIFT.] *trans.* To thrust off.

1470-85 MALORY *Arthur* (1817) I. 91 She coude not beskyfte hym by no meane.

beslab, beslap, beslash, etc.: see BE- *pref.*

beslabber, beslaber, variants of BESLOBBER.

beslave (bɪ'sleɪv), *v.* [f. BE- 5 + SLAVE.]

1. *trans.* To make a slave of, enslave. *lit.* and *fig.*

1615 BP. HALL *Contempl. N.T.* IV. iv. 198 He that..hath beslaved himself to a bewitching beauty. **1645** QUARLES *Sol. Recant.* IV. 51 Or if thy droyling hand should once beslave Thy glorious freedome.

2. To address as a slave, to call 'slave.'

1630 J. TAYLOR (Water P.) *Wks.* II. 158/1, I will not rayle, or rogue thee, or be-slaue thee. **1713** ADDISON *Guardian* No. 153 He is now chiding and beslaving the emmet that stands before him.

3. To fill with slaves, pollute with slavery.

1862 J. SPENCE *Amer. Union* 246 Texas would not have been annexed and beslaved.

Hence **be'slaved** *ppl. a.*, **be'slaving** *vbl. sb.*

1656 S. H. *Gold. Law* 54 Redeeming of many poor beslaved souls. **1641** LD. DIGBY *Sp. in Ho. Com.* 19 Jan. 16 Our beslaving since the Petition of Right.

beslaver (bɪ'slævə(r)), *v.* [f. BE- 1 + SLAVER *v.* Cf. also BESLOBBER.] *trans.*

1. To slaver upon or over, to bedrivel; to cover with anything suggesting slaver.

1589 *Pappe w. Hatchet* C iij, Giue the infant a bibbe, hee all to beslauers his mother tongue. **1602** *Return fr. Parnass.* I. ii. (Arb.) 14 One of your reumaticke Poets, that beslauers all the paper he comes by. **1870** SWINBURNE *Ess. & Stud.* (1875) 38 Unconscious if any reptile beslaver its base.

2. To cover with fulsome flattery.

1861 *Life Ld. Bacon* xxii. 498 He was ready to beslaver Majesty infinitely.

Hence **be'slavered** *ppl. a.*

1598 E. GILPIN *Skial.* (1878) 5 To thinke so well of a scald railing vaine, Which soone is vented in beslauered writs.

†**be'sleeve,** *v. nonce-wd.* [BE- 6 c. + SLEEVE.] *trans.* To take the sleeves from (a bishop). Hence **be'sleeving** *vbl. sb.*

1589 NASHE *Almond for P.* 16 a, Am not I old *Ille ego qui quondam* at y[e] besleeuing of a sichophant.

beslime, beslipper, beslow, etc.: see BE-.

beslobber (bɪ'slɒbə(r)), *v.* Also 4-5 bislaber. [f. BE- 1 + SLOBBER *v.*] To wet and befoul with saliva (= to BESLAVER), or with portions of liquid food escaping from the mouth; to kiss like a drivelling child; *hence*, to kiss childishly or effusively; *fig.* to cover with fulsome flattery.

1393 LANGL. *P. Pl.* C. VIII. 1 Tho cam sleuthe al by-slobered [B. v. 392 bislabered] with two slymed eyen. **1828** MACAULAY *Hallam, Ess.* (1851) I. 84 The salaried Viceroy of France..beslobbering his brother and courtiers in a fit of maudlin affection. **1868** *Blackw. Mag.* Aug., When a man is beslobbered by high and by low, In our senates and schools deemed a light of the age.

beslombre, beslomere, *v. Obs.*: see next.

beslubber (bɪ'slʌbə(r)), *v.* Also 4-5 beslombre, beslomer. [f. BE- 1 + SLUBBER *v.* The early *beslom(b)er* is probably merely a phonetic variant: Mätzner would make it distinct, comparing it with 'Du. *slommeren* to trouble'; but see the sense.]

trans. To wet and soil with a thick liquid; to bedaub, bedabble, besmear. Hence **be'slubbered.**

c **1394** *P. Pl. Crede* 427 His hosen..Al beslombred [*v.r.* beslomered] in fen as he þe plow folwede. **1587** GOLDING *De Mornay* xviii. (1617) 317 A certain common conceiuing of God, howbeit so defaced and beslubbered. **1596** SHAKS. *1 Hen. IV*, II. iv. 341 To beslubber our garments with it, and sweare it was the blood of true men. **1621** MOLLE *Camerar. Liv. Libr.* I. xv. 64 Perfumes..wherewith he vsed to sweeten and beslubber himselfe. **1748** SMOLLETT *Rod. Rand.* iv. (1804) 14 A countenance beslubbered with tears. **1863** BARING-GOULD *Iceland* xi. 197 The boiling jets squirt suddenly at one over the red beslubbered rim.

beslur, beslurry, etc.: see BE- *pref.*

besme, obs. form of BESOM.

besmear (bɪ'smɪə(r)), *v.* Forms: 1 bismierwan, besmyrwan, 3 bismeoruwien, 6 besmeere, -smere, -smire, 6-7 besmeare, 7-8 besmeer, 6- besmear. [OE. *bismierwan*, late WSax. *besmyrwan*, Anglian *besmerwan*, f. *bi-*, BE- 1 + *smierwan*, *smerwan* (pa. t *smierede*):—OTeut. **smerwjan* to SMEAR, f. **smerwo-(m)*, in OE. *smeoru*, *smeru*, ointment, grease.] *trans.* To smear over or about; to cover the surface generally or largely *with* any greasy, viscous, or sticky substance; usually with the notion of soiling or staining: to bedaub.

c **1050** *Gloss. Cott. Cleop.* in Wr.-Wülcker *Voc.* 422/14 *Interlitam*, besmyred. *a* **1225** *Ancr. R.* 214 Kumeð forð biuoren his Louerde bismitted & bismeoruwed. **1535** JOYE *Apol. Tindale* 50 Besmering and dawbing eche other with dirte and myer. **1596** SPENSER *F.Q.* I. ii. 42 The divelish hag ..With wicked herbes and oyntments did besmeare My body. **1601** SHAKS. *Twel. N.* v. 55 That face of his..was besmear'd As blacke as Vulcan in the smoake of warre. **1777** ROBERTSON *Hist. Amer.* (1783) II. 145 They besmear their children with the blood. **1837** W. IRVING *Capt. Bonneville* (1849) 42 He..caused the bodies of the wagons to be..besmeared with a compound of tallow and ashes.

b. predicated of the unguent or viscous matter.

a **1700** DRYDEN (J.) Her gushing blood the pavement all besmear'd. **1725** POPE *Odyss.* XXII. 329 His batter'd front and brains besmear the stone.

c. *intr.* (for *refl.*) To become besmeared.

1587 TURBERV. *Louer confess.* (R.) If face besmear with often streames.

2. *fig.* To sully, defile, pollute.

1579 TOMSON *Calvin's Serm. Tim.* 245/2 That they bee not besmeered with any blame. **1596** SHAKS. *Merch. V.* v. 219 My honor would not let ingratitude So much besmeare it. **1612** T. TAYLOR *Comm. Titus* i. 10 (1619) 216 With the black coales of enuious and slanderous inuectiues striuing to besmeare them. **1867** *Sat. Rev.* 5 July, Ministers vie with each other in getting themselues besmeared.

besmeared (bɪ'smɪəd), *ppl. a.* [f. prec. + -ED[1].] Smeared over, covered with anything greasy or nasty; befouled.

1592 NASHE *P. Penilesse* (ed. 2) 10 b, Mistris Minx..that lookes as simperingly as if she were besmeard. *c* **1600** SHAKS. *Sonn.* lv, Unswept stone besmear'd with sluttish time. **1655** GURNALL *Chr. in Arm.* x. 208/1 Thy filthy garments, and besmeared countenance. **1805** SOUTHEY *Madoc Azt.* xvi, His face, besmeared And black with gore.

besmearer (bɪ'smɪərə(r)). [f. as prec. + -ER[1].] One who besmears.

1611 COTGR., *Barbouilleur*..a blotter, smutter, besmearer.

besmearing (bɪ'smɪərɪŋ), *vbl. sb.* [f. as prec. + -ING[1].] A smearing or daubing over; also *fig.*

1580 BARET *Alv.* B 571 A Besmeering, or annoynting. **1611** COTGR., *Enduisement*, a plaistering, dawbing.. besmearing. **1653** A. WILSON *Jas. I.* Proem., The defacing and besmearing of Virtue and Innocence.

besmell, besmile, etc.: see BE- *pref.*

besmirch (bɪ'smɜːtʃ), *v.* Also 7 besmerch, -smyrch. [f. BE- 1 + SMIRCH *v.*] To soil, discolour, as with smoke, soot, or mud; also *fig.* to sully, dim the lustre of.

1602 SHAKS. *Ham.* I. iii. 15 And now no soyle nor cautell doth besmerch The vertue of his feare. *a* **1700** *Bride's Bur.* in Percy *Reliques* III. (R.) Fair Helen's face Did Grecian dames besmirche. **1881** *Daily Tel.* 14 Nov., You cannot permanently besmirch a work of art. Time is sure to rub off the stain. **1882** *Garden* 21 Jan. 33/3 The first shower of rain would..besmirch the velvet of their petals.

Hence **be'smirched** *ppl. a.*

1599 SHAKS. *Hen. V*, IV. iii. 110 Our Gaynesse and our Gilt are all besmyrcht. **1864** *Spectator* 618 The toiling, and besmirched priesthood of the world. **1868** MORRIS *Earthly Par.* I. (1870) 94 In besmirched array Some met us.

besmire, obs. form of BESMEAR.

†**be'smit,** *v. Obs.* Also 3 bismit, 4 besmet, 5 bismyt. [f. BE- 2 + SMIT *v.*] *trans.* To stain, infect (as with disease), contaminate. (Mostly *fig.*)

[**971** *Blickl. Hom.* 85 þu woldest symle þone besmitan þe þu nan wiht yfles on nystest.] *a* **1225** *Ancr. R.* 214 Kumeð forð biuoren his Louerde bismitted [*v.r.* bismudded] and bismeoruwed. **1340** *Ayenb.* 32 A uice huerof al þe wordle is besmet. *Ibid.* 229 þet ne is naȝt besmetted ine herte mid kueade þoȝtes. **1480** CAXTON *Trevisa's Descr. Brit.* 52 His is bismytted with their treson also.

besmoke (bɪ'sməʊk), *v.* Forms: 4-5 bysmoke, 5 bismoke, 6-9 besmoak, 7 besmoake, 6- besmoke. [f. BE- 4 + SMOKE *v.*] *trans.* To fill with smoke, to act on with smoke, to fumigate.

1398 TREVISA *Barth. De P.R.* XVIII. liii. (1495) 813 Yf a man bismokith the hous of the ampte wyth byrmstoon. **1574** HYLL *Bees* xv, Besmoke the hive with flaxe. **1598** SYLVESTER *Du Bartas* (1608) 1133 Mists of Rome, That have so long besmoaked Christendom. **1611** FLORIO, *Affumare*, to besmoake, to drie in the smoake as bacon. **1823** W. TAYLOR in *Month. Mag.* LVI. 126 They besmoak us with a disgusting mixture of sacrifice and frankincense.

Hence **be'smoked** *ppl. a.*, **be'smoking** *vbl. sb.*

c **1374** CHAUCER *Boeth.* 5 It is wont to dirken by-smoked ymages. **1611** COTGR., *Enfumement*, a smoaking, a besmoaking. **1854** DICKENS *Hard Times* xxii. (D.) The besmoked evergreens were sprinkled with a dirty powder.

besmooth, besmother, besmouche, besmudge: see BE- *pref.*

†**be'smottered,** *ppl. a. Obs. rare.* In 4 bi-, bysmotered, -erd, 6 *Sc.* besmotterit. [A simple *smotered* or *smoteren* does not occur: though Chaucer has an adj. *smoterlich*, which Prof. Skeat takes as = '*dial.* smutty, wanton.' The Du. *smodderen* to smut, and LG. *besmaddern*, have been compared, but do not quite answer phonetically. The form looks like a freq. or dim. of *besmut*, but neither this nor *smut* is found so early. Douglas evidently took the word from Chaucer.]

trans. To bespatter as with mud or dirt.

c **1386** CHAUCER *Prol.* 76 Of ffustian he wered a gypon Al bismotered with his habergeon. **1513** DOUGLAS *Æneis* V. vi. 124 His face he schew besmotterit.

be-smut (bɪ'smʌt), *v.* [f. BE- 1 + SMUT *v.*] *trans.* 'To blacken with smoke or soot' (J.), to dirty; also *fig.*

1610 HOLLAND *Camden's Brit.* I. 154 That blot wherewith Chalcondilas hath besmutted our nation. **1656** EARL MONM. *Advt. fr. Parnass.* 438 The flash did so singe his face, having monstrously besmutted him.

Hence **be'smutted** *ppl. a.* (also said of wheat blackened by smut).

1829 *Blackw. Mag.* XXVI. 33 We see the 'rara avis,' with beak and claws begrimed and besmutted. **1837** CARLYLE *Fr. Rev.* III. v. iii. (D.) One besmutted, redbearded corn-ear in this which they cut.

be-smutch (bɪ'smʌtʃ), *v.* [f. BE- 1 + SMUTCH.] *trans.* To besmirch.

1832 CARLYLE in *Fraser's Mag.* V. 258 Her siren finery has got all besmutched. **1856** R. VAUGHAN *Mystics* VI. i. (ed. 2) I. 151 Ruffling and besmutching all his gay feathers.

† **be'snare,** *v. Obs.* [f. BE- 4 + SNARE *v.*] *trans.* To take in a snare, to entrap.

1571 GOLDING *Calvin on Ps.* ix. 17 God fulfilleth the part of a Judge, as often as he besnareth [*printed* besnarleth] the wicked in their wickednesse.

besnivel, besnowball, besnuff, besob: see BE- *pref.*

besnow (bɪs'nəʊ), *v.* Forms: 1 besniwan, 4 bi-, by-, besnywe(n, -snewe(n, 6- besnow. [OE. *besníwian*, f. BE- 1 + *sníwan* to SNOW.] *trans.* To snow on; to cover or whiten with, or as with, snow; also *fig.* Hence **be'snowed** *ppl. a.*

a **1000** ÆLFRIC *Gloss.* in Wr.-Wülcker *Voc.* 175 *Ninguidus*, besniwod. **1340** *Ayenb.* 81 Non vayr body ne is bote..ase a donghel besnewed. **1393** GOWER *Conf.* III. 51 He was with yiftes all besnewed. **1597** DRAYTON *Mortimer.* 26 The battered Caskes..Besnow the soyle with drifts of scattered plumes. **1633** *True Trojans* I. iii, Foam besnows the trampled corn. **1849** LYTTON *Caxtons* II. IX. xxxix, A fourth, all besnowed and frozen, descends from the outside.

† **be'sogne.** *Obs.* Also besognie, bessogne. [a. Fr. *bisogne*, '*bisongne*, a filthie knaue, or clowne; a raskall, bisonian, base humoured scoundrell' (Cotgr.), ad. It. *bisogno*, cf. BESONIO.] **a.** A raw recruit. **b.** A low worthless fellow; = BEZONIAN.

1615 CHAPMAN *Odyss.* Ep. Ded. 50 Against this host, and this invincible commander, shall we have every besogne and fool a leader? **1633** T. STAFFORD *Pac. Hib.* xi. (1821) 352 There were but a few Besognies amongst them. **1658** BROME *Covent Gard.* v. iii, Beat the Bessognes that lie hid in the Carriages.

† **be'sognier.** *Obs. rare.* An adapted form of BESOGNE or BISOGNIO, with English ending; = prec.

1584 WHETSTONE *Mirr. Mag.*, These be no bashful Besogniers. **1588** J. HARVEY *Disc. Probleme* 71 Bribing copesmates and incroching Bisogniers.

† **be'soigne.** *Obs.* Also 5 boesyngne, besoynye, 6 besone. [a. OF. *besoigne* business, mod. *besogne* = Pr. *besonha*, It. *bisogna*, fem. forms found alongside of the masc. *besoin, besonh, bisogno*; see Diez, Littré.] Business, affair, ado.

1474 CAXTON *Chesse* IV. ii, Thynges that aperteyne to the counceyl & to the besoyngne of the royame. **1653** A. WILSON *Jas. I*, 142 Fitted for those little besoignes of Accounts, and Reckonings.

besoil (bɪ'sɔɪl), *v.* Forms: 3-4 bisuele, -suyle, 5 beswyle, 4-6 besoyle, 7- besoil. [f. BE- 1 + SOIL *v.*] *trans.* To soil, stain, sully; also *fig.* Hence **be'soiled** *ppl. a.*

a **1300** *Pains of Hell* 91 in *O.E. Misc.* 225 And summe he sauȝ bi-suyled · as souwes..vp to þe brouwes. *c* **1315** SHOREHAM 108 Thys men by-soyled beth. *c* **1450** *Merlin* x. 165 His swerde all besoyled with blode of men and of horse. *a* **1670** HACKET *Abp. Williams* II. 164 The Remonstrance..came forth..to besoil his Majesty's reign. **1798** SOUTHEY *Sonn.* xii, Cobwebs and dust thy pinions white besoil. **1831** CARLYLE *Sart. Res.* III. iv, All weather-tanned, besoiled.

besom (biːzəm), *sb.* Forms: 1-2 besma, 1 besema, 3-4 besem, 3-5 besme, 4 beesme, bisme, 4-5 besum, 5 besumme, bessume, besowme, 5-7 besome, 6 bysom, beasome, bessem, 6-8 beesom(e, 7 beesum, beasom, (6 *Sc.* boosome, 7 bissome, 9 *dial.* bezom, bizzim, buzzom), 5- besom. [Com. WGer.: OE. *besema, besma* (= OFris. *besma*, OHG. *besamo*, MHG. *besme, besem*, mod.G. *besen*, Du. *bezem*):—OTeut. **besmon-* (not found in EGer.). Ulterior derivation obscure.]

† **1.** A bundle of rods or twigs used as an instrument of punishment; a birch. *Obs.* (L. *fascis.*)

c **893** K. ÆLFRED *Oros.* II. iii. §2 He..hy..het ȝebindan, and..mid besman swingan. *a* **1225** *St. Marher.* 5 [He] strupeth hire steorcnaket..ant beateth hire bare bodi with bittere besmen. *a* **1225** *Juliana* 16 Þu schalt beon ibeaten mid besmes.

2. An implement for sweeping, usually made of a bunch of broom, heather, birch, or other twigs bound together round a handle; a broom. (Dialectally, as in Scotland, the generic name for sweeping implements of any material, e.g. a *heather, birch,* or *broom besom,* a *hair besom*; but in literary Eng. 'broom' is now generic, and 'besom' specific.)

c **1000** *Ags. Gosp.* Matt. xii. 44 He ȝemet hyt æmtiȝ, and ȝeclænsod mid besmum [*v.r.* besemum]. *c* **1200** *Trin. Coll. Hom.* 87 Mid beseme clene swopen. **1382** WYCLIF *Matt.* xii. 44 Clensid with bismes [**1388** besyms]. **1398** TREVISA *Barth. De P.R.* XVII. clix. (1495) 708 Of the bowes and braunches of the byrche ben besomes made. *c* **1440** *Promp. Parv.* 33 Besme or besowme [**1499** besym], *scopa.* **1493** *Churchw. Acc. Walberswicke, Suffolk* (Nichols, 1797) 185 A bessume of pekoks fethers. **1552** HULOET, *Beasome*, Loke in *browme.* **1580** LYLY *Euphues* (Arb.) 309 There is no more difference betweene them, then betweene a Broome, and a Beesome. **1641** H. BEST *Farm. Bks.* (1856) 104 Wee make the miller take a besome and sweepe a place. **1697** POTTER *Antiq. Greece* II. iii. (1715) 208 He swept the Temple with a Beasom of Lawrel. **1756** C. LUCAS *Ess. Waters* III. 51 The..bath is scrubbed all over with a birchen beesom. **1857** Bohn's *Handbk. Prov.*, There is little for the rake after the besom.

3. *fig.* Any agent that cleanses, purifies, or sweeps away things material or immaterial.

c **1380** WYCLIF *De Papa* Wks. (1880) 468 ȝif he & his secte be..clensid wiþ besumms. *c* **1440** HYLTON *Scala Perf.* (W. de W. 1494) I. xlviii, Swepe thy soule clene wyth the besome of the drede of god. **1611** BIBLE *Isa.* xiv. 23, I will sweepe it with the besome of destruction. **1639** FULLER *Holy War* I. xix. (1840) 35 The riuer Kishon, God's besom to sweep away Sisera's great army. **1837** CARLYLE *Fr. Rev.* I. III. ix. 139 With steel-besom, Rascality is brushed back into its dim depths. **1862** TYNDALL *Mountaineer.* iv. 30 Grandly the cloud-besom swept the mountains.

4. *fig.* Anything resembling a besom in shape; *spec.* applied to a comet.

1566 KNOX *Hist. Ref.* Wks. 1846 I. 254 A comet..called 'The fyrie boosome.' *a* **1639** SPOTTISWOOD *Hist. Ch. Scot.* II. (1677) 94 A Comet of that kind which..the vulgars [call] a firie Bissome.

5. Applied dialectally to heath and broom, plants used for besoms. (Cf. *broom*, in its two senses.)

1796 MARSHALL *Econ. W. Devon.* (E.D.S.), Beesom, bizzom, *spartium scoparium*, the broom plant. **1864** CAPERN *Devon Prov.*, *Bizzim*, Heath. **1878** BRITTEN *Plant-n.* 26 Basam, Basom, Bassam or Bisom, *Sarothamnus scoparius.*

6. *Comb.* and *attrib.*, as ***besom-handle, -staff***, etc.; also **besom-head**, *fig.* a foolish or stupid person, a blockhead, whence ***besom-headed***; **besom-heath**, heath used for making besoms; **besom-rider**, a witch, from the popular notion that they rode on broom-sticks; **besom-tail**, a tail formed like a besom, a bushy tail, whence ***besom-tailed***; **besom-weed** = BESOM 5.

1864 ATKINSON *Whitby Gloss.* s.v. *Bezom*, 'He's as fond as a bezom,' or '*bezom-headed,' very foolish indeed. **1756** *Phil. Trans.* XLIX. 829 *Erica brabantica*..Low Dutch Heath, or *Besom Heath. **1664** H. MORE *Myst. Iniq.* 161 Defaming them for *Besom-riders or witches. **1678** *Lond. Gaz.* No. 1356/4 Lost or stolen..one of the King's Setting Dogs..a long *beesum tail. **1695** —— No. 3086/4 A dark Iron grey Mare..Silver Eyed, and *Besome Tailed. **1578** LYTE *Dodoens* 628 *Bessem weede, or the herbe serving for Bysoms. **1642** FULLER *Holy & Prof. St.* v. iii. 368 By a Witch-bridle they can make a fair of horses of an acre of *besome-weed.

7. A contemptuous or jocular designation for a woman. *Sc.* and *dial.* (Pronounced 'bɪzəm; also † 'bʌzəm).

1808-1929 in *Sc. Nat. Dict.* **1816** SCOTT *Old Mort.* viii, To set up to be sae muckle better than ither folk, the auld besom. **1930** J. BUCHAN *Castle Gay* xvi. 255 She's a determined besom. **1936** W. HOLTBY *South Riding* v. i. 276 Gosh! The little besom!

'besom, *v.* [f. BESOM *sb.* Cf. *to brush.*]

† **1.** *intr.* To sweep with force or violence. *Obs.*

? *a* **1400** *Morte Arth.* 3662 The..wynde owte of the weste rysses, Brethly bessomes with byrre in berynes sailles.

2. *trans.* To sweep. Often with *away, out,* etc.

1791 COWPER *Odyss.* XXII. 526 They cleansed The thrones and tables, while Telemachus Beesom'd the floor. **1842** MRS. BROWNING *Grk. Chr. Poets* 13 Besom away the thick dust which lies upon their heavy folios. **1866** KINGSLEY *Herew.* xix. 244 He would besom you all out.

besomer. [f. prec. + -ER[1].] One who uses a besom.

besonard, obs. form of BEZOAR.

besone, -ian, variants of BESOIGNE, BEZONIAN.

† **be'sonio, be'sognio.** *Obs.* [var. of BISOGNIO, a. It. *bisogno* 'need, want; also, a fresh needy souldier. *Bisogni*, new leuied souldiers such as come needy to the war' (Florio). 'Applied in derision to young soldiers who landed in Italy from Spain ill accoutred and in want of everything' (*Vocab. della Crusca.*) Hence also Sp. *bisoño*, Pg. *bisonho*, F. *bisogne.* (The conjecture that *bisogno* was an It. corruption of F. '*becjaune*, BEJAN, is baseless.) Cf. BESOGNE.] **a.** A raw soldier. **b.** (term of contempt) A needy beggar; a base worthless fellow. See BEZONIAN.

[**1591** GARRARD *Art of Warre* 170 A raw souldier and Bisognio.] **1603** R. JOHNSON *Kingd. & Commw.* 55 A base Besonio, fitter for the spade then the sword. **1611** FLETCHER *Four Pl.* 28 Draw my sword of Fate on a Pesant, a Besognio! **1622** R. HAWKINS *Voy. S. Sea* (1847) 78 The souldiers..who after the common custome of their profession (except when they be besonios), sought to pleasure him. **1820** SCOTT *Monast.* xvi, Base and pilfering besognios and marauders.

besonnet, besoothe, etc.: see BE- *pref.*

† **be'soop,** *v. Obs. rare.* [App. f. BE- 1 + *soop*, earlier form of SWOOP: though the application is not quite clear.] *trans.* ? To thrash, lay about.

1589 *Hay any Work* B, I wil so besoop you..as al the world shal cry shame vppon you. *Ibid.* 36, I will so besoop thee, as thou neuer bangedst John Whitgift.

besoot (bɪ'sʊt), *v.* [f. BE- 6 + SOOT.] *trans.* To soil or blacken with (or as with) soot. Hence **be'sooting** *vbl. sb.*

1611 COTGR., *Poislure*, a smutting, smeering, besooting. **1622** MABBE *Aleman's Guzman d'Alf.* I. 12 Was it fit that hee should besoot his face with the same paintings? **1661** EVELYN *Misc. Writ.* I. (1805) 228 This coale..flies abroad..besoots all the leaves.

besoothment (bɪ'suːðmənt). *rare.* [f. BESOOTHE: see BE- *pref.* 2.] The fact of soothing; its means or resulting state.

OGILVIE cites *Q. Rev.*

† **be'sort,** *v. Obs.* [f. BE- + SORT *sb.* or *v.*; cf. ASSORT *v.*] To assort, match, or agree with; to befit.

1605 SHAKS. *Lear* I. iv. 272 Such men as may besort your Age.

† **be'sort,** *sb. Obs.* [? from prec. vb.; cf. ASSORT *sb.*] Suitable company.

1604 SHAKS. *Oth.* I. iii. 238 Such Accomodation, and besort, As leuels with her breeding.

besot (bɪ'sɒt), *v.* [f. BE- + SOT; cf. ASSOT.]

1. *trans.* To affect with a foolish, blinding affection; to cause to dote *on*; to infatuate *with.*

1581 CAMPION in *Confer.* IV. (1584) A a iiij b, He might be taken with the loue of his eies towards her, to be besotted with her. **1637** HEYWOOD *Dial.* ii. Wks. 1874 VI. 118 It shall besot thee on some sordid Swaine. **1675** *Art Contentm.* viii. §5. 217 The kind aspects of the world are very enchanting, apt to inveigle and besot us. **1748-1864** [see BESOTTED 1.].

2. To make mentally or morally stupid or blind; to stupefy in mind.

1615 BP. HALL *Contempl. N.T.* IV. iv, Impiety is wont to besot men. **1660** FULLER *Mixt Contempl.* (1841) 231 Till they besot their understandings. **1822** HAZLITT *Men & Mann.* Ser. II. v. (1869) 122 Such persons are in fact besotted with words. **1877** SPARROW *Serm.* xix. 249 To besot the minds of men with ignorance and superstition.

3. To stupefy in the brain, make a sot of. (Said of narcotics.) Also *absol.*

1627 DRAYTON *Agincourt, etc.* 134 They no sooner tooke this drinke; But nought into their braines could sinke, Of what had them besotted. **1692** TRYON *Good House w.* xxvi. 209 Opium..stupifying and besotting them, even as the superfluous drinking of..strong Drinks does. **1755** YOUNG *Centaur* ii. Wks. 1757 IV. 137 Pleasure..has an opiate in it; it stupefies, and besots. **1852** THACKERAY *Esmond* I. xiv, I besotted myself and gambled and drank.

besotted (bɪ'sɒtɪd), *ppl. a.* [f. prec. + -ED.]

1. Having the affections foolishly or dotingly engaged; infatuated.

1580 NORTH *Plutarch* (1676) 964 Antonius..besotted by Cleopatra. *a* **1618** RALEIGH *Instr. Son* ii. (1651) 6 Haue..ever more care, that thou be beloved of thy wife, rather than thyself besotted on her. **1748** RICHARDSON *Clarissa* xxxii. (1811) I. 246 If you are not besotted to that man..you will like it. **1864** BURTON *Scot Abr.* I. iii. 137 Never did besotted lover abandon himself to wilder folly.

2. Intellectually or morally stupefied or blinded.

1634 MILTON *Comus* 790 Swinish gluttony..with besotted base ingratitude Crams and blasphemes his feeder. **1687** *Reflect. on Hind & P.* 25 The gross Ignorance and besotted Superstition of Italy. **1877** MOZLEY *Univ. Serm.* xvi. 271 A stupid besotted indifference to everything spiritual.

3. Intoxicated or muddled by a narcotic.

1831 SCOTT *Cast. Dang.* ix, You besotted villains, you have been drinking. **1832** MARRYAT *N. Forster* v, Newton went down to rouse the besotted Thompson.

be'sottedly, *adv.* [f. prec. + -LY[2].] Infatuatedly, stupidly, with mental or moral blindness.

1660 MILTON *Free Commw.* Wks. 1738 I. 591 Basely and besottedly to run their necks again into the Yoke. **1849** C. BRONTË *Shirley* i. 4 He was..besottedly arrogant.

be'sottedness. [f. as prec. + -NESS.] The state of being besotted; infatuation; intoxication.

1628 BP. HALL *Old Relig.* 11 The World..stood amazed to see its owne slauerie and besottednesse. **1673** MILTON *True Relig.* Wks. (1851) 419 Hardness, besottedness of heart, and Idolatry. **1862** J. LUDLOW *Hist. U.S.* 240 The besottedness or demoralisation of a portion of the North.

be'sotting, *ppl. a.* [f. BESOT + -ING[2].] Infatuating, stupefying.

1762 FIELDING *Ess. Convers.* Wks. (1840) 636 The beastly custom of besotting and ostentatious contention for pre-eminence in their cups. **1863** GEO. ELIOT *Romola* in *Cornh. Mag.* VI. 435 To steal over my senses like besotting wine.

besought (bɪ'sɔːt), pa. t. and pple. of BESEECH.

besouled (bɪ'səʊld), *ppl. a.* [f. BE- + SOUL *sb.* + -ED.] Endowed with a soul, ensouled.

1843 CARLYLE *Past & Pr.* 388 Besouled with earnest human Nobleness. **1862** SIMON *tr. Dorner's Pers. Christ* II. (1874) I. 199 His..besouled humanity was not done away with by the deification.

be'souling, *vbl. sb.* [f. as prec. + -ING[1].] The endowing with a soul.

1862 SIMON tr. *Dorner's Pers. Christ* I. (1875) II. 399 To reduce the incarnation to a besouling..of this man.

besour, besow, bespaded, etc.: see BE- *pref.*

besouth (bɪˈsaʊθ), *prep.* now *Sc.* Also 5–6 besowth. [f. BE- + SOUTH: cf. *be-east*, *be-north*.] On the south side of; to the south of.

c **1410** *Sir Cleges* 473 A gest.. Of a knyght there be-sowth. **1530** LYNDESAY *Papyngo* 918 The borrow mure, Besouth Edinburgh. **1551** RECORDE *Cast. Knowl.* (1556) 85, 29 degrees besouthe the tropike of Capricorne. **1650** *Act Seder.* 10 Jan. 64 (JAM.) This present Act shall.. take effect for those besouth the water of Die. **1862** M. NAPIER *Life Dundee* II. 342 Perth besouth the river Earn.

besowme, besoyle, obs. form of BESOM, BESOIL.

besoyngne, -soynye, var. of BESOIGNE.

bespall, var. of BESPAWL *v. Obs.*

bespangle (bɪˈspæŋg(ə)l), *v.* [f. BE- 6 + SPANGLE.]

1. *trans.* To set about with spangles; to besprinkle or adorn with small glittering objects.

1612 DRAYTON *Poly-olb.* xiii. Notes 214 Every lofty top, which late the humorous night Bespangled had with pearle. **1722** WOLLASTON *Relig. Nat.* v. 80 [Stars] to adorn and bespangle a canopy over our heads. **1862** G. LLOYD *Tasmania* iii. 36 The genial morning dews.. that used to glisten upon and bespangle the vernal-leaved kangaroo grass?

2. *fig.*

1675 BROOKS *Gold. Key* Wks. 1867 V. 115 Being bespangled with holiness and clad with the royal robe of righteousness. **1800** W. TAYLOR in *Month. Mag.* X. 425 Other admirable similies bespangle this book. **1846** PRESCOTT *Ferd. & Is.* I. viii. 374 The subtilties and conceits with which the ancient Castilian verse is so liberally bespangled.

Hence **beˈspangled** *ppl. a.*, **beˈspangling** *vbl. sb.*

1593 NASHE *Christ's T.* (1613) 144 Women.. sumptuously pearled and bespangled. **1611** COTGR., *Papillottement*, a bespangling. **1634** SIR T. HERBERT *Trav.* 118 Under a bespangled Canopie, the Firmament. **1848** KINGSLEY *Saint's Trag.* v. i. 226 Uprushing pillars, star-bespangled roofs.

bespankle (bɪˈspæŋk(ə)l). = BESPANGLE.

1621 QUARLES *Argalus & P.* (1678) 89 Garments.. bespankled ore With Stars of purest Gold. **1853** G. JOHNSTON *Nat. Hist. E. Bord.* I. 227 So she tastefully.. bespankles every branchlet and every spine with a daisy flower.

†**beˈspar,** *v. Obs.* Forms: 1 besparri-an, 3 bisparr-en, 4 -sperr-en, -speren. [f. BE- 2 + SPAR *v.* to bolt, shut.] *trans.* To shut in; to lock up.

a **1100** in Wr.-Wülcker *Voc.* 459 *Oppilate*, besparrade. *a* **1225** *Ancr. R.* 94 Ancren þet bisparreð [*v.r.* bituneð] her. **1377** LANGL. *P. Pl.* B. xv. 139 And þat he spared and bispered [bi-sperred, bisperde, bispared] spene we in murthe.

†**beˈsparage,** *v. Obs.* [f. DISPARAGE, by exchange of prefixes (cf. *distain*, *bestain*), and mistake of *sparage* for the stem.] *trans.* To disparage.

1592 NASHE *P. Penilesse* (N.) These men.. should come to besparage gentlemen and chuff-headed burghomasters.

†**beˈsparkle,** *v. Obs.* [f. BE- + SPARKLE *v.* Cf. BYSPARKIT.] *trans.* To bespatter, to spot.

1485 CAXTON *St. Wenefryde* 5 The stones.. al besparklyde with blood. **1633** AMES *Agst. Cerem.* Pref. 26 He besparckles the worshippers therof with disdaine.

†**beˈsparkling,** *ppl. a. Obs.* [f. as prec. + -ING².] Sparkling, throwing out sparks.

1648 HERRICK *Hesper.* App. 449 In his desires More towring and besparkling than thy fires.

bespatter (bɪˈspætə(r)), *v.* [f. BE- 1 + SPATTER.]

1. *trans.* To spatter over; to cover with small spots of wet mud or anything of like consistency.

1674 *Govt. of Tongue* v. §9. 123 Those who will not take vice into their bosoms, shall yet have it bespatter their faces. **1844** THIRLWALL *Greece* VIII. lxvi. 447 They.. were even bespattered with mud.

2. To spatter about; to scatter or cast (anything) so that it sticks in spots on surrounding objects.

1813 *Examiner* 1 Feb. 80/1 [He] had.. literally bespattered his brains about the floor.

3. *fig.* To asperse (*with* abuse, blame, flattery, praise, etc.). Generally in a bad sense even when *praise* is in question.

1644 JESSOP *Angel of Eph.* 24 Bishop Halls titles of honour wherewith he doth bespatter them. **1759** *Let. to Methodists*, Bespattering with your dirty hints and innuendoes the whole body of its Clergy. **1819** SOUTHEY *Lett.* (1856) III. 150, I shall get plentifully bespattered with abuse. **1851** RUSKIN *Mod. Paint.* I. Pref. 19 He.. bespatters with praise the canvass which a crowd concealed from him. **1858** ROBERTSON *Lect.* 244 Bespattered with applause.

4. *spec.* To cover with abuse; to vilify or slander.

1653 A. WILSON *Jas. I*, Proeme 4 If Ignorance or Malice attempts to hack, hew, or bespatter it. **1709** STEELE *Tatler* No. 115 ¶1 Punch who takes all opportunities of bespattering me. **1748** RICHARDSON *Clarissa* (1811) II. xxxiii. 208, I will convince you that I am basely bespattered.

beˈspattered, *ppl. a.* [f. prec. + -ED.] Covered with small spots of mud or the like.

1667 H. MORE *Div. Dial.* iii. §28 (1713) 250 The whole Keys were all bespattered with Letters. **1831** CARLYLE *Sart. Res.* II. vii, Every window of your Feeling, even of your Intellect, as it were, begrimed and mud-bespattered.

beˈspatterer. [f. as prec. + -ER¹.] One who bespatters with mud, or abuse.

a **1849** H. COLERIDGE *Ess. & Margin.* (1851) II. 90 It defiles the bespatterer, whether it hit the object or not.

beˈspattering, *vbl. sb.* [f. as prec. + -ING¹.] The action of covering with spots of mud, or the like, thrown at an object; or *fig.* with abuse.

a **1677** BARROW *Serm.* Wks. 1716 I. 169 The bespattering our neighbours good name. **1862** *Sat. Rev.* 5 July 4 Pitching the filthiest mud that he could find.. and naturally receiving a liberal bespattering in return.

beˈspatterment. *rare.* = prec.

1870 C. SMITH *Syn. & Antonyms, Adulation.. Ant.* Traducement.. bespatterment.

†**beˈspattle,** *v. Obs.* [f. BE- 1 + SPATTLE *v.*] *trans.* To bespatter with anything dirty. Hence **beˈspattling** *vbl. sb.*

1546 BALE *Eng. Votaries* II. (1550) 107 They rated hym.. byspatled hym, and byspitted him. **1611** COTGR., *Papilloter* .. to bespattle, or spot with durt. —— *Papillottement*, a bespangling; also, a bespattling.

†**beˈspawl,** *v. Obs.* Also 7 bespaul, bespall. [f. BE- 1 + SPAWL *v.*] *trans.* To bespatter with saliva; also *fig.*

1602 B. JONSON *Poetast.* v. i, Bespawls The conscious time, with humours, foam, and brawls. **1641** MILTON *Animadv.* iii. 63 This Remonstrant would invest himself conditionally with all the rheum of the town.. to bespaul his brethren. **1647** R. STAPYLTON *Juvenal* 215 Whose slipping guests are ready still to fall, He doth his Spartan marble so bespall.

Hence **beˈspawled** *ppl. a.*

1612 DRAYTON *Poly-olb.* ii. 33 His foame-bespawled beard.

bespeak (bɪˈspiːk), *v.* Pa. t. **bespoke,** and (*arch*). **-spake.** Pa. pple. **bespoken, bespoke.** For other forms see SPEAK. [Com. WGer.: OE. *bi-, besprecan* = OS. *bisprecan* (Du. *bespreken*), OHG. *bisprehhan* (MHG. and mod.G. *besprechen*), f. *bi-*, BE- + *sprecan* (*specan*) to SPEAK. The connexion of the senses is very loose; some of them appear to have arisen quite independently of each other from different applications of BE- *pref.*]

I. *intransitive.*

†**1.** To call out, exclaim, complain *that.* Only OE.

c **893** K. ÆLFRED *Oros.* I. x. §6 Hu unȝemetlice ȝe Romware bemurcniað & besprecað þæt, etc. *Ibid.* II. iv. §7 Ond nu ure Cristne Roma bespricð þæt.. etc.

†**2.** To speak up or out, to exclaim: orig. with some notion of objection or remonstrance; in later times, simply, to raise one's voice, to speak. *Obs.* or *arch.*

c **1314** *Guy Warw.* 185 Than bispac Otous of Pavi, To Gii he bar gret envie. *c* **1440** *Erle Tolous* 877 Then bespake an olde Knyght, Y have wondur, be goddys myght, That syr Autore thus was bestedd. *c* **1500** *Deb. Carpenters' T.* in Halliw. *Nugæ P.* 17 Than be-spake the polyff With gret strong wordes and styffe. **1590** MARLOWE *Edw. II*, III. ii, The Earl of Pembroke mildly thus bespake; 'My lords,' etc. **1629** MILTON *Nativ.* vi, Until their Lord himself bespake, and bid them go. **1791** COWPER *Iliad* II. 201 And thus the chief bespake.

†**b.** quasi-*trans. rare. Obs.*

1579 SPENSER *Sheph. Cal.* Feb., Whatever that good old man bespake.

II. *transitive.*

†**3.** To speak against: to charge, accuse; oppose.

a **1000** *Laws of Ethelb.* ii. 8 (Bosw.) Hit besprecen biþ. *a* **1000** *Psalms* (Lamb.) xliii. 17 (Bosw.) Fram stefne besprecendre. *c* **1250** *Gen. & Ex.* 1444 And sȝe ne bi-spac him neuere a del. **1297** R. GLOUC. 524 He was of churche inome, thu clergie bispek it vaste.

†**4.** To speak about: **a.** To discuss, advise upon, determine upon. (Also *intr.* with *infin.* of purpose.)

c **1175** *Lamb. Hom.* 91 Heo bispeken heom bitweonen þet heo walden ibuȝen. **1297** R. GLOUC. 200 þo þys was syker & byspeke. *c* **1300** *K. Alis.* 94 Wel thrytty ygedred beoth, And byspekith al his deth. **1489** CAXTON *Faytes of A.* IV. ix. 250 She hathe traytted or bespoken for to make hym dey other by poyson or by som other secrete dethe.

†**b.** To promise. *Obs. rare.* (Ger. *versprechen.*)

c **1320** *Cast. Loue* 221 For so hit was to Adam bi-speke, And God nolde no forward breke.

5. To speak for; to arrange for, engage beforehand; to 'order' (goods).

1583 STANYHURST *Aeneis* II. (Arb.) 68 Theare doe lye great kingdooms.. bespoken For the. **1602** *Return fr. Parnass.* III. v. (Arb.) 46 A lodging bespoken for him.. in Newgate. **1688** in Ellis *Orig. Lett.* II. 367. IV. 143 The six thousand pair of Shoes which he bispoke at Exeter. **1709** STEELE *Tatler* No. 16 ¶2 She bespoke the Play of Alexander the Great, to be acted by the Company of Strollers. **1712** ARBUTHNOT *John Bull* (1755) 2 His tradesmen.. waited upon him to.. bespeak his custom. **1793** SMEATON *Edystone L.* §255 A new set of chains was bespoke. **1839** DE QUINCEY *Murder* Wks. IV. 43 You may have.. bespoken a murder.

b. To stipulate or ask for (a favour or the like).

1677 *Quest. conc. Oath of Alleg.* 11, I must humbly bespeak your pardon. **1786** T. JEFFERSON *Writ.* (1859) II. 69, I bespeak, beforehand, a right to indulge my natural incredulity. **1818** COBBETT *Pol. Reg.* XXXIII. 54 With the view.. of bespeaking a friendly reception for himself. **1846** GROTE *Greece* II. xxiv. 572 Whose patience I have to bespeak.

†**c.** To request or engage (a person) *to do* (something). *Obs.*

1590 SHAKS. *Com. Err.* v. i. 233 Then fairely I bespoke the Officer To go in person with me to my house. **1667** PEPYS *Diary* (1877) V. 35 Who I feared did come to bespeak me to be Godfather to his son. **1670** WALTON *Lives* IV. 293, I must .. bespeak the Reader to prepare for an almost incredible story. **1764** SMELLIE *Midwif.* III. 80, I was bespoke.. to attend a woman in her first child.

6. To speak to (a person), to address. (Now chiefly *poet.*)

1590 MARLOWE *Edw. II*, I. iv, My gentle lord, bespeak these nobles fair. **1597** *North. Mothers Bless.* xiii, When folks thee bespeaken curtesly hem grete. **1677** HALE *Contempl.* II. 124 From this high Mountain he bespeaks Mankind. *a* **1703** BURKITT *On N.T.* Luke xxiii. 31 These Christ thus bespoke: 'Weep not for me, but for yourselves.' **1725** POPE *Odyss.* XXIV. 508 Medon first th' assembled chiefs bespoke. **1870** BRYANT *Iliad* II. xv. 75 The Father of immortals.. Frowned upon Juno and bespake her thus.

7. To speak of, tell of, be the outward expression of; to indicate, give evidence of.

1628 EARLE *Microcosm.* 43 His very countenance and gesture bespeaks how much he is. **1671** FLAVEL *Fount. Life* viii. 20 Long preparations bespeak the.. greatness of the work. **1778** HAN. MORE *Florio* II. 184 Gorgeous banquets oft bespeak A hungry household all the week. **1814** WORDSW. *Excurs.* I. 855 But her house Bespake a sleepy hand of negligence. **1863** MRS. C. CLARKE *Shaks. Char.* iii. 65 Hamlet's proneness to soliloquy bespeaks the reflective man.

b. with *compl.*

a **1704** T. BROWN *Pr. Drunkenness* Wks. 1730 I. 31 Those whose smiling aspect bespeaks them friends. **1762** STERNE *Tr. Shandy* (1802) VI. xxxii. 356 Did that bespeak me cruel? **1815** *Scribbleomania* 18 Symptoms bespeaking me rash.

c. To tell of or betoken beforehand; to prognosticate, augur.

1719 YOUNG *Revenge* III. i, Anguish, and groans, and death bespeak to-morrow. *a* **1745** SWIFT (J.) They started fears, bespoke dangers, and formed ominous prognosticks. **1851** HAWTHORNE *Snow Im.* (1879) 167 Circumstances that bespeak war and danger.

†**d.** (as prec. with reverse construction.) *Obs. rare.*

1655 FULLER *Ch. Hist.* VI. III. 511 My tongue is so farre from bespeaking such lands with any ill successe.

†**e.** To bear witness, to declare to. *Obs. rare.*

1674 N. FAIRFAX *Bulk & Selv.* 144 We have.. only reason to bespeak us, that bulk has a least part.

†**8.** To speak (a person) into some state. *Obs.*

1604 *Gallants at Ordin.* 19 How a young fellow was even bespoke and jested to death by harlots.

bespeak (bɪˈspiːk), *sb.* [f. the vb.]

1. A bespeaking; *esp.* the bespeaking of a particular play to be performed; *hence*, a benefit night, when the actor's friends and patrons choose the play.

1807 A. C. HOLBROOK *Memoirs of Actress* 24 The first families in the neighbourhood, who had come to attend a bespeak that evening. **1839** DICKENS *Nich. Nick.* xxiv, On her bespeak night... The night of her bespeak. Her benefit night, when her friends and patrons bespeak the play. **1880** MISS BRADDON *Just as I am* lii. 347 He had given his bespeak to the theatre, and Mr. Montmorency was to act Claude Melnotte.

2. An application made to a lending library for the loan of a book when it shall become available.

1922 *Glasgow Herald* 28 Dec. 9 In the past year the number of 'bespeaks' was 4153, an increase of 650 on the previous year.

beˈspeaker. [f. BESPEAK *v.* + -ER¹.] He who or that which bespeaks.

1624 WOTTON *Archit.* (1672) 51 The Bespeaker of the Work. **1686** GOAD *Celest. Bodies* I. xvii. 111 Infallible Bespeakers of a showre.

beˈspeaking, *vbl. sb.* [f. as prec. + -ING¹.] The action of speaking to, for, about, or of.

1661 *Origen's Opin.* in *Phœnix* (1721) I. 1 Custom, which sends few Books into the world.. without some fair bespeaking of the Reader. **1687** DRYDEN *Hind & P.* To Rdr., A Preface.. which is but a bespeaking of Favour. **1711** SWIFT *Lett.* (1767) III. 243 The dinner was my bespeaking.

beˈspecked, *ppl. a.* [f. BE- 1 + SPECKED: cf. *besmottered*.] Spotted or specked over the surface.

1565 GOLDING *Ovid's Met.* IV. (1593) 84 The berrie is bespect With colour tending to a blacke. **1598** SYLVESTER *Du Bartas* II. i. II. (1641) 90/2 A Dragons skin All brightbespect. **1745** *Phil. Trans.* XLIII. 296 Broad yellow spots [that] her whole body had been bespecked with.

bespeckle (bɪˈspɛk(ə)l), *v.* [f. BE- 1 + SPECKLE *v.*] To speckle over, to variegate with specks or spots. Hence **beˈspeckled** *ppl. a.*, **beˈspecklement.**

1607 TOPSELL *Four-f. Beasts* 340 The colour yellowish, but bespeckled on the sides with blew spots. **1641** MILTON *Ch. Discip.* I. Wks. (1851) 23 They.. bespeckl'd her with all the gaudy allurements of a Whore. **1655** FULLER *Ch. Hist.* IX. vi. §15. V. 76 A Translation.. everywhere bespeckled

with hard words. **1860** *Encycl. Brit.* XXI. 976/2 Minute black points..bespeckle the anterior extremity. **1883** *Chamb. Jrnl.* 631 [They] threw the white foam from their bits..to the bespecklement of the groom's hat and coat.

be'spectacled, *ppl. a.* [f. BE- 7 + SPECTACLES.] Having spectacles on.

1742 JARVIS *Quix.* II. II. xvi. (D.) A white-veiled, lank, and bespectacled duenna. **1848** J. H. NEWMAN *Loss & Gain* 60 He was a little, prim, smirking, bespectacled man.

bespeech, bespend, besperple, bespew: see BE- *pref.*

bespeed (bɪ'spiːd), *v. rare.* [f. BE- 2 + SPEED *v.*] *trans.* To speed, help on, prosper. Hence **besped** (bɪ'spɛd), *ppl. a.*, prospered, having got on (well or ill).

c **1630** JACKSON *Creed* B IV. iv. vi, Men set to woo..for others take often opportunity to bespeed themselves. **1796** COLERIDGE *To Unfort. Woman* i, Myrtle leaf, that ill besped Pinest in the gladsome ray.

bespell (bɪ'spɛl), *v.* [f. BE- 6 + SPELL *sb.*[1] 3.] *trans.* To cast a spell on; to bewitch literally or figuratively. Hence **be'spelled** *ppl. a.*

1894 MEREDITH *Ld. Ormont* iv, If his glory bespells her. **1897** A. NUTT in K. Meyer *Voy. Bran* II. 6 A bard..had threatened to bespell his land. **1902** —— *Leg. Holy Grail* 58 The bespelled kinsman appears in a hideous guise. **1926** *Contemp. Rev.* Oct. 503 We were gazing, bespelled at the fair scene.

† **be'spete,** *v. arch.* Forms: *Inf.* 3-4 bi-, byspete, -speete, (6 bespette). *Pa. t.* 4 byspet, bispatte. *Pa. pple.* 3-4 bispat, 4 bispet, 5 by-, 6 bespetted, 9 bespate. [ME. *bespeten*, f. BE- 1 + *speten*, OE. *spǽtan* to spit.] = BESPIT.

a **1225** *Ancr. R.* 122 ȝif me mis-seið þe, þenc þæt tu ert eorðe..ne bispet me þe eorðe? *a* **1240** *Orison* 32 in *O.E. Misc.* 140 Bi-spat þu were and al myd wowe. *c* **1315** SHOREHAM 84 Hy..Byspet hym that swete semblant. **1382** WYCLIF *Mark* xv. 19 Thei smyten his heed with a reede, and bispatten him. *c* **1386** CHAUCER *Pers. T.* ⁋205 Thanne was his visage..vileynsly bispet [*v.r.* bespit]. **1496** *Dives & Paup.* (W. de W.) VI. xv. 259 That blyssfull bodye..was..by-spetted for our synne. **1580** BARET *Alv.* B 576 To Bespette one all ouer. **1855** BROWNING *Ch. Roland* xix, Its [a river's] black eddy bespate with flakes and spumes.

bespice (bɪ'spaɪs), *v.* [f. BE- 1 and 4 + SPICE.] **1.** *trans.* To season with (or as with) spice.

1575 CHURCHYARD *Chippes* (1817) 191 Sweete words did walke, bespyest [? bespyset] with fained cheere. **1601** HOLLAND *Pliny* XIX. viii, Seasoned also and bespiced with the costly root of the plant Laserwoort. **1611** SHAKS. *Wint. T.* I. ii. 316 Thou His Cup-bearer..might'st be-spice a cup. **1611** RICH *Honest. Age* (1844) 50 So be-spiced, and be-poudered, that a man may well vent them the breadth of a streete.

†**2.** To sprinkle as spice or seasoning. *Obs.*

1567 MAPLET *Gr. Forest* 49 b, This root..being bespiced or bestrewed vpon their meate..killeth the Panther.

bespill (bɪ'spɪl), *v.* [f. BE- 1 + SPILL.] Intensive of SPILL.

1556 ABP. PARKER *Psalter* lxxxiii, And let theyr fames all shame bespill. *a* **1843** SOUTHEY *Poems Slave-tr.* II. 60 By every drop of blood bespilt..Awake! arise! avenge!

bespin, bespirt, besplit, etc.: see BE- *pref.*

bespirit (bɪ'spɪrɪt), *v.* Also 6 besprite. [f. BE- 5 + SPIRIT.] *trans.* **a.** To possess with a (familiar) spirit. **b.** To fill or endow with spirit.

1574 HELLOWES *Gueuara's Ep.* (1577) 55 The letter had no spirit in it: but he aduised me, that he which wrote it should be beesprited. **1862** SIMON *Dorner's Pers. Christ* I. (1875) II. 399 To reduce the incarnation to a..bespiriting of this man.

be'spit, *v. arch.* Pa. t. and pple. bespit. For forms see SPIT. [f. BE- 1 + SPIT *v.*] *trans.* To spit upon, cover or defile with spitting. Rarely *intr.* with *upon.* (Cf. BE-SPETE.)

a **1300** *Cursor M.* 17771 Jesus..was Bath bi-scurget and bi-spit. **1382** WYCLIF *Mark* xiv. 65 Summe bigunnen for to bispitte him. *c* **1460** *Towneley Myst.* 223 Thus have thay dight me drerely And all by-spytt me spytusly. **1546** BALE *Eng. Votaries* II. (1550) 107 They..byspatled hym, and byspitted him. **1629** GAULE *Pract. The.* 22 Christ was..crowned with Thornes, bespit vpon. **1678** HICKES in Ellis *Orig. Lett.* II. 319 IV. 51 They railed at my black coat, for so they called my gown, and bespit it all over.

bespite (bɪ'spaɪt), *prep. rare*⁻¹. Despite.

1842 R. I. WILBERFORCE *Rutil. & Lucius* 96, I have had friends who, bespite my ignorance and penury, are ready to receive me as their equal.

be-splash (bɪ'splæʃ), *v.* [f. BE- 1 + SPLASH *v.*] *trans.* To splash all over, to wet by splashing. Hence **be'splashed** *ppl. a.*

1804 W. TAYLOR in *Ann. Rev.* II. 288 He besplashes and bemires the ladies who are walking near. **1845** *Whitehall* xlvi. 329 Dismounting from his besplashed steed.

bespoke (bɪ'spəʊk), *ppl. a.* [See BESPEAK *v.*] = BESPOKEN *ppl. a.* 2; *spec.* of goods; ordered to be made, as distinguished from READY-MADE; also said of a tradesman who makes goods to order. Also *sb.*, a bespoke article.

1755 MRS. C. CHARKE *Life* 203 At length the bespoke Play was to be enacted. **1866** *Chambers's Encycl.* VIII. 691/1 The shoemaking trade..is divided into two departments—the bespoke and the ready-made or sale business. **1884** *Birmingh. Daily Post* 24 Jan. 3/3 Boot Trade.—Wanted..Saleswoman, accustomed to Bespoke Trade. **1907** W. DE MORGAN *Alice-for-Short* xlvii, His boots may have been 'bespokes' for anybody, except himself. **1908** *Daily Chron.* 13 June 4/7 A 'bespoke tailor'. **1928** *Punch* 30 May p. xv (Advt.), Lotus Bespoke Model Shoes. **1965** *Ibid.* 29 Sept. 478/1 A 'Special Collection' which is, in harsh reality, a collection of bargain bespokes. **1966** *Economist* 16 July 239/2 Although there is a lot of bespoke work in this [steel] plant, management would prefer some element of payment by results.

bespoken (bɪ'spəʊkən), *ppl. a.* Also BESPOKE *ppl. a.*. [See BESPEAK *v.*]

†**1.** Spoken, of speech; as in *well bespoken. Obs.*

1474 CAXTON *Chesse* III. vi. (1860) H iv b, The hostelers ought to be wel bespoken and curtoys of wordes. **1483** —— *Gold. Leg.* 387/4 A mayden wel bespoken.

2. Ordered, commissioned, arranged for. See also BESPOKE *ppl. a.*

1607 HEYWOOD *F. Mayde Exch.* Wks. 1874 II. 31 Here is bespoken work. **1807** W. TAYLOR in *Ann. Rev.* V. 577 Which gives to his treatise an appearance of bespoken work.

3. Spoken of, talked of.

1871 BLACKIE *Four Phases* i. 59 The much-bespoken utilitarianism of the most recent ethical school.

besport (bɪ'spɔət), *v.* [Alteration of DISPORT *v.*, by exchange of prefix (BE- 1).] *refl.* To disport oneself. Also *intr.* (for *refl.*).

1855 *Chambers's Jrnl.* IV. 65 Living gems of light, besporting themselves on the bosom of the lake. **1906** *Westm. Gaz.* 7 June 9/2 And surely Shylock never besported himself more ostentatiously. **1925** A. S. ALEXANDER *Tramps across Watersheds* viii. 256 The famous golf course, where ladies and gentlemen besported in the glowing sun.

bespot (bɪ'spɒt). [ME., f. BE- 1 + SPOT *v.*] *tr.* To cover or mark over the surface with spots; to cover with blots or blemishes. Hence **be'spotted** *ppl. a.*, **be'spottedness** *sb.*, **be'spotting** *vbl. sb.*

c **1374** CHAUCER *Boeth.* III. iv. 73 Whan þei byspotten and defoulen dignites wiþ hire vylenie. **1483** CAXTON *G. de la Tour* A vij, The vessel of siluer whiche was foully bespottyd of the donghylle. **1532** MORE *Confut. Barnes* VIII. Wks. 802/2 Theyr continuall newe byspottyng and wrinclyng. **1622** HEYLIN *Cosmogr.* II. (1682) 213 Marble curiously bespotted. **1684** CHARNOCK *Attrib. God.* I. 331 It soils our duties, and bespots our souls. **1720** ROWE *Amb. Step-Mother* V. i. 78 Com'st thou bespotted with the recent slaughter? **1814** WORDSW. *Excurs.* VII. 788 The Danube..like a serpent, shows his glittering back Bespotted—with innumerable isles. *a* **1882** SIR R. CHRISTISON *Autobiog.* I. xviii. 349 The degree of the Sun's bespottedness.

† **be'spouse,** *v. Obs.* In 2-3 bispusen. [f. *bi-*, BE- + ME. *spusen* to SPOUSE.] *trans.* To espouse, marry.

c **1175** *Lamb. Hom.* 133 Ða þe..beon bispused richtliche to gedere. *c* **1200** *Trin. Coll. Hom.* 13 ȝef he ben laȝeliche bispusede.

bespout (bɪ'spaʊt), *v.* [f. BE- + SPOUT *v.*] *trans.* To besprinkle by spouting. *fig.* **a.** To utter or recite with pompous elocution. **b.** To recite to, to plague with oratory.

1575 TURBERV. *Falconrie* 84 Take wine and water and therewith bespout hir well with your mouth. **1828** *Blackw. Mag.* XXIV. 591 It has been bespouted, bequoted, and beparodied. **1857** CARLYLE *Misc.* IV. 138 Woe for the age, woe for the man, quack-ridden, bespeeched, bespouted.

† **be'spray,** *v. Obs. rare*⁻¹. [f. BE- 6 + SPRAY *sb.*] *trans.* To besprinkle, bespatter. Hence **be'spraying** *vbl. sb.*

1593 NASHE *Christ's T.* (1613) 62 Her Alablaster wals were all furred and fome-painted..with the bespraying of mens braines dung out against them.

bespread (bɪ'sprɛd), *v.* [ME. *bi-*, *bespred(en*, f. *bi-* BE- 4, 1 + *spreden* to SPREAD *v.* Cf. MHG. *bespreiten.*] *trans.*

1. To cover, mark, or diversify (a surface) *with* (things spread over it); to spread *with.*

c **1205** LAY. 16521 He..mid ærmen hine bisprædde and forð hine lædde. **1393** GOWER *Conf.* III. 364 A see-foule she becam, And with her winges him besprad. *c* **1450** *Crt. of Love* xii, High pinacles..With plate of gold bespred on every side. **1561** T. NORTON *Calvin's Inst.* III. 252 Ther are euident foule blots where with the workes of the holy are bespred. **1610** HOLLAND *Camden's Brit.* II. 32 The coasts are well bespred with prety townlets. *a* **1764** R. LLOYD *New-Riv. Head* Poet. Wks. (1774) II. 68 Bespread her hospitable board With what she had. **1871** PROCTOR *Light Sc.* 110 A wide continent bespread with volcanic mountains.

2. Said of things: To spread over, to cover by spreading over.

1641 M. FRANK *Serm.* (1672) 253 When our graces..bespread and cloth this earth we carry. **1779** FORREST *Voy. N. Guinea* 297 Mats bespreading the floor of a large hall. **1832** *Fraser's Mag.* V. 148 The ' giant graves' that bespread the shore of the Hellespont.

3. To spread (anything) *over* or *upon* (a surface).

1598 YONG *Diana* 207 But with a teint, like the Vermillion Rose, Bespred vpon her face as white as snowe.

4. To spread out.

1557 TOTTELL'S *Misc.* (Arb.) 242 With armes bespred abrode. **1646** J. HALL *Poems* 25 Since for thy sake so brisk they're grown And such a Downy carpet have bespred.

† **be'spreng,** *v. Obs.* exc. in pa. pple. *pa. pple.* besprent. Forms: 1 besprengan, 2-4 bisprenge(n, 5 besprenge(n. *Pa. t.* 3-5 bi-, bysprengede, 5 besprenged, 6 besprent. *Pa. pple.* 3-5 bi-, bysprenged, 4-6 besprenct, 5 bysprincte, 4-5 bi-, bespreynt, 6 besprinct, -spraynte, -sprint, spreigned, 6-7 spreinct, -spreint, 6- besprent. [OE. *besprengan*, f. BE- 1 + *sprengan* to sprinkle:—OTeut. *sprangjan*, causal of *springan* to SPRING. MHG., mod.G., MDu., and Du. have all *besprengen* in same sense. No part appears after 1600, exc. the pa. pple., and this mostly as ppl. adj. See BESPRING and BESPRENT *v.*; also BESPRINK.]

1. *trans.* To sprinkle (anything) over: **a.** *with* moisture or powder: To besprinkle, asperse.

c **1000** *Sax. Leechd.* I. 190 Besprenge hyne mid þam wætere. *c* **1175** *Lamb. Hom.* 73 Bi-spreng me lauerd mid buhsumnesse. **1388** WYCLIF *Isa.* lii. 15 He schal bisprenge many folkis. *c* **1430** *Syr Generides* 7068 Asshes with the water she menged And her white legges al be-sprenged. **1494** FABYAN VI. clxxxv. 185 Whome she besprent with many a salte tere. **1600** FAIRFAX *Tasso* XII. ci, His siluer locks with dust he foule besprent. **1601** HOLLAND *Pliny* II. 126 Being bespreint, dashed, and drenched quite therewith. **1606** —— *Sueton.* 150 As himselfe sacrificed, bespreint he was with the bloud.

b. *with* spots or patches of colouring: To speckle.

1388 WYCLIF *Gen.* xxx. 39 Spotti beestis, and dyuerse, and bispreynt with dyuerse colour. **1486** *Bk. St. Albans* A viij b, Euery tercellis braylis been bysprenged with blake speckes.

2. To sprinkle (a substance or things) about.

a **1529** SKELTON *Vox Pop.* 182 From Scotland to Kent This preachyng was bysprennt. —— *Epit. Dk. Bedforde* 76 Deth wyth me doloure So hath bespraynte. **1567** MAPLET *Gr. Forest* 28 *Insecta*..having for all this life proportionably and equally besprent throughout the whole bodie. **1820** BYRON *Juan* V. xlvi, O'er the front There seemed to be besprent a deal of gilding.

besprent (bɪ'sprɛnt), *ppl. a.* [f. prec., where see forms.] Besprinkled.

a. *with* moisture of any kind, or dust.

c **1368** CHAUCER *Compl. Pity* 10 To Pite ran I all bespreynt [*v.r.* besprente] with teres. **1483** CAXTON *Gold. Leg.* 269/1 Thre stones besprenct with his bloode. *Ibid.* 353/1 Stones bespryncte and specled as it were with blood. **1535** JOYE *Apol. Tindale* (Arb.) 17 Euen unto the bespreigned bloude. **1561** JR. HEYWOOD *Seneca's Herc. Furens* (1581) 19 My body thus with wicked bloud besprinct. **1579** SPENSER *Sheph. Cal.* Nov. 111 Morne now my muse..with teares besprint. **1634** MILTON *Comus* 542 Knot-grass dew-besprent. *a* **1866** LONGF. *Sir Christopher* 133 His boots with dust and mire besprent.

b. *with* points, or objects dotted about: Strewed.

1556 ABP. PARKER *Psalter* cii[i], My soule with cares was full besprenct. **1837** WORDSW. *At Vallombrosa*, The flowerbesprent meadows. **1873** BROWNING *Red Cott. Night-c.* 162 The tawdry tent..besprent with hearts and darts.

2. Scattered, strewed about.

1567 MAPLET *Gr. Forest* 15 Having certain blottes besprent upon it. **1870** MORRIS *Earthly Par.* II. III. 139 He lay upon the flowers besprent about.

† **be'sprent,** *v. Obs. rare*⁻¹. [improperly f. prec.] *trans.* To besprinkle.

1573 TWYNE *Æneid* XII. Mm iv, Latinus rentes His hoarie head..and auntient beard with durt besprentes.

† **be'spring,** *v. Obs.* Forms: 4 bispringen, 4-5 -sprynge(n, 5 be-. *Pa. t.* 5 bysprang. *Pa. pple.* 4 bispronge(n, 4-5 by-, 5 besprong. [A late ME. variant of BESPRENG, in which the strong verb *spring* is substituted for the causal *spreng.*] *trans.* To besprinkle; = BESPRENG. Hence **be'springing** *vbl. sb.*

1387 TREVISA *Descr. Brit.* (Caxton) 54 With mylke of a cowe that is of one yeer bespringe the welle. **1398** —— *Barth. De P.R.* XI. iv, Ofte as a cloude byspryngeþ þe erþe with droppynge, he wasteþ him selfe in þat bispryngynge [ed. **1582** bespringing]. *c* **1420** *Pallad. on Husb.* I. 678 Barly coct and colde, and wyne besprong. **1483** CAXTON *Gold. Leg.* 291 Thou art al besprongen with the blood. *c* **1575** *Jacob & Sonnes* (Collier) 20 Their meat cloth they besprang all with gotes blood.

† **be'sprink,** *v. Obs. rare.* [Shortened from BESPRINKLE, probably under the influence of *bespring*, *bespreng*, and esp. of the pa. pple. *besprinct*, *besprenct*: see BESPRENG.] = To BESPRINKLE.

1609 HEYWOOD *Brit. Troy* in Farr's *S.P.* 330 With Hipprocrenes drops besprinke my head.

besprinkle (bɪ'sprɪŋk(ə)l), *v.* Also 5 besprengil, 6 by-, besprincle, -ckle, -ckel. [ME. *besprengil*, **besprenkel*, f. BE- 1 and 4 + *sprenkel*, freq. of *sprengen* to asperse; *besprinkle* is therefore in form the freq. of BESPRENG.] Hence **be'sprinkled** *ppl. a.*

1. *trans.* To sprinkle all over *with* small drops (of liquid), or *with* powdery substance, as flour, salt.

c **1440** *Gesta Rom.* (1879) 26 That was all besprengild with his blessyd blode. **1534** MORE *On the Passion* Wks. 1295/2 They shoulde bysprincle the postes..with the bloud. **1622** R. HAWKINS *Voy. S. Sea* (1847) 58 To keepe cleane the shippe; to besprinkle her ordinarily with vineger. **1781** GIBBON *Decl. & F.* III. lii. 273 The walls were besprinkled

with holy water. **1835** PAUL *Antiq. Greece* I. II. iv. §8 [He] was also thrice besprinkled with water.

b. predicated of the fluid.

1738 GLOVER *Leonidas* v. 657 The gory drops besprinkle all his shield. **1872** SPURGEON *Treas. Dav.* Ps. lxvi. 14 Scarce a drop of rain would venture to besprinkle their splendour.

2. *fig.* To strew *with* (comparatively) small things scattered about; to spot, to dot; to intersperse *with* any elements diffused throughout.

1561 T. NORTON *Calvin's Inst.* III. 258 All our good workes are continually besprinckled with many filthy spottes. **1646** SIR T. BROWNE *Pseud. Ep.* I. viii. (1686) 22 [He] hath besprinkled his work with many fabulosities. **1670** EACHARD *Cont. Clergy* 40 Besprinkling all their sermons with plenty of Greek and Latin. **1842** DICKENS *Amer. Notes* (1850) 54/1 Sloping banks besprinkled with pleasant villas. **1861** LADY WALLACE *Mendelssohn's Lett.* 303 We.. besprinkled each other mutually with great praise.

†**3.** *transf.* To water, moisten (as streams). *Obs.*

1611 SPEED *Theat. Gt. Brit.* xxx. (1614) 39/1 Vallies besprinkled with many sweet springs. **1623** FAVINE *Theat. Hon.* II. xiii. 202 A million of Riuers that water and besprinkle France.

be'sprinkler. [f. BESPRINKLE *v.* + -ER[1].] He who or that which besprinkles.

1611 COTGR., *Arroseur*, a bedeawer; a besprinkler.

be'sprinkling, *vbl. sb.* [f. as prec. + -ING[1].] The action of the vb. BESPRINKLE.

1580 HOLLYBAND *Treas. Fr. Tong, Aspersion* and *arrousement*, besprinckling or bedewing. **1680** H. MORE *Apoc. Apocal.* 186 The besprinkling of Sheep and other Cattle with holy Water.

besprong, pa. pple. of BESPRING *v. Obs.*

bespue, variant of BESPEW: see BE- *pref.* 4.

†**be'spurt,** *v. Obs.* [f. BE- 4 + SPURT *v.*] *trans.* To asperse or befoul *with* anything spurted or spirted on; also *fig.*

1579 TOMSON *Calvin's Serm. Tim.* 834/1 To walke through the myre and durt, and not bespurt himselfe. **1603** HOLLAND *Plutarch's Mor.* 1232 The city of the Corinthians ..he hath..bespurted and dashed..with a most grievous slander. **1641** MILTON *Animadv.* Wks. (1851) 185 To send home his haughtinesse well bespurted with his owne holy-water.

†**be'spurtle,** *v. Obs.* [f. BE- 4 + SPURTLE.]

1. A frequentative variant of prec.

1618 BOLTON *Florus* (1636) 245 Merula..bespurtled the eyes of Iove himselfe, with the blood. *a* **1655** T. ADAMS *Pract. Wks.* (1861) III. 21 (D.) They sputter their venom abroad, and bespurtle others.

2. *fig.* To asperse with reproach or abuse; to spot or sully with vice.

1604 MARSTON *Malcontent* I. ii. (D.) Trot about, and bespurtle whom thou pleasest. **1629** J. MAXWELL tr. *Herodian* 77 He bespurtled his life with foule Vices.

besputter (bɪ'spʌtə(r)), *v.* [f. BE- 4 + SPUTTER.] To sputter (anything) over; 'to dawb anything by sputtering, or throwing spittle over it.' (J.)

1730 BAILEY, *Besputter*, to spirt or flirt spittle upon.

bespy, besquatter, besqueeze, besquib, etc.: see BE- *pref.*

†**be'squirt** (bɪ'skwɜːt), *v. Obs.* [f. BE- 4 + SQUIRT *v.*] *trans.* To asperse or befoul by squirting; also *fig.* in reference to abuse or defamation.

1611 COTGR., *Foirer*, to besquirt or beray with squirting. **1682** *Roxb. Bal.* (1884) V. 195 Celliers, that Midwife-Slut, Who Dangerfield doth so besquirt.

besquite, obs. form of BISCUIT.

bessant, bessaun, obs. forms of BEZANT.

Bessarabian (ˌbɛsə'reɪbɪən), *a.* and *sb.* [f. *Bessarabia*, a province of south-west Russia + -AN.] **A.** *adj.* Of or pertaining to Bessarabia. **B.** *sb.* An inhabitant of Bessarabia.

1835 *Penny Cycl.* IV. 340/1 Its [*sc.* the Dniester's] chief tributaries on the Bessarabian side are, the Reut..and the Botna. *Ibid.* 341/1 The majority of the Bessarabians are Moldowans or Moldavians. **1852** H. W. DULCKEN tr. *Pfeiffer's Visit to Holy Land* ii. 37 Tehussa, a Bessarabian village of most miserable appearance. **1908** KIPLING *Lett. Travel* (1920) 160 You are always talking of the second generation of your Smyrniotes and Bessarabians. **1925** *Chambers's Jrnl.* Apr. 214/2 The traditional Bessarabian hospitality. **1959** E. H. CARR *Socialism in One Country* II. xxiii. 394 When a Bessarabian division was enrolled in the Ukraine, desertions amounted to 50 per cent. **1963** *House & Garden* Mar. 73/2 This room, with its handsome Bessarabian rug.

Bessel ('bɛsəl). The surname of F. W. *Bessel* (1784–1846), a German astronomer, used *attrib.* or in the possessive in ***Bessel('s) function***: a solution of Bessel's differential equation $x^2\frac{d^2y}{dx^2} + x\frac{dy}{dx} + (x^2 - n^2)y = 0$. So **Be'sselian** *a.* (Cent. Dict., 1889).

1872 *Phil. Mag.* XLIV. 328 The value of Bessel's functions is becoming generally recognized. **1894** *Ann. Math.* IX. 27 (*heading*) Roots of the Second Bessel Function. **1939** *Nature* 22 July 162/2 Results calculated.. by the Besselian method. **1963** G. TROUP *Masers & Lasers* (ed. 2) vii. 117 The cut-off parameters u_{om} for these modes are the *m*th roots of the zero order Bessel function J_0.

Bessemer ('bɛsɪmə(r)). [From the name of the inventor, Sir H. *Bessemer*, in 1856.] **Bessemer process**: a process for decarbonizing and desiliconizing pig-iron so as to convert it into steel or malleable iron, by passing currents of air through the molten metal. Hence **Bessemer iron, steel**, briefly *Bessemer*; and *attrib.*, as in ***Bessemer converter, flame, maker, method, slag***, etc.

[**1856** *Encycl. Brit.* XII. 574/2 The ingots derived from Mr. Bessemer's process.] **1864** PERCY *Metall.* 819 Analyses ..of the pig-irons and Bessemer irons made therefrom. **1875** URE *Dict. Arts* III. 905 The enormously high temperature developed by the action of cold air on molten cast iron in the Bessemer process. *Ibid.* 907 The exact chemical character of the spectrum of the Bessemer flame. *Ibid.* 909 Good pig iron, such as that employed for Bessemer steel-making. **1881** *N.Y. Nation* XXXII. 404 The generic term Bessemer steel denotes a steel made essentially by blowing air through molten iron, in a vessel called a converter. **1883** *Daily News* 3 Sept. 2/7 Bessemer makers are very busy.

bessemerize ('bɛsɪməraɪz), *v.* [f. BESSEMER + -IZE.] *trans.* To treat by the Bessemer process.

1888 in *Amer. Speech* (1960) XXXV. 267. **1901** *Prospectus Mond Nickel Co.*, Plant of the most modern type for Roasting, Smelting and Bessemerizing this ore.

besset, early Kentish form of BESHUT.

besshe, variant of BISSE *sb. Obs.*

bessome, obs. form of BESOM.

best (bɛst), *a.* and *adv.* Forms: 1 betost, betast, betest, betst (3 bezst, 3–4 beist, 4–5 beste, 5 beest), 2– best. [Com. Teut.: OE. (adv.) *bętst*, earlier *bętest, bętost* = OFris., OS. (MDu., Du.) *best*, OHG. *bezzist* (MHG., mod.G. *best*), ON. *bazt, bezt* (Da. *best*, Sw. *bäst*), Goth. *batist*, OTeut. **batist*, superlative belonging to the comp. **batiz*, BETTER, q.v. The adj. differed from the adv. only in its inflexions; as nom. sing. masc. str. OTeut. **batisto-z*, Goth. *batist-s*, ON. *bazt-r*, OE. *bętest*, wk. *se bętsta, þæt bętste*, etc. By assimilation of *t* to following *s*, the word has been reduced to *best* in Eng., as in all modern Teut. langs.]

A. *adj.* The superlative degree of GOOD: Most good. (*Goodest*, in 17th c. in Dryden, etc., was merely analogical; no such form is found in OTeut.)

I. As simple adjective.

1. Of the highest excellence, excelling all others in quality.

a. Said of persons, in respect of physical, mental, or esp. moral qualities; or as regards social standing, as in 'the best people in the town.'

891 *O.E. Chron.* (Parker MS.), Se betsta lareow þe on Scottum wæs. *c* **893** K. ÆLFRED *Oros.* v. iv. §3 Scipia, se besta and se selesta Romana witena. *a* **1000** *Crist* 1012 (Gr.) Æð-elduguð betast. *a* **1075** *O.E. Chron.* (Laud MS.) an. 1052 Ealle þa eorlas and þa betstan menn. *a* **1300** *Cursor M.* 12619 þe beste maistris of þat toun. **1382** WYCLIF *Dan.* v. i, Balthasar, Kyng, made a grete fest to his best men a thousand. *c* **1435** *Torr. Portugal* 2752 Beste of bone and blood. **1591** SHAKS. *Two Gent.* I. ii. 102 Of many good, I thinke him best. **1601** CHESTER in *Shaks. C. Praise* 43 The best and chiefest of our moderne writers. **1693** W. PAYNE *Pract. Disc.* i. §2. 18 Some..failures and imperfections will stick to the best of Men. **1749** FIELDING *Tom. Jones* IX. iv, I will fight the best man of you all for twenty pound. **1848** MACAULAY *Hist. Eng.* II. 267 The best Roman Catholic families in England. **1856** FROUDE *Hist. Eng.* (1858) I. i. 62 Henry VIII..was the best rider, the best lance, and the best archer in England.

b. Said of things, in respect of their essential qualities. Applied to a room that is furnished especially well, often one reserved for special use. In U.S., *best room*, spec. a parlour.

a **1075** *O.E. Chron.* (Laud MS.) an. 1052 Eall þæt æfre betst wæs. **1297** R. GLOUC. 370 Edgar Aþelyng þat best kunde in Engelond adde to be Kyng. **1382** WYCLIF *Gen.* xliii. 11 Take ȝe of the beste fruytis of the loond. **1398** TREVISA *Barth. De P.R.* IX. xxvi. (1495) 363 In the Saturdaye men weren aournyd..with theyr beest clothes. **1552** *Bk. Com. Prayer, Commun.* (Rubr.) The best and purest Wheat Bread that conveniently may be gotten. **1653** WALTON *Angler* 179 The Pearch..and the Pike are..the best of fresh water fish. **1702** C. FIENNES *Journeys* (1947) I. ix. 56 These doores open through to the end one way the best bed chamber..the other side a visto. **1719** S. SEWALL *Diary* 30 Oct. in *Mass. Hist. Soc. Coll.* (1882) 5th Ser. VII. 233 Had a very good Dinner..in the best room. **1751** JORTIN *Serm.* (1771) VII. i. 13 Acting according to their best judgement. **1800** JANE AUSTEN *Let.* 8 Nov. (1952) 83 The little Table..has most conveniently taken itself off into the best bedroom. **1834** SOUTHEY *Doctor* cxcix. (1862) 532 Best ..in the shopkeeper's vocabulary..is at the bottom of his scale of superlatives. **1839** F. A. KEMBLE *Jrnl. Residence on Georgian Plantation* Jan. 80 In all establishments..some disparity exists between the comforts of the drawing-room and best bed-rooms, and the servant's hall and attics. **1849** MACAULAY *Hist. Eng.* I. 172 The best years of his life. **1872** *Harper's Mag.* Oct. 684/2 A parlor, or 'best room'. **1911** BEERBOHM *Zuleika D.* ii. 7 The sun streamed through the bay-window of a 'best' bedroom in the Warden's house. **1967** J. SPEIGHT *Till Death us do Part* i. 22 I've always wanted a best room, somewhere you could put all your decent bits of furniture.

c. *spec.* denoting a certain grade of wrought iron; also ***best best*** adj., of a higher quality than best; ***best best best*** adj., of the highest quality.

1888 *Lockwood's Dict. Terms Mech. Engin., Best, or B.*—A brand of wrought-iron plate or bar equivalent to No. 3 quality, or that grade which is only just superior to the commonest... The 'best' plates of the first-class houses are, however, equal to the 'best, best' and 'treble best' of other firms. *Ibid., Best, Best, or B.B.*...obtained by piling, reheating, and rerolling 'best' or No. 3 bars. *Ibid., Best, Best, Best, or Treble Best, B.B.B.* **1940** *Chambers's Techn. Dict.* 67/1 *B.* and *B.B.*, brand-marks signifying *Best* and *Best Best*, placed on wrought-iron to indicate the maker's opinion of its quality.

d. *spec.* in ***best boat***, a racing boat on the Thames, as distinguished from the heavier types; esp. used attrib. in ***best-boat race, racing, regatta, rowing***. Also ***best-and-best boat, punt***: a boat of the lightest and narrowest construction, used for racing.

1890 *Lock to Lock Times* 23 Aug. 162/2 This year the amateur oarsmen have ungrudgingly given up their boats to the watermen, who have been rowing in the past regatta; wager, or 'best' boats, being in special demand by the fleet of scullers, who were attracted by the liberal programme. **1894** *Daily News* 5 May 6/5 The race will..be decided in best-and-best punts. **1897** *Ibid.* 30 Aug. 5/1 No best-boat racing will be attempted. **1927** *Observer* 24 July 26/2 The best-boat rowing season..is all too short.

2. a. Of persons: Most kind or beneficent. Of persons and things: Most advantageous or suitable for the object in view; most appropriate or desirable.

a **1000** *Beowulf* 6007 Nu is ofost betost, þæt we þeodcyning þær sceawian. *a* **1240** *Ureisun* 129 in *Lamb. Hom.* 197 Nim nu ȝeme to me so me best a beo ðe beo. **1297** R. GLOUC. 504 To loki, wat were best to do. *a* **1300** *Cursor M.* 5287 He þat til his in nede es beste. **1377** LANGL. *P. Pl.* B. v. 299 As best is for the soule. **1523** LD. BERNERS *Froiss.* I. cv. 126 It was thought nat beste to employ his people then. **1569** J. ROGERS *Gl. Godly Love* 187 [He] knoweth what is beste for you. **1605** SHAKS. *Macb.* III. iv. 4 In best time We will require her welcome. **1716** in *Lond. Gaz.* No. 5445/3 To be sold to the best Purchaser. **1879** LOCKYER *Elem. Astron.* iii. §28. 157 The best way to obtain a knowledge of the various constellations. *Mod. colloq.* Which of your brothers is best to you?

b. ***best friend***, one's favourite friend (of persons and *transf.* of things); also in colloq. phr. ***to be 'best friends' with*** (a person).

c **1374** CHAUCER *Troylus* II. 412 When he, that for my beste freend I wende. **1609** BEAUMONT & FLETCHER *Kn. Burn. Pestle* 111, *Luce.* No my best friend. **1671** [see FRIEND *sb.* 5 d]. **1796** M. EDGEWORTH *Parent's Assistant* (ed. 2) I. 23 Ay, go along with its best friend, and take care it does not get into a scrape. **1885** C. M. YONGE *Two Sides of Shield* II. vii. 130 'I want to be friends with both. One can have two friends.' 'No! no! no! not two *best* friends. And you are my best friend, Nysie.' **1905** F. H. BURNETT *Little Princess* iii. 36 Lavinia and Jessie are 'best friends'... I wish we could be 'best friends'. **1967** E. MCGIRR *Here lies my Wife* v. 149 Our mothers are on best-friend terms.

c. ***best girl*** (GIRL *sb.* 2 c), a man's favourite female companion. orig. *U.S.* Also *ellipt.* (U.S. slang) for *best girl*.

1887 *Texas Siftings* 7 May 11/2 You can't convince a young man whose best girl has just said 'Yes' that this country is going to wreck and ruin. **1904** *Democrat* (Celina, Ohio) in *Daily Chron.* 23 Feb. 5/2 Wm. Londen and best were at church Sunday evening. **1904** *Indicator* (Merriweather, Georgia) in *Daily Chron.* 21 May 4/5 Messrs. Bub Peary and Pierce Biggers called on their best girls last Sunday afternoon. **1918** *Punch* 16 Jan. 38/3 When he [*sc.* a Tommy] gave me an unprovoked smile..I hoped that perhaps I reminded him of his best girl. **1944** *Sat. Rev.* 8 July 16/2 To pluck a bouquet for his best girl.

3. Largest, most; esp. in ***best part***.

1538 *Lisle Papers* XI. 49 Twenty nobles, of which I think he doth owe the best part for his rent. **1647** W. BROWNE *Polex.* I. 215 The Artillery plaid, the best of an houre, on both sides. **1697** POTTER *Antiq. Greece* II. x. (1715) 293 Fiery foam..which cover'd the best part of its natural Azure. **1834** BECKFORD *Italy* II. 265, I..rode the best part of the way. **1877** A. B. EDWARDS *Up Nile* xii. 318 The best part of three days.

4. In the idiomatic *I, you,* etc. ***had best*** (formerly ***me were best***, afterwards ***I were best***): it would be most advantageous for me, you, etc. For the history see BETTER.

c **1330** *Lay le Freine* 107 Yete me is best take mi chaunce. **1393** GOWER *Conf.* II. 306 What thing him were best to do. **1483** *Cron. Englonde* (1510) Q 6 b, He wyste not what he was beste to do. **1509** FISHER *Fun. Serm.* Wks. 1876 I. 292 Doubtfull in her mynde what she were best to do. **1584** LYLY *Campaspe* IV. i, He were best be as cunning as a bee. **1591** SHAKS. *Two Gent.* I. iii. 24 Tell me, whether were I best to send him? **1611** —— *Cymb.* III. ii. 59 Madam, you're best consider. **1628** *Powerf. Fav.* 77 Liuia may..resolue whether she were best to marry againe. **1636** *Ariana* 102 Ignorant of what hee was best to doe.

1559 CUNINGHAM *Cosmogr. Glasse* 61 You had best omit the worke. *c* **1590** MARLOWE *Faust* (1st. vers.) ix, Stand aside, you had best. **1639** MASSINGER *Unnat. Combat* V. ii, Thou hadst best follow her. **1710** ADDISON *Tatler* No. 221 ¶2 Whether I had best sell my Beetles in a Lump. **1777** GARRICK *Sheridan's Sch. Scand.* Prol. 21 A certain Lord had best beware. **1608** SOUTHEY *Lett.* (1856) II. 52 The 'Monthly' must needs be sore, and had best be civil. **1877** MALLOCK *New Rep.* (1878) 145, I had best not give her any.

5. *Phrases* and *locutions*. **a.** ***best work***: a miner's term for the best class of ore. Also BEST-MAN. *to*

put one's best foot or ***leg foremost***: to do one's best to get on. ***to turn the best side outward***: to make the best appearance possible. ***at the best-hand***: see HAND. ***best end***, the end of a neck of lamb, mutton, or veal consisting of the ribs; opp. *scrag-end*.

1663 PEPYS *Diary* 9 Nov., A conceited man, and one that would put the best side outward. **1670** COTTON *Espernon* II. VIII. 364 Espernon..endeavour'd nevertheless all he could to turn the best side outward. **1840** BARHAM *Ingol. Leg., St. Odille* vi, She set off and ran, Put her best leg before. **1728, 1874** Best end [see SCRAG *sb.*[1] 2]. **1936** MENCKEN *Amer. Lang.* (ed. 4) vi. 236 What we call the *rib* chops are [in England] the *best end of the neck* or *best end*. **1962** *House & Garden* Nov. 93/1 *Crown roast of lamb.* Ingredients: 2 best ends of neck (there are usually 6 cutlets in each).

b. ***to give*** (a person or thing) ***best***: to admit the superiority of, give way to. Also *absol.*

1888 'R. BOLDREWOOD' *Robbery under Arms* I. vii. 94, I could hardly stand for laughing till the calf gave him best and walked. **1895** A. B. PATERSON *Man from Snowy River* (1906) 71 My country joker, are you going to give it best? Are you frightened of the fences? **1911** J. MASEFIELD *Everlasting Mercy* 31 In all the show from birth to rest I give the poor dumb cattle best. **1927** T. E. LAWRENCE *Let.* 1 Dec. (1938) 549 Those people who have compared the versions generally give me best with the new one. **1959** *Times* 20 Nov. 18/5 It was now the turn of the young professionals to give best.

II. *absol.* (rarely passing into *sb.*)

6. *pl.* (formerly also *sing.*) The best people.

c **1050** *Ags. Gloss.* in Wr.-Wülcker *Voc.* 466 *Prestantissimus*, se betesta, and se fyrmesta. **1091** *O.E. Chron.* (Laud MS.), Ðas forewarde ȝesworan xii þa betste of þes cynges healfe. *c* **1205** LAY. 707 Brutus þe wes cnight mid þane beste. *c* **1325** *E.E. Allit. P.* A. 279 I-wyse quoth I my blysfol beste. **1737** POPE *Hor. Epist.* ii. i. 286 Observe how seldom e'en the best succeed.

7. *sing.* **a.** The best thing, point, circumstance, element.

c **1175** *Lamb. Hom.* 3 Heo nomen heore claþes and þe beste þet heo hefde. **1562** J. HEYWOOD *Prov. & Epigr.* (1867) 166 Prouyde for the woorst, the best wyll saue it selfe. **1591** SHAKS. *Two Gent.* III. i. 349 The best is, she hath no teeth to bite. **1597** DANIEL *Civ. Wares* II. xxiv, We neede must take the seeming best of bad. **1654** JENKYN *On Jude* (1845) 30 The best is best cheap. *a* **1693** KILLIGREW *Chit-chat* I. i, I confess bad is the best.

b. individualized, or with indef. article *a*. *spec.* = RECORD *sb.* 5 d.

c **1600** SHAKS. *Sonn.* xci, All these I better in one generall best. **1765** TUCKER *Lt. Nat.* I. 617 That unknown best appointed by divine provision. *Ibid.* The best we may attain by the road of virtue and discretion will be..a better best, than any we can arrive at [otherwise]. **1881** *Sportsman's Year-bk.* 192 [Cortis] has accomplished bests on record at 10 and 20 miles. **1884** *Christmas Illus. Lond. News* 19/3 For certainly if I have a best I have not put it on. **1930** F. A. M. WEBSTER *Athletics of to-day for Women* vi. 86 Miss M. A. Gunn..ripped through her heat in 14⅗ secs., thus equalling the world's record and beating Miss Hatt's British best. **1963** G. F. D. PEARSON et al. *Athletics* I. ii. 40 Snell was obviously not deterred by having to set personal bests *en route* to..the Gold Medal in Rome. *Ibid.* iv. 85 Lord Burghley, who produced a best of 14·5 sec. in 1930. *Ibid.* II. vii. 154 A stupendous new world's best of 63 ft. 1½ in.

c. ***all the best***: an expression of goodwill, used as a toast or a valediction.

1937 M. SHARP *Nutmeg Tree* xv. 192 All the best, Fred. **1951** J. B. PRIESTLEY *Fest. Farbridge* I. ii. 78 Let's drink to it. All the best!

d. ***best of*** (a specified odd number): (applied to) a series of games, contests, etc., between two parties in which the first to gain a majority of successes (points, etc.) is declared the overall winner; usu. *attrib.* (hyphened).

1895 H. W. W. WILBERFORCE *Lawn Tennis* 77 All matches shall be the best of three advantage-sets. **1933** LD. ABERDARE *Rackets, &c.* ix. 109 A match shall consist of the best of five games. **1957** *Encycl. Brit.* XIII. 792/2 A match in England and the U.S. consists ordinarily of the best of three or the best of five sets. **1977** *Time* 19 Sept. 56/1 Among the eagle-eyed yachting fraternity that swarmed into historic Newport for the best-of-seven series, there was nearly unanimous agreement.

8. With possessive. ***one's best***: †**a.** what is best for one; **b.** the best one can (do); esp. in ***to do one's best***, formerly, ***the best of one's power***.

a **1300** *Cursor M.* 2456 (Gött.), Þai most nede part to seke þair beste [*Fairf.* to do þaire best]. **1423** JAS. I. *Kings Q.* v, My best was more to loke Vpon the writing of this noble man. *c* **1530** LD. BERNERS *Arth. Lyt. Bryt.* (1814) 235, I shall do the best of my power. **1579** SPENSER *Sheph. Cal.* May 225 Ne for all his worst, nor for his best Open the dore at his request. **1585** ABP. SANDYS *Serm.* (1841) 112 When a man hath done his best, he must then begin again. **1590** SHAKS. *Mids. N.* II. ii. 145 Do thy best To pluck this crawling serpent from my brest. **1599** SANDYS *Europæ Spec.* (1637) 247, I have..also, to my best, avoyded that rashnesse. *c* **1620** Z. BOYD *Zion's Flowers* (1855) 42 To turne to him's our best. **1733** POPE *Hor. Sat.* II. vi. 173 He did his best to seem to eat. **1863** KINGSLEY *Water Bab.* 7 [He] would have done and behaved his best.

c. Best state, point, or condition.

1571 GOLDING *Calvin on Ps.* xxxix. 6 When man seemeth to bee at his best, hee is altogither nothing. **1828** STEUART *Plant. Guide* 489 Whatever is at its best..can admit of no further improvement. **1832** *Athenæum* 197 She was at her best both as to voice and exertion on Tuesday last. **1871** SMILES *Charac.* i. (1876) 1 It exhibits man at his best.

d. Best clothes.

1790 BURNS *Tam O'Shanter*, It was her best, and she was vauntie. **1794** SOUTHEY *Bot. Bay Eclog.* ii, To go to fair I drest..in my Sunday's best. **1830** GALT *Lawrie T.* v. viii. (1849) 227 Mr. Herbert joined me, also in his modest best. **1859** JEPHSON *Brittany* xvi. 271 Little family parties dressed in their Sunday best.

e. *Ellipt.* for 'best wishes'; usu. ***one's best.*** *U.S. colloq.*

1922 F. SCOTT FITZGERALD *Let.* Jan. (1964) 332 Zelda sends best. **1953** W. STEVENS *Let.* 28 Jan. (1967) 770 My best to Marianne Moore. **1969** *Rolling Stone* 28 June 13 Billy Jean came here tonight, too, and she sends her best.

III. Phrases. **9.** With *verbs.*

a. ***to have the best*** (obs.), ***to have the best of it***: to have the advantage in a contest, or greatest possible advantage in a transaction, and *hence*, the least possible disadvantage or loss; so **b.** ***to make the best of.*** **c.** ***to make the best of one's way***: to go by the most advantageous route, hence, to go with the greatest possible speed.

a. **1593** SHAKS. *3 Hen. VI*, v. iii. 20 We hauing now the best at Barnet field. **1647** W. BROWNE *Polex.* II. 343, I see well that Polexander must have the best..of his Enemies. **1832** MOORE *Wks.* (1862) 561 Those who had the best of the joke. **1846** BROWNING *Luria* I. i, You have so plainly here the best of it. **1871** TYNDALL *Fragm. Sc.* viii. 135 To conclude that the other had the best of it.

b. *a* **1626** BACON (J.), Carry their commodities where they may make the best of them. **1694** R. LESTRANGE *Fables* (1708) II. 75 Making the Best of a Bad Game. **1836** DICKENS *Sk. Boz* (C.D. ed.) 36 Accustomed to take things as they came, and to make the best of a bad job. **1862** TROLLOPE *Orley F.* i. (1874) 11 Making the best of it for herself.

c. **1704** ADDISON *Italy* 4 The next Day we again set Sail, and made the best of our way. **1716** *Lond. Gaz.* No. 5450/2 Captain Vernon was ordered..to make the best of his Way to Sheerness. **1868** FREEMAN *Norm. Conq.* (1876) II. vii. 154 The two brothers made the best of their way towards Bristol.

10. With *prepositions*:

a. †***at the best, at best***: at the best possible pitch, in the best possible way, manner, or condition; see also quot. 1812. *Obs.* ***at best***: (taken) in the best circumstances, in the most favourable aspect, making every allowance, at most; also in *Finance*, at the best possible pitch or price. ***at one's best***: see 8 c. † ***at the best hand*** (see HAND *sb.* 10 b). ***at the best of times***: even in the most advantageous conditions or circumstances.

c **1325** *Coer de L.* 132 The wynd..servede hem atte the best. *c* **1386** CHAUCER *Prol.* 29 And wel we weren esed atte beste [*v.r.* at the beste]. *c* **1399** *Pol. Poems* (1859) II. 6 To stere peace oghte every man alyve..Ffor so this world mai stonden ate beste. **1485** CAXTON *Trevisa's Higden* I. xxx. (1527) 31 Of whiche cleye men make erthen vessell at beste. **1586** COGAN *Haven Health* (1636) 169 Shell fishes be at the best when the moon increaseth, as the Poet Horace noteth. **1604** SHAKS. *Oth.* I. iii. 171 Good Brabantio, take up this mangled matter at the best. **1812** VAUX *Flash Lang.* 155 *To get your money at the best*, signifies to live by dishonest or fraudulent practices, without labour or industry.

1629 H. BURTON *Truth's Tri.* 133 Our inherent righteousnesse, call it Christs merits, or what you will, is at the best but as *Piscis in arido.* **1645** QUARLES *Sol. Recant.* III. 48 Thy days are ev'll at best. **1722** DE FOE *Col. Jack* (1840) 286 Man is a shortsighted creature at best. **1796** BURKE *Regic. Peace* Wks. 1845 IV. 513 'Tis a random shot at best. **1841** MYERS *Cath. Th.* IV. §19. 276 External Evidence must at the very best be but partial and secondary. **1938** *Times* 29 Sept. 19/1 Numerous orders to sell 'at best' have been given recently in respect of small amounts of rubber.

1936 BENTLEY & ALLEN *Trent's Own Case* iv. 30 A shifty-looking character at the best of times, thought the Inspector; and now looking sick and frightened. **1966** M. KELLY *Dead Corse* x. 162 Allie could not take drink at the best of times.

b. ***for the best***: intended for, aiming at, tending to, the best result. †***for my, his,*** etc. ***best***: for my, his, etc. greatest advantage (*obs.*). †***for best***: finally; cf. 'for good (and all),' 'for better or for worse' (*obs.*).

c **1386** CHAUCER *Melib.* ¶ 271, I speke for youre beste. —— *Frankl. T.* 158 Al is for the best. *c* **1450** *Why I can't be Nun* 156 in *E.E. Poems* (1862) 142, I hope hyt schalle be for the best. **1593** SHAKS *3 Hen. VI*, III. iii. 170, I hope all's for the best. **1607** —— *Cor.* IV. vi. 144 That we did we did for the best. **1794** SOUTHEY *Bot. Bay Eclog.* iii, But all's for the best. *a* **1674** MILTON (Webster), Those constitutions..are now established for best, and not to be mended.

c. ***in the best*** = ***at best*** (see 10 a).

1602 SHAKS. *Ham.* I. v. 27 Murther most foule, as in the best it is.

d. ***of the best***: of the best quality or sort. In colloq. phrases: (i) (a specified number, esp. ***six***) ***of the best***, a thrashing; (ii) referring to a sum of money: pounds or dollars; (iii) ***one of the best***: a good fellow.

1338 R. BRUNNE *Chron.* (1725) I. 183 Ten sergeanz of þe best his targe gan him bere. *c* **1420** *Anturs of Arth.* lv, Bokelornut byrners and bischoppus of the beste. *c* **1510** SKELTON *E. Rummyng* (1568) line 265 And dame Elinoure entreaet To byrle them of the best. **1534** in EDW. PEACOCK *Eng. Ch. Furniture* (1866) 185 Itm ix cusshions of the best wherof.. be backyd wt red lether. **1828** C. CROKER *Fairy Leg.* 481 After a supper which was of the best, they embarked.

1912 'SAKI' *Unbearable Bassington* ii. 29 You'll get six of the very best, over the back of a chair. **1923** KIPLING *Land & Sea Tales* 110, I got nine cuts of the best from the Senior Sub for occupying the bathroom ten seconds too long. **1929** WODEHOUSE *Mr. Mulliner Speaking* ix. 297 He was..an officious little devil who needed six of the best with a fives-bat.

1911 E. WALLACE *Sanders of River* v. 103, I wouldn't take a half-share of the trouble he's going to find for five hundred of the best. **1920** WODEHOUSE *Let.* 28 Feb. in *Perf. Flea* (1953) 15 Heaven knows what a women's magazine wants with my sort of stuff, but they are giving me fifteen thousand of the best for it. **1928** GALSWORTHY *Swan Song* II. xii. 204 The walrus put down five thousand of the best.

1917 'CONTACT' *Airman's Outings* 238 The brigades are directed by the General-Officer-Commanding.., one of the best, who treats us like brothers. **1959** *Listener* 22 Jan. 155/1 Harry Truman was one of the best.

e. ***to the best***: in the best sense, for the best. (*obs.*) Also, To the utmost effort or extent (of one's power, knowledge, belief, etc.).

1503-4 *Act 19 Hen. VII.* xxxiv. Pream., To helpe and assiste hym to the best of their power. **1531** TINDALE *Exp. & Notes* (1849) 175 He taketh it to the best, and is not offended. **1843** C. BRONTË in *Life* (1857) I. 290 She..will always serve you..to the best of her abilities. **1863** FR. KEMBLE *Resid. Georgia* 132 To the best of his belief. **1885** *Law Rep.* XIV. *Q. Bench Div.* 891 There was no such inspector to the best of our knowledge.

f. ***with the best*** (***of them***): as well as anyone.

1748 M. W. MONTAGU *Let.* 5 Jan. (1966) II. 393, I can ass[ure you] she jumps and Gallops with the best of them. **1864** TENNYSON *Grandm.* 20 Only at your age, Annie, I could have wept with the best. **1935** 'L. LUARD' *Conquering Seas* 32, I can make tea with the best of 'em, Peter. **1957** I. CROSS *God Boy* (1958) xxii. 187, I can drag my share out of the old girls with the best of them.

11. a. *Comb.* with sbs. used attrib., as ***best-quality***.

1906 *Westm. Gaz.* 12 Nov. 2/3 It is on the best-quality produce, not the second quality..that the British agriculturalist can make the most money. **1960** *Farmer & Stockbr.* 29 Mar. 116/3 The production of the best-quality wood.

b. *Comb.* with advbs. used attrib., as ***best-ever***.

1959 *News Chron.* 23 Nov. 3/4 Twelve of Duke Ellington's best-ever pop up on..a set of re-issues from the early 'forties. **1960** *Times* 6 Feb. 9/1 Many a game book received its best-ever entry.

B. *adv.* Superlative of WELL.

1. With *vbs.* In the most excellent way, in the most eminent degree; in the most suitable manner, with the greatest advantage, to the fullest extent. (For the obs. *alder-best*, best of all, see ALL.)

c **888** K. ÆLFRED *Boeth.* ii, Ða bereafodon ælcere lustbærnesse þa ða ic him æfre betst truwode. *a* **1067** *Chart. Eadweard* in *Cod. Dipl.* IV. 208 Swa freolice swa hit ic meseolf betst habbe. *c* **1175** *Lamb. Hom.* 7 Þenne þu wenest þu scalt libben alre best. *c* **1205** LAY. 26606 þe bezst [**1250** best] þat lond cneowen. *c* **1380** WYCLIF *De Dot. Eccl.* Sel. Wks. III. 433 Ensaumple of siche deds exponeþ best Cristis lawe. *c* **1420** *Sir Amadace* xl, He that furst is inne the feld, And best thenne justus thare. **1596** SPENSER *F.Q.* II. i. 59 But after death the tryall is to come, When best shall be to them, that liued best. **1602** T. SCOTT *Four Parad.* in Farr's *S.P.* II. 315 He that knowes thee best, knowes nought at all. **1615** BRATHWAIT *Love's Labyr.* (1878) 276 A Countrie lasse best fits a Countrie Swaine. *c* **1655** MILTON *Sonn.* xix, Who best Bear his mild yoke, they serve him best. *c* **1680** BEVERIDGE *Serm.* 1729 I. 358 Cannot but..believe it to be well done, yea the best that could be. **1715** BURNET *Own Times* (1823) I. 391 He excused himself the best he could. **1797** COLERIDGE *Anc. Mar.* VII. xxiii, He prayeth best, who loveth best All things both great and small. **1843** MACAULAY *Ess.* (1850) 686 The man who does best what multitudes do well.

2. With *adjs.* and *pples.* written (for syntactical distinctness) with the hyphen.

a. In the most excellent manner; as, ***best-aimed***, ***-bred***, ***-built***, ***-clad***, ***-conducted***, ***-considered***, † ***best-consulted*** (most prudent, or best-advised), ***-cultivated***, ***-dressed***, ***-established***, ***-grounded***, ***-kept***, ***-laid***, ***-looking***, ***-made***, ***-managed***, ***best-meaning*** (most well-meaning), ***-meant***, ***-moving***, ***-preserved***, ***-trained***, etc.

1588 SHAKS. *L.L.L.* II. 29 We single you As our best-mouing faire soliciter. *a* **1659** OSBORN *Observ. Turks* (1673) 288 Queen Elizabeth..the best consulted Monarch that ever filled the English Throne. **1711** SHAFTESB. *Charac.* II. 327 The best-meaning person in the world may err. **1762** HUME *Hist. Eng.* (1806) V. lxx. 253 Multitudes struck with the best-grounded terror. **1765** TUCKER *Lt. Nat.* II. 155 Counter to the clearest best-established principles of reason. **1785** BURNS *To Mouse* vii, The best-laid schemes o' mice an' men Gang aft agley. **1790** BEATSON *Nav. & Mil. Mem.* 241 To frustrate all our best-laid plans. **1794** COLERIDGE *Relig. Musings* 119 In her best-aimed blow Victorious murder a blind suicide. **1837** LOCKHART *Scott* (1839) VIII. 12 The best looking of her daughters. **1844** MARG. FULLER *Wom. 19th C.* (1862) 147 The best-considered efforts have often failed. **1856** *Farmer's Mag.* Nov. 384 The prizes given..for the best regulated farms. **1863** LYELL *Antiq. Man* 69 The best-preserved human skulls. **1903** A. BENNETT *Leonora* viii. 206 We are relying on you to be the best-dressed woman in the place. **1956** *Nature* 4 Feb. 214/1 In a night they [*sc.* worms] may cover a best-kept green with little piles of earth. **1964** *McCall's Sewing* I. 1/1 There are several ways to earn a place in the list of 'best-dressed' women in your town. **1968** *Guardian* 10 Aug. 6/2 You would certainly never win a best-kept village competition that way.

b. To the fullest extent, most: forming comb. differing little from ordinary superlatives; now usually written with the hyphen; as, ***best-abused***, ***-accomplished***, ***-beloved***, ***-described***, ***-discussed***, ***-esteemed***, ***-frequented***, ***-hated***, ***-known***, ***-loved***, ***-read***, ***-skilled***, etc.; including many obs. or arch. uses, as ***best able***, ***agreeable***, ***best-betrust*** (most to be trusted), ***learned***, ***nourishing***, ***pleasing***, ***valiant***, ***worthy***, etc.

c **1435** *Torr. Portugal* 786 Let Torrent her have, For best worthy ys he. **1526** *Pilgr. Perf.* (W. de W. 1531) 17 b, He sente his..best beloved sone into this worlde. **1571** ASCHAM *Scholem.* I. (1863) 12 The best learned, and best men. **1579**

E. K. in *Spenser's Sheph. Cal.* Gen. Argt. §2 The vsed and best knowen name. **1596** SHAKS. *Merch. V.* II. ii. 181, I doe feast to-night My best-esteemd acquaintance. **1601** *Downfall Earl Huntington* v. i, And you Lord Ely! and old best-betruss'd? **1620** VENNER *Via Recta* iii. 66 They are best agreeable to cholericke bodies. **1622** BACON *Hen. VII.* 124 Best-bee-trust-Spies. **1641** HINDE *J. Bruen* 114 The first and best, and best worthy to be first. **1685** OTWAY *Windsor Cast.*, The ugliest snakes, and best lov'd favourites there. **1724** WATERLAND *Eucharist* (1737) 41 The generality of the best learned Men interpret it of the Eucharist. **1742** JARVIS *Quix.* I. I. vii, To give me what I am best able to bear. **1844** MARG. FULLER *Wom. 19th C.* (1862) 56 Binding the emblem of faith on the heart of the best-beloved. **1848** *Punch* XV. 155/1 We have heard certain persons whose claims to distinction arose from their being the 'best abused men in the world'. **1866** G. MACDONALD *Ann. Q. Neighb.* viii. (1878) 128 Will better know what is best to know than the best-read bishop. **1869** *Church Times* 26 Feb., [Pusey] for years and years the best abused man in England. **1872** JENKINSON *Guide Eng. Lakes* (1879) 4 One of the best-frequented houses in the district. **1900** *Daily News* 16 Feb. 7/2 Englishmen are the best-hated people in the world. **1903** 'A. MCNEILL' *Egregious Eng.* 100 The best-discussed and best-described man in England.

c. In parasynthetic comb. (where the hyphen is always used), meaning 'having the best thing of its kind'; as, ***best-conditioned***, i.e. *best condition* + *-ed*, having or being in the best condition; so ***best-graced***, ***-humoured***, ***-intentioned***, ***-minded***, ***-natured***, ***-policied***, ***-principled***, ***-resolved***, ***-sighted***, ***-tempered***, etc. *best-graced* (1580), *best-tempered* (1594), may really belong to a., but lead to such as *best-minded* (1586), *best-natured* (1690).

1580 SIDNEY *Arcadia* 144 One of the proprest and best-graced men that euer I sawe. *a* **1586** —— in Farr's *S.P.* I. 75 Lest the best minded..Bend to abuses. **1594** T. B. *La Primaud. Fr. Acad.* II. 381 Those natures that are most moderate and best tempered. **1627** BP. HALL *Char. Virtues & V.* 174 Blind in no mans cause, best-sighted in his owne. **1690** NORRIS *Beatitudes* (1692) 134 He had the Best-natured ..Soul in the World. **1774** GOLDSM. *Retal.* Postscr., Thou best humoured man with the worst humoured muse. **1789** M. HUBER in *Ld. Auckland's Corr.* (1861) II. 326 The two best-intentioned..of their order. **1840** CARLYLE *Heroes* vi. 369 The best-conditioned of kings! **1863** J. JEAFFRESON *Sir Everard's Dau.* 208 The best-natured fellow alive.

3. a. With *agent-nouns*, as *best-wisher* (cf. *well-wisher*).

1876 MISS YONGE *Womankind* viii. 58 Their best wishers are thankful if half are lost.

b. best seller (orig. *U.S.*), one of the books having the largest sale of the year or the season; also, a writer of such books; also *transf.* and *attrib.*; hence (as a back-formation) **best-sell** *v. intr.*, to be or become a best seller; **best-sellerdom**, **-sellership**, the state or achievement of being a best seller; **best-sellerism**, concentration on best sellers; **best-selling** *a.*, that is a best seller.

1889 *Kansas Times & Star* 25 Apr., Kansas City's literary tone is improving. The six best sellers here last week were 'Fools of Nature' [etc.]. **1895** *Bookman* July 429/2 The best selling new book is Mr. Stockton's *Adventures of Captain Horn.* **1905** *Out West* (U.S.) Sept. 363 To be able to discuss the Six Best Sellers has become as much an article of faith as any in the Longer Catechism. **1913** R. W. CHAMBERS *Gay Rebellion* ii. 28 Go on with the dolly dialogue..you third-rate best seller. **1920** *Chambers's Jrnl.* 8 May 363/2 [He] promised to reach the doubtful altitude of best-sellership without difficulty. **1922** JOYCE *Ulysses* 450 He has cribbed some of my bestselling books. **1925** *Punch* 20 May 560/1 Fiction of best-seller quality and little more. **1926** W. R. INGE *Lay Thoughts* 190 Best-selling novels. **1928** *Daily Express* 1 June 5/3 'A house can be full of sweet scents..' writes one of our best-sellers, and he is perfectly right. *Ibid.* 16 July 8 A 'best-selling' biography. **1928** *Publishers' Weekly* 24 Nov. 2184/2 Two books that almost made the Best Seller List. **1928** WESEEN *Dict. Eng. Gram.* 120 *Coined Words...* Bestsellerdom. **1931** O. H. CHENEY *Economic Surv. Book Industry* I. iii. 126 Best-sellerism is an intolerable curse on the industry. **1937** *Observer* 8 Aug. 6/5 And, in the words of the elderly, this is a thoroughly 'nice' book. I think it may best-sell. **1938** H. GRANVILLE-BARKER *Quality* 11 Authors..who set out in a businesslike way to supply what is supposed to be most in demand..taking example by the latest best seller. **1946** *Sat. Rev. Lit.* 19 Jan. 7/1 It is one of those rare books which, fated for bestsellerdom, will at the same time interest..the serious, adult reader. **1956** A. WILSON *Anglo-Saxon Attitudes* II. i. 200 All the bad writers and painters who aren't even best-sellers.

best (bɛst), *v. colloq.* [f. prec. Of dialectal origin, from the idea of 'getting the better of,' 'having the best of it'; but the form is hardly in accordance with the sense, which is nearly equivalent to the existing vb. *to worst*, i.e. 'to make worst, put to the worst'; cf. also *to better*, to make better, improve.] *trans.* To get the better of, get an advantage over, outdo; to outreach, outwit, circumvent.

1863 TRAFFORD *World in Ch.* II. 77 As I am a staunch Churchman I cannot stand quiet and see the Dissenters best the Establishment. **1885** MAY in *Fortn. Rev.* Oct. 578 The quack broker who piles up money by besting his clients.

best, obs. f. BEAST; obs. Sc. f. *based*, see BASE *v.*¹; obs. 2nd. sing. indic. of BE *v.*

bestab, bestamp, etc.: see BE- *pref.*

†**bestad, -stadde**, *v. Obs.* Earlier form of BESTED *pa. pple.* Used only in passive voice: but by Spenser made a pa. t. and active pple. = BESET.

1579 E. K. in *Spenser's Sheph. Cal.* Aug. 7 What the foule euill hath thee so bestadde? [*gloss.* disposed, ordered.] **1596** SPENSER *F.Q.* III. v. 22 But both attonce on both sides him bestad.

bestail(le, obs. form of BESTIAL *sb.*¹

bestain (bɪˈsteɪn), *v.* [f. BE- 1 + STAIN *v.*] *trans.* To stain (a thing) over its surface, to mark with stains. Hence **beˈstained** *ppl. a.*

1559 *Mirr. Mag.* 360 (R.), His skin with blood and teares so sore bestain'd. **1595** SHAKS. *John* IV. iii. 24 We will not lyne his thin bestained cloake With our pure Honors. **1869** BALDW. BROWN *Div. Myst.* I. iv. 93 The blood-drops that bestain His steps. **1877** PLUMPTRE *Sophocles* 133 With his spears all blood-bestained.

†**beˈstand**, *v. Obs.* For forms see STAND. [Com. Teut.: OE. *bestanden* = OS. *bistân* (*Du. bestaan*), OHG. *bistân*, *pistantan* (MHG. *bestân*, *bestên*, mod.G. *bestehen*), Goth. (and OTeut.) *bistandan*, f. *bi-*, BE- about + *standan* to stand.]

1. *trans.* To stand by or near; to stand over (in solicitude); *esp.* to stand by (the dead), to mourn for. Also *absol.*

c **1000** ÆLFRIC *Gen.* xxiii. 2 Abraham hiȝ bestod on þa ealdan wisan. *c* **1250** *Owl & Night.* 1438 He cumeþ and fareþ and beod and bid, And heo bistant [*v.r.* bistarte] and oversit. *c* **1250** *Gen. & Ex.* 3857 Ðor wæs Moyses sister dead; Ðat folc..after wune faire hire bistod Mid teres.

2. To stand round in hostility; to beset, press hard upon, harass.

c **1000** *Ags. Gosp.* John x. 24 Ða bestodon [*c* **1160** *Hatton* be-stoden] þa iudeas hyne utan. *c* **1205** LAY. 30323 Swa bið a bar wilde..bistonden mid hunden. *c* **1320** *Sir Tristr.* I. xxxiv, Stormes hem bistode. **1470–85** MALORY *Arthur* (1816) II. 417 In all my life was I never thus bestood. *Ibid.* II. 466 He is full straitly bestood with a false traitor.

3. To surround, encompass (as a wall, water, etc.).

c **1205** LAY. 23726, I þan aitlonde þat mid watere is bistonde. *Ibid.* 17175 Ich wat a wærc mid wundere bistonde.

bestar (bɪˈstɑː(r)), *v.* [f. BE- + STAR.] *trans.* To spangle or adorn as with stars.

1612 SYLVESTER *Trophies* Wks. (1877–80) 274 (D.), O ladycow, Thou shalt no more bestar thy wanton brow With thine eyes rayes. **1851** S. JUDD *Marg.* III. (1871) 398 The dandelions that bestar the grass.

bestare, bestay, etc.: see BE- *pref.*

bestarred (bɪˈstɑːd), *ppl. a.* [f. prec. + -ED¹.]

1. Spangled or studded as with stars.

c **1655** MENNIS *Oberon's Appar.* in Arb. *Garner* I. 18 A rich mantle..Bestarred over with a few Diamond drops of morning dew. **1876** BLACK *Madcap V.* xlvi. 390 Sheltered woods, bestarred with anemones.

2. Decorated with the star of an order.

1860 *All Y. Round* No. 52. 34 The bestarred,..jewelled, .. throng. **1861** SALA *Tw. round Clock* 298 A crowd of.. bestarred and be-ribboned ministers.

3. *ill-bestarred*, for the more usual *ill-starred*.

a **1834** COLERIDGE *Charac.*, Alas poor Bird! and ill-bestarred.

beste, earlier form of BEAST *sb.* and *v.* Still often used in sense 8.

1874 H. H. GIBBS *Ombre* 35 When the Ombre loses bodille, his loss is the same as if he had been Bested. *Ibid.* 37 If the Defender is bested, there are of course two Bestes to be paid.

bestead (bɪˈstɛd), *v.*¹ Also 7 bested, -steed. *Pa. t.* besteaded. *Pa. pple.* 6 bestedde, 9 bested, bestead. [f. BE- 2 + STEAD *v.*¹ to prop, support, help.]

1. *trans.* To help, assist, relieve.

1581 SIR H. SAVILE *Tacitus* III. xxxii. (1591) 133 They were thought to haue bestedde and helped Vitellius side. **1627** R. PERROT *Jacobs Vowe* 56 Better able by his purse.. to bestead his neighbours, than they him. **1662** FULLER *Worthies* (1840) I. 520 Who besteaded him with the kings favour. **1874** HOLLAND *Mistr. Manse* xxi. 96 Sapphire nought without the red, Ruby still by blue bested.

2. To be of service or use to; to avail.

1589 *Sir F. Drake's Voy. W. Ind.* (R.) Great store of dry Newfoundland fish..did very greatly bestead us. **1669** WOODHEAD *St. Teresa* II. xix. 128 All nights..our mantles of thick Cloth which many times besteaded us. **1805** SOUTHEY *Madoc in Azt.* xv, Little did then his pomp of plumes bestead The Azteca..Against the tempered sword. **1862** CLOUGH in *Macm. Mag.* Aug. 321 Thou vain Philosophy! Little hast thou bestead, Save to perplex the head.

†**beˈstead**, *v.*² *Obs.* [f. BE- 6 + STEAD *sb.* place.] To go instead of, take the place of.

1596 NASHE *Saffron Wald.* 111 Hys missing of the Vniuersitie Oratorship, wherin Doctor Perne besteaded him.

†**beˈsteal**, *v. Obs.* For forms see STEAL. [OE. *bestelan*, f. BE- + *stelan* to STEAL. Parallel compounds in the other mod.Teut. langs. are Du. *bestelen*, Ger. *bestehlen*, Da. *bestiæle*, Sw. *bestjäla*, all meaning 'to steal, rob.'] *intr.* (and *refl.*) To steal or move stealthily (*away* or *on*).

a **725** *Laws of Ina* §39 (Bosw.) Gif hwa on oðre scire hine bestele. *c* **893** K. ÆLFRED *Oros.* I. x. §4 And þa nihtes on unȝearwe hi on bestæl. *c* **1175** *Moral Ode* 15 in *Lamb. Hom.* 161 Elde me is bistolen on . er ich hit wiste. *c* **1380** *Sir Ferumb.* 3876 On of hem..ys by-stole awaye. **1597** DOWLAND *Lyrics* in Arb. *Garner* IV. 47 Worn soul! That living dies, till thou on me bestoule!

bested, bestead (bɪˈstɛd), *pa. pple.* Forms: 2–3 bistaðed, -et, 3–5 bistad, 4 bisted, 4–5 bestedd(e, 4–6 bestadd(e, 4–7 bestad, 5 bistadde, bystedde, -stade, 6 bestade, 6– bestead, 8– bested. [ME. *bistad*, f. *bi-*, BE- 2 + *stad*, later *sted*, 'placed.' a. ON. *staddr* pa. pple. of *steðja* to stop, place: see STED *v.* and *pa. pple.* (ME. had also *bistaðed*, ultimately f. ON. *staðr* 'place,' which might itself have become *stad*: cf. history of *clad.*) The later spelling *bestead* is merely due to analogy, cf. BESTEAD *v.* and STEAD *sb.* Hence Spenser's BESTAD *pa. t.* and *pa. pple.*]

†**1.** Placed, located, situated. *Obs.*

a **1300** *Cursor M.* 5254 Qua-so had ben be-stadd þat day, And had þat suete meting sene. *Ibid.* 1045 Now adam is in erþe bi stad. *c* **1300** in Wright *Lyric P.* xi. 38 Of al this world namore y bad Then beo with hire myn one bistad. *c* **1430** *Syr. Tryam.* 1461 In worlde where ever he be bestedd.

†**2.** Settled, constituted, arranged. *Obs.*

c **1300** in Wright *Lyric P.* xii. 41 So hit wes bistad, That nomon hem ne bad huere lomes to fonde. *a* **1400** *Cov. Myst.* 77 We xal make us so mery, now this is bestad.

†**3.** Set about, set *with* (ornaments), etc. *Obs.* Cf. BESET, BELAY.

1558 PHAËR *Æneid* v. M iv b, A harneys coat..with heauy hookes of gold bestad.

4. Beset *by* (formerly *with*, enemies), *with* (dangers, fears, troubles).

1303 R. BRUNNE *Handl. Synne* 3365 Wyþ hys enmys he was bestedde. **1393** GOWER *Conf.* I. 77 For he with love was bestad. **1493** *Festivall* (W. de W. 1515) 6 Bestad with dethe on euery syde. **1598** R. BERNARD tr. *Terence's Andria* III. v, See you not how I am bestead by your devices. **1616** *Manifest. Abp. Spalato's Motives* App. iii. 2 Bestead with feare of a more mortall blow. **1839** GLEIG *Only Dau.* (1859) 103 Bested by the dangers of a Highland sheeptrack.

5. Placed in some situation, situated, circumstanced; generally with *ill*, and the like. ***to be hard bested***: to be hard put to it, hard pressed.

a **1225** *Ancr. R.* 264 Hwon we beoð so bistaðed & so stronge bistonden. *c* **1330** R. BRUNNE *Chron.* (1810) 190 Þe þrid eschele fulle hard was bisted. *c* **1400** *Epiph.* (Turnb. 1843) 145 On the all wemen wyl call When thei with chylde ben by stedde. *a* **1420** OCCLEVE *De Reg. Princ.* 704 There rekkethe none how harde I be bystade. **1523** LD. BERNERS *Froiss.* I. cccxcviii. 690 They that were lefte behynde were hardly bestadde. **1593** SHAKS. *2 Hen. VI*, II. iii. 56, I never saw a fellow worse bestead. **1596** SPENSER *F.Q.* VI. i. 4 On his way, Uppon an hard adventure sore bestad. *a* **1618** J. DAVIES in Farr's *S.P.* (1845) I. 247 Since by ill we are so well bestad, We cannot greeue for ill. **1730** T. BOSTON *Mem.* App. 49 Luther found himself hardly bestead in the several conflicts within his own breast. *a* **1850** ROSSETTI *Dante & Circ.* I. (1874) 157 Poor barque, so ill bested! **1881** SHAIRP *Asp. Poetry* vi. 166 Men of his kind..are often sore bestead.

†**b.** In an evil sense, without an adverb expressing it: To be in trouble, to be hard pressed; to be 'in hard plight set' (*Promp. Parv.*). *Obs.*

1393 GOWER *Conf.* III. 194 Whan they ben glad I shall be glad, And sory whan they ben bestad. *c* **1400** *Rom. Rose* 1227 Were a man for hir bistadde, She wolde ben right sore adradde. **1513** DOUGLAS *Æneis* X. xi. 16 All efferd of thy fatal dreidfull wordis I am bestad. **1587** TURBERV. *Trag. Tales* (1837) 104 Shee was bestead, when that at last she sawe Gentile there.

besteer, bestench, etc.: see BE- *pref.*

besteill, obs. form of BESTIAL.

†**beˈstented**, *ppl. a. Obs. rare*⁻¹. [f. BE- 2 + STENT *v.*] Distended.

1648 HERRICK *Hesper.*, *Oberon's Feast*, The sag And well bestented bees sweet bag.

bester (ˈbɛstə(r)). *slang.* [f. BEST *v.* + -ER¹.] One who gets the better of others by fraudulent means; a sharper.

a **1852** MAYHEW *Lond. Labour* Extra vol. (1862) 32/1 The '*Bouncers*' and '*Besters*' obtain what they want by betting, intimidating, or talking people out of their property. **1862** MAYHEW *Crim. Prisons* 46 'Bouncers and besters, who cheat by laying wagers. **1906** *Daily Chron.* 15 Nov. 6/5 An Action for slander had been commenced against him by the Hoopers for calling them 'two besters'. **1941** BAKER *Dict. Austral. Slang* 9 Bester, a fraudulent bookmaker.

bestest (ˈbɛstɪst), *a.* and *adv. dial.* and *joc.* [f. BEST *a.* + -EST.] Used emphatically as superl. of GOOD *a.* and of WELL *adv.*: very best.

1868 S. LYSONS *Vulgar Tongue* 49 Our word 'best' is a syncope of 'beltistos'; and our Gloucestershire people stick to the 'bestest', which is nearer to the Greek than the modern pronunciation. **1905** E. PHILLPOTTS *Secret Woman* I. iv. 36 It all comes back to Him, though you may try your bestest to make a case. **1922** JOYCE *Ulysses* 419 The bestest puttiest longbreak yet.

bestial (ˈbɛstɪəl), *sb.*¹ *Obs.* exc. *Sc.* Forms: 4 beestaile, 4–5 bestayle, -lle, 4–7 bestaile; also 5–7 beastial, bestiall(e, -yal(l, (7 beastal, bestuall), 8

bestail, -eill, 6- bestial. (As *sing.* 6 bestyll.) [Two forms: α. ME. *bestaile*, a. OF. *bestaille* (sing. fem.):—L. *bestiālia*, used in late L. in sense of L. *pecudes* cattle, beasts of the farm, pl. neut. of *bestiālis* adj. (see below), f. *bestia* BEAST; β. mod.Eng. and Sc. *bestial*, a. OF. *bestial* (still in 17th c., now dial.), sing. of mod.F. *bestiaux*, later substantive use of *bestial* adj., ad. L. *bestiālis.*]

1. A collective term for domestic animals, especially of the bovine kind, kept for food or tillage. It took the place of the OE. *féoh*, ME. *fee*; and has, since 17th c., been displaced in England by *cattle*, but is retained in Scotland as a legal and technical word of the farm.

α. *a* **1300** *Cursor M.* 2444 Be-twyx him and loth · his neuow Of bestaile [*Cott.* fee, *Fairf.* bestayle, *Trin.* beestaile] hade þai plente enow. **1393** GOWER *Conf.* II. 138 And that they shulde also forth drawe Bestaile. **1433** *E. E. Wills* (1882) 95 Alle the meuable Catell of bestall that y haue in Sussex. **1481** EARL WORC. *Tulle on Friendsh.* C j b, To gete them grete plente of bestaylle. [**1607** COWELL has Bestaile; **1678** PHILLIPS Beastal; **1721** BAILEY Bestail; *obs.*]

β. *a* **1470** TIPTOFT *Cæsar* xiii. (1530) 18 There was found a great nomber of bestyall. *c* **1470** HENRY *Wallace* III. 5 Als bestiall.. Weyle helpyt ar be wyrken of natur. **1510** *Act 1 Hen. VIII*, xx. § 1 Every maner of fresshe fysshe, bestyall and wyne. **1611** SPEED *Hist. Gt. Brit.* IX. xv. 41 Leauing the Country bare of men and bestiall. **1631** HEYLIN *Sabbath* II. (1636) 171 Hee might.. kill and skinne his bestiall which were fit for sale. *a* **1670** SPALDING *Troub. Chas. I*, (1829) 96 They.. lived royally upon the corns and bestial of the said ground. **1828** SCOTT *F.M. Perth* I. 22 It is not my business where they get the bestial, so I get the hides. **1833** *Act 3 & 4 Will. IV*, xlvi. §83 No person shall drive cattle or bestial of any description on Sunday through.. such burgh.

2. A single beast; (with *plural.*)

c **1430** LYDG. IV. in Cleveland *Wks.* (1687) 388 Void of Discretion that other Beastial. *a* **1450** *Knt. de la Tour* (1868) 103 Alle his bestailes and richesses. **1562** J. HEYWOOD *Prov. & Epigr.* (1867) 56 A good bestyll is woorth a grote. **1670** BLOUNT *Law Dict.*, *Bestials*, Beasts or Cattle of any sort.. generally and properly used for all kind of Cattle. **1725** BRADLEY *Fam. Dict.*, *Besteills.* *a* **1788** MICKLE *Ode* i. (R.) No joy, no hope it knows Above what bestials claim. **1813** *Sismondi's Lit. Eur.* (1846) II. xxxviii. 523 And each lulled in his shade, The bestials sleep. **1863** J. KEBLE *Bp. Wilson* viii. 280 The produce of the island, their 'bestials' especially.

† **'bestial**, *sb.*² *Obs. Sc.* [Erron. form of *bastaille*, *-ailʒe*: see BASTILLE 2 a.; prob. after the substitution of *bestial* for *bestaile* in prec. word.] A wooden tower used in sieges.

c **1470** HENRY *Wallace* VII. 977 Ramsay gert byg strang bestials [ed. 1570 bastailʒeis] off tre. *Ibid.* XI. 877 On the north syd his bestials had he wrocht.

bestial ('bɛstɪəl), *a.* Forms: 4-7 **bestyall(e**, **-iall(e**, 6 **beestyal**, 6-8 **beastial(l**, (7 **beastual**), 5- **bestial**. [ME.: a. OF. *bestial* (13th c. in Littré), ad. L. *bestiāl-is* like a beast, f. *bestia* beast.]

1. Of or belonging to the lower animals, esp. four-footed beasts.

1393 GOWER *Conf.* I. 140 To take a mannes hert aweie And sette there a bestiall, So that he lich an oxe shall Pasture. **1470** HARDING *Chron.* xxxvi, Moruile, Kyng of Britaine, was slayne.. with a fysshe bestyall of the sea. **1528** PAYNELL *Salerne Regim.* O ij b, Bestiall fysshe as the see swyne, dogge fyshe, and dolphin. **1549** *Compl. Scot.* vi. 64 The scheip and nolt.. pronuncit there bestial voce. **1607** TOPSELL *Four-f. Beasts* (1673) 29 At length her parents.. found their little Daughter in the Bears den, who delivered her from that savage and beastual captivity. **1687** DRYDEN *Hind & P.* I. 167. **1706** PHILLIPS s.v., Bestial Signs of the Zodiack are Aries, Taurus, Leo, and Capricornus. **1709** STEELE *Tatler* No. 49 ⁋3 A Satyr; of Shape, part Humane, part Bestial. **1831** CARLYLE *Sart. Res.* I. v, Lurking for his bestial or human prey.

2. *transf.* Like a beast in its want of intelligence; 'below the dignity of reason or humanity' (J.); brutish, untaught, irrational; rude, barbarous.

c **1400** MANDEV. xxii. 224 Thei weren but bestyalle folk, and diden no thing but kepten Bestes. *c* **1400** *Rom. Rose* 6718 If a man be so bestial, That he of no craft hath science. **1484** CAXTON *Chyualry* 16 They gyue doctryne to the peple laye and bestiall. **1538** STARKEY *England* 10 Men were brought from theyr rudenes and beestyal lyfe to thys cyvylyte. **1547** BAULDWIN *Mor. Philos.* (Palfr.) ii. 2 There is no nation so savage and beastiall. **1615** G. SANDYS *Trav.* I. 60 To please beastiall Ignorance. **1816** SCOTT *Bl. Dwarf* iv, The slavish and bestial doctrine.

3. *esp.* Like a beast in obeying and gratifying the animal instincts and sensual desires; debased, depraved, lustful, cruel, brutal, beastly, obscene.

1447 BOKENHAM *Seyntys* (1835) 95 That he wold be so bestyal To forsakyn hys glorye pontifical. **1509** BARCLAY *Shyp of Folys* (1570) 245 Thy faythfull felowe is bestiall dronkennes. **1594** SHAKS. *Rich. III*, III. v. 80 Beastiall appetite in change of Lust. **1755** YOUNG *Centaur* vi. Wks. 1757 IV. 267 The bestial abyss of a few year's debauch. **1878** S. COX *Salv. Mundi* i. (ed. 3) 13 Sodom was a synonym for the most utter and bestial corruption.

4. quasi-*sb.* The nature of a beast or animal.

1667 H. MORE *Div. Dial.* iii. §24 (1713) 238 That more full and sensible Sweetness of the Animal or Bestial. **1878** B. TAYLOR *Deukalion* I. iv. 36, I see the bestial, base unpurified, Its hideous features smeared with filth and blood.

'bestialism. [f. prec. + -ISM.] The state or condition of beasts; irrationality.

1871 M. F. ROSSETTI *Shad. Dante* v. 52 That Bestialism which seems to correspond to the Folly of Holy Writ.

'bestialist, *nonce-wd.* One who makes a study of bestiality.

1881 SWINBURNE in *Fortn. Rev.* Feb. 129 The sect or school known among its members as the school of realists, among men at once of sounder and more sensitive organs as the sect of bestialists.

bestiality (bɛstɪ'ælɪtɪ). [ME. *bestialite*, a. F. *bétialité*: see BESTIAL and -ITY.]

1. The nature or qualities of a beast; want of intelligence, irrationality, stupidity, brutality.

c **1374** CHAUCER *Troylus* I. 735 For that he [an ass] So dul is in his bestialite. **1563** GRAFTON *Chron. Mary* an. 5 (R.) Espiyng well the beastiality of the Fleminges his neighbours. **1649** MILTON *Eikon.* xviii. Wks. (1851) 468 As Politicians oft times.. handle the matter, there hath bin no where found more bestialitie. **1714** ARBUTHNOT, etc. *Mart. Scribl.* (J.) What can be a greater absurdity than to affirm bestiality to be the essence of humanity? **1874** MIVART in *Contemp. Rev.* Oct. 773 The great doctrine concerning the essential Bestiality of Man.

2. Indulgence in the instincts of a beast; brutal lust; *concr.* a disgusting vice, a beastly practice.

a **1656** BP. HALL *Remains* 189 (L.) They tickle themselves with the wanton remembrances of their younger bestialities. **1659** *Gentl. Call.* (1696) 77 The sordid bestialities of the most abject of men. **1710** *Tatler* No. 241 ⁋4 The unhappy Consort of his Bestiality. **1728** MORGAN *Algiers* II. iii. 241 Their Wives and Children.. [were] not safe from Bestialities, even in their most retired Apartments.

b. Filthy language, obscenity.

1879 FROUDE *Cæsar* xv. 241 Filthy verses.. about Clodius and Clodia, ribald bestiality, delightful to the ears of Tully.

†**3.** Unnatural connexion with a beast. *Obs.*

1611 BIBLE *Lev.* xx. Argt., Of Sodomie. Of Beastialitie. Of vncleannesse. **1649** DRUMM. OF HAWTH. *Fam. Ep.* Wks. (1711) 143 A poor miserable fellow accused of bestiality. **1765** GOLDSMITH *Ess.* xiv. ⁋5 Bestiality [was] sanctified by the amours of Jupiter.

†**4.** = BESTIAL *sb.*¹ *Obs.*

1549 *Compl. Scot.* vi. 43 To keip bestialite and to manure corne landis. *Ibid.* 44 Paris.. vas ane scheiphird, and kepit bestialite on montht ydea.

bestialize ('bɛstɪəlaɪz), *v.* [f. BESTIAL *a.* + -IZE.] *trans.* To change into the form or nature of a beast; to brutalize, debase in character. Hence **'bestialized, 'bestializing** *ppl. a.*

1684 CHARNOCK *Attrib. of God* (1834) I. 231 The most famous guides of the heathen world.. bestialized him [God] in the form of a brute. **1751** *Phil. Lett. Physiogn.* 87 (T.) Humanity is debased and bestialized where it is otherwise. **1845** *Edin. Rev.* July 11 While he bestializes men and humanizes beasts, he is a great moralist. **1866** FELTON *Anc. & Mod. Gr.* I. vii. 114 Circe and her enchanting bestializing cup.

† **'bestiallich**, *a. Obs.* [f. BESTIAL *sb.* or *a.* + *lich*, OE. *-lic*: see -LY¹.] = BESTIAL *a.* 1.

c **1400** *Test. Loue* II. (R.) These liues be thorow names departed in three maner of kinds as bestialliche, manlyche, and reasonabliche.

bestially ('bɛstɪəlɪ), *adv.* Also 5 **bestyally**, 7 **beastially.** [f. as prec. + -LY².] In the manner of a beast or brute; brutishly, brutally.

c **1440** *Gesta Rom.* xlvi. 411 Bestialle men that leuyn bestially. **1640** *Case Ship Money* 23 Why the French Pesants are so beggarly, wretched, and bestially used. **1679** J. SMITH in Jenison *Narr. Popish Plot* 48 How inhumanely and beastially.. they dyed. [**1755** in JOHNSON; and in mod. Dicts.]

† **'Bestian**, *a. Obs.* Also 7-8 **beastian.** [f. L. *bestia*, BEAST + -AN.] Of or belonging to the 'Beast' of the Apocalypse (cf. BEAST 7). **'Bestianism**, the power of the Beast; **'Bestianize**, to be a follower of the 'Beast.'

1652 CULVERWELL *White Stone* (1661) 134 This Bestian Empire, (for so 'tis stil'd in the Revelation,) delights only in sensuals, and strikes at spirituals. **1660** H. MORE *Myst. Godl.* 208 It does not follow, because the number of the Beast is not upon us, that we do not Bestianize. **1691** BEVERLEY *Mem. Kingd. Christ.* 9 Even as if It were the Bestian Power. **1701** —— *Apoc. Quest.* 30 The Life, and Bestianism, Idolatrous Supremacy, shift from one Head to another.

bestiarian (ˌbɛstɪ'ɛərɪən). Also **beast-**. [f. as prec. (by Prof. Owen) after *humanitarian.*] A name given to anti-vivisectionists, as 'friends of the beast.' **ˌbesti'arianism**, the principles of those who uphold the 'rights of animals.'

1882 OWEN *Exper. Phys.* 56 The advantage of signifying the second group to which my present work relates by the word 'bestiarian.' *Ibid.* 57 That arises from abuse of true bestiarianism. **1883** *Amer. Naturalist* Feb. 175 The antivivisectionists, or beastiarians.

bestiary ('bɛstɪərɪ). [ad. L. *bestiārius* 'a fighter with beasts in the public spectacles,' and med.L. *bestiārium* a menagerie, also 'liber de bestiis compositus,' etc., f. *bestia* beast: see -ARY.]

†**1.** A beast-fighter in the Roman amphitheatre. (L. *bestiarius.*) *Obs.*

1625 T. GODWIN *Rom. Antiq.* 20 The Amphitheatre was full of hollow passage.. for the convenient keeping of wilde beasts, and beastiaries.

2. A treatise on beasts: applied to the moralizing treatises written during the Middle Ages.

[**1834** *Gentl. Mag.* CIV. I. 190 The Bestiarium in the Ashmolean library.] **1840** WRIGHT *Reliq. Antiq.* I. 208 (*title*) A Bestiary. **1865** —— *Hist. Caricat.* vi. (1875) 95 The earliest Bestiaries, or popular treatises on natural history. **1871** *Sacristy* I. 7/1 The Bestiaries.. are natural histories of animals treated so that the peculiarities of animals shall convey a wholesome moral.

† **'bestiate**, *v. Obs.* Also 7 **beastiate.** [f. L. *bestia* beast + -ATE.] To bestialize.

1628 FELTHAM *Resolves* I. lxxxiv. (1647) 259 Drunkennesse.. bestiates even the bravest spirits. **1639** *Junius' Sin Stigmat.* 235 (L.) Drunkenness beastiates the heart. **1655** R. YOUNGE *Agst. Drunkards* 5.

bestick (bɪ'stɪk), *v.* [f. BE- 1 and 4 + STICK *v.*] Chiefly in pa. pple. **bestuck.**

1. *trans.* To stick about, to cover all over; to bedeck, adorn. Also *fig.*

1623 H. HOLLAND in *Shaks. Wks.* (1st folio) Pref. Verses, That coffin now besticke those bayes, Which crown'd him Poet first. **1698** FRYER in *Phil. Trans.* XX. 340 The Rocks.. are bestuck with Oyster-Shells. **1838** HAWTHORNE *Amer. Note-Bks.* (1871) I. 117 Coats of linen covered with pitch and bestuck with flax.

2. To pierce through, transfix.

1667 MILTON *P.L.* XII. 536 Truth shall retire, Bestuck with slandrous darts. **1823** LAMB *Elia* (1860) 106 No emblem is so common as.. the bestuck and bleeding heart.

bestill (bɪ'stɪl), *v.* [f. BE- 2 + STILL *v.*] *trans.* To make quiet, to still, to hush.

1770 ARMSTRONG *Imit.* 80 Each brook that wont to prattle to its banks Lies all bestilled. *a* **1842** A. CUNNINGHAM *Eleg. Ode* (R.) Commerce bestill'd her many-nationed tongue. **1871** G. MACDONALD *Wks. Fancy & Imag.* II. 107 The solemn looks, the awful place, Bestill the mother's joy.

¶ In the following the quartos and mod. edd. read *distilled*; but it may belong to this with the sense 'made motionless, stiffened, congealed.'

1602 SHAKS. *Ham.* I. ii. 204 Whilst they bestil'd Almost to Jelly with the Act of feare, Stand dumbe and speake not.

bestinch, bestink, etc.: see BE- *pref.*

† **'bestious**, *a. Obs. rare*⁻¹. In 5 **bestyous.** [f. L. *bestia* BEAST + -OUS.] Beast-like, monstrous.

1470 HARDING *Chron.* xxxvi, Then come fro the Yrishe sea, A bestyous fyshe.

bestir (bɪ'stɜː(r)), *v.* For forms see STIR. [OE. *bestyrian*, f. BE- 2 + *styrian* to STIR.]

†**1.** ? To heap or pile (a thing) about *with.* (OE.)

c **890** K. ÆLFRED *Bæda* III. ii. (Bosw.) His þeȝnas mid moldan hit bestyredon and ȝefæstnedon.

2. To stir up, 'to put into vigorous action' (J.).

a. *refl.* To begin to move actively, to manifest activity, to busy oneself.

c **1300** *K. Alis.* 3078 Alle they wolde heom bysteorre, Agayns him with ryght to weorre. *c* **1330** *Arth. & Merl.* 6248 Bestir the and hardiliche fight. **1393** GOWER *Conf.* III. 295 The shipmen stood in such a fere, Was none that might him self bestere. **1581** J. BELL *Haddon's Answ. Osor.* 512 Not much otherwise this good man Osorius here doth besturre himselfe agaynst the Lutherans. **1611** BIBLE *2 Sam.* v. 24 Then thou shalt bestirre thy selfe. **1767** FORDYCE *Serm. Yng. Wom.* I. vi. 215 She bestirs herself with the utmost activity. **1832** HT. MARTINEAU *Weal & Woe* i. 11 Just bestir yourself to plant your potatoes. **1867** SMILES *Huguenots Eng.* vi. (1880) 93 The townspeople.. bestirred themselves in aid of the poor refugees.

b. *trans.* To rouse into activity, make active. *to bestir one's stumps* (obs.): to move one's limbs actively, to exert oneself: see STIR.

1549 COVERDALE *Erasm. Par. Heb.* xii. 1 Bestyre youre werye handes. **1579** GOSSON *Sch. Abuse* 41 The duety of every man in a common wealth one way or other to bestirre his stoomps. **1581** J. BELL *Haddon's Answ. Osor.* 407 This raungyng Rhetorician besturreth his stumps so earnestly. **1605** SHAKS. *Lear* II. ii. 58 No Maruel, you haue so bestir'd your valour. **1663** GERBIER *Counsel* 59 Bestirring their Hand and Tools. **1873** BROWNING *Red Cott. Night-c.* 178 More need that heirs, His natural protectors, should assume The management, bestir their counsinship.

c. *intr.*

1610 SHAKS. *Temp.* I. i. 3 Speake to th' Mariners: fall too't, yarely, or we run our selues a ground, bestirre, bestirre.

3. To move, stir, agitate (a thing).

1813 BYRON *Giaour* 377 Methought Some motion from the current caught Bestirr'd it more.

bestirring (bɪ'stɜːrɪŋ), *vbl. sb.* [f. prec. + -ING¹.] Movement, motion, emotion.

1340 *Ayenb.* 263 Þe wyl of skele, to huam be-longeþ moche mayné, þoȝtes and his besteriinge. **1674** N. FAIRFAX *Bulk & Selv.* 154 The tiny bestirrings of the least atoms.

be'stirring, *ppl. a.* [f. as prec. + -ING².] Moving, actuating.

1628 RUTHERFORD *Lett.* iii. (1862) I. 40 The bestirring power of the life of God.

best man ('bɛst 'mæn). [Of Scotch origin.] The groomsman or 'friend of the bridegroom' at a wedding. So **best maid** *Sc.*, the bridesmaid or chief bridesmaid.

1814 *Discipline* III. 21 (JAM.) Mr. Henry was the best man himself. **1823** ELIZA ACTON *St. Johnstoun* III. 90 (JAM.) The two bridegrooms entered, accompanied each by his friend, or best man, as this person is called in Scotland. **1861** S. LYSONS *Claudia & P.* 170 Whether they had any bridesmaids; whether there was a best man.

bestness (ˈbɛstnɪs). [f. BEST + -NESS.] The quality of being best.

1557 CHEKE *Let.* in *Ascham's Scholem.* (Arb.) Pref. 5, I am verie curious in mi freendes matters, not to determijn, but to debaat what is best. Whearin, I seek not the bestnes haplie bi truth. *a* **1659** BP. MORTON *Episcop. Assert.* §4 (T.) Generally the bestness of a thing (that we may so call it) is best discerned by the necessary use. **1820** J. WILSON in *Mem. Chr. North* ix. 327 We are now speaking not on the question of bestness, but as to fact.

bestock, bestore, etc.: see BE- *pref.*

bestorm (bɪˈstɔːm), *v.* [f. BE- 1 + STORM *v.*] *trans.* To storm on all sides, to assail with storms or storming. Hence **beˈstormed** *ppl. a.*

1651 DAVENANT *Gondibert* III. vi, In Boats bestorm'd all check at those that row. **1742** YOUNG *Nt. Th.* IV. 560 All is sea besides; Sinks under us; bestorms, and then devours. **1837** CARLYLE *Fr. Rev.* II. III. VII. v. 363 Betocsined, bestormed; overflooded by black deluges of Sans-culottism.

†**beˈstourn,** *v. Obs.* [a. OF. *bestourne-r*, f. *bes-* pejorative + *tourner* to turn.] *trans.* To turn upside down, overthrow.

1483 CAXTON *G. de la Tour* cxlii, Toke reason fro us, and bestourned our wytte. *Ibid.* E iv b, The stenche of it.. bestorrneth [Fr. *bestourne*] all the ordre of nature.

bestow (bɪˈstəʊ), *v.* Forms: 4-6 bistow(e, 5 bystow(e, 5-7 bestowe, (6 bestoe), 5- bestow. *Pa. pple.* bestowed, (7 bestowne). [ME. *bistowen*, f. *bi-*, BE- 2 + *stowen* to place, STOW.]

1. *trans.* To place, locate; to put in a position or situation, dispose of (*in* some place). *arch.*

c **1374** CHAUCER *Troylus* I. 967 The god of love hath the bystowid In place digne unto thy worthines. **1528** MORE *Conf. agst. Trib.* III. Wks. 228/1 As rowmes and liuinges fal voyde to bestowe them in. **1567** DRURY *Let.* in Tytler *Hist. Scot.* (1864) III. 412 Bills bestowed upon the church doors. **1598** SHAKS. *Merry W.* IV. ii. 48 How should I bestow him? Shall I put him into the basket againe? **1610** GWILLIM *Heraldry* III. i. (1660) 96 Under what heads each peculiar thing must be bestowed. **1713** POPE *Iliad* IX. 284 Glittering canisters.. Which round the board Menœtius' son bestow'd. **1873** BROWNING *Red Cott. Night-c.* 116 The white domestic pigeon.. does mere duty by bestowing egg In authorized compartment.

2. To stow away; to place or deposit (anywhere) for storage, to store up. *arch.*

1393 GOWER *Conf.* II. 84 The leed after Satorne groweth, And Jupiter the brass bestoweth. **1494** FABYAN VII. 466 Lancastre.. bestowed suche ordenaunce as the Frenshemen for haste lafte behynde. **1526** TINDALE *Luke* xii. 17, I have noo roume where to bestowe my frutes. **1590** SHAKS. *Com. Err.* I. ii. 78 **1630** J. TAYLOR *Gt. Eater Kent* 13 His storehouse, into which he would stow and bestow any thing that the house would afford. **1853** KANE *Grinnell Exp.* xxix. (1856) 247 Bestowing away my boots in a snugly-lashed bundle.

3. To lodge, quarter, put up; to provide with a resting- or sleeping-place. Also *refl. arch.*

1577 HOLINSHED *Chron.* III. 813 They were all bestowed aboord in Spanish ships. **1605** SHAKS. *Macb.* III. vi. 23 Sir, can you tell, Where he bestowes himselfe? **1665** MANLEY *Grotius' Low-C. Wars* 295 To bestow the wearied men into Garrisons. **1821** BYRON *Sardan.* III. i. 121 See that the women are bestow'd in safety In the remote apartments. **1851** LONGF. *Gold. Leg.* IV. iv, Shall the Refectorarius bestow Your horses and attendants for the night.

†**b.** To bring to bed, confine. *Obs. rare.*

c **1320** *Sir Beves* (Halliw.) 132 And Iosiane, Christ here be milde! In a wode was bestoude of childe.

†**4.** To settle or give in marriage. Also *refl. Obs.*

c **1386** CHAUCER *Reeves T.* 61 To bystow hir hye Into som worthy blood of ancetrye. **1530** PALSGR. 452/1 He hath bestowed his doughter well. *c* **1550** CHEKE *Matt.* xxiv. 38 Eating and drinking, marijng, and bestowing yeer children. **1600** SHAKS. *A.Y.L.* v. iv. 7 You will bestow her on Orlando heere. *c* **1670** MRS. HUTCHINSON *Mem. Col. Hutchinson* (1806) 9 Only three daughters who bestowed themselves meanly. **1714** ELLWOOD *Autobiog.* (1765) 100 He bestowed both his Daughters there in Marriage.

5. To apply, to employ (*in* an occupation); to devote (*to*, *of* obs.) *for* a specific purpose.

c **1315** SHOREHAM 95 Thenche thou most wel bysyly, And thy wyȝt thran by-stowe. *c* **1386** CHAUCER *Wyf's Prol.* 113, I wol bystowe the flour of myn age In the actes and in the fruytes of mariage. **1530** PALSGR. Introd. 2 Many.. shall also herafter bestowe theyr tyme in such lyke exercise. **1541** R. COPLAND *Guydon's Quest. Cyrurg.*, Howe to bestowe his remedyes to the body of man. **1580** BARET *Alv.* B 580 Thou haste well bestowed thy paynes. **1653** WALTON *Angler* i. 39 Bestow one day with me and my friends in hunting the Otter. **1655** FULLER *Ch. Hist.* VI. 279 These.. onely bestowed themselves in prayer. **1851** DIXON *W. Penn* xv. (1872) 125 How he intended to bestow his day.

†**b.** *esp.* To apply money to a particular purpose; to lay out, expend, spend. *Obs.*

1377 LANGL. *P. Pl.* B. II. 75 In þe stories he techeth To bistowe þyn almes. **1526** TINDALE *2 Cor.* xii. 15, I will very gladly bestowe, and wilbe bestowed for youre soules. **1583** STUBBES *Anat. Abus.* 56 But nowe it is a small matter to bestowe.. a hundred pounde of one payre of Breeches. (God be mercifull unto us!) **1590** SHAKS. *Com. Err.* v. v. 11, I would haue bestowed the thousand pound I borrowed of you. **1611** BIBLE *Deut.* xiv. 26 Thou shalt bestow that money for whatsoeuer thy soule lusteth after. **1631** WEEVER *Anc. Fun. Mon.* 225 He bestowed much in building.

†**c.** *refl.* To acquit oneself. *Obs.*

1591 SHAKS. *Two Gent.* III. i. 87. **1600** —— *A.Y.L.* IV. iii. 87 The boy is faire, Of femall fauour, and bestowes himselfe Like a ripe sister. **1606** SYLVESTER *Du Bartas* (1633) 320 He all assayls and him so brave bestowes, in his Fight, etc.

6. *tr.* (& *absol.*). To confer as a gift, present, give.

1580 BARET *Alv.* B 580 To bestowe and giue his life for his country. **1583** STANYHURST *Æneis* II. (Arb.) 45 Thee Greeks bestowing theyre presents Greekish I feare mee. **1613** SHAKS. *Hen. VIII*, IV. ii. 56 In bestowing, madam, He was most princely. **1632** BROME *Novella* II. i, To brag of benefits one hath bestowne Doth make the best seeme lesse. **1750** JOHNSON *Rambl.* No. 38 ¶11 You here pray for water, and water I will bestow. **1802** MAR. EDGEWORTH *Moral T.* I. i. 7 The importance that wealth can bestow. **1870** BRYANT *Iliad* I. III. 83 Whatever in their grace the gods bestow.

b. Const. *on*, *upon* (*of* obs.) a person.

1535 COVERDALE *2 Chron.* xxiv. 7 All that was halowed for the house of the Lorde, haue they bestowed on Baalim. **1601** SHAKS. *Twel. N.* III. iv. 2 How shall I feast him? What bestow of him? **1628** WITHER *Brit. Rememb.* Pref. 112 What freedomes on the Muses are bestowne. **1817** JAS. MILL *Brit. India* II. IV. v. 205 The steadiness.. of the English.. bestowed upon them a complete and brilliant victory. **1876** GREEN *Short Hist.* vi. §4 (1882) 301 He bestowed on him a pension of a hundred crowns a year.

†**c.** (rarely) *to* or *dat. pronoun.* (Cf. 1541 in 5.)

1588 SHAKS. *Tit. A.* IV. ii. 163 You must needs bestow her funerall. **1605** —— *Lear* II. i. 128 Bestow Your needfull counsaile to our businesses.

†**beˈstow,** *sb. Obs. rare.* [f. prec. vb.] Bestowing, lodgement, stowage.

1589 WARNER *Alb. Eng.* v. xxvii, They find as bad Bestoe as is their Postage beggerly.

bestowable (bɪˈstəʊəb(ə)l), *a.* [f. BESTOW *v.* + -ABLE.] Capable of being bestowed or given.

1882 *Fraser's Mag.* July 112 The greatest blessing bestowable.

†**beˈstowage,** *sb. Obs. rare.* [f. as prec. + -AGE.] Stowage.

a **1656** BP. HALL is cited by Webster.

bestowal (bɪˈstəʊəl). [f. as prec. + -AL[2].] The action of bestowing; **a.** disposal, location; **b.** presentation, gift.

1773 *Gentl. Mag.* XLIII. 633 If the bestowal of necessaries be a task fruitless as the fabled labour of Sisyphus. **1867** FREEMAN *Norm. Conq.* (1876) I. App. 660 The bestowal of the earldom on Eric I have mentioned.

bestowed (bɪˈstəʊd), *ppl. a.* [f. as prec. + -ED.]

1. Placed, located; employed, applied, given; often with qualifying adv., as *well-*, *ill-bestowed.*

1483 CAXTON *G. de la Tour* E j, Hit is wel bestowed. *a* **1603** T. CARTWRIGHT *Confut. Rhem. N.T.* (1618) 178 Our Sauiour Christs friends are euill bestowed and thrust into his scalding house. **1667** MILTON *P.L.* v. 317 Well we may afford Our givers their own gifts, and large bestow From large bestowed. **1814** SCOTT *Ld. of Isles* v. xxi, In silvan lodging, close bestow'd.

†**2.** Filled, stowed *with. Obs.*

1621 R. BOLTON *State Irel.* 168 (*Act 28 Hen. VIII*), Boates, Scowts.. and other vessels loden and bestowed with goods.

bestower (bɪˈstəʊə(r)). Also 6 -ar. [f. as prec. + -ER[1].] One who bestows.

1548 UDALL, etc. *Erasm. Par. 1 Cor.* iv. 1 Stewardes and bestowars of other mennes goodes. **1612** T. TAYLOR *Comm. Titus* ii. 11 Gifts and good turnes haue great power to hold mens hearts to the bestower. **1721** R. KEITH *Kempis' Vall. Lillies* xxxi. 95 The Bestower of eternal Rewards. **1879** R. DOUGLAS *Confuc.* iii. 77 The.. bestower of destiny.

bestowing (bɪˈstəʊɪŋ), *vbl. sb.* [f. as prec. + -ING[1].] The action of the verb BESTOW.

a. Placing, stowing away, putting up. **b.** Employment, expenditure. **c.** Conferment, presentation.

1532 FRITH *Mirror* (1829) 277 As touching the bestowing of thy goods. **1542** BRINKLOW *Complaynt* iv. (1874) 17 Ye shal gyue account.. for the bestowyng of your ryches. **1608** HIERON *Wks.* I. 751 Knowledge and discretion are Thy bestowings. **1709** STEELE *Tatler* No. 9 ¶2 So hurried away with that strong Impulse of Bestowing, that he confers Benefits without Distinction. **1802** PALEY *Nat. Theol.* (1817) 129 The bestowing of the liquor in the hogsheads.

bestowment (bɪˈstəʊmənt). [f. BESTOW *v.* + -MENT.]

1. The action of bestowing; bestowal.

1754 EDWARDS *Freed. Will* IV. v. (ed. 4) 314 God's bestowment of the benefit. **1871** BROWNING *Balaust.* 1536 Such things as bear bestowment, those thou hast.

2. *concr.* That which is conferred; a gift.

1837-40 HALIBURTON *Clockm.* (1862) 118. **1856** R. VAUGHAN *Mystics* III. iv. (1860) I. 81 Angels and Archangels have at their command only subordinate bestowments.

†**beˈstract,** *ppl. a. Obs. rare*[−1]. [See next.] Distracted.

1581 J. STUDLEY *Seneca's Medea* 123 b, Bestract of wits, with wauering minde perplext.

bestraddle, bestraw, etc.: see BE- *pref.*

†**beˈstraught,** *v.* and *ppl. a. Obs.* Also 6 bestrought. [f. BE- *intensive* + STRAUGHT (found as early as 1520); cf. also *astraught*, *distraught.* The genesis of these forms seems to have been thus: L. *distractus* gave *distract*, and (on some Eng. analogies) DISTRAUGHT; thence *astraught* and STRAUGHT; hence *be-straught* and (with reference again to *distract*) *be-stract*; finally *bestraughted.* Found as pa. pple. and also as pa. t. of a vb., of which the present ought analogically to have been *bestract.* But this is app. not found; and the later inflexions *bestraughted*, *-ing*, imply that *bestraught* was itself assumed as the present.]

1. as *pa. t.* of a vb. Distracted, bereft (*of* wits).

1580 NORTH *Plutarch* (1676) 278 An Oracle.. whose spirit possessed many Inhabitants thereabouts, and bestraught them of their wits.

2. *pa. pple.* and *adj.* Distracted, distraught.

a **1547** SURREY *Æneid* IV. 360 Æneas with that vision striken down Well nere bestraught. **1586** WARNER *Alb. Eng.* I. ii, 'Till she, as one bestrought Did crie. **1603** HOLLAND *Plutarch's Mor.* 459 His wits were bestraught. **1642** T. TAYLOR *God's Judgem.* I. I. vii. 14 Like a man bestraught he ranne after them. **1748** RICHARDSON *Clarissa* (1811) VIII. 248, I have been, to use an old word, quite bestraught.

†**beˈstraughted,** *ppl. a. Obs. rare*[−1]. [See prec.; cf. also *astraughted*, *distraughted.*] Distracted.

a **1650** *Song to Lute* in Percy I. (R.) Be-strawghted hedes relyfe hath founde By musickes pleasaunte swete delightes.

†**beˈstraughting,** *vbl. sb. Obs.* [See BESTRAUGHT.] Distracting, distraction (of the wits).

1585 *Nomenclator* s.v. *Delirium, Resuerie, radotement*, a bestraughting of the mind. **1621** MOLLE *Camerar. Liv. Libr.* III. xvii. 202 The losse of ones wits, and bestraughting.

bestraw, obs. f. BESTREW. See also BE- 6 b.

bestreak (bɪˈstriːk), *v.* [f. BE- 1 + STREAK *v.*] *trans.* To overspread with streaks, to streak. Hence **beˈstreaked** *ppl. a.*

a **1600** BUREL in Watson *Coll. Scot. P.* II. 12 (JAM.) Thair girtens wer of gold bestreik. **1659** CLEVELAND *Sing-song* ix, Her Cheeks bestreak'd with white and red. **1725** POPE *Odyss.* xv. 65 When the dawn bestreak'd the east. **1849** W. IRVING *Capt. Bonneville* 86 The animal is bestreaked with vermilion, or with white clay.

bestream: see BE- *pref.*

bestrew (bɪˈstruː), *v.* Also **bestrow** (bɪˈstrəʊ), and **bestraw** (*obs.*). Pa. pple. **bestrewed; bestrewn, bestrown.** For the forms see STREW. [OE. *bi-*, *bestréowian*, f. *bi-*, BE- 1 + *stréowian* to STREW. Cf. MHG. *beströuwen*, Du. *bestrooijen*, Da. *bestrøe*, Sw. *beströ.* Orig. a weak verb: the pple. *bestrewn* is recent, and due to analogy.]

1. To strew (a surface) *with*; to cover more or less with things scattered about and lying flat. Often in pa. pple. as adj.

a **1000** *Job* ii. 12 Ettm. 5. 38 Hi mid duste heora heafod bestreowodon. *c* **1175** *Lamb. Hom.* 5 Heo.. nomen þa twigga and.. bistreweden al þane weye. *c* **1420** *Pallad. on Husb.* III. 889 On a floor with chaf bystrowed. **1555** *Fardle Facions* I. v. 75 They all to bestrawe the carckesse with salte. **1596** SHAKS. *Tam. Shr.* Ind. ii. 42 Say thou wilt walke: we wil bestrow the ground. **1697** POTTER *Antiq. Greece* II. iv. (1715) 231 Having bestrawed their heads with the Fruits of Ceres. **1725** POPE *Odyss.* XXII. 273 Yon' fierce man no more With bleeding Princes shall bestrew the floor. **1815** WORDSW. *White Doe* I. 140 The dewy turf with flowers bestrewn. **1837** HAWTHORNE *Amer. Note-Bks.* (1871) I. 40 The brook is bestrewn with stones.

b. *transf.* and *fig.*

1611 SPEED *Theat. Gt. Brit.* (1614) 131/1 The Kingdom of Scotland.. every where bestrewed with cities, townes, and borroughes. **1660** T. WATSON in Spurgeon's *Treas. Dav.* Ps. xxxii. 1 He who is pardoned, is all bestrewed with mercy. **1859** HELPS *Friends in C.* Ser. II. I. i. 30 His daily work thickly bestrewed with trouble and worry.

2. To strew or scatter (things) about.

1667 MILTON *P.L.* I. 311 So thick bestrown Abject and lost lay these, covering the Flood. **1787** J. BARLOW *Hasty Pudding*, The yellow flour, bestrew'd and stirr'd with haste.

3. Of things: To lie scattered over (a surface).

1718 POPE *Iliad* II. 266 Thin hairs bestrew'd his long misshapen head. **1794** WORDSW. *Guilt & Sorr.* Wks. I. 107 In a dry nook where fern the floor bestrows. **1832** HT. MARTINEAU *Ella of Gar.* vii. 83 To sweep away the sand and rubbish which bestrewed it.

beˈstrewment. *rare.* [f. prec. + -MENT.] A strewing about or over.

1833 *Blackw. Mag.* XXXIII. 137 From beneath all their sweet and sad bestrewments she who is their sister revives. **1845** *Ibid.* LVII. 526 The call for the bestrewment of flowers.

bestrid, bestridden, ppl. a. of BESTRIDE.

1651 H. MORE in *Enthus. Tri.* (1656) 175 Like some bestrid Pythonick or hackneyed Enthusiastick.

bestride (bɪˈstraɪd), *v.* Pa. t. **bestrode;** also **bestrid.** Pa. pple. **bestridden;** also **-strid, -strode,** (8 **-strodden**). For other forms see STRIDE. [OE. *bi-*, *bestrídan*, f. *bi-*, BE- 4 + *strídan* to STRIDE. Cf. MHG. *bestrîden*, MDu. *bestryden.*]

1. To sit upon with the legs astride. **a.** To ride, mount (a horse, etc.). The original use.

c **1000** ÆLFRIC *Hom.* II. 136 He his hors bestrad. *c* **1300** *K. Alis.* 706 Bulsifal that hors het.. No dorste no mon him bystryde. *c* **1386** CHAUCER *Sir Thopas* 192 His goode Steede al he bistrood. *c* **1450** *Laud MS.* 595 f. 1 The worthiest wyght in wede That ever by-strod any stede. **1593** SHAKS. *Rich. II*, v. v. 79 That horse that thou so often hast bestrid. **1630** *Tink. Turvey* 17, I never bestrad any one beast in my life but a mare. *a* **1771** GRAY *Fatal Sisters* 63 Sisters, hence with spurs of speed.. Each bestride her sable steed. **1817**

BYRON *Manfred* II. ii. 7 The Giant steed, to be bestrode by Death. **1853** KINGSLEY *Hypatia* xxii. 281 Ostriches.. bestridden each by a tiny cupid.

b. To sit across (other things) as on a horse.

c **1205** LAY. 28020 þa halle ich gon bistriden Swulc ich wolde riden. **1592** SHAKS. *Rom. & Jul.* II. ii. 31 When he bestrides the lasie pacing cloudes. **1785** COWPER *Task* II. 439 Through the pressed nostril, spectacle-bestrid. **1793** SOUTHEY in *Life* (1849) I. 180 The driving blast, bestrodden by the spirit of Ossian. **1822** SCOTT *Nigel* i, Who can say what nose they [the barnacles] may bestride.

fig. **1752** BP. WARBURTON *Lett. Emin. Prelate* (1809) 119 The Church, bestrid by some bumpish minister of state, who turns and winds it at his pleasure. **1865** BUSHNELL *Vicar. Sacr.* III. vi. 320 The wrath that is to bridle and bestride everlastingly His will and counsel.

2. To stand over (a place) with the legs astride; to straddle over, to bestraddle. Also *fig.*

1601 SHAKS. *Jul. C.* I. ii. 135 He doth bestride the narrow world like a Colossus. **1606** —— *Ant. & Cl.* v. ii. 82 His legges bestrid the Ocean. **1787** BENTHAM *Def. Usury* xiii. 131 Your formidable image bestriding the ground. **1872** YEATS *Growth Comm.* 53 A statue..called the Colossus of Rhodes, is said to have bestridden the mouth of the harbour.

b. To stand over, as a victor over the fallen.

1526 *Pilgr. Perf.* (W. de W. 1531) 97 b, His crucifyers bestrydynge hym. **1719** YOUNG *Revenge* v. ii, How I bestride your prostrate conqueror! **1826** SCOTT *Woodst* ix, He seemed already to bestride the land which he had conquered.

c. To stand over (a fallen man) in order to defend him; also *fig.* to defend, protect, support.

1580 NORTH *Plutarch* 236 A Romaine souldier being thrown to the ground euen harde by him, Martius straight bestrid him, and slew the enemie. **1590** SHAKS. *Com. Err.* v. i. 192 When I bestrid thee in the warres, and tooke Deepe scarres to saue thy life. **1605** —— *Macb.* IV. iii. 4. **1642** CHAS. I *Answ. 19 Prop.* 2 They have..bestridde Sir John Hotham in his bold-faced Treason. **1847** TENNYSON *Princ.* ii. 224 As he bestrode my Grandsire, when he fell, And all else fled.

†**d.** *intr.* To stand astride. *Obs.*

1526 *Pilgr. Perf.* (W. de W.) 254 His turmentours or crucifyers moost unreuerently bestrydynge ouer his blessed face.

3. *transf.* of things (e.g. a rainbow, bridge). *trans.*

1728 THOMSON *Spring* 203 Bestriding earth, the grand ethereal bow Shoots up immense. **1785** COWPER *Task* IV. 3 Yonder bridge That with its wearisome, but needful length Bestrides the wintry flood. **1860** HAWTHORNE *Marb. Faun* (1878) II. xix. 222 Bestridden by old, triumphal arches.

4. To stride across, to step across with long strides. Also *fig.*

c **1600** *Rob. Hood* (Ritson) II. x. 62 Deepe water he did bestride. **1607** SHAKS. *Cor.* IV. v. 124 When I first my wedded Mistris saw Bestride my Threshold. **1814** BYRON *Corsair* III. xix. 13 He..Strives through the surge, bestrides the beach. **1824** DIBDIN *Libr. Comp.* 615, I shall bestride the sixteenth and seventeenth centuries.

Hence **be'strider, be'striding** *vbl. sb.* and *ppl. a.*

1618 BOLTON *Florus* II. vi. 95 If his Sonne..had not rescued his Father from certaine death itselfe with bold bestriding him. **1830** SOUTHEY *Yng. Dragon* II. 77 The fiercest steed that e'er To battle bore bestrider. **1849** DICKENS *Dav. Copp.* xiii, A third animal laden with a bestriding child.

†**be'stride,** *prep. Obs. rare*⁻¹. For ASTRIDE, influenced by the vb.

1813 J. C. HOBHOUSE *Journey* 408 A marble lion..with the legs of a man bestride him.

†**be'strike,** *v. Obs. rare.* Also bestryke. [f. BE- 1 + STRIKE to rub, stroke; cf. LG. *bestrîken*, G. *bestreichen* to overspread, do over:—OHG. *bistrîhhan*, f. *bi-* BE- 1 + *strîhhan* to stroke.] *trans.* To overspread, do over, anoint, smear, daub, rub over *with.*

1527 ANDREW *Brunswyke's Distyll. Waters* B iv b, Rounde aboute the panne ye shal lay sande and bestryke that above with claye. **1563** HYLL *Art Garden.* (1593) 33 If you bestrike the lowar part of your tree with redde Oker.

†**be'strip,** *v. Obs.* [OE. *bestrýpan*, f. BE- 1, 2, + **strýpan* to STRIP; cf. MHG. *bestroufen.*] *trans.* To strip clean: to deprive *of* or take away entirely.

1065 *O.E. Chron.* (MS. C.) Ealle þa bestrypte þe he ofer mihte æt life and æt lande. **1340** *Ayenb.* 150 Þes yefþe.. bestrepþ and kest out þe rote and þe zenne of ire. **1622** MABBE *Guzm. d'Alf* II. 87 Be-stript of all manner of vice.

bestripe (bɪ'straɪp), *v.* [f. BE- 1 + STRIPE *v.*] To cover with stripes. Hence **be'striped** *ppl. a.*

1618 BOLTON *Florus* (1636) 271 As if his faire successes were..to be bestryped, and inter-woven with crosse accidents. **1821** CLARE *Vill. Minstr.* I. 75 Vales Bestriped with shades of green and gray.

bestrode, pa. t. and pple. of BESTRIDE *v.*

bestroke: see BE- *pref.*

bestrought, var. of BESTRAUGHT *v. Obs.*

bestrow, bestrown, variants of BESTREW, -N.

be'strut, *v.* In 6 bestrout. [f. BE- 4 + STRUT *v.*] *trans.* To strut or walk pompously over.

1594 CAREW *Tasso* (1881) 74 With sauage insteps some the soyle bestrout.

†**be'strut,** *ppl. a. Obs.* Also bestrutted. [Cf. ASTRUT, and STRUT, whence this seems to have been formed on the analogy of compounds in BE- found only in pa. pple.] Swollen.

1603 HOLLAND *Plutarch's Mor.* 632 Pappes bestruct with milke. **1648** HERRICK *Oberon's Feast, Poems* (1869) 127 He.. eates the sagge And well bestrutted bees sweet bag.

bestual, Obs. form of BESTIAL.

bestuck, pa. t. and pple. of BESTICK.

bestud (bɪ'stʌd), *v.* [f. BE- 1 + STUD *v.*] *trans.* To stud the surface of, set with or as with studs.

1601 HOLLAND *Pliny* I. 258 This Purple is bestudded (as it were)..with sharpe knobs pointed. **1634** MILTON *Comus* 734 The unsought diamonds Would so emblaze the forehead of the deep, And so bestud with stars. *c* **1800** K. WHITE *Poems* (1837) 85 The glittering host bestud the sky.

Hence **be'studded** *ppl. a.*

1601 WEEVER *Mirr. Mart.* E iij, This starre-bestudded vaile. **1870** ROLLESTON *Anim. Life* 253 The ectoderm is very richly bestudded with the thread cells.

‖**bestuur** (bə'styːr). [Du.; = government, f. *besturen* to govern.] Government, administration; i.e. in the Dutch-speaking parts of South Africa.

1885 *Pall Mall G.* 12 May 8/2 Stellaland will..be governed by the Bestuur under the advice of Captain Trotter and Vincent. **1885** *Daily News* 13 Feb 3/2 A member of the Goshen bestuur.

bestyly, bestysshe, obs. form of BEASTLY, -ISH.

besugar, besuit, etc.: see BE- *pref.*

besully (bɪ'sʌlɪ), *v.* [f. BE- 1 + SULLY *v.*] *trans.* To sully or soil badly.

a **1635** CORBET *Fairef. Wind.* (D.) The limber corps, besully'd o'er With meagre paleness. **1820** *Blackw. Mag.* VII. 190 Cheeks are besullied with unused brine.

besumme, obs. form of BESOM.

†**besure** (bɪ'ʃʊə(r)), *adv. phr. Obs.* = Be sure; you may be sure; ? surely, certainly.

1743 APPLETON *Serm.* 95 And besure, this bids fair for a certain Mark of a good Christian. **1754** RICHARDSON *Grandison* III. 322 Get away as soon as you can. Besure do.

†**be'swaddle,** *v. Obs. rare.* [f. BE- 1 + SWADDLE *v.*] *trans.*

1. To envelop in swaddling-clothes.

1755 P. WHITEHEAD *Ep. Thomson* (R.) Infant limbs beswaddled in the lawn.

2. To beat, thrash, 'swaddle.'

1598 FLORIO, *Pestare*..to bang, to bebast, to beswaddle with a cudgell.

†**be'swak,** *v. Sc. Obs.* Pa. pple. **beswakkit.** [f. BE- 1 + SWAK *v.*] *trans.* To dash, strike.

c **1505** DUNBAR *Flyting* 188 Oft beswakkit with ane ourhie tyd.

†**be'swape,** *v. Obs. rare.* [OE. *beswápan*, f. *be-*, BE- 1 + *swápan* to sweep, brush.] *trans.* To envelop, entangle.

c **980** K. ÆLFRED *Bæda* II. xii, Hi hi mid scytan besweop. *c* **1175** *Cott. Hom.* 239 Him selfe bi sandlice senne beswapen.

beswarm, besweeten, beswelter: see BE-.

†**be'sweat,** *pa. pple. Obs.* exc. *arch.* Also 5 beswette. [f. BE- 7 + SWEAT.] Covered with sweat. (Revived by William Morris.)

c **1205** LAY. 9315 Al his burne wes bi-swæt [*c* **1250** bi-swat]. *c* **1460** *Lybeaus Disc.* 108 All beswette for hete. **1470–85** MALORY *Arthur* (1816) II. 206 Her horse was all to besweat. **1574** HELLOWES *Gueuara's Ep.* (1577) 53 Your letters..come wrinckled like linnen..besweat like a doublet. **1876** MORRIS *Sigurd* IV. 316 Lo, lord, our spurs are bloody, and our brows besweat with haste.

†**be'swike,** *v. Obs.* Forms: *Inf.* 1 beswícan, 2–4 biswike(n, 4 by-, beswyke(n, (bisuike, bisquyke), 5 bi-, byswyke, (beeswik). *Pa. t.* 1 beswác, 2–3 biswak, (3–4 -suak), 3–5 -swok(e. *Pa. pple.* 1–3 biswicen, 2–5 -swiken, 4–5 -swike. [OE. *beswícan* to evade, betray, deceive, = OS. *biswîcan*, OHG. *biswîhhan* (MHG. *beswîchen*), f. BE- 1 + *swícan*:—OTeut. **swîqan* to cease, go away, leave off.]

trans. To betray, cheat, deceive.

971 *Blickl. Hom.* 5 Deofol..beswac þone ærestan wifmon. *c* **1000** *Ags. Gosp.* Matt. xxiv. 4 Warniað þæt eow nan ne beswice [**1160** *Hatton* beswike]. *a* **1240** *Lofsong* in *Lamb. Hom.* 213 Þat te hope of ham bi-swoc me. *c* **1250** *Gen. & Ex.* 3861 He ben bi-swiken. *a* **1300** *Cursor M.* 818 Þe find..bi-suak adam. *Ibid.* 19231 Ilk suik it-self bisuikes. *c* **1380** *Sir Ferumb.* 4164 Y wil ȝou noȝt be-swyke. **1470** HARDING *Chron.* clxxviii, Sir Archbald Douglas and erle Patrike.. their kyng thought to bee swik.

be'swiker (in 4 bezuikere), deceiver; **be'swiking** *vbl. sb.*, cheating, deception.

1340 *Ayenb.* 23 Bezuykynges and euel red and uele oþre zennes. *Ibid.* 171 Ase his þyef, ase his manslaȝþe, ase his bezuykere.

beswim, beswitch, etc.: see BE- *pref.*

†**be'swing,** *v. Obs.* [f. BE- 4 + SWING *v.*] *trans.* To swing about; to hang.

1571 R. EDWARDES *Damon & P.* in Hazl. *Dodsley* IV. 84 Such lackeys make me lack; an halter beswinge them!

†**be'swinge,** *v. Obs.* Also 6 beswindge. [f. BE- 2 + SWINGE *v.*] *trans.* To swinge, beat soundly. Also *fig.*

[*c* **1000** ÆLFRIC *Ex.* v. 16 We ðine ðeowas synd beswungene. *c* **1175** (see next, 2).] **1568** T. HOWELL *Arb. Amitie* (1879) 45 With better words beswindge this dame, let no perswasion lacke. **1590** GREENE *Orl. Fur.* (1599) 56 You had best..least I beswinge you.

†**be'swink,** *v. Obs.* [OE. *beswincan*, f. BE- 4 + *swincan* to toil, to labour: see SWINK.]

1. *trans.* To labour for, work for. (Cf. *betravel.*)

[*c* **1000** *Ags. Gosp.* John iv. 38 Ich sende eow to ripene, þæt þæt ȝe ne beswuncon [*c* **1160** *Hatton* beswuncen]. **1377** LANGL. *P. Pl.* B. VI. 216 Bolde beggeres and bigge þat mowe her bred biswynke. **1393** GOWER *Conf.* I. 131 They hadden that they have beswunke. *c* **1400** *Test. Love* (1560) 272/2 With sweate thy sustenaunce to beswinke.

2. To chastise. *rare.* (Prob. for *beswinge.*)

c **1175** *Lamb. Hom.* 111 Ec þet mon biswinke þene stunte lichome for steore.

†**be'swinkful,** *a. Obs. rare*⁻¹. Toilsome.

a **1225** *Ancr. R.* 188 Goð nu þeonne gledluker bi stronge wei, & biswincfule, touward þe muchele feste of heouene.

beswyle, obs. form of BESOIL.

besy, -ly, -nes, obs. forms of BUSY, etc.

besym, obs. form of BESOM.

bet (bɛt), *sb.* Also 7–8 **bett.** [Of uncertain origin; nor is it clear whether the sb. or the vb. was the starting-point; if the sb., we may perhaps see in it an aphetic form of ABET *sb.* in the sense of 'instigation, encouragement, support, maintaining of a cause': see the quotation from Spenser under ABET *sb.* 2. The vb. would then be derived from the sb., as in the case of WAGER *sb.* and *v.* It is less easy to get from the sense of ABET *v.* to that of BET *v.*, since the original construction ought then to be, not 'to bet money on a champion,' etc., but 'to bet (i.e. abet) a champion with money,' of which no trace is found. See however ABET *v.* 4 in sense of 'to bet that.'

(The suggestion that *bet* is:—early ME. BEOT, 'vow, promise, threat,' has no support in the history or phonology.)]

1. a. The backing of an affirmation or forecast by offering to forfeit, in case of an adverse issue, a sum of money or article of value, to one who by accepting, maintains the opposite, and backs his opinion by a corresponding stipulation; the staking of money or other value on the event of a doubtful issue; a wager; also, the sum of money or article staked. ***an even bet*** (fig.): an equal chance, a balance of probabilities. ***a good bet, best bet*** (fig.) (orig. *U.S.*): a satisfactory choice; the person, thing, or course most likely to succeed. ***my bet is*** (colloq.): = 'I bet', my opinion is.

(The first quotation is quite uncertain in meaning.)

[*c* **1460** *Towneley Myst.* 87 Ye fyshe before the nett, And stryfe on this bett, Siche folys never I mett.] **1592** GREENE *Art Conny catch.* II. 7 Certaine old sokers, which are lookers on, and listen for bets, either euen or od. *c* **1614** DRAYTON *Mis. Q. Margaret* (1748) 151 For a long time it was an even bet..Whether proud Warwick or the Queen should win. **1646** BUCK *Rich. III*, II. 60 Might have brought the odds of that day to an even bet. **1735** POPE *Mor. Ess.* I. 86 His pride was in Piquette, Newmarket fame, and judgment at a Bett. **1818** BYRON *Beppo* xxvii, And there were several offer'd any bet, Or that he would, or that he would not come. **1871** KINGSLEY in *Life & Lett.* (1879) II. 271 Plenty of bets pass on every race, which are practically quite harmless.

1906 H. GREEN *Actors' Boarding House* 224 He hailed his juicy jay as the one best bet of a good afternoon. **1923** WODEHOUSE *Inimit. Jeeves* vi. 71 'The fact is, Sir Roderick is being rather troublesome.' 'Thinks I'm not a good bet? Wants to scratch the fixture? Well, perhaps he's right.' **1941** L. A. G. STRONG *Bay* viii. 190 Keep that up... It's our best bet. **1947** 'N. BLAKE' *Minute for Murder* viii. 168 On the face of it, he's the best bet... He provided the poison. **1958** *Times Rev. Industry* May 52/3 Speculating on possible markets... Packaging film and pipes are considered the 'best bet'.

1954 J. B. PRIESTLEY *Magicians* vi. 134 My bet is there's been a fair amount of swift dirty work round here while poor little hubby's been kept at his lab. **1958** *Listener* 25 Sept. 468/2 My bet is that the listening audience would decrease rapidly.

b. An amount staked on the result of a card-game; *spec.* in faro (see quot. 1909); ***heeled bet***: see HEELED *ppl. a.*

1796 C. JONES *Hoyle's Games Improved* (new ed.) 276 *The Game of Faro...* He may masque his Bets, or change his Cards whenever he pleases. **1810** *Sporting Mag.* XXXVI. 32/1 The dealer [at Lansquenet]..proceeds to play, having first *covered*, that is, placed an equal sum near the sums staked by the players, to demonstrate to each that he has accepted his bet. **1844** [see ANTE *sb.*[2]]. **1880** J. BLACKBRIDGE *Compl. Poker-Player* xix. 129 When a player makes a bet, the next player must either *see him*..or *go better, i.e.*, make the previous bet good..or he must pass out. **1891** 'L. HOFFMANN' *Cycl. Card Games* 202 If a player bets, or raises a bet, and no other player goes better, or calls him, he wins the pool. **1909** *Cent. Dict.* Suppl., *Bet*, in faro, a card which is a case, that is, the only one of that denomination

remaining in the box: so called because the player cannot be split.

2. A challenge contest.

1843 *Proc. Berw. Nat. Club* II. xi. 59 A great *bet*, as a game [at bowls] was called, came off on Cockburnspath Green in 1807 or 1808.

bet (bɛt), *v.* Also 7-8 bett. Pa. t. and pple. bet; also betted. [See prec.] **a.** *trans.* To stake or wager (a sum of money, etc.) in support of an affirmation or on the issue of a forecast.

1597 SHAKS. *2 Hen. IV*, III. ii. 50 Iohn of Gaunt loued him well, and betted much Money on his head. ? *a* **1600** *Rob. Hood* (Ritson) II. xii. 105 Said the bishop then, Ile not bet one peny. **1727** POPE, etc. *Bathos* 110 These on your side will all their fortunes bet. **1849** DICKENS *Dav. Copp.* ii. (C.D. ed.) 16 I'll as good as bet a guinea.. that she'll let us go. **1876** O. W. HOLMES *How Old Horse won Bet* Poems (1884) 309 I'll bet you two to one I'll make him do it.

b. *absol.* To lay a wager. ***you bet*** (*slang*, chiefly in U.S.): be assured, certainly; also ***you bet you***.

1609 ROWLANDS *Knaue Clubbes* 4 At Bedlem-bowling alley late, Where Citizzens did bet: And threw their mony on the ground. **1628** EARLE *Microcosm.* xlviii. 101 He enjoys it [gambling] that looks on and bets not. **1711** *Act 9 Anne* in *Lond. Gaz.* No. 4863/2 If such Person.. shall.. at any one time.. Play or Bett for any Sum. **1857** HUGHES *Tom Brown*, Brandy punch going, I'll bet. **1857** *Phoenix* (Sacramento) 22 Nov. 2/2, I saw all the 'boys', and distributed to them the papers and 'you bet', they were in great demand. **1858** THACKERAY *Virgin.* II. xv. 114, I don't bet on horses I don't know. **1868** O. W. HOLMES *Once More* Poems (1884) 224 'Is it loaded?' 'I'll bet you! What doesn't it hold?' **1868** [see sense c]. **1872** 'MARK TWAIN' *Roughing It* xx. 152 'I'll get you there on time' and you bet you he did, too. **1882** *Sk. Texas Siftings* 131 'Are you drunk?' 'You bet.' 'Then you move off from here.' **1910** S. E. WHITE *Rules of Game* v. xxxiv, 'He's a quick thinker, then,' said Bob. 'You bet you!' **1928** D. L. SAYERS *Lord Peter views Body* iv. 68 'Can you handle this outfit?' 'You bet,' said the scout.

c. In various (orig. *U.S.*) slang asseverative phrases meaning: to stake everything or all one's resources (upon the truth of an assertion).

1852 *San Francisco Sun. Dispatch* 18 Jan. 1/5 He's around when there's money in the pipe—bet your life on t-h-a-t. **1856** *Spirit of Times* (N.Y.) 6 Sept. 3/3 You may bet your old boots on that. **1865** BRET HARTE *Poet. Wks.* (1872) 81 Smart! You bet your life 'twas that! **1866**, etc.[see *bottom dollar* s.v. BOTTOM *sb.* 20]. **1868** *All Year Round* 31 Oct. 489/2 'You bet' or 'You bet yer life', or 'You bet yer bones', while to 'bet your boots' is confirmation strong as holy writ—in the mines, at least. **1913** WODEHOUSE *Little Nugget* I. i. 14 'You will order yourself something substantial, marvel-child?' 'Bet your life,' said the son and heir tersely. **1933** M. LOWRY *Ultramarine* 39 'You bet your boots,' he replied. **1957** P. FRANK *Seven Days to Never* i. 22 He would bet his bottom dollar.. that his target would be one of those bases.

Also in corrupt forms (*I, you,* etc.) ***betcha***, ***betcher***, representing colloq. pronunciation of ***bet you*** or ***your*** (***life***).

1922 'R. CROMPTON' *Just—William* ix. 174 You betcher life! **1936** WODEHOUSE *Laughing Gas* v. 61 'You're home-sick, what?' 'You betcher.' **1936** F. CLUNE *Roaming round Darling* xxii. 219 Andrew Hume.. had said one day to the governor of the prison, 'Betcher I know where to find the sole survivor of the Leichhardt expedition.' 'Betcher!' mocked the governor. **1940** G. BUTLER *Kiss Blood off Hands* v. 82, I collared a kid.. and asked him if he wanted to earn a shilling. 'You betcha, mister,' he said. **1962** J. LUDWIG in R. Weaver *First Five Years* 29 Your tea's cold, I betcha.

†**bet**, *adv.* (and *a.*) *Obs.* Forms: 1-7 **bet** (3-6 bet, 4-6 bette). [Com. Teut.: OE. *bęt* = OFris. *bet*, OS. *bat*, *bet* (MDu. *bat*, *bet*, Du. *bet-*), OHG., MHG. *baz* (mod.G. *basz*), ON. *betr*, Goth. *batis*:—OTeut. **batiz* adv., the uninflected comparative stem, whence was formed the adj. **batizon-*, in OE. *bętera*, BETTER. In the adv. the comparative ending *-iz* underwent the same phonetic changes as the formative *-iz* of nouns, and was thus reduced to *-e*, or lost entirely before the OE. period. (*Bęt*, for the expected *bęte*, probably followed *lęng*, *sęft*, etc.) About the end of the OE. or beginning of the ME. period, *bet(e)re*, the neuter gender of the adj., began to be used, in certain constructions, in the place of *bet*, and, after a long existence side by side, gradually superseded it about 1600: instances of *bet* just before, and especially after, 1600 are archaisms. This encroachment of *betere*, *beter*, *better* upon *bet* began in phrases where the adj. and adv. are not easily separated, as in *hit is bet* or *betere* (positive 'it is *well*' or '*good*'), and gradually extended to others; the final ascendancy of *better* was doubtless helped by the fact that *bet* and other comparatives of the same type (e.g. *leng*, *near*) had not the ordinary comparative sign, and were thus less definite in expression. As in similar cases, during the time that *bet* and *better* were interchangeable as adverbs, *bet* was by compensation sometimes used for *better* as adjective.]

I. *adv.* (and *predicative adj.*)

1. The earlier form of BETTER, the comparative of WELL.

c **888** K. ÆLFRED *Boeth.* xxiii, Ðæt se hwæte mæȝe ðy bet weaxan. *a* **1200** *Moral Ode* 15 in *Trin. Coll. Hom.* 220 Ich mihte habben bet idon. *c* **1205** LAY. 28560 Wha dude wurse, no wha bet. **1297** R. GLOUC. 209 Hys men truste þe bet to hym. **1377** LANGL. *P. Pl.* B. VIII. 123 Where do-wel, do-bet, and do-best ben in lond. **1393** GOWER *Conf.* I. 126 One justeth wel, another bet. **1423** JAS. I, *King's Q.* ci, Ȝe knaw the cause of all my peynes smert Bet than myself. **1466** *Pol. Rel. & L. Poems* (1866) 109 And graunt me grace ai bett & bett. *c* **1570** THYNNE *Pride & Lowl.* (1841) 20 No Auditor, ne Clerke of Check Can penne it bet then he. **1586** FERNE *Blaz. Gentrie* 71 We dezerue full bet then they.

2. As predicate after *be*; interchanging with the neuter adj. *betere*. (In quots. 1386, 1575, its adjective function is distinct.) Cf. BETTER A 4.

c **1175** *Lamb. Hom.* 145 Him is wel.. him is ec muchele bet þet is ilaðed from muchele wowe. *c* **1200** ORMIN 5548 þatt hemm baþe beo þe bett. *c* **1205** LAY. 870 Hit is þe bet mid us. *c* **1386** CHAUCER *Pers. T.* ¶465 Therfore saith a wise man, that ire is bet than play. **1430** LYDG. *Chron. Troy* I. vi, Bett were me to deye, Than liue ashamed. *c* **1575** GASCOIGNE *Fruites Warre* (1831) 209, I termed have all strife To be no bet than warres. *a* **1643** W. CARTWRIGHT *Ordinary* in *Dodsley* (1780) X. 251 Sin it may be no bet now gang in peace.

II. *absol.* and quasi-*sb.*

3. ***the bet***: the advantage: cf. BETTER A. 8.

c **1340** *Cursor M.* 7642 (Trin.) Wiþ þat folke soone he met And wiȝtly wan of hem þe bet [*v.r.* his dete]. **1592** WYRLEY *Armorie* 118 It seemd the Frenchmen had the bet.

4. ***one's bette***: cf. BETTER A. 7. *rare*.

1494 FABYAN VII. ccxl 281 No man I thought my bette.

†**bet**, *adv.*² *Obs.* [Origin and meaning doubtful.] In *go bet*. (Prof. Skeat takes it as = go better, i.e. go quicker.)

c **1386** CHAUCER *Pard. T.* 339 Go bet, quod he, and axe redily what cors is this. *c* **1425** *Seven Sag.* (P.) 1005 The maystir made hys hor go bete. *a* **1528** SKELTON *El. Rummyng* 331 And bad Elynour go bet, And fyll good met. *c* **1600** *Parl. Byrdes* 148 in Hazl. *E.P.P.* III. 174 Here is nought els with friende nor foe, But go bet peny go bet go. **1617** *Frere & Boye* 300 *ibid.* III. 73 Ye hath made me daunce, maugre my hede, Amonge the thornes, hey go bette.

bet, obs. and Sc. pa. t. of BEAT *v.*¹; dial. form of BEET *v.*

beta ('biːtə). [a. L. *beta*, Gr. βῆτα.]

1. The second letter of the Greek alphabet, Β, β.

a **1300** *Cursor M.* 12425 Bot sai þou me first o betha, And siþen i sal þe sai alpha.

2. In various scientific uses; *esp.* **a.** *Astron.* Used to mark the second star in a constellation. **b.** *Chem.* The second of two or more isomerous modifications of the same organic compound. **c.** *Nat. Hist.* The second sub-species or permanent variety of a species. **d.** In various other classifications. Cf. ALPHA.

1867 CHAMBERS *Astron.* VI. ii. (1877) 492 Amongst the conspicuous stars β Libræ (green) appears to be the only instance. **1877** WATTS *Fownes' Chem.* II. 497 Beta-orcin is obtained by dry distillation of usnic acid. **1877** —— *Dict. Chem.* IV. 235 Stenhouse designated the acid obtained from South American Roccella.. as α-orsellic, and that prepared.. from South African Roccella as β-orsellic.

e. Math. ***beta distribution***, a distribution of a variate *x* of the form

$$dF = x^{p-1}(1-x)^{q-1}dx/\mathrm{B}(p, q),$$

where $0 \leqq x \leqq 1$, $p, q > 0$; ***beta function***, the function $\mathrm{B}(p, q) = \int_0^1 x^{p-1}(1-x)^{q-1}dx$, where $p, q > 0$; also called the ***complete beta function*** and the ***first Eulerian integral***; also, the function $\mathrm{B}_x(p, q) = \int_0^x x^{p-1}(1-x)^{q-1}dx$ (the ***incomplete beta function***).

1888 W. W. R. BALL *Hist. Math.* xviii. 368 The Beta and Gamma functions were invented by Euler. **1924** C. H. FORSYTH *Introd. Math. Anal. Statistics* iv. 61 The value of any Beta function for positive values of *m* and *n* can be expressed directly in terms of Gamma functions. **1941** *Biometrika* XXXII. 153 The special character of the Beta-distribution.. makes it necessary to vary the method of computation in different parts of the range of variables covered. **1967** A. BATTERSBY *Network Analysis* (ed. 2) 319 The method of calculating the expected value and variance of the duration of a job depends on the assumption that the duration follows a Beta distribution. The Beta distribution is derived from the Beta function.

f. *Physics.* ***beta*** (or β) ***radiation***, the second of three types of radiation emitted by radioactive substances, having greater penetrating power than alpha radiation. So ***beta*** (or β) ***particle***, ***ray***.

1899 RUTHERFORD in *Phil. Mag.* XLVII. 116 These experiments show that uranium radiation is complex, and that there are present at least two distinct types of radiation—one that is very readily absorbed, which will be termed for convenience the α radiation, and the other of a more penetrative character, which will be termed the β radiation. **1902** RUTHERFORD & GRIER in *Phil. Mag.* IV. 325 For brevity and convenience we will call the non-deviable rays of *all* radioactive substances α *rays* and the deviable rays β *rays*. **1904** RUTHERFORD in *Nature* 10 Mar. 437/1 It is to be expected that Röntgen rays would be set up at the sudden *starting* as well as the sudden stopping of the electron or β particle. **1909** SODDY *Interpr. Radium* 55 In ordinary circumstances radium appears to be expelling both α- and β-particles together. **1922** A. S. EDDINGTON *Theory of Relativity* 19 The β particles shot off from radioactive substances are negative electrons which sometimes attain speeds of 100,000 miles a second. **1933** *Discovery* Feb. 45/1 Beta radiations, which are streams of electrons. **1957** *Technology* Mar. 14/2 Both beta and gamma rays can also be used for gauging thickness or height in the examination, for instance, of red-hot sheets of steel.

Hence denoting a process in which, or a substance from which, beta particles are emitted, as ***beta decay***, ***disintegration***, ***emission***, ***emitter***.

1931 RUTHERFORD in *Proc. R. Soc.* A. CXXXII. 674 There will be a broadening of the line by the Doppler effect due to recoil of the nucleus from the immediately preceding β-disintegration. **1933** C. D. ELLIS & MOTT *Ibid.* CXLI. 502 The.. upper limit of the β-ray spectrum is a significant parameter with which to classify a β-disintegration. **1934** G. GAMOW *Ibid.* CXLVI. 217 Every theory treating the β-decay as the transformation of a nuclear neutron into a proton. **1935** *Internat. Conference Physics 1934* I. 41 The final state of the nucleus after a β-emission is an excited one. **1947** C. D. CORYELL in C. Goodman *Sci. & Engin. Nuclear Power* I. 248 (*heading*) Long-lived β emitters without γ radiation. **1955** *Gloss. Terms Radiology* (*B.S.I.*) 6 *Beta decay*, the radioactive decay process characterized by the emission of a beta particle. The parent atom involved is called a beta emitter.

g. *Metallurgy.* (*a*) Applied to the second of a series of allotropic forms of iron (see quot. 1949); (*b*) applied to the second of a range of alloys, as ***beta brass***, the second of a series of alloys of copper and zinc, containing less copper than in alpha brass. Cf. ALPHA 3 d.

1885, etc. [see ALPHA 3 d]. **1895** *Jrnl. Iron & Steel Inst.* XLVIII. 258 A special strong, hard, brittle, allotropic state called β iron. **1914** *Jrnl. Inst. Metals* XI. 105 Plane sections through a bees' honeycomb.. a benzene water-foam, and an over-annealed β brass are all very similar in appearance. **1949** R. T. ROLFE *Dict. Metallogr.* (ed. 2) 24 *Beta iron*, formerly, a supposed allotropic form of i[ron] stable between.. 768° and about 900° C., of body-centred cubic form, and only very feebly magnetic. In reality, the change in magnetic susceptibility of α-iron occurring at 768° C. is not associated with any structural transformation and β-iron is no longer recognized as a distinct variety.

h. ***beta rhythm***, ***waves***, fast activity of the brain recorded in an electroencephalogram, having a frequency of fourteen to twenty-four cycles per second. Cf. ALPHA 3 f.

[**1935** *Brain* LVIII. 349 Berger describes a definite series of small oscillations—the *b* waves—superimposed on the primary *a* waves of the 10 a second rhythm. The frequency of the *b* waves is given as 35 a second.] **1936** *Archives Neurol. & Psychiatry* XXXVI. 1215 Less prominent, because lower in voltage, is a faster rhythm, with a frequency of about 25 waves a second, called by Berger the 'beta waves'. *Ibid.* 1220 A prominent fast (beta) rhythm. **1943** *Electronic Engin.* XVI. 237 Faster rhythms, sometimes called 'beta' rhythms, have been described in the EEG.

i. ***beta receptor*** (Physiol.), one of two categories of adrenergic receptor on organs innervated by sympathetic nerves, which when stimulated increases cardiac action and blood flow and relaxes smooth muscle; ***beta-blocker*** (Pharm.), a drug that prevents the stimulation of beta receptors; so ***beta-blocking*** adj.

1948 R. P. AHLQUIST in *Amer. Jrnl. Physiol.* CLIII. 596 One type of [adrenotropic] receptor is associated with most of the excitatory functions and with at least one of the inhibitory functions (intestine). The other type is associated with most of the inhibitory functions and with one.. excitatory function (myocardium)... Because of the opposite effects.. the customary signs, *E* (excitatory) and *I* (inhibitory) cannot be applied. Therefore, for convenience they have been designated as the *alpha* adrenotropic receptors and the *beta* receptors. **1965** J. H. BURN *Lect. Notes Pharmacol.* (ed. 8) 8 The β-blocking agents are those which prevent adrenaline from causing relaxation in smooth muscle. **1970** *Biol. Abstr.* LI. 96372 Beta blockers exert a powerful physiological effect primarily on the cardiovascular system. **1977** *South China Morning Post* (Hong Kong) 22 July 16/4 We're hoping that beta blockers will calm performers without taking the edge off their performance. **1983** *Oxf. Textbk. Med.* II. xiii. 64 Inhibition of the beta receptor in bronchial smooth muscle is likely to produce a significant increase in airways resistance in asthmatic subjects. *Ibid.* 66/1 Beta-blocking agents may produce depression and other central nervous system side-effects, such as sleep-disturbances, insomnia, and nightmares. **1986** *Here's Health* Dec. 28/3 With the advent of calcium channel blockers advertising has mentioned side-effects from beta blockers which were never mentioned during their peak of acceptability.

3. An examiner's second-class mark. Also *transf.*

1902 [see ALPHA 4]. **1936** 'N. BLAKE' *Thou Shell of Death* I. 104 He's quite a decent old trot, but definitely in the Beta class. **1958** *Oxf. Mag.* 13 Mar. 362/1, I have mentioned twenty recent pictures.. four have some *alpha* about them; the rest are gamma minus to beta plus (I have not mentioned deltas).

betacism ('biːtəsɪz(ə)m). [ad. mod.L. *betacismus*, f. *beta* (see BETA), after L. *iotacismus*, etc.] (See quot. 1926.)

[**1885** *Amer. Jrnl. Philol.* VI. 501 Even these forms were threatened with destruction by the spread of Betacismus, whereby *amavit* was pronounced like *amabit* and vice versa.] *Ibid.*, In Africa, especially where betacism flourished, the need of new substitutes for the future made itself early felt. **1926** PLATER & WHITE *Gram. Vulgate* 43 What is called betacism (the interchange of *b* and *v*) causes great confusion in verbs of the first conjugation.

betafite ('biːtəfaɪt). *Min.* [a. F. *betafite* (A. Lacroix 1912, in *Compt. Rend. Acad. Sci.*

CLIV. 1042), f. *Betafo* in Madagascar, one of its localities + -ITE[1].] A niobate and titanate of uranium, etc.

1912 *Jrnl. Chem. Soc.* CII. II. 567 Radioactive Uraniferous Columbotantalotitanites from Pegmatites of Madagascar... Betafite, D 4·17, is dark green, and shows rudimentary cubic faces. 1921 *Brit. Mus. Return* 155 Minerals from..Madagascar (chrysoberyl, betafite, columbite, etc.).

betag: see BE- *pref.*

betaght(e, -ȝt(e, pa. t. of BETEACH *v. Obs.*

betaikin, obs. Sc. form of BETOKEN.

betail (bɪˈteɪl), *v. nonce-wd.* [on analogy of *behead*.] *trans.* To deprive of the tail.

18.. TROLLOPE (O.) [The sportsman] puts his heavy boot on the beast's body, and there beheads and betails him.

betailed (bɪˈteɪld), *ppl. a.* [f. BE- 7 + TAIL.] Furnished with a tail.

1760 GOLDSM. *Cit. W.* iii, Thus betailed and bepowdered, the man of taste fancies he improves in beauty. 1854 H. MILLER *Footpr. Creat.* ix. (1874) 165 The betailed reptiles.

betaine (ˈbiːteɪaɪn). *Chem.* [anomalously f. L. *bēta* BEET *sb.* + -INE[4].] A chemical base ($C_5H_{11}NO_2$) found in beet and mangold-wurzel.

1879 WATTS *Dict. Chem.* VI. 340 Betaine crystallizes in large shining hydrated crystals.

betaine, betani, obs. forms of BETONY.

†**be'taint**, *v. Obs.* [f. BE- 1 + TAINT.] *trans.* To tinge. Hence (short for **betainted**) *ppl. a.*

1594 CAREW *Tasso* (1881) 60 Her beguil[d]ed lockes this slightest wound With some few drops, such wise betainted red, As gold growes ruddie. 1598 GREENE *James IV* (1861) 195 Where every wean is all betaint with blood.

betake (bɪˈteɪk), *v. str.* Pa. t. betook. Pa. pple. betaken. For forms see TAKE *v.* [ME *be-*, *bitake(n*, f. *bi-*, BE- + TAKE. There seems to have been an early confusion of *betake* with *betæce*, *betæche*, BETEACH, which extended in part also to the simple *take*, so that this had the sense of 'deliver, hand over, give in charge,' not found in ON., and not logically developed in Eng. from its proper sense of 'seize, grasp, catch hold of, make oneself holder or owner of.' In any case, in ME., *betake*, *betôk*, *betaken* was identified in sense with *beteach*, *betaughte*, *betaught*; and only since the latter became obs., has *betake* tended to revert toward the normal sense of *take*. See TAKE.]

†**1.** *trans.* To hand over, deliver, give up, grant, place at a person's disposal; = BETEACH 2. Const. with *dat.* or *to*, *unto*, etc. *Obs.*

c1205 LAY. 6251 Heo sculleð eow, þat lond bi-taken. c1250 *Ibid.* 22791 He was bi-take [c1205 iȝefen] Arthur! in stede of hostage. a1300 *Havelok* 1226 Gold and siluer and oþer fe Bad he us bi-taken þe. c1400 *Destr. Troy* IV. 1391 Ercules..Betoke hir to Telamon. 1534 MORE *On Passion* Wks. 1338/2 The onely sacrifice betaken by Chryst vnto his christen church. 1618 ROWLANDS *Sacred Mem.* 24 Then bread he brake, And that to his Disciples did betake. 1621 QUARLES *Esther* (1638) 89 Zedechia..Into Serajahs peacefull hand betooke The sad contents of a more dismall Booke.

†**b.** To hand over to the care of; to entrust, commit, give in charge *to*; = BETEACH 3. *Obs.*

1297 R. GLOUC. 354 He bytoc hym Engelond, þat he yt wel wuste To Wyllammes byofþe. a1300 *Cursor M.* 1126 (Gött.) He was noght bitan [*C.* bi-taght, *F.* betaȝt, *T.* bitake] to me. c1375 WYCLIF *Wks.* (1880) 365 þe whiche god hadde bytake to her gouernance. c1440 *Promp. Parv.* 34 Betakyn' a thynge to anothere, *committo, commendo.* 1596 SPENSER *F.Q.* III. iv. 28 Phœbe to a nymphe her babe betooke To be upbrought in perfect maydenhed. 1649 SELDEN *Laws Eng.* I. lix. (1739) 110 The Empress perceiving the power of the Clergy, betakes her case to them.

†**c.** To give in marriage. *Obs.*

1382 WYCLIF *Ecclus.* vii. 27 Bytac a doȝtir and a gret werk thou shalt do; and to a wel felende man ȝif hyr.

†**2.** To commit or commend (one), by the expression of a wish, *to* (God, the devil, etc.); often as an appreciation or imprecation. Also in leave-taking: To bid adieu, say good-bye. *Obs.*

1297 R. GLOUC. 475 God & Seinte Marie, & Sein Denis al so..Ich bitake min soule. c1386 CHAUCER *Milleres T.* 564 My soule bitake I vn to Sathanas. c1400 *Apol. Loll.* 24 Petre be tok Anani..to þe fend to be tormentid perpetuali. 1493 *Festyvall* (W. de W. 1515) 115 He betoke them to god & Mary maudeleyne to kepe & wente his way. 1526 SKELTON *Magnyf.* 406 Nowe to the Devil I the betake. 1642 EVELYN *Mem.* (1857) III. 4 To God Almighty I betake it for support and speedy good success.

†**3.** To allot, to assign; = BETEACH 5. *Obs.*

c1300 *Cursor M.* 4001 (Gött.) þe fiss to water als we finde, þe foul he bitok [*C.* be-taght, *F.* be taȝt] to þe wind.

4. *refl.* To commit oneself, have recourse or resort *to* any kind of action. ***to betake oneself to one's heels***: to retreat in flight, to run away.

15.. *Sc. Metr. Ps.* lvii, My soule doth her betake unto the helpe of the. 1593 HOOKER *Eccl. Pol.* I. vii. §3 When we betake ourselves unto rest. 1598 GREENWEY *Tacitus' Ann.* XII. viii. (1622) 166 The enemy betooke him to his heeles with small losse. 1601 SHAKS. *Twel. N.* III. iv. 240 That defence thou hast, betake the too't. 1684 BUNYAN *Pilgr.* II. 22 They betook themselves to a short debate. 1762 HUME *Hist. Eng.* (1806) III. 220 To betake themselves to other expedients for supporting authority. 1794 BURKE *Sp. W. Hastings* Wks. 1842 XV. 166 They saw him..betaking himself to flight. 1833 HT. MARTINEAU *Briery Creek* v. 107 The Irish betake themselves to rebellion when stopped in their merry-makings.

†**b.** *intr.* (for *refl.*) *Obs.*

1596 SPENSER *F.Q.* I. v. 28 Then to her yron wagon she betakes. 1606 SYLVESTER *Du Bartas* (1633) 320 All be-take to flight. 1641 MILTON *Ch. Govt.* II. Introd., Whether aught was imposed me by them, or betaken to of mine own choice.

c. *passive.*

1601 T. WRIGHT *Passions of Minde* (1620) 303 The matter whereunto I am betaken.

5. *refl.* To resort, make one's way, turn one's course, go. (Here the notion of 'taking' or 'conveying' oneself becomes distinct.)

1612 WOODALL *Surg. Mate* Wks. 1653 Pref. 3 It was of old a custome..for the sick to betake themselves unto the..Temple of Aesculapius. 1667 MILTON *P.L.* x. 922 Whither shall I betake me, where subsist? 1714 ELLWOOD *Autobiog.* 3 He betook himself to London. 1815 L. HUNT *Feast Poets* 21 So off he betook him the way that he came.

b. with *obj.* = *refl. pron.*

1861 DICKENS *Gt. Expect.* II. 307 They betook their little quickened hearts behind the panels.

†**6.** To take; to take in some sense. *Obs.*

c1420 *Pallad. on Husb.* I. 639 The xth day the IIII away betake And other IIII enscore her place into. a1555 LATIMER *Wks.* (1844–5) I. 73 (D.) As the blanchers have blanched it and wrested it, and as I myself did once betake it. 1591 SPENSER *M. Hubberd* 69 Ere that anie way I doo betake, I meane my Gossip privie first to make.

†**7.** (?) To pursue; to overtake. *Obs.*

a1000 ÆLFRIC *Colloquy* ⁋34 Mid swiftum hundum ic betæce [*MS.* betæcc] wildeor [*insequor feras*]. 1375 BARBOUR *Bruce* III. 159 Now may ȝe se Betane the starkest pundelan. 1583 STANYHURST *Æneis* II. (Arb.) 52 When slumber sweetlye betaketh Eech mortal person.

betaken, -in, obs. forms of BETOKEN.

be'taking, *vbl. sb.* [f. BETAKE + -ING[1].] Taking (*obs.*); in mod. senses chiefly gerundial.

c1449 PECOCK *Repr.* I. xx. 128 The bitaking of these bookis..into her vce.

betalde, obs. pa. pple. of BETELL.

betalk, betallow, betask, betaxed, see BE-.

†**betall**, *v. Obs.* [a. Du. *betal-en* to pay: used in Eng. in 17th c.] *trans.* To pay.

1630 J. TAYLOR (N.) Our host said we had foure shilling to betall or pay. 1631 HEYWOOD *Fair Maid W.* I. II. i, With one word of my mouth I can tell them what is to be-tall.

betan(e, north. dial. f. *betaken*: see BETAKE.

betan(y, obs. form of BETONY.

be'tanglement. [f. BE- 2 + TANGLE *v.* + -MENT.] Tangled condition.

1881 J. HAWTHORNE *Fortune's Fool* I. ii, The riotous betanglement of his brown hair.

†**betas.** *Obs. rare*[−1]. [a. ON. *beiti-áss* sailyard, ? f. *beita* to make the ship catch the wind, to tack + *áss* pole, yard; cf. *windlass*, in ME. *windas*, in ON. *vindáss*.] A sailyard.

c1330 R. BRUNNE in *Layamon* III. 396 Som aforced the wyndas, Som the lofe, som the betas.

betassel (bɪˈtæs(ə)l), *v.* [f. BE- 1 + TASSEL.] *trans.* To hang round or decorate with, or as with, tassels. Hence **be'tasselled, -eled** *ppl. a.*

1648 EARL WESTMLD. *Otia Sacra* (1879) 16 The Lustfull Clusters..Betasseling Autumn. 1778 MRS. DELANY *Lett.* Ser. II. II. 341 Her bridal apparel..festooned and betassel'd. 1812 *Examiner* 12 Oct. 653/1 One cannot be always..devising patterns, and betasselling dragoons.

betatron (ˈbiːtətrɒn). [f. BETA + -TRON.] A machine designed for the acceleration of β particles.

Kerst first spoke of the machine (1940) as an 'Induction Accelerator'.

1941 *Time* 29 Dec. 44/3 A new electron-hurling machine ..its brilliant young inventor, Donald William Kerst, 30, who calls the machine a 'betatron'. *Ibid.*, 'The heart of the betatron,' explains Inventor Kerst, 'is a doughnut-shaped glass vacuum tube between the poles of a large electro-magnet.' 1942 D. W. KERST in *Rev. Sci. Instr.* XIII. 387 (*title*) A 20-Million Electron-Volt Betatron or Induction Accelerator. 1960 *Gloss. Atomic Terms* (*H.M.S.O.*) 6 *Betatron*, a machine for accelerating a continuous beam of electrons to high speeds in a circular path by means of the electric field produced by a changing magnetic flux.

betattered (bɪˈtætəd), *ppl. a.* [f. BE- 1 + TATTER *v.*] All in tatters, ragged.

1618 WITHER *Motto* Wks. (1633) 553 The beggarliest And most betattered Pesant. a1704 T. BROWN *Wks.* (1760) I. 240 (D.) She brought a gown..bepatch'd and betatter'd.

betaughte, -tauhte, etc., pa. t. of BETEACH *v.*

†**be'tawder**, *v.* ? *nonce-wd.* [f. BE- + ? TAWDR(Y).] *trans.* To bedizen with tawdry finery.

a1689 MRS. BEHN *City-heiress* II. ii, Trick and betawder yourself up, like a right City-Lady, rich but ill-fashion'd.

betayne, obs. form of BETONY.

betcha, betcher: see BET *v.* c.

bete, obs. form of BEAT and BEET.

†**be'teach**, *v. Obs.* Forms: *Inf.* 1 betǽcan, 2 -en, 3 bitæchen, -teachen, 3–4 biteche(n, 3–5 biteche, 4 byteche, beteiche, -teyche, 5 beteche, 6 *Sc.* beteiche, 7 beteach. *Pa. t.* 1 betǽhte, 2 betahte, -tehte (-tohte, -tacte), 2–4 bitaht(e, -hhte, -ȝte, 3 biteihte, 3–5 bi-, by-, betaght(e, -ȝt(e, (4 bitahut, biteched), 4–5 bi-, by-, betauȝt(e, -ht(e, -ght(e, -wght, -wt, 4–6 *Sc.* betaucht, -wcht, 7 beteached. *Pa. pple.* analogous to pa. t. [OE. *betǽc(e)an*, f. BE- 2 + *tǽc(e)an* to show (:—OTeut. type **taikjan*, from same root as **taikno-*, OE. *tácn* token). Cf. BETAKE.]

1. *trans.* To show, point out.

c1000 *Ags. Gosp.* Luke xxii. 12 And he eow betæcð mycele healle gedæfte.

2. To hand over, deliver, give up, yield. Const. with *dat.*, or *to*, *till*, *unto*.

a1000 ÆLFRIC *Colloquy* ⁋21 Ic betæce hiȝ ðam yrthlincge. c1000 *Ags. Gosp.* Luke i. 2 Swa us betæhtun ða þe hyt of frymðe ȝesáwon. c1175 *Lamb. Hom.* 11 Drihten him bitahte twa stanene tables breode. c1175 *Cott. Hom.* 221 Alle hi beoð þe betéhte. a1225 *Ancr. R.* 300, I chulle ower foes lond bitechen in his honden. a1300 *Cursor M.* 3539 þe mete mi moder me bi-taght. 1375 BARBOUR *Bruce* I. 610 The king betaucht hym in that steid The Endentur. c1400 MAUNDEV. v. 63 That is the Place where oure Lord be-taughten the Ten Comandementes to Moyses. 1513 DOUGLAS *Æneis* XI. xi. 124 To ane onhappy chance betaucht is sche.

3. To hand over as a trust; to entrust, commit, give in charge *to*.

c1000 *Ags. Gosp.* Matt. xxv. 15 [He] betǽhte hym hys æhta. 1160 *Hatton G.* ibid., Betacte [*v.r.* betahte]. c1205 LAY. 11503 Ich him wulle bitæchen [c1250 bi-teche] mine kine-riche. a1300 *Cursor M.* 4254 þe wardeinscipp of al his aght Has putifar ioseph bi-taght [*v.r.* betaȝt, bitauȝt]. c1425 *Seven Sag.* (P.) 324 The emperour..byddis ȝow..bryng with ȝow his son dere, That he betauȝt ȝow to lere. 1513 DOUGLAS *Æneis* II. xii. [xi.] 113 Our Troiane Goddis..Onto my feris betawcht I, for to keip.

4. To commit or commend (one), by the expression of a wish, *to* (God, the devil, etc.). As a formula of leave-taking: To bid adieu or good-bye.

c1314 *Guy Warw.* (A) 1248 Fader, god y þe biteche And mi leue moder al-so; For hastiliche ichil nov go. c1330 *Amis & Amil.* 328 Aither bitaught other heuen king And went in her iurnè. 1375 BARBOUR *Bruce* XV. 538 Quhen wiffis vald thar childir ban Thai wald..Beteche thame to the blak douglass. c1386 CHAUCER *Melib.* Prol. 6 Now swich a Rym the deuel I biteche. 1535 STEWART *Cron. Scot.* (1856) III. 65 Beteichand hir to him that bocht ws deir. 1685 G. SINCLAIR in R. Law *Memor.* (1818) 124 He beteached himself strongly to God.

b. Hence, by confusion, ***to beteach one good day***: to wish or bid one good day.

c1400 *Gamelyn* 338 Whan his gestes took her leue..[they] bitaughte Gamelyn god & good day. a1440 *Ipomydon* 568 They toke leve..And bytaught the lady gode day. a1500 *Kyng & Hermit* 513 in Hazl. *E.P.P.* 33 Ather betauȝt other gode dey.

5. To allot, assign.

a1300 *Cursor M.* 400 þe fuxol [? fuȝol] be-taght he to þe wind. *Ibid.* 5412 (Trin.) þat was bitauȝte prestes to fede.

6. To TEACH, instruct.

a1300 *Cursor M.* 15669 Quen he ha þus-gat þam bi-taght, stil he left þam þare. c1435 *Torr. Portugal* 1664 He is of the deville betaught.

7. in *pa. pple.* Related.

a1300 *Cursor M.* 13222 Of hei oxspring þan es þis ion.. Nere be-taght to mild mari.

beteam(e, obs. form of BETEEM *v. Obs.*

†**be'tear**, *v.*[1] *Obs.* [f. BE- 6 + TEAR *sb.*] *trans.* To suffuse with tears. Hence **be'teared** *ppl. a.*

1580 SIDNEY *Arcadia* I. 81 When I lift my beteard eyes. 1635 J. HAYWARD *Banish'd Virg.* 44 Staring about them with beteared eyes.

betear, *v.*[2]: see the ppl. a. BETORN.

†**be'tee**, *v. Obs.* For forms see TEE, draw, lead. [Com. Teut.: OE. *betéon* (:—*bitéohan*), pa. t. *betéah*, *betuȝon*, pple. *betoȝen*, = OHG. *biziohan*, MHG. *beziehen*, Goth. *bitiuhan*; f. *bi-*, BE- + *tiuhan* in OE. **téohan*, *téon* to draw.]

1. To draw over (as a covering), to cover, veil.

c893 K. ÆLFRED *Oros.* v. vii. §2 Heora scyldas wæron be-toȝene mid [elpenda] hydum. c1250 *Gen. & Ex.* 3796 Ðor [h]aueth a skie hem wel bitoȝen. c1380 *Sir Ferumb.* 4539 He was þanne to-be-toȝe With an hard crested serpentis fel.

2. To pull or tug at.

c1205 LAY. 7536 And þus heo [Julius & Nennius] hit [þe sweord] longe bituȝen.

3. To employ, spend, bestow (time, pains, etc.).

c1175 *Lamb. Hom.* 31 On sum stude þer hit beoð wel bi-toȝen for cristes luue. c1205 LAY. 13010 Ȝe scullen..eowre while wel biteon. c1250 *Gen. & Ex.* 3626 Here swinc wel he biten.

4. To bring about, manage, arrange.

c1205 LAY. 23253 Wælle wel wes hit bitoȝen þat Walwai wes to monne iboren.

†**beteela.** *Obs.* Also (6 beatillia), 7 beteela, betille, 7–8 bettily, bettillee, bettelle, betellee, 8 betelle, betteela. [A word without any fixed form written or spoken, of constant occurrence in the East Indian trade in 17–18th c. It appears to be identified with the Pg. *beatilha* 'linen to make

white veils for women,' Sp. *beatilla* 'sort of fine thin linen'; but whether this is = med.L. *beatilla*, dim. of *beata* a nun, a religious 'sister' (see Du Cange, and cf. BATTALIA [pie]), or whether it was originally an oriental word, which assumed that form in Pg. under the influence of pop. etymol., is uncertain.] A kind of muslin formerly imported from the East Indies.

1598 W. PHILLIPS *Linschoten's Trav. Ind.* 28 (Y.) This linnen..is called..Beatillias, Satopassas. **1685** in J. T. WHEELER *Madras in O.T.* I. 149 (Y.) To servants, 3 pieces beteelaes. **1687** *Lond. Gaz.* No. 2269/3, 2000 pieces of Betilles Otisaeles, 1400 pieces of Betilles Calemapho, etc. *Ibid.* No. 2273/7 Bettelles. **1696** *Merchants Wareho.* 2 Musling called Bettilies, which is of general use for cravats. *Ibid.* 3 Very thin, but..very little worse than the first Bettily that I have mentioned. **1703** *Lond. Gaz.* No. 3933/4 The Cargo..consisting of Long Cloth, Sallampoores, Betelles. **1721** C. KING *Brit. Merch.* I. 310 Betellees or fine Muslins. **1727** A. HAMILTON *Acc. E. Ind.* I. 264 (Y.) This country [Sundah] produced the finest Betteelas or Muslins in India.

†**be'teem**, *v.*[1] *Obs.* Also 6–7 beteeme, 7 beteam(e, betemme, (*erron.* beterme). [App. f. BE- 2 + TEEM, to think fit; but the rarity of the simple vb., and its non-occurrence in ME. or OE. (though in OS. *teman*, OHG. *zeman*) raise historical difficulties of which there is at present no solution. *Beteem* is parallel to Du. *betamen*.]

1. *trans.* To think fit or proper; to vouchsafe, grant, consent. Const. *inf.* or *obj. clause.*

1565 GOLDING *Ovid's Met.* x. 157 (R.) Yet could he not beteeme The shape of any other bird than eagle for to seeme. **1641** MILTON *Animadv.* Wks. 1738 I. 95 He could have well beteem'd to have thank'd him of the ease he profer'd. **1642** ROGERS *Naaman* 170 He cannot beteame to promote his Master's with the losse of his owne. **1647** WARD *Simp. Cobler* 25 Gray Gravity it selfe can well beteam, That Language be adapted to the Theme.

2. To vouchsafe, accord, grant, concede. (*Const.* To beteem a person a thing, a thing *to* a possessor.)

1590 SHAKS. *Mids. N.* I. i. 131 Raine, which I could well Beteeme them, from the tempest of mine eyes. **1642** ROGERS *Naaman* 53 Still I can beteame thee that same loue, if thou wert not weary of it. **1654** TRAPP *Comm. Ezra* i. 6 David..could beteeme God more love and service then he is able to bestow. **1674** N. FAIRFAX *Bulk & Selv.* 108 We can no more betemme wholeness to the one, than to the other.

b. To allow, permit (*to do* something). *rare.*

1602 SHAKS. *Ham.* I. ii. 141 That he might not beteene [*v.r.* beteeme] the windes..Visit her face too roughly.

3. To think (a person) worthy, to admit the worth of.

1627 W. SCLATER *Expos. 2 Thess.* (1632) 221 Grace may be emulous, is not envious; easily, willingly, fainely beteemes another.

†**be'teem**, *v.*[2] *Obs. rare*[−1]. [f. BE- 1 + TEEM *v.* to empty, pour.] *trans.* To pour all about.

1618 T. ADAMS *Gener. Serp.* Wks. I. 75 These..beteem their poison..to the overthrow of all.

beteem (bɪ'ti:m), *v.*[3] *rare*[−1]. [f. BE- 2 + TEEM, to bring forth.] *trans.* To give birth to.

1855 SINGLETON *Virgil* I. 88 Then earth with cursed birth both Ceus and Iapetus Beteems [*creat*].

be'teeming, *vbl. sb. rare*[−1]. [f. BETEEM *v.*[2] + -ING[1].] Copious outpouring, profusion.

1871 R. ELLIS *Catullus* lxvi. 17 The parents' joy dashes a showery tear, When to the nuptial door they come in rainy beteeming.

betel ('bi:t(ə)l). Forms; 6 betola, bettel(l, 6–7 bettele, 7 betele, betell, bethel, betre, bettaile, bettle, 7–9 betle, beetle, 8 betelle, 7– betel. [Prob. immed. a Pg. *betel* (Varthema 1510), *betele*, formerly also *vitele*, *betle*, *betre*, ad. Malayâlam *vettila* (in Tamil *vettilei*; cf. Skr. *vîti* 'betel').]

1. a. The leaf of a plant, which is wrapped round a few parings of the areca nut (see 2) and a little shell lime, and chewed by the natives of India and neighbouring countries as a masticatory. **b.** Also the shrubby evergreen plant (*Piper betle* or *Chavica betel*, N.O. *Piperaceæ*) which yields this leaf; called also ***betel-pepper***, ***betel-vine***. **c.** Hence *comb.* and *attrib.*, as ***betel-box***, ***-carrier***, ***-server***; ***betel-leaf***, etc.

1585 LLOYD *Treas. Health* N iij, Take of Cloves..of bettels, of Galingale. **1598** W. PHILIPS *Linschoten's Trav. Ind.* (1864) 183 They doe nothing, but sit and chaw Leaues or Herbes, called Bettele with Chaulke and a certaine Fruit called Arrequa. *a* **1626** BACON *Sylva* §738 Betell is but champed in the Mouth, with a little Lime. **1697** DAMPIER *Voy.* (1729) II. I. 24 The Betle of Tonquin is said to be the best in India. **1851** R. BURTON *Goa* 106 The Gentoo will..chew his betel, and squirt the scarlet juice all over the floor. **1871** MATEER *Travancore* 97 Betel is the dark green heart-shaped leaf of a kind of climbing pepper plant, which grows like hops on poles.

b. 1553 EDEN *Treat. New Ind.* (Arb.) 21 The herbe called Betola. **1606** E. SCOTT *E. Indians* N ij, A certaine hearbe called bettaile. **1611** COTGR., *Tambu*, the bastard Pepper plant called Bettle or Betre. **1633** H. COGAN *Pinto's Trav.* (1663) 263 Bethel, an herb whose leaves..these Pagans are accustomed to chaw. **1859** R. BURTON *Centr. Afr.* in *Jrnl. R.G.S.* XXIX. 47 *note*, The betel pepper..resembles the piper betel, or betel vine of India. **1866** *Treas. Bot.* 88 These nuts are rolled up with a little lime in leaves of the betle-pepper.

c. 1681 R. KNOX *Hist. Ceylon* 18 The Tree that bears the Betel-leaf..grows like Ivy. **1779** FORREST *Voy. N. Guinea* 14 The beetle leaf, which all East Indians chew.

2. betel nut: the nut or fruit of the Areca Palm (see ARECA); so misnamed (by Europeans) because it is chewed with the betel leaf. Hence ***betel-nut-tree***, ***betel-tree***, Areca Catechu; **betel(nut) palm**, the Areca palm, *Areca catechu*, from which the 'betel nut' or areca nut is obtained.

1673 FRYER *New Acct. E. Ind.* 40 [Calls *areca* beetle, and *v.v.*]. **1681** R. KNOX *Hist. Ceylon* 97 Betle-nuts, 4000 nine pence Currant price. **1697** DAMPIER *Voy.* (1729) I. 318 The Betel-Tree grows like the Cabbage-Tree..On the top of the Tree among the Branches the Betel-Nut grows. **1772** LD. CLIVE in *Weekly Mag.* 117/2 The privilege of free trade in beetle-nut being taken away. **1858** CARPENTER *Veg. Phys.* §370 Betel-nuts are chewed by the natives of Hindoostan. **1861** BENTLEY *Man. Bot.* 684 The Catechu or Betel Nut Palm. **1875** *Encycl. Brit.* III. 616/2 The betel nut is the fruit of the Areca or betel palm, *Areca Catechu*.

betel, -ll(e, obs. form of BEETLE.

Betelgeuse ('bɛtəldʒu:z, ‖-ɛlʒœz, 'bi:-). *Astr.* Also **Betelgeux** (-ʒœ). [Fr. *Bételgeuse*, f. Arab.] A yellowish-red variable star of the first magnitude, the brightest in the constellation of Orion.

1796 C. HUTTON *Math. & Philos. Dict.* I. 205/1 *Betelgeuse*, a fixed star of the first magnitude in the right shoulder of Orion. **1820** H. BROOKE *Guide to Stars* 12 A line from the Pleiades..will give Bellatrix in the western shoulder of Orion, and the bright star immediately to the eastward is Betelgeux in the right or eastern shoulder. **1866** J. N. LOCKYER tr. *Guillemin's Heavens* II. viii. 355 Betelgeuse, the brightest star in Orion, and Aldebaran show a decided red tint. *a* **1930** D. H. LAWRENCE *Last Poems* (1932) 49 The heavens are wandering The moon and the earth, the sun, Saturn and Betelgeuse. **1938** R. GRAVES *Coll. Poems* 121 We have no truck either with the forebeings Of Betelgeux or with the atom's git. **1955** *Oxf. Jun. Encycl.* III. 109/2 On Orion's shoulder the giant orange star Betelgeuse shines. **1962** *Listener* 31 May 950/1 Betelgeux in Orion..is a typical Red Giant.

†**be'tell,** *v. Obs.* Forms: *Inf.* 1 betellan, 2–4 bitelle(n, 4 bitele, 5 betelle, (6 betele). *Pa. t.* 3 bitald(e, -told(e. *Pa. pple.* 3 bitald, 5 betolde. [OE. *betęllan*, f. BE- 1 + *tęllan* to TELL.]

1. *trans.* To speak for, answer for, justify.

1048 *O.E. Chron.* (Laud MS.) þæt he [Godwin] moste hine betellan. *a* **1250** *Owl & Night.* 263 Lust hu ich con me bi-telle Mid riȝte sothe.

2. To speak of, declare, narrate.

c **1205** LAY. 15868 Ȝif ich..mid soðe hit bitelle · þat heore talen sinde lese. *c* **1425** WYNTOUN *Cron.* II. viii. 128 As yhe haf herd before be-talde.

3. To lay claim to; to win; to rescue.

c **1205** LAY. 7894 Bi-ðencheð eow ohte cnihtes to bi-tellen eowere rihtes. *Ibid.* 18099 þu hauest Brutlond al bitald To þire hond. *c* **1250** *Gen. & Ex.* 920 Loth was fifti winter hold Quan Abram him bitold.

4. To calumniate, deride, deceive. [Perh. there is here properly a vb. *bitelen*, f. OE. *tælan* to speak ill of, calumniate: esp. in the last quot.]

a **1225** *Ancr. R.* 226 He þeonne mid tet, birleð [*v.r.* bitelleþ] him ilome. *a* **1240** *Lofsong* in *Lamb. Hom.* 205 þet heo hire ne muwen bitellen. *a* **1300** *Cursor M.* 6890 He..wrat þe nam, and sett to sele, þat man suld oþer nan bitele. *a* **1460** *Towneley Myst.* 217 He shalle with alle his mawmentry No longere us be telle. **1567** HARMAN *Caveat* 67 She sayth that they be her children, that beteled be babes borne of such abhominable bellye.

betemme, variant of BETEEM *v.*[1] *Obs.*

beten, obs. f. BEATEN, also of BEAT, BEET *v.*

‖**bête noire** (bɛ:t nwɑ:r, beɪt nwɑ:(r)). [Fr., lit. 'black beast'; *fig.* insufferable person.] A person or thing that is the bane of a person or his life; an insufferable person or thing; an object of aversion.

1844 THACKERAY *Barry Lyndon* xvii. in *Fraser's Mag.* XXX. 235/1 Calling me her bête noire, her dark spirit, her murderous adorer, and a thousand other names indicative of her extreme disquietude and terror. **1850** *Household Wds.* 6 July 359/1 You or any one else's *bête noire* is apt to get polished off with a few extra touches of blacking. **1860** W. H. RUSSELL *Diary India* I. 209 Jung Bahadoor, who is evidently the present *bête noir* of our General's life. **1866** MRS. H. WOOD *Elster's Folly* xiv, It was the bête noire of Clerk Gum's life. **1905** *Spectator* (Lit. Suppl.) 28 Jan. 118/2 [His] *bête-noire* is the submission of military affairs to the control of 'political exigencies'. **1961** L. MUMFORD *City in History* x. 290 As for the disposal of ordure, this has always been the bête noire of close urban settlements.

beter(e, obs. form of BEATER, BETTER.

‖**bête rouge** (bɛ:t ru:ʒ, beɪt ru:ʒ). [Fr., lit. 'red beast'.] A species of *Trombidium* (see quots.).

1909 *Cent. Dict.* Suppl., *Bête-rouge*,..probably a larval *Trombidium*, which in the West Indies corresponds to the so-called 'red bug' or 'jigger' of the southern United States. **1932** DORLAND *Med. Dict.* (ed. 16) 191/1 *Bête rouge*, the red mite of Martinique and Honduras which burrows into the skin. It is probably a species of *Trombidium*. **1934** E. WAUGH *Handful of Dust* v. 267 He had picked up bêtes rouges in the bush and they were crawling and burrowing under his skin.

beth(e, = shall be, is, are, be(ye): see BE *v.*

†**be'thank,** *v. Obs. rare*[−1]. [f. BE- 2 + THANK.] *trans.* To thank.

1593 BARNES *Eleg.* in Arb. *Garner* V. 412 They must climb Into your bosom, to bethank their friend.

bethankit, ellipt. for *God be thanked* (Sc. *thankit*), as grace after meat.

1787 BURNS *To Haggis*, Then auld guid man, maist like to rive, Bethankit hums.

Beth Din (beɪt 'di:n). Also **Beth-Din, Bethdin.** [Heb. *bēth* house, *dīn* judgement.] A Jewish court composed of the Chief Rabbi and two or more assistants, responsible for matters of Jewish ecclesiastical law and the settlement of disputes between Jews.

1795 WILLIAM SCOTT in J. Haggard *Rep. Cases Consist. Crt.* (1822) I. 244 The Answers of the Bethdin to the Questions proposed by the Court. **1897** *Daily News* 30 Jan. 3/3 Are you in competition with the Chief Rabbi in his Court the Beth Din? **1928** *Sunday Dispatch* 30 Dec. 7/2 Should the proceedings of London's Jewish House of Judgment—the Beth-Din—be kept secret?

bethel ('bɛθəl). [Heb. *bēth-ēl* house of God.]

1. A hallowed spot; a place where God is worshipped; the pillar that marks such a place. (See *Gen.* xxviii. 17.)

a **1617** HIERON *Wks.* II. 241 Whence it is that such places are termed *Bethels*, 'Gods houses.' **1641** HINDE *J. Bruen* xv. 50 Raising up an altar for Gods worship in his family, and so making it a little Bethel. **1840** S. F. ADAMS *Hymn 'Nearer my God'* iv, Out of my stony griefs Bethels I'll raise.

2. Sometimes used (esp. by some Methodists and Baptists) like 'Zion,' 'Zoar,' 'Bethesda,' etc., as the designation of their chapel or meeting-house; sometimes applied *fig.*, or as in 'Little Bethel,' in contempt, to any place of worship other than those of the established church. Also a place of worship for seamen (a sense apparently first used in U.S.)

1840 R. DANA *Bef. Mast* 145 The establishment of Bethels in most of our own seaports..where the gospel is regularly preached. **1865** *Reader* 15 Apr. 415/3 The class contemptuously described as dividing its energies between business and bethels. **1867** SMYTH *Sailor's Wd. Bk.*, *Bethel, Floating Bethel*, an old ship fitted up in a port for the purpose of public worship. **1875** EMERSON *Lett. & Soc. Aims* iii. 93 You may find him in some lowly Bethel, by the seaside.

bethel, *v. nonce-wd.* (See quot.)

a **1733** NORTH *Exam.* 93 (D.) In the year 1680 Bethel and Cornish were chosen sheriffs. The former..kept no house, but lived upon chops, whence it is proverbial for not feasting to Bethel the city.

bethel, obs. form of BETEL.

Bethell ('bɛθəl). The name of John *Bethell*, a nineteenth-century American inventor, used *attrib.* or in the possessive to designate a process of wood preservation (see quot. 1940).

1838 *Brit. Pat.* 7731 (*title*) Rendering wood, cork, and other articles more durable, &c. Bethell's specification. **1901** *Trans. Amer. Soc. Civil Engin.* XLV. 503 All the French roads [*i.e.* railways] but one have creosoting by the 'Bethell' process. **1940** *Chambers's Techn. Dict.* 88/2 *Bethell's process*, a process for preserving timber, which is first dried, then subjected to a partial vacuum within a special cylinder, and finally impregnated with creosote under pressure. **1962** W. P. K. FINDLAY *Preservation of Timber* iii. 38 Bethell's process is often called the Full Cell Process because it results in filling the cells of the treated zone with a liquid.

bethenche, -thenke, obs. forms of BETHINK.

betheral, -el, variants of BEDRAL, beadle.

Bethesda (bɛ'θɛzdə). [The name of a healing pool mentioned at John 5. 2–4, perh. representing *Bethzatha*, and understood to mean 'house of grace'.] Occasionally (chiefly in the nineteenth cent.) adopted by Methodists, Baptists, Independents, etc., as the name of a particular chapel or meeting-house. Hence also as a synonym for 'Nonconformist chapel'.

1857 TROLLOPE *Barchester T.* I. vii. 100 They would..stick him up in some new Sion or Bethesda, and put the cathedral quite out of fashion. **1911** A. BENNETT *Odd Volume* 14 Ye must come to th' Bethesda down yon, on Sunday morning, and hear the word o' God. **1953** DYLAN THOMAS *Under Milk Wood* (1954) 20 Look, over Bethesda grave-stones one hoots and swoops and catches a mouse by Hannah Reese, Beloved Wife. **1976** D. MORGAN *Thomas the Fish* xi. 126 Bethesda (a split from Zion) had a sermon about the Congregation.

Beth Hamidrash (beɪt hamɪ'drɑ:ʃ). Also **Bet Hamidrash, Beth Hamedrash, Beth Hammidrash.** [Heb. *bēth hammidhrāsh*, lit. 'house of study'.] (See quot. 1962.)

1874 *Jewish Directory* 17 Beth Hamedrash. Smith's Buildings, 75, Leadenhall Street, E.C. For the study and exposition of the Scriptures and Commentaries and Hebrew Literature generally. **1887** *Encycl. Brit.* XXII. 811/2 The school (*bēth hammidrāsh*) trained scholars, but the synagogue..was the means of popular instruction. **1892**

ZANGWILL *Childr. Ghetto* (1893) I. v. 57 The learned Rabbonim, who sat shaking themselves all day in the Beth Hamidrash. **1962** BRIDGER & WOLK *New Jewish Encycl.* 51/1 *Bet Ha-Midrash*, Hebrew term meaning 'house of study', applied to a place where Jews congregate for prayer and study... The term is also applied to a rabbinical school for higher studies.

bethink (bɪˈθɪŋk), *v.* Pa. t. and pple. **bethought** (bɪˈθɔːt). In OE. *biþencan*, ME. *bithenchen*, *bithenke*: for variants see THINK. [Com. Teut.: OE. *biþęncan* = OS. *bithenkjan*, OHG. *bidenchan* (MHG., mod.G., Du. *bedenken*), Goth. *biþagkjan*:—OTeut. **biþaŋkjan*, f. *bi-*, BE- + *þaŋkjan* to THINK. The sense-development may be compared with that of ADVISE *v.* and F. *aviser*.]

I. *trans.*

1. To think of or about, bear in mind; to call to mind, recollect. *Obs.* exc. with clause.

a **1000** *Guthlac* 1270 (Gr.) Tid is, þat þu fere and þa ærendu eal biþence. *c* **1250** LAY. 8257 Biþench þat he was Lud kinges sone. *c* **1374** CHAUCER *Troylus* I. 982 Her bewte to bythenkyn, and her youthe. **1597** J. PAYNE *Royal Exch.* 33 Bethinck that the crowne of glorie is set forthe.. in the end of the race. **1601** SHAKS. *Per.* V. i. 44 'Tis well bethought. **1885** E. ARNOLD *Secr. Death* 10 Bethink How those of old, the saints, clove to their word.

†**b.** To think upon or remember (a person). *Obs.*

c **1320** *Cast. Loue* 482 And to habben me bi-þouht. *c* **1350** *Leg. Rood* (1871) 19 A bi-heste he hedde Whon þe tyme weore folfuld vr lord him wolde biþenche. *c* **1449** PECOCK *Repr.* II. v. 164 We bithenken tho persoones.

†**2.** To think of, imagine, conceive. *Obs.*

c **1175** *Lamb. Hom.* 25 Biþenchen mid his fule heorte þe heo wulle underfon swa heȝ þing. *c* **1386** CHAUCER *Wyf's T.* 772 He spak moore harm than herte may bithynke.

†**3.** To think over (a thing) with a view to decision or action; to consider. *Obs.*

c **1220** *Bestiary* 94 Or he it biðenken can hise eȝen weren mirke. **1297** R. GLOUC. 289 Hii.. byþoȝte hou hii myȝte best myd þe holy body do. *c* **1350** *Will. Palerne* 2747 þe werewolf ..biþout how were best þe bestes to help. **1577** NORTHBROOKE *Dicing* (1843) 10 Al things which he hath.. either intended, bythought, said, or done. **1614** R. WILKINSON *Paire Serm.* Ep. Ded., Bethinking by what meanes I might best either expresse or deserve thankes. **1647** F. BLAND *Souldiers March* 32 If they should.. seriously bethink what clemencie..they would desire, if in the same case.

†**4.** To devise, contrive, plan, arrange. *Obs.*

a **1225** *Juliana* 67 Greiðe al þat þu const grimliche biþenchen. *c* **1320** *Cast. Loue* 698 Seue berbicans.. Wiþ gret ginne al bi-þouht. *c* **1440** *Gesta Rom.* 35 Go we alle anon to the Emperour, and be-thynke vs a remedye. **1593** SHAKS. *3 Hen. VI*, III. iii. 39 We bethinke a meanes to breake it off.

†**5.** To regret, repent, grudge (= OE. *ofþęncan*.)

1682 NORRIS *Hierocles* 24 Neither ought we to bethink what we spend upon them. **1687** in *Lond. Gaz.* No. 2252/5 That Your Majesty may never have cause.. to withdraw or bethink the.. Liberty given us. **1696** LOCKE in F. Bourne *Life* II. xiii. 338, I can never bethink any pains or time of mine in the service of my country.

†**6.** *causal.* To remind (one) *of*, *that*. *Obs.*

1340 *Ayenb.* 100 þis word uader þe beþengþ þet þou art zone.

II. *refl.*

†**7.** To collect one's thoughts; to take thought; to recollect oneself, return to oneself. *Obs.*

c **1000** *Ags. Gosp.* Luke xv. 17 þa beþohte he hine and cwæð. *a* **1200** *Moral Ode* 43 in *Lamb. Hom.* 161 Wel late ich habbe me bi-þocht. **1483** CAXTON *Gold. Leg.* 244/1 She bethoughte her and prayed thus in her self. **1611** BIBLE *1 Kings* viii. 47 If they shall bethinke themselues.. and repent. **1649** MILTON *Eikon.* ad. fin., The rest..may find the grace ..to bethink themselves and recover.

8. To occupy oneself in thought; to reflect, consider, think; *also*, to call to mind, recollect.

c **1205** LAY. 7664 Ælc Frensc mon þe wes aht hæfð hine seolfne biþoht. *a* **1225** *Ancr. R.* 200 ȝif heo hire wel bi-ðouhte. *c* **1330** *Arth. & Merl.* 893 The iustice him gan bi-thenche, And thus aposed that wenche. *a* **1450** *Knt. de la Tour* (1868) 56 Eve..ansuered to lightely withoute bethenkinge her. **1575** LANEHAM *Let.* (1871) 51 Ile tell yoo if I can, when I haue better bethought me. **1603** SHAKS. *Meas. for M.* II. ii. 145, I will bethinke me: come againe to morrow. **1740** L. CLARKE *Hist. Bible* VIII. 525 Advising them to bethink themselves, and to take soberer measures. **1820** W. IRVING *Sketch Bk.* I. 83 Rip bethought himself a moment.

b. with *inf.* (obs.) or *obj. clause*, esp. indirect interrogative.

c **1175** *Lamb. Hom.* 155 Hwenne ho hom biðohten þet heo isuneȝed hefden. *c* **1386** CHAUCER *Pers. T.* ¶228 Bythynke him wel that he hath deserved thilke peynes. **1634** HEYWOOD *M'head lost* IV. Wks. 1874 IV. 148 Bethinke thee what thou vndertak'st. **1851** HELPS *Comp. Solit.* vi. (ed. 1874) 84 To bethink themselves how little they may owe to their own merit.

c. with *of* (formerly *on*, *upon*).

c **1200** ORMIN 2917 þatt Godess þeoww himm ȝeorne birrþ Biþennkenn & bilokenn, Off all þatt tatt he wile don. **1297** R. GLOUC. 368 Kyng Wyllam byþoȝte hym ek of þe volc, þat was verlore. *c* **1380** WYCLIF *Wks.* (1880) 372 He by-þouȝte hym on þis swerde. **1413** LYDG. *Pylgr. Sowle* V. v. (1859) 76 Thenne I bethought me vppon the byrdes. **1603** SHAKS. *Meas. for M.* V. i. 461, I haue bethought me of another fault. **1870** BRYANT *Iliad* I. IV. 113 The Greeks will.. Bethink them of their country.

9. To take it into one's head, propose to oneself, resolve. (F. *s'aviser*.)

c **1325** *E.E. Allit. P.* B. 125 þe mayster him biþoȝt, þat he wolde se þe semblé. **1387** TREVISA *Higden* I. 139 þanne þe lordes byþouȝte hem..oþerwise to fiȝte. **1601** SHAKS. *Jul. C.* IV. iii. 251 It may be I shall otherwise bethinke me. **1712** STEELE *Spect.* No. 264 ¶5 A Fellow..has bethought himself of joining Profit and Pleasure together. **1884** COURTHOPE *Addison* iv. 58 Charles naturally bethought himself of calling literature to his assistance.

III. *intr.*

10. To consider, reflect, meditate, think. *arch.*

c **1300** *Beket* 43 He moste bithenche, For he was stronge adrad ȝut. **1382** WYCLIF *Gen.* xxiv. 63 He was goon out to bithenk in the feeld. **1413** LYDG. *Pylgr. Sowle* I. xiv. (1859) 11, I gan to bythenke to me yf euer I had seruyd ony seynt. **1590** SWINBURN *Testaments* Ded., Bethinking vvith myselfe (most reuerende Father). **1817** BYRON *Manfred* I. i. 167 Bethink ere thou dismiss us, ask again.

†**b.** with *of*, *on*, *upon*; = 1-4. *Obs.*

a **1200** *Moral Ode* 162 in *Trin. Coll. Hom.* 224 He biðohte an helle fur. *c* **1205** LAY. 5021 Biðenc o ðire monschipe. *a* **1300** *Floriz & Bl.* 428 While i biþenche of sume ginne. **1384** CHAUCER *H. Fame* 1176 On this Castell to bethynke. **1597** J. PAYNE *Royal Exch.* 10, I wyshe..the exchange..to bethinck on the wayters..on there..soules. **1608** J. KING *Serm.* 38 His Eie-liddes haue considered and bethought of the means. **1647** W. BROWNE *Polex.* II. 75 He bethought on the meanes.

IV. *passive.*

11. *to be bethought*: to bethink oneself (in senses 7, 8, 9). See also BETHOUGHT.

c **1250** *O.E. Misc.* 166 To bidden his milce to late we beoð biþohte. *c* **1386** CHAUCER *Prol.* 767 Of a myrthe I am right now bythoght To doon yow ese. *c* **1420** *Pallad. on Husb.* I. 1080 It is not strange..An husbonde on his baathe to be bethought. **1605** SHAKS. *Lear* II. iii. 6 And am bethought To take the basest, and most poorest shape.

bethinking (bɪˈθɪŋkɪŋ), *vbl. sb.* [f. prec. + -ING¹.] The action of thinking, considering, reflecting, or remembering.

1340 *Ayenb.* 233 þou sselt louye god..mid al þine beþenchinge wyþoute uoryetinge. *a* **1520** *Myrr. Our Ladye* 246 Sorowe..that came of the bethynkynge of payne and of dethe. **1592** SHAKS. *Ven. & Ad.* 1024 Trifles vnwitnessed.. Thy coward heart with false bethinking greeues. **1873** MRS. WHITNEY *Other Girls* xxi. 290 The footstep suddenly checked; then, as if with..swift bethinking, it went by.

bethlehem, bethlem: see BEDLAM.

†**'Bethlehemite.** *Obs.* Also **Bethlemite.** [f. BETHLEHEM + -ITE.] One of an order of monks existing in England in the 13th century; they wore a five-rayed star upon the breast, in memory of the star which announced the Nativity of Christ at Bethlehem.

1721 in BAILEY.

bethorn, bethreaten, bethunder: see BE-.

bethought (bɪˈθɔːt), *pple.* and *a.* [f. BETHINK.]

†**1.** Of a thing: Intended, purposed, contrived. *Obs.*

c **1200** *Trin. Coll. Hom.* 63 Beten [we] for þat we hauen agilt her biforen..oðer recheluste ðe is erueðer to betende, oðer to biþohte þinge þe is swiþe erueðer to betende.

†**2.** Of a person: Minded, disposed; chiefly in comb. with *well-*, *ill-*, etc. *Obs.*

c **1205** LAY. 8831 Nu is min eam wel biðoht. *a* **1250** *O.E. Misc.* 69 Nere we nouht so ofte bicherd ne so vuele by-þouhte. *c* **1430** *Syr Tryam.* 1539 Now am y welle bethoght.

bethout, variant of BYTHOUT, without.

†**'bethphany, -ie.** *Obs.* [ad. med.L. *bethphania*, made up of Heb. *beth* house, and *-phania*, Gr. -φάνεια showing, manifestation, in ἐπιφάνεια EPIPHANY.] A term invented by the Schoolmen for the 'third divine manifestation' commemorated in the feast of Epiphany, viz. the miracle 'in the house' at Cana of Galilee.

1635 AUSTIN *Medit.* 55 By three Apparitions our Saviour was manifested this day..the third was the Bethphania *in Domo* when at a Marriage hee turned Water into Wine in a House..Though the Feast bee of all the three Manifestations, yet the Epiphany hath carried away the name both from the Theophanie and the Bethphanie. **1875** SMITH *Dict. Chr. Antiq.* I. 619/1. **1883** STALLYBRASS tr. *Grimm's Teut. Mythol.* II. 586 That miracle [turning water into wine] to which was given a special name, *bethphania*.

bethral, -el, var. of BEDRAL, beadle. Hence, **bethrelian**, *a. nonce-wd.*

1870 RAMSAY *Remin.* (ed. 18) Introd. 36 The *esprit de corps* of the bethrelian mind.

†**be'thrall,** *v. Obs. rare*⁻¹. [f. BE- 5 + THRALL.] *trans.* To enthrall, enslave.

1596 SPENSER *F.Q.* I. viii. 28 She..did my lord bethrall.

†**be'through,** *prep. Obs. rare*⁻¹. In 5 *Sc.* be throwch. [f. BE- + THROUGH.] Throughout.

c **1425** WYNTOUN *Cron.* VII. vi. 355 Be throwch þe Land traweland.

†**be'throw,** *v. Obs. rare.* [f. BE- 1 + THROW *v.*] *trans.* To 'throw' or twist about, to torture.

1393 GOWER *Conf.* III. 5, I with loue am so bethrowe.. That I am veriliche dronke.

bethumb (bɪˈθʌm), *v.* [f. BE- 1 + THUMB *v.*] To take hold of or mark with the thumbs. Hence **be'thumbed** *ppl. a.*

1657 H. CROWCH *Welsh. Trav.* 19 The bread and butter so bethums. **1822** *Blackw. Mag.* XI. 64 Bethumbing and bequoting their beauties into triteness and commonplace. **1840** POE *W. Wilson* Wks. I. 420 Much-bethumbed books.

bethump (bɪˈθʌmp), *v.* [f. BE- 2 + THUMP *v.*] *trans.* To thump soundly. Also *fig.* Hence, **be'thumped** *ppl. a.*, **be'thumping** *vbl. sb.*

1595 SHAKS. *John* II. i. 466, I was neuer so bethumped with words. **1657** H. CROWCH *Welsh Trav.* 6 Those stones did so bethump her bones. **1826** SCOTT *Woodst.* (1832) I. 92 Bethumping us with his texts. **1831** *Fraser's Mag.* III. 102 Here's a bethumping of words, with a vengeance.

bethwack (bɪˈθwæk), *v.* [f. BE- 2 + THWACK.] *trans.* To pelt, thrash, or cudgel soundly.

1555 *Fardle Facions* I. vi. 92 They..haue a good sporte to all to bethwacke it with stones. **1598** R. BERNARD tr. *Terence Andr.* I. ii. (1629) 16, I will all to becurry thee, or bethwacke thy coate. **1848** LOWELL *Poet. Wks.* (1879) 143 He bangs and bethwacks them.

bethwine (ˈbɛθwaɪn). Also **bethwyn, pethwind.** [Of unknown derivation: the second element is perh. *wind*: the whole looks like a perversion of *bend-with* or *bind-with*.] A name given locally to various twining plants: **a.** The Great Hedge Convolvulus (*C. sepium*). **b.** The Bear-bind (*Polygonum Convolvulus*). **c.** The Traveller's Joy (*Clematis Vitalba*).

1609 C. BUTLER *Fem. Mon.* (1623) iii. F iij, And then with a small pliant Garth or Belt of Bethwyn, Bramble, Brier, or the like, gird the Hackle close to the Hiue. **1863** KINGSLEY *Water Bab.* (1878) 187 There was no more hope of rooting out them than of rooting out peth-winds [*convolvulus*]. **1875** PARISH *Sussex Gloss.*, *Bethwine*, the wild clematis.

betide (bɪˈtaɪd), *v.* Forms: 2-3 bitiden, 3-4 bi-, bytyden, 4-5 bi-, bytide, 4-7 betyd(e, 4- betide. *Pa. t.* 3-4 bitidde, 4 bitide, 4-5 bi-, bytidd, -tydde, 5 bytid, beted, 5-6 betyd, -tid, 6 -tyded, -tided. *Pa. pple.* 3-4 bitid, 4-5 betyd, 5-6 betid, 4-5 bi-, betyde, 5-7 betide, 6 betidde, -tidd, (-tight), 7 -tyded, 6- betided, 9 betid. [ME. *bitide-n*, f. *bi-*, BE- 2 + *tide-n* to happen; see TIDE *v.*]

1. *intr.* To happen, befall. Only in 3rd pers. and often *impers.*

c **1250** *Gen. & Ex.* 2358 Sone it was king pharaon kid Hu ðis newe tiding wurð bi-tid. **1297** R. GLOUC. 418 He nolde non lenger abyde..tyde wat so bytyde. *a* **1300** *Cursor M.* 21723 Has bitid oft mani quar, þat less folk ouercummen þe mar. *c* **1380** WYCLIF *Wks.* (1880) 377 þe casis þat bitydden bytwene..naaman and heliȝe. *c* **1420** *Anturs Arth.* i, In the tyme of Arther thys antur be-tydde. **1591** SPENSER *M. Hubberd* 37 A strange adventure, that betided Betwixt the Foxe and th' Ape. **1647** W. BROWNE *Polex.* II. 199 The wounded man..about to aske what was betided. **1765** H. WALPOLE *Otranto* iii. (1798) 55 The death of my son betiding while my soul was under this anxiety. *a* **1802** *Pop. Rime attrib. to T. of Erceld.* in Scott *Minstr.* III. 209 Betide betide, whatever betide, Haig shall be Haig of Bemerside. **1870** MORRIS *Earthly Par.* III. IV. 3 Who 'gan to tell Mishaps betid upon the winter seas.

b. Const. *dative object*; occas. *to*, *unto*.

c **1175** *Lamb. Hom.* 71 Ac ȝif us eni ufel bitit: þonke we gode in ure wit. *c* **1250** LAY. 2237 Wel þe sal bityde. *c* **1386** *Miller's T.* 264 A man woot litel what him schal betyde. *c* **1430** *How Gd. Wijf tauȝte D.* 174 in *Babees Bk.* (1868) 45 What-sum-euere þee bitide, Make not þin husbonde poore with spendinge. **1579** SPENSER *Sheph. Cal.* Nov. 174 As if some euill were to her betight [*gloss.* happened]. **1603** KNOLLES *Hist. Turks* (1621) 122 Which calamitie betided unto the Christians. **1832** HT. MARTINEAU *Hill & Vall.* ix. 139 Whatever fortune betides you.

c. *esp.* in the expression of a wish. Now almost exclusively in 'Woe betide!'

c **1325** *E.E. Allit. P.* B. 522 Multyplyez on þis molde, & menske yow bytyde. **1393** LANGL. *P. Pl.* C. IV. 157 Er ich wedde suche a wif· wo me by-tyde. **1633** HEYWOOD *Eng. Trav.* IV. Wks. 1874 IV. 70 A happy Morning now betide you Lady. **1808** SCOTT *Marm.* III. xxiii, But woe betide the wandering wight. **1868** G. DUFF *Pol. Surv.* (1868) 194 Woe betide the unfortunate shipmaster.

†**2.** To become *of* (rarely *on*). *Obs.*

a **1300** *Cursor M.* 3274 For be þis well sal i habide Quat o mi nerrand mai be tide. **1494** FABYAN VII. ccxxii. 246 Howe so it betyde of the kynge. **1594** SHAKS. *Rich. III*, I. iii. 6 If he were dead, what would betide on me? **1675** HOBBES *Iliad* (1677) 189 What is betide Of th' Argive threats.

†**3.** To fall to as a possession. *Obs.*

a **1300** *Cursor M.* 4035 þir breþer tuain þam tok to red To dele þair landes þam bi-tuix..Til esau bitid ebron. *c* **1430** *Syr Gener.* 4384 Twoo the best knightes of all oure side, Such twoo shal neuer vs betide. **1587** BYRD *Sonn.* in Arb. *Garner* II. 88 If I had Davids crown to me betide.

†**4.** To become or befit (any one). *Obs.*

1554 PHILPOT *Exam. & Writ.* (1842) 327 It betideth no man to doubt of the authority..of thilk things. **1566** J. STUDLEY *Seneca's Medea* (1581) 136 She threates our king more then doth her betyde.

5. In *pa. pple.* Circumstanced, beset, begone.

1470 HARDING *Chron.* ci. vii, Then with his staffe he slewe hym so betyd.

¶ *catachr.* To bode, betoken.

[Not in JOHNSON 1773.] *a* **1799** COWPER *Morn. Dream* 41 Awaking, how could I but muse At what such a dream should betide? **1850** PRESCOTT *Peru* (1856) II. 251 The Spaniards doubted..whether it betided them good or evil.

†**be'tide**, *sb. Obs. rare*⁻¹. [f. prec.] Befalling, event, fortune, chance.

1590 GREENE *Neuer too late* (1600) 87 My wretched hart wounded with bad betide.

†**be'tider.** *Obs. rare*⁻¹. [f. BETIDE *v.* + -ER.] That which betides or befalls; an accident.

1674 N. FAIRFAX *Bulk & Selv.* 196 'Tis clear that darkness or Sun-light, are such narrow betiders of body.

†**be'tiding,** *vbl. sb. Obs.* [f. BETIDE *v.* + ING[1].] Happening, occurrence.

c **1374** CHAUCER *Boeth.* v. iii. 155 Þe bytidyng of þinges y-wist byforn is necessarie.. al þouȝ þat it ne seme nat þat the prescience brynge in necessite of bytydynge of þinges to comen.

†**be'tie,** *v. Obs.* [f. BE- 1 + TIE *v.*] *trans.* To tie round, bind fast.

1578 *Parad. Dainty Dev.* B ij, I turne, I chaunge from side to side, And stretch me oft in sorrowes linkes betyde.

betight, incorrect form of pa. pple. of BETIDE.

betill(e, obs. f. BEADLE, BEETLE, BETEELA.

†**be'timber,** *v. Obs.* [OE. *betimbr(i)an*, f. BE- 1 + *timbr(i)an* to build.] *trans.* To build.

a **1000** *Beowulf* 6299 And betimbredon on tyn daȝum beadu-rofes beacn. [**1829** SOUTHEY in *Q. Rev.* 362 Finan built, or, in Saxon phrase, betimbred, a humble edifice.]

be'timbered, *ppl. a.*[f. BE- 7 + TIMBER *sb.*] Furnished with timber.

1848 H. MILLER *First Impr.* xi. (1857) 172 Its old venerable dwellings betimbered with dark oak.

†**be'time, bitime,** *v. Obs.* [f. *bi-*, BE- + *time(n* to happen: see TIME *v.*] *intr.* To betide.

a **1225** *Ancr. R.* 324 Ȝif sunne bitimeð bi nihte. *Ibid.* 340 Uorði þet swuch cas, and swuch auenture bitimeð to summe monne. *a* **1225** *St. Marher.* 2 Bitimde umbe stunde þat ter com ut of asie toward antioche þes feondes an foster.

¶ In the following the Folio of 1623 and many editions have *be time* in two words: the chronology of the verb supports their reading.

1588 SHAKS. *L.L.L.* IV. iii. 382 No time shall be omitted, That will betime [be time], and may by vs be fitted.

†**be'time,** *adv. Obs.* Also 3–4 **bitime,** 4 **bityme,** 4–6 **betyme,** 6 **bytime, -tyme.** [properly a phrase: ME. *bi-, by-time*, i.e. *by time.*]

1. In good time, early, seasonably.

a **1300** *Cursor M.* 4321 Bettur it es bi-time to stint þan folu þi prai þat es bot tint. *c* **1385** CHAUCER *L.G.W.* 452 ffor who so ȝeuyth a ȝifte or doth a grace, Do it be tyme his thank is wel the more. **1509** HAWES *Conv. Swearers* 20 Amende by tyme lest I take vengeaunce. **1595** SHAKS. *John* IV. iii. 98 Put vp thy sword betime. *a* **1632** BP. M. SMYTH *Serm.* 274 She was very betime.. lewd or naught.

2. *spec.* At an early hour, early in the day.

c **1250** *Gen. & Ex.* 1088 Elles sulen he brennen and forfaren, If he ne bi time heðe[n] waren. *a* **1300** *K. Horn* 965 For ischal beo þer bitime, A soneday bi pryme. **1558** WARDE *Alexis' Secr.* (1568) 42 a, In the morninge betime take some of the foresaied preservatives. **1606** SHAKS. *Ant. & Cl.* IV. iv. 20 To businesse that we loue, we rise betime. **1630** PAGITT *Christianogr.* III. (1636) 78 Upon Saturday morning betime.

†**be'timely,** *a. Obs. rare*⁻¹. [f. BETIME, after *timely*. Cf. Da. *betimelig* adv.] Early.

1594 CAREW *Tasso* (1881) 96 We see the morning ryse In his fresh blooming, and betimely howres.

betimes (bɪ'taɪmz), *adv.* Forms: 4 **bitimes, -tymes,** 4–5 **be-, bytymys,** 5–6 **bytymes,** 6 **betymes, bytimes,** (8–9 **by times**), 6– **betimes.** [f. BETIME + advb. genitive *-s*; cf. *beside, besides.*]

1. At an early time, period, or season; early in the year; early in life.

c **1314** *Guy Warw.* 1212 Al bi times þou miȝt wende; Ȝete no hastow ben here a moneþ to þende. **1578** LYTE *Dodoens* 208 The flowers of the first kinde, do shewe bytymes, as in Marche or before. **1611** BIBLE *Prov.* xiii. 24 He that loueth him, chasteneth him betimes. **1791** J. WILSON in Sparks *Corr. Amer. Rev.* (1853) IV. 388 Good principles.. should be laid betimes, as the foundation. **1875** HELPS *Ess.* 59 He [man of business] must learn betimes to love truth.

2. *spec.* At an early hour, early in the morning.

1481 CAXTON *Reynard* 43, I wil to morow bytymes as the sonne riseth take my way to rome. **1535** COVERDALE *Bible* Josh. vii. 16 Iosua gat him vp by tymes in the mornynge. **1601** SHAKS. *Twel. N.* II. iii. 2 Not to bee a bedde after midnight, is to be vp betimes. **1663** PEPYS *Diary* 1 Sept., Up pretty betimes, and after a little at my violl, to my office. **1828** SCOTT *F.M. Perth* III. 59, I will ride to Perth to-morrow by times.

3. In good time, in due time; while there is yet time, before it is too late.

c **1380** WYCLIF *Wks.* (1880) 372 And it wer nede þat cristis chirche toke tente to þis word by-tymys. **1545** BRINKLOW *Complaynt* (1874) 95 Repent betymes, and.. fall diligently to prayer. **1667** MILTON *P.L.* III. 186 To appease betimes Th' incensed Deitie. **1794** G. ADAMS *Nat. & Exp. Philos.* II. xvii. 298 Happy those who learn this lesson betimes. **1860** HAWTHORNE *Marb. Faun* (1879) II. xxv. 254 It is wise, therefore, to come back betimes, or never.

4. In a short time, soon, speedily, anon, forthwith.

c **1400** *Destr. Troy* XIV. 5966 So hit tid hom tensiche betymys þat day. **1593** SHAKS. *Rich. II*, II. i. 36 He tyres betimes, that spurs too fast betimes. **1707** FREIND *Peterboro's Cond. Sp.* 180 We hope for a Maritine Force betimes in these Seas.

†**be'tine,** *v. Obs. rare*⁻¹. [f. BE- 2 + *tine*, late form of TIND, to kindle.] To set fire to.

1659 FULLER *App. Inj. Innoc.* (1840) 612 Bishop Williams fell foul on the books, moving they might be burned. Let every one betine his share herein.

betinge, betipple, betire, etc.: see BE- *pref.*

‖**bêtise** (bɛːtiːz, beɪ'tiːz). [Fr. = stupidity, f. *bête* foolish, OF. *beste* BEAST.] A foolish, ill-timed remark or action; a piece of folly.

1827 LADY GRANVILLE *Lett.* (1894) I. 406, I think it is an *enfantillage*, a *bêtise*, on the part of the Austrian Government. **1831** DISRAELI *Young Duke* II. III. xix. 256 This *bêtise* of a war has made us all serious. **1849** GEO. ELIOT *Let.* 9 Feb. (1954) I. 278, I will not dilate on the book or on your criticism for I am so sleepy that I should write nothing but bêtises. **1893** HENRY JAMES *Let.* 2 May in C. Mackenzie *Life* (1963) II. 309 If your public.. can't see any of that charm, and wants such a *bêtise* instead, we are engaged in a blind-alley. **1948** 'J. TEY' *Franchise Affair* i. 9 In spite of her *bêtise* about striped suits he saw her point of view.

betitle (bɪ'taɪt(ə)l), *v.* [f. BE- 6 + TITLE.] *trans.* To give a name or title to; to entitle. Hence **be'titled** *ppl. a.*, furnished with a title.

1654 CROMWELL *Lett. & Sp.* (Carl. 1871) IV. 28 But for men on this principle to betitle themselves, that they are the only men, etc. **1832** CARLYLE *Misc.* III. 82 A milder second picture was painted over the canvas of the first, and betitled, Glorious Revolution. **1858** —— *Fredk. Gt.* (1865) II. VI. iii. 163 A mere betitled, betasselled military gentleman.

Betjeman ('bɛtʃəmən). The surname of John *Betjeman* (1906–), English author and poet, applied *attrib.* to a style of Victorian architecture that he is known to admire. Hence **'Betjemanic, ˌBetjema'nesque, 'Betjemanish,** *adjs.*, of or pertaining to Betjeman; resembling the style admired by Betjeman; **'Betjemanite,** a supporter of Betjeman or his views.

1956 L. E. JONES *Edwardian Youth* viii. 182 We emerged from those grim Betjemanic halls. **1958** *Observer* 14 Dec. 9/2 Betjeman belongs to that eccentric group of people.. whose names have become adjectives. Betjeman country, Betjeman houses, and Betjeman streets seem to have changed from gloomy Victoriana into charming antiquities since he started writing about them. **1959** M. BRADBURY *Eating People is Wrong* i. 22 He found himself getting more and more a Betjemanesque *frisson* from Victoriana. **1959** *Spectator* 20 Feb. 258/3 The Beauregard Hotel.. is a frowsty, tragi-comic, Betjemanish place with permanent 'residents', stained-glass lozenge windows, and the aspidistras and gentility and ghastliness no more exaggerated than you find them in such places. **1959** *Listener* 11 June 1031/2 The neo-Victorian Age is upon us. The Law Courts have become a shrine for the Betjemanites. **1963** *Punch* 9 Oct. 527/2 A Betjemanesque society dedicated to the preservation of fairground lettering.

betle, obs. form of BETEL, BEETLE.

betocne, obs. form of BETOKEN.

†**be'toil,** *v. Obs.* Also 7 **betoyl.** [f. BE- + TOIL *sb.* and *v.*] *trans.* To worry or exercise with toil. Hence **be'toiled** *ppl. a.*

1622 ROWLANDS *Good Newes & Bad* 36 This is better farre then scurvy wooing, Betoyl'd about a wife, and cannot get her. *a* **1683** EVELYN *Hist. Relig.* (1850) I. 243 Why, then, do we any longer perplex and betoil ourselves in macerating studies? **1837** CARLYLE *Fr. Rev.* I. I. IV. iii. Poor Lackalls, all betoiled, besoiled, encrusted into dim defacement.

betoken (bɪ'təʊk(ə)n), *v.* Forms: 2–3 **bitacnien, bitocnen,** 3 *Orm.* **bitacnenn,** 3–4 **be-, bi-, bytaken(en, -in(en,** 3–6 **be-, bi-, bytoken(e,** 3 **-on(e,** 4–5 **-yn(e),** 4 **bytokne, betocne,** 6 *Sc.* **betakin, -taikin** (? **betoke**), 4– **betoken.** [Early ME. *bitacnien*, later *bitok(e)nen*, prob. OE. **betácnian*, not recorded (but cf. OHG. *bizeichanôn* mod.Ger. *bezeichnen*, Du. *beteekenen*), f. *bi-*, BE- + *tácnian* to signify, f. *tácn* TOKEN.]

†**1.** *trans.* To signify, mean; to denote, express in words. *Obs.*

c **1175** *Lamb. Hom.* 79 Ierusalem bitacneð griþes sihþe. *c* **1200** *Trin. Coll. Hom.* 17 Ich wille.. segge ou þe crede word after word, and þarmid hwat elch word bitocneð. **1502** *Ord. Crysten Men* (W. de W. 1506) I. ii. 11 Or in other langage or wordes betokenynge the same sentence. **1587** FLEMING *Contn. Holinshed* III. 1333 When men intend to betoken the exceeding huge greatnesse of Rome, they terme it the triumphant Rome. **1612** BRINSLEY *Lud. Lit.* vi. (1627) 68 When two Substantives come together, betokening divers things.

†**b.** *absol. Obs.*

1561 T. NORTON *Calvin's Inst.* III. 232 Many that bost themselues to be Christians.. tremble at euery mention of it [death], as of a thing betokening vnluckely and vnhappy. **1674** N. FAIRFAX *Bulk & Selv.* 200 World, may betoken plurally or indefinitely.

†**2.** To be a type or emblem of; to typify, symbolize. (Sometimes with *obj. clause.*) *Obs.*

c **1175** *Lamb. Hom.* 89 Þet lomb bitacnede cristes þrowunge. *a* **1300** *Cursor M.* 41 Þis ilke tre Bytakens man .. þis fruit bitakens alle oure dedis Both gode and ille. **1393** LANGL. *P. Pl.* C. xx. 118 The paume.. bytokneþ trewely.. The holy gost of heuene. *c* **1440** *Gesta Rom.* 71 Þe rook.. betokenyth okerers and false merchauntz. **1534** MORE *On the Passion* I. Wks. 1331/2 Thys excellente high sacrament.. betokeneth also manyfold merueilous mysteries. **1667** MILTON *P.L.* XI. 867 In the Cloud a Bow.. Betok'ning peace from God and Cov'nant new.

3. To be a token, sign, or omen of; to give promise of, augur, presage.

c **1205** LAY. 16008 What bitacnieð þa draken þe þene dune makeden. *a* **1300** *Cursor M.* 4598 Þas oþer seuen nede nett Bitakens seuen yer of hunger. *c* **1460** *Towneley Myst.* 124 Yond starne betokyns.. The byrthe of a prynce. **1592** SHAKS. *Ven. & Ad.* 453 Like a red morn, that ever yet betoken'd Wreck to the seaman, tempest to the field. **1635** SWAN *Spec. M.* v. §2 (1643) 125 They betoken rain and moist weather. **1853** KANE *Grinnell Exp.* xxix. (1856) 249 Everything betokened a crisis.

4. To give evidence of, point to, indicate, show.

1486 *Bk. St. Alban's* A viij b, And much it betokynis hardenes. **1602** SHAKS. *Ham.* v. i. 242 This doth betoken The Coarse they follow did with disperate hand Fore do it owne life. **1814** CARY *Dante's Inf.* VII. 114 All naked, and with looks Betokening rage. **1863** HAWTHORNE *Old Home* (1879) 302 As he talked.. he betokened in many ways a fine .. sensibility. **1871** MACDUFF *Mem. Patmos* iv. 44 This symbolic number further betokens, that the epistolary addresses were designed as a directory of perpetual obligation.

b. *With of.* To give indication.

1793 HOLCROFT *Lavater's Physiog.* xl. 203 As weak hair betokens of fear, so does strong hair courage.

†**5.** Used by Wyclif in the sense of 'set a mark upon' (L. *signare*), and 'presage, predict, prophesy.'

1382 WYCLIF *Isa.* Prol., And thoȝ.. he betocne [*v.r.* betokeneth] the aȝeencomyng of the puple in to Iewerie. —— *John* vi. 27 God the fadir bitokenede or markede him [*Vulg.* signavit].

betokener (bɪ'təʊk(ə)nə(r)). [f. BETOKEN *v.* + -ER[1].] He who or that which betokens or indicates.

1587 GOLDING *De Mornay* ix. 123 This worde *forego* being a betokener of time, excludeth.. eternitie. **1662** J. CHANDLER *Van Helmont's Oriat.* 332 Anatomy.. as if it were the undoubted betokener, and healer of all Diseases.

betokening (bɪ'təʊk(ə)nɪŋ), *vbl. sb.* [f. prec. + -ING[1].] The giving of a sign or token; signification, meaning; emblem, symbol; omen, portent.

c **1175** *Lamb. Hom.* 51 Ȝe habbeð iherd of þis putte þe bitacninge. *a* **1225** *Ancr. R.* 50 Þe blake cloð also tekeðe bitocnunge. *a* **1400** *Cursor M.* 2682 (Trin.) Þe werke of circumcisyng Bereþ greet bitokenyng [*Gött.* forbisining]. **1489** CAXTON *Faytes of A.* II. vi. 103 Hys folke toke hit for an euyll betoknynge. **1532** MORE *Confut. Tindale* Wks. 374/1 He mocketh not the sacramentes but the mynysters that openeth not the betokeninges thereof. **1674** N. FAIRFAX *Bulk & Selv.* To Rdr., If you.. lay their betokenings to the things whose names they bear.

be'tokening, *ppl. a.* [f. as prec. + -ING[2].] Significant, symbolic.

1584 FENNER *Def. Ministers* (1587) 106 It is a signe, a betokening signe, which men doe worship. **1646** G[REGORY] *Notes & Obs.* (1650) 109 A glorious and betokening Light shined round about this Holy Child.

betombled, obs. form of BETUMBLED.

‖**beton** (betɔ̃, 'bɛtən). [F. *béton*:—OF. *betun* rubble, rubbish, dirt, app. a. Pr. *betun* cement:—L. *bitūmen* mineral pitch (which was used as a cement).] A kind of concrete, composed of sand, lime, and hydraulic cement.

1819 *Pantologia*, Beton, a name given by the French engineers to a kind of mortar, which they use in raising the foundations of masonry under water. **1877** WRAXELL *Hugo's Miserables* v. xix. 12 With a coating of concrete on a foundation of beton. **1885** *N. York Weekly Sun* 29 Apr. 3/5 A monolithic block of beton containing the vast quantity of 400 cubic yards.

betongue (bɪ'tʌŋ) *v.* [f. BE- 6 + TONGUE *sb.*] *trans.* To assail with the tongue; to flout, rally.

1639 AINSWORTH *Annot. Ps.* ci. 5 Hurteth with tongue —traduceth, or (as the Hebrew phrase is) betongueth. **1859** MASSON *Milton* I. 33 How Ben and Shakespeare betongued each other, while the others listened and wondered.

betony ('bɛtənɪ). *Bot.* Forms: (1 **betonice**), 4–6 **betone,** 5 **betan, batany,** 5–6 **betany, betayne, betonye,** 6 **bittonie, byten, bytone, betain(e,** 6–7 **betonie,** 7 **bettony,** 5– **betony.** [a. F. *bétoine*, ad. late L. **betonia* for *betonica*, written by Pliny (*N.H.* xxv. 46) *vettonica*, and said by him to be a Gaulish name for a plant discovered by a Spanish tribe called Vettones. (Previously in OE. in the Latin form *betonica.*)]

1. *prop.* A plant (*Stachys Betonica*) of the Labiate order, having spiked purple flowers and ovate crenate leaves. In former days medicinal and magical virtues were attributed to it.

[*c* **1000** *Ags. Leechd.* II. 58 Wyl ón ealað.. betonican.] *a* **1275** in Wr.-Wülcker *Voc.* 554 Bethonica, beteine. *c* **1375** ? BARBOUR *St. Baptista* 760 In þe prouince of þe sare (= tzar?).. Quhare mene makis drink of spycery—Of betone þare is gret copy. *c* **1440** *Promp. Parv.* 34 Betayne, herbe [**1499** batany or betony], *betonica*. **1483** *Cath. Angl.* 30 Betan, harba. **1519** HORMAN *Vulg.* in *Promp. Parv.* 34 Nesynge is caused with byten (*betonica*) thrust in the nostril. **1586** COGAN *Haven Health* lxxiii. (1636) 79 Betaine, though it grow wilde, yet it is set in many Gardens. **1621** BURTON *Anat. Mel.* III. iv. II. vi. (1676) 721 All which [herbs].. expel Devils.. The Emperour Augustus.. approves of Betony to this purpose. **1821** CLARE *Vill. Minstr.* I. 114 Wild-woad on each road we see; And medicinal betony.

b. Applied (with qualification) to other British plants supposed to resemble the preceding in some respect: **St. Paul's betony**, a small species of Speedwell (*Veronica serpyllifolia*); **water-betony**, a figwort (*Scrophularia aquatica*) having crenate leaves. In contradistinction to these, betony itself was called *Head Betony*.

1741 *Compl. Fam.-Piece* I. iv. 244 Take.. Leaves of.. Lung-wort.. Paul's Betony, Self-heal. **1796** MORSE *Amer. Geog.* I. 189 Head Betony (*Betonica officinalis*).

†**be'torn**, *ppl. a. Obs.* [f. BE- 1 + TORN.] **a.** Torn. **b.** Torn about the sides, tattered.

a **1300** *Cursor M.* 24045 Al his flexs it was be-torn [*v.r.* bitorn(e]. **1561** NORTON & SACKV. *Gorboduc* IV. i. 47 Whose hart betorne out of his panting brest. **1599** *Parismus* II. (1661) 218 Her ornaments all betorn and tattered.

betoss (bɪ'tɒs), *v.* [f. BE- 1 + TOSS *v.*] *trans.* To toss about. Hence **be'tossed** *ppl. a.*

1582 T. WATSON *Hekatompath.* lxxxv. (Arb.) 121 With grieusome wars, with toyles, with storms betost. **1592** SHAKS. *Rom. & Jul.* v. iii. 76 My betossed soule. **1630** J. TAYLOR (Water P.) *Wks.* II. 256/2 Man doth man within the Law betosse. **1845** *Whitehall* lix. 410, I am betossed on a sea of perplexities.

betoure, betoyl, obs. ff. BITTERN, BETOIL.

betowel, betowred, betrace, etc.: see BE-.

†**be'track**, *v. Obs.* [f. BE- 2 + TRACK *v.*] *trans.* To trace or track carefully. Hence **be'tracker**, *spec.* one who searches cloth for faults.

1578 in Stow *Survey* (Strype 1754) II. v. xx. 403/2 If the owner thinketh his baye to be better, he doth appeal to another company called Betrackers.

†**be'trade, bytrade**, *v. Obs. north.* Pa. t. bytradit, betrat. (Cf. BETRAUT.) A variant of BETRAY; perhaps influenced by L. *tradere*.

c **1375** BARBOUR *Troy-bk.* II. 849 Thy contre þow bytradit has. *c* **1400** *Destr. Troy* XXIX. 12026 The couenand to kepe ..þat betrat hom þe toun.

betrai(e, etc., obs. form of BETRAY, etc.

betrail (bɪ'treɪl), *v.* [f. BE- 4 + TRAIL.] *trans.* To trail round or over.

1640 FULLER *Joseph's Coat* (1867) 221 As loving ivy on an oak did wind And with her curling flexures it betrail.

betrainted: see BETRAYNTED.

†**betraise, -traish**, *v. Obs.* Forms: 4 bi-, betrais(e, -trayse, bitrissh, bytrassh, betreyss, *Sc.* betrese, 4–6 betrais(s, 5 betraishe, -trayshe, -trasche, 6 betrassh, -traysshe, *Sc.* betrase. [f. BE- 2 + *traïss-*, *trahiss-*, lengthened stem of F. *trahir* to BETRAY, q.v.] A by-form of BETRAY, chiefly northern.

1. *trans.* To deliver treacherously into the hand or power of an enemy; = BETRAY 1.

a **1300** *Cursor M.* 15272 He þat etes o mi dische, He sal be-trais [*v.r.* betrays, -traye] me. *c* **1386** CHAUCER *Pers. T.* 195 He hadde be bitraysed of his disciple. **1430** LYDG. *Chron. Troy* IV. xxxv, This priest.. For golde and good betrayshed the cytye. **1558** KENNEDY *Compend. Treat.* in *Misc. Wodrow Soc.* 136 The devyll possessit the hart of Judas to betrais his Lorde.

2. To act treacherously towards (a person); to deceive (the trustful or innocent).

c **1374** CHAUCER *Troylus* v. 1780 For wommen that betraised be Thorwgh fals folk. **1375** BARBOUR *Bruce* IV. 17 Worthy crystoll off Seytoune In-to Loudon betresyt was. *c* **1400** *Rom. Rose* 1648 In the snare I felle anoon, That hath bitrisshed many oon. **1501** DOUGLAS *Pal. Hon.* I. lx, Thou.. hes.. Hir sone.. For till betrais awaitit heir sen prime.

3. To seize or entrap (the unsuspecting).

c **1400** *Epiph.* (Turnb. 1843) 136 Yf he may askape Or deth betrasche hym with hys sodeyn rape. **1535** LYNDESAY *Satyre* 3282 Haif I nocht maid ane honest schift That hes betrasit common Thift? **1583** STANYHURST *Æneis* IV. (Arb.) 108 A tarbreeche quystroune.. with phrensye betrasshed.

4. To reveal, disclose incidentally. Cf. BETRAY 6.

c **1400** *Rom. Rose* 1520 He therof was alle abasshed; His owne shadowe was hym bytrasshed.

†**be'traising**, *vbl. sb. Obs.* = BETRAYING.

c **1385** CHAUCER *L.G.W.* 2460 3e han wel herd of Theseus deuyse In the betraysynge [*v.r.* betraying] of fayre Adryane.

betrample (bɪ'træmp(ə)l), *v.* [f. BE- 2 + TRAMPLE.] *trans.* To affect the state of (anything) by trampling; to crush, mark, dirty with the feet. Hence **be'trampled** *ppl. a.*

1565 GOLDING *Ovid's Met.* VI. (1593) 134 A field.. Betrampled every day with horse. **1624** F. WHITE *Reply Fisher* 113 They betrample their rule with vile manners. **1866** FELTON *Anc. & Mod. Gr.* I. xiii. 264 Olympus, thou by robber-feet betrampled.

betrap (bɪ'træp), *v.*[1] *Obs.* Also 1 betræppan, 3–4 bi-, betrappe(n, 5–6 betrappe. [OE. *betreppan*, *-træppan*, f. BE- 1 + *treppan* to TRAP. Cf. the later ATTRAP from Fr.] *trans.* To catch in a trap, entrap, ensnare, circumvent, enclose.

a **1000** *O.E. Chron.* an. 992 (MS. C), Meahton hy þone here betreppan [*MS. F.* betræppan, *E.* betræppen]. *a* **1225** *Ancr. R.* 174 Beo heo bitrappet [MS. C. bitreppet] þer ute. *c* **1490** CAXTON *Four Sons Aymon* xvi. (1885) 384 Ha, ha Reynawde, by my soule ye be now taken & betrapped! **1570** LEVINS *Manip.* 27 To Betrappe, *irretire, circumuenire.* **1575** CHURCHYARD *Chippes* (1817) 154 Betrapt in penfold close. [**1848** *Petrie & Stev.* tr. *O.E. Chron.* (1853) 75 Could anywhere betrap the army about.]

b. *fig.*

1393 GOWER *Conf.* III. 257 Her innocence to betrappe. **1556** ABP. PARKER *Psalter* cxl. 403 Let theyr lippes in crafty wickednes Betrap themselfe.

†**be'trap**, *v.*[2] *Obs.* [f. BE- 1 + TRAP *v.*[2]] *trans.* To furnish (a horse, etc.) with trappings; to deck, adorn. *lit.* and *fig.*

1509 HAWES *Past. Pleas.* XXVII. lviii, Wyth haute courage betrapped fayre and gaye. **1593** NASHE *Christ's T.* Wks. 1883 I. 4 *note*, Was neuer whore of Babylon so betrapt with abhominations. **1597** R. JOHNSON *Sev. Champ.* I. xii. 87 A sable-coloured steed, betrapped with bars of burnished gold.

betrasche, -trase, -trassh, var. BETRAISE *v.*

†**be'traut**, *v. Obs. north.* A synonym of BETRAY, of unexplained form. [? *betrant*.]

c **1400** *Destr. Troy* III. 731 So fals to be founden.. To betraut soche a trew, þat þe trust in. *Ibid.* XXVIII. 11767 And the troiens betrautid with his triet wit.

†**be'travail**, *v. Obs.* Also 4 bitrauel, bytrauaile, -uaille, 5 -vaylle. [f. BE- 1 + TRAVAIL *v.*]

1. *trans.* To work at; to compose (a book).

1387 TREVISA *Higden* (1865) I, þis storie is bytrauailled by cause of Brytayne. *Ibid.* I. xlviii. (1527) 47 b, Cyte of legyons there this Cronycle was bytravaylled.

2. To work for; to earn by labour.

1393 LANGL. *P. Pl.* C. IX. 242 With swot and swetynge face By-tulye and by-trauaile treuly oure lyf-lode. *Ibid.* XVI. 210 For no bred þat ich by-trauaile.

3. To do violence to, to violate.

1388 WYCLIF *Judg.* xx. 5 Thei bitraueliden my wijf with vnbileueful woodnesse of letcherie.

betravel: see BE- *pref.*

betray (bɪ'treɪ), *v.* Forms: 3–5 bitrai(e, -y(e, by-, betraye, 4–7 betrai(e, 4- betray. *Pa. pple.* 5 betrayne. [ME. *bi-*, *betraien*, f. *bi-*, BE- 2 + *traien* TRAY, a. OF. *traïr*:—L. *tradĕre* to deliver, hand over.]

1. a. *trans.* To give up to, or place in the power of an enemy, by treachery or disloyalty.

c **1275** *Passion Our Lord* 93 in *O.E. Misc.*, On me scal bi-traye · þat nv is vre yuere. *a* **1300** *Cursor M.* 16514 Iudas.. come als traitur ful fals his lauerd for to be-trai. **1382** WYCLIF *Jer.* xxvi. 15 An ynnocent blod 3ee shul betra3e a3en 3ou self. *c* **1400** *Destr. Troy* XXVIII. 11196 The toune to be-tray, truly, þai thoght. **1526** TINDALE *Matt.* xxvi. 21 Verely I saye vnto you, that one of you shall betraye [WYCLIF, bitraye] me. **1584** POWEL *Lloyd's Cambria* 374 Lhewelyn was betraied by the men of Buelht. **1718** POPE *Iliad* x. 521 Once a traitor, thou betray'st no more. **1862** STANLEY *Jew. Ch.* (1877) I. xiii. 265 The faithless guardian.. tempted to betray the sacred treasure.

†**b.** To give up or expose *to* punishment. *Obs.*

1590 SHAKS. *Com. Err.* v. 90 She did betray me to my owne reproofe. **1598** —— *Merry W.* III. iii. 207 To betray him to another punishment. **1660** STANLEY *Hist. Philos.* (1701) 87/1 Circumvented and betrayed to excessive Punishments.

2. a. To be or prove false to (a trust or him who trusts one); to be disloyal to; to disappoint the hopes or expectations of.

a **1300** *Cursor M.* 1634 'Noe,' God said, 'i tell till þe, All þis world bitrais me.' *c* **1384** CHAUCER *H. Fame* 294 Let us speke of Eneas How he betrayed hir allas. *c* **1430** *Syr Tryam.* 165 (Halliw.) Syr, he sayde, for certenté, Your quene hath you betrayne. *c* **1590** MARLOWE *Dido* v. i, Why wilt thou so betray thy sons good hap? **1791** BURKE *Corr.* (1844) III. 278 People who.. betray every cause that they have in hand. **1844** A. WELBY *Poems* (1867) 24 Those whom I trust are the first to betray.

b. *fig.* To prove false to, let go weakly or basely.

1614 LODGE *Seneca* I Without any election we rather betray than bestow our benefits. **1624** QUARLES *Job* (1717) 171 Worn bare with grief, the patient Job betraid His seven-days silence. **1765** H. WALPOLE *Otranto* iii. (1798) 51 Scorning.. to betray the courage he had always manifested.

†**3.** *loosely.* To cheat, disappoint. *Obs.*

1588 SHAKS. *Tit. A.* v. ii. 146 Reuenge now goes To lay a complot to betray thy foes. *a* **1704** T. BROWN *Sat. Quack* Wks. I. 65 Her much wrong'd child was of its life betray'd.

4. a. To lead astray or into error, as a false guide; to mislead, seduce, deceive (the trustful).

c **1250** LAY 8924 He wende [þat Andr]ogius bi-traie [*c* **1205** swiken] hi[ne wo]lde. *c* **1385** CHAUCER *L.G.W.* 137 Had hem bitraied with his sophistrye. **1604** SHAKS. *Oth.* v. ii. 6 Yet she must dye, else shee'l betray more men. **1647** COWLEY *Mistr., Bargain* i, Take heed, take heed, thou lovely Maid, Nor be by glittering ills betraid. **1775** JOHNSON *Tax. no Tyr.* 35 Their wit has not yet betrayed them to heresy. **1860** PUSEY *Min. Proph.* 239 Pride and self-confidence betray man to his fall.

b. *spec.* To induce (a woman) to surrender her chastity by false promises; to seduce. Also *absol.*

1766 GOLDSMITH *Vicar* xxix, When lovely Woman stoops to folly, And finds too late that men betray. **1891** HARDY *Tess* xvi, A conviction not so entirely unknown to the 'betrayed' as some amiable theorists would have us believe. **1926** J. BLACK *You can't Win* v. 52 Betrayed and deserted, she stole enough of her father's money to take her to the city and into a hospital where her baby was born.

5. To disclose or reveal with breach of faith (a secret, or that which should be kept secret).

1735 POPE *Prol. Sat.* 298 Who tells whate'er you think, whate'er you say, And, if he lie not, must at least betray. **1798** FERRIAR *Illustr. Sterne* v. 150 The officious doctor.. betrayed his patient's confidence. **1848** MACAULAY *Hist. Eng.* II. 65 He betrayed to Barillon all the schemes adverse to France. **1855** TENNYSON *Maud* II. v. 34.

6. To reveal or disclose against one's will or intention the existence, identity, real character of (a person or thing desired to be kept secret).

1588 SHAKS. *L.L.L.* I. ii. 138, I do betray my selfe with blushing. **1667** MILTON *P.L.* IV. 117 Ire, envie and despair ..betraid Him Counterfet. **1697** DRYDEN *Virg. Georg.* II. 650 Antick Vests; which, thro' their shady fold, Betray the Streaks of ill-dissembl'd Gold. **1759** JOHNSON *Rasselas* xv, Lest they should betray their rank by their unusual behaviour. **1822** PROCTOR (B. Cornwall) *A Voice*, She tries to hide The love her eyes betray.

7. To reveal, disclose or show incidentally; to exhibit, show signs of, to show (a thing which there is no attempt to keep secret).

1697 DRYDEN *Virg. Georg.* IV. 426 His Bowels bruis'd within, Betray no Wound on his unbroken Skin. **1711** ADDISON *Spect.* No. 106 ¶3 If he coughs, or betrays any Infirmity of Old Age. **1774** J. BRYANT *Mythol.* II. 174 A temple of this sort, which betrayed great antiquity. **1841** MYERS *Cath. Th.* III. §14. 51 An irreverence which betrays an utter unconsciousness of our due position. **1856** FROUDE *Hist. Eng.* (1858) I. ii. 92 No prince of the house of Lancaster betrayed a wish to renew the quarrel with the Church.

†**be'tray**, *sb. Obs. rare*[−1]. [f. prec. vb.] = next.

1600 CHAPMAN *Iliad* XXIV. 74 O thou that to betray and shame art still companion!

betrayal (bɪ'treɪəl). [f. as prec. + -AL[2].]

1. A treacherous giving up to an enemy.

1816 SOUTHEY *Ess.* (1832) I. 354 The betrayal and imprisonment of Toussaint. **1871** FREEMAN *Norm. Conq.* (1876) IV. xviii. 108 An attempted betrayal of the country into the hands of an invader. *Hymn* The dark betrayal night.

2. A violation of trust or confidence, an abandonment of something committed to one's charge.

1826 SOUTHEY in *Q. Rev.* XXXIV. 346 Tempted to such betrayal of his trust by habits of reckless expenditure. **1856** FROUDE *Hist. Eng.* (1858) I. iv. 292 He must justly have resented the betrayal of his confidence.

3. A revelation or divulging of something which it is desirable to keep secret.

1873 BLACK *Pr. Thule* 23 Men.. not to be led into these betrayals of their secret opinions.

betrayed (bɪ'treɪd), *ppl. a.* [f. as prec. + -ED.] Treacherously given up or exposed.

1597 SHAKS. *Lover's Compl.* xlvii, That borrowed motion ..Would yet againe betray the fore-betrayed. **1660** T. M. *Walker's Hist. Indep.* IV. 2 The sacred Reliques of betrayed Majesty.

betrayer (bɪ'treɪə(r)). Also 6–7 **betraier**. [f. as prec. + -ER[1].] One who betrays: in various senses of the vb.

1526 TINDALE *John* xiii. 11 For he knewe his betrayer. **1552** HULOET, *Betrayer*, bewrayer, or trayter. **1678** WANLEY *Wond.* II. xviii, Shamefacedness [is] many times a.. betrayer of the mind. **1738** WARBURTON *Div. Legat.* I. 157 Betrayers of the Mysteries were punished capitally. **1767** FORDYCE *Serm. Yng. Wom.* I. iv. 144 She met a betrayer, and lost her honour. **1828** D'ISRAELI *Chas. I*, I. viii. 253 The betrayer of his patron in his turn was betrayed.

betraying (bɪ'treɪɪŋ), *vbl. sb.* [f. as prec. + -ING[1].] The action of the vb. BETRAY in various senses; betrayal.

1382 WYCLIF *Wisdom* xvii. 11 No thing forsothe is drede, but.. betra3yng of the helpis of tho3t. **1483** *Cath. Angl.* 30 A Betraynge, *delatura, prodicio.* **1579** FULKE *Heskins' Parl.* 35 The conception of Sampson was a figure of the incarnation of Christ. Ioseph, of his betraying. **1647** W. BROWNE *Polex.* I. 105 We will.. never more finde fault with her betrayings. **1678** *Yng. Man's Call.* 8 It were no betraying of the sacred principles of religion.

be'traying, *ppl. a.* That betrays.

1628 EARLE *Microcosm.* xliv. 96 Affectation is the most betraying humour. **1814** WORDSW. *Excurs.* VI. 163 A betraying sickliness was seen To tinge his cheek.

betrayment (bɪ'treɪmənt). *rare.* [f. as prec. + -MENT.] = Betrayal.

1548 UDALL, etc. *Erasm. Par. Matt.* xxvii. 4 (R.) Confessing him to be innocent, whose betraiment they had bought. **1863** J. COLEMAN in Spurgeon *Treas. Dav.* Ps. lv, Betrayment of the Messiah by one of the twelve.

†**be'traynted**, *pple. Obs. rare*[−1]. [Of doubtful formation; perhaps an erroneous form: cf. TRAIN *v.* 'draw, drag.'] Borne or carried away.

1583 STANYHURST *Aeneis* II. 62, I thus muttred, with roystring phrensye betraynted [Virgil *furiata mente ferebar*].

betrays(e, -traysh, var. BETRAISE *v. Obs.*

betre, obs. form of BETTER, BETEL.

be'tread, *v.* In 5 bitrede. Now only in pa. pple. betrodden. [ME. f. *bi-*, BE- 4 + ME. *treden* TREAD *v.*] *trans.* To tread over or walk upon.

1398 TREVISA *Barth. De P.R.* XIV. ii. (1495) 465 Erthe hyghte terra in latyn · and hath that name of the ouer party that tredyth other bitredeth the erthe. **1828** CARLYLE in Page *De Quincey* I. 279 Betrodden by picturesque tourists.

†**be'trench**, *v. Obs. rare.* [f. BE- 2 + TRENCH.] *trans.* To cut up, carve, slash.

1656 *Sheph. Cal.* viii, The most horrible and fearfull butchers of hewed, and betrenched them with their glaives.

† **be'trend**, *v. Obs.* Pa. pple. 4 betrend, bitrent. [f. BE- 4 + TREND.] To wind or draw round; to encompass.

c **1374** CHAUCER *Troylus* III. 1182 Aboute a tre.. Bitrent and writhen is the swete woodbynde. *Ibid.* IV. 842 Aboute hire eyen two a purpre rynge Bytrent. *c* **1380** *Sir Ferumb.* 4006 Sorwe hym gan betrende.

betrese, -treyss, Sc. var. of BETRAISE *v. Obs.*

betreuþe, obs. form of BETROTH.

betrim (bɪ'trɪm), *v.* [f. BE- 1 + TRIM *v.*] *trans.* To trim (anything) about.

1610 SHAKS. *Temp.* IV. i. 65 Thy bankes.. Which spungie Aprill, at thy hest betrims. **1812** TENNANT *Anster F.* III. xxxix, Yon mastlike pole.. betrimm'd with clout. **1855** SINGLETON *Virgil* II. 21 With green bay Betrims his brows.

betroth (bɪ'trəʊð, -'trɒθ, -ɔ:-), *v.* Forms: 4 bitreuthien, betreuþe, -trouþe, -treuthy, 5-6 betrouth(e, 6 betrothe, troughth, 7 betroath, 6- betroth. [ME. *bitreuðien*, f. *bi-*, BE- 6 + ME. *treuðe, treowðe*, TRUTH *sb.*; Mätzner suggests after the analogy of OE. *tréowsian* to give one's word, pledge. Subsequently assimilated to the form *trouthe*, TROTH; since this is now shortened to *trǫþ*, the same sound is by many extended to the vb., but the historical and analogical pronunciation is as in *clothe, loathe.*]

1. *trans.* To engage (a woman) in contract of marriage, to plight one's troth to. *arch.*

1303 R. BRUNNE *Handl. Synne* 1704 Þou shal nat betrouþe a womman wyþ hande þe whylys here husbande ys lyvande. *c* **1315** SHOREHAM 70 Ȝef thou myd word.. Aryȝt bitreuthest one. *c* **1380** *Sir Ferumb.* 2105 By þe hond þanne he tok hur sone: & be-treuþede þat swete wiȝt. **1426** *Pol. Poems* (1859) II. 136 Herry.. Of Englond kyng.. Betrouthed hath my lady Kateryne. **1611** BIBLE *Deut.* xx. 7 What man is there that hath betrothed a wife. **1653** HOLCROFT *Procopius* I. 15 Having betroathed a handsome Maid, an Inheritrix. [**1844** LINGARD *Anglo-Sax. Ch.* viii. (1858) II. 6 (transl. of an OE. law) If a man wish to betroth a maiden.]

2. To contract two persons to each other in order to marriage; to affiance. (More usually, but not exclusively, said of contracting the female to her future husband.)

1566 PAINTER *Pal. Pleas.* I. 21 They had betrouthed their doughter, to one L. Icilius. **1592** SHAKS. *Rom. & Jul.* v. iii. 288 You.. betroth'd, and would haue married her perforce to Countie Paris. **1684** BUNYAN *Pilgr.* II. 130 Let Christiana look out some Damsels for her Sons; to whom they may be Betroathed. **1798** FERRIAR *Illustr. Sterne* v. 151 The lovers were soon after betrothed. **1839** KEIGHTLEY *Hist. Eng.* II. 80 She was soon after betrothed to the Dauphin. **1864** D. MITCHELL *Sev. Stor.* 225 He was very early betrothed to a daughter of the Contarini.

b. In the *passive*, now commonly used, senses 1 and 2 are blended.

c **1590** GREENE *Fr. Bacon* v. 108 They'll be betrothed each to other. **1685** BAXTER *Paraphr. Luke* i. 26 Not married, but betrothed.

3. *fig.* Said of God and his Church or people. Also, said of the relation of a bishop to a church before consecration.

1611 BIBLE *Hosea* ii. 19, I will betroth thee vnto me for euer. **1726** AYLIFFE *Parergon* 195 If any Person be consecrated a Bishop to that Church, whereunto he was not before betrothed, he shall not receive the Habit of Consecration, as not being canonically promoted. **1860** PUSEY *Min. Proph.* 13 God made the soul for Himself; He betrothed her to Himself through the gift of the Holy Spirit.

†**4.** *transf.* **a.** To pledge, engage. **b.** To pledge or engage oneself to, to espouse (a cause). *Obs.*

1566 GASCOIGNE *Jocasta* Wks. (1587) 102 To privat fight they have betrotht themselves. **1575** *Brieff Disc. Troub. Franckford* 202 They will not slack to vowe and betrothe their whole diligence. **1599** SHAKS. *Much Ado* I. iii. 49 What is hee for a foole that betrothes himselfe to vnquietnesse? **1670** WALTON *Lives* I. 13 At that time [he] had betrothed himself to no religion.

b. 1658 T. WALL *Comm. Times* 68 While he thought to betroth a Deity, he betrayed humanity. **1674** N. FAIRFAX *Bulk & Selv.* Ep. Ded., Those that have betrothed the Way.

betrothal (bɪ'trəʊðəl: see vb). [f. prec. + -AL[2].] The act of betrothing; the fact of being betrothed; engagement for marriage, affiance.

1844 *Mem. Babylon. Pr'cess.* II. 103 Here, as in Assyria and Chaldea, betrothals take place at a very early age. **1858** LONGF. *M. Standish* IX. 12 Softly the youth and the maiden repeated the words of betrothal.

attrib. **1872** YEATS *Techn. Hist. Comm.* 188 Betrothal rings, set with pearls and gems. **1878** B. TAYLOR *Deukalion* I. iii. 32 Our betrothal-kiss.

be'trothed, *ppl. a.* [f. as prec. + -ED[1].]

1. Engaged for marriage, affianced. Often *subst.*

1540 SURREY *Frailtie of Beautie* (R.) The new betrothed birdis ycoupled how they went. **1588** SHAKS. *Tit. A.* I. 286 That iustly may Beare his Betroth'd, from all the world away. **1825** SCOTT *Betrothed* xxxi, [Thus] ended the trials and sorrows of The Betrothed. **1884** L. WALFORD *Baby's Grandm.* 171 One of the three was his betrothed bride.

†**2.** Plighted, pledged. *Obs.*

1651 HOBBES *Govt. & Soc.* xiv. §18. 226 No conscience of contracts and betrothed faith can withhold them.

betrothing (bɪ'trəʊðɪŋ: see vb), *vbl. sb.* [f. as prec. + -ING[1].] The action of giving a pledge or engagement to marry; affiancing. Also *fig.*

c **1315** SHOREHAM 59 Wythoute speche and by-treuthynge, And alle manere othe. **1552** HULOET, Betroughthyng, or plyghtynge of troughth betwene man and wyfe. *a* **1639** W. WHATELEY *Prototypes* II. xxxiv. (1640) 158 Betrothing is nothing but a serious promise of future marriage. **1805** SCOTT *Last Minstr.* v. xxvi, For this is your betrothing day.

be'trothment (see BETROTH). = BETROTHAL.

1585 *Expos. Canticles* (R.) Making as it were thereby the betrothment. **1741** RICHARDSON *Pamela* II. 175, I said after Mr. Peters.. the words of Betrothment. **1847** TENNYSON *Princess* v. 463 How the strange betrothment was to end. **1871** HAWTHORNE *Sept. Felton* (1879) 50 When he gave her the kiss of betrothment.

† **be'trow**, *v. Obs.* [f. BE- 2 + TROW *v.*] *trans.* To trust.

1556 ABP. PARKER *Psalter* civ. 294 O hym betrow, Hys larges note.

† **be'trump**, *v. Obs. rare.* [f. BE- 2 + TROMP *v.*, a. F. *tromper* to deceive.] *trans.* To deceive, cheat; to elude, slip from. (= L. *fallere.*)

1513 DOUGLAS *Æneis* II. xii. (xi.) 105 Sche was away, and betrumpit suthlie Hir spous, hir son, and all the cumpany. *Ibid.* IV. xi. 14 Sall he.. my realm betrump on thes maneir?

betrumpet (bɪ'trʌmpɪt), *v. rare.* [f. BE- 6 + TRUMPET.] *trans.* To trumpet the praises of. Hence **be'trumpeting** *vbl. sb.*

1828 CARLYLE *Misc.* (1857) I. 156 Betrumpeted and beshouted from end to end of the habitable globe. **1866** —— *Remin.* I. 92 All this betrumpeting of Irving to me.

† **be'trust**, *v. Obs.* Also 5-6 betrist. *Pa. pple.* betrusted; also 5 betrost, 6 betrust, -trist. [f. BE- 2 + TRUST *v.*]

1. *trans.* To trust, place confidence in (a person).

c **1440** *Generydes* 3615 He was right weel betrost both ferr and neere. **1556** ABP. PARKER *Psalter* civ. 294 O marke hys wyll: Hys care betrist. *a* **1577** GASCOIGNE *Wks.* (1587) 114 Not best betrust among the worthyes nine. **1649** MILTON *Eikon.* 128 Maisters.. of the People that betrusted them.

2. To entrust.

1619 J. DYKE *Caveat* (1620) 45 If.. man.. should betrust vs with such a businesse of weight, etc. **1702** C. MATHER *Magn. Chr.* III. iv. (1852) 328 Those who are betrusted to receive men unto ordinances in churches. *a* **1748** WATTS (J.) Whatsoever you would betrust to your memory.

† **be'trust**, *sb. Obs.* [f. prec. vb.] An entrusting, a trust.

1656 S. H. *Gold. Law* 42 This impowering him.. was only a betrust, a redelivery being expected when exacted. *Ibid.* 43 Their engagements and be-trusts forbade.

† **be'trusted**, *ppl. a. Obs.* [f. as prec. + -ED.] **a.** Trusted, or confided in. **b.** Given in trust.

a **1461** *Paston Lett.* 423 II. 66 Ryght reverent and most be trusted maister. **1691** E. TAYLOR *Behmen's Theos. Phil.* 188 His betrusted Talents. **1692** HACKET *Abp. Williams* II. 195 To pluck his best betrusted from him.

† **be'trustment.** *Obs. rare*$^{-0}$. [f. as prec. + -MENT.] An entrusting, a trust.

(In modern Dicts.)

‖ **'betso.** *Obs.* [It. *bezzo.*] 'A small brass coin in Venice.' Barretti.

1641 *Antiquary* III. i. in Hazl. *Dodsl.* XIII. 460 Thirty livres: I'll not bate you a betso.

Betsy ('bɛtsɪ). *slang* or *dial.* (orig. *U.S.*). Also Bessy, Betsey, and with lower-case initial. [Var. BETTY *sb.*] A gun or pistol; *spec.* one's favourite gun; freq. *old Betsy.*

1856 *Spirit of Age* (Sacramento) 4 Nov. 3/1 Jest let them raise that check agin me, and if I don't shoot why old Betsy won't blizzard. **1869** *New No. West* (Deer Lodge, Mont.) 20 Aug. 2/7 Mr Fredericks proceeded immediately on the horse, loaded 'Betsey', (his shot gun). **1895** P. H. EMERSON *Marsh Leaves* liv. 137 Potter had a long-barrelled gun, his 'old Bessy', and I took my eyes along with me. **1965** J. P. CARSTAIRS *Concrete Kimono* v. 48 'You've noticed I'm toting a Betsy.' 'Betsy?' 'Equalizer, rod, gat, iron.' **1969** *Win* 15 May 12/2 Emotionally, the satisfying thing to fantasize is grabbing ole betsy and going to join my black brothers in Wayne County.

bett- in various words: see BET-.

bett(e, obs. pa. t. and pple. of BEAT *v.*

bettaile, obs. form of BETEL.

bettant, var. of BATAND.

c **1400** *Rowland & Ot.* 356 Thay.. Broghte hym ane helme of bettant.

bettee, obs. form of BETTY *sb.* 4.

better ('bɛtə(r)), *a.*, (*sb.*), and *adv.* Forms: 1-2 betera, 1-4 betere, 3-4 betre, 3-6 bettre, 4 beter, bettar, -ur, -yr, 4-5 bettir, 5 bettere, bettyrer (*Cath. Angl.*). [Com. Teut.: OE. (sing. masc.) *betera* = OFris. *betera*, OS. *betiro* (Du. *beter-*, OHG. *beziro*, mod.G. *besser-e*), Goth. *batiza*:—OTeut. **batiz-on-*, used as the compar. of *gôdo-z* GOOD, but itself pointing to a positive stem extant in no Teutonic lang., and prob. wanting also in OTeut. The root *bat-* was prob. related to *bôt-*: see BEET *v.* and BOOT *v.* Fick and Kluge have compared Skr. *bhadrá-s* salutary, benign.]

A. *adj.* The comparative degree of GOOD (which see for phrases and idiomatic uses in which the force of *better* corresponds with that of the positive adj.): more good.

I. As simple adjective.

1. Of greater excellence, of superior quality.

a. Said of persons, in respect of physical, mental, or *esp.* moral qualities; also, of social standing.

c **893** K. ÆLFRED *Oros.* IV. ix. §6 þæt hie þa wæron beteran þegnas þonne hie nu sien. **1382** WYCLIF *1 Kings* ii. 32 He slewȝ two riȝtwise men betere than hym self. **1596** SHAKS. *1 Hen. IV*, v. iv. 104, I could haue better spar'd a better man. **1617** MORYSON *Itin.* III. I. iii. 38 Fat men, as the Northerne, are better men then those who are leane, as the Southerne men be. **1632** MASSINGER *City Mad.* III. iii, Be confident your better angel is Entered your house. **1709** STEELE *Tatler* No. 164 ¶6 Looking upon my self as no better than a dead Man. **1856** HALLIWELL *Shaks.* V. 323 A person who exceeds another in wealth is said to be a better man than the other.

b. Said of things, in respect of their essential qualities.

c **1230** *Hali Meid.* 19 To ȝiuen ham stude & betere nome þen sunen & dohtren. *a* **1300** *Cursor M.* 2363 Ȝee sal weind til a better land. *Ibid.* 12088 Till bettir theues þu suld him wune. **1485** CAXTON *Paris & V.* 33 Yf the sayd Iewellys were better the half than they be. *c* **1550** BALE *K. Johan* (1838) 73 Lyke Lorde, lyke chaplayne, neyther barrell better heryinge. *a* **1555** RIDLEY *Wks.* 130 Oftentimes the greater part overcometh the better. **1611** COTGR., *A bon iour bon œuvre*.. as we say, the better day the better work. **1722** DE FOE *Plague* (1754) 9 Coaches fill'd with People of the better Sort. **1823** BYRON *Island* III. ii, Their better feelings, if such were, were thrown Back on themselves. *a* **1847** MRS. SHERWOOD *Lady of M.* III. xix. 86 The poor woman had been accustomed to what is called better life.

c. *Comb.* with sbs. used attrib., as ***better-class, -quality, -type.***

1890 W. F. BUTLER *Sir Chas. Napier* 7 Merchants or local better-class farmers. **1965** K. GILES *Some Beasts No More* ii. 30 The better-class houses of 1910 vintage with area steps now unwhitened. **1908** *Westm. Gaz.* 12 Aug. 11/3 Better-quality teas. **1958** *Spectator* 8 Aug. 196/1 The better-type delivery library.

d. In phrases used *attrib.*, as ***better-than-average, better-than-chance.***

1922 A. BENNETT *Let.* 8 Nov. (1966) I. 317 The respectable better-than-average English plays. **1938** J. HILTON *To You, Mr. Chips* i. 21 The school was perhaps a better-than-average example, both educationally and structurally, of its type. **1964** *Language* XL. 262 A better-than-chance probability that a language will possess certain features.

2. Of persons and things: More profitable, useful, or suitable for a purpose; more eligible or desirable. Of persons: Kinder, more beneficent.

c **1175** *Lamb. Hom.* 17 Betere hit is þet heo beon ispilled. **1297** R. GLOUC. 367 So þat after betere wynd hii moste þere at stonde. **1362** LANGL. *P. Pl.* B. Prol. 195 Better is a litel losse þan a longe sorwe. *c* **1375** WYCLIF *Sel. Wks.* I. 138 þe more þat an herd is lyke to Crist he is þe better.. in þis office. **1394** *P. Pl. Crede* 762 A great bolle-ful of benen · were betere in his wombe. **1591** SHAKS. *Two Gent.* I. i. 159, I must goe send some better Messenger. *Ibid.* II. i. 145 Oh excellent deuise, was there euer heard a better? **1615** LATHAM *Falconry* (1633) 136 There is not a more better thing for any new swelling. **1703** ROWE *Fair Penit.* I. i. 7 Thy better Stars Are join'd to shed their kindest Influence on thee. **1810** HENRY *Elem. Chem.* (1826) II. 532 We have much better indicators of both these acids.

3. Of greater amount: **a.** More. **b.** Larger, greater; esp. in ***better half, part,*** etc.

a. 1587 FLEMING *Cont. Holinshed* III. 1382/2 Woorth one hundred and twentie pounds and better. **1603** R. JOHNSON *Kingd. & Commw.* 129 Able to furnish better then ten thousand men with horse. **1630** WADSWORTH *Sp. Pilgr.* iii. 15 Vntill nine and better they are exercised in repeating. **1679** PLOT *Staffordsh.* (1686) 239 The bodies.. being better than an inch long. **1769** GRAY in *N. Nicholls' Corr.* (1843) 87 It is better than three weeks since I wrote to you. **1823** SCOTT *Peveril* vii, Pursued by half a score of horsemen and better. **1823** LAMB *Some old Actors, Elia* 399, I think it is now better than five-and-twenty years ago.

b. 1580 SIDNEY *Arcadia* III. 334, I.. shall thinke the better halfe of it alreadie atchieued. **1586** COGAN *Haven Health* (1636) 60 Let it boile untill the better part of the liquour be consumed. **1667** MARVELL *Corr.* xxxvi. Wks. 1872-5 II. 81 Your businesse is the better-halfe done. **1707** FREIND *Peterboro's Cond. Sp.* 197 That the Forces shou'd be divided, and the better half march immediately into Valencia. **1739** SWIFT *Let.* Wks. 1745 VIII. 376 Forced to sell the better half of his estate. **1805** WORDSW. *Prel.* v. (1850) 130 For the better part Of two delightful hours we strolled along.

c. Hence, ***better half***: orig. ***my better half***, the more than half of my being; said of a very close and intimate friend (cf. 'the better part of me' Shaks.; 'meæ partem animæ,' 'animæ dimidium meæ' Horace; 'animæ partem... nostræ majorem' Statius); esp. (after Sidney) used for 'my husband' or 'wife'; now, jocularly appropriated to the latter. Formerly also applied to the soul, as the better part of man.

1580 SIDNEY *Arcadia* III. 280[*Argalus to Parthenia, his wife*] My deare, my better halfe (sayd hee) I find I must now leaue thee. [*c* **1600** SHAKS. *Sonn.* xxxix. 2 When thou art all the better part of me. **1646** BUCK *Rich. III*, II. 61 As if his [Richard's] body must suffer more, because they could not

kill his better part.] **1709** J. Stevens *Quevedo's Wks.* 33 [*A woman to her husband*] Thou dear better-half of my soul. *a* **1720** Sheffield (Dk. Buckhm.) *Wks.* (1753) I. 274 My dear and better half is out of danger. **1742** R. Blair *Grave* 733 The lag flesh Rests, in hope of meeting once again Its better half [the soul]. **1842** T. Martin in *Fraser's Mag.* Dec. 241/2, I..shall look out for a better-half.

4. a. In the predicate, after *be*, the neuter adj. formerly interchanged with the adv. *bet*, and its grammatical character is still dubious: the positive of 'it is better to go' may be either 'it is good' or 'it is well.' Cf. bet *adv.* 2. The dubiety is still greater in elliptical expressions, as in quot. 1553, 1667, 1837. See below, B 3.

c **888** K. Ælfred *Boeth.* xxxviii. §7 Hit is betere þæt mon wreȝe þone scyldiȝan. *c* **1000** *Ags. Gosp.* Mark ix. 43 Betere þe is þæt þu wanhal to life ga. *c* **1175** *Lamb. Hom.* 49 Betre hit is þet mon ne iknawe noht þe wei. *c* **1386** Chaucer *Melib.* ¶180 You is better hyde youre counseil in youre herte. **1470–85** Malory *Arthur* (1817) I. 242 Whether is me better to treate with Kynge Arthur, or to fyghte. **1553** Udall *Roister D.* (Arb.) 81 Better (they say) a badde scuse than none. **1667** Milton *P.L.* I. 263 Better to reign in Hell than serve in Heav'n. **1821** Keats *Isabel* xi, Better had it been for ever so. **1837** J. H. Newman *Par. Serm.* I. iii. 44 Better be a little too strict than a little too easy.

b. In the idiomatic *I, we, you, he*, etc. *had better*, the original construction was *me, us*, etc. *were betere* (or *bet*) = it would be more advantageous for me, etc. (Cf. *me is betere*, etc. in 4.) The dat. pronoun was subsequently changed into the nominative, *I, we, were better* (perh. because in sbs. the two cases were no longer distinguished). Finally this was given up for the current *I had better* = I should have or hold it better, to do, etc. (Mr. F. Hall has shown that in these changes, *better* followed in the main the analogy of *liefer* and *rather*.) See have. ***you'd better believe***: you may be assured. *colloq.* (orig. *U.S.*).

971 *Blickl. Hom.* 25 Him wære betere þæt he næfre ȝeboren nære. *c* **1160** *Hatton Gosp.* Mark ix. 42 Betere him wære þæt [he] wære on sæ ȝeworpen. *a* **1320** *Maximon* in *Rel. Antiq.* I. 122 Betere me were ded þen þus alyve to be. **1393** Gower *Conf.* III. 241 Him were better go beside. *a* **1450** *Knt. de la Tour* 31 Hem were better take the furre. **1465** Marg. Paston *Lett.* 534. II. 250 The Duck [= duke] had be beter..that it had never be don.

c **1370** *K. Robt. Cicyle* 55 Bettur he were..So to do then for hunger dye. **1470–85** Malory *Arthur* (1816) I. 33 Ye were better to give me a gift..than to lose great riches. **1594** T. B. *La Primaud. Fr. Acad.* 512 We were better to support the domesticall imperfections of our brethren. **1601** Shaks. *Twel. N.* ii. ii. 27 She were better loue a dreame.

[*c* **1435** *Torr. Portugal* 1186 Better he had to have be away.] **1537** *Thersytes, Four O. Plays* (1848) 69 They had better haue set me an errande at Rome. **1594** Harington in *Nugæ Ant.* (1804) I. 168 Who livethe for ease had better live awaie[from Court]. **1613** Shaks. *Hen. VIII*, v. iii. 132 He had better starue Then but once thinke his place becomes thee not. **1875** Jowett *Plato* I. 15, I had better begin by asking you a question.

1856 *Yale Lit. Mag.* XXI. 171 (Th.), You'd better believe, I'll live in the clover. **1872** O. W. Holmes *Poet. Breakf.-t.* x, My old gentleman means to be Mayor or Governor or President..you'd better b'lieve. **1968** *Globe & Mail* (Toronto) 17 Feb. 42 (Advt.), You'd better believe it. .. We've got 'em.

(*b*) With *had* omitted (occas. with pronoun also omitted). *colloq.* (orig. *U.S.*).

1831 S. Smith *Major Downing* (1834) 65 My clothes had got so shabby, I thought I better hire out a few days and get slicked up a little. **1846** J. J. Hooper *Some Adv. Simon Suggs* (1851) i. 154 You better mind the holes in them ere rocks. **1865** *Major Jack Downing of Downingville Militia* (1867) ix. 70 You better believe we've been in an awful excitement here. **1904** A. Bennett *Great Man* xii. 120 Miss Foster she says her name is. Better show her in here, hadn't I? **1910** C. E. Mulford *Hopalong Cassidy* xi. 73, I reckon you better pull out—you ain't needed around here. **1946** K. Tennant *Lost Haven* (1947) i. 15 Well, we better get back to the house. *Ibid.* iii. 53 Brace better meet that train. **1968** *Listener* 9 May 596/2 You better get those two guys inside.

c. *to be better* (in health, estate, etc.): see B 4.

5. Phrases. †*(to have) the better hand*: i.e. 'the upper hand,' the superiority. ***to be better than one's word***: to do more than one has promised. ***better cheap***: see cheap *sb.* ***no better than*** (one) ***should*** (or ***ought to***) ***be***, of doubtful moral character, (usu.) of easy virtue.

1523 Ld. Berners *Froiss.* I. ccxv. 272 The marques..had the better hande. **1587** Whetstone *Cens. loy. Subj.* (Collier) 30 Q. Marie..had the better hand against her rebels. **1604** *Pasquils Jests* sig. C, A Man, whose wife was no better then she should be. **1684** T. Burnet *Th. Earth* II. 167 God may be better than His word. *Mod.* I have usually found him better than his word. **1764, 1780** [see shall v. 18]. **1815** C. Lamb *Let.* 28 Apr. (1935) II. 158 To term her a poor outcast seems as much as to say that poor Susan is no better than she should be. **1871** Trollope *Eust. Diamonds* (1873) I. xxiii. 305 He..almost believed that she was not now, and hadn't been before her marriage, any better than she should be. **1882** J. Morison *Macaulay* 105 They are all no better than they should be. **1904** A. Bennett *Great Man* xiii. 139 Her ..suspicion that the self-styled Miss Foster was no better than she ought to be. **1937** A. L. Rowse *Sir R. Grenville* xix. 346 The one was a brute, and the other a vixen, and no better than she should be into the bargain.

II. *absol.* passing into a *substantive*.

6. *absol.* Something better; that which is better. ***for better, for worse***: see worse B. 3 a; ***to go (one) better***: see go *v.* 36.

1535 Coverdale *Heb.* vi. 9 We trust to se better of you [Wyclif, We tristen of ȝou betere thingis]. **1594** Shaks. *Rich. III*, iii. v. 50, I never look'd for better at his hands. **1699** Dryden *Fables* Pref., If I have altered him any where for the better. **1879** Geo. Eliot *Coll. Breakf. P.* 485 A possible Better in the seeds of earth. —— *Theo. Such* ii. 51 They feed the ideal Better.

7. *sb.* with *possessive pron.*: One's superior: **a.** in some personal quality or attainment; **b.** in rank or station. In the latter sense, now only in the plural, which was however from 16th to 18th c. often applied to a single person.

a. *c* **1325** *Coer de L.* 1650 In al Yngelond was non hys beter. **1526** *Pilgr. Perf.* (1531) 88 To be instructe and taught of my better. **1594** Shaks. *Rich. III*, i. ii. 140 His better doth not breath vpon the earth. **1859** Tennyson *Vivien* 349 To help herself By striking at her better.

b. [*c* **1205** Lay. 3749 Heora sunen..þa weren hire beteren.] **1432–50** tr. *Higden* Rolls Ser. IV. 325 Ȝiffenge not contrarious wordes and answeres to their betters. *c* **1500** in *Babees Bk.* (1868) 25 When thi better spekes to the Do offe thi cape & bow þi kne. **1549** *Bk. Com. Prayer* Catech., To ordre myself lowely and reuerently to al my betters. **1600** Shaks. *A.Y.L.* ii. iv. 68 *Cor.* Who cals? *Clo.* Your betters Sir. **1712** Steele *Spect.* No. 266 ¶4 A Squire or a Gentleman, or one that was her Betters. **1742** Fielding *J. Andrews* iv. i, I look upon myself as his betters. **1866** Kingsley *Herew.* xiv. 182 She will grow as proud as her betters.

8. ***the better***: the superiority or mastery; now chiefly in ***to get the better of***. Also *fig.* (Cf. best 9 a.)

1461 *Paston Lett.* 396 II. 21 The blyssyd Trinite..send yow the better of all your adversariis. **1586** Warner *Alb. Eng.* iii. xvii. 79 Little wanted that the Brutes the better did not win. **1630** M. Godwyn *Annales Eng.* 197 We alwayes came of with the better. **1660** Stanley *Hist. Philos.* (1701) 10/2 Sometimes the Medes had the better of the Lydians. **1675** Hobbes *Odyssey* viii. 320 The slow has gotten of the swift the better. **1718** Hickes & Nelson *J. Kettlewell* 55 App., The worst Causes are likely to have the better, at this way of Reasoning. **1839** Thirlwall *Greece* VI. xlviii. 137 Prudence..got the better of his pride.

†**9.** ***with the better***: with addition; and more. *Obs.*

1601 Holland *Pliny* I. 163 When his father was 62 yeares old with the better. **1690** W. Walker *Idiom. Anglo-Lat.* 333 To pay what one hath borrowed with the better.

B. *adv.*

[The original adverbial form was bet, which survived till *c* 1600. See that word as to its gradual displacement by *better*.]

1. In a more excellent way, in a superior manner.

c **1240** *Lofsong* in *Lamb. Hom.* 215 þu wult..don betere bi me þen is þet ich wilni. *c* **1250** *Gen. & Ex.* 1585 Ðu salt ðe betre sped. *c* **1394** *P. Pl. Crede* 95 Fond to don betere. *c* **1400** *Apol. Loll.* 26 Mak hem to drede synne & to do bettar. **1530** Palsgr. 147, I drinke better than I syng. **1677** Moxon *Mech. Exerc.* (1703) 194 The better to come at it with the Tool. **1797** Ld. Nelson in Duncan *Life* (1806) 44 The sooner the better. *Mod.* Until he learns to behave better.

2. a. In a superior degree.

a **1225** *St. Marher.* 4 Aðet he hefde betere biþoht him. *c* **1230** *Hali Meid.* 37 þat ha..witen þe beter hwat ham beo to don. *a* **1300** *Cursor M.* 2438 He loued hir..better þan he did are. *c* **1400** *Destr. Troy* xix. 8083 For to hold hym in hope, & hert hym the bettur. **1471** *Paston Lett.* 681 III. 23 That shall dysse avayll him better than a CC. marc. **1475** Caxton *Jason* 77 b, They had him better in grace than zethephius. **1577** B. Googe *Heresbach's Husb.* (1586) 65 Where-by it [sage] prospereth the better. **1666** Bunyan *Grace Ab.* ¶50, I better considering the matter. **1771** *Junius Lett.* lii. 266, I know that man much better than any of you. **1848** Macaulay *Hist. Engl.* I. 435 But there were in the palace a few persons who knew better.

†**b.** Rather. *Obs.*

c **1340** *Cursor M.* (Laud MS.) 9815 His hert ought bettyr breke in iijᵉ Then fro his byddynges to fle. **1475** Caxton *Jason* 17 b, He semed better a thing of that other worlde thenne an humayne persone. **1801** Southey *Life* (1850) II. 168 He..prefers books better than official papers.

c. More, in addition. *arch.* and *dial.*

1538 Bale *Thre Lawes* 1351 He swore, and better swore, yea he did sweare and sweare agayne. **1830** James *Darnley* vii. 36/2 On this he wondered, and better wondered.

3. In the predicate, after *be*, the adv. and adj. run together: see A 4. In some cases the adverbial character seems more prominent.

1570–87 Holinshed *Scot. Chron.* (1806) II. 75, I will here (being better late than never) set down this.

4. a. ***to be better***: to be improved in health, *esp.* of convalescence after an illness. (In northern use, to be well again, as in *quite better*, quite well again, fully recovered.) ***to get better*** : to amend, recover. (The orig. const. was 'him is bet or better,' i.e. it is better to or with him. See well.)

c **1000** *Ags. Gosp.* John iv. 52 Ða acsode he, to hwylcum timan him bet wære. *c* **1160** *Hatton G.* ibid., Hym bet wære [*Lindisf. & Rushw.*, þæt betre hæfde = *Vulg.* melius habuerit; **1382** Wyclif, He axide of hem the our, in which he hadde betere, **1388** was amended; **1611** began to amend.] **1686** J. Davies in R. Ward *Life H. More* (1710) 215 He had been let Blood, and seem'd after it much better than before. **1745** Shaftesb. in *Lett. 1st Earl Malmesbury* (1870) I. 9 Poor Handel looks something better. **1771** Johnson in *Mrs. Piozzi's Lett.* (1788) I. 42 Dr. Taylor is better, and is gone out in the chaise. **1863** T. Thompson *Ann. Influenza* 95 [He] was blooded and got better, went abroad got well. **1872** Geo. Eliot *Middlem.* (1875) 587 She is better this morning, and..she will be cheered by seeing you again.

†**b.** ***to be the better***: to be profited or advantaged. *arch.* and *dial.*

1619 J. Dyke *Counterp.* (1620) 37 What are we the better to know our disease? *a* **1620** —— *Sel. Serm.* (1640) 282 What is man the better for eating the Sacrament, if hee eate not Christ? *Mod. Sc.* What the better would you be, if you had it?

5. *Comb.* With *adjs.* and *pples.*: usually (for syntactical clearness) written with a hyphen. **a.** With past and pres. pples. as compar. of well: as, ***better-advised, -affected, -balanced, -behaved, -born, -considered, -dressed, -informed, -regulated, -seasoned***, etc.; ***better-becoming, -knowing, -liking, -looking***; sometimes approaching the sense 'more fully, more.' **b.** In parasynthetic comb. formed on a sb. with attribute; as, ***better-humoured***, i.e. (*better humour*) + *-ed*; so ***better-natured, -omened, -principled, -witted***, etc.

1609 Newes in *Shaks. C. Praise* 87 And have parted better-wittied then they came. **1616** Surfl. & Markh. *Countr. Farme* 549 To resort to the better-knowing husbands. **1677** *Govt. Venice* 23 Such Gentlemen..as thereby become better-affected to the Venetian Nobility. **1680** *Spir. Popery* 48 A great, and better Principled Lady. **1697** Dryden *Virg. Georg.* iv. 142 For Empire he design'd Is better born. **1711** Shaftesb. *Charac.* I. 254 His better-humour'd and more agreeable successor. *Ibid.* I. 310 Growing better-natur'd, and enjoying more..the pleasures of society. **1792** Bentham *Wks.* (1843) X. 276 There was not a better-behaved young woman in the whole parish. **1818** Scott *Rob Roy* x, Neglecting the minor and better-balanced chances of the game. **1820** —— *Abbot* xxiii, To cumber our better-advised devotions. **1826** Syd. Smith *Wks.* (1859) II. 113 His awe of better-dressed men and better-taught men. **1827** Carlyle *Misc.* (1857) I. 2 Richter was much better-natured than Johnson. **1833** Marryat *P. Simple* (1863) 95, I was by far the better-looking chap of the two. **1854** Mrs. Gaskell *North & S.* v, To learn his change of opinion.. from her better-informed child. **1856** *Farmer's Mag.* Nov. 431 A more matured and better-considered measure. **1860** Gen. P. Thompson *Audi Alt.* III. clxxi. 198 The move of a better-omened man.

6. Phrases. ***to think better of***: **a.** (a thing); to give it reconsideration with the result of deciding more wisely. **b.** (a person): to form a better opinion of him.

1607 Shaks. *Cor.* ii. iii. 15 To make us no better thought of, a little helpe will serve. **1752** Bp. Warburton *Lett. Emin. Prel.* (1809) 116, I resolved to be prepared for them (who, by the way, thought better of it). **1812** *Examiner* 21 Sept. 596/1 The enemy's General thought better of it,—beat a retreat. **1884** J. Hawthorne in *Harper's Mag.* Feb. 430/1 The.. gentleman seems to have thought better of his contrariness. *Mod.* I think better of him for his present conduct.

7. ***better off***, comp. of *well off*: see off *adv.* 11. Also as *adj. phr.* and *absol.* as *sb.*

1865 [see off *adv.* 11]. **1865** Mill *Auguste Comte* 167 The better-off classes. **1940** F. Kitchen *Brother to Ox* i. 15 The 'better offs' sat in the chairs. **1959** B. Wootton et al. *Soc. Sci. & Soc. Path.* 366 The better-off, or those who still have better-off standards, can deal with the unmarried mother and the illegitimate child more easily.

better, bettor ('bɛtə(r)), *sb.* [f. bet *v.* + -er¹. As in other cases where a general agent-noun becomes somewhat specific, the tendency is to spell with *-or*; cf. *abettor*.] One who makes bets.

1609 B. Jonson *Sil. Wom.* i. i. (1616) 531 Able to giue 'hem the character of every bowler, or better [*ed.* **1640** bettor] o' the greene. **1628** Earle *Microcosm.* xlvii. 102 The betters are the factious noise of the alley, or the gamesters beadsmen that pray for them. **1711** Addison *Spect.* 126 ¶9 Notwithstanding he was a very fair Bettor, no Body would take him up. **1859** Sala *Tw. round Clock* (1861) 182 Like the honourable betters inside, and the thievish touts outside. **1878** H. Smart *Play or Pay* xi. 234 Some of the big bettors of the Turf.

better ('bɛtə(r)), *v.* [ME. *bet(e)re(n*:—OE. **bet(e)rian* (only *ȝebetrod* is found) = OFris. *beteria*, Du. *beteren*, ON. *betra*, OHG. *bazirôn*, *bezzerôn*, MHG. *bezzern*, mod.G. *bessern*:—OTeut. **batizojan*, f. **batiz-* better.]

1. *trans.* To make better; to improve, amend, ameliorate.

[*c* **897** K. Ælfred *Past. Care* 204 þa scamfæstan bioð oft mid ȝemetlicre lare ȝebetrod.] **1384** Wyclif *De Eccl.* v. Sel. Wks. III. 349 Siþ þei witen not who is beterid by entryng into þes ordris. **1470–85** Malory *Arthur* ii. xvii, I did it to this entent that it sholde better thy courage. **1585** Abp. Sandys *Serm.* (1841) 95 Granted that some rites..might be bettered, or omitted. **1650** Gell *Serm.* 8 Aug. 48 He will improve and better the land he holds. **1711** J. Greenwood *Eng. Gram.* 10 As to our daily borrowing abundance of Words, I cannot think our Language is better'd by it. **1752** Hume *Ess. & Treat.* (1777) I. 283 It is difficult for labourers and artisans to better their condition. *a* **1850** Wordsw. *Sonn.* i. xxv, Love betters what is best, Even here below. **1869** Freeman *Norm. Conq.* (1876) III. xiii. 311.

b. To make morally better.

1587 Fleming *Cont. Holinshed* III. 1351/1 Are you not resolued to better your life? *a* **1593** H. Smith *Wks.* (1867) I. 486 If we will be bettered..by the word, we must be as new-born babes. **1641** Milton *Ch. Govt.* ii. Wks. (1851) 148 Instructing and bettering the Nation at all opportunities. **1849** Ruskin *Sev. Lamps* vii. §8. 194 We think too much.. of bettering men by giving them advice and instruction.

c. To make better in health; to make better off in worldly condition.

1581 W. Stafford *Exam. Compl.* iii. (1876) 91 Oure Townes myght be soone..farre bettered. **1611** Bible *Mark* v. 26 A certaine woman which..had spent all that she had, and was nothing bettered. **1655** Gouge *Comm. Heb.* xiii. 5 So great hope of bettering himself. **1792** Mary Wollstonecr. *Rights Wom.* iv. 164 Girls marry merely to

'better themselves,' to borrow a significant vulgar phrase. **1840** MARRYAT *Poor Jack* i, She left to better herself, and obtained the situation of nurse.

†**2.** *intr.* To be better, have the mastery. *Obs.*

a **1300** *E.E. Psalter* xii. [xiii.] 5 Les when mi wither-win he sai, I betred againes him ai. *Ibid.* lxiv. [lxv.] 4 Wordes of wike bettred over us nou.

3. *trans.* To do better than, surpass, excel.

1548 UDALL, etc. *Erasm. Par.* Pref. 15 Begrieued to see his thing bettered. **1593** SHAKS. *Rich. II*, I. i. 22 Each day still better others happinesse! **1623** COCKERAM III. s.v. *Isæan*, Salmon, which is.. not to be betterd in any part of the world. **1821** KEATS *Lamia* 229 Jove heard his vows, and better'd his desire. **1848** RUSKIN *Mod. Painters* II. III. xiv. §15. 114 It hardly betters the blocks.. in barbers' windows.

†**4.** *absol.* To be better, to be an improvement.

1592 WARNER *Alb. Eng.* VIII. xxxviii. (1612) 189 It betters not to tarrie.

5. *intr.* To grow better, improve. Cf. BETTERING *vbl. sb.* 2.

1839 CARLYLE *Chartism* ii. 116 The general condition of the poor must be bettering instead of worsening. **1883** MISS BROUGHTON *Belinda* II. II. viii. 113 The day has bettered.

†**'betterance.** *Obs. rare*$^{-1}$. [f. BETTER *v.* + -ANCE.] Process of bettering; amelioration.

1614 RALEIGH *Hist. World* I. III. 93 For their securitie and betterance in time to come.

bettered ('bɛtəd), *ppl. a.* [f. as prec. + -ED.]

1. Improved, amended, rendered more excellent.

1660 H. MORE *Myst. Godl.* II. vi. 40 The bettered soil answers the swain's desire. **1874** S. COX *Pilgr. Ps.* i. 21 Let me find a bettered world when I come back to it.

b. *esp.* Improved in health or condition.

1632 SIR J. ELIOT in *Four C. Eng. Lett.* 65, I find myself bettered but not well. **1856** MRS. BROWNING *Aur. Leigh* III. 960 They certainly felt bettered unaware, Emerging from the social smut of towns.

2. Advantaged, that has got the better of another.

a **1659** OSBORN *Observ. Turks* (1673) 343 Here the bettered Party is left so little to boast of.

betterer ('bɛtərə(r)). One who makes better.

1862 TRENCH *Miracles* i. 116 Not a betterer of the old life of man, but the bringer in of a new.

†**'betterhood.** *Obs.* [f. BETTER *a.* + -HOOD.] The state or condition of being better; superiority.

1611 MARKHAM *Countr. Content.* I. ix. (1668) 48 In every contention there must be a better-hood or super-excelling.

bettering ('bɛtərɪŋ), *vbl. sb.* [f. BETTER *v.*]

1. The action of making better or improving; amelioration, amendment, improvement.

c **1375** WYCLIF *Serm.* Sel. Wks. I. 55 Men may.. take of hem þere just dettis for beterynge of þese dettours. **1529** MORE *Comf. agst. Trib.* I. Wks. 1156/1 For the bettering of his sinful soul. **1594** PLAT *Jewell-ho.* I. 3 The manuring, or bettering of all barren grounds. **1690** NORRIS *Beatitudes* (1694) I. 78 Nor.. Does it tend to the bettering of others. **1711** ADDISON *Spect.* No. 124 ¶6 After having consulted many Oculists for the bettering of his Sight. **1776** ADAM SMITH *W.N.* I. I. viii. 86 The hope of bettering his condition animates him. **1862** TRENCH *Miracles* xix. 320 It was no true bettering of the disciples which they desired.

2. The process of becoming better; improvement, progress in a right direction.

c **1600** SHAKS. *Sonn.* xxxii, Compare them with the bettering of the time. *a* **1656** BP. HALL *Occas. Med.* §40 (1851) 48 O God, thou art not capable, either of bettering, or of change. **1718** WODROW *Corr.* (1843) II. 373 Your remark upon the bettering of my style in my History. **1872** BLACKIE *Lays Highl.* 191 Not they who err are damned; but who being wrong.. Refuse all bettering.

3. *bettering-house*, †*-mansion*, a reformatory.

1735 BERKELEY *Querist* Wks. 1871 III. 360 Whether there are not such things in Holland as bettering houses for bringing young gentlemen to order? **1740** CHEYNE *Regimen* iii. 107 If they are reckon'd only Correction and Bettering Mansions. **1854** MRS. S. AUSTIN *Germany* 83 Fit only for a penal colony or a bettering-house.

'bettering, *ppl. a.* [f. as prec. + -ING².] That makes or grows better; improving.

c **1600** SHAKS. *Sonn.* lxxxii, Some fresher stampe of the time bettering dayes. **1876** MRS. WHITNEY *Sights & Ins.* II 639 The struggling, distracted, half-blind, bettering earth.

'betterish, *a.* Somewhat better, of somewhat superior sort.

Mod. colloq. and in newspapers.

betterment ('bɛtəmənt). [f. as prec. + -MENT.]

1. The fact of making or becoming better; the condition of being better; amendment, improvement, amelioration, reformation.

1598 SYLVESTER *Agst. Libertie* in *Du Bartas* (1608) 628 What may most availe unto his betterment. **1649** BLITHE *Eng. Improv. Impr.* (1652) 250 Why we should not.. raise our Flax to a great betterment too, I know not. **1669** WOODHEAD *St. Teresa* I. 293, I find not this betterment of my health. **1865** MISS CARY *Bal. & Lyrics* 304 Each man should live for all men's betterment.

2. *spec.* **a.** Improvement of property. (In U.S.)

1785 in *Vermont State P.* (1823) 501 The value of the improvements and betterments made on such lands by such possessor or possessors. **1809** KENDALL *Trav.* III. lxxiv. 160 These men.. demand either to be left owners of the soil, or paid for their betterments. **1830** GALT *Lawrie T.* III. i. (1849) 81 He sold off his land and betterments in Vermont.

b. Enhanced value (of real property) by reason of local improvements. So *betterment tax*, an assessment made on this.

1890 *Spectator* 28 June 893/2 It was hoped that the principle of 'betterment' might become the means for raising considerable sums of money. **1890** *Contemp. Rev.* May 644 The betterment tax. **1896** J. H. B. BROWNE & ALLAN *Compensation* 683 'Betterment' as a principle is only a proposal to tax the increment when it clearly and directly arises from an improvement carried out by a public authority and at the public expense. *Ibid.* 684 A betterment charge in respect of improvements effected by local authorities. **1902** *Encycl. Brit.* XXVII. 182/2 The principle of 'betterment', according to which promoters would be allowed to set off against an owner's claim for compensation any enhancement of the value of his land by the use of the land taken by the promoters. **1960** *Spectator* 15 July 88 The 1947 Silkin Town and Country Planning Act.. introduced a system of development charges—or betterment tax, based on the value of a particular planning permission.

†**3.** = BETTERNESS 1; difference for the better. *Obs.*

1678 BUNYAN *Pilgr.* I. 35 It will appear there is no betterment 'twixt him [Pliable] and my self.

bettermost ('bɛtəməʊst, -məst), *a. colloq.* [f. BETTER *a.*, after *uppermost*, *uttermost*, etc.: see -MOST.] Best (relatively, rather than absolutely).

1762 *Gentl. Mag.* 403 Some of our bettermost neighbours. **1849** ROCK *Ch. Fathers* I. ii. 141 The bettermost sort of wine. **1879** G. MEREDITH *Egoist* I. v. 69 Men, after their fashion, as well as women, distinguish the bettermost, and aid him to succeed.

betterness ('bɛtənɪs). Also 5 bettirnes. [f. BETTER *a.* + -NESS.]

1. The quality of being better, having more good qualities, or excelling; superiority.

a **1300** *E.E. Psalter* li[i]. 5 Þou loved ivelnes ovre betternes. **1492** *Act. Dom. Conc.* 247–8 (JAM.) The bettirnes of the said tercis [of land]. **1580** SIDNEY *Arcad.* 407 Your vnmatched betternesse. **1607** HIERON *Wks.* I. 305 There is no betternesse or precedence of one place aboue another for the administration of holy things. **1611** CHAPMAN *Iliad* II. Comm. (1857) 56. **1856** RUSKIN *Mod. Paint.* III. IV. x. §4 An infinity of Betterness above other human effort.

b. *spec.* Fineness of the precious metals beyond the standard.

c **1530** in Gutch *Coll. Cur.* II. 287, Item for the betternes of the golde that went to the same Rings—iiijs. **1820** G. CAREY *Funds* 99 If gold or silver be finer than standard, the difference is termed betterness by the trade.

2. Improvement, amendment, betterment. *dial.*

1864 ATKINSON *Whitby Gloss.* s.v. *Betterness*.. As for my ailment I find no betterness in it.

better-to-do, *adj. phr.* [Comparative of WELL-TO-DO.] Above the well-to-do in social condition or worldly circumstances; more prosperous. Also *absol.*

1890 W. BOOTH *In Darkest England* II. vi. 217 His better-to-do neighbour will often assist him by providing the capital. **1898** *Daily News* 6 Dec. 5/6 To the new L.C.C. buildings there had come many better-to-do workmen. **1905** *Daily Chron.* 1 Feb. 6/2 Children.. of the better-to-do. **1940** *Manch. Guardian Weekly* 9 Feb. 116 Even among the better-to-do there is greater simplicity of living and independence of service than among their compeers in England. **1965** in P. Jennings *Living Village* (1968) 133 Many of the better-to-do people send their children away to school.

bettily, obs. form of BETELLEE.

betting ('bɛtɪŋ), *vbl. sb.*¹ [f. BET *v.* + -ING¹.]

1. The making of bets, wagering. Also (*Racing*), the odds offered. *to change the betting*, i.e. the course of the betting on an event, put for 'the chances, the way things are going.'

1599 SHAKS. *Hen. V*, II. i. 98 You'l pay me the eight shillings I won of you at Betting? **1855** MACAULAY *Hist. Eng.* III. 548 Gambling and betting were his amusements. **1858** GEN. P. THOMPSON *Audi. Alt.* II. lxxx. 38 It is not hiding the head as is the wont of the ostrich and the turkey, that will change the betting. **1901** C. RICHARDSON *Eng. Turf* i. 2 In the North-country towns, too, a single sheet is everywhere on sale shortly before noon, filled with telegrams from the course,.. and the little regarded 'latest betting', which is an epitome of the prices offered on the day's races. **1922** JOYCE *Ulysses* 632 Betting 5 to 4 on *Zinfandel*, 20 to 1 *Throwaway* (off). **1939** P. R. CHALMERS *Racing England* vi. 88 Not to be mentioned in the betting has never yet stopped a horse from winning.

2. *Comb.*, as **betting-book**, a book in which a better enters his bets; **betting-house**, a house where betting is carried on; **betting-man**, one who makes bets, a better, *usually* a professional gambler; **betting office**, an establishment licensed to handle bets (on horse-races, dog-races, etc.); **betting-post**, (?) a post or station for betting-men; **betting ring** = RING *sb.*¹ 14 b; **betting room**, a room where betting is carried on; **betting shop** *colloq.* = *betting office*; **betting-slip**, a slip of paper on which a bet is entered.

1813 *Sporting Mag.* XLII. 141/1 By a recent exposition of his betting-book at Tattersall's, it appeared that he lost 1200 guineas. **1836** R. S. SURTEES *Let.* in E. K. Mathews *Mem. C. Mathews* (1839) IV. 194 As soon as ever he got to town he would advertise for a man that could keep a betting-book. **1855** *Ess. Intuit. Morals* 154 Making up their lives as sagaciously as a black-leg does his betting book. **1853** *Act 16 & 17 Vict.* c. 119 (*title*) An Act for the Suppression of Betting Houses. **1819** *Sporting Mag.* V. 3/2 The betting men have all agreed to pay and receive accordingly. **1825** P. EGAN *Life of Actor* iv. 140 Sir Henry was.. not.. acknowledged as a betting man in the sporting circles. **1864** *Soc. Sc. Rev.* 386 If he be a betting-man the race-course.. calls him into the open air. **1939** A. CHRISTIE *Ten Little Niggers* xi. 162 I'm not a betting man. And anyway if you were dead I wouldn't get paid. **1852** *Chambers's Edin. Jrnl.* XVIII. 57/1 'Commission Office', 'Racing Bank',.. 'Betting-Office', are the styles of announcement adopted by speculators who open what low people call Betting-shops. **1951** *R. Commission on Betting, Lotteries & Gaming 1949–51 Rep.* (*Cmd. 8190*) 65 We were told by one police witness that the licensing of betting offices would merely be regularising what is a fact in his city. **1961** *Economist* 6 May 565/1 Nobody has any real idea of how many bookmakers in Britain have taken advantage of the new Betting and Gaming Act.. to open betting shops—or.. Licensed Betting Offices. **1771** P. PARSONS *Newmarket* II. 148 Let us walk a little about the betting-post. **1822** *Sporting Mag.* X. 4/1 He was well known in the betting ring. **1954** W. FAULKNER *Fable* 57 A hard-faced jockey-sized man who seemed to have brought on his warped legs.. something of hard, light, razor-edge horses and betting-rings. **1793** *Sporting Mag.* II. 124/1 In the betting-room, at Tattersall's the horse was so little thought of, that he had never been mentioned. **1857** DICKENS & W. COLLINS in *Househ. Words* XVI. 410/1 A complete choke and stoppage of the thoroughfare outside the Betting Rooms. **1852** Betting-shop [see *betting-office* above]. **1961** *Daily Tel.* 2 May 13/5 The Betting and Gaming Act came into force yesterday, but.. betting shops are not easy to find. **1927** W. E. COLLINSON *Contemp. Eng.* 37 Betting agents or touts are often had up before the courts for passing betting-slips in the streets to would-be backers. **1959** J. BRAINE *Vodi* xxv. 264 The action was surreptitiously executed, as if he were passing a betting-slip in the street.

†**betting,** *vbl. sb.*² *Obs.* [variant of BEETING.] Material for a fire, fuel.

1521 Item payd for viij*li.* of pyche for the bettyngs to the Cressets, viij*d.*

‖**bettong.** A species of Kangaroo rat, a nocturnal animal about the size of a hare.

1839 *Penny Cycl.* XIV. 462/1 Mr. Ogilby describes (*Zool. Proc.* 1831) a fourth species, *Hypsiprymnus setosus*, known in the colony of New South Wales by the native name of Bettong Kangaroo.

bettony, obs. form of BETONY.

bettor. †**1.** Aphetic form of ABETTOR. *Obs.*

1671 *True Non-Conf.* 490 Having solemnly vowed a detestation thereof, and a non-conjunction with all their bettors.

2. Variant form of BETTER *sb.*

Betty ('bɛtɪ), *sb.* [dim. of *Bet*, abbreviation of *Elizabet*, *-beth*.]

1. A female pet name or familiar name, once fashionable (as in Lady Betty), but now chiefly rustic or homely. Hence,

2. Given in contempt to a man who occupies himself with a woman's household duties. (So MOLLY.)

3. 'A pear-shaped bottle covered round with straw, in which olive oil is sometimes brought from Italy; called by chemists a Florence flask.' Webster. (? Only in U.S. The quot. seems to refer to some kind of vessel; cf. BELLARMINE.)

1725 L. WELSTED *Oikogr.* 12 No Bellarmine, my Lord, is here; Elisa none, at hand to reach, A Betty call'd in common speech!

4. Cant name formerly given to a short bar of iron used by burglars as a lever to force open doors: also called a *Jenny*, and now a *Jemmy*.

1700 LUTTRELL *Brief Rel.* (1857) IV. 687 One of the persons that broke open the exchequer was taken.. he was discovered by the smith who made the betty and saw. **1707** E. WARD *Hud. Rediv.* II. ix. 7 Ruffians, who, with Crows and Betties, Break Houses. **1712** ARBUTHNOT *John Bull* (J.) Describing the powerful betty or the artful picklock. **1721** BAILEY, *Bettee.* **1755** JOHNSON, *Betty.*

5. *Betty lamp* (see quots.).

1893 A. EARLE *Customs Old New England* iv. 125 Betty lamps.. were a shallow receptacle.. with a projecting nose an inch or two long.. they were filled with tallow or grease, and a wick.. was placed so that the lighted end could hang on the nose. **1952** J. GLOAG *Dict. Furn.* III. 141 *Betty lamp*, a type of lamp used in America during the 18th century... It resembles the Scottish type of hanging lamp known as a cruisie. **1957** *Encycl. Brit.* XIV. 101/2 The Betty lamp of the Pilgrims (1620).. was equipped for hanging from mantelpieces or shelves.

betty ('bɛtɪ), *v. colloq.* [f. prec. sb.] *to betty about*: to fuss about, like a man who busies himself with a woman's duties. Hence **'bettying** *vbl. sb.*

1851 T. PARKER in Weiss *Life* II. 105, I am only an old maid in life after all my bettying about in literature and philosophy.

Betty Martin. In slang phr. (*all*) *my eye* (*and*) *Betty Martin*: 'all my eye' (see EYE *sb.*¹ 2 h).

1781 S. CRISPE *Let.* 16 Oct. in W. H. Hutton *Burford Papers* (1905) iv. 69 Physic, to old, crazy Frames, like ours, *is all my eye and Betty Martin*—(a sea phrase that Admiral Jemm frequently makes use of). **1785** [see EYE *sb.*¹ 2 h]. **1812** J. & H. SMITH *Rej. Addr.* 104 The knife that I thought that I saw, Was nought but my Eye Betty Martin. **1859** HOTTEN *Dict. Slang* 1 All my eye, answer of astonishment to an improbable story; All my eye and Betty Martin, a vulgar phrase with similar meaning. **1930** W. DE LA MARE *On Edge* 108 You might be suggesting that both shape and scarecrow too were all my eye and Betty Martin.

betuckered, beturbaned, betutor, betwattle, etc.: see BE- *pref.*

betuix, obs. form of BETWIXT.

betulin ('bɛtjʊlɪn). [f. L. *betula* birch + -IN.] 'A resinous substance extracted from the outer bark of the birch-tree (*Betula alba*), or from the tar prepared therefrom.' Watts *Dict. Chem.* 1879.

betuline ('bɛtjʊlaɪn), *a. rare*[−1]. [f. L. *betula* + -INE[1].] Pertaining to the birch, or birch-rod.
1873 M. COLLINS *Miranda* III. 22 He had been bullying boys all his life with betuline despotism.

†**be'tumbled,** *ppl. a. Obs. rare*[−1]. In 6 betombled. [f. BE- 2 + TUMBLE *v.*] Tossed in confusion, disordered.
1593 SHAKS. *Lucr.* 1037 From her betombled couch shee starteth.

betumen, -une, obs. forms of BITUMEN.

†**beturn,** *v. Obs.* For forms see TURN. [ME. f. *bi-*, BE- + *turnen* to TURN.] To turn about.
a **1225** *Ancr. R.* 394 Biturn þe and cum aȝean. *a* **1300** *Pains of Hell* 119 in *O.E. Misc.* 226 Seynt Poul þo bitornd his face. **1594** CAREW *Tasso* (1881) 110 To their aduises the disdainefull hart, Of this audacious youth, beturning plies.

†**be'tweche,** *v. Obs. rare*[−1]. [? for BETEACH.] (The context suggests 'exorcize, deliver, or rid.')
c **1450** *Pol. Rel. & L. Poems* (1866) 23 Dominus deus sabaot, emanuel, þe gret gods name, I be-tweche þes place from ratones & from alle oþer schame!

between (bɪt'wiːn), *prep.* and *adv.* Forms: α. 1 bi-, betweonum, -an, -twinum, -an, -twynum, -an, 2–3 bitweone(n, -twene(n, bitwine, 3 bitweounen, 3–4 bituene, 4 bituine, bytwyne, betwene. β. 1 bi-, betwion, -tuien, bitwien, -twen, -twin, betweon, 2 bitweon, -twon, 2–3 bitwien, 3–4 bitwen, -tuen, (bitwhen, beþwen). α. β. (4–5 betweyn(e), 4–6 bi-, betwen(e, (5 bytwyen, betwyn), 5–7 betweene, 6– between. [The modern *between* combines two earlier forms: α. OE. *bi-*, *betwéonum*, etc., ME. *bitwenen*, *-twene*; β. OE. *bi-*, *betwéon*, etc., ME. *bitwēn*; see BE-. In *betwéonum*, Mercian *betwínum*, the second element represents an original OE. dative **twīhnum*, **tweohnum*. In *betwéon* (only a northern form, Rushworth Gosp. *bi-*, *betwion*, *betweon*, Lindisf. *bi-*, *betuien*, *bitwén*, Durh. Ritual *bitwien*, *-twén*, *-twín*), the second element points back, according to Sievers, through earlier **twīhen*, **twīhon*, to an orig. OE. acc. *twīhn* (cf. *bituichn* in Erfurt Gloss.). These, **twīhnum*, **twīhn*, answer respectively to Goth. *tweihnaim* dat. pl., and *tweihna* acc. pl. neuter, of the distributive numeral *tweih-nai* 'two each', a derivative of *twa* TWO *sb.* (= L. *bī-nī*, for **dvī-nī* 'two each'), which appears also, but with the simple sense of 'two' (nom. masc.), in OS. and OFris. *twêne*, OHG., MHG. *zwêne* (early mod.G. *zween*). *Betwéonum*, later *betwéonan*, gave the prevailing ME. form *bitwenen*, reduced before a consonant, and at length generally, to *bitwene*; *bitwen* was mostly northern. But after 1400, when final *-e* became mute, and was omitted in writing, or retained only as a sign of a preceding long vowel, both forms necessarily coalesced in *betwene* (= betwēn), whence mod. *between*. In OE. the original construction was *bi sǽm twéonum*, lit. 'by seas twain'; thence through constructions like *frið freondum bi twéon* 'peace friends between,' *bi twéonum*, *bi twéon* coalesced into prepositions. (Cf. the history of *to(us)-ward*, *to-ward*, *toward*.)
Intimately related to *between*, alike in their elements, and in the process by which these coalesced, are its synonyms BETWIXT, in ME. *betwix*, and †BETWIXEN, †BITWIH, †BITWIHEN, †BITWEIES. *Bitwih* was actually, in its origin, a doublet of OE. *betwéon*, and *betwihen* an expansion of that, on the analogy of *betweonen*. *Betwixen* and *betwix* were a parallel pair, formed on the OTeut. adj. *twiski-* 'two-fold'. (See Sievers *Misc. zur Ags. Gram.* §329.) *Bitwih* died *a* **1100**, *bitwihen a* **1300**, *betwixen a* **1500**; *betwixt* is now archaic, *between* is the living word.]

¶ Instances of the original construction:
Beowulf 1720 Suð ne norð be sǽm tweonum. **971** *Blickl. Hom.* 139 And hie [Peter and Paul] ȝesawon be him tweonum þæt heo wæs ȝewuldrod. *Ibid.* 143 Heo bið swiþor ȝestrangod be us tweonum þurh Drihtnes gehát.

A. *prep.*

I. Of simple position. * *Of a point.*

1. The proper word expressing the local relation of a point to two other points in opposite directions from it (i.e. if a point has two other points on opposite sides of it, it is said to be *between* them): In the space which separates two points; in the direct line which joins two points; hence, in any line of communication which passes from one point, place, or object, to another.
c **1200** *Trin. Coll. Hom.* 171 Noðer on heuene · ne on eorðe · ac bitwien two · on þe wolcne. *c* **1250** *Gen. & Ex.* 760 An oðer alter Abram made bi-twen Betel and Ai. **1297** R. GLOUC. 371 At þere hii gonne abyde Bytuene þe water of Trente & of Ouse. **1398** TREVISA *Barth. De. P.R.* VIII. xxiii. (1495) 335 Mystes other clowdes sette bytwene hym and the syghte. **1535** COVERDALE *Gen.* xiii. 3 The place where his tent was at yᵉ first, betwene Bethel and Ay [ÆLFRIC, betwux; WYCLIF, bytwix, bitwixe]. **1592** SHAKS. *Ven. & Ad.* 194, I lie between that sun and thee. **1667** MILTON *P.L.* I. 387 Jehovah..thron'd Between the Cherubim. **1838** ARNOLD *Hist. Rome* (1845) I. xxiv. 517 They..established themselves between the Danube and Greece. *Mod.* Any station on the Inner Circle Railway between Gower Street and The Temple.

2. *fig.* Used of a similar relation to two immaterial objects figured as lying in space; or of a relation, figured as spatial, to two material objects.
c **1325** *E.E. Allit. P.* A. 140 A deuyse Bytwene myrþez by merez made. *a* **1400** *Cursor M.* 723 (Trin.) Now mon is sett bitwene [*v.r.* bituix] two, On eiþer side he haþ a fo, Bitwene sathan & his wif. **1621** BURTON *Anat. Mel.* I. ii. III. x, Thus between hope and fear, suspicions, angers..we bangle away our best days. **1641** J. JACKSON *True Evang. T.* iii. 200 While these Sermons were betweene the Pulpit, and the Presse. **1742** H. WALPOLE *Lett.* (1857) I. 128 To hold the balance between liberty and prerogative. *c* **1815** MISS AUSTEN *Northang. Ab.* (1848) 168 The General, between his cocoa and his newspaper, had luckily no leisure for noticing her. **1826** DISRAELI *Viv. Grey* III. iv. 102 Between astonishment and fear the lady was tearless. *Mod.* The choice lies between the two last-named applicants.

b. In many phrases, which see under the substantives concerned: e.g. † ***between the beetle and the block***; ***between the cup and the lip***; ***between the devil and the Dead*** (or ***deep***) ***Sea***. ***between wind and water***: along the line where anything is submerged in water or in damp soil, *esp.* on the load-line of a ship, which, as the vessel tosses, is alternately above and below the water's surface.
1580 LYLY *Euphues* (Arb.) 471 Manye thinges fall betweene the cup and the lippe. **1613** HAYWARD *Norm. Kings* 274 Earle William being thus set as it were betweene the beetle and the block—was nothing deiected. **1627** CAPT. SMITH *Seaman's Gram.* xiii. 60 Wee are shot thorow and thorow, and betweene wind and water. **1642** ROGERS *Naaman* 22 Nothing shall come betweene cup and lip to defeat thee. **1692** LUTTRELL *Brief Rel.* (1857) II. 637 Having received a shot between wind and water, [she was] forced to lye by to stop her leake. *Mod.* An oaken gate-post always decays between wind and water.

3. Of time: In the interval following one event or point of time and preceding another.
c **1131** *O.E. Chron.* an. 1124 Betweonen Cristes messe and Candel-mæsse. *c* **1205** LAY. 24274 Bitwene þis and domes-dæi. *c* **1330** *Amis & Amil.* 992 He cam bitven the day and the night. *c* **1485** *Digby Myst., Mor. Wisd.* (1882) 167 And at the paroyse I wyll be..be-twyn two and three. **1601** SHAKS. *Jul. C.* II. i. 63 Betweene the acting of a dreadfull thing And the first motion, all the interim is Like a phantasma. **1790** BOSWELL *Johnson* (1826) I. 321 Between one and two in the morning. **1848** MACAULAY *Hist. Eng.* II. 51 The nine months which elapsed between the death of Charles and the commencement of the viceroyalty of Clarendon.

b. ***between hands*** (Sc.): in the intervals of regular occupation; also = BETWEENWHILES.
c **1817** HOGG *Tales & Sk.* II. 222 Always, between hands, thanked Heaven for her health. **1881** J. YOUNGER *Autobiog.* vi. 54 Retiring to sit and work between hands.

4. Of the relation of a number, quantity, degree, or quality to two others above and below it, or differing from it in opposite ways; Intermediate to.
1711 STEELE *Spect.* No. 49 ⁋3 Persons..such as are between these two sorts of Men. **1711** ADDISON *Ibid.* No. 108 ⁋3 He is now between Forty and Fifty. **1712** PARNELL *Ibid.* No. 501 ⁋6 Rivulets that had a colour between red and black. **1816** MISS AUSTEN *Emma* (1849) 123 The atmosphere in that unsettled state between frost and thaw. **1838** ARNOLD *Hist. Rome* (1845) I. iii. 33 Between five and six miles from the city. **1885** *Law Rep.* XV. *Q. Bench Div.* 170 To the value of between 30,000*l.* and 40,000*l.*

** *Of a line of motion.*

5. Expressing the relation that motion along a line bears to two points on opposite sides of it; as, 'to steer between Scylla and Charybdis.'
c **1205** LAY. 20948 Swa heo liðen æfter sæ..swa longe þat heo commen bitwiȝe Ænglelonde & Normandie. **1535** COVERDALE *Josh.* xviii. 11 The border of their lot wente out betwene the children of Iuda and the children of Ioseph. **1590** SHAKS. *Com. Err.* III. ii. 132 The salt rheume that ranne betweene France and it. **1799** SOUTHEY *Ebb Tide* Lyr. Poems II. 193 Yet little way they made, though labouring long Between thy winding shores. **1812** BYRON *Ch. Har.* I. xxxiii, But these between a silver streamlet glides. **1864** TENNYSON *Brook* 28 By thirty hills I hurry down Or slip between the ridges.

II. Of intervening space. * *As separating or connecting.*

6. Expressing the relation of the continuous space, or distance, which extends from one point to another, and separates them, or of a line which passes from one to the other and unites them.
c **1205** LAY. 30017 Nas heom bi-tweounen bute bare twa milen. **1790** BURNS *Tam O'Shanter* 9 We think na on the lang Scots miles That lie between us and our hame. **1858** SEARS *Athan.* III. 280 The vast distance between heaven and hell. **1884** *Manch. Exam.* 19 Mar. 4/7 A scheme was mooted ..for a plateway between Liverpool and Manchester. *Mod.* To stretch a rope between the two rafters.

7. Used in reference to any objective relation uniting two (or more) parties, and holding them in a certain connexion.
a **1300** *Cursor M.* 3338 þe mariage þan did he make, Bi-tuene Rebecca and ysaac. **1690** LOCKE *Hum. Und.* (1777) II. 150 A vital union between the soul and body. **1758** JOHNSON *Idler* No. 12 ⁋4 A marriage celebrated between Mr. Buckram..and Miss Dolly Juniper. **1815** *Scribbleomania* 197 The close alliance which has lately existed between this country and the Peninsula. **1848** MACAULAY *Hist. Eng.* I. 123 A coalition was formed between the Royalists and a large body of Presbyterians.

8. Used with the subjective relations of difference, diversity, likeness, equality, proportion, comparison.
a **1225** *Ancr. R.* 70 Ancre & huses lefdi ouh muche to beon bitweonen. **1340** *Ayenb.* 210 Zwych difference ase þer is be-tuene þe cheue and þe corn. **1530** PALSGR. Introd. 43 Dyvers other sortes of phrasys betwene our tong and theyrs. **1692** E. WALKER *Epictetus' Mor., Life*, Bear and Forbear, Words which in Greek have a peculiar Elegance, there being but the Difference of a single Letter between them. **1785** PALEY *M. Philos.* III. III. ix, There is no comparison between a fortune which a man acquires by well-applied industry, and one.. received from another. **1802** MAR. EDGEWORTH *Moral T.* (1816) I. i. 1 Inequality between the rich and the poor. **1837** NEWMAN *Par. Serm.* (ed. 2) III. xx. 327 Is there no difference between a chance and a certainty?

** *Of motion across intervening space.*

9. Expressing motion or communication from one body or place to another.
1598 SHAKS. *Merry W.* II. ii. 130 You must send her your Page..hee may come and goe betweene you both. **1629** MASSINGER *Emperor of E.* I. ii, You are..the go-between This female and that wanton sir. **1696** LUTTRELL *Brief Rel.* (1857) IV. 142 All clipt money shal goe between man and man at 5*s.* 2*d.* per ounce. **1712** STEELE *Spect.* No. 263 ⁋5 Two Letters which passed between a Mother and Son lately. **1812** MISS AUSTEN *Pride & Prej.* (1846) 301 Not a word passed between the sisters concerning Bingley. *Mod. Newspaper.* Carried backwards and forwards between the police station and the workhouse. Tenders for carrying the mails between Great Britain and New Zealand.

10. Expressing reciprocal action or relation maintained, by two (or more) agents towards each other.
971 *Blickl. Hom.* 221 Swylce ða ȝesceafta twá him be-tweonan ȝefeohtan sceoldan. **1038–50** *Chart. Godwine* in *Cod. Dipl.* IV. 118 [Ða forew]eard ðe Godwine eorl worhte betweonan Ælfstáne abbod..and Leófwine preóste. *c* **1175** *Lamb. Hom.* 41 Haldeð broþerredene eow bitwenen. *c* **1205** LAY. 22968 Feond-scipe..bitweone twom monnen. *c* **1300** *Beket* 281 The love that bituene hem was. *c* **1380** *Sir Ferumb.* 986 þan comencede a batail newe *!* by-twene þes hostes two. **1478** SIR J. PASTON *Lett.* 815 III. 223 Suche cawsys as ar nowe bygunne by twyen my Lorde off Suffolke and me. **1503** WRIOTHESLEY *Chron.* (1875) I. 5 A peace made betwene the Emperoure and the Kinge. **1611** BIBLE *Gen.* iii. 15, I will put enmitie betweene thee and the woman, and betweene thy seed and her seed. **1779–84** HORNE *Disc.* (1799) III. iv. 73 A friendly intercourse is opened between the most distant lands. **1857** BUCKLE *Civilis.* I. x. 607 To talk of sympathy existing between the two classes is a manifest absurdity. **1875** JOWETT *Plato* (ed. 2) I. Pref. 19 The same opposition between science and religion.

III. Of relation to things acting conjointly or participating in action.

11. Expressing the position of anything confined or enclosed by objects on opposite sides.
c **1175** *Lamb. Hom.* 185 Hwine warpe ich me bitweone þe ilke earmes. **1340** *Ayenb.* 210 þou sselt bidde God betuene þine teþ þet is to zigge ine þine herte. *c* **1380** WYCLIF *Wks.* (1880) 19 þe sacrament of þe auter þat men seen bitwen þe prestis hondis. **1593** SHAKS. *Lucr.* 390 The pillow..Between whose hills her head entombed is. **1643** DENHAM *Coopers H.* 224 Between the Mountain and the Stream embrac'd. **1682** DRYDEN *Medal* 121 This new Jehu..Instructs the beast.. To take the bit between his teeth and fly. **1853** KANE *Grinnell Exp.* i. (1856) 13 The Arctic Ocean is enclosed between the northern shores of Asia, Europe, and America.

12. Expressing confinement or restriction to two (or more) parties; especially used of privacy or secrecy in conversation. ***between ourselves***: as a matter not to be communicated to others.
c **1000** *Ags. Gosp.* John vii. 35 þa iudeas cwædon betweonan him sylfum. *c* **1205** LAY. 25963 þer heo heom bi-twenen [*c* **1250** bi-twine] heolden heore runen. *c* **1300** *K. Alis.* 1556 Tel me..pryvely bytweone thè and me! **1470–85** MALORY *Arthur* (1816) II. 112 Pray him to speak with me between us two. **1526** TINDALE *John* xi. 56 And spake bitwene [**1611** among] them selves. **1588** J. UDALL *Diotreph.* (Arb.) 12 This I tel you between you and me, but I would haue it go no further. **1711** STEELE *Spect.* No. 118 ⁋3 Between you and me, I am often apt to imagine it has had some whimsical Effect upon my Brain. **1840** MARRYAT *Poor Jack* xix, I was desired to ask you a question..between ourselves.

13. By the joint action of, done by, shared in by, belonging to (two parties) jointly. (Sometimes said of more than two, when it is desired to mark the participation of all the parties more defintely than can be done by *among*; cf. 19.)
1297 R. GLOUC. 32 þat heo myȝte som eyres bitwene hem forþ bringe. *a* **1400** *Cursor M.* 2443 (Laud) By-twene [*v.r.* bituix] hym and his nevew lot Bestayle they had y-now y wot. **1512** *Act 4 Hen. VIII*, xi, The heires of the bodies of the seid Countesse and..hir late Husbond decessed bytwene theym laufully begoten. **1590** SHAKS. *Com. Err.* v. i. 177 Betweene them they will kill the coniurer. **1785** MACKENZIE *Lounger* No. 36 They had but one pair of silk stockings between them. **1812** MISS AUSTEN *Mansf. Pk.*

(1847) 160 We brought home six brace between us. **1867** FREEMAN *Norm. Conq.* (1876) I. App. 776 Between the two we get a full and consistent narrative.

14. Expressing division and distribution to two (or more) partakers.

1758 JOHNSON *Idler* No. 19 ¶5 By this ingenious distribution of himself between two houses. **1771** R. HENRY *Hist. Gt. Brit.* I. I. vi. 383 The British trade was thus divided between Marseilles and Narbonne. **1788** J. POWELL *Devises* (1827) II. 627 Her personal estate..should go and be equally divided between her said two grandsons. *Mod.* They had it between them.

IV. Of separation.

15. Expressing the relation of a line to two spaces which it separates or divides from each other.

*c***1385** CHAUCER *L.G.W.* 713 There was but a ston wal hem be-tweene. *c***1400** MAUNDEV. xi. 124 By twyne the Cytee of Darke and the Cytee of Rophane, ys a Ryvere. **1590** SHAKS. *Mids. N.* v. 176 O vvall..That stands betweene her fathers ground and mine. **1770** BURKE *Pres. Discont.* Wks. 1845 I. 383 No man can draw a stroke between the confines of day and night. **1855** DICKENS *Dorrit* i, The line of demarcation between the two colours.

16. Expressing the relation of motion or action to bodies or surfaces which it forces apart. ***between the bark and the wood*** or ***tree***: see BARK.

*c***1000** *Ags. Ps.* cv. 9 And [ðu] hi betweonum wætera weallas læddest. *a***1120** *O.E. Chron.* (Laud MS.) an. 1101 Þa heafod men heom betwenan foran. **1642** ROGERS *Naaman* 490 Let none of them come betweene barke and tree to defeat your faith. **1837** CARLYLE *Fr. Rev.* (1872) II. II. vi. 80 Stand between them, keeping them well separate. **1843** *Penny Cycl.* XXV. 81/2 The boots..(in which the torture was applied by driving in wedges with a hammer between the flesh and iron rings drawn tightly upon the legs).

17. *fig.* ***to be, come, stand between*** a person and any object desired, or anything threatening him; between combatants, etc.

*c***1325** *E.E. Allit. P.* A. 657 Now is þer noȝt in þe worlde rounde Bytwene vus & blysse. **1580** BARET *Alv.* B 602 To go betweene or to be betweene..to make intercession; to let: to prohibite. **1774** BLACKLOCK *Graham* I. xxiv, With pallid cheek, and trembling frame, Between the combatants she came. **1816** J. WILSON *City of Plague* I. iii. 103 A sinful wretch implores That thou would'st stand between him and the wrath Of an offended God. **1884** W. C. SMITH *Kildrostan* 55 How could Doris come between us two?

18. After verbs and nouns of action expressing: **a.** separation, division; **b.** subjective separation, distinction, discrimination, discernment, judgement.

a. 1340 HAMPOLE *Pr. Consc.* 1691 Gastely ded es twynyng thurgh synne, Bitwene God and man saule within. **1689** SELDEN *Table T.* (Arb.) 71 'Twas an unhappy Division that has been made between Faith and Works. **1848** MACAULAY *Hist. Eng.* I. 300 A complete separation between the naval and military services.

b. 1340 *Ayenb.* 82 Hi ne conne deme betuene zuete and byter. **1526** *Pilgr. Perf.* (W. de W. 1531) 32 To discerne bytwene the inspiracyon of the holy goost and the illusyon of the ennemy. **1593** HOOKER *Eccl. Pol.* I. vi. §5 To judge rightly between truth and error. **1771** *Junius Lett.* lxi. 319 The public must determine between us. **1848** MACAULAY *Hist. Eng.* I. 640 In cases of felony, a distinction..is made between the principal and the accessory after the fact.

V. 19. In all senses, *between* has been, from its earliest appearance, extended to more than two. In OE. and ME. it was so extended in sense 1, in which AMONG is now considered better. It is still the only word available to express the relation of a thing to many surrounding things severally and individually, *among* expressing a relation to them collectively and vaguely: we should not say 'the space lying among the three points,' or 'a treaty among three powers,' or 'the choice lies among the three candidates in the select list,' or 'to insert a needle among the closed petals of a flower.'

971 *Blickl. Hom.* 229 Þa apostoli wæron æt-somne; and hie sendon hlot him betweonum. *c***1175** *Lamb. Hom.* 61 And cristes wille bo us bitwon. *c***1205** LAY. 26936 Heo..sweoren heom bitwænen [*c***1250** bi-twine] þat heo wolden. *a***1225** *Ancr. R.* 358 In unkuðe londe, & in unkuðe earde, bitwhen unðeode. *c***1250** *Gen. & Ex.* 1601 And wulde noȝt ðat folc bi-twen Herberȝed..ben. *a***1300** *Cursor M.* 10244 Ga heþen, he said, fra vs bituin. *c***1380** *Sir Ferumb.* 1255 Bytwene hymen þanne euerechon: þay lift vp þat bodi faste. *a***1400** *Cov. Myst.* 352, I xalle telle ȝow why In ȝoure erys prevyly Betweyn us thre. **1755** JOHNSON *Dict.*, *Between* is properly used of two, and *among* of more; but perhaps this accuracy is not always preserved. **1771** JOHNSON in *Boswell* (1826) II. 127, I..hope, that, between publick business, improving studies, and domestick pleasures, neither melancholy nor caprice will find any place for entrance. **1828** SOUTHEY *Ess.* (1832) II. 436 Between the prior, the boatmen, and a little offering to St. Patrick, he had not as much money left, etc. **1885** J. COWPER in *N. & Q.* Ser. VI. XII. 148/2 There were six, who collected between them 15*s.* 4*d.*

†**VI. 20.** ***between and*** (an adaptation of *betwix and*: see BETWIXT A. 3): until, till; with *sb.* or *clause*.

*a***1400** *Cursor M.* 16583 (Trin.) Þei alle ne myȝt stir þe cros of þat stede Bitwene & [*v.r.* bituix and; til] oure lord crist was þider him self lede. *Ibid.* 20181 (Fairf.) I walde wite gladli bi-twene [*v.r.* tuix] & quen to take leue atte my kinnismen.

B. *adv.* (Mostly the preposition with object understood.)

1. Of place: In an intermediate position or course, midway, in the midst. *lit.* and *fig.*

*c***890** K. ÆLFRED *Bæda* IV. ix. (Bosw.) Ne si lang fæc betweonum. *c***1205** LAY. 276 Heo wepen heore leoten þe scucke wes bitweonen. **1297** R. GLOUC. 355 Þo þat water was bytuene. *c***1430** *Stans Puer* 77 in *Babees Bk.* (1868) 31 Schewe out þi visage, To glad, ne to sory, but kepe þee euene bitwene. **1606** SHAKS. *Ant. & Cl.* III. iv. 12 A more unhappie Lady ne're stood betweene. **1667** MILTON *P.L.* IV. 699 Roses, and Gessamin Rear'd high thir flourisht heads between. **1795** SOUTHEY *Joan of Arc* VII. 216 The man of lowly line That instant rush'd between. **1858** SEARS *Athan.* III. ii. 268 Looking into the immense vacuum between.

†**2.** ***to go between***: to act as a medium or mediator; see GO-BETWEEN. *Obs.*

*c***1320** *Sir Trist.* II. 101 A bischop yede bitvene. **1523** LD. BERNERS *Froiss.* cccviii. 580/1 Certayne good people of Gaunte..went so bytwene in this mater. **1606** SHAKS. *Tr. & Cr.* I. i. 72, I haue..gone betweene and betweene, but small thankes for my labour.

3. Of time: In the interval, at intervals.

*a***1240** *Ureisun* 28 in *Lamb. Hom.* 193 Murie dreameð engles..Pleieð. and sweieð. and singeð. bitweonen. *a***1300** *Cursor M.* 3572 Þe nese it droppes ai bi-tuine. *c***1374** CHAUCER *Troylus* v. 1086 How longe it was betweyne That she forsoke hym. **1611** BIBLE *Acts* iii. 42 *margin*, In the sabbath between. **1661** *Bk. Com. Prayer, Priv. Baptism* Rubr., The first or second Sunday next after their birth, or other Holy-day falling between. **1742** R. BLAIR *Grave* 589 Visits, Like those of angels, short and far between. **1830** TENNYSON *Merman* iii, They would pelt me with starry spangles and shells, Laughing and clapping their hands between.

4. *Comb*, as **between-lens shutter** *Photogr.*, a type of shutter that is fitted between the components of a double lens; †**between-lier**; †**between-light**, twilight; †**between-space**, **between-time**, intervening time, interval; **between-times** *adv.*, in the intervals of time: = BETWEEN-WHILES; **between-war(s)** *adj. phr.*, of or belonging to the period between two wars, spec. the world wars of 1914–18 and 1939–45.

1674 N. FAIRFAX *Bulk & Selv.* 94 A change of the world in the suchness of the *between-lyers, begetting a change in my nearness as answering that suchness. **1821** CLARE *Vill. Minstr.* I. 154 As *'tween-light was cheating the view. *a***1641** BP. MOUNTAGU *Acts & Mon.* 341 In the betweene-space of Festus his death and Albinus his succession. **1580** SIDNEY *Arcadia* II. 119 Those great Lords & little kings who in those *between-times of raigning..had brought in..the worst kind of oligarchie. *a***1641** BP. MOUNTAGU *Acts & Mon.* 118 All that Interval and between-time, interceding the first and second comming of our Saviour. **1909** *Westm. Gaz.* 20 Feb. 14/2 The popular *between-lens shutters. **1950** G. L. WAKEFIELD *Your Camera Lens & Shutter* 86 A between-lens shutter exposes the whole of the film at once; the focal-plane shutter..exposes it piecemeal in strips. **1909** *Westm. Gaz.* 10 Aug. 6/3 There is no question of any between-time. Immediately the day ends, the night's work begins. **1952** E. BOWEN *Demon Lover* 222 These are between-time stories. **1907** *Westm. Gaz.* 13 Sept. 2/1 The Fairy Queen sat *between-times, when she was aweary, beside the Fairy King. **1941** 'G. ORWELL' *Lion & Unicorn* 44 The stagnation of the Empire in the *between-war years. **1945** J. B. PRIESTLEY *Three Men in New Suits* viii. 142 Those bright successful novels of the between-wars period.

C. quasi-*sb.*

1. Anything occupying an intermediate position; an interval of time.

1611 SHAKS. *Wint. T.* III. iii. 62 There is nothing (in the betweene) but stealing, fighting. **1851** R. TRENCH *Steadf. Prince* xxxix, All the dreary and the dread Between Was gone, like aught which had not ever been.

2. An intermediate size of sewing-needle.

1849 LONGFELLOW *Kavanagh* v. 22 If I do not like the sizes, he offers to exchange them for others, either sharps or betweens. **1862** MORRALL *Needle Making* 39 The Betweens are still shorter than the Ground downs, half a size thicker, and with stronger points. **1955** J. E. LIBERTY *Pract. Tailoring* (ed. 2) i. 2 There are several types of needles, chief of which (for tailoring) are ground downs, betweens and sharps... Betweens, as the name implies, are medium pointed.

between-decks (bɪˈtwiːndɛks), *adv.* and *sb.* [f. BETWEEN *prep.* + DECK.] **A.** *adv.* In the space or spaces between the decks of a ship.

1725 DE FOE *Voy. round World* (1840) 77 One or two of them..got between decks among our men. **1844** *Regul. & Ord. Army* 340 No washing between decks is to take place oftener than once a week.

B. *sb.* The space or spaces themselves.

1769 FALCONER *Dict. Marine* (1789) *Couradoux*, between-decks; the space betwixt any two decks of a ship. **1840** R. DANA *Bef. Mast.* xxii. 67 These between-decks were holy-stoned regularly. **1852** ROSS *Humboldt's Trav.* iii. 141 They considered the between-decks of the ship as infected.

betweenity (bɪˈtwiːnɪtɪ), [A playful formation on BETWEEN, after words from L., such as *extremity*, *vicinity*: see -ITY.] Intermediateness of kind, quality, or condition; anything intermediate.

1760 H. WALPOLE *Corr.* (1820) II. 174 (D.) The house is not Gothic, but of that betweenity that intervened when Gothic declined and Palladian was creeping in. **1824** MISS MITFORD *Village* (1863) 20 A little ruinous cottage, whitewashed once, and now in a sad state of betweenity. **1824** *Q. Rev.* XXXI. 167 It is really provoking to find [Miss Mitford using] such low and provincial corruptions of language as 'transmogrified,' 'betweenity,' 'dumpiness.' **1836** SOUTHEY *Lett.* (1856) IV. 448 To rejoin heads, tails, and betweenities, which Hayley had severed.

be'tween-maid. A maidservant who assists both the cook and the housemaid; = TWEENY. Also ***between girl***, ***servant***.

1890 *Daily News* 23 June 7/5 Between servant..to assist cook and housemaid. *Ibid.* 9 Dec. 7/6 Between-maid wanted. **1891** *Ibid.* 11 Nov. 8/4 Wanted..good Plain Cook, also Between Girl. **1914** J. M. BARRIE *Admirable Crichton* I, A tweeny; that is to say, my lady, she is not at present, strictly speaking, anything; a between maid; she helps the vegetable maid. **1923** *Daily Mail* 25 Jan. 5 All of the general servant class masquerading as parlour-maids, cooks, between-maids, or others of experience.

betweenness (bɪˈtwiːnnɪs). [f. BETWEEN + -NESS.] The condition or fact of being between; *spec.* in *Math.*, the ordinal quality possessed by one of every three points on a straight line, in virtue of which it may be said to lie between the other two points.

1892 *Monist* II. 243 In reality there are not two things and, in addition to them a betweenness of the two things. **1904** *Science* 11 Mar. 410/2 Of Hilbert's betweenness assumptions, axioms of order, one of the five is redundant. **1966** *Mathematical Rev.* Jan. 18/1 The author lists fifteen possibilities for a betweenness relation on a lattice.

between-whiles (bɪˈtwiːnhwaɪlz), *adv.* [f. BETWEEN *prep.* + WHILE.] In the intervals of time; at intervals.

1678 J. PHILLIPS *Tavernier's Trav.* v. xviii. 242 Between whiles they have Sweetmeats, Coffee, and Fruits. **1838** DICKENS *Nich. Nick.* xxx, Regaling the social circle between-whiles. **1850** L. HUNT *Autobiog.* xv. (1860) 237 Betweenwhiles he would walk in the garden.

b. quasi-*adj.*

1859 G. MEREDITH *R. Feverel* iii. (1885) 17 A monotonous betweenwhiles kind of talk.

betwih, betwihen: see BITWIH, -EN.

†**be'twine.** *Obs. rare*$^{-1}$. [f. BE- 1 + TWINE *v.*] To entwine, twine together.

1661 HICKERINGILL *Jamaica* 87 There's no such joy in this betwin'd State.

betwinen, -um, obs. form of BETWEEN.

†**be'twit,** *v. Obs. rare*$^{-1}$. In 7 betwitt. [f. BE- 2 + TWIT.] Emphatic of TWIT.

1661 PEPYS *Diary* 2 Apr. (D.) Strange how these men.. betwitt and reproach one another with their former condition.

†**be'twixen, -twixe,** *prep. Obs.* Forms: 1 **betweoxn,** 2 **bitwuxan, -twixan, -tweoxe, -twuxe,** 2–4 **bitwixen,** 3 **bituxe(n,** 3–5 **bitwixe,** 4 **betwixen, -twyxen, -twexen,** 4–5 **by-, betwixe,** (9 **betwixen**). [ME. *bi-*, *betwixe(n*, 12th c. *bitwixan*, *-twuxan*, *-tweoxe*, pointing to an OE. **betweoxan* (for which the *Pastoral Care* has *betweoxn*), app. for earlier **be-tweoxum*, *-tweohsum*, orig. OE. **bi-twihsum*:—**-twicsum*, **-twiscum*; f. *bi-*, BE- *prep.* + **twiscum*, dat. pl. of **twisc* adj., in OS. *twisc*, OHG. *zuiski*, MHG. *zwisc*, *zwisch*:—OTeut. *twiskjo-* 'two-fold,' f. *twa*, TWO *sb.* + -ISH *(i)sc.* The same idea (*inter duos*, *entre deux*) was expressed in OHG. by the dat. pl. *zuiskên*, MHG. *zwischen*, with a preceding prep., *untar*, *undar*, *in*, *en* (cf. mod.G. *zwischen* from *'nzwischen*, Du. *tusschen*). The ordinary form in OE. was *betweox* (see next); but *bitweoxan*, *bitwixan*, became frequent *a*1200, prob. because of its analogy to the numerous other prepositions in *-an*, ME. *-en*. For the subsequent history see BETWIXT.] Betwixt, between.

*c***897** K. ÆLFRED *Gregory's Past.* 121 Ne sie hit ðonne na sua betweoxn eow. *c***1160** *Hatton Gosp.* Matt. xxi. 25 Beotweoxe heom. *c***1175** *Lamb. Hom.* 91 Ne þer nas nan wone bi-twuxan heo. *Ibid.* 115 Bitwixen godes wrecchan. *c***1205** LAY. 5012 Bi-twixen hire ærmes. *Ibid.* 30618 Bitwixe Dinan and þære sæ. *a***1250** *Owl & Night.* 1747 That maister Nichole..Bi-tuxen us deme schulde. *a***1300** *Cursor M.* 21840 (Edinb.) Bituixin us and helles here. *c***1325** *Metr. Hom.* 166 A derne priuite..bytwixe me and the. *c***1384** CHAUCER *H. Fame* (Fairf. MS.) 715 Betwexen heuene and erthe and see. *c***1386** —— *Prol.* 277 Bitwixe Middleburgh and Orewelle. *c***1449** PECOCK *Repr.* I. xiii. 69 Bitwixe me and ȝou..Bitwixe Poul and the Cristen. [**1865** SWINBURNE *Christm. Carol* 52 The manger shall be straw two spans Betwixen kine and kine.]

betwixt (bɪˈtwɪkst), *prep.* and *adv.* Forms: 1 **betwihs, betweohs, -tweox, -twiux, -twyx, -twux, -tux,** (**-twuxt, -twyxt**), 3 **bitwex,** 3–5 **bitwix,** (4 **bituex, -tuix, -tuixs, -þwex, bytwyste, -tuixte**), 4–5 **betwex,** 4–7 **betwix, -tuix, tuyx, -twyx,** 5 **bituxst, bytwex, by-twyxte,** 6 **betwyxte, -twixte,** (8 *Sc.* **betwisht, -tweesht**), 5– **betwixt,** 7– **'twixt.** [mod.Eng. *betwixt*, ME. *betwix*:—OE. *betweohs*, *-tweox*, *-twux*, *-twyx*, *-tux*: prob. shortened from the dative form **be-tweoxum*, *-tweox(a)n*; see the prec. (Cf. the shortened *wolc* from *wolcen*, also history of BITWIH.) It is however also possible that *be-tweox* goes back through **tweohsu* to **twiscu* acc. pl. neuter. Much more common in OE. than the preceding. In ME. *betwix* seems to have been more northern, *betwixen*, *betwixe*,

more southern; in the 15th c. the loss of the final syllable of the latter finally levelled both as *betwix*. Already in OE., there appeared occasional instances of *betwuxt*, *-twyxt*, with a *-t*, either phonetic or analogical, but having no significance. This was also rare in ME., but after 1500 became the regular form, except in the north, which retained *betwix*, in 18th c. Sc. *betwish*, *betweesh*; cf. G. *zwischen*. (ME. had occasionally *bitwixte*, prob. a confusion between *bitwixt* and *bitwixe*.) There is a late shortened form *'twixt*.]

A. *prep.*

1. = BETWEEN, in the various senses of that word. Now somewhat arch. in literary Eng. and chiefly poetical. Still in colloquial use in some dialects.

a. of local position. *lit.* and *fig.*

931 *Chart. Æðelstan* in *Cod. Dipl.* V. 207 Andlang hærepaðes; ðonne betweox ða twéȝen weȝas þurh ðone leá. *a* **1300** *Cursor M.* 725 Bi-tuix þe warlau and his wijf, Adam es stad in strang strijf. **1330** R. BRUNNE *Chron.* 18 Ouer alle þe londes bituex Douer & Tuede. *a* **1400** *Cursor M.* 14233 (Fairf.) Be-twix ierusalem & þis castel..is mylis nane bot bare xv. *a* **1450** *Knt. de la Tour* (1868) 19 She ansuered hem no thinge but bituxst her tethe. **1512** *Act 4 Hen. VIII*, xix. §14 Peynes [= pennys] beryng lyke dyuers Rowles of Spurres betwyxte the barres of the Crosse. **1632** MILTON *L'Allegro* 82 A cottage chimney smokes From betwixt two aged oaks. **1660** BARROW *Euclid* I. Def. iv, A Right Line is that which lies equally betwixt its Points. **1663** BUTLER *Hud.* I. i. 68 He could distinguish, and divide A hair 'twixt south and south-west side. *a* **1758** A. RAMSAY *Poems* (1844) 89 Betwisht twa's shoulders. **1798** COLERIDGE *Anc. Mar.* III. vii, When that strange shape drove suddenly Betwixt us and the sun. **1865** DICKENS *Mut. Fr.* viii, If Mrs. B. had not thrown herself betwixt us.

b. of time.

c **1250** LAY. 24274 Bitwix [*c* **1205** bitwene] þis and domesday. *c* **1400** *Sowdone Bab.* 41 Hit bifelle by-twyxte March and Maye. **1709** STEELE *Tatler* No. 78 ¶10 Betwixt the Hours of Eight and Ten at Night. **1860** HAWTHORNE *Marb. Faun* xxxiii, A tolerable journey betwixt now and to-morrow noon.

c. of other relations.

c **975** *Rushw. Gosp.* Matt. xxi. 25 Hi þa þohtun betwihs heom cwæþende [*Lindisf.* betuih, *Ags. Gosp.* betwux, -tweox, *Hatton G.* beotweoxe]. *a* **1300** *K. Horn* 345 Wiþ him ȝe wolden pleie Bitwex ȝou selue tweie. *a* **1300** *Cursor M.* 2443 Be-twyx him and loth his neuow Of bestaile hade þai plente enow. *c* **1315** SHOREHAM 77 Thet hol assent By-tuixte man an wyf. **1489** CAXTON *Faytes of A.* III. xix. 211 A generall werre..betwyx oure kynge and yours. **1578** *Forlorne Son* iii. in *Gude & Godely Ball.* 31 The Father did his gude deuyde Betuix them. **1596** SPENSER *F.Q.* II. iv. 33 Betwixt them both, they haue me doen to dye. **1607** HIERON *Wks.* I. 239 That great separation which shall be betwixt the sheepe and the goates. **1622** R. HAWKINS *Voy. S. Sea* (1847) 149 Betwixt threescore and fourescore leagues from the shore. **1689** SELDEN *Table T.* (1847) 222 You must look into the Contract betwixt him and his People. **1732** LAW *Serious C.* i. (ed. 2) 12 Can you find any farther difference betwixt them? **1779** J. MOORE *View Soc. Fr.* (1789) I. xv. 110 They have but three legs betwixt them. **1838** DICKENS *O. Twist* xxiii, 'Betwixt you and me, ma'am,' returned Mr. Bumble, 'that's the great principle.' **1860** HAWTHORNE *Marb. Faun* (1879) II. x. 106 The bond betwixt you.

2. In reference to more than two: in early use = AMONG.

a **1000** *Ags. Gosp.* Luke vii. 28 Betwux wifa bearnum. *a* **1000** *Nat. S. Greg.*, Ða ȝeseah Gregorius betwuxt ðam warum cypecnihtas ȝesette. *c* **1000** ÆLFRIC *Ex.* xxxiv. 10 Betweohs him. *a* **1300** *E.E. Psalter* vi. 8 Bitwix my faes al elded I. **1711** POPE *Temple F.* 11, I stood, methought, betwixt earth, seas, and skies. **1788** J. POWELL *Devises* (1827) II. 759 Her legacy..equally to be divided betwixt them all. **1878** G. MACDONALD *Phantastes* xii. 184 Betwixt grey stones on the side of a hill.

†3. ***betwix and, betuix and, betwixt and*** (prob. elliptical for ***betwixt this and***...: cf. the similar ON. *milli ok*) *north. dial.*: between this (or that) and..., until, till. **a.** with *till*; **b.** with *sb.*, or *prep. phrase*; **c.** with *subord. clause. Obs.*

a. *a* **1300** *Cursor M.* 21100 He lenthid his sermon, Bituixand til his passion.

b. *a* **1300** *Cursor M.* 8614 Sco slep bituix and dai. *Ibid.* 17322 And bad þam do him up..in prisun state, Bituix and efter þair sabat. **1641** *Kirkcudbr. War-Comm. Min. Bk.* (1855) 129 In caice betwixt and that they get not a supplie. *Ibid.* 153 It is necessar that the haile common burdens..be prepared and in rediness..betwixt and the tyme foirsaid.

c. [*a* **1300** *Cursor M.* 1437 All þat deid bi-tuix and þan þat iesus ras. *Ibid.* 11074 Al þe land þat heþen lijs, Bituixand [*Gött.* by-tuix and] þar þe sun it rijs. *Ibid.* (Gött.) 16583 Betuix and þat [*Cott.* til] ur lauerd crist was þedir ledd.] *Ibid.* 1103 Bituixand þai þe southe had sene. *Ibid.* 3763 Mi hert bes neuer in rest, bituixand þis Iacob be slan.

B. *adv.*

1. Of space: = BETWEEN I.

a **1300** *E.E. Psalter* xxviii [ix]. 7 Laverdes steven of bi-twix falland low of fire. **1611** BIBLE *Job* xxxvi. 32 The cloud that commeth betwixt. **1697** DRYDEN *Virg. Georg.* IV. 516 And leave a Space betwixt.

b. *fig.* In an intermediate position or attitude.

1659 HAMMOND *On Ps.* cviii. 4 To the lowest and meanest of us, and to all betwixt. **1816** BYRON *Ch Har.* III. xxxvi, Extreme in all things! hadst thou been betwixt, Thy throne had still been thine, or never been.

2. Of time: = BETWEEN 3.

a **1300** *Cursor M.* 13521 Noght lang bi-tuix bot alson, A-noþer he did. **1685** DRYDEN *Thren. August.* 27 With scarce a breathing space betwixt. **1697** —— *Virg. Past.* v. 19, I writ, and sung betwixt.

3. **betwixt and between** (*colloq.* and *dial.*): in an intermediate or middling position; neither one thing nor the other. Also as *adj.*: Middling, indifferent, so-so.

1832 MARRYAT *N. Forster* xliv, [He] took the lease of a house in a betwixt and between fashionable street. **1877** BESANT & RICE *Son of Vulc.* I. iv. 53 She's the fool, and he's the knave, so it's betwix and between. **1884** *Point-blank* III. xv. 226 There are very few who marry into our sort of set. We are just betwixt and between.

C. *Comb.* †**betwixt-hands, betwixt-times** (obs.), between-whiles, at intervals, now and then.

c **1568** tr. *Let. Mary Q. Scots* in H. Campbell *Love-lett.* (1824) App. 24 At the leist, to dissemble so weill—and to tell hym the treuth betwix handis. **1607** TOPSELL *Four-f. Beasts* 270 Neither let him drink much nor often, but betwixt times.

†**betwynde**, *v. Obs.* [Perh. there is some error; cf. ATWIND to escape.] ? To escape.

1493–1535 W. DE WORDE *Communyc.* B iij, Out of thy tene to betwynde Mercy and loue thyn helpe were thyse.

betyde, betyl(le, betymes, betyn, betys; obs. ff. BETIDE, BEETLE, BETIMES, BEATEN, BEET.

betyng(e, obs. form of BEATING, BEETING.

c **1440** *Promp. Parv.* 34 Betynge [**1499** instrument], *instrumentum, verberaculum.*

beu, obs. form of BEAU *a.* fair.

beuch, beugh, Sc. forms of BOUGH.

beuchit, bewchit, Sc. forms of BOWED.

beudantite ('bjuːdəntaɪt). *Min.* [f. *Beudant*, name of a French mineralogist, + -ITE.] A mineral occurring in modified acute rhombohedrons, containing sesquioxide of iron and oxide of lead, with phosphoric or arsenic acid, or both. (Dana.)

1826 A. LEVY in *Ann. Philos.* II. 194 The two [specimens]..belong, I believe, to two new species. For one of them I propose the name of Beudantite, in honour of Mr. Beudant. **1850** *Phil. Mag.* XXXVII. 167 Beudantite is *chiefly* composed of sesquioxide of iron and oxide of lead. **1960** *Mineral. Mag.* June 423 Carminite and beudantite are both rare minerals for which very few localities have hitherto been recorded.

beuer, obs. form of BEAVER.

†'**beugle.** *Obs.* [cf. Du. *beugel* bow, hoop, bail; f. *buigen* to bow; cf. BEGUEL.] In **beugle-backed** *Sc.*, crook-backed.

a **1709** in Watson *Collect. Sc. Poems* II. 54 (JAM.) Beugle-back'd, bodied like a beetle.

beuk, Sc. form of BOOK, and obs. pa. t. of BAKE *v.*

beulcer, beuniformed, beurine, etc.: see BE-.

‖**beurre** (bœr). [Fr., butter.] In phrases: ***beurre manié*** (man*ie*) [F. *manié* handled], a mixture of flour and butter used for thickening sauces or soups; ***beurre noir*** (nwar) [F. *noir* black], a sauce made by heating butter until it is brown, usually mixing it with vinegar; = *black butter* (b).

1856 E. ACTON *Mod. Cookery* ii. 53 Skate..is..sauced with *beurre-noir* (burned or browned butter). **1939** A. L. SIMON *Concise Encycl. Gastronomy* 8/1 A 'beurre manié'..is a piece of butter the size of a large walnut, rolled and indeed 'squashed' in flour. **1960** *Times* 1 Aug. 9/3 Beurre Manié. For thickening a sauce quickly just before serving. *Ibid.*, Beurre Noir. Heat 1½ oz. butter till it is brown, but not black.

‖**beurré** (bœre). Also 8 berry, beury. [Fr.; f. *beurré* buttered, buttery, f. *beurre* butter.] A mellow variety of pear. Also *attrib.*

1741 *Compl. Fam.-Piece* II. iii. 352 And these Pears..Martin Sec, Winter Beurre. **1750** MRS. DELANY *Autobiog.* (1861) II. 594, I have just been gleaning my autumn fruits—melon, figs, beury pears. **1866** MRS. GASKELL *Wives & Dau.* I. 197 She had eaten some brown beurré pears.

beuscher, variant of BEAUSIRE, *Obs.*

beute, -tie, etc., obs. form of BEAUTY *sb.*, etc.

beutefeau, beutifew, obs. forms of BOUTEFEU.

BeV, B.E.V., bev: see B III.

Bevanism ('bɛvənɪz(ə)m). *Pol.* [f. the name of Aneurin *Bevan* (see below) + -ISM.] The political policy expounded by, or associated with, Aneurin Bevan (1897–1960), Labour politician and leader of a left-wing group within the Labour Party; advocacy of this policy.

1951 R. CROSSMAN *Diary* 5 Dec. in M. Foot *Aneurin Bevan* (1973) II. ix. 373 The fact is that Bevanism and the Bevanites seem much more important, well organized and Machiavellian to the rest of the Labour Party, and indeed to the U.S.A., than they do to us who are in it. **1951** *Nation* (N.Y.) 15 Dec. 513/1 Bevanism, it seems, has spread to the United States and is becoming respectable. **1963** *Times* 8 Feb. 11/2 Mr. Wilson's one-time Bevanism..makes him look more a man of the left than he would probably prove to be as leader of the party. **1979** M. JENKINS (*title*) Bevanism: Labour's high tide.

So '**Bevanite** *sb.*, an adherent of Bevanism; also as *adj.*, of, pertaining to, or characterized by Bevanism.

1951 *Here & Now* (N.Z.) May 31/2 The few Bevanites have won little support. **1952** *Times* 8 Mar. 6/1 Although the Bevanite amendment was defeated by a majority of three to one, the Parliamentary Committee was not confident that the matter would end there. **1956** A. WILSON *Anglo-Saxon Attitudes* I. iii. 90 'She's a Bevanite,' he added with a grunt of disapproval. His own position as M.P. had been Right-Wing Radical. **1958** *New Statesman* 28 June 825/1 It was even suggested that another Bevanite MP, who confined his broadcasting activities to sports quizzes, should be barred even from them unless he was balanced by a rota of five orthodox Labour MPs. **1977** *Economist* 25 June 119/3 His friend and fellow Bevanite..tries to fill in some of the gaps in a brief..postscript. **1980** *Ibid.* 15 Nov. 115/3 Note the word 'Bevanite'. The left-right divisions of the Labour party remain.

bevapid, obs. f. *bewhaped*: see BEWHAPE.

†'**bevar**, ? *a.* or *sb. Obs.* In 3 beuir, 5 *Sc.* bevar. [Of doubtful origin and meaning: most conjectures refer it to BEVER *v.* to tremble, shake.] Known only in *bevar hore*. Since ME. *hore* (now HOAR, q.v.) was both adj. 'hoary,' and sb. 'grey-beard' (Ger. *greis*), it remains uncertain whether *bevar* was an adj. 'feeble, worn-out,' or a sb. 'old man' or ? 'feeble old man.'

a **1275** *Prov. Alfred* 627, And þu þen beuir hore sixst þe biforen stonden. *c* **1450** HENRYSON *Age & Youth*, The bevar hoir said to this birly berne. [**1808** JAMIESON *Sc. Dict.* s.v., 'We still say a *bevir-horse* for a lean horse, or one worn out with age or hard work.']

bevatron ('bɛvətrɒn). [f. *BeV* (see B III) + -TRON.] A synchrotron designed to accelerate protons to energy levels in the BeV range.

1947 E. O. LAWRENCE in *Centennial of Sheffield Sci. School* (1950) 24 The Bevatron..a high-energy multi-billion volt proton accelerator. **1947** *Sci. News Let.* 25 Oct. 259/1 A new monster atom-smashing 'bevatron' to attain 10 billion electron volts was also shown.

be'veiled, *ppl. a.* [f. BE- 7 + VEIL *sb.* + -ED².] Covered, or furnished, with a veil.

1583 STANYHURST *Æneis* II. (Arb.) 55 With darcknesse nightye beueyled. **1826** MISS MITFORD *Village* Ser. II. (1863) 327 Leading Miss Reid beflounced and be-scarfed and beveiled and be-plumed..up the aisle.

bevel ('bɛvəl), *a.* and *sb.*¹ Forms: 7 beuell, 8–9 bevil, 8– bevel; in *Her.* 6 beuile, 7–9 bevil(e. [App. a. OF. **bevel*, not found, but implied in the mod.F. *beveau*, *beauveau*, *beuveau* (in Boiste's Dict.), *biveau* (Littré), *buveau* (Cotgr., Littré, Boiste); of unknown derivation. Godefroy cites a single instance of a vb. *bever*, which he explains as '*biaiser* (i.e. to slope, make slanting): architectural term'; but this seems insecure. It is uncertain whether the adj. or sb. is earlier: the order here is provisional.]

A. *adj.*

1. *Her.* Of a line: Broken so as to have two equal acute alternate angles; composed of two parallel portions joined at acute angles by an intermediate piece.

1562 LEIGH *Armorie* (1579) 78 b, Hee beareth party per pale Beuile, Or and purpure..He beareth party per Bend Beuile, Argent, and purpure.

2. Oblique; *esp.* at more than a right angle; sloping, slant, inclined from a right angle, or from a horizontal or vertical position.

c **1600** SHAKS. *Sonn.* cxxi, I may be straight though they them-selues be beuel. **1677** MOXON *Mech. Exerc.* (1703) 89 The Bevil..is used..for the striking such Bevil lines. **1679** PLOT *Staffordsh.* 368 The walls of the Chappel stand quite bevil to those of the Church. **1733** TULL *Horse-hoeing* xxii. 148 The Mortise is bevel. [See *bevel edge*, etc., in C.] **1943** L. MACNEICE in *Penguin New Writing* XVI. 41 A bevel hill with..a cairn of stones. **1944** AUDEN *For Time Being* (1945) 55 With bisson eye and bevel course.

B. *sb.* 1. A common joiner's and mason's tool, consisting of a flat rule with a moveable tongue or arm stiffly jointed to one end, for setting off angles.

1611 COTGR., *Buveau*, a kind of Squire or Squire-like Instrument, hauing mouable, and compasse, branches; or th' one branch compasse and th' other straight; some call it a Beuell. **1677** MOXON *Mech. Exerc.* (1703) 89 The Bevil..having its Tongue movable upon a Center, may be set to strike Angles of any..numbers of Degrees. **1823** P. NICHOLSON *Pract. Build.* 386 The Bevel is employed in drawing the soffit line on the face of the bricks. **1876** BLACKIE *Songs Relig. & Life* 221 Time 'tis none for square and bevel.

2. A slope from the right angle, an obtuse angle; a slope from the horizontal or vertical; a surface or part so sloping. In the mechanical arts, the defined slope or curve to which timber, etc. must be cut. (Sometimes *bevel* is technically applied to any angle exc. 90° and 45°.)

1677 MOXON *Mech. Exerc.* (1703) 110 Any sloping Angle that is not a square, is called a Bevil. **1787** BURNS *Tam Samson's El.* iii, The brethren o' the mystic level May hing their head in wafu' bevel. **1793** SMEATON *Edystone L.* §53 The upper bevil, or projection by way of cornice for throwing off the sea. **1851** RUSKIN *Stones Ven.* I. xvi. §13 In

the outlook window the outside bevel downwards is essential. **1863** WYNTER *Subtle Brains, etc.* 274 [It] cut the plank to the exact size and bevil it was required to take.

3. Short for *bevel-wheel* (see C).

1870 in *Eng. Mech.* 18 Mar. 652/3 This bevel gears with a horizontal bevel underneath the base.

4. *Typogr.* (A piece of metal used by stereotypers to form) the bevelled edge of a plate.

a **1877** KNIGHT *Dict. Mech.* I. 278/2 *Bevel*.., a slug cast nearly type-high and with chamfered edges. Used by stereotypers. **1900** H. HART *Cent. Typogr.* 8 The above and also the plate used as a Frontispiece to the 1695..and 1706 *Specimens*, have no flanges or bevels, but are almost straight-cut at the edges.

C. *Comb.* and *Attrib.*, as **bevel-angle** (see quot.); **bevel edge**, the oblique edge of a chisel or similar tool; hence **bevel-edged** *a.*; **bevel-gear, -gearing**, gear for conveying motion by means of bevel-wheels from one shaft to another at an angle (usually a right angle) with it; **bevel-joint**, a sloping joint for uniting pieces of timber end to end; **bevel-square** (see B 1); **bevel-tool**, a turner's tool with a bevel-edge for forming grooves and tapers in wood; **bevel-wheel**, a toothed wheel whose working face, consisting of a frustum of a cone, is oblique with the axis, used to work in connexion with another bevel wheel, the shafts of the two being usually at right angles to each other; **bevel-ways, -wise**, *adv.* at a bevel.

1727–51 CHAMBERS *Cycl.*, **Bevel-angle* is used among the workmen, to denote any other angle but those of ninety or forty-five degrees. **1833** PHILLIPS *Fam. Cycl.* 1339/1 Wheels are denominated spur, crown, or *bevel-gear, according to the direction or position of the teeth. *c* **1790** IMISON *Sch. Art* I. 34 The Principle of *Bevel Geer, consists in two cones, rolling on the surface of each other. **1823** P. NICHOLSON *Pract. Build.* 120 Other modes of continuing the length of timbers or beams is, by splicing them with a long *bevel-joint.

†ˈ**bevel**, *sb.*² *Sc. Obs.* A staggering blow.

1603 *Philotus* cxxxiv, Indeid thow sall beir mee a beuell. **1715** PENNECUIK *Poems* 92 (JAM.) And gave him..Three bevels till he gard him beck.

ˈ**bevel**, *v.* Also 8 bevil. [f. BEVEL *sb.*¹]

1. *trans.* To cut away or otherwise bring to a slope; to reduce (a square edge) to a more obtuse angle; often with *away*, *off*, etc.

1677 MOXON *Mech. Exerc.* (1703) 109 You may..Bevil away the outer edges of the Pannels. **1802** PALEY *Nat. Theol.* x. (1827) 474/2 The same rings are bevelled off at the upper and lower edges. **1851** RUSKIN *Stones Ven.* I. xvi. §11 The wall is to be bevelled on the outside so as to increase the range of sight as far as possible. **1884** TENNYSON *Becket* 171 All was planed and bevell'd smooth again.

fig. **1874** BLACKIE *Self-Cult.* 16 To bevel down the corners of a character so constituted by a little æsthetical culture.

2. *intr.* To recede in a slope from the right angle; to slant.

1679 PLOT *Staffordsh.* 168 In the whole length it did not bevel, or depart from a true level, above an inch. **1727** SWIFT *Gulliver* III. ii. 188 Their houses are very ill built, the walls bevil, without one right angle in any apartment. **1862** TYNDALL *Mountaineer.* vii. 63 At one place, however, the precipice bevels off to a steep incline of smooth rock.

bevele, early Kentish form of BEFILE.

bevelled, beveled (ˈbɛvəld), *ppl. a.* Also bevilled. [f. BEVEL *v.* + -ED¹.] Made or cut to a bevel; sloped off. **a.** *gen.*

1757 *Phil. Trans.* L. 105 The bevilled roof of the south-west corner. **1822** IMISON *Sc. & Art* I. 453 Bevelled-wheels are much used for changing the direction of motion in wheel-work. **1860** TYNDALL *Glac.* II. §11. 292 The precipice, upon a bevelled slope of which some blocks long continued to rest. **1865** LUBBOCK *Preh. Times* iv. (1878) 98 Brought to a bevelled edge.

b. *spec.* in *Archit.*; in *Crystallog.* (see quot.); in *Heraldry* = BEVEL A 1.

1840 T. HOPE *Ess. Archit.* xii. (ed. 3) I. 123 The porch.. affords five bevilled entrances. **1851** RUSKIN *Stones Ven.* (1874) I. xvi. 175, I do not like the sound of the word 'splayed'; I always shall use 'bevelled' instead. **1878** GURNEY *Crystallog.* 51 An edge is bevelled when replaced by two faces which are respectively equally inclined to the adjacent faces.

beveller (ˈbɛvələ(r)). [f. BEVEL *v.* + -ER¹.] An operative in various trades, esp. one who bevels the edges of plate glass or steel plates; one who cuts stereotype, electrotype, or process plates and bevels them; one who cuts, bevels, and (when necessary) gilds cards.

1881 *Instr. Census Clerks* (1885) 55 Plate and Looking Glass Silverer: Beveller, Dipper. *Ibid.* 83 Card, Pattern-card..Perforator, Beveller. **1890** W. J. GORDON *Foundry* 131 We may as well follow the plate to the bevellers, where the edges are again ground and smoothened. **1921** *Dict. Occup. Terms* (1927) §558 Card beveller..arranges a pile of cards so that edge of pile slopes at required bevel angle..and scrapes sloped edge with sharp knife. **1961** *Evening Standard* 19 July 19/4 (Advt.), Wanted Beveller..Gt. Yarmouth.

ˈ**bevelling, beveling**, *vbl. sb.* Also bevilling. [f. as BEVELLED, BEVELED *ppl. a.* + -ING¹.]

1. A cutting to an oblique angle; the oblique angle or slant so given; a bevelled portion or surface: *esp.* in *Shipbuilding*.

1769 FALCONER *Dict. Marine* (1789), *Bevelling*, in ship building, the art of hewing a timber with a proper and regular curve. **1853** KANE *Grinnell Exp.* xviii. (1856) 138 A sort of beveling prevented the ice-mass from actual contact with the bottom. **1869** SIR E. REED *Shipbuild.* xx. 430 Care has to be taken in bringing the flanges to the correct bevilling.

2. *Comb.*, as **bevelling-board** (*Shipbuild.*), see quot.; **bevelling-machine**, a book-binder's machine for bevelling the edges of a book-cover.

c **1850** *Rudim. Navig.* (Weale) 96 *Bevelling-board*, a piece of deal on which the bevellings or angles of the timbers, etc. are described.

ˈ**bevelling**, *ppl. a.* [f. as prec. + -ING².] Slanting, oblique, cut to an obtuse angle. *bevelling edge* (Shipbuilding): 'the edge of a ship's frame, which is in contact with the skin, and which is worked from the moulding-edge, or that which is represented in the draft.'

1677 MOXON *Mech. Exerc.* (1703) 91 You Saw the Bevilling Angles. *c* **1850** *Rudim. Navig.* (Weale) 154 *Syphered*, a mode of joining,..with a bevelling edge.

bevelment (ˈbɛvəlmɛnt). Also **bevillment**. [f. as prec. + -MENT.] The process of bevilling; *spec.* in *Crystallog.*, the replacement of the edge of a crystal by two similar planes equally inclined to the adjacent faces.

1804 R. JAMESON *Mineral.* I. 204 There is formed a four-sided prism bevilled on both extremities,..and the edge of the bevillment is truncated. **1870** H. MACMILLAN *Bible Teach.* xvi. 313 The truncatures of their [*i.e.* crystals'] angles, and the bevelment of their edges.

bevenom, etc.: see BE- *pref.*

†ˈ**bever** (ˈbiːvə(r)), *sb.* Forms: 5–7 beuer, 6 beuoir, boeuer, boyuer, 6–7 boier, 7 beauer, 7–9 beaver, bever. [a. OF. *beivre* (also *baivre*, *beivere*, *boivre*) drinking, drink, subst. use of OF. *beivre*, *boivre* (now *boire*) pres. inf.:—L. *bibĕre* to drink. (In med.L. *biber*, *bibera*, *biberis*.) With sense 3, cf. the parallel OF. form *beverie*, *beverry*, in the sense of a lunch or collation in a monastery.]

†1. Drink, liquor for drinking. *Obs.*

1451 MARG. PASTON *Lett.* 149 (1872) I. 201, I can gett none ell [eels] yett; as for bever ther is promysid me somme.

†2. A potation, a drinking; a time for drinking.

1499 *Promp. Parv.* 34 Beuer, drinkinge tyme, *biberrium*. **1552** HULOET, Beuer, or drinckyng, or potacion. **1580** BARET *Alv.* B876 A Boeuer or drinking betweene dinner and supper. **1626** H. MASON *Epicure's Fast* iii. 25 Their custome of drinking which I call a continuall Bever.

3. A small repast between meals; a 'snack,' nuncheon, or lunch; *esp.* one in the afternoon between mid-day dinner and supper. Chiefly *dial.*

1500 *Ortus Voc.* in *Promp. Parv.* 34 *note*, *Merendula*, a beuer after none. **1573** COOPER *Thesaurus*, *Merenda*..a collation, a noone meale, a boyuer. *c* **1590** MARLOWE *Faust.* vi, Thirty meals a-day and ten bevers. **1599** HAKLUYT *Voy.* II. I. 60 As they vse to ring to dinner or beuoir in cloisters. **1602** FULBECKE *2nd Pt. Parall.* Introd. 3 The booke of Littletons tenures is there breakfast, their dinner, their boier, their supper, and their rere-banquet. **1650** BULWER *Anthropomet* xxii. 246 Children of Princes..were to be allowed their Bevers or afternoons Nuncians. **1679** PLOT *Staffordsh.* 286 Sent hungry with a bever to her Father in the field. **1750** W. ELLIS *Mod. Husb.* V. iii. 146 They eat wholly on this [cheese] and bread at one time of the day, which they call their beaver, and this is commonly about four of the clock in the afternoon. **1884** M. MORRIS in *Eng. Illustr. Mag.* Nov. 73 [At Eton], Came up from cricket in the summer afternoons for 'bever.'

fig. *a* **1640** JACKSON *Creed* XI. xxxv. Wks. XI. 99 Are our daily sermons but as so many bevers of wind whose efficacy vanisheth with the breath that uttereth them.

†ˈ**bever**, *v.*¹ *Obs.* [f. prec. sb.] *intr.* To partake of bever. See prec.

1607 *Lingua* II. i. in Hazl. *Dodsl.* IX. 366 Your gallants never sup, breakfast, or bever without me. **1632** SHERWOOD, To beuer..*collationner*. **1783** AINSWORTH *Lat. Dict.* (Morell) I, To beaver, *merendam sumere*.

†**bever** (ˈbɛvə(r)), *v.*² *Obs.* exc. *dial.* [Frequentative f. OE. *beofian* to tremble (see BIVE): as *glimmer* f. *gleam*. Cf. LG. *beveren*, Du. *bibberen* to tremble.] *intr.* To tremble, shake, quiver. (Still widely spread in the dialects.)

1470–85 MALORY *Arthur* I. xv, And they were so couragyous that many knyghtes shoke and beuerd for egrenes. **1808** JAMIESON *Sc. Dict.*, *Bever*, *baiver*, *bevver*, to shake, tremble, esp. from age or infirmity. **1864** CAPERN *Devon Provinc.*, *Bevver*, to shake with the cold.

beverage (ˈbɛvərɪdʒ). Forms: 3–7 beuerage, beverege, 5 beuereche, -iche, 5–7 beuurage, 7 beueridge, beurage, beuvrage, beauvrage, biverage, 7–8 beveridge, 8 beuverage, 4– beverage. [ME. a. OF. *bevrage*, *buverage* (mod.F. *breuvage*), a com. Romanic formation, in Pr. *beurage*, Sp. *bebrage*, Pg. *beberagem*, It. *beveraggio*; f. the sb. *bevere*, *bevre* (in OF. *beivre*, see BEVER *sb.*) 'drinking' + -AGE: L. type **biberāticum*.]

1. Drink, liquor for drinking; *esp.* a liquor which constitutes a common article of consumption.

c **1325** *E.E. Allit. P.* B. 1433 Bryng hem now to my borde, of beuerage hem fylles. *c* **1400** MAUNDEV. xii. 141 Gode Beuerage and swete and norysshynge that is made of Galamelle. **1475** CAXTON *Jason* 52 Metes delicious and with al beuurages and drynkes sumptuous. **1611** SHAKS. *Wint. T.* I. ii. 346 If from me he haue wholesome Beueridge. **1615** G. SANDYS *Trav.* 74 Sherbet-men (who make the fore-said beurage). **1791** BOSWELL *Johnson* (1831) I. 297 Tea..that elegant and popular beverage. **1870** YEATS *Hist. Comm.* 116 Cocoa and maté, or Paraguay tea, are the beverages of South America.

fig. **1647** W. BROWNE *Polex.* II. 309 The soules of the Embassadors lay..drown'd in that delicious bev'rage wherein Polexander's Eloquence had throwne them.

2. *fig.* A 'draught' which has been brewed, and must be drunk; the bitter or sorrowful sequel of any conduct. Cf. BREW.

1297 R. GLOUC. 26 A luþer beuerage to here bihofþe þei browe. *c* **1325** *Coer de L.* 4365 A sorye beverage ther was browen.

†3. **a.** Drinking, a drink or draught. *Obs.*

1362 LANGL. *P. Pl.* A. v. 189 Bargeyns and beuerages · bigonne to aryse. **1628** DIGBY *Voy. Medit.* (1868) 56 New wines which were naught for beuurage. **1697** DRYDEN *Virg. Georg.* I. 170 The standing Waters..yield Too large a Bev'rage to the drunken Field.

b. = BEVER *sb.* 3.

1577 HARRISON *England* II. vi. (1877) 162 We had beuerages or nuntions after dinner.

4. *spec.* Various kinds of drink: **a.** The liquor made by pouring water over the pressed grapes, after the wine has been drawn off. **b.** West Indian term for lemonade. **c.** In Devonshire, small cider.

1627 CAPT. SMITH *Seaman's Gram.* viii. 36 The Cooper is ..to..repaire the..hogsheads, etc. for wine, beare, sider, beverage, fresh water. **1705** *Lond. Gaz.* No. 4159/4 About 5 Tun of Beveridge at 20s. per Tun. **1721** C. KING *Brit. Merch.* I. 7 They generally drink..a sort of Liquor they call Beuverage (which is Water pass'd thro the Husks of Grapes after the Wine is drawn off). **1796** W. MARSHALL *W. England*, Beverage, water cider, or small cider. **1834** M. SCOTT *Cruise Midge* (1859) 389 The bottle of Lemonade or Beverage as it is called in Jamaica.

†5. A drink, or drink-money, demanded on certain occasions, as *e.g.* from one who for the first time wears a new suit of clothes, etc. Now *dial.*

1721 BAILEY, *To pay Beverage*, to give a treat upon the first wearing of a new Suit of Cloths. **1755** JOHNSON, *Beverage*, a treat at first coming into a prison, called also *garnish*. **1808** JAMIESON s.v., 'She gat the *beverage* o' his braw new coat.'

6. *attrib.*, as **beverage room**, in Canada, a bar-room in which beer is served; = *beer-parlor*.

1936 L. A. MCKAY in F. R. Scott & A. J. M. Smith *Blasted Pine* (1957) 23 'Taprooms' and 'taverns' and 'pubs' are absurd; Give us..A respectable name like 'Beverage Room'. **1968** *Globe & Mail* (Toronto) 10 July 6/4 All the hotel beverage rooms within the City of Sudbury are operating with ale and lager supplied by the local brewery.

†ˈ**beveren, -yn(e**, *a. Obs.* [prob. f. BEAVER *sb.*¹ + -EN¹. Cf. OHG. *bibirîn*, L. *bebrīnus*, *fibrīnus*.] *prob.* Beaver-coloured, reddish-brown.

?*a* **1400** *Morte Arth.* 3631 Alle bare-hevvede for besye with beveryne lokkes. *c* **1420** *Anturs Arth.* xxviii, His ene, that gray were and grete With his beueren berd. Cf. next.

Beveren (ˈbɛvərən). [Name of a town in Belgium.] A breed of rabbit.

1919 *Bazaar, Exchange & Mart* 18 Jan. Suppl. 14 Beverens for sale, bucks and does. **1920** *Ibid.* 19 Mar. Suppl. 24/2 Unique snow white Beverens, with sky blue eyes. **1946** *Nature* 13 July 68/1 A small feeding trial was started with twenty young Beveren rabbits.

†**beverhued**, obs. form of *beaver-hued*.

c **1340** *Gaw. & Gr. Knt.* 845 Brode bryȝt watz his berde & al beuerhwed.

†ˈ**bevering**, *vbl. sb. Obs.* [f. BEVER *v.*² + -ING¹.] Trembling, shaking, quivering.

1398 TREVISA *Barth. de P.R.* XVII. cviii, Feueres, þat comeþ with beueringe [**1535** sheuerynge] and colde. *Ibid.* VII. xxxvii, Thereof comyth gryllynge, beverynge, and colde.

beverneck, -nex. *Obs.* Also 6 barnnecks. Some fabric.

1567 *Richmond. Wills* (1853) 197 Beds, hangings of bucherame, and a teaster of bevernexe. **1567** *Ibid.* 221 A tabill clothe barnnecks, *vs.*

beveroy, variant form of BAVAROY.

1713 *Lond. Gaz.* No. 5185/4 A sandy colour Beveroy broad Cloth Coat.

beverse, bevesselled, beveto, bevillain, bevined, bevomit, etc.: see BE- *pref.*

beves, -is, obs. f. *beeves*, pl. of BEEF.

bevil(e, bevilled, variants of BEVEL, -ELLED.

Bevin (ˈbɛvɪn). [f. the name of Ernest *Bevin* (1881–1951), Minister of Labour and National Service 1940–5.] Used *attrib.* in **Bevin boy**, a

young man of age for military service, but selected by lot to work in a coal-mine.

1944 *Manpower* 53 The 'Bevin boys' selected by ballot undergo preliminary training. **1947** L. MACNEICE *Dark Tower*, etc. 158 *Hare.* Excuse me. Are you a Bevin Boy? *Miner.* I am not. I am a professional. **1969** *Peace News* 5 Dec. 9/2 The Bevin boys who were conscripted to go down the mines.

bevin, obs. form of BAVIN.

†**beviss.** *Obs.* [Etymol. unknown: see conjecture in Britten's *O.C. and Farm. Wds.*]

*a***1722** LISLE *Husb.* (1757) 259 A cow-calf would make very pretty beef, at three years old, but, if killed sooner, they called it beviss.

‖**bevue** (bevy). In 8 **bevew**. [Fr. *bévue*, f. *bé-*, *bes-*, pejorative prefix + *vue* VIEW *sb.* Naturalized in 18th c.] An error of inadvertence.

1716 M. DAVIES *Ath. Brit.* I. Pref. 3 The Follies of the Ignorant, the bevews of Government. **1813** SCOTT in *Lockhart* (1839) IV. 71 He will content himself with avoiding such bevues in future.

bevvy (ˈbɛvɪ). *slang.* Also **bevali, bevie, bevy.** [f. BEV(ERAGE + -Y⁶.] A drink, esp. beer.

1889 BARRÈRE & LELAND *Dict. Slang* I. 110/1 *Bevy* or *bevali* (common), beer; abbreviation of beverage. **1925** FRASER & GIBBONS *Soldier & Sailor Words* 22 *Bevvy*, beer. Any drink. **1934** P. ALLINGHAM *Cheapjack* vi. 59 'I think this calls for a bevvy,' I said, and we walked off to the nearest pub together. **1960** K. AMIS *Take Girl like You* vi. 87 Dindin. The old scoff. Bevvy too. **1963** *New Statesman* 18 Oct. 537/1 The police..accuse the public of a lack of civic responsibility—a phrase that's good for a laugh over a bevy.

Hence as *v. intr.*, to drink. So ˈ**bevvied** *a.*, drunk, intoxicated.

1934 P. ALLINGHAM *Cheapjack* x. 111 They just sit in the 'ouse and talk and bevvy till all the money's gone. **1960** J. MACLAREN-ROSS *Until Day she Dies* ii. 28 Lon and Carl coming backstage, both of them bevvied. **1966** 'L. LANE' *ABZ of Scouse* 8 The Scouser's favourite excuse for an act of hooliganism is *I wuz bevvied.* **1966** F. SHAW et al. *Lern yerself Scouse* 77 Ard cases who could bevvy by the jug.

bevy (ˈbɛvɪ). Forms: 5 **bevey, beuye, beue,** 5–7 **beuy,** 6 **beve, (bevvy),** 6–7 **beavie, beauie, beuie, bevie,** 7–9 **beavy,** 5– **bevy.** [Derivation and early history unknown; ME. *bevey, beue* answers in form to OF. *bevee, buvee* 'drink, drinking' (in mod.F., a drink of water thickened with meal for beasts). This seems to correspond, with difference of conjugation (*bevée:— *bevāta*), to It. *bevuta* 'drinking-bout, a draught'; cf. also *beva* 'drink, liquor, potion, drench' (Baretti) with *beva* 'a beavie' in Florio. To explain the Eng. sense, it has been conjectured that *bevy* may have passed from the sense of 'drinking-bout' to 'drinking-party,' and to 'party' or 'company' generally: but of this there is no known evidence. These old names for companies of men and animals are however very fantastical and far-fetched, as may be seen in the first three works quoted.]

1. The proper term for a company of maidens or ladies, of roes, of quails, or of larks.

*c***1430** *Bk. Hawkyng* in *Rel. Ant.* I. 296 A covey of pertrich, a bevey of quayles, and eye of fesaunts. *c***1470** *Hors, Shepe, & G.* (1822) 30 A beuye of larkes, A beuye of ladyes, A beuye of quayles, A beuye of roos. **1486** *Bk. St. Albans* F vj, A Beuy of Ladies, a Beuy of Roos, a Beuy of Quaylis. **1579** E. K. in *Spenser's Sheph. Cal.* Apr. 118 *gloss.*, They say a Beuie of Larkes. **1613** SHAKS. *Hen. VIII*, I. iv. 4 None heere he hopes In all this Noble Beuy. **1667** MILTON *P.L.* XI. 582 A Beavie of fair Women, richly gay. **1678** PHILLIPS s.v. *Bevy*, The Foresters say a Bevy of Roes. **1725** POPE *Odyss.* VI. 98 Around, a beavy of bright damsels shone. **1725** BRADLEY *Fam. Dict.*, *Beavy of Quails*, a Term that imports only a Brood of young Quails. **1808** SCOTT *Marm.* II. xiv, A bevy of the maids of heaven.

2. *transf.* A company of any kind; *rarely*, a collection of objects.

1603 B. JONSON *Entertm.* Wks. (1692) 314 A bevy of Fairies. **1611** BEAUM. & FL. *King & No K.* v. 59 What a beavy of beaten slaves are here? **1688** VILLIERS (Dk. Buckhm.) *Chances* Wks. (1714) 110 When you've purchas'd A Beavy of those Butter-prints. *a***1774** GOLDSM. *Double Transf.* 53 She kept a bevy Of powder'd coxcombs. **1848** MACAULAY *Hist. Eng.* II. 365 The whole bevy of renegades. **1861** A. B. HOPE *Eng. Cathedr.* 164 A basilica sheltering a bevy of minor altars.

3. *Comb.*, as †**bevy-grease**, the fat of a roe-deer.

1610 GWILLIM *Heraldry* III. xiv. (1660) 166 The fat of a Roe is termed Bevy Greace. **1616** BULLOKAR, *Beuiegreace*, the fat of a row Deere.

bevyr, obs. form of BEAVER.

bew, obs. form of BEAU *a.* fair, and BOUGH.

bewail (bɪˈweɪl), *v.* Forms: 4 **bi-, byweile(n, -weylen, -wayle, bywaile,** 4–5 **biwaill, -wayle, bywaylen,** 4–6 **bewayll,** 6–7 **bewaile, -wayle,** 6– **bewail.** [f. BE- 4 + WAIL.]

1. *trans.* To wail over, to utter wailings or cries of sorrow over, *esp.* over the dead. Also *refl.*

*c***1300** *K. Alis.* 4395 Ded he is of sadel y-falle; Perciens hit byweileth alle. **1475** CAXTON *Jason* 18 How they bewaylled eche other. **1611** BIBLE *Jer.* iv. 31 The daughter of Zion that bewaileth herself. **1822** B. CORNWALL *Flood Thess.* I. 364 Pyrrha, sheltered in a cave, bewail'd Her child which perished.

2. To express great sorrow for; to lament loudly, mourn. Also *refl.*

*c***1374** CHAUCER *Troylus* IV. 1223 Bywaylynge ay the day that they were borne. **1388** WYCLIF *2 Cor.* xii. 21 Y biweile many of hem, that bifor synneden. **1549** *Bk. Com. Prayer, Commun. Serv.*, We knowledge and bewaile our manifold sinnes and wickednes. **1649** MILTON *Eikon.* Wks. 1738 I. 395 He bewails his want of the Militia. **1758** JOHNSON *Idler* No. 3 ¶8 These miseries I have often felt and often bewailed. **1880** DIXON *Windsor* III. xiv. 128 Other bards bewailed the dead poet.

b. To mourn or lament the want of.

1795 SOUTHEY *Joan of Arc* VI. 437 Then wild with joy speeds on to taste the wave So long bewail'd.

3. *intr.* To utter lamentations; to lament, mourn.

*c***1374** CHAUCER *Boeth.* I. vi. 26 For þe same þing songe þou..byweyledest and byweptest. **1611** J. FIELD in Coryat *Crudities* Pref. Verses, Tom-Piper is gone out and mirth bewailes. **1820** SOUTHEY *Wesley* II. 38 Instead of bewailing for him and for herself.

b. with cognate object; see BEWAILED.

¶ In the following passage, the use of *bewaile* is either very forced (? suggested by the consequences of a wreck), or it is a mere error. The suggestion that it was meant for a derivative of *wale* 'to choose' is worthless.

1590 SPENSER *F.Q.* I. vi. 1 As when a ship..An hidden rocke escaped hath unwares, That lay in waite her wrack for to bewaile.

bewailable (bɪˈweɪləb(ə)l), *a.* [f. prec. + -ABLE.] Fit or proper to be bewailed; lamentable.

1611 COTGR., *Larmoyable*, bewaylable, lamentable, wofull, worthie of teares. **1757** RICHARDSON in Mrs. Barbauld *Life* (1804) IV. 158 Tho' the consequences..are so very bewailable. **1775** ADAIR *Amer. Ind.* 187 The Hebrew ladies..reckoned their virginity a bewailable condition.

beˈwailed, *ppl. a.* [f. BEWAIL + -ED¹.]

1. Lamented with wailing.

1600 SHAKS. *Sonn.* xxxvi, Lest my bewailed guilt should do thee shame.

†**2.** Expressed by wailing, wailed forth. *Obs.*

1624 CAPT. SMITH *Virginia* v. 176 His much bewailed sorrow for his death.

bewailer (bɪˈweɪlə(r)). [f. as prec. + -ER¹.]

1. One who bewails or laments.

1614 R. TAILOR *Hog lost Pearl* IV. in *Dodsley* (1780) VI. 433 O blest bewailer of thy misery! **1710** WARD *Life H. More* 186 A great bewailer of the late troublesome times. **1851** MRS. BROWNING *Casa Guidi* 2 Bewailers for their Italy enchained.

2. *Zool.* A species of monkey, the white-throated Sajou, also called Weeper.

1774 GOLDSM. *Nat. Hist.* (1862) I. VII. i. 508 Called..the Bewailer, from its peculiar manner of lamenting.

†**beˈwailful**, *a. Obs. rare.* [f. BEWAIL + -FUL, after *wailful*.] Wailing, mournful.

1592 HARVEY *Foure Lett.* iii. 30 The bewailefull moane of that sobbing and groning Muse.

beˈwailing, *vbl. sb.* [f. as prec. + -ING¹.] The utterance of wails; loud lamentation, mourning.

1485 CAXTON *St. Wenefr.* 3 The fader & moder..desyred to make bewaillynges. **1599** HAKLUYT *Voy.* II. I. 93. **1635** WITHER *Lord's Prayer* (1665) 82 Else his bewailings had not proceeded from true compassion.

beˈwailing, *ppl. a.* [f. as prec. + -ING².] That bewails or laments. Hence **beˈwailingly** *adv.*

1613 SHAKS. *Hen. VIII*, III. ii. 255 Thy Ambition..robb'd this bewailing Land Of Noble Buckingham. **1862** THORNBURY *Turner* II. 234 He alludes bewailingly to the November fog, that stops his painting.

beˈwailment. [f. BEWAIL + -MENT.] A bewailing, a lamentation.

1607 BEAUMONT *Wom. Hater* III. i. Wks. 477 These lamentations, these lowsie love-layes, these bewailements. **1828** *Blackw. Mag.* XXIII. 33 A general bewailment of the 'inconsistency'..of human nature.

†**beˈwake,** *v. Obs.* [ME. *biwak(i)en*, f. *bi-*, BE- + WAKE; cf. G. *bewachen*, Du. *bewaken*. For the strong and weak pa. tense, see AWAKE.]

1. *trans.* To keep watch over; to guard.

*c***1200** *Trin. Coll. Hom.* 35 þe herdes biwakeden here oref. *c***1200** ORMIN 3339 Hirdess..þatt nihht Biwokenn þezzre faldess. **1393** GOWER *Conf.* II. 350 My lady..Nis better ȝemed and bewaked.

2. *spec.* To watch a corpse. Cf. WAKE *sb.*

*c***1250** *Gen. & Ex.* 2444 Egipte folc him bi-waken xl. niȝtes and .xl. daiȝes. *c***1320** *Seuyn Sag.* (W.) 2578 He was bi-waked richeliche And wel faire browt on erthe.

3. To spend waking; to watch through.

1393 GOWER *Conf.* II. 244 That night was wel bewaked.

4. *intr.* To keep awake; to watch.

*a***1450** *Knt. de la Tour* c. (1868) 131 Magdalene..bewaked and wepte for her synnes.

bewall, bewallow, etc.: see BE- *pref.*

bewandered (bɪˈwɒndəd), *ppl. a. rare.* [f. BE- 1 and 4 + WANDER + -ED.] †**a.** Made to wander, bewildered (*obs.*). **b.** Wandered over.

1574 HELLOWES *Gueuara's Ep.* (1577) 188, I go..so bewandred in my businesse, that scarcely I knowe any man. **1863** W. BARNES *Poems Dorset Dial.* Ser. III. 83 The stream be-wandered dell did spread Vrom height to woody height.

bewape, variant of BEWHAPE *v. Obs.*

beware (bɪˈwɛə(r)), *v.*¹ Forms: 2 **ben war,** 3–6 **be war, be-war,** 3–7 **bewar,** 3–5 **be-warr,** 5 **by-war,** 5–6 **be ware,** 6 **bewarre, be wayre,** 6– **beware.** [The origin of this is involved: 1. OE. had a trans. vb. *warian* 'to guard, take care or charge of,' with a compound *bewarian* 'to defend.' The latter is not certainly found in ME. (where it would have been *bewaren*); the former survived as WARE, common till 1500 with a dative refl. const., esp. in the imperative *ware thee!* 'cave tibi, take care of thyself, be on your guard, beware!'; and has been retained down to the present day in the simple imperative *ware!*, as 'Ware holes!' (although in this form it has often since 1600 been mistaken for a contraction of *beware!* or an interjectional use of the adjective). 2. OE. had also an adj. *wær* 'cautus, cautious, on one's guard,' which survived in ME. as *war*, *ware*, common in the phrase *to be ware* 'to be on one's guard,' of which the imperative *be ware!* was practically = *ware thee!* aforesaid. 3. From this equivalence of meaning, *be ware* early began to be treated in some respects as a single word, viz. as a compound of the vb. *ware*, thus stepping into the place of the OE. *bewarian*. As early as 1300 we find it written as one word, and even with *by* as the prefix, and in 14–15th c. it often followed the verbal constructions of the simple *ware*, even to taking a direct object, as in 'beware that train' (*c* 1500 in 1 e). But on the other hand it was used only in those parts of the vb. where *be* is found, viz. the imper., infin., and pres. subj. (the indic. being *I am ware, thou art ware*, etc.). After 1600, the verbal aspect so far prevailed that the inflexions *bewares, bewared, bewaring*, were used by good writers; but these have again been discarded, and *beware* is now used only where *be ware* would be a possible construction, viz. in the imper. (chiefly), the infin., and pres. subj. (rarely). The full evidence of these statements will be found under WARE: the following quotations show the relations of *to be ware, to ware oneself, ware thee, ware to thee, be ware to thee, beware thee, beware thyself*, before 1500.

*c***1200** *Trin. Coll. Hom.* 5 [He] muneȝed us alle to ben warre þarof. *a***1300** *Cursor M.* 62 He þat stitthest wenis at stand, Warre hym! his fall is nexst his hand. **1377** LANGL. *P. Pl.* B. v. 452 Ware þe fram wanhope wolde þe bitraye. **1388** WYCLIF *Ecclus.* xiii. 16 Be war [*v.r.* war] to thee, and take heede..to thin heryng. **1470–85** MALORY *Arthur* (1816) II. 399 Be you beware also what ye do. **1477** EARL RIVERS(Caxton) *Dictes* 11 b, Ware the of the wordes of lyers. **1483** *Vulgaria abs Terentio* 2 b, Ware thy hede thy handys or fete. **1483** CAXTON *G. de la Tour* G iv, A woman ought to beware herself.]

I. Without inflexions.

1. To be cautious or on one's guard, to be wary; to take care, take heed, in reference to a danger.

a. *simply.*

*a***1300** *Cursor M.* 17432 Bot we ne be-warr [*Gött.* be-war] wit-stand in time. *c***1440** *Promp. Parv.* 34 Be ware, *caveo.* **1535** COVERDALE *Eccles.* iv. 13 An olde Kinge that doteth and cannot bewarre in tyme to come. **1610** SHAKS. *Temp.* II. i. 304 Shake off slumber and beware.

b. with *of* (*from, with*, obs.): To be on one's guard against.

1297 R. GLOUC. 547 Hii miȝte bewar of hor fon. *c***1340** *Cursor M.* 4425 (Fairf.), Be-war of treson of womman. **1557** NORTH *Gueuara's Diall Pr.* (1582) 269 a, There are such malices from the which wee ought to beware. **1624** HEYWOOD *Gunaik.* II. 74 From Sophists we must altogether beware. **1711** ADDISON *Spect.* No. 128 ¶1 Men should beware of being captivated. **1712** POPE *Rape Lock* I. 114 Beware of all, but most beware of Man. **1836** J. GILBERT *Chr. Atonem.* ix. (1852) 293 Let us then beware of self-deception.

†**c.** with infinitive. *Obs.*

*c***1325** *E.E. Allit. P.* B. 292, I schal wayte to be-war her wrenchez to kepe. *c***1386** CHAUCER *Truth* 11 Bywar therfore to spurne ageyns an al.

d. with clause: *lest, that not, how.*

1523 FITZHERB. *Husb.* §21 Let hym beware, that he trede not to moche vppon the corne. **1549** COVERDALE *Erasm. Par. 2 Cor.* 53 Beware, leste your cleannes be defiled. **1770** *Junius Lett.* xli. 219 Beware how you indulge..your resentment. **1870** MORRIS *Earthly Par.* I. I. 376 Beware lest..in thy mirth, Thou tell'st the story of thy love unseen.

e. with simple object; = b.

*c***1500** *Doctr. Gd. Servaunts* in *Anc. Poet. Tr.* (Percy Soc.) 4 Beware that trayne, For it standeth in grete daungere. **1596** SHAKS. *Merch. V.* III. iii. 7 Since I am a dog, beware my phangs. **1605** —— *Macb.* IV. i. 72. **1697** DRYDEN *Virg. Past.* III. 145 Ye Boys..Beware the secret Snake that shoots a Sting. **1842** LONGF. *Excelsior* vi, Beware the pine-tree's withered branch! Beware the awful avalanche!

†**2.** To take care, have a care of: **a.** with *of.* *Obs.*

c **1386** CHAUCER *Frankl. T.* 813 But euery wyf be war of hire biheeste [*v.r.* be ware, bewar]. **1611** BIBLE *Ex.* xxiii. 21, I send an Angel.. Beware of him, and obey his voice.

†**b.** with simple object. *Obs.*

1566 STAPLETON *Ret. Untr. Jewel* iii. 70 When the Fox preacheth, beware your geese. **1591** SHAKS. *1 Hen. VI*, I. iii. 47 Priest, beware your Beard, I meane to tugge it. *a* **1600** *Rob. Hood* (Ritson) II. xii. 136 Now, bishop, beware thy purse. **1713** ADDISON *Cato* IV. ii. 19 Have at thy heart. *Juba.* Nay, then beware thy own.

c. with infin. or clause. *arch.*

a **1569** KINGESMYLL *Man's Est.* xii. (1580) 80 Christ is sent unto us, let us beware that we receive him. **1599** GREENE *Alphonsus* (1861) 245 Beware you follow still your friends advice. **1697** DRYDEN *Virg. Georg.* IV. 595 The more he varies Forms, beware To strain his Fetters with a stricter Care. **1860** [see II].

†**3.** To take warning *by*. *Obs.*

c **1500** *New Notbr. Mayd* 52 Beware by dedes dampnable. **1536** WRIOTHESLEY *Chron.* (1875) I. 40, I beseche God.. that all you may be wayre by me. **1581** W. STAFFORD *Exam. Compl.* ii. (1876) 65, I pray God this Realme may beware by that example. **1605** CAMDEN *Rem.* (1637) 300 It is good to beware by other mens harmes. **1700** [see II].

II. As an inflected verb.

1598 FLORIO, *Raueduto*, bewared, espied. **1606** N. BAXTER *Sidney's Ourania* K iij, Bewaring of too hot combustion. **1661** MILTON *Accedence* Wks. 1738 I. 613, I had bewar'd if I had foreseen. **1672** NEWTON in Rigaud *Corr. Sci. Men* (1841) II. 316, I stirred them a little together, bewaring.. that I drew not in breath near the pernicious fumes. **1700** DRYDEN *Cock & Fox* 799 Once warn'd is well bewar'd. **1860** EMERSON *Cond. Life* i. (1861) 32 We beware to ask only for high things. **1870** *Echo* 17 Oct., Showing the greatest respect.. and bewaring of the slightest insubordination.

†**be'ware**, *v.*[2] *Obs.* [First *c* 1400; f. BE- 2 + WARE *v.* to spend (still in every-day use in the north).] *trans.* To lay out (money, etc.), expend, spend.

c **1374** CHAUCER *Troylus* I. 636 Thus oght wyse men beware by folis: If so thow do thy wit is wele by waryd. **1393** GOWER *Conf.* I. 262 If the clerk beware his faith In chapmanhode at such a faire. *c* **1460** *How March. dyd Wyfe betray* 244 in Hazl. *E.P.P.* 207 Yf thou thynke hyt not wele besett, Gyf hyt another can be ware hytt bett. *c* **1460** *Childe of Bristowe* 220 *ibid.* 119 He let never, til he had bewared alle the tresour his fader spared. **1472** MARG. PASTON *Lett.* 689 III. 37 If ye bewar any mor money.. I shall pait you ageyn.

bewash, bewasted, bewater, etc.: see BE- *pref.*

†**be'wave**, *v. Obs.* Also 6 bywaif. [f. BE- 1 + WAVE *v.*] To blow about, to blow or waft away.

1501 DOUGLAS *Pal. Hon.* III. xxxix, How that Eneas.. In countreis seir was be the seyis rage Bewauit oft. **1513** —— *Æneis* I. iv. 44 Quhilk lait to fore the wyndis hed biwavit. *Ibid.* VI. xiv. 42 The fervent luif of his kynd native land.. Mot al evil rumour fra his lawd bywaif.

†**be'wayne**. *Obs. rare.* Also bewanȝe. [f. BE- + WAIN, gain. Perh. there was a vb. of the same form: it is even possible that we have a vb. in the first quot.] Profit, advantage.

c **1375** BARBOUR *St. Ninian* 754 Mene cummis þar of landis sere.. Of þe pardone for be-wanȝe. *Ibid.* 1279 Sir, ȝe ma haf na bewayne Vith sanctis þis [= þus] to mak bargane.

bewe, obs. form of BOUGH.

beweary, etc.: see BE- *pref.*

†**be'wed**, *v. Obs.* [OE. *beweddian*, f. *bi-*, BE- 2 + *wedden* to WED.]

1. *trans.* To wed, to marry.

c **1000** ÆLFRIC *Ex.* xxi. 9 Gif he hiȝ his suna beweddaþ. *c* **1205** LAY. 11033 Custance hauede Ælene biwedded to quene. **1513** DOUGLAS *Æneis* III. v. 74 Art thou, or na, to Pirrhus ȝit bywed?

2. *fig.* To unite closely and intimately.

1674 N. FAIRFAX *Bulk & Selv.* 10 Bewedding to body the things that belong to ghost. **1720** W. GIBSON *Diet Horses* vii. (ed. 3) 105 They will be so much bewedded to Custom.

Hence **bewedded** *ppl. a.*

c **1205** LAY. 31960 His biweddede wif.

beweep (bɪˈwiːp), *v.* Forms: 1 bewépan, 2–4 biwepen, -weopen, 4–6 bi-, by-, bewepe, 7 beweepe, 6– beweep. *Pa. t.* 1–4 beweop, 2 biwiep, 4–6 bywepte, 6– bewept. See BEWEPT. [OE. *bewēpan* = OFris. *biwêpa*, OS. *biwôpian*, f. *be-*, *bi-*, BE- 4 + *wôpian*, *wêpan* to WEEP.]

1. *trans.* To weep for, weep over, deplore (the dead, losses, sins, etc.).

c **1000** ÆLFRIC *Deut.* xxxiv. 8 And Israhela bearn hine beweopon þritiȝ daȝa. *c* **1175** *Lamb. Hom.* 39 þu scalt bi wepen þine sunne. **1388** WYCLIF *Matt.* ii. 18 Rachel biwepynge hir sones. **1494** FABYAN VII. ccxxv. 252 The kynge.. bewepte y[t] vnskylfull dede. **1561** VERON *Hunt. Purgat.* 25 b, The Egiptians bewept him seventye dayes. *c* **1600** SHAKS. *Sonn.* xxix, I all alone beweepe my out-cast state. **1678** SHADWELL *Timon* v, I'll beweep these comforts. **1876** SWINBURNE *Erecth.* 81 Boast me not blameless nor beweep me wronged.

2. To wet or moisten with, or as with, tears.

c **1420** *Pallad. on Husb.* IV. 61 Yf lukewarm hem by-wepe, Thai wol be greet. **1530** PALSGR. 453/2, I bewepe, I slubber a thynge with wepyng. **1587** TURBERV. *Trag. T.* (1837) 178 Which bones he long bewept with teares. **1848** KINGSLEY *Saint's Trag.* v. i. 230 And passing clouds bewept.. Those wasted limbs.

†**3.** *intr.* To weep. *Obs.*

c **1374** CHAUCER *Boeth.* I. vi. 26 For þe same þing songe þou a lytel here.. byweyledest and byweptest. **1388** WYCLIF *Rev.* xviii. 9 The kingis of the erthe schulen biwepe, and biweile hem silf on hir.

†**be'weeper**. *Obs.* One who beweeps.

1388 WYCLIF *Wisd.* xviii. 10 Wepeful weilyng of biweperis of ȝonge children was herd.

bewelcome, etc.: see BE- *pref.*

beweld(e, variant of BEWIELD *v. Obs.*

†**be'well**, *v. Obs.* [f. BE- 2 + ME. *wellen* to WELL *v.*] *intr.* To well up.

1387 TREVISA *Higden* (1865) I. 111 Makeþ þe brook torrentem Cedron wexe and bewel þe more.

beweltered (bɪˈwɛltəd), *ppl. a.* [f. BE- 4 + WELTER.] Besmeared by weltering (in blood, etc.).

1565 GOLDING *Ovid's Met.* IV. (1593) 83 Beweltred in his bloud her lover she espide. **1865** CARLYLE *Fredk. Gt.* VI. xv. xi. 75 The beweltered broken harness-gear.

†**be'wend**, *v. Obs.* Also 1 bewendan, 3–4 bi-, by-, bewende(n. [Common Teut.: OE. *bewęndan* = OS. *biwendian*, OHG. *biwentan* (MHG. and mod.G. *bewenden*), Goth. *biwandjan*, f. *bi-*, BE- 1 + OTeut. *wandjan* to turn, causal of *windan* to WIND; *bewend* is thus the causal of BEWIND.]

1. *trans.* To turn round, turn away.

c **1000** *Ags. Gosp.* Mark v. 30 He cwæð bewend to þære meniȝu. *a* **1300** *Cursor M.* 825 Alkin blis was þan bi-went, Fra þaim. *c* **1314** *Guy Warw.* (1849) 253 Sir Gii his stede biwent tho.

2. *refl.* To turn oneself round.

c **1000** *Ags. Gosp.* Matt. ix. 22 And se Hælend bewende hyne. *c* **1205** LAY. 18084 Hiȝendliche he hine biwent. *c* **1314** *Guy Warw.* (1840) 187 Biwende the, seyd Herhaud fre.

3. *intr.* (for *refl.*)

a **1300** *Body & Soul* in *Map's Poems* (1841) 334 Wan the gost it scholde go, yt biwente and withstod. *c* **1330** *Kyng of Tars* 1026 Theos fyf kynges forth bewent.

bewept (bɪˈwɛpt), *ppl. a. arch.* Also 4 biwope, -weped, -wepen, 5–6 by-, bewepte. [f. BEWEEP.] Drowned in tears; marked or disfigured by weeping.

c **1320** *Seuyn Sag.* (W.) 1186 He fond his emperice.. here visage al biwope. *c* **1350** *Will. Palerne* 661 Al bi-weped for wo. *c* **1374** CHAUCER *Troylus* IV. 888 That he yow nat biwepen thus ne fynde. **1490** CAXTON *Eneydos* iv. 24. **1531** ELYOT *Gov.* (1580) 128 Wash cleane your visage and eyen thus bewepte. **1858** CARLYLE *Fredk. Gt.* II. VIII. v. 337 The Prince, all bewept and in emotion, followed his Father.

bewer, var. BUER.

bewest (bɪˈwɛst), *adv.* and *prep.* [OE. *bewestan*, f. BE- *prep.* + *westan* from the west: cf. BE-EAST.]

†**A.** *adv.* On or to the west. *Obs.*

1016 *O.E. Chron.* (Laud MS.), Be westan. **1106** *ibid.* *a* **1225** *Ancr. R.* 232 Hu þe holi mon.. iseih biwesten aȝan him so muchel uerde of deoflen. **1475** *Bk. Noblesse* (1860) 9 The regions be west of Rome.

B. *prep.* To the west of. Now only *Sc.*

a **855** *O.E. Chron.* an. 709 Be westan wuda. **1535** STEWART *Cron. Scot.* 28936 In Inchchennane, schort gait bewest Glasgw. **1676** W. ROW *Contn. Blair's Autobiog.* x. (1848) 276 The sea be-west Inverkeithing. **1883** *Blackw. Mag.* Nov. 636 Bewest North Berwick Law.

bewet (bɪˈwɛt), *v.* Also 5 bywet. *Pa. t.* and *pa. pple.* 4–8 by-, bewet(te, 7 bewetted. [f. BE- 2 + WET *v.*] *trans.* To wet profusely.

c **1400** *Test. Love* I. (1560) 272 b/2 The beames.. of thyne eyen arne so bewet. **1491** CAXTON *Vitas Patr.* (W. de W.) I. xxxv. 30 a/1 Saynt Anthonye.. wepte and alle bywette his face wyth teeres. **1528** A. DALABER in Froude *Hist. Eng.* (1856) II. 52 We all bewet both our faces. **1588** SHAKS. *Tit. And.* III. i. 146 His Napkin with her true tearess all bewet. **1643** BURROUGHES *Exp. Hosea* iii. (1655) 55 As Gideons fleece bewetted with the tempest of Gods wrath. **1718** ROWE *Lucan* v, The crow bewets her, and prevents the rain.

bewet, bewit (ˈbjuːɪt), *sb. Falconry.* Also 5 bewette. [Appar. a. OF. *beuette, an unrecorded dim. of *beue*, *bue*, orig. *buie*, *boie* collar, bond, chain, fetter:—L. *boia*, in pl. *boiæ* collar for the neck (of leather, wood, or iron); but perh. the dim. is of Eng. formation.] A ring or slip of leather for attaching the bell to a hawk's leg.

1486 *Bk. St. Albans* B vj a, Thessame letheris that be putt in hir bellis: to be fastyned a boute hir leggys ye shall calle Bewettis. **1575** TURBERV. *Falconrie*, With belles and Bewets, Vernels eke, to make the falcon fine. **1753** CHAMBERS *Cycl. Supp.*, Bewits, in Falconry, denote pieces of leather, to which a hawk's bells are fastened, and buttoned to his legs. **1875** 'STONEHENGE' *Brit. Sports* I. IV. i. §3 A running noose in which the leg of the hawk together with the 'bewit' of the bell is inserted.

bewetye, bewgle, bewgrye, obs. form of BEAUTY *sb.*, BUGLE, BUGGERY.

†**bewh**, *v. Obs.* exc. *dial.* [Imitative of the sound.] *intr.* To bark in a thin voice, to yelp.

1581 T. HOWELL *Deuises* (1879) 262 A little bewhing Curre.

†**be'whape**, *v. Obs.* Only in pa. pple. 4 bewhaped, -whapped, -waped, -vapid. [f. BE- + *whape*: see AWHAPE, WHAP.] *trans.* To bewilder, amaze, confound utterly.

c **1320** *Sir Beves* 1689 The porter was al bewaped. Alas! queth he, is Beues ascaped. **1380** *Sir Ferumb.* 3037 þai buþ neȝ be-vapid. **1393** GOWER *Conf.* III. 4 So bewhapped and assoted. *Ibid.* 378 Thus bewhaped in my thought.

†**be'whatled**, *ppl. a. Obs. rare*[−1]. [Cf. *betwattle* in BE- 2.] Bewildered, out of one's wits.

1641 CARTWRIGHT *Siege* v. iii, She looks as if she were bewhatled.

bewhete, -whethe, obs. ff. BEQUEATH.

bewhig, bewhisker, bewhisper, bewhistle, bewhite(n, bewidow, etc.: see BE- *pref.*

†**be'whore**, *v. Obs.* [f. BE- 5.] **a.** To call whore. **b.** To make a whore of; to prostitute.

1604 SHAKS. *Oth.* IV. ii. 115 My Lord hath so bewhor'd her, Throwne such dispight, and heauy termes vpon her. **1623** FLETCHER *Maid in Mill* III. i. 9 Had you a daughter stoln, perhaps bewhor'd.

†**be'wield**, *v. Obs.* Also 3 biwelden, 4–5 by-, bewelde, 6 bewylde. [ME. *biwelden*, f. *bi-*, BE- 2 + *welden*, to WIELD.] *trans.* To hold in hand, rule, control, manage, handle, wield. *refl.* To use one's limbs.

c **1200** *Trin. Coll. Hom.* 25 þe holie þremnesse þe shop and biwalt alle shafte. **1393** GOWER *Conf.* III. 377 (MS. Harl. 3490) And may my selven nought bewelde, What for sikenesse and what for elde. **1483** CAXTON *Gold. Leg.* 99/1 Thyse ii.. toke of theyr clothes.. to thende that they myght better & lyghtlyer bywelde them to stone hym. **1494** FABYAN V. cxxviii. 110 To bewelde his lande when his fader dyed. **1530** PALSGR. 453/2, I bewylde my selfe, I styrre my selfe. **1577** HARRISON *Descr. Brit.* v. (R.) Gerards staffe.. which.. no man can beweld.

bewig (bɪˈwɪg), *v.* [f. BE- 6, 7 + WIG.] To furnish or cover with a wig. Hence **be'wigged** *ppl. a.* **a.** Wearing a wig. **b.** Under the influence of bureaucracy or 'red-tape.' (In Germany *Zopf* = cue, pigtail, is the symbol of official pedantry or red-tape.)

1774 *Westm. Mag.* II. 600 Suppose me now be-wigg'd and seated here. **1851** MARIOTTI *Italy* vii. 416 A paltry Baden, a bewigged Prussia. **1866** *Lond. Rev.* 9 June 640/1 It drives him to bewig his bald head. **1876** GEO. ELIOT *Dan. Der.* I. i. 3 An old bewigged woman, with eyeglasses pinching her nose.

bewilder (bɪˈwɪldə(r)), *v.* [f. BE- 2 + WILDER, to lead one astray, *refl.* to stray, to wander (found 1613 and common in 17th c.).]

1. *lit.* 'To lose in pathless places, to confound for want of a plain road.' J. *arch.*

1685 [see next]. **1752** JOHNSON *Rambl.* No. 195 ¶3 He was so much bewildered in the enormous extent of the town. **1772–84** COOK *Voy.* (1790) I. 36 An unfrequented wood, in which they might probably be bewildered till night. **1856** KANE *Arct. Exp.* II. xxviii. 282 The berg that had bewildered our helmsman.

2. *fig.* To confuse in mental perception, to perplex, confound; to cause mental aberration.

1684 CHARNOCK *Attrib. God* (1834) I. 37 We must come to something at length.. or else be bewildered. **1709** POPE *Ess. Crit.* 26 Some are bewilder'd in the maze of schools. **1742** H. BAKER *Microsc.* I. xv. 64 Let no.. honest Observer.. bewilder his Brains in following such idle Imaginations. **1823** T. JEFFERSON *Writ.* (1830) IV. 372 A vain and useless faculty, given to bewilder, and not to guide us.

be'wildered, *ppl. a.* [f. prec. + -ED[1].]

1. Lost in pathless places, at a loss for one's way; *fig.* confused mentally.

1685 DRYDEN *Lucretius* II. 11 (R.) Human-kind Bewilder'd in the maze of life, and blind. **1703** MAUNDRELL *Journ. Jerus.* (1732) 142 We rambled about for seven hours thus bewildred. **1762** BEATTIE *Triumph Mel.* xli, The bewilder'd soul. **1810** SCOTT *Lady of L.* I. xv, Should each bewildered stranger call To friendly feast and lighted hall. **1843** J. MARTINEAU *Chr. Life* (1857) 384 The new generation may grow up with bewildered vision.

2. *transf.* Pathless, trackless, mazy; utterly confused or tangled.

1729 M. BROWNE *Pisc. Eclog.* VII. (1773) 96 And oft would to bewilder'd shades retire. **1820** KEATS *Hyperion* III. 9 Wandering in vain about bewilder'd shores. **1840** CARLYLE *Heroes* i. 10 A bewildered heap of allegories.

bewilderedly (bɪˈwɪldədlɪ), *adv.* [f. prec. + -LY[2].] In a bewildered manner; in uncertainty as to one's way or perceptions.

1846 *R. de Coverley* I. 20 The fox.. speeding bewilderedly away. **1883** A. FORBES *Soc. Char. Australia*, Asking oneself bewilderedly how or whence they get it.

be'wilderedness. [f. as prec. + -NESS.] The quality of being bewildered; bewilderment.

1847 in CRAIG; and in other Dicts.

bewildering (bɪˈwɪldərɪŋ), *vbl. sb.* [f. BEWILDER + -ING[1].] The causing one to lose his way; the losing of oneself in a maze.

1806 WORDSW. *Redbreast & B.*, The bird.. That, after their bewildering, Covered with leaves the little children.

be'wildering, *ppl. a.* [f. as prec. + -ING[2].] That causes one to lose his way; mentally confusing or perplexing.

1792 WORDSW. *Descr. Sk.* Wks. I. 82 At once bewildering mists around him close. **1860** TYNDALL *Glac.* I. §12. 90 A bewildering mass of crags and chasms.

be'wilderingly *adv.* [f. prec. + -LY².] In a bewildering manner; so as to bewilder.
1838 *New Monthly Mag.* LIII. 524 Our bark is bewild'ringly blown back, forward, or sideways. **1865** *Athenæum* No. 1974. 285/1 Bewilderingly multitudinous.

bewilderment (bɪ'wɪldəmənt). [f. BEWILDER + -MENT.] The state or condition of bewildering or being bewildered: **a.** Confusion arising from losing one's way; mental confusion from inability to grasp or see one's way through a maze or tangle of impressions or ideas.
1820 IRVING *Sketch Bk.* I. 85 In the midst of his bewilderment. **1861** GEO. ELIOT *Silas M.* 13 Thought was arrested by utter bewilderment.
b. A tangled or labyrinthine condition of objects, an inextricable confusion or medley.
1844 *Proc. Berw. Nat. Club* II. 109 The entangled bewilderment of oak and pine, birch and hazel. **1884** BLACK *Jud. Shaks.* xxxi, What a bewilderment of light and color met her eyes!

bewill (bɪ'wɪl), *v.* [f. BE- 2 + WILL *v.*] To will. Hence, **be'willed** *ppl. a.*
1864 J. GROTE *Mor. Ideals* 32 The past is the experienced and already bewilled.

bewimple, etc.: see BE- *pref.*

† **be'win, bi'win**, *v. Obs.* For forms see WIN. [ME. *biwinnen*, f. *bi-*, BE- + *winnen* to WIN.] To gain, to win, get possession of.
c **1175** *Lamb. Hom.* 41 Hwa erest bi-won reste þam wrecche saule. *c* **1205** LAY. 25067 He biwon [*c* **1250** biwan] Rome. *a* **1225** *Ancr. R.* 228 þe tur nis nout asailed, ne þe castel, ne þe cite hwon heo beoð biwunnen. *c* **1325** *Chron. Eng.* 465 in Ritson *Met. Rom.* II. 289 With is host.. Engelond to bywynne. *c* **1330** R. BRUNNE *Chron.* 323 Of alle þat grete tresoure þat euer he biwan. ? *a* **1400** *MS. Camb.* v. 48. 24 þat catell was wo begon, So be-wunne was neuer non.

† **be'wind**, *v. Obs.* Also bi-. For forms see WIND. [Com. Teut.: OE. *bewindan*, f. *be-*, *bi-*, BE- 1 + *windan* to WIND; cf. Goth. *biwindan*, OHG. *bewintan*, mod.G. *bewinden*.]
1. *trans.* To wind (a thing) about; to involve, envelop *with* (bands, etc.).
c **1000** *Ags. Gosp.* Matt. xxvii. 59 Joseph ʒenam þone lichoman, & bewand hyne mid clænre scytan. *c* **1200** *Trin. Coll. Hom.* 95 þe crisme cloð . þe þe prest biwindeð þat child mide. *c* **1280** *Christ on Cross* in *E.E.P.* (1862) 20 Loke to is heued . wiþ þornis al be-wonde.
b. *fig.*
a **1000** *Beowulf* 6097 Iu-monna gold galdre bewunden. *c* **1200** *Trin. Coll. Hom.* 11 ȝet is sume þarfore of unbileue ifild..and swo faste bunden . and swo biwunde þarinne. *c* **1340** *Cursor M.* 22492 So soiled in oure synne And al bi-wounden now þer Inne.
2. To wind or twine oneself round.
c **1200** *Trin. Coll. Hom.* 87 And þanne ferde þe fule gost . and seuen oðre gostes..and bitrumede þat child..and biwunden it . and biwalden it al. **1393** GOWER *Conf.* II. 295 A gret serpent it hath bewounde.

bewing, dial. form of BOWING.

bewinged, bewinter, bewire, etc.: see BE-.

† **be'wist(e, biwist(e.** *Obs.* Also 1 biȝwist, 3 biwest, buwist, beowust, beoust, bywist(e, -wyste. [OE. *'biwist*, fem., f. *bi-*, BE- 1 + *wist* 'being' = OS., OHG., *wist*, Goth. *wists*:—OTeut. **wisti-z* 'being,' f. *wesan* to be. *'Biwist* is the sb. answering to a vb. **bi-'wesan*; cf. Goth. *bi-wisan* to be together, to feast, make merry, f. *bi-*, BE- 1 + *wesan* to be, remain. This word survived longest in the north; in later times the stress was shifted to the root-syllable, as in verbal *be-* compounds; cf. *behote*, *beot*, etc. With the senses cf. BEING.]
1. Food, provision, victual, a living.
c **888** K. ÆLFRED *Boeth.* xvii, He habban sceal þam þrym ȝeferscipum biwiste. *c* **1000** ÆLFRIC *Oswald* in *Saints' Lives* (Sweet *Reader* 102/228) He wolde..him biȝwiste syllan.
2. State or condition of life.
c **1200** *Trin. Coll. Hom.* 133 Oðer [his] he[r] biwist. *Ibid.* 167 þis holi man [Job] hadde þre biwistes. *c* **1205** LAY. 17809 Lauerd hu mid þe ! hu beoð þine beouste. *a* **1300** *Cursor M.* 13832 He hates to cum to vr bewist.
3. Abiding, dwelling, sojourn, living.
c **1200** *Trin. Coll. Hom.* 149 Wumme..þat min biwist is teȝed here swo longe. *a* **1225** *Ancr. R.* 160 He was isuiled þuruh beouste [*MS.* T. ifuled þurh bewiste] among men.
4. Dwelling-place, abode, habitation.
c **1200** *Trin. Coll. Hom.* 161 Ðis woreldes biwest is efned to wastene. *c* **1325** *Metr. Hom.* 69 To heuen, that bese thi beste bewyste. *c* **1375** BARBOUR *St. Cristofore* 269 Hame he passit til his bewist. —— *St. Catharine* 1118.

bewit, -wytt, obs. northern ff. of BEQUEATH.
1587 *Test. Ebor.* (1868) 28, I bewit to the gyld of Seynt John Baptiste in York vjs. viij*d*.

bewit (*Falconry*), variant of BEWET.

bewitch (bɪ'wɪtʃ), *v.* Also 3 biwucch, 4 biwich, bywicch, bewycche, 5-6 by-, bewytch. [ME. *biwicchen*, f. *bi-*, BE- 2 + *wicchen*:—OE. *wiccian* to enchant, to WITCH, f. *wicca* masc., *wicce* fem., WITCH. **Bewiccian* may have been in OE.]
1. *trans.* To affect (generally injuriously) by witchcraft or magic. Sometimes with complemental phrase defining the result.
c **1205** LAY. 24275 Summe bokes suggeð..þat þa burh wes biwucched. *c* **1315** SHOREHAM 71 Thaȝ that on bi-wiched be. *c* **1400** MAUNDEV. xiv. 159 ȝif ony cursed Wycche..wolde bewycche him. **1581** J. BELL *Haddon's Answ. Osor.* 149 b, Least he bewitche into stones all the whole ancient race of the Old Testament. **1594** SHAKS. *Rich. III*, III. iv. 70 Looke how I am bewitch'd. **1702** POPE *Wife of B.* 301 He had bewitch'd me to him. **1864** KINGSLEY *Rom. & Teut.* i. 2 The Trolls have bewitched him.
2. *fig.* To influence in a way similar to witchcraft; to fascinate, charm, enchant. Formerly often in a bad sense; but now generally said of pleasing influences.
1526 TINDALE *Gal.* iii. 1 O folisshe Galathyans: who hath bewitched [WYCLIF disceyuede] you? **1596** SHAKS. *1 Hen. IV*, II. ii. 18, I am bewitcht with the rogues company. **1712** PARNELL *Spect.* No. 460 ¶6 The breeze that played about us bewitched the Senses. **1815** *Scribbleomania* 165 (g) Our author..can never fail of bewitching the reader. **1876** GREEN *Short Hist.* vii. §4. 376 There was in Mary 'some enchantment whereby men are bewitched.'

bewitched (bɪ'wɪtʃt), *ppl. a.* [f. prec. + -ED¹.]
1. Influenced by witchcraft; under, or having, magical influence.
1387 TREVISA *Higden* II. 423 To ȝeue chese þat was by-wicched to men. **1571** GOLDING *Calvin on Ps.* lx. 5 A bewitched drink, that bereeveth mennes myndes of wit. **1606** G. W[OODCOCKE] *Ivstine* 101 a, The flattering and bewitcht enticements of a harlot. **1694** S. JOHNSON *Notes Past. Let. Bp. Burnet* I. Pref. 2 There was not one drop of Wine in it, it was all Water Bewitch't. **1876** BANCROFT *Hist. U.S.* II. xxx. 261 The bewitched persons pretended to be dumb.
2. *fig.* Under a fascination; fascinated.
1579 LYLY *Euphues.* (Arb.) 103 Lucilla, either so bewitched that she could not relent, or, etc. **1670** MARVELL *Corr.* cxlvii. II. 325 At any other but so bewitched a time as this.

be'witchedness. [f. prec. + -NESS.] Bewitched quality or condition.
1847 in CRAIG.

be'witcher. [f. BEWITCH + -ER¹.] One who bewitches or charms.
1545 JOYE *Exp. Dan.* v. (R.) Oure..subtyle sorcerers.. and bewitchers. **1611** A. STAFFORD *Niobe* 117 (T.) These bewitchers of beautie.

be'witchery. [f. BEWITCH + -ERY.]
1. Bewitching action or influence; charm, fascination; witchery.
1664 H. MORE *Myst. Iniq.* 281 There is something further observable in this golden Cup, wherein the force of its bewitchery may consist. *a* **1716** SOUTH *12 Serm.* (1717) III. 456 There is a certain bewitchery, or fascination in Words. **1868** HAWTHORNE *Amer. Note-Bks.* (1879) II. 161 There was a great bewitchery in the idea.
2. = BEWITCHMENT.
1711 *Spect.* No. 250 ¶7 Oblique vision..was anciently the mark of bewitchery and magical fascination. **1727** BRADLEY *Fam. Dict.* s.v. *Falling-Sickn.*, Good Housewives took it for a Bewitchery of their Poultry.

† **be'witchful**, *a. Obs.* [f. BEWITCH + -FUL.] Having power to bewitch; fascinating, alluring.
1631 MILTON *Let.* in *Wks.* (1738) I. 4 There is on the other side ill more bewitchfull to entice away.

bewitching (bɪ'wɪtʃɪŋ), *vbl. sb.* [f. BEWITCH + -ING¹.] The action of influencing by witchcraft; enchantment, fascination.
1535 COVERDALE *Wisd.* iv. 12 For yᵉ craftie bewitchinge [WYCLIF, desceyuyng] of lyes make good thinges darck. **1563** HYLL *Arte Garden.* 120 It doth also greatly auaile against all bewitchings. **1646** GAULE *Cases Consc.* 129 Some worke their bewitchings only by way of Invocation or Imprecation.

be'witching, *ppl. a.* [see -ING².] That bewitches; enchanting; charming, captivating.
1561 *Calvin's Foure Serm.* ii. (R.) Such a bewitching and furiouse madness. **1595** T. EDWARDES in *Shaks. C. Praise* 18 His bewitching pen. **1603** DRAYTON *Heroic Ep.* xiii. 27 Poys'ning Philters, and bewitching Drinke. **1749** SMOLLETT *Regic.* I. vi, The bewitching music of thy tongue. **1827** KEBLE *Chr. Y.* 3rd Sund. East., In Spring's bewitching hour.

be'witchingly, *adv.* [f. prec. + -LY².] In a bewitching manner; charmingly.
1673 HALLYWELL *Acc. Familism* 106 (T.) He is wonderful eloquent and bewitchingly taken. **1862** MISS BRADDON *L. Audley* xxx. 203 My lady..smiled most bewitchingly. **1883** G. BOUGHTON in *Harper's Mag.* Dec. 94/2 The bows and the ribbons became more bewitchingly tied.

be'witchingness (bɪ'wɪtʃɪŋnɪs). [f. as prec. + -NESS.] Bewitching quality.
1846 WORCESTER cites BROWNE. **1879** G. MEREDITH *Egoist* II. xi. 219 The attitude had its bewitchingness.

be'witchment (bɪ'wɪtʃmənt). [See -MENT.]
1. The fact or power of bewitching; 'fascination, power of charming.' J.
1607 SHAKS. *Cor.* II. iii. 108, I will counterfet the bewitchment of some popular man. **1830** MACKINTOSH *Eth. Philos.* Wks. 1846 I. 135 The seductions of paradox..the intoxication of fame..the bewitchment of prohibited opinions. **1876** MISS BRADDON *J. Haggard's D.* III. 10 When weighed against the bewitchment of fair looks and winning ways.
2. The fact or state of being bewitched.
1810 COLERIDGE *Friend* (ed. 3) I. 40 The evil day of his sensual bewitchment.

bewith ('biːwɪð). *Sc.* [lit. 'what one can *be with*,' equivalent to the Eng. *do with*; '*To be wi*' to tolerate, to bear with.' (Jamieson.)] A makeshift, stopgap, substitute.
1724 RAMSAY *Tea-t. Misc.* (ed. 9) I. 105 This bewith, when cunzie is scanty Will keep them frae making din.

bewizard, bewomanize, etc.: see BE- *pref.*

† **be'wonder**, *v. Obs.* [f. BE- + WONDER *v.* Cf. Ger. *bewundern*, Du. *bewonderen*, both modern.]
1. *trans.* To fill with wonder, or admiration; *esp.* in **bewondered.**
1580 SIDNEY *Arcadia* II. 184 A while we stood bewondred, another while delighted with the rare beautie thereof. —— III. 357 That childish stuffe..bewonder[s] gasing eye. **1600** FAIRFAX *Tasso* X. xvii. 182 How he bewondred was.
2. To wonder at, regard wonderingly, admire.
1610 HEALEY *St. Aug. City of God* Ded. 2 But men given to learning doe not so much bewonder your wealth or your power. *a* **1628** F. GREVILLE *Cælica* VI. lxxi, My soule, you know, onely be-wonders you.

† **be'word**, *v. Obs. rare*⁻¹. [For *beworth*, f. BE- 2 + WORTH *v.*, OE. *weorðan*.] To happen, come to pass.
c **1570** THYNNE *Pride & Lowl.* (1841) 61 Wee mused all what would hereof beword.

† **be'work**, *v. Obs.* Pa. pple. **bewrought.** [OE. *bewyrcan*, f. BE- 1 + *wyrcan* to WORK; cf. Ger. *bewirken*, Du. *bewerken*.]
1. *trans.* To work round about, to surround.
a **1000** *Beowulf* 6303 Beadu-rofes beacn..wealle beworhton.
2. To work, adorn, embroider (cloth, etc.).
c **1000** *Sax. Leechd.* I. 326 Hy..bewind and on golde oþþe on seolfre bewyrc. *a* **1450** *Syr Eglam.* 1152 The mantelle and the gyrdylle bothe That rychely was bewroght. *a* **1637** B. JONSON *Masque of Owles* (R.) Smocks all bewrought With his thread.

beworn, beworship, etc.: see BE- *pref.*

† **bewound** (bɪ'wuːnd), *v. Obs.* [f. BE- 1 + WOUND *v.*] *trans.* To cover or afflict with wounds. Hence **be'wounding** *ppl. a.*
1556 ABP. PARKER *Psalter* xxxviii. 108 Bewound me not. **1612** J. DAVIES *Muse's Sacr.* 16 (D.) With wounded spirit I salute Thy wounds, O all-bewounding Sacrifice for sinne!

bewound (bɪ'waʊnd), pa. pple. of BEWIND.

bewpere, -pers, -pleader, etc.; see BEAU-.

bewrap (bɪ'ræp), *v.* Also in 3 biwrabbe. [ME. f. BE- 1 + WRAP *v.*]
1. *trans.* To wrap up, clothe, cover, envelop.
a **1225** *Ancr. R.* 260 Heo leiden hine up on heih in one crecche, mid clutes biwrabled [C. biwrabbet]. *c* **1350** *Will. Palerne* 1735 Alisaundrine..in þat oþer bereskyn bewrapped William. **1491** CAXTON *Vitas Patr.* (W. de W.) II. (1495) 230 b/1 Why he had bewrapped her handes in his mauntell. **1578** BANISTER *Hist. Man* v. 65 The nature of fleshes, which so plentifully bewrapped the frame of man. **1609** J. DAVIES *Holy Roode* (1875) 17 Loe, a Wreath of Thornes bewraps thy Browes.
2. *fig.* **a.** To envelop, involve, clothe. **b.** To cover up, conceal.
a **1430** WYCLIF *Job.* xviii. 11 (MS. S), Dredis..schulen bewrappe [**1388** biwlappe] hise feet. **1481** CAXTON *Reynard* (Arb.) 71 He can bywrappe and couere his falshede. **1596** J. NORDEN *Progr. Pietie* (1847) 54 Our corruptions..have bewrapped us in bondage to sin.

bewrapped (bɪ'ræpt), *ppl. a.* [f. prec. + -ED.] Wrapped up, enveloped; involved; absorbed.
1447 BOKENHAM *Seyntys* (1835) 169 Thou lyist.. Bewrappyd in clothys of sylk and gold. **1589** R. ROBINSON *Gold. Mirr.* (1850) 20 Loe thus bewrapt in viewing this prospect. **1643** HORN & ROB. *Gate Lang. Unl.* xxi. §258 The breech bewrapped about with buttocks.

bewrathed, etc.: see BE- *pref.*

bewray (bɪ'reɪ), *v. arch.* Forms: 4 by-, bewreie(n, bywryghen, biwray, 4-5 bi-, by-, bewrey(e, 4-6 by-, bewrie, -ye, 4-7 bewraie, -ye, 6- bewray. [ME. *bewreien*, f. BE- + *wreien*: see WRAY. Probably more or less of a conscious archaism since the 17th c.; the ordinary modern equivalent is *expose*.] Always *trans.*
† **1.** To accuse, malign, speak evil of. *Obs.*
c **1314** *Guy Warw.* (A.) 3379 Ac biwrayed þou war to me, & þerfore haue he maugre..þat ouȝt sigge bot gode of þe. *c* **1400** *Rom. Rose* 3879 Wikkid-Tunge hath custome ay, Yonge folkis to bewreye.
† **2.** To expose (a person), by divulging his secrets, or telling something that one knows to his discredit or harm. Hence passing into, To expose or reveal (the unknown doer of an act.) *Obs.* or *arch.*
c **1300** *K. Alis.* 4116 That ye no schal me bywryghen Of that Y wol to yow sayn. *c* **1330** *Arth. & Merl.* 1336 Alle the sothe sche gan hem say, And bad hem nought hir biwray. *c* **1440** *Promp. Parv.* 34 Bewrethyn, or wreyyn [**1499**

bewreyen], *prodo, recelo, revelo.* **1481** CAXTON *Reynard* (Arb.) 36 They were of my next kynne· whom gladly I wold not bewraye. **1510** LOVE *Bonavent. Mirr.* xiv. E iv b, Say nat this now and bewrye me nat. **1587** FLEMING *Cont. Holinshed* III. 1321/2 That who so would bewraie the dooers thereof, should haue fortie crownes for their labour. **1603** KNOLLES *Hist. Turks* (1621) 7 For feare to be enforced by torments to bewray his confederates.

†**b.** To expose (a deception). *Obs.*

1548 UDALL, etc., *Erasm. Par.* Pref. 11 In bewraiyng the iugleyng sleightes. *a* **1601** NOWELL in Strype *Ann. Ref.* I. I. xxxix. 451 Finding therein certain notable untruths . . he did bewray them to the auditors.

3. To divulge or reveal (secrets) prejudicially.

c **1386** CHAUCER *2nd Nun's T.* 147 A conseil . . Which that night fayn I wolde vn to yow seye So that ye swere ye shul it nat biwreye. *c* **1440** *Gesta Rom.* 182 (2nd vers.), Happely . . thou woldest be-wreye my counsaile. **1525** LD. BERNERS *Froiss.* II. cxxi. [cxvii.] 345 None shulde issue out to bewray their entreprice. **1599** *Pass. Pilgr.* 352 Yet will she blush . . To hear her secrets so bewray'd. **1600** DEKKER *Fortun.* 109 The talke of kings none dare bewray. **1819** SCOTT *Ivanhoe* xxxiv, Villain! . . thou wouldst not bewray our counsel?

†**4.** Less specifically: To reveal, divulge, disclose, declare, make known, show. *Obs.*

c **1386** CHAUCER *Frankl. T.* 226 Ne dorste he nat to hire his wo biwreye. **1430** LYDG. *Chron. Troy.* I. ii, His entent there can no man bewreye. *c* **1500** DUNBAR *Tua mariit Wem.* 41 Bewrie, said the Wedo, ȝe weddit wemen ȝing Quhat mirth ȝe fand in maryage. **1576** THYNNE *Ld. Burghley's Crest* 218 The horn'd Diana chaste, is silver brighte Whiche waninge moone dothe unto us bewraye. **1588** SHAKS. *Tit. A.* II. iv. 3 Write downe thy mind, bewray thy meaning so. **1611** BIBLE *Prov.* xxix. 24 Hee heareth cursing, and bewrayeth it not.

†**5.** To reveal the presence of, or expose (a fugitive) *to* his enemies, or *to* justice; to betray. *Obs.*

1535 COVERDALE *Isa.* xvi. 3 Bewraye [WYCLIF, betraȝe; **1611** bewray] not them that are fled. **1548** HALL *Chron.* in Ellis *Orig. Lett.* III. I. 100 He . . bewrayed his guest and master to John Milton then sherif of Shropshire. **1628** HOBBES *Thucyd.* (1822) 65 He was bewrayed unto them.

6. To reveal, expose, discover (unintentionally, and usually what it is intended to conceal); = BETRAY 6. **a.** the existence or presence of (something).

1579 LYLY *Euphues* (1636) D vj, Thy hot words bewray thy heauy wrath. **1611** BIBLE *Prov.* xxvii. 16 The ointment of his right hand which bewrayeth it selfe. **1644** BULWER *Chirol.* 2 The blushes of Aurora bewray the early approach of the bright Emperour of the day. **1738** WESLEY *Psalms* xxxvi. 1 My heart to every Vice inclin'd, The Sinner's closest Sin bewrays. *a* **1849** H. COLERIDGE *Ess. & Marg.* (1851) II. 168 A smoke and a crackling that bewrayed the ligneous and carbonaceous quality of the fuel. **1863** MRS. C. CLARKE *Shaks. Char.* xii. 311 The mental bias in every writer will casually bewray itself.

b. the true character of.

1535 COVERDALE *Matt.* xxvi. 73 Thy speach bewrayeth the. **1585** ABP. SANDYS *Serm.* (1841) 395 A mans speech and gesture will bewray his thoughts. **1624** CAPT. SMITH *Virginia* III. ix. 79 The extremity of his feare bewrayed his intent. **1645** MILTON *Colast.* Wks. (1851) 345 His very first page notoriously bewraies him an illiterat and arrogant presumer. **1867** FREEMAN *Norm. Conq.* I. App. (1876) 610 A touchstone to bewray the half-learned.

c. a fact (expressed by a *clause*).

1607 SHAKS. *Cor.* v. iii. 95 Our raiment And state of bodies would bewray what life We haue led since thy exile. **1649** R. HODGES *Plain Direct.* 27 The childe did bewray, that hee would beray himself. **1692** WASHINGTON tr. *Milton's Def. Pop.* x, Your very speech bewrays you to be a right Balaam.

†**7.** To exhibit incidentally; = BETRAY 7. *Obs.*

1575 *Laneham's Let.* (1871) 56 Nothing more bewraying hiz age then hiz wit. **1600** TOURNEUR *Transf. Metam.* To Rdr. 14 This Pluto-visag'd world hell doth bewray. *a* **1631** DONNE *Poems* (1650) 106 O foole, which yesterday Might'st have read more than all thy books bewray. **1763** KAMES *Elem. Crit.* II. xii. 43 He never once bewrays a smile.

bewray, erroneous form of BERAY.

bewrayer (bɪˈreɪə(r)). *arch.* [f. BEWRAY + -ER[1].] He who or that which bewrays or reveals.

c **1440** *Promp. Parv.* 34 Bewrayer of counsel, *recelator.* **1535** COVERDALE *2 Macc.* iv. 1 This Symon . . beynge a bewrayer of the money and of his owne naturall countre. **1598** GREENWEY *Tacitus' Ann.* XI. xi. 153 Certaine writings, bewrayers of hir lusts and lasciuiousnes. **1652** GAULE *Magastrom.* 342 Lest they might be the bewrayers of his secrets. **1711** ADDISON *Spect.* No. 225 ⁋2 When a Friend is turned into an Enemy, and a Bewrayer of Secrets.

beˈwraying, *vbl. sb. arch.* or *Obs.* [f. as prec. + -ING[1].] The action of revealing or exposing.

c **1386** CHAUCER *Melib.* ⁋174 Biwrey nat youre conseil to no persone but if so be that ye wenen sikerly that thurgh youre biwreyyng youre condicion shal be to yow the moore profitable. **1553-87** FOXE *A. & M.* (1596) 38/2 By the bewraieng or confession of him. **1597** HOOKER *Eccl. Pol.* v. xlii. §2 By bewraying their affection towards him.

beˈwrayingly, *adv. arch.* or *Obs.* [f. *bewraying* pr. pple. + -LY[2].] By way of disclosing secrets.

beˈwrayment. *arch.* or *Obs.* [f. BEWRAY + -MENT.] The fact of bewraying, disclosure.

1864 in WEBSTER.

†**beˈwreak**, *v. Obs.* Forms: 4-6 bewreke, 6 -wreake, -wrecke. [ME. *bewreke*, f. BE- 2 + *wreke*, WREAK *v.*] *trans.* To avenge; to give vent in action to (incensed feelings). Cf. AWREAK.

c **1325** *Coer de L.* 6283, I wole me off hym so bewreke. **1430** LYDG. *Chron. Troy* II. xvi, Our iuste sorowe Compelleth vs . . On Troyan our harmes to bewreke. **1523** LD. BERNERS *Froiss.* I. ccxlvii. 368 He thought it shulde be a great crueltie, if he shulde bewreke his displeasur on them. **1559** *Mirr. Mag.* 120 (T.) Yet was I, or I parted thence, bewreckt. **1586** J. HOOKER *Irel.* in *Holinshed* II. 59/1 Euen with that weapon . . they will . . bewreake their malice.

bewreath, etc.; see BE- *pref.*

beˈwrite, *v.* †**1.** Intensive of WRITE. *Obs.*

1660 Z. CROFTON *St. Peter's Fett.* 74 Bewritten in such sensible Acts, and legible Characters.

2. *trans.* To write about. In *pa. pple.*

1875 SWINBURNE in *Times Lit. Suppl.* (1909) 3 June 204/2, I have probably been more be-written and belied than any man since Byron. **1895** *Critic* 1 June 396/2 Tammany has been much be-written of late. **1931** *Times Lit. Suppl.* 5 Nov. 864/3 The track covered by Mr. Waugh has been . . thoroughly bewritten in recent years.

bewrought, pa. pple. of BEWORK.

†**beˈwry**, *v.*[1] *Obs.* Also 1 bewréon, bewría, 3 biwreo, bywryen. *Pa. pple.* 1-3 be-, biwriȝen, 3 bi-wrie(n, 6 bewry. [OE. *bewréon, -wréan, -wría* for **bewríhan*, f. BE- 1 + *wréon* to cover: see WRY *v.*[1]] *trans.* To cover up, or over; to overlay.

a **1000** *Sal. & Sat.* (G.) 301 Forhwon fealleð se snaw, foldan behydeð, bewrihð wyrta cið. *c* **1205** LAY. 5366 Ha leopen on heore feire hors: biwriȝen [**1250** biwreȝe] mid færie palle. *c* **1300** *K. Alis.* 6453 Whan theo sonne to hote schyneth . . his eren with, Al his body he bywryeth. **1513** DOUGLAS *Æneis* IV. iv. 16 Ane brusit mantill of Sydony With gold and perle the bordour all bewry [circumdata].

b. *fig.*

c **1000** *Metr. Boeth.* iv. 93 Bið þæt lease lot . . bewriȝen mid wrencum. *a* **1250** *Owl & Night.* 673 Ȝif muþ wiþute mai biwreo þat me þe heorte noht niseo.

†**bewry**, *v.*[2] *Obs.* [f. BE- 1 + WRY *wk. v.* ME. *wrien*, OE. *wriȝian* to stretch.] To wrest, distort.

1513 DOUGLAS *Æneis* x. i. 80 Quhy that ony mycht pervert or ȝit bewry Thy commandmentis?

†**ˈbewscher, -schyre, -sher.** **1.** Northern form of BEAUSIRE. **2.** *pl.* The buttocks.

? *a* **1400** *Morte Arth.* 1047 His bakke and his bewschers, and his brode lendez.

bewte, -tee, -tiful, -tious, obs. ff. BEAUTY *sb.*, etc.

bewter, Scotch form of BITTERN.

†**ˈbewtynes.** *Obs. rare.* = BEAUTY *sb.*

c **1511** *1st Eng. Bk. Amer.* (Arb.) Introd. 27 All with feders bounden for there bewtynes and fayrenes.

[**bewunus** (Hall.), error for *bewunne*; see BEWIN.]

bex, obs. plural of BEAK.

bey (beɪ), *sb.* Forms: 6 by(e, 7 beye, bei, 7- bey. [a. Osmanli *bey* 'prince, governor,' mod. pronunciation of *beg*: see BEG *sb.*[1]]

A Turkish governor of a province or district: also a title of rank.

1599 HAKLUYT *Voy.* II. 168 The By who is the gouernour of the Iland. *Ibid.* II. I. 176 You goe to the Bye, onely for that he will inquire newes of you. **1649** *Alcoran* A iv b, Bashaws, or Vice-Roys, Beyes, or Governors. **1687** RYCAUT *Hist. Turks* I. 250 Letters sent to the young Bei at Tunis. **1768** *Hist. Europe* in *Ann. Reg.* 27/2 The Basha of Bosnia being joined by the Bey of Romelia. **1813** BYRON *Br. Abydos* II. xxi, And wouldst thou save that haughty Bey?

Hence **beydom, beyship.**

1860 TRISTRAM *Gt. Sahara* ii. 37 The semi-independent beydom of Tittery. **1867** *Standard* 2 Mar., We . . kept our remarks to his titles, his colonelcy, and his beyship.

†**bey**, *v. Obs.* Forms: 1 béȝan, bíeȝan, bíȝan, býȝan, 2 beiȝen, 2-4 beien, 3-4 beie, beighe(n, beyghe(n, 4 bie, buyen, buȝen, 9 *dial.* bay. [Com. Teut.: OE. Anglian *béȝan*, WSax. *bíeȝan, bíȝan, býȝan* wk. vb. = OFris. *bêja*, ON. *beygja* (Sw. *böja*, Da. *böie*), OHG. *bougen* (MHG. *böugen*, mod.G. *beugen*), MDu. *bôghen*, Goth. *baugjan*, causal of *biugan, baug*, in OE. *búȝan, béah* to bow (intr.). In the 13th c. there was confusion between this verb, and the primary *buȝen* to BOW, partly because both verbs began to be used both transitively and intransitively, partly because of the ambiguity of the letter *u* (= *ū* or *ü*), so that *buȝen* might be for OE. *búȝan*, or OE. *býȝan*. At length the strong verb took also a weak past *buȝede, buhde*: see BOW. *Bey, bay*, is not found in literature after the 14th c., but seems to have survived in dialects.]

1. *trans.* To bend, cause to bow.

c **888** K. ÆLFRED *Boeth.* xxv, Hwelcne boh . . swelce þu beȝan mæȝe. *c* **1000** *Ags. Gosp.* Mark xv. 19 [Hi] heora cneow biȝdon. *c* **1160** *Hatt. G.* ibid., Hire cneow beiȝdon. *a* **1225** *Juliana* 77 Wið [þat] ilke ha beide hire & beah duuelunge adun bihefdet to þer eorðe. *c* **1230** *Hali Meid.* 3 Bei þin eare, þat is beo buhsum to mi lare. *c* **1300** *Beket* 1529 Whan i ne mai his hurte so buye. *a* **1325** *Maximon* in *Rel. Ant.* I. 122 He chaungeþ al my ble, Ant buȝeþ me to grounde. [**1851** *Cumberl. Gloss.*, *Bay*, to bend.]

2. *intr.* To bend, bow.

c **1205** LAY. 1051 Ah he mot nede beien þe mon þe ibun den bið. *a* **1225** *St. Marher.* 7 Buh nu ant bei to me. *Ibid.* 22 Ant te bodi beide . ant beh to þer eorðe. *c* **1230** *Hali Meid.* 15 þat hit ne breke ne beie. *c* **1300** *K. Alis.* 4373 Theo spere was styf and nought no beyghed.

bey, obs. form of BOY (*Promp. Parv.*).

beyape, variant of BEJAPE *v. Obs.*

beyard, obs. form of BAYARD *sb.*[1]

beye = both; see BO.

†**beˈyelp**, *v. Obs.* In 4 biȝelp. [ME. *biȝelp(en* f. *bi-*, BE- + *ȝelp(en* to YELP.] *trans.* To talk loudly of, boast of, glory in. Also *refl.* with *of.*

c **1314** *Guy Warw.* (A.) 1455 þat tow schalt it biȝelp nouȝt þat he is to deþ y-brouȝt. **1393** GOWER *Conf.* III. 155 How shulde I thanne me beyelpe . . of thy largesse.

beyend(e, obs. form of BEYOND.

beyer = of both: see BO.

beyete, obs. form of BEGET *v.*

beyght, obs. form of BAIT.

beyke, -ynge, obs. form of BEEK *v.*, -ING.

beyl(e, obs. form of BAIL *sb.*[2], [5].

beyld, obs. form of BIELD, BUILD.

‖**beylic, -lik** (ˈbeɪlɪk). Also beglick. [a. Osmanli *beglik, beylik*, jurisdiction of a *beg* or BEY.] The dominion or jurisdiction of a bey.

a **1733** NORTH *Lives* III. 84 To Morat he left the beylic. **1869** RAWLINSON *Anc. Hist.* 77 The modern Beylik of Tunis.

Hence **ˈbeylical** *a.*, of or belonging to a beylic. **ˈbeylicat** = beylic.

1884 *Weekly Times* 4 Jan. (Tunis), The Beylical doing of justice in times past. **1884** *Pall Mall G.* 20 Dec. 1 The beylicat was afterwards annexed.

beyme, obs. form of BEAM.

beyn, obs. form of BAIN *a.*, and BEEN *pa. pple.*

beyne = both: see BO.

beyond (bɪˈjɒnd), *adv.* and *prep.* Forms: 1 be-, biȝeondan, beiundan, 2 beȝeonden, 3 biȝeonde(n, biȝonndenn, 3-5 bi-, byyond(e, -ȝonde, biȝende, 4 beȝonde(n, be-, biȝunde, 4-6 beyend(e, 5-6 beyonde, 6 by yonde, byȝend, 5- beyond. [OE. *beȝeondan*, not found in other Teut. langs.: f. *bi-*, BE- indicating position + *ȝeondan* from the farther side:—OTeut. **jandana*, f. **jand* (in OE. *ȝeond* across, through, beyond. Cf. Goth. *jaind* yonder) + *-ana* advb. suffix: cf. BEHIND. The advb. **jand*, (*jaind*,) *ȝeond*, belongs to the demonstr. pron. **jano-z*, Goth. *jains*, OHG. *jenêr* (stem *jani-*), OE. *ȝeon*, YON. Other derivatives in Gothic were *jainar* there; *jaindre* thither, *jainþro* thence. The literal meaning of *beȝeondan* was thus 'on yon side, on the farther side.' Used either without (adv.) or with (prep.) an object.]

A. *adv.*

1. On the farther side, farther away, at a greater distance.

c **1000** ÆLFRIC *Gram.* 232 *Ulterius*, feor beȝeondan. **1362** LANGL. *P. Pl.* A. III. 105 Ichaue a kniht hette Concience com late from bi-ȝonde [B. biȝunde]. *c* **1400** MAUNDEV. xxxi. 314 With outen ony more rehercyng of . . marvaylles that ben beȝonde. *c* **1440** *York Myst.* xvii. 59 And be-yonde is Bedleem. **1596** SPENSER *F.Q.* III. i. 38 Lo, where beyond he lyeth languishing. **1610** SHAKS. *Temp.* II. i. 242 So high a hope, that euen Ambition cannot pierce a winke beyond. **1842** TENNYSON *Pal. Art* 82 Beyond, a line of heights.

2. In addition, besides, over and above. *rare.*

1886 *Law Times* LXXX. 193/1 This amount and £5, his own damages beyond, he sought to recover in this action.

B. *prep.*

1. Of position in space: On the farther side of. **a.** of a boundary, barrier, or intervening space. *beyond seas*: out of the country; abroad.

a **1000** ÆLFRIC *Deut.* i. 5 Beiundane Iordane on Moab lande. *c* **1000** *Ags. Gosp.* John i. 28 On beþania beȝeondan iordanen. *c* **1205** LAY. 28274 Al biȝeonde þerere Humbre. *a* **1300** *Cursor M.* 11396 Bi-yond þam ar wonnand nan. *c* **1440** *Gesta Rom.* 1 Myn husbond, quod she, is biȝende þe see. **1599** SHAKS. *Hen. V*, III. vi. 180 Beyond the Riuer wee'le encampe our selues. **1644** MILTON *Educ.* ad init., Both here and beyond the seas. **1725** DE FOE *Voy. round World* (1840) 258 The new world beyond the hills. **1792** S. ROGERS *Pleas. Mem.* II. 51 Beyond the western wave. **1848** MACAULAY *Eng.* I. 173 From 1646 to 1660 he had lived beyond sea.

b. of an object regarded simply as a point in space: Past, further on than, at a more distant point or position than.

1382 WYCLIF *1 Sam.* xx. 22 The arowis ben beȝonde [**1388** biȝende] thee. **1610** SHAKS. *Temp.* II. i. 247 She that is Queene of Tunis, she that dwels Ten leagues beyond mans life. **1821** BYRON *Cain* II. i. 14 Thou shalt behold The worlds beyond thy little world. **1846** RUSKIN *Mod. Paint.* I. II. §4. iii. 296 Out of which rise the soft rounded slopes of mightier mountains, surge beyond surge. **1873** KINGSLEY *Prose Idylls* 96 While high overhead hung, motionless, hawk beyond hawk, buzzard beyond buzzard, kite beyond kite, as far as eye could see.

2. a. Of motion: To the farther side of, farther than, past, so as to leave behind. (Cf. 10.)

a **1075** *O.E. Chron.* an. 1048 Godwine eorl and Sweȝen ..ȝewendon heom beȝeondan sæ. *c* **1205** LAY. 29149 Sum fleh bi-ȝeonden sæ. *c* **1305** *St. Dunstan* 103 in *E.E.P.* (1862) 37 Biȝunde see he drouȝ. **1529** RASTELL *Pastyme, Hist. Brit.* (1811) 97 Drove them..by yonde Doram. **1556** *Chron. Grey Friars* (1852) 35 Barnes..brake aways from them and went beyend see unto Luter. **1709** POPE *Ess. Crit.* 49 Launch not beyond your depth, but be discreet. **1821** KEATS *Lamia* 429 His spirit pass'd beyond its golden bourn Into the noisy world. **1862** SPALDING *Hist. Eng. Lit.* (1876) 372 Never able to pass a step beyond the self-drawn circle.

b. *fig.*

1690 LOCKE *Hum. Und.* (1777) I. 275 It can proceed and pass beyond all those lengths. **1797** WASHINGTON *Writ.* (1858) 213 That France has stepped beyond the line of rectitude cannot be denied. *a* **1849** J. MANGAN *Poems* (1859) 450 All-baffled reason cannot wander Beyond her chain. **1860** HAWTHORNE *Marb. Faun.* iv. (1883) 47 The story of this adventure..made its way beyond the usual gossip of the Forestieri.

c. = BESIDE 5 a. *rare.*

1834 M. SCOTT in *Blackw. Mag.* XXXVI. 814 The excess of her joy..had driven her beyond herself.

†**d.** *to go beyond*: to 'get round,' circumvent.

1602 *Life T. Cromwell* IV. v. 120 We must be wary, else he'll go beyond us. **1611** BIBLE *1 Thess.* iv. 6 That no man goe beyond and defraud his brother in any matter. **1613** SHAKS. *Hen. VIII*, III. ii. 409 The king has gone beyond me.

3. Towards the farther side of, farther than, past. (With *look* and equivalent verbs.) *to look beyond* (quot. 1597): to misconstrue, misunderstand.

1597 SHAKS. *2 Hen. IV*, IV. iv. 67 My gracious Lord, you looke beyond him quite. **1712** STEELE *Spect.* No. 302 ¶7 Looking beyond this gloomy Vale of Affliction and Sorrow into the Joys of Heaven and Immortality. **1768** BEATTIE *Minstr.* I. (R.) Lofty souls who look beyond the tomb.

4. Of time: Past, later than.

1597 SHAKS. *2 Hen. IV*, IV. iv. 57 My griefe..Stretches it selfe beyond the howre of death. *c* **1600** —— *Sonn.* cxxii, Which shall..remain Beyond all date, even to eternity. **1747** GRAY *Ode Eton Coll.* 54 No care beyond to day. **1762** HUME *Hist. Eng.* (1826) V. xli. 228 Those who should remain beyond that time..should be guilty of treason. **1816** J. WILSON *City of Plague* II. ii. 15, I have been kept from home, beyond my promised hour. **1853** C. BRONTË *Villette* xx. 236 We arrived safe at home about an hour and a half beyond our time.

5. *fig.* **a.** Outside the limit or sphere of, past; out of the grasp or reach of.

1535 COVERDALE *Num.* xxii. 18 Yet could I not go beyonde yᵉ worde of the Lorde my God. **1595** SHAKS. *John* IV. iii. 117 Beyond the infinite and boundlesse reach of mercie. **1596** —— *1 Hen. IV*, I. iii. 200 Imagination of some great exploit Driues him beyond the bounds of Patience. **1597** —— *2 Hen. IV*, I. iii. 59 The Modell of a house Beyond his power to builde. **1605** HEYWOOD *If know not me* Wks. 1874 I. 210 Shoomaker, you goe a little beyond your last. **1651** HOBBES *Leviath.* III. xxxiii. 201 A time past, beyond the memory of man. **1760** GOLDSM. *Cit. W.* lxx. (Globe) 202 It was beyond one man's strength to remove it. **1856** FROUDE *Hist. Eng.* (1858) I. i. 53 A detail of the working of the trade laws would be beyond my present purpose. **1869** J. MARTINEAU *Ess.* II. 76 Some offences..are beyond detection. **1885** SIR L. CAVE in *Law Times' Rep.* LII. 629/2 We cannot go beyond the written agreement.

b. *to be beyond a person* (colloq.): to pass his comprehension.

1812 MISS AUSTEN *Mansf. P.* (1847) III. i. 280 This is beyond me, said he. **1928** E. O'NEILL *Strange Interlude* VII. 250 Why Gordon should take such a fancy to that old sissy is beyond me. **1966** *Listener* 12 May 699/1 How someone like Anthony de Lotbinière, its producer, could make Japan boring is beyond me, but he succeeded.

6. *esp.* with nouns expressing an action or a state of mind, as *belief*, *doubt*, *endurance*, *expectation*, *question*, etc.: Not within the range of, not according to, past, surpassing.

1601 SHAKS. *Jul. C.* II. ii. 25 These things are beyond all vse. **1610** —— *Temp.* II. i. 59 Which is indeed almost beyond credit. **1692** BENTLEY *Boyle Lect.* iv. 135 'Tis beyond even an Atheist's Credulity. **1701** W. WOTTON *Hist. Rome* 285 His Spectacles were almost beyond belief. **1758** BP. NEWTON *Dissert.* xvii. Wks. II. 400 Adversity..often procures friends beyond hope and expectation. **1848** MACAULAY *Hist. Eng.* I. 197 France was now, beyond all doubt, the greatest power in Europe.

7. Exceeding in quantity or amount, more than. (As with *above*, the phrase *beyond a hundred*, etc. may be the subject of a sentence.)

? *a* **1500** *Battle Egyngec.* 238 in Hazl. *E.P.P.* II. 102 There dyed by yonde .vii. score vpon a day. **1605** *Lond. Prodigal* I. i. 220 Doth he spend beyond the allowance I left him? **1653** WALTON *Angler* i. 34 When he was beyond Seventy years of age he made this description. **1885** *Law Rep.* XXIX. Chanc. Div. 528 To an amount far beyond their value.

8. a. Surpassing in quality or degree, exceeding, superior to; more than.

1593 SHAKS. *3 Hen. VI*, II. v. 51 The Shepherd's homely Curds..Is farre beyond a Princes Delicates. **1628** DIGBY *Voy. Medit.* 55 Were so much beyond our vessels in sayling. **1634** MILTON *Comus* 813 Delight Beyond the bliss of dreams. **1749** FIELDING *Tom Jones* (1836) I. I. xi. 52 His shoulders were broad beyond all size. **1873** TRISTRAM *Moab* ii. 35 Our guide, looking on game as far beyond names in importance.

b. *beyond measure* (advb. phr.): more than what is meet or moderate; exceedingly, excessively.

1526 TINDALE *Mark* vii. 37 They..were beyonde measure astonyed [so **1611**]. **1596** SHAKS. *Tam. Shr.* I. ii. 90 Shrow'd and froward, so beyond all measure. **1875** JOWETT *Plato* (ed. 2) I. 89, I am delighted beyond measure.

9. In addition to, besides, over and above; in negative and interrog. sentences almost = Except; cf. BESIDES B 2 and 3.

c **1449** PECOCK *Repr.* III. i. 281 Ouer and biȝende the citees. **1593** HOOKER *Eccl. Pol.* I. xi. §4 Somewhat beyond and above all this. **1613** SHAKS. *Hen. VIII*, III. i. 135 Bring me a constant woman to her Husband, One that ne're dream'd a Ioy, beyond his pleasure. **1761** HUME *Hist. Eng.* (1826) II. cxi. App. 112 The Conqueror ordained that the barons should be obliged to pay nothing beyond their stated services. **1831** CARLYLE *Sart. Res.* II. vi, No prospect of breakfast beyond elemental liquid. **1851** DIXON *W. Penn* xvi. (1872) 134 Beyond his labours as a preacher, he composed..twenty-six books of controversy.

10. When *beyond* = 'farther than,' 'more than,' introduces an adverbial extension of the predicate, the clause in which it occurs is often contracted; *They prospered beyond other men* = 'beyond the measure in which other men prospered'; *I went a step beyond Whiston* = 'beyond the point to which he went.'

1578 *Gude & Godely Ball.* 127 His bemis send he hes out far Beȝond vther sternis all [*i.e.* beyond the distance to which all other stars have sent theirs]. **1631** GOUGE *God's Arrows* i. §29. 44 They go in inhumane cruelty beyond the Heathen. **1667** MILTON *P.L.* x. 805 That were to extend His Sentence beyond dust and Natures Law. **1758** BORLASE *Nat. Hist. Cornw.* xix. §7. 232 The plant grows luxuriant beyond what we have in Cornwall. **1766** GOLDSM. *Vic. Wakef.* ii. (1806) 6, I even went a step beyond Whiston in displaying my principles. **1848** MACAULAY *Hist. Eng.* I. 154 The discarded warriors prospered beyond other men.

C. quasi-*sb.* **a.** That which lies on the other side or farther away, the remote or distant; that which lies beyond our present life or experience.

1581 SAVILE *Tacitus' Hist.* IV. viii. 174 Beyond [*ulteriora*] he honored and admired, but professed to follow the present estate. **1835** LYTTON *Rienzi* X. viii, Each is the yearning for the Great Beyond, which attests our immortality. **1876** MOZLEY *Univ. Serm.* iii. 47 Love..wants a beyond, and no being that is without this beyond can duly answer to it as an object. **1885** J. MARTINEAU *Eth. Theory* I. 281 They are the All, with no beyond.

b. *the back of beyond*: a humorous phrase for ever so far off, some very out of the way place.

1816 SCOTT *Antiq.* I. 37 (JAM.) You..whirled them to the back of beyont to look at the auld Roman camp. **1853** DE QUINCEY *Sp. Mil. Nun* Wks. III. 12 Which port (according to a smart American adage) is to be looked for at the back of beyond. **1883** STEVENSON *Silv. Squatters* 151 In the fastnesses of Nature, forests, mountains, and the back of man's beyond.

D. *Comb.* **beyond-man**, an early synonym of SUPERMAN; †**beyond-sea** *a.* (cf. B 1), ultramarine, outlandish, foreign; *hence* †**beyond-sea-ship**, humorously applied to a foreign prince (cf. *lordship*).

1498 *Will. of Petyt* (Somerset Ho), Ij paire of beyond see shetes. **1534** *Eng. Ch. Furniture* 209 A paynted cloth of beyond see werk. **1578** LYTE *Dodoens* 580 The garden Mallow called the winter or beyond see roose. *Ibid.* 682 The red beyondsea Gooseberie. **1611** BEAUM. & FL. *Philaster* IV. ii, I never loved his beyond-sea-ship. **1639** FULLER *Holy War* IV. viii. (1840) 192 Henceforward the beyond-sea world took notice of him. **1711** J. GREENWOOD *Eng. Gram.* 10 Excessive Lust of Novelty..has stung many with an Itch of bringing in beyond-Sea words. **1896** A. TILLE tr. *Nietzsche's Thus spake Zarathustra* in *Wks.* VIII. 5 Behold, I teach you beyond-man! Beyond-man is the significance of earth. Your will shall say: beyond-man shall be the significance of earth. *Ibid.* 129 Never yet beyond-man existed. I have seen them both naked, the greatest and the smallest man. **1896** T. COMMON tr. *Nietzsche's Twilight of Idols* in *Wks.* XI. 198 To be set up..as a 'higher man', as a kind of beyond-man. **1908** *Athenæum* 13 June 729/1 The 'Super-tramp' is..the opposite of the 'oversoul' or 'beyond-man'. *a* **1917** G. B. SHAW *Let.* in *Trans. Philol. Soc. 1916–20* (1932) 8 Some of our most felicitous writers..had been using such desperate and unspeakable forms as Beyondman, when the glib Superman was staring them in the face all the time.

beyondness (bɪ'jɒndnɪs). [f. BEYOND *adv.* and *prep.* + -NESS.] The condition or quality of being beyond.

[**1848** A. STEINMETZ *Hist. Jesuits* I. III. 283 Oh! 'twas a glorious prospect—a spirit-stirring something-beyondness!] **1923** W. DEEPING *Secret Sanct.* xvi. 164 There was the beyondness of growing cabbages, the secret life of a cabbage patch. **1963** *Times* 26 Apr. 8/1 Will it not still be a relation to a Beyond? Call it deep down, but it always means a Beyondness.

†**be'yonds**, *prep. Obs.* Only in Wyclif, as **biȝendis, biȝondis, byȝondes.** [f. BEYOND *adv.* and *prep.* + advb. suffix *-s.*] = BEYOND.

1382 WYCLIF *Mark* iii. 8 Fro Ydume and biȝendis [**1388** biȝondis] Jordan. —— *2 Cor.* x. 16 Also for to preche into tho thingis that ben byȝondes ȝou.

beyre = of both: see BO.

beysaunce, obs. form of BEISANCE.

beysc, beȝȝsc, obs. forms of BASK *a.* bitter.

beyt(e, obs. form of BAIT.

bez, beze: see BES- and BEZANTLER.

bezaar, bezahar, obs. forms of BEZOAR.

Bezaleelian, -elian (bɛzə'liːlɪən), *a.* [f. *Bezaleel, -lel*, the name of the artificer mentioned in *Exod.* xxxi., sometimes used connotatively.] Worthy of Bezaleel, or of a cunning workman.

[**1609** C. BUTLER *Fem. Mon.* v. (1623) Kiv, Their Hexagonia no Bezaleel For curious Art may passe or imitate.] **1878** T. SINCLAIR *Mount* 289 They all are bezaleelian, skill within skill.

†**be'zan**, *sb.*[1] *Obs. rare*⁻¹. [a. Du. *bezaan* mizen sail, ad. Sp. *mesana* or It. *mezzana* mizen.] Apparently used in Eng. in the sense of a small sailing vessel.

1662 PEPYS *Diary* 5 Sept., Saw the yacht..set out from Greenwich with the little Dutch bezan.

bezant, byzant ('bɛzənt, bɪ'zɑːnt, -æ-). Forms: 3 (*Ormin*) **beȝȝsannt**, 3–7 **besand(e**, 4 (*pl.*) **besaunce**, 4–5 **besaund(e, -unt(e, -wnt, bessant, -aun**, 4–9 **besant(e, bezaunde, -nt**, 6 **besaunte, beisand**, 6–7 (*pl.*) **basence, beazance**, 7–9 **bi-, byzant**, 7– **bezant.** [a. OF. *besan* (pl. *besanz*):—L. *byzantius* (sc. *nummus*) Byzantine (coin), from *Byzantium*, where it was first struck; cf. *Byzantine.* Poems *c* 1400 show the accentuation '*bezant.*]

1. A gold coin first struck at Byzantium or Constantinople, and seemingly identical with the Roman *solidus* or *aureus*, but afterwards varying in value between the English sovereign and half-sovereign, or less. It was current in Europe from the 9th century, and in England, till superseded by the noble, a coin of Edw. III. There were also silver bezants worth from a florin to a shilling. Used by Wyclif to translate both the Latin words *talentum* and *drachma.*

c **1200** ORMIN 8102 He ȝaff hise cnihhtess þa Fifftiȝ beȝȝsannz to mede. **1297** R. GLOUC. 409 Vyfty þousend besans, he sende hem. *a* **1300** *Cursor M.* 4194 þar was ioseph in seruage sald, For tuenti besands [*v.r.* besaundes, besauntis]. *c* **1314** *Guy Warw.* (A.) 2474 An hundred bessauns gif Y the. **1382** WYCLIF *Matt.* xxv. 15 To oone he ȝaue fyue talentis or besauntis. **1388** —— *Luke* xv. 8 What womman hauynge ten besauntis. ? *a* **1400** *Morte Arth.* 3253 Bruches and besauntez and oþer bryghte stonys. *c* **1400** *Roland* 411 Tok of the hethyn broche or bessant. **1494** FABYAN VII. 374 One is called a bezaunde imperiall, & yᵉ other a bezaunt ducall. *c* **1500** KENNEDY *Agst. Mouth-thankl.* iii, Brotches, beisands, robbis, & rings. **1577** *Test. 12 Patriarchs* (1604) 144 They ask two basences of gold. **1611** SPEED *Hist. Gt. Brit.* IX. vii. 32 They should pay twentie thousand Bizants. **1653** URQUHART *Rabelais* I. xxxi, A thousand besans of gold. **1820** SCOTT *Ivanhoe* vii, Here, Isaac, lend me a handful of byzants. **1875** JEVONS *Money* ix. 97 In Anglo-Saxon times gold byzants from Byzantium were used in England.

2. The offering made by the kings of England at the sacrament, or at festivals.

1667 E. CHAMBERLAYNE *St. Gt. Brit.* I. II. xii. (1743) 98 The gold offered by the King at the Altar, when he receives the Sacrament..is still called the Byzant. **1762** *Gentl. Mag.* 599 The King's [offering] is a byzant, or wedge of gold, value 30*l.*

3. *Her.* A gold roundel representing the above coin plain and unstamped: according to Littré, originally signifying that the bearer had been in the Holy Land. Also *attrib.*

1486 *Bk. St. Albans, Her.* C iij b, This is calde a besant cros for it is made all of besanttis..He berith gowles a cros besauntid. **1572** BOSSEWELL *Armorie* II. 79 Plates are of dignitie nexte vnto the besauntes..whiche are alwayes of a golden colour. **1610** GUILLIM *Heraldry* IV. xix. (1660) 352 If they [Roundles] be Or, then we call them Besants. **1864** BOUTELL *Her. Hist. & Pop.* v. 25 In the instances of the Bezant and the Plate.

Bezantin(e, obs. form of BYZANTINE.

bez-antler (beɪ-, beɪz'æntlə(r)). Forms: 7 **bezantelier, beas antlier, beantler**, 7–9 **bez-antler, bezantler**, 8–9 **bes-antler**, 9 **bees-antler, bis-antler.** [f. *bez-*, BES- secondary + ANTLER. A word of unfixed form, also called *bay antler*, and varied as *bay-*, *bez-*, *beze-tyne.*] The second branch or 'start' of a deer's horn, next above the brow-antler (or antler proper).

1598 MANWOOD *Lawes Forest* iv. §6 (1615) 46 The Brow-antlier, or Beasantlier. **1610** GUILLIM *Heraldry* III. xiv. (1660) 168 Skilfull Woodmen describing the head of a Hart do call the Next above there unto [i.e. the Browanteliers].. Bezanteliers. [**1611** COTGR., *Surandoillier*, the beankler or second branch of a Deeres head. *Ibid.*, *Surentouiller*..the Beancler of a Bucke.] **1664** POWER *Exp. Philos.* I. 11 With little branches and twigs (like Bezanteliers) springing out of them. **1678** PHILLIPS (App.) *Bezantler*, the..next branch of the Harts-horn to Browantler, which is the lowest. **1855** OWEN *Vertebr. An.* (1868) III. 618 Its branches are the 'tynes'..the first or lowest branch is the 'brow-tyne,' the second is the 'beze' or 'bez tyne.' **1874** T. BELL *Brit. Quadrup.* 349 The branches or antlers..as the *brow-antler*, *bez-antler*, and *royal.* **1884** JEFFERIES *Red Deer* iv. 71 Above the 'burr' came the brow-antlier, now the brow-point; next the bez-antlier, now the bay.

bezanty (bɪ'zɑːntɪ, -æ-), *ppl. a. Her.* Also 7–9 **bezantee.** In 5 englished as **besantid, besauntid.** [a. F. *besantée*, f. *besant*, BEZANT.] Charged with or formed of bezants.

1486 *Bk. St. Albans, Her.* C iij b, He berith gowles a cros besauntid. *c* **1630** RISDON *Surv. Devon* §192 (1810) 206 These Vaultorts bear a border bezantee in their coat-armour. **1864** BOUTELL *Her. Hist. & Pop.* xv. (ed. 3) 174 The brothers De La Zouche severally bear gules bezantée,

and azure bezantée. **1877** L. JEWITT *Half-hrs. Eng. Antiq.* 194 The lion rampant within a bordure bezanty.

bezaor, -zar(d, -zas, obs. forms of BEZOAR.

bezaunce, obs. form of BEISANCE, BEZANTS.

beze: see BES- and BEZ-ANTLER.

bezeche, bezeik, obs. forms of BESEECH.

bezel ('bɛzəl). Forms: 7 bezell, -ill, beasel, bizel, bezle, 7–8 beazil, 8 bezil, bazil, (9 beazel), 7– basil, bezel, 8– bezil. [a. OF. *besel, *bezel, in mod.F. *biseau, bizeau* (cf. Sp. *bisel*), also *basile*; of unknown origin: it may be dim. of *bis, bez*, or contain that word. (It does not represent med.L. *bisalus*.) Cf. BELEF, BEVEL.]

1. A slope, a sloping edge or face: *esp.* that of a chisel or other cutting tool (commonly *basil*.)

1611 COTGR., *Biseau*, a bezle, bezeling, or scuing; such a slopenesse, or slope form, as is in the point of an yron leauer, chizle, &c. **1677** MOXON *Mech. Exerc.* (J.) These chissels are not ground to such a basil as the joiner's chissels. **1721** BAILEY, *Basil* is the Sloping edge of a chissel. **1823** NICHOLSON *Pract. Build.* 225 Edge-tools are sharpened, by applying the basil to the convex surface [of a grind-stone].

2. The oblique sides or faces of a cut gem; *spec.* the various oblique faces and edges of a brilliant, which lie round the 'table' or large central plane on the upper surface, comprising the 8 star-facets, 16 skill-facets, and 8 lozenges. [Cf. Sp. *bisel* 'edge of a looking-glass, or crystal plate.']

1839–75 URE *Dict. Arts* II. 25 Upper skill-facets are wrought on the lower part of the bezil, and terminate in the girdle; star-facets are wrought on the upper part of the bezil, and terminate in the table; lozenges are formed by the meeting of the skill- and star-facets on the bezil.

3. 'The groove and projecting flange or lip by which the crystal of a watch or the stone of a jewel is retained in its setting.'

1616 BULLOKAR, *Bezill.* **1623** COCKERAM, *Bezell*, the broad place of a Ring where the stone is set. **1658** ROWLAND *Mouffet's Theat. Ins.* 968 In the uttermost part of the wings, as if it were four Adamants glistering in a beazil of Hyacinth. **1680** *Lond. Gaz.* No. 1499/4 One silver [watch]..the hours in form of Diamonds, the Out-case holes with Bizels for the sound of the Bell. **1783** AINSWORTH *Lat. Dict.* (Morell) IV. s.v. *Gyges*, When he turned the beazil to the palm of the hand. **1826** KIRBY & SP. *Entomol.* III. 496 The partitions that separate the lenses, or rather Bezels in which they are set. **1877** W. JONES *Finger-ring* 12 A long oval bezel chased in intaglio.

4. *Comb.* **bezelwise** *adv.*, sloping, bevelled.

1727 BRADLEY *Fam. Dict.* s.v. *Chimney*, The Sides of the Frame and Trap are made slope or bezelwise.

bezel ('bɛzəl), *v.* Also 7 **basil.** [f. prec. sb.] *trans.* To grind (a tool) down to an edge; to cut to a sloping edge, to bevel.

1677 MOXON *Mech. Exerc.* (1703) 185 The Chissels..are Basil'd away on both the flat sides. **1715** DESAGULIERS *Fires Impr.* 122 Instead of rabbiting the Frame and Trap-Door, let both be bezell'd or sloap'd.

bezel(l, variant of BEZZLE *v. Obs.*

bezelling ('bɛzəlɪŋ), *vbl. sb.* Also 7 **bezeling,** 9 **bezilling.** [f. BEZEL + -ING[1].] Collective appellation of that which forms a bezel.

1611 COTGR., *Biseau*, a bezle, bezeling, or scuing. **1866** BLACKMORE *Cradock N.* xxviii, No bezilling, no jewel whatever.

bezenge, obs. form of BESINGE.

bezer, obs. form of BEZOAR.

‖**bezesteen** ('bɛzɪstiːn). Also 7 **besestano, bisestano,** 7–8 **besestein,** 8 **bezestan,** 9 **bezestein.** [a. (directly or through Fr. or It.) Turk. *bazistān*, originally a Pers. word meaning 'clothes market.'] An exchange, bazaar, or market-place in the East.

1656 BLOUNT *Glossogr.*, *Besestein*, an Exchange or the chief Market-place among the Turks. **1696** PHILLIPS, *Besestano*, a Burse or Exchange for Merchants. **1736** BAILEY, *Bezestan*..a Burse or Exchange. **1849** CURZON *Visits Monast.* 35 Some of the bezesteins and principal bazaars are closed at twelve o'clock. **1864** SALA *Tw. round Clock* 267 Behold the Bezesteen of borrowed money.

‖**bezetta** (bɪ'zɛta). [Corruption of It. *pezzetta*, dim. of *pezza* a PIECE of cloth; defined in Tommaseo's Dict. as 'piece of cloth, usually of cotton, which when rubbed gives a red stain, and is used for rouging.'] 'A dye or pigment prepared by dipping linen rags in solutions of certain colouring matters' Watts *Dict. Chem.* I. 583.

1863 WATTS *Dict. Chem.* I. 583 Red bezetta is coloured with cochineal, and is used as a cosmetic. *Ibid.*, Blue bezetta ..chiefly used for colouring the rind of Dutch cheeses.

bezil, variant of BEZZLE *v. Obs.*

bezique (bə'ziːk). Also 9 **bazique.** [corruption of F. *besigue, besy*: of unknown origin.] A game of cards, in which the name 'Bezique' is applied to the occurrence in one hand of the knave of diamonds and queen of spades.

1861 *Macm. Mag.* Dec. 138 Bazique is a game, probably of later invention, and of quite a novel kind..The knave of diamonds and queen of spades together, form Bazique, and score four. **1869** *Eng. Mech.* 24 Dec. 367/1 Bézique is a very amusing game for two or four persons.

bezle, obs. form of BEZEL.

bezoar ('biːzɔə(r), 'bɛzəʊɑː(r)). Forms: 6 besert, bezer, 6–7 bezahar, 6–8 bezaar, bezar, 7 besohard, besar, beazar, beazer, bazar, bezor, beazoar, bezaor, boezar, 8 besaar, bezard, 7–9 -oard, -oart, 7– bezoar. [Like mod.L. *bezahar, bezaar, bezoar* (*bezardicum, lapis bezoarticus*), Sp. *bezaar, bezar, bezoar*, F. *bezahar, bezar, bezoar, bezoard*, ad. Arab. *bāzahr* or *bādizahr*, ad. Per. *pād-zahr* counter-poison, antidote, bezoar stone; f. *zahr* poison. In 17th c. Eng., as in F. and Sp., *bezahar, bezaar* was reduced to two syllables, *bezar, beazar, beazer* ('beːzər), of which the mod. pronunc. would be regularly ('biːzə(r)). The spelling *bezoar* (for *bezaär*) appears to be of mod.L. origin; it has influenced the pronunciation given in dictionaries since the end of last century.]

†**1.** *gen.* A counter-poison or antidote. *Obs.* (In later writers taken as a *fig.* use of sense 2 a: hence, also, ***bezoar-stone.***)

1597 GERARD *Herbal* II. cclxxiv. (1633) 969 This root Anthora is the Bezoar or counterpoison to that Thora. **1607** TOPSELL *Serpents* 775 The juice of Apples being drunk, and Endive, are the proper Bezoar against the venom of a Phalangie. **1637** EARL MONMOUTH *Rom. & Tarquin* 208 Valour is a kinde of Besar, which comforts the hearts of subjects, that they may the better endure a Tyrants venome. **1750** tr. *Leonardus' Mirr. Stones* 78 Every Thing that frees the Body from any Ailment, is called the Bezoar of that Ailment.

b. 1658 ROWLAND *Mouffet's Theat. Ins.* 929 A Hornet is the Bezoar stone for its own wound.

2. Various substances formerly held as antidotes: *spec.* **a.** A calculus or concretion found in the stomach or intestines of some animals, chiefly ruminants, formed of concentric layers of animal matter deposited round some foreign substance, which serves as a nucleus. Often called ***bezoar-stone.*** (The ordinary current sense.)

The original sort was the *lapis bezoar orientale*, obtained from the wild goat of Persia and various antelopes, etc.; the *lapis bezoar occidentale*, obtained from the lamas of Peru, was less valued; the chamois yielded *German bezoar*.

1580 FRAMPTON *Joyf. News* 126 The stone is called the Bezaar, beyng..approved good against Venome. **1585** in Nichols *Progr. Q. Eliz.* II. 420 Item, a besert stone. **1615** CROOKE *Body of Man* 230 Diuisible into many shels or huskes like a Bezoar stone. **1622** R. HAWKINS *Voy. S. Sea* (1847) 74 The becunia, and other beasts, which breed the beazer stone. **1638** SHIRLEY *Mart. Soldier* III. iv. in Bullen *O. Pl.* (1882) I. 217 A true rare Quintessence Extracted out of Orientall Bezar. **1670** J. NARBROUGH in Burney *Discov. S. Sea* III. xiii. (1813) 333, I had his [a guanaco's] paunch opened to search for the Bezoar stone. **1749** *Phil. Trans.* XLVI. 120 Rhinoceros-Bezoars, which I supposed were taken out of the Stomach or Guts of that large Animal. **1774** GOLDSM. *Nat. Hist.* (1862) I. II. iii. 307 The concretion sometimes found in the stomach of these animals [the chamois], called the German Bezoar. **1849** TODD *Cycl. Anat. & Phys.* IV. 85/1 The oriental bezoard, a resinous intestinal calculus. **1882** *Catal. Museum St. Barthol. Hosp.* I. 542 (No. 293) Section of a Bezoar, composed chiefly of Pinic Acid. Its nucleus is a date-stone.

†**b.** Alleged stones or concretions of various kinds. (Usually due to ignorance of the origin of the prec.) *Obs.*

1477 NORTON *Ord. Alch.* in Ashm. v. (1652) 72 Bezoars of the Mine. **1594** BLUNDEVIL *Exerc.* v. ix. (ed. 7) 550 This stone Bezar groweth in a concavity in manner of a girdle about two handfull long and three inches broad. **1607** TOPSELL *Four-f. Beasts* 100 The hart..sendeth forth certain tears, which are turned into a stone called 'bezahar.' **1618** *Rep. E. Ind. Comp.* in Jas. Mill *Brit. India* I. I. ii. 23 On the island of Borneo, diamonds, bezoar stones, and gold, might be obtained. **1634** SIR T. HERBERT *Trav.* (1677) 358 The soil ..uberous in rich Stones, as Diamonds, Chrysolites, Onyx, Magnets and Bezoars.

†**c.** Applied to various medicinal preparations.

1706 PHILLIPS, *Bezoar Minerale*, a Chymical Preparation of Butter of Antimony. *Ibid.*, *Bezoar-Animale*, the Livers and Hearts of Vipers dry'd in the Sun and powder'd. **1710** T. FULLER *Pharm. Extemp.* 309. **1807** AIKIN *Dict. Chem.*, *Bezoard Mineral* is a perfect oxyd of Antimony.

†**3.** *transf.* The wild goat of Persia, the best-known source of the calculus (2 a). In later times called **bezoar-goat**; so **bezoar antelope**. *Obs.* (Early writers confound *beazer* and *beaver*.)

1611 COTGR., *Bezoard*..breeds in the maw of the Goat called a Beazer. **1620** FORD *Linea V.* 60 Their places and honours are hunted after as the beazar for his preservatiues. **1670** *Phil. Trans.* V. 1177 The Oriental Bezoar..being a Savage Animal like a kid. **1774** GOLDSM. *Nat. Hist.* (1862) I. II. iii. 308 The Bezoar goat..is the animal famous for that concretion in the intestines..called the oriental bezoar. **1781** tr. *Buffon's Nat. Hist.* VI. 407 *note*, The bezoar antilope..is one of the animals which produce the bezoar.

4. *Attrib.* and *Comb.*, as ***bezoard-extract***, etc.

1641 FRENCH *Distill.* ii. (1651) 60 Which may be called a Bezoard extract. **1676** *Phil. Trans.* XI. 743 The Bezoar-like virtue of such stones. **1709** G. WILSON *Chym.* i. (ed. 3) 13 One Pound more of new Bezoart Spirit of Nitre.

bezoardic, -artic (bɛzəʊ'ɑːdɪk, -'ɑːtɪk), *a.* and *sb.* [ad. mod.L. *bezoardicus, -articus*; a. F. *bezoard, bezoart*, BEZOAR; see -IC.]

A. *adj.* Of the nature of, or pertaining to, bezoar; having its properties; serving as antidote.

1670 *Phil. Trans.* V. 2082 Wont to breed Bezoardick stones. **1712** tr. *Pomet's Hist. Drugs* I. 39 Angelica is.. Cordial, Bezoartick, and Alexipharmack. **1835** *Penny Cycl.* IV. 361 Any substance..thought to possess important qualities was termed bezoardic, to indicate its value.

B. *sb.* A bezoardic drug; an antidote; a remedy.

1671 SALMON *Syn. Med.* III. xxii. 396 The Bezoartick..is the present cure for all poysons and Feauers. **1684** tr. *Bonet's Merc. Compit.* III. 92 Guaiacum..I have used..as the Bezoardick of this Disease. **1727** BRADLEY *Fam. Dict.* s.v. *Bezoar Stone*, All Medicines contrary to Poison are called Bezoardicks. **1819** REES *Cycl.* s.v.

†**bezo'ardical, -tical,** *a.* = prec. *Obs.*

a **1644** CHILLINGW. *Serm.* v. §52 The healing Bezoartical Virtue of Grace. **1693** SIR T. BLOUNT *Nat. Hist.* 36 Every thing good against Poysons, is commonly term'd Bezoardical.

†**bezonian** (bɪ'zəʊnɪən). *Obs.* Also 6 **bezonion,** 6– **bi-, besonian.** [f. It. *bisogno*, Sp. *bisoño* (see BESONIO). The ending is perh. -AN, as in *Oxonian*, etc.]

a. A raw recruit. **b.** (as a term of contempt) Needy beggar, base fellow, knave, rascal.

1592 NASHE *P. Penilesse* Wks. 1883–4 II. 86 Trod vnder foote of euery inferior Besonian. **1593** SHAKS. *2 Hen. VI*, IV. i. 134 Great men oft dye by vilde Bezonions. **1597** —— *2 Hen. IV*, V. iii. 115 *Bezonian*, speake, or dye. **1611** COTGR., *Bisongne* [see BESOGNE], a raskall, bisonian, base humored scoundrell. **1632** MASSINGER *Maid of Hon.* IV. i, For half a mouldy biscuit, sell herself To a poor bisognion. **1843** LYTTON *Last Bar.* I. xi, Out on ye, cullions and bezonians!

bez tyne: see under BEZ-ANTLER.

†'**bezzle,** *v. Obs.* exc. *dial.* Forms: 5 besil, 6 beizle, 7 beezel, bezel, bezzel, bizle, bizel, 8 bezil, bezzil, 7– bezzle. [Late ME. *besil*, a. OF. *besiler, besillier, beziller*, to lay waste, ravage, destroy; shortened form of *embesillier*: see EMBEZZLE.] General sense: To make away with wastefully.

†**1.** *trans.* To plunder, spoil; to make away with (the property of others). *Obs.* Cf. EMBEZZLE.

c **1430** LYDG. *Bochas* V. xvi. (1554) 132 b, That he should haue besiled the Of Chartage. **1594** CAREW *Tasso* (1881) 94 Her sweet showes and faire lookes shall beizle harts. **1611** BEAUM. & FL. *Knt. Burn. Pest.* I. iii, I have laid up a little for my younger son Michael, and thou think'st to 'bezzle that. *c* **1612** FLETCHER *Woman's Prize* IV. i. 115/2, I must be shut up and my substance bezel'd. **1720** *Stow's Surv.* (Strype 1754) II. VI. iii. 626/2 To suffer no manner of person to bezil or purloin..out of the said park any timber.

2. *intr.* To make away with a large quantity of food or especially drink; to drink to excess, to guzzle, to revel.

1604 DEKKER *Honest Wh.* Wks. 1873 II. 113, I wonder how the inside of a Tauerne lookes now. Oh when shall I bizle, bizle? **1612** T. TAYLOR *Comm. Titus* i. 7 (1619) 143 It is too much for a minister to lie bezelling in the delight of his tast. **1633** T. ADAMS *Exp. 2 Peter* ii. 12 (1865) 453/1 He that will be sober when others bezzle..is branded with the name of puritan. **1721** BAILEY, *Bezzle* (*q.d.* to Beastle), to guzzle, tipple, or drink hard. **1875** *Whitby Gloss.* (E.D.S.), *Beb* or *Bezzle*, to drink.

b. *trans.* To make away with or consume (drink), waste or squander (one's money). *Obs.* or *dial.*

1617 J. TAYLOR (Water P.) *Trav.* Wks. (1630) 78/2, 13 or 14 brewings haue beene..stayed in the Towne, as not sufficient to be beezeled in the Country. [**1775** COLLIER (Tim Bobbin) *Tummus & Meary* Wks. (1862) 54, I drank meh Pint o Ele..I cawd for another, on [= and] bezzilt tat too. *Ibid.* 55 In i'dd'n [= an ye had] bezzilt owey moor brass inney [= than ye] hadd'n. **1875** *Lanc. Gloss.* 37 *Bezzle*, to waste, to squander; generally applied to drinking].

†'**bezzle,** *sb. Obs. rare.* Also 7 **bezell.** [f. prec.] A hard drinker, a bouser.

1592 NASHE *P. Penilesse* (ed. 2) 12/1 Foule drunken bezzle. **1597** BP. HALL *Sat.* V. ii, The swolne bezell at an alehouse fyre, That tonnes in gallons to his bursten paunch.

†'**bezzled,** *ppl. a. Obs.* exc. *dial.* Also **beazled.** [f. as prec. + -ED.] ? Wasted, spent, worn out, exhausted; muddled (with drinking).

1604 MARSTON *Malcont.* (T.), Wonder of thy errour will strike dumb Thy bezel'd sense. **1875** PARISH *Sussex Gloss.* s.v. *Beazled*, He comes home tired of an evening, but not beazled like boys who go to plough.

†'**bezzler.** *Obs.* Also 7 **beazler.** [f. as prec. + -ER.] One who drinks much, a tippler, bouser.

a **1593** H. SMITH *Serm.* (1637) 473 If they had been Epicures, and Libertines, and Beazlers, God would not have heard his prayer for them. **1601** *Jack Drum's Entert.* (1616) A iij. (R.) The shewing horne bezelers discourse.

†'**bezzling,** *vbl. sb. Obs.* Also 6 **bezeling,** 7 **bezelling, bezzeling, bisseling.** [f. as prec. +

-ING[1].] Drunken revelry or dissipation, bousing.

1599 MARSTON *Sc. Villanie* II. vii. 206 That diuine part is soak't away in sinne, In sensuall lust, and midnight bezeling. **1641** MILTON *Animadv.* Wks. (1851) 196 They that spend their youth in loitering, bezzling, and harlotting.

†**bezzling**, *ppl. a. Obs.* [f. as prec. + -ING[2].] That drinks hard; bousing, swilling.

1617 J. TAYLOR (Water P.) *Trav.* Wks. (1630) 80/1 Gogmagog, or our English Sir John Falstaff were but shrimps to this bezzeling Bombards latitude, altitude, and crassitude.

B-girl ('bi:gɜ:l). *U.S. slang.* [Abbrev. of *bar-girl* (BAR *sb.*[1] 29 c).] A woman employed to encourage customers to buy drinks at a bar.

1936 *San Francisco News* 31 July 3/6 No B Girls buzzing around you here to sip tea you think is a highball. **1938** *True Story* Dec. 66/2 'B-girls?' I repeated, 'What are they?' ..'That's just short for bar girls.' **1964** 'F. ARCHER' *Out of Blue* (1966) v. 76 If I stand here, I'm a waitress, see? If I sit down, I'm a B-girl, and this joint doesn't pay for that kind of protection.

‖**bhajan** ('bʌdʒən). *Hinduism.* Also **bhajana, bhajjan.** [Skr.] A devotional song.

1914 A. H. FOX-STRANGWAYS *Music of Hindostan* xi. 286 The oldest forms of Hindu song are the *Pada* and *Bhajana.* **1925** A. B. FYZEE-RAHAMIN *Music of India* iii. 32 Bharat Math..sang religious songs called *Bhajans.* **1968** *Observer* 25 Feb. 3/5 The singing of devotional songs called *bhajans.*

‖**bhakta** ('bʌktə). *Hinduism.* [Skr.] A religious devotee; a worshipper, believer.

1828 H. H. WILSON in *Asiatic Researches* XVI. 12 The *Bháktas* worshipped Vishnu as Vásudeva, and wore no characteristic marks. **1886** *Encycl. Brit.* XXI. 290/2 The *Bhaktas*, a Vaishṇava sect founded, towards the end of the 15th century, by Chaitanya. **1910** *Ibid.* XIII. 511/1 His doctrine of Bhakti distinguishes five grades of devotional feeling in the *Bhaktas*, or faithful adherents. **1930** V. ELWIN *R. Rolle* i. 7 Rolle himself is a typical *bhakta*..his wandering sannyāsī life; his glowing, burning heart—all mark him as a *bhakta* after the mind of Jesus.

‖**bhakti** ('bʌktɪ). *Hinduism.* [Skr.] Religious devotion, piety, or devoted faith, as a means of salvation.

1832 H. H. WILSON in *Jrnl. Asiatic Soc.* (Bengal) I. 220 Expatiating upon the different degrees of *Bhakti*, or faith, and the various kinds of *Mukti*, or salvation. **1877** MONIER-WILLIAMS *Hinduism* ix. 115 The doctrine of *bhakti*, or 'salvation by faith'. **1911** E. B. HAVELL *Ideals Ind. Art* 117 *Bhakti* is the moving spirit in all great religious art, in the West as in the East. **1915** N. MACNICOL *Ind. Theism* 30 Those in India whose hearts are filled with *bhakti* or 'loving faith'. **1921** T. R. GLOVER *Jesus Exper. Men* iii. 41 Tuka and other mystics of India believed that from this a man might be saved by *Bhakti*, by self-annihilating devotion to a friendly god. *Karma* and *Bhakti* are the two poles of Indian religious thought. **1953** E. M. FORSTER *Hill of Devi* 117 Sivaji..believed in bhakti, in our union with the Divine through love.

b. *attrib.* and *Comb.*, as **bhakti-marga** [Skr. *mārga* path], the way to salvation through religious devotion or faith.

1936 *Times Lit. Suppl.* 18 Jan. 57/4 The *bhakti* movement, the movement of emotional religion. **1937** A. HUXLEY *Ends & Means* xiii. 234 In India it is known as *bhakti-marga*, the path of devotional faith, as opposed to *karma-marga*, the path of duty or works, and *jñana-marga*, the path of knowledge. **1959** *Chambers's Encycl.* XIV. 798/2 *Bhakti yoga* or devotion to God is also advocated as an additional means. **1963** *Listener* 28 Mar. 550/2 In the last centuries B.C. a second way, *Bhakti-marga* or the way of devotion came into prominence, seeking to obtain union with the chosen god through love and service.

‖**bhang, bang** (bæŋ). Forms: 6–9 **bangue**, 7–9 **bang**, 9 **bhang**; (also 7 **bange**, 7–8 **banque**, 8 **bank**, 9 **beng, benj, bhung**). [A word widely spread in Eastern langs.: in Urdū, and various Indian langs., *bhāng, bhang, bhung*; in Pers., *bang* (whence Arab. *banj, benj*); all from Skr. *bhaṅgā* hemp. Its first European form was the Pg. *bangue*, also the earliest form in Eng.; *bang* (representing the Pers.) has prevailed since *c* 1675; *bhang* became frequent during the 19th century, and is etymologically preferable.]

The native name of the Indian variety of the common Hemp, which in warm countries develops narcotic and intoxicating properties. In India the leaves and seed-capsules are chewed or smoked, or eaten mixed up into a sweetmeat, and sometimes an infusion of them is drunk. The name is sometimes extended to an intoxicating substance prepared from the resinous exudation of the plant, called by the Arabs *hashish.*

[**1563** GARCIA DE ORTA *Simples e Drogas* 26 (transl.), All he had to do was to eat a little bangue.] **1598** W. PHILLIPS *Linschoten's Trav. Ind.* 19 Many kinds of Drogues, as Amfion, or Opium, Camfora, Bangue. **1621** BURTON *Anat. Mel.* II. v. I. v. (1651) 392 Another [herb] called Bange, like in effect to Opium. *c* **1645** HOWELL *Lett.* (1650) II. 72 In the orientall countries—as Cambaia, Calicut..ther is a drink call'd 'Banque,' which is rare and precious. **1673** FRYER *Acc. E. India* (1698) 91 (Y.) Bang (a pleasant intoxicating Seed mixed with Milk). **1727** A. HAMILTON *Acc. E. Ind.* I. 131 (Y.) Before they engage in fight they drink Bang. **1782** T. ARNOLD *Insanity* II. 254 A preparation of a poisonous vegetable called Banque. **1838** LOUDON *Encycl. Plants* 1083 The..intoxicating Turkish drug called Bang or Haschisch. **1839** E. W. LANE tr. *Arab. Nts.* I. ii. 107 She contriveth to defraud him by means of the cup of wine..putting benj into it. **1850** C. KINGSLEY *Alton Locke* I. xxi. 291 Mesmerism and magic-lanterns, benj and opium, winna explain all facts. **1859** LANG *Wand. India* 47, I took to opium and smoking *bhung* (hemp). **1866** LIVINGSTONE *Jrnl.* i. (1873) I. 29 Bhang is not smoked, but tobacco is. **1934** F. STARK *Valley of Assassins* v. 284 An aromatic sage-like plant they call generically *Benj.*

bharal ('bʌrəl). Also **b(h)arhal, burhel, burrell, burrhal, burrhel.** [Hindi *bharal.*] The wild or blue sheep of the Himalayas and Tibet, *Pseudois nayaur.*

1838 *Proc. Zool. Soc.* 79 A skin of the Burrhal Sheep from the Himalaya Mountains. **1840** *Ibid.* 68 The Burrhel would seem to inhabit a much loftier region of the Himalaya than the Nahoor. **1881** *Encycl. Brit.* XII. 742/2 The *barhal*, or blue wild sheep. **1886** *Ibid.* XXI. 785/1 A species..with smaller and more spreading horns, the burrhel, *O[vis] nahoor.* **1887** *Field* 19 Feb. 243/2, I had a shot at a small burrell and missed. **1924** H. WHISTLER *In High Himalayas* xiii. 165 We found the tracks of burhel on some bare soil. **1937** H. W. TILMAN *Ascent of Nanda Devi* xi. 129 A herd of bharal, or wild sheep, was seen traversing..the..cliffs. **1965** S. H. PRATER *Bk. Indian Animals* 252 In structure and habits the Bharal holds a place intermediate between sheep and goats.

bhasmatti, var. BASMATI.

‖**bheesty, bheestie** ('bi:stɪ). Also 8– **beasty**, 9 **beestie.** [Urdū *bhīstī*, a. Pers. *bihishtī*, f. *bihisht* paradise; prob. of jocular origin.] In India, the servant who supplies an establishment with water, which he carries in a skin slung on his back.

1781 *India Gaz.* 24 Nov. (Y.) With the loss of only 1 sepoy, 1 beasty, and a cossy. **1810** T. WILLIAMSON *Vade-Mec.* I. 229 (Y.) If he carries the water himself in the skin of a goat,..he then receives the designation of Bheesty. **1859** LANG *Wand. Ind.* 63 Jehan, the bheestie's daughter, was a virtuous girl. **1883** W. BAXTER *Winter in Ind.* ii. 22 Bheesties pressing water out of their pigskins to lay the dust.

‖**bhikku** ('bɪku:). [Pali *bhikku*, f. Skr. *bhikṣú* (see next).] A Buddhist mendicant or religious devotee. Cf. next.

1846 *Jrnl. R. Asiatic Soc.* (*Ceylon Branch*) 84 The original formulary of introduction into the priesthood, after the shaving of the head and beard and putting on the yellow garment, being simply 'Approach, O Bikkhu', the Bikkhu being necessarily from his appellation a religious mendicant. **1903** *Nature* 17 Dec. 163/2 Bhikkus of occidental nationalities..would be able to return to their own countries, there to spread the knowledge of Buddhism. **1927** J. P. ARENDZEN *Whom do You Say—?* v. ii. 284 Buddhist Bhikkus when in England would..assume this title [Reverend]. **1959** *Times* 3 Feb. 11/6 There is now a separate order of English *bhikkus* near Swiss Cottage.

‖**bhikshu** ('bɪkʃu:). Pl. **-shook, -shu, -shus.** [Skr. *bhikṣú* a beggar, f. *bhikṣ* to beg, ask alms.] A Brahmanical or Buddhist mendicant or religious devotee.

1811 W. WARD *Acc. Hindoos* III. vi. 400 He becomes a Bhikshookŭ, literally a beggar, but his person is supposed to be distinguished by his having become..insensible to all human things, and to be absorbed in thinking on God. **1827** A. STEELE *Law & Custom of Hindoo Castes* II. 86 Bhikshook or professional beggars may be Gruhust, and may marry and have children, which the Sunyasees may not. **1876** *Encycl. Brit.* IV. 204/2 *Sannyāsin* (or *bhikshu*), or religious mendicant. **1924** W. B. SELBIE *Psychol. Relig.* vii. 138 This transforming experience..made men Sannyasi or Renouncers, and Bhikshu or beggars. **1962** *Times Lit. Suppl.* 10 Aug. 609/3 The self-complacency which he had previously remarked in Hinayana bhikshus.

Bhil (bi:l). Also **Bheel.** [Hindi *Bhīl*, f. Skr. *Bhilla.*] (A member of) a central Indian people. Also *attrib.*

1823 J. MALCOLM *Mem. Central India* I. xi. 517 The Bheels are quite a distinct race from any other Indian tribe. *Ibid.* xii. 551 The Bheel chiefs have a power over the lives and property of their own subjects. **1848** J. D. HOOKER *Let.* in L. Huxley *Life* (1918) I. xii. 246 The monkey, man, Bhil, and all the other common tropical animals. **1891** KIPLING *From Sea to Sea* (1899) I. vii. 54 The little Bhil is an aborigine. **1937** L. BROMFIELD *Rains Came* I. v. 35 The wild Bhils who inhabited the rocky hills. **1964** R. PERRY *World of Tiger* xii. 177 The Gonds and Bhils and other aboriginal hunting tribes. *Ibid.* xiv. 210 The elephant was mounted, and with a Bheel walking by his side to track, proceeded into cover.

‖**Bhoodan** (bu:'dɑ:n). Also **bhoo-dan, bhoodan.** [Hindi, f. *bhū* earth, land + *dān* gift.] A movement in India initiated by Vinoba Bhave in 1951 for landowners to make free gifts of land to the poor.

1953 *Times* 15 Apr. 7/3 The *bhoodan* (land-gift) movement..is attempting to help the thirty million to forty million landless cultivators of India. **1958** *Times of India* 3 June 6 Many of them had not even heard of bhoo-dan or gram-dan before Vinoba and his men came along and asked them to give a part of their land as a gift or pool their land in the interest of the whole village. **1960** KOESTLER *Lotus & Robot* I. i. 19 His..solemn pledge to devote the rest of his life to the service of the Bhoodan movement.

‖**bhoosa** ('bu:sə). *India.* Also **bhoos, bhusa.** [Hindi *bhus, bhusā.*] Husks and broken straw, used as food for cattle. Also *attrib.*

1829 TOD *Annals* I. 700 *Bhoos* stacks are erected to provide provender for the cattle in scanty rainy seasons. **1888** KIPLING *Plain Tales* 148 A pinch of *bhusa* or cattle-food. **1901** —— *Kim* iii. 80 Grain and cotton and timber, bhoosa, lime and hides. **1920** *Blackw. Mag.* Oct. 449/2 Having to wait weary hours sitting on a bhoosa bale. **1954** J. MASTERS *Bhowani Junction* xxvi. 222 The explosives that had been found..under bhoosa stacked in cattle sheds.

bhoot, var. BHUT.

B-horizon, see HORIZON *sb.*

Bhotanese, var. BHUTANESE *sb.* and *a.*

Bhotia ('bəʊtɪə), *sb.* (and *a.*). Also **Bhooteah, Bhooteea, Bhotea, Bhotiya, Bhutia.** [ad. Skr. *Bhoṭiya* Tibetan, f. *Bhoṭa* Tibet.] A native or inhabitant of Bhutan (see BHUTANESE *sb.* and *a.*) or southern Tibet; the language(s) of this region; also, (one of) a breed of pony native to the Himalayas. Also *attrib.* or quasi-*adj.* Hence '**Bhotian** *a.*

[**1826** F. C. G. SCHRŒTER *Dict. Bhotanta Lang.* (*heading*) A Grammar of the Bhotan Language. *Ibid.*, A Dictionary of the Bhota Language.] *a* **1826** R. HEBER *Narr. Journey Upper Provinces of India* (1828) I. xviii. 493 The Bhooteahs, a Mongolian tribe, worshippers of the Delai Lama. **1835** R. B. PEMBERTON *Rep. Eastern Frontier Brit. India* ii. 81 The Bhooteeas imported woollen cloths, gold-dust, salt, musk, horses, the celebrated Thibet chowries, and Chinese silk... In 1833, two Bhooteea merchants only came down from the hills..of Thibet and Bhootan. **1848** J. D. HOOKER *Let.* 10 June in L. Huxley *Life* (1918) I. xiii. 253 The people (Bhoteas) are a disagreeable and morose race. *Ibid.* 25 Apr. xiv. 287 My lower extremities cased in Bhotea boots. **1875** *Encycl. Brit.* III. 631/2 Physically the Bhutiás are a fine race, although dirty in their habits and persons. *Ibid.* 632/2 Several raids in British territory headed by Bhutiá officials. **1884** *Ibid.* XVII. 341 The Bhotiyas..are..Buddhists. **1899** L. J. TROTTER *Hist. India* VII. ii. 383 The Bhotia highlanders had made frequent inroads into British ground. **1937** H. W. TILMAN *Ascent of Nanda Devi* i. 7 The Bhotia..has little respect for things sacred. **1939** R. GODDEN *Black Narcissus* i. 8 They rode on Bhotiya ponies that were small and thick-set like barbs. *Ibid.* 11 They were only ponies like the Bhotiyas. **1948** D. DIRINGER *Alphabet* II. vi. 352 The Indian term Bhotia has been accepted..to designate the group of languages, of which Tibetan is a member; other Bhotian dialects are spoken in Bhutan, [etc.]. **1963** *Times* 13 June 13/6 The Bhutias, people from Tibet and Bhutan who have been Sikkimese for centuries.

b'hoy. *colloq.* (orig. *U.S.*). Also **bhoy, bo-hoy.** [Supposed Irish pronunc. of BOY *sb.*[1]] = BOY *sb.*[1] 6 b; a gay or spirited fellow.

1846 *Knickerbocker* XXVII. 467 A smile on his lip peculiar to 'one of the bo-hoys'. *Ibid.* XXVIII. 557 A friend of ours..was much struck..by '*The B'hoys*', returning from their Sunday drives. **1850** C. A. BRISTED *Upper Ten Thousand* (1852) 29 Of not-to-be-mistaken Bowery cut—veritable 'bhoys'. **1866** *Atlantic Monthly* Dec. 727 'I want', said the stranger, 'to see a b'hoy,—a real b'hoy.' **1929** R. ALDINGTON *Death of Hero* I. i. 39 George Augustus..thought himself rather a hell of a bhoy because he occasionally sneaked off to a play or a whore.

‖**bhut** (bu:t). Also **bhoot, bhuta.** [Hindi *bhūt*, f. Skr. *bhūtá* lit. 'become, been, existing'.] In India, a spirit; a demon or goblin.

1785 C. WILKINS tr. *Bhăgvăt-Gēētā* ix, The servants of the *Bhōōts*, or spirits, go unto the *Bhōōts*; and they who worship me go unto me. **1838** H. H. WILSON in *Jrnl. R. Asiatic Soc.* V. 290 These superterrene realms, the Lokas or spheres, inhabited by various orders of beings, as the Bhútas. **1883** D. C. J. IBBETSON *Rep. Rev. Settlt. Karnal* ix. 154 People who have died violent deaths..are specially likely to become *bhúts.* **1909** *Westm. Gaz.* 11 Aug. 8/3 These 'bhutas' are the devils or goblins of our mediæval fairy tales. **1939** R. GODDEN *Black Narcissus* xvi. 147 'Probably He's a dragon, a bhût in the shape of a child...' They were all afraid of bhûts, Hindus and Buddhists alike.

Bhutanese (bu:tə'ni:z), *sb.* and *a.* Also **Bhotanese.** Pl. **-ese.** [f. *Bhutan* (see below) + -ESE.] **A.** *sb.* A native or inhabitant of Bhutan, a country in the south-east of the Himalayas; the language of Bhutan. **B.** *adj.* Of or pertaining to Bhutan, its inhabitants or its language.

1813 C. STEWART *Hist. Bengal* 47 Kurmputtun..was inhabited by Brahmans and Bootaneers. **1848** J. D. HOOKER *Let.* 10 June in L. Huxley *Life* (1918) I. xiii. 254 Trisected ..by the Goorkhas, Bhotanese and Thibetans. **1854** —— *Himalayan Jrnls.* I. v. 136 The Bhotanese, natives of Bhotan, or of the Dhurma country, are called Dhurma people. **1880** J. T. WHEELER *Short Hist. India* III. xxvi. 674 In reality the Bhutanese authorities did not want to receive a mission at all. **1960** 'S. HARVESTER' *Chinese Hammer* xxv. 203 They were married according to a mixture of Tibetan and Bhutanese custom.

Bhutia, var. BHOTIA.

bi (baɪ), *a.* and *sb.* Colloq. abbrev. of BISEXUAL *a.* 2 and *sb.* Also in *Comb.*, *esp.* as *bi-guy.* orig. *U.S.*

1966 M. DUFFY *Microcosm* 194 My luck she should turn out to be bi. Don't expect it in a butch. **1967** WENTWORTH & FLEXNER *Dict. Amer. Slang* Suppl., Bi n., adj., bisexual. **1970** A. REID *Confessions of Hitch-Hiker* xxi. 207 Raphael was bi. Or perhaps it was us who had lured him over to the other side of the fence. **1972** *Screw* 12 June 32/4 (Advt.), Attractive, broad-minded, uninhibited, bi-minded couple.

1973 *Nation Rev.* (Melbourne) 31 Aug. 1466/2 (Advt.), Camp or bi-guy wanted to share large flat with two likewise. **1977** *Gay News* 24 Mar. 34/1 (Advt.), Good looking bi-guy, 30s.. wants friendship with similar couple. **1983** *Listener* 14 Apr. 2/3 Some were gay, many apparently bi, and a few were so hard that they would be given a wide berth in a Gorbals pub.

bi, ME. variant of BY, a town.

bi, freq. ME. spelling of BY *prep.*, *adv.* (*a.*, *sb.*[1]): the same as next.

bi- *pref.*[1], the early OE., and the ordinary ME., form of the prefix BE-; under which spelling see most of the words. Those alone are left under BI-, which did not survive long enough to be spelt with *be-*.

bi- *pref.*[2], a. L. *bi-* (earlier *dui-*, cogn. with Gr. δι-, Skr. *dvi-*) 'twice, doubly, having two, two-,' which is in Latin a prefix of adjs., occas. of sbs., rarely of vbs. (e.g. *bipertīre*). The earliest Latin adjs. of this type are formed by simply prefixing *bi-* either to adj.- (and verb-) stems, as *bifer*, *bifidus*, *bijugus*, *bisonus*, or to sb.- (and adj.-) stems, as *bicolor*, *biceps*, *bifrons*, *bifurcus*, *bigener*; later in all probability, and more evidently mere compounds, are those in which *bi-* is prefixed to an adj. with a thematic suffix, as *bicorniger*, *bicubitālis*, *bilongus*, *bipatens*, and these are occas. participial in form, as *bicamerātus*, *biformātus*. The Latin sbs., ending usually in *-ium*, are formed on the prec. adjs., or possible ones of corresponding type, as *biennium* a space of two years, *biennis* lasting two years, *biclīnium*, **biclīnus*.

The prefix entered Eng. in composition, e.g. in *bigam* (= med.L. *bigamus*), found *c* 1300, *bicorne*, *c* 1420; *bifront*, *biforked* occur late in 16th c.; and from the 17th c. onward, by a wide extension of the Latin analogy, especially in its later phases, *bi-* has been prefixed to any adj. conveniently indicating the thing or quality which is to be described as doubled or occurring twice, principally to those of Latin etymology, as in *biangular*, *bicavitary*, *bicentral*, *bivaulted*, *bivoluminous*, but also to others as *birainy*, *biweekly*. In modern scientific terminology, adjs. in *-ate*, *-ated* are most frequently employed, as *biauriculate*, *bicarinate*, *bilamellate*, *bipinnate*, *biunguiculate*, *bimaculated*; and the attrib. use of sbs. as adjs. tends to such modern forms as *bichord*, *biwhirl*. (See also the form BIN-.)

Bi- is therefore used in Eng. to form:—

I. Adjectives, with the sense:—

1. Having or furnished with two —, two-—, as **bi-angular, -ate, -ated, -ous,** having two angles; **bibracteate,** having two bracts; **bibracteolate,** having two small bracts; **bicallose, -ous,** having two callosities; †**bicapited, bicapitate,** having two heads, two-headed; **bicapsular**; **bicavitary,** having two cavities; **bicentral**; **bichord,** having two strings; **biciliate,** having two cilia or hairs; **bicoloured, bicolumnar, biconsonantal**; **bicorporal, -ate, -ated, -eal,** having two bodies; **bicristate,** having two crests; **bifanged**; **biglandular,** having two glands; **bimarginate, bimembral, bimuscular**; **binodal,** having two nodes; **binuclear,** having two nuclei; **bi-ovulate, bipetalous**; **biporose,** having or opening by two pores; **bipupillate,** having two pupil-like markings; **biradiate,** having two rays; **birainy,** having two rains or rainy seasons; **bispinous, bistipuled**; **bitentaculate,** having two tentacles; **bituberculate, -ated,** having two tubercles; **bivascular,** having two vessels; **bivaulted**; **bivoluminous,** consisting of two volumes; **biwhirl.**

1870 HOOKER *Stud. Flora* 259 Peduncles *bi-bracteate at the forks. *Ibid.* 345 Scale peltate, *bi-bracteolate. **1572** BOSSEWELL *Armorie* II. 42 [Lions] are borne in armes ..*Bicapited, Bicorporated, Tricorporated. **1679** PLOT *Staffordsh.* (1686) 196 The *bicapsular seed vessel of *Digitalis ferruginea.* **1870** ROLLESTON *Anim. Life* Introd. 101 Nerve-centres.. spoken of as '*bicavitary.' **1854** MAXWELL in *Life* viii. 231 Full of ellipses—*bicentral sources of lasting joy. **1857** BERKELEY *Cryptog. Bot.* §136 *Biciliate spores. **1862** R. PATTERSON *Ess. Hist. & Art* 34 A *bi-coloured uniform. **1884** M. RULE *Eadmeri Hist. Nov.* Pref. 84 The pages are *bicolumnar. **1861** MAX MÜLLER *Sc. Lang.* vii. 251 A *bi-consonantal root. **1839** BAILEY *Festus* viii. (1848) 94 Luxurious, violent, *bicorporate. **1686** GOAD *Celest. Bodies* II. iv. 201 Airy Signs, or Signs *Bicorporeal. **1882** R. BROWN *Law Kosmic Ord.* 57 A gigantic *bicorporeal Scorpion-couple. **1852** DANA *Crust.* I. 212 Fourth [joint] prominently *bicristate, the crests thin. **1851** RICHARDSON *Geol.* viii. 315 Small *bifanged molar teeth. **1876** HARLEY *Mat. Med.* 441 Terminal panicles.. supported by *biglandular bracts. **1812** J. JEBB *Corr.* (1834) II. 77 In these stanzas, each line is obviously *bimembral. **1835** KIRBY *Hab. & Inst. Anim.* I. viii. 237 The first [order] is *Bimuscular, having two attaching muscles. **1835** LINDLEY *Introd. Bot.* (1848) I. 324 The cyme.. may be *binodal, trinodal. **1880** *Times* 24 Nov. 10 A small *bi-nuclear, gaseous, planetary nebula. **1881** *Gard. Chron.* No. 411. 621 Spores.. cylindrical, *binucleate. **1858** W. CLARK *Van der Hoeven's Zool.* II. 145 Ventral fins *biradiate. **1855** MAURY *Phys. Geog. Sea* v. §296 Bogota is within the *birainy latitudes. **1852** DANA *Crust.* I. 621 The preceding segment is *bispinous. **1877** HUXLEY *Anat. Inv. An.* iii. 131 A ciliated *bitentaculate body. **1849** *Proc. Berw. Nat. Club* II. vii. 371 A minutely *bituberculated wart. **1809** J. BARLOW *Columb.* IX. 15 In this *bivaulted sphere. **1870** LOWELL in *Athenæum* 19 Mar. 380 That *bivoluminous shape in which dullness overtakes.. genius at last. **1882** in *Nature* XXVI. 546 The formation of whirl and *biwhirl systems.

2. Doubly ——; —— in two ways or directions, on both sides; as **bi-bisalternate** (see quot.); **bicleft**; **biconic,** conical in two directions; **biconcave, biconstant, biconvex**; **bicrescentic,** crescent-shaped on both sides; **bicurvate, bifusiform, bipyramidal, birectangular, birefracting, -ive, birefringent, birhomboidal, bi-sphero-concave**; **bisubstituted.**

1817 R. JAMESON *Char. Min.* 210 When there are two rows of bisalternate planes on each side, as in the *bibisalternate cinnabar. **1627** DRAYTON *Agincourt, etc.* 216 Those sacred springs, which from the *by-clift hill Dropt their pure Nectar. **1854** WOODWARD *Mollusca* (1856) 285 Shell inversely conical, *bi-conic, or cylindrical. **1833** LYELL *Elem. Geol.* xvii. (1874) 291 This Bird approaches the reptilian type in possessing *biconcave vertebræ. **1836** TODD *Cycl. Anat. & Phys.* I. 409/1 A *biconcave disc. **1880** *Nature* XXI. 289 A *bi-constant dispersion formula. **1849–52** TODD *Cycl. Anat. & Phys.* IV. 1438/2 When the rays pass out from a *bi-convex lens. **1854** J. HOGG *Microsc.* II. ii. (1867) 400 Spicula having both extremities bent alike —*bicurvate. **1831** BREWSTER *Optics* xxix. 243 The *bipyramidal dodecahedron. **1869** TYNDALL *Notes Light* 75 A *birefracting prism of Iceland spar. *Ibid.* 66 This crystal is *birefractive. **1880** *Nature* XXI. 204 A *birefringent crystal. **1817** R. JAMESON *Char. Min.* 202 A crystal is said to be *bi-rhomboidal, when its surface consists of.. two different rhomboids. **1849–52** TODD *Cycl. Anat. & Phys.* IV. 1469/1 *Bi-sphero-concave lenses. **1880** CLEMENSHAW *Wurtz' Atom. Th.* 303 In a *bisubstituted derivate of marsh gas, the third substitution may take place on either side.

3. *Bot.* and *Zool.* Twice over, re- ——; *i.e.* having characteristically divided parts which are themselves similarly divided; as BILACINIATE, BIPINNATE, BISERRATE, BITERNATE, q.v.

4. Lasting or continuing for two ——; occurring or appearing every two ——; as BIENNIAL, **bi-hourly, bi-monthly, bi-weekly.**

1843 in *Proc. Amer. Philos. Soc.* II. 247 *Bi-hourly observations.. had ceased with the first of the present year. **1879** GLADSTONE in *Daily News* 1 Dec. 6/5 Annual as opposed to *bi-monthly or tri-monthly budgets.

b. Occurring or appearing twice in a ——; as in **bi-diurnal, bi-monthly, bi-quarterly, bi-weekly, bi-winter, bi-yearly.** (The ambiguous usage is confusing, and might be avoided by the use of *semi-*; e.g. *semi-monthly*, *semi-weekly*; cf. *half-yearly*.)

1854 WOODWARD *Mollusca* (1856) 32 A *bi-diurnal visit from the tide. **1878** *Print. Trades Jrnl.* xxv. 4 A new Spanish *bi-monthly journal. **1884** *Pall Mall G.* 15 Feb. 16 To issue these etchings in *bi-quarterly numbers. **1885** FARRAR *Camb. Bible Sch.* Luke xviii. 12 The *bi-weekly fast of the Pharisees.. The days chosen were Thursday and Monday. **1884** *Harper's Mag.* Feb. 394/1 The mail-carriers are making one of their *bi-winter trips. **1879** *Print. Trades Jrnl.* XXVIII. 9 A *bi-yearly calendar.

c. The prec. adjs. in *-ly* are also used adverbially.

1864 *Even. Standard* 29 Oct., Sixpenny parts, to be issued bi-monthly. **1865** *Reader* 12 Aug. 188/3 To be held bi-weekly, on Mondays and Thursdays.

d. The adjs. are also used substantively: **bi-weekly,** a newspaper, magazine, etc., published once every two weeks.

1890 in WEBSTER. **1978** *Daily Tel.* 2 Dec. 1/7 The remainder are weeklies, bi-weeklies and three provincial Sunday newspapers.

5. Joining or connecting two ——; as BI-ACROMIAL, BI-ISCHIATIC, BI-PARIETAL, q.v.

6. Occasionally in other senses, as **bimanual,** employing two hands; BISERIATE, arranged in two series; **bitaurine,** belonging to two bulls.

1872 F. THOMAS *Dis. Women* 73 The practice of *bimanual palpation. **1882** VINES *Sachs' Bot.* 430 The *biseriate segmentation of the apical cell. **1864** E. SWIFTE in *N. & Q.* V. 142 The *bitaurine bellow.

II. Adverbs, verbs, and substantives; chiefly **a.** derivatives from the adjectives in I, as **bicleavage** (cf. *bicleft* in 2), **bicoloration** (cf. L. *bicolor* and *bicoloured* in 1), BIVOCALIZE *v.*; but also **b.** substantives formed after Latin analogies, in which *bi-* has the force of 'double, two'; as **bimillionaire,** the owner of property valued at two millions of money; **binomenclature,** double naming; **biprong,** a two-pronged fork.

a. 1847–9 TODD *Cycl. Anat. & Phys.* IV. 676/2 A *bicleavage of the azygos ventral rays. **1877** COUES *Fur Anim.* iv. 120 [The] animal.. resumes its *bicoloration.

b. 1838 *New Month. Mag.* LIV. 314 The millionaire.. becomes a *bi-millionaire. **1873** TRISTRAM *Moab* vii. 120 Another instance of *binomenclature, a duplicate name occurring on the east side. **1872** M. COLLINS *Pr. Clarice* I. xii. 114 The ancient *biprong of steel.

III. *Chem.* Substantives and adjectives, in which *bi-* signifies the presence in a compound of twice that amount (usually two equivalents) of the acid, base, etc. indicated as present by the word to which it is prefixed. Thus *carbonate of soda* was viewed as containing one equivalent of carbonic acid, *bicarbonate of soda* as containing two. In recent chemical nomenclature, *bi-* has been systematically superseded by *di-*.

1863 WATTS *Dict. Chem.* I. 584 **Bi-compounds*: see *Di-compounds*. **1819** BRANDE *Chem.* v. §306 *Bicarbonate of Potassa is formed by passing a current of carbonic acid into a solution of the subcarbonate. **1869** ROSCOE *Elem. Chem.* 210 The *bicarbonate [of soda] is chiefly used.. for the production of refreshing drinks. **1826** HENRY *Elem. Chem.* II. 45 The second sulphuret, or *bi-sulphuret of tin. **1850** DAUBENY *Atom. Th.* x. (ed. 2) 342 *Bisulphuretted hydrogen is.. decomposed by the action of alkalies. **1863** TYNDALL *Heat* i. 14, I wet a pellet of cotton-wool with liquid *bi-sulphide of carbon. **1879** G. GLADSTONE in *Cassell's Techn. Educ.* IV. 213/1 Tartar emetic—the *bitartrate of antimony and potash.

biace, obs. form of BIAS.

biacid (baɪˈæsɪd), *a.* [f. BI- *pref.*[2] III + ACID.] Of a base: Capable of combining with an acid in two different proportions.

1864 in WEBSTER.

biacromial (baɪəˈkrəʊmɪəl), *a. Phys.* [f. BI- *pref.*[2] 5 + ACROMIAL.] Joining the extremities of the two shoulder-blades.

1878 BARTLEY *Topinard's Anthrop.* 83 The biacromial line.

biacuminate (baɪəˈkjuːmɪnət), *a.* [f. BI- *pref.*[2] 1, 2 + ACUMINATE.] (See quot.)

1880 GRAY *Bot. Text-bk.* 398 *Biacuminate*, two-pointed, as malpighiaceous hairs, fixed by the middle and tapering to each end.

Biafran (biːˈæfrən, baɪ-), *a.* and *sb.* [f. *Biafra* + -AN.] **A.** *adj.* Of or pertaining to Biafra, a region in West Africa that seceded from federal Nigeria in 1967 and was reunited with it in 1970. **B.** *sb.* A native or inhabitant of Biafra.

1967 *Guardian* 19 June 1/4 The Biafrans naively thought them dead, ambled up, and were themselves killed. **1967** *Times* 27 July 4/2 Enugu radio claimed today that the Biafran air force.. had killed about 1,000 federal troops. **1969** *Listener* 8 May 634/2 They have British armoured cars which are almost invulnerable to Biafran weapons. They have so many big guns and mortars that they can lay continuous barrages on the Biafrans.

biaften, biæften, early form of BAFT *adv.*

bi-alate (baɪˈeɪlət), *a.* [f. BI- *pref.*[2] 1 + ALATE.] Having two wings or wing-like membranous expansions.

1852 DANA *Crust.* II. 1360 Posterior segment bi-alate.

†**bially,** *a. Obs. Her.* [Suggests an OF. **biallé* (f. *bi-* two), not known.] (See quots.)

1486 *Bk. St. Albans, Her.* B v b, Byally. **1586** FERNE *Blaz. Gentrie* 212 Bially, that is a barre betweene two Cheuerons.

‖**bianco sopra bianco** (ˈbjanko ˈsopra ˈbjanko). Also **sopra bianco.** [It., lit. 'white upon white'.] A form of white decoration on white porcelain (see quots.). Also *attrib.*

1856 OWEN JONES *Grammar of Ornament* xvii, *Sopra-bianco* was a painting in white upon a white-lead ground, with green or blue borders round the margin of the plate. **1870** W. CHAFFERS *Marks & Monogr. Pott.* (ed. 3) 55 *Sopra bianco*, white upon white, palmette ornaments of opaque white enamel upon milky white ground. **1877** A. BECKWITH *Majolica & Fayence* 51 The work is notable for exquisite finish.. *Bianco sopra Bianco* ornament was much used. **1896** C. D. E. FORTNUM *Maiolica* 273 A large plate.. painted in blue relieved with white on a white ground; on the upright sides a diaper pattern in *bianco sopra bianco*. **1932** W. CHAFFERS *Marks & Monogr. Pott.* (ed. 14) 873 A peculiarity to be noticed in the Bristol ware is a charming effect produced by painting part of the design in white opaque enamel on the white ground of greenish tint. This process has been called *bianco sopra bianco*.

biangulate, -ated, -ous, etc.: see BI- *pref.*[2] 1.

biannual (baɪˈænjuːəl), *a.* and *sb.* [f. BI- *pref.*[2] 4, 4 b + ANNUAL.] **A.** *adj.* Used as = Half-yearly. **B.** *sb.* = BIENNIAL *sb.* Hence **biˈannually** *adv.*

1877 OUIDA *Puck* xii. 123 Every half-year his lawyers transmitted him.. the biannual rental. **1884** *Illustr. Sydney News* 26 Aug. 15/1 Plant out.. annuals and bi-annuals. **1882** *Century Mag.* XXIII. 647 A change in the fashion of her clothes bi-annually at least.

biarchy (ˈbaɪɑːkɪ). [f. BI- *pref.*[2] II + *-archy* = Gr. -αρχια; cf. *monarchy*.] Dual sovereignty, government by two.

1847 in CRAIG. **1862** M. HOPKINS *Hawaii* 141 To terminate the biarchy, and leave Kaméhaméha sole ruler of Hawaii.

biarticulate (baɪɑːˈtɪkjʊlət), *a.* [f. BI- *pref.*[2] 1 + ARTICULATE.] Having two joints, two-jointed.

1816 KIRBY & SP. *Entomol.* (1843) II. 268 Their biarticulate tarsi. **1852** DANA *Crust.* II. 909 *note*.

bias ('baɪəs), *a.*, *sb.*, and *adv.* Forms: 6–7 biace, (? 6 byess), 6–8 **byas**, (7 biais, biase, biaz), 7–8 biass, byass, 6– bias. Pl. biases; also 6 bias, 6–9 biasses, 7 byasses. [a. F. *biais*, in 14th c. 'oblique, obliquity', = Pr. *biais* (cf. OCat. *biais*, mod. *biaise*, *biase*; also Sardinian *biasciu*, It. *s-biescio* awry, in Piem. *sbias*); of unknown origin. The conjecture of Diez that it is:—L. *bifax*, *bifacem*, explained by Isidore as *duos habens obtutus* 'looking two ways,' is rejected by later Romanic scholars as phonetically untenable. Originally an adjective, as in Pr. *via biayssa* cross or oblique road; but early used as a sb. in French, so that the first quotable example in Eng. is of the subst. use. The latter became a technical term at the game of bowls, whence come all the later uses of the word. With pl. *biases*, cf. *atlases*, *crocuses*.]

A. *adj.* (Sense 1 is original; 1 b and 2 appear to be derived from senses of the sb.)

†**1. a.** Slanting, oblique. ***bias line***: (in early geometry) a diagonal or hypotenuse. [Cf. OF. (Oresme, 14th c.) une figure quarrée et le dyametre qui la traverse biais.] *Obs.* Cf. BIAS-WISE, -WAYS.

1551 RECORDE *Pathw. Knowl.* II. xxxii, By the Bias line, I meane that lyne, whiche in any square figure dooth runne from corner to corner. **1601** HOLLAND *Pliny* 953 (R.) Her oblique and byass declination. **1688** R. HOLME *Acad. Arm.* II. 351 Some shells are crooked and byas.

b. *spec.* in dress (cf. B 1): Cut across the texture, slanting.

1815 *La Belle Assemblée* in Jane Austen *Persuasion* (Chapman, 1933) 274 This pelisse is trimmed..with byas white satin laid on in folds. **1883** *Daily News* 22 Sept. 3/3 A wide bias band of wall-flower velvet. **1884** *Girl's Own Paper* Aug. 681/1 Plain skirts, trimmed with flat bias bands.

2. 'Swelled as the bowl on the biased side' J.

1606 SHAKS. *Tr. & Cr.* IV. v. 8 Thy sphered Bias cheeke.

B. *sb.*

1. An oblique or slanting line; cf. A 1. Now app. only in the spec. sense of a wedge-shaped piece or gore, cut obliquely to the texture of a woven fabric. ***on the bias***: diagonally, across the texture.

1530 PALSGR. 198/1 Byas of an hose, *bias*. **1538** BALE *Thre Lawes* 513 Take me a napkyn folte, With the byas of a bolte. *c* **1570** LD. SEMPLE *Three Taverners* ix, Now gif ye..shape it precyslie, The ellwand wald be grit & lang, Gif the byess be wyde, gar lay it on side. **1880** *Melbourne Bulletin* 29 Oct. 5/1 The clothing..may not be cut on the bias. **1884** *West. Daily Press* 2 June 7/2 All skirts are..cut with a curved bias.

2. a. A term at bowls, applied alike to: The construction or form of the bowl imparting an oblique motion, the oblique line in which it runs, and the kind of impetus given to cause it to run obliquely. Thus a bowl is said 'to have a wide or narrow bias,' 'to run with a great' or 'little bias'; the player 'gives it more' or 'less bias' in throwing it.

It is difficult to decide in which sense exactly *bias* was here first used. A priori we think of the oblique line of motion: this is favoured also by the quotations under C. and BIAS-WISE; yet early quotations here point rather to the oblique one-sided structure or shape of the bowl. Formerly bias was given by loading the bowls on one side with lead, and this itself was sometimes called the *bias*; they are now made of very heavy wood, teak or ebony, and the bias given entirely by their shape, which is that of a sphere slightly flattened on one side and protuberant on the other, as if composed of the halves of an oblate and a prolate spheroid.

1570 tr. *Life 70 Abps. Canterb.* B v. *marg.*, As you haue sett youre bias, so runneth your bowle. **1596** SHAKS. *Tam. Shr.* IV. v. 25 Well, forward, forward, thus the bowle should run, And not vnluckily against the Bias. **1643** T. GOODWIN *Wks.* (1861) III. 492 A bowl..is swayed by the bias, and lead that is in it. **1692** BENTLEY *Boyle Serm.* ii. 71 If it [the Bowl] be made with a Byas, that may decline it a little from a straight line. **1692** SOUTH *12 Serm.* (1697) I. 444 A bowl may lie still for all its Byass. **1710** NORRIS *Chr. Prudence* i. 22 The Bowl will run, not as the Hand directs, but as the Bias leads. **1728** POPE *Dunciad* I. 170 O thou, of business the directing soul, To human heads like byass to the bowl. **1753** CHAMBERS *Cycl. Suppl.*, *Bias* of a bowl is a piece of lead put into one side, to load and make it incline towards that side. **1822** HAZLITT *Men & Manners* Ser. II. iv. (1869) 89 The skittle-player bends his body to give a bias to the bowl he has already delivered from his hand. **1851** A. W. HARE *Serm.* viii. I. 133 Just as a bowl with a bias, if you try to send it straight, the longer it rolls, the further it will swerve. **1864** *Athenæum* No. 1920. 209/1 A bias that should reach the jack.

b. Figurative senses taken from the game of bowls.

1589 PUTTENHAM *Eng. Poesie* III. xix. (1811) 205 Her bosome sleake as Paris plaster, Helde vp two balles of alabaster, Eche byas [i.e. nipple] was a little cherrie. **1593** SHAKS. *Rich. II*, III. iv. 5 'Twill make me thinke the World is full of Rubs, And that my fortune runnes against the Byas. **1581** SIDNEY *Apol. Poetrie* (Arb.) 66 To finde a matter quite mistaken, and goe downe the hill agaynst the byas, in the mouth of some such men. **1618** MYNSHUL *Ess. Prison* (1638) 17 To bee a bowle for every alley, and run into every company, proves thy mind to have no bias. **1625** BACON *Ess., Wisd. Man's Self* (Arb.) 185 Which set a Bias vpon the Bowle, of their owne Petty Ends. **1714** C. JOHNSON *Country Lasses* II. ii, Joy shall be the jack, pleasure the bias, and we'll rowl after happiness to the last moment of life.

c. *Cricket.* The turning of a ball in its course from the leg side towards the off after pitching. Also *attrib.*

1833 J. MITFORD in *Gent. Mag.* Sept. 238 The plan adopted by good batters against slow bias bowling was successful. *Ibid.* 239/1 His balls..have a very perplexing bias. **1921** LD. HARRIS *Few Short Runs* v. 135 The bowler was not slow to take advantage of the opening by developing anew the old 'bias' or break from leg.

3. *transf.* **a.** An inclination, leaning, tendency, bent; a preponderating disposition or propensity; predisposition *towards*; predilection; prejudice.

1572 tr. *Buchanan's Detect. Mary* in *Love-lett.* (1824) 125 She cometh to her own bias, and openly showeth her own natural conditions. **1577** HOLINSHED *Chron.* I. 166/1 They cease their crueltie for a time, but within a-while after fall to their bloudie bias. **1620** QUARLES *Jonah* (1638) 38 To change the byas of her crooked wayes. **1643** SIR T. BROWNE *Relig. Med.* II. §1 Though..the byas of present practise wheel another way. **1768** BLACKSTONE *Comm.* III. 361 The law will not suppose a possibility of biass or favour in a judge. **1827** HARE *Guesses* (1859) 13 A proof of our natural bias to evil. **1829** SOUTHEY *Inscript.* xlv, My intellectual life received betimes The bias it hath kept. **1830** SIR J. HERSCHEL *Stud. Nat. Phil.* III. i. (1851) 241 If the bricks..had all a certain leaning or bias in one direction out of the perpendicular. **1878** LECKY *England in 18th C.* II. vi. 179 They could have no possible bias in favour of the Irish.

b. *Statistics.* A systematic distortion of an expected statistical result due to a factor not allowed for in its derivation; also, a tendency to produce such distortion.

1900 *Phil. Mag.* L. 167 The results show a bias from the theoretical results, 5 and 6 points occurring more frequently than they should do. **1911** G. U. YULE *Introd. Theory Statistics* xiv. 277 Such an examination may be of service.. as indicating one possible source of bias, viz. great heterogeneity in the original material. **1943** M. G. KENDALL *Adv. Theory Statistics* I. viii. 189 If the observer was unbiased the digits should appear in approximately equal numbers; but there is a bias in favour of all the even numbers and against the odd numbers 1, 3 and 9.

†**4.** Set course in any direction, ordinary 'way.' ***from*** or ***out of the bias***: out of the way. ***to put out of*** or ***off one's bias***: to put out, disconcert, confuse, put into disorder. *Obs.*

1588 *Marprel. Epist.* (1843) 51 Marke what wil be the issue..if you still keep your olde byas. **1600** DEKKER *Gentle Craft* Wks. 1873 I. 30 Well Master all this is from the bias, doe you remember the Shippe. *c* **1619** R. JONES *Serm.* in *Phenix* (1708) II. 478 Such strange opinions as would turn the whole world out of bias. **1642** HOWELL *For. Trav.* 142 Here it will not be much out of the byas, to insert a few verses. **1741** RICHARDSON *Pamela* (1824) I. 272 There is no putting him out of his bias. He is a regular piece of clock-work. **1752** HUME *Pol. Disc.* ii. 30 Superstition, which throws the Government off its bias. **1799** WOLCOTT (P. Pindar) *Nil Adm.* Wks. 1812 IV. 266 And turn even Bishops off from Wisdom's bias.

5. a. A swaying influence, impulse, or weight; 'any thing which turns a man to a particular course, or gives the direction to his measures' (J.)

1587 TURBERVILLE *Trag. T.* (1837) 206 That to the end he might the maid Unto his bias bring. **1595** SHAKS. *John* II. 577 This vile drawing byas, This sway of motion, this commoditie. **1642** FULLER *Holy & Prof. State* IV. iv. 254 In his prime he [Wolsey] was the bias of the Christian world, drawing the bowl thereof to what side he pleased. *a* **1659** CLEVELAND *Wks.* (1687) 82 In what a puzzling Neutrality is the poor Soul, that moves between two such ponderous Biasses! **1660** W. SECKER *Nonsuch Prof.* 430 The love of God is the byas of a Volunteer. **1705** STANHOPE *Paraphr.* II. 196 The Bribery and Byass of Sense and Flesh. **1851** GLADSTONE *Gleanings* IV. xxxix. 28 He could not possibly be under any bias.

†**b.** Centre of gravity (as that which determines the direction of motion in a falling body). *rare.*

1674 PETTY *Disc. bef. R. Soc.* 126 I suppose in every atom ..two poles in its superficies, and a Central point within its substance, which I call its Byas.

6. *Telegr.* (See quot. 1940.)

1885 W. WILLIAMS *Man. Telegr.* c. 47 The force of restitution is no longer effected simply by the bias of the tongue but by an opposite current drawing it back. **1902** *Encycl. Brit.* XXXIII. 221/2 With the tongue set neutral, having no bias either to the spacing or marking side—the relay will give good signals with $1\frac{1}{2}$ milliamperes of current. **1940** *Chambers's Techn. Dict.* 89/1 *Bias*, the adjustment of a telegraph relay so that it operates for currents greater than a given current (against which it is biased), or for a current of one polarity.

7. *Electr.* A steady voltage or current applied to an electronic device (see quot. 1960); also *attrib.*

1922 *Electrical Review* 30 June 928/1 Security from undesired operation is obtained by the introduction of a controlling bias, and distinction is made between earth faults..and phase faults. **1926** [see GRID 5 b]. **1932** F. E. TERMAN *Radio Engin.* xi. 392 The regeneration increases as the total amplification A_1A_2 and the bias impedance *Zc* are increased. **1940** *Chambers's Techn. Dict.* 89/1 *Bias voltage*, generally, the mean potential of any electrode in a thermionic tube, measured with respect to the cathode. Specially applied to that of the control grid. **1942** *Electronic Engin.* XV. 9 The sensitivity of the receiver is adjusted by varying the bias of the..amplifiers. **1960** H. CARTER *Dict. Electronics* 28 *Bias*, steady direct voltage applied between the cathode and control electrode of a thermionic tube in order to determine its working point. *Ibid.* 119 *Grid bias*, steady negative potential applied to the control grid of a thermionic valve or other tube in order to pre-set the no-signal value of the cathode current.

C. *adv.* [Cf. *on the bias*, F. *en biais*, *de biais*.]

1. Obliquely, aslope, athwart. *Obs.* exc. of dress.

1575 LANEHAM *Lett.* (1871) 25 Wold run hiz race byas among the thickest of the throng. **1598** SYLVESTER *Du Bartas* I. iv. (1641) 33/1 That rich Girdle..Which God gave Nature..To weare it biaz, buckled over-thwart-her. **1601** HOLLAND *Pliny* XXVII. iv. (R.) The leaves be..chamfered or chanelled biais all along. **1616** SURFL. & MARKH. *Countr. Farm* 349 It should be..cut byas, as wedges are. **1656** FINETT *For. Ambass.* 32 Placed..on the King's right hand, not right out but byas forward. **1878** NAPHEYS *Phys. Life Women*, A body-case of strong linen, cut bias.

†**2.** *fig.* Off the straight, awry, wrong, amiss. ***to run bias on, to***: to fall foul of, attack. *Obs.*

1600 ROWLANDS *Let. Humours Blood* i. 47 His tongue runs byas on affaires. **1606** SHAKS. *Tr. & Cr.* I. iii. 15 Euery action that hath gone before..Triall did draw Bias and thwart, not answering the ayme. **1618** BOLTON *Florus* (1636) 264 Metellus..who always ranne bias to the mighty, detracted Pompey. **1633** G. HERBERT *Constancie* vii. in *Temple* 64 When the wide world runnes bias.

D. *Comb.* **bias binding**, a narrow strip of cloth cut on the bias and used for binding (cf. sense A 1 b); **bias-cut** *a.*, cut on the bias; **bias-drawing** *vbl. sb.*, a turning awry or from the truth; **bias-eyed** *a.*, oblique-eyed. Also BIASWISE, q.v.

1606 SHAKS. *Tr. & Cr.* IV. v. 169 Faith and troth, Strain'd purely from all hollow bias drawing. **1883** *Glasgow Wkly. Her.* 12 May 2/7 The bias-eyed son of the sun [Chinaman] manipulated the gummy mass. **1927** *New Butterick Dressmaker* xix. 174 Bias bindings make attractive finishes either in the same or in a contrasting material or color. **1931** *Times Lit. Suppl.* 29 Oct. 844/3 The teacher..may perhaps think that in these days of 'bias bindings' it is not worth while to put children to the pains of making curved hems. **1960** *Woman's Realm* 2 Apr. 36/4 Bind napkin all round with red bias binding. **1960** *Lebende Sprachen* V. 35/1 Bias-cut. **1969** *Guardian* 30 July 7/4 Bias cut skirts flare out from the hips.

bias ('baɪəs), *v.* Also 7 biace, 7–8 byas, byass, 7–9 biass. [f. prec. sb. Cf. F. *biaiser*, Pr. *biaisar*. In inflexions, often spelt *biasses*, *biassed*, *biassing*; though the single *s* is more regular; cf. the sb.]

1. *trans.* To give bias to (a bowl); to furnish with a weight or bias; cf. BIASED 1.

1662 DRYDEN *Wild Gallant* IV. i, Your Bowl must be well bias'd to come in.

2. *transf.* and *fig.* **a.** To give a bias or one-sided tendency or direction to; to incline to one side; to influence, affect (often unduly or unfairly).

a **1628** F. GREVILLE *Sidney* (1652) 60 To biace Gods immortal truth to the fantasies of mortall Princes. **1646** S. BOLTON *Arraignm. Err.* 239 Beware of being byassed with carnall and corrupt affections. **1683** BURNET tr. *More's Utopia* (1685) 122 Men whom no Advantages can byass. *a* **1711** KEN *Hymnar.* Poet. Wks. 1721 II. 108 By Grace our Wills may byass'd be. **1855** MACAULAY *Hist. Eng.* IV. 89 If his judgment had not been biassed by his passions. **1875** HAMERTON *Intell. Life* II. iii. 66 Artists are seldom good critics of art, because their own practice biasses them, and they are not disinterested.

b. To incline *to* or *towards*; to cause to swerve.

1643 T. GOODWIN *Wks.* (1861) III. 488 We shall..not be biassed aside. **1712** STEELE *Spect.* No. 491 ⁋2 Without any Vice that could biass him from the Execution of Justice. **1801** STRUTT *Sports & Past.* Introd. 4 Such exercises as.. biased the mind to military pursuits. **1862** LYTTON *Str. Story* I. 216 Whether..it was the Latin inscription..that had originally biased Sir Philip Derval's literary taste towards the mystic jargon.

†**c.** To influence or incline (one) *to do* anything.

1722 DE FOE *Moll Fl.* (1840) 255 She soon biassed me to consent. **1747** GOULD *Eng. Ants* 93 Mr. Ray..and other Naturalists, are hence byassed to believe the Curiosity.

†**3.** *intr.* To incline to one side, to swerve from the right line. *Obs.*

1622 HEYLIN *Cosmogr.* II. (1682) 191 Without partiality, or byassing on either hand. **1640** SANDERSON *Serm.* II. 158 The hearts of such as byass too much that way. **1645** *City Alarum* 20 Many great Patriots in the beginning have since byased. **1687** A. LOVELL *Bergerac's Comic Hist.* II. 21 That made me imagine that I byassed towards the Moon.

4. *trans.* To cut bias. *U.S.*

1883 *Century Mag.* XXVI. 960/1 You may baste, you may bias the Gore if you will.

5. *Electr.* To apply bias (BIAS *sb.* 7) to. Hence **'bias(s)ing** *ppl. a.* and *vbl. sb.*

1922 *Electrical Review* 30 June 928/1 The equipment for each end of the line of a 3-phase system comprises three protective transformers, a biasing transformer, an earth fault relay, [etc.]. **1923** MEARE & NEALE *Electr. Engin. Practice* (ed. 4) XV. 511 Illustrating the principle of the biassed transformer. *Ibid.*, The 'restraining' or 'biassing' winding *BB* produces a flux as shown on the dotted line. **1930** *Engineering* 31 Oct. 543/2 The multiplier circuits are heavily biassed. **1944** *Electronic Engin.* XVI. 336 Bias the valve so that the anode current is normally zero or small. **1953** AMOS & BIRKINSHAW *Telev. Engin.* (1957) I. vi. 117 The signal plate is biased approximately 30 volts positive with respect to the cathode. **1962** SIMPSON & RICHARDS *Junction Transistors* ix. 213 (*heading*) Other biasing methods.

biased ('baɪəst), *ppl. a.* Also biassed. [f. prec. + -ED.]

1. Of bowls: Having a bias.

1611 MARKHAM *Countr. Content.* i. (1615) 108 Your round byazed bowles for open grounds. **1877** EG.-WARBURTON *Poems* 15 The bias'd bowl roll'd circling to the jack.

2. a. Influenced; inclined in some direction; unduly or unfairly influenced; prejudiced.

1649 G. DANIEL *Trinarch, Rich. II*, lxxv, How byassed all humane Actions are! **1662** FULLER *Worthies* III. 110 If he were a Biassed and Partiall writer. **1681** DRYDEN *Abs. & Achit.* I. 79 When to Sin our byast Nature leans. **1870** *Pall Mall G.* 18 Aug. 2 Abstention from biassed language.

b. spec. in *Statistics*. Containing a bias or error which will not balance itself out on average.

1911 G. U. YULE *Introd. Theory of Statistics* xiv. 276 Any sample, taken in the way supposed, is likely to be definitely *biassed*, in the sense that it will not tend to include, even in the long run, equal proportions of the A's and α's in the original material. **1931** *Economist* 18 July 127/2 What statisticians describe as 'biassed errors' in company accounting (the term is used without any derogatory sense) are made cumulative.

3. Of fabric: (see quot.). Cf. BIAS *sb.* 1.

1919 W. B. FARADAY *Dict. Aeronaut. Terms* 55 *Biassed fabric*, fabric laid with its threads inclined to the length of the piece of cloth.

biasing ('baɪəsɪŋ), *vbl. sb.* [f. as prec. + -ING[1].]

1. Inclination towards one side; propension.

1646 J. HALL *Horæ Vac.* 7 The best course to keepe his judgement from biasing. **1865** CARLYLE *Fredk. Gt.* V. XIII. vii. 74 The question is intricate, and there are many secret biassings concerned in the solution of it.

2. In needlework: A kind of work resembling 'gathering.'

1838 *Workwoman's Guide* I. i. 7.

3. See BIAS *v.* 5.

'biasing, *ppl. a.* [f. as prec. + -ING[2].] **a.** That gives a bias. †**b.** That moves obliquely, oblique.

1658 USSHER *Ann.* vi. 98 The Loxodromie, or biassing motions of the stars, in the Zodiac. **1861** H. MACMILLAN *Footn. Page Nat.* 242 [These] operate as biassing influences.

c. See BIAS *v.* 5.

†**'biasness.** *Obs. rare.*[—0] Obliquity.

1611 COTGR., *Biaiseure*, slopenesse, byasnesse, obliquenesse, or obliquitie.

'bias-,wise, -way-s, *adv.* In a slanting manner, aslant, obliquely; also *fig.*

1540 RAYNALD *Birth Man* I. iii. (1634) 22 Two Byasswise descending muscles. **1551** RECORDE *Cast. Knowl.* (1556) 111 A little altering of the one side, maketh the boul to run biasse waies. *c* **1618** J. SMYTH *Berkeleys* (1883) 149 A man that from the font to the grave..walked alwayes byaswise. **1660** HEXHAM *Dutch Dict., Schuyn*, crosse, Oblique, or Byas wise. **1702** W. J. tr. *Bruyn's Voy. Levant* xxxvii. 148 The roof.. was not flat, but rising Bias way. **1888** M. W. HUNGERFORD *Mrs. Vereker* II. xi. 129 They have pulled it bias-wise, and cross-wise, and straight-wise.

biathlon (baɪ'æθlən). [f. BI-[2] II + Gr. ἄθλον contest, after PENTATHLON.] An athletic event consisting of skiing and shooting performed by the same contestants.

1958 *Times* 6 Nov. 14/4 Events new to the Olympic Games are the biathlon, a 20 kilometres combined skiing and shooting competition, and a speed skating contest for women. **1966** *Daily Mail* 22 Dec. 11/5 The biathlon is a 20-kilometre race with a pause every five kilometres, when the competitor has to fire five rounds at a target 150 yards away.

biauricular (baɪɔː'rɪkjʊlə(r)), *a.* [f. BI- *pref.*[2] I + AURICULAR.] Having two auricles. **biauriculate** *a.* the same.

1835 KIRBY *Hab. & Inst. Anim.* II. xxii. 414 Heart..bi-auriculate. **1839** TODD *Cycl. Anat.* III. 991 A bi-auricular structure of the heart, as in the Siren.

bi'axal, *a.* = next. **bia'xality**, biaxial character.

1837 WHEWELL *Hist. Induct. Sc.* (1857) II. 296 Its crystalline symmetry is biaxal. **1869** TYNDALL *Notes Light* §423 Biaxal crystals, or those which possess two optic axes. **1864** *Reader* 85. 206/2 The biaxality ascribed to it.

biaxial (baɪ'æksɪəl), *a.* [f. BI- *pref.*[2] I + AXIAL.]

1. Having two (optic) axes.

1854 J. HOGG *Microsc.* I. ii. (1867) 146 Topaz, a biaxial crystal. *c* **1865** J. WYLDE in *Circ. Sc.* I. 84/1 Nitre..is..a biaxial crystal.

2. *Geom.* (See quot.)

1889 CAYLEY *Math. Papers* (1897) XIII. 13 Each conic meets each axis in two points; and at each of these points the axis and the tangent to the conic form with the lines to I, J a harmonic pencil. The binodal quartic is in this case said to be biaxial.

bib (bɪb), *v.* Forms: 4–6, 9 *dial.* beb, 6 bibb, byb, bybbe, 6–7 bibbe, 4– bib. [Possibly an adaptation of L. *bib-ĕre*, to drink; but it may have originated independently, in an imitation of repeated movements of the lips; cf. the variant *beb.*] *trans.* & *intr.* To drink; keep on drinking, tipple.

c **1325** *E.E. Allit. P.* B. 1499 A boster on benche bibbes þer-of. *c* **1386** CHAUCER *Reeve's T.* 242 This Millere hath so wisely bibbed [*v.r.* bebbed] Ale That as an hors he snorteth in his sleepe. **1566** DRANT *Horace Sat.* vii. Eiv b, Thou thinkes by sleepe, and bibbinge wyne, to banishe out all woes. **1641** *Vox Borealis* in *Harl. Misc.* (Malh.) IV. 433 If they cannot byte of a bannock, and bibbe of the brooke. *c* **1645** HOWELL *Lett.* II. 48 As soon a little little Ant Shall bib the Ocean dry. **1879** BROWNING *Ned Bratts* 5 Folks kept bibbing beer While the parsons prayed for rain.

b. *bib-all-night*: a drunkard, confirmed toper.

1612 SYLVESTER *Lacrym. Lacr.* Wks. (1621) 1150 Bats, Harpies, Sirens, Centaurs, Bib-all-nights.

bib (bɪb), *sb.*[1] Also 6 bibbe, 7–8 bibb. [Prob. from BIB *v.*; but whether because worn by a child when drinking (cf. *feeder*), or because a bib imbibes moisture (Skeat), is purely conjectural.]

1. a. A cloth placed under a child's chin, to keep the front of the dress clean, esp. at meals.

1580 BARET *Alv.* B634 A Bibbe for a childes breast: a gorget. **1589** *Pappe w. Hatchet* C iij, Giue the infant a bibbe. **1613** BEAUM. & FL. *Captain* III. v, We'll have a bib, for spoiling of thy doublet. **1785** COWPER *Task* IV. 226 Misses, at whose age their mothers wore The back-string and the bib. **1840** HOOD *Kilmansegg* xxxii, Her best bibs were made Of rich gold brocade.

b. A similar article worn over the breast by adults, frequently as the upper part of an apron. *best bib and tucker*: put for 'best clothes' as a whole, properly of girls or women, but also of men. *bib-and-brace*, applied *attrib.* to a type of overall having the upper part supported by braces.

1687 B. RANDOLPH *Archipelago* 52 Before their breasts hangs a bibb which reaches a little below their wast. **1737** G. SMITH *Cur. Relat.* I. ii. 132 The Driver is dressed in his best Band and Bib. **1747** tr. *Marquis d'Argens' New Memoirs establishing a True Knowledge of Mankind* II. 264 The Country-woman..minds nothing on Sundays so much as her best Bib and Tucker. **1793** [see TUCKER *sb.* 3]. **1855** *Sharpe's Lond. Mag.* V. 92/2 All-London..puts on its best bib and tucker. **1865** DICKENS *Mut. Fr.* iv, She girded herself with an apron, and contrived a bib to it. **1875** *Lanc. Gloss.* (E.D.S.) 37 An' put him his best bib-an-tucker on, an' went to look for a place for him. **1959** *Manchester Guardian* 13 July 5/6 The engine-driver, a dapper figure in bib-and-brace overalls.

c. *attrib.*, as in *bib-apron, -cravat.*

1674 DRYDEN *Prol. Open. New House* 27 Only fools..Th' extremity of modes will imitate, The dangling knee-fringe and the bib-cravat. **1750** LADY FEATHERSTONH. in *Mem. Ld. Gambier* (1861) I. ii. 31 A laced bib-apron was brought to me. **1880** KINGLAKE *Crimea* VI. xi. 440 The gracious bib-apron seemed to fold her in honour.

2. A patch of feathers resembling a bib under the bill of a bird.

1854 *Poultry Chron.* I. 391/1 A dark bib under the bill. **1948** *Brit. Birds* XLI. 156 A distinct bib..contrasted with white under-parts.

bib (bɪb), *sb.*[2] [from BIB *sb.*[1]: see quot. 1836.] A fish; the whiting-pout (*Gadus luscus*).

1674 RAY *Fishes* 101 The Bib or Blinds. **1766** PENNANT *Zool.* (1769) III. 149 The Bib (*Gadus luscus*)..is esteemed a good eating fish, not unlike the whiting in taste. **1836** YARRELL *Brit. Fishes* II. 159 From a singular power of inflating a membrane which covers the eyes and other parts about the head, which, when thus distended, have the appearance of bladders, it is called Pout, Bib, Blens, and Blinds. **1880** GUNTHER *Fishes* 541.

bibacious (bɪ-, baɪ'beɪʃəs), *a.* [f. L. *bibāci-* (nom. *bibax*) given to drinking + -OUS.] Addicted to, or fond of, drinking; bibulous.

1676 BULLOKAR, *Bibacious*, given much to drinking. **1834** *Blackw. Mag.* XVI. 650 The middle [class are] bibacious more than health requires.

bibacity (bɪ'bæsɪtɪ). [f. as prec.: see -ACITY.] Addictedness to drinking; tippling.

1623 COCKERAM II, Outragious drinking, *Bibacity*. **1642** T. TAYLOR *God's Judgem.* I. vii. 105 This Sinne of Bibacity and Vinosity. **1804** T. TROTTER *Drunkenness* iv. §2. 111 The evils which follow bibacity.

bibasic (baɪ'beɪsɪk), *a. Chem.* [f. BI- *pref.*[2] I + BASE *sb.*[1] + -IC.] Having two bases. *bibasic acid*: one which contains two atoms of displaceable hydrogen (*e.g.* H_2SO_4), and can therefore form two series of salts, normal (*e.g.* K_2SO_4) and acid (*e.g.* $KHSO_4$). Now more commonly DI-BASIC.

1847–9 TODD *Cycl. Anat. & Phys.* IV. 80/2 The bibasic phosphate of ammonia and magnesia. **1876** HARLEY *Mat. Med.* 314 Oxalic acid is bibasic.

bibation (bɪ'beɪʃən). [Humorously f. BIB *v.*: see -ATION: cf. BIBITION.] Bibbing; potation.

1830 *Fraser's Mag.* I. 217 Wilson had lost his five senses, only retaining that of whisky bibation. **1843** CARLYLE *Past & Pr.* (1858) 127 He of the frequent bibations.

bibatory: see BIBITORY.

bibb (bɪb). *Naut.* Also 8 bib. [variant of BIB *sb.*[1]] A bracket under the trestle-tree of a mast, resembling in position a child's bib.

1779–80 COOK *Voy.* (1785) II. 271 The foremast..to be unrigged, in order to fix a new bib. **1867** in SMYTH *Sailor's Word-bk.*

bibbed (bɪbd), *ppl. a.* Furnished with a bib.

1883 *Sunday Mag.* 483 The lady in neat white cap and bibbed apron.

bibber ('bɪbə(r)). [f. BIB *v.* + -ER[1].] One who drinks frequently; a tippler. (Frequent in comb., as *wine-*, *beer-bibber*, etc.)

1536 *Remed. Sedition* 20 b, Bibbers wil be offended with hym. **1756** C. LUCAS *Ess. Waters* I. 185 The subjects of the Gout are generally..wine, cider, and beer bibers. *a* **1845** HOOD *Drink. Song* x, Look at the bibbers of wine.

Hence **bibbership**.

1670 EACHARD *Cont. Clergy* 31 That would much better fit some old soker at Parnassus than his sipping unexperienced bibbership. Alas, poor child!

'bibbery. *rare.* [f. as prec. + -Y.] Bibbing, drinking; a bibbing-house.

1653 URQUHART *Rabelais* I. xl, I never eat any confections ..whiles I am at the bibbery. **1831** J. WILSON in *Blackw. Mag.* XXX. 541 The high and palmy state of wine-bibbery.

bibbing ('bɪbɪŋ), *vbl. sb.* [f. BIB *v.* + -ING[1].] Continued or repeated drinking; tippling.

a **1400** *Alexander* (Stev.) 154 Bacus he was braynewode for bebbing of wynes. **1563** *Homilies* II. *Agst. Gluttony* (1859) 298 They that give themselves..to bibbing and banqueting. **1835** L. HUNT *Jrnl.* No. 70. 256 The bibbing of bad water.. meets with encouragement.

b. *attrib.*, as in *bibbing-house* (= tippling-house).

1587 CHURCHYARD *Worth. Wales* (1876) 14 The Danes likewise, doe lead a bibbing life. **1687** T. BROWN *Lib. Consc.* in *Dk. Buckhm's. Wks.* (1705) II. 131 It wou'd sound oddly to turn it [the Meeting-house] into a Bibbing-House.

'bibbing, *ppl. a.* [f. BIB *v.* + -ING[2].]

1. That bibs; given to drinking.

1594 CAREW *Huarte's Exam. Wits* xiv. (1596) 253 If the same be gluttonous, greedy, and bibbing. **1656** DU GARD *Gate Lat. Unl.* §623 Ravening and bibbing belly-gods. **1833** *Fraser's Mag.* VIII. 44 He is now a..port-bibbing, gout-bemartyred believer in the Tory faith.

2. Of things: Absorbent; = BIBULOUS I.

1633 P. FLETCHER *Purple Isl.* v. xvii. 51 Unto a bibbing substance down convoying. *Ibid.* v. xxvi, The bibbing third draws it together nigher.

bibble ('bɪb(ə)l), *v.* Also 6 bible, bibil, bybyll. [f. BIB + -LE, freq. ending; cf. *prattle, tipple.*]

†**1.** To keep drinking, to drink: **a.** *trans. Obs.*

1583 STANYHURST *Æneis* I. (Arb.) 33 His fierce steeds.. Xanth stream gredilye bibled.

†**b.** *intr. Obs.*

a **1529** SKELTON *Elyn. Rumming* 550 Let me wyth you bybyll. **1581** MARBECK *Bk. of Notes* 326 An Eagles olde age for necessitie, compelleth him to be ever bibling.

2. *intr.* To dabble with the bill like a duck. **b.** *trans.* To drink with a dabbling noise.

1552 HULOET, Bubblyng, or bybblyng in water, as duckes do, *amphibolus*. **1861** M. B. EDWARDS *Tale of Woods* II. ii, *Eider-duck*, How pleasant it is to glide through the grass And bibble the dew-drops as I pass!

bibble-babble ('bɪb(ə)l,bæb(ə)l), *sb.* Also 6 bybell-babbel, byble-, bible-bable, bybble-babble. [Intensive reduplication of BABBLE: cf. *tittle-tattle, pit-pat*, etc.] Idle or empty talk; prating. (Very common in 16th c.)

1532 MORE *Confut. Barnes* VIII. Wks. 754/1, I..will cutte of all his bybell babbel. **1593** G. HARVEY *Pierce's Super.* 48 His phantasticall bible-babbles and capricious panges. **1601** SHAKS. *Twel. N.* IV. ii. 105 Endeauour thy selfe to sleepe, and leaue thy vaine bibble babble. **1656** TRAPP *Comm. Matt.* xxii. 29 [The Athenians] therefore counted all that St. Paul could say to it, bibble babble. **1701** SEDLEY *Grumbler* I. i. (1766) 205 Bibble babble, give the goose more hay! **1866** *Reader* 21 Apr. 397 Terrible philippics against wit-frittering, froth-whipping, and vain bibble-babble.

'bibble-,babble, *v.* [f. the sb.] *trans.* and *intr.* To indulge in bibble-babble or idle talk; to babble.

1888 DOUGHTY *Trav. Arabia Deserta* I. 256 They all love to bibble-babble their infirmities in the wholesome ears of the hakîm. *Ibid.* 596 They sat out long hours bibble-babbling.

bibbler ('bɪblə(r)). Also 6 bibbiler. [f. BIBBLE + -ER[1].] A drinker, a tippler.

a **1553** UDALL *Royster D.* III. v. (Arb.) 58 Fare ye well bibbler, and worthily may ye speede. **1566** GASCOIGNE *Supposes* Wks. (1587) 5 An excellent good bibbiler. **1773** *Gentl. Mag.* XLIII. 196 Each idle bibbler is now such a ninny.

†**'bibbles, bibles.** ? *Obs. rare.* [f. BIBBLE *v.*] Strata of clay containing water.

1747 HOOSON *Miner's Dict.* M iv, He comes..from common Earth, the first into Clay, from Clay to Bibles, etc.

bibbling ('bɪblɪŋ), *ppl. a.* [f. BIBBLE + -ING[2].] **a.** Drinking; tippling. **b.** Dabbling with the bill like a duck drinking.

1552 HULOET, Bybblyng with the byll, *bibulus*. **1565** GOLDING *Ovid's Met.* III. (1593) 60 Little bibling Phyale, and Pseke that pretie mops. **1619** GORGES tr. *Bacon's Wisd.* 270 An age..that is dull, bibling and reeling.

bib-cock. [? f. BIB *sb.*[1]] A cock or tap with a turned-down nozzle, as distinguished from a stop-cock. So *bib-nozzle, -valve.*

1797 J. CURR *Coal Viewer* 63, 1 Piston cock (bib)..1 Air cock (bib) to fix in the sink pipe. **1853** *Dict. Archit., Bib-cock*, a term used..to distinguish a cock which delivers fluids out of a pipe, from a stop-cock which is placed in the length of a pipe. *a* **1877** KNIGHT *Dict. Mech.* s.v., *c* is a bib-valve, the closure being by a reciprocating slide. **1909** WEBSTER, Bib nozzle. **1951** *Good Housek. Home Encycl.* 281/2 *Screw-down bib cock*: this is the best-known type of tap.

†**bi'bede,** *v. Obs.* [OE. *bebéodan*, f. BE- + *béodan* to BID.] *trans.* To bid, command.

c **1000** ÆLFRIC *Deut.* iii. 28 Bebeod Iosue. *c* **1000** *Ags. Gosp.* Luke iv. 10 He hys englum be þe bebyt [**1160** *Hatton* bebeot] þæt hiȝ þe ȝehealdon. *c* **1175** *Cott. Hom.* 225 He [Noe] dede þa swa him god bebead.

‖**bibelot** (biblo). [Fr.] A small curio or article of *virtù*.

1873 LADY C. SCHREIBER *Jrnl.* (1911) I. 185 After 3, walked up to Lady Hopetoun's to amuse her with some of our little bibelots. *Ibid.* 231 Van Minden had a lovely little bibelot of Cupid with drums. **1882** 'OUIDA' *Resurgo* vi. in *Belgravia* XLVI. 453 His soul never rises above brocades and *bibelôts*! **1886** F. M. CRAWFORD *Tale Lonely Parish* xviii, The spectacle of her pictures, her furniture and her bibelots. **1900** H. HARLAND *Cardinal's Snuff-Box* xix, The table, with its books and bibelots. **1936** *Burlington Mag.* Apr. 186/1 A Chinese *bibelot* on the table shows the influence of the fashion for lacquer.

bibenella, obs. form of PIMPINELLA, a herb. [Cf. med.L. *pipinella*, G. *bibernelle* = the same.]

1631 SPEED *Prosp. Parts World* 43 Silke..dyed with certaine knots of Bibenella.

†**'biberage**. *Obs. rare*$^{-1}$. Also **-idge**. [ad. med.L. *biberagium*, f. *bibĕre* to drink: see -AGE.] A drink given by way of fee. Cf. BEVERAGE.

1687 *England's Jests*, Collecter general of foys and biberage [*v.r.* biberidge].

†**bi'bergh**, *v. Obs.* [OE. *bebeorȝan* to defend, f. BE- + *beorȝan*, BERGH *v.*] *trans.* To protect oneself from, ward off.

*a***1000** *Beowulf* 3497 Him bebeorȝan ne con wom-wundor-bebodum werȝan gastes. *c***1205** LAY. 1462 Corineus bleinte and þene scute bi-berh [*c***1250** him seolf werede].

†**'biberon**[1]. *Obs. rare*$^{-1}$. [a. F. *biberon*, f. L. *bibĕre* to drink.] A tippler.

1637 BASTWICK *Litany* I. 19 Corporations of biberons and tiplers.

‖**biberon**[2] (bibrɔ̃). [Fr.] A drinking-vessel with elongated spout, formerly used by travellers, invalids, and children.

*a***1853** MAYNE *Expos. Lex.* (1860) 120/2 *Biberon*, name proposed for a feeding-bottle for infants. **1862** *Catal. Internat. Exhib., Brit.* II. II. xvii. 127 The Biberon, a new patent invention, adapted for a lady's travelling companion. **1905** *Westm. Gaz.* 27 May 15/3 The biberon is wrought in rock-crystal..and is in the form of a grotesque animal, of which the head is utilised as the spout.

†**biberot**. *Obs.* (See quot.)

1706 PHILLIPS, *Biberot*, minc'd Meats made of the Breasts of Partridges and fat Pullets. **1731-90** in BAILEY.

†**bibesy**. *Obs.*$^{-0}$ [ad. L. *bibesia* the 'drink-land' (Plautus).] 'A too earnest desire after drink.' Bailey 1731, Vol. II.

‖**bibi** ('biːbiː), var. BEEBEE.

1842 in Yule & Burnell *Hobson-Jobson* (1886) s.v. *Beebee*. **1921** *Spectator* 14 May 627/2 They get..one or two tomans when the carpet is finished..according to whether the Bibi (the chief's wife) is pleased with the result or not. **1935** *Discovery* June 164/2 *Bibi* (mistress of the household).

bibition (bɪ'bɪʃən). [ad. late L. *bibitiōn-em*, f. *bibĕre* to drink: see -TION.] Drinking.

1852 G. S. FABER *Diff. Romanism* (1853) lvi, The gross carnal sense of..an actual bibition.

bibitory ('bɪbɪtərɪ), *a. rare.* [ad. mod.L. *bibitōrius*, f. *bibit-* ppl. stem of *bibĕre* to drink; see -ORY.] Of or pertaining to drinking; *spec.* in ***bibitory muscle***, synonym for 'rectus internus oculi.'

1696 PHILLIPS, *Bibitory Muscle*, the Muscle that draws down the Eye towards the Cup when we drink. **1834** *Fraser's Mag.* IX. 586 This is not a question amatory—it is a consideration bibatory [*sic*].

Bible ('baɪb(ə)l). Forms: 3-4 bibul, 4 bibel, 4-6 bibil(l, 5 bybulle, bybylle, 5-6 byble, 6 bybill, bybul, 4- bible. [a. F. *bible*, 13th c. (= Pr. *bibla*, Sp. and Pg. *biblia*, It. *bibbia*; whence also Ger. *bibel*, Du. *bijbel*, all fem.):—late L. *biblia* fem. sing., for earlier *biblia* neut. pl., the Scriptures, a. Gr. τὰ βιβλία, lit. 'the books,' in later Christian writers *spec.* 'the canonical books, the Scriptures.'

The Gr. βιβλία was pl. of βιβλίον, dim. of βίβλος (1. the inner bark of the papyrus, 'paper'; 2. a paper, scroll, roll, or book), which had ceased to have a diminutive sense, and was the ordinary word for 'book,' whether as a distinct treatise, or as a subdivision of a treatise, before its application to the Jewish and Christian Scriptures. In reference to the former, see τὰ βιβλία τὰ ἅγια 'the holy books,' in *1 Macc.* xii. 9: in Clemens Alex. probably, and Origen (*in Joannem* v. iv., ed. Lomm. I. 168) *c* 223, certainly, τὰ βιβλία include the N. Test. books. In Latin, the first appearance of *biblia* is not ascertained. Jerome uses *bibliothēca* for the Scriptures, and this name continued in literary use for several centuries. Of *biblia*, Becker, *Catal. Biblioth. Antiq.* 42, has a 9th c. example (see also those under sense 1 below); but the evidence of the Romanic langs. shows that *biblia* must have been the popular name, and have been treated as a fem. sing., much earlier than this. The common change of a Lat. neuter pl. into a fem. sing. in *-a* (as in *arma, battalia, folia, gaudia, gesta, opera*, etc.) was in the case of *biblia* facilitated by the habit of regarding the Scriptures as one work. In OE. *bibliopéce* alone occurs; in Anglo-Latin *biblia* and *bibliothēca* interchange in the 11th c. catalogue of the library of Lindisfarne; in the 13th c. catalogue of the Durham books only *biblia* occurs.]

I. 1. a. The Scriptures of the Old and New Testament. (Sometimes in early use, and still dial., used for the Old Testament; *e.g.* 'neither in the Bible nor the Testament.') ***the open Bible***: the Bible accessible to all in the vernacular.

[**1095** *Catal. Lindisfarne* (Becker *Catal. Biblioth. Antiq.* 172) Unum bibliam in duobus voluminibus..Bibliotheca, id est vetus et novum testamentum in duobus libris. **1266** *Catal. Eccles. Dunelm* (*ibid.* 256) Unam bibliam in IV magnis voluminibus..aliam bibliam in duobus voluminibus.] *a* **1300** *Cursor M.* 1900 As þe bibul [*v.r.* bibil, bibel, bible] sais. **1330** R. BRUNNE *Chron.* 290 þe bible may not lie. *c* **1430** LYDG. *Min. Poems* 179 Like as the bibylle rehersith. **1528** MORE *Heresyes* I. Wks. 154/1 He lerned the articles of his beleue in the byble. **1530** RASTELL *Bk. Purgat.* I. i, Neyther of the bokys of the olde byble nor of the newe testament. **1587** GOLDING *De Mornay* xxiv. 357 Certaine bookes which we call the Bible or Olde Testament. **1798** SOUTHEY *Eng. Eclog.* v, Is that the charity your Bible teaches? **1837** *Ch. Eng. Mag.* 9 Dec., Bear witness, martyrs of the olden days, How your true hearts the open Bible priz'd. **1850** PRESCOTT *Mexico* I. 363 [They] carried with them the sword in one hand and the Bible in the other. **1908** TILBY *Eng. People Overseas* I. 48 The persecution of Mary and the open Bible worked a change.

b. A copy of the Scriptures.

1468 SIR J. PASTON *Lett.* 592 II. 329 As for the Byble that the master hath, I wend the uttermost pryse had not passyd v. mark. **1539** COVERDALE *Let. Cromwell* in *Bible* (Bagster) Pref. 18 License and privilege for the sale of his Bibles and New Testaments. **1704** NELSON *Fest. & Fasts* xviii. (1739) 227 To force from Christians their Bibles. **1852** H. COTTON *Edit. Bible* Pref. 8 Mutilated church Bibles.

c. A particular edition, or a copy of it.

1538 COVERDALE *Let. Cromwell* in *Bible* (Bagster) Pref. 16, I may know your pleasure concerning the annotations of this Bible. **1644** EVELYN *Mem.* (1857) I. 120 They are described in some of St. Hierom's bibles. **1835** *Penny Cycl.* IV. 374/2 This [Geneva] edition is often called the 'Breeches Bible' on account of a rendering given in Gen. iii. 7. **1842** MACAULAY *Fred. Gt., Ess.* (1854) 659/2 To Frederic William, this huge Irishman was what a brass Otho, or a Vinegar Bible, is to a collector of a different kind.

2. Hence *fig.* A text-book, an authority (of religion, politics, etc.); a sacred book.

1804 SOUTHEY in Robberds *Mem. W. Taylor* I. 517 The Annual..bids fair to become my political bible. **1856** EMERSON *Eng. Traits* Wks. 1874 II, The poets who have contributed to the Bible of existing England sentences of guidance. **1883** M. WILLIAMS *Relig. Thought Ind.* ii. 21 This phase of the Brahmanical system has for its special bible the sacred treatises called Brāhmaṇas.

†**3.** *transf.* A large book, a tome, a long treatise.

1377 LANGL. *P. Pl.* B. xv. 87 Of þis matere I myȝte make a longe bible. **1384** CHAUCER *H. Fame* 1334 Men myght make of hem a bible xx^{ti}. foote thykke. **1542** UDALL *Erasm. Apophth.* 205 a, When he had read a long bible writen and sent to hym from Antipater. **1629** Z. BOYD *Last Battell* 656 (JAM.), I would gladlie know what a blacke bible is that which is called, the Book of the wicked.

4. *Nautical slang.* (See quots.) Cf. PRAYER-BOOK 2.

1867 SMYTH *Sailor's Word-Bk.* 98 *Bible*,..a squared piece of freestone to grind the deck with sand in cleaning it; a small holystone, so called from seamen using them kneeling. **1906** *Voy. of 'Scotia'* iii. 25 Holy-stones for polishing decks..are commonly known to sailors as 'Bibles'.

II. A collection of books; a library. [One of the senses of Gr. βιβλία: not cited by Du Cange in med.L.; but cf. the converse use of *bibliothēca* in sense of *biblia*.]

1382 WYCLIF *2 Macc.* ii. 13 He makynge a litil bible [Vulgate *bibliothecam*] gadride of cuntrees bokis. *c* **1425** in Wr.-Wülcker *Voc.* 648 *Bibleoteca*, bybulle. **1483** *Cath. Angl.* 31 A Bybylle, *biblia, bibliotheca.*

III. *Comb.*, chiefly attrib., as ***Bible-black***, ***-composition***, ***-distributor***, ***-lore***, ***-matter***, ***-reader***, ***-reading***, ***-seller***, ***-story***, ***-student***, ***-tone***, ***-version***; and ***Bible-bearing***, ***-reading***, adjs. Also **Bible-banger**, **-basher** *Austral. and N.Z. slang*, = *Bible-pounder*; hence ***Bible-banging***, ***-bashing*** ppl. adjs.; **Bible belt**, a designation of those parts of the United States reputed to be fanatically puritan or fundamentalist; also *attrib.*; **Bible-bigot**, **-moth**, a person who is obstinately devoted to the Bible; esp. applied to the Methodists, sometimes contemptuously (cf. quot. 1820); **Bible-box**, a box with a flat lid, esp. one of the 17th century, large enough to hold a family Bible; **Bible class**, a class for the study of the Bible; **Bible-leaf**, (*a*) a thin slice of whale-blubber for heating in a try-pot; (*b*) *U.S.* (see quot. 1931); **Bible-moth**: see *Bible-bigot*; **Bible-oath**, a solemn oath taken upon the Bible; **Bible paper**, a very thin but strong opaque printing-paper; cf. INDIA PAPER 2; **Bible-pounder**, **-puncher** *slang*, one who expounds or follows the Bible in a vigorous or aggressive manner, esp. a clergyman; hence **Bible-pounding**, **-punching** *ppl. adjs.* and *vbl. sbs.*; **Bible-press**, **bibble-**, *Naut.* a hand rolling-board for cartridges, rocket-cases, etc.; **Bible-reader**, a reader of the Bible; also, one employed to read the Bible from house to house; **Bible-thumper** *slang*, = *Bible-pounder*; **Bible-woman**, one employed to read the Bible from house to house.

1942 M. HARCOURT *Parson in Prison* iii. 35 We don't want any damned *Bible bangers around here! **1945** BAKER *Austral. Lang.* vi. 131 Here are some self-explanatory Australianisms: *bible banger, bible basher*, [etc.]. **1948** D. BALLANTYNE *Cunninghams* (1963) I. xxiv. 106 Gil reckoned Kent was better than most of the Bible-bangers who visited the hospital. **1964** O. E. MIDDLETON *Walk on Beach* 40 That *Bible-banging, psalm-singing old crawler. **1958** R. STOW *To Islands* iv. 74 They were *Bible-bashers and humourless clods. **1944** L. GLASSOP *We were Rats* xxi. 124, I doan want any *bible-bashing bastard..mumblin' any bull—over me. **1624** BP. MOUNTAGU *App. Caesarem* in Forster *Sir J. Eliot* I. 256 Saint-seeming, *bible-bearing, and hypocritical. **1926** *Amer. Mercury* Feb. 141/2 The *Baptist Record*, of Jackson, Miss., [is] in the heart of the *Bible and Lynching Belt. **1926** S. LEWIS in G. Frankau *My Unsent. Journey* xi. 148 I'm collecting parsons, Gilbert... That's why I've been living in Kansas City. It's the centre of the Bible belt. **1960** *20th Cent.* Dec. 558 Nashville is..the Bible Belt capital. **1766** J. WESLEY *Jrnl.* (1938) 5 June, I am a *Bible-bigot. I follow it in all things, both great and small. **1789** —— *Sermon* no. xlviii, in *Arminian Mag.* Jan. 7 They were continually reproached for this very thing: some terming them in derision, *Bible-bigots*; others *Bible-moths*: feeding, they said, upon the Bible, as moths do upon cloth. **1820** SOUTHEY *Wesley* I. 47 They were called, in derision, the Sacramentarians, Bible-bigots, Bible-moths. **1953** DYLAN THOMAS *Under Milk Wood* (1954) 1 It is spring, moonless night in the small town, starless and *bible-black. **1904** P. MACQUOID *Hist. Eng. Furniture* I. vii. 190 Boxes..with a flat lid..were termed *Bible or lace boxes, and used for these purposes. **1966** A. W. LEWIS *Gloss. Woodworking Terms* 48 Jacobean period (1603–1649)... Gate-legged tables and Bible boxes first appeared. **1824** *Amer. Baptist Mag.* IV. 371, I intimated my intention to establish..*Bible classes. **1888** C. M. YONGE *Our New Mistress* xvii. 161 She was so fond of her church and her Bible class. **1851** MELVILLE *Moby Dick* III. ix. 69 Arrayed in decent black; occupying a conspicuous pulpit; intent on '*Bible leaves'..what a lad for a Pope were this mincer! **1931** W. N. CLUTE *Plants* 60 More appealing names are..bible-leaf (*Chrysanthemum balsamita*) for that fragrant-leaved plant whose leaves were often carried to church. **1698** CONGREVE *Way World* v. ii. (D.) So long as it was not a *Bible-oath, we may break it with a safe conscience. **1859** THACKERAY *Virginians* (1876) 539 He would take his Bible oath of that. **1926** *Paper Terminol.* (*Spalding & Hodge*) 2 **Bible paper*, see *India paper*. **1889** BARRÈRE & LELAND *Dict. Slang* I. 111/1 **Bible-pounder* (popular), a parson. **1890** FARMER *Slang* I. 186/2 *Bible-pounder*, a clergyman..from the practice indulged in by some excitable exponents, of pounding or beating their hands upon the book or desk while preaching. **1951** C. SIMAK *Time & Again* (1956) xxxvi. 173 The old-time Bible-pounding preachers. **1917** *Tiki Talk* (N.Z.) 10 Synonyms: clergyman, parson..preacher, *bible-puncher. **1938** X. HERBERT *Capricornia* (1939) xxxii. 486 You horse-faced bible-puncher. **1933** P. FLEMING *Braz. Adv.* II. iii. 205 It seemed..that *bible-punching was a bit of a racket. **1961** *John o'London's* 13 Apr. 415/2 An earnest evangelist..denouncing the devil with bible-punching relish. **1538** BALE *Thre Lawes* 1204 Then I holde it best that we always condempne The *Byble readers. **1874** M. ARNOLD in *Contemp. Rev.* Oct. 806 These two things achieved by us..for the Bible-reader's benefit. **1849** STOVEL *Introd. Canne's Necess.* 53 The demands of its *Bible-reading members. **1827** CUNNINGHAM *N.S. Wales* II. xxx. 252 None remained but the old *fence*, who continued Bible-reading to the end of the voyage. **1863** M. L. WHATELY *Ragged Life Egypt* xi. 99 This Bible-reading continued for several months. **1707** *Lond. Gaz.* No. 4342/4 Robert Whitledge, *Bible-seller, at the Bible in Creed-lane. **1888** C. M. YONGE *Our New Mistress* xvi. 152 The tinies..answered about their *Bible stories as prettily as could be wished. **1967** 'M. UNDERWOOD' *Man who died on Friday* xv. 139 He could remember a picture, in a children's book of Bible stories, of..'Elijah being taken up to heaven'. **1853** LYNCH *Self-Improv.* (1859) 43 No *Bible-student can mistake Christianity. **1923** J. MANCHON *Le Slang* 61 *Bible-pounder* (or *-*thumper*), un prêtre. **1942** A. L. ROWSE *Cornish Childhood* 31 It's always the Bible-thumpers who are the greatest hypocrites. **1859** MRS. GASKELL *Let.* 7 Nov. (1966) 587 Just before I left Manchester I heard of search being made for a '*Bible-woman' to work there; doubtless suggested by the success in London. **1862** MAYHEW *London Labour* Extra vol. p. xix, This void has been admirably supplied by the 'Bible women' of the nineteenth century. **1908** *Daily Chron.* 27 Mar. 27/2 £200 to Mrs. Wilson, her Biblewoman in London.

'bible-back. *U.S.* and *dial.* [BIBLE III.] A hump-backed or round-shouldered person.

1873 G. W. PERRIE *Buckskin Mose* x. 145 Pitching our camp in the Lassen Meadows, at La Due Very's, generally known as Old Bible-back. **1896** NORTHALL *Warwickshire Word-Bk.*, *Bible-back*, a person with broad, rounded shoulders. 'Here comes old bibleback!' **1903** *Dial. Notes* II. 349 *Bible-back*, Rockland Co. N.Y. Bergen Co. N.J.

So **bible-backed** *a.*

1857 *Olympia* (W.T.) *Pioneer & Democrat* 11 Dec. (Th.), We might, in consequence, become somewhat round-shouldered and 'bible-backed'. **1873** *N. & Q.* XII. 227 What kind of shoulders? Rather high. Anything else? He was humpy or bible-backed.

Bible-'Christian.

1. A Christian according to Scriptural standard.

1766 WESLEY *Jrnl.* 31 Oct., A real Bible Christian. **1788** —— *Wks.* (1872) VII. 203 The Methodists..were one and all determined to be Bible-Christians.

2. The name of a Protestant sect founded in 1815 by William O. Bryan, a Wesleyan preacher in Cornwall; chiefly in the south-west of England.

a **1860** WHATELY *Com.-pl. Bk.* (1864) 267 Still more objectionable is the title of Bible-Christians assumed by a sect. **1860** VENABLES *Isle Wight* 389 The 'Bible Christians,' or 'Bryanites,' were peculiarly active in gathering congregations in the outlying hamlets.

Bible-'clerk. a. A student of the Bible. **b.** *spec.* The title of a class of students in certain colleges

at Oxford, having the duty of reading the lessons in chapel, and of saying grace in Hall.

1626 BERNARD *Isle of Man* (ed. 10) 12 Thus Hue and Crie is written by the Bible-clarke. **1650** J. COTTON *Sing. Psalms* 21 In some Cathedrall Churches..the Bible-Clerks doe sing their Chapters out of the old and New Testament. *a* **1672** WOOD *Life* (1848) 112 The bible-clerks of Merton Coll. **1845** J. PYCROFT *Collegian's Guide* 42 In All Souls there are none but fellows who have already graduated, except four Bible Clerks. **1889** [see CLERK *sb.* 2 b]. **1965** *Oxf. Univ. Calendar* 213 Hertford College...Bible Clerks.

bi-bleed, -bloody, -blot: see BE-BLEED, etc.

Bibler (ˈbaɪblə(r)). [f. BIBLE + -ER[1].] †**a.** A student or reader of the Bible. †**b.** A Bible-clerk. **c.** *Sc.* One of the older scholars in a Scotch country school, so called because the Bible was their class-book.

1538 COVERDALE *N.T.* Ded., New-fangled fellows, English biblers, coblers of divinity. **1569** in *Etoniana* (1865) 220 The Bibler's office seems to have been to read a portion of Scripture in the hall at dinner. In the accounts for 1569 there is a charge 'for making ii halfpaces in the hawle for the Bybelers to stand upon, *vs.*' **1625** tr. *Gonsalvio's Sp. Inquis.* 170 Many would scornfully..tearm him a good Bibler. **1883** NASMYTH *Autobiog.* ii. 20 The 'Bibler's Seat' is marked [i.e. a seat on the Castle rock to which the bigger boys used to climb].

bibless (ˈbɪblɪs), *a.* Without a bib.

1865 DICKENS *Mut. Fr.* III. iv. 27 Bibless and apronless.

†**ˈbiblet.** *Obs. rare*[−1]. [f. BIBLE + -ET[1], ? dim.] ? A book, or ? library.

1388 WYCLIF *Ezra* v. 17 Now therfor if it semeth good to the king, rikene he in the biblet [*v.r.* biblet, *that is, the book of cronicling,* biblet *of cronyclis;* **1382** librarie; Lat. *bibliotheca*] of the king.

biblic (ˈbɪblɪk), *a.* ? *Obs.* [ad. med.L. *biblic-us,* f. *biblia* or Gr. *βίβλος*.] = next.

1684 N. S. *Crit. Enq. Edit. Bible* App. 294 A late Writer..in his Biblic Inquisitions. **1725** tr. *Dupin's Eccl. Hist.* I. v. 180 Biblick Exercitations. *c* **1811** FUSELI *Lect. Art* iv. (1848) 443 The Biblic expression..'the Ancient of Days.'

biblical (ˈbɪblɪkəl), *a.* [f. as prec. + -AL[1].] Of, relating to, or contained in, the Bible. ***biblical theology:*** see THEOLOGY.

1790 PORSON *Lett. Travis* 305 (T.) Augustine and Jerome corresponded upon biblical subjects. **1849** MACAULAY *Hist. Eng.* I. 331 Deeply versed in biblical criticism.

bibliˈcality. [f. prec. + -ITY.] Biblical quality; *concr.* a biblical matter or fact.

1851 CARLYLE *Sterling* I. xv. 125 He would study theology, biblicalities. **1920** GALSWORTHY *In Chancery* I. x. 91 'I must live again—live and move and have my being.' And in answer to that queer biblicality church-bells chimed the call to evening prayer. **1946** *Scrutiny* XIV. 103 The wastes of biblicality and fervid enthusiasm..devoted to Mordecai.

ˈbiblically, *adv.* [f. as prec. + -LY[2].] In biblical style, according to the Bible.

1838 G. S. FABER *Inquiry* 475 Conrad..might..be ignorant of the biblically-recorded circumstance.

Biblicism (ˈbɪblɪsɪz(ə)m). [f. BIBLIC + -ISM.] Adherence to the letter of the Bible.

1851 CARLYLE *Sterling* III. vi, As rampant as Biblicism was in the Seventeenth Century. **1874** tr. *Oosterzee's Chr. Dogmatics* 223 Biblicism, or idolatry of the letter.

Biblicist (ˈbɪblɪsɪst). [f. BIBLIC + -IST.] A professed adherent of the letter of the Bible.

1837 G. S. FABER *Justification* 276 The speculations of the Schoolmen were strongly opposed by the Biblicists of the Old Theology. **1862** *West. Rev.* XLI. 78 The extravagant claims of Biblicists with more zeal than discretion.

biblicize (ˈbɪblɪsaɪz), *v.* [f. as prec. + -IZE.] *trans.* To subject to the Bible. Hence **ˈbiblicized** *ppl. a.*

1865 *Pall Mall G.* 23 Sept. 10/1 The more recent creed of the biblicized Chinese.

biblico- (ˈbɪblɪkəʊ), comb. form of BIBLIC, -AL[1], as in **biblico-literary** *a.*, relating to the literature of the Bible; **biblico-poetic** *a.*, of or relating to scriptural poetry; **biblico-psychological**, etc.

1800 *Month. Mag.* X. 433 Under his biblico-poetic banner. **1863** TREGELLES in *N. & Q.* Ser. III. III. 342 His biblico-literary preparations. **1869** R. WALLIS *Delitzsch' Bibl. Psychol.* 15 A biblico-psychological investigation.

biblio- (ˈbɪblɪəʊ), repr. Gr. *βιβλίο-* stem and comb. form of *βιβλίον* book. In compounds formed in Greek itself, as *bibliography, βιβλιογραφία;* and in many of mod. formation, as *bibliogony, biblioklept, bibliophagist,* etc., some of which are merely pedantic or ponderously humorous.

biblioclasm (ˈbɪblɪəʊˌklæz(ə)m). [f. BIBLIO- + Gr. *-κλασμος* breaking.] Destruction of books, or of the Bible. **biblioclast** (-ˌklɑːst, -æ-) [Gr. *-κλάστης* breaker], a destroyer of books, or of the Bible. Also **biblioˈclastic** *a.* (Little more than nonce-words.)

1864 T. GRIFFITH *Plea Scripture* 8 The Biblioclasm of the 'higher criticism.' **1880** BLADES *Enemies Bks.* 96 Such a wicked old biblioclast as John Bagford. **1884** *Athenæum* 7 June 724 Made bonfires of the Maya and Aztec manuscripts..May these bishops expiate their crimes in the purgatory of biblioclasts! **1887** *Longman's Mag.* Dec. 239 The biblioclastic dead.

bibliognost (ˈbɪblɪəˌgnəʊst, -ɒst, -ɔː-). [a. F. *bibliognoste,* f. BIBLIO- + Gr. *γνώστης* one who knows.] One who knows books and bibliography. Hence **biblioˈgnostic** *a.*

a **1824** D'ISRAELI *Cur. Lit.* (1839) III. 343 A *bibliognoste*..is one knowing in title-pages and colophons..and all the minutiæ of a book. **1863** *Sat. Rev.* 505 A priggish bibliognostic air.

bibliogony (bɪblɪˈɒgənɪ). [f. BIBLIO + Gr. *-γονία* generation.] The production of books.

1843 SOUTHEY *Doctor* Interch. xiii. (D.) The various schemes of bibliogony..devised for explaining its phenomena.

bibliograph (ˈbɪblɪəʊgrɑːf, -æ-), *sb.* [prob. a. F. *bibliographe,* ad. Gr. *βιβλιογράφος* book-writer.] = BIBLIOGRAPHER.

1815 T. JEFFERSON *Writ.* (1830) IV. 263 Mr. Ticknor is..the best bibliograph I have met with. **1872** J. HATTOW *Vall. Poppies* I. ix. 118 You find the old bibliograph in some corner of the room, amidst a heap of books.

ˈbibliograph, *v.* [Back-formation from BIBLIOGRAPHY.] *trans.* To compile a bibliography of (an author or subject).

1961 B. MALAMUD *New Life* (1962) 120 Goddam, imagine bibliographing Civil War fiction.

bibliographer (bɪblɪˈɒgrəfə(r)). [f. as BIBLIOGRAPH *sb.* + -ER[1].]

†**1.** A writer of books, a copyist. *Obs.*

1656 BLOUNT, *Bibliographer,* a writer of books, a Scrivener. **1761** FENNING *Eng. Dict., Bibliographer,* one who writes or copies books.

2. One who writes about books, describing their authorship, printing, publication, etc.

1810 E. BRYDGES (*title*) The British Bibliographer. Vol. I. **1814** DIBDIN *Bibl. Spencer.* I. Pref. 6 One of the most celebrated of modern Bibliographers. **1869** BUCKLE *Civilis.* II. viii. 480 Antonio the most learned bibliographer Spain ever possessed.

bibliographic (ˌbɪblɪəʊˈgræfɪk), *a.* [f. Gr. *βιβλιογράφ-ος* (see above) + -IC: cf. F. *bibliographique,* perh. the immediate source.] Of or pertaining to bibliography.

1847 in CRAIG. **1890** A. W. VERRALL in *Class. Rev.* XII. 109/1 All of them originated in times which we should now call pre-historic, or at least pre-bibliographic. **1948** H. E. BLISS in *Rev. Docum.* XV. 93 Books and articles on the organization of knowledge and bibliographic classification (a select bibliography).

ˌbiblioˈgraphical, *a.* [f. as prec. + -AL[1].] Of, relating to, or dealing with bibliography.

1679 (*title*) Baconiana, Or Certain Genuine Remains of Sr. Francis Bacon..in Arguments Civil and Moral, Natural,..and Bibliographical. **1802** DIBDIN *Introd. Class.* Advt., The English Nation..is without a Bibliographical and Typographical Dictionary. **1846** GEO. ELIOT tr. *Strauss's Life of Jesus* I. p. xii, The author has not..aimed to give a complete bibliographical view of this department of theological literature, but..has adhered to the chief works in each separate class of opinions. **1868** PATTISON *Academ. Org.* §4. 117 An assistant qualified by professional bibliographical knowledge. **1961** T. LANDAU *Encycl. Librarianship* (ed. 2) 38/2 *Bibliographical note.* 1. A note, often a footnote, containing a reference to one or more works used as sources for the work. 2. A note in a catalogue or a bibliography, relating to the bibliographical history or a description of a book.

ˌbiblioˈgraphically, *adv.* [f. prec. + -LY[2].] With respect to bibliography.

1824 DIBDIN *Libr. Comp.* 40 There is little, bibliographically speaking, which can be advanced on the subject.

bibliographize (bɪblɪˈɒgrəfaɪz), *v.* [f. as prec. + -IZE.] *trans.* To write a bibliography of.

1824 DIBDIN *Libr. Comp.* 770 To bibliographise the article Voltaire. **1881** *Daily News* 15 Feb., Catalogues are catalogued and bibliographies are bibliographised.

bibliography (bɪblɪˈɒgrəfɪ). [a. Gr. *βιβλιογραφία* book-writing: cf. F. *bibliographie.*]

†**1.** The writing of books. *Obs.*

1678 in PHILLIPS (App.)

2. The systematic description and history of books, their authorship, printing, publication, editions, etc.

1814 DIBDIN *Bibl. Spencer.* I. Pref. 5 The Study of Bibliography in this country is perhaps in its infancy. **1854** ALLIBONE *Dict. Eng. Lit.* Pref. 5 Some other manuals of a similar character are very defective in bibliography. **1870** EMERSON *Soc. & Solit.* viii. 168 The annals of bibliography afford many examples of the delirious extent to which book-fancying can go.

3. A book containing such details.

1838 HALLAM *Hist. Lit.* I. I. iii. 184 *note,* No such book appears in any of the bibliographies.

4. A list of the books of a particular author, printer, or country, or of those dealing with any particular theme; the literature of a subject.

1814 T. H. HORNE *Introd. Study Bibliography* I. II. iii. §4. 365 *Professional,* or..*special bibliography,* has reference only to one class of books, and comprehends every work published on the subject of which it treats... Special bibliographies may be disposed either alphabetically, or systematically. **1869** W. ROWLANDS (*title*) Cambrian Bibliography. **1879** R. H. SHEPHERD (*title*) The Bibliography of Ruskin. **1882** *Nature* XXVI. 26 The literature or bibliography of the species of the Orthocerata. **1930** K. MALONE in *English Jrnl.* XIX. 646 The term *bibliography* is also used, unhappily, I think, to mean 'list of writings germane to a given topic'.

biblioklept (ˈbɪblɪəʊklɛpt). [f. BIBLIO- + Gr. *κλέπτης* thief.] A book-thief. **ˌbiblioˌkleptoˈmaniac,** a book-thief regarded as insane.

1881 *Athenæum* 25 June 842/3 Besides the direct biblioklept there is the indirect thief, who borrows and never returns the book. **1881** A. LANG *Library* 53 Catherine de Medici..was a biblioklept. *Ibid.* 46 A great Parisian book-seller who..was a bibliokleptomaniac.

bibliolatry (bɪblɪˈɒlətrɪ). [f. BIBLIO- + Gr. *λατρεία* worship.] **a.** Extravagant admiration of a book. **b.** Excessive reverence for the mere letter of the Bible. **bibliˈolater** [cf. *idolater*], one who entertains such excessive admiration or reverence. **bibliˈolatrist** = prec. **bibliˈolatrous** *a.*, given to, or characterized by, bibliolatry.

a **1763** BYROM *Bp. Glo'ster's Doctr. Grace,* If to adore an image be idolatry, To deify a book is bibliolatry. **1826** C. ROBINSON *Diary* (1869) II. 330 Coleridge had convinced him that he was a bibliolatrist. **1847** DE QUINCEY *Protest.* Wks. VIII. 110 They..charge upon us Bibliolatry, or a superstitious allegiance—an idolatrous homage—to the words, to the syllables, and to the very punctuation of the Bible. *Ibid.* 116 It leaves the dispute with the bibliolaters wholly untouched. *Ibid.* 135 Bibliolatrous madness. **1865** ELLICOTT *Destiny Creat.* Pref. 6 Interpretations of scripture..narrow and bibliolatrous.

bibliology (bɪblɪˈɒlədʒɪ). [f. BIBLIO- + -LOGY, Gr. *-λογία* discourse.] **a.** Scientific description of books, book-lore; bibliography. **b.** 'Biblical literature, doctrine, or theology' (Worcester 1859). **bibliological** (ˌbɪblɪəʊˈlɒdʒɪkəl), *a.* [f. prec. + -ICAL], of or pertaining to bibliology. **bibliˈologist** [see -IST], a professed student of bibliology.

1807 SOUTHEY *Life* (1850) III. 108 There is a sort of title-page and colophon knowledge—in one word, bibliology. —— *Lett.* (1856) II. 34 'Prince Arthur'..in which I design to give the whole bibliology of the Round Table. **1843** —— *Doctor* Interch. xviii. (D.) Careful investigation by the most eminent bibliologists.

bibliomancy (ˈbɪblɪəʊˌmænsɪ). [f. BIBLIO- + Gr. *μαντεία* divination; cf. F. *bibliomancie.*] Divination by books, or by verses of the Bible.

1753 CHAMBERS *Cycl. Supp., Bibliomancy*..amounts to much the same with what is otherwise called *sortes biblicae*..F. J. Davidius, a jesuit, has published a bibliomancy. **1864** *N. & Q.* Ser. III. V. 195/2 Bibliomancy or Divination by Books, was known to the ancients under the appellation of Sortes Homericæ and Sortes Virgilianæ. The practice was to take up the works of Homer and Virgil, and to consider the first verse that presented itself as a prognostication of future events.

bibliomane (ˈbɪblɪəʊˌmeɪn). [a. F. *bibliomane,* f. BIBLIO- + Gr. *-μανής* mad.] = BIBLIOMANIAC *sb.*

1809 FERRIAR *Bibliomania* 5 The Bibliomane exclaims..'No Margin!' turns in haste, and scorns to buy. *a* **1824** D'ISRAELI *Cur. Lit.* (1866) 503/1 A *bibliomane* is an indiscriminate accumulator. **1827** DE QUINCEY *Wks.* XIII. 235 The regular literator or blackletter bibliomane. **1960** C. DAY LEWIS *Buried Day* ii. 32 He has been writing..to other bibliomanes.

bibliomania (ˌbɪblɪəʊˈmeɪnɪə). [f. BIBLIO- + Gr. *μανία* madness, after F. *bibliomanie.*] A rage for collecting and possessing books.

1734 T. HEARNE *Diary* 9 Nov. (1921) XI. 389, I should have been tempted to have laid out a pretty deal of money without thinking my self at all touched with Bibliomania. [**1750** CHESTERF. *Lett.* 220 II. 348 Beware of the Bibliomanie.] **1809** DIBDIN (*title*) Bibliomania, or Book-madness; containing some account of the history, symptoms, and cure of this fatal disease. **1835** T. HOOK *G. Gurney* (1850) II. i. 153 The bibliomania which appeared to engross my friend.

bibliomaniac (ˌbɪblɪəʊˈmeɪnɪæk), *sb.* and *a.* [f. prec. + -AC.] **A.** *sb.* One affected with bibliomania. **B.** *adj.* Given to bibliomania; mad after books; also = next.

1816 SCOTT *Antiq.* iv, The most determined, as well as earliest bibliomaniac upon record..Don Quixote de la Mancha. **1865** RUSKIN *Sesame* 75 If a man spends lavishly on his library, you call him mad—a biblio-maniac. **1834** *Fraser's Mag.* IX. 146 Biblio-maniac and genealogical inquiry. **1883** *Athenæum* 17 Nov. 629/3 The bibliomaniac Ptolemies.

bibliomaniacal (-məˈnaɪəkəl), *a.* [f. prec. + -AL[1].]

1. Of, relating to, or characterizing, a bibliomaniac.

1816 SCOTT *Antiq.* iii. *note,* This bibliomaniacal anecdote is literally true. **1861** *National Rev.* Oct. 275 Societies

(Roxburghe..Camden &c.)..tainted with bibliomaniacal exclusiveness.

2. = BIBLIOMANIAC *a.*

1822 SCOTT *Nigel* xxiv, The bibliomaniacal reader. **1856** J. STRANG *Glasgow & Clubs* 249 A few bibliomaniacal acquaintances.

ˌbiblioˈmanian, *a.* and *sb.* [f. BIBLIOMANIA + -AN.] = BIBLIOMANIAC.

Hence **ˌbiblioˈmanianism**, bibliomania.

1836 HOR. SMITH *Tin Trump.* 67 A hint which has not been thrown away upon our Bibliomanians.

bibliomanism (bɪblɪˈɒmənɪz(ə)m). [f. as BIBLIOMANE + -ISM.] = BIBLIOMANIA. So **bibliˈomanist**, a bibliomaniac.

1820 *Blackw. Mag.* VII. 693 During the highest rage of Bibliomanism. **1823** LAMB *Lett.* xiv. 132, I..am not bibliomanist enough to like black-letter. *a* **1828** BEWICK in *Century Mag.* XXIV. 663 The whimsies of the bibliomanists.

biblioˈpegia. *rare.* = BIBLIOPEGY.

1835 J. A. ARNETT (*title*) Bibliopegia; or, the art of bookbinding, in all its branches.

biblioˈpegically, *adv.* [f. BIBLIOPEGIC *a.*: see -ICALLY.] As regards bookbinding. So **bibliˈopegism** = BIBLIOPEGY.

1817 DIBDIN *Decam.* II. 513 The art and craft of bibliopegism. **1896** GOSSE in *Contemp. Rev.* Jan. 98 His own library..was not conspicuous bibliopegically.

bibliopegy (bɪblɪˈɒpɪdʒɪ). [f. BIBLIO- + Gr. -πηγία, f. πηγ-νύναι to fix.] Bookbinding as a fine art. **bibliopegic** (ˌbɪblɪəʊˈpɛdʒɪk), *a.*, of or pertaining to bookbinding. **bibliopegist** (bɪblɪˈɒpɪdʒɪst), a bookbinder. **bibliopeˈgistic** *a.*, of, relating to, or befitting a bookbinder. **bibliopeˈgistical** *a.*, = prec.

1835 J. A. ARNETT *Bibliopegia* p. iv, A record of the present state of the Bibliopegistic Art. **1876** *Encycl. Brit.* IV. 42/1 Contemporary masterpieces of French, Italian, and German bibliopegy. **1885** *Pall Mall G.* 10 Sept. 15 The Exhibition of what is known as bibliopegy. **1882** *Bibliographer* II. 15 The handsomest of covers by the first of bibliopegic artists. **1824** DIBDIN *Libr. Comp.* 591 The choicest morocco coverings of Charles Lewis, the renowned bibliopegist. *Ibid.* 605 The workshop of that bibliopegistical Coryphæus. **1882** *Times* 18 July 4/4 A fine specimen of bibliopegistic skill. **1958** 'M. INNES' *Long Farewell* 72 Appleby, although hazy about bibliopegy, was quite certain he wasn't a distinguished student of it. **1968** *Oxf. Mag.* 22 Nov. 88 (*caption*) A sad case of bibliopegistical elephantiasis.

bibliophagist (bɪblɪˈɒfədʒɪst). [f. BIBLIO- + Gr. -φάγος devouring + -IST.] A devourer of books. So **biblioˈphagic** *a.*

1881 *Sund. at Home* 27 Aug. 552 That eminent bibliophagist, and printer of scarce tracts. **1884** *Ibid.* May 329 Men of enormous bibliophagic appetite.

bibliophil(e (ˈbɪblɪəʊfɪl). [a. F. *bibliophile*, f. BIBLIO- + Gr. φίλος friend.] A lover of books; a book-fancier; also as adj. **ˌbiblioˈphilic** *a.*, of or pertaining to a bibliophile. **bibliophilism** (bɪblɪˈɒfɪlɪz(ə)m), the principles and practice of a bibliophile. **bibliˈophilist**, a bibliophile. **ˌbibliophiˈlistic** *a.*, of or befitting a bibliophilist. **bibliophilous** (bɪblɪˈɒfɪləs), *a.*, addicted to bibliophily. **bibliˈophily** [F. *bibliophilie*], love of books, taste for books.

1824 DIBDIN *Libr. Comp.* 780 The work..has been reprinted by the Society of *Bibliophiles at Paris. **1883** *Pall Mall G.* 12 Oct. 5/1 A *bibliophil, an autograph and print collector. **1883** *American* VI. 25 A *bibliophilic rarity and treasure. **1824** DIBDIN *Libr. Comp.* 4 Manias which sometimes..bring disgrace upon the good old cause of *bibliophilism. **1883** *Daily News* 1 Mar. 5/1 This quaint rule of *bibliophilistic morality, 'no harm in stealing a book if he does not mean to sell it, but to keep it.' **1882** STEVENSON *Men & Bks.* 277 Odd commissions for the *bibliophilous Count. **1877** SWINBURNE *Let.* 9 Oct. (1960) IV. 24, I have lately had two noble windfalls in the way of dramatic *bibliophily (if there is such a word). **1883** *Athenæum* 2 June 702/2 The old reputation of France as the true home of elegant bibliophily.

bibliophobia (ˌbɪblɪəʊˈfəʊbɪə). [f. BIBLIO- + Gr. -φοβία dread.] Dread of, or aversion to, books.

1832 DIBDIN (*title*), Bibliophobia, remarks on the present languid and depressed state of Literature.

bibliopoesy (-ˈpəʊɪsɪ). [f. BIBLIO- + Gr. ποιησία making.] The making of books.

1832 CARLYLE in Froude *Life* (1882) 310 Bibliopoly, bibliopoesy in all their branches are sick, sick, hastening to death.

bibliopole (ˈbɪblɪəʊpəʊl). [ad. L. *bibliopōla*, Gr. βιβλιοπώλης, f. βιβλίο-ν book + πώλης seller, dealer.] A dealer in books, a bookseller. **bibliopolar** (-ˈpəʊlə(r)), **bibliopolic** (-ˈpɒlɪk), **ˌbiblioˈpolical** *a.*, of or belonging to booksellers; hence **ˌbiblioˈpolically** *adv.* **bibliopolism** (bɪblɪˈɒpəlɪz(ə)m), the principles or trade of bookselling. **bibliˈopolist**, a bookseller (16th c.). **ˌbibliopoˈlistic** *a.*, of, pertaining to, or befitting a bookseller. **bibliopoly** (bɪblɪˈɒpəlɪ), **bibliopolery** (ˈbɪblɪəʊˌpəʊlərɪ), bookselling.

1775 JOHNSON in *Boswell* (1831) III. 220 He..kept a shop in the face of mankind, purchased copyright, and was a *bibliopole, Sir, in every sense. **1826** DISRAELI *Viv. Grey* II. xi. 55 The ancient and amusing ballad purchased..of some itinerant *bibliopole. **1822** BYRON in Moore *Life* (1866) 485 The *bibliopolar world shrink from his Commentary. **1825** *Blackw. Mag.* XVII. 477 It shows some *bibliopolic liberality. **1856** MASSON *Chatterton* II. iii. (1874) 187 The *bibliopolic powers of Paternoster Row. **1823** HONE *Anc. Myst.* Pref. 10 To a *bibliopolical friend I am indebted for the notice of the Castle of Good Preservance. **1834** *Fraser's Mag.* X. 363 The *bibliopolically baptised Contarina Fleming or the Wondrous Tale of Alroy. **1792** S. WHYTE in Hone *Table Bk.* I. 128 Initiation into the mysteries of *bibliopolism and the state of authorcraft. **1813** SHELLEY in *Contemp. Rev.* (1884) Sept. 388 With all the pomp of empirical *bibliopolism. **1541** *Guydon's Quest. Cyrurg.* ad. fin., Henry Dalbe stacyoner and *byblyopolyst in Poules churche yarde. **1852** HAWTHORNE *Blithed. Rom.* xvii. (1879) 171 A novel purchased of a railroad *bibliopolist. **1824** DIBDIN *Libr. Comp.* 340 A constant ingress and egress of *bibliopolistic Mercurii. **1831** *Fraser's Mag.* IV. 4 Similar complaints..from the highest quarters of *bibliopoly. **1881** RUSSELL *Hesperothen* I. 63 *Bibliopolery and bibliomania are rather rampagious in America.

bibliotaph (ˈbɪblɪəʊtæf). [a. F. *bibliotaphe*, f. BIBLIO- + Gr. τάφος tomb.] One who buries books by keeping them under lock and key. So **biblioˈtaphic** *a.*, **bibliˈotaphist** (Crabbe).

a **1824** D'ISRAELI *Cur. Lit.* (1866) 503/1 A *bibliotaphe* buries his books, by keeping them under lock. **1880** *St. James's Gaz.* 5 Nov. 14 The last species of 'enemy' treated of by Mr. Blades, is the 'bibliotaph' or book-burier.

bibliothec (bɪblɪˈɒθɪk), *a.* and *sb.* [f. next.] Belonging to a library or librarian; *sb.* a librarian.

[*a* **1641** BP. MOUNTAGU *Acts & Mon.* (1642) 152 Diodorus Siculus, that generall Bibliothec.] **1816** COLMAN *Lumin. Hist.* ix. in *Br. Grins* (1872) 309 Cadell..exclaimed in bibliothec state, 'Who sells great authors must himself be great.' **1859** CUNNINGHAM *Hist. Ch. Scotl.* II. 317 Never had a burgess of St. Andrews been capable of winning his bread by learning save one, and that was their present bibliothec.

bibliothec, library: see BIBLIOTHEQUE.

‖**bibliotheca** (ˌbɪblɪəʊˈθiːkə). [L. *bibliothēca* library, collection of books, ad. Gr. βιβλιοθήκη book-case, library, f. βιβλίον book + θήκη repository; used also by Jerome, and after him, commonly in med.L., for the BIBLE, being evidently in earlier literary use than *biblia*: hence OE. *bibliopéce* was the original name of the Bible in Eng.] **a.** (in OE.) The Scriptures, the Bible. **b.** *mod.* A collection of books or treatises, a library. **c.** A bibliographer's catalogue.

c **1000** ÆLFRIC *Test.* (Gr.) 16 Hieronimus ure biblioþecan ȝebrohte to Ledene of Greciscum bocum and of Ebreiscum. *Ibid.* 14 Se saltere ys an boc on ðære biblioþecan. *a* **1824** D'ISRAELI *Cur. Lit.* (1839) III. 344 Literary bibliothèques (or bibliothecas) will always present to us..an immense harvest of errors. **1879** MACLEAR *Celts* viii. 133 The Old and New Testaments, in the form of a Bibliotheca, or Bible.

bibliothecal (ˌbɪblɪəʊˈθiːkəl), *a.* [ad. L. *bibliothēcālis.*] Belonging to a library.

1811 W. TAYLOR in *Month. Rev.* LXIV. 131 The Bibliothecal shelves of pedants.

†**bibliothecar.** *Obs. Sc.* Also mod., in Fr. form, *bibliothecaire.* [See BIBLIOTHECARY *sb.* and *a.*] A librarian.

1581 N. BURNE *Dispot.* 97 a (JAM.) Anastasius, bibliothecar of the Kirk of Rome. [**1839** D'ISRAELI *Cur. Lit.* (1866) 502/2 The bibliothecaire is too delightfully busied among his shelves.]

bibliothecarial (ˌbɪblɪəʊθiːˈkɛərɪəl), *a.* [-AL.] = BIBLIOTHECARY *a.*

1889 *Athenæum* 27 Apr. 539/2 Of the two sets of terms that are so constantly confounded, one may be said to be bibliographical or scientific, the other bibliothecarial or practical. **1893** F. MADAN *Bks. in MS.* vii. 75 The one great bibliothecarial fact of antiquity is the Library of Alexandria. **1918** *Bodleian Q. Rec.* II. 156 So little has happened in Bodley in this Long Vacation that it is lawful to extravagate a little in Oxonian (and not purely bibliothecarial) pastures.

bibliothecary (bɪblɪˈɒθɪkərɪ), *sb.* and *a.* [ad. L. *bibliothēcārius, -um*; see BIBLIOTHECA and -ARY[1]. Cf. F. *bibliothécaire.*]

A. *sb.* †**1.** A library. *Obs.* [= L. **bibliothēcārium.*]

1553–87 FOXE *A. & M.* I. 5/1 Taken out of the Popes bibliothecary, a suspected place.

2. A librarian. [= L. *bibliothēcārius.*]

1611 CORYAT *Crudities* 477 Mr. James Gruterus the Princes Bibliothecarie. **1700** in *Misc. Cur.* (1708) III. 400 Il Signior Abbate Bencini, Bibliothecary of the Propaganda. **1887** O. W. HOLMES *Hundred Days* vi. 218 These two experts in books, the bibliopole and the bibliothecary.

B. *adj.* Of or belonging to a library or librarian.

1820 *Blackw. Mag.* VIII. 252 These biographical jewels should not lie locked up in a bibliothecary cabinet.

Hence **bibliotheˈcarian** *a.* and *sb.* = prec.

1685 tr. *Bossuet's Doctr. Cath. Ch.* Advt. 7 M. l'Abbe Gradi..Bibliothecarian of the Vatican. **1701** *Lond. Gaz.* No. 3708/4 Ecclesiastical Historians and Bibliothecarians. **1716** M. DAVIES *Ath. Brit.* III. 92 A third well orderd Bibliothecarian Closet of Medals.

‖**bibliothèque.** In 6 biblyotheke, 7 bibliotheicke, -theke, -thec, thek. [a. F. *bibliothèque*, ad. L. BIBLIOTHECA; formerly quite naturalized in Eng. (with -θeːk, θɛk), but now again treated as French (biblijɔtɛk).]

A library; a collection of books or treatises.

1549 BALE *Concl. Leland's Itin.* (T.) He [Alcuinus] muche commendeth a biblyotheke or library in Yorke. **1601** HOLLAND *Pliny* II. 523 Asinius Pollio, by dedicating his Bibliotheque, containing all the books that euer were written. *a* **1631** DONNE *Aristeas* 16 How many thousand volumes he had gotten together in his Bibliotheicke. **1657** COLVIL *Whigs Supplic.* (1751) 67 Tho' with these two ye join in one The bibliothec of Prester John. **1755** JOHNSON in *Boswell* (1816) 265, I intend in the winter to open a Bibliotheque.

fig. **1685** SIR G. MACKENZIE *Relig. Stoic* xi. 105 In the bibliotheck of his head.

bibliotherapy (ˌbɪblɪəʊˈθɛrəpɪ). [f. BIBLIO- + THERAPY.] The use of reading matter for therapeutic purposes in the treatment of nervous disorders.

1920 C. MORLEY *Haunted Bookshop* 10 The young man had heard of none of these books prescribed by the practitioner of bibliotherapy. **1929** *U.S. Veterans' Bur. Med. Bull.* V. 440 (*title*) Bibliotherapy; Use of Books as Form of Treatment in Neuropsychiatric Hospital. **1931** *Library Assoc. Rec.* June 198 The articles have been roughly arranged..according to the particular aspect of hospital library work with which they deal:—1. General Works. 2. Bibliotherapy. **1961** *New Scientist* 26 Oct. 253/3 Books on science..and..science fiction, appear to be the most effective types of reading matter in bibliotherapy.

bibliothetic (ˌbɪblɪəʊˈθɛtɪk), *a.* [f. BIBLIO- + Gr. θετικός concerned with placing or setting.] Relating to the placing and arrangement of books on the shelves of a library.

1901 E. C. RICHARDSON *Classification* 93 The systems for classifying books on the shelves of a library, which, if you need a technical name, may be called 'bibliothetic'. **1959** in L. M. HARROD *Librarians' Gloss.* (ed. 2) 37.

ˈBiblism [f. BIBLE + -ISM.] Adherence to the Bible as the sole rule of faith.

1879 M. ARNOLD *Equality, Mixed Ess.* 77 The mind-deadening influence of a narrow Biblism.

Biblist (ˈbaɪblɪst, ˈbɪblɪst). [f. BIBLE + -IST.] **a.** One who makes the Bible the sole rule of faith. **b.** A biblical student.

1562 A. SCOTT *New Y. Gift Quene*, And ar bot biblistis fairsing full their bellie. **1653** in *Phenix* (1708) II. 320 The Biblists..confess that a Man may not pray for the Holy Spirit as he ought. **1836** CDL. WISEMAN *Sc. & Relig.* II. x. 207 All the pretended improvements of modern biblists.

biblodge, biblodke, var. of BEBLOODY *v. Obs.*

‖**biblus, -os** (ˈbɪbləs, -əs). Also byblus. [L. *biblus*, Gr. βίβλος.] The papyrus or paper-reed; the inner bark of this plant.

1656 COWLEY *Davideis* I. Wks. 1710 I. 316 Some writ in tender Barks..Some in Beasts Skins, and some in Biblos Reed. **1863** LD. LYTTON *Ring Amasis* I. II. i. v. 261 Some crumbling byblus or papyrus. **1875** SCRIVENER *Lect. G.T.* 8 'Bring with thee the books' (of the *biblus* or *papyrus* plant).

†**biˈbod.** *Obs.* [OE. *bebod*, f. *bebéodan*, BIBEDE (pa. pple. *beboden*) to command.] Commandment.

c **1000** *Ags. Gosp.* Matt. xxii. 38 Ðis ys þæt mæste and þæt fyrmyste bebod. *a* **1175** *Cott. Hom.* 221 Gif þu þanne þis litle bebód to brecst. *c* **1175** *Lamb. Hom.* 125 Ðis is min bibode and min heste, þet ȝe luuian eou.

biˈborate. *Chem.*: see BI- *pref.*[2] III.

bibosity (bɪˈbɒsɪtɪ). [f. L. *bibōs-us* fond of drink + -ITY.] Capacity for drinking.

1823 *Blackw. Mag.* XIV. 528 Vast ideas of stupendous bibosity.

bibovine (baɪˈbəʊvaɪn), *a. Zool.* [f. BI-[2] + BOVINE *a.*] Designation of the group of bovine ruminants which includes the Oriental species, gaur, gayal, and banteng (forming the subgenus *Bibos*).

1889 NICHOLSON & LYDEKKER *Palæontol.* (ed. 3) II. lviii. 1351 The genus *Bos*..may be divided into the Bibovine and Taurine groups. In the former are included the wild Oxen of India and Burma. **1891** FLOWER & LYDEKKER *Mammals* ix. 365 The Bibovine group.

†**biˈbufenn, biˈbuven**, *adv. Obs.* [f. *bi-*, BE- + *bufen*, OE. *bufan*, later BOVE. If this had survived, it would have become BEBOVE.] = ABOVE.

c **1200** ORMIN 17970 Hе þatt fra bibufenn comm.

†**biˈbugh**, *v. Obs.* [OE. *bebúȝan*, f. BE- + *búȝan* to BOW.] *trans.* To avoid, abandon.

a **1000** *Elene* (Gr.) 609 Ne meahte he þa gehðu bebuȝan. *c* **1205** LAY. 8193 Al þat folc he bi-beah. *Ibid.* 10569 Æuere ælcne ut-laȝe þe his lond hadde bi-boȝen.

bibulate, *v.* [A bombastic or humorous diminutive from L. *bib-ĕre* to drink, with

reference to BIBBLE, BIBULOUS.] *trans.* To bibble or tipple. So **'bibulant** *a.* and *sb.*, **bibu'lation** *sb.*

1767 A. CAMPBELL *Lexiph.* (1774) 29 I bibulated [it]. 1828 *Blackw. Mag.* XXIV. 866 We bibulate gin and water with the housekeeper. 1883 *Boston Herald* Corresp., Bibulants will even buy alcohol, dilute it and drink it. 1882 *St. James's Gaz.* 12 Apr. 5 The extraordinary capacity for bibulation displayed by the regular soldier.

bibu'losity. [See BIBULOUS *a.* and -OSITY.] Addiction to tippling. Also **'bibulousness** (cf. BIBULOUS *a.* 1, 2).

1844 *Jrnl. R. Agric. Soc.* V. I. 125 Their colour;..their bibulousness; all these properties conspire to the determination of the temperature of a given soil. 1901 RASHDALL & RAIT *New College* 207 The common-room which Spence occasionally adorned could not have been wholly given up to uncultivated bibulosity. 1928 *Daily Express* 2 Oct. 6 He caught the man under the arm and affected a slight bibulousness himself.

bibulous ('bɪbjʊləs), *a.* [f. L. *bibul-us* freely or readily drinking (f. *bibĕre* to drink) + -OUS.]

1. Absorbent of moisture.

1675 EVELYN *Terra* (1729) 18 If the Soil be exceeding bibulous. 1790 COWPER *Odyss.* I. 138 With bibulous sponges those Made clean the tables. 1827 FARADAY *Chem. Manip.* ii. 43 Remove the excess by bibulous paper.

2. Addicted to drinking or tippling.

1861 THORNBURY *Turner* I. 116 The..irregular hours of a careless bibulous age, had undermined Girtin's health.

3. Relating to drink.

1825 *Blackw. Mag.* XVII. 322 Unskilled in bibulous lore, if he knows not the value set upon the claret of Ireland.

Hence **'bibulously** *adv.*

1858 DE QUINCEY *Goldsm.* Wks. VI. 226 The arid sands that bibulously absorbed all the perennial gushings of German enthusiasm.

biburien, variant of BEBURY *v. Obs.*

bicachen, bical, see BECATCH, BECALL.

bicalcarate (baɪ'kælkəreɪt), *a.* [f. BI- *pref.*² 1 + CALCARATE, f. L. *calcar* spur.] Furnished or armed with two spurs.

1876 HARLEY *Mat. Med.* 381 Anther..bicalcarate at base.

bicallose, -ous, bicapsular: see BI- *pref.*² 1.

bicameral (baɪ'kæmərəl), *a.* [f. BI- *pref.*² 1 + L. *camera* chamber + -AL¹; L. had *bicamerātus.*] Having two (legislative) chambers. **bi'camerist**, an advocate of two legislative chambers.

a 1832 BENTHAM is cited by WEBSTER. 1863 *Sat. Rev.* 140 [This] reduced our Houses to two, and..created that 'bi-cameral' system which the rest of the world has been content to imitate. 1872 FREEMAN *Growth Eng. Const.* ii. (1876) 97 The form of government which political writers call *bi-cameral.* 1884 GOLDW. SMITH in *Contemp. Rev.* Sept., The only valid argument in favour of the retention of the House of Lords is, in fact, the difficulty which the Bi-Camerists find in devising any [substitute].

bicarb (baɪ'kɑːb). Colloq. abbrev. of BICARBONATE (of soda).

1922 S. LEWIS *Babbitt* xxxiii. 361 Bad indigestion? Shall I get you some bicarb? 1947 WODEHOUSE *Full Moon* ii. 35 The sort of hangover which makes a man lose interest in anything but bicarb of soda. 1952 M. STEEN *Phoenix Rising* iii. 61 Tell me where I can find the bi-carb., and I'll mix you a charge that will jolt your ridiculous stomach into order.

bicarbide, -onate, -uret, etc.: see BI- *pref.*² III.

bicarinate (baɪ'kærɪneɪt), *a. Bot.* [f. BI- *pref.*² 1 + CARINATE, f. L. *carina* keel.] Furnished with two keels or axial ridges. So **bi'carinated.**

1872 OLIVER *Elem. Bot.* App. 310 The pale..bicarinate with inflexed margins. 1880 *Jrnl. Linn. Soc.* XV. 226 Shell ..conical, with bicarinated contracted whorls.

bicas, by chance: see CASE.

bicast(e, obs. form of BECAST.

bicaudal (baɪ'kɔːdəl), *a.* [f. BI- *pref.*² 1 + CAUDAL, f. L. *cauda* tail.] Having two tails.

bicause, obs. form of BECAUSE.

†**'bicched**, *ppl. a. Obs.* Also 5-6 **byched**, 6 **bychyde, biched.** Origin (see below) and precise meaning unknown: in general the sense 'Cursed, execrable, shrewed,' suits the context.

a 1400 *Alexander* (Stev.) 165 [The basiliske] A straȝtill and a stithe worme stinkande of elde, And es so bitter, and so breme, and bicchid in himselfe, That..quat he settes on his siȝt, he slaes in a stonde. *a* 1400 *Cov. Myst.* 395 Faste, harlotys, go youre gate, And brynge me that bychyd body, I red. 1522 *Worlde & Chylde* (Roxb.) C ij b, That bychyde Conscyence. 1533 MORE *Apol.* xxii. Wks. 884/2 Helpe me vp agayne with this bichede burdayne & lay it in my necke. —— *Debell. Salem* v. Wks. 941/1 Anye of the blessed byched newe broched bretherhead..playnelye proued heretikes.

b. *bicched bones*: opprobriously applied to dice.

c 1386 CHAUCER *Pard. T.* 328 This fruyt cometh of the bicched bones two, fforsweryng, Ire, falsnesse, Homycide [*So* 2 *MSS.*; 2 *read* bicche, 1 becched, *Wr.* bicchid]. *c* 1460 *Towneley Myst.* 241, I was falsly begylyd withe thise byched bones, Ther cursyd thay be. *Ibid.*, The byched bones that ye be, I byd you go bett.

[*Bicched* appears rather early to be certainly referable to BITCH in an opprobrious sense, from which moreover the formation is not easily explained (for *shrewed* there was a verb to *shrew.*) The conjecture has been offered that it was a contracted form of ME. *biwicced* 'bewitched'; but for this no evidence or analogy has been found. In *bicched bones* applied to dice, some have suggested a corruption of Du. *bikkel* 'knuckle-bone, astragalus, cockal, bone-plaything, dice, marbles,' Ger. *bickel* 'ankle, ankle-bone, astragalus, die, dice'; this is possible, but would suppose an Eng. series **bikkel*, **bicchel, bicche, bicched* bone, of which the most important links are neither represented nor accounted for, and it would only show assimilation of **bikkel* to the opprobrious *bicched*, leaving the latter unexplained. That *bicched bone* could be for a Du. **bikked been* 'bone picked with holes or pips,' is highly improbable: moreover, this would not connect the expression with Du. *bikkel*, since the latter (whether or not connected with *bikkel* a pickaxe, *bikken* to pick, or notch) certainly did not mean 'bone picked with holes,' but was a name of the ankle, and of the astragalus or knuckle-bone used in play, long before it passed over to dice. See Grimm s.v.]

bice (baɪs), *a.* and *sb.* Forms: 4-5 **bis**, 5-6 **byce**, 6 **byse, bysse, bisse, bize**, 5-7 **bise**, 6- **bice.** [a. F. *bis* brownish-grey, dark-coloured = Pr. *bis*, It. *bigio*; of unknown origin: see Diez and Littré. From the combination *azur bis* dark blue, 'blew byce,' *vert bis* dark green, 'green bice,' *bice* was erroneously transferred in Eng. to blue or green pigments, and the shades of blue or green which they yield.]

†**A.** *adj.* Brownish grey, dark grey. ***blewebis***: dark or dull blue. *Obs.*

1330 R. BRUNNE *Chron.* 230 At Westmynstere he lis toumbed richely, In a marble bis of him is mad story. *c* 1450 *Sloane MS.* 73 lf. 201 b, Triste wel þ^t it is not lapus lazuly, but it is lapis almanie of whiche men maken a blewe bis azure.

B. *sb.* (also *attrib.*) **1.** Short for *blewe bis* 'blue bice': indicating a shade of blue obtained from smalt, duller or inferior to ultramarine or azure, with which however it was often loosely identified.

c 1430 LYDG. *Bochas* IV. xv. (1554) 116 There is a difference of colours..Twene gold and gold, atwene bis and asure, All is not gold that shineth bright. 1490 *Will of Bukwell* (Somerset Ho.), Canapie colowrid with goold and bise. 1519 HORMAN *Vulg.* 81 b, Scryueners write with blacke, redde, purple, gren, blewe or byce. 1523 SKELTON *Garl. Laurel* 1158 The margent was illumyned with golden railles And byse. 1598 FLORIO, *Turchino*, blue, azure, watchet, or bisse colour. 1753 CHAMBERS *Cycl. Supp.*, *Bice* ..of all bright blues..is the palest in colour.

2. The pigment which yields this colour, prepared from smalt; also a green pigment (***green bice***) made by adding yellow orpiment to smalt.

1548 HALL *Chron.* 605 The Florishyng Bise was comparable to the riche ammel. 1573 *Art Limming* 4 Grinde azure or bize on a painters stone with clene water. 1634 J. BATE *Myst. Nature* 132 Colours to be used..blew and greene Bise. 1676 NEWTON in Rigaud *Corr. Sci. Men* (1841) II. 391 Red and blue powders (as Minium and Bice). 1875 URE *Dict. Arts* I. 341 Bice, a light blue colour prepared from smalt. There is a green bice prepared by mixing some yellow orpiment with smalt.

bicentenary (baɪ'sɛntɪnərɪ, -sɪn'tiːnərɪ), *a.* and *sb.* [f. BI- *pref.*² 1 + CENTENARY, ad. L. *centēnārius* consisting of or relating to a hundred, f. *centēni* a hundred each. As to the form and pronunciation, see CENTENARY.] **A.** *adj.* Consisting of or relating to two hundred (in use, confined to *years*, as if confused with *bicentennial*). **B.** *sb.* Used for: The bicentennial, or two hundredth anniversary (of an event); also *attrib.*

1862 *Congreg. Year Bk.* 72 The 24th day of August, 1862 the Bicentenary day of the ejectment of 2000 ministers. 1872 *Daily News* 18 June 5/5 The bi-centenary of Czar Peter's birth. 1884 *Athenæum* 4 Oct. 441/2 The bicentenary festival of the founder of Danish literature.

bicentennial (baɪsən'tɛnɪəl), *a.* and *sb.* [f. BI- *pref.*² 4 + CENTENNIAL, f. L. **centennium* (cf. *biennium*) space of a hundred years.] **A.** *adj.* Occurring every two hundred years; lasting two hundred years. Also, of or pertaining to a 200th anniversary; = BICENTENARY *a.*

1883 'MARK TWAIN' *Life on Miss.* 297 The bicentennial anniversary of this illustrious event. 1901 GOLDWIN SMITH *Let.* 18 Oct. in *Oxf. Univ. Gaz.* 12 Nov. 140/2 On my way to your [*sc.* Yale University's] bicentennial celebration I am unfortunately arrested by sickness. 1959 *Times* 13 May 5/1 She paid her homage to bi-centennial Handel.

B. *sb.* = BICENTENARY (and etymologically more correct than that word).

1883 *Harper's Mag.* Dec. 160/1 Bicentennial of German Colonisation in the United States.

bicephalous (baɪ'sɛfələs), *a.* [f. BI- *pref.*² 1 + CEPHALOUS, f. Gr. κεφαλή head.] Two-headed.

1803 WILLOUGHBY in *N. & Q.* Ser. III. III. 17 Two other bicephalous monsters. 1869 *Sat. Rev.* 13 Feb. 215 The bicephalous calf..of the showman.

biceps ('baɪsɪps), *a.* and *sb.* [a. L. *biceps, bicipit-*, f. *bi-* two + *-ceps* = *caput* head.]

A. *adj.* Having two heads or summits; *spec.* applied to muscles (see B).

1634 READ *Body of Man* 77 The I. muscle of the cubit, cald Biceps. 1717 BERKELEY in Fraser *Life* (1871) 588 In Strabo's time it [Vesuvius] seems to have been neither biceps, nor to have had a hollow. 1863 READE in *All Y. Round* 3 Oct. 123/2 A gentle timidity that contrasted prettily with her biceps muscle.

B. *sb.* A muscle with two heads or tendinous attachments; *spec.* that on the front of the upper arm, which bends the fore arm; also the corresponding muscle of the thigh; the former of these is often humorously referred to as the type or standard of physical strength.

1650 READ *Muscles of Body*, The ulna is bended by two [muscles], to wit, biceps and brachiæus internus. 1865 *Daily Tel.* 8 Nov. 4/5 The training which gives him back his healthy sleep, his appetite, and his biceps. 1873 MIVART *Elem. Anat.* viii. 293 The biceps is the well known muscle used in flexing the arm.

bich(e, obs. form of BITCH and PITCH.

†**bi'chant**, *v. Obs.* [f. *bi-*, BE- 4 + CHANT.] *trans.* To enchant, bewitch.

c 1330 *Arth. & Merl.* 721 And the eldest [soster] to bichaunte Yong mannes loue for to haunte.

†**bi'charre, bi'cherre**, *v. Obs.* Forms: 1 becerr-an, -cierran, -cyrran, 2-3 bicherr-en, 2-4 bicharren, 3 bichearr-en, bicheorr-en. [OE. *becęrran*, f. BE- 1 + OE. *cęrran, cięrran* to turn; cf. OHG. *bikêrjan*, mod.G. *bekehren.*]

1. *trans.* To turn, turn round. (Only in OE.)

a 1000 *Boeth. Metr.* xiii. 156 Wonne hio ealles wyrð utan becerred.

2. To turn from duty or right; to pervert, seduce.

a 1100 *O.E. Chron.* (Cotton MS.) an. 1011 Ælfmær hí becyrde þe se arceb' Ælfeah ær ȝenerede æt his life. *c* 1200 *Trin. Coll. Hom.* 105 þeh þe deuel muȝe man bi-charre, he ne mai no man neden. *c* 1305 *Old Age* in *E.E.P.* (1862) 149 Ic wene he be bi-charred þat trusteþ to ȝuþe.

3. To entice, wile.

c 1175 *Lamb. Hom.* 53 þurh þe sweate smel of þe chese: he bicherreð monie mus to þe stoke.

biched: see BICCHED.

bicherm: see BE- *pref.*

bichloride (baɪ'klɔəraɪd). *Chem.* [see BI- *pref.*² III.] A compound in which two equivalents of chlorine are combined with a metal, etc.

1810 HENRY *Elem. Chem.* (1826) II. 136 Bi-chloride of mercury..is a violent poison.

bichop, obs. form of BISHOP.

bichotomously, erroneously f. DICHOTOMOUSLY.

1830 LINDLEY *Nat. Syst. Bot.* 204 Cymes, branched bi- or trichotomously.

bichromate (baɪ'krəʊmət). *Chem.* [see BI- *pref.*² III.] **a.** A salt containing two equivalents of chromic acid, *e.g.* the ***bichromate of potash***, used in photography and other arts; whence **bi'chromated, bi'chromatized** *ppl. a.*

1854 SCOFFERN in *Orr's Circ. Sc.* Chem. 447 Heating bichromate of potash to whiteness. 1869 *Echo* 15 Dec., The bichromated gelatine. 1870 *Eng. Mech.* 14 Jan. 428/3 A second bichromatised film is poured upon the first.

b. *attrib.*, as **bichromate battery** or **cell**, a zinc-carbon cell containing an electrolyte of an acid bichromate solution.

1873 *Eclectic Engin. Mag.* VIII. 220/1 Next, I try the bichromate battery, without porous cells; small resistance, high potential, but soon losing its power..destroying itself by a single night's action. 1875 J. T. SPRAGUE *Electr.* iv. 108 The bichromate cell..furnishes a most powerful current for a very short time. *Ibid.* 111 The cost per unit is..2·16 with the simple bichromate solution. 1886 L. M. FISHBACK tr. *Niaudet's Electric Batteries* (ed. 4) viii. 213 (*heading*) Chemical action in the bichromate battery. 1892 *Daily News* 25 Oct. 3/1 Casting zinc rods for the bichromate cells.

bichrome ('baɪkrəʊm), *sb.*¹ *Chem.* [Shortened form of BICHROMATE.] Bichromate of potassium or sodium. Also *attrib.* (see quot. 1904).

1896 G. DUERR *Bleaching* iv. 56 The following colours.. require to be passed through a solution of bichrome in order to develop or raise the colours. 1904 *Westm. Gaz.* 31 Dec. 14/2 Another improvement..is the 'Bichrome' lamp, in which the light is filtered through a tank containing a solution of bichromate with certain selected aniline dyes.

bichrome ('baɪkrəʊm), *a.* and *sb.*² [f. BI-² + Gr. χρῶμα colour.] **A.** *adj.* Having two colours. **B.** *sb.* A two-coloured design, etc.

1921 M. C. BURKITT *Prehistory* xix. 265 Bichromes produced by restoring an animal painted in one colour in another. 1929 *Gryphon* (Univ. Leeds) Feb. 155 To hurl the completed bichrome palimpsest in my face with a hideous oath. 1948 KROEBER *Anthrop.* xviii. 830 Mochica ceramics are only bichrome. 1959 J. D. CLARK *Prehist. S. Afr.* x. 278 This monochrome group is followed by shaded polychromes and bichromes. 1960 K. M. KENYON *Archæol. in Holy Land* viii. 200 The decoration is bichrome, nearly always red and black.

bicipital (baɪ'sɪpɪtəl), *a.* [f. L. *bicipit-* (see BICEPS) + -AL¹.]

1. Having two heads; = BICEPS *a.*

1646 SIR T. BROWNE *Pseud. Ep.* 77 The bicip[i]tall muscle of either parties arme. 1843 J. WILKINSON *Swedenborg's Anim. Kingd.* I. ii. 59 Sometimes a bicipital muscle.

2. Of or pertaining to the biceps (muscle).
1831 R. KNOX *Cloquet's Anat.* 207 The bicipital tuberosity.

bicipitous (baɪ'sɪpɪtəs), *a.* [f. as prec. + -OUS.] Having two heads or terminal extremities.
1646 SIR T. BROWNE *Pseud. Ep.* III. v. 141 Bicipitous Serpents with the head at each extreme. *Ibid.* 140 A bicipitous conformation.

bi'circular, *a. Math.* [BI-[2] 1 and 2.]
Applied to a class of quartic curves each of which passes twice through each of the circular points at infinity, and thus resembles (analytically, and sometimes in form) a pair of circles.
1867 J. CASEY *Bicircular Quartics* in *Trans. R. Ir. Acad.* XXIV. I. 458 A bicircular quartic; that is, .. a quartic having the two circular points at infinity as double points. **1872** B. WILLIAMSON *Diff. Calc.* xi. 195 A curve of the fourth degree of the class called 'bicircular quartics'. **1879** G. SALMON *Higher Plane Curves* (ed. 3) 241 Quartics with two nodes, in the case where these are the circular points at infinity, have been extensively studied under the name of bicircular quartics. **1880** *Athenæum* 20 Nov. 678/3 Bicircular Quartics.

bick. Short for *bick-iron* (see BEAK-IRON) or BICKERN.
1896 *Farriers' Price List* Suppl., Farriers' Anvils, with Steeled Bick. **1953** A. JOBSON *Househ. Crafts* x. 112 The real hoops are made on a bick or beck-iron, which is an anvil mounted about 3 feet 6 inches high. **1957** R. LISTER *Dec. Wrought Ironwork* ii. 12 The pointed cone at the opposite end is variously called a *beak-iron, bickern, pike, bick, beak* or *horn*.

bick, Sc. form of BITCH, female dog.
1808 in JAMIESON. **1826** J. WILSON *Noct. Ambr.* Wks. 1855 I. 217 See how the wee bick is worrying him again now.

bicker ('bɪkə(r)), *sb.*[1] Also 5 biquere, 6 biquour. [Sc. form of BEAKER.] 'A bowl or dish for containing liquor, properly one made of wood.' Jamieson. Formerly, a drinking cup of any material; in modern Scotch applied also to vessels made of wooden staves for holding porridge, etc.
1458 *Will of Russel* (Somerset Ho.), Meum biquere argenti. *c* **1505** DUNBAR *Test. Kennedy* 47 But and I hecht to tume a Bicker. *a* **1774** FERGUSSON *Farmer's Ing.* Poems (1845) 37 The cheering bicker gars them glibly gash. **1814** SCOTT *Rob Roy* xxiv, 'It will be a heavy deficit—a staff out o' my bicker, I trow.' **1884** *U.P. Mag.* July 337 Coopers found employment in making or mending 'bickers' for brose or porridge.
b. *attrib.* and *comb.*, as *bickerful, bickermaker*.
1813 W. BEATTIE *Tales* 37 (JAM.) A brown bickerfu' to quaff. **1822** SCOTT *Pirate* I. 265 (JAM.) A bickerfu' of meal. **1851** J. M. WILSON *Tales Borders* VIII. 162 He followed the profession of a cooper or bicker-maker.

bicker ('bɪkə(r)), *sb.*[2] Forms: 3–4 biker, 4–5 bekir, bikre, bykkyr, 4–6 byker, 5 bekur, bikir, -kyr, bykere, bykker, bikkar, 6 bikker, bikar, 6– bicker. [ME. *biker*, like the associated verb *bikeren*, of uncertain origin: nor can it be said whether the sb. is derived from the verb or *vice versâ*. So far as evidence goes, the sb. appears earlier, and might, as in *battle, quarrel, skirmish*, be the source. On the other hand, the verb has the form of a frequentative, as in *sputter, totter, flutter*, etc., which is in favour of its priority. Mätzner and Skeat would see in it the freq. of the rare and somewhat doubtful *bike* '? to thrust, strike with a pointed weapon,' noted under BEAK *v.* 3, q.v. The obs. Welsh *bicra* is not native.]
1. Skirmishing; a skirmish, encounter, fight; exchange of blows.
1297 R. GLOUC. 538 Bituene the castel of Gloucetre & Brumefeld al so Ther was ofte biker gret, & muche harm ido. *c* **1400** *Destr. Troy* xx. 8363 Mony bold in the bekur were on bent leuit! **1440** *Promp. Parv.* 35/2 Bikyr of fytynge [**1499** bykere or feightinge], *pugna*. **1530** PALSGR. 198/1 Bicker fightyng, *escarmovche*.
2. *esp.* An encounter with missiles; anciently an attack with arrows; in later Sc., a street or school fight with stones and the like.
c **1470** HENRY *Wallace* IV. 547 Twenty he had yat nobill archars war.. On Wallace sett a bykker bauld and keyne. *c* **1505** DUNBAR *Gold. Terge* 145 A wonder lusty bikkir [*v.r.* bikar] me assayit. **1535** STEWART *Cron. Scot.* III. 322 With tha stanis thir stalwart carlis strang Ane bikker maid. **1810** SIR A. BOSWELL *Edinb.* 164 From hand and sling now fly the whizzing stones.. The bicker rages. **1861** J. HANNAY *Ess. fr. Q. Rev.* 371 He went to the High School, and joined in the street fights called bickers.
3. Quarrel, contention; angry altercation.
1330 R. BRUNNE *Chron.* 79 Gospatrik þat suffred biker, he reft boþe lond & liþe. *c* **1385** CHAUCER *L.G.W.* 2661 If thou sey nay we two shul have a bekyr [*v.r.* byker, biker, bekir, bikre, bykkyr]. *c* **1430** *Hymns Virg.* (1867) 46 Þe bolder in bikir y bidde him bataile. **1883** *Academy* 15 Sept. 175/2 The rise and progress of the colony, its bickers with autocratic Governors and Chief Justices.
4. Noise as of contention, rattle of light guns, sound of a rapid stream descending over a stony channel, etc. Cf. BICKER *v.* 4.
1870 *Daily News* 7 Dec., No bicker of mere field artillery. **1872** BLACKIE *Lays Highl.* 47 Leap the white-maned fountains With lusty bicker to the vale below.
b. *Sc.* A short rapid run.
1785 BURNS *Dr. Hornbook* v, Leeward whyles, against my will, I took a bicker.

bicker ('bɪkə(r)), *v.* Forms: 4–5 bi-, byker(e, 4 bi-, bykkir, -yr, 4–6 beker, -ir, 5 bekyre, bikre, bickre, byccer, -ker, bykre, -kir, bykker, -kyr, byger, 6 becker, bikker, -ar, 5– bicker. [See BICKER *sb.*]
1. *intr.* To skirmish, exchange blows; to fight.
1330 R. BRUNNE *Chron.* 256 Þan is tyme to bikere with þe kyng of France. **1393** LANGL. *P. Pl.* C. XXIII. 78 Ther to abyde and bykere · aȝeyns beliales children. *c* **1440** *Promp. Parv.* 36 Bekeryn or fyghtyn, *pugno, dimico*. **1630** J. TAYLOR (Water P.) *Wks.* I. 100/1, I have bickered with the French at Brest and Deepe. **1635** N. R. tr. *Camden's Hist. Eliz.* III. 231 After they had bickered together a little while.. and neither of them hurt, they dranke a carowse and so parted friends. **1848** KINGSLEY *Saint's Trag.* II. xi. 138 Slaughtered bickering for some petty town.
†**b.** Said esp. of archers and slingers, before battle was joined. *Obs.*
c **1400** *Destr. Troy* XVII. 7400 Paris.. With his bowmen full bold bykrit with the grekes. *c* **1470** HENRY *Wallace* IV. 556 Ynglis archaris.. Amang ye Scottis bykkeryt with all thair mycht. *c* **1505** DUNBAR *Gold. Terge* 194 Thay.. bikkerit vnabaisitly: The schour of arowis rappit on as rain. *c* **1534** tr. *Pol. Verg. Eng. Hist.* (1846) I. 67 Bee fore hand strokes thei firste bickered with dartes and slinges.
c. *fig.*
1593 *Bacchus Bountie* in *Harl. Misc.* (1809) II. 264 Bickering with the broth of bountifull Bacchus. **1647** W. BROWNE *Polex.* II. 46 They [passions] have not such ability as to bicker with absence.
†**2.** *trans.* To attack with repeated strokes; *esp.* to assail with missiles. *Obs.*
1352 MINOT *Poems* 51 A bore es boun ȝow to biker. **1375** BARBOUR *Bruce* IX. 152 Thair archaris.. thai send To bykkir thame. *c* **1400** *Destr. Troy* 10685 Þan he braid out a brand, bikrid hym hard. *a* **1550** *Christis Kirke Gr.* xix, The buschment haill about him brak And bikkerit him with bowis.
3. *intr.* To dispute, quarrel, wrangle.
a **1450** *Chester Pl.* (1847) II. 51 All againste us boote he not to becker. **1614** B. JONSON *Barth. Fair* v. iii, You'd have an ill match on't, if you bicker with him here. **1641** MILTON *Ch. Discip.* II. Wks. (1851) 46 Though their Merchants bicker in the East Indies. **1753** MISS COLLIER *Art Torment.* 157 To keep on bickering on this irksome subject, till you have put her in a passion. **1859** TENNYSON *Enid* 1174 Tho' men may bicker with the things they love.
4. *transf.* Applied to the making of any rapidly repeated noisy action, suggesting the showering of blows, as the brawling of a rapid stream over a stony channel, the pattering of rain, etc.
1748 THOMSON *Cast. Indol.* iii. 26 Glittering streamlets play'd.. as they bicker'd thro' the sunny glade. **1817** COLERIDGE *Sibyl. Leaves* (1862) 218 Against the glass The rain did beat and bicker. **1820** SCOTT *Monast.* ix, At the crook of the glen, Where bickers the burnie. **1855** TENNYSON *Brook* 26 And sparkle out among the fern, To bicker down a valley. **1874** HOLLAND *Mistr. Manse* v. 33 The swallow bickered 'neath the eaves.
b. *Sc.* To make a short quick run; describing the rapid vigorous action of the feet. Cf. *pelt, skelp*.
1792 BURNS *Wks.* II. 404 The dreary glen through which the herd-callan maun bicker. **1879** JAMIESON s.v., I met him coming down the gait as fast as he could bicker.
5. *poet.* Applied to the quick movement of flame and light: To flash, gleam, quiver, glisten. Cf. *flicker*.
1667 [see BICKERING *ppl. a.* 3]. **1813** SHELLEY *Q. Mab* IX. 154 The restless wheels.. Whose flashing spokes Bicker and burn to gain their destined goal. **1827** KEBLE *Chr. Y.* Matrim., Those fires That bicker round in wavy spires. **1859** TENNYSON *Enid* 1298 She saw Dust, and the points of lances bicker in it. **1876** BROWNING *Pacchiarotto* 150 And bicker like a flame.

bickerer ('bɪkərə(r)). [f. prec. + -ER[1].]
1611 COTGR., *Escarmoucheur*, a bickerer, skirmisher. **1755** in JOHNSON.

'bickering, *vbl. sb.* [f. as prec. + -ING[1].]
1. Skirmishing, a skirmish.
1297 R. GLOUC. 540 Ther was ofte bituene hom gret bikering. **1494** FABYAN VII. 373 Atwene theym were had many bykeringes and skyrmysshes. **1530** PALSGR. 197 Beckeryng, scrimysshe. **1622** HEYLIN *Cosmogr.* II. (1682) 198 The first bickering between the Soldiers of Cæsar and Pompey. **1670** MILTON *Hist. Eng.* II. Wks. (1851) 55 Then was the Warr shiverd.. into small frayes and bickerings. *a* **1763** BYROM *3 Black Crows* 19 Disputes of ev'ry size.. from bick'ring, up to battle. **1867** FREEMAN *Norm. Conq.* (1876) I. iv. 229 Smaller wars and bickerings still went on.
2. Wordy sparring, wrangling, altercation.
1573 G. HARVEY *Letter-bk.* (1884) 5 Ful oft hath he bene at gud whot bickerings with sum others. **1593** SHAKS. *2 Hen. VI*, I. i. 144 If I longer stay, We shall begin our ancient bickerings. **1742** RICHARDSON *Pamela* IV. 54 The Tears a poor Wife might shed in matrimonial Bickerings. **1821** SYD. SMITH *Wks.* (1867) I. 349 The parchment bickerings of Doe and Roe. **1882** E. GOSSE *Gray* iv. 81 The.. bickering which went on in the combination-room.

'bickering, *ppl. a.* [f. as prec. + -ING[2].]
1. That bickers; wrangling, contentious.
1808 J. BARLOW *Columb.* x. 60 With bickering strife inflame their furious bands. **1811** SCOTT *Roderick* I. xxxv, From court intrigue, from bickering faction far. **1843** CARLYLE *Past & Pr.* (1858) 80 Such waste-bickering Saxondom.
2. That makes a bickering sound.
1789 D. DAVIDSON *Seasons* 156 (JAM.) The once bick'ring stream.. low-growling, runs. **1821** JOANNA BAILLIE *Elder Tree* xvii. 3 Rattle the windows with bickering hail.
3. Coruscating, flashing, quivering.
1667 MILTON *P.L.* VI. 767 Smoak and bickering flame, and sparkles dire. **1786** tr. *Beckford's Vathek* (1868) 112 Their bickering sabres. **1825** SCOTT *Talism.* (1854) 475 Spread not the flax before a bickering torch. **1876** FARRAR *Marlb. Serm.* xxxiv. 343 Who.. played with the red fire and the bickering flames.

bickerment ('bɪkəmənt). [f. as prec. + -MENT.] = BICKERING *sb.*
1586 WEBBE *Eng. Poetrie* (Arb.) 46 Dreery byckerments of warres. **1682** BUNYAN *Holy War* 91. 25 Thus the bickerment went awhile: at last they passed from words to blows. **1876** BLACKIE *Songs Relig. & Life* 142 The priesthood.. rent the ears O' the fevered time with fretful bickerment.

bickern ('bɪkən). Forms: 6 bycorne, 8 bickhorn, 9 bickorne, 7– bickern. [a. F. *bigorne* (= Sp. *vigornia*, It. *bicornia*):—L. *bicornia*, pl. of *bicornis* two-horned, f. *bi-* two + *cornu* horn.] *orig.* An anvil with two projecting taper ends; *later* (under the influence of popular etymology; see BEAK-IRON) applied to: One such taper end of an anvil.
1547 SALESBURY *Welsh Dict.*, *Eingion gyrioc*, a bycorne. **1677** MOXON *Mech. Exerc.* (1703) 3 A Black Smith's Anvil.. is sometimes made with a Pike, or Bickern, or Beak-iron, at one end of it. **1781** J. T. DILLON *Trav. Spain* 145 They have no other word in the Spanish language for a bickhorn, or a bench vice, than *Vigornia*. **1814** *Archæol.* XVII. 292 And nails with a bickorne.

bickiron, var. BEAK-IRON.

bicky, bikky ('bɪkɪ). *colloq.* [dim. of BISCUIT; see -Y[6].] A diminutive or affectedly childish form of BISCUIT.
1930 R. BLAKER *Medal without Bar* iv. 303 Sammy.. said there was some breakfast. 'Only "bikkies" again, I'm afraid,' he apologised. **1947** *Mod. Lang. Rev.* July 356 Eng[lish] stands almost alone with *bicky* for 'biscuit'. **1954** C. P. SNOW *New Men* viii. 56 The Minister pulled out a bag.. It contained grey oatmeal cakes. 'Bikkies,' explained the Minister. **1955** B. MOORE *Judith Hearne* i. 11 Have a bikky, Bernie? **1963** M. ALLINGHAM *China Governess* xiv. 171 He's going to be asked to share Eustace's boiled milk and bickies.

bi-clagged, -clart, -clepe, come, etc.: see BE-CLAGGED, etc.

bicollateral (ˌbaɪkə'lætərəl), *a. Bot.* [BI-[2].] Of a vascular bundle: having two masses of phloem on opposite sides of the xylem. (See COLLATERAL A. 1 e.) Hence ˌ**bicoˌllate'rality**.
1881 *Encycl. Brit.* XII. 18/1 In *Cucurbita, Solanum*, and others the bundles are 'bicollateral', there being an additional phloem portion inside the xylem. **1882** VINES tr. *Sachs's Bot.* 949 *Bicollateral bundles*, in which.. there is a layer of phloëm on the inner as well as on the outer side of the xylem. **1884** BOWER & SCOTT tr. *De Bary's Phaner.* 319 A special subordinate form, to be called the double collateral or bicollateral, is distinguished from the usual one by the fact that two phloem groups lie on opposite sides of one xylem group. **1900** W. WALLACE in *Ann. Bot.* Dec. 640 Most Cucurbitaceæ have bicollateral bundles. *Ibid.* 641 Weiss adopts this conception of bicollaterality. **1953** K. ESAU *Plant Anat.* xv. 355 The presence of phloem on both sides of the xylem makes the bundle bicollateral.

bicolligate (baɪ'kɒlɪgeɪt), *a.* [f. BI- *pref.*[2] 2 + COLLIGATE, ad. L. *colligātus* bound together.] In *Ornith.* of the anterior toes of birds: United by a basal web; web-footed.
1847 in CRAIG.

bicolour, -color ('baɪkʌlə(r)), *a.* and *sb.* [ad. L. *bicolor* or F. *bicolore* adj.: see BI-[2].] **A.** *adj.* Having two colours. **B.** *sb.* A two-coloured blossom or animal.
1889 *Cent. Dict.*, *Bicolor* a., same as *bicolored*. **1898** C'TESS VON ARNIM *Elizabeth & Germ. Gard.* 56 The Persian Yellows and Bicolors have been, as I predicted, a mistake among the teas. **1911** R. C. PUNNETT *Mendelism* (ed. 3) vii. 74 The proportion in which the three classes of purples appeared was 9 bicolors, 3 deep purples, 4 picotees. **1931** *Antiquity* V. 430 The second variety of new faience beads are the bicolour inverted drop pendants. **1967** *Guardian* 18 Dec. 5/1 The Bi Colour Longhair, long observed about Britain, has only been recognised as a breed since 1966.

bicoloured, -concave, -vex: see BI- *pref.*[2] 1, 2.

biconditional (ˌbaɪkən'dɪʃənəl). *Logic.* [f. BI-[2] + CONDITIONAL *sb.*] The relation between two propositions when one is true only if the other is true, or false if the other is false; the symbolic or verbal representation of such a relation. Also *attrib.* or as *adj.*
1940 W. V. QUINE *Math. Logic* i. §3. 20 This binary mode of composition may be called the biconditional. **1941** —— in P. A. Schilpp *Philos. A. N. Whitehead* II. iv. 141 '≡' is the *biconditional* sign. **1950** —— *Methods of Logic* §3. p. 16 The idiom '*p* if and only if *q*', called the biconditional, amounts obviously to the conjunction of two conditionals, 'if *p* then *q*' and 'if *q* then *p*'. **1961** R. R. STOLL *Sets, Logic, &c.* ii. 58 The words 'if and only if' are used to obtain from two sentences a biconditional sentence. **1962** *Gloss. Automatic Data Processing* (*B.S.I.*) 30 Equivalence operation.. biconditional.

bicone ('baɪkəʊn). [f. BI-² + CONE *sb.*¹] An object having the form of two cones placed base to base; esp. of beads. Also *attrib.*

1928 H. C. BECK in *Archæologia* LXXVII. 7 Bicone. Beads in which the profile consists of two straight lines, at an angle to one another, which meet the perforation. *Ibid.* 25 (*caption*) Bicone fluted bead. Agate, Ur. **1931** *Antiquity* V. 428 The faience beads include all the simple forms such as oblate, spherical..bicone..and cylindrical. **1937** MOND & MYERS *Cemeteries of Armant* I. v. 70 It is often difficult to tell whether a bead is..a long barrel [or]..a long truncated convex bicone.

bi'conical, *a.* [f. BI-² + CONICAL *a.*] Similar in shape to two cones placed base to base. Hence **biconically** *adv.*

1870 ROLLESTON *Anim. Life* Introd. 71 The biconical cavity thus formed. **1875** *Encycl. Brit.* III. 775/1 Eggs of the Grebes..which also have both ends nearly alike but pointed, are so wide in the middle as to present a biconical appearance. **1881** *Jrnl. Linn. Soc.* XV. No. 87. 390 Shell..biconically fusiform. **1928** V. G. CHILDE *Most Anc. East* viii. 191 Biconical faceted beads. **1963** H. N. SAVORY in Foster & Alcock *Culture & Environment* iii. 42 The biconical Cinerary Urn of Hilversum affinity which accompanied the primary burial in the round cairn.

biconjugate (baɪ'kɒndʒ(j)ʊgət), *a.* [f. BI- *pref.*² 2 + CONJUGATE, ad. L. *conjugātus* united, paired.] Twice paired: applied *e.g.* in *Bot.* to a petiole that forks twice.

1847 in CRAIG. **1880** GRAY *Bot. Text-bk.* 398.

bicorn ('baɪkɔːn), *a.* (and *sb.*) [ad. L. *bicornis* two-horned, f. *bi-* two + *cornu* horn, prong.] **A.** *adj.* Having two horns or horn-like processes. **B.** *sb.* A two-horned animal; cf. *unicorn.*

[**1753** CHAMBERS *Cycl. Supp.*, Bicorne os, or two-horned bone, in anatomy, the same with the *os hyoides.*] **1823** LAMB *Elia, Vis. Horns*, Bicorns, Tricorns, and so on up to Millecorns. **1847–9** TODD *Cycl. Anat. & Phys.* IV. 209 The divided and bicorn uterus. **1872** NICHOLSON *Palæont.* 426 Rhinoceros Etruscus is also bicorn.

†**bi'corne.** *Obs. rare*⁻¹. In 5 bycorne. [a. OF. *bicorne*:—L. *bicorn-is* (see prec.) two-pronged (fork).] A two-pronged fork, a pitchfork.

c **1420** *Pallad.* I. 1161 Crookes, adses and bycornes.

bicorned ('baɪkɔːnd), *a.* [see -ED.] = BICORN.

1606 SYLVESTER *Columnes* Wks. 1879 I. 379 In form of Ram with golden Fleece they put The bi-corn'd Signe. *a* **1652** BROME *To Potting Pr.* (R.) Your body being revers'd did represent (Being forked) our bicorned government. **1859** TODD *Cycl.* V. 614 The..bi-corned condition of the uterus.

bicornous (baɪ'kɔːnəs), *a.* [f. as prec. + -OUS.] Two-horned; = BICORN.

1646 SIR T. BROWNE *Pseud. Ep.* (1650) 263 The letter Y, or bicornous element of Pythagoras. **1690** RAY *Philos. Lett.* (1718) 232 *Alpinum luteum* is..only bicornous. **1851** BALFOUR *Bot.* 625.

bicornute (ˌbaɪkɔː'njuːt), *a.* [f. BI- *pref.*² 1 + CORNUTE, ad. L. *cornūtus* horned.] = BICORN.

1880 in GRAY *Bot. Text-bk.* 398. **1881** *Jrnl. Linn. Soc.* XVIII. 312 The peculiar bicornute labellum.

bicorporal, -ate, -eal: see BI- *pref.*² 1.

bicrenate (baɪ'kriːˌneɪt), *a.* *Bot.* [f. BI- *pref.*² 3 + CRENATE.] Of (leaf-) margins: Crenate or scolloped, with the scollops themselves crenate.

1835 LINDLEY *Introd. Bot.* (1848) II. 358. **1870** BENTLEY *Bot.* 152.

bicrescentic, -cristate: see BI- *pref.*² 2.

bicrural (baɪ'krʊərəl), *a.* [f. BI- *pref.*² 1 + CRURAL, f. L. *crūs* (*crūr-*) leg.] Two-legged.

1847 in CRAIG.

bicultural (baɪ'kʌltjʊərəl), *a.* [f. BI-² + CULTURAL *a.*] Having or combining two cultures. So **bi'culturalism, biˌcultu'ration.**

1940 C. F. WARE *Cultural Approach Hist.* II. 67 The assumption of a single culture with a common language, rather than the bicultural tradition of Quebec. **1953** *Internat. Jrnl. Amer. Linguistics Memoir* VIII. 40 Weinreich considered Lounsbury's point important for bilingualism and biculturalism. **1955** W. E. COLLINSON in *Archivum Linguisticum* VII. 143 In..the socio-cultural setting of linguistic contact all kinds of different factors emerge, e.g...biculturation, religious differences, [etc.]. **1958** *Jrnl. Abnormal & Soc. Psychol.* LVI. 242/1 A comparison was made between those who acquired their two languages in geographically distinct cultures (bicultural experience) and those who acquired both languages in separated contexts within one geographical region (unicultural experience). **1963** *Times* 25 Feb. (Canada Suppl.) p. v/7 Officially Canada has been a bilingual and a bicultural country since 1867, but in fact this bilingualism and this biculturalism do not exist.

bicursal (baɪ'kɜːsəl), *a.* *Geom.* [f. BI-² + L. *cursus* course + -AL.] Of a curve: having two paths.

1873 CAYLEY *Math. Papers* (1895) VIII. 181 A curve of deficiency 1 may be termed bicursal. **1876** *Ibid.* (1896) IX. 582 The bicursal sextic has in general 9 nodes.

bicuspid (baɪ'kʌspɪd), *a.* and *sb.* [f. L. *bi-* two + *cuspid-em* point, spike, CUSP.] **A.** *adj.* Having two cusps or points. **B.** *sb.* A premolar tooth in man. **bi'cuspidate** [see -ATE] = prec. adj.

1836–9 TODD *Cycl. Anat. & Phys.* II. 533/1 From being more decidedly divided into two lips [this valve of the heart] is termed bicuspid. **1873** MIVART *Elem. Anat.* vii. 252 The fourth and fifth teeth of the lower jaw are called bicuspid molars. **1878** T. BRYANT *Pract. Surg.* I. 579 The enamel on the bicuspid. **1847** CRAIG, *Bicuspidate*, having two points. **1870** HOOKER *Stud. Flora* 417 Beak bicuspidate.

bicuspidal (baɪ'kʌspɪdəl), *a.* *Geom.* [f. BI-² + CUSPIDAL *a.*] Of a curve: having two cusps.

1867 CAYLEY *Math. Papers* (1893) VI. 528 A bicuspidal or Cartesian curve. **1879** G. SALMON *Higher Plane Curves* (ed. 3) 241 Quartics having the two circular points as cusps have also been much studied under the name of Cartesians, the properties of which may similarly be generalized and stated as properties of bicuspidal quartics.

bi-cweðe, obs. form of BEQUEATH.

bicycle ('baɪsɪk(ə)l), *sb.* [mod.f. (first in Fr.) BI- *pref.*² II. + Gr. κύκλος circle, wheel.] **a.** A machine for rapid riding, consisting of a saddle-seat surmounting two wheels, to which the rider communicates motion by means of treadles; a two-wheeled velocipede.

1868 *Daily News* 7 Sept., Bysicles and trysicles which we saw in the Champs Elysées and Bois de Boulogne this summer. **1869** MRQ. HARTINGTON in *Daily News* 14 May, The practice of riding or driving upon bicycles does not form any part of the examination of the Civil Service Commissioners.

b. *attrib.* and *Comb.*, as ***bicycle-basket, -gymkhana, -lamp, -polo, -pump, -race, -ride, -riding, -shed, -trade, -tyre***; **bicycle-chain**, the chain which transmits the driving power from the pedals of a bicycle to its rear wheel; also, one used as a weapon in gang-warfare, etc.; **bicycle-clip**, a clip used to hold a cyclist's trouser-leg firmly around the ankle; **bicycle-rickshaw**, a rickshaw drawn by a person on a bicycle.

1870 *Belgravia* X. 445 A novel feature in connection with bicycle races is taken from a donkey race... A prize is frequently given for the rider who can go, say, 100 yards in the *longest time. Ibid.* 446 Physicians of all nations have had time to judge of the effects of bicycle-riding on the human frame. **1882** *Pall Mall G.* 20 June 5/2 The bicycle trade is particularly brisk. **1896** Bicycle gymkhana [see GYMKHANA]. **1897** *Illustr. London News* 27 Mar. 433 (Advt.), The 20th century bicycle lamp. **1898** G. B. SHAW *Let.* 7 May in J. Dunbar *Mrs. G.B.S.* (1963) x. 169, I went for a bicycle ride. **1899** M. BEERBOHM *Around Theatres* (1924) I. 59 We watched four..men riding round the stage on bicycles and trying to project with their front-wheels a small ball into one or other of two small goals. 'Bicycle Polo' was the name given to this cheerful pastime. **1899** W. JAMES *Talks* 222 Just as a bicycle-chain may be too tight, so may one's carefulness and conscientiousness be so tense as to hinder the running of one's mind. **1905** E. M. FORSTER *Where Angels fear to Tread* iv. 104 There were bicycle gymkanas, and on the 30th Mrs Herriton would be holding the annual bazaar..for the C.M.S. **1907** *Yesterday's Shopping* (1969) 124/1 Bicycle Baskets, for fixing to handle-bar of Bicycle. **1908** *Sears, Roebuck Catal.* 170/2 Bicycle Pumps..including hose connection which will fit all valves. **1922** H. WILLIAMSON *Dandelion Days* 157 If you had a pin stuck..in a bicycle tyre. **1923** R. MACAULAY *Told by Idiot* x. 97 Her bicycle basket was full of primroses. *a* **1930** D. H. LAWRENCE *Phoenix II* (1968) 177 Do you think he'd flown over, with bicycle-clips round his trouser-ankles and spots of mud on his nose? **1936** *Punch* 12 Aug. 190/2 He [*sc.* the Headmaster] was venturing to ask friends of the School for subscriptions towards the cost of a new bicycle-shed to replace the old one. **1939** C. DAY LEWIS *Child of Misfortune* II. i. 144, I could hear you playing bicycle-polo in the yard below. **1960** KOESTLER *Lotus & Robot* I. i. 78 The bicycle-rickshaw—whose half-starved operator must pedal single-legged up to four passengers. **1960** C. DAY LEWIS *Buried Day* vi. 124 Thomas Hardy..was living only a bicycle-ride away. **1962** *John o'London's* 1 Nov. 404/2 The bicycle-chain Teds. **1963** P. M. HUBBARD *Flush as May* i. 11 The constable..took out a pair of bicycle clips, which he adjusted round his ankles.

'bicycle, *v.* [f. prec.] To ride on a bicycle.

1869 [cf. BICYCLING]. **1883** *Harper's Mag.* Apr. 692/2 Many enterprising souls..would have..bicycled, or canoed.

Hence **'bicycler, bicyclian, 'bicycling.**

1869 *Latest News* 5 Sept. 15 (*paragraph heading*), Bicycling. **1876** B. RICHARDSON in *Good Wds.* 716 Rowing, or gymnastics, or bicycling. **1880** *Scribn. Mag.* Feb. 497 Bicyclers sped along its shore. **1880** J. G. DALTON *Lyra Bicyclica*, Bicyclian bards. **1884** *Harper's Mag.* Jan. 304/2 You wish to be a bicycler.

bicyclette (baɪsɪ'klɛt). [Fr., dim. of *bicycle.*] A low-wheeled or safety bicycle (see SAFETY 9).

1895 *Columbus* (Ohio) *Dispatch* 17 Jan. 4/3 There were two-seated and four-seated vehicles and a petroleum bicyclette. **1895** *Blackw. Mag.* Nov. 646/2 If Nature..be more to you than bicyclettes and German bands.

bicyclic (baɪ'sɪklɪk), *a.* [f. BICYCLE *sb.* + -IC.] Of or connected with bicycles. So **bicyclical.**

1876 *Daily News* 8 Nov. 5/3 Parties of bicyclic enthusiasts.

'bicyclism. [see -ISM.] The practice or art of bicycling.

1876 *World* V. 12 That *ne plus ultra* of snobbishness—bicyclism. **1881** *Philada. Rec.* No. 3466. 2 Great and valuable principles are emphasized by bicyclism.

bicyclist ('baɪsɪklɪst). [see -IST.] One who rides a bicycle.

1869 *Porcupine* XI. 72/3 Jeered and hooted by the mob, the 'bicyclists' pushed along. **1876** *Daily News* 8 Nov. 5/2 Bicyclists sometimes make themselves a dangerous nuisance. **1881** *Philada. Rec.* No. 3466. 2 The bicyclist realizes..the old myth of the Centaur.

bicycular (baɪ'sɪkjʊlə(r)), *a.* [f. BICYCLE, after *vehicular.*] Of the nature of a bicycle or pertaining to bicycling.

1869 *Sci. American* 20 Feb. 117 Her skilful management of the bicycular velocipede. **1886** *Cyclist* 21 Apr. 618/2 Matters bicycular appear to be progressing..in Norway.

bid (bɪd), *v. str.* Pa. t. bad, bade, (bæd), bid. Pa. pple. bidden, bid. Here there are combined two originally distinct verbs; viz.

I. *béodan*; *beden, bede.* Forms: 1 béodan, 2–3 beoden, 3–5 beden, 3–6 bede, 4–5 beede, 7 *dial.* bede. *Pa. t. sing.* 1 béad, 2–3 bead, 2–4 bed, 3–4 bedd, 4–5 bede; also 3–6 bod, 4–6 bode. *pl.* 1 budon, 2–3 buden; also 3–4 bedde(n, 4 bede, beode, 5 beede; also 3–4 boden, 5–6 bode. *Pa. pple.* 1–6 boden, 4 -in, -un, 4–5 -yn, bode, 5 bodden, -yn, 6 bouden, bod, 9 *dial.* bodden, *Sc.* budden.

II. *biddan*; *bidden, bidde*; *bid.* Forms: 1 biddan, 2–5 bidden, (2–3 biden, 3 bedden), 3–6 bidde, 4–6 bydde, (4 bedde, bide), 4–5 bidd, 4–6 byd, (5 byde), 4– bid. *Pa. t. sing.* 1 bæd, 2–9 bad, 3–5 badd, 4 baad, 4–6 badde, (6 *Sc.* bald), 4– bade; also 3–6 bed, 4 bedd, 5 bede, *Sc.* baide; also 6 bidde, bydd, 7–9 bid. *pl.* 1 bǽdon, 2–3 beden, 3–5 bede; also 3 badden, 4–5 baden, 4–9 bad, bade; also 6–9 bid. *Pa. pple.* 1–5 beden, 3–5 -in, -yn, (y)bede, 4–5 bedun, 4 bedd; 3– bidden, (4 -in, 5 bed, byden, 6 bad), 7–9 bid.

[I. OE. *béodan, béad, budon, boden,* = OS. *biodan* (MDu. and Du. *bieden*), OHG. *biotan* (MHG. and mod.G. *bieten*), ON. *bioða*, Goth. *biudan* (pa. t. *bauþ, budum,* pple. *budans*):—OTeut. **beudan* 'to stretch out, reach out, offer, present,' hence 'to communicate, inform, announce, proclaim, command'; pre-Teutonic **bheudh-*, cogn. with Skr. *budh* to present, and perh. with Gr. πυθ- (for φυθ-) in πυθέσθαι 'to inform oneself.' From the pa. pple. *boden* was derived the sb. *boda* messenger, whence the vb. *bodian* to BODE, announce. The normal ME. forms were *bēde(n*, pa. t. *bead, bēd, beed*, pl. *buden*, pa. pple. *boden.* But by form-levelling, the pa. t. had also pl. *bēden, bēd(e* from the sing.; and later also *bod(e*, by assimilation to the pa. pple.

II. OE. *biddan, bæd, bǽdum, beden,* = OS. *biddian* (MDu. and Du. *bidden*), OHG. and mod.G. *bitten*, ON. *biðja*, Goth. *bidjan* (pa. t. *baþ, bêdum,* pple. *bidans*):—OTeut. **bidjan*, assigned to a pre-Teutonic **bhedh-* 'to press' (cf. Skr. *bâdhate* to press), whence the senses 'to ask pressingly, beg, pray, require, demand, command.' (Osthoff would connect *bidjan* with Gr. πείθω.) The normal ME. forms were *bidde(n*, pa. t. *bad*, pl. *beaden, bede(n*, pa. pple. *beden.* By form-levelling the pa. t. had also occasionally sing. *bead, bēd, beed*, and at length pl. *baden, bade, bad*; and the pa. pple. became *bidden*, whence also a later pa. t. *bid.*

III. Thus the sense 'command' had been developed in both verbs already in OE. The past tenses were further confused in form in ME. The result was the frequent substitution of the forms of one verb for the other, in other senses also, and their total confusion after 1400–1500. As a whole, the forms of *biddan, bid* are those which survive in literary Eng., but in the dialects these are quite mixed, in such conjugations as *bid, bad* or *bod, bodden* or *budden.* Senses survive from both verbs, though mostly archaic, or in certain unanalysed phrases, as to 'bid farewell,' 'bid a truce,' 'bid fair'; the chief modern use is that of 'bid at an auction,' 'bid for votes or support,' which belongs to *bede.* The senses of 'invite' and 'order' are in every-day use in the north, but archaic in southern speech, where 'bid him do it' is regularly made 'tell him to do it.' Particular forms of the pa. t. and pa. pple. are preferred with particular senses.]

I. Senses originating from OE. *béodan*, ME. *bede*, (but taking eventually the form *bid*).

The *bede* quotations are marked α, the *bid* quotations β.

* To offer, present.

†**1. a.** *trans.* To offer. *Obs.* in the general sense.

α. *a* **1000** *Cædmon's Gen.* (Gr.) 2435 Hafa árna þanc ðara, ðe ðu unc bude. *c* **1000** ÆLFRIC *Deut.* xx. 10 Beod him ærest sibbe. *a* **1225** *Ancr. R.* 156 Heo wule..ȝein þe smitare beoden uorð hire cheoken. *a* **1240** *Ureisun* in *Cott. Hom.* 201

þu beodest þin elning al wið-ute bone. c1250 *Gen. & Ex.* 1069 Loth hem bead is doȝtres two. a1300 *Cursor M.* 12360 Leons..bede til him þus þair seruise. c1386 Chaucer *Clerkes T.* 304 Thilk honour that ye me bede. c1440 *York Myst.* ix. 170 Som bote us bede.

β. c1250 *Gen. & Ex.* 2653 He bad ðis child brennen to colen. c1430 *How Gd. Wijf tauȝte D.* 32 in *Babees Bk.* (1868) 39 If ony man biddiþ þe worschip, and wolde wedde þee. c1435 *Torr. Portugal* 794 A knyghtes dowghttyr wase hym bed.

†**b.** *intr.* with *dative infin. Obs.*

α. a1225 *Ancr. R.* 390 He..bead for to makien hire cwene of al þet he ouhte.

†**c.** *spec.* (*trans.*) To offer (treatment); *intr.* to offer to act. *Obs.* With *dat.* of person.

α. c1175 *Lamb. Hom.* 13 Þet uuilc mon scal beoden oðre alswa he wile þet me him beode. 1314 *Chart.* in Arnold *Chron.*, I nyl suffer, yt ony man you any wrongis beed.

2. a. *trans.* †*to bid* (any one) ***battle, arms***: to offer battle to, challenge to fight. *Obs.* ***to bid defiance*** (still in use). (With pa. t. *bade*, pple. *bidden*.)

α. a1300 *Cursor M.* 7472 Ilk dai he come..and batail bede [*v.r.* bed, bedd] wiþ sli[k] manace. c1330 *K. of Tars* 1018 Uppon the soudan thei bede bataile. c1450 Lonelich *Grail* xlvi. 517 Aȝens the miscreantz bataille to bede.

β. 1570 *Marr. Wit. & Sc.* iv. i. in Hazl. *Dodsl.* II. 364 When you feel yourself well able to prevail, Bid you the battle. 1590 Marlowe *2nd Pt. Tamburl.* ii. ii, An hundred Kings..will bid him arms. 1611 Speed *Hist. Gt. Brit.* vii. xlv. 371 Edmund..two dayes after at Brentford bad them battaile. 1626 Massinger *Rom. Act.* iv. i, We, undaunted yet..bid defiance To them and fate. 1639 Fuller *Holy War* ii. xxxvi. (1840) 98 Whom he bade battle, and got the day. 1848 Macaulay *Hist. Eng.* II. 15 That spirit which had bidden defiance to..the House of Valois.

†**b.** *ellipt.* To challenge, defy. *Obs.*

α. 1375 Barbour *Bruce* vii. 103, I trow he suld be hard to sla, And he war bodyn all evynly.

†**c.** ***to bid the base***: to challenge to a run at prisoners' base; hence *fig. Obs.* See base *sb.*²

β. 1591 Shaks. *Two Gent.* i. ii. 98 Indeede I bid the base for Protheus.

3. a. *trans.* To offer (a certain price) *for*, to offer as a price one is prepared to give *for*. (Sometimes with dative obj. of person: 'you bid me too little.')

¶ In this sense the pa. t. and pa. pple. are now *bid*; Scotch writers retain the past, *bad, bade*, used by Dr. Johnson.

α. c1200 *Trin. Coll. Hom.* 213 Þe sullere loueð his þing dere..þe beȝer bet litel þar fore. 1297 R. Glouc. 378 He sette hys londes to ferme wel vaste Wo so mest bode vore.

β. c1470 Henry *Wallace* ii. 38 For a strak he bad hym grottis thre. 1530 Palsgr. 454/2 You bydd me money and fayre wordes. 1602 Shaks. *Ham.* ii. ii. 372 There was..no mony bid for argument. a1704 T. Brown *Two Oxf. Scholars* Wks. 1730 I. 9 If I..farm out my Tythes, my Parishioners will bid me half the worth of them. 1751 Johnson *Rambl.* No. 161 ⁋10 [They] bade her half the price she asked. 1832 Ht. Martineau *Each & All* iii. 37 Starving thousands..bid their labour against one another for bread. *Mod.* Who bids five shillings for this lot?

b. *intr.* (*ellipt.*) To offer (any one) a price, to make an offer (*for* a thing), as 'to bid at an auction.' ***to bid against*** (a person): to compete with (him) in offers. Often *fig.* as in 'to bid for the Irish vote.' Also with indirect pass., ***to be bid for***; and with complemental object, ***to bid*** (a thing) ***up***: to raise its price by successive bids.

β. 1611 Shaks. *Cymb.* iii. vii. 71, I bid for you, as I do buy. 1776 Adam Smith *W.N.* I. 90 Masters bid against one another in order to get workmen. 1777 Sheridan *Sch. Scand.* v. iii, I stood a chance of..being knocked down without being bid for. 1848 Macaulay *Hist. Eng.* I. 669 The intolerant king and the intolerant church were eagerly bidding against each other for the support of the party. 1851 J. M. Wilson *Tales Border* XX. 256 Some other individuals bade, and the bodes had arrived at £14,000. 1864 Burton *Scot. Abr.* ii. 264 They bade them up until they reached 10,000 livres.

c. *Card-playing.* (*a*) *intr.* To make a bid (see bid *sb.* 2). (*b*) *trans.* To make a bid of or in (a number of tricks, a specified suit, etc.). Cf. declare *v.* 11 c.

1880 'Trumps' *American Hoyle* 229 When the eldest hand makes a bid of five or more tricks, and another player bids the *same number* of tricks, the eldest hand may bid over him, or abandon his bid. 1897 R. F. Foster *Complete Hoyle* 270 If a player proposes to win all five tricks he bids *nap*, which is the highest bid possible. 1908 L. Hoffmann *Five Hundred* 14 A player who has once 'passed' cannot again bid. 1910 *Encycl. Brit.* IX. 878/1 *Bid Euchre*... Each player 'bids', *i.e.* declares and makes a certain number of tricks. 1929 [see biddable *a.* 2]. 1933 C. Vandyck *Contract Contracted* i. 15 If there have been two no-bids before your turn to bid, you should [etc.]. *Ibid.* ii. 17 Always bid a suit in preference to No Trumps. 1958 [see bidding *vbl. sb.* 1 b].

4. *intr.* ***to bid fair***: to offer with reasonable probability, to present a fair prospect, seem likely. Orig. with *for* and object; now also with *infin.* (With pa. t. *bade*, pa. pple. *bidden*.)

β. 1646 S. Bolton *Arraignm. Err.* 360 Two things would bid fair for it, if not wholly accomplish this desired accommodation. 1738 J. Keill *Anim. Œcon.* 24 The Bones of all the Parts..seem to bid the fairest for Solidity. 1786 T. Jefferson *Corr.* (1830) 4 The present reign bids fair to be a long one. 1869 Freeman *Norm. Conq.* (1876) III. xiv. 334 The proposed expedition..bade fair to be successful.

** To announce, proclaim, threaten.

†**5. a.** To proclaim, announce. *Obs.* exc. in one or two arch. phrases, as 'to bid the saints' days': see 1725. In ***bid the banns***, it is doubtful whether the original sense was 'proclaim,' or 'ask' as in 7; the phrase seems to go back only to the 16th c., and thus exists only in the β form.

α. a1000 *Guthlac* (Gr.) 716 Geácas ȝear budon. c1340 *Cursor M.* 13363 (Fairf.), A bridale was þer bodin an. 1398 Trevisa *Barth. De P.R.* xii. viii, [The stork] is messanger of spryngynge tyme, and in hire comynge sche bedeþ [1535 tokeneth, *Lat.* prædicat] nouelte of tyme. c1440 *Morte Arth.* (Roxb.) 2 A turnement the kinge lett bede.

β. 1483 *Cath. Angl.* 31 To byde halydayes, *Indicere.* 1599 Bp. Hall *Sat.* iv. i. 124 Go bid the baines and point the bridall day. 1622 Sparrow *Bk. Com. Prayer* (1661) 150 Upon the Sundaies before these Fasts, the Priests..bid the solemn Fast. 1725 Pope *Odyss.* xvii. 148 The herald..To bid the banquet interrupts their play. 1725 tr. *Dupin's Eccl. Hist. 16th C.* I. v. 67 This Custom of bidding the Passover on the Day of the Epiphany. 1603 —— *Const. & Canons Ch. Eng.* 64 Ministers solemnly to bid Holy-days.

†**b.** To proclaim, declare, threaten (war). *Obs.* Preserved in *to bid a truce* (in *fig.* sense).

α. 1330 R. Brunne *Chron.* 49 Now is Eilred biried, þat mykelle wo beade [*printed* bade].

β. c1590 *1st Pt. Jeronimo* in *Dodsley* (1780) III. 77, I bid you sudden wars. 1596 Chapman *Iliad* i. 155, I was not injur'd so By any Trojan, that my powers should bid them any blows. 1805 Southey *Madoc in Azt.* iii, At this late hour, When even I shall bid a truce to thought.

†**6.** To make known, indicate, declare. *Obs.*

α. a1300 *Cursor M.* 8026 (Gött.), þat stede þat him was bodin in his bede. c1430 *Syr Gener.* 1160 The Quene..most nede To Generides hir folie bede.

II. Senses originating from OE. *biddan*, (afterwards occasionally expressed by forms from *bede*).

*** To ask pressingly.

7. To ask pressingly, beg, entreat, pray.

†**a.** *trans.* with acc. of person and genitive of thing; with dative of person and acc. of thing; passing into two objects. *Obs.*

c893 K. Ælfred *Oros.* vi. xxxiv. §4 Hi hiene bædon ryhtes ȝeleafan and fulwihtes bæðes. 971 *Blickl. Hom.* 21 Ne bidden we urne Drihten þyses lænan welan. a1000 *Andreas* (Gr.) 353 Þá..Andreas ongann mereliðendum miltsa biddan. c1175 *Lamb. Hom.* 13 3e..helpes me biddað. c1200 *Trin. Coll. Hom.* 139 A maiden bad te kinge his heued. c1305 *St. Edward* in *E.E.P.* (1862) 106 Me ne scholde him noþing bidde.

b. To press, entreat, beg, ask, pray (a person). Const. *for* a thing, or *inf.*, *subord. cl.*, or *object sentence*; also *simply*, to pray to (God, saints, etc.).

c1000 *Ags. Gosp.* John iv. 31 His leorning-cnihtas hine bædon [*Rushw.* bedon] and þus cwædon. c1175 *Lamb. Hom.* 17 Bide hine lueliche þet he þe do riht. a1240 *Lofsong* in *Lamb. Hom.* 207 Ich bide þe..bi þe þornene crununge. c1250 *Gen. & Ex.* 2509 For godes luue ȝet bid ic ȝu..wið ȝu ben mine bones boren. 1297 R. Glouc. 337 Icham Swythyn, wam þou byst. a1300 *E.E. Psalter* cv[i]. 19 And a kalf in Oreb maked þai, And baden þe grave. c1300 *Beket* 1085 And wepinge ech halewe bad: hir help forto beo. c1314 *Guy Warw.* (MS. A.) 1628 Ich þe bidde, par charite þat þou this bodi vnder-fo. c1374 Chaucer *Troylus* iii. 826, I bidde god I neuere mot haue Ioye.

†**c.** To ask, beg (a thing); to ask, beg, or pray for. Const. *simply*, or *of, from* a person, etc. *Obs.*

971 *Blickl. Hom.* 21 Se blinda..bæd his eaȝena leohtes. c1000 *Ags. Gosp.* Luke xiv. 32 He sent ærynd-racan and bitt sibbe. —— Matt. xx. 20 Sum þingc fram him biddende. c1200 *Trin. Coll. Hom.* 103 Forlet þine sunnes..and bide milce þerof. c1250 *Gen. & Ex.* 3011 Moyses bad meðe here on. c1300 *Beket* 1678 Thider ich wole wende And bidde mi mete for Godes love. c1330 *Roland & V.* 534 Roland..þo bad leue to fiȝt. c1340 *Cursor M.* 19054 (Trin.) He bad of hem som gode. c1420 *Chron. Vilod.* 65, To haue of God what yt he bedde. 1513 Douglas *Æneis* xi. xv. 55, I ask na trophe..Nothir byd I therof spulȝe nor renown. [1678 Phillips App., To *Bid a boon* (old word), to ask a Boon.]

†**d.** *intr.* To beg, entreat, pray; to offer prayer. Const. *simply, for* a person or thing, *subord. cl.* or with *so, thus*, etc. *Obs.*

971 *Blickl. Hom.* 19 He..ȝeornor bæd þæt Hælend him miltsade. c1175 *Lamb. Hom.* 17 Bide for him duwamliche. *Ibid.* 167 He is wis þe beet and bit and bet bi-fore dome. a1225 *Ancr. R.* 228 Ure Louerd sulf..techeð us to bidden, 'Et ne nos inducas in tentationem.' c1300 *Beket* 423 We biddeth niȝt and dai For the. 1377 Langl. *P. Pl.* B. vii. 68 He þat beggeth or bit but if he haue nede, He is fals. 1387 Trevisa *Higden* (1865) I. 115 Criste went ynne ful ofte for to bidde and praye. c1400 *Prymer* in Maskell *Mon. Rit.* II. 11 Preie for the peple: bidde for the clergie. 1458 in *Dom. Archit.* III. 43 Now every good body that gothe on this brige, Bid for the barbour gentil Jeffray.

†**e.** *trans.* (with cognate obj.) To bid a *bene, bone, bede, prayer*, etc.: *orig.* to pray, or offer a prayer; *later* 'to move the people to join in prayer,' as in bidding prayer. *arch.*

c1175 *Lamb. Hom.* 67 Hu maȝen heo bidden eni bene. c1305 *St. Christoph.* 71 in *E.E.P.* (1862) 61 Þu most..to churche go: & þi beden bidde also. c1375 Wyclif *Serm.* Sel. Wks. II. 270 Men bidden to God þer preier. c1386 Chaucer *Milleres T.* 455 Stille he sitt, and biddeth his preyere. c1400 *Rom. Rose* 7374 A peire of bedis eke she bere Upon a lace, alle of white threde, On which that she her bedes bede. c1420 *Avow. Arth.* xiii, To Jhesu a bone he bede. 1535 Coverdale *Jer.* vii. 16 Thou shalt nether geue thankes, nor byd prayer for them. 1562 J. Heywood *Prov. & Epigr.* (1867) 108 Commaundid By his Curate his pater noster to bid. 1621 Bolton *Stat. Irel.* 134 (*Act 28 Hen. VIII*), [They] shall bid the beades in the English tongue. 1764 Gray in Mason *Life* (ed. 2) 381 And bidding his beads for the souls of his benefactors. [1859 Jephson *Brittany* ii. 15, I observed persons 'bidding their beads,' or engaged in silent devotion.]

α. Forms from OE. *beoden. Obs.*

c1250 *Gen. & Ex.* 3169 Quat-so he boden..Egipte folc hem lenen ðat. a1300 *Leg. Rood* (1871) 22 Bede him þat ich deie mote. 1330 R. Brunne *Chron.* 29 Þat he wild bede his bone, vntille þe Trinite. 1362 Langl. *P. Pl.* A. ix. 96 3if Dobest beede [*v.r.* bede, bidde] for [hem]. c1380 Wyclif *Wks.* (1880) 167 Bi louynge & bedynge as who wold selle a worldly þing. c1440 *Morte Arth.* (Roxb.) 90 An holy man had boddyn that bone. 1691 Ray *N.C. Words, Bid, Bede*, to pray.

8. To ask (any one) to come, to invite (*to* a feast, wedding, burial, etc.). *arch.* but common *dial.*

The double sense of bid is played on in Shirley's *Wedding* i. i, where Belface asks his servant Isaac whether he has invited the guests:—*Isaac.* I have commanded most o' them. *Belf.* How, sir? *Isaac.* I have bid them, sir.

α. a1225 *Ancr. R.* 414 Ane beggare..þet bede men to feste. a1300 *Cursor M.* 7250 Sampson was to þe bridal bedd. c1300 *K. Alis.* 5823 Alisaundre, and his meygnee, Comen, and badden hem entree. 1393 Langl. *P. Pl.* C. iii. 56 Al þe riche retynaunce..Were bede [*v.r.* beden, ibede, boden] to þat brudale. 1483 *Cath. Angl.* 31/1 To byd to mete, *Invitare.* 1577 Northbrooke *Dicing* (1843) 102 They vsed commonly to bidde their guestes a whole yeare before. 1580 Baret *Alv.* B 644, I was bidde to an other place to dinner. 1611 Bible, *Zeph.* i. 7 He hath bid his ghests. —— *Luke* xiv. 9 He that bade thee and him. 1632 Brome *North. Lasse* i. i. I hope you'l see our Marriage. I sent indeed to bid you. a1810 Tannahill *Kebbuckston Wed.*, I'se warrant he's bidden the half of the parish. 1842 Tennyson *Sisters* iii, I made a feast; I bad him come.

α. Forms from OE. *beoden. Obs.*

c1200 *Trin. Coll. Hom.* 159 We ben alle boden þider. 1377 Langl. *P. Pl.* B. ii. 54 Alle þe riche retenauns..were boden [*v.r.* bede, a-bede] to þe bridale. 1483 Caxton *Gold. Leg.* 209/2 Gladder therof than he were boden to a feste. 1541 Elyot *Image Gov.* 96 She bode the emperour unto a supper. 1546 Langley *Pol. Verg. de Invent.* ii. vi. 45 b, He was boden to a banket. 1864 Atkinson *Whitby Gloss.* s.v. *Bid*, I nivver was bodden.

9. In ***to bid welcome, adieu, farewell, good bye, good morning***, the original notion was probably that of 'pray,' 'invoke,' or 'wish devoutly'; the phrases are now used without analysis, 'bid' being little more than = 'say, utter, express.'

a1300 *Cursor M.* 15060 [Vr lauerd] biddes þe welcum hame. 1413 Lydg. *Pylgr. Sowle* ii. lxv. (1859) 59, I bad hym adyeu. 1485 Caxton *St. Wenefryde* 9 She toke leue of this holy man and bad hym fare well. 1579 Spenser *Sheph. Cal.* Sept. 1, I bidde her God day. 1593 Shaks. *Rich. II*, i. iv. 32 A brace of Dray-men bid God speed him well. 1632 Milton *L'Allegro* 46 At my window bid good morrow. 1711 Steele *Spect.* No. 27 ⁋4 He'll bid adieu to all the Vanity of Ambition. 1844 *Mem. Babylonian Pr'cess* II. 311, I now..respectfully bid the British public farewell.

α. 1600 Fairfax *Tasso* vii. xiii. 119, I bod the court farewell.

III. Senses originating independently from the two verbs. (Now referred in form to *biddan*.)

**** To command, enjoin.

10. To command, enjoin, order, tell with authority. (Still literary; also in every-day use in the north; but in the south colloquially expressed by *tell*, as 'tell him to sit down,' for 'bid him sit down.')

a. with personal obj. (sometimes absent), and clause with *that*, or object sentence.

α. 971 *Blickl. Hom.* 15 Þa fore-ferendan him budon þæt he swiȝade. 1398 Trevisa *Barth. De P.R.* vi. xxiv. (1495) 215 It is boden that they..sholde not slepe. 1598 Sylvester *Du Bartas* (1608) 385 And then he bod..That daily once they all should march the round About the city.

β. c1000 Ælfric *Ex.* xxxiii. 12 Ðu bitst me þæt ic læde ut tis folc. c1200 *Trin. Coll. Hom.* 41 He..bit us..þat we shule þis notien. 1297 R. Glouc. 29 Ich bidde þe Sey me al clene þin herte. a1400 *Relig. Pieces fr. Thornton MS.* 2 He byddes ..þat þay here and lere þise ilke sex thynges. c1460 *Towneley Myst.* 50 Another [commandment] bydes thou shall not swere. a1520 *Myrr. Our Ladye* 89 The same Pope ordeyned and badde that so yt shulde be done. 1593 Shaks. *Rich. II*, i. i. 164 Obedience bids I should not bid agen.

b. with personal obj., and infin.

α. c1200 *Trin. Coll. Hom.* 87 Þis laȝe sette ure drihten bi þe patriarche abraham, and bed him holden hit. c1250 *Gen. & Ex.* 3544 Aaron and vr..boden hem swilc ðhowtes leten. a1300 *K. Horn* 504 Horn he bidde knighte..And bed him beon a god kniȝt. c1375 Wyclif *Serm.* Sel. Wks. I. 259 As God haþ bodyn hem to do. c1400 *Destr. Troy* ii. 389 The Kyng..Bede his doughter come downe. 1477 Earl Rivers (Caxton) *Dictes* 57 He that wil holde his peas till he be boden speke is to be preysed. 1529 More *Comf. agst. Trib.* iv. Wks. 263/1 Who hath not bod them do wel. 1592 Warner *Alb. Eng.* viii. xli. 199 He bod me buy thy loue.

β. c1175 *Lamb. Hom.* 109 Godes laȝe bit ec mon wurðie efre his feder and his moder. c1200 *Trin. Coll. Hom.* 139 Þe king..bad binden him · and don him into prisune. a1300 *Cursor M.* 3177 Þe angel..bade him..tak A scepe his sacrifice to mak. c1470 Henry *Wallace* iv. 763 He..baide hyr haiff no dreide. 1549 *Compl. Scot.* vi. 40 The maister bald the marynalis lay the cabil to the cabilstok. 1581 Marbeck *Bk. Notes* 91 Christ bidde the Church to baptise in the name of the Father, the Sonne and the holie Ghost. 1592 Shaks. *Rom. & Jul.* ii. v. 83 Thou..bad'st me bury Loue. 1684 Bunyan *Pilgr.* ii. 71 [He] bid them turn aside. 1751 Johnson *Rambl.* No. 171 ⁋10 He..bad me cant and whine in another place. 1833 Ht. Martineau *Briery Cr.* ii. 24 Bid them begone. 1848 Thackeray *Van. Fair* vii, Having wakened her bedfellow, and bid her prepare for departure. 1871 Freeman *Norm. Conq.* (1876) IV. xvii. 73 The two Earls were..bidden to be diligent. 1876 Green *Short Hist.* i. 3 Custom bade him blow his horn.

c. with the thing bidden as obj., with or without dative of person. (Formerly used also in sense of 'to order' goods, dinner, etc.)

α. *c* **1000** *Ags. Gosp.* John xv. 17 Đas þing ic eow beode; þæt ʒe lufion eow ʒemænelice. **1393** GOWER *Conf.* Prol. I. 12 When Criste him self hath bode pees. *c* **1400** *Rom. Rose* 2721 Whanne Love alle this hadde boden me.

β. **971** *Blickl. Hom.* 39 Ne bæd he nó þæs forþon þe him æniʒ þearf wære. *a* **1300** *Cursor M.* 12639 þat þai comaund wald or bide..he dide. *c* **1375** WYCLIF *Serm.* Sel. Wks. II. 229 He is not dispensour of service þat God haþ beden. **1401** *Pol. Poems* (1859) II. 35 How might ye for shame pray the pope undo that the Holy Ghost bit. **1559** *Mirr. Mag., Worcester* viii, Did execute what euer my king did byd. **1610** SHAKS. *Temp.* I. ii. 195 Hast thou, Spirit, Performd to point, the Tempest that I bad thee. **1632** MASSINGER *City Mad.* III. i, A chapman That in courtesy will bid a chop of mutton.

d. with personal obj. only; treated at length as the direct obj.

α. *c* **1430** *Life St. Katherine* (1884) 19 Than Adrian baptized hir as our lady had bode hym. **1541** ELYOT *Image Gov.* (1556) 143 b, So philosophie beadeth you.

β. *a* **1300** *Cursor M.* 5202 Quat art þou me beddes sua? **1375** BARBOUR *Bruce* VI. 91 Thai did as he thame biddin had. **1483** *Cath. Angl.* 31/1 To bydde, *admonere.* **1535** COVERDALE *2 Kings* iv. 24 Do as I byd the. **1599** SHAKS. *Much Ado* III. iii. 32 He will not stand when he is bidden. **1601** —— *All's Well* IV. ii. 53 Ile be bid by thee. **1647** SANDERSON *Serm.* II. 216 They that were about Him, though bidden and chidden too, could not hold from sleeping. *c* **1680** BEVERIDGE *Serm.* (1729) I. 529 Nobody.. bad him.

e. with no object; often with *so, as,* and the like.

β. *a* **1000** *Beowulf* 2467 Druncne dryht-guman dóð swa ic bidde. *a* **1300** *Cursor M.* 387 He baad, and it was don. **1340** HAMPOLE *Pr. Consc.* 2069 Haf God in mynde..Als þe prophet biddes.

†**11.** To bid not to do, to forbid, interdict, ban.

α, and β. *c* **1400** *Apol. Loll.* 31 As þe olde Testament to þe redars, so is bedun to dekunnis to prech þe newe. *Ibid.* 45 Till þu lefe þis þat þu art bodun bi þo bidding of Crist, what þing þat þu werkyst is vnþankful to þe Holi Goost. **1622** HEYLIN *Cosmogr.* III. (1673) 104/2 And by so doing did bid entrance unto the rest, till it were removed.

†**bid,** *v.*[2] *Obs.* exc. *dial.* Also bidde. [A variant of BUD, *behod, behoved.* Still in mod.Sc. as a present tense.)] = Must (by moral obligation, logical or natural necessity).

a **1300** *Havelok* 1733 Of the mete for to telle, Ne of the metes bidde I nout dwelle; That is the storie for to lenge. [*Mod. Sc.* (*Roxb.*), 'The man bid be a fuil to gang on that way.' 'It's a bid-be,' i.e. a must-be, a natural necessity.]

bid (bɪd), *sb.* [f. BID *v.*[1] 3.]

1. a. The offer of a price, the amount offered; *spec.* at an auction.

1788 T. JEFFERSON *Corr.* (1830) 342 He..thought to obtain a high bid by saying he was called for in America. **1837** *Penny Mag.* 1 Apr. 124 The salesman rapidly naming a lower price until he gets a bid. **1850** MRS. STOWE *Uncle Tom* xii. 101 Half-a-dozen bids simultaneously met the ear of the auctioneer.

fig. **1858** GEN. P. THOMPSON *Audi Alt.* II. lxxvii. 31 This time it will be a 'bid' between two opposite political parties.

b. Phr. ***to make a bid for***: to make an attempt to secure; to 'have a try' at getting. Hence the simple sb. is freq. used, esp. in journalese, for: an attempt to win or secure something.

1885 *Century Mag.* Dec. 179/2 He was a little ashamed of making such a bare-faced bid for her sympathy. **1893** *Cassell's Fam. Mag.* Apr. 357/2 The Colonel makes a good bid for the hole with the odd, and lies by the rim. **1895** *Geogr. Jrnl.* May 415 To make a bid himself for the throne. **1935** *Punch* 21 Aug. 204/2 'Britain's Bid for War-Plane Supremacy.'—*Daily Mirror...* 'Campbell's Bid for Record.' *All the Papers.* **1942** *Sunday Express* 14 June 1/6 Here they [*sc.* the German army] are now making a determined bid to move on Acroma.

2. *Card-playing.* The statement of an undertaking which a player makes; *spec.* in *Bridge*, an announcement of the number of tricks in a specified suit or 'no-trumps' by which a player proposes to beat his opponents. Cf. CONTRACT *sb.*[1] 1 g, DECLARATION 8 b, and see APPROACH *sb.* 12.

1880, 1897 [see BID *v.* 3 c]. **1908** L. HOFFMANN *Five Hundred* 14 A player who has been over-bidden is entitled to make a further bid. **1913** W. DALTON *Royal Auction Bridge* ii. 48 You should never make a bid unless you are prepared to play the hand with that suit as trumps. **1928** [see SCORE *sb.* 22].

†**'bid-ale.** *Obs.* Also 5 bede-ale. [See BID *v.* 8 and ALE.] An 'ale' or entertainment for the benefit of some person, to which a general bidding or invitation was given.

c **1462** in *N. & Q.* (1865) VIII. 436/1 None hereafter.. shall make or procure to be made, any Ale commonly called 'Bede Ale' within the lib[ty] nor within this Towne. **1534** *Act 26 Hen. VIII*, vi. (§5) No person..shall..within Wales.. gather or leuie any Commorth, Bydalle, tenauntes ale, or other collection or exactions. **1656** BLOUNT, *Bid-ale* is when an honest man decayed in his estate is set up again by the liberal benevolence and contribution of friends at a Feast, to which those friends are bid or invited. **1733** NEAL *Hist. Purit.* II. 246 The Justices assembled at Bridgwater ordered That no Church Ale, Clerk Ale, or Bid Ale be suffered. **1857** TOULM. SMITH *Parish* 504.

bidarka (baɪ'dɑːkə). Also baidarka, baidarke, bidarkee. [ad. Russ. *baĭdárka*, pl. *-ki*, dim. of *baĭdára* an oomiak.] In Alaska and adjacent regions, a portable canoe for one or more persons; a kayak.

1834 W. F. TOLMIE *Jrnl.* 20 June (1963) 283 The youth took his departure—soon after a bidarka approached—paddled by two men—the officer sitting in the middle seat. **1868** F. WHYMPER *Trav. Alaska* 137 Their 'baidarkes' are similar to the Greenland 'kyack'. **1894** *Outing* (U.S.) XXIII. 389/1 A one-hatch *bidarka*, or hunting boat, of the Aleutian Islands. **1898** *Century Mag.* LV. 672 Their kayaks and bidarkees. **1967** J. C. BEAGLEHOLE in *Cook's Jrnls.* (1967) III. I. 412 The small *baidarka* [was] the same as the Eskimo *kayak.*

bidaw, early form of BEDAW.

bidax(e, dial. var. *beat-axe* (see BEAT *sb.*[3]).

1778 PRYCE *Min. Cornub.* IV. i. 226 Then it is digged and broken to pieces with a bidax, or hedging tool. **1806** R. POLWHELE *Hist. Cornwall: Population* 31 Where a man of York or Kent would employ a shovel or a spade, a Cornishman uses a bidaxe.

'bidcock. 'The Water-rail.' Halliwell.

1613 DRAYTON *Polyolb.* xxv. 107 The pallat-pleasing Snite The Bidcocke, and like them the Redshanke.

ˌbiddaˈbility. [f. BIDDABLE *a.* (see -ILITY).] The state or quality of being biddable; obedience.

1947 W. F. BROWN *Field Trials* xxii. 148 There is not the pronounced emphasis on biddability, kindly handling response. **1948** L. A. G. STRONG *Trevannion* iii. 49 There were limits to Mrs. Wishart's biddability. **1958** *Times* 13 Dec. 7/6 The modern Labrador..was selectively bred.. with speed, style, and biddability in mind.

biddable ('bɪdəb(ə)l), *a.* Also bidable. [f. BID + -ABLE. Of Scotch origin.] **1.** Ready to do what is bidden, obedient, willing, docile.

1826 J. WILSON *Noct. Ambr.* Wks. 1864 I. 259 Judicious, regular..and biddable contributors. **1848** DICKENS *Dombey* (C.D. ed.) 61, I never saw a more biddable woman. **1862** H. KINGSLEY *Ravenshoe* xliv. (1864) 265 A more gentle and biddable invalid..can hardly be conceived.

2. *Card-playing.* Of a hand, suit, etc.: capable of being bid; strong enough to warrant a bid.

1926 M. C. WORK *Auction Bridge Complete* I. vi. 56 Either suit is biddable because both have length. **1929** —— *Compl. Contract Bridge* v. 79 If he has a biddable suit,..he unhesitatingly bids two of his best suit. **1959** *Listener* 22 Jan. 189/2 The slam is hardly biddable.

Hence **'biddableness, 'biddably** *adv. Sc.*

biddakil, obs. form of BINNACLE.

biddance ('bɪdəns). [f. BID *v.* + -ANCE, Romanic suffix: cf. ABIDANCE.] Bidding, invitation.

1836 *Fraser's Mag.* XIV. 495 The proud are humbled at his biddance. **1857** *Blackw. Mag.* LXXXI. 123 Right quickly did she send To lords and ladies biddance her son's marriage to attend.

bidde, obs. form of BED.

†**Bi'ddelian, -'ellian, Bidellian.** *Obs.* exc. *Hist.* A follower of John Biddle (died 1662), styled the father of the English Unitarians.

1780 KIPPIS *Biogr. Brit.* II. 307/2 *note*, The adherents to Mr. Biddle were called Biddellians; but this name was lost in the more common appellation of Socinians, or, what they preferred, Unitarians. **1882-3** SCHAFF in *Herzog's Encycl. Rel. Knowl.* I. 296.

bidden, pa. pple. of BID and BIDE.

bidden ('bɪd(ə)n), *ppl. a.* [f. BID + -EN[1].] Invited; commanded, ordered.

1614 KING *Vitis Palat.* 12 And Christ must bee a bidden guest. **1637** MILTON *Lycidas* 118 The worthy bidden guest. **1718** POPE *Iliad* v. 890 On the bright axle turns the bidden wheel of sounding brass. **1837** CARLYLE *Fr. Rev.* (1872) III. I. i. 2 Where Force is not yet distinguished into Bidden and Forbidden. **1875** *Lanc. Gloss.* (E.D.S.) 38 *Bidden-wedding* (N. Lanc.), a wedding to which it was formerly the custom in North Lanc. to invite the whole country-side.

bidder ('bɪdə(r)). [f. BID *v.* + -ER[1].]

†**1.** One who asks or begs; ***bidders and beggars*** is frequent in *P. Plowman*, referring to those who made a trade of begging. *Obs.*

1362 LANGL. *P. Pl.* Prol. 40 Bidders [*v.r.* byddere s] and Beggers · faste a-boute eoden. **1393** *Ibid.* C. x. 61 Beggers and bydders beþ nat in [þat] bulle.

2. One who commands or orders.

1340 HAMPOLE *Pr. Consc.* 3679 Onence þe bidder it standes in nede. **1632** SHERWOOD, A bidder, *commandeur.*

3. One who invites, or delivers an invitation.

1548 UDALL, etc. *Erasm. Par. Matt.* xxii. 4 They agayne neglected the bidder. **1705** STANHOPE *Paraphr.* III. 205 On the Bidder's Part every Circumstance conspires to magnify his Condescension. **1876** *Whitby Gloss.* Pref. 9 To the burying the parish clerk was the usual Bidder.

4. One who makes an offer for a thing, *esp.* at a public auction; also *fig.* (The usual sense.)

1685 *Lond. Gaz.* No. 2050/4 The Bidder to advance 6*d.* per Gross upon each bidding. **1702** *Ibid.* No. 3832/4 To be sold to the highest Bidder. **1710** STEELE *Tatler* No. 195 ¶5 This over-stock of Beauty, for which there are so few Bidders. **1776** GIBBON *Decl. & F.* I. 109 The Roman world was to be disposed of to the best bidder by public auction. **1868** M. PATTISON *Academ. Org.* §5. 203 The Universities will be the only bidders for such eminent qualities.

5. *Card-playing.* One who makes a bid (see BID *sb.* 2) (see also quot. 1908). Cf. DECLARER 3 b.

1880 'TRUMPS' *American Hoyle* 230 The bidder may at his option call for a lead of any suit from the player whose proper lead it is. **1897** R. F. FOSTER *Complete Hoyle* 271 The hands are usually abandoned when the bidder succeeds in his undertaking. **1908** L. HOFFMANN *Five Hundred* 14 The player who has bid highest is thenceforth known as 'the bidder' for that hand. **1929** M. C. WORK *Compl. Contract Bridge* ii. 9 The exact strength of the bidder's hand is of vital importance.

biddery, variant form of BIDRI.

biddikil, obs. form of BINNACLE.

bidding ('bɪdɪŋ), *vbl. sb.* [f. BID *v.* + -ING[1].]

1. a. The offering of a price for an article; a bid.

a **1300** *Cursor M.* 8819 (Gött.) Bot for na biding [*v.r.* beting, beding, profur] þat þai bide Ne miht þai do it stand in stede. **1685** *Lond. Gaz.* No. 2050/4 The Bidder to advance 6*d.* per Gross upon each bidding. **1863** GEO. ELIOT *Romola* (1880) I. I. i. 15 Let me have the bidding for that stained suit of yours, when you set up a better. **1878** BLACK *Gr. Past.* 310 He had listened to one or two of the biddings.

b. *Card-playing.* The act or process of making a bid or bids (see BID *sb.* 2). Also *attrib.*

1880 'TRUMPS' *American Hoyle* 229 A player having the highest bid, must declare the suit he plays in as soon as the bidding ceases. **1908** W. DALTON *Auction Bridge* vii. 103 The bidding is quite the most interesting, as well as the most exciting, feature of Auction Bridge. **1908** L. HOFFMANN *Five Hundred* 14 The bidding is continued till no player will go any further. **1928** [see SCORE *sb.* 22]. **1929** M. C. WORK *Compl. Contract Bridge* p. xii, To claim that any sound bidding system can be reduced to the simplicity of a multiplication table. **1958** *Listener* 6 Nov. 753/2 Over Two Diamonds I bid Two Hearts rather than Three Diamonds to preserve bidding space.

†**2.** The action of asking pressingly, of begging or requesting; request, desire, entreaty. *Obs.*

a **1225** *Ancr. R.* 108 Er þen þet biddunge arere eni schaundle. *c* **1340** *Cursor M.* 7131 (Trin.) þat bruyd was of biddyng bolde, Sampson al þe soþe hir tolde. **1340** *Ayenb.* 194 No þing ne is zuo diere y-boȝt; ase þet me heþ be biddinge.

†**3.** The action of praying; prayer. *Obs.*

1297 R. GLOUC. 280 þoru byddynge of Seyn Dunston, ys soule com to blys. **1340** *Ayenb.* 219 Moyses ouercom amalec . be his holy biddinges. *c* **1440** *Promp. Parv.* 35 Byddynge or praynge, *oracio, deprecacio, supplicacio.*

4. Invitation, summons.

1810 TANNAHILL *Kebbuckston Wed.*, We a' got a bidding, To gang to the wedding. **1869** *Times* 18 Aug., The Pope sent a bidding to the Patriarch of Constantinople..the Patriarch returned a distinct refusal.

attrib. **1863** MISS SEWELL *Chr. Names* II. 401 The beed-stick—bidding-stick, or summons to the muster.

5. A command, order, injunction. *to sit any one's bidding* (Sc.): to neglect his order to go.

a **1300** *Cursor M.* 3093 þi biding wil we do ful fayn. **1398** TREVISA *Barth. De P.R.* xv. xxix. (1495) 499 By byddynge of his fader. **1526** *Pilgr. Perf.* (W. de W. 1531) 34 b, I haue not founde the disobedyent to my byddynges. **1601** SHAKS. *All's Well* II. v. 93, I shall not breake your bidding, good my Lord. **1634** RUTHERFORD *Lett.* xliii. (1862) I. 132, I would.. swim through the water ere I sat His bidding. **1867** FREEMAN *Norm. Conq.* (1876) I. App. 790 Whatever Godwine did he did at the bidding of his lord.

6. ***bidding of beads, beads-bidding; bidding of prayers, bidding prayer.*** As to these expressions there has been a series of curious misapprehensions. The original meaning down to the Reformation was 'praying of prayers,' i.e. saying of prayers, praying; cf. BID *v.* 7 e. From an early date in the Christian church, it was the custom to request the prayers of the faithful in behalf of certain persons and things; and in the 16th c., in England, forms of allocution or direction to the congregation, telling them whom and what to remember in 'bidding their beads' or 'prayers' were authoritatively put forth. As *bid* in the sense of 'pray' was now becoming obsolete, the meaning of the expression was forgotten after the Reformation, and *bid* taken in the sense of 'order, direct,' so that in the reign of Elizabeth the 'bidding of prayers' was applied to the allocution itself, as if = 'the directing or injoining of prayers.' With the later use of the vbl. sb. as a gerund directly governing an object, we have in the 17th c. 'the form of bidding prayers' or 'prayer' (= *precationem hortandi*); and later still, a misunderstanding of the grammatical construction in this phrase has given rise to the vulgar error of calling this exhortation to the people (in which 'concionatores populum hortabuntur ut secum in precibus concurrat' Sparrow *Collect. Articles*, 1671) 'the bidding-prayer,' as if it were itself a kind of prayer qualified by the attribute 'bidding.'

c **1175** *Lamb. Hom.* 69 þurh festing and þurh wacunge, and ec þurh ibodenes biddunge. [**1349** in Coxe *Forms Bid. Prayer* 11 Ye shulle stonde up and bydde your bedys..Ye shull also bydde for the stat of Holy Cherche, etc.] **1535** *Act 27 Hen. VIII*, xxv, In al..their sermons, collacions, biddinges of the beades. **1539** HILSEY *Primer*, An order and form of bydding by the Kynges Commandment. Ye sholl praye for the whole congregasion, etc. **1563** *Homilies* II. *Idolatry* (1859) 236 For the which [the cross] they pray in their beads bidding. *a* **1746** LEWIS in Coxe *Forms Bid. Prayer* Pref. 12 Two ancient forms of bidding the bedes or praying the prayers on Sundays and Holydays 1349, 1483. *c* **1550** *Injunct. Edw. VI.* in *R. Glouc.* (Hearn) 624 *The fourme of biddyng of the common prayers.* Fyrst you shall pray for the whole congregatyon of the true chrysten and catholyke churche of Chryste. And specyally for the churche of Englande and Irelande, etc. **1559** *Injunct.* D iv, The fourme of bidding the prayers to be used generally in this uniforme sorte. Ye shall praye for Christs holy catholic

church, etc. **1622** SPARROW *Bk. Com. Prayer* (1661) 257 This form of bidding Prayers is very ancient. **1680** *Old Puritan Detect.* 5 A Form..of Bidding Prayer, wherein the Priest was not to speak to God, but only to the people, exhorting them to pray instantly for such and such persons and things. **1685** STILLINGFL. *Orig. Brit.* iv. 224 At the Bidding of Prayers, which was a direction for the People what to pray for in their private Devotions. **1732** NEAL *Hist. Purit.* I. 49 The custom of bidding prayer, which is still in use in the Church, is a relick of Popery. **1782** PRIESTLEY *Corrupt. Chr.* II. VIII. 126 What they call bidding prayers, or an exhortation to pray for such and such things. **1885** *Oxford Univ. Cal.* 31 The Form of Bidding Prayer before the Latin Sermons.

1753 CHAMBERS *Cycl. Supp.*, We have a form of these bidding-prayers in the apostolical constitutions. **1840** COXE *Forms Bid. Prayer* Pref., A concise view of the history of the Bidding Prayer. **1879** WACE *Bampt. Lect.* vi. 157 The bidding prayer read at the commencement of these Lectures is but an echo of this ancient supplication. **1885** *Public Opin.* 9 Jan. 36/2 That there should not be wanting, in the language of the bidding prayer, a due supply of fit persons qualified to discharge the functions of Royalty.

biddle, dial. var. BEETLE *sb.*[1]

1876 G. L. GOWER *Surrey Prov.* 82 A 'stake-*biddle*' is that which is used for driving stakes, a long or dumb-*biddle* for cleaving wood. **1937** *John o'London's* 30 Apr. 197 The 'biddle' itself is a huge wooden mallet. *Ibid.*, Peculiar to Devon, sometimes used as a term of endearment, but not always, is 'biddle head'. **1941** H. J. MASSINGHAM *Remembrance* xiii. 133 He was a thatcher..with biddle, leggatt, [etc.].

biddy[1] ('bɪdɪ). [Familiar abbrev. of *Bridget.*]
1. Used chiefly in U.S. for an Irish maid-servant.

[**1708** SWIFT (*title of poem*) To Mrs. Biddy Floyd. **1858** O. W. HOLMES *Aut. Breakf.-t.* xii. 363 Poor Bridget, or Biddy, our red-armed maid of all work!] *a* **1861** T. WINTHROP *Life in Open Air* (1863) 261 Our thousand [*sc.* soldiers] did the Capitol little harm that a corporal's guard of Biddies with mops and tubs could not repair in a forenoon's campaign. **1902** BRET HARTE in *Harper's Mag.* Apr. 733 He's..puttin' up a high-toned house on the hill..with a Chinese cook, and a Biddy. *a* **1953** E. O'NEILL *More Stately Mansions* (1965) II. iii. 120 A mother of children, our Irish biddy nurse girl and house servant.

2. A woman, usu. with derogatory implication (see quots.). *slang.*

1785 GROSE *Vulg. Tongue, Biddy*, or *Chick-a-biddy*, a chicken, and figuratively a young wench. **1947** *Horizon* XVI. 205 Few of our chaps have a biddy [*sc.* Italian girl] up the alley here. **1958** *Observer* 10 Aug. 11/3 He is already installed as the local delinquent, using his considerable charm on the local biddys. **1960** C. P. SNOW *Affair* xl. 368, I believe she's the bloodiest awful specimen of a party biddy.

biddy[2] ('bɪdɪ). *Obs.* exc. *dial.* [Of uncertain origin: it has been variously conjectured to be an instinctive sound used in calling chickens, a form of Gaelic *bîdeach* 'very small,' and the same word as prec. Cf. CHICKABIDDY.] A chicken, a fowl. Also *dial.*, a louse.

1601 SHAKS. *Twel. N.* III. iv. 128 *To.* Why how now my bawcock? how dost y^u^ chuck. *Mal.* Sir. *To.* I biddy, come with me. **1875** *Lanc. Gloss.* (E.D.S.), *Biddy*, a louse. **1881** *Isle of Wight Gloss.* (E.D.S.), *Biddy* or *Chickabiddy*, a chick. **1884** *Harper's Mag.* May 930/2 When a biddy wished to sit, she was removed at night upon the nest.

biddy[3] ('bɪdɪ). = *red biddy.*

1940 DYLAN THOMAS *Portrait of Artist* 228 He used to drink a pint of biddy before his breakfast.

biddy-biddy. Also bid-a-bid, biddy-bid, bidi-bid, bidy-bidy. [Corruption of Maori *piripiri.*] The New Zealand name for the troublesome burr of the piripiri. Also *attrib.*

1866 G. MUELLER *My Dear Bannie* (1958) iv. 110 We shall have..after that 'bidy-bidy' tea..without sugar. **1880** T. H. POTTS in *N.Z. Country Jrnl.* XII. 195 (Morris), Piri-piri (*acaena sanguisorbe*) by the settlers has been converted or corrupted into *biddy-biddy*. **1896** *Otago Witness* 23 Jan. II. 36 (Morris), Biddybids detract very materially from the value of the wool, and the plant should not be allowed to seed where sheep are depastured. **1944** D. STEWART in *Coast to Coast 1943* 96 Scrape them off like sand or bid-a-bid seeds. **1951** J. FRAME *Lagoon* 19 Father shook the bidi-bids off the big red and grey rug.

bide (baɪd), *v.* Forms: 1 bídan, 2–6 biden, 3– bide; also 3–6 byde(n, 4 bidde, 5 *Sc.* byd. *Pa. t.* 1 bád, *pl.* bidon, 3–5 bad(e, *pl.* 2–4 biden, 3–6 bod, 4–5 bood, 5 boode, 6–7 boad, 3– bode; 6 bid, 7– bided; also *north.* 3–4 badd, 3–6 baid, 4 badde, 5 bayd, 6 bed, 8 bade. *Pa. pple.* 1–4 biden, 4–7 bidden, 6 bid; also 3–4 biden, 4–6 bydden, 5 beddyn, 6 byden, 9 *dial.* bodden. [Com. Teut.: OE. *bídan* (pa. t. *bád, bidon*; pple. *biden*) = OS. *bîdan* (MDu. *bîden*), OHG. *bîtan* (MHG. *bîtan*, mod. dial. G. *beiten*), ON. *bíða*, Goth. *beidan*:—OTeut. **bîdan* to wait. Mostly replaced in mod.Eng. by its compound ABIDE, but regularly preserved in northern Eng. and Sc., and also employed by 19th c. poets, partly perhaps as an archaism, partly as an aphetized form of *abide*.]

I. *intr.*

1. To remain in expectation, to wait. Often with an adverbial adjunct of time. (Chiefly northern, but used by modern poets.)

c **1000** *Ags. Ps.* lv[i]. 6 Swa min sawl bad. *a* **1300** *Cursor M.* 10991 Quen þai had beden til þai war irk þai com þamself in-to þe kyrk. *c* **1325** *E.E. Allit. P.* B. 982 Ones ho bluschet to þe burȝe, bot bod ho no lenger. *a* **1400** *Sir Perc.* 569 The childe thoghte he longe bade That he ne ware a knyghte made. **1483** *Cath. Angl.* 31 To Byde, *expectare.* **1634** MALORY *Arthur* (1816) II. 307 He shall receive by thee his health, the which had bidden so long. **1816** SCOTT *Old Mort.* xxiii, 'Bide a wee, bide a wee,' said Cuddie. **1864** TENNYSON *En. Ard.* 435 Will you not bide your year as I bide mine? **1865** DICKENS *Mut. Fr.* xvi, 'Bide a bit.'

†**b.** Const. *for, to*; *on, upon* (north.). *Obs.*

a **1300** *Vox & Wolf* 135 Ich hedde so ibede for the. **1609** SKENE *Reg. Mag.* 124 Except he fraudfullie absent himselfe, and in that case, he sal be bidden vpon..be the space of fourtie dayes.

2. To remain or continue *in* some state or action; to continue to be (something). *arch.*

c **893** K. ÆLFRED *Oros.* III. iii. §3 Seo eorþe giniende bád. *c* **1000** *Ags. Ps.* ciii[iv]. 11 Bídað assan eac onþurste. *a* **1300** *Cursor M.* 1907 Yeit he baid seuen dais in rest. *c* **1340** *Ibid.* 19836 (Trin.) In orisoun he lay and bode. **1413** LYDG. *Pylgr. Sowle* v. i. (1859) 68 Ful longe there I boode in my torment and peyne. *c* **1530** *Jacob & 12 Sonnes* (Collier) 12 Rachel bod long barrain. **1611** BIBLE *Rom.* xi. 23 If they bide not still in vnbeliefe. **1633** P. FLETCHER *Purple Isl.* VI. xliv, And thirstie drinks, and drinking thirstie bides. **1871** R. ELLIS *Catullus* viii. 10 Nor follow her that flies thee, or to bide in woe Consent.

b. *to bide by* (rarely *at*): to stand firm by, adhere to, stick to, maintain. † *to bide upon*: to dwell or insist upon (a point). *Obs.*

1494 FABYAN VI. cciv. 214 For this [battle] was so strongly bydden by, that men coude nat iudge whiche parte had the better. **1526** TINDALE *Mark* x. 7 And for this thingis sake shall a man leve father and mother and byde by his wife. **1536** SIR R. MORYSON in Strype *Eccl. Mem.* I. App. lxxii, Many things..which be both truly spoken and cannot but do good being bydden bye. **1559** KENNEDY *Let.* in *Misc. Wodrow Soc.* (1844) 266 He gaif me nevir answir to my wryttingis, nor ȝit baid at his sayingis. **1611** SHAKS. *Wint. T.* I. ii. 242 To bide upon 't: thou art not honest. **1847** TENNYSON *P'cess* v. 316 Worthy reasons why she should Bide by this issue.

Cf. *to be a bidden by*, prop. *abidden by*: to be maintained; also *advb.* = undoubtedly, we may be sure.

1549 LATIMER *Serm. bef. Edw. VI*, v. (Arb.) 133 To be a bidden by he would have done much good in that part.

3. To remain in a place, or with a person, as opposed to going away; to stay. Often with the idea of remaining behind when others go. *arch.*

c **893** K. ÆLFRED *Oros.* II. v. §7 þonne he þær leng bide. [*c* **1000** *Ags. Gosp.* Matt. xxvi. 38 Gebídaþ her and waciaþ mid me.] *c* **1200** *Trin. Coll. Hom.* 149 Wuo is mi soule þat ich bide here swo longe. *a* **1300** *Cursor M.* 16744 Durst naman wit him bide. **1482** *Monk of Evesham* (Arb.) 34 Y thought to haue byddyn ther in the same place tyl the mornyng. **1515** BARCLAY *Egloges* i. (1570) A v/4 Better were for suche to have bid at home. **1560** ROLLAND *Crt. Venus* II. 399 He baid..Vpon that hill..Him to refresche. **1596** SPENSER *F.Q.* VI. xi. 40 So there all day they bode, till light the sky forsooke. **1668** CULPEPPER & COLE *Barthol. Anat.* I. ii. 3 Such as dive and bide long under the Water. **1857** EMERSON *Poems* 89 Who bides at home, nor looks abroad. **1868** MORRIS *Earthly Par.* I. 68 While we bided on that flowery down.

4. Of things: To remain, be left. *to let a thing bide*: to leave it where it is; to leave it alone for the present, to let it stand over.

c **1325** *E.E. Allit. P.* B. 449 þaȝ þe kyste in the cragez wern closed to byde. **1398** TREVISA *Barth. De P.R.* XIX. lxxix. (1495) 913 Yf they byde in the stomak they torne sone to fumosyte and corrupcion. *c* **1470** HENRY *Wallace* v. 166 A gret power at Dipplyn still thar baid. **1581** MARBECK *Bk. of Notes* 154 Heauen and earth shal sooner perish, then one iot bide behind of that he hath promised. *a* **1631** DONNE *Poems* (1650) 72 Waters stinke soone, if in one place they bide. **1866** KINGSLEY *Herew.* iv. 97 We will let the crow bide.

5. To remain in residence; to sojourn, dwell, reside. *arch.*

c **1280** *Fall & Passion* 40 in *E.E.P.* (1862) 13 Nedis he most wend to helle..þere he most bide an dwelle. *c* **1386** CHAUCER *Cokes T.* 35 This ioly prentys with his maister bood [*v.r.* bode]. **1482** *Monk of Evesham* (Arb.) 26 Than bode with hym a certeyn brother. **1591** SPENSER *M. Hubberd* 400 The world, in which they bootles boad. **1621** BURTON *Anat. Mel.* II. ii. III. (1651) 258 Some..will know..what God did..Where did he bide. **1667** MILTON *P.L.* III. 321 All knees to thee shall bow, of them that bide In Heaven, or Earth, or under Earth in Hell. **1798** COLERIDGE *Anc. Mar.* v. xxv, The spirit who bideth by himself In the land of mist and snow. **1821** JOANNA BAILLIE *Met. Leg., Lady G. B.* xii. 9 Many his wants who bideth lonely there.

II. *trans.*

6. To wait for, await. Now only in the phrase, *to bide one's time*: to await one's opportunity.

c **950** *Lindisf. G.* Matt. xi. 3 Oðer we bidas. **971** *Blickl. Hom.* 7 Drihtnes engel bideþ þinre ȝeþafunga. *c* **1230** *Hali Meid.* 11 Eauer bide his grace. *c* **1325** *E.E. Allit. P.* B. 622 We byde þe here. **1382** WYCLIF *Ps.* cxviii. [cxix.] 166, I bod thin helthe ȝiuere, Lord. *c* **1420** *Avow. Arth.* xxii, Atte Tarnewathelan Bidus me Sir Gauan. **1513** DOUGLAS *Æneis* VII. x. 122 Now at the dur deyd redy bydis me. **1611** BIBLE *Wisd.* viii. 12 When I hold my tongue they..shal bide my leisure. **1853** ROBERTSON *Serm.* Ser. III. xvii. 218. §1 They bide their time and then suddenly present themselves. **1873** SMILES *Huguenots Fr.* I. ix. (1881) 191 They held their peace and bided their time.

7. To await in resistance, to face, encounter, withstand; = ABIDE 14.

[*a* **1000** *Beowulf* 3241 Se þe ǽr æt sæcce gebád wíȝ-hrýre wraðra.] *c* **1340** *Gaw. & Gr. Knt.* 376 He baldly hym bydez. **1480** *Robt. Devyll* 23 None durst hym byde there at all. **1523** LD. BERNERS *Froiss.* I. cccxxxix. 532 Some of the capitayns wolde that thenglisshmen shulde be byden, and some other sayd nay, bycause they were nat strong ynough to abyde them that were fresshmen. **1664** *Floddan F.* ix. 83 Yet for defence they fiercely frame And narrow dint with danger boad. **1813** SCOTT *Rokeby* v. xxxii, They dare not, hand to hand, Bide buffet from a true man's brand. **1877** BRYANT *Odyss.* v. 583 Two men and three, in that abundant store, Might bide the winter storm.

†**8.** To await submissively, submit to. *Obs.*

c **1205** LAY. 4721 þæt ne sulde he nauere ibiden þe while þe he mihte riden. *c* **1400** *Ywaine & Gaw.* 545 The kynges wil wald he noght bide, Worth of him what may bityde.

†**9.** To endure, suffer, bear, undergo; = ABIDE 16. *Obs.* exc. *dial.*

c **1200** *Trin. Coll. Hom.* 33 Ne wot no man hwat blisse is þe naure wowe ne bod. *c* **1250** *Gen. & Ex.* 3105 Maniȝe ðor sorȝe on liue bead. *c* **1400** *Sir Perc.* 627 The sorowe that the kinge bade Mighte no tonge telle. **1530** PALSGR. 454/2, I can nat byde this payne. **1601** SHAKS. *Twel. N.* II. iv. 304 There is no womans sides Can bide the beating of so strong a passion. **1671** MILTON *P.R.* I. 59 Wherein we Must bide the stroak of that long threatn'd wound. **1748** THOMSON *Cast. Indol.* I. xxii, Who bides his grasp will that encounter rue. **1816** SCOTT *Antiq.* xl, I wonder how younger folk bide it—I bide it ill.

†**b.** *to bide out*: to endure to the end. *Obs.*

1637 RUTHERFORD *Lett.* 85 I. 217 To bide out the seige.

10. To tolerate, endure, put up with; = ABIDE 17.

c **1250** *Gen. & Ex.* 1594 If iacob took her also a wif, Ne bode ic no lengere werldes lif. **1325** *E.E. Allit. P.* B. 32 For he..May not byde þat burne. **1810** TANNAHILL *Poems* (1846) 25, I cou'dna bide the thought. **1816** SCOTT *Antiq.* xii, I could never bide the staying still in ae place. **1884** TENNYSON *Becket* 84 Tho' I can drink wine I cannot bide water, my lord.

†**bide, byde**, *sb. Obs.* [f. prec. vb.]
1. A dwelling, dwelling-place, habitation.

a **1300** *Salomon & Sat.* (1848) 273 Ne make þe nout for þy to wroþt, þaȝ þou byde borewe. *c* **1435** *Torr. Portugal* 1463 With wyld bestis to have byde.

2. Delay, stay.

a **1000** *Riddles* iv. 3 (Gr.) Hwilum mec min frea..on bid wriceð. *a* **1300** *Cursor M.* 1761 Quen al was tift was þar na bide, þe stormes ras on ilka side. *c* **1325** *Leg. Rood* (1871) 113 Vp he rase wiþ-outen bide.

bidel, obs. form of BEADLE.

bidele, ME. form of BEDEAL.

†**bi'deme**, *v. Obs. rare*[-1]. [f. *bi-*, BE- + ME. *demen*:—OE. *déman* to DEEM.] *trans.* To condemn.

a **1200** *Moral Ode* 107 in *Lamb. Hom.* 167 Ech Mon scal him solue þer biclepie and bidemen.

bident ('baɪdənt). [ad. L. *bident-em* (nom. *bidens*) adj. 'having two teeth, two pronged, forked,' sb. 'a two-pronged fork, a sheep or other animal for sacrifice whose two rows of teeth are complete,' f. *bi-* two + *dentem* tooth.]

1. An instrument or weapon with two prongs.

1675 COTTON *Poet. Wks.* (1765) 232 The blust'ring Aeo for his Bident. **1850** LAYARD *Nineveh* v. 94 A half-moon, a bident, and a horned cap.

2. A two-year-old sheep. *rare.*

1881 THURN in *Academy* No. 491. 252 The timid bident has usurped the place of the bellower.

bidental (baɪ'dɛntəl), *a.* [f. L. *bident-em* (see prec.) + -AL[1].] 'Belonging to a Fork, or Instrument with two teeth.' Bullokar, 1676.

‖**bi'dental**, *sb. Rom. Antiq.* [L. *bidental*, f. *bident-em* (see BIDENT), according to some called from the forked lightning (see *bidental = fulmen bifidum* in Du Cange), according to others from the *bidens* or sheep sacrificed at its consecration.] A place struck by lightning, consecrated by the haruspices, and enclosed. Also *fig.*

1692 COLES, *Bidental*..also a place where sheep were sacrificed. **1753** CHAMBERS *Cycl. Supp.* s.v., Festus represents the bidental as a temple, where sheep of two years old were offered in sacrifice. **1794** MATHIAS *Purs. Lit.* (1798) 29, I would only set up the bidental at the bookseller's door at Wimbledon. **1873** BLACKMORE *Cradock N.* xxvii, The scene of his ruin and despair,—the 'bidental' of his destiny.

bidentate, -ated (baɪ'dɛnteɪt, -ɪd), *a.* [f. L. *bident-em* (see BIDENT) + -ATE.] Having two teeth or tooth-like processes.

1826 KIRBY & SP. *Entomol.* III. xxxii. 314 The male mandible is more bidentate at the apex than the female. **1866** TATE *Brit. Mollusks* iv. 76 The uncini of *Limax agrestis* are bidentated.

†**bi'dented** *a.* = prec.

1756 P. BROWNE *Jamaica* 321 The seeds are all bidented. **1828** SOUTHEY *Life* (1850) V. 366 A fork bidented, and a trenchant knife.

bidential (baɪ'dɛnʃəl), *a.* [f. L. *bident-em* (see BIDENT) + -IAL.] Two-pronged.

1730 SWIFT *Let. Gay* 10 Nov., Ill management of forks is not to be helped when they are only bidential.

bider ('baɪdə(r)). [f. BIDE *v.* + -ER[1].] One who stays or remains.

1535 STEWART *Cron. Scot.* III. 440 [Seldom is] ane mydding tulȝear in ane battell bydar. **1577** NORTHBROOKE *Dicing* (1843) 95 Saint Paule admonisheth women—to be byders and tariers at home.

bidery, variant of BIDRI.

bidet (bidɛ, bɪˈdɛt). [a. F. *bidet* pony; of unknown origin: cf. OF. *bider* (Godefroy) to trot. In 16th c. the F. word meant also some small kind of dagger. (The Celtic comparisons made by Diez and Littré are rejected by Thurneysen.)]

1. A small horse.

1630 B. JONSON *Chlorid.* Wks. (1838) 656, I will return to myself, mount my bidet, in a dance, and curvet upon my curtal. **1828** DISRAELI *Chas. I*, I. ii. 18 Then there are thanks for two bidets which Henry sends him. **1863** SALA *Capt. Dangerous* II. vi. 202, I trotted behind on a little Bidet.

2. (ˈbiːdeɪ). ‘A vessel on a low, narrow stand, which can be bestridden’ (*Syd. Soc. Lex.*) for bathing purposes. Now usu. a shallow oval basin fitted in a bathroom, used for washing the perineum.

1766 SMOLLETT *Trav.* I. v. 64 Will custom exempt from the imputation of gross indecency a French lady, who shifts her frousy smock in presence of a male visitant, and talks to him of her *lavement*, her *medecine*, and her *bidet!* **1785** GROSE *Dict. Vulg. Tongue, Bidet*, commonly pronounced biddy, a kind of tub, contrived for ladies to wash themselves, for which purpose they bestride it like a little French poney, or post horse, called in France bidets. **1801** *Ann. Reg. 1799* 401/1 A machine answering the purposes of a portable water-closet, or bidet, and easy chair. **1959** R. GANT *World in Jug* 60 We checked into our hotel near the Opéra and the boys joked about the bidets.

bid-hook, variant of BEAD-HOOK.

1607 DEKKER *Knts. Conjur.* (1842) 43 He has split one of his oares and broken his bid-hook. **1867** SMYTH *Sailor's Word-Bk.*, *Bid-hook*, a small kind of boat-hook.

bidialectal (ˌbaɪdaɪəˈlɛktəl), *a. Linguistics.* Also bi-dialectal. [BI-²; after BILINGUAL *a.*] Of a person: having command of two regional or social dialects of a language, one of which is commonly the standard language; of a speech community or language teaching: in which two varieties of a language are used for different functions.

1954 *Word* X. 390 A ‘diasystem’ is experienced in a very real way by bilingual (including ‘bidialectal’) speakers and corresponds to what students of language contact have called ‘merged system’. **1969** *Language* XLV. 603 Bidialectism in this sense has never been observed by the present writer, even in children cited..as prototypic examples of bidialectal speakers. **1971** C. M. KERNAN *Lang. Behaviour in Black Urban Community* 7 In a linguistic community which is bilingual or bidialectal..the code..is likely to be highly salient to.. members of the community. **1976** *Scotsman* 20 Nov. 8/6 Sociolinguists..have been advocating a ‘bidialectal’ approach for the teaching of standard English to non-standard speaking pupils. **1985** *English World-Wide* VI. 131 Until about thirty years ago Norfolk Islanders with few exceptions were bidialectal. *Ibid.* 143 Islanders live in a bidialectal society.

Hence ˌ**bidiaˈlectalism**, the state of being bidialectal; also, advocacy of bidialectal education; ˌ**bidiaˈlectalist** *sb.* and *a.*, (one) advocating bidialectalism; **biˈdialectism** = *bidialectalism* above.

1959 *Word* XV. 144 The result of these adaptations made by the newcomers was either bidialectism or dialect mixture. **1968** *Zeitschr. für Mundartforschung* Beihefte IV. 549 Such a situation we might call one of functional bidialectalism, analogous to the functional bilingualism so common in such nations as Switzerland and Luxemburg. **1973** *English Jrnl.* May 770/2 The bidialectalist does not argue that one language or dialect may in itself be better than another. **1975** *Language* LI. 728 A number of the assumptions underlying the bidialectalists' position have been questioned by linguists and educators, including some who were or are in the bidialectalist camp. **1982** *English World-Wide* III. 162 Studies exclusively or mainly concerned with the (language) education of minority children, the ‘deficit hypothesis’ or the concept of ‘bidialectalism’. **1984** *Ibid.* IV. 255 A continued period of bilingualism and bidialectism.

bidigitate (baɪˈdɪdʒɪteɪt), *a.* [f. BE- *pref.*² 1 + DIGITATE, f. L. *digitus* finger.] Having two digits, fingers, or finger-like processes. **biˈdigital** *a.* = prec.

1852 DANA *Crust.* I. 649 Small bi-digitate sacs. **1881** MIVART *Cat* 103 The skeleton of the fore-leg..is divisible into a tri- and a bi-digital series, placed side by side.

ˌ**bidiˈmensional**, *a.* [BI-².] Having or perceived in two dimensions. Also *transf.*

1927 N. T. BURROW *Social Basis of Consciousness* I. v. 92 Depending on whether the child ‘succeeds’ or ‘fails’ as judged by the bidimensional standard of good and bad. **1937** H. F. BRANDT in *Amer. Jrnl. Psychol.* XLIX. 666 A bidimensional eye-movement camera. *Ibid.* 669 This new instrument provides laboratory equipment which is essential for all types of ocular photography in the bidimensional plane.

biding (ˈbaɪdɪŋ), *vbl. sb.* [f. BIDE *v.* + -ING¹.]

1. Awaiting, expectation; remaining, tarrying.

1340 HAMPOLE *Pr. Consc.* 4708 And men sal wax dry..for lang bydyng þar-in. **1483** *Cath. Angl.* 31 A Bydynge, *expectacio, perseuerancia.* *a* **1657** SIR J. BALFOUR *Ann. Scot.* (1825) II. 315 His longe delay and bydinng out. **1862** BARNES *Rhymes Dorset Dial.* II. 182 But bidin up till dead o'night..do soon consume The feäce's bloom.

†**b.** *concr.* The object of expectation. *Obs.*

1382 WYCLIF *Jer.* xiv. 8 Thou biding [*Vulg.* expectatio] of Israel, his saueour in tyme of tribulacioun.

2. Stay, residence, dwelling.

c **1400** *Cov. Myst.* 22 In erthliche paradys withowtyn wo I graunt the bydyng. **1653** MILTON *Ps.* v. 11 Evil with thee no biding makes. **1713** ROWE *J. Shore* I. ii, At Antwerp has my constant biding been. **1866** [see 3].

†**b.** *concr.* An abode, dwelling, habitation. *Obs.*

1600 HAKLUYT *Voy.* III. 809 (R.) They brought us to their bidings about two miles from the harborough. **1605** SHAKS. *Lear* IV. vi. 228 I'll lead you to some biding. *a* **1687** COTTON *Voy. Irel.* I. 66 Three miles ere we met with a biding.

3. *attrib.*, as **biding-place**, place of abode.

1557 PAYNELL *Barclay's Jugurth* 17b, They had no certayne bydinge place. **1626** MILTON *Death Fair Inf.* 21 He ..Unhoused thy virgin soul from her fair biding-place. **1866** MRS. WHITNEY *L. Goldthwaite* i, How many different little biding-places there are in the world.

ˈ**biding**, *ppl. a.* [f. as prec. + -ING².] Lasting, continuing, enduring. (Now usually ABIDING.)

1430 LYDG. *Chron. Troy* I. ii, And though the ginning be but casuell The biding frete is passingly cruell. **1536** LYNDESAY *Answ. Kyngis Flyting* 38 Beleif richt weill, it is ane bydand gam. **1633** W. STRUTHER *True Happ.* 5 We have need of some biding substance to supply these losses.

ˌ**bidiˈrectional**, *a.* [BI-².] Functioning in two directions; *spec.* of a microphone (see quot. 1962¹).

1941 A. E. CRAIG *Speech Arts* (ed. 2) xxxix. 509 A bidirectional microphone, with the speech directed into either, or both, the openings or faces, is the kind deemed best for the production of radio plays. **1960** *Aerodrome Lighting (B.S.I.)* 29 Light fittings..may be bi-directional or uni-directional according to whether they are to cover both directions of landing and take off or not. **1962** A. NISBETT *Technique Sound Studio* 243 *Bi-directional microphone*, one which is live on the front face and back, but which is dead at the sides and above and below. **1962** SIMPSON & RICHARDS *Junction Transistors* xvi. 384 A bi-directional switch using four silicon junction diodes.

Hence ˌ**bidiˈrectionally** *adv.*

1966 *Jrnl. Compar. Neurol.* CXXVII. 71/1 The rate of flow may be as high as 30–70 mm per day, streaming bidirectionally. **1973** *Nature* 26 Oct. 459/2 These findings are consistent with the Yin Yang hypothesis that the two cyclic nucleotides have opposing actions in bidirectionally controlled systems. **1984** *Freetime* Autumn 49/2, I liked the versatility it offers: lots of features and the ability to print text bi-directionally.

‖**bidon** (bidɔ̃). [Fr.] A container for liquids: *spec.* (*a*) a wooden cup; (*b*) a bottle or canteen for water, wine, etc.; (*c*) an oil drum or petrol tin. Hence **bidonville** [F. *ville* town], a shanty-town built of oil drums or petrol tins.

1867 ‘OUIDA’ *Under Two Flags* II. i. 13 ‘Take a draught of my burgundy...’ He..took the *bidon.* **1922** E. E. CUMMINGS *Enormous Room* iii. 48 Tilting their *bidons* on high and absorbing the thin streams which spurted therefrom. *Ibid.*, He remarked: ‘Bread without wine doesn't taste good,’ and proffered his *bidon.* **1933** ‘G. ORWELL’ *Down & Out* xv. 115 She had picked up an empty oil *bidon.* **1955** *Times* 21 July 6/6 Huge fires destroyed two Moroccan bidonvilles (shanty towns) in the suburbs of Fedala. **1961** *Times* 6 May 9/7 Elsewhere the *bidonvilles*, or petrol can shanty towns, spread like a rash. **1964** E. AMBLER *Kind of Anger* vi. 164 Get the car filled up. Adèle left me two *bidons* for emergencies.

†ˈ**bidowe.** *Obs. rare*⁻¹. [Referred by Prof. Skeat (*Notes to Piers Plowman*) to med.L. *bidubium*, a bill-hook or bush-hook (which has been conjectured to be of Celtic origin, from Gaulish **vidu* wood); others have compared Welsh *bidog* dagger: but the meaning and derivation are alike uncertain.] ? A weapon of some kind.

1362 LANGL. *P. Pl.* A. XI. 211 A bidowe or a baselard he beriþ be his side.

bid-prayer = *bidding prayer*: see BIDDING 6.

1691 WOOD *Ath. Oxon.* (R.) He lays by the text for the present and..addressed himself to the bid-prayer.

bidrep(e, -ripe, var. BEDRIP, *Obs.*, boon service.

‖**bidri, bidree, bidry** (ˈbɪdrɪ). Also 8–9 biddery, bidery. [Urdū *bidrī*, f. *Bidar* or *Bedar* a town in the Nizam's dominion in India.] An alloy of copper, lead, tin, and zinc, used as a ground for inlaying with gold and silver, in the manufacture of *bidri-* or *biddery-ware.*

1794 *Europ. Mag.* 209 You may have heard of Bidry Work. **1813** *Ann. Reg.* 499/1 The alloys for the gurry and the Biddery ware. **1875** URE *Dict. Arts* I. 341 Bidery does not rust, yields little to the hammer, and breaks only when violently beaten. **1883** *Daily News* 3 July 2/2 The ‘bidri’ ware is now almost as well known in England.

†ˈ**bidstand.** *Obs.* [One who *bids* travellers *stand* and deliver.] A highwayman.

a **1637** B. JONSON is cited by Halliwell. **1863** SALA *Capt. Dang.* II. vii. 225 Rogues, Thieves..Bidstands, and Clapper-dudgeons..infested the outskirts of the Old Palace.

biduous (ˈbɪdjuːəs), *a.* [f. L. *bīdu-um* space of two days (f. *bi-* two + *dies, diu-* day) + -OUS.] Lasting for two days.

1866 in *Treas. Bot.*

bidweolien, early form of BEDWELE *v. Obs.*

bie, obs. form of BEE *sb.*², BUY, BY.

bieberite (ˈbiːbəraɪt). *Min.* [ad. G. *bieberit* (Haidinger 1845), f. *Bieber*, near Hanau, Germany: see -ITE¹.] Sulphate of cobalt, found as a red crust on other minerals.

1854 DANA *Syst. Min.* 385 *Bieberite*... Lustre vitreous. Color flesh and rose-red. **1882** —— *Mineral. & Lithol.* 168 Bieberite or Cobalt Vitriol.

Biedermeier (ˈbiːdəmaɪə(r)). Also **-maier, -meyer.** [The name of a fictitious poet, Gottlieb *Biedermaier* (see below).] Applied *attrib.* to the period between 1815 and 1848 in Germany and to styles, furnishings, etc., characteristic of that period, esp. to a type of furniture derived from the French Empire style. Also *transf.* with derogatory implication: conventional, bourgeois.

[**1854** [L. EICHRODT] in *Fliegende Blätter* XXI. 102/1 (*title*) Auserlesene Gedichte von Weiland Gottlieb Biedermaier, Schulmeister in Schwaben. *Ibid.* 103/1 Die ästhetischen Begriffe des Biederschönen und Bidermaiern.] **1905** A. S. LEVETUS *Imperial Vienna* xvi. 245 The Biedermaier period also produced landscape-painters. **1914** EBERLEIN & MCCLURE *Pract. Bk. Period Furniture* xv. 323 Following the prevalence of the Empire style we see the advent of the Biedermeyer type of painted decoration. **1924** G. B. STERN *Tents of Israel* i. 8 A true son of the Biedemeyer period, in his long, tight pantaloons, his cambric frills. **1956** *English Studies* XXXVII. 183 The examples..from the early Victorian age may be regarded as contradictions of the ‘Biedermeier’ dominance in literature. **1957** *Encycl. Brit.* IX. 948E/2 The Biedermeier style..is characterized by chairs with curved legs and sofas with rolled arms and generous upholstery. **1963** *Listener* 24 Jan. 161/1 A hill close to the centre of the city [*sc.* Darmstadt] where there was a piece of Biedermeier park and a Russian church.

bief(e, obs. form of BEEF.

bieften, early form of BAFT.

biel, obs. form of BEAL, BOIL *sb.*

bield (biːld), *sb. Obs.* exc. *dial.* Forms: 1 byldo, 4–5 beld(e, 5 beelde, 6 beald, 5–7 beeld, 4–9 beild(e, 5– bield, (6 beill, bele, beale, 8–9 biel). [Common Teut.: OE. *bęldo*, in WSax. *bięldo, byldo* boldness, courage = OHG. *baldî*, MHG. *belde* confidence, feeling of security, Goth. *balþei* boldness, confidence:—OTeut. **balþjôn-*, n. of quality from **balþo-z*, Goth. *balþs*, OHG. *bald*, OE. *bald, beald*, BOLD. The evidence appears to show that mod.Sc. *bield, beild* is the same as the ME. *belde*, the connexion being through sense 3. But the matter is not without difficulty, and the derivation of Sc. *bield* has been sought elsewhere, esp. in connexion with *build*, though without much success.]

†**1.** Boldness, courage. *Obs.*

c **890** K. ÆLFRED *Bæda* I. vii, He sceolde ða byldo anescian. *a* **1300** *Cursor M.* 12237 A barn wit-uten beild [*v.r.* beilde, belde]. *c* **1340** *Gaw. & Gr. Knt.* 649 Quen he bluschel þerto, his belde neuer payred. **1470** HARDING *Chron.* clxxxv. iv, His brother bastard, with strong beeld, Had putte hym out.

†**2.** Confidence, assurance, feeling of security; *hence*, comfort. Often in alliterative connexion with *bliss. Obs.*

a **1300** *Cursor M.* 605 A land o lijf, o beld, and blis, þe quilk man clepes paradis. *c* **1325** *Metr. Hom.* 162 This tronchoun for relic scho held Al hir lif, with worschip and beld. *Ibid.* 166 Ic haf tinte werdes, mensc, and belde. *c* **1400** *Melayne* 324 With mekill blysse & belde.

†**3.** Resource, help; often in alliterative connexion with *bote* (BOOT); succour, defence, relief.

c **1325** *Metr. Hom.* 7 Mankind in prisoun he held, With outen help, wit outen belde. *c* **1360** *Yesterday* in *E.E.P.* (1862) 136 Vnswere I schal, Whi god sent suche men boote and belde. *c* **1440** *Bone Flor.* 1721 A woman dyscownfortyd sare, Wythowten bote or belde. **1535** STEWART *Cron. Scot.* II. 549 Mony berne wist nother of bute no beild. **1570–87** HOLINSHED *Scot. Chron.* (1806) II. 51 Quhan Kings and princes hes na other beild bot in thair awin folks.

†**b.** A means of help or succour. *Obs.* (Often transferred to a *person.*)

a **1300** *Cursor M.* 20815 Ogain þat fa scho be vr beild. *c* **1352** MINOT *Poems* vi. 27 Alweldand god..He be his beld. *c* **1425** WYNTOUN *Cron.* VII. vi. 15 He wes þe Beld of all hys kyn. *c* **1440** *Bone Flor.* 762 Sche cryed to hym..Thou be my fadurs belde.

†**4.** Resource against hunger; ‘cheer,’ sustenance. (Only Sc.) *Obs.*

1513 DOUGLAS *Æneis* XII. ix. 50 His fader eyrit and sew ane peice of feild, That he in hyregang held to be his beild. **1552** LYNDESAY *Monarche* 1087 For fude thow gettis none uther beild Bot eait the herbis upone the feild.

5. a. Refuge, shelter. **b.** A place of shelter. (Only Scotch and north. dial.).

1450 HENRYSON *Mor. Fab.* 82 He ran restlesse, for hee wist of no bield. **1513** DOUGLAS *Æneis* II. x. (ix.) 16 Hecuba thidder..for beild Ran all in vane. **1570–87** HOLINSHED *Scot. Chron.* (1806) I. 8 The Scotishmen call it [Cromart haven] beill of shipmen. **1594** *Scot. Peoms 16th C.* II. 352 Argyll..Wpone ane hill had tane beild. **1600** FAIRFAX *Tasso* II. lxxxiv. 36 This is our beild, the blustring windes to shun. **1691** RAY *N. Country Wds.* 7 *Beeld*, shelter. **1792** BURNS *Wks.* II. 397 Better a wee bush than nae bield. *Ibid.* III. 216 Jamaica bodies, use him weel, An' hap him in a cozie biel.

1818 SCOTT *Rob Roy* xxv, 'The oppressors that hae driven me to tak the heather-bush for a bield.' **1822** W. NAPIER *Pract. Store-farm.* 117 The most valuable..shelter..is derived from the bield of a close, well built, stone dike. **1864** ATKINSON *Whitby Gloss.*, *Bield*, a shelter or shed. 'A bit of a bield in a field neuk.'

c. A lodging, dwelling; a den.

1570 LEVINS *Manip.* 207 A Beale, den, *spelunca.* **1585** ABP. SANDYS *Serm.* iii, The fox will not worry near his beeld [*v.r.* bele]. **1815** SCOTT *Guy M.* viii, 'There's thirty yonder ..that ye have turned out o' their bits o' bields.'

bield (biːld), *v. Obs.* exc. *dial.* Forms: 1 **bieldan, byldan, beldan,** 2–5 **belden,** *Orm.* **beoldenn,** 3–5 **beld(e,** 5 **bylde, beilde, beelde, beled, beyld, bild,** 6 **beald,** 7–9 **beal,** 4– **beild, bield.** *Pa. pple.* **beld, beilded, bealed, bield.** [Com. Teut.: OE. (Anglian) *bęldan*, (WSax.) *bieldan, byldan* = OS. *beldjan*, OHG. *baldên*, MHG. *belden*, Goth. *balþjan* 'to make bold,' f. OTeut. **balþ-oz* BOLD. The sense-development in ME. was evidently influenced by that of the cognate sb. (see prec.), which it closely follows. In senses 1 and 2, ME. had another vb. of precisely the same meaning, *bealden, balden, bolden*:—OE. *bealdian* (see BOLD *v.*); but the latter never got the senses of 'protect, shelter.']

†**1.** *trans.* To make bold, encourage; to confirm.

c **897** K. ÆLFRED *Past. Care* xviii. 128 Ne tyht nan man his hieremonna mod ne ne bielt [*v.r.* bilt] to gastlicum weorcum. **993** *Byrhtnoð* 209 Swa hi bylde forð bearn Ælfrices. *c* **1200** ORMIN 2614 Wiþþ iwhillc mahht To beoldenn itt and strengenn. —— 2745 þurrh Godess millce beldedd. *a* **1225** *Ancr. R.* 162 Ure Louerd sulf stont þer bi þe uihte, and beldeð [*v.r.* bealdeð] ham. *c* **1330** *Lai Le Freine* 231 The abbesse her gan teche & beld. *c* **1400** *Destr. Troy* x. 4541 Of the Bisshop þo buernes beldid were þen.

†**2.** *intr.* To grow bold or strong; to be bold, have confidence. *Obs.*

1330 R. BRUNNE *Chron.* 135 Long myght he not regne, ne on his lif belde. *a* **1400** *St. Alexius* (Laud) 29 As he bigon to Belde And was i-come to monnes elde. *a* **1500** *MS. Harl.* 1701, lf. 64 (Halliw.) Thys mayde wax and bygan to belde Weyl ynto womans elde.

3. *trans.* To defend, protect, shelter. *Sc.* and *north. dial.*

c **1300** in Wright's *Lyric P.* iv. 24 He shal him birewen that he hire belde. *c* **1400** *Ywaine & Gaw.* 1220 None es so wight wapins to welde, Ne that so boldly mai us belde. *c* **1440** *York Myst.* i. 35, I beelde þe here baynely in blys for to be. —— 107 We þat ware beelded in blys, in bale are we nowe. **1470** HARDING *Chron.* cxl. vii, Kyng Philip cowardly with royall hoste hym beld. **1570** LEVINS *Manip.* 208 To Beald, succour, *adumbrare, protegere.* ? *a* **1600** *Felon Sow of Rokeby*, The fryar leaped..And bealed him with a tree. **1828** SCOTT *F.M. Perth* xii, That..bielded me as if I had been a sister.

4. *intr.* (for *refl.*) To find refuge, protection, or shelter; to shelter oneself; to lodge, dwell. (In this sense possibly confused with BUILD, q.v.)

c **1400** *Destr. Troy* XIV. 5864 And bowet fro the batell.. ffor to beld hym on þe bent, & his brethe take. ? *a* **1400** *Morte Arth.* 8 Ewyre to belde and to byde in blysse with hyme selvene. *Ibid.* 1242 Thi baronage, that bieldez thare-in. *c* **1400** *Melayne* 1496 Under the cante of a hille Oure Bretons beldis & bydis stille. *c* **1440** *York Myst.* i. 61 All blys es here beeldande a-boute vs. —— xxxii. 1 Pees, bewscheres, I bidde you, þat beldis here aboute me. *c* **1460** *Towneley Myst.* 135 Alas! Where may we beyld?

†**5.** *transf.* To cover, cover over. (Only Sc.)

a **1455** HOLLAND *Houlat* xix. 9 Braid burdis & benkis, ourbeld with bancouris of gold. *c* **1495** DUNBAR *Tua Mariit Wemen* 164 Now sall the byle all out brist, that beild has bein so lang. *c* **1550** SIR J. BALFOUR *Practicks* 618 To see the ship tyit and beiled.

†**6.** To sustain, nourish, feed. *Obs.*

c **1470** HENRY *Wallace* XI. 43 This land is purd off fud that suld ws beild. **1513** DOUGLAS *Æneis* I. xi. 21 Fyfty damicellis ..To graith the chalmeris, and the fyris beild.

bield, *ppl. a. Sc.* Also **biel.** [f. prec. verb.] Sheltered, comfortable, cosy.

1792 BURNS *Bessie & Spin. Wheel* i, And haps me biel and warm at e'en. **1795** MACNEILL *Will & Jean* 92 Neat and bield, a cot-house stood.

bielding ('biːldɪŋ), *vbl. sb. north.* Also 5 **beel-, beyldyng.** [f. as prec. + -ING¹.] Protection; shelter.

c **1440** *York Myst.* I. 38 In þis blis sall be ȝhour beeldyng. *c* **1460** *Towneley M.* 122 That I may have som beyldyng by In my travaylle. **1724** RAMSAY *Tea-t. Misc.* (1733) II. 198 Nae beilding can she [the hare] borrow In Sorrel's field.

†**'bieldly,** *a. Obs. north. dial.* In 5 **beyldly.** [f. BIELD *sb.* + -LY¹.] Of the nature of a shelter.

c **1440** *York Myst.* XLI. 336 Welcome to thy beyldly boure.

bieldy ('biːldɪ), *a. Sc.* Also 8 **beildy, biely.** [f. as prec. + -Y¹.] Affording shelter.

a **1758** RAMSAY *Poems* II. 485 (JAM.) Beildy holes when tempests blaw. **1789** D. DAVIDSON *Seasons* 176 (JAM.) An' Spring peeps cautious on the biely braes. **1822** SCOTT *Nigel* xxvii, When I came here first..England was a bieldy bit.

Bielid ('biːlɪd). *Astr.* [f. the name *Biela* (see below) + -ID², as in *Leonid*, etc.] An Andromede. So called because supposed to come from the remains of Biela's comet (named after the Austrian astronomer, W. von Biela). Also *attrib.*

1885 *Science* VI. II. 496/2 The Bielid meteors were observed here in considerable numbers. **1899** *Edin. Rev.* Oct. 318 Displacements of the Bielid orbit are no abnormal events. **1899** *Sci. Amer.* 9 Dec. 379/3 A Shower of Bielids. A well-marked shower of Bielid meteors was observed at Princeton on the evening of November 24.

bi-emarginate: see BI- 3.

‖**bien** (bjɛ̃), *adv.* The French word for 'well'; used in certain French phrases:

bien entendu (bjɛ̃nɑ̃tɑ̃dy). [F. *entendu*, pa. pple. of *entendre* to hear, understand.] Of course; that goes without saying.

1844 THACKERAY *Barry Lyndon* vii. in *Fraser's Mag.* Apr. 396/1 Burgundy and velvet are the best, *bien entendu.* **1863** C. READE *Hard Cash* I. vi. 190 And I was not penniless, bien entendu. **1904** H. O. STURGIS *Belchamber* x. 136, I could never call her that to her face, *bien entendu.* **1927** B. MALINOWSKI *Sex & Repression in Savage Society* I. ix. 77 First of all—and that has, *bien entendu*, nothing to do with matriliny—there is no condemnation of sex.

bien-être (bjɛ̃nɛtr). [Fr. (16th) c.); *être* to be.] A state of well-being; comfort.

1849 GEO. ELIOT *Let.* 26 Oct. in J. W. Cross *Life* (1884) I. iv. 189, I never enjoyed a more complete *bien être* in my life than during the last fortnight. **1873** W. JAMES *Let.* 11 May in R. B. Perry *Thought & Char. W.J.* (1935) I. 344 Your letter..seemed to reveal a great physical *bien être.* **1883** C. M. YONGE *Stray Pearls* I. x. 112 There was an indefinable bliss and *bien-être* in their very presence. **1946** WODEHOUSE *Joy in Morning* i. 3 No inkling of the soup into which I was to be plunged came to mar my perfect *bien-être.*

bien pensant (bjɛ̃ pɑ̃sɑ̃), *a.* [Fr. *pensant*, pr. pple. of *penser* to think.] Right-thinking; orthodox, conservative. Also as *sb.*

1923 A. HUXLEY *On Margin* 113 If you are rich, of good family and *bien pensant.* **1938** *Times Lit. Suppl.* 1 Oct. 622/3 A Nationalist rising in Spain, which not only M. Maurras but all the French *bien-pensants* supported. **1958** *Listener* 7 Aug. 209/2 The pitiful, hasty funeral from which the local *bien-pensants* remain away. **1962** N. MITFORD *Water Beetle* 136 In her world, Catholic, royalist, *bien pensant.*

bien, variant of BEIN.; obs. f. of BUY.

biend, obs. form of BEND *sb.*¹

bienfait, -volence: see BENE-.

†**bi'ennal.** *Obs.* [ad. late L. *biennāl-e* (sc. *officium*), neuter of *biennālis* of two years (see next).] The saying of masses for a departed soul during the period of two years.

1362 LANGL. *P. Pl.* A. VIII. 156 Bienals [*v.r.* biennales, byennals] and Trienals and Busschopes lettres.

biennial (baɪ'ɛnɪəl), *a.* and *sb.* [f. L. *bienni-s* of two years, *bienni-um* space of two years (f. *bi-* two + *annus* year) + -AL¹.] **A.** *adj.*

1. Existing or lasting for two years; changed every two years.

1621 HOWELL *Lett.* I. I. xli, The Duke is there [at Genoa] but Biennial, being chang'd every two years. *a* **1711** KEN *Hymnoth.* Poet. Wks. 1721 III. 12 Biennial Stores they [ants] treasure under Earth. **1854** WOODWARD *Mollusca* (1856), The land-snails are mostly biennial.

b. *esp.* of plants; see B.

1691 RAY *Creation* I. (J.), Some..very long lived, others only annual or biennial. **1755** *Gentl. Mag.* XXV. 69 The common hemlock is biennial. **1805** KNIGHT in *Phil. Trans.* XCV. 262 Annual and biennial plants.

2. Recurring, happening, or taking place once in every two years.

1750 JOHNSON *Rambl.* No. 61 ⁋6 Whom he condescends to honour with a biennial visit.

B. *sb. Bot.* A plant which springs from seed and vegetates one year (or growing season), and flowers, fructifies, and perishes the next.

1770 WARING in *Phil. Trans.* LXI. 385 Biennials..are the natural..product of such places. **1815** *Encycl. Brit.* (ed. 5) III. 610 Of the esculent kinds, the cabbage, savoy, carrot, parsnip, beet, onion, leek, etc., are biennials.

bi'ennially, *adv.* [f. prec. + -LY².] Every two years; once in two years.

1775 BURKE *Sp. Conc. Amer.* Wks. III. 98 Through whose hands the acts pass biennially in Ireland, or annually in the colonies. **1820** SCOTT *Abbot* iv, The Professor's cast-off suit, which he disparts with biennially.

‖**bienseance** (bjɛ̃seɑ̃s). [Fr., f. *bienséant*, f. *bien* well + *séant*, pr. pple. of *seoir* to befit. Rather common in Eng. use about end of 18th and beginning of 19th c.] Decorum; propriety.

[**1665** BOYLE *Occas. Refl.* (1675) Pref. 20 The Laws of Decorum or, as the French call it *Bien-seance*.] **1788** *Walpoliana* lxviii. 34 Those northern countries are rigid in the *bienséance.* **1818** SCOTT *Rob Roy* xiv, Bred in a country where much attention is paid..to *bienséance.* **1823** BYRON *Juan* XIV. lxvii, At least as far as *bienséance* allows.

‖**bienvenue.** *Obs.* Also 5 **beneveneuew,** 6 **bienveneu,** 6–7 **benvenue,** 7 **bienvenu.** [Fr. (bjɛ̃v(ə)ny), f. *bien* well + *venue* coming. Formerly as frequent in Eng. use as *adieu.*]

1. Welcome.

1393 GOWER *Conf.* I, To ben upon his bienvenue The firste, which shall him salue. *c* **1440** *York Myst.* xxx. 280 Now bene-veneuew, beuscher, What boodworde haste þou brought? **1599** NASHE *Lent. Stuffe* (D.), I having no great pieces to discharge for his ben-venue. **1629** MASSINGER *Picture* II. ii, They have..given him the bienvenu.

2. A fee exacted from a new workman.

1793 *Ann. Reg.* 251/1 The compositors demanded of me Bienvenue afresh.

bier (bɪə(r)). Forms: 1 **bǽr, ber,** 2–3 **bære,** 2–6 **bere,** 3 **bare,** 4–7 **beer(e,** 5–6 *Sc.* **beyr,** 5–7 **bear(e,** 6 **beir(e,** 6–7 **biere,** 6– **bier.** [Com. Teut.: OE., WSax. *bǽr*, Anglian *bér*, = OS., OHG. *bâra* (MHG. *bâre*, mod.G. *bahre*), OTeut. **bêrâ* fem. f. *beran* to bear; cf. ON. *barar* fem. pl., also BARROW. The modern spelling (since 1600) appears to be due to imitation of the F. form *bière*, ad. OHG. *bâra* (cf. Pr. *bera*, It. *bara*).]

†**1.** A framework for carrying; a handbarrow; a litter, a stretcher. *Obs.* exc. *Hist.*

c **890** K. ÆLFRED *Bæda* v. xix. (Bosw.), On his þegna handum on bære boren wæs. *c* **975** *Rushw. G.* John v. 8 Aris & ȝinim bere ðine & gaa. *c* **1300** *Beket* 899 Ibare in barewe other in bere. **1535** COVERDALE *2 Macc.* iii. 27 They toke him vp and bare him out vpon a beare. **1583** STANYHURST *Æneis* IV. (Arb.) 108 On beers her softlye reposing. *c* **1600** SHAKS. *Sonn.* xii, Sommers greene all girded vp in sheaues Borne on the beare with white and bristly beard. **1851** TURNER *Dom. Arch.* I. iv. 140 Horse litters or beres were also in use.

2. The movable stand on which a corpse, whether in a coffin or not, is placed before burial; that on which it is carried to the grave.

a **1000** *Elene* (Gr.) 873 And ȝefarenne man [hi] Brohton on bære. *c* **1200** ORMIN 8167 All the bære wass bileȝȝed With bæten gold and silferr. *a* **1300** *Cursor M.* 20703 Four of þapostles ber þe bere. **1382** WYCLIF *2 Sam.* iii. 31 Forsothe Dauid folwide the bere [Cov. bere]. **1565** JEWEL *Repl. Harding* (1611) 211 Whosoeuer was chosen Bishop there, should come to the Beare, and lay his Predecessours hand upon his head. **1611** BIBLE *2 Sam.* iii. 31 King Dauid himselfe followed the biere. —— *Luke* vii. 14 Hee came and touched the beere. **1658** SIR T. BROWNE *Hydriot.* i. 7 Feretra or Beers of Wood. **1703** MAUNDRELL *Journ. Jerus.* 100 He had seiz'd the Bier. **1877** BRYANT *Lit. People Snow* 303 Following the bier, Chanted a sad and solemn melody.

b. Put for the corpse on the bier. *rare.*

1596 SPENSER *Astroph.* 149 The dolefulst beare that euer man did see, Was Astrophel.

3. *transf.* A tomb, a sepulchre.

1513 DOUGLAS *Æneis* III. i. 116 To Polidorus wp a beir We ereckit. **1535** STEWART *Cron. Scot.* II. 600 Tuke the Scottis in the feild war slane, To Crissin bereis in the tyme thame buir. **1596** SPENSER *F.Q.* III. iii. 11 He was surprisd, and buried under beare. **1808** SCOTT *Marm.* I. Introd., Drop upon Fox's grave a tear, 'Twill trickle to his rival's bier.

†**4.** *to bring to, on,* or *upon (one's) bier*: to bring to the grave or to death, to put to death; in *passive*, to meet one's death, die. *Obs.*

c **1480** *Childe Bristowe* 132 in *E.P.P.* (1864) 116 Sone, now y pray the, myn attourney that thu be, when y am broght to bere. **1513** DOUGLAS *Æneis* x. x. 138 This Dardane prince Sa mony douchty corpsis brocht on beyr. **1530** LYNDESAY *Papyngo* 405. **1559** *Mirr. Mag., Dk. Suffolk* xvi, Through privy murder we brought him to his beere. *Ibid. Mempr.* v, When I had my brother brought on beire.

5. *Comb.* and *Attrib.*, as *bier-carrier*; †**bier-balk,** a balk in a field where there is a right of way for funerals; **bier-cloth,** a pall; †**bier-right,** an ordeal in which a person, accused of murder, was required to approach the corpse, and clear himself on oath; †**bier-tree,** the frame of a bier.

1563 *Homilies* II. *Rogation Wk.* IV. (1640) 237 Where their ancestors left of their land a broad and sufficient *beere-balke to carry the corps to the Christian sepulture. **1654** TRAPP *Comm. Job* xxxiii. 22 His life..to the *Bier-carryers, say the Tigurines. **1549** *Invent. Ch. Goods* in *Norfolk Archæol.* (1865) VII. 34 Itm ij *beer clothes, whereof the on is of blacke worsted, the other of canvasse. **1693** *Lond. Gaz.* No. 2845/4 Two black *Bier Cloths. **1828** SCOTT *F.M. Perth* II. 237 I have heard of the *bier-right, Sir Louis. *c* **1440** *Bone Flor.* 1350 Broght hym home on a *bere-tree.

bier, obs. form of BEAR, BEER, BIRR, BUYER.

bierd, variant of BURD, *Obs.*, lady.

bierdly, bierly, variants of BUIRDLY *a.*

‖**bierhaus** ('biːrhaʊs). [G.] A German public house or ale-house.

1930 G. GREENE *Name of Action* viii. 219 A bierhaus with an open door. **1963** —— *Sense of Reality* 83, I imagined myself drinking my way through the festival itself in some *bierhaus* decorated with holly. **1967** J. LEASOR *Passport in Suspense* 2 His father ran a *bierhaus* behind Hamburg railway station.

bierlin, variant of BIRLING, a galley.

biern, -en, variants of BERNE, *Obs.*, warrior.

‖**bierstube** ('biːrʃtuːbə). Also **Bierstube.** Pl. -**ben** or -**bes.** [G.] A German tavern, taproom or bar.

1909 in WEBSTER. **1922** *Glasgow Herald* 6 May 9 Here [*sc.* in Berlin], in the streets, hotels, and bierstubens, many languages..can be heard. **1952** KOESTLER *Arrow in Blue* x. 84 Our fraternity marched..to our favourite Bierstube. **1956** E. BERCKMANN *Strange Bedfellow* xii. 111 She would wait for him in the *Bierstube.*

bies, variant of BYSS, *Obs.*, fine linen.

bieste, biestings, obs. ff. BEAST, BEESTINGS.

bieu, obs. form of BEAU *a.* fair.

bieves, obs. form of *beeves*, pl. of BEEF.

biewaie, obs. form of BY-WAY.

bif, biff, *int.* orig. *U.S.* An exclamation uttered when something strikes an object, or a sound imitative of such a blow. Cf. BIFF *v.* 3.
1847 J. S. ROBB *Squatter Life* 137, I hit him, *biff*, alongside his smeller. **1905** H. G. WELLS *Kipps* I. iv. §1 When I go to turn, if I don't remember, Bif!—and I'm *in* to something. **1917** H. A. VACHELL *Fishpingle* xi, Hamlin bowled straight and true for the middle stump. The youth smote and missed. 'Bif!' yelled Lionel. *a* **1930** D. H. LAWRENCE *Phoenix II* (1968) 109 He..took the poker with satisfaction. Biff! A well-aimed blow.

biface (ˈbaɪfeɪs). *Archæol.* [f. BI-² + FACE *sb.*] A type of prehistoric stone implement flaked on both faces. Also *attrib.*
1934 A. C. HADDON *Hist. Anthropol.* vii. 89 Throughout all Africa a core-tool, or 'biface', is the oldest known technique, and the same applies to India; in Africa it developed from a chipped-pebble industry. **1937** *Proc. Prehist. Soc.* III. 15 The lower Palaeolithic industries may be roughly divided into two main groups:—biface cultures and flake cultures. **1946** F. E. ZEUNER *Dating the Past* vi. 164 The bifaces are mostly made on flakes. **1953** J. PROCHÁZKA tr. *B. Hrozný's Anc. Hist. W. Asia, India & Crete* iv. 12 The so-called flint flakes and more massive bifacial tools ('bifaces') have been uncovered in the early palaeolithic strata.

biˈfacial, *a.* [BI-².] Having two faces; spec. *Bot.*, having distinct dorsal and ventral surfaces; *Archæol.*, of a flint: worked on both sides. Hence **biˈfacially** *adv.*
1884 BOWER & SCOTT *De Bary's Phanerog. F.* 48 Firm, leathery..bifacial leaves. **1952** V. G. CHILDE *New Light on Most Anc. East* ii. 19 Bifacial trimming in which the primary flake is thinned and shaped by the removal of fine secondary flakes from both sides or faces and along both edges. **1953** [see BIFACE]. **1957** V. G. CHILDE *Dawn Europ. Civ.* (ed. 6) vii. 111 The Bükkians made from the volcanic glass knives and scrapers, but no bifacially worked arrow-heads.

bifanged: see BI- *pref.*² 1.

bifarious (baɪˈfɛərɪəs), *a.* [f. L. *bifāri-us* two-fold, double.]
1. Two-fold, double, ambiguous. *arch.* or *Obs.*
1656 BLOUNT *Glossogr.*, *Bifarious*, that which may be spoken two ways. **1707** E. WARD *Hud. Rediv.* II. VII. 3 Some strange, mysterious Verity In old bifarious Prophesy. **1770** *Month. Rev.* 18 To exercise her bifarious talents.
2. *Bot.* Ranged in two rows.
1846 DANA *Zooph.* (1848) 645 Polyps seriate, or bifarious. **1876** HARLEY *Mat. Med.* 380 Turmeric.—Leaves bifarious.

biˈfariously, *adv.* [f. prec. + -LY².] In a bifarious manner: **a.** In two ways; ambiguously. **b.** In two rows. *bifariously pubescent* in *Bot.*: having the hairs on each internode ranged in two opposite rows at right angles to the rows on the two adjacent internodes.
1657 TOMLINSON *Renou's Disp.* 556 Polypody must be bifariously prepared. **1870** HOOKER *Stud. Flora* 268 *Veronica arvensis*..branches..bifariously pubescent.

†**biˈfel-e**, *v. Obs.* [Com. WGer.: OE. *befeolan* = OS. and OHG. *bifelhan* (MHG. *bevelhen*, mod.G. *befehlen*, MDu. and Du. *bevelen*), f. *bi-*, BE- + *felhan*, in ON. *fela* to hide, bury, entrust, Goth. *filhan* to hide, bury. An important vb. in Ger. and Du., but early lost in Eng.]
trans. To commit, entrust, consign, grant.
c **1000** *Ags. Ps.* lxxii. 14 [lxxiii. 18] þu him for inwite, yfel befæle. *c* **1175** *Lamb. Hom.* 123 On helle þe we weren in bifolen þurh ure eldra gult.

bifer (ˈbaɪfə(r)). [a. L. *bifer* adj. 'bearing fruit twice in the year,' f. *bi-* twice + *-fer* bearing.] A plant which produces fruit or flowers twice a year.

biferous (ˈbɪfərəs), *a.* [f. as prec. + -OUS. Cf. F. *bifère*.] **a.** *Bot.* Bearing fruit or flowers twice in a year. **b.** *Crystallog.* (see quot.)
1656 in BLOUNT *Glossogr.* *a* **1682** SIR T. BROWNE *Tracts* 70 Some are biferous and triferous which bear twice or thrice in the year. **1816** R. JAMESON *Char. Min.* (1817) 220 Biferous (*bifère*), when every angle and edge suffers two decrements. Example, Biferous grey copper-ore.

biff (bɪf), *v. slang.* [Imitative.] **1.** *trans.* To hit, strike. Also *to biff* (a person) *one*.
1888 *Judy* 18 Jan. 27 He playfully biffed him with a brick. **1894** KIPLING *Day's Work* (1898) 71 Ef we all biffed you now, these same men..'u'd call us off. **1903** CLAPIN *Dict. Amer.* 50 *Bif, biff, bift*, current in several parts of the States in sense of to strike, and especially to give a quick blow. 'He biffed him on the ear.' **1908** G. H. LORIMER *J. Spurlock* i. 19 If she had biffed me one it would have been all right. **1950** A. BARON *There's no Home* 181 Where'd you get that bruise on your forehead? Girl friend been biffing you with the old rolling pin?
b. *fig.* To deal a blow to, to refute, to 'stump' (see also quot. 1895).
1895 W. C. GORE in *Inlander* Nov. 60 *Biff*, to refuse; to repulse; to slight. **1914** T. E. LAWRENCE *Let.* June (1938) 174 To biff that, Woolley & I walked over next day to Mesopotamia. **1915** C. MACKENZIE *Guy & Pauline* v. 263 'Oh, it's in old French, is it?' said Brydone in a disappointed voice. 'That would biff me.' A silence fell upon the room, a silence that seemed to symbolize the 'biffing' of the doctor's son by old French.
c. To throw. Also *intr. Austral.* and *N.Z.*
1941 BAKER *Dict. Austral. Slang* 9 *Biff*, to throw. **1964** *N.Z. Listener* 1 May 4/2 'All I can do is biff.' 'Then just biff —as hard as you can. You're a natural [at putting the shot].'
2. *intr.* To go, proceed. Esp. with *off*, to leave, depart.
1923 WODEHOUSE *Inimit. Jeeves* i. 9 Bingo biffs about London on a pretty comfortable allowance. *Ibid.* xv. 189, I can't go chucking all my engagements..in order to biff down to Twing. **1929** —— *Mr. Mulliner Speaking* viii. 250 Biffed off a trifle abruptly.
3. The verb used adverbially with *go*, in the sense of 'with a violent blow'. Cf. BIF, BIFF *int.*
1904 *Daily Chron.* 15 Dec. 4/7 There might go biff through the glass the occasional plank.
Hence **ˈbiffing** *vbl. sb.*, the action of the verb *biff*.
[**1894** KIPLING in *Century Mag.* Dec. XLIX. 295/2 S'pose we want the Back Pasture turned into a biffin'-ground on our only day er rest?] **1915** [see sense 1 b above]. **1959** I. & P. OPIE *Lore & Lang. Schoolch.* xvii. 374 The miscreant receives..a..biffing.

biff, *sb. slang.* Also bif. [f. the vb.] A blow, whack. Also *fig.* Cf. BAFF *sb.*
1889 BARRÈRE & LELAND *Dict. Slang*, *Biff* (Americanism), to give [one] a 'biff in the jaw'. **1890** *Dialect Notes* I. 72 *Bif*, ..oftenest used in such phrases as 'to give one a biff in the ear'. **1904** W. H. SMITH *Promoters* x. 165 What an idiot a man can be when he gets a biff that takes his wind. **1926** *Blackw. Mag.* Feb. 224/1 Contusions on top of head..biff on the — bruise on inside of knee. **1935** L. A. G. STRONG *Tuesday Afternoon* 45 A biff that made him bite his tongue.

biff, *int.*: see BIF *int.*

biffin (ˈbɪfɪn). Also beefen, -in, -ing, beaufin. [A dial. pronunc. of *beefing*, f. BEEF, in reference to the deep red colour of the apple; see -ING. The spelling *beaufin* has been fabricated to give colour to a fictitious derivation from F. *beau* beautiful + *fin* fine.]
1. A variety of cooking apple, cultivated especially in Norfolk.
1794 GODWIN *Cal. Williams* 63 Frost-bitten cheeks, as red as a beefen from her own orchard. **1829** PEACOCK *Misf. Elphin* 180 This archetype of a Norfolk beefin. **1834** *Penny Cycl.* II. 190/1 For drying, the Norfolk Beaufin. **1844** DICKENS *Christm. Carol* 82 Norfolk Biffins, squab and swarthy, setting off the yellow of the oranges and lemons.
2. A baked apple, of the preceding variety, flattened in the form of a cake.
1822 KITCHINER *Cook's Orac.* 500 Dried Biffins from Norfolk. **1837** *New Month. Mag.* XLIX. 555 Beat his enormous head as flat as a biffin. **1858** R. HOGG *Veg. Kingd.* 308 Baked in ovens, and flattened in the form of round cakes, they [apples] are called Beefings.

bifid (ˈbaɪfɪd, ˈbɪfɪd), *a.* Also 8 biffid. [ad. L. *bifidus*, f. *bi-* two + *fid-*, stem of *findĕre* to cleave, split.] Divided into two parts by a deep cleft or notch. **ˈbifidly** *adv.*, in a bifid manner.
1661 LOVELL *Hist. Anim. & Min.* Introd., Amongst serpents..the tongue is..bifid in the end. **1766** *Phil. Trans.* LVI. 213 A land tortoise in which was found a biffid wind-pipe. **1834** MRS. SOMERVILLE *Connex. Phys. Sc.* (1849) 404 The bifid tail of the comet. **1849** *Proc. Berw. Nat. Club* II. 371 Bifidly divided at the apex.

bifidate (ˈbɪfɪdeɪt), *a.* [f. prec. + -ATE.] A bad variant of prec.
1847 in CRAIG.

bifidated, *a.* [f. as prec. + -ED.] = prec.
1755 in JOHNSON; hence in mod. Dicts.

bifidity (baɪ-, bɪˈfɪdɪtɪ). [f. BIFID + -ITY.] The quality of being bifid.
1870 ROLLESTON *Anim. Life* 106 Antero-posterior bifidity.

ˈbifidous, biˈfideous, *a.* Obsolete by-forms of BIFID.
1657 TOMLINSON, *Renou's Disp.* 456 Bifideous hoofes. *Ibid.* 457 Bifidous ungles, like a Goat. **1715** *Phil. Trans.* XXIX. 307 Quadrupeds..multifidous and bifidous.

bifilar (baɪˈfaɪlə(r)), *a.* [f. BI- *pref.*² 1 + FILAR, f. L. *fīl-um* thread + -AR.] Fitted or furnished with two threads; *spec.* applied to apparatus for measuring minute distances or angles; also for suspending a body so that it has a very slight directive force in a definite plane, with a view to the measurement of minute forces, etc. Also as *sb.* **biˈfilarly** *adv.*, in a bifilar manner, by means of two threads.
[**1836** W. S. HARRIS in *Trans. R. Soc.* CXXVI. 417 A new species of balance; it may be termed, from the peculiar mechanical principle on which it depends, a bifile balance.] **1839** WHEWELL *Let. to Quételet* 17 Jan. (1876) II. 275 Airy has just put up his Gaussian apparatus..at Greenwich, including a *Bifilar*. **1846** *Penny Cycl.* Suppl. II. 256/1 The horizontal force magnetometer at the Greenwich Observatory is bifilar. **1848** W. S. HARRIS *Rudimentary Electricity* iii. 83 *The Bifilar Balance.* In this electrometer.. a re-active force is obtained by means of a lever at the extremity of two parallel and vertical threads of unspun silk. **1870** R. FERGUSON *Electr.* 26 Gauss's bifilar magnetometer. **1879** THOMSON & TAIT *Nat. Phil.* I. I. §435 The Bifilar Suspension..was used also by Gauss in his bifilar magnetometer for measuring the horizontal component of the terrestrial magnetic force. **1884** *Harper's Mag.* Sept. 644/1 A copper disc suspended bifilarly.

bifistular (baɪˈfɪstjʊlə(r)), *a.* [f. BI- *pref.*² 1 + FISTULAR, f. L. *fistula* tube.] Having two tubes.
1870 HOOKER *Stud. Flora* 224 *Lobelia Dortmanna*; leaves all radical, submerged, subcylindrical, bifistular.

biflecnode (baɪˈflɛknəʊd). *Math.* [f. BI-² + FLECNODE.] A point on a curve that is both a node and a point of inflexion for each branch passing through it. Hence **biflecˈnodal** *a.*
1874 G. SALMON *Analyt. Geom.* (ed. 3) p. xvii, Number of points at which two tangents are biflecnodal. *Ibid.* 521 Biflecnodal points. **1879** —— *Higher Plane Curves* (ed. 3) 217 Such a node may be considered as the union of an ordinary node with (in the first case) a point of inflexion, and with (in the second case) two points of inflexion; and the node may be termed a flecnode or a biflecnode in the two cases respectively.

biflete, *v.*, to flow round: see BE- *pref.* 4.

biflorate (baɪˈflɔəreɪt), *a.* [f. as next + -ATE.] = next.
1864 in WEBSTER.

biflorous (baɪˈflɔərəs), *a.* [f. mod.L. *biflōr-us* two-flowered (f. BI- + *flōr-em* flower) + -OUS.] Bearing two flowers or blooms; two flowered.
1794 MARTYN *Rousseau's Bot.* xxv. 357 Tangier Pea, another of the biflorous section. **1880** GRAY *Bot. Text-bk.* 399.

biˈfocal, *a.* and *sb.* orig. *U.S.* [BI-².] **A.** *adj.* Having two foci; *spec.* designating spectacles with two segments of different focal lengths.
1888 G. M. GOULD in *Med. & Surg. Reporter* LIX. 545 (*title*) A new style of bi-focal lenses. **1895** *Pop. Sci. Monthly* Aug. 470 Ordinary bifocal glasses. **1938** E. AMBLER *Cause for Alarm* ii. 29 A..man of about fifty with rimless, bi-focal spectacles. **1968** *New Scientist* 21 Mar. 619/2 Bifocal and trifocal spectacles have been a blessing.
B. *sb. pl.* Bifocal spectacles.
1899 *Ophthalmic Rev.* XVIII. 270 Dr. G. C. Harlan..had shown..a pair of bi-focals made by Borsch in which the reading part is formed of a circular lens 15 mm. in diameter ..sunk into the distant lens. **1936** G. B. SHAW *Simpleton* 31 Wears glasses. Bi-focals. **1960** J. WAIN *Nuncle* 6 Harley Street types looking at me through their bifocals.

†**ˈbifoil.** *Obs. Herb.* [ad. med.L. *bifolium*, f. *bi-* two + *folium* leaf; cf. *trefoil*, *cinquefoil*.] Obs. name of the Twayblade (*Listera ovata*).
1633 GERARD *Herbal.* II. lxxxvii. 402 Of Twayblade, or herbe Bifoile. **1860** MAYNE *Med. Lex.* 121.

bifold (ˈbaɪfəʊld), *a.* [f. BI- *pref.*² + FOLD.] Double, twofold; of two kinds, degrees, etc.
1609 SHAKS. *Tr. & Cr.* v. ii. 144 (*Qo.*) O madnesse of discourse, that cause sets up with and against it selfe, By-fould authority. [1 *Fol.* By foule authoritie. *Globe* Bi-fold authority!] **1818** J. BROWN *Psyche* 85 Like Janus with his bifold faces. **1876** EMERSON *Ess.* Ser. I. vii. 186 The scholar shames us by his bifold lie.

bifole, obs. form of BEFOOL.

bifoliate (baɪˈfəʊlɪət), *a.* [f. mod.L. *bifoli-us* two-leafed (f. BI- + *folium* leaf) + -ATE.] Having or consisting of two leaves.
1836 *Penny Cycl.* V. 251. **1870** BENTLEY *Bot.* 164 A leaf is said to be binate, bifoliate, or unijugate, if it consists of only 2 leaflets springing from a common point.

bifoliolate (baɪˈfəʊlɪəleɪt), *a.* [f. BI- *pref.*² 1 + mod.L. *foliol-um*, dim. of *folium* leaf + -ATE.] Having or composed of two leaflets: see quot.
1835 LINDLEY *Introd. Bot.* (1848) II. 360 Bifoliolate, when in leaves the common petiole is terminated by two leaflets growing from the same point.

bifolium (baɪˈfəʊlɪəm). *Palæogr.* Pl. -ia. [f. BI-² + L. *folium* leaf.] A pair of conjoint leaves.
1938 E. A. LOWE *Codices Latini Antiquiores* III. 283 Foll. 3..composed of a bifolium and a single leaf. *Ibid.* 284 Ruling on the hair-side central opening, four bifolia at a time before folding. **1957** N. R. KER *Catal. MSS. containing Anglo-Saxon* 407 A bifolium followed by three singletons. **1960** E. A. LOWE *English Uncial* 11 The following Insular, at least non-Italian, features were enumerated: pricking and ruling of the bifolia after folding, [etc.].

bifollicular: see BI- *pref.*² 1.

bifor, -an, -en, obs. forms of BEFORE.

biforate (baɪˈfɔərət, ˈbɪfəreɪt), *a.* [f. BI- *pref.*² 1 + FORATE, ad. L. *forātus* pierced.] 'Having two openings' (Gray *Bot. Text-bk.* 1880); having two perforations, as the anther of the rhododendron.
1842 in BRANDE.

biforine (ˈbɪfəraɪn). *Bot.* [f. L. *bifor-is* having folding doors or two openings (f. *bi-* two + *foris* door) + -INE.] A minute oval sac found in the green pulpy part of some leaves; so called from discharging its contents by an opening at each end.
1842 in BRANDE. **1870** BENTLEY *Bot.* 34 Such cells have been called Biforines.

biforked (ˈbaɪfɔːkt), *a.* [f. BI- *pref.*² 1 + FORKED.] Having, or divided into, two forks, branches, or peaks; = BIFURCATE *a.*
1578 BANISTER *Hist. Man* I. 20 The same posteriour Processe of the second Vertebre is clouen or biforked. **1685** MORDEN *Geog. Rect.* 198 A steep biforked mountain. **1873** LONGF. *Aftermath* Prel. 72 [Birds that] flying write upon the sky the biforked letter of the Greeks. **1878** BROWNING *Poets Croisic* xlviii, The biforked hill betwixt.

biform (ˈbaɪfɔːm), *a.* [ad. L. *biformis*, f. *bi-* two + *forma* shape, form.] Having, or partaking of, two distinct forms.
1816 R. JAMESON *Char. Min.* (1817) 202 A crystal is said to be bi-form, when it contains a combination of two remarkable forms. **1825–36** MONTAGU tr. *Bacon's Sap. Vet.* (1860) 209 Of a biform figure, human above, half brute below. **1864** SWINBURNE *Atalanta* 1253 The biform bull.

ˈbiformed, *a.* [f. as prec. + -ED.] = prec.
1586 WARNER *Alb. Eng.* III. xviii. 81 Bi-formed Janus. **1607** TOPSELL *Four-f. Beasts* 437 The Epithets of a Mule are . . dirty, Spanish, rough, and bi-formed. **1656** in BLOUNT *Glossogr.*; and in mod. Dicts.

biˈformity. [f. as prec. + -ITY.] Biform nature.
1611 COTGR., *Biformité*, biformitie, double forme. **1642** H. MORE *Song of Soul* I. III. lxx, Strange things he spake of the biformity Of the Dizoians.

biforn(e, obs. form of BEFORE.

†biˈfornys, *adv. Obs.* [= *beforn-es*, f. *beforn*, BEFORE + *-es* of advb. genitive.] Before, in front.
c **1420** *Pallad. on Husb.* VII. 43 This teeth wol bite hem so that the bifornys And fere hem in.

bifront (ˈbaɪfrʌnt), *a.* Also 7 byfront. [ad. L. *bifront-em*, f. *bi-* two + *front-em* (nom. *frons*) forehead, face.] Having two faces or aspects; double; *absol.* = Janus.
1598 MARSTON *Pigmal.* i. 141 This Ianian-bifront hypocrisie. **1640** T. CAREW *Poems* 111 But, Byfront, open thou no more, In his blest raigne, the temple dore. **1658** COKAINE *Poems* (1669) 1 The bifront hill. **1880** SWINBURNE *Gard. Cymodoce* 244 One sheer thread of narrowing precipice Bifront.

bifrontal (baɪˈfrɒntəl), *a.* = prec.
1876 HUMPHREYS *Coin Coll. Man.* xxi. 259 Bifrontal Janus.

biˈfronted, *a.* [f. as prec. + -ED.] = prec.
1598 MARSTON *Pigmal.* i. 137 Yee vizarded-bifronted-Ianian rout. **1680** *Protest. Petit. agst. Popery* in *Roxb. Ball.* (1881) IV. 207 A bi-fronted Conscience. **1817** GODWIN *Mandev.* II. 106 The bifronted imputation of cowardice and treachery.

‖**bifteck** (biftɛk). Also biftek. [Fr., adaptation of BEEF-STEAK.] = BEEF-STEAK.
[**1825** *French Domestic Cookery* 50 Bifteck au Beurre d'Anchois.—*Beef-Steaks with Anchovy Butter.*] **1861** MRS. BEETON *Bk. Househ. Managem.* 264 There is in every *carte* at every French restaurant . . *biftek d'Angleterre.* **1941** KOESTLER *Scum of Earth* 16 To become a Deputy or Minister was only a form of earning one's *bifteck* and rather a fat one at that. **1969** *Guardian* 30 Aug. 3/4 With meat the price it is, it is unlikely that it will be a very good biftek in a 27s 6d meal.

bifurcal (baɪˈfɜːkəl), *a. rare.* [f. L. *bifurc-us* two-forked, two-pronged + -AL¹.] = BIFURCATE *a.*
1861 READE *Cloister & H.* III. 145 A little bifurcal dagger to hold the meat.

bifurcate (ˈbaɪfɜːkeɪt), *v.* [f. med.L. *bifurcāt-us* two-forked (cf. BIFURCOUS and -ATE); at first only in the pa. pple., which is also generally used as an adj.] To divide into two forks, branches, or peaks: **a.** *trans.*
1615 CROOKE *Body of Man* 905 The utter of these two vneqvall branches . . is presently byfurcated.
b. *intr.*
1831 R. KNOX *Cloquet's Anat.* 746 Sometimes, at its termination, it [Vena Azygos] bifurcates.
Hence **ˈbifurcated, ˈbifurcating** *ppl. a.*
1615 CROOKE *Body of Man* 977 The spinall processes of the necke are byfurcated. **1811** PINKERTON *Petral.* II. 345 Which renders the summit of Etna properly bifurcated. **1845** DARWIN *Voy. Nat.* xx. (1873) 478 [The] atoll is divided by a bifurcating channel. **1853** TH. ROSS *Humboldt's Trav.* III. xxv. 17 The northern branch of the bifurcated river.

bifurcate (baɪˈfɜːkət), *a.* [f. med.L. *bifurcāt-us*: see prec.] = BIFORKED; see also quot. 1880.
1835 LINDLEY *Introd. Bot.* (1848) I. 342 The filament . . is in Crambe bifurcate. **1880** GRAY *Bot. Text.-bk.* 399 *Bifurcate*, two-forked . . But it may mean *bis furcatus*, forked and again forked.

bifurcation (baɪfɜːˈkeɪʃən). [n. of action f. BIFURCATE *v.*: see -ATION.]
1. Division into two forks or branches (viewed either as an action or a state).
1646 SIR T. BROWNE *Pseud. Ep.* 93 A byfurcation or division of the roote into two parts. **1879** RUTLEY *Stud. Rocks* ix. 79 A bifurcation of the rays is no longer induced.
b. *fig.*
1849 GROTE *Greece* II. xlv. *marg.*, Bifurcation of Grecian politics between Sparta and Athens. **1876** DOUSE *Grimm's Law* App. E. 206 An incipient bifurcation of meaning.
2. *concr.* **a.** The point at which the division into two forks takes place. **b.** The bifurcating branches or one of them.
1615 CROOKE *Body of Man* 905 The greater and vtter part of that byfurcation . . descendeth along the Brace. **1761** STILES in *Phil. Trans.* LV. 263 The tube . . lessens gradually as far as the bifurcation. **1855** MAURY *Phys. Geog. Sea* ii. §128 To regard them as bifurcations of the Gulf Stream. **1860** MOTLEY *Netherl.* (1868) II. ix. 23 The island . . at the bifurcation of the Rhine and the Waal.

biˈfurcous, *a.* ? *Obs.*⁻⁰ [f. L. *bifurc-us* two-forked (f. BI- 1 twice + *furca* fork) + -OUS.] = BIFURCATE *a.*
1656 in BLOUNT *Glossogr.* **1847** in CRAIG and mod. Dicts.

bi-furked, *a.* A mixture of *biforked* and *bifurcate*.
a **1563** BALE *Sel. Wks.* (1849) 440 The disciples of Antichrist with their bifurked ordinaries. **1879** DIXON *Windsor* II. i. 5 His beard . . was bi-furked and short.

big, *sb. Obs.* exc. *dial.* Also bigg, bigge. [Deriv. unknown. (Some refer it to BIG *a.*; some compare Cornish *begel*, Breton *bégél* the navel.)]
1. A teat. Now *dial.*
1573 TUSSER *Husb.* xxxiii. (1878) 74 Lamb, bulchin, and pig, geld vnder the big. **1601** HOLLAND *Pliny* I. 558 With bigs or dugs. **1705** HICKERINGILL *Priest-Cr.* II. v. 48 If they had suckt in the Whimsie from the Bigg with their Mother's Milk. **1727** BRADLEY *Fam. Dict.*, *Bigg*, a Pap or Teat in some Country Places. **1875** *Lanc. Gloss.* (E.D.S.) *Big*, a teat, where the 'familiar' was said to draw blood from the body of a witch.
†2. A boil. *Obs.*
1601 HOLLAND *Pliny* II. 444 Good for the swelling piles and bigs. **1646** GAULE *Cases Consc.* 6 If you will not admit a big, or a boyl.

big (bɪg), *a.* Forms: 4 byge, 4–6 byg(g, bygge, 4–7 bigg(e, 3– big. [ME. *big*, *bigg*, *bigge*, first known in end of 13th c. in writers of Northumbria and north Lincolnshire: hence perh. of Norse origin; but its derivation is entirely unknown. (See Skeat: E. Müller's suggestion that it may be short for BIGLY *a.* is not favoured by the history of the senses; but the latter is itself uncertain, and the arrangement here may require change.)]
A. † 1. a. Of living beings: Of great strength or power; strong, stout, mighty. *Obs.* L. *validus*, *potens*.
a **1300** *Havelok* 1774 Bernard stirt up, þat was ful big. **1352** MINOT *Poems* vi. 29 To batail er thai baldly big. *a* **1375** *Joseph Arim.* 452 A-non tholomers men · woxen þe biggore; Sone beeren hem a-bac · and brouhten hem to grounde. **1377** LANGL. *P. Pl.* B. VI. 216 Bolde beggeres and bigge þat mowe her bred biswynke. *c* **1400** *Destr. Troy* VIII. 3971 A felle man in fight, fuerse on his enimys, And in batell full bigge. **1470–85** MALORY *Arthur* (1816) II. 367 Within four or five days, sir Launcelot was big and strong again. **1530** PALSGR. 306/1 Bygge of strength, *robuste*. Bygge of power or myght, *puissant*. **1599** SHAKS. *Hen. V*, IV. ii. 43 Bigge Mars seemes banqu'rout in their begger'd Hoast.
† b. Powerful in resources, rich, wealthy. (Cf. OE. *ríce*.) *Obs. rare.*
1340 HAMPOLE *Pr. Consc.* 1460 Now er we bigg [*v.r.* riche], now er we bare.
† 2. Of things: Strong, stout; stiff; forceful, violent, vehement. (This passes into the sense of 'great,' cf. 'a great or violent storm.') *Obs.*
c **1325** *E.E. Allit. P.* B. 43 Ful bygge a boffet. *Ibid.* A. 374 Much þe bygger ȝet watz my mon. *c* **1400** *Destr. Troy* xv. 6548 Big was the batell vpon bothe haluys. **1477** EARL RIVERS (Caxton) *Dictes* 84 He is of bygge & strong corage. **1523** FITZHERB. *Husb.* § 10 Bigge and styffe grounde, as cley, wolde be sowen with bigge stuffe, as beanes. **1574** HYLL *Weather* vii, The redder the Rainbow appeareth, even so much the bigger doth the winde ensue. **1604** SHAKS. *Oth.* III. iii. 349 Farewell the bigge Warres That makes Ambition Vertue!
3. a. Of great size, bulk, or extent; large. (The first appearance of this sense is doubtful. Quot. 1386 probably, 1490 possibly belong to 1.)
[*c* **1386** CHAUCER *Prol.* 548 Ful byg he was of brawn and eek of bones. **1490** CAXTON *Eneydos* xv. 60 The grete cytees and bygge townes. **1494** FABYAN V. cxxxi. 114 Precious stones of a great bygnesse and value.] **1552** HULOET, Bigger parte or syde, *bona pars.* **1580** BARET *Alv.* B 648 The Epistle was as bigge or as great as a booke. **1597** SHAKS. *2 Hen. IV*, III. ii. 277 Care I for . . the stature, bulke, and bigge assemblance of a man? **1642** MILTON *Apol. Smect.* Wks. (1851) 305 The biggest and the fattest Bishoprick. **1665** BOYLE *Occas. Refl.* IV. iii. (1675) 185 For the loss of the biggest Fortune in the East. **1719** W. WOOD *Surv. Trade* 220 In a Condition to have a bigger Trade. **1816** BYRON *Ch. Har.* III. xciii, The big rain comes dancing to the earth. **1859** TENNYSON *Enid* 489 Apt at arms and big of bone. **1884** JESSOP in *19th Cent.* Mar. 389 Big ships, big hotels, big shops, big drums, big dinners.
b. *esp.* Grown, large, tall, grown up.
1552 HULOET, Bygge to be, or waxe of stature lyke a man. **1607** SHAKS. *Cor.* V. iii. 128 Ile run away Till I am bigger, but then Ile fight. **1653** WALTON *Angler* 133 The Salmon . . never grows big but in the Sea. **1871** M. COLLINS *Mrq. & Merch.* I. iv. 127 After some years of bullying by big girls . . Amy . . became a 'big girl' herself.
c. 'Having comparative bulk, greater or less.'
1547 BOORDE *Introd. Knowl.* 198 Sardyns . . a lytle fyshe as bydg [? bygg] as a pylcherd. **1570** DEE *Math. Pref.* 21 The vnskillfull man, would iudge them [Sun and Moon] a like bigge. **1592** SHAKS. *Rom. & Jul.* I. iv. 55 She comes In shape no bigger than an Aggat stone. **1642** MILTON *Apol. Smect.* Wks. (1851) 311 Seeming bigger then they are through the mist and vapour. **1753** HOGARTH *Anal. Beauty* xi. 85 Statues . . bigger than life. **1847** TENNYSON *Princ.* iv. 7 No bigger than a glow-worm shone the tent.
d. quasi-*adv.*
1563 HYLL *Art Garden.* (1593) 7 Made more fruitfull and plentifuller or bigger yeelding. **1658** ROWLAND *Mouffet's Theat. Ins.* 928 The Hornets . . dig their nests bigger and bigger, as the family growes greater and greater. **1871** MORLEY *Voltaire* (1886) 48 Such enormities bulked big in the vision of the father.
e. Fig. phr. *to get, grow*, etc., *too big for one's boots* (*breeches*, etc.), to become conceited, put on airs.
1835 D. CROCKETT *Tour to North* 152 When a man gets too big for his breeches, I say Good-bye. **1879** [see BOOT *sb.*³ 1 c]. **1893** H. MAXWELL *Life of W. H. Smith* I. ii. 57 Sometimes a young man, 'too big for his boots', would . . sniff at being put in charge of a railway bookstall. **1905** H. G. WELLS *Kipps* III. ii. § 1 He's getting too big for 'is britches. **1929** W. FAULKNER *Sound & Fury* 270 You're getting a little too big for your pants. **1952** M. LASKI *Village* xv, A young man who was getting too big for his boots.
f. In the collocations ***big brother, sister***, elder (cf. 3 b). Also *transf.* (see BIG BROTHER below). Hence ***big-brotherly*** adj.
1851 MAYHEW *London Lab.* I. 151/1 I've a big sister, and a brother and a sister younger than I am. **1863** *Harper's Mag.* Apr. 693/1 In a modern story, a big brother would have kicked the noble lord out of the front door. **1873** J. H. H. ST. JOHN *Pakeha Rambles through Maori Lands* viii. 149 Little mud volcanoes . . aped the customs of their big brothers, and blobbed out their stenches with as much complacency as Tongariro. **1902** A. BENNETT *Anna of Five Towns* i. 4 Your big sister isn't out of school yet? **1922** JOYCE *Ulysses* 497 Big Brother up there, Mr. President, you hear what I done just been saying to you. **1937** H. G. WELLS *Star Begotten* v. 84 If there is such a thing as a Martian . . he's humanity's big brother. *Ibid.* viii. 157 Out of these cravings come all these impulses towards slavish subjection to Gods, Kings, leaders, heroes, bosses, mystical personifications like the People, My Country Right or Wrong, the Church, the Party, the Masses, the Proletariat. Our imaginations hang on to some such Big Brother idea almost to the end. **1947** *Landfall* I. 293 Lachlan was in splendid fettle . . radiating big-brotherly goodwill. **1961** *Listener* 24 Aug. 293/3 For the Czechs and Slovaks . . Russia . . was the big sister to whom they looked . . for deliverance from the Austrian and Hungarian oppressors.
g. ***Big Brother Movement*** (see quots.).
1925 *Times* 24 Oct. 9/5 Mr. Richard Linton, the originator of the 'Big Brother' Movement. *Ibid.*, Mr. Linton had conceived the idea of providing 'Big Brothers' for boys who were emigrating to Australia. **1958** *Oxf. Mail* 14 Aug. 3/1 The Big Brother movement—a voluntary organisation founded in 1925 to assist the settlement of British boys in Australia.
h. Of a letter: capital. Cf. CAPITAL *a.* 5 b.
1874 TROLLOPE *Way we Live* I. i. 1 She spoke of herself . . as a woman devoted to Literature, always spelling the word with a big L. **1894** MRS. H. WARD *Marcella* III. IV. vi. 374 'You had spoken of "*marriage*"!' she said. 'Marriage in the abstract, with a big *M.*' **1964** *Times* 11 Jan. 5/5 An attempt to impose Culture, with a big 'C', on the . . people.
4. Great with young, far advanced in pregnancy; ready to give birth. Const. *with*, rarely *of*.
1535 COVERDALE *Hos.* xiii. 16 Their women bygg with childe. **1593** DONNE *Sat.* iv, Like a big wife . . ready to travail. **1611** SHAKS. *Cymb.* I. i. 39 His gentle Lady Bigge of this Gentleman. **1711** ADDISON *Spect.* No. 7 ¶ 3 One of our female companions was big with child.
5. *transf.* and *fig.* Filled, full so as to be ready to burst out or bring forth; distended, swoln; teeming, 'pregnant' *with*.
[**1580** BARET *Alv.* B 648 Bigge vaines standing out.] **1598** SHAKS. *Merch. V.* II. viii. 44 His eye being big with teares. **1672** DRYDEN *Conq. Granada* II. i, Shining Mountains big with Gold. **1713** ADDISON *Cato* I. i, Th' important day, big with the fate Of Cato and of Rome. **1790** BURKE *Fr. Rev.* 79 The mind of this political preacher . . big with some extraordinary design. **1876** BLACKIE *Songs Relig. & Life* 169 Fateful moments, Big with issue.
6. Full in voice or sound, loud. †*to speak* or *talk big*: to speak or talk loudly, or with full voice. *Obs.* (Cf. also 8 b.)
1581 J. BELL *Haddon's Answ. Osor.* 360 b, They . . fashion theyr voyces bigge like olde men. **1591** SPENSER *Virgil's Gnat.* ii, This Muse shall speak to thee In bigger notes. **1656** DUGARD *Gate Lat. Unl.* § 701 The voice of striplings, before they begin to speak bigg. **1709** *Col. Records Penn.* II. 501 It was necessary to talk bigg & sound aloud that usefull Language. **1859** TENNYSON *Enid* 1390 [He] cried out with a big voice.
7. a. Of high position or standing; great, important. (Colloquial or humorous, for *great.*)
1577 HOLINSHED *Chron.* III. 1146/1 Such . . vtterance, as pulled manie teares out of the eies of the biggest of them. **1588** SHAKS. *L.L.L.* V. ii. 555, 'I Pompey am, Pompey surnam'd the big.' **1670** PENN *Liberty Consc.* Wks. I. 446 Let no Man therefore think himself too big to be admonish'd. **1879** TROLLOPE *Thackeray* 50 Thackeray had become big enough to give a special éclat to any literary exploit.
b. *spec.* In phrases with numerals, as ***big three, four, five***, designating a combination of three, etc., important things, persons, companies, nations, etc. (see quots.); also *attrib.* orig. *U.S.*
1886 *Outing* (U.S.) Nov. 156/1 The trial races . . proved beyond a doubt that the *Mayflower* was the queen of the 'big four'. **1890** WHEELER & CARDWILL *W.A.W.* p. vi, Big 4 Route . . Best Modern Day Coaches on all Trains. **1922** *Encycl. Brit.* XXX. 397/2 The resources of the 'big five' [*sc.* banks] were . . very substantial. **1924** *Golfers' Guide to Happy Holidays* 25 Golf's 'Big Four' are: Skill, Temperament, Experience, Luck. **1931** H. G. WELLS *Work*,

Wealth & Happiness of Mankind (1932) xii. 635 Both China and Japan are members of the League [of Nations] and Japan is one of the Big Five. The Council..has five permanent members (Britain, France, Germany, Italy, and Japan). **1932** Wodehouse *Louder & Funnier* 283 The Big Four at Scotland Yard..hold a round-up of the novelists. **1934** *Ann. Reg. 1933* II. 68 The 'big five' banks—Barclay's, Lloyds, the Midland, the National, and the Westminster. **1934** Webster, *Big Three, Gr. Brit.*, the industrial alliance (formed 1919) of the miners' federation, the national transport workers' federation, and the national union of railwaymen. **1945** *Ann. Reg. 1944* 314 A further 'Big Three' meeting which could concert policy on common problems. **1946** *News Chron.* 8 July 1 The decisions laboriously reached..by the Big Four. **1968** *Globe & Mail* (Toronto) 17 Feb. 26 Toronto is already in the first line of orchestras after the big five in the United States.

c. In designations of operatives, denoting the chief or senior men.

1910 *Westm. Gaz.* 9 Mar. 4/1 There are over 40,000 male cotton-piecers who earn from 8s. 6d. to 15s. 6d. as little-piecers (youths), and from 13s. 6d. to 22s. 6d. as big-piecers (young men). **1921** *Dict. Occup. Terms* (1927) §363 Big tenter. *Ibid.* §365 Big piecer..big spinner.

8. a. Haughty, pompous, pretentious, boastful.

1570 Ascham *Scholem.* (1863) 43 To the meaner man..to seeme somewhat solemne, coye, big, and dangerous of looke. **1581** J. Bell *Haddon's Answ. Osor.* 495b, Not dasht out of countenaunce for any bygge lookes. **1624** Massinger *Renegado* I. iii, For all your big words, get you further off. **1705** Stanhope *Paraphr.* I. 243 All such big Pretensions are false and groundless. **1862** Burton *Bk. Hunter* II. 142 A mere platitude delivered in the most superb climax of big words.

b. *esp.* in the quasi-*advb.* use, ***to talk, look big***.

1596 Shaks. *Tam. Shr.* II. ii. 230 Nay, looke not big, nor stampe, nor stare. **1685** Baxter *Paraphr. Matt.* xviii, How big soever he now look and talk. **1741** Middleton *Cicero* II. vii. 248 Pompey..always talked big to keep up their spirits. **1812** *Examiner* 5 Oct. 631/2 He heads his troops and looks big. **1841** [see talk *v.* 3c]. **1865** Dickens *Mut. Fr.* II. xii. 274 You talk big, you do, but things look pretty black against yourself.

9. *colloq.* (orig. *U.S.*). Generous, magnanimous; freq. ironical, esp. in phr. ***that's big of you***.

1934 Webster s.v. *big*, He is big enough to overlook the slight; he can be depended upon to do the big thing. **1942** N. Coward *Blithe Spirit* I. ii. 39 *Ruth.* You can come in and say good night to me if you feel like it. *Elvira.* That's big of her, I must say. **1951** N. Marsh *Opening Night* iv. 92 You will be really generous won't you? Really big? You won't bring me into it, will you? **1959** H. Hamilton *Answer in Negative* vi. 82 That's big of you... I ought to lead a..sober life, and if I do you'll consent to be seen about with me. Thank you.

10. *slang* (orig. *U.S.*). In various quasi-*advb.* uses. **a.** With pronounced success, esp. in phr. ***to go (over) big*** (see go *v.* 19b and 87h). **b.** Feelingly; emotionally. Cf. sense 8b.

1912 J. London *Let.* 7 Sept. (1966) 363 That the book should sell big, I have all the confidence in the world. **1932** Wodehouse *Hot Water* xvii. 300, I see now why you took it so big when I mentioned that Soup Slattery was in the neighbourhood. **1936** M. Allingham *Flowers for Judge* i. 12 The ridiculous task of putting himself over big. **1958** I. Cross *God Boy* xiv. 110 My actually seeing God would put me in big with Father Gilligan.

B. *Comb.*, chiefly adjectives. **1.** General: **a.** parasynthetic, as (of size or bulk) ***big-bearded, -bodied, -boned*** (also ***-bone*** obs.), ***-bosomed, -brained, -bulked, -eye(d), -hearted, -wombed***; (of sound, etc.) ***big-voiced, worded***; also ***big-heartedness, -wordiness*** sb. **b.** quasi-*advb.* with ppl. adjs., as ***big-buzzing, -looking, -made, -sounding, -swollen***.

1857 Hughes *Tom Brown* I. v, A great *big-bearded man. **1611** Speed *Theat. Gt. Brit.* ix. (1614) 17/1 Many *bigge-bodied streames. **1610** Rowlands *Martin Mark-all* 11 A stout sturdie and *bigbone knaue. **1588** Shaks. *Tit. A.* IV. iii. 46 *Big-bon'd men, fram'd of the Cyclops size. **1818** Scott *Hrt. Midl.* iii, Handcuffs..too small for the wrists of a man so big-boned. **1915** E. R. Lankester *Divers. Nat.* xxix. 270 We compare the actual mental accomplishments of the highest civilized races of man with those of *big-brained savages. **1599** Marston *Sco. Villanie* II. vi. 201 Ye *big-buzzing little-bodied Gnats. **1885** G. Meredith *Diana* I. v. 118 He was a *big-chested fellow. **1818** *Amer. Jrnl. Sci.* I. 79 The *big-eye herring (*Clupea megalops*) begin to be seen at the fish-market. **1885** J. S. Kingsley *Standard Nat. Hist.* III. 187 The *big-eyed scad,..the *Trachurops crumenophthalmus* of naturalists. **1957** T. Hughes *Hawk in Rain* 23 Now he rides the morning mist With a big-eyed hawk on his fist. **1868** Trollope *He knew he was Right* I. xiii. 106 Had he not been so manly and *big-hearted, he would have taken such pressure as a sign that she wished him to ask her again. **1914** D. H. Lawrence *Let.* 18 Dec. (1962) I. 300 You are so bighearted, we think of you with great affection. **1872** W. F. Butler *Great Lone Land* (ed. 2) xvii. 282 After such a present no man can possibly entertain..a doubt upon the subject of the *big-heartedness of the donor. **1953** *Scrutiny* XIX. 143 Implying that you are a rather inferior creature if you do not share his manly big-heartedness. **1634** *Malory's Arthur* (1816) I. 360 A young man, and a *big made. **1874** F. Hall in *N. Amer. Rev.* CXIX. 328 The gratuitous *big-wordiness of Sir Thomas Browne and Henry More.

2. a. Special combinations: ***big bird, board, deal, drink, hand, idea, noise, pot, shot, talk, way*** (see the sbs.); **Big Apple**, (*a*) a ballroom dance for a group of people, popular in the 1930's; (*b*) *slang*, the city of New York; **big band**, a large band of musicians playing jazz, dance-music or the like (as distinct from a small group or 'combo'); freq. *attrib.*; **big bang**, (*a*) a great or loud explosion; *spec.* the explosion of a single compact mass, in which (according to one cosmological theory) the universe originated; freq. *attrib.*; (*b*) *Stock Exchange*, a colloq. name for the deregulation of the London Stock Exchange on 27 October 1986, when a number of complex changes in trading practices were put into effect simultaneously (see quots.); **big-bellied** *a.*, having a large belly, corpulent; pregnant; **big bore**, a rifle of large calibre *U.S.*; also *attrib.* or quasi-*adj.*, having a large calibre, large-bore; **big boy** *colloq.* (orig. *U.S.*) = *big bug* (see bug *sb.*^{1} 1b); freq. used as an ironical form of address; also *transf.*; **big buck(s)** *U.S. slang* [buck *sb.*^{8}] = *big money* below; also *attrib.*; **big bud**, a disease of plants caused by the gall-mite; **big bug**: see bug *sb.*^{1} 1b; **big business** (orig. *U.S.*), (those in control of) large mercantile organizations or transactions collectively; also *attrib.*, esp. ***big-business man***; **big C** *colloq. euphem.* (orig. *U.S.*), cancer; **big city** (orig. *U.S.*), a large city; esp. *attrib.* or quasi-*adj.*, of, pertaining to, or characteristic of a large city; **big crunch** *Astr.*, a contraction of the universe to a singular state of extreme density and temperature (a hypothetical opposite of a *big bang*); **Big Daddy**, a paternal, dominating, or influential person; also *attrib.*; **Big Dipper**, (*a*) *U.S.* = dipper 5b; (*b*) (also with lower-case initials) a switchback at a place of amusement; also *fig.*, *transf.*, and *attrib.*; **big end**, the end of the connecting-rod that encircles the crank-pin, esp. in a motor-vehicle engine; also *attrib.*; cf. *small end*; **big-endian** (also **Big-endian**), in Swift's 'Gulliver's Travels', a person who believed that eggs should be broken at the larger end before they are eaten (cf. *little-endian* s.v. little *a.* 14); hence allusively and as *adj.*; **big figure** *U.S. slang* (see quot. 1848); **big game**, large animals hunted as game; freq. *attrib.*; **big gun**: see gun *sb.* 7b; **big-horn, bighorn**, a species of sheep inhabiting the Rocky Mountains; **big inch**, also *attrib.*, (of) an oil or natural gas pipe-line 20 inches in diameter or larger; **big laurel** *U.S.*, (*a*) a species of large magnolia, *M. grandiflora*; (*b*) the rose-bay *Rhododendron maximum*; **big league** *U.S.*, a major American baseball league (hence ***big leaguer***); also *transf.* and *attrib.*; **(the) big lie** [cf. G. *grosse lüge*], (an instance of) falsehood on a large scale, *spec.* used in (Nazi) propaganda; **Big Mac** *U.S.*, (*a*) a proprietary name for the largest in a range of hamburgers sold by McDonald's fast-food outlets; also *fig.*, the biggest or best of a number of related things; (*b*) a nickname for the Municipal Assistance Corporation of New York City; **big man** (see sense 7a); **big money** (orig. *U.S.*), a large amount of money; high salary, large profit; also *attrib.*; **big mouth** (orig. and chiefly *U.S.*), a very talkative or boastful person; also, loquacity, boastful talk; **big-mouthed** *a.*, (*a*) having a big mouth; (*b*) loquacious or boastful (cf. *big mouth*); **big name** (orig. *U.S.*), a famous or celebrated person, esp. in the field of entertainment; also *attrib.*; **big picture** *colloq.*, the main film in a cinema programme; **big science**, term used of scientific and technological investigation that requires large resources; **big smoke**, (*a*) *Austral.*, an Aboriginal name for a town or city; (*b*) London (see smoke *sb.* 1d); **big stick** (orig. *U.S.*), (a display of) force or power; hence ***big-sticker, -stickism***; **big stuff**, in various *slang* uses (see quots.); **big thing** *colloq.*, a promising affair, a good prospect; something magnanimous; **big ticket** *slang* (orig. *U.S.*), used *attrib.* of merchandise that is highly priced or whose purchase would constitute a major expense; esp. as ***big-ticket item***: see ticket *sb.*^{1} 2c; **big time** (orig. and chiefly *U.S.*), an excellent time; hence (often *attrib.*), (of) the best kind or the highest rank; so **big-timer**, a top-ranker; **big top** (orig. *U.S.*), the main tent of a circus; the circus in general; also *transf.*; **big wheel**, (*a*) a Ferris wheel; (*b*) *slang* (orig. and chiefly *U.S.*) = *big shot* (see shot *sb.*^{1} 22c). Also in various collocations which have come to have specific force, as **big drum, big game, big toe; big coat** (*Sc.*), an over-coat; **big daisy**, the Ox-eye daisy, and similar flowers; **big dog**, a watch dog; also *fig.*; **big trees**, the Sequoias or Wellingtonias of the Sierra Nevada, N. America. See also bigwig.

1928 *N.Y. Times* 11 Mar. VIII. 6 *The *big apple*, New York City. **1937** *Dancing Times* Nov. 170/1 The rage of the winter is the *Big Apple and its related steps... Such steps as the Shag, the Flea Hop, the Strut, and the Walk, are combined with the new Big Apple notes. **1946** Mezzrow & Wolfe *Really Blues* (1957) ix. 170 As soon as we hit The Big Apple we'll ditch the buggy, and when the New York cops find it your insurance company will have to..ship it back to you. **1958** *Publ. Amer. Dial. Soc.* XXX. 48 This term [Apple = New York] gave its name to that defunct dance, the Big Apple. **1979** *United States 1980/81* (Penguin Travel Guides) 114 Many Broadway-bound shows play Chicago before heading for the Big Apple. **1984** *New Yorker* 6 Aug. 21/1 Mr. Charles Gillett, the president of the New York Convention & Visitors Bureau, Inc., spoke..on..the value of the image of New York as 'the Big Apple'... It was his organization that plucked the term from the jazz lingo of the twenties... The phrase in the jazz world, he said, had been 'playing the Big Stem in the Big Apple'—the Big Stem being Broadway. (Another saying that we subsequently picked up from a dictionary of slang was 'There are many apples on the tree, but New York is the big apple.') **1926** *Melody Maker* Feb. 35 [It] gives the lie to those who say that a '*big band' is unwieldy. **1947** R. de Toledano *Frontiers of Jazz* xiii. 137 It remains the best big band jazz. **1955** *Jazzbook 1955* 6 He [*sc.* Duke Ellington] is the only man who has consistently created big band jazz of more than ephemeral value. *Ibid.* 7 In James Crawford the band possessed perhaps the finest of big band drummers. **1950** F. Hoyle *Nature of Universe* v. 102 One [idea] was that the Universe started its life a finite time ago in a single huge explosion... This *big bang idea seemed to me to be unsatisfactory. **1957** Big bang [see bang *sb.*^{1} 2c]. **1964** *Listener* 3 Sept. 340/2 The man who comes to astrophysics with a belief in after-life might be expected to have some thoughts about the 'big-bang theory'. **1969** *Observer* (Colour Suppl.) 2 Feb. 16/1 A unique and inscrutable primeval atom, out of which all matter was born in some mysterious First Explosion—the famous 'Big Bang'. *Ibid.* 16/4 A mysterious radio hiss, which may be the dying echoes of the original big bang. **1983** *Financial Times* 19 Sept. 16/8 It is argued that a 'big bang' approach, with all changes in Stock Exchange rules taking place on a single day.., would allow firms to make rational plans. **1984** *Times* 14 Feb. 19/7 The removal of the minimum commissions guaranteed to the 250-member firms of the [Stock] Exchange is now likely to happen in one go—by what is known as the 'big bang' approach. **1986** *Sunday Express Mag.* 26 Oct. 12/1 After the Big Bang tomorrow, the City will never be the same again... From tomorrow,..the distinction between brokers and jobbers disappears. **1561** Stow *Eng. Chron.* an. 1087 (R.) [William Rufus] was..not of any great stature, though somewhat *big bellied. *c* **1660** *Sea Crabb* in *Bp. Percy's Folio MS. Loose & Humorous Songs* (1963) 99 This goodwiffe was bigbellyed, & with a lad. **1670** Brooks *Wks.* (1867) VI. 174 A big-bellied mercy, a mercy that has many thousand mercies in the womb of it. **1711** Addison *Spect.* No. 127 ¶6 Waddling up and down like big-bellied Women. **1794** Burns *Wks.* III. 299 A big-bellied bottle's a heav'n of care. **1812** J. Sinclair *Syst. Husb. Scot.* I. 357 When they [*sc.* calves] are allowed to drink much water at an early age, they will become big-bellied. **1916** R. Graves *Goliath & David* 14 Big-bellied, spectacled, crop-haired. **1843** 'R. Carlton' *New Purchase* II. xxxvi. 31, I had a powerful *big bore to fix for a feller going out West. **1960** *Farmer & Stockbreeder* 23 Feb. 45/2 Big-bore, short-stroke engine—high power at low piston speeds. **1918** A. P. McKishnie *Willow* xx. 279 'Hold on, *Big Boy,' he called. **1925** Fraser & Gibbons *Soldier & Sailor Words* 22 *Big boys*, large guns. 'Heavies'. **1929** W. R. Burnett *Little Caesar* I. i. 12 The Big Boy can't fix murder. He can fix anything but murder. **1939** J. B. Priestley *Let People Sing* iv. 94 'Am I right, sirs?' 'You sure are, big boy.' **1940** *Times Weekly* 27 Nov. 10 We had one of the really 'big boys' on board—the brother of the one I dropped at Munich. **1970** in *Dict. Amer. Regional Eng.* I. 406/2 He's in the *big buck bracket. **1972** E. A. Butler (*title*) The big buck and the new business breed. **1975** *Forbes* (N.Y.) 1 July 26 They could afford big bucks for advertising and theater rentals and still come out way ahead. **1986** *Los Angeles Times* 19 May v. 1/3 Neither government was behind it, nor were there any sponsors, angels, captains of commerce or industry, no big bucks or big francs flowing from anywhere or anybody. **1900** G. Nicholson *Dict. Gardening* Suppl. 274/1 Currant-Bud Mite (*Phytoptus ribis*), or Black Currant Gall Mite, is responsible for the condition of the bushes known as '*Big Bud'. **1958** *Spectator* 10 Jan. 58/2 Mites cause the swelling of blackcurrant buds at this time of year and give rise to what is commonly called Big Bud, a destructive thing resulting in a poor crop. **1905** *McClure's Mag.* 49 The stench of the vice graft did not repel, it attracted *big business. **1912** J. H. Moore *Ethics & Educ.* vi. 32 These are big-business times. **1913** T. Roosevelt *Autobiogr.* (Appendix A) 615 We demand that big business give the people a square deal; in return we must insist that when any one engaged in big business honestly endeavors to do right he shall himself be given a square deal. **1922** J. M. Murry *Things we Are* 23 Mr. Thomson, whom nature had modelled after the physical pattern of the dour American big-business man. **1930** G. B. Shaw *Apple Cart* I. 22 The political encroachments of big business. **1968** J. D. MacDonald *Girl in Plain Brown Wrapper* iv. 35, I..might look almost as well this year too, except for a little problem known familiarly as *Big C. A year ago they thought they took it all out, but then they used cobalt [etc.]. **1979** *Time* 29 Jan. 69 John Wayne..accepted the news with true grit. 'I've licked the Big C before,' he said. **1984** H. D. Weaver *Confronting Big C* ii. 22 He is no longer afraid; he knows it is possible to conquer 'the big C'. **1909** 'O. Henry' *Options* 110 The *big city is like a mother's knee to many who have strayed far and found the roads rough beneath their uncertain feet. **1929** D. Hammett *Red Harvest* xxiii. 235 A big-city paper or two are sending in special correspondents. **1960** *New Left Rev.* Mar.–Apr. 45/1 A big-city airport. **1981** J. Ellis in J. H. Mulvey *Nature of Matter* vi. 143 If..it does not contain a sufficient density of matter to cause it to collapse back on itself into a *Big Crunch then the Universe will continue to expand forever. **1984** Barrow & Silk *Left Hand of Creation* 234 *Closed universe*, a model of the universe that is finite in total volume and in total age. It evolves from a 'big bang' to a point of maximum expansion before contracting back to a 'big crunch' of high density and temperature. **1752** in *Scots Mag.* (1753) June 290/2 The said Allan Breck had no *big coat on. [**1955** T. Williams *Cat on Hot Tin Roof* (1966) p.

xi, Characters of the play... *Big Daddy, [etc.].] **1958** *Spectator* 29 Aug. 278/2 Mr. Francis Williams, journalism's Big Daddy. **1959** N. MAILER *Advt. for Myself* (1961) 348 The Fuehrer's tone will be heard in the Twenty-First Century as the Big Daddy voice of all virile and velvety broadcasters. **1869** 'MARK TWAIN' *Innoc. Abr.* 19 Constellations that never associate with the '*Big Dipper'. **1936** J. L. HODSON *Our Two Englands* vi. 111 [They] spend a pound a day on the Big Dipper when on holiday at Blackpool. **1957** R. HOGGART *Uses of Literacy* v. 127 Thus one arrives at the 'big-dipper' style of singing, the style used by working-class entertainers... Here the voice takes enormous lifts and dips to fill out the lines of a lush emotional journey. **1960** *Spectator* 21 Oct. 601 It has been a week on the big dipper—plunging below the surface of farce into tragedy and then jerking back up again. **1833** J. S. JONES *Green Mt. Boy* I. iii, For the rale genuine grammar larnin' I am a six-horse team and a *big dog under the wagon. **1846** J. J. HOOPER *Adv. Simon Suggs* x. 126 Pointing to the reverend gentleman who.. was the 'big dog of the tanyard'. **1884** *Gd. Words* June 400/1 He was 'big-dog' to a disorderly house. **1906** W. P. ADAMS *Motor-Car Mechanism* 160 **Big end*, the lower end of an engine connecting-rod enlarged to carry the big end bearing or brasses which surround the crank pin. **1909** *Westm. Gaz.* 4 Feb. 4/2 The big-end bearings can be examined and adjusted. **1726** SWIFT *Gulliver* iv, The books of the *Big-endians have been long forbidden. *Ibid.* I. I. vii. 120 All the People of that Empire, who would not immediately forsake the *Big-Endian* Heresy. **1726** MRS. HOWARD *Let.* Nov. in *Swift's Wks.* (1824) XVII. 81 Many disputes have arisen here, whether the big-endians, and lesser-endians, ever differed in opinion about the breaking of eggs, when they were to be either buttered or poached? **1832** CARLYLE in *Fraser's Mag.* V. 254 Its dome is but a foolish Big-endian or Little-endian chip of an egg-shell compared with that star-fretted Dome. **1888** Big-endian [see *little-endian* s.v. LITTLE *a.* 14]. **1905** *Westm. Gaz.* 29 Aug. 10/2 The quarrel between the Big-Endians and the Little-Endians promises to be a merry one. **1961** Y. OLSSON *Syntax Eng. Verb* ii. 18 Though what Jonathan Swift might have called the Small-Endian view seems to be in a certain vogue, the procedure here followed is Big-Endian. **1831** *Boston Transcript* 28 Oct. 2/2 The opponents of the existing militia system.. are 'going it' at New York 'on the *big figure'. **1848** BARTLETT *Dict. Amer., Big figure.* To do things on the big figure, means to do them on a large scale. **1864** *Spectator* No. 1874. 627 Versed in wood craft and the destruction of '*big game.' **1890** LD. LUGARD *Diary* 10 Nov. (1959) I. 362 Endless big-game tracks led westwards now. **1905** *Daily Chron.* 25 May 5/2 President Roosevelt's love of big-game hunting. **1966** J. BINGHAM *Double Agent* ii. 32 In the old days, a jilted man might go big game shooting. **1805** W. CLARK *Jrnl.* 4 Apr. in *Lewis & Clark Exped.* (1905) I. vii. 240 The horns of the mountain ram, or *big horn. **1849** W. IRVING *Astoria* 240 The bighorn is so named from its horns; which are of a great size, and twisted like those of a ram. **1926** *Chambers's Jrnl.* July 449/1 It had been the regular route traversed by large droves of bighorn. **1943** *Times* 19 May 3/5 An oil line known as the '*Big Inch', which was laid from Texas oilfields to Illinois.. was broken to-day. **1960** *Times Rev. Industry* Dec. 79/2 The construction of two big-inch pipelines from the North Sea ports of Wilhelmshaven and Rotterdam... The first pipeline.. is 28 in. dia... The second.. is 24 in. dia. **1810** F. A. MICHAUX *Hist. des Arbres* I. 32 The large magnolia.. [or] *Big laurel. **1853** D. H. STROTHER *Blackwater Chron.* vii. 89 This dale is girt round.. by a broad belt of the Rhododendron—commonly called the *big laurel* out here. **1899** *Chicago Daily News* 10 May 6/1 One of Chicago's crack players new in the big league. **1946** *Ibid.* 31 Aug. 6/6 Let's train our men to be big leaguers if they are to compete, as our representatives, in the big leagues! **1947** *Time* 14 Apr. 66/3 They announced a prize book contest baited with enough cash to make big-league authors sit up and take notice. **1910** *Amer. Mag.* May 6/1 College players stop eight out of nine grounders and *big leaguers stop 15 out of 16. **1946** 'G. ORWELL' in *Polemic* Jan. 7 The friends of totalitarianism in this country usually tend to argue that since absolute truth is not attainable, a *big lie is no worse than a little lie. **1948** *News* (San Francisco) 30 July 2/5 This is a continuation of the Nazi theory of the 'big lie', expounded by Hitler and Goebbels, that the bigger the lie and the more frequently it is told the more people who would accept it. **1951** in *Amer. Speech* XXVI. 293/2 Gloomy Washington prophets are forecasting a period of 'the big lie', of the furtive informer... They lump the whole under the term McCarthyism. **1970** *Forbes* (N.Y.) 1 Nov. 21/3 It [*sc.* McDonald's] tested big burgers—today's big seller—for years before adopting the *Big Mac. **1974** *Official Gaz.* (U.S. Patent Office) 5 Nov. 48 McDonald's Corporation... Filed Apr. 30, 1973. *Big Mac.* For Sandwich... First use at least as early as 1957. **1974** *Florida FL Reporter* XIII. 52/3 It would be a lot easier for mainstream society if the annoying non-Standard speakers would learn to speak mainstream too—the verbal Big Mac. **1975** *Times* 12 June 18/4 Now that 'Big Mac', the new state agency nicknamed after a hamburger, has swung into action, there seems little chance that New York will really go bankrupt. **1977** *Rolling Stone* 21 Apr. 15/4 It's possible now for a lot of them to live a normal Big Mac existence, but the middle class is the great nebbish class of the world. **1981** P. CAREY *Bliss* v. 198 David Joy arrived home with his two Big Macs at eight o'clock. **1985** *N.Y. Times* 2 July A18/4 When in July 1975, Big MAC, as it was called, offered its first bond issue. **1874** TROLLOPE *Way we Live* II. liii. 14 A moment's private conversation with the *big man. **1886** *Lantern* 3 Nov. 3/1 Who is supposed to be a big man in the boot and shoe trade. **1936** *Amer. Speech* XI. 118/2 *Big man*, the brains behind a dope ring; the one who seldom takes the rap... The *big man* wholesales dope to peddlers. **1880** in *Amer. Speech* (1942) XVII. 65/2 '*Big money' to be made in cattle and sheep. **1907** *Westm. Gaz.* 16 Aug. 2/1 The skilled artisan has always been.. well paid in Belfast. He makes what he calls 'big money'. **1950** J. DEMPSEY *Championship Fighting* 10 My five big-money bouts. **1889** BARRÈRE & LELAND *Dict. Slang* I. 113/2 **Big mouth* (American), a very common expression applied to any man who talks too much. **1890** FARMER *Slang* I. 190/2 *Big mouth* (American), excessive talkativeness; loquacity. **1938** M. K. RAWLINGS *Yearling* xxiii. 288 Now mister impudent big-mouth. **1940** R. CHANDLER *Farewell, My Lovely* xxxiii. 154, I didn't have any idea of getting tough in the first place, except just the routine big mouth. **1951** E. COXHEAD *One Green Bottle* i. 9 He was a big mouth. He picked up strangers ..and told them the story of his life. **1642** MILTON *Apol. Smect.* Wks. 1738 I. 125 It was *big-mouth'd, he says; no marvel, if it were fram'd as the Voice of three Kingdoms. **1914** C. MACKENZIE *Sinister Street* II. IV. iv. 930 Fancy going off.. with that big-mouthed five-to-two. **1919** MASEFIELD *Reynard the Fox* 27 Bill, that big-mouthed smiler. **1926** *Amer. Cinematographer* Dec. 5 A '*big name' actor. **1932** Q. D. LEAVIS *Fiction & Reading Public* I. ii. 32 *Nash's* in search of 'big names' ran the last Forsyte epic as a serial. **1942** BERREY & VAN DEN BARK *Amer. Thes. Slang* §144/7 Famous, *big-name, blown to the skies*, [etc.]. **1949** L. FEATHER *Inside Be-Bop* vi. 43 A big-name policy at the Roost. **1927** *Melody Maker* Sept. 933/3 A score specially composed for each '*big picture'. **1961** A. M. WEINBERG in *Science* 21 July 161/1 She [*sc.* history] will find in the monuments of *Big Science—the huge rockets, the high-energy accelerators, the high-flux research reactors—symbols of our time. **1848** H. W. HAYGARTH *Bush Life Australia* i. 6 As he gradually leaves behind him the '*big smoke' (as the aborigines picturesquely call the town). **1917** E. MILLER *Diary* 24 Apr. in *Camps, Tramps & Trenches* (1939) x. 61 My first day in 'the Big Smoke'. **1968** *Tel.* (Brisbane) 14 Aug. 54/1 He falls for a beautiful blonde who wants him to stay in the Big Smoke—but city life has no appeal. [**1900** T. ROOSEVELT *Let.* 26 Jan. (1951) II. 1141, I have always been fond of the West African proverb: 'Speak softly and carry a big stick; you will go far.'] **1904** *Springfield Weekly Republ.* 26 Aug. 1 Happily the revolution in Paraguay is too far down in South America to arouse the '*big stick' in Washington. **1912** KIPLING *Diversity of Creatures* (1917) 171 The secret of power.. is not the big stick. It's the liftable stick. **1956** A. WILSON *Anglo-Saxon Attitudes* I. iii. 65 Elvira's on the side of the big stick in these things. **1905** *Springfield Weekly Republ.* 9 June 1 A *big-sticker after Mr. Roosevelt's own heart. **1926** *Spectator* 2 Jan. 19/1 There is nothing in the British record to compare with Roosevelt's robust *big-stickism in the Alaska boundary case. **1925** FRASER & GIBBONS *Soldier & Sailor Words* 22 **Big stuff*, heavy shells. **1927** R. W. HINDS in *Flynn's Weekly* 19 Feb. 9/2 'Bagler's big stuff.' I got his slang. Big stuff meant that Bagler was a crook who conducted extensive deals. **1942** BERREY & VAN DEN BARK *Amer. Thes. Slang* §20/4 Something important.. *big stuff.* *Ibid.* §388/1 *Big stuff*.. persons of importance. **1948** PARTRIDGE *Dict. Forces' Slang* 15 *Big stuff.* In the Navy, a battleship or an aircraft carrier; or collectively.—In the Army, heavy guns, and the exploding shells from them. Heavy vehicles such as tanks. **1953** R. LEHMANN *Echoing Grove* 36, I played the lead, and it was big stuff; supporting roles are less rewarding. **1859** G. W. MATSELL *Vocabulum*, **Big thing*, a rich booty. **1862** *Campfire Songster* 48 (D.A.), There's a big thing coming, boys. **1935** *Times* 13 Feb. 7/7 He appealed to the Minister of Labour, who had no responsibility for the muddle and who had done the big thing, to go on doing the big thing in his constructive proposals. **1956** *Business Week* 8 Sept. 27/2 Charge account credit seems more liberal than ever—except for *big-ticket items such as appliances. **1967** *Economist* 7 Jan. 64/1 'Big ticket' items, carpets, bedding, furniture and other consumer durables, which did so very badly before Christmas are selling quite well at cut prices. **1975** *U.S. News & World Rep.* 14 Apr. 17 Very few plan to use the rebate as part of a down payment on a big-ticket purchase. **1985** *Investors Chron.* 8–14 Nov. 11/1 The edge-of-town DIY chains.. rely on big-ticket leisure purchases. **1863** O. W. NORTON *Army Lett.* (1903) 183 The brigade was flying round, getting into line, drums beating and a *big time generally. *Ibid.* 190 We had big times that night for fires. **1910** R. GRAU *Business Man in Amusement World* 36 The 'big time', as such theatres as Percy Williams' and William Morris' are termed. **1914** in *Amer. Speech* (1957) XXXII. 209 Here are huge ledgers that tell the past movements and future bookings of every good act and every artist deemed worthy of 'big time'. *Ibid.*, They buy and sell for all 'big time' acts and all 'big time' theaters. **1921** *Collier's* 25 June 3/3 Like as not I will have to go back pitchin' baseball in some bush league on the account I am too old for the Big Time. **1935** M. M. ATWATER *Murder in Midsummer* xxviii. 261 Of the big-time news-hawks who had gathered in Keedora, only Matter remained. **1936** *Amer. Speech* XI. 117 Big-time gangsters, racketeers, and the criminal aristocrats do not use narcotics. **1951** J. B. PRIESTLEY *Fest. Farbridge* 52 From now on it's Big Time stuff. **1966** *Crescendo* Feb. 9 (Advt.), Scores of drummers who hit the big time play Premier. **1932** E. WALLACE *When Gangs came to London* xxiii. 233 Only the *big timers—I'll interpret that, gentlemen: it means the more important armies—would be employed. **1959** F. USHER *Death in Error* vii. 99 Do you know what sort of criminals he associates with?.. Big-timers? **1895** *McClure's Mag.* V. 49/2 Having settled where the '*big top' will stand, the location of the other eleven tents is determined with mathematical precision. **1946** *Univ. of Chicago Mag.* Dec. 9/2 The fact is that he was not really a good showman under the academic big-top. **1962** *Radio Times* 2 Aug. 37/1 Whatever type of act you prefer under the Big Top, whether it's clowns, jugglers or acrobats. **1853** *Placer Times* (S.F.) 27 June 2/2 The *Big Tree at the World's Fair. **1865** J. M. HUTCHINGS *Scenes Calif.* i. 13 The starting-point for the Big-Tree Grove. *Ibid.* iv. 77 A sketching tour to the Big Trees. **1883** *Harper's Mag.* Jan. 193/1 The 'big trees' proper are confined to certain groves on the western flank of the Sierra Nevada. **1908** *Chambers's Jrnl.* Mar. 271/1 Sensational amusements invariably associated with exhibitions, such as the water-chute, *big-wheel, [etc.]. **1942** BERREY & VAN DEN BARK *Amer. Thes. Slang* §388/2 Person of importance or self-importance.. *big cog* or *wheel.* **1952** AUDEN *Nones* 57 They met some big wheels, and do not Let you forget it. **1958** C. FREMLIN *Hours before Dawn* xx. 168 The Big Wheel, which rose with strange dignity into the quiet sky. **1958** M. DICKENS *Man Overboard* i. 17 He was evidently quite a big wheel at the studio.

b. In collocations used *attrib.*

1909 *Westm. Gaz.* 29 Jan. 2/2 Whether we be 'big-Navy' men or 'little-Navy' men. *Ibid.* 27 Apr. 11/2 Big-print headlines in newspapers. **1909** *Daily Chron.* 7 May 1/4 The big-fleet party in Vienna. **1930** *Economist* 13 Dec. 1110/1 To ascertain the view of manufacturers with regard to big-scale amalgamations. **1947** 'G. ORWELL' *English People* 30 The big-circulation newspapers. **1961** *Sunday Express* 2 Apr. 18/6 The film.. is not a big-budget one. **1962** 'J. LE CARRÉ' *Murder of Quality* v. 62 Smiley was fascinated by Fielding.. by his whole big-screen style.

big, bigg (bɪg), *v. Obs.* exc. *north. dial.* Forms: 3–5 bigg(en, (3 biggenn), 4 big(en, 4–6 byg(e, 5 bygg(en, 4– big, bigg. [ME. *biggen*, *bygge*, a. ON. *byggja* to inhabit, dwell in, build, cognate with OE. *búian* to dwell, inhabit, cultivate, from same root as BE.]

†**1.** *trans.* To dwell in, inhabit. *Obs.*

*c*1300 *E.E. Psalter* xxxvi[i]. 3 (Mätz.) Big þe erþe [*Vulg.* inhabita terram] and best fede in his riches.

†**2.** *intr.* To dwell; to have an abode. *Obs.*

*c*1200 ORMIN 12734 Lef maȝȝstre, whære biggest tu. **1330** R. BRUNNE *Chron.* 339 Biside his broþer to bigge. *Ibid.* 330 To biggen in pays.

†**3.** *refl.* (and *passive*). To place or locate oneself, take up one's position. *Obs.*

*c*1352 MINOT *Poems* vii. (1795) 35 Bigges him right by ȝowre side. *c*1400 *Destr. Troy* v. 1598 With barburs bigget in bourders of the stretes. *c*1485 *Digby Myst.* (1882) III. 2024 þou hast byggyd þe here among spynys.

4. *trans.* To build. Still in Sc. and north. dial.

*a*1300 *E.E. Ps.* lxviii. 36 God.. sal.. bigge þe cites of Jude. *c*1325 *Allit. P.* B. 1666 I haf bigged Babiloyne. **1375** BARBOUR *Bruce* v. 453 To byg the castell vp agane. *c*1440 *Promp. Parv.* 35 Byggyn, or bildyn, *edifico.* **1458** *Test. Ebor.* II. 225 The chapell.. bigged and made be the said sir Thomas. **1609** SKENE *Reg. Maj.* 83 Gif ane man.. hes there bigged houses and biggings. **1646** ROW *Hist. Kirk* (1842) 12 Down with those crow nests, else the crowes will big in them againe! **1869** WAUGH *Lanc. Sk.* 205 in *Lanc. Gloss.*, They bigged yon new barn. **1884** *U.P. Mag.* Apr. 156 Bigging the fold dyke.

5. *transf.* and *fig.* To erect, rear, pile up.

*a*1300 *E.E. Psalter* xxvii[i]. 5 In þair hand-werkes þam fordo, And noght big þam þou salt als so. *c*1430 LYDG. *Min. Poems* (1840) 264 Thy place is biggyd above the sterrys cleer. **1513** DOUGLAS *Æneis* IV. xii. 73 This funerall fire with thir handis biggit I. **1663** SPALDING *Troub. Chas. I*, (1829) 14 Seats of deals, for the purpose bigged of three degrees. **1716** in *Wodrow Corr.* (1843) II. 134 A young lad.. was bigging corn in the wain.

†**6.** To construct, form, fashion. *Obs.*

*c*1325 *E.E. Allit. P.* C. 124 Hit may not be þat he is blynde þat bigged vche yȝe. **1430** LYDG. *Chron. Troy* II. x, So ryche coloures byggen I ne may.

big, variant of BIGG, barley.

‖**biga** (ˈbaɪgə) *Rom. Antiq.* [L.; later form of *bigæ*, contr. from *bijugæ*, f. *bi-* two + *jug-um* yoke, collar.] A two-horsed chariot.

1850 LEITCH *Müller's Anc. Art* §245. 253 A biga, the king therein. **1857** BIRCH *Anc. Pottery* (1858) II. 202 A man standing in a biga.

†**bi'gale**, *v. Obs.* Also 1 begalan. [OE. *begalan*, f. BE- + *galan* to sing, GALE *v.*] *trans.* To charm with incantations, etc.; to enchant.

*c*1000 *Sax. Leechd.* I. 190 Gyf hwylc yfel dæde man þurh æniȝne æfþancan oþerne begaleþ. *c*1200 *Trin. Coll. Hom.* 197 And te londes-men hire bigaleð. *c*1205 *Lay.* 19255 Heo bigolen þat child mid galdere swiðe stronge.

†**'bigam(e**, *a.* and *sb. Obs.* Also 5–6 **bygame**. [a. OF. *bigame*, ad. med.L. *bigamus*, f. *bi-* two, twice + Gr. -γαμος married.] Having at the same time two wives or husbands. *sb.* A man or woman so married. In *Eccl. Law* applied also to one who marries a second time.

*a*1300 *Cursor M.* 1528 Lamech.. was þe first o liue þat bigam was wit dubul vijfe. *a*1460 PECOCK in Lewis *Life* 286 (T.) St. Paul's ordaining that a bigam should not be a deacon. **1491** CAXTON *Vitas Patr.* (W. de W.) I. cxvii. 140a/1 In the sayd cite was a man bygame. **1502** *Ord. Crysten Men* (W. de W.) IV. xxi (1506) 234 If he were.. excommunycate, bygame, illegittime.

‖**'bigama.** *Obs. rare*[−1]. [med.L., fem. of BIGAMUS.] A woman living in bigamy.

1597 WARNER *Alb. Eng. Æneidos* 320 Greater is the wonder of your strickt chastitie, than it would be a nouell to see you a Bigama.

bi'gamic, *a.* Of or belonging to bigamy.

1868 *Newspaper*, Not with any bigamic intentions.

bigamist (ˈbɪgəmɪst). [f. as BIGAMY + -IST.] A man or woman living in bigamy: **a.** in the usual acceptation; cf. BIGAMY 1. Hence **biga'mistic** *a.*

*a*1631 DONNE *Septuagint* 202 (T.) Lamech the prime bigamist and corrupter of marriage. **1840** THACKERAY *Paris Sk. Bk.* (1872) 237 Old La Vauballière was a bigamist. **1834** *Fraser's Mag.* IX. 332 He had actually gone through a bigamistic sham with her.

b. in *Eccl. Law*; cf. BIGAMY 2. *Obs.* exc. *Hist.*

[**1656** BLOUNT *Glossogr.*, *Bigamist*, he that hath marryed two wives.] **1726** AYLIFFE *Parerg.* 116 Much less can a Bigamist have such a Benefice. **1844** LINGARD *Anglo-Sax. Chr.* (1858) II. i. 17 The bigamist, though he were a widower.. was excluded.. from the rank of bishop, etc.

bigamous (ˈbɪgəməs), *a.* [f. med.L. *bigam-us* (see BIGAM) + -OUS.] Living in bigamy; involving bigamy. **'bigamously** *adv.*, so as to commit or involve bigamy.

1864 *Times* 17 Aug. (reviewing 'Enoch Arden'), Arden's bigamous wife. **1866** *Standard* 2 June 7/4 He deserted her and contracted a bigamous marriage. **1882** *Ibid.* 14 Oct. 2/7 Charged with bigamously intermarrying with one L——.

‖**ˈbigamus**, *a.* (*sb.*) *Obs.* Pl. bigami. [med.L.] = BIGAM(E.

c **1375** WYCLIF *Sel. Wks.* (1869) I. 87 Crist was not bigamus ne brake not his matrimonye. **1543** BERTHELET *Act 4 Edw. I*, Concerning men twise maried, called Bygamy. *c* **1555** HARPSFIELD *Divorce Hen. VIII*, (1878) 43 So doth he dispense with a bygamus. **1706** tr. *Dupin's Eccl. Hist. 16th C.* II. 395 Tonsured Clerks, provided they be not Bigami.

bigamy (ˈbɪgəmɪ). Forms: 3–7 **bigamie**, 4 **bygamye**, 6 **bygamy**, 6– **bigamy**. [a. F. *bigamie*, f. *bigame*: see BIGAM(E and -Y.]

1. Marriage with a second wife or husband during the lifetime of the first; the crime of having two wives or husbands at once.

c **1250** *Gen. & Ex.* 449 Bigamie is unkinde ðing, On engleis tale, twie-wifing. *c* **1386** CHAUCER *Wife's Prol.* 54 Of shrewed Lamech and his bigamie. **1460** CAPGRAVE *Chron.* (1858) 5 Lamech, that broute in first bigamie. **1660** STANLEY *Hist. Philos.* (1701) 97/2 The occasion, whereupon the Athenians..allowed bigamy. *c* **1725** POPE *Mart. Scribl.* xiii, A suit against Martin for Bigamy. **1884** *Pall Mall G.* 4 Mar. 3/2 Bigamy cases seldom have any legal interest for lawyers at the present day.

b. (Used *fig.* or *loosely*.)

1635 J. TAYLOR (Water P.) *Old Parr* D j, Each man had many wives, which Bigamie, Was such increase to their Posterity. *a* **1658** CLEVELAND *Gen. Poems* (1677) 70 But is this Bigamy of Titles due? Are you Sir Thomas and Sir Martin too?

2. *Eccl. Law.* Re-marriage after the death of a first wife (*or* husband); marriage of, or with, a widow (*or* widower). *Obs.* exc. *Hist.*

[**1345** *Act* [in Rastell 1557] *18 Edw. III*, ii, De trier par enquestes ou en auter maner la bygamie.] **1528** MORE *Conf. agst. Trib.* III. Wks. 229/1 The forbidding of bigamy by yᵉ wedding of one wife after another. **1543** GRAFTON *Cont. Harding* 504 It is..a greate blemishe to the sacred maiestie of a prince..to bee defiled wᵗ bigamy in his first mariage. **1594** SHAKS. *Rich. III*, III. vii. 189 Seduc'd..To base declension, and loath'd Bigamie. **1752** FIELDING *Amelia* VI. vii, I shall not enter into the question concerning the legality of bigamy. Our laws certainly allow it. **1865** NICHOLS *Britton* II. 25 *note*, Bigamy (in the ancient and proper sense of the word) involved the loss of the benefit of clergy.

bigan(e: see BEGIN and BEGO.

†**biˈgape**, *v. Obs. rare*⁻¹. [f. *bi-*, BE- + ME. *gapen* to GAPE; cf. Du. *begapen*, LG. *begaffen*.] *trans.* To gape or stare at.

a **1225** *Leg. Kath.* 1262 Þes keiser bigapede ham, as mon þæt bigon to weden.

‖**bigarade** (biːgarɑːd). [Fr.] The Spanish bitter orange. Freq. *attrib.*, as ***bigarade sauce***, a sauce flavoured with this orange; also applied to a dish (usu. roast duck) having this sauce as a dressing.

1703 tr. *H. van Oosten's Dutch Gardener* v. xiii. 289 Among the sour ones [*sc.* oranges], the Bigarade are the best, the handsomest, and the most esteemed. **1753** N. TORRIANO tr. *Chomel's Hist. Diss. Sore Throat* 78 The Bigarades, (*i.e.* large Oranges),..are very wholesome in such Cases. **1757** A. COOPER *Compl. Distiller* III. xxxix. 205 Take of the outer or yellow Part of the Rinds of fourteen Bigarades. **1877** E. S. DALLAS *Kettner's Bk. of Table* 68 *Bigarade sauce.*— Bigarade is the French name for a Seville orange, and the sauce is described under its English name of Orange Gravy Sauce. **1911** A. FILIPPINI *Internat. Cook Bk.* 651 *Bigarade duckling*..roast forty minutes... Pour a bigarade sauce over. **1930** *Times Educ. Suppl.* 25 Jan. 31/2 The bitter or bigarade oranges are used for making marmalade. **1957** R. POSTGATE *Good Food Guide 1957–1958* 297 Duck Bigarade.

bigarreau, -roon (ˈbɪgəˌrəʊ, -ˈruːn). Also 7 biguar, 7–8 bigarro, 7–9 biguarreau. [a. F. *bigarreau*, pl. *-eaux*, f. *bigarré* variegated. *Bigarroon* seems to be an Eng. change.] The large white heart-cherry, one side of which is pale yellow, and the other red. See also quot. 1859.

1629 PARKINSON *Parad.* III. xii. 572 The Biguarre Cherrie is..sometimes discoloured halfe white and halfe reddish. **1675** *Phil. Trans.* X. 494 Cherry of that kind which we call Bigarreaux. **1688** HOLME *Armory* II. iii. 49 The Biguar Cherry is a fair kind. **1693** EVELYN *De la Quint. Compl. Gard.* I. 73 The backward Cherries or Bigarros. **1719** LOUDON & WISE *Compl. Gard.* 87 The Biggaro, or Heart-Cherry, is a Fruit both firm and crackling. **1859** LOUDON *Encycl. Gard.* §4485 At the present time all the heart-shaped cherries which have the flesh firm..are arranged under the head of Bigarreaux. **1875** M. COLLINS *Sweet & Tw.* I. I. xii. 166 Under the great bigaroon cherry-trees. **1925** BLUNDEN *Eng. Poems* 117 From this fine orchard, branches sprawl And bigarreaus and blackhearts fall.

†**ˈbigate**, *a.* (*sb.*). [ad. L. *bigātus*, f. *biga*: see BIGA.] (A coin) bearing the figure of a biga.

1600 HOLLAND *Livy* XXXIII. xxiii. 838 Hee had..of silver coine in bigate pieces [L. *bigāti*] 532000. **1656** BLOUNT *Glossogr.*, Bigat (*bigātus*) was a piece of Roman silver Coyn.

Big Brother. [Cf. BIG *a.* 3 f.] The head of state in George Orwell's novel *1984*; hence, an apparently benevolent, but ruthlessly omnipotent, state authority. Also *attrib.* Hence **Big Brotherdom**, the rule or position of Big Brother; **Big Brotherism**, behaviour characteristic of Big Brother; **Big Brotherly** *a.*, of or pertaining to Big Brother.

1949 'G. ORWELL' *1984* I. 5 On each landing..the poster with the enormous face gazed from the wall... *Big Brother is watching you*, the caption beneath it ran. *Ibid.* II. 209 One could infer..the general structure of Oceanic society. At the apex of the pyramid comes Big Brother. Big Brother is infallible and all-powerful... Nobody has ever seen Big Brother. He is a face on the hoardings, a voice on the telescreen. **1953** *Economist* 12 Sept. 683/1 The distrust of the *concierge* who is also a police spy, of the admirable focusing device which the big block provides for the watchful eye of Big Brother. **1957** *Ibid.* 19 Oct. 208/2 The reporting to the Privy Council of any evidence discovered by this court of 'misconduct in the administration of security organisations' would usefully discourage the Big Brother mentality. **1958** *Listener* 9 Oct. 566/3 Mr. Harold Wilson's ingenious but ridiculous variant of 'big-brotherism'. **1959** *Glasgow Herald* 17 Apr. 8/5 One sight of that terrible big-brotherly finger and we will redouble our efforts to find a litter basket. **1964** *Punch* 7 Oct. 547/2 The growth of Big Brotherdom. **1967** *Boston Sunday Globe* 9 Apr. 28 We must take these measures to protect every citizen's privacy before 'Big Brotherism' and the police state take over.

bigeminal (baɪˈdʒɛmɪnəl), *a.* [f. BI- *pref.*² 6 + GEMINAL, f. L. *geminus* twin.] Existing or arranged in two pairs; *spec.* in *Phys.* applied to the *corpora quadrigemina* of the brain, lying beneath the cerebral hemispheres.

1836 TODD *Cycl. Anat. & Phys.* I. 583/1 Their medullary fibres..enter the bigeminal bodies. **1870** ROLLESTON *Anim. Life* Introd. 53 The bigeminal hollow optic lobes.

biˈgeminate (-meɪt), *a.* [f. as prec. + GEMINATE, ad. L. *gemināt*us doubled, f. *geminus* twin.] = prec. (Chiefly in *Bot.*) Also **biˈgeminated** *ppl. a.* (See quot.)

1817 R. JAMESON *Char. Min.* 205 Bi-geminated calcareous spar is a combination of two rhomboids and two dodecahedrons. **1835** LINDLEY *Introd. Bot.* (1848) II. 361 [Decompound leaves are] bigeminate, when each of two secondary petioles bears a pair of leaflets.

bigener (ˈbaɪdʒɪnə(r)). *Bot.* [a. L. *bigener*, f. *bi-* two + *gener-* (nom. *genus*) kind.] A cross or hybrid between two genera.

1835 LINDLEY *Introd. Bot.* (1848) II. 242 Bigeners, that is to say mules between different genera. **1883** *Nature* XXVII. 570 A true bigener.

bigeneric (baɪdʒɪˈnɛrɪk), *a. Bot.* [f. BI-² + GENERIC *a.*] Of, pertaining to, or produced from two distinct genera.

1885 *Gardeners' Chron.* XXIII. 631/3 How will these bigeneric crosses affect the stability of the genera as at present circumscribed? **1952** A. G. L. HELLYER *Sanders's Encycl. Gardening* (ed. 22) 205 *Gaulnettya*...Bigeneric hybrid between Pernettya and Gaultheria. **1964** *Guardian* 6 June 5/5 Bigeneric hybrids are plants whose parents belong to entirely separate genera..this type of cross seldom occurs in nature.

†**biˈgenerous**, *a. Obs.* [f. as BIGENER + -OUS.] Partaking of two genera or species; hybrid.

1610 GUILLIM *Heraldry* III. xxv. (1660) 255 A bigenerous beast of unkindly procreation. **1688** HOLME *Armory* II. 208 Bigenerous Creatures, Monsters by Natures Generation.

†**ˈbigeng**. *Obs. rare*⁻¹. [OE. *bígeng* 'worship, cultus,' the subst. form belonging to *begán*, in sense of *colĕre* to worship: see BEGO *v.*] Worship.

c **1000** ÆLFRIC *Gram.* xi. 79 *Cultus*, bigeng. *c* **1175** *Lamb. Hom.* 119 We beoð þurh crist to heouene ibroht, ȝif we his bigenge haldað.

bigent, variant of BEJAN.

bigential (baɪˈdʒɛnʃəl), *a.* [f. BI- *pref.*² 1 + L. *gent-em* race + -IAL.] Composed of or containing two races or peoples.

1846 WORCESTER cites *N. Amer. Rev.*

†**biˈgern**, *v. Obs. rare.* [f. *bi-*, BE- 2 + *girn*, GRIN to snare.] *trans.* To ensnare.

c **1400** *Apol. Loll.* 64 Þer oune findingis..bi gernyn hem þat þey may not out.

†**biˈgeten, biȝeoten**, *v. Obs. Inf.* 1 beᵹéotan, 3 biȝeoten. *Pa. t.* 1 beᵹéat. *Pa. pple.* 1 begoten, 3 bigoten, -ȝoten. [Com. WGer.: OE. *bigéotan*, *beᵹéotan* = OS. *bigiotan* (Du. *begieten*), OHG. *bigiozan* (MHG. *begiezen*, mod.G. *begieszen*), f. *bi-*, BE- 1 + *giutan*, in OE. *ᵹéotan* to pour. (The mod. form would be *be-yeet*.)]

trans. To pour about or over; to suffuse.

a **1000** *O.E. Chron.* an. 734 Swelce he wære mid blode begoten. *a* **1225** *Juliana* 27 Þat ha al were bigoten of þe blode. *a* **1240** *Sawles Warde* in *Lamb. Hom.* 261 Ich iseh þe apostles..biȝoten al of unimete blisse.

bigeten, -ȝe(o)ten, -ȝiten, obs. ff. BEGET.

bigg, big (bɪg). *Sc.* and *dial.* Also 5 byge, 6 bygg(e, 6–7 bigge. [a. ON. *bygg* barley (Da. *byg*, Sw. *bjug*), corresp. to OE. *béow* grain:—OTeut. **beuwo-m*, f. Old Aryan root **bheu* to grow, to be (whence BE; cf. Gr. *φύω*, Skr. *bhū*).]

1. The four-rowed barley, an inferior but hardier variety of the six-rowed or winter barley (*Hordeum hexastichon*), of rapid growth, and suited to inferior soils and more northern latitudes. (*Barley* is generic; *bear* includes the six-rowed and four-rowed kinds; *bigg* the four-rowed only. But *bear* interchanges in local use, now with *barley*, now with *bigg*.)

c **1450** in Wr.-Wülcker *Voc.* 726 *Hoc exaticum, hec mixtilio*, byge. **1547** *Wills & Invent. N.C.* (1835) 127 I gyue to George Bayts a chaldre of Bygg & a chalder of hauer. **1562** TURNER *Herbal* II. (1568) 16 The seconde kinde is called in Latin Hordeum Tetrastichum, in Englishe, bigge barley or beare or bigge alone. This kind groweth muche in yᵉ North country. **1570** LEVINS *Manip.* 118 Bigge, corne, *hordeum quadratum*. **1633** *Acts Durham High Commiss. Crt.* 57 And did violently carrie awaie the tieth beare or bigge. **1845** *Statist. Acc. Scotl.* XII. 453 Oats & bear or big with a little barley, are the kinds of grain. **1882** *Proc. Berw. Nat. Club* IX. 444 Used for husking big, or four-rowed barley.

2. *attrib.*, as in *bigg-barley*, *-market*, *-riddle*.

1597 GERARD *Herbal.* I. xliv. §2. 64 Called..of our English northerne people..Big Barly. **1864** *Sat. Rev.* 29 May, Most strangers would be inclined to think that the 'Bigg Market' meant the large one. **1446** *Wills & Inv. N.C.* (1835) I. 95 Item j whetridell, j bigridell.

bigg(e, obs. form of BIG.

†**ˈbiggand**, *ppl. a. Obs.* [north. dial. pres. pple. of BIG *v.*] Building; *sb.* a builder.

a **1300** *E.E. Psalter* cxvii[i]. 22 Þe stane whilk biggand forsoke. [*a* **1340** HAMPOLE *Psalter* cxlvi[i]. 2 Biggand ierusalem oure lord.]

†**bigge.** *Obs. rare*⁻¹. [Of unknown etymology and doubtful genuineness, like most of the words in the list quoted.] An alleged name of the hare.

c **1300** *Names of Hare* in Wright *Rel. Ant.* I. 133 The hare, the scotart, The bigge, the bouchart.

bigge(n, obs. form of BUY.

†**biggel.** *Obs.* Apparently the Nyl-Ghau.

1745 PARSONS *Quadr.* in *Phil. Trans.* XLIII. 465 Among the Horses in the Stables of the Viceroy of Goa, he saw a Beast called a *Biggel*, a creature much about the Colour and Bigness of a Rain-deer. **1771** PENNANT *Synop. Quadr.* 29 *Antilope Tragocamelus*, Biggel.

biggen (ˈbɪg(ə)n), *v. Obs.* exc. *dial.* [f. BIG *a.* + -EN². Perh. sense 3 was the earliest.]

1. *trans.* To make big; to increase, enlarge.

1643 TUCKNEY *Balm of G.* 35 Our sinnes..are very great, and if circumstances can biggen them, of the largest size. **1674** N. FAIRFAX *Bulk & Selv.* 185 Those things feed and biggen us. **1862** MISS CHARLESWORTH *Minist. Children* ii. 22, I can biggen them a bit when they get too small.

2. *intr.* To become big, to increase in size.

1649 BLITHE *Eng. Improv. Impr.* (1652) 53 All waters biggen the further they run. **1674** N. FAIRFAX *Bulk & Selv.* 127 Some bigning or growing. **1701** STEELE *Chr. Hero* (1711) 45 His great heart..rose and biggened in proportion to any growing danger that threatened him. **1830** GALT *Laurie T.* v. vii. (1849) 222 My heart biggened in my bosom.

†**3.** To recover strength after confinement. *dial. Obs.* Cf. BIG *a.* 1. Hence **ˈbiggening** *vbl. sb.*

1674 RAY *N.C. Wds.* 6, I wish you a good biggening. **1721** BAILEY, *Biggenning*, the Up-rising of Women after Child-Birth. *Country Word.*

ˈbigger, *sb. Obs.* exc. *north. dial.* Also **biggar(e**. [f. BIG *v.* + -ER¹.] A builder.

c **1440** *Bone Flor.* 8 The furste byger of Anteoche. **1552** ABP. HAMILTON *Catech.* (1884) 28 Ane biggare can nocht make ane evin up wal without direction of his lyne.

bigger (ˈbɪgə(r)), *a.*, compar. of BIG. Also *sb.* One who is bigger; a superior in size.

1562 J. HEYWOOD *Prov. & Epigr.* (1867) 39 His biggers or betters. **1582** N. T. (Rhem.) *Acts* xiv. 22 *note*, As if they should translate..Maior of London, the Bigger of London. **1869** MRS. WHITNEY *Hitherto* iv. 50 Its own capacity to take in sunshine as fast, in proportion, as its biggers and betters.

ˈbiggermost, *a. dial.* = Biggest.

1803 S. PEGGE *Anecd. Eng. Lang.* 102 The biggermost man in the parish.

†**ˈbiggerness.** *Obs. rare*⁻¹. [f. as prec. + -NESS.] The quality of being bigger; larger size.

1674 PETTY *Disc. bef. R. Soc.* 27 Wetting of Sails..doth make the Sail, as it were, bigger; which biggerness may be known and measured.

biggie (ˈbɪgɪ). *slang.* Also **biggy**. [f. BIG *a.* + -IE.]

1. a. An important person; a 'big shot'. orig. *U.S.*

1931 H. MUTSCHMANN *Gloss. Americanisms* 8/1 *Biggie*, important person, celebrity. **1941** AUDEN *New Year Let.* III. 69 Each biggie in the Canning Ring An unrobust lone Fisher-King. **1969** *Melody Maker* 13 Sept. 12/7 It's time for me to be a biggie... My aim now is to get..on to the front page.

b. Anything impressively large or influential; an important organization, event, etc. orig. *U.S.*

[**1942** BERREY & VAN DEN BARK *Amer. Thes. Slang* §20/12 *Important*, big, big-bore, biggie, big-league, [etc.].] **1945** MENCKEN *Amer. Lang.* Suppl. I. v. 338 It [sc. *Variety*] converts all the other parts of speech into nouns, e.g.,..*pink* (a sexy picture), *clicky* (a picture making money), *cheapie*, *biggie*, *brush-off* and *vocal* (a song). **1965** 'LAUCHMONEN' *Old Thom's Harvest* xii. 149 Make that order a biggie. **1977** *Chicago Tribune* 2 Oct. III. 8/1 Football... Next Saturday's Midwestern biggies on the college scene include Michigan at Michigan State. **1981** *Pop. Hi-Fi* Mar. 15/3 The only development that I would class as the 'biggy' for 1980 was

the introduction of reasonably priced active systems. **1983** *Sunday Express* 17 Apr. 8/4 Over 300 organisations.. ranging from biggies like the National Trust to smaller, personal favourites like the Dachshund Club. **1985** A. BLOND *Book Bk.* i. 5 The firm needs a blockbuster... I've got to have a biggy.

2. *pl.* A children's word or euphemism for 'excrement'.

1953 E. SIMON *Past Masters* IV. iii. 233 You're used to having biggies all over your floor, aren't you? **1967** A. WILSON *No Laughing Matter* II. 103 He's a bit erratic where he does his biggies, now he's a grown up parrot.

biggin[1] ('bɪgɪn). Also 6 begin, byggen, 7 biggon, -ging, 6-9 biggen. [a. F. *béguin* child's cap. See BEGUINE, *note*.]

1. A child's cap.

1530 PALSGR. 198/1 Byggen for a chyldes heed, *beguyne*. **1532** MORE *Confut. Tindale* Wks. 577/2. **1639** MASSINGER *Unnat. Combat* IV. ii, Would you have me Transform my hat to double clouts and biggings? **1755** *Connoisseur* No. 80 (1774) III. 71 Such a store of clouts, caps..biggens..as would set up a Lying-in Hospital. **1819** SCOTT *Ivanhoe* xxviii, My brain has been topsy-turvy..ever since the biggin was bound first round my head.

b. Taken as the sign of infancy.

1609 B. JONSON *Sil. Wom.* III. vi, [You have] beene a courtier from the biggen, to the night-cap. **1638** QUARLES *Hieroglyph.* iii. 215 How many dangers meet Poor man between the biggin and the winding sheet.

2. A cap or hood for the head, a night-cap; also the coif of a Serjeant-at-law.

1562 BULLEYN *Bk. Simples* 10 a, Put into a Forhead clothe or Biggen. **1589** *Pappe w. Hatchet* B ij b, [His] head is swolne so big, that he had neede send to the cooper to make him a biggin. **1597** SHAKS. *2 Hen. IV*, IV. v. 27 Hee whose Brow (with homely Biggen bound) Snores out the Watch of Night. **1610** MARKHAM *Masterp.* II. xvii. 245 Make the horse a biggen of canuase to close in the soare. **1639** *City-Match* IV. vii. in Hazl. *Dodsley* XIII. 288 Ha' made him barrister, And rais'd him to his satin cap and biggon. **1828** SCOTT *F.M. Perth* xvii, Reduced..to biggen and gown, in a night brawl.

†**3.** The amnion enveloping the fœtus. *Obs.*

1611 COTGR., *Agneliere*..called by some Midwiues, the Coyfe, or Biggin of the child; by others, the childs shirt.

biggin[2]. [See quot.] A kind of coffee-pot containing a strainer for the infusion of the coffee, without allowing the grounds to mix with the infusion.

1803 *Gents. Mag.* LXXIII. 1094 Mr. Biggin some years ago invented a new sort of coffee pot which has been ever since extensively sold under the name of coffee biggins. **1817** *Specif. of Ogle's Patent* No. 4173, for Improvements in tea and coffee pots or biggins.—'The tea or coffee being put into the canister, placed within the pot or biggin, the boiling water is then poured upon it, and the extract is filtered through the strainer into the exterior pot or biggin.' *a* **1803** MOORE in *Mem. & Corr.* (1853) I. 97, I had yesterday a long visit from Mr. Biggin..By the bye it is from him the coffee biggins take their name.

†'**biggined**, *a. Obs.* Wearing a biggin.

1607 R. C. tr. *Stephens's World Wond.* 235 To see a man bigginned with a hood vpon his head. **1655** tr. *Francion* 24 This old Biggin'd ape?

†'**bigging**, *vbl. sb. dial.* [f. BIG *v.* + -ING[1].]

†**1.** The fact of dwelling; sojourn, stay.

c **1250** *Gen. & Ex.* 718 Long bigging is here noȝt god.

b. Dwelling-place, habitation, home. *Obs.*

c **1250** *Gen. & Ex.* 3163 Ðo was non biging of al egipte lichles. *c* **1400** *Epiph.* (Turnb. 1843) 156 Bryng hus all to that bygyng bryghth. *c* **1425** *Emare* 709 When he come to his byggynge, He welcomed fayr that lady yynge.

2. The action of building. *north. dial.*

c **1440** *Promp. Parv.* 35 Byggynge, or beeldynge, *edificatio, structura.* **1527** *Lanc. & Chesh. Wills* (1854) 34 Sufficiant reparations and bydgynges of howses. *c* **1550** SIR J. BALFOUR *Practicks* (1754) 34 For the bigging, mending and reparatioun of paroche kirkis. **1816** SCOTT *Antiq.* iv, 'Prætorian here, Prætorian there, I mind the bigging o't.'

3. *concr.* A building, an edifice; also, an outbuilding as distinguished from a house. *north. dial.*

a **1300** *Cursor M.* 1774 Þe bigginnes fel bath hey and lau. *c* **1400** *Destr. Troy* xxxv. 13452 Betwene the biggyng on þe buerne & þe burgh riche. *c* **1440** *Promp. Parv.* 35 Byggynge ..*edificium.* **1533** BELLENDEN *Livy* v. (1822) 432 Magnificent housis and biggingis. **1681** BLOUNT *Glossogr.*, *Biggin*, or *Bigging* in the northern parts is used for a fair house or Gentlemans Seat. **1790** BURNS *Capt. Grose* iii, By some auld houlet-haunted biggin' Or kirk deserted by its riggin'. **1849** C. BRONTË *Shirley* xxx. 442 About to fall asleep wi' the length of the sermon and the heat of the biggin'. **1876** GRANT *Burgh Sch. Scot.* I. i. 25 Certain houses, crofts, biggings, lands and gardens.

'**biggish**, *a.* [f. BIG *a.* + -ISH.] Rather big.

a **1626** W. SCLATER *Exp. 2 Thess.* (1632) 150 The volumne growes biggish. **1867** CARLYLE *Remin.* (1881) I. 100 A biggish, simple house on the sands.

†'**biggit**, *ppl. a. Obs. Sc.* [f. BIG *v.*] **a.** Inhabited, cultivated (*obs.*). **b.** Built, erected. *north. dial.*

1375 BARBOUR *Bruce* XIV. 383 Quhen thai come in biggit land, Wittale and mete yneuch thai fand. **1815** SCOTT *Guy M.* III. 150 (JAM.) 'Bred in biggit wa's.'

biggity ('bɪgɪtɪ), *a.* orig. and chiefly *U.S. dial.* Also biggety. [f. BIG *a.* + -Y[1]; *-it-*, *-et-* unexplained, but cf. BIGOTED *a.* and UPPITY *a.*] Vain, conceited, boastful; assertive, impudent. Also as *adv.*

1880 J. C. HARRIS *Uncle Remus* xviii, Like po'in' spring water on one er deze yer biggity fices. **1898** *Westm. Gaz.* 11 Mar. 3/2 John Bull naturally talks 'biggity' about his Navy. **1938** M. K. RAWLINGS *Yearling* xxxi. 382 You mighty biggety now you're a yearlin'. **1940** C. MCCULLERS *Heart is Lonely Hunter* (1943) I. iii. 42 From the biggity way you been acting lately it seem to me like you already got one toe in the pit. **1946** MEZZROW & WOLFE *Really Blues* i. 5 We had a yen..to strut and act biggity.

'**biggonet.** *Sc.* [Dim. of BIGGIN; cf. OF. *beguinet* in same sense.] A woman's cap or headdress.

1725 RAMSAY *Gent. Sheph.* I. ii, Good humour and white bigonets shall be Guards to my face, to keep his love for me. **1818** SCOTT *Hrt. Midl.* xxiv, The queen tore her biggonets for perfect anger.

biȝ: see under BIY-.

bigha ('bi:gə). Also beega(h, begah, biggah. [Hindi.] A measure of land-area in India varying locally from ⅓ acre to 1 acre.

1763 in Gleig *Mem. Hastings* (1841) I. 129, I never seized a boga [*sic*] or a beswa of the land belonging to Calcutta. **1823** MALCOLM *Central India* II. 15 A Begah has been computed at one third of an acre, but its size differs in almost every province. The smallest Begah may perhaps be computed at one third, and the largest at two thirds of an acre. *a* **1876** MEADOWS TAYLOR *My Life* (1878) xii. 251 It would be a noble sheet of water, and very profitable, as it would irrigate upwards of 10,000 *beegahs* of rice. **1895** MRS. CROKER *Village Tales* (1896) 167 Two biggahs of land, planted in rape and linseed. **1905** *Statesman* 22 Aug. 2/4 All that piece or parcel of vacant land containing by measurement one bigha fifteen cottahs more or less.

big-head. Also big head, bighead. [BIG *a.* 3.]

1. Any of certain diseases of cattle, horses, sheep, etc., characterized by swelling of the head. orig. *U.S.*

1805 *Lancaster* (Pa.) *Intelligencer* 3 Dec. Advt. (Th.), A Brown Steer, having 'what they call the Big Head'. **1868** *Rep. Iowa Agric. Soc. 1867* 130, I have not lost but two of the bovine species..; one in 1861 had big head or jaw. **1888** in FARMER *Americanisms.* **1955** GAIGER & DAVIES *Vet. Path. & Bacteriol.* (ed. 4) xxxvii. 711 The condition [*sc.* osteofibrosis] is also known..in England, as 'big head'.

2. *U.S.* and *Austral.* A popular name for various fish having large heads (see quots.).

1820 C. S. RAFINESQUE SCHMALTZ *Ichth. Ohiensis* 49 Vulgar names, Chub, Big-mouth, and Big-head. **1889** *Cent. Dict.*, *Bighead*, a local name of a Californian species of sculpin, *Scorpænichthys marmoratus*, a fish of the family *Cottidæ*. **1909** *Ibid.* Suppl., *Bighead*, a fish, *Eleotris nudiceps*, of the family *Gobiidæ*. [Australia.]

3. *fig.* 'Swelled head'; an inflated opinion of oneself; conceit, arrogance. *U.S. colloq.*

1850 H. C. LEWIS *Louisiana 'Swamp Doctor'* 157 Pride.. lets human nature die of the big-head before common sense can bleed freely. **1857** B. YOUNG in *Jrnl. Discourses* IV. 69/2 They need to be careful, or they will have the 'big head', and become as dead..as old pumpkins. **1896** *Congress. Rec.* Mar. 3030/2 [Such] men holding subordinate places in the government of the U.S. to-day..have got the 'big head' and got it bad. **1902** G. H. LORIMER *Lett. Self-Made Merchant* 226 A boss with a case of big-head will fill an office full of sore heads.

b. A conceited or arrogant person. *colloq.*

[**1846** *Warsaw* (Ill.) *Signal* 6 Feb. 3/1 A certain Jack-mormon of Hancock county, we won't call him big-head, (but the Saints used to) is in the habit of shaving the hair off his forehead, in order to give it an intellectual appearance. **1863** W. STOKES tr. *Creation of World* 107 in *Trans. Philol. Soc. 1864*, The Father's anger hath gone with me For slaying Abel (the) big-head.] **1932** J. CARY *Aissa Saved* 106 He is simply a fool, a conceited bighead who thinks he knows better than the oldest and most experienced men in the whole country. **1955** E. BLISHEN *Roaring Boys* IV. 238 Saying..'This man was a bighead,' in baffled parody of Shakespeare's funeral speeches.

4. (A person wearing) a large and grotesque mask covering the head.

1895 ROBERTS & MORTON *Adv.* vi. 73 Everybody gagged, even the supers and the big-heads. **1933** P. GODFREY *Back-Stage* iv. 53 'You 'ad *real* pantos—..'Arliquinades, and a chorus of Big 'Eads.' From the litter of the bygone he produces a specimen 'Big Head'. It is a fantastic object nearly three feet high.

big-headed, *a.* [BIG *a.* 3; cf. prec.]

1. Having a large head.

1869 A. R. WALLACE *Malay Archipelago* I. xvi. 376, I killed two [snakes] of a very abundant species, big-headed and of a bright green colour. **1921** E. STEP *Brit. Insect Life* vii. 103 A commoner example of these devouring Insects is the Big-headed Broscus (*Broscus cephalotes*)... Its big-headed appearance is helped largely by the size and convexity of the fore-body. **1960** M. BURTON *Wild Animals* 155 Their form is more graceful and not 'big headed'.

2. Conceited, arrogant. *colloq.*

1942 in BERREY & VAN DEN BARK *Amer. Thes. Slang* §301/5. **1959** J. BRAINE *Vodi* xii. 166 The selfish big-headed, hard-hearted young lover. **1960** P. HASTINGS *Sandals for my Feet* I. vii. 71 It was the duty of a sister not to let her sister get big-headed.

biȝeme, *v.*: see BIYEME.

big house. [BIG *a.* 3.] **1.** A large house, a mansion; *spec.* (freq. with capital initials) the principal house of an estate. Also *attrib.* orig. *U.S.*

1823 J. F. COOPER *Pioneers* xli, The big house has rung with merriment this month past! **1848** A. SOMERVILLE *Autobiogr. Working Man* i. 13 The stack-yard..and cattle sheds..were at Thriepland Hill, while the 'big house', the stables, and some other offices..were at Branxton. **1867** TROLLOPE *Claverings* II. xxiii. 287 We might as well stay with them at the big house. **1926** J. DEVANNY *Butcher Shop* 15 A passage leading to the 'big house' as the homestead is generally called. **1941** L. MACNEICE *Poetry of Yeats* v. 102 Yeats's cult of the Big House is to be correlated with his dislike for democracy. **1959** L. LEE *Cider with Rosie* vii. 138 There were other stories of Big House life.

2. The workhouse. (Cf. HOUSE *sb.*[1] 2 a.) *slang.*

1851 MAYHEW *London Lab.* I. 48/2 As long as they kept out of the 'big house' (the workhouse) she would not complain. **1868** J. HARTLEY *Yorks. Ditties* (1873) 13 But him 'ats as poor as a maase..He mun point his noas up to th' big haase.

b. A prison. *slang* (orig. *U.S.*).

1916 *Lit. Digest* 19 Aug. 424/3 The malefactor is sent away to the 'big house'. **1940** F. SCOTT FITZGERALD *Let.* 11 Apr. (1964) 68, I feel like a criminal who has been in a hideout, been caught, and has to go back to the Big House. **1942** 'D. HUME' *Destiny is my Name* ii. 21 You'll land yourself in the big house for fourteen years.

bight (baɪt). Also 4 byȝt, 5 bycht, 6 byght, 7 beight, 7-9 bite. [OE. *byht* bend, masc., corresp. to MLG. *bucht* (whence mod.G. *bucht* 'bay, bight,' mod.Du. *bocht*, also Da., Sw. *bugt*):—OTeut. **buhti-z*, f. *būgan* to BOW. OE. *byht* 'bend' appears to occur in *Cod. Dipl.* 538 and App. 308. It is to be distinguished from the poetic *byht* abode, corresp. to ON. *bygð*, from *byggja* to dwell, inhabit. See also BOUGHT *sb.*]

1. A bending or bend; *esp.* an angle, hollow, or fork in the human or animal body; a corner.

? **967** *Cod. Dipl.* 538 (Bosw.), Andlang norþȝeardes ðæt hit cymþ in ðone byht. *c* **1340** *Gaw. & Gr. Knt.* 1349 Bi þe byȝt al of þe byȝes. *c* **1400** *Rel. Ant.* I. 190 In the byȝt of the harme. **1523** FITZHERB. *Husb.* §132 Dresse the wodde and bowe it clene and cutte it at euery byghte. **1674** RAY *N.C. Words.*, *Beight* of the Elbow: Bending of the Elbow. *Cheshire.* **1721** BAILEY, *Bight* [of a Horse] is the inward bent of the Chambrel: also the bent of the Knees in the Fore-legs. [So in subseq. Dicts.]

2. *esp.* The loop of a rope, as distinguished from its ends; the part between the ends.

1622 R. HAWKINS *Voy. S. Sea* (1847) 132 With our capsten [we] stretched the two byghtes. **1769** FALCONER *Dict. Marine* (1789), *Bight*, the double part of a rope when it is folded..as, her anchor hooked the bight of our cable. **1812** *Examiner* 9 Nov. 720/1 The bite of a whale-line having ..caught his leg. **1833** MARRYAT *P. Simple* (1863) 242 To put the little beast into the bight of a rope, and tow him overboard. **1875** BUCKLAND *Log-bk.* 290 Catch him round the neck with the bight of a rope.

3. a. A bend or curve as a geographical feature, *e.g.* an indentation in a coast line, a corner or recess of a bay, a bend in a river, etc. Also, an indentation or bay in a mass of ice.

1481 in *Ripon Ch. Acts* 344 Sleningford Bygh. **1555** EDEN *Decades W. Ind.* (Arb.) 381 In the byght of a bay. **1622** HAWKINS *Voy. S. Sea* (1847) 180 We found presently in the westerne bight of the bay a deepe river. **1725** DE FOE *Voy. round World* (1840) 146 In the very bite or nook of the bay there was a great inlet of water. **1818** W. SCORESBY in *Memoirs Wernerian Nat. Hist. Soc.* II. 266 A *bight* signifies a bay or sinuosity, on the border of any large mass or body of ice. **1852** CONYBEARE & H. *St. Paul* (1862) I. v. 135 The town was situated on a bight of the coast. **1876** MORRIS *Sigurd* II. 165 The bight of the swirling river. *Ibid.* III. 326 Far off in a bight of the mountains. **1956** ARMSTRONG & ROBERTS *Illustr. Ice Gloss.* 5 *Bight*, an extensive crescent-shaped indentation in the *ice-edge*, formed either by wind or current.

b. *transf.* and *fig.*

1851 SIR F. PALGRAVE *Norm. & Eng.* I. 30 Bights and bends in the great stream of Time. **1878** *Masque Poets* 121 Larded with talk and tallow In the bight of the afternoon.

4. The space between two headlands, a bay, generally a shallow or slightly-receding bay; *spec.* in the Bights of Benin and Biafra, and the Australian Bight; also *transf.* a bay-like segment.

1555 EDEN *Decades W. Ind.* (Arb.) 380 There is a byght or bay as thowgh it were a harborowe. **1725** DE FOE *Voy. round World* (1840) 194 We ran boldly into the bay, and came to an anchor in that which they call the Bite, or little bay. **1769** FALCONER *Dict. Marine* (1789), *Bight*, is also a small bay between two points of land. **1833** M. SCOTT *Tom Cringle* xvii. (1859) 447 The glowing mirror of the calm bight. **1864** D. MITCHELL *Wet Days Edgew.* 43, I see there is a bight of blue in the sky. **1878** K. JOHNSTON *Africa* xi. (1884) §15 Fernando Po, near the head of the Bight of Biafra. **1879** STEVENSON *Trav. Cevennes* 190, I spied a bight of meadow.. in an angle of the river.

†**biȝule**, *v. Obs.* [for *bi-ȝuhele(n*, f. *bi-*, BE- + *ȝuhele(n*:—OE. **ȝéoȝelian*, in *ȝéoȝelere* a juggler, cogn. w. OHG. *gougulâri*, mod.G. *gaukler.*] *trans.* To BEGUILE.

a **1225** *Ancr. R.* 268 Vor þet is his unwrench..þet he haueð monie holi men grimliche biȝuled. *a* **1225** *Leg. Kath.* 1054 Þurh wiheles & wicchecreftes wurcheð Sume wundres & biȝuleð [*v.r.* biȝulið] unwiten.

bigin(e, -ne, bigirde, obs. f. BEGIN, BEGIRD.

biglandular: see BI- *pref.*[2] 1.

biglot (ˈbaɪglɒt), *a. rare.* [f. BI- *pref.*[2] 6 + Gr. γλῶττα, tongue, language; cf. Gr. δίγλωττος, Eng. *polyglot*.] In two languages, bilingual.

1883 *N. & Q.* 29 Sept. 254/2 The biglot edition..is a translation into Italian..with the Latin text in parallel columns.

† **ˈbigly**, *a. Obs.* Also bygly, byggly. [f. BIG *v.* to inhabit + -LY[1].] Habitable, fit or pleasant to dwell in; hence *gen.* pleasant.

c **1325** *E.E. Allit. P.* A. 962 Bryng me to þat bygly bylde, & let me se þy blysful bor. *c* **1440** *York Myst.* vi. 42 To byggly blys we bothe were brought. *c* **1440** *Bone Flor.* 220 He wyll dystroye thy bygly landys. *c* **1450** HENRYSON *Bludy Serk* 13 Scho wynnit in a bigly bour, On feld wes none so fair. [*a* **1803** *Erlington* i. in Child *Ball.* I. (1882) 107/1 He has built a bigly bower, An a' to put that lady in.]

bigly (ˈbɪglɪ), *adv.* [f. BIG *a.* + -LY[2].]

†**1.** With great force or violence; firmly, strongly, violently. *Obs.*

c **1325** *E.E. Allit. P.* C. 321 þe barrez of vche a bonk ful bigly me haldes. *c* **1400** *Destr. Troy* XIV. 6035 Knyt hom with cables..And bound hom full bigly on hor best wise. **1470–85** MALORY *Arthur* (1816) I. 416 So roughly and so bigly, that there was not one that might withstand him. **1556** J. HEYWOOD *Spider & F.* lxxviii. 140 A serius argument: Whether I should liue or die, was biglie bent.

2. Loudly, boastfully, haughtily, pompously.

1532 MORE *Confut. Tindale* Wks. 397/1 And bereth it out bigly wᵗ shameles deuelyshe heresie. **1585** ABP. SANDYS *Serm.* (1841) 104 Goliah thought bigly of himself. **1602** WARNER *Alb. Eng.* IX. xlvi. 218 Oftentimes Authoritie lookes biglier than a Bull. **1741** JOHNSON *Debates in Parl.* (1787) II. 246 Talking bigly, indeed, of vindicating foreign rights. **1846** LANDOR *Exam. Shaks.* Wks. II. 299 He spoke as bigly and fiercely as a soaken yeoman at an election feast.

bigness (ˈbɪgnɪs). [f. BIG *a.* + -NESS.]

1. Large size or bulk.

1494 FABYAN V. cxxxi. 114 Most precious stones of a great bygnesse and value. **1509** HAWES *Past. Pleas.* XXXVIII. viii. 197 A poynted dyamonde of mervaylous bygnes. **1614** MARKHAM *Cheap Husb.* I. i. (1668) 4 Not grosse with much flesh but with the bignesse of his bones. **1827** HARE *Guesses* (1859) 381 Bigness with the bulk of mankind is the nearest synonym for greatness. **1878** TAIT & STEWART *Unseen Univ.* ii. §85 But we must not be terrified at mere bigness.

b. *fig.* Haughtiness, pompousness, swagger.

1681 H. MORE *Exp. Dan.* Pref. 57 The worldly bigness and downbearing Dominion of a tyrannical Clergy. **1847** L. HUNT *Men, Women, & Bks.* II. i. 15 A puffed and uneasy pomp, a bigness instead of greatness.

2. Size, magnitude, bulk (large or small).

1529 RASTELL *Pastyme* (1811) 105 They be of one bygnes. **1667** MILTON *P.L.* II. 1052 This pendant world, in bigness as a Starr. **1779** JOHNSON *Blake* Wks. IV. 375 Seven forts with cannon proportioned to the bigness. **1826** KIRBY & SP. *Entomol.* III. xxix. 78 The bigness of a large pea.

‖ **bignonia** (bɪgˈnəʊnɪə). *Bot.* [Named by Tournefort after the Abbé Bignon, librarian to Louis XIV.] A genus of plants, N.O. *Bignoniaceæ*, natives of hot climates, remarkable for the beauty of their trumpet-shaped flowers. Hence **bignoniˈaceous**, **bigˈnonial** *a.*

[**1700** TOURNEFORT *Inst. Rei Herb.*, Bignoniam appellavi.] **1785** H. MARSHALL *Amer. Grove* 22 Ever-green Bignonia, or Yellow Jasmine. **1802** M. CUTLER in W. P. & J. P. Cutler *Life & Corresp.* (1888) II. 104 Magnolias, bignonias, liriodendrons. **1826** T. FLINT *F. Berrian* I. v. 155 Beautiful stone cottages, clustered with the bignonia in full flower. **1835** *Penny Cycl.* IV. 391/2 The..Bignonia, many species of which are common in our gardens. **1865** PARKMAN *Huguenots* iv. 52 The scarlet trumpets of the bignonia.

† **bigold.** *Obs. rare*[−1]. *Bot.* [perh. f. BY- in sense of 'inferior' + GOLD.] The Corn Marigold.

1636 GERARD *Herbal* Supp., Bigold, *Chrysanthemum segetum*. **1863** PRIOR *Plant-n.* 21 Bigold, tinsel, false gold, applied to a plant that is not the genuine *Golde*.

bigonial (baɪˈgəʊnɪəl), *a.* [f. BI-[2] 5 + mod.L. *goni-on* the outer point of the jaw-bone (Gr. γωνία angle) + -AL.] Of or relating to the distance between the points at the angle of the lower jaw on each side.

1895 tr. *Lombroso & Ferrero's Female Offender* i. 25 The bigonial diameter of female criminals is much greater than in women and men of moral lives. **1937** *Nature* 16 Jan. 120/2 The bigonial breadth, 108·6 mm. is below the Eskimo measurement of 130 mm.

bigot (ˈbɪgət), *sb.* and *a.* [a. F. *bigot*, of unknown origin: see below.] **A.** *sb.*

†**1. a.** A hypocritical professor of religion, a hypocrite. **b.** A superstitious adherent of religion.

1598 SPEGHT *Chaucer*, *Bigin, bigot*, superstitious hypocrite [**1602** *adds* or hypocriticall woman]. **1653** URQUHART *Rabelais* I. xl, He is no bigot or hypocrite. **1656** BLOUNT *Glossogr.*, *Bigot* (Fr.), an hypocrite, or one that seems much more holy then he is, also a scrupulous or Superstitious fellow. **1664** H. MORE *Myst. Iniq.* 436 One part of their Church becomes Sotts and Bigots.

2. A person obstinately and unreasonably wedded to a particular religious creed, opinion, or ritual.

1661 COWLEY *Cromwell* Wks. II. 655 He was rather a well-meaning and deluding Bigot, than a crafty and malicious Impostor. **1741** WATTS *Improv. Mind* I. Wks. (1813) 14 A dogmatist in religion is not a long way off from a bigot. **1844** STANLEY *Arnold* II. viii. 13 [Dr. Arnold] was almost equally condemned, in London as a bigot, and in Oxford as a latitudinarian.

b. *transf.* (Of other than religious opinions.)

1687 CONGREVE *Old Bach.* I. v, Yet is adored by that bigot Sir Joseph Wittol as the image of valour. **1838** HALLAM *Hist. Lit.* I. vii. §14 I. 395 Lord Bacon, certainly no bigot to Aristotle. **1863** KINGSLEY *Water-Bab.* vi. 290 The children of Prometheus are..the bigots, and the bores.

3. *Comb.*, as ***bigot-maker***.

a **1720** SHEFFIELD (Dk. Buckhm.) *Wks.* (1753) II. 155 The best of all the Bigot-makers that ever I read of.

B. *adj.* [Often merely ***attrib.*** use of sb.]

1623 LD. HERBERT in Ellis *Orig. Lett.* I. 298 III. 164 The most common censure, even of the bigot party. **1680** DRYDEN *Kind Kpr.* Ep. Ded., In a Country more Bigot than ours. **1751** SMOLLETT *Per. Pic.* lxii, The crazed Tory, the bigot Whig. **1844** KINGLAKE *Eothen* xxvii. (1878) 345 Old bigot zeal against Christians.

[In OF. *Bigot* appears first in the romance of *Girart de Roussillon* (12th c.) as the proper name of some people, apparently of the south of Gaul. Hence already in the 17th c. it was suggested by Caseneuve, that it might be an OF. form of *Wisigothus*, Visigoth; the relations between the Visigoths of Toulouse who were Arians, and the Franks who were Catholics, being such as readily to attach to the name of the former the connotation of 'detestable foreigner' or 'foreign heretic.' But modern Romanic scholars find phonetic difficulties, besides that there is no evidence that the name *Wisigothi* was preserved in the vulgar tongue. Slender support to some connexion with the Goths is suggested by the med.L. form *Bigothi* (Du Cange). Whether the Sp. *bigote*, moustache, is in any way connected, cannot be decided. According to Wace *bigoz, bigos* was applied opprobriously by the French to the Normans, which shows that the word had then acquired some connotative force; the legend that it originated in the refusal of Hrolf or Rollo to kiss the foot of Charles the Simple, when, in the words of the 12th c. chronicler, 'lingua Anglica (!!!) respondit *Ne se, bi got*, quod interpretatur *Ne per Deum*' (No by God!), is absurdly incongruous with facts. The opprobrious sense in Wace was certainly not that of 'superstitious' or 'hypocrite,' as in later F. and Eng.; materials to show how the latter was developed are wanting, but there is evidence to show that the feminine *bigote* was subsequently applied in opprobrium to the *Beguines* (see *Beguta, Bigutta*, in Du Cange): our first quotation identifies *bigot* with *bigin* or *beguine*. In early times the word became a Norman family name as in Roger Bigod earl of Norfolk.]

‖ **biˈgote.** [Sp.] The moustache.

1623 MABBE *Aleman's Guzman d'Alf.* II. 332 It seeming perhaps unto them that..the bearing their Bigotes high, turn'd vp with hot yrons..should be their saluation and bring them to heauen.

bigoted (ˈbɪgətɪd), *a.* Also 7–8 big(g)otted. [f. BIGOT + -ED[2]. (In 17th c. pronounced *biˈgotted*.)] Obstinately and blindly attached to some creed, opinion, or party; unreasonably devoted to a system or party, and intolerant towards others.

1645 EVELYN *Mem.* (1857) I. 192 Though the least bigoted of all Roman Catholics. **1682** S. PORDAGE *Medal Rev.* 336 One bigotted in the Romish way. **1759** DILWORTH *Pope* 69 A bigotted Jacobite. **1848** H. MILLER *First Impr.* vii. 107 His bigoted, weak-minded sister, the bloody Mary. **1875** H. E. MANNING *Mission H. Ghost* ix. 236 We are thought to be intolerant and bigoted, because we will keep no peace with heresy.

b. Const. *to*.

a **1704** T. BROWN *Sat. Antients* Wks. 1730 I. 22 Men who are biggoted to the opinions they have imbibed under their teachers. **1782** MISS BURNEY *Cecilia* IV. v. (1783) 199 Mr. Harrel has been so strangely biggotted to his friend. **1816** BYRON *Ch. Har.* III. xliv, So nursed and bigoted to strife.

ˈbigotedly, *adv.* In a bigoted manner.

1831 J. WILSON in *Blackw. Mag.* XXX. 405 Your notions ..are as bigotedly aristocratic as ever.

† **biˈgotic**, *a. Obs.* [f. BIGOT + -IC.] = BIGOTED. So **biˈgotical** *a.*, **biˈgotically** *adv.*, **ˈbigotish** *a.*

1678 CUDWORTH *Intell. Syst.* I. iii. §38. 177 Some noble and generous truth which the bigotick religionists endeavour to smoother and oppress. *Ibid.* I. i. §19. 18 Some Bigotical Religionists. *Ibid.* I. iv. §15. 274 Bigotically zealous for the worship of the gods. **1652** EVELYN *State France* Misc. Writ. (1805) 82 The Roman Catholicks of France are nothing so..bigotish as are..the Recusants of England.

† **ˈbigotism.** *Obs.* [a. F. *bigotisme*.] Bigotry.

1681 HICKERINGILL *Vind. Naked Truth* II. 24 'Tis this Bigottism that undoes us. **1705** —— *Priest-cr.* I. (1721) 52 The additional Bigotism of Sabbathising.

† **ˈbigotly**, *adv. Obs.* [f. BIGOT *a.* + -LY[2]].

1646 BAILLIE *Anabapt.* (1647) Pref. A. 2 a, The most of the Cantons are bigotly popish.

bigotry (ˈbɪgətrɪ). Also 7 bigottry. [a. F. *bigoterie*, f. *bigot*: see -RY.] The condition of a bigot; obstinate and unenlightened attachment *to* a particular creed, opinion, system, or party.

a **1674** CLARENDON *Hist. Reb.* XIV. (1706) III. 423 The present Duke was with more than ordinary Bigottry zealous in the Roman Religion. *a* **1755** WATTS (J.), Bigotry to our own tenets. **1800** T. JEFFERSON *Writ.* (1859) IV. 319 We see the bigotry of an Italian to the ancient splendor of his country. **1876** GREEN *Short Hist.* vii. §6 (1882) 406 The bigotry of Philip was met by a bigotry as merciless as his own.

b. *concr.* A specimen or act of bigotry.

1715 BENTLEY *Serm.* x. 351 These Bigotries were yet without any mixture of Craft and Knavery.

big-side. (See quot. 1900.)

1845 *Rules Footb. Rugby School* §21 Two big-side balls must always be in the Close during a match or big-side. **1848** C. H. NEWMARCH *Recoll. Rugby* 133 'The Laws of Football', which were 'sanctioned by a Levee of Big Side', on the 7th of September, 1846. **1856** GOULBURN *Bk. Rugby School* 154 Allowing the blood to flow out freely in that most glorious channel—a Big-Side Match. *Ibid.* 157 The tuft of trees.. bordering Big-side. **1900** J. S. FARMER *Public Sch. Word-Bk.* 21 *Big-side* (Rugby and elsewhere). The combination of all the bigger fellows in the school in one and the same game or run. Also the ground specially used for the game so denominated.

biguanide (baɪˈgwɑːnaɪd). *Chem.* [f. BI-[2] + GUAN(IDINE + -IDE.] = DIGUANIDE.

1881 *Jrnl. Chem. Soc.* XL. 896 By the action of an ammoniacal solution of cupric oxide on dicyandiamide, biguanide is produced. **1960** *Diabetes* IX. 227/1 Phenformin is a biguanide which..has a blood-sugar-lowering effect in certain diabetic patients.

bigurdel, -gyrdel, variants of BYGIRDLE, *Obs.*, a moneysack.

bigurt, obs. form of BEGIRT.

biˈguttate, *a.* [BI-[2].] Having two guttate spots.

1887 PHILLIPS *Brit. Discomycetes* 161 Sporidia..shortly fusiform, biguttate.

biˈguttulate, *a.* [BI-[2].] Having two drops or spots.

1887 PHILLIPS *Brit. Discomycetes* 25 Sporidia.. biguttulate. **1940** *Chambers's Techn. Dict.* 90/1 *Biguttulate*, containing two vacuoles or two oil drops.

bigwig (ˈbɪgwɪg). [f. BIG + WIG, from the large wigs formerly worn by men of distinction or importance.] A man of high official standing, or of note or importance. (*humorous* or *contemptuous*.) Hence **ˈbigwigged** *ppl. a.*, wearing officially a big wig; **bigˈwiggedness**, **bigˈwiggery**, **bigˈwiggism**, official display of importance.

a **1731** E. WARD in Partridge *Dict. Slang* [context not given]. **1781** G. SELWYN *Let.* in *15th Rep. Hist. MSS. Commission* (1897) App. VI. 526 A new point of discussion for the lawyers, for our big wigs, for their Lordships. **1792** SOUTHEY *Lett.* (1856) I. 12 Though those big-wigs have really nothing in them, they look very formidable. **1815** *Scribbleomania* 221 As poet-translator, no big wig ranks stouter. **1865** TROLLOPE *Belton Est.* vii. 75 Some big-wig has come in his way who is going to dine with him. **1862** MRS. H. WOOD *Channings* iii. 17 If any big-wigged Lord Chancellor could take away the money. **1884** *Athenæum* 28 June 831/3 Characteristic big-wiggedness..pervades many of these pages. **1855** *Househ. Wds.* XII. 250 All this solemn bigwiggery—these triumphs, ovations, sacrifices, orations. **1872** GEO. ELIOT *Middlem.* (1878) I. II. 265, I didn't like.. so much empty bigwiggism. **1945** AUDEN *Coll. Poetry* 121 O beggar, bigwig, mugwump.

bigyle, obs. form BEGUILE.

† **biˈhalve, -en, -es**, *adv.* and *prep. Obs.* [OE. *be healfe* 'by (the) side,' a phrase construed with a dative; treated in ME. as an adv. and prep. The ME. ending *-en* seems due to form-association with words like *beforen*, *betwixen*, etc., in which the *-en* was historical; *-es* imitated the advb. genitives. Cf. BESIDE, *bisiden*, BESIDES (perhaps the direct model for *bihalven*, *bihalves*).]

A. *phrase.* By the side, beside.

a **1000** *Metr. Boeth.* xxix. 43 (Gr.) Be healfe heofones þisses. —— *Byrhtnoth* 152 Him be healfe stód hyse unweaxen cniht. *Ibid.* 318 Be healfe mínum hláforde.

B. *adv.* Beside, near, by.

c **1205** LAY. 571 þe bi-halues were. *Ibid.* 8170 Enne hendlicne mon þe þer stod bi-haluen. *c* **1305** *St. Katherine* in *E.E.P.* (1862) 90 Heo stod bihalues and bihuld.

C. *prep.* Beside, close to, by.

c **1205** LAY. 8436 Enne gume..him bihalfues. *Ibid.* 9313 Bihælues þan fihte.

† **biˈhalven**, *v. Obs.* [f. *bi-*, BE- + *halve*, HALF, side: cf. OHG. *behalbôn* surround.] *trans.* To surround on all sides.

c **1250** *Gen. & Ex.* 3355 Harde he bi-haluen ðer moyses. *a* **1300** *Havelok* 1834 A red thei taken hem bitwene, That he sholde him bi-halue, And brisen.

Bihari (bɪˈhɑːrɪ). [Hindi *bihārī*, f. *Bihār* the state of Bihar or Behar in north-eastern India.] **a.** (Also **Behari**.) A native or inhabitant of Bihar. **b.** An Indo-Aryan language of north-eastern India.

1882 G. A. GRIERSON *Let.* 24 Jan. in *Seven Grammars of the Bihárí Lang.* (1883) Pref., The first or introductory part of the series of Bihárí grammars which I was deputed to compile in the early part of 1881. **1897** *Jrnl. R. Asiatic Soc.* XXIX. 471 The Behāri women's ceremony for producing rain. **1899** KIPLING *From Sea to Sea* I. v. 238 The street.. ought to have been full of Beharis. **1910** *Encycl. Brit.* III. 924/1 *Bihari*..the name of the most western of the four forms of speech which comprise the Eastern Group of modern Indo-Aryan Languages. *Ibid.* 924/2 The Bihari vocabulary calls for few remarks. **1933** BLOOMFIELD *Lang.* iv. 63 Indic..include[s] such great languages as..*Bihari* (36 millions), *Bengali* (50 millions).

biˈharite. *Min.* [f. the Biharberg, in Hungary, where found.] A hydrous silicate of magnesium and aluminium, of yellowish, green, or brown colour, and greasy feeling.

bihate, variant of BEHATE.

†**bi'heald**, *v. Obs.* [f. *bi-*, BE- 1 + ME. *healden.*] *trans.* To pour over, to sprinkle.

a **1225** *Leg. Kath.* 1400 þæt tes meiden moste..wið halwende wettres bihealden [*v.r.* biheolden] ham alle.

†**bi'hede**, *v. Obs. Pa. t.* and *pple.* bihedde. [OE. *behēdan*, f. BE- + *hēdan* to HEED; cf. OFris. *bihûda* (Du. *behoeden*, LG. *behöden*), OHG. *bihuotan* (mod.G. *behüten*).]

1. *trans.* To take notice of, notice, perceive.

c **1205** LAY. 27672 þe eorl þat bihædde, an heorte him wes unneðe. *Ibid.* 28398 Arður þat bihedde, þe king wes abolȝe.

2. To pay attention to, take care of.

c **1250** LAY. 25900 Ich was hire fostermoder and faire hire bihedde [*c* **1205** uostredde]. *a* **1400** in *Rel. Ant.* II. 225 Thorou wyldernesse ich ladde the, And vourty ȝer bihedde the.

3. To guard against.

a **1250** *Owl & Night.* 635 Hwat can þat ȝongling hit bihede ȝif hit misdeþ hit mot nede.

4. To procure or prepare (for), offer, give (to).

c **1205** LAY. 12101 Melga nom Oriene..and scorne hire bihedde. *c* **1420** *Chron. Vilod.* 1113 Wherfore þe kyng by hedde hym no grace.

biheet(e, -hete, -hight, hiȝt, hote, etc.: see BEHIGHT.

bihelve, obs. form of BEHALF.

†**bi'heve**, *a. Obs.* Forms: 1 behoefe, behefe, 3 biheue. [OE. *behéfe*, earlier *bihóefe*:—**bihofio-*, adj. f. **bihóf-* BEHOOF, meaning 'of behoof, of use.'] Profitable, useful, needful.

c **975** *Rushw. Gosp.* Mark xi. 3 Cweoðas ðætte drihtne bihoefe [*Lindisf.* behoflic] *vel* ned-ðarf is. *c* **1000** *Ags. G.* Luke xiv. 28 þa and-fengas þe him behefe synt. *a* **1225** *Juliana* 46 Nis nawt þe biheve.

†**bi'heve**, *sb. Obs.* Forms: 1 behéfe, 3 biheue. [subst. use of prec. adj.] Behoof; advantage.

a **1225** *Ancr. R.* 96 Vor moni vuel ich iseo þerinne, & none biheue. *c* **1320** *Cast. Love* 1425 Ac heore doute was vre biheue. *c* **1320** *Assump. Virg.* 676 He wist he was to godes biheue.

†**bi'hofth(e.** *Obs.* Forms: 2–3 bihofþe, 3 bihouþe, biofte, byefþe, 3–4 byofþe, 4 byhofþe. [f. OE. *bi-*, *behofian* to need, BEHOVE + -TH[1].] Need, behoof; use, service.

c **1175** *Lamb. Hom.* 19 To þere saule bihofðe. *c* **1250** *Gen. & Ex.* 1408 Rebecca wile ic hauen, To ysac-is bi-ofte wile ic crauen. **1297** R. GLOUC. 348 To hys byefþe. *Ibid.* 354 To Wyllammes byofþe. **1393** LANGL. *P. Pl.* C. XIII. 187 To mannes byhofthe. *a* **1400** *Eng. Gilds* 354 To here owne byofþe.

†**bi'hoȝi-en**, *v. Obs.* [OE. *behoȝian*, f. BE- 1 + *hoȝian* to think, consider: see HOWE *v.*] *trans.* To be anxious about, be careful for.

a **1000** *Benedict. Rule* 58 (Bosw.) Behoȝian, *solicitum esse.* *c* **1175** *Lamb. Hom.* 113 Ðe lauerd scal bihohȝian þet he habbe godes fultum. *c* **1205** LAY. 17369 Bruttes..heore gode wepnen · wurðliche bihoȝeden.

†**bi'howe**, *v. Obs.* [OE. *behawian*, f. BE- + OE. *hawian* to look, view.] *trans.* To view; to see.

c **1000** *Ags. G.* Matt. vii. 5 þu liccetere..behawa [**1160** *Hatton* behawe]..þæt mot of þines broður eagan. **1330** R. BRUNNE *Chron.* 11165 (Stratm.) þe folk to bihowe.

bihynde, bii, obs. f. of BEHIND, BUY.

biis, bijce, bijs, var. BYSS, *Obs.*, fine linen.

bi-ischiatic (ˌbaɪɪskɪ'ætɪk), *a. Phys.* [f. BI- *pref.*[2] 5 + ISCHIATIC, f. Gr. ἰσχίον hip-joint.] Joining the two hip-joints.

1878 BARTLEY tr. *Topinard's Anthrop.* ii. 83 The biischiatic line, or width of the seat.

‖**bijou** ('biːʒuː). Pl. bijoux. [F. *bijou* (16th c. in Littré): prob. a. Breton *bizou*, formerly *besou* 'ring with a stone' (cf. Cornish *bisou* 'finger-ring' in 13th c.), f. Bret. *biz*, *bez* = Cornish *bis*, *bys*, *bes*, Welsh *bys* finger. See other conjectures in Diez, Littré, Scheler.] A jewel, a trinket; a 'gem' among works of art. Also *attrib.* Loosely as *adj.*: small and elegant, luxurious (applied esp. to houses).

1668 LADY CHAWORTH in *12th Rep. Hist. MSS. Commission* (1889) App. v. 10 Perfumed gloves, fans, and all sorts of delicate bijoux for each lady to take att her pleasure. **1747** H. WALPOLE *Let.* 5 June (1857) II. 86, I..may retire to a little new farm... This little rural *bijou* was Mrs. Chevenix's. **1838** MACAULAY *Let.* in Trevelyan *Life* (1881) 269 The bijou of his gallery. **1860** *Players* I. I. 7 The new theatre will be a perfect bijou temple of Thalia. **1865** 'OUIDA' *Strathmore* I. xxi. 311 Her bijou theatre. **1868** MISS BRADDON *Dead-Sea Fr.* II. i. 3 Owner of..the bijou house in Park Lane. **1876** GEO. ELIOT *Dan. Der.* III. xx. 154 The farthing buckles were bijoux. **1878** M. JEWRY *Warne's Model Cookery* (Advt.), Warne's Bijou Books are handy for the waistcoat pocket. **1904** *Society in New Reign* iii. 73 The London *pied-à-terre* consisted..of a bijou residence in Mayfair. **1911** A. BENNETT *Card* ii. 34 An apartment so tiny that an auctioneer would have been justified in terming it 'bijou'. **1952** WODEHOUSE *Pigs have Wings* i. 14 The Empress lived in a bijou residence not far from the kitchen garden.

‖**bijouterie** (biː'ʒuːtərɪː). [Fr.; f. prec. + *-erie* see -RY. The *-t-* is analogical.] Collective appellation for jewelry, trinkets, and articles of vertu.

1815 J. SCOTT *Visit to Paris* (ed. 2) 315 They have improved every article of *bijouterie* to the highest pitch of excellence. **1826** DISRAELI *Vivian Grey* II. ii. 97 Her Ladyship was not remarkable for anything, save a correct taste for poodles, parrots, and bijouterie. **1831** DISRAELI *Yng. Duke* (1878) 317 The furniture, and the bijouterie, produced a most respectable fund. **1863** R. BURTON *Abeokuta* I. 106 The bijouterie was coral, in necklaces and wristlets.

bijugate ('baɪdʒ(j)uːgeɪt), *a.* [f. BI- *pref.*[2] + L. *jugāt-us* yoked.]

1. Of a coin: Bearing two heads side-facing, one overlapping the other.

1725 W. STUKELEY in *Mem.* (1882) I. 87 Bijugate coin of Carausius.

2. Two-paired, 'as a pinnate leaf of two pairs of leaflets' (Gray *Bot. Text-bk.* 1880).

1846 in WORCESTER.

bijugous ('baɪdʒ(j)uːgəs, bɪ-), *a.* [f. L. *bijug-us* yoked two together (f. *bi-* two + *jugum* yoke) + -OUS.] = BIJUGATE 2.

1836 *Penny Cycl.* V. 252.

bik, bikalle, see BIKH, BECALL.

bike (baɪk), *sb.*[1] *north. dial.* Also 5–9 byke, 6 byik, byk, 8 beik. [Etymology unknown. The sense 'bees' nest' is the original; hence a conjecture that it represents an OE. *béoc*, contr. from **béowic* 'bee-dwelling,' but the phonetic repr. of that would have been *beke*, *beek*. The sense 'building' (4) is apparently erroneous; some, assuming it to be the original, compare *big*, *bike* with *dig*, *dike*.]

1. A nest of wasps, hornets, or wild bees, as distinct from the *hive* or *skep* of domestic bees. Also, the whole nestful of bees; a swarm.

a **1300** *Cursor M.* 76 Suetter..þon hony o bike. *c* **1460** *Towneley Myst.* 325 Wormes shalle in you brede as bees dos in the byke. *a* **1500** *MS. Cott. Calig.* A. ij. 109 (Halliw.) A byke of waspes bredde in his nose. **1536** BELLENDEN *Cron. Scot.* (1821) II. 271 Ane tod was ouirset with ane bike of fleis. *a* **1758** RAMSAY *Poems* (1844) 89 Like bumbees frae their bykes. **1790** BURNS *Tam O'Shanter*, As bees bizz out wi' angry fyke, When plundering herds assail their byke. **1883** BLACK *Black Bothy* v, They had thoroughly dug out that wasps' byke.

2. *fig.* A place likened to a bees' nest, e.g. a subterranean retreat or 'hole,' a well-filled storehouse.

1513 DOUGLAS *Æneis* VIII. iv. 26 Ȝone fendlych hole..A hellis byke, quhair sonnis beme nevyr schane. **1806** R. JAMIESON *Pop. Ballads* I. 293 (JAM.) Nocht but a house-wife was wantin' To plenish his weel foggit byke.

3. *fig.* Applied contemptuously to a swarm of people; a teeming crowd, a 'crew.'

1552 LYNDESAY *Monarche* 5803 In that court sall cum mony one Off the blak byik of Babilone. **1785** BURNS *Jolly Beggars*, The glowrin' byke. **1818** SCOTT *Hrt. Midl.* xii, A bonny bike there's o' them! **1818** —— *Rob Roy* xxvi, A bike o' the maist lawless unchristian limmers that ever disturbed a douce, quiet..neighbourhood.

†**4.** ? 'A building, a habitation.' Jamieson. *Obs.* (But the quotation may mean 'populous centre,' or 'swarm of men.')

c **1440** *Gaw & Gologras.* II. viii, Mony burgh, mony bour, mony big bike; mony kynrik to his clame cumly to knaw.

†**5.** (See quot.) *Obs.* or *local.*

1771 PENNANT *Tour Scotl.* (1794) 202 The corn is thrashed out and preserved in the chaff in bykes, which are stacks in shape of bee-hives, thatched quite round.

bike (baɪk), *sb.*[2] **1.** Colloq. abbrev. of BICYCLE. Also used for *motor bike* (see MOTOR *sb.* 6).

1882 *Wheelman* I. 189 Much I should like To know why you..take such a header from off your bike. **1886** W. RALEIGH *Let.* 8 Oct. (1926) I. 96 The people..dress in European fashion and go about with bikes and parasols. **1913** G. B. SHAW *Let.* 20 Mar. in *Corresp. B. Shaw & Mrs. P. Campbell* (1952) 98 In the morning I brave the bike [*i.e.* motor-bicycle] at last. **1924** T. E. LAWRENCE *Let.* 3 Mar. in J. Dunbar *Mrs. G.B.S.* (1963) xvii. 269 The bike [*i.e.* motor-bicycle] was raw & new, a man-killer. I'm afraid to death of it. **1939** T. S. ELIOT *Fam. Reunion* II. i, So I slipped along on my bike. **1968** *Guardian* 2 Apr. 5/3 The ceremonial riding of the last Automobile Association motor-cycle patrol combination..took place yesterday... 'The bikes were fine and ideally suited to the times in which they served,' Inspector Hatfield said.

b. *to get off one's bike* (usu. in negative contexts), to get rattled, to get annoyed. *Austral.* and *N.Z. colloq.*

1939 X. HERBERT *Capricornia* xxxiv. 521 'I tell you I saw no-one.' 'Don't get off your bike, son. I know you're tellin' lies.' **1943** J. A. W. BENNETT in *Amer. Speech* XVIII. 90 'Don't get off your bike' (from 'don't get off your horse', via a music-hall song?) means 'don't get rattled, excited'. **1944** J. H. FULLARTON *Troop Target* ix. 75 Don't get off your bike, Jock.

c. In dismissive slang phr. ***on your bike!***, go away, 'push off'; now also with implication that the hearer should busy himself with something, 'shake a leg'.

The latter implication was popularized by a speech given by Employment Secretary Norman Tebbit at the Conservative Party Conference in October 1981, in which he pointed out that his father had not rioted in the 1930s when unemployed, but had 'got on his bike and looked for work'.

1967 *Listener* 2 Mar. 299/3 Next time we'll have *on your bike* and *choc-ice* and other new mintings. **1980** J. GARDNER *Garden of Weapons* II. xi. 219 'On your bike then, son,' one of the policemen told him...He couldn't take any pictures of that particular building. **1981** *Times* 4 Feb. 14/1 'On your bike, Khomeini', the crowd shouted outside the Iranian Embassy during the siege. **1983** *Economist* 22 Oct. 25 He 'got on his bike' and looked for work. 'On yer bike, Tebbit!' became the slogan of right-to-work marchers, to the delight of Mr Tebbit's supporters. **1985** *Punch* 16 Oct. 44/3 On your bike Jake, I said, this joke has gone far enough, when I caught him taking huge slices from the fridge.

2. a. *attrib.*

1899 A. C. GUNTER *M.S. Bradford Special* II. xiv. 185 The ting-ting-ting of bike bells. **1951** E. COXHEAD *One Green Bottle* vi. 173 If I climbed to please you, you'd have to..do a few bike-rides to please me. **1958** BETJEMAN *Coll. Poems* 133 As slow the weary clergyman subsides Tired with his bike-ride from the parish church.

b. Special Comb. **bikeway** orig. *N. Amer.* = *cycleway* s.v. CYCLE *sb.* 12.

1967 *Britannica Bk. of Year* (U.S.) 802/1 **Bikeway*, a thoroughfare (as in a park) restricted to bicycles. **1971** *Daily Tel.* 4 Oct. 4/8 The bikeways have been labelled a dangerous fraud by a group called 'bike for a better city'. **1974** *Globe & Mail* (Toronto) 6 Sept. 5/1 It was explained at the city parks committee that the bikeway system is composed entirely of main routes without feeder pathways from the midtown to the downtown area. **1978** WATSON & GRAY *Penguin Bk. Bicycle* vi. 276 There is a similar kind of contrast between American and British attitudes to 'bikeways'. **1983** *Metro* (Auckland) Feb. 68/2 Basically the bikeway was already there; the Council simply painted a stripe down the centre of the old footpath.

Hence **bike** *v.*[2] *intr.*, to ride a bike; also *to bike it.* So **'biker, 'biking.**

1883 *Wheelman* I. 336 Nature had rallied all her forces for one grand attack on us three poor, miserable 'bikers'. *Ibid.*, We very modestly declined, informing them that 'biking' and drinking are inconsistent. **1895** *Daily News* 10 Sept. 7/1 Young girls..who are learning to 'bike'. **1895** *Westm. Gaz.* 14 Oct. 7/2 The 'biking' craze seems to grow... Lady Warwick..was one of the 'bikers'. **1897** R. S. S. BADEN-POWELL *Matabele Campaign* xix, The other..can use his revolver—which cannot be done by single bikers. **1901** W. R. H. TROWBRIDGE *Lett. her Mother to Eliz.* vi. 25 Daisy biked over to Exeter this morning with Mr. Frame. **1931** M. FRANKLIN *Old Blastus of Bandicoot* xv. 188 'How did you come?' 'I biked it from the turn-off.' **1940** AUDEN *Another Time* 74 She was biking through a field of corn. **1960** BETJEMAN *Summoned by Bells* v. 48 All that was crumbling, picturesque and quaint..sent me biking off..for Architecture bound.

bike, *v.*[1] *Sc.* [f. BIKE *sb.*[1]] To swarm like bees.

1805 A. SCOTT *Poems* 16 (JAM.) The lads about me biket.

bike, obs. form of BEAK *v.*

bikeche, variant of BECATCH.

biken, obs. form of BEACON, BECKON.

†**bi'kenned**, *pa. pple. Obs. rare.* [f. *bi-*, BE- + ME. *kennen* to beget: cf. AKENNED.] Begotten.

a **1250** *Creed* in *Rel. Ant.* I. 234 Ðatt of de holigost bikennedd was.

biker, bikkyr, obs. ff. BEAKER, BICKER.

‖**bikh.** Also bik, bish. [Hindī, Nepālī, *bikh*, Bengālī, *bish* poison:—Skr. *visha* poison.] The poison of various species of Aconite, esp. *Aconitum ferox*; also the root or plant yielding it.

1830 LINDLEY *Introd. Bot.* 7 The root of the Aconitum of India, one of the substances called Bikh, or Bish, is a most virulent poison. **1833** *Penny Cycl.* I. 88/1 The dreadful *Bikh* or *Bish* of Nepaul, the *Aconitum ferox.*

(The same name is given by the natives to the effect of the rarefied atmosphere at great heights in the Himālaya, which they attribute to poisonous exhalation from the ground or from plants.)

bikie ('baɪkɪ). *Austral.* and *N.Z. slang.* [f. BIKE *sb.*[2] + -IE.] A motor-cyclist; *spec.* a member of a gang of motor-cyclists, usu. leather-jacketed, notorious for disturbing civil order. Cf. *hell's angel* s.v. HELL *sb.* 12.

1967 *Sunday Mail* (Brisbane) 23 Apr. 2 Maria was abnormally addicted to what are called 'bikies' around The Cross. **1968** *Everybody's Mag.* (Austral.) 20 Mar. 4/2 Before the bikies came to the Wayside Chapel, they spent most of their spare time drinking in hotels and other places. **1972** *Salient* (Wellington, N.Z.) 27 Apr. 1/1 These cops..display gross cowardice when a few 'bikies' or other thugs start throwing bottles. **1975** *Australasian Express* 7 Nov. 11/7 A sole policeman took on 22 'bikies' in the main street of the sea-side resort and ordered them to leave town. **1984** *Sydney Morning Herald* 10 Nov. 3/8 The NSW police are still seeking a member of the Bandido bikie gang over the Milperra massacre on September 2.

bikini (bɪ'kiːnɪ). [f. *Bikini*, name of an atoll in the Marshall Islands where an atomic bomb test was carried out in July, 1946.] **a.** A large explosion. (? *Obs.*)

1947 *Daily Tel.* 19 Apr. 6/6 Those in [the troopship] must have had a splendid view of what..was a miniature Bikini.

b. [a. Fr., app. f. prec. sense.] A scanty two-piece beach garment worn by women. Also *attrib.* and *Comb.* Hence **bi'kinied** *a.*, clad in a bikini.

[**1947** *Le Monde Illustré* Août 929/1 Bikini, ce mot cinglant comme l'explosion même..correspondait au niveau du vêtement de plage à un anéantissement de la surface vêtue; à une minimisation extrême de la pudeur.] **1948** *Newsweek* 14 June 33 This..French beauty..shows the 1948 countertrend against the skimpy 'Bikini' style..which swept French beaches and beauty contests last year. **1950** *News of World* 25 June 5/6 —— made an unsuccessful attempt yesterday to swim in a Hampstead Heath pond in her home-made 'Bikini' costume. **1955** *Times* 6 July 12/7 The Watch Committee there..has never yet lost a night's sleep over a bikini. **1957** *Times* 2 July 11/6 'What is a bikini?' ..'A small pair of pants and a brassière.' **1959** *N.Z. Listener* 9 Jan. 4/2 The bikinied beauties of the Redleaf Pool. **1959** *Times* (Suppl. Britain's Food) 9 Mar. p. xii/5 The wrapping is not a bikini-sized tissue. **1963** *Economist* 3 Aug. 422/2 Our bikini-clad assaults on Spanish beaches. **1967** C. DRUMMOND *Death at Furlong Post* xi. 131 He accidentally lodged a ball-bearing in the navel of a bikinied damsel.

bikky: see BICKY.

biknaw, bikome, etc.: see BEKNOW, etc.

bil(e, obs. form of BILL.

bilabial (baɪˈleɪbɪəl), *a.* **1.** = next.
1862 DANA *Man. Geol.* i. v. 160 Having a bilabial form.

2. *Phonetics.* Of certain consonants (e.g. *p, b, m, v, w*): produced by the juncture or apposition of the lips. Also *sb.*, a bilabial consonant.
1894 W. M. LINDSAY *Lat. Lang.* 47 At some time before the fifth cent. A.D...initial *v*..seems to have passed from the bilabial spirant (Spanish *b*) to the labio-dental spirant (our *v*). **1899** W. RIPPMANN *Elem. Phonetics* 82 The labio-dentals and the bilabials. *Ibid.* 90 In general the lip stops are bilabial, *i.e.* formed by a closure of both lips. **1911** *Encycl. Brit.* XXVII. 830/1 The Latin V..was not a labio-dental spirant like the English *v*, but a bilabial semivowel like the English *w*.

bilabiate (baɪˈleɪbɪət), *a.* [f. BI- *pref.*² 1 + LABIATE, f. L. *labi-a* lip + -ATE¹.] Two-lipped.
1794 MARTYN *Rousseau's Bot.* xxxi. 479 The nectaries are bilabiate. **1839** TODD *Cycl. Anat. & Phys.* II. 113/2.

†**biˈlacche,** *v. Obs.* Pa. t. bela(u)ght. [f. *bi-*, BE- + ME. LACCHE to take.] To take away.
[*c* **1000** *Ags. Gosp.* Mark ix. 18 Swa he hine ȝelæcð.] *c* **1250** *Gen. & Ex.* 773 Sone him was sarray bilaȝt.

bilaciniate (baɪləˈsɪnɪət), *a. Bot.* [f. BI- *pref.*² 3 + LACINIATE, f. L. *lacinia* lappet, flap.] Of leaves: Doubly laciniate; *i.e.* divided into flaps or lappets which are themselves similarly divided.

biˈlamellar, *a.* = next.
1852 DANA *Crust.* II. 1035 The organ has a bilamellar termination.

bilamellate, -ated (baɪˈlæmɛleɪt, -eɪtɪd), *a.* [f. BI- *pref.*² 1 + LAMELLATE, f. L. *lāmella*, dim. of *lāmina* thin plate.] Having or consisting of two lamellæ or small thin plates.
1846 WORCESTER cites BRANDE. **1870** HOOKER *Stud. Flora* 260 Verbascum..stigma undivided or bilamellate. **1876** HARLEY *Mat. Med.* 476.

biˈlaminar, *a.* = next.

bilaminate, -ated (baɪˈlæmɪneɪt, -eɪtɪd), *a.* [f. BI- *pref.*² 1 + LAMINATE, f. L. *lāmina* thin plate.] Having or consisting of two thin plates.
1839–47 TODD *Cycl. Anat. & Phys.* III. 568/1 The fascia on reaching its anterior edge, is bi-laminated.

biland, variant of BYLAND *Obs.* peninsula.

bilander (ˈbɪləndə(r), ˈbaɪləndə(r)). Also 7 billander, 7–9 bylander, 8 belande, belandre, billinder. [ad. Du. *bijlander* 'a vessel with one large mast, sailing on the coast,' 'a lighter,' f. Du. *bij* BY + *land* LAND. Adapted in Fr. as *bélandre*.] A two-masted merchant vessel, a kind of hoy, distinguished by the trapezoidal shape of the mainsail; used in Holland for coast and canal traffic.
1656 *(title)*, The Opening of Rivers for Navigation..a Mediterranean Passage by Water for Billanders of thirty tun, between Bristol and London. **1666** *Lond. Gaz.* No. 37/4 Here are three small Billanders from Bruges in Flanders. **1676** TEMPLE *Let.* Wks. 1731 II. 351 Their baggage is already laden in a By-lander in this Canal. **1687** DRYDEN *Hind & P.* I. 128 Like bilanders to creep Along the coast. **1731** BAILEY, *Belande, belandre.* **1755** *Mem. Capt. P. Drake* II. iii. 62, I agreed for a Billinder, which is a kind of Dutch Vessel. **1833** SOUTHEY *Naval Hist. Eng.* IV. 295 In little boats and bylanders to steal along the shore by night.

†**ˈbilary,** *a. Obs.* = BILIARY.
1681 tr. *Willis' Med. Wks.* Voc., *Bilary*, belonging to bile or choler. **1727–51** CHAMBERS *Cycl.*, The bilary pore.

bilateral (baɪˈlætərəl), *a.* [f. BI- *pref.*² 1, 6 + LATERAL, f. L. *later-* (nom. *latus*) side.] **a.** Of, pertaining to, affecting, or arranged upon two sides; disposed on opposite sides of an axis.
1775 ASH *Bilateral*, Having two sides, both by the father and mother's side. **1854** H. MILLER *Footpr. Creat.* ix. (1874) 162 That bilateral symmetry of the skeleton.

b. *Law.* Pertaining to or affecting two parties.
1818 COLEBROOKE *Obligations* I. 16 Contracts are either unilateral or bilateral. **1850** ALISON *Hist. Europe* V. xxvii. §99. 78 Bound to perform the other side of the bilateral engagement.

c. Pertaining to or concerning two countries (only), esp. of the trade and financial agreements made between them. Cf. MULTILATERAL *a.*
1935 *Economist* 2 Feb. 279/2 Those countries with which bilateral trade agreements have been concluded. **1937** *Sunday Times* 24 Jan. 19/3 The Duce now pins his faith to bi-lateral agreements.

d. *Education.* Of a secondary school or its educational system: providing two of the three possible types of course ('grammar', 'modern', or 'technical').
1947 *Min. Educ. Circular* CXLIV. 1/2 Combinations of two or more types of secondary education are often referred to as bilateral, multilateral or comprehensive... A bilateral school means one which is organised to provide for any two of the three main elements of secondary education, i.e. modern, technical or grammar. **1957** *Economist* 12 Oct. 103/1 Surrey is developing many grammar school courses in 'bilateral schools'.

Hence **biˈlaterally** *adv.*, in a bilateral manner, on both sides. **biˈlateraˌlism, bilateˈrality, biˈlateralness,** bilateral condition, arrangement on opposite sides of an axis.
1852 TODD *Cycl. Anat. & Phys.* IV. 850/1 The idea of bilateralism is by no means included in our definition of symmetry. **1949** *Times* 10 Sept., *Bilateralism*..has acquired a special meaning from..recent trade and financial agreements between this country and other individual countries..marked by two main principles: (1) that an equal value of trade on each side is aimed at; (2) that the proceeds of each country's exports can be spent only in the country concerned. **1959** *Times Rev. Industry* Sept. 100/2 Bilateralism..aims at securing a market for each of the partners' products. **1884** W. JAMES in *Mind* Apr. 282 Neither rightness nor leftness, except through bi-laterality. **1901** G. N. CALKINS *Protozoa* vi. 172 In *Dileptus*..where bilaterality and asymmetry are well established. **1849** MURCHISON *Siluria* App. D. 540 Growing bilaterally and branching regularly. **1875** POSTE *Gaius* I. (ed. 2) Introd. 8 A judgement may be bilaterally penal..may both impoverish the defendant and enrich the plaintiff. **1880** *Nature* XXI. 262 The phenomenon of bilateralness in the prothallia of ferns.

†**biˈlauh, -lauȝ,** *v. Obs.* Forms see LAUGH. [Com. Teut.: OE. *bihliehhan, -hlehhan* = OHG. *bihlahhian* (MHG. and mod.G. *belachen*, Du. *belagchen*), Goth. *bihlahjan* to laugh at, deride, f. *bi-*, BE- 4 + *hlahjan*, in OE. *hliehhan*, to LAUGH.] *trans.* To laugh at; mock, deride.
a **1000** *Guthlac* (Gr.) 1331 Huru ic swiðe ne þearf hinsið bihlehhan. **1297** R. GLOUC. 64 Atte laste ys tricherie wel lutel he by lowȝ. *a* **1300** *K. Horn* 681 þe fys me so bylaucte [= lauhte] þat ich nawt ne kaucte.

bilaw, obs. form of BY-LAW.

bilbaocatch: see BILBOQUET.

bilbergia, variant of BILLBERGIA.

bilberry, billberry (ˈbɪlbɛrɪ). Also 7 bilbery. [App. of Norse origin; cf. Da. *böllebær*, f. *bölle* (used separately for bilberry) + *bær* BERRY. (The origin of Da. *bölle* is unknown; the suggestion that it is:—ON. *bǫllr* BALL is phonetically improbable, since this gives Sw. *boll*, Da. *bold*.)]

1. The fruit of a dwarf hardy shrub (*Vaccinium Myrtillus*), abundant on heaths, on stony moors, and in mountain woods, in Great Britain and Northern Europe; the berry is of a deep blue black, and about a quarter of an inch in diameter. So called chiefly in the Midlands; other names are WHORTLEBERRY and BLAEBERRY. The name is applied also to the plant, and used *attrib.*
1577 DEE *Relat. Spir.* I. (1659) 171 The cloth, Hair-colourd, Bilbery juyce. **1594** BARNFIELD *Aff. Sheph.* II. xii, Straw-berries or Bil-berries, in their prime. **1598** SHAKS. *Merry W.* v. v. 49 There pinch the Maids as blew as Bill-berry. **1810** WORDSW. *Descr. Lakes* I (1823) 29 The bilberry, a ground plant, never so beautiful as in early spring. **1821** CLARE *Vill. Minstr.* I. 87 In misty blue, Bilberries glow on tendrils weak. **1860** TYNDALL *Glac.* I. §6. 45, I lay down upon the bilberry bushes.

2. Applied with or without qualification to other species of *Vaccinium*; e.g. in Britain to the Great Bilberry or Bog Whortleberry (*V. uliginosum*).
1640 PARKINSON *Theat. Bot.* 1455 *Vaccinia nigra fructu majore.* The greater Billberry. **1859** R. BURTON *Centr. Afr.* in *Jrnl. R.G.S.* XXIX. 84 Garlands of small red bilberries. **1864** WEBSTER s.v., The species of American bilberry are referred to the sub-genus *Eu-vaccinium.*

Hence **ˈbilberrying** *vbl. sb.*, gathering bilberries.
1859 W. COLEMAN *Woodlands* (1866) 92 A party of rustic children 'a bilberrying.'

bilbo¹ (ˈbɪlbəʊ). Forms: 6 bilboa, 6–7 bilboe, -bowe, 7 bilbow, 6– bilbo. [App. (as stated by Blount in 1656) from *Bilbao* in Spain, long called in Eng. *Bilboa*. 'Bilbow blades' were, according to a marginal note to Drayton *Agincourt* (1631) p. 10, 'blades accounted of the best temper.' Cf. *Damascus blade, Toledo blade.* The swords of Bilbao, according to Moll's *Geogr.* 1701, 'are famous over all Europe.']

1. A sword noted for the temper and elasticity of its blade. Now only *Hist.*
1598 SHAKS. *Merry W.* III. v. 112 Compass'd like a good Bilbo in the circumference of a Pecke, hilt to point. **1603** DRAYTON *Odes* xvii. 81 Downe their Bowes they threw And forth their Bilbowes drew. **1625** MARKHAM *Souldiers Accid.* 2 Sharpe and broad Swords (of which the Turkie or Bilboe are best). **1826** SCOTT *Woodst.* iii, My tough old Knight and you were at drawn bilbo. **1860** J. KENNEDY *Rob of Bowl* xv. 174 We shall come to bilbo and buff before long.

b. Often used as the proper name of a sword personified; esp. that of a bully or swash-buckler.
1676 SHADWELL *Libertine* I. Wks. 1720 II. 106 Stand, you dog!.. I'll put Bilbo in your guts. **1749** ABP. RHYS *Spain* (1760) 20 Bilbo is an humourous term for a Bully's Sword.

c. Phrase. *bilbo's the word.*
1687 CONGREVE *Old Bach.* III. vii, Bilbo's the word and slaughter will ensue. **1713** *Guardian* No. 145 Bilbo is the word, remember that and tremble. **1859** THACKERAY *Virgin.* xxxvii. 294.

2. *transf.* ? One who bears a bilbo. (Doubtful.)
1598 SHAKS. *Merry W.* I. i. 165, I combat challenge of this Latine Bilboe. **1690** CROWNE *Eng. Frier* v. 41 This bilboe has shew'd more brains then our Statesmen do.

3. *Attrib.* and *Comb.*, as *bilbo-blade, -man, -mettle, -smith*; **bilbo-lord,** a bully, swash-buckler.
1592 GREENE *Disput.* Wks. (Grosart) X. 236 Let them doe what they dare with their *bilbowe blades. **1656** BLOUNT *Glossogr.*, **Bilbo blade* from Bilboa..in Spain where the best blades are made. **1621** FLETCHER *Wild-G. Chase* III. i, That this *bilbo-lord shall reap that maidenhead That was my due. **1611** BEAUM. & FL. *King & No King* v. 59 You are much bound to your *Bil-bow-men. **1632** B. JONSON in Brome *North. Lasse* Pref. Verses, An honest *Bilbo-Smith would make good blades.

bilbo². Pl. bilboes (ˈbɪlbəʊz). Also 6 bilbows, 7 bilbowes, bylboes, 8 (*comb.*) bilboo-. [Of uncertain derivation. It is usually, like the prec., referred to *Bilbao*, on the alleged ground that many of these instruments were manufactured there, and shipped on board the Spanish Armada, for the confinement of English prisoners expected to be made; but the word occurs in English many years before 1588.] A long iron bar, furnished with sliding shackles to confine the ankles of prisoners, and a lock by which to fix one end of the bar to the floor or ground.
1557 in Hakluyt's *Voy.* I. 295, I was also conueyed to their lodgings..where I saw a pair of bilbowes. **1591** J. HORTOP *Narr.* in Arb. *Garner* V. 316 Whom he presently commanded to be set in the bilbows. **1602** SHAKS. *Ham.* v. ii. 6 Me thought I lay Worse then the mutines in the Bilboes. **1723** MRS. CENTLIVRE *Basset-Table* I. i. 205 For every fault that she commits, he'll condemn her to the Bilboes. **1879** SALA in *Daily Tel.* 26 June, The..prisoner kneeling to show how..the bilboes and the neckstocks were put on him.

b. *attrib.*
1772–84 COOK *Voy.* (1790) V. 1597 Carrying with him the shackle of the bilboo-bolt that had been put about his leg.

bilboquet (bɪlbəʊˈkɛt). Corrupted forms in sense 2, 9 bilboketch, -catch, bilbaocatch, bilverketch, biblercatch. [a. Fr. *bilboquet*, in same senses and various intermediate ones; in OF. *billeboquet, -bauquet*, of doubtful origin: see Diez, Littré.]

†**1.** 'A cord or line, having at either end, and in the middle, a sticke fastened vnto it wherwith Gardeners measure out their beds.' Cotgr.
1616 SURFL. & MARKH. *Countr. Farm* 256 For round workes, you must haue an instrument, commonly called the Gardners Bilboquet. **1688** R. HOLME *Acad. Armory* II. 118 A Bilboquet, an Instrument made of Lines and sharp pointed Sticks or Iron Pins, to square out Beds.

2. The plaything called Cup-and-ball; the game played with it, which consists in catching the ball either on the cup or spike end of the stick.
[A typical example of popular etymology is afforded by the corruption of *-quet* = *ket*, to *ketch, catch*, so as to associate it with the action of the game; in *Bilbao catch* we have the more deliberate perversion of pseudo-scholarship.]
1743 WALPOLE *Lett. H. Mann* (1834) I. lxix. 253 To set up the noble game of bilboquet. **1801** MAR. EDGEWORTH *Good Fr. Gov.* (1832) 109 Bilboquets, battledores, and shuttle-cocks. **1808** JANE AUSTEN *Lett.* (1884) II. 26 Bilbocatch, at which George is indefatigable. **1812** *Month. Mag.* XXXIII. 26 He made great use of a bilbao-catch (*note*, said to have come hither from Bilbao, in Spain, and thence to have its name) or ivory cup and spike. **1832** HONE *Year Bk.* 1297 To the hautboy succeeded the bilbo-catch, or bilver-ketch. **1875** PARISH *Sussex Gloss.*, *Bibler-catch.*

bilby (ˈbɪlbɪ). [Prob. Australian Aboriginal name.] An Australian nocturnal burrowing marsupial with blue-grey fur; rabbit-bandicoot. Also *attrib.*, as *bilby-hole.*
1903 'T. COLLINS' *Such is Life* 240 There happened to be a bilby-hole close in front, and she fell in the sort of trough, with her head down the slope. **1945** BAKER *Austral. Lang.* iii. 58 Holes made by the Australian marsupial 'rabbit' or *bilby.*

bilcock ('bɪlkɒk). A bird: the Water-rail.
1678 Ray *Willughby's Ornith.* 314 The Water-Rail, called by some the Bilcock or Brook-Ouzel. **1841** *Penny Cycl.* XIX. 283/1 The..Bilcock..of the modern British.

bild, etc., obs. form of BUILD, etc.

†**'bilder.** *Obs. rare.* A kind of horse, a nag.
1570 Levins *Manip.* 71 A Bilder, horse, *equulus, equila.* **1653** Urquhart *Rabelais* I. xii. I. 48 That suffer your bilder [Fr. *courtaud*] to fail you, when you need him most.

bilders ('bɪldəs). *Herb.* Forms: 5 **byllerne, billere, 6 bylders, bilders, 6–8 belders;** *mod. dial.* **bilders, billers, bellers.** [It has been shown by the Rev. A. L. Mayhew, in *N. & Q.* Ser. vii. III. 365, that the etymological form is (in the sing.) *biller*, adopted from the Irish *biolar*, a late variant of *biorar* water-cress:—OIr. *biror* (corresp. to Welsh *berwr* water-cress), f. *bior, bir* water, well, spring. The forms *billern* and *billers, bilders* are plural. The word appears in med.L. as *berula*, and is the F. *berle* = *Sium angustifolium* (Littré). It is also discussed by J. L. G. Mowat in *Alphita* (Anecd. Oxon.), 21, s.v. *Berula.*]
A name given by the old herbalists to some water plant or plants, cruciferous or umbelliferous (perh. *Helosciadium* or *Nasturtium*). In modern dialects applied locally to Water Cress, co. Derry; Water Dropwort (*Œnanthe crocata*), Cornwall; Cow Parsnip, Devon. See Britten and Holland.
c **1425** in S. B. Liljegren *Agnus Castus* (Essays & Studies Engl. Lang. & Lit. Upsala) (1950) VI. 138 Bursula, is an herbe þat men clepe billere...it growyȝt in water. *c* **1440** *Promp. Parv.* 36 Byllerne, watyr herbe, *berula.* **1545** Elyot *Dict., Lauer,* an herbe growyng in the water, lyke to alysaunder, but hauyng lesse leaues. Some do call it bylders. [**1548** Cooper *Bibl. Eliota,* bilders; **1573** —— *Thesaurus,* belders.] **1598** Florio, *Gorgogliestro,* of some called.. belders, or bell-rags.

bildge, obs. form of BILGE.

‖**Bildungsroman** ('bɪldʊŋzrəʊ,mɑːn). [G., f. *bildung* education + *roman* novel.] A novel that has as its main theme the formative years or spiritual education of one person (a type of novel traditional in German literature). Hence **Bildungs(roman)-hero**, the main character in such a novel.
1910 *Encycl. Brit.* XII. 185/1 Its flashes of intuitive criticism and its weighty apothegms add to its value as a *Bildungsroman* in the best sense of that word. **1938** *Times Lit. Suppl.* 10 Sept. iii/1 The story is then a kind of *Bildungsroman.* **1956** C. Wilson *Outsider* iii. 51 The *Bildungsroman* is a sort of laboratory in which the hero conducts an experiment in living. **1962** *Listener* 3 May 778/1 The *Bildungs*-heroes lead in a fairly straight line from Simplicissimus to the Ks of Kafka. *Ibid.* 778/2 Musil's heroes..are all *Bildungsroman*-heroes.

bile (baɪl). [a. F. *bile*, ad. L. *bīlis.*]
1. The fluid secreted by the liver, and poured into the duodenum, as an aid to the digestive process. It is bitter, of a brownish yellow colour, passing sometimes into green, and of a highly complex structure. (It was one of the 'four humours' of early physiology, and was, till the beginning of the 18th c., commonly termed *choler.*)
1665 G. Thomson *Med. Ignor.* 147 Blood, Bile, Phlegme and Melancholy. **1700** Dryden *Cock & Fox* 147 These foolish Fancies..Are certain Symptoms..Of boiling Choler, and abounding Bile. **1732** Arbuthnot *Rules of Diet* 267 Livers of Animals, because of the Bile which they contain. **1810** Henry *Elem. Chem.* (1826) II. 441. **1861** Hulme tr. *Moquin-Tandon* II. III. iii. 95 Bile..is secreted by the liver, and is received into a special receptacle termed the gall-bladder.
b. Excess or derangement of the bile.
1803 Pitt in G. Rose *Diaries* (1860) II. 10, I am..quite free both from gout and bile.
2. *fig.* Anger, ill temper, peevishness. Cf. CHOLER, GALL, SPLEEN.
1836 Marryat *Midsh. Easy* viii, His bile was raised by this parade and display in a lad. **1838** Hallam *Hist. Lit.* I. I. iv. §45. 289 After all this bile against those whom the royal bird represents.
3. black bile = *atrabilis, choler adust,* or *melancholy*, the fourth of the 'humours' of early physiology; see ATRABILE.
1797 Godwin *Enquirer* I. x. 88 He had been.. accumulating..black bile.
4. *Comb.* and *Attrib.*, as ***bile-cell, -cyst, -duct,*** etc.; **bile-pigment**, one of the colouring substances of bile; **bile-stone**, a calculus formed in the gall-bladder, a gall-stone.
1674 Grew *Anat. Trunks* III. ii. §17 In the Liver, it were hard to say, which is a Blood-Vessel, and which is a Bile-Vessel..if it were not for the Contents of them both. **1774** E. Darwin in *Phil. Trans.* 346 The bile-duct was tied before it was taken out of the body. **1796** —— *Zoon.* II. 4 Where these bile-stones are too large to pass. **1880** J. W. Legg *Bile* 87 In health no bile-pigment can be detected in the blood.

bile, obs. f. BOIL tumour, and BUILD.

bilection, variant of BOLECTION, a moulding.

bilefy, obs. form of BILIFY.

bilek, biloc, biloken, biluken, etc.: see BELOOK and BELOUKE.

bileman, etc.: see BY-.

†**bi'lenge**, *a.* *Obs. rare*⁻¹. [Only in Ormin, taking place of OE. *ȝelęnge*, f. *ȝe-* prefix + *lęnge*, secondary form of *lang* long:—OTeut. **langjo-*. Cf. *bilong*, BELONG *a.* for OE. *ȝelang.*] Belonging, related to (with *dat.*).
c **1200** Ormin 2230 Bitwenenn þatt Iudisskenn þeod þatt Iacob wass bilenge.

bileue, -leve, variants of BELEAVE *v. Obs.*

†**bi'leven.** *Obs. rare*⁻¹. [perh. for *biliven*, pa. pple. of BELIVE, to remain; perh. a plural sb.] That which is left; remainder, remains.
c **1250** *Gen. & Ex.* 3154 Ðe bi-leuen brennen he bead.

†**'bilewhit**, *a. Obs.* Forms: 1 **bilewit(e, bilwit,** 1–2 **bylewite,** 2 **bylehwit(t),** 3 **bilewhit, -ehwit.** [Etymology doubtful: prob. f. OTeut. **bili-*, cogn. w. OIr. *bil* good, mild, and found in OHG. *billich*, mod.G. *billig* just, reasonable + WIT; giving the sense 'mild of wit or mind.' Cf. G. *bilwiz* 'a good friendly house-spirit,' Grimm *Germ. Myth.* (ed. 4) III. 137 (Eng. ed. II. 473), and BILLY-BLIND. The interpretation 'white of bill,' like a young bird (f. OE. *bile* + *hwít*), was current at an early date, as shown by 12th c. spellings; cf. F. *bec-jaune*, G. *gelb-schnabel*, though these are depreciative rather than laudatory; and it must be noted that the earlier spellings had not *hwit*, but *wite.*]
Mild, gentle, clement; innocent, simple.
c **890** K. Ælfred *Bæda* IV. xxiv. in Sweet *Reader* 50 Swa swa he hluttre mode and bilewite ond smyltre willsumnesse Dryhtne ðeowde. *c* **950** *Lindisf. Gosp.* Matt. xi. 29 Biluit [ic] am. [*c* **975** *Rushw. G.* mild, *c* **1000** *Ags. G.* bilwite, *v.r.* bylewite, *c* **1150** *Royal MS.* bylewit, *c* **1160** *Hatton* bylehwit.] *c* **975** *Rushw. G.* Matt. x. 16 Bilwite swa swa culfra. [*c* **1000** *Ags. G.* bylwite, *c* **1150** *Royal MS.* bylewitte, *c* **1160** *Hatton* bylehwitte.] **1123** *O.E. Chron.* (Laud MS.) an. 1041 He wæs swiðe god man and swiðe bilehwit. *c* **1200** Ormin 6654 Shepisshe & bilewhit, All clene off ille þohhtess. *a* **1225** *St. Marher.* 22 Þe engles..sungen on hire bodi bilehwit and blesceden hit.

bilge (bɪldʒ), *sb.* Also 7–8 **bildge, billage.** [Prob. a corruption of BULGE, ad. OF. *boulge* = mod.F. *bouge*, shown not only by the occurrence of BULGE and BULCH as synonyms of BILGE, but also by the fact that *bouge* in F. still means 'bilge' both with reference to a cask and to a ship. *Billage* must be a further corruption, due to the rarity of the ending *-lge* in Eng.; this form seems in later times to be preferred where the word denotes a measure, from form-association with *tonnage, stowage*, and other abstracts in *-age.*]
1. a. The bottom of a ship's hull, or that part on either side of the keel which has more a horizontal than a perpendicular direction, and upon which the ship would rest if aground; also the lowest internal part of the hull.
1513 Douglas *Æneis* v. iv. 78 The mychty kervell schudderit..Doun swakkand fludis ondir hir braid bilge of aik. **1692** in *Capt. Smith's Seaman's Gram.* I. xvi. 75 The *Bilge*, the breadth of the place the Ship rests on when she is a ground. **1696** Phillips, *Billage* of a Ship is the breadth of the Floor when she lies aground; and billage-water is that which cannot come to the pump. **1786** Cowper *Odyss.* xv. 579 She pitched headlong into the bilge Like a sea coot. **1866** *Daily Tel.* 7 Nov., We were only blown over on our other bilge, and remained fast.
b. The foulness which collects in the bilge.
1829 Southey *O. Newman* iii, To breathe again the air With taint of bilge and cordage undefiled. **1856** Emerson *Eng. Traits* ii. 35 Nobody likes to be..suffocated with bilge, mephitis, and stewing oil.
c. Nonsense, 'rubbish', 'rot'. *slang.*
1908 D. Coke *House Prefect* viii. 99 Let's go... This [*sc.* an excursion] is awful bilge. **1921** A. S. M. Hutchinson *If Winter Comes* II. vii. §6 And they didn't talk any of this bilge about fighting us in England. **1954** Wodehouse *Jeeves & Feudal Spirit* i. 11 She wrote this novel and it was well received by the intelligentsia, who notoriously enjoy the most frightful bilge.
2. The 'belly' of a cask or other vessel of similar shape; cf. BELLY 10, 11.
1513 Douglas *Æneis* II. i. 11 Of chost men..thai tuik Ane greit numir, and hid in bilgis derne Within that best. **1797** Nelson in Nicolas *Disp.* VII. 143 The great weight of stores laid on the casks..has pressed the bilges.
3. *Comb.* and *Attrib.*, as ***bilge-block, -board, -coad, -keelson, -plank;*** **bilge-fever** (see quot.); **bilge-free** *a.* (of a cask), stowed so that the bilge does not come in contact with the floor; **bilge-piece** = BILGE-KEEL; **bilge-pump**, a pump to draw off the bilge-water; **bilge-stringer**, a shelf or line of beams running round the bilge; **bilge-ways** (see quot.). Also BILGE-KEEL, -WATER.
1862 *Catal. Internat. Exhib. Industrial Dept.* II. xii. 7 A new method of adjusting *bilge-blocks on the arms of the cradle. **1961** F. H. Burgess *Dict. Sailing* 27 *Bilge blocks*, supports placed at the bilges when a ship docks. **1867** Smyth *Sailor's Word-bk.*, **Bilge-fever*, the illness occasioned by a foul hold. **1869** Sir E. Reed *Ship-build.* ii. 47 The iron-clad frigates of our Navy..have numerous ..*bilge-keelsons. **1880** *Times* 25 Dec. 7/5 The vessel rolled 'deeper' than before the removal of the *bilge-pieces, the increase of the ballast, etc. **1867** Smyth *Sailor's Word-bk.*, **Bilge-planks*, certain thick strengthenings on the inner and outer lines of the bilge. **1866** G. Macdonald *Ann. Q. Neigh.* xi. (1878) 226 It's better..to keep a look-out on the *bilge-pump. **1869** Sir E. Reed *Ship-build.* i. 10 The butts of the angle-irons forming the fore and aft *bilge-stringers, were not sufficiently connected. **1769** Falconer *Dict. Marine* (1789) Hiij b, The *bilge-ways or cradles, placed under the bottom, to conduct the ship..into the water whilst lanching.

bilge, *v.* [f. prec. sb.]
1. *trans.* To stave in a ship's bottom, cause her to spring a leak.
1557 A. Jenkinson in Hakluyt *Voy.* I. 333 The Trinitie came on ground..and was like to be bilged and lost. **1658** Ussher *Ann.* 662 Euphranor..had bilged and sunck one of the enemies ships. **1762–9** Falconer *Shipwr.* III. 642 A second shock Bilges the splitting vessel on the rock. **1836** Marryat *Midsh. Easy* xxxi, It was one of the Sicilian government galleys bilged on the rocks.
2. *intr.* (for *refl.*) To suffer fracture in the bilge; to be broken or stove in, spring a leak. Also *fig.*
1728 Morgan *Algiers* II. v. 301 The Ships..were running ashore and bilging on the Rocks. **1748** Anson *Voy.* II. iii. 146 She struck on a sunken rock, and soon after bilged. **1870** Lowell *Among my Bks.* Ser. I. (1873) 223 On which an heroic life..may bilge and go to pieces.
3. *trans.* and *intr.* To bulge or swell out.
1807 Vancouver *Agric. Devon* (1813) 369 These narrow ways are..by the traffic of the lime-carts, bilged, and forced out upon their sides. **1849–52** Todd *Cycl. Anat. & Phys.* IV. 941/2 The whole apparatus is capable of bilging outwards in the movements of respiration.

bilged, *ppl. a.* In 6 *Sc.* **bilgeit.** [f. BILGE *sb.* + -ED².] Having a large bilge; broad-bottomed.
1513 Douglas *Æneis* II. iv. [iii.] 65 Alkyn portage quhilk was hidder brocht In barge or bilgeit ballingare our se.

bilge-keel ('bɪldʒ-kiːl). See quot. 1850.
c **1850** *Rudim. Navig.* (Weale) 97 Bilge-Keels, the pieces of timber fastened under the bilge of boats or other vessels, to keep them upright when on shore, or to prevent them falling to leeward when sailing. **1884** E. Fishbourne in *Pall Mall G.* 23 Sept. 2/2 A large number of our ships have deep bilge-keels to reduce their rolling propensities.

'bilge-water. a. The water that collects in the bilge of a ship through leakage or otherwise, and becomes disgustingly foul and noxious.
1706 Phillips, *Bildge-Water*, that water which..cannot come to the Well in the Ship's Hold. **1751** Smollett *Per. Pic.* lx, May I be bound to eat oakum and drink bilge-water for life. **1840** R. Dana *Bef. Mast* ii. 3 That inexpressibly sickening smell, caused by the shaking up of the bilge-water in the hold.
b. = BILGE *sb.* 1 c. *slang.*
1878 G. M. Hopkins *Let.* 13 May (1935) 50 Write no bilgewater about it.

†**bilgres.** *Obs.* A plant: perhaps = BILDERS.
c **1460** J. Russell *Bk. Nurture* in *Babees Bk.* (1868) 185 Scabiose, Bilgres, wildflax, is good for ache.

bilgy ('bɪldʒɪ), *a.* [f. BILGE *sb.* + -Y¹.] Characteristic of a bilge: e.g. 'a bilgy smell.' Also *fig.*
1878 G. M. Hopkins *Let.* 13 May (1935) 51 You *drew off* your criticisms all stinking..and bilgy. **1890** *Harper's Mag.* Sept. 594/2 Living in quarters as crowded and bilgy as a slaver's hold.

Bilharzia, bilharzia (bɪl'hɑːzɪə). [mod.L., f. the name of Theodor *Bilharz* (1825–62), a German physician who discovered the parasite in 1852.] **a.** A genus of trematode worms parasitic in the veins of the pelvic region and urinary organs of human beings, esp. in Egypt and other parts of Africa. Also *attrib.*
1859 T. S. Cobbold in *Trans. Linnean Soc.* XXII. IV. 364 *Bilharzia magna* (mihi)... Up to the time of Bilharz's discovery of *Distoma hæmatobium*, all the flukes were considered hermaphrodite... Trematodes possessing so marked a structural peculiarity as *D. hæmatobium*..deserve, I think, to be generically separated from Distomata properly so called, and I have therefore employed the indefatigable discoverer's name for this purpose. **1864** —— *Entozoa* 203 The blood..forms the proper habitat of the *Bilharzia.* **1877** Huxley *Anat. Inv. Anim.* 202 Diœcious Trematodes are very rare, the most important being the formidable *Bilharzia.* **1916** *Brit. Med. Jrnl.* 18 Mar. 411/1 Three species..were infected with certain cercariae, which developed in mice under experimental conditions into bilharzia worms. **1963** *Times* 16 May 14/7 Perennial streams which are clear and cool to the eye but full of *bilharzia.*
b. By extension = BILHARZIASIS.
1889 *Brit. Med. Jrnl.* 20 Apr. 891/2 *Cases of Bilharzia.* Mr. Anthony Bowlby showed..organs..from two cases of this disease. **1937** C. L. Leipoldt *Bushveld Doc.* ii. 44 To-day bilharzia is as easily curable as malaria. **1961** *New Scientist* 21 Sept. 714/1 Bilharzia..is a widespread disease in many tropical countries.
Hence **bil'harzial, bil'harzic** *adjs.*; **bilharz'iasis, -'osis**, the disease produced by the presence of this worm in the bladder; = SCHISTOSOMIASIS.
1893 *Lancet* 9 Sept. 622/1 The rules I laid down many years ago for the prevention of bilharzial infection..are still

appropriate. **1900** DORLAND *Med. Dict.* 109/2 Bilharziasis, bilharziosis. **1903** *Philad. Med. Jrnl.* 31 Jan. 208/1 Bilharziosis of the kidney may show primary bilharzic lesions and secondary bilharzic lesions. **1906** *Lancet* 27 Oct. 1178/2 The liver proved to be a typical specimen of advanced bilharzial cirrhosis. *Ibid.*, A remarkable case of bilharziasis. **1913** *Glasgow Med. Jrnl.* Jan. 15 Egypt has well been termed the 'home of bilharziosis'. **1959** J. CLEGG *Freshwater Life* (ed. 2) xix. 312 Bilharziasis..in some parts of the world has been said to affect every third person.

bili- (baɪlɪ), combining form of the L. *bīlis* bile, used in various compounds and derivatives, *esp.* in the names of bile-pigments; as ***bili-cyanin***; BILIRUBIN, BILIVERDIN, etc. **bili'ation**, 'the production or secretion of bile.' *Syd. Soc. Lex.* 1880. **bi'liferous** *a.*, producing bile. †**,bilifi'cation**, the action or process of making bile. †**'bilify**, *v.* to form bile; **'bilifying** *ppl. a.* bile-forming.

1880 J. W. LEGG *Bile* 49 Bilicyanin they always find in human gall-stones. **1836-9** TODD *Cycl. Anat. & Phys.* II. 483/2 In many insects..the biliferous organs consist of fluid sacs. **1692** SIR T. BLOUNT *Ess.* 113 The nature of sanguification, Bilification, Separation of Urine. **1657** TOMLINSON *Renou's Disp.* 526 So much Vinegar must be added..as will correct that bilefying faculty.

bilian ('bɪlɪən). Also **balean, billian, bulean.** [Malay.] The ironwood of Borneo.

1812 J. HUNT in H. Keppel *Exped. Borneo* (1846) II. p. xxxi, The woods about Pontiana for carpentry and joinery are, kayu bulean, chena, [etc.]. **1846** J. BROOKE *Ibid.* viii. 167 The Chinese export considerable quantities of timber from Sambas and Pontiana, particularly of the kind called Balean by the natives, or the lion-wood of the Europeans. **1882** DE WINDT *Equator* 63 Loading 'bilian' or iron wood. **1887** DALY *Digging S. Austr.* 272 Forests of bilian..in British North Borneo. **1902** *Encycl. Brit.* XXXII. 417/1 With the exception of billian (iron wood) from the river Rejang, very little is exported. **1906** *Macm. Mag.* Nov. 42 That wonderful wood *billian*, the Bornean ironwood.

biliary ('bɪlɪərɪ), *a.* [ad. F. *biliaire*; cf. mod.L. *biliāris*, and see -ARY².]

1. Of or pertaining to the bile.

1731 ARBUTHNOT *Ailments* i. §4 Voracious Animals..have the Biliary Duct inserted into the Pylorus. **1827** CARLYLE *Misc.* (1857) 51 Derangement in the biliary organs.

2. = BILIOUS 2.

1837 CARLYLE *Fr. Rev.* (1871) III. VI. vi. 234 The biliary face seems clouded with new gloom. **1860** —— *Remin* I. 97 Not sanguine and diffusive he, but biliary and intense.

†**bi'libre.** *Obs. rare.* [ad. L. *bilībra*, f. *bi-* two + *lībra* pound.] A weight of two pounds.

1382 WYCLIF *Rev.* vi. 6 A bilibre of whete, *that is a weyȝt of two pound*, for oo peny, and thre bilibres of barly for oo peny.

bilif, -liue, var. ff. of BYLIFE, *Obs.*, sustenance.

‖**bilimbi** (bɪ'lɪmbɪ). Also 8 **blimbi**, 9 **bilimby, blimbing.** [Tamul *bilimbi*, Malay *bilimbing*, Cingalese *bilin.*] A tree (*Averrhoa Bilimbi*, N.O. *Oxalidaceæ*), growing in India and Ceylon, which yields a juice used by the natives for the cure of skin-diseases; also its fruit.

1772-84 COOK *Voy.* (1790) I. 247 There are fruits of various kinds, and particularly the blimbi, which has a sharp taste, and is a fine pickle. **1852** F. NEALE *Resid. Siam* xii, To see the fruit trees..the callacca, and the bilimby, the custard apple and the pomegranate. **1866** *Treas. Bot.* 112 *Averrhoa Bilimbi*, the Blimbing.

†**'biliment.** *Obs.* Forms: 6 **beliment, bellementte, billament, billemente, billyment, bylli(a)ment**, 6-7 **billiment(e**, 7-8 **billement**, 8 **biliment.** [aphetic form of ABILIMENT, HABILIMENT (also *abillement*, *habillament*, *abyllyment*, etc., etc.); used in specific senses of that word.]

1. *gen.* An ornamental article of (female) attire, an ornament worn by women; = HABILIMENT 5.

[*c* **1530** LD. BERNERS *Arth. Lyt. Bryt.* (1814) 8 Pyers.. bought for them abylementes and jewelles.] **1589** *Lanc. Wills* (1861) 155, I give unto my said wiefe all her chaynes of goolde..billimentes and all apparell. **1611** COTGR., *Dorlot*, a iewell, or prettie trinket, as..aglet, button, billement, etc. wherewith a woman sets out her apparell, or decks herselfe. **1720** *Stow's Surv.* (ed. Strype 1754) II. v. ix. 270/1 Many Biliments, Chains, Tablets, Buttons, and such like which were commonly worn. **1721-90** BAILEY, *Billements* [*i.e.* the Habilliments], Ornaments and Cloaths of a Woman.

2. *spec.* in 16th c.: 'The attire or ornaments of a woman's head or neck: or a bonnet: a French hood: a paste or such like.' Baret *Alvearie* 1580. 'The jewelled fronts of the ladies' head-dresses, as we see them in the portraits of Queen Anne Boleyne, etc.' J. G. Nicholls.

[**1555** *Fardle Facions* II. vii. 161 The abillementes of their heades are much like the frontlettes that their Magi doe weare.] *a* **1553** UDALL *Royster D.* II. iii. (Arb.) 35 We shall go in our frenche hoodes..In our tricke ferdegews and billiments of golde. *a* **1556** *Chron. Gr. Friars* (1852) 43 Thene [1539] beganne alle the gentylwomen of Yngland to were Frenche whooddes with bellementtes of golde. **1583** GOLDING *Calvin on Deut.* lxxvii. 472 Women weare billiments of gold, and other costly attyres vpon their heades. **1611** COTGR., *Bavolet*, a Billiment, or head-attire, worne by the women of Picardie.

3. ***biliment lace***: an ornamental lace used in the 16th c. for trimming.

1578 *Inv. Jas. Backhouse* in *Draper's Dict.* 187 Lace 5*d* to 9*d* per dozen. vij doz. and a d. of bylliament, 8*s*...x owncis of sylke bylliment, 12*s*. **1588** *Lanc. Wills* (1861) 139 One velvett jerkin laid one wth billimt lace. **1600** *Queen's Wardrobe* in Nichols *Progr. Q. Eliz.* III. 501 One frocke of clothe of golde..with a billament lace of Venice Golde.

bilimien, -limpen, etc.: see BE-.

bilin ('baɪlɪn). [f. BILE + -IN.] A gummy pale yellow mass, formerly considered to be the principal constituent of the bile.

1849-52 TODD *Cycl. Anat. & Phys.* IV. 844/2 Bilin and biliary colouring matter. **1872** HUXLEY *Phys.* v. 122 Bilin.. is a mixture of two acids in combination with soda.

bilinear (baɪ'lɪnɪə(r)), *a.* [f. BI- *pref.*² 6 + LINEAR, L. *linea* line.] 1. Of, pertaining to, or contained by, two (straight) lines.

1851 MANSELL *Proleg. Log.* (1860) 24 There is no difficulty in understanding the meaning of the phrase 'bilinear figure'..though the object is inconceivable. **1851** *Phil. Mag.* I. 132 There are *three* points of contact..where the two right lines meet. This, then, is a case of triple contact. I distinguish it by the name of bilinear-contact. **1866** *Math. Questions from 'Educational Times'* V. 76 Any equation expressed in Cartesian language may immediately be transformed into another expressed in bilinear (perpendicular) coordinates. **1885** S. NEWCOMB *Elem. Analytic Geom.* ii. 13 (*heading*) Cartesian or bilinear co-ordinates.

2. Linear in two ways; chiefly in *Math.*: linear and homogeneous in each of two sets of independent variables. Also *absol.*, a bilinear form.

1886 G. S. CARR *Synopsis Pure & Appl. Math.* I. II. 851/1 Bilinear forms. *Ibid.*, Bilinear functions. **1923** T. MUIR *Theory Determinants* IV. xx. 428 The corresponding theorem for the general bilinear is easily anticipated. **1938** A. D. CAMPBELL *Adv. Analytic Geom.* viii. 121 This choice of new fundamental circles amounts to a so-called bilinear transformation of the parameter. **1967** GRUENBERG & WEIR *Linear Geom.* v. 91 A bilinear form is orthosymmetric if, and only if, it is either symmetric or skew-symmetric.

bilingual (baɪ'lɪŋgwəl), *a.* [f. L. *bilingu-is* speaking two languages (f. *bi-* two + *lingua* tongue, language) + -AL¹.]

1. a. Having, or characterized by two languages.

1862 ANSTED *Channel Isl.* 543 A constitution of bilingual islands. **1871** EARLE *Philol.* §20 *Cock-boat* is probably a bilingual compound.

b. In extended use: speaking two forms of the same language.

1955 T. H. PEAR *Eng. Social Diff.* iii. 97 In London, many waitresses and shop assistants are bi-lingual. **1961** PARTRIDGE *Dict. Slang* Suppl. 997/2 He's bilingual—speaks both English and American.

c. As *sb.*, one who can speak two languages.

1949 *Archivum Linguisticum* I. 155 'Foreign accent' in the speech of bilinguals. **1959** J. C. CATFORD in Quirk & Smith *Teaching of English* vi. 164 The teaching of English or of any language as a foreign language may be described as a process of creating bilinguals.

2. *spec.* Of inscriptions, etc.: Written or inscribed simultaneously in parallel versions in two different languages. Also quasi-*sb.*

1845 *Proc. Philol. Soc.* I. 193 The bilingual inscriptions furnish the meanings of a certain number of Lycian words. **1847** GROTE *Greece* II. xxxiv. IV. 352 The inscriptions were bilingual, in Assyrian characters as well as Greek. **1869** BALDWIN *Preh. Nations* viii. (1877) 340 The bilingual stone of Thugga. **1881** *Athenæum* 1 Oct. 433/3 Our bilinguals are as yet scanty.

Hence **bi'lingually** *adv.*, in two languages. So **bi'linguar** *a.* = BILINGUAL. **bi'linguist**, one who speaks two languages. **bi'linguous** *a.* = BILINGUAL.

1871 EARLE *Philol.* §77 Not an unfrequent thing in Chaucer for a line to contain a single fact bilingually repeated. **1839** *Fraser's Mag.* XX. 202 The bilinguar monument of Rosetta. **1884** *Pall Mall G.* 4 Jan. 3/1 A genuine bilinguist is as rare a prodigy as a two-headed calf. **1730** BAILEY *Bilinguous*; (whence also in mod. Dicts.).

bi'lingualism. [f. BILINGUAL *a.* + -ISM.] Ability to speak two languages; the habitual use of two languages colloquially. Hence **bi'lingualist** = BILINGUIST.

1873 J. EARLE *Philol. Eng. Tongue* (ed. 2) 85 The Bilingualism of King's English... Words run much in couples, the one being English and the other French. **1897** A. J. BUTLER tr. *Ratzel's Hist. Mankind* II. 20 The bi-lingualism of the Carib tribes, whose women speak Arawak and the men Carib. **1926** *Encycl. Brit.* III. 114 The effects of bilingualism deserve attention, especially in those areas where permanent contact is established between two different families of speech, as in India. **1927** *British Weekly* 12 May 125/4 Welsh bilingualists [decreased] by more than two per cent. **1960** *Guardian* 7 Mar. 5/4 The progress in bilingualism shown by the Welsh children.

b. The use of two forms of the same language. (See also quot. 1940.)

1940 J. H. JAGGER *Eng. in Future* ii. 38 It [*sc.* Elizabethan English] suffered from two literary fashions... The first..is known to literary historians as Bilingualism, and consisted in the incessant employment of a pair of synonyms to convey a single idea. **1955** T. H. PEAR *Eng. Social Diff.* iii. 105 For the great majority of pupils, bilingualism is to be preferred to the replacement of their native speech by a colourless standard dialect.

bilin'guality. *Linguistics.* [f. BILINGUAL *a.* + -ITY.] = BILINGUALISM (usu. in sense a).

1953 U. WEINREICH *Lang. in Contact* ii. 67 The external factors include..the bilinguality of the interlocutors, emotional involvement of the speaker, etc. **1968** W. E. LAMBERT et al. in J. A. Fishman *Readings Sociol. of Lang.* 484 Fundamental differences exist between our two samples of Franco-American students in terms of their experience with French, their degree of bilinguality, and their adjustment to the American society as ethnic minority groups. **1977** BOURHIS & GILES in H. Glass *Lang., Ethnicity & Intergroup Relations* v. 121 A number of Welshmen are assuming a new pride in their bilinguality. **1984** *Guardian* 1 Feb. 10/3 He instinctively reverted to what middle-class mothers of children in state schools have long termed 'bilinguality'; he assumed a Cockney accent as protective colouring.

†**bili'ose**, *a. Obs.* [ad. L. *bīliōs-us*.] = next.

1710 *Phil. Trans.* XXVII. 34 The Biliose Liquor..being of a whitish yellow colour.

bilious ('bɪlɪəs), *a.* Also 6 **bilius, bylyous**, 7 **bileous**, 8 **biliose.** [ad. F. *bilieux*:—L. *bīliōs-us*, f. *bīli-s* BILE: see -OUS.]

†1. Of, pertaining to, or connected with, the bile; = BILIARY. *Obs.*

1541 R. COPLAND *Gaylen's Terap.* 2 Gijb, Cankers cometh of bylyous excrementes. **1651** CULPEPPER *Astrol. Judgem. Dis.* (1658) 133 Caused by cholerick or bilious matter. **1697** DOWNING *Disord. Horned Cattle* 35 This medicine..cleanses the bilious passages.

2. Of diseases and temperament: Affected by, or arising from, too great a secretion of bile, or from bilious derangement.

1651 BIGGS *New Disp.* 74 Bilious diseases. **1671** H. STUBBE *Def. Phlebot.* 36 His natural habit, be it bilious, melancholy, or phlegmatick. **1732** ARBUTHNOT *Rules of Diet* i. 245 An excellent Drink in bilious Fevers. **1826** DISRAELI *Viv. Grey* IV. v. 159 Rise in the morning as bilious as a Bengal general. **1842** DICKENS *Lett.* (1880) I. 67.

3. Choleric, wrathful, peevish, ill-tempered.

1561 T. FORTESCUE *Forest* (1571) 52 A great note of temperancie is it not to waxe or bilius or angrie for the injurie that is done us. **1662** FULLER *Worthies* (1840) III. 374 Here bilious Bale lets fly without fear. **1866** *Sat. Rev.* 20 Jan. 76/1 The outpouring of a bilious cynicism.

'biliously, *adv.* [f. prec. + -LY².] In a bilious or ill-tempered manner.

1865 *Pall Mall G.* 27 July 11/1 He wishes heartily—if not biliously—that some biped English boas might come to the same fate.

'biliousness. Bilious quality or condition; *fig.* peevishness, ill-temper.

1821 DE QUINCEY *Confess.* I. 67 The suffering from biliousness. **1884** GEN. GORDON *Jrnl. Kartoum* 8 Oct., I hope Stewart will cut out all this biliousness.

bilirubin (,bɪlɪ'ruːbɪn). *Biochem.* [a. G. *bilirubin* (G. Städeler 1864, in *Ann. d. Chem. und Pharm.* CXXXII. 326), f. BILI- + L. *ruber* red + -IN¹.] A reddish pigment, $C_{33}H_{36}O_6N_4$, occurring in bile. Also *attrib.*

1871 *Jrnl. Chem. Soc.* IX. 419 An alcoholic solution of biliverdin or of bilirubin and ammonia, was decomposed. **1878** GAMGEE tr. *Hermann's Phys.* (ed. 2) 138 Yellow bile becomes green through the oxidation of bilirubin to biliverdin. **1961** *Lancet* 12 Aug. 376/2 The table lists all the bilirubin levels available.

bilis, obs. form of BYLES, a game.

biliteral (baɪ'lɪtərəl), *a.* [f. BI- *pref.*² 1 + LITERAL, f. L. *lītera* or *littera* letter.] 1. Having or consisting of two letters; quasi-*sb.* a linguistic root consisting of two letters. **bi'literalism**, a biliteral condition of language.

1787 SIR W. JONES *Anniv. Disc.* iv. (1824) I. 43 It is the genius of the Sanscrit..that the roots of verbs be almost universally biliteral. **1863** R. TOWNSEND *Mod. Geom.* I. 2 The former or biliteral notation is..more convenient. **1874** SAYCE *Compar. Philol.* ii. 78 The so-called biliterals are.. the result of phonetic decay. **1860** FARRAR *Orig. Lang.* x. 212 The supposition of an original biliteralism.

2. Of an inscription: written in two different scripts. Also *sb.*, a biliteral inscription.

1877 SKENE *Celtic Scot.* II. 450 Several of those [*sc.* ogham inscriptions] in Wales being biliteral, and having a corresponding inscription in debased Roman characters. **1878** PETRIE & STOKES *Christian Inscript.* II. 165 The biliteral inscriptions on our stone monuments. *a* **1886** S. FERGUSON *Ogham Inscript.* (1887) 114 Other biliterals of.. mere British origin.

-bility [F. *-bilité*, L. *-bilitātem*], a termination forming abstract substantives from adjectives in -BLE.

biliverdin (,bɪlɪ'vɜːdɪn). *Biochem.* Also **-dine.** [a. G. *biliverdin* (Berzelius 1840, in *Ann. d. Chem. und Pharm.* XXXIII. 140), f. BILI- + *verd-* (as in VERDURE) + -IN¹.] A green pigment, $C_{33}H_{34}O_6N_4$, occurring in bile.

1845 WOOD & BACHE *Dispensatory of U.S.A.* (ed. 6) 1285 Biliverdin, a green colouring matter resulting from the absorption of oxygen. **1856** *Fownes' Man. Chem.* (ed. 6) 672 *Biliverdin*..is dark green, amorphous, without taste or smell. **1863** W. O. MARKHAM tr. *Neubauer & Vogel's Anal. Urine* xxiv. 86 *Biliverdine* (green-pigment) is the form of pigment into which cholepyrrhine often passes, and into which, indeed, it may be converted. **1878** [see BILIRUBIN].

1963 *New Scientist* 25 July 182/1 Biliverdin is formed by biological degradation of the red blood pigment hemin.

bilk (bılk), *sb.* [Of uncertain origin; nor can it be determined whether the sb. or the vb. was first in use. The verb was at first a technical term in the game of Cribbage, where it interchanged with *balk*; hence a conjecture that it may have originated in a mincing pronunciation of the latter. Blount's assertion that the word is Arabic is altogether erroneous; and the derivation 'from Mœso-Goth. *bi-laikan* to mock, to deride,' given in some dicts., belongs to a pre-scientific age.]

1. *Cribbage.* A balking or spoiling of an adversary's score in his crib.

1791 J. WILLIAMS (A. Pasquin) *Cribbage* 63 To assist your own Crib better, or to throw a greater bilk into that of your adversary. *Ibid.* 65 A King is, in general, a great bilk with almost any other card.

†**2.** A statement having nothing in it. *Obs.*

1633 B. JONSON *T. Tub* I. i, *Tub.* He will have the last word, though he talk bilk for 't. *Hugh.* Bilk! what's that? *Tub.* Why, nothing: a word signifying Nothing; and borrowed here to express nothing. **1681** BLOUNT, *Bilk* is said to be an Arabick word, and signifies *nothing*: cribbage-players understand it best. *a* **1733** NORTH *Exam.* I. iii. ¶139. 213 Bedloe was sworn, and, being asked what he knew against the Prisoner, answered, Nothing..Bedloe was questioned over and over, who still swore the same Bilk. *Ibid.* I. iii. ¶46 The Words in a common Acceptation are a meer Bilk, and signify nothing.

3. A hoax, a deception, a 'take in.' ? *Obs.*

1664 BUTLER *Hud.* II. III. 376 Spells, Which over ev'ry month's blank-page In th' Almanack strange Bilks presage. **1694** CONGREVE *Double Deal.* III. x, There he's secure from danger of a bilk. *a* **1733** NORTH *Lives* I. 260 After this bilk of a discovery was known.

4. A person who bilks or cheats; a cheat.

1790 SHERIDAN in *Sheridaniana* 109 Johnny W——lks, Johnny W——lks, Thou greatest of bilks. **1836** MARRYAT *Japhet* ix, The wagoner drove off, cursing him for a bilk.

†**bilk**, *a. Obs.* [See prec.]

a **1733** NORTH *Exam.* I. iii. ¶10. 129 To that and the Author's bilk account of it, I am approaching.

bilk (bılk), *v.* [See BILK *sb.*]

1. *trans.* In *Cribbage*: To balk or spoil any one's score in his crib.

1651 CLEVELAND *Poems* 24 So many Cards, i'th stock, and yet be bilkt? **1680** COTTON *Compl. Gamester* viii, If he find no Games in them, nor help by the Card that was turn'd up, which he takes into his hand, then he is bilkt, and sometimes it so happens that he is both bilkt in hand and crib. **1791** J. WILLIAMS (A. Pasquin) *Cribbage* 65 Bilking the Crib of your adversary is a very essential part of the game of Cribbage.. any cards which are not likely to make sequences, are proper cards to bilk your adversary. **1850** Bohn's *Hand-bk. Games*, 'Baulking' or 'bilking' the crib.

2. To balk (hope, expectation); to cheat, deceive, betray.

1672 MARVELL *Reh. Transp.* I. 27 When we have search'd all over, we find ourselves bilk'd in our expectation. *a* **1683** OLDHAM *Wks. & Rem.* (1686) 48 Hopes often bilkt, and Sought Preferment lost. **1774** *Westm. Mag.* II. 145 Hapless woman..Bilk'd while she's young, and ancient without friends! **1822** HAZLITT *Table-t.* II. xv. 351 Native talents at work..to bilk their consciences, and salve their reputation. **1829** CARLYLE *Misc.* (1857) I. 293 Fate..may be to a certain extent bilked.

3. To 'do (a person) out' *of* (his due); to cheat, defraud; to evade payment of (a debt).

1672 LOCKE in Fox Bourne *Life* I. v. 268 A man that had bilked one of the most considerable men of the place. **1692** LUTTRELL *Brief Rel.* (1857) II. 412 Beleiving the persons therein would bilk the coachman. *a* **1704** T. BROWN *Praise Poverty* Wks. 1730 I. 98 A..scoundrel who knows no pleasure beyond..bilking bauds and coaches. **1723** DE FOE *Col. Jack* (1840) 198 We bilked the captain of his ransom money. **1766** *New Bath Guide* vi. (1807) 40 'Tis hard to be bilk'd of our fare. **1785** COWPER *Tiroc.* 327 His skill..In bilking tavern bills. **1853** MERIVALE *Rom. Rep.* viii. (1867) 224 In bilking a creditor or negotiating a loan.

4. To elude, evade, escape from, 'give the slip' to.

1679 R. W. *Cromwell's Ghost* 2, I bilkt my Keeper, and.. Once more I mount my Native Soyl again. **1713** *Guardian* No. 124 (1756) II. 159 The country lass! who, her cow bilking, leaves her milking, For a green gown on the grass. **1720** GAY *Poems* (1745) II. 64 She scorn'd to bilk her assignation. **1826** SCOTT *Woodst.* xxviii, I bilked Everard in order to have my morning draught. **1852** THACKERAY *Esmond* II. i. 161 T'other recollected how a constable had been bilked.

'bilked. Also bilkt. [f. prec. + -ED[1].] Cheated, 'done out' of one's due or expectation.

1682 DRYDEN *Mac Fl.* 104 Bilkt stationers for yeomen stood prepar'd. ——(J.) The pleasing sight Of your bilk'd hopes.

bilker ('bılkə(r)). *slang.* [f. BILK *v.* + -ER[1].] One who practises cheating; *esp.* one who evades payment of a cabman's fare.

1717 *Daily Courant* 27 Dec., A Dramatick Entertainment of Dancing, call'd, The Cheats, or, The Tavern Bilkers. **1887** *Tit-Bits* 25 June 172 Cab Bilkers. **1892** *Daily News* 6 May 6/5 Fares who tried to evade payment, known as 'bilkers'. **1898** *Ibid.* 8 Jan. 3/5 The London Cab Act, 59 and 60 Victoria, chapter 27, commonly known as the Bilkers' Act. **1909** H. G. WELLS *Ann Veronica* xvi. 336 Ann Veronica, you're a bilker!

'bilking, *vbl. sb.* [f. as BILKED + -ING[1].] The action of cheating or 'doing out' of one's due.

1687 T. BROWN *Saints in Upr.* Wks. 1730 I. 77 A pack of vermin, bred up to..bilking of their landladies. **1756** *Gray's-Inn Jrnl.* I. 177 The..bilking of Waiters at Places of Entertainment.

'bilking, *ppl. a.* [f. as prec. + -ING[2].] Balking, disappointing, cheating.

1731 FIELDING *Lottery* ii. Wks. 1784 II. 140 Dear Madam, be not in such a passion, I am no bilking younger brother.

bill (bıl), *sb.*[1] Forms: 1–7 bil, 5–6 byl, bylle, bille, 1– bill. [Com. WGer.: OE. *bil, billes* neut., sword, falchion = OS. *bil*, the same, OHG. *bill* neut. (MHG. *bil* neut., mod.G. *bille* fem., pickaxe) prob.:—OTeut. **biljo-(m* (with WGer. *ll* for *lj*), connected by some with Skr. *bhil* to split, cleave. Applied to various cutting weapons and implements, the relations of which to each other are not satisfactorily ascertained. (Ger. *beil*, OHG. *bîhal*, is an entirely different word.)]

†**1.** A weapon of war mentioned in OE. poetry, a kind of broadsword, a falchion. *Obs.* (Probably passing with modified shape into sense 2.)

a **1000** *Beowulf* 4126 Æfter billes bíte. *c* **1050** *Ags. Gloss.* in Wr.-Wülcker *Voc.* 376 *Chalibem*, bill. **1205** LAY. 1740 þer wes bil ibeat ; þer wes balu muchel. [**1867** FREEMAN *Norm. Conq.* (1876) I. v. 273 *note*, The bill here [in *Death of Brihtnoth*] spoken of was a sword and not an axe.]

2. An obsolete military weapon used chiefly by infantry; varying in form from a simple concave blade with a long wooden handle, to a kind of concave axe with a spike at the back and its shaft terminating in a spear-head; a halberd.

Distinct forms of bills seem to have been painted or varnished in different colours; hence the ***black*** and ***brown bills*** of the 16th and 17th centuries.

c **1300** *K. Alis.* 1624 With longe billes..They carve heore bones. **1465** MARG. PASTON *Lett.* 518 II. 215 The tenauntes ..havyng rusty polexis and byllys. **1495** *Act 11 Hen. VII*, lxiv. Pream., Armours Defensives, as..Bowes, Billes, Hauberts. **1593** SHAKS. *Rich. II*, III. ii. 118 Distaffe-Women manage rustie Bills. **1598** BARRET *Theor. Warres* I. i. 2 Inveterate opinion..touching blacke bils and bowes. **1603** DRAYTON *Bar. Warres* II. xxxvii, Wer't with the Speare, or Browne Bill, or the Pike. **1813** SCOTT *Trierm.* I. xiii, When the Gothic gateway frown'd, Glanced neither bill nor bow. **1834** PLANCHÉ *Brit. Costume.* 33.

b. A similar weapon used by constables of the watch till late in the 18th cent. Also *attrib.*

1589 *Pappe w. Hatchet* (1844) 28 All weapons from the taylors bodkin, to the watchmans browne bil. **1599** SHAKS. *Much Ado* III. iii. 44 Haue a care that your bills be not stolne. **1616** FLETCHER *Cust. Country* II. i. 9, I. *Off.* He was still in quarrels, scorned us Peace-makes, And all our bill-authority. **1799** S. FREEMAN *Town Off.* 176 Every watchman carries a staff with a bill fastened thereon.

3. Short for BILL-MAN.

1495 HEN. VII. in Ellis *Orig. Lett.* I. 11. I. 21 For..an archer or bille on horsback viijd. by the day. **1513** HEN. VIII. in Strype *Eccl. Mem.* I. II. App. i. 4 A hundred able men..wherof threescore to be archers and forty bills on foot. **1532** HERVET *Xenophon's Househ.* (1768) 35 Billes, and archers, the which folowe their capitaynes in good arraye. **1825** SCOTT *Talism.* x, A strong guard of bills and bows.

4. An implement used for pruning, cutting wood, lopping trees, hedges, etc., having a long blade with a concave edge, often ending in a sharp hook (cf. BILL-HOOK), and a wooden handle in line with the blade, which may be long as in the *hedging-bill*, or short as in the *hand-bill*. (The form of the 'bill' varies greatly in different localities.)

c **1000** ÆLFRIC *Gloss.* in Wr.-Wülcker *Voc.* 106 *Falcastrum*, siþe, *uel* bill. **1481** CAXTON *Reynard* xxxiii. §1 The men..cam out with stauys and byllis, with flaylis and pyk-forkes. **1552** HULOET, Byl called a forest bil, or bushsithe. **1570** *Wills & Inv. N.C.* (1835) 334 Ij paire of wood skeles, one bilstaffe iiijs. *a* **1604** HANMER *Chron. Irel.* (1633) 103 Having a forrest Bill on his shoulders. **1643** W. GREENHILL *Axe at Root* 19 It is not Falx, a Bill or Hooke, to chop off some Armes or Bowes. **1740** SOMERVILLE *Hobbinol* ii. 80 And with his crooked Bill Cut sheer the frail Support. **1862** TRENCH *Monk & Bird* xxxiii. Poems 28 The woodman's glittering bill.

†**5.** A digging implement; a mattock or pickaxe.

[*c* **1050** *Ags. Gloss.* in Wr.-Wülcker *Voc.* 361 *Bidubium, marra*, bill.] *c* **1325** *Pol. Songs* (1839) 151 Thah y sulle mi bil ant my borstax. *c* **1400** *Ywaine & Gaw.* 3223 Thai had broght bath bill and spade. **1468** *Medulla Gram.*, *Fossorium*, a byl or a pykeys. **1483** *Cath. Angl.* 31 A Bille (a Byll or a pycoss), *fossorium, ligo.*

6. *Comb.* †**bill-hager** (?); BILLMAN, q.v.

c **1460** *Towneley Myst.* 85 Both bosters and bragers God kepe us fro..From alle bylle hagers with colknyfes that go.

bill, *sb.*[2] Forms: 1–4 bile, 4 beele, bil, 4–5 bylle, 5–6 bille, 6 byll, 4– bill. [OE. *bile* ? masc., not found elsewhere in Teut.; prob.:—OTeut. **bili-*, and possibly a derivative of the same root as BILL *sb.*[1]]

1. a. The horny BEAK of certain birds, especially when slender, flattened, or weak.

In Ornithology, *beak* is the general term applicable to all birds; in ordinary language *beak* is always used of birds of prey, and generally when striking or pecking is in question; *beak* and *bill* are both used of crows, finches, sparrows, perching birds and songsters generally, *bill* being however more frequent; *bill* is almost exclusively used of humming-birds, pigeons, waders, and web-footed birds.

a **1000** *Ags. Gloss.* in Wr.-Wülcker *Voc.* 318 *Rostrum*, bile. *c* **1200** *Trin. Coll. Hom.* 49 Duue ne harmeð none fugele ne mid bile ne mid fote. **1387** TREVISA *Higden* Rolls Ser. II. 421 þe bryddes woundeþ hem wiþ hire grete beeles. *c* **1440** *Promp. Parv.* 36 Bylle of a byrde, *rostrum.* **1486** *Bk. St. Albans* A vj b, Ye shall say this hauke has a large beke..And call it not bille. **1563** B. GOOGE *Eglogs* (Arb.) 109 To moue the Byll and shake the wings. **1601** DENT *Pathw. Heaven* D d, As the Eagle renueth her bill. **1642** HOWELL *For. Trav.* (Arb.) 80 Noah's dove brought the branch of Olive in her Bill. **1847** CARPENTER *Zool.* §454 The duck tribe are distinguished by the breadth and depression of the bill. **1862** WOOD *Nat. Hist.* II. 3 A peculiar horny incrustment, called the beak or bill. This bill is of very different shape in the various tribes of birds.

b. The horny beak of the *Platypus.*

1847 CARPENTER *Zool.* §317 (*Ornithorhynchus*) Its muzzle is converted into a bill, closely resembling that of a duck.

†**c.** ***to hold (one) with his bill in the water***: to keep him in suspense. *Obs.* = Fr. *tenir le bec dans l'eau*, Littré.

1579 TOMSON *Calvin's Serm. Tim.* 1041/1 What meant God to holde the fathers with their billes in the water (as wee say) so long, and sent not the Redeemer sooner?

†**2.** *trans.* The beak, muzzle, or snout of other animals; the human mouth or nose (cf. BEAK).

a **1000** ÆLFRIC *Gloss.* in Wr.-Wülcker *Voc.* 118 *Promuscida*, ylpes bile *vel* wrot. *c* **1330** *Poem temp. Edw. II.* 353 Ne triste no man to hem, so false theih beth in the bile. *c* **1380** *Sir Ferumb.* 2654 To hewe þe Sarasyns boþe bok & bil. **1611** SHAKS. *Wint. T.* I. ii. 183 How she holds vp the Neb, the Byll to him! *a* **1625** BOYS *Wks.* (1630) 498 A third most resembled his progenitors, having his fathers bill and his mothers eye.

3. A beaklike projection; a spur, tooth, spike. Applied to some narrow promontories, as *Portland Bill, Selsea Bill. Naut.* in *pl.*, see quot. 1850.

1382 WYCLIF *Zech.* iv. 12 The two eris..of the olyues that ben bysidis the two golden bilis [*Vulg.* rostra aurea.] **1388** —— *Isa.* xli. 15 A newe wayn threischynge, hauynge sawynge bilis. *c* **1400** *Destr. Troy* xv. 6407 He braid out a brond with a bill felle. **1770** WITHERING *Brit. Plants* (1796) I. 43 Beak, or Bill (rostrum), a long projecting appendage to some seeds like the beak of a bird. *c* **1850** *Rudim. Navig.* (Weale) 97 Bills, the ends of compass or knee timber.

4. *Naut.* The point of the fluke of an anchor. Hence **bill-board**, a board fastened edgewise to the side of a ship for the bill of the anchor to rest upon; also a board to protect the timbers of the ship from being damaged by the bill when the anchor is weighed.

1769 FALCONER *Dict. Marine* (1789) *Bill*, the point or extremity of the fluke of an anchor. **1825** H. GASCOIGNE *Nav. Fame* 51 Another tackle on the Bill they place. *c* **1860** H. STUART *Seaman's Catech.* 70 What are the bill-boards for? For the flukes of the anchors to rest on. **1875** BEDFORD *Sailor's Pocket Bk.* x. (ed. 2) 364 The strain is applied..on the palm, at a spot which, measured from the extremity of the bill, is one-third of the distance between it and the centre of the crown.

5. *Comb.* ***bill-clappering, -fencing, -snapping.*** **bill-fish** (*Belone truncata*), a small anadromous sea-fish of N. America. Also called Sea-pike, Silver Gar-fish, etc.; †**bil-fodur**, ? bill-fodder; **bill-twisted** *a.*, having a twisted bill.

c **1350** *Will. Palerne* 1858 His bag wiþ his bilfodur wiþ þe best be lafte. **1649** G. DANIEL *Trinarch* To Rdr. 148 From some Trees Byll-twisted Barnacles, ripen to Geese. **1782** P. H. BRUCE *Mem.* XII. 424 The sea hereabouts [Bahamas, etc.] abounds with fish unknown to us in Europe..bill-fish, hound-fish, etc. **1936** *Brit. Birds* XXIX. 327, I have had the opportunity of seeing 'bill-fencing'. **1937** *Brit. Birds* XXXI. 239 The weird bill-clappering and strident cries of old and young Herons. **1949** *Ibid.* XLII. 286 Bill-snapping: loud snapping of the mandibles is used as a threat when attempting to drive other birds—of any species—from food, or as a prelude to attack. **1957** BANNERMAN *Birds Brit. Isles* VI. 13 One or two days later..courtship [of white storks] begins. This takes the form of bill-clappering and the assumption of curious postures.

bill (bıl), *sb.*[3] Forms: 4–7 byll(e, bille, 6–7 byl, bil, 4– bill. [ME. *bille*, in AFr. *bille*, (AngloL. *billa*, an alteration of L. *bulla* in its mediæval sense. In cl.L., *bulla* was 'a bubble, a boss, a stud, an amulet for the neck'; whence, in med.L., 'a seal' esp. 'the seal appended to a charter,' etc.; thence, *transf.* 'a document furnished with a seal' e.g. a charter, a papal 'bull'; and, by extension, any official or formal document, 'a bill, schedule, memorandum, note, paper.' It was in these latter senses that *bulla* became in England *billa, bille.* Being a word of common use (see Du Cange), *bulla* was probably pronounced with *ü*, passing into Eng. *y, i*; though no direct evidence of this has been found.]

†**1. a.** A written document (originally sealed), a statement in writing (more or less formal); a letter, note, memorandum (cf. BILLET *sb.*) *Obs.* in general sense, but retained in numerous legal and commercial terms: see 10.

[H. KNYGHTON *Chron.* III. i. an. 1272 Decanus Lincolniensis proposuit unam billam excusatoriam.] *c* **1374**

CHAUCER *Troylus* II. 1081 Scripe nor bill..that touchith suche matere, Ne bring me none! **1393** GOWER *Conf.* III. 304 But eche of hem to make a bille He bad and write his own wille. **1424** *E.E. Wills* (1882) 55 I..declare my last will in þis bille. **1425** *Paston Lett.* 5 I. 21, I send you, closed in this bille the copie of un frendly lettre. *c* **1460** *Stans Puer* 92 in *Babees Bk.* (1868) 32 Go, litel bille, bareyn of eloquence, Pray yonge children that the shal see or Reede, etc. **1512** *Act 4 Hen. VIII*, xi, Every thing..expressed in this bill of peticion. **1531** W. T. *Epist. John* 10 It is called..an Epistle because it is sent as a letter or a byll. **1599** HAKLUYT *Voy.* II. I. 25 To cast ouer the wals into the campe of the Christians, certaine bils written in Hebrue, Greeke, and Latine. **1727** SWIFT *Furth. Acc. E. Curll* Wks. 1755 III. I. 156 To whom he gave the following bill of directions, where to find them. **1755** MAGENS *Insurances* II. 122 A Bill containing the Reasons of the Citation shall be left with the Person that is summoned, or at his House.

†**b.** A letter or 'bull' of the Pope. *Obs.*

1450 MYRC 709 All þat falsen the popes lettres or billes or seales. *c* **1500** *Cocke Lorelles B.* 7 The pope darlaye hath graunted in his byll That euery brother may do what he wyll.

†**c.** A writing circulated reflecting upon any person; the analogue of the later printed pamphlet or lampoon. *Obs.*

1424 *Paston Lett.* 4. I. 13 Manaces of deth..maden..by ..billes rymed in partye. **1532** MORE *Confut. Tindale* Wks. 622/1 By sclaunderous bylles blowe abrode an euyl noughty tale. **1542** UDALL *Erasm. Apoph.* (1877) 273 Augustus had written a great ragmans rewe, or bille, to be soung on Pollio in derision and skorne of hym by name. **1553–87** FOXE *A. & M.* (1596) 812/2 Many billes and rimes were set forth in diuers places against them.

†**d.** A deed. *Obs.*

1548 FORREST *Pleas. Poes.* 95 And then I dare to this Byll sett my hande. *c* **1590** MARLOWE *Faust.* v. 74 Consummatum est; this bill is ended. **1613** R. C. *Table Alph., Scedule*, obligation, or bill of ones hand.

†**2. a.** A formal document containing a petition to a person in authority; a written petition. *Obs.*

[**1321** *Liber Custum.* (Rolls Ser.) 379 Come ils eient requis par bille a voz Justices eiraunz en la Tour de Loundres remedie dun tort.] **1377** LANGL. *P. Pl.* B. XIII. 247 Hadde iche a clerke þat couthe write I wolde caste hym [the pope] a bille. **1423** JAS. I. *King's Q.* lxxxii, A warld of folk..With billis in thaire handis, of one assent Vnto the Iuge thaire playntis to present. **1555** *Fardle Facions* I. v. 56 In the morning..it behoued him to peruse al lettres supplicacions, and billes. **1681** NEVILE *Plato Rediv.* 111 That no Parliament should be dismist, till all the Petitions were answered; That is..till all the Bills (which were then styled Petitions) were finished. **1728** POPE *Dunc.* II. 89 All vain petitions..Amus'd he reads, and then returns the bills.

†**b.** A supplicatory address (not necessarily in writing); a prayer, supplication, request. *Obs.*

c **1386** CHAUCER *Doctor's T.* 166 Doth me right upon this pitous bille, In which I pleyne upon Virginius. *c* **1430** LYDG. *Bochas* VI. i. (1554) 145 b, This was the bille which y John Bochas Made unto Fortune. **1570** *Scot. Poems 16th C.* II. 234 Diligent to heir the pure mannis bill.

†**c.** *to put (up) a bill*: to present a petition.

1387 TREVISA *Higden* Rolls Ser. V. 141 The bishops at Nicæa, putte up billes to þe emperour. **1414** BRAMPTON *Penit. Ps.* xxviii. 11 And mekely puttyth to the this bylle. **1450** *Paston Lett.* I. 153, I cend yow a copy of the bylle that my Lord of Yorke put unto the Kynge.

3. The draft of an Act of Parliament submitted to the legislature for discussion and adoption as an 'Act.' Historically, this has passed through the senses of **a.** A petition to the Sovereign, as in sense 2; **b.** A petition, containing the draft of the act or statute prayed for; **c.** The draft act without the petitionary form, as is now the case with all *public bills*, or such as affect the interests of the public generally. *Private bills*, i.e. such as grant relief to or confer privileges upon individuals or corporations, are still introduced in the form of petitions. The nature and scope of a bill is expressed by such phraseology as 'a bill to reform the representation of the people,' 'a Bill of Indemnity,' a 'Reform Bill,' 'Manchester Waterworks Bill.'

[**1362** LANGL. *P. Pl.* A. v. 45 Thenne cam pees in-to parlement and putte vp a bylle, How þat wrong wilffullich hadde hus wif for-leyen. **1484** *Act 1 Hen. VII* (1780) X. App. 103 Item quædam alia Billa..cum cedula eidem annexa exhibita fuit coram Domino Rege in Parliamento prædicto.] **1512** *Act 4 Hen. VIII*, viii. Pream., To putte forth certeyn bylles in this present parliament. **1577–87** HARRISON *England* II. viii. (1877) 176 The clerke of the parlement, whose office is to read the billes. **1598** SHAKS. *Merry W.* II. i. 29 Ile Exhibit a Bill in the Parliament for the putting downe of men. **1709** *London Gaz.* No. 4534/1 A Message to the House of Commons..to desire the House to come up..to be present at the passing the said Bills into Acts. **1798** T. JEFFERSON *Writ.* (1859) IV. 217 Congress has nothing of any importance before them, except the bill on foreign intercourse. **1813** *Parl. Deb.* in *Examiner* 21 May 328/1 [He] moved, that the Insolvent Debtors' Bill be re-committed. **1858** LD. ST. LEONARDS *Handy Bk. Prop. Law* xxi. 163 The bill..passed the House of Lords. **1884** GLADSTONE in *Standard* 29 Feb. 2/7 We knew..that the Bill must remain a Bill, and could never have become an Act of Parliament.

†**4. a.** *Law.* A written statement of a case; a pleading by the plaintiff or defendant (but generally by the former), e.g. a ***bill of complaint*** in Chancery; an indictment. *Obs.* exc. in certain phrases, chiefly, ***to find a true bill, to ignore the bill***, said of a Grand Jury, whose duty it is, in criminal Assizes, to declare that there is, or is not, sufficient evidence to justify the hearing of a case before the judge and ordinary jury.

c **1400** MAUNDEV. xv. 172 Both partyes writen here Causes in 2 Billes. *c* **1480** *Black Bk. Admiralty* (Rolls) I. 305 [Les querelles et billes de lappellant et du deffendant seront plaidees a la court.] *transl.* The quarell and the billes of the appellant and of the defendant shall be pletid in the Court. **1495** *Act 11 Hen. VII*, vii, Justices..have auctorite..to here and determyn the reherced causes..upon bill before theym. **1531** *Act 23 Hen. VIII*, xv, Any accion, bill, or playnt of trespace. **1607** COWELL *Interpr., Bille* is..a declaration in writing, that expresseth either the griefe and the wrong that the complaynant hath suffered, by the party complayned of, or els some fault, that the party complayned of, hath committed against some law or statute of the common wealth. *Ibid., Ignoramus*, is a word properly vsed by the Grand Enquest..and written vpon the bill. **1660** STANLEY *Hist. Philos.* (1701) 89/1 Anytus..procured Melitus to prefer a bill against him. **1788** J. POWELL *Devises* (1827) II. 485 Sir T. Plumer, M.R...accordingly dismissed the bill.

b. *Scotch Law.* Any summary application by way of petition to the Court of Session.

†**5. a.** A written list or catalogue, an inventory. *Obs.* exc. in specific combinations.

a **1340** HAMPOLE *Prose Tr.* (1866) 7 The abbotte tuke þat byll þat þay ware wrettyn in and lukede thareone. *a* **1400** *Cov. Myst.* (1841) 41 Synne..scrapyth hym out of lyvys bylle, That blyssyd book. *a* **1500** *E.E. Misc.* (1855) 64 Thay schalle be wryttyne in a bylle. **1523** LD. BERNERS *Froiss.* I. xviii. 26 Than the knyghtis..made a byll of their horses, and suche other stuffe as they had lost. **1605** SHAKS. *Macb.* III. i. 100 Whereby he does receiue Particular addition, from the Bill, That writes them all alike.

†**b.** *Med.* A list of drugs, etc. to be mixed to form a medicine, a medical prescription or recipe.

1529 MORE *Comf. agst. Trib.* I. Wks. 1142/2 After the billes made by the greate physicion God, prescrybynge the medicines hymselfe. **1602** WARNER *Alb. Eng.* IX. xliv. (1612) 209 Physitians bylles not Patients but Apothecaries know. **1663** BUTLER *Hud.* I. I. 603 Like him that took the Doctor's Bill And swallow'd it instead o' th' Pill. **1754** SMELLIE *Midwif.* III. 540 The Apothecary..went home to bring the bills.

c. *Naut.* A list of persons appointed to duties.

1830 MARRYAT *King's Own* xiii, Turn the hands up to muster by the quarter-bill. **1840** R. DANA *Bef. Mast* xxiii. 69 Each man had his station. A regular tacking and wearing bill was made out.

d. *Typogr.* A scale or list of the proper quantities of each letter required for a fount.

1824 J. JOHNSON *Typogr.* II. 29 We will now give..a regular bill, perfect in all its sorts. **1875** URE *Dict. Arts* III. 640 Typefounders have a scale or bill, as it is called, of the proportional quantity of each letter required for a fount.

e. At Harrow School, properly, the list of boys; hence, the calling-over of the list. Also *attrib.*

1814 W. C. TREVELYAN *Diary* 25 Jan. in G. T. Warner *Harrow in Prose & Verse* (1913) 107 Locked up at 8 o'clock, placed at the 2 bill. **1815** *Ibid.* 2 Mar. 113 Dr. B showed us a bill of Harrow School for 1770. **1818** N. CARLISLE *Descr. Endowed Gram. Sch. Eng. & Wales* II. 148 The Absences for Bills..are regularly called every Two hours by The Head Master. **1894** *Harrovian* 15 Nov. 103/2 From the Bill-yard to the Old Station. **1894** R. C. WELCH *Harrow Sch. Reg.* 17 Our present Bill Books. **1898** HOWSON & WARNER *Harrow School* 275 The 4 bill in summer is called, part on the cricket-ground (cricket-bill)... At yard-bill the boys pass one by one in bill order before the bill-master of the week, answer their names, touch their hats, and walk on.

f. At Eton College, the punishment-list.

a **1877** SWINBURNE *Lesbia Brandon* (1952) iii. 53, I and another fellow..were so used to our flogging every after twelve, the praepostor of our division wouldn't have dared show up a bill without our two names in it. **1883** J. BRINSLEY-RICHARDS *Seven Yrs. at Eton* v. 46 A perfume which told its tale to their tutors, and caused them to be put in the Bill.

6. A note of charges for goods delivered or services rendered, in which the cost of each item is separately stated; also known as a ***bill of parcels***.

In modern use, confined in this sense to the professions and to retail trade, and implying a demand for payment. In wholesale transactions, an 'invoice,' containing the usual particulars of a bill, is supplied on delivery of the goods, and the formal demand for payment is made by a 'statement of account' sent in when the money is due. *Bill* is however often loosely used for 'invoice,' and *vice versa*.

1420 *E.E. Wills* (1882) 53 þat [they] be paied of their billes for makyng off a liuerey. **1526** TINDALE *Luke* xvi. 6 Take thy bill..and wryte fiftie. **1600** B. JONSON *Ev. Man out of Hum.* IV. v, Farewell, good haberdasher. Well, now, Master Snip, let me see your bill. **1671** *Lex Talionis* 10 Apothecaries Bills, which..amount to very great Sums. **1712** *Lond. Gaz.* No. 5079/3 Several other Notes and Bills of Parcels. **1748** SMOLLETT *Rod. Rand.* lv, I did myself the pleasure of discharging the bill. **1837** DICKENS *Pickw.* x, Call a hackney-coach directly, and bring this lady's bill.

†**7.** A label. *Obs.*

1474 CAXTON *Chesse* 130, I haue put on eche keye a bylle and writyng. **1600** SHAKS. *A.Y.L.* I. ii. 131 Three proper yong men..With bils on their neckes.

8. a. A written or printed advertisement to be passed from hand to hand (hence also called *hand-bill*), or posted up or displayed in some prominent place; a poster, a placard.

1480 CAXTON *Chron. Eng.* ccxiii. 199 The scottes made a bylle that was fastned vpon the chirche dores of seynt petre. **1563** GRINDAL in Strype *Life* (1821) 122 [They] did then daily, but especially on the holidays, set up their bills, inviting to plays. **1599** SHAKS. *Much Ado* I. i. 39 He set vp his bils here in Messina, and challenged Cupid at the flight. **1621** MOLLE *Camerar. Liv. Libr.* IV. xv. 291 It was cried to be hired or sold, and Bils were set up to that purpose. **1666** PEPYS *Diary* (1879) IV. 193 Walked..to the Temple thinking to have seen a play..but there missing of any bills concluded there was none. **1678** N. WANLEY *Wond.* VI. xxix. 619/2 Bills set upon the Church-doors to inquire for things lost. **1710** ADDISON *Tatler* No. 240 ¶6 To be seen both upon the Sign where he lived, and in the Bills which he distributed. **1727** SWIFT *Gulliver* II. ii, Put out bills in the usual form, containing an exact description. **1836** DICKENS *Sk. Boz* iii, A newly-posted bill informed us the house was again 'To Let.'

†**b.** An announcement to be publicly read. *Obs.*

1642 *Scots Scouts Disc.* in *Phœnix* (1732) I. 464 One Sunday, at one Mr. Shute's Parish Church, a Bill was delivered that John Commonwealth of England, being sick of the Scots Disease, desires the Prayers of the Congregation. **1727** SWIFT *Furth. Acc. E. Curll* Wks. 1755 III. I. 155 She privately put a bill into several churches, desiring the prayers of the congregation for a wretched stationer.

c. A list of the items on a (theatre) programme; hence, the entertainment itself; a group of entertaining items. orig. *U.S.* Cf. quot. 1666 for sense 8 a, and PROGRAM(ME *sb.* 2 a (esp. quot. 1823). So ***double bill***, a programme consisting of two plays, films, etc.; so ***triple bill***; also *transf.*

1851 H. MELVILLE *Moby Dick* I. i. 8 This part of the bill ..must have run something like this: 'Grand Contested Election for the Presidency of the United States. Whaling Voyage by one Ishmael. Bloody Battle in Affghanistan.' **1855** W. B. WOOD *Recoll. Stage* 155 Warren had prepared.. a strong bill..and announced the 'Foundling of the Forest', with the 'Budget of Blunders'. **1875** *Chicago Tribune* 13 Sept. 7/3 Hooley's Theatre..California Minstrels, in a Bill of Rare Ethiopian Sketches. **1891** G. B. SHAW *Quint. of Ibsenism* 147 Mr Thorne..was the first leading manager who ventured to put a play of Ibsen's into his evening bill. **1895** —— in *Sat. Rev.* 11 May, I hope I have not conveyed an impression that the triple bill makes a bad evening's entertainment. **1938** *Encycl. Brit. Bk. of Yr.* 423/1 Theatres widely adopted the 'double bill policy', which meant offering two picture dramas on a programme for a single admission. **1956** C. B. PURDOM in *Shaw's Lett. to Granville Barker* 184 The dramatist was proposing that the piece should go with Galsworthy's *Eldest Son* into the bill at the Kingsway. **1959** T. S. ELIOT *Elder Statesman* II. 73 It's a very long time since the name of Maisie Mountjoy Topped the bill in revue. **1962** *Listener* 27 Sept. 495/2 Apple jam by itself can be dull, but there are plenty of variations... For a triple bill there is apple, pear, and quince.

d. ***to fill the bill***: to fulfil the necessary requirements; to come up to the requisite standard. orig. *U.S.* (Cf. FILL *v.* 7 c.)

1861 *Trans. Ill. Agric. Soc. 1860* IV. 471 Austin.. Seedling, Dr. W. hopes well from because of its great vigor, but doubts if it fills the bill. **1880** A. A. HAYES *New Colorado* (1881) ii. 23 With this requirement in view does Colorado 'fill the Bill'? **1890** *Harper's Mag.* Feb. 441/1 They filled the bill according to their lights. **1904** W. H. SMITH *Promoters* i. 20, I don't think I ever saw a word used that..filled the bill quite so completely as this word 'experimentally' will do for us. **1954** W. S. MAUGHAM *Ten Novels* iv. 75 He felt that he owed it to himself to have a mistress he could love, and whose position would add to his prestige. He decided that Alexandrine Daru, Pierre's wife, would fill the bill.

e. *slang.* (See quots.)

1930 'A. ARMSTRONG' *Taxi!* xii. 164 The 'bill' is the driver's licence, generally with reference to the original held by the man's proprietor, and to 'draw your bill' is to ask your employer for your licence, i.e., leave his employment. **1939** H. HODGE *Cab, Sir?* xv. 217 'The Bill' is the Metropolitan Police Cab-driver's licence—as distinct from the ordinary County Council driving licence.

9. a. (More fully **bill of exchange**). A written order by the writer or 'drawer' to the 'drawee' (the person to whom it is addressed) to pay a certain sum on a given date to the 'drawer,' or to a third person named in the bill, known as the 'payee.'

A true bill of exchange is given in consideration of value received (and this is usually stated upon the bill), but a bill is sometimes drawn, not against value received, but merely as a means of raising money on credit, and is then known as an *accommodation bill* (see ACCOMMODATION 8).

1579 FENTON *Guicciard.* VI. (1599) 237 The merchants making difficultie..to accept the billes of exchange that were sent out of Fraunce. **1661** PEPYS *Diary* 27 Mar., I did get him to promise me some money upon a bill of exchange. **1682** SCARLETT *Exchanges* 23. **1713** STEELE *Guardian* No. 2 He gave me a bill upon his goldsmith in London. **1768** BLACKSTONE *Comm.* II. 466. **1809** R. LANGFORD *Introd. Trade* 20 An Inland Bill is when the drawer and person drawn upon live in the same country or kingdom. **1848** THACKERAY *Van. Fair* xviii, His bills were protested; his act of bankruptcy formal. **1880** B. PRICE in *Fraser's Mag.* May 668 Bills impart a valuable convenience to trade..they borrow the goods without payment for a time more or less long.

†**b.** Loosely used for: A promissory note. *Obs.* Hence, ***bill of debt*** or ***bill obligatory***: a bill acknowledging a debt and promising to meet it at a specified date. Also applied (with specification) to various promises to pay at a future date, or at sight, issued by Banks, and by the Government; cf. BANK-BILL, EXCHEQUER BILL.

1613 DEKKER *Bankrouts Banq.* Wks. 1884–5 III. 371 Next, came in Bils obligatory, a thousand in a cluster. **1685** BAXTER *Paraphr. Philemon* 19, I here give thee a Bill under my hand, that I will repay all that he oweth thee. **1711** *Lond. Gaz.*, No. 4869/3 Navy, Victualling, Ordnance, and Transport Bills. **1721** *King's Sp.* 19 Oct. in *Lond. Gaz.*, The Navy and Victualling Bills are at very high Discount.

c. = NOTE *sb.*[2] 18 a. Cf. *dollar-bill*. orig. and chiefly *U.S.*

1682 in A. McF. Davis *Tracts Mass. Bay* (1902) 7 Credit pass'd in Fund, by Book, & Bills, (as afore) will fully supply the defect of Money. 1790 *Deb. Congress* II. 2055 The bills and notes of the bank .. shall be receivable in all payments to the United States. 1852 Mrs. Stowe *Uncle Tom's C.* 438 She unlocked the desk, took from it a roll of bills, which she counted over rapidly. 1854 A. E. Baker *Gloss. Northants Words* I. 49 *Bills*, bank notes; all kinds of paper money. 1924 E. O'Neill *Welded* II. 145 He takes a bill from his pocket and holds it out to her—contemptuously. 1947 —— *Iceman Cometh* I. 46, I t'rows down a fifty-dollar bill like it was trash paper. 1953 *Manch. Guardian Weekly* 29 Oct. 7 This bold proclamation can be found on every dollar bill.

10. With specification: **bill of costs** (see quot. 1911); **bill of fare**, a list of dishes to be served at a banquet, or which may be ordered at a restaurant (in the latter case with the prices attached), a 'menu'; often *fig.* a programme; **bill of goods** (orig. and chiefly U.S.), a consignment of merchandise; so in colloq. phr. *to sell* (someone) *a bill of goods*: to persuade (someone) to accept something undesirable; to swindle; **bill of health**, an official certificate given to the master of a vessel sailing from a port liable to infection, stating whether at the time of sailing any infectious disease existed on board or in the port (hence a *clean bill*: one certifying total absence of infection; *suspected* or *touched bill*, *foul bill*); also a similar document required of travellers in some foreign ports; **bill of lading**, an official detailed receipt given by the master of a merchant vessel to the person consigning the goods, by which he makes himself responsible for their safe delivery to the consignee. This document, being the legal proof of ownership of the goods, is often deposited with a creditor as security for money advanced; cf. CHARTER-PARTY; †**bill of mortality** or **weekly bill**, a periodically published official return of the deaths (later, also of the births) in a certain district; such a return began to be published weekly by the London Company of Parish Clerks in 1592 for 109 parishes in and around London; hence this district (the precise limits of which were often modified) became known as 'within the bills of mortality'; **bill of sale**, a written instrument effecting a transfer of personal property; *spec.* a document given as security for money borrowed, authorizing the lender to seize the property in case of the non-payment of the money by a specified time; **bill of sight**, permission from the custom-house officers to land goods for inspection in their presence, when, from want of precise information, the consignee is unable to enter them accurately; **bill of store** (see quots.); †**bill of sufferance** (see quot.). Also *bill of attainder*, *attorney* (= letter of attorney), *bill of conformity*, *credit*, *debt*, *discharge*, *exceptions*, *indictment*, *payment*, *receipt*, *remembrance*, *review*, *rights*, etc. for which see these words.

1815 (*title*), *Bills of costs and allowances, in the Court of King's Bench, according to the present scale of allowance; with a precedent for affidavits of increase. 1826 *New Monthly Mag.* II. 109 [He] made the invitation an item in his bill of costs. 1869 *Yng. Men Gt. Brit.* 14 May 260/2 An attorney, about to furnish a bill of costs. 1911 *Encycl. Brit.* III. 932/2 A *Bill of Costs* is an account setting forth the charges and disbursements incurred by a solicitor in the conduct of his client's business. The delivery of a bill of costs is by statute a condition necessary before the solicitor can sue upon it. [1577–87 Harrison *England* II. xv. (1877) 272 Which bill [of dishes] some doo call a memoriall.] 1636 Massinger *Bashf. Lovers* Prol., 'Tis no crime .. To please so many with one *bill of fare. 1748 Mrs. S. Harrison *House-kprs. Pocket-bk.* Pref., The Bill of Fare is a new and admirable contrivance. 1861 Mrs. Beeton *Bk. Househ. Managem.* 954 A menu or bill of fare should be laid by the side of each guest. 1927 E. O'Neill *Marco Millions* I. 41 Selling a big *bill of goods hereabouts, I'll wager, you old rascals? 1945 E. Ford *Larry Scott* xii. 120 Don't let Jim sell you a bill of goods. 1968 *Globe & Mail* (Toronto) 17 Feb. 8/3 There was no production bonus... We were sold a bill of goods. 1644 Evelyn *Mem.* 12 Oct., Having procur'd a *bill of health (without which there is no admission at any towne in Italy) we embarq'd on the 12th. 1753 Hanway *Trav.* (1762) I. v. lx. 279 Upon his giving us a bill of health, I went on board. 1851 McCulloch *Dict. Comm.* 1084 Were the said bills of health clean, unclean, or suspected? 1599 Hakluyt II. II. 44 We .. caused one of them to fetch vp his *bils of lading. 1627 Capt. Smith *Seaman's Gram.* xiii. 62 Come aboord .. with their .. cocket, or bils of loading. 1875 Jevons *Money* (1878) 207 A bill of lading entitles the legal holder of it to certain cases or packages of goods. 1645 Bp. Hall *Remed. Discontent.* 26 Pleasure dies in the birth, and is not therefore worthy to come into this *bill of Mortality. 1681 *Lond. Gaz.* No. 1651/4 The second of September was taken up within the Bills of Mortality, a Deal Box. 1698 Congreve *Way of W.* III. xv, We could have the gazette .. and the Weekly Bill. 1709 Steele *Tatler* No. 54 ¶7 Living within the Bills of Mortality. 1724 *Abstr. Act 10 Geo. I.* in *Lond. Gaz.* No. 6270/7 All Chocolate .. must be brought to be stamped .. within the Weekly Bills in 14 Days. 1854 Thackeray *Newcomes* viii, He was as scrupulously whited as any sepulchre in the whole bills of mortality. 1608 Dekker *Belman Lond.* Wks. (Grosart) III. 150 By *bils of sale .. get the goods of honest Citizens into their hands. 1765 *Phil. Trans.* LV. 46 He sold the boy to his present master .. I saw the bill of sale. 1875 Bedford *Sailor's Pocket Bk.* (ed. 2) 225 The Bill of Sale is the instrument by which a Vessel is transferred to a purchaser. 1852 McCulloch *Dict. Comm.* 147 The East India Company are authorised .. to enter goods by *bill of sight. 1670 Blount *Law Dict.*, **Bill of Store*, is a kind of Licence granted at the Custom-house to Merchants, or others, to carry such Stores or Provision as are necessary for their Voyage Custom-free. 1833 *Act 3 Will. IV*, lii, It shall be lawful to re-import into the United Kingdom .. any goods .. which shall have been legally exported .. and to enter the same by bill of store. 1670 Blount *Law Dict.*, **Bill of sufferance*, is a Licence granted at the Custom-house to a Merchant, to suffer him to trade from one English Port to another, without paying Custom.

11. *Comb.* and *Attrib.*, as (in sense 3) ***bill-drafter***, ***-drafting***; (in sense 8) ***bill-poster***, ***-posting***, ***-sticker***, ***-sticking***, ***-patched***, etc.; (in sense 9) ***bill-book***, ***-broker***, ***-broking***, ***-discounter***, ***-holder***, ***-trade***; (in sense 2) †***bill-maker***; **bill-book**, *spec.* in U.S., a pocket-book; **bill chamber** (sense 4), a department of the Scottish Court of Session, to which suitors may repair at all times (including vacations) in emergencies requiring summary proceeding; **bill-clerk** *U.S.*, a clerk who deals with the bills at a hotel; **billfold(er** *U.S.*, a note-case or wallet; **bill-head** (sense 6), paper ruled for a tradesman's bills, having his name, etc. printed at the top; **bill-holder**, (*a*) a person who holds a bill or acceptance; (*b*) *U.S.* a container for bank-notes, etc.

1774 Henley in *Phil. Trans.* LXIV. 426 A large book .. ruled in the manner of a *bill-book, used by tradesmen. 1895 *Montgomery Ward Catal.* 101/1 Seal grain leather bill book, size $3\frac{1}{2} \times 8$ inches. 1833 Ht. Martineau *Vanderput & S.* iv. 58 The *bill-brokers can tell how nearly the debts of different countries balance each other. 1764 Wesley *Jrnl.* 2 July (1827) III. 179 That wretched trade of *bill-broking. 1857 *Sat. Rev.* III. 345 To create a fortune by banking, brewing, or bill-broking. 1699 Lord Reay *Let.* 10 Oct. in *Pepys Corr.* (1926) I. 190 Direct it to the care of Mr Robert Menzies, to be found att the *Bill Chamber in Edinburgh. 1838 W. Bell *Dict. Law Scotl.* 99 By 53 Geo. III. c. 64, §2, it is enacted that the junior judge in the Court of Session shall officiate permanently in the Bill Chamber during the sitting of the court. 1901 *Daily Chron.* 10 Oct. 3/5 Paying such surplusage to the *bill-clerk, or the head-porter. 1866 Crump *Banking* 135 A very common custom among bankers .. who style themselves *bill-discounters. 1886 P. Robinson *Teetotum Trees* 65 The most experienced of *bill-draughters. 1894 *Westm. Gaz.* 6 Feb. 2/2 The kind of mistake for which even a Bill-drafter can hardly be expected to provide. 1895 *Ibid.* 8 Jan. 2/2 Ministers have led .. a quiet, if busy and *Bill-drafting, existence. 1895 *Montgomery Ward Catal.* 100/3 Pocket books .. 4 pockets and *bill fold. 1914 C. E. Walk *Green Seal* xxii. 283 Here, perhaps, was a surer passport to my goal than the tickets reposing in my bill-fold. 1919 H. Leverage *White Cipher* 43 Sir Richard drew from his inner vest-pocket a thin bill-fold. 1951 *Catal. of Exhibits, Festival of Britain* 57/2 Woman's billfold. 1961 J. Steinbeck *Winter of our Discontent* I. 40 From his side pocket he brought a billfold, a rich and beautiful affair of pin seal. 1909 'O. Henry' *Options* (1916) 35 He drew out his *bill-folder to pay the cabman. 1845 J. W. Norris *Chicago Directory* 136 (D.A.E.), Circulars, *Bill Heads, Hand Bills. 1910 A. Bennett *Clayhanger* I. iii. 21 Nobody heard romance in the puffing of the hidden steam-engine multiplying catalogues and billheads. 1830 G. Colman *Random Rec.* I. viii. 271 The *bill-holders .. were to be paid. 1847 C. Addison *Contracts* II. v. §1 (1883) 783 Securities .. available to the bill-holders if both drawer and acceptor become insolvent. 1890 Webster, *Bill holder*, .. a device by means of which bills, etc., are held. 1929 E. Rice *Street Scene* II. 176 He .. carries a large black-covered bill-holder. 1529 More *Supplic. Souls* Wks. 302 They had leuer see theire *bylmaker burned, than their supplicacion spedde. 1599 Marston *Sco. Villanie* III. ix. 218 Th' Ape .. is as malecontent As a *bill-patch't doore. 1864 *Times* 24 Dec., A corps of *bill-posters, painters, etc., to put advertisements on the prominent rocks. 1869 J. R. Browne *Adv. Apache Country* 352 *Bill-posting is one of the fine arts. 1895 in *N. & Q.* (1941) CLXXXI. 159/1 One of the largest Bill-posting Firms in the World. 1774 *Westm. Mag.* II. 323 *Bill-stickers, pickpockets, and chimney-sweepers. 1862 Shirley *Nugæ Crit.* §2. 117 Written in large and prominent type, like that employ'd by bill-stickers. 1851 Dickens *Bill-sticking* in *Househ. Words* 22 Mar. 604/1 Several *bill-sticking companies have started. 1864 *Realm* 23 Mar. 6 With .. the progress of civilisation, bill-sticking has expanded into bill-posterism. 1791 Wesley *Wks.* 1872 VIII. 309 That base practice of raising money by coining notes (commonly called the *bill-trade).

bill, *sb.*^{4} *rare.* [For *beel*, *beeal*, dial. form of BELL, BELLOW.] Bellowing; the boom of the bittern.

1789 Wordsw. *Even. Walk* 21 When first the bittern's hollow bill Was heard.

Bill, *sb.*^{5} *slang.* [Shortened f. OLD BILL 2.] The police-force; a policeman. Freq. preceded by *the*.

[1939 H. Hodge *Cab, Sir?* xv. 217 'Old Bill' is an extraordinarily profitable fare—someone who not only wants to go a long way, but also gives a big tip... '*The* Bill' is the Metropolitan Police Cab-driver's licence—as distinct from the ordinary County Council driving licence.] 1969 *Daily Mirror* 10 Oct. 18/3 *Bill*, the police. 1975 *Daily Express* 4 Apr. 6/8, I listened to this banging and I said: 'That's no cat, that's the Bill'. 1979 *Brit. Jrnl. Photogr.* 1 June 523/1 There wasn't going to be no questions asked in the House about some working-class kid getting hisself duffed up by the Bill if said Bill got his old man too chicken-shit to say a dicky-bird about it. 1986 *Telegraph* (Brisbane) 31 July 35/3 'The Bill' takes place in the tough streets of Wapping, where .. a policeman's day may begin catching a pickpocket and end up saving a life.

bill (bɪl), *v.*^{1} [f. BILL *sb.*^{1}] *trans.* To work at or on with a bill; to hoe, hack, chop, lop.

c 1440 *Promp. Parv.* 36 Byllen wythe mattokys, *ligonizo, marro.* 1647 H. More *Ad Paron.* Poems 319 Busily billing the rough outward rinde. 1833 M. Scott *Tom Cringle* xix. 534 A small footpath that had been billed in the bush.

bill, *v.*^{2} Forms: 3 **billen**, 4 **bilen**, 5 **byll-en**, **-yn**, (**bollyn**), 7 **bile**, 6– **bill**. [f. BILL *sb.*^{2}]

†**1.** *intr.* To strike with the bill; to peck. *Obs.*

c 1220 *Bestiary* 82 in *O.E. Misc.* 3 Đanne goð he [the eagle] to a ston, and he billeð ðer on, billeð til his bec biforn haueð ðe wrengðe forloren. 1398 Trevisa *Barth. De P.R.* XII. xxxii, The sparow .. biteþ and bileth [1535 byllyth] for to haue nestes of swalowes. *c* 1440 *Promp. Parv.* 36 Bollyn or jowyn [*v.r.* byllen or iobbyn] wythe the bylle as byrdys, *rostro.* *a* 1678 Marvell *Unfort. Lover* 51 As one cormorant fed him, still Another on his heart did bill.

†**b.** *trans.* with *out*, *away*, etc.

1496 *Dives & Paup.* (W. de W.) IV. iii. 163/1 She [the Pellycane] beteth & bylleth and casteth them out of her company.

2. To stroke bill with bill (as doves).

1592 Shaks. *Ven. & Ad.* 366 Like two silver doves that sit a-billing. 1637 Heywood *Dialogues* 309, I observ'd but late Two Turtles bill, and either court it's mate. 1687 Dryden *Hind & P.* III. 950 Voracious Birds, that hotly Bill and breed. 1850 Mrs. Jameson *Leg. Monast. Ord.* (1863) 20 Two doves billing upon the roof above.

3. *transf.* To caress, make show of affection; usually (of reciprocal action) ***to bill and coo***.

1606 Shaks. *Tr. & Cr.* III. ii. 60 What, billing againe? 1678 Butler *Hud.* III. i. 687 Still amorous, and fond, and billing, Like Philip and Mary on a shilling. 1712 Steele *Spect.* No. 300 ¶1 Tom Faddle and his pretty spouse wherever they come are billing at such a Rate. 1854 Thackeray *Newcomes* I. 295 Jenny and Jessamy .. billing and cooing in an arbour.

bill, *v.*^{3} [f. BILL *sb.*^{3}]

†**1. a.** *trans.* To enter (in a bill, book, catalogue, account, or reckoning). *Obs.*

c 1305 *Leg. Holy Rood* (1871) 138 Pardoun in book is billed. 1615 Bp. Hall *Content.* (1645) 58 There is none of all our cates here, but must be billed up. 1629 H. Burton *Babel no Beth.* 52 The Authours billed and catalogued by Brierly. 1656 Jenkyn *On Jude* (1845) 85 The impenitent are billed and booked by God, and at length God will call in his debts.

b. *U.S.* To enter in a railway book or way-bill; to 'book.'

1867 *Vermont Rep.* XL. 326 The station agent .. billed the plaintiff's goods through to C. 1881 *Chicago Times* 16 Apr., There were four hundred cars of grain billed to St. Louis. 1883 *St. James's Gaz.* 15 Mar., It was a young lady .. about nineteen years of age, and billed from Selma, Alabama, to New York.

2. To enter (a person) in a list (e.g. of soldiers for service), to enroll. *Obs.* exc. *arch.*

1460 Capgrave *Chron.* (1858) 278 And officeres inquired whi he was so bold for to bille hem. 1542 Udall *Erasm. Apoph.* 190a There was one persone bewraied, that had billed hymself in the noumbre of the sickefolkes. 1567 Grindal *Let.* Wks. (1843) 292 He might bill three or four grave men, whereof her Majesty might make choice. 1633 T. Adams *Exp. 2 Pet.* ii. 3 As if they were booked, enrolled, and billed to this confusion. 1910 Masefield *Pompey* 22 Send out your press. Bill every able-bodied man. Bill the women if the men won't come.

†**3.** To make (one) the subject or object of a bill; to libel, lampoon; to indict; to petition. *Obs.*

c 1450 *Pol. Poems* (1859) II. 228 Yt is myche lesse harme to bylle thanne to kylle. 1537 *State Papers Hen. VIII*, I. 547 We haue neither billed any suche nomber of persounes .. ne purpose to call uppe any oon persoune. 1728 Ramsay *Wks.* (1848) III. 137 Poor Pousies .. bill'd the judge, that he wad please To give them the remaining cheese.

4. To announce or advertise by bill. Also *fig.*

1694 R. L'Estrange *Fables* cccc. (ed. 6) 429 A Composition that he Bill'd about, under the name of a Sovereign Antidote. 1871 *Daily News* 21 Mar., At the Opera to-night Flick und Flock is 'billed.' 1884 *Manch. Exam.* 1 Oct. 5/5 The leading feature of the Pall Mall Gazette 'special' .. so loudly billed to-night. 1934 E. Bowen *Cat Jumps* 159 She was billed, it appeared, for yet another confession. 1963 *Listener* 21 Mar. 484/2 He [*sc.* Kenyatta] is so much more the Kikuyu, and the older Kikuyu, than the national leader he is billed to become.

5. To plaster over, occupy, or crowd with bills.

1821 P. Egan *Real Life in London* ix. 158 The practice of advertising and billing the town has become so common. 1851 *Househ. Wds.* II. 601 All traces of the broken windows were billed out, the doors were billed across. 1884 *Harper's Mag.* Sept. 509/2 The .. agent thought this town .. would be a good place for his man, and so he 'billed' it.

6. To send a bill or account to; to charge.

1867 Trollope *Last Chron.* xxxii, As for billing my first cousin, which your wife is, I should as soon think of sending in an account to my own. 1953 'S. Ransome' *Hear no Evil* (1954) vi. 65 If the money doesn't come through, please bill me. 1956 'N. Shute' *Beyond Black Stump* 40 If there's a scratch on it, I'll bill you for it. 1960 *Times* 12 Aug. 14/4 It [*sc.* photocopying] is used by doctors to bill their patients.

bill, obs. Sc. form of BULL.

billable ('bɪləb(ə)l), *a.* *rare*$^{-1}$. [f. BILL *v.*^{3} + -ABLE.] Liable to be served with a bill; indictable.

1579 *Rep. Commis. Border Causes* in *Egerton Papers* 234 Certifying such as shall resett the same upon their ground, that they shalbe billable for their so doing.

billabong ('bɪləbɒŋ). *Austral.* Also 9 **billibong**, **billy-bonn**. [ad. *Billibang*, Aboriginal name of Bell River, f. *billa* water + *bang* of uncertain

meaning.] A branch or effluent of a river, forming a blind channel, backwater, or stagnant pool.

[**1836** T. L. MITCHELL *Jrnl.* 11 Apr. in *Three Exped. Interior E. Australia* (1838) II. ii. 30 A small watercourse, then dry, and named Billibang, skirts the eastern side of the hill.] **1865** W. HOWITT *Discov. Australia* I. 298 Their way on was intercepted..by..what the Major calls.. anabranches of the river, but which the natives call billibongs, channels coming out of a stream and returning into it again. **1866** W. LANDSBOROUGH *Explor. Australia* vi. 31 In the south, such a creek as the Macadam is termed a *billy-bonn*, from the circumstance of the water carrier returning from it with his pitcher (*billy*) empty (*bong*, literally *dead*). **1896** H. LAWSON *While Billy Boils* (1897) 91 While out boating one Sunday afternoon on a billabong across the river. **1911** C. E. W. BEAN *'Dreadnought' of Darling* xiv. 133 Australian rivers..often have a long arm or two wandering off into the plain, and either coming back to the river again in the end or else straying off for perhaps a hundred miles and ending nowhere in particular. Those arms are what they call billabongs. *a* **1917** A. B. PATERSON *Waltzing Matilda* 1 Once a jolly swagman camped by a billabong. **1950** 'N. SHUTE' *Town like Alice* iii. 81 You get a sandy billabong, and you'll get water there by digging.

billage ('bɪlɪdʒ), *sb.* A variant of BILGE.

1627 CAPT. SMITH *Seaman's Gram.* ii. 4 A ships Billage is the breadth of the floore when she doth lie aground. **1708** HARRIS *Lexicon Techn., Bildge,* of a Ship, is the bottom of her Floor..and *Billage* is the breadth of her Floor when she lies aground.

'billage, *v.* [See prec.] To BILGE.

1627 CAPT. SMITH *Seaman's Gram.* ix. 41 The ship may.. Billage on a rocke. **1628** DIGBY *Voy. Medit.* 43 My boate was billaged and all of vs tumbled in the sea.

billament, variant of BILIMENT, *Obs.*

billander, obs. form of BILANDER.

†**'billard.** *Obs.* or *dial.* [Derivation unknown: it is not easy to connect it in sense with F. *billard* stick with a knob or hook.]

1. The Coal-fish, a fish allied to the Cod; cf. BILLET *sb.*³

1661 RAY *Itin.* (1760) 173 There are the same sorts of Fish taken at Whitby as at Scarborough; and some others they named to us, as Dabs, Billards. **1753** CHAMBERS *Cycl. Supp., Billard,* in ichthyology, an English name for the young fish of the coal-fish..up to a certain size. **1865** COUCH *Brit. Fishes* III. 84.

2. (See quot.) [probably distinct from 1.]

1669 WORLIDGE *Syst. Agric.* (1681) 322 *Billard* is in some places used for an imperfect or Bastard Capon. **1674** RAY *S. & E.C. Wds.* 59 *Billard,* a Bastard Capon. *Suss.*

billards, obs. form of BILLIARDS.

bill'bergia, bil'bergia. [Named after Billberg, a Swedish botanist.] A genus of ornamental and fragrant epiphytes (N.O. *Bromeliaceæ*), natives of the forests of tropical America.

1858 *Penny Cycl.* 2nd Supp. 66/1 Billbergia, a genus of plants..all natives of South America. **1882** *Garden* 17 June 428/2 The cultivation of Bilbergias is so very simple.

billberry, variant of BILBERRY.

bill-board, billboard ('bɪlbɔəd). orig. *U.S.* [f. BILL *sb.* 8 + BOARD *sb.* 2 b.] **1.** A board to which notices, posters, advertisements, etc., are affixed; a notice-board or hoarding.

1851 W. K. NORTHALL *Bef. & Behind Curtain* 15 The bill-boards of the Park..still continued to style the Park 'The Theatre'. *a* **1877** in Bartlett *Dict. Amer.* (ed. 4) 44 People who fail to edit a bill-board are firmly convinced that they could edit a newspaper. **1950** *Manch. Guardian Weekly* 19 Jan. 10/3 Billboards bearing the strange advice: 'Go East, Young Man, Go East!' **1950** O. NASH *Fam. Reunion* 131, I think that I shall never see A billboard lovely as a tree. Indeed, unless the billboards fall I'll never see a tree at all. **1954** N. COWARD *Future Indef.* IV. 247 Outside a canteen was a billboard announcing 'To-Nite Bing Crosby and Dorothy Lamour'.

b. *attrib.*; **bill-board pass,** a free theatre ticket issued to tradespeople who allow advertisements to be displayed on their premises.

1890 'BIFF' HALL *Turnover Club* 100 The holder of a bill-board pass addressed the Count Bozenta as 'Mr. Modjeska'. **1902** W. N. HARBEN *Abner Daniel* 58 Jack Ass in bill-board letters would come nearer to it than anything that occurs to me now. **1963** *New Yorker* 1 June 24/1 Exquisitely faithful duplications of bill-board lettering. **1967** *Listener* 3 Aug. 156/2 Garish and absurd as a billboard likeness.

2. An aerial array resembling a bill-board in appearance, consisting of a number of dipoles mounted in front of a large vertical metal reflector. Freq. *attrib.*

1950 J. D. KRAUS *Antennas* iv. 118 A 'billboard' type of array..having many dipole antennas carrying equal currents. *Ibid.* xii. 327 (*caption*) Array of ½-wavelength elements with flat sheet reflector (billboard or mattress antenna). **1963** *Life* 1 Mar. 20/1 Dye Main's 60-foot-high radio antennas—the technicians call them 'billboards'—make sure these warning signals get through. **1966** *Electronics* 17 Oct. 138/3 The tropo routes use 60-foot billboard antennas. At some of the stations in Turkey, the tropo paths require 120-foot billboards.

billed, *ppl. a.*¹ [f. BILL *sb.*¹ and ².] Furnished with a bill; having a beak, spike, etc. (Usually in composition, as ***long-, broad-, soft-billed,*** etc.)

1399 LANGL. *Rich. Redeles.* iii. 37 All billid breddis þat þe bough spareth. **1513** DOUGLAS *Æneis* XI. xiii. 20 The weill stelit and braid billit ax. **1582** D. INGRAM *Narr.* in Arb. *Garner* V. 257 It is bigger than a goose, billed like a showeler. **1625** BACON *Goodness, Ess.* (Arb.) 201 A longe Billed Fowle. **1770** G. WHITE *Selborne* xxxvi, Hard-billed birds subsist on seeds. **1847** CARPENTER *Zool.* §385 *Dentirostres,* or toothed-billed Birds, which are characterized by a notch or tooth near the extremity of the upper mandible.

billed (bɪld), *ppl. a.*² [f. BILL *v.*³]

1. Entered in a bill or list; *spec.* (see quot.).

1873 W. W. KNOLLYS *Dict. Mil. Terms, Billed,* a term exclusively confined to the Foot Guards. It means that a man's name is placed in the list or bill of those who are to undergo drill and confinement to barracks. Hence a 'billed man'.

2. Announced or advertised by a bill. (See BILL *v.*³ 4.)

1895 *Westm. Gaz.* 18 July 8/1 The..train reached Aberdeen at 6.46..or fourteen minutes before the billed time of arrival. **1897** *Daily News* 22 May 5/7 The establishment of a boldly billed enclosure for lost children.

billement(e, variant of BILIMENT. *Obs.*

†**'biller.** *Sc. Obs.* [? a. F. *belier*, in 16th c. also *bellier* ram.] ? A ram.

c **1560** A. SCOTT *Moneth May,* In May gois damosells and dammis In gardynnis grein to play lik lammis, Sum at the barris thay brace like billers.

billers, variant of BILDERS.

billet ('bɪlɪt), *sb.*¹ Forms: 5 bylet, 5–6 billette, 6 billot, billotte, 7 bullet, 6– billet. [ME. and AF. *billette,* AngloL. *billetta,* dim. of *billa, bille,* BILL *sb.*³ (But *billete* occurs also in continental OF., apparently as a variant of *bullete,* in med.L. *bulletta,* dim. of L. *bulla*; and this may have contributed to the Eng. form.)]

†**1.** *gen.* **a.** A short written document; a small paper, notice, or note; a label. *Obs.*

[**1317** in Dugdale's *Monast. Angl.* I. 654 Secundum quod continetur in quadam billetta inter sigillum & scriptum ante consignationem affixa.] *c* **1440** *Promp. Parv.* 36 Bylet, scrowe [*v.r.* Bille], *matricula.* **1495** *Act 11 Hen. VII,* x. §2 Acquietaunce, writynges, billes, or billettis, wherby it may appere..[that] the seid Commyssioners..have receyved the somme. **1555** *Fardle Facions* II. iv. 142 Thei caried vppon their foreheades..pretie billettes of Paper..these were called their Philacteries.

†**b.** A bill of fare. *Obs. rare.*

1577 HARRISON *England* II. xv. (1877) 272 Which bill [of dishes] some doo call a memoriall, other a billet.

2. *spec.* A short informal letter, a 'note'. *arch.*

1579 FENTON *Guicciard.* v. (1599) 218 Writing to him billets and letters full of office and humanitie. *a* **1674** CLARENDON *Hist. Reb.* III. x. 58 The King..receiv'd little Billets, or Letters..without any Name, which advertised him of wicked designs upon his life. **1712** STEELE *Spect.* No. 306 ¶2 The Lady..writ this Billet to her Lover. **1807** T. JEFFERSON *Corr.* (1830) 78 Once in a winter, he usually wrote him a billet of invitation to dine. **1849** MACAULAY *Hist. Eng.* II. 49 Carrying billets backward and forward between his patron and the ugliest maids of honour. **1877** MERIVALE *Rom. Triumv.* viii. 166 They thrust billets into his hand, inscribed 'Brutus, thou sleepest.'

†**3.** A written permission to enter a theatre, public place, etc.; an order, a pass. *Obs.* or *arch.*

1697 *C'tess D'Aunoy's Trav.* (1706) 33 Although I had a Pasport..I was oblig'd to take a Billet from the Toll-House. **1816** J. SCOTT *Vis. Paris* 335 The conductor examined the billets of admission [to the catacombs]. **1823** LAMB *Elia* Ser. I. xvi. (1865) 124 A pretty liberal issue of those cheap billets in Brinsley's easy autograph.

4. *Mil.* **a.** An official order requiring the person to whom it is addressed to provide board and lodging for the soldier bearing it. (The ordinary modern sense.) Hence **billet-master,** the official whose duty it is to make out billets; **billet-money,** the cost of quartering soldiers; also fig. ***every bullet has its billet*** (i.e. its destination assigned): only those are killed whose death Providence has ordained.

1644 in Rushw. *Hist. Coll.* III. II. 649 That no Billet shall be granted upon any of the Inhabitants without their consent. **1723** *Lond. Gaz.* No. 6152/3 His Officers and Soldiers; who were by those Billets dispersed into Quarters in several Parts of the Town. **1811** WELLINGTON *Let.* in Gurw. *Disp.* VII. 140 A Billet is a legal order from a competent authority to the person to whom it is addressed to provide lodging for the bearer of it. **1640–4** *King's Sp.* in Rushw. *Hist. Coll.* III. (1692) I. 614 That which is owing to this County for Billet-Money. **1765** WESLEY *Jrnl.* 6 June, He never received one wound. So true is the odd saying of King William, that 'every bullet has its billet.' **1837** [see BULLET *sb.*¹ 7]. **1922** JOYCE *Ulysses* 366 The ball rolled down to her as if it understood. Every bullet has its billet.

b. A place in which a soldier is billeted; a soldier's lodging or quarters. Also *gen.*, spec. in the war of 1939–45, quarters assigned to civilian evacuees.

1830 E. S. N. CAMPBELL *Dict. Mil. Sci.* 26 Any Justice may, at the request of the Officer or Non-commissioned Officer commanding any Soldiers requiring Billets, extend the Routes or enlarge the District within which Billets shall be required. **1858** *Billets & Bivouacs* 246 Thou long-suffering reader,..tarry with me yet a moment in the last billet we shall ever share together—my dark abode on the dreary shores of Old Father Thames. **1875** *Encycl. Brit.* II. 571/2 The army lived in barracks, camps, or billets. **1919** WODEHOUSE *Damsel in Distress* vii, So George took up his abode..in the plainly-furnished but not uncomfortable cottage... He might have found a worse billet. **1942** E. WAUGH *Put out more Flags* iii. 161 Getting harder to find billets, particularly since the anti-aircraft battery had come to South Grappling. **1946** [see BILLETEE, BILLETTEE]. **1968** A. SILLITOE in B. S. Johnson *Evacuees* 238 We were allotted to four different houses, and taken by car to our separate billets.

c. *transf.* An appointment, post, or 'berth'.

1870 *Cassell's Mag.* II. 58/1 The private..doesn't see why ..he should give up his billet as pioneer or canteen waiter. **1887** 'HOPEFUL' *'Taken-in'* 135 If you are out of work, or out of a situation, as we say, here [*sc.* in N. Zealand] it is called 'out of billet'. **1890** HORNUNG *Bride fr. Bush* xvii, If ever she went back to Australia, she'd remember my young man, and get him a good billet. **1890** *Lippincott's Monthly Mag.* XLV. 384 A billet as clerk in the recruiting rendezvous. **1941** BAKER *Dict. Austral. Slang* 10 *Billet,* a position or job.

†**5.** A voting-paper used in voting by ballot. *Act of Billets* (Scotch Parl. 1662): a measure by which the twelve persons excepted from the King's Indemnity were to be chosen by secret voting.

1627 *Lisander & Cal.* IX. 195 Three billets were made with their three names which were all put into a cask. **1676** W. ROW *Contn. Blair's Autobiog.* 450 That..unjust, unreasonable, and illegal Act of Billets. *c* **1690** LAUDERDALE *Speech* in Mackenzie *Mem.* 85 Some Republicks use the Billet, or the Ballot, in giving places. **1781** J. MOORE *View Soc. It.* (1790) I. xi. 121 Each elector..throws a little billet into an urn..On this billet is inscribed the person's name.

‖**6.** A bank-note. [French; used by Carlyle for local colouring.]

1837 CARLYLE *Fr. Rev.* I. v. iii. 207 Billets of a new National Bank.

¶ See other senses which may belong here, at the end of BILLET *sb.*²

'billet, *sb.*² Also 4–6 billette, 5 bylet, 5–6 belet, 6 byllet, 8 billot. [a. F. *billette* (OF. *billete*), and *billot,* diminutives of *bille* 'trunk of a tree, length of round timber'; in 12th c. med.L. *billa* and *billus* 'branch, trunk of a tree': of unknown origin. (The Celtic derivation given by Littré and others is erroneous. The alleged Irish *bille* 'trunk of a tree,' is only one of the innumerable figments of O'Reilly's Dictionary. Whitley Stokes.)]

1. a. A thick piece of wood cut to a suitable length for fuel.

[**1361** in Rymer's *Fœdera* VI. 316 Quatuor Milia Billetorum..Emi & Provideri.] *c* **1440** *Promp. Parv.* 36 Bylet, schyde, *tedula.* **1635** W. AUSTIN *Medit.* 36 Surely many stickes together, burne more vehemently, then a single Billet. **1748** ANSON *Voy.* II. ii. 133 Some of our men ..were employed in cutting down trees, and splitting them into billets. **1846** PRESCOTT *Ferd. & Is.* II. v. 349 He slept on the ground with a billet of wood for his pillow.

†**b.** *collect.* Wood so cut for fuel; billet-wood. *Obs.*

1465 *Mann. & Househ. Exp.* 482 Payd fore a cartfulle of belet at Eltam, iijs. viij*d.* **1559** FABYAN VII. 705 The maior.. solde to the poore people billet and faggot, by the peniworthe. **1642** CHAS. I in *Let. Student Oxf.* 1 Where.. was fuell and billet enough. **1664** EVELYN *Sylva* (1679) 27 The smaller trunchions..make billet, bavine, and coals.

†**c.** Fire-wood of size regulated by law. *Obs.*

1502 ARNOLD *Chron.* (1811) 98 Item that euery Esex belet of one [shide] contayn in length with the Carf iij fote and half of assise and in gretnes in yᵉ middes xv inches. **1542–3** *Act 34–35 Hen. VIII,* iii, The vntrewe lengthe and quantitie of faggotte talwood, and billette. **1581** LAMBARDE *Eiren.* II. vii. (1588) 208.

2. A (thick) stick used as a weapon. † ***single billet***: single stick.

1603 SHAKS. *Meas. for M.* IV. iii. 58 Or they shall beat out my braines with billets. **1613** BEAUM. & FL. *Captain* II. i. 53/1 Fighting at single billet with a barge-man. [**1741** RICHARDSON *Pamela* (1824) I. 88 Nan..was taking up a billet to knock me on the head.]

3. A small bar of metal. †**a.** A 'bar' or ingot of gold or silver. **b.** Of iron or steel: see quot.

[**1353** *Act. 27 Edw. III,* ii. §14 Plate dargent, billettes dor et tut autre maner dor.] **1670** BLOUNT *Law Dict., Billets of Gold,* Wedges or Ingots of Gold. **1881** RAYMOND *Mining Gloss., Billet* 1. Iron or steel, drawn from a pile, bloom, or ingot, into a small bar for further manufacture. 2. A small bloom. **1883** *Daily News* 8 Oct. 2/5 In Bessemer steel.. hoops and billets are somewhat easier to buy.

4. *Arch.* An ornamental moulding used in Norman architecture, consisting of short cylindrical pieces placed lengthwise at regular intervals in hollow mouldings; sometimes in two or more rows, breaking joint. Also *attrib.*

1835 T. HOPE *Hist. Ess. Archit.* xiii. (1840) I. 139 Never extended beyond the jejune form of the lozenge..or the zig-zag, and the billet. **1845** R. FORD *Handbk. Trav. Spain* II. xiii. 980/2 Observe the singular billet patterns on the arches. **1870** F. WILSON *Ch. Lindisf.* 69 Their billet ornamentation and its chequered shade. **1879** SIR G. SCOTT *Lect. Archit.* II. 86 The chamfers of a string or label relieved with the billet or short piece of roll left projecting from them at intervals. **1926** R. GLAZIER *Man. Hist. Ornament* (ed. 4) 45 Later Norman work is very rich, the mouldings being well carved with..the Chevron,..Billet,..or Key Patterns.

5. *pl.* The excrements of a fox. (cf. BILLETING 3.)

¶ The following senses belong doubtfully to this or the prec. word.

6. *Her.* A bearing of the shape of a rectangle placed on end. (Variously conjectured by early writers to represent a folded letter, a brick, and cloth of gold.)

1592 WYRLEY *Armorie* 153 A siluer fes 'tween many billets gold. **1610** GUILLIM *Heraldry* iv. v. (1660) 279 This Billet in Armory is taken for a paper folded up in form of a letter. **1724** *Ibid.* (ed. 6) Dict., *Billets*.. Tresor Heraldique says, most Authors take them for Bricks. **1727–41** CHAMBERS *Cycl.*, *Billets*, in Heraldry, are supposed to represent pieces of cloth of gold or silver. **1852** MISS YONGE *Cameos* (1877) II. ii. 24 The eleven argent billets on their azure shield.

†**7.** *transf.* and *fig. Obs.*

1548 HALL *Chron.* (1809) 613, xii persones all ridyng on coursers barded and apparelled in white Sattin and blacke broched with gold and silver with cuttes and culpynes muche after tawny and blacke Sattin Billottes. *c* **1600** G. WYATT in *Cavendish's Wolsey* (1825) II. 200 So many cross billets of cunning polities, surmounted by the guiding providence of God.

8. *Saddlery.* **a.** A strap which enters a buckle. **b.** A pocket or loop which receives the end of a buckled strap.

1481–90 *Howard Househ. Bks.* 195, Ij. peyr of brode reynys, and ij. new bellet-thongs. **1794** W. FELTON *Carriages* (1801) I. 137 The tassels, the plated buckles, and the leather billets. *Ibid.* 138 The tassel, and the billet and buckle to complete it, is also 3*s.*

9. *Comb.* and *Attrib.*, as ***billet-dealer***, ***-wood***, etc.; **billet-head**, a piece of wood at the bow of a whale-boat, round which the harpoon line runs; also 'a carved prow bending in and out, contrariwise to the fiddle-head (scroll-head)' Smyth *Sailor's Word-bk.*; **billet mill** (see quot. 1910); **billet moulding** = BILLET *sb.*^{2} 4.

a **1625** FLETCHER *Noble Gent.* III. i. 35 There's not the least of the *billet dealers But have it in measure delicate. **1840** R. DANA *Bef. Mast* xxxv. 134 The cornucopia which ornamented her *billet-head. **1910** H. P. TIEMANN *Iron & Steel* 282 Billets, blooms, small slabs, and sheet bars are produced on a mill called a *billet mill, blooming mill, or cogging mill. **1958** *Times* 7 Jan. 15/1 The billet mill should be completed before the end of the current financial year. **1851** RUSKIN *Stones Ven.* I. xxiv. §3 What is called the Norman *billet moulding. **1759** B. MARTIN *Nat. Hist. Eng.* II. Norf. 70 A Fire of clean *Billet-wood. **1772** *Phil. Trans.* LXII. 90 Billet-wood for fewel.

ˈ**billet**, *sb.*^{3} Also billit. [perh. a corruption of BILLARD; perh. the correct form, and identical with prec. word.] A coal-fish, when one year old. Cf. BILLARD 1.

1769 PENNANT *Zool.* III. 153 They [the fry of the coalfish] are called at Scarborough *Parrs*, and when a year old, *Billets*. **1832** J. COLE *Scarbor. Guide* 108 The principal fish.. for sale are.. parr, billits, cole fish. **1883** *Fisheries Exhib. Catal.* 10 Mounted Lines for.. Billet, and all surface fish.

billet (ˈbɪlɪt), *v.* Also 7 **billit**, **billett**. Pa. t. and pple. **billeted**. [f. BILLET *sb.*^{1}]

†**1.** *trans.* To enter in a list; to enroll. *Obs.*

1607 SHAKS. *Cor.* IV. iii. 48 The Centurions, and their charges distinctly billetted.. and to be on foot at an houres warning. **1618** *Select. Harl. Misc.* (1793) 218 He billetted the said pioneers for several ships. **1629** R. HILL *Pathw. Piety* I. Pref. 11 Blessed and billeted up be they in Heaven.

2. a. To assign quarters to (soldiers) by a note or ticket; to quarter (troops) *in, at, on, upon, with.*

1599 NASHE *Lent. Stuffe* (1871) 10 For ten weeks together this rabble-rout.. are billetted with her. **1604** SHAKS. *Oth.* II. iii. 386 Go where thou art Billited. *a* **1674** CLARENDON *Hist. Reb.* I. I. 33 They refused to suffer the Soldiers to be billetted upon them. **1849** MACAULAY *Hist. Eng.* I. i. 85 Companies of soldiers were billeted on the people.

b. *gen.* To assign or appoint quarters to; to locate. (With 1837 cf. BILLET *sb.*^{1} 4.) *spec.*, in the war of 1939–45, to assign quarters to (civilian evacuees). Freq. const. *on.*

1606 SYLVESTER *Du Bartas, Columnes* IV. II. ii. 643 In what bright starry Signe, th' Almighty dread, Dayes Princely Planet's dayly billeted. **1650** R. GELL *Serm.* 15 We finde the twelve Tribes.. billeted according to the four Quarters of heaven. **1837** DICKENS *Pickw.* xix, Shots.. cast loose upon the world and billeted nowhere. **1939** *Punch* 6 Dec. 631/3 It was when you first heard that little Sidney and the others were to be billeted on you. **1942** E. WAUGH *Put out more Flags* iii. 165 Wait till the gentleman billets you. **1955** *Times* 2 Aug. 8/6, I dimly recognized one of the children who had been billeted on us during the wartime evacuation, and who had gone back to London 10 years ago.

†**c.** To give quarters to, lodge. *Obs.*

1637 QUARLES *Elegy* Wks. 1881 III. 15 Sorrow is the Guest Which I must entertaine, and billet in my brest.

†**3.** *intr.* (for *refl.*) To have quarters. *Obs. rare.*

1628 in *Parr's Lett.* 400 (L.) He billets in my lodgings.

4. *trans.* To serve (a person) with a billet.

1833 MARRYAT *P. Simple* xxiv, 'Conscripts!' said the woman of the house.. 'I am billeted full already.'

†**5.** To select by billet (see BILLET *sb.*^{1} 5); to ballot. *Obs.*

c **1690** SIR G. MACKENZIE *Mem. Aff. Scotland* 75 Lauderdale.. askt the King, 'What if they billet me, Sir?'.. Then Lauderdale told him that he was billeted.

‖**billet-doux** (bijɛdu). [Fr.; = sweet note.] A love-letter. (Now usually *jocular.*)

1673 DRYDEN *Marr. à la Mode* II. i. 261 He sings and dances en François, and writes the billets doux to a miracle. *a* **1688** VILLIERS (Dk. Buckhm.) *Ep. Julian* Wks. 1705 II. 94 Strephon's Billet douxe's have made them sport. **1712** POPE *Rape Lock* I. 138 Here files of pins extend their shining rows, Puffs, powders, patches, bibles, billet-doux. **1848** THACKERAY *Van. Fair* iv, To see whether there was a billet-doux hidden among the flowers.

billeté, -etté, -etty (ˈbɪlɪtɪ). Also 6 bil-, billettie, 9 billetée, billettée. [a. F. *billeté*, in same sense, f. *billet*: see BILLET *sb.*^{2} 7.]

Her. Charged with billets: see quot. 1766.

1572 BOSSEWELL *Armorie* II. 27 He beareth quarterly, Sable and Argent engrayled, Billettie. **1766** PORNY *Heraldry* (1787) Gloss., *Billeté*, Billetty.. is used in blazoning Billets that exceed ten. **1864** BOUTELL *Heraldry Hist. & Pop.* vii. 33 A field *semée* of Billets is *Billetée.*

billeted (ˈbɪlɪtɪd), *ppl. a.* [f. BILLET *v.* and *sb.*]

†**1.** Furnished with billets or strips of metal. *Obs.*

1626 T. H. *Caussin's Holy Crt.* 189 The Cymball was.. composed of thinne plates of brasse, with certayne small barres of iron, fastned, and crosse billeted in the plates.

2. Quartered by billet.

1628 *Moundeford MSS.* in Forster *Gr. Remonstr.* 221 The billeted souldiers. **1866** *Morn. Star* 12 July, In Saxony each billeted soldier pays five silbergroschen.

billetee, billettee (bɪlɪˈtiː). [f. BILLET *v.* + -EE.] A person who is billeted.

1939 *Times* 12 Oct. 9/4 Mrs. M[iniver].. will cope in a wonderful manner with refractory billetees. **1946** A. PHELPS *'I couldn't care Less'* xv. 120, I sought out the billet that had been arranged for me. I am not a good billettee. **1958** D. WALLACE *Forty Years On* xv. 185 A lot of our dear billettees weren't even house-trained.

ˈ**billeter.** [f. BILLET *v.* + -ER.] **a.** An officer who makes out billets. †**b.** A soldier with a billet. †**c.** One who selects by billet: see BILLET *v.* 5.

1640–4 in *Rushw. Hist. Coll.* III. (1692) I. 206 Officers or Billiters of Souldiers, dead or run away. **1643** BRAMHALL *Wks.* 1842–4 III. 450 So soon as he was gotten into Hull to fill their house with billetters. **1663** W. SHARP in *Lauderd. Papers* (1884) I. 127 The billeters may be disappoynted.

d. A person who receives a billetee into his or her household.

1939 *Picture Post* 18 Nov. 44 The Government pays billeters 10s. a week for one child or 8s. 6d. each for more than one. **1966** *New Statesman* 11 Feb. 202/2 First, there's evacuation. 'Are they coloured?' asks a billeter. 'I can't take eight people,' says another.

billeting (ˈbɪlɪtɪŋ), *vbl. sb.* [Consists of what are really different words f. BILLET *v.* and *sb.*]

1. a. The quartering of soldiers by billet.

1640 *Petit. to King* in *Harl. Misc.* (1811) VII. 215 Your subjects burdened with.. billeting of soldiers, and other military charges. **1810** WELLINGTON in Gurw. *Disp.* VI. 72 As long as the system of billeting continues.

b. The provision of quarters for civilian evacuees, esp. in the war of 1939–45. Freq. *attrib.*

1936 in R. M. Titmuss *Probl. Social Policy* (1950) iii. 25 The evacuation of London needs to be thought out in terms, not of transport only but of reception, housing (by compulsory billeting if necessary) and feeding. **1938** *Hansard Commons* 12 May 1703, I assume that my hon. Friend has in mind what are sometimes called billeting surveys. **1939** *Punch* 11 Oct. 400/2 The children were deposited on her doorstep by an apologetic but helpless billeting-officer. **1940** *Ann. Reg. 1939* 112 Evacuation necessarily caused a good deal of inconvenience... There were many 'misfits' in the billeting. **1969** A. CALDER *People's War* ii. 45 In spite of all the fuss, there had been many cases of successful billeting. *Ibid.* vi. 409 There had been many allegations that billeting officers, usually 'respectable' people themselves, had let other 'respectable' people off lightly.

†**2.** Selection by billet or voting-paper. *Obs.*

1662 R. LAW *Mem.* (1817) 12 An act of billating, by which he would have cut off some nobles in the land from all public trust. **1662** W. SHARP in *Lauderd. Pap.* (1884) I. lvi, The billeting being agreed to in the articles yesterday.

3. See quot. (Cf. BILLET *sb.*^{2} 5.)

1706 PHILLIPS, *Billiting*, (among Hunters), the Ordure, or Dung of a Fox. [So in BAILEY and later Dicts.]

4. *billeting-roll* (Iron-working), a set of rollers for reducing smelted iron to the form of bars.

ˈ**billetless**, *a.* Without a billet.

1868 *Once a Wk.* No. 14. 300 A billetless bullet from the old flint rifle.

bill-fish: see BILL *sb.*^{2}

billful (ˈbɪlfʊl). As much as fills a bird's bill.

1616 SURFL. & MARKH. *Countr. Farm* 718 Giue her a birds bill full foure times a day. **1863** BUCKLAND *Cur. Nat. Hist.* Ser. II. 329 He takes a billfull of mud.

bill-hook (ˈbɪlhʊk). [f. BILL *sb.*^{1} + HOOK *sb.*^{1}] A heavy thick knife or chopper with a hooked end, used for pruning, cutting brushwood, etc.

1611 COTGR., *Rivereau*.. a Welsh hooke, or hedging bill made with a hooke at the end.. we call it a Bill-hooke. **1837** HOWITT *Rur. Life* VI. xviii. (1862) 608 The billhook of the Midland counties, with a back edge as well as a front one. **1857** S. OSBORN *Quedah* ix. 118 Each carried a sharp bill hook, with which to cut his way through the underwood.

billian, var. BILIAN.

ˈ**billiardist.** [f. BILLIARD(S + -IST.] A billiard-player.

1865 *Philadelphia Sun. Mercury* 15 Oct. 6/3 Nelms, the great billiardist, covered himself with glory. **1888** *St. Louis Globe Democrat* 24 Jan. (Farmer), Each competitor has put up fifty dollars entrance money in Billiardist Daly's hands. **1901** *Daily Chron.* 3 Apr. 6/6 A player, like a billiardist, would require practice to be successful. **1921** *Glasgow Herald* 18 Jan. 6 Smith's rise to fame as a billiardist.

billiards (ˈbɪljədz), *sb. pl.* Also 6–7 **balliards**, 7 **billards**, **billiars**, **billyards**. The sing. **billiard** is used only in comb. (see 2). [a. F. *billard*, OF. also *billart*, the game; so named from *billard* 'a cue,' orig. 'a stick with curved end, a hockey-stick,' dim. of *bille* piece of wood, stick: see BILLET *sb.*^{2} and -ARD. In Eng. introduced only as the name of the game, and made pl. as in *draughts*, *skittles*, *bowls*, and other names of games.]

1. A game played with small solid ivory balls on a rectangular table having a smooth cloth-covered horizontal surface, the balls being driven about, according to the rules of the game, by means of long tapering sticks called cues.

1591 SPENSER *M. Hubberd* 803 With all the thriftles games that may be found.. With dice, with cards, with balliards. **1598** FLORIO, *Trucco*, a kinde of play with balles vpon a table, called billiards. **1606** SHAKS. *Ant. & Cl.* II. v. 3 Let it alone, let's to billiards. **1611** COTGR., *Billiard*, a short and thicke trunchion, or cudgell: hence.. the sticke wherewith we touch the ball at billyards. **1712** ARBUTHNOT *John Bull* (1755) 5 You sot, says she, you.. spend your time at billiards, etc. **1873** BENNETT & CAVENDISH *Billiards* 2 Nothing is known about Billiards prior to the middle of the sixteenth century.

2. *Comb.* and *Attrib.*, as ***billiard-ball***, ***-club***, ***-cue***, ***-hall***, ***-player***, ***-playing***, ***-room***, ***-sharper***, ***-sharping***, ***-stick***; **billiard-cloth**, fine green woollen cloth used for covering billiard-tables; **billiard-mace**, or †**-mast**, a rod furnished with a head or knob used to propel the ball in billiards; **billiard-marker**, a person who marks the 'points' made by each player, and keeps account of the progress of the game; *also*, a counting apparatus for registering results; so **billiard-marking**; **billiard-table**, the large table on which the game of billiards is played; usually 12 ft. by 6, covered with fine green cloth, surrounded by a cushioned ledge, and provided with six 'pockets' at the corners and sides for the reception of the balls; also used *attrib.* to describe a perfectly smooth green, road, etc.

a **1637** B. JONSON *Celebr. Charis*, And cheek.. Smooth as is the *billiard-ball. **1871** TYNDALL *Fragm. Sc.* (ed. 6) II. xv. 408 Not all the sense of pain or pleasure in the world could lift a stone or move a billiard-ball. **1873** *Winfield* (Kansas) *Courier* 18 Jan. 3/2 The lower room will soon be occupied.. as a saloon and *billiard hall. **1939** JOYCE *Finnegans Wake* (1964) 125 And uses noclass billiardhalls with an upandown ladder? **1775** SHERIDAN *Rivals* II. i, Seven.. waiters, and thirteen *billiard-markers. **1785** COWPER *Task* IV. 221 What was an hour-glass once Becomes a dice-box, and a *billiard-mast [**1806** -mace] Well does the work of his destructive scythe. **1790** T. WILKINSON *Mem.* IV. 228 This was of infinite service to Mr. Fleetwood as a *billiard player. **1872** GEO. ELIOT *Middlem.* I. II. xviii. 321 The Vicar was a first-rate billiard-player. **1807** J. R. SHAW *Life* (1930) 76 Men of diabolical principles.. employed in.. horse-racing, *billiard-playing, [etc.]. **1890** W. JAMES *Princ. Psychol.* I. xiii. 509 Billiard-playing, rifle-shooting, tight-rope-dancing, demand the most delicate appreciation of minute disparities of sensation. *c* **1702** C. FIENNES *Journeys* (1947) III. iv. 172 Out of the *billiard roome the first was with gravell walks and a large fountaine. **1814** JANE AUSTEN *Mansf. Park* I. xiii. 259 Maria, Julia, Henry Crawford, and Mr. Yates, were in the billiard room. **1848** THACKERAY *Van. Fair* viii, Tall doors with stags' heads over them, leading to the billiard-room and the library. **1865** *Pall Mall G.* 11 Aug. 2/2 He meant to climb in the world to all that was pure and heroic by *billiard-sharping. **1588** in *N. & Q.* (1915) XI. 227 Three *billyard stickes and one porte and ij balles of yvery. *a* **1700** EVELYN *Diary* 4 Dec. (1955) IV. 190 They for the most part use the sharp & small end of the billiard-stick, which is shod with brasse or silver. **1817** COLERIDGE *Biog. Lit.* (1817) 52 When.. the billiard-stick strikes the first or white ball. **1641** in *N. & Q.* (1915) XI. 227 A *billiard table and three bearers. **1677** EVELYN *Mem.* 10 Sept., The gallery is a pleasant, noble room: in the.. middle, is a billiard-table. **1711** STEELE *Spect.* No. 54 ¶4 Bowling-Greens, Billiard-Tables, and such like Places. [**1851** J. PYCROFT *Cricket Field* vii. 107 We do not play cricket.. on billiard tables.] **1867** BAKER *Nile Tribut.* viii. 190 An immense tract of high grass, as level as a *billiard-table. **1887** F. GALE *Game Cricket* 183 Pougher.. got seven wickets.. for 116 runs, on a billiard-table ground. **1905** *Westm. Gaz.* 6 June 4/2 A land of billiard-table roads.

billie, variant of BILLY^1.

billiken (ˈbɪlɪkɪn). Also -kin. [Prob. f. BILLY^2 + -KIN.] A small, squat, smiling figure used as a mascot.

1914 WODEHOUSE *Man Upstairs* 257 When you send a girl three bouquets, a bracelet, and a gold Billiken with ruby eyes, you do not expect an entire absence of recognition. **1927** A. HUXLEY *Proper Studies* 225 We now worship, under the name of mascots, lucky pigs, billikens, swastikas, and the like, a whole pantheon of fetishes which stand for nothing beyond themselves. **1927** W. E. COLLINSON *Contemp. Eng.* 100 Before the war.. there was a craze for Billikins or little oriental gods of luck. **1932** *Times Lit. Suppl.* 10 Nov. 829/3 Are there not modern airmen who will not go up without the moral support.. from some grinning Billiken or 'Fumsup'?

billimente, variant of BILIMENT. *Obs.*

billinder, obs. form of BILANDER.

† **'billing**, *vbl. sb.*[1] *Obs.* [f. BILL *v.*[1] + -ING[1].] Working with a bill or mattock; hoeing.
c **1440** *Promp. Parv.* 36 Byllynge of mattokys, *ligonizacio.*

billing ('bɪlɪŋ), *vbl. sb.*[2] [f. BILL *v.*[2] + -ING[1].]
† **1.** The pecking of a bird. *Obs.*
c **1440** *Promp. Parv.* 36 Byllynge of byrdys, *rostratus.* **1598** FLORIO, *Imbeccata*..an embilling, a billing or feading. **1599** *Broughton's Lett.* i. 6 The billing of such filthie garbage.
2. The caressing of doves; kissing; love-making.
1587 WARNER *Alb. England* VI. xxxi. (1612) 153 First blend they heards, and forthwith lips, and after billing fell To other Sport. c **1630** DRUMM. OF HAWTH. *Poems* Wks. (1711) 21 Come, let us teach new billing to the dove. **1732** FIELDING *Miser* I. iii, Here's fine billing, and cooing, I warrant. **1815** L. HUNT *Feast of Poets* 10, I never much valued your billings and cooings.

'billing, *vbl. sb.*[3] [f. BILL *v.*[3] + -ING[1].] **a.** The action of entering in a list, enrolling, indicting, lampooning, etc.
1884 *Manch. Exam.* 14 Nov. 5/4 The proceedings in connection with the billing of the Sheriffs.
b. Announcing or advertising by bill or poster; publicity. Also *attrib.* So *top billing*, the most prominent position on a poster, advertisement, or the like; stardom.
1875 *Chambers's Jrnl.* 132/1 Advertisements, which most likely took the form of 'billing'. **1900** *Daily News* 4 Dec. 3/2 No billing is attempted in the City, and hence the urgent necessity for a thorough distribution of election literature. **1902** *Daily Chron.* 20 Mar. 7/4 If plaintiff did not send.. particulars of her performance for billing purposes. **1905** *Ibid.* 28 June 6/2 The defence was that Mr. Elen did not send on 'billing matter' two weeks in advance of his engagement. **1957** L. F. R. WILLIAMS *State of Israel* 145 English plays of recent date, in Hebrew translations, figure more frequently in the billings. **1968** *Globe & Mail* (Toronto) 13 Jan. 24/1 He made his Broadway debut as Lancelot in Camelot, with billing below the title; now, he is returning to Broadway, with top billing. **1969** *Times* 14 Feb. 10/7 He and other dance band leaders..vied with Gracie Fields for the top billing on the music halls and radio.
c. *Comm.* The act of making out or sending a bill, invoice, etc. Also *attrib.*, as *billing machine*.
1908 *Westm. Gaz.* 26 Feb. 9/2 The billing machine..will produce half a dozen business documents at one operation, and will total up automatically the various items entered. *Ibid.* 29 Feb. 7/1 The special Oliver for Billing and Invoicing... Combined Billing and Adding Machines. **1959** *Economist* 4 Apr. 68/2 The two industries might profitably co-operate in such things as meter reading, billing and collection of accounts.
d. The total amount of business or investment, esp. of an advertising agency, during a given period. *U.S.*
1958 M. MAYER *Madison Ave.* iii. 53 We've grown from $2,900,000 in billings in 1940 to about $100,000,000 in 1957. **1959** I. ROSS *Image Merch.* (1960) viii. 134 Their gross billing was $150,000 in 1951.

'billing, *ppl. a.* [f. BILL *v.*[2] + -ING[2].] That bills or caresses like a pair of doves.
1720 GAY *Espousal*, Let me be The billing dove, and fondling lamb to thee. **1729** T. COOKE *Tales, etc.* 67 Hear the billing Turtles coo. **1801** MOORE *The Kiss*, Give me, my love, that billing kiss I taught you.

Billingsgate ('bɪlɪŋsgeɪt). Also 3 **Bellingesȝate**, 7 **Bellings gate, Belin'sgate**, 7–8 **Billinsgate**. [The proper name (presumably from a personal name *Billing*) of one of the gates of London, and hence of the fish-market there established. The 17th c. references to the 'rhetoric' or abusive language of this market are frequent, and hence foul language is itself called 'billingsgate.']
1. One of the gates of the city of London; the fish-market near it; the latter noted for vituperative language.
c **1250** LAY. 15070 And ladde to Londene..bisides Bellinges-ȝate [c **1205** Bælȝes-]. **1585** PILKINGTON *Exp. Nehem.* (1841) 345 The gates of cities have their names..of them that builded them, as Lud-gate and Billings-gate, of Lud and Billinns. **1658** R. NEWCOURT *Title Map Lond.*, Billings gate Founded by Belen yᵉ 23ᵗʰ Brittish Kinge. **1672** MARVELL *Reh. Transp.* I. 167 There is not a scold at Billinsgate but may defend herself. **1705** HICKERINGILL *Priest-cr.* I. (1721) 56 The Rhetorick of Billingsgate, viz. Lying and Slandering. **1795** WINDHAM *Speeches Parl.* (1812) I. 266 The scolding of a fishwoman in Billingsgate. **1848** THACKERAY *Van. Fair* xiii, Mr. Osborne..cursed Billingsgate with an emphasis worthy of the place.
b. *attrib.* (in reference to language.)
1652 CULPEPPER *Eng. Physic.*, With down-right Billingsgate-Rhetoric. **1726** AMHERST *Terræ Fil.* x. 48, I know nothing that he is fit for, but Billinsgate sermons. **1750** WESLEY *Wks.* (1872) IX. 87 Low, Billingsgate invectives.
2. Scurrilous vituperation, violent abuse.
1676 WYCHERLEY *Pl.-Dealer* III. i. (1678) 35 With sharp Invectives —— *Wid.* (Alias Belin'sgate). **1710** SHAFTESB. *Charac.* (1737) III. ii. 15 Philosophers and Divines, who can be contented to..write in learned Billinsgate. **1799** T. JEFFERSON *Writ.* (1859) IV. 289 We disapprove the constant billingsgate poured on them officially. **1867** FREEMAN *Norm. Conq.* (1876) I. App. 625 This is mere Billingsgate.
† **3.** A clamouring foul-mouthed person, a vulgar abuser or scold. *Obs.*
1683 TRYON *Way to Health* 480 Neither have we any Billings-gates, all that sort of People are our hewers of VVood and drawers of Water. **1715** *Bowes' Trag.* in *Yorksh. Anthol.* (1851) 18 Words not fit for a Billingsgate. **1721–90** BAILEY, *Billingsgate*, a scolding impudent Slut.
Hence † **Billingsgate** *v. rare.* † **Billingsgatry**, scurrilous language.
1673 *Remarks upon Rem.* 56 (Boucher) A great deal of Billingsgatry against poets. **1715** A. LITTLETON *Lat. Dict.*, To Billingsgate it. *Arripere maledictum ex trivio.*

billion ('bɪljən). [a. F. *billion*, purposely formed in 16th c. to denote the second power of a MILLION (by substituting BI- *pref.*[2] for the initial letters), *trillion* and *quadrillion* being similarly formed to denote its 3rd and 4th powers. The name appears not to have been adopted in Eng. before the end of the 17th c.: see quot. from Locke. Subsequently the application of the word was changed by French arithmeticians, figures being divided in numeration into groups of threes, instead of sixes, so that F. *billion*, *trillion*, denoted not the second and third powers of a million, but a thousand millions and a thousand thousand millions. In the 19th century, the U.S. adopted the French convention, but Britain retained the original and etymological use (to which France reverted in 1948).
Since 1951 the U.S. value, a thousand millions, has been increasingly used in Britain, especially in technical writing and, more recently, in journalism; but the older sense 'a million millions' is still common.]
1. *orig.* and still commonly in Great Britain: A million millions. (= U.S. *trillion.*)
1690 LOCKE *Hum. Und.* II. xvi. §6 But to show how much distinct names conduce to our well reckoning, let us see all these following figures in one continued line:—
Nonillions Octillions..Trillions Billions Millions Units
857324, 162486 .. 235421, 261734, 368149, 623137.
The ordinary way of naming this number in English, will be the often repeating of millions of millions of millions, etc. a **1711** KEN *Prepar.* Poet. Wks. 1721 IV. 67 A Star..will run, Of Miles a Billion round the Sun. **1778** MASERES in *Phil. Trans.* LXVIII. 897 A billion, or the square of a million. **1870** PROCTOR *Other Worlds* ix. 200 The aggregate weight of the various meteoric systems..must be estimated by billions of tons.
2. In U.S., and increasingly in Britain: A thousand millions.
1834, etc.: see *D.A.E.* **1864** See WEBSTER, s.v. *Numeration.* **1983** *Dict. Computing* (O.U.P.) 156 *Giga-*,..a prefix indicating a multiple of one billion, 10^9.

billionaire (bɪljə'nɛə(r)). [f. prec., after *millionaire.*] The possessor of property worth a billion or more of the recognized standard coin of the realm; (see next).
1861 O. W. HOLMES *Elsie V.* vii, One would like to give a party now and then, if one could be a billionnaire. **1865** E. LOTT *Gov'ness Egypt* 7 The billionaire merchant Prince.

billionism ('bɪljənɪz(ə)m). *nonce-wd.* [f. as prec. + -ISM.] The financial position of a billionaire.
1861 O. W. HOLMES *Elsie V.* vii, Billionism, or even millionism, must be a blessed kind of state.

billionth ('bɪljənθ), *a.* and *sb.* [f. as prec. + -TH[1].] **A.** *adj.* The ordinal adjective corresponding to 'billion.' **B.** *sb.* The billionth part.
1778 MASERES *Converg. Series* in *Phil. Trans.* LXVIII. 900 The billionth root of 10 will be = 1.000,000,000,002,302,585,093. **1865** DRAPER *Int. Devel. Europe* xxv. 607 The vibrations which thus occasion light are, at a mean, 525 in the billionth of a second.

billitonite ('bɪlɪtənaɪt). *Min.* [G. (Suess 1901, in *Jahrb. d. K.K. Geol. Reichsanstalt 1900* L. 194), f. *Billiton* the name of an Indonesian island + -ITE[1] 2 b.] A form of tektite found in the East Indies.
1909 SOLLAS tr. *Suess's Face of Earth* IV. v. xv, The acid felspar rocks of the earth are represented among the meteorites..by the once completely molten tektites (Moldavite, Australite, Billitonite). **1944** PALACHE et al. *Dana's Syst. Min.* (ed. 7) 121 *Tektites*..include..the billitonites of the East Indies.

billman ('bɪlmən). [f. BILL *sb.*[1] + MAN.] **a.** A soldier armed with a bill. **b.** A watchman similarly armed. **c.** A labourer using a bill.
1530 PALSGR. 198 Bylman in a batayle, *halebardier.* **1552** HULOET, Byll man, *falcarius.* **1581** SAVILE *Tacitus' Hist.* I. xxiv. (1591) 15 Cocceius Proculus, a bilman of the Garde. **1604** DEKKER *Honest Wh.* Wks. 1873 II. 163 Enter Constable and Bilmen. **1606** SYLVESTER *Captaines* 242 A sort of lusty Bill-men, set..to fell a Cops. **1801** STRUTT *Sports & Past.* II. i. 62 Four thousand whifflers and billmen. **1861** DIXON *Bacon* iv. §17 The Bowmen of Cressy, the billmen of Boulogne.

billon ('bɪlən). [a. F. *billon* 'debased metal,' originally certainly meaning 'mass' (Littré), i.e. 'l'or et l'argent en bille,' billon, f. *bille*, BILLET of wood, etc.: cf. BILLOT. F. *billon* is cogn. w. Pr. *billo*, Sp. *vellon*, It. *biglione*, med.L. *billi-ōnem.* In Eng., of modern adoption from French, where its sense-development has not been clearly traced; it had at one time the sense now expressed by Eng. *bullion*, med.L. *bulliōnem*, and the two words have mutually influenced each other, though they are distinct in origin: see BULLION.]
1. A mixed metal used in coinage, consisting of gold or silver with a preponderating admixture of a baser metal. Also *attrib.*
1727 CHAMBERS *Cycl.*, *Billon*, *Billio*, in coinage a kind of base metal either of gold or silver, in whose mixture copper predominates. *Note.* We don't find 'tis naturaliz'd among us: but the necessity we are frequently under of using it in the course of this work, requir'd its being explain'd. **1797** *Encycl. Brit.* s.v. *Billon*, Gold under twelve carats fine, is called billon of gold. **1876** MATHEWS *Coinage* xxii. 231 For Martinique..small coins of silver and gold washed billon were struck in France during parts of the last century.
2. *esp.* An alloy of silver with copper, tin, or other base metal, in which the latter predominates.
1819 REES *Cycl.* s.v. *Billon*, The writers on numismatic science appropriate the term billon to signify metals of copper alloyed with a very small quantity of silver. **1852** WRIGHT *Celt, Rom. & Saxon* (1861) 378 Of these Richborough coins..fifteen [are] of billon or debased silver. **1883** *Antiquary* July, James III..issued several denominations of billon coins, as placks, half-placks, farthings.

billot ('bɪlət). [a. Fr. *billot* a wooden block.]
1. Obs. form of BILLET *sb.*[2]
2. 'Bullion in the block or bar previous to being coined.'
1846 in WORCESTER; and in mod. Dicts.

billow ('bɪləʊ), *sb.* Also 6 bellow(e, 6–7 billowe. [Not known bef. 1550, but may have been in dial. use. App. a. ON. *bylgja* billow (in Da. *bölge*, Sw. *bölja*); cf. MHG. *bulge*; OHG. **bulga* and OE. **bylge* are not found; f. com. Teut. *belgan* to swell, swell up: see BELL *v.*[1]]
† **1.** The swell on the ocean produced by the wind, or on a river or estuary by the tide. *Obs.*
1560 JENKINSON in Hakluyt *Voy.* (1589) 358 And much adoe to keepe our barke from sinking, the billowe was so great. **1614** RALEIGH *Hist. World* I. iii. §13 That branch of Indus..[is] so large and deepe, and by reason thereof so great a billow, as it endangered his whole Fleet.
2. a. *prop.* A great swelling wave of the sea, produced generally by a high wind; but often used as merely = Wave, and hence poetically for 'the sea.'
1552 HULOET, Bellowe or waue of water. **1566** GASCOIGNE *Jocasta* III. (1575) 99 b, His barke with many a billowe beaten. **1596** SPENSER *Prothal.* 48 The gentle stream..bad his billowes spare To wet their silken feathers. **1601** SHAKS. *Jul. C.* v. i. 67 Why now blow winde, swell Billow, And swimme Barke. **1611** BIBLE *Ps.* xlii. 7 All thy waues, and thy billowes [WYCLIF flodis, COVERD. waterflouds] are gone ouer me. **1712** HUGHES *Spect.* No. 467 ¶2 The Waves and Billows thro' which he has steered. **1799** *Scotland Descr.* (ed. 2) 12 The appulse of the billows of the open Atlantic. **1817** WOLFE *Burial Sir J. Moore*, The foe and the stranger would tread o'er his head, And we far away on the billow.
b. *fig.* esp. of death as an overwhelming flood.
1592 tr. *Junius on Rev.* xii. 18 And provoke the nations that they might with their furious bellowes toss up and down. **1807** CRABBE *Par. Reg.* III. 15 Till the last strong billow stops the breath. **1857** HEAVYSEGE *Saul* (1869) 429 The billows black of death's deep gulf.
3. *transf.* A great wave of flame, air, sound; a body of men sweeping onward, etc.
1677 MILTON *P.L.* I. 224 On each hand the flames..rowld In billows, leave i' th' midst a horrid Vale. **1854** RUSSELL *The War* xxvi. (ed. 17) 173 Huge stately billows of armed men. **1860** TYNDALL *Glac.* I. §25. 185 Billows of air..rolled over us with a long surging sound. **1872** BLACKIE *Lays Highl.* 104 Let the billow of your pæans To Dunolly's tower be borne.
4. *Comb.* and *Attrib.*, as *billow-crest*, *-roll*, *-swell*, *billow-beaten*, *-like* adjs.; **billow-bred** *a.*, reared or brought up on the sea; **billow-rife** *a.*, full of, or beset with many, billows.
1597 MIDDLETON in Farr's *S.P.* (1845) II. 536 The swans forsooke the quire of billow-roule. **1749** WEST *Pindar* in Johnson *Life* Wks. IV. 202 The billow-beaten side Of the foam-besilver'd main. **1851** H. MELVILLE *Moby Dick* I. ix. 65 How billow-like and boisterously grand! **1855** SINGLETON *Virgil* I. 229 Upon the billow-crest hang these. **1904** W. DE LA MARE *Henry Brocken* 95 The hosts of our pursuers paused, billow-like, reared, and scattered.

'billow, *v.* [f. prec. sb.]
1. *intr.* To rise in billows; to surge, swell.
1597 DRAYTON *Mortimer.* 94 A poole of tears..Billow'd with sighes, like to a little maine. **1655** H. VAUGHAN *Silex Scint.* 39 When his waters billow thus, Dark storms and wind Incite them. **1794** COLERIDGE *Dest. Nations*, Ocean behind him billows. **1868** TENNYSON *Lucretius* 31 A riotous confluence of watercourses Blanching and billowing in a hollow of it.
2. *fig.* and *transf.* To surge, swell, undulate, roll with wavy motion.
1628 FELTHAM *Resolves* I. xxxvi. (1647) 119 Vexations when they daily billow upon the minde. **1713** YOUNG *Last Day* III. 249 It soars on high, Swells in the storm, and billows through the sky. **1795** SOUTHEY *Joan of Arc* v. 120 The yellow harvest billow'd o'er the plain. **1865** G. MACDONALD *A. Forbes* xviii. 75 A laugh..billowed and broke thro' the whole school. **1871** ROSSETTI *Last Confess.* 407 The pain comes billowing on like a full cloud of thunder.

ˈbillowiness. [f. BILLOWY + -NESS.] Undulating nature; succession of crested elevations.
1826 CARRINGTON *Dartmoor* Pref. 12 The singular billowiness of the ground causes..some delicious varieties of light and shade.

billowing (ˈbɪləʊɪŋ), *ppl. a.* [f. BILLOW *v.* + -ING[2].] Rolling or rising in billows; undulating.
1718 PRIOR *Solomon* III. 129 The billowing Snow. **1812** SIR R. WILSON *Diary* I. 42 The background..was formed by billowing mountains. **1854** DE QUINCEY *Joan of Arc* Wks. III. 242 The fiery smoke rose in billowing volumes.

ˈbillowlet. [See -LET.] A small billow.
1867 J. MACGREGOR *Rob Roy Baltic* 99 The dancing billowlets of the lake. **1892** *Temple Bar* Oct. 292 The bay.. with its sheltered succession of crescent-shaped billowlets.

billowy (ˈbɪləʊɪ), *a.* [f. BILLOW *sb.* + -Y[1].]
1. Characterized by billows.
c **1615** CHAPMAN *Odyss.* v. 345 The billowie ocean. **1798** *Anti-Jacobin* 21 May (1852) 142 Biscay's billowy bay. **1865** GEIKIE *Scen. & Geol. Scot.* ii. 75 Crests and troughs of a billowy sea.
2. Of, pertaining to, or of the nature of billows.
1791 HUDDESFORD *Salmag.* i. 24 And elevate his trembling mast Above the billowy precipice. **1860** TYNDALL *Glac.* I. §4. 36 The..horizon of the lake presented a billowy tumultuous appearance. **1884** W. C. SMITH *Kildrostan* 87 The bounding sea, And billowy roll of life.
3. *transf.* Cf. BILLOW *sb.* 3.
1726 THOMSON *Winter* 273 O'er the hapless flocks..The billowy tempest whelms. **1789** COLERIDGE *Nose*, On billowy flames of fire I float. **1847** L. HUNT *Men, Women, & Bks.* I. viii. 133 The great blue billowy domains of heather.
4. *comb.* (advb. and parasynthetic.)
1855 BROWNING *Men & Wom., Last Ride*, Some western cloud All billowy-bosomed. **1876** SWINBURNE *Erechth.* (ed. 2) 45 Broad strength of billowy-beating war.

billy[1], **billie** (ˈbɪlɪ). *Sc.* and *north. dial.* [Of unknown derivation. (It has been compared with BULLY and G. *buhle*, but to little purpose.)]
1. Fellow; companion, comrade, mate.
c **1505** DUNBAR *In secreit place* 31 Be nocht our bosteous to ȝour billie. ? *a* **1750** *Graeme & Bewick* in Scott *Minstr.* (1812) II. 292 Your son..is but bad, And billie to my son he canna be. **1786** BURNS *Let. J. Tennant*, My auld schoolfellow, preacher Willie, The manly tar, my mason Billie. **1808** *Cumbrian Ball.* xlii. 96 My billy Aye thought her the flow'r o' them aw. **1863** ATKINSON *Provinc. Danby*, *Billy*, a comrade, familiar acquaintance.
2. 'Fellow,' in the wider sense (*familiar*).
a **1774** FERGUSSON *Hallowfair*, Here chapman billies take their stand And show their bonny wallies. **1790** BURNS *Tam O'Shanter*, When chapman billies leave the street. **1815** SCOTT *Guy M.* xxv, 'There I met wi' Tam o' Todshaw, and a wheen o' the rest o' the billies on the water side.'
3. Brother. (The corresponding feminine is *tittie*. Both are now considered rude.) Hence **billyhood**, brotherhood.
1724 RAMSAY *Tea-t. Misc.* (1733) I. 22 His minny Meg upo' her back Bare baith him and his billy. *a* **1748** *Dick O' the Cow* ii. (in Scott *Minstr.*), Johnie Armstrang to Willie did say—'Billie, a riding we will gae.' **1818** HOGG *Brownie* II. 31 (JAM.) That's a stretch of billyhood that I was never up to afore.

billy[2] (ˈbɪlɪ). [f. *Billy*, familiar perversion of *Willie*, hypocoristic or pet form of *William*: cf. *Bobby* = *Robby* = *Robert*.]
1. A term applied to various machines and implements: as, **a.** a slubbing or roving machine; **b.** a highwayman's club; a bludgeon; also (*U.S.*), a policeman's truncheon; see also quot. 1848; also ***billy club***. Cf. uses of BETTY, JACK, JEMMY, JENNY.
1795 *Edin. Advert.* 6 Jan. 15/1 Five common carding engines..four pickers, four roving billies, twenty-one spinning jeannies. **1848** 'NED BUNTLINE' *Myst. N.Y.* iv. 49 The foremost villain..broke down her guard with a short iron crowbar, or 'billy' as the burglars term it. **1856** *Santa Barbara* (Calif.) *Gaz.* 14 Feb. 2/5 He was knocked down by a blow from a 'billy'. **1865** *Times* 28 Apr., The man struck Mr. Seward on the head with a billy. **1875** URE *Dict. Arts* III. 1165 The slubbing machine, or billy. **1889** *Weekly Scotsman* 21 Sept. 3/5 He was felled by Marshal Glade's billy, which stunned him. **1903** *N.Y. Times* 11 Sept., Eight men set upon a policeman this morning,..taking his revolver and billy away from him. **1931** L. STEFFENS *Autobiogr.* I. II. v. 214, I felt the ache they [*sc.* policemen] conveyed to rap some head with the handy little billy. **1949** *Amer. Speech* XXIV. 262 By 1859 the billy club was demanding order in American cities. **1967** M. PROCTER *Exercise Hoodwink* ix. 67 Lying in the other bunk was a shark club or 'billy'. *Ibid.*, He had not taken his shark billy. **1969** *Listener* 3 July 11/2 He thought it necessary, this pig, this racist, to take his billy club out and crush her skull.
c. = BILLY-GOAT.
1849 C. J. PHARAZYN *Jrnl.* 17 Dec. (MS.) 137 Hunting goats Robin shot a Billy. **1928** *Daily Tel.* 9 Oct. 4/6 The Ministry of Agriculture, through the agency of its stud goat scheme, has now placed 103 'billies' at the disposal of smallholders.
2. *Comb.* In names of animals, plants, etc., mostly local: as **billy-biter**, the Blue Titmouse; **billy-button**, local name of the Bachelor's Button, Field Scabious, Double Daisy, Red Campion, and various other plants; **billy roller**, the wooden roller of a slubbing 'billy' (see quot.); **billy-wix**, the Tawny Owl. See also the following words.
1843 *Penny Cycl.* XXV. 4/1 Draws back his hand..well pecked by the irritated matron. Hence he calls it 'Billy Biter.' **1834** *Blackw. Mag.* XXXV. 297 Down came on his head..the patriotic billy-roller. **1875** URE *Dict. Arts* III. 1166 This is the billy-roller, so much talked of in the controversies between the operatives and masters in the cotton-factories, as an instrument of cruel punishment to children, though no such machine has been used in cotton-mills for half a century at least.

billy[3] (ˈbɪlɪ). *Austral.* and *N.Z.* [Origin uncertain: perh. f. Austral. Aboriginal *billa* river, water (cf. BILLABONG).] A cylindrical container, usu. of tin or enamel ware, with a close-fitting lid and a wire handle, used for making tea and for cooking over fires in the open, and for carrying food or liquid.
1839 J. HEBERLEY *Autobiogr.* (MS.) 87 [We] boiled the Billy and made some Tea out of tawa bark. **1853** J. ROCHFORT *Adv. Surveyor in N.Z.* viii. 63 We must needs purchase a 'billy' (a tin pot for boiling tea, coffee, meat or anything you may have the luck to get). **1858** *Jrnl. R. Geogr. Soc.* XXVIII. 310 We are..boiling our flesh or fowl in our tea-can (called a *billy*). **1872** BADEN POWELL *New Homes* 48 Men travelling about..invariably carry their billy or quart tin pot, wherein to make tea. **1881** *Cheq. Career* 361 To cook dampers..and boil a 'billy' are works of art. **1940** F. SARGESON *Man & Wife* (1944) 10 She was letting them have milk at half the town price... And my last job each day was to take a billy up to the back fence. **1943** D. STEWART in *Coast to Coast 1942* 212 The girls began to pluck handfuls of the berries and carry them to the billies the boys were filling. **1950** G. WILSON *Brave Company* xi. 179 The billy is boiled and the tea made.
attrib. Also **ˈbillyful**.
1865 G. MUELLER *My Dear Bannie* (1958) ii. 55 Price had a billy lid for a plate. **1866** A. H. WILLIAMSON in R. P. Whitworth *Martin's Bay Settlement* 23/1 Gathered a billyful of mussels..which we had for supper. **1897** D. McK. WRIGHT *Station Ballads* 17 The spuds and meat were nicely done, the billy tea was made. **1934** *Bulletin* (Sydney) 12 Sept. 9/2 'Billy tea,' says a paragraph issued by the Melbourne Centenary Committee, 'will be served to H.R.H. the Duke of Gloucester in the East Gippsland forest.' **1950** G. WILSON *Brave Company* xi. 179 First we boil a billyful of water.

billyards, obs. form of BILLIARDS.

billy-blin(d (ˈbɪlɪ-blaɪnd). *Sc.* [Of uncertain origin: see BELLY-BLIND.]
1. In ballads, the name of a benevolent household demon or familiar spirit. (See Child *Eng. & Sc. Ballads* I. 67, Grimm *Teut. Myth.* (Eng. ed.) II. 473.)
a **1802** *Willie's Ladye* xiv. (in Scott *Minstr.*), Then out and spak the Billy Blind, He spak aye in a gude time. *a* **1806** R. JAMIESON *Pop. Ball.* II. 130 (JAM.) Up it starts the Billy Blin, And stood at her bed feet.
2. The game of 'Blind-man's-buff'; = BELLY-BLIND. Hence, **billyblinder**, he who blindfolds the chief actor in this game; *fig.* a hoodwinker.
1822 HOGG *Perils Man* III. 387 (JAM.) Ay weel I wat that's little short of a billyblinder.

billyboy (ˈbɪlɪbɔɪ). [Derivation unknown: it has been conjecturally compared with BILANDER; also with BULLY-BOY.]
'A Humber or east-coast boat, of river-barge build, and a try-sail; a bluff-bowed north-country trader, or large one-masted vessel of burden.' Smyth.
1855 R. KNOX *E. Yorksh.* 62 Small flat-bottomed sloops called Billy-boys or Humber-keels. **1879** *Hertf. Merc.* 1 Mar. 2/7 The large tanned-sail barges, sometimes called billy-boys,..coming from Rochester or other places on the Kentish coast. **1884** *Mehalah* viii. 116 The pay was too small to entice a youth, who owned a vessel, a billy-boy, and oyster pans.

Billy Bunter (ˌbɪlɪ ˈbʌntə(r)). The name of a schoolboy in stories written between 1908 and 1961 by 'Frank Richards' (Charles Hamilton, 1875–1961), used allusively to indicate fatness, gluttony, clumsiness, etc.
1939 L. MACNEICE *Autumn Jrnl.* x. 41 Our little jokes of Billy Bunter dirt. **1959** *Times* 7 Mar. 7/4 'It is better for Britain,' declared an M.P. recently, 'to have a few more Billy Bunters than the kind of hunger which was caused to many children before milk in schools.' **1961** A. WILSON *Old Men at Zoo* ii. 72 Strawson, whose fat, self-satisfied Billy Bunter form waddled towards me at that moment. **1966** B. COOPER *Drown him Deep* xviii. 147 The full moon..stared down with a Billy Bunter's curious face.

billy-can (ˈbɪlɪˌkæn). *Austral.* and *N.Z.* [f. BILLY[3] + CAN *sb.*[1]] = BILLY[3].
1885 C. PRAED *Head Stat.* xxiii, I lost the billy-can-lid. **1899** 'S. RUDD' *On our Selection* 96 He carried no swag or billycan. **1933** *Bulletin* (Sydney) 26 Apr. 21/4 It contains half a dozen fire-blackened billy-cans. **1951** *Here & Now* (N.Z.) May 27/1 In many suburbs billy cans are still used for deliveries, the milk being ladled out of a container that is open to germs and dust.

billycock (ˈbɪlɪkɒk). [App. the same as *bully-cocked*, used 1721, prob. meaning 'cocked after the fashion of the *bullies*' or hectoring blades of the period: see BULLY and COCKED.] A colloquial term for a round low-crowned felt hat worn by men, and sometimes also by young women. Also *attrib.*
1721 AMHERST *Terr. Fil.* No. 46. 246 He [the Oxford 'smart'] is easily distinguish'd by a stiff silk gown..a flaxen tie-wig..a broad bully-cocked hat, or a square cap of above twice the usual size. **1862** *Life among Colliers* 35, I was told to take off my bonnet, and tie a billy-cock (wide-awake) tight down. *Mod. Newspaper.* She..is masculine from the crown of her billycock hat, to the point of her laced-up double-soled boots.

Billy Fairplay or **Playfair**. *Coal-mining.* (See quot. 1883.)
1876 *Brit. Pat. 4387*, Machines for weighing small coal known by the name of 'Billy fair play'. **1883** GRESLEY *Gloss. Coal Mining*, *Billy Playfair* or *Fair-play*,..a mechanical contrivance for weighing coal, consisting of an iron trough with a sort of hopper bottom, into which all the small coal passing through the screen is conducted and weighed off and emptied from time to time. **1889** *Law Rep.* (*Appeal Cases*) XIV. 231 The coal was shot down on a screen called Billy Fairplay.

billy-goat (ˈbɪlɪgəʊt). [f. *Billy* (a male name) + GOAT.] Familiar term for: A male goat.
1861 T. PEACOCK *Gryll Gr.* 108 There is nothing to eat in Greece but tough billy goats. **1882** *Standard* 11 Feb. 3/2 Hair turning grey, hazel eyes, billygoat beard.

billyment, obs. form of BILIMENT.

billy-o. *colloq.* Also -oh. Used in the intensive phr. ***like billy-o*** (see LIKE *adv.* 1 b) = like the devil (see DEVIL *sb.* 16); also in other intensive phrases.
1885 *Referee* 9 Aug. 7/4 Shure it'll rain like billy-oh! **1914** W. J. LOCKE *Fortunate Youth* iii, 'And they fight?' 'Like billy-o,' said Paul. **1927** *Punch* 25 May 584/3 He would take a team anywhere... He would take a team to Billy-O. **1927** *Observer* 11 Dec. 26 The Holy Rollers were going it like billy-oh to a tune which sounded like 'My old man's a fireman'. **1934** *Bulletin* (Sydney) 25 July 21/4 With the price of copra and rubber all to billyoh, Papua has been in the doldrums lately. **1969** *Sunday Mail Mag.* (Brisbane) 1 June 6/3 There was Amundsen..with his dogs going like billyo for the Pole.

bilobate (baɪˈləʊbeɪt), *a.* [f. BI- *pref.*[2] 1 + LOBATE, f. mod.L. *lobus*, Gr. λοβός.] = BILOBED.
1794 MARTYN *Rousseau's Bot.* xxi. 293 The petals are.. bilobate. **1877** COUES *Fur Anim.* iii. 77 Bilobate tips.

ˈbilobated, *a.* [f. as prec. + -ED.] = next.
1770 PENNANT *Zool.* IV. 85 Nose bilobated. **1837** *Penny Cycl.* VII. 78/2 The anterior lamella being deeply bilobated.

bilobed (baɪˈləʊbd), *ppl. a.* [f. BI- *pref.*[2] 1 + LOBED.] Having, or divided into, two lobes.
1756 P. BROWNE *Jamaica* 214 They..contain each a bilobed kernel. **1880** BASTIAN *Brain* 97 The Brain of the Crab is represented by a rather small bilobed ganglion.

bilobular (baɪˈlɒbjʊlə(r)), *a.* [f. BI- *pref.*[2] + LOBULE + -AR.] Having, or divided into, two lobules or small lobes.
1859 TODD *Cycl. Anat. & Phys.* V. 540/1 Slightly cleft so as to indicate a bilobular tendency.

bilocation (baɪləʊˈkeɪʃən). [f. BI- *pref.*[2] II + LOCATION.] The fact or power of being in two places at the same time.
1858 FABER *Life Xavier* 336 It was in fact a case of bilocation. **1871** TYLOR *Prim. Cult.* i. 404 The word 'bilocation' has been invented to express the miraculous faculty of being in two places at once.

bilocellate (baɪˈlɒsɪleɪt), *a.* [f. BI- *pref.*[2] 1 + *locellus*, dim. of *loculus*: see next.] Having, or divided into, two minute cells.
1880 GRAY *Struct. Bot.* vi. §6. 254 The cells of anthers.. are bilocellate.

bilocular (baɪˈlɒkjʊlə(r)), *a.* [f. BI- *pref.*[2] 1 + LOCULAR, f. L. *loculus*, dim. of *locus* place.] Having, divided into, or consisting of two cells or small receptacles.
1783 DAVIDSON in *Phil. Trans.* LXXIV. 455 The germen is..bilocular. **1836** TODD *Cycl. Anat. & Phys.* I. 107/2 The molluscous classes..[have] a bilocular heart.

biˈloculate, *a.* [f. as prec.; see -ATE[2].] = prec.
1874 JONES & SIEV. *Pathol. Anat.* 365 This kind is of more frequent occurrence than the biloculate.

biloculine (baɪˈlɒkjʊlaɪn), *a.* *Zool.* [ad. mod.L. *Biloculīna*, f. *bi-* BI-[2] + L. *loculus*, dim. of *locus* place: see -INE[1].] Having two chambers or compartments; characteristic of the foraminiferous genus *Biloculina*.
1898 SEDGWICK *Zool.* I. 9 In the genus *Biloculina* (*Miliolidæ*), while the mode of growth of the megalospheric form is..on the biloculine plan from the first, that of the microspheric form is at first on the quinqueloculine plan, and it is not until many chambers have been formed that the biloculine plan, characteristic of the genus, is assumed.

bilong, obs. form of BELONG.

biloöghe, obs. form of BELOW.

bilophodont (baɪˈlɒfədɒnt), *a.* *Zool.* [f. BI-[2] + *lophodont* (see LOPHO-).] Of the molar teeth in

certain ungulates: having two transverse crests or ridges on the grinding surface.

1868 OWEN *Anat. Vertebr.* III. 343 The 'bilophodont' sub-type becomes more marked in *Dinotherium*. *Ibid.* 358 Certain huge fossil bilophodont grinders, which seemed to indicate a gigantic Tapir. **1891** FLOWER & LYDEKKER *Mammals* 373 Molars brachydont and bilophodont.

biloquial (baɪˈləʊkwɪəl), *a.* [f. BI- *pref.*² II + *-loquial*, after *colloquial*.] Speaking with two different voices.

a **1810** C. B. BROWN *Carwin* (1822) I. 135 The confession of my biloquial powers.

biloquist (ˈbɪləkwɪst). [f. BI- *pref.*² II + *-loquist*; cf. *ventriloquist*.] One who can speak with two different voices.

a **1810** C. B. BROWN (title) *Carwin, the Biloquist.* **1884** *Sat. Rev.* 12 July 54 As a biloquist Mr. Maccabe's powers are very considerable.

bilouen, -lufen, -luuen, etc., obs. ff. BELOVE.

‖**biltong** (ˈbɪltɒŋ). Also (corruptly) **beltong, bell-tongue.** [S. African Dutch, f. *bil* buttock + *tong* tongue, 'because it is mostly cut from the buttock, and in appearance somewhat resembles a smoked neat's-tongue' (Changuion).] Strips of lean meat (of antelope, buffalo, etc.) dried in the sun.

1815 A. PLUMTRE *Lichtenstein's Trav.* II. 77 He lived almost entirely upon dried mutton and biltong. **1863** BALDWIN *Afr. Hunting* 111, I..converted the most of them into bell-tongue. **1879** ATCHERLEY *Boërland* 149 Cut up into strips, and hung to dry on the tree for biltong.

bilverketch: see BILBOQUET.

†**ˈbilwise,** *a. Obs.* App. *bill-wise* wise or clever of mouth, as opposed to *poll-mad*.

1577 STANYHURST *Descr. Irel.* in *Holinsh.* II. 12/1 Marcus Cicero..perceiving his countrimen to become changelings, in being bilwise and polmad, and to sucke with the Greeke [tongue] the conditions of the Grecians, as to be in words talkative, in behaviour light.

bilyne, variant of BLIN *v. Obs.* to cease.

†**ˈbilynge.** *Obs. rare*⁻¹. [Cf. OE. *bile* beak of a ship.] ? The beak or prow of a ship.

? *a* **1400** *Morte Arth.* 3664 The bilynge and the beme brestys in sondyre.

Bim¹ (bɪm). Also **Bimm.** Colloq. name for an inhabitant of Barbados. So **ˈBimshire,** Barbados.

1852 C. W. DAY *Five Yrs. W. Indies* I. 15 The Barbadians are familiarly known as 'Bimms'. **1859** TROLLOPE *W. Indies* xiii. 207 One soon learns to know a—Bim. That is the name in which they themselves delight, and therefore, though there is a sound of slang about it, I give it here. *Ibid.* 208 The Bims..are generally stout fellows. **1887** W. A. PATON *Down the Islands* (1888) xii. 135 Barbadoes is known to the initiated as Bimshire—a Barbadian as a Bim. **1902** *Daily Chron.* 1 Feb. 5/1 Mr. Bosanquet's team of English cricketers, which has lately been playing in Barbados, and making but an indifferent show before the doughty 'Bims'.

bim². *U.S. slang.* [Abbrev. of BIMBO².] A girl, woman; a whore.

1925 *Eng. Jrnl.* Nov. 700 John took his bim to a dance. **1935** J. T. FARRELL *Studs Lonigan* (1936) III. i. 467 Studs Lonigan copped off a bim whose old man is lousy with dough. **1953** W. R. BURNETT *Vanity Row* ix. 71 I'd hate to turn you loose on a desert island with that big bim.

bim³. *slang.* = BUM *sb.*¹ 1.

1935 I. MILLER *School Tie* vi. 59 Fligg never hits you properly on the bim, always below it. **1948** C. DAY LEWIS *Otterbury Inc.* ix. 119 He slid gracefully down it on his bim.

bimaculate, -ated (baɪˈmækjʊlət, -eɪtɪd), *a.* [f. BI- *pref.*² 1 + L. *macŭlātus* spotted, f. *macŭla* spot.] Marked with two spots.

1769 PENNANT *Zool.* III. 205 Bimaculated Wrasse. **1848** C. JOHNS *Week at Lizard* 333 Bimaculated Duck.

‖**Bimana** (ˈbɪmənə, ˈbaɪ-), *sb. pl. Zool.* [mod.L. neut. pl. of **bimanus* two-handed (sc. *animalia*), the latinized form of Buffon's *bimane*, f. L. *bi-* two + *manus* hand.] Two-handed animals: Cuvier's name for the highest order of Mammalia, of which man is the type and only species.

[**1766** BUFFON *Hist. Nat.* XIV. 18 Faisons pour les mains un nom pareil à celui qu'on a fait pour les pieds, et alors nous dirons avec vérité et précision que l'homme est le seul qui est bimane et bipède. **1785** SMELLIE *Transl.* (1791) VIII. 52 We might then say that man was the only biped and *bimanus*.] **1839** *Penny Cycl.* XIV. 353/2 Class *Mammifères*. Order I. *Bimana*, Man. **1871** DARWIN *Desc. Man* I. vi. 190 The greater number of naturalists..have placed man in a separate order, under the title of *Bimana*.

ˈbimanal, *a. Zool.* = BIMANOUS.

1859 TODD *Cycl. Anat. & Phys.* V. 172/2 The bimanal.. Reptiles. **1882** OWEN in *Longman's Mag.* I. 67 The highest (Caucasian) variety of the Bimanal order.

bimane (ˈbaɪmeɪn). *Zool.* [a. F. *bimane*; see BIMANA, to which this supplies a singular.]

A two-handed animal; one of the *Bimana*.

1835 KIRBY *Hab. & Inst. Anim.* II. xvii. 215 He [man] is the only Bimane. **1880** *Libr. Univ. Knowledge* III. 632 Bimanes, including mankind.

bimanous (ˈbɪmənəs, baɪ-), *a.* [f. mod.L. *biman-us* or F. *bimane* + -OUS.] **a.** Two-handed. **b.** Of or belonging to the *Bimana*.

1832 LYELL *Princ. Geol.* II. 15 Transformed into bimanous animals. **1878** BARTLEY tr. *Topinard's Anthrop.* ii. 79 The anthropoid ape..is bimanous, but he has the assistance of his hands in walking.

bimanual (baɪˈmænjuːəl), *a.* [f. BI-² + MANUAL *a.*] Performed with both hands; in which both hands are employed. Hence **biˈmanually** *adv.*, by means of both hands.

1898 G. E. HERMAN *Dis. Women* 59 Bimanual examination. *Ibid.* 63 There are cases in which..you cannot bimanually feel the distinction. **1902** D. J. CUNNINGHAM *Anat.* 1233 By the bimanual examination the pelvic organs are steadied and pushed downwards towards the pelvic outlet by the pressure of the left hand applied in the hypogastric region.

bimarginate, bimembral: see BI- *pref.*² 1.

†**biˈmarian,** *a. Obs. rare*⁻⁰. [f. L. *bimari-s* (see BIMARINE) + -AN.] 'Of or pertaining to two seas.' Bailey 1731, vol. II.

†**biˈmarical,** *a.* 'Of two seas.' Coles.

1692 in COLES, etc.

bimarine (baɪməriːn), *a.* [f. L. *bimaris* (f. *bi-* two + *mare* sea) after *marine*.] Between two seas.

1852 GROTE *Greece* II. lxxiv. IX. 425 *note*, The bimarine road or region [Gr. τὴν ἀμφίαλον].

†**biˈmatical.** *Obs.*⁻⁰ [f. L. *bimāt-us* the age of two years.] 'Two yeeres space.' Cockeram 1623.

bi-matter, obs. form of BY-MATTER.

bimbashi (bɪmˈbɑːʃɪ, -æ-). Also **bimbashee, binbashi.** [Turk., lit. 'one who is head of a thousand' (*bin* thousand, *baş* head; cf. BASHAW).] A Turkish major, naval commander, or squadron-leader. Also formerly in Egypt, an English officer in the service of the Khedive.

1819 T. HOPE *Anastasius* II. xv. 329 A Bimbashee [*note* Turkish colonel], with about eighteen hundred men. **1876** GLADSTONE *Bulgarian Horrors* 31 Their Bimbashis and their Yuzbachis, their Kaimakams and their Pashas. **1896** *Daily News* 28 Mar. 5/3 'Bimbashi' is the general name for the English officers attached to the Egyptian army. **1899** KIPLING *Stalky* 197 He did not know that Wake..would be a bimbashi of the Egyptian Army ere his thirtieth year. **1922** *Blackw. Mag.* Apr. 519/1 Let me be the Bimbashi of the Hakim's river watchers.

bimbo¹ (ˈbɪmbəʊ). A kind of punch.

1880 *Barman's Man.*, Bimbo is made nearly in the same way as Arrack punch, except that Cognac brandy is substituted for arrack. [See also BUMBO.]

ˈbimbo². *slang* (orig. *U.S.*). Pl. **-os, -oes.** [It., = little child, baby; cf. BAMBINO.] **a.** A fellow, chap; usu. contemptuous.

1919 *Amer. Mag.* Nov. 69/1 Nothing but the most heroic measures will save the poor bimbo. **1924** WODEHOUSE *Bill the Conqueror* xx. 285 The bimbo Pyke arrived. **1936** R. CHANDLER *Killer in Rain* (1964) 53 There's a thousand berries on that bimbo. A bank stick-up, ain't he? **1947** WODEHOUSE *Full Moon* v. 90 Bimbos who went about the place making passes at innocent girls after discarding their wives.

b. A woman; esp. a whore.

1929 *Amer. Speech* IV. 338 *Bimbo*, a woman. **1937** *Detective Fiction Weekly* 3 Apr. 20/2 We found Durken and Frenchy LaSeur, seated at a table..with a pair of blonde bimboes beside them. **1952** S. KAUFFMANN *Philanderer* (1953) xii. 194 Not that you were just a bimbo to me... I've discovered that I'm a little in love with you, too.

bimeane, -mene, obs. ff. BEMOAN.

bimeby (ˈbaɪmbaɪ), *adv. dial.* Also **bimby(e, bimebye, bymeby,** etc. Reduced form of BY AND BY A. 4.

[**1549** [see BY AND BY A. 4]. **1708** *Deplorable State of New Eng.* 35 Altho'..one Day it was voted, That the Fort should be attack'd, it was by 'nd by, unvoted again.] **1722** in O. E. Winslow *Broadside Verse* (1930) 115/2 Indian bimeby take Captain Westbrook's fort. **1824** *Nantucket Inquirer* 5 Jan. (Th.), Well, bimeby he took notion to hab my daughter... Well, bimeby I found em out. **1825** J. JENNINGS *Obs. Dial. West of Eng.* 26 *Bimeby*, by-and-by; some time hence. **1825** etc. [see BY AND BY A. 4]. **1850** 'N. HOGG' *Lett. in Devonshire Dial.* (ed. 2) 6 Bim-bye, in com'd a wacking hoss. **1857** J. G. HOLLAND *Bay-Path* xiv. 156 It's a thing that'll come round byme-by. **1873** 'MARK TWAIN' & WARNER *Gilded Age* ii. 32 But bymeby she roused up like, and looked around wild. **1899** R. WHITEING *No. 5 John St.* vii. 64, I s'pose everybody all over the world 'll know our patter bimeby. **1907** E. WHARTON *Fruit of Tree* I. ii. 27 A small boy who said breathlessly: 'Mr. Truscomb wants you to come down bimeby.' **1952** *Amer. Speech* XXVI. 26 Common expressions in the pidgin of Hawaii are..*bimeby* (by-and-by), *wasamatta* (what's the matter?), [etc.].

bimedial (baɪˈmiːdɪəl), *a.* (and *sb.*) [f. BI- *pref.*² + MEDIAL, f. L. *medi-us* middle.]

†**a.** *Algeb.* (See quot. 1557.) *Obs.* **b.** *Geom.* The sum of two medial lines; a medial line being the geometric mean between two incommensurable lines, which have commensurable squares.

1557 RECORDE *Whetst.* Ppiv, The nombers that be compounde with +, be called *Bimedialles*..And if the Bimedialles haue all their nombers and partes of one denominations, then bee thei called onely by their general name Bimedialles. But if their partes be of 2 denominations, then are thei named Binomialles properly. Howbeit, many vse to call Binomialles all compounde nombers that haue +. **1570** BILLINGSLEY *Euclid* x. lxvii. 278 A line commensurable in length to a bimediall line, is also a bimediall lyne and of the selfe same order. **1727** CHAMBERS *Cycl.* s.v. *Bimedial*, When two medial lines, as AB and BC, commensurable only in power, and containing a rational rectangle, are compounded; the whole AC shall be irrational, and is called a first bimedial line. [So in later Encycl.]

†**biˈmelden,** *v. Obs. rare*⁻¹. [f. *bi-*, BE- + ME. *melden*:—OE. *meldian* to indicate, inform against, betray. Cf. Ger. *bemelden*.] *trans.* To inform against, betray.

a **1300** *Siriz* 37 (Mätz.) Bote on that thou me nout bimelde, Ne make the wroth, Min hernde willi to the bede.

†**biˈmen.** *Obs. rare*⁻¹. [ME.: f. *bimenen* = BEMOAN.] A complaint, a lament.

c **1250** *Gen. & Ex.* 2894 [He] to god made hise bimen.

†**biˈmensal,** *a. Obs.*⁻⁰ [f. BI- *pref.*² 4 + L. *mensis* month.] 'During the space of two moneths.' Bullokar 1676.

†**bimensical.** 'Two moneths space.' Cockeram.

bimeridian (baɪməˈrɪdɪən), *a.* [f. BI- *pref.*² 4, 6 + MERIDIAN.] Belonging to, or recurring at, midday and midnight.

1869 PHILLIPS *Vesuv.* vi. 169 Before accepting as probable bimeridian influences.

bimestrial (baɪˈmɛstrɪəl), *a.* [f. L. *bimestri-s* (f. *bi-* two + *mensis* month) + -AL¹.] Of two months' duration; occurring every two months.

1846 WORCESTER cites *Q. Rev.* **1870** LOWELL *Among my Bks.* Ser. II. (1873) 11 An office which the Florentines had made bimestrial in its tenure.

bi-metal (ˈbaɪmɛtəl). [f. BI-² + METAL *sb.*] A bimetallic material or object. Freq. *attrib.* or as *adj.*, = next.

1935 *Discovery* Dec. 369/1 The word 'bi-metal' is used for a composition of two metals with different expansion coefficients. *Ibid.*, The 'Rototherm' bi-metal thermometer. *Ibid.* 369/2 Making the bi-metal in the form of a single spiral. **1938** *Jrnl. Marine Res.* I. 95 A Bathythermograph... Mounted on the movable end of the pressure element is a straight bi-metal strip, and thus motion with pressure is at right angles to the deflection of the strip with temperature. **1946** D. DE CARLE *Pract. Watch Repairing* xii. 119 A bi-metal balance of steel with brass fused on the outer edge is used. **1953** *Electronic Engin.* XXV. 78 The loop is provided by a spiral bi-metal strip which tends to coil and uncoil with change of temperature.

bimetallic (baɪmɪˈtælɪk), *a.* [ad. F. *bimétallique*, f. *bi-* two, twice, double + *métallique* METALLIC: used for the nonce by M. Cernuschi in addressing the Soc. of Pol. Econ. in Paris, on Jan. 5, 1869; and in its Eng. form in his paper, 'Silver Vindicated,' read before the Social Sc. Assoc. at Liverpool in 1876, after which it was universally adopted as the proper word for the system in question.] **1.** Of, pertaining to, or using a 'double standard' of currency, i.e. one based upon the two metals gold and silver, in opposition to a mono-metallic currency based upon gold or silver alone.

1876 (*title*) 'La Monnaie bimetallique,' par Henri Cernuschi, Paris—*Eng. Transl.* 'Bi-metallic Money and its bearing on Monetary Crises in Germany, France, England and the United States.' **1876** S. WILLIAMSON *Let. S. Smith* 19 We may find no satisfactory adjustment..without adopting a dual or bimetallic standard. **1877** S. HORTON *Silver & Gold* 149 The relative amounts of the stock of Bi-metallic countries and of Mono-metallic countries. **1879** H. H. GIBBS *Silver & Gold* 33 In point of fact the world is already bimetallic; but it is an unregulated and haphazard bimetallism which prevails among us.

2. Composed of two different metals; ***bimetallic strip***: a sensitive element in some thermostats, made of two bands of different metals, one of which expands more than the other when the temperature rises, and so causes the strip to bend.

1907 *U.S. Pat.* *851,684*, The process..of making bimetallic products such as ingots, sheets, tubes, wires and the like, of different metals welded together. **1922** *Jrnl. Amer. Chem. Soc.* XLIV. 2504 Bimetallic electrode systems in electrometric analysis. I. Systems comprising two dissimilar metals. **1930** *Engineering* 31 Oct. 543/1 The smaller ovens are controlled by a bimetallic-strip thermostat.

bimetallism (baɪˈmɛtəlɪz(ə)m). [f. as prec. + -ISM.] The system of allowing the unrestricted currency of two metals (*e.g.* gold and silver) at a fixed ratio to each other, as coined money.

1876 H. CERNUSCHI *Silver Vind.* 9 The Anglo Indian Exchange, thanks to French bi-metallism, would still be at its old level. **1881** *Times* 7 May, If bimetallism be adopted, the ratio of gold and silver apparently should be 1 to 15½.

bi'metallist, *sb.* [f. as prec. + -IST.] An advocate or supporter of bimetallism. Also *attrib.* or as *adj.*

1879 *Sat. Rev.* 20 Sept. 355 Mr. Gibbs and all reasonable bi-metallists admit this. **1885** D. BARBOUR *Bimetallism* Introd. 12 The bimetallists.. advocate a system of currency which has the advantage of rendering the market ratio of gold and silver nearly constant.

bimeta'llistic, *a.* [f. BIMETALLIST + -IC.] Relating or inclining to bimetallism.

1889 in *Cent. Dict.* (citing *Contemp. Rev.*). **1897** *Daily News* 5 Feb. 10/5 The Agriculturists, with their.. bimetallistic hankerings.

bimillenary (baɪ'mɪlɪnərɪ). [f. BI- *pref.*² II + MILLENARY, f. L. *millēnārius* containing a thousand.] Properly (like *millenary*) an adj., meaning: Of or pertaining to two thousand, two thousand strong; but taken to express: A space of two thousand years (for which *bimillennium* or some derivative of it would be the proper term). Also, the two-thousandth anniversary of an event.

1850 J. H. NEWMAN *Diffic. Anglic.* 130 To testify the very truth of revelation to a fallen generation, or rather to almost a bi-millenary, which has been in unintermittent traditionary error. **1961** in WEBSTER. **1965** G. MCINNES *Road to Gundagai* xi. 192, I didn't meet the full force of his authority until the celebration of the Bimillenary of Virgil. **1971** *Bookseller* 13 Nov. 2234/3 The only country to commemorate the recent bimillenary of the death of Lucretius was the Soviet Union. **1981** *N.Y. Times* 31 Dec. A23/5 The exact date on which we should celebrate 'the bimillenary' (2,000th anniversary) of Virgil's death was a subject of controversy.

bimodal (baɪ'məʊdəl), *a.* [f. BI-² + MODAL *a.*] Having two modes, esp. in *Statistics* (MODE *sb.* 8 d).

1903 *Amer. Naturalist* 302 The tendency to bilateral symmetry here in the number of teeth is very strong and so gives a bimodal curve with apices at 10 and at 12. **1903** *Bot. Gaz.* Dec. 477 Field studies showed that the stamens vary from 0 to 13, forming a bimodal curve with principal maximum on 3 and secondary minimum on 5. **1925** F. C. MILLS *Statistical Methods* iv. 129 In Table 9, representing the distribution of wages, there are two definite modal points. A distribution of this type is called bi-modal; when plotted, a frequency curve having two humps is obtained. **1935** R. S. WOODWORTH *Psychology* (ed. 10) iii. 37 When only a small number of individuals is tested, the distribution often looks bimodal. **1968** *Brit. Med. Bull.* XXIV. 212/1 The corresponding histogram of conjugated bilirubin is markedly bimodal.

bimodality (baɪməʊ'dælɪtɪ). [f. BI-² + MODALITY.] The quality or fact of being bimodal, esp. in *Statistics*.

1903 *Amer. Naturalist* 308 As in the case of the curve for the prosternal teeth, which is strongly bimodal, the bimodality is due to the tendency towards bilateral symmetry. **1928** S. A. RICE *Quantitative Methods in Politics* viii. 113 Bimodality is invariably regarded as evidence of absence of homogeneity in the data which is distributed. **1932** J. S. HUXLEY *Problems of Rel. Growth* ii. 70 A similar but less-marked bimodality occurs in this species.

bimodulus (baɪ'mɒdjʊləs). *Math.* [f. BI- *pref.*² II + MODULUS.] The double of the modulus of a system of logarithms. **bi'modular** *a.*, of or pertaining to the bimodulus.

1881 *Nature* XXIII. 379 A bimodular method is one founded on the familiar proposition, that if the bimodulus.. be multiplied by the difference and divided by the sum of two numbers, the result would be approximately the difference of their logarithms. **1881** *Athenæum* 12 Feb. 237/2 An Improved Bimodular Method.

bimolecular (baɪməʊ'lɛkjʊlə(r)), *a.* [BI-².] Involving two molecules.

1899 J. WALKER *Introd. Physical Chem.* 256 Saponification of ethereal salts by alkalies affords us an example of a bimolecular reaction. *Ibid.* 257 A bimolecular reaction, which is, strictly speaking, a balanced action, but proceeds very nearly to an end in aqueous solution, is the formation of urea from ammonium cyanate. **1904** J. W. MELLOR *Chem. Stat. & Dynam.* 35 The hydrolysis of ethyl acetate by sodium hydroxide is a bimolecular reaction. **1946** *Nature* 20 July 94/1 Those bimolecular and unimolecular substitutions in which a nucleophilic reagent displaces halogen as halide ion from an alkyl halide. **1957** *Encycl. Brit.* XIX. 3D/1 If a kinetic study shows that two molecules (of the same or of different compounds) react with one another directly, then the reaction is said to be bimolecular.

† **bi'mong, by'mong**, *prep. Obs.* [A parallel form to AMONG, IMONG; f. *bi, be,* BY *prep.* + *mong*, aphetic f. IMONG, OE. *ʒemang* 'mingling, concourse, crowd.'] Among.

a **1225** *Ancr. R.* 102 þu ueir bimong wummen. *a* **1225** *St. Marher.* 1 Bimong worldliche men. *c* **1300** in Wright *Lyric P.* ix. 35 Baloynge mengeth al by-mong.

bi-monthly, *a.*, *sb.*, and *adv.* [BI-² 4.] (Occurring or produced) every two months; *sb.*, a bi-monthly periodical. Also used = occurring (etc.) twice a month (cf. *semi-monthly* s.v. SEMI- 6 b).

1846 *Punch* 31 Jan. 61/1 Bi-monthly breakneck expresses between the Punjaub and Cheapside. **1864** *Even. Standard* 29 Oct., Sixpenny parts, to be issued bi-monthly. **1878** *Print. Trades Jrnl.* xxv. 4 A new Spanish bi-monthly journal. **1879** GLADSTONE in *Daily News* 1 Dec. 6/5 Annual as opposed to bi-monthly or tri-monthly budgets. **1926** (*title*) Vogue Fashion Bi-Monthly. **1959** *Times* 10 Jan. 7/7 A bi-monthly called *Recorded Folk Music*.

bimorph ('baɪmɔːf). *Electr.* [f. BI-² + Gr. μορφή form.] A device consisting of two piezo-electric crystals, used in sound reproduction.

1932 *Electronics* May 166/2 The bimorph or opposed action types [of crystal units] have been adapted and used for loudspeakers, phonograph pickups and microphones. **1962** A. NISBETT *Technique Sound Studio* 247 A crystal bimorph—two plates cut from different planes of a crystal of Rochelle Salt and held together in the form of a sandwich.

bimorphemic (baɪmɔː'fiːmɪk), *a.* [f. BI-² + MORPHEMIC *a.*] Consisting of or pertaining to two morphemes.

1942 *Amer. Speech* XVII. 168 In 168 oscillograph records of such homophonic pairs [as *tide, tied; rise, rye's*].. the average duration of the vowel in the bimorphemic words is about ·030 sec. greater than that of the vowel in the monomorphemic words. **1947** *Language* XXIII. 339 Some may.. prefer to reinterpret portmanteaus as bimorphic as well as bimorphemic, even though to do so one must extend the definition of 'morph' to cover elements of other than overt phonemic content. **1964** R. H. ROBINS *Gen. Linguistics* v. 205 The bimorphemic structure of all English noun plurals.

bimuscular: see BI- *pref.*² 4, 1.

bin (bɪn), *sb.* Forms: 1 binn(e, 2–8 binne, 4–6 bynne, byn, 5–7 bene, 7–8 binn, 1– bin. [OE. *binn(e* str. fem. 'manger, crib, hutch, bin.' In later times a good deal confused with BING.

Franck compares Du. *beun*, MDu. *bunne* fem. 'fish-cauf.' Others would refer OE. *binn(e* directly to late L. *benna*, applied to various vessels or receptacles, among others to a 'hamper' and a 'vivarium' for fish, and apparently identical with *benna*, given by Festus as a Gaulish name for a kind of vehicle (cf. Welsh *ben* 'cart, wagon'), inferred to have been a wicker- or basket-cart, which sense, with that of 'panier for pack-horse,' 'large creel,' etc., is preserved in It. *benna* wicker-work sleigh, dung-cart, F. *benne* 'grape-gatherer's creel, fish-cauf, basket-cart for charcoal,' *banne* panier, basket-cart (also mod.G. *benne*, Du. *benne, ben*, large basket, adopted from Fr., It., or med.L.). If OCeltic *benna* orig. meant a wicker-work panier (with or without wheels), a root **ben-*, **bun-* to twist, plait, may as Franck suggests have been common to Celtic and Teutonic. (See Diez, Du Cange *benna*, in Littré, Scheler *benne*, in Franck *ben, beun*.)]

1. *gen.* A receptacle (*orig.* of wicker- or basket-work): still used dialectally and technically in the most diverse senses, as seen in the following quotations.

1570 LEVINS *Manip.*, A Binne, *scrinium vimineum*. **1676** WORLIDGE *Cider* (1691) 101 The boards that descend from the hopper or bin. **1787** W. MARSHALL *Rural Econ. E. Norf.* (E.D.S.) *Bins*, applied provincially to the receptacles of straw in a farm-yard; cow-cribs. **1802** J. SIBBALD *Chron. Sc. Poetry* Gloss. (JAM.) *Binne*, a temporary inclosure or repository made of boards, twigs, or straw-ropes for containing grain or such like. **1863** MORTON *Cycl. Agric.*, *Bin* or *Bing*, a space in a barn partitioned off at the side: also a wooden receptacle of any kind.

The following are the chief specific uses:

†**2.** The receptacle in a stable for the provender of the beasts; the manger or crib; *loosely* (?) a stall. *Obs.* exc. ? *dial.*

c **950** *Lindisf. Gosp.* Luke ii. 7, And eft ʒebeʒ hine in binnæ [*Rushw., Ags., & Hatton G.* binne]. **971** *Blickl. Hom.* 11 Arweorþian we Crist on binne asetene. *a* **1000** ÆLFRIC *Colloq.* Q. 8 Ic sceal fyllan binnan oxan mid hiʒ. *c* **1305** *Leg. Rood* (1871) 145 Beestes gan Belwe in ueeri binne. *a* **1400** *Cov. Myst.* 159 In a bestys bynne Bestad in a stalle. *c* **1425** *Leg. Rood* 211 God was borne with beest in bynne.

3. A receptacle for holding corn, meal, bread, fruit, and other articles of consumption; a hutch. Also, in later use, for dust (*dust-bin*), coal, or other things requiring storage for a time.

c **1386** CHAUCER *Prol.* 595 Wel cowde he kepe a gerner and a bynne. **1481–90** HOWARD *Househ. Bks.* 407 A pece of tymbir for the bene in the pantrey iij*d*. **1580** BARET *Alv.* B 700 A Binne or place to put bread in. **1648** HERRICK *Poems* (1869) 267 A little bin best fits a little bread. *a* **1682** SIR T. BROWNE *Tracts* 43 They put up their corn in granaries and binns. **1695** KENNETT *Par. Antiq.* Gloss. s.v. *Abunda, Bin*, or *Bing*, a Safe, an Aumbry or Cupboard in a Buttery or Lardar. **1871** J. WALSH ('Stonehenge') *Horse* xiii. (1877) 193 A bin for oats, beans, and chaff.

4. a. A partitioned case or stand for storing bottles in a wine-cellar; *transf.* wine from a particular bin. Also *attrib.*

1758 T. WARTON in *Idler* No. 33 ¶5 To remove the five-year-old Port into the new bin on the left hand. **1828** KIRBY & SP. *Entomol.* III. xxix. 80 Piled on their sides like bottles of wine in a bin. **1864** TENNYSON *Aylmer's F.* 405 His richest beeswing from a bin reserved For banquets. **1872** LEVER *Ld. Kilgobbin* lxix. 380 He tasted that 'bin.'

b. in a forcing-house for plants.

1861 DELAMER *Kitch. Gard.* 104 Though less convenient than the open bins, it is a good plan for economizing space.

5. A large receptacle used in hop-picking. (Cf. Fr. *benne* 'hotte a l'usage de vendangeurs.')

1737 MILLER *Gard. Dict.* s.v. *Lupulus*, A long square Frame of Wood call'd a Binn, with a Cloth hanging on Tenter-hooks within it, to receive the Hops. **1880** *Times* 10 Sept. 9/5 Merry parties of pickers round the bins. **1883** J. STRATTON *Hops & Hop-pick.* 20 The hops are picked into bins or baskets.

6. One of a number of receptacles in a wool-shed where wool is stowed by classes after sorting. *Austral.* and *N.Z.*

1865 LADY BARKER *Let.* 1 Dec. in *Station Life N.Z.* (1870) v. 33 Armfulls of rolled-up fleeces [were] laid on the tables before the wool-sorters who.. pronounced.. to which bin they belonged. **1891** R. WALLACE *Rural Econ. Austral. & N.Z.* xxix. 383 Bins of fleeces awaiting pressing. **1933** L. G. D. ACLAND in *Press* (Christchurch) 23 Sept. 13/7 A man or boy.. carries the fleeces from the wool table to their bins after the wool-classer has classed them.

7. Short for *loony bin* (see LOONY *a.* and *sb.*). *slang.*

1938 E. WAUGH *Scoop* I. i. 10 To my certain knowledge she's driven three men into the bin. **1942** L. A. G. STRONG *Unpractised Heart* 77 The chaps who certified you and popped you in the bin.

8. Special Comb. **bin end**, one of the last bottles from a bin of wine; **bin-liner**, a strong plastic or paper bag designed to be used inside a dustbin or other waste-bin, and lifted out with the rubbish still inside it when the bin is full.

1968 *Times* 21 Sept. 23/2 Pleasant wine can often be found in Fine Wine and *Bin End sales. **1976** *Norwich Mercury* 19 Nov. 12/7 (Advt.), Collective sale of inexpensive Fine Wines and Bin Ends, in all approx. 750 dozen. **1984** *Times* 17 Nov. 9/7 My local supermarket has several bottles clearly labelled 'Beaujolais Nouveau 1984' in a basket marked.. 'bin ends'. [**1972** *Exchange & Mart* 14 Dec. 43/1 (Advt.), Polythene waste bin liners.] **1976** *S. Wales Echo* 26 Nov. 20/7 You may get free *bin liners, free bins, or neither; collections may be once or twice a week, from the kerb-side or back or front of your house. **1985** *Listener* 9 May 17/2 Another moment I see a sour-looking man, like Marley's Ghost, washing out his bin-liner.

¶ By confusion of spelling = BING.

1695 KENNETT *Par. Antiq.* Gloss. s.v. *Abunda*, A Binne of hides or skins is in some countries a quantity for common sale, consisting of thirty three skins or hides.

bin, *v.* [f. prec. sb.] *trans.* To stow in a bin.

1841 MARRYAT *Poacher* xxxviii, You may bottle and bin it here. **1844** R. E. WARBURTON *Hunt. Songs, Sawyer* v, We binn'd him like a bottle of old Sherry in sawdust.

† **bin, binne**, *adv.* and *prep. Obs.* Forms: 1 binnan, (*north.* binna, bionna), 2–3 binnen, 2 binnon, 3 binnenn, 2–4 binne, 4–5 bynne, 5 byn. [Com. WGer.: OE. *binnan, binna* = OFris. *binna*, OS. **binnan* (MDu., Du. *binnen*), OHG. *binnana, binnân* (MHG., mod.G. *binnen*):—**bi-innana*, f. *bi-*, BE- of position + OTeut. **innana* (in Goth. and OHG.) within, from within, f. *in* prep. + *-ana* advb. suffix. Both adv. and prep.: the latter in OE. with dat. and acc. motion. (Cf. BEN.)]

A. *adv.* Within, inside. Hence † **binward** *adv.*

c **950** *Lindisf. G.* Matt. xxxiii. 25 Binna fulle sint nednima [*Rushw.* binne, *Ags. G.* innan]. —— *John* xx. 26 Uoeron ðeʒnas his binna [*Rushw.* bionna]. **1123** *O.E. Chron.* (Laud. MS.) an. 1122 Ealle þa gersumes þe þær binnen wæron. *c* **1205** LAY. 5920 Binnen heo i-wenden. *c* **1325** *E.E. Allit. P.* B. 452 þat þe burne bynne lorde byhelde þe bare erþe. *c* **1425** *Seven Sag.* (P.) 3058 He lokyd both forth and bynne.

B. *prep.* **1.** Within, inside of; in, into.

c **1000** *Ags. Gosp.* John xi. 30 Ne com se hælend binnan þa ceastre. *c* **1175** *Cott. Hom.* 225 þa þe binnon þane arce were. *a* **1250** *Prov. Alfred* 24 in *O.E. Misc.* 133 Swich mon mai.. ofte binnen þine burie bliþe wenden.

2. Of time: Within, in the course of, during.

c **1000** *Ags. Gosp.* John ii. 19 Ic hit arære binnan þrym daʒum. *c* **1175** *Cott. Hom.* 235 Eft bine fece and þes lare and laʒe swiðe acolede. *c* **1250** *Gen. & Ex.* 1731 Ten siðes ðus binnen . vi . ʒer. *c* **1400** *Ywaine & Gaw.* 1214 Byn this fowretenyght.

bin, obs. and dial. form of *been*, pa. pple. etc. of BE *v.*, and obs. f. BEN, peak.

bin-, *pref.*, treated as a euphonic form of BI- *pref.*², used before vowels. Not found in L.: it seems to have originated in Fr. with the word *binocle*, which was probably formed from L. *bīnī* two together, a pair of (*boves bini* a pair of oxen yoked together). From *binocle, binocular, bin-* has been extended in English to other words, esp. chemical compounds (see BI- *pref.*² III) as *binacetate, biniodide, binoxalate, binoxide* (for which Fr. has *bioxyde*). The phonetic analogy of *a-, an, co- con-*, has probably influenced this Eng. use.

1808 WOLLASTON in *Phil. Trans.* XCVIII. 100 The common binoxalate, or salt of sorrel. **1810** HENRY *Elem. Chem.* (1826) II. 107 Binacetate of copper. *c* **1860** FARADAY *Forces Nat.* iii. 3. 195 *note*, Binoxide of nitrogen. *c* **1865** J. WYLDE in *Circ. Sc.* I. 375/1 The proto-, and biniodide.

binacid (bɪ'næsɪd), *a.* ? *Obs.* = BIACID.

1808 WOLLASTON in *Phil. Trans.* XCVIII. 99 Examples of binacid salts.

binacle, obs. form of PINNACLE.

c **1325** *Coer de L.* 4150 Thomas.. another stone i-slong To Ser Mahouns habitacle, And smot out a gret binacle.

binacle, obs. form of BINNACLE.

binal ('baɪnəl), *a.* [mod.L. *bīnālis* twin, f. L. *bīn-i* two together, a pair: see -AL¹.] Twin, double, twofold.

1658 FORD *Witch Edmond.* III. ii. Wks. (1811) 457, I have 'em already.. Binal revenge, all this. **1806** W. HERSCHEL in *Phil. Trans.* XCVI. 227 Periodical binal revolution of stars about a common centre of gravity.

binam, obs. pa. t. of BENIM.

binant ('baɪnənt). [f. BIN- + *-ant* as in QUADRANT.] A half of a circle or circular body; ***binant electrometer***, an electrometer in which the index moves through half a circle.

1908 *Chem. Abstr.* 2492 (*title*) A Binant Electrometer for Pointer and Meter Reading... Description of a new form of electrometer which has many advantages over the quadrant form. **1936** *Nature* 21 Nov. 866/1 After the Great War, still more sensitive electrometers were designed; for example.. a binant electrometer of high sensitivity by Hofmann. **1938** R. W. LAWSON tr. *Hevesy & Paneth's Man. Radioactivity* (ed. 2) 290 Semicircular hollow plates or dees, resembling the duants or binants of an electrometer. **1952** F. K. HARRIS *Electr. Measurements* x. 447 Electrometers (Hoffman) have been constructed using binants instead of quadrants and having an unsymmetrical needle position... Instability increases with increasing voltage between the binants.

†**'binarchy.** *Obs.*—⁰ [a. F. *binarchie* (Cotgr.), f. L. *bīn-ī* twin + *-archie*, ultimately Gr. -αρχία rule: form influenced by *monarchie*.] = BIARCHY.

1656 in BLOUNT *Glossogr.* **1678–96** in PHILLIPS.

†**bi'narious,** *a.* *Obs.*—⁰ = BINARY.

1656 in BLOUNT *Glossogr.* **1721** in BAILEY, etc.

binarium: see BINARY *sb.*

binary ('baɪnərɪ), *a.* and *sb.* [ad. L. *bīnāri-us*, f. *bīnī* two together.]

A. *adj.* Of, pertaining to, characterized by, or compounded of, two; dual: **a.** *gen.* ***binary system*** (of classification): one by which each group and sub-group is perpetually divided into two, the one with a positive and the other with a negative character, till individuals (or genera) are reached.

1766 CROKER, etc. *Compl. Dict.*, The *cubitus*.. is composed of a binary number of bones. **1835** W. SWAINSON *Geogr. & Class. Anim.* §250 Binary or dichotomous systems, although regulated by a principle, are among the most artificial arrangements that have been ever invented. **1885** J. LECKY in *Proc. Philol. Soc.* 19 Dec., A stress-group might have a ternary effect when only containing two syllables, and a binary effect when containing three.

b. in *Music.* ***binary measure***: that which has two beats to a bar. ***binary form***: the form of a movement which is founded on two principal themes or subjects.

1597 MORLEY *Introd. Mus.* Annot., That circle.. with the binarie cipher following it, signified the lesse moode perfect, and time vnperfect. **1609** DOULAND *Ornithop. Microl.* 50 The Song is.. [to] end in a Binarie measure. **1782** BURNEY *Hist. Mus.* II. v. 454 All measure was then, as at present, reducible to two standards of proportion, the Ternary and Binary, or perfect and imperfect, which we now call Triple and Common Time. **1875** OUSELEY *Mus. Forms* 70 Handel's longer airs are written in.. the ancient binary form.

c. in *Astron.* ***binary stars*** or ***system***: two stars or suns, one of which revolves round the other, or both of which revolve round a common centre.

1802 W. HERSCHEL in *Phil. Trans.* XCII. 481 The binary sidereal system which we are now to consider. **1878** LOCKYER *Star-gaz.* xxiv, The binary stars, those compound bodies, those suns revolving round each other.

d. in *Chem.* and *Min.* ***binary compound***: one consisting of two elements. ***binary theory***: that which considers all acids as compounds of hydrogen with a radicle simple or compound (as $H + Cl$, $H + NO_3$), and all salts as similar compounds with a metal replacing hydrogen (as $K + Cl$, $K + NO_3$).

1812 SIR H. DAVY *Chem. Philos.* Pref. 12 Acidiferous substances.. and their binary combinations with oxygene. **1833** LYELL *Princ. Geol.* III. 365 Mica-schist.. is a binary compound of quartz and mica. **1863** WATTS *Dict. Chem.* I. 42 In 1816 Dulong proposed the theory, since known as the binary or hydrogen-theory of acids.

e. in *Crystallog.* (See quot.)

1816 R. JAMESON *Char. Min.* (1817) 216 A crystal is named binary, bibinary, tribinary, when it experiences one, two, or three decrements by two rows.

f. in *Math.* ***binary arithmetic***: a method of computation in which the binary scale is used, suggested by Leibnitz. ***binary scale***: the scale of notation whose ratio is 2, in which, therefore, 1 of the ordinary (denary) scale is expressed by 1, 2 by 10, 3 by 11, 4 by 100, etc. ***binary logarithms***: a system invented by Euler for use in musical calculations, in which 1 is the logarithm of 2, and the modulus is 1·442695. Cf. j below.

1796 C. HUTTON *Math. & Philos. Dict.* I. 206/1 *Binary number*, that which is composed of two numbers. *Binary arithmetic*, that in which two figures or characters, viz, 1 and 0, only are used; the cipher multiplying every thing by 2, as in the common arithmetic by 10: thus, 1 is one, 10 is 2, 11 is 3, 100 is 4, 101 is 5. **1823** J. MITCHELL *Dict. Math. & Phys. Sci.* 327/2 Therefore 1810 = 11100010010 in the binary scale. **1858** CAYLEY *Math. Papers* (1889) II. 527 Certain binary quantics, viz. the quadric, the cubic, and the quartic. **1860** [see TERNARY *a.* 1 e]. **1861** Binary scale [see SCALE *sb.*³ 6 b]. **1871** CAYLEY in *Messenger of Math.* V. 53 A covariant of the binary form U. **1898** —— *Math. Papers* (Suppl.) 78 Tables of Binary Quadratic Forms. **1929** L. E. DICKSON *Introd. Theory Numbers* v. 63 The function $q = ax^2 + bxy + cy^2$ is called a *binary quadratic form.* **1941** D. H. LEHMER *Guide to Tables in Theory of Numbers* 37 These tables give the primes also in the binary scale, or rather in a condensed form of binary scale. **1957** *Encycl. Brit.* I. 607/2 Forms in two variables are called binary... Consider a binary quadric:—$f(x) = x_1^2 - x_2^2$.

g. ***binary colour*** U.S. (see quots.).

1876 S. R. KOEHLER tr. *von Bezold's Theory of Color* p. xxiii, The other colors of the spectrum are called secondary or binary, since.. each is composed of two primary colors. **1919** H. D. EBERLEIN et al. *Interior Decorating* II. ii. 192 The primary colours are yellow, red and blue, and the binary colours (those composed of two) are orange (yellow and red), violet (red and blue) and green (yellow and blue). **1937** *Discovery* July 217/1 Binary colours, that is to say, colours obtained by combining two of the above [*sc.* the primary colours].

h. In *Biol.*, ***binary fission***: the division of a cell or organism into two (see FISSION *sb.* 2).

1897 PARKER & HASWELL *Textbk. Zool.* I. I. 14 It is mainly by this simple process of division into two, or *binary fission* as it is called, that reproduction or multiplication takes place in the Amœba. **1910** *Encycl. Brit.* IX. 317/1 The division of the nucleus is effected by the process called binary fission; that is to say, it divides into two, then each of these divides simultaneously again into two, giving four nuclei; each of these after a pause again simultaneously divides into two.

i. *Logic.* Involving two items or terms.

1933 *Mind* XLII. 203, $a \times b$, or simply ab, is the result of a binary operation on *a* and *b*. **1951** QUINE *Math. Logic* i. 13 Conjunction and alternation are *binary*, in that they combine statements two at a time. **1956** A. CHURCH *Introd. Math. Logic* 33 A connective is called singulary, binary, ternary, etc., according to the number of its operands.

j. ***binary digit***, one of the two digits (conventionally 0 or 1) in a binary system of notation; also = BIT *sb.*¹ ***binary number, system***, esp. with reference to electronic computers.) Cf. f above.

1946 A. W. BURKS et al. *Electr. Computing Instr.* in *von Neumann's Works* (1963) V. 42 An accuracy of ten decimal digits requires at least 40 binary digits. **1946** *Electronic Engin.* XVIII. 373/1 The internal working of the machine will be entirely in the binary system, in which a number is represented by a series of 1's and 0's, the 1's being pulses and the 0's the spaces between them. **1948** *Ibid.* XX. 209 For mathematical reasons.. it was decided to make provision for 34 binary digits in each number. **1948** [see BIT *sb.*⁴]. **1951** Electronic Engin. XXIII. 140 Binary numbers can be conveniently represented in electrical circuits. **1953** *Sci. News* XXX. 83 Elemental areas of the track magnetized with positive and negative polarity represent the binary digits. **1957** *Encycl. Brit.* XII. 350A/1 The simplest type of choice is a choice from two possibilities, each with probability ½... It is convenient to use the amount of information produced by such a choice as the basic unit and it has been called a binary digit or, more briefly, a 'bit'.

k. *Linguistics.* Having two elements or aspects.

1921 E. SAPIR *Language* ii. 25 We may.. analyze the words *sings, singing,* and *singer* as binary expressions involving a fundamental concept of subject matter (*sing*), and a further concept of more abstract order. **1953** C. E. BAZELL *Linguistic Form* 6 The modern fashionability of the binary opposition. **1953** J. B. CARROLL *Stud. Lang.* ii. 34 These distinctive features [of the phoneme] consist of binary, two-valued oppositions or contrasts, such as *voiced/unvoiced, high/low, rounded/unrounded.*

l. Designating a system of higher education (see quot. 1965).

1965 *Sun* 2 Nov. 11/5 The present Government have decided.. to establish what they call a binary system of education. On the one hand would be the universities and the colleges of education. On the other hand would be the local authority regional and area colleges of technology, cut off from the universities and getting their degrees and other diplomas and certificates from a quite independent source. **1969** *Listener* 27 Mar. 414/1 People complain of what they call the binary system of higher education. It's quite wrong, we're told, to set the universities apart from other institutions of advanced education.

m. *Mil.* Designating a weapon in which two harmless chemicals are combined after firing to form the charge.

1973 *Nature* 5 Oct. 231/1 Binary weapons open up the possibility of getting rid of the stockpiles of lethal nerve gases that are now stored in army depots throughout the United States. **1980** *Sci. Amer.* Apr. 34/2 Requests by the U.S. Army for funds to build production facilities for a new generation of poison-gas artillery projectiles, called binary munitions, have been rejected by Congress and the Administration. **1981** *Observer* 19 July 6/9 The two men shipped binary liquid explosives from America through Britain to.. Uganda.

B. *sb.*

1. A combination of two things; a couple, pair, "two"; duality. ? *Obs.*

1460 CAPGRAVE *Chron.* 3 Make eke thre binaries. As for the first, think that ye be mad of to natures—body and soule. *aa* **1619** FOTHERBY *Atheom.* II. x. §4 (1622) 307 If you desire to make Two, or a Binary. [**1627** BACON *Sylva* §608 This same Binarium of a Stronger and a Weaker.. doth hold in all Living Bodies.] **1782** BURNEY *Hist. Mus.* I. 65 The Alpha, or unit.. and the Beta, or binary. **1837** *Fraser's Mag.* XVI. 405 The invariable opposition.. of the binaries of boats and Anubises.

2. *Astron.* A binary star or system. Cf. A c.

1868 LOCKYER *Heavens* 351 The elliptical or oval form of this binary [ξ in Ursa Major]. **1882** *Athenæum* 27 May 670/1 Binaries, or stars known to be physically double.

3. *Mil.* A binary weapon.

1974 *Nature* 5 Apr. 467/1 The weapons, which are called binaries,.. will consist of two chemical components neither of which is lethal by itself, but which will form a highly potent nerve agent when they are mixed together. **1981** *Observer* 19 July 4/8 Binaries stored.. in Europe would make resupply much easier. **1986** *City Limits* 29 May 8 The new generation of 'binaries' (delivered by missile or any other operational delivery system) are as significant a military event as the plan to build neutron bombs in the late 1970s.

binate ('baɪneɪt), *a.* [ad. mod.L. *bīnāt-us* (cf. late L. *combīnātus*), f. L. *bīnī*: see BINAL.] Arranged in couples. **'binately** *adv.*, in pairs.

1807 J. E. SMITH *Bot.* 176 *Binatum*, binate, is a fingered leaf consisting of only two leaflets, as in Zygophyllum. **1857** BERKELEY *Cryptog. Bot.* §119. 147 The binate ramification. **1870** HOOKER *Stud. Flora* 4 Leaves binately pinnate.

bi'national, *a.* [BI-².] Concerning or consisting of two nations. Hence **bi'nationalist** *a.*

1888 *Blackw. Mag.* Sept. 391 Another piece of binational work. **1922** *Glasgow Herald* 15 July 4 Alsace and its historic capital.. bi-lingual and bi-national.. as they are. **1949** KOESTLER *Promise & Fulf.* III. i. 298 An Arab-Jewish binational state in which the 'toiling masses' of the two races were to unite against the Arab effendis and the Jewish capitalists... The idealists of the Zionist left.. dropped all binationalist pretences.

binaural (bɪ'nɔːrəl), *a.* [f. BIN- (or L. *bīnī* two by two) + AURAL, f. L. *auris* ear.] **1.** Of or pertaining to one's two ears; used with both ears, as the ***binaural stethoscope***.

1861 [see STETHOSCOPE *sb.*]. **1878** *Engineering* XXIV. 151/3 Mr. S. P. Thompson.. read his paper 'On Binaural Audition'. **1881** LE CONTE *Light* 265 A kind of binaural audition, by means of which we judge imperfectly of direction of sound. **1881** *Nature* XXV. 208.

2. Applied to a system of sound reproduction that uses two separated microphones and two transmission channels to achieve a stereophonic effect; *esp.* one in which the sound is delivered to each ear separately by earphones.

1933 *Electronics* July 196/2 Ready-made equipment for an experiment with binaural transmission. **1952** *N.Y. Times* 26 Oct. II. 11/6 In binaural transmission, the sound is broadcast on both the standard radio wave length and on FM. In the home two receivers are necessary to achieve the effect of 'three dimensional' sound. **1958** *N.Z. Listener* 10 Oct. 21/3 In a binaural recording of an orchestral performance, two microphones would be placed some distance apart among the players and the output from each microphone recorded separately. Both sound tracks would then go onto a single tape or onto a single record.

Binche (bɛ̃ʃ). The name of a town in Belgium, applied *attrib.* or *absol.* to a type of lace originally made there.

1888 A. S. COLE tr. *Lefébure's Embroidery & Lace* 325 List of laces according to their names and local origins... Binche. **1902** B. PALLISER *Hist. Lace* vii. 135 The first Binche lace has the character of Flanders lace. *Ibid.*, The characteristic peculiarities of Binche are, that there is either no cordonnet at all outlining the pattern, or that the cordonnet is scarcely a thicker thread than that which makes the *toilé.* **1908** N. H. MOORE *Lace Book* III. 108 Binche Lace of the old make resembles the old Valenciennes very closely. .... Modern Binche lace is machine-made net with bobbin sprigs applied. **1966** 'E. KYLE' *Love is for Living* iii. 27, I just bought a few handkerchiefs bordered with Binche. *Ibid.* vi. 51 Binche.. is made at a small village on the other side of Brussels... Binche makes the best bordering.

bind (baɪnd), *v.* Pa. t. and pple. **bound** (baʊnd). Forms: 1 **bind-an,** 2–4 **bind-en,** 2–7 **binde,** (3–6 **bynd(e,** 4 **bynd-en,** 5 **-yn),** 3– **bind.** *Pa. t. sing.* 1–6 **band,** 1–5 **bond,** (3–5 **bonde,** 4–5 **boond(e,** 4–6 **bande, bounde),** 5– **bound,** (7 **binded;** *Sc.* **band, ban');** *pl.* 1 **bundon,** 2–3 **-en,** 3 **-e,** 3–4 **bounden,** (4–5 **bonde(n,** 5– **bound,** (*north.* 4–5 **bande,** 5– **band, ban').** *Pa. pple.* 1–4 **bunden,** (1–2 **ȝebunden,** 2–3 **ibunde(n,** 3–4 **ibounde(n,** 4 **ybounde(n,** 6 **ybound),** 4– **bounden,** 4–6 **bounde,** 5– **bound,** (also 3–4 **bonden,** 4 **-in, boundoun,** 4–5 **bonde, -yn, boundon, -yn,** 4–6 **bownde(n,** 5 **bowndene, -yn(e,** 6 **-on,** 7 **binded;** *north.* 4–6 **bundin,** 5 **-yn, bwndyn,** 6–7 **bund,** 5– **bun).** [Com. Teut.: OE. *bindan*, pa. t. *band* (*bǫnd*), pl. *bundon*, pple. *bunden* = OS. *bindan* (MDu., Du. *binden*), OFris., ON. *binda* (Sw. *binda*, Da. *binde*), OHG. *bintan* (MHG., mod.G. *binden*), Goth. *bindan*, pa. t. *band, bundum*, pple. *bundans*; cogn. with Skr. *bandh*:—Aryan **bhendh* to bind. As in other words with *-nd*, the originally short vowels of *bind, bunden* (still retained in the north. dial., as in the cognate langs.) have been lengthened and diphthongized in midl. and south. Eng. The north. dial. also retains the original past form *band* (which it has extended to the pl.), while in the standard speech *band* was supplanted already in the 15th c. by *bound*, proper to the pl. and to the pa. pple.] *General sense*: To make fast with a band or bond.

I. To tie fast.

1. a. *trans.* To make fast with a tie; to fasten, tie up.

[*c* **1000** ÆLFRIC *Gen.* xlii. 24 He.. nam Simeon and band hine beforan him.] *c* **1250** *Gen. & Ex.* 2216 Ðo breðere seckes hauen he filt.. And bunden ðe muðes. *a* **1300** *Cursor M.* 15871 His hend þai band and ledd him forth. **1535** COVERDALE *Gen.* xxii. 9 Abraham.. bande his sonne Isaac, layed him on the altare. **1562** J. HEYWOOD *Prov. & Epigr.* (1867) 7 Fast binde fast finde. **1804** ABERNETHY *Surg. Observ.* I. 215 The fascia, which binds it down in its situation. **1855** THACKERAY *Rose & Ring* xvii, They.. bound his legs tight under his horse.

b. To tie fast *to* (*on, upon*).

1205 LAY. 16684 Samuel.. lette hine swiðe sterke to ane stake binde [**1250** bynde]. **1480** CAXTON *Chron. Eng.* xcv. 75

They . . take pyeces of tunder and of fire, and bonde it to the sparwes fete. **1611** BIBLE *Deut.* vi. 8 Thou shalt bind them for a seal upon thine hand.

c. *fig.*

1382 WYCLIF *Prov.* vi. 21 Bind hem bisili in thin herte. **1563** *Mirr. Mag.* Induct. xxxviii, To this poore life was Miserie ybound. **1610** HEALEY *St. Aug. City of God* 438 To binde incomprehensible effectes to the lawes of nature. **1720** OZELL *Vertot's Rom. Rep.* II. XIV. 328 To bind Cæsar faster to their Interest. **1810** SCOTT *Lady of L.* II. xxx, Distrust, and grief, Will bind to us each Western Chief. **1866** *Ecce Homo* xiv. (ed. 4) 166 To bind men to their kind.

d. *esp.* said of spiritual or ecclesiastical binding. (In reference to Matt. xvi. 19.)

c **975** *Rushw. Gosp.* Matt. xvi. 19 Swa hwæt swa þu bindes on eorðan ȝebunde biðon and in heofunum. *c* **1200** *Trin. Coll. Hom.* 65 Al þat prest bindeð soðliche buð ibunden. *a* **1340** HAMPOLE *Pr. Consc.* 3850 'Alle þat þou byndes in erthe,' says he, 'Sal in heven bunden be.' **1340** *Ayenb.* 172 He ssel zeche zuch ane confessour þet conne bynde and onbynde. *c* **1400** *Apol. Loll.* 28 If ilk prest mai vse þe key . . to assoile him, or ellis to bind him fro grace. **1611** BIBLE *Matt.* xvi. 19 Whatsoeuer thou shalt bind on earth, shall be bound in heauen.

¶ See also Branch IV.

2. *esp.* **a.** To make fast (any one) with bonds or fetters; to deprive of personal liberty, make a captive or prisoner.

971 *Blickl. Hom.* 23 Hie hine swungon, & bundon, & spætledon on his onsyne. *c* **1200** *Trin. Coll. Hom.* 23 He ferde in to helle and . . bond þe deuel. **1382** WYCLIF *Jer.* xxxix. 7 He . . bond [**1388** boond] hym in gyues. —— *Matt.* xiv. 3 Forsothe Eroude helde Joon, & bounde hym, & putte him in to prisoun. **1535** COVERDALE *Isa.* lxi. 1 Yᵗ I might . . open the preson to them that are bounde. **1697** DRYDEN *Virg. Georg.* IV. 574 Surprize him first, and with hard Fetters bind. **1742** POPE *Dunciad* IV. 32 Too mad for mere material chains to bind. **1875** JOWETT *Plato* (ed. 2) I. 318 My father bound him hand and foot and threw him into a ditch.

b. *fig.* Said of sickness, sin, passion, affection, intellectual embarrassment, a magic spell, etc.

[*c* **1000** *Ags. Gosp.* Luke xiii. 16 þas abrahames dohtor þe satanas ȝeband nu eahtatyne ȝear.] *c* **1200** *Trin. Coll. Hom.* 63 þenne bie we bunden of wiðerfulnesse. *a* **1225** *Ancr. R.* 408 Luue bint so ure Louerd. **1382** WYCLIF *Luke* xiii. 16. *c* **1400** *Destr. Troy* XXIII. 9542 Achilles . . lay in his loge all with loue boundon. *c* **1450** *York Bid. Prayer* in *Layfolks Mass Bk.* 70 We sall pray . . for all þaes þat er bun in dette or in dedely syn. **1634** CANNE *Necess. Separ.* (1849) 174 The magistrate (say they) . . hath no power to bind the conscience. **1853** LYTTON *My Novel* VIII. ii, The magician will release the fair spirit he has bound to his will.

¶ See also Branch IV.

II. To tie about, bandage, gird, encircle.

3. To tie (a knot *obs.*); hence *fig.* to conclude (a story *obs.*, a bargain or agreement), to make (any contract) fast or sure. † ***to bind an end*** (*Naut.*): to finish up (*obs.*).

a **1300** *Sarmun* 53 in *E.E.P.* (1862) 6 þe last word bint þe tale. *c* **1320** *Sir Tristr.* I. v, A forward fast thai bond. *c* **1375** BARBOUR *Bruce* x. 825 That cunnand band thai sekirly. **1567** *Declar. Lordis Quarrel* (Dalzell) II. 274 Syne with his Burrio band ane new mariage. **1591** SHAKS. *1 Hen. VI*, v. i. 16 The sooner to effect, And surer binde this knot of amitie. *a* **1649** DRUMM. OF HAWTH. *Hist. Scot.* (1655) 7 None of the Subjects should bind up a league together. **1677** *Act Frauds* xvii, Give something in earnest to bind the bargain. **1883** T. HARDY in *Longm. Mag.* July 259 A shilling is passed to bind the bargain.

4. 'To hinder the natural flux of the bowels, to make costive.' J. Cf. *to confine.*

[*c* **1050** *Ags. Gloss.* in Wr.-Wülcker *Voc.* 342 *Astringentes*, ȝebindende.] **1597** GERARD *Herbal* I. xxix. §2. 40 It heateth moderately and bindeth. **1626** BACON *Sylva* §19 Rubarb hath manifestly in it . . parts that bind the body. **1683** SALMON *Lond. Disp.* I. i. (1702) 11/1 Hyacinthi . . bind the Belly. **1815** *Encycl. Brit.* (ed. 5) IV. 197/1 The fruit [Medler-tree] . . is somewhat austere, and binds the bowels.

5. To bandage (the body, etc. *with* something); to put a bandage on (any part of the body); to 'swaddle' a child, to 'wind' a corpse.

c **1000** *Ags. Gosp.* John xi. 44 Hys nebb wæs mid swat-line ȝebunden. *c* **1175** *Lamb. Hom.* 121 Summe þer weren þet his eȝan bundan. *a* **1300** *Cursor M.* 11236 Wit suilk [clathes] sco suedeld him and band. **1382** WYCLIF *John* xix. 40 Thei token the body of Jhesu, and bounden it in lynnen clothis. **1694** SALMON *Iatrica* I. v. 284/1 To bind her Belly with a large swathing-band. **1837** *Penny Mag.* No. 335 A schöppe . . bound his eyes and led him to where the court was sitting. **1838** S. COOPER *Surg. Dict.* 691 This graduated compress is then to be bound on the part with a roller.

6. 'To cover a wound with dressings and bandages.' J. Usually with *up.*

c **1175** *Lamb. Hom.* 79 An helendis Mon . . bond his wunden. **1377** LANGL. *P. Pl.* B. XVII. 70 [The Samaritan] embawmed hym and bonde his hed. **1382** WYCLIF *Luke* x. 34 He comynge nyȝ bond to gidere his woundis. **1490** CAXTON *Eneydos* li. 145 He made his thye to be dressed and bounden vp. **1568** BIBLE (Bishops') *Hosea* vi. 1 Hee hath wounded vs, and hee will binde vs vp. **1594** SHAKS. *Rich. III*, v. iii. 177 Giue me another Horse, bind vp my Wounds. **1786** T. JEFFERSON *Corr.* (1830) 50 Who can so softly bind up the wound? **1816** CRABBE *Eng. Synon.* 161/2 A wounded leg is bound but not tied; a string is tied but not bound.

7. To fasten round, to gird, encircle, wreathe (the head, etc. *with* something; something *about*, *round* the head, etc.).

c **1000** ÆLFRIC *Lev.* viii, And band his heafod mid claþe. *c* **1386** CHAUCER *Reeves T.* 33 His typet y-bounde aboute his heed. **1552** HULOET, Bynde vp, as a woman doth her heade. **1594** SHAKS. *Rich. III*, IV. iv. 333 Bound with Triumphant Garlands will I come. **1607** —— *Cor.* I. iii. 16 His browes bound with Oake. **1697** DRYDEN *Virg. Past.* VIII. 89 Bind those Altars round With Fillets. **1704** POPE *Windsor For.* 178 A belt her waist, a fillet binds her hair. **1870** TENNYSON *Holy Grail* 159, I, maiden, round thee, maiden, bind my belt.

8. To secure with a border or edging of some strengthening material, as a box or jewel with metal, a garment with braid, etc.; also *fig.*

c **1380** WYCLIF *Wks.* (1880) 349 Hem failen charite to bynde her schelde in ordre. **1464** *Inv. Dk. Suffolk* in *Dom. Archit.* III. 113 A gret standard of the chapell bounde with ierne. **1535** COVERDALE *Ecclus.* xlv. 11 A worke . . set with costly precious stones, all bounde with golde. **1667** MILTON *P.L.* XI. 881 A flowrie verge to binde The fluid skirts of that same watrie Cloud. **1682** DRYDEN *Mac Fl.* 64 Close to the walls which fair Augusta bind. **1808** R. PORTER *Trav. Sk. Russ. & Swed.* ii. (1813) I. 17 A sort of low beef-eater hat bound with yellow. *Mod.* Silk binding to bind coats and vests.

III. To tie together, to unite.

9. a. To tie (a number of things) so as to hold them together, or to form them into a single mass; *esp.* to tie up (sheaves of corn).

c **1000** *Ags. Gosp.* Matt. xiii. 30 Gadriað ærest þonne coccel, and bindað sceafmælum. *a* **1225** *Ancr. R.* 254 Heo schulen beon ibunden togederes. **1382** WYCLIF *Matt.* xiii. 30 Gedre ȝee to gedre dernels, and byndeth hem to gidre in knytchis [**1611** binde them in bundels] for to be brent. **1580** BARET *Alv.* B 686 To binde with osiers or twigs, as hoopers do. **1611** BIBLE *Ps.* cxxix. 7 Hee that bindeth sheaues. **1632** MILTON *Allegro* 87 Her bow'r she leaves, With Thestylis to bind the sheaves. **1750** FRANKLIN *Wks.* (1840) 238 Bind the pieces of glass together from end to end with strong silk thread. *a* **1832** CRABBE *Posth. Tales* Wks. 1834 VIII. 162 What time the reaper binds the burden'd sheaf. **1861** O. W. HOLMES *Elsie V.* xxviii, Old Sophy . . bound up her long hair for her sleep.

absol. **1770** A. YOUNG *Tour N. Eng.* I. 189 A man follows every two scythes to bind.

b. *fig.*

1568 BIBLE (Bishops') *1 Sam.* xxv. 29 The soule of my lorde shal be bounde in the bundel of the liuing. **1697** DRYDEN *Virg. Past.* IV. 20 The jarring Nations he in peace shall bind. **1785** T. JEFFERSON *Corr.* (1830) 417 Friendships which had bound their ancestors together. *c* **1854** STANLEY *Sinai & Pal.* ii. (1858) 116 The situation of Palestine is remarkably bound up with its future destinies.

10. a. To cement (particles) together, or cause them to cohere in a firm mass. *spec.* in *Cookery.*

a **1000** *Exon.* 78a (Bosw.) Hrusan [*MS.* hruse] bindeþ wintres wôma. *a* **1300** *Cursor M.* 355 þis elementz þat al thinges bindes Four er þai. *c* **1440** *Anc. Cookery* in *Househ. Ord.* (1790) 435 Qwhen the sawse is bounden to the felettes, then take hom out of the pot. *c* **1760** SMOLLETT *Blue ey'd Ann* 3 When Lybian sands are bound in frost. **1787** WINTER *Syst. Husb.* 218 Stiff and loamy soils, which become hardened and bound. **1861** MRS. BEETON *Bk. Househ. Managem.* x. 199 Pound well, and bind with 1 or 2 eggs. **1871** RUSKIN *Fors Clav.* II. xvi. 10 That rain and frost of heaven; and the earth which they loose and bind. **1962** *Listener* 29 Nov. 943/2 You will need . . beaten egg (to bind). **1963** *Ibid.* 14 Mar. 479/1 Mix together the stuffing ingredients, binding with beaten egg.

b. *intr.* (for *refl.*) To stick together, cohere in a mass.

1674 GREW *Luctation* II. §15 Their Alkaly binds in with some preternatural Acid in the Stomach. **1677** PLOT *Oxfordsh.* 240 Soiling it [chalk land] with the best mould . . to keep it from binding. **1677** MOXON *Mech. Exerc.* (1703) 37 The Mettal running close to the Spindle will bind on that place. **1709** STEELE *Tatler* No. 179 ¶8 A spacious Walk of the finest Gravel, made to bind and unite so firmly. **1838** N. PATERSON *Manse Gard.* III. 210 The coarse [gravel], it is true does not bind.

c. *intr. Hawking.* To grapple or close *with.*

1575 TURBERV. *Falconry* 255 As diuers times it happeneth to the falcon . . when they binde together in the ayre. **1615** G. SANDYS *Trav.* 76 Nothing flieth in the aire that they will not bind with. **1826** SEBRIGHT in 'Stonehenge' *Brit. Sports* I. IV. i. § 10 When one of the hawks seizes his prey, the other soon binds to him.

11. a. *trans.* To fasten together the sheets of (a book), and put it into a stiff cover. Technically 'binding' is covering with leather, vellum, or other durable material; though in ordinary language we say 'bound in cloth.' A book is ***half-bound*** when it has a leather back, and the sides covered with cloth or paper.

?a **1400** *Morte Arth.* 3317 The sexte had a sawtere semliche bowndene. **1509** BARCLAY *Shyp of Folys* (1874) I. 20 I haue them [my books] in great reuerence . . Full goodly bounde in pleasaunt couerture. **1588** *Marprel. Epist.* (Arb.) 34 That no Byble should be bounde without the Apocripha. **1637** *Decree Star-Chamb.* §7 in *Milton's Areop.* (Arb.) 13 No person . . shall bind, stitch, or put to sale, any such booke. **1727** SWIFT *Further Acc. E. Curll* Wks. 1755 III. I. 156 He always binds in sheep. **1851** LONGF. *Gold. Leg.* II. 113 A huge tome, bound In brass and wild-boar's hide.

b. ***to bind up***: i.e. together into one volume.

1650 R. STAPYLTON *Strada's Low C. Warres* IV. 95 It is printed, and bound up with her life. **1682** GREW *Anat. Plants* Ep. Ded., An Animal is . . several Plants bound up into one Volume. **1875** E. WHITE *Life in Christ* II. xvi. (1878) 183 The fragment on Hades, formerly bound up with the works of Josephus.

12. *Hedging.* To interlace stakes with edder.

1523 FITZHERB. *Husb.* (1534) 54 Set thy stakes within ii. foote and a halfe together, excepte thou haue very good edderynge, and longe, to bynde with. *Ibid.* The better the stake wil be dryuen, whan he is wel bounden.

13. *transf.* To fasten together or connect in various ways, as to harness a horse or chariot (*obs.*), to fasten parts of dress (*poetic*), to connect distant places (*rhet.*); and in various *fig.* uses.

1535 COVERDALE *Ecclus.* vii. 8 Bynde not two synnes together. —— *Ex.* xiv. 6 He bounde his charetts fast [WYCLIF, ioynede the chare]. **1611** BIBLE *Micah* i. 13 Bind the chariot to the swift beast. **1720** GAY *Ep. T. Snow*, A sharpen'd skewer cross his bare shoulders bound A tattered rug. **1836** O. W. HOLMES *Poems, My Aunt*, She strains the aching clasp That binds her virgin zone. **1855** MOTLEY *Dutch Rep.* (1884) I. 3 To bind by watery highways with the furthest ends of the World, a country disinherited by nature of its rights. **1860** KEBLE *Hymn 'The voice that,'* Thou didst bind two natures In Thine eternal bands.

IV. To restrain or unite by non-material bonds. (Closely connected with the *fig.* uses of 1, 2, from which these senses spring.)

14. To tie, restrain, confine, restrict by a non-material bond or force of any kind.

a **1300** *Cursor M.* 23748 We ar bunden vnder þair au. **1330** R. BRUNNE *Chron.* 35 þe Walsch men he band With homage and feaute. **1606** SHAKS. *Ant. & Cl.* II. ii. 90 When poysoned houres had bound me vp From mine owne knowledge. **1647** CAMPION *Art Descant.* II. 27 No Tune . . can have any grace or sweetness unless it be bounden within a proper Key. **1713** DERHAM *Phys. Theol.* VIII. ii, The great Contriver of Nature is not bound up to one Way only. **1838** MACAULAY in Trevelyan *Life* (1876) II. vii. 14, I have no official business to bind me.

15. a. To tie (a person, oneself) up in respect to action; to oblige by a covenant, oath, promise or vow. Const. *to*, *from*, an action, *to do* something.

a **1225** *Ancr. R.* 6 Hwoa se . . bihat hit God alse heste to donne, heo bint hire þerto. *c* **1374** CHAUCER *Compl. Mars* 47 He bynt him to perpetuall obeisaunce. *c* **1440** *York Myst.* xxxii. 217, I will me bynde to be your man. **1535** COVERD. *Numb.* xxx. 2 Yf eny man . . sweare an ooth, so that he binde his soule. **1651** HOBBES *Leviath.* 71 A Covenant, if lawfull, binds in the sight of God, without the Oath. **1654** EARL ORRERY *Parthenissa* (1676) 640 What I bind my self from now, I will abjure for ever for your sake. **1832** CHALMERS *Pol. Econ.* v, A landed proprietor may bind himself to a future payment, in a written deed.

†**b.** *intr.* (for *refl.*) To agree, pledge oneself.

c **1470** HENRY *Wallace* VI. 927 Than bund thai thus; thar suld be no debait. *c* **1817** HOGG *Tales & Sk.* II. 215 He would voluntarily bind for it.

16. *trans.* To oblige or constrain with legal authority.

1463 *Paston Lett.* 473 II. 133 Your certificat . . shall bynd any of the parties to sey the contrary. **1526** *Pilgr. Perf.* (W. de W. 1531) 161 For the lawe of the chirche . . byndeth vs to synge or saye our seruyce diligently. **1583** STANYHURST *Æneis* II. (Arb.) 48 What law can bynd mee, to be trew to so wycked a countrye? **1775** JOHNSON *Tax. no Tyr.* 45 Whether the English laws could bind Ireland. **1849** MACAULAY *Hist. Eng.* I. 375 Every parish was bound to repair the highways which passed through it.

17. To subject to a specific legal obligation.

a. To make (a person or estate) liable for the payment of a debt, or fulfilment of an obligation. Usually *passive*: To be made or become surety.

1462 *Mann. & Househ. Exp.* 149 My mastyre and Thomas Howe are bowndyne . . to my lord of Esex, lx, *li.* **1596** SHAKS. *Merch. V.* I. iii. 5 For the which, as I told you, Anthonio shall be bound. **1650** T. B[AYLEY] *Worcester's Apoph.* 69 Offering to bind her estate for the repayment. **1727** SWIFT *Wonder of W.* Wks. 1755 II. II. 54 He has hardly one acquaintance, for whom he hath not been bound. **1772** MACKENZIE *Man of World* II. ix. (1823) 476, I will become bound to make up all your losses.

b. To lay under obligation to answer or prosecute a charge (usually ***to bind over to appear***, etc.), or *gen.* to perform a stated act or pursue a line of conduct. Freq. ***to bind over*** (used without following *to* and dependent phrase): to oblige (a person) to undertake to do, or abstain from, a particular act; *spec.* to make (someone) give a recognizance not to commit a breach of the peace, usu. for a specified period.

1549 *Bk. Com. Prayer, Matrim.*, Yf any man . . will be bound, and sureties with him to the parties. **1592** GREENE *Art Conny-catch.* II. 12 They were apprehended, and bound ouer to the Sessions at Westminster. **1610** W. YONGE *Diary* 28 May (1848) 21 Being asked by Mr. Drake wherefore he was bound over, he said for a private grudge borne him by the bishop. **1642** FULLER *Holy & Prof. St.* IV. xii. 299 He is not to be bound to the peace. *c* **1702** J. P. *New Guide Constables* 106 Such Parents may be bound over . . to answer their sad default. **1764** T. CUNNINGHAM *Law-Dict.* s.v. *Good behaviour*, This statute . . seems to impower them, not only to bind over those, who seem to be notoriously troublesome, . . but also those who are publickly scandalous. **1820** TOMLINS *Law-Dict.* (ed. 3) s.v. *Surety of the peace*, A Peer or Peeress cannot be bound over in any other place than the Courts of King's Bench or Chancery. *Ibid.*, A justice may bind over all night-walkers. **1837** DICKENS *Pickw.* xiii. 109 The Mayor . . declared he would . . bind them over to keep the peace. **1917** *Oxford Jrnl. Illustr.* 17 Jan. 8/3 The prisoner was bound over for twelve months. **1970** *Oxf. Mail* 6 Jan. 5 Judge Mais told him that in binding him over there was no possible slur cast upon him.

c. ***to bind one*** (***over***) ***to his good behaviour.*** lit. and fig.

1642 ROGERS *Naaman* 40 Till the Lord binde the soule to her good behaviour. **1644** MILTON *Areop.* (Arb.) 79 It pretended to bind books to their good behaviour. **1760** *Life of Cat* 108 Sufficient . . to bind him down to his good behaviour. **1829** SOUTHEY *Sir T. More* I. 142 The members would virtually be bound to their good behaviour. **1855** MACAULAY *Hist. Eng.* III. 559 He thought it unjust . . to bind him over to his good behaviour.

d. colloq. ***I dare***, or ***will be bound***: I undertake the responsibility of the statement, I feel certain.

1557 NORTH *Gueuara's Diall Pr.* (1582) 399 b, I dare be bound . . he shal not want infinit troubles. **1589** *Theses Martinianæ* Introd., Ile bee bounde hee shall not loose his labour. **1611** SHAKS. *Cymb.* IV. iii. 18, I dare be bound hee's true. **1773** GOLDSM. *Stoops to Conq.* v. ii, I'll be bound that no soul here can budge a foot to follow you. **1850** MRS.

STOWE *Uncle Tom* xxviii, You've been stealing something, I'll be bound.

18. *to be bound*: to be under obligation, to have it as a duty, moral or legal, *to do* something.

c **1360** *Deo Gratias* in *E.E.P.* (1862) 125 To þonke and blesse hym we be bounde. *c* **1386** CHAUCER *Knts. T.* 291 Thou art ybounden..To helpen me. **1484** CAXTON *Chyualry* 15 So moche arte thow more bonde and bounden to be good. **1595** SHAKS. *John* II. i. 522 That she is bound in honor still to do. **1607–12** BACON *Counsel, Ess.* (Arb.) 318 Princes are not bound to communicate all matters. **1771** *Junius Lett.* liv. 283, I am not bound to assign the..motives of his..hatred. **1852** MᶜCULLOCH *Taxation* II. i. 158 Government..is bound to treat all its subjects alike.

19. To engage or unite in matrimony.

1330 R. BRUNNE *Chron.* 40 He wild him bynd to som berde in boure. **1382** WYCLIF *1 Cor.* vii. 27 Thou art boundyn to a wyf. **1580** BARET *Alv.* B 1027 Moreouer I am bounde to my wife. **1600** SHAKS. *A.Y.L.* v. iv. 59 As mariage binds and blood breakes. **1807** CRABBE *Par. Reg.* I. 338 To bind in law, the couple bound by love.

20. To indenture (any one) to a master, or to a trade, as an apprentice or learner; to apprentice. Sometimes with *out* or *over*.

c **1500** in Halliw. *Nugæ P.* 20 The preste that bounde me prentys. **1586** in Wadley's *Bristol Wills* (1886) 251 Twenty shillings to John Stinchcome yf he be bownde. **1602** *Life T. Cromwell* I. ii. 80 Had I bound him to some honest trade. *a* **1672** WOOD *Life* (1848) 89 *note*, Imploying the yearly profits..in binding forth apprentices into other parishes. **1710** STEELE *Tatler* No. 196 ⁋3 [I] have bound him to a Shoe-maker. **1845** STEPHEN *Laws Eng.* II. 230 Apprentices are usually bound out by their friends; though their own consent is essential. **1848** THACKERAY *Van. Fair* ii, Rebecca ..was bound-over as an articled-pupil.

21. To attach *to* (a person) by ties of duty, gratitude, affection, etc.

1530 PALSGR. 362, I am bownden to no man. **1595** SHAKS. *John* III. iii. 29, I am much bounden to your Maiesty. **1634** W. WOOD *New Eng. Prosp.* Ded. Note, The good assurance of your native worth..hath so bound my thankfull acknowledgement. **1682** *Pepys' Diary* VI. 147, I am infinitely bound to my friends..for their thoughts of me. **1765** BURKE *Corr.* (1844) I. 71 The way in which you take up my affairs binds me to you in a manner I cannot express. **1828** SCOTT *F.M. Perth* II. 181 Simon Glover, to whom the Fair City is so much bounden.

V. *slang.* **22.** *trans.* To bore, weary.

1929 T. E. LAWRENCE *Lett.* (1938) 640 Voyages are binding things, & I'm lucky to have had this job to keep me busy. **1943** C. H. WARD-JACKSON *Piece of Cake* 13 *Bind*, a depressing job or situation, one who is a bore. Used as a verb it suggests a petty or depressing order or regulation... Thus, 'It's a perfect bind, old boy', or 'Smith's got his tapes: I suppose he'll be binding everyone now', or 'He's the worst binder I ever served under'... *Binds you rigid, binds you stiff*, bores you completely. **1944** E. PARTRIDGE in *19th Cent.* CXXXV. 184 To *bind* a person is to bore him stiff; probably from the ill-temper that so often results from being *bound* or constipated; but perhaps from the fact that such a duty as is a *tie* may easily become boring.

23. *intr.* To complain. (In quot. 1942 used transitively, to complain to, to admonish.)

1942 I. GLEED *Arise to Conquer* i. 11 We stayed sitting in our cockpits listening to Pat binding the ground station on the radio telephone. **1943** *Penguin New Writing* XVII. 18 'Stop binding,' said Ginger mechanically... 'When I get back to civvy street I'll never moan about my job again.' **1948** *Jrnl. R. Aeronaut. Soc.* LII. 719 It is useless to expect information on maintenance difficulties..because usually the operator 'binds' to himself or his mates on encountering a snag. **1955** W. FINK in P. Chambers & A. Landreth *Called Up* vi. 115, I dare say we would have binded more about all this bull if it hadn't been that there was a system by which the best hut got a forty-eight hour pass. **1959** 'D. BUCKINGHAM' *Wind Tunnel* viii. 73 Eddy's been binding to Vic about you.

bind (baınd), *sb.* Also 4–6 bynde: see BINE. [f. BIND *v.*]

1. a. Anything used to bind or tie; a band or tie. ***Our Lady's binds*** (obs.): confinement at childbirth. Cf. BEND *sb.*[1] 1 d, BAND *sb.*[1] 1 c.

a **1000** *Cod. Dip.* (Kemble) VI. 133 (Bosw.), Hio an Ceoldryþe hyre betstan bindan. *c* **1400** *Bidding Prayer* in *York Manual* (1874) App. 221 Wymmen þat bethe in oure lady byndes.

b. A connecting timber in a ship.

1803 *Hull Advert.* 9 Apr. 2/1 The ship..had new binds and new top sides. **1833** RICHARDSON *Merc. Mar. Arch.* 6 The best place for the upper bind is about ⅜ of the midship height.

c. *Music.* 'A curved line (also called *tie*) placed between two notes of the same degree, to denote the continuance of the sound, during the value of both, instead of the repercussion of the second note.' Grove *Dict. Mus.* 1880. Also applied by some to the BRACE or ACCOLADE.

1880 GROVE *Dict. Mus.* I. 242/2 The employment of the bind is a necessity whenever a sound is required to be of a duration which cannot be expressed by any single note.

2. A twining or climbing stem of a plant; a flexible shoot. **a.** *esp.* The climbing stem of the hop-plant. **b.** Used to name varieties of the hop, as ***grey-bind, red-bind, white-bind***. Now BINE.

c **1325** *E.E. Allit. P.* C. 444 God..ded growe of þat soyle þe fayrest bynde..þat euer burne wyste. *c* **1440** *Promp. Parv.* 36 Bynde, a twyste of a vyne. **1792** *Gentl. Mag.* Apr. 343 Hop Stalks or Binds. **1815** *Encycl. Brit.* III. 618 *Bind*, a country word for a stalk of hops. [See BINE.]

3. Hence, used as the name of certain climbing plants that wind round the stems of other plants or trees. †**a.** Honeysuckle or WOOD-BINE. **b.** = BINDWEED (*Convolvulus* and *Polygonum*).

c **1440** *Promp. Parv.* 36 Bynde or Wode bynde, *corrigiola, vitella*. **1575** GASCOIGNE *Wks.* (1587) 189 Tares and Byndes can pluck good grayne adowne. **1878** BRITTEN & HOLLAND *Plant-n.*, *Common Bind*, Convolvulus [wild].

4. a. Indurated clay, occurring between coal-strata.

1799 KIRWAN *Geol. Ess.* 297 Indurated clay, which the miners commonly call clunch, and when much mixed with calx of iron, bind. *Ibid.* 301 Black shale, iron stone, shale, blue bind. **1844** H. HUTCHINSON *Pract. Drainage* 173 Red clay and skerry or bine. **1864** *Derby Merc.* 7 Dec., The fall of bind suddenly liberating a quantity of bad air.

b. A thin stratum of shale or stone.

1748 *Phil. Trans.* XLV. 126 The upper Pillars..lying between two Binds of Stone like Seams of Coal.

5. A measure of quantity in salmon and eels.

1477 *Sc. Act Jas. III.* (1597) §76 Of the bind of Salmond. **1487** *Ibid.* §131 The Barrell bind of Salmound sould.. contein the assyse and mesour of fourteene gallonis. **1667** E. CHAMBERLAYNE *St. Gt. Brit.* I. III. ii. (1743) 154 Eels have 25 to the Strike; 10 Strikes to the Bind. *a* **1728** KENNETT *Gloss.* (MS. Lansd. 1033) A Bind of eels..consisted of ten sticks, and every stick of twenty five eels. [In mod. Dicts.]

6. Capacity, measure, limit, size. ***aboon my bind***: beyond my power. *Sc.* Cf. BEND.

1551 *Acts Mar.* xi. (JAM.) The wylde Guse of the greit bind, iis. **1560** ROLLAND *Crt. Venus* I. 122 His hois they war ..Of biggest bind. **1823** SCOTT *St. Ronan's* i, Their bind was just a Scots pint over-head, and a tappit-hen.

7. A bruise on a horse's foot caused by the pressure of a nail on the sensitive parts.

1908 *Animal Managem.* 239 'Pricks', wounds from nails driven into the fleshy part, and 'presses', or 'binds', from their being so close that they bruise them.

8. A bore, nuisance (cf. BIND *v.* 22). *slang.*

1930 T. E. LAWRENCE *Lett.* (1938) 676 Letter writing is what the R.A.F. call a 'bind'. **1942** *Penguin New Writing* XIII. 24 Occasionally..it publishes a serious article... But this is regarded as a 'bind', i.e. boring and tiresome. **1943** [see BIND *v.* 22]. **1953** 'N. SHUTE' *In Wet* viii. 272 But it's an awful bind for you, at such a time as this.

9. A difficult situation, a predicament. (In quot. 1851, = '(tight) squeeze'.) Cf. *double bind* s.v. DOUBLE *a.* 6. *colloq.* (orig. and chiefly *U.S.*).

1851 *Let.* 27 Mar. in N. E. Eliason *Tarheel Talk* (1956) iv. 127, I scuffle hard but can not get along... It is a very tight bind for me to live... I am not worth five dollars. **1946** *Sat. Even. Post* 30 Mar. 45/2 Amon Carter was out of the state at the time, but when he heard Dallas would get the centennial, it threw him in a hard bind. **1969** D. ACHESON *Present at Creation* (1970) xxix. 258 Seeking..American help in escaping from the bind in which British treaties with Egypt and Jordan placed him. **1974** K. MILLETT *Flying* (1975) III. 355 He is nonplussed. Has probably been in this bind a hundred times. Whole movie business runs on credit. **1986** *Sunday Times* 23 Feb. 21/1 Mrs. Thatcher and Tebbit..are clearly in a bind.

†**bindbalk.** *Obs. rare.* A tie-beam.

c **1425** *Voc.* in Wr.-Wülcker *Voc.* 668 *Trapecula*, a byndbalk.

†**'bindcorn.** *Herb. Obs.* [f. BIND *v.* + CORN.] Black or Corn Bindweed (*Polygonum Convolvulus*).

1577 HOLINSHED *Chron.* II. 16/2 It will bring foorth weeds, bindcorne, cockle, darnell. **1580** BARET *Alv.* B 1424 Renning Bucke, or binde corne..like vnto withwinde.

†**bind-days.** *Obs.* Days on which tenants were bound to render stated unpaid service to their feudal lord; boon-days.

1664 SPELMAN *Gloss., Precariæ*..vulgo bind dayes. **1706** PHILLIPS, *'Bind-Days.* See Precaria.'

†**'binded,** *ppl. a. Obs. rare.* [A weak pa. pple. of BIND.] Bound together, connected.

1650 J. G[REGORY] *Notes & Obs.* Pref. 7 That invisible Harmony and binded discord of the Parts.

bindei, var. BINDI-EYE.

binder ('baındə(r)). [f. BIND *v.* + -ER[1].]

I. Of persons.

1. *gen.* One who binds. (See senses of the verb.)

a **1000** *Riddles* (Gr.) xxviii. 6 Ic eom bindere and swingere. *a* **1300** *Havelok* 2050 Bynderes loue ich neuere mo. *c* **1450** *Gloss.* in Wr.-Wülcker *Voc.* 688 *Hic ligator*, a bynder. **1651** HOBBES *Govt. & Soc.* viii. §4. 129 The binder supposes him that is bound not to be sufficiently tyed by any other obligation. **1846** TRENCH *Huls. Lect.* Ser. II. vi. 235 The true binder up of the bleeding hurts of humanity.

2. *spec.* **a.** A bookbinder.

1556 *Chart. Stationers' Comp.* in Entick *London* (1766) IV. 227 Any..printer, binder or seller of any manner of books. **1705** HEARNE *Diary* (1885) I. 57 This was discovered by the binder. **1862** BURTON *Bk.-hunter* I. 26 There are binders who have immortalized themselves.

b. One who binds sheaves behind the reapers.

1611 CHAPMAN *Iliad* XVIII. (J.) Three binders stood, and took the handfuls reapt From boys that gather'd quickly up. **1799** J. ROBERTSON *Agric. Perth.* 159 One man follows the two binders, to stook the corn. **1870** BRYANT *Iliad* XVIII. II. 226 Binders tied them fast With bands, and made them sheaves.

c. 'One who undertakes to keep a mine open.' Weale *Dict. Terms* 1849.

II. Of things.

3. a. Anything used to bind; a band, bandage, etc.; in *Med.*, a piece of calico or a special apparatus used in obstetric surgery.

1695 MOTTEUX *St. Olon's Morocco* 94 Nothing on their Heads but a single Veil or Binder. **1787** MRS. TRIMMER *Œcon. Charity* 79 Plain linen caps, with binders herring-boned with coloured cruel. **1861** *Year-bk. Med. & Surg.* 359 The use of the obstetric binder. **1868** *Daily News* 3 Sept., The binder and wimple were placed on the head [of a nun]. **1885** *Cheshire Gloss.* (E.D.S.), *Binders*, narrow strips of thick hempen cloth..put round cheeses..to prevent them bulging.

b. *fig.* (Cf. 4.)

1621–31 LAUD *Sev. Serm.* (1847) 99 Justice and judgment is the greatest binder up of a State. **1627** BP. HALL *Medit. & Vows* ii. 29 Performance is a binder. **1643** CARYL *Sacr. Covt.* 5 A Covenant is a binder of affection.

4. A connecting piece that holds the several parts of any structure together; as, **a.** A long pliant withe or branch used in fencing, etc. (cf. BIND *v.* 12); **b.** *Carpentry.* A tie-beam or binding joint; **c.** A principal part of a ship's frame, such as keel, transom, beam, etc.; **d.** A long stone that passes quite through a wall, and gives support to the smaller stones, a 'bond' stone.

1642 FULLER *Holy & Prof. St.* III. xxii. 212 Though batchelours be the strongest stakes, married men are the best binders in the hedge of the Commonwealth. **1666** J. SMITH *Old Age* (ed. 2) 207, I compare..the Sinews or Nerves to the binders of the hedge; which fasten and unite all the other parts. **1842** GWILT *Archit.* (1876) 601 By the 14th century the system of girders, binders, and joists was perfected. **1845** *Proc. Berw. Nat. Club* II. 122 It makes an admirable binder of the moveable sands. **1919** MASEFIELD *Reynard the Fox* 55 The binders crashed as hounds went over.

5. In various technical applications:

a. A band of straw, etc. for binding sheaves of corn; **b.** A contrivance attached to a reaping-machine to bind up the grain as cut into sheaves; also, a separate machine used for binding up the grain (Knight, *Dict. Mech.* Suppl.); **c.** An appliance attached to a sewing-machine for putting binding on cloth; **d.** *Weaving.* A lever fixed in the shuttle-box to arrest the shuttle and prevent its recoil; **e.** A detachable cover or binding for unbound magazines, music, papers, etc.

1837 *U.S. Patent* 26 Dec., Binder for newspapers. **1857** *Trans. Illinois Agric. Soc.* II. 120 A self raker, and even a binder, may be just as simple..as some hand raker. **1865** *Morn. Star* 30 May, A policeman produced a steel binder belonging to a sewing machine. *a* **1877** KNIGHT *Dict. Mech.* II. 1891/2 1850. Heath's binder, with a reciprocating rake beneath the platform. 1851. Watson's automatic binder. **1891** R. WALLACE *Rural Econ. Austral. & N.Z.* v. 89 The light steel binder..is produced wholesale in..[Canada] for £28 each. **1945** 'G. ORWELL' *Animal Farm* v. 39 Electricity ..could operate threshing machines..and reapers and binders. **1964** *Which?* July 224/1 All new members get an index when they join CA (which can be kept in the binder pocket).

†**6.** *Med.* Anything which produces astriction or constipation of the bowels. *Obs.*

1528 PAYNELL *Salerne Regim.* N iv, Hit scoureth away the dropsye..neuer the lesse it is a bynder. **1621** BURTON *Anat. Mel.* II. iv. I. i. (1651) 364 They would prescribe..binders for purgatives. **1678** SALMON *New Lond. Disp.* I. vi. (1702) 140/1 Where binders and strengthners are used.

7. a. Anything which causes bodies to adhere or stick together; a cement.

1678 SALMON *New Lond. Disp.* III. xii. (1702) 416/2 The Bone-Binder..speedily glews broken Bones together. **1727–51** CHAMBERS *Cycl.* s.v. *Elements*, The elements of metals..and sulphur as the binder, or cement. **1940** [see *binding agent* s.v. BINDING *ppl. a.* 3]. **1957** *Brit. Commonw. Forest Terminol.* 23 *Binder*,..the component of a glue primarily responsible for the adhesive forces.

b. In road-making (see quot. 1911).

1901 G. W. TILLSON *Street Pavements* viii. 230 It was deemed best to change..the method of construction and for the cushion-coat to substitute a so-called binder, made up of coarse stones held together by asphaltic cement. This binder has been laid of different thicknesses, sometimes 1½ or even 2 inches. Its object..is simply to serve as a medium between the wearing surface and the concrete. **1908** *Chambers's Jrnl.* 29 Aug. 624/1 A light binder of clay and gravel is added to the second coating of stone. **1911** *Encycl. Brit.* XXIII. 392/1 Upon the concrete foundation is first spread a layer of fine bituminous concrete called 'binder', 1½ in. thick, to unite the wearing surface to the concrete foundation. Upon the binder the asphalte is laid to a thickness of 2 in. **1937** *Times* (Brit. Motor No.) 13 Apr. viii/3 The principle is the same as that of the ordinary tar-macadam road, but cement mortar is used as the 'binder' in the place of tar.

c. A binding medium used in painting to cause pigment to cohere and set.

1922 M. TOCH *How to paint Permanent Pictures* 33 The decorations made by the Egyptians were made without any binder other than the lime naturally found in the soil, and in a few cases the glue was used. *Ibid.* 34 There are some really wonderful decorative [Egyptian] paintings in which binders were used. The portraits..in the second century were done with wax and resins. **1934** H. HILER *Notes on Technique of Painting* iii. 144 These media, or binders, each require a different manner and method in their use. **1951** R. MAYER *Artist's Handbk. Materials & Techniques* i. 19 Tempera paint films are adequately strong and durable, but when dry the volume of binder in relation to the volume of pigment is less than that of oil paints.

8. *Comb.*, as **binder's-board**, hard smooth pasteboard used in bookbinding; **binder twine**, twine used in a binder or for binding.

1890 *Moose Jaw* (Sask.) *Times* 18 July 4/6 The local situation in Binder twine is somewhat interesting. **1899** *Westm. Gaz.* 12 June 9/2 The fibre was chiefly used in the United States for binder twine for harvesting. **1950** *N.Z. Jrnl. Agric.* Mar. 227/3 Tying them [*sc.* the leaders of a vine] with binder twine is preferable to twisting the leaders around the wires [of the trellis].

9. A large quantity, esp. of food; a satisfying meal. *dial.* and *N.Z. colloq.*

1881 H. & C. R. SMITH *Isle of Wight Words* 46 Binder, a quantity. 'A pretty good binder of it.' **1917** *Chrons. N.Z.E.F.* 19 Sept. 55/1, I was hungry so I turned my eyes away from the promising binder. **1943** F. SARGESON in *Penguin New Writing* XVII. 59, I shouted him a bob dinner and I could tell by the way he ate he was in need of a binder. **1967** —— *Hangover* vi. 42, I am so devilish hungry I must first spend half an hour in the kitchen putting away a binder.

10. A last drink (see also quot. 1953). *slang.*

1899 A. BINSTEAD *Gal's Gossip* 15 He joyfully fell in with her suggestion to step inside and take a 'binder'. **1953** *Word for Word* (*Whitbread & Co.*) 13/1 *Binder*, colloquial expression for the last drink... Also used to describe the person who orders a drink after closing time.

11. *slang.* **a.** A boring person or thing (see BIND *v.* 22). **b.** One who 'binds' or complains (see BIND *v.* 23).

1930 T. E. LAWRENCE *Lett.* (1938) 679 More books go to you almost at once. You'll find some of the packets have quite decent things amongst them—though generally they are what the troops call my 'binders'. **1937** PARTRIDGE *Dict. Slang* 54/1 *Binder*, a bore (person). **1943** [see BIND *v.* 22]. **1944** PARTRIDGE in *19th Cent.* CXXXV. 184 A person.. who is a grouser or a fault-finder is termed a *binder*.

12. *pl.* Brakes. *slang.*

1942 'H. W.' *What's the Gen?* 19 *To jump on the binders*, to apply the brakes. **1962** *Amer. Speech* XXXVII. 267 *Binders*, brakes. Most often used in referring to emergency stops. 'Hit the binders!'

bindery ('baɪndərɪ). [f. prec. + -Y: see -ERY.] A bookbinder's workshop or establishment. (First in use in U.S.)

1810 I. THOMAS *Hist. Printing in Amer.* I. 402 At Worcester, he.. set up a bindery. **1828** In WEBSTER. **1833** *Penny Cycl.* I. 449/1 s.v. *Americanism*; *Bindery*, meaning 'a place where books are bound'.. is not a bad word. **1879** *Academy* 11 Oct. 265 The bindery at the Boston Public Library. **1882** *Encycl. Brit.* s.v. *Libraries*, Provision.. for work-rooms, librarians' offices, cataloguing rooms, and a Bindery.

bindi-eye ('bɪndɪ,aɪ). Also **bindei, bindyi.** [Origin unknown.] The popular name in Australia of a small perennial herb, *Calotis cuneifolia*, with burr-like fruit.

1911 C. E. W. BEAN '*Dreadnought*' *of Darling* v. 50 They swung their legs over the saddle and rode off over the grass and the twigs and the bindyi. **1923** *Census Plants of Victoria & Vernacular Names* 64 Calotis cuneifolia.. Bindi-eye. N.W. **1925** *Austral. Encycl.* I. 231/2 Calotis... *C. cuneifolia* (with blue flowers) and *C. lappulacea* (with yellow flowers) are known in the west as bindieyes (or bindeïs—the spelling is doubtful). Their burr-like flower-heads become entangled by the barbed bristles in the wool of sheep. **1934** *Bulletin* (Sydney) 13 June 19/3 Bindei burr, which was one of their favourite foods. **1941** K. TENNANT *Battlers* xiii. 147 Some comfortable little parking-place that was neither.. full of bindi-eyes and other assorted prickles, nor the home of ants.

binding ('baɪndɪŋ), *vbl. sb.* [f. BIND *v.* + -ING[1].]

I. Abstract.

1. a. The action of the vb. BIND in various senses.

a **1240** *Lofsong* in *Lamb. Hom.* 207 Ich bede þe.. bi his nimunge. and bindunge. *c* **1440** *Promp. Parv.* 36 Byndynge, *ligacio.* **1517** in Glasscock *Rec. St. Michael's, Stortford* 35 Pd. for flower and woode for the bynding of the books, ijd. **1633** G. HERBERT *Temple, Sacrifice* xii, I suffer binding, who have loos'd their bands. **1651** HOBBES *Govt. & Soc.* xvii. §25. 324 What binding and loosing, or remitting and retaining of sinnes, is, admits of some scruple. **1706** PHILLIPS, etc., *Binding* (in Falconry) signifies tiring or when a hawk seizes [cf. BIND *v.* 9 c]. **1832** C. HOWARD *Sel. Farms* 8 By.. large sheaves, and tight binding. **1881** GREENER *Gun* 257 The wood screws.. are always soaped before turned in, to prevent their binding in the wood.

b. Engagement for service, or as an apprentice.

1834 *Penny Cycl.* II. 194/1 The binding is to a carpenter for six years. **1858** *Lond. Rev.* Oct. 42 At the annual bindings [for service].

2. The state or condition of being bound (in various senses of the vb.).

c **1380** WYCLIF *De Dot. Eccl.* Sel. Wks. III. 431 Byndyng to siche signes lettiþ fredom of Crist. **1620** VENNER *Via Recta* vii. 115 In case of binding they are best to be eaten before meate. **1632** RUTHERFORD *Lett.* (1862) I. 83 What think ye to take binding with the fair Corner-stone, Jesus?

†**3.** A quantity bound up; a bundle, bunch. *Obs.*

1388 WYCLIF *1 Sam.* xxx. 12 Twei byndyngis [*Vulg.* ligatura] of dried grapis.

II. Concrete.

4. That with which anything is bound; a bond, band, bandage; a fastening.

a **1300** *E.E. Psalter* cxxiv. [cxxv]. 5 Heldand in bindinges Laverd lede sal. **1398** TREVISA *Barth. De P.R.* xvii. xlv. (1495) 629 The tame cucurbita.. byndyth it self wyth certen fastnynges and byndynges as a vyne dooth. **1607** TOPSELL *Four-f. Beasts* 379 The same bindings being again bound upon the wound.. infect it. **1611** BIBLE *Dan.* v. 6 The joints [*marg.* bindings or knots] of his loins were loosed.

5. *spec.* **a.** The strong covering of a book, which holds the sheets together, and protects the volume.

1647 CRASHAW *Steps Temp.* 61 A little volume, but great book.. the rest of a rich binding. **1709** STEELE *Tatler* No. 80 ¶1 Provided always, that the Binding be of Calves-Skin. **1787** BURNS *Book Worm* i, Spare the golden bindings. **1854** *N. & Q.* IX. 423 Receipt for varnishing the binding of old books.

b. A protective covering for the raw edges of a fabric; the braid or other material of this.

1598 FLORIO, *Cordicella*, a little cord.. an inkle, a binding. **1747** *Gentl. Mag.* XVII. 284 The boys and girls hats are white, and tied round with red binding. **1885** *Price List*, Bindings.. Silk, 2*d.* per yard.

c. *Arch.* and *Shipbuilding.* A band of masonry and brickwork; a connecting timber, etc.

1626 CAPT. SMITH *Accid. Yng. Seamen* 10 Plankes, bindings, knees, boults. **1730** A. GORDON *Maffei's Amphit.* 223 The three Fasciæ or Bindings, which serve as a Parapet. *c* **1850** *Rudim. Navig.* (Weale) 97 Bindings, the iron links which surround the Dead-Eyes. **1884** *Congregational Year Bk.* 401 The ceiling of roof over the nave is.. divided by arched bindings.

d. An arrangement of straps or springs holding the ski to the boot.

1911 *Encycl. Brit.* XXV. 186/2 The feet.. are fastened to the middle of the skis by an arrangement of straps, called the binding. **1924** *Tourist* (Winter Sports) 12/1 There are many varieties of 'rigid' or 'spring' bindings, which hold the ski to the foot.

6. *Attrib.* and *Comb.*, as ***binding factory***, ***shrub***; **binding-cloth**, fancy cloth (usually dyed and stamped muslin) for covering books; **binding copy** (see quot. 1951); **binding-guide**, a contrivance fitted to sewing-machines for adjusting the binding to the material to be bound; †**Binding-Tuesday**, the Tuesday in Hocktide, the second Tuesday after Easter. (See also the *ppl. adj.*)

1591 PERCIVALL *Sp. Dict.*, *Retama*, a kinde of binding shrubbe or broome, *Genista.* **1664** SPELMAN *Gloss.* s.v. *Hocday*, Alii in hac celebritate alios obsident, capiunt, ligant (præsertim viros fœminæ) atque inde, binding Tuesday, i. Diem Martis ligatoriam appellant. **1845** STRUTT *Sports & Past.* IV. iii. 350 [tr. Spelman]. **1936** *Rogers' Catalogue* (*Newcastle upon Tyne*), [Item] 249.. is really a binding copy. **1951** J. CARTER *ABC for Book-Collectors* 33 *Binding copy*, this means.. a copy whose covers are in a very poor state, but whose interior is clean and which is worth re-binding.

'binding, *ppl. a.* [f. as prec. + -ING[2].]

1. That binds together or up; causing or tending to cohere; astringent, styptic.

1382 WYCLIF *Dan.* iii. 69 Byndynge frost and colde, blesse ȝe to the Lord. **1398** TREVISA *Barth. De P.R.* VII. lxix. (1495) 289 Byndyng medycynes.. as.. Acacia. **1606** B. JONSON *Hymenæi*, We see The binding force of Vnitie. **1616** SURFL. & MARKH. *Countr. Farm* 539 As for the mixt soyles, if they be binding, as the clayes. **1824** LOUDON *Cycl. Garden*, §1958 Choosing the best coloured good binding gravel.

2. *fig.* Obligatory, restrictive, coercive.

1611 BIBLE *Num.* xxx. 13 Euery binding othe to afflict the soule. **1782** PRIESTLEY *Corrupt. Chr.* II. IX. 224 No promise made to an heretic is binding. **1859** MILL *Liberty* iv, Laws of conduct binding on ourselves and on all others.

3. *Comb.* (some of them perh. from the *vbl. sb.*), as **binding agent**, a substance that assists cohesion (cf. BIND *v.* 10); **binding energy** *Physics*, the energy required to break up a nucleus into its constituent particles; **binding-joist**, a joist resting on the wall-plates and carrying other joists; †**binding-note**, a bind or tie in musical notation; **binding-plate**, one of a series of iron plates used to strengthen or arm a puddling-furnace; **binding-rafter**, a longitudinal timber lying upon the principals of a roof and enabling them to support the covering; **binding-screw**, a screw used in various instruments for purposes of clamping or adjustment; **binding-twine**, twine used for binding sheaves of corn; **binding wire**, wire used for binding.

1933 *Burlington Mag.* Mar. 123/2 Egg, milk, or size, was used as a *binding-agent. **1940** *Chambers's Techn. Dict.* 91/1 *Binding agent* or *binder*, the basic material of disc records, chiefly shellac, which causes the various materials to adhere together and form, after heating, a solid mass. **1932** J. CHADWICK in *Proc. R. Soc.* A. CXXXVI. 708 This suggests that the neutron consists of a proton and an electron in close combination, the *binding energy being about 1 to 2 × 10^6 electron volts. **1933** E. WIGNER in *Physical Rev.* XLIII. 253/2 One of the remarkable facts about the mass defects in the very first elements is the very great binding energy of the He nucleus. *Ibid.* 256/1 We now come to the calculation of the binding energy of the He nucleus, 1 and 2 are neutrons, 3 and 4 protons. **1957** *Encycl. Brit.* XVI. 593D/1 The binding energy is a negative energy in the sense that one has to add energy to decompose a helium nucleus into neutrons and protons. **1958** W. K. MANSFIELD *Elem. Nucl. Physics* ii. 15 It should require, roughly, 28/4 = 7 MeV to detach a single nucleon. This amount of energy is known as the average *binding energy* per nucleon. **1677** MOXON *Mech. Exerc.* (1703) 132 The *binding Joysts marked *cc.* **1879** SIR G. SCOTT *Lect. Archit.* I. 266 The beams and binding-joists are shown. **1782** BURNEY *Hist. Mus.* II. 454 Semicircular marks, called *binding-notes, and slurs. **1875** URE *Dict. Arts* II. 997 Bolted upon both sides to the cast-iron *binding plates of the furnace. **1842** GWILT *Archit.* Gloss., **Binding Rafters*, The same as Purlins. **1828** F. WATKINS *Electro-Magnetism or Electro-Dynamics* 74 Two wooden.. troughs are secured by *binding-screws. **1839** *Annals Electr., Magn. & Chem.* IV. 65 The result is a method whereby solder.. and binding screws are dispensed with. *c* **1865** J. WYLDE in *Circ. Sc.* I. 258/1 From these springs the two wires proceed, ended by binding-screws. **1890** *U.S. Congress. Record* Aug. 9260/1 The observations of.. [Senator Davis] in respect to *binding-twine are very important to the people of La. **1767** H. M. BROOKS *Olden Time Series* (1886) IV. 31 *Binding wire; Brass and Iron ditto. **1843** C. & J. J. HOLTZAPFFEL *Turning* I. xx. 424 The soft iron binding-wire used in soldering. **1920** *Whittaker's Electr. Engin. Pocket-Bk.* (ed. 4) 363 The binding wire should be wrapped round the conductor where it rests against the insulator.

bindingly ('baɪndɪŋlɪ), *adv.* [f. prec. + -LY[2].] In a binding manner; so as to be obligatory.

1851 G. S. FABER *Many Mansions* 10 Nothing is bindingly to be received and believed as an Article of Faith, unless, etc.

'bindingness. [f. as prec. + -NESS.] Binding or obligatory quality.

1874 SIDGWICK *Meth. Ethics* viii. 87 The truth and bindingness of.. these current rules.

'bindle[1]. *Sc.* [Cf. OE. *bindele* a binding, a tying.] 'The cord or rope that binds anything, whether made of hemp or of straw.' Jamieson.

bindle[2] ('bɪnd(ə)l). *U.S.* and *Canadian slang.* [Prob. a corruption of BUNDLE *sb.*, but cf. prec.]

a. A bundle containing clothes and possessions, *esp.* a bedding-roll carried by a tramp. Hence **bindle-man, -stiff**, a tramp who carries such a bundle.

1900 'FLYNT' *Itinerant Policeman* 167 Among the 'Bindle Men', 'Mush Fakers', and 'Turnpikers' of the middle West, the East, and Canada, there exists a crude system of marking 'good' houses. **1901** J. LONDON *Let.* 6 Dec. (1966) 126 Wyckoff only knows the workingman, the stake-man, and the bindle-stiff. **1925** *Forum* Aug. 232 Carrying his 'bindle roll' or roll of blankets on his back, he is prepared to make his home wherever night finds him. *Ibid.* 235 *Bindle stiff*, a western hobo, who carries his blankets in a roll or bindle. **1927** *Glasgow Herald* 24 July 8 In his stride he took almost all the experiences that can befall bums, bindle stiffs.. and all other variously designated knights of the moonlight. **1937** J. STEINBECK *Of Mice & Men* 4 George unslung his bindle and dropped it gently on the bank. **1952** —— *East of Eden* vii. 46 Before he knew it he was a bindlestiff himself.

b. Any package or bundle, spec. one containing narcotics (see quot. 1923).

1916 *Lit. Digest* 19 Aug. 425/1 A package is a 'bindle'. **1922** E. MURPHY *Black Candle* (1926) xi. 214 The pedlars would buy it [*sc.* morphine] in big amounts; would.. dish it out in small packages. We would call these 'decks', but some people call them 'bindles'. **1923** *Dialect Notes* VI. vi. 246 *Bindle*, a package containing either morphine or cocaine. 'Give me a bindle of snow.'

bindweed ('baɪndwiːd). *Bot.* Also 6 **bind(e)-weede, bynd-,** 7 **binde-,** 9 **bine-.** [f. BIND *v.* + WEED. (Perh. sometimes for BINDWITH.)]

1. The English name for the species of the N.O. *Convolvulus*; as Greater Bindweed (*C. sepium*), Lesser Bindweed (*C. arvensis*), Seaside Bindweed (*C. Soldanella*).

1548 TURNER *Names of Herbes* (1881) 30 Conuoluulus is called.. in english wythwynde or byndeweede. **1562** —— *Herbal* II. 128 Byndweed.. is as it wer an vnperfyt worke of nature lerning to make lilies. **1616** SURFL. & MARKH. *Countr. Farm* 531 Bind-weed, both great and small, do proceed partly of drinesse. **1783** AINSWORTH *Lat. Dict.* (Morell) 1, Sea bells, sea bind weed, or withwand, *Soldanella.* **1814** WORDSW. *Excurs.* I. 761 The cumbrous bind-weed, with its wreaths and bells.

attrib. **1855** TENNYSON *Brook* 203 The fragile bindweed-bells and briony rings.

2. Applied dialectally or vaguely to various other climbing plants, as species of *Smilax*, *Honeysuckle*, *Tamus*, etc. See also BINWEED.

1601 HOLLAND *Pliny* XVI. xxxv, Like unto Ivie is that plant which they call Smilax, or rough Bindweed. **1671** SALMON *Syn. Med.* III. xxii. 432 Smilax.. Bindweed; it opens the belly, disolves hard swellings.

3. black, corn, or **ivy bindweed**, *Polygonum Convolvulus*; **blue bindweed**, Bittersweet or Woody Nightshade.

1617 B. JONSON *Vis. Delight*, The blue bindweed doth itself infold With honey-suckle. **1794** MARTYN *Rousseau's Bot.* xix. 261 Black Bindweed.. frequent weed among corn.

bindwith ('baɪndwɪθ). *Bot.* [f. BIND + WITH(E a flexible twig: cf. BENDWITH.] A name given by some recent writers (perhaps erroneously) to *Clematis Vitalba*, or Traveller's Joy.

1797–1804 MILLER *Gard. Dict.* (ed. Martyn). **1863** PRIOR *Plant-n.* 21 *Bind-with*, a with used to bind up faggots, the Traveller's Joy.

'bindwood. *Bot.* Also **binwood.** [f. BIND + WOOD.] Scotch and north Eng. name for Ivy; also *occas.* for Honeysuckle.

1790 TELFORD in *Burns' Wks.* I. 370 The rocky how Where binwood bushes o'er them flow. **1808** JAMIESON *Sc. Dict.*, *Bindwood*, the vulgar name for ivy.

bine (baɪn). Also 4–5 **bynde,** 8–9 **bind.** [A dial. form of BIND *sb.*, recently adopted as the literary form in the following senses.]

1. A flexible shoot of any shrub, a shoot of the year's growth; the flexible stem of a climbing plant.

1807 VANCOUVER *Agric. Devon* (1813) 186 When the crop is heavy, the lower parts of the bines [of vetches] will be less inviting than the upper part. **1880** *Standard* 12 Nov., The

first frosts..shrivel the bines of white bryony. **1880** JEFFERIES *Gr. Ferne F.* 194 A trailing bine of honeysuckle.

b. *spec.* The climbing stem of the hop.

1727 BRADLEY *Fam. Dict.* s.v. *Hop Gard.*, When you find the Binds very vigorous..you must forbear giving them any more Earth. *a* **1845** HOOD *Ode R. Wilson*, What Kentish boor would tear away the prop So roughly as to wound, nay, kill the bine? **1864** TENNYSON *Aylmer's F.* 112 When burr and bine were gather'd. **1884** G. ALLEN in *Longm. Mag.* V. 43 The 'fly'..on hops, is an aphis specialized for that particular bine.

c. Hence, used to name varieties of the Hop; e.g. ***white-bine*** (formerly ***-bind,*** corruptly ***-vine***).

1732 MILLER *Gard. Dict.* s.v. *Lupulus*, The grey Bind..is a large square Hop. **1835** *Penny Mag.* 453 The hop-plant.. has several varieties, such as the red-bind, the green-bind, the white-bind. **1866** *Treas. Bot.* 602 Several varieties are known, the finest of which are the White Bines, etc.

2. Entering into names of plants: e.g. WOODBINE. Cf. BIND *sb.* 3.

bine, obs. form of BIN, within.

binervate (baɪ'nɜːveɪt), *a.* [f. BI- *pref.*² 1 + NERVATE, f. L. *nerv-us* NERVE.] Having two nerves: applied **a.** in *Bot.* to leaves having two longitudinal ribs; **b.** in *Ent.* to insect-wings supported by two nerves only.

1842 in BRANDE *Dict. Sc.*

binethe, obs. form of BENEATH.

Binet-Simon (biːneɪsiː'mɔ̃). The names of the French psychologists A. *Binet* (1857–1911) and T. *Simon* (1873–1961), applied *attrib.* to a form of intelligence test which they devised. ***Binet-Simon scale***, the measurement of intelligence by such a test. Also ***Binet('s) scale, test.*** Also *ellipt.*

1910 G. M. WHIPPLE *Man. Mental & Physical Tests* 278 There are marked differences in the *amount of work* (number of additions) done..*e.g.*, in Binet's tests, from 40 to 96 numbers. *Ibid.* 491 (*heading*) Application of the 1905 Binet-Simon Tests to Defectives. **1912** *Jrnl. Educ. Psychol.* III. 70 The following chart..throws into relief the periods of rapid, normal and slow mental growth as measured by the Binet scale. *Ibid.* 63 The Binet tests of 1908 are the only set hitherto devised covering any considerable variety of functions. **1914** M. DRUMMOND in W. B. Drummond tr. *Binet & Simon's Mentally Defective Children* 147 Part of the interest of this work on defective children consists in the fact that in it we find the origin of those ideas and investigations which culminated in the formation of the Binet-Simon Scale of Intelligence, now so widely known throughout Europe and America. **1921** C. L. BURT *Mental & Scholastic Tests* 3 The Binet-Simon scale consists of about sixty graded tests for measuring the intelligence of school children. **1963** M. MCCARTHY *Group* iv. 87 She wished he would let her give him the Binet and some of the personality tests she had tried on the group at Vassar.

bineweed, variant of BINDWEED.

bing (bɪŋ), *sb.*¹ Also 5–6 bynge, 6–7 binge, byng, 7 bingg. [a. ON. *bing-r* masc. 'heap'; cf. Sw. *binge* masc. 'heap.' Da. *bing* has the sense not of 'heap,' but of 'bin'; and in Eng. *bing* has also been used dialectally for BIN in various senses since the 15th c. In Da. this change can only be explained by transference of the name from a 'heap' to the place where a heap is contained; the Eng. use of *bing* for *bin* may be partly of Danish origin, but is prob. largely due to phonetic contact of the two words.]

1. A heap or pile: formerly of stones, earth, trees, dead bodies, as well as of corn, potatoes, and the like, as still in northern dial.

1513 DOUGLAS *Æneis* IV. ix. 45 Of treis thow big a bing To be a fyre. *Ibid.* IV. vii. 80 Lyk emetis gret Quhen thai depulȝe the meikle bing of quheit. **1528** LYNDESAY *Dream* ii. 173 The men of Kirk lay boundin into byngis. *a* **1547** SURREY *Æneid* IV. 529 Like ants when they do spoile the bing of corne. **1787** BURNS *Brigs of Ayr* 27 Potato-bings are snugged up frae skaith Of coming Winter. **1880** *Antrim & Down Gloss.* (E.D.S.), *Bing*..a heap of potatoes in a field covered with earth: a heap of grain in a barn.

2. *spec.* A heap of metallic ore, of alum; a definite quantity (8 cwt.) of lead ore.

1815 *Encycl. Brit.* III. 619 Bing in the alum-works denotes a heap of alum thrown together in order to drain. **1876** *Mid Yorks. Gloss.* (E.D.S.), *Bing*, a bing of ore contains eight weighs, a weigh being a hundred weight, *Nidd.* **1885** *Trans. Cumbrld. & Westm. Archæol. Soc.* VIII. 19 In one year eighty workmen raised 12,000 bings of ore in this mine.

b. ***bing ore*** (or simply ***bing***): the best lead ore.

1679 PLOT *Staffordsh.* (1686) 166 The best [lead-ore] being call'd Bing. **1851** TAPPING *Manlove's Chron.* Gloss., *Bing*..ore is the Derbyshire mining term for the purer, richer, and cleaner part of the fell or boose.

3. = BIN, in various applications. Now *dial.*

c **1325** *Metr. Hom.* 97 King hafs riueli gold in bing. *c* **1440** *Promp. Parv.*, Bynge, *theca, cumera.* **1539** *Indent. Berwick Castle* in *Archæol.* XI. 440 In the pantre, a large bynge of okyn tymbar with 3 partitions. **1575** TURBERV. *Venery* 28 Pretty little Binges or baskettes of woodde to put theyr breade in. **1617** MARKHAM *Caval.* v. 6 In..the stable shall be placed close binggs or hutches for the keeping of prouender. **1695** KENNETT *Par. Antiq.* Gloss. s.v. *Abunda*, The Cistern into which they throw their crystallized Allom, for the water to drain from it, is call'd a Bing. **1775** E. BARRY *Observ. Wines* 82 To cover the Bottles in the Bings with Saw-Dust. **1879** MISS JACKSON *Shropsh. Word-Bk.* (E.D.S.), *Bing*, a place railed off from the cow-house in which fodder is kept.

4. 'The kiln of the furnace wherein they burn their Charcoal for the melting of metals.' Kennett *Par. Antiq.* 1695.

1658 RAY *Itin.* (1760) 127 Then they carry it [silver ore].. to each Smelter's several Bing, where it is melted with Black and White Coal. **1674** —— *Prep. Tin* Coll. 123 Throwing on Charcoal, then upon that Black Tin, and so interchangeably into a very deep bing (which they call the house).

5. *Comb.* †**bing-ale**; †**bing-brine**, brine of a pickling trough; **bing-hole** (see quot.); **bing-place, bing-stead**, the place to which the 'bing' or round lead ore is brought to be crushed; also, a place for ashes.

1735 PEGGE *Kenticisms* (E.D.S.), **Bing-ale*, the liquour which the fermor of a parsonage gives to the fermours.. when he has gathered their tythe. **1745** W. THOMPSON *R.N. Advoc.* (1757) 9 *Bing Brine..composed of the entire Juices of the Flesh and Salt, when boiled..is of a sweet Smell, and quite transparent. **1881** RAYMOND *Mining Gloss.*, **Bing-hole*, a hole or shoot through which ore is thrown. **1653** MANLOVE *Lead Mines* 129 To fine such..as..digg or delve in any Mans *Bing-place. **1747** W. HOOSON *Miner's Dict.* B ij b, **Bingstead*, the place where the largest and best of the ore..is thrown. **1793** SMEATON *Edystone L.* 198 Cinders are thrown..into a *Bing-stead in the court-yard.

‖**bing**, *sb.*² *Obs.* [Chinese *bing*, dial. form of *ming*, the name of a Chinese character often denoting the leaves of the tea-plant, and especially the tender leaves or leaf-buds. Prof. Legge.] A kind of tea.

1701 *Phil. Trans.* XXIII. 1205 The Bohe..is the very first bud gather'd..The Bingtea is the second growth in April. **1721** *Lond. Gaz.* No. 5934/3 One Chest Bing per Carnarvan.

bing (bɪŋ), *sb.*³ and *int. dial.* and *colloq.* [Echoic, representing a sudden banging noise or blow.] **a.** *sb.* A thump or blow. *dial.* (See *E.D.D.*) **b.** *int.* All of a sudden; in a flash; with a bang.

1922 JOYCE *Ulysses* 506 Now I do this kind of thing On the wing, on the wing! Bing! **1924** WODEHOUSE *Ukridge* iii. 57 Always getting ideas—*bing*—like a flash. **1925** C. MORLEY *Thunder on Left* xi. 140 And then the train..smashes into a lot of people, bing! **1946** WODEHOUSE *Joy in Morning* xxix. 264 She looked round and—*bing*—a pillar of salt. **1959** 'A. GILBERT' *Death takes Wife* xv. 187 Money saved..and then bing! everything vanished into thin air.

Also **bing-bang** *colloq.*, an onomatopœic reduplication expressing a repeated heavy thump or a continued banging noise.

1914 W. J. LOCKE *Fortunate Youth* xiii, Lets 'em have it bing-bang in the eye. Don't he, Jane? **1926** *Glasgow Herald* 1 Mar. 10 Bing-bang, cling-clang clatter.

bing (bɪŋ), *v.*¹ To pile or put up in a bing.

1513 DOUGLAS *Æneis* VIII. Prol. 57 The burges byngis in his buith, the broun and the blak. **1822** *Blackw. Mag.* Dec. (JAM.) The hairst was ower..The 'tatoes bing'd.

bing, *v.*² *dial.* Also **byng**. *intr.* Of milk: To begin to turn sour, to be on the turn.

1867 HARLAND *Lanc. Folk-lore* 165 in *Lanc. Gloss.* (E.D.S.) The milk is bynged or will not churn, though a hot poker has been used to spoil the witchery. [cf. BLINK.]

†**bing**, *v.*³ *Obs.* [Slang. ? Gipsy.] *intr.* To go.

1567 HARMAN *Caueat* 84 Bynge a waste, go you hence. **1609** DEKKER *Lanth. & Candle-Lt.* Wks. 1884–5 III. 198 And bing we to Rome vile. **1652** BROME *Jov. Crew* IV. ii. 431 Bing awast. **1815** SCOTT *Guy M.* xxviii, 'Bing out and tour, ye auld devil.' **1822** —— *Nigel* xxiii, 'You shall be carted for bawd..and bing off to Bridewell.'

binge, *v. Sc.* Also 6 bynge, 8 beenge, 9 beenje. [Of late formation, app. with a feeling for the initial sound of *bow, bend, beck*, and the closing sound of *cringe*; cf. *whinge*. The dial. *binge* to soak (Lincoln.) appears to be a different word.]

intr. To make a low obeisance, to curtsey; also to fawn, cringe. **bingeing** *vbl. sb.* and *ppl. a.*

1562 A. SCOTT *N. Yere Gift Quene*, Thay bad thame bek and bynge at deid mennis banes. **1712** ARBUTHNOT *John Bull* II. iv. (1755) 51, I mun stand becking and binging, as I gang out and into the hall. **1724** RAMSAY *Tea-t. Misc.* (1729) 17 The Maiden blusht and bing'd fu' law. **1805** J. NICOL *Poems* I. 187 (JAM.) Beenjin slaves ca' them divine. **1879** JAMIESON *Sc. Dict.* s.v. *Beck*, 'A great deal of becking and beenging' is a phrase still used among the vulgar.

binge, *sb.*¹ *Sc.* In 5 bing, 6 benge, 7 beinge. [f. prec. vb.] A servile bow or obeisance.

c **1450** HENRYSON *Mor. Fab.* 24 (Quod hee) with many bing and many becke. **1535** STEWART *Cron. Scot.* III. 105 With mony benge and bek, He salust him. **1681** R. LAW *Mem.* (1818) 190 With many a scrape, beck and beinge.

binge (bɪndʒ), *sb.*² *slang* (orig. *dial.*: see E.D.D.). [Special use of dial. *binge* to soak (a wooden vessel).] A heavy drinking-bout; hence, a spree.

1854 A. E. BAKER *Gloss. Northampt. Words* s.v., A man goes to the alehouse to get a good binge, or to binge himself. **1889** BARRÈRE & LELAND *Dict. Slang*, *Binge* (Oxford), a big drinking bout. **1922** *Chambers's Jrnl.* Sept. 569/1 This is only a binge—just a jolly old bachelor-party. **1928** WODEHOUSE in *Strand Mag.* July 4 Eh? What about our Monte Carlo binge?

So **binge** *v.*² *refl.* and *pass.*, to drink heavily, 'soak'; *intr.* to have a 'binge'; *trans.* to enliven, const. *up* (cf. 'pep up').

1854 [see *sb.*]. **1910** BELLOC *On Something* xxii. 195 It is plainly evident that they know how to binge. **1914** EARL BEATTY *Let.* 17 Nov. in W. S. Chalmers *Life & Lett.* (1951) 163 And one has to be cheerful and encouraging to the others and binge them up to live in hope every time that this is *the* time. **1925** *Sunday at Home* Dec. 146/1 One man was so binged in drink and so enchained by the craving for it. **1935** E. BAGNOLD *National Velvet* xiv. 224 The information having been looked over and binged up here and toned down there..Reuter sent round the world the following message.

binghi, Binghi ('bɪŋgaɪ). *Austral. slang.* Also bingy, etc. [Aboriginal.] An Aboriginal.

Recorded earlier in the general sense 'brother': *e.g.* 1831 R. DAWSON *Present State of Australia* 221, I was received by them with the greatest cordiality, and greeted by the term bingeye, or brother.

1933 *Bulletin* (Sydney) 15 Feb. 20 One good idea that far inlanders..learnt from Binghi. *Ibid.* 2 Aug. 21/4 Binghi's legend is some evidence that it existed there. *Ibid.* 13 Dec. 37/1 A binghi wife the Chinaman had. **1934** T. WOOD *Cobbers* 34 The home for a floating population of Japanese, Chinese, Malays..binghis, half-castes and whites.

bingle ('bɪŋg(ə)l). [f. B(OB *sb.*¹ 5 b + SH)INGLE *sb.*¹ 1 e.] A short hairstyle for women, between a bob and a shingle. Hence as *v. trans.*, to cut (hair) in this style. So '**bingled** *ppl. a.*, '**bingling** *vbl. sb.*

1925 *Punch* 11 Mar. 256 This lady complains that you have—ah—completely bungled her bingle. **1925** *Westm. Gaz.* 13 Apr. 5/3 The shingled or bingled head is firmly established in popularity. **1927** *Daily Express* 2 Mar. 3/7 Of course, shingled hair goes with any of this kit, or it may be bobbed, Eton cropped, or bingled. **1927** W. E. COLLINSON *Contemp. Eng.* 63 Bobbing..shingling..and a combination of the two, bingling. **1959** W. GOLDING *Free Fall* xii. 228 Bobbing, bingling, Eton crops. **1960** *News Chron.* 11 Oct. 8/3 Bingle it [*sc.* your hair] yourself.

bingle-bangle ('bɪŋg(ə)l'bæŋg(ə)l), *a. dial.* [A reduplicate formation from BANGLE *v.*] Fickle, vacillating, irresolute; cf. *shilly-shally.*

1825 R. WARD *Tremaine* II. xxvi. 234 He is but a bingle bangle man..no good will come on him.

bingo¹ ('bɪŋgəʊ), *sb.* [App. a humorous formation from B. for 'brandy' (cf. 'B. and S.') and STINGO.] A slang term for brandy.

1699 B. E. *Dict. Cant. Crew*, *Bingo*, c. Brandy. *Bingo-boy*, c. a great Drinker or Lover thereof. *Bingo-club*, c. a set of Rakes, Lovers of that Liquor. **1750** B.-M. CAREW *Apol. for Life* 337 *Bingo-Mort*, a female drunkard, a she brandy drinker. **1839** G. W. M. REYNOLDS *Pickwick Abroad* xxvi. 224 From morn to night we'll booze a ken, And we'll pass the bingo round. **1861** HUGHES *Tom Brown Oxf.* xxxiii. (D.) Some soda water with a dash of bingo clears one's head in the morning.

bingo² ('bɪŋgəʊ). [Of obscure origin, but cf. next.] A modern development of LOTTO (sense 1), often played in public halls, etc., for prizes. Also *attrib.*

1936 *Time* 21 Dec. 26/2 In many a U.S. Catholic diocese during the past few years the simple gambling game of bingo ..has served as a prime money-raiser. **1949** N. STREATFEILD *Painted Garden* vi. 57 Such heavenly things were happening on deck... There was a game called Bingo. **1953** *Oxford Mail* 21 Nov. 4/9 For some time now Bingo drives have been gaining in popularity at Oxford social gatherings. Bingo..is very closely akin to what used to be known as 'Housey Housey'. **1958** *Economist* 29 Nov. 798/1 While the essential elements of the game have provided amusement and diversion for centuries, bingo was named and introduced as a modern parlour game in 1929 by a toy manufacturer, Mr. Edwin Lowe. Each player has a card with 25 numbers between 1 and 75 arranged in a square, and the first to get five in a row as the numbers are called out cries 'bingo'. **1964** A. WYKES *Gambling* x. 250 British entrepreneurs have converted most of the nation's failing cinemas into thriving bingo halls.

bingo ('bɪŋgəʊ), *int.* [Echoic, cf. BING.] = BING b; *spec.* an exclamation made by someone winning a game of bingo (see prec.). Also in the colloq. intensive phr. ***like bingo*** (see LIKE *adv.* 1 b), = 'like billy-o'.

1927 E. WALLACE *Ringer* (1952) xxiii. 93, I just laid my hands on him when—bingo! I was on the ground with four inches of good knife in me. **1931** WODEHOUSE *If I were You* xi. 125 What ensued? Bingo! Eaten by bears! **1933** M. ALLINGHAM *Sweet Danger* iv. 50, I just 'ad one look at 'im and came back 'ere like bingo. **1951** J. B. PRIESTLEY *Fest. Farbridge* II. ii. 222 If he can't do it, I will. Do it on my head —bingo! **1958** [see prec.]. **1959** N. MARSH *False Scent* (1960) i. 33 I've been drinking with The Management. Only two small ones, but on an empty tum: Bingo!

bingy ('bɪŋɪ), *a. north. dial.* [f. BING *v.*² + -Y.] Said of milk: In the incipient stage of sourness.

1857 MRS. GASKELL *C. Brontë* (1857) I. 70 The milk, too, was often 'bingy,' to use a country expression for a kind of taint which is far worse than sourness. **1884** *Cheshire Gloss.* (E.D.S.), *Bingy*, a peculiar clouty or frowsty taste in milk. The first stage of turning sour.

bingy ('bɪndʒɪ), *sb. Austral. slang.* Also bingee, bingie, bingey, binjy. [Aboriginal.] The stomach, belly. Also *attrib.*

[**1851** REV. D. MACKENZIE *Ten Years in Australia* xiv. 140 They lay rolling themselves on the ground, heavily groaning in pain,..exclaiming, 'Cabonn buggel along bingee' (that is, I am very sick in the stomach).] **1859** H. KINGSLEY *Recoll. G. Hamlyn* II. vi. 94 Don't you fret your bingy, boss; he'll be as good a man as his father yet. **1908** E. J. BANFIELD *Confessions of Beachcomber* I. iv. 143 Bingie (belly) belonga you, sore fella. *Ibid.* II. ii. 301 His 'debil-debil all the same

like dead man', had 'sat down' in 'Little Jinny's bingey'. **1924** D. H. LAWRENCE & SKINNER *Boy in Bush* 85 Success is t'grow a big bingy like a bloke from town. **1929** K. S. PRICHARD *Coonardoo* xv. 150 Give them a bit of pain killer or a dose of castor oil when they've got a bingee ache. **1931** I. L. IDRIESS *Lasseter's Last Ride* ii. 18 Micky landed, whoof! on his bingy. **1963** *Australasian Post* 20 June 44 Plenty tucker here. Just look at those binjies!

† **'binhead.** *Obs.* A kind of fresh-water fish; perh. the Bull-head or Miller's-thumb.

1581 LAMBARDE *Eiren.* IV. iv. (1588) 450 Angling is excepted, and so is the taking of Smelts, Loches, Minews, Binheads, Gudgeons, and Eeles.

Bini, var. BENIN.

binime(n, var. BENIM *v. Obs.* to take away.

biniou ('bɪnjuː). [Breton, pl. of *benvek* tool, (musical) instrument.] The form of bagpipe used in Brittany.

1902 *Westm. Gaz.* 20 Mar. 10/1 A toast was followed by such music as the native biniou can produce. **1925** *Blackw. Mag.* Sept. 359/2 When Lommic took the biniou under his arm he made the pipes sing.

binit ('bɪnɪt). [Abbrev. of BIN(ARY DIG)IT.] A binary digit (occas. distinguished from BIT *sb.*[4]); also, a probability expressed as the logarithm to the base two of the odds (also called ***binit weight***).

1953 S. GOLDMAN *Information Theory* i. 4 We shall use the contractions *decit* for decimal digit and *binit* for binary digit. *Ibid.* 5 The author does not know who originated the term *binit*, but he first heard it used by Dr. E. W. Samson. *Ibid.* 7 The total amount of information necessary to locate the cow is thus 6 binits. **1959** *Science* CXXX. 956/3 It is conventional practice in information theory to use logarithms to the base 2 of the probabilities expressed in the form of the 'odds', for or against. The units are known as 'binits'. **1963** N. ABRAMSON *Information Theory & Coding* i. 7 It is important to make a distinction between the binit (binary digit) and the bit. *Ibid.* ii. 18 If the 0s and 1s are not equally probable, then the amount of information provided by a given binit will be either less than or greater than 1 bit, depending upon its probability. **1965** H. B. NEWCOMBE in *Math. in Biol. & Med. (Med. Res. Council)* II. 46 We have found logarithms to the base 2 especially convenient and have called these 'binit weights'.

binitarian (baɪnɪ'tɛərɪən), *a.* and *sb. Theol.* [f. L. *bīnī*(pl.) twofold, double, after TRINITARIAN. Cf. G. *binitarisch* (Loofs 1898).] **A.** *adj.* Of or belonging to a belief in a Godhead of two persons only. **B.** *sb.* A believer in this doctrine. Hence **bini'tarianism**.

1908 W. R. NICOLL in T. H. Darlow *Life* (1925) 360 There are Trinitarians, Binitarians, Arians, and Unitarians. **1910** SANDAY *Christologies Anc. & Mod.* i. 12 The same alternation of Trinitarian and Binitarian language (the conjunction of Father, Son, and Spirit by the side of Father and Son). **1928** K. E. KIRK in A. E. J. Rawlinson *Ess. Trin. & Incarn.* 207 The two strains of thought—the binitarian and the trinitarian. *Ibid.* 215 The binitarianism of Tertullian's earlier Catholic thought.

† **'binity.** *Obs. rare*⁻¹. [f. L. *bīnī* two by two + -ITY; cf. *trinity*.] A pair.

1575 LANEHAM *Let.* (1871) 54 What a sort of fréendly binitéez we oour seluez doo consist & stond vpon, Fyrst, oour too féet, too legs, too knéez, so vpward.

bink (bɪŋk). *Sc.* and *north. dial.* Forms: 3 **bennk**, 3– **benk(e**, 3–4 **binc, binck**, 4 **bengk, bynk**, 5 **bynke**, 4– **bink**. [Later form of ME. *benk* = BENCH *sb.*]

1. A bench or form to sit on; = BENCH 1.

c **1200** ORMIN 15231 Wiþþ þrinne bennkess bennkedd. *a* **1300** *Cursor M.* 5321 He kist and sett on binc him bi [*Gött.* binck, *Fairf.* benk, *Trin.* bench]. **1375** BARBOUR *Bruce* VII. 238 The gud vif on the bynk sytand. *c* **1440** *York Myst.* XXVI. 188, I schall buske to þe benke. *a* **1548** *Thrie Priests Peblis* 24 (JAM.) Hal binks ar ay slidder. **1603** *Philotus* xvii, His wyfe may ay sit formest doun, At eyther burde or bink. **1855** *Whitby Gloss.* s.v., The summer binks, a benched alcove or summer-house in a garden.

2. A seat of justice; = BENCH 2.

1330 R. BRUNNE *Chron.* 58 At London at þe benke schewe þer þin askyng. *c* **1460** *Towneley Myst.* 317 When ye were set as syres on bynke. **1862** *Hislop Prov. Scot.* 63 For faut o' wise men fools sit on binks.

3. A shelf; particularly, a long flat slab of stone fixed to a wall, used either as a seat or as a shelf; also, a plate-rack; a dresser.

1535 *Richmond. Wills* (1853) 12 A cobbord with a dysbynk. **1657** COLVIL *Whigs Supplic.* (1751) 67 The Goodman keeps it, as we think, Behind a dish, upon the bink. **1816** SCOTT *Antiq.* xxvi, Ony thing . . frae the roof-tree down to a crackit trencher on the bink. **1818** —— *Hrt. Midl.* xiv, Nor the bowies put up on the bink. **1864** ATKINSON *Whitby Gloss.*, *Bink*, a bench. Upon those of stone at cottage doors, the fresh scoured milkpails and other dairy utensils are oft seen placed to dry and sweeten.

4. A bank (of earth); = BENCH 6.

c **1500** DUNBAR *Flyting* 289 Na fowlis . . amangis tha binkis Biggis, nor abydis. **1807** HEADRICK *Arran* 153 On putting down a bore in moss binks, water spouted up.

5. = BENCH 7, BANK *sb.*[1] 7.

1679 PLOT *Staffordsh.* (1686) 136 A Workman in another *Bink* hard by fear'd the roof would have fallen in. **1797** J. CURR *Coal Viewer* 15 The long way of working collieries, where the roads along the benk faces are narrow. **1940** *Chambers's Techn. Dict.* 87/1 *Benk*, the place underground where coal is being broken from the face of the coal seam.

† **6.** = BING, in sense of BIN. *Obs.*

1534 *Eng. Ch. Furniture* 190 A bynke to ley colis in.

¶ In south of Scotland = BIKE, wasps' nest.

'binman. Also **binsman. 1.** The man in charge of a bin during hop-picking.

1883 J. STRATTON *Hops & Hop-pick.* 31 The pickers are divided into companies . . the chief of which is the binman, who is commonly the pole-puller. **1884** *Sunday Mag.* Sept. 578/2 The 'bin-man' . . is alone permitted thus to go backwards and forwards.

2. *local* (esp. *North.*) and *colloq.* = DUSTMAN.

a **1966** 'M. NA GOPALEEN' *Best of Myles* (1968) 300 'Where else could that happen but in Ireland!' That's his supreme and universal apothegm. It embraces, defines and explains . . the following occasions: Late arrival and departure. . . Discovery that bin-man's brother is Field Marshal in army forces of a Great Power unnamed. **1968** *Guardian* 20 Sept. 24/6 The main problem is the 800 tons a day of domestic and shop refuse which the binmen collect. **1977** P. JOHNSON *Enemies of Society* viii. 105 Dustmen (or binmen in the North of England) become refuse-collectors. **1986** *Daily Tel.* 15 Sept. 6/1 Another common request was for . . a waste-disposal system that would eliminate the need for bin men.

binna, Sc. form of *be not*: see BE *v.*

binnacle ('bɪnək(ə)l). Forms: α. 7 **biticle, bittake, -kle, -kell, biddikil**, 7–8 **bittackle**, 7–9 **bittacle**; β. 8– **binacle, binnacle**. [The current *binnacle* first appears after 1750, as a corruption of the earlier *bittacle* (still found 1839), apparently ad. Sp. *bitácula, bitácora* 'a place where the compasse or light is kept in a ship' (Minsheu), or Pg. *bitácola*, cogn. w. It. *abitacolo*, Pr. *abitacle, habitacle*, F. *habitacle*:—L. *habitāculum* habitation, lodge, f. *habitāre* to inhabit. (A direct adoption of F. *habitacle*, and subseq. shortening to *bittacle* in Eng., is phonetically less probable.) The 17th c. *biddikil* appears to be a transitional form.]

A box on the deck of a ship near the helm, in which the compass is placed.

1622 *Recov. Ship Bristol* in Arb. *Garner* IV. 584 Watch the biticle, attend the compass. **1627** CAPT. SMITH *Seaman's Gram.* ii. 11 A square box nailed together with woodden pinnes, called a Bittacle, . . and in it alwaies stands the Compasse. **1684** I. MATHER *Remark. Provid.* (1856) 65 The compass in the biddikil. **1762** FALCONER *Shipwr.* II. 458 Companion, binnacle, in floating wreck, With compasses and glasses strew'd the deck. [**1769** —— *Dict. Marine* (1789) F 2 This is called *bittacle* in all the old sea-books.] **1836** MARRYAT *Midsh. Easy* xiii, Then they went aft to the binnacle again. **1839** —— *Phant. Ship* xli, The . . shrine of the saint at the bittacle. **1870** R. FERGUSON *Electr.* 24 To place pieces of soft iron or magnets in the immediate neighbourhood of the binnacle.

b. *attrib.*

1834 H. MILLER *Scenes & Leg.* xxviii. (1857) 422 In inventing binnacle lamps. **1856** OLMSTED *Slave States* 142 The binnacle-compass was a sort of fetish to him.

binn-an, -en, obs. forms of BIN, within.

binny ('bɪnɪ). *Ichthyol.* The barbel of the Nile (*Barbus bynni*).

binocle ('bɪnək(ə)l). [a. F. *binocle* (= It. *binocolo*), f. L. *bīnī* two each + *oculī* eyes.] A field-glass or opera-glass having tubes for both eyes.

1696 PHILLIPS, *Binocle* (Fr.), a double Prospective glass . . to see at a distance with both eyes at the same time. **1721** in BAILEY. **1871** *Echo* 18 Jan., My friend took his umbrella and I my binocle.

binocular (bɪ'nɒkjʊlə(r)), *a.* and *sb.* [f. L. *bīnī* two each + *oculī* eyes + -AR; cf. F. *binoculaire*.]

A. *adj.* † **1.** Having two eyes; binoculate. ? *Obs.*

1713 DERHAM *Phys. Theol.* VIII. iii. (1754) 361 Most animals are binocular, Spiders for the most Part octonocular.

2. Performed by or adapted to both eyes. In *Photogr.* = stereoscopic.

1738 R. SMITH *Opticks* 387 A binocular telescope. **1876** FOSTER *Phys.* III. ii. (1879) 509 Binocular vision . . affords us a means of judging of the solidity of objects. **1879** RUTLEY *Stud. Rocks* vii. 47 Many observers prefer to work with binocular microscopes. **1879** ROOD *Chromatics* 160 Binocular mixture of colours produces more or less lustre. **1889** E. J. WALL *Dict. Photogr.* 18 *Binocular Camera*, another name for Stereoscopic Camera. **1901** *Amateur Photographer* 26 July 70/1 The binocular portraits of M. Fred. Boissonnas. *Ibid.*, Binocular photography. *Ibid.* 70/2 Binocular photographs.

B. *sb.* (Short for *binocular glass*.) A field-glass or opera-glass in the use of which both eyes are employed in viewing an object; a BINOCLE. Also applied to a binocular microscope. Now usu. *pl.*

1871 M. COLLINS *Mrq. & Merch.* III. iv. 114, I shall keep this binocular. **1877** W. THOMSON *Voy. Challenger* I. i. 15 One of Smith and Beck's binoculars is more convenient for observing . . large foraminifera, by reflected light. **1928** E. O'NEILL *Strange Interlude* VIII. 272 Looking up the river through a pair of binoculars. *Ibid.* 295 Raising the binoculars as he goes to the rail, he looks up the river. **1932** *Bird Lore* XXXIV. 124 Tests to determine quality of binoculars. **1935** *Discovery* Nov. 330/2 We were busy watching the parties of cormorant through the binoculars.

bi'noculared, *a.* [f. BINOCULAR *sb.* + -ED[2].] Furnished or provided with binoculars.

1959 *Landfall* XIII. 130 Becket, grey-suited and binoculared, seemed to stand beside him. **1962** *Punch* 26 Sept. 458/2 Spied on by binoculared office workers. **1962** *Times* 20 Dec. 5/4 A binoculared naval man.

binocularity (bɪ,nɒkjʊ'lærɪtɪ). [f. BINOCULAR *a.* + -ITY.] Binocular quality or conditions; simultaneous employment of both eyes.

1854 J. HOGG *Microsc.* I. ii. (1867) 113 Obtaining binocularity with the compound achromatic microscope. **1881** LE CONTE *Light* 120 Perception of depth of space, so far as this is connected with binocularity.

bi'nocularly, *adv.* [f. as prec. + -LY[2].] By the simultaneous employment of both eyes.

1881 LE CONTE *Light* 146 Where we . . binocularly perceive depth of space.

binoculate (bɪ'nɒkjʊleɪt), *a.* [f. as BINOCULAR + -ATE[2].] Having two eyes.

1847 in CRAIG.

binodal: see BI- pref.[2] 1.

binode ('baɪnəʊd). *Geom.* [BI-[2].] A point on a surface at which there are two tangent planes.

1869 CAYLEY in *Phil. Trans. R. Soc.* CLIX. 201 Conical and biplanar nodes, or, as I call them, cnicnodes, and binodes. **1874** G. SALMON *Analyt. Geom.* (ed. 3) 457 The quadric cone may degenerate into a pair of planes. Such a node may be called a *binode*. **1934** D. M. Y. SOMMERVILLE *Anal. Geom. Three Dimensions* xvii. 375 If the double-point at *D* is a binode, $ax^2 + \ldots = 0$ breaks up into two planes and the discriminant Δ of this quadratic vanishes.

binom, -nume(n, etc.: see BENIM *v. Obs.* to take away.

binomial (baɪ'nəʊmɪəl), *a.* and *sb.* [f. late L. *binōmi-us* (see BINOMY) + -AL[1]; cf. F. *binôme*.]

A. *adj.*

1. *Math.* Consisting of two terms; see B. Also, relating to or derived from the binomial theorem or the binomial distribution; ***binomial coefficient***: a coefficient of a term in a binomial expansion; ***binomial distribution***: a frequency distribution of the possible number of successful outcomes in a given number of trials in each of which there is the same probability of success; ***binomial equation***: an equation reducible to the form $x^n - A = 0$; ***binomial expansion***: an expansion of a power of a binomial; ***binomial series***: an infinite series obtained by expanding $(x + y)^n$, where *n* is not a positive integer or zero; also, a binomial expansion; ***binomial theorem***: the general algebraic formula, discovered by Newton, by which any power of a binomial quantity may be found without performing the progressive multiplications..

1570 BILLINGSLEY *Euclid* X. xxxvi. 258 If two rationall lines commensurable in power onely be added together: the whole line is irrationall, and is called a binomium, or a binomiall line. **1706** PHILLIPS s.v., A binomial Quantity or Root, i.e. a Quantity or Root that consists of two Names or Parts joyn'd together by the Sign + as $a + b$, or $3 + 2$. **1725** J. KERSEY *Algebra* 137 Production of Powers from Roots Binomial, Trinomial, etc. **1755** J. LANDEN *Math. Lucubrations* ix. 132 By the Binomial Theorem $\frac{p}{1+x}$ is $= 1 + px + \frac{p.p-1}{2}x^2 + \frac{p.p-1.p-2}{2.3}x^3$ &c. **1796** C. HUTTON *Math. & Philos. Dict.* I. 208/2 He [*sc.* Newton] happily discovered that, by considering powers and roots in a continued series, . . the same binomial series would serve for them all, whether the index should be fractional or integral. **1814** P. BARLOW *New Math. & Philos. Dict.*, *Binomial equation*, is any equation of two terms, but more commonly applied to the higher order of equations of the form $x^n = 1$. **1848** A. DE MORGAN in *Camb. & Dublin Math. Jrnl.* III. 239 Use the binomial expansion up to the term in $(x - b)^{-(n-1)}$. **1870** BOWEN *Logic* xii. 410 The Binomial Theorem . . is a true Law of Nature according to our definition. **1889** *Cent. Dict.*, Binomial coefficient. **1911** G. U. YULE *Introd. Theory Statistics* xv. 305 The binomial distribution, . . only becomes approximately normal when *n* is large, and this limitation must be remembered in applying the table . . to cases in which the distribution is strictly binomial. **1914** *Biometrika* X. 36 Binomial frequencies belong to the teetotum class of chances. **1925** R. A. FISHER *Statistical Methods* iii. 65 The binomial distribution is well known as the first example of a theoretical distribution to be established. **1948** J. V. USPENSKY *Theory Equations* i. 26 The particular binomial equation $x^n = 1$, defining the so-called roots of unity of degree *n*, is of special interest. **1949** W. L. FERRAR *Higher Algebra Schools* v. 73 The binomial expansion can be used to find the value of expressions such as $(1{\cdot}002)^{13}$, $(1{\cdot}01)^7$ to any desired number of significant figures. **1959** G. & R. C. JAMES *Math. Dict.* 31/1 The $(r + 1)$th binomial coefficient of order *n* (*n* a positive integer) is $n!/[r!(n - r)!]$, the number of combinations of *n* things *r* at a time. **1961** P. G. GUEST *Numer. Meth. Curve Fitting* iv. 72 The binomial distribution for rare events . . approximates to the Poisson form. **1966** *McGraw-Hill Encycl. Sci. & Technol.* XII. 191/2 One of the most important power series is the binomial series.

2. Having or characterized by two names; = BINOMINAL.

1656 in BLOUNT *Glossogr.* **1850** *Gard. Chron.* 404 The binomial system adopted in every department of science since the days of Linnæus. **1880** HUXLEY *Crayfish* 16 The terms of this binomial nomenclature.

B. *sb.* **1.** An algebraic expression consisting of two terms joined by the sign + or −: formerly only when connected by +. (Cf. *binomium*, BINOMY.) Also *ellipt.* for *binomial distribution*, *theorem*, etc.

1557 RECORDE *Whetst.* Pp iv a, The nombers that be compounde with + be called Bimedialles... If their partes be of 2 denominations, then are thei named Binomialles properly. Howbeit many vse to call Binomialles all compounde nombers that haue +. **1720** RAPHSON *Arith.* 223 The Binomial $a - \frac{q}{3a}$, or $a + b$. **1806** HUTTON *Course Math.* I. 214 To extract any Root of a Binomial. **1835** *Penny Cycl.* IV. 412/2 The general theorems of which the binomial is a particular case. **1914** *Biometrika* X. 64 The binomial is built up on the assumption of the repetition *n* times of a number of independent events, of which the chance of occurrence is identical and equal to *q*. **1966** MEYER & HANLON *Fun with New Math* viii. 105 Perhaps you have forgotten how to multiply a binomial (an algebraic expression of two terms) by a binomial. **1968** P. A. P. MORAN *Introd. Probability Theory* ii. 77 If we require a distribution with a variance smaller than that of a binomial we can use a hypergeometric distribution.

2. *Biol.* The two-part Latin name of a plant or an animal.

1945 *Rhodora* XLVII. 372 Binomials had appeared sporadically in the publications of Bauhin, Cornut and others. **1957** W. T. STEARN *Linnæus's Species Plantarum* i. 2 In Linnaeus's work the binomial became more than a two-word label; it functioned as a point of reference within a vast logically devised and integrated system.

3. *Philol.* An expression consisting of two words of the same form-class.

1959 *Lingua* VIII. 113 In the typical newspaper headline *Cold and snow grip the nation* it is proper to set off the segment *cold and snow* as a binomial. **1964** *Linguistics* May 69 In A-Tokharian texts we find numerous combinations of two synonymous words or words expressing nearly related—or, in some cases, opposite—conceptions. The meaning of such a binomial obviously approaches that of a dvandva.

† **bi'nomical**, *a. Obs.* [f. as prec. + -ICAL.] 'Of two names.' Coles 1692.

binominal (baɪ'nɒmɪnəl), *a.* [f. L. *binōmin-is*, f. *bi-* two + *nōmin-* (nom. *nōmen*) name + -AL[1].] Having or characterized by two names, *esp.* those of genus and species in scientific nomenclature.

1880 GUNTHER *Fishes* 10 Applying binominal terms to the species. **1881** *Trans. Vict. Inst.* 24 In this way the binominal system is growing.

binominated (baɪ'nɒmɪneɪtɪd), *a.* [f. BI- *pref.*[2] + L. *nomen* name, *nōmindruat-us* named: cf *nominated.*] Having or bearing two names.

1857 M. LOWER *Eng. Surnames* (ed. 4) II. App. 170 A binominated person.

bi'nominous, *a.* [f. L. *binōmin-is* (see BINOMY) + -OUS.] = prec.

1612 T. JAMES *Jesuits' Downef.* 52 Hee was binominous; sometimes called Rob. Parsons, sometimes Rob. Cowbucke. **1662** FULLER *Worthies* II. 274 Many of them are binominous. [In mod. Dicts.]

† **bi'nomious**, *a. Obs.* [f. late L. *binōmius* (see BINOMY) + -OUS.] 'Of two names.' Coles 1692.

† **'binomy.** Also 6–7 in L. form **binomium**. [ad. mod.L. *binōmius, -um*, in algebraical use in 16th c., but common in late Latin in the general sense of 'having two personal names'; see Du Cange. For this, the classical L. word was *binōminis*: *binōmius* may be compared with *homicīda.*] = BINOMIAL *sb.* 1

1571 DIGGES *Pantom.* Y ij b, An irrationall called Binomium, reteining proportion to the side, as $\sqrt{z}\,\frac{1}{4} + \frac{1}{4}$ vnto 1. *Ibid.* C c j a, His conteyned Icosaedrons side is an irrationall Binomye. *Ibid.* C c iij b, By reduction of the former Trinomye to a Binomye. **1670** NEWTON in Rigaud *Corr. Sc. Men* (1841) II. 298 The extraction of cubic roots out of imaginary binomiums.

binormal (baɪ'nɔːməl). *Math.* [f. BI- *pref.*[2] II + NORMAL.] (See quot. 1848.)

1848 SALMON *Analyt. Geom.* (1865) §353 The normal perpendicular to that [the osculating] plane.. being normal to two consecutive elements of the curve, has been called by M. Saint-Venant the Binormal. **1857** PRICE *Infin. Calculus* I. 512 The former [line] has the distinctive name of binormal.

‖ **binot** (bino). [F.] (Not in Eng. use.)

1825 LOUDON *Encycl. Agric.* §2620 The binot is almost the same thing as the double mould-boarded plough.

binoternary (baɪnəʊ'tɜːnərɪ), *a.* [f. L. *bīnī* two by two + TERNARY; cf. F. *binoternaire.*] Combining binary and ternary characteristics.

1817 R. JAMESON *Haüy's Crystallog.* in *Min.* 217 Binoternary (*binoternaire*), when there is one [decrement] by two, and the other by three rows.

binotonous (baɪ'nɒtənəs), *a.* [f. L. *bīnī* (see BIN-) + *ton-us*, Gr. τόν-ος TONE + -OUS; ? after *monotonous.*] Consisting of two tones or notes.

1802 G. MONTAGU *Ornith. Dict.* (L.) During the breeding season their [the Lesser Pettychaps] binotonous cry is incessant. **1847** in CRAIG.

binous ('baɪnəs), *a.* [f. L. *bīn-i* + -OUS.] = BINATE.

1832 in WEBSTER.

binovular (bɪn-, baɪ'nəʊvjuːlə(r)), *a. Biol.* [f. BIN- (or L. *bīnī* two by two) + OVULAR *a.*] Pertaining to or derived from two ova.

1900 in DORLAND. **1917** C. BERKELEY *Midwifery* xxxii. 376 *Binovular twins* are developed from two ova. **1961** *Lancet* 30 Sept. 743/2 Two cases of goitre are described in the binovular twins of a mother who for years had taken 'Felsol' powders.

binoxalate, binoxide: see BIN-.

† **bint, binte**, *sb.*[1] *Obs.* (Meaning and derivation doubtful: cf. Du. *bindte* 'joint, crossbeam.')

1629 *S'hertogenbosh* 21 The French were.. very busie, making that night three bints of their Gallery neere the great Sconce. *Ibid.* 28 The ninth binte of the other Gallery on the South side of the said Bulwarke.

bint (bɪnt), *sb.*[2] *colloq.* [Arab. *bint* daughter.] A girl or woman (usu. derog.); girl-friend.

The term was in common use by British servicemen in Egypt and neighbouring countries in the wars of 1914–18 and 1939–45.

1855 R. F. BURTON *Pers. Narr. Pilgrimage to Meccah* I. v. 121 'Allah! upon Allah! O daughter!' cry the by-standers, when the obstinate 'bint' of sixty years seizes their hands. **1888** C. M. DOUGHTY *Trav. Arabia Deserta* I. viii. 231 Hirfa sighed for motherhood: she had been these two years with an husband and was yet *bint*, as the nomads say, 'in her girlhood'. *Ibid.* xiii. 374 The homesick Beduin bint. **1919** *Athenæum* 25 July 664/2 *Bint*, girl. **1930** E. RAYMOND *Jesting Army* I. ii. 24 Damned jolly little bint, that one, too! **1938** 'R. HYDE' *Godwits Fly* xi. 169 Fancy turning in a smoke for a bint. **1941** *New Statesman* 30 Aug. (*list of war slang*) *Bint*—Girl friend. **1942** N. STREATFEILD *Table for Six* 151 I'd like her to grow up a lush bint. **1946** *Penguin New Writing* XXVIII. 175 What are the bints like round here, Tom? **1958** K. AMIS *I like it Here* xiii. 162 As the R.A.F. friend would have put it, you could never tell with these foreign bints.

binturong ('bɪntjʊrɒŋ). Also **benturong**. [Malay.] A prehensile-tailed civet, *Arctictis binturong*, found in southern Asia.

1822 T. S. RAFFLES in *Trans. Linnean Soc.* XIII. 253 Intermediate between *Viverra* and *Ursus* is an animal called Binturong, found at Malacca by Major Farquhar. **1838** *Penny Cycl.* XII. 434/1 The newly discovered forms, the Benturong and the Panda. **1883** *Encycl. Brit.* XV. 436/1 The Binturong, an inhabitant of southern Asia from Nepal through the Malay peninsula to the islands of Sumatra and Java. **1930** *Times Educ. Suppl.* 16 Aug. iv/2 A female binturong with two young. **1964** G. DURRELL *Menagerie Manor* i. 16 The binturong.. suggests a badly-made hearth-rug, to one end of which has been attached a curiously oriental-like head with long ear-tufts and circular, protuberant and somewhat vacant eyes.

binuclear, -ate: see BI- *pref.*[2] 1.

binweed, corruptly **bindweed**: see BUNWEED.

binwood, variant of BINDWOOD.

biny ('baɪnɪ), *a.* [f. BINE + -Y[1].] Of hops: abounding in bine, running much to bine.

1881 C. WHITEHEAD *Hops* 36 It will be found in 'biny' years that many of the hops are light and 'white livered' from sheer lack of sunshine.

bio ('baɪəʊ), colloq. or slang abbrev. of BIOGRAPHY (occas. of BIOGRAPHICAL *a.*).

1961 in WEBSTER. **1965** J. M. CAIN *Magician's Wife* (1966) v. 37 Fisher's credit department did me your bio sketch. **1967** *Sat. Rev.* 25 Nov. 50/3 Paul Gallico's bios are, as one would expect of such a gifted journalist, clear and revealing.

bio- ('baɪəʊ), repr. Gr. βίο- stem and comb. form of βίος 'life, course or way of living' (as distinct from ζωή 'animal life, organic life'). Hence, in compounds formed in Greek itself, as *biography*, βιογραφία; and in modern scientific words in which *bio-* is extended to mean 'organic life.'

bio-a'ssay = *biological assay* (see ASSAY *sb.* 6 b); **bio-astro'nautic** *a.*, of or pertaining to bio-astronautics; **bio-astro'nautics** *sb. pl.* (see quots.); **bio-biblio'graphical** *a.*, dealing with the life and writings of an author; **bio-bibli'ography**, a bibliography containing biographical information about the author or authors; **bioblast** [Gr. βλαστός sprout, germ], (*Biol.*) a minute mass of amorphous protoplasm having formative power; **bio'centric** *a.*, treating life as a central fact; **bio'chemic** *a.*, pertaining to the chemistry of life; **'biochrome**, any natural colouring matter of plants or animals; hence **bio'chromic** *a.*, **bio'chromy** (see quot. 1944[1]); **bio'colloid** *Chem.* [contracted form of *biological colloid*: cf. G. *biokolloid*], a colloid derived from an organic substance; **'biodata** *sb. pl.* (chiefly *U.S.* and *Anglo-Indian*) = *curriculum vitae* s.v. CURRICULUM; biographical details, esp. those supplied by candidates applying for a job; **biode'gradable** *a.*, susceptible to the decomposing action of living organisms, esp. of bacteria; occas., broken down by biochemical processes in the body; so **ˌbiodegrada'bility**, **biodegra'dation**; **ˌbiodeterio'ration**, deterioration of a substance or material caused by the action of living organisms; so **biode'teriorative** *a.*; **biody'namic, -al** *a.*, of or relating to biodynamics; **biody'namics**, that part of biological science which treats of vital force, or of the action of living organisms; **bio-e'cology** (see quot. 1957); **bioelectric(al** (baɪəʊɪ'lɛktrɪk, -əl) *a.*, of or pertaining to electrical phenomena produced in living organisms; hence **bioelec'tricity**, electrical phenomena produced in living organisms; **bio-ener'getics**, the study of the transformation of energy in living organisms; **bioengi'neering**, the application of engineering techniques to biological processes; so **bioengineer**; **bio'flavonoid** = FLAVONOID; **biogeo'chemistry** [f. GEOCHEMISTRY, after Russ. *biogeokhimiya*], the branch of biochemistry that deals with the relation of chemicals found in the soil to living organisms; the biological application of geochemistry; hence **biogeo'chemical** *a.*; **bi'ognosy**, a proposed general term for the 'life-sciences'; **bioherm** ('baɪəʊhəm), *Geol.* [Gr. ἕρμα sunken rock, reef], a reef (as a coral reef) formed from organic material; **bioki'netics** (see quot.); **'biolith** *Geol.* [ad. G. *biolith* (C. G. Ehrenberg, 1854): -LITH], a rock formed from organic material; **bio'lytic** *a.*, life-destroying; **biomag'netic** *a.*, of or pertaining to animal magnetism; **bio'magnetism**, animal magnetism; **'biomass**, the total weight of the organic substance (as plankton) or organisms in a given area; **biomathe'matics** (see quots.); **bio'medical** *a.*, pertaining or relating to both biology and medicine; *spec.* pertaining to the biological effects of space-travel; **bi'ometer**, a measurer of life; **bio'molecule** (see quot.); hence **biomo'lecular** *a.* (1909 in *Cent. Dict.* Suppl.); **biophysi'ologist**, an investigator of the physiology of living beings; **'biosatellite** (orig. *U.S.*), an artificial satellite containing living organisms for experimental purposes; **'bioscience**, a collective term for the biological sciences; hence **bioscientist**; **bio'social** *a.*, of or pertaining to the interaction of biological and social factors; relating to both biology and sociology; **biosoci'ology** (see quot. 1901); so **biosocio'logical** *a.*, involving both biological and sociological factors; **biospelæ'ology, -eology** [ad. F. *biospéléologie* (A. Vire 1904, in *Comptes rendus Acad. Sci. Paris* CXXXIX. 992), f. SPELÆOLOGY.], the study of the fauna of caves; hence **biospelæo'logical** *a.*; **bio'static, -al** *a.*, of or pertaining to biostatics; **bio'statics**, that part of biological science which treats of structure as adapted to act, as distinguished from *biodynamics* or *biokinetics*; **biostrome** ('baɪəstrəʊm), *Geol.* [Gr. στρῶμα mattress, bed]: see quots.; **bio'synthesis**, the production of a chemical substance by a living organism; hence **biosyn'thetic** *a.*, pertaining to biosynthesis; (of a substance) produced by a living organism; **'biotech**, colloq. abbrev. of BIOTECHNOLOGY 2; also *attrib.*; **bio'technics**, the practical application of discoveries in the biological sciences; so **bio'technic** *a.*; **'biozone** *Geol.* (see quot.).

1912 H. C. WOOD in *Jrnl. Amer. Med. Assoc.* LIX. 1433/2 The underlying principle of physiologic standardization, or as those engaged in this work prefer to call it, the bio-assay, is to determine the quantity of a given sample of drug required to produce some easily recognizable effect on a lower animal. *Ibid.* 1434/1 The bio-assay must be acknowledged as a great step forward in the direction of accuracy in our materia medica. **1939** *Nature* 8 July 76/2 A bioassay on the isolated benzoate.. gave an 80 per cent response in a group of ten mice, each receiving a single dose of 0·5 γ in nut oil. **1955** *New Biol.* XIX. 52 The suitability of an inbred strain of mice for the bio-assay of oestrogens. **1961** *Flight* LXXIX. 344/2 American bio-astronautic activities. **1957** *N.Y. Times Mag.* 20 Oct. 12/1 The third phase has a wholly new name, 'bioastronautics'—the study of man's capabilities and needs, and the means of meeting those needs, for travel in outer space. **1959** H. STRUGHOLD in *Space Weapons* 136 Space medicine.. can.. be considered a branch of the more general field which we call 'bioastronautics', the investigation of every aspect of life in the universe, as it may be encountered by men from this planet in the future. **1809** SOUTHEY *Lett.* (1856) II. 162 This collectanea may be formed into a biobibliographical and critical account. **1880** *Athenæum* 25 Dec. 845/3 One more instalment will complete the biobibliographical part. **1959** L. M. HARROD *Librarians' Gloss.* (ed. 2) 39 *Biobibliography*, a bibliography which contains brief biographical details about the authors. **1944** D. L. FOX in *Science* C. 470/2 From the standpoint of the biochemist.. concerned with the metabolic significance of natural coloring matters, the designation of these by a discriminating scientific term has long been desirable. In response to an inquiry, Dr. George M. Calhoun.. suggested to the writer [in a personal communication, 1936] the descriptive and self-explanatory term *biochrome*, with an adjective *biochromatic* (*biochromic* is perhaps preferable), and a collective noun *biochromy*. *Ibid.* 471/1 Biochromes.. possess two chief characteristics in common, *i.e.*, their origin and occurrence in living organisms and their reflection of a fundamental chemical

property, the selective absorption of light waves in the visible spectrum. *Ibid.*, Our present understanding of the parts played by..biochromic compounds in the metabolic economy of organisms leaves much to be desired. **1954** *Sci. News* XXXIV. 91 [Porphyrins] probably serve in this role, as well as a biochrome, in insects. **1917** *Chem. Abstr.* 3283 (*title*) Effect of acids and salts on 'bio-colloids'. *Ibid.*, An extension of the tests..was made to include mixts. of the 'bio-colloid' agar. **1932** *Ibid.* 19 (*title*) Studies of the combination of biocolloids. **1956** *Nature* 24 Mar. 562/2 General behaviour of biocolloids and polyelectrolytes in aqueous solution. **1968** *Amer. Psychologist* XXIII. 782/2 The best prediction of what a man will do in the future is what he has done in the past. It is precisely what a subject has done that bio-data measure. **1971** *Hindustan Times Weekly* (New Delhi) 4 Apr. 8/6 (Advt.), Candidates with agricultural spraying experience need only apply..giving complete bio-data, qualifications and experience. **1981** *Amer. Speech* 1977 LII. 219 There are now in hand the replies of 1000 informants..together with the requisite biodata. **1986** *Sunday Observer* (Sri Lanka) 24 Aug. 5 (Advt.), Vacancies exist for General Clerks...Apply with full bio-data. **1960** *Biochim. & Biophys. Acta* XLIII. 348 (*heading*) Biodegradation of dehydro-L-ascorbic acid; 2, 3-diketo-aldonic acid decarboxylase from rat liver. **1961** Nelson et al. in *Devel. Industrial Microbiology* II. 93 The present study was initiated to provide information on the effect of molecular structure on the biodegradability of synthetic detergents. *Ibid.* 101 Compounds with strictly linear side chains and those containing one or two methyl branches on the carbon atom attached to the benzene ring are readily biodegradable. **1962** *Chem. & Engin. News* 10 Sept. 38/3 Feedstock..suitable for the production of a completely biodegradable detergent. *Ibid.* 24 Dec. 36/1 Biodegradability has so far been tested mainly in flask tests. **1969** *Nature* 19 July 230/2 Biodegradable detergents are now a reality. **1961** W. M. Bejuki in *Devel. Industrial Microbiology* II. 265 The bacteria..are microorganisms being newly introduced into biodeterioration evaluations. **1964** *Nature* 5 Sept. 1084/1 These thermophilic fungi may play a significant part in the biodeterioration of oil palm produce during processing and storage. **1966** D. G. Coursey in *Microbiological Deterioration in Tropics* (Soc. Chem. Industry Monograph XXIII) 44 (*title*) Biodeteriorative processes in palm oil stored in West Africa. *Ibid.* 55 Purely chemical changes..are slow compared with the biodeteriorative process. **1874** Lewes *Prob. Life & Mind* I. 129 The biostatical and the biodynamical—i.e. the consideration of the structure ready to act; and the consideration of the structure acting. **1923** F. E. Clements et al. in *Carnegie Inst. Washington Year Book 1922* 355 The concept of the biome was advanced in 1915 to emphasize the importance of treating plants and animals together as mutually interacting members of a community... The entire field of bio-ecology has been sketched in outline to serve as a guide for further work. **1927** W. P. Taylor in *Ecology* VIII. 280 If the botanists persist in appropriating the term ecology as synonymous with plant ecology we shall be forced to domesticate the new term bio-ecology to take its place as referring to the whole field. **1939** F. E. Clements & Shelford (*title*) Bio-Ecology. **1957** *Encycl. Brit.* XVIII. 29B/1 Other aspects of general ecology are animal ecology, human ecology and bio-ecology, which is defined provisionally as the ecology of plant and animal interrelations. **1918** *Science* 22 Nov. 518/2 Bioelectric phenomena constitute a group of facts for which adequate and satisfactory explanations have hitherto been lacking. **1927** Lund & Kenyon in *Jrnl. Exper. Zoöl.* XLVIII. 333 (*title*) Relation between continuous bio-electric currents and cell respiration. **1943** *Electronic Engin.* XV. 519 The above facts suggest that the alpha rhythm..may possibly be due to the same cause as that producing slow bio-electric rhythms in other organs. **1962** *IRE Trans. Bio-Medical Electronics* IX. 85/1 Bioelectrical brain reactions arising in response to certain stimuli are often very poorly expressed. **1949** *Blakiston's New Gould Med. Dict.* 136/1 *Bio-electricity*, electric phenomena occurring in living tissues; effects of electric currents upon living tissues. **1969** *Listener* 15 May 688/1 A bioelectricity, which originates in the abdominal cavity. **1945** S. Brody *Bioenergetics & Growth* ii. 12 Bioenergetics, concerned with energy transformations in living things, is a branch of general energetics generalized briefly by the first and second laws of thermodynamics. **1947** *Ann. Reg. 1946* 388 The Timiriazeff Institute [U.S.S.R.], which is divided into sections dealing with photosynthesis,..comparative physiology, bioenergetics. **1960** *Appl. Microbiol.* VIII. 122/1 The real problem may exist near the cell surfaces where flow..may depend upon capillary action. Herein may lie one of the real challenges for the bioengineer. *Ibid.* 124/1 This bioengineering approach has been most fruitfully applied to microbiological processes. **1964** *New Scientist* 30 July 262/1 Bio-engineering to help in converting new crops into human food. **1952** *Chem. Abstr.* 10215/1 (*title*) Effect of bioflavonoids on radiosensitivity of transplanted tumors. **1955** *Sci. News Let.* 26 Feb. 141/1 Nature's yellow dyestuff and related chemicals..promise to help fight certain artery troubles and other ailments of man. The chemicals are now called bioflavonoids. **1938** tr. *Vernadsky's On some Fundamental Probl. Biogeochem.* 5 Life in the biogeochemical aspect is the living matter of the biosphere, that is, the total of all the living organisms present in the biosphere at a given moment. **1956** *Nature* 25 Feb. 353/1 To further the study of biogeochemical cycles. **1938** tr. *Vernadsky's On some Fundamental Probl. Biogeochem.* 5 Biogeochemistry, which is a part of geochemistry and has peculiar methods and peculiar problems of its own, may be finally reduced to a precise quantitative mathematical expression of the living nature in its indissoluble connection with the external medium, in which the living nature exists. **1940** *Chem. Abstr.* 3769 (*title*), Problems of bio-geochemistry. **1883** C. A. Cutter (Boston) *Classif. Nat. Sci.* 4 In Biognosy the specials [Phytognosy, Zoognosy] contain subdivisions brought together in a group for convenience of treatment. **1928** E. R. Cumings & R. R. Shrock in *Bull. Amer. Geol. Soc.* XXXIX. 599 *Coral reef* encourages the misconception that reefs are largely made of coral, whereas many of them were formed by other organisms... The authors have for some time used the term 'bioherm'. **1939** W. H. Twenhofel *Princ. Sedimentation* ix. 329 Colonial corals have been among the chief contributions to the building of the reefs or bioherms. **1954** W. D. Thornbury *Princ. Geomorphology* xviii. 480 The term 'bioherm' (organic mould) is a more appropriate name for such structures, but they have been called reefs so long that the name persists despite its inadequacy. **18..** Long in *Education* III. 587 Biokinetics will consider them [organisms] in the successive changes through which they pass during the different stages of their development. **1906** H. Potonié in *Rep. Brit. Assoc. Advancem. Sci.* 748, I set aside those combustible biolithes which are pyromonimites, such as amber. **1920** A. W. Grabau *Textbk. Geol.* (1921) I. xii. 269 The organic or biogenic rocks... The true organic rocks are conveniently termed *bioliths*. **1934** B. G. Bogorov in *Jrnl. Marine Biol. Assoc.* XIX. 585 Weighing is the main method of obtaining the biomass. The conception 'biomass' may be applicable also to the quantity of substance, characteristic for a given species at its different stages of development. **1937** W. Pickles in *Jrnl. Animal Ecol.* VI. 54 In order to determine the biomass of each species, it was necessary to weigh the ants, larvae, pupae, etc., of each nest. *Ibid.* 60 The success of species..can also be expressed as the biomass, i.e. the total weight per unit area. **1957** *Encycl. Brit.* VII. 919/2 The biomass could be determined for each link of a food chain, or for each stratum of a community or for the whole community. *Ibid.* XVIII. 237/1 This method uses weights of population samples (biomass) instead of counts of individuals. **1923** W. M. Feldman *Biomath.* i. 1 Biomathematics is the science and art of rapid and accurate computation applied to the study and investigation of biological problems. **1963** *New Scientist* 10 Jan. 72/2 There are now strong indications that biomathematics and medicomathematics are emerging as distinctive scientific disciplines. **1955** *Bull. Atomic Sci.* May 200/2 The only biomedical data which remains classified is in piecemeal or incomplete form and therefore inadequate for use by the medical profession. **1962** S. Carpenter in *Into Orbit* 160 Next, you run a check on the intercom and the bio-medical leads to make sure they are working. **1963** C. D. Green in J. H. U. Brown *Physiol. of Man in Space* 257 (*title*) Biomedical capsules. **1865** *Reader* 25 Feb. 213/1 A life table ..is an instrument of investigation; it may be called a *biometer*, for it gives the exact measure of the duration of life under given circumstances. **1946** *Nature* 28 Sept. 440/2 A later technique is beautifully illustrated by the exhibit from the Department of Biomolecular Structure of the University of Leeds. **1901** J. G. McKendrick in *Rep. Brit. Assoc. Advancem. Sci.* 810 The conception of a biomolecule, or living molecule, that is to say the smallest quantity of living matter that can exhibit some of the chemical phenomena of life. **1882** *Pop. Sci. Monthly* XXII. 169 The eminent biophysiologist, William B. Carpenter. **1958** *Newsweek* 17 Feb. 95/1 The NACA sphere could be ready within a year as a bio-satellite to test space stresses on small laboratory animals. **1966** *Daily Tel.* 19 Dec. 1/4 They were millions of insects and bacteria in a 'biosatellite' that went astray. **1964** (*title of periodical*) BioScience. **1966** I. Asimov *Fantastic Voyage* i. 12 Tell him I want some crumbs for the bio-sciences. **1959** *Listener* 14 May 834/2 Most physical scientists can be rather precise in their measurements and in the predictions based on them. Not so the bio-scientists. [**1894** J. Izoulet *La Cité Moderne* I. i. 1 (*title*) Livre Premier. Exposé de notre hypothèse bio-sociale.] **1927** L. L. Bernard *Introd. Social Psychol.* I. v. 79 The physico-social and bio-social environments are intimately connected with human behavior. **1935** L. Bloomfield in *Language* XI. 98 The bio-physical description, in terms of speakers' movements, or of sound-waves,..must be left to the laboratory. The biosocial description consists in a statement of the combinations in which these phonemes occur. **1937** C. W. Morris *Log. Positivism* ii. 22 Pragmatism..is not falsely described as a biosocial positivism. **1942** C. F. Hockett in *Language* XVIII. 6 Phonological equivalence involves, generally, the two factors of *a*-phonetic similarity and biosocial equivalence. **1936** E. van Loo tr. *Bouger's Introd. Criminol.* iv. 77 'Every crime is the resultant of individual, physical and social conditions.'.. This view was shared by several later authors... Its adherents form what is called the 'biosociological school'. **1949** Koestler *Insight & Outlook* xvi. 221 The biosociological significance of these upheavals is rarely appreciated. [**1894** J. Izoulet *La Cité Moderne* IV. i. 544 Je crois que la psycho-morale et la bio-sociologie ne peuvent coexister parallèlement, sans agir et réagir l'une sur l'autre.] **1901** G. Gissing *Our Friend Charlatan* ii. 22 'It's uncommonly suggestive,' said Dyce... 'The best social theory I know. He [*sc.* J. Izoulet] calls his system Bio-Sociology, a theory of society founded on the facts of biology.' **1953** Hazelton & Glennie in C. H. D. Cullingford *Brit. Caving* ix. 248 British biospeleological literature is necessarily scanty. **1947** *New Biol.* III. 103 Small bands of enthusiastic workers, like those who laid the foundations of biospelæology, can hardly be expected to produce rapid results. **1965** B. E. Freeman tr. A. Vandel (*title*) Biospeleology: the biology of cavernicolous animals. **1874** Lewes *Prob. Life & Mind* I. 115 These may be classed (by a serviceable extension of the term Statics) under the heads of Biostatics and Psychostatics. **1885** *Athenæum* 28 Feb. 285/1. The inquiry was limited to the biostatics and anthropometry of the Ashkenasim Jews. **1932** E. R. Cumings in *Bull. Geol. Soc. Amer.* XLIII. 334 For purely bedded structures, such as shell beds, crinoid beds, coral beds, etcetera, consisting of and built..by sedentary organisms..I propose the name *biostrome*... *Biostrome* means literally an organic layer. **1961** J. Challinor *Dict. Geol.* 23/1 Where the biolith is a more or less extensive bed it is sometimes called a 'biostrome'. **1930** *Brit. Chem. Abstr.* A. 479/2 The closely related structure of natural anthocyanins, [etc.]..is discussed on the basis of biosynthesis from the simple components formaldehyde and its condensation products. **1949** E. Chain in H. W. Florey *Antibiotics* II. xvii. 695 The strain 1984. A is more exacting in its requirements for the biosynthesis of penicillin. **1959** *Sci. News* LII. 17 The presence of iron is essential to the biosynthesis of chlorophyll. **1948** *Biol. Abstr.* 304 The dominant opinion was that biosynthetic processes were to be considered as cascades. **1974** *Bioscience* May 310/1 Project *Biotech*..was designed to provide training opportunities for the so-called middle manpower needs in the life sciences. **1980** *N.Y. Times* 29 June III. 5/1 In addition to Bethesda Research Laboratories, there is Biotech Research, in Rockville, Md. **1982** *Sunday Times* 4 Apr. 51/2 CLS [is] the first UK 'biotech' business to go public. **1986** *Courier-Mail* (Brisbane) 26 June 40/1 Three short years ago there was considerable concern in Japan over the lead held in biotech by the US. **1938** L. Mumford *Culture of Cities* 495 *Biotechnic*, refers to an emergent economy..pointing to a civilization in which the biological sciences will be freely applied to technology... The application of bacteriology to medicine and sanitation, [etc.]..are further marks of this order. **1925** Geddes & Thomson *Biol.* 245 (*heading*) The Applications of Biology (Biotechnics). **1902** J. J. Buckman in *Geol. Mag.* IX. 556 Why cannot we call this a *biozone*, using the term to signify the range of organisms in time as indicated by their entombment in the strata? Thus we might have the biozone of a species, of a genus, of a family, or of a larger group.

biocellate (baɪˈɒsɪleɪt), *a.* [f. Bi- *pref.*² 1 + ocellate, ad. L. *ocellātus* marked with eyelets, f. *ocellus* eyelet, dim. of *oculus* eye.] Marked with two small eye-like spots, as a butterfly's wing.

1847 in Craig.

bio'central, *a.* = biocentric *a.*

1905 *Athenæum* 8 Apr. 436/2 The study of synthetical chemistry from the biocentral point of view.

biocentric (baɪəˈsɛntrɪk), *a.* [f. bio- + centric *a.*] Centring in life; regarding or treating life as a central fact. Hence **bio'centrically** *adv.*, from a biocentric point of view.

1889 in *Cent. Dict.* **1899** R. Meldola in *Nature* 5 Jan. 217/1 In brief, there has arisen a set of ideas which are even broader than 'anthropocentric', and which might fairly be designated *biocentric*. **1904** —— *Vital Products* I. 6 Organic Chemistry from the Biocentric Standpoint. **1913** L. J. Henderson *Fitness Environm.* 110 Water is the one fit substance for its place in the process of universal evolution, when we regard that process biocentrically. *Ibid.* 312 The biologist may now rightly regard the universe in its very essence as biocentric. **1952** V. A. Demant *Relig. & Decl. Capitalism* vii. 169 Bio-centric living supplants logo-centric living when the latter claims too much.

biochemical (baɪəˈkɛmɪkəl), *a.* [f. bio- + chemical, after G. *biochemisch.*] Of or pertaining to biochemistry. Hence **bio'chemically** *adv.*

1851 T. Laycock in tr. *J. A. Unzer's Princ. Physiol.* p. vi, He repudiated all histological,..and bio-chemical researchers, as worse than useless in medicine. **1867** R. E. Wallis tr. *Delitzsch's Bibl. Psychol.* 273 Without wishing to substitute for Scripture a knowledge of that bio-chemical process. **1887** A. M. Brown *Anim. Alkaloids* 147 That which might seem *a priori* evident, is now biochemically proved to demonstration. **1897** A. B. Griffiths *Respir. Proteids* 107 The foundation of all life, the biochemical processes. **1904** R. Meldola *Vital Products* I. 5 It is doubtful whether this compound [*sc.* furfural] is really a biochemical product. **1969** N. W. Pirie *Food Resources* iv. 122 Processes of this type are sometimes referred to as 'chemurgy'; 'biochemical engineering' seems a preferable term.

biochemist (baɪəˈkɛmɪst). [f. next.] One who is versed in biochemistry.

1897 *Amer. Naturalist* XXXI. 272 In bacteriology the biochemist has a wide field of work. **1913** [see biophysics]. **1935** *Discovery* Apr. 98/2 A problem for a physical chemist, assisted by a bio-chemist. **1957** *Encycl. Brit.* III. 591/1 The biochemist..must know the chemical structure of the myriads of substances present in living material. *Ibid.* 591/2 Biochemists have long been interested in the chemical composition of the food of animals.

biochemistry (baɪəˈkɛmɪstrɪ). [f. bio- + chemistry, after biochemical *a.* Cf. G. *biochemie.*] The science dealing with the substances present in living organisms and with their relation to each other and to the life of the organism; biological or physiological chemistry.

1881 M. D. Walker tr. *Schüssler's Cure of Diptheria by Biochemic Treatment* 16 My system, or method of Procedure, is direct Biochemistry, because I use *only* tissue-cell-salts. **1902** *Nature* 14 Aug. 381/2 The chair of biochemistry recently founded in University College [Liverpool]. **1904** R. Meldola *Vital Products* I. p. v, I am not without hope that it may be found of service as a step towards the foundation of a more exact science of Biochemistry. **1926** *Encycl. Brit.* I. 373/2 Biochemistry may be defined as the study of the chemical or physico-chemical processes which play a part in the life phenomena of plants and animals. **1943** *Endeavour* Apr. 41/1 Dramatic progress ..continues to be made in the applications of biochemistry to the eradication of disease.

'biochore (-kɔː(r)). *Ecol.* [G. *biochore* (W. Köppen 1900, in *Geogr. Zeitschr.* VI. 675).]

a. (In the use of Köppen and Raunkiaer) the climatic boundary of a region (see quot. 1934). **b.** A group of similar biotopes; the largest division or region of animal and plant environment, as forest, desert, grassland, etc.

1913 *Jrnl. Ecology* I. 20 These climate-zones..are limited by *biochores* or plant-climate boundaries as suggested by Köppen. **1934** A. G. Tansley in tr. *Raunkiaer's Life Forms of Plants* p. xiii, The 'biochore'.., originally Köppen's term and analogous to the climatological terms isotherm and isohyet, is the line passing through all the areas whose floras show the same percentage number of a characteristic life-form: biochores can only be determined by the analysis of a large number of adjacent local floras. **1937** Allee & Schmidt tr. *Hesse's Ecol. Animal Geogr.* ix. 137 Regions with a general similarity of habitus are recognized as biochores, which may be united as superbiochores or subdivided into subbiochores; areas within the biochores which have uniform external habitat conditions are biotopes. **1957** P. Dansereau *Biogeography* iii. 125 The biochore is the geographical environment where certain dominant life-forms appear to be adapted to a particular conjunction of meteorological factors... Each biochore is

characterized by a major type of vegetation... Within each biochore there develops one or more formations which extend over an entire province.

biocide ('baɪəsaɪd). [f. BIO- + -CIDE.] (See quots.); *spec.* a pesticide.

1947 E. M. GREENBERG in *Sat. Rev. Lit.* 30 Aug. 21/3 'Biocide', or destruction of the tissues of the human body, is caused by all the unphysiologic habits that civilization has imposed upon the human race. **1963** W. G. HOLBROOK in *Sat. Rev.* 19 Jan. 23, I have encountered the term 'biocide' used in a context similar to genocide..namely, the destruction of living species by indirect chemical, or, for that matter, nuclear, poisons. **1963** R. L. CARSON *Silent Spring* ii. 7 Can anyone believe it is possible to lay down such a barrage of poisons on the surface of the earth without making it unfit for all life? They should not be called 'insecticides', but 'biocides'. **1968** *Proc. 1st Int. Biodeterioration Symposium* IX. 511 The toxicity and hazards of the biocide to higher forms of life must be considered.

bioclimatic (baɪəʊklaɪ'mætɪk), *a.* [f. BIO- + CLIMATIC *a.*] Pertaining to the study of climate in relation to the seasonal activities and geographical distribution of living organisms. Hence **biocli'matics** (= next).

1918 A. D. HOPKINS in *Monthly Weather Rev. Suppl.* IX. 9/1 We have in this proposed bioclimatic law of latitude, longitude and altitude, a fundamental guide to lines of research and practice as related to any periodical phenomena in life activity including that of man. **1921** —— in *Jrnl. Washington Acad. Sci.* XI. 223 (*title*) International problems in bioclimatics with special reference to natural and artificial distribution of plants and animals. *Ibid.* 223 *The bioclimatic law* is a law of life and climate as related to the geographical coordinates *latitude, longitude* and *altitude*. **1929** W. C. COOK in *Ecology* X. 283 In bioclimatic studies it is impossible to demonstrate the effect of climate upon insect distribution outside the economic range of the species. **1938** A. D. HOPKINS (*title*) Bioclimatics. A Science of Life and Climatic Regions. **1938** *Nature* 25 June 1146/1 The bioclimatic zone and zonal types of a place, area, or local region are the most reliable indexes to the species of animals and plants, and to the types of agriculture, that are best adapted to the local conditions. **1959** *Times* 9 Nov. (Ghana Suppl.) p. iv/4 Ghana's agricultural production naturally is related directly to her major bioclimatic regions.

bioclima'tology. [f. BIO- + CLIMATOLOGY.] The study of climate in relation to living organisms and esp. to human health. Hence **bioclimato'logical** *a.*, of or pertaining to bioclimatology.

1922 *Readers' Guide Periodical Lit. 1919–21* V. 146/1 (*heading*) Bioclimatology... Bioclimatics. **1949** W. G. MOORE *Dict. Geogr.* 22 *Bioclimatology*, the study of climate in relation to life and health, one of its objects being to determine the climatic conditions most favourable to human habitation, especially for invalids, and to define the areas where such climates exist. **1961** *Lancet* 23 Sept. 706/2 The factor which primarily actuates this seasonal variation [of poliomyelitis] is unknown; but it is evidently bioclimatological.

biocœnosis (baɪəʊsiː'nəʊsɪs). *Ecol.* Also biocenose, biocœnose. [mod.L., ad. Ger. *biocönose* (K. Möbius 1877, *Die Auster und die Austernwirthschaft*), f. BIO- + Gr. κοίνωσις sharing (κοινός common).] An association of organisms forming a biotic community; the relationship that exists between such organisms.

1883 H. J. RICE tr. *Möbius' Oyster & Oyster Culture* in *Rep. U.S. Comm. Fish & Fisheries 1880* VIII. 723 Science possesses, as yet, no word..for a community where the sum of species and individuals..have, by means of transmission, continued in possession of a certain definite territory. I propose the word *Biocœnosis* for such a community. Any change in any of the relative factors of a biocönose produces changes in other factors of the same. **1925** I. W. BAILEY in *Bot. Gaz.* LXXX. 93 (*title*) The 'Spruce Budworm' Biocoenose. **1957** *Encycl. Brit.* III. 607/2 The idea of the animal community and of the fully integrated biological community or biocoenosis is largely the result of the study of shallow water populations in the sea. *Ibid.* VII. 917/2 Such assemblages..have been called biocoenoses, if the interrelations are especially closely knit, and they are known generally as communities. **1957** *Sci. News* XLIII. 71 A fossil 'community'..is seldom identical with the original biocoenose (or life community).

Hence **biocœ'nology**, the study of biocœnosis; **biocœ'no tic** *a.*, of or pertaining to biocœnosis.

1927 *Biol. Abstr.* 593/1 Small associations should be known as biocöenotic complexes. **1931** R. N. CHAPMAN *Animal Ecol.* ix. 203 From the viewpoint of biocenology the population, or biocenose, may be classified on the basis of the bond which is of primary importance in holding the population together as an ecological unit. **1939** CLEMENTS & SHELFORD *Bio-Ecology* i. 10 [Gams (1918).] To him, 'vegetation research' is synonymous with his new term 'biocenology'. **1957** *Encycl. Brit.* III. 607/1 The first contributions to what is now called *synecology*, or perhaps better *biocoenology*, or the study of biological communities ..were devoted solely to plants. **1967** *Oceanogr. & Marine Biol.* V. 489 The whole population of the *Posidonia* meadows..cannot be considered as a single biocoenotic unit or entity.

bioethics (baɪəʊ'ɛθɪks), *sb. pl.* (const. as *sing.*) [f. BIO- + *ethics* s.v. ETHIC *sb.*[2]] The discipline dealing with ethical questions that arise as a result of advances in medicine and biology.

1971 V. R. POTTER *Bioethics* p.vii, The purpose of this book is to contribute to the future of the human species by promoting the formation of a new discipline, the discipline of Bioethics. *Ibid.* i. 26 Bioethics would attempt to balance cultural appetites against physiological needs in terms of public policy. **1977** *Annals R. College Physicians & Surgeons of Canada* X. 130/1 Because of its strong component of moral and religious values, bioethics is a delicate and difficult subject. **1978** *Observer* 30 July 9/3 The first successful completion of a pregnancy begun in the laboratory does raise some interesting issues. They fall into that area of debate which the Americans call..'bio-ethics'. **1984** *New Scientist* 9 Aug. 34/1 A professional philosopher with a particular interest in bioethics.

Hence **bio'ethical** *a.*; **bioethicist** (-'ɛθɪsɪst), an expert in or student of bioethics.

1973 *Hastings Center Studies* I. I. 73/1 The discipline of bioethics should be so designed..that it will directly..serve those physicians and biologists whose position demands that they make the practical decisions. This requires, ideally, a number of ingredients as part of the training..of the bioethicist. **1974** *Jrnl. Amer. Med. Assoc.* 8 July 177 Maintaining a critical tension between the individual and the bioethical dimensions. **1977** *Lancet* 13 Aug. 347/2 It seems that in the United States, notwithstanding legislative attempts to settle bioethical issues, the courts will have the final say. **1978** *Brit. Med. Jrnl.* 4 Nov. 1270/1 A decade ago there was only a handful of bioethicists in the country — small numbers of theologians, philosophers, sociologists and others. **1983** *Church Times* 28 Jan. 7/2 A bioethicist examines the ethical implications of the IVF method against the background of general human ethics.

biofeedback (baɪəʊ'fiːdbæk). [f. BIO- + FEEDBACK, FEED-BACK *sb.*] A technique in which electronic equipment is used to enable a person to monitor bodily processes and parameters that are normally involuntary or unperceived, so that he or she can learn to modify them.

1970 *Jrnl. Transpersonal Psychol.* I. 3 Gardner Murphy must be given due credit for stimulating and promoting bio-feedback research..and for his effort..to establish the Bio-Feedback Research Society, which met for the first time in 1969. **1977** H. J. EYSENCK *You & Neurosis* iv. 135 The third group was given a course in 'biofeedback', a technique which uses electrical recording devices to measure the functioning of various bodily systems. **1979** *Time* 2 Apr. 40/1 At one end of this therapeutic spectrum are such exuberant exercises in self-help as biofeedback and Transcendental Meditation. **1984** A. SMITH *Mind* IV. xiv. 275 A system of 'biofeedback' is being used, apparently successfully, to help with rehabilitation, the patient learning how to tense and relax muscles properly. **1987** *Oxf. Textbk. Med.* (ed. 2) II. XIII. 367/2 Several groups have now reported successful use of biofeedback in the voluntary control of heart rates or blood pressure.

biofte, var. f. BIHOFTHE. *Obs.*

biog ('baɪɒg), colloq. or slang abbrev. of BIOGRAPHY.

1942 BERREY & VAN DEN BARK *Amer. Thes. Slang* §522/11 Biography, *biog, close-up. Ibid., Puff biog*, a laudatory biographical sketch. **1967** P. MCGERR *Murder is Absurd* iii. 44 If he should drop out—well, 'replaced Mark Kendall' will sound good in your biog.

biogen ('baɪədʒɛn). *Biol.* Also **-gene**. [See BIO- and -GEN.]

1. (See quot.)

1882 E. COUES *Biogen* (1884) 62 The substance of the soul, to which I apply the name 'biogen,' seems to correspond closely to what Prof. Crookes calls the 'fourth state of matter';..It is the 'od' of Prof. Reichenbach.

2. [G. *biogen* (M. Verworn 1895, *Allgemeine Physiologie* vi. 468).] A hypothetical protoplasmic unit. (Cf. BIOPHOR.)

1899 F. S. LEE tr. *Verworn's Gen. Physiol.* vi. 481 In order to distinguish this body..from dead proteid and to indicate its high significance in the occurrence of vital phenomena, it appears fitting to replace the term 'living proteid' with that of *biogen*. **1909** *Westm. Gaz.* 23 Oct. 6/3 First, the biogene, ..secondly, the cell, composed of a great number of biogenes. **1911** *Encycl. Brit.* XXI. 557/2 These combinations have been termed 'biogens'. **1915** W. M. BAYLISS *Physiol.* i. 18 A certain theory, that of 'biogen molecules', has attracted many investigators. **1916** A. P. MATHEWS *Physiol. Chem.* 261 A molecule which may be called a biogen. *Ibid.* 844 The biogenes or large molecules of the cell.

biogenesis (baɪəʊ'dʒɛnɪsɪs). [f. Gr. βιο-, BIO- + γένεσις birth, production.] **1.** (See quot.)

1870 HUXLEY *Addr. Brit. Assoc.* in *Nature* 15 Sept. 401 The hypothesis that living matter always arises by the agency of pre-existing living matter..to save circumlocution, I shall call the hypothesis of Biogenesis. **1878** TAIT & STEWART *Unseen Univ.* vii. §243 To receive the law of Biogenesis as expressing the present order of the world.

2. = *biosynthesis* (see BIO-).

1933 *Chem. Rev.* XIII. 479 Attempts to explain the biogenesis of the terpenes on the basis of occurrence side by side in one or more species of plants have not been wanting. **1959** *New Scientist* 27 Aug. 302/2 The mode of biogenesis of cellulose still remains one of the major unsolved problems of carbohydrate chemistry.

3. The biochemical evolution of living matter, esp. its hypothetical development from complex but inanimate substances.

1960 *Science* 19 Feb. 479 The possibility of recurring biogenesis and the abiotic origin of optical activity are considered. **1965** J. B. S. HALDANE in S. W. Fox *Orig. Prebiological Syst.* 11 Some particular group may have been the limiting factor in biogenesis. Perhaps amino acids.. were present in adequate amounts, but high-energy phosphates were only rarely so. **1967** J. D. BERNAL *Orig. Life* 192 The molecular biology of biogenesis consists of successive stages of topochemical reactions.

Hence **bio'genesist**, one who holds the theory of biogenesis.

biogenetic (ˌbaɪəʊdʒɪ'nɛtɪk), *a.* [f. as prec. + Gr. *γενετικός, f. γένεσις: see prec.] Of or pertaining to biogeny or biogenesis; **biogenetic law** (G. *biogenetisches grundgesetz*): the theory, formulated by Haeckel, that evolutionary stages are repeated in the growth of a young animal; also called *recapitulation theory* (see RECAPITULATION[1] 1 b).

1879 tr. *Haeckel's Evol. Man* I. i. 8 The text of the biogenetic first principle is vitiated. **1879** tr. *K. Semper's Anim. Life* Pref., The popular cant about Biogenetic principles. **1882** R. MELDOLA tr. *Weismann's Studies Theory Descent* III. 611 A corollary to the 'fundamental biogenetic law' first enunciated by..Haeckel. **1933** *Chem. Rev.* XIII. 481 The coëxistence of compounds in a few instances out of many..may indicate nothing as to their biogenetic relationship. **1934** *Nature* 10 Feb. 199/1 In our judgment the formulation of this biogenetic law was the greatest service which Haeckel did to the science of zoology. **1962** E. M. KOSOWER *Molec. Biochem.* i. 47 The correlation of the structures of many classes of natural products by 'biogenetic' schemes has long been a successful intellectual pastime in organic chemistry.

biogenic (baɪə'dʒɛnɪk), *a.* [f. BIOGENY + -IC.]

1. = BIOGENETIC *a.*

1904 G. S. HALL *Adolescence* I. ii. 55 The great biogenic law that the individual recapitulates the growth stages of his race.

2. Produced by living organisms.

1913 A. W. GRABAU *Princ. Stratigraphy* x. 384 Biogenic rocks, or *Bioliths* as Chr. G. Ehrenberg has termed them, are deposits of organic material, or material formed through the physiological activities of the organisms. **1957** *Encycl. Brit.* XX. 274/2 *Foraminifera* and *Radiolaria* are examples of biogenic sediments. **1958** F. E. ZEUNER *Dating Past* (ed. 4) 430 He..upholds the biogenic character of *Corycium*, possibly an alga, from the pre-Cambrian of Finland.

biogenist (baɪ'ɒdʒɪnɪst). [f. next + -IST.] One skilled in biogeny.

biogeny (baɪ'ɒdʒɪnɪ). [mod. f. Gr. βιο-, BIO- + -γένεια birth.]

1. The history of the evolution of living organisms.

1879 tr. *Haeckel's Evol. Man* I. 6 Biogeny (or the history of organic evolution in the widest sense).

2. = BIOGENESIS 1.

1870 HUXLEY *Crit. & Addr.* x. (1873) 233 If the doctrine of Biogeny is true, the air must be thick with germs.

ˌbioge'ography. [BIO-.] The science of the geographical distribution of living things, animal and vegetable. Hence **bioge'ographer**, one versed in biogeography; **biogeo'graphic, -ical** *adjs.*

1895 C. H. T. TOWNSEND in *Geogr. Jrnl.* (1896) VII. 333 (*title*) On the bio-geography of Mexico, Texas..and Arizona, with special reference to the limits of the life areas, and a provisional synopsis of the bio-geographic divisions of America. **1899** H. R. MILL *Internat. Geogr.* 4 Living things possess the world, and the purpose of Biogeography is to trace out the reasons why particular species occupy the regions where they are now found. **1909** WEBSTER, Biogeographic. **1910** H. R. MILL *Guide Geogr. Bks.* 110 This is also the aspect of biogeography usually dealt with in ordinary text-books. **1922** L. R. DICE in *Science* LV. 335/2 Biogeographers have long made use of floral and faunal areas for the classification of distribution. **1928** *Funk's Stand. Dict.*, Biogeographical. **1958** *New Scientist* 10 Apr. 12/2 The southern Pacific area presents several fascinating biogeographical problems. One..is the affinity between the flora and fauna of South America and that of Australasia. **1961** *Ibid.* 15 June 636/3 The biogeographer's task is to explain how this contact [between plants and animals] was achieved, and how it gave rise to the present pattern of distribution.

biograph ('baɪəʊgrɑːf, -æ-), *sb.* [Cf. *biography*, and *photograph.*] **1.** A biographical sketch or notice. *rare*

1865 E. BURRITT *Walk Land's End* 8 The thoughts submitted on the subject of biographs.

2. An earlier form of cinematograph, introduced from the U.S. (Cf. ANIMATOGRAPH.) Also *attrib.*

1897 *Westm. Gaz.* 19 Mar. 3/3 The exhibition of the American biograph at the Palace Theatre..is another step towards the perfection of the animatograph. *Ibid.*, It cannot be claimed that the biograph is free from vibration, nor do the pictures rest as steadily on the screen as they might. **1898** *Brit. Jrnl. Photogr. Alm.* 655 The exhibition of animated photographs on a larger scale than usual, by the biograph, the invention of an American, Mr. Casler. **1901** W. R. H. TROWBRIDGE *Lett. her Mother to Eliz.* xviii. 89 The Palace [music-hall] in place of the ballet [at the Empire] has a Biograph, which wiggles and makes you feel cross-eyed. **1912** C. N. & A. M. WILLIAMSON *Heather Moon* II. iv, They're going to take photographs of a Gretna Green wedding..for a biograph show.

'biograph, *v. rare.* [f. prec., after *photograph*; or ? deduced from *biograph-er.*] **1.** *trans.* To write or prepare a biography of.

1883 *Kendal Merc. & Times* 19 Oct. 5/1 It will be.. impossible to 'biograph' these great men, without, etc.

2. To make a biograph (sense 2) of.

1898 *Westm. Gaz.* 27 May 4/2 The finish of the Derby on Wednesday was 'biographed' for the Palace Theatre. **1901** *Ibid.* 14 Jan. 8/2 The experiment of biographing a battle is not absolutely new.

biographee (baɪˌɒgrəˈfiː). [Formed as the correlative of BIOGRAPHER: see -EE.] One who is the subject of a biography.

1841 *Blackw. Mag.* XLIX. 757 The family..are too nearly connected with the biographee. **1879** *Athenæum* 29 Nov. 687/1 There is too much of the biographer in it, and not enough of the biographee.

biographer (baɪˈɒgrəfə(r)). [f. BIOGRAPHY *sb.* (or its Gr. source) + -ER (cf. *astronomer*): taking the place of the earlier *biographist*.] A writer of biographies, or of the 'life' of a particular person.

1715 ADDISON *Freeholder* No. 35 (1751) 209 Grub-street Biographers..watch for the Death of a great Man. **1790** BOSWELL *Johnson* (1831) I. Introd. 48, I flatter myself that few biographers have entered upon such a work as this with more advantages. *a* **1849** H. COLERIDGE *North. Worthies* (1852) Introd. 18 He would be a local biographer. **1855** MILMAN *Lat. Chr.* VIII. viii, The seven or eight contemporary biographers of Becket.

biographic (baɪəʊˈgræfɪk). *a.* [f. as BIOGRAPH + -IC: cf. Gr. γραφ ικ-ός of or pertaining to writing.] Of, pertaining to, or of the nature of biography.

c **1794** WOLCOTT (P. Pindar) *Bozzy & P.* Wks. I. 352 He now could meet more biographic scrap. *a* **1859** DE QUINCEY *Bentley* Wks. VI. 178 A biographic record. **1879** FARRAR *St. Paul* I. 206 The biographic retrospect in the Epistle to the Galatians.

biographical (baɪəʊˈgræfɪkəl), *a.* [f. as prec. + -AL[1].] Of, relating to, or dealing with biography.

1738 OLDYS *Life Ralegh* Wks. 1829 I. 13 As the biographical fry who follow have nibbled out of him. **1747** *Biogr. Britan.* Pref. 13 In this Biographical Dictionary. **1860** *Sat. Rev.* IX. 301 This is the true biographical temper.

bioˈgraphically, *adv.* [f. prec. + -LY[2].] After the manner of, or with reference to, biography.

1760 STERNE *Tr. Shandy* II. viii. 57 This plea, tho' it might save me dramatically, will damn me biographically. *a* **1849** H. COLERIDGE *North. Worthies* (1852) Introd. 19 The facts of the same life may be considered either biographically or historically.

biographist (baɪˈɒgrəfɪst). [See BIOGRAPHY *sb.*: and cf. -IST.] = BIOGRAPHER.

1662 FULLER *Worthies* iii, The Biographists of these Saints. **1877** MRS. OLIPHANT *Makers Flor.* i. 30 Wanton biographists assailed her with..slanders.

biographize (baɪˈɒgrəfaɪz), *v.* [f. as BIOGRAPHY *sb.* + -IZE.] *trans.* To write a biography of. Also *intr.*

1800 SOUTHEY *Lett.* (1856) I. 115 As a Latin poet, I biographise him. **1868** *Spectator* 14 Nov. 1340 The Royal Family of England has been quite sufficiently biographized. **1897** W. RALEIGH *Let.* 13 Mar. (1926) I. 192 If I biographize it should be on a literary gent.

biography (baɪˈɒgrəfɪ), *sb.* [This word and its numerous connexions (see above) are recent. No compounds of the group existed in Old Greek: but βιογραφία 'writing of lives' (f. βίο-ς life + -γραφία writing, f. γράφ-ειν to write, -γράφος writer), is quoted from Damascius *c* 500, and βιογράφος 'writer of lives' is cited by Du Cange as med.Gr. *Biographus, biographia*, were used in mod.L. before any words of the group appeared in Eng., where *biographist* was used by Fuller 1662, *biography* by Dryden 1683, *biographer* by Addison 1715, *biographical* by Oldys 1738; all the others are later. It is doubtful whether *biographist* was formed directly from the Gr. elements, or after mod.L. *biographus*; *biography* appears to have been an adaptation of L. *biographia*. The first appearance of *biographe, biographie* in Fr. is not recorded; so that their immediate relation to the Eng. words is not yet determined.]

1. The history of the lives of individual men, as a branch of literature.

1683 DRYDEN *Life Plutarch* (1712) 55 Biographia, or the History of particular Mens Lives, comes next to be considered. *Ibid.* 59 In all parts of Biography..Plutarch equally excell'd. *a* **1724** FIDDES *Life Wolsey* Introd. 15 That Distinction or particular Branch of History, which is termed Biography. **1803** SCOTT in *Lockhart* XI, Biography, the most interesting perhaps of every species of composition. **1883** HALLIWELL-PHILLIPPS *Life Shaks.* Pref. 1, At the present day, with biography carried to a wasteful and ridiculous excess.

2. A written record of the life of an individual.

c **1791** WOLCOTT (P. Pindar) *Bozzy & P.* (1812) 361 Bid her a poor biography suspend, Nor crucify through vanity a friend. **1814** PINKERTON *Voy.* XVII. Index, Biography of Haller. **1883** HALLIWELL-PHILLIPPS *Life Shaks.* Pref. 12 John Aubrey..was the author of numerous little biographies.

b. *Comb.*

1860 *Sat. Rev.* IX. 301 If it had come from the hands of a regular biography-monger.

3. *transf.* The life-course of a man or other living being; the 'life-history' of an animal or plant.

1854 H. MILLER *Footpr. Creat.* xv. (1874) 268 In studying the biography, if I may so express myself, of an individual animal. **1883** HALLIWELL-PHILLIPPS *Life Shaks.* Pref. 8 The scanty records of the poet's biography that yet remain.

biˈography, *v.* [f. the sb.] *trans.* To write the life of; to make the subject of a biography. So **biˈographied** *ppl. a.* (also *absol.*).

1844 *Fraser's Mag.* XXX. 518/1 If..the biographied be of low birth. **1858** [see BIOGRAPHYING *vbl. sb.*]. **1887** *L'pool Merc.* 10 Mar. 4/5 Captain Burton is to be biographied. **1908** *Fabian News* XIX. 22/2, I cannot help a sneaking regret that G.B.S. has mounted above us into the regions of the biographied. **1909** *Westm. Gaz.* 29 May 5/3 Diane de Poitiers, Lola Montez [etc.] are nearly all much-biographied ladies.

biˈographying, *vbl. sb.* [f. BIOGRAPHY *sb.*: cf. *speechifying*.] The writing of biographies.

1858 CARLYLE *Fredk. Gt.* II. x. ii. 579 Endless writing and biographying..about this man.

biologic (baɪəʊˈlɒdʒɪk), *a.* [f. BIOLOGY + -IC.] Of, belonging to, or of the nature of biology.

1864 H. SPENCER *Illustr. Univ. Progr.* 374 The biologic history of the supposed new continent. **1884** J. B. THOMAS in *Homiletic Monthly* June 532 Features so conspicuous in the biologic realm.

biological (baɪəʊˈlɒdʒɪkəl), *a.* (and *sb.*) [f. prec. + -AL[1].] **A.** *adj.* **1.** Of, or relating to, biology or (quot. 1874) 'electro-biology.'

1859 G. WILSON *E. Forbes* ii. 43 Natural History..the biological half of natural science. **1874** CARPENTER *Ment. Phys.* (1876) 555 The psychical phenomena manifested during the persistence of the Biological state. **1877** W. THOMSON *Voy. Challenger* I. i. 5 The physical and biological conditions of the sea-bottom.

2. In various specific combs.: ***biological assay*** (see ASSAY *sb.* 6 b); ***biological chemistry*** = BIOCHEMISTRY; ***biological clock***, an innate mechanism that regulates various cyclic and rhythmic activities of an organism; ***biological control*** (see quot. 1930); ***biological hole***, a cavity in a nuclear reactor designed to permit the placing of animals or plants near the core in order to test the biological effects of radiation; ***biological race, species*** (see quot. 1916); ***biological shield***, a shield round a nuclear reactor or cyclotron as a protection against radiation; ***biological spectrum*** (see SPECTRUM); ***biological value*** [G. *biologische wertigkeit*, K. Thomas 1909, in *Archiv f. Physiologie* 219]: of a protein (see quots.); ***biological warfare***, warfare involving the use of toxins, germs, etc., harmful to plants, animals, or human beings; a more comprehensive term than *bacteriological warfare*.

1897 A. B. GRIFFITHS (*title*) Respiratory proteids. Researches in biological chemistry. **1957** *Encycl. Brit.* III. 589/2 The terms 'biochemistry', 'biological chemistry' and 'physiological chemistry' are often used interchangeably. **1955** *Proc. Nat. Acad. Sci.* XLI. 99 Such a biological clock would seem theoretically to be a necessary component in the mechanism of the normally precise rhythms of solar and lunar frequency. **1967** *Guardian* 1 Sept. 16/4 We do not have one biological clock, but many working together, and after a long flight to east or west or after a change of working shift, they may take from one to five days to synchronize again. **1923** *Jrnl. Econ. Entomology* XVI. 506 (*title*) What may we expect from Biological Control? **1926** A. D. IMMS in *Ann. Appl. Biol.* XIII. 402 (*title*) The biological control of insects and injurious plants in the Hawaiian Islands. **1930** *Times Lit. Suppl.* 18 Dec. 1078/3 The saving of the copra industry is as complete an example of what is now called 'biological control', the subduing of a living pest by the introduction of a living enemy of the pest, as the saving of the citrus industry of California by the introduction of a lady-beetle from Australia. **1957** *Gloss. Terms Nucl. Sci.* (*A.S.A.*) 19/2 Biological hole. **1916** B. D. JACKSON *Gloss. Bot. Terms* (ed. 3) 50/1 *Biological* (*races*, or) *species*, those species which differ only by their physiological behaviour, being morphologically identical. **1941** J. S. HUXLEY *Uniqueness of Man* v. 157 What are called 'biological races' of parasites adapted to different hosts. **1942** —— *Evolution* v. 166 Groups..remain separate in spite of the complete or almost complete absence of morphological differences. In many such cases (e.g. in 'biological' or 'physiological races'), the allocation of specific rank must be a mere matter of opinion and convenience. **1953** *Times* 31 Oct. 6/1 The reactor core would be enclosed in a mild steel shell within the biological shield. **1957** *Financ. Times Ann. Rev. Brit. Ind.* 1 July 66/1 Reinforced concrete also provides the vital barrier against the insidious dangers of radiation. This 'biological shield' must totally enclose the reactor. **1902** H. M. WARD in *Ann. Bot.* XVI. 236 Various names have been proposed for these physiologically, but as yet not morphologically, different varieties... Rostrup names them 'Biological species' (*biologische Arten*). **1924** H. H. MITCHELL in *Jrnl. Biol. Chem.* LVIII. 878 The 'biological value' of a protein, as the term was applied originally by Karl Thomas, referred to the utilization by the body of the products of protein digestion. *Ibid.* 901 The biological value of the protein is taken as the percentage of the absorbed nitrogen that is not eliminated. **1960** A. E. BENDER *Dict. Nutrition* 17/2 The biological value of a protein is the amount, when fed under standard conditions, that is retained in the body for synthesis of body protein. It is expressed on the percentage scale; 100% is the perfect protein. **1946** *Life* 18 Nov. 118/2 Biological warfare, using scourges of disease and famine as weapons, is as dreadful as the atomic bomb and far more difficult to control. **1951** 'J. WYNDHAM' *Day of Triffids* ii. 31 The United States Government took the suggestion seriously enough to deny emphatically that it controlled any satellites designed to conduct biological warfare directly upon human beings. **1959** Biological warfare [see BACTERIOLOGICAL *warfare*].

B. as *sb.* (After *chemical*, chiefly in *pl.*) A biological product used for therapeutic purposes.

1921 *Lancet* 5 Mar. 497/2 A report..to consider the effective control of therapeutic substances which cannot be tested by direct chemical means. On the analogy of 'chemicals' we propose, for want of a better term, to call these substances 'biologicals'. **1937** *Times* 28 July 16/5 The manufacture of fine chemicals and biologicals. **1957** *New Scientist* 21 Nov. 12/3 In recent years there has been a shortage of these biologicals.

bioˈlogically, *adv.* [f. prec. + -LY[2].] In a biological manner; with reference to biology.

1875 *N. Amer. Rev.* CXX. 255 Human nature, either biologically or psychologically considered. **188.** G. ALLEN *Vignettes, Fall of Year*, Africa..cut almost in two, biologically speaking, by the..Sahara.

biologism (baɪˈɒlədʒɪz(ə)m). [f. BIOLOGY + -ISM.] The interpretation of human life from a strictly biological point of view.

Motley's use of the word (= ELECTRO-BIOLOGY 2) is *Obs. rare.*

1852 MOTLEY *Corr.* 18 May (1889) I. 143 Whenever a charlatan can't find any to believe in his tricks of mesmerism or biologism, or whatever may be the latest neologism. **1924** *Public Opinion* 25 Jan. 81/3 When we try to force all the facts of human society into frameworks of zoology we are guilty of a biologism. **1926** J. A. THOMSON *Man in Light Evol.* 32 A biologism is an attempt to ignore the uniqueness of man by forcing his activities in their entirety into the framework of mammalian physiology... It is a biologism to picture an average man as the slave of his hormones. **1967** *Guardian* 20 Oct. 6/3 Much of the biologism of this and other of his recent books is mere accretion concealing his own experiential progress.

Hence **bioloˈgistic** *a.*, of or relating to biologism.

1948 K. DAVIS *Human Society* (1959) xx. 556 So ingrained is the old biologistic approach to human fertility. **1959** *New Scientist* 17 Dec. 1266/1 A Neo-Freudian who has tried to correct Freud's biologistic approach to behaviour by stressing some of its cultural determinants.

biologist (baɪˈɒlədʒɪst). [f. BIOLOGY + -IST.] One who studies biology or (quot. 1874) a 'professor' of 'electro-biology.'

1813 J. STANFIELD *Biography* ii. 57 If the Biologist (should a distinctive term be allowed) come not to his study with the same spirit of impartiality that is required from the Biographer. **1874** CARPENTER *Ment. Phys.* (1876) 553 In the public exhibition of professed Biologists. **1879** WRIGHT *Anim. Life* 2 The Biologist has to study both Plants and Animals.

biˈologize, *v.* [f. BIOLOGY + -IZE. In sense 1, referring to 'electro-biology.'] Hence **biˈologized** *ppl. a.*, **biologizer**.

† **1.** *trans.* To mesmerize. *Obs.*

1862 LYTTON *Str. Story* 26 A select few, whom he first fed and then biologized. **1874** CARPENTER *Ment. Phys.* (1876) 553 The Mind of the Biologized 'subject' seems to remain entirely dormant. *Ibid.* The relationship between the Biologizer and his 'subject.'

2. *intr.* and *trans.* To cultivate biology; to deal with biologically.

biology (baɪˈɒlədʒɪ). [mod. f. Gr. βίο-ς life + -λογία discoursing (see -LOGY); according to Littré invented by the German naturalist Gottfried Reinhold (Treveranus) in his *Biologie* 1802, and adopted in Fr. by Lamarck in his *Hydrologie* 1802; it was used in Eng. by Stanfield in 1813, but in a sense directly repr. Gr. βίος (see BIO-), and βιολόγος 'one who represents to the life.']

† **1.** The study of human life and character. *Obs.*

1813 J. STANFIELD *Biography* Introd. 12 There exists, what might be called *biology*, as well as *biography*.

2. The science of physical life; the division of physical science which deals with organized beings or animals and plants, their morphology, physiology, origin, and distribution; sometimes, in a narrower sense = Physiology; see Rolleston *Brit. Assoc. Rep.* 1870, II. 96.

1819 LAWRENCE *Lect. Man* ii. (1844) 42 A foreign writer has proposed the more accurate term of biology, or science of life. **1847** WHEWELL *Philos. Induct. Sc.* I. 544 The term Biology..has of late become not uncommon, among good writers. **1880** A. WALLACE *Isl. Life* I. i. 9 One of the most difficult and interesting questions in geographical biology—the origin of the fauna and flora of New Zealand.

† **3.** = 'ELECTRO-BIOLOGY,' or 'animal-magnetism,' a phase of mesmerism.

1874 CARPENTER *Ment. Phys.* (1876) 551 'Electro biology,' or 'Biology' (as it came to be very commonly designated).. became a fashionable amusement in some circles, at ordinary evening parties.

ˌbioluminˈescence. *Biol.* [BIO-.] The emission of light by living organisms; also, the light so produced. Hence **ˌbioluminˈescent** *a.*

1916 E. N. HARVEY in *Amer. Jrnl. Physiol.* XLI. 449 (*title*) Studies on Bioluminescence. **1929** *Biol. Abstr.* (*Index*) 2366/3 Bioluminescent bacteria. **1936** *Mind* XLV. 69 Bioluminescent fluids. **1953** J. RAMSBOTTOM *Mushrooms & Toadstools* xiv. 157 The phenomenon of bioluminescence is widespread in the animal kingdom, examples occurring in at least thirty-nine orders. **1954** *Lancet* 25 Dec. 1317/1 Several substances, under the appropriate stimulus, can emit light,

and so far the compounds responsible for bioluminescence have not been conclusively identified.

biolysis (baɪ'ɒlɪsɪs). [f. BIO- + Gr. λύσις dissolution.] Chemical decomposition of organic matter brought about by bacteria, etc.

1897 SCOTT-MONCRIEFF in *Prof. Papers Corps R. Engineers* XXIII. 213 *(heading)* Purification of Sewage by Biolysis. **1922** H. E. BABBITT *Sewerage & S. Treatment* xii. 366 The biolysis of sewage is the term applied to the changes through which its organic constituents pass due to the metabolism of bacterial life. *Ibid.* 367 In the biolysis of sewage there is no destruction of matter.

biolytic, -magnetic, etc.: see BIO- *pref.*

biome ('baɪəʊm). *Ecol.* [f. Gr. βίος life + -OME.] A biotic community of plants and animals; *spec.* such a community in a prehistoric period.

1916 F. E. CLEMENTS *Plant Succession* 319 Human evidence of past climates and biotic communities, or biomes, must come to be of very great value. **1918** —— in *Bull. Geol. Soc. Amer.* XXIX. 372 In paleo-ecology the concept of the biome, or biotic community, seems to have peculiar value, as it directs special attention to the causal relations and reactions of the three elements—habitat, plant, and animal. *Ibid.* 374 Climatic changes and biotic movements..are involved in..the appearance of new biomes and the disappearance of preceding ones. **1931** *Ecology* XII. 456 Because the larger and more influent animals tend to range throughout units of largest (formational) size including their seral stages, the biome or biotic formation is the natural ecological unit with some properties which are well illustrated by comparison with an organism. **1935** *Ibid.* XVI. 399 Migratory species..are frequently seasonal influents classed in seasonal communities in two biomes. **1957** G. CLARK *Archæol. & Society* (ed. 3) vi. 175 All the forms of life, including man himself, that together constitute the biome. **1957** *Encycl. Brit.* VII. 434/2 A biome is based on the concept that the plants and animals associated together in the same area have a certain unity. The biome is thus a plant-plus-animal formation that is composed of a plant matrix together with all associated animals.

ˌbiome'chanics. [BIO-.] The study of the mechanical laws relating to the movement or structure of living organisms. So **ˌbiome'chanical** *a.*, pertaining or relating to biomechanics.

1933 STEDMAN *Med. Dict.* (ed. 12) 134/1 *Biomechanics*, the science of the action of forces, internal or external, on the living body. **1941** J. S. HUXLEY *Uniqueness of Man* i. 9 Specialization is one-sided progress, and after a..time, reaches a biomechanical limit. The horse stock cannot reduce its digits below one;..feathered flight cannot become aerodynamically more efficient than in existing birds. **1951** *Engineering* 23 Feb. 226/2 Their subject covers what have been described as biotechnology, biomechanics, human engineering,..engineering psychology. **1970** *Physics Bull.* June 264/1 A biomechanical investigation of the human hearing mechanism.

b. *Russ. Theatre.* [cf. Russ. *biomekhanika.*] Also **bio'mechanism**. (See quots.)

1924 H. CARTER *New Theatre & Cinema in Soviet Russia* vi. 67 He [*sc.* Meierhold] established a studio of bio-mechanics [in 1921]. *Ibid.* 70 The principles of bio-mechanics..became systematically applied by him in the R.S.F.S.R. theatre in Petrograd from 1918 to 1922. *Ibid.*, The laws of bio-mechanics are founded on the study of the physiological construction of man. The system aims to produce men who understand the mechanism and laws of their structure and can, therefore, use it perfectly. It has established a principle of analysis by which each movement of the body can be differentiated and made fully expressive. **1930** P. ENGLAND tr. *Fülöp-Miller & Gregor's Russ. Theatre* 68 The classical example of bio-mechanism is the comedy *The Magnificent Cuckold.* In this the movements of the performers were so standardized that they seemed to obey some geometric law... Large revolving wheels were also employed, in order to register the various emotions that prevailed from time to time in the breasts of the actors.

biometric (baɪə'mɛtrɪk), *a.* and *sb.* [f. BIO- + METRIC *a.*[1]]

A. *adj.* Of or pertaining to biometry. So **bio'metrical** *a.*

1901 *Biometrika* I. 2 The collection of biometric data. *Ibid.* 6 Biometric workers. **1902** *Encycl. Brit.* XXVIII. 344/2 Biometric investigation. *Ibid.*, Biometrical inquiry. **1936** *Discovery* Jan. 32/2 The application of biometric methods to the study of the composition of ethnic groups. **1937** R. H. LOWIE *Hist. Ethnol. Theory* ix. 130 He has done a full-fledged professional's work in physical anthropology ..investigating growth by biometrical techniques.

B. *sb. pl.* = BIOMETRY 2.

1902 in *Encycl. Brit.* XXVIII. 344/1. **1923** W. M. FELDMAN *Biomath.* xxi. 327 Biometrics is the application of modern statistical methods to the measurements of biological (variable) objects. **1935** HUXLEY & HADDON *We Europeans* ii. 61 The work of Karl Pearson and his school in the study of statistical methods as applied to biological and anthropological problems ('Biometrics').

biometrician (ˌbaɪəmɪ'trɪʃən). [f. BIOMETRIC *a.* + -IAN: cf. *metrician.*] One who is versed in biometry; one who applies statistics to the problems of biology, esp. that of variation. So **bio'metricist**.

1901 F. GALTON in *Biometrika* I. 10 Biology could soon be raised to the status of a more exact science.., if each of many biometricians would thoroughly work out his own particular plot. **1902** *Encycl. Brit.* XXVIII. 344/2 The biometricist demands statistics to show the range of the variations and the mode of their distribution. **1914** K. PEARSON *(title)* Tables for Statisticians and Biometricians. **1922** W. R. INGE *Outspoken Ess.* 263 It seems to be established by the biometricians that children who are born after their fathers are fifty seldom attain distinction. **1948** *Mind* LVII. 294 They [*sc.* two cats] certainly differ slightly in various measurements, and it is the business of a biometrician to describe such differences.

biometry (baɪ'ɒmɪtrɪ). [See BIO- and -METRY.] †**1.** The measurement of life; the calcuation of the average duration and expectation of life. *Obs.*

1831 WHEWELL *Let.* 12 Nov. (1876) II. 135 By the way there is a problem in *Biometry* (if you choose to call your calculations on lives by a Greek name) which may perhaps be included. **1875** *Med. Rec.* X. 481 Biometry: its relations to the practice of medicine. **1881** *Index-Catal. Libr. Surg-Gen. U.S.* II. 66/2 *Biometry*, see anthropometry; longevity.

2. The application of mathematics to biology, esp. the study of resemblances between living things by statistical methods.

1901 F. GALTON in *Biometrika* I. 9 The primary object of Biometry is to afford material that shall be exact enough for the discovery of incipient changes in evolution which are too small to be otherwise apparent. **1927** HALDANE & HUXLEY *Anim. Biol.* ii. 72 When we take the averages of large numbers these irregularities become smoothed out, and we find a strong average resemblance, due to heredity, between parent and offspring, or between brothers and sisters. The science of biometry deals with studies of this sort. **1942** *Nature* 18 Apr. 428/2 Thus with Pearson defending biometry and Bateson advocating Mendelism a feud arose.

biomorph ('baɪəmɔːf). [f. BIO- + Gr. μορφή form.] A decorative form representing a living object. Hence **bio'morphic** *a.*

1895 HADDON *Evol. Art* 126 The biomorph is the representation of anything living in contradistinction to the skeuomorph. *Ibid.* 188 Biomorphic Pottery. **1954** *Archit. Rev.* CXV. 272/2 Leaden echoes of lively biomorphs with a sinister absence of meaning. **1959** P. & L. MURRAY *Dict. Art* 27 *Biomorphic art* is a form of abstract art which purports to take its abstract forms from living organisms rather than from the geometrical basis of such abstract movements as constructivism. **1960** H. READ *Forms of Things Unknown* III. x. 165 Some are biomorphic, reminiscent of cellular structures as revealed by the microscope.

bionic (baɪ'ɒnɪk), *a.* [f. Gr. βίος life + *-onic* (in sense 2 after ELECTRONIC *a.*).] †**1.** *Geol.* (See quot. 1901.) *rare.*

1901 H. S. WILLIAMS in *Jrnl. Geol.* IX. 578 The enduring power of organisms, expressed by the repetition of like characters in successive fossil forms, is the time quality..to which we must look for the making of a scientific time-scale. In order to isolate this time quality I have proposed to speak of it as the bionic quality or value of the organism. The bionic quality of an organism may, then, be defined as its quality of continuing, and repeating in successive generations, the same morphologic characters. *Ibid.* 579 *(heading)* Order of magnitude of bionic units.

2. Of or pertaining to bionics; having or being an artificial, esp. electromechanical, device that replaces part of the body; having ordinary human capabilities increased (as if) by the aid of such devices.

1963 *IEEE Trans. Military Electronics* VII. 91/1 Sometimes in evolving a mathematics appropriate to a biophysical or bionic problem one can use stock mathematical treatments in unconventional combinations to surprisingly good effect. **1965** *Johns Hopkins Mag.* Mar. 6 Their goal was to design and construct a machine with built-in behavioral responses... The group decided to attack the problem from a 'bionic' approach, i.e. applying knowledge of a biological system—in this case, man—to an engineering problem. **1970** *Encycl. Sci. Suppl.* (Grolier) 115 In building a submarine, designers wish to determine the most efficient shape for the hull. The bionic approach..consists of studying organisms that exhibit the desired characteristic of moving through water with the least amount of resistance. **1976** *Daily Tel.* 30 Jan. 3/3 He was always playing at being the Six Million Dollar Man... There should be a warning at the end of each programme telling children not to attempt the stunts carried out by the bionic man. **1978** *Guardian* 10 June 22/5 Artificial 'bionic' hands will be fitted free under the National Health Service under a trial programme. *Ibid.* 22/6 The 'bionic' hands look and work like real ones, responding to tiny electronic impulses from the body. **1979** *Daily Tel.* 27 Aug. 3/1 'Bionic' racehorses—with carbon fibre implants in injured tendons—are expected to compete in this year's National Hunt season. **1980** *Brit. Med. Jrnl.* 12 July 126/1 Examples of the 'bionic arms' made in Sweden and fitted to young children with congenital upper-limb deficiencies. *Ibid.*, The 'bionic arm', or more accurately the myoelectric hand. **1986** *Christian Science Monitor* 24 Oct. 23 A brainy young man plants a computer chip in his next-door neighbor's cranium and comes up with a bionic murderer.

b. *transf.* Outstandingly gifted or competent. *slang.*

1976 *Guardian* 2 Dec. 10/6 Among the splendid women in the cast, Prunella Gee stands out..as a bionic Julie Christie who proves to be the unprincipled Eternal Female Principle. **1976** *Horse & Hound* 10 Dec. 77/3 (Advt.), Bionic twosome required as groom/gardener and housekeeper. **1977** *Private Eye* 1 Apr. 16/3 Am I not right in thinking that the Faraday catchment area includes the delightful Ealing home of Margaret Jay, lovely daughter of Stoker Jim Callaghan and wife of the bionic Peter? **1984** *Washington Post* 2 May D1/6No one in the emergency room seemed to speak English... After two hours, the woman who is frequently described as 'unflappable' and 'bionic' did the appropriate thing. She sat down and cried.

bionics (baɪ'ɒnɪks). [f. BIO- + ELECTR)ONICS.] (See quots.)

1960 J. E. KETO in *Proc. Nat. Aeronaut. Electronics Conference* 218 The title of this session is Bionics. This is a new term referring to a relatively new but rapidly expanding area of activity—the study of systems which function after the manner of or in a manner characteristic of or resembling living systems. **1962** *New Scientist* 29 Mar. 737/3 Much of the emphasis in 'bionics'—study of animals by engineers in an attempt to learn 'dodges' from nature—has been on sense organs and nervous systems. **1966** *Ibid.* 10 Mar. 626/1 Engineering bionics is a relatively new science aimed at making machines which behave like living systems.

bionomic (baɪə'nɒmɪk), *a.* and *sb.* [f. BIO-, after ECONOMIC.] **A.** *adj.* Of or pertaining to the conditions under which an organism lives in its natural habitat; of or pertaining to bionomics (see B).

1899 J. A. THOMSON in H. R. Mill *Internat. Geogr.* 85 Bionomic Relations. **1920** *Rep. Brit. Assoc. Advancem. Sci.* 1919 207 The formation of a great collection of butterflies —a most valuable asset for bionomic research. **1956** *Nature* 25 Feb. 359/1 A number of his systematic papers contain bionomic and ecological observations.

B. *sb. pl.* The branch of biology which deals with the mode of life of organisms in their natural habitat, their adaptation to their surroundings, etc.; ecology.

1888 E. R. LANKESTER in *Encycl. Brit.* XXIV. 803/2 *Bionomics*..including thremmatology, or the science of breeding. **1895** *Naturalist* 337 The old out-door ornithologists are to-day's sportsmen, who study the bionomics of their quarry that they may outwit them. **1902** *Westm. Gaz.* 6 Dec. 8/1 The bionomics of the North Sea; in other words, the relationships of the various forms of life to one another and to their surroundings. **1947** *New Biol.* III. 57 This study of the mode of life of any animal and of its relationships to its surroundings and to other animals is called the study of the bionomics of the animal.

bio'nomical, *a.* Of or pertaining to bionomics (see prec. B); ecological.

1902 *Encycl. Brit.* XXVIII. 344/1 Bionomical investigators. **1909** *Athenæum* 17 July 72/1 The bionomical stores contained in its pages. **1930** *Jrnl. Ecol.* XVIII. 81 *(title)* Bionomical investigation of English mosquito larvae with special reference to their algal food.

biophor ('baɪəfɔː(r)). *Biol.* Also **-phore**. [G. *biophor*, f. Gr. βίος life + -φορος -bearing.] In Weismann's theory of heredity: a supposed ultimate unit of living protoplasm.

1893 PARKER & RÖNNFELDT tr. *Weismann's Germ-Plasm* I. i. 40 We have to imagine that..protoplasm..consists of groups of molecules, each of which is composed of different kinds of chemical molecules. I shall call these units the 'bearers of vitality' ('Lebensträger') or 'biophors', because they are the smallest units which exhibit the primary vital forces, viz. assimilation and metabolism, growth, and multiplication by fission. **1894** *Nat. Sci.* Sept. 185 His [*sc.* Weismann's] germ-plasm is made up of primary units, the biophores, which are built up into determinants, a determinant existing for each independently varying cell or group of cells in the adult organism. **1959** A. HUGHES *Hist. Cytol.* iv. 83 His [*sc.* Weismann's] ideas on development.. are as outdated as the peculiar terminology in which the postulated structure of the germ-plasm was expressed. The 'Biophor' has long been extinct, and the 'Id' has acquired a new meaning in another science.

bio'physics. The science dealing with the mechanical and electrical properties of the parts of living organisms. Hence **bio'physical** *a.*, of or pertaining to biophysics; **bio'physicist**, one who is versed in biophysics.

1892 K. PEARSON *Gram. Sci.* 470 This branch of science which endeavours to show that the facts of Biology.. constitute particular cases of general physical laws has been termed *Ætiology*. It would perhaps be better to call it *Bio-physics.* **1913** L. J. HENDERSON *Fitness Environm.* 310 While biophysicists like Professor Schäfer follow Spencer in assuming a gradual evolution of the organic from the inorganic, biochemists are more than ever unable to perceive how such a process is possible. **1913** *Science Progress* VIII. 319 The bio-physical and bio-chemical conditions underlying normal physiological processes in the organ of mind. **1926** *Encycl. Brit.* Suppl. II. 675/1 His main work is on the fundamental problem of biophysics—the stimulation of living matter. **1926** J. PRYDE *Rec. Advances Biochem.* v. 137 *(heading)* Biophysical Aspects of the Lipides and their Significance in Biology. **1958** A. R. RADCLIFFE-BROWN *Meth. Soc. Anthrop.* I. iv. 103 The nature of multicellular organisms is determined by the nature of the living cell which it is the business of the cytologist, the biochemist and the biophysicist to study. **1959** *New Biol.* XXX. 112 The study of the forces which mould a developing egg..is a comparatively new branch of biophysics. **1961** *Lancet* 22 July 190/2 Our American colleagues are fully aware of the importance of integrating basic biochemical, biophysical, and physiological effort.

biopic ('baɪəʊpɪk). *colloq.* (orig. *U.S.*). Also **bio-pic.** [f. BIO(GRAPHICAL *a.* + PIC[4] b.] A biographical film; a film biography.

1951 *Memphis* (Tennessee) *Commercial Appeal* 22 Dec. 6/3 'Variety' coins another word for show biz—'biopic', meaning a biographical film. **1975** *Globe & Mail* (Toronto) 16 Aug. 29/5 Warners..dares to document the social problems of the time..educating an unsophisticated audience with its historical and medieval bio-pics. **1976** *Time Out* 2 Apr. 47/2 Old fashioned Hollywood biopic. **1984** *Listener* 19 Apr. 35/1 It has most of the classic attributes of the anti-fascist biopic—predictability, smugness and 20-20 hindsight.

bioplasm ('baɪəʊplæzm). *Biol.* [f. BIO- + Gr. πλάσμα a thing moulded.] Prof. Beale's term for: The germinal matter of all living beings; living 'protoplasm.'

1872 BEALE *Bioplasm* i. §14 As the germ of every living thing consists of matter having the wonderful properties

already mentioned, I have called it germinal matter; but the most convenient and least objectionable name for it is living plasma or bioplasm. **1882** *Spectator* 30 Sept. 1251 A bit of bioplasm, or a minute parasitical organism.

Hence **bio'plasmic** *a.*

1872 Nicholson *Biol.* 71 Bioplasmic matter is colourless, transparent, and apparently wholly destitute of structure. **1883** Wright *Dogm. Sceptic.* 12 Bioplasmic theories.

bioplast ('baɪəʊplæst). *Biol.* [f. bio- + Gr. πλαστ-ός moulded, formed.]

A small separate portion of Bioplasm generally less than the thousandth of an inch in diameter. (Beale).

1883 Wright *Dogm. Scept.* 9 Lionell Beale, who originated the valued method of staining red all bioplasts in living tissues. **1884** Hayward in *Daily News* 19 Sept. 7/3 Some maintaining that the germs were vegetable spores, whilst others assert that they were animal bioplasts.

Hence **bioplastic** *a.*

1877 Saintsbury in *Academy* 10 Feb. 112 The third volume, where a Woman's College and a bioplastic professor are introduced.

biopoesis (baɪəʊpəʊ'iːsɪs). [f. bio- + Gr. ποίησις making.] The (hypothetical) origination or evolution of living or lifelike structures from lifeless matter; abiogenesis. Hence **bio'poeic** *a.*, pertaining to, causing, or resulting from biopoesis.

1953 N. W. Pirie in *Discovery* Aug. 239/1 Biopoesis (the cognate adjective is biopoeic) seems a more suitable word than Huxley's *abiogenesis* for the making of life *de novo*. Words ending in *genesis* carry a sense of generation as in animals; the making of like by like. *Ibid.*, Perhaps..there is no need to postulate any special biopoeic agency at all. **1967** J. D. Bernal *Orig. Life* viii. 137 The modern view of biopoesis includes elements both of deterministic character and of the older teleological character.

biopsy ('baɪɒpsɪ, baɪ'ɒpsɪ). [ad. F. *biopsie* (Besnier), f. Gr. βίος life + ὄψις sight. After necropsy.] Examination of tissue, etc., removed from the living body; also, the removal of such tissue.

1895 E. Besnier in J. J. Pringle *Pict. Atlas Skin Dis.* 88 Clinical teaching will now find in a 'biopsy' a valuable means of confirming or invalidating a dubious diagnosis. **1902** *Brit. Jrnl. Dermatol.* XIV. 56 A certain diagnosis was probably impossible without a biopsy. **1910** *Practitioner* Apr. 453 More definite evidence of the existence of gastrostaxis, apart from gastric ulcer, is obtained from biopsies and necropsies. **1955** *Brit. Med. Jrnl.* 31 Dec. 1590/1 (*title*) Serial biopsy in ulcerative colitis. **1966** *New Statesman* 11 Mar. 328/1 This is called a biopsy, wherein a cone of the infected cervical cell-tissue is surgically removed.

biordinal (baɪ'ɔːdɪnəl), *a.* (*sb.*) *Math.* [f. bi- *pref.*[2] II + ordinal, f. L. *ordo*, *ordin-*, rank, order.]

A. *adj.* Of the second order.

1853 De Morgan *Camb. Philos. Trans.* IX. iv. 2 It is desirable to invent single words to stand for the phrases 'of the first order,' 'of the second order,' etc. I propose *primordinal*, *biordinal*, etc. The word *differential* may be dispensed with, since these adjectives are understood to apply to differential equations only.

B. *sb.* A linear differential equation of the second order: see ordinal.

1881 Sir J. Cockle in *Athenæum* 268 [Paper entitled] 'Supplement on Binomial Biordinals.'

biorhythm ('baɪəʊrɪð(ə)m). [f. bio- + rhythm *sb.*] An endogenous cyclic variation in some aspect of an organism's bodily functioning, as the daily cycle of sleeping and waking, or the annual cycle of dormancy and activity in some animals; *spec.* each of three alleged cycles of different periods involving a person's physical, emotional, and intellectual activity, as used to explain or predict behaviour.

1960 *New Scientist* 29 Sept. 849/2 Hibernation is not simple sleep, nor is it continuous sleep. It proceeds in a biorhythm of the same sort as causes Man to sleep and waken at regular intervals. **1968** *Science Year World Bk. Science Ann.* 115 Symptoms of biorhythm upset, known popularly as the jet syndrome, are experienced by jet airplane travelers who fly through several time zones in 12 hours or less. **1972** Manaka & Urquhart *Layman's Guide Acupuncture* (1977) i. 77 The concept of biorhythm, of an internal 'biological clock' that regulates the organism's functioning in relation to both solar and lunar time measurement, is now an accepted part of Western physiology. **1976** *National Observer* (U.S.) 24 Jan. 9/2 The biorhythms theory..holds that a person's three key cycles begin running in a regular pattern at the moment of birth. The physical cycle is 23 days, the sensitivity cycle is 28 days, and the intellectual cycle is 33 days. **1985** F. O'Neill *Agents of Sympathy* vi. 71 Bach..breathed God's own Lutheran music over Transcendental Meditators, biorhythm fetishists, and aging Maoists. **1986** *New Health* Oct. 82/3 An exclusively prepared biorhythm chart will help you at a glance to overcome those 'off' days and capitalize your energies during periods of peak performance.

Hence **bio'rhythmic** *a.*, of, pertaining to, or indicating biorhythms; **bio'rhythmically** *adv.*; **bio'rhythmicist**, one who advocates or employs biorhythmics; **bio'rhythmics** *sb. pl.* (const. as *sing.*), the study of biorhythms, esp. one's own in order to improve one's efficiency and self-knowledge.

1966 *Sci. Amer.* Aug. 99/1 It is important in computing the 'biorhythmic compatibility' between two individuals. **1969** *Cumulated Index Medicus* IX. 1484/3 (*heading*) Biorhythmics and blood pressure regulation. **1972** *Time* 10 Jan. 48/3 Although there has been no rational explanation so far for the claims of biorhythmicists, variations of the concept have been put to practical use in at least two countries. **1972** *Times* 30 June 18/1 The new biorhythmic watch,..individually coded (by the retailer) according to the date of your birth, charts the state of your physical, psychological and intellectual health. **1973** *Nursing Times* 15 Feb. 207/2 Biorhythmics is the modern study of the three main biological functions. **1975** *Drive* New Year 85/1 He came to the startling conclusion that 70% of accidents happen on biorhythmically critical days. **1979** *London Rev. Bks.* 25 Oct. 14/1 (Advt.), How can you construct your own biorhythmic chart? **1985** *Observer* (Colour Suppl.) 21 Apr. 7/3, I have done yoga, reflexology, biorhythmics, aromatherapy and EST.

biorlinn, variant of birlinn.

bios ('baɪɒs). *Biochem.* [Gr. βίος life.] The name given by E. Wildiers to the factor or factors stimulating the growth of yeast.

[**1901** E. Wildiers in *Cellule* XVIII. 322 Qu'il nous soit permis d'adopter un nom commode pour désigner cette substance inconnue..nommons-la 'bios'.] **1907** *Chem. Abstr.* 1311 The active principle of the 'Bios' is contained in lecithin. **1919** *Jrnl. Biol. Chem.* XXXVIII. 466 The possibility presented itself that the substance which Wildiers called 'bios' might be the same as the vitamine known to be contained in yeast. **1936**, **1937** [see biotin]. **1953** J. Ramsbottom *Mushrooms & Toadstools* viii. 81 It was found that bios is a complex substance and components bios I, bios II, [etc.]..were recognised; later they were identified with known growth substances.

bioscope ('baɪəskəʊp). [See bio- and -scope.]

†**1.** A view or survey of life. *Obs.*

1812 G. Penn (*title*) The Bioscope, or Dial of Life, explained. **1824** W. Bayley (*title*) Bagman's Bioscope: Various Views of Men and Manners.

2. An earlier form of cinematograph (cf. biograph *sb.* 2); retained in South Africa as the usual term for a cinema or a moving film.

1897 *Wall's Dict. Photogr.* (ed. 7) 75 *Bioscope*. See *Zoetrope*. **1901** *Daily Chron.* 27 Dec. 6/1 The Bioscope views are not so much incidents of the day as exciting adventures. **1904** J. Joyce *Let.* 28 Dec. (1966) II. 75 The other evening we went to a bioscope. There were a series of pictures about betrayed Gretchen. **1925** *Public Opinion* 4 Sept. 234/3 No use to try and blame your poor digestion Nor yet the bioscope's unnerving scene. **1968** D. Braithwaite *Fairground Archit.* 21 In the early 1900's there were 'Bioscope Shows'.

1908 *Cape Times* 14 Jan. 6 The Electro-Chrono ('King of Bioscopes'). A Machine for exhibiting Living Pictures of exceptional brilliance. *Ibid.* 22 Jan 6 The Bioscope will project 'The Boxer Rebellion in China'. **1915** *The Cape* I. no. 10. p. 11 They extended to her facetious invitations to the theatre and the bioscope. **1919** S. G. Millin *Dark River* xxii. §2. 148 The Novelty was one of the Cape Town bioscopes that boasted a small orchestra and occasional variety turns. **1935** *Quandary* Sept. 20 When a bioscope company comes to the village. **1950** L. G. Green *Land of Afternoon* i. 12 He denounced newspapers and bioscopes. **1958** *Observer* 12 Jan. 15/4, I saw the film..on the quivering screen of a Central African bioscope.

Hence **bio'scopic** *a.*

1903 *Athenæum* 12 Dec. 799/1 The utility of the bioscopic camera in zoological work. **1928** *Daily Tel.* 18 Sept. 6 It is excellent to have bioscopic presentations of the eminent, but Herr Ludwig's film is too long.

biose ('baɪəʊs). *Chem.* [f. bi-[2] + -ose[2].] (See quots.)

1892 E. F. Smith tr. *Richter's Org. Chem.* (ed. 2) 507 Only the disaccharides of the hexoses, $C_6H_{12}O_6$, are known. They consist of two molecules of the glucoses or monoses..and therefore are called bioses. **1903** *Jrnl. Chem. Soc.* LXXXIV. i. 713 By the action of alcoholic hydrogen chloride on bioses, hydrolysis occurred and glucosides of the monoses were formed. **1916** A. P. Mathews *Physiol. Chem.* 18 The monosaccharides are in their turn classified by the number of carbon atoms, or more properly by the aldehyde, ketone and alcohol groups they contain into bioses, trioses, tetroses, pentoses, hexoses, heptoses, octoses, nonoses, etc.

biosphere ('baɪəsfɪə(r)). [ad. G. *biosphäre* (E. Suess 1875, *Entstehung d. Alpen* 159), f. bio- + sphere.] The regions of the earth's crust and atmosphere that are occupied by living organisms; occas., the living organisms themselves; also *transf.*

1899 H. R. Mill *Internat. Geogr.* 4 Some geographers even bring in the layer of living matter to complete four parts of the physical globe—the lithosphere, hydrosphere, atmosphere and biosphere. **1909** H. B. C. Sollas tr. *Suess's Face of Earth* IV. 637 It brings with it the idea of a biosphere, which assigns to life a place above the lithosphere. **1931** J. A. Thomson in W. Rose *Outl. Mod. Knowl.* vi. 204 The Biosphere of living organisms, both plants and animals. **1949** W. C. Allee et al. *Princ. Animal Ecol.* xxxv. 729 Life and habitat are integrated into an evolving ecosystem, ultimately incorporating the entire biosphere of the earth. **1957** P. Dansereau *Biogeography* iii. 125 The biosphere is that part of the earth's crust and atmosphere which is favorable to at least some form of life. **1962** F. I. Ordway et al. *Basic Astronautics* vi. 297 A mature civilization..would possibly create an artificial biosphere at a comfortable distance from its star to sustain a greatly expanded population. **1968** *Guardian* 16 Sept. 1/8 The biosphere, i.e. living things and the milieu in which they exist.

biostatic, biotaxy, etc.: see bio- *pref.*

biota (baɪ'əʊtə). *Ecol.* [mod.L.: cf. Gr. βιοτή life.] A collective term for the animal and plant life of a region.

1901 L. Stejneger in *Amer. Naturalist* XXXV. 89 The author, like many other writers..has felt the need of a comprehensive term to include both fauna and flora which will..designate the total of animal and plant life of a given region or period..also any treatise upon the animals and plants of any geographical area... As such a term I would suggest *Biota*. **1939** *Nature* 25 Mar. 504/2 In Natal, the population [of animals and algæ] consists partly of 'Cape' species, but a high percentage of the biota belongs to the great tropical Indo-West-Pacific group, and includes reef corals and many species which characteristically inhabit coral reefs. **1957** *Ibid.* 4 May 892/2 The need for planned observational work on the airborne biota still remains.

ˌbiotech'nology. [bio-.] **1.** The branch of technology concerned with the development and exploitation of machines in relation to the various needs of human beings.

1947 *Science* CV. 217/2 Hours of work, on-the-job feeding, rest periods, etc. are also phases of the physiology of work which form an important part of a comprehensive biotechnology. **1969** *Sci. Jrnl.* June 50/1 Biotechnology is just as concerned with the provision of tools for medical research as with the development of equipment for medical service.

2. The branch of technology concerned with modern forms of industrial production utilizing living organisms, esp. micro-organisms, and their biological processes.

1972 (*title of periodical*) Biotechnology and bioengineering symposium. **1975** A. Wiseman (*title*) Handbook of enzyme biotechnology. **1982** *Times* 11 May 17/2 Biotechnology appeared to have staked out half a dozen major industries, each of which would be transformed by new manufacturing processes based on cell culture, genetic engineering, or the catalysing powers of enzymes. **1982** *Economist* 20 Mar. 68/1 More than 200 new biotechnology firms in Europe and America are losing money and are unable to bring new wonder-drugs to the market. *Ibid.*, Insulin is one of the few products which could soon be made commercially by using the latest in biotechnology. **1983** *Times* 9 June 22/6 Conventional brewing and wine making are not usually regarded as biotechnology but many other fermentation processes are. **1985** I. J. Higgins in I. J. Higgins et al. *Biotechnol.* i. 2 It is..the discovery of genetic engineering techniques via recombinant DNA technology..which is responsible for the current 'biotechnology boom'.

Hence **ˌbiotechno'logical** *a.*

1947 *Science* CV. 218/2 Biotechnological functions either are being performed by inadequately or narrowly trained individuals or are neglected entirely.

bi'otic, *a.* [ad. L. *biōtic-us*, a. Gr. βιωτικός pertaining to life, f. βίος life.]

†**1.** Of or pertaining to (common) life, secular. *Obs. rare.*

1600 J. Melvill *Diary* (1842) 331 The quhilk to serve for all those biotik matters, I thought weil to be heir insert.

2. Of animal life; vital. So **bi'otical**. Also, pertaining to, produced, or influenced by living organisms, esp. in their ecological relations.

1847 Carpenter in Todd *Cycl. Anat. & Phys.* III. 151 Organization and biotical functions arise from the natural operations of forces inherent in elemental matter. **1868** Martin *Keil's Min. Proph.* I. 408 The idea that there is a biotic *rapport* between man and the larger domestic animals. **1882** *Pop. Sc. Monthly* XXII. 168 The phenomena of irritability, assimilation, growth, and reproduction, which we may comprehensively designate as biotical. **1907** F. E. Clements *Plant Physiol. & Ecol.* i. 5 Cases of abnormal response are due to biotic factors, particularly parasitic fungi and insects. **1923** A. G. Tansley *Pract. Plant Ecol.* iv. 48 Man is constantly stopping or modifying the development... Where he has introduced a more or less permanent modifying factor or set of factors, we have biotic (anthropogenic) climaxes. **1949** *New Biol.* VI. 54 British grasslands represent neither a climatic nor an edaphic climax, but are a *biotic climax*. They are maintained as grassland *per se* under the influence exerted upon them by the biota, i.e. by living organisms, in particular by man and his domestic animals.

biotin ('baɪətɪn). *Biochem.* [a. G. *biotin* (F. Kögl & B. Tönnis 1936, in *Zeitschr. physiol. Chem.* CCXLII. 50), f. Gr. βιότος (βίος) life (see bios) + -in[1].] A crystalline growth vitamin, $C_{10}H_{16}O_3N_2S$, occurring esp. in yeast and egg-yolk, that is inactivated by combination with avidin; vitamin H.

1936 *Chem. Abstr.* XXX. 7624 (*heading*) The bios problem. Isolation of crystalline biotin from egg yolk. **1937** *Nature* 24 July 161/1 'Biotin', a sulphur-containing substance of great potency which may be the chief component of 'bios', originally described by Wildiers as a necessary growth factor for yeast. Biotin has also been shown to have an effect on the growth of higher plants. **1944** *Lancet* 24 June 826/2 The egg-white injury demonstrated in rats is not a direct toxic effect but the result of biotin deficiency.

biotite ('baɪətaɪt). *Min.* [after *Biot*, a French mineralogist.] Hexagonal or magnesia mica.

1862 Ansted *Channel Isl.* ii. x. (ed. 2) 259 *note*, The ordinary varieties of mica (not biotite). **1878** Lawrence *Cotta's Rocks Class.* 21 The geological area of biotite.

biotope ('baɪətəʊp). *Ecol.* Also biotop. [ad. G. *biotop*, f. Gr. τόπος place.] The smallest subdivision of a habitat, characterized by a high

degree of uniformity in its environmental conditions and in its plant and animal life.
1927 *Biol. Abstr.* 593/1 A true association is the population of a biotop. Distinction is made between biotop and habitat. **1936** *Proc. Prehist. Soc.* II. 64 Taken as a whole this assemblage suggests a tundra biotope. **1937** ALLEE & SCHMIDT tr. *Hesse's Ecol. Animal Geogr.* ix. 135 The primary topographic unit is the 'niche' or 'biotope'. Such a unit is an area of which the principal habitat conditions and the living forms which are adapted to them are uniform. **1937** [see BIOCHORE]. **1962** H. HANSON *Dict. Ecol.* 55 *Biotope*, the smallest geographic unit of a habitat..e.g., a decaying stump, a sandy beach.

biotype ('baɪətaɪp). *Biol.* [f. BIO- + TYPE *sb.*[1]] A group of organisms having a common genotype. Hence ˌ**bioty'pology** [-OLOGY], the study of biotypes.
1906 W. JOHANNSEN in *Rep. Third Internat. Conference Genetics* 98 It remains quite uncertain whether the numbers ..contain a multitude, or a few, or only one single 'sort' of organism—'biotypes' as I have called them. *Ibid.* 111 To elucidate the origin and conduct of the veritable types of organism, the 'biotypes'. **1937** *Nature* 11 Sept. 471/2 One section of the International Congress was devoted to matters coming under such heads as biometry, biotypology and heredity. **1955** *New Biol.* XVIII. 114 Evidently the East Anglian colony [of *Nymphæa alba*] contains a far greater range of biotypes than this particular Irish one. **1957** *Encycl. Brit.* XXI. 177/2 *Biotype*..is used for a population of individuals with identical genotypical constitution under similar conditions... Parallel mutation may possibly account for some biotypes.

biouac, biovac, obs. forms of BIVOUAC.

bioue, obs. form of BEHOVE.

'**bi-pack.** [BI-[2].] In colour photography, a pack of two sensitive plates or films used to obtain colour separation.
1924 *Brit. Jrnl. Photogr.* Suppl., Sept. 35/2 The staining of the front member of a bi-pack with aniline orange. **1935** *Discovery* July 192/1 Using two films in the form known as 'bi-pack'.

bipalmate (baɪ'pælmeɪt), *a. Bot.* [f. BI- *pref.*[2] 3 + PALMATE, f. L. *palma* palm (of the hand).] Doubly or subordinately palmate: applied to compound leaves having a palmate arrangement on secondary petioles which are themselves palmately arranged on the primary petiole.
1864 in WEBSTER. **1878** MASTERS *Henfrey's Bot.* 63 Bi- or tripalmate leaves are very rare (*Araliaceæ*).

bipa'rental, *a.* [BI-[2].] Of, pertaining to, or derived from, two parents.
1900 K. PEARSON *Gram. Sci.* (ed. 2) 469 These are the questions of bi-parental heredity. *Ibid.* 473 The variability of the individual makes itself felt not only in bi-parental reproduction but in autogamic and parthenogenetic reproduction. **1903** *Biometrika* Nov. 396 The existence of this assortative mating most substantially modifies the form of biparental inheritance. **1929** B. RUSSELL *Marriage & Morals* xvi. 187 Easy divorce..must be regarded as a transitional stage on the way from the bi-parental to the purely maternal family. **1955** *New Biol.* XIX. 7 Biparental reproduction is the main cause of variation in most species.

biparietal (ˌbaɪpə'raɪɪtəl), *a.* [f. BI- *pref.*[2] 5 + PARIETAL, f. L. *pariet-em* wall.] Joining the two parietal bones of the skull.
1857 [see BITEMPORAL]. **1859** TODD *Cycl. Anat. & Phys.* V. 183/1 The bi-parietal diameter of the fœtal head.

biparous ('bɪpərəs), *a.* [f. BI- *pref.*[2] 2 + L. *-parus* producing (*parĕre* to produce) + -OUS.] Producing two at once (in time or place).
1731 in BAILEY II. **1880** GRAY *Bot. Text-bk.* 399 Biparous, as a cyme of two rays or axes.

†**bipar'tation,** *Obs.* f. BIPARTITION.

biparted (baɪ'pɑːtɪd), *a.* [f. BI- *pref.*[2] 1 or 6 + PART, -ED; cf. following words.] = BIPARTITE.
1586 J. HOOKER *Girald. Irel.* in *Holinshed* II. 5/2 His armes and ensigne..were biparted, being of two sundrie changes. **1586** WARNER *Alb. Eng.* IV. xx. (1597) 93 Our byparted crowne, of which the Moyetie is mine. **1725** BRADLEY *Fam. Dict.* s.v. *Umbone*, An *Umbone* which they call double-pointed, or biparted, as in the Peony.

bipartible (baɪ'pɑːtɪb(ə)l), *a.* [f. L. *bipartīre* after L. *partībilis*.] Divisible into two parts.
1847 in CRAIG. **1880** in GRAY *Bot. Text-bk.* 399.

bipartient (baɪ'pɑːtɪənt), *a.* and *sb.* [ad. L. *bipartient-em*, pr. pple. of *bipartīre* to divide into two parts, bisect, f. *bi-* two + *partīre* to divide.]
A. *adj.* That divides into two parts.
1678 in PHILLIPS. **1857** FALCONER in *Q. Jrnl. Geol. Soc.* 318 The longitudinal, mesial, bipartient cleft.
B. *sb.* A number which divides another into two equal parts, without leaving any remainder.
1819 REES *Cycl.* s.v., Thus 2 is a bipartient to 4.

bipartile (baɪ'pɑːtaɪl), *a.* [f. L. *bipartīre* (see prec.), after L. *partīlis*.] = BIPARTIBLE.
1847 in CRAIG.

biˌparti'san, *a.* [BI-[2].] Of, representing, or composed of members of, two (political or other) parties.
1909 in WEBSTER. **1920** *Glasgow Herald* 13 Feb. 10 The 14 Republican reservations, as modified by the Bipartisan Conference. **1947** *Times* 13 Dec. 5/2 That rare thing in American public life a bi-partisan policy. **1959** *Ann. Reg. 1958* 32 Mr. Gaitskell..showed a determination to cling as long as possible to a bipartisan foreign policy.
Hence **bipartisanship.**
1950 *Congressional Dig.* Feb. 36 Bipartisanship in the balance. **1952** *Oxf. Mag.* 27 Nov. 108/1 This House sees no sufficient cause to abandon bipartisanship in British foreign policy.

bipartite (baɪ'pɑːtaɪt), *a.* Also 6 bipertite, **bypartite.** [ad. L. *bipartītus*, pa. pple. of *bipartīre*; see BIPARTIENT.]
1. a. Divided into or consisting of two parts.
1574 NEWTON *Health Mag.* Pref. 1 Such indications [are] bipartite and devided into two partes, that is to witte Conservation, and Preservation. **1602** FULBECKE *Pandectes* 3 A bipartite diuision of the yeare into winter and sommer. **1635** SWAN *Spec. M.* viii. §2 (1643) 386 A bipartite hoof. **1836** TODD *Cycl. Anat.* I. 307/2 A corresponding gland..of large size and bipartite.
b. Divided between or shared by two.
1618 BOLTON *Florus* I. ix. 22 The authoritie..should bee now but from yeere to yeere and bipartite. **1658** W. BURTON *Itin. Anton.* 65 This bipartite, or joint-power.
c. *Bot.* Divided into two parts nearly to the base.
1864 in WEBSTER. **1872** OLIVER *Elem. Bot.* II. 162 Observe also the..bipartite calyx of Common Furze.
d. *Math.* Of a curve (see quot. 1879).
1858 CAYLEY *Math. Papers* (1889) II. 527 Bipartite binary quantics. **1869** *Ibid.* (1893) VI. 464 The quantic is unipartite, bipartite, tripartite, &c., according as the number of sets is one, two, three, &c. **1879** G. SALMON *Higher Plane Curves* (ed. 3) 168 We shall then call the curve we have been considering a bipartite curve, as consisting of two distinct continuous series of points.
2. in *Law*, of a contract, indenture, etc.: Drawn up in two corresponding parts, one for each party.
1506 *Bury Wills* (1850) 106 My present testament and last will bipertite. **1592** WEST *Symbol.* I. §47 These deedes indented are not only bypartite..but may be tripartite.

bi'partitely, *adv.* [f. prec. + -LY[2].] In a bipartite manner; in or into two parts.
1656 DU GARD *Gate Lat. Unl.* §584 A Man is divided bipartitely into Soul and Body.

bipartition (baɪpɑː'tɪʃən). [n. of action f. *bipartīre*: see prec. and -TION.] Division into two parts; (viewed either as action or result).
1652 SPARKE *Prim. Devot.* (1663) 321 These imitating fire ..may easily be conceived to spread into a bipartation. **1684** T. BURNET *Th. Earth* II. ix. 284 The form, qualities, and bipartition of the Primæval Earth. **1789** BENTHAM *Princ.* xvi. §1 n. on p. cci, This can only be done in the way of bipartition, dividing each superior branch into two. **1865** W. PALGRAVE *Arabia* I. 352 The fact of the great bipartition of the Arab race is certain.

'**bi-ˌparty.** Used *attrib.* = consisting of, or representing, two (political or other) parties.
1898 *Westm. Gaz.* 17 Feb. 3/1 British institutions presuppose the British character, with..its faithful adherence to the bi-party system. **1900** *Ibid.* 2 July 3/1 Philosophers cling with the same pathetic insistence as members of Parliament to their traditional bi-party system. **1926** *Contemp. Rev.* Apr. 454 The bi-party system [in Canada].

bipaschal (baɪ'pɑːskəl, -æ-), *a. Theol.* [f. BI-[2] + PASCHAL *a.*] Including two consecutive passover feasts: applied to the view that limits Christ's public ministry to a little over one year.
1883 SCHAFF *Hist. Ch., Apostol. Chr.* I. 131 The bipaschal scheme confines the public ministry to one year and a few weeks or months. **1893** BROADUS *Harm. Gospels* 243 The Bi-paschal theory makes the time of the public life of Jesus one year, allowing only two Passovers to the Gospel of John. **1908** J. HASTINGS *Dict. Christ* II. 185/1 Between these two Passovers lay the whole ministry, hence this theory is called the *bipaschal* view.

†**bipatent,** *a. Obs.* [ad. L. *bipatēnt-em*, f. *bi-* twice, in two ways + *patēnt-em* lying open.] 'Open on both sides.' Blount *Glossogr.* 1656.

†**bi'peche,** *v. Obs.* Forms: 1 bepǽcan, 2–3 bipeche(n. *Pa. t.* 2–3 **bipehte.** *Pa. pple.* 1 **bepǽht,** 2–3 **be-, bipaht, -pauht,** 3 **bipeiȝte.** [OE. *bepǽcan*, f. *bi-*, BE- + *pǽcan* to deceive.]
trans. To cheat, deceive, delude.
c **1000** *Ags. Gosp.* Matt. ii. 16 For þam þe he bepæht wæs fram þam tungel-witeȝum. **1154** *O.E. Chron.* (Laud MS.) an. 1132 Te king was welneh bepaht. *c* **1200** *Trin. Coll. Hom.* 213 In chepinge man bipecheð oðer. *a* **1300** *Fragm. Sev. Sins* in *E.E.P.* (1862) 19 þer is mani man bipeiȝte.
Hence †**bi'peching** *vbl. sb.*, deception, fraud.
c **1200** *Trin. Coll. Hom.* 213 þe grune of hindre. þat is of bipeching.

bipectinate, -ated (baɪ'pɛktɪneɪt, -eɪtɪd), *a.* [f. BI- *pref.*[2] 1 + PECTINATE, f. L. *pecten, pectin-em* comb.] Having two margins toothed like a comb.
1836–9 TODD *Cycl. Anat. & Phys.* II. 892 The bipectinated antennæ of many moths. **1870** ROLLESTON *Anim. Life* 40 The four bipectinate gills.

biped ('baɪpɛd), *sb.* and *a.* [ad. L. *biped-em*, f. *bi-* two + *pedem* (nom. *pēs*) foot; cf. F. *bipède*.]
A. *sb.* A two-footed animal.
1646 SIR T. BROWNE *Pseud. Ep.* III. iv. 114 Neither biped nor quadruped oviparous have any [stones] exteriorly. **1699** TYSON *Orang-Out.* 91 Our Pygmie is..tho' a Biped, yet of the Quadrumanus-kind. **1824** MISS MITFORD *Village* Ser. I. (1863) 39 Those fastidious bipeds, men and women.
B. *adj.* Having two feet; two-footed.
1793 SOUTHEY *Nondesc.* i. Wks. III. 59 His drivers goad the biped beast. **1849–52** TODD *Cycl. Anat. & Phys.* IV. 1297/1 The purely biped progression of Man.

bipedal ('baɪpɪdəl), *a.* [ad. L. *bipedālem* two feet long, f. *bi-* two + *pedem* (*pēs*) foot. The modern senses are derived from prec. sb.]
†**1.** Two feet long. *Obs. rare.*
c **1420** *Pallad. on Husb.* VI. 185 Brik bipedal chaneled bryng on lofte.
2. Having two feet, two-footed, biped; *spec.* designating a reptile that uses its two hind feet for walking or running; also denoting this method of movement. Hence **bi'pedalism;** **bi'pedally** *adv.*
1607 TOPSELL *Four-f. Beasts* 425 Three kindes of Mice, of the which some are called Bipedal or two-footed. **1760** *Life of Cat* 106 His bipedal fellow-creatures. **1854** *Fraser's Mag.* Sept. 273/2 Clergymen may still be found..in an easy association with their flocks, quadrupedal and bipedal. **1870** T. H. HUXLEY in *Q. Jrnl. Geol. Soc.* XXVI. p. xlviii, These Bird-reptiles or Reptile-birds were more or less completely bipedal. **1896** *Nature* 27 Feb. 397/1 The absurdly grotesque appearances these lizards presented when progressing in this bipedal fashion. **1898** *Ibid.* 10 Feb. 341/1 The Mexican Iguanoid Lizard..also runs bipedally. *Ibid.* 341/2 Several varieties of these bipedal lizards are now on view in the Reptile House. **1907** *Proc. Zool. Soc.* Feb. 231 The most primitive Dinosaurs are bipedal in their habits. *Ibid.* 234 A bipedal animal never could or did develop a patagium without giving up bipedalism. **1908** *Westm. Gaz.* 17 Oct. 5/1 Having once lost the prize in the overture With his bipedal rival. **1969** *Times* 6 Feb. 10/8 Palaeo-anthropologists still do not know what factors influenced the adoption of bipedalism.
3. Of, pertaining to, or caused by a biped.
1833 LYELL *Elem. Geol.* xxi. (1874) 371 The bipedal impressions are for the most part trifid. **1872** NICHOLSON *Palæont.* 467 Man is distinguished..by his..bipedal progression.

bipedality (baɪpɪ'dælɪtɪ). [f. prec. + -ITY.] The quality of being two-footed.
1847 LEWES *Hist. Philos.* (1853) 301 Rationality, morality, bipedality, and all the other substantial attributes. **1882** *Academy* 15 July 41/2 Personality no more 'involves' mortality..than it involves bipedality.

†**bipe'daneous,** *a. Obs.*[−0] [f. L. *bipedāneus*.] = BIPEDAL. Blount *Glossogr.* 1656.

†**bi'pedical(l,** *a. Obs.*[−0] 'Two foot long.' Cockeram 1623.

bipeltate (baɪ'pɛlteɪt), *a.* [f. BI- *pref.*[2] 1 + PELTATE, ad. L. *peltātus*; f. L. *pelta*, a. Gr. πέλτη shield.] Having a defence like a double shield.
1846 in BRANDE.

bipennate, -ated (baɪ'pɛneɪt, -eɪtɪd), *a.* [f. BI- *pref.*[2] 1 + PENNATE, ad. L. *pennātus*, f. *penna* feather, wing.] Two-winged.
1713 DERHAM *Phys. Theol.* VIII. iv. *note*, All bipennated Insects have Poyses joyn'd to the body.

bipenniform (baɪ'pɛnɪfɔːm), *a.* [f. BI- *pref.* 1 + PENNIFORM.] Feather-shaped on both sides.
1842 E. WILSON *Anat. Vade M.* 136 Or bipenniform, converging to both sides of the tendon.

bi'personal, *a.* Of the godhead: existing in two persons; also, relating to this system of belief, binitarian.
1928 K. E. KIRK in A. E. J. Rawlinson *Ess. Trin. & Incarn.* 162 'Bipersonal', 'ditheistic', or 'dyarchian' are occasionally employed also as synonyms [of binitarian]. *Ibid.* 196 The cosmogony of *Poimandres* is fantastically pluralist..; its religion is strictly bipersonal.

bipertite, obs. f. BIPARTITE; cf. L. *bipertīre*.

bipetalous: see BI- *pref.*[2] 1.

bi'phasic, *a.* [BI-[2].] Having two phases.
1909 in *Cent. Dict.* Suppl. **1956** *Nature* 3 Mar. 431/2 Fluoride changed only the slope, but not the linearity, except for sodium, which developed a biphasic curve. **1961** *Lancet* 23 Sept. 684/2 Case 5 showed a biphasic neurological illness. **1964** M. HYNES *Med. Bacteriol.* (ed. 8) xxv. 395 When disease does appear, it is biphasic, a viræmia with influenza-like symptoms subsiding to be followed by signs of CNS involvement.

†**bi'phyllous,** *a. Obs. rare*[−1]. [f. BI- *pref.*[2] 1 + Gr. φύλλ-ον leaf + -OUS.] Two-leaved, bifoliate.
1756 P. BROWNE *Jamaica* 153 A very small exterior biphyllous cup.

†**bi'pil(en,** *v. Obs.* [f. BE- 3 + ME. *pilen* to PEEL.] *trans.* To deprive of the peel or bark. Hence **bi'piliung** *vbl. sb.*, peeling.
a **1225** *Ancr. R.* 148 Heo haueð bipiled mine figer. *Ibid.* 150 Vor þe uormeste bipiliunge..nis buten of prude.

bipinnate (baɪ'pɪneɪt), *a.* [ad. mod.L. *bipinnātus*: see BI- *pref.*[2] 3 and PINNATE, f. *pinna* wing.]
1. Doubly or subordinately pinnate; see quot.

1794 MARTYN *Rousseau's Bot.* xxi. 301 The leaves are doubly winged or bipinnate. **1872** OLIVER *Elem. Bot.* I. vii. 77 A leaf becomes twice pinnate (bi-pinnate) when the common petiole, instead of bearing leaflets, bears secondary petioles upon which the leaflets are pinnately arranged.

2. *Zool.* Having feathery appendages in opposed pairs.

1856-8 W. CLARK *Van der Hoeven's Zool.* II. 63 Tail.. without spur, bipinnate above. **1868** WRIGHT *Ocean World* vi. 142 Pennatula.. with polypes on bipinnate wings.

bi'pinnated, *a.* [f. as prec. + -ED.] = prec. 1.

1842 RICHARDSON *Geol.* (1856) 182 Leaves bipinnated.

bipinnatifid (baɪpɪ'nætɪfɪd), *a. Bot.* [f. BI- *pref.*² 3 + PINNATIFID.] Of leaves: Pinnatifid, with the primary lobes or pinnæ themselves similarly divided. So **bipinnati'parted, -'partite, bipi'nnatisect, -'sected.**

1830 LINDLEY *Nat. Syst. Bot.* 83 Leaves.. sinuate-pinnatifid, or bipinnatifid. **1870** BENTLEY *Bot.* 153 If the divisions are themselves divided in a similar manner to the lamina itself, the leaf is said to be bipinnatifid, bipinnatipartite, or bipinnatisected.

biplanar (baɪ'pleɪnə(r)), *a.* (and *sb.*) *Math.* [f. next + -AR¹: cf. *planar*.] Lying or situated in two tangent planes. Also *sb.*, a biplanar node.

1849 G. SALMON in *Cambr. & Dublin Math. Jrnl.* IV. 257 The two tangent planes at the biplanar point. *Ibid.*, One [plane] through both conical points (1 × 4), one through the biplanar alone (3). **1927** H. P. HUDSON *Cremona Transformations* xii. 238 With a d[ouble] p[oint], the parts are both planes, and the singularity is called a binode or biplanar point.

biplane ('baɪpleɪn). [f. BI-² + PLANE *sb.*³]

1. *Math.* Each of the pair of planes tangential to a surface at a binode.

1870 CAYLEY in *Phil. Trans. R. Soc.* CLIX. 206 The binode.. is a biplanar node, where instead of the proper quadricone we have two planes; these may be called the biplanes, and their line of intersection, the edge of the binode. The biplanes form a plane-pair. **1905** W. H. BLYTHE *Models Cubic Surfaces* p. xii, When the biplanes coincide the node is said to be uniplanar.

2. An aeroplane having two 'planes' or main supporting surfaces, one above the other.

1874 D. S. BROWN in *Ann. Rep. Aeronaut. Soc.* 14 The bi-plane when elevated will proceed for a considerable distance. **1908** *Westm. Gaz.* 14 Aug. 10/2 Mr. Wilbur Wright is busy experimenting with his greatly successful bi-plane. **1910** R. FERRIS *How it Flies* 12 In March [1908], Delagrange flew in a Voisin biplane 453 feet. **1911** GRAHAME-WHITE & HARPER *Aeroplane* 17 He [*sc.* Lilienthal] abandoned the monoplane type of glider in favour of a biplane. *Ibid.* 18 One of Chanute's biplane gliders was fitted with a stern rudder. **1957** P. KEMP *Mine were of Trouble* iv. 70 A formation of Fiat CR 42 bi-planes.

biplate ('baɪpleɪt). *Optics.* [BI-².] A combination of two glass plates used in polariscopic observations.

1890 T. PRESTON *Th. Light* 121 Bi-plates.—A beam of light may be subdivided by refraction through two plates, of the same nature and equal thickness, placed at an angle. **1904** A. SCHUSTER *Th. Optics* iv. 80 The 'bi-plate'.. serves either to separate or to bring together two parallel beams of light. It consists of two plane parallel plates of glass cemented together at an angle.

biplicate ('bɪp-, 'baɪplɪkeɪt), *a.* [f. BI- *pref.*² 2 + *-plicate*, ad. L. *plicātus* folded.] Twice folded.

1861 in HENSLOW.

biplicity (baɪ'plɪsɪtɪ). [f. BI- *pref.*² II; cf. *duplicity*.] Twofold state or quality.

1731 in BAILEY II; whence in mod. Dicts.

bipod ('baɪpɒd). [f. BI-² + *-pod*, after TRIPOD.] A two-legged support or structure, esp. one for a light machine-gun. Also *attrib.*

1938 *Jrnl. R. Aeronaut. Soc.* XLII. 868 Later I introduced a gaff mainsail.. and still later (1930) I rigged a bipod mast. **1940** *War Illustr.* 2 Feb. 41 It [*sc.* the Bren gun] may be mounted either on a tripod or a bipod, or fired direct from the shoulder. **1950** *Archit. Rev.* CVII. 262/2 The first floor consists of a series of boxes suspended from steel bipods, and connected by corridors in the form of enclosed bridges.

bipolar (baɪ'pəʊlə(r)), *a.* [f. BI- *pref.*² 1 + POLAR.] **a.** Having two poles or opposite extremities; in *Phys.* applied to nerve-cells connected with the nerve-fibres by two prolongations.

1859 TODD *Cycl. Anat. & Phys.* V. 282/1 The vaso-ganglions of the eel.. are bipolar. **1865** MANSFIELD *Salts* 4 This bipolar, two-membered system. *fig.* **1810** COLERIDGE *Friend* ix. (ed. 3) III. 171 Philosophy being necessarily bipolar. **1875** E. WHITE *Life in Christ* III. xix. (1878) 254 The Divine Nature is revealed as bi-polar, or of double aspect.

b. Of, pertaining to, or occurring in both polar regions.

1896 A. E. ORTMANN in *Proc. Acad. Nat. Sci. Philad. 1895* 191 The examples of bipolar distribution of crustacea. **1951** *Jrnl. Ecol.* XXXIX. 209 The term 'bipolar' is not precise. What is intended is taxa with widely discontinuous ranges to the north and to the south of the tropics.

bipolarity (baɪpəʊ'lærɪtɪ). [f. prec. + -ITY.]

1. Bipolar quality or state. Also *transf.* and *fig.*

1865 MANSFIELD *Salts* 63 The voltaic bipolarity of each. **1917** C. R. PAYNE tr. *Pfister's Psychoanal. Method* I. xii. 361 As a result of the 'bipolarity of all psychic phenomena', each of the two possible interpretations.. may be correct. **1955** M. BELOFF *Foreign Policy* 9 We have been taught to view things in the light of the rivalry between two powers and two powers only.. 'bipolarity', as it is called.

2. The occurrence of the same species in each of the polar regions but not in the intervening zones (see also quot. 1959).

1896 A. E. ORTMANN in *Proc. Acad. Nat. Sci. Philad. 1895* 191 Neither in this species is.. a bipolarity of the genus probable. **1959** *New Biol.* XXIX. 117 Bipolarity.. has undergone some change of meaning... In a very short period of time, the sharpness of its meaning was lost and bipolarity came to include those cases where organisms occurred in the north and south temperate zones but were absent from the tropics. The term underwent still further changes and was used to cover not only species, but genera and even higher classification categories provided they had a discontinuous distribution with northern and southern forms.

'bipont, bi'pontine, *a.* [ad. L. *Bipontīnus*, f. *Bipontium*.] Of editions of the classics, etc.: Printed at Zweibrücken (Deuxponts, *Bipontium*) in Bavaria, in the latter half of the 18th c.

biporose: see BI- *pref.*² 1, 2.

bipp (bɪp). *Med.* Also bip, B.I.P.P. [f. the initials of *B*ismuth *I*odoform *P*araffin *P*aste.] A paste containing bismuth subnitrate, iodoform, and (sometimes) paraffin, used as a dressing for wounds. Also *attrib.* Hence as *v. trans.*, to treat or cover with bipp.

1916 R. MORISON in *Lancet* 12 Aug. 268 The paste: Bismuth subnitrate, 1 oz. by weight; iodoform, 2 oz. by weight; paraffin liq. q.s. to make thick paste. I suggest for this the name 'Bipp'. **1917** *Lancet* 10 Mar. 378/1 Excellent results with 'Bipp' in compound comminuted fractures. *Ibid.*, I 'Bipped' the sloughing surface and renewed the 'Bipp' every ten days. **1933** *Ibid.* 4 Feb. 250/1 The wound was swabbed with ether and smeared with B.I.P.P., the surplus being removed on a dry gauze swab. **1939** *Times* 11 Jan. 12/3 The 'Bip' treatment of wounds.

†bi'prene, -preone, *v. Obs.* [ME., f. *bi-* BE- pref. 2 + *preon-en* to PREEN.] To pin, or nail fast, to fasten down.

c **1275** *Signs Death* 10 in O.E. Misc. (1872) 101 Leyþ be on bére . And bi-preoneþ þe on here . And doþ þe ine putte.

'biprism. [BI-².] A glass prism with a refracting angle of nearly 180 degrees, used in observing the interference of light.

1884 A. DANIELL *Princ. Physics* 486 Such a beam may be divided in two parts.. by refraction through a biprism. **1890** T. PRESTON *Th. Light* 119 Fresnel's Bi-prism... Let CDE represent a glass prism with a very obtuse angle E... The whole prism is as if made up of two prisms CE and DE of very small angle (at C and D) placed base to base at E, and hence the name bi-prism. **1904** A. SCHUSTER *Th. Optics* iv. 60 (*heading*) Fresnel's Biprism.

bipunctate (baɪ'pʌŋkteɪt), *a.* [ad. mod.L. *bipunctātus*, f. *bi-* twice + *punctātus* pointed.] Having or marked by two punctures or points.

1864 in WEBSTER.

bipunctual (baɪ'pʌŋktjuːəl), *a.* [f. BI- *pref.*² 1 + PUNCTUAL, f. as in prec.] **1.** = prec.

1731 in BAILEY; whence in mod. Dicts.

2. *Math.* Having certain specified properties in relation to two points.

1878 *Amer. Jrnl. Math.* I. 152 As long as the direction of reference remains fixed, the only change that can be made in a system of bipunctual coordinates is an alteration in the position of the initials. **1922** H. F. BAKER *Princ. Geom.* II. iii. 123 To speak of the latter conic as being bipunctual.

bipupillate, -pyramidal: see BI- pref.² 1.

biquadrate (baɪ'kwɒdreɪt), *a.* and *sb. Math.* [f. BI- *pref.*² + QUADRATE, ad. L. *quadrātus* squared.] The square of the square (power or root); the fourth power in arithmetic and algebra; = BIQUADRATIC.

1706 PHILLIPS, *Biquadrate*,..the fourth Power in Arithmetic and Algebra. **1806** HUTTON *Course Math.* I. 171 Its.. cube (a^3), or biquadrate (a^4). *Ibid.* I. 203 The biquadrate root of $16a^4 - 96a^3x + 216a^2x^2 - 216ax^3 + 81x^4$.

bi'quadrate, *v. Math.* [f. prec.] *trans.* To raise (a number) to its fourth power.

1694 *Phil. Trans.* XVIII. 70 Performed by squaring, cubing, biquadrating, etc. of the terms.

biquadratic (baɪkwə'drætɪk), *a.* and *sb. Math.* [f. BI- *pref.*² + QUADRATIC: see prec.]

A. *adj.* Pertaining to the square of a square, or fourth power, of a number.

biquadratic equation: an equation in which the unknown quantity is raised to the fourth power. ***biquadratic parabola***: a curve of the third order, having two infinite legs tending the same way. ***biquadratic root***: the square root of the square root (of a number).

1668 PELL in Rigaud *Corr. Sci. Men* I. 132 The Latin paper concerning biquadratic equations. **1694** *Phil. Trans.* XVIII. 70 By extracting.. the Cubick, Biquadratick Roots, etc. of the Terms. **1804** YOUNG in *Phil. Trans.* XCV. 74 Determined by the solution of a biquadratic equation.

B. *sb.* **a.** The fourth power of a number. **b.** A biquadratic equation.

1661 PELL in Rigaud *Corr. Sci. Men* I. 132 This biquadratic hath not four possible roots. **1727** CHAMBERS *Cycl.*, *Biquadratick*, the next Power above the Cube. **1798** WOOD in *Phil. Trans.* LXXXVIII. 369 In cubics and biquadratics, the imaginary roots were found to be of this form, $a + \sqrt{-b^2}$. **1838** HALLAM *Hist. Lit.* I. I. ix. §5 The method of solving biquadratics.

biquarterly: see BI- *pref.*² 4.

biquartz ('baɪkwɔːts). *Optics.* [BI-².] A double quartz plate used for detecting polarization.

1878 LOCKYER *Stargazing* 452 There is also another instrument for detecting polarization which is perhaps more commonly used than the biquartz. **1884** A. DANIELL *Princ. Physics* 510 A double-quartz plate, or Biquartz. **1890** T. PRESTON *Th. Light* 373 The biquartz.. consists of two semicircular plates of quartz placed in juxtaposition. **1911** *Encycl. Brit.* XXI. 938/1 The chief features of Soleil's saccharimeter are the biquartz and the compensator.

biquaternion (baɪkwɒ'tɜːnɪən). *Math.* [BI-².] **1.** A quaternion with complex coefficients.

1852 *Rep. Brit. Assoc.* (1853) Notices & Abstracts 2 On Biquaternions. By Sir William R. Hamilton. **1853** W. R. HAMILTON *Lect. Quatern.* p. lxviii, A biquaternion may be considered generally as the sum of a biscalar and a bivector. **1905** C. J. JOLY *Man. Quaternions* ii. 21 The tensor of a biquaternion may vanish.

2. (See quots.)

1873 W. K. CLIFFORD in *Proc. London Math. Soc.* IV. 386 In this way the ratio $\frac{\gamma+\omega\delta}{\alpha+\omega\beta}$ is expressed in the form $q + \omega r$, which expression may conveniently be called a biquaternion. **1876** —— *Math. Papers* (1882) 394 The ratio of two motors is a quantity of the form.. $s + \omega t$ (if $2s = p + q$, $t = 2p - q$), where p, q, s, t are quaternions. This combination of two quaternions I have called a Biquaternion. **1910** *Encycl. Brit.* I. 614/2 Clifford's biquaternions are quantities $\xi q + \eta r$, where q, r are quaternions, and ξ, η are symbols (commutative with quaternions) obeying the laws $\xi^2 = \xi$, $\eta^2 = \eta$, $\xi\eta = \eta\xi = 0$.

biqueste, biquethe: see BEQ-.

bi'quinary, *a.* [BI-².] Designating a type of code for use in computers or the like (see quot. 1962).

1946 O. CESAREO in *Bell Lab. Rec.* XXIV. 457/2 In bi-quinary notation, a digit is always represented by two numbers: a quinary part consisting of one of the digits 0 to 4 inclusive, and a binary part consisting of either 0 or 5. **1949** D. R. HARTREE *Calculating Instrum.* vii. 80 The machines work in a scale of ten, with number [*sic*] expressed in the so-called 'bi-quinary' system of coding decimal digits. **1962** *Gloss. Terms Autom. Data Processing (B.S.I.)* 21 *Biquinary code*, a code in which a decimal numeral n is represented by the pair of numbers a and b where: $n = 5a + b$ in which $a = 0$ or 1 and $b = 0, 1, 2, 3$ or 4.

biquintile (baɪ'kwɪntaɪl, -ɪl). *Astrol.* [f. BI- *pref.*² + QUINTILE.] An aspect of the planets, when they are distant from each other twice the fifth part of a great circle, i.e. 144 degrees.

1647 LILLY *Chr. Astrol.* iii. 32 Kepler.. hath added some new ones [aspects], as follow.. A Biquintill *B q* consisting of 144 degrees. **1686** GOAD *Celest. Bodies* I. ii. 39 The Biquintile will look for some Respect. **1727** in CHAMBERS *Cycl.*; and in mod. Dicts.

biquour, obs. form of BICKER *sb.*¹

†bir, *v. Obs. impers.* Forms: *Pres.* 1 **byreð**, 3 **burþ, birþ,** 4 **birt, birs, beres, bers.** *Pa. t.* 1 **byrede,** 3-4 **burd(e, bird(e, byrd.** [OE. *byrian* impers. (more usually *ȝebyrian*), cogn. w. ON. *byrja*, OHG. *purjan*, MHG. *buren*, *bürn* to lift or hold up, MDu. *bören*, *boren*, Du. *beuren* to lift:—OTeut. **burjan*; f. root *ber-* BEAR. Franck connects the primitive sense of 'lift, raise' with that of OE. *ȝebyrian* (*byrian*), Ger. *gebühren*, by supposing the latter to have been orig. 'to arise, come up (as an event), occur, happen, befall, fall *to* as an occurrence, whence "fall *to* as a share, right, duty, etc."'] To fall *to*, pertain, belong; to behove, be proper.

c **950** *Lindisf. G.* Mark iv. 38 Ne to ðe byreð [*Rushw.* ȝibyreð] þæt we sie dead? *c* **975** *Rushw. G.* Matt. xii. 4 þa þe ne byrede him [*Lindisf.* neron ȝelefed, *Ags. G.* nærun him alyfede] to etanne. *a* **1300** *Cursor M.* 17164 Birt þe thinc apon mi pine. *c* **1325** *Metr. Hom.* 2 On the bird be his mast thouht. *Ibid.* 10 Forthi bers us trow thaim. *Ibid.* 84 Wel birs us blis the derworthelye. *c* **1375** ? BARBOUR *St. Martha* 152 Me byrd be blyth þat sycht to se.

bir, obs. form of BIRR.

bi-'racial, *a.* [BI-².] Concerning or containing (members of) two races.

1922 *Contemp. Rev.* Feb. 243 Belgium is bi-lingual and bi-racial. **1960** *Guardian* 11 Apr. 1/7 Decent business men form bi-racial committees.

biradiate, -ated: see BI- *pref.*² 1.

birall, -ell, obs. forms of BERYL.

biramose (baɪ'reɪməʊs), *a. Zool.* [f. BI-² + RAMOSE *a.*] = BIRAMOUS *a.*

1877 H. WOODWARD in *Encycl. Brit.* VI. 652/1 Behind these are six pairs of powerful biramose natatory feet. **1888** ROLLESTON & JACKSON *Anim. Life* 539 With a bivalve shell and large natatory biramose second antennæ.

biramous (baɪˈreɪməs), *a.* [f. BI- *pref.*[2] 1 + L. *rāmus* branch.] Two-branched.

1877 HUXLEY *Anat. Inv. An.* vi. 276 Biramous swimming feet. *Ibid.* 277 The first pair of biramous appendages.

birational (baɪˈræʃənəl), *a. Math.* [f. BI-[2] + RATIONAL *a.*] Applied to a transformation in which each of two sets of variables is expressed rationally in terms of the other, or to a correspondence between two sets of variables that can be so related. Hence **biˈrationally** *adv.*

1894 C. A. SCOTT *Introd. Plane Analyt. Geom.* xi. 240 The transformations hitherto considered are birational transformations of the whole plane. **1915** R. A. P. ROGERS *Salmon's Analyt. Geom.* (ed. 5) II. 268 Such a correspondence is called birational. *Ibid.*, Any surface which can be birationally transformed into a unicursal surface is itself unicursal. **1954** HODGE & PEDOE *Methods Algebraic Geom.* III. xviii. 224 An irreducible correspondence between two varieties *U* and *U'* in which to a generic point of each there corresponds a unique point of the other is called a birational correspondence.

†**birb.** *Obs. rare*[−1]. A minute barb or beard.

1658 R. FRANCK *North. Mem.* (1821) 183 Their..birbs as stiff and as strunt as bristles.

birbine, variant form of BEARBINE.

1860 PIESSE *Lab. Chem. Wond.* 113 Wild roses and birbine, two stragglers of my walk.

birch (bɜːtʃ), *sb.* Forms: α. 1 berc, beorc (? beorch), byrc. β. 1 birciae, byrce, birce, 3–6 birche, 5–6 byrch(e, 4– birch; *north.* 4–5 byrk(e, 4– birk. [OE. had two forms: (1) *berc, beorc* str. fem. = ON. *bjǫrk* (Sw. *björk*, Da. *birk*):—OTeut. **berkâ-* str. fem.; (2) OE. *bierce, byrce, birce*, in Epinal Gl. *birciae*, wk. fem. = OHG. *bir(i)cha* (MHG., mod.G. *birke*):—OTeut. **birkjôn-* wk. fem., a derivative of **berkâ-* (cf. the two forms *bôkâ-* and *bôkjôn-* BEECH). An Indo-Germanic tree name:—OAryan **bherĝo-*, **bherĝā-*: cf. Skr. *bhūrja* a species of birch, Lith. *beržas*, OSlav. *brěza*. The OE. *birce* gave ME. *birche*, mod. *birch*; the northern form *birk* reaches to Morecambe Bay and Lincoln: cf. CHURCH, KIRK.]

1. A genus of hardy northern forest trees (*Betula*), having smooth tough bark and very slender branches. **a.** *esp.* The common European species (*B. alba*) which grows from Mt. Etna to Iceland, and from Greenland to Kamtschatka, and is distinguished among the other forest trees by its slender white stem; its twigs, bound in bundles, have furnished brooms, and the 'birch' for flogging. Also called Lady Birch, Silver B., White B.; the Weeping or Drooping Birch (*B. pendula*) is a variety.

(In OE. Vocabularies *berc, birce*, translate both L. *betula* and *populus*.)

a **700** *Epinal Gl.* 132 (also *Erf. & Cott.*), *Bet[ul]a*, berc *arbor dicitur.* —— 792 *Populus*, birciae [*Corpus* birce]. *a* **1000** *Rune-poem* 18 Beorc byð bleda leás. *a* **1000** ÆLFRIC *Gloss.* in Wr.-Wülcker *Voc.* 138 *Populus*, byrc. *Betulus*, byrc. *c* **1000** *Sax. Leechd.* II. 332 Nim æps rinde..berc rinde. *c* **1050** Wr.-Wülcker *Voc.* 361 *Betulus*, byrce. —— 469 *Populus*, byrce. *c* **1300** *K. Alis.* 5242 Beches, birches of the fairest. **1375** BARBOUR *Bruce* XVI. 394 Byrkis on athir syde the way. *c* **1386** CHAUCER *Knts. T.* 2063 As oke, fir, birch, aspe, alder, holm, poplere. **1398** TREVISA *Barth. De P.R.* XVII. clix. (1495) 708 Therwyth houses ben swepte and clensyd . and many called this tree Byrche. **1551** TURNER *Herbal* (1568) 66 Byrche..serueth..for betynge of stubborne boyes. **1577** B. GOOGE *Heresbach's Husb.* (1586) 102 Birch..is a tree very meete for woodes. **1801** SOUTHEY *Thalaba* XI. xxiii, The Birch so beautiful, Light as a lady's plumes. **1829** SOUTHEY *Sir T. More* I. 121 Directly opposite there are some..steps of herbage, and a few birch. **1830** TENNYSON *Dirge* i, Shadows of the silver birk Sweep the green that folds thy grave. **1874** BLACKIE *Self-Cult.* 42 The fragrant breath of birches blowing around him.

b. Dwarf Birch (*B. nana*), a low wiry shrub found on Scottish moorlands and in continental Europe and North America; **Paper Birch** or **White B.** of America (*B. papyracea*), a North American species, so called from the brilliant white colour of the bark, of which the Indians build birch-bark canoes; **Cherry Birch** (*B. lenta*), also called **Sweet Mahogany**, or **Mountain B.**, a native of N. America, with fragrant leaves. Numerous other species are known: and the name is popularly applied to other genera, as the **West Indian Birch** (*Bursera gummifera*, NO. *Amyridaceæ*).

1875 HIGGINSON *Yng. Folks' U.S. Hist.* iii. 17 The canoe was made of the bark of the white-birch.

c. The wood of this tree.

a **1400** *Sir Perc.* 772 A fyre brynnande Off byrke and of akke. **1823** P. NICHOLSON *Pract. Build.* 262 Birch is also a very common wood.

d. The plural *birks* is often used in the north in the name of a wood or grove of birches.

a **1724** D. MALLET *Song* 'The Birks of Endermay.' **1794** BURNS *Birks Aberfeldy*, Let us spend the lightsome days In the birks of Aberfeldy. **1855** *Whitby Gloss.*, *Birks*, a coppice or small wood in which the growth chiefly consists of birches.

2. A bunch of birch-twigs bound together to form an instrument for the flagellation of school-boys and of juvenile offenders; a birch-rod.

[*c* **1440** *Bone Flor.* 1518 He bete hur wyth a yerde of byrke.] **1603** SHAKS. *Meas. for M.* I. iii. 24 The threatning twigs of birch.] **1648** HERRICK *Upon Pagget, Hesp.* (1869) 67 Pagget, a school-boy, got a sword, and then He vow'd destruction both to birch and men. **1730** SWIFT *Sheridan's Subm.* Wks. 1755 IV. I. 260 I've nothing left to vent my spleen But ferula and birch. **1831** CARLYLE *Sart. Res.* II. iii, Were he [the Schoolmaster] to walk abroad with birch girt on thigh. **1835** MARRYAT *Jac. Faithf.* v.

3. A canoe made of the bark of the Canoe or Paper Birch (*Betula papyracea*).

1864 LOWELL *Fireside Trav.* 129 Never use the word *canoe* ..if you wish to retain your selfrespect. *Birch* is the term among us backwoodsmen. **1884** E. HALE *Christmas in Narrag.* i. 10 To paddle a birch across the lake.

4. *Comb.* and *Attrib.*, as *birch-broom, -knowe, -leaf, -stalk, -tree, -wand, -wood*; *birch-fringed, -shaded* adjs.; **birch bark**, the bark of a birch-tree (also *attrib.*); (*U.S.*) a birch-bark canoe; **birch beer** *U.S.*, a beverage of slight alcoholic content prepared with an extract from the birch-tree; also a carbonated soft drink flavoured to resemble this; **birch camphor**, a resinous substance obtained from the bark of the Black Birch (*B. nigra*); **birch oil**, an oil extracted from the bark of the birch, and used in the preparation of Russia leather, to which it gives its smell; **birch partridge**, a North American name for the ruffed grouse, *Bonasa umbellus*; **birch-rod** = BIRCH 2; **birch-water**, the sap obtained from the birch-tree in spring; **birch-wine**, wine prepared from birch-water.

1643 WILLIAMS *Key Lang. Amer.* 67 Others make slighter doores of *Burch or Chestnut barke. **1771** PENNANT *Tour Scotl.* 97 The materials [of the nest were] moss, worsted, and birch bark. **1829** J. MACTAGGART *Three Yrs. Canada* II. 54 Thus we can run a rapid of the Rideau River with a birch-bark canoe heavily laden. **1843** 'R. CARLTON' *New Purchase* 175 To float in birch bark canoes on..free waters. **1868** F. WHYMPER *Trav. & Adv. in Alaska* 212 Birch-barks are.. easily navigated. **1927** E. V. GORDON *Introd. Old Norse* 225 They used birch-bark for leggings. **1883** *Wheelman* (U.S.) I. 392 We reached Bushkill at 12:30 P.M., stopping—for *birch beer—at odd places. **1933** E. C. GUILLET *Early Life in Upper Canada* iv. 100 There was..a considerable manufacture of birch beer, a very popular drink among those who did not aspire to social heights. **1762** CHURCHILL *Ghost* II. 306 Hark! something scratches round the room! A cat, a rat, a stubb'd *birch-broom. **1796** MRS. GLASSE *Cookery* xxii. 348 Scrub them well with a little birch-broom or brush. **1823** *Gen. Descrip. Nova Scotia* iii. 31 A list of most of the known birds of the Province with their popular names... *Birch Partridge. **1834** *Chambers's Edinb. Jrnl.* 21 June 168/1 A bird, called the partridge,..is found all over the American continent; they are of two sorts, the spruce and the birch, so called from the different buds which they select for their food. **1880** *Encycl. Brit.* XI. 223/2 *B. umbellus*, the Ruffed Grouse or Birch-Partridge. **1831** CARLYLE *Sart. Res.* II. iii, That it [the soul]..could be acted on through the muscular integument by appliance of *birch rods. **1879** *Act 42–3 Vict.* xlix. § 10 Such young person to be..privately whipped with not more than twelve strokes of a birch rod by a constable. **1530** PALSGR. 198/1 *Byrche tree, *boulliav.* **1578** LYTE *Dodoens* VI. lxxvii. 758 The Birche tree hath taglettes or Chattons for his blossom, lyke as the Hazell. **1924** C. OMAN *Road Royal* xiv. § 2 She was made ready for bed and was all white as a moonlit birch tree. **1876** GRANT *Burgh Sch. Scot.* II. v. 196 Striking some on the hand with a *birch-wand. **1663** BOYLE *Usefulness Nat. Philos.* II. iv. 103 The great commendation..given to this *Birch-water. **1769** MRS. RAFFALD *Eng. Housekpr.* (1778) 325 Boil twenty gallons of birch water. **1681** *Lond. Gaz.* No. 1616/4 *Birch-Wine rightly prepared, and made of the Sap of Birch Trees. **1853** LINDLEY *Veg. Kingd.* (ed. 3) 252 Birch Wine has a popular reputation as a remedy for stone and gravel. **1849** SOUTHEY *Com-pl. Bk.* Ser. II. 615 Horns made of *birch-wood. **1860** G. H. K. *Vac. Tour* 135 The old birch-woods still linger here and there.

birch, *v.* [f. prec. sb.]

1. *trans.* To punish with a birch rod; to flog.

[Not in RICHARDSON; nor in TODD 1818.] **1830** MARRYAT *King's Own* xlvii, Like a school-boy ordered up to be birched. **1845** THACKERAY *Bk. Snobs* v, At Eton..he was birched with perfect impartiality.

2. To drive (knowledge) *into* (a boy) by flogging.

1883 *American* VI. 214 Greek and Latin were birched into them while they were young.

birchen (ˈbɜːtʃ(ə)n), *a.* Forms: 5–6 birkin, byrchen, -in, 6–7 birchin, 7 burchin, 5– birchen, (*north.*) birken. [f. BIRCH *sb.* + -EN[1].] Of, pertaining to, or composed of birch; of or pertaining to the birch used in flogging.

c **1440** *Gaw. & Gologras* I. 3 (Mätz.) Birkin bewis about boggis and wellis. **1481** CAXTON *Reynard* (Arb.) 41 Two birchen trees. **1536** TINDALE *Wks.* (1573) 166 We say of a wanton child..he must be annoynted with byrchin salve. **1556** J. HEYWOOD *Spider & F.* iii. 19 Our maide with hir birchin broome. **1611** BEAUM. & FL. *Knt. Burn. Pestle* IV. 64 And now the Burchin Tree doth bud that makes the Schoolboy cry. **1749** FIELDING *Tom Jones* v. xi, Unless you had the same birchen argument to convince me. **1808** J. MAYNE *Siller Gun* 28 (JAM.) Birken chaplets not a few And yellow broom. **1833** *Fraser's Mag.* VII. 137 Boyhood sheds its flood of birchen tears. **1865** PARKMAN *Champlain* ix. (1875) 300 Canoe-men, in their birchen vessels.

bircher[1] (ˈbɜːtʃə(r)). [f. BIRCH *v.* + -ER[1].] One who administers a birch-rod; a flogger.

1888 *Ch. Times* 13 July 622 The renowned bircher [*sc.* Dr. Keate]. **1908** *Daily Chron.* 18 June 4/7 The vicarious cane is considered by birchers of experience to be an unsatisfactory substitute for the birch rod itself. **1953** L. PAUL *Sir T. More* ii. 30 Erasmus relates that often after a common meal a schoolmaster would pick out a boy and hand him over for punishment to a bircher.

Bircher[2] (ˈbɜːtʃə(r)). [f. the name of John *Birch*, a U.S.A.F. officer killed in 1945, sometimes referred to as 'the first casualty of the Cold War'.] A member or supporter of the John Birch Society, an extreme right-wing American organization founded in 1958 by Robert Welch. Also **ˈBirchite** *sb.* and *a.*; **John Bircher**.

1961 in *Amer. Speech* (1962) XXXVII. 145 'Birchers' active in S.F. *Ibid.*, In Birchite circles. *Ibid.* 146 We have a lot of near John Birchers right here in Nebraska. **1961** *Guardian* 25 Nov. 7/2 Robert Welch, the Birchites' leader. **1962** *Economist* 17 Nov. 666/1 Two veterans of Congress whose Birchite connections had been unknown in previous elections. **1963** *Ibid.* 5 Oct. 43/2 Shrugging off the Birchers has not prevented the Senator [*sc.* Mr. Goldwater] from continuing to denounce some of the President's leading advisors. **1968** J. UPDIKE *Couples* iv. 299 A lot of melancholy fill-in about Dallas the Birchers' paradise.

ˈbirching, *vbl. sb.* [f. BIRCH *v.* + -ING[1].] A whipping with a birch rod, a flogging. † *to send one to Birching* (*Birchin, Birchen*) *Lane*: i.e. for a whipping (with a punning reference to Birchin Lane in London). Nares.

a **1845** HOOD *To I. Walton* 33, I poked his rods and lines in the fire, and his father gave him a birching.

bird (bɜːd), *sb.* Forms: 1–5 brid, 1 *north.* bird, 3–5 bridd, 3–6 bryd, 4–5 bridde, bred(e, 4 berd, 4–6 byrd(e, 5 brydde, 5–7 birde, 5– *dial.* brid, 5– bird. Pl. birds: formerly briddas, -es, -is, -ys, -us; birdas, -es. [ME. *byrd, bryd*:—OE. *brid* masc. (pl. *briddas*), in Northumbrian *bird, birdas* 'offspring, young,' but used only of the young of birds. There is no corresponding form in any other Teutonic lang., and the etymology is unknown. If native Teut., it would represent an original **bridjo-z*: this cannot be derived from BROOD, BREED, and even the suggestion that it may be formed like these from the root **bru-* (see BROOD) appears to be quite inadmissible.]

†**I. 1. a.** *orig.* The general name for the young of the feathered tribes; a young bird; a chicken, eaglet, etc.; a nestling. The only sense in OE.; found in literature down to 1600; still retained in north. dial. as 'a hen and her birds.'

a **800** *Corpus Gl.* (*O.E. Texts*) 1687 *Pullus*, brid. *c* **1000** *Ags. Gosp.* Luke ii. 24 Twa turtlan oððe twegen culfran briddas [*Lindisf. & Rushw.* birdas, *Hatton* briddes]. *a* **1100** in Wr.-Wülcker *Voc.* 318 *Pullus*, cicen oððe brid. *c* **1200** *Trin. Coll. Hom.* 49 Duue fedeð briddes. *a* **1300** *E.E. Psalter* lxxxiii[iv]. 4 And þe turtil [findes]..a neste þar he mai with his briddes [WYCLIF, briddis, bryddis] reste. **1377** LANGL. *P. Pl.* B. XI. 348 Some..bredden, and brouȝten forth her bryddes so · al aboue þe grounde. **1526** *Pilgr. Perf.* (W. de W. 1531) 13 He..cheryssheth vs, as the egle her byrdes. **1592** WARNER *Alb. Eng.* VIII. cxli. (1597) 200 The Pellicane theare neasts his Bird. **1593** SHAKS. *3 Hen. VI*, II. i. 91 That Princely Eagles Bird. **1822** GALT *Entail* lxv, The craw thinks its ain bird the whitest.

†**b.** The young of other animals. *Obs.*

1388 WYCLIF *Matt.* xxiii. 33 Ȝe eddris, and eddris briddis. **1398** TREVISA *Barth. De P.R.* XII. v. (1495) 415 In temperat yeres ben fewe byrdes of been [= bees]. *Ibid.* XIII. xxvi. (1495) 458 All fysshe..fede and kepe theyr byrdes. *c* **1440** *Gesta Rom.* I. vii. 16 A serpent—made his nest..and broȝt forthe his briddis there. **1591** BRUCE *11 Serm.* Y viij a (JAM.) They wald ever be handled as Tods birds. **1597** *Act 7 Jas. I*, 1427 (*title*) The Woolfe and Woolfe-birdes suld be slaine.

†**c.** *transf.* A young man, youngster, child, son. *Obs.* (In later times only *fig.*: cf. chick, chicken.)

a **1300** *Cursor M.* 22381 [Anticrist] þat ilk warlau bridd [*Fairf.* warlagh brid, *Trin.* þulke fendes brid]. *Ibid.* 9811 Qua-sum on suilk a bird [Jesus] wald thinc [*Gött.* brid]. *c* **1330** *Amis & Amil.* 15 The berdes bold of chere. **1559** *Homilies* I. *Good Wks.* II. (1859) 54 To follow his own phantasie, and (as you woulde saye) to fauoure his owne byrde. **1566** KNOX *Hist. Ref.* Wks. 1846 I. 125 His bastard byrdis bear some witness. **1571** *Scot. Poems 16th C.* (1801) II. 280 Thea dispard birds of Beliall.

d. A maiden, a girl. [In this sense *bird* was confused with *burde*, BURD, originally a distinct word, perhaps also with *bryd(e* BRIDE; but later writers understand it as fig. sense of 1 or 2.] In mod. (revived) use: a girl, woman (often used familiarly or disparagingly) (*slang*).

a **1300** *Cursor M.* 7131 [Delilah] þat birde [*v.r.* bride, bryde, bruyd] was biddande bald. *Ibid.* 10077 [Mary] þat blisful bird [*v.r.* berde, byrd, buyrde] of grace. *c* **1325** *E.E. Allit. P.* A. 768 Maskellez bryd þat bryȝt con flambe. *c* **1400** *Ywaine & Gaw.* 3313 That he ne might wed that bird bright. *c* **1485** *Digby Myst.* (1882) III. 356 Ȝe bewtews byrd [Luxuria], I must yow kysse. **1611** SHAKS. *Cymb.* IV. ii. 197 The Bird is dead That we haue made so much on. **1804** CAMPBELL *Ld. Ullin's Dau.* vi, And by my word! the bonny bird In danger shall not tarry. **1816** SCOTT *Old Mort.* xli, 'Peggy, my bonny bird,'..addressing a little girl of twelve years old. **1915** P. MACGILL *Amat. Army* v. 62 There's another bird there—and cawfee! **1927** COLLINSON *Contemp. Eng.* 96 Bird (used like Ger. *Biene* especially for a more

flirtatious or less reputable type of girl). **1935** 'G. ORWELL' *Clerg. Daughter* ii. 161 He kept a sharp eye open for the 'birds'. **1958** *Observer* 14 Dec. 7/6 The birds.. get 'emselves into trouble, let 'em get 'emselves out. **1960** *News Chron.* 16 Feb. 6 Hundreds more geezers were taking their birds to 'The Hostage' and 'Make me an Offer'. **1961** *New Statesman* 26 May 830/2 Victor is an ex-seaman in his twenties, who deserted in South Africa and got in law trouble out there for shacking up with a coloured bird.

e. *jocularly.* A man, a 'cove'; esp. in *old bird* (see OLD *a.* 5 b). Cf. quots. 1799 and 1875 under senses 4 a and b below.

Often in the punning collocation *downy bird*: see DOWNY *a.*² 5.

1852 BRISTED *Upper Ten Th.* vi. 128 The same reason.. kept Mr. Simpson, and other 'birds' of his set, out of the exclusive society. **1853** 'C. BEDE' *Verdant Green* vi, I suppose the old bird was your governor. **1873** [see DOWNY *a.*² 5]. **1877, 1890** [see OLD *a.* 5 b]. *a* **1885** 'H. CONWAY' *Living or Dead* (1886) vii, After all, Philip,.. your father must be a queer bird—excuse slang, mother. **1899** KIPLING *Stalky* 131 The Head's a downy bird. **1928** [see *coffin-nail*, COFFIN *sb.* 13]. **1930** E. POUND *XXX Cantos* xi. 49 And that gay bird Piero della Bella. **1939** J. B. PRIESTLEY *Let People Sing* 358 He's one of them queer birds that aren't human until they're properly pickled.

2. Any feathered vertebrate animal: a member of the second class (*Aves*) of the great Vertebrate group, the species of which are most nearly allied to the Reptiles, but distinguished by their warm blood, feathers, and adaptation of the fore limbs as wings, with which most species fly in the air.

Now used generically in place of the older name FOWL, which has become specialized for certain kinds of poultry, and by sportsmen for wild ducks and wild geese. In this sense, *bird*, ME. *brid*, is found in the south *c* 1300; it appears to have been extended from the young of birds (sense 1) at first to the smaller kinds, Chaucer's 'smale foules.' So late as a century ago, Dr. Johnson says (1755–73) 'In common talk *fowl* is used for the larger, and *bird* for the smaller kind of feathered animals'; and this distinction still obtains to some extent dialectally. (In Scotland *large birds* e.g. hawks, herons, are ' fowls,' *small birds*, as well as chickens, are 'birds.') A further process of specialization (cf. the histories of *fowl, deer, beast*), seems still to be in progress in regard to *bird*, as witness its technical use by game-preservers (sense 3).

a **1225** *Ancr. R.* 102 Eni totilde ancre.. þet bekeð euer utward ase untowe brid ine cage. *Ibid.* 134 þeos briddes habbeð nestes. *c* **1385** CHAUCER *L.G.W.* 1753 On morwe, whanne the brid began to synge. **1398** TREVISA *Barth. De P.R.* v. xxviii. (1495) 138 Amonge birdes the popyniaye and the pellycan vse the fote in stede of an honde. *c* **1432–50** tr. *Higden* (1865) I. 99 A brydde callede fenix. **1475** *Bk. Noblesse* 59 By augures and divinacions of briddis. **1526** TINDALE *Matt.* viii. 20 The bryddes of the aier have nestes. **1613** SHAKS. *Hen. VIII*, IV. i. 89 The Rod, and Bird of Peace, and all such Emblemes. **1631** T. POWELL *Tom All Trades* 166 As free as bird in ayre. **1770** M. BRUCE *Cuckoo* v Sweet bird! thy bower is ever green. **1798** COLERIDGE *Anc. Mar.* v, He loved the bird that loved the man Who shot him with his bow. **1850** TENNYSON *In Mem.* cxiv, The happy birds that change their sky To build and brood.

3. *Sport.* A game bird; with game-preservers *spec.* a partridge. *fig.* Prey, object of attack.

1596 SHAKS. *Tam. Shr.* v. ii. 46 Am I your Bird, I meane to shift my bush. **1609** DEKKER *Lanth. & Candle-Lt.* Wks. 1884–5 III. 243 The Bird that is preid vpon, is Money. **1833** M. SCOTT *Tom Cringle*, The lieutenant.. was my bird, and I had disabled him by a sabre-cut. **1877** *Daily News* 1 Oct. 5/1 It is impossible to avoid admiring the bird—for although the partridge has usurped the designation, after all the pheasant is a bird—which can inspire such master-pieces of felonious skill. *Mod.* Reports from the northern moors say the birds are very wild.

4. a. In various *fig.* applications, chiefly from sense 2; as in reference to the winged or noiseless flight, or soaring of birds; to their confinement in cages (cf. GAOL-BIRD); to their song; to the Latin *rara avis* rare fowl, rarity. ***Arabian bird*** = phœnix. Also, referring to a (pretended) private or secret source of information; esp. in phr. ***a little bird.***

1546 J. HEYWOOD *Dial. cont. Prouerbes* folio Hiii. *recto*, I dyd lately here.. By one byrd, that in myne eare was late chauntyng. **1588** *Marprel. Epist.* (Arb.) 30, I hope to see you in for a bird. **1593** *Pass. Morrice* 79 She song ere long like a bird of Bedlam. **1597** SHAKS. *2 Hen. IV*, v. v. 113 We beare our Ciuill Swords.. As farre as France. I heare a Bird so sing. **1606** —— *Ant. & Cl.* III. ii. 12 Oh Anthony, oh thou Arabian Bird! **1610** —— *Temp.* IV. i. 184 *Prosp.* This was well done (my bird). **1711** SWIFT *Jrnl. to Stella* 23 May (1948) I. 277 You quarrelled this morning..: I heard the little bird say so. *c* **1799** MISS ROSE in Rose *Diaries* (1860) I. 212 There were strange birds getting about my father. **1833** MARRYAT *P. Simple* xxxix, A little bird has whispered a secret to me. **1853** C. BRONTË *Villette* III. xxxi. 47 'Who told you I was called Carl David?' 'A little bird, monsieur.' **1872** GEO. ELIOT *Middlemarch* III. VI. lix. 314, I know all about it. I have a confidential little bird. **1875** B. TAYLOR *Faust* I. xvi. 159 There must be such queer birds however.

b. An exceptionally smart or accomplished person (freq. ironical); a first-rate animal or thing. *U.S. slang.*

1839 *Spirit of Times* 21 Dec. 498/2 If you jist could see one man what the Gineral Government sent out with an office to these parts,—he is a bird! **1840** *Ibid.* 27 June 199 An Ivanhoe has been winner and a second. Kendall has made a good beginning, and Sufferer may yet prove a 'bird'. **1852** *Knickerbocker* Oct. 320 Talking of fast men, that Williams is a bird. **1856** *Ibid.* Apr. 429 A sleigh, drawn by a 'perfect bird' of a three-mile bay mare. **1907** S. E. WHITE *Arizona Nights* I. vii. 129 A little place.. in the Colorado mountains. Fellows, she was a bird. **1911** H. QUICK *Yellowstone N.* ix. 230 He's got a disguise that's a bird.

c. A prison sentence; prison. Cf. BIRD-LIME 2.

1924 E. WALLACE *Room 13* ix. 90 He's just out of 'bird'—that's jail. **1931** *Police Jrnl.* Oct. 501 This, with Jack's previous convictions (bird), caused him to be sentenced.. to five years' penal servitude.. at Parkhurst. **1938** J. CURTIS *They drive by Night* ii. 22 Hell of a long time the next bit of bird was going to be unless he got done for suspect. **1953** *Listener* 3 Sept. 366 Having done his bird, as imprisonment is called in the best circles. **1961** [see BIRD-LIME 2].

d. An aeroplane. Also, a guided missile, rocket, or space-craft. *slang.*

1933 H. G. WELLS *Shape of Things to Come* III §11. 332 We had no gas masks on our bird, so I didn't take part in the landing party which seized the new 'planes. **1951** *Time* 21 May 34/1 The military phrase of the day is 'guided missiles'. .. These 'birds' (so the missilemen call them) are the heirs presumptive of war. **1962** A. SHEPARD in *Into Orbit* 100, I really enjoy looking at a bird that is getting ready to go.

e. An obscene gesture of contempt (see quots.). *U.S. slang.*

1968–70 *Current Slang* (Univ. S. Dakota) III–IV. 10 *Bird*, an upward thrust with the index or middle finger.—New Mexico State. **1971** E. E. LANDY *Underground Dict.* 33 *Bird*. .. Term for the middle finger when raised alone, which means Fuck you—eg. *That guy gave me the bird.*

5. a. Phrases. †*a bird of one's own brain*: a conception of one's own. †*the bird in the bosom*: one's own secret or pledge, one's conscience. *birds of a* (= one) *feather*: those of like character. †*John Grey's bird* (see quot.).

1550 HALL *Chron.* 2 Saiyng, when he was diyng: I haue saued the birde in my bosome: meaning that he had kept both his promise and othe. *c* **1575** GASCOIGNE *Fruites Warre* cxxxi, The Greene knight was amongst the rest Like John Greyes birde that ventured withe the best. **1580** in Hazlitt *Prov.* (1869) 263 Perceiving them to cluster togither like John Grayes bird, *ut dicitur*, who always loved company. **1594** T. B. *La Primaud. Fr. Acad.* II. 523, I take it to be a bird of their owne braine. **1600** HOLLAND *Livy* XXVI. xl. 615 As commonly birds of a feather will flye together. **1608** D. T[UVILL] *Ess. Pol. & Mor.* 90 b, A prying eye, a listning eare, and a prating tongue are all birds of one wing. **1632** D. LUPTON *Lond. & Carbon.* 57 The Tayler and Broker are Birds of a feather. **1757** W. THOMPSON *R.N. Advoc.* 13 *note*, Birds of a Feather flock together. **1818** SCOTT *Hrt. Midl.* xxxii, I trow thou be'st a bird of the same feather. **1820** —— *Abbot* viii, Thou hast kept well.. the bird in thy bosom.

b. Phr. *the big bird*, cf. GOOSE *sb.* 1 g; esp. in *to get the* (*big*) *bird*: of an actor, to be hissed by the audience; hence *gen.* to be dismissed, get the sack. Similarly, *to give* (a person) *the bird*, *to get the bird.* orig. *Theatr. slang.*

1825 P. EGAN *Life of Actor* p. xii, And the end of their folly marked by the attacks of the big birds (*geese*) driving them off the stage. **1846** PLANCHÉ *Aristophanes' Birds* 6 So hear him patiently before you frown Nor let his first shot bring the 'Big Bird' down. **1865** HOTTEN *Slang Dict.* s.v., 'To get the big-bird', *i.e.* to be hissed, as actors occasionally are by the 'gods'. **1884** in Ware *Passing Eng.* (1909) s.v., Professor Grant, Q.C., had both 'the bird' and 'the needle' at the Royal on Monday. **1886** *Graphic* 10 Apr. 399/2 To be 'goosed', or, as it is sometimes phrased, to 'get the big bird', is occasionally a compliment to the actor's power of representing villainy. **1895** *People* 13 Jan. 7/2 Three or four of the most prominent artistes.. have been.. threatened with.. 'the bird'—that is, hissing. **1924** GALSWORTHY *White Monkey* 56 Mr. Danby had 'given him the bird'. *Ibid.* 255 When you were ill, I stole for you. I got the bird for it. **1927** *Daily Express* 4 Feb. 6/4 Britons in Hollywood will get what is locally known as the 'razzberry', which may be translated as 'the bird'. **1928** WODEHOUSE *Money for Nothing* vii. 137 Would a Rudge audience have given me the bird a few years ago? **1957** P. KEMP *Mine were of Trouble* iii. 35 She gave him the bird—finally and for good. So he came to Spain to forget his broken heart.

c. *like a bird*: with swift and easy motion onwards; easily; without resistance, difficulty, or hesitation.

1825 J. NEAL *Bro. Jonathan* I. xiii. 421 Away she went, like a bird. **1873** W. S. GILBERT *More Bab Ballads* 118 'Miss Emily, I love you—Will you marry? Say the word!' And Emily said 'Certainly, Alphonso, like a bird!' **1879** *Cassell's Fam. Mag.* Mar. 197/2 Over he went like a bird, and, with his fair burthen yet in the saddle. **1914** G. B. SHAW *Fanny's First Play* Induction, I told him Trotter would feel lonely without him; so he promised like a bird.

d. Phr. (*strictly*) *for the birds*: trivial, worthless; appealing only to gullible people. orig. and chiefly *U.S. colloq.*

1951 J. D. SALINGER *Catcher in Rye* i. 6 'Since 1888 we have been moulding boys into splendid, clear-thinking young men.' Strictly for the birds. **1953** *Time* 7 Sept. 2/1 Kinsey's book is strictly for the birds. **1955** J. POTTS *Death of Stray Cat* vii. 79 He's the jerk that brought you home tonight, isn't he? Strictly for the birds. **1957** *Amer. Speech* XXXII. 240 In 1942, when I entered the U.S. Army.. the disparaging term *that's for the birds* was in common use among officers and enlisted men.. . The metaphor alludes to birds eating droppings from horses and cattle. **1958** OSBORNE & CREIGHTON *Epit. G. Dillon* II. 49 'You aren't very impressed with Geoffrey..?' 'Right. What the Americans call "strictly for the birds".' **1963** *Listener* 14 Feb. 301/2 Our answer, at that age, would have been that Stanley Matthews was for the birds. Football was just not mobile enough.

6. In many proverbial expressions.

c **1440** *Generydes* 4524 Some bete the bussh and some the byrdes take. **1523** SKELTON *Garl. Laurel* 1452 Who may have a more ungracious lyfe Than a chyldis bird and a knavis wyfe? *a* **1529** —— *Agst. Garnesche* 197 That byrd ys nat honest That fylythe hys owne nest. *c* **1530** R. HILLES *Com.-pl. Bk.* (1858) 140 A byrde yn honde ys better than three yn the wode. *c* **1530** H. RHODES *Bk. Nurture* 579 in *Babees Bk.* (1868) 98 A byrd in hand.. is worth ten flye at large. *c* **1600** *Timon* IV. ii. (1842) 62 Tis well.—An olde birde is not caught with chaffe. **1652** ASHMOLE *Theatr. Chem.* lxii. 225 A Chyldys Byrde, and a Chorlys Wyfe, Hath ofte sythys sorow and mischaunce. **1655** GURNALL *Chr. in Arm.* (1845) 46 Man.. knows not his time.. he comes when the bird is flown. **1656** HOBBES *Liberty, etc.* (1841) 117 T. H. thinks to kill two birds with one stone, and satisfy two arguments with one answer. **1823** GALT *Entail* lvi, It's a foul bird that files it's ain nest. *Prov.* The early bird catches the worm.

II. In combinations.

7. With some defining word connected by *of*, as **Bird of Freedom** *U.S.*, the emblematic bird of the U.S. (see EAGLE *sb.* 1); **bird of Jove**, the eagle; **bird of Juno**, the peacock; also, a hawk; **bird of paradise**, (*a*) a bird belonging to the family *Paradiseidæ*, found chiefly in New Guinea, and remarkable for the beauty of their plumage; also *fig.*; (*b*) *Astron.* (see quot. 1659); (*c*) **bird-of-paradise flower**, a perennial musaceous plant, *Strelitzia reginæ*, having scapes of purple and orange flowers; **bird of passage**, any migratory bird; (see also PASSAGE *sb.* 1 e); **bird of prey** (see PREY *sb.* 4 b); **Bird of Washington**, the American Eagle (*Falco leucocephalus*); **bird of wonder**, the phœnix.

1848 LOWELL *Biglow P.* Ser. I. ii. 28 Yourn, Birdofredom Sawin. **1854** B. F. TAYLOR *Jan. & June* 120 The Bird of Freedom inclined his body forward. **1906** *Harper's Mag.* Mar. 638 The short story is peculiarly an American institution, and we are as proud of it as we are of the 'Bird of Freedom'. **1667** MILTON *P.L.* XI. 185 The Bird of Jove, stoopt from his aerie tour. **1733** POPE *Song Person Qual.*, See the bird of Juno stooping. **1606** J. CARPENTER *Solomon's Solace* xxi. 86 The bird of Paradise, which being taken in a snare is neuer quiet. **1638** WILKINS *New World* I. (1684) 175 The Birds of Paradise.. reside Constantly in the Air. *a* **1649** CRASHAW *Carmen Deo Nostro* (1652) f. a. ij *verso*, With heauenly riches: which had wholy call'd His thoughtes from earth, to liue aboue in'th aire A very bird of paradice. **1659** MOXON *Tutor Astron.* I. iii. §10. 19 There are in Heaven yet twelve Constellations more, posited about the South Pole, which were added by Frederico Houtmanno,.. who.. named them as follows.. 4 The *Peacock*, 5 The *Bird of Paradice*, 6 The *Fly*. **1663** T. KILLIGREW *Parsons Wedding* III. ii, *Wild.* A Bird of Paradise, what's that? *Capt.* A Girl of Fifteen, smooth as Satten, White as her Sunday Apron, Plump, and of the first down. **1850** *Jrnl. Ind. Archipel.* IV. 182 The birds of paradise are natives of New Guinea. **1884** W. MILLER *Dict. Eng. Names of Plants* 253/2 *Strelitzia.* Bird's-tongue-Flower, Bird-of-Paradise-Flower. **1926** D. H. LAWRENCE *Glad Ghosts* 5 She showed off a bit, it is true, playing bird of paradise among the pigeons. **1791** E. DARWIN *Bot. Gard.* II. 26 *note*, The arrival of certain birds of passage. **1868** WOOD *Homes without H.* xxviii. 532 The well known Bald-headed Eagle, sometimes called the Bird of Washington. **1613** SHAKS. *Hen. VIII*, V. v. 41 The Bird of Wonder dyes, the Mayden Phoenix. **1620** MELTON *Astrolog.* 21 Impostors.. like the Bird of Wonder, flye the light of the Citie.

8. General combinations: **a.** objective with pres. pple., vbl. sb., or agent-noun, as ***bird-alluring***, ***-angler***, †***-batting*** (= BAT-FOWLING), ***-catcher***, ***-catching***, ***-echoing***, ***-fancier***, ***-keeper***, ***-lover***, ***-marking***, ***-netting***, ***-seller***, ***-snaring***, ***-stuffer***, ***-stuffing***, ***-tenting***. **b.** instrumental, as ***bird-conjurer***, ***-divination***, ***-diviner***, ***-ridden***, †***-speller***; ***bird-haunted***. **c.** parasynthetic and similative, as ***bird-black***, ***-blithe***, ***-clear***, ***-eyed***, ***-fingered***, ***-headed***, ***-high***, ***-voiced***, ***-winged***. **d.** attrib. (of or pertaining to birds), as ***bird-architecture***, ***-chorus***, ***-claw***, ***-flight***, ***-migration***, ***-music***, ***-note***, ***-skin***, ***-voice***; (connected with the scaring, catching, selling, or training of birds), as ***bird-boy***, ***-box***, ***-fair***, ***-net***, ***-pole***, ***-rock***, ***-shop***. Also ***bird-like*** adj.

1653 WALTON *Angler* xi. 206 This *Bird-Angler standing upon the top of a steeple to [catch swallows]. **1742** FIELDING *J. Andrews* II. x, *Bird-batting.. is performed by holding a large clap-net before a lanthorn, and at the same time beating the bushes. **1918** E. SITWELL *Clowns' Houses* 10 Amid thick leaves I saw the wink Of *bird-black eyes. **1917** D. H. LAWRENCE *Look! We have come Through!* 84 You *bird-blithe, lovely Angel in disguise. **1869** A. R. WALLACE *Malay Archipelago* I. iii. 46 We took with us.. insect and *bird boxes,.. guns and ammunition. **1914** W. M. WEBB in *Bird-Lover* I. 3 The requests for bird-boxes.. led to the keeper being employed in autumn and winter in making them. **1850** *Househ. Wds.* I. 545 You shall be *bird-boy when the sowing season comes on. **1580** HOLLYBAND *Treas. Fr. Tong.*, *Pippe*, a little pipe the which *bird catchers doe vse. **1909** *Westm. Gaz.* 8 July 8/1 The cruel trade carried on by the bird-catcher. **1687** R. LESTRANGE *Answ. Diss.* 7 The Skill and Address of *Bird-catching. **1889** W. B. YEATS *Wanderings of Oisin* III. 38 Golden the nails of his *bird-claws. **1922** W. DE LA MARE *Down-adown-Derry* 8 Never so much as a bird-claw print Of footfall to be seen. **1838** —— *Memory* 16 Her glistening *bird-clear eyes. **1382** WYCLIF *Deut.* xviii. 14 Thes gentils.. *brydd coniurers and dyuynours heren. —— *Jer.* xxvii. 9 Sweueneres, and *brid deuyneres. **1670** GALE *Crt. Gentiles* II. III. 68 Now this *Bird-divination was gathered chiefly by the flying or singing of Birds. **1928** C. DAY LEWIS *Country Comets* 24 We let The brave, *bird-echoing sunlight in. **1564** BULLEIN *Dial. agst Pest* f. 43 *recto*, He is a *burde iyed iade, I warrant you. **1590** *Pasquil's Apol.* I. C iij, The fellowe is bird eyed, he startles and snuffes at euery shadow. **1933** W. DE LA MARE *Fleeting* 80 In your bird-eyed wonder. **1773** BARRINGTON in *Phil. Trans.* LXIII. 283 The *bird-fanciers will not keep them. **1852** ARNOLD *Empedocles*, etc. 88 Some wet *bird-haunted English lawn. **1897** *Daily News* 29 June 6/3 The bird-haunted estuary of a river falling into Lake Tanganyika. **1916** *Jrnl. R. Anthrop. Inst.* XLVI. 184 The human figure with the two supporting *bird-headed *manaias*, a design recurring.. through the whole field of Maori carving. **1958** Bird-headed [see *bird-mask* under

sense 9]. **1920** E. SITWELL *Wooden Pegasus* 81 *Bird-high voices shrill and chatter. **1880** JEFFERIES *Gt. Estate* i. 4 Should anyone in authority ask where that gun went off, the labourer 'thenks it wur th' *birdkippur up in th' Dree Vurlong'. **1938** *British Birds* XXXI. 375 A Common Partridge..was taken to St. James's Park and handed over to the bird-keeper. **1587** GOLDING *De Mornay* xvii. 270 Reteyning nothing..of her *birdlike nature. **1876** GEO. ELIOT *Dan. Der.* VIII. lxi. 550 His bird-like hope..soared again. **1866** C. M. YONGE *Dove in Eagle's Nest* I. iv. 83 The gentle Minnesinger and *bird lover, Walther von Vogelweide. **1938** *British Birds* XXXI. 383 Richmond Park has much to interest the bird-lover. **1909** *British Birds* I Apr. 364 To show the value of *bird-marking I conclude by giving short summaries of the results obtained at Rossitten. **1908** *Westm. Gaz.* 1 Feb. 16/1 The *bird-migration routes. **1533-4** *Act 25 Hen. VIII*, vii, By means of any wele, butte, net, *berd net of heare. **1908** *Westm. Gaz.* 26 June 4/1 A different *bird-note seems to come from every bush and corner. **1835** BECKFORD *Recoll.* 163 These *bird-ridden dominions. **1898** R. KEARTON *Wild Life at Home* iii. 99 Ailsa Craig..is a capital *bird-rock. **1778** J. COOK *Jrnl.* 26 Oct. (1967) III. II. 1142 Their dress consists of a *bird skin Frock. **1904** *Daily Chron.* 7 May 5/6 Birdskin garments from the islands of the South Pacific. **1933** *Brit. Birds* XXVII. 174 For over forty years I have been collecting bird-skins for various scientific purposes. **1571** GOLDING *Calvin on Ps.* xiv. 4 *Birdspellers and other heathen soothsayers. **1899** *Daily News* 10 June 8/5 Go bird-nesting or *bird-snaring in one of the parks. **1838** AUDUBON *Ornith. Biogr.* IV. 271 A *bird-stuffer whom I knew at Camden had many fine specimens. **1861** DU CHAILLU *Equat. Afr.* xv. 274 After dinner *bird-stuffing goes on. **1864** *Times* 18 May, '*Bird-tenting' in England means shooting birds or scaring them away..in Australia..preserving birds with the most assiduous care. **1904** W. H. HUDSON *Green Mansions* iii. 41 Hearing nothing except the usual *bird voices. **1923** R. GRAVES *Whipperginny* 68 Now a bird-voice sings, And a loud throat bellows. **1925** E. SITWELL *Troy Park* 48/1 *Bird-voiced fire screams. **1869** A. R. WALLACE *Malay Archipelago* II. xxx. 199 One of the most magnificent insects the world contains, the great *bird-winged butterfly, Ornithoptera poseidon. **1903** KIPLING *Five Nations* 41 The blazoned, bird-winged butterflies. **1936** *Discovery* Dec. 367/1 The *Troides* or *Ornithoptera*, the magnificent bird-winged butterflies, are the glory of the eastern tropics.

9. Special comb.: **bird-band**, an identifying band fixed on to a bird's leg; so ***bird-bander***, ***-banding***; **bird bath**, a vessel, usu. in a garden, for birds to bathe in; **bird brain**, (a person with) a small brain; so **bird-brained** *a.*, having a small brain; *fig.* inattentive, flighty (cf. *bird-witted*); **bird-call**, an instrument for imitating the note of birds, in order to attract or decoy them; **bird-catching, -eating spider** = *bird-spider*; **bird-** (or **bird's**) **cherry**, a wild fruit tree or shrub (*Prunus Padus*) bearing a small astringent drupe; but formerly, the Wild Cherry (*P. Avium*); **bird dog** *U.S.*, a gun dog trained to retrieve birds; **bird-fly**, a fly (*Ornithomyia*) which lives under the plumage of birds; **bird-fountain**, a glass vessel of special construction for caged birds to drink out of; †**bird-gaze**, auspice; †**bird-gazer**, an augur; **bird-glasses**, field-glasses for observing birds; **bird-land**, the land or realm of birds; so **bird-folk**, **bird-world**; **bird-life** = AVIFAUNA; also, the life and habits of birds; **bird-lore**, the facts and beliefs concerning birds and their life and habits (see also LORE *sb.*[1] 5 a); **bird-louse**, any of the small wingless insects of the family *Mallophaga*, parasitic on birds and mammals; **bird-mask**, a mask resembling a bird's face; hence ***bird-masked*** adj.; **bird-mouthed** *a.*, having a mouth like a bird; *hence*, unwilling to speak out, inclined to mince matters (*obs.*); †**bird-nut**, a variety of walnut; **bird-organ**, a small organ used in teaching birds to sing; **bird-pepper**, kinds of capsicum (*C. baccatum* and *frutescens*); **bird-ringing** = *bird-banding*; so ***bird-ringer***; **bird sanctuary**, a piece of land where birds are protected, and encouraged to build and breed; **bird-seed**, canary-seed, hemp, millet, plantain, or other seeds given to caged birds; **bird-shot** orig. *U.S.* = *dust-shot* s.v. DUST *sb.*[1] 8 e; **bird-snake**, a S. African tree-snake, *Thelotornis capensis*, that preys on birds; **bird-song** (see SONG 3); **bird-spider**, a large hairy spider (*Mygale* or *Avicularia*) of tropical America, which kills small birds; **bird-spider fly** (see quot. 1844); **bird-spit**, a spit for roasting birds on, †*fig.* a rapier; **bird-stone** *U.S.* (see quot. 1907); **bird-strike** (see quots.); **bird table**, a raised platform on which food for birds is placed; **bird-tick**, a fly (*Olfersia*) parasitic upon birds (*Riverside Nat. Hist.* 1888 II. 433); **bird-watching**, the study of birds in their homes and haunts by a naturalist or bird-lover; also as *ppl. a.*; also **bird-watcher**, one who thus observes the ways of birds; **bird-witted** *a.*, lacking the faculty of attention, flitting from subject to subject; **bird-wittedness**, the condition of being bird-witted; **bird-world** (see *bird-land* above). Also BIRD-BOLT, BIRD-CAGE.

1939 *Nat. Geogr. Mag.* Mar. 368 My companion placed *bird bands around their legs and released them one by one. **1914** *Country Life* July 36/2 One of the first questions asked of the *bird-bander, is 'How do you get hold of the bird in order to band it?' **1912** *Technical World Mag.* 214/1 The *Bird Banding Association of America has just been formed in New York. **1954** BANNERMAN *Birds Brit. Isles* III. 209 As we have learned from the results of bird-banding, the ring-ouzel..has many miles to travel before it reaches our shores. **1895** *Montgomery Ward Catal.* 545 *Bird baths, white or opal for large sized birds. **1912** JEKYLL & WEAVER *Gardens for Small Country Houses* xiv. 165 A shallow bird bath made of lead. **1933** *Boys' Mag.* xlvii. 106/1 Some gardens boast of superb and ornamental bird baths. **1943** *Gen* 2 Jan. 28/1 There are more *birdbrains and dim-wits outside the boxing ring..as ever stepped around in it. **1948** H. LAWRENCE *Death of Doll* iv. 87 Jewel has a bird brain. You know what a bird brain is? Teeny-weeny. **1922** M. A. VON ARNIM *Enchanted April* xii. 176 *Bird-brained... Not an idea in her head. *a* **1625** FLETCHER *Bl. Brother* IV. ii, 'Tis Pippeau That is your *bird-call. **1773** BARRINGTON in *Phil. Trans.* LXIII. 272 Easily imposed upon by that most imperfect of all instruments, a bird-call. **1805** BINGLEY *Anim. Biog.* III. 489 The *Bird-catching Spider. **1871** KINGSLEY *At Last* xvii, A live 'Tarantula', or bird-catching spider. **1597** GERARD *Herbal* III. cxxx. §9 The *Birds Cherry-tree, or the blacke Cherry-tree..vsed for stockes to graft other Cherries vpon. **1863** KINGSLEY *Water Bab.* (ed. 2) 15 The bird-cherry with its tassels of snow. **1888** in *Amer. Speech* (1960) XXXV. 267 **Bird-dog*, a dog which accompanies a bird-hunter for the purpose of scenting the game and picking it up after it falls. **1923** J. MINER *J. M. & Birds* xv. 61 He went for his bird dog, thus giving the drake nearly an hour to make his escape. **1792** M. RIDDELL *Voy. Madeira* 73 The *aranea avicularia*, and the *aranea venatoria*, the *great hairy *bird-eating spider* of Brasil. **1934** HALDANE & HUXLEY *Animal Biol.* xii. 277 South American bird-eating spider. **1901** F. T. BULLEN *Sack of Shakings* 10 The hovering *bird-folk gathered in myriads. *c* **1865** LETHEBY in *Circ. Sc.* I. 110/1 Constructed on the principle of the *bird-fountain. **1587** GOLDING *De Mornay* xxii. 335 Cato wondered how two *Birdgazers could meet..or looke one vpon another without laughing. **1924** A. D. SEDGWICK *Little French Girl* I. vi, Yes, I can see him... And with his *bird-glasses. He would have been watching birds. **1924** R. MACAULAY *Orphan Island* iii, William..produced his bird-glasses and said no, it would, on the other hand, be a frigate-bird. **1900** O. G. PIKE (*title*) In *Bird-Land with Field Glass and Camera. **1940** C. DAY LEWIS tr. *Virgil's Georgics* II. p. 48 And blood-red berries like rubies adorn the untilled bird-land. **1874** E. COUES *Field Ornith.* iii. 30 *Bird-life is too beautiful a thing to destroy to no purpose. **1910** W. H. HUDSON *Shepherd's Life* p. x, Bird-life on the Downs. **1934** *Discovery* Oct. 293/1 It is not true..that bird-life in this country is decreasing and that the future of British bird-life is one of depleted numbers. **1830** 'DILETTANTE' [= W. Barnes] in *Gent. Mag.* June 503/2 Ornithology, should be *birdlore. **1826** KIRBY & SPENCE *Entomol.* III. xxix. 97 The egg..of some *bird-louse attached to the golden pheasant..resembles the purest wax. **1887** *Buck's Handbk. Med. Sci.* V. 751/1 *Mallophaga* (Bird-lice). Distinguished from the lice by possessing three- to five-jointed antennæ. **1930** E. SITWELL *Coll. Poems* 88 The Sun, that blackamoor, Comes in a *bird-mask With a bird-flute. **1958** E. A. ARMSTRONG *Folklore of Birds* i. 11 Some of the other human figures are indeed bird-headed and presumably wearing bird masks. *Ibid.* i. 16 A group of people..including apparently bird-masked officiants. **1610** HEALEY *St. Aug. Citie of God* 746 They [the disciples] were not *bird-mouthed unto him [Christ]. **1837** GALT in *Fraser's Mag.* XVI. 24 I am not deemed bird-mouthed on peremptory occasions. **1676** WORLIDGE *Cyder* (1691) 227 Called the *Bird-nut, from the resemblance the kernel hath to a bird, with its wings displayed..after the nut is slit in the middle. **1851** *Bird organ [see *minuet-tune*, MINUET *sb.* 3]. **1786** P. BROWNE *Jamaica* 176 *Bird Pepper. The capsule and seeds..are used by most people in these colonies. **1949** *British Birds* XLII. 102 *Bird ringers generally state the size of the brood when ringing nestlings. **1927** *Ibid.* XXI. 134 (*title*) Traps for *Bird Ringing. **1936** *Ibid.* XXIX. 226 The bird-ringing trap in the garden..was missing a great deal of the visible small bird migration. **1887** *Leisure Hour* 69/1 Mr. Maynard..has suggested the establishment of '*bird sanctuaries' along Cape Cod and other coast regions. **1922** (*title*) Bird sanctuaries in Royal Parks. **1840** DICKENS *Old C. Shop* I. xiii. 163, I can buy some *birdseed. **1909** *Daily Chron.* 25 Sept. 5/3 A bird-seed company. **1630** J. WINTHROP *Let.* 14 Aug. in *Winthrop Papers* (1931) II. 310 We have powder and peeces enough, but want flintes and *birdshott. **1761** *Boston Gaz.* 28 Sept. 3/3 To be sold by George Deblois..best gun powder and flints, bird, pigeon, duck, and goose shot. **1874** R. H. COLLINS *Kentucky* I. 217/2, 7 Radical negroes, at 2 A.M., called out of his house one who voted the Democratic ticket, and kukluxed him by shooting him with bird-shot. **1936** R. CAMPBELL *Mithraic Emblems* 58 A wind..Shook opals from the vernal palms Birdshot of the silver huntress By which the nightingale was slain. **1986** *Philadelphia Inquirer* 11 July A4/4 Birdshot and tear gas were fired toward the attacking prisoners, he said. **1910** F. W. FITZSIMONS *Snakes S. Afr.* iii. 57/1 *Thelotornis kirtlandii.* *Bird Snake. .. Distribution Tropical Africa. All over South Africa. **1954** J. A. PRINGLE *Common Snakes* 4 The Bird-snake has a long thin body which is admirably suited for its arboreal life... It is common in the Lowveld of the Transvaal. **1896** R. L. STEVENSON *Songs of Travel* 15 *Bird-song at morning. **1927** E. M. NICHOLSON *How Birds Live* iv. 39 It has become impossible now to treat the subject of territory without taking into consideration bird-song. **1826** KIRBY & SPENCE *Entomol.* III. xxviii. 40 In the class *Arachnida*, the *bird-spiders (*Mygale*) are amongst the principal giants. **1840** J. & M. LOUDON tr. *Köllar's Treat. Insects* I. 67 The Bird Spider-Fly..is scarcely half as large as the forest fly. **1844** H. STEPHENS *Bk. Farm* III. 856 The smallest insect on the same cut is the Bird-spider fly, *Ornithomyia avicularia*. **1607** *Miseries Enf. Marr.* in Hazl. *Dodsl.* IX. 563 Put up your *bird-spit, tut, I fear it not. **1881** C. C. ABBOTT *Primitive Industry* 365 The curious carved '*bird stones', common to our Atlantic coast states. **1907** F. W. HODGE et al. *Amer. Indians* I. 148/1 *Bird-stones*, a name given to a class of prehistoric stone objects of undetermined purpose, usually resembling or remotely suggesting the form of a bird. **1963** *Daily Tel.* 19 June 19/2 The..search..to find the answer to the growing menace of what they call '*birdstrike', the paralysing, sometimes fatal, effect of a bird being drawn into a jet engine. **1967** *Idle Moments* Oct. 15 The (RN) Air Station at Lossiemouth..had the worst record of any airfield in the United Kingdom for birdstrikes—collisions between birds and aircraft. [**1894** *Nature Notes* V. 5 A pair of hedge-sparrows frequented the shrubs surrounding the table..content to pick up the crumbs underneath, dropped by the other birds.] **1905** *Country-side* I. 82/3 A cock chaffinch will often play the bully at your *bird-table. **1931** *Boys' Mag.* XLV. 140/2 The large platform a little way beneath the bird table is a safeguard against cats. **1905** E. SELOUS (*title*) The *Bird Watcher in the Shetlands. **1930** J. S. HUXLEY *Bird-Watching* i. 13 From the bird-watcher pure and simple it is but a step to the bird-watcher naturalist. **1901** E. SELOUS (*title*) *Bird Watching. **1920** *Edin. Rev.* Jan. 63 Bird-Watching as a Hobby. **1930** J. S. HUXLEY *Bird-Watching* iii. 52 Accompanying Mr. Eliot Howard..on his bird-watching rounds. *Ibid.* iv. 64 A party of bird-watching friends. **1605** BACON *Adv. Learning* II. (1861) 228 If a child be *bird-witted, that is, hath not the faculty of attention, the Mathematics giveth a remedy thereunto. **1658** USSHER, *Ann.* vi. 360 [He] proved..but a bird-witted man. **1904** RAYMONT *Princ. Educ.* x. 231 The deliberate cultivation of mere irrelevance and *bird-wittedness. **1910** 'MARK RUTHERFORD' *More Pages fr. Jrnl.* 90 The birdwittedness, the absence of resistance and of difficulty, were intolerable. **1881** A. LESLIE tr. *Nordenskiöld's Voyage of Vega* II. xi. 42 The acquaintance I had made..with the *bird-world of the high north. **1904** *Westm. Gaz.* 20 Aug. 2/3 In the bird-world the lark has an exclusive and singular reputation for early rising. **1907** *Daily Chron.* 16 Feb. 6/7 The albinos—those freaks of nature in the bird-world.

10. Combinations of *bird's* (chiefly similative): **a.** *gen.*, as **bird's-beak moulding** (see quot.); **bird's-mouth**, an interior or re-entrant angle cut out of the end of a piece of timber.

1823 P. NICHOLSON *Pract. Build.* 191 Fitted..to its bearings, and to the newel, with a re-entrant angle, or bird's mouth. **1862** RICKMAN *Goth. Archit.* 15 The most complex of all mouldings is the birds-beak. **1876** GWILT *Archit.* Gloss., *Bird's-beak moulding*, a moulding which in section forms an ovolo or ogee with or without a fillet under it followed by a hollow.

b. *esp.* in plant-names; e.g. **bird's bill**, *Trigonella ornithorhynchus*; **bird's bread**, the Small Yellow Stone-crop (*Sedum acre*); **bird's eggs**, the Bladder Campion (*Silene inflata*); **bird's orchis**; **bird's pease**; **bird's tare**, a species of Arachis; **bird's tongue**, applied to numerous plants, usually in reference to the shape of their leaves, as the Greater Stitchwort (*Stellaria holostea*), the Common Maple, Scarlet Pimpernel, Great Fen Ragwort (*Senecio paludosus*), Ornithoglossum; also the fruit of the ash-tree. See also BIRD'S EYE, BIRD'S FOOT, BIRD'S NEST.

1597 GERARD *Herbal* I. cxiii. (1633) 213 **Birds Orchis.* The flowers..like in shape unto little birds, with their wings spread abroad ready to fly. **1713** J. PETIVER in *Phil. Trans.* XXVIII. 211 Winged *Birds Pease or Ochre. **1597** GERARD *Herbal* Table Supp., *Birds Tongue is Stitch-wort. *Ibid.* II. clxi, Knot grasse is called..in the North *Birds tongue. **1770** WITHERING *Brit. Plants* (1830) III. xix. 939 *Senecio paludosus.* *Bird's-tongue Groundsel.

bird (bɜːd), *v.* Also 6 **bryd.** [f. prec.]

1. *intr.* To pursue birdcatching or fowling.

1576 GASCOIGNE *Steel Gl.* Epil., Till they have caught the birds for whom they bryded. **1580** BARET *Alv.* B 707 To birde, foule, or hauke.

†**2.** *to bird off*: to 'pick off' with a musket, etc. (as a sportsman a bird). *Obs. rare.*

1700 RYCAUT *Hist. Turks* iii. 151 Their Men wading over a marshy Ground..sticking in the Mire, were birded off and killed with Musquet-shot.

3. *trans.* To give the bird to (an actor, entertainer, etc.): see BIRD *sb.* 5 b. *colloq.*

1936 N. COWARD *Red Peppers* 93 Lot of hooligans birding the poor old man.

bird, pa. t. of BIR *v. Obs.* to pertain, befit.

†**'bird-bolt.** *Obs.* Also 6-7 **burbolt**, 7 **birdboult.** [f. BIRD *sb.* + BOLT.] A kind of blunt-headed arrow used for shooting birds.

c **1440** *Promp. Parv.* 50 Brydbolt or burdebolt, *epitilium.* *a* **1553** UDALL *Royster D.* (1869) 43 *Mery.* He hath in his head. *Custance.* As much braine as a burbolt. **1601** SHAKS. *Twel. N.* I. v. 100 To take those things for Bird-bolts, that you deeme Cannon bullets. **1659** in Burton *Diary* (1828) III. 541 You can never make a bird-bolt of a pig's tail. **1865** TYLOR *Early Hist. Man.* viii. 209 The wooden headed bird-bolts of the Middle Ages.

b. *attrib.*, as in *birdbolt-shot*.

1553-87 FOXE *A. & M.* (1596) 1887/1 Only one, which was a byrdbolt shot off. **1626** BACON *Sylva* §249 Some Bird-bolt shot, or more, from the River of Seane.

bird-bolt, variant of BURBOT *sb.*

bird-cage ('bɜːdkeɪdʒ). [f. BIRD *sb.* + CAGE *sb.*]

1. A cage or coop for a bird or birds. ***bird-cage clock*** (see quot.). Hence **bird-cage-like** *a.*

1490 *Test. Ebor.* (Surtees Soc. 1869) IV. 57 De j lez bird-cage, cum ij lez ald bordes, j d. **1662** GERBIER *Princ.* 17 Those who seem to have had for Models Bird-Cages. **1663** —— *Counsel* 46 Fit for substantial Structures, but not usual in Lime and Haire Birdcage-like-Buildings. **1691** MOSES PITT *Cries of the Oppressed* 105, I built a great House in Duke street, just against the Bird-Cages in St. James's Park. [Hence the name *Birdcage Walk.*] **1784** COWPER *Acc. Hares* in *Poems* (1811) II. 425, I was cleaning a bird-cage while the hares were with me. **1851** MAYHEW *London Labour* (1861) II. 65 Some twenty empty bird-cages of different sizes hung against the walls. **1952** GLOAG *Dict. Furniture* 144 *Birdcage clock*, a modern term sometimes used to describe the iron or

brass weight-driven wall clocks which were made in large numbers during the 17th century.

2. *Sporting.* The paddock at the Newmarket race-course in which horses are generally saddled. Also, a similar paddock at other race-courses.

1884 *St. James' Gaz.* 1 May 7/1 All the favourites were brought into the birdcage. **1934** *Evening Post* (Wellington) 13 June 6/3 The stewards' stand, however, has not yet been touched, and only the birdcage will be used at this portion of the course. **1940** F. SARGESON *Man & Wife* (1944) 64 And didn't Fred and me get a kick out of taking the horses into the birdcages and leading them round. **1952** M. DUGGAN in D. M. Davin *N.Z. Short Stories* (1953) 246 In the birdcage the horses for the first race circled and danced.

'bird-dom. *nonce-wd.* [f. as prec. + -DOM.] Birds collectively; 'the feathered creation.'

1884 G. FENN *Sw. Mace* i. 5 All bird-dom breaks into song.

†**birde.** *Obs.* [App. short for **ȝebirde*:—OE. *ȝebyrd(o* 'birth, lineage'; cf. BIRTH (of which Mätzner and Stratmann treat this as a variant).]

1. Birth; offspring. (ME. instances doubtful.)

[*a* **1000** *Crist* (Gr.) 65 Witȝan cyþdon Cristes ȝebyrd.] *a* **1225** *Ancr. R.* 158 þauh þe engel Gabriel hefde his burde [*other MSS.* burðe] ibocked. *a* **1300** *Cursor M.* 20281 (Gött.) He þat I bare, þat blisful bird [*Cott.* brid, *Laud* breth, *Trin.* birþe. But see BIRD *sb.* 1 c.]

2. Family; nation.

[*c* **890** K. ÆLFRED *Bæda* II. vii. (Bosw.), Of ðære cynelican ȝebyrdo.] *c* **1200** ORMIN 2052 An þatt wass off hire kinn, & all off hire birde. *Ibid.* 8358 Far till Issrææless land Inntill þin aȝhenn birde.

birdeen (bɜːˈdiːn, ˈbɜːdiːn). [f. BIRD *sb.* + *-een*, Ir. *-ín* dim. suffix: cf. *colleen*.] A young bird; also, a young girl (used as a playful form of address).

1895 'FIONA MACLEOD' *Mount. Lovers* 47 She was like a birdeen lured by the dancing sunrays. *Ibid.* 61, I am sure, birdeen. **1916** C. A. RENSHAW *England's Boys* 58, I can hear your sleepy birdeens in their swaying moonlit nest. **1922** I. J. POSTGATE (*title*) Robin in khaki: a book of birdeens.

birder (ˈbɜːdə(r)). [f. BIRD *v.* + -ER¹.]

†**1.** A bird-catcher, a fowler. *Obs.*

1481–90 *Howard Househ. Bks.* 379 My Lord gaff to a byrder of the Quenes xx. *d.* **1551** TURNER *Herbal* I. Fvb, Byrders..lyme the twygges and go a batfolynge wyth them. **1622** BRETON *Strange Newes* (1876) 13 And like good birders kindly knew a Bunting from a Larke.

2. A breeder of birds.

1827 CARLYLE *Germ. Rom.* III. 151 His father..who in winter had been a birder.

3. A local name for the wild cat.

1864 *Northampton Herald* 2 July, In the woods of Rockingham and Burghley, it is known by the name of birder.

4. A bird-watcher. orig. *U.S.*

1945 *Audubon Mag.* XLVII. 212/2 As a birder and a soldier, I've wandered up and down the country. **1965** *Times* 22 Dec. 7/1 Bird watchers—known in America as birders. **1967** *Boston Sunday Globe* 23 Apr. B59/2 Some time ago an assembly of Audubon enthusiasts rejected the term 'bird watchers' by which they had been commonly known, and adopted the designation 'birders'. **1975** *Globe & Mail* (Toronto) 8 Oct. S6/1 Ottawa birders have seen 17 grey jays so far this fall. **1980** *Daily Tel.* 13 Nov. 16/8 Mr Oddie is a serious bird-watcher, or 'birder' as he prefers to be called. **1985** *Birds* Autumn 38/2 The proficient birder can identify birds by song as easily as by sight.

'birdery. *nonce-wd.* [f. BIRD *sb.* + -ERY.] A collection of birds; birds collectively.

1831 *Blackw. Mag.* XXX. 260 The Birdery of North America, it may be said, belonged to him.

'birdhood. *rare.* [f. BIRD *sb.* + -HOOD.] The state or condition of a bird.

1884 *Cent. Mag.* XXVIII. 483 The vigor of waxing birdhood thrills my throat.

birdie (ˈbɜːdɪ), *sb.* [f. BIRD *sb.* + -IE, -Y⁴.]

1. a. A little bird, a dear or pretty little bird.

1792 BURNS *Braes o' Ballochmyle*, Ye birdies dumb, in with'ring bowers. **1864** TENNYSON *Sea Dreams* 281 She sang this baby song. What does little birdie say In her nest at peep of day?

b. = BIRD *sb.* 1 d. Cf. BIRDEEN.

1889 *Cent. Dict.*, *Birdie*.., a term of endearment for a child or a young woman. **1915** P. MACGILL *Amateur Army* v. 62 'Cup of coffee, birdie!' he cried,..trying to grip her [*sc.* the waitress's] hand.

2. In golf: the fact of doing a hole in one under the par score. (Cf. BIRD *sb.* 4 b.)

[**1911** *Maclean's Mag.* Sept. 205/1 Lanesborough followed with a 'bird' straight down the course, about two hundred and fifteen yards.] **1921** *Glasgow Herald* 14 Sept. 10 Brown squared with a 'birdie' 3 at the second. **1923** *Daily Mail* 13 June 10 Then he went all out to 'shoot birdies'..the American colloquialism for aiming at doing holes in a stroke under the par scores. **1960** *Times* 23 May 5/1 She..at last got down a birdie putt.

'birdie, *v. Golf.* [f. the sb. (sense 2).] *trans.* To play (a hole) in one under the par score.

1956 H. W. WIND *Story Amer. Golf* VI. 545 Fleck had been faced with birdieing that hole the day before. **1968** *Times* 11 Oct. 13/2 He birdied the 14th, and missed three six-foot putts. **1975** *New Yorker* 5 May 103/1 This was the championship in which Palmer got back into the fight by birdieing six of the first seven holes on that final round. **1984** *News* (Mexico City) 12 Mar. 32/2 She was within one shot of the lead before double-bogeying 13—a hole Johnson birdied to go back up by five strokes.

birdikin (ˈbɜːdɪkɪn). *rare.* [f. BIRDIE *sb.* + -KIN, dimin.] A little bird.

a **1864** THACKERAY is cited by WEBSTER.

birding (ˈbɜːdɪŋ), *vbl. sb.* [f. BIRD *v.*]

1. The action or sport of bird-catching or fowling. *arch.*

1569 J. SANFORD *Agrippa's Van. Artes* 122 An other exercise of Hunting, which is termed Fouling, or Birding. **1605** VERSTEGAN *Dec. Intell.* iii. (1628) 63 The great pleasure hee tooke in his youth in birding. **1729** M. BROWNE *Pisc. Eclog.* VIII. (1773) 110 Two Swains who are exercised in Birding. [**1852** THACKERAY *Esmond* I. iv, Lord Castlewood would take the lad..a-hunting or a-birding.]

b. *fig.* and *transf. arch.*

[*c* **1460** *Towneley Myst.* 79, I have..of hir byrdyng hir upbrade, And she not gylty is.] **1624** FLETCHER *Rule a Wife* V. i. (1776) 55 Do you go a birding for all sorts of people? **1656** in Burton *Diary* (1828) I. 178 They..go a birding for sheriffs every year. **1708** MRS. CENTLIVRE *Busie Body* I. i, A birding thus early!

c. *colloq.* The activity of bird-watching. Also *attrib.*

[**1927** *Daily News* 16 June 6/5 Miss Fry plays the flute and joins in the arduous sport of 'birding'. This consists in following across country any strange species of bird, and of playing the flute beneath the tree on which the melodious songster performs.] **1934** *Brit. Birds* XXVII. 345, I wrenched up the gorse-bush by means of a hooked stick-crowbar, a tool which sometimes forms part of my 'birding' equipment with such an emergency in view. **1956** PETERSON & FISHER *Wild Amer.* xxxiii. 356 Bill did more pure birding than the rest of us. **1977** *New Yorker* 12 Sept. 31/3 Top of the Point..has for years been a popular birding spot. **1980** *Daily Tel.* 13 Nov. 16/8 The book gives a glossary of 'birding' terms and advice on identification. **1986** *Bird Watching* May 9/4 Membership of a bird club can open the door to the whole wonderful world of birding probably quicker than by any other means.

†**2.** A taking aim, as at a bird. *Obs.*

a **1678** MARVELL *Loyal Scot*, [He] entertains..his time,.. With birding at the Dutch.

3. *attrib.*

1588 *Lanc. & Chesh. Wills* III. 12 To Robt. Leftwiche my birdinge piece with a little horne flaske. **1598** SHAKS. *Merry W.* IV. ii. 59. **1613** J. [DENNYS] *Angling* in Arb. *Garner* I. 153 Like to the pellet of a birding bow. **1669** J. ROSE *Eng. Vineyard* (1675) 28 When the fruit is of the size of birding-shot. **1673** *Lond. Gaz.* No. 751/4 A plain Birding Gun, in a Red Leather Case. **1816** SCOTT *Antiq.* xxxv, To crack off his birding-piece at a poor covey of partridges.

birding, -yne, obs. forms of BURDEN *sb.*

birdinsek, obs. form of BURDENSAK.

birdless (ˈbɜːdlɪs). [f. BIRD *sb.* + -LESS.] Void of birds; deserted or unfrequented by birds.

1508 *Balade* in Sibbald's *Scot. Poetry* I. 155 A birdless cage; a key withouten lok. **1797** HOLCROFT *Stolberg's Trav.* (ed. 2) II. lxiii. 426 The Greeks gave it the appellation of *Aornos*: or birdless. **1906** *Westm. Gaz.* 14 Apr. 18/1 The Yellow Cat's paw is out, after a birdless winter. **1955** P. LARKIN *Less Deceived* 20 A huge and birdless silence.

birdlet (ˈbɜːdlɛt). [f. as prec. + -LET.] A little or tiny bird.

1867 LONGF. *Dante's Purg.* XXXI. 61 The callow birdlet.

bird-lime (ˈbɜːdlaɪm), *sb.* [f. as prec. + LIME *sb.*] **1. a.** A glutinous substance spread upon twigs, by which birds may be caught and held fast.

c **1440** *Promp. Parv.* 50 Brydelyme, *viscus.* **1578** LYTE *Dodoens* 701 With the barkes of Holme they make Birdlyme. **1697** *Phil. Trans.* XIX. 368 It would draw out into long tough strings, like Bird-lime. **1863** THORNBURY *True as Steel* II. 152 Love..is like birdlime; the more we struggle, the more entangled our wings get.

b. *fig.* and *transf.* Also *attrib.*

1562 A. SCOTT *N. Yere Gift*, Kirk-mennis cursit substance semis sweet Till land-men, with that leud burd-lyme are knyttit. **1626** T. H. tr. *Caussin's Holy Crt.* 86 O what a strong birdlyme is a benefit! All generous birds are taken with it. **1705** VANBRUGH *Confeder.* v. 2 That birdlime there stole it. *Ibid.* III. ii, My rogue of a Son has laid his birdlime fingers on it.

2. *Rhyming slang.* Time; often *spec.* a term of imprisonment (cf. TIME *sb.* 7 b (*d*)).

1857 'DUCANGE ANGLICUS' *Vulgar Tongue* 2 *Bird-lime*, time. **1961** *John o' London's* 16 Nov. 551/2 Time is *bird lime*, but this is shortened to *bird* and..imprisonment is often called *bird*. **1962** *Radio Times* 20 Sept. 35 In the past Charley's done his 'birdlime' but he was given time off for good behaviour.

'bird-lime, *v.* [f. prec. sb.] *trans.* To smear or catch with (or as with) bird-lime. Hence **bird-limed** *ppl. a.*

1580 HOLLYBAND *Treas. Fr. Tong*, *Englué*, birdlimed. **1618** HOLYDAY *Juvenal* vi. 100 It bird-limes her poor husbands lips. **1791** WOLCOTT (P. Pindar) *Rights of Kings* Wks. 1812 II. 427 Some..bird-limed Fly. **1802** SOUTHEY *Lett.* (1856) I. 195 If..any very desirable house were vacant ..that would perhaps birdlime me.

'bird-limy, *a.* [f. as prec. + -Y¹.] Of the nature of bird-lime; sticky.

1658 ROWLAND *Mouffet's Theat. Ins.* 1069 They smeer it over with a birdlimy glutinous spittle.

birdling (ˈbɜːdlɪŋ). [f. BIRD *sb.* + -LING.] A little or young bird, a nestling.

1856 MRS. BROWNING *Aur. Leigh* 250 Nestled birdlings. **1878** *Masque Poets* 36 The birdling in the tree.

bird-man, birdman. Also birdsman. **1.** A man concerned with birds; an ornithologist.

1697 *Lond. Gaz.* No. 3269/4 At Black Joe's, the German Bird-man..canary-birds. **1729** M. BROWNE *Pisc. Eclog.* VIII. (1773) 119 The Fisher on the green-sea-deep, And Birdsman in the osier copse. **1796** MORSE *Amer. Geog.* II. 17 The birdmen or climbers..bringing away the birds and their eggs. **1844** C. WATERTON *Ess. Nat. Hist.* (ed. 3) p. lxviii, These birdmen outwardly had the appearance of Italian banditti, but it was all outside and nothing more. **1969** *Observer* 16 Feb. 7/5 The Smithsonian staff itself is.. envious of the birdmen for getting so much money. Those involved in the ornithological expedition have had to receive military clearance.

2. An aviator, airman. *colloq.*

1909 *Daily Chron.* 27 Oct. 4/4, I shall say: 'I saw the first bird-men in England, my dears.' **1917** 'CONTACT' *Airman's Outings* 244 Even intrepid birdmen (war correspondentese for flying officers) tire of trying to be offensive on a patrol. **1957** J. BRAINE *Room at Top* iv. 44 You were both intrepid birdmen, weren't you?

bird-nest: see BIRD'S-NEST.

bird's-eye, *sb.* and *a.* Also bird-eye.

I. *sb.* **1.** A name given to several plants with small round bright flowers.

a. A species of Primula (*P. farinosa*) having pale lilac flowers with a yellow eye; formerly called ***bird's eyen***, and now also more fully ***bird's-eye primrose***. The ***American bird's-eye*** is a kindred species (*P. pusilla*).

b. Germander Speedwell (*Veronica chamædrys*).

c. Species of *Adonis* (more usually *Pheasant's eye*).

d. Robert's Geranium, and many other plants locally: see Britten and Holland.

1597 GERARD *Herbal* II. ccIxi. 638 In the middle of euery small flower appeereth a little yellowe spot, resembling the eie of a bird, which hath mooued the people..to call it Birds Eine. **1731** MILLER *Gard. Dict.*, *Adonis*, or Flos Adonis, Bird's-Eye, or Pheasant's-Eye. **1771** *Ibid.* Primula (Farinosa), called Birds' eyen. **1859** C. JOHNS *Flowers Field* 465 *Veronica Chamædrys*. A well-known plant, which, under the popular names of Blue Speedwell and Birds-eye, is a favourite with every one. **1868** BURGESS *Old Eng. Wild Fl.* 104 The Bird's eye Primrose is..somewhat like an auricula. **1885** *Longm. Mag.* 311 Blue Veronica..sometimes called germander speedwell, sometimes bird's-eye.

2. A variety of manufactured tobacco in which the ribs of the leaves are cut along with the fibre.

1857 TROLLOPE *Three Clerks* I. ii. 29 Mary, my dear, a screw of bird's-eye! *Ibid.* 33 An ample allowance of gin-and-water and bird's-eye tobacco. **1861** SALA *Tw. round Clock* 40 A pipeful of the best Bristol Bird's-eye. **1922** JOYCE *Ulysses* 444 Gaudy dollwomen loll in the lighted doorways.. smoking birdseye cigarettes.

II. *attrib.*

3. Of or belonging to a bird's eye; as in ***bird's-eye view***: a view of a landscape from above, such as is presented to the eye of a bird; a perspective representation of such a view; also *fig.* a résumé of a subject.

1762–71 H. WALPOLE *Vertue's Anecd. Paint.* (1786) II. 145 It exhibits an almost birds-eye view of an extensive country. **1790** BURKE *Fr. Rev.* 96 A bird-eye landscape of a promised land. *a* **1797** —— *Let.* Wks. 1845 V. 148 The government..have..as it were a bird's eye view of everything. **1859** C. BARKER *Assoc. Princ.* i. 2 Presenting a *résumé* or bird's-eye view of a subject.

4. Marked as with bird's eyes; spotted. ***bird's-eye limestone***: a lower Silurian rock of North America, with eye-like markings. ***bird's-eye maple***: the wood of the sugar maple when full of little knotty spots, used in cabinet-making. ***bird's-eye primrose, tobacco***: see 2, 3.

1665 PEPYS *Diary* (1879) III. 156 My wife very fine in a new yellow bird's-eye hood, as the fashion is now. **1689** *Lond. Gaz.* No. 2440/4 A third [pair of stays] of Olive coloured Birds-eye Silk. **1793** E. P. SIMCOE *Diary* 26 Apr. (1911) xi. 161 Capt. Shaw has given me a tea-chest in bird's-eye maple. **1837** HAWTHORNE *Amer. Note-bks.* (1871) I. 81 Finished off with bird's-eye maple and mahogany. **1841** THACKERAY *Yellowpl. P.* 22 He wore a white hat, a bird's-eye handkerchief, and a cut-away coat. **1848** MRS. GASKELL *Mary Barton* I. iii. 37 Her business was duly announced in gold letters..enclosed in a bird's-eye maple frame. **1916** A. BENNETT *Lion's Share* xxx. 221 A table of bird's-eye maple.

bird's-eyed, *a.* [f. BIRD'S-EYE.] Of maple: having small eye-like markings.

1855 *Trans. Mich. Agric. Soc.* VI. 528 Much of this maple timber is curled and some bird's-eyed.

'bird's-foot, 'bird-foot.

1. Applied to objects having the shape of a bird's foot, as various plants. **a.** A small yellow vetch (*Ornithopus*); **b.** A small fern (*Cheilanthes radiata*); **c.** = Bird's-foot Trefoil.

1578 LYTE *Dodoens* 486 Birdes foote is lyke to..the wilde vetche, but far smaller. **1794** MARTYN *Rousseau's Bot.* xxv. 366 The wild species [*Lotus corniculatus*] is called common Bird's foot. **1859** MISS YONGE *T. Thumb* xiv. 91 There the scented thyme..the glowing bird's-foot, and the tufted milk-wort grow. **1865** GOSSE *Land & Sea* (1874) Among Ferns of humbler pretensions, the pretty little Bird-foot.

d. Applied to the delta of a river (see quot. 1944).
1939 A. K. LOBECK *Geomorphology* vii. 230 (*caption*) Three types of delta; arctuate, estuarine, and bird's foot. *Ibid.* 231 Bird's foot delta. Still a third type of delta is built by streams carrying large amounts of extremely fine material. **1944** A. HOLMES *Princ. Physical Geol.* x. 171 The Mississippi..extends its mouths seaward by way of deep channels..which are outstretched like fingers. This part of its delta is the chief example of the *bird's foot* type.

2. ***bird's-foot trefoil*** or ***lotus***: a yellow leguminous plant (*Lotus corniculatus*), a native of Britain; also applied to other species. So ***bird's-foot fenugreek, bird's-foot violet.***
1833 *Proc. Berw. Nat. Club* I. 29 *Lotus decumbens*, Spreading Bird's-foot Trefoil. **1861** MISS PRATT *Flower. Pl.* II. 97 *Trigonella ornithopodioides*, Bird's Foot Fenugreek.. a very little plant..and bearing very small yellow flowers. **1882** *Garden* 29 Ap. 286/2 The Bird's-foot Violet [is] one of the sweetest flowers we have seen.

3. ***bird's-foot star, sea-star***: an echinoderm related to the star-fish.
1855 KINGSLEY *Glaucus* (1878) 167 The bird's foot star (*Palmipes membranaceus*)..crawling by its thousand sucking-feet..a pentagonal webbed bird's foot, of scarlet and orange shagreen. **1862** ANSTED *Channel Isl.* II. ix. (ed. 2) 237 The Cribella, the sun-stars..and the birds' foot sea-star, are all represented.

'bird's-nest, bird-nest, *sb.*
1. a. (Usually two words): The nest of a bird; *spec.* the edible nest of certain species of swallow found in the Chinese Sea. Also *attrib.*, as in ***bird's-nest soup.***
1599 SHAKS. *Much Ado* II. i. 229 A Schoole-boy.. ouerioyed with finding a birds nest. **1760** GOLDSM. *Cit. W.* xcvii, I am for a Chinese dish of bear's claws and bird's nests. **1865** LONGF. *Hiaw.* Introd. 25 In the bird's-nests of the forest. **1864** R. REID *Glasgow & Env.* 354 The [cotton] yarns..were imported in globular balls, pretty similar to a bird's nest, and got the name of Bird-nest Yarns. **1871** M. COLLINS *Mrq. & Merch.* II. iii. 82 Ideas..as strange to an ..Englishman's brain as bird's-nest soup to his palate.
b. *transf.* Also *attrib.*
1931 R. CAMPBELL *Georgiad* ii. 32 A bird's-nest wig, a melancholy face. **1950** A. CHRISTIE *Murder is Announced* i. 16 Her curly bird's nest of grey hair was in a good deal of disorder. **1961** *Sunday Express* 19 Feb. 14/3 Worn with dark legs and a bird's nest hair style.
2. A cask or similar shelter fixed at the mast-head of ships in the Arctic regions to protect the man on the look-out; a crow's nest.
1867 SMYTH *Sailor's Word-bk.*
3. A name given to several plants: **a.** The Wild Carrot (or its concave umbel); **b.** *Monotropa Hypophitys*; **c.** = Bird's-nest Orchid.
1597 GERARD *Herbal* I. cccxci, Wilde Carrot..The whole tuft is drawne together when the seede is ripe, resembling a birdes nest, whereupon it hath been named of some Birds nest. *Ibid.* I. cvi. 176 *Nidus avis*, Birdes nest..hath many tangling rootes platted or crossed one ouer another verie intricately..It is esteemed a degenerate kinde of Orchis. **1848** W. GARDINER *Flora Forfar.* 84 *Wild Carrot.* This is the origin of our garden carrot, and is sometimes called Bird's nest. **1861** MISS PRATT *Flower. Pl.* V. 200 Order. *Orchideæ* ..(Common Bird's nest). **1870** HOOKER *Stud. Flora* I. xliv. §12 *Monotropa*, Bird's-nest..a saprophyte feeding on decayed vegetable matter.
4. bird's-nest fern, a name given to various exotic ferns from their habit of growth; **bird's-nest orchid** (*Neottia Nidus-avis*), a plant, wild in Britain, entirely of a brown feuillemort colour.
1858 W. ELLIS *Vis. Madagascar* xi. 285 The large bird's nest ferns might sometimes be seen at the end of the trunk of a dead tree. **1875** MISS BIRD *Sandwich Isl.* (1880) 82 The glossy, tropical-looking bird's-nest fern, or Asplenium Nidus. **1883** *Good Words* Dec. 791/1 The Birds'-Nest Orchid wears the livery of withered leaves.
5. *Path.* (See quots.)
1879 *St. George's Hosp. Rep.* IX. 500 A tubular epithelioma..consisting of numerous tracks of epithelial cells (without any birds' nests). **1879** *Syd. Soc. Lex.*, *Bird's nest bodies*, a name given to a condition of arrangement of the scaly cells of epithelial cancer, in which they are placed in nest fashion around a circular central space, which contains amorphous colloid matter or degenerated cells. **1885** *Buck's Handbk. Med. Sci.* I. 771/1 Concentric formations known as 'birds' nests', which characterize the typical squamous epithelioma. **1894** GOULD *Dict. Med.*, *Bird's-nest Bodies*, or *Cells*, the cells of certain forms of carcinoma, distinguished by the concentric arrangement of their cell-walls.
6. bird's-nest spider = *bird-spider* (BIRD *sb.* 9).
1910 *Encycl. Brit.* II. 307/1 The larger species of Bird's Nest Spiders (*Avicularia*)..undoubtedly attack young birds.

'bird's-ˌnest, bird-nest, *v.* [Inferred from the gerund *bird's nesting*, which was much earlier in use; cf. *nutting*, *to nut*, etc.] *intr.* To search for bird's nests.
1856 J. GRANT *Black Drag.* xlvi, A thicket of fir-trees, in which I had often bird-nested. **1875** A. HOPE *My Schoolboy Fr.* 148 They went to birdnest in the morning. **1877** *Hon. Miss Ferrard* II. ii. 227 A solitary magpie, birdsnesting.

'bird's-ˌnester. One who goes bird's-nesting.
c **1825** (*title*) Ben the Birdsnester. **1896** *Brit. Birds, Their Nests & Eggs* I. 35 A trick which..renders the birds-nester more satisfied that he is on the right scent.

'bird's-ˌnesting, bird-nesting, *vbl. sb.* [f. BIRD'S NEST *sb.* + -ING[1]; cf. *nutting*.] **1. a.** The action or occupation of searching for bird's-nests.
1772 BARRINGTON in *Phil. Trans.* LXII. 314 *note*, Birds-nesting is confined almost entirely to hedges, and low shrubs. **1806** DUNCAN *Nelson* 9 He..went out a bird's-nesting. **1881** *Macm. Mag.* XLIV. 347 Where is the schoolboy who has not a strong love for bird-nesting?
b. *attrib.* and *ppl. a.*
1848 *Proc. Berw. Nat. Club* II. 273 A man..whose bird-nesting days were spent in the woods near Gifford. **1859** HELPS *Friends in C.*, Ser. II. II. viii. 157 Not that he is a birds'-nesting boy.
2. Furring of a passage.
1901 *Daily Mail* 26 Aug. 3/5 The cap ferrules of the Minerva's tubes were found to be partially choked from 'bird-nesting'. **1930** *Engineering* 9 May 597/3 To overcome the trouble of 'birdnesting' originally experienced in the lower rows of boiler tubes.

†'bird's-nie, -nye. *Obs.* [*Nye* for EYE, as in *my nye* = *myn eye*.] An obsolete vulgar term of endearment; cf. *pig's-nie*.
1661 R. DAVENPORT *City Night-C.* II. in *Dodsley* (1780) XI. 289 Oh, my sweet birds-nie! What a wench have I of thee! *Ibid.* 306 Pr'ythee, sweet birds-nye, be content.

bire, obs. form of BYRE.

bireade, -rede, birein: see BEREDE, BERAIN.

†bi'redien, *v. Obs.* [ME., f. *bi-*, BE- + *redien* to make READY.]
c **1205** LAY. 4198 We scullen ous bi-redien.

birefringence (baɪrɪ'frɪndʒəns). *Optics.* [Cf. F. *biréfringence*, *-ent.*] = *double refraction* (see REFRACTION 2). Also **bire'fringent** *a.*
1889 *Cent. Dict.*, Birefringent. **1898** E. S. DANA *Text-bk Min.* (ed. 2) II. 172 The wide separation of the two refracted rays by calcite..is a consequence of the large difference in the values of its indices of refraction, in other words, as technically expressed, it is due to the *strength* of its double refraction, or its *birefringence*. **1949** *New Biol.* VII. 73 The spindle is birefringent (i.e. it has different refractive indices in different transecting planes). **1957** *Ibid.* XXII. 67 The polarizing microscope..is a device for detecting and measuring optical anisotropy, commonly referred to as birefringence (or double refraction), because the value of the refractive index varies systematically in different directions.

bireme ('baɪriːm), *a.* and *sb.* [ad. L. *birēmis*, adj. and sb., f. *bi-* two, twice + *rēmus* oar.] **A.** *adj.* Having two banks of oars. **B.** *sb.* A galley having two banks of oars.
1600 HOLLAND *Livy* VII. vi. 1399 *note*, The forme of a bireme gally. **1662** J. BARGRAVE *Pope Alex. VII.* (1867) 118 Their byremes & tyremes being but pitiful boats. **1697** POTTER *Antiq. Greece* III. xiv (1715) 125 Betwixt an Unireme and Bireme, consisting of a Bank and a Half. **1858** RAWLINSON *Herodotus* I. 290 *note*, Biremes were probably a Phœnician invention.

†bi'reme, *v. Obs.* [ME., f. *bi-*, BE- + *remen*:—OE. *hrémen* (in WSax. *hrieman*, *hrýman*) to cry out.] *trans.* To call out at.
c **1200** *Trin. Coll. Hom.* 29 Nu shalt [þu]..biremen him mið euel wordes.

biretta (bɪ'rɛtə). Also 6 **berretta, barretta,** 9 **beretta, birretta.** [a. It. *berretta* and Sp. *birreta* (= Pr. *berreta*, *barreta*, F. *barette*), found beside the masc. forms Pr. *birret*, Béarn. *berreto*, Catalan *baret*, F. *béret*:—late L. *birretum* cap, f. *birrus* (*byrrhus*) a cloak or cape of silk or wool, prob. ad. Gr. πυρρός flame-coloured, yellow.] The square cap worn by clerics of the Roman Catholic Church; that of priests being black, of bishops purple, of cardinals red.
1598 BP. HALL *Sat.* IV. vii. 52 Or his berretta [**1599** Barretta] or his towred felt. **1865** *Pall Mall G.* 3 Oct. 11 Near his church, he should of course wear the beretta or priest's cap. **1881** *Athenæum* 21 May 693/2 He has a black shock of hair escaping under a red biretta.

†bi'reusing, *vbl. sb. Obs.* Also 1 **behréowsung,** 2 **bireusinge, bireusunke,** 3 **bireousinge, -unge, birewsunge.** [f. prec. + -ING[1].] Repentance, compunction, ruth.
c **1000** ÆLFRIC *Gram.* xxxiii. 207 *Pœnitentia*, behréowsung. *c* **1200** *Trin. Coll. Hom.* 49 Bireusinge of ure fule sinnes. *a* **1225** *Ancr. R.* 372 Þe uormeste bitternesse is bireousunge & dedbote uor sunne.

†bi'reusy, *v. Obs.* Forms: 1 **behréowsian,** 2 **bireusien,** 3 **bireowsen,** *Orm.* **bireowwsenn, -rewwsenn, bi-, byreusy(e.** [OE. *behréowsian*, f. BE- + *hréowsian* to be sorry: cf. MHG. *beriuwesen*, *beriusen* to be sorry for.]
1. *trans.* To be sorry for, repent of (a sin, etc.)
c **1000** ÆLFRIC *Gram.* xxxiii. 207 *Pœnitere*, behréowsjan. *c* **1175** *Lamb. Hom.* 97 Þa þet heore sunnan bireusiaδ. *c* **1200** ORMIN 13631 Birewwseþþ inn hiss herrte..hiss missdede. *c* **1315** SHOREHAM 43 Ac senne..To bi-reusy he proveth.
2. To feel sorry for, have pity on (a person).
c **1275** *Sinners Beware* 341 in *O.E. Misc.* 83 Þe milde and þe clene..Nulleþ heo neuer ene By-reusy ne bimene.

†bi'rewe, *v. Obs.* Forms: 3 **bireowen, birewen,** 4 **birue,** 4–5 **birewe,** 5 **biriwe.** [ME. *bireowen*, *birewen*, f. *bi-*, BE- 4 + *reowen*, *rewen*:—OE. *hréowan* to RUE.]
1. *trans.* To repent of, rue; also *impers.*
c **1200** ORMIN 4506 Whase maȝȝ..innwarrdliȝ bireowenn itt. **1377** LANGL. *P. Pl.* B. XII. 250 Þough þe riche..birewe þe tyme þat euere he gadered so grete and gaf..so litel.
2. To feel sorry for, pity (a person).
a **1300** in Wright *Pop. Treat. Sc.* 137 Thu makest the se [= so] heȝ her, and noman nelt bi-rue. *c* **1449** PECOCK *Repr.* II. xvii. 253 Y schal neuere biriwe ȝou.

†bi'rewness. *Obs.* Only in 3 **bireaunesse.** [f. ME. *rewnesse*, after the prec. vb. Cf. MHG. *beriuwenisse.*] Commiseration, compassion, ruth, pity.
a **1225** *Ancr. R.* 66 Uor þi þæt [he]..þurh þe bireaunesse crie Crist inwardliche merci uor ou.

birgand(er, obs. form of BERGANDER.

birges, obs. form of BRUGES (satin).

birie(n, biriel(e, obs. ff. BURGH, BURY, BURIAL.

birimose (ˌbaɪraɪ'məʊs), *a.* [f. BI- *pref.*[2] 1 + RIMOSE, ad. L. *rīmōsus* full of cracks.] 'Opening by two slits.' Gray *Bot. Text-bk.* 1880.

†bi'ripe, *v. Obs.* [ME., f. *bi-*, BE- + *ripen*:—OE. *ripan* to REAP.] *trans.* To pluck the fruit of.
a **1300** *E.E. Psalter* lxxix. 13 [lxxx. 12] And bi-ripe it [the vineyard] alle þat gane for-bi þe wai.

†bi'rise, *v. Obs.* [ME., f. *bi-*, BE- + **risen* = ONorthumb. *rísa*, short for *ȝerísa*, OE. *ȝerísan* to become.] To become, befit (only in 3rd pers.).
c **1175** *Lamb. Hom.* 111 Wisdom, biriseδ weran and clenesse birisaδ wifan. *c* **1205** LAY. 9821 Þingges þe biriseδ [*c* **1250** bi-comeþ] to ælche kinge.

birk, -en, -in, north. forms of BIRCH, BIRCHEN.

birk, var. BERK.

†'birken, *v. Obs. rare.* [f. *birken*, north form of BIRCHEN]. *trans.* To beat with a birch-rod, to birch.
1675 J. SMITH *Chr. Relig. Appeal* 91 (L.) They..birkened those they met with, from the rump to the crown of the head.

birkie ('bɜːkɪ, Sc. 'bɪrkɪ), *sb.* and *a. Sc.* Also **birky.** [Connexion has been suggested with ON. *berkja* to bark, boast, which might do for the sense, but the form is uncertain.]
A. *sb.* **1.** A familiar or jocular term for a man, often connoting self-assertion, crustiness, or the 'having a mind of his own'; sometimes slightly depreciatory = 'strutting fellow,' but often, like 'fellow,' 'carle,' 'chield,' without definable force.
1724 RAMSAY *Poems* (1800) 92 (JAM.) Spoke like ye'rsell, auld birky; never fear. **1795** BURNS *A Man's a Man* iii, Ye see yon birkie ca'd 'a lord,' Wha struts, an' stares, an' a' that. **1816** SCOTT *Old Mort.* xli, Folks may speak out afore they birkies now. **1836** J. MAYNE *Siller Gun* in Chambers' *Hum. Sc. Poems* 126 Auld birkies, innocently slee, Wi' cap and stoup.
2. A game at cards, 'Beggar-my-neighbour.'
1777 BRAND *Pop. Antiq.* (1849) II. 396. **1827** J. WILSON *Noct. Ambr.* Wks. 1855 I. 302 Catch me at the cards, unless it be a game at Birky, for I'm sick o' Whust itself.
B. *adj.* Somewhat irrepressible, active, spirited.
1821 *Ann. Par. Dalmailing* 40 (JAM.) Kate, being a nimble and birky thing, was..useful to the lady. **1822** *Steam-Boat* 38 (JAM.) A gay and birky callan, not to be set down by a look or a word. **1830** GALT *Lawrie T.* VI. viii. (1849) 289 A very fashious trade that of school-mastering either hardy lasses or birkey boys.

†birl, *v.*[1] *Obs.* [Etymology unknown; perhaps two words: with the latter quot. cf. PIRL.] *trans.* To prick, pierce, or stab; to cover with punctures.
c **1400** *Destr. Troy* XXII. 9061 Mony birlt on the brest, & the backe þirlet. **1552** HULOET, Birled, powldred, or spangled, *clauus* [ed. **1572** *clauatus*].

birl (bɜːl, Sc. bɪrl), *v.*[2] *Sc.* [A modern word: apparently onomatopœic; having probably association with *birr*, *whirr*, *whirl*, *hurl*, and Sc. *dirl*, *pirl*, in all of which there is a reference to vibration or rotation and its sound.]
1. *intr.* To move on with rotatory motion, as a rifle bullet; also *fig.*
1789 D. DAVIDSON *Seasons* 39 (JAM.) Now through the air the auld boy birl'd.
2. To revolve or rotate rapidly and with characteristic noise.
1790 MORISON *Poems* 6 (JAM.) The temper pin she gi'es a tirl, An' spins but slow, yet seems to birl. **1806** R. JAMIESON *Pop. Ball.* II. 356 (JAM.) Coming frae the hungry hill, He hears the quernie birlin.
3. *trans.* To cause anything to rotate rapidly; to spin (a coin in the air or on the table); hence to toss a coin on the table as one's contribution to a joint fund, to contribute one's share.
1724 RAMSAY *Poems* I. 262 Now settled gossies..Did for fresh bickers birle. *a* **1774** FERGUSSON *Cauler Oyst.* Poems (1845) 8 There we adjourn wi' hearty foulk To birle our bodles. **1818** SCOTT *Rob Roy* xxviii, I'll pay for another.. and then we'll birl our bawbees a' round. **1879** JAMIESON *Sc.*

Dict. s.v. *Birl*, Children put half-pence on their fingers to birl them..in the low game of Pitch-and-toss.

birlady, -lakin: see BYRLADY, -LAKIN.

birlaw, obs. form of BYRLAW.

†**birle**, *sb. Obs.* Also 1 byrele, byrle, 2–3 birle, 3 borle, (*Orm.*) birrle. [OE. *byrele*, *byrle*, str. masc., of uncertain etymology (perh. for earlier *byrel*:—OTeut. type **burilo-z*, f. *beran* to BEAR). The ON. *byrli* 'cupbearer,' *byrla* 'to pour out,' were prob. adopted from OE.] One who pours out drink; a cupbearer, butler.

a **1000** *Beowulf* 2327 Byrelas sealdon win of wunder-fatum. *c* **1000** ÆLFRIC *Gen.* xl. 20 þæra byrla ealdor. *c* **1200** ORMIN 14053 Acc wel þe birrless wisstenn. *c* **1205** LAY. 24604 Beduer, þas kinges hæȝe birle [*c* **1250** borle, *and so always*].

birle (bɜːl), *v. Obs.* except *dial.* Forms: 1 byrlian, 3 (*Orm.*) birrlenn, 3–4 birlen, 5 bryllyn, 5–6 byrle, 6 birll, 8 birle (9 *dial.* burl), 6– birl. [OE. *byrelian*, f. *byrele*: see prec.]

1. To draw or pour out (drink, *to* or *for* any one).

a **1000** *Guthlac* (Gr.) 840 þone bitran drync, þone Ewe fyrn Adame ȝeaf, byrelade bryd ȝeong. *c* **1200** ORMIN 15396 þuss birrleþþ defell & hiss þeww Aȝȝ werrse & werrse drinnchess. *c* **1380** WYCLIF *Sel. Wks.* III. 43 þei drinke.. and birlen it to oþere men. *c* **1435** *Torr. Portugal* 292 Sche byrlyd whyt wyne and rede. *c* **1510** SKELTON *Elynour Rum.* 268 Dame Elynour entrete To byrle them of the best. **1548** HALL *Chron.* (1809) 605 Bacchus birlyng the wyne which by the Conduytes in therth ranne to all people. **1851** *N. & Q.* Ser. I. III. 204/2 'Told me to burl out the beer..and I burled out a glass and gave it to him.' **1875** *Lanc. Gloss.* (E.D.S.) 40 'Birl out th' beer.'

2. To supply or ply *with* drink.

a **1225** *Anc. R.* 226 He þeonne mid tet, birleð him ilome. *a* **1325** *Metr. Hom.* (1863) 121 Than birles he thaim wit waikere [win]. *a* **1800** *Earl Richard* iii. in Scott *Minstr.*, She birled him wi' the ale and wine.

3. *intr.* To carouse; *trans.* to drink and pass (the cup). (A modern pseudo-archaism.)

a **1800** *Ballad Sir P. Spens* i, Hie sits oor king in Dumfermline, Sits birlin at the wine. **1816** SCOTT *Old Mort.* x, Birling the brown bowl wi' the fowler and the falconer. **1818** —— *Rob Roy* xiv, The twa loons that did the deed birling and drinking wi' him.

†ˈ**birler.** *Obs.* or *dial.* Also **burler.** [f. BIRLE *v.* + -ER[1].] One who pours out drink.

c **1440** *Promp. Parv.* 51 Bryllare of drynke, or schenkare [**1499** drinkshankere], *propinator.* *c* **1450** in Wr.-Wülcker *Voc.* 685 *Hic exelerarius*, byrler. **1857** WRIGHT *Dict.*, *Birler*, the master of the revels at a bidding-wedding in Cumberland. **1873** R. FERGUSON *Cumberld. Gloss.*, *Burler*, who carries round the ale at the festivities in the Lake district.

birlet, variant of BURLET, a coif or kerchief.

ˈ**birlie,** ˈ**birley.** *Sc.* A corrupted form of BYRLAW, used in comb. **birley-court, birlie-man.** (See also BURLEY-.)

1609 SKENE *Reg. Maj.* 74 Birlaw courts, the quhilks are rewled be consent of neighbours. **1609** HUME *Admon.* in *Wodr. Soc. Misc.* 587 Birlay Courtis. **1750** C. CAMPBELL in *Scots Mag.* (1753) 454/2 I think it is quite right to have birlie-men. **1791–9** *Statist. Acc. Scot.* IV. 512 (JAM.) *Crawford* This towne consists of above 20 freedoms.—This little republic was governed by a birley court, in which every proprietor of a freedom had a vote. **1798** D. GRAHAM *Hist. John C.* Wks. 1883 II. 102 The good man being a sworn birley-man of that barony. **1814** SCOTT *Wav.* xlii, Jamie Howie, wha's no fit to be a birlieman, let be a bailie. **1866** *Proc. Berw. Nat.* 261 Birley Courts, in the traditions of the Borders a name for any particularly stormy meeting.

birling (ˈbɜːlɪŋ), *vbl. sb. Obs.* exc. *dial.* [f. BIRLE *v.* + -ING[1].] The action of drawing or pouring out liquor; also *fig.*

a **1340** HAMPOLE *Psalter* lxxiv. 7 [lxxv. 8] Chalis of clere wyn that is, birlynge of rightwis dome. *c* **1440** *Promp. Parv.* 51 Bryllynge of drynke, *propinacio.* **1818** SCOTT *Br. Lamm.* xxiii, The Tod's-hole, an house of entertainment where there has been mony a blithe birling.

‖**birlinn** (bɪərlɪn). Forms: 6– birling, 7– birlin, 8 birline, bierlin, 9 berlin, birlinn, biorlinn. [Gaelic *birlinn*, *bierlinn*.] A large barge, or rowing boat, used by the chieftains of the Western Islands of Scotland.

1595 in Tytler *Hist. Scot.* (1864) IV. 236 Running their galleys, boats and birlings into a little harbour. *a* **1639** SPOTTISWOOD *Hist. Ch. Scot.* VI. (1677) 468 With a number of Birlings (so they call the little vessels those Isles-men use). **1792–9** *Statist. Acc. Scot.* VI. 292 He..kept always a bierlin or galley in this place with 12 or 20 armed men, ready for any enterprise. **1815** SCOTT *Guy M.* xl, A place where their berlins and galleys, as they ca'd them, used to lie. **1873** BURTON *Hist. Scot.* VI. lxv. 39 No single chief should keep more than one birling. **1883** STEWART *Nether Lochaber* lxi. 398 Receiving in return an eight-oared birlinn.

Birman, var. BURMAN.

birmbank, variant of BERMBANK.

birme, obs. form of BARM.

Birmingham (ˈbɜːmɪŋ(h)əm). A town in Warwickshire, in England. Used as a nickname for the supporters of the Exclusion Bill in 1680; cf. ANTI-BIRMINGHAM. Also, **Birminghamize**, to artificialize, make up artificially. Cf. BRUMMAGEM.

1849 MACAULAY *Hist. Eng.* I. 343 In allusion to their spurious groats, the Tory party had fixed on demagogues who hypocritically affected zeal against popery, the nickname of Birminghams. **1856** EMERSON *Eng. Traits* v. 102 The manners and customs of society are artificial—made-up men with made-up manners; and thus the whole is Birminghamized.

birn[1] (bɜːn). *Mus.* [a. Ger. *birn* pear, from the resemblance in shape.] The portion of a clarionet or similar musical instrument into which the mouth-piece is inserted.

birn[2] (bɜːn, Sc. bɪrn). *Sc.* The charred stem of burnt heath, which remains after moor-burning. Hence **birny** *a.*, abounding in birns.

1715 PENNECUIK *Poems* 25 (JAM.) Toasting bannocks at the birns. **1848** W. GARDINER *Flora Forfar.* 88 The fuel used for boiling the water is either peats or birns. **1789** D. DAVIDSON *Seasons* 4 (JAM.) O'er the birny brae.

birn(e: see BERNE, BURN *v.* and *sb.*

birneist, obs. form of BURNISHED.

birnie, birny, variant of BYRNIE, *Obs.*, cuirass.

Biro (ˈbaɪərəʊ). [f. the name of László *Biró*, the Hungarian inventor.] The proprietary name of a particular make of ball-point pen; also (with lower-case initial) applied loosely to any ball-point pen. Hence ˈ**biro** *v. trans.*, to write (something) with a biro; ˈ**biroed** *ppl. a.*, written with a biro.

1947 *Trade Marks Jrnl.* 29 Oct. 660/2 (*heading*) Biro. Writing instruments and parts thereof, not included in other classes. **1948** 'G. ORWELL' *Let.* 2 Jan. in *Coll. Ess.* (1968) IV. 393 Thanks ever so for sending the pen... It'll do just as well as a Biro. **1952** J. CANNAN *Body in Beck* ii. 39 Price jumped and dropped his Biro pen. **1958** *Oxf. Univ. Gaz.* 1 Dec. 299/1 A table 7 ft. 6 in. long, and biro pens were installed. **1962** L. DEIGHTON *Ipcress File* i. 12 The biro'd message, 'Inquiries third floor..'. **1962** *Observer* 4 Mar. 13/2 Most White Papers, editorials and poems are now not penned, but biro'ed. **1967** M. DRABBLE *Jerusalem the Golden* vii. 169 Even the sight of a broken biro on his windowsill was of interest to her.

birostrate, -ated (baɪˈrɒstreɪt, -ɪd), *a.* [f. BI- *pref.*[2] 1 + ROSTRATE, ad. L. *rostrātus*, f. *rostrum* beak.] Two-beaked; having a double beak or two beak-like processes.

1847 in CRAIG.

birotate (baɪˈrəʊteɪt), *a.* [f. BI- *pref.*[2] 1 + ROTATE *a.*, f. L. *rota* wheel.] Two-wheeled.

1880 *Scribner's Mag.* XIX. Feb. 483 The birotate chariot.

birotation (baɪrəˈteɪʃən). *Physical Chem.* [BI-[2].] The power possessed by certain sugars of changing their rate of optical rotation according to the length of time they have been in solution. Now usually called MUTAROTATION.

1882 ROBB & VELEY tr. *Landolt's Handbk. Polariscope* IV. 62 A peculiar case of variation of specific rotation occurs in crystallized milk-sugar... As the initial rotation is nearly twice as great as the constant rotation, the name of *birotation* has been applied to this peculiarity. **1893** *Jrnl. Chem. Soc.* LXIV. I. 125 Birotation and Hydrazone Formation of some Sugars. **1896** *Ibid.* LXX. II. 139 The birotation phenomena of glucose. **1907** J. B. COHEN *Org. Chem.* 100 Freshly prepared solutions of certain sugars change in rotation on standing. The specific rotation of glucose sinks to one-half before becoming constant. The phenomenon was therefore termed *birotation.* **1955** J. G. DAVIS *Dict. Dairying* (ed. 2) 78 *Birotation ratio*..certain sugars when dissolved in water gradually change in their optical rotation.

birr (bɜː(r), *Sc.* bɪrr), *sb.* Forms: 4 bur, burre, bire, 4–6 bir, 4–5 bure, byre, 5 byrre, ber(e, beere, beare, 5–6 byr, birr, 7 burr(e, beir(e, biere, 7–8 birre, *dial.* beer, 9 bir, *dial.* ber, 8– birr. [a. ON. *byrr* favouring wind (Sw., Da. *bör* fair wind, foul gale):—OTeut. **burjo-z* (or *buri-z*), f. *beran* to bear. Sense 3 is, in part at least, of independent origin, imitating the sound which it names, and is to be compared with BURR.]

†**1.** A strong wind; *esp.* one that carries a vessel on. *Obs.*

a **1325** *Conception* in *Metr. Hom.* Introd. 17 The bir it blew als he wald bid. *c* **1325** *E.E. Allit. P.* C. 148 þe bur ber to hit baft, þat braste alle her gere. *c* **1400** *Destr. Troy* 12488 Thai..puld vp hor sailes, Hadyn bir at þere backe.

2. The force of the wind, or of any moving body; momentum, impetus; rush. ***to take*** or ***fetch one's birr***: to gather impetus for a leap by a short run or 'ram-race.'

1382 WYCLIF *Isa.* v. 28 His wheles as the byre [**1388** feersnesse] of the tempest. —— *Matt.* viii. 32 Loo! in a greet bire, al the droue wente heedlynge in to the see. ?*a* **1400** *Morte Arth.* 3662 Brethly bessomes with byrre in berynes sailles. *c* **1450** LONELICH *Grail* xlv. 419 And to hire he ran with a ful gret ber. **1580** SIDNEY *Arcadia* 54 Carried with the Beere of violent loue. **1609** HOLLAND *Amm. Marcel.* XXII. viii. 197 And giving way backward fetch their feese or beire againe. **1611** COTGR. s.v. *Saulter*, *Il recule pour mieux saulter*, He goes backe to take burre, or to leape the better. **1790** BURNS *Election Ball.* iii, Thus I break aff wi' a' my birr. **1867** E. WAUGH *Owd Blanket* ii. 37 in *Lanc. Gloss.*, Thae'd no need to come i' sich a ber.

†**b.** A charge in battle; an attack, a fight. *Obs.*

c **1340** *Gaw. & Gr. Knt.* 290 I schal bide þe fyrst bur, as bare as I sitte. **1382** WYCLIF *2 Sam.* xi. 23 We, the bure made [Vulg. *impetu facto*], pursueden hem into the ȝate. *c* **1400** *Destr. Troy* 11141 All the bent of þat birr blody beronnen. *c* **1440** *Bone Flor.* 659 Garcy..arayed hys batels in that bere.

c. A thrust, a violent push or blow; also *fig.*

c **1325** *E.E. Allit. P.* A. 176 Such a burre myȝt make myn herte blunt. *c* **1400** *Destr. Troy* 1244 A ȝonge knight..suet to þe Duke With a bir on þe brest, þat backeward he ȝode. **1830** GALT *Lawrie T.* III. xvi. (1849) 137 Dashed my head with such a bir against the branch of a prostrate tree.

d. Bodily force exerted against anything, might.

c **1340** *Gaw. & Gr. Knt.* 2261 With alle þe bur in his body he ber it on lofte. **1382** WYCLIF *James* iii. 4 Shippes..ben born aboute of a litel gouernayle, where the bire [*impetus*] of a man dressinge shal wole. **1674** RAY *N.C. Wds.* 5 *Beer, Birre, Beare*, force, might. *With aw my beer* (Chesh.), with all my force. **1823** GALT *Entail* III. vii. 70 Ye need na mair waste your bir about it.

e. Force of pronunciation, energetic utterance.

1825 LD. COCKBURN *Mem.* ii. 133 What the Scotch call the Birr..the emphatic energy of his pronunciation. **1827** J. WILSON *Noct. Ambr.* Wks. 1855 I. 118 Just such a voice.. in its laigh notes there's a sort of birr..that betokens power. **1883** W. JOLLY *J. Duncan* xvii. 181 He told Charles the story with great birr.

3. An energetic whirring sound, such as that of a moor-fowl's flight, the running-down of a clock, or the vigorous trilling of the letter *r*.

1837 R. NICOLL *Poems* (1842) 82 The birr o' Scotland's spinnin'-wheel. **1856** STRONG *Glasgow & Clubs* 207 Never did a Parisian badaud rattle the R with greater birr. **1876** SMILES *Sc. Natur.* viii. (ed. 4) 136 The birr of the moorcock and the scream of the merlin.

birr (bɜrr), *v.* [f. prec.] *intr.* To emit a whirring noise; to move rapidly with such a noise. Hence ˈ**birring** *ppl. a.*

1513 DOUGLAS *Æneis* IX. ix. 134 Ane gret staf slung, byrrand wyth felloun wecht. **1786** BURNS *Tam Samson's El.* viii, Rejoice ye birring paitricks a'. **1791** A. WILSON *Laurel Disp.* Poet. Wks. 125 The lasses' wheels, thrang birring round the ingle. **1802** A. CAMPBELL in *Tales Borders* (1863) I. 157 They were both seated in the gig, and birring it on merrily towards Carlisle.

Birrell (ˈbɪrəl). The name of Augustine *Birrell* (1850–1933), English writer and politician, used in various formations (see quots.) alluding to his easy and discursive style, his beliefs, etc.

1894 *Westm. Gaz.* 4 Apr. 3/1 'Birrelling.' Mr. Birrell followed with a speech of quips and cranks, pleasantly diverting in a Scotch debate. **1896** *Ibid.* 6 Feb. 2/3 How would he like the future chronicler to have to say that Birrellism and Trilbyism were the marked features of 1896? *Ibid.* 18 June 2/3 He was in the habit..of 'birrelling' his examiners. **1898** G. W. E. RUSSELL *Coll. & Recoll.* 212 To 'birrell' is now a verb as firmly established as to 'boycott', and it signifies a style, light, easy, playful, pretty, rather discursive, perhaps a little superficial. Its characteristic note is grace. **1906** *Daily Chron.* 16 Feb. 4/7 It's a two to one chance..Religion, Irreligion, and Birreligion. **1906** *Westm. Gaz.* 23 Feb. 3/1 The House rejoiced to hear a new Birrellism. **1906** *Daily Chron.* 29 Dec. 3/5 A Birrelline Christmas card. **1937** *Times Lit. Suppl.* 10 Apr. 271 Birrelled out of his pose of sympathy. *Ibid.*, The Birrellian *obiter dictum*, fatal to a political reputation. **1960** *Times* 9 May 16/2 Barrie-isms became even more popular than once Birrellisms had been.

birretta, variant of BIRETTA.

birse (bɜːs, *Sc.* bɪrs), *sb.*[1] *Sc.* Forms: 1 byrst, 4 brust, 6 byrs(s, birs. Pl. birses; also 6–7 byrss. [In 16th c. *birs*, *birss*, for earlier *birst*:—OE. *byrst*, cogn. with OHG. *burst*, *bursti*, ON. *burst* (Sw. *borst*, Da. *börste*) 'bristle.' Only Sc. in later times.]

1. = BRISTLE. (***to lick the birse***: to pass a small bunch of hog's bristles through the mouth—as is done on being made a 'soutar of Selkirk.')

a **700** *Epinal Gl.* 905 *Seta*, byrst. *c* **1000** *Sax. Leechd.* I. 156 Swylce swinene byrst. *c* **1330** *Rouland & V.* 860 No is worþ þe brust of a swin. **1513** DOUGLAS *Æneis* VIII. iv. 181 The rouch byrsis on the brest and crest Of that..beist. **1721** J. KELLY *Sc. Prov.* 338 (JAM.) The souter gae the sow a kiss; 'grumph,' quo she, 'its a' for the birse.' **1724** RAMSAY *Ever-Green* (1761) I. 253 Knichts of the Birs and Thumble. **1815** SCOTT in *Lockhart* xxxvi. (1839) V. 123 I am still puzzled to dispose of the Birse. *Note.* A birse or bunch of hog's bristles forms the cognizance of the Sutors. **1882** *Society* 14 Oct. 5/1 Mr. G. O. Trevelyan..will require to 'lick the birse' at Selkirk.

b. Short hair of the beard or body.

a **1572** KNOX *Hist. Ref.* Wks. 1846 I. 147 Many of thame lacked beardis..and therefore could not bukkill other by the byrse. **1786** BURNS *Addr. Beelzebub*, They lay aside all tender mercies, An' tirl the hallions to the birses.

2. *fig.* In the phrase ***to set up the birse***, etc.: Temper, rage, anger, in allusion to animals that bristle up when irritated.

1622 *Course Conformitie* 153 (JAM.) Now his birse rise when he heareth the one. **1816** SCOTT *Antiq.* xxi, He wad set up the tother's birse, and maybe do mair ill nor gude. **1830** GALT *Lawrie T.* III. xi. (1849) 122 To smooth the birsses of their husbonds. **1871** GUTHRIE *Speech Westm. Hotel* 19 July, This set up my birse.

Hence **birsit** *a. Sc.*, bristled, bristly.

1513 DOUGLAS *Æneis* VII. i. 35 The birsit baris and beris in thair styis Roring all wod.

birse, *sb.*² *Sc.* Also 9 birz. [as prec.]
a. A bruise. **b.** 'The act of pressing; the pressure made by a crowd.' (Jamieson.)
1821 SIR A. WYLIE III. 292 (JAM.) My brother has met wi' a severe birz and contusion.

birse, *v. Sc.* [Sc. variant of *briz* = BRUISE.]
trans. **a.** To bruise, crush. **b.** To press, push.
1513–75 *Diurn. Occurr.* (1833) 293 Borne to jybbit, becaus he wes birsit with the buttis [the 'Boots']. **1790** SHIRREF *Poems* 348 (JAM.) For they're ay birsing in their spurs Whare they can get them. **1879** JAMIESON s.v. *Birse*, I saw Sisyphus . . Birzing a heavy stane up a high brae.

birsle ('bəs(ə)l, *Sc.* 'bɪrs(ə)l), *v. Sc.* Also 6 brissle, brissil, byrsle, 7 *north. dial.* brusle. [Derivation and etymological form uncertain: the mod. Sc. is *birsle*, but 16th c. Eng. had *brissill*, and 17th c. north. dial. *brusle*.]
trans. To scorch (the surface) with radiant heat; to toast hard; also *fig.* Hence **'birsled** *ppl. a.*
1513 DOUGLAS *Æneis* VII. xiii. 36 Feill echirris of corn thik growing, Wyth the new sonnys heit byrsyllit. *Ibid.* VII. ix. 109 Blunt styngis of the byrsillit [**1553** brissillit] tre. **1691** RAY *North Co. Wds.*, *Brusle*, to dry; as 'the sun *brusles* the hay'; and '*brusled* pease,' parch'd pease. **1716** *Wodrow Corr.* (1843) II. 137 He was sorry he got not the old dog's bones to birsle in the flames. **1818** MISS FERRIER *Marriage* II. 132 Than ye maun sit an' birsle yoursels afore the fire at hame. **1833** M. SCOTT *Tom Cringle* xvi. (1859) 409, I trained best on birsled peas and whiskey.

'birsle, *sb. Sc.* [f. prec.] 'A hasty toasting or scorching' (Jam.); the toasted or scorched surface (of a potato, etc.).

birst, **birstit**, obs. forms of BURST.

birsy ('bəsɪ, *Sc.* 'bɪrsɪ), *a. Sc.* [f. BIRSE *sb.*¹ + -Y¹.] = BRISTLY, BRISTLING *lit.* and *fig.*
1513 DOUGLAS *Æneis* X. iv. 127 The monstre . . With byrsy body. **1810** TANNAHILL *Poems* (1846) 145 His black birsie beard. **1836** *Scot. Month. Mag.* July 183 The creature was a birsie bodie.

†**birt, burt.** *Obs.* Forms: 6 birte, byrte, burte, 7 byrt, berte, 6–8 birt, burt. [Derivation and etymological form uncertain: written also *brit(e, brut, brytte*, BRET, q.v. Cotgrave has '*bertonneau* a bret or turbot. Norman.' This may be related.] A fish identified with the Turbot.
1552 HULOET, Byrte, fyshe, *rhombus*. **1573** in Nichols' *Progr. Q. Eliz.* I. 362 Item, for a burte . . 3*s.* 8*d.* . . for two brites . . 6*s.* **1620** VENNER *Via Recta* iv. 74 Turbut or Birt is meetly pleasant to the taste. **1678** R. HOLME in *Babees Bk.* (1868) 157 *note*, He beareth Azure a Birte (or Burt, or Berte). **1706** PHILLIPS, *Bret, Brut*, or *Burt*, a Fish of the Turbot-kind. **1783** AINSWORTH *Lat. Dict.* (Morell) II, *Rhombus*, a fish called a birt, or turbot.

birth (bɜːθ), *sb.*¹ Forms: 3 **burðe(y)**, **birðe**, 3–4 **burþe**, **birþ(e**, 4 **byrþe**, **burþ**, **berþe**, (**briþ**, **breth**,) 4–5 **burth(e**, **birthe**, 4–6 **byrth(e**, 5 **bryth**, 6–7 **berth**, 3– **birth**. [Early ME. *byrþ(e, burð(e, birþ(e*, probably, since the form is foreign to OE., a. ON. **byrð(i)r* str. fem. (OSw. *byrþ*, Da. *byrd*), genit. *burðar* (on which Icelandic formed a new nominative *burðr* masc.); = Goth. *ga-baurþs*:—OTeut. **(ga-)burþi-z*, f. the stem of *ber-an* to BEAR, with suffix *-þi-* (= Aryan *-ti-s*, cf. Skr. *bhrtís*, OIr. *brith*). The OTeut. word had shifting stress, and consequently, according to Verner's law, *þ* and *d* interchanged in the inflexion: in ON. and Goth. these were levelled under *þ*, but in WGer. under *d* (High G. *t*), in OS. *giburd*, OHG. *giburt*, *burt* (MHG., mod.G. *geburt*), OE. *ȝebyrd*. The latter was prob. the source of ME. BIRDE, *burde*, 'race, descent'; but could hardly be that of *birth*, unless the latter was assimilated to sbs. in *-þ*, *-þe*, or influenced by ON. For the final *-e* of ME. *byrþe*, cf. ME. *derþe* a. ON. *dyrð*, and see -TH¹.]
1. The bearing of offspring. Viewed as an act of the mother: **a.** Bringing forth, giving birth. Now chiefly in '(several young) *at a birth*.'
a **1300** *Cursor M.* 10575 Quen Anna was cummen to time of birþ, Sco bar þat maiden. **1382** WYCLIF *Gen.* xxxv. 17 For the hardnes of birth [**1388** childberyng] she biganne to perishe. **1593** SHAKS. *2 Hen. VI*, IV. ii. 147 By her he had two children at one birth. **1631** MILTON *Epit. M'chess. Winchester* 67 Who, after years of barrenness The highly-favoured Joseph bore . . And at her next birth . . Through pangs fled to felicity. **1749** FIELDING *Tom Jones* II. ii, The birth of an heir by his beloved sister. **1787** GARTHSHORE in *Phil. Trans.* LXXVII. 357 The lady . . produced at one birth eight perfect children. **1881** W. GREGOR *Folk Lore N.E. Scot.* 4 One . . wished God speed to the birth.
†**b.** Conception or gestation. *Obs.*
c **1375** WYCLIF *Serm.* cxxvii. Sel. Wks. II. 7 Boþe in birþe in wombe and in birþe of þe wombe.
c. Viewed as a fact pertaining to the offspring: The fact of being born, nativity, beginning of individual existence, coming into the world. *to give birth to*: to bear, bring forth (offspring).
c **1200** *Trin. Coll. Hom.* 47 On þe ehteðe dai efter his burþe. *c* **1250** *Gen. & Ex.* 1484 Ðe fader luuede esau wel for firme birðe & swete mel. *a* **1340** HAMPOLE *Pr. Consc.* 2193 Better es þe day of dede þan þe day of burthe. *c* **1387** CHAUCER *Mother of God* 74 The birthe of Cryst our thraldom putte vs fro. **1595** SHAKS. *John* III. i. 51 At thy birth, deere boy, Nature and Fortune ioyn'd to make thee great. **1732** POPE *Hor. Sat.* II. ii. 97 Why had not I in those good times my birth? **1855** TENNYSON *Maud* I. xix. iv, Mine by a right, from birth till death.
2. *fig.* Of things: Origin, origination, commencement of existence, beginning.
[**1588** SHAKS. *L.L.L.* v. ii. 521 When great things labouring perish in their birth.] **1611** —— *Wint. T.* IV. iv. 80 Not yet on summers death, nor on the birth Of trembling winter. **1712** ADDISON *Spect.* No. 267 ¶6 Æneas's Settlement . . gave Birth to the Roman Empire. **1789** BENTHAM *Princ. Legisl.* xvii. §17 Offences which owe their birth to the joint influence of indolence and pecuniary interest. **1875** HAMERTON *Intell. Life* X. viii. 376 The birth of a powerful idea.
3. a. The product of bearing, that which is born; offspring, child; young (of animals). *arch.* (Cf. AFTERBIRTH.)
a **1400** *Cursor M.* 10886 (Trin.) For þi of þe beþ born a burþ. **1483** CAXTON *Gold. Leg.* 433/2 The moder shold be delyuerd of hyr byrthe. **1597** SHAKS. *2 Hen. IV*, IV. iv. 122 Vnfather'd Heires, and loathly Births of Nature. **1647** CRASHAW *Poems* 129 Saturn . . devour'd that birth he fear'd. **1703** FARQUHAR *Inconst.* III. (1728) 43 The woman's birth was spirited away. **1711** ADDISON *Spect.* No. 120 ¶5 Others hatch their Eggs and tend the Birth, 'till it is able to shift for it self. **1883** W. G. BLACK *Folk-Med.* viii. 128 The next birth will be a boy.
†**b.** That which is borne in the womb; 'fruit of the womb.' *Obs.*
c **1250** *Gen. & Ex.* 1697 Rachel non birðe ne nam. **1500** *Will of Treffry, Cornwall* (Somerset Ho.), I bequeth to the byrth being in the bely of Elyn Danyel. **1535** COVERDALE *Jer.* xx. 15 That the byrth might not haue come out, but remayned still in her. **1657** W. COLES *Adam in Eden* liv, It expelleth the dead Birth.
†**c.** *collect.* Children, offspring. *Obs.*
1614 CHAPMAN *Odyss.* VIII. 337 When you come To banquet with your wife and birth at home.
d. *fig.* Of things: Product, creation, 'offspring.'
1625 BACON *Innovations, Ess.* (Arb.) 526 Innouations, which are the Births of Time. **1697** DRYDEN *Virg. Georg.* I. 196 The fruitful Earth Was free to give her unexacted Birth. **1742** YOUNG *Nt. Th.* II. 476 Teaching we learn; and, giving, we retain The births of intellect. **1884** W. C. SMITH *Kildrostan* 66 It was a foolish jest, The birth of vacant brains.
†**4.** A race, a nation. (transl. L. *natio.*) *Obs. rare.*
a **1300** *E.E. Psalter* lxxviii[ix]. 10 And in berthes unknawen be, Bi-fore oure eghen þat we se. *Ibid.* cxlix. 7 In birthes wrekes for to do.
5. a. Parentage, lineage, extraction, descent; *esp.* rank, station, position inherited from parents.
a **1240** *Wohunge* in *Cott. Hom.* 269 Noblesce and hehnesse of burðe. *c* **1374** CHAUCER *Boeth.* III. vi. 78 Al þe linage of men þat ben in erþe ben of semblable burþe. **1599** SHAKS. *Much Ado* II. i. 172 She is no equall for his birth. *a* **1687** PETTY *Pol. Arith.* x. (1691) 115 To live according to their Birth and Breeding. **1752** JOHNSON *Rambler* No. 201 ¶9 A young man whose birth and fortune give him a claim to notice. **1839** THIRLWALL *Greece* xii. II. 94 Marriages contracted between parties of unequal birth.
b. *spec.* Good family, noble lineage.
1595 SHAKS. *John* II. i. 430 If loue ambitious fought a match of birth. **1752** HUME *Ess. & Treat.* (1777) I. 96 Birth, titles, & place, must be honoured above industry & riches. **1876** J. H. NEWMAN *Hist. Sk.* I. iv. 201 There is nothing men more pride themselves on than birth.
†**c.** *transf.* One born in such a position. (Cf. 3.)
1602 WARNER *Alb. Eng.* XI. lxii. 270 Such Births as she not else must loue, but as they licens't are.
†**6.** Nature, kind, sex; natural character. *Obs.*
c **1230** *Hali Meid.* 13 þis mihte . . athalt hire burðe i licnesse of heuenliche cunde. *c* **1374** CHAUCER *Boeth.* III. vi. 79 ȝif he norisse his corage vnto vices and forlete his propre burþe. **1382** WYCLIF *Wisd.* xiv. 26 The mischaunging of birthe [**1611** changing of kinde, *marg.* sexe]. **1558** Q. ELIZ. in Strype *Ann. Ref.* I. II. App. vi. 11 Her highness, beyinge a woman by birthe and nature. **1592** SHAKS. *Rom. & Jul.* II. iii. 20 Nor ought so good, but strain'd from that faire vse, Reuolts from true birth.
7. Conditions or relations involved in birth.
c **1400** *Destr. Troy* XXXII. 12826 Teucro . . þat was brother of birthe to þe bold Thelamon. **1697** DRYDEN *Æneid* VII. 1001 A foe by birth to Troy's unhappy name. **1816** J. WILSON *City of Plague* II. iii. 346 By my very birth I am a creature sinful as yourselves. **1875** JOWETT *Plato* (ed. 2) V. 31 He was an Athenian by birth, and a Spartan citizen.
†**8.** *first* (*firme*) *birth*: rights of primogeniture; BIRTHRIGHT. *Obs.*
c **1250** *Gen. & Ex.* 1497 Ðat ic ðin firme birðehe gete. *Ibid.* 1501 Firme birðe was wurði wune ðe fader dede ðe firme sune. **1387** TREVISA *Higden* Rolls Ser. II. 301 þe furste burþe [*primogenita*] were special profiȝtes and worschippes to the eldest sones. **1527** *Ibid.* II. xi. 69 Jacob . . had boughte the firste byrthes and slyly geten his faders blessynge.
†**9.** Nativity; 'fortune' as influenced by the aspect of the planets at the moment of birth. *Obs.*
1593 SHAKS. *2 Hen. VI*, IV. i. 34 A cunning man did calculate my birth, And told me that by Water I should dye.
10. *Theol.* in phr. *new birth*: regeneration.
1535 COVERDALE *Tit.* iii. 5 He saued vs by the fountayne of the new byrth. **1597** HOOKER *Eccl. Pol.* v. l. §1 The Church is to us that very Mother of our new birth. **1678** R. BARCLAY *Apol. Quakers* v. §24 (1701) 175 The New Birth cometh not by the outward Knowledge of Christ. **1875** H. E. MANNING *Mission H. Ghost* i. 16 Baptism confers a new birth.
11. (See quot.)
1616 SURFL. & MARKH. *Countr. Farm* 141 In the paine of the bellie [of a horse], vvhich some call the Birth, you shall take the seeds of vvild Rue, etc.
12. *attrib.* = 'native, natal,' and in *comb.*: **a.** relating to sense 1, as ***birth-carol***, ***-city***, ***-date***, ***-hour***, ***-land***, ***-note***, ***-notice***, ***-pang***, ***-peal***, ***-robe***, ***-song***, ***-spot***, ***-stead*** (obs.), ***-struggle***, ***-throe***, ***-town***, ***-trauma***, ***-year***, also BIRTHDAY, BIRTHPLACE; ***birth-brought***, ***-favouring***, ***-strangled*** adjs.; **b.** in sense of 'belonging to one from birth,' as ***birth-blindness***, ***-blot***, ***-mark*** (also *fig.*), ***-name***, ***-poison*** (= original sin), ***-sin***, ***-tongue***, BIRTHRIGHT; ***birth-marked*** adj. **c.** with astrological reference, as ***birth-planet***, ***-sign***, ***-star***.
1864 *Soc. Sc. Rev.* I. 302 A case of *birth blindness. **1589** WARNER *Alb. Eng.* VI. xxix. 142 Whose *birth-brought Nature. **1641** J. JACKSON *True Evang. T.* iii. 190 That Angelicall *birth-Caroll of our blessed Lord. **1935** C. DAY LEWIS *Time to Dance* 11 Birth-carol of spring. **1593** SHAKS. *Lucr.* 537 Worse than a slavish wipe or *birth-hours blot. **1580** NORTH *Plutarch* (1676) 150 A certain *birth-marke he had upon one of his lips, like a little wart. **1869** SWINBURNE in *Fortnightly Rev.* July 74 Here too the birth-mark of the great race is visible. **1934** 'G. ORWELL' *Burmese Days* ii. 21 His birthmarked cheek. **1925** L. P. SMITH *Words & Idioms* v, The *birth-notices in *The Times*. **1821** BYRON *Sardan.* II. i. 66 'Tis thy natal ruler—thy *birth-planet. **1528** TINDALE *Doctr. Treat.* (1848) 301 By the reason of original sin, or *birth-poison, that remaineth in him. **1566** DRANT *Horace Sat.* I. vii. E b, What unstable starres, what *byrthe-sygnes once he had. **1562** 39 *Articles* ix. (*title*) Of Original or *Birth-sin. **1842** H. E. MANNING *Serm.* (1848) I. 8 All that lies wrapped up in his birth-sin. **1641** J. JACKSON *True Evang. T.* ii. 140 [Homer] whom nine Cities strove about, which should be his *birth-spot. **1583** STUBBES *Anat. Abus.* II. 64 Neither fate, destonie, *birthstar, signe or planet. *a* **1300** *Cursor M.* 22092 Right sua sal þe feind . . ches him a *birth-sted i-wiss. **1605** SHAKS. *Macb.* IV. i. 30 Finger of *Birth-strangled Babe. **1837** CARLYLE *Fr. Rev.* I. IV. iv. 164 And so, with death-throes and *birth-throes, a new one is to be born. **1387** TREVISA *Higden* in Craik *Lit. & Learn. Eng.* (1844) 109 This apayringe of the *birthe tonge is by cause of twey thinges. **1929** O. RANK *Trauma of Birth* p. xiii, The to all appearances purely physical *birth trauma with its prodigious psychical consequences for the whole development of mankind.
13. Special comb.: †**birth-bearing**, parturition; †**birth-brief**, a genealogical table, a family tree; **birth certificate**, a certificate of birth (CERTIFICATE *sb.* 3); †**birth-child**, child by birth (in a place), native; **birth control**, the prevention of conception; also *attrib.*; hence ***birth controller***; †**birth-cord**, the umbilical cord; †**birth-gazer**, †**birth-lotter**, a calculator or caster of nativities; **birth parent**, a natural (as opposed to an adoptive) parent; **birth-puffed** *a.*, proud of one's descent; **birth-rate**, the ratio of the number of births per year to the population (usually calculated per thousand); **birth-roll**, a list of persons born in one place; **birth-root**, the *Trillium erectum* or Indian Balm; **birth-state**, condition by birth; **birthstone**, a gemstone associated with the month of one's birth; **birth-stool**, a stool for assisting in parturition; †**birth-tide** = BIRTH-TIME; **birth-weight**, the weight of a baby at birth.
a **1300** *Pains of Hell* 135 in *O.E. Misc.* 215 Slowyn here childer in *burþberyng. **1708** J. CHAMBERLAYNE *St. Gt. Brit.* II. II. iv. (1743) 374 All . . Legitimations, *Birthbrieves, Presentations, etc. **1900** *Whitaker's Almanack 1901* 4 (*Index*) *Birth certificates. **1928** W. C. & J. C. HALL *Law of Adoption* I. 47 The production of a birth certificate is necessary for candidates for nearly all important examinations and for many kinds of employment. **1608** SHAKS. *Per.* IV. iv. 41 The earth Hath Thetis *birth-child on the heavens bestow'd. *c* **1630** RISDON *Surv. Devon* §104 (1810) 99 Very notable hath this town been for her birthchild Winefride. **1914** *The Woman Rebel* June 39/2 (*heading*) The *Birth Control League. **1922** LD. DAWSON (*title*) Love—Marriage—Birth Contol. **1936** D. V. GLASS *Struggle for Population* iii. 35 Condoms are listed as preventatives of disease and not as birth-control appliances, and are thus easily available. **1937** V. GOLLANCZ in 'G. Orwell' *Road to Wigan Pier* p. xvii, Birth control clinics up and down the country. **1921** A. HUXLEY *Crome Yellow* v. 45 The indignation of a convinced *birth-controller. **1923** M. EDGE *Artificial Birth Control* 15 Another reason the Birth Controller gives in support of his theory is, that we are over-populated. **1586** T. B. *La Primaud. Fr. Acad.* (1594) 40 *marg.*, Sorcerers, magitians, and *birth gazers. **1549** CHALONER *Erasm. Moriæ Enc.* A jv, An evident argument and token of good lucke, as these *byrthlotters saie. **1977** *N.Y. Times* 30 Jan. IV. 8 A small but apparently growing number of adults . . have started searching for their biological parents, or their '*birth parents', as some prefer it. **1984** *Gainesville* (Florida) *Sun* 3 Apr. 10A/2 Father No. 1 is my real father. He never married my real mother. She gave me up for adoption, but I have become acquainted with my birth parents in the last year or so. **1859** *Ann. Rep. Registr. Gen.* p. ii, The marriage rate and the *birth rate were above, the death rate was below the average. **1919** W. R. INGE *Outspoken Ess.* 69 In the Rhondda Valley the birth-rate is still about forty. **1822** *Amer. Jrnl. Science* IV. 62 Plants collected . . around the great Lakes . . [include] *Birth root. **1867** A. GRAY *Man. Bot.* (ed. 5) 523 *Trillium erectum*, Purple T. or Birth-root. **1861** MAINE *Anc. Law* iv. (1876) 94 The current language concerning the *birth-state of men. **1907** *Ladies Home Jrnl.* Sept. 65/2 September's *birthstone is the sapphire, and stands for constancy, truth and virtue. **1913** G. F. KUNZ *Curious Lore Precious Stones* ix. 317 The substitution of a new schedule for the time-honored list of

birth-stones has received the approval of the National Association of Jewellers. **1978** *N.Y. Times* 30 Mar. B10/1 (Advt.), 50% discount. Pearl Rings. Birthstone Rings. Star Sapphire. **1627** DRAYTON *Agincourt, etc.* 154 Bring forth the *Birth-stoole. *a* **1240** *Wohunge* in *Cott. Hom.* 277, I þi *burðtid. *a* **1631** DRAYTON *Dudley to Lady J. Gray* (R.) No ominous star did at thy birthtide shine. **1949** M. MEAD *Male & Female* xiii. 268 It is taken to its mother, at the proper hour for its *birth-weight,..and persuaded to suck. **1985** *New Yorker* 11 Feb. 34/2 Taped to each crib was a..card telling mother's name, the time of birth, and birth weight.

† **birth**, *sb.*² *Obs.* [Perh. the same word as prec. with the general sense of 'bear'; perhaps a. ON. *byrðr* burthen: the derivation being the same.] Burthen, weight, ? bulk.

c **1425** WYNTOUN *Cron.* I. xiii. 17 (JAM.) Thare bwyis bowys all for byrtht. **1513** DOUGLAS *Æneis* v. iii. 31 The busteus barge..Sa huge of birth a cetie semit sche. **1535** STEWART *Cron. Scot.* II. 246 For birth and wecht, hir furing wes so hie, With thame ilkane scho sank into the se.

'**birth**, *v.* [f. BIRTH *sb.*¹: the ME. vb. may be *birthen.*] **1.** *intr.* To have birth, be born. *rare.*

c **1250** *Gen. & Ex.* 1471 He wroȝten and fiȝt, Queðer here sulde birðen bi-foren. **1865** J. H. STIRLING *Secret Hegel* I. 147 It is difficult to perceive how I am related to it, how I birth from it, or decease into it.

2. *trans.* To give birth to; to give rise to. Chiefly *dial.* and *U.S. dial.*

1906 V. MCNABB in F. Valentine *Fr. V. McNabb* III. iii. §7. 300 Salute the sail that birthed you free. **1928**, etc. in H. Wentworth *Amer. Dial. Dict.* **1945** in *Amer. Speech* (1946) XXI. 303 The plan for UNO was birthed at Dumbarton Oaks. **1958** J. CAREW *Wild Coast* ii. 22 The night his mother birthed him.

birth, obs. form of BERTH *sb.*

birthday ('bɜːθdeɪ). [f. BIRTH *sb.*¹ + DAY.]

1. The day on which any one is born; also *fig.* that of regeneration; *transf.* (of things), the day or date of origin or beginning.

1580 BARET *Alv.* B 711 The daye that the citie was first founded on, the birth day. **1599** DAVIES in Farr's *S.P.* (1845) I. 102 We..That haue bene euer from our birth-day blind. **1709** STEELE *Tatler* No. 130 ¶10 The Anniversary of the Birth-day of this Glorious Queen. **1784** COWPER *Task* I. 18 The birthday of Invention. **1858** SEARS *Athan.* viii. 68 Now therefore comes the second birthday of man.

2. The anniversary or annual observance of the day of birth of any one; sometimes *spec.* that of the sovereign.

[*c* **1000** *Ags. Gosp.* Matt. xiv. 6 On Herodes gebyrd-dæȝe]. **1382** WYCLIF *Mark* vi. 21 Eroude in his birthe day [**1388** birthdai] made a soper to the princes. **1579** FULKE *Refut. Rastel* 796 To celebrate his Martyrs byrth day. **1601** SHAKS. *Jul. C.* v. i. 71 This is my Birth-day; as this very day Was Cassius borne. **1755** *Connoisseur* No. 117 This suit..was made up for a noble lord on the last birthday. **1859** TENNYSON *Enid* 633 A costly gift..given her on the night Before her birthday.

3. *attrib.* and *comb.*, as ***birthday boy, card, dress, feast, finery, gift, girl, ode, party, present, treat, wish,*** etc.; **birthday book**, a book in diary form with spaces for recording birthdays; usu. having quotations for each day from the works of a particular author; also, a book suitable for a birthday present; a book compiled to honour someone's birthday; **birthday honours**, the titles of honour conferred by the sovereign on each anniversary of his or her official birthday; so ***birthday gazette***; † **birthday('s mind**, the commemoration of a birthday; **birthday suit**, a dress worn on the King's birthday; also (humorous): the bare skin; so ***birthday attire, clothes, gear.***

1860 'G. & P. WHARTON' *Wits & Beaux of Society* I. 127 In 'birthday attire'. **1859** (*title*) The boy's birth-day book; a collection of tales, essays, and narratives of adventure. **1881** C. DIXON (*title*) The Longfellow birthday book. **1884** *Spectator* 12 Jan. 58/1 Mr. Arnold does not describe classes of men sufficiently numerous and various to supply apt quotations for a birthday book. **1967** *Listener* 25 May 690/1 Garlands, festschrifts and birthday books tend to be tedious. **1959** H. PINTER *Birthday Party* 11, Shine it on the birthday boy. **1902** *Little Folks* Oct. 287/2 Miss Shaw seemed to appreciate Moya's birthday card very much. **1961** H. S. TURNER *Something Extraordinary* ii. 39 My birthday was on Sunday... I have got six birthday cards. **1732** LD. EGMONT *Diary* 2 June (1920) 279 Mr. Spencer was a man of extraordinary breeding to acknowledge the favour of a common visit in his birthday clothes. **1801** M. EDGEWORTH *Belinda* I. v. 148 (*title*) Birthday Dresses. **1856** C. M. YONGE *Daisy Chain* I. xxiii. 244 Mrs. Charles Wilmot's little girl was to have a birth-day feast, at which Mary, Blanche, and Aubrey were to appear. **1749** J. CLELAND *Mem. Woman of Pleasure* II. 84, I now stood..in all the truth of nature... The figure I made..outshone all other birth-day finery whatever. **1910** BEATRIX GATACRE *General Gatacre* xvii. 262 On the 24th in the *Birthday Gazette*, his name appeared as a recipient of the Gold Medal of a New Order, the Kaiser-i-Hind. **1734** SWIFT *Strephon & Chloe* in *Poems* (1958) II. 591 To see some radiant nymph appear In all her glitt'ring birthday gear. **1868** W. COLLINS *Moonst.* (1871) 61 Your uncle's birthday gift. **1909** E. NESBIT *Daphne in Fitzroy St.* i. 3 (*title*) Birthday Girl. **1886** KIPLING *Departm. Ditties* (ed. 2) 8 Then the Birthday Honours came. Sad to state and sad to see, Stood against the Rajah's name nothing more than *C.I.E.*! **1897** *Sat. Rev.* 5 June 626/2 In any list of Birthday honours or New Year honours one expects to see the name of at least one distinguished man. **1606** HOLLAND *Sueton.* 265 Because he had celebrated the Birth-dayes-minde, of Otho the Emperour. *Ibid.* 101 His birth-day-mind [*natalem suum*] falling out in the time of the Plebeian games. **1803** C. WILMOT *Let.* 6 Mar. in *Irish Peer* (1920) 146 The composition of a birthday Ode. **1942** E. BLOM *Music in England* vi. 104 Purcell in his birthday-ode and welcome-song mood. **1830** GEN. P. THOMPSON *Exerc.* (1842) I. 314 The time that a birthday ox takes in roasting. **1852** MRS. GASKELL *Let.* 4 Sept. (1966) 198 Yesterday..we had a birthday party for Julia. **1796** M. EDGEWORTH *Parent's Assistant* (ed. 2) II. II. (*title*) The Birth-Day Present. **1854** C. M. YONGE *Castle Builders* xxii. 342 Her immense wax-doll, a birthday present from her papa. **1753** SMOLLETT *Ferd. Count Fathom* II. xli. 43 He made an apology for receiving the count in his birth-day suit. **1809** [see SUIT *sb.* 19 e]. **1727** SWIFT *What Pass. Lond.* Wks. 1755 III. I. 184 So many birth-day suits were countermanded the next day. **1922** BLUNDEN *Bonadventure* xxvii. 167 A dancing saloon, where birthday suits were the fashion. **1851** *Sharpe's London Jrnl.* XIII. 200/1 Father alwaies gives us a birthdaye treat. **1902** A. BENNETT *Grand Babylon Hotel* i. 12 I'll be content this year with the cheapest birthday treat you ever gave me.

† '**birthdom.** *Obs. rare*⁻¹. [f. BIRTH *sb.*¹ + -DOM.] Inheritance, birthright.

1605 SHAKS. *Macb.* IV. iii. 4 Let vs..like good men, Bestride our downfall Birthdome.

† '**birthel**, *a. Obs.* [f. BIRTH + -EL.] Fruit-bearing.

c **1250** *Gen. & Ex.* 119 Ilk gres, ilc wurt, ilc birðheltre, His owen sed beren bad he.

birthen, -an, obs. forms of BURDEN *sb.*

† '**birthful**, *a. Obs. rare.* [f. BIRTH *sb.*¹ + -FUL.] Prolific, productive.

1483 *Cath. Angl.* 33 Birthfulle, *fetosus.* **1596** J. DALRYMPLE *Leslie's Hist. Scot.* (1884–5) 9 The ane parte lyeng to the South is mekle birthfuller, throuch fertilitie of the ground.

† '**birthhood.** *Obs.* = BIRTHDOM.

1653 T. WHITFIELD *Treat. Sinf. Men* ix. 42 That Jacob should get the birth-hood and blessing.

birthing ('bɜːθɪŋ), *vbl. sb.* [f. BIRTH *v.* + -ING¹.]

1. The action or process of giving birth; childbirth, labour; now esp. 'natural' childbirth, in which there is a minimum of medical intervention. Also, the moment of birth, the fact of being born (*lit.* or *fig.*).

1901 [see sense 2 below]. **1928** J. PETERKIN *Scarlet Sister Mary* viii. 72 The whole earth was full of birthing and growth. **1942** M. K. RAWLINGS *Cross Creek Cookery* xviii. 261 Unfortunately, the spring birthings also mean pigs. **1956–60** A. R. AMMONS *Coll. Poems* (1972) 42 The birthing and aging of Life's all-clustered grief. **1978** I. M. GASKIN *Spiritual Midwifery* (rev. ed.) III. 343 If you are the midwife chiefly responsible for the welfare of the baby and the mother, you must make sure that the presence of everyone attending the birthing is beneficial. **1981** S. KITZINGER *Experience of Childbirth* (ed. 4) viii. 180 To give support..means really sharing what the mother is feeling..and *enjoying* the whole adventure of birthing. **1985** S. VANAUKEN *Under Mercy* x. 262 Birthing and dying will alike be forgotten.

2. *attrib.*

1901 *Westm. Gaz.* 3 Oct. 10/1, I, the changer, I Who make the rose's grave the birthing-bed For scarlet turban-lilies. **1928** J. PETERKIN *Scarlet Sister Mary* xxii. 253 The birthing lesson was over, the teacher was going away. **1971** D. PRYDE *Nunaga* (1972) xi. 105 Angulaalik came over and..sang a birthing song to it, a special little chant specially for new-born children. **1977** *Spare Rib* June 45/2 If all women had an epidural, freely available and theirs by right, all birthing problems could be solved. **1978** *Tucson Mag.* Dec. 57/1 St. Joseph's..was the first Tucson hospital with a home-like birthing room. **1982** *Brit. Med. Jrnl.* 28 Aug. 637/1 The obstetricians felt threatened because the birthing process had been taken out of their hands.

birthing, variant of BERTHING *vbl. sb.*

birthless ('bɜːθlɪs), *a.* [f. BIRTH *sb.*¹ + -LESS.]

a. Abortive. **b.** Without the advantages of 'birth.'

1649 OWEN *Serm.* Wks. 1851 VIII. 234 Their plots have proved tympanous and birthless. **1859** TROLLOPE *Dr. Thorne* 238 Poor Mary was such a birthless foundling.

birthnight ('bɜːθnaɪt). [f. BIRTH *sb.*¹ + NIGHT.]

1. The night on which any one is born.

1671 MILTON *P.R.* IV. 506 The Angelic Song in Bethlehem field, On thy birth-night. **1849** SOUTHEY *Com.-pl. Bk.* Ser. II. 420 The fire..was extinguished on the birth-night of the Prophet.

2. 'The night annually kept in memory of anyone's birth' (J.).

1628 DRYDEN *Relig. Laici* Pref., Now they celebrate Queen Elizabeth's birthnight. **1798** T. JEFFERSON in *Harper's Mag.* (1885) Mar. 536/2 Subscription for General Washington's birth night 5 D. *a* **1845** HOOD *Sea of Death*, They lay in loveliness, and kept the birthnight of their peace.

† **3.** *spec.* The evening of a royal birthday (see BIRTHDAY 2); the court-festival held thereon. *Obs.*

1712 BUDGELL *Spect.* No. 277 ¶9 That you may not be surprised at my appearing a la mode de Paris on the next Birth-night. **1730** SWIFT *Vind. Carteret* Wks. 1755 V. II. 181 To..dance at a birth-night.

b. *attrib.*

1712 POPE *Rape Lock* I. 23 More glitt'ring than a Birth-night Beau. **1800** MAR. EDGEWORTH *Belinda* iii, The crape petticoat of her birthnight dress. **1818** SCOTT *Hrt. Midl.*, Dropped a curtsy as low as a lady at a birth-night introduction.

birthplace ('bɜːθpleɪs). [f. BIRTH *sb.*¹ + PLACE.] The place where a person (or *fig.* a thing) is born.

1607 SHAKS. *Cor.* IV. iv. 23 My Birth-place hate I, and my loues vpon This Enemie Towne. **1789** BURNS *Farew. Highlands* i, The birth-place of valour, the country of worth. **1814** WORDSW. *Excurs.* III. 90 How gracefully that slender shrub looks forth From its fantastic birthplace! **1849** W. IRVING *Goldsm.* 19 In this house Goldsmith was born, and it was a birthplace worthy of a poet.

birthright ('bɜːθraɪt). [f. BIRTH *sb.*¹ + RIGHT.]

1. Right by birth; the rights, privileges, or possessions to which one is entitled by birth; inheritance, patrimony. (Specifically used of the special rights of the first-born.)

1535 COVERDALE *Gen.* xxv. 31 Sell me this daye thy byrth-right. **1593** SHAKS. *2 Hen. VI*, II. ii. 62 Be we the first That shall salute our rightfull Soueraigne With honor of his Birth-right to the Crowne. **1651** HOBBES *Leviath.* II. xxi. 110 Their Private Inheritance and Birthright. **1718** POPE *Iliad* xv. 185 Our elder birthright and superior sway. **1849** MACAULAY *Hist. Eng.* I. 445 The prince whom a faction..had tried to rob of his birthright.

attrib. **1652** T. HODGES *Hoary Head Cr.* 18 Jacob..got the birth-right blessing. **1810** SCOTT *Lady of L.* II. x, In Scotland's court, thy birthright place.

fig. **1684** R. WALLER *Nat. Exper.* To Rdr., Among all the Creatures of Divine Wisdom, the Birthright doubtless belongs to the Idea of Truth.

2. Native right; lot to which birth entitles.

1659 MILTON *Civ. Power* Wks. 1738 I. 555 The new Birth-right of every true Believer, Christian Liberty. **1719** W. WOOD *Surv. Trade* 296 Freedom of Trade is their undoubted Birth-right. **1810** COLERIDGE *Friend* (1865) 157 The laws of the land are the birth-right of every native. **1875** FARRAR *Silence & V.* viii. 136 Work is the best birthright which man still retains.

birth-time ('bɜːθtaɪm). Also 3 birde-, 3–4 bur-, buyr-, burþe-. Date or moment of birth.

1297 R. GLOUC. 9 From oure Lordes burþe time to þe worldes ende. *Ibid.* 443 Oure Louerdes burtyme. *c* **1300** *Life of Jesus* 295 (Mätz.) þet oþur buyrtyme þat scholde beo þo he gan hem þat lere. *a* **1564** BECON *Com.-pl. Holy Script.* Wks. (1844) 302 If they did perceive in the birth-time that it was a boy. **1860** HAWTHORNE *Marble Faun* (1879) I. xviii. 183 The birth-time of Christianity.

birthun, obs. form of BURDEN *sb.*

birthwort ('bɜːθwɜːt). *Bot.* [f. BIRTH *sb.*¹ + WORT.] The genus of shrubs ARISTOLOCHIA.

[**1548** TURNER *Names Herbes* (1881) 15 Astrolochia or round hertworte.] **1551** —— *Herbal* (1568) 43 *Aristolochia rotunda*..may be called in Englyshe..round byrthwurte: because it helpeth wymen to brynge furth theyr byrth. **1712** tr. *Pomet's Hist. Drugs* I. 44 The long Birthwort is a Root like a Radish. **1861** DELAMER *Fl. Gard.* 110 Birthwort—Aristolochia.

'**birthy**, *a. Sc.* [f. BIRTH *sb.*¹ + -Y¹.] Prolific.

1680 R. LAW *Mem.* (1818) 159 The last year's crop..was not birthie.

† '**birtle.** *Obs.* Forms: 5 birtylle, byrtyl, 6 brytyl. A sweet apple. Also in comb. *birtle-tree.*

1483 *Cath. Angl.* 33 A Birtylle, *malomellum*; a Birtylle tre, *malomellus.* **1500** *Ortus Voc.*, *Malomellus*, a brytyl tre. [**1847** HALLIWELL, *Birtle*, a summer apple. *Yorksh.*]

biry, etc., obs. form of BURY, etc.

biryani (bɪr'jɑːnɪ, bɪrɪ'ɑːnɪ). *Cookery.* Also biriani, biriyani, etc. [a. Hindi *biryānī*, ad. Pers. *biryān* fried, roasted.] A highly-spiced Indian dish made of meat or vegetables cooked with rice, saffron, and usu. brown lentils.

1932 M. R. ANAND *Curries* 81 (*heading*) Biriani (lamb pulao). *Ibid.* 83 (*heading*) Chicken biriani. **1956** H. DEUTROM *Ceylon Daily News Cookery Bk.* (ed. 4) 192 An Onion Sambol usually accompanies Buriani. **1958** S. NOORDEEN *Muslim Cookery* 9 The Buriyani dish is a mixture of a savoury and rice (or string hoppers) prepared separately. **1958** [see CARPET-BAG *sb.* 3]. **1967** L. DEIGHTON *London Dossier* 43 A *birianee* is an assembly of a pilau and a meat dish. **1969** *Eve's Weekly* (Bombay) 20 Dec. 67/3 Idd to us meant palatable biryanis and seviyian. **1978** J. PASSMORE *All Asian Cookbk.* (1979) 34/1 Mutton biriyani.

‖ **bis**, *adv.* [Fr. and It., a. L. *bis* twice.] Encore, again: used **a.** in *Music* as a direction that a phrase or passage is to be repeated. **b.** Twice; calling attention to the occurrence of a number, word, etc., twice.

1819 REES *Cycl.* s.v. *Bis*, The word *bis* placed over such passage,..implies that the whole is to be repeated. **1837** CARLYLE *Fr. Rev.* (1872) III. III. vii. 127 Marat like a musical *bis* repeating the last phrase. **1877** F. HALL *Eng. Adjs. in -able* 48 See for the verb, pp. 175 (*bis*), 302.

bis: see BICE, BYSS.

bis-, *pref.*¹ The prec. adv. used in late L., Fr., It., before *s*, *c*, or a vowel, in place of BI- *pref.*²; hence occas. in Eng., as in *bisacromial* = BIACROMIAL, *bisalternate* alternate in two ways.

bis-, *pref.*², *Chem.*, abbreviation of BISMUTH, used in comb., as *bisethyl*, C_2H_5Bi, *bistriethyl*, etc.

1863 WATTS *Dict. Chem.* I. 596.

bisaccate (baɪˈsækeɪt), *a.* [f. BI- *pref.*² 1 + SACCATE, f. L. *saccus* bag.] Having two sacs, or pouches.
1864 WEBSTER cities LOUDON.

†**bisalt** (ˈbaɪsɔːlt). [f. BI- *pref.*² III + SALT.]
1810 HENRY *Elem. Chem.* (1826) II. ix. 110 This certainly does away with an anomaly..that all the salts of copper are bi-salts, or contain 2 atoms of acid united to one of base.

†**biˈsannual**, *a.* and *sb.* *Obs.* [f. BIS- + ANNUAL.] = BIENNIAL.
1725 BRADLEY *Fam. Dict.*, *Scabious*..are call'd Bis-Annual, hardy plants, by reason they seldom Flower till the Second Year after Sowing and then Dye. *Ibid.* s.v. *Herb*, Which bear the Name of Bis-annuals.

biˈsantler. [variant of BEZANTLER.] The second branch of a deer's horn.
1863 KITTO & ALEX. *Cycl. Bibl. Lit.* 99/1 Barbary stag—distinguished by the want of a bisantler.

†**biˈsaumple**, *v.* *Obs.* [f. *bi-*, BE- 6 + *saumple*, ME. form of SAMPLE.] To moralize (about); bring forward 'instances' in illustration, palliation, etc.
a **1225** *Ancr. R.* 88 Bisaumpleð longe abuten uor te beon þe betere ileued. *Ibid.* 316 Schrift ȝet schal beon naked: þet is, nakedliche imaked, and nout bisaumpled feire.

bisawe, variant of BYSAWE, *Obs.*, proverb.

†**biˈsay, bisey**, *v.* *Obs.* [f. *bi-*, BE- 2 + *saȝen*, *seȝen*:—OE. *sǽgan* to cause to sink = OS. *sêgjan*, OHG. *seigan*:—OTeut. **saigjan*, causal of *sîgan* to sink.] *trans.* To cause to fall or stumble, to entrap.
c **1200** *Trin. Coll. Hom.* 213 Biswikeð her aiðer oðer, and beð þanne bisaid in þe grune of hinder. *Ibid.* 215 Mid fele folde grunen þe werse hine biseið and henteth.

‖**biscacha** (bisˈkatʃa). *Zool.* Also biz-, vis-. [a. Sp. *biscacho*.] A species of the *Chinchillidæ*, a burrowing rodent of South America.
a **1837** BENNETT in *Penny Cycl.* VII. 88/1 The Biscachas live in society, in burrows. **1847** CARPENTER *Zool.* §235 The burrows of the Viscacha are also inhabited by..small owls. **1859** DARWIN *Orig. Spec.* xiv. (1878) 379 Of all Rodents the bizcacha is most nearly related to the Marsupials.

Biscainer, obs. form of BISCAYNER.

†**ˈbiscake.** *Obs.* Also 7 biskake. [f. *biscuit* and *cake*.] = BISCUIT.
1657 TOMLINSON *Renou's Disp.* 171 Little long masses of bread..which they commonly call Biskakes. **1681** *Lond. Gaz.* No. 1606/4 William Marshal, a Sea-Biscake Baker.

Biscayan (ˈbɪskeɪən), *a.* Also 7 biscan, 8 biskaine. [f. *Biscay* + -AN.] Belonging to, or characteristic of, the province of Biscay; also as *sb.*, an inhabitant or native of Biscay. So **Biscayanism** (6 biscanism), the Basque language. **Biscayen** [ad. F. *biscaïen*], (*a*) A long heavy musket, first used in Biscay; (*b*) One of its balls (see quot.). **Biscayner (Biskiner, Biscainer, Biscayneer)**, a native of Biscay, a Biscayan ship.
1634 MASSINGER *Very Wom.* IV. iii, *Almira.* What country are you of? *Antonio.* A Biscan, lady. **1769** PENNANT *Zool.* III. 39 The cargo of two great Biskaine ships. **1875** URE *Dict. Arts* II. 936 There are three varieties of this forge [in which malleable iron is obtained directly from the ore], the Catalan, the Navarrese, and the Biscayan. **1596** NASHE *Haue With You* Wks. (Grosart) III. 78 Biscanism the most barbarous Spanish. **1812** *Examiner* 14 Sept. 581/2 He was struck on the shoulder by a Biscayen. *Ibid.* 588/1 A Biscayen is a cannon ball of a small calibre. **1601** J. KEYMOR *Dutch Fish.* in *Phenix* II. 225 Fish taken by the..Biscainers. **1813** *Sismondi's Lit. Europe* (1846) I. xii. 342 From the wicked Biscayneer.

biscent, -schent, obs. pa. pples. of BESHEND.

bisceop, bischop, obs. ff. BISHOP.

bischadwe, and other obs. vbs. in **bi-**: see BE-.

†**biˈschun**, *v.* *Obs.* Also 3 biscunien, bisunien. [ME., f. *bi-*, BE- 2 + *schunien* to SHUN. The mod. repr. would have been *beshun*.] *trans.* To shun, avoid (a thing); also with refl. pron.
c **1200** *Moral Ode* 132 in *Lamb. Hom.* 169 Wið þet þe mihte helle pine biflien and bisunien [*Egerton MS.* biscunien]. *a* **1250** *Prov. Alfred* 368 in *O.E. Misc.* 124 From lesynge þu þe wune And alle vnþewes þu þe bischune.

biscoct, -cot, obs. forms of BISCUIT.

†**biscot**, *v.* *Obs. rare*⁻¹. [a. F. *biscoter*.] *trans.* To caress amorously.
1653 URQUHART *Rabelais* II. xxiii, Wheresoever they should biscot and thrum their wenches.

†**ˈbiscot**, *sb.* *Obs.* [f. SCOT = payment: the prefix is doubtful: see the authorities cited.] A fine formerly exacted from the owners of marsh lands for failure to repair banks, ditches, etc.
1662 DUGDALE *Hist. Embanking and Draining Fens* 254 *a.* **1691** BLOUNT *Law Dict.* s.v., And if he should not by a second day given him, accomplish the same; then he should pay for every Perch ijs, which is called Bi-scot. **1790** BAILEY, *Biscot*, a Fine..to be paid on Default of repairing of Banks, Ditches, etc.

†**biscotin.** *Obs.* [a. F. *biscotin*, ad. It. *biscottino* little biscuit, f. *biscotto*: cf. BISCUIT.] A kind of sweet biscuit made of flour, sugar, eggs, etc.
1727 BRADLEY *Fam. Dict.* s.v. *Gimbels*, Bake 'em in the same manner as you do Biscotins. **1819** *Banquet* 17 Biscuit, bisk, and biscotin Swam in one indescribable tureen.

biscuit (ˈbɪskɪt). Forms: 4 besquite, 5 bysqwyte, -cute, 5–6 bysket, 6–8 bisket, 8– biscuit. (Also, casually, 6 biskett, -kette, -ked, -kitte, -kott, -ky, -quette, -quite; 6–7 bisquet; 7 bisquett, biscot, -coct.) [a. OF. 12th c. *bescoit*, 13th c. *bescuit*, 16th c. *biscuit*, mod.F. *biscuit*, a common Romanic word (= Pr. *bescueit*, Cat. *bescuyt*, Sp. *bizcocho*, Pg. *biscuto*, It. *biscotto*) on L. type **biscoctum* (*panem*), bread 'twice baked,' from the original mode of preparation. The regular form in Eng. from 16th to 18th c. was *bisket*, as still pronounced; the current *biscuit* is a senseless adoption of the mod. French spelling, without the Fr. pronunciation.]

1. a. A kind of crisp dry bread more or less hard, prepared generally in thin flat cakes. The essential ingredients are flour and water, or milk, without leaven; but confectionery and fancy biscuits are very variously composed and flavoured. Even the characteristic of hardness implied in the name is lost in the sense 'A kind of small, baked cake, usually fermented, made of flour, milk, etc.' used, according to Webster, in U.S.
1330 R. BRUNNE *Chron.* (1810) 171 Armour þei had plente, & god besquite to mete. *c* **1440** *Promp. Parv.* 48 Bysqwyte..*biscoctus.* **1555** *Fardle Facions* II. vii. 159 Their daiely foode..is hard Bisquette. **1569** CRAWLEY *Soph. Dr. Watson* ii. 169 The bread was such as was prouided to serue at neede, or in warres, for it was Bisket, that is twice baked, and without leauen or salt. **1595** SIR J. GILBERT in *N. & Q.* Ser. III. (1864) Feb. 109/1, 1400 tones off corn too be bakyd ynto bysky. **1600** SHAKS. *A.Y.L.* II. vii. 39 As drie as the remainder bisket After a voyage. **1697** DAMPIER *Voy.* (1729) I. 303 Bread of fine Wheat Flower, baked like Bisket, but not so hard. **1755** JOHNSON, *Bisket*: see BISCUIT. **1770** FITZ-HENRY *Observ. Baretti's Journ.* i. 90, I call for a bisket and a glass of Madeira. **1818** J. PALMER *Jrnl. Trav. N. Amer.* ix. 125 Hot short cakes, called biscuits. **1828** WEBSTER, *Biscuit*, ..a composition of flour and butter, made and baked in private families. **1843** 'R. CARLTON' *New Purchase* v. 27 Hot rolls.., a novelty then, but much like biscuits in parts of the Far West. **1860** *All Y. Round* No. 63. 302 Munching an Abernethy biscuit. **1903** *N.Y. Sun* 1 Dec. 8 Did he never spread cream ham gravy on his hot biscuits?

b. *transf.* (*a*) (see quot.).
1881 *Encycl. Brit.* XII. 836 The flat rounded cakes of [South American] rubber made in this manner are known in the London market as 'biscuits'.

(*b*) *Military slang.* A square brown palliasse or mattress.
1915 'IAN HAY' *First Hundred Thous.* v. 33 'Got the biscuits here, Sergeant-Major?'.. The Sergeant-Major dives into a pile of brown blankets and presently extracts three small brown mattresses, each two feet square. **1917** *Times* 21 Nov. 11/4 Sleeping on the floor on army 'biscuits'—as they had already learned to call the military mattress. **1919** *Athenæum* 22 Aug. 791/2 'Biscuits.' These were the palliasses—square in form and brown as to colour—of which three went to each bed. *a* **1935** T. E. LAWRENCE *Mint* (1936) III. v. 173 The mattresses are three little square brown canvas cushions, rammed solid with coir. Biscuits they call them.

c. The characteristic light-brown colour of biscuits; biscuit colour; often *attrib.* = of this colour.
1884 Biscuit colour, biscuit satin [see sense 3]. **1892** *Daily News* 16 Sept. 3/3 A biscuit straw hat. **1896** *Ibid.* 18 July 6/3 White, cream, and biscuit-fawn. **1897** *Ibid.* 15 Sept. 6/6 Biscuit-tinted lace insertion. **1923** *Daily Mail* 15 Jan. 6 Newest shades, including: Pale Pink..Scarlet Fuchsia, Biscuit, Mauve.

d. Colloq. phr. ***to take the biscuit***: to 'take the cake' (see CAKE *sb.* 7).
1907 G. B. SHAW *John Bull's other Island* III. 76 All you know is ah to ahl [howl] abaht it. You take the biscuit at that, you do. **1930** WODEHOUSE *Very Good, Jeeves!* vi. 167 Of all the absolutely foul sights I have ever seen, this took the biscuit with ridiculous ease. **1961** *Listener* 16 Nov. 825/2 For the sheerest idiocy, it's the comparative 'as contemporary as...' that takes the biscuit.

2. *Pottery.* The name given to porcelain and other pottery-ware after having undergone the first firing, and before being glazed, painted, or otherwise embellished; also *fig.*
1791 E. DARWIN *Bot. Gard.* I. 87 The kneaded clay refines, The biscuit hardens, the enamel shines. **1864** J. HARFORD *Recoll. Wilberforce* i. 21 'What an interesting creature is Dunn! he is formed of the finest biscuit.' **1880** CH. M. MASON *Forty Shires* 158 Potter's 'Biscuit' is the dough after it has been made into vessels and baked.

3. *Comb.* and *attrib.* **a.** attrib., as (in sense 1) *biscuit-bag, -box, -cask, -figure, -manufactory, -sack, tin, -worm*; (of the colour of a biscuit, light-brown), as ***biscuit satin***; also ***dry-biscuit-jest, -rogue***; (in sense 2) *biscuit-body, -china, clay, oven, stage, state, ware, warehouse* (hence ***b. warehouseman***). **b.** objective, as *biscuit-baker, -baking, -beater, -cast, -maker, -making, -throw, -toss* (cf. STONE'S THROW). **c.** parasynthetic and similative, as *biscuit-brained, -coloured, -like, -shaped.* **biscuit barrel**, a barrel used to contain biscuits; *spec.* a small domestic barrel-shaped container for biscuits; **biscuit root** *N. Amer.*, the quamash (*Camassia esculenta*) of North America, or other esculent roots similar to this.
1837 CARLYLE *Fr. Rev.* I. III. viii. 132 A sinking pilot will fling out..his very *biscuit-bags. **1707** *Lond. Gaz.* No. 4332/8 Caleb Claggett, *Biscuit Baker. **1865** L. SIMPSON *Handbk. Dining* ii. (ed. 3) 27 Biscuit bakers..hold a middle path between pastry cooks and confectioners. **1787** T. JEFFERSON *Let.* 18 Sept. in *Writings* (1853) II. 269 He has contrived a varnish..for lining *biscuit barrels. **1840** N. HAWTHORNE in *Harper's Mag.* XLV. 690/2 Sometimes I..warmed myself by a red-hot stove, among biscuit-barrels..and kettles. **1886** F. H. BURNETT *Little Lord Fauntleroy* (1887) ii. 21 You said..that you wouldn't have them sitting 'round on your biscuit barrels. **1935** D. SAYERS *Gaudy Night* xi. 174 People *still* give plated biscuit-barrels! **1783** WEDGWOOD in *Phil. Trans.* LXXIII. 285 Mixed with porcelain *biscuit body. **1886** *Times* 24 Feb. 9/6 Constructing the *biscuit-box redoubt under fire at Gubat. **1853** KANE *Grinnell Exp.* xlix. (1856) 461 Within short *biscuit-cast. **1862** MAYHEW *Crim. Prisons* 129 As white as slabs of *biscuit-china. **1599** B. JONSON *Ev. Man out Hum.* Grex 157 [He] breaks a drie *bisquet-jest, Which..He steepes in his owne laughter. **1836** TODD *Cycl. Anat. & Phys.* I. 746/1 The rough *biscuit-like surface of the bone. **1835** *Penny Cycl.* IV. 452/1 Our description of *biscuit-making. *Ibid.* The largest *biscuit-manufactories are those ..for supplying the navy. **1768** J. WEDGWOOD *Let.* 13 June (1965) 65 We..cannot keep Pace with the *Biscuit oven. **1902** A. BENNETT *Anna of Five Towns* viii. 172 There's the biscuit oven, but we can't inspect it because it's just being drawn. **1904** GOODCHILD & TWENEY *Technol. & Sci. Dict.* 52/2 *Biscuit oven*, is that in which the clay articles are placed, and the heat of which renders them more or less vitrified. **1620** FLETCHER *Fr. Lawyer* II. i. 58 Ze dry *bisket rogue! **1837** W. IRVING *Capt. Bonneville* III. i. 9 The cowish, also, or *biscuit root, about the size of a walnut, which they reduce to a very palatable flour. **1847** DE SMET *Oregon Missions* 116 The bitter root..grows in light dry, sandy soil as also the caious or biscuit root. **1779** JOHNSON *Drake* Wks. IV. 410 A sail made of a *bisket sack. **1884** *Pall Mall G.* 8 Apr. 4/2 In dinner and evening dresses the biscuit colour is equally popular. An evening dress of *biscuit satin. **1865** *Daily Tel.* 3 Nov. 5/5 It is fired for about sixty hours..and is then in what is called the '*biscuit' state. **1833** MARRYAT *P. Simple* (1863) 340 Running the brig within *biscuit-throw of the weather schooner. **1901** KIPLING *Five Nations* (1903) 114 We stumble on refuse of rations, The beef and the *biscuit-tins. **1891** *Pall Mall Gaz.* 26 Jan. 3/1 This was but a *biscuit-toss from Crown Office-row. **1896** KIPLING *Seven Seas* 29 And north, amid the hummocks, A biscuit-toss below. **1960** *Listener* 18 Aug. 250/2 Daughters of 'rails' and raised within biscuit-toss of the 'big rust'—the main line. **1782** WEDGWOOD in *Phil. Trans.* LXXII. 307 The kiln in which the *biscuit ware is fired. **1902** A. BENNETT *Anna of Five Towns* viii. 173 Mynors took the plate..to the *biscuit-warehouse... A solitary biscuit-warehouseman was examining the ware. **1798** COLERIDGE *Anc. Mar.* I. xvii, The mariners gave it *biscuit-worms.

4. biscuit bread. Formerly used as = BISCUIT.
c **1440** *Promp. Parv.* 37 Byscute brede, *biscoctus.* **1555** EDEN *Decades W. Ind.* I. III. (Arb.) 77 The vytayles (especially the byskette breade) corrupted. **1616** SURFL.& MARKH. *Countr. Farm* 583 Physitians appoint bisket bread for such as are troubled with rheumes. **1684** tr. *Bonet's Merc. Compit.* x. 364 Adust humours, which are increased by Biscoct Bread.

Hence **ˈbiscuiting** *vbl. sb.*, the first baking of earthenware or similar material.
1871 *Echo* 6 Jan., This first burning is technically termed 'biscuiting.'

biscuity (ˈbɪskɪtɪ), *a.* [f. BISCUIT + -Y¹.] Biscuit-like in texture, flavour, colour, etc.
1892 *Eng. Illustr. Mag.* IX. 859 The pleasant 'biscuity' flavour of the atmosphere. **1925** *British Weekly* 22 Oct. 127/1 In Germany and Austria..*Zwieback* comprises a vast variety of small crunchy biscuity cakes. **1961** *Guardian* 27 Sept. 3/6 Warm, biscuity, hand-shaped stone.

biscutate (baɪˈskjuːteɪt), *a.* [f. BI- *pref.*² 1, 6 + SCUTATE, ad. L. *scūtātus*, f. *scūtum* shield.] Having two shields; resembling two bucklers.
1838 LOUDON *Encycl. Pl. Biscutella*, Silicle flat, biscutate.

‖**bise** (biz, biːz). Also 6 bisa. [a. F. *bise*, in same sense. Also found in med.L., Pr., Piedmontese *bisa*; OHG. *bîsa*, MHG. *bîse*, mod.G., Swiss *bîse*, *beiswind*, Breton *biz*. Origin and native lang. unknown: Diez (s.v. *Bigio*) and Scheler incline to refer it to *bis* dark, blackish. In mod.Eng. only an alien French word.]
A keen dry N. or NNE. wind, prevalent in Switzerland and the neighbouring parts of France, Germany, and Italy.
a **1300** *Havelok* 724 That it ne bigan a wind to rise Out of the north, men calleth bise. **1594** GREENE *Look. Glasse* (1861) 134 Our sails were split by Bisas bitter blast. **1834** MRS. SOMERVILLE *Connex. Phys. Sc.* xxvi. (1849) 292 The cutting north wind called the bise in Switzerland. **1885** RUSKIN *Præter.* II. 38 The bise, now first letting one feel what malignant wind could be.

bise, obs. f. BICE.

bisect (baɪˈsɛkt), *v.* Also 7 bissect. [Apparently of Eng. formation, from *bi-*, *bis-* two + *sect-* ppl. stem of *secāre* to cut: cf. *intersect*, etc.]
1. *trans.* To cut or divide into two equal parts. (The earlier and usual sense.)

1646 SIR T. BROWNE *Pseud. Ep.* 292 The rationall Horizon..bissecteth the Globe into equall parts. 1660 BARROW *Euclid* I. x, To bisect a right line. 1879 WALLACE *Australas.* xviii. 347 Borneo is nearly bisected by the equator.

2. To cut in two, divide into any two parts.

1789 BENTHAM *Princ. Legisl.* xviii. §56 The logical whole ..has been bisected in as many different directions as were necessary. 1853 GROTE *Greece* II. lxxxv. XI. 249 Attacking them while thus disarrayed and bisected by the river.

3. *intr.* To divide in two; to fork.

1870 *Daily News* 5 Oct., On the *chaussée* just before it bisects, is a village named Belle-Croix.

bisect (ˈbaɪsɛkt), *sb. Ecol.* [f. BISECT *v.*] (See quots.)

1916 F. E. CLEMENTS *Plant Succession* xv. 432 It is proposed to indicate the vertical and lateral relations of individuals by means of a cross-section showing both shoots and roots in their normal position. Such a cross-section may be termed a *bisect.* 1919 J. E. WEAVER *Ecol. Relations Roots* 32 Schematic bisect showing the root and stem relations of ..prairie plants. 1926 TANSLEY & CHIPP *Stud. Vegetation* iv. 66 When a profile chart includes the root systems of the plants it is called a *bisect.* 1962 H. HANSON *Dict. Ecol.* 55 *Bisect,* a line transect which shows the vertical and lateral distribution of roots along the side of a trench in the soil and the above-ground parts of the plants along the line.

biˈsected, *ppl. a.* [f. BISECT *v.* + -ED.]

a. Divided into two (usually equal) parts. **b.** Forked (as a road).

1656 in BLOUNT *Glossogr.* 1794 T. TAYLOR *Pausanias* III. 5 The bisected road belonging to the Phocenses. 1806 HUTTON *Course Math.* I. 312 The two other Sides including the Bisected Angle. 1880 GRAY *Bot. Text-bk.* 399 Bisected, completely divided into two parts.

bisection (baɪˈsɛkʃən). [n. of action f. BISECT *v.*, after L. *sectiōnem*; see -TION.]

1. Division into two equal parts.

1656 tr. *Hobbes's Elem. Philos.* (1839) 307 By perpetual bisection of an angle. 1837 WHEWELL *Hist. Induct. Sc.* II. 209 Continued bisection and other aliquot subdivisions.

2. Division into any two parts.

1822 DE QUINCEY *Confess.* (1862) 97, I wished to bisect the journey..such a bisection was attained in a clean roadside inn. 1876 E. MELLOR *Priesth.* iv. 182 The theory which requires the bisection of the chapter into two unequal parts.

3. Division into two branches; forking.

1870 *Daily News* 5 Oct., It stands a little to the south of the great chaussée from Metz to Saarlouis and Saarbruck, while as yet the bisection has not taken place.

bisectional (baɪˈsɛkʃənəl), *a.* [f. prec. + -AL¹.] Of, pertaining to, or of the nature of bisection. **biˈsectionally** *adv.*, by bisection, so as to divide into two equal parts.

1809 TROUGHTON in *Phil. Trans.* XCIX. 109 How to render the usual divisions of the quadrant bisectional. *Ibid.* 110 Contrived the means of dividing bisectionally.

bisector (baɪˈsɛktə(r), -tɔː(r)). [f. BISECT *v.*] One who or that which bisects; a bisecting line.

1864 *Reader* 5 Oct. 483/2 The internal and external bisectors of the angle. 1883 PROCTOR in *Knowledge* 6 July 14/2 The bisector of the vertical angle.

bisectrix (baɪˈsɛktrɪks). [f. prec.: see -TRIX.] = prec.; *spec.* in biaxial polarization, the line bisecting the angle between the two axes of polarization (= *linea bisectrix*).

1854 DANA *Min.* Introd. 20 A line bisecting the..angle between these optical axes is called a bisectrix.

bisee, bisege, -seige: see BESEE, BESIEGE.

bisegment (baɪˈsɛgmənt). [f. BI- *pref.*² + SEGMENT: the sense follows that of BISECT.] One of the two equal parts into which a line or other magnitude is divided.

1847 in CRAIG.

biseke, biseme, obs. ff. BESEECH, BESEEM.

bisemar(e, -mere, obs. forms of BISMER.

bisen, variant of BISSON and BYSEN.

bisench, bisend, etc., see BE-.

bisensory (baɪˈsɛnsərɪ), *a.* [BI-².] Of an hallucination: affecting two senses.

1894 *Proc. Soc. Psych. Research* X. 194 In these 'bisensory' or 'trisensory' cases, the constructive imagination seems to have reached a higher point than in simple visual or auditory hallucinations. *a* 1901 F. W. H. MYERS *Hum. Pers.* (1903) I. 254 Visual, auditory, bisensory, and trisensory hallucinations.

biseptate (baɪˈsɛpteɪt), *a.* [f. BI- *pref.*² 1 + SEPTATE, f. L. *septum* enclosure, wall.] Having two *septa* or partitions.

1871 M. COOKE *Fungi* (1874) 40 Similar biseptate spores.

biserial (baɪˈsɪərɪəl), *a.* [f. BI- *pref.*² 6 + SERIAL, f. L. *series* SERIES.] Arranged in two rows or series. **biˈseriate** *a.* = prec. **biˈseriately** *adv.*, in biseriate order, in a double row.

1839 *Proc. Berw. Nat. Club* I. 199 Suckers of the arms biserial. 1870 ROLLESTON *Anim. Life* 144 Biserial rows of ambulacral ampullæ. 1846 DANA *Zooph.* (1848) 215 With cellules interruptedly uniseriate, and occasionally biseriate. *Ibid.* 223 Septa biseriately cellular.

biserrate (baɪˈsɛreɪt), *a.* [f. BI- *pref.*² 3 + SERRATE, ad. L. *serrātus* notched like a saw, f. *serra* saw.] Notched like a saw, with the notches themselves similarly minutely notched.

1835 LINDLEY *Introd. Bot.* II. 358 When these teeth are themselves serrate, we say *biserrate.* 1870 BENTLEY *Bot.* 252.

‖**biset** (bizɛ, ˈbɪzɪt). [a. Fr. *biset*, f. *bis* dark-grey, greyish brown.] The wild rock-pigeon.

1834 R. MUDIE *Feather. Tribes* (1841) I. 74 Biset, a kind of fancy pigeon. 1837 *Penny Cycl.* VII. 370/1 The ring pigeon ..and the rock pigeon or biset (*Columba livia*).

bisetous (baɪˈsiːtəs), *a.* [f. BI- *pref.*² + L. *sæta, sēta* bristle + -OUS. (L. had *bisētus-a* and *setōsus.*)] Having or furnished with two *setæ* or bristles. So **biseˈtose** *a.* the same.

1842–52 BRANDE *Dict. Sc.*, *Bisetous*, in Zoology, when an animal or part is furnished with two bristle-like appendages. 1847 CRAIG, *Bisetose.*

†**ˈbisexed**, *a. Obs.* [f. BI- *pref.*² 1 + SEX.] Of both sexes. So **biˈsexous.**

1606 SYLVESTER *Du Bartas* (1608) 267 Our bisexed Parents, free from sin, In Eden did their double birth begin. 1646 SIR T. BROWNE *Pseud. Ep.* 149 That the whole species or kinde should be bisexous. 1656 in BLOUNT *Glossogr.*

bisexual (baɪˈsɛksjuːəl, -ʃ(j)ʊəl), *a.* and *sb.* [f. BI- *pref.*² 1 + SEXUAL, f. L. *sexus.*] **A.** *adj.* **1.** Of two sexes; *spec.* having both sexes in the same individual.

1824 COLERIDGE *Aids Refl.* (1848) I. 204 The very old tradition of the *homo androgynus,* that is, that the original man..was bi-sexual. 1859 TODD *Cycl. Anat. & Phys.* V. 116/2 In all the bisexual Crustacea the ova are fecundated while still within the body of the female parent. 1880 GRAY *Struct. Bot.* vi. §3. 191 A flower which possesses stamens and pistils is Bisexual.

2. Sexually attracted to individuals of both sexes. Cf. AMBISEXUAL *a.*

1914 *Amer. Med.* IX. 531/1 By nature all human beings are psychically *bisexual* — capable of loving a person of either sex. 1955 R. LINDNER *Fifty-Minute Hour* 213 Persons like Anton are neither homosexual nor heterosexual, but bisexual. 1956 E. FROMM *Art of Loving* ii. 33 Just as physiologically man and woman each have hormones of the opposite sex, they are bisexual also in the psychological sense. 1966 M. DUFFY *Microcosm* 252 Then she asked me to come back but so many things she'd done had left a taste in my mouth, and besides she was bi-sexual and I've never been interested in that. 1979 R. JAFFE *Class Reunion* III. ii. 238 It was the Seventies now, and the rock stars and Beautiful People had made it suddenly chic to be bisexual. 1986 P. BOOTH *Palm Beach* x. 172 Jo-Anne tells me there's another problem, Lisa. I didn't know you were bisexual.

B. *sb.* **a.** A hermaphrodite. *rare.* **b.** A person who is sexually attracted to members of both sexes.

1922 'R. WERTHER' *Female Impersonators* I. iv. 43 As a result, male bisexuals are goody-goody boys who develop into ultra-religious adolescents. 1931 *Med. Jrnl. & Rec.* CXXXIII. 382/1, I have heard this 'history' many times, not only from normal men..., but also from bisexuals and homosexuals. 1942 BERREY & VAN DEN BARK *Amer. Thes. Slang* § 405/1 *Effeminate man or masculine woman*..bisexual, eerquay, freak. 1970 N. SAUNDERS *Alternative London* xx. 145 True bi-sexuals, who can have emotionally warm relationships with either sex are very rare. 1978 *Globe & Mail* (Toronto) 17 Aug. T7/4 She was also upset, she said, that so many people had assumed she was a lesbian or bisexual because her character in the movie, Tanya, was bisexual.

bisexuˈality. [f. prec. + -ITY.] **1.** Bisexual quality or condition.

1859 TODD *Cycl. Anat. & Phys.* V. 595/2 The elements of the male, as well as of the female, reproductive apparatus, without any true exhibition of bi-sexuality.

2. The state or condition of being sexually attracted to members of both sexes.

1892 C. G. CHADDOCK tr. *R. von Krafft-Ebing's Psychopathia Sexualis* (ed. 7) III. 187 Careful investigation of the so-called acquired cases makes it probable that the predisposition also present here consists of a latent homosexuality, or, at least, bi-sexuality. 1914 S. A. TANNENBAUM tr. *W. Stekel's Masked Homosexuality* in *Amer. Med.* IX. 537/1 Only the careful study of the masked forms of homosexuality will enable us to understand the tremendous significance of bisexuality in our psychic life. 1931 *Med. Jrnl. & Rec.* CXXXIII. 381/2 The homosexual phase of development..still leaves some traces in the mentality of boys between the ages of seventeen and twenty-five. They are still nearer bisexuality than older boys. 1956 C. WILSON *Outsider* iii. 63 Haller admits that a part of his new 'life of the senses' is smoking opium; and there is bisexuality too. (Pablo suggests a sexual orgy for three: himself, Harry and Maria; and Maria and Hermine have Lesbian relations.) 1965 G. MELLY *Owning Up* ii. 12, I moved slowly from homosexuality to bisexuality and from there to heterosexuality. 1983 J. BANCROFT *Human Sexuality* 175 With changing attitudes to homosexuality and to sex in general we should also prepare ourselves for a weakening of the polarisation of homo- and heterosexuality. Bisexuality, or ambisexuality, may become more a part of the human experience.

ˈbisgay. *dial.* [var. of BESAGUE.] Somersetshire name for a double axe, having the two faces opposite and transverse to each other.

bish (bɪʃ), *sb.*¹ and *v.*¹ Jocular abbrev. of BISHOP *sb.* and *v.*

1875 A. PORSON *Quaint Words* 20 To be *bish'd*.. confirmed. 1927 WODEHOUSE *Meet Mr. Mulliner* iii. 88 He turned appealingly from one to the other. 'Vicar! Bish!' 1930 *Outlook & Independent* 29 Oct. 328/3 Some one.. asked in amazement, 'When does the Bishop bish?' 1958 I. MURDOCH *Bell* 247, I suppose I'd better leave the way clear for the bish's Rolls Royce.

bish (bɪʃ), *sb.*² *slang.* [Etym. unknown.] A mistake, blunder.

1937 PARTRIDGE *Dict. Slang* 55/2 *Bish*,..a mistake: Seaford Preparatory School: from ca. 1925. 1955 F. SWINNERTON *Sumner Intrigue* xx. 198 He's always making bishes like this! 1956 B. GOOLDEN *At Foot of Hills* x. 236 She ..suddenly realised she'd made an [*sic*] complete bish.

bish (bɪʃ), *v.*² *Austral.* and *N.Z. slang.* [Imitative.] *trans.* To throw.

1940 N. MARSH *Surfeit of Lampreys* (1941) X. §1. 142 They'd just sort of bished them into the cupboard. 1945 BAKER *Austral. Lang.* xi. 205 To throw is *to bish, biff* or *peg.*

bish, variant of BIKH.

bishemel, obs. form of BECHAMEL.

bishop (ˈbɪʃəp), *sb.* Forms: 1 biscop, -sceop, -scep, 2–3 biscop, 3–6 bischop, 4–5 bisshop, 3– bishop. Also 1 biscob, 2 bish-, bisshup, 2–3 biscopp, bisscop, -kop, 2–4 (*s.e.*) bissop, 3 byssop, 3–7 bishoppe, 4 bisschop(e, -oppe, bi(s)shope, -opp, -up, busschop, 4–5 byschop, 4–6 bisch-, bisshopp, busshop, bysshop, bishope, -opp, 4–7 byshop, 5 bis-, byschope, -oppe, -upp, -yp, buschop(e, 5–6 bysch-, bysshopp, -ope, -oppe, 6 bischoipp, biszhop, -oppe, bushopp(e, byshe-, bys-, bysshopp(e, 6–7 bisshope, bushop, 7 biship, busschope. [OE. *biscop* (also in North. *biscob*), *bisceop, biscep*, an early adopted word (cf. OS. *biskop*, MDu. *bisscop*, Du. *bisschop*), OHG. *biscof, piscof* (MHG., mod.G. *bischof*), ON. *biskup* (Sw *biscop*, Da. *bisp*), a. Romanic **biscopo* or vulgar L. (*e*)*biscopus*:—L. *episcopus*, a. Gr. ἐπίσκοπος overlooker, overseer, f. ἐπί on + -σκοπος looking, σκοπός watcher; used in Greek, and to some extent also in Latin, both in the general sense, and as the title of various civil officers; with the rise of Christianity it gradually received a specific sense in the Church, with which it passed into Slavonic, Teutonic, and Celtic. With the form *biscopo, biscobo*, which passed into Teutonic, cf. also It. *vescovo*, OF. *vesque*, Pg. *bispo*, Pr. *vesque, bisbe*. Cf. BISP.]

1. A spiritual superintendent or overseer in the Christian Church.

a. Used in the New Testament versions to render the Gr. word ἐπίσκοπος, applied to certain officers in early Christian churches, either as a descriptive term, or as their actual title. In Wyclif, the Rhemish, and Revised Versions, the Gr. word is so rendered in every instance; but in the other versions from Tindale to 1611, it is in Acts xx. 28 (where applied to the πρεσβύτεροι or 'elders' of Ephesus) rendered 'overseers.' Also applied to Christ, as descriptive of his office. (Sometimes applied by those who do not recognize the episcopal order, to their pastor or chief elder, but only as a descriptive term, or as identifying his office with that of the New Testament 'bishop.')

1382 WYCLIF *Acts* xx. 28 Al the folk in which the Hooly Gost sette ȝou bischopis. [TINDALE oversears, CRANMER ouersears, *Geneva* Ouersears, *Rhem.* bishops, 1611 ouerseers, 1881 bishops (*marg.* or overseers).] —— *1 Peter* ii. 25 Ȝe ben conuertid now to the sheperde and bischop of ȝoure soulis [1881 the Shepherd and Bishop (*marg.* or Overseer) of your souls]. *c* 1383 —— *Sel. Wks.* III. 310 Crist veriest bischop of alle. 1535 COVERDALE *Phil.* i. 1 Paul & Timotheus..vnto all the payntes..with the Biszhoppes & mynisters. 1647 JER. TAYLOR *Lib. Proph.* vii. 130 The Holy Ghost hath made them Bishops or Over-seers.

1868 LIGHTFOOT *Philippians* 93 It is a fact now generally recognized by theologians of all shades of opinion, that in the language of the New Testament the same officer in the Church is called indifferently 'bishop' ἐπίσκοπος and 'elder' or 'presbyter' πρεσβύτερος.

b. *spec.* In the Eastern, Western, Anglican, and other churches of episcopal order: A clergyman consecrated for the spiritual government and direction of a 'diocese,' ranking beneath an archbishop (where these exist) and above the priests or presbyters, and deacons. (This is the sense in which the word passed with Christianity into all the Teutonic langs., and thus the earliest sense in English.)

***bishop in partibus* (*infidelium*)** in R.C. Ch., one dignified with the title of a bishopric, whose district or diocese is in the possession of infidels or heretics; originally applied to those expelled from the Holy Land by the Saracens.

c 897 K. ÆLFRED *Gregory's Past.* (Hatton MS.) 1 Ælfred kyning hateð gretan Wærferð biscep. 1121 *O.E. Chron.* 984 (Laud MS.) Her forðferde se halȝa biscop Aðelwold. *c* 1175 *Cott. Hom.* 237 Archebiscopes . and biscopes. 1297 R. GLOUC. 376 He huld..Byssopes & abbotes to hys wylle echon. *c* 1380 WYCLIF *Wks.* 417 Bischops..shulden not amersy pore men. 1473 WARKW. *Chron.* 3 The Kyng put

oute of the Chauncelerschepp the Bysshope of Excetre. **1548** PATTEN *Exped. Scotl.* Arb. *Garner* III. 68 That venemous *aspis*..the Bishop of Rome. *c* **1600** NORDEN *Spec. Brit.* (1728) 32 Former times afforded Cornwall a peculiar Bushop. **1641** SMECTYMNUUS *Vind. Answ.* §16. 208 King James of blessed memory said, *no Bishop, no King*: it was not he, but others that added, *No Ceremony, no Bishop.* **1738** BOLINGBR. *On Parties* 170 Another Man wears..Lawn Sleeves, and sits in a purple Elbow-Chair, to denote that he is a Bishop. **1753** CHAMBERS *Cycl. Supp.* s.v. *Bishop*, By the canon law, a bishop *in partibus* is qualified hereby to be a coadjutor of another bishop. **1844** LINGARD *Anglo-Sax. Ch.* (1858) I. iv. 133 These ministers [of religion] were at first confined to the three orders of bishops, priests, and deacons. **1882** FARRAR *Early Chr.* I. 529 James lived to furnish the nearest approach to a bishop to be found in the Apostolic age.

†**2.** *transf.* Formerly applied to: A chief priest of any religion; *e.g.* a chief priest or High Priest of the Jews, a Roman pontiff ('high' or 'principal bishop' = *pontifex maximus*), Mohammedan Caliph, etc. *Obs.*

c **893** K. ÆLFRED *Oros.* v. iv. §1 Lucinius Crassus..wæs eac Romana ieldesta biscep. *c* **950** *Lindisf. Gosp.* Mark xv. 11 Ða biscobas ðonne ȝeegedon ðone ðreat. *c* **1200** ORMIN 1022 Te biscopp sellf Wiþþ blod..þær sholde cumenn. **1382** WYCLIF *Mark* xv. 11 Forsothe the bischopis stireden the cumpenye of peple, that more he schulde leeue to hem Barabas. **1447** BOKENHAM *Seyntys* 49 At that tyme byschop was isakar In the temple. *c* **1460** *Towneley Myst.* 57 Now am I set to kepe..Byschope Jettyr shepe. **1541** PAYNELL *Catiline* xvii. 24 b, P. Scipio, the hyghe bysshope..slewe Tiberius Gracchus. **1586** T. B. *La Primaud. Fr. Acad.* 597 The caliphaes of the Sarasins were chiefe bishops in their religion. **1600** HOLLAND *Livy* XXII. ix. 437 e, The Colledge of the Bishops or Prelates [*pontificum*]. **1615** BEDWELL *Arab. Trudg.* Sultan, The Byshop of Egypt is called the Souldan. **1647** R. STAPYLTON *Juvenal* 101 Supposititious children, bishops pull'd From the foule lake.

†**3.** As a literalism of translation:

a. Overlooker, inspector, watchman.

1592 ANDREWES 96 *Serm.* v. (1843) 516 No pinnacle so high but the devil is a bishop over it, to visit and overlook it.

b. for L. *episcopus* in its most common civil sense of: Superintendent or overseer of the public victualling. [Cf. Charisius in *Roman Digest*, 'Episcopi qui præsunt pani et ceteris venalibus rebus quæ civitatum populis ad quotidianum victum usui sunt.']

1808 *Month. Mag.* XXVI. 109 They gave away corn, not cash; and Cicero was made bishop, or overseer, of this public victualling.

4. Applied ludicrously to the chief of the company in the 'Festival of Fools.' Cf. the *Boy Bishop* of St. Nicholas Day: Brande *Pop. Antiq.* I. 232.

1801 STRUTT *Sports & Past.* IV. iii. 303.

5. One of the pieces in the game of chess, having its upper part carved into the shape of a mitre; formerly called *archer*, and in still earlier times *alfin* or *aufyn*.

1562 ROWBOTHAM in *Archaeol.* XXIV. 203 The Bishoppes some name Alphins, some fooles, and some name them Princes; other some call them Archers. **1581** SIDNEY *Def. Poesie* (1622) 520 Giuing a peece of wood the reuerend title of a Bishop. **1656** F. BEALE *Chesse-play* 2 A Bishop or Archer, who is commonly figured with his head cloven. **1801** STRUTT *Sports & Past.* IV. ii. 275 The alfin was also denominated..with us an archer, and at last a bishop.

6. a. 'The little spotted beetle commonly called the Lady-cow or Lady-bird.' Ray *S. & E. Country Wds.* 1674.

1875 PARISH *Sussex Dial.* s.v., 'Bishop, Bishop-Barnabee, Tell me when my wedding shall be; If it be to-morrow day, Ope your wings and fly away.

b. = *bishop-bird.*

1934 in WEBSTER. **1953** D. A. BANNERMAN *Birds W. & Equat. Afr.* II. 1415 When not breeding the Fire-crowned Bishops go about in small flocks.

†**7.** (See quot.) *Obs.*

1611 FLORIO, *Fungo*..that firy round in a burning candle called the Bishop.

8. A sweet drink variously compounded, the chief ingredients being wine, oranges or lemons, and sugar; mulled and spiced port.

1738 SWIFT *Wom. who cry Oranges* Wks. 1755 IV. I. 278 Well roasted, with sugar and wine in a cup, They'll make a sweet bishop. **1790** BOSWELL *Johnson* (1831) I. 235 A bowl of that liquor called bishop, which Johnson had always liked. **1801** COLERIDGE *Poems* II. 169 Spicy bishop, drink divine. **1834** CAMPBELL *Mrs. Siddons* II. viii. 191 Unacquainted with the language of taverns, Miss Burney made her King exclaim, in an early scene, 'Bring in the Bishop!' and the summons filled the audience with as much hilarity as if they had drank of the exhilarating liquor.

9. Articles of attire: **a.** A bustle (*U.S.*). **b.** A smock or all-round pinafore worn by children (*north. dial.*).

a **1860** *The Bustle* (Bartlett), I sing the bishop, alias the bustle. *a* **1860** SAXE *Progress* (Bartlett) If, by her *bishop*, or her 'grace' alone, A genuine lady or a church is known. **1874** E. WAUGH in *Lanc. Gloss.* (E.D.S.) Here; tak him, an wesh him; an' put him a clen bishop on.

10. a. *Comb.*, as *bishop-coadjutor, -commissioner, -seat, -see*; **bishop-bird**, any of various African weaver-birds the males of which have scarlet, orange or black plumage during the breeding-season; **Bishops' Bible**, the version of the Bible published in 1568 under the direction of Abp. Parker; **bishop's court**, an ecclesiastical court held in the cathedral of a diocese; **bishop-designate** (see quot.); **bishop-elect**, a bishop elected, but not yet consecrated; **bishop's length** (*Painting*), a certain size of canvas; **bishop('s) sleeve**, a sleeve in a woman's dress made full and gathered in at the wrist like the lawn sleeves of an Anglican bishop.

1835 *Penny Cycl.* IV. 375/1 The instructions..were, that they should adhere to the *Bishops' Bible. **1884** LAYARD & SHARPE *Birds S. Afr.* 462 Pyromelana Oryx (*Linn.*). Red *Bishop Bird. *Ibid.* 463 We have not thought it necessary to separate these two Bishop Birds specifically. *Ibid.*, Pyromelana Capensis, *Linn.* Black and Yellow Bishop Bird. **1931** R. C. BOLSTER *Land & Sea Birds S.W. Cape* 133 The Bishop Birds are also known as 'Kaffir Finks'. **1883** *Manch. Guardian* 18 Oct. 4/6 The representative clergy and laity..assembled in conference..under the presidency of *Bishop-coadjutor Ryan. **1751** CHAMBERS *Cycl. Supp.*, **Bishop-designed* (*designatus*) denoted a coadjutor of a bishop, who in virtue of his office is to succeed at the incumbent's death. **1883** FREEMAN in *Longm. Mag.* II. 488 The *Bishop Designate is one who has simply received a letter from the Prime Minister, which as yet makes no difference whatever in his actual legal or ecclesiastical position. **1844** LINGARD *Anglo-Sax. Ch.* (1858) I. ii. 86 The two *bishops-elect gave satisfaction. *c* **1870** *Winsor & Newton's Advt.*, *Bishop's ½ length, 4 ft. 8 in. by 3 ft. 8 in.; whole length, 7 ft. 10 in. by 4 ft. 10 in. **1330** R. BRUNNE *Chron.* 248 Þe olde chartres & titles..Of ilk a *bisshopse & ilk a priourie. **1650** R. STAPYLTON *Strada's Low-C. Warres* I. 18 He appointed fourteen Cities..for Bishops-sees. **1829** *Mirror of Lit.* 26 Sept. 205/2 The mistress..conceived the idea of *bishops' sleeves, an article of dress which precludes all hope..of imitation in the kitchen. **1846** D. CORCORAN *Pickings from 'Picayune'* 56 Instead of making the sleeves tight they are the old fashioned *bishop* sleeves. **1861** *Englishwoman's Dom. Mag.* III. 69/1. 1. A bishop sleeve, with a narrow wristband. 2. A bishop sleeve, the fulness gathered in to a band the length of the arm, this band being shown on the upper part of the sleeve. **1958** *Vogue* Sept. 109 The bishop sleeves are a widely-seen revival.

b. Plant-names: **bishop's-cap**, the genus *Mitella* or Mitre-wort; **bishop's elder** = **bishop-weed**; **bishop's-hat**, *Epimedium alpinum*; **bishop's-leaves**, Water Figwort (*Scrophularia aquatica*); **bishop's weed, bishop-weed**, a name for the genus AMMI; also *Ægopodium*; **bishop('s wort**, Wood Betony, *Stachys betonica*; also Devil-in-a-bush, *Nigella damascena.*

1839 LONGF. *Voices of Nt.* Prel. viii, When..*Bishops-caps have golden rings. **1597** GERARD *Herbal* II. ccxliv. 715 Called in English Water Betonie, in Yorkeshire *Bishops leaves. **1614** MARKHAM *Cheap. Husb.* I. Table, Ameos, Comin royal, is a Herb of some called Bulwort, *Bishops-weed, or Herb-william. **1861** MISS PRATT *Flower. Pl.* III. 26 Order Umbelliferæ..(Common Gout-weed, or *Bishop's-weed.) *c* **1000** *Sax. Leechd.* I. 2 Betonica þæt is *biscopwyrt. *c* **1450** *Roy. MS.* 18 A. vi. f. 68 in *Promp. Parv.* 34 *note*, [Betony] also clepyd *byschuppyswort. **1863** PRIOR *Plant-n.* 23 *Bishop's-wort..is now..applied to the Devil-in-a-Bush.

Hence **'bishopful** *a.* (cf. *worshipful, masterful*). †**'bishopist**, an adherent of episcopacy. **bishopless** *a.*, without bishops. **bishoplet, -ling**, a little or petty bishop. **bishopship**, the office or dignity of a bishop. †**bishopwick** = BISHOPRIC.

1866 NEALE *Seq. & Hymns* 116 O ye, His chosen servants, in bishopful array. **1590** J. DAVIDSON *Repl. Bancroft* in *Wodr. Soc. Misc.* 516 This sort of the generation of Bishopists. **1662** FULLER *Worthies* II. 560 (D.) Landaff..lay Bishopless for three years. **1838** *Fraser's Mag.* XVIII. 546 The doctor was totally ignorant of this custom, ours being a bishopless land. **1878** *All Y. Round* 9 Nov. 449 What a bishoplet it must have been that presided there. **1570** LEVINS *Manip.* 141 Byshopship, *episcopatus.* **1641** MILTON *Ch. Govt.* iii Wks. (1851) 110 The superiority of Bishopship. **1837** CARLYLE *Fr. Rev.* (1857) I. II. I. vii. 258 The abolition of Most-Christian Kingship and Most-Talleyrand Bishopship. **1570** LEVINS *Manip.* 121 Bishopwick, *diocesis.*

'bishop, *v.*[1] *arch.* [OE. *bisceopian* to exercise the office of a bishop, f. *bisceop* BISHOP.]

1. To administer the rite of confirmation to (a person); to confirm. *arch.* or *Obs.*

c **1000** *Thorpe's Laws* II. 348 (Bosw.) Se bisceop biþ ȝesett..to bisceopȝenne cild. *c* **1315** SHOREHAM 5 Wanne the bisschop, bisschopeth the, Tokene of marke he set on the. **1393** LANGL. *P. Pl.* C. XVIII. 268 [Christ] baptisede, and busshoppede · with þe blode of hus herte. **1622** W. YONGE *Diary* (1848) 50 The Marquis of Buckingham and his wife were both bishopped, or confirmed by the Bishop of London. **1786** J. ROBERTS *Life* 29 How many of them have been bishop'd?

b. *jocularly.* To confirm.

1602 WARNER *Alb. Eng.* x. liv. (1612) 241 Why sent they it by Felton to be bishoped at Paules? **1648** HERRICK *Hesper.* I. 87 'Tis good confirm'd, for you have bishop't it. **1700** DRYDEN *Cymon & Iph.* 243 He..chose to bear The name of fool confirm'd and bishop'd by the fair.

2. To appoint to the office of bishop.

1549 LATIMER *Serm. bef. Edw. VI* (Arb.) 138 *marg.*, Thys hathe bene often tymes..sene in prechers, before they were byshoppyd. **1641** MILTON *Prel. Episc.* 6 This tradition of Bishoping Timothy over Ephesus was but taken for granted. **1861** *Sat. Rev.* 23 Nov. 537 There may be other..matters to occupy the thoughts of one about to be bishopped.

3. To supply with bishops.

1865 *Daily Tel.* 6 Dec. 5/3 Italy would be well bishoped if her episcopacy..did not exceed fifty-nine.

4. *to bishop it*: to act as bishop.

1655 FULLER *Ch. Hist.* IX. ii. §12 *marg.*, Harding and Saunders bishop it in England. *Ibid.* XI. ii. §7 He bishoped it over all the Romish Catholiques.

5. To let (milk, etc.) burn while cooking. In allusion to the proverb 'The bishop has put his foot into it.' *north. dial.*

[*a* **1536** TINDALE *Wks.* 166 (T.) If the porage be burned to, or the meate ouer rosted, we say the bishop hath put his foote in the potte or the bishop hath played the cooke, because the bishops burn who they lust and whosoever displeaseth them. **1641** MILTON *Animadv.* §1 (D.) It will be as the bishop's foot in the broth. **1738** SWIFT *Polite Conv.* i. (D.) This Cream is burned too—why Madam, the bishop has set his foot in it.] **1863** MRS. GASKELL *Sylvia's L.* (ed. 2) I. 64 She canna stomach it if it's bishopped e'er so little. **1875** in *Lanc. Gloss.* 40 Th' milk's bishopped again!

'bishop, *v.*[2] [f. the name of persons who initiated the several practices.]

1. *trans.* To file and tamper with the teeth of (a horse) so as to make him look young; to improve his appearance by deceptive arts.

1727 [see BISHOPING]. **1840** E. NAPIER *Scenes & Sp. For. Lands* I. v. 138, I found his teeth had been filed down and bishoped with the greatest neatness and perfection. **1884** *Illust. Lond. News* 23 Aug. 171/2 To bishop..a term..signifying the use of deceptive arts to make an old horse appear like a young one.

2. To murder by drowning. [From one Bishop who, with a confederate, drowned a boy in Bethnal Green in 1831, in order to sell his body for dissection.] ? *Obs.*

1840 BARHAM *Ingol. Leg.* 201, I Burked the papa, now I'll Bishop the son. **1864** *Athenæum* 559/1 We have 'to Burke' and 'to Bishop.'

bishopdom ('bɪʃəpdəm). Also 6 **-dome.** [f. BISHOP + -DOM; cf. OE. *bisceopdóm* bishopric.]

†**1.** = BISHOPHOOD. *Obs.*

a **887** *O.E. Chron.* an. 660 Wine heold þone biscepdom iii ȝear. **1635** J. SKIDMORE in Lee *Valid. Anglic. Ord.* (1869) 86 He giveth power of bishopdom to the party consecrated.

2. Episcopal order; episcopate; also *concr.* bishops collectively.

1641 MILTON *Animadv.* Wks. (1851) 194 The succession, and divine right of Bishopdom. **1807** W. TAYLOR in *Ann. Rev.* V. 578 A real bishopdom prevails in the allied sect. **1858** GEN. P. THOMPSON *Audi Alt.* I. xxxix. 150 Bishopdom is up in arms.

†**3.** The personality of a bishop. *Obs.*

1589 *Marprel. Epit.* (1843) 4 The Puritans..Crushe the very braine of your Bishopdomes. **1589** *Hay any Work* (1844) 60 Though they have none of your Bishopdomes.

bishopess ('bɪʃəpɪs). [f. BISHOP *sb.* + -ESS.]

1. The wife of a bishop. (Only a nonce-word.)

1672-5 COMBER *Comp. Temple* (1702) 240 The Councils of that age call their Wives by the name of (*Episcopa*) the Bishopess. **1748** MRS. DELANY *Life & Corr.* 489 We..found the bishop and his bishopess very well. **1885** *Q. Rev.* July 184 *note*, Sophia did not take the title of Bishopess or even Princess of Osnabruck.

2. A female- or she-bishop. (Here used jestingly.)

1854 THACKERAY *Newcomes* I. 30, I enclose you a rude scrap representing the bishopess of Clapham. **1880** *Macm. Mag.* Dec. 149 Can you conceive such a thing as the notion of a bishopess?

bishophood ('bɪʃəphʊd). Forms: 1-3 **-had(e**, 3-5 **-hed(e**, 4-5 **-od, -hode**, 4- **-hood.** [OE. *bisceophad*; cf. -HOOD, -HEAD.] The office, condition, dignity, or rank of a bishop.

c **1000** *Ags. Ps.* cviii[ix]. 8 His bisceophad brucan feondas. *a* **1300** *Cursor M.* 21248 For his liuelade Siþen þan toke he bischophade. **1382** WYCLIF *1 Tim.* Prol., The apostle..techith of the ordynaunce of byschophood. *c* **1383** —— *Sel. Wks.* III. 315 He mynistride [*MS.* mysurde] þe ordre of bischopod. *c* **1400** *Apol. Loll.* 2 He þat desiriþ bischophed, he desiriþ a good werk. *c* **1449** PECOCK *Repr.* III. xvi. 380 Officis of bischophode or louȝer preesthode. **1849** ROCK *Ch. of Fathers* IV. ii. 47 Before he may reach the bishophood.

'bishoping, *vbl. sb.*[1] [f. BISHOP *v.*[1] + -ING[1].]

†**1.** The action or rite of confirmation. *arch.*

c **1175** *Lamb. Hom.* 101 Heom com to þe halȝa gast þurh heore bisceopunge. *c* **1315** SHOREHAM 7 Cristendom, and bisschopynge. *a* **1535** MORE *Wks.* (1557) 378 That they call confirmacion, yᵉ people call *bishopping.* **1732** NEAL *Hist. Purit.* I. 505 Bishoping of children, Organs, etc. **1884** *Chr. Commonw.* 13 Nov. 63/2 A considerable time often elapsed between the baptism and the bishopping.

2. *colloq.* The performing of the duties of a bishop.

1857 TROLLOPE *Barchester T.* (1861) 28 The archdeacon..really understood the business of bishoping.

'bishoping, *vbl. sb.*[2] [cf. BISHOP *v.*[2]] The deceptive treatment of the teeth of horses.

1727 BRADLEY *Fam. Dict.* s.v. *Horse*, This way of making a Horse look young is..called Bishoping. **1847** YOUATT *Horse* viii. 200 A method of prolonging the mark in the lower nippers..is called bishoping.

bishoplike ('bɪʃəplaɪk), *a.*, *adv.* [see -LIKE.]

A. *adj.* Like a bishop; *formerly*, of or pertaining to a bishop, episcopal.

[*c* **890** (see BISHOPLY).] **1544** *Suppl. Hen. VIII*, 28 This..worldely byshoplike estate. **1584** FENNER *Def. Ministers* (1587) 73 Bishoplike iurisdiction. **1641** PRYNNE *Antip.* 260 A Bishop like application. **1868** FREEMAN *Norm. Conq.* (1876) II. vii. 114 The new prelate did nothing bishoplike.

B. *adv.* After the manner of a bishop.

c **1555** HARPSFIELD *Divorce Hen. VIII*, (1878) 115 He did full well and bishoplike. **1621** P. BAYNES *Dioces. Tryall* Pref. 3 Telling him very bishoplike, that it were a good turn to lay him by the heels for so doing.

ˈbishoply, *a.* [f. BISHOP *sb.* + -LY[1]:—OE. *bisceoplic.*] Episcopal.

c **890** K. ÆLFRED *Bæda* v. xviii. (Bosw.) Ðæt biscoplíce líf. *c* **1475** *Found. St. Barthol. Ch.* I. vii. (1886) 55 Bysshoply auctoryte. **1549** LATIMER *Serm. bef. Edw. VI* (Arb.) 25 Byshoplye dutyes and orders. **1600** HOOKER *Eccl. Pol.* VII. iv. §3 The same kind of bishoply power. **1642** SIR E. DERING *Sp. Relig.* 88, I never liked the bishoply injunctions.

bishopric (ˈbɪʃəprɪk). Also formerly -rice, -riche, -rich, -rick, -rik. [OE. *bisceopríce*, f. *bisceop* + *ríce* realm, province. Cf. ON. *biskups-ríki.*]

1. The province of a bishop; a diocese.

c **890** K. ÆLFRED *Bæda* II. vii. (Bosw.) Mellitus feng to ðam bisceopríce. *c* **1150** *Gloss.* in Wright *Voc.* 87 *Diocesis* uel *parochia*, biscopriche. **1297** R. GLOUC. 417 Þe byssopryche of Salesbury. **1533–4** *Act 25 Hen. VIII*, xx, Archebishopriches and bishopriches. **1777** WATSON *Philip II*, (1839) 107 The regular clergy still continued to complain as loudly as ever of the new erection of bishoprics.

2. The office or position of a bishop.

1394 *P. Pl. Crede* 360 Þey biʒʒeþ hem bichopryches · wiþ bagges of golde. **1565** JEWEL *Repl. Harding* (1611) 166 To him Bishopricke was first giuen in the Church of Christ. **1711** ADDISON *Spect.* No. 89 §7 A vertuous woman should reject the first offer of marriage as a good man does that of a bishoprick. **1790** BURKE *Fr. Rev.* Wks. V. 271, I know well enough that the bishopricks..are sometimes acquired by unworthy methods. **1851** KINGSLEY *Yeast* xiv. 276 They promised him something—some prince-bishopric, perhaps.

†**3.** Overseership, office. (for Gr. ἐπισκοπή.) *Obs.*

a **1300** *Cursor M.* 18892 Anoþer most haf his biscop-rike. **1382** WYCLIF *Acts* i. 20 Another take the bisshopryche of him. **1535** COVERDALE *ibid.*, His biszhoprike another take. **1611** *ibid.*, His Bishopricke [*marg.* office: or, charge] let another take. [**1881** *Revised* ibid., His office [*marg.* Gr. overseership] let another take.] **1592** BP. ANDREWES 96 *Serm.* v. (1843) 515 He may see Ananias..buying his bishopric for money.

†**4.** High-priesthood: see BISHOP 2. *Obs.*

1480 CAXTON *Chron. Eng.* I. (1520) 6 b/1 Heleazar succeded in the bysshopryche.

†**5.** The seat or residence of a bishop. *Obs.*

1623 LISLE *Ælfric on O. & N.T.* 35 He entertained him.. at yᵉ bishopricke.

†**ˈbishopry.** *Obs. Sc.* [f. BISHOP + -RY.] **a.** = BISHOPRIC. **b.** Episcopacy.

1535 LYNDESAY *Satyre* 3045 That thair be giuen to na man bischopries. **1665** BROWN *Apologet. Relation* 35 (JAM.) They did protest against bishopry and bishops.

bishopstool (ˈbɪʃəpstuːl). [OE. *bisceopstól* bishop's seat: see STOOL.] The throne, seat, or see of a bishop. *Obs.* since 13th c., but taken up by some recent historical writers.

c **1065** *Chart. Eadweard* in *Cod. Dipl.* IV. 197 Ðe ðone bisceopstol ʒestaðeloðon. *a* **1300** *O.E. Misc.* 145 Wes.. imaked þer [at Bath] Bisscop stol. **1868** FREEMAN *Norm. Conq.* (1876) II. App. 604 The Bishop had his see, his Bishopstool, in some particular church. **1876** GREEN *Short Hist.* i. §3 (1882) 31 The old bishop-stool of the West-Saxons had been established..at..Dorchester.

biside, bisie, obs. ff. BESIDE, BUSY.

†**biˈsiliquous**, *a. Obs.* [f. BI- *pref.*[2] 1 + L. *siliqua* pod.] Two-podded.

1731 BAILEY II. *Bisiliquus* (Bot.), plants..whose seed is contained in two distant pods succeeding one flower, as in.. Periwinkle, etc. Hence **1775** ASH, *Bisiliquous*; and in mod. Dicts.

bisin(e, -sink, -sit: see BYSEN, BESINK, BESIT.

bis-ischiatic, *a.* = BI-ISCHIATIC.

1857 BULLOCK *Cazeaux' Midwif.* 32 The bis-ischiatic space.

bisk (bɪsk), *sb.* Forms: 7 biske, 8–9 bisque, bisk. [a. F. *bisque* crayfish soup.]

a. A rich soup made by boiling down birds, etc. **b.** *spec.* Crayfish soup.

1647 R. STAPYLTON *Juvenal* 267 Beccafico..one of the greatest rarities they [the Italians] can put into a bisk or ollio. **1715** *Pancirollus' Rerum Mem.* I. IV. x. 181 A Bisk of all sorts of Fish. **1731** BAILEY, *Bisk, Bisque* [in Cookery], a rich kind of pottage, made of Quails, Capons, fat Pullets, and more especially of pigeons roasted. **1741** *Compl. Fam.-Piece* I. ii. 138 To make a Bisque of Pidgeons. **1882** MRS. H. REEVE *Cookery* xiii. 90 Bisque or Crayfish Soup.

†**bisk**, *v. Obs.* [No etymology known: perhaps an error of Calamy's, followed by Southey.]

a **1732** E. CALAMY *Nonconf. Mem.* 581 (Boucher) To be bisk'd, as I think the word is, that is to be rub'd over with an inky brush. **1847** SOUTHEY *Doctor* chap. extra. (D.) The chapter..has not been bisked but semiramised.

bisk, variant of BISQUE.

biskaine, biskake, bisket, etc.: see BISC-.

biskop (ˈbɪskɒp). *S. Afr.* [Afrikaans, lit. BISHOP.] Either of two species of S. African fishes, namely the white biskop, *Sparodon durbanensis*, and the black, or blue, biskop, *Cymatoceps nasutus*.

1902 J. D. F. GILCHRIST in *Trans. S. Afr. Philos. Soc.* XI. 227 Biscop, Poeskop..*Chrysophrys, sp.* **1930** C. L. BIDEN *Sea-Angling Fishes of Cape* 257 *The Biskops or Mussel-crushers*..White Biskop..Black Biskop. **1957** S. SCHOEMAN *Strike!* 60 In False Bay and Hermanus it is called white musselcracker or white biskop, or simply biskop.

bismar (ˈbɪsmə(r)). *Sc. dial.* Also bismer, -more, bysmer, bissimar. [a. Da. *bismer*, ON. *bismari* steelyard; in LG. of Holstein *besemer*, Sw. *besmar*; a Slavo-Lithuanic word; in Lettish *besmens, besmers*, Lith. *bẽzmēnas*, Russ. *bezmen'*, Pol. *bezmian.*]

1. A kind of steelyard used in the north-east of Scotland, and in Orkney and Shetland.

1805 G. BARRY *Hist. Orkney* (1808) 220 The bysmer is made use of for ascertaining the weight of butter, oil, salt, wool. **1814** *Statist. Acc. Scot.* VII. 563 (Kirkwall) The instruments they have for the purpose of weighing, are two in number; and the one of them is called a pundlar and the other a bismar. **1880** TYLOR in *Academy* 18 Sept. 204/1 A rude kind of steelyard or bismar, to weigh out pounds of cheese with.

2. The fifteen-spined stickle-back: (see quot.).

1805 BARRY *Hist. Orkney* 289 (JAM.) The Fifteen-spined stickleback (*gasterosteus spinachia*) is here denominated the bismer, from the resemblance it is supposed to bear to the weighing instrument of that name. **1859** YARRELL *Brit. Fishes* I. 101 Bismore.

Bismarck (ˈbɪzmɑːk). [The name of the German statesman Prince Otto von *Bismarck* (1815–98).]

1. In full ***Bismarck brown***: = VESUVIN.

1885 J. J. HUMMEL *Dyeing Textile Fabrics* xix. 413 Phenylene Brown..also bears the commercial names: Bismarck Brown, Vesuvine, Cannelle, Manchester Brown. **1886, 1897** [see VESUVIN].

2. A drink consisting of a mixture of champagne and stout.

1910 *Daily Chron.* 7 Apr. 6 The formidable drink compounded of champagne and stout, and known in the Colonies as 'Bismarck' has..an intimate connection with the German Chancellor. **1958** A. L. SIMON *Dict. Wines* 31/1 *Bismarck*, another name for *Black Velvet*—half Champagne and half stout; a pick-me-up which Bismarck is said to have favoured.

3. ***Bismarck herring***: a marinaded herring served cold. Hence ***Bismarcked*** ppl. adj.

1931 D. RUNYON *Guys & Dolls* (1932) vii. 155, I set him down and get him a cup of coffee and a Bismarck herring to revive him. **1945** *Times* 2 Oct. 5/6 Herrings, which appear in various forms including fresh, kippered, bismarcked, klondyked, and home smoked.

Bismarckian (bɪzˈmɑːkɪən), *a.* [f. prec.: see -IAN.] Of, designating, or typical of Bismarck or his policy.

1878 H. J. COLERIDGE in *Month* XIII. 263 The principles of State persecution—principles which have been repudiated by the civilization of modern Europe, even though the new Bismarckian phase of that civilization seems to tend to their re-adoption. **1901** G. B. SHAW *Three Plays for Puritans* p. xx, The strong-minded Bismarckian man of action. **1914** *Chambers's Jrnl.* 3 Jan. 78/1 Germany's policy is the Bismarckian policy of 'blood and iron'.

Also **Bisˈmarckianism**; **ˈBismarckism**.

1870 *Fortn. Rev.* 1 Dec. 640 To substitute Bismarckism for Napoleonism would be a very small gain to civilisation. **1889** *Voice* (N.Y.) Feb. 7 The general expression of the public loss..may serve to check a too rampant Bismarckianism. **1931** *Times Lit. Suppl.* 19 Feb. 122/1 Commercial and territorial expansion—Bismarckism in Germany, Imperialism in England. **1954** A. J. P. TAYLOR *Struggle for Mastery in Europe 1848–1918* xx. 467 It was Bismarckianism run mad for Kiderlen to suppose that Caillaux would find it easier to compromise if he was first threatened.

bismarine (bɪsməˈriːn), *a. rare.* [f. BIS- + MARINE, L. *marīnus*, f. *mare* sea.] Between or washed by two seas.

1806 G. S. FABER *Gen. & Connect. View* (1808) II. 191 In the same bismarine region.

†**bisme.** *Obs.* [aphetic form of *abisme*, ABYSM.] An abysm; a deep pit.

1513 DOUGLAS *Æneis* VI. v. 3 Fra thine strekis the way.. Deip onto hellis flude..With holl bisme, and hidduus swelth wnrude. **1663** GERBIER *Counsel* 51 For burning of Bricks..Noblemen care not to make a Bisme in their Parks.

bisme, bismeoruwe, obs. ff. BESOM, BISSON, BESMEAR.

†**ˈbismer**, *sb. Obs.* Also 1 bysmer, -mor, bismor, 3–4 bisemar, busemare, 3–5 bis-, bysmar(e, 4 bissemare, busmar, 4–6 bismere, 6 (*Sc.*) bysmeyr, bismeir. [West Germanic: OE. *bísmer, -or* (str. neut.), identical with OHG. *bísmer* 'ridicule,' f. *bí*, BY (in its strong or accented form) + *-smer*, which Schmeller connects with MHG. *smier* a smile, laughing, *smieren* to smile. Others have compared OHG. *smero*, OE. *smeoru*, OTeut. **smerwo-(m*, 'fat, grease, butter,' which seems, on phonetic as well as other grounds, less probable.]

1. Shame, disgrace; reproach, mockery; scorn.

c **893** K. ÆLFRED *Oros.* III. vii. §1 Seo stow [Caudine Forks] ʒewearþ swiþe mære..for Romana bismere. *c* **1175** *Lamb. Hom.* 91 Þa seiden þa iudeiscen men a bismer, þas men beoð mid miste fordrencte. *a* **1225** *Ancr. R.* 132 He lauhweð hire to bisemare. *c* **1325** *E.E. Allit. P.* B. 653 Þenne þe burde byhynde þe dor for busmar laʒed. *c* **1386** CHAUCER *Reeves T.* 45 As ful of hokir, and of bissemare. *c* **1460** *Launfal* 923 Thy barouns dryveth the to bysmare.

2. A reproach, taunt, insult.

971 *Blickl. Hom.* 23 He..æt þæm unlædum Iudeum maniʒ bysmor ʒeþrowade. **1393** LANGL. *P. Pl.* C. XXII. 294 Bold of abydyng · busemares to suffren.

3. A person worthy of scorn; a lewd person, a pander or bawd. Cf. BESOM[2].

a **1300** *Cursor M.* 22029 Anticrist..sal be born..of bismer brem and bald. *a* **1400** *Cov. Myst.* (1841) 140 Se this bolde bysmare wolde presume, Ageyn God to preve his myght. **1513** DOUGLAS *Æneis* IV. Prol. 191. *Ibid.* VIII. Prol. 72 Get ane bysmeyr ane barn, than all hir blys gane is. **1535** LYNDESAY *Satyre* 4234 That bismair, war scho thair, withoutin dowt Out of hell the Devill scho wald ding out.

†**ˈbismer**, *v. Obs.* Forms: 1 bysmerian, bysm-, bismrian, bismærian, bysmorian, bysmriʒan, 2 bysmerian, 4 bismere. [OE. *bysmerian*, f. prec.] *trans.* To treat with scorn, mock, deride, insult.

c **1000** *Ags. Gosp.* Mark iii. 29 Se þe ðone halʒan gast bysmerað [*Hatton* bysmerieð]. *c* **1160** *Hatton G.* Matt. xxvii. 41 Eac þare sacerde ealdres hyme bysmeredon. **1340** *Ayenb.* 22 [Þe proude] bisemereþ and scorneþ þe guode men.

bismethyl: see BIS- *pref. Chem.*

‖**biˈsmillah.** [Arab. *bi-'sm-illah(i* 'in the name of God.'] In the name of Allah or God.; a common Mohammedan exclamation.

1813 BYRON *Giaour* 568 They reach the grove of pine at last: Bismillah! now the peril's past. **1850** THACKERAY *Pendennis* liii, He..is all for the sack practice, Bismillah!

†**ˈbisming**, *ppl. a. Sc. Obs.* ? Abysmal.

1513 DOUGLAS *Æneis* VII. vi. 110 Pluto..reputtis That bismyng belch haitfull to se.

bismite (ˈbɪsmaɪt, bɪz-). *Min.* [f. BISM(UTH + -ITE.] The native oxide of bismuth, called also *bismuth-ochre*, an earthy, or foliated mineral, of yellowish or dirty white colour.

bismite, bismoke, etc.: see BE-.

bismuth (ˈbɪsməθ, bɪz-). Also 7 bismute, bismuto, biˈsmutum, 8 bizmuth. [a. Ger. *bismuth*; the present Ger. form is *wismuth* or *wismut*, a reversion to *wissmuth*, the form in which the word first occurs in G. Agricola (1629), though he latinized it as *bisemūtum*. Derivation unknown.]

a. One of the elementary bodies; a reddish white metal, found native, and also in combination in numerous ores; it is brittle and melts at a low temperature. (Chemically, bismuth (Bi) is closely allied to ANTIMONY, and is, in different combinations, a triad and a pentad. Its chief use in the arts is as an alloy; the oxide and some salts are used in medicine.)

acicular b. = AIKINITE, also called *needle-ore*; † ***butter of b.***, bismuth chloride; ***flowers of b.***, an efflorescence of the oxide on minerals containing metallic bismuth; ***magistery of b.***, ***white b.***, the subnitrate or basic nitrate of bismuth, used as a paint and cosmetic under the name of Pearl White, Pearl Powder; ***regulus of b.***, an old name for the metal; ***telluric b.*** (see 2); ***mineral b.***, ***native b.***, bismuth occurring as a brittle mineral in crystals, etc.

1668 WILKINS *Real Char.* 66 Imperfect kinds of Metal.. used for Making of Pewter, being of shining brittle substance: *Bismute*, Tin-glass. **1674** *Phil. Trans.* IX. 189 In the mountains of Sudnos in Bohemia there was some years ago found a metal, by them called Bismuto. **1678** PHILLIPS, *Bismutum*, that which is called Tinglosse, differing both from Tin and Lead. **1755** *Gentl. Mag.* XXV. 454 It perfectly resists the destructive power of lead, bismuth, and the antimonial semi metal. **1870** R. FERGUSON *Electr.* 42 Among diamagnetic substances is bismuth.

b. *attrib.* Of or combined with bismuth, as ***bismuth alloys***, ***compounds***, ***ores***, ***salts***, etc.; esp. in *Chem.*, in systematic names of compounds, as ***bismuth carbonate***, ***pentoxide***, ***silicate***, ***trisulphide***; and in *Min.*, **bismuth-blende**, native silicate of bismuth or EULYTITE; **bismuth-glance** = BISMUTHINITE; **bismuth-nickel**, a native ore of bismuth and nickel in union with sulphur, = GRÜNAUITE; **bismuth-ochre**, the native oxide of bismuth, = BISMITE; **bismuth-silver**, a native alloy of bismuth and silver, Ag_6Bi, = CHILENITE; **bismuth-tellurium** (**telluric bismuth**), a native alloy, Bi_2Te_3, = TETRADYMITE.

1796 R. KIRWAN *Elem. Min.* (ed. 2) II. 265 *Bismuth*. Mineralized by Oxygen, with or without Sulphur. Bismuth Ochre. **1839** URE *Dict. Arts* 119 Bismuth..is a rare substance, occurring native..as a sulphuret, called bismuth glance. **1847** E. SEYMOUR *Severe Dis.* I. 8, I recommended the bismuth mixture. **1863** WATTS *Dict. Chem.* I. 597 A bismuth-silver from the mine of San Antonio, Chili. **1869** *Daily News* 12 June, Those wondrous demoiselles with low hair [and] bismuth eyebrows.

bismuthal (ˈbɪsməθəl, ˈbɪzmjʊθəl), *a.* [f. prec. + -AL[1].] Of or pertaining to bismuth.

So †**ˈbismuthane**, Davy's name for chloride of bismuth. **ˈbismuthate**, a salt of bismuthic acid. **bismuthic** (bɪzˈmjuːθɪk), *a.*, of bismuth, applied to compounds in which bismuth combines as a pentad, as ***bismuthic oxide***, Bi_2O_5. **ˈbismuthide** (*Chem.*), a primary compound of bismuth with

another element or an organic radical, as ***bismuthide of potassium*** or of ***ethyl***; (*Min.*) Beudant's name for a family of minerals of the bismuth type. **'bismuthine**, a compound of bismuth having the structure of an amine, as ***triethyl-bismuthine*** (cf. ARSINE[1]); also = next. **bi'smuthinite** (*Min.*), native sulphide of bismuth, or *bismuth-glance*, a lead-grey lustrous mineral, isomorphous with stibnite. **'bismuthous** *a.*, combined with bismuth as a triad, as ***bismuthous oxide***, Bi_2O_3. **'bismutite, bismuthite** (*Min.*), the native hydrous carbonate of bismuth, Bi_2C, of various forms and colours.

1812 SIR H. DAVY *Chem. Philos.* 407 It has been called butter of bismuth. It may be called bismuthane. **1799** KIRWAN *Geol. Ess.* 428 Bismuthic, cobaltic, arsenical pyrites. **1854** J. SCOFFERN in *Orr's Circ. Sc.* Chem. 469 The peroxide of bismuth, or bismuthic acid. **1881** *Athenæum* 12 Nov. 634/3 The synthesis of bismuthous iodide.

† **bisocne.** *Obs.* Also 3 bisockne, -sokne. [ME., an analogical formation upon *besechen, beseken*, BESEECH, after the relation that *socne*, SOKEN, OE. *sócn*, already bore to *sechen, seken*, SEEK.]

1. Beseeching entreaty.

a **1225** *Ancr. R.* 376 þuruh Marie bone & bisocne was water..iwent to wine. **1297** R. GLOUC. 495 Ac thoru bisokne of the king delayed it was ȝute.

2. Visiting, frequenting, attendance.

c **1175** *Lamb. Hom.* 45 Ne beo in hire naþing iwrat bute chirche bisocnie and beode to criste.

‖ **bi'sognio, bisogno.** *Obs.* [a. It. *bisogno* 'need; also, a needy fellow, a raw recruit'; also in Sp. *bisoño*, Pg. *bisonho*, in same sense.] Early form of BESONIO, BEZONIAN.

1591 GARRARD *Art Warre* 170 The name of a raw souldier, and Bisognio. **1598** BARRET *Theor. Warres* II. i. 17 Many inconueniences and disorders which rawe Bisognios will commit. *Ibid.* Gloss. 249 Bisognio or Bisonnio, a Spanish or Italian word. **1612** CHAPMAN *Widdowe's T.* Plays 1873 III. 17 Spurn'd out by Groomes like a base Bisogno. **1636** ABP. WILLIAMS *Holy T.* (1637) 218 Being as yet Gods Bisognos, as it were, *Tyrones Dei.*

bison ('baɪsən, 'bɪsən, 'bɪzən). Pl. 4-6 in Latin form, **bisontes, bisountes**; sing. 7- **bison**. [Adopted, directly or through F. *bison*, (Cotgr. 1611) from L. *bison* (pl. *bisontes*), ad. OTeut. **wisand, wisund* str. masc., the native name, in OHG. *wisunt, -ant, -int*, MHG. *wisant, -ent, -en*, MGer. *wesant*, OE. *wesend*, ON. *visundr*, pl. *visundar* (with *i* afterwards lengthened). The Old English *wesend* having been long obsolete, the word has come back to us through Latin, in which guise it can hardly be looked upon as Eng. before the 17th c., and has become familiar only in connexion with the American Bison. It is in Minsheu, Coles, Phillips 1678-1706, and Kersey; but not in Cockeram, Blount, Bailey 1721-90, Johnson, nor Richardson 1836-55: it was added by Todd to Johnson, 1818. Etymologically ('bɪsən) is the most correct, but ('baɪsən) is the prevailing pronunciation.]

The name of two species of Wild Oxen, which some naturalists separate from the genus *Bos*, and make a distinct genus *Bison* or *Bonasus*.

1. *orig.* A species of Wild Ox (*Bos Bison* Gesn., *B. bonasus* Linn.), formerly prevalent in Europe, including Great Britain, and still existing in a protected state in forests of Lithuania. (This was the *βίσων* of Pausanias and Oppian, the *βόνασος* of Aristotle and Ælian, the *bĭson* and *bonăsus* of Pliny and Solinus, the *bison* of Seneca and Martial; pl. *bisontes*, in later writers *visontes, vesontes, bissontes*. It is now sometimes called the *Aurochs*, a name belonging rightly to the extinct *Bos Urus*, the Urus of Cæsar. See the exhaustive article *Wisunt*, in Schade, *Altdeutsches Wbch.*)

1398 TREVISA *Barth. De P.R.* XV. xxx. (1495) 499 There ben many bestes of dyuers kynde in Beme [= Bohemia] as beeres, hartes..bubali and bisontes. *Ibid.* XV. lxxxiii. (1495) 521 In Karinthia ben many beers, bysountes and other wonderful beestis. **1601** HOLLAND *Pliny* II. 323 Those neat or buffles called uri or bisontes. **1611** BIBLE *Deut.* xiv. 5 The pygarg [*marg.* bison], and the wild ox, and the chamois. **1617** MINSHEU s.v. *Bison*, a wilde oxe, great eied, broad-faced, that will neuer be tamed. **1661** LOVELL *Hist. Anim. & Min.* 23 Hereto may be referred the Bison: and Ureoxe. **1860** GOSSE *Rom. Nat. Hist.* 203 In the forests of Lithuania there yet linger a few herds of another enormous ox, which at one time roamed over the whole of Europe, including even the British Isles—the European bison.

2. The North American species *B. Americanus*, popularly called 'Buffalo,' which formerly roamed in vast herds over the interior of the continent, chiefly in the neighbourhood of the Rocky Mountains.

[**1693** RAY *Synops. Animal.* 71 *Bison*..hujusmodi bovem aliquando vidimus in vivario regio Westmonasteriensi unde allatum nescio; ni forte ex Florida regione Americana.] **1774** GOLDSM. *Nat. Hist.* II. 12. **1777** ROBERTSON *Hist. Amer.* (1783) II. 107 The bison of America. **1810** CAMPBELL *Poems* II. 16 We launch'd our quivers for the bison chace. **1841** CATLIN *N. Amer. Ind.* (1844) I. iv. 24 The buffalo (or more correctly speaking bison) is a noble animal, that roams over the prairies. **1877** J. ALLEN *Amer. Bison* 449 The height of the American bison..is found to be sixty-six inches.

'bisonant, *a.* [f. BI- *pref.*[2] 1 + SONANT, ad. L. *sonantem* sounding.] Having two sounds.

1876 F. DOUSE *Grimm's L.* §16. 31 Which attributes to the primitive aspirates a bisonant and oscillating character.

bisonian, obs. form of BEZONIAN.

bisontine ('baɪsɒntaɪn), *a.* [ad. L. **bisontinus*, f. *bison, bisont-* BISON, after *elephantinus* ELEPHANTINE *a.*] Pertaining to or resembling the bison.

1885 E. BALFOUR *Cycl. India* (ed. 3) III. 1104/1 The general aspect of the yak is distinctly bisontine. **1887** *Blackw. Mag.* CXLI. 795 They belong to the same sub-family, Cattle (Bovinæ), but are members of the Bisontine group.

bisouȝte, obs. pa. t. of BESEECH.

† **bisp**, *sb. Obs.* Also bysp, bissp, bysb. [A phonetically contracted form of *biscop*, BISHOP, in early ME.: cf. mod.Da. *bisp* with ON. *biskup*, Sw. *biskop*; also Pg. *bispo.*] = BISHOP.

a **1300** *Passion Our Lord* 76 in *O.E. Misc.* 39 þe byspes and þe maystres hi were swiþe wroth. *Ibid.* 471 þe bispes of þe Gywes seyden Pilatus to. [*Biscop* occurs in sing. in this poem.] **1330** R. BRUNNE *Chron.* 114 Thurstan sent his sond, tille a bissp [*printed* bissh] sauuage, Rauf of Orkeney.

Hence **bispriche, -ryche** = BISHOPRIC.

a **1300** *Shires & Hundr.* in *O.E. Misc.* 145 þis bispryche wes hwylen two bispriche. [*Biscopryche* also occurs.]

† **bisp, bysp, bysb**, *v. Obs.* [Cf. prec.] *trans.* To bishop, to confirm.

c **1450** MYRC 158 Do þat they I-bysbede were. Tyl the byschope haue bysbede hyt.

bispel, variant of BYSPEL, *Obs.*, parable.

bisperre: see BESPAR *v. Obs.* to shut up.

bispinose, -ous: see BI- *pref.*[2] 1.

bisque[1] (bɪsk). Also 7 biscaye, 8 bisk. [a. F. *bisque*, of same meaning; of unknown origin. Littré compares It. *bisca* a gaming-place, a 'hell.']

1. *Tennis.* A term for the odds which one player gives the other in allowing him to score one point once during the 'set' at any time he may elect. Also in *Croquet*: An extra turn allowed to a weaker player.

[**1611** COTGR., *Biscaye*, a vantage at Tennis. *Bisque*, a fault at Tennis.] **1656** BLOUNT *Glossogr.*, and **1678** PHILLIPS, Bisque (Fr.), a fault at Tennis. **1679** SHADWELL *True Widow* I. Wks. 1720 III. 124 We'll play with you at a bisk, and a fault, for twenty pound. **1721** BAILEY, *Bisk, Bisque*, odds at the play of Tennis; a stroke allowed to the weaker player. *French.* **1872** PRIOR *Croquet* 56 Mr. Hale made the happy suggestion of adopting the bisque as a means of equalizing a strong and a weak player. **1874** HEATH *Croquet Pl.* 77 Example of how to take the Bisque.

2. fig. † ***to have a bisque in one's sleeve***: to have something to fall back upon, another resource, another string to one's bow. ***to give one fifteen***, etc. ***and a bisque***: to give him long odds, to 'leave him nowhere' in a contest or comparison.

1713 *Flying-Post* 24 Nov. 26 He (like a compleat Politician) reserves always a Bisk in his sleeve (a Phrase we Tennis-players use). **1717** BULLOCK *Wom. a Riddle* II. 18 Before the game's up, I have a Bisk in my sleeve, an appeal to the House of Peers. **1881** *Sat. Rev.* 30 July 136/2 If alliteration be a mark of study and finish, the latest school of English poetry can give Byron thirty and a bisque.

bisque[2]. [f. BISCUIT.]

1. ? BISCUIT (bread).

2. In *Pottery*, = BISCUIT 2; also a variety of unglazed white porcelain used for statuettes, etc. Also *attrib.*, as ***bisque oven***.

1664 EVELYN *Sylva* (1776) 619 Be sure never to carry your Bottle and Bisque into the field without your Style and Tablet. **1853** URE *Dict. Arts* (ed. 4) II. 454 The quantity of coals necessary for a 'bisque' oven is from 16 to 20 tons. **1864** *Daily Tel.* 28 Sept., He had..seen vast numbers of statuettes in plaster of Paris and in bisque.

3. A light brown colour or tint. (Cf. BISCUIT 1 c.)

1922 *Glasgow Herald* 17 Aug. 6 A dress of pale bisque. **1923** *Daily Mail* 15 Jan. 1 In Navy, Bisque, Rust, Champagne, Orchid, Flesh, Silver, Nattier Blue, Black, Jade & Ivory.

bisque, variant of BISK, soup.

bisquet(te, -quit(e, obs. forms of BISCUIT.

biss, var. of BYSS *v. Obs.* to sing to sleep.

bisschop(e, -choppe, -cop, obs. ff. BISHOP.

† **bisse**[1]. *Obs.* [a. med.L. (also OF.) *bisse*, L. *bes* two thirds of an as, etc., explained as *be-is* = *binæ partes assis.*] Two thirds.

1398 TREVISA *Barth. De P.R.* VIII. xvii. (1495) [The mone] abydeth in euery signe ii dayes & vi houres and bisse. *Ibid.* And full endyth his course in xxvij dayes and viij houres.

† **bisse**[2]. *Obs. rare.* [a. OF. *bisse, bisce, bische*, mod.F. *biche* hind, doe.] A female deer, a hind.

c **1450** *Venery de Twety* in *Rel. Ant.* I. 154 Bestes of venery? Sire, of hertis, of bisses, of bukkes, and of doos.

† **bisse**[3]. *Obs. rare.* [Watts *Dict. Chem.* I. 597 has '*bissa-bol* a gum-resin from Arabia, resembling myrrh.'] Some odoriferous substance.

1608 R. JOHNSON *Seven Champ.* II. C iij b, As though the heavens had rained downe showers of Campheare, Bisse or Amber greece.

bisse, obs. form of BICE, BYSS.

bisseling, bissemare: see BEZZLING, BISMER.

† **'bisset.** *Sc. Obs.* [a. F. *bisette* 'plate of gold, silver, or copper, wherewith some kindes of stuffe are striped' (Cotgr.). Cf. Littré.] Lace or binding of gold, silver, silk, etc.

1561 *Invent.* (1815) 154 (JAM.), Thre curtenis of crammosie dames..enrichet upoun the seames with a litle bisset of gold. *Ibid.* 221 And wrocht with small silver bissettis wantand bodeis. **1568** in Chalmers *Life Q. Mary* (1818) I. 285, 300 elns of small silken bissetis.

† **bi'ssext.** *Obs.* In 4-6 bisext(e, 6 (bisex), bysext. [ad. L. *bi(s)sextus (dies)*, f. *bis* twice + *sextus* sixth, the name given to the intercalary day inserted by the Julian calendar every fourth year after the *sixth* day before the calends of March, or 24th of February.] *prop.* The intercalary day in leap-year; but also taken as = BISSEXTILE.

1398 TREVISA *Barth. De P.R.* IX. iii. (1495) 348 The Bisexte is gaderynge of eyghtene houres whyche comyth in thre yeres wyth syxe houres of the fourth yere to make a ful daye..and the yere Bisextilis hath that name. **1530** ELYOT *Gov.* I. xxv. (1883) 265 Bisext, called the lepe yere. **1618** *Sheph. Kal.* (1656) ii, In four years, there is one Bysext.

bissextile (bɪ'sɛkstɪl), *a.* and *sb.* [ad. L. *bi(s)sextilis (annus)*, i.e. (the year) of the *bissextus*: see prec.]

A. *adj.* Containing the *bissextus* or extra day which the Julian calendar inserts in leap-year. ***bissextile day*** (= L. *bissextus dies*; see above).

[**1398** The yere Bisextilis (see prec.).] **1594** BLUNDEVIL *Exerc.* III. I. xli. (ed. 7) 355 The Bissextile or leape yeere, containing 366 daies. **1696** WHISTON *Th. Earth* II. (1722) 158 The Julian Calendar..intercalates the Bissextile Day immediately after the Terminalia. **1768** BLACKSTONE *Comm.* II. 140 In bissextile or leap-years. **1854** TOMLINSON *Arago's Astron.* 189 Thus 1600 was bissextile, 1700 and 1800 were not so.

B. *sb.* Leap-year.

1581 LAMBARDE *Eiren.* IV. v. (1588) 491 The Bissextile (or Leepe yeere) which hapneth once in every foure yeeres. **1601** HOLLAND *Pliny* I. 586. **1834** MRS. SOMERVILLE *Connex. Pys. Sc.* xii. 95 If in addition to this, a bissextile be suppressed every 4000 years, the length of the year will be nearly equal to that given by observation.

bissh-: see BISH-.

bissie, bissy, obs. forms of BUSY.

bissome, obs. form of BESOM.

† **'bisson**, *a. Obs.* Also 1 bisene, 1-4 bisne, 4 bisen, 5 byson(e, bysom, 6 bysome, bisme, 7 beasom, beesome, (*north. dial.* beesen, beezen.) [OE. (Northumb.) *bísene*, a difficult word, of doubtful etymology. Comparison with Du. *bijziend* short-sighted, lit. 'near-seeing, seeing (close) by,' has suggested that it was a corruption of *bíséonde*, f. *bi-*, BY + *séonde* seeing. Another suggestion is that the original form was *bisénе*, f. *bi-* pref. + *(ȝe)siéne, -sýne, -séne* manifest, conspicuous, visible. See Skeat. The former explanation has various etymological difficulties; the latter appears to fail in the sense, since 'visible close by' is not = 'seeing only close at hand,' still less = 'blind.']

1. Destitute of sight; blind.

c **950** *Lindisf. Gosp.* Matt. ix. 27 Gefylȝdon hine tuoeȝe bisene. *c* **1250** *Gen. & Ex.* 2822 Quo made bisne, and quo lockende? *c* **1420** *Chron. Vilod.* 682 A byson mon dwelt fast hym by; þe whyche hadde ben bleynte alle his lyve. **1548** UDALL *Erasm. Par. Mark* viii. 22 Not poreblynde, or a litell appayred, and decayed in sight, but as bysome as was possible to be. **1552** HULOET, Blynde or beasom borne, *cæcigenus.* **1559** *Mirr. Mag.* 478 As thou art bisme, so are thy actions blind.

b. In the following the sense is perh.: Purblind.

a **1250** *Owl & Night.* 243 A dai thu art blind other bisne. *c* **1450** in *Rel. Ant.* II. 240 Now the bysom ledys the bleynde. **1607** SHAKS. *Cor.* II. i. 70 What harme can your beesome Conspectuities gleane out of this Charracter.

2. ? Blinding.

1602 SHAKS. *Ham.* II. ii. 529 [The mobled queen] Threatning the flame With Bisson Rheume.

† **'bisson,** *v. Obs. rare.* In 7 bizen, byzon. [f. prec.] To make blind. Only in ppl. adj. **bissoned.**

c 1600 DAY *Begg. Bednell Gr.* iv. 2 Peace; heaven may give my byzon'd eyes their light. **1674** RAY *N.C. Words* 6 *Bizen'd*, blinded.

† **bissursolid.** *Math. Obs. rare.* [f. L. *bis* twice, double + SURSOLID.] The second or double sursolid, the seventh power of a number.

1557 RECORDE *Whetst.* H iv. a, Those nombers.. commonly are called bsursolides, or bissursolides, that is, seconde sursolides, or double sursolides.

bissyllable. *Obs.* = DISYLLABLE.

1589 PUTTENHAM *Eng. Poesie* (Arb.) 82 To euery bissillable they allowed two times, and to a trissillable three times, and to euery polisillable more.

bist, obs. or dial. = *art*: see BE *v.*

bistable (baɪ'steɪb(ə)l), *a.* [BI-².] Having two stable states.

1949 D. SAYRE in B. Chance et al. *Waveforms* v. 164 The basic plate-to-grid-coupled bistable multivibrator is illustrated. *Ibid.*, Bistable circuits have also been called 'scaling' circuits, 'scale-of-two' circuits, and in England 'lockover' circuits. **1951** *Wireless Engineer* XXVIII. 101/2 Two-position (bistable) trigger circuits. **1952** *Proc. Inst. Radio Engineers* XL. 1531/2 The operation of this circuit may be monostable, bistable, or astable (oscillatory), depending on the nature of the emitter load. **1962** *Gloss. Automatic Data Processing* (*B.S.I.*) 58 *Toggle*, bistable trigger circuit, a trigger circuit which has two quasi-stable or stable states and which requires an appropriate excitation in each state to cause a transition to the other. **1970** *Nature* 24 Oct. 319/2 It is, however, possible to obtain bistable switching action in which the device remains indefinitely in the desired 'on' or 'off' state until specifically switched out of it.

bistard, obs. form of BUSTARD.

bistare, bister, -sterre: see BESTARE, BESTIR.

† **bi'steke,** *v. Obs.* [f. *bi-*, BE- 2 + *steke*, STEEK to fix, shut; cf. Du. and LG. *besteken*, mod.G. *bestechen.*] *trans.* To shut (firmly).

a 1225 *Ancr. R.* 62 þæt heo muhten bisteken deað þer vte. *a* 1240 *Sawles Warde* 247 Alle.. bisteken þrute.

† **bi'step,** *v. Obs.* [ME. *bisteppen*, f. *bi-*, BE- + *steppen* to STEP.] *intr.* To step, walk, go.

a 1225 *Ancr. R.* 174. Vor beo heo bistepped þer ute.

† **'bistighe.** *Obs. rare.* [f. *bi-*, BY *prep.* + *stiȝe* path: see STYE.] By-way, by-path.

c 1340 SHOREHAM *Ps.* xxii[i]. 3 in *Wyclif's Bible* Pref. 4 The bistiȝes of riȝtfulnes.

† **bi'stint,** *v. Obs.* [ME. *bistinten*, f. *bi-*, BE- 4 + *stinten* to be dull or weary, to slacken; cf. STINT.] *trans.* To cause to slacken, to check.

c 1300 *K. Alis.* 1183 Was nere lambe in no land lower of chere.. þen was þe blonk to þe beurn þat hym bistint.

bistipuled: see BI- *pref.*² 1.

bistort ('bɪstɔːt). [(a. F. *bistorte*), ad. L. *bistorta*, f. *bis* twice + *torta* twisted, fem. pa. pple.]

1. A species of Polygonum (*P. bistorta*), named from the twisted form of its large root, bearing a cylindrical spike of small flesh-coloured flowers; also called *Snakeweed.* See ADDERWORT.

1578 LYTE *Dodoens* 21 There be two sortes of Bistorte.. the Great Bistorte [and] the Small Bistorte. **1712** tr. *Pomet's Hist. Drugs* I. 44 Bistort is a Plant that has a Root roll'd upon itself. **1872** H. MACMILLAN *True Vine* v. 180 The common bistort.. is supposed to have bloomed on Calvary, and to have been sprinkled with the drops of blood that fell from Christ's side. Hence the pink stains on its white flower-heads, and the dark blotches on its green leaves.

2. *Surgery.* = BISTOURY.

1655 CULPEPPER *Riverius* VI. vii. 143 Open the imposthume with a crooked incision Knife called a Bistort.

bistoury ('bɪstərɪ, 'bɪstʊrɪ). Also 5 bystorye, 8–9 bistory, 9 bistouri. [a. OF. *bistorie* (in sense 1), ad. mod.F. *bistouri* (in sense 2): origin uncertain: see Littré. (Said in some books to be from *Pistorium*, now *Pistoja*; but this is merely a conjecture from the similarity of the words.)]

† **1.** A mediæval weapon, a large knife or dagger.

1490 CAXTON *Eneydos* xvi. 65 Eneas had a bystorye or wepen crysolite, as it were a lityl swerde crosseles.

2. *Surgery.* A scalpel; made in three forms, the straight, the curved, and the probe-pointed (which is also curved).

1748 *Phil. Trans.* XLV. 133 An Incision made with a Bistory. **1764** SMELLIE *Midwif.* I. Introd. 31 He must.. amputate with a bistory. **1804** ABERNETHY *Surg. Observ.* 214 They were divided by the crooked bistoury. **1859** F. MAHONEY *Rel. Father Prout* ii. 546 The surgeon's bistouri. **1873** TRISTRAM *Moab* v. 92 Screwing my courage to use a bistory.

bistre ('bɪstə(r)). Also bister. [a. F. *bistre*, in same sense: see below.] A brown pigment prepared from common soot; the colour of this.

1727–51 CHAMBERS *Cycl.*, *Bister*, or *Bistre*, among painters.. a colour made of chimney-soot boiled, and afterwards diluted with water. **1808** SOUTHEY *Lett.* (1856) II. 58 One set, of six folios, is lettered in gold upon bister. **1853** KANE *Grinnell Exp.* xlix. (1856) 467 A dark sky, something between the bistre of the frost-smoke and the indigo of our thunder clouds at home.

b. *attrib.* and in *comb.*

1853 KANE *Grinnell Exp.* xxix. (1856) 241 The frost-smoke is all around us in bistre-colored vapor. **1862** THORNBURY *Turner* I. 79 Published in aqua-tinta, in imitation of bistre or India-ink drawings. **1881** *Nature* XXIII. 223.

[In form, *bistre* comes near to a series of Teutonic words, ON. *bistr* angry, knitting one's brows, Sw., Da. *bister* angry, fierce, raging, grim, Du. *bijster* bewildered, LG. *biester* having lost one's way; also 'dark, dismal, gloomy' Flügel. Of these Franck takes the Flemish *bijstier* as apparently the most etymological form, and would refer it to an OTeut. **bi-stiuri* with the notion of 'deranged, disturbed, amazed.' If this be the derivation, these words can hardly be related to the Fr. *bistre*, as they might be if 'gloomy, dark' were the radical notion. Mr. H. Bradley compares OF. *behistre*, *beïstre*, var. of *besistre* bissextile, meaning, 1. the bissextile day in February, 2. unlucky event, disaster, calamity, 3. 'a horrible storm or tempest in the aire' (Cotgr.); whence the notions of 'dismal, gloomy, grim, raging, etc.' might be plausibly derived; but historical evidence as to connexion between the various words is wanting.]

bistred ('bɪstəd), *ppl. a.* [f. prec. + -ED².] Stained with or as with bistre.

1876 MISS BROUGHTON *Joan* xx. 186 A keener look in her stained and bistred eyes.

bistrete, bistrood: see BESTREW, BESTRIDE.

‖ **bistro** (bistro, 'biːstrəʊ). Also bistrot. [Fr.] A small wine-shop, bar, or restaurant.

1922 C. BELL *Since Cézanne* 213 Perhaps the best painter in France, one of the best musicians, and an obscure journalist were sitting in a small *bistrot* on the Boulevard St. Germain. **1924** *Blackw. Mag.* Nov. 649/1 The cook of our little bistro restaurant. **1941** 'R. WEST' *Black Lamb* I. 144 A restaurant which though small was not a mere bistrot. **1954** KOESTLER *Invis. Writing* 249 He bought me a real hot dinner in a *bistro.* **1959** *Spectator* 31 July 134/3 Candle-lit Chelsea *bistros.*

† **'bisulc,** *a.* (and *sb.*) *Obs.* Also 7 bisulk(e. [ad. L. *bisulcus* two-furrowed, two-cleft, f. *bi-* two + *sulcus* furrow.] **A.** *adj.* Cleft in two; *spec.* having a cloven hoof. **B.** quasi-*sb.* A cloven-hoofed animal.

1650 BULWER *Anthropomet.* xiv. 142 The tongue of man is not double, or trisulke or bisulke. **1661** LOVELL *Hist. Anim. & Min.*, Those that are horned, are commonly bisulks. **1693** *Phil. Trans.* XVII. 850 The Cloven-hoof'd are either Bisulc.. or Quadrisulc.

So **bi'sulcate, bi'sulcated, bi'sulcous** *a.*, in same sense.

1833 LYELL *Elem. Geol.* xvi. (1874) 256 Tracks of the Anoplotherium with its bisulcate hoof. **1839–47** TODD *Cycl. Anat. & Phys.* III. 241/2 Feet bisulcate. **1657** TOMLINSON *Renou's Disp.* 468 A Scorpion hath.. arms and fore-cleyes bisulcated. **1646** SIR T. BROWNE *Pseud. Ep.* III. xxv. §5. 175 The Swine.. being bisulcous.. is farrowed with open eyes as other bisulcous animals.

† **bi'sulien,** *v. Obs.* [f. BE- 1 + *sulien*, OE. *sulian* to pollute, soil; perh. in OE.: cf. OHG. *bisullan*, MHG. *besuln.*] To pollute, make filthy.

c 1200 *Trin. Coll. Hom.* 37 þan he fulle ben, [he] bisulieð hem on þe fule floddri of drunkennesse.

bisuyle, obs. form of BESOIL.

† **bi'sweligh,** *v. Obs.* Pa. pple. bisuelid. [f. *bi-*, BE- 2 + ME. *swelȝen*, OE. *swięlȝan*, *swelȝan* to SWALLOW.] To swallow up.

a 1300 *Cursor M.* 16484 (Gött.), Allas! þat þe erd þe time þat i was born ne had bisuelid me.

bisy, biszhop, obs. form of BUSY, BISHOP.

bit (bɪt), *sb.*¹ Forms: 1–4 bite, 3–5 bytt, 4 byte, 4–6 byt, bitte, 6 bytte, 7–9 bitt, 6– bit. [Com. Teut.: OE. *bite* str. masc., 'bite, biting,' OFris. *bit, bite, biti*, OS. *biti*, (MDu. *bete*, Du. *beet*), OHG., MHG. *biz* 'piece bitten off,' mod.G. *bisz* 'biting,' ON. *bit* 'bite, biting' (Sw. *bett*, Da. *bid, biden* 'bite'):—OTeut. **biti-z* str. masc., f. *bītan* to BITE. As will be seen on comparing the next word, there were two OTeut. sbs. derived from this verb, of which the senses 'act of biting,' 'piece bitten off,' were not uniformly distinguished in the different langs. In OE., *bite* 'act of biting, bite,' and *bita* 'piece bitten off, morsel, bit,' were distinct, but both became *bĭte*, *bit* in ME., and both are now *bit*, so that they can be distinguished only by tracing the history of their senses. In the general sense the former is now represented by the later sb. BITE, but *bit* is retained in numerous specific uses, esp. that of the biting part of a tool.]

† **I.** Biting; what one bites. All *Obs.* or *dial.*

† **1. a.** The act or action of biting; a BITE. ***at a bit***: at one bite; also *fig. Obs.*

c 893 K. ÆLFRED *Orosius* I. vii, Gnættas comon ofer eall þæt land.. mid fýrsmeortendum bitum. *c* 1000 *Sax. Leechd.* I. 370 Hundes heafod ȝebærned to acxan.. þa wedendan bitas ȝehæleþ. *a* 1300 *Cursor M.* 8500 Adam.. thoru a bitte [*v.r.* bitt, bite, bit] broght all in blam. *c* 1300 *K. Alis.* 5436 Her bytt envenymed was. *c* 1440 *Promp. Parv.* 37 Bytt, or bytynge, *morsus.* **1577** tr. *Bullinger's Decades* (1592) 735 The fretting bit of the tooth of sin. **1639** FULLER *Holy War* III. xviii. (1647) 138 He.. requested their aid only for forty days, hoping to chop up those Albigenses at a bit. **1653** WALTON *Angler* 55 You may, if you stand close, be sure of a bit, but not sure to catch him.

† **b.** *fig.* The 'bite' or 'sting' of death, disease, etc.; hence, ***to be one's bit***: to be inimical or destructive to one. *Obs.*

c 1175 *Lamb. Hom.* 123 *Morsus tuus ero inferne*.. þu helle ic wulle beon þin bite. *a* 1225 *Ancr. R.* 288 þeonne he.. bit deaðes bite. *c* 1449 PECOCK *Repr.* II. x. 204 A bitte to helle [*inferni morsus*]. **1609** BIBLE (Douay) *Hosea* xiii. 14 Thy bitte wil I be ô hel.

† **2.** *transf.* **a.** The cutting or penetrating action of an edged weapon. *Obs.*

a 1000 *Beowulf* 4126 Æfter billes bite blod-faȝ swefeð. *a* 1000 *Fata Apost.* (Gr.) 34 þurh sweordes bite. *a* 1225 *Leg. Kath.* 2436 Ich abide her þe bite of swordes egge. *c* 1400 *Destr. Troy* xv. 6494 Two speirus.. of fell bite.

† **b.** A catching hold with a sharp edge: grip.

c 1400 *Destr. Troy* XI. 4702 þai.. cast ancres with cables þat kene were of byt.

† **3.** The action of biting food; eating; grazing. Hence † *bit-grass.* *Obs.*

1523 FITZHERB. *Surv.* 4 The whole commen is his owne, and his tenauntes haue.. onely bytte of mouthe with their catell. *a* 1600 in Risdon's *Surv. Devon* §308 (1810) 315 Bitt grass for all hys beasts. **1624** SANDERSON *Serm.* (1681) I. 244 An heifer.. going alwayes at full bit. **1635** —— *2 Serm. St. Paul's* i. 57 An idle servant.. good at bit, and nothing else.

4. Food to bite, victuals. Chiefly *dial.*

1719 *Scot. Presbyt. Eloq.* 36 (JAM.) He desires no more in the world, but a bit and a brat; that is only as much food and raiment as nature craves. *a* 1845 HOOD *Sweep's Compl.*, Here's a precious merry Christmas; I'm blest if I can earn either bit or sup! **1863** KINGSLEY *Water Bab.* i. 41 Some one will give me a bit and a sup.

II. The 'biting' part of anything.

† **5.** The cutting blade or edge of an edged tool, axe, spade, etc. (*obs.*); the point of a pickaxe.

c 1330 *Arth. & Merl.* 4808 The Bite was to fot long. *c* 1400 *Destr. Troy* XVI. 7316 With the bit of his blade.. He clefe hym to the coler. **1660** SHARROCK *Vegetables* 109 Get a strong hoe, of a good broad bit. **1677** GREW *Anat. Seeds* iv. §14 The Lobes.. are shaped like the Bitt of a Spade. **1747** HOOSON *Miner's Dict.* O iij, We strike or hit.. with the Bit or Point of the Hack.

6. a. The biting or cutting end or part of a tool; *spec.* the movable boring-piece of a drill (e.g. brace and bit, stock and bit), or a similar tool for use with the ratchet, drilling machine, boring machine, etc.; the borer for clearing the vent of a gun; the cutting-iron of a plane, the nipping parts or jaws of tongs, pincers, and similar tools.

1594 PLAT *Jewell-ho.* I. 27 A long Auger or Percer, with seuerall large bittes which he may put on and take off at his pleasure. **1677** MOXON *Mech. Exerc.* (1703) 94 The Gimblet.. hath a Worm at the end of its Bitt. **1693** LISTER in *Phil. Trans.* XVII. 869 The superlative hardning of the Heads and Bitts of Tools. **1769** FALCONER *Dict. Marine* (1789) K, The bit, or priming-iron, is a kind of large needle.. serving to clear the inside of the touch hole. **1823** P. NICHOLSON *Pract. Build.* 253 The Stock is accompanied with several bits, or cutters, made of steel. **1881** GREENER *Gun* 234 The fine-boring bit.. tends in a great measure to set the barrel tolerably straight.

b. *Comb.*, as ***bit-brace, -holder, -stock.***

1881 *Mechanic* §266. 100 The bit-brace or stock-and-bit is the.. principal tool in the second division of boring tools.

7. The part of a key, at right angles to the barrel or shank, which grips the levers of the lock.

1644 *MS. Louth* (*Lincoln.*) *Churchw. Acc.*, For one new bit for a key 4*d.* **1677** MOXON *Mech. Exerc.* (1703) 24 To every Ward on the Plates, you must make a Slit, or Ward in the Bit of the Key. **1855** A. HOBBS *Locks* v. (1868) 58 Bit or Bitt, is the name given, somewhat indefinitely, either to the whole flat part of a key, or to the small stepped portions of it.

8. a. The mouthpiece of a horse's bridle, consisting of the metal *bit-mouth*, and adjacent parts, to which the reins are attached. (It is not clear whether the word in this sense signifies that which the horse bites, or that which bites or grips the horse's mouth. OE. had *bitol* bridle, *frænum*; ON. *bitull, bitill* bit of a bridle; the Da. is *bid*, Sw. *bett*, Du. *gebit*, Ger. *gebisz.*)

c 1340 *Gaw. & Gr. Knt.* 2310 With þe barbe of þe bitte bi þe bare nek. *c* 1385 CHAUCER *L.G.W.* 1208 The fomy brydil with the bit [*v.r.* bitte] of gold. *c* 1440 *Promp. Parv.* 37 Bytt of a brydylle, *lupatum.* **1613** SHAKS. *Hen. VIII*, v. iii. 23 Stop their mouthes with stubborn Bits & spurre 'em. **1731** BAILEY *Dict.*, *Bitt* [with Horsemen], in general signifies the whole machine of a bridle, as the bit-mouth, the branches, the curb, the sevil holes, the tranchefil, and the cross-chains; sometimes it is used only for the bit-mouth in particular. **1850** MRS. BROWNING *Prometh. Bd.* I. 160 Steeds that love the bit They champ at.

b. *fig.*

1562 J. HEYWOOD *Prov. & Epigr.* (1867) 139, I wyll brydell the with rough byt, wife. *a* 1649 DRUMM. OF HAWTH. *Wks.* 8/1 Not feeling honour's bit, nor reason's rein. **1789** WOLCOTT (P. Pindar) *Wks.* (1812) II. 118 Now calmly Camden takes the bit, And trots so mildly under Master Pitt.

c. *transf.* A like contrivance in any apparatus.

1660 MRQ. WORCESTER *Water-comm. Engine* 15 The.. Engine [has] A Helm or Stern with Bitt and Reins, wherewith any Child may.. controul the whole Operation.

d. ***to draw bit***: to stop one's horse by pulling at the reins; hence *fig.*, to stop, slacken speed; ***on the bit***: (of a horse) pulling at the bit or ridden on a tight rein; also *transf.*: ***off the bit***: ridden on a

loose rein; ***to take the bit in his teeth*** (of a horse): i.e. so that it cannot hurt the mouth; hence, to become unmanageable, to be beyond restraint; also *fig.*; ***up to the bit***: up to full speed allowed by the degree of restraint in which a horse is held by the bit; also *transf.* (Cf. BRIDLE *sb.* 1.)

1600 ABP. ABBOT *Exp. Jonah* 521 Neither yet taking the bit perversely in his teeth. **1664** BUTLER *Hud.* II. III. 560 And for three years has rid your Wit And Passion without drawing Bit. **1782** COWPER *Table Talk* 685 Spend-thrift.. never drawing bit. **1857** RUSKIN *Pol. Econ. Art* 28 If he takes the bit fairly in his teeth. **1859** J. S. RAREY *Modern Art of Taming Wild Horses* (ed. 2) viii. 126 Your legs are to be used to force your horse forward up to the bit... Unless a horse rides up to the bit you have no control over him. **1878** WHYTE MELVILLE *Riding Recoll.* v. 92 Keeping the rebel up to his bit with legs and spurs if necessary. **1889** LADY C. CAMPBELL *D. Blake* v. 95 'It's the only way to treat women,' he thought; 'they will always come up to the bit if you show who is the master.' **1890** *Field* 6 Sept. 393 At the top of the hill we cast off our leader, the remaining four go in their collars and up to their bits. **1928** *Daily Tel.* 16 Oct. 19/1 He was going so strongly and 'on the bit' that it took Dines nearly two furlongs to pull him up in his own time. **1958** J. HISLOP *Start to Finish* vi. 35 All work except trials or semi-trials.. is done 'on the bit'. This means that the horse is being ridden on a tight rein and is not galloping flat out. *Ibid.* viii. 66 There is a vast difference between sitting against a horse when he is on the bit and riding him out when he is off the bit. **1962** *Listener* 1 Nov. 739/3 North remained on the bit for so long [in Bridge bidding] that his partner's interest in a slam could not be awakened.

e. *comb.*, as ***bit-bridle***, ***bit-chain***, ***-maker***, ***-mouth***, ***-rein***.

1577 HELLOWES *Gueuara's Ep.* 72 Alexander the Great did write unto Pulion his Bitmaker. **1676** *Lond. Gaz.* No. 1078/4 A brown leather Saddle.. and a Bitt Bridle. **1766** ENTICK *London* IV. 73 This company of Loriners or Bitt-makers. **1833** *Regul. Instr. Cavalry* I. 44 The bridoon is to be taken in the same manner as the bit reins. **1902** *Daily Chron.* 26 Sept. 3/6 Something wrong with the bit-chain. **1908** *Westm. Gaz.* 5 June 10/1 Bombardier Mueller deposed that Thamme had struck him several times with his fist and bit-chains.

9. *techn.* Applied to parts of various mechanical contrivances; *e.g.* the copper head of a soldering-iron; a short sliding piece of tube in a cornet for modifying the tone; the joint connecting the stretcher and rib of an umbrella; the earlike projections above the bowl of a spoon.

1703 *Lond. Gaz.* No. 3895/4, 7 Silver Spoons, no Marks, but branched on the tops, and the outsides of the Bits, etc. *a* **1877** KNIGHT *Dict. Mech.* I. 289/2 The copper piece of a soldering-tool riveted to an iron shank. A copper-bit. **1893** [see SOLDERING *vbl. sb.* 5]. **1944** *Electronic Engin.* XVI. 343 The handle does not tend to become unduly hot in spite of the user's hand being so near the copper bit.

bit, *sb.*[2] Forms: 1 bita, 2 bite, 3–6 byte, 6 bytte, 6– bit. [Com. Teut.: OE. *bita* wk. masc., morsel, bit = OFris. *bita*, OS. **bito*, (MDu. *bete*, Du. *beet* bit, morsel), OHG. *bizzo* biting, MHG. *bizze*, mod.G. *bisse*, *bissen* piece bitten off, bit, ON. *biti* bit, mouthful (Sw. *bit*, Da. *bid* bit, morsel):—OTeut. **biton-* wk. masc., f. *bītan* to bite. As to the relation of this to BIT *sb.*[1], see that word; both became in ME. *bite*, mod.Eng. *bit*, so that the two words can now be separated only in sense. In the strict sense of 'the portion bitten off,' the later sb. BITE is now used.]

†**1. a.** The portion of food bitten off at once; as much as is taken in the mouth at once; a mouthful; = BITE *sb.* 4. *Obs.*

c **1000** *Ags. Gosp.* John xiii. 27 þa æfter þam bitan [*Hatton*, bite] satanas eode on hyne. **1297** R. GLOUC. 207 And yspyted hym þoru out myd an yrene spyte, And rostede in þys grete fure to abbe þe folle byte. **1377** LANGL. *P. Pl.* B. XVIII. 200 þe bite þat þei eten. **1570** LEVINS *Manip.* 148 Bit, *buccella, minutal.* **1590** SPENSER *F.Q.* I. viii. 41 His bare thin cheekes for want of better bits. **1622** FLETCHER *Span. Curate* II. iv. 33 He'll eat but half-a-dozen bits, and rise immediatly. **1665** BOYLE *Occas. Refl.* iii. ad fin., When we dip them in vinegar, we may, for sauce to one bit, devour alive a schole of little animals.

†**b.** A bite or mouthful of grass for cattle. *Obs.*

1523 FITZHERB. *Husb.* §70 And there be to moche grasse in a close, the cattel shall fede the worse, for a good bytte to the erthe is suffycyente. **1579** TOMSON *Calvin Serm. Tim.* 151/2 The verie asses may haue a bit there, as we say in common prouerbes.

This passes into the sense of:

2. Morsel, small piece (of food), without actual reference to biting. Hence *dainty bit*, *tit-bit*, etc.

c **1200** ORMIN 8640 He badd tatt ȝho shollde himm ec An bite brædess brinngenn. *c* **1550** *Scot. Poems 16th C.* II. 197 Gif God was made of bits of breid. **1588** SHAKS. *L.L.L.* I. i. 26 Dainty bits Make rich the ribs, but bankerout the wits. *c* **1626** *Dick of Devon* I. ii. in Bullen *O. Pl.* II. 15 England that yeare was but a bit pickd out To be layd on their Kinges Trencher. **1684** BUNYAN *Pilgr.* II. 67 Come, said Christiana, will you eat a bit? *c* **1850** *Arab. Nts.* (Rtldg.) 615, I had not had a bit of meat for a long time in my house. **1860** TYNDALL *Glac.* I. §11. 80 We had not a bit of bread nor a drop of wine left.

By extension to other things:

3. a. A small piece formed by cutting, breaking, or other process; a morsel, a fragment.

1606 SHAKS. *Tr. & Cr.* v. ii. 159 The fragments, scraps, the bits, & greazie reliques, Of her ore-eaten faith. **1611** COTGR., *Piecette*, a shred, bit, morsell, manmocke; a small parcell, or peece. **1694** SALMON *Iatrica* I. v. 303/1 Cut also the root of Peony into little bits. **1716–18** LADY M. W. MONTAGUE *Lett.* I. x. 35 There is not the least bit of linen to be seen. **1838** COOPER *Surg. Dict.* 1470 To remove [from the wound] any extraneous matter, such as gravel, bits of glass or china.

b. ***by bits***: a little at a time; ***bit by bit***: = prec., gradually, piecemeal; also *attrib.* and quasi-*sb.*; †***at bits and starts***: irregularly, intermittingly (cf. *by fits and starts*); ***bits and bats*** (or ***bobs***, ***pieces***): fragments, oddments, odds and ends; small articles, personal belongings, bric-à-brac; (***all***) ***to bits***: (reduced) to the condition of fragments; ***to go to bits***: to go to pieces (see PIECE *sb.* 1 c).

1596 SPENSER *F.Q.* IV. ii. 33 Workes of heavenly wits Are quite devourd, and brought to nought by little bits! **1624** GATAKER *Transubst.* 176 His grace is not consumed by bits. **1632** SHERWOOD, By bitts, *par morceaux.* **1704** SWIFT *T. Tub* (1768) I. 142 He writ it in a week at bits and starts. *a* **1720** [see TO *prep.* 11 a]. **1849** HARE *Par. Serm.* II. 189 To pick it up in this way bit by bit. **1859** E. FITGERALD *Omar Khayyam* lxxiii. 16 This sorry Scheme of Things entire, Would not we shatter it to bits. **1871** FREEMAN *Hist. Ess.* Ser. I. ii. 45 This sort of bit-by-bit reform, going on for six hundred years. **1896** *Yorks. Weekly Post* 7 June, Ah've sammed up a toathry oddments—bits an' bats mi mother ud call em. **1896** NORTHALL *Warwicks. Word-Bk.* 29 Gather up your bits-and-bobs, and let me lay the tea. **1905** G. B. SHAW *Let.* 31 July (1946) 21 We have withdrawn the play there because it went to bits. **1931** S. JAMESON *Richer Dust* xv. 427 His right leg and his stomach had been full of what he called bits and pieces. **1933** W. S. MAUGHAM *Sheppey* III. p. 91 I'm not going to stand by and see you sneak his bits and pieces. **1936** G. POLLETT *Song for Sixpence* III. iv. 239 A shop of artistic 'bits and pieces' standing alongside the close. **1940** *New Statesman* 9 Nov. 466/1 There was still only the rubble, the bits and bats of broken furniture. **1955** 'E. C. R. LORAC' *Ask Policeman* ii. 25 She'd taken all her bits and pieces to uncle long ago. **1958** M. ALLINGHAM *Hide my Eyes* xv. 151 Give those chaps half an hour in here with their bits and bobs and there's no telling what they might be able to find. **1959** *Listener* 16 July 107/1 Is it all bits and pieces, a mosaic of images?

4. a. A small portion or quantity, a little (of anything material or immaterial). Also applied to complete objects, viewed as portions or samples of a substance. ***to give any one a bit of one's mind***: (colloq.) to express one's candid (and uncomplimentary) opinion of his conduct, etc.

1740–61 MRS. DELANY *Life & Corr.* (1861) III. 239, I shall be only allowed bits and scraps of time for it. **1815** SCOTT *Guy M.* xi, There was never a prettier bit o' horseflesh in the stable o' the Gordon Arms. **1859** JEPHSON *Britanny* xv. 244 Picturesque little bits of scenery. **1867** FREEMAN *Norm. Conq.* (1876) I. App. 696 The vigorous little bit of English. **1873** H. SPENCER *Stud. Sociol.* vii. (1877) 154 The peasant was called from his heavily-burdened bit of land. **1876** TREVELYAN *Macaulay* II. ix. 122 This bit of criticism shews genuine perspicacity. **1864** LD. CAMPBELL in *Times* 12 Apr. (Hoppe) He had given the house what was called a 'bit of his mind' on the subject.

b. *ellipt.*

1862 ANSTED *Channel Isl.* I. iv. (ed. 2) 63 The rocky bits to be seen at the back of Herm. **1879** FURNIVALL *Rep. E. Eng. Text Soc.* 6 The Preface has an interesting bit.. about Wine-growing in England.

c. Used depreciatively or pitifully in Sc. and north Eng., as in 'bits of children' = poor little children. Also in colloquial Eng., in singular, as 'a bit of a coward' = somewhat of a coward; 'a little bit of a place' = a place comparatively petty; and in understatements, in the sense of 'a considerable; quite a (lot of)'. Cf. *to take a bit of doing* (sense 4 h, below).

1677 RUTHERFORD *Lett.* lxxix. (1862) I. 201 What is behind.. but that sinners warm their bits of clay houses at a fire of their own kindling. *c* **1771** S. FOOTE *Maid of Bath* I. 20 Your beauty is a little bit of a jilt. **1815** SCOTT *Guy M.* xxvi, When Ailie has had her new gown and the bairns their bits o' duds. **1836** T. HOOK *G. Gurney* i. 7 My young companion was a bit of a poet, a bit of an artist, a bit of a musician, and.. a bit of an actor. **1855** CARLYLE in Froude *Life* (1885) II. xxii. 170 Thy bits of debts paid. **1861** GEO. ELIOT *Silas M.* 110 As to washing its bits o' things. **1866** J. E. BROGDEN *Prov. Words in Lincolnshire* 229 We'd six little mouths ta fill.. 'twer a-bit-on-a-pill [pull]. **1885** *Illustr. Lond. News* 9 May 491/1 A bit of a landslip somewhere down the line. **1885** *Manch. Exam.* 28 May 5/3 If Riel proved himself to be a bit of a coward. **1913** 'G. A. BIRMINGHAM' *Gen. John Regan* vi. 99 He may have been a bit of a lad in his early days. **1930** 'J. J. CONNINGTON' *Two Tickets* viii. 109 'That was a bit of a job,' he said ruefully. **1966** G. W. TURNER *Eng. Lang. Austral & N.Z.* iii. 48 Faced with tragedy, what can one say except 'It's a bit of a cow'?

d. = TIT-BIT b; esp. in *pl.*, a number of short items in a popular periodical.

1884 (*title*) Illustrated bits. **1892** *Idler* May 483 Once on board ship, I tried a course of 'bits', pictorial, philosophical, scientific, conundrumistic, and otherwise. **1896** *Daily News* 4 Nov. 2/7 This is a weekly journal called 'Gems'. As its title suggests, the new paper will be of the 'bits' order. **1928** *Granta* 30 Nov. 172/1 If the editor of the *Review* were to ask me to write a little bit about Christmas I should laugh in his face.

e. ***a bit***: a sum of money; money. (Cf. 8 a.) *slang.*

1894 A. MORRISON *Mean Streets* 214 Bill had been 'left a bit', and 'a bit' means money, all the world over. **1909** WARE *Passing Eng.* 31/1 *To have a bit on* (Sporting), to have a bet on—a 'bit' of money on—a race. **1928** GALSWORTHY *Swan Song* II. iii. 124 He knew that everybody had 'a bit on' something now-a-days. For one person who ever went racing there were twenty.. who didn't, and yet knew at least enough to lose their money.

f. A woman or girl (perh. ellipt. for *a bit of muslin*, etc.: see 4 h); cf. PIECE *sb.* 9 b. *slang.*

1923 in J. MANCHON *Le Slang* 62. **1931** GALSWORTHY *Maid in Waiting* v. 34 He had seen the girl pass twice or three times—had noticed her specially as a 'nice bit'. **1953** B. GOOLDEN *China Pig* xiii. 195 If I want a common little bit for a best girl that's my look-out, too.

g. A small part in a play or film; freq. *attrib.* and *Comb.*, as ***bit part***, ***player***; also *transf.* orig. *U.S.*

1926 *Amer. Speech* I. 437/1 *Bit*, any small part. It may be a thinking part or the character may have a few lines. Occasionally a bit in the hands of a capable actor.. is the outstanding hit of the show. **1936** F. SCULLY *Bedside Manna* 155 So I got a job as a bit-player in Hollywood. **1937** *Kansas City Star* 17 Oct. 4 The bass horn player.. getting ready to do a bit part. **1940** *Manch. Guardian Weekly* 14 June 469 He spotted Cagney when Cagney was a 'bit' player, and was early in recognising Bette Davis's.. talents. **1946** J. B. PRIESTLEY *Bright Day* v. 138 They gave her a test and a couple of bit parts. **1954** M. ALLINGHAM *No Love Lost* 108 Francia had been spotted playing 'bits' in Sweden.

h. In various colloq. and slang uses containing ***a bit of*** = a small amount or a small specimen of (see quots.). So ***a bit of blood***: a mettlesome horse; ***a bit of cavalry***: a horse; ***a*** (***little***) ***bit of all right***: something or somebody regarded as highly satisfactory; esp. applied to a pretty or obliging woman; ***a bit of muslin***: see MUSLIN 2; similarly ***a bit of fluff***, ***a bit of goods***, ***a bit of mutton*** (see FLUFF *sb.*[1] 1 d, MUTTON 4); ***to take a bit of doing***: see DOING *vbl. sb.* 1 a; ***not a bit of it*** = '*not a bit*' (see sense 5). Also ***to do one's bit***: to play one's part; to fulfil one's responsibilities or obligations; to make one's contribution to a cause or the like, esp. by serving in the armed forces.

1787 'G. GAMBADO' *Acad. Horsem.* (1809) 20 Nothing now is to be seen but bred horses; every apprentice must bestride a bit of blood. *c* **1810** W. HICKEY *Mem.* (1960) xx. 329 If you be a lord, it must be a bit of bastard business. **1819** MOORE *Tom Crib* (ed. 3) 11 A showy, but hot and unsound, *bit of blood.* **1821** MONCRIEFF *Tom & Jerry* I. vi, I shall here buy a bit of cavalry—that is a prad. **1828** *Subaltern's Log Bk.* II. 164, I entered the house in great spirits, fancying myself, to make use of a slang phrase, a very good bit of stuff. **1844** DICKENS *Mart. Chuz.* xxxvi, We rather put the bits of blood upon their mettle. **1847** A. & H. MAYHEW *Greatest Plague* vii. 86 When the conceited bit of goods came after the situation, she looked *so* clean, tidy, and respectable. **1853** C. R. READ *Austral. Gold Fields* 123 A good paddock, in which are a few *bits of blood.* **1854** LEVER *Dodd Fam. Abr.* xxii, 'I'm sorry,' said he, 'that the "bit of stiff",' meaning the bill, 'wasn't for five thousand francs.' **1855** *Harper's Mag.* May 791/1 'She is too good for me, or for the world!' 'Not a bit of it, Philip.' **1874** HOTTEN *Slang Dict.*, *Bit-of-Stuff*, overdressed man; a man with full confidence in his appearance and abilities; a young woman, who is also called a *bit of muslin.* **1882** *Papers for People* 7 June 102 The convicts almost to a man set such a high value on a 'bit of leaf'. **1889** BARRÈRE & LELAND *Dict. Slang*, *Bit of blood*, a spirited horse that has some blood. *Bit of cavalry*, a saddle horse. *Bit of leaf* (prison), a small quantity of tobacco. *Bit of mutton* (common), a nice woman, generally in a questionable sense... *Bit of sticks* (sporting), a copse... *Bits of stiff* (popular), bank notes. **1889** G. B. SHAW in *Star* 13 Apr. 4/3 The generosity with which 'the industrial classes' audience applaud you if they think you have 'done your bit' heartily. **1898** J. D. BRAYSHAW *Slum Silhouettes* 109 She was a nice little bit o' goods. There's her portrait. .. A nice little bit of orlright, ain't she? **1902** KIPLING in *Windsor Mag.* Dec. 4/2 'This,' said Pyecroft.. 'is a bit of all right.' **1903** YEATS *Let.* 1 Aug. (1954) III. 408 Archbishop Walsh has 'a little bit of all right' for the Chester Cup. **1904** A. BENNETT *Great Man* xii. 120 It's a girl... She's a bit of all right. **1905** H. G. WELLS *Kipps* I. iv. §1 That was a Fair Bit of All Right. **1910** —— *Mr. Polly* ix, This beef is a Bit of All Right, Ma'm. **1911** KIPLING in *Windsor Mag.* Aug. 261/2 'He's a raging blight!' 'Not a bit of it,' said Stalky cheerfully. **1915** *Punch* 12 May 362/1 For these our Army does its bit. **1917** *Ladies' Home Jrnl.* June 78/2 Every man beyond the military age can and should do his 'bit'. **1919** GALSWORTHY *Saint's Progress* III. ii. §2 These young women are 'doing their bit', as you call it; bringing refreshments to all those who are serving their country. **1919** G. B. SHAW (*title*) Augustus does his bit. **1932** T. S. ELIOT *Sweeney Agonistes* 18 Yes we did our bit, as you folks say, I'll tell the world we got the Hun on the run. **1957** *Listener* 24 Oct. 671/1 The B.B.C. has done its bit to restore the balance.

i. (See quot. 1960.) *slang* (orig. *U.S.*).

1958 G. LEA *Somewhere there's Music* 69 What's the Mister Musician bit? **1959** F. ASTAIRE *Steps in Time* (1960) vi. 45 We were in Detroit—stranded—and that is where Mother did the pawning-of-the-jewels bit. **1960** WENTWORTH & FLEXNER *Dict. Amer. Slang* 39/2 *Bit*, any expected or well-defined action, plan, series of events, or attitudes, usu., but not necessarily, of short duration; one's attitude, personality, or way of life; fig., the role which one assumes in a specif. situation or in life. Orig. bop and cool use. **1961** 'I. T. ROSS' *Requiem for Schoolgirl* xi. 179 'The Gestapo bit,' she told her friends bitterly. *Ibid.* 182 'I don't dig the bit,' Monty muttered. **1968** *Scottish Daily Mail* 3 Jan. 6 They're crazy about this psychological bit. **1969** *Gandalf's Garden* IV. 9/1, I was originally on the jazz scene and in a terrible state. You know, doing the whole bit, being on the phoney junkie trip which nearly every jazz musician was on.

5. *colloq.* A very small measure or degree, a jot, a whit; used *advb.* in the expressions ***a bit***: a little, somewhat, rather; ***not a bit***: not in the least, not at all; ***every bit***: entirely, quite; ***a bit much***: a little too much (to have to endure); something excessive or very annoying.

1675 COTTON *Poet. Wks.* (1765), I had not wrong'd the Gods a bit. **1719** T. GORDON *Cordial Low Spir.* 174 An Aspect every Bit as terrible. **1749** FIELDING *Tom Jones* IX. vi, He loves her not a bit the worse. **1860** GEO. ELIOT *Mill on Fl.* ii. II. 71 You should have sent me to school a bit more. **1865** TROLLOPE *Belton Est.* iii. 26 The old tower out there. It isn't changed a bit! **1869** TREVELYAN *Horace at Univ. Athens* 61 He sings a sparkling song, can write a bit. **1885** *Illustr. Lond. News* 14 Feb. 184/1, I am a little bit afraid of him. **1939** 'N. BLAKE' *Smiler with Knife* iv. 70 This is a bit much, isn't it, darling?.. I don't approve of baby-snatching. **1954** I. MURDOCH *Under Net* xviii. 248 This is a bit much! .. I was asleep.

6. a. *colloq.* A short while; a short space of time.

1653 WALTON *Angler* 211 There we sit For a bit Till we fish intangle. **1794** GODWIN *Cal. Williams* (1849) 86, 'I think we may as well stop here a bit.' **1800** MAR. EDGEWORTH *Cast. Rackrent* Wks. 1832 I. 70 'It's no time for punch yet a bit.' **1884** *P'cess Alice Mem.* 41, I cannot tell you what pleasure it has been to have that dear child a little bit.

b. *Sc.* The exact point or 'nick' of time.

1785 BURNS *Addr. Deil* xi, When the best wark-lume i'the house.. Is instant made no worth a louse, Just at the bit.

c. A prison sentence. *slang.*

1871 *Session Paper: Central Criminal Court* 10 July 156 Bill, how do they know of your bit in Dover? **1884** A. GRIFFITHS *Chron. Newgate* II. ix. 407 All three.. passed on .. to Leicester, where they did their 'bit'. **1917** *New Republic* 13 Jan. 294/1 Ferrati, whose 'bit' was three to seven years. **1951** J. H. SMYTH *I, Mobster* xii. 133 The only question was how much of a bit Lucky would get.

7. *Sc.* A small piece of ground, a 'spot.'

1814 SCOTT *Wav.* III. 237 It's a bieldy enough bit. **1816** —— *Antiq.* xxv, What gars ye stop [digging] now?—ye're just at the very bit for a chance. **1879** JAMIESON *Sc. Dict.* s.v., He canna stan' in a bit [i.e. still, in one spot].

8. In reference to money:

a. *Thieves' slang.* Money. Cf. BITE *sb.* 5.

1607 DEKKER *Jests to make Merie* Wks. (Grosart) II. 328 If they.. once knew where the bung and the bit is.. your purse and the money. **1608** —— *Belm. Lond.* III. 122 To learne.. what store of Bit he hath in his Bag. **1832** *Mirror* 17 Nov. 333 Coiners.. *vulgus*, Bit-makers.

b. Applied in the Southern States of N. America, in the West Indies, etc., to small silver coins forming fractions of the Spanish dollar, or (when these are obsolete) to their value in current money. Now usu. applied in the U.S. to a unit of value equivalent to an eighth of a dollar; used only in even multiples, as ***four bits***, ***six bits***.

In the eighteenth century the *bit* was generally the old Mexican real = $\frac{1}{8}$ of a dollar or about $6\frac{1}{2}d.$ sterling; later values assigned are a half pistareen or $\frac{1}{10}$ of a dollar, $\frac{1}{16}$ of a dollar, and (in some colonies) the value of $1\frac{1}{2}d.$ sterling.

1683 *Col. Rec. Penn.* I. 85 Their Abuse to y^e Governm^t, in Quining of Spanish Bitts and Boston money. **1730** SOUTHALL *Bugs* 8, I would give him.. a Bit, (a Piece of Spanish Money, there current at Seven-pence Half-Penny). **1780** COOK *Voy.* (1785) I. 18 The meat is.. sold for half a Bit (three pence sterling) a pound. *c* **1782** T. JEFFERSON *Autobiog.* Wks. 1859 I. App. 165 The tenth [of the dollar] will be precisely the Spanish bit, or half-pistareen. *a* **1848** MARRYAT *R. Reefer* liii, I.. gave my sable nurses a handful of bits each. **1873** BARRY & PATTEN *Men & Mem. San Francisco* xiii. 132 Two bits for a cup of coffee; two bits for a piece of pie; or if hunger and economy were to be considered, two doughnuts for a quarter of a dollar. **1883** *Century Mag.* XXVII. 29 With six bits in his pocket and an axe upon his shoulder. **1909** WEBSTER, *Bit*.. now, usually, the sum of $12\frac{1}{2}$ cents (generally in the phrases two *bits*, four *bits*, six *bits*). **1938** RUNYON *Furthermore* xiv. 281 She has.. a smile like six bits. **1939** STEINBECK *Grapes of Wrath* xvi. 224 If you wanta pull in here an' camp it'll cost you four bits.

c. *colloq.* A small coin or 'piece' of money, the value being generally named, as ***seven-shilling bit*** (an obs. Eng. gold coin), ***sixpenny***, ***fourpenny***, and ***threepenny bit***. In slang = fourpence.

1829 MARRYAT *F. Mildmay* ii, A seven shilling bit would be thought handsome.

9. In Scotch *bit* is used for *bit of* ('a bit bread'; cf. Ger. *ein Stück Brod*), and for *bit of a* ('a bit bairn'); in the latter use it approaches the nature of an adj. = little, tiny, small.

1785 BURNS *Cotter's Sat. Nt.* iii, His wee bit ingle blinkin bonilie. **1787** BEATTIE *Scotticisms* 13 A bit bread, a bit paper. —A bit of bread, a bit of paper. **1816** SCOTT *Antiq.* vii, I heard ye were here, frae the bit callant ye sent. **1883** J. HAWTHORNE in *Harper's Mag.* Nov. 926/1, I can take a bit draw of the pipe.

10. *Comb.* **bit-wise**, little by little, a bit at a time, piecemeal.

1832 AUSTIN *Jurispr.* (1879) II. 1064 Codified law does not adapt itself to the successive wants of successive ages so easily as law made bit-wise.

† **bit** *sb.*[3] *Obs.* Forms: 1 byt, bytt, 2 butte, 3–5 bitte, 4 bit. [OE. *byt(t)* str. fem., cogn. w. ON. *bytta* pail, MDu., MLG. *butte* (Du. *but*, LG. *but*, *büt* water-bucket, cask; adopted, at some period, from med.L. *buttis*, *butta* (cf. It. *botte*, Sp., Pr. *bota*, F. *botte*, *boute*), of uncertain origin: see Diez, Littré, Scheler. OE. had also *byden* fem., a butt, cogn. w. OHG. *butina*, MHG. *büten*, *bute*, mod.G. *bütte*, adopted from med.L. *butīna*, **budīna*, dim. of *butta*. The phonetic forms show that these words are not Teutonic. Cf. BUTT, BOTTLE.] A leathern bottle or flask; the uterus or womb; a fire-bucket.

c **1000** *Ags. Gloss.* in Wr.-Wülcker *Voc.* 336 *Uter*, byt. *c* **1000** *Ags. Gosp.* Matt. ix. 17 Ne hiȝ ne doð niwe win on ealde bytta.. ȝyf hi doð, þa bytta beoð tobrokene. *a* **1200** in Wr.-Wülcker *Voc.* 552 *Uter*, butte. *c* **1230** *Hali Meid.* 35 Inwið þi wombe swelin þe bitte [*v.r.* butte]. *c* **1467** *E.E. Gilds* 382 That the bitters be redy with hur horses and bittes to brynge water.. when eny parelle of fuyre ys.

bit (bɪt), *sb.*[4] [Abbrev. of *binary digit*.] **1.** A unit of information derived from a choice between two equally probable alternatives or 'events'; such a unit stored electronically in a computer.

1948 C. E. SHANNON in *Bell Syst. Techn. Jrnl.* July 380 The choice of a logarithmic base corresponds to the choice of a unit for measuring information. If the base 2 is used the resulting units may be called binary digits, or more briefly *bits*, a word suggested by J. W. Tukey. **1952** *Sci. Amer.* Sept. 135/1 It is almost certain that 'bit' will become common parlance in the field of information, as 'horsepower' is in the motor field. **1957** *New Scientist* 9 May 14/1 One 'bit' is the smallest amount of data which can exist, and corresponds to the answer to a yes-or-no question. On this basis, a decimal numeral can be described with four bits and an alphabetic letter with five... Existing electronic computers can store, in their normal memories, up to about one million bits.

2. Special Comb.: **bit map**, a representation, e.g. of a computer memory, in which each item is represented by one bit; *spec.* a graphic display in which characters are formed by assigning to each individual pixel a bit value; so **bit-mapped** *ppl. a.*, employing or involving a bit map; **bit mapping** *vbl. sb.*, the use of a bit map.

1973 *Computing Surveys* June 112/1 In a *bit map scheme, a Boolean form of the matrix *M* is the basic indexing reference. Whenever a non-zero entry occurs in the sparse matrix, a 1 bit is placed in the bit-map. **1981** *High Technol.* Sept. 20 All have headend electronics that takes the input character stream and makes a 'bitmap', a point-by-point representation of a page. **1983** *Your Computer* (Austral.) June 94/2, I have included a program.. which when run will provide a bitmap of the specified disk. **1978** *Proc. Micro-Delcon* (Delaware Bay Microcomputer Conf.) 21/2 The system features a *bit-mapped display. **1983** *Electronics* 1 Dec. 139 High-performance bitmapped graphics. **1979** *Computer* Oct. 25/1 The RTBM—real-time *bit mapping —scan for the same parameters shows the detailed effect that the failure mechanism has on each memory cell. **1984** J. HILTON *Choosing & using your Home Computer* 265/1 'Bit-mapping'.. enables the programmer to control each individual pixel within a given area of the screen.

bit (bɪt), *v.* [f. BIT *sb.*[1]]

1. *trans.* To furnish with a bit, to put the bit into the mouth of (a horse); to accustom to the bit.

1583 GOLDING *Calvin on Deut.* clvi. 962 Wee be as coltes that were neuer sadled nor bitted. **1602** WARNER *Alb. Eng.* XII. lxxii. (1612) 298 Till when the Horse was neuer back't nor bitted. **1814** SCOTT *Wav.* xxxix, The horses were not trained to the regular pace.. nor did they seem bitted (as it is technically expressed) for the use of the sword.

2. *fig.* To curb, restrain.

1824 COLERIDGE *Aids Refl.* (1848) I. 82 It is not women and Frenchmen only that would rather have their tongues bitten than bitted. **1858** BRIGHT *For. Pol., Sp.* (1876) 468 At the Revolution the monarchy of England was bridled and bitted.

bit, pa. t. and pple. of BITE *v.*

bitacnie, bitaght, etc.: see BE-.

bitale, variant of BYTALE, *Obs.*, parable.

† **bi'talt**, *v.* *Obs. rare*[−1]. [ME., f. *bi-*, BE- + *talten*:—OE. *tealtian* to shake.] *trans.* To shake.

c **1325** *E.E. Allit. P.* A. 1160 Bot of þat munt I watz bitalt.

bitamen, obs. form of BITUMEN.

bitangent (baɪ'tændʒənt). *Geom.* [BI-[2]. Cf. F. *bitangente*.] A line that touches a curve or surface at two different points; a double tangent. Hence **bitan'gential** *a.*, designating a curve that passes through the points of contact of the bitangents of a given curve; also *ellipt.*

1873 G. SALMON *Treat. Higher Plane Curves* (ed. 2) vi. 218 Through the four points of contact of any two bitangents we can describe five conics. *Ibid.* ix. 336 The equation of the bitangential curve of a quartic. *Ibid.* 340 If the equation of this tangential curve were once formed, then, by forming the condition that the given tangent should touch this curve, we should immediately have the equation of the bitangential. **1948** J. W. ARCHBOLD *Introd. Algebr. Geom. Plane* vii. 271 The only 'multiple lines' of the tangent envelope $\overline{C}$ are β bitangents of C and the tangents at ι simple inflexions.

† **bi'tavelen**, *v.* *Obs. rare*[−1]. [f. *bi-*, BE- + TAVELEN, ? to talk.] To overthrow (in argument).

a **1225** *Leg. Kath.* 1284 An anlepi meiden, wið hire anes muð, haueð swa biteuelet [*v.r.* bitaulet ow], itemet, and iteiet.

bitch (bɪtʃ), *sb.*[1] Forms: 1 bicce, bicge, 3–4 bicche, 4 bycche, biche, 5 bych(e, (begch), 5–6 bytch(e, 9 *Sc.* bich, 6– bitch. [OE. *bicce*, elsewhere in Teutonic only in ON. *bikkja*: it is altogether uncertain what is the relation of the two words, whether they are cognate, or if not, which is adopted from the other. If the ON. *bikkja* was the original, it may, as shown by Grimm, be ad. Lapp. *pittja*: but the converse is equally possible. Ger. *betze*, *petze* (only modern), if related at all, must be a germanized form of *bitch*. The history of the F. *biche* bitch, and *biche* fawn, and their relation, if any, to the Eng. word, are unknown. There is a Sc. form *bick* sometimes affected in the pronunciation of sense 1, to avoid association with sense 2.]

1. a. The female of the dog.

c **1000** ÆLFRIC *Gloss.* in Wr.-Wülcker *Voc.* 120 *Canicula*, bicȝe. *c* **1000** *Sax. Leechd.* I. 362 Biccean meolc. *c* **1300** *K. Alis.* 5394 Comen tigres many hundre; Graye bicchen als it waren. **1387** TREVISA *Higden* Rolls Ser. III. 141 He fonde a bicche ȝeue þe childe souke. **1398** —— *Barth. De P.R.* XVIII. i. (1495) 742 The bytche bringeth forth blynde whelpes. **1542** BRINKLOW *Complaynt* xxiv. (1874) 63 As chast as a sawt bytch. **1598** SHAKS. *Merry W.* III. v. 11 A blinde bitches Puppies, fifteene i'th litter. *a* **1680** BUTLER *Rem.* xvii. (1759) 12. **1842** LEVER *Handy Andy* ii. 14 All the dogs are well, I hope, and my favourite bitch.

b. The female of the fox, wolf, and occasionally of other beasts; usually in combination with the name of the species. (Also as in sense 2.)

1555 EDEN *Decades W. Ind.* III. II. (Arb.) 144 The dogge tiger beynge thus kylled they.. came to the denne where the bytche remayned with her twoo younge suckynge whelpes. **1569** SPENSER *Sonn.* vii. *a* **1687** COTTON *Aeneid Burlesqued* (1692) 70 I saw Mischievous bitchfox Helena. **1749** FIELDING *Tom Jones* x. vii, We have got the dog fox, I warrant the bitch is not far off. **1820** SCOTT *Monast.* xxxvi, As if ye had been littered of bitch-wolves, not born of women. **1825** *Bro. Jonathan* III. 265 The whelp of a bitch-catamount.

2. a. Applied opprobriously to a woman; strictly, a lewd or sensual woman. Not now in decent use; but formerly common in literature. In mod. use, *esp.* a malicious or treacherous woman; of things: something outstandingly difficult or unpleasant. (See also SON OF A BITCH.)

?*a* **1400** *Chester Pl.* (1843) 181 Whom calleste thou queine, skabde biche? **1575** J. STILL *Gamm. Gurton* II. ii, Come out, thou hungry needy bitch. **1675** HOBBES *Odyssey* XVIII. 310 Ulysses looking sourly answered, You Bitch. **1712** ARBUTHNOT *John Bull* (1755) 9 An extravagant bitch of a wife. **1790** WOLCOTT (P. Pindar) *Adv. Fut. Laureat* Wks. 1812 II. 337 Call her Prostitute, Bawd, dirty Bitch. **1814** *Byron Let.* 15 Oct. (1830) I. 586 It is well that *one* of us is of such fame, since there is a sad deficit in the *morale* of that article upon my part,—all owing to my 'bitch of a star', as Captain Tranchemont says of his planet. **1833** MARRYAT *P. Simple* (1834) 446 You are a.. son of a bitch. **1904** KIPLING *Traffics & Discoveries* 165 After eight years, my father, cheated by your bitch of a country, he found out who was the upper dog in South Africa. **1913** D. H. LAWRENCE *Sons & Lovers* I. iv. 60 'Look at the children, you nasty little bitch!' he sneered. **1931** T. E. LAWRENCE *Let.* 10 June (1938) 722 'She' says the incarnate sailor, stroking the gangway of the *Iron Duke*, 'can be a perfect bitch in a cross-sea.' **1931** R. ALDINGTON *Colonel's Daughter* I. 50 What a preposterous old bitch that woman is. **1944** WYNDHAM LEWIS *Let.* 20 Aug. (1963) 378 For it may be a bitch of a Peace. **1956** S. BECKETT *Godot* I. p. 37 That's how it is on this bitch of an earth.

b. Applied to a man (less opprobrious, and somewhat whimsical, having the modern sense of 'dog'). Not now in decent use.

a **1500** *E.E. Misc.* (1855) 54 He is a schrewed byche, In fayth, I trow, he be a wyche. **1749** FIELDING *Tom Jones* XVII. iii, Landlord is a vast comical bitch. **1893** STEVENSON *Catriona* xi. 123 Ay, Davie, ye're a queer character.. a queer bitch after a', and I have no mind of meeting with the like of ye. **1916** JOYCE *Portrait of Artist* v. 203 Is your lazy bitch of a brother gone yet?

c. A primitive form of lamp used in Alaska and Canada.

1904 E. ROBINS *Magnetic North* I. 233 'I'll light a piece of fat pine,' shouted the Boy... 'Where's your bitch?' said Dillon... 'Haven't you got a condensed milk can with some bacon grease in it, and a rag wick?' **1927** C. M. RUSSELL *Trails plowed Under* 159 In the long winter nights their light was coal oil lamps or candles—sometimes they were forced to use a 'bitch', which was a tin cup filled with bacon grease and a twisted rag wick. **1961** *Canadian Geogr. Jrnl.* Jan. 14/2 'Office' work was done by candlelight and sometimes by nothing better than a 'bitch'—a wick in a shallow tin of tallow.

3. *Comb.* and *attrib.*, as (sense 1) ***bitch-puppy***, ***-whelp***; (sense 2) ***bitch-baby***, ***-clout***, ***-daughter***, ***-hunter***, ***-son***; † **bitch-daughter** (*obs.*), the nightmare; **bitch-fou** *a.* (*Sc.*), as drunk and sick as a bitch, 'beastly' drunk; **bitch-goddess**, in William James's phr. (see quot. 1906); cf. SUCCESS *sb.* 3.

a **1400** *Cov. Myst.* 218 Come fforthe, thou hore, and stynkynge *byche-clowte. **1483** *Cath. Angl.* 31 Þe *Bych-doghter, *epialta*, *noxa*. **1786** BURNS *Interv. Ld. Dare*, I've been.. *bitch-fou 'mang godly priests. **1906** W. JAMES *Let.* 11 Sept. (1920) II. 260 A symptom of the moral flabbiness born of the exclusive worship of the *bitch-goddess *success*. **1928** D. H. LAWRENCE *Lady Chatterley* ix. 125 He realized now that the bitch-goddess of success had two main appetites: one for flattery, adulation, stroking and tickling such as writers and artists gave her; but the other a grimmer appetite for meat and bones. **1960** *Cambr. Mag.* 21 May 554/2 The pursuit, in our time, in the University and outside, of the Bitch Goddess Success, of a 'better living' without quality. **1787** HUNTER in *Phil. Trans.* LXXVII. 255 My Lord Clanbrassil purchased a *Bitch-puppy. *c* **1330** *Arth. & Merl.* 8487 *Biche sone! thou drawest amis. *c* **1480** *Gloss.* in Wright *Voc.* 251 *Hec catula*, a *byche qwelpe. **1601**

HOLLAND *Pliny* I. 220 The *bitch-whelpe that commeth of the first litter.

bitch, *sb.*[2] *Mining.* Also biche, BECHE, q.v.

1747 HOOSON *Miner's Dict.* s.v. *Boring,* For drawing up the Rods, we have, to hold them, an Iron Instrument called a Bitch, and, for unscrewing them, two more we call Dogs. **1881** RAYMOND *Mining Gloss., Biche,* a tool ending below in a conical cavity, for recovering broken rods from a bore-hole.

bitch, *v.*[1] [f. BITCH *sb.*[1] sense 2.]

†**1.** *intr. Obs.* **a.** To frequent the company of lewd women. **b.** To call any one 'bitch.'

1675 C. COTTON *Poet. Wks.* (1765) 177 Jove, thou now art going a Bitching. **1687** —— *Aeneid Burl.* (1692) 43. **1709** *Ramb. Fuddle-Caps* 6 In wonderful Rage went to Cursing and Bitching.

2. *trans.* and *intr.* To behave bitchily towards (a person); to be spiteful, malicious, or unfair (to); to deceive (in sexual matters).

1934 E. WAUGH *Handful of Dust* ii. 58, I quite enjoy coping—in fact I'm bitching him rather. **1936** D. POWELL *Turn, Magic Wheel* II. 125 She'd been bitched by everyone else..so that she wouldn't be surprised to have me leave her there in the rain. **1948** G. GREENE *Heart of Matter* II. III. i. 199 She said, 'I thought you were never coming. I bitched you so.' **1955** P. WILDEBLOOD *Against Law* III. 105 They're absolute hell, all having affairs with the Officers and bitching everybody like mad. **1958** B. HAMILTON *Too Much of Water* xi. 248 She'd started bitching him from the beginning, with every man in sight. **1963** *Listener* 7 Feb. 263/1 A very Mayfair cast of a new play bitched and intrigued at a rehearsal with much verisimilitude and some wit.

bitch *v.*[2] [perh. f. BITCH *sb.*[1] sense 1.]

1. *trans.* To hang back. *rare.*

1777 BURKE *Letter* in *Corresp.* (1844) II. 157 Norton [Speaker] bitched a little at last; but though he would recede, Fox stuck to his motion.

2. *trans.* To spoil, to bungle. Also const. *up.* Cf. BOTCH *v.*[1] Hence **'bitched(-up)** *ppl. a.*, spoilt, bungled. *colloq.*

1823 'JON BEE' *Slang* 10 To *bitch* a business, to spoil it, by aukwardness, fear, or want of strength. **1856** C. READE *Never too Late to Mend* III. iii. 18 You will bitch my schemes and lose your fifty pounds. **1928** HECHT & MACARTHUR *Front Page* III. 150 You've just bitched up my whole life! **1929** J. B. PRIESTLEY *Good Companions* II. vi. 400 She [*sc.* a bus-engine] was bitching 'erself up all along. **1931** KIPLING *Limits & Renewals* (1932) 197 'Reg'lar lower-deck palaver. Jemmy damned 'em all for bitchin' the evolution. **1932** H. NICOLSON *Public Faces* viii. 201 Yes, that charming M. Cocquebert has, for you will excuse the word, bitched the whole business. **1937** E. ST. V. MILLAY *Conv. at Midnight* ii. 58 Can't you let the poor benighted bitched-up country go to hell in peace? **1958** J. WAIN *Contenders* 188, I was in a hurry to..begin the hunt for Ned, before Robert had a chance to do anything to bitch it up. **1960** R. DANIEL *Death by Drowning* xv. 225 But for a squall bitching his escape route..he would be in France.

3. *intr.* To grumble, to complain. *colloq.* (orig. *U.S.*). Hence **'bitching** *vbl. sb.*

1930 *Amer. Speech* V. 238 He bitched about the course. **1941** B. SCHULBERG *What makes Sammy Run?* vi. 96 What the hell have you got to bitch about when I'm putting the money in your pocket? **1953** C. M. KORNBLUTH *Syndic* (1964) xiv. 145 If you'll quit me set off the explosion, I'll quit my bitching. **1954** J. CHRISTOPHER *22nd Cent.* 68 Tele did a damned fine job. It'll be a long time before I bitch at Saguki again. **1961** B. CRUMP *Hang on a Minute* i. 12 Nothing to do but go home and listen to the bitching. *Ibid.* xiii. 147 Couples bitching at each other is human nature.

'bitchery. [f. BITCH *sb.*[1] + -ERY.] **1.** Lewdness, harlotry.

1532 MORE *Confut. Tindale* Wks. 648/1 Such mariage is very vnlawfull lechery and plain abhominable bychery. **1599** MARSTON *Sco. Villanie* I. iv. 188 He will vnline himselfe from bitchery. *a* **1704** T. BROWN *Wks.* (1760) III. 94 (D.) The roguery of their lawyers, the bitchery of their paramours. **1929** A. HUXLEY *Do what you Will* 85 Here is a happy mean between bitchery and virginity. **1932** W. FAULKNER *Light in Aug.* (1933) vi. 119 Womansinning and bitchery.

2. Malice, vindictiveness, bitchiness.

1936 C. DAY LEWIS *Friendly Tree* i. 22 How I hate the Womanly woman and all her bitchery! **1962** *Times* 27 Sept. 15/2 Fausto's fiancée is an admirable study in feminine bitchery.

bitchily ('bɪtʃɪlɪ), *adv.* [f. next.] In the manner of a bitch; sensually; also, maliciously.

1938 G. GREENE *Brighton Rock* II. ii. 83 A little Jewess sniffed at him bitchily and then talked him over with another little Jewess on a settee. **1961** J. B. PRIESTLEY *Saturn over Water* viii. 119 All no good. That's why I've behaved so bitchily. **1963** I. FLEMING *On H.M. Secret Service* vi. 66 He still, rather bitchily, flirted with her.

bitchy ('bɪtʃɪ), *a.* [f. BITCH *sb.*[1]] **1.** Belonging to or resembling a bitch.

1948 J. CREASEY in B. Vesey-Fitzgerald *Bk. of Dog* II. 694 The full-grown dog is termed 'bitchy' in head. **1961** C. H. D. TODD *Pop. Whippet* iv. 55 Avoid a bitchy 'pretty pretty dog' [for stud] no matter how brilliant his show record may be.

2. *transf.* **a.** Sensual, sexually provocative. **b.** Malicious, catty.

1928 A. HUXLEY *Point Counter Point* xii. 215 It was different in the past... The liveliness wasn't..so exclusively bitchy, to put it bluntly. **1933** E. A. ROBERTSON *Ordinary Families* iv. 65 Ronald said proudly that the bits not dull were bawdy... Lester pronounced them 'bitchie', having..acquired the term from an American art critic. **1941** *Time* 13 Oct. 100/1 Two bitchy strip queens are murdered with their own G-strings. **1947** J. STEINBECK *Wayward Bus* vii. 94 There wasn't anything mean or bitchy about her. **1958** P. MORTIMER *Daddy's gone A-Hunting* xxxiii. 186 There's no need to be bitchy.

Hence **'bitchiness,** the quality of being 'bitchy'; sensuality; maliciousness.

1934 DYLAN THOMAS *Let.* 9 May (1966) 120 Let me raise one nasty growl about your unparalleled bitchiness in pinching my letter. **1951** E. AMBLER *Judgment on Deltchev* xvii. 198 Do I detect a note of bitchiness and distrust? **1954** KOESTLER *Invis. Writing* xv. 174 A great lady..who constantly fought a losing battle against her own innate bitchiness. **1957** W. CAMP *Prospects of Love* III. i. 150 A girl ..with none of Lucinda's exhausting 'come-and-get-me' bitchiness.

bite (baɪt), *v.* Pa. t. bit (bɪt). Pa. pple. bitten ('bɪt(ə)n); also bit. *arch.* Forms: *Inf.* 1-2 **bítan**, 2-4 **biten**, (4-6 **byte**, 6-7 **bight**), 4- **bite**. *Pa. t.* 1-4 **bát**, 3-5 **bot**, 4-5 **boot**, 4-6 (and 9 *dial.*) **bote**, (5 **boght**); 7- **bit**; *pl.* 1 **biton**, 2-4 **biten**; also *sing.* 4 **bett, bited**, 5 **bete**; *Sc.* 4 **bayte**, 6 **bait**, 6- **bate**. *Pa. pple.* 1-4 **biten**, 4 **byten**, **bittin**, (**ybite**, **ibyten**), 8-9 **bit**, 7- **bitten**. [Com. Teut.: OE. *bítan*, pa. t. *bát*, *biton*, pa. pple. *biten* = OS. *bîtan* (MDu. *bîten*, Du. *bijten*), OFris. *bîta*, ON. *bíta* (Sw. *bita*, Da. *bide*), OHG. *bîzan* (MHG. *bîzen*, mod.G. *beiszen*). Goth. *beitan*, pa. t. *bait*, *bitum*, pple. *bitans*:—OTeut. **bîtan*, cogn. w. Skr. *bhid-*, L. *fid-* (*findere*) 'to cleave, split.' Originally inflected like *write*; but since 16th c. the regular pa. t. *bote*, still used in Lancashire, etc., has been superseded in standard Eng. by the form *bit*, which (though it has the original vowel of the plural) is not a continuation of that form, but formed either after the pa. pple., or on the analogy of some other verbs of the same class.]

I. Said of the teeth.

1. a. *trans.* To cut into, pierce, or nip (anything) with the teeth.

To bite is the function of the front teeth (incisors and canines); the back teeth (molars) chew, crush, or grind.

a **1000** *Beowulf* 1488 He ȝefeng hraðe..slæpendne rinc bát bán-locan. *a* **1400** *Cov. Myst.* (1841) 29 Adam ffor thou that appyl boot Agens my byddyng. *c* **1420** *Anturs Arth.* xliii, The burlokkest blonke ther euyr bote brede. *a* **1500** in *Restrosp. Rev.* (1853) Nov. 104 The appulle that Adam bett. **1526** *Pilgr. Perf.* (W. de W. 1531) 208 b, He that doth byte a thynge dothe not vtterly destroye it but mynysshe it. **1592** SHAKS. *Ven. & Ad.* 316 He stamps and bites the poor flies in his fume. **1733** SWIFT *On Poetry* 90 Be mindful, when invention fails, To scratch your head and bite your nails.

b. with adverbial complement. *to bite away* or *off*: to remove or detach by biting. *to bite through, asunder, in two*, etc.: to divide by biting. *to bite back*: to restrain (speech) by biting the lips.

c **1250** *Gen. & Ex.* 2926 Here aldre heuedes he of bot. *c* **1374** CHAUCER *Boeth.* II. vi. 53 Þis free man boot of hys owen tunge, and cast it in þe visage of þilke wode tyraunte. **1460** CAPGRAVE *Chron.* (1858) 178 His hed was byten fro the body. **1480** *Robt. Devyll* 155 in Hazl. *E.P.P.* I. 225 Hys teeth grewe so peryllousslye, That the norysshe nypples he bote a waye. *a* **1529** SKELTON *P. Sparowe* 302 The selfe same hounde..Myght byte asondre thy throte. [**1861** E. WAUGH *Birtle Carter's T.* 11 His wife bote her tung i' two.] **1870** GEO. ELIOT *Armgart.* ii, Truth has rough flavours if we bite it through. **1881** MRS. RIDDELL *Senior Partner* II. xi. 221 Hot and strong was the reply which rose to Robert's lips, but he bit it back. **1923** 'JOAN SUTHERLAND' *Garland of Olive* xxv, Hunt bit back his sharply released breath.

c. with cognate object.

c **1320** *Cast. Love* 1343 A gret bite he bot of helle.

2. a. *intr.* or *absol.* in same sense. Const. *of, on, upon* (obs.). *to bite at*: to make an attempt to bite, to snap with the teeth at.

c **1175** *Lamb. Hom.* 123 Ne nom he na alle..ah ane dale alswa me bit of ane epple. *a* **1300** *Cursor M.* 18732 He..þat neuer o þat appel bate. **1398** TREVISA *Barth. De P.R.* v. xx. (1495) 126 Sharpe teeth growen or the brode teeth . for it nedyth to byte rather than to grynde. *c* **1450** *Knt. de la Tour* (1868) 148 She bote upon the appille. **1596** SPENSER *State Irel.* 46 [They] byte at the dugge from which they sucked life. **1668** PEPYS *Diary* 11 Feb., [It] makes me mad to see them bite at the stone, and not at the hand that flings it.

b. *to bite on* (fig.): to 'get one's teeth into', to take or get hold of (something substantial).

1904 W. H. SMITH *Promoters* i. 20 They'll bite on anything that promises water west of either of those places. **1920** *Times Lit. Suppl.* 25 Nov. 770/2 These two writers are not..'Academics'..and there is plenty to 'bite on' in their criticisms.

3. a. *trans.* To wound or lacerate with the teeth.

a **1000** *Riddles* (Gr.) lxvi. 4 Æghwa..biteð mec on bær lic. *c* **1300** *K. Alis.* 5435 Hy biten [*pa. t.*] bothe man and hors. **1340** *Ayenb.* 66 Þe felle dog þet byt and beberkþ alle þo þet he may. *c* **1400** *Destr. Troy* XXIX. 12150 Scho bete hom bitturly with hir bare teth. *c* **1440** *Gesta Rom.* (1879) 399 The grewhonde..grevously bote hym. **1557** *K. Arthur* (Copland) III. v, The whyte brachet bote hym by the buttocke and pulled out a pece. **1640** SHAKS. *Temp.* II. ii. 10 Sometime like Apes, that moe and chatter at me, And after bite me. **1766** GOLDSM. *Elegy Mad Dog,* The dog..Went mad, and bit the man. **1845** FORD *Handbk. Spain* i. 42 The last man is the one the dog bites.

b. with cognate object.

1607 TOPSELL *Serpents* 613 The Spider..biteth into his head a mortal wound.

c. *fig.* (cf. *wound, sting, prick.*)

c **1200** ORMIN 15580 Hat lufe towarrd godess hus Me biteþþ i min herrte. *c* **1325** *Metr. Hom.* 105 Penanz bites man ful sare. **1531** ELYOT *Gov.* I. ix. (1557) 24 Hym a lytle chydyng sore byteth. **1649** FULLER *Just Man's Fun.* 18 An affrighted conscience..biting of them. **1675** HOBBES *Odyss.* VIII. 186 So much your words me bite.

d. *absol.* or *intr.*

c **1380** WYCLIF *Sel. Wks.* III. 440 Lettiþ [þe houndis] boþe to berke and to byte. **1530** PALSGR. 456/1 A woman can defende her selfe no better than to scratche and byte. **1580** NORTH *Plutarch* (1676) 829 A dead man biteth not. **1591** SPENSER *M. Hubberd* 424 Yet spite bites neare. **1647** MAY *Hist. Parl.* I. vii. 73 Would faine be at something were like the Masse, that will not bite; a muzzled Religion. **1720** WATTS *Div. & Mor. Songs* xvi, Let dogs delight to bark and bite. **1855** MACAULAY *Hist. Eng.* IV. 666 It was better to die biting and scratching to the last.

4. *trans.* To 'sting' as a serpent, or an insect that sucks blood.

a **1300** *Cursor M.* 5955 (Gött.) Hungri flies..þat bath þai bat bath man and best. **1382** WYCLIF *Prov.* xxiii. 32 It [wine] shal bite as a shadewe eddre [**1535** COVERD. it byteth like a serpent. So **1611**]. **1483** CAXTON *Gold. Leg.* 113/4 Saynt machaire kylde a flee that bote hym. **1535** COVERDALE *Numb.* xxi. 6 Fyrie serpentes..which bote [*Genev.* and **1611** bit] the people. **1730** SOUTHALL *Bugs* 19 This Sucking the Wound.. is what we improperly call biting us. **1793** T. BEDDOES *Calculus* 185 He employed more than three thousand vipers, and caused to be bit more than four thousand animals. **1871** B. TAYLOR *Faust.* I. v. (1886) 64 We crack them [fleas] and we crush them, At once, whene'er they bite.

†**5. a.** *trans.* To go on nipping (portions of food), to nibble; to eat. *Obs.*

c **1205** LAY. 15340 Ne moste he nauere biten mete. *c* **1250** *Bestiary* 262 Ne bit ȝe nowt ðe barlic beren abuten. **1590** SPENSER *F.Q.* I. i. 23 As gentle shepheard..Markes which doe byte their hasty supper best.

†**b.** *absol.* or *intr.* Const. *on, upon. Obs.*

c **1386** CHAUCER *Pard. Prol.* 36 Her at this alestake I wil both drynke and biten on a cake. **1535** COVERD. *Micah* iii. 5 When they haue eny thinge to byte vpon. *c* **1620** Z. BOYD *Zion's Flowers* (1855) 49 He..Shall..neither have to bite, nor yet to sup. **1640** BP. HALL *Chr. Moder.* (Ward) 28/2 Fain to bite upon beans to keep himself from sleeping.

†**c.** *trans.* Of liquid food: To taste, to drink.

a **1225** *Ancr. R.* 364. *a* **1300** *K. Horn* 1130 No beer nullich ibite Bote of coppe white. *a* **1300** *Havelok* 1731 No page so lite, That euere wolde ale bite.

6. a. *intr.* Of fish: To seize or snap *at* the bait of the angler.

1653 WALTON *Angler* 86 He thought that Trout bit not for hunger but wantonness. *Ibid.* 131 He will bite both at the Minnow, the Worm, and the Fly. **1711** ADDISON *Spect.* No. 108 ¶2, I intend to..see how the Perch bite in the Black River. **1878** JEVONS *Prim. Polit. Econ.* 29 The angler..in the early morning..when the fish will bite.

b. *fig.* To take or be caught by any bait. Also *absol.*

1752 CARTE *Hist. Eng.* III. 247 The council bit eagerly at the proposal. **1786** T. JEFFERSON *Corr.* (1830) 51 Do not bite at the bait of pleasure till you know there is no hook beneath it. **1917** WODEHOUSE *Uneasy Money* ix. 99 'Nutty, he's bitten.'.. 'Good gracious! What by?' 'You don't understand. What I meant was that I invited your Mr. Chalmers to help me open a hive, and he said "Rather!"' **1948** D. BALLANTYNE *Cunninghams* 48 He'd just touched Sydney to start a scrap, but Sydney wouldn't bite.

†**7.** *to bite in*: to repress (what one has to say); to restrain (one's feelings, etc.). *Obs.*

1608 BP. HALL *Epist.* I. v, How manly he could bite-in his secret want; and dissemble his over-late repentance. **1650** —— *Cases Consc.* 380 Content to bite in their hidden grievances.

II. Said of other things.

8. a. *trans.* To cut into or penetrate as a sharp-edged weapon. Also *fig.*

a **1000** *Riddles* (Gr.) lxxxviii. 13 Blod ut ne com..þeah mec heard bite stið-ecȝ style. *c* **1374** CHAUCER *Anel. & Arc.* 270 The swerde of sorowe byte My wooful harte. *a* **1450** *Syr. Eglam.* 490 Ther was no knyfe that wolde hym byte. **1611** SHAKS. *Wint. T.* I. ii. 157 My Dagger muzzel'd, Least it should bite it's master. **1700** DRYDEN *Meleager & A.* 86 No sounding ax presum'd those trees to bite. **1859** TENNYSON *Enid* 573 Who heaved his blade aloft, And crack'd the helmet thro', and bit the bone.

b. *absol.* or *intr.*

a **1000** *Beowulf* 5150 Sio ecȝ ȝewac bat unswiðor. *c* **1314** *Guy Warw.* 123 He hem smot With his fauchon that wele bot. *c* **1386** CHAUCER *Sqrs. T.* 150 Þoruhe oute his armour it wil kerue and bite. *c* **1400** *Epiph.* (Turnb. 1843) 743 Gret axes..full scharpe bytond. **1535** STEWART *Cron. Scot.* II. 35 The fedderit flanis..Outthrow thair birneis bait. **1598** SHAKS. *Merry W.* II. i. 136, I haue a Sword: and it shall bite vpon my necessitie. **1842** MACAULAY *Battle Lake Reg.* viii, Camerium knows how deeply The sword of Aulus bites.

†**c.** Const. *in, into, to, of, on, upon. Obs.*

c **1205** LAY. 7513 Þet swerd in bat. *c* **1340** *Gaw. & Gr. Knt.* 426 Þe bit of þe broun stel bot on þe grounde. *c* **1386** CHAUCER *Knts. T.* 1776 The jelous strokes on here helmes byte. *c* **1430** *Syr. Tryam.* 1221 To hys herte hys spere can byte. **1596** SPENSER *F.Q.* II. v. 7 There the steel stayd not, but inly bate Deepe in his flesh. **1634** *Malory's Arthur* (1816) II. 255 There would no sword bite on him, no more than upon a gad of steel.

9. a. *trans.* and *intr.* To cause a sharp smarting pain (to): as a sharp stroke, a blister, caustic, etc.

c **1325** *E.E. Allit. P.* C. 373 Heter hayrez þay hent þat asperly bited. **1377** LANGL. *P. Pl.* B. xx. 359 Fro lenten to lenten He lat hise plastres bite. *c* **1485** *Digby Myst.* (1882) III. 735 Thys hard balys on þi bottokkys xall byte! **1594** LYLY *Moth. Bomb.* I. i. 73 These medecines bite hot on great mischiefes. **1637** RUTHERFORD *Lett.* lxxxiv. I. 215 Our crosses would not bite upon us if we were heavenly-minded.

b. To make (the mouth, throat, etc.) smart.

1552 HULOET, *Bite* as..ginger and peper the tonge. **1580** BARET *Alv.* B 731 This mater biteth me by the stomacke. **1803** R. DALLAS *Hist. Maroons* I. iv. 92 Offering a..man.. his choice of wine or rum..he chose the latter, with this answer: 'Oh! Sir, any thing that bites the throat.'

†**c.** *intr.* To have a 'nip'; to taste *of*. *Obs.*

1713 *Lond. & Countr. Brew.* I. (1742) 47 It makes the Ale bite of the Yeast.

10. *trans.* and *absol.* To affect painfully or injuriously with intense cold. Cf. *frost-bitten.*

1552 Huloet, Bite, as frost biteth the grasse. **1553** Eden *Treat. New Ind.* 19 Thei are nether bytten with colde in winter nor burnt with heate in somer. **1600** Shaks. *A.Y.L.* II. vii. 186 Freize, freize, thou bitter skie that dost not bight so nigh as benefitts forgot. **1609** Dekker *Guls Horn-bk.* Wks. 1884–5 II. 219 Vnlesse that Freezeland Curre, cold winter, offer to bite thee. **1866** Tennyson *Window*, Frost is here And has bitten the heel of the going year.

11. a. *trans.* and *intr.* To corrode, or eat into, as a strong acid or other chemical agent; to act upon chemically as a mordant.

1623 Favine *Theat. Hon.* II. xiii. 236 An Antique inscription, but bitten and worne with age. **1677** Moxon *Mech. Exerc.* (1703) 242 Being washed three or four times, it Bites or Eats not, but dries quickly. **1684** T. Burnet *Th. Earth* II. 44 And stony mountains, which no fire can bite upon. **1822** Imison *Sc. & Art* II. 428 Those lines which are not intended to be bit any deeper must now be stopped up. **1875** Ure *Dict. Arts* II. 286 The sal-ammoniac..has the peculiar property of causing the aqua-fortis to bite more directly downwards. **1879** *Cassell's Techn. Educ.* IV. 299/2 The workman immerses the articles..in this solution, until the acid no longer 'bites' the metal.

b. *to bite in* in *Engraving*: to eat out the lines of an etching on metal with an acid.

1821 Craig *Lect. Drawing* vii. 401 The cracks..when bit in, form..the grain of the work. **1875** Ure *Dict. Arts* II. 283 Dürer's etching appears to have been bitten in, or corroded with the acid at once.

c. *refl.* (*fig.*)

1876 Geo. Eliot *Dan. Der.* II. xxix. 238 A man whose slight relations with her had..bitten themselves into the most permanent layers of feeling.

d. *intr.* To have a (desired) adverse effect. *colloq.*

1976 in *Conc. Oxf. Dict.* **1979** *Economist* 26 May 77/2 Today's refugee problem may look like a minor inconvenience compared with the exodus that may come when the food crisis begins to bite. **1985** *Times* 2 Apr. 5 (*heading*) Danish hospitals suffer as strike bites. **1986** *Ibid.* 24 July 40/3 The date was March, 1983—the drought began to bite.

12. *trans.* and *intr.* Used to express the proper or improper action of various tools, implements, and parts of mechanism, in gripping or taking hold, either by penetrating or by friction. **a.** Of a plough: To run too deeply into the ground. **b.** Of a file, saw, etc.: To make an impression upon (the substance). **c.** Of an anchor: To enter and take hold of the bottom. **d.** Of the wheels of a locomotive and other parts of machinery depending for their effectiveness upon friction: To 'grip' the rails or surface. **e.** Of a skate on the ice.

1523 Fitzherb. *Husb.* §4 A reste balke is where the plough byteth at the poynte of the culture and share, and cutteth not the ground cleane to the forowe. **1635** Swan *Spec. M.* vi. (1643) 291 Of such hardnesse that the file can scarcely bite it. **1762** tr. *Duhamel's Husb.* I. ix. (ed. 2) 49 If the share is apt to bite, or run too deep into the ground. **1769** Falconer *Dict. Marine* (1789), *To bite*, to hold fast in the ground; expressed of the anchor. **1849** J. R. Jackson *Min. & Uses* xxvi. 308 So hard that a steel tool will hardly bite upon it. **1864** *Daily Tel.* 23 Dec., The engines did not bite, owing to the 'greasiness' of the metals. **1883** *Harper's Mag.* Jan. 192 His anchor biting in the golden sand. **1884** *Sunday Mag.* May 307/1 The oil..prevented the driving-wheels from 'biting.'

f. *Typogr.* (see quot.)

1824 J. Johnson *Typogr.* II. 521 He examines whether the frisket bites; that is, whether it keeps off the impression from any part of the pages. **1882** *Print. Times* 15 Feb. 36/1.

g. Of a cricket ball: to get a grip of the surface of the ground on pitching.

1867 *J. Lillywhite's Cricketers' Companion* 7 If the ground is soft, slow bowlers will tell best, the ball hangs or bites. **1904** P. F. Warner *Recov. Ashes* iii. 56 When Jennings came in Rhodes was making the ball 'bite' a bit. **1960** E. W. Swanton *West Indies Revisited* 231 The occasional ball that hopped or bit.

h. *Palæogr.* Of the strokes of part of two letters: to converge (cf. biting *vbl. sb.* 1 b).

1957 N. R. Ker *Catal. MSS. containing Anglo-Saxon* p. xix, *d* and *o* occasionally 'bite'..but not apparently *d* and *e*.

13. *fig.* (*trans.* and *intr.*) **a.** To take hold of (the mind, etc.), seize, impress, come home to. *arch.*

c **1325** *E.E. Allit. P.* A. 356 Þy prayer may his pyte byt. **1532** Frith *Mirror* (1829) 273, I will allege another text of the wise man, which shall..bite them better. **1535** Joye *Apol. Tind.* 18 This reason did so byght Tindal and stoke so fast upon him. **1642** Rogers *Naaman* 198 That worship which bites not the spirit, is most specious to the eye. **1627** tr. *Bacon's Life & Death* (1651) 24 Those thoughts, which seeing they are severed from the affairs of the world, bite not. **1864** *Macm. Mag.* Oct. 467 Speaking of Algebra, in comparison with..Geometry, he [Chalmers] said..he could not take to it, for he could not make it bite like the other.

b. To exercise, excite; to worry, perturb; esp. in phr. ***what's biting you?*** *colloq.* (orig. *U.S.*).

1909 *Sat. Even. Post* 27 Mar. 7/3 Say! what's biting you? **1928** E. Scott *War among Ladies* II. xii. 173 'What's biting her?' she thought idly... Miss Pearson's grievances were so frequent. **1929** 'G. Daviot' *Man in Queue* v. 59 'Where the hell's my hat!' 'It's on the chair behind you,' she said, amazed. 'What's biting you?' **1932** C. Williams *Greater Trumps* xiii. 229 I'll pop up and see what's biting him now. **1959** 'A. Gilbert' *Death takes Wife* xvii. 220 'What's biting Dad?'.. 'Nothing to what'll bite you if he hears you.'

†**14.** *trans.* To speak sharply or injuriously against; to calumniate (cf. *backbite*); to carp at. *intr.* To find fault sharply or severely, speak bitterly, jibe.

1330 R. Brunne *Chron.* 335 Here now þe grete despite ..þat to þer bak, gan bite of Scotlond þe clergie. **1586** T. B. *La Primaud. Fr. Acad.* To Rdr., Seeking out what to bite at, and to reprehend in other mens works. **1605** Verstegan *Dec. Intell.* (1628) Pref. Verses, If Enuie bite what thou hast here set foorth. **1683** J. Barnard *Life Heylyn* 40 It does not become any Son of the Church..to bite and snarl at the Name of Protestant.

15. a. *trans.* (*colloq.*) To deceive, to overreach, 'take in.' Now only in *passive*. Cf. bite *sb.* 9.

1709 Steele *Tatler* No. 12 He has bit you fairly enough. **1732** Pope *Ep. Bathurst* 143 The judge shall job, the Bishop bite the town. **1798** W. Hutton *Autobiog.* 31 The work-men saw my ignorance, and bit me as they pleased. *a* **1847** Mrs. Sherwood *Lady of Manor* V. xxxii. 330 Both parties had been in some degree bitten in the reciprocal attempt to deceive each other. **1852** Thackeray *Esmond* III. iii. 340 Miss Beatrix was quite bit (as the phrase of that day was). *Mod. phrase.* 'The biter bit.'

b. To cadge or borrow (money, etc.) from. *Austral. slang.*

1919 W. H. Downing *Digger Dialects* 11 *Bite*, to borrow. **1919** [see hum *sb.*[2]]. **1934** *Bulletin* (Sydney) 7 Nov. 10/1 Think not I'm throwing 'biting' hints. **1935** *Ibid.* 6 Mar. 48/2 The feud had begun when the bagmen sallied forth to 'bite' the town for old coats. **1941** K. Tennant *Battlers* vi. 63 The Stray trotted back bemoaning her lack of success in 'biting' housewives. It was only dole-day, and those wise women knew that travellers could not be really destitute.

16. Phrases. † ***to bite upon the bridle***: to champ the bit like a restless horse, to wait impatiently; ***to bite the dust, ground, sand,*** etc.: to fall in death, to die; also, to fall to the ground, to fall wounded; to be abased; also *fig.*; ***to bite the lip,*** or (obs.) ***upon the lips***: to press the lip between the teeth, in order to restrain the expression of anger or mirth; † ***to bite one's tongue***: to hold it between the teeth so as to repress speech (cf. 'to hold one's tongue'); † ***to bite the thumb at***: 'to threaten or defie by putting the thumbe naile into the mouth, and with a ierke (from the upper teeth) make it to knack,' (Cotgr. s.v. *Nique*); to give the 'fico,' to insult; † ***to bite the teeth***: to gnash or grind them; ***to bite one's ear*** or ***one by the ear***, † (*a*) i.e. as a sign of fondness, to caress fondly; (*b*) (*slang*), to borrow money from (someone); cf. 15 b and bite *sb.* 1 i; ***to bite one's head*** (or ***nose***) ***off***: to snap one's head off (see snap *v.* 7 b); ***to bite the hand that feeds one***: to injure a benefactor; to act ungratefully; ***to bite off more than one can chew*** (orig. *U.S.*): to undertake too much, to be too ambitious; ***to bite*** (***on***) ***the bullet***: to behave courageously; to avoid showing fear or distress.

1330 R. Brunne *Chron.* 155 Philip bote on his lippe. **1362** Langl. *P. Pl.* B. v. 84 His body was to-bolle for wratthe þat he bote his lippes. **1475** Caxton *Jason* (1477) 52 He frowned ..and bote on his lippe. **1514** Barclay *Cyt. & Uplondyshm.* (1847) 41 These courtiers..Smelling those dishes, they bite upon the bridle. **1535** Coverdale *Lament.* ii. 16 Thine enemies..bytinge their teth sayenge: let vs deuoure. **1592** Shaks. *Rom. & Jul.* I. i. 58 No, sir, I do not bite my Thumbe at you sir: but I bite my Thumbe sir. **1592** *Ibid.* II. iv. 81, I will bite thee by the eare for that iest. **1593** —— *2 Hen. VI*, I. i. 230 So Yorke must sit, and fret, and bite his tongue. **1599** [see nose *sb.* 9 c]. **1600** Abp. Abbot *Exp. Jonah* 342 Bite upon the bridle, that..he may be wiser afterward. **1610** B. Jonson *Alch.* II. iii, Slave, I could bite thine Ear. **1611** Cotgr., *Mordre l'oreille à*, as much as *flatter ou caresser mignonnement*, wherein the biting of th' eare is, with some, an vsuall Action. **1613** Shaks. *Hen. VIII*, III. ii. 113 He bites his lip, and starts, Stops on a sodaine. **1697** Dryden *Virg. Æneid* XI. 528 So many Valiant Heros bite the Ground. **1718** Pope *Iliad* v. 51 First Odius falls, and bites the bloody sand. **1750** Smollett *Gil Blas* I. III. ii. 223 We made two of them bite the dust, and the others betake themselves to flight. **1770** Burke *Pres. Discont.* 3 This..proposition..that we set ourselves to bite the hand that feeds us; that with.. insanity we oppose the measures..whose sole object is our own peace and prosperity. *a* **1771** Gray *Poems, Ode* viii, Soon a King shall bite the ground. **1813** Byron *Giaour* xxii, The foremost Tartar bites the ground! **1820** Keats *Isabella* xxii, And many times they bit their lips alone. **1855** *Golden Era* 18 Mar. 1/5 We..made one bite the dust every crack. **1856** [see dust *sb.*[1] 4]. **1857** Trollope *Barchester T.* III. xiii. 229 That ecclesiastical knight before whose lance Mr. Slope was to fall and bite the dust. **1857** Lytton *What will he do with It?* III. iv. in *Blackw. Mag.* Sept. 301/2 He will never bite the hand that feeds him now. **1857** Dickens *Dorrit* II. xv. 456 You make one bite your head off, when one wants to be soothing beyond everything. **1870** Bryant *Iliad* I. II. 55 May his fellow warriors..Fall round him to the earth and bite the dust. **1878** J. H. Beadle *Western Wilds* ii. 42 You've bit off more'n you can chaw. **1879** *Macm. Mag.* Oct. 502/1 He used to want to bite my ear (borrow) too often. **1887** *Lantern* (New Orleans) 5 Mar. 3/1 If he ain't careful, he'll bite the dust [get broke and go begging]. **1891** Kipling *Light that Failed* xi. 219 Bite on the bullet, old man, and don't let them think you're afraid. **1916** G. B. Shaw *Pygmalion* 195 The mistake we describe metaphorically as 'biting off more than they can chew'. **1923** Wodehouse *Inimit. Jeeves* ii. 27 Brace up and bite the bullet. I'm afraid I've bad news for you. **1925** —— *Carry on, Jeeves!* ii. 36 His principal source of income..was derived from biting the ear of a rich uncle. **1927** H. T. Lowe-Porter tr. *Mann's Magic Mountain* I. v. 282 Thus ungrateful is immature youth! It takes all that is offered, and bites the hand that feeds it. **1940** Wodehouse *Eggs, Beans & Crumpets* 229, I was not dreaming of biting your ear... What I require is something far beyond your power to supply. Five pounds at least. **1943** S. V. Benét *Western Star* 70 The treacherous redskins always bite the dust. **1946** R. Lehmann *Gipsy's Baby* 126 He'd bite my head off if I asked him to come on the committee. **1955** *Times* 11 May 14/6 'Better men than Mr. Strachey have bit the dust in Dundee,' was how the Tory hopes were summed up by one Conservative. *a* **1960** J. L. Austin *Sense & Sensibilia* (1962) i. 1 They [*sc.* doctrines] all bite off more than they can chew.

bite (baɪt), *sb.* Also 5 byte. [f. bite *v.* Taking the place of bit *sb.*[1] and [2], in several of their original and more literal senses, first in 15th c. in sense 1, and at various later dates in the other senses. (As bit was earlier spelt *bite*, with short *ĭ*, it is not possible always to distinguish the two words, at the period when *bīte* was coming in.)]

1. a. The act or action of cutting, piercing, or wounding, with the teeth; also *fig.*

1499 *Promp. Parv.* (Pynson), Byte, *morsus*. **1570** Levins *Manip.* 150 A Byte, *morsus, rictus*. **1697** Dryden *Virg. Georg.* II. 522 Their venom'd Bite [*durique venenum Dentis*]. **1735** Pope *Prol. Sat.* 106 Of all mad creatures..It is the slaver kills, and not the bite. **1799** Southey *King Crocod.* II, King Crocodile..show'd his teeth, but he miss'd his bite. *Mod. Provb.* His bark is worse than his bite.

b. The keen cutting effect of a harsh wind.

1881 *Daily Tel.* 28 Jan., A thin scattering of sleet in the air which gave a peculiar edge to the bite of the wind.

c. The action of a machine indenting metal, etc.

1876 E. Clark *Japan* 192 Stamping machines..closed upon each of them [blank coins] with a 'bite.'

d. The corrosive action of acid upon the metal plate in etching.

1875 Ure *Dict. Arts* II. 286 If..the engraver finds that the acid has acted as he wishes, he has secured what is technically termed 'a good bite.'

e. A downward jerk of a horse's head.

1861 Whyte-Melville *Market Harb.* xii. (ed. 12) 98 'Hold up, you brute,' he added, as Hotspur made an egregious 'bite,' that nearly landed him on his nose.

f. = occlusion 3. Also, the imprint of the occlusion in a plastic material.

1848 J. Tomes *Lect. Dental Physiol. & Surg.* xvi. 367 The *bite*, or closure of the upper and under teeth, must be adjusted. **1878** C. Hunter *Mech. Dentistry* vi. 74 (*heading*) Taking the 'Bite' in wax and plaster. *Ibid.* 79 Bites..may be cast by first cutting a perpendicular groove on the back of the model, then filling plaster into the impression of the teeth in the wax block. **1880** N. W. Kingsley *Treatise on Oral Deformities* v. 84 The object was, not to protrude the lower teeth, but to change or jump the bite in the case of an excessively retreating lower jaw. **1902** [see occlusion]. **1904** V. H. Jackson *Orthodontia* xi. 201 An apparatus..was utilized for opening the bite and moving the upper incisors outward. **1968** J. Woodforde *False Teeth* 126 Having decided which is the proper relationship, or bite, the dentist attaches the upper and lower casts of the jaw to a machine called an articulator, which reproduces chewing motions.

g. *Cricket.* The quality in a cricket-pitch that helps a ball to 'bite' (see bite *v.* 12 g).

1905 *Daily Chron.* 5 May 8/3 Aided by the trifle of 'bite' in the pitch, the Surrey bowler always appeared likely to get wickets.

h. *fig.* Incisiveness, pungency; point or cogency of style, language, etc.

1899 R. Whiteing *No. 5 John St.* xxiii. 228 There seems no 'bite' in their pretty ways, their soft voices, their allusive turns of phrase. **1921** J. Agate in *Sat. Rev.* 24 Dec. 708/2, I want to hear..common Spanish speech interpreted and made real. I want tang and bite which I can translate into actuality. **1939** *Punch* 11 Oct. 398/1 There is an unexpected and genuine satirical bite in the whole treatment of the story. **1946** H. Foss in A. L. Bacharach *Brit. Music* iv. 70 The quality of 'bite', of urgency, or, as I would call it, of single-minded artistic sincerity. **1957** *Listener* 19 Sept. 416/1 The party's election propaganda lacked bite and purpose.

i. Slang phr. ***to put the bite on***: to borrow money from (someone); to ask (someone) for a loan; also, to threaten, to blackmail, to extort money from. orig. and chiefly *U.S.*

1933 D. Runyon *Furthermore* (1938) v. 81 He once tries to put the bite on Sorrowful for a sawbuck. **1934** Wodehouse *Thank You, Jeeves* v. 61 For years and years I have been trying to lend him of my plenty, but he has always steadfastly refused to put the bite on me. **1939** R. Chandler *Big Sleep* xxvi. 232 You can put the bite on the peeper and be on your way. **1950** 'S. Ransome' *Deadly Miss Ashley* iii. 33 Everybody keeps putting the bite on me for money I haven't got.

2. a. The biting of food or victuals; *concr.* food to eat; chiefly in the phrase ***bite and sup***. Also, a small meal; a snack.

1562 J. Heywood *Prov. & Epigr.* (1867) 34 One peny.. That euer might either make me bite or sup. **1816** Scott *Old Mort.* vi, There's puir distressed whigs enow about the country will be glad to do that for a bite and a soup. **1861** Miss Braddon *Trail Serp.* VI. vi. 301 He had lain concealed for fourteen days without either bite or sup. **1899** Ade *Fables in Slang* (1900) 188 He would be reading the Menu Card to her, and telling her how different it is when you have Some One to join you in a Bite. **1929** 'G. Daviot' *Man in Queue* iv. 46 Have a bite before you go to bed. **1952** M. Laski *Village* xi. 166 Come back for a bite, just a scratch meal. **1959** 'C. Carnac' *Death of Lady Killer* xi. 124, I..had a bite with my friend at the fish and chips stall.

b. The biting of grass; herbage to bite.

1765 Tucker *Lt. Nat.* I. 618 Little seeds, each whereof cannot throw up herbage enough to make a bite for a sheep. **1799** J. Robertson *Agric. Perth* 302 It..gives sheep a good bite early in the season. **1834** *Brit. Husb.* I. viii. 216 They are

then again turned out as soon as there is a bite of grass in the spring. **1881** *Daily News* 4 June 5/5 Grass lands were terribly backward; there was little bite for cattle.

3. *Angling.* The seizure of the bait by a fish.

1653 WALTON *Angler* 169, I have knowne a very good Fisher angle..for three or four dayes together for a River Carp, and not have a bite. **1836** MARRYAT *Midsh. Easy* vi, I have another bite..ah! he's off again. **1863** BURTON *Bk. Hunter* 102 The chance of these excites him, like the angler's bites and rises, and gives its zest to the pursuit.

4. a. A piece bitten off (usually to eat); a mouthful.

1535 STEWART *Cron. Scot.* III. 476 To mak him remeid, Or him support with ane byte of gra breid. **1784** MRS. A. ADAMS *Lett.* (1848) 203 Although he longs for a morsel, he has not yet agreed for a single bite. *a* **1817** *Ballad 'Susan Pye'* xx. *ibid.* 472/2 Tell him to send one bite of bread. **1827** SCOTT *Two Drovers* Take it all, man—take it all—never make two bites of a cherry.

b. A share (of profits, etc.), a 'cut'; an exaction or amount exacted. *N. Amer. slang.*

1925 *Dialect Notes* V. 326 *Bite*, share of money. **1946** *Sun* (Baltimore) 5 Aug. 12/5 Some turfmen have openly predicted that the tax, which increases the total official 'bite' on the betting handle to about 16 per cent. would threaten the future of racing at the Spa. **1968** *Globe & Mail* (Toronto) 17 Feb. 8/1 Horsemen have agreed to boycott Assiniboia Downs..until the provincial Government reduces its bite on the pari-mutuel intake. **1976** *National Observer* (U.S.) 24 Jan. 20/3 Whatever the price, the weekly bite goes on... A hundred pesos for water [etc.].

†**5.** *Thieves' slang.* Cash, money. *Obs.* Cf. BIT *sb.*[2] 8 a.

1532 *Dice Play* (1850) 30 So proud..because he hath gotten a new chain..and some store of byte. **1592** GREENE *Def. Conny-catch.* Wks. 1881–3 XI. 44 Some..would venter all the byte in their boung at dice.

6. A wound made with the teeth.

1736 BAILEY, *Bite*, an hurt made by the teeth. **1766** GOLDSM. *Elegy Mad Dog*, The man recovered of the bite, The dog it was that died. **1830** TENNYSON *Dream Fair Wom.* 160 Thereto [her breast] she pointed with a laugh, Showing the aspick's bite. **1838** *Penny Cycl.* XII. 400/1 The bite of a rabid animal generally heals up like that of a healthy one.

7. The grip or hold of an edge surface in various mechanical contrivances. Also *fig.*

1865 MASSON *Rec. Brit. Philos.* iii. 176 His system..may have lost its bite upon the British mind. *Mod.* In wet weather sand is sprinkled under the wheels of a locomotive to increase their bite upon the rails.

8. *Typogr.* A blank left in printing through the accidental covering of a portion of the 'forme' by the frisket.

1677 MOXON *Mech. Exerc.* in Savage *Dict. Print.* s.v. *Bite*, If the frisket is not sufficiently cut away, but covers some part of the form, so that it prints on the frisket, it is called a bite. **1882** BLADES *Caxton* 130 In 'Speculum Vitæ Christi' we actually find 'a bite,' half of the bottom line remaining unprinted.

†**9.** *slang.* **a.** An imposition, a deception; what is now called a 'sell'; passing from the notion of playful imposition or hoax, to that of swindle or fraud. *Obs.* (Cf. BITER, 2.)

1711 STEELE *Spect.* No. 156 ¶2 It was a common Bite with him, to lay Suspicions that he was favoured by a Lady's Enemy. **1726** AMHERST *Terræ Fil.* ix. 43 Sharpers would not frequent gaming-tables, if the men of fortune knew the bite. **1755** M. MASTERS *Lett. & Poems* 260 What the witlings term'd Bite in the Spectator's time is now call'd Humbug. **1815** SCOTT *Guy M.* iii, What were then called bites and bams, since denominated hoaxes and quizzes. **1860** *Sat. Rev.* 14 Apr. 475/2 That form of practical joking which in the time of 'The Spectator,' was known as a *bite*..in the popular slang of the day, is designated 'a sell.'

b. A sharper, a swindler: see also quot. 1846.

1742 FIELDING *Miss Lucy* (1762) 176 Is this wench an idiot, or a bite? marry me, with a pox! *a* **1787** S. JENYNS in *Dodsley* III. 169 The fool would fain be thought a bite. **1846** BRACKENRIDGE *Mod. Chiv.* 21 The jockeys suspected that the horse was what they call a bite, that under the appearance of leanness and stiffness, was concealed some hidden quality of swiftness.

10. *slang.* A nickname for a Yorkshireman. (Origin disputed: see *Daily News* 11 Sept. 1883; *Yorksh. Post* 9 Jan. 1884.)

1883 *Daily News* 4 Sept. 5/6 The great and puissant race known indifferently as 'tykes' or 'bites.'

11. *Comb.* **bite-beast** (*nonce-wd.*), a beast that bites; **bite-free** *a.*, free from, or not liable to, bites; **biteless** *a.*, that does not bite, unbiting.

1730 SOUTHALL *Bugs* 30 They will no longer think themselves bite-free. **1850** BLACKIE *Æschylus* I. 163 A torpedo, that with biteless touch Strikes numb who handles. **1877** BROWNING *Agamem.*, Calling her the hateful bite-beast. **1884** *Century Mag.* XXVII. 780 Speechless and biteless.

biteable, bitable (bɛˈɪtəb(ə)l), *a. rare.* [f. BITE *v.* + -ABLE.] That may be bitten.

1483 *Cath. Angl.* 33/1 Biteabylle, *morsalis.*

biteach, -teche, var. of BETEACH *v. Obs.*

†**ˈbitel,** *a. Obs.* [ME., prob. representing an OE. **bitol* 'mordacious,' f. *bītan* to BITE; cf. *etol, drincol*, etc.] Biting, cutting with a sharp edge.

c **1200** ORMIN 10073 Wiþþ bitell wræchess axe. *c* **1205** LAY. 19503 Mid bitele stelen.

bitel(e, -le, -yl, obs. forms of BEETLE, BETELL.

bitemporal (baɪˈtɛmpərəl), *a.* [f. BI- *pref.*[2] 5 + TEMPORAL, f. *tempora* (sb. pl.) temples.] Joining the two temporal bones.

1857 BULLOCK *Cazeaux' Midwif.* 221 The transverse diameters are two..the Bi-parietal, and the Bi-temporal.

biten, -teon, variants of BETEE *v. Obs.*

biter (ˈbaɪtə(r)). [f. BITE *v.* + -ER[1].]

1. One who or that which bites. (See the vb.)

c **1300** *Names of Hare* in *Rel. Ant.* I. 133 The hare..The gras-bitere, the goibert. **1496** *Bk. St. Albans, Fysshynge* 28 A stately fysshe..a stronge byter. **1594** CAREW *Tasso* (1881) 42 A biter at the backe, of such quaint wayes As when he carpeth most, he seemes to prayse. **1607** TOPSELL *Four-f. Beasts* 445 Otters are most accomplished biters. **1696** J. EDWARDS *Exist. Prov. God* II. 22 These biters, these cutters, are made with a very acute edge. **1870** SPURGEON *Treas. Dav.* Ps. vii. 15 This biter who has bitten himself.

2. *spec.* A deceiver; one who amuses himself at another's expense; a sharper. (*Obs.* exc. in 'the biter bit,' a traditional quotation.)

1680 COTTON *Compl. Gamester* 333 Shoals of huffs, hectors, setters, gilts, pads, biters, etc...may all pass under the general appellation of rooks. **1693** D'URFEY *Richmond Heiress* Epil. p. 64 Is't not fit Once in an age the Biter should be bit. **1710** E. WARD *Nuptial Dial.* II. ix. 179, I think she merits equal Praise That has the Wit to bite the Biter. **1711** ADDISON *Spect.* No. 47 ¶8 An ingenious Tribe of Men..who are for making April Fools every Day in the Year. These Gentlemen are commonly distinguished by the name of Biters. **1712** STEELE *ibid.* No. 504 §3 A Biter is one who thinks you a Fool, because you do not think him a Knave. **1812** COMBE (Dr. Syntax) *Picturesque* XIX, To think we have so little wit, As by such biters to be bit. **1826** M. KELLY *Reminiscences* (ed. 2) I. 336 Delighted at seeing the biter bit. **1885** *Illustr. Lond. News* 14 Nov. 492/2 An excellent instance of 'the biter bit' was furnished.

biter, obs. form of BITTER.

biternate (baɪˈtɜːneɪt), *a.* [f. BI- *pref.*[2] 3 + TERNATE.] Doubly or subordinately ternate; see quot. 1870. Hence **biˈternately** *adv.*

1794 MARTYN *Rousseau's Bot.* xxi. 304. **1870** BENTLEY *Bot.* 166 If the common petiole divides at its apex into 3 partial ones, each of which bears 3 leaflets, the leaf is termed biternate. **1870** HOOKER *Stud. Flora* 167 Leaves biternately pinnate.

†**bite-sheep.** *Obs.* Forms: 6 **bitesheepe, byteschiep,** 7 **bite-shappe,** 6–7 **bite-sheep.** [f. BITE *v.* + SHEEP *sb.* Cf. Ger. *beiszschaf, beischaf.*] A once-favourite pun upon *bishop*, as if = One who bites the sheep which he ought to feed. Also *attrib.*

1553–87 FOXE *A. & M.* II. 466 Ye are become rather bite-sheeps than true bishops. *c* **1575** *Leg. Bp. St. Androis* (Dalyell) II. 313 Then to the court this craftie lown, To be a byteschiep maid him boun. **1683** J. BARNARD *Life Heylyn* 184 Your Bishops are bite-Sheep, Your Deans are Dunces.

†**biˈthecche,** *v. Obs.* 1 be-, **biþeccan.** *Pa. t.* 1 **-þeahte,** 3 **-þehte, -þæhte, -þahte.** [Com. WGer.: OE. *biþecc(e)an* = OS. *bithekkjan*, OFris. *bithekka, bidekka*, OHG. *bidecchan* (MHG. and mod.G. *bedecken*); f. *bi-*, BE- + OTeut. **þakjan* (ON. *þekja*, OE. *þecc(e)an*) to cover, THETCH.] *trans.* To cover over; to bedeck.

c **1000** *Guthlac.* 1255 þystrum biþeahte. *c* **1205** LAY. 19216 Al mid pælle bi-þæht [*c* **1250** bi-þehte]. *Ibid.* 22338 Arðures men weoren mid wepnen al bi-þehte.

bitheism (baɪˈθiːɪz(ə)m). *rare.* [f. BI- *pref.*[2] II + THEISM.] A recognition of two deities (i.e. a good and an evil).

1884 L. TOLLEMACHE *Stones of Stumbl.* 83 *note*, At bottom, every such system is Bitheism.

bithink, bithoght, etc.: see BETHINK, etc.

†**biˈthret(t,** *ppl. a. Obs. rare.* [f. *bi-*, BE- + ME. *threten* to THREAT.] Menaced, threatened.

a **1300** *Cursor M.* 10102 Wit thrin fas bi-thrett.

†**biˈthring,** *v. Obs.* Only in pa. pple.: 1–3 **be-, biþrungen,** 3 **biþronge(n.** [OE. *beþringan*, f. *bi-*, BE- 1 + *þringan* to THRONG; cf. MHG. *bedringen.*] *trans.* To throng about, to press hard. Also *fig.*

c **1000** *Elene* 1245 (Gr.) Ic wæs..bysgum beþrungen. *c* **1200** ORMIN 14825 Wiþþ waundraþ biþrungenn. *c* **1205** LAY. 9435 þer binnen wes Aruiragus ærmliche biþrungen [**1250** biþronge].

†**biˈthynch, bethunch,** *v. Obs.* [f. *bi-*, BE- 2 + *punchen*, OE. *þyncan*, THINK *v.*[2] Cf. Ger. *bedünkt.*] *impers.* To seem right or good.

a **1225** *Ancr. R.* 346 Sum lutel hwat he mei leggen on þe ȝif him so biðuncheð.

biticle, obs. form of BINNACLE.

†**biˈtight,** *pa. pple. Obs. rare.* In 3 **bitiȝt, bituht.** [Cf. BETEE, TIGHT.] Clad, attired.

a **1250** *Owl & Night.* 1013 Hi goþ bituht [*MS. Cot.* bitiȝt] mid ruȝe felle.

bitime, -s, var. of BETIME, BETIMES.

biting (ˈbaɪtɪŋ), *vbl. sb.* [f. BITE *v.* + -ING[1].]

1. a. The action of the vb. BITE in its various senses.

c **1175** *Lamb. Hom.* 33 A þer [in helle] is waning and graming..and feonda bitinga. *c* **1440** *Promp. Parv.* 37 Bytynge, *morsura.* **1534** LD. BERNERS *Gold. Bk. M. Aurel.* (1546) E viii, It is like the bitynge of a madde dogge. **1577** tr. *Bullinger's Decades* (1592) 48 The enuenomed bytinges of the Serpents. **1867** F. FRANCIS *Angling* ii. (1880) 70 The fish begin to slacken in their biting.

b. *fig.*

1382 WYCLIF *Isa.* Prol. 224 Opene to the bitingus of manye men. **1398** TREVISA *Barth. De P.R.* v. xxvi. (1495) 136 By the sharpenes and bytynge therof ache bredyth in the synewe of felynge. *c* **1440** HYLTON *Scala Perf.* (W. de W. 1494) I. xxxiv, Bityng of conscience. **1627** J. DOUGHTY *Serm.* (1628) 17 Hence those bitings and censures against others.

c. *spec.* in *Palæogr.* The convergence of part of two letters, esp. *d* with *e* or *o*, in some medieval manuscripts. Cf. BITE *v.* 12 h.

1957 N. R. KER *Catal. MSS. containing Anglo-Saxon* p. xix, The earliest dated English example of biting of *d* and *e* known to me is in the form of profession of Bishop Sefrid of Chichester in 1180 (Muniments of the Dean and Chapter of Canterbury, C.115, no. 43). **1960** —— *English MSS. Cent. after Norman Conquest* 39 This *de* ligature is perhaps the earliest of the numerous bitings of converging strokes which characterize the formal book-hand throughout the rest of its long existence.

†**2.** The wound made by a bite; the part bitten.

1527 ANDREW *Brunswyke's Distyll. Waters* Cjv, Cloutes wet therin and layd upon the bytynge. **1607** TOPSELL *Serpents* 788 Spiders applyed and laid upon their own bitings..do heal and help those hurts. **1669** WORLIDGE *Syst. Agric.* (1681) 192 The same it will effect on the bitings or stingings of Snakes..and on the bitings of mad Dogs.

3. *biting in* (cf. BITE *v.* 11 b).

1821 CRAIG *Lect. Drawing* vii. 390 The corroding with the aquafortis is also called biting in. **1822** IMISON *Sc. & Art* II. 428 The biting-in of the plate is the most uncertain part of the process.

ˈbiting, *ppl. a.* [f. BITE *v.* + -ING[2].]

1. That bites (in the various senses of the vb.).

a **1300** *Cursor M.* 5954 Hungre flees, sare bitand. **1483** *Cath. Angl.* 33 Bytynge, *mordens, mordax.* **1607** HIERON *Wks.* I. 234 A sharpe axe, which hath a byting edge. **1607** TOPSELL *Four-f. Beasts* 445 It hath very sharp teeth, and is a very biting Beast. **1865** DICKENS *Mut. Fr.* 114 The bitingest and tightest screw in London.

2. That causes pain or smart; keen, pungent.

1340 *Ayenb.* 143 þet zed o mostard is wel smal..hit is wel strang and wel bitinde. **1552** HULOET, Bytynge..as gynger or Peper. **1579** E. K. in *Spenser's Sheph. Cal.* Feb. 231 The byting frost nipt his stalke dead. **1802** SOUTHEY *Thalaba* x. vi, Louder grows the biting wind. **1843** DICKENS *Christm. Carol* i. 12 It was cold, bleak, biting weather.

b. In names of plants: Acrid, hot, pungent.

1597 GERARD *Herbal* II. cccxxvii. 890 White Clematis or Biting Periwinkle. **1861** MISS PRATT *Flower. Pl.* II. 324 The Biting Stonecrop.

3. That wounds the mind or feelings; stinging, caustic; bitter, painful.

c **1374** CHAUCER *Boeth.* III. vii. 79 Of whiche children how bitynge is euery condicioun. *c* **1400** *Apol. Loll.* 105 þei are..glosandist flaterars & bitandist bacbitars. **1598** SHAKS. *Merry W.* v. v. 178 To repay that money will be a biting affliction. **1611** RICH *Honest. Age* (1844) 29 They will say wee are too bitter, too byting, too satiricall. **1711** SWIFT *Lett.* (1767) III. 187, I writ him lately a biting letter. **1749** FIELDING *Tom Jones* I. xiii, So biting a calamity. **1868** FREEMAN *Norm. Conq.* (1876) II. vii. 129 Full of the insolent and biting wit of their nation. **1872** BLACK *Adv. Phaeton* xii. 171 Casting about for some biting epigram.

ˈbitingly, *adv.* [f. prec. + -LY[2].] In a biting manner; bitterly, sorely; caustically, acridly; keenly, penetratingly.

c **1374** CHAUCER *Boeth.* II. vii. 59 þat oþer man answered[e] aȝein ful bityngly. **1562** JEWEL *Apol. Ch. Eng.* IV. vi. (1845) 74 To utter these things more bitterly and bitingly, than it becometh divines to do. **1673** HICKERINGILL *Greg. Greyb.* 302 With teeth bitingly set. **1705** —— *Priest-cr.* IV. (1721) 211 To be bitingly wise as Serpents. **1873** GEIKIE *Gt. Ice Age* xxx. 427 Every wind..is bitingly cold.

ˈbitingness. [f. BITING *ppl. a.* + -NESS.] Biting quality.

1894 *Contemp. Rev.* July 43 His article, by its very sharpness and bitingness, will help to wake our people up.

bitle, obs. form of BEETLE.

bitless (ˈbɪtlɪs). [f. BIT *sb.*[1] 8 + -LESS.] Not having a bit.

1605 SYLVESTER *Du Bartas* (1621) 102 The..bit-less Horse I ride. **1859** *Blackw. Mag.* Sept. 270/1 With his bitless halter. *Ibid.* 271/1 The Anazeh, bitless, and almost reinless.

†**ˈbitling.** [f. BIT *sb.*[2] + dim. -LING.] A very small bit, a particle.

1674 N. FAIRFAX *Bulk. & Selv.* 56 The cleavesom bitlings of body..can never make up an Immensity.

bitogen, -ȝe(n, -wen, pa. pple. of BETEE *v. Obs.*

bitok, bitoken: see BETAKE, BETOKEN.

bitonality (baɪtəʊˈnælɪtɪ). *Mus.* [f. BI-[2] + TONALITY.] The simultaneous use of two keys in a musical composition. So **biˈtonal** *a.*, characterized by bitonality.

1927 A. E. HULL *Mus. Class. Romantic & Mod.* xvii. 317 *Atonality, Bi-tonality* and *Polytonality* are the technical catch-words of the day... Bi-tonality is a richer kind of counterpoint (or harmony), produced by two melodies (or harmonic streams) which proceed simultaneously, each in its own key. *Ibid.* 318 Bi-tonality in two harmonic streams

arose from the isolated bi-tonal chords, so frequently found in the works of Strauss and the French impressionists of the period 1900–10. **1945** *Times* 28 Sept. 7/5 His [*sc.* Bartok's] Fourteen Bagatelles (1908), trifles maybe, but exploiting modern devices like bitonality and irregular rhythm, are fairly well known. **1956** W. MELLERS in A. Pryce Jones *New Outl. Mod. Knowl.* 360 The result is a bitonal ambiguity between major and minor.

† **'bitop**, *a. Obs. rare*⁻¹. [f. BI- *pref.*² + TOP.] With two tops.

1681 COTTON *Poet. Wks.* (1765) 338 She took a greater Leap, against her Will, Than Pegasus from t'other Bi-top Hill.

bitorn, -tourne, obs. forms of BETURN.

† **bi'tought**, *pa. pple. Obs. rare.* [Cf. BITIGHT.] Attired, arrayed.

c **1314** *Guy Warw.* (1840) 232 With armes the maiden him had bitought.

bitour(e, obs. form of BITTERN.

bitraie, -traise, -trap, etc.: see BE-.

bi-tri- (baɪtraɪ), *pref.* compounded of BI- *pref.*² and TRI-, expressing a possibility of either a double or triple degree of the conformation specified; as in **bitripartite**, divided into two or three parts, **bitripinnatifid, bitriseptate**, etc.

1845 LINDLEY *Sch. Bot.* iv. (1858) 28 Leaves tripartite, or bi-tripartite. **1851** RICHARDSON *Geol.* (1855) 182 Leaves bi-tripinnatifid. **1870** HOOKER *Stud. Flora* (1878) 490. **1871** M. COOKE *Fungi* (1874) 40 The spores are bi-triseptate.

† **bi'trufle**, *v. Obs. rare*⁻¹. [ME., f. *bi-*, BE- 4 + *truflen* to TRIFLE.] *trans.* To befool, delude.

c **1225** *Ancr. R.* 106 Þeos ant oðre trufles þet he bitrufleð monie men mide.

† **bi'trum**, *v. Obs.* Forms: 1 **betrymian**, 2 **betremien**, 3 **bitrum(i)en (y)**. [Late OE. *betrymian*, f. BE- 1 + **trymian*, earlier *trymman* to strengthen, fortify, f. *trum* firm, strong. Cf. the earlier OE. *ymb-trymman, ymb-trymian*. The sense passed from that of 'fortify all round' to that of 'surround' simply, and 'beset, besiege.'] *trans.* To surround, beset.

c **1000** *Ags. Gosp.* Luke xix. 43 Þine fynd þe betrymiaþ. *Ibid.* xxi. 20 Þonne ʒe ʒeseoð hierusalem mid here betrymede [*Hatton* betremed]. *a* **1225** *St. Marher.* 6 Helle houndes .. habbeð bitrumet me. *a* **1225** *Leg. Kath.* 1659 A burh .. al abuten bitrumet wið a deorewurðe wal.

bitsy ('bɪtsɪ), *a. colloq.* Also **bittsie**. [f. pl. of BIT *sb.*² or f. BITTY *a.*: see -SY.] = ITSY-BITSY; tiny, (charmingly) small. Freq. preceded by 'little'.

1905 *Dialect Notes* III. 87 They was little-bitsy fellers. **1906** 'O. HENRY' *Four Million* 110 Oh, oo's um oodlum, doodlum, woodlum, toodlum, bitsy-witsy skoodlums? **1919** F. HURST *Humoresque* 147 Wouldn't I just love to .. hang some great big headlight earrings in them little bittsie ears. **1959** W. GOLDING *Free Fall* xiv. 251 A bitsy village with reed thatch and wrought-iron work.

bitt, usually in *pl.* **bitts** (bɪts). *Naut.* Also 6 **beetes**, 7–9 **bits**. [Derivation uncertain: some form of the word is now found in most European languages, but its history is not clear in any: in Fr. *bitte*, Sp. *bita*, It. *bitta*; cf. med.L. *bitus* a whipping-post, 'lignum quo vincti flagellantur' Erfurt Gloss. In Sw. *beting*, Da. *beding*; LG. and Du. *beting*, Ger. *bäting* (perh. from Sw.) 'bitts'; with which cf. OE. *bæting*, *béting* 'a cable, a rope, anything that holds or restrains.' Cf. also ON. *biti* 'a cross-beam in a house or ship, *transtrum*,' according to Vigfusson, the same word as *biti* bit, mouthful = OE. *bita*, BIT *sb.*²

(Franck concludes that the word is of Teutonic origin, and from the root of *bitan* to bite.)]

One of the strong posts firmly fastened in pairs in the deck or decks of a ship, for fastening cables, belaying ropes, etc.; generally used in the plural. The chief pair, the ***riding bitts***, are used for fastening the cable while the ship rides at anchor; others are the ***topsail-sheet bitts***, ***carrick-bitts***, ***wind-lass bitts***, etc. Also *attrib.*, as *bitt-head*, *-pin*.

1593 P. NICHOLS *Drake Revived* in Arb. *Garner* V. 509 Two or three yonkers, which were found afore the beetes. **1612** WOODALL *Surg. Mate* Wks. (1653) 398 A Cable as it was running out of the bits of the ship (as the Sea-men terme it). **1627** CAPT. SMITH *Seaman's Gram.* ii. 10 The Bits are two great peeces of timber, and the Crospeece goeth thorow them. **1769** FALCONER *Dict. Marine* (1789), *Tour-et-choque*, a weather-bit of the cable, or a turn and half-turn about the bits. **1836** MARRYAT *Midsh. Easy* ix, Jack stood .. not far from the main bitts. *c* **1850** *Rudim. Navig.* (Weale) 97 *Bitts* .. It consists of two upright pieces of oak, called *Bitt-Pins*, when the bitts are large, or of knees, when the bitts are small, with a cross piece fastened horizontally near the head of them. **1869** SIR E. REED *Shipbuild.* xv. 276 To keep the bitt in its proper position.

bitt (bɪt), *v.* [f. prec.]

trans. To coil or fasten (a cable) upon the bitts.

1769 [see BITTING *vbl. sb.*²] **1833** MARRYAT *P. Simple* xv, See it [the Cable] double bitted. **1840** R. DANA *Bef. Mast.* x. 24 The chain is then passed round the windlass, and bitted.

b. *Sailor's slang.*

1833 MARRYAT *P. Simple* iii, Come, Mr. Bottlegreen, rouse and bitt. **1836** —— *Midsh. Easy* (1863) 130 'Come, Easy, you are not on board now. Rouse and bitt.'

bittacle, obs. form of BINNACLE.

bittayne, obs. form of BETONY.

bitted ('bɪtɪd), *ppl. a.* [f. BIT *sb.*¹ + -ED².] Furnished with or having a bit.

c **1420** *Pallad. on Husb.* I. 1162 And double bited axes for thees thornes. *c* **1615** CHAPMAN *Odyss.* XXI. 8 The key, Bright, brazen, bitted passing curiously.

bitten ('bɪt(ə)n), *ppl. a.* [pa. pple. of BITE *v.*]

1. Cut into, pierced, or wounded with the teeth.

1613 SHAKS. *Hen. VIII*, v. iv. 64 Youths that .. fight for bitten Apples. **1789** J. O'DONNEL in *Med. Commun.* II. 299 His face on the bitten side was .. swelled.

2. *fig.* Infected, seized with a mania.

1847 L. HUNT *Men, Women, & B.* II. vii. 89 Readers not bitten with the love of verse. **1873** MORLEY *Rousseau* II. 186 Readers of the Social Contract, and .. bitten by its dogmatic temper.

3. Often combined with instrumental sbs., as ***frost-***, ***hunger-***, ***vice-bitten*** (***-bit***), etc.

1599 H. C. in *Greenham's Wks.* To Rdr., The thirstie soule .. Or hunger-bit. **1669** WORLIDGE *Syst. Agric.* (1681) 93 The leaves .. before they are frost-bitten. **1754** RICHARDSON *Grandison* VI. xxvii. 164 A man vice-bitten.

† **4.** *actively.* Having bitten, biting. (Used with qualifying adverb: cf. *fair-spoken*.) *Obs. rare.*

1616 SURFL. & MARKH. *Countr. Farm* 674 They [Greyhounds] are of all dogs the sorest bitten and least amased with any crueltie in their enemie.

5. In engraving, ***bitten-in***: see BITE *v.* 11 b.

1878 ABNEY *Treat. Photogr.* 183 The plate has to be .. again heated to slightly melt the bitumen, so as to allow it to flow down the sides of the bitten-in lines.

6. ***bitten-off***: abruptly terminated (as if by the action of biting).

1829 T. CASTLE *Introd. Bot.* 20 The eroded or bitten-off appearance. **1937** V. WOOLF *Years* 288 Baxter gave a queer little bitten-off smile.

bitter ('bɪtə(r)), *a.* and *sb.*¹ Forms: 1–4 **biter**, 1– **bitter**. (Also 1 **bitor, -yr, bittor**, 3 *Orm.* **bitterr**, 3–5 **bittir, -ur**, 4 **byter**, 4–5 **byttyr**, 4–6 **bytter**, 5 **-ir, -ur, bittyr**. *Definite* 1–4 **bitre**, 1–5 **bittre**.) [Com. Teut.: OE. *biter* = OS. and OHG. *bittar*, ON. *bitr* (MDu., Du., MHG., mod.G., Sw., Da. *bitter*), Goth. (with different vowel) *baitrs*; prob. f. root of *bîtan* to BITE, with the original meaning 'biting, cutting, sharp,' but within the historical period only used of taste, and in modern use no longer even 'biting' or 'acrid' in taste: see sense 1.]

A. *adj.*

1. a. One of the elementary sensations of taste proper (i.e. without any element arising through the nerves of touch): obnoxious, irritating, or unfavourably stimulating to the gustatory nerve; disagreeable to the palate; having the characteristic taste of wormwood, gentian, quinine, bitter aloes, soot: the opposite of *sweet*; causing 'the proper pain of taste' (Bain).

a **1000** *Guthlac* (Gr.) 840 Þone bitran drync. *c* **1175** *Lamb. Hom.* 129 Ðet weter of egipte .. þe wes sur and bitere. *a* **1300** *Cursor M.* 6349 Water bitter sum ani brin. *c* **1400** MAUNDEV. viii. 99 A lytille Broke of Watre, that was wont to ben byttre. **1591** SHAKS. *Two Gent.* II. iv. 149 When I was sick, you gaue me bitter pils. **1626** BACON *Sylva* §21 The Second [water will have] more of the Tast, as more bitter or Biting. **1756** BURKE *Subl. & B.* Introd. Wks. I. 100 All men are agreed to call vinegar sour, honey sweet, and aloes bitter. **1868** BAIN *Ment. & Mor. Sc.* I. ii. 38 Taste proper comprehends sweet and bitter tastes .. The acrid combines the fiery with the bitter. **1884** *Cornh. Mag.* 628 Bitter things in nature .. are almost invariably poisonous.

b. *fig.* Unpalatable to the mind; unpleasant and hard to 'swallow' or admit.

1810 COLERIDGE *Friend* (1865) 166 Some bitter truths, respecting our military arrangements.

c. bitter lake = *salt lake* (see SALT *sb.*¹); *spec.* as the name of certain lakes in Egypt; (see also quot. 1882).

1843 E. CLARKSON *Suez Navigable Canal* 7 The Bitter Lakes would fill up at any time from the Red Sea. **1882** A. GEIKIE *Text-bk. Geol.* III. II. 395 Saline lakes, considered chemically, may be grouped as *salt lakes*, where the chief constituents are sodium and magnesium chlorides with magnesium and calcium sulphates: and *bitter lakes*, which usually are distinguished by their large percentage of sodium carbonate as well as chloride and sulphate. **1957** *Encycl. Brit.* XXI. 517/2 Finally in the summer of 1869 the waters of the Mediterranean and the Red Sea were united [by the Suez Canal] in the Bitter lakes.

2. *transf.* **a.** Of anything that has to be 'tasted' or endured: Attended by severe pain or suffering; sore to be borne; grievous, painful, full of affliction.

971 *Blickl. Hom.* 229 Þu me ne syle on Þone biterestan deað. *c* **1205** LAY. 9685 Her heo sculeð ibiden bittrest alre baluwen. *c* **1340** *Cursor M.* 4827 (Trin.) For bittur hongur þat is bifalle. *c* **1400** *Destr. Troy* VI. 2502 Soche bargens are bytter þat hafe a bare end. **1583** STANYHURST *Æneis* II. (Arb.) 65 Soom Greeks shal find yt bitter, before al we be slaghtred. **1828** SCOTT *F.M. Perth* xxvi, The time of separation now approached. It was a bitter moment. **1839** THIRWALL *Greece* VII. 285 For Eurydice she still reserved what she thought a bitterer death. **1850** TENNYSON *In Mem.* VI, That loss is common, would not make My own less bitter, rather more.

b. ***to the bitter end***: to the last and direst extremity; to death itself. So commonly used: but the history is doubtful: see BITTER *sb.*³ Cf. BIBLE *Prov.* v. 4.

1849 *Congress. Globe* 12 Dec. 23, I am unfortunately among those who voted for the gentleman from Indiana, even 'to the bitter end'. **1850** *Ibid.* 9 Apr., App. 434 Our defence is a just one, and will be maintained by us to the 'bitter end'. **1921** L. STRACHEY *Q. Victoria* vi. 210 He would go on, working to the utmost and striving for the highest, to the bitter end. **1955** G. GREENE *Loser takes All* I. ix. 62 A wife ought to believe in her husband to the bitter end.

3. a. Hence, of a state: Intensely grievous or full of affliction; mournful; pitiable.

c **1485** *Digby Myst.* III. 997 Thys sorow is beytterar þan ony galle. **1588** SHAKS. *Tit. A.* v. iii. 89 Nor can I vtter all our bitter griefe. **1611** BIBLE *Job* iii. 20 Wherefore is light giuen to him that is in misery, and life vnto the bitter in soule? **1816** WORDSW. *White Doe* II. 115 Concealing In solitude her bitter feeling.

† **b.** 'Sour,' morose, peevish. *Obs.*

a **1225** *Ancr. R.* 118 Aȝein bittre ancren Dauid seið þis uers.

4. Expressing or betokening intense grief, misery, or affliction of spirit.

c **1230** *Hali Meid.* 43 Marie Magdalene wið bittre wopes bireowseð hare gultes. *c* **1330** *Arth. & Merl.* 1018 His moder .. swithe bitter ters lete. **1611** BIBLE *Gen.* xxvii. 34 Esau .. cried with a great and exceeding bitter cry. **1650** R. STAPYLTON *Strada's Low-C. Warres* II. 29 No complaints were bitterer then the Abbots and Monks. **1853** KINGSLEY *Hypatia* iv. 42 Bursting into bitter tears. **1884** (*title*) 'The Bitter Cry of Outcast London.'

† **5. a.** Causing pain or suffering; injurious, baleful, cruel, severe. *Obs.*

a **1000** *Beowulf* 5377 Draca .. heals ealne ymbefeng biteran bánum. *a* **1225** *St. Marher.* 11 Þet balefulle wurm ant þet bittre best. *a* **1300** *Cursor M.* 697 Þe nedder was noght bitter. **1330** R. BRUNNE *Chron.* 35 He tok bittere Estrild, dukes douhter Orgare. **1603** SHAKS. *Meas. for M.* IV. ii. 81 It is a bitter Deputie. **1635** N. R. *Camden's Hist. Eliz.* II. 183 The government of the French was bitter.

b. of instruments of torture.

a **1225** *Juliana* 17 Ibeaten wið bittere besmen. **1596** SHAKS. *1 Hen. IV*, I. i. 27 Nail'd For our aduantage on the bitter Crosse.

6. a. Characterized by intense animosity or virulence of feeling or action; virulent.

971 *Blickl. Hom.* 25 Onbærnde mid þære biteran æfeste. **1377** LANGL. *P. Pl.* B. XVIII. 64 For a bitter bataille .. Lyf and deth in þis derknesse her one fordoth her other. **1382** WYCLIF *James* iii. 14 If ȝe han bittir zeel, *or enuy*, and striuynges ben in ȝoure hertis. **1655** FULLER *Ch. Hist.* III. 44 No medium betwixt not loving and bitter hating. **1737** WHISTON *Josephus' Hist.* II. iii. §1 Sabinus .. made a bitter search after the kings money. **1838** MACAULAY in Trevelyan *Life* (1876) I. vii. 9 In politics a bitter partisan. **1848** —— *Hist. Eng.* I. 446 The bitter animosity of James.

b. Const. *to*, *against*.

1382 WYCLIF *Col.* iii. 19 Men, loue ȝe ȝoure wyues, and nyle ȝe be bitter to hem [**1611** against them]. **1606** SHAKS. *Tr. & Cr.* IV. i. 67 You are too bitter to your country-woman. **1833** HT. MARTINEAU *Tale of Tyne* i. 20 She had .. been bitter against them.

7. Of words (or the person who utters them): Stinging, cutting, harsh, keenly or cruelly reproachful, virulent.

c **1175** *Lamb. Hom.* 95 He ne remde ne of bitere speche nes. *c* **1200** ORMIN 9786 Fulle off bitterr spæche. **1589** PUTTENHAM *Eng. Poesie* (Arb.) 41 To taxe the common abuses and vice of the people in rough and bitter speaches. **1600** SHAKS. *A.Y.L.* III. v. 69 As fast as she answeres thee with frowning lookes, ile sauce her with bitter words. **1605** —— *Lear* I. iv. 150 A bitter Foole! **1611** BIBLE *Job* xiii. 26 For thou writest bitter things against mee. **1712** ADDISON *Spect.* No. 433 ⁋6 They would reproach a Man in the most bitter Terms. **1828** CARLYLE *Misc.* (1857) I. 124 Faust is no longer the same bitter and contemptuous man.

8. Of wind, cold, etc.: Sharp, keen, cutting, severe; hence of the weather: Bitingly cold.

1600 SHAKS. *A.Y.L.* II. vii. 184 Freize, freize, thou bitter skie. **1667** BOYLE *Orig. Formes & Qual.*, The Night proving very bitter .. I found the Glasse crack'd .. by the violence of the Frost. **1697** DRYDEN *Virg. Georg.* III. 466 To fend the bitter Cold. **1796** MORSE *Amer. Geog.* II. 308 The frosts are consequently bitter in winter. **1837** CARLYLE *Fr. Rev.* (1871) III. v. ii. 180 A cold bitter drizzling rain. **1875** M. PATTISON *Casaubon* 255 He caught his death in the boat on a bitter Palm Sunday.

B. quasi-*sb.*¹

1. a. That which is bitter; bitterness. *lit.* and *fig.*

a **1000** *Elene* (Gr.) 1245 Weorcum fah, synnum asæled, sorȝum ȝewæled, bitrum ȝebunden. *a* **1240** *Lofsong* in *Lamb. Hom.* 215 Euer bið ðet swete abouht mid twofold of bittre. **1362** LANGL. *P. Pl.* A. v. 99 Þat al my breste Bolleþ · for bitter of my galle. **1690** LOCKE *Hum. Und.* II. xxi, A little bitter mingled in our Cup, leaves no relish of the sweet. **1749** FIELDING *Tom Jones* III. vi, Surfeited with the sweets of marriage, or disgusted by its bitters. **1830** TENNYSON *Dream Fair Wom.* 286 All words .. Failing to give the bitter of the sweet.

b. A bitter part.

1860 O. W. HOLMES *Prof. Breakf.-t.* iv. 104 When you can get the bitter out of the partridge's thigh, you can make an enlightened commonwealth of Indians.

2. A bitter medicinal substance: now usually in pl. BITTERS, q.v.

1711 SWIFT *Lett.* (1767) III. 101, I still drink Dr. Radcliffe's bitter. **1711** *Vind. Sacheverell* 63 He..might.. be provok'd to mix a little Bitter with his Wine. *Mod.* Camomile yields a useful bitter.

3. (A glass of) bitter beer. *colloq.*

1857 'C. BEDE' *Verdant Green Married* x. 78 Mr. Verdant Green and Mr. Bouncer..turned into the coffee-room of 'The Mitre' to 'do bitters', as Mr. Bouncer phrased the act of drinking bitter beer. **1862** TROLLOPE *Rachel Ray* I. iii. 41 Going into Parliament..just as they pleased, like the modern heroes of the bitter cask. **1865** HOTTEN *Slang Dict.*, *Bitters*, 'to do bitters', to drink beer.— *Oxford.* **1874** *Ibid.* s.v., 'To do a bitter', to drink beer.—Originally Oxford, but now general. **1894** G. MOORE *Esther Waters* xxx. 236 A dozen pots of beer..and a few glasses of bitter. **1896** H. G. WELLS *Wheels of Chance* ix, Every public-house..meant a lemonade and a dash of bitter. *Ibid.* xviii, A lemonade and bitter, please. **1901** *Westm. Gaz.* 8 June 6/3 A bitter having been brought, he quaffed it to his second's health. **1942** *Penguin New Writing* XIV. 133 The barmaid..replied there was nothing left but bitter and old-and-mild.

C. *Comb.*: see after the *adv.*

bitter ('bɪtə(r)), *adv. arch., poet.*, and *dial.* Forms: 1-4 **bitre, bittre, bitere,** 4 **bittere, byttere,** 2- **bitter.** [OE. *bitere, bitre*, f. BITTER *a.* with which it is now identified in form.] = BITTERLY.

971 *Blickl. Hom.* 195 Hit weorþeþ þe swiþe bitere forȝolden. *a* **1300** *Sarmun* xxxvii. in *E.E.P.* (1862) 5 Þou salt hit rew bitter and sore. **1393** LANGL. *P. Pl.* C. XVII. 220 The biterour he shal a-bygge bote yf he [wel] worche. **1602** SHAKS. *Ham.* I. i. 7 'Tis bitter cold, And I am sicke at heart. **1721** CIBBER *Doub. Gallant* I. Sp. 63 [A servant says] 'my Lady's bitter young and gamesome.' **1824** CAMPBELL *Wound. Hussar*, How bitter she wept o'er the victim of war! **1886** STEVENSON *Dr. Jekyll* viii. 73 [A butler says] 'This drug is wanted bitter bad, sir.'

bitter-, *a.* and *adv.* in *combination.*

1. adverbial and parasynthetic, as ***bitter-biting*** (biting bitterly), ***bitter-blessed, -hearted, -heartedness, -pungent, -rinded, -tasted, -well.***

1749 FIELDING *Tom Jones* IV. ii, *Bitter-biting Eurus. **1786** BURNS *Daisy* iii, The *bitter-biting north. **1848** KINGSLEY *Saint's Trag.* II. xi. 135 The day I found the *bitter-blessed cross. **1775** ADAIR *Amer. Ind.* 277 *Bitter-hearted foes. *Ibid.* 43 Their word, which expresses 'sharp,' conveys the idea of *bitter-heartedness. **1884** BROWNING *Ferishtah* 3 Sage-leaf is *bitter-pungent. **1831** CARLYLE *Sart. Res.* II. ii. 107 A prickly, *bitter-rinded stone-fruit. **1850** MRS. BROWNING *Poems* II. 71 He laughed out *bitter-well.

2. (*adj.*) In many names of plants and other productions, some merely denoting a particular bitter variety of that to which the name is properly given, ***bitter almond, bitter bay, bitter beer*** (also *fig.*), ***bitter oak***; in others specifying a distinct plant or substance, as **bitter-apple** (= *bitter-gourd*); **bitter-ash**, a West Indian tree, *Simaruba excelsa*; **bitter bark**, a popular name for any of various shrubs and small trees (see quots.); **bitter-blain**, a name given by the Dutch Creoles in Guiana to *Vandellia diffusa* (Treas. Bot.); **bitter-cress**, a book-name for the genus *Cardamine*, and esp. the species *C. amara*; **bitter-cucumber** or **gourd**, the Colocynth (*Citrullus Colocynthus*), a plant of the gourd family, which furnishes a well-known cathartic drug; **bitter-cup**, a cup made of quassia wood to impart some of its bitter principle to water poured into it; **bitter-damson**, a West Indian tree, *Simaruba amara*; **bitter earth**, magnesia; **bitter-fitch** (= *bitter-vetch*); **bitter herb**, the British plant *Erythræa Centaurium*; **bitter-king**, a tree, *Soulamea amara*, of the Eastern Archipelago, excessively bitter in all its parts; **bitter-nut**, the Swamp Hickory, *Carya amara*, of North America; also ***bitter-nut hickory***; **bitter root**, a popular name for a plant of the species *Apocynum androsæmifolium*; also a plant of the N. American species *Lewisia rediviva*; (see also quot. 1909); **bitter-vetch**, a book-name for species of *Lathyrus* and *Vicia* formerly *Orobus*; †**bitter-weed**, obs. name of species of poplar, also, a N. American species of wormwood; **bitter-wood**, the timber of a tropical American genus of trees *Xylopia*, or the trees themselves; **bitter-wort**, species of gentian, esp. the Fell-wort (*G. amarella*); and in other general collocations, as **bitter-ender** *colloq.*, one who fights or holds out 'to the bitter end' (see BITTER *a.* 2b); one who refuses to yield, give way, or compromise; hence ***bitter-enderism***; **bitter pit**, a disease of apples, characterized by brown spots; †**bitter-salt**, obs. name of Epsom salts; **bitter-spar**, a mineral, a variety of dolomite; BITTER-SWEET, q.v.;

1632 MASSINGER *City Mad.* IV. ii, Quite forget their powders And *bitter almonds. **1865** *Morn. Star* 23 June, He gave the bearer half an ounce of powdered colocynth commonly called *bitter-apple. **1884** W. MILLER *Dict. Eng. Names Plants* 231/1 *Pinckneya pubens*, *bitter-bark-tree, Fever-tree of Georgia. **1889** J. H. MAIDEN *Native Plants Australia* 198 Petalostigma quadriloculare, *F.v.M.*..Bitter bark... The bark contains a very powerful bitter, said to have the same properties as cinchona. **1898** MORRIS *Austral Eng.* 31/2 *Bitter-bark*, an Australian tree, *Petalostigma quadriloculare*,..N.O. *Euphorbiaceæ*... The name is also applied to *Tabernæmontana orientalis*..N.O. *Apocyneæ*, and to *Alstonia constricta*..N.O. *Apocyneæ*. **1955** *Times* 26 May 9/2 *Alstonia constricta*, or 'bitter bark', a new source of supply of the drug known as 'reserpine'... Supplies have also been found in the roots of 'bitter barks' grown in India. **1755** SMOLLETT *Quix.* (1803) I. 98 Crowned with garlands of cypress and *bitter-bay. **1850** THACKERAY *Pendennis* II. xx. 200 The *bitter beer hot and undrinkable. **1871** M. COLLINS *Mrq. & Merch.* I. vi. 161, I supped on..cold beef and bitter beer. **1890** KIPLING *Barrack-r. Ballads* (1892) 4 'I've drunk 'is beer a score o' times,' said Files-on-Parade. ''E's drinkin' bitter beer alone,' the Colour-Sergeant said. **1876** HARLEY *Mat. Med.* 675 *Bitter cups turned out of the wood are used as a ready means of furnishing the infusion. **1850** *Congress. Globe* 12 Mar., App. 303 The disunionist looks forward to a southern confederacy; the *bitter-ender to the triumph of his party. **1906** H. SPENDER *General Botha* vii. 127 In these discussions their leaders still proved the most obstinate 'Bitter-enders'—just as now..they still resist most obstinately the mingling of their racial influence with that of the British stock. **1926** *Contemp. Rev.* June 687 The trade union world lies shattered and in ruins [after the General Strike]. There is fierce controversy between volunteers, 'scabs', 'hands-uppers', and 'bitter-enders'. **1918** *N.Y. Times* 15 Sept. III. 2/1 An unreasoning '*bitter enderism'. **1551** TURNER *Herbal* P iv a, *Bitter fitches, or bitter tares. **1585** LLOYD *Treas. Health* G iv, Decoctyon of Lichepeasen or bitterfitch. **1755** *Gentl. Mag.* XXV. 408 If we plant cucumbers..near the *bitter-gourd, the fruits of the first will be as bitter as gall. **1810** MICHAUX *Arbres* I. 19 *Bitter nut hickory.., seul nom en usage dans N.Y. **1832** D. J. BROWNE *Sylva Amer.* 170 This species is generally known in New Jersey by the name of Bitternut Hickory. *Ibid.*, The inhabitants of New Jersey give it the name of Bitternut, which..indicates one of the peculiar properties of the fruit. **1898** *Agric. Gaz. N.S. Wales* I. 683 **Bitter Pit.* This disease appears in the form of small sunken brown pits having a bitter taste. **1960** *New Scientist* 24 Nov. 1392/3 The incidence of bitter pit [in Australia]..has been reduced in a spectacular manner by spraying with calcium salts. **1838** S. PARKER *Expl. Tour* 204 The racine amère, or *bitter root, which grows on dry ground, fusiform, and though not pleasant to the taste, yet it is very conducive to health. **1909** *Cent. Dict.* Suppl. 138/3 *Natal bitter root*, a climbing vine of the gourd family, *Gerrardanthus macrorhiza*, having tuberous roots..which are intensely bitter and are used by the natives in medicine. *a* **1918** G. STUART *40 Years on Frontier* (1925) I. 178 The wild flax and bitter-root are in full bloom. **1945** B. MACDONALD *Egg & I* (1946) 18 The bitter-root daisies, the Montana State flower. **1843** PORTLOCK *Geol.* 214 *Bitter spar, or Brown spar, occurs in small but well-defined crystals. **1661** LOVELL *Hist. Anim. & Min.* 44 The simples are Vineger, Betony..*bitter vetch with Wine. **1878** in BRITTEN & HOLL. *Plant-n.* 45 Fir, saugh, and *bitterweed. **1597** GERARD *Herbal* c. §4. 352 Named in English Felwoort Gentian; *Bitterwoort; Baldmoyne, and Baldmoney.

†'**bitter,** *sb.*^{2} *Obs.* [f. BIT *sb.*^{3} + -ER^{1}.] One who has charge of a 'bit' or fire-bucket; a fireman.

c **1467** *E.E. Gilds* 371 That the Bitters be redy when eny parylle of fuyre ys. *Ibid.* 382 That the bitters be redy with hur horses and bittes to brynge water.

'**bitter,** *sb.*^{3} *Naut.* [f. BITT + -ER (prob. as in *header, rounder, cropper, whopper*).] (See quots.)

1627 CAPT. SMITH *Seaman's Gram.* vii. 30 A Bitter is but the turne of a Cable about the Bits, and veare it out by little and little. And the Bitters end is that part of the Cable doth stay within boord. **1630** J. TAYLOR *Wks.* (N.) To let fall an anchor, which being done, the tide running very strong, brought our ship to so strong a bitter, that the fast which the Portugals had upon us brake. **1867** SMYTH *Sailor's Word-bk.* 103 A ship is 'brought up to a bitter' when the cable is allowed to run out to that stop..When a chain or rope is paid out to the bitter-end, no more remains to be let go.

Hence, perh. *bitter end*: but cf. BITTER *a.* 2b.

bitter ('bɪtə(r)), *v.*^{1} [ME. *bitt(e)re(n*:—OE. *biterian*, f. *biter*, BITTER *a.*; = OHG. *bittaren*, MHG. *bittern* to be bitter.]

†**1.** *intr.* To be or become bitter. (Only in OE.)

897 K. ÆLFRED *Gregory's Past.* 425 Ðætte us biteriȝe sio hreowsung.

2. *trans.* To make bitter; *fig.* to embitter (*obs.*).

c **1175** *Lamb. Hom.* 23 A lutel ater bittere[h] muchele swete. *a* **1225** *Ancr. R.* 308 Uour þinges, ȝif me þencheð.. muwen makien him to seoruwen, & bittren his heorte. *a* **1619** FOTHERBY *Atheom.* I. xii. §5 (1622) 132 Men in sad taking, bitter[d] with affliction. **1622** H. SYDENHAM *Serm. Sol. Occ.* (1637) 309 Shall I bitter vertue, & sweeten vice? **1713** *Lond. & Country Brew.* I. (1742) 7 Such hasty Dryings, or Scorchings, are also apt to bitter the Malt. **1815** *Encycl. Brit.* (ed. 5) IV. 131 This plant [Bog-bean] is used in the north of Europe to bitter the ale.

bitterbump, var. of BUTTERBUMP, bittern.

†'**bitterful,** *a. Obs.* [f. BITTER *sb.* + -FUL.] Full of bitterness.

a **1500** *Lament. Mary Magd.* 53 (Chaucer's Wks.) Remembryng this bitterfull departing. **1552** HULOET, Bytterful, or full of bytternes. **1618** *Sheph. Cal.* (1656) xlviii, Pilate condemned him to the most bitterfull death.

†'**bitterhede, biterhede.** *Obs.* [f. BITTER + *-hede*, -HEAD: cf. Da. *bitterhed.*] = BITTERNESS.

1340 *Ayenb.* 28 Þe mouþ of þe enuious is uol of corsinge and of biterhede.

'**bittering,** *sb.* [f. BITTER + -ING^{1}.] A preparation used to adulterate beer; = BITTERN *sb.*^{2} 2.

1864 in WEBSTER.

bitterish ('bɪtərɪʃ), *a.* Rather or somewhat bitter. Hence '**bitterishness** *sb.*

1605 TIMME *Quersit.* II. vii. 141 The bitterish Guaiacum. **1684** BUNYAN *Pilgr.* II. 194 The Water..tasted a little Bitterish to the Palat. **1849-52** TODD *Cycl. Anat. & Phys.* IV. 858/1 A slightly bitterish sensation is produced. **1702** FLOYER in *Phil. Trans.* XXIII. 1164 Its..taste, which is crude and styptic, with a bitterishness in the Seed.

bitterling ('bɪtəlɪŋ). [G., f. *bitter* BITTER *a.* (transl. L. *amārus*) + *-ling*, -LING^{1}.] A small carp-like freshwater fish, *Rhodeus amarus*, of Central Europe.

1880 GÜNTHER *Fishes* 601 The European species is known in Germany by the name of 'Bitterling'. **1911** *Encycl. Brit.* XX. 794/2 *Rhodeus amarus*, the bitterling,..injects its eggs into the mantle-cavity of pond-mussels, where the fry develop. **1959** J. CLEGG *Freshwater Life Brit. Isles* (ed. 2) xvi. 266 The Bitterling..uses one species [of mussel] in particular, the Painter's Mussel..as a nursery for its young.

bitterly ('bɪtəlɪ), *adv.* [ME. *bit(t)erliche, -like*, OE. *biterlíce*, f. *biter*, BITTER *a.* + *-líce, -liche*, -LY^{2}.] In a bitter manner; with bitterness. (See the senses of BITTER *a.*)

c **1000** *Ags. Gosp.* Matt. xxvi. 75 Petrus..eode ut, and weop biterlice [*v.r.* bytyrlice]. *c* **1200** ORMIN 9726 Forrþi toc Johan wiþþ hemm Full bitterrliȝ to mælenn. *c* **1250** *Gen. & Ex.* 3896 Hem cam wirm-kin among, ðat hem wel bitterlike stong. *c* **1275** *Serving Christ* 56 in *O.E. Misc.* 92 Hwo ysayh euer blisse byterluker ibouht. *c* **1400** *Gamelyn* 198 And bigan bitterly his hondes for to wrynge. *c* **1440** *Bone Flor.* 1628 A scharpe knyfe..That bytterly wolde byte. **1593** SHAKS. *Rich. II*, I. iv. 7 The Northeast wind Which then grew bitterly against our face. **1611** BIBLE *Ruth* i. 20 For the Almightie hath dealt very bitterly with me. **1709** ADDISON *Tatler* No. 152 ¶12 Achilles is not more bitterly lamented among us than you. **1847** GROTE *Greece* II. xlv. (1862) IV. 94 Exiles..bitterly hostile to Athens. **1856** FROUDE *Hist. Eng.* (1858) I. iii. 265 He complained bitterly of the Italians. **1865** TROLLOPE *Belton Est.* xxii. 263 It came on to rain bitterly,—a cold piercing February rain.

bittern ('bɪtən), *sb.*^{1} Forms: α. 4 **botor, -ur(e,** 5 **botore, -oore, -owre, butturre, -ir,** 5-7 **butor,** 6 **buttour, buttur, -our, buture,** 7 **bewter, boter.** β. **bitoure, biture,** 4-5 **bi-, bytore, betoure,** 5 **betore, -owre, bytturre,** 5-7 **bittor,** 6 **bi-, bytture, bittarde, byture, byter, bytter,** 6-7 **bitter, bitour, byttour,** 6-8 **bittour,** 7 **byttur.** γ. 6 **bittorn,** 7 **bitturn, -erne, -orne,** 7- **bittern.** (Also *dial.* 7- *bitterbump*, BUTTERBUMP.) [ME. *botor*, a. OF. *butor*, of obscure origin, perhaps related to rare L. *būtiōn-em* in same sense. (The med.L. *butorius, bitorius* are f. the mod. langs.) The Eng. forms in *byt-, bit-* prob. represent Fr. *ü*. The Fr. had a fem. *butorde*, with which cf. 16th c. Eng. *bittarde*. The final *-n* in 16th c. *bittorn*, mod. *bittern*, is due to some mistaken analogy: cf. *alder, aldern, elder, eldern*, etc. The mod.L. zoological name *botaurus*, is an adaptation of the OF. and ME. *botor*, with a reference to a fanciful derivation from *bos taurus, taurus* being applied by Pliny (x. xlii), to a bird that bellows like an ox, and the bittern being called *taureau d'etang, boeuf de marais, meerrind, moosochse*, and similar names in many langs.]

A genus of grallatorial birds (*Botaurus*), nearly allied to the herons, but smaller. *spec.* The species *B. stellaris*, a native of Europe and the adjoining parts of the Old World, but now rare in Great Britain on account of the disappearance of the marshes which it frequents. It is noted for the 'boom' which it utters during the breeding season, whence its popular names *mire-drum*, and *bull of the bog*, and the scientific term *botaurus* (see above). With qualifying adj., as **American bittern**, *Botaurus lentiginosus* of N. America; **least bittern**, *Ixobrychus exilis* of N. America; **little bittern**, any of several small bitterns of the genus *Ixobrychus*; **sun bittern** (see SUN *sb.*^{1} 13b).

α, β. [*c* **1000** in Wr.-Wülcker *Voc.* 131 *Bitorius, pintorus*, wrenna. (App. some mistake.)] *c* **1330** *Arth. & Merl.* 3130 Swannes, pecokes and botors. *c* **1386** CHAUCER *Wife's T.* 116 As a Bitore [*v.r.* bytore, bitor, betoure] bombleth in the Myre. **1388** WYCLIF *Isa.* xiii. 22 And bitouris [**1382** ȝellende foules; *Vulg.* ululæ; **1611** wild beasts of the islands] schulen answere there. *c* **1420** *Liber Cocorum* (1862) 35 To wodcok, snype, curlue also, The betore in fere with hom schalle goo. *c* **1430** LYDG. *Min. Poems* (1840) 202 The botoore that etith the greet eel. **1486** *Bk. St. Alban's* F vj. A Sege of betouris. *a* **1529** SKELTON *Ph. Sparowe* 432 The bitter with his bumpe. **1530** PALSGR. 202/1 Buttour a byrde, *butor.* **1533-4** *Act 25 Hen. VIII*, xi. §5 Euery egge of euery bittour, heroune, or shoulearde. *viiid.* **1543** TRAHERON *Vigo's Chirurg.* II. ix. 42 Cranes, geese, bittardes. **1627** P. FLETCHER *Locusts* I. viii, Their hoarse-base-hornes like fenny Bittours sound. **1646** SIR T. BROWNE *Pseud. Ep.* III. xxv. §4 That a Bittor maketh that mugient noyse, or as we terme it Bumping by putting its bill into a reed.

γ. **1515** BARCLAY *Eglog.* ii, The partriche, plover, bittorn and heronsewe. **1611** BIBLE *Isa.* xxiv. 11 The cormorant and the bitterne shall possesse it. **1638** SUCKLING *Aglaura* III. i, A Bittorne whooping in a reed is better music. **1641** J. JACKSON *True Evang. T.* iii. 209 The Hawk hath struck down the Bitturn. **1770** GOLDSM. *Des. Vill.* 44 The hollow-sounding bittern guards its nest. **1776** T. PENNANT *Brit. Zool.* II. 537 The Little Bittern..was shot as it perched on

one of the trees in the Quarry or public walks in Shrewsbury. **1810** SCOTT *Lady of L.* I. xxxi, And the bittern sound his drum, Booming from the sedgy shallow. **1813** WILSON *Amer. Ornith.* VIII. 35 American Bittern, *Ardea Minor*.. is another nocturnal species, common to all our sea and river marshes. *Ibid.* 37 Least Bittern: *Ardea exilis*.. is commonly found in fresh water meadows. **1831** Least bittern [see LEAST *a.* 1 c]. *a* **1857** LONGF. *Sunr. on Hills* 18 The noisy bittern wheeled his.. way. **1957** BANNERMAN *Birds Brit. Isles* VI. 115 It seems to be generally conceded that the whole European population of little bitterns winters in Africa. *Ibid.* 134 *American bittern*.. An Accidental Visitor which has occurred about fifty times in Britain.

bittern ('bɪtən), *sb.*[2] [f. BITTER *a.* (perh. dial. form of *bittering*).]

1. The mother water or lye which remains after the crystallization of common salt from sea-water or the brine of salt-springs. It contains sulphate and chloride of magnesium, bromine, iodine, etc.

1682 COLLINS *Salt in Eng.* 54 The Bittern in Refining of French Salt, is a Liquor separated from it, that resembles Sack in Colour, but Gall in Tast. **1810** HENRY *Elem. Chem.* I. 415 The uncrystallizable part called bittern. **1879** G. GLADSTONE *Salt* in *Cassell's Techn. Educ.* IV. 354 The deliquescent and non-crystallisable ingredients constitute.. the bitterns which drain from the stacks of sea salt. **1883** *Knowledge* 15 June 354/2 The.. bittern is employed as a source from which other substances are prepared, as.. bromine.

b. *attrib.*

1755 HALES in *Phil. Trans.* XLIX. 327 The saline spirit arises chiefly from the bittern salt. **1772** MONRO *ibid.* LXII. 30 Sea salt mixed with a bittern and oily matter.

2. A name applied to bitter substances used for different purposes; *spec.* (also *bitterin*, *bittering*) an old trade name for a mixture of quassia and other drugs employed in adulterating beer.

1775 ADAIR *Amer. Ind.* 403 The water is sufficiently impregnated with the intoxicating bittern.

bitterness ('bɪtənɪs). [OE. *biternys*, f. *biter*, BITTER + -NESS.] The quality or state of being bitter: **a.** to taste; **b.** to the mind or feelings; **c.** deep sorrow or anguish of heart; **d.** animosity, acrimony of temper, action, or words; **e.** intensity of frost or cold wind.

971 *Blickl. Hom.* 115 þes middanȝeard flyhþ from us mid mycelre biternesse. *c* **1000** ÆLFRIC *Ex.* xv. 23 Mara.. þæt ys on ure Lyden biternys. *c* **1200** *Trin. Coll. Hom.* 45 Mirre for ure biternesse. **1382** WYCLIF *Isa.* xxxviii. 15 In the bitternesse of my soule. —— *Rom.* iii. 14 The mouth of whom is ful of cursyng, *or wariyng*, and bitternesse. **1477** EARL RIVERS (Caxton) *Dictes* 68 The bittrenesse of the aloe tre. **1535** COVERDALE *1 Sam.* xv. 32 Thus departeth the bytternesse of death. **1597** SHAKS. *2 Hen. IV*, I. ii. 198 You measure the heat of our Liuers with the bitternes of your gals. **1617** MARKHAM *Caval.* I. 4 All the bitternesse and sharpenesse.. of the Winter. **1711** STEELE *Spect.* No. 262 ¶6 The Bitterness of Party. **1732** ARBUTHNOT *Rules of Diet* i. 249 A small degree of Bitterness, extremely agreeable to the Stomach. **1814** SCOTT *Wav.* xxxiii, A sentiment of bitterness rose in his mind against the government. **1851** DIXON *W. Penn* xxvi. (1872) 237 A prince who had tasted the bitterness of persecution.

†**f.** *concr.* A trait of bitterness, anything bitter.

1382 WYCLIF *Job* xiii. 26 Thou writist aȝen me bitternessis [**1611** bitter things]. **1790** G. WALKER *Serm.* II. xx. 104 The disappointments, vexations, and bitternesses of life.

bitters ('bɪtəz), *sb. pl.* [f. BITTER *sb.*[1]] **1.** Bitter medicines generally, as Peruvian bark, quinine, etc.; *spec.* alcoholic (or other) liquors, impregnated with the extract of gentian, quassia, wormwood, orange peel, etc. and used as stomachics, anthelmintics, etc. (Also in singular: see BITTER *sb.*[1] 2.)

1713 *Guardian* No. 131 (1756) II. 188 Two hogsheads of bitters. **1784** J. SIMS in *Med. Commun.* I. 422 He took vomits, purgatives and bitters. **1822** J. FLINT *Lett. Amer.* 54 Some Americans drinking their morning's bitters (spirits with rice, wormwood, or other vegetable infusion). **1880** *New Syd. Soc. Lex.* s.v. *Bitters*, Medicinal substances.. distinguished into the aromatic, pure, and styptic bitters.

2. *fig.*, esp. in *U.S.* colloq. phr. ***to get one's bitters***: to get one's deserts. *Obs.*

1812 in *Maryland Hist. Mag.* (1914) IX. 70 You might get your bitters in Baltimore Town. **1836** HOR. SMITH *Tin Trump.* I. 16 Misfortunes are moral bitters, which frequently restore the healthy tone of the mind. *a* **1846** in W. T. Porter *Quarter Race Ky.* (1846) 194 The seal soon got his bitters, and the captin cut a big hunk off the tail eend.

bitter-sweet ('bɪtəswiːt), *a.* and *sb.*

A. *adj.* Sweet with an admixture or aftertaste of bitterness. *fig.* agreeable or pleasant with an alloy of pain or unpleasantness.

1611 COTGR., *Amer-doux*, a bitter-sweet apple. **1633** ROWLEY *Match Midn.* in *O. Pl.* VIII. 373 (N.) Till then adieu, you bitter-sweet one. **1641** MAISTERTON *Serm.* 18 Bitter-sweet delights, or pleasures mixt with pain. **1749** FIELDING *Tom Jones* v. iii, To compose a draught that might be termed bitter-sweet. **1855** BRIMLEY *Ess.* 92 It awakes all the fountains of bitter-sweet memory.

B. *sb.*

1. A thing which is bitter-sweet; sweetness or pleasure alloyed with bitterness.

1386 CHAUCER *Chan. Yeom.* Prol. & T. 325 Vn-to hem it is a bitter-swete. **1627** FELTHAM *Resolves* 295 'Tis something like Love, a kinde of bitter-sweet. **1878** SYMONDS *Sonn. M. Angelo* xl, A bitter-sweet sways here and there my mind.

2. A kind of apple.

1393 GOWER *Conf.* III. 281 Lich unto the bitter swete, For though it thenke a man first swete, He shall well felen ate laste, That it is soure. **1483** *Cath. Angl.* 33 A Bittyrswete, *amarimellum, musceum.* **1552** HULOET, Apple called a bytter swete, *amarimellum.* **1727** BRADLEY *Fam. Dict.* s.v. *Cyder*, The best sort of Cyder.. made of.. the Bitter-sweet.

3. *Herb.* The Woody Nightshade, *Solanum Dulcamara*, a common shrubling plant in Britain. (A translation by Turner of the med.Latin name.)

1568 TURNER *Herbal* III. 2. **1597** GERARD *Herbal* lviii. 278 Bitter sweete bringeth foorth wooddie stalks as doth the Vine. **1671** SALMON *Syn. Med.* III. xxii. 390 Bittersweet helps the Jaundies. **1821** CLARE *Vill. Minstr.* II. 198 Ramping woodbines and blue bitter-sweet. **1882** *Times* 6 July 10/4 The bitter-sweet is a twining shrub with scarlet berries.

† '**bitter-,sweeting.** *Obs.* [f. prec. + -ING[1].] The Bitter-sweet Apple. (In Shaks. allusively.)

1592 SHAKS. *Rom. & Jul.* II. iv. 83 Thy wit is a very Bitter-sweeting, It is a most sharpe sawce.

bittil(l, bittle, obs. forms of BEETLE.

bitting ('bɪtɪŋ), *vbl. sb.*[1] [f. BIT *v.* + -ING[1].] The putting of the bit in a horse's mouth.

1611 COTGR., *Embouchement*.. the bitting, or bridling of a horse. **1833** *Regul. Instr. Cavalry* I. 83 On first bitting, the bridoon is to be used.

Comb. **bitting-rigging** (*Saddlery*), a bridle, surcingle, back-strap, and a crupper placed on young horses to give them a good bearing. (Knight.)

'**bitting,** *vbl. sb.*[2] *Naut.* [f. BITT *v.* + -ING[1].]

1769 FALCONER *Dict. Marine* (1789), *Tour de bitte au cable*, a turn of the cable about the bits; the bitting of a cable.

† '**bittlock.** *Obs.* [f. BIT *sb.*: the rest is doubtful; cf. next, for which it may be an error.] A fragment, a small piece.

? *a* **1400** *Chester Pl.* I. 124 [Call] after Trowle And byde hym some of our bittlockes.

bittock ('bɪtək). *north. dial.* [f. BIT *sb.* + -OCK, dim. suffix.] A little bit, a small piece or portion.

1802 J. WILSON (Congleton) *MS. Let. to J. Boucher*, *Bittock*, a small Piece or small Bit; *Cheshire.* **1815** SCOTT *Guy M.* i, The 'three mile' diminished into 'like a mile and a bittock.' **1818** —— *Rob Roy* xviii, 'My ain parish of Dreepdaily, that lies a bittock farther to the west.'

bittonie, -y, obs. forms of BETONY.

bittor, -our, etc., obs. ff. BITTERN, the bird.

bitts, *sb. Naut.*: see BITT *sb.*

bitty ('bɪtɪ), *a.* [f. BIT *sb.*[2] + -Y[1].]

1. Made up of little bits (used disparagingly); consisting of (too many) unrelated parts; scrappy.

1892 *Idler* May 484 It is an awful thing to be shut up for a week with all the 'bitty' papers of the day. *c* **1909** in C. W. Cunnington *Eng. Women's Clothes* (1952) iii. 91 The bitty dress is entirely relegated to the mercantile mind. **1924** N. COWARD *Rat Trap* II. p. 30 She doesn't dress smartly enough—too bitty. **1928** *B.B.C. Handbk.* 71/2 At the risk of the programme being called 'bitty' by sections of the audience with specially marked and developed tastes—it is necessary to compound the programmes.. of diverse elements. **1952** E. R. JANES *Flower Garden* 31 Unless there is enough width, a double path.. gives a bitty appearance. **1963** *Times* 18 May 5/7 The costumes are gaudier.. and the whole thing is rather bitty.

2. Covered with or containing bits or scraps (of a material).

1902 *Little Folks* Jan. 58/2 'Oh Ted; you are *bitty*!' she remarked.. while she.. picked off the shavings that clung to his clothes. **1953** *Gloss. Paint Terms* (*B.S.I.*) 5 *Bitty*, a description applied to paints or varnishes containing bits of skin or flocculated material which project above the surface when the paint or varnish is applied.

3. = BITSY *a.* *U.S. colloq.*

1905 *Dialect Notes* III. 87 They was little-bitty fellers. **1908** *Ibid.* 291. **1940** R. CHANDLER *Farewell, My Lovely* x. 78 That toy... It's just a little bitty gun, a butterfly gun.

So '**bittiness**, the state of being bitty, scrappiness.

1950 M. PEAKE *Gormenghast* 182 Unknown to her the 'bittiness' that resulted gave to the salon a certain informality far from her intentions. **1957** R. HOGGART *Uses of Literacy* vii. 179 Little tablets of curious information are scattered throughout... This is bittiness run riot.

bitueiȝen, var. form of BITWIHEN, betwixt.

bituen, -tuex, -twix, obs. ff. BETWEEN, -TWIXT.

bituȝen, pa. pple. of BETEE *v.* *Obs.*

Bitumastic (,bɪtjʊ'mæstɪk). Also **bitumastic.** [Trade-name.] A protective coating (see quot. 1889). Also *attrib.* or as *adj.*

1889 *Trade Marks Jrnl.* 23 Jan. 77 *Bitumastic.* Asphaltic and Composite Paints for Protecting from Corrosion the interior parts of Iron or Steel Ships.. Bridges, and other structures of Iron and Steel. **1933** *Archit. Rev.* LXXIII. p. liv (Advt.), The flat roofs are constructed from.. bitumastic felt sheeting. **1940** *Manch. Guardian Weekly* 12 Apr. 292 The enameller did not take sufficient care to see that the test cock hole was kept clear of bitumastic. **1960** *Farmer & Stockbreeder* 19 Jan. Suppl. 19/2 Painting houses with bitumastic paint greatly helps to keep them clean and free from pests.

†**bitume,** *v.* *Obs. rare.* [f. *bitume*, obs. form of BITUMEN.] To smear or spread with bitumen.

1601 SHAKS. *Per.* III. i. 72 We have a chest beneath the hatches, caulk'd and bitumed ready. *Ibid.* III. ii. 56 How close 'tis caulk'd and bitumed [*Other edd.* bottomed].

bitumen (bɪ'tjuːmɪn, 'bɪtjʊmɪn). Forms: 5 **bithumen, bethyn,** (**betune**), 6 **betumen,** 7 **bitamen, bitum(e, bittumen, bytumen,** 6– **bitumen.** [a. L. *bitūmen* (stem *bitūmin-*). Cf. F. and It. *bitume*, Pg. *betume*, Pr. *betum*, Sp. *betun*, from which some of the obs. Eng. forms were taken.]

1. Originally, a kind of mineral pitch found in Palestine and Babylon, used as mortar, etc. The same as asphalt, mineral pitch, Jew's pitch, *Bitumen judaicum.*

1460 CAPGRAVE *Chron.* 30 A vessel of wykyris, filled the joyntis with tow erde, cleped bithumen. **1480** CAXTON *Ovid's Met.* xv. iv, The.. bethyn & sulphur brennyng. **1577** J. FRAMPTON *Joyf. Newes* 6 Betumen which is a kind of Pitch. **1601** HOLLAND *Pliny* I. 101 Asphaltites, or the lake of Sodom.. bringeth forth nothing but Bitumen. **1609** BIBLE (Douay) *Gen.* vi. 14 Thou.. shalt pitch it [the arke] within, and without with bitume. **1610** HOLLAND *Camden's Brit.* I. 519 Coles, being of the nature of hardned Bitamen. **1656** BLOUNT *Glossogr.*, *Bitume*, a kind of clay or slime naturally clammy, like pitch, growing in some Countries of Asia. **1817** BYRON *Manfred* I. i. 90 The lakes of bitumen Rise boilingly higher. **1849** GROTE *Greece* II. lxx. (1862) VI. 239 [The Wall of Media] was of bricks cemented with bitumen.

2. a. In modern scientific use, the generic name of certain mineral inflammable substances, native hydrocarbons more or less oxygenated, liquid, semi-solid, and solid, including naphtha, petroleum, asphalt, etc. ***elastic bitumen***: mineral caoutchouc or Elaterite.

1605 TIMME *Quersit.* I. xiii. 52 There are also manie kindes of.. bitumen. **1635** SWAN *Spec. M.* vi. (1643) 297 Naphtha, is a liquid Bitume. **1677** MOXON *Mech. Exerc.* (1703) 243 Morter used.. at Rome.. called Maltha, from a kind of Bitumen Dug there. **1835** *Penny Cycl.* IV. 473/2 Elastic bitumen is soft and elastic like caoutchouc. **1857** PAGE *Adv. Text-bk. Geol.* xx. (1876) 441 The bitumens—naphtha, petroleum, asphalt—have been long known and used in the arts.

b. ***the bitumen***: a tarred road; *spec.* the road from Darwin to Alice Springs. *Austral. colloq.*

1953 BAKER *Australia Speaks* v. 137 *One for the bitumen*, a final round of drinks, i.e. 'one for the road'. **1954** B. MILES *Stars my Blanket* xxv. 219 We had not seen another vehicle since we turned off the bitumen at Elliott. **1958** A. J. TOYNBEE *East to West* xiv. 44 'The bitumen', running dead straight for hundreds of miles without a swerve, is an impressive symbol of the modern world. **1963** V. B. CRANLEY *27,000 Miles through Australia* ii. 19 The minute you left the 'bitumen', as tarred roads are called here, you were back in the bush.

3. A pigment prepared from asphalt.

1855 J. EDWARDS *Paint. in Oil* 26 *Bitumen*.. is Asphaltum ground in strong drying oil.. for the painter's use.

†**4.** Used by Turner, for the sap of the birch-tree.

1551 TURNER *Herbal* (1568) F v b, The frenche men seth out of it a certain iuce or suc otherwise called bitumen.

5. *attrib.* **bitumen process**, a photographic process using a metal plate coated with bitumen which is rendered insoluble by the action of light.

1816 SHELLEY *Alastor* 85 Bitumen lakes. **1837** CARLYLE *Fr. Rev.* III. III. i. 150 Here lay the bitumen stratum, there the brimstone one. **1858** T. SUTTON *Dict. Photogr.* 329 Mr. Macpherson is not the *inventor* of the bitumen process; M. Nicéphore Niépce first used bitumen in photography. **1960** A. L. M. SOWERBY *Dict. Photogr.* (ed. 19) 40 Half-tone or Process Blocks by the Bitumen Process. A copper or zinc plate is coated with bitumen, and it is exposed... After development, or the removal of the superfluous bitumen, the plate is etched.

bitumene ('bɪtjʊmiːn). *Chem.* [f. BITUM-EN + -ENE, suffix of the hydrocarbon class.] Name given by Berthelet to the least volatile of the hydrocarbons obtained by passing benzene vapour through a red-hot porcelain tube. Watts *Dict. Chem.*

1873 FOWNES *Chem.* 758 Bitumene, a blackish liquid, remains in the retort at a dull red heat, and solidifies on cooling.

bituminate (bɪ'tjuːmɪneɪt), *v.* [f. L. *bitūmināt-* ppl. stem of *bitūmināre*, to treat with BITUMEN.] Hence **bi'tuminated** *ppl. a.*

†**1.** *trans.* To cement with bitumen (as mortar).

1628 FELTHAM *Resolves* I. xlvi. (R.) The bituminated walls of Babylon. **1656** BLOUNT *Glossogr.*, *Bituminated*, soldered or done with bitumen.

2. To convert into or impregnate with bitumen.

1799 KIRWAN *Geol. Ess.* vi. 294 Trees carbonated, or bituminated sometimes repose on Coal. *Ibid.* 297 A bituminated clay. *Ibid.* 319 This carbonaceous part would never be bituminated and converted into coal if real bitumen were not present.

bituminiferous (bɪˌtjuːmɪˈnɪfərəs), *a.* [f. L. *bitūmin-* + -(I)FEROUS.] Yielding bitumen.

1799 KIRWAN *Geol. Ess.* xiv. 259 Bituminiferous and Cupriferous Sand. **1857** PAGE *Adv. Text-bk. Geol.* xiv. (1876) 251 Caking or coking coal, a highly bituminiferous sort.

bituminization (bɪˌtjuːmɪnaɪˈzeɪʃən). Also **bitumenization.** [f. next + -ATION.] The process or state of conversion into bitumen.

1804 in *Phil. Trans.* XCIV. 407 The process of bituminization (if I may be allowed to employ such a term). **1884** *Harper's Mag.* Mar. 522/1 Hard jet is of two distinct formations, being both wood and petroleum, now in a high state of bitumenization.

bituminize (bɪˈtjuːmɪnaɪz), *v.* Also **bitumenize.** [f. L. *bitumin-* + -IZE.] *trans.* To convert into, or impregnate with, bitumen; to cover or varnish with bitumen. Hence **biˈtuminized, biˌtumiˈnizing** *ppl. adjs.*

1751 STACK in *Phil. Trans.* XLVII. 273 Wax bituminized by burning. **1816** *Edin. Rev.* XXVI. 165 Trunks of bituminized wood. **1854** H. MILLER *Footpr. Creat.* x. (1874) 193 Injured by compression or the bitumenizing process. **1861** GLADSTONE in *Times* 3 May 6/3 This is a bitumenized pipe.

bituminoid (bɪˈtjuːmɪnɔɪd), *a.* [f. as prec. + -OID.] Approaching the character of bitumen.

1878 GREEN *Coal* v. 167 It differs very widely from the adjoining bituminoid portions.

†**biˌtumiˈnose,** *a.* ? *Obs.* [ad. L. *bitūminōsus,* f. *bitūmin-* BITUMEN: see -OSE.] = BITUMINOUS.

1691 RAY *Creation* (1714) 87 They [the waters] are.. bituminose.

bituminous (bɪˈtjuːmɪnəs), *a.* Also 7 -enous. [a. F. *bitumineux,* ad. L. *bitūminōs-us*: see -OUS.]

1. Of the nature of or resembling bitumen, consisting of or containing bitumen. (Sometimes with reference to the 'burning lake' of Hell.)

1620 VENNER *Via Recta* Introd. 8 Which rise from sulphurous, bituminous, or metalline places. **1649** JER. TAYLOR *Gt. Exemp.* II. x. 133 The liquid flames of pitch and a bituminous bath. **1667** MILTON *P.L.* XII. 41 The Plain, wherein a black bituminous gurge Boiles out from under ground, the mouth of Hell. **1774** J. BRYANT *Mythol.* I. 279 In Seleucia..there was a like bituminous eruption. **1826** SCOTT *Woodst.* xvi, Others swore they had smelt savours of various kinds, chiefly bituminous **1830** M. DONOVAN *Dom. Econ.* I. 135 This coal..has a bituminous fracture.

b. *spec.* in the scientific or technical names of various minerals, manufactures, etc., as ***bituminous coal, limestone, schist, shale; cement, mastic.***

1830 LYELL *Princ. Geol.* I. 219 Bituminous shales. **1842** MILLER *O.R. Sandst.* ii. (ed. 2) 55 Dark-coloured bituminous schist. **1875** URE *Dict. Arts* I. 755 The bituminous or black cement for bottle-corks consists of pitch hardened by the addition of resin and brick-dust. *Ibid.* III. 119 Bituminous limestone..containing various hydrocarbon compounds, diffusing by the action of fire a bituminous odour. **1879** *Cassell's Techn. Educ.* I. 67 Bituminous coals..burn..with a brilliant flame.

†**2.** ? Cemented with bitumen. *Obs.*

1658 J. BURBERY *Christina Q. Swedl.* 112 The walls..are strong and bituminous and abound with ancient towers.

3. *fig.* (Cf. *sulphurous.*)

1878 *N. Amer. Rev.* 329 It is only about a hundred years since Jonathan Edwards dropped his bituminous rhetoric upon the tender sensibilities of the unconverted.

†**biˈtun,** *v. Obs.* Forms: 1 betýnan, 2–3 bitun(en, -tuinen(*ü*). [OE., f. *bi-* BE- + *týnan* (:—*OTeut. *tûnian*), f. *tún* enclosure, TOWN; cf. Du. *betuinen,* OHG. *bizûnen,* MHG. *beziunen.*] *trans.* To enclose; to shut up.

c **1000** *Ags. Gosp.* Matt. xxi. 33 Sum hiredes ealdor wæs, se plantode win-ȝerd, and betynde hyne. *c* **1175** *Lamb. Hom.* 83 Þe muchele lauerd..bitunde him solue in ane meidenes inneþe. *a* **1225** *Ancr. R.* 164 Ancren wise, þet habbeð wel bituned ham aȝein þe helle leun. **1250** LAY. 19191 Ȝe þisne castel; bituneþ swiþe faste.

biturn(en, obs. form of BETURN.

bituxe(n, -tweoxe, -twixe(n, -twuxe, variants of BETWIXEN *prep. Obs.*

†**biˈtweies,** *prep. Obs.* [ME. for **bitwihes,* **bitwiȝes,* f. *bitwih, betweoh* + genitival *-es*: it is the *-es* form corresponding to *bitueiȝ-en*: see BITWIHEN.] = BETWIXT, BETWEEN.

c **1300** *Thrush & Night.* 7 in Hazl. *E.P.P.* 50 Hic herde a strif bitweies two.

†**bitwih,** *prep. Obs.* [OE. Anglian *bi-, betwih,* Saxon *betwīh, -tweoh, -twuh, -tuh, -twioh, -twyh,* f. *bi-,* BE *prep.* + *twih,* etc., prob. shortened from the old accusative form **twīhn* (*twihn, tweohn; twīhen, twīhon*) mentioned as one of the sources of BETWEEN. The original construction of *twih* is seen in the phrase *mid unc twih* 'amid us twain,' i.e. 'between us'; from a parallel *bi (unc) twih, bi twih,* came the combined *betwih.* In *bitwuht,* the *-t* must have been added on the analogy of *betwixt.* Only in OE.; superseded in ME. by the expanded form BITWIHEN.] = BETWIXT, BETWEEN.

c **888** K. ÆLFRED *Boeth.* xxxix. §13 Sio sunne and se mona habbaþ todæled butwuht him þone dæȝ and þa niht. *c* **893** —— *Oros.* I. iii. §1 Betuh Arabia and Palestina. *c* **950** *Lindisf. Gosp.* Luke x. 3 Ic sendo iuih sua lombro bituih [*Rushw.* bitwih] ulfum. *a* **1000** *Boeth. Metr.* xxviii. 104 Betweoh him.

†**biˈtwihen, -twihe,** *prep. Obs.* Forms: 2 bitwihan, 2–3 bitwihen, 3 bitueiȝen, -twiȝe, -tuh(h)en, -tuh(h)e, -twhwe. [First found in 12th c. as *bitwihan*; it took the place of OE. *bitwih,* of which it was apparently a later extension, in accordance with the analogy of *betwix, betwixan, betweon, betweonan.* The variant *bitueiȝen* appears to have been influenced by *tweȝen* TWAIN; cf. also BITWEIES.] = BETWIXT, BETWEEN.

c **1175** *Lamb. Hom.* 37 He is iset bi-twihan god almihtin and þe. *c* **1205** LAY. 784 Lufe þe us bi-tueiȝen lið. *Ibid.* 20947 Bitwiȝe Ænglelonde and Normandie. *a* **1240** *Sawles Warde* in *Cott. Hom.* 255 Bituhhen heard ant nesche, bituhhe wa of þis world ant to moche wunne. *a* **1250** *Owl & Night.* 1747 Maister Nichole..Bitwihen us deme schule.

bityl, bityme, obs. forms of BEETLE, BETIME.

biuncinate (baɪˈʌnsɪneɪt), *a.* [f. BI- *pref.*[2] 1 + UNCINATE, ad. L. *uncinātus* hooked, f. *uncus* hook, barb.] Having two hooks or barbs.

1852 DANA *Crust.* II. 905 Biuncinate at apex.

biune (ˈbaɪjuːn), *a. rare.* [f. BI-[2] + L. *ūnus* one, after *triune.*] Two in one.

1897 F. THOMPSON *Orient Ode* in *New Poems* 34 Yea, biune in imploring dumb, Essential Heavens and corporal Earth await. **1900** G. W. ALLEN *Mission of Evil* 75 This Edenic Man was..male and female in one; that is, 'bi-une'.

biunguiculate (baɪʌŋˈgwɪkjʊleɪt), *a.* [f. BI- *pref.*[2] 1 + UNGUICULATE, f. L. *unguiculus,* dim. of *unguis* nail, claw.] Having two little claws.

1852 DANA *Crust.* II. 935 The outer [branch]..at apex bi-unguiculate, claws recurved.

bi-unial (baɪˈjuːnɪəl), *a.* [f. BI- *pref.*[2] 6 + L. *ūnus* one + -(I)AL.] Consisting of two (*e.g.* optic tubes) combined in one.

1883 *Eng. Mechanic* 6 Apr. 104 The expensive lanterns of the bi-unial and triple types.

biunique (baɪjuːˈniːk, ˈbaɪjuːniːk), *a.* Chiefly *Math.* and *Linguistics.* [f. BI-[2] + UNIQUE *a.*] Consisting of, pertaining to, or being a one-to-one correspondence, *spec.* between phonemic and phonetic representations.

1941 O. HELMER tr. *Tarsk's Introd. Logic* xxiii. 103 One-to-one relations or biunique functions. **1944** Z. S. HARRIS in *Language* XX. 187 We are preserving the bi-unique one-to-one correspondence of phonemic writing. (The term bi-unique implies that the one-to-one correspondence is valid whether we start from the sounds or from the symbols: for each sound one symbol, for each symbol one sound.) **1953** A. A. FRAENKEL *Abstract Set Theory* i. 31 We pointed out the difference between biunique (one-to-one) and merely unique correspondence. **1956** *Nature* 11 Feb. 283/2 The combination of solutions that bring about the disappearance of the abnormal symptom defines the element responsible, because elements and combinations are in a biunique correspondence. **1968** P. M. POSTAL *Aspects Phonol. Theory* iii. 51 He argues fallaciously that a biunique phonemic level (called 'C-phonemics') is necessary to distinguish those phonetic features which are distinctive from those which are not. **1975** N. CHOMSKY *Logical Struct. Linguistic Theory* vii. 187 By definition, the set of ρ-derivations is uniquely determined by **P**. Thus if ρ^r is defined to uniqueness in terms of ρ, one part of this biunique relation will hold.

Hence **ˌbiuˈniqueness, ˌbiuˈniquely** *adv.*

1959 F. W. HOUSEHOLDER in Saporta & Bastian *Psycholinguistics* (1961) 22/1 Segmentation in morphology is also troubled by the stipulation of biuniqueness. **1968** P. M. POSTAL *Aspects Phonol. Theory* iii. 51 Most crucially, perhaps, Lamb states quite clearly as justification of the Biuniqueness Principle..the fallacious argument documented and analyzed in Chapters 1 and 2. **1975** N. CHOMSKY *Logical Struct. Linguistic Theory* vii. 187 We.. require that **P** be related biuniquely to ρ^r, in the sense that **P** be uniquely recoverable from ρ^r, and ρ^r be uniquely constructible from **P**. **1981** *Amer. Speech 1977* LII. 171 The insistence upon phonemic biuniqueness must be given up.

bi-ˈunity. ? *Obs.* [f. BI- *pref.*[2] II + UNITY.] A unity or oneness of two members or parts.

1646 *Game at Scotch & Eng.* 8 This unity..admits of no addition; for so the property of that Bi-unity were lost.

biurate (baɪˈjʊərət). *Chem.* [f. BI-[2] + URATE.] An acid salt of uric acid.

1891 F. TAYLOR *Pract. Med.* (ed. 2) 702 They [*sc.* urates] are decomposed in the presence of water into free uric acid and biurates. **1908** *Practitioner* Apr. 517 The writer is doubtful that the cause of the pain, in gouty arthritis, is the result of the deposit of crystals of sodium biurate.

biuret (ˈbaɪjʊrɛt). *Chem.* [a. G. *biuret* (G. Wiedemann 1847, in *Jrnl. f. prakt. Chem.* XLII. 256), f. BI-[2] + UREA: see -URET.] A compound formed by heating urea. Also *attrib.,* as ***biuret base, test***; **biuret reaction,** the reaction of biuret, proteins, and some other substances containing the –CO · NH– group with an alkaline solution of cupric sulphate, which gives a red or violet coloration.

1869 ROSCOE *Elem. Chem.* xxxv. 354 When heated to 120°, urea fuses and begins to decompose, forming substances termed ammeline and biuret. **1877** ROSCOE & SCHORLEMMER *Chem.* I. 652 Biuret, $C_2O_2H_5N_3$. This compound, discovered by Wiedemann, is formed when urea is heated for some time to 150–160°. **1883** *Jrnl. Chem. Soc.* XLIV. 1019 The author..described a substance..obtained from peptones, which gives conspicuously the biuret reaction of those bodies. **1895** D. C. BLACK *Urine in Health & Dis.* iv. 153 The albumen is separated by filtration and the biuret test applied to the filtrate. **1907** J. B. COHEN *Org. Chem.* 410 Triglycylglycine (biuret base). **1916** A. P. MATHEWS *Physiol. Chem.* 145 Biuret, a substance..formed by the condensation of two molecules of urea (hence biurea or biuret) with the elimination of ammonia. **1956** *Nature* 4 Feb. 234/2 A number of amino-acids..which appear to constitute a polypeptide moiety yielding a weak biuret reaction.

biurne, -an, -on, pa. t. & pple. of BERUN *v. Obs.*

bivalence (ˈbɪvələns, ˌbaɪˈveɪləns). [f. BIVALENT *a.*; see -ENCE.] In various subjects: the quality of being bivalent; bivalency; *spec.* in *Logic,* ***principle of bivalence*** (see quots.).

1889 *Cent. Dict., Bivalence* (Chem.), a valence or saturating power which is double that of the hydrogen atom. **1909** *Ibid.* Suppl., *Bivalence of the chromosomes,* the double as distinguished from the single (univalent) condition of the chromosomes, for example, in the oöcytes and spermatocytes of one of the forms of *Ascaris megalocephala.* **1951** J. ŁUKASIEWICZ *Aristotle's Syllogistic* iv. 82 The so-called principle of bivalence, which states that every proposition is either true or false, i.e. that it has one and only one of two possible truth-values: truth and falsity. **1962** W. & M. KNEALE *Devel. Logic* ii. 47 The principle that every statement is true or false is called the Principle of Bivalence.

bivalency (ˈbɪvələnsɪ). *Chem.* [f. next; see -ENCY.] The quality of being bivalent.

1880 CLEMENSHAW *Wurtz' Atom. The.* 181 The bivalency of certain metals.

bivalent (ˈbɪvələnt), *a.* and *sb.* [f. BI- *pref.*[2] III + *-valent,* ad. L. *valēntem,* pr. pple. of *valēre* to be worth.] **1.** *Chem.* Combining with two atoms of an element or radicle; also *divalent.*

1869 *Eng. Mechanic* 12 Nov. 198/3 The elements are classified as..diatomic or bivalent..as sulphur. **1880** CLEMENSHAW *Wurtz' Atom. The.* 121 Mercury, cadmium, and probably other bivalent metals.

2. *Biol.* Applied to homologous chromosomes united in pairs at the first division of meiosis. Hence as *sb.*

1899 J. H. MCGREGOR in *Jrnl. Morphology* XV. (Suppl.) 81 The only possibility of a true reduction..is by conceiving the chromosomes to be 'bivalent'..and to assume that the halves of these bivalent chromosomes form new connections before the final mitosis. **1937** *Nature* 30 Oct. 760/2 When the bivalent..attempts to divide, the 'dicentric' chromatid forms a bridge between the daughter nuclei. **1949** DARLINGTON & MATHER *Elements of Genetics* i. 30 The compact paired, or *bivalent,* chromosomes..lie evenly in the nucleus. **1952** *New Biol.* XIII. 35 Sometimes during the nuclear divisions, four chromosomes similar to each other all 'pair' together, forming a quadrivalent, instead of the usual two pairs of bivalents.

bivallate (baɪˈvæleɪt, -ət), *a.* [f. BI-[2] + VALLATE *a.*] Having two encircling ramparts.

1930 *Antiquity* IV. 198 This 'bivallate ditch' is a good example of a type of earthwork found commonly in Wessex. **1936** *Proc. Prehist. Soc.* II. 216 The enclosure appeared to have been built on to a ditch of the bivallate meandering variety. **1963** G. DANIEL in Foster & Alcock *Culture & Environment* ii. 20 The building of the bivallate and multivallate hillforts of Wales.

bivalve (ˈbaɪvælv), *a.* and *sb.* [f. BI- *pref.*[2] 1 + VALVE, ad. L. *valvæ* folds of a door, folding-doors.] **A.** *adj.*

1. Having two leaves or folding parts, as a shutter or door.

1677 PLOT *Oxfordsh.* 271 Great bivalve wooden Windows. *a* **1877** KNIGHT *Dict. Mech.* s.v. *Speculum,* Webber's magnifying bivalve ear-speculum. **1908** *Practitioner* Aug. 284 There was no appreciable difference obtained in the results by using a bivalve speculum in order to avoid contact with the external meatus.

2. *Zool.* Having two shells united by a hinge.

1661 LOVELL *Hist. Anim. & Min.* Introd., Fishes which are..bivalve, as the Chama, oister, pectines. **1756** C. LUCAS *Ess. Waters* III. 123 Several small bivalve shells. **1848** CARPENTER *Anim. Phys.* 33 The ligament which holds together the shells of the bivalve Mollusca.

3. *Bot.* (A seed vessel) Having two valves.

1737 MILLER *Gard. Dict.* s.v. *Chelidonium majus,* The Flowers..are succeeded by many bivalve Pods. **1794** MARTYN *Rousseau's Bot.* xvi. 191 The capsule bivalve.

B. *sb.* **1.** *pl.* Folding-doors. *Obs.* exc. *Hist.*

1832 GELL *Pompeiana* I. ii. 22 Doors seem to have been called bivalves where only formed of two folds.

2. *Zool.* A molluscous animal having a shell consisting of two halves joined together by an elastic ligament at the hinge, so as to open and shut like a book: such as the oyster, mussel, etc. Also the shell of such animal.

1683 *Phil. Trans.* XIV. 507 Distinction of shells into Univalves Bivalves and Turbinated. **1771** *Ibid.* LXI. 230 Four..species, like the sea bivalve. **1847** CARPENTER *Zool.* §876 Lamellibranchiata..To this group belong all ordinary

bivalves. **1865** TYLOR *Early Hist. Man.* viii. 192 The refuse-mounds consist of oysters, mussels, and other bivalves.

3. *Bot.* A bivalve capsule or seed-vessel.

'bivalved, *a.* [f. as prec. + -ED.] = BIVALVE *a.*: **a.** in *Zool.*; **b.** in *Bot.*

a. 1755 *Gentl. Mag.* XXV. 31 A shell is said to be bivalved when it consists of two parts or leaves. **1872** NICHOLSON *Palæont.* 159 Small Bivalved Crustaceans.
b. 1852 E. HAMILTON *Flora Homœop.* 185 A thin, bivalved, white, ligneous shell (endocarp).

bi'valvian. *rare.* = BIVALVE *sb.* 2.

1863 RUSSELL *Diary North & S.* 274 We went into one of the great oyster saloons, and..had the opportunity of tasting those great bivalvians.

bivalvous (baɪ'vælvəs), *a.* [f. BIVALVE + -OUS.] = BIVALVE *a.*

1696 *Phil. Trans.* XIX. 188 Testaceous Animals of the turbinated and bivalvous kinds. [In mod. Dicts.]

bivalvular (baɪ'vælvjʊlə(r)), *a.* (and *sb.*) [f. BI- *pref.*^{2} 1 + VALVULAR.] = BIVALVE: **a.** in *Zool.*; also quasi-*sb.*; **b.** in *Bot.*

a. 1677 PLOT *Oxfordsh.* 100 The bivalvular Conchæ, such as Cockles. 117 Bivalvulars..found with their shells apart.
b. 1830 LINDLEY *Nat. Syst. Bot.* 294 Those species of Panicum that have the lower flower neuter and bivalvular.

bivariant (baɪ'vɛərɪənt), *a.* *Physical Chem.* [BI-^{2}.] Having two degrees of freedom (see FREEDOM 10 b).

1902 [see TRIVARIANT *a.*]. **1904** A. FINDLAY *Phase Rule* ii. 16 We may also speak of the variability or variance of a system, and describe a system as being invariant, univariant, bivariant, multivariant, according as the number of degrees of freedom is nought, one, two, or more than two.

bivariate (baɪ'vɛərɪət), *a.* *Statistics.* [f. BI-^{2} + VARIATE *a.*] Involving or depending upon two variables.

1920 *Biometrika* XIII. 37 Thus in 1885 Galton had completed the theory of bi-variate normal correlation. **1923** *Ibid.* XV. 77 (*title*) On the general forms of bivariate frequency distributions. **1951** D. R. WHITNEY *Ann. Math. Statistics* XXI. 274 (*title*) A bivariate extension of the *U* statistic.

bivaulted: see BI- *pref.*^{2} 1.

†**bive,** *v.* *Obs.* Forms: 1 bifian, befian, byfian, beofian, 3 beouien, buuien, biuien. [Com. Teut.: OE. *bifian* = OS. *bibon* (MDu., Du. *beven*), OHG. *bibên* (MHG. *biben*, mod.G. *beben*), ON. *bifa*:—OTeut. **bibai-*, identified by Kluge with Skr. *bibhêmi*, reduplicated pres. of *bhî* to fear. Cf. BEE, BEVER *v.*^{2}] *intr.* To shake, tremble.

c **888** K. ÆLFRED *Boeth.* xxxv. §6 Þa wudas bifodon. *c* **1000** *Ags. Ps.* xcv[i]. 9 For his ansyne sceal eorðe beofian. *c* **1160** *Hatton Gosp.* Matt. xxvii. 51 Syo eorðe befode [*v.r.* byfode], and stanes toburston. *c* **1205** LAY. 23530 Burhmen gunnen beouien [**1250** buuie]. *Ibid.* 28084 Þa gon ich to biuien: swulc ich al fur burne. *c* **1250** *Gen. & Ex.* 2280 Wot ic ðor mon ðat he ne biueð.

biventer (baɪ'vɛntə(r)). *Phys.* [f. BI- *pref.*^{2} II + L. *venter* belly.] A muscle, distinguished by its two bellies or bulges; *esp.* the digastric muscle.

1706 in PHILLIPS. **1740** B. MARTIN *Bibl. Technol.* xi. (ed. 2) 371 Muscles..as the Biventer, which hath two Bellies. **1843** J. WILKINSON *Swedenborg's Anim. Kingd.* I. ii. 62 The biventer, or digastricus..arises from the incisure under the mastoid process.

biventral (baɪ'vɛntrəl), *a.* *Phys.* [f. BI- *pref.*^{2} 1 + VENTRAL; see prec.] Having two bellies; digastric.

1706 in PHILLIPS. **1839–47** TODD *Cycl. Anat. & Phys.* III. 689/2 Behind the amygdala is the biventral lobe.

†**bi'ventrous,** *a.* *Phys.* *Obs.* [See prec.] Having two ventricles.

1702 W. COWPER in *Phil. Trans.* XXIII. 1182 All Animals, that have Biventrous Hearts.

biverb ('baɪvɜːb). *rare.* [f. BI- *pref.*^{2} + L. *verbum* word.] A name composed of two words.

1831 SIR W. R. HAMILTON in *Life* (1882) I. 457 [In a letter to *Lord* Adare] My dear Adare (you see that..your name is not with me, a biverb any longer).

biverbal (baɪ'vɜːbəl), *a.* *rare.* [f. BI- *pref.*^{2} 6 + VERBAL; cf. prec.] Relating to two words; punning.

1823 LAMB *Elia* Ser. II. xxiv. 411 This biverbal allusion.

bivial ('bɪvɪəl), *a.* *Phys.* [f. BIVI-UM + -AL^{1}.] Of or pertaining to the *bivium*.

1877 HUXLEY *Anat. Inv. An.* 570 The bivial ambulacra.

bivious ('bɪvɪəs), *a.* [f. L. *bivi-us* having two ways or passages (f. *bi-* two + *via* way) + -OUS.] 'That leadeth (two) different ways' (T.); having or offering two ways or courses.

a **1644** QUARLES *Virgin Wid.* III. i, I stand even balanc'd.. Beneath the burden of a bivious brest. **1682** SIR T. BROWNE *Chr. Mor.* (1756) 86 In bivious theorems..let virtuous considerations state the determination. **1719** J. AUBREY *Surrey* IV. 189 This Vault is bivious.

‖**bivium** ('bɪvɪəm). *Phys.* [a. L. *bivium* a place where two ways meet; see prec.] The two hinder ambulacra of Echinoderms.

1870 [see TRIVIUM 2]. **1877** HUXLEY *Anat. Inv. An.* ix. 570 It is possible in any of the Echinidea, to separate the three anterior ambulacra, as the *trivium*, from the two posterior, the *bivium*; and in the fossil genus Dysaster, this separation of the ambulacra into trivium and bivium exists naturally.

bivocal (baɪ'vəʊkəl). [f. BI- *pref.*^{2} II + VOCAL, ad. L. *vocālis* adj. 'of the voice, vocal,' sb. 'a vowel,' f. *vox* VOICE.] A combination of two vowels, a diphthong. **bi'vocalized** *ppl. a.*, placed between two vowels.

1813 J. C. HOBHOUSE *Journey* 1098 Vossius..the principal advocate of the ancient bivocals. **1876** DOUSE *Grimm's L.* App. D. 199 The softening process clearly originated..in the interior or bivocalized position.

bivoltine (baɪ'vɒltɪn), *a.* Also -in. [a. F. *bivoltin*, f. *bi-*, BI-^{2} + It. *volta* time.] Of certain silkworms: producing two broods per annum. Also as *sb.*

1874 [see *multivoltine* s.v. MULTI- 1 a]. **1888** E. A. BUTLER *Silkworms* 69 Most of the other species produce two, three, four, six, or even eight broods per annum, and in the commercial world are..distinguished as 'bivoltins', 'trivoltins', 'quadrivoltins', etc. **1932** *Proc. 6th Internat. Congress Genetics* I. 377 The bivoltine breeds also show less growth than the univoltine ones.

bivon, variant of BEFONG *v.* *Obs.* to grasp.

bivouac ('bɪvwæk, 'bɪvuːæk). Forms: 8 biouac, bihovac, biovac, 9 bivuack, bivouack, (bivouake), bivouaque, 8– bivouac. [In Dictionaries since *c* 1700, but hardly in use before the French War: a. F. *bivouac*, *bivac*, generally said to have been introduced during the Thirty Years' War. It has with probability been referred to a dialectal (Swiss) Ger. *beiwacht*, according to Stalder, *Versuch eines Schweizerischen Idiotikon* (1812) II. 426, used in Aargau and Zürich to denote the patrol of citizens (*Schaarwache*) added (*beigegeben*) to assist the ordinary town watch by night at any time of special commotion. This remaining of a large body of men under arms all night explains the original sense of bivouac.]

1. *Mil.* Originally, a night-watch by a whole army under arms, to prevent surprise; now, a temporary encampment of troops in the field with only the accidental shelter of the place, without tents, etc.; also the place of such encampment.

1706 PHILLIPS, *Biouac or Bihovac*, an extraordinary Guard perform'd by the whole Army, when..it..continues all night under Arms..to prevent Surprize, etc. *To Raise the Biovac*, is to return the Army to their Tents, or Huts, some time after break of Day. **1753** CHAMBERS *Cycl. Supp.*, *Biouac, bivouac, biovac*..is formed by corruption from the German *weywacht*, a double watch or guard; *Trevoux.* **1755** JOHNSON, *Biovac, bihovac, bivouac* [as in Phillips]. 'Not in use.' **1772** SIMES *Milit. Guide*, *Biovac*, a night guard, performed by the whole army, when there is any danger from the enemy. **1811** WELLINGTON in Gurw. *Disp.* VIII. 21 The bivouac which Hill quitted this morning appears to be an excellent situation for the cavalry to-morrow. **1813** *Examiner* 7 June 356/1 (transl. from French), The army had taken its bivouaques. **1850** PRESCOTT *Peru* II. 151 Almagro, afraid of stumbling on the enemy's bivouac. **1885** *Times* 16 May 7/1 Our troops recrossed..and went into bivouac.

fig. **1839** LONGF. *Ps. Life* v, In the world's broad field of battle, In the bivouac of Life.

2. *transf.* An encampment for the night in the open air; a camping out.

1853 DE QUINCEY *Sp. Mil. Nun* §6. 11 Withered leaves, which furnished to Kate her very first bivouac. **1872** C. KING *Sierra Nev.* iii. 49 Morning dawned brightly upon our bivouac among a cluster of dark firs.

bivouac, *v.* [f. prec. sb.]

1. *Mil.* Of troops: To remain, *esp.* during the night, in the open air, without tents or covering. Also *to be bivouacked*: to be so posted or disposed.

1809 SIR J. MOORE *To Ld. Castlereagh* 13 Jan., In two forced marches, bivouacing for six or eight hours in the rain, I reached Betanzos on the 10th instant. **1815** J. CROKER in *Croker Papers* (1884) I. iii. 61 The Carrousel, where about 2000 Prussians are bivouacked. **1882** PEBODY *Eng. Journalism* xxii. 180 As if the British army were bivouacked on the Hog's Back.

2. *transf.* To rest or pass the night in the open air.

1814 SCOTT *Wav.* II. i. 8 These distinguished personages bivouacked among the flowery heath, wrapped up in their plaids. **1860** TYNDALL *Glac.* I. §3. 29 That night we bivouacked together.

Hence **'bivouacking** *vbl. sb.*

1812 *Examiner* 7 Dec. 771/2 Night bivouacings are very injurious. **1861** C. ANDERSON *Okavango Riv.* xvii. 192 We could not have selected a worse spot for bivouacking.

bivvy, bivy ('bɪvɪ). *Army slang.* [Shortened f. BIVOUAC *sb.*] A temporary shelter for troops; a small tent.

1916 *Anzac Book* 142 We lays down in the open W'en our 'bivvies' isn't dug. **1918** *N.Z.E.F. Chrons.* 13 Feb. 9/1 We arrived at our allotted spot, somewhere in Palestine, and erected our bivvies. **1920** *Blackw. Mag.* May 596/2 The Egyptian Camel Corps and Gurkhas arrived, bringing 'Bivies' and other luxuries. *Ibid.* 606/1 Tying his horse to my bivy-pole. **1925** *Glasgow Herald* 30 Mar. 10 That word was 'tambu', meaning a rough and ready shelter made of branches, planks, corrugated iron, a 'bivvy', in fact. **1947** D. M. DAVIN *Gorse blooms Pale* 199 Snow and me were sitting outside the bivvy.

biw-: see BEW-, BYW-.

†**bi'wait,** *v.* *Obs.* [f. *bi-*, BE- + WAIT; cf. AWAIT *v.*] **a.** *trans.* To watch, look at. **b.** *intr.* To look about or out, be circumspect.

a **1250** *Owl & Night.* 1322 Hwat canstu wrecche þing of steorre Bute þat þu biwaitest [*MSS.* bihaitest] hi feorre. *c* **1456** *How wise Man taught Son* 92 in Hazl. *E.P.P.* I. 173 Thou wyse bywayt, and wele awyse.

biway, biword: see BY-.

biweekly, biwhirl: see BI- *pref.*^{2} 4, 1.

biweile, biweep, etc.: see BEWAIL, etc.

†**bi'were,** *v.* *Obs.* Forms: 1 bewerian, 2–3 biwerien. [OE. *bewerian* = OHG. *biwarjan*, *biwerjan*, MHG. *beweren*, mod.G. *bewehren*, f. *bi-*, BE- + OTeut. *warjan*, OHG. *warian*, *werian*, ON. *verja*, OE. *werian* to defend, protect: see WERE.] *trans.* To defend, shield, protect.

c **1000** ÆLFRIC *Ex.* ii. 17 Þa aras Moises & bewerode þa mædenu. *c* **1175** *Lamb. Hom.* 115 He scal biwerian widewan and steopbern. *a* **1250** *Owl & Night.* 1126 Þu..mid þine ateliche sweore Biwerest manne corn from deore.

†**bi'wern(e,** *v.* *Obs.* [f. *bi-*, BE- + WERN *v.* to refuse.] *trans.* To refuse or deny.

1413 LYDG. *Pylgr. Sowle* I. xv. (1859) 14 Was neuer done yet, to whom it was biwernyd.

†**bi'weve,** *v.*^{1} *Obs.* Forms: 1–2 bewǽfan, (2 bewafen), 3 biwefen, -weauen, -wæiuen, 3–5 bi-, byweuen, -ven. [OE. *bewǽfan* = Goth. *biwaibjan*, f. *be-*, *bi-*, BE- 1 + *waibjan*, in OE. *wǽfan* to wind.]

1. *trans.* To wrap up, envelop, clothe.

c **1000** ÆLFRIC *Gen.* xxiv. 65 Heo nam raþe hyre wæfels and bewæfde hiȝ. *c* **1205** LAY. 28475 Me hire hafd bi-wefde mid ane hali rifte. *c* **1314** *Guy Warw.* 303 Poverliche he was biweved.

fig. *c* **1205** LAY. 130 Mid wintre he wes biweaued. *c* **1275** in *O.E. Misc.* 55 Fort ye beon byweued of heueliche myhte.

2. To entwine, weave.

c **1300** *K. Alis.* 4085 The croune, of gold byweved, He set on his fadir heved. *c* **1400** *Rowland & Ot.* 1202 With golde abowte it was by-wevede.

†**biweve,** *v.*^{2} *Obs.* [f. *bi-*, BE- + ME. *weven* to twist, hurl: see WEVE.]

1. *trans.* To whirl or drive away.

a **1300** *Cursor M.* 24109 Mi soru..Biweft þat word awai.

2. *intr.* To hurry away.

c **1205** LAY. 30856 Forð he bi-wafde, þene pic he bilæfde.

†**bi'wihele,** *v.* *Obs.* Also biwiȝelien. [f. *bi-*, BE- + ME. *wiȝelien*:—OE. *wiȝelian* to soothsay.] To overcome by witchcraft; to bewitch.

c **1205** LAY. 969 Heo wlleð us biwiȝelien [*c* **1250** bi-cheorre] þurh heora wiðere craftes. *a* **1225** *Juliana* 56 Wenestu þat we beon so eð to biwihelen [*v.r.* biwihelin].

†**bi'wile,** *v.* *Obs.* Also 4 bi-, bywylen. [f. *bi-*, BE- 1 + WILE *v.* Cf. BEGUILE.] *trans.* To overcome with wiles, ensnare, beguile.

a **1275** *Prov. Alfred* 327 in *O.E. Misc.* 123 Hue weped oþer wile, þen hue þe wille biwilen. *a* **1300** *Cursor M.* 28522 Wende i womman to be wile. *c* **1340** *Gaw. & Gr. Knt.* 2425 Alle þay were biwyled With wymmen.

†**bi'wit,** *v.* *Obs.* Pa. t. biwiste, -wuste. Pa. pple. biwist, -wust. [OE. *bewitan*, f. *bi-*, BE- + OE. *witan* to look.] *trans.* To look after, keep, take charge of, guard, protect, keep in safety.

c **1000** ÆLFRIC *St. Oswald* in Sweet *Reader* 97/76 An ðæs cyninges þeȝna ðe his ælmessan bewiste. *c* **1175** *Lamb. Hom.* 23 Þu scoldest heo [þi limen] biwiten al swa clenliche swa crist ha þe bitahte. *c* **1275** *Pass. Our Lord* 538 in *O.E. Misc.* 52 Hyne biwusten knyhtes voure oþer vyue.

¶ Also found with strong inflexions, apparently by form-association: see next, and cf. AT-WITE.

c **1205** LAY. 13028 He..spæc wið þæne abbod: þe þat munster biwat. *Ibid.* 20505 Twa hundred scipene: þer weoren wel biwitene.

†**bi'wite,** *v.* *Obs.* [A strong vb.: cf. OE. *ȝewitan* to depart.] *intr.* To go, go away.

c **1300** *K. Alis.* 5203 That no man ne shulde y-wite, Whiderward hy were biwite.

†**bi'witi(e,** *v.* *Obs.* Also biwittien, -witeȝen, -witteȝen. [OE. *bewitian*, f. *bi-*, BE- 1 + *wittian*: see WITIE.] *trans.* To watch over, observe, guard, keep.

c **1000** *Beowulf* 2860 Ða [nicras] on undern mæl · oft bewitiȝað sorhfulne sið on sæȝl-rade. *c* **1200** *Trin. Coll. Hom.* 195 Ðe deuel..is gredi uppen woreld richeise..and ȝiep him to biwitiende. *c* **1205** LAY. 27198 Bi-halues he sende..wel iwepnede men · þene wude to bi-witteȝen.

† **bi'wlappe**, *v. Obs.* [A confusion of *bewrappe* and *lap*, ME. *lappen.*] = BEWRAP.

1388 WYCLIF *Job* xviii. 11 Dredis..schulen biwlappe hise feet [*v.r.* bewrappe].

† **bi'wrench(e**, *v. Obs.* [OE. *bewrencan*, f. BE- 1 + *wrencan* to WRENCH.] To cheat, deceive.

a **1225** *Ancr. R.* 92 Ȝe schulen iseon alle þes deofles wieles: hu he biwrencheð & bicherreð wreches.

biwreo, -wrien, var. BEWRY *v. Obs.* to cover.

† **bi'wrixle**, *v. Obs.* [ME., f. *bi-*, BE- 1 + WRIXLEN, OE. *wrixlan*, *-ian*, to change.] *trans.* To change, transform.

a **1225** *Ancr. R.* 262 He..scheaweð him to ou flesliche and licamliche iðe messe, biwrien [biwrixlet] þauh, in oðres like—under breades heouwe. *Ibid.* 310 He is him sulf al biwrixled, & bicumen, of Godes child, þes deofles bearn.

‖ **bixa** ('bɪksə). [Native name in Central America.] A genus of small trees, natives of tropical America, from the fruits of one species of which (*B. orellana*) the dye anatta is prepared. Hence **bixin**, (*a*) The colouring principle of anatta; (*b*) A variety of anatta of greatly increased colouring power.

1879 WATTS *Dict. Chem.* I. 600. **1880** *Syd. Soc. Lex.* s.v.

[**bixwort**, 'an herb,' is apparently an error of some kind, in Phillips 1706, and Bailey's Folio of 1730, whence copied by Johnson and modern dictionaries. It is unknown to the herbalists.]

biys, var. of BYSS 'fine linen.' *Obs.*

biz (bɪz). Colloq. abbrev., orig. *U.S.*, of BUSINESS. So *show biz* (see SHOW *sb.*[1]).

1862 C. F. BROWNE *Artemus Ward His Bk.* 222, I must forth to my Biz. **1873** LELAND *Egypt. Sketch-Bk.* 35 No. IV. made it his 'biz' to fall upon the old hands. **1878** J. H. BEADLE *Western Wilds* iii. 46 He had what he called a 'big biz' at each successive terminus town. **1890** *Harper's Mag.* Apr. 813/1 I'll go Down to the sale, if I can leave my biz. **1909** WODEHOUSE *Mike* xx. 115 As the poet has it, 'Pleasure is pleasure, and biz is biz, and kep' in a sepyrit jug.' **1941** F. SCOTT FITZGERALD *Last Tycoon* (1947) iii. 36 The cleverest plagiarist in the biz.

bizant, bizantine, obs. ff. BEZANT, BYZANTINE.

bizarre (bɪ'zɑː(r), or as Fr. bizar), *a.* and *sb.* Also 7 bizare, bizarr. [mod.Eng. (17th c.), a. F. *bizarre* 'odd, fantastic,' formerly 'brave, soldier-like'; cf. Sp. and Pg. *bizarro* 'handsome, brave,' It. *bizzarro* 'angry, choleric,' dial. Fr. (Berry) *bigearer* to quarrel. Littré suggests that the Spanish word is an adaptation of Basque *bizarra* beard, in the same manner as *hombre de bigote* moustached man, is used in Sp. for a 'man of spirit'; but the history of the sense has not been satisfactorily made out.

1667 EVELYN *Mem.* (1857) III. 161 We have hardly any words that do so fully express the French..*naivete, ennui, bizarre, concert..emotion, defer, effort*..let us therefore (as the Romans did the Greek) make as many of these do homage as are like to prove good citizens.]

1. At variance with recognized ideas of taste, departing from ordinary style or usage; eccentric, extravagant, whimsical, strange, odd, fantastic.

a **1648** LD. HERBERT *Life*, Her attire seemed as bizare as her person. **1668** DRYDEN *Maid. Queen* Pref., The Ornament of Writing, which is greater, more various and bizarre in Poesie than in any other kind. **1757** HUME *Stand. Taste, Ess.* (1875) I. 270 Ariosto pleases; but not..by his bizarre mixture of the serious and comic styles. **1825** SCOTT *Talism.* (1863) 42 Such oddity of gestures and manner as befitted their bizarre and fantastic appearance. **1879** FARRAR *St. Paul* I. 352 The bizarre superstitions by which he was surrounded.

b. *esp.* At variance with the standard of ideal beauty or regular form; grotesque, irregular.

1824 DIBDIN *Libr. Comp.* 577 The bizarre wooden cuts of Caxton. **1851** RUSKIN *Stones Ven.* I. xi. §14 If the arch be of any bizarre form, especially ogee. **1861** N. WOODS *Pr. Wales in Canada* 359 The capitol is a bizarre Græco-American building which runs much to windows.

c. *absol.* or quasi-*sb.*

1850 LEITCH tr. *Müller's Anc. Art* §99 An intentional striving at the bizarre. **1851** R. WORNUM *Exhib. a Lesson in Taste* 5/2 In the Renaissance [architecture], we have..a prevalence of the bizarre and a love of profusion of parts.

2. *Hort.* Applied to variegated species of garden flowers, as tulips and carnations. Often as *sb.*

1753 CHAMBERS *Cycl. Supp.*, *Bizarre*, a term used among the florists for a particular kind of carnation, which has its flowers striped or variegated with three or four colours. **1843** *Penny Cycl.* XXV. 343/2 Bizarre tulips have a yellow ground marked with purple or scarlet of different shades. **1883** *Athenæum* 30 June 825/3 The 'streaked gillyflower' is the clove so crossed as to become a 'bizarre.'

bi'zarrely, *adv.* [f. BIZARRE *a.* + -LY[2].] In a bizarre manner. So **bi'zarreness** = BIZARRERIE.

1884 RIDER HAGGARD *Dawn* v, This woman so bizarrely beautiful. **1920** *Edin. Rev.* Oct. 255 Of his faults he was perfectly conscious—the over-intensities, the dualities, sometimes the bizarreness, which we have shadowed. **1953** QUINE *From Logical Point of View* iii. 54 A reaction suggesting bizarreness of idiom. **1960** *20th Cent.* Oct. 366 Rilke waffles bizarrely on about Arabian poetry.

‖ **bizarrerie** (bizarəri, bɪ'zɑːrərɪ). [F. *bizarrerie.*] Bizarre quality.

1741-70 *Lett. Mrs. Carter* (1808) 207 The bizarreries which arise from the mixture of good and bad which makes up the composition of most folks. **1828** SCOTT *Tapestr. Chamber*, Rich in all the bizarrerie of the Elizabethan school. **1844** *For. Q. Rev.* XXXIII. 60 Bizarreries. **1858** BAGEHOT *Lit. Studies* II. 194 The bizarrerie of Mr. Dickens's genius.

bizcacha variant of BISCACHA.

bize, obs. form of BICE.

bizel, -le, obs. forms of BEZEL, BEZZLE.

bizygomatic (,baɪzɪgəʊ'mætɪk), *a.* [f. BI- *pref.*[2] 5 + ZYGOMATIC.] Joining the two zygomatic arches.

1878 BARTLEY tr. *Topinard's Anthrop.* II. ii. 252 The maximum transverse or bizygomatic diameter of the face.

bizz, -ard, -ie, Sc. ff. of BUZZ, BUZZARD, BUSY.

bla(a, blaad: see BLAE, BLAD, BLADE.

‖ **blaasop** (blɑː'sɒp). *S. Afr.* [Afrikaans, f. *blaas* to blow + *op* up.] A puff-fish: see PUFF *sb.* 9 b.

[**1853** L. PAPPE *Edible Fishes Cape Good Hope* 8 This fish (*Blaasopvisch*; *Balloonfish*; *Toadfish*) is never found in Table Bay, but is very common in the bays to the east of it.] **1902** J. D. F. GILCHRIST in *Trans. S. Afr. Philos. Soc.* XI. 227 Blassop, Toad-fish (E. London). *Tetrodon honkenyi.* **1913** W. W. THOMPSON *Sea-Fisheries Cape Colony* 159 Tetrodon honkenyi..Blaasop; Toad-fish (East London). **1947** K. H. BARNARD *Pict. Guide S. Afr. Fishes* 209 *Globe-Fishes or Puffers.* Known at the Cape as Blaasops and in England and America as Puffers from their habit of 'blowing up' or puffing out the body; called Tobies in Natal. **1947** L. G. GREEN *Tavern of Seas* iv. 37 The blaasop's liver contains a deadly poison.

blab (blæb), *sb.*[1] Forms: 4-7 blabbe, 6- blab. [The history of *blab* and *blabber*, and the question of their mutual relations, if any, is very obscure. *Blabbe* sb. 'chatterer' occurs in Chaucer *c* 1374, and is very common thenceforth; *blab* sb. 'chatter, loose talk' is in *Tale of Beryn* (*c* 1400), but has not been found elsewhere before the 16th c., when appears also *blab* vb. 'to chatter' (1535), followed in course by its agent noun *blabber*. But the vb. *blabber* is earlier than any of these; it occurs in *Piers Ploughman* (1362), and is (with its deriv. *blabberer*) very common in Wyclif; the facts thus forbid us to take *blabber* as a frequentative derivative of *blab* vb.; while no analogy exists for the formation of either (of the only two early words) *blabbe* sb., *blabber* vb., from the other. It would be hardly justifiable to assume *blabbe* to be a 14th c. abbreviation of *blabberer*. For forms akin to *blabber* in other langs. see that word. With *blabbe* we have to compare a sb. *labbe* 'revealer of secrets, blabber,' in Chaucer, and a vb. *labbe* of same age in P. Ploughman, with pple. *labbyng* 'blabbing, open-mouthed,' also in Chaucer, identical with ODu. *labben* to chatter 'garrire' (Stratm.). *Blabbe* might be a mixed form due to association of *labbe* and *blabber*; but may also be purely onomatopœic. Cf. BABBLE.]

1. An open-mouthed person, one who has not sufficient control over his tongue; a revealer of secrets or of what ought to be kept private; a babbler, tattler, or tell-tale; used also of the tongue. (Exceedingly common in 16th and 17th c.; unusual in literature since *c* 1750.)

c **1374** CHAUCER *Troylus* III. 251 Proverbis canst thi self ynow, and wost Ayenst that vice for to bene a blabbe. *c* **1440** *Promp. Parv.* 37 Blabbe, labbe, wreyare of cownselle, *futilis, anubicus.* **1496** *Dives & Paup.* (W. de W.) v. iv. 199/2 Thou shalt be noo tale teller ne blabbe to defame man or woman falsely. **1535** COVERDALE *Prov.* xvi. 29 He yᵗ is a blabbe of his tonge, maketh deuysion amonge prynces. **1577** HOLINSHED *Chron.* IV. 933 Now I will plaie the blab. **1583** STANYHURST *Æneis* IV. (Arb.) 105 Fame, the blab vnciuil. **1600** HEYWOOD *2 Edw. IV*, 148 This tongue was never knowne to be a blab. **1656** DUGARD *Gate Lat. Unl.* §644. 197 A long-tongued blab, uttering the secrets committed to him. **1671** MILTON *Samson* 491 To be excluded all friendship, and avoided as a blab. **1853** *C. Auchester* I. 290 Miss Lawrence is a blab. **1869** SPURGEON *J. Ploughm. Talk* 42 Some men are quite as bad blabs as the women.

2. Loose talk or chatter; babbling; divulging of secrets.

c **1400** *Beryn* 3022 Leve thy blab, lewd fole! **1548** HALL *Chron. Rich. III* an. 2 If he had taryed styl, the duke had not made so many blabbes of his counsail. *a* **1604** HANMER *Chron. Irel.* (1633) 127 Thus the blabbe of his tongue, turned to his confusion. **1679** *Observ. last Dutch Wars* 8 You with your blustring blabs. **1863** W. WHITMAN *Elem. Drifts* 2 All that blab whose echoes recoil on me.

† **3.** ? as *adj.* Incontinent of speech. *Obs.*

1552 HULOET, Blabbe, *linguax.* **1590** GREENE *Mourn. Garm.* (1616) 20 Fame is blab. **1598** SYLVESTER *Du Bartas* (1621) 250 Phrenzie, that makes the vaunter insolent; The talk-full, blab.

4. *Comb.* See after BLAB *v.*

† **blab**, *sb.*[2] *Obs.* exc. *dial.* [A variant of BLEB, BLOB.] A bubble; a blister, a swelling.

1656 TRAPP *Comm. Acts* viii. 9 Such a blab the devil had blown up there, as a small wind may blow up a bubble. **1861** RAMSAY *Remin.* v. (ed. 18) 115 I've had..the blabs [*note*, Nettle-rash].

Hence **blab-lipped** = BLABBER-LIPPED.

c **1430** *Chester Pl.* (1818) 41 If any blabb-lipped boyes be in my way They shall rue it by mighty Mahowne. **1591** HARINGTON *Orl. Fur.* XLIII. cxxviii, Blab-lipt, beetle-browd, and bottle-nozed.

blab, *v.*[1] Also 6-7 blabb(e, (6 blobbe). [App. f. *blabbe*, BLAB *sb.*[1]; prob. under the influence of BLABBER *v.*] To talk or utter as a blab.

† **1.** *trans.* To utter with open mouth; usually with *out*. Also *absol.* To talk much or ineptly; to chatter, babble, 'blether.' *Obs.*

1535 COVERDALE *Prov.* xv. 2 A foolish mouth blabbeth out nothinge but foolishnesse [**1568** *Bishops'*, bableth: **1611** poureth out, *marg.* Heb. belcheth or bubbleth]. **1570** LEVINS *Manip.* 1 Blab, *garrire, multiloqui.* **1598** DELONEY *Jacke Newb.* vii. 87 He blabbed out this broken English.

2. a. *trans.* To open one's mouth about (a thing better kept in); to tell, or reveal indiscreetly.

1583 STANYHURST *Æneis* II. (Arb.) 48, I do hold yt lawful ..to blab theyre secrecye priuat. **1589** *Pappe w. Hatchet* B iij b, Ile blabb all, and not sticke to tell. **1591** *Troub. Raigne K. John* (1611) 22 Must I recount my shame, Blab my misdeeds? **1612** R. CARPENTER *Soules Sent.* 101 To blab or blaze a dead mans follies. **1620** *Swetnam Arraign'd* (1880) 28 What will not women blab to those they love. **1741** RICHARDSON *Pamela* I. 38 It will be said I blab every thing. **1834** PRINGLE *Afr. Sk.* xiv. 459 One of the Boors.. afterwards blabbed the real facts of the transaction. **1848** MACAULAY *Hist. Eng.* II. 179 This pushing talkative divine, who was always blabbing secrets.

b. Often with *out* (*forth, abroad*).

1548 UDALL *Erasm. Par. Matt.* xiii. 44 He blabbeth it not abrode to others. **1580** NORTH *Plutarch* (1676) 822 He blabbed not out all the conspiracy. **1635** *Camden's Hist. Eliz.* III. 269 He had blabbed forth somewhat to the prejudice of the King. **1742** R. BLAIR *Grave* 433 Oh! that some courteous ghost would blab it out. **1869** DIXON *Tower* (1870) II. xiv. 141 He blabbed out the secret to his priest.

3. *intr.* To talk indiscreetly about what should be kept secret, to reveal or betray secrets.

1601 SHAKS. *Twel. N.* I. ii. 63 When my tongue blabs, then let mine eyes not see. **1733** SWIFT *Poetry* Wks. 1755 IV. I. 188 If you blab, you are undone. **1747** B. HOADLY *Suspic. Husb.* III. ii, Mum's the Word, I never blab. **1865** CARLYLE *Fred. Gt.* IV. II. i. 18 His Brother..had blabbed upon the Prince. **1870** LOWELL *Among my Bks.* Ser. I. (1873) 202 We certainly should not have guessed it, if he had not blabbed.

4. *trans.* (*transf.*) To reveal otherwise than by talking; to betray, bewray.

1597 SHAKS. *2 Hen. IV*, III. i. 154 Beaufords red sparkling eyes blab his hearts mallice. **1646** J. HALL *Poems* I. 14 His age is blab'd by silver haires. **1654** E. JOHNSON *Wond.-wkg. Provid.* 103 Least his watry eyes should blab abroad the secret conjunction of his affections.

5. *Comb.*, as *blab-mouth, -tongue*; so *blab-mouthed* adj.; **blab-off** *attrib.* (see quot. 1953).

1600 S. NICHOLSON *Acolastus* (1876) 14 O blab-tongue Tantalus, why dost not eate? **1683** CHALKHILL *Thealma & Cl.* 34 Report, the blab-tongue of those tell-tale times. **1865** *Washington Star* 29 Apr., Such a shallow-pated blab-mouth. **1913** D. H. LAWRENCE *Sons & Lovers* I. i. 16 He was blab-mouthed, a tongue-wagger. **1953** *Daily Mail* 20 Nov. 7/2 A member suggested that the Chamber of the House [of Commons] should be fitted with 'blab-off switches'... These 'popular devices enabled American viewers [of television] to switch off advertisers' announcements'. **1958** A. SILLITOE *Sat. Night & Sun. Morn.* vi. 82 She was known as a blab-mouth in all the pubs. **1962** *Punch* 5 Dec. 834/2 Others..ignore the commercial interference..without benefit of blab-off devices.

† **blab**, *v.*[2] *Obs.* [f. BLAB *sb.*[2]; cf. BLEB, BLOB.] *trans.* To swell, make swollen (the cheeks). Hence **blabbed** *ppl. a.*

1601 HOLLAND *Pliny* I. 427 Some of them looke pale, with a paire of flaggie blabd-cheekes. **1719** RAMSAY *Content* Wks. 1848 I. 148 [She] Blabs her fair cheeks till she is almost blind. Poor Phillis' death the briny pearl demands.

blabber ('blæbə(r)), *sb.* [f. BLAB *v.* + -ER[1].] One who blabs; one who reveals secrets, a tell-tale.

1557 NORTH *Gueuara's Diall Pr.* (1582) 94 a, He was..a great blabber of his tongue. **1624** HEYWOOD *Captives* v. iii, in Bullen *O. Pl.* IV, Peace, fellowe Godfrey. I'l now play the blabber. **1793** T. JEFFERSON *Writ.* (1830) IV. 491 The indiscretion of this blabber. **1841** D'ISRAELI *Amen. Lit.* (1867) 236 Time, that blabber of more fatal secrets.

† '**blabber**, *a.* Also 5 blabyr, 6-7 blaber. [First in comb. *blabyr-lyppyd*, in the *Catholicon* 1483, the *Prompt.* *c* 1440 having the earlier *babbyr-lyppyd*, used also by Langland 1377 (see BABBER-LIPPED). But there was also a 15-17th c. form *blab-lipped* (see BLAB *sb.*[2]), which is of more simple explanation: cf. BLOB, BLOBBER, BLUBBER, BUBBLE, all expressing the sense of swelling or inflation.] Swollen, protruding; said of the lips (e.g. of negroes), and sometimes the cheeks.

1552 HULOET, Blabber lyppes, *dimissa labra.* **1610** HOLLAND *Camden's Brit.* I. 530 The divels of Crowland, with their blabber lips [*labiis pendentibus*]. *a* **1627** MIDDLETON *Sp. Gipsy* IV. iii, She has full blabber cheeks. **1687** SHADWELL *Juvenal* 108 What ugly blabber-lipps had he! **1833** COLERIDGE in *Fraser's Mag.* VII. 177 A waxy face and a blabber lip. [In *Poems* III. 87 (1834) 'blubber lip.']

Hence **blabber-lipped** *ppl. a.*

[1377, 1440, 1607; see BABBER-LIPPED.] **1483** *Cath. Angl.* 33 Blabyrlyppyd, *broccus, labrosus.* *c* **1485** *Digby Myst.* III. 927 Ye..blabyr-lyppyd bycchys. **1601** HOLLAND *Pliny* XI. xxxvii, Others againe who are blabber-lipped are named in Latine *Labiones.* **1653** GREAVES *Seraglio* 101 The most.. blabber-lipped, and flat nosed girles that may be had through all Egypt. **1704** *Lond. Gaz.* No. 4034/4 Run away ..a short Negro Man..blabber Lip'd..long Heel'd.

† **blabber,** *v. Obs.* Forms: 4 **blaberen, blaiberen,** 5 **blaberyn, -veryn, blabir, -yr,** 5–6 **blaber,** 6 **blabbar,** 7 **-or,** 6–7 **blabber.** [ME. *blaberen*, late 14th c. Words of similar form appear in other Teut. langs.: cf. ON. *blabbra* (cited by Rietz), Da. *blabbre* to babble, gabble, Sw. dial. *blaffra* to prattle, G. *blappern* (Grimm), *plappern* to blab, babble, prate. But the evidence is not sufficient to show whether any of these were actually connected with the English word, or whether they agree only in being natural expressions of the action involved, which seems to be essentially that of producing a confused repetition or combination of labial (*b*) and lingual (*l, r*) sounds. It is noteworthy that in the earliest instance quoted, *blaberde* varies in the MSS. with *babeled, bablide*, etc.: cf. BABBLE. See further under BLAB.]

1. *intr.* To make sounds with the lips and tongue as an infant (cf. sense 3); to speak inarticulately or indistinctly; to babble, to mumble.

1362 LANGL. *P. Pl.* A. v. 8 So I blaberde [*v.r.* blaberid, babelide, -ed, bablide] on my Beodes. **1382** WYCLIF *1 Esdr.* Prol., The tunge kut of it shal blaberen. *c* **1505** KENNEDIE *Flyting* 344 And blaberis that noyis mennis eris to here. **1530** PALSGR. 456 My sonne dothe but blabber yet, he can nat speke his wordes playne. *a* **1800** *Ballad 'Ld. Ingram'* xxi, in Child's *Ballads* III. 131/2 A' was for the bonnie babe That lay blabbering in her bleed.

b. *trans.*

c **1505** DUNBAR *Flyting* 112 Fairar Inglis..Than thow can blabbar with thy Carrik lippis.

2. *intr.* To chatter, babble, talk idly or senselessly.

c **1375** WYCLIF *Serm.* Sel. Wks. I. 376 þei blaiberen þus for defaute of witt. *a* **1400** *Cov. Myst.* 164 Boys now blaberyn. *c* **1430** *Life St. Kath.* (1884) 53 þat oþer cristen peple presume not to blaber aȝenst oure goddes. *c* **1440** *Promp. Parv.* 37 Blaberyn, or speke wythe-owte resone, *blatero.* **1483** *Cath. Angl.* 33 To Blabyr, *blaterare.*

b. *trans.*; also with *out, forth.* Cf. *blab, blurt.*

c **1380** WYCLIF *Wks.* (1880) 168 Prestis..blabren out matynys and masse..wiþ-outen deuocion and contemplacion. *Ibid.* 73 þei prechen not cristis gospel..but blaberen forþe anticristis bullis. **1580** SIDNEY *Arcadia* IV. 417 Did blabber out what he had found. **1624** A. H. in *J. Davies' Wks.* (1878) II. 81 And blabber forth His Funerall, in Rimes.

† **3.** To move the tongue between the lips in mockery. *Obs.* Cf. BLEAR *v.*²

1530 PALSGR. 456, I blaber, I put forthe the lyppe, as one dothe his tonge in his heed..his tonge blabred in his heed, *Je baboye.* **1611** COTGR., *Baboyer*, to blabber with the lips: to famble, to falter. **1629** *Schoole Gd. Manners* (Halliw.) To mocke anybody by blabboring out the tongue is the part of ..lewd boyes.

† **ˈblabberer.** *Obs.* One who blabbers.

c **1375** WYCLIF *Serm.* Sel. Wks. II. 234 For to speke as blaborers may take here.

† **ˈblabbering,** *vbl. sb.* [f. BLABBER *v.* + -ING¹.] Inarticulate, imperfect or foolish speaking; babble.

c **1375** WYCLIF *Serm.* Sel. Wks. I. 127 And so to blaberynge in þis speche mannis voicis ben not sufficient. *a* **1400** *Cov. Myst.* 384 Ces now youre blaberyng in the develis name. **1513** DOUGLAS *Æneis* Prol. 33 This ignorant blabring imperfyte. **1795** T. TAYLOR *Apuleius* (1822) 234 The vain blabbering of that iniquitous knave.

† **ˈblabbering,** *ppl. a.* [f. as prec. + -ING².] Speaking inarticulately or irrationally; babbling.

c **1410** LOVE *Bonavent. Mirr.* xl. 88 (Gibbs MS.) He þat is vnknowynge and blaberynge. *c* **1430** *Hymns Virg.* (1867) 108 þat blaberyng are wiþ oþes blent. **1509** BARCLAY *Shyp of Folys* (1570) 38 Blabbering fooles superflue of language. **1549** *Compl. Scot.* vi. 38 Blaberand eccho.

blabber-mouth, blabbermouth (ˈblæbə maʊθ). *slang* (orig. *U.S.*). = BLABBER *sb.*

1936 STEINBECK *In Dubious Battle* xiii. 249 One minute he's a blabber-mouth kid. **1956** D. KARP *All Honorable Men* 174 No, Burney isn't a blabbermouth. He tells you a lot less than he knows. **1959** I. & P. OPIE *Lore & Lang. Schoolchildren* x. 189 One who blabs to a teacher or to a senior is a 'blabber-mouth'.

ˈblabbing, *vbl. sb.* [f. BLAB *v.*¹ + -ING¹.] Indiscreet talking; publishing or revealing of secrets.

1602 WARNER *Alb. Eng.* XII. lxxv, For his blabbing him to her the which had had his Ring. **1716** ADDISON *Free-holder* No. 9 (1751) 52 Many here wish you would forbear blabbing. *a* **1791** WESLEY *Husb. & Wives* iii. §8 Wks. 1811 IX. 67 Be strange to one whom experience has convinced of blabbing. **1878** SEELEY *Stein* II. 536 Blabbing of secrets.

blabbing (ˈblæbɪŋ), *ppl. a.* [f. as prec. + -ING².] That blabs or publishes secrets.

1593 SHAKS. *2 Hen. VI*, IV. i. 1 The gaudy, blabbing, and remorsefull day. **1637** MILTON *Comus* 138 The blabbing eastern scout, The nice morn. **1705** HICKERINGILL *Priest-Cr.* II. viii. 85 This blabbing and talkative old Fellow. **1855** TENNYSON *Maud* II. v. vi, Curse me the blabbing lip.

† **ˈblabbish,** *a. Obs.* [f. BLAB *sb.* + -ISH¹.] Of the nature of a blab, given to blabbing.

1604 T. WRIGHT *Passions* IV. i. 119 So simple and blabbish.

blabery, obs. form of BLAEBERRY.

blab-lipped: see after BLAB *sb.*²

blacche, obs. form of BLATCH, blacking.

black (blæk), *a.* Forms: 1 **blæc** (*def.* **blace**), 1–4 **blac,** 2–6 **blake,** 3–5 **blak,** 5 **blaak(e,** 4–7 **blacke,** 5– **black.** [OE. *blæc, blac* (def. *blace*) = OHG. *blah-, blach-* (in comb.); a word of difficult history. In OE., found also (as the metres show) with long vowel *blāc, blācan*, and thus confused with *blác* shining, white:—OTeut. **blaiko-* (see BLAKE), as is shown by the fact that the latter also occurs with short vowel, *blăc, blăcum*; in ME. the two words are often distinguishable only by the context, and sometimes not by that. (Cf. ¶7.) ON. *blakkr* is not an exact phonetic equivalent, but, if native, points to an OTeut. **blakko-* (for *blak'no*: see Kluge *Beitr.* ix. 162). Sievers suggests that the original Teutonic types were *'*blăkno-*, **blak'ko-*, subsequently levelled to *blăko-, blako-, blakko-*, giving the OE. and ON. words; in this case **blăk-no-* might be pa. pple. of a vb. **blăkan* to burn (cogn. w. Gr. φλέγειν), and the original sense 'burnt, scorched.' Cf. BLATCH, which points to an OTeut. **blakkjo-*, from *blakko-*. In Eng. *black* has quite displaced the original colour-word SWART, which remains in the other Teutonic languages.]

I. *literal.* The proper word for a certain quality practically classed among colours, but consisting optically in the total absence of colour, due to the absence or total absorption of light, as its opposite *white* arises from the reflection of all the rays of light.

1. a. As a colour pertaining to objects, even in full light: Absorbing all light; 'of the colour of night' (J.); 'of the colour of soot or coal'; 'of the darkest possible hue'; swart. (Perfect blackness being a rare attribute of objects, those from the surface of which very little light is reflected are commonly called *black.*)

Beowulf 3606 Hrefn blaca heofenes wynne. *c* **890** K. ÆLFRED *Bæda* II. xvi. (Bosw.) He hæfde blæc feax, and blacne andwlitan. *c* **1000** ÆLFRIC *Gram.* vi. 12 *Niger coruus*, blac hrem. *c* **1205** LAY. 17699 Ane blake claðe. *c* **1300** *K. Alis.* 6259 Al blak so colebrond. *c* **1380** *Sir Ferumb.* 2461 þan lai he þar so blac so pych. **1382** WYCLIF *Song Sol.* v. 11 Blac [**1388** blake] as a crowe. *c* **1440** *Promp. Parv.* 38 Blak, *niger, ater.* *c* **1440** *York Myst.* xlviii. 143 In helle to dwelle with feendes blake. **1536** WRIOTHESLEY *Chron.* (1875) I. 51 Hattes of blake velwett and whyte feethers. **1588** SHAKS. *L.L.L.* IV. iii. 266 To look like her are Chimney-sweepers blacke. **1611** BIBLE *Matt.* v. 36 Thou canst not make one haire white or blacke. **1674** R. GODFREY *Inj. & Ab. Physic* 71 She had been in the black Box (meaning the Coffin) e're now. **1710** J. CLARK *Rohault's Physique* (1729) I. 223 The Black Body..absorbs and choaks all the Rays. **1807** ROBINSON *Archæol. Græca* v. v. 425 They put on mourning garments, which were always black. **1842** TENNYSON *Gardener's D.* 28 That hair More black than ashbuds in the front of March. **1885** LD. BLACKBURN in *Times* 9 July 3/2 It has been observed..that no number of black rabbits would ever make a black horse.

b. Of a very dark colour closely approaching black.

c **1420** *Liber Cocorum* 7 Take black sugur for mener menne. **1718** POPE *Iliad* I. 608 The priest himself..Pours the black wine. **1853** C. KNIGHT *Once upon Time* (1859) 417 On every road-side was what was familiarly termed 'the black ditch.' In every alley was a lesser black ditch. **1859** JEPHSON *Brittany* i. 3 The blackest of port-wine.

c. Having an extremely dark skin; strictly applied to negroes and negritos, and other dark-skinned races; often, loosely, to non-European races, little darker than many Europeans.

890 [see 1]. *a* **1225** *Ancr. R.* 234 Blac as a bloamon. *a* **1225** *St. Marher.* 10 Muchele del blaccre þen euer eni blamon. *c* **1380** *Sir Ferumb.* 2785 Among þe Sarsynz blake. **1553** EDEN *Treat. New Ind.* (Arb.) 14 The bodyes of men begin to waxe blacke and to be scorched. **1591** [See BLACK MAN 1]. **1666–7** [See BLACK BOY 1]. **1782** *India Gaz.* 30 Mar. (Y.) The black officers..were drummed out of the cantonments. **1842** PRICHARD *Nat. Hist. Man* 24 Forrest says the Pappua Caffres are as black as the Caffres of Africa. **1856** [See BLACK BOY 1].

d. *fig.* Of or pertaining to the negro race.

1852 T. HUGHES in *J. Ludlow's Hist. U.S.* 342 The 'black law,' by which coloured people were excluded from the territory. **1885** STEVENSON *Dynamiter* 152 The black blood that I now knew to circulate in my veins.

2. With the names of various objects prefixed, by way of comparison, as *coal-, jet-, pitch-, raven-black.*

c **1600** SHAKS. *Sonn.* cxxvii, My mistress eyes are raven-black. **1710** *Lond. Gaz.* No. 4782/4 Stolen or stray'd..a cole black Horse. **1771** P. PARSONS *Newmarket* II. 89 On his head, observe the jett-black glossy velvet cap.

3. Characterized in some way by this colour.

a. Having black hair; dark-complexioned. (Cf. the surnames *Black, Blackie.*) *arch.* or *Obs.*

a **1067** *Chart. Eadweard* in *Cod. Dipl.* IV. 242 And Ælfwynes ȝherde ðe blake. *c* **1190** *Vita S. Godrici* §510 (1845) 417 Mulier pedissequa..cognomento Blache, id est Nigri, mercenaria. *c* **1375** BARBOUR *Bruce* XIX. 556, I dred me sair for the blak dowglass. **1604** SHAKS. *Oth.* II. i. 133 How if she be Blacke and Witty? **1661** PEPYS *Diary* 30 Apr., Took up Mr. Hater and his wife..I found her to be a very pretty, modest, black woman. **1715** R. NELSON *A Kempis' Chr. Exerc.* vii. 13 The Fair, the Black, the Learned, the Unlearned, do all pass away. **1815** *Hist. Univ. Camb.* I. 144 The portrait in the Master's lodge represents him as a handsome black man.

b. Wearing black clothing, armour, etc.

1298 [see BLACK MONK]. *c* **1305** *Edmund Conf.* 184 in *E.E.P.*, Blake monekes he seȝ, As hit crowen and choȝen were. *a* **1400** *Sir Perc.* 49 The rede kynghte ne the blake. **1750** CARTE *Hist. Eng.* II. 73 Clement..retained only 200 horse and 2000 foot of the black bands so called from their being clad in mourning. **1877** BROCKETT *Cross & Cr.* 154 The black, or monastic clergy.

c. Of coffee: see COFFEE *sb.* 1.

1796, 1867 [see COFFEE *sb.* 1 γ]. **1913** *Lancet* 29 Nov. 1563/2 Coffee is often made with a generous proportion of the powdered bean as in the case of after dinner 'black' coffee, the view being that the secret of good coffee is to make it strong. **1940** AUDEN *Another Time* 77 Kept awake with black coffee.

d. Applied to spades and clubs in a pack of cards. Cf. RED *a.* 16 e.

1676 [see ACE 1 b]. **1714** POPE *Rape of Lock* III. 23 The Club's black Tyrant first her Victim dy'd. **1860** 'PERSEVERANCE' *Patience* 9 Remembering to place a black 3 upon a red 3, a red 6 upon a black 6. **1953** A. CHRISTIE *Pocket Full of Rye* viii. 52 Miss Ramsbottom continued with her patience.. 'Red seven on black eight. Now I can move up the King.'

4. Characterized by absence of light.

a. Enveloped in darkness; dark, dusky, swart.

1393 GOWER *Conf.* I. 81 The blacke winter night. *c* **1400** *Rom. Rose* 5359 The blak shadowes. **1595** SHAKS. *John* v. vi. 17 Heere walke I, in the black brow of night. **1637** MILTON *Comus* 61 In thick shelter of black shades imbower'd. **1790** BURNS *Tam O'Shanter* 69 That hour, o'night's black arch the key stane. **1840** R. DANA *Bef. Mast* x, The rain fell fast, and it grew black. **1883** J. PARKER *Apost. Life* II. 168 Storms howling down the black chimney in the blacker night.

b. Of deep water, clouds, the clouded sky, etc.: Reflecting and transmitting little light; dark, sombre, dusky, gloomy.

c **1374** CHAUCER *Boeth.* v. ii. 153 þe nyȝt ne wiþstondeþ nat to hym by þe blake cloudes. *c* **1400** *Ywaine & Gaw.* 369 The weder wex than wonder blak. **1611** BIBLE *1 Kings* xviii. 45 The heauen was blacke with cloudes. **1626** BACON *Sylva* §874 Water of the Sea..looketh Blacker when it is moved, and Whiter when it resteth. **1646** BUCK *Rich. III*, III. 84 The young Princes were imbarqued in a Ship at Tower wharfe, and conveyed..to Sea, so cast into the Blacke deeps. **1818** BYRON *Juan* I. lxxiii, The blackest sky Foretells the heaviest tempest.

5. Deeply stained with dirt; soiled, dirty, foul.

a **1300** *Havelok* 555 In a poke ful and blac. *c* **1384** CHAUCER *H. Fame* 1637 But he [i.e. Eolus] Toke out hys blake trumpe of bras That fouler than the Devill was. **1387** TREVISA *Higden* Rolls Ser. V. 229 Blake flokkes of Scottes [*tetri Scotorum greges*]. *Mod. Proverb. Rime.* I'd rather have black hands, and plenty of meat, Than never such white ones, and nothing to eat.

6. a. *Black* is used in naming varieties or species of animals naturally distinguished by this colour, as *black bear, beetle, duck, rat*; also varieties or species (or what are popularly so considered) of plants characterized by darkness of stem, leaf, etc., as *black bindweed, hellebore, parsley, spleenwort*, etc. See these and the like under the generic names BEAR, BEETLE, BINDWEED, HELLEBORE, etc.

b. In the names of artificial flies used in fly-fishing.

1496 [see LOUPER]. **1655** WALTON *Angler* (ed. 2) v. 145 There are twelve Kinds of Artificial made Flies to Angle with upon the top of the water... The sixth is, the black-fly .., the body made of black-wool and lapt about with the herle of a Peacocks tail. **1799** [see MIDGE 2]. **1837** KIRKBRIDE *Northern Angler* 35 The Black Midge, or Gnat,..cannot be made too fine and small. *Ibid.* 51 The Black Palmer..is made with a body of black ostrich harle, ribbed with silver thread. *Ibid.* 57 The Black Spinner..has acquired a high reputation, both as a lake and a river-fly. **1923** *Daily Mail* 11 Aug. 7 The Lea should yield some good specimens of these fish to the black gnat.

¶ **7.** In ME. it is often doubtful whether *blac, blak, blake*, means 'black, dark,' or 'pale, colourless, wan, livid' = OE. *blác*; see farther under BLAKE.

c **1205** LAY. 19890 Ænne stunde he wes blac and on heuwe swiðe wak. Ane while he wes reod. *a* **1240** *Sawles Warde* in *Cott. Hom.* 249 His leoc deaðliche ant blac and elheowet. *c* **1325** *E.E. Allit. P.* B. 747, I am bot erþe ful euel, & vsle so blake. *c* **1330** *Roland & V.* 434 [Charlemagne was] of a stern sight, Blac of here and rede of face. [He had 'la chevelure belle' (Martin, from Eginhard.)] *c* **1420** *Anturs of Arth.* ix, Alle bare was the body, and blak by the bone.

II. *fig.*

8. a. Having dark or deadly purposes, malignant; pertaining to or involving death, deadly; baneful, disastrous, sinister.

1583 STUBBES *Anat. Abus.* II. 22 Many a black curse haue they of the poore commons for their doing. **1599** SHAKS. *Hen. V*, II. iv. 56 That black Name, Edward, black Prince of Wales. **1640** HABINGTON *Castara* II. II. xxxii, The blacke edict of a tyrant grave. *Ibid.* II. II. xi, By Fate rob'd even of that blacke victory. **1713** STEELE *Guardian* No. 18 ¶1 Think it madness to be unprepar'd against the black moment. **1758** H. WALPOLE *Catal. R. Authors* (1759) I. 142 The throne..usurped by the Queen's black enemy, Philip. **1821** BYRON *Sardan.* v. i. 195 That's a black augury!

b. *spec.* Of comedy: macabre. Cf. Fr. *pièce noire*.

1963 *Listener* 14 Feb. 310/1, I prefer my black comedy a little blacker. **1964** *Ibid.* 13 Feb. 287/3 His recent group of Swiftean black comedies. **1964** *Guardian* 8 July 7/6 [It is] 'black comedy'. Death's kind of fashionable nowadays. **1965** *Listener* 11 Mar. 379/3 The whole form of 'Berck-Plage', a poem about a seaside funeral, is a most remarkable piece of black cinema.

9. Foul, iniquitous, atrocious, horribly wicked.

1581 LAMBARDE *Eiren.* (1588) App., You wil haue a blacke soule..if you doe not the sooner forsake the Queene..and her heresies. **1592** GREENE *Groatsw. Wit* (1617) 33 Black is the remembrance of my blacke works. *c* **1600** J. DAVIES in Farr's *S.P.* I. 255 Red Seas to drowne our blacke Egyptian Sins. **1692** BENTLEY *Boyle Lect.* 23 The portion of the blackest criminals. **1713** S. PYCROFT *Free-thinking* 25 He has vented the blackest Calumnies. **1738** A. M'AULAY in *Swift's Lett.* clix, I shall never be guilty of such black ingratitude. **1749** FIELDING *Tom Jones* XVII. vii, Concealing facts of the blackest dye. **1839** BAILEY *Festus* v, Die with the black lie flapping on your lips.

10. a. Clouded with sorrow or melancholy; dismal, gloomy, sad.

1659 HAMMOND *On Ps.* xlii. 9 What a black gloomy condition am I now in? **1715** BURNET *Own Time* (1766) II. 234 He had also very black fits of the spleen. **1809** J. BARLOW *Columb.* I. 16 The slow, still march of black despair.

b. Of the countenance, the 'look' of things, prospects: Clouded with anger, frowning; threatening, boding ill; the opposite of *bright* and *hopeful*.

1709 STANHOPE *Paraphr.* IV. 190 When the Face of affairs looked blackest and no glimpse of Comfort appeared. **1832** HT. MARTINEAU *Each & All* ii. 25 His countenance was black as night. **1840** E. ELLIOTT *Corn-Law Rhymes* 119 The crew will no longer regard my child with black looks.

c. Hence *to look black*: to frown, to look angrily (*at* or *upon* a person).

1814 MISS AUSTEN *Mansf. Pk.* (1870) I. vi. 50 My brother-in-law..looked rather black upon me. **1855** THACKERAY *Rose & Ring* xv, Black as thunder looked King Padella at this proud noble. **1855** BROWNING *Fra Lippo*, The monks looked black.

11. a. Indicating disgrace, censure, liability to punishment, etc. Cf. BLACK BOOKS, BLACK LIST *sb.*, etc. Often accompanied by some symbol actually black, as in quot. 1840.

1612 BRINSLEY *Lud. Lit.* 286 To punish by a note, which may be called, the Black Bill. *c* **1830** A. PICKEN *Chang. Charlie*, When mounted..on the top of the black stool, he seemed..delighted. **1840** DICKENS *Barn. Rudge* viii, Write Curzon down, Denounced..Put a black cross against the name of Curzon.

b. Short for BLACK-LEG 3c: of persons or of work performed by 'blackleg' labour. Hence in extended use, of work boycotted by trade unions during a dispute, also of products, supplies, etc., which they refuse to handle.

1927 *Daily Tel.* 22 Nov. 12/2 The Waterside Workers' Federation to-day declared as 'black' the steamer Kakakiri. **1935** *Economist* 8 June 1302/2 [Work books] will facilitate the control of the labour market and the prevention of 'double-earning' and 'black labour'. **1956** *Times* 24 Aug. 8/4 Two more freighters..were declared 'black' to-day by the boilermakers' union because of work being done by members of the crew. **1959** *New Statesman* 11 July 34/1 Meanwhile, as magazines and provincial papers progressively close down, tension is increasing in those offices where arrangements have been made to produce 'black' editions. **1963** *Times* 28 May 5/1 When supervisory staff took over maintenance and transport driving duties, all the firm's production men quickly classified their work as 'black' and walked out.

c. Existing in contravention of economic regulations, as the 'black market'; hence, bought or sold by illicit trading.

1937 S. & B. WEBB *Soviet Communism* (ed. 2) II. 1199 There was always in Moscow and Leningrad, Kharkov and Kiev, the so-called 'Black Exchange', where native speculators illegally offered to the tourist, for American dollars or British pound notes, five, ten or twenty times as many roubles as the State Bank would give. **1938** *Baltimore Sun* 18 Mar. 3/1 We're expected to buy 'black' rubles or bootleg rubles which are available..at a fraction of the standard rate. We used to get them in what we call the Black Bourse... It's..a name applied to the 'bootleg' circles; to channels through which we bought black rubles. **1942** *Ann. Reg. 1941* 175 Contravention of war economic decrees, *e.g.* black slaughtering, were frequently punished with death. **1946** *Times* 18 Apr. 5/6 There are some things—food bought 'black' and services—which are not to be had for Reichsmarks.

III. Phrases and combinations.

12. Phrases. *to say black is anyone's eye* (*eyebrow, nail*, etc.): to find fault with, to lay anything to his charge (? *obs.*) *black in the face*: having the face made dark crimson or purple by strangulation, passion, or strenuous and violent effort.

1528 ROY *Sat.* (1845) They eate their belies full..And none sayth blacke is his eye. **1589** *Hay any Work* 36 If you were my chaplains once, I trowe John Whitgift..durst not once say blacke to your eies. **1675** BROOKS *Gold. Key* Wks. 1867 V. 250 He knew that the law could not say black was his eye, and that the judge upon the bench would pronounce him righteous. **1720** *Vade-mec. Malt-Worms* 11 None can say that black's his eyebrow to him. **1749** FIELDING *Tom Jones* IX. iv, I defy anybody to say black is my eye. **1789** WOLCOTT (P. Pindar) *Ep. Falling Minist.* Wks. 1812 II. 121 Swore himself black in the face. **1828** CARR *Craven Dial.* II. 2 'Thou cannot say black's my nail'..*Cui tu nihil dicas vitii*. Ter. **1836** DICKENS *Pickw.* v, Mr. Winkle pulled..till he was black in the face. **1870** LOWELL *Study Wind.* 67 Though we should boast..till we were black in the face.

13. black and blue, orig. *blak and bla*, *blak and blo*, of which the present form is a corruption arising when *blo* became obsolete after 1550. The proper *black and blae* remains in the north, though often supplanted there also by the literary form.

esp. Of the human body: Discoloured by beating, bruising, or pinching, so as to have black and 'blue' or livid bruises: as *to beat* (*any one*) *black and blue*. Also *absol.*

a **1300** *Cursor M.* 8073 Four sarzins..Blac and bla [*Trin.* blak and blo] als led þai war. *c* **1314** *Guy Warw.* (A.) 506 Þe leches ben to him y-go, Gy þai finde blaike and blo. *c* **1460** *Towneley Myst.* 206 Bett hym blak and bloo. **1552** HULOET, Beaten blacke and bloo, *suggilatus*. **1563** HYLL *Arte Garden.* (1593) 68 The black and blewe of a stripe. **1663** BUTLER *Hud.* I. ii. 942 Flew To rescue Knight from black and blue. **1690** *Lond. Gaz.* No. 2577/4 His right Eye black and blue with a Blow. **1785** BURNS *Twa Herds* xii, Aft hae made us black and blae. *a* **1845** HOOD *Happy New Year* xii, He's come home black and blue from the cane.

14. a. black and tan (of a kind of terrier dog): Having black hair upon the back, and tan (yellowish brown) hair upon the face, flanks, and legs. Also *ellipt.* as *sb.*

1850 C. M. YONGE *Langley School* vi. 41 Oscar, the bloodhound, that monster of a black-and-tan dog. **1863** KINGSLEY *Water-Bab.* vi. 272 Out jumped a little black and tan terrier dog. **1870** D. J. KIRWAN *Palace & Hovel* (1963) xiii. 118 The dog-fancier may be noticed with..a black and tan under one arm and a spaniel under the other. **1884** *Harper's Mag.* Aug. 464/1 A jealous little black-and-tan stood by. **1948** C. L. B. HUBBARD *Dogs in Britain* III. xx. 271 Since 1925 Black-and-Tan Miniature Terriers may exceed the previous weight limit of 7 pounds.

b. *black and tan*: a drink composed of porter (or stout) and ale. *slang.*

1889 in BARRÈRE & LELAND *Dict. Slang.* **1955** G. FREEMAN *Liberty Man* I. iv. 60 He asked for a pint of black and tan, and had to explain to the waiter what it was. **1958** A. SILLITOE *Sat. Night & Sun. Morn.* vi. 93 Gin-and-orange? I'll have a black-and-tan.

c. *Black and Tans*: popular name for an armed force specially recruited to combat the Sinn-Feiners in 1921, so named from the mixture (black and khaki) of constabulary and military uniforms worn by them. Also *attrib.* Hence *black-and-tannery*: the principles or activities of the Black and Tans.

1921 *Times* 28 Jan. 7/5 'God Save the King' and 'God Bless the Black and Tans'. **1921** LD. BRAYE in *Hansard Lords* XLIV. 792, I rise to ask His Majesty's Government.. whether they will..recall the Black and Tans. **1922** W. B. YEATS *Lett.* (1954) 680 The Black and Tans flogged young men and then tied them to their lorries by the heels. **1923** *Weekly Disp.* 4 Mar. 9 'How can I,' concluded Sir John Simon, 'defend black-and-tannery?' **1958** *Spectator* 8 Aug. 183/2 The only way would be a reversion to Black-and-tannery, to forcible coercion and repression.

15. black and white: **a.** *adj.* Having a surface diversified with black and white. Also applied *spec.* to a type of house painted white and having black timbers.

1612 W. STRACHEY *Hist. Trav. Virginia* (1849) I. x. 123 Squirrells they have..some blackish, or black and white. **1811** A. WILSON *Amer. Ornith.* III. 23 Black and White Creeper. *Certhia Maculata.* **1819** KEATS *Let.* 3 Jan. (1958) II. 29 Mrs. Dilke has two cats... The Mother is a tabby and the daughter a black and white. *c* **1830** E. GROSVENOR in G. Huxley *Lady Eliz. & Grosvenors* (1965) ii. 45 The house black and white outside and good carved oak within. **1848** MRS. GASKELL *Mary Barton* I. i. 2 One of those old-world, gabled, black and white houses. **1878** STEVENSON *Inl. Voy.*, Black-and-white cattle fantastically marked. **1936** M. ALLIS *Eng. Prelude* xv. 116 The same holds true of old houses, in which Shrewsbury is very rich, especially the type called 'black and white'. **1959** *New Biol.* XXX. 50 The Black and White Hawk-Eagle, *Spizaetus alboniger*. **1968** 'R. SIMONS' *Death on Display* xi. 171 High Tor was a black and white two-car-garage type, with a weedy drive, and..a large wooden cross above the front porch.

b. *sb.* Black characters upon white paper; writing. *in* (†*under*) *black and white*: in writing or in print. (*Black on white* is a fanciful alteration.)

1599 SHAKS. *Much Ado* v. i. 314 Moreouer sir, which indeede is not vnder white and black, this plaintiffe here.. did call me asse. *a* **1656** BP. HALL *Rem. Wks.* (1660) 136 We stay not till we have gotten it under black and white. **1712** STEELE *Spect.* No. 286 ¶3 Give us in Black and White your Opinion in the Matter. **1830** GALT *Lawrie T.* IV. x. (1849) 180 A confirmed black and white agreement. **1845** CARLYLE *Cromwell* (1871) IV. 117 In Authentic black-on-white against them. **1866** W. COLLINS *Armadale* IV. xv, The whole story of her life, in black and white.

c. *Art.* (A sketch or drawing in) black or dark tint on white paper, or with white colour used. Also *attrib.*, as in *black-and-white art, artist, drawing, sketch*.

1885 *Athenæum* 21 Feb. 251/1 Pictures and drawings in black and white. **1889** *Pall Mall Gaz.* 2 Jan., The modern work in which black-and-white art is seen in its most perfect stage of development... Many of the best black-and-white men of the day are represented. **1892** C. G. HARPER *Eng. Pen Artists* 60 Such excellent black-and-white renderings of dog life. *Ibid.* 178 The arts of black-and-white drawing. *Ibid.*, Colourists or black-and-white artists. **1895** PENNELL *Mod. Illustr.* Introd. 3 The amount of black-and-white work which he [*sc.* Dürer] produced. **1896** *Daily News* 29 Sept. 6/6 The well-known black-and-white artist, Mr. Fred Barnard.

d. *Photogr.* and *Television.* Applied to monochrome photographs, photographic reproductions, films, etc., opp. 'colour'.

1890 *Portfolio* XXI. Art Chron. xviii/2 In so far as small photographic black-and-white versions can be satisfactory they are very good. **1940** GRAVES & HODGE *Long Week-End* xxv. 434 American advertising carried far more photographs than British, both coloured and black and white. **1958** *Amateur Photographer* 31 Dec. 914/2 A 35-mm camera, with which it is undesirable to use the very fastest black-and-white films unless forced. **1961** *Guardian* 7 Feb. 6/4 Black-and-white television in cinemas.

16. Often prefixed to other adjectives of colour, indicating a blackish shade of the latter, as *black-brown, -green, -grey*, etc.

c **1000** ÆLFRIC *Gloss.* in Wr.-Wülcker *Voc.* 152 *Ferrugo*, blac purpur. **1462** *Test. Ebor.* II. 254 Unum equum coloris le blak-gray. **1685** *Lond. Gaz.* 2037/4 Stolen or strayed..a black-brown Gelding. **1844** KINGLAKE *Eothen* xxvii. (1878) 343 A long low line of blackest green. **1849** D. CAMPBELL *Inorg. Chem.* 257 This oxide separates after some time as a black-green hydride. **1863** BROWNING *Pippa P.* I, Its black-blue canopy seemed let descend. **1877** G. NEVILE *Horses* xv. 105 A black-chestnut will clip the same colour he was before. **1923** D. H. LAWRENCE *Birds, Beasts & Flowers* 180 The black-green skirts of a yellow-green old Mexican woman.

17. quasi-*adv.* with an adj., as in **black babbling**, babbling maliciously, slanderous; **black boding**, of ill omen, inauspicious; **black fasting**, enduring a very severe fast; *blacklooking*, etc.

1910 J. BUCHAN *Prester John* v. 97, I'll admit the truth to you, Davie. I'm *black afraid. **1915** —— *Salute to Adventurers* iii. 47, I had been sore at my imprisonment, I was *black angry at this manner of release. **1624** QUARLES *Job* (1717) 168 Earths *black-babling daughter (she that hears And vents alike, both truth and forgeries). **1742** YOUNG *Nt. Th.* iv. 8 *Black-boding man Receives, not suffers, death's tremendous blow. **1938** E. BOWEN *Death of Heart* I. i. 24 His father was *black depressed. **1664** *Floddan F.* vii. 66 *Black fasting as they were born. **1824** SCOTT *St. Ronan's* xvi, To sit for ten hours thegither, black fasting. **1854** J. ABBOTT *Napoleon* (1855) I. xx. 328 He was a little, *black-looking man.

18. In parasynthetic comb., as *black-aproned, -backed, -bearded, -berried, -bodied, -bordered, -breasted, -capped, -clothed, -coated, -coloured, -cornered, -draped, -edged, -favoured, -footed, -gowned, -hafted, -haired, -hearted, -hilted, -hoofed, -legged, -lipped, -maned, -margined, -necked, -orbed, -plumed, -rimmed, -robed, -scarved, -shawled, -skinned, -souled* (also *absol.*), *-spotted, -stoled, -striped, -tailed, -throated, -veiled, -veined, -visaged, -winged* adjs. etc., etc. Most of these are later than 16th c.: their number may be increased indefinitely, and they may have derivatives, as *blackheartedness*.

1776 PENNANT *Brit. Zool.* II. 445 *Black backed Gull.. Larus marinus. **1858** *U.S. War Dept. Rep. Explor. Railroad Route* IX. 98 Black-backed Three-toed Woodpecker. **1874** COUES *Birds N.W.* 368 Black-backed Eagle. **1833** TENNYSON *Dream Fair Women* in *Poems* 130 The stern *blackbearded kings with wolfish eyes. **1881** WILDE *Poems* 107 Grim watchmen on their lofty seats..strained black-bearded throats across the dusky parapet. **1838** DICKENS *Nickleby* i. 2 A *black-bordered letter to inform him how his uncle..was dead. **1815** STEPHENS in Shaw *Gen. Zool.* IX. I. 205 *Black-breasted woodpecker. **1854** *Poultry Chron.* I. 544/2 Game (Black-breasted and other Reds). **1873** W. CORY *Lett. & Jrnls.* (1897) 322 Our parson bends his *black-clothed back in the sun. **1871** *Member for Paris* II. 67 A sort of *black-coated Mephistopheles. **1528** PAYNELL *Salerne Regim.* Fiv, *Blacke colered wyne. **1607** SHAKS. *Timon* v. i. 47 When the day serues, before *blacke-corner'd night. **1898** *Westm. Gaz.* 28 May 10/1 The bowed, *black-draped figure passing sadly from the shadows in the Abbey. **1904** *Daily Chron.* 8 Dec. 3/2 The black-draped scaffold at Whitehall. **1865** MISS YONGE *Clever Wom. of Fam.* I. i. 5 Hurry to the drawing-room, and tear open the *black-edged letter. **1681** *Lond. Gaz.* No. 1668/4 A middle siz'd, *Black Favour'd [man]. *c* **1400** *Destr. Troy* VIII. 3780 Telamon truly was a tulke full faire, *Blake horit. **1771** BURKE *Powers of Juries* Wks. X. 122 Whether a *black-haired man or a fair-haired man presided in the Court. **1849** EASTWICK *Dry Leaves* 175 The *black-hearted gibes of a portion of our English press. **1863** *Times* 10 Apr., The 'black-hearted traitors' of the North..worse than the 'black-hearted miscreants' of the South. **1872** *Rep. Vermont Board Agric.* I. 94 A dry, dead knot is left when they [*sc.* the branches] are cut off, which sometimes kills the center of the tree, making it 'black-hearted'. **1932** A. J. WORRALL *Eng. Idioms* iii. 20 He is a black-hearted villain. **1871** MORLEY *Crit. Misc.* Ser. I. (1878) 250 Downright malignity and *blackheartedness. **1850** CUMMING 5 *Yrs. in S. Afr.* (1902) 115/2 The most magnificent old *black-maned lion. **1839** W. B. O. PEABODY in *Mass. Zool. & Bot. Surv., Rep. Ornith.* 358 The *Black

Necked Stilt, *Himantopus nigricollis.* **1910** F. W. FitzSimons *Snakes of S. Afr.* 73/2 Naia nigricollis. Black-necked Cobra... Average length 5 to 6 ft. Distribution: Natal, Zululand, Transvaal, [etc.]. **1934** *Discovery* Oct. 294/2 There has been a marked increase in the nesting of the black-necked grebes in Britain and Ireland. **1938** W. de la Mare *Memory* 73 Prowling, *black-orbed, disconsolate, Questing antennae, quivering wing. **1729** *Black-rimm'd [see rimmed *a.* 1] . **1922** Joyce *Ulysses* 128 Staring through his blackrimmed spectacles. **1858** M. Arnold *Merope* 9 This *black-rob'd train. **1863** Black-robed [see black *sb.* 5 c]. **1917** D. H. Lawrence *Look! We have come Through!* 81 *Black-scarved faces of womenfolk. **1929** R. Graves *Poems* 27 The *black-shawled peasant woman. **1840** Whitman *Uncoll. Poetry & Prose* (1921) I. 15 All lie earth's spreading arms within, The pure, the *black-souled, proud and low. **1944** E. Blunden *Shells by Stream* 43 And forth from black-souled hurricanes Conjures glad day. **1591** *Troub. Raigne K. John* I. iv, *Black-spotted Periure as he is. **1662** R. Smith (*title*) A Wonder of Wonders: .. an Invective against Black-spotted Faces. **1783** Latham *Gen. Syn. Birds* II. II. 633 Black-spotted P[igeon]. **1901** *Westm. Gaz.* 27 June 3/2 Black-spotted white foulard. **1932** D. Gascoyne *Roman Balcony* 9 A tattered projection of black-spotted leaves On a branch. **1815** Scott *Ld. of Isles* II. xxii, The *black-stoled brethren. **1908** *Westm. Gaz.* 21 Nov. 16/2 The finest perch of the week (2½ lb.) also hails from this part, though some nice specimens of the *black-striped fish have been secured from the Thames. **1923** D. H. Lawrence *Birds, Beasts & Flowers* 167 She [*sc.* the goat] .. reaches her black-striped face up like a snake. **1806** Lewis in *L. & Clark Exped.* (1905) IV. 87 The *black tailed fallow deer. **1863** Black tailed [see Godwit]. **1916** E. Blunden *Harbingers* 32 And black-tailed chub still shoal below. **1785** Pennant *Arctic Zool.* II. 363 *Black-throated Bunting. **1860** G. H. K. *Vac. Tour* 126 Hearing the hoarse cry of the black-throated diver. **1631** Weever *Anc. Fun. Mon.* 238 An house of *blacke veyled Nunnes. **1906** *Westm. Gaz.* 18 Aug. 11/2 These black-veiled children of the East. **1906** B'ness von Hutten *What became of Pam* III. i, A black-veiled nursing-sister. **1775** M. Harris *Eng. Lepidoptera* 7 *Papilio.* English Names... White, *black veined. **1903** *Westm. Gaz.* 1 Dec. 8/2 Black-veined marble. **1710** *Lond. Gaz.* No. 4695/3 This William Charlton is a *black visag'd Man. **1628** Feltham *Resolves* (1647) 41 Styx, and *black-wav'd Acheron. **1817** Shelley *Laon & Cythna* I. xxx. 16 *Black winged demon forms. **1953** E. Sitwell *Gardeners & Astronomers* 41 Only her sisters, harpy winds, black-winged like flies.

19. a. Specialized comb. (For such as *black cattle*, *black coal*, *black draught*, etc. see cattle, coal, draught, etc.) **black-about** *a.* (*nonce-wd.*), black all around; **Black Africa**, the part of the African continent, esp. south of the Sahara, (ruled and) inhabited predominantly by Blacks; **black-apronry**, the wearers of black aprons, the clerical and legal professions; **black arm**, a bacterial disease of cotton plants characterized by angular discolorations; **black bag** *adj. phr.* (U.S. colloq.), applied to activities of the Federal Bureau of Investigation involving illegal entry into premises; **black-band**, an earthy carbonate of iron found in the coal measures, and containing coaly matter sufficient for calcining the ore; **black bean**, (*a*) a bean of the genus *Phaseolus*, having black seeds; (*b*) an Australian hardwood tree (*Castanospermum australe*); also its timber; **black body** *Physics*, a body or surface that absorbs all radiation falling upon it; also *attrib.*, esp. in ***black-body radiation***, the radiation emitted by a black body; **black bomber** *slang*, an amphetamine tablet (see quot. 1964); † **black bowl**, a drinking bowl; **black box**, orig. Royal Air Force slang for a navigational instrument in an aeroplane; later extended to denote any automatic apparatus performing intricate functions (cf. quot. 1674 under black *a.* 1 a); also *fig.* and *attrib.*; **black bread**: see bread *sb.* 2 e; **black-buck**, a name used by sportsmen for the antelope proper (*Antilope cervicapra*); also, the South African *Hippotragus niger*; **black bun**, a rich fruit cake in a pastry case, eaten in Scotland, etc., at New Year; cf. *Hogmanay cake* s.v. Hogmanay; **black butter**, † (*a*) = *apple-butter*; (*b*) butter browned in a pan and mixed with vinegar and parsley to make a sauce; † **black canon**, a canon regular of St. Augustine; **black character** = black-letter; † **black-choler**, one of the four humours of early physiologists, melancholy; see choler; **black-clock** [clock *sb.*[3]], any black beetle, esp. the cockroach (*north. dial.*); **black-coat**, (*a*) a depreciative term for clergyman, parson; (*b*) any black-coated worker (see *black-coated* adj.); also *attrib.*; **black-coated** *a.*, spec. defining clerical or professional as distinguished from industrial or commercial occupations; hence, of or composed of persons engaged in such occupations; **black code** *U.S.*, a code or body of laws relating to Negroes in some Southern States, esp. before the abolition of slavery; **black cotton ground** or **soil**, a dark, rich soil found esp. in the Deccan region of India, produced by the disintegration of a black lava; = regur; **Black Country**, parts of Staffordshire and Warwickshire grimed and blackened by the smoke and dust of the coal and iron trades; **black-crop**, a crop of peas or beans as opposed to one of corn; **black curlew** (see quot.); **black damp**, the choke-damp of coal mines: see damp; **black disease**, a fatal disease of sheep characterized by necrosis of the liver (see quot. 1918); **black doctor** (see quot.); **black dress** *attrib.* (see quot.); **black dwarf** *Astr.*, a small, very dense star composed of degenerate matter which has cooled and become non-luminous; **black earth**, (*a*) = chernozem; also *attrib.*; (*b*) *attrib.* in ***black-earth country*** = black belt 2; **black economy**, (*a*) *U.S.*, the economy of the U.S. Black population; (*b*) = *underground economy* s.v. underground *a.* 4 e; see sense 11 c; **Black English**, the form of English spoken by many Blacks, esp. as an urban dialect of the U.S.; **black fast** *Eccl.*, a fast which includes abstinence from milk and eggs (cf. *black fasting* under sense 17); **black fellow**, an Australian aboriginal; also *gen.* = black man 1; **blackfellow's bread** = *native bread* (see bread *sb.*[1] 2 e); **black-figure** *Archæol.*, applied *attrib.* to a type of Greek pottery ornamented with figures in black silhouette; also *absol.*; so ***black-figured*** adj.; **black fox**, the red fox, *Vulpes fulva* , of northern America, during a colour phase in which its fur is black; **black frost**: see frost *sb.* 1; **black gang**, a gang employed on such work as coaling, stoking, etc.; **black gold** *colloq.* (chiefly *U.S.*), oil; also *transf.*; **black gown**, a collegian or learned man; *U.S.*, an Indian name for a Roman Catholic priest; **black growth** *U.S.* (see quots.); **Black Hand**, (*a*) defining a Spanish revolutionary society of anarchists; (*b*) defining a secret society of Italian immigrants in U.S., concerned chiefly in levying blackmail; hence **Black Hander**, a member of such a society; **black heart**, (*a*) (for *black* heart-cherry), a dark sort of cultivated cherry; (*b*) *Metallurgy*, used *attrib.* or *ellipt.* of a type of malleable cast iron having a core of graphite or the process for making this; **black heat** (see quots.); **black helmet**, a mollusc shell used in the making of shell-cameos; **black hole**: see as main entry; † **black-hood**, a non-regent member of the senate of the University of Cambridge; † **black humour**, black choler, melancholy: see humour; **black ice**, a thin hard transparent ice; **black Jew** (see Jew *sb.*); **black job** *slang* (*Obs.*), a funeral; **black joke**: see joke *sb.* 1; **black knot**, (*a*) any of certain kinds of fungus in the U.S.; (*b*) a fast knot as distinguished from a running knot (Ogilvie, 1881); **black larch** *U.S.*, an American variety of larch, the hackmatack; **black-lark** (see quots.); **black level** *Television*, the level of the picture signal that corresponds to black in the transmitted picture; also *attrib.*; **black light**, light-rays beyond the two ends of the visible spectrum; invisible ultra-violet or infra-red light; **black liquor**, acetate of iron used instead of green copperas as a mordant in dyeing (*Cent. Dict.* 1889); † **black literature**, that printed in 'black letter'; **black magic** (see magic *sb.* 1 b); **black money**, (*a*) see money *sb.* 1 d; (*b*) chiefly *India*, money not declared for tax purposes; cf. *black economy* (b) above; **Black Mountain**, used *attrib.* of a school of projective poets (cf. projective *a.* 7) led by Charles Olson (1910–70), who taught at Black Mountain College, N. Carolina; hence **Black Mountaineer**, one of these poets; **Black Museum**, the name given to a collection preserved at Scotland Yard of exhibits connected with crimes of the past; **Black Muslim**, a member of the Nation of Islam, an American Negro sect, established in 1931 by 'Wallace Farad' and developed from 1934 by Elijah Muhammad, which preaches a form of Islam and proposes principally the separation of Negroes and Whites; **Black Nationalism**, advocacy of the national civil rights of U.S. (also occas. of South African and other) Blacks; hence **Black Nationalist** *sb.* and *a.*; **black oil**, any of various dark-coloured oils, *spec.* heavy crude oil used for lubrication; **Black Panther**, a member of an American Negro organization which adopts a militant attitude to the promotion of the Negro cause; **black-plate** (see quot. 1858); **black pod**, a disease of the cocoa tree caused by the fungus *Phytophthora faberi*; **black pope**: see pope *sb.*[1] 1; **black power**, power for black people; used as a slogan of varying implication by, or in support of, Negro civil rights workers and organizations; **black print** *Photogr.* [print *sb.* 13], a print giving black lines on a white ground; **black propaganda**, falsified or unacknowledgeable propaganda, esp. that disseminated among the enemy, purporting to come from the enemy's own sources, and designed to lower morale; **black quarter**, a disease of cattle (= black-leg *sb.* 1); **black rent**, black mail, an illegal tribute; **Blackrobe** *Canad.*, [sense 3 b] a North-American Indian term for a Christian (missionary) priest; **black root**, any of various American plants with dark-coloured roots; **black root rot**, any of various diseases of plants characterized by black lesions of the root; spec. a disease of tobacco and other plants caused by the fungus *Thielaviopsis basicola*; **black rot**, any of various diseases of plants characterized by dark discoloration and decay; **black rubber vine**, an African plant producing a black juice which is used as rubber; **black rust** [rust *sb.*[1] 6 b], a plant rust producing black discoloration; **Black Sash**, applied *attrib.* to a women's anti-apartheid organization in South Africa; **black scab** (see quot. 1915); **black scale**, a destructive scale (*Lecanium oleæ*) infesting olive, citrus, and other cultivated plants; **black scour(s)** [scour *sb.*[2] 5], a hæmorrhagic diarrhœa of sheep, pigs, and cattle; **black-seed**, a popular name of the black Medick; **Black September**, the name adopted by a Palestinian Arab paramilitary group [from the month in 1970 when Jordan attacked Palestinian commandos]; hence **Black Septembrist**; **black sheet**, (a piece of) ungalvanized sheet iron; **black silk**, used *attrib.* to define a period of mourning during which black silk is worn instead of crape; **black soil** = chernozem; **black-sole** (*Sc.*) = blackfoot; **black southeaster** *S. Afr.* (see quots.); **black spring** *Austral.* (see quot.); **black step** *Printing* (see quot.); **black strap**, an inferior kind of port wine, also a mixture of rum and treacle taken as a beverage; **black stripe**; (*a*) = *black strap*; (*b*) a disease of the tomato-plant, produced by the fungus *Alternaria solani*; **black studies** chiefly *U.S.*, the investigation of African or Afro-American culture, history, etc., as a school or college course; **black stump** *Austral. colloq.*, a place imagined to be the last outpost of civilization, usu. in phr. ***this side of the black stump***; [the black stump has been variously but inconclusively identified since 1826 (cf. 1970 *Sun-Herald* (Sydney) 22 Feb. 27)]; **black sugar** (*Sc.*), Spanish or Italian (liquorice) juice; **black theology**, an interpretation of Christianity having special relevance to the aspirations of (esp. U.S.) Blacks; **black tie**, *spec.* a man's black bow-tie worn with a dinner-jacket; also *ellipt.*, evening dress including a black tie; so **black-tied** *a.*, wearing a black tie; **black tongue** chiefly *U.S.*, any of various diseases in human beings or animals characterized by a dark discoloration of the tongue; **black tooth** *U.S.*, a condition of pigs in which the teeth become black; **black tracker** *Austral.*, an Aboriginal employed to help the police in tracking down fugitives or persons lost in the bush; **black tripe**, unbleached tripe; **black turf (soil)**, a dark-coloured soil found in the Transvaal (see quots.); **black velvet**, (*a*) a drink made by mixing stout and champagne; (*b*) *Austral.* and *N.Z. slang*, a black-skinned or coloured woman; such women collectively; **black wart** = *black scab*; **Black Watch**, the 42nd Highland regiment of the British army (see quot.); **black widow (spider)** (see quots.); **black willow**, any of various willows (see quots.), esp. the *Salix nigra* of N. America; **black work**, (*a*) iron-work; also spec. (see quot. 1888); (*b*) blacked leather; (*c*) a kind of embroidery (see quot. 1910); (*d*) undertakers' work (cf. black man 3 and blackmaster); **black-wort**, a popular name of the common Comfrey (*Symphytum officinale*).

1876 G. M. Hopkins *Wr. Deutschland* (1918) st. xxiv, She to the *black-about air .. Was calling. **1938** L. Hughes *New Song* 10 Torn from *Black Africa's strand I came. **1947** A. Keppel-Jones *When Smuts Goes* viii. 139 Mishka and Nakovalny, whose country was now an Indian Ocean Power, regarded Black Africa as a very promising field for Muscovite missionary work. **1958** *Observer* 2 Nov. 7/4 The key to Black Africa lies in the vast territory of Nigeria. **1975** E. Shils in H. M. Patel et al. *Say not Struggle Nought Availeth* 83 In Black Africa, between 1954 and 1970, they have increased the number of pupils in primary schools threefold. **1832** Maginn in *Blackw. Mag.* XXXII. 427 The absurd etiquette which prevents [them] from following any profession save the Army, the Navy, *Black-apronry, and Black-leggery. **1907** W. A. Orton *U.S. Farmers' Bull.* CCCII. 41 There is a bacterial disease of cotton (*Bacterium malvacearum*) .. producing various symptoms and receiving various names, such as angular leaf-spot, *black-arm, boll-

spot, etc. 1939 Nature 14 Oct. 676/2 (title) Genetics of Blackarm Resistance in Cotton. 1973 Telegraph (Brisbane) 25 Aug. 4/1 An [F.B.I.] agent.. said he engaged in about a dozen illegal '*black bag jobs' during his career. 1977 Time 21 Nov. 50/3 As head of the domestic intelligence division for a decade, Sullivan was involved in many abuses including 'black bag' operating and illegal wiretapping of National Security Council phones. 1857 PAGE Adv. Text-bk. Geol. xiv. (1876) 252 Admixture of coaly matter which confers on these *black-bands their especial value. 1863 SMILES Indust. Biog. 160 The Black Band ironstone. 1792 E. RIOU tr. J. van Reenen's Jrnl. Journey from Cape Good Hope 29 Extensive handsome gardens, planted with kaffer corn, maize,.. *black beans. 1863 A. GRAY Man. Botany (ed. 4) p. xliv, Egyptian or Black Bean, cultivated for ornament, rarely for its beans.. seeds black or tawny with a white scar. 1895 J. H. MAIDEN in Agric. Gaz. N.S.W. V. 1 Because of the dark colour of the wood, and partly by way of distinction from the red bean, it is usually known by timber merchants as black bean. 1912 C. H. B. QUENNELL in L. Weaver Home & Equipm. 58 The bookcase illustrated has been made in a new Australian wood called 'black bean'. 1937 E. HEMINGWAY To have & have Not I. ii. 35, I had black bean soup and a beef stew. 1710 *Black body [see BLACK a. 1 a]. 1895 H. F. REID in Astrophysical Jrnl. II. 161 It is curious that a really black body, the most important in the theory of radiation, has not so far been used by experimenters. 1919 T. PRESTON Theory of Heat (ed. 3) vi. 559 The intensity of black-body radiation. 1923 GLAZEBROOK Dict. Appl. Physics IV. 568/1 Suppose that we have a substance with the property that all radiation falling on its surface is completely absorbed. This is called a black body. 1928 F. K. RICHTMYER Mod. Physics vii. 183 The 'black body' may radiate, as well as absorb, energy. Such radiation is called 'black body' radiation. 1957 Encycl. Brit. III. 679/1 The black-body temperature of a source like the sun is the temperature at which a black body would emit radiation of the same intensity. 1963 Daily Tel. 16 Oct. 23/1 Police who raided the house found.. 100 methydrine tablets and 99 '*Black Bomber' pills. 1964 Lancet 29 Aug. 452/1 The preparations in circulation apparently included 'black bombers' ('Durophet', a mixture of the two amphetamines). 1509 HAWES Past. Pleas. xxix. 136 He never dranke but in a fayre *blacke boule. 1568 Like to Like in Hazl. Dodsl. III. 324 From morning till night I sit tossing the black bowl. 1945 PARTRIDGE Dict. R.A.F. Slang 16 *Black box or gen box, instrument that enables bomb-aimer to see through clouds or in the dark. 1947 Jrnl. R. Aeronaut. Soc. LI. 432/1 These British night fighters were crammed with 'black boxes' all of which had to be operated by the pilot or his navigator. 1948 A. P. ROWE One Story of Radar i. 6 For many years the 'death ray' had been a hardy annual among optimistic inventors. The usual claim was that by means of a ray emanating from a secret device (known to us in the Air Ministry as a Black Box) the inventor had killed rabbits at short distances. 1953 Jrnl. Brit. Interplan. Soc. XII. 223 As far as the layman is concerned, a phantastron is a 'black box' which will divide the frequency of its output pulses by any integral number between 2 and 20. 1956 W. R. ASHBY Introd. Cybernetics vi. 86 Black Box theory is.. even wider in application than these professional studies. Ibid., In our daily lives we are confronted at every turn with systems whose internal mechanisms are not fully open to inspection, and which must be treated by the methods appropriate to the Black Box. 1962 Daily Tel. 14 Nov. 1/3 Russia advocated the use of unmanned seismic detection stations, known as 'black boxes' to Western scientists, as a means of avoiding inspection. 1964 Ibid. 3 July 25/5 The flight recorder is an indestructible 'black box' which automatically records the key functions in the aircraft... The 'black box' can.. tell what went wrong in a crash. 1964 Economist 25 July 356/1 Silent 'black boxes'—electronic computers which measure the varying demand for power of the Savannah. 1888 W. T. BLANFORD Mammalia 521 Antilope cervicapra. The Indian Antilope or *black Buck. 1902 Encycl. Brit. XXV. 453/2 Antelope.. properly denotes the Indian black buck, which alone constitutes the genus Antilope, with the title of A. cervicapra. 1898 J. L. WAUGH 'Mumper' 104 I'se warrant ye hae nae *black bun or currant loaf to first-fit wi'. 1929 F. M. MCNEILL Scots Kitchen 188 Black bun, a festive cake at Hogmanay. Big blue raisins, currants, sweet almonds; orange, lemon, and citron peel; flour, Demerara sugar, ground cloves or cinnamon, ground ginger, Jamaica pepper, black pepper, baking soda, buttermilk or eggs, brandy; crust; flour, butter, water. 1958 Spectator 30 May 698/2 We could have done with something more like a haggis and less like a black bun. 1808 JANE AUSTEN Let. 27 Dec. (1932) I. 241 Our *black butter.. was neither solid nor entirely sweet... Miss Austen had said she did not think it had been boiled enough. 1877 E. S. DALLAS Kettner's Bk. of Table 96 Black Butter—the French Beurre noir, much used for skate, for calf's brains, and the like. 1895 G. A. SALA Thorough Good Cook 470/1 Black butter sauce. 1906 MRS. BEETON Bk. Househ. Managem. x. 273 Black Butter Sauce. Ingredients—1½ ozs. of butter, 1 teaspoonful of chopped parsley, ½ a teaspoonful of vinegar. 1962 Listener 23 Aug. 299/1 Serve them [sc. mackerel] hot with black-butter sauce. To make the sauce.. melt 2 ounces of butter until it is dark brown but not burnt, and then throw chopped parsley into it and let it fry for a few seconds only. a 1672 WOOD Life (1848) 156 The abbey there, originally built for *Black Canons. 1722 J. STEVENS Addit. Dugdale's Monast. II. 69 By reason of their black Habit, worn over their white Surplices.. generally call'd either Black Canons, or Canons of St. Augustin. 1751 JOHNSON Rambl. No. 177 ¶6 Books.. printed in the *black character. 1620 *Black Clock [see CLOCK sb.[3]]. 1886 in F. PODMORE Apparitions & Thought Transf. (1894) vii. 169 He found a 'blackclock' (i.e. cockroach) floating in his coffee. 1944 S. CHAPLIN in Penguin New Writing XXII. 106 Living in that rat, mice, bug and blackclock infested area. 1627 R. PERROT Jacob's Vow 52 Let us take heed how these *blackcoates get the day of us. 1818 SCOTT Hrt. Midl. i, You are the black-coat's son of Knocktarlitie. 1870 EMERSON Soc. & Solit. ix. 197 The black-coats are good company only for black-coats. 1920 Times Weekly 19 Nov. 427 (heading) Rights of 'Black Coats'. 1940 Archit. Rev. LXXXVII. 110/1 Both these sorts of public house are essentially working class; the blackcoat's pub is another sort of place. 1945 H. J. MASSINGHAM in F. Thompson Lark Rise to Candleford p. ix, It was the vanguard of the city black-coats and proletariat, governed by the mass-mind. 1893 Jrnl. Soc. Arts 14 Apr. 506/1 The young fellow who will devote himself to agriculture.. in New Zealand.. may do even better than the youth who wins his way to the *black-coated servitude of a bank. 1902 Westm. Gaz. 11 Aug. 7/3 A serried rank of the black-coated. 1928 Britain's Industr. Future III. xiv. §6. 158 The workers are apt to be suspicious of 'black-coated' unions. 1932 D. L. SAYERS Have his Carcase i. 12 He can't be a fisherman or anything of that kind; they don't waste time snoozing. Only the black-coated brigade does that. 1937 Daily Herald 5 Jan. 3 London's blackcoated workers are to hold a mass meeting in the Albert Hall. 1840 Daily Picayune (New Orleans) 30 July 2/1 A black man.. [will] be tried before Judge Preval, under the *Black Code. 1876 Congress. Rec. 9 Aug. 5347/2, I hold in my hand the laws of the Legislature of South Carolina passed in the session of 1865–'66... Among the very first acts that they passed was the act which is known all over this country and all over the world as the 'black code' of South Carolina, a code that should disgrace every one of its authors. [a 1826 R. HEBER Narr. Journey India (1828) II. xxv. 168 A black soil, with many deep cracks, chiefly cultivated in cotton.] 1838 Penny Cycl. XII. 205/1 On the whole surface of the table-land [of the Deccan] a black soil prevails, which, from being favourable to the growth of cotton, has been called the *black cotton ground, or regur. 1844 W. H. SLEEMAN Rambles & Recoll. I. xiv. 123 The soil of the valley of the Nerbudda.. is formed for the most part of the detritus of trap-rocks... This basaltic detritus forms what is called the black cotton soil by the English, for what reason I know not. 1882 GEIKIE Text-bk. Geol. III. II. 442 The 'regur', or rich black cotton soil of India. 1935 THOMAS & SCOTT Uganda vii. 116 The top soil is very sticky when wet and cracks badly on drying... In its extreme form it is almost uncultivable and is known (quite erroneously since it will not grow cotton) as 'black cotton soil'. 1960 M. PERHAM Lugard 1898–1945 iii. 51 The black cotton-soil plains of Bornu [Nigeria], flat dry land patched with thorn-scrub. 1834 J. C. YOUNG Mem. C. M. Young (1871) 212 In the densely-populated *black country. 1864 Daily Tel. 12 Dec., By night the Black Country blazes up lurid and red with fires which.. are never extinguished. 1889 H. SAUNDERS Man. Brit. Birds 379 The Glossy Ibis. Plegadis falcinellus (Linnæus).. was known to gunners and fishermen as the '*Black Curlew'. 1911 M. HENRY in Agric. Gaz. N.S.W. XXII. 111 The post-mortem appearances in general are all indicative of '*black disease'. Ibid., In 'black disease', so far as is known, sheep about 20 months and 2 years old are principally affected. 1918 S. DODD in Jrnl. Comp. Path. & Therap. XXXI. 2 Two explanations of the origin of the term black disease are given, viz., (1) on account of the dark appearance of the liver of animals dead of the disease; (2) because of the dark colour assumed by the under surface of the skin. 1932 Discovery Dec. 401/2 Research on the black disease of sheep.. showed that the malady is caused through infection following injury to the liver by the young fluke. 1909 Westm. Gaz. 22 Oct. 4/2 When.. there is no possibility of catching a salmon except by that engine of death, the '*Black Doctor'—the three big hooks tied back to back and dragged along the floor of a pool. 1899 Daily News 3 July 5/6 The convict Billinge is what is known as a '*Black dress' man, being thus distinguished because of his bad conduct. 1966 C. HAYASHI in Stein & Cameron Stellar Evolution III. 199 These stars evolve towards *black dwarfs along the surface condition. 1978 PASACHOFF & KUTNER University Astron. x. 284 Some black dwarfs come from featherweight stars.., stars that were not massive enough to begin hydrogen burning; others are cooled white dwarfs. 1982 Sci. Amer. Jan. 69/2 Virtually all stars and galaxies will have yielded to internal gravitational forces and collapsed to form black dwarfs, neutron stars or black holes. 1842 Proc. Geol. Soc. III. 712 (title) On the Tchornoi Zem, or *Black Earth of Central Russia. 1905 Athenæum 5 Aug. 175/1 The black-earth country of the south. 1935 HUXLEY & HADDON We Europeans vii. 198 The black-earth belt of Russia. 1955 G. V. JACKS Multiling. Vocab. Soil Sci. 310 Black earth, general term including chernozem and dark plastic clays of tropics. 1969 T. L. CROSS Black Capitalism VI. 162 Another special need of the *black economy is for loans. 1972 2nd Nat. Symposium State of Black Econ. 21 Far too many black Americans find it easier to praise the black economy than to live in it. 1978 Washington Post 18 Jan. A1 When placed against the statistics of blacks still in poverty, they indicate the disturbing quality of the black economy—a slow-growing black middle-class and an increasingly jobless lower economic class. 1978 Financial Times 31 May 18/1 The existence of a black economy does lead to the understatement of activity when we are concerned with such things as decorating, building, motor repairs and the like. 1985 Daily Tel. 30 Mar. 16/2 There are.. many ways in which we are not like those.. Americans, but the rise of the black economy suggests that indifference to financial gain is not one of them. [1734 S. Carolina Gaz. 30 Mar. 3/2 To be sold... Four young Negroe Men Slaves and a Girl, who.. speak very good (Black-)English.] 1969 WOLFRAM & FASOLD in Baratz & Shuy Teaching Black Children to Read 139 Even in the rural South, *Black English is characteristically different from the speech of the lower socio-economic class white. 1978 English Jrnl. Dec. 7/1 There are dozens of standard kinds of Black English, which vary from Detroit to Chicago to Mobile to Albuquerque. 1981 Amer. Speech LVI. 163 Others deny that such a creole played a role in the development of modern black English. 1577 R. BARNES Charge 16 in Newcastle Tracts (1847) VI. 16 That no.. superfluous faste be vsed as those called the Lady fast saint trinyons fast, the *black faste. 1738 F. MOORE Trav. Africa 191 Natives, who had been got up together at the Persuasion of a *Black Fellow. 1828 New Monthly Mag. XXIII. 220 The fish are so abundant that a black fellow with a seine, can load a bullock-cart at one or two hauls. 1831 TYERMAN & BENN. Voy. & Trav. II. xxxvii. 158 In his opinion, the best use which could be made of 'the black fellows' would be, to shoot them all. 1865 Intell. Observ. No. 37. 15 Panther-like approach of the Blackfellow. 1925 Austral. Encycl. I. 496/1 Near decaying stumps or roots of eucalypts rounded lumps varying in size from a pin's head to a human head, and known to most people as 'blackfellows' bread' are often found. 1935 Bulletin (Sydney) 8 May 21/1 Quite good pipes can be carved out of a fungus known as 'blackfellow's bread', which can be dug up almost anywhere on the far South Coast of N.S.W. 1891 Jrnl. Hellenic Stud. XII. 164 Small fragment of a *black-figure cylix. 1930 J. D. BEAZLEY in Proc. Brit. Acad. XIV. 217 (title) Attic Black-Figure. 1948 A. LANE Gk. Pottery iii. 19 This orientalising phase of the seventh century saw also the introduction of polychrome painting and the 'black figure' technique, wherein black-painted silhouette figures were enriched with detail incised in the yet unfired clay. 1858 S. BIRCH Hist. Anc. Pottery I. iii. 224 The subjects represented on the *black figured vases. 1890 VERRALL & HARRISON Anc. Athens 432 It [sc. the vase] is of the finest early black-figured style, not later than the time of the sixth and fifth centuries B.C. 1602 J. BRERETON Discov. Virginia 13 Beares. Luzernes. *Blacke Foxes. 1826 J. D. GODMAN Amer. Nat. Hist. I. 276 The black fox is found throughout the northern parts of America.. where it is considered among the richest and most valuable of furs. 1922 C. T. BARNES Mammals of Utah 120 Black Fox, Silver Fox, Vulpes fulva argentata.. [is] uniform lustrous black with a distinct white tip to the tail. 1918 L. E. RUGGLES Navy Explained 24 The engineer's division is always known as the '*black gang'. 1923 R. D. PAINE Comr. Rolling Ocean iii. 44 There wasn't a smarter man in the black gang. 1910 Sunset XXV. 173 (title) California's *black gold: the romance of the oil gushers. 1926 H. C. WITWER Roughly Speaking 27 Gold—black gold—this farm is a hotbed of oil! 1948 South Bend (Ind.) Tribune 3 Apr. 5/1 The 'Black Gold' of the farm belt—grunting hogs—is beginning to tarnish. 1969 Punch 19 Mar. 401/3 Tankers which leave the Gulf with 200,000 tons of black gold come to Milford Haven with nothing but a cargo of pullulating bacteria. 1710 TOLAND Refl. Sacheverell's Serm. 12 That great Company of *Black-Gowns, commanded in chief by.. Doctor Lancaster. 1804 C. B. BROWN tr. Volney's Climate & Soil U.S.A. 409 This is as difficult to the black gowns as to ourselves. 1872 Amer. Naturalist VI. 94 Everywhere among the western Indians the Jesuits were known by the name of Blackgowns. 1814 in Mass. Hist. Soc. Coll. (1815) III. 121 The wood is chiefly *black growth, viz. hemlock and spruce. 1851 S. JUDD Margaret (ed. 2) I. xvii. 215 Yet there are, what by a kind of provincial misnomer is called the black growth, pines and firs. 1898 Harper's Weekly 12 Nov. 1100/2 The secret society called—from its picturesque method of warning its victims—the '*Black Hand' is a political organization known to have existed in the island before the beginning of the American war with Spain. 1904 N.Y. Tribune 31 July 2 For months the black hand society has been forcing Italians to contribute to its treasury with threats of death. 1905 Westm. Gaz. 5 Jan. 6/3 The notorious Italian blackmailing gang which has been given the name of the 'Black Hand Society'. 1906 Ibid. 2 June 9/3 La Mano Negra, the famous revolutionary Black Hand Society. 1923 L. J. VANCE Baroque viii. 49 The Wop detective that used to play horse with the Black Handers. 1707 MORTIMER Husb. 546 In June are ripe the White, Red, *Black and Bleeding Hearts. 1833 TENNYSON Blackbird 7 The unnetted black hearts ripen dark.. against the garden wall. 1910 Jrnl. Iron & Steel Inst. LXXXII. 477 In the American black-heart process low sulphur-irons are used. 1917 Ibid. XCVI. 330 For the most part, Americans do not machine their malleable castings, and hence they use 'black-heart', which is ordinary cast iron when the decarburised skin is taken off... 'Black-heart' castings were not suitable for certain purposes. 1962 B.S.I. News June 12/2 Methods of test for blackheart, whiteheart and pearlitic malleable iron. 1910 H. P. TIEMANN Iron & Steel 22 *Black heat; black hot, a temperature just below a visible red. 1958 Good Housekeeping Oct. 133/2 Most electric convectors give what is known as a black heat, which means that the element is made from a special, low resistance, thick wire which does not glow. 1962 Newnes Encycl. Electr. Engin. 365/2 Infra-red rays may be produced electrically by utilizing a 'dull emitter' resistance element operating at black heat. 1861 Chambers's Encycl. s.v. Cameo, The *Black Helmet.. has a dark onyx ground. 1876 Encycl. Brit. IV. 740 The black helmet (Cassis tuberosa) of the West Indian seas. 1797 Camb. Univ. Calend. 147 The Non-Regents or *Black-hoods are those who have taken their master of arts' degree five years or upwards. 1829 J. MACTAGGART Three Years in Canada I. 66 The most compact *black ice anywhere to be found. 1922 WRIGHT & PRIESTLEY Glaciology x. 325 Large sheets of fresh 'black' ice a very few inches thick.. had evidently formed between the floes. 1941 T. A. H. PEACOCKE Mountaineering v. 64 There is white ice which is really a form of very hard snow, and there is black ice, the real thing. Ibid., Black ice is seldom met with.. except.. when the snow has been stripped from the peaks by the fierce heat of the sun. [Black] ice slopes can generally be detected by a glint or gleam, for they reflect the sun's rays much like a piece of glass. 1961 Guardian 28 Dec. 1/3 Roads in many places were covered with black ice which was hard to detect at night. 1849 THACKERAY Lett. (1887) 91 An expatriated parson.. who gets his living by *black jobs entirely and attends all the funerals of our country-men. 1876 LORD LENNOX Celebrities I. xii. 313 The 'black job' business. 1851 P. BARRY Fruit Garden 364 The Plum Wart or *Black Knot.. originates.. from an imperfect circulation of the sap. 1884 W. MILLER Dict. Names Plants 252 Sphæria mortosa, 'Black knot' fungus. 1915 Board Agric. & Fisheries Leaflet No. 213 Gooseberry Black-knot (Plowrightia ribesia, Sacc.). The fungus.. causing this disease is closely related to Plowrightia morbosa, Sacc., the widely distributed 'black-knot' of plum and cherry trees in the United States and Canada. [1785 H. MARSHALL Amer. Grove 104 Black American Larch-Tree.] 1803 LAMBERT Descr. Genus Pinus I. 56 *Black Larch, P[inus] pendula,.. shews itself only in the cold mountainous parts of North America. 1907 Westm. Gaz. 11 Mar. 13/1 At the last meeting of the British Ornithologists' Club, three examples of the *black-lark (Melanocorypha yeltoniensis) were exhibited. 1953 BANNERMAN Birds Brit. Isles II. 4 Black lark.. is another very large lark, more closely resembling a blackbird in size but with a short stumpy bill and a short tail. 1936 E. J. G. LEWIS Television 80 In high definition systems signals below about 37·5 per cent (Baird) or 30 per cent (Marconi–E.M.I.) of the peak carrier represent synchronizing signals and occur below the 'artificial *black' level. 1938 Jrnl. Inst. Electr. Engineers LXXXIII. 744/2 The intermediate amplifier received the output from the master oscillator and raised it to a level of 1·2 kW at black level. 1942 Electronic Engin. XV. 127 Among the novel features of the design are.. keyed diodes for black-level setting. 1953 AMOS & BIRKINSHAW Television Engin. I. i. 17 The picture signal voltage at any point in a television system varies between two limits, one representing the maximum brightness it is intended to transmit and known as white level and the other representing zero tonal value or black and known as black level. 1927 Daily Tel. 21 Feb. 7/4 Mr. John L. Baird.. described what he calls '*black light'... This.. makes it possible to see without any visible light. 1933 Trans. Illumin. Engineering Soc. XXVIII. 618 The 'black bulb'

ultraviolet lamp..can be easily concealed..projecting invisible radiations of 'black light' on to luminous designs painted on the walls. **1937** *Discovery* Nov. 348/2 'Black light' contains a large proportion of ultra-violet rays, which, when they impinge upon specially prepared surfaces, cause these to luminesce. **1957** *Encycl. Brit.* IX. 426D (Plate 1: *caption*) Photograph of white girl made in the dark by black light. **1797** *Month. Rev.* XXII. 345 Multitudinous porers in *black literature. **1972** *Guardian* 19 Sept. 13/7 *Black money is a vast parallel economy of billions of rupees in cash transactions that never reach the tax collector. **1977** *N.Y. Rev. Bks.* 23 June 16/4 Erlich has also promised an amnesty for those who reveal their black money and pay a tax on it. **1981** S. Rushdie *Midnight's Children* iii. 418 All sorts of things happen during an Emergency: trains run on time, black-money hoarders are frightened into paying taxes. **1964** *Review* Jan. 3 (*heading*) The *Black Mountain poets. **1966** *New Statesman* 11 Feb. 198/1 The latest school of American poets..goes by the name of 'Black Mountain', from a small college in North Carolina where in the early Fifties Charles Olson..taught. **1977** *Fontana Dict. Mod. Thought* 67/2 The key to the Black Mountain poetics is to be found in American pragmatism as exemplified by John Dewey, with its accompanying blind optimism. **1983** *Christian Science Monitor* 13 May 88 Along with his associates of the Black Mountain School, Creeley strove to invigorate and enlarge midcentury American writing. **1966** *New Statesman* 198/3 The good *Black Mountaineers are still internationalists. **1970** *Listener* 23 July 122/2 It is worth noting in Dorn's favour that not all the Black Mountaineers can write, viz. Robert Duncan's atrocious hodge-podge of Yeats and Bridges. **1877** *Littell's Living Age* 24 Nov. 501/1 In one of the houses in Scotland Yard..is the '*Black Museum', in which, during the last three years, *pièces de conviction*, which until then had been kept indiscriminately with the other property of criminals, have been arranged and labelled, forming a ghastly, squalid, and suggestive show. **1902** A. Griffiths *Myst. Police & Crime* III. xxxiii. 124 Some very beautiful implements are now exhibited in the Black Museum of New Scotland Yard... Amongst these ..are some of the tools used by the notorious Charles Peace. **1926** G. Dilnot *Story Scotl. Yard* xxxvii. 303 Round about 1875 the Black Museum came into being, ostensibly for the instruction of young officers, though for long afterwards it was, in fact, little more than a show place, wherein privileged visitors might see the grim relics of great crimes. **1960** *San Francisco News-Call Bulletin* 11 Oct. 4/2 *Black Muslim leaders concede there are many ex-convicts, former prostitutes, drug addicts, and alcoholics in the movement, but they put a different interpretation on this than the police. **1961** C. E. Lincoln *Black Muslims in Amer.* p. iv, The racial emphases peculiar to this rapidly growing, Chicago-centred movement suggested the descriptive phrase 'Black Muslims', which I coined in 1956... Theretofore they had been variously known as the 'Temple People', 'the Muhammadans', 'the Muslims', 'the Voodoo Cult' and 'the Nation of Islam'. **1964** *Punch* 1 Apr. 505/1 Black Muslim claims to an African heritage. **1968** E. Cleaver *Soul on Ice* ii. 96 A racist Black Muslim heavyweight champion is a bitter pill for racist white America to swallow. **1968** M. A. Malik *From Michael de Freitas to Michael X* xv. 131, I read as much as I could about the Black Muslims in the Press, but they were presented more or less as a bunch of lunatics. **1962** E. U. Essien-Udom (*title*) *Black nationalism: a search for identity in America. **1963** *N.Y. Times* 23 Apr. 2/1 A new assertive mood, characterized by some Negro leaders as 'Black Nationalism' is spreading throughout the United States. **1967** *New Yorker* 7 Jan. 20/1 In one form or another, it [*sc.* the theme] has nearly always been—black nationalism—from the West Indian brand of Marcus Garvey and his followers to the more militant brand of Charles (Morriss). **1977** *Washington Post* 11 Jan. A1 It is failing to provide the Afrikaners with a 'moral alternative' to the use of force in containing black nationalism. **1983** *N.Y. Times* 9 Nov. C23/4 In the breadth of her concept, the playwright was prescient, touching on such issues as black nationalism and capitalism at the same time that she links her characters to their enslaved ancestors. **1963** *Life* 24 May 4/2 The Negro's feeling that the white man's law has failed him is polarized by extreme *black nationalists. **1970** *New Society* 5 Mar. 384/3 For journalists it was like covering American Black Nationalists in 1963. **1974** *Encycl. Brit. Macropædia* II. 1093/1 The Black Muslims..are a quasi-religious black nationalist organization among Afro-Americans. **1874** W. Gregor *Echo of Olden Time* iii. 22 The oil used was made from the livers of the haddock, cod, ling, and other fish caught on the coast, and was distinguished by the name of **black oil*. **1896** B. Redwood *Petroleum* II. ix. 532 Lubricating Oils..'pale' oils..'black' oils..'compound' oils. *Ibid.* 532 Black oils should be free from solid matter in suspension. **1904** Goodchild & Tweney *Technol. & Sci. Dict.* 54/1 *Black oils*, mineral oils which have not been chemically purified. **1962** *Listener* 10 May 796/1 The consumption of oil, to be exact of the so-called black oils, rose 249 per cent. **1965** *San Francisco Examiner* 20 Dec. 53/8 SNCC has chosen a black panther to adorn its party emblem—a requirement of parties in Alabama..SNCC's '*black panther' movement is viewed by some as a form of black nationalism at the local level. **1966** *Economist* 19 Nov. 807/3 Good sense (or fear of white retaliation) led Negroes in Lowndes County, Alabama, to reject the 'Black Panthers', who stand for 'black power'. **1969** E. Cleaver *Post-Prison Writings* 23, I fell in love with the Black Panther Party immediately upon my first encounter with it. **1970** *Idiot International* Jan. 11/1 The Black Panthers put before the June Convention a proposal for community control of police. **1858** Simmonds *Dict. Trade*, **Black plates*,..thin sheets of iron not coated with tin. **1962** *Engineering* 16 Mar. 372/1 Continuous annealing of blackplate has been made more than ten times faster. **1927** *Bull. Dept. Agric. Gold Coast* No. 11, p. 15 In the early morning..pods suffering from *black pod disease are covered by mildew. **1945** *Rep. Cocoa Research Conf.* 76 'Black pod' accounted for a loss in Nigeria now of not much less than 10,000 tons... Places which were most susceptible to 'black pod' were the wetter areas in Ife and Oyo Provinces. **1953** *Economist* 19 Dec. 917/1 The outlook for the Nigerian [cocoa] crop is uncertain... The poor weather..increases the risk of black pod disease. **1966** *Times* 27 June 1/4 Young Negroes.., supporters of the '*black power' group led by Mr Stokely Carmichael. **1966** *Guardian* 28 June 8/1 The emergence of the slogan 'black power', proclaimed by the supporters of the Student Non-violent Coordinating Committee. **1967** Carmichael & Hamilton *Black Power* ii. 44 The concept of Black Power..is a call for black people in this country to unite, to recognize their heritage, to build a sense of community. It is a call for black people to begin to define their own goals, to lead their own organizations and to support those organizations. It is a call to reject the racist institutions and values of this society. **1967** *Listener* 5 Oct. 423/1 The word 'black power'..for most Negroes..means the exercise of legitimate power of numbers at the polls, in the market-place and in the community, whereas for many whites it means an open threat to use physical force to gain objectives. **1968** W. Safire *New Lang. Politics* 40/1 *Black power*, a deliberately ambiguous Negro slogan, meaning antiwhite rebellion to some, the use of political and economic 'muscle' to others. **1888** *Lockwood's Dict. Terms Mech. Engin.*, *Black Print. **1962** *Guardian* 16 Nov. 7/5 The '*black' propaganda of 'Lord Haw-Haw'. **1965** B. Sweet-Escott *Baker St. Irregular* i. 29 Neither of these bodies had the job of doing 'black' or unacknowledgeable propaganda in neutral countries or for that matter anywhere else. **1972** F. Fitzgerald *Fire in Lake* iii. 76 Their tactics were promises and 'black propaganda', or the falsification of enemy reports. **1976** Black propaganda [see propaganda 3]. **1834** W. Youatt *Cattle* xi. 356 Inflammatory fever..is termed *black quarter, quarter evil, [etc.]. **1879** Wrightson in *Cassell's Techn. Educ.* I. 78 Land drainage is..followed by the disappearance of 'black-quarter,' or inflammatory fever. **1533** *Calend. Carew MSS.* (Rolls Ser.) No. 39 The *black rents and tributes which Irishmen by violence have obtained of the King's subjects. **1612** Sir J. Davies *Why Ireland etc.* 179 To abolish the black-rents and tributes exacted by the Irish upon the English colonies. **1827** Hallam *Const. Hist.* (1876) III. xviii. 359 The inhabitants ..were hardly distinguishable from the Irish, and paid them a tribute called black-rent. **1811** J. Black tr. *Humboldt's Political Essay* I. 116 The Canadian savages call themselves Metoktheniakes, born of the sun, without allowing themselves to be persuaded of the contrary by the **black robes*, a name which they give to missionaries. **1840** N. P. Willis *Canad. Scenery* I. 24 They exhorted her to take it into the woods, where the blackrobes, as they called the Christian priests, would not be able to find her. **1907** J. W. Schultz *My Life as Indian* xvii. 189 'I will pray to those gods for you. Long ago..a Blackrobe..taught me the way,' and she began... 'Twas the Lord's prayer! **1976** *Canad. Collector* (Toronto) Jan.–Feb. 20/1 Most of these French Canadians remembered the religion they had learned at home and were eager for the Men of Prayer or Blackrobes to come to..minister to them. **1709** W. Byrd *Secret Diary* 13 Feb. (1941) 4, I sent him some *blackroot..for the gripes. **1833** A. Eaton *Man. Bot.* (ed. 6) 288 *Pterocaulon pycnostachya*, black root. **1843** T. Talbot *Jrnl.* 8 Sept. (1931) 45 We traded some Kooyah or Black root,..a black, sticky, suspicious looking compound, of very disagreeable odor. **1851** C. Cist *Sk. & Stat. Cincinnati* 211 Concentrated extracts of vegetable medical articles..such as ..leptandrin or black-root extracts. **1910** G. Massee *Dis. Cultiv. Plants* 160 *Black root rot* (*Thielavia basicola*,..) was first met with in England on the roots of peas. **1954** A. G. L. Hellyer *Encycl. Gard. Work & Terms* 208/2 Black root rot ..is found most commonly on peas, violas and violets. **1850** *Rep. Comm. Patents: Agric. 1849* (U.S.) 438 In the southern part of the State winter apples are very liable to the *black-rot, spots, [etc.]. **1957** *Encycl. Brit.* X. 640/1 Europeans imported the American varieties [of grape-vine], and thereby unwittingly imported phylloxera..and black rot (*Guignardia bidwellii*). **1887** Moloney *Forestry W. Afr.* 90 The *black-rubber vine, known to the natives as 'Duah Kurrie'. **1790** S. Deane *New-Eng. Farmer* 20/1 The pods are liable to be hurt by a *black rust, if they are exposed much to the sun. **1931** *Discovery* Aug. 260/1 The problem in Kenya with regard to wheat is that two different strains of black rust occur in the main wheat-growing areas. **1957** *Ann. Reg. 1956* 91 The '*Black Sash' movement, consisting of women pledged to 'defence of the Constitution', organized 'vigils' of protest in the larger towns. **1908** *Black scab [see scab *sb.* 2 b]. **1915** *Board Agric. & Fisheries Leaflet* (1916) No. 105. 1 Wart Disease (Black Scab) of Potatoes. (*Synchytrium endobioticum*.)..In recent years a variety of other names such as Black Wart and Potato Wart have been given to it. **1881** J. H. Comstock in *Rep. U.S. Dept. Agric. 1880* 336 Lecanium Oleae Bernard. The *Black Scale of California. **1930** *Discovery* Apr. 135/2 The little ladybird has been enlisted to fight the black-scale pest in California. **1942** C. G. Grey & Dale *U.S. Dept. Agric. Farmers' Bull.* MCMXIV. 15 Swine Dysentery is also known as..bloody diarrhea, bloody scours, bloody dysentery, bloody flux, *black scours, and colitis. **1947** *New Biol.* III. 59 Species of Trichostrongylus often cause a blackish-green diarrhoea, which is called 'black scour' by some farmers. **1863** Prior *Plant-n.* 24 *Black-seed, the Nonesuch, from its black head of legumes. **1972** *Times* 6 Sept. 7/3 The *Black September organization, the secret cell of Al Fatah, has links with Germany's revolutionary underground movement. **1972** *Guardian* 4 Oct. 3/7 The Black Septembrists, like most Palestinians, cannot seriously believe that sporadic letter bombs, kidnappings, and hijackings..can ever liberate Palestine. **1983** *Washington Post* 27 Nov. B1 Two guerrillas from Black September wanted to visit the castle at the top of Bkechtine. **1895** *Daily News* 18 Feb. 2/5 *Black sheets for galvanisers. **1930** *Engineering* 21 Feb. 254/3 In the black-sheet trade. **1894** *Daily News* 22 Nov. 8/1 Deep crape and distinctive headgear have been dropped at the end of six months, the period known technically as '*black silk' then setting in. **1845** R. I. Murchison et al. *Geol. Russia in Europe* I. xxii. 559 The *black soil does not, however, occupy all the vast country alluded to. **1908** N. M. Tulaïkoff in *Jrnl. Agric. Sci.* III. 82 *Black soils* (*Tchernozem*)..cover generally the grassy steppe or prairies of the temperate zone. **1914** H. I. Jensen *Soils of N.S.W.* x. 47 In Australia we can find..black-soil plains (pasture and agriculture, maize and gourds). **1936** W. Lawson *When Cobb & Co. was King* xiv. 263 The black-soil plains, which can be so bare in drought-time..were green with short grass. **1959** M. Hastings *Hour-Glass to Eternity* i. ii. 40 What we call black soil areas. They're covered in kunai grass ..no trees will grow in that soil. **1725** Ramsay *Gentle Sheph.* iii. iii, This too fond heart o' mine..a *black-sole true to thee. [**1861** Lady Duff-Gordon *Let.* 18 Nov. in *Last Lett. fr. Egypt* (1875) 227 Alas! next day came the south-easter —blacker, colder, more cutting than ever.] **1870** *Cape Monthly Mag.* Dec. 357 Then we are sometimes blessed with a **black* south-easter... The mountain is then *quite buried* in cloud, the air is laden with moisture, the winds run howling hither and thither,..the rain descends. **1950** L. G. Green *Daybreak for Isles* vi. 74 In the middle of January 1844 a 'black south-easter', the wind most feared in summer on this coast, forced most of the fleet to run for open sea. **1848** H. W. Haygarth *Bush Life Australia* ix. 98 A narrow rill, rising out of some rich dark soil, known in Australia as a '*black spring'. **1946** A. Monkman in H. Whetton *Pract. Printing* iv. 56/2 Another style of signature which has become popular in bookwork offices is known as the *black-step method... A piece of rule, about 6 points thick and 24 points long, is placed between the first and last pages (or spine) of each section... For the first section the rule would be positioned opposite the top line of text. The next section would have the rule stepped down, say 24 points, and so on through the sections. **1785** Grose *Dict. Vulg. Tongue*, **Black strap*, bene carlo wine, also port. **1821** *Blackw. Mag.* X. 105 What champaigne is to homely black strap. **1823** Lockhart *Reg. Dalton* i. x. 60 Do they give you good black strap at Oxford? **1842** Orderson *Creol.* i. 5 The planter being content to..make an evening's finish with bub or black-strap. **1880** *Black stripe [see stripe *sb.* 9]. **1927** *Smallholder* 26 Mar. 104/2 If any [*sc.* tomato plants] have very finely cut, lace-like leaves, take them out... These plants have contracted Black Stripe disease. **1968** *Economist* 28 Dec. 24/1 They also demand '*black studies' classes, devoted to Negro culture, history or arts. **1973** Baskin & Runes *Dict. Black Culture* 53 Black studies..now include courses in African history and religions, Swahili, and Afro-American literature, economics, and social and political thought. **1983** *Sunday Tel.* 4 Dec. 14/3 The attempts to force schoolchildren to learn about reggae and Rastafarianism in schools as part of 'Black studies'. **1954** T. Ronan *Vision Splendid* 264 The best bloody station bookkeeper this side of the *black stump. **1973** *Guardian* 5 Mar. 14/1 Douglas Gas Light Company, arguably the smallest gas works this side of the black stump. **1975** X. Herbert *Poor Fellow my Country* 1149 I've been played for the biggest mug this side o' the Black Stump. **1787** Beattie *Scotticisms* 15 *Black sugar, Licuorice juice. **1864** J. Brown *Plain Wds. Health* v. 76 A bit of black sugar. **1969** J. H. Cone *Black Theol. & Black Power* ii. 31 There is, then, a desperate need for a **black theology*, a theology whose sole purpose is to apply the freeing power of the gospel to black people under white oppression. **1976** *Christian Believing* 31 We see this spirit still at work in such new guises as the Latin-American 'theology of liberation' and in 'Black theology', which employ the biblical writings as aids to a dialogue with and illumination of their own existential situation. **1983** J. H. Cone in Richardson & Bowden *New Dict. Christian Theol.* 74/1 The publication of the 'Black Power' statement [in July 1966] may be regarded as the beginning of the conscious development of a black theology in which black ministers consciously separated their understanding of the gospel of Jesus from white Christianity. **1856** C. M. Yonge *Daisy Chain* ii. xxiii. 603 Tom..had sent on his *black tie and agate studs. **1933** J. B. Priestly *Wonder Hero* iv. 102 Not tails, I think... Not in character. Essentially a black tie part. **1936** R. C. K. Ensor *England, 1870–1914* xv. 555 Till some time after 1914 there was no rigorous division between a white-tie and a black-tie *ensemble*, such as now compels gentlemen to keep two sets of evening dress. **1951** I. Shaw *Troubled Air* x. 165 Mary Lowell called to ask us..for dinner next Wednesday. Black tie. **1848** A. H. Clough *Bothie of Tober-na-Fuosich* 5 Hope was the first, *black-tied, white-waistcoated. **1834** *Amer. Railroad Jrnl.* III. 120/3 A disease in horses and cattle [is] called the **Black Tongue* or *Burnt Tongue*. **1845** W. Bagley *Let.* 20 Mar. in N. E. Eliason *Tarheel Talk* (1956) 260 A very fatal disease has been ravaging the counties of Edgecomb & Northampton, it is called the 'black tongue', the patient dies in six hours after he is taken & very few cures are effected. **1858** C. Flint *Milch Cows* (1860) 281 Typhoid fever..is sometimes followed by diseases known as black tongue, black leg, or quarter evil. **1919** J. P. Dunn *Indiana* II. 804 In 1842–3 epidemic erysipelas prevailed in a number of counties in southern Indiana, and was known by a number of popular names, as 'black tongue', 'sore throat', etc. **1960** Runnells & Monlux *Princ. Vet. Path.* (ed. 6) 65/2 Dogs fed exclusively on a cereal diet..develop a niacin deficiency disease called blacktongue. **1877** *Rep. Vermont Dairym. Assoc.* VIII. 107 *Black tooth is a popular disease of swine. **1867** J. Morison *Australia as it Is* 88 The native police, or '*black trackers',..are a body of aborigines trained to act as policemen. **1952** R. E. Robinson in *Coast to Coast 1951–52* 213 The black-tracker, in his police boy's shirt, trousers, and hat, was with them. **1937** 'G. Orwell' *Road to Wigan Pier* i. i. 7 The grey flocculent stuff known as '*black tripe'. **1961** *Guardian* 29 Sept. 13/6 Yorkshiremen know how succulent it [*sc.* tripe] is—and how varied:..there are ..'black' tripe (unbleached), [etc.]. **1939** A. L. du Toit *Geol. S. Afr.* (ed. 2) xix. 442 *Black 'Cotton' Soils*..This type is known to the Dutch farmer under the name of '**Black Turf*' from its peaty aspect. *Ibid.* 443 (*heading*) Black turf soils. **1955** J. H. Wellington *S. Africa* I. ii. xi. 329 The norite soils are heavy black clays with a much lower magnesium content (12 mg.). These 'black turf' soils occur along the outcrop of the Great Dyke. **1929** K. S. Prichard *Coonardoo* vii. 79 'No "*black velvet" for you, I suppose?' 'I'm goin' to marry white and stick white,' Hugh said. **1930** H. Craddock *Savoy Cocktail Bk.* i. 29 *Black velvet.* Use long tumbler. ½ Guinness Stout. ½ Champagne. **1942** E. Waugh *Put out more Flags* 45 Young men..gulping Black Velvet. **1948** D. Ballantyne *Cunninghams* 263 I'd like a nice piece of black velvet. One of those quarter-castes, boy. **1861** *Trans. Ill. Agric. Soc.* IV. 454 It is sometimes affected by the *black wart. **1822** D. Stewart *Sk. Highlanders* III. § 1 The 42nd Highland Regiment..was originally known by the name of *Black Watch. It arose from the colour of their dress. **1830** Scott *Tales Grandf.* lxxiv, Another measure.. was the establishment of independent companies to secure the peace of the Highlands..Black soldiers as they were called, to distinguish them from the regular troops, who wore the red national uniform. **1871** P'cess Alice *Mem.* 12 Sept. (1884) 273 We did not see the 42nd Highlanders, the 'Black Watch,' to-day. **1915** *Jrnl. Parasitology* I. 107 The not-infrequent occurrence of the notorious '*black widow' spider, *Latrodectes mactans*, in the vicinity of Stanford University. **1927** *Daily Express* 21 July 2/7 A small black spider known to entomologists as '*latrodectus mactans*', and commonly called the 'black widow' or 'shoe-button', which has been introduced from Oriental ports into North America. **1803** A. Ellicott *Jrnl.* x. 284 *Black-willow..

becomes more scarce as you descend the river. **1841** W. A. LEIGHTON *Flora of Shropshire* 485 *Salix Pentandra*, Linn. *Sweet Bay-leaved Willow*... Much sought after by the Irish harvestmen, who call it 'the black willow', and cut it for their *shillelahs*. **1884** C. S. SARGENT *Rep. Forests N. Amer.* 170 *Salix flavescens*.. Black Willow. **1569–1595** *Blak wark (work), see D.O.S.T. **1859** SALA *Gaslight & Daylight* xxvi, A florid man who..sometimes takes a spell in the black work, or undertaking line of business. *a* **1877** KNIGHT *Dict. Mech.*, *Black-work*, the work of the blacksmith in contradistinction to bright-work or the work of the silversmith. **1888** *Lockwood's Dict. Terms Mech. Engin.*, *Black work*, work which has not been machined or polished. In some instances the term would apply to metal work which had been machined on a bearing section, but not elsewhere. And in other cases where no portion, working or otherwise, had been machined. **1910** *Encycl. Brit.* IX. 311/2 A kind of embroidery known as 'black work', done in black silk on linen, was popular during the same reign [*i.e.* of Elizabeth I]. **1597** GERARD *Herbal* II. cclxxiv, It is called..in English, Comfrey..of some Knitbacke, and *Black-woort. **1611** in COTGR.

b. Esp. in *Ceramics*.

1766 WEDGWOOD in L. Jewitt *Wedgwoods* (1865) 187 Basaltes or black ware; a black porcelain biscuit. **1787** *Ibid.* 332 The black basaltes having the appearance of antique bronze..is excellently adapted for busts, sphynxes, small statues, etc. **1832** [see BASALT 2]. **1865** [see BLUE PRINTING, vbl. sb.]. **1875** METEYARD *Wedgwood Handbk.* 391 *Black Marble*. A crystalline terra-cotta body. The colour is black shaded. *Black painted*. Single stems and flowers painted on black glazed ware... *Black printed*. Cream-ware printed over or under the glaze with patterns in black. *a* **1884** KNIGHT *Dict. Mech.* Suppl., *Black-basalt Ware*. **1885** *Encycl. Brit.* XIX. 615/1 Etruscan Black Ware. *Ibid.* 618/2 Black Pottery is usually made from a very silicious or sandy clay. *Ibid.* 619/1 Roman black ware decorated with groups of dots in relief. **1934** V. G. CHILDE *New Light on most Anc. East* iii. 79 The rare Black Incised ware, a fabric principally found in Nubia. **1936** *Discovery* Sept. 289/1 This 'black burnished' pottery is identical with the black ware found in Mohenjodaro and not dissimilar to the black ware..of the earlier Chalcolithic periods of Baluchistan and Persia.

black, *sb.* [The adj. used absol. or elliptically.]

1. a. Black colour or hue. It may have a plural, as in 'different blacks,' i.e. kinds or shades of black.

a **1225** *Ancr. R.* 282 Biholden euer his blake & nout his hwite. **1526** *Pilgr. Perf.* (W. de W. 1531) 229 b, Knowe what whyte is, and it is soone perceyued what blacke is. **1645** RUTHERFORD *Tryal & Tri. Faith* (1845) 56 All his blacks are white. **1821** CRAIG *Lect. Drawing* iii. 175 We must take black and white into our list, as colours with the painter though not with the optician. **1856** RUSKIN *Mod. Paint.* IV. v. iii. §14. 45.

b. ***black is beautiful***: a slogan asserting pride in Blackness and Black self-awareness. Freq. *attrib.*

1965 *Liberation* (N.Y.) Sept. 25/1 Radical blacks turn inward to united fronts and to 'black is beautiful' stated as an ideological principle. **1967** *Black Panther* 20 July 24/3 The hangup is that they have tried to sweep 'Black' under the rug for all these years and can't stand us digging 'Black is Beautiful'. **1971** *Black Scholar* Apr.–May 15/2 These prisons boast Soul Shows, Black is Beautiful days, and bongo sessions in the yard. **1973** A. DUNDES *Mother Wit* 231 In 'The Language of Soul' we find an important reversal in attitude, a reversal which is..in harmony with the general 'Black is Beautiful' philosophy. **1983** *Washington Post* 22 Sept. DC1/1, I remember how black was beautiful 10 years ago and have since been struck with how abruptly the Afro was cut short.

2. A black paint, dye, or pigment. In senses **a**, **b**, see also BLECK, BLATCH, BLETCH.

†**a.** Black writing fluid, ink. *Obs.* ***black and white***: see BLACK *a.* 15, a, b, c.

a **1000** *Canons K. Edgar* in *Anc. Laws* II. 244 And we læræð þæt hi..habban blæc & bóc-fel to heóra gerædnessum. *c* **1000** ÆLFRIC *Gloss.* in Wr.-Wülcker *Voc.* 164 *Incaustum vel atramentum*, blæc.

b. A preparation used by shoemakers, curriers, etc. for staining leather black.

1661 LOVELL *Hist. Anim. & Min.* 277 Shoomakers black with vineger.

c. A black pigment, dye, or varnish; many different preparations are used by artists, as ***ivory black***, ***lamp black***, ***Spanish black***, etc.; in the industrial arts several black varnishes and pigments are similarly distinguished, as ***Berlin black***, ***Brunswick black***.

1573 HULOET, Blacke, called paynters blacke, *atramentum tectorium*. **1581** *Act 23 Eliz.* ix. §3 Clothes..dyed with a galled and mathered Black. **1670** W. SIMPSON *Hydrol. Ess.* 75 Dyers in the making of their Blacks, use not Alom but Vitriol. **1815** *Specif. J. Taylor's Patent* No. 3929. 2 Bones converted either into ivory or bone black. **1846** G. WRIGHT *Scientif. Knowl.* 46 Ivory black is..ivory or bones thoroughly burnt, and afterwards ground. *c* **1860** WINSOR & NEWTON *Handbk. Water-Col.* 31 Lamp Black is not quite so intense, nor so transparent, as that made from ivory.

d. ***to be in the black***: to show a profit; to have a credit balance. (From the practice of recording credit items and balances in black.) Cf. *in the red* (RED *sb.*[1]). orig. *U.S.*

1928 *N.Y. Times* 11 Mar. VIII. 6/2 *In the black*, showing a profit. **1940** *Jrnl. R. Aeronaut. Soc.* XLIV. 734 With but few exceptions American air carriers are..operating 'in the black'. **1955** *Times* 30 Aug. 9/5 On an overdraft, understandably, the banks charge their customers a percentage; but when we are 'in the black' nothing is ever added. **1958** *Times* 24 July 5/1 All the independent television companies are well in the black. A.T.V. made a profit of over £3,500,000 for the past year.

3. A particle of some black substance, a black speck; **a.** *spec.* the dark-coloured fungus which attacks wheat, smut.

1303 R. BRUNNE *Handl. Synne* 11869 Yche blak, y dar wel telle þat hyt was a fende of helle. **1607** TOPSELL *Four-f. Beasts* 259 They have also little blacks in the middle of their teeth. **1615** MARKHAM *Eng. Housew.* (1660) 110 You shall take the blacks of green Corn either Wheat or Rye. **1783** AINSWORTH *Lat. Dict.* I. s.v. *bean*, The black of a bean, *Hilum*. **1883** *Gd. Words* 735 Who has not observed the smut, or blacks, among corn?

b. A small particle or flake of soot, a smut. Usually in *plural*.

c **1816** *Yng. Woman's Comp.* 196 Let the blamange settle before you turn it into the forms, or the blacks will remain at the bottom. **1843** F. PAGET *Pageant* 84 She carefully covered over..any articles that were likely to be damaged by blacks. **1862** GOULBURN *Pers. Relig.* III. viii. (1873) 223 The blacks of the world have settled down upon it. **1865** DICKENS *Mut. Fr.* II. 149 If you see a black on my nose, tell me so.

c. A deposit of dirt on the body, esp. under the finger-nails. *dial.*

1753 WASHINGTON *Diaries* (1925) I. 49 You say this land belongs to you, but there is not the Black of my Nail yours. **1870** J. P. ROBSON *Evangeline* Introd. (E.D.D.), Aw ha'e wesht baith maw feet frae the black. **1889** *Brighouse News* 14 Sept. (E.D.D.), He weant pairt wi' t'black afore his finger-nails.

4. The dark spot in the centre of the eye, the pupil. *Obs.*

1387 TREVISA *Higden* Rolls Ser. II. 189 þese hauen in eueriche yȝe tweie blakkes. **1398**— *Barth. De P.R.* v. vii. (1495) 113 The blacke of the eye syttyth in the mydle as a quene. **1541** R. COPLAND *Guydon's Quest. Chirurg.*, In the region of the blacke of the eye. *a* **1648** DIGBY (J.) As big as the black or sight of the eye.

5. Black fabric or material.

a. Black clothing, especially that worn as a sign of mourning, in which sense the plural was formerly used, as still in Lowland Sc. (*Blacks*, in modern use, sometimes = black or dress trousers.)

c **1400** *Rom. Rose* 4759 And eke as wel be amorettes In mourning blacke, as bright burnettes. *c* **1500** *Merch. & Son* in Halliw. *Nugæ P.* 28 Fadur, why appere ye thus in black, ar not yowre synnys foryevyn? **1580** NORTH *Plutarch* (1656) 20 Ten moneths..was the full time they used to wear blacks for the death of their fathers. **1636** FEATLY *Clavis Myst.* xix. 247 Neither are all that weare blackes his mourners. **1641** R. BROOKE *Eng. Episc.* I. iv. 17 Some to Ministers, as Cassockes, Gownes..Canonicall Coats, Blackes. **1699** LUTTRELL *Brief Rel.* (1857) IV. 557 The King..has ordered all his subjects to go into black. **1748** RICHARDSON *Clarissa* (1811) VI. 52 Whom dealest thou with for thy blacks? **1862** THACKERAY *Philip* I. 174 My old blacks show the white seams so, that you must..rig me out with a new pair.

b. *pl.* Hangings of black cloth used in churches, etc., at funerals; funereal drapery.

1608 MIDDLETON *Mad World* II. ii, I'll pay him again when he dies in so many blacks; I'll have the church hung round with a noble a yard. **1611** COTGR., *Littre*..the blacke wherewith the vpper part of a Church is compassed, at the funerall of a great person. **1711** J. DISTAFF *Char. Sacheverellio* 16 The Company of Upholders are not able to furnish Blacks enough for the Deceased.

c. Often in comb., as ***black-robed***.

1602 WARNER *Alb. Eng.* x. lvi. 250 The black-clad Scaffold. **1863** MISS WHATELY *Ragged Life Egypt* iv. 23 Her black-robed female relatives support her on each side. **1870** MORRIS *Earthly Par.* I. I. 375 Her friends black-clad and moving mournfully.

6. = Black man or woman.

a. A person of 'black' skin; an African negro, or Australasian negrito, or other member of a dark-skinned race. In this sense it appears to be a translation of *Negro*, which was in earlier use.

1625 PURCHAS *Pilgrims* IX. xiii. §1. 1570 The mouth of the Riuer [Gambra], where dwell the Blackes, called Mandingos. **1679–88** *Secr. Serv. Moneys Chas. & Jas.* (1851) 58 To Randall Mc Donnell, for a black his sl Matie bought of him, 50*l.* **1682** BUNYAN *Holy War* 20 This giant was one of the Blacks or Negroes. **1789** GEORGE PR. WALES in *Cornwallis' Corr.* II. 29 (Y.) The Adaulet of Benares..now held by a Black named Alii Caun. **1805** *Ann. Rev.* III. 289 They exclude from suffrage the blacks and the paupers. **1856** OLMSTED *Slave States* 129 The free black does not, in general, feel himself superior to the slave.

†**b.** One of a band of poachers who went about their work with blackened faces. *Obs.* *attrib.* in ***black-act***, a severe law (9 Geo. I. xxii) against poaching, trespassing, etc.

1722 *Act 9 Geo. I*, xxii, Whereas several ill-designing and disorderly Persons have of late associated themselves under the name of Blacks. **1785** G. WHITE *Selborne* vii, The Waltham blacks..committed such enormities, that Government was forced to interfere with that severe and sanguinary Act called the Black Act. **1809** TOMLINS *Law Dict.* s.v., A virtual repeal of the punishment inflicted by the Black Act.

†**c.** A black-haired person. *Obs.*

c **1686** *Yng. Mans C.* in *Roxb. Ball.* II. 558 The pleasant Blacks and modest Browns, their loving Husbands please.

†**d.** A mute or hired mourner at a funeral. *Obs.*

1619 FLETCHER *M. Thomas* III. i, I do pray ye To give me leave to live a little longer: Ye stand before me like my Blacks.

7. In various elliptical applications: **a.** *Typogr.* (see quot.) **b.** *Chess & Draughts*. The player using the black or coloured pieces. **c.** *Archery*. A shot which hits the target in the black ring surrounding the inner white circle. **d.** A pigeon of a black variety. **e.** A black postage stamp. **f.** The black colour in roulette or rouge-et-noir. Cf. RED *sb.*[1] 1 b.

a. **1882** *Print. Times* 15 Feb. 36/1 *Blacks* is a term applied to any mark on a sheet made by pieces of furniture, catches, etc. rising to the level of the form.

b. **1837** *Penny Cycl.* VII. 52/1 Black's fourth move was a very bad one.

c. **1882** *Standard* 31 Aug. 6/4 The Vice-President's Prize to ladies for most blacks.

d. **1855** *Poultry Chron.* II. 515/2 A pen of short-faced bald head Tumblers, Blues, Blacks,..Almond, of rare quality.

e. **1890** S. C. SKIPTON *Auction Epitome 1889* 28, 1d. black sheet of 240, used. **1907** *Daily Chron.* 12 Dec. 6/6 A 12d. black of Canada, 1851. **1936** R. GRAVES *Antigua, Penny, Puce* x. 149, I specialize in the archetype and grandmother of all stamps—the Penny Black of 1840. **1970** *Times* (Sat. Rev.) 31 Jan. p. v/2 (Advt.), Over 250 lots of One Penny Blacks, incl. all Plates, many with matched 1d. Reds.

f. **1868** [see RED *sb.*[1] 1 b]. **1928** [see NOIR 2 b]. **1950** [see INVERSE *sb.* 3]. **1975** *Way to Play* 279/1 If the opposite characteristic (eg black) comes up, the bet is lost.

8. In Italian history. **a.** A member or supporter of the political faction of the Neri, the opponents of the Bianchi (Whites), in a feud which began in Pistoia in 1300 and later spread to Florence. **b.** In Rome, a supporter of the Vatican as opponents of the Italian monarchy; one of the clericals.

1680, etc. [see WHITE *sb.* 19]. **1802** C. WILMOT *Let.* 17 Dec. in *Irish Peer* (1920) 134 The blacks and the whites form'd opposite parties which totally disorganized the Republick. **1877** *Encycl. Brit.* VI. 811/2 A quarrel had arisen in Pistoia between the two branches of the Cancellieri,—the Bianchi and Neri, the Whites and the Blacks. The quarrel spread to Florence, the Donati took the side of the Blacks, and Cerchi of the Whites. **1902** *Academy* 11 Oct. 390/1 Were you a White and for the people, or a Black and for the nobles? **1903** [see WHITE *a.* 6 b]. **1909** *Daily Chron.* 29 Jan. 4/6 Most of the skaters are of the Vatican party... 'Black' is the local name.

9. A black horse.

1846 J. J. HOOPER *Taking Census* in *Adv. Simon Suggs* I. 153 Mounting our old black, we determined to give the old soul a parting fire. *a* **1861** T. WINTHROP *John Brent* (1883) iii. 26 The black was within the corral, pawing the ground, neighing, and whinnying. **1874** *Rep. Vermont Board Agric.* II. 211 They are able to ride in grand carriages with their three minute blacks hitched thereto.

10. Short for BLACK-LEG 3. (Cf. BLACK *a.* 11 b.)

1866 *Sat. Rev.* 20 July 59 The lists of 'blacks', and the victims of the picket system.

11. Short for BLACKMAIL 2. ***to put the black*** (***on a person***), to blackmail. *slang*.

1923 E. WALLACE *Missing Million* xii. 95 I've been paying 'black' for years. *Ibid.* xiv. 115, I don't know the 'black' people; they're not the kind of folk I like to meet. 'Black's' dirty and always will be. **1924** —— *Room 13* iii. 38 Are you trying to put the black on me? **1928** —— *Gunner* xxiii. 190 I've never known you put the black before. **1951** J. B. PRIESTLEY *Fest. Farbridge* III. iii. 561 Got a lovely pub..and yet wants to start putting the black on people!

12. A serious mistake or blunder, esp. ***to put up a black***: to make a blunder. *colloq.* or *slang* (orig. *Services*'). (Cf. BLACK MARK.)

1939 *Flight* 26 Oct. 335/2 Last week's special black. The ex-civil pilot..who thought that the ripcord of his parachute was a carrying handle specially provided by the kind manufacturers. **1941** *English Digest* Feb. 38/1 A glaring error is a 'black'. 'I have put up a black,' they will say. **1943** *Word Study* Apr. 6/1 Far from committing the black they expected, she showed great heroism. **1946** G. GIBSON *Enemy Coast Ahead* xi. 142 One day she put up a black... She had fried our salmon in batter. **1948** 'N. SHUTE' *No Highway* v. 142 Probably I should have to..leave Government service altogether, having put up such a black as that.

black (blæk), *v.* Forms: 3–4 blak-en, blakk-in, black-en, 3–6 blake, 5 blak-, black-yn, 5–7 blacke, 7– black. [f. BLACK *a.*]

†**1.** *intr.* To be or become black. *Obs.*

a **1225** *Juliana* 48 þat him eoc euch neil & blakede of þe blode. *c* **1340** *Cursor M.* (Trin.) 14747 To blake [*Cott.* blaken] þo bigan her brewes. *c* **1380** *Sir Ferumb.* 2388 Wanne þe nyȝt gynt blake. *a* **1400** *Syr Percyv.* 688 Now sone ..salle wee see Whose browes schalle blakke! *c* **1460** *Towneley Myst.* 107 So my browes blaky To the doore wylle I wyn.

2. a. *trans.* To make black; now *esp.* to put black colour on. Also with *up*; spec. *intr.*, to colour one's face black in order to play the role of a Negro (orig. *U.S.*). Cf. BLACKEN.

c **1315** SHOREHAM 155 The wyte the vayrer hyt maketh, And selve more hyt blaketh. *c* **1386** CHAUCER *Monkes T.* 141 Til that his fleisch was for the venym blaked. *a* **1400** *Syr Percyv.* 1056 Thare he and the sowdane salle mete, His browes to blake. **1532–3** *Act 24 Hen. VIII*, i. §6 Every coriar shall well and sufficiently corie and blacke the said Lether tanned. **1650** R. STAPYLTON *Strada's Low-C. Warres* IX. 26 Having blackt his face, and died his hair. **1748** FRANKLIN *Wks.* (1840) 207 The paper will be blacked by the smoke. **1823** J. BADCOCK *Dom. Amusem.* 49 Crown-glass, blacked on one side. **1842** TENNYSON *Simeon Styl.* 75, I lay..Black'd with thy branding thunder. **1877** W. R. ALGER *Life of E. Forrest* I. 109 He blacked himself up and rigged his costume quite to his content. **1890** 'BIFF' HALL *Turnover Club* 197 They barely had time to get back to the theater to black up for the evening performance. **1934** WODEHOUSE *Thank You, Jeeves* xv. 212 Old Glossop isn't blacking up?

b. *spec.* To clean and polish shoes and other black leather articles with BLACKING.

1557 NORTH *Guevara's Diall Pr.* (1582) 369 a In varnishing hys sword and dagger, blacking his bootes. **1684** *Foxe's A. & M.* III. 907 Causing his shoos to be blacked.

1812 J. & H. SMITH *Rej. Addr.* ii. (1873) 12 My uncle's porter, Samuel Hughes, Came in at six to black the shoes.

†**c.** To drape with black. *Obs.*

1664 LAMONT *Diary* 25 Nov., The isle being blacked—with a number of dependants on the pall of black velvet.

d. *to black (a person's) eye*: to bruise or discolour the eye by a blow (cf. BLACK EYE 2).

1902 E. NESBIT *Five Children & It* viii. 203 The baker's boy blacked his other eye. **1950** G. GREENE *Third Man* ii. 26 I'd rather make you look the fool you are than black your bloody eye.

e. To blackmail (cf. BLACK *sb.* 11). *slang.*

1928 E. WALLACE *Gunner* xxx. 244 If I 'blacked' you after this I should be cutting my own throat. **1964** G. SIMS *Dreadful Door* xxiii. 124 He..took naughty photos of them and then blacked them.

3. *trans.* **a.** To draw or figure in black.

1840 BROWNING *Sordello* IV. 374 The grim, twynecked eagle, coarsely blacked With ochre on the naked wall.

b. *to black out*: to obliterate with black.

1850 BROWNING *Christmas Eve* Wks. 1868 V. 175 If he blacked out in a blot Thy brief life's pleasantness. **185.** GEN. GORDON *Lett.* 121 The Russian censor who blacks out all matter that is displeasing to the Government. **1905** *Westm. Gaz.* 2 Mar. 10/2 A memorial..urging that betting news should be 'blacked out' from the newspapers in the libraries. .. Ultimately the Committee decided to 'black-out' horse-racing news.

c. *to black out* (*trans.* and *intr.*), to extinguish or obscure (lights), esp. during a stage performance, or as a precaution against air-raids; also *intr.* of lights, etc.: to be so extinguished or obscured. Also in extended uses.

1921 GALSWORTHY *Six Short Plays* 127 Mr. Foreson!.. Black out! *The lights go out.* **1928** *Amer. Speech* IV. 70 To *black out* is to cut off all light, footlights, borders, and spot. **1934** *Baltimore Sun* 15 Aug. 4/6 There will be a burst of music, and the lights will 'black out'. This will form the prelude to the pageant. **1935** N. MARSH *Enter A Murderer* v. 62 We black out for a little before the curtain goes up. *Ibid.* xxii. 264, I am not going to black-out the lights. **1939** *Daily Mail* 12 Sept. 5/3 It took about three visits from courteous wardens before my house was properly blacked out. **1939** E. AUGUST *Black-out Book* 18/2 (*heading*) You can't black-out the Stars. **1940** *Ann. Reg. 1939* 377 In many countries the lamps of science were dimmed, and in Austria, Czechoslovakia, Poland, and Finland they were blacked out. **1944** in Zandvoort *Wartime Eng.* (1957) 36 Look how the windows are hastily blacking out. **1965** in M. McLuhan *Medium is Massage* (1967) 149 The largest power failure in history blacked out nearly all of New York City.

4. *fig.* **a.** To stain, sully; to defame, represent as 'black.' (Usually *blacken.*)

c **1440** *Promp. Parv.* 38 Blackyn' or make blake, *vitupero, increpo.* **1625** FLETCHER *Nt. Walker* II. 216 Thy other sins which black thy soul. **1683** D. A. *Art Converse* 16 To black his repute. *a* **1845** HOOD *Trumpet* xxx, Not that elegant ladies..ever detract, Or lend a brush when a friend is black'd.

b. To declare to be 'black' (see BLACK *a.* 11 b). Hence ***blacked*** ppl. adj.

1958 *Times* 20 Jan. 5/4 The firm's 1,500 employees are 'blacking' work in the fettling shop. **1960** *Guardian* 21 Dec. 2/4 Four men who refused to repair 'blacked' machinery. **1961** *Daily Tel.* 11 Dec. 11/6 (*heading*) Equity 'blacks' TV programme.

†**5.** *intr.* To poach as one of the 'Blacks': see BLACK *sb.* 6 b. *Obs. rare.*

1789 G. WHITE *Selborne* vi, As soon as they began blacking, they [the deer] were reduced to about fifty head.

6. *to black out*, to suffer a 'black-out' (see BLACK-OUT 4); esp. in flying, to be temporarily blinded through the effect of a sudden sharp turn or acceleration; to lose consciousness. Cf. BLACKING *vbl. sb.* 1 c.

1940 *Illustr. London News* CXCVI. 449/1 The blood in his head seeks to fly outwards, and, as his body and feet are away from the centre of the turn, runs towards his legs and drains from behind his eyes, so that he becomes temporarily blind, or 'blacks out'. **1940** *Times* 30 Mar. 9/6 The pilot's body weight would soar, to six, eight, or more times normal. At 8g he would black-out, and at 10g faint. **1940** *Flight* 7 Nov. 387/1 So I went into a steep left-hand turn and blacked out. **1957** 'C. E. MAINE' *High Vacuum* x. 84 'How did you react to the take-off?' 'I blacked out. Don't remember much about it.' **1958** P. MORTIMER *Daddy's gone A-Hunting* vii. 36 The child, dizzy with speed, was blacking out.

†**7.** *Comb.* **black-shoe (boy)** = SHOE-BLACK.

1732 FIELDING *Covent Gard. Jrnl.* No. 61 A rebuke given by a blackshoe boy to another. **1746** W. HORSLEY *The Fool* (1748) I. 5 [He] reduces himself to the Level of Highwaymen, Footmen, and Black-shoe Boys.

†**'black acre.** *Law. Obs.* An arbitrary name for a particular parcel of ground, to distinguish it from another denominated 'white acre'; a third parcel being, when necessary, similarly termed 'green acre' (= parcel *a*, parcel *b*, parcel *c*). The choice of the words 'black,' 'white,' and 'green' was perhaps influenced by their use to indicate different kinds of crops.

1628 COKE *On Litt.* 148 b. **1698** [R. FERGUSSON] *View Eccles.* 10 Foolish comparisons, of..the Exchanging of Black-Acre by A for White-Acre from B.

Hence **black-acre,** *v. Obs.* to litigate about landed property. (Wycherley's *Double Dealer* has a Mrs. Blackacre, a litigious widow, whose name may be immediately alluded to in the quotation.)

1751 MRS. DELANY *Life & Corr.* 67 She is now gone to town, black-acreing, to her lawyers.

†**black-a-lyre.** *Obs.* A fabric. See LYRE.

Blackamoor ('blækəmʊə(r), -mɔə(r)). Forms: 6 blake More, Blacke Moryn, black a Moore, 6–7 blacke Moore, blackmoor(e, 7 Black-Moor(e, -More, -moor, black Moor, Blackmore, -moore, Blackemore, Black-a-Moore, Black-amoore, blackeamoore, 7–8 Blackamore, Blackamoor(e, 7– blackamoor. [= *Black Moor*, a form actually used down to middle of 18th c. *Blackamoor* is found 1581: of the connecting *a* no satisfactory explanation has been offered. The suggestion that it was a retention of the final *-e* of ME. *black-e* (obs. in prose before 1400) is, in the present state of the evidence, at variance with the phonetic history of the language, and the analogy of other *black-* compounds. Cf. *black-a-vised.*]

1. A black-skinned African, an Ethiopian, a Negro; any very dark-skinned person. (Formerly without depreciatory force; now a nickname.)

1547 BOORDE *Introd. Knowl.* 212, I am a blake More borne in Barbary. **1548** THOMAS *Ital. Gram., Ethiopo*, a blacke More, or a man of Ethiope. **1552** HULOET, Blacke Moryns or Mores. **1581** T. HOWELL *Deuises* (1879) 184 Like one that washeth a black a Moore white. **1599** SANDYS *Europæ Spec.* (1632) 239 Shee is painted like a blackmoore. **1604** DEKKER *Honest Wh.* Wks. 1873 II. 98 This is the Blackamore that by washing was turned white. **1606** SHAKS. *Tr. & Cr.* I. i. 80, I care not and she were a Black-a-Moore. **1614** RALEIGH *Hist. World* I. 95 The Negro's, which we call the Blacke-Mores. **1631** BRATHWAIT *Eng. Gentlew.* (1641) 308 The Blackmoore may sooner change his skin, the Leopard his spots. **1666** PEPYS *Diary* (1879) VI. 46 For a cook maid we have used a blackmoore. **1702** C. MATHER *Magn. Chr.* III. III. (1852) 576 The instruction of the poor blackamores. **1771** SMOLLETT *Humph. Cl.* Lett. Ap. 26 The first day we came to Bath, he..beat two black-a-moors. **1856** R. VAUGHAN *Mystics* (1860) I. 271 As far below the reality as a blackamoor is unlike the sun.

b. *attrib.*

1580 SIDNEY *Arcadia* 36 A Coach drawne with foure milke white horses..with a black-a-Moore boy vpon euery horse. **1676** HOBBES *Iliad* I. 403 To Blackmoor-land the Gods went yesterday. **1706** *Lond. Gaz.* No. 4238/8 A Blackamore Man called Cæsar. **1716** *Ibid.* No. 5434/3 Run away..a Black Moore Boy.

†**c.** ***blackamoor's teeth***: cowry shells. *Obs.*

1700 W. KING *Transactioneer* 36 He has Shells called *Blackmoors Teeth*, I suppose..from their Whiteness. **1719** W. WOOD *Surv. Trade* 334 Known by the Name of Cowries amongst Merchants, or of Blackamore's Teeth among other Persons.

2. *fig.* A devil.

1663 COWLEY *Cut. Coleman St.* IV. vi, He's dead long since, and gone to the Blackamores below.

3. *attrib.* Black-skinned, quite black.

1813 J. FORBES *Orient. Mem.* I. 325 The first blackamoor pullen I ever saw was here: the outward skin of the fowl was a perfect negro. **1856** CAPERN *Poems* (ed. 2) 90 Some blackamoor rook.

†**blacka'morian,** *sb.* and *a. Obs.* [f. BLACK + MORIAN (in Coverdale).] Ethiopian, Negro.

1526 *Pilgr. Perf.* (W. de W. 1531) 78 b, Out of the chirche þou blacke moryan, out of the chirche thou man of ynde. *a* **1563** BALE *Sel. Wks.* (1849) 177 When the blackamorian change his skin, and the cat of the mountain her spots. **1631** HEYWOOD *F. Maide West* Wks. 1874 II. 328 To the black a Morrian king.

black art. [Probably 'black' refers primarily to the dark and secret nature of the magician's art, or to the popular belief in the association of the magician with the devil; but the name is also associated with the med.L. *nigromantīa*, corruption of *necromantīa* (= Gr. νεκρομαντεία, f. νεκρός dead body), as if this contained L. *niger, nigro-* black.]

1. The art of performing supernatural acts by intercourse with the spirits of the dead or with the devil himself; magic, necromancy.

c **1590** MARLOWE *Faust.* ix. 53, I have heard strange report of thy knowledge in the black art. **1611** COTGR., *Nigromance*, nigromancie, coniuring, the blacke Art. **1674** R. GODFREY *Inj. & Ab. Physic* 178 He useth Astrology, (which the Vulgar call the Black Art). **1775** SHERIDAN *Rivals* I. ii, I'd as soon have them taught the black art as their alphabet! **1831** BREWSTER *Nat. Magic* iv. (1833) 69 A native of Pistoia, who cultivated the black art.

†**2.** *Thieves' slang.* Lock-picking, burglary. *Obs.*

1591 GREENE *Conny-Catch.* II. Wks. 1883 X. 72, I can set downe the subtiltie of the blacke Art, which is picking of lockes. **1608** DEKKER *Belman Lond.* Wks. 1884–5 III. 137 This Blacke Art..is called in English Picking of Lockes.

Hence, †**black-'artist,** *Obs.*, a necromancer. †**black-'artship,** *Obs. nonce-wd.*

1620 SYLVESTER *Lit. Bartas* (1877–80) 408 (D.) Those Black-Artists that consult with Hell. **1697** MOUNTFORT *Faustus* I. ad fin., I came only to ask your Black Artship a Question. **1825** CARLYLE *Schiller* II. (1845) 66 Spectres..the terror-struck black-artist cannot lay them.

black ash. *U.S.* [BLACK *a.* 6.] A North American species of ash (*Fraxinus nigra*), also called *basket-ash* and *hoop-ash.*

1673 in *Essex Inst. Hist. Coll.* (1864) VI. 178/2 A forked Black ash which is alsoe osmund trask his bound. **1728** *Boston Town Rec.* (1883) III. 222 We are of Opinion That no Popler,..Black ash, Basswood, or Ceder Shall be Corded up. **1872** *Rep. Vermont Board Agric.* I. 154 An experiment had been tried by a Cornwall farmer, packing butter in spruce, oak and black ash tubs.

†**'black-a-top,** *a. Obs.* Black-headed.

1733 BAILEY *Erasm. Colloq.* (1877) 31 (D.) Can you fancy that black-a-top, snub-nosed,..paunch-bellied creature?

black-a-vised ('blækəˌvaɪst), *a. north. dial.* Also -viced, -vized. [f. BLACK *a.* and F. *vis* face; perh. originally *black-à-vis*, or *black o' vis*; but this is uncertain.] Dark-complexioned.

a **1758** RAMSAY *Poems* (1800) II. 362 (JAM.) A black-a-vic'd snod dapper fallow. **1816** SCOTT *Old Mort.* xi. **1848** C. BRONTË *J. Eyre* (1857) xvii, I would advise her black aviced suitor to look out. **1881** BLACK *Sunrise* (ed. 5) III. 99 The fat black-a-vised Italian.

'blackback. A species of sea-gull; the black-backed gull (*Larus marinus*).

1855 KINGSLEY *Westw. Ho.* xxxii. (D.) The great black-backs laughed querulous defiance at the intruders. **1863** *Reader* 29 Aug., Mer and shearwater, blackback and herring-gull.

black-ball, 'blackball, *sb.*

1. A composition, also called *heel-ball*, used by shoemakers, etc., and also for taking rubbings of brasses and the like.

1847 in CRAIG.

2. A black ball of wood, ivory, etc. put into the urn or ballot-box to express an adverse vote; *hence*, an adverse secret vote, recorded in any way.

1869 *Spectator* 3 July 779 They have exercised precisely the same right which is exercised by every man who drops a blackball into the urn. **1884** *Harper's Mag.* June 148/2 Three blackballs used to make a gentleman wince.

3. *dial.* A hard sweetmeat. Also, in N.Z., *spec.* a humbug.

1851 MAYHEW *Lond. Labour* I. 203/2 'Hard-bake', ..'black balls',..and 'squibs' are all made of treacle. **1877** *N. & Q.* VIII. 481 'Black-ball' is a delicacy compounded of black treacle and sugar boiled together in a pan. **1943** *Amer. Speech* XVIII. 87 The peppermints described in England as *humbugs* become *blackballs* in New Zealand. **1957** J. FRAME *Owls do Cry* xi. 47 Also a sixpenny shout from her pay for blackballs or acid drops or aniseed balls.

blackball ('blækbɔːl), *v.* [see prec.]

1. To exclude (a person) from a club or other society by adverse votes, recorded by the placing of black balls in the ballot-box, or in other ways.

1770 MRS. DELANY *Lett.* Ser. II. I. 262 The Duchess of Bedford was at first black-balled, but is since admitted. **1826** DISRAELI *Viv. Grey* IV. i. 135, I shall make a note to blackball him at the Athenæum. **1880** BESANT & RICE *Seamy Side* xi. 83 There are no rules in this club..nobody is ever blackballed, nobody is ever proposed.

2. To exclude from society; to ostracize, taboo.

1840 MACAULAY *Clive, Ess.* (1854) 534 The Dilettante sneered at their want of taste. The Maccaroni blackballed them ['nabobs'] as vulgar fellows. **1861** *Crt. Life Naples* 88 All foreigners are not to be blackballed.

3. To blacken with black-ball.

1818 COBBETT *Pol. Reg.* XXXIII. 92 With big blackballed whiskers under his nose.

Hence **'blackballer, 'blackballing** *vbl. sb.* and *ppl. a.*

1869 *Spectator* 3 July 779 The blackballer declines to associate with the person blackballed, if he can help it. **1826** SCOTT in *Lockhart* (1839) IX. 43 Here is an ample subject for a little blackballing in the case of Joseph Hume. **1865** *Times* 23 Aug., The most inexorable blackballing club.

'black-bean, *v.* ? *Obs.* [f. *black beans*, used instead of black balls in balloting.] = BLACKBALL *v.*

1829 T. C. CROKER *Leg. Lakes* I. 94 Geoffry Lynch of Drummin, who was black beaned at the Club-room. **1838** *New Month. Mag.* LIII. 122 To have ruined half a score of tailors..does not black-bean, in the very best company.

black belt. [BLACK *a.*] **1.** That portion of the southern United States (see quot. 1905) in which the coloured population is most numerous. Also *transf.*

1875 *Congress. Rec.* Jan. 342/1 During this campaign I made a number of speeches in Georgia. I spoke in what is known as the 'Black Belt'. **1898** *Ibid.* Feb. 1594/1 The Fourth Alabama Congressional district..was composed entirely of Black belt counties. **1905** *N.Y. Even. Post* 21 Nov. 3 The Black Belt has a curiously irregular shape. Extending from Virginia across North and South Carolina, Georgia, Alabama, to Mississippi and Southern Louisiana, it stretches a narrow arm across the river and up into southern and central Arkansas. **1960** *Guardian* 8 Dec. 8/3 Would it have been possible for you to have lived with your white wife in the North reasonably unmolested? If we had kept within the Black Belt.

2. A belt of fertile black soil.

1870 *Q. Jrnl. Geol. Soc.* XXVI. 120 The black soil lies in an extensive bed..the black belt running from the head of the Gulf in a north-westerly direction. **1883** E. A. SMITH *Rep. Alabama Geol. Surv. 1881–82* 268 The Black Belt or Canebrake Region. This division of the prairie region is underlaid by the Rotten Limestone before described. **1901** B. T. WASHINGTON *Up from Slavery* 108 The term 'Black Belt'..was first used to designate a part of the country which was distinguished by the colour of the soil.

3. The belt worn by one who has attained a certain degree of proficiency in judo; also, a person qualified to wear such a belt.

1913 E. J. HARRISON *Fighting Spirit of Japan* iv. 59 Costume in the practice of *judo*... The only outward distinction of rank in the Kano school lies in the colour of the belt... From *shodan* upwards a black belt is worn. **1954** E. DOMINY *Teach yourself Judo* vii. 75 If unable to obtain the usual grip, you will find it almost as effective—many Black Belts consider it better—to place one or both your arms outside your opponent's arms. **1960** *Oxf. Mail* 10 Mar. 8/2 The Cambridge captain, D. J. Mason..a black belt of 1st dan (teacher grade). **1967** 'J. MUNRO' *Money that Money can't Buy* vii. 81 His black belt Loomis knew all about, but what dan he held was a secret.

blackberry (ˈblækbɛrɪ).

1. The fruit of the bramble (*Rubus fruticosus*) and its varieties. This being almost the commonest wild fruit in England is spoken of proverbially as the type of what is plentiful and little prized.

c **1000** ÆLFRIC *Gloss.* in Wr.-Wülcker *Voc.* 139 *Flaui, uel mori*, blaceberian. *c* **1250** *Gloss.* ibid. 558 *Murum*, blakeberie. *c* **1350** *Will. Palerne* 1809 Blake-beries þat on breres growen. *a* **1420** OCCLEVE *De Reg. Princ.* 4715 He settethe not therby a blakberie. **1555** EDEN *Decades W. Ind.* III. viii. (Arb.) 172 Bramble busshes bearynge blacke berries or wylde raspes. **1596** SHAKS. *1 Hen. IV*, II. iv. 265 If Reasons were as plentie as Black-berries, I would giue no man a Reason vpon compulsion. **1713** GAY *Past.* vi, Blackberries they pluck'd in deserts wild. **1852** *Gard. Chron.* 3 A real novelty..in the form of what is called a White Blackberry.

b. *attrib.*

1578 LYTE *Dodoens* VI. iv. 661 The Bramble or Blacke berie bushe. **1580** BARET *Alv.* B 1111 Bramble, the blacke bery tree. **1846** SOWERBY *Brit. Bot.* (1864) III. 164 Who.. has not in his day, been a Blackberry-gatherer? **1847** HALLIWELL *Dict.*, *Blackberry summer*, the fine weather..at the latter end of September and the beginning of October, when the blackberries ripen. *Hants.* **1880** BESANT & RICE *Seamy Side* xxiii. 290 'Real jam, blackberry-jam.'

2. The trailing shrub which bears this fruit; the bramble.

1579 LANGHAM *Gard. Health* (1633), Bramble breer or Blackberry. **1688** R. HOLME *Acad. Armorie* II. 119 Spinous or thorny shrubs..Bramble, Blackberry, Rose. **1849** MRS. SOMERVILLE *Phys. Geog.* II. xxvi. 163 Of the seven species of bramble which grow at the Cape, one is the Common English bramble or blackberry.

3. Now, in the north of England and south of Scotland, the Black Currant (*Ribes nigrum*), the 'blackberry' of sense 1 being there called 'Brambleberry'; formerly in some localities the Bilberry, or Blaeberry; also, according to some, but perhaps erroneously, the sloe or fruit of the Blackthorn.

1567 MAPLET *Gr. Forest*, The blackberie tree is after his sort bushy bearing that fruite that eftsones refresheth the Shepherde. **1597** GERARD *Herbal* (1633) 1417 We in England [call them] Worts, Whortleberries, Black-berries, Bill-berries. **1721** BAILEY, *Black-berries*..the Berries of the Black-thorn. **1783** AINSWORTH *Lat. Dict.* (Morell) II. *Vaccinium*, a blackberry, as some say. **1852** *Gard. Chron.* 54 In speaking of blackberries about Kelso, black currants are understood. **1885** *Scot. Border Rec.* 6 June, The red currant and blackberries have suffered somewhat.

ˈblackˌberrying, *vbl. sb.* [Really formed directly on BLACKBERRY *sb.*, but coming to be treated as a gerund, implying a vb. to *blackberry*. See NUTTING.] The gathering of blackberries.

1861 J. BENNET *Winter Medit.* I. i. (1875) 35 The days when they go blackberrying. **1885** MISS YONGE *Two Sides Shield* i, We never had such a blackberrying.

black birch. *U.S.* [BLACK *a.* 6.] One or other of several North American species of birch, esp. *Betula lenta* and *B. occidentalis*.

1674 JOSSELYN *Two Voyages* 69 The Birch-tree is of two kinds, ordinary Birch, and black Birch. **1711** *Boston Town Rec.* (1883) III. 86 A black burch on the Side of a Swamp. **1832** D. J. BROWNE *Sylva Amer.* 118 Wherever it grows in the United States, it is known by the name of Black Birch. **1957** M. HADFIELD *Brit. Trees* 174 The wood of some birches..produces wood alcohol. For this purpose the sweet or black birch..of the north-eastern U.S.A. is much used.

blackbird (ˈblækbɜːd). [The only BIRD in an earlier sense (before crows and rooks were included) which is *black* (or rather dark brown).] A well-known European song-bird, a species of thrush (*Merula turdus*, L.). In North America the name is given to other birds, e.g. the *Gracula quiscala*, and *Oriolus* (*Agelaius*) *phœniceus*.

1486 *Bk. St. Albans* D j a, For the blacke bride and the thrushe. **1552** HULOET, blacke byrde or owsyl, *turdus*. **1616** SURFL. & MARKH. *Countr. Farm* 729 The strongest and stoutest bird that can be, is the Blacke-bird. **1766** PENNANT *Zool.* (1768) I. 412 The blackbird continues in Italy the whole year. **1879** JEFFERIES *Wild Life S. County* 131 In glass cases are..a white blackbird, and a diver. *Nursery Rime*, Four and twenty blackbirds baked in a pie.

b. *loosely* = Songster.

1634 MASSINGER *Very Wom.* III. i, You never had such black-birds.

2. *fig.* Cant name for a captive negro or Polynesian on board a slave or pirate ship.

1881 *Chequered Career* 180 The white men on board knew that if once the 'blackbirds' burst the hatches..they would soon master the ship.

blackbirder (ˈblækbɜːdə(r)). [f. BLACKBIRDING + -ER[1].] A man or a vessel engaged in BLACKBIRDING or slave-traffic.

1883 *All Year Round* 22 Sept. 355 Blackbirders, the kidnappers for labour purposes on the islands of the Pacific. **1888** W. B. CHURCHWARD *Blackbirding* 126 You see the harm those cussed blackbirders do in the islands. *Ibid.* 163 That chap whose throat I cut on board the blackbirder. **1928** *New Statesman* 28 July 507/2 Polynesians in their wild state ..were..shipped to Australia by enterprising gentlemen called blackbirders. **1969** *Sunday Mail Mag.* (Brisbane) 9 Feb. 4/1 After 20 years as a 'blackbirder', Buttray had returned to the more respectable coastal service.

ˈblackbirding, *vbl. sb.* [f. BLACKBIRD (sense 2): the verb is recorded later.] The kidnapping of negroes or Polynesians for slavery. Also as ppl. adj. Hence (as a back-formation) **blackbird** *v.*

1873 HOTTEN *Slang Dict.* 84 *Blackbirding*, slave-catching. Term most applied nowadays to the Polynesian coolie traffic. **1883** *Academy* 8 Sept. 158 [He] slays Bishop Patteson by way of reprisal for the atrocities of some 'black-birding' crew. **1884** *Pall Mall G.* 19 Aug. 2/2 Years ago blackbirding scoundrels may have hailed from Fiji. **1888** W. B. CHURCHWARD (*title*) 'Blackbirding' in the South Pacific. *a* **1889** in BARRÈRE & LELAND *Dict. Slang.* I. 125/1 But sometimes—we are glad to say in the past—iniquitously blackbirded or kidnapped, and practically sold into slavery. **1897** W. C. MORROW *The Ape, the Idiot* (1898) 314 'Blackbirding' (which is kidnapping Gilbert Islanders and selling them to the coffee-planters of Central America). **1908** *Daily Chron.* 6 Nov. 4/6 'Blackbirding'..is not yet an entirely extinct industry [in the Pacific Islands]. **1946** K. TENNANT *Lost Haven* (1947) 4 He had really made it [*sc.* money] blackbirding natives from the Pacific Islands to the Queensland sugar plantations.

black board, ˈblackboard. **a.** A large wooden board, a tablet of papier-maché, etc., painted black, and used in schools and lecture-rooms to draw or write upon with chalk. Now also used of a similar board in any colour.

1823 PILLANS *Contrib. Cause Educ.* (1856) 378 A large black board served my purpose. On it I wrote in chalk. **1835** *Musical Libr.* Supp., Aug. 77 The assistant wrote down the words..on a blackboard. **1846** *Rep. Inspect. Schools* I. 147 The uses of the black board are not yet fully developed.

b. *attrib.* and *Comb.* **blackboard jungle**, an undisciplined or unpleasant school.

1870 MEDBERY *Men & Myst. Wall St.* 21 The 'marker' or black-board clerk writes off the prices upon the tablet. **1880** *Plain Hints Needlework* 33 These three strips can be sewed ..together, and thus form a dish-cloth or black-board rubber. **1890** W. J. GORDON *Foundry* 89 To see the service complete we should have been in the great hall, and heard the blackboard lesson. **1895** *Daily News* 26 Apr. 3/2 'Black-board Drawing'..seemed to him to be useful..for..the student, the teacher, and the child. **1905** H. H. STEPHENS (*title*) Black-board and free-arm drawing. **1954** E. HUNTER (*title*) Blackboard jungle. **1958** *Economist* 29 Nov. 784/1 This is a variation, *andante moderato*, on the theme of the blackboard jungle. Mr Townsend describes the teacher's end of the stick—now used more and more sparingly—in the new system of secondary modern education.

black book.

1. An official book bound in black.

1624 BEDELL *Lett.* xi. 141 The Copie of the record of Doctor Parkers Consecration..which..you saw in a blacke Booke. **1815** *Encycl. Brit.* (ed. 5) III. 261/1 He keeps the black book of receipts, and the treasurer's key of the treasury. **1823** T. LANE *Stud. Guide Lincoln's Inn* 122 Curious regulations..are to be found in their Black Books.

2. The distinctive name of various individual books of public note, referring in some cases to the colour of the binding.

a. *Black Book of the Exchequer*: a book preserved in the Exchequer Office, containing an official account of the royal revenues, etc. at the time of its compilation (? *c* 1175).

1479 *Mem. Ripon* (1885) II. 158 In libro..nuncupato blakboke. **1561** STOW *Eng. Chron.* an. 1176 (1615) 154 This yeere was compiled a booke of the orders and rules of the Exchequer, nowe commonly called there the Blacke booke. **1605** CAMDEN *Rem.* 6 It is written in the Blackebooke of the Exchequer, that our Auncestors termed England, a Storehouse of Treasure. **1631** T. POWELL *Tom All Trades* 169 Search the Blacke Booke in the Exchequer.

b. *Black Book of the Admiralty*: an ancient code of rules for the government of the navy, said to have been compiled in the reign of Edw. III.

1769 FALCONER *Dict. Marine* (1789), *Oleron*..a code of.. rules relating to naval affairs..formed by Richard I..are still preserved in the black book of the admiralty.

3. An official return prepared during the reign of Henry VIII, containing the reports of the visitors upon the abuses in the monasteries.

1581 T. NORTON *Let.* in Dugdale *Warw.* (1730) II. iiii, T. Cromwell..having..thus searcht into their lives, which by a Black Book, containing a world of enormities, were represented in no small measure scandalous. **1815** *Encycl. Brit.* (ed. 5) III. 641/1 The black-book of the English monasteries was a detail of the scandalous enormities practised in religious houses. **1878** DIXON *Hist. Ch. Eng.* I. v. 341.

4. A book recording the names of persons who have rendered themselves liable to censure or punishment.

1592 GREENE *Black Bks. Messenger* Wks. 1881–3 XI. 5 Ned Brownes villanies..are too many to be described in my Blacke Booke. **1595** SPENSER *Sonn.* x, Al her faults in thy black booke enroll. **1657** REEVE *God's Plea* 20 This Day-book will prove a black-book to him. **1726** AMHERST *Terræ Fil.* 115 The black book is a register of the university, kept by the proctor, in which he records any person who affronts him, or the university; and no person, who is so recorded, can proceed to his degree. **1816** C. JAMES *Mil. Dict.* (ed. 4) 57/2 The black book is a sort of memorandum which is kept in every regiment to describe the character and conduct of non-commissioned officers and soldiers.

b. † *to be in the black book*(*s*: to be in disgrace. *to be in* (*any one's*) *black books*: to have incurred his displeasure, to be out of his favour.

1785 GROSE *Dict. Vulg. Tongue*, s.v., He is down in the black book, i.e. has a stain in his character. **1881** PAYN *From Exile* 89 This unfortunate youth is so deep in your black books.

5. A book of the 'black art,' of necromancy.

1842 BARHAM *Ingol. Leg., Raising the Devil*, A 'Magician' ..has brought him [Cornelius Agrippa] and his terrible 'Black Book' again before the world.

black bottom. **1.** [BLACK *a.* 1 c, BOTTOM *sb.* 5.] A low-lying area inhabited by a coloured population. *U.S.*

1915 *Lit. Digest* 4 Sept. 500/2 Uncle Mose aspired to the elective office of justice of the peace in the 'black bottom' part of town.

2. The name of a dance, esp. popular in and for a time after 1926. Also as *v.* orig. *U.S.*

1926 *N.Y. Times* 19 Dec. VII. 4/6 It occurred to the producer that if you could dance before the beat you would have a new rhythm... The result is the Black Bottom. **1927** *Observer* 6 Feb. 15/7 The accounts of the new dances are discouraging. There is the Black Bottom, the very name of which spoils a spring morning. **1927** *Daily Express* 25 May, Miss Bradhurst had black bottomed nineteen miles..before she collapsed. **1928** 'SAPPER' *Female of Species* v. 76 'What matter that his Black Bottom is the best in London.' 'My Gawd! sir,' gasped the other. 'His 'ow much?' **1968** D. BRAITHWAITE *Fairground Archit.* viii. 137 The mock elegance and good taste of the Victorian *soirée* gave place to the rumbustious 'Charleston' and the 'Black Bottom'.

black boy. Also black-boy, blackboy. **1.** A boy having a black or very dark skin; spec. (*a*) = BLACK MAN 1; (*b*) a Negro manservant (cf. BOY *sb.*[1] 3).

1635 *Relation of Maryland* v. 28 The Children live with their Parents; the Boyes untill they come to the full growth of men..then they are put into the number of Bow-men, and are called Black-boyes. **1666–7** PEPYS *Diary* 27 Jan., Her little black boy came by him. **1681** [see BOY *sb.*[1] 3 c]. **1738** F. MOORE *Trav. Inland Afr.* 64 *Creague* saved himself in his Boat, with the Help of his black Boy. *Ibid.* 175 As he was chastising his BlackBoy. **1774** J. HARROWER *Diary* 24 May in *Amer. Hist. Rev.* (1900) VI. 78 There was a gray Mare started with the Bay a black boy ridder but was far distant the last heat. **1829** B. HALL *Trav. N. Amer.* I. 122 His first assistant was a sharp-faced, well-tanned, old woman in spectacles; next came a black boy. **1856** OLMSTED *Slave States* 141 The 'old Ab' was manned by one black boy, sixty years old. **1923** D. H. LAWRENCE *Birds, Beasts & Flowers* 178 The fully fathomless, shining eyes of an Australian black-boy. **1948** V. PALMER *Golconda* xviii. 148 I had a trip over there with a blackboy and a couple of camels.

2. An Australian grass-tree of the genus *Xanthorrhœa*, having a thick dark trunk and a head of grass-like leaves, exp. *Xanthorrhœa preissii*.

1840 *Jrnl. Bot.* II. 344 One of the most striking plants to a stranger is our common *Blackboy*, a fine arborescent species of *Xanthorrhœa*. **1840** PEREIRA *Elem. Mat. Med.* II. 658 A red resin, probably from *X*[*anthorrœa*] *arborea*.., has been recently imported under the name of *black-boy gum*. **1846** J. L. STOKES *Discov. in Australia* II. 132 Black boy.. gum on the spear—resin on the trunk. *Ibid.* 380 *note*, These trees, called Blackboys by the colonists, from the resemblance they bear, in the distance, to natives. **1870** W. H. KNIGHT *W. Australia* 46 A resin got from the 'black-boy', or grass tree, (*xanthorrhea drummondii*). **1956** S. HOPE *Diggers' Paradise* 59 The 'blackboys' several times taller than a man with twisted coal-black stems crowned by massive raffia-like tufts in green and white.

3. A kind of black tobacco.

1898 *Daily News* 8 Oct. 3/3 She had been addicted to the use of the weed, in the specific shape of 'black boy', for over forty years. **1908** *Daily Chron.* 10 Apr. 4/7 A black boy tobacco much in favour with mariners.

black-browed (ˈblækbraʊd), *ppl. a.* **a.** Having a dark brow or front; frowning, scowling.

1590 SHAKS. *Mids. N.* III. ii. 387 They..must for aye consort with blacke browd night. **1687** DRYDEN *Hind & P.* III. 1144 Black-brow'd, and bluff, like Homer's Jupiter. **1826** *Sheridaniana* 317 Sheridan was dining with the black-browed Chancellor. **1882** *Athenæum* 1 Apr. 421/3 A ruffian is not of necessity a black-browed..scoundrel.

b. *black-browed albatross*, an albatross, *Diomedea melanophrys*, found in the south Atlantic Ocean.

[**1865** GOULD *Handbk. Birds Australia* II. 438 *Diomedea Melanophrys*..Black-eyebrowed Albatros.] **1883** *Encycl. Brit.* XV. 334/2 All the rest of the plumage is white, except a dusky superciliary streak, whence its name of Black-browed Albatros. **1968** T. STOKES *Birds of Atlantic Ocean* 26/2 The black-browed albatross is a beautiful bird of regular, clear-cut marking.

Blackˈburnian, *a. U.S.* [f. the name of Mrs. Hugh *Blackburn*, fl. 18th c.] ***Blackburnian***

warbler, a North American warbler (*Dendroica blackburniæ*). Also *ellipt.* as *sb.*

1783 LATHAM *Gen. Syn. Birds* II. II. 461 Blackburnian Warbler. **1868** *Amer. Naturalist* II. 179 The Blackburnian Warbler (*D. Blackburniae*) is one of the most beautiful. **1893** B. TORREY *Footpath-Way* 6 We..soon were in the old forest listening to bay-breasted warblers, Blackburnians, black-polls, and so on. *Ibid.* 16 A Blackburnian warbler perched as usual, at the very top of a tall spruce. **1936** T. S. ELIOT *Coll. Poems 1909–35* 152 Leave to chance The Blackburnian warbler, the shy one. **1947** *Harper's Mag.* May 480/1 The orange flittings of a Blackburnian in the treetops.

blackbutt (ˈblækbʌt). *Austral.* Also **black butt, black-butt.** [BLACK *a.*, BUTT *sb.*[3] 2.] An Australian timber tree, *Eucalyptus pilularis*. Earlier, ***black-butted gum***.

1801 C. GRIMES in *Hist. Rec. Austral.* (1915) 1st Ser. III. 414 The finest stringy-bark and black-butted blue-gum trees I ever saw. **1820** J. OXLEY *Jrnls. Two Exped. N.S.W.* 331 The timber was chiefly black butted gum. **1847** LEICHHARDT *Jrnl.* ii. 49 The range..having, with the exception of the Blackbutt, all the trees..of Moreton Bay. **1901** *Daily Chron.* 3 Sept. 7/4 Fencing post of blackbutt, forty-five years in the ground. **1934** *Archit. Rev.* LXXVI. 70/2 In addition jarrah, blackbutt, mountain ash and blackwood from Australia..are all good flooring timbers.

black cap, 'black-cap, 'blackcap.

1. ***black cap***: spec. that worn by English judges when in full dress, and consequently put on by them when passing sentence of death upon a prisoner.

1838 DICKENS *O. Twist* lii, The jury returned..The judge assumed the black cap.

2. One who wears a black cap or head-dress.

1856 J. GRANT *Bl. Dragoon* v, The old blackcaps frowned terribly at..this fashion.

3. ***blackcap***: A name given to various birds having the top of the head black; esp. by English writers to the small bird also called Blackcap Warbler, *Curruca* (or *Motacilla*) *atricapilla*.

Also applied locally to: **a.** Several species of *Parus*, as *P. major* the Great Tit, *P. palustris* the Marsh Tit, *P. ater* the Cole Tit, and in U.S. *P. atricapillus* the Blackcap Tit, or Chickadee; **b.** the Black-headed Bunting; **c.** the Black-headed Gull; **d.** the Stonechat; and casually to others.

1678 RAY *Willughby's Ornith.* 241 The Marsh Titmouse or Black-cap. *Ibid.* 347 The Pewit or Black-cap, called in some places, the Sea-Crow and Mire-Crow. **1768** PENNANT *Zool.* II. 262 The black cap is a bird of passage, leaving us before winter. **1789** G. WHITE *Selborne* (1853) 145 The black-cap has..a full sweet deep loud and wild pipe. **1802** G. MONTAGU *Ornith. Dict.* (1833) 350 Great Black-headed Tomtit, Blackcap. *Ibid.* 415 *Black-bonnet*, *Black-cap*, prov. names for the Black-headed Bunting, *Emberiza schœniclus*. **1863** *Yng. England* Aug. 127 In Wiltshire I have heard the red-backed shrike..called the black cap. **1883** G. ALLEN in *Knowledge* 25 May 304/1 Blackcaps are above everything hangers-on of civilisation.

4. a. ***black-cap pudding***: a boiled batter pudding into which a handful of currants or raisins is dropped before boiling, which sink to the bottom, and form a black capping when the pudding is reversed out of the basin or mould.

1822 KITCHINER *Cook's Oracle* 517.

b. A halved apple baked with the flat side downwards and a 'cap' of sugar.

1723 J. NOTT *Cook's & Confectioner's Dict.* No. 103 B, *Black Cap.* Take..large Pippins..cut them in halves..squeeze a Lemon..over them..grate over them..Sugar..put them into a quick Oven. **1958** *Listener* 27 Nov. 903/1 Sprinkle a 'cap' of caster sugar on each [*sc.* apple]. Bake for twenty or twenty-five minutes above the chicken, and when the bird goes to the top of the oven, put the 'blackcaps' in its place.

5. A variety of raspberry; the Black Raspberry, *Rubus occidentalis*. *U.S.*

1847 W. DARLINGTON *Agric. Bot.* 127 *Rubus occidentalis*..Wild or Black Raspberry. Thimble-berry. Black Caps. **1886** *Harper's Mag.* July 281/2 There is another American species of raspberry (*Rubus occidentalis*) that is almost as dear to memory as the wild strawberry—the thimble-berry, or black-cap. **1946** B. MACDONALD *Egg & I* (1947) vi. 85 Alder, salal, wild raspberry and blackcaps.

black-capped, *a.* **1.** [Cf. BLACK CAP 3.] Of birds: having the top of the head black.

1781 J. LATHAM *Gen. Synop. Birds* I. 727 Black-Capped Cr[eeper]..head is black. *Ibid.* 748 Black-Capped H.B. [Humming-Bird]. **1808** A. WILSON *Amer. Ornith.* I. 134 [The] Black-Capt Titmouse, *Parus Atricapillus*,..is one of our resident birds. **1868** *Amer. Naturalist* II. 175 The Green Black-capped Warbler (*Myiodioctes pusillus*). **1870** *Ibid.* III. 74 The cries and habits of all these black-capped species. *Ibid.* IV. 543 In the depths of winter they and..the Black-capped Titmouse (*Parus Atricapillus*), enliven the woods.

2. Wearing a black cap.

1908 *Westm. Gaz.* 15 Jan. 3/1 Moors in turbans..and black-capped Jews. **1930** BLUNDEN *Summer's Fancy* 22 And black-capped and gowned The sour-tongued master stared.

blackcock (ˈblækkɒk). The male of the black grouse or BLACK GAME.

1427 *Scot. Acts Jas. I* (1597) § 108 Patricks, plovers, black-cockes. **1753** *Stewart's Trial* App. 21 He would make black cocks of them, before they entered into possession, by which the deponent understood shooting them. **1815** SCOTT *Ld. Isles* v. xiii, The black-cock deem'd it day, and crew. **1832** *Proc. Berw. Nat. Club* I. 5 The blackcock (*Tetrao tetrix*) was heard harshly calling to his mates.

black currant. a. The fruit of the *Ribes nigrum*; also the shrub. Often used *attrib.*, as in ***black-currant jam, jelly, tea, wine***, etc.

1629 PARKINSON *Parad.* III. ii. 558 The blacke Curran bush riseth higher than the white. **1768** WALES in *Phil. Trans.* LX. 119 These shrubs consist of willows..gooseberry, and black currants. **1769** MRS. RAFFALD *Engl. Housekpr.* (1778) 211 To make Black Currant Jelly. **1836** DICKENS *Sk. Boz* ii. (1850) 5 Anonymous presents of black-currant jam, and lozenges.

b. ***black currant (gall) mite***, an insect pest that attacks currant and gooseberry bushes, but especially the black currant bush, living chiefly inside the buds and producing the disease known as 'big bud' (BIG *a.* B. 2).

1890 E. A. ORMEROD *Man. Injurious Insects* (ed. 2) III. 303 The details of those of the Black Currant Gall Mite have not been described. **1918** *Board Agric. & Fisheries Leaflet* No. 1. The disease known as 'big bud' in Black Currants, caused by the Black Currant Mite, was first recorded in these islands in the year 1869.

Black death: see DEATH *sb.*

black dog.

†**1.** A cant name, in Queen Anne's reign, for a bad shilling or other base silver coin. *Obs.*

1706 LUTTRELL in Ashton *Reign Q. Anne* II. 225 The Art of making Black Dogs, which are Shillings, or other pieces of money made only of Pewter, double Wash'd. **1724** SWIFT *Drapier's Lett.* Wks. 1755 V. II. 44 Butchers' half-pence, black-dogs, and others the like.

2. *fig.* Melancholy, depression of spirits; ill-humour; (in some country places, when a child is sulky, it is said 'the black dog is on his back').

1826 SCOTT in *Lockhart* (1839) VIII. 335 A great relief from the black dog which would have worried me at home. **1882** STEVENSON *New Arab. Nts.* II. 111 He did not seem to be enjoying his luck..The black dog was on his back, as people say, in terrifying nursery metaphor.

black drop.

1. *Med.* A dark-coloured liquid medicine, chiefly composed of opium, with vinegar and spices.

1823 BYRON *Juan* IX. lxvii, A quintessential laudanum or 'black drop.' **1878** *Cycl. Med.* XVII. 844 Black drops, Godfrey's Elixir..etc. all contain opium.

2. *Astron.* A dark drop-like appearance observed at solar transits of Venus and Mercury immediately after apparent internal contact at ingress, and before it at egress, giving to the planet a pear-shaped appearance, elongated towards the sun's edge.

1869 E. DUNKIN *Midn. Sky* 252 The formation of the black-drop..was very clearly observed at..Greenwich. **1878** NEWCOMB *Pop. Astron.* II. iii. 189 Father Hell's black drop, seen before the limbs [of Sun and Venus] were in contact.

blacked (blækt), *ppl. a.* [f. BLACK + -ED[1].]

1. Made or coloured black, blackened.

1552 ABP. HAMILTON *Catech.* 122 Gif thai see thair face blekkit. **1716** ADDISON *Drummer* v. Mourning paper, that is black'd at the edges. **1815** SCOTT *Guy M.* liii, Do you see that blackit and broken end of a sheeling?

2. ***blacked out***, (*a*) obliterated with black; also *fig.*; (*b*) with lights extinguished or obscured; (*c*) of an aircraft pilot, temporarily blinded (see BLACK *v.* 6).

1919 *Illustr. London News* 27 Sept. 482 (*caption*) No longer 'blacked out': London herself again. **1930** E. POUND *XXX Cantos* vii. 26 Time blacked out with the rubber. **1933** *Flight* 2 Feb. 100/1 Tight turns had been made for much longer periods than 10 sec., while the pilot was 'blacked out', without any tendency whatsoever to lose consciousness. **1938** *San Francisco Examiner* 27 Sept. 3/7 (*headline*) City blacked out in raid test. **1939** *Punch* 8 Nov. 504/2 We must still endure the totally blacked-out nights. **1940** C. DAY LEWIS tr. *Virgil's Georgics* I. 23 At the South pole..it's dead of night,..the shadows shrouded in night, blacked out for ever. **1940** *New Statesman* 19 Oct. 371 Most unfavourable conditions—crowded shelters, stuffy, blacked-out factories and offices. **1967** V. NABOKOV *Speak, Memory* (ed. 2) xiv. 292 Opaque curtains separated me from blacked-out Paris.

blacken (ˈblæk(ə)n), *v.* [ME. *blakne(n, blackone(n* f. BLACK *a.* + -EN.]

1. *intr.* To become or grow black. *lit.* and *fig.*

a **1300** *Cursor M.* 17430 To blacken þan bigan þair brous. *c* **1400** *Destr. Troy.* XXII. 9134 Blaknet with bleryng all hir ble qwite. *Ibid.* XXVI. 10706 All blakonet his blode, & his ble chaunget. **1758** JOHNSON *Idler* No. 17 ¶2, I..believe that rain will fall when the air blackens. **1871** MORLEY *Crit. Misc.* Ser. I. (1878) 193 It may blacken into cynicism.

2. *trans.* To make black or dark. *lit.* and *fig.*

1552 HULOET, To make blacke, or blacken, *denigro*. *a* **1649** DRUMM. OF HAWTH. *Jas. V*, Wks. (1711) 85 Calumnies, tho' they do not burn, yet blacken. **1660** *Trial Regic.* 45 To draw up that Impeachment so, as to Blacken Him. **1712** STEELE *Spect.* No. 518 ¶2 You ought to have blackened the edges of a paper which brought us so ill news. **1863** KINGSLEY *Water Bab.* vi, The Birds..blackening all the air.

Hence **'blackened** *ppl. a.*, **'blackening** *vbl. sb.* and *ppl. a.*

c **1400** *Apol. Loll.* 55 Corrumping cold and blakning. **1513** DOUGLAS *Æneis* III. i. 122 Crownit..with the bleknyt cipres deidlie bewis. **1660** *Trial Regic.* 55 The Blackning of the King. **1725** POPE *Odyss.* VII. 161 Some dry the black'ning clusters in the sun. **1793** HOLCROFT *Lavater's Physiog.* xxix. 144 Smellfungus views all objects through a blackened glass. **1818** BYRON *Ch. Har.* IV. xxiv, The blight and blackening which it leaves behind. **1842** MIALL *Nonconf.* II. 249 More than they fear a blackened reputation.

'blackener. [f. prec. + -ER[1].] He who or that which blackens.

1632 [see next]. **1748** RICHARDSON *Clarissa* (1811) VII. 364 A partial whitener of his own cause, or blackener of another's.

'blacker. [f. BLACK *v.* + -ER[1].] One who or that which blacks.

1632 SHERWOOD, A Blacker, or Blackener, *noircisseur*. **1882** *Punch* 1 Mar., An elderly lady had had her boots blackt, And gave to the blacker a nice little tract.

blacketeer: see BLACK MARKET.

blackey, var. of BLACKY, a black man.

black eye.

1. An eye of which the iris is black or very dark-coloured; *esp.* as a mark of beauty, a dark lustrous eye.

a **1667**, **1775** [Implied at BLACK-EYED *a.* 1 a.] **1839** *Penny Cycl.* XIV. 363/2 The Mongolian variety:—characterised by olive colour..and black eyes. **1842** TENNYSON *May Queen* ii, There's many a black black eye, they say, but none so bright as mine.

2. a. A discoloration of the flesh around the eye produced by a blow or contusion.

1604 DEKKER *Honest Wh.* II. Wks. 1873 II. 122, I doe not bid you beat her, nor giue her blacke eyes. **1819** BYRON *Juan* II. cxii, Just like a black eye in a recent scuffle. **1886** C. COBORN (*title of song*) Two lovely black eyes. **1926** GALSWORTHY *Silver Spoon* II. iii. 132, I thought they'd have a row... Hadn't Michael a black eye? **1937** D. L. SAYERS *Busman's Honeymoon* i. 54 At this moment I could have been tramping at your heels with five babies and a black eye.

b. *fig.* A severe blow or rebuff.

1744 C. CIBBER *Another Occas. Let. to Mr. P[ope]* 8 If you had not been a blinder Booby, than myself, you would have sate down quietly with the last black Eye I gave you. **1813** J. ORROK *Let.* 1 Oct. (1927) 167 The young folks gave the Jelly and Jam a black eye. **1900** *Congress. Rec.* Jan. 1004/2, I hope the Pension Committee will give a black eye to every bill of that kind. **1962** *Listener* 29 Nov. 895/1 A black eye for the Indian Army.

black-eyed, *a.* [BLACK *a.* 18.]

1. Having black eyes. Cf. BLACK EYE 1.

1598 CHAPMAN *Iliad* I. p. 4 Nor will containe..his heauie hand before: The blacke eyde virgin be releast. *a* **1667** COWLEY *Lover's Chron.* ix, Black-eyed Bess, her viceroy-maid. **1775** SHERIDAN *Duenna* I. v, Egad, a very pretty black-eyed girl!

b. *spec.* Of a variety of pea: having a black speck.

1728 W. BYRD *Hist. Dividing Line* in *Writings* (1901) 74 Each Cell [of N.C. pine cone] contains a Seed of the Size and Figure of a black-ey'd Pea. **1786** WASHINGTON *Diaries* (1925) III. 56 They proceeded to sow the small black eyed pea. **1857** *Texas Almanac* 13 Plant Black-Eyed..Peas. **1862** *Chambers's Encycl.* s.v. *Dolichos*, *D. sphaerospermus* (Calavana or Black-eyed Pea), a native of the West Indies.

2. ***black-eyed Susan***: **a.** A name applied to various plants having pale flowers with dark centres, esp. *Thunbergia alata* and *Rudbeckia hirta*.

1891 *Cent. Dict.* s.v. *Thunbergia*, The hardy annual *T. alata*, known locally by the name *black-eyed Susan* from its buff, orange, or white flowers with a purplish black center. **1900** C. BENNETT in W. D. Drury *Bk. Gardening* xv. 696 *T. alata*, with a buff-yellow corolla, and a very dark eye nearly approaching black (hence the common name Black-eyed Susan). **1906** H. D. PITTMAN *Belle of Blue Grass C.* xvi. 241, I found all of the waste places now covered with black-eyed susans. **1956** A. M. COATS *Flowers & their Histories* 226 'Black-eyed Susan' (the annual *R. hirta*) immigrated in 1714.

b. *U.S. slang.* (See quots.)

1869 in M. Mathews *Beginnings Amer. Eng.* (1931) 153 Among names of revolvers I remember the following: Meat in the Pot,..Black-eyed Susan. **1888** FARMER *Americanisms*, *Black-eyed Susan.*—Texan for a revolver.

'black-face. Also black face. **1.** One who has a black face; a black-faced sheep or other animal.

1844 W. H. MAXWELL *Sports & Adv. Scotl.* i. (1855) 21 We..added a black-face to our sea-stock. **1879** WRIGHTSON *Sheep* in *Cassell's Techn. Educ.* IV. 321/1 The Black Faces are found on the moors of Yorkshire.

2. †(*a*) A Negro. *Obs. U.S.* (*b*) The exaggerated make-up worn by an actor playing a Negro role. Also *attrib.* orig. *U.S.*

(*a*) **1704** S. KNIGHT *Jrnl.* (1825) 40 Order the master to pay 40s to black face. **1899** H. B. CUSHMAN *Hist. Choctaw Indians* 312 Do they not even now kick and strike us as they do their black-faces?

(*b*) **1869** F. DUMONT *Benedict's Congress Songster* 9 Lew made his first bow before the public at the Metropolitan Theatre in a black face. **1895** *N.Y. Dramatic News* 16 Nov. 7/4 An old-time black-face actor died in Bellevue hospital. **1969** C. HIMES *Blind Man with Pistol* xii. 129 Two big rugged black men clad in belted leather coats, looking for all the world like Nazi SS troopers in blackface.

'black-faced, *a.*

1. Having a black or dark-coloured face; *spec.* of sheep. Also *fig.*

1594 SHAKS. *Rich. III*, i. ii. 159 Black-fac'd Clifford shooke his sword at him. **1773** G. WHITE *Selborne* lvi. (1851) 172 The black-faced poll-sheep have the shortest legs. **1801** *Farmer's Mag.* Nov. 394 The Cheviot breed of sheep will succeed fully as well in the North, if not better, than the common Black-faced. **1878** TENNYSON *Q. Mary* II. i. 54 The

black-faced swains of Spain. **1886** C. SCOTT *Sheep-Farming* 113 Blackfaced stocks [are letting] at about 2s 6d per sheep.

2. Of things: Dark, dismal, gloomy.

1592 SHAKS. *Ven. & Ad.* 773 This black-faced night, desires foul nurse. **1611** R. CHESTER *Ann. Gt. Brit.* (1878) 79 The Sunne did frowne, Fore-shewing to his men a blacke-fac't day.

black fish.

1. A name given to several varieties of English and American fishes; e.g. the Black Ruff (a kind of perch), *Centrolophus pompilus* (a kind of mackerel), *Tautoga Americana* (a species of wrasse).

1754 BORLASE *Cornwall* 271 Black ruffe, *synonym* Black-fish. **1765** R. ROGERS *Acct. N. Amer.* 68 In the sea adjacent to this island [*sc.* Long Island] are sea-bass and black-fish in great plenty. **1861** J. BLIGHT *Week Land's End* 142 During the mackerel-season the blackfish of Gesner, *Coryphæna Pompilus*, is not of rare occurrence. **1888** GOODE *Amer. Fishes* 39 The Sea Bass is also known south of Cape Hatteras as the 'Blackfish'. **1897** *Outing* (U.S.) XXX. 160/2 These fishermen, who think that God made blackfish for them exclusively.

2. A small species of whale.

1688 S. SEWALL *Diary* (1878) I. 239 [We saw] a number of Fishes called Bottle-noses. Some say they are Cow-fish or Black-fish. **1796** MORSE *Amer. Geog.* I. 398 Black fish, a sort of whale 'of about five tons weight.' **1879** WALLACE *Australas.* 428 The people of Solor..capture the small whales called black-fish.

3. A name given to salmon just after spawning. Hence **black-fisher**, one who catches salmon when in this condition. **black-fishing**, the taking of such salmon; especially applied in Scotland to their capture at night by torchlight, whence the term is sometimes explained.

1808 WALKER *Prize Essays* II. 364 (JAM.) The salmon in these states are termed in our acts of Parliament, *Red* and *Black* Fish. **1841** *Penny Cycl.* XX. 363/1 The females are dark in colour and are as commonly called black-fish. **1809** *St. Patrick* III. 42 (JAM.) Ye took me aiblins for a black-fisher. **1848** *Life Normandy* (1863) II. 55 Black-fisher..is the name given to the poachers who kill salmon when they are out of season. **1794** *Forfar Statist. Acc.* XII. 294 (JAM.) Black-fishing is so called because it is performed in the night-time, or perhaps because the fish are then black or foul. **1815** SCOTT *Guy M.* ii, The holding of a black-fishing, or poaching court.

4. The freshwater fish *Gadopsis marmoratus*, found in Australia.

1850 CLUTTERBUCK *Port Phillip* iii. 44 The Schnapper, blackfish and eel. **1879** MCCOY *Zool. Victoria* I. III. 39 *Gadopsis gracilis*... The Yarra Blackfish. **1890** *Melbourne Argus* 9 Aug. 4/5 You could catch a few blackfish in the pools. **1962** L. WEDLICK *Fishing in Australia* III. 76 The blackfish is a poor fighter.

black flag. A flag of black cloth, used with some reference to death or deadly purpose: e.g. as a sign that no quarter will be given or asked, as the ensign of pirates, and as the signal of the execution of a criminal. Also in *plur.* applied to the pirates of the Chinese Sea, the opponents of the French in Tonquin, etc.

1593 NASHE *Christ's T.* (1613) 7 The black-flag was set vp, which signified there was no mercy to be looked for. **1720** DEFOE *Capt. Singleton* xiii, We let them soon see who we were, for we hoisted a black flag, with two cross daggers on it. **1821** SCOTT *Pirate* xl, Up goes the Jolly Hodge, the old black flag, with the death's head and hour-glass. **1827** P. CUNNINGHAM *N.S.W.* II. xiii. 302 Every effort ought to be made to impress..upon..the multitude the terrible nature of our punishments, without permitting them to be.. spectators... The having..a black flag with emblems of death hung out [etc.]. **1840** MARRYAT *Poor Jack* xliv, I would hoist the black flag. **1870** BREWER *Dict. Phrase & Fable* 301/1 *To unfurl the black flag*, to declare war. **1887** *Longm. Mag.* Nov. 105 Mr. Brander Matthews alleges that certain English publishers can also run up the 'Jolly Roger' on occasion, and sail under the Black Flag.

black fly. [BLACK *a.* 6.] **1.** Any of various dark-coloured flying insects.

1608 [see FLY *sb.*[1] 1 a]. **1716** J. LOWTHORP *Phil. Trans. Abridged* II. 338 In the Cross-Bath the Guides have observed a certain Black Fly with Sealed Wings, in the form of a Lody-Cow, but somewhat bigger. **1789** B. LINCOLN in *Mass. Hist. Soc. Coll.* (1795) IV. 148 Objections have been made to these counties, on account of the black flies, and other insects. **1876** *Fur, Fin & Feather* Sept. 139 At Calais, Maine, last fall rugged grouse were as thick as black flies in August. **1889** [see FLY *sb.*[1] 2]. **1959** *Times* 30 Oct. 15/1 Blackfly or buffalo gnat, but coming to be known in West Africa by the ominous name of 'eye flies'.

2. A name given to various insects infesting plants, esp. to an insect of the species *Frankliniella robusta* (formerly *Thrips pisivora*) and *Aphis rumicis*: used *collect.* in *sing.* for thripses or aphides when infesting certain plants and giving a blackish appearance to the part affected.

1743 ELLIS *Mod. Husb.* July iv. 31 But when the Black Bug, or Fly..takes the Ear..they do a great deal of harm. **1850** *Working Man's Friend* 13 July 55/1 To Remove the Aphides, or black fly. **1884** *Sutton's Cult. Veget. & Flowers* 269 The Blue and the Black Fly are common plagues of the Peach-house and the orchard. **1919** *Board Agric. & Fisheries Leaflet* No. 104. 2 The Bean Aphis, known variously as Black Fly, Collier, and Black Dolphin. **1951** *New Biol.* XI. 50 Many a garden crop of beans..has been saved from the devastating 'black-fly' by early pinching-out of the growing tips.

black foot.

1. A (member of a) North American Indian people; their language. Also *attrib.*

1794 *Mass. Hist. Soc. Coll.* (1810) 1st Ser. III. 24 The Blackfeet tribe. **1834** J. TOWNSEND *Jrnl.* 17 July in A. B. Hulbert *Overland to Pacific* (1934) IV. 192 The Blackfoot is a sworn and determined enemy to all white men. **1836** IRVING *Astoria* I. xv. 246 Colter..[had] some knowledge of the Blackfoot language. **1842** PRICHARD *Nat. Hist. Man* 404 The Black-feet are a very powerful and numerous people. **1933** BLOOMFIELD *Lang.* iv. 72 A few detached languages in the west: Blackfoot, Cheyenne, and Arapaho. **1962** *Listener* 26 Apr. 721/2 He was captured by Blackfeet Indians. **1969** *Observer* (Colour Suppl.) 18 May 22/4 Among the Blackfoot, stealing an enemy's weapons was the highest exploit. *Ibid.* 25/2 Yet calling a Blackfoot, for example, 'warlike' reveals nothing. The entire Blackfoot tribe did not habitually engage in war because individual members possessed 'warlike' personalities.

2. *Sc.* A go-between in a love affair; a match-maker.

1814 *Saxon & Gael* I. 161 (JAM.) Thinkin' ye might be black-fit, or her secretar. **1822** SCOTT *Nigel* xxxiv, I could never have expected this intervention of a *proxeneta*, which the vulgar translate blackfoot, of such eminent dignity. **1830** GALT *Lawrie T.* VII. ix. (1849) 344.

Black friar. A member of the order of Dominican friars, founded at the beginning of the 13th century by St. Dominic, so called from the colour of their dress.

c **1500** *God speed Plough* 55 Then commeth the blak freres. **1530** PALSGR. 198/2 Blacke frere, *jacobin*. **1556** *Chron. Grey Friars* (1852) 95 The bysshopp of Rochester, Morys, that was some tyme a blacke freere. **1655** FULLER *Ch. Hist.* vi. III. 269 Of these, Dominicans were the first friars which came over into England anno 1221..they were commonly called Black friars, Preaching friars, and Jacobin friars. **1786** *Ann. Reg.* 210/2 He was originally a Black-friar.

Hence, in *pl.*, the quarters of these friars in various cities and towns, e.g. the part of London where their convent was.

1583 PLAT *Divers New Exp.* (1594) 32 An expert Jeweller, dwelling..in the Black friers. **1613** SHAKS. *Hen. VIII*, II. ii. 139 The most conuenient place, that I can thinke of For such receipt of Learning, is Black-Fryers.

black game. Black grouse (*Tetrao tetrix*), of which the male is called BLACKCOCK, and the female *grey hen.*

1678 RAY *Willughby's Ornith.* 173 The Heathcock or Black game or Grous, called by Turner the Morehen. **1787** G. WHITE *Selborne* vi. **1818** SCOTT *Rob Roy* vii, The law against unauthorized destroyers of black-game, grouse, partridges, and hares. **1879** *Daily News* 12 Aug. 5/1 The Twentieth when black game are (legally) fair game.

black-grass. [BLACK *a.* 1.]

1. A species of rush (*Juncus Gerardi*) growing in salt-marshes. *U.S.*

1782 H. ST. JOHN DE CRÈVECŒUR *Lett. of American Farmer* vi. 159 The best mowing grounds in the island, yielding four tons of black grass per acre. **1872** SCHELE DE VERE *Americanisms* 408 *Salt-hay*, a very important product of salt-marshes, is of two principal sorts, called *salt-grass* and *black-grass*.

2. A species of foxtail grass, *Alopecurus agrestis.*

1798 W. CURTIS *Flora Lond.* II. Plate 16 *note*, The Farmer also distinguishes the *Alopecurus agrestis*..by the name of Black Grass. **1840** *Farming at Scoreby* in *Husbandry* (*Libr. Useful Knowl.*) III. 6 'The black grass'..is a very noxious weed.

blackguard ('blægəd), *sb.* and *a.* (Written 6–8 as two words, 7–8 with hyphen, 8–9 as one word.) [lit. *Black Guard*, concerning the original application of which there is some doubt. It is possible that senses 1 and 2 began independently of each other; or the one may have originated in a play upon the other, *black* being taken with a different sense; it would be difficult to assign priority to either. It is even possible that there may have been a guard of soldiers at Westminster called the *Black Guard*, or that, as some suggest, the attendants or torch-bearers at a funeral, or the link-boys of the streets, may have had this name.]

The following quotations, including the earliest known, show this uncertainty: they may belong to ascertained senses, but cannot be certainly located:

1532 *MS. Churchw. Acc. St. Marg. Westm.* (Receipts for burials), Item Receyvid for the lycens of iiij. torchis of the blake garde vjd. **1568** FULWELL *Like wil to like* B iij, Thou art serued as Harry hangman captain of the black garde. Nay, I am serued, as Haman, etc. **1578** H. KILLIGREW in *Cal. State Pap., Dom. Add.* Rolls Ser. 530 A woman has been murdered in Court by the black guard [*cf.* p. 532 certain soldiers, for the murder of a woman were condemned to die]. **1621** BURTON *Anat. Mel.* I. ii. I. ii. (1651) 42 Inferiour to those of their own rank..as the black guard in a Princes Court. **1633** SHIRLEY *Tri. Peace* 280 There rush in a carpenter, a painter, one of the black guard.

A. *sb.* I. A body of persons.

†**1.** The lowest menials of a royal or noble household, who had charge of pots and pans and other kitchen utensils, and rode in the wagons conveying these during journeys from one residence to another; the scullions and kitchen-knaves. *Obs.*

1535 SIR W. FITZWILLIAMS 17 Aug. in *Cal. State Pap.*, Two of the ring-leaders had been some time of the Black Guard of the Kings kitchen. **1579** FULKE *Refut. Rastel* 779 They ought not, nor yet any of the scullerie or blacke garde. **1612** WEBSTER *White Devil* I, A lousy slave, that..rode with the black guard in the dukes carriage, 'mongst spits and dripping-pans. **1631** BRAITHWAIT *Whimzies* 56 In progresse time..shee followes the court; and consorts familiarly with the black-guard. **1678** BUTLER *Hud.* III. I. 1407 Thou art some paltry Black-guard Sprite, Condemned to drudgery in the night.

†**b.** Those who held a similar position in an army; the servants and camp-followers; the rabble of irregular hangers-on and followers. Also *fig. Obs.*

1560 JEWEL *Corr. Cole* iii, Haue the learned men of your side none other Doctors? for alas these that ye alleage..are scarcely worthy to be allowed amongst the blacke garde. *a* **1640** DAY *Parl. Bees* iv. (1881) 29 Such silken clownes, When wee with bloud deserve, share our reward—We held scarce fellow-mates to the blacke guard. **1640** FULLER *Joseph's Coat* (1867) 46 The black guard of Romish traditions, which lag still behind. **1654** TRAPP *Comm. Ps.* xviii. 13 Ye have lyen among the Pots, black and sooty, as the black guard of an army. **1702** *Eng. Theophrast.* 8 The Muses Black-guard, that like those of our Camp, have no share in the Danger or Honour, yet have the greatest in the Plunder.

†**2.** A guard of attendants, black in person, dress, or character; a following of 'black' villains. *Obs.*

1563 FOXE *A. & M.* (1583) II. 801 The Blacke gard of the Dominike friers..were not all mute, but laide lustily from them. **1583** FULKE *Defence* x. 386 Pelagius, Celestius, and other like heretics of the devils black guard. **1609** DEKKER *Lanth. & Candle-Lt.* Wks. 1884–5 III. 214 The great Lord of Limbo did therefore commaund all his Blacke Guard that stood about him, to bestirre them. **1676** HALE *Contempl.* 97 An Apostle, one of the twelve, he it is that conducts this black Guard. **1705** HICKERINGILL *Priest-Cr.* II. iii. 28 This Black-guard [Jaylors and Hangmen] is the only Life-guard of a High-flown, Persecuting..Ceremony-monger.

†**3.** The vagabond, loafing, or criminal class of a community; the blackguardry. *Obs.*

1683 in *N. & Q.* Ser. I. (1854) IX. 15/2 A sort of vicious idle and masterless boyes and rogues commonly called the Black-guard..do usually haunt and follow the Court. **1688** SIR J. KNATCHBULL *Diary* in *N. & Q.* Ser. III. (1864) VI. 2/2 For fear of some of the black guard of Canterbury that had horsed themselves, and had been padding on the road ever since Sunday. **1704** in *Stow's Surv.* (ed. Strype) I. xxvi, Such who are commonly known by the name of the Black Guard, who too commonly lived upon Pilfering Sugar and Tobacco on the Keys, and afterwards became Pickpockets and House Breakers. **1768** TUCKER *Lt. Nat.* II. 143 How prevent your sons from consorting with the blackguard?

†**b.** *esp.* The vagrant children of great towns; the 'city Arabs,' who run errands, black shoes, etc.

1715 NELSON *Addr. Pers. Qual.* 214 The distressed Children called the Black-guard. *Ibid.* App. 53 The Children commonly call'd, Blackguard Boys, are destitute of all manner of Provision for Instruction. **1725** DE FOE *Everybody's Bus.* 20 Above ten thousand wicked idle pilfering vagrants..called the black-guard, who black your honour's shoes, etc. **1736** BAILEY, *Black-guard*, dirty tatter'd Boys, who ply the Streets to clean shoes.

II. An individual.

†**4.** A guard or soldier black in person, dress, or character. Also *fig.* Cf. 2. *Obs.*

1563 R. BAKER in Hakluyt *Voy.* (1589) 133 The Captein now past charge of this brutish blacke gard. **1696** BROOKHOUSE *Temple Open.* 6 Satan..placed his Black Guards there. **1745** *Lond. Mag.* 391 He was oblig'd to set up his corps of Black-Guards to escorte him to and from the Senate.

†**5.** A soldier's boy; a street shoe-black; a 'city Arab' picking up a living by blacking boots, and other jobs, or in less honest ways. *Obs.*

1698 BOYER *Fr. Dict.* (1719), *Goujat*, a soldiers boy, a Black-guard. **1725** SWIFT *Wood's Petit.* Wks. 1755 IV. I. 285 The little black-guard Who gets very hard His halfpence for cleaning your shoes. **1785** GROSE *Dict. Vulg. Tongue*, *Black guard*, a shabby dirty fellow; a term said to be derived from a number of dirty tattered and roguish boys, who attended at the horse guards..St. James's park, to black the boots and shoes of the soldiers, or to do any other dirty offices, these..were nick-named the black guards.

6. One of the idle criminal class; a 'rough'; hence, a low worthless character addicted to or ready for crime; an open scoundrel. (A term of the utmost opprobrium.)

1736 HERVEY *Mem. Geo. II*, I. 284 This step so strengthened his majesty's enmity that 'scoundrel, rascal or black-guard' never failed of being tacked to his name. **1773** BARRINGTON in *Phil. Trans.* LXIII. 259 If the singing of the ploughman in the country is..compared with that of the London blackguard. *c* **1780** BURNS *Twa Dogs*, And cheat like ony unhang'd blackguard. **1830** MACAULAY *Bunyan*, A man whose manners and sentiments are decidedly below those of his class deserves to be called a blackguard. **1836** MARRYAT *Midship. Easy* x, You impudent blackguard, if you say another word, I'll give you a good thrashing.

7. A name for a kind of snuff. Also called ***Irish blackguard.***

[The story runs, that Lundy Foot, the Dublin snuff-merchant, when a shop-boy, made a mistake in the preparation of some snuff, for which his master called him an 'Irish Blackguard': but the mistake turning out a fortunate one, the new preparation obtained the name given to its author.]

1792 WOLCOTT (P. Pindar) *Odes K. Long* Wks. 1812 III. 155 An ounce of blackguard or a yard of cloth. **1812** L. HUNT in *Examiner* 12 Oct. 643/1 Knowing the snuff to be real blackguard. **1871** FORSTER in *Lit. World* 370/1 Taking in moderate quantities the snuff called Irish blackguard.

B. *attrib.* or *adj.*

†**1.** Of or pertaining to the shoe-black or street Arab class. *Obs.* (In 1670 applied to a link-boy.)

c **1670** EARL DORSET *Song* 'Dorinda's sparkling wit,' Her Cupid is a blackguard boy, That runs his link full in your face. **1724** SWIFT *Drapier's Lett.* Wks. 1755 V. II. 91 What is written we send to your house by a black-guard boy. *c* **1735** —— *Direct. Servants, Cook*, Let a blackguard boy be always about the house to send on your errands. **1822** H. MACKENZIE *Life Home*, Idle and blackguard boys bawl through the streets.

2. Of or pertaining to the dregs of the community; of low, worthless character; brutally vicious or scurrilous; blackguardly.

1784 CORNWALLIS *Corr.* (1859) I. vi. 166 The Duchess of Devonshire is indefatigable in her canvas for Fox; she was in the most blackguard houses in Long Acre by eight o'clock this morning. **1786** BURNS *Earnest Cry & Pr.* viii, A blackguard smuggler right behint her. **1788** WOLCOTT (P. Pindar) *Peter's Pens.* Wks. 1812 II. 13 Instead of that vile appellation, Devil, So blackguard, so unfriendly, and uncivil. **1818** BYRON *Let.* Wks. (1846) 397/2, I have heard him use language as blackguard as his action. **1857** HUGHES *Tom Brown* viii. (1871) 163 Marking certain things as low and blackguard.

blackguard ('blægɑːd), *v.* [f. prec. sb.]

1. *intr.* To act the blackguard (sense 3, 6); to 'loaf,' play the vagabond.

1786 BURNS *Holy Fair* ix, An' there a batch of wabster lads, Blackguardin frae Kilmarnock, For fun this day.

2. *trans.* To treat as a blackguard; to abuse or revile in scurrilous terms.

1823 COBBETT *Weekly Reg.* XLVIII. 642/2 You, in your quality of Saint, may claim a right to becall and to blackguard, as much as you please, any portion of the rest of mankind. **1837** SOUTHEY *Lett.* (1856) IV. 518 The 'Monthly Review,'..turned against me afterwards and literally blackguarded 'Madoc.' **1872** LEVER *Ld. Kilgobbin* xxi. (1875) 130 I'd bear a deal of blackguarding from the press.

Hence '**blackguarding** *vbl. sb.* (see above).

blackguardism ('blægədɪz(ə)m). [see -ISM.]

1. The characteristic behaviour or manner of a blackguard; blackguardly conduct, ruffianism.

1785 G. A. BELLAMY *Apology* I. lxii. 311 He had the meanness, servility, and blackguardism of a Buckhorse. **1813** *Edin. Rev.* XXI. 283 There is a tone of blackguardism both in his indecency and his profanity. **1828** MACAULAY *Hallam, Ess.* (1854) I. 87 This..blackguardism of feeling and manners. **1869** *Athenæum* 28 Aug. 265 The blackguardism which is making horse-racing..detestable.

2. Blackguardly language.

1799 T. JEFFERSON *Writ.* (1859) IV. 281 They wish to hear reason instead of disgusting blackguardism. **1827** *Blackw. Mag.* XXI. 754 The revolting scurrilities, and brutal blackguardism..heaped upon Lord Eldon.

'**blackguardize**, *v.* [f. as prec. + -IZE.] *trans. rare.* To reduce to the condition of a blackguard.

1846 *Blackw. Mag.* LX. 594 At last we became..a good deal blackguardised in our taste.

'**blackguardly**, *a.* and *adv.* [f. as prec. + -LY.]

A. *adj.* Characteristic of a blackguard; ruffianly, brutal; scurrilous, 'low.'

1847 in CRAIG. **1863** DICEY *Federal St.* II. 17 The essentially blackguardly nature of the..war. **1881** MISS YONGE *Lads & L.* v. 177 The most blackguardly boys in the place.

B. *adv.* After the manner of a blackguard.

1827 SCOTT in *Lockhart* (1839) IX. 146 Want of that article blackguardly called pluck.

'**blackguardry.** *rare.* Also **blackguardery** *U.S.* [see -RY.] **1.** The community of blackguards; = BLACKGUARD *sb.* 3.

1853 *Blackw. Mag.* LXXIV. 669 The impertinent question at one time current amongst the blackguardry of London.

2. = BLACKGUARDISM 1.

1881 G. M. HOPKINS *Let.* 14 May (1935) 129, I have in me a great vein of blackguardry and have long known I am no gentleman. **1883** —— *Let.* 14 Jan. (1956) 251 Blackguardry stamps my whole behaviour. **1936** M. MITCHELL *Gone with Wind* x. 202 The blackguardery of the Irish who were being enticed into the Yankee army by bounty money.

black gum. *U.S.* (Also hyphened and as one word.) [BLACK *a.* 6.] A North American tree of the genus *Nyssa*. Also *attrib.*

1709 LAWSON *Carolina* 95 Of the Black Gum there grows, with us, two sorts. **1785** WASHINGTON *Diary* 28 Feb. (1925) II. 346 Planted all the..Blackgums in my Serpentine Walks. **1868** [see GUM *sb.*[2] 5]. **1868** *Amer. Naturalist* II. 122 When mast is not plenty, they [*sc.* bears] lap black-gum berries. **1901** C. MOHR *Plant Life Alabama* 32 Chestnut..and black gum (*Nyssa sylvatica*) are common.

black-head ('blækhɛd).

1. A name given to various black-headed birds; e.g. a kind of white pigeon with a black head, the Black-headed Gull (*Larus ridibundus*), etc.

1658 ROWLAND *Mouffet's Theat. Ins.* 1088 Meal-worms..seem to be bred to catch black-heads and Nightingales. **1741** *Compl. Fam. Piece* III. 512 The Black-Head is a white Pidgeon with a black Head. **1806** P. NEILL *Tour Orkn. & Shetl.* 201. **1844** W. H. MAXWELL *Sports & Adv. Scotl.* xx. (1855) 174 What obliging birds the blackheads are!

2. *Angling.* A variety of the Marsh-worm.

1875 'STONEHENGE' *Brit. Sports* I. v. ii. §3 A variety of this [the marsh] worm..is called in Scotland the Black-head.

3. *pl.* Name for the Reed Mace (*Typha latifolia*).

4. = COMEDO.

1837 J. F. PALMER *Gloss.* in 'A Lady' *Dialogue Devonshire Dial.* 30 *Blackhead*, a boil or pinswell, from the black spot which appears at the apex. **1885** [see COMEDO]. **1910** *Daily Chron.* 15 Jan. 9/1 Sometimes blackheads gather in the forehead lines,..they must be pressed out with the blackhead instrument, if steaming and massage fail to remove them. **1949** E. DE MAUNY *Huntsman in Career* III. iii. 160 His skin was tanned deep brown, which somehow accentuated the blackheads.

5. *Vet.* An infectious disease of turkeys and other birds caused by the protozoon parasite *Histomonas meleagridis*, producing a bluish-black discoloration of the head.

1902 *U.S. Dept. Agric. Experiment Station Rec.* XIII. 287. **1906** *U.S. Dept. Agric. Bureau Animal Ind. Circular* No. 5 (*title*) Blackhead, or infectious entero-hepatitis in turkeys. **1955** GAIGER & DAVIES *Vet. Path. & Bacteriol.* (ed. 4) xxiii. 468 In dealing with blackhead emphasis should be placed on prevention.

6. *attrib.* = BLACK-HEADED *a.*

1827 J. L. WILLIAMS *View W. Florida* 30 Black-head fly catcher. **1835** J. MARTIN *Gaz. Virginia* 483 A great variety of ducks as..the red head shoveler, the black head shoveler.

'**black-,headed**, *a.* Having a black head: used in the names of animals, esp. birds.

1774 G. WHITE *Selborne* xli. 106 The great black-headed titmouse. **1783** LATHAM *Gen. Syn. Birds* II. I. 198 Black-headed B[unting]. *Emberiza melanocephala.* **1785** PENNANT *Arct. Zool.* II. 398 Black-headed Warbler. **1870** *Amer. Naturalist* III. 75 The habits of the Black-headed grosbeak are quite different. *Ibid.* 234 The Black-headed Gull, a southern and somewhat rare species. **1902** *Encycl. Brit.* XXXII. 109/2 The Black-headed Rock Snake (*Aspidiotes*), one of the Pythons. **1931** *Discovery* Mar. 87/1 Black-headed gulls, the little red-legged, red-beaked sea birds so familiar to Londoners as winter visitors to the metropolitan parks and riverside. **1964** C. WILLOCK *Enormous Zoo* ix. 165 A black-headed heron picks for grubs in the garden.

black-hole, black hole. (Beside obvious application to any dark hole or deep cell:)

1. *Mil.* The punishment cell or lock-up in a barracks; the guard-room. (The official designation till 1868.)

(The name has become historic, in connexion with the horrible catastrophe in 1756 at the black hole of the barracks in Fort William, Calcutta, into which 146 Europeans were thrust for a whole night, of whom only 23 survived till the morning.)

1758 J. HOLWELL *Black Hole Calcut.* 8 The guard..ordered us to go into the room at the southernmost end of the barracks, commonly called the Black-Hole prison. **1758** J. BLAKE *Plan Mar. Syst.* 49 What happened lately in the black-hole at Bengal. **1816** C. JAMES *Mil. Dict., Black-hole*, a place in which soldiers may be confined by the commanding officer..In this place they are generally restricted to bread and water. **1844** *Regul. & Ord. Army* 121 Confinement to the Black Hole..to be reserved for cases of Drunkenness, Riot, Violence, or Insolence to Superiors. **1868** *Ibid.* ¶789 *note*, The term lock up room and black hole is to be abolished.

2. *gen.* A place of confinement for punishment. (Often with allusion to that at Calcutta.)

1831 A. WATTS *House-Hunt.*, The bed-chambers (the black-holes of her establishment). **1848** THACKERAY *Van. Fair* ii, Do you think Miss Pinkerton will come out and order me back to the black hole?

3. The deep dark pool under a waterfall; as 'the Black Hole at Aira Force.'

4. *Astr.* (As two words.) A region within which the gravitational field is so strong that no form of matter or radiation can escape from it except by quantum-mechanical tunnelling, and thought to result from the collapse of a massive star; also *fig.*

1968 J. A. WHEELER in *Amer. Scientist* LVI. 9 Light and particles incident from outside emerge and go down the black hole only to add to its mass and increase its gravitational attraction. **1971**, **1974** [see s.v. SCHWARZSCHILD 2]. **1977** *Sci. Amer.* Jan. 34/3 A black hole weighing a billion tons..would have a radius of about 10^{-13} centimeter. **1978** PASACHOFF & KUTNER *University Astron.* xii. 326 Once matter is inside a black hole, it loses its identity in the sense that from outside a black hole, all we can tell is the mass of the black hole, the rate at which it is spinning, and what electric charge it has. **1980** *Time* 16 June 64 To the 1.7 million people added to the jobless rolls in April and May, the U.S. economy may well seem to have..been sucked into a black hole. **1986** *Nature* 8 May 111/1 Quantum mechanics allows a particle to tunnel out of a black hole... Eventually it evaporates to such a small size that the semiclassical approximation becomes invalid, and quantum mechanics must be applied to the gravitational field of the black hole itself.

Hence **black-hole** *v.*, to confine to the black-hole.

1866 *Pall Mall. G.* 9 He was blackholed for twelve hours.

black house. †**1.** A prison; also a place of business where working-hours are long and wages are very small. *Obs. slang.*

1848 *Flash Dict.* in *Sinks of London laid Open* 99/1 *Black houses*, prisons. **1861** MAYHEW *Lond. Labour* III. 224/2 The black houses, or linendrapers at the west end of London, were principally supplied from the east end.

2. *Sc.* Also *black-house*. (*a*) A turf house; (*b*) a house built of unmortared stone, found esp. in north-western Scotland and the Hebrides.

1824 J. MACCULLOCH *Highlands & Western Isles* I. 112 The genuine, pure black house is built entirely of turf; walls and roof: it is a 'good black house' when the roof is of thatch. **1870** *Proc. Soc. Antiq. Scotl.* VII. 154 The native structure is a Black-house or Tigh-dubh. **1911** W. C. MACKENZIE in N. Munro *Home Life of Highlanders* 38 In some of the outlying districts..there are phases of life that have apparently remained unaltered since the Middle Ages. They are typified by the 'black houses', many of which are still to be found in the Long Island. **1931** W. C. MACKENZIE *Sc. Place-Names* viii, 'Black-houses' of the Outer Hebrides, *i.e.* the houses built of turf [as contrasted with] the 'white' or stone houses, by which they are rapidly being replaced. **1951** *Antiquity* XXV. 200 The roof had doubtless been the normal blackhouse roof with no smoke-hole.

blackie, var. BLACKY *sb.*

blacking ('blækɪŋ), *vbl. sb.* [f. BLACK *v.*]

1. a. The action of making black by applying some substance.

1609 DOULAND *Ornithop. Microl.* 45 The blacking of the Notes. **1823** J. BADCOCK *Dom. Amusem.* 49 This blacking may be effected with the smoke of a lamp.

b. *blacking-out*: see BLACK *v.* 3 b and 3 c.

1905 *Academy* 27 May 562/1 Maternal censorship is rigid, the Russian blacking-out system not more so. **1919** *Illustr. London News* 27 Sept. 482 After the war-years.., the great 'blacking-out' to deceive enemy aircraft, London is herself again.

c. *blacking-out*: see BLACK *v.* 6.

1932 *Flight* 1 Apr. 272/1 With the speed of modern fighters when on the dive, it might happen that the fighter pilots would experience 'blacking out' at the critical moment of the turn and zoom. **1933** *Jrnl. R. Aeronaut. Soc.* XXXVII. 397 The effect most frequently noticed is the well-known phenomenon of 'blacking-out', wherein the subject without losing consciousness becomes momentarily blind.

†**2.** The unconsumed carbon of flame; 'lamp-black.' *Obs.*

1594 PLAT *Jewell-ho.* III. 72 The blacking of a Lampe tempered with oyle.

†**3. a.** Any preparation used for making black, as 'shoemakers' black,' which is a stain used to blacken the originally brown leather. *Obs.*

1571 *Buchanan's Detect. Mary* in H. Campbell's *Love-lett. Mary Q. Scots* (1824) 127 As it were washed with sowters blacking. **1580** HOLLYBAND *Treas. Fr. Tong., Encre, ou noire peincture*..blacking. **1603-4** *Act 1 Jas. I*, xx. §2 It shall..be lawfull..for any of the Companie of Plaisterers..to lay and use Whitinge, Blacking, Red Leade. **1611** COTGR., *Noir*, blacke colour; blacking.

b. *spec.* A preparation for giving a shining black surface to boots and shoes.

1598 FLORIO, *Folligine*, blacking for shooes. **1712** STEELE *Spect.* No. 461 ¶13 The ingenious Authors of Blacking for Shoes, Powder for colouring the Hair. **1814** MOORE *Parod. Let.* vi. 94, Like the vendor of Best Patent Blacking.

c. *attrib.*, as in ***blacking ball, bottle, brush, manufacturer***, etc.; **blacking leather**, leather which is to be blacked, as distinct from patent leather.

1753 *Scots Mag.* Oct. 490/2 My pumps were varnished..with the new German blacking ball. **1837** DICKENS *O. Twist* (1838) I. v. 78 His 'prentice..sent 'em some medicine in a blacking-bottle. **1850** —— *Dav. Copp.* xxvii. 283 His blacking-brushes and blacking were among his books. *c* **1860** H. STUART *Seaman's Catech.* 81 Scrubbing brush, and blacking brushes. **1893** YEATS *Celtic Twilight* 184 A fiddle made apparently of an old blacking-box. **1896** *Daily News* 2 July 8/7 High glacé boots have patent leather goloshes, and others have plain 'blacking' leather.

†'**blacking**, *sb. dial.* A black pudding.

1674 N. FAIRFAX *Bulk & Selv.* 159 Thus shall we sort out eternity..as the Darbyshire huswife does her puddings, when she makes whitings and blackings and liverings.

blackish ('blækɪʃ), *a.* [f. BLACK *a.* + -ISH.] Somewhat black; inclining to black.

1486 *Bk. St. Albans* B iij, As longe as yowre hawkes fete be blakysh and rough: she is full of grece. **1611** BIBLE *Job* vi. 16 As the streame of brookes..Which are blackish by reason of the yce. **1803** HATCHETT in *Phil. Trans.* XCIII. 65 A blackish-brown colour. **1884** BROWNING *Ferishtah* 109 Till blackish seems but dun, and whitish—grey.

Hence **blackishly** *adv.*, '**blackishness** *sb.*

1580 HOLLYBAND *Treas. Fr. Tong., Noircissure*, blackishnesse. **1627** GREW *Anat. Plants* vii. §17 By their Blackishness well enough remark'd. **1670** H. STUBBE *Plus Ultra* 147 But the blood turned blackishly-red.

Black Jack, 'black-jack.

1. A large leather jug for beer, etc. coated externally with tar.

1591 NASHE *Prognost.* 24 Cuppes, cannes, pots, glasses, and black iacks. **1619** *Pasquil's Palin.* (1877) 157 The great blacke Iack well fild with Sack. **1645** MILTON *Colast.* Wks. (1851) 367 Hee runs to the black jack, fills his flagon, spreds the table, and servs up dinner. **1672** DAVENANT *Unfort. Lovers* (1673) 121 He looks as if he had a black Jack under His Cloak. **1822** SCOTT *Nigel* xxii, Ale which he brought in a large leathern tankard or black-jack. **1854** C. M. YONGE *Heartsease* I. ii. 31 She was enchanted with St. Cross..in raptures at the black jacks, dole of bread and beer. **1921** O. BAKER *Black Jacks & Leather Bottells* iii. 67 The black jack was..a kind of leathern pitcher or jug, always lined with pitch or metal. **1965** *Harper's Bazaar* 49 Black Jack jugs in two sizes, £4 7s. 6d. and 6 gns. (waterproof leather).

2. A miner's name for zinc sulphide or blende.

1747 HOOSON *Miner's Dict.* N iij b, It is most commonly found in hard Veins and Pipes, some do call it Black-Jack. **1762** *Gentl. Mag.* 400 Blende, called by the miners black-jack or mock ore. **1812** SIR H. DAVY *Chem. Philos.* 373 Zinc is procured..from blende or black-jack.

3. *U.S.* A shrubby kind of oak (*Quercus nigra*).
1765 J. BARTRAM *Diary* 31 July in *Trans. Amer. Philos. Soc.* (1942) XXXIII. 17/1 Ye oaks black which is reconed ye best fire wood thay have thay call them black Jacks seldom grow above A foot diameter. **1782** JEFFERSON *Notes Virginia* (1787) 62 Black jack oak. Quercus aquatica. **1856** OLMSTED *Slave States* 383 The gray beech, and the shrubby black-jack oak. **1863** *Times* 16 June The intrenchments and abbatis in the black jack thicket. **1879** TOURGEE *Fool's Err.* xv. 75 The wide fire-place, in which the dry hickory and black-jack was blazing brightly.

†**4.** *Sc.* A black leather jerkin: see JACK. *Obs.*
1513 DOUGLAS *Æneis* VIII. Prol. 99 Some garris wyth a ged staf to jag throw blak jakkis. **1820** SCOTT *Monast.* x, With their glittering steel caps, and their black-jacks.

5. A popular name of the mustard beetle.
1886 *Standard* 24 May 2/1 The mustard beetle (*Phædon betulæ*), commonly known as the Black Jack.

6. The black caterpillar of the turnip saw-fly, *Athalia centifolia* or *A. spinarum*.
1840 [see NIGGER *sb.* 2].

7. The South African plant *Bidens pilosa*; also its hooked seed.
1877 LADY BARKER *Year's Housekeeping S. Africa* vii. 130 An innocent-looking plant..bearing a most aggravating tuft of little black spires, which lose no opportunity of sticking to one's petticoats in myriads. They are familiarly known as 'black jacks'. **1932** *Discovery* Jan. 24/2 The seeds of the horrible weed 'Black Jack' are eaten by a serin-finch.

8. = BLACK FLAG as the ensign of a pirate. Cf. JACK *sb.*[3]
1867 in SMYTH *Sailor's Word-bk.*

9. A weapon consisting of a weighted head and short pliable shaft, used as a bludgeon. Hence as *vb.*, to strike with a blackjack. *U.S.*
1889 in *Cent. Dict.* **1895** *Denver Times* 5 Mar. 8/5 During the scuffle Miss Alderfer, Knapp's niece, saw the 'black jack' up his sleeve,..and as a result, swore out the concealed weapons charge. **1904** *N.Y. Even. Post* 10 Mar. 1 This position..was not such as the body would have taken had Newman been struck with a blackjack or other weapon. **1905** *Ibid.* 2 Sept., 'I got a partner there [*sc.* in the penitentiary],' Red said,..'blackjacked a man.' **1934** J. M. CAIN *Postman always rings Twice* iv. 31 She was to..clip him from behind with a blackjack I had made for her out of a sugar bag with ball bearings wadded down in the end. **1946** 'P. QUENTIN' *Puzzle for Fiends* (1947) xv. 106 Perhaps you gave a ride to a hitchhiker who blackjacked you.

10. = VINGT-ET-UN.
1910 R. W. SERVICE *Trail of '98* (1911) IV. iv. 316 A tall fair-moustached man whom I recognized as a black-jack booster. **1931** *Kansas City Star* 28 Dec. 16 The governor knows his politics and is too poor a black jack player to mingle with gobs, anyway. **1937** J. STEINBECK *Of Mice & Men* 117 I seen guys nearly crazy with loneliness for land, but ever' time a whore-house or a blackjack game took what it takes. **1954** *Encounter* Oct. 8/1 Roulette and dice and blackjack were available. **1967** *Guardian* 25 Feb. 8/1 The proprietors must not be allowed..unfair advantage of their customers by keeping the bank to themselves in..roulette, chemin de fer and blackjack.

black lead, black-'lead, 'blacklead, *sb.*
†**1.** A black ore of LEAD. *Obs.*

2. The ordinary name of the mineral called also plumbago or graphite; a substance of greyish-black colour and metallic lustre, consisting of almost pure carbon with a slight admixture of iron; it is chiefly used (made into pencils) for drawing and writing, and for giving a black metallic polish to iron-work. (The name dates back to days before the real composition of the substance was known.)
1583 PLAT *Divers New Exp.* (1594) 39 Some..draw thereon with blacke lead. **1610** HOLLAND *Camden's Brit.* I. 767 That minerall kind of earth or hardned glittering stone (we cal it Black-lead). **1612** BRINSLEY *Lud. Lit.* 47 Note them with a pensil of black lead. **1683** PETTUS *Fleta Min.* II. *Lead*, Of late it [black lead] is curiously formed into cases of deal or cedar, and so sold as dry pencils. **1732** DE FOE, etc. *Tour Gt. Brit.* (1769) III. 320 The Black-lead is found in heavy Lumps, some of which are hard, gritty, and of small Value, others soft and of a fine Texture. **1866** RUSKIN *Eth. Dust.* 18 There is a little iron mixed with our black lead.

b. This substance in the form of a pencil.
1656 DUGARD *Gate Lat. Unl.* §725. 225 Have with you alwayes a table-book (or black-lead and paper). **1832** CARLYLE in *Fraser's Mag.* V. 390 Boswell is there with ass-skin and black-lead to note thy jargon.

c. Writing done with a black-lead pencil.
1667 PEPYS (1877) V. 276 Having done it without looking on my paper, I find I could not read the black-lead.

d. A preparation of inferior quality for domestic use in polishing grates and other cast-iron utensils.
a **1849** CHAMBERS *Inform. People* II. 788/2 Stove-grates are cleaned with black-lead mixed with turpentine.

3. *attrib.* and *Comb.* ('black-lead), as ***black-lead pen, pencil, study***, etc.; †**black-lead comb**, a comb used to darken the hair.
1655 GURNALL *Chr. in Arm.* ix. §3 (1669) 145 He could not bear the sight of his own grey hairs, and therefore used a *black-lead-comb to discolour them. **1716** SWIFT *Progr. Beauty* Wks. 1755 III. II. 166 To think of *black-lead combs is vain. **1612** BRINSLEY *Lud. Lit.* 247 Being noted with a line with a *blacklead pen. **1687** M. CLIFFORD *Notes Dryden* ii. 5, I..put up my *Black Lead Pen. **1677** MOXON *Mech. Exerc.* (1703) 36 With a *Black-lead Pencil, draw a line from that Mark to the second Mark. **1790** BOSWELL *Johnson* (1831) I. 162 He had marked the passages with a *black-lead pencil. **1813** *Examiner* 17 May 311/2 S. Terry..*black-lead-maker. **1862** THORNBURY *Turner* I. 87 His..*blacklead studies of trees.

black'lead, black-'lead, *v.* [f. prec.] **a.** *trans.* To colour or rub with black-lead; to trace or draw in black-lead. Hence **black-'leaded** *ppl. a.*, **black-'leading** *vbl. sb.*
1839 C. BRONTË *Let.* 21 Dec. in *Life*, I am much happier black-leading the stoves. **1861** PYCROFT *Agony Point* (1862) 154 The same hands that had black-leaded the grate. *c* **1865** G. GORE in *Circ. Sc.* I. 220/1 Zinc deposits spread over blackleaded surfaces. *Ibid.* 234/1 The mould may..be prepared..by blackleading.

b. In *Electrotyping*, to brush (the mould) over with blacklead.
1888 *Encycl. Brit.* XXIII. 703/2 The mould, having been finished, has to be blackleaded... To facilitate this operation, a blackleading machine is used in large establishments... The process of depositing a copper solution upon the blackleaded surface of the mould is continued until a solid plate is formed.

'black-leg, -legs, *sb.* Also blackleg.
1. a. A disease in cattle and sheep which affects the legs. (Better *black-legs.*)
a **1722** LISLE *Observ. Husb.* (1757) 347 They have a distemper in Leicestershire frequent among the calves, which in that country they call the black-legs.. It is a white jelly settling in their legs, from whence it has its name of black-legs. **1884** *Illustr. Sydney News* 26 Aug. 15/2 A cattle disease, known as blackleg, is stated to have killed a number of cattle in the Mount Alexander district.

b. Any of various diseases that attack vegetables (see quots.).
1880 *Encycl. Brit.* XII. 281/1 To prevent the cauliflowers from getting the disease of 'black legs'. **1916** B. D. JACKSON *Gloss. Bot. Terms* (ed. 3) 52/1 *Black Leg*, a bacterial disease of potatoes due to *Bacillus phytophthorus*. **1918** *Board Agric. & Fisheries Leaflet* No. 23. 17 Diseases of the Potato.. Black-Leg or Black-Stalk Rot. **1956** *Nature* 10 Mar. 465/2 *Phoma betae*..the cause of black leg in sugar beet.

2. A turf swindler; also, a swindler in other species of gambling. (Formerly also *black-legs.*) [As in other slang expressions, the origin of the name is lost: of the various guesses current none seem worth notice.]
1771 B. PARSONS *Newmarket* II. 163 The frequenters of the Turf, and numberless words of theirs are exotics everywhere else; then how should we have been told of *black-legs*, and of *town-tops..taken-in, beat-hollow*, etc. **1774** R. CUMBERLAND *Note of Hand* II. i, Gentlemen of the turf; what sort of gentlemen are they? *Francis.* These fellows are gamblers, black-legs, sharpers. **1812** *Examiner* 14 Sept. 591/1 Any blackleg or pickpocket in the land. **1813** *Ibid.* 17 May 319/1, I was..posted as a black-legs. **1857** THACKERAY *Eng. Hum.* v. (1858) 245 You see noblemen and black-legs bawling and betting in the Cockpit.

3. a. A local name of opprobrium for a workman willing to work for a master whose men are on strike. (Also called *black-neb.*) Now *gen.*
1865 *Pall Mall G.* 29 Oct. 7 If the timber merchants persist in putting on 'blacklegs,' a serious disturbance will ensue. **1875** R. J. HINTON *Eng. Rad. Leaders* IV. xix. 333 The police were used to watch the strikers or to protect the blacklegs, as those are called who work outside the Union movement. **1890** W. BOOTH *In Darkest England* I. iv. 34 Men hungering to death..are the materials from which 'black-legs' are made.

b. A person who fails or refuses to join his fellows in combination for a given purpose, or breaks the rules of a particular trade or group.
1889 *Pall Mall Gaz.* 21 Nov. 5/1 The question of the preparation of a list of master-baker 'blacklegs' was also touched upon. These men are selling bread at 4½d. the quartern, and at even a lower rate. **1913** 'A. R. HOPE' *Half & Half* 275 We abused him as a 'blackleg' because his industry set too high a standard to the rest. **1955** *Times* 3 Aug. 9/4 Any milkman delivering outside his boundaries would be regarded as 'a blackleg' (their own expression). **1971** *Times* 28 Jan. 7/8 The clause was known as the black-legs' charter.

c. *attrib.* or as *adj.*
1890 *Daily News* 8 Sept. 6/1 There were hundreds of men ..being subjected to blackleg competition. **1894** *Ibid.* 31 May 7/5 There were two 'blackleg' cabs discovered on the rank. **1955** *Times* 3 June 6/6 Members of the Amalgamated Engineering Union in the Swindon Railway Works have been recommended by their district committee not to do any 'blackleg' work such as repairing and servicing engines and rolling stock.

4. *Sc.* = BLACKFOOT, a match-maker. *rare.*
Hence (in sense 2) **black-'leggery, black'legism**, the profession or practice of a black-leg.
1832 MAGINN in *Blackw. Mag.* XXXII. 427 From following any profession save the Army, the Navy, Black-apronry, and Black-leggery. **1882** *Pall Mall G.* 9 Dec. 20 The two baronets resemble each other only in cowardice, spite, and blackleggery. **1845** *Blackw. Mag.* LVIII. 204 There was a fair amount of black-legism on both occasions.

blackleg ('blæklɛg), *v.* [f. BLACK-LEG *sb.*]
a. *trans.* To take the place of (a worker who is on strike), thereby helping the employer to carry on his business and defeat the ends of the strike.
1897 *Daily News* 1 Sept. 2/4 They would be able to get many German engineers to 'blackleg' their English brethren. **1904** *Daily Chron.* 23 Apr. 5/7 The employers are permitted to persuade other workmen to 'blackleg' the men on strike.
fig. **1893** *Daily News* 10 July 5/2 Is it fair to 'blackleg' these industrious men, as it were,..and adapt their researches to the needs and purposes of romance? **1906** G. B. SHAW in *Fabian News* XVII. 2/2 One result is that the dead dramatist blacklegs the live one: Shakespeare can charge no royalty.

b. *intr.* To act or work as a blackleg. So ***to blackleg it***: to return to work before a strike is settled (said of a trade-union workman).
1888 *Baltimore Herald* 6 May (Farmer), Knights of Labor who had determined to blackleg it, regardless of the jeers and threats of their companions. **1892** *Chambers's Jrnl.* 17 Feb. 98/1 Volunteers were also obliged..to satisfy the leaders that they never 'black-legged' in any Australian strike. **1907** *Daily Chron.* 9 Mar. 6/6 If the alternative is to 'blackleg' or to starve. **1952** *Granta* 15 Nov. 12/2 In the General Strike of 1926, for instance, most Cambridge and Oxford students either blacklegged or were prepared to blackleg.

So **blacklegging** *vbl. sb.* [partly from BLACKLEG *sb.*]
1839 THACKERAY in *Misc.* (1856) II. 454 Blacklegging is as bad a trade as can be. **1894** G. B. SHAW *Let.* 20 Mar. (1965) 421 As there is no Trade Union of dramatic authors, and I am going into the business, I can only avoid black-legging by asking you what are the list prices, so to speak, for the work. **1909** H. G. WELLS *Ann Veronica* x, It's a sort of blacklegging to want to have a life of one's own. **1955** *Times* 19 July 9/6 Should all good trade unionists boycott any blacklegging?

'blacklet. [f. BLACK *sb.* + -LET, dim. suffix.] A tiny speck of soot or dirt.
1861 WYNTER *Soc. Bees* 25 Those finer blacklets that invisibly permeate the air.

'black-letter, black letter, 'blackletter.
1. A name (which came into use about 1600) for the form of type used by the early printers, as distinguished from the 'Roman' type, which subsequently prevailed. A form of it is still in regular use in Germany, and in occasional use (under the name of 'Gothic' or 'Old English') for fancy printing in England.
1640-4 *Charge agst. Abp. Canterb.* in Rushworth *Hist. Coll.* III. (1692) I. 115 His diligence to send for the Printer, and directing him to prepare a Black Letter, and to send it to his Servants at Edenburgh, for Printing this Book. **1712** ARBUTHNOT *John Bull* II. vii. (1727) 60 The Seven champions in the black-letter. **1871** EARLE *Philol. Eng. Tong.* §99 The form which is known to us as 'Black Letter,' and which was hardly less rectilinear than the old Runes themselves.

2. That which is printed in this type.
1811 BYRON *Hints fr. Hor.* 101 *note*, This is the millennium of black letter. **1860** HAWTHORNE *Marb. Faun* I. xxiv. 263 Like a page of black letter, taken from the history of the Italian republics.

3. *attrib.* (Usually with hyphen, or as one word.)
1791 MAXWELL in Boswell *Johnson* an. 1770, He loved.. the old black-letter books. **1800** RITSON *Rob. Hood* II. iv, From an old black-letter copy. **1808** W. IRVING *Salmag.* xviii. (1860) 410 There was a certain black-letter dignity in the name. **1820** —— *Sketch Bk.* II. 90 He was a complete black-letter hunter. **1845** LD. CAMPBELL *Chancellors* (1857) IV. lxxiv. 6 Not much of a lawyer compared with the black-letter men of these days. **1855** MACAULAY *Hist. Eng.* III. 31 He scornfully thrust aside..all that blackletter learning. **1862** BURTON *Bk. Hunter* I. 18 He was not a black-letter man, or a tall-copyist, or an uncut man. **1864** *Reader* 23 July 105/1 The collection of black-letter ballads.

4. ***black letter day***: an inauspicious day; as distinguished from a red letter (or auspicious) day: the reference being to the old custom of marking the saints'-days in the calendar with red letters.
1757 SMOLLETT *Reprisal* I. ii. (1777) 135 O! the month of November, She'll have cause to remember, As a black letter day all the days of her life.

Hence **'black-,lettered** *ppl. a.*
1820 SCOTT *Abbot* xxxii, Endeavouring..to fix her.. attention on the black-lettered Bible which lay before her.

black list, *sb.*
1. a. A list of persons who have incurred suspicion, censure, or punishment; cf. BLACK *a.* 11. Also *transf.* (Cf. sense 2)
c **1619** MASSINGER *Unnat. Combat* (1639) II. i, The blacke list of those That have nor fire nor spirit of their owne. **1692** WASHINGTON tr. *Milton's Def. Pop.* x. Wks. (1851) 228 If ever Charles his Posterity recover the Crown..you are like to be put in the Black List. **1774** MRS. A. ADAMS *Lett.* (1848) 36 Mr. Boylston and Mr. Gill the printer, are held upon the black list. **1788** GIBBON *Decl. & F.* V. xlviii. 82 His memory was stored with a black list of enemies and rivals. **1920** *Nature* 27 May 392/2 A chapter is devoted to beasts which the author would place in a black list as having many undesirable proclivities.

b. *Naut.* A list of delinquents to whom extra duty is assigned as a punishment. Also, the punishment of being put on the black list.
1834 'OLD SAILOR' *Tough Yarns* 34 Almost every ship had a black list as long as the main-top bowline. **1837** *United Service Jrnl.* II. 10 The cleaning, polishing and black-list methods of wasting time. **1902** W. KENNEDY *Sport in Navy* 76 Ten days black list for the boat's crew for not giving way. **1914** LD. C. BERESFORD *Mem.* I. 120 Such a process [*sc.* the spit-and-polish system] involves perpetual extra bother and worry and black-list.

c. (*a*) An employers' list of workmen whom it is considered undesirable to employ. (*b*) A trade union list of employers for whom their members are instructed not to work.
1888 *Atlantic Monthly* Nov. 611/2 He had got his name taken off from the black-list. **1888** *Encycl. Brit.* XXIII. 786/2 The..dreaded weapon known as the 'black list', by which combinations of employers..drove employees inclined to 'agitation' out of employment. **1923** *Management*

Engin. May 343/1 *Blacklist*, a list of union workmen circulated by employers to prevent such workers from being hired.

d. A list of persons convicted as habitual drunkards under the Licensing Act of 1902. Hence **black-lister**, one who is put on the black list.

[Cf. **1902** *Act 2 Edw. VII* c 28 §6 [Habitual drunkards] Whether an order of detention is made or not, the court shall order that notice of the conviction, with such particulars as may be prescribed by a Secretary of State, be sent to the police authority (within the meaning of the Police Act, 1890) for the police area in which the court is situate.] **1903** *Daily Chron.* 7 Jan. 5/2 A..suitable word is wanted by magistrates ..to denote a drunkard on the 'black list' under the new Act. .. The word 'blacklister' is one that readily occurs. **1903** *Ibid.* 19 Jan. 2/7 The first number of the 'Black List', issued under the new Licensing Act, was sent out from Scotland-yard on Saturday. **1904** *Ibid.* 16 Feb. 6/7 It was suggested that on the approach of a known 'black-lister' the police should give warning to the publican.

2. *fig.* A list of bad cases.

1853 Kane *Grinnell Exp.* xxxi. (1856) 267 Eight cases of scorbutic gums were already upon my black-list.

Hence **'black-list** *v.*, to enter in a black list. So **black-listed** *ppl. a.*; **black-listing** *vbl. sb.* (also *attrib.*).

1718 Hickes & Nelson *J. Kettlewell* III. §10. 212 This Method of Black-Listing had its original from a certain notion. **1884** *Milnor* (Dakota) *Teller* 30 July, All the clerks making application [for work at other stores] were spotted and blacklisted and many have been dismissed. **1888** *Atlantic Monthly* Nov. 608/1 The manufacturers..had retaliated for some 'labor troubles'..by 'black-listing' about thirty men. *Ibid.*, Mr. H. informed us that he was a 'black-listed' man. *Ibid.* 608/2 The increase of evil in the world thus resulting from the black-listing scheme. **1892** *Daily News* 13 Feb. 6/1 Calling on members of the Society to 'black list' men for life just because they offended their employers. **1892** *Pall Mall Gaz.* 29 Nov. 7/2 There are heavy penalties, too, for black-listing, or in any other way trying to induce persons to leave their employment [in Russia]. **1899** *Daily News* 18 Jan. 4/5 The Plasterers' Union ..prohibiting their members from working for certain black-listed firms. **1903** *Westm. Gaz.* 8 Jan. 7/2 A stoker in the Royal Navy, who has been black-listed for several weeks as a deserter. **1955** *Times* 5 May 11/3 The recent blacklisting of two British and one Italian cargo steamers by the Alexandria customs administration.

blackly ('blækli), *adv.* [f. black *a.* + -ly[2].] In a black, gloomy, or frowning manner; darkly, gloomily, dismally.

1563 *Mirr. Mag.* (Induct.) lvi, With visage grym, sterne lookes and blackeley hewed. **1639** Fuller *Holy War* v. xi. (1840) 262 This project so blackly blasted with perjury. *a* **1824** Campbell *Dead Eagle* 38 His shape distinct Was blackly shadow'd on the sunny ground. **1876** Geo. Eliot *Dan. Der.* iv. xxx, The pool blackly shivering. **1876** Ruskin *Fors Clav.* VI. lxix. 283 A perfect example of the special type of youthful blackguard now developing generally in England; more or less blackly pulpous and swollen in all the features. **1894** H. Nisbet *Bush Girl's Rom.* 195 Mysterious ledges high up, which yawned blackly at the spectator below. **1898** H. S. Salt in *Dict. Nat. Biogr.* LVI. 256/2 His writings are blackly pessimistic in the main. **1900** H. Lawson *Over Sliprails* 27 He went and stood before the fire ..and looked blackly at a print against the wall before his face.

† **'black-mack.** *Obs.* A blackbird.

1519 Horman *Vulgaria* 101 §10 The blackmacke or an osyll [*merula*] fleeth alone. **1598** Florio, *Merula*, a birde called a black-mack, and owzell, a mearle, a black bird.

blackmail, *sb.* Also **black-mail, black mail.** [f. mail = rent, tribute.]

1. *Hist.* A tribute formerly exacted from farmers and small owners in the border counties of England and Scotland, and along the Highland border, by freebooting chiefs, in return for protection or immunity from plunder.

1552 Abp. Hamilton *Catech.* (1884) 98 Quhay takis ouer sair mail, ouer mekle ferme, or ony blake maillis, fra thair tennands. *c* **1561** R. Maitland *Thievis Liddesd.* vi, Commoun taking of blak maill. **1567** *Scot. Act Jas. VI*, (1597) xxi, Diuers subjects of the Inland, takis and sittis vnder their assurance, payand them black-maill, and permittand them to reif, herrie, and oppresse their Nichtbouris. **1601** *Act 43 Eliz.* xiii, Sundry of her Maiesties louing Subiects within the sayd [4 northern] Counties.. have been inforced to pay a certaine rate of money, corne, cattell, or other consideration, commonly there called by the name of Blacke maile. **1707** *Addr. fr. Cumbrld.* in *Lond. Gaz.* No. 4334/2 There is, now, no Debatable Land to contend for; no Black Mail to be paid to the Leaders of the Robbers, as a Ransom. **1768** Blackstone *Comm.* IV. 263. **1814** Scott *Wav.* I. 222 The boldest of them will never steal a hoof from any one that pays black-mail to Vich Ian Vohr. **1875** Stubbs *Const. Hist.* II. xvi. 344 Preferring to pay blackmail to the Scots.

2. By extension: Any payment extorted by intimidation or pressure, or levied by unprincipled officials, critics, journalists, etc. upon those whom they have it in their power to help or injure. Now usu. a payment extorted by threats or pressure, esp. by threatening to reveal a discreditable secret; the action of extorting such a payment. Also *fig.*

a **1826** R. Heber *Narr. Journey Upper Prov. India* (1828) I. xvi. 441 The country is burdened with a crowd of lazy, profligate, self-called suwarrs, who..obtain for the most part a precarious livelihood by spunging on the industrious tradesmen and farmers, on whom they levy a sort of 'black-mail'. **1840** Macaulay *Clive, Ess.* (1854) II. 503 Even the wretched phantom who still bore the imperial title stooped to pay this ignominious black-mail. **1860** Mrs. Harvey *Cruise Claymore* II. 216 Arabs infesting the country, and levying blackmail on all passers-by. **1863** Longf. *Birds Killingw.* 36 Marauders who, in lieu of pay, Levied black mail upon the garden beds. **1927** F. W. Crofts *Inspector French & Starvel Tragedy* viii. 121 Was it credible that a man would really pay blackmail for fear of having an obviously forged confession produced? *Ibid.* 122 Philpot's admission that he had submitted to blackmail was actually in his favour. **1940** A. Christie *One, Two, Buckle my Shoe* 70 He's believed to have done a spot or two of blackmail. **1969** *Woman* 19 Apr. 20/1 That old moan: 'You'll be sorry when I've gone' is a very common one. It's an emotional blackmail to keep loved ones on their toes.

†**3.** *Law.* Rent reserved in labour, produce, etc., as distinguished from 'white rents,' which were reserved in 'white money' or silver. *Obs.* (Coke's and Blackstone's explanation of *redditus nigri*, which Camden appears to have taken for rents in 'black money' or copper.)

1605 Camden *Rem.* 205 Black money (what that was I know not, if it were not of Copper, as *Maill* and *Black-maill*). **1642** Coke *Inst.* ii. *Magna Ch.* viii, Work-days, rent cummin, rent corn, etc...called *Redditus nigri*, black maile, that is, black rents. **1768** Blackstone *Comm.* II. 42.

'blackmail, *v.* [f. prec.] *trans.* To levy black mail upon; to extort money from by intimidation, by the unscrupulous use of an official or social position, or of political influence or vote. *spec.* to extort money from (a person) by threatening to reveal a discreditable secret.

1880 L. Oliphant *Gilead* ix. 265 The sheikh..blackmails travellers. **1882** W. Weeden *Soc. Law Labor* 176 The chief..would protect and blackmail him.

Hence **'blackmailed** *ppl. a.*, that is subjected to blackmail; also *absol.* (with *the*), the person on whom blackmail is levied; **'blackmailer, 'blackmailing** *vbl. sb.* and *ppl. a.* (modern words referring chiefly to the levying of blackmail in sense 2.)

1868 *N. York Herald* 24 Apr., The Quixotic enterprise of the lobbyists and blackmailers. **1879** J. Hawthorne *Laugh. Mill* 108 Were I to lose all my fortune, I could, by turning black-mailer, ensure a permanent income twice as large. **1884** *Pall Mall G.* 27 Feb. 4/1 Introducing a system of blackmailing even worse than that which prevailed before. **1884** *Harper's Mag.* Mar. 567/1 The black-mailing vixen. **1895** *Westm. Gaz.* 18 Feb. 2/1 There must be a distinct threat, a direct menace of the blackmailed by the black-mailer. **1898** *Ibid.* 10 June 6/1 The blackmailer naturally keeps his own counsel as well as the money, and the black-mailed submits in silence. **1950** A. Christie *Murder is Announced* xxiii. 238 He hadn't the faintest idea he knew anything to blackmail her about.

black man.

1. A man having a black or very dark skin. (Cf. quot. 1815 for black *a.* 3 a.)

1591 Shaks. *Two Gent.* v. ii. 12 Blacke men are Pearles, in beauteous Ladies eyes. **1738** F. Moore *Trav. Africa* 102 After which came on Shore the Captain, four Writers, one Apprentice,..and one Black Man. **1820** *Hist. N. Amer.* II. 10 Two slaves, the one a black man, a native of the place. **1894** F. A. Steel *Potter's Thumb* iv, He wondered..what certain politicians at home would say to this candid distrust of the black man.

2. An evil spirit; also, the evil one, the devil; also, a spirit or bogey invoked in order to terrify children. *colloq.* or *dial.*

[**1591** in Pitcairn *Crim. Trials Scot.* (1833) I. 246þe Dewill start vp in þe pulpett, lyke ane mekill blak man, with ane blak baird stikand out lyke ane gettis baird.] **1658** tr. *Bergerac's Satyr. Char.* xii. 48, I send the Goblins..the nightbats,..the black men. **1851** *Fraser's Mag.* Feb. 240/2 'The foreigner', who is to the farmers what the black man and the sweep of nurse-maids are to children. **1861** G. Meredith *Evan Harrington* iii, Rich as Crœsus, and as wicked as the black man below! **1873** J. Ogg *Willie Waly* 123 Nor will the black man get ye. **1878** *Folk-lore Rec.* I. 19 What nights of misery does that name, the black man, bring back to my memory! **1886** Elworthy *W. Somerset Word-bk.*, *Black-man*, a terrible object; a bogy; a nursery terror. (Very com.) Now you be good chillern, else the black-man 'll come down the chimley arter ee. **1969** J. C. Faris in Halpert & Story *Christmas Mumming in Newfoundland* 138 One would seldom, even in jest, call someone a Devil... circumlocutions are used, such as 'Black Man', [etc.].

3. A local equivalent of blackmaster.

1921 *Dict. Occup. Terms* (1927) §925 Undertaker; blackman (Lancashire).

Black Maria. *colloq.*

1. A van for the conveyance of prisoners. orig. *U.S.*

1847 *Boston Even. Traveller* 25 Sept. 2/3 A new Black Maria,..a new wagon for the conveyance of prisoners to and from the courts of justice. **1869** J. Greenwood *Seven Curses of London* ii. vi. 87 The van that conveys prisoners to gaol —*Black Maria.* **1924** *Punch* 17 Sept. 309 A Black Maria containing twelve prisoners.

2. A name used by soldiers in the war of 1914–18 for a German shell that on bursting emitted volumes of dense smoke, and for a German gun.

1914 *Scotsman* 12 Oct. 10/5 The 16-inch 'Black-Maria' shells of the heaviest German artillery. **1916** Ld. E. Hamilton *First 7 Div.* 125 The enemy were all this time steadily outranging our artillery with its big eleven-inch guns, popularly known as 'Black Marias'. **1919** *Athenæum* 11 July 583/2 For high or low velocity German shells, as substitutes for 'marmite', the British soldier came out with 'coalbox', 'Black Maria', 'Jack Johnson', 'heavy stuff'.

black mark. A black cross or other mark made against the name of a person who has incurred censure, penalty, etc. Also *fig.*

1845 Disraeli *Sybil* (1863) 129 Who's pushing on there? I see you, Mrs. Page. Won't there be a black mark against you? **1874** Blackie *Self-Cult.* 60 Note such a fellow..with a black mark, as a disloyal and disaffected subject.

Hence **black-mark** *v.*

1873 Masson *Drumm. of Hawth.* xiii. 278 Ostracise and black mark all who do not come into their confederacy.

black market. [black *a.* 11.] Unauthorized dealing in commodities that are rationed or of which the supply is otherwise restricted. Freq. *attrib.* Hence **black marke'teer,** (less commonly) **'marketer,** one engaged in such dealing; also abbrev. **blacke'teer** (cf. racketeer). Hence also **black-'market** *v.*, **black-marke'teering, black-'marketing, blacke'teering** *vbl. sbs.*, to deal, dealing, in the black market.

1931 *Economist* 10 Jan. 60/1 The growth of an unofficial or 'black' market in sterling exchange. **1935** *Ibid.* 5 Oct. 662/2 'Black market' quotations of Lit. 65–75 are reported in London. **1941** *New Statesman* 26 Apr. 430/2 There is evidence of a 'black market' where food can be bought without restriction if the price is high enough. **1942** *Ann. Reg. 1941* 96 The Government..took active steps to suppress the so-called 'black market' transactions in foodstuffs [etc.]..which..were also a matter of grave scandal in the country, particularly to those who could not afford 'black market' prices. **1942** *Time* 9 Mar. 29/1 The British people..favor outright imprisonment of guilty 'blacketeers'. **1942** *New Republic* 13 Apr. 490/2 The most skilled black marketer..is the sort of man who used to be a confidence man or other City hanger-on. **1942** *New Statesman* 11 July 25/1 If Jewish black-marketeers flourish in England, it is an indication of the inefficiency of the Government in checking this pursuit. **1942** *Times Lit. Suppl.* 15 Aug. 401/3 The profits of black marketeering. **1943** *Ann. Reg. 1942* 22 The penalties for 'black marketing' were also made more severe. **1943** E. M. Almedingen *Frossia* ii. 81 People black-marketed in currency, in timber ..in leather and in steel. **1944** *Daily Express* 6 Dec. 4/3 Alleged blacketeering by Paris 'Gestapo'. **1957** *Economist* 7 Sept. 788/2 By some means it must be made more attractive to sell through legal channels than through the black market. Vigorous use of powers of deportation against the black marketeers would help. **1957** *New Statesman* 2 Nov. 554/1 Scruffy black-marketeers..offered me wads of *escudos* for my ticket.

black mass. [mass *sb.*[1]] A mass for the dead, at which the vestments and drapings are black. Also, a travesty of the mass, used in the cult of Satanism.

1893 *Nation* 2 Feb. 84/3 He resorted to a sort of benevolent parody of the Christian sacrifice—a sort of White Mass, as one might call it, in contradistinction to the Black Mass of the Kabalists. **1896** A. E. Waite *Devil-worship in France* 4 To say..that Black Masses are celebrated..will not enhance the credibility or establish the intelligence of the speaker. **1904** Rolfe *Hadrian the Seventh* (1929) 61 My first Mass must be a black mass, Excellency. **1961** A. Christie *Pale Horse* v. 64 She's very occult... Goes in for spiritualism and trances, and magic. Not quite black masses, but that sort of thing.

blackmaster ('blæk,mɑːstə(r)). ? *Obs.* [black *sb.* 5.] A funeral furnisher, an undertaker.

1901 *Daily Chron.* 14 May 12/2 To Blackmasters and Undertakers. **1904** *Ibid.* 12 Nov. 6/7 'What is a black-master?'..'That's a well-known term in London,' said the applicant, 'and means an undertaker.' **1905** *Ibid.* 11 Feb. 9/3 Goodwill of a Black Master's Business.

Black Monday, black money: see Monday, money.

Black Monk. A monk of the order of St. Benedict, so called from the colour of the habit worn. See monk.

1297 R. Glouc. 433 þe priorye..of blake monekes. **1517** Torkington *Pilgr.* (1884) 10 The Monastery of blake monkys callyd Seynt Nicholas De Elio. **1722** J. Stevens *Addit. Dugdale's Monast.* I. 169 The Benedictine Monks in England, who were call'd Black Monks.

black moor, more: see blackamoor.

'black-mouth. A black-mouthed person or animal; *fig.* a foul-mouthed person, a slanderer.

1642 *Lond. Apprent. Decl.* in *Harl. Misc.* (Malh.) V. 307 As some blackmouths have uncharitably belched out against us. **1656** Trapp *Comm. John* ix. 28 Every black-mouth cast dirt upon Christ's disciples.

black-mouthed (-'maʊðd), *a.* †**a.** Having a black mouth; *fig.* slanderous, calumnious.

1595 *Polimanteia* (1881) 33 Blackemouthed enuie. **1633** T. Stafford *Pac. Hib.* iii. (1821) 256 Blacke mouthed railing Rabshakeh. **1689** *Lond. Gaz.* No. 2427/4 One black brindled Bull-Bitch..Black Mouth'd. **1697** *Snake in Gr.* (ed. 2) 281 All the Black-Mouth'd and Hellish Venom.

b. Applied to a fish having a black-mouth: *black-mouthed dog-fish* (*Pristiurus melanostomus*).

1862 J. Couch *Hist. Fishes Brit. Isl.* I. 18 The Black-mouthed or Eyed Dogfish is better known in the Mediterranean than with us. **1903** G. Sim *Vertebrate Fauna of 'Dee'* 272 Pristiurus melanostomus. Black-mouthed Dog-fish... One was caught by trawl four miles off Aberdeen.

'black-neb. *dial.* [See NEB, beak, bill.]
1. A popular name for various black-billed birds, as the Crane and the Common Crow.
1802 G. MONTAGU *Ornith. Dict.* (1833) 47. **1837** MACGILLIVRAY *Hist. Brit. Birds* I. 516. **1884** *Chamb. Jrnl.* 29 Mar. 204/2 Swarms of diminutive 'black nebs.'
†**2.** *Sc.* A person charged with democratic sympathies at the time of the French Revolution. *Obs.*
1816 SCOTT *Antiq.* vi, Take care, Monkbarns! we shall set you down among the black nebs by and by. **1821** GALT *Ann. Parish* 269 (JAM.) Many of the heritors considered me a black-neb. **1864** M^c^KAY *Hist. Kilmarnock* 107.

blackness ('blæknɪs). [f. BLACK *a.* + -NESS.] **a.** The quality or state of being black.
c **1340** *Cursor M* 8077 (Fairf.) Foure sarasinis con þai mete ..of þaire blaknes hit was selcouþis. **1382** WYCLIF *Nahum* ii. 10 The face of alle as blacnesse of a pott. **1606** SHAKS. *Ant. & Cl.* I. iv. 13 The Spots of Heauen, More fierie by nights Blacknesse. **1611** BIBLE *Jude* 13 The blacknesse of darkenesse. **1710** H. BEDFORD *Vind. Ch. Eng.* 35 The different blackness of the Ink. **1712** ADDISON *Spect.* No. 459 ¶ 13 The Blackness and Deformity of Vice. **1856** KANE *Arct. Expl.* I. xv. 167 You steer through the blackness for a lump of greater blackness.
b. (Often with capital initial.) The quality of being Black (sense 1 c); *spec.* the racial self-consciousness of (U.S.) Blacks, considered as a matter of pride.
1961 L. HUGHES *Ask your Mama* 8 They asked me right at Christmas if my blackness, would it rub off? I said, *Ask your mama.* **1968** *N.Y. Times* 12 Mar. 45/4 A sweeping change taking place in Harlem that emphasizes blackness and African heritage. **1971** *Black World* Mar. 87/2 'Blackness' is a political/cultural concept which calls the individual to view the nobility of his ancestral civilization. **1973** S. HENDERSON *Understanding New Black Poetry* 4 If there is such a commodity as 'blackness' in literature (and I assume that there is), it should somehow be found in concentrated or in residual form in the poetry. **1983** *Sunday Tel.* 4 Dec. 14/2 An attempt to build up something called 'Black culture'—coupling the idea of 'Blackness' to a general sense of rebellion against all forms of authority.

black nob, ox: see NOB, OX.

black-out ('blækaʊt). [f. phr. *to black out* (BLACK *v.* 3 b).] **1.** *Theatr.* The darkening of a stage during a performance; a darkened stage.
1913 G. B. SHAW *Let.* 3 Apr. (1956) 188 The more I think of that revolving business the less I see how it can be done. .. There will have to be a black-out. **1918** E. T. DENT in R. Brooke *Coll. Poems* p. xxxii, The elder generation were scandalized almost before the play began: no scenery..no music, no footlights, frequent 'black-outs'. **1932** A. J. WORRALL *Eng. Idioms* iii. 20 Immediately after the murder there is a black-out; when the lights come on again the stage is empty. **1952** GRANVILLE *Dict. Theatr. Terms* 28 In revue a *black out* serves as a quick curtain to a sketch.
2. *transf.* and *fig.* A condition of (temporary) obscuration; *spec.* (*a*) a temporary loss of memory; (*b*) suppression of information or news; (*c*) loss of a radio signal (because of an electrical storm, etc.).
1924 GALSWORTHY *Forest* III. i, What do you think death really is?.. Change of trains, or a black-out, eh? **1934** *Atlantic Monthly* Mar. 350/1 'Black-out'..is now used of a temporary loss of memory, or failure of the electric light. **1935** C. DAY LEWIS *Time to Dance* 55 The arctic winter and black-out of your dreams. **1940** H. G. WELLS *Babes in Darkling Wood* IV. iii. 356 There's not a trace now of the original concussion... But there is still a black-out in the memory. **1941** WYNDHAM LEWIS *Let.* 17 Oct. (1963) 301 If my eyes go I go too. Loathsome as the world is, I do like to *see* it. *That* sort of blackout I could not live in. **1942** *Mind* LI. 257 It is only when we reach the rarefied air of high theology that this particular intellectual black-out occurs. **1945** *Daily Express* 19 Apr. 1/1 There is still a news blackout in Moscow. **1958** *Listener* 25 Dec. 1072/1 The normal reflections from the *F*-layer [of the ionosphere] cease and there is prolonged disturbance of short-wave reception. This is what has been called the radio 'black-out'.
3. The action of extinguishing, covering, or obscuring lights as a precaution against air-raids, etc.; the resulting darkness; the time or period of compulsory covering of lights; the material used to obscure the lights. Also *attrib.*
1935 *Lancet* 3 Aug. 281/1 Mr. Harcourt Johnstone asked the Prime Minister whether instructions for compulsory 'black-outs' in districts where experiments were being carried out against air attacks were issued by authority of any Government department. **1939** L. MACNEICE *Autumn Jrnl.* 35 Black-out practice and A.R.P. **1939** *Archit. Rev.* LXXXVI. lvi/3, I slept right through the 'black out' on August 10th. **1940** *Ann. Reg. 1939* 127 Of the inconveniences the most serious continued to be the 'black-out'. **1940** *Flight* 8 Aug. 102/2 Also fitted are special 'black-out blinds' controlled from the pilot's compartment, which completely cover all the windows within the passenger cabin. **1940** 'N. SHUTE' *Landfall* i. 7 No parking allowed on these common roads after black-out. **1941** *New Statesman* 17 Aug. 154/2 Sick people cannot be nursed in wards with broken windows or with damaged black-out. **1942** E. WAUGH *Put out More Flags* 252 It's like walking in the blackout with a shaded torch. You can see just as far as the step you're taking. **1960** J. LEHMANN *I am my Brother* i. 3 That night—the first night of black-out—I struggled out in the slithery rainy darkness to dine up in Highgate.
4. Temporary complete loss of consciousness; also, in flying, temporary blindness resulting from physical derangement produced by a sudden sharp turn or acceleration.
1940 *Hutchinson's Pict. Hist. War* 14 Feb.–9 Apr. 217 The problems of future fighters of over 400 m.p.h. are: to defeat the pilot's 'black-out' [etc.]. **1940** *Times* 30 Mar. 9/6 The actual black-out the Germans..call the 'curtain'. There is no loss of consciousness..merely this 'curtain' of black before the eyes. And so soon as the turn is eased and the *g* brought down, sight returns. **1959** *Daily Mail* 2 Apr. 10/5 The man-carrying centrifuge at the Farnborough Institute of Aviation Medicine..tests pilots for 'black-outs'. **1961** *Lancet* 5 Aug. 322/1 He had had several 'black-outs' resembling epilepsy.

black-poll. *U.S.* [BLACK *a.* 1.] A North American warbler (*Dendroica striata*), the male of which has a black head when in full plumage. In full, ***black-poll warbler.***
1783 J. LATHAM *Gen. Synop. Birds* II. 460 Black-poll Warbler... Crown black... Found at New York and Newfoundland. **1868** *Amer. Naturalist* II. 180 It is very quick, scarcely less so than the black-poll. **1872** COUES *Key N. Amer. Birds* 100 Blackpoll Warbler..*Dendrœca striata.* **1893** B. TORREY *Footpath-Way* 6 We..were in the old forest listening to bay-breasted warblers, Blackburnians, black-polls and so on.

'black-pot. Also blackpot, black pot. **1.** A beer-mug (cf. BLACK-JACK); a toper.
c **1590** GREENE *Fr. Bacon* v. 122 I'll be Prince of Wales over all the blackpots in Oxford. **1636** HEYWOOD *Love's Mistr.* 11, Iugg, what's shee but sister to a black-pot. **1818** SCOTT *Ht. Midl.* xxxii, A whole whiskin, or black pot of sufficient double ale.
2. A black pudding. (Cf. POT *sb.*[1] 8.) *s.w. dial.*
1825 JENNINGS *Observ. Dial. W. Eng.*, *Black-pot*, black-pudding. **1880** HARDY *Trumpet-Major* xvi, Seventy rings of black-pot. **1891** —— *Tess* I. i, I should like for supper,—well, lamb's fry if they can get it; and if they can't, black-pot. **1895** —— *Jude* VI. viii, I shall have to make black-pot and sausages.
3. Coarse Danish crockery-ware exposed to dense smoke in baking as a substitute for glazing.
1889 in *Cent. Dict.* **1904** in R. HUNTER et al. *Encycl. Dict. Suppl.*

Black Prince.
1. A name given (apparently by 16th c. chroniclers) to the eldest son of Edward III. [As to the origin of the appellation, many guesses are current, but published sources afford no evidence.]
1563 GRAFTON *Chron.* (1569) 324 Edward prince of Wales, who was called the blacke Prince. **1587** HOLINSHED *Hist. Eng.* 348 b. **1599** SHAKS. *Hen. V*, II. iv. 56 All our Princes captiu'd, by the hand Of that black Name, Edward, black Prince of Wales. **1611** SPEED *Theat. Gt. Brit.* IX. xii. an. 1329 By-named (not of his colour, but of his dreaded acts in battell) the Blacke Prince. **1688** J. BARNES *Hist. Edw. III*, I. iii. §5. 46 Sirnamed by the French le Neoir, or the Black-Prince. [But cf. **1724** COSTE *Ess. de Montaigne* I. i. (1836) I. 3 *note*, Edouard, prince de Galles, que les Anglois nomment communément the *black prince.*] **1762** HUME *Hist. Eng.* (1770) II. xvi. 513 Denominated the Black Prince, from the colour of his armour. *a* **1854** E. M. STEWART *Lond. City T.Q. Phillipa* xvi. 139 The surcoat of black velvet emblazoned with three white ostrich feathers, and the motto 'Ich Dien,' which gave rise to the epithet of the Black Prince.
†**2.** The prince of darkness, the devil. *Obs.*
1589 R. HARVEY *Pl. Perc.* 7 To entitle those *Browne sectaries* of the *Blacke Prince*, with the name of traytors.

black pudding. (Also with hyphen.) A kind of sausage made of blood and suet, sometimes with the addition of flour or meal.
1568 FULWEL *Like to like* B j, Who comes yonder puffing as whot as a black pudding. **1634** HEYWOOD *Maidenh. lost* III. Wks. 1874 IV. 142 We will haue..sixe Black-Puddings to bee served vp in Sorrell-sops. **1664** BUTLER *Hud.* II. III. 380 In Lyrick numbers write an Ode on His Mistress eating a Black-pudden. **1873** E. SMITH *Foods* 80 Sausages and black puddings.

Black Rod. Short for *Gentleman Usher of the Black Rod* (so called from the black wand surmounted by a golden lion which he carries as his symbol of office). The chief Gentleman Usher of the Lord Chamberlain's department of the royal household, who is also usher to the House of Lords and to the Chapter of the Garter. Also, a similar functionary in colonial legislatures.
1632 in SHERWOOD. **1646** EVANCE *Noble Ord.* 1 Ely is committed to the Black Rod. **1668** MARVELL *Corr.* ci. Wks. 1872–5 II. 257 The Lords..sentenced Sir Samuel Barnardiston..to pay 300 *li.* fine, and be under black rod without baile till he payd it. **1724** *Lond. Gaz.* No. 6284/1 The Black Rod kneeling held the Gospels. **1861** HUGHES *Tom Brown Oxf.* I. iii. 40 Lords and ladies in waiting, white sticks or black rods. **1865** *Times* 25 Aug. (Quebec), The Usher of the Black Rod..was directed, after the manner of St. Stephen's, to summon the members of the Lower House.

black rubric. An inaccurate term for the declaration explanatory of the rubric concerning kneeling at the reception of the Holy Communion, which was first inserted at the end of the Communion Office in the Book of Common Prayer of 1552 (omitted in 1559, and restored in 1662) (see quot. 1957).
1866 J. H. BLUNT *Annot. Bk. Com. Prayer* 199 They retained the protest against Transubstantiation, whilst they removed all risk of the Declaration, or 'Black rubric' as it was sometimes called. **1877** E. DANIEL *Prayer-Book* 333 The Black Rubric explains the intention of the rubric, which prescribes that communicants should receive the Holy Communion kneeling. **1957** *Oxf. Dict. Chr. Ch.* 176/1 The expression 'Black Rubric' dates only from the 19th cent. when the practice of printing the BCP with the rubrics in red was introduced and the fact that the 'Declaration' was really not a rubric at all was marked by printing it in black. In modern two-colour reprints of the BCP it will be found, however, printed in red.

black salts. In the old potash-making process: Wood ashes after lixiviation and evaporation; impure potassium hydrate. Hence **'black-salter**, one who makes black salts.
1880 E. KIRKE *Garfield* 6 Our future President became prime-minister to a black-salter. **1881** THAYER *Log Cab. to White Ho.* x, Potash..in its crude state, was called 'black-salts.' The manufacturer of the article was called a 'black-salter.'

†**black sanctus.** *Obs.* A burlesque hymn or anthem; 'rough music.' See SANCTUS.

black sand. [BLACK *a.* 1.] Dark-coloured sand, esp. that on beaches in Australia and New Zealand; also *attrib.* Hence **black-sander**, a beach-comber who washes the black sand of the beach for gold; **black-sanding** *vbl. sb.*, this process or occupation.
1778 D. SAMWELL *Jrnl.* 27 June in Cook *Jrnls.* (1967) III. II. 1120 We came to an Anchor in about 30 fath^ms^ Water with bottom of black sand and shells. **1849** *Rep. Comm. Patents* (*U.S.*) (1850) 405 Much of the black sand now in use is colored, and is common silicious sand, but the best article is a ferruginous sand. **1874** A. BATHGATE *Colonial Experiences* xi. 147 It promised well from the quantity of black sand visible in the dish. **1882** *Jrnl. Iron & Steel Inst.* I. 251 It was found very difficult to work this black sand, on account of the large percentage of titanic acid it contains. **1906** in P. Galvin *N.Z. Mining Handbk.* 122 (*heading*) Black-sand beaches on the West Coast. *Ibid.*, At present there are small parties who earn a good average living by what is known as 'blacksanding'..between Jackson's Bay and Karamea. *Ibid.* 124 The 'black-sanders' reaped their harvest. *Ibid.*, What old leads there were were then washed out in detail and most of the gold secured by the busy 'blacksanders' in the process. **1965** G. J. WILLIAMS *Econ. Geol. N.Z.* ix. 130/2 A 'blacksand' is material containing opaque iron-bearing grains in sufficient quantity to impart at least a grey colour to the whole.

black sheep: see SHEEP.

blackshirt, black shirt. [tr. It. *camicia nera.*] A black shirt as the distinctive mark of the uniform of the Fascist party of Italy; hence *transf.* and *gen.* = FASCIST. So **black-shirted** *a.*
1922 *Youth's Companion* 30 Nov. (ed. L. Thompson, 1954) 84 The 'black shirts' have beaten down Communism by force of arms. **1923** P. PHILLIPS (*title*) The 'Red' Dragon and the Black Shirts. **1923** *Weekly Dispatch* 28 Jan. 9 The 'scotching' of Bolshevism in Italy by the black-shirted Fascisti. *a* **1930** D. H. LAWRENCE *Phoenix II* (1968) 534 She cares terribly because far-off, invisible, hypothetical Italians wear black shirts. **1934** H. G. WELLS *Exper. Autobiogr.* II. ix. 782 It was a gathering of Mosley's black-shirts. **1935** *Ann. Reg. 1934* 17 The wearing of a distinctive uniform—in this case a black shirt. *Ibid.* 51 Next day the whole of England was ringing with the cry of 'blackshirt brutality'.

blacksmith ('blæksmɪθ). **a.** A smith who works in iron or black metal, as distinguished from a 'whitesmith' who works in tin or white metal.
1483 *Act 1 Rich. III*, xii. §1 Artificers of the said Realm.. Bladesmiths, Blacksmiths, Spurriers, Goldbeaters. *c* **1500** *Cocke Lorell's B.* 9 Brydel bytters, blacke smythes, and ferrars. **1709** STEELE *Tatler* No. 31 ¶3 Having got a Black-Smith of Lemnos to make her Son's Weapons. **1813** *Parl. Debate in Examiner* 24 May 326/2 If this should be decided to be a valid marriage, the poor Gretna green Blacksmith would be ruined. **1860** TYNDALL *Glac.* II. §19 A clever blacksmith can make a nail red-hot by hammering it.
b. ***blacksmith's*** (*U.S.* ***blacksmith***) ***shop***, a smithy.
1752 in *New Hampshire Probate Rec.* (1915) III. 454 The Blacksmiths Shop which stand[s] on the home lot. **1795** P. M. FRENEAU *Poems* 421 Unless the [stage-]driver..Has made some business for the black-smith-shop. **1845** F. DOUGLASS *Life* (1846) 94 Fred, go to the blacksmith's shop and get me a new punch. **1889** *Harper's Mag.* Aug. 390/1 Perhaps he had better ride over to the blacksmith shop.
Hence **'blacksmithing** *sb.*
1830 GALT *Lawrie T.* II. i. (1849) 43 For blacksmithing a prime hammer. **1861** DU CHAILLU *Equat. Afr.* xxvi. 464 In their blacksmithing operations. **1876** GEO. ELIOT *Dan. Der.* IV. lvii. 169 If he doesn't like the blacksmithing.

blacksmithery (ˌblæksˈmɪθərɪ). [f. BLACKSMITH + -ERY; cf. SMITHERY.] **1.** A smithy. *U.S.*
a **1854** J. F. KELLY *Humors of Falconbridge* (1856) 303 The town—of some four houses, six 'groceries', a *store* and blacksmithery—was aroused. **1872** *U.S. Office Indian Affairs Rep. 1871* 327 The fixed property of this reservation consists of agents quarters, 3 dwellings, 2 blacksmitheries.
2. Blacksmith's work. orig. *U.S.*
1869 *Overland Monthly* III. 10 In North Carolina, as in the North, blacksmithery, wagon-making, coopery, and other sorts of hard-handed industry, were in noisy blast. **1936** J. GRIERSON *High Failure* vi. 134 Altering its rake—a tricky piece of blacksmithery. **1938** *Antiquity* XII. 8 The blacksmithery of their simple ironwork.

black-snake.
1. A name given to several dark-coloured snakes; as in U.S. to the *Coluber constrictor* and *C. Alleghaniensis*; in Jamaica to the *Natrix atra.*
1688 J. CLAYTON *Virginia* in *Phil. Trans.* XVIII. 135 The Black Snake, is the largest I think. **1802** BINGLEY *Anim.*

Biog. (1813) II. 462 The black snake.. able to fascinate birds. **1883** *Harper's Mag.* Oct. 708/1 None of my venomous acquaintances.. black-snake, whip-snake, coral-snake, or viper.

2. *U.S.* A long whip-lash. Also *attrib.*

1864 J. FISK *Exped. Rocky Mts.* 5 A 'black snake'.. brought him on his legs. **1883** *Harper's Mag.* Mar. 495/1 The.. drivers trudged beside them.. cracking huge 'black-snakes' at the animals. **1901** S. E. WHITE *Westerners* xxxiv. 310 He snapped the lash of his black-snake whip.

Hence **'blacksnake** *v. trans.*, to flog with a black-snake whip.

1870 'MARK TWAIN' in *Galaxy* Dec. 878/2, I lay I'll black-snake you within an inch of your life!

†**'blacksome,** *a. Obs. rare*⁻¹. [f. BLACK + -SOME.] Of black character, dusky, darksome.

1597 TOFTE *Laura* in *Alba* (1880) Introd. 29 Like to the blacksome night I may compare My Mistres gowne.

blacksploitation, var. BLAXPLOITATION.

black spot. 1. Any of various diseases of plants or animals, producing black spots upon the diseased portions; esp. a disease of roses (see quot. 1889).

1889 *Cent. Dict.* I. 571/1 *Black-spot*, a disease of rose-bushes, characterized by diffuse, dark-colored spots on the upper surface of the leaves. It is caused by a parasitic fungus, *Asteroma Rosæ*. **1906** M. C. COOKE *Fungoid Pests* 50 Chrysanthemum Leaf-Spot... The black spot (*Cylindrosporium Chrysanthemi*) is very destructive in Canada. *Ibid.* 134 Peach Freckle.. is known in the United States as 'scab' or 'black spot'... The fungus is a kind of black mould which attacks ripe Peaches. **1910** F. C. STEWART in *N.Y. Agric. Exper. Station Bull.* CCCXXVIII. 364 Maple, Silver.. Black Spot, *Rhytisma acerinum*.. the characteristic tar-colored spots of which may be detected at a considerable distance. **1933** *Jrnl. R. Hort. Soc.* LVIII. 253 Black spot, the worst enemy of the rose. **1966** *Punch* 30 Mar. 462/1 Huge stocks of the munitions of bacterial warfare, of mildew and rust, black spot, botrytis and scab, are being made ready for immediate use at call.

2. A place or area of trouble, anxiety, or danger; esp. a dangerous section of a road.

1925 *Daily Herald* 30 June 2/3 Against general and protracted depression in the 'black spots', they might.. set .. improvement in the trades. **1936** *Discovery* Nov. 355/2 The development of newer industries is vital to the recovery of our distressed areas, which remain the one black spot in the otherwise remarkable position of Great Britain. **1937** *Daily Herald* 5 Jan. 7/4 Road-crossing improvements at 'black spots' throughout London. **1940** R. MORRISH *Police & Crime-Detection* i. 20 'Black spots' are easily recognized by recording the districts and streets where, for example, housebreaking takes place. **1959** *Listener* 6 Aug. 208/2 You begin to see what are the black spots, that is to say, where accidents do in fact happen.

'black-tail.

†**1.** A sea fish not identified; the μελάνουρος, *melanurus*, of ancient writers. *Obs.*

1661 LOVELL *Hist. Anim. & Min.* 232 Black-taile, *Melanurus*.. Was counted a poore fish.

2. A name for certain varieties of the perch.

1734 MORTIMER in *Phil. Trans.* XXXVIII. 316 *Perca marina, cauda nigra*, the Black-Tail.

3. The black-tailed deer. Also *attrib.* with *deer*, *buck*. *U.S.*

1828 H. G. ROGERS *Jrnl.* 20 June in H. C. Dale *Ashley-Smith Explor.* (1918) 259, I killed a fine black tail buck. **1848** J. W. ABERT *Exam. New Mexico* 23 Of the latter there are two varieties, the common deer, and the black tail. **1872** SCHELE DE VERE *Americanisms* 371 The variety found on the Pacific coast (*Cervus columbianus*) is more commonly designated as the Black-tail Deer, from the black tip to its tail. **1895** *Outing* (U.S.) XXVII. 45/2 We.. had two large black-tail bucks and a doe.

4. = DASSIE *sb.*² *S. Afr.*

1905 *East London Dispatch* 29 July 7/3 A few friends, fishing in the Buffalo River.. had some excellent sport, taking.. *black-tail* of about 21/2 lbs. **1906** *Ibid.* 6 Mar. 7/5 The biggest I caught on these rocks was a fine *dasje* (black-tail) weighing 7¼ lbs.

'black-thorn ('blækθɔːn).

1. a. A common thorny shrub, bearing white flowers before the leaves and very small dark purple plums; called also the Sloe (*Prunus spinosa*): the name is probably due to the dark colour of the naked branches, with which the white flowers strongly contrast. Its wood is prized for walking-sticks.

1388 WYCLIF *Dan.* xiii. 58 Vndur a blak thorn [**1382** plum tree]. **1496** *Bk. St. Albans, Fysshynge* 8 Take a fayr shote of blacke-thorn; crabbe tree; medeler. **1578** LYTE *Dodoens* VI. xlvii. 721 The wilde Plumme tree, Blacke thorne, and Sloo tree. **1634** HABINGTON *Castara* II. §2. xix, Love shall in that tempestuous showre Her brightest blossome like the blacke-thorne show. **1842** TENNYSON *May Queen* II. 8, I shall never see The blossom on the black-thorn, the leaf upon the tree. **1882** *Garden* 8 Apr. 241/1 One of the best flowering shrubs we know is the double-flowered Blackthorn.

b. A walking-stick or cudgel made of the stem of this shrub.

1849 W. H. MAXWELL *Stories Waterloo*, An hundred blackthorns rattled above my head.

c. *attrib.*, as in ***blackthorn leaves, winter***. Also *Comb.*, as ***blackthorn-fleeced*** adj.

1789 G. WHITE *Selborne* (1813) II. 292 Blackthorn.. usually blossoms while cold N.E. winds blow; so that the harsh rugged weather obtaining at this season, is called by the country people, blackthorn-winter. **1824** SCOTT *St. Ronan's* xv, Tea, madam! I saw none. Ash leaves and black-thorn leaves were brought in. **1898** C. M. YONGE *John Keble's Parishes* xvi. 214 Black-thorn winter is supposed to bring fresh cold in spring, when the bushes almost look as if covered by hoar-frost. **1905** *Daily Chron.* 11 Apr. 4/7 'Blackthorn winter' is the Gloucestershire name for the fit of January weather that almost always follows the flowering of the beautiful wild sloe blossom. **1946** L. B. LYON *Rough Walk Home* 28 Pray blackthorn-winter's dawn may rediscover us. **1948** C. DAY LEWIS *Poems 1943–47* 84 Walking by blackthorn-fleeced Hedges to church.

2. *U.S.* A species of hawthorn (*Cratægus tomentosa*), also called Pear-thorn. Webster 1864, and Miller *Plant-n.* 1884. In W. Indies, a species of Acacia (*A. Farnesiana*).

1737 J. BRICKELL *Nat. Hist. N. Carolina* 79 The Black Thorn.. grows plentifully in several parts of this Province. **1798** *Trans. N.Y. State Soc. Agric.* I. III. 18 The black thorn has been destroyed by a worm that preys upon its twigs. **1848** A. GRAY *Man. Bot.* 128 Black or Pear Thorn.

black-throat. *U.S.* [BLACK *a.* 1.] A black-throated warbler. In full, ***black-throat warbler***.

1785 PENNANT *Arct. Zool.* II. 399 Black-throat Warbler. .. Inhabits, during summer, Canada and other parts of America, to the south. **1902** S. E. WHITE *Blazed Trail* xlii. 296 Wilson's warblers.. pine creepers, black-throats.. passed silently or noisily.

black-top. *U.S.* [BLACK *a.* 1.] A blackish material used for surfacing roads, etc.; a road, etc., surfaced with this material. Freq. *attrib.* Hence as *v.*, to surface (a road) with black-top; **black-topping** *vbl. sb.*

1931 *Amer. City* Oct. 112/1 This was done by adding a black border for the letters and other characters, which for black top pavements are yellow. **1940** *Topeka Jrnl.* 22 Apr. 3 Strewed some of the victims on the blacktop. **1947** J. STEINBECK *Wayward Bus* 112 Juan.. turned right into the black-top road. **1957** 'F. RICHARDS' *Practise to Deceive* ii. 18 Next spring would be time enough to think of black-topping. *Ibid.* 26 She took it easy, backing up the narrow blacktop.

black vomit. The dark matter vomited in the last stage of yellow fever; also, the fever itself. See VOMIT *sb.* 2 b.

'black-wash, *sb.* Also **black wash**.

1. *Med.* A lotion composed of calomel and lime-water; grey lotion.

1818 A. COOPER *Surg. Ess.* I. (ed. 3) 166 Under the black-wash poultice. **1854** J. SCOFFERN in *Orr's Circ. Sc.* Chem. 495 The lotion known in medical and surgical practice, as the *black wash*.

2. Any black composition used for washing over and blackening. (Also *blackwash.*)

1861 *Times* 12 July, The blackwash was removed from the paintings; bad taste and want of means caused the white-wash to be left. [See next.]

3. The opposite of WHITEWASH *sb.* 3. Also **'black,washing** *vbl. sb.*

1859 KINGSLEY *Misc.* II. 48 To remove.. the modern layers of 'black-wash', and to let the man himself, fair or foul, be seen. **1877** *Chambers's Jrnl.* 28 Apr. 258/2 A skilful counsel.. using as much whitewash as he can for the accused, and applying plentiful blackwash to the witnesses for the prosecution. **1890** *Literary World* XLI. 388/1 By giving Cromwell another plentiful coating of black-wash. **1905** *Contemp. Rev.* Oct. 552 (*title*) The Blackwashing of Dante.

'blackwash, *v.* [f. prec. sb.]

1. *trans.* To wash or colour with a black liquid.

c **1770** Used by H. WALPOLE. **1861** *Times* 12 July, The Gueux.. whitewashed the façades. But they also blackwashed the paintings of Van Eyck and Memlinc.

2. *fig.* To blacken the character of; to asperse, calumniate. (Cf. *whitewash.*)

1869 ST. CLAIR & BR. *Resid. Bulgaria* Pref. 7 The Rayah has been too much whitewashed.. whilst the Turk has been too much blackwashed by his enemies. **1875** HELPS *Soc. Press.* xii. 160 He 'black-washes'.. the whole human race.

black water.

1. A stream stained brown by the peat of the mosses from which it flows.

1676 COTTON *Walton's Angler* II. ii. 14 This River [Trent] from its head for a Mile or two is a black water. *Ibid.* 16 The River Wye.. a black water too at the Fountain... Derwent, a black water too.

2. A disease incident to sheep and cows.

1800 TUKE *Agric. N. Riding Yorks.* 272 There is another disorder to which lambs are liable in autumn; it is called the black-water. **1825** LOUDON *Encycl. Agric.* §6263 The black water is only the aggravated and latter stages of [red water]. **1879** J. LUCAS in *Zoologist* 3rd Ser. III. 356 Many [sheep] die in cold nights, when they contract a disease known as 'blackwater'.

3. In full ***blackwater fever***. A tropical fever to which chiefly white people are subject, characterized by a brown or blue-black colour of the urine.

1884 J. F. EASMON (*title*) The nature and treatment of blackwater fever. **1897** MARY KINGSLEY *W. Africa* 645 Two extremely deadly forms of fever have come into notice here, malarial typhoid and blackwater. **1926** *Blackw. Mag.* Nov. 663/1 The doctor had died three weeks before of blackwater. **1965** B. SWEET-ESCOTT *Baker St. Irreg.* viii. 249 Musgrave had known Burma well before the war, and had twice suffered from blackwater fever.

4. [tr. Hindi *kālā pānī*.] A term used by Indians, esp. Hindus, for the sea.

1818 M. M. SHERWOOD *Hist. Little Henry & his Bearer* (ed. 12) 79 He could never follow him through the black water, as the Hindoos call the seas. **1898** KIPLING *Day's Work* 7 A sea-priest—one who had never set foot on Black Water, but had been chosen as ghostly counsellor by two generations of sea-rovers. **1940** M. R. ANAND (*title*) Across the black waters. **1966** P. SCOTT *Jewel in Crown* v. 209 Unclean by traditional Hindu standards and custom because I had crossed the black water. **1977** —— *Staying On* xv. 199 He would spend his remaining years like a little dog at Lila's heels, panting after her all round India and perhaps beyond the black water.

'black-wood, blackwood¹. **a.** A name applied in different parts of the world to various trees and their timber: in New South Wales, *Acacia melanoxylon*; East Indies, *Dalbergia latifolia*; St. Helena, *Melhania melanoxylon*; West Australia, *Acacia penninervis*. (Miller *English Plant-names.*)

1631 SPEED *Prosp. Fam. Parts World* 43 Cedars, Palmetoes, Black-wood, White-wood. **1693** *Phil. Trans.* XVII. 621 The.. Blackwood of those of Barbados. **1779** FORREST *Voy. N. Guinea* 381 They carry to China great quantities of blackwood, which is worked up there into furniture, &c. **1841** ELPHINSTONE *Hist. India* I. 9 Sissoo (or blackwood trees). **1883** MISS BRADDON *Gold. Calf* xi. 144 The pretty carved Indian tea-table—a gem in Bombay blackwood.

b. = *black growth* (see BLACK *a.* 19). Also *attrib. U.S.*

1812 F. A. MICHAUX *Hist. Arbres de l'Amérique* II. 220 On désigne ces terreins sous le nom de *Black wood lands*, terreins à essence noire. **1848** BARTLETT *Dict. Amer.* 33 *Black wood*, hemlock, pine, spruce, and fir. Maine. **1872** SCHELE DE VERE *Americanisms* 420 Black Wood is, in the Northern States, used as a generic term for the evergreens, hemlock, pine, spruce, and fir.

'Blackwood². *Bridge.* The name of an American, E. F. *Blackwood*, used *attrib.* or *absol.* of a bidding system that he devised, whereby a bid of four no-trumps is used as an asking bid to which the partner's reply in five of a suit shows the number of aces that he holds.

1938 E. CULBERTSON *Contract Bridge Complete* (1939) xxvi. 321 A four and five no-trump convention known in most parts of the country as the Blackwood Convention has a number of sturdy adherents. **1958** *Listener* 16 Oct. 611/2 Assuming the use of Blackwood, my auction would be [etc.].

blacky ('blækɪ), *sb. colloq.* Also **blackie, -ey.** [f. BLACK, with -Y⁴, dim., as in *Tommy.*]

1. A black, a negro: often used without the article after the fashion of a proper name. Cf. *darky.*

1815 MOORE *Epist. Tom Crib* 1 Aye, even Blackey cries shame. **1854** THACKERAY *Newcomes* I. 35 He swore he would demolish blackey's ugly face. **1863** *Athenæum* No. 1858 737/2 Overseers who.. flog their blackies unmercifully.

2. *dial.* and *colloq.* = Black one; also = blackbird.

1876 MRS. FRANCIS in W. W. Skeat *S. Warwickshire Words* 124 *Blackie*, a blackbird. **1890** A. J. ARMSTRONG *Ingleside Musings* 84, I listen to the blackie's note. **1940** F. KITCHEN *Brother to Ox* i. 3 Every bush along the carriage drive owned a blackie or a thrush.

blacky ('blækɪ), *a.* [f. BLACK *a.* + -Y¹.] Somewhat black, blackish.

1594 CAREW *Tasso* (1881) 75 From his fell mouth such blacky belches came. **1877** *Hon. Miss Ferrard* I. vii. 234 Of jute and blacky-brown silk.

blad, *sb.*¹ *Sc.* [f. BLAD *v.*] A firm flat blow.

a **1715** *Jacobite Relics* II. 139 (JAM.) They lend sic hard and heavy blads, Our Whigs nae mair can craw, man. **1789** D. DAVIDSON *Seasons* 79 (JAM.) Wha gied them mony a donsy blaad.. that day.

blad (blad), *sb.*² Chiefly *Sc.* Also **blaud.** [Possibly the same as prec., or at least from BLAD *v.*: thus there is also *dad* vb. to beat, thump, and *dad* a large piece, a 'thumping' piece.] **1.** A fragment, portion, piece, bit, or lump.

c **1527** STEWART *Soutars Answ.* in *Evergreen* I. 121 Grit blads and bitts thou staw [= stole] full oft. **1574** J. MELVILL *Autobiog.* (1842) 33 He [John Knox] was lyk to ding that pulpit in blads. **1573** in Thomson's *Invent.* 187 (JAM.) Take the fyve bladdis of tapestrie. **1785** BURNS *2nd Ep. Lapraik* iv, I'll write, and that a hearty blaud, This vera night. **1824** SCOTT *Redgaunt.* xi, Dougal would hear nothing but a blaud of Davie Lindsay. **1842** *Blackw. Mag.* LI. 181 Dabs of gum, blads of orange, and lumps of putty.

2. a. A portfolio (Jamieson, 1808).

1813 E. PICKEN *Poems* II. 132 He staps in his warks in his pouch in a blink, Flang by a' his warklooms, his blaud an' his ink.

b. A blotting-pad or writing-pad.

1837 *Tait's Mag.* IV. 103/2 As if I were merely amusing myself with my pen on my blad. **1923** G. WATSON *Roxb. Word-bk.* 58 *Blad*, a blotting pad.

c. [cf. Sw., Du. *blad* leaf.] In non-dial. use: see quots.

1933 PARTRIDGE *Slang Today & Yesterday* III. iii. 181 Blad.. is applied to a sheaf of specimen pages or to other 'illustrative matter' liked by the bookseller, especially the bookseller resident abroad. **1960** G. A. GLAISTER *Gloss. of Bk.* 28 *Blad*, a sample of a book, made up for the publisher's traveller to show to the trade. It usually consists of the first thirty-two pages, including prelims, bound up in the same cloth as the finished book.

blad, *v. Sc.* Also 8 **blaud.** [prob. onomatopœic.] *trans.* To deal a blow to, to slap heavily.

1524 *Vision* xiv. in *Evergreen* I. 220 Theyil jade hir and blad hir Untill scho brak hir Tether.

1786 BURNS *Ordination* ii, He's the boy will blaud her! **1837** R. NICOLL *Poems* 110, I like the healthfu' gale That blads fu' kindly there.

Hence '**blading** (also **blauding**), *ppl. a.*

1785 BURNS *Ep. J. M. Math* i, The shearers cowr To shun the bitter blaudin' show'r.

bladder ('blædə(r)), *sb.* Forms: 1 **blédræ**, (**blédre**), **blǽdre**, **-ddre**, 3–4 **bleddre**, 4–5 **bleddere**, **bladdre**, 5 **bled-**, **bladdyr**, **bladdur(e**, ? **blowre**, 5–6 **bledder**, 6 **blader**, **bladdare**, 6–7 **blather**, (*Sc.* 6 **bleddir**, 8– **blather**, **blether**), 5– **bladder**. [Com. Teut.: OE., WSax. *blǽdre*, *blæddre*, Anglian *blédre*, wk. fem. = OSax. **blâdra*, (MLG. *blâder*, *bladder*, MDu. *blâder*(*e*, Du. *blaar*, Flem. *bladder*), OHG. *blâtara* (MHG. *blâtere*, *blâttere*, mod.G. *blatter*), ON. *bláðra* (Sw. *bläddra*, Da. *blære*):—OTeut. **blǣ-drôn-*, f. verb. stem *blǣ-* to BLOW + *-drôn* suffix denoting instrument, cogn. w. Gr. *-τρα*, *-τρον*. The dialectal variation in OE. *blédre*, *blǽdre*, remained in the ME. *bledder*, *bladder* (both having the vowel shortened by position); *blather*, *blether* (still used in Scotland) may represent the ON. form, but is more probably an instance of the fluctuation of *d* and *ð* in conjunction with *r*, seen in comparing *father*, *mother*, *feather*, *hither*, with ME. *fader*, *moder*, *feder*, *hider*.]

1. A membranous bag in the animal body.

a. *orig.* The musculo-membranous bag which serves as the receptacle of the urinary fluid secreted by the kidneys. Called also *urinary bladder*.

a **700** *Epinal Gloss.* (*O.E. Texts*) 1077 *Vessica*, bledrae. *Corpus Gl.* 2101 *Vesica*, bledre. *c* **1000** *Sax. Leechd.* I. 360 Wið blæddran sare ȝenim eoferes blædran mid þam micȝan. **1398** TREVISA *Barth. De P.R.* v. xliv. (1495) 161 Euery beest that gendryth hath a bladder. *Ibid.* VII. lv. 268 Yf they come of the bledder. *c* **1420** *Pallad. on Husb.* I. 54 Yf langoure in thaire bledders ought awake. **1519** HORMAN *Vulg.* iii. 32 The payne of the stone that cometh of dropynge of the bladder. **1530** PALSGR. 904 The bledder, *la uessie.* **1570** LEVINS *Manip.* 28 Bladdare, Blader, *vesica.* **1607** TOPSELL *Four-f. Beasts* 546 The bladder of a wilde Boar..The blather of a Goat. **1718** POPE *Iliad* v. 88 Between the bladder and the bone it pass'd. **1782** BURNS *Death Poor Mailie* 64 For thy pains, thou'se get my blather. **1785** —— *Sc. Drink* xvii, May gravels round his blather wrench! **1842** E. WILSON *Anat. Vade M.* 541 The Bladder is an oblong membranous viscus of an ovoid shape.

b. Any membranous bag in the animal body; usually with distinctive adjunct, as ***gall-***, ***air-***, ***swimming-bladder***.

1661 LOVELL *Hist. Anim. & Min.* 232 A bladder in them full of spawn. **1668** CULPEPPER & COLE *Barthol. Anat.* II. vi. 106 The first bladder of the Heart. **1797** BAILLIE *Morb. Anat.* (1807) 250 The gall-bladder is sometimes distended with bile. **1847** CARPENTER *Zool.* §527 In the organisation of Fishes..the swimming bladder is situated in the abdomen. **1869** NICHOLSON *Zool.* xxv. (1880) 250 *Rotifera*..In the hinder part of the body..is a sac or vesicle, which is termed the 'contractile bladder.'

†**2. a.** A morbid vesicle containing liquid or putrid matter; a boil, blister, pustule. *Obs.*

c **1000** ÆLFRIC *Ex.* ix. 9 On mannum and on nytenum beoð wunda and swellende blæddran. *c* **1000** *Sax. Leechd.* I. 86 Uncuþum blædrum ðe on mannes nebbe sittað. **1388** WYCLIF *Ex.* ix. 10 Woundis of bolnynge bladdris weren maad in men & in werk beestis. **1523** FITZHERB. *Husb.* §62 A bladder full of water two inches longe and more. **1577** B. GOOGE *Heresbach's Husb.* (1586) 167 All swelling as it were with little blathers. **1606** SHAKS. *Tr. & Cr.* v. i. 24 Dirt rotten livers..bladders full of imposthume. **1607** TOPSELL *Four-f. Beasts* 419 The pimples or bladders which arise in the bites of a Shrew. **1880** *Syd. Soc. Lex.* s.v., *Bladder in the throat*, old American term for cynanche.

b. (see quot.)

a **1722** LISLE *Observ. Husb.* (1757) 343 (E.D.S.) A distemper that falls on a bullock in the spring..which they in their country call the bladder; the bullock will be taken with a swelling of his lips, and running of his mouth, and swelling of his eyes, and running of them.

3. The prepared bladder of an animal, which may be inflated and used from its buoyancy as a float; also as the wind-bag of a simple kind of bag-pipe, as a receptacle for lard, etc.

a **1225** *Ancr. R.* 282 A bleddre ibollen ful of winde ne duueð nout. *c* **1425** *Seven Sag.* (P.) 2181 Grete blowen bladdyrs he brake And thay gave a gret crake. *a* **1520** *Myrr. Our Ladye* 17 Though hys harte were stretched out..as a blather full of wynde. **1595** SPENSER *Col. Clout* 717 Bladders blowen up with wynd, That being prickt do vanish into noughts. **1613** SHAKS. *Hen. VIII*, III. ii. 359 Little wanton Boyes that swim on bladders. **1717** LADY M. W. MONTAGU *Lett.* xxxvii. I. 145 As if a foreigner should take his ideas of English music from the bladder and string. **1782** WOLCOTT (P. Pindar) *3rd Ode to R.A.'s*, Learn to squeeze the colours from the bladders. **1783** COWPER *Task* I. 585 With dance, And music of the bladder and the bag. **1862** MRS. BEETON *Cookery Bk.* §194 Put it [lard] into small jars or bladders for use.

4. The substance of a sheep's or ox's bladder used for air-tight coverings.

1769 MRS. RAFFALD *Eng. Housekpr.* (1778) 347 Tie them down with a bladder and paper over it. **1796** MRS. GLASSE *Cookery* xviii. 294 Cover them close with a bladder and leather. **1827** FARADAY *Chem. Manip.* xviii. 477 Moistened bladder is in constant requisition.

5. A filmy cavity full of air, a vesicle, a bubble.

1702 *Lond. Gaz.* No. 3776/4 Looking-Glass Plates..free from Bladders, Veins, and Fowlness. **1761** CHURCHILL *Rosciad* 870 Behold the pipe-drawn bladders circling swim. **1856** *Enquire Within* (1862) 82 If little bladders appear, it has attained that degree.

6. a. *fig.* Anything inflated and hollow, like a blown-up bladder.

1589 *Pappe w. Hatchet* (1844) 27 A bladder of worldlie winde which swells in their hearts. **1627** SANDERSON *Serm.* I. 283 Prick the bladder of our pride. **1649** G. DANIEL *Trinarch., Rich. II*, clxxvii, Hee..With former Titles swolne, vnwillingly Would loose that Bladder. **1734** POPE *Donne Sat.* iv. 205 Such as swell this bladder of a court.

b. An inflated pretentious man; 'a wind-bag.'

1579 TOMSON *Calvin's Serm. Tim.* 279/2 Them that are harebraines and bladders full of winde. **1616** R. C. *Times' Whis.* iii. 1115 Thou bladder full puft vp with vanity. **1840** DICKENS *Barn. Rudge* lxii, My friend the noble captain—the illustrious general—the bladder.

c. ***bladder of lard***: a bald-headed or fat person. *slang.*

1864 in HOTTEN *Slang Dict.* **1886** *Athenæum* 31 July 142/1 An elderly Jew money-lender, whom she afterwards describes to her admiring friends as a 'bladder of lard', a graceful reference to his baldness and tendency to stoutness. **1943** W. DE LA MARE *Magic Jacket* 24 Here's that bladder-of-lard, schoolmaster Smiles, saying exactly the same thing.

d. *slang* (chiefly *U.S.*). A newspaper, esp. a poor one. Cf. BLAT *sb.*[2]

1936 MENCKEN *Amer. Lang.* (ed. 4) 159 Other etymologists..have discerned German influences..in the common use of *Bladder* as a derisory title for a small and bad newspaper [cf. G. *blätter* newspapers]. **1937** D. RUNYON in *Collier's* 16 Jan. 8/2 In a bundle of old magazines and newspapers.., he comes upon a bladder that is called the Matrimonial Tribune. **1973** *Observer* 7 Jan. 9/1 The news of your return has caused hardly a ripple in the daily bladders.

7. *Bot.* **a.** The inflated pericarp of some plants.

1578 LYTE *Dodoens* III. xc. 444 The flowers bring foorth rounde balles, or blasted bladders. **1867** BAKER *Nile Tribut.* ii. 30 This vegetable silk is contained in a soft pod or bladder about the size of an orange.

b. A hollow vesicle occurring as an appendage of several plants, as the genus *Utricularia*, and various sea-weeds. Cf. AIR-BLADDER.

1789 LIGHTFOOT *Flora Scot.* II. 904 Bladder Fucus..In the disc or surface are immersed hollow sphærical or oval air-bladders. **1854** BALFOUR *Bot.* §973. 473 Bladderworts..so called on account of the utricles or bladders connected with the leaves. **1875** DARWIN *Insect. Pl.* xvii, The real use of the bladders is to capture small aquatic animals.

†**8.** ? A plant. *Obs.*

a **1500** in Wr.-Wülcker *Voc.* 568 *Berula*, Bleddere. [*Berula* = 'a herb, called also cardamine.']

9. *attrib.* and *Comb.*, as ***bladder chops***; ***bladder-less***, ***-like***, ***-puffed***, adjs.

1549 LATIMER *Serm. bef. Edw. VI*, (Arb.) 66 These bledder puffed vp wylye men. **1610** HEALEY *St. Aug. Citie of God* 607 All the bladder-like humors of vaine glory. **1611** *Wom. is Weather Cock* IV. ii, in Hazl. *Dodsl.* II. 67 Thy bladder-chops and thy robustious words. **1698** J. PETIVER in *Phil. Trans.* XX. 324 A turgid bladder-like Pod. **1847** TODD *Cycl. Anat. & Phys.* III. 253/2 The bladder scirrhus of Dr. Benedict is nothing more than this form of hydatid disease. **1881** *Jrnl. Botany* X. 28 Bladderless and thick-leaved.

10. Special comb., as **bladder-angling**, fishing with a hook fixed to an inflated bladder; **bladder-brand**, a local name of the Bunt; **bladder-campion**, the common book-name of *Silene inflata*, from the inflated calyx; **bladder-fern**, a fern of the genus *Cystopteris*, from their bladder-like indusia; **bladder-fish**, apparently a variety of the globe-fish, *Tetraodon ocellatus*; **bladder-glass**, a glass vessel covered at one end with a piece of bladder, for showing the atmospheric pressure, by the bursting in of the bladder when the air is exhausted from the vessel; **bladder-green**, a green pigment obtained from the Common Buckthorn (*Rhamnus catharticus*), sap-green; **bladder-herb**, a name of the Winter Cherry, from its inflated calyx; **bladder-hole** (see quot.); **bladder-kelp** (= *bladder-wrack*); **bladder lard**, lard put up for sale in bladders, used spec. as the trade name for lard of the best quality; **bladder-nose**, a species of seal; **bladder-nut**, the fruit of a kind of shrub, *Staphylea pinnata*, contained in bladder-like pods; also the shrub itself; **bladder-plum** (see quot.); **bladder-pot**, English name of the *Physolobium*, a species of Leguminosæ of South-west Australia; the American Bladder-pod is *Vesicaria Shortii*; **bladder-seed**, English name of the *Physospermum*, from the loose outer coating of the undeveloped fruit; **bladder-senna**, the *Colutea arborescens*, so called from its distended pods, and the fact that its leaves are sometimes mixed with senna leaves; *Sutherlandia frutescens*, a showy shrub of the Cape of Good Hope is found in English gardens under the name of the Cape Bladder-senna (*Treas. Bot.*); **bladder-snout** (= *bladder-wort*); **bladder-tangle** (= *bladder-wrack*); **bladder-tree**, the North American species of the Bladder-nut tree (*Staphylea trifoliata*); **bladder-weed** (= *bladder-wrack*); **bladder worm**, the larva of a tapeworm in its encysted state; a hydatid; **bladder-wort**, a genus of water-plants, *Utricularia* [of which the word is a mod. transl.], distinguished by the small bags on roots, stems, and leaves, filled with air, which keep them afloat during the period of flowering; **bladder-wrack**, a species of sea-weed (*Fucus vesiculosus*), with air bladders in the substance of the fronds.

1883 *Gd. Words* Nov. 736/1 Bunt..is known by various names..as smut-balls, *bladder-brand, stinking-rust, &c. **1828** J. E. SMITH *Eng. Flora* IV. 297 *Cystea.* *Bladder-fern. *Ibid.* 298 *C. fragilis.* Brittle Bladder-fern. **1961** R. W. BUTCHER *Brit. Flora* I. 154 The Common Bladder Fern grows in walls and rocky woods on the basic soils commonly in highland Britain and rarely in the eastern and southern portions. **1770** in *Phil. Trans.* LX. 526 The..property of rendring the poison of the *bladder-fish..more virulent. **1854** J. SCOFFERN in *Orr's Circ. Sc.* Chem. 296 If a bladder-glass..be laid flat on the plate of an air-pump..the full force of atmospheric pressure will take place externally on the tense membrane. **1830** LINDLEY *Nat. Syst. Bot.* 114 The green colour known under the name of *Bladder-green. **1789** MILLS in *Phil. Trans.* LXXX. 97 Higher up the hill is an hard chert, with a kind of *bladder-holes. **1835** KIRBY *Hab. & Inst. Anim.* I. ix. 294 [Periwinkles] appear to make the *bladder-kelp..a kind of submarine pasture. **1872** *Eng. Mech.* 11 Oct. 82/3 The fourth [sample] (a *bladder lard) contained 10 per cent. of water. **1578** LYTE *Dodoens* VI. lx. 735 Of the *Bladder Nut. **1741** *Compl. Fam. Piece* II. iii. 374 Several other Trees and Shrubs..are now in Flower, as.. Bladder Nut. **1869** MASTERS *Veg. Terat.* 465 The stone of plums is occasionally deficient, as in what are termed *bladder-plums; some of these, consisting merely of a thin bladder, are curiously like the pods of Colutea. **1794** MARTYN *Rousseau's Bot.* xxv. 360 Common *Bladder-Sena has an arboreous stem..It grows twelve or fourteen feet high. **1857** KINGSLEY *Two Y. Ago* I. 259 Every sea-snail crept to hide itself under the *bladder-tangle. **1858** *Bladder worm [see CYSTICERCAL *a.*]. **1949** *New Biol.* VII. 116 If pigs swallowed the eggs of *Taenia solium*, bladder-worms (*Cysticercus cellulosae*) developed in their flesh. **1815** *Encycl. Brit.* (ed. 5) IV. 90/1 Common *bladder-wort, or hooded milfoil, grows in stagnant waters. **1839** G. FRANCIS *Eng. Flora* 1 The curious Bladderwort, the roots of which are furnished with little air bags. **1789** LIGHTFOOT *Flora Scot.* II. 904 *Bladder Fucus or Common Sea Wrack. **1810** *Edin. Rev.* XVII. 146 The prickly tang..often grows intermixed with the bladder-wrack.

bladder, *v.* Also 6 **blader**, 7 **blather**. [f. prec.]

†**1.** *intr.* To swell out like, or into, a bladder.

c **1440** in Halliw. *Nugæ P.* 66 Avaryssia ys a souking sore, He bladdyrth and byldeth alle in my boure. **1543** TRAHERON *Vigo's Chirurg.* II. x. 23 Everye..pustle that bladereth.

†**2.** *trans.* To inflate; to puff *up*, swell *out*.

1610 G. FLETCHER *Christ's Vict.* II. lviii, A hollow globe of glasse..She full of emptiness had bladdered. *Ibid.* I. lxxii, Bladder'd vp with pride of his own merit. *a* **1625** BEAUM. & FL. I. li. (Halliw.) Fame Gathers but wind to blather up a name. **1649** G. DANIEL *Trinarch., Hen. IV*, xxiv, To amuse the world, and bladder out Light Braines. *Ibid. Rich. II*, xv, Bladder'd with Ambition.

3. To put into a bladder, as 'bladdered lard.' Hence '**bladdered** *ppl. a.*, '**bladdering** *vbl. sb.* and *ppl. a.*

1633 P. FLETCHER *Elisa* I. xxvi, Lest these goods might swell my bladder'd minde. **1672** DRYDEN *Conq. Granada* V. i. 168 'Till they have burst the bladder'd Cloud. **1697** —— *Vergil* Ded., They affect greatness in all they write: but it is a bladdered greatness. **1885** *Pall Mall G.* 3 Sept. 4 A line of glittering bladdered olive-green seaweed. **1612** WOODALL *Surg. Mate* (1653) 32 Bladderings of the skin.

'**bladderdash.** (A mixture of *bladder* and *balderdash.*)

1826 J. WILSON *Noct. Ambr.* Wks. 1855 I. 221 His Spital sermon..the most empty bladderdash that ever attempted to soar without gas.

bladderet ('blædərɛt). *Phys. rare.* [f. BLADDER *sb.* + -ET[1].] A small bladder; a vesicle.

1615 CROOKE *Body of Man* 200 Many vesicles or bladderets. **1656** DUGARD *Gate Lat. Unl.* §230. 63 The longish bladderet of the gall. **1883** W. JOLLY *Life J. Duncan* xvii. 172 The utricles or bladderets that give it its name.

bladderskate, obs. form of BLETHERSKATE.

bladdery ('blædərɪ), *a.* [f. BLADDER *sb.* + -Y[1].]

1. Of the nature of a bladder; thin and inflated; inflated and hollow. *lit.* and *fig.*

1794 MARTYN *Rousseau's Bot.* xxv. 370 A berry..with a bladdery pulp. **1810** CRABBE *Borough* ix, Th' entangled weeds..upborne on bladdery beads. **1831** *Fraser's Mag.* III. 343 Bladdery laudations. **1870** HOOKER *Stud. Flora* 51 Calyx bladdery.

2. Abounding in bladders or vesicles.

1798–9 COLERIDGE *Lines to Lady* ii, In dim cave with bladdery seaweed strewed. **1880** BROWNING *Pan & Luna* 60 The bladdery wave-worked yeast.

bladdry, -ie, variant of BLATHERY *Sc.*

blade (bleɪd), *sb.* Forms: 1 **blæd**, 4–5 **blad**, 5 **bladde**, **blaad(e**, **blayd**, 6 **blaid**, 3– **blade**. [Com. Teut.: OE. *blæd*, neut., (pl. *blado*, *bladu*) = OFris. *bled*, OS. *blad* (MDu. *blat*, Du. *blad*, LG. *blad*), OHG., MHG. *blat* (mod.G. *blatt*), ON. *blað* (Sw., Da. *blad*):—OTeut. **blado-*(*m*; perh. a ppl. formation (with suffix *-ðo- do*:—Aryan *-tó-*) from OTeut. verbal stem **blō̆-*, see BLOW *v.*[2], cognate with L. *flos*. The long vowel in ME. and modern Eng. appears to be derived from the oblique cases and plural, *blăd-es*, *blăd-o*, made in ME. into *blā-des*, *blā-de*. The 15th c. northern

spellings *blayd*, *blaid*, and Chaucer's dissyllabic *blade*, *bladde*, require explanation. The sense-history is notable: in German *blatt* is the general word for 'leaf,' *laub* being the foliage collectively of trees; in Norse 'herbs or plants have *blað*, trees have *lauf*'; but in OE. *léaf* is the general word for 'leaf' and 'foliage'; *blæd* occurs only once, (as it happens, poetically, in the *brád blado* of the plant of wickedness), and this sense is quite absent in ME., while that of the 'blade' of an oar (also in OE.), of a sword or knife, is frequent. It would almost seem then that the modern 'blade' of grass or corn is a later re-transfer from 'sword-blade'; while in regard to corn, there is some reason to suspect influence of med.L. *bladum*, OF. *bled* corn, wheat; at least these were evidently supposed to be the same word. The mod.Sc. 'cabbage-blade' also is prob. not directly connected with the OE.; but Norse influence may possibly have contributed to a retention of the vegetable sense in the north.]

I. Of plants.

1. The leaf of a herb or plant; originally perhaps (as in Icelandic) applied to those of all herbs, while *leaf* was used of the foliage of trees. Now applied *dial.* (e.g. in south of Scotland) to a broad flat leaf, as the outer leaves of cabbage or lettuce, the leaves of rhubarb, tobacco, etc.; in literary Eng. only poetically and vaguely for 'leaf.'

a **1000** *Cædmon's Gen.* (Gr.) 994 Brád blado. **1785** BURNS *Dr. Hornbook* xix, In a kail-blade..send it. **1864** SWINBURNE *Atalanta* 1357 The low lying melilote And all of goodliest blade and bloom that springs. **1877** BRYANT *Lit. People of Snow* 350 In shape like blades and blossoms of the field.

2. *spec.* **a.** The flat lanceolate leaves of grass and cereals; esp. such as spring from the root and appear first above ground; also the whole of such plants before the spike or ear appears. (Cf. 4: botanically the leaves of grass are all 'blade.')

c **1450** *Gloss.* in Wr.-Wülcker *Voc.* 583 *Festuca*, the blaad of corn or a strawe. **1523** FITZHERB. *Husb.* §84 Red wheate ..is the greatteste corne, and the brodeste blades, and the greatest strawe. **1577** B. GOOGE *Heresbach's Husb.* I. 27 The eare..fyrst appeareth enclosed in the blade. **1597** GERARD *Herbal* I. xl, From whence shoot foorth grassie blades or leaues. **1611** BIBLE *Mark* iv. 28 First the blade, then the eare, after that the full corne in the eare. **1670** *Janua Ling.* xii. §92 Corn raiseth it self up into a blade. **1727** SWIFT *Gulliver* II. vii, Who ever could make two ears of corn, or two blades of grass, to grow..where only one grew before, would deserve better of mankind..than the whole race of politicians. **1849** ROBERTSON *Serm.* Ser. I. ii. (1866) 37 Disappointed at the delay which ensues before the blade breaks the soil.

b. ***in the blade***: while there is as yet only blade or leaf, not yet in the ear. Also *fig.*

1584 R. SCOT *Disc. Witchcr.* I. iv, Transferre corne in the blade from one place to another. **1589** *Pappe w. Hatchet* D iij b, Vnripened youthes, whose wisedomes are yet in the blade. **1601** SHAKS. *All's Well* v. iii. 6 Naturall rebellion done i'th blade of youth. **1834** PRINGLE *Afr. Sk.* xiv. 472 His corn was in the blade. **1847** TENNYSON *Princess* I. 31, I had been, While life was yet in bud and blade, betroth'd.

†**c.** The grassy leaves of other endogens. *Obs.*

1578 LYTE *Dodoens* II. xxxvi. 195 The small floure Deluce, hath narrow long blades, almost like the leaues of the right Gladyn. *Ibid.* v. lxxiii. 640 Onyon hath leaues or blades almost like garlike. **1585** LLOYD *Treas. Health* Qj, Take borage and leke blades. **1611** GUILLIM *Heraldrie* III. x. 115 The field is sable, three Lilies slipped, their..blades argent.

†**d.** Corn, growing corn, corn-crop. *Obs.* [Taken as a translation of med.L. *bladum*, F. *bled*, *blé*.]

1553 EDEN *Treat. New Ind.* (Arb.) 26 Nere vnto the citie of Caigui groweth plentie of blade and ryce. **1555** —— *Decades W. Ind.* II. ix. (Arb.) 130 Lykewyse blades, settes, slippes, grasses, suger canes.

†**3. a.** ? A pointed shoot or 'spire' of any plant. *Obs.*

c **1440** *Anc. Cookery* in *Househ. Ord.* (1790) 445 Take the blades of fenell. *c* **1440** *Promp. Parv.* 37 Blade of an herbe [**1499** blad or blade], *tirsus.* **1552** HULOET, Blade of a chiboll or oynion, *talia.* **1570** LEVINS *Manip.* 8 Blade of an herb, *talia.* **1634** T. HORNE *Janua Ling.* Index post., The blade of an hearb, *talea.*

†**b.** Applied by Grew to the 'style' of composite flowers. *Obs.*

1674 GREW *Anat. Plants* v. §20 The Sheath, after some time, dividing at the top, from within its Concave the Third and innermost part of the Suit, sc. the Blade, advances and displays itself.

4. *Bot.* The broad, thin, expanded part of a leaf, as opposed to the petiole or foot-stalk; the lamina or limb; also the corresponding part of a petal.

1835 LINDLEY *Introd. Bot.* (1848) I. 260 The Blade..is subject to many diversities of figure and division. **1870** HOOKER *Stud. Flora* 52 Petals with an appendage at the base of the blade. **1872** OLIVER *Elem. Bot.* I. i. 5 Foliage-leaves.. consist of petiole and blade, or of blade only; the blade being spread out horizontally.

II. Of other things.

5. a. The broad, flattened, leaf-like part (as distinguished from the shank or handle) of any instrument or utensil, as a paddle, oar, battledore, bat, spade, forceps; from that of a paddle or oar (a very ancient sense) extended to the parts of a whale's tail, a paddle wheel, or screw propeller, which act similarly upon the water.

c **1000** ÆLFRIC *Gloss.* in Wr.-Wülcker *Voc.* 167 *Palmula*, roðres blæd. *c* **1050** *Ags. Gloss.* ibid. 182 *Palmula*, arblæd. **1674** PETTY *Disc. bef. R. Soc.* 59 Suppose, that the Oars remain the same length, but that the Blade be doubled. **1770** ROBERTSON in *Phil. Trans.* LX. 321 The tail, as in all the whale tribe, was placed horizontal a little forked; the blades were of a wedge shape, and fourteen feet from tip to tip. **1835** TODD *Cycl. Anat. & Phys.* I. 224/2 Seized between the blades of a forceps. **1854** G. B. RICHARDSON *Univ. Code* v. 7602 How many blades have you to screw propeller? **1880** V. L. CAMERON *Fut. Highw.* II. xiii. 274 A spade with a blade the size of the palm of one's hand. **1886** HOLMES *Mortal Antip.* ii, Their blades flashed through the water.

b. The front flat part of the tongue.

1877 SWEET *Handbk. Phonetics* 2 Of the tongue we distinguish..the 'blade' which includes the upper surface of the tongue immediately behind the point. 'Lower blade' implies..the lower..surface.

c. A vane upon the circumference of a revolving cylinder or disc of a turbine.

1887 *Encycl. Brit.* XXII. 517/1 Attempts have been made ..to devise steam-engines of the turbine class, where rotation of a wheel is produced..by impact of a jet [of steam] upon revolving blades. **1900** [see TURBINE 1 b]. **1904** GOODCHILD & TWENEY *Technol. & Sci. Dict.* 795/2 [In an impulse turbine]..the water rushes with high velocity through a series of jets or nozzles and impinges on suitably shaped blades.

d. *Aeronaut.* A part of the propeller of an aeroplane or rotary-wing aircraft which acts upon the air. Also *attrib.*

1907 W. M. VARLEY tr. *Moedebeck's Aeronautics* xxv. 421 A screw-propeller is built up usually of two or more blades. **1916** H. BARBER *Aeroplane Speaks* iv. 115 The propeller screws through the air, and its blades..secure a reaction. **1920** *Flight* XII. 1309/1 Sketch of a sectioned blade root. **1958** *Chambers's Techn. Dict.* 960/2 *Blade loading*, the thrust of a helicopter rotor divided by the total area of the blades.

e. = ***switch-blade*** (see SWITCH *sb.* 9).

1920 *Whittaker's Electr. Engin. Pocket-Bk.* (ed. 4) 323 The blades of isolating switches should be locked in position.

6. a. The thin cutting part of an edged tool or weapon, as distinguished from the handle.

1330 R. BRUNNE *Chron.* I. 350 Caliborne, þat gode brond .. Ten fote longe was þen þe blade. *c* **1386** CHAUCER *Reeves T.* 10 And of a swerd ful trenchaunt was the blade. *c* **1450** *Nominale* in Wr.-Wülcker *Voc.* 735 *Sindula*, a blayd [among parts of a knife]. **1530** PALSGR. 198/2 Blade of a knyfe, *alumelle.* **1611** BIBLE *Judges* iii. 22 The haft also went in after the blade. **1677** MOXON *Mech. Exerc.* (1703) 114 Pricker. Is vulgarly called an Awl: Yet..it hath most commonly a square blade, which enters the Wood better than a round blade will. **1720** *Lond. Gaz.* No. 5852/12 Lost..a..Sword ..the Blade a little rusty. **1831** J. HOLLAND *Manuf. Metals* I. 280 A penknife blade is formed at two heats. **1849–52** TODD *Cycl. Anat. & Phys.* IV. 913 The blade of the sutorial tooth. **1880** BIRDWOOD *Ind. Art* II. 3 The blades of Damascus..were in fact of Indian iron.

b. *Archæol.* A long, narrow flint-flake, used esp. as a tool in prehistoric times (see quot. 1959). Freq. *attrib.*, as ***blade-axe***, ***-culture***, ***-tool***.

1921 M. C. BURKITT *Prehistory* iv. 65 While long flakes or blades are being struck off a core, vibrations transverse to the blow itself are set up in the flake or blade. **1926** R. A. SMITH *Flints* 29 (*caption*) A blade-scraper. *Ibid.* 30 Graving-tools..are generally made from flakes, preferably blades (flakes with the side-edges parallel and longer than the ends). **1935** HUXLEY & HADDON *We Europeans* ii. 53 Various types of Homo sapiens from Africa and Asia whose implements are typically..blade tools, a form of flake technique. **1937** *Discovery* Sept. 287/2 Blade-axes, chisels, spear-heads. **1943** J. & C. HAWKES *Prehist. Britain* i. 21 The late Palæolithic hunters had a much more delicate and specialized equipment than their predecessors, that is distinguished from the core and flake forms by the general name of 'blade' culture. **1959** J. D. CLARK *Prehist. S. Afr.* v. 111 The lump is called a *core*..and the pieces removed are known as *flakes* or, if they are long and narrow, they are called *blades*.

7. a. The blade being the essential part of such weapons etc. is often put for the whole, esp. in poetry and literary language.

c **1325** *E.E. Allit. P.* B. 1105 Nauþer to cout ne to kerue, with knyf ne wyth egge, For-þy brek he þe bred blades wythouten. *c* **1386** CHAUCER *Prol.* 618 A long surcote of pers vp on he hade [*v.r.* haade, hadde] And by his syde he baar a rusty blade [so 4 MSS.; *v.r.* blaade, bladde]. *c* **1460** *Towneley Myst.* 40 The shynyng of youre bright blayde It gars me quake for ferd to dee. **1583** STANYHURST *Æneis* I. (Arb.) 23 Theyre blades they brandisht. **1599** SHAKS. *Much Ado* v. i. 190 You breake iests as braggards do their blades. **1776** GIBBON *Decl. & F.* I. 13 He drew his sword..a short well-tempered Spanish blade. **1832** MACAULAY *Armada* 28 Ho! gunners, fire a loud salute: ho! gallants, draw your blades.

b. *fig.* (Cf. *weapon.*)

1692 A. PITCAIRNE *Babell* 287 He did his trustie tongue unsheath..It was a blade that he could trust. **1735** OLDYS *Life Raleigh* Wks. 1829 I. 384 Cecyll..play'd a smooth edge upon Ralegh throughout the trial; his blade seemed ever anointed with the balsam of compliment or apology.

c. Usu. *pl.* Hand shears for shearing sheep. Also *attrib. Austral.* and *N.Z.*

1905 A. B. PATERSON *Old Bush Songs* 26 All among the wool, boys, Keep your wide blades full, boys. **1917** *N.Z. Jrnl. Agric.* 20 Sept. 134 The majority of the larger sheep-owners..have come to recognize the advantages of 'machines' over 'blades'. **1923** W. PERRY et al. *Sheep Farming in N.Z.* vi. 83 In some parts there is a reaction in favour of blade shearing. **1945** BAKER *Austral. Lang.* iii. 64 Shearers have also been called..*bladesmen*, although the last term is going out of fashion because most shearing is now done with machines.

8. a. A broad flattened bone or part of a bone, as the ***cheek blades***, ***jaw-blades***; esp. the flat, triangular-shaped bone of the shoulder called the ***shoulder-blade*** or ***blade-bone***, the scapula; also the corresponding bone of the fore leg of animals.

b. One of the scythe-shaped plates in which whalebone occurs.

a **1300** *Havelok* 2644 Bi the shudre-blade The sharpe swerd let wade. **1398** TREVISA *Barth. De P.R.* v. xxvi. (1495) 135 Sholder blades ben..hight blades for they ben sharpe as a brode swerde. **1535** COVERDALE *Tob.* vi. 3 Take him by the cheke blade, and drawe him to the. **1600** CHAPMAN *Iliad* v. 577 Atrides' lance did gore Pylemens shoulder in the blade. **1663** BUTLER *Hud.* I. i. 20 Nor put up Blow, but that which laid Right worshipful on Shoulder-blade. **1802** BINGLEY *Anim. Biog.* (1813) II. 22 A Whale, the longest blade of whose mouth measures nine or ten feet. **1878** J. MARSHALL *Anat. Artists* 17 The two scapulæ, shoulder bones, or blade-bones.

9. Used of other things; as a ***blade of mace***.

1653 WALTON *Angler* 158 Mixt, with a blade or two of Mace. **1677** MOXON *Mech. Exerc.* (1703) 231 Put the blades of the Quadrants into two Slits. *a* **1718** PENN *Tracts* Wks. 1726 I. 498 That he ever took..one Clove, Nutmeg, Blade of Mace, or Skain of Silk..I utterly deny. **1825** S. & S. ADAMS *Compl. Servant* 97 Put a blade of mace, and a quartered nutmeg into a quart of cream. **1856** KANE *Arct. Exp.* II. i. 17 Take a blade of bone, and scrape off all the ice from your furs.

10. Senses of doubtful origin: **a.** *Arch.*

1851 *Dict. Archit.*, *Blade*, a word sometimes applied, as well as Back, to the principal rafter of a roof. **1879** *Shropshire Gloss.* (E.D.S.), *Blade*, that timber in a roof which goes at an angle from the top of the 'king-post' to the beam of the 'principal.'

†**b.** A staff, pole, shaft. Also found as *blede.*

1559 *Wills & Inv. N.C.* (1853) 170 Two long wayne blayds ..9 ashilltresse and a plowe. **1627** JACKSON *Creed* VII. xviii. §12 To receive the prize, or (as the original word imports) to snatch it from the blede or staff whereto they run.

†**c.** ***blades***: a spindle for winding yarn upon.

c **1475** *Gloss.* in Wr.-Wülcker *Voc.* 794 *Hoc girgillum*, a bladys. *Hic virgillus*, a yerwyndylleblad. **1530** PALSGR. 184 *Vnes tournettes*, a payre of wyndynge blades. *Ibid.* 646, I ontwyne yarne of the spyndel or blades. **1552** HULOET, Blades or yarne wyndles, an instrumente of huswyfery, *girgillus, volutorium.*

III. Applied to a man. [Prob. connected with senses 6, 7, though whether as a fig. use of these, or as a wielder of a blade, does not appear from the 83 earliest quotations examined.]

11. a. A gallant, a free-and-easy fellow, a good fellow; 'fellow', generally familiarly laudatory, sometimes good-naturedly contemptuous. (The original sense is difficult to seize: Bailey 1730 says, 'a bravo, an Hector; also a spruce fellow, a beau'; Johnson 'a brisk man, either fierce or gay, called so in contempt.') (Now colloquial or slangy: in literature, chiefly a reminiscence of the eighteenth century.)

1592 SHAKS. *Rom. & Jul.* II. iv. 31 By Iesu a very good blade, a very tall man. **1640** NABBES *Bride* II. i, Go carry the blades in the Lion a pottle of Sack from me. **1658** USSHER *Ann.* 159 Sending for such..as he knew to be blades, and had good hearts and head-peeces of their owne. **1667** PEPYS *Diary* (1879) IV. 354 As the present fashion among the blades is. **1705** HICKERINGILL *Priest-Cr.* II. v. 57 These are the Blades must do all, though they do all ill. **1760** *Lond. Mag.* XXIX. 224 Gentlemen of the town, as a sort of Blades may be well y'clep'd. **1818** COBBETT *Resid. U.S.* (1822) 354 A blade whom I took for a decent tailor.

b. usually taking force and colour from an attribute: e.g. *brave*, *stout*, *gallant*, *fighting*, *swaggering*, *swashing*, *bullying*, *blustering*, *dashing*, *rattling*, *roaring*, *roistering*, *jolly*, *lively*, *wild*, *comical*, *fantastical*, *cynical*, *crafty*, *knowing*, *saucy*, *worthy*, *old*, *young*, etc.

c **1600** *Rob. Hood* (Ritson) II. vi. 73 This is a mad blade, the butchers then said. **1629** FORD *Lover's Melanch.* I. ii. (1839) 4 He's an honest blade, though he be blunt. **1646** EVELYN *Mem.* (1857) I. 243 A true old blade, and had been a very curious virtuoso, etc. **1649** C. WALKER *Hist. Indep.* II. 184 Those free spirited Blades whom Oliver raised into a Mutiny. **1682** N. O. tr. *Boileau's Lutrin* I. Argt. 2 Three swashing Blades. **1714** ELLWOOD *Autobiog.* (1765) 143 These two Baptists were topping Blades. **1726** AMHERST *Terræ Fil.* 185 [In] All-Souls college one afternoon, several jovial blades..were sitting there over a pipe and a bottle. **1779** JOHNSON *Lett.* II. ccxviii. 75 When we meet we will be jolly blades. **1818** SCOTT *Hrt. Midl.* i, Two dashing young blades. **1822** W. IRVING *Braceb. Hall* ix. 75 He was one of the most roaring blades of the neighbourhood. **1840** DICKENS *Barn. Rudge* v, He's a knowing blade. **1857** SIR F. PALGRAVE *Norm. & Eng.* II. 443 The clever old crafty blade spoke out with..a thorough knowledge.

c. sometimes with local or official attribute.

c **1626** *Dick of Devon* II. i. in Bullen *O. Pl.* II. 26 My Devonshire blade, honest Dick Pike. **1638** SUCKLING *Goblins* in *Fragm. Aur.* (1646) 35 [He] askes much after certaine Brittish blades, One Shakespeare and Fletcher. **1663** *Hist. Cromwell* in *Select. Harl. Misc.* (1793) 367 [Cromwell] packs up a juncto of army blades..who constitute a high court of justice. **1755** CARTE *Hist. Eng.* IV. 406 Exposed to any sudden attempt from..the Buckinghamshire blades. **1882** J. GREENWOOD *Tag, Rag & Co.* xiii. 106 Adventures of a keen Yorkshire blade.

IV. **12.** *Comb.* and *Attrib.*, as ***blade-forger***, ***-metal***, ***-mill***, ***-smith***, etc.; ***blade-like***, ***-wise*** adj.

and adv.; also **blade-bone**, the shoulder-blade, the corresponding bone of animals and 'joint' of meat; **blade-consonant** *Phonetics*, a consonant formed with the blade of the tongue; also **blade-point** (see quot. 1890); **blade-fish**, one of the Ribbon-fishes (*Trichiurus lepturus*); **blade-spring**, a form of spring used to hold piston rings in place; **blade-work**, work done with the blade of an oar.

a **1678** MARVELL *Life* Wks. 1776 III. 463, I shall have the sweet *blade-bone broiled. **1845** DISRAELI *Sybil* III. iv, A deformity occasioned by the displacement of the bladebone. **1877** SWEET *Handbk. Phonetics* 48 A blade consonant rather advanced. **1890** SWEET *Primer of Spoken Eng.* 8 The *blade*-consonant *s* is formed with the 'blade' or flattened point of the tongue; if the tongue is retracted from this position, and the point raised, we get the *blade-point* consonant ʃ in 'fish'. **1831** J. HOLLAND *Manuf. Metals* I. 300 Hammers..used by the *blade-forgers. **1859** TODD *Cycl. Anat. & Phys.* V. 157/1 The shaft being long and *blade-like. **1645** MILTON *Colast.* Wks. (1851) 357 The men of Toledo had store of good *blade-mettle. *c* **1400** *Destr. Troy* v. 1592 Bochers, *bladsmythis, baxters. **1569** *Wills & Inv. N.C.* I. (1835) 301 John Tedcastle of Gatisheid, blaidsmith. **1863** CAMPIN *Mech. Engin.* 130 Four arms, which serve a double purpose, connecting the boss with the top and bottom of the piston, and carrying at their extremities the *blade-springs. **1905** *Daily Chron.* 30 Mar. 6/7 Their *blade work is not pretty, the finish not being clean, and the feather frequently under water. **1959** *Times* 13 Mar. 18/1 They [*sc.* the Cambridge crew] went up quickly, in spite of some dirty bladework.

blade (bleɪd), *v.* [f. prec. sb. Cf. Ger. *blatten* in sense 1.]

1. *trans.* To take off the blades (senses 1, 3). *dial.*

c **1440** *Promp. Parv.* 37 Bladyn herbys, or take away the bladys, *detirso.* **1818** *Edin. Mag.* Sept. 155 (JAM.) When she had gane out to blade some kail for the pat. **1880** *Antrim & Down Gloss.* (E.D.S.), *To Blade mangles*, to take the outside leaves off growing mangolds.

2. To provide with a (cutting) blade.

c **1440** *Promp. Parv.* 37 Bladyn haftys, *scindulo.* **1801** W. TAYLOR in *Month. Mag.* XII. 590 To blade the prow of the gondola of embassy.

3. *intr.* To put forth blades or leaves.

1601 HOLLAND *Pliny* XVIII. xvii, Otherwise the corn would never spindle, but blade still, and run all to leafe. **1633** P. FLETCHER *Elisa* II. xxxv, Down falls her glorious leaf, and never more it bladeth. **1869** BLACKMORE *Lorna D.* iv, Grass was blading out upon it.

†**4.** *to blade it*: to fight. *to blade it out*: to fight a matter out with the sword. *Obs.*

1571 R. EDWARDS *Damon & P.* in *Dodsley* (1780) I. 194 Rather than I wyll lose the spoyle, I wyll blade it out. **1589** *Pappe w. Hatchet* 15 None dare blade it with thee.

bladed ('bleɪdɪd), *ppl. a.* [f. BLADE *sb.* + -ED.]

1. Formed as a blade, lanceolate.

1578 LYTE *Dodoens* II. xxxvii. 195 The stinking flagge or Gladyn hath long narrow bladed leaves.

2. Having, producing, or abounding in blades.

1590 SHAKS. *Mids. N.* I. i. 211 Decking with liquid pearle the bladed grasse. **1687** DRYDEN *Hind & P.* I. 225 Nor bladed grass, nor bearded corn succeeds. **1727** THOMSON *Summer* 57 From the bladed field the fearful hare limps, awkward. **1814** WORDSW. *Excurs.* I. 740 The soft and bladed grass, Springing afresh.

b. *Her.* Having blades distinctly tinctured.

1611 GUILLIM *Heraldry* III. ix. 111 He beareth..three Wheate stalkes, Bladed and Eared.

3. ? Enclosed in the blade, not yet in full ear. (Cf. 'in the blade'; and see discussion in Furness.)

1605 SHAKS. *Macb.* IV. i. 55 Though bladed Corne be lodg'd, and Trees blown downe.

4. Stripped of the blades.

1611 COTGR., *Porreau sectil*, the cut Leeke..bladed Leeke. *Mod. Sc.* A bladed cabbage.

5. Having a blade, as an oar, a sword, etc.

1837 *New Month. Mag.* XLIX. 477 The broad bladed spear. **1859** *Merc. Mar. Mag.* (1860) VII. 17 The *Prince* was supplied with a three-bladed fan.

6. *Min.* Having a structure characterized by long narrow plates.

bladeless ('bleɪdlɪs), *a.* [f. BLADE *sb.* + -LESS.] Without or lacking a blade.

1857 *Blackw. Mag.* Oct. 486/1 Only the bladeless [*i.e.* grassless] rocks rang hollow mocking replies to his despairing 'Allah!' **1896** J. A. MITCHELL *Amos Judd* viii. 161 A bladeless jack-knife. **1927** *Glasgow Herald* 16 Apr. 9 A bladeless safety razor.

bladelet ('bleɪdlɪt). [see -LET.] A small blade.

1859 TODD *Cycl. Anat. & Phys.* V. 288/2 The corresponding secondary veins on the opposite side of the bladelet.

†**'blader.** *Obs.* [f. BLADE *sb.* + -ER.]

1. A maker of blades; a blade-smith.

1598 STOW *Surv.* xxviii. (1603) 247 Ordinances..made betwixt the Bladers, and the other Cutlers. **1766** ENTICK *London* IV. 357 Smiths, forgers of blades, and therefore called bladers.

2. The user of a blade; a swordsman.

1577 tr. *Bullinger's Decades* (1592) 398 That the sanctuaries should be a safegarde..not to bladers and cutters.

3. *Comb.*, as ***three-blader*** = three-bladed (knife).

1870 *Daily News* 12 July, Fancy the embarrassment of.. having to cut anything with a twenty blader.

blader, obs. form of BLADDER *sb.*

blading ('bleɪdɪŋ), *vbl. sb.* [f. BLADE *v.* + -ING[1].]

1. The shooting out into blade; sprouting.

1548 UDALL, etc. *Erasm. Par. Luke* viii, In the first bladyng it perished. **1653** T. BAILEY *Life Fisher* i. (1655) 7 The bladeing of the Field.

†**2.** Fighting with blades or swords. *Obs.*

1577 HOLINSHED *Descr. Irel.* in *Chron.* II. 17/2 He maketh blading his dailie breakefast. *a* **1624** BP. M. SMITH *Serm.* (1632) 278 Whence are quarrels, blading, wounds without cause?

3. *collect.* The blades of a turbine.

1905 W. J. A. LONDON *Brit. Pat. 13,883*, The blading of the high pressure section is mounted on a drum. **1955** *Times* 12 July 4/4 By extensive use of ceramics and liquid-cooled blading..the engine will operate at much higher temperatures than any other marine gas turbine being developed.

bladish (bleɪdɪʃ), *a. rare.* [f. BLADE *sb.* + -ISH.] Of or belonging to a 'blade'; blade-like.

1819 R. RABELAIS *Abeillard & Hel.* 15 That old beaux with bladish tricks.

blady ('bleɪdɪ), *a.* [f. BLADE *sb.* + -Y[1].] Characterized by a blade or blades; blade-like. Esp. in ***blady grass***; spec. the coarse grass *Imperata arundinacea* of Australia, Indonesia, etc.

1612 DRAYTON *Poly-olb.* xix. (1748) 333 The blady grass unwholesome..and harsh. **1645** DIGBY *Nat. Bodies* xxiv. (1658) 267 How should a bone here be hollow, there be blady. *a* **1758** J. DYER *To Aaron Hill* 41 With curling moss and blady grass o'ergrown. **1827** P. M. CUNNINGHAM *N.S. Wales* II. xxvii. 170 The roof being..thatched with blady grass. **1847** L. LEICHHARDT *Jrnl. Exped. Australia* iii. 59 The blady-grass had..begun to show its young shoots. **1864** G. M. HOPKINS *Poems* (1948) 120 I'll take in hand the blady stone And to my palm the point apply. **1918** *Chambers's Jrnl.* Feb. 140/1 Utilising the lalang or 'blady' grass, for the manufacture of paper-pulp.

blae (bleː, blɪə, bliː), *a.* (*sb.*) *Obs.* exc. *Sc.* and *north. dial.* Forms: 3-5 **bla, blaa,** 3 **bloa,** 3-6 **blo,** 4 **blowe,** 4-6 **bloo,** 5 **bloe,** 6- **blae,** (*dial.* 7 **bley,** 9 **blay, bleea,** 7- **blea**). [ME. *blo, bloo*, in north. dial. *bla, blaa*, a. ON. *blá* (sing. masc. *blár*) dark blue, livid (Sw. *blå*, Da. *blaa* blue), cogn. w. OHG. *blâo*:—**blâw* (MHG. *blâ, blâwer*, mod.G. *blau*), MLG. *blâ*(*w*, OFris. *blâw, blâu* (MDu. *blâ, blâu*, Du. *blaauw*), OE. (rare) *bláw* (or *blǽw*, whence *blǽwen*:—*bláwin*):—OTeut. **blǽwo-z* blue. The German *blâw* was adopted in Romanic (med.L. *blāvus*, OSp. *blavo*, Pr. *blau, blava*, F. *bleu*), whence it also passed into Eng. in the form *blew*, now BLUE, with the sense 'cæruleus,' while *bla, blo* retained the ONorse sense 'lividus.' The midland and southern Eng. form was *blo, bloe*, which survived till the 16th c.; but the word is now only northern Eng. and Sc. in the forms *blae, blea, bleae, bley, blay*. (These dialects have also *blue* in its ordinary sense, distinct from *blae*.)]

A. *adj.* **1.** Of a dark colour between black and blue; blackish blue; of the colour of the *blaeberry* (*Vaccinium Myrtillus*); livid; also, of a lighter shade, bluish grey, lead-coloured. (Sometimes perh., in early writers, simply = Blue.)

c **1250** *Gen. & Ex.* 637 Rein-bowe, men cleped reed and blo. **1330** R. BRUNNE *Chron.* 173 Þe sailes..som were blak & blo, Som were rede & grene. *c* **1375** ? BARBOUR *St. Justine* 733 Blac pic gert & brynstane bla. *c* **1384** CHAUCER *H. Fame* 1647 Suche a smoke gan out wende..Blak bloo [*v.r.* blo] grenyssh swart rede. *c* **1440** *Promp. Parv.* 40 Bloo, coloure, *lividus, luridus.* *c* **1460** *Towneley Myst.* 224 My barne..Bete as blo as lede. **1513** DOUGLAS *Æneis* VII. xiv. 10 That wondrus monstre, wyth wyd chaftis bla. **1565** GOLDING *Ovid's Met.* III. (1593) 56 Licking with his blo And blasting toong their sorie wounds. **1641** BEST *Farm. Bks.* 99 It is usually a blea, flinty, wheate..the meale of it is of a darkish, bley, and flinty colour. **1781** J. HUTTON *Tour to Caves* Gloss. (E.D.S.), *Blea*, a lead colour. **1796** J. MARSHALL *Yorksh.* (ed. 2) II. 65 The blue, blow, or lead-coloured flax—provincially, 'blea-line.' **1833** *Smuggler* 34 Knee-breeches and blay-thread stockings. **1875** ROBINSON *Whitby Gloss.* s.v. *Bleea*, As bleea as a whetstone. [Hence, the names of the *Blea* or *Blae Tarns*, in Langdale, Eskdale, and Borrowdale, of *Blea Water* in Mardale, and the *Bleas* by Ullswater, in the Lake district.]

b. *esp.* Applied to the complexion or colour of the human body, as affected by cold, or contusion: Livid. Hence ***black and blae***, now altered to *black and blue*: see BLACK *a.* 13.

? *a* **1200** *Leges Quat. Burgorum* (*Acts Parl. Sc.* I.) Si quis verberando fecerit aliquem blaa et blodi [cf. transl. 1609]. *c* **1300** in Wright *Lyric P.* xxix. 86 Ant thi bodi colde, thi ble waxeth blo. *a* **1340** HAMPOLE *Pr. Consc.* 5260 Alle bla and blody als he þan was, When he deyhed for mans trespas. *a* **1400** *Isumbras* 311 Made his flesche fulle blaa! *c* **1430** *Hymns to Virg.* (1867) 10 Hise sidis bloo and blodi were. *a* **1529** SKELTON *Prayers* Wks. I. 140 Thy body wan & blo. **1609** SKENE *Reg. Maj.* 130 Gif ane man strikes ane other, and makes him blae and bloudie. **1709** M. BRUCE *Soul-Conf.* 11 (JAM.) You will stand with a blae countenance before the tribunal of God. **1785** BURNS *Twa Herds* xii, Aft ha'e made us black and blae, Wi' vengefu' paws. *Mod. Sc.* Blae wi' cauld.

Hence † ***blae-making***.

1538 *Aberd. Reg.* V. 16 (JAM.) Conwict [= convicted] for the blud drawing, blamaking & strublens.

c. Applied to the colour of the sea.

c **1325** *E.E. Allit. P.* C. 134 Blowes boþe at my bode vpon blo watteres. *c* **1400** *Emare* 318 in Ritson *Metr. Rom.* II, The water so blo. **1503** HAWES *Examp. Virt.* x. 180 Ner lettynge of this water blo.

2. Of the weather: Bleak, sunless. [From the prevailing colour of the landscape.]

1513 DOUGLAS *Æneis* VII. Prol. 130 The mornyng bla, wan, and har. **1789** BURNS *Ep. J. Tennant* 3 This blae eastlin wind. **1818** *Edin. Mag.* 503 (JAM.) It was in a cauld blae hairst day. **1821** CLARE *Vill. Minstr.* II. 119 Though floods of winter bustling fall Adown the arches bleak and blea.

†**3.** Dark, black: only in the early comb. **blamon,** BLOMAN 'a blackamoor' [ON. *blámaðr*].

†**4.** Tawny. *Obs. rare.*

a **1400** *Gloss.* in *Rel. Ant.* I. 8 *Fulvus*, bloo.

5. Dingy-coloured, 'grey', as opposed to white; unbleached. [So OSp. *blavo*, though = F. *bleu*, meant 'yellowish grey.'] Usu. in form BLAY *a.*

B. *sb.* A bluish grey indurated clay occurring in thin slaty strata.

[*c* **1440** *Promp. Parv.* 40 Blo erþe, *argilla.*] **1724** FRASER in *State* 345 (JAM.) The mettals I discovered were a coarse free stone and blaes. **1757** *Phil. Trans.* L. 145 Another mineral that the miners call blaes is a cliffery stratum of a blueish colour. ? **1811** *Statist. Acc. Hebrides* 149 (JAM.) Blae (which is a kind of soft slate).

blae, Sc. form of BLEA *v.* to bleat.

blaeberry ('bleɪbərɪ, 'blɪə-). Also (5 **blabery**), 6 **ble-,** 9 **blea-, blay-, bleeaberry.** [f. BLAE + BERRY: in ON. *bláber*, Sw. *blåbär*, Du. *blaabær*.]

1. The common name in Scotland and the north of England of the BILBERRY or whortleberry (*Vaccinium Myrtillus*). Applied to fruit and plant.

[**1483** *Cath. Angl.* 33 A Blabery.] **1562** TURNER *Herbal* II. Lj, Takyng the bleberries or hurtel berries. *a* **1758** RAMSAY *Poems* (1800) II. 107 (JAM.) Gif I could find blae-berries ripe for thee. **1822** BEWICK *Mem.* 256 The creeping groundlings, the blea-berry, the wild strawberry, the hare-bell. **1861** GEIKIE in *Gd. Words* Feb. 76/1 Yonder pastoral glens, where we boys were wont to gather blaeberries and junipers. **1862** *Corn. Mag.* V. 457 Branches loaded with the tiny purple blae berry, the bloom yet fresh on them.

2. Also applied to cognate species.

1853 KANE *Grinnell Exp.* xix. (1856) 143 Here I saw the bleaberry (*vaccinium uliginosum*) in flower and in fruit. **1861** MISS PRATT *Flower. Pl.* III. 353.

†**blæd-fast**, *a. Obs.* [OE. *blǽd-fæst*, f. *blǽd* prosperity + *-fæst*, -FAST.] Prosperous; glorious.

a **1000** *Beowulf* 2602 Heo..abreat blæd-fæstne beorn. *c* **1205** LAY. 6986 Blæð-fest king. *Ibid.* 10100 He wes swiðe blæðfæst.

'blaeness. *north. dial.* (Frequent in ME. in the form **blonesse.**) [f. BLAE + -NESS.] 'Blae' quality; lividness as of a wound or stripe.

1382 WYCLIF *Ex.* xxi. 25 Wounde for wounde, blones for blones. **1398** TREVISA *Barth. De P.R.* V. xvii. (1495) 122 Bloones of lyppes. *Mod. Sc.* The blaeness of his lips.

†**blaff**, *v. Obs.* [perh. a. Du. and LG. *blaffen*, an imitative word (cf. BAFF *v.*[1]): cf. also ME. *wlaffen* in same sense.] To bark (as a dog).

1699 CAPT. COWLEY *Voy.* (1729) 6 Seals, which would rise out of the water, and blaff like a dog.

'blaflum, *sb. Sc.* Also **bleflum, blephum, blawflum, blafum.** Deception, imposition, hoax.

a **1661** RUTHERFORD *Lett.* (1765) I. ii. (JAM.) Many..when they go to take out their faith, they take out a fair nothing.. a bleflume. *a* **1662** R. BAILLIE *Lett.* (1775) I. 201 (JAM.) All his act was but a blephum. **1788** E. PICKEN *Poems* 63 (JAM.) Fine blaw-flums o' teas That grow abroad. **1880** PATTERSON *Antrim & Down Gloss.* (E.D.S.), *Blaflum, blafum*, nonsense; something said to mislead.

Hence **blaflumry, blaeflummery.**

1819 A. BALFOUR *Campbell* I. 328 (JAM.) A' that blaeflummery that's makin sic a haliballoo in the warld.

'blaflum, *v. trans. Sc.* To impose upon.

1728 RAMSAY *Wks.* (1848) I. 221 The chair Which bears him to blaflum the fair.

blag (blæg), *sb. slang.* [Etym. unknown.] Robbery (with violence); theft.

1885 *Session Paper* 30 July 471 There has been another *blag* down round here. **1936** J. CURTIS *Gilt Kid* 22, I don't want to say 'O.K.' and then find out that I've let myself in for..doing a blag on the crown jewels. **1960** *Observer* 24 Jan. 5/1 The top screwing teams, the ones who went in for the really big blags, violent robberies.

Hence **blag** *v.*, to rob (with violence); to steal. So **'blagger**, one who blags.

1933 C. E. LEACH *On Top of Underworld* x. 137 *Blag*, snatch a watch chain right off. **1938** F. D. SHARPE *S. of Flying Squad* i. 15 Blaggers, screwsmen, [etc.]..abound in the Underworld of London. *Ibid.* 329 'Johnny blagged the till'—Johnny took the till. **1945** J. HENRY *What Price Crime?* 93 Another is known as the 'blagger' or 'snatcher'. These are usually young louts who specialize in snatching ladies' handbags and bolting off.

‖**blague** (blag), *sb.* [Fr.] Pretentious falsehood, 'humbug.'

1837 CARLYLE *Fr. Rev.* (1857) II. III. v. vi. 313 The largest, most inspiring piece of blague manufactured, for some centuries. **1865** *Day of Rest* Oct. 580 That is all blague. **1886** HUXLEY in *Pall Mall G.* 13 Apr. 13/2 It believes in shibboleths and sentimental blague.

‖**blague**, *v.* [F. *blaguer*, f. the sb.] To tell lies.

1883 *Century Mag.* 743 She laughed and said I blagued.

‖**blagueur** (blagœ:r). [Fr. (Robert, 1808), f. *blague* BLAGUE *sb.* + *-eur* -ER[1].] One who talks pretentiously; a joker or teller of tall stories.

1883 *Sat. Rev.* 14 Apr. 467/2 [It is] not the laughter of the true humourist, but that of the professional *blagueur*. *c* **1903** WYNDHAM LEWIS *Lett.* (1963) 8, I went to a cabman in the rank, and he asked 5/–; so I left him as a blageur [*sic*]; but it appears that it is without the 4 mile radius, and it is 1/- a mile. **1950** A. L. ROWSE *Eng. of Elizabeth* xii. 515 That marvellous adventurer and *blagueur* Anthony Shirley of All Souls.

blah (blɑ:), *sb. colloq.* (orig. *U.S.*). Also **bla**, **blaa.** [Imitative.] Meaningless, insincere, or pretentious talk or writing; nonsense, bunkum. Also used as a derisive interjection. Freq. reduplicated.

1918 *Wine, Women & War* (1926) 136 [He] pulled old blah about 'service', 'doing one's bit', etc. **1921** *Collier's* 15 Jan. 10/3 Then a special announcer begin a long debate with himself which was mostly blah blah. **1922** S. LEWIS *Babbitt* xxx. 359 Why the dickens they want to put in their time listening to all that blaa. **1924** M. ARLEN *Green Hat* vi. 164 So you heard about it from that *femme fatale*, did you? Damn that man! Bla, bla, bla! **1927** *Observer* 10 July 28/1 England isn't fooling anyone with so much 'blah' about the world's greatest tournament. **1943** 'G. ORWELL' in *New Road* 151 Exactly similar blah is being written about the Red Army at this moment. **1958** E. H. CLEMENTS *Uncommon Cold* 229 A good deal of blah about waste of public money.

Hence **blah, blah-blah** *v. intr.*, to talk or write 'blah'.

1924 'W. FABIAN' *Sailors' Wives* iv. 56, I was just blahing to hear myself blah. **1931** ST. JOHN ERVINE in *Time & Tide* 12 Sept. 1057 That schoolmasters should permit him to blah-blah about his ignorance is a crime against the mind. **1942** 'G. ORWELL' *Diary* 18 Apr. in *Coll. Ess.* (1968) II. 419 The tactless utterances of Americans who for years have been blahing about 'Indian freedom' and British imperialism. **1945** —— in *Tribune* 14 Dec. 10/3 Instead of blah-blahing about the clean, healthy rivalry of the football field..it is more useful to inquire how and why this modern cult of sport arose.

blah, *a. slang.* [Cf. BLAH *sb.*]

1. Mad. (? orig. *U.S.*)

1924 *Telegr. & Teleph. Jrnl.* X. 68/2 The third class is hopeless... It consists of the people who, in New York slang, have gone 'blah'. **1928** A. E. W. MASON *Prisoner in Opal* xxiii. 276 More of your questions and I am blah.

2. Dull, unexciting; pretentious.

1937 N. MARSH *Vintage Murder* xi. 122 That fascinating blah stuff of hers goes down with the nitwits. **1955** H. ROTH *Sleeper* ix. 68 You must..have come to realize how blank and blah he made himself. **1959** J. VERNEY *Friday's Tunnel* iv. 49 One of those blah sneery voices like a butler in a film.

blahs (blɑ:z), *sb. pl. slang* (orig. and chiefly *U.S.*). [f. BLAH *a.* 2 (perh. infl. by *blues*).] Depression, despondency, low condition, esp. of spirits. Usu. ***the blahs.***

1969 *Life* 12 Dec. 40/1 The radicals are suffering from a case of the blahs, the liberals are frustrated. **1970** *Sunday Tel.* (Brisbane) 22 Feb. 92/1 Thursday was a day for the 'Blahs'—a lovely descriptive American expression for feeling washed out and down in the dumps and cranky. **1974** *Courier-Mail* (Brisbane) 25 July, I've got the Monday blahs. **1978** *Detroit Free Press* 5 Mar. D12/4 A good haircut, maybe some streaking to lift the winter blahs. **1982** *Fortune* 5 Apr. 54/2 The town's 4,800 first-class casino-hotel rooms are a long way from the 10,000 needed to attract the big conventions that would cure the off-season blahs.

blaik(e, var. BLAYK(E *a.* bleak, pale.

'**blaiken**, *v. Sc.* [f. prec.] To make pale.

1570 *Sempill Ballates* (1872) 50 Paill of the face, baith blaiknit, blude and ble.

blain (bleɪn). Forms: 1 **bleȝen**, 3 **blein(e**, 3–5 **bleyn(e**, 3–8 **blane**, 5–6 **blayn(e**, 6–7 **blaine**, 6– **blain.** [OE. *bleȝen* str. fem., = MDu. *bleine*, Du. *blein*, LG. *bleien*, Da. *blegn*; OTeut. form possibly **bleganâ-*: cf. OHG. *blehin-ougi* 'lippus.']

1. An inflammatory swelling or sore on the surface of the body, often accompanied by ulceration; a blister, botch, pustule; applied also to the eruptions in some pestilential diseases. Cf. CHILBLAIN.

c **1000** *Sax. Leechd.* I. 380 Wið þa bleȝene ȝenim niȝon æȝra and seoð hiȝ fæste. *a* **1225** *St. Marher.* 18 Barst on to bleinen þæt hit aras up oueral. *c* **1250** *Gen. & Ex.* 3027 Blein on erue and man. **1382** WYCLIF *Job* ii. 7 He smot Iob with the werste stinkende bleyne [**1388** wickid botche, COVERD. sore byles]. *c* **1440** *Bone Flor.* 2024 The fowlest mesell bredd Of pokkys and bleynes bloo. **1529** MORE *Comfort agst. Tribulat.* III. Wks. 1224/1 Yf his fynger dooe but ake of an hoate blaine. **1544** ASCHAM *Toxoph.* (Arb.) 49 A litle blayne ..in his finger, may kepe him. **1583** STUBBES *Anat. Abus.* (1877) 96 It bringeth ulcerations, scab, scurf, blain. **1612** WOODALL *Surg. Mate* Wks. (1653) 332 The third manifest and demonstrative sign of [the Plague]..is the Pestilential Blain. **1667** MILTON *P.L.* XII. 180 Botches and blaines must all his flesh imboss. **1850** LAYARD *Nineveh* vii. 154 Children ..covered with discoloured blains.

fig. **1866** *Lond. Rev.* 10 Mar. 276/1 Some moral blain has suddenly broken out on..a fair character.

2. 'A distemper incident to beasts, consisting in a bladder growing on the root of the tongue against the wind-pipe, which at length swelling, stops the breath' (Chambers *Cycl.* 1727–51).

¶ Jamieson's sense 'A mark left by a wound,' is apparently erroneous.

3. *Comb.* †**blain-grass**, ? clover; †**blain-worm**, some parasitic insect; also *fig.*

1570 LEVINS *Manip.* 35 Blaynegrasse, *trifolium.* **1657** BROME *Queen* v. viii. 123 Are you so tart, Court Blain-worm? **1658** ROWLAND *Mouffet's Theat. Ins.* 1000 In English it [the Buprestis] is called a Blainworm, or Troings. *a* **1722** LISLE *Husb.* (1752) 342 If the blain-worm be broken in the mouth of the cow..he knows no cure for it.

blain, *v.* [f. prec.] *trans.* To affect with blains; to blister. Hence **blained** *ppl. a.*, '**blaining** *vbl. sb.*

[*c* **1000** *Sax. Leechd.* II. 4 Wiþ ȝebleȝnadre tungan.] **1394** *P. Pl. Crede* 299 Nou han þei bucled schon for bleynynge of her heles. **1830** GALT in *Fraser's Mag.* I. 269 The recoiling boughs had..sorely blained..his cheeks.

blaise, -ze, blait, Sc. var. BLAZE, BLATE, BLEAT.

blait, obs. form of BLATE.

blaithrie, -dry, variants of BLATHERY.

blak, obs. form of BLACK and of BLAKE.

†**blake**, *a. Obs.* exc. *dial.* Also 3–4 **blac**, **blak.** [Chiefly northern: probably therefore, since OE. *á* remained in the north as *ā* (e.g. *ake, stane, mare*), *blake* was the direct phonetic descendant of OE. *blác* pale (in early southern ME. *bloc*, BLOKE), a common Teut. adj. = OS. *blêc*, ON. *bleikr*, OHG. *bleih*, OTeut. **blaiko-z* shining, white, pale, f. root of *blîkan* to shine, BLIK. Cf. the synonyms BLEAK, BLEYKE, BLOKE. In Eng. the notion of 'shining,' i.e. white from excess of light, passed entirely into that of 'pale,' i.e. white from deficiency of colour, dead white. This added to the formal confusion with BLACK, since 'dark' and 'pale' alike express deficiency or loss of colour.]

1. Pale, pallid, wan: implying deficiency or loss of colour, esp. of the ruddy hue of health, or of the full green of vegetation; of a sickly hue: thus passing on one side into 'ash-coloured, livid,' on another into 'withered yellow,' whence sense 3.

(Many early instances of *blake* may be examples of *blak* black, with final *e* inflexional or phonetic, the context leaving the sense uncertain. Some early forms written *blac, blak*, also stand for *blāk, blake*, and belong here. See what is said under BLACK of the confusion of the forms of *blæc* and *blác* already in OE.)

c **1205** LAY. 1888 Whil heo weoren blake..whil heo weoren ræde. —— 19890 Ænne stunde he wes blac..while he wes reod. *c* **1400** *St. Alexius* (Cott.) 236 So was he lene and blake of hewe. *c* **1420** *Anturs Arth.* li, Thayre blees weren so blake. Alle blake was thayre blees. *c* **1420** *Pallad. on Husb.* I. 187 The vynes blake awaie thowe take, eke greene And tender vynes kytte. **1530** PALSGR. 306 Blake, wan of colour. *c* **1596** *King & Barker* 7 in Hazl. *E.P.P.* I. 4 Blake kow heydys sat he apon.

2. Yellow. (Current in north England, from Cumberland to the Humber; but app. unknown in Scotland, and in the Eng. midlands.)

1691 RAY *N.C. Wds.*, *Blake*, Yellow, spoken of Butter and Cheese. As blake as a Paigle. **1851** *Cumberland Gloss.* s.v., As blake as a marigold. **1864** ATKINSON *Whitby Gloss.* s.v., As blake as butter. **1877** *Holderness Gloss.* 30 *Blake* [Hornsea and Bridlington], of a light yellow colour.

†**blake**, *v. Obs.* Forms: 1 **blácian**, 2–3 **blakien**, 3–4 **blaken**, 3–5 **blake.** [ME. *blāke(n*, was app. the north. repr. of OE. *blácian* to become pale, f. *blác* shining, white, pale: see BLAKE *a.* The normal southern form would have been *blokien, bloke(n*, of which there are a few 13th c. instances: see BLOKE *v.* In spelling, this vb. was confounded with *blǎkien, blǎken* to grow black or dark (see BLACK *v.*); and at length became obs., its place being taken by *bleyke(n, bleike(n* from ON. and by the cognate *bleke(n* and BLEACH.]

1. *intr.* To become pale.

1205 LAY. 19799 His neb bigon to blakien [**1250** blokie]. *Ibid.* 7524 He ne blakede no. *a* **1225** *St. Marhar.* 9 Hire bleo bigon to blakien. **1330** R. BRUNNE *Chron.* 183 Þo Normans ..of contenance gan blaken. *c* **1460** *Bone Flor.* 579 Hur ble beganne to blake.

2. *trans.* To make pale.

(Doubtful: Mätzner's example belongs to BLACK *v.* 2.)

Blake (bleɪk). The name of Lyman *Blake*, the inventor of a sewing-machine for boots and shoes, as in ***Blake-sewn***, whence ***Blake-sewer***, etc.

1895 *Daily News* 26 Mar. 6/7 A Levant goat quarter, whole satin golosh, blake sewn. **1921** *Dict. Occup. Terms* (1927) §414 *Machine operator, Blake*; *Blake sewer, Blake sole sewer*, a sole attacher who stitches sole of boot or shoe on to insole..with a Blake sewing machine, i.e. heavy sewing machine worked by power.

blake, early ME. form of BLACK *a.* and *v.*

†**blakeberyed.** *Obs.* Used by Chaucer with uncertain meaning. Skinner in 17th c. suggested 'sent to the realms of darkness'; others would connect it with BLACKBERRY.

c **1386** CHAUCER *Pard. Prol.* 78, I rekke neuere whan they been beryed, Though that hir soules goon a blakeberyed [so 5 MSS., *Lansd.* a blakberied, *Petw.* o blakburied].

Blakeian ('bleɪkɪən), *a.* Also **Blakean, Blakian.** [-IAN.] Of, pertaining to, or characteristic of William *Blake* (1757–1827), poet and painter, or his work.

1906 E. J. ELLIS *Poet. Wks. W. Blake* 337 In more Blakean terms, they are Albion as Ijim, bearing Tiriel on his shoulders between East and West. **1907** *Daily Chron.* 27 June 3/2 There is something Blakean in his artistic conception of the human form as typifying abstract energy. **1930** T. E. LAWRENCE *Lett.* (1938) 687 The idea of 'genitals being beauty' in the Blakian sense. **1952** S. SPENDER *Shelley* v. 40 The beautiful poem *To William Shelley*..has a Blakian simplicity and innocence. **1954** *Essays & Studies* VII. 110 Blake's 'Jerusalem'..is betrayed by Parry's tune, the inimitable Blakeian imagery being obliterated by the prevalent vociferation.

blakenes(s, obs. f. of BLACKNESS.

Blakey ('bleɪkɪ). Also **blakey.** The name of the manufacturer of a kind of metal protector for a boot (esp. a heel- or toe-cap), used *absol.* and †in the possessive, to designate such a protector. Cf. SEG *sb.*[3] (Formerly a proprietary name.)

1887 *Trade Marks Jrnl.* 9 Mar. 307 Blakey's boot protectors No. 58,882... John Blakey, trading also as E. Blakey and Sons, Lady Lane, Leeds; Manufacturer of boot protectors, machinist, and leather factor. **1889** *Ibid.* 3 July 617 Blakey... Metal boot protectors. John Blakey.., Leeds. **1969** *Daily Tel.* 15 Feb. 16/1 Their footsteps sounded each alike—no tip-tap of a high-heeled Miss, no rasp of the farmhand's blakeys. **1974** P. CAVE *Mama* (new ed.) ix. 71 Tucked into the waistband of his trousers was a wicked-looking knife, and heavy metal blakeys had been driven in to the front of his boots. **1980** *Times Lit. Suppl.* 20 June 717/4, I always wore Blakeys (the iron plates fixed to the heels of boots which struck wonderful sparks from the pavements) because they saved cobbler's bills.

blaky, obs. form of BLEAKY.

blamable: see BLAMEABLE.

blamange, -manger, obs. forms of BLANCMANGE.

blame (bleɪm), *v.* Also 3–4 **blam**, 3–6 **blamen**, (5 *Caxton* **blasmen**). [a. OF. *blâmer, blasmer* (= Pr. and OSp. *blasmar*, It. *biasimare* (:—*blasimare*) to blame):—late L. *blasphēmāre* to revile, reproach, ad. Gr. βλασφημεῖν to BLASPHEME; introduced into L. in the lang. of the New Test. The phonetic changes in *blasphemāre, blasimāre, blasmar, blasmer, blâmer*, and the modified sense, are due to the continuous popular use of the word; the original form and sense are reproduced in the learned or semi-popular *blaspheme*.]

1. *trans.* To find fault with; to censure (an action, a person *for* his action): the opposite of *to praise.*

c **1200** *Trin. Coll. Hom.* 73 Drede letteð þe mannes shrifte ..swiche men blameð þe prophete on þe sealm boc. *a* **1225** *Ancr. R.* 64 Ne he ne cunne ou nouðer blamen [*v.r.* lastin, laste] ne preisen. *c* **1386** CHAUCER *Man Lawes T.* 8 Thow blamest crist, and seist ful bitterly, He mysdeparteth richesse temporal. **1483** CAXTON *Cato* B iij, Thow oughtest not to blame ne dyspreyse other. **1523** LD. BERNERS *Froiss.* I. clxxxvi. 221 Of this aduenture the prouost was greatly blamed. **1596** SHAKS. *Tam. Shr.* III. ii. 27 Goe girle, I cannot blame thee now to weepe. **1633** HEYWOOD *Eng. Trav.* III. i. Wks. 1874 IV. 43 Who can blame him to absent himselfe from home? **1676** RAY *Corr.* (1848) 123, I had not blamed him had he acknowledged his authors. **1727** DE FOE *Syst. Magic* I. iii. (1840) 84 All they can blame him for. **1848** MACAULAY *Hist. Eng.* II. 77 To blame the revocation of the Edict of Nantes. **1875** JOWETT *Plato* (ed. 2) I. 80 We blame our fathers for letting us be spoiled.

†**2.** To address with rebuke; to reprove, chide, scold. *Obs.*

1297 R. GLOUC. 163 Bi fore hym he lette brynge ys men, & bi gan hem faste blame. **1382** WYCLIF *Luke* viii. 24 And he risynge blamyde the wynd, and the tempest of watir. **1483** CAXTON *G. de la Tour* F iv b, She shalle not make herself to be blamed ne to be bete. **1528** MORE *Heresyes* I. Wks. 116/1 The good kinge Dauyd..blamed his folishe wife. **1559** *Mirr. Mag., Jack Cade* v, No reproche can be to much to blame her.

†**3.** To bring into disrepute or discredit. *Obs.*

1596 SPENSER *F.Q.* VI. iii. 11 This ill state..To which she for his sake had weetingly Now brought herselfe, and blam'd her noble blood. **1611** BIBLE *2 Cor.* vi. 3 Giuing no offence in any thing, that the ministery be not blamed.

†**4.** To charge; to accuse (*of, with* a fault, etc.).

c **1340** *Cursor M.* 13027 (Trin.) He coom to blame þe kyng of synne. *c* **1400** MAUNDEV. vi. 69 A fayre Maiden was blamed with wrong, and sclaundred, that sche hadde don Fornycacyoun. **1483** *Cath. Angl.* 34 To Blame, *accusare, culpare.* **1583** GOLDING *Calvin on Deut.* viii. 44 So would men blame him of unfaithfulnesse. **1649** DRUMM. *Jas. III*, Wks. (1711) 61 He is blam'd of avarice.

5. To lay the blame on, reproach; to fix the responsibility upon; to make answerable. Also, *to blame* (something) *on* (or *on to*) (someone).

a **1300** *Cursor M.* 1102 To blam þe broiþer was þam laith. **1393** GOWER *Conf.* III. 158 Wherof full ofte netheles A king is blamed gilteles. **1481** CAXTON *Reynard* I. viii. (Arb.) 14, I shold be blasmed yf they dyde you ony harme. **1601** SHAKS. *All's Well* III. vi. 54 That was not to be blam'd in the command of the seruice: it was a disaster of warre. **1651** HOBBES *Leviath.* III. xl. 255 Blaming sometimes the Policy, sometimes the Religion. **1711** ADDISON *Spect.* No. 89 ¶2 She has no Body to blame for it but herself. **1835** *Fraser's Mag.* XI. 617, I call this bad management, and I blame it upon you. **1903** KIPLING *5 Nations* 22 We will blame it on the deep. **1910** —— *Rewards & Fairies* 175 If you can keep your head when all about you Are losing theirs and blaming it on you. **1955** A. L. ROWSE *Expans. Eliz. Eng.* viii. 283 Naval historians have all blamed the failure on to the Queen.

6. The dat. infin. *to blame* is much used as the predicate after *be*. In the 16–17th c. the *to* was misunderstood as *too*, and *blame* taken as adj. = blameworthy, culpable.

a **1225** *Ancr. R.* 232 [He] is swuðe to blamen. **1393** LANGL. *P. Pl.* C. IV. 308 If yt be payed prestliche the payer is to blame. **1594** SHAKS. *Rich. III*, II. ii. 13 The King mine Vnckle is too blame for it. **1596** —— *1 Hen. IV*, III. i. 177 In faith, my Lord, you are too wilfull blame. **1631** W. SALTONSTALL *Mayde* iv, Perhaps Potentia wanted to be blame. **1633** HEYWOOD *Eng. Trav.* III. Wks. 1874 IV. 58 The Girle was much too blame. **1633** HARINGTON *Epigr.* I. 84 b, Blush and confesse that you be too too blame. *c* **1710** LADY M. W. MONTAGU *Lett.* xciv. II. 154, I am not so much to blame as you imagine. **1875** JOWETT *Plato* (ed. 2) I. 93, I was to blame in having put my question badly.

7. *dial.* and *U.S.* Used as an imprecation.

a. In the imperative mood.

1830 R. FORBY *Vocab. E. Anglia* I. 27 *Blame*, *v.* a very decent and commendable evasion of the horrible word *damn*. Ex. '*Blame* me', or 'I will be *blamed*, if', &c... Nobody ever heard so mild an imprecation as '*blame* you for a rascal', or 'John Smith be *blamed* for a fool'. *a* **1832** R. C. SANDS *Writings* (1834) II. 149 Goy blame it all. **1876** 'MARK TWAIN' *Tom Sawyer* vii. 67 Blame it, I ain't going to stir him much. **1886** *Harper's Mag.* June 52/2 Blame me if them ain't the darnedest beans *I* ever seen! **1897** KIPLING *Capt. Cour.* ix. 210 Blame that boy! He never told. I'd ha' listened to *that*. **1905** G. H. GIBSON in A. B. Paterson *Old Bush Songs* 70 But blame my cats if I know what else They'll find for Bill to do.

b. In passive, in phr. (*I'm*) *blamed if* (etc.).

1830 [see 7 a above]. **1844** 'J. SLICK' *High Life N.Y.* I. iii. 31 I'll be blamed if you've the least bit of Yankee in you. **1876** 'MAX ADELER' *Elbow-Room* xv, Blamed if I haven't forgotten that word. **1905** H. R. MARTIN *Tillie* 322 I'm blamed if I dare adwise you.

c. as *adv.* = BLAMED 2.

1843 'R. CARLTON' *New Purchase* xvii. 134 'Blamed close, stranger,' said the old hero. **1876** 'MARK TWAIN' *Tom Sawyer* vii. 67 He's my tick and I'll do what I blame please with him or die! **1905** G. H. LORIMER *Old Gorgon Graham* 160 You know blame well that I don't understand any French.

d. as *adj.* = BLAMED 1.

1876 'MARK TWAIN' *Tom Sawyer* vi. 65 Talk about trying to cure warts with spunk-water such a blame-fool way as that! **1897** KIPLING *Capt. Cour.* vi. 129 You.. go hoggin' the road on the high seas with no blame consideration fer your neighbours. **1917** —— *Diversity of Creatures* 263 The blame thing jarred off—spiteful as a rattler! **1934** *Amer. Ballads & Folk Songs* 155 Them blame little children is all crying yet.

blame (bleɪm), *sb.* Also 3–4 blam. [a. OF. *blâme*, *blasmer* (= Pr. *blasme*, OSp. *blasmo*, It. *biasimo*), on Romanic type **blasimo*, f. **blasimare*:—L. *blasphēmāre*: see prec. Cf. L. *blasphēmus*, Gr. βλάσφημος adj. 'blasphemous, reviling.']

1. The action of censuring; expression of disapprobation; imputation of demerit on account of a fault or blemish; reproof; censure; reprehension.

c **1325** *E.E. Allit. P.* B. 43 With mony blame, ful bygge a boffet, peraunter. **1393** GOWER *Conf.* I. 347 Thus more and more arose the blame Ayein Egiste on every side. **1526** *Pilgr. Perf.* (W. de W. 1531) 8 Moche worthy blame is that chrysten man. **1709** STEELE & SWIFT *Tatler* No. 67 ¶12 The contrary to Fame and Applause, to wit, Blame and Derision. **1856** FROUDE *Hist. Eng.* (1858) I. iii. 282 Even Henry himself he [Latimer] did not spare where he saw occasion for blame.

†**b.** The condition of being blamed. *Obs.*

c **1230** *Hali Meid.* 33 Wið unworð ne wið uuel blame. *c* **1374** CHAUCER *Ann. & Arc.* 278 And putte yowe in sclaundre nowe and blame.

†**2.** A charge, an accusation. *Obs.*

c **1340** *Cursor M.* 19335 (Trin.) Wol ȝe dryue on vs þe blame þat we haue slayn him wiþ wronge. **1382** WYCLIF *Titus* ii. 3 Not bacbiteris, or seyinge fals blame on othere men. *c* **1386** CHAUCER *Man Lawes T.* 542 Immortal god þat sauedest susanne ffro false blame. *c* **1450** *Merlin* 121 She was ledde to be brente for a blame that was put upon hir. **1581** SIDNEY *Apol. Poetrie* (Arb.) 71 The blames laid against it [Poesie], are either false or feeble.

3. Blameworthiness, culpability; fault. *arch.*

1297 R. GLOUC. 432 Þy louerd ssal abbe an name.. vayr wyþout blame. *c* **1314** *Guy Warw.* 1737 Gij of Warwike.. a kniȝt he was wiþ-outen blame. **1398** TREVISA *Barth. De P.R.* I. xix, He enticeth or enflameth vnto crymes and blames. **1586** WARNER *Alb. Eng.* II. ix. (1597) 38 Oftner thought she it more blame not to haue erred so. **1601** SHAKS. *All's Well* V. iii. 36 My high repented blames Deere soueraigne pardon to me. **1611** BIBLE *Ephes.* i. 4 That we should be holy and without blame before him. **1859** TENNYSON *Merl. & Viv.* 648 Is thy white blamelessness accounted blame?

4. Responsibility for anything wrong, culpability; esp. in *to lay the blame on*, *to bear the blame*.

1393 GOWER *Conf.* I. 76 The blame upon the duke they laide. **1542** UDALL *Erasm. Apoph.* 62 b, I am not in the blame, quoth he, but Dionisius. **1580** BARET *Alv.* B 777 The faulte and blame is in thee. **1665** MANLEY *Grotius' Low-C. Warres* 87 He.. casts the blame upon the Prince of Aurange. **1873** MORLEY *Rousseau* I. 274 He took all the blame on himself. **1883** FROUDE *Short Stud.* IV. 53 They laid the blame of the quarrel on the archbishop's violence.

†**5.** ? Injury, hurt. *Obs.*

1549–62 STERNHOLD & H. *Ps.* l. 15 Then call to me When ought would worke thee blame. **1596** SPENSER *F.Q.* I. ii. 18 Glauncing down his shield from blame him fairly blest.

blameable, blamable (ˈbleɪməb(ə)l), *a.* [f. BLAME *v.* + -ABLE. Cf. F. *blâmable*, and see -BLE.] Worthy to be blamed; giving cause for fault-finding or reproach; faulty, culpable; reprehensible.

1387 TREVISA *Higden* VI. xxv, I am nouȝt blamable ne gilty in þise þinges. **1530** PALSGR. 306/2 Blameable, *coulpable*. **1586** W. WEBBE *Eng. Poetrie* (Arb.) 55 It is their foolysh construction, not hys wryting that is blameable. **1711** ADDISON *Spect.* No. 256 ¶2 In the blameable Parts of his Character. **1784** FRANKLIN *Autobiog.* Wks. 1840 I. 104 My conduct might be blameable. **1848** MACAULAY *Hist. Eng.* I. 160 Such feelings, though blamable, were natural. **1857** RUSKIN *Pol. Econ. Art* 36 One fault which.. is unnecessary, and therefore a real and blameable fault.

Hence ˈ**blameableness, ˈblamableness.**

1654 WHITLOCK *Manners Eng.* 505 (T.) Without the least blameableness. **1684** J. GOODMAN *Wint. Even. Conf.* 3 (R.) If he had not freedom of will.. there could be no.. blamableness. **1838** ARNOLD *Life & Corr.* II. viii. 123 The degree of blameableness in those who do not embrace this belief.

blameably, blamably (ˈbleɪməblɪ), *adv.* [f. prec. + -LY².] In a blamable manner; culpably.

1726 AYLIFFE *Parerg.* 181 A Person, that is maliciously or blameably absent. **1766** GOLDSM. *Vic. W.* xiv. (1806) 69 Blameably indifferent as to doctrinal matters. **1836** *Fraser's Mag.* XIII. 458 Blamably democratic in tone.

blamed (bleɪmd), *ppl. a.* and *adv. dial.* and *U.S.* [Cf. BLAME *v.* 7.]

1. *ppl. a.* = BLASTED *ppl. a.* 3.

1840 HALIBURTON *Clockm.* 3rd Ser. vi. 84 Yes, John Bull is a blamed blockhead. **1876** 'MARK TWAIN' *Tom Sawyer* ix, Drunk, same as usual, likely—blamed old rip! **1905** G. H. LORIMER *Old Gorgon Graham* 200 They've an ache or a pain in every blamed joint. **1946** K. TENNANT *Lost Haven* (1947) i. 14 I've stood the ugly, blamed thing long enough.

2. *adv.* Confoundedly, excessively.

1833 *Knickerbocker* I. 303 Which I now look upon as a blamed foolish notion. **1876** 'MARK TWAIN' *Tom Sawyer* viii. 79 Well, it's blamed mean—that's all. **1884** W. CUDWORTH *Yorks. Dial. Sk.* 27, I knaw they wor blamed nice. **1904** G. STRATTON-PORTER *Freckles* 51, I am.. so blamed ignorant I don't know which ones go in pairs.

blameful (ˈbleɪmfʊl), *a.* [f. BLAME + -FUL.]

1. Imputing or conveying blame or censure; blaming, fault-finding.

c **1386** CHAUCER *Melibeus* ¶161 He þat is Irous and wroþ, as seith Senek, ne may nat speke but blameful thynges. **1860** RUSKIN *Mod. Paint.* V. IX. xii. §4, I never saw him look an unkind or blameful look; I never knew him let pass.. a blameful word spoken by another.

2. Fully meriting blame; blameworthy; guilty.

c **1430** WYCLIF *Esther* xvi. 6 (MSS. I. & S.) Malicious men gessynge othere men bi her owen kynde blameful. *c* **1430** *Life St. Katherine* (Gibbs MS.) 106 For þe blamefull chaungeablenesse of þe queene. **1594** SHAKS. *Rich. III*, I. ii. 119 Is not the causer of the timelesse deaths.. As blamefull as the Executioner. **1738** GLOVER *Leonidas* x. 95 To die, uncalled, is blameful. **1838** *New Month. Mag.* LIV. 374 'Now Venus screen us!' sobb'd the blameful dame.

Hence ˈ**blamefully** *adv.*, ˈ**blamefulness.**

c **1400** *Apol. Loll.* 112 Ne man schuld blamfuly bi idulnes.. bring him silf to swilk nede. **1642** MILTON *Apol. Smect.* Wks. 1738 I. 130 Those who.. blamefully permitted the old leven to remain.

blameless (ˈbleɪmlɪs), *a.* [f. BLAME + -LESS.]

†**1.** Exempt from censure or blame; free from charge or reproof; uncensured. *Obs.*

1377 LANGL. *P. Pl.* B. XI. 306 Neyther is blamelees · þe bisshop ne þe chapleyne, For her eyther is endited. **1526** TINDALE *Matt.* xii. 5 The prestes in the temple breake the saboth daye and yet are blamlesse. So **1611.**

2. Giving no cause for blame; undeserving of reproach; faultless, guiltless.

1535 COVERDALE *Titus* i. 6 Yf eny be blamelesse, the huszbande of one wife.. A Bisshoppe must be blamelesse. **1641** J. JACKSON *True Evang. T.* II. 124 The blameless behaviour of the Christians. **1851** DIXON *W. Penn* xxviii. (1872) 262 John Hough, a man of blameless life. **1859** TENNYSON *Merl. & Viv.* 162 The blameless King.

b. Const. *of*.

1611 BIBLE *Josh.* ii. 17 Wee will bee blamelesse of this thine oath. **1747** MALLET *Amynt. & Theod.* I. 9 Blameless still of arts That polish to deprave.

†**3.** Not imputing or containing blame. *Obs.*

1595 SPENSER *Col. Clout* 749 Blame is.. more blamelesse generall, Then that which private errours doth pursew.

ˈ**blamelessly**, *adv.* In a blameless manner.

1611 COTGR., *Irreprehensiblement*.. blamelesly, vnreprouably. **1645** MILTON *Tetrach.* Wks. 1738 I. 256 As blamelesly as They in Heauen. **1861** MILL *Utilit.* v. 66 That any law, judged to be bad, may blamelessly be disobeyed.

ˈ**blamelessness.** Blameless quality or condition.

1670 BAXTER *Narrative* III. §35 A man of the Primitive sort of Christians for Humility, Love, Blamelessness. **1754** EDWARDS *Freed. Will* IV. iii. (ed. 4) 293 The notion of plain and manifest Blamelessness. **1873** SYMONDS *Grk. Poets* iii. 77 The soul be restored to its pristine blamelessness.

blamer (ˈbleɪmə(r)). [f. BLAME *v.* + -ER¹.] He who blames or finds fault; a censurer, reprover.

1387 WYCLIF *Isa.* l. 6 My face I turnede not awei fro the blameres [*ab increpantibus*]. **1566** T. STAPLETON *Ret. Untr. Jewel* Ep., Blamers shoulde allwaie be Blamelesse. *c* **1610** DONNE *To C'tess Bedford* iii, Blamers of the times they mard. **1867** SWINBURNE *Ess. & Stud.* (1875) 110 Casual praisers and blamers.

blameworthy (ˈbleɪmwɜːðɪ), *a.* Worthy or deserving of blame, culpable.

1387 TREVISA *Higden* VI. xxvii, Bote he was i-founde blameworþy in his answere. *c* **1440** *Promp. Parv.* 38 Blame-worthy, *culpabilis*. **1533** MORE *Apol.* xi. Wks. 869/2, I am not greatlye blame woorthye therein. **1699** BURNET 39 *Art.* xvii. (1700) 167 All men are so far free as to be praise-worthy or blame-worthy for the Good or Evil that they do. **1876** J. GROTE *Eth. Fragm.* iii. 58 Every action which is wrong or blameworthy.

Hence ˈ**blameworthiness.**

1580 SIDNEY *Arcadia* (1622) 15 The blame-worthinesse is, that to heare them, he rather goes to solitarinesse. **1754** EDWARDS *Freed. Will* IV. xiii. (1762) 282 The nature of Blame-worthiness or Ill-desert. **1868** BROWNING *Ring & Bk.* 1355 Blame I can bear, though not blameworthiness.

blaming (ˈbleɪmɪŋ), *vbl. sb.* [f. BLAME *v.*] The action of the verb BLAME; censure, reproach.

1382 WYCLIF *Job* xxiii. 4 My mouthe I shal fille with blamyngis. **1393** GOWER *Conf.* II. 176 In blaminge of the Grekes feith. **1613** R. C. *Table Alph.* (ed. 3), *Castigation*, chastisment, blaming.

attrib. **1583** FOXE *A. & M.* 337 The Captayne.. in blaming wise sayde vnto hym: Did I not, etc.

ˈ**blaming,** *ppl. a.* That blames. Hence ˈ**blamingly** *adv.*, with imputation of fault.

1832 CARLYLE in *Fraser's Mag.* V. 380 Speak blamingly of 'Carteret being used as a dactyl.'

blamischere, obs. form of BLEMISHER.

blamon, var. of BLOMAN, *Obs.*, negro.

blan(ne, pa. t. of BLIN *v. Obs.* to cease.

blanc, obs. form of BLANK.

‖**blanc** (blɑ̃). [F. *blanc* white: see BLANK.]

1. White paint (*esp.* for the face). Cf. BLANCH *sb.* 1. *blanc fixe*: sulphate of barium used esp. as an extender in paint.

1764 MRS. HARRIS in *Priv. Lett. 1st Ld. Malmesbury* I. 112 She.. would look very agreeable if she added blanc to the rouge instead of gamboge. **1866** ROSCOE *Elem. Chem.* xx. 179 *Barium Sulphate*.. is used as a paint, and the precipitated salt is termed *blanc fixé*. **1869** *Pall Mall G.* 29 Sept. 10 Tattooed blue with woad instead of being smeared with rouge and blanc. **1904** GOODCHILD & TWENEY *Technol. & Sci. Dict.* 54/1 *Blanc fixe*, an artificial sulphate of barium, very white and fine and somewhat heavy. Principally used in papermaking and in the manufacture of wallpaper colours. **1963** R. HIGHAM *Handbk. Papermaking* iv. 90 Blanc fixe is still used in the preparation of photographic base papers because of its soft powder structure and slightly higher opacity than the barytes form.

2. A rich stock or gravy in which tripe, etc. is stewed.

1845 BREGION & MILLER *Pract. Cook* 40 *Blanc*, a rich broth or gravy, in which the French cook palates lamb's head, and many other things. **1869** M. JEWRY *Warne's Model Cookery* 20/1 First-rate cooks preserve the whiteness of their boiled meats.. by.. using.. a sort of broth.. called *blanc*. **1952** F. WHITE *Good Eng. Food* II. iii. 130 To Make a Blanc.. do not take off the fat as the *blanc* cooks.

3. See BLANK.

blancard (ˈblæŋkəd). [a. F. *blancard* (also *blanchard*), f. *blanc* white + -ARD.] A kind of linen cloth manufactured in Normandy, the thread of which is half bleached before it is woven.

1848 in WEBSTER.

‖**blanc-bec** (blɑ̃ bɛk). [Fr., lit. 'white beak'.] A raw youngster, greenhorn.

c **1845** C. BRONTË *Professor* (1857) I. xii. 219 It was nonsense for her to think of taking such a 'blanc-bec' as a husband, since she must be at least ten years older than I. **1853** —— *Villette* I. ix. 172 You should have seen what a *blanc-bec* he looked.. how he hesitated and blushed. **1923** CONRAD *Rover* viii. 132, I may be *disparu* but I am too solid yet for any blancbec that loses his temper.

‖**blanc de blanc(s)** (blɑ̃ də blɑ̃). [Fr., lit. 'white of (or from) white(s)'.] A still or sparkling French white wine made from white grapes only.

1952 A. LICHINE *Wines of France* xviii. 218 Some of the wine of the Côte de Blancs is made into a Champagne called Blanc de Blancs, white Champagne from the white Pinot only... Blanc de Blancs is not often sold under firm names, but under the village or commune name, called Blanc de Blancs of Cramant, or Avize, or Mesnil. **1953** I. FLEMING *Casino Royale* viii. 71 The Blanc de Blanc Brut 1943 of the same marque is without equal. **1961** *Observer* 7 Jan. 26/6 Hence the growing popularity of blanc de blancs, the champagne that is made of the juice of white grapes only,

instead of the more usual three or four parts black to one of white. **1963** I. FLEMING *On H. M. Secret Service* ii. 26 He ..ordered..a bottle of the Taittinger Blanc de Blanc that he had made his traditional drink. **1978** W. M. SPACKMAN *Armful of Warm Girl* 27 He uttered judgements concerning this blanc de blancs, which he described as 'Heidsieck'. **1984** *Washington Post Mag.* 15 Jan. 25/1 For a sparkler, try the Paul Cheneau for $60, or splurge on the Brut Royal blanc de blanc for about $85.

‖**blanc de Chine, chine** (blɑ̃ də ʃin). [Fr., lit. 'white of China'.] White glazed porcelain made at Te-hua in south-eastern China, esp. during the Ming period.

1888 F. HIRTH *Anc. Porcelain* xi. 44 Tê-hua has since the Ming dynasty furnished porcelains of a fascinating creamy white, a distinct class, which I believe constitutes together with the Ting-chou white pottery the article known as 'blanc de Chine'. **1910** S. W. BUSHELL *Chinese Art* (ed. 2) II. 26 The velvety white porcelain sometimes known as *blanc de Chine*. **1955** *Times* 19 July 10/7 An eighteenth-century Chinese blanc-de-chine vase.

‖**blanc de perle** (blɑ̃ də pɛːrl). [Fr.] Pearl-white (see PEARL *sb.*¹ 18).

1881 *Queen* 12 Mar. (Advt.), Eyebrow pencils, 12 stamps; ..Blanc de Perle, 30. **1897** M. CORELLI *Ziska* viii. 164 She managed to produce a delicate shudder of her white shoulders without cracking the *blanc de perle* enamel. **1919** FIRBANK *Valmouth* xi. 189, I gave her my little precious volume of *blanc de perle* in order to rub her nose.

blanch (blɑːnʃ, -æ-), *sb.* [partly from BLANCH *a.* (or its French source), partly from BLANCH *v.*]

†**1.** White paint, *esp.* for the face. *Obs.* Cf. BLANC 1.

1601 HOLLAND *Pliny* II. 520 This..serueth to make an excellent blanch for women that desire a white complexion. *Ibid.* 529 Their blanch of cerusse for complexion. **1610** FOLKINGHAM *Art of Survey* I. xi. 35 Woad and Blaunch would haue a strong ground.

†**2.** A white spot on the skin. *Obs.*

1607 TOPSELL *Serpents* 765 In the neck thereof are two blanches. **1609** *Man in Moone* (1849) 38 Ulcers, filth and blanches, will breed upon you.

3. *Min.* 'Lead ore mixed with other minerals.' Raymond *Mining Gl.* 1881.

1747 HOOSON *Miner's Dict.* M ij, They break by following some Blanch of Ore or Spar.

blanch, *a. Obs.* exc. *Hist.* Forms: 4–6 blaunch(e, 4– blanche, 6– blanch; *Sc.* 7 blensch, blenshe, 7– blench. [a. OF. *blanche*, fem. of *blanc* white; see BLANK. Occurring originally only where the fem. would be used in French.]

†**1.** White, pale. Chiefly in specific uses, as ***blanch fever, blanch powder, blanch sauce.*** *Obs.*

1330 R. BRUNNE *Chron.* 40 (Mätz.) He wedded þe dukes douhter, faire Emme þe blaunche. *c* **1374** CHAUCER *Troylus* I. 916 And some þow seydist had a blaunch feuere. **1393** GOWER *Conf.* III. 9 Thanne cometh the blanche fever With chele. *c* **1420** *Liber Cocorum* 28 Blaunche sawce for capons. *c* **1460** J. RUSSELL *Bk. Nurture* in *Babees Bk.* (1868) 122 Aftur sopper, rosted apples, peres, blaunche powder, your stomak for to ese. **1475** CAXTON *Jason* 17 Affayted with the blanche feures. **1586** COGAN *Haven Health* (1636) 125 A very good blanch powder, to strow upon rosted apples.

2. *Her.* White, argent.

1697 *Lond. Gaz.* No. 3287/4 Robert Dale, Gent., Blanch-Lion Pursuivant. **1805** SCOTT *Last Minstr.* IV. xxx, For who ..Saw the blanche lion e'er fall back?

3. *Blanch*, Sc. *blench*; more fully ***blanch farm, blench ferme*** [OF. *blanche ferme*]; according to Spelman and Coke, Rent paid in silver, instead of service, labour, or produce; in Scottish writers extended to a merely nominal quit-rent, not only of money, as a silver penny, but of other things, as a white rose, pair of gloves, pair of spurs, etc. paid in acknowledgement of superiority.

1609 SKENE *Reg. Maj.* 36 Frie tennents, haldand their lands, be blenshe ferme. [**1627** SPELMAN 232 *Firma alba*, ea est quae argento penditur, non pecude.] **1642** COKE *Inst.* II. 19 Redditus albi, White rents, blanch farmes, or rents, vulgarly and commonly called quit rents..called white rents, because they were paid in silver, to distinguish them from work-days, rent cummin, rent corn, etc. **1768** BLACKSTONE *Comm.* II. 42. **1864** *Glasgow Daily Her.* 24 Sept., Changing the tenure of the castle..to free blench farm, for payment of a penny silver, if asked only.

1602 K. JAS. I *Law Free Mon.* in *Life* (1830) I. ix. 294 The King changeth their holdings from tack to feu, from ward to blanch, etc. **1609** SKENE *Reg. Maj.* 31 Gif anie man hes lands haldin in frie soccage (in *blensch* or few). **1670** BLOUNT *Law Dict.* s.v., To hold Land in Blench, is, by payment of a Penny, Rose, Pair of Gilt Spurs, or such like thing, if it be demanded; In name of Blench. **1799** J. ROBERTSON *Agric. Perth* 45 The blanch, feu, and other casualties of superiority payable to the crown. **1814** SCOTT *Wav.* III. 8 The holding of the Barony of Bradwardine is of a nature alike honourable and peculiar, being blanch. **1868** *Act 31–32 Vict.* ci. §6 The lands are..to be holden of the grantor in free blench.

b. as *adv.* = In blench.

1828 TYTLER *Hist. Scot.* (1864) I. 254 A grant of land.. either for military service or to be held blench for the payment of a nominal feu-duty. **1860** J. IRVING *Dumbartonsh.* 386 The coronatorship of the County to be held blench of the crown for one penny.

c. So ***blanch duty, blanch holding, blanch kane; blanch holden*** adj.

1634–46 ROW *Hist. Kirk* (1842) 345 All blench holden lands. **1723** W. BUCHANAN *Fam. Buchanan* (1820) 245 Payment of four pennies of blench-duty if demanded. **1753** *Scots Mag.* XV. 49/1 To change all ward holdings of the principality of Scotland into blanch holdings. **1754** ERSKINE *Princ. Sc. Law* (1809) 150 Blanch-holding..is that whereby the vassal is to pay to the superior an elusory yearly duty, as a penny money, a rose, a pair of gilt spurs, &c. merely in acknowledgment of the superiority, *nomine albæ firmæ*. **1872** E. ROBERTSON *Hist. Ess.* 137 *note*, The obligations.. commuted for a money payment, known as Blanche Kane.

blanch (blɑːnʃ, -æ-), *v.*¹ Forms: 4–6 blaunche, 5 blawnche, blanch-yn, 6 blanche, 7 blaunch, 6– blanch. [a. F. *blanch-ir* to whiten, f. *blanc* white. Cf. also BLANK *v.*]

1. a. *trans.* To make white, whiten: chiefly, in mod. use, by depriving of colour; to bleach. Also *fig.*

? *a* **1400** *Morte Arth.* 3040 Chirches and chapelles chalke whitte blawnchede. **1607** DEKKER *Sir T. Wyatt* 126 Patience has blancht thy soule as white as snow. **1727** BRADLEY *Fam. Dict.* s.v. *Guiacum*, The Salt of Guaiacum, which you may blanch by calcining it with a great Fire in a Crucible. **1805** SOUTHEY *Madoc in W.* viii, His bones had now been blanch'd. **1859** MERIVALE *Rom. Emp.* (1865) VII. lv. 15 Age had blanched his hair. **1875** BROWNING *Aristoph. Apol.* 120 All at once, a cloud has blanched the blue.

b. To make (metals) white: in *Alchemy* by 'albation,' or 'albification'; in *techn.* use, to tin.

1582 HESTER *Secr. Phiorav.* III. civ. 130 Orpiment..doeth blanche all mettals. **1710** PALMER *Proverbs* 102 Like them that pass base money, blanch it to cover the brass. **1728** RUTTY *Tin-Plates* in *Phil. Trans.* XXXV. 635 Till..you would tin them, or in the Term of Art, blanch them.

c. To remove the dark crust from an alloy after annealing. *spec.* in coining money.

1803 *Phil. Trans.* XCIII. 187 Gold alloyed with one-twelfth of silver..may be stamped without being annealed; it consequently does not require to be blanched. **1868** [see BLANCHING *vbl. sb.*¹]. **1883** *Encycl. Brit.* XVI. 489/2 The removal of a small portion of the alloying metal in this way constitutes 'blanching' or 'pickling' the coin.

2. a. *Cookery.* To whiten almonds, or the like, by taking off the skin; *hence* (as this is done by throwing them into boiling water), to scald by a short rapid boil in order to remove the skin, or for any other purpose.

1398 TREVISA *Barth. De P.R.* XVII. cix, They [Hazel-nuts] engender moche ventosite, yf þey ben ete with þe small skynnes; þerfore..it is good to blaunche hem in hoot water. *c* **1440** *Promp. Parv.* 38 Blanchyn almandys, or oþer lyke. *dealbo, decortico.* **1530** PALSGR. 456/2 He can blandysshe better..than blanche almondes. **1681** CHETHAM *Angler's Vade-m.* xxxix. §5 (1689) 257 Before you put on the Sawce, blanch off very neatly the skins of the Pearch and Tench. **1769** MRS. RAFFALD *Eng. Housekpr.* (1778) 88 Blanch your tongue, slit it down the middle, and lay it on a soup plate. **1796** MRS. GLASSE *Cookery* v. 41 After boiling your palates very tender..blanch and scrape them clean.

b. *humorously.* To strip.

1675 COTTON *Poet. Wks.* (1765) 261 Come, Ladies, blanch you to your Skins.

3. To whiten plants by depriving them of light, so as to prevent the development of chlorophyll.

1669 WORLIDGE *Syst. Agric.* (1681) 169 If you have a desire to have them white, or *blanch* them, (as the French term it)..you may cover every Plant with a small Earthen-pot, and lay some hot Soyl upon them. **1807** J. E. SMITH *Phys. Bot.* 206 The common practice of blanching Celery. **1861** DELAMER *Kitch. Gard.* 73 Blanching the shoots by a covering of sweet earth.

4. To make pale with fear, cold, hunger, etc.

1605 SHAKS. *Macb.* III. iv. 116 And keepe the naturall Rubie of your Cheekes When mine is blanch'd with feare. **1791** COWPER *Iliad* III. 41 Fear blanches cold his cheeks. **1857** RUSKIN *Pol. Econ. Art* 17 The famine blanches your lips.

5. To give a fair appearance to by artifice or suppression of the truth; to palliate, to 'whitewash.' Now only with *over* (with reference to 1 b.).

1549 LATIMER *Ploughers* (Arb.) 37 Blanchers..that can blanche the abuse of Images. **1601** DENT *Pathw. Heaven* 165 Howsoeuer you mince it and blanch it ouer. **1611** SPEED *Hist. Gt. Brit.* III. xlv. 373 The Author..blancheth the matter, saying, that he died a naturall death. **1641** MILTON *Ch. Discip.* I. (1851) 11 To blanch and varnish her deformities. **1709** SACHEVERELL *Serm.* 15 Aug. 10 Men.. that..can Hypocritically Blanch and Palliate..Iniquities. **1880** RUSKIN *Lett. Clergy* 367 To take the punishment of it [wrong], not to get it blanched over by any means.

6. *intr.* To turn or become white (chiefly by loss of colour); to bleach; to pale.

1768 TUCKER *Lt. Nat.* I. 12 If wax blanches in the sun. **1839** MARRYAT *Phant. Ship.* xxix, Their cheeks blanched. **1862** BRIGHT *Amer. Sp.* (1876) 111 Left the bones of her citizens to blanch on a hundred European battlefields. **1863** TENNYSON *Boadicea* 76 As when the rolling breakers boom and blanch on the precipices.

blanch (blɑːnʃ, -æ-), *v.*² [A variant of BLENCH, which see for the derivation and history.]

†**1.** *trans.* To deceive, cheat, bilk. Cf. BLENCH *v.* 1. ***to blanch of***: to cheat or do out of. *Obs.*

1592 WARNER *Alb. Eng.* VII. xxxix. 193 But so obscurely hath beene blancht of good workes elsewheare done. **1602** *Ibid.* XII. lxxi. (1612) 296 Dallying Girles..that intertaine.. All Louers..And hauing blaunched many so, in single life take pride.

†**2.** To shut the eyes to, leave unnoticed, shirk, 'blink' (a fact); to pass without notice, miss, omit. *Obs.* (Cf. BLANCH *v.*¹ 5.)

1605 BACON *Adv. Learn.* II. 69 In Annotacions..it is ouer vsual to blaunch the obscure places, and discoarse vpon the playne. **1618** RALEIGH *Prerog. Parl.* (1628) 52 You blanch my question, and answere mee by examples. **1638** SIR H. WOTTON in *Four C. Eng. Lett.* 53, I suppose you will not blanch Paris in your way. **1671** EVELYN *Mem.* (1857) III. 240 Whether I am to blanch this particular?

3. *intr.* To shrink, start back, give way. *arch.* (Later users apparently mix it up with BLANCH *v.*¹ 6, in sense of 'turn pale, change colour for fear.')

1572 in Neal *Hist. Purit.* (1732) I. 285 'Tis no time to blanch. **1632** MASSINGER & F. *Fat. Dowry* II. i, What! Weep ye, soldiers? Blanch not! **1640–1** LD. DIGBY *Parl. Sp.* 9 Feb. 13 A man of a sturdy conscience, that would not blanch for a little. **1870** EDGAR *Runnymede* 126 The saints forbid that I should ever blanch at the thought of battle.

4. *trans.* To turn (anything) off, aside, or away; in *Venery*, to 'head back' the deer in his flight.

1592 LYLY *Galathea* II. i. 231 Saw you not the deare come this way..I beleeve you have blancht him. **1627** F. E. *Hist. Edw. II*, (1680) 117 He would not blaunch the Deer, the Toyl so near. **1741** *Compl. Fam.-Piece* II. i. 310 When he [the deer] swarves, or is blanched by any Accident. **1793** SMEATON *Edystone L.* §323 The lantern was secured by..the Cornice; which, when the sea rose to the top of the house, blanched it off like a sheet. **1875** 'STONEHENGE' *Brit. Sports.* I. x. §1.

†**blanch,** *v.*³ *Obs.* [App. worn down from *blandish* (like *blench* from BLEMISH *v.*); but approaching certain senses of both BLENCH *v.*¹ and BLENCH *v.*², with which it was probably confounded.] *intr.* = BLANDISH *v.* 2.

1572 R. H. *Lavaterus' Ghostes* (1596) 19 b, Men which blaunche and flatter with us, are alwayes suspitious. *a* **1587** FOXE *Serm. 2 Cor.* v. 10 If I shoulde say that nothing therein were amisse, I should indeede blanch and flatter too much. **1612** BACON *Counsel, Ess.* (Arb.) 326 Books will speake plaine, when Counsellors Blanch [*in adulationem lapsuri*].

†'**blanchard, -art,** *a. Obs.* [a. OF. *blanchart* whitish, bordering upon white, also as name of a white horse; f. *blanc, blanch*-white; see -ARD.] White; a white horse; often as a *quasi*-proper name. (Cf. *bayard* = bayhorse.)

c **1440** *Generydes* 2458 Vppon my stede blanchard thu ridest here. *c* **1440** *Gaw. & Gol.* ii. 19 (JAM.) On stedis stalwart and strang, Baith blanchart and bay.

blanche, obs. form of BLANCH.

blanched (blɑːnʃt, -æ-), *a.* [f. BLANCH *v.*¹ + -ED.]

1. Whitened (now, chiefly, by loss of colour).

1401 *Pol. Poems* (1859) II. 50 Blaunchid graves ful of dede bones. **1633** P. FLETCHER *Purple Isl.* XII. xxxi, Her loathsome face, blancht skinne and snakie hair. **1820** KEATS *St. Agnes* xxx, Blanched linen, smooth and lavendered.

b. ***blanched copper***: an alloy of copper and arsenic (cf. BLANCH *v.* 1 b.).

1603 KNOLLES *Hist. Turkes* (1621) 1203 A cup of blancht copper.

2. Whitened (as almonds) by removal of the skin; peeled.

c **1420** *Liber Cocorum* (1862) 28 Take blanchid almondis and small hom grynde. *a* **1666** A. BROME *Horace's De Arte P.* (1671) 391 Him that buys chiches blanch't.

3. Of plants: Whitened by exclusion of light.

1793 T. BEDDOES *Calculus* 199 Blanched plants lose their green colour, and become whitish and sickly. **1834** MRS. SOMERVILLE *Connex. Phys. Sc.* xxvii. (1849) 301 They [Plants] are found in caverns almost void of light, though generally blanched and feeble.

4. Pale with fear or other emotion, hunger, etc.

1828 SCOTT *F.M. Perth* I. 50 They looked on each other with fallen countenances and blanched lips.

†**5.** ? Colourless, feeble; or ? perverted. *Obs.*

1553–87 FOXE *A. & M.* (1596) 86/2 Now marke (good reader) what blanched stuffe here followeth.

†**blancheen.** *Obs.* [f. F. *blanc, blanche* white.] ? White flour of fine quality.

1601 HOLLAND *Pliny* I. 564 A Modius of meale comming of the French Siligo, called Blancheen, or Ble-blanch.

blancher¹ ('blɑːnʃə(r), -æ-). Also 6 blauncher, branchar, 7 -er. [f. BLANCH *v.*¹ + -ER.]

1. He who or that which blanches or makes white.

1852 D. MOIR *Miner Peru* Wks. II. 171 The tottering step, Proclaimed Time's ravages, blancher of the hair.

2. *spec.* One who blanches metals or money (see BLANCH *v.*¹ 1 b. and c.).

1578 *Ord. R. Househ., 2 Eliz.* 256 The Mynte..Branchars 2; fee apeece 13*l.* 6*s.* 8*d.* **1647** HAWARD *Crown Rev.* 23 Two Blanchers [in the Mint]. **1728** RUTTY in *Phil. Trans.* XXXV. 635 Kept..a Secret by the Blancher. **1766** ENTICK *London* IV. 342 Melters, blanchers, moniers.

b. A chemical agent used for blanching.

1477 NORTON *Ord. Alch.* iii. in Ashmole (1652) 39 In Malgams, in Blanchers and Citrinacions. **1594** PLAT *Jewell-ho.* I. 20 The Alcumists giue a blauncher vnto Venus with the salt of Tartar. **1667** BOYLE *Orig. Formes & Qual.*, To make Blanchers for Copper.

'**blancher**². Forms: 6 blawnsher, blawnsherr, blawnshere, blaunsher, 6– blancher. [f. BLANCH *v.*² + -ER.]

†**1.** One who causes to turn aside; a perverter; an obstructor, hinderer. *Obs.*

1549 LATIMER *Ploughers* (Arb.) 33 Not for the continuaunce of the Masse as the blaunchers have

blaunched it and wrested it. *Ibid.* 36 Certeyne blanchers longyng to the markette, to lette and stoppe the lyght of the Gospel.

†**2.** *Venery.* A person or thing placed to turn the deer from a particular direction. *Obs.*

1535 R. Layton in Ellis *Orig. Lett*, Ser. II. II. 61 Getheryng up part of the said bowke leiffs..to make him sewells or blawnsherrs to kepe the deere within the woode. **1580** Sidney *Arcadia* 64 Zelmane was like one that stood in a tree waiting a good occasion to shoot, and Gynecia a blancher, which kept the dearest deere from her. **1602** Warner *Alb. Eng.* IX. li. (1612) 230.

3. One who starts or balks *at* (any thing).

a **1659** Osborn *Q. Eliz.* Wks. (1673) 465 So as the wall-eyed blanchers at them [ceremonies] were followed more out of reproach than approbation.

†'**blanchet.** *Obs.* Also **blaunchette.** [ME., a. OF. *blanchet* dim. of *blanc*: see -ET¹.] White flour or powder for the face.

c **1175** *Lamb. Hom.* 53 Heo smurieð heom mid blanchet þet is þes deofles sape. *c* **1330** R. Brunne (MS. Bowes) 20 (Halliw.) With blaunchette and other flour, To make thaim qwytter of colour.

blanchet, obs. form of BLANKET.

blanchimeter (blɑːn'ʃɪmɪtə(r), -æ-). [f. BLANCH + -METER.] An instrument for measuring the blanching power of chloride of lime and potash; a chlorometer.

1847 in Craig, etc.

blanching ('blɑːnʃɪŋ, -æ-), *vbl. sb.*¹ [f. BLANCH *v.*¹] The action of making white: see the vb. Also in *Cookery*: see BLANCH *v.*¹ 2 a.

1600 Holland *Livy* XL. 1091 b, The polishing, blaunching and whiting..of the temple of Iupiter. **1657** *Phys. Dict., Blanching*, is the separation of the skins and hulls from divers seeds and kernels. **1868** Seyd *Bullion* 545 The furnaces for..blanching are on the first floor. **1951** *Good Housek. Home Encycl.* 357/2 *Blanching*..in which food is treated with boiling water. **1960** *Times Rev. Industry* Aug. 22/3 Another operation applied to vegetables is blanching—immersion in near-boiling water for a few minutes.

'**blanching,** *vbl. sb.*² [f. BLANCH *v.*² + -ING¹.]

†**1.** Telling of falsehoods. *Obs.*

1581 J. Bell *Haddon's Answ. Osor.* 73 These blasphemous flatteries, detestable and horrible blaunchyngs. *Ibid.* 155 Your impudent usage in lyeng and blaunchyng.

†**2.** Shirking, evasion. *Obs.*

1642 Rogers *Naaman* 529 [Balaam] should have returned home, and abhorred his blanching with Gods command.

'**blanching,** *ppl. a.* [f. BLANCH *v.*¹ + -ING².] Whitening; becoming white.

c **1800** K. White *Poet Wks.* (1837) 77 When old age shall shed Its blanching honours on thy weary head. **1847** Tennyson *Princ.* ii. 182 On the blanching bones of men.

blanck(e, obs. form of BLANK.

blancket, obs. form of BLANKET, BLUNKET.

blancmange, -manger (blə'mɑːnʒ, -'mɒnʒ, -'mɑ̃ːʒ). Forms: 4 **blancmanger(e, blank(e)manger(e, bla-, blam-, blan-, blaumanger, blamyngere,** 5 **blanc maungere, blaunche-, blonc-, blawemanger, blanger mangere,** 6 **blowmanger,** 7 **bla-, blanch-, blanck-, blankemanger,** 8 **blomange,** 9 **blamange,** 8- **blancmange, -manger.** [In 14th c. *blancmanger*, a. OF. *blanc-manger* (earlier *-mangier*), lit. 'white food or dish,' f. *blanc* white + *manger* to eat, eating, food. *Blanc* fell already in 14th c. to *blam-, bla-, blau-*, later *blawe-, blow-, blo-, bla-*, and *manger* was in 18th c. abridged to *mange*. The present spelling is a half attempt at restoring the French, but the pronunciation is that of the 18th c. *blomange, blamange*, often garnished with a French nasal, by those who know French.]

†**a.** Formerly: A dish composed usually of fowl, but also of other meat, minced with cream, rice, almonds, sugar, eggs, etc. *Obs.*

b. Now: A sweetmeat made of dissolved isinglass or gelatine boiled with milk, etc., and forming an opaque white jelly; also a preparation of cornflour and milk, with flavouring substances.

1377 Lang. *P. Pl.* B. XIII. 91 Þat neither bacoun ne braune · blan[c]mangere ne mortrewes Is noither fisshe [ne] flesshe · but fode for a penaunte. *c* **1386** Chaucer *Prol.* 387 ffor blankmanger [*v.r.* blankemangere] that made he with the beste. *c* **1420** *Liber Cocorum* 19 Blanc maungere of fysshe. *c* **1460** J. Russell *Bk. Nurture* in *Babees Bk.* (1868) 165 Two potages, blanger mangere, & Also Iely. **1483** *Cath. Angl.* 34 Blawemanger, *peponus*. **1530** *Ortus Voc.*, Blowmanger. **1603** Holland *Plutarch's Mor.* 680 Their blamangers, jellies, chawdres. **1626** Bacon *Sylva* §48 Blanch-Manger or Jelly. **1769** Mrs. Raffald *Eng. Housekpr.* (1778) 195 To make Blomange of Isinglass. **1772–84** Cook *Voy.* (1790) I. 54 Its flavour was something like blanc mange. **1801** Wolcott (P. Pindar) *Ep. Ct. Rumford* Wks. 1812 V. 137 Soap-suds to Syllabubs and Trifles change, And Bullocks' Lights and Livers to Blamange. **1812** L. Hunt in *Examiner* 21 Dec. 801/1 Trembling at it's fate, like blanc-manger. **1862** Mrs. Beeton *Cookery Bk.* 44/1 Loosen the edges of the blanc-mange from the mould.

c. *fig.* (cf. '*flummery*.')

1790 Burke *Corr.* (1844) III. 157 Whenever that politic prince made any of his flattering speeches..when he served them with this, and the rest of his blanc-mange, of which he was sufficiently liberal.

blanco ('blæŋkəʊ). [Trade name, f. F. *blanc* white.] A white preparation for whitening accoutrements; also, a similar preparation of khaki colouring. Hence '**blanco** *v. trans.*, to treat with blanco; '**blancoed** *ppl. a.*

1895 in *Army & Navy Co-op. Soc. Price-list.* **1906** *Daily Chron.* 30 Mar. 3/7 The sleeves get covered with 'blanco' off the belt. **1912** E. Wallace *Pte. Selby* viii. 75 One unhappy mortal, 'warned' for guard..was lugubriously 'blancoing' his straps. *a* **1918** W. Owen *Coll. Poems* (1963) 79 Boots dubbined; rifles clean and oiled; Belts blancoed. **1948** A. Baron *From City* 32 For half a crown he would blanco the whole of a man's equipment. *a* **1953** Dylan Thomas *Quite Early One Morning* (1954) 30 Gym-shoes white as the blanco'd snow. **1955** *Times* 25 June 6/5 Since the war they have worn British battle-dress and blancoed web equipment. **1966** D. Holbrook *Flesh Wounds* 37 They covered their webbing with the watery yellow blanco.

†**bland,** *sb.*¹ *Obs.* [a. ON. *bland*, in phr. *í blana* in union, together, whence ME. *in bland*: cf. OE. *bland* mixture, f. stem of BLAND *v.*¹]

In phr. ***in bland***: in mixture, in union, **a.** *adv.* together; **b.** *prep.* among.

c **1325** *E.E. Allit. P.* B. 885 Þay blwe a buffet in blande þat banned people. *c* **1340** *Gaw. & Gr. Knt.* 1205 Boþe quit and red in-blande. *a* **1400** *Alexander* (Stev.) 2786 In batail..in-bland with þe Grekis.

bland (blænd), *sb.*² [a. ON. *blanda* (fem.) a mixture of fluids, *spec.* 'a beverage of hot whey mixed with water,' Vigfusson: cf. OE. *bland* (neut.) 'mixture.'] The name in Orkney and Shetland of a beverage made of buttermilk and water.

1703 M. Martin *Descr. W. Isles* (1716) 374 Their drinking of bland [in Shetland]. **1732** De Foe, etc. *Tour Gt. Brit.* (1769) IV. 337. **1822** Scott *Pirate* vi. (D.) She filled a small wooden quaigh from an earthen pitcher which contained bland, a subacid liquor made out of the serous part of the milk. **1837** R. Dunn *Ornith. Ork. & Shet.* 13.

bland (blænd), *a.* [ad. L. *bland-us* soft, smooth, caressing.]

1. Of persons, their actions, etc.: Smooth and suave in manner; mildly soothing or coaxing: gentle.

1661 Pepys *Diary* 12 Sept., With some bland counsel of his. **1667** Milton *P.L.* IX. 855 With bland words at will. **1774** Goldsm. *Retal.* 140 His manners were gentle, complying, & bland. **1801** Southey *Garci Ferrand.* II. iii, Winning eye and action bland. **1828** Carlyle *Misc.* (1857) I. 93 Bland satire on his friends. **1855** Macaulay *Hist. Eng.* III. 439 A bland temper and winning manners. **1878** Black *Green Past.* xv. 120 A bland and benevolent face.

2. Of things: Soft, mild, pleasing to the senses; gentle, genial, balmy, soothing.

1667 Milton *P.L.* v. 5 Temperat vapours bland. **1820** Keats *St. Agnes* xi, The sound of merriment and chorus bland. **1872** C. King *Sierra Nev.* vi. 122 The air was bland, the heavens cloudless.

b. Of medicines: Mild, unirritating. Of food: Not stimulating. (Cf. quot. 1667 in 2).

1836 Todd *Cycl. Anat. & Phys.* I. 671/2 A very small force only is requisite to cause bland fluids to follow the course of blood. **1876** Duhring *Dis. Skin* 92 Bland oils are serviceable in softening scales and crusts. **1878** Holbrook *Hyg. Brain* 111 The food should be bland.

¶ quasi-*advb.* (in poetry).

1596 Spenser *Hymn to Beauty* 171 That base affection, which your eares would bland Commend to you by Loves abused name. **1850** Mrs. Browning *Poet's Vow* II, They clasping bland his gift.

†**bland,** *v.*¹ *Obs.* Also **blonden.** [Common Teut. str. vb.: OE. *blandan, blǫndan*, pa. t. *bléond*, pple. *blanden* = OS. *blandan*, OHG. *blantan*, ON. (and Sw.) *blanda*, Goth. *blandan, baibland, blandans*, to mix. Only once exemplified in OE., and in ME. superseded by BLEND *v.*² The two later instances here may be accidental; if genuine, they perh. represent the ON. rather than the OE. vb.] *trans.* To mix, intermingle, blend.

a **1000** *Riddles* (Gr.) xli. 59 Swétra, þonne þu beobread blénde mid hunige. *c* **1340** *Gaw & Gr. Knt.* 1931 Blande[n] al of blaunner were boþe al aboute. *c* **1420** *Liber Cocorum* 24 Blonde hit with mylke and put alle in panne. **1513** Douglas *Æneis* III. ix. 83 Blude blandit with wyne.

†**bland,** *v.*² *Obs.* Also **blaund, blond.** [a. OF. *bland-ir*:—L. *blandīri* to soothe, flatter: see BLANDISH.] *trans.* To soothe, flatter; a by-form of BLANDISH.

c **1315** Shoreham 73 Ac blondeth. *c* **1505** Dunbar '*Schir, ȝit remembir*' 77 Nor ȝit with benifice am I blandit.

bland, var. of BLEND(E *pa. pple.* and *ppl. a.*

blandander (blæn'dændə(r)), *v. colloq.* [cf. Ir. *blanndar* dissimulation, flattery.] *trans.* To tempt by blandishment (*into*); to cajole. Hence **blan'dandering** *ppl. a.*

1888 Kipling *Soldiers Three* (1895) 70 I've blandanthered thim through the night somehow. **1896** G. B. Shaw in *Sat. Rev.* 1 Feb. 123/1 Boucicault was a coaxing, blandandhering sort of liar. **1898** *Link* 3/1 When you bullied and blandandered me into learning how to ride. **1914** *Times Lit. Suppl.* 4 June 267/2 [European diplomacy] refused to be blandandered by King Nicholas.

†**blan'dation.** *Obs. rare.* [app. carelessly formed from BLAND *v.*² (or ? BLAND *a.*) + -ATION.]

1. Flattery.

1605 Camden *Rem.* (1637) 325 One had flattered William Longchampe..with this blandation.

2. A deception, illusion.

1612 Chapman *Widowes T.* v, For the corpse, sir..there's no body; nothing. A mere blandation; a *deceptio visus.*

†'**blander.** *Obs. rare.* Only in ME. form blondere. [f. BLAND *v.*² + -ER.] A flatterer.

1340 *Ayenb.* 60 Þe blonderes byeþ þe dyeules noriches. *Ibid.* 61 Huanne þe blondere defendeþ and excuseþ and wryeþ þe kueades and þe zennes of ham þet he wyle ulateri.

blandiloquence (blæn'dɪləkwəns). *rare.* [ad. L. *blandiloquentia*, f. *blandi-loquent-em* smooth-talking; cf. next and -ENCE.] Smooth speech, flattering talk. So **blandiloquent** *a.* = next.

1656 in Blount *Glossgr.* **1779** T. Twining in *Parr's Wks.* (1828) VIII. 264 Even the blandiloquence of Mr. Bland is now converted into railing. **1865** *Pall Mall G.* 9 May 9/2 He swallows a great quantity of blandiloquence.

†**blan'diloquous,** *a. Obs. rare.* [f. L. *blandiloqu-us* (f. *blandus* BLAND + stem of *loqui* to speak) + -OUS.] Smooth-speaking, flattering, fair-spoken. So (in same sense) **blandi'loquious** *a.* [f. L. *blandiloquium*.]

1615 T. Adams *Blacke Dev.* 44 Though he flatter..and give blandiloquous proffers. **1689** T. Plunket *Char. Gd. Command.* 1 As hath that Blandiloquious Colonel R.

†**blan'diloquy.** *Obs. rare*⁻⁰. [ad. L. *blandiloquium.*] 'Flattering speech.'

1623 in Cockeram. **1699** in Coles.

†'**blandiment.** *Obs.* Also 6 **blandimente, blandymente.** [a. OF. *blandiment*, ad. L. *blandīmentum*; see -MENT.] By-form of BLANDISHMENT.

c **1510** Barclay *Mirr. Good Mann.* (1570) Aj, Sweete blandiment of wordes amiable. *c* **1510** More *Picus* Wks. 4/2 Womens blandimentes. **1569** Newton *Cicero's Old Age* 32 These blandiments of pleasure.

b. *fig.* Soothing or healing action. (So L.)

1684 tr. *Bonet's Merc. Compit.* XIV. 509 Upon the first Blandiment of the Fomentation the pain grows milder.

†'**blanding,** *vbl. sb. Obs.* [f. BLAND *v.*² + -ING¹.] Flattery, blandishment.

c **1315** Shoreham 14 That he may nauȝt y-weid be With blanding ne with boste. **1340** *Ayenb.* 10 Þet is zenne of blondingge, oþer of lozengerie.

†'**blanding,** *ppl. a. Obs.* [f. as prec. + -ING².] Flattering, blandishing.

c **1315** Shoreham 59 The fend Wyth hys blaundynge stevene.

blandish ('blændɪʃ), *v.* Forms: 4 **blandise, -isshe, -isсhe, blaundise, -isshe, bloundise, -iss,** 4-6 **blaundysh,** 5 **blandysh(e, -yss, -yssh, blaundish, -iss, -yssh,** 6 ? **blandesh,** *Sc.* **blandyis,** 5- **blandish.** [a. F. *blandiss-* lengthened stem of *blandir*:—L. *blandīri* to flatter, f. *blandus* smooth, soft: see -ISH². Rare in 17th and 18th c.: Johnson says 'I have met with this word in no other passage' than the quotation from Milton (see BLANDISHED).]

1. *trans.* To flatter gently by kind words or affectionate actions, to coax; to act upon with caressing action or complaisant speech; to cajole.

c **1305** [see BLANDISHING *vbl. sb.*] *c* **1430** Lydg. *Bochas* I. viii. (1544) 15 b, She can them blandishen with her flatery. *c* **1530** *Proverbs* in *Pol. Rel. & L. Poems* (1866) 31 Allso repelle that seruavnte that vsith to blaundysh the. **1748** Richardson *Clarissa* II. xi. 68 You must then blandish him over with a confession, that all your past behaviour was maidenly reserve only. **1831** Carlyle *Sart. Res.* II. v, By this fairest of Orient Light-bringers must our Friend be blandished. **1837** —— *Fr. Rev.* II. III. VII. ii. 353 To blandish down the grimness of Republican austerity.

b. *fig.* Of things.

1758 J. G. Cooper *Aristippus* i. (R.) In former days a country life..Was blandish'd by perpetual spring.

2. *intr.* (*absol.*) To use blandishments; to act or speak with gentle allurement or flattery.

a **1340** Hampole *Psalter* i. 1 He spekis of crist & of his folouers, bloundisand til vs. *Ibid.* xc. 13 The dragoun..that bloundiss with the heuyd and smytes with the tayle. *c* **1386** Chaucer *Parson's T.* 302 If he flatere or blandise [*v.r.* blaundise, blandisshe, blaundisshe, blandische] moore than hym oghte for any necessite. **1612** Drayton *Poly-olb.* xiii. 220 How shee blandishing, By Dunsmore drives along.

†**3.** *trans.* To offer blandly (cf. *to smile thanks*).

c **1630** Drumm. of Hawth. *Wks.* 11 Though they [flowers] sometime blandish soft delight. *a* **1638** R. James *Wks.* (1880) 254 That knew not how to menace speare, Or blandish words that ravish sense.

†'**blandish,** *sb. Obs. rare.* Blandishment.

c **1475** *Found. St. Barthol.* I. ix. (1886) 91 When with flaterynge blandysh, a goodwhyle she hadde flateryd.

ˈblandished, *ppl. a.* [f. as prec. + -ED[1].] Invested with flattery or blandishment.

1671 MILTON *Samson* 403 With blandish'd parleys, feminine assaults.

blandisher (ˈblændɪʃə(r)). [f. as prec. + -ER[1].] One who blandishes, a flatterer.

1611 COTGR., *Blandisseur*, a blandisher, gloser, soother.

blandishing (ˈblændɪʃɪŋ), *vbl. sb.* [f. as prec. + -ING[1].] Blandishment, flattery.

c **1305** *St. Kath.* 165 in *E.E.P.* (1862) 94 Al þi blandisinge Ne þi tourmentz ne schulle ene fram him myn hurte bringe. *a* **1340** HAMPOLE *Psalter* ii. 3 Dispise we thaire bloundisynges & thaire manaunces. **1485** CAXTON *Curial* I b, Fayr langage..or blandysshing of flaterers. **1648** JOS. BEAUMONT *Psyche* VI. iii. (T.) Double-hearted friends, whose blandishings Tickle our ears, but sting our bosoms.

ˈblandishing, *ppl. a.* [f. as prec. + -ING[2].] Softly flattering, soothing, coaxing.

c **1374** CHAUCER *Boeth.* II. i. 30 þe see..calme and blaundyshing wiþ smoþe water. **1483** CAXTON *Gold. Leg.* 117/2 The blaundissyng wordes of wymen. **1566** STUDLEY *Seneca's Medea* (1581) 135 With countnaunce bright and blandishing. **1840** DICKENS *Humphrey's Clock* 48 Would the blandishing enchanter still weave his spells around me.

blandishment (ˈblændɪʃmənt). [f. as prec. + -MENT: cf. OF. *blandissement*.]

1. Gently flattering speech or action; cajolery.

1591 SPENSER *M. Hubberd* 1274 He gan enquire..of the Foxe, and his false blandishment. **1622** BACON *Henry VII*, Wks. (1860) 477 He..would use strange sweetness and blandishments of words. **1711** ADDISON *Spect.* No. 128 ¶4 Nature has given all the Arts of Soothing and Blandishment to the Female. **1880** L. STEPHEN *Pope* iv. 96 He was not..inaccessible to aristocratic blandishments.

2. *fig.* Attraction, allurement. *concr.* Anything that pleases or allures.

1594 GREENE *Look. Glasse* (1861) 142 Bear hence these wretched blandishments of sin (Taking off his crown and robe). **1660** STANLEY *Hist. Philos.* (1701) 609/1 If any external blandishments happen, they increase not the chief good. **1875** J. BENNET *Winter Medit.* II. xi. 369 His thoughts ..were ever on the blandishments of imperial Rome.

†**ˈblanditude.** *Obs. rare.* [f. L. *blandus* BLAND *a.* + -TUDE; but with reference to BLANDISH.] Flattering or blandishing behaviour; blandness.

1689 T. PLUNKET *Char. Gd. Command.* Ded., Yet shall you meet with..Rubs, Censures, Cavils, and base blanditude. —— 24 Blanditude Desert shall overthrow. **1922** *Observer* 16 Apr. 10/5 Then Mr. Lloyd George rose.. in wise fun and paternal blanditude.

blandly (ˈblændlɪ), *adv.* [f. BLAND *a.* + -LY[2].] In a bland manner; with gently flattering or soothing words or actions; mildly, gently, pleasingly.

1827 CARLYLE *Misc.* (1857) I. 7 It is seldom so much rugged energy can be so blandly attempered. **1853** C. BRONTË *Villette* i. 2 Time always flowed..blandly, like the gliding of a full river through a plain. **1863** LANDOR *Heroic Idylls, Myrtis,* Friends whom she lookt at blandly from her couch.

blandness (ˈblændnɪs). [f. as prec. + -NESS.] The quality or state of being bland; suavity, mild or soothing quality.

1846 BROWNING *Luria* II. i, This hating people, that hate each the other, And in one blandness to us Moors unite. *a* **1859** MACAULAY *Hist. Eng.* V. 82 Envy was disarmed by the blandness of Albemarle's temper. **1862** G. WILSON *Relig. Chem.* 10 What water is among liquids, in blandness, neutrality, and indifference, nitrogen is among gases.

blane, pa. t. of BLIN *v. Obs.*; and obs f. BLAIN.

blank, (blæŋk), *a.* Forms: 5-7 blanke, 6-7 blanck(e, 7-8 blanc, 5- blank. [F. *blanc* white, a common Romanic adj. (Pr. *blanc, blanca,* Sp. *blanco,* Pg. *branco,* It. *bianco,* med.L. *blancus*), a. OHG. *blanch* (MHG. *blanc*):—OTeut. **blanko-z* shining, referred by etymologists generally to the verbal stem BLINK, as a nasalized form of *blik-* in *blîkan,* OHG. *blîchan,* OE. *blícan* to shine. But **blink,* **blinch* is not actually found in any of the old dialects; and the origin of **blanko-z* thus remains obscure.]

A. *adj.* **1.** White (*obs.*, and chiefly in specific uses, e.g. *blank plumb* white lead, *blank falcon* a 'white hawk,' i.e. one in its third year); pale, colourless.

c **1325** *Coer de L.* 6526 A robe i-furryd with blaun [? blaunc] and nere. *c* **1440** *Promp. Parv.* 38 Blanke plumbe [*K.H.* blavmblumbe, **1499** blawnblumb, otherwyse called whyte lede.] *a* **1500** in *Rel. Ant.* I. 108 Tempur blank chalke, plum or ceruse, with gleyre. **1562** LEIGH *Armorie* (1597) 133 b, The Herehaught..in a chemise blanke, powdred and spotted with mullets Sable. **1575** TURBERV. *Bk. Falconry* 212 The blancke falcons are flegmaticke. **1615** LATHAM *Falconry* (1633) 25 In your blanke Hawks. **1667** MILTON *P.L.* x. 656 To the blanc Moone Her office they prescrib'd. **1726** THOMSON *Winter* 124 Rising slow, Blank, in the leaden-colour'd east, the moon. **1821** BYRON *Juan* IV. ix, The blank grey was not made to blast their hair.

2. a. Of paper, etc.: Left white or 'fair'; not written upon, free from written or printed characters, 'empty of all marks' (J.); said also of orders, cheques, deeds, and official documents left with an empty space for special signature or instruction; not 'filled up'. See 10.

1547 LYNDESAY *Trag. Cdl. Betoun* 121 Ane paper blank his Grace I gart subscrive. **1598** SHAKS. *Merry W.* II. i. 77, I warrant he hath a thousand of these Letters, writ with blancke-space for different names. **1687** *Lond. Gaz.* No. 2209/4 A Copy-Book of Letters..about one half of it being Blank paper. **1708** *Ibid.* No. 4499/3 His Grace sent him a blank Passport. **1712** ADDISON *Spect.* No. 549 ¶1 When I look upon the Creditor-side, I find little more than blank Paper. **1855** MACAULAY *Hist. Eng.* IV. 178 Requesting the King to send a blank safe conduct in the largest terms.

b. Const. *of*.

1842 TENNYSON *St. Simeon* 156 That God hath now Sponged and made blank of crimeful record.

c. *in blank*: without names specified.

1836 KENT *Comm. Amer. Law* xliv. (1873) III. 89 A note endorsed in blank is like one payable to bearer. **1845** STEPHEN *Laws Eng.* II. 129 Policies being made in blank, that is, without specifying the names of the persons, for whose benefit they were made. **1861** GOSCHEN *For. Exch.* 37 Bills which are technically said to be drawn in blank.

3. a. *gen.* Empty, without contents, void, bare.

1748 THOMSON *Cast. Indol.* I. xxix, Wide o'er this ample court's blank area. **1840** HOOD *Up Rhine* (1869) 245 The Figure..strode forth into the blank darkness. **1849** RUSKIN *Sev. Lamps* 201 The blank lancet arch on the one hand, and the overcharged cinquefoiled arch on the other. **1855** BAIN *Senses & Int.* II. ii. §6 The blank sensation of the naked body is owing principally to the deprivation of touch. **1856** DOVE *Logic Chr. Faith* v. i. §1. 261 Issuing out of a universe in which there was only blank space.

b. *blank practice*: practice with 'blank' or empty cartridges (see 10). Also *fig.*

1873 MORLEY *Rousseau* I. 66 Rousseau..changed the blank practice of the elder philosophers into a deadly affair of ball and shell.

4. *fig.* **a.** Void of interest or event; vacant, 'having nothing in it;' as *a blank look-out*.

1729 BUTLER *Serm.* Wks. 1874 II. 189 Various kinds of amusements..serve to fill up the blank spaces of time. **1803** BRISTED *Pedest. Tour* II. 481 They..suffered us to talk Irish to ourselves all the evening, without the least interruption, so that we had but a blank night of it. **1867** FREEMAN *Norm. Conq.* (1876) I. App. 753 A year which the Chronicles leave quite blank.

b. Void of result, unsuccessful, fruitless, nugatory; amounting to or producing nothing.

a **1553** UDALL *Royster D.* II. ii. (Arb.) 34, I weene I am a prophete, this geare will proue blanke. **1627** E. F. *Hist. Edw. II,* (1680) 47 The King doubles his pace homewards; instead of Triumph, glad he had got loose from so imminent a danger..This blank return filled the Kingdom with a fretting murmur. **1643** *Lanc. Tracts* 165 The two Colonells being blank in their treaty, spent their stay in wise instructions. **1699** BOYER *Fr. Dict.* (1753), A blank (or bad) come-off, *Une méchante defaite.* **1832** EG.-WARBURTON *Hunt. Songs* ii. (1883) 7 The man..Whose heart heaves a sigh when his gorse is drawn blank. *Ibid.* 163 But I felt inclin'd in my inmost mind, To wish for a blank day.

c. Of the face or look: Void of expression, expressing no attention, interest, or emotion; vacant. Also const. *of.*

1859 TENNYSON *Elaine* 816 While he roll'd his eyes Yet blank from sleep. **1884** MRS. EWING *Story Short Life* i, Lady Jane's face was blank because she was trying not to laugh. **1884** W. C. SMITH *Kildrostan* I. iii. 85 To look with blank fixed gaze at these old books. **1924** A. E. W. MASON *House of Arrow* viii. 97 Hanaud's eyes..were blank of all expression.

5. Of persons: (Looking) as if deprived of the faculty of speech or action; 'shut up,' utterly disconcerted, discomfited, resourceless, or non-plussed; now chiefly in *to look blank*: cf. prec.

1542 UDALL *Erasm. Apoph.* 61 a, Beeyng confounded and made blanke in a disputacion of a certain feloe. **1580** BARET *Alv.* B 781 These fellowes be blanke or out of hart and courage. **1649** MILTON *Eikon.* 184 The Damsell of Burgundy at sight of her own letter, was soon blank. **1652** BP. HALL *Invis. World* III. §3 How blank must Moses needs have looked to see his great works patterned by those presumptuous rivals! **1667** MILTON *P.L.* IX. 890 Adam.. amaz'd, Astonied stood and Blank. **1711** ADDISON *Spect.* No. 7 ¶1 Upon this I looked very blank. **1727** THOMSON *Summer* 1050 The blank assistants seem'd, Silent, to ask, whom Fate would next demand. **1853** KINGSLEY *Hypatia* xi. 134 The two old men looked at each other with blank and horror-stricken faces.

6. Of emotions: Prostrating the whole faculties; unrelieved, helpless, stark, sheer.

1634 MILTON *Comus* 452 Noble grace that dashed brute violence With sudden adoration and blank awe. **1717** POPE *Eloisa* 148 'Tis all blank sadness, or continual tears. **1809** W. IRVING *Knickerb.* VII. xi. (1849) 437 Blank terror reigned over the community. **1837** DICKENS *Pickw.* v, Gazing on each other with countenances of blank dismay. **1875** HAMERTON *Intell. Life* I. vii. 39, I well remember the blank despair which I felt.

7. a. *gen.* Pure, unmixed, utter, downright, sheer, absolute (with a negative or privative force).

1839 DE QUINCEY *Murder* Wks. 1862 IV. 59 The blank impossibilities of Lilliput. **1856** KANE *Arct. Exp.* I. xviii. 222 The red sandstones contrast most favorably with the blank whiteness. **1871** FARRAR *Witn. Hist.* ii. 54 The blank atheism..of recent controversialists.

†**b.** Mere, bare, simple. *Obs.*

1596 NASHE *Saffron-Wald.* Wks. (1883-4) 103 None is priuy to a blank maintenance he hath, and some maintenance of necessity he must haue. **1640** BROME *Antip.* v. iv. Wks. III. 327 Did you not warrant me upon that pawne..your blanck honour, That you would cure his jealousie?

c. *Cards.* Unsupported by other cards of the same suit (see quots.).

1895 MANSON *Sporting Dict., Blank,* a card in hand is said to be blank when there is no other card of the same suit in hand with it. The term is also applied to a king and queen of the same suit, in which case the twenty of that suit is blank. **1934** [see BLANK *v.* 8]. **1958** *Listener* 16 Oct. 611/3 The blank honour combination in diamonds takes the bloom off West's hand.

8. a. *blank verse*: verse without rime; *esp.* the iambic pentameter or unrimed heroic, the regular measure of English dramatic and epic poetry, first used by the Earl of Surrey (died 1547).

1589 NASHE in Greene *Menaph.* Pref. (Arb.) 6 The swelling bumbast of bragging blanke verse. **1602** SHAKS. *Ham.* II. ii. 339 The Lady shall say her minde freely; or the blanke Verse shall halt for't. **1739** CHESTERF. *Lett.* I. xxv. 93 Those that have no rhymes are called blank verses. **1784** COWPER *Lett.* 13 Dec., Blank verse is susceptible of a much greater diversification of manner than verse in rhyme. **1874** SAYCE *Compar. Philol.* ix. 385 Our greatest poems have been written in blank verse.

b. Hence *blank versifier*.

1746 W. HORSLEY *The Fool* (1748) II. 96 Rebus-Men, Punsters, and Blank Versifiers.

9. *Comb.*, as *blank-eyed, blank-faced, blank-looking* adjs.

1881 H. JAMES *Portr. Lady* xxxvi, It was her habit to interpose a good many blank-looking pauses. **1882** J. PARKER *Apost. Life* (1884) III. 63 The blank-eyed villagers. **1887** G. MEREDITH *Ballads & Poems* 61 He raced..across a ground Flint of breast, blank-faced. **1921** V. WOOLF *Writer's Diary* 8 Apr. (1953) 31 This diary being a kindly blankfaced old confidante.

10. In various specific collocations: as (in sense 2) **blank acceptance**, one not having the amount filled in; **blank bar**, 'a Plea in Bar, which in an Action of Trespass is put in to compel the Plaintiff to assign the certain place where the Trespass was committed' (Blount *Law Dict.* 1670); **blank bond**, a bond in which a blank is left for the creditor's name; **blank charter**, a document given to the agents of the crown in Richard II.'s reign, with power to fill it up as they pleased; hence *fig.* liberty to do as one likes; **blank cheque**, one not having the amount filled in (see also CHEQUE, CHECK 3); **blank credit**, 'an authorized permission given to draw on an individual or firm to a certain amount' (Ogilvie); **blank flange** (see quot. 1940); **blank indorsement**, a bill in which the indorsee's name is omitted. Also (in sense 3) **blank-cartridge**, a cartridge containing no ball; **blank-door** (*Arch.*), an imitation of a door; **blank-tire**, a tire without a flange; **blank-tooling** = blind-blocking; see BLIND 14; **blank wall**, (*a*) a wall without an opening in it; (*b*) an apparently impenetrable obstacle, esp. in phr. *to come up against a blank wall* (cf. BRICK WALL *sb.*[1] 2). **blank-window**, an imitation-window. Also **blank-form**: see BLANCH; **point blank**: see POINT.

1826 *Gentl. Mag.* May 458/2 Their carbines..were only loaded with *blank cartridges. **1398** *Hist. Croyland. Cont.* in *Rer. Angl. Script. Vet.* (1684) I. 493 Quadam alba charta vocata *Blankechartre..quod utique Regis Richardi in posterum causa exitii magna fuit. **1593** SHAKS. *Rich. II,* I. iv. 48 Our Substitutes at home shall haue Blanke-charters. **1593** DONNE *Sat.* iii, That God hath with his hand Sign'd kings blank-charters, to kill whom they hate. **1940** *Chambers's Techn. Dict.* 94/2 *Blank flange,* a disc, or solid flange, used to blank off the end of a pipe. **1904** GOODCHILD & TWENEY *Technol. & Sci. Dict.* 54/1 **Blank wall,* a wall without an opening in it. **1930** *Economist* 9 Aug. 290/1 Restriction proposals in the rubber-growing industry have apparently come up against a blank wall. **1958** *Times* 17 Nov. 11/3 The Advisory Council on Standards for Consumer Goods..has continued to come up against a blank wall of opposition on matters which were clearly worrying it a year ago.

†**B.** quasi-*adv.* Absolutely, unreservedly. *Obs.*

1677 TEMPLE *Let.* Wks. 1731 II. 434 The Allegations on either side are blank contrary one to the other.

blank (blæŋk), *sb.* Forms: 6-7 blanc, blanke, blanck(e, 7- blank. [f. prec. The senses consist of a number of absolute or elliptical uses of the adj., not mutually connected. (The arrangement here is chiefly chronological.)]

†**1.** A small French coin, originally of silver, but afterwards of copper; also a silver coin of Henry V current in the parts of France then held by the English. According to Littré, the French *blanc* was worth 5 deniers. The application of the name in the 17th c. is uncertain. *Obs.*

a **1399** ARNOLD *Chron.* (1811) 14 Yeldyng therof by yere CCC *li.* of sterlynge of blankis. **1480** CAXTON *Chron. Eng.* ccxliv. 298 The frensshmen playde owre kyng and his lordes at the dise and an archer alwey for a blank of hir money. For they wenden al had ben heres. **1523** LD. BERNERS *Froiss.* I. ccccxli. 776 Whosoeuer brought a fagot before the kynges tent, he shulde haue a blanke of Fraunce. **1577** HELLOWES *Gueuara's Chron.* 204 He did rather leaue his woode vnsolde, then abate one blanke of his price. **1629** *S'hertogenbosh* 45 Candles 12 stiuers a pound, an Egge two blancks. **1670** BLOUNT *Law Dict., Blancks,* a kinde of Money, coyned by King Henry the Fifth, in the parts of

France, which were then subject to England, the value whereof was 8*d*.. The reason why they were called Blanks, was because..this of Silver, was in name distinguished by the colour. **1753** CHAMBERS *Cycl. Supp.*, *Blank* also denotes a small copper coin, formerly current in France, at the rate of five deniers Tournois. **1863** *Spring & Sum. in Lapland* 81 A specie dollar, or 'blank,' as they call it here, will rouse the apathy and greed of a Lap when paper currency will have no effect.

2. a. The white spot in the centre of a target; hence *fig.* anything aimed at, the range of such aim.

1554 *Interl. Youth* in Hazl. *Dodsl.* II. 35 Pink and drink, and also at the blank, And many sports mo. **1598** BARRET *Theor. Warres* III. i. 35 To cause them to leuell, and discharge at the blancke thereof. **1837** CDL. WISEMAN *Fun. Orat. Cdl. Weld* 23 Rome, the very blank and aim of religious partizanship in our country.

Cf. the following with b, as illustrating its origin:

1602 SHAKS. *Ham.* IV. i. 42 (Globe) As level as the cannon to his blank Transports his poisoned shot. **1604** —— *Oth.* III. iv. 128, I haue stood within the blanke of his displeasure.

b. 'Level line mark for cannon, as point-blank, equal to 800 yards.' Smyth *Sailor's Wrd.-bk.*

1747 *Gentl. Mag.* XVII. 398 Fired at the Bellona, which Capt. Barrington..did not return (being but just within blank).

†**3.** A nonplus. *Obs.*

1542 UDALL *Erasm. Apoph.* 61 a, Aristippus was nothyng greued to take a blanke in disputacion. **1548** UDALL, etc. *Erasm. Par. Acts* vi. 10 The inwarde griefe..whiche thei had conceiued for the blancke they wer put unto. **1580** LYLY *Euphues* (Arb.) 362 Such a place, as turned them all to a blanke.

4. A lottery ticket which does not gain a prize. ***to draw a blank***: see DRAW *v.* 52 b.

1567 in Kempe *Loseley MSS.* (1835) 188 A verie rich Lotterie..without any blancks. **1607** SHAKS. *Cor.* v. ii. 10 It is Lots to Blankes, My name hath touch't your eares. **1779** J. MOORE *View Soc.* II. xcv. 426 All the tickets he had in the lottery had proved blanks. **1824** W. IRVING *T. Trav.* I. 4 When one has drawn a blank.

5. a. A blank space in a written or printed document.

c **1570** *Leg. Bp. St. Andrews* in *Scot. Poems 16th C.* II. 343, I sall leive blankis for to imbrew thame. **1632** *Star Chamb. Cases* (1886) 119 Warrantes..with blankes for names of plaintiff and defendant. *c* **1677** MARVELL *Growth Popery* Wks. I. 555 Which blanck..shall be filled up with the Christian name of such King or Queen. *a* **1745** SWIFT (J.) I cannot write a paper full as I used to do; and yet I will not forgive a blank of half an inch from you. *a* **1859** MACAULAY *Hist. Eng.* V. 138 Full powers must be sent..with blanks left for the names of the plenipotentiaries.

b. Provisional words printed in italics (instead of blank spaces) in a bill before Parliament, being matters of practical detail, of which the final form will be settled in Committee.

1817 *Parl. Debates* 583/2 The blanks of the bill were then filled up in the committee. **1863** H. COX *Inst.* I. ix. 167 In going through the bill[in committee], words printed in italics, commonly called 'blanks,' stand, unless objected to.

c. ***in blank*** [after F. *en blanc*]: with blank spaces for the filling in of details.

c **1814** A. REES *Cycl.* (1819) XXVIII. sig. H1r/2 Inconvenience having been experienced from having marine insurances in blank. **1842** STEPHEN *Comm. Laws Eng.* II. II. v. 164 A bill, payable to order, is indorsed in *blank* by the payee. **1858** J. W. SMITH *Law of Bills* 27 Another way in which the holder of a bill or note indorsed to him *in blank* may transfer it without incurring personal liability, is by writing over the indorser's signature the words, 'Pay A. B. or order'. **1882** BITHELL *Counting-ho. Dict.* 45 Bills and Notes of this description are said to be drawn 'in Blank'.

6. a. A document, 'paper,' or 'form' with spaces left blank to be filled up at the pleasure of the person to whom it is given (*e.g.* a blank charter), or as the event may determine; a blank form. Now chiefly *U.S.*, freq. with defining term.

1586 T. B. *La Primaud. Fr. Acad.* 708 The citie of Athens..was constrained to sende a blanke for capitulations of peace. **1593** SHAKS. *Rich. II*, II. i. 250 And daily new exactions are deuis'd, As blankes, beneuolences, and I wot not what. **1611** BEAUM. & FL. *Maid's Trag.* v. iii, Throw him the blank. Melantius, write in that Thy choice. **1711** in *Lond. Gaz.* No. 4817/7 The several Blanks..are printed..at the Crown and Scepter. **1780** J. REED in Sparks *Corr. Amer. Rev.* (1853) III. 23 We have furnished the Commissioners with blanks of various kinds of returns, and directed them to send us a weekly account. **1805** D. MCCLURE *Diary* (1899) 83 Dr. Wheelock..had given us blanks, for bills of Exchange, on the School's funds, in Scotland. **1860** HOLLAND *Miss Gilbert's Career* x. 181 You've had to write the whole of this. How long have we been out of blanks? **1904** P. H. HANUS *Mod. School* 128 By means of question blanks sent to the parents, much information..is secured by the teachers. **1904** *N.Y. Times* 24 Nov. 1 The messages were always on regular telegraph blanks. **1963** *P.M.L.A.* LXXVIII. IV. ii. 15/1 These committees required applicants to send in a completed application blank together with academic transcripts.

b. An empty form without substance; anything insignificant; nothing at all.

a **1700** DRYDEN (J.) She has left him The blank of what he was. **1704** PENN in *Pa. Hist. Soc. Mem.* IX. 308 People might have thought..I was gone with him a blank, he being called governor. **1742** YOUNG *Nt. Th.* II. 80 No blank, no trifle, nature made, or meant. **1818** SCOTT *Hrt. Midl.* i, His debts amount to blank—his losses to blank—his funds to blank—leaving a balance of blank in his favour.

c. An unprinted leaf of a book.

1952 J. CARTER *ABC for Book-Collectors* 36 Blanks sometimes occur at the beginning of the book, sometimes at the end of a clearly marked division, more often at the end of the last gathering.

7. *fig.* A vacant space, place, or period; a void.

1601 SHAKS. *Twel. N.* II. iv. 113 *Duke.* And what's her history? *Vio.* A blanke, my lord. **1667** MILTON *P.L.* III. 48 For the Book of knowledg fair Presented with a Universal blanc Of Natures works to mee expung'd and ras'd. **1759** FRANKLIN *Ess.* Wks. 1840 III. 525 The remainder of that day was wasted..The next was a blank likewise. **1793** LD. SPENCER in *Ld. Auckland's Corr.* (1862) III. 124 The interval till then will be a complete blank in my life. *c* **1815** J. HISLOP *Scott. Sacr. Sabb.* vii, The blanks in family circles fill'd again. **1876** MOZLEY *Univ. Serm.* vi. 142 The future is a blank, or a dark enigma to them.

8. Blank verse; cf. BLANK *a.* 8.

1589 GREENE *Menaph.* Wks. 1881–3 VI. 27 Lest..they bewaile in weeping blankes the wane of their Monarchie. **1627** FELTHAM *Resolves* I. lxx. Wks. (1677) 108, I hold it better put in Prose, or Blanks. **1793** SOUTHEY *Nondescr.* i. Wks. III. 58 In Miltonic blank bemouth'd. **1809** BYRON *Bards & Rev.* ix, Rhyme and blank maintain an equal race.

9. *Mech.* **a.** A piece of metal, cut and shaped to the required size of the thing to be made, and ready for the finishing operations; *esp.* in *Coinage*, the disc of metal before stamping.

1596 J. BUREL *Entry Q. Edinb.*, Braid blancis hang above thair eis, With jewels of all histories. *c* **1695** in Ruding *Ann. Coinage* (ed. 2) III. 423 The Blanks for Farthings cast. **1753** CHAMBERS *Cycl. Supp.*, *Blank*, in coinage, a plate, or piece of gold, or silver, cut and shaped for a coin, but not yet stamped. **1831** J. HOLLAND *Manuf. Metals* I. 201 The blanks for wood screws are generally forged by the nailors. **1881** GREENER *Gun* 296 The blank [for a cartridge case] is..forced by a descending plug through a tapering aperture.

b. (See quot. 1962.)

1899 *Daily News* 14 June 9/1 In the blowing of the opal glass surface of the 'blank' a blister or bubble may be caused. **1962** *Gloss. Terms Glass Ind.* (*B.S.I.*) 23 *Blank*, any article of glass on which subsequent processing is required.

c. *Electric recording.* (See quot.)

1940 *Chambers's Techn. Dict.* 94/2 *Blank*, the shaved wax ready for placing on a recording machine for making wax records with a stylus.

10. The $\frac{1}{230400}$ of a grain.

1680 MORDEN *Geog. Rect.* (1685) 279 The Monyers Divide the Perit into 24 Blanks. **1725** BRADLEY *Fam. Dict.* II. s.v. *Weights*, The Moneyers subdivide the grain thus: 24 Blanks make 1 Perrot; 20 Perrots 1 Dwit; 24 Dwits 1 Mite; 20 Mites 1 grain.

11. In the game of dominoes: A piece which is without points on one or both of its divisions.

12. a. A dash written in place of an omitted letter or word. Thus, —— —— Esq. of —— Hall, read *Blank Blank* Esquire of *Blank* Hall. Cf. DASH.

1773 GOLDSMITH *Stoops to Conq.* v. 106 Anthony Lumpkin, Esquire, of BLANK place. **1818** SCOTT *Rob Roy* xi, A dispensation..to Diana Vernon to marry *Blank* Osbaldistone, Esq. **1836** DICKENS *Pickw.* xxiv. 251 Here's my authority. Blank Tupman, blank Pickwick—against the peace of our sufferin Lord the King. **1861** *Two Cosmos* II. IV. ix. 83 She was married, though—blank—years younger than Miss Lambert. **1888** *Co-operative News* 24 Mar. 266 Our adjoining neighbours at blank—the place shall be nameless. **1968** *Listener* 4 Apr. 445/2 It was not practicable to print anecdotes week after week about Lord Blank's personality and foolish views.

b. Used euphemistically as a verbal representation of a dash put instead of an oath or profane word. Cf. BLANK *v.* 5 c. So (as *adjs.* or *advs.*) **blankety** ('blæŋkɪtɪ), which represents an adj. derivative, such as *bloody*; less freq. **blanked** (blæŋkt), **blanky** ('blæŋkɪ).

1854 'C. BEDE' *Further Adv. Verdant Green* iv. 28, I wouldn't give a blank for such a blank blank. I'm blank, if he doesn't look as if he'd swallowed a blank codfish. **1874** M. CLARKE *His Natural Life* II. III. xiii. 236 'My blank!' cried Burgess. 'You blank blank, is that your blank game? I'll blank soon cure you of that!' **1876** BRET HARTE *Gabriel Conroy* VI. vi, Blank me, if she was inclined to show some attention to Colonel Starbottle. *Ibid.* vii, But what in blank are you waiting for? **1886** BAUMANN *Londinismen* 11/1 Blanked. **1888** *Troy Daily Times* 3 Feb. (Farmer), He had known vessels to be hindered thirty days; yes, even three months, by that blankety blankety bar! **1892** *Photogr. Ann.* II. 42 The blankety blankness that ensues when the tyro..finds that he has forgotten..his tripod top, &c.! **1896** *Daily News* 15 Feb. 5/1 He..is called 'a blanky capitalist'. **1900** *Westm. Gaz.* 25 May 2/2 Then he lay back, swearing at the blankety blank young blanker. **1900** H. LAWSON *On Track* 31 And do you think I'd tell you a blanky lie? *Ibid.* 40 'What does he want to do that for?' 'To get it blanky well analysed! You ass!' **1902** —— *Children of Bush* 12 Let 'em go to ——! I'm blanked if I give a sprat. **1908** M. DIVER *Great Amulet* xviii, Colonel Stanham Buckley..inquired picturesquely of a passing official when the blank this blankety blank train was supposed to start. **1914** W. J. LOCKE *Fortunate Youth* i, What cared he for the blankety little blanks who gibed at him? **1952** A. GRIMBLE *Pattern of Islands* 8 Never springing a blanky leak anywhere. **1959** in N. Mailer *Advts. for Myself* (1961) 345 Mailer? He's an incorrigible blank.

13. A zero score in a game. *U.S.*

1867 *Ball Players' Chron.* 6 June 2/2 Sharp fielding should have disposed of the Harvards for a blank. **1888** *Outing* (U.S.) May 119/2 The tenth innings had seen both sides retire for blanks.

14. Short for *blank cartridge* (see BLANK *a.* 10).

1896 KIPLING *Seven Seas* 202 For it's 'Three rounds blank' an' follow me. **1935** N. MARSH *Enter Murderer* iv. 52 The report comes from the wings. A blank was never used on the stage, as it would have scorched Surbonadier's clothes.

blank (blæŋk), *v.* Forms: 6 blanck(e, 6–7 blanke, 6– blank. [f. prec. Cf. ONFr. *blankir*, -*quir*, F. *blanchir*, OCat. *blanquir* to make white.] The senses are mixed up with those of BLANCH $v.^1$ and ^{2}, and BLENCH, BLENK, BLINK.

†**1.** *trans.* To make white, whiten; to make pale.

1483 CAXTON *G. de la Tour* liv, A baronnesse..the whiche as men saide blanked and popped or peynted her self. **1605** SYLVESTER *Du Bartas* I. vi. (1621) 119 His brow Was never blankt with pallid fear. **1652** BENLOWES *Theoph.* IX. li, The coral die is blankt at lips so red.

2. To put out of countenance; to nonplus, disconcert, 'shut up.' Cf. BLANK *a* 5. *arch.*

1548 UDALL, etc. *Erasm. Par. Mark* xii. 28 The Saduceis were put to a foyle and blanked. **1587** GOLDING *De Mornay* xxix. 464 At this R. Eliezer was blankt and held his peace. **1611** COTGR., *Bejaune*..a doult, noddie; one that's blankt, and hath nought to say, when hee hath most need to speak. —— *Confuter vn tesmoing*, to disgrace, confound, puzle, blanke him; to put him out of countenance, or, driue him to a Non-plus. **1653** URQUHART *Rabelais* (1807) I. 179 If I do not blank and gravel you..and put you to a non plus. **1820** SCOTT *Abbot* xviii, Which fairly blanked the bold visage of Adam Woodcock.

3. a. To frustrate, make void, invalidate, bring to nought, disconcert (plans, etc.). *arch.*

1566 T. STAPLETON *Ret. Untr. Jewell*, iv. 104 To dasel the Readers eyes withall, or to blancke his..Argument. **1596** SPENSER *State Irel.* Wks. (1862) 536/1 All former purposes were blancked. *a* **1659** CLEVELAND *To Ald. Hoyle* 8 And thus..blanks the Reckning with their Host. **1814** SCOTT *Wav.* II. i, Their sports blanked by the untoward accident.

b. To dismiss (a sports team) without a score; to prevent from scoring. *N. Amer.*

1870 *N.Y. Herald* 2 July 5/4 St. John..again blanked the Mutuals and then scored two. **1887** *Courier-Jrnl.* 26 May 2/6 In the eighth and ninth innings both [baseball] teams were blanked. **1951** *Amer. Speech* XXVI. 230 Michigan Normal blanks Ball State. **1968** *Globe & Mail* (Toronto) 5 Feb. 18/7 Oakville Oaks came up with their best effort of the season last night to blank Toronto Marlboros 3–0.

†**4.** To turn away. *Obs.* (Cf. BLANCH $v.^2$ 4.)

1640 YORKE *Union Hon.* 49 This unexpected aversion..blanckt the Scots. **1659** GAUDEN *Tears Ch.* 139 Nor are people to be blanked or scared from any thing which they list to call their Religion.

5. a. To render blank or void; to veil from sight. Also const. *out*.

1763–5 CHURCHILL *Gotham* III. Poems II. 20 When dreary Night..blank'd half the Globe. **1881** MISS BRADDON *Asph.* III. 331 An obelisk..blanking out earth and heaven with its gigantic form. **1937** *Times* 16 Apr. 8/6 A smoke screen by howitzers to blank out hostile observation posts and machine-guns.

b. To indicate by a blank or dash (——).

1789 BENTHAM *Wks.* X. 189 Dele *Foxical*, I doubt it is hardly safe; or blank it thus *F——ical*.

¶**c.** *Blank* (often printed ——, but read 'blank') is also, for decorum's sake, substituted for a word of execration.

1873 C. READE *Simpleton* xxiii. Blank him! that is just like him; the uneasy fool! **1878** MRS. EDWARDES *Jet* iii. 272 '—— the colonel of the regiment!' exclaims Mark..'Blank the colonel of the regiment!' With slow unmistakable gusto she lingers over the monosyllable 'Blank.'

d. To seal or render inoperative. Const. *off*, *up*.

1928 *Daily Tel.* 6 Mar. 5/6 The steam inlet and exhaust passages are blanked up and the cylinder subjected to a hydraulic pressure. **1932** *Amer. Speech* VII. 264 *Blank off*, to case off (a portion of an oil sand). **1940** [see *blank flange* s.v. BLANK *a.* 10]. **1963** *Guardian* 7 Mar. 3/2 Three-wheeled vehicles with the reverse gear 'blanked off'..remain Group 'A' vehicles..attracting a higher rate of duty.

e. *intr.* To become blank or empty.

1955 J. CHRISTOPHER *Year of Comet* i. 11 The callscreen blanked.

†**6.** *intr.* To be disconcerted; to blench; to shrink back. *Obs.*

1655 GURNALL *Chr. in Arm.* xiii. §2 (1669) 49/1 If thou canst..blank no more than a cold suitor doth, when he hears not from her whom he never really loved. **1642** ROGERS *Naaman* 423 But these would shed the bloud of such and no whit blanke.

†**7.** (?) To blanch = to strip off the skin. *Obs.*

1515 J. ROBSON *Scot. Field* in *Chetham Misc.* II, We blancked them with billes, through all their bright armor.

8. *Cards.* To leave (a card) unsupported by another card of the same suit. Cf. BLANK *a.* 7 c.

1884 'CAVENDISH' *Whist* (ed. 14) 100 It is dangerous to unguard an honour, or to blank an ace. **1934** *Amer. Speech* IX. 11/1 A *blank* King is a King without a guard and to *blank* a King is to discard its guard.

9. To cut or prepare a blank (see BLANK *sb.* 9); often const. *out*. Hence ***blanked*** ppl. a., ***blanking*** vbl. sb.

1914 *Amer. Machinist* 19 Feb. 342/1 The finished articles..are pierced, embossed, bent at a right-angle, and blanked in one operation. *Ibid.* (European ed.) 28 Mar. 66E/2 Describing their guard [for power presses] the firm classify press operations under blanking, clipping, and raising. **1943** F. D. JONES *Engineering Encycl.* (ed. 2) 136 A blanking die consists essentially of: a die-block..which has an opening that conforms to the shape of the part to be cut or blanked out. **1958** C. D. HANBURY *Industr. Efficiency Rural Labour* viii. 89 *Small dish blanking*... Strip metal is..fed into the machine, which blanks one disk every time a foot pedal is operated.

blank book, blank-book. orig. *U.S.* [BLANK *a.* 2.] A book of clean writing-paper in which to make entries, keep accounts, etc.

1713 C. MATHER *Diary* 12 Apr. in *Mass. Hist. Soc. Coll.* (1912) VIII. 199 To transcribe..into a blank Book, some instructive Passage. **1802** in C. Cist *Cincinnati: Early Annals*, etc. 193 For a blank-book to record ordinances.

1831 *Boston Directory* 18 (Advt.), Blank book manufacturers. **1886** S. W. MITCHELL *R. Blake* ii. 14 He spent a few minutes more over the details of daily duty set out in a little blank-book. **1952** J. B. OLDHAM *Eng. Blind-Stamped Bindings* i. 2 Sometimes what appears at first to be a blank book is not really one at all. *Ibid.* iii. 34 Blank-book binderies.

blanked (blæŋkt), *ppl. a.*
†**1.** Whitened, made white. *Obs.*
a **1529** SKELTON *Elyn. Rum.* in *Harl. Misc.* (Malh.) III. 479 She hobbles like a goose, with her blanked hose.
†**2.** Nonplussed. *Obs.*
1611 COTGR. s.v. *Camus*, *Des harangueurs bien camus*, blanked, grauelled, or driuen to a Non-plus.

blanked: see BLANK *sb.* 12 b.

blanket (ˈblæŋkɪt), *sb.* Forms: 4 blenket, 4–6 **blankette**, 5–7 **blankett**, 6–7 **blanquet**, **blanchet**, **blancket**, 3– **blanket**. [a. OF. *blankete*, *blanquette* blanket, f. *blanc* white + dim. suffix *-ette*; see *blanchētus*, *-um* in Ducange. Cf. BLUNKET. (The *Thomas Blanket* to whom gossip attributes the origin of the name, if he really existed, doubtless took his name from the article.)]
†**1.** A white or undyed woollen stuff used for clothing. *Obs.*
c **1300** *Beket* 1167 Blak was his cope above: his curtel whit blanket. *c* **1420** *Anturs Arth.* xxix, Her belte was of blenket . . Beten with besandus, and boculf ful bene. *c* **1440** *Promp. Parv.* 38 Blankett, lawngelle, *langellus*. [**1866** ROGERS *Agric. & Prices* I. xxii. 575 Blanket being undyed stuff. *Ibid.* 576 Blanket, or coarse woollen cloth, was woven at Witney nearly 500 years ago.]
2. a. A large oblong sheet of soft loose woollen cloth, used for the purpose of retaining heat, chiefly as one of the principal coverings of a bed; also for throwing over a horse, and, by savages or destitute persons, for clothing. ***tossing in a blanket*** was a rough irregular mode of punishment.
'*Blankets*' are now also made of cotton, of paper, etc.
1346 *Test. Ebor.* I. (1836) 23, Ij. lintheamina cum uno blanket. **1392** LANGL. *P. Pl.* C x. 254 Noþer blankett in hus bed. **1444** *Test. Ebor.* II. (1855) 111 A pair of blankettis. **1597** SHAKS. *2 Hen. IV*, II. iv. 241 A rascally Slaue, I will tosse the Rogue in a Blanket. **1606** HOLLAND *Sueton.* 17 Annot., A light blanquet or quilt. **1639** J. W. tr. *Guibert's Char. Physic* II. 66 Three or foure blanchets of Cotton hemmed. **1682** DRYDEN *Mac. Fl.* 42 The like was ne'er in Epsom blankets tost. **1711** BUDGELL *Spect.* No. 150 ¶3 Had Tully himself pronounced one of his Orations with a Blanket about his Shoulders. **1713** STEELE *Guardian* No. 72 (1756) I. 319, I have . . more than once seen the discipline of the blanket administred to the offenders. **1876** JEVONS *Logic Prim.* 9 People are so accustomed to use blankets to make themselves warm that they are surprised to see blankets used to keep ice cold.
b. *fig.*
1605 SHAKS. *Macb.* I. v. 54 Nor Heauen peepe through the Blanket of the darke, To cry, hold, hold. **1782** WOLCOTT (P. Pindar) *Ode R. Acad.* v. Wks. 1812 I. 23 The black blanket of Old Mother Night. **1828** CARLYLE *Misc.* (1857) I. 215 The blanket of the Night is drawn asunder.
c. A large number of bombs dropped to cover a wide area.
1944 *Flight* 22 June 661/2 A blanket of bombs is dropped to smother the whole of the area.
d. *Nuclear Engin.* (See quot. 1960.)
1955 S. VISNER in *Reactor Handbk.: Engin.* iv. 533 The conversion ratio increases with decreasing core diameter owing to increasing neutron leakage from the core to the blanket. **1960** *Gloss. Atomic Terms (H.M.S.O.)* 7 *Blanket*, fertile material put round a reactor core to breed new fuel, e.g. thorium becomes uranium by absorption of spare neutrons.
3. Phrases. **a.** ***a wet blanket***: a person or thing that throws a damper over anything, as a wet blanket smothers fire. ***born on the wrong side of the blanket***: said of an illegitimate child; also (***on***) ***the right side of the blanket***.
1771 SMOLLETT *Humph. Cl.* II. 185 (D.) I didn't come on the wrong side of the blanket, girl. **1815** SCOTT *Guy M.* I. 83 (D.) 'Frank Kennedy,' he said, 'was a gentleman, though on the wrong side of the blanket.' **1830** GALT *Lawrie T.* III. xiii. (1849) 128, I have never felt such a wet blanket before or syne. **1842** MARRYAT *P. Keene* II. i. 100 The Captain marrying and having children on the right side of the blanket as they call it. **1879** H. SPENCER *Data of Ethics* xi. §72. 194 He [a melancholy man] is called a wet blanket. **1919** D. ASHFORD *Young Visiters* (1951) v. 34 An old friend of mine not quite the right side of the blanket as they say.
b. ***on the blanket*** (slang): applied to supporters of the Irish Republican cause held in the Maze prison (near Belfast) and elsewhere, who wear blankets instead of prison clothes, as a form of protest against being treated as a criminal rather than as a political prisoner. Cf. *dirty protest* s.v. DIRTY *a.* 6 b.
1977 *New Statesman* 30 Sept. 439 (*heading*) The men on the blanket. **1978** *Economist* 19 Aug. 15 The boys on the blanket have never won the same support beyond their immediate circle of friends and families that those who were interned could rely on. **1979** *Guardian* 23 Jan. 7/1 Provisional IRA prisoners . . are 'on the blanket', refusing to wear clothes, wash, or slop out their cells. **1979** *An Phoblacht* 29 Sept. 2/3 The latest organisation in Co. Meath to come out in support of the prisoners on the blanket in H-Block is the Meath County Board of the G.A.A. **1982** M. WALLACE *Brit. Govt. in N. Irel.* viii. 158 The first prisoner had gone 'on the blanket' in September 1976, refusing to wear prison clothing.

4. *Printing.* A woollen cloth used to cover the platten, so as to deaden and equalize its pressure.
1824 J. JOHNSON *Typogr.* II. 648 The blankets must be of fine broad-cloth, or kerseymere. **1846** *Print. Apparatus Amat.* 11 The platten is therefore covered with a piece of thick woollen cloth called the blanket.
5. (See quot.)
1816 C. JAMES *Mil. Dict.* (ed. 4) 53 Blankets, combustible things made of coarse paper steeped in a solution of salt-petre, which, when dry, are again dipt in a composition of tallow, resin, and sulphur. Used only in fire-ships.
6. *transf.* A layer of blubber in whales.
1885 WOOD in *Longm. Mag.* V. 548 The layer of blubber . . called by whalers the 'blanket.'
7. a. *attrib.* and *Comb.*, as ***blanket-bag***, ***-cloth***, ***-making***, ***blanket-tossing***; etc.; ***blanket-hidden***, ***-tossed***, ***-wrapped*** adjs.; **blanket bath**, the washing of an invalid in bed; **blanket bog** (see quot.); **blanket coat** *N. Amer.* (see quot. 1872); **blanket finish**, a finish of a race in which the contestants are so close together that they could be covered with a blanket; **blanket fish** *U.S.* (see quot.); **blanket flower**, popular name of the Gaillardia; †**blanket-love**, illicit amours; **blanket overcoat** *U.S.* = *blanket coat*; **blanket pack**, a pedestrian traveller's kit with his blanket rolled about it; **blanket-piece** = BLANKET *sb.* 6; **blanket-roll** *Mil.* (*U.S.*), a soldier's equipment of blanket and kit made into a roll for use on active service; **blanket shawl**, a thick woollen shawl; **blanket sheet** *U.S.*, a newspaper in folio form; also *attrib.*; **blanket-sluice**; (see quot.) **blanket stitch**, a buttonhole stitch worked on the edge of a blanket or other material too thick to be hemmed; hence **blanket-stitched** *a.*, sewn with a blanket stitch. **blanket-weed** (see quots.).
1856 KANE *Arct. Exp.* I. xvi. 193 Skins and *blanket-bags. **1917** A. M. ASHDOWN *Compl. Syst. Nursing* ii. 11 Points to bear in mind when giving a *blanket bath. **1962** C. WATSON *Hopjoy was Here* xvi. 180 An ambulent case, no bed pans or blanket baths. **1939** A. G. TANSLEY *Brit. Islands* xxxiv. 676 Where the rainfall is high and the air so constantly moist that bog is the *climatic formation*, not necessarily arising in fen basins but covering the land continuously except on steep slopes and outcrops of rocks. This is the third type of bog met with in the British Isles and may be called **blanket bog*, because it covers the whole land surface like a blanket. **1520** SIR R. ELYOT *Will* in Elyot's *Gov.* (1883) App. A, *Blanket cloth for blankettes. **1761** A. HENRY *Trav. & Adv. Canada* (1901) iii. 35 A molton, or *blanket coat. **1775** *Pennsylvania Even. Post* 31 Oct. 497/1 Our people had taken from the regulars some blanket coats. **1872** SCHELE DE VERE *Americanisms* 194 Mackinaw blankets . . being very thick and well made, . . served not only for beds but also for overcoats, which were called Blanket-Coats. *c* **1683** (*Title of Ballad*) A true description of *Blanket Fair upon the river Thames in the time of the Great Frost. [**1793** *Sporting Mag.* II. 52/1 Of the nineteen [race-horses] that started, the judge could only place the first four, for not only those, but four or five others, might have been nearly covered with a blanket.] **1934** WEBSTER *s.v.*, A *blanket finish. **1960** *Times* 1 Sept. 4/3 Black was beaten by a hairsbreadth in a blanket finish for the silver and bronze medals. **1870** *Amer. Naturalist* IV. 597 Large numbers of '*blanket fish' (a species of *Thymallus*) were to be seen ascending the small rivers. **1879** T. MEEHAN *Native Flowers of U.S.* II. 182 In the settled parts of Texas . . the *Gaillardia* is known as the '*Blanket-flower'. **1884** W. MILLER *Dict. Eng. Plants* 14/2 *Blanket flower*, blunt-toothed. *Gaillardia amblyodon* [etc.]. **1963** *Oxf. Bk. Garden Flowers* 146/2 *Gaillardia*, . . they are sometimes called 'blanket flower' because the margins of the petals are like the edging of a blanket. **1903** KIPLING *Five Nations* 131 The funerals through the market (*Blanket-hidden bodies). **1649** G. DANIEL *Trinarch.*, *Rich. II*, ccxvi, Such *Blanket-Love. **1857** RUSKIN *Pol. Econ. Art* i. 72 It is *blanket-making and tailoring we must set people to work at. **1822** J. A. QUITMAN *Let.* 16 Jan. in J. F. H. Claiborne *Life J.A.Q.* (1860) I. iv. 72 In winter coarse shoes and *blanket overcoats. **1920** *Chambers's Jrnl.* Apr. 220/1 Only one small tin of corned beef remained in his *blanket-pack. **1851** H. MELVILLE *Moby Dick* II. xxv. 181 The longer upper strip, called a *blanket-piece. **1854** *Chambers's Jrnl.* I. 54 The strip of blubber thus in course of separation is about four feet in length, and is called a blanket-piece. **1868** H. C. JOHNSON *Argent. Alps* 113 Learning we had no beef, he ordered a fine 'blanket piece' to be cut off the entire side of the animal. **1891** *Harper's Mag.* June 8/1 His bridle hand is raised by the *blanket roll. **1899** *Scribner's Mag.* XXV. 27/1 These men . . were . . making ready to disembark, carrying their blanket-rolls and rifles with them. **1837** *Southern Lit. Messenger* III. 660 The *blanket shawls with their varied coloring looked pretty and comfortable. **1839** *Boston Wkly. Mag.* 2 Feb. 175 [The] Baltimore Athenæum . . is a **blanket sheet*, very well executed. **1870** A. MAVERICK *Raymond & N.Y. Press* 36 The heavy, old-fashioned, 'blanket sheet' newspaper. **1881** RAYMOND *Mining Gloss.*, **Blanket-sluices*, sluices in which coarse blankets are laid, to catch the fine but heavy particles of gold, amalgam, etc., in the slime passing over them. **1880** L. HIGGIN *Handbk. Embroidery* iii. 23 *Blanket stitch is used for working the edges of table-covers, mantel valances, blankets, etc. . . It is simply a button-hole stitch. **1882** CAULFEILD & SAWARD *Dict. Needlework*, *Blanket Stitch*, used in crewel work and other embroideries for edging woollen, linen, and silk materials, and for forming ornamental lines. It is a variety of button-hole worked wide apart in long loops. **1960** *House & Garden* May 113/1 The quilt . . is in a soft lime green . . with a blanket-stitched edge. **1881** DUFFIELD *Don Quixote* I. 374 The *blanket-tossed Squire. *Ibid.* 369 Never a word did he say of the blanket tossing. **1711** *Lond. Gaz.* No. 4862/7 Her Majesty . . hath been . . pleased to Incorporate the *Blanket Weavers. **1879** G. FENNELL in *Cassell's Techn. Educ.* IV. 153 Weeds are often . . troublesome in tanks or ponds . . particularly the green filmy weed Cladophera, known as '*blanket-weed.' **1923** D. H. LAWRENCE *Birds, Beasts & Flowers* 197 Mountains *blanket-wrapped Round a white hearth of desert.
b. Used *attrib.*, (*a*) to designate American Indians who use the blanket as a garment, remaining in a primitive state of civilization and keeping tenaciously to their old tribal customs.
1859 BARTLETT *Dict. Amer.* (ed. 2), *Blanket-Indian*, a wild Indian, whose principal article of dress is the blanket. **1866** *Rep. Indian Affairs* (U.S.) 173 There is . . great ignorance concerning the location of the prairie or blanket tribes. **1891** M. E. RYAN *Told in Hills* III. iii. 166 You should hear her talking Chinook to a blanket brave. **1906** *Atlantic Monthly* Mar. 328/2 Only 26,000 blanket Indians are left in the United States.
(*b*) Similarly in South Africa to designate Africans who wear a blanket; hence, by extension, *blanket vote*, the vote of such Africans.
1892 MITFORD *'Tween Snow & Fire* xxxvi, There were a few muttered jeers about . . getting into the Assembly on the strength of 'blanket votes'. **1904** *Daily Chron.* 13 May 3/3 The 'compound' system is essentially degrading even for 'blanket' Kaffirs.
c. Used adjectivally in the sense: covering or including all, or a number of, cases, contingencies, requirements, things, etc.; all-embracing; indiscriminate. orig. *U.S.*
1886 *Rep. Sec. U.S. Treasury* I. p. xli, Suitable annual appropriations . . require no blanket-clause to justify or cover them. **1896** *Congress. Rec.* May 4783 Messrs. Morgan & Co. had given a blanket bid to cover the whole amount. . . Under the terms of the blanket bid, which covered all bids [etc.]. **1908** W. JAMES *Let.* 2 Jan. (1920) II. 300 The general blanket-word pragmatism covers so many different opinions. **1926** *Mind* XXXV. 251 The German habit of ascribing everything to '*Vorstellungen*', and using this vague and futile blanket-term to cover all the manifestations of mind. **1930** M. MEAD *Growing up in New Guinea* xvi. 277 Once we lose faith in the blanket formula of education . . we can turn our attention to the vital matter of developing individuals. **1933** *Brit. Jrnl. Psychol.* Oct. 161 Observers . . generalize and agglomerate under a few 'blanket' epithets the immense complexities and inconsistencies of behaviour. **1935** *Economist* 13 Apr. 848/1 The . . Appropriations Bill . . is virtually a blanket authorisation for the President to expend £5,000 millions for any purposes which he considers desirable. **1949** 'G. ORWELL' *1984* 305 Countless other words such as honour, justice, morality . . had simply ceased to exist. A few blanket words covered them, and, in covering them, abolished them. **1951** *Ann. Reg. 1950* 68 With . . the 'blanket-powers' under regulation 55, the country would approach the Reichstag method of government by order.

ˈblanket, *v.* Pa. t. and pple. **-eted**. [f. the sb.]
1. *trans.* To cover with or as with a blanket.
1605 SHAKS. *Lear* II. iii. 10 My face Ile grime with filth, Blanket my loines, elfe all my haires in knots. **1865** PARKMAN *Champlain* i. (1875) 194 The rocks, the shores, the pine-trees . . all alike were blanketed in snow. **1875** TENNYSON *Queen Mary* III. ii. 122 Blanketed In ever-closing fog. **1884** ROE in *Harper's Mag.* Feb. 452/2 The horses were sheltered as well as possible, and heavily blanketed. **1895** KIPLING *2nd Jungle Bk.* 198 The face of the water was blanketed with wild bees buzzing sullenly and stinging all they found. **1910** J. SIMON in *Times* 11 Oct. 10/2 It was a free country, . . and he had no intention to blanket his opinion. **1962** *Economist* 3 Nov. 456/1 The energetic campaign . . with which Mr Kennedy was blanketing the country.
2. a. *Yachting.* To cover a yacht with the sail of another passing to windward; to take the wind out of the sails of. Also *fig.*
1884 G. C. DAVIES *Norfolk Broads* xxv. 191 It is difficult to pass to leeward while blanketed by the sail of a yacht to windward. **1900** ADE *More Fables* (1902) 44 She had her Upper Rigging set, and was trying to Blanket everything on the Street. **1923** *Weekly Dispatch* 1 Apr. 2 Lord Curzon's chief ambition has been to become Prime Minister, and he has been known to complain to his intimates that he has always been blanketed by Arthur Balfour, who was just a little ahead of him.
b. To exclude (a radio signal) from reception by the use of a stronger signal. Const. *out*.
1938 *Nation* 12 Mar. 301/1 The blanketing out of American broadcasts to South America by Berlin and Rome. **1952** *Economist* 26 July 235/1 The Soviet Union had just extended its jamming operations to blanket not only BBC programmes in Russian but also those in Polish and Finnish.
3. To toss in a blanket (as a rough punishment.)
1609 B. JONSON *Sil. Wom.* v. iv. (1616) 595 Wee'll haue our men blanket 'hem i' the hall. **1634** HEYWOOD *Maidenh. lost* III. Wks. 1874 IV. 143, I would tosse him, I would blanket him i' th' Ayre, and make him cut an Italian caper in the Clouds. **1867** *Cornh. Mag.* Apr. 455 The memorable inn . . where Sancho was blanketed.
4. To supply with blankets; to furnish with blankets.
1874 *Contemp. Rev.* XXIII. 466 Schemes of clothing and blanketing whole districts. **1899** *Daily News* 21 July 8/6 The beds are amply blanketed hammocks.

blanket, *a.*: see BLONKET, BLUNKET.

blanketed (ˈblæŋkɪtɪd), *ppl. a.* [f. prec.]
1. Covered with, or wrapped in or as in, a blanket.
1864 SALA in *Daily Tel.* 5 May, 'A horde of blanketed banditti.' **1878** TENNYSON *Q. Mary* III. ii, Who dream'd us blanketed In ever-closing fog.
2. Applied in U.S. to cattle having a broad belt of white round the middle, also called *belted* and *sheeted cattle*.

3. Tossed in a blanket.

†**blanke'teer.** *Obs.* [f. BLANKET + -EER[1].]
a. One who uses a blanket. One who tosses in a blanket. **b.** *plur.* A body of operatives who met at the so-called Blanket Meeting in St. Peter's Fields near Manchester, on 10th March 1817, provided with blankets or rugs, in order to march to London and press their grievances upon the attention of the Government. Hence **blanke'teering** *vbl. sb.*
1755 SMOLLETT *Quix.* (1803) I. 156 God grant there may be neither blankets nor blanketeers. **1822** COBBETT *Rural Rides* (1885) I. 222 These base landlords laughed..at the blanketeers. **1830** MORIARTY *Husband Hunter* III. 230 On returning from her blanketeering adventure. **1833** SOUTHEY in *Life & Corr.* VI. 203 The projected expedition of the Blanketeers.

†**'blanketer.** *Obs.* A blanket-maker.
1677 PLOT *Oxfordsh.* 278 The Blanketers, whereof there are at least threescore in this Town [Witney]. **1707** *Lond. Gaz.* No. 4393/4 John Brookes, of Witney..and Thomas Brookes..Blanketers.

blanketing ('blæŋkɪtɪŋ), *sb.* [f. BLANKET.]
1. Material for blankets; supply of blankets. Also, as a dress material.
1677 PLOT *Oxfordsh.* 25 No place yields Blanketing so notoriously white, as..Witney. **1735** *Phil. Trans.* XXXIX. 42 A narrow Ring of thick Blanketting. **1839** F. BARHAM *Adamus Exul* 42 Love Night's pitchy blanketing. **1879** McCARTHY *Own Times* II. xxvii. 317 Clothing, blanketing, provisions..were destroyed in vast quantities. **1903** *Daily Chron.* 20 June 8/4 Wraps..made of fine cream blanketing with big sleeves brought into high cavalier cuffs. **1908** *Ibid.* 21 Sept. 7/2 The warm Witney blanketing..makes exceedingly cosy coats for girls.
2. Taking the wind out of the sails of a yacht by passing to windward of it. Cf. BLANKET *v.* 2.
1883 *Times* 27 Aug. 8/2 The Marjorie then went on and gave the Neptune a blanketing.
3. The punishment of tossing in a blanket.
1577 HOLINSHED *Chron.* II. 547 Iesting, plaicing, blanketing, and..such other filthie and dishonorable exercises. **1621** FLETCHER *Thierry* II. Wks. 457 The worst that can come Is blanketing; for beating..I have been long acquainted with. *a* **1754** FIELDING *To keep Wife at H.* I. i, This affair, Sir, may end in a blanketing. **1808** HURSTONE *Piccadilly Ambul.* II. 53 The chance of undergoing a blanketting.
4. *Mining.* The catching of ore in suspension by a blanket-sluice; the ore thus caught.
1884 *Athenæum* 3 May 570/3 Yield of gold..from pyrites and blanketings operated on 4,387 ounces.
5. The action of covering with, or as with, a blanket.
1896 *Pop. Sci. Monthly* L. 245 There's a blanketing of the earth's heat.

blanketing ('blæŋkɪtɪŋ), *ppl. a.* [f. BLANKET *v.* + -ING[2].] That covers as with a blanket. Also *transf.*
1904 FARRER *Garden Asia* 244 The smoke descends densely upon the volcano in blanketing clouds. **1925** JOLY *Surface-Hist. Earth* vi. 103 The blanketing effects of continental radioactivity.

'blanketless, *a.* Without a blanket.
1863 S. L. J. *Life in South* II. ii. 36 Footsore soldiers, campless and blanketless. **1880** *Daily Tel.* 4 Nov., The blanketless bed on the floor.

blankety ('blæŋkɪtɪ), *a.* Of or like a blanket.
1872 MISS SEDGWICK *Hope Leslie* II. 132 Kept on her Indian mantle in that blankety fashion.

blankety, blanky: see BLANK *sb.* 12 b.

blankish ('blæŋkɪʃ), *a.* [f. BLANK *a.* + -ISH[1].] Somewhat blank; hence (*obs.*) whitish, palish.
1580 HOLLYBAND *Treas. Fr. Tong, Besané*, dried vp, withered, blanckish.

†**'blankless,** *a. Obs.* [f. BLANK *sb.* + -LESS.] Without spot or blemish.
1589 R. ROBINSON *Gold. Mirr.* (1851) 4 No blotte of blame Their banners blanckles, of any euill part.

blankly ('blæŋklɪ), *adv.* [f. BLANK *a.* + -LY[2].]
1. In a blank manner, vacuously; with helpless passivity, resourcelessly, aimlessly.
1863 FROUDE *Hist. Eng.* VIII. 65 They were looking blankly in each other's faces. **1867** MORLEY *Burke* 63 The once blind souls of men and women who had laboured blankly, as brute beasts labour. **1881** H. JAMES *Portr. Lady* xxxvii, The latter smiled blandly, but somewhat blankly.
2. Starkly, utterly (in privative sense).
1823 LAMB *Elia* (1860) 213 So blankly divested of all meaning. **1870** E. J. B. BROWN *Eccl. Truth* 230 Blankly atheistic doctrines.
3. Point-blank, flatly, nakedly, merely.
a **1859** DE QUINCEY *Mackintosh* Wks. XIII. 89 It could not be blankly denied.

blankmanger, obs. form of BLANCMANGE.

blankness ('blæŋknɪs). [f. BLANK *a.* + -NESS.] Blank quality or condition.
1850 *Fraser's Mag.* XLI. 503 The pale silver, midway between the lustre of the gold and the blankness of the lead. **1868** HOLME LEE *B. Godfrey* xviii. 105 Kempe's..face fell into final blankness and silence. **1876** GLADSTONE *Synchr. Homer* 134 The blankness and vagueness of Greek tradition.

blann(e, pa. t. of BLIN *v. Obs.* to cease.

blanquet, obs. form of BLANKET.

‖**blanquette** (blɑ̃kɛt). Also 8 blanquet. [Fr. (see BLANKET *sb.*).] A dish of light meat (esp. veal) in a white sauce.
1747 H. GLASSE *Art of Cookery* ii. 29 Veal Blanquets. Roast a Piece of Veal..cut it into little thin Bits..put in some good Broth... Keep it stirring. **1846** 'A LADY' *Jewish Man. Cookery* p. xiii, *Blanquette*, a kind of fricassee with a white sauce. **1906** MRS. BEETON *Bk. Househ. Managem.* xv. 435 Blanquette of veal. *Ibid.* xviii. 560 Blanquette of lamb. *Ibid.* 719 Blanquette of turkey. **1923** *Harmsworth's Househ. Encycl.* III. 2404/3 *Lamb Blanquette.* This is an entrée composed of scallops of cold roast lamb heated in a rich white sauce, with the addition of mushrooms. **1960** *Times* 1 Aug. 9/3 It is hard to distinguish clearly between a *blanquette* and a *fricassee*. Both should be made from fresh meat (usually chicken, veal or lamb) cooked in a flavoured white stock... For a *blanquette* the meat is more often blanched with herbs and seasoning.

Blanquism ('blɑ̃kɪz(ə)m). [From the name of Louis Auguste *Blanqui* (1805–81), French revolutionary communist + -ISM.] The doctrine or practice of Blanqui and his followers (see quots.). So **'Blanquist,** one who advocates Blanquism; also as *adj.*
1879 *Nation* 15 May 333/2 There was, last Sunday, another trial of electoral strength, out of which the Blanquists emerged the victors. **1922** R. W. POSTGATE *Out of Past* 7 Very attentive students of modern revolutionary literature may have noticed recently a few references—generally ill-informed—to 'Blanquism'. *Ibid.* 67 The independent history of the Blanquist Party begins with the fall of the Parish Commune... Almost immediately after the Commune's fall and the scattering of the Blanquists, questions of policy arose. **1949** I. DEUTSCHER *Stalin* iii. 55 To the Menshevists this sounded like an ominous repetition of Blanquism, the doctrine of the leader of the Paris Commune, who believed that the only method of achieving revolution was direct action by a small conspiratorial minority ignoring the will of the majority. **1950** E. H. CARR *Bolshevik Rev.* I. i. 18 'Blanquism' in nineteenth-century revolutionary parlance meant addiction to the isolated revolutionary conspiracy or *putsch* and neglect of methodical organization.

blare (blɛə(r)), *v.* Forms: 5 bleren, 6 blear, *Sc.* bleir, 8–9 blair, 8– blare. [Identical in form and sense with MDu. *blaren*, LG. *blaren* (*blarren, blaeren*), MHG. *blêren, blerren* (mod.G. *plärren*); not found in the older stages of Teutonic, and generally taken as an imitative word. Cf. BLEA.]
1. *intr.* To roar with prolonged sound in weeping, as a child; to bellow as a calf. Now chiefly *dial.*
c **1440** *Promp. Parv.* 40 Bloryyn, or wepyn [**1499** bleren], *ploro, fleo.* **1535** COVERDALE *Isa.* xv. 4 The worthies also of Moab bleared and cried for very sorow. —— *1 Sam.* vi. 12 The kyne..wente on blearynge. *a* **1586** R. MAITLAND *New Year*, Thoch all thair barnes suld bleir. **1677** LITTLETON *Lat. Dict.*, To blare, *clamitare, muginari.* **1783** AINSWORTH *Lat. Dict.* (Morell) 1, To blare like a cow, *mugio.* **1791** COWPER *Odyss.* x. 499 Blaring oft, With one consent all dance their dams around. **1862** BARNES *Rhymes Dorset Dial.* I. 162 The calves did bleäry to be sar'd.
2. a. To sound a trumpet, to trumpet. (Now the ordinary word for this sound.)
1782 COWPER *Lett.* 27 Apr., Blairing like trumpeters at a fair. **1837** CARLYLE *Fr. Rev.* II, I. x. 60 Innumerable regimental bands blare off. **1865** —— *Fredk. Gt.* V. XIII. ix. 97 Those 'subsidised 6,000,' who go blaring about on English pay. **1863** TENNYSON *Welcome Alexandra* 14 Warble O bugle and trumpet blare.
b. Of a gramophone, loudspeaker, etc.: to sound loudly and stridently. Also of the sound transmitted and with *out.*
1955 B. PYM *Very Private Eye* (1984) III. 194 We passed Westbourne Grove Baptist Church and heard records of hymns blaring out. **1956** *People* 13 May 10/3 The record-player blaring, the liquor, gin punch and the vodka. **1969** D. ACHESON *Present at Creation* (1970) xv. 130 He would, his voice blared through powerful amplifiers, announce the speakers of the evening as they came to the platform. **1975** R. P. JHABVALA *Heat & Dust* (1976) 66 Devotional songs blared from a loudspeaker. **1986** P. BARKER *Century's Daughter* xv. 271 The juke box blared.
3. a. *trans.* To utter in blaring.
1859 TENNYSON *Elaine* 939 A tongue To blare its own interpretation. **1863** *Tyneside Songs* 4 He blaired oot his last Cuckoo.
b. Of a gramophone, loudspeaker, etc.: to utter (a sound) loudly and stridently. Freq. with *out.*
1939 F. THOMPSON *Lark Rise* iv. 72 The wireless blares out variety and swing music. **1956** R. MACAULAY *Towers of Trebizond* viii. 76 From cafés and squares loud speakers blared across the water to us the eternal Turkish erotic whine. **1964** E. HUXLEY *Back Street New Worlds* vi. 65 A radio blares out pop music at full blast. **1980** B. PLAIN *Random Winds* xxviii. 394 A fat man got out of a taxi, fumbling in the pocket of his bulky overcoat, while traffic behind the taxi blared furious horns.
†**4.** 'To sweal, or melt away, as a Candle does.' Bailey 1721 [cf. *flare*]. *Obs.*—[0]

blare (blɛə(r)), *sb.*[1] [f. the vb.] **1.** The weeping of a child, the bellowing of calves (*dial.*); the noise of trumpets and similar instruments. Also of loud music or other noise.
1809 J. BARLOW *Columb.* III. 22 Sigh for battle's blare. **1855** TENNYSON *Ode Wellington* 115 With blare of bugle, clamour of men. **1861** LYTTON *Str. Story* II. 369 One cry alone more wild than their own savage blare [said of a herd of bisons]. **1924** WODEHOUSE *Bill the Conqueror* xv. 242 The blare of the music and the restlessness of the chorus afflicted his nerves. **1953** J. CARY *Except the Lord* xviii. 80, I drifted through the heat, the noise,..The ear-splitting blare of steam organs,..and the ground bass of voices. **1961** A. HOPKINS *Talking about Symphonies* iv. 63 With a great thump of timpani and a blare of brass, the whole band come sweeping in with the main theme.
2. *transf.* of 'loudness' of colour; cf. *glare.*
1880 TENNYSON *Ballads & other Poems* 149 Lured by the light from afar,..Lured by the glare and the blare. **1884** G. H. BOUGHTON in *Harper's Mag.* Sept. 530/2 The womenkind did not..put on much 'blare' of color. **1957** C. DAY LEWIS *Pegasus* 18 A pure pale blare of distance.

blare, *sb.*[2] A paste of hair and tar for caulking the seams of boats. Smyth *Sailor's Word-bk.* 1867.

blaring ('blɛərɪŋ), *vbl. sb.* [f. BLARE *v.* + -ING[1].]
1. = BLARE *sb.*[1].
c **1440** *Promp. Parv.* 40 Bloryynge or wepynge, *ploratus, fletus.* **1641** BEST *Farm. Bks.* (1856) 118 That they [kyne] may not hear the rowtinge and blaringe one of another. **1855** *Whitby Gloss.*, *Blairing*, bellowing, crying or squalling as a child. **1879** JEFFERIES *Wild Life S. County* 104 The blaring of trumpets, the tootling of pan-pipes.
2. *fig.* Clamour, noise, outcry.
1837 *Fraser's Mag.* XVI. 129 No people..make such a blaring about apostasy, and such a clamour about consistency, as the Liberals. **1840** CARLYLE *Heroes* iii. 158 What uproar and blaring he made in this world.

blaring, *ppl. a.* [f. as prec. + -ING[2].]
1. Uttering a loud noise: bellowing. As said of the *tongue* cf. also BLEARING.
1566 J. STUDLEY *Seneca's Medea* (1581) 133 In fiery foming blaring mouth his forked tongue hee wags. **1615** *Curry-c. for Coxe-c.* v. 237 Blareing label-lolling tongue. **1814** SOUTHEY *Roderick* XVIII. 8 The blairing horn.
2. *transf.* of a 'loud' colour; cf. *glaring.*
1866 *Sat. Rev.* 4 Aug. 146 A painter who should exclude every colour but a blaring red.

blarney ('blɑːnɪ), *sb.* [f. *Blarney*, name of a village near Cork. In the castle there is an inscribed stone in a position difficult of access. The popular saying is that any one who kisses this 'Blarney stone' will ever after have 'a cajoling tongue and the art of flattery or of telling lies with unblushing effrontery' (Lewis *Topog. Dict. Ireland*).] Smoothly flattering or cajoling talk. (*Colloquial.*) Also, nonsense.
[**1766** GOLDSMITH *Vicar* I. xi. 95 Our two great acquaintances from town, Lady Blarny and Miss Carolina..Skeggs!] **1796** SCOTT *Let.* 26 Sept. (1932) I. 55, I hold it (so to speak) to be all *Blarney.* **1819** CRABBE *T. of Hall* xx 378 Bah!—bother!—blarney! What is this about? **1833** MARRYAT *P. Simple* (1863) 71 With promises and blarney he got credit for all I wanted. **1884** RUSKIN in *Pall Mall G.* 17 Nov. 11/2 It was bombastic English blarney—not Irish. **1925** D. H. LAWRENCE *Refl. Death Porcupine* 178 Perfect love, I suppose, means that a married man and woman never contradict one another... What blarney! **1955** *Times* 18 June 6/6 You do not want to come here every day to listen to a lot of blarney.

'blarney, *v.* [f. prec.] **a.** *trans.* To assail with blarney, to overcome or beguile with flattery. **b.** *intr.* To use flattering speech.
1803 SOUTHEY *Lett.* (1856) I. 246 On the occasion of some prize, blarneying (Mrs. King will explain the word), and assuring him that he must get it. **1833** MARRYAT *P. Simple* (1863) 302 But I won't blarney you, Peter. **1837** HAWTHORNE *Amer. Note-Bks.* (1871) I. 43 Then would she wheedle and laugh and blarney.
Hence **'blarneyed** *a.*, seasoned with blarney. **'blarneyer,** one who blarneys, a flatterer. **'blarneyfied** *a.* (*slangy*), blarneyed. **'blarneying** *vbl. sb.*, flattering talk; *ppl. a.* flattering.
1861 CLINGTON *Frank O' Don.* 12 Whose blarneyed tongues and good looks proved irresistible passports. **1882** *Cornh. Mag.* June 671 All these avocats are arch blarneyers. **1830** *Fraser's Mag.* I. 508 No balderdash of blarneyfied botheration. **1884** MARY HICKSON *Irel. in 17th C.* I. 162 To follow..in the wake of their blarneying orators.

blart (blɑːt), *v. dial.* [? corruption of BLEAT *v.*] *intr.* **1.** Of sheep and cattle: to bleat, low, bellow. (See *Eng. Dial. Dict.*)
2. Of a child, etc.: to cry, whimper, howl. Also quasi-*trans.* Hence **'blarting** *vbl. sb.* and *ppl. a.*
[**1824** W. CARR *Horae Momenta Cravenae* 59 *Blaat, Blate*, To bleat.] **1896** G. F. NORTHALL *Warwickshire Word-bk.* 30 *Blart*, to cry or holloa vociferously. **1898** *Eng. Dial. Dict.* I. 289/1 He was blartin away for all the world like a babby. *Ibid.*, Stop that child's blarting. **1959** I. & P. OPIE *Lore & Lang. Schoolch.* x. 186 Other local terms for crying are:..blahing or blarting (Birmingham, Hanley, Wolverhampton). **1976** A. HILL *Summer's End* ii. 30 A very young kid..blarting its eyes out. *Ibid.* vi. 88 He went home blarting. **1977** *Punch* 31 Aug. 350/1 Real folk singers were great tough hard-handed ploughmen with strong blarting voices that could be heard against the thumping of pewter pots on old oak tables in drunken harvest feasts.

†**blas.** *Obs.* Also 3–4 bles, 7 blass. [In ME. use either a phonetic variant or parallel form of BLAST, f. OE. *blǽsan, ON. *blása*, etc. to blow. In sense 2 it was invented by Van Helmont,

probably with a reference to the same root; cf. his other term GAS.]

1. A blast, breath.

c **1205** LAY. 27818 þa eorðe gon beouien for þon vnimete blase. *a* **1225** *Ancr. R.* þes deofles bles, & his owene stefne. *c* **1370** *Clene Maydenh.* 30 Hit wendeþ away as wyndes bles. *c* **1380** *Sir Ferumb.* 2648 þay herde þat blas [of horns].

2. Van Helmont's term for a supposed 'flatus' or influence of the stars, producing changes of weather.

1662 J. CHANDLER *Van Helmont's Oriat.* 78 The Stars.. cause the changes, seasons, and successive courses or interchanges. To which end, they have need of a twofold motion.. I signifie both these by the new name of Blas. **1669** W. SIMPSON *Hydrol. Chym.* 129 The next arbitrary Blass or flatus. **1812** SIR H. DAVY *Chem. Philos.* 19 Van Helmont has used a term not so applicable or so intelligible as gas, viz. Blas. **1875** WHITNEY *Life Lang* vii. 120.

blase, earlier form of BLAZE *sb.* and *v.*

blasé ('blɑːzeɪ), *a.* [Fr.; pa. pple. of *blaser* to exhaust by enjoyment, a modern word of unknown etymol.: see Littré, Scheler.]

a. Exhausted by enjoyment, weary and disgusted with it; used up.

1819 BYRON *Juan* XII. lxxxi, A little 'blasé'—'tis not to be wonder'd At, that his heart had got a tougher rind. **1860** *All. Y. Round* No. 46. 474 Blasé, knowing airs. **1884** LADY VERNEY in *Contemp. Rev.* Oct. 554 The somewhat blasé, artificial, conventional stage of [society] in the old world.

b. Bored or unimpressed through over-familiarity; insensitive, supercilious.

1930 N. COWARD *Private Lives* I. 2 Don't laugh at me, you mustn't be *blasé* about honeymoons just because this is your second. **1962** M. TWEEDY in *Mirfield Ess. Christian Belief* III. ii. 170 The Romans of the Empire were far too cynical and blasé to worship anything. **1978** *Radio Times* 18 Mar. 77/2, I potted them up and for a time was quite blasé about the whole business of gardening. **1984** *N.Y. Times* 1 Jan. I. 18/3 You don't feel so blasé anymore going out on your [firefighting] calls.

† **'blaseness.** *Obs.* [f. *blase* obs. form of BLAZE *sb.*[1] + -NESS.] Brilliancy, brightness.

1398 TREVISA *Barth. De P.R.* XIX. xix. (1495) 875 Blacke tempryth the shedynge blasenesse of redde [*rubedinis disgregatiuam claritatem*].

blasfeme, etc., obs. form of BLASPHEME, etc.

blash (blæʃ). *dial.* [A modern word or series of words of onomatopœic formation; with reminiscences of *plash*, *splash*, *dash*, etc., and probably of *blow*; in sense 4 perhaps of *blaze* and *flash*.]

1. A dash or plash of liquid, as when rain appears to fall in sheets; a mixture of *blow* and *splash*.

[**1725** cf. BLASHY.] **1805** A. SCOTT *Harvest* Poems 36 (JAM.) Where snaws and rains wi' sleety blash. **1827** J. WILSON *Noct. Ambr.* Wks. I. 156 A snaw storm came down frae the mountains.. noo a whirl, and noo a blash.

2. Watery stuff; said of very liquid mud, poor tea, watered milk. *fig.* Wishy-washy talk. *dial.*

1835 MRS. CARLYLE *Lett.* (1883) I. 52 Dear Mother, excuse all this blash. **1864** ATKINSON *Whitby Gloss.* s.v., 'It's all blash,' or 'blish blash'; nonsense. *Mod.Sc.* No proper meal; only a blash of tea.

3. A gash or smash due to a blow; a bash.

1860 G. H. K. *Vac. Tour* 169 A.. skull, with a tremendous blash across it.

4. A broad flash; a blaze flashing up.

1875 *Lanc. Gloss.* (E.D.S.), *Blash*, a sudden flame. *Ibid.*, *Blash-boggart*, a fire-goblin, or flash-goblin; that is, a goblin that flashes and disappears. It is more commonly used figuratively, and is applied to persons who are fiery, wild, or strange in appearance.

blash (blæʃ), *v. dial.* [f. as prec.] *trans.* To dash a quantity of liquid; to dash (a thing) broadly with liquid. *intr.* To plash, to splash heavily in, work in, water.

1788 PICKEN *To Cowslip* Poems 91 (JAM.) Whan.. blashan rains, or cranreughs fa'. **1861** *Fam. Herald* 16 Feb. 672 'How much water does your mistress.. put in our.. milk?' 'I'm sure,' replied the rogue, 'I don't know.. she just blashes it in.' **1864** ATKINSON *Whitby Gloss.*, *Blash*, to splash with water. Also in sense of going or having gone to sea. 'What he has got, he has blash'd for, ' as property obtained by a seafaring life.

'blashy, *a. dial.* [f. BLASH *sb.* + -Y[1].]

1. Of or characterized by sudden heavy showers; heavily splashy.

1725 RAMSAY *Gent. Sheph.* I. ii, Thick-blawn wreaths of snaw, or blashy thows. **1863** *Robson's Bards of Tyne* 487 The day was drizzly wet an' drear, And blashy under feet, man. **1864** ATKINSON *Whitby Gloss.* s.v., Blashy weather.

2. Consisting too much of liquid; watery, thin.

1820 *Blackw. Mag.* Nov. 154 (JAM.) Thae blashy vegetables are a bad thing. **1857** CHAMBERS *Inform. People* II. 677 When a young man.. fills his stomach with a great blashy meal. **1864** ATKINSON *Whitby Gloss.* s.v., Blashy ale.

blason, obs. form of BLAZON.

† **blasphe'mation.** *Sc. Obs.* [ad. L. *blasphēmātiōn-em* (in Tertullian), f. *blasphēmāre.*]

1. Insult, reviling, calumniation.

1533 BELLENDEN *Livy* II. (1822) 176 To the mair schame and blasphemacioun of Romane linage. **1538** LYNDESAY *Papyngo* 881 Thay.. bostit hir, with blasphematioun. *a* **1560** ROLLAND *Crt. Venus* IV. 182 Caus Ladeis to get blasphematioun.

2. Blasphemy.

1549 *Compl. Scot.* xvii. 155 Ther blasphematione of the name of god corruptis the ayr. **1552** ABP. HAMILTON *Catech.* 284 It can nocht be said without blasphematioun.

† **blas'phematory**, *a. Obs.* [f. on type of a L. **blasphēmātōri-us*, f. *blasphēmātor*: see prec. and -ORY: cf. F. *blasphématoire.*] Blasphemous.

1611 COTGR., *Blasphematoire*, blasphematorie, blasphemous. **1725** tr. *Dupin's Eccl. Hist. 16th C.* I. VII. i. 285 He would have no part in their Blasphematory Doctrine.

† **blasphematour.** *Obs.* Also 6 **-ature.** [a. F. *blasphémateur*, ad. late L. *blasphēmātōr-em*, agent noun f. *blasphēmāre*: see below.] A blasphemer.

1483 CAXTON *Gold. Leg.* 431/3 Swerars and blasphematours. **1581** N. BURNE *Admon. Deform. Kirk Scotl.*, That drunken blasphemature.

blaspheme (blɑːs'fiːm, -æ-), *v.* Forms: 4 **blasfeme(n, 5 -yn, (blasefleme), 7 blaspheam,** 4– **blaspheme.** [ME. *blasfeme-n*, a. OF. *blasfeme-r* (= Pr., Sp. *blasfemar*), ad. L. *blasphēmā-re*, ad. Gr. βλασφημέειν to speak profanely, f. βλάσφημος evil speaking, blasphemous (-φημος speaking). Transferred to L. in the Vulgate and eccles. writers, and preserved liturgically in the modern langs. The same word became popular in late L. in sense of 'revile, reproach,' whence Romanic **blasimāre*, It. *biasimare*, Pr. *blasmar*, F. *blasmer*, *blâmer*, Eng. *blame.*]

1. *intr.* To utter profane or impious words, talk profanely. Const. *against* (in Wyclif also *in*, *upon*).

1340 *Ayenb.* 30 Ha.. blasfemeþ aye god and his halȝen. **1382** WYCLIF *Mark* iii. 29 He that shal blasfeme aȝeins [**1611** blaspheme against] the Holy Gost. —— *Sel. Wks.* III. 170 ȝif freres by gabbingis blasfeme upon Crist. *Ibid.* 349 þei blasfemen in Crist. *c* **1440** *Gesta Rom.* 381 Then the soule began to blasefleme. **1595** SHAKS. *John* III. i. 161 Brother of England, you blaspheme in this. **1711** ADDISON *Spect.* No. 99 ¶7 One may tell another he whores, drinks, blasphemes. **1821** BYRON *Cain* I. i. 35 Blaspheme not; these are serpents' words. **1835** J. G. DOWLING *Lett. Dr. Maitland* 17 They.. blaspheme against the precious cross.

2. *trans.* To speak irreverently of, utter impiety against (God or anything sacred.)

1382 WYCLIF *Isa.* i. 4 Thei blasfemeden the hoeli of Israel. **1526** *Pilgr. Perf.* (W. de W. 1531) 4 b, They not onely despysed hym, but also they blasphemed the holy goost. **1593** SHAKS. *2 Hen. VI*, III. ii. 372 Blaspheming God, and cursing men on earth. **1795** BURKE *Let.* Wks. VII. 350 He is ready to blaspheme his God, to insult his king. **1872** RUSKIN *Eagle's N.* §240 New foulness with which to blaspheme the story of Christ.

3. *gen.* To speak evil of, revile, calumniate, abuse.

c **1386** CHAUCER *Sompn. T.* 475 As that this olde cherl with lokkes hoore Blasphemed hath oure hooly Couent eke. **1605** SHAKS. *Macb.* IV. iii. 108 Since that the truest Issue of thy Throne.. do's blaspheme his breed. **1654** EARL ORRERY *Parthen.* (1676) 327 As soon as this fatal news came to Pacorus's knowledge, he blasphem'd them for it. **1725** POPE *Odyss.* XIV. 462 While those who from our labours heap their board, Blaspheme their feeder and forget their lord. **1847** TENNYSON *Princ.* IV. 119 So they blaspheme the muse!

† **b.** *intr.* To rail, to utter words of abuse. *rare.*

a **1592** GREENE *Arbasto* vi, Doralicia chafed much in her choller, blaspheming bitterly both against me and her sister.

† **blaspheme**, *a.* and *sb.*[1] *Obs.* Also 4–5 **blasfem(e.** [a. F. *blasphème*, ad. L. *blasphēmus*, ad. Gr. βλάσφημος; see prec.] **A.** *adj.* Blasphemous.

1382 WYCLIF *2 Macc.* x. 4 To barbaris, or heithen, and blasfeme men. *c* **1410** LOVE *Bonavent. Mirr.* xxxiv. 66 (Gibbs MS.), To haue stoned hym as blaspheme [**1530** a blasphemer].

B. *sb.* A blasphemer.

1382 WYCLIF *Sel. Wks.* III. 347 Shulden siche blasfemes be stoned to deeþ. **1401** *Pol. Poems* (1859) II. 93 The Pharisees, pursuwed Crist to the dethe, ȝe, callid hym a blasfeme.

† **blas'pheme**, *sb.*[2] *Obs.* [a. F. *blasphème* (in 12th c. also *blafeme*:—L. *blasphēmia* BLASPHEMY. (In Chaucer also accented '*blaspheme.*)] The earlier word for BLASPHEMY.

1384 CHAUCER *Env. Scogan* 15 In blaspheme of the goddis? *c* **1386** —— *Pard. T.* 265 Cursed forswerynges, Blaspheme of crist, manslaughter. **1526** *Pilgr. Perf.* (W. de W. 1531) 138 With many suche blasphemes and prouocacyons to impacyence. **1583** T. WATSON *Poems* (Arb.) 153 Yet glorious heauns, ô pardon my blaspheme.

† **blasphemely**, *adv. Obs.* In 4–5 **blasf-.** [f. BLASPHEME *a.* + -LY[2].] Blasphemously.

c **1380** *Serm. agst. Mir.-Plays* in *Rel. Ant.* II. 55 And therefore blasfemely thei seyen, that siche pleyinge doith more good than the word of God. **1395** PURVEY *Remonstr.* (1851) 45 Principlis.. applied blasfemeli to a synful man.

† **blasphement.** *Obs. rare.* Blasphemy.

1544 BALE *Chron. Sir J. Oldcastell* in *Harl. Misc.* (Malh.) I. 249 Romish blasphement—long hyd in the darke.

blasphemer (blɑːs'fiːmə(r), -æ-). Forms: 4 **blasfemer(e, blasphemour, -femour,** 5 **blasfemare,** 6 – **blasphemer.** [a. OF. *blasfemeor*, *-eur* (AF. *-our*), in nom. *blasphemère*:—L. *blasphēmātor -em.*] One who blasphemes.

c **1386** CHAUCER *Sompn. T.* 505 This false blasphemour that charged me To parte that wol nat departed be. *c* **1400** *Apol. Loll.* 27 þus was Crist callid a synnar & blasfemer. **1535** COVERDALE *2 Macc.* ix. 28 That murthurer and blasphemer of God. **1770** BURKE *Pres. Discont.* Wks. II. 298 A common slaughter of libellers and blasphemers. **1870** R. ANDERSON *Missions Amer. Bd.* III. xx. 348 The recent blasphemer cried out in agony.

blas'phemeress. *rare.* [a. OF. *blasphemeresse*: see -ESS.] A woman who blasphemes.

1548 HALL *Chron.* 158 A diabolicall Blasphemeresse of God.

blaspheming (blɑːs'fiːmɪŋ, -æ-), *vbl. sb.*

1. The uttering of blasphemy; profane speaking.

c **1430** *Life St. Kath.* (1884) 30 þe blasfemynge whiche she spake aȝenst his goddes. **1514** BARCLAY *Cyt. & Uplondyshm.* (1847) 26 There is blaspheming of Gods holy name. **1648** JENKYN *Blind Guide* iv. 105 Take heed.. of blaspheming.

† 2. Railing, calumniation. *Obs.*

1677 GALE *Crt. Gentiles* II. III. 18 Blasphemings of each others reputation.

blas'pheming, *ppl. a.* That blasphemes.

1569 SPENSER *Visions* i, The vile blaspheming name. **1605** SHAKS. *Macb.* IV. i. 26 Liuer of Blaspheming Iew. **1805** SOUTHEY *Madoc in Azt.* x, These blaspheming strangers.

blasphemous ('blɑːsfɪməs, -æ-), *a.* Also 6 **blasphemose.** [f. L. *blasphēm-us* (see BLASPHEME *a.*) + -OUS, or perh. immed. a OF. *blasphemeus*, AF. *-ous.* Marlowe and Milton accented it, after L., *blas'phēmous.*]

1. Uttering or expressing profanity, impiously irreverent.

1535 COVERDALE *Isa.* lviii. 9 Yf thou.. ceasest from blasphemous talkinge. **1590** MARLOWE *2nd Pt. Tamburl.* II. i, And scourge their foul blasphemous paganism. **1667** MILTON *P.L.* v. 809 O argument blasphemous, false and proud! **1782** PRIESTLEY *Corrupt. Chr.* II. ix. 187 John.. pronounced it to be a.. blasphemous doctrine. **1871** MORLEY *Voltaire* (1886) 42 The history of a prolonged outrage upon these words by blasphemous and arrogant persons.

† 2. Abusive, slanderous, defamatory. *Obs.*

1604 SIR D. CARLETON in Winwood *Mem.* II. 52 (L.) Stone was well whipped in Bridewell, for a blasphemous speech, 'that there went sixty fools into Spaine besides my lord admiral and his two sons.' **1610** SHAKS. *Temp.* I. i. 43 You bawling, blasphemous incharitable Dog.

'blasphemously, *adv.* [f. prec. + -LY[2].] In a blasphemous manner; impiously, profanely.

1531 FRITH *Judgm. Tracy* (1829) 245 Against the which many men.. have blasphemously barked. **1611** BIBLE *Luke* xxii. 65 And many other things blasphemously spake they against him. **1665** WITHER *Lord's Prayer* 99 A woman, blasphemously termed her self the Virgin Mary. *a* **1745** SWIFT (J.) He would blasphemously set up to controul the commands of the Almighty. **1874** SPURGEON *Treas. Dav.* Ps. xcviii. 5 'This infectious frenzy of psalm-singing,' as Warton almost blasphemously describes it.

'blasphemousness, [f. as prec. + -NESS.] The quality of being blasphemous.

1854 DUFF in *Life* xxi. (1881) 342 Such God-defying blasphemousness.

blasphemy ('blɑːsfɪmɪ, -æ-), Forms: 3 **blasphemie,** 4 **blasfemie, -y(e, blasfamye, blassefemy,** 4–6 **blasphemye,** (5 **blaseflemy**), 6–7 **blasphemie,** 7 **blasfemy,** 5– **blasphemy.** [ME. *blasfemie*, *blasphemie*, a. OF. *blasfemie*, a learned adaptation of L. *blasphēmia*:—Gr. βλασφημία slander, blasphemy, abstr. sb. f. βλάσφημος BLASPHEMOUS. In Spenser accented *blas'phe·my* (F.Q. VI. xii. 25). Cf. BLASPHEME *sb.*[2]]

1. Profane speaking of God or sacred things; impious irreverence.

a **1225** *Ancr. R.* 198 þe seoueðe hweolp is Blasphemie. þisses hweolpes nurice is þe þet swereð greate oðes. *c* **1325** *E.E. Allit. P.* B. 1661 þenne blynnes he not of blasfemy on to blame þe dryȝtyn. **1488** CAXTON *Chast. Goddes Chyld.* 46 Some haue fallen in to blasphemie whiche ben they that speken unhonestly of god. **1526** *Pilgr. Perf.* (W. de W. 1531) 118 b, Mocyons of infidelite, and blasphemyes. **1659** MILTON *Civil Power in Eccl. Causes* Wks. 1738 I. 548 Blasphemy or evil speaking against God maliciously. **1768** BLACKSTONE *Comm.* IV. 59 Blasphemy against the Almighty, by denying his being or providence. **1853** ROBERTSON *Serm.* Ser. IV. v. (1876) 64 It is all blasphemy; an impious intrusion upon the prerogatives of the One Absolver.

b. *fig.* (against anything held 'sacred.')

1605 BACON *Adv. Learn.* I. ii. §9 (1873) 17 He was well punished for his blasphemy against learning. **1873** MORLEY *Rousseau* I. 165 You are drawing an indictment against nature,—no trifling blasphemy in those days. **1875** HAMERTON *Intell. Life* IX. i. 302 This doctrine sounds like blasphemy against friendship.

† 2. *gen.* Slander, evil speaking, defamation. *Obs.*

1656 WHALLEY in Burton *Diary* (1808) I. 103 To speak evil of any man is blasphemy. *a* **1656** BP. HALL *Tracts* 5 Blasphemy.. is a blasting the fame or blaming of another.

† **b.** *transf.* A thing evil spoken of, an occasion of evil speaking. *Obs.*

1609 BIBLE (Douay) *Ezek.* v. 15 Thou shalt be a reproch, and blasphemie.

3. *Comb.*

1828 E. IRVING *Last Days* 68 A blasphemy-enduring ear.

†**blasphemy**, *a. Obs.* [perh. f. ME. BLASPHEME *sb.*² + -Y.] Blasphemous.

c **1384** WYCLIF *Wks.* (1880) 158 A more blasphemye ground. *Ibid.* 1 But on this blasphemye heresie schullen alle cristene men crien out.

blast (blɑːst, -æ-), *sb.*¹ Forms: 1-3 **blǽst**, 3- **blast**, 4 **blest**, 6 (*Douglas*) **blist**, 4-6 **blaste**. [Com. Teut.: OE. *blǽst* str. masc. = OHG. *blâst*, ON. *blǫ́str*:—OTeut. **blǣs-tu-z* str. m.; f. OTeut. **blǣsan*, (Goth. *-blêsan*, ON. *blása*, WGer. *blâsan*) to blow: see BLAZE *v.*² Cf. L. *flā-tu-s*. (The original long vowel was shortened by position in ME.)]

1. A blowing or strong gust of wind.

a **1000** *Cædmon's Ex.* 290 (Gr.) Sæ grundas suþ wind fornam bæþweȝes blæst. *a* **1300** in Wright *Pop. Treat. Sc.* 136 A dunt other a blast of grete miȝte. **1340** *Ayenb.* 203 Be zuych blest and be zuych wynd. *c* **1374** CHAUCER *Troylus* II. 1338 Reed that boweth dowen with every blaste. *c* **1440** *Promp. Parv.* 38 Blaste of wynde, *flatus*. **1573** G. HARVEY *Lett.-bk.* (1884) 34 Two March blasts. **1603** KNOLLES *Hist. Turks* (1621) 1336 Those that fortune advanceth by the favour of her blastes. **1697** DRYDEN *Virg. Georg.* I. 325 Frosts and Snows, and Bitter Blasts. **1840** R. DANA *Bef. Mast* xxxiv. 132 Broken by the blast of a hurricane. **1847** LONGF. *Ev.* II. III. 184 Blown by the blast of fate like a dead leaf over the desert.

2. a. A puff or blowing of air through the mouth or nostrils; a breath. *Obs.* or *arch.*

c **1250** *Gen. & Ex.* 201 His licham of erðe he nam, And blew ðor-in a liues blast. *c* **1325** *Coer de L.* 1779 Unnethe he might draw his blast. **1387** TREVISA *Higden* (1865) I. 223 A lanterne brennynge alway, þat no man couthe quenche wiþ blast noþer wiþ water. **1594** T. B. *La Primaud. Fr. Acad.* II. 567 As when we breathe, we make a blast. **1611** BIBLE *Ex.* xv. 8 With the blast of thy nostrils the waters were gathered together. **1642** T. TAYLOR *God's Judgem.* I. II. xxvi. 276 Breathing his last blast. **1741** MIDDLETON *Cicero* (1742) III. 304 The empty blast of popular favor.

†**b.** Angry breath, rage. *Obs.*

1535 COVERDALE *Jud.* viii. 2 Whan he had sayde this, their blast was swaged from him.

3. a. The sending of a continuous puff of breath through a wind-instrument, so as to make it sound; the blowing (of a trumpet, or the like); hence, the sound so produced; any similar sound. Also *fig.*

c **1205** LAY. 19926 Þa wes bemene blæst. *a* **1300** *Cursor M.* 18075 Þar come a steuen als thoner blast. *a* **1340** HAMPOLE *Pr. Consc.* 4990 When þai here þe grete bemes blast. *c* **1400** *Destr. Troy* XI. 4614 Iche buerne to be bun at the blast of a trumpe. **1509** HAWES *Past. Pleas.* i. xiv, Of a grete horne I harde a royal blast. **1513** DOUGLAS *Æneis* II. vii. [vi.] 31 Wpsprang the cry of men and trumpis blist [*clangorque tubarum*]. **1611** BIBLE *Josh.* vi. 5 When they make a long blast with the rammes-horne. **1667** MILTON *P.L.* XI. 76 Th' Angelic blast Filld all the Regions. **1782** HAN. MORE *Daniel* VII. 114 Were thy voice Loud as the trumpet's blast. **1851** D. MITCHELL *Fresh. Glean.* Wks. (1864) 304 The postilion had given two blasts on his bugle.

†**b.** *fig.* Boasting: cf. the phrase *to blow one's own trumpet*. *Obs.*

1494 FABYAN v. cxl. 127 To kele somwhat theyr hyghe corage, or to oppresse in partye theyr brutisshe blastis.

†**c.** *at one blast* (L. *uno flatu*): at once, at the same time. *for a blast*: for once.

c **1380** *Sir Ferumb.* 2487 Hure hornes þai gunne þo to blowe: ful many at one blaste. **1579** TOMSON *Calvin's Serm. Tim.* 94/2 Let vs glorifie him .. and that not onely for a blast, but let vs continually preach and set forth the praises of God. **1638** T. WHITAKER *Blood of Grape* 57 Both indeed at the first view or blast will seeme to shake both my foundation and edifice also. **1790** BEATSON *Nav. & Mil. Mem.* I. 193 Plunging a number of gallant men at one blast into eternity.

†**d.** A company (of huntsmen). *Obs.*

1486 *Bk. St. Albans* F vij a, A Blast of hunters.

4. a. A strong current of air produced artificially.

a **1618** RALEIGH *Rem.* (1644) 137 The Organ hath many Pipes, all which are filled with the same blast of wind. **1667** MILTON *P.L.* I. 708 As in an Organ from one blast of wind To many a row of Pipes the sound-board breaths. **1827** FARADAY *Chem. Manip.* iv. 97 By which the blast was to be thrown in.

b. *spec.* The strong current of air used in iron-smelting, etc.

1697 *Phil. Trans.* XIX. 482 To give very strong and lasting Blasts for Iron Forges. **1725** BRADLEY *Fam. Dict.* s.v. *Steel*, As soon as the Coal is thoroughly kindled .. give the Blast. **1875** URE *Dict. Arts.* II. 945 The blast is conducted through sheet-iron or cast-iron pipes .. into the tuyères.

c. ***in blast, at*** or ***in full blast*** (also *transf.*): at work, in full operation; also ***full blast***: at full pitch; *esp.* very loudly. ***out of blast***: not at work, stopped.

1780 in *Virginia State Papers* (1875) I. 370 If Mr. Ross can get in Blast time enough .. he shall be paid for Shot Twenty five pounds pr: ton. **1796** MORSE *Amer. Geog.* I. 652 At present there are four or five furnaces in the state that are in blast. **1832** HT. MARTINEAU *Hill & Vall.* vii. 114 The day when yonder furnaces are out of blast will be the day of your ruin. **1839** MARRYAT *Diary* II. 229 In *full blast*—something in the extreme. 'When she came to meeting, with her yellow hat and feathers, was'n't she in *full blast*?' **1853** A. BUNN *Old & New England* I. v. 86 Oyster-saloons .. to use an American phrase 'in full blast' (*Anglicè*, having a great run of business). **1854** J. ABBOT *Napoleon* (1855) I. xxvi. 412 All the foundries of France were in full blast. **1858** HAWTHORNE *Fr. & It. Jrnls.* II. 143 The organ .. was in full blast in the church. **1874** SPURGEON *Treas. Dav.* lxxxviii. I. IV. 130 They burned perpetually like a furnace at full blast. **1936** H. MILLER *Black Spring* (1938) 84 A penny arcade is going full blast. **1938** E. BOWEN *Death of Heart* II. ii. 191 Even when the wireless was not on full blast, Daphne often shouted as though it were. **1957** I. CROSS *God Boy* (1958) xxi. 183 If it had come through a radio going full blast[etc.].

d. *fig.* A severe or violent reprimand, outburst, or the like. *colloq.* (orig. *U.S.*).

1874 'MARK TWAIN' *Let.* 4 Sept. (1917) I. 226, I gave the P.O. Department a blast in the papers. **1930** E. RAYMOND *Jesting Army* II. iv. 203 If he but heard them, he charged up to revile them... Fred Roberts came under his blast. **1935** *Time* 11 Mar. 23/3 Despite blast and counterblast between President Roosevelt and Soviet Foreign Minister Litvinoff. **1936** *Variety* 1 July 35/5 Would You Like a Nice 15-Minute Blast at President Roosevelt? **1954** *New Yorker* 31 July 48/2 A typical blast comes from the West Renfrewshire group, which concludes its resolution by saying tartly that the 'blind folly' of the official Party shows that the leadership is completely divorced from the feelings of the majority of the Labour movement.

†**5.** The sudden stroke of lightning, a thunderbolt. *Obs.*

1650 MRS. HUTCHINSON *Mem. Col. Hutchinson* (1846) 351 He .. died by a blast of lightning. **1751** FRANKLIN *Lett.* Wks. 1840 V. 224 The end entered by the electric blast points north.

6. A sudden infection destructive to vegetable or animal life (formerly attributed to the blowing or breath of some malignant power, foul air, etc.). **a.** Blight; also an insect which causes blight. **b.** *spec.* A disease of the sugar cane. *arch.* or *Obs.*

1577 B. GOOGE *Heresbach's Husb.* (1586) 29 b, To preserve it from blast and mildew. **1702** C. MATHER *Magn. Chr.* v. iv. (1852) 316 Our wheat and our pease, fell under an unaccountable blast. **1750** G. HUGHES *Barbados* 245 It [the sugar-cane] is liable to one disorder hitherto incurable, the Yellow Blast. **1756** P. BROWNE *Jamaica* 435 The Blast. This insect .. is generally pernicious to all the plants on which it breeds. **1815** *Encycl. Brit.* (ed. 5) III. 658/2 Blast is also used in agriculture and gardening, for what is otherwise called a blight.

c. *transf.* and *fig.* Any blasting, withering, or pernicious influence; a curse.

1547 BOORDE *Brev. Health* C 21 b, A Blast in the Eye. **1559** T. BRYCE in Farr's *S.P.* (1845) I. 176 When shall thy spouse and turtle-doue Be free from bitter blaste? **1659** HAMMOND *On Ps.* xxxiv. 14 Must needs be the forfeiting of God's protection, and bring his blasts and curses. **1727** DE FOE *Eng. Tradesm.* (1745) I. xiii. 101 Turns the blessing into a blast. **1752** JOHNSON *Rambl.* No. 204 ¶2 Resistless as the blasts of pestilence.

d. A dialectal name of erysipelas. **e.** A flatulent disease in sheep.

1845 W. BUCHAN *Domest. Med.* xxv. 202 The country people .. call this disease [erysipelas] a blast, and imagine it proceeds from foul air, or ill wind.

†**7.** A blasted bud or blossom; blasted state.

1579 LYLY *Euphues* (Arb.) 190 Thou shalt hang like a blast among the faire blossomes. *Ibid.* 196 As in all gardeins, some flowers, some weedes, and as in al trees some blossoms, some blasts. **1795** SOUTHEY *Occas. Pieces* i, Thy youth in ignorance and labour past, And thine old age all barrenness and blast.

8. a. A 'blowing up' by gunpowder or other explosive; an explosion.

1635 J. BABINGTON *Pyrotechn.* lvi. 63 Holding your head under the horizontal line of your Piece, for feare the blast annoy you. **1748** ANSON *Voy.* I. vii. 72 The blast was occasioned by a spark of fire from the forge. **1853** KANE *Grinnell Exp.* xxxiii. (1856) 285 A noise like a quarry blast, explosive and momentary.

b. The quantity of gunpowder or other explosive used in a blasting operation.

1885 *Daily News* 12 Oct 5/2 When Hallett's Reef in Hell Gate was destroyed .. the blast was the largest ever used.

c. A destructive wave of highly compressed air spreading outwards from an explosion. Also *attrib.* and *Comb.*, as ***blast wall*** (see quot. 1852), ***wave***; ***blast-proof*** adj.

1852 *Harper's Mag.* Apr. 644/2 A structure of black timber .. set up in the shape of an acute angle. This is a 'blast-wall', intended to offer some resistance to a rush of air in case of an explosion [at the powder-mill]. **1923** [see *back-blast* s.v. BACK- A. 11]. **1939** *Jrnl. R. Aeronaut. Soc.* XLIII. 225 Blast is a non-translational shock wave that is transmitted through the air to considerable distances from an exploding bomb... In the blast wave a phase of positive pressure is followed by a phase of negative pressure. **1940** GRAVES & HODGE *Long Week-end* xxiv. 420 The Government was planning .. to provide blast-proof steel shelters for every house in the country. **1941** *Flight* 10 Apr. 272/2 Even some of the machines .. are protected against bombing by blast walls.

d. A party, esp. one that is very noisy or wild. Also, a good time, an enjoyable or exciting experience (chiefly *U.S.*). *slang.*

1953 D. HARRIS in *Wentworth & Flexner's Dict. Amer. Slang* (1975) 42/1 Maybe it's a little early in the day for their first blast. **1959** *Times* 9 Mar. 13/4 *A blast*, a great party. **1966** *N.Y. Times* 9 Sept. D9 I've been a lucky girl... In 'Dolittle' I'm having a blast. **1967** W. MURRAY *Sweet Ride* vi. 89 Man, they're throwing a monster blast over on the East Latego later... Everybody's going. **1970** *Harper's Mag.* July 37 Meyer himself had a blast. An entirely unpretentious man,.. he had dreaded this confrontation with sophisticated, distinguished Yale. **1972** J. S. GUNN in G. W. Turner *Good Austral. Eng.* iii. 56, I found that the effect of a drug can be a *bang, blast, boot*. **1979** *Navajo Times* (Window Rock, Arizona) 24 May 15/5 Johnson said playing in the pros and in Oakland has been a blast and baseball had been good to him.

9. *Sc.* A smoke (of tobacco). Cf. K. James's *Counterblast to Tobacco* (1604).

Mod. South Sc. He takes his blast after dinner.

10. *Comb.* and *attrib.*, as (in sense 1) ***blast-borne***, ***-puff***; (in sense 3) ***blast-horn***; (in sense 4) ***blast-bloomery***, ***-cylinder***, ***-engine***, ***-machine***, ***-meter***; also †**blast-bob**, the stroke of a blast of wind; **blast bomb**, a bomb whose effect depends mainly on its blast, *esp.* a home-made or hand-held one; **blast-fan**, a fan for producing a blast of air; **blast-hearth**, a hearth for reducing lead-ore; **blast-hole**, the hole by which water enters a pump, the wind-bore; **blast-lamp**, (*a*) see quot. *a.* 1884; (*b*) a lamp in which the flame is driven on to a surface by a current of air; a blow-lamp; **blast-pipe**, in a locomotive, a pipe conveying the steam from the cylinders into the funnel and so increasing the draught; **blast-pot** (see quot.).

1860 W. FORDYCE *Hist. Coal.* 110 Besides the orifice or chimney at the top, there were two openings, one large in front, the other of smaller dimensions behind, for the insertion of the bellows pipe. Such was the *Blast Bloomery. **1582** STANYHURST *Æneis* IV. (Arb.) 110 Thee boughs frap whurring, when stem with *blastbob is hacked. **1976** *Economist* 21 Feb. 17/2 One man was killed when a *blast bomb he was assembling on Saturday night went off too early. **1981** *N.Y. Times* 13 July A2 The police reported a blast bomb was thrown at an army patrol. **1830** TENNYSON *Poems* 124 *Blastborne hail. **1875** URE *Dict. Arts* II. 949 There are 3 *blast-engines .. They have 96-inch blast- and 40-inch steam-cylinders. **1879** *Cassell's Techn. Educ.* IV. 339/2 To .. blow either hot or cold air through it by means of a *blast-fan. **1844** *Camp of Refuge* I. 27 Sounding all the *blast-horns on the house-top. *a* **1884** KNIGHT *Dict. Mech.* Suppl., **Blast Lamp*, one with an artificially produced draft of air to aid combustion. **1902** MRS. BARNES-GRUNDY *Thames Camp* 57 A benzoline blast lamp which would fetch off any varnish in the world. *c* **1865** J. WYLDE in *Circ. Sc.* I. 315/1 The combustion .. is rapidly effected by means of the *blast-pipe of the cylinder. **1887** *Harper's Mag.* Apr. 670/2 Before the war only seven small furnaces—'*blast-pots' they were called—having a total capacity of 20,000 tons, were in operation in all Tennessee.

blast (blæst), *sb.*² [f. Gr. βλαστ-ός: see -BLAST.] A primitive undifferentiated blood-cell, esp. one found in acute leukæmia. In full ***blast cell***.

1947 H. A. CHRISTIAN *Osler's Princ. & Practice Med.* (ed. 16) 965 Monocytic Leucemia... The cell is a monocyte or monocyte blast. **1952** *Science* CXV. 357/2 The inhibitor activity of the primitive blast cells from acute leukemia was close to zero. **1961** *Lancet* 9 Sept. 603/1 Leukæmic cells, particularly the blast cells, contain no inhibitor whatever.

blast (blɑːst, -æ-), *v.* Also 3, 7 **blaste**. [f. the sb.]

I. †**1. a.** *intr.* To blow, to puff violently. *Obs.*

c **1300** *K. Alis.* 5438 Dragouns .. grisely whistleden and blasten. **1483** CAXTON *Gold. Leg.* 397/3 Ther came a grete multytude of fendes blastyng and roryng. **1530** PALSGR. 457/1 To blaste with ones mouthe or with belowes. **1768** ROSS *Helenore* 23 (JAM.) Twa shepherds out of breath, Rais'd-like and blasting.

†**b.** *trans.* To blow (*out*, *forth*, *abroad*); to breathe (*out*), utter loudly, proclaim. *Obs.*

1536 LATIMER *Serm. bef. Convoc.* i. 35 Counterfeit doctrine, which hath been blasted and blown out by some. **1548** HALL *Chron.* Hen. VI. an. 14 (R.) They blasted emongest themselfes, that the Calisians would leaue the town desolate. **1631** WEEVER *Anc. Fun. Mon.* 712 The winde .. whereby this fire was .. blasted abroad.

c. *nonce-wd.* To emit blasts.

1842 DICKENS *Amer. Notes* (1850) 14/1 The engine which had been clanking and blasting in our ears incessantly for so many days.

†**2. a.** *intr.* To blow (on a trumpet or other wind instrument). **b.** *trans.* To blow (a trumpet, etc.). **c.** with the hearers as object.: To din or denounce by trumpeting. *Obs.*

1384 CHAUCER *H. Fame* 1866 Toke his blake trumpe faste And gan to puffen and to blaste. **1530** PALSGR. 457/1 He blasted his horne so hygh that all the wodde dyd shake. **1606** SHAKS. *Ant. & Cl.* IV. viii. 36 Trumpetters With brazen dinne blast you the Citties eare. **1858** POLSON *Law & L.* 197 'Blasting you at the horn,' 'poinding your estate.'

3. *intr.* To boast, 'blow one's own trumpet.' *Sc.*

1814 *Saxon & Gael* I. 100 (JAM.), I am no gien to blast.

†**4. a.** *trans.* To blow (*up*), inflate. **b.** *intr.* (for *refl.*) To swell up. *Obs.* exc. *dial.*

1578 LYTE *Dodoens* I. xcv. 137 The same herbe .. slaketh the [bowels] whan they are blasted vp and swollen. *Ibid.* II. xxv. 177 A yong Catt whereunto I haue giuen of these floures to eate .. blasted immediatly, and shortly after died. **1874** HARDY *Madding Crowd* I. xxi. 228 [A rustic says] 'They [the sheep] be getting blasted.' .. 'Joseph,' he said, 'the sheep have blasted themselves.'

5. a. *trans.* To blow up (rocks, etc.) by explosion.

1758 BORLASE *Nat. Hist. Cornwall* xv. §1. 161 The miner is generally obliged to blast the rock. **1858** FROUDE *Hist. Eng.* III. xv. 314 His shallow schemes were blasted to atoms. **1859** HAWTHORNE *Fr. & It. Jrnls.* II. 279 The ledge of rock had been blasted and hewn away.

b. *intr.* Of a rocket or spacecraft: to take off, be launched into space; usu. const. *off*. Also used of any powered phase of flight. Also of an astronaut.

1951 R. BRADBURY *Silver Locusts* 190 You could still smell the hard, scorched smell where the last rocket blasted off when it went back to Earth. **1953** H. HABER *Man in Space* 262 The moment the big ship blasts off there is no allowance for the slightest failure. **1956** R. HEINLEIN *Double Star* (1958) ii. 38, I was spacesick.. as soon as the rocket ship quit blasting and went into free fall. **1969** *Times* 17 May 8/1 It only remains for three veteran space travellers.. to blast off on Sunday.

c. To create *from* or *out of* rock, etc., by means of explosion.

1951 R. CAMPBELL *Light on Dark Horse* vi. 96 In many of these places swimming baths had been blasted out of the rocks. **1978** B. BAINBRIDGE *Young Adolf* i. 11 The train plunged into the hills surrounding the city and entered a massive tunnel blasted from yellow sandstone.

6. a. (*dial.*) To smoke (tobacco). Cf. *blow*. (The usual word in S. Scotl.)

b. To smoke (marijuana). Also *intr.* Cf. BLASTED *ppl. a.* 4. *slang* (chiefly *U.S.*).

1959 J. E. SCHMIDT *Narcotics Lingo & Lore* 17 *Blast Mary Jane to kingdom come*, to smoke hemp or Mari Huana cigarettes 'by the pack', i.e., furiously. **1960** R. G. REISNER *Jazz Titans* 151 *Blast*, to get high. **1961** RIGNEY & SMITH *Real Bohemia* p.xiii, *Blast crap, to*, to smoke marijuana. **1970** C. MAJOR *Dict. Afro-Amer. Slang* 27 *Blast*,.. smoke marijuana.

II. To blow on perniciously.

7. *trans.* To blow or breathe on balefully or perniciously; to wither, shrivel, or arrest vegetation; to blight. Said of a malignant wind, lightning, flame and (formerly) of a 'malignant' planet.

1532 FRITH *Mirror* (1829) 277 By blasting thy fruits, or such other scourges. **1576** LAMBARDE *Peramb. Kent* (1826) 271 This lately advaunced building was blasted with flame. **1580** BARET *Alv.* B 786 To be Blasted or striken with a planet. **1625** MILTON *Death Fair Inf.* i, O fairest flower, no sooner blown but blasted. **1634** T. JOHNSON *Parey's Chirurg.* XXVIII. (1678) 682 Every body that is blasted or stricken with lightning. **1697** DRYDEN *Virg. Past.* II. 84 Southern Winds to blast my flowry Spring. **1862** STANLEY *Jew. Ch.* (1877) I. ii. 38 The fertile vale of Siddim was blasted with eternal barrenness.

8. *transf.* and *fig.* (Blasting withers up the brightness, freshness, beauty, vitality, and promise of living things: hence) **a.** To blight or ruin (hopes, plans, prosperity).

1639 FULLER *Holy War* III. iv. (1840) 121 Oftentimes heaven blasteth those hopes which bud first and fairest. **1759** ROBERTSON *Hist. Scot.* I. II. 90 The death of Henry blasted all these hopes. **1834** PRINGLE *Afr. Sk.* x. 338 My personal prospects in the colony were for the present entirely blasted. **1871** R. ELLIS *Catullus* lxiv. 397 When heinous sin earth's wholesome purity blasted.

b. To bring infamy upon (character, reputation); to discredit effectually, ruin, destroy.

1596 DRAYTON *Leg.* iv. 21 Would you forbeare to blast Me with Defame. **1660** WINSTANLEY *Engl. Worthies* (1684) 174 So hath this worthy Princes fame been blasted by malicious traducers. **1713** STEELE *Englishm.* No. 5. 31 This Query.. is designed to blast the Memory and Title of King William. **1769** *Junius Lett.* xxxiv. 148, I did not attempt to blast your character. **1877** CONDER *Bas. Faith* iv. 194 To blast this evidence with suspicion of untrustworthiness.

†**c.** To affect injuriously or perniciously *with*.

1605 CAMDEN *Rem.* (1637) 166 Some of the greatest Romans were a little blasted with this foolerie. **1750** JOHNSON *Rambl.* No. 157 ¶6, I was blasted with sudden imbecility.

d. To strike (the eyes or vision) with dimness or horror. *arch.*

a **1771** GRAY *Poems* (1775) 24 He saw; but blasted with excess of light, Clos'd his eyes in endless night. **1803** MISS PORTER *Thaddeus* ix. (1831) 83 Wherever he turned his eyes they were blasted with some object which made them recoil. **1817** COLERIDGE *Sibyl. Leaves* (1862) Still Edmund's image rose to blast her view.

†**9.** *intr.* To wither or fall under a blight. *Obs.*

1580 LYLY *Euphues* (Arb.) 236 The Easterly winde maketh the blossomes to blast. *a* **1618** RALEIGH in Farr's *S.P.* (1845) I. 235 Tell Beauty how she blasteth. *c* **1630** RISDON *Surv. Devon* §44 (1810) 51 This bud soon blasted in the blossom. **1748** J. ELIOT *Field-Husb. New England* (1760) I. 14, I have been told that Summer Wheat sowed with Barley is not apt to blast. **1838** E. FLAGG *Far West* II. 217 All of the smaller grains.. being liable to blast before the harvesting.

10. a. *trans.* To strike or visit with the wrath and curse of heaven; to curse. Often in imprecations in the imperative or optative form (for *God blast*...); also as an exclamation of annoyance.

a **1634** CHAPMAN *Revenge for Hon.* v, And thus I kiss'd my last breath. Blast you all. **1640–4** in Rushworth *Hist. Coll.* III. (1692) I. 130 Blasted may that tongue be, that shall.. derogate from the glory of those Halcyon days. **1659** HAMMOND *On Ps.* iv. 3 His enemies.. blasted him as a man of blood. **1706** ADDISON *Rosamond* I. i, My wrath like that of heav'n shall.. blast her in her Paradise. **1752** FIELDING *Amelia* IV. x. v, But, blast my reputation, if I had received such a letter, if I would not have searched the world to have found the writer. **1762** GOLDSMITH *Cit. W.* cv, 'Blast me!' cries Tibbs, 'if that be all, there is no need of paying for that.' **1793** T. HASTINGS *Regal Rambler* 74 Leaving all the ladies below to blast or bless their eyes, no matter which. **1824** SCOTT *St. Ronan's* viii, 'As I think, he laid hands on your body...' 'Hands,.. no, blast him—not so bad as that neither.' **1849** MACAULAY *Hist. Eng.* I. iii, Calling on their Maker to curse them.. blast them, and damn them. **1916** E. F. BENSON *David Blaize* ix. 158 'I say, Blazes, there's extra confirmation class this evening.'.. 'Oh, blast!' said David. **1936** AUDEN & ISHERWOOD *Ascent of F6* I. iii, Give it here, blast your eyes! **1955** N. MARSH *Scales of Justice* ix. 209 'Damnation, blast and bloody hell!' Alleyn said.

b. *absol.* To curse, to use profane language.

1762 *Gentl. Mag.* 130 On they go.. swearing, blasting, damning.

-blast [ad. Gr. βλαστ-ός sprout, shoot, germ], used as the second element in technical terms, esp. in Biology, in sense of 'germ, embryo' as in *epiblast*, *mesoblast*, and *hypoblast*; cf. BLASTODERM.

blasted ('blɑːstɪd, -æ-), *ppl. a.*

1. Balefully or perniciously blown or breathed upon; stricken by meteoric or supernatural agency, as parching wind, lightning, an alleged malignant planet, the wrath and curse of heaven; blighted.

1552 HULOET, Blasted corne. **1594** SHAKS. *Rich. III*, III. iv. 71 A blasted Sapling, wither'd vp. **1605** —— *Macb.* I. iii. 77 Vpon this blasted Heath you stop our way. **1667** MILTON *P.L.* x. 412 The blasted Starrs lookt wan. **1727** THOMSON *Summer* 1152 Stretched below A lifeless groupe of blasted cattle lie. **1850** MRS. STOWE *Uncle Tom* xxxvi. 318 A black, blasted tree.

2. *transf.* and *fig.*; cf. BLAST *v.* 8.

1742 COLLINS *Ode to Fear*, Lest thou meet my blasted view. **1762** HUME *Hist. Eng.* (1806) V. lxix. 168 The blasted credit of the Irish witnesses. **1855** MACAULAY *Hist. Eng.* IV. 548 Driven.. from public life with blasted characters.

3. Cursed, damned. In low language as an expression of reprobation and hatred. Also used adverbially.

1682 DRYDEN *Medal* 260 What Curses on thy blasted Name will fall. **1750** CHESTERF. *Lett.* 8 Jan. (1870) 169 Colonel Chartres.. who was, I believe, the most notorious blasted rascal in the world. **1854** M. J. HOLMES *Tempest & Sunshine* (1858) xv. 204 Lord's sake be spry, for I'm blasted hungry! **1874** PUSEY *Lent. Serm.* 79 Balaam, after the success of his blasted counsel. **1884** *Gd. Words* Nov. 767/1 Jim Black states that the 'blasted' railway has done away with those journeys. **1886** *Leslie's Pop. Monthly* Jan. 67/2 He's too blasted smart for an Indian.

4. Under the influence of drugs or alcohol, intoxicated. Cf. BLAST *v.* 6 b. *slang* (chiefly *U.S.*).

1972 *Sunday Sun* (Brisbane) 2 July 14/3 Today they [*sc.* addicts] get blasted. **1973** *To Our Returned Prisoners of War* (U.S. Office of Secretary of Defense) 2 *Blasted*, under the influence of drugs including alcohol... Usually indicates very high, but pleasantly so. **1978** J. CARROLL *Mortal Friends* II. vi. 205 Den O'Coole forced his way to the bar... He was already blasted. **1985** S. BOOTH *True Adventures Rolling Stones* xxv. 255 He seemed as fog-bound as I was, a sweet-tempered English boy staying blasted on grass and coke.

‖**blastema** (blæ'stiːmə). Pl. bla'stemata. [a. Gr. βλάστημα a sprout, also, in Hippocrates, a morbid humour causing scab or disease, f. vbl. stem βλαστε-, βλαστα- to sprout, bud.]

1. *Biol.* The primary formative material of plants and animals; protoplasm. Now applied *spec.* to the initial matter or growth out of which any part is developed.

1849 TODD *Cycl. Anat. & Phys.* IV. 100/2 The structureless fluid just referred to is termed blastema. **1855** OWEN *Skel. & Teeth* 5 The primitive basis, or 'blastema,' of bone is a subtransparent glairy matter. **1879** tr. *De Quatrefages' Human Spec.* 124 Adam, who sprang from a primordial blastema called clay in the Bible.

transf. **1870** HUXLEY *Lay Serm.* xiii. (1874) 309 A nebular blastema.

2. *Bot.* The budding or sprouting part of a plant; the thallus of a lichen.

1880 GRAY *Bot. Text-bk.* 399.

bla'stemal, *a.* [f. prec. + -AL[1].] Of or pertaining to blastema.

1849 TODD *Cycl. Anat. & Phys.* IV. 102/1 The blastemal elements within the vessels.

blaste'matic, *a.* [f. as prec. + -IC.] = prec.

1879 *Syd. Soc. Lex.*, *Blastematic mass*, a name given by some.. to organs still in a state of imperfect development.

blaster ('blɑːstə(r), -æ-). [f. BLAST *v.* or (in sense 7) *sb.* + -ER[1].]

1. One who blows or emits blasts.

1664 COTTON *Poet. Wks.* (1765) 18 You there [Boreas], Goodman Blaster. **1854** BLACKIE in *Blackw. Mag.* LXXVI. 261 That fiery blaster, Typhon.

†**2.** A trumpeter. *Obs.*

1575 LANEHAM *Let.* (1871) 33 Triton, Neptunes blaster.

3. He who or that which blights, or ruins.

1599 MARSTON *Sco. Villanie, To Detract.* 165 Vile blaster of the freshest bloomes on earth.. Detraction. **1760** FOOTE *Minor* I. i, Dead to pleasures themselves, and the blasters of it in others.

†**4.** One of the sect of free-thinkers in Ireland about 1738. *Obs.*

c **1738** *Rep. Irish Comm. Relig.* in Fraser *Berkeley* vii. 254 Loose and disorderly persons have of late erected themselves into a Society or Club under the name of Blasters.

5. One who blasts rocks.

1776 PENNANT *Tour Scotl.* (1790) III. 34 A blaster was kept in constant employment, to blast with gunpowder the great stones. **1884** *Pall Mall G.* 10 Oct. 8/2 A rock blaster.. explaining the working of a dynamite cartridge.

6. An iron borer used for rocks to be blasted.

7. Anything designed to produce a blast or draught of air.

1830 M. DONOVAN *Dom. Econ.* I. 353 The smoke and soot.. are carried up the funnel over the mouth of the oven, the ascent being promoted by laying a blaster over the mouth: the blaster is a large piece of sheet-iron.

8. *dial.* (*Sc.*) A smoker.

9. *Science Fiction.* A weapon that emits a destructive blast.

1950 I. ASIMOV *Pebble in Sky* xvii. 179 It was a full-size blaster that could shred a man to atoms. **1958** *Listener* 13 Nov. 775/2 Elijah Baley, the human detective, with a blaster-pistol.

10. *Golf.* = *sand-iron* (b) s.v. SAND *sb.*[2] 10.

1937 H. LONGHURST *Golf* I. xxii. 198 The blaster gives no margin for error above the ball, but an almost infinite margin below it. **1948** *Chambers's Jrnl.* July 337/2 If you were a lovely young girl whose father had been a golf champion, would you touch a knock-kneed bowler even with a blaster? **1960** R. LARDNER *Out of Bunker* ix. 146, I bent my blaster into a sharp V and hurled it end over end high up into the branches of a nearby tree. **1975** *Oxf. Compan. Sports & Games* 429/2 Sand-wedge (formerly 'blaster'), 36 in. (912 mm.), 56°.

blasterand, obs. Sc. form of BLUSTERING.

†'**blasterous**, *a. Obs. rare.* In 6 -terus. Blasting, blighting.

1583 STANYHURST *Æneis* II. (Arb.) 53 Corneshocks singded with blasterus hurling of Southwynd whizeling.

blastful ('blɑːstfʊl, -æ-), *a.* [f. BLAST *sb.*[1] + -FUL.] Full of or exposed to blasts of wind.

1883 *Blackw. Mag.* Oct. 520 Breezy hills and blastful mountains.

'**blast-'furnace.** A furnace in which a blast of air is used; *spec.* the common furnace for iron-smelting, into which a blast of compressed and highly heated air is driven by a blowing-engine. Also *attrib.*

1706 *Lond. Gaz.* No. 4241/2 A new Invention of Smelting.. of Black Tin-Ore into White Tin.. in a Blast Furnace. **1827** FARADAY *Chem. Manip.* iv. 94 The wind-furnace may generally be replaced with advantage by the blast-furnace. **1860** W. FORDYCE *Hist. Coal, etc.* 116 The blast furnace consists of two truncated cones, united at their bases. **1877** *Practical Mag.* VII. 248 (*title*) The utilization of blast furnace slag. **1902** *Encycl. Brit.* XXVIII. 601/2 (*heading*) Blast-furnace gases. **1906** *Westm. Gaz.* 19 July 8/2 The blast-furnacemen at Workington. **1930** *Engineering* 17 Jan. 68/1 Mortar, with the exception of blast-furnace cement, ceased to change in strength.

blastid ('blæstɪd). *Palæont.* [f. Gr. βλαστ-ός sprout, bud; cf. BLASTEMA.] (See quot.)

1877 LE CONTE *Elem. Geol.* (1879) 299 Stemmed Echinoderms, or Crinoids may be divided into three families, viz.: 1. Crinids; 2. Cystids; 3. Blastids. *Ibid.* 301 Blastids.. had a bud-shaped body, with five petalloid spaces.. radiating from the top, and reaching half way down the body.

'**blastide.** *Biol.* [f. Gr. βλαστ-ός germ + εἶδος resemblance.] 'The clear space in each segment of a dividing impregnated ovum, which precedes the appearance of a nucleus' (*Syd. Soc. Lex.* 1880).

'**blastie.** *Sc. rare.* [f. BLAST *v.* + -IE, -Y[4] dim. suffix.] A little blasted creature; a dwarf.

1787 BURNS *To Louse* vii, Ye little ken what cursed speed The blastie's makin!

blasting ('blɑːstɪŋ, -æ-), *vbl. sb.* [f. as prec. + -ING[1].]

†**1. a.** The production of blasts of wind or breath.

1535 COVERDALE *Isa.* lvii. 16 Ye blastinge goeth fro me, though I make the breath. —— *Ps.* xvii. 15 At the blastinge & breth of thy displeasure.

†**b.** Flatulence; breaking of wind. *Obs.*

c **1460** J. RUSSELL *Bk. Nurture* 304 in *Babees Bk.* (1868) 136 Alle wey be ware of þe hyndur part from gunnes blastynge. **1579** LANGHAM *Gard. Health* (1633) 28 Windinesse, belching, and blasting of the stomach and belly.

2. a. The blowing of a wind-instrument.

1862 *Guardian* 23 Apr. 403/3 The ruthless blasting of horns and beating of drums.

b. *Radio.* (See quot. 1926.)

1926 S. O. PEARSON *Dict. Wireless Techn. Terms*, *Blasting*, term used to denote the distortion which takes place in loudspeaker or telephone signals on extra loud notes, due to working beyond the straight portion of valve characteristic. **1928** *Observer* 29 Jan. 22/5 When the definite minimum level of sensitivity is given, so that the softer passages are not lost, heavy passages cause most distressing blasting.

3. a. Withering or shrivelling up caused by atmospheric, electric, or unseen agency.

1535 COVERDALE *Hagg.* ii. 17, I smote you with heate, blastinge & hale stones. **1552** HULOET, Blastynge or Searynge, as of corne, herbes, fruite, and trees. **1607** HIERON *Wks.* I. 452 In thy husbandry, blasting may vndoe thee. **1616** SURFL. & MARKH. *Countr. Farm* 313 Blasting, which is a corruption happening to hearbes and trees by some euill constellation. **1669** WORLIDGE *Syst. Agric.* (1681) 15 Blasting hath commonly been mistaken for Mildew. **1870** H. MACMILLAN *Bible Teach.* vi. 114 Blasting and mildew.. had no place in the Divine ideal of a pure and holy world.

†**b.** A similar affection of the animal body. *Obs.*

1579 LANGHAM *Gard. Health* (1633) 1, To heale inflamations, blastings and swellings of the eyes. **1607** TOPSELL *Four-f. Beasts* 387 The fat..doth keep the skin of the face free from all blastings and blemishes. **1661** LOVELL *Hist. Anim. & Min.* 43 It cureth shrinking of the joints, and blasting.

c. *fig.* and *transf.*

1677 GILPIN *Dæmonol.* (1867) 286 They have also so great a blasting upon their understanding.

†**4.** Calumnious whisper; scandal. (Cf. next word quot. 1603.) *Obs.*

a **1628** F. GREVILLE *Sidney* (1652) 89 Saves Sir Francis Drake from blastings of Court. **1665** *Surv. Aff. Netherl.* 169 About which matter there are not a few blastings and Factions.

5. The operation of blowing rocks to pieces; also its result or material produce. Also, the operation of breaking up ice.

1824 *Encycl. Brit.* Suppl. II. 317 *Blasting*..the application of the explosive force of gunpowder, in opening or rending rocks. **1856** E. K. KANE *Arctic Explor.* I. xxvi. 340 The blasting had succeeded; one canister cracked and uplifted two hundred square yards of ice with but five pounds of powder. **1885** R. CHRISTISON *Autobiog.* I. iv. 96 Finding prehnite among the blastings of a trap cliff.

6. *Comb.* and *attrib.* (sense 5), as ***blasting-charge, -fuse, gelatine, -powder, -tools***; **blasting cartridge**, a cartridge containing a blasting charge, usually exploded by electricity; **blasting-needle**, a taper piece of metal to make an aperture for a fuse; **blasting-oil**, nitro-glycerine.

1881 RAYMOND *Mining Gloss.*, *Blasting-stick*, a simple form of fuse. **1883** *Fortn. Rev.* May 645 Blasting gelatine.. consists of nitro-cotton..dissolved in nitro-glycerine. **1884** *Pall Mall G.* 5 Sept. 11/1 An article on the manufacture of dynamite and nitro-glycerine, and..the still more powerful 'explosive of the future'—blasting gelatine. **1889** *Cent. Dict.*, Blasting cartridge. **1899** *Westm. Gaz.* 1 June 4/1 Several cavalry horses have been injured by blasting cartridges exploded under their feet.

blasting, *ppl. a.* [f. as prec. + -ING².]

1. That blasts, in various senses of the vb.; blighting, striking with baleful effect, defaming, etc.

1591 PERCIVALL *Sp. Dict.*, *Sereno*, the blasting aire ..*sideratio*. **1603** SHAKS. *Meas. for M.* V. i. 122 A blasting and a scandalous breath. **1667** MILTON *P.L.* IV. 929 The blasting volied Thunder. **1810** SOUTHEY *Kehama* III. ii, Is he left..alone, To bear his blasting curse? **1861** GEN. P. THOMPSON *Audi Alt.* III. cxlv. 131 Every blasting abomination to be raked up in the middle ages.

2. *fig.* Boastful. (*Sc.*)

1786 *Har'st Rig.* in Chambers *Pop. Scot. Poems* (1862) 44 When in a blasting tift.

blastment ('blɑːstmənt, -æ-). [f. as prec. + -MENT.] = BLASTING *vbl. sb.* (sense 3).

1602 SHAKS. *Ham.* I. iii. 39 In the Morne and liquid dew of Youth, Contagious blastments are most imminent. **1803** BRISTED *Pedest. Tour* II. 368 The pestilential blastments of contagion. **1817** COLERIDGE *Prel. Zapolya* ii. Wks. IV. 193 False glory, thirst of blood and lust of rapine..Shall shoot their blastments on the land.

blasto- (blæstəʊ), repr. Gr. βλαστο- stem and comb. form of βλαστός sprout, germ. Used as the first element in many technical terms, chiefly in Biology, with the sense of 'germ' or 'bud.' Thus **blasto'carpous** *a. Bot.* [Gr. καρπός fruit], of the nature of a seed which germinates before escaping from the pericarp. **'blastocele** (-siːl), [κελίς spot], the germinal spot. **'blastocheme** (-kiːm), [ὄχημα vehicle], a Medusa in which a generative body is developed in the radiating canals. **'blastochyle** (-kaɪl), [χυλός juice], the clear mucilaginous fluid in the embryonal sac of the ovule of plants. **'blastocœle** (-siːl) [κοῖλος hollow], the central cavity which forms in the ovum after segmentation. **blasto'colla**, *Bot.*, [κόλλα glue], the gummy substance which coats certain buds, as those of the horse-chestnut. **'blastocyst** (-sɪst), **blasto'cystinx** (-'sɪstɪŋks), [κύστις bladder, κύστιγξ little bladder], the germinal vesicle, BLASTODERM. **'blastodisc**, the germinal disc of the ovum of birds. **blasto'genesis**, reproduction by buds. **bla'stogeny** (-'ɒdʒɪnɪ), Hæckel's term for the evolution of bodily form, the 'germ-history of persons.' **bla'stography**, the scientific description of the buds of plants. **'blastomere** (-mɪə(r)), [Gr. μέρος part], each of the segments into which the impregnated ovum at first divides. **blastomy'cosis** [MYCOSIS], a disease caused by infection with pathogenic fungi, affecting either the skin or the organs generally. **bla'stophagine** *a.*, of or belonging to the *Blastophaga*, a genus of fig-insects. **'blastophor** (-əfɔ(r)), [Gr. -φορος -bearing, -bearer], a more or less centrally placed portion of the spermatospore, which is not used up in the process of division to form spermatoblasts, but serves to carry these; hence **bla'stophoral** *a.*, as in *blastophoral cell*. **'blastophore** (-əfɔə(r)), *Bot.*, Richard's name for the part of the embryo with a large radicle which bears the bud. **bla'stophyly** ('ɒfɪlɪ), [Gr. φυλή tribe], Hæckel's term for the 'tribal history of persons.' **bla'stoporal** *a.*, of or pertaining to the blastopore. **'blastopore** [πόρος passage], the orifice produced by the invagination of a point on the surface of a blastula, or blastosphere, to form the enteron. **'blastosphere**, a name for the impregnated ovum, when after segmentation, it has acquired a blastocœle and blastoderm. **blasto'stroma** [Gr. στρῶμα a stratum, a bed], the germinal area. **'blastostyle** [στῦλος pillar], a stalk upon which gonophores or generative buds are developed in the Hydrozoa.

1877 HUXLEY *Anat. Inv. An.* iv. 213 The central cavity of the body of the embryo Tænia simply represents a *blastocœle. **1883** *Knowledge* 24 Aug. 123/2 A mass of nucleated cells..within which there is a cavity or blastocœle. **1876** *Encycl. Brit.* (ed. 9) IV. 81 The *blastocolla, which covers the bud. **1877** HUXLEY *Anat. Inv. An.* Introd. 16 Tracing the several germ layers back to the *blastomeres of the yelk. **1881** *Jrnl. Microsc. Soc.* Jan. 147 There are two kinds of blastomeres, the larger form the lower half of the egg, the smaller ones the upper half. **1900** DORLAND *Med. Dict.* 113/1 *Blastomycosis. **1901** H. T. RICKETTS in *Jrnl. Boston Soc. Med. Sci.* V. 453 (*title*) A new mould-fungus as the cause of so-called blastomycosis or oïdiomycosis of the skin. **1903** *Brit. Jrnl. Dermatology* XV. 121 A case of blastomycosis. **1921** *Brit. Mus. Return* 133 Notes on Fig Insects, including..a new *Blastophagine Genus. **1881** *Encycl. Brit.* XII. 557 The ciliated 'planula'.. fixes itself, probably by the *blastoporal pole. **1933** *Discovery* Feb. 55/2 A small piece of the blastoporal lip [was] ..cut out of the gastrula of a species of newt. **1880** HUXLEY *Cray-Fish* iv. 409 Its external opening termed the *blastopore. **1877** —— *Anat. Inv. An.* iii. 131 In some *blastostyles..the ectoderm splits into two layers.

blastoderm ('blæstəʊdɜːm). *Biol.* [f. BLASTO- + Gr. δέρμα, δέρματ- skin.] The germinal skin or membrane surrounding the yolk in the impregnated living ovum, and constituting the superficial layer of the embryo in its earliest condition. It divides into two and afterwards three layers of cells (the *epiblast*, *mesoblast*, and *hypoblast*: cf. -BLAST), from one or other of which all the parts of the new animal are developed.

Hence **blastoder'matic**, **blasto'dermic** *a.*, of or pertaining to the blastoderm.

1859 TODD *Cycl. Anat. & Phys.* V. 46/1 A layer of nucleated organised cells, named by Pander Blastoderm or germinal membrane. **1877** HUXLEY *Anat. Inv. An.* iii. 110 The cells of the blastoderm give rise to the histological elements of the adult body. **1881** MIVART *Cat* 319. **1836** TODD *Cycl. Anat. & Phys.* I. 786/2 The arteries begin to show themselves..in the substance of this same blastodermic lamina. *Ibid.* IV. 975/1 In one germinal membrane or blastodermatic vesicle. **1877** HUXLEY *Anat. Inv. An.* iv. 200 The homologue of the blastodermic disk or vesicle.

'blast-off. [f. BLAST *v.* 5 b.] The initial thrust required to launch a rocket or the like into space; the launching of the rocket itself. Also *attrib.*

1951 M. GREENBERG *Travelers of Space* 20 *Blast-off*, the initial expenditure of energy by a space ship leaving a planet, or in emergency takeoffs. **1952** A. C. CLARKE *Islands in Sky* viii. 125 We were supposed to keep out of the pilot's way at blast-off. **1958** *Observer* 2 Feb. 1/3 This stage developed a blast-off thrust of 78,000 lb.

blastogenesis (blæstəʊ'dʒɛnɪsɪs). *Biol.* [f. BLASTO- + GENESIS.] **1.** Reproduction by gemmation or budding.

1889 in *Cent. Dict.* **1966** *Immunology* X. 281 Chapman and Dutton..demonstrated a similar blastogenesis when cells from spleens or lymph nodes of two non-related rabbits were cultured together.

2. The theory of the transmission of inherited characters by germ-plasm, as distinguished from 'pangenesis'.

1893 in *Funk's Stand. Dict.*

blastogenic (blæstəʊ'dʒɛnɪk), *a. Biol.* [ad. G. *blastogene* (Weismann 1888, in *Biologisches Centralblatt* VIII. 106); f. BLASTO- + -GENIC.] Of or pertaining to blastogenesis; pertaining to origin from, or that originates in, the germ-cell or germ-plasm.

1889 E. B. POULTON et al. tr. *Weismann's Ess. Heredity* vii. 412 'Acquired characters'..we might also call ..'*somatogenic*'..; while all other characters might be contrasted as '*blastogenic*', because they include all those characters in the body which have arisen from changes in the germ. *Ibid.* 413 Among the *blastogenic* characters, we include not only all the changes produced by natural selection operating upon variations in the germ, but all other characters which result from this latter cause. **1912** A. DENDY *Outl. Evol. Biol.* xi. 157 Blastogenic modifications are from their very nature as attributes of the germ cells handed on by heredity. **1966** *Immunology* X. 283 An intrinsic difference may exist in the blastogenic potential of adult rabbit and rat thymus glands.

blastoid ('blæstɔɪd), *a.* and *sb.* [f. mod.L. *Blastoidea*, f. Gr. βλαστός sprout, germ + εἶδος form: see BLASTO- and -OID.] **A.** *adj.* Of or belonging to the *Blastoidea*, a group of fossil echinoderms. **B.** *sb.* An echinoderm of this group.

1876 *Q. Jrnl. Geol. Soc.* XXXII. 112 The Blastoid affinities of *Astrocrinites* (= *Zygocrinus*) have been pointed out. **1882** GEIKIE *Text-bk. Geol.* IV. II. 722 The blastoids or pentremites, which now took the place in the Carboniferous waters that in Silurian times had been filled by the Cystideans. **1914** *Brit. Mus. Return* 202 Newly-described Blastoids from Somerset. **1962** D. NICHOLS *Echinoderms* viii. 96 Tubercles have not been found in cystoids, blastoids and heterosteles. *Ibid.* xii. 149 The *steganoblastidae* are superficially blastoid-like.

blastophthoria (blæstəʊf'θɔːrɪə). *Path.* [mod.L., f. BLASTO- + Gr. φθορά destruction (φθείρειν to destroy): see -IA.] The hypothetical degeneration of germ cells caused by chronic poisoning as from alcoholism or other diseases. Hence **blastoph'thoric** *a.*, of or relating to blastophthoria.

1908 *Index Medicus* VI. Index 112/2 Blastophthoria. **1913** STEDMAN *Med. Dict.* (ed. 2) 114/2 Blastophthoria... Blastophthoric. **1914** *Proc. Soc. Exper. Biol. & Med.* XIV. 14 The continued administration of small doses of lead produces a definite blastophthoric effect in male guinea pigs; and..the lead blastophthoria thus induced manifests itself [etc.]. **1938** *Nature* 16 July 107/2 Forel's contributions to the study of the alcohol problem were then considered under the headings of blastophthoria, alcoholism and the sexual question.

blastous ('blæstəs), *a.* [f. Gr. βλαστ-ός (see above) + -OUS: cf. F. *blasteux*.] Belonging to a germ or bud; germinal.

1880 in *Syd. Soc. Lex.*

blastula ('blæstjʊlə). *Embryol.* [mod.L., f. Gr. βλαστός sprout + dim. suffix (see -ULE). Cf. BLASTULE.] An embryo, typically composed of cells arranged in a sphere enclosing the blastocœle. Hence **blastu'lation**, the formation of the blastula.

1887 A. C. HADDON *Introd. Study Embryol.* ii. 21 The result of segmentation is the formation of a multicellular body, usually enclosing a central cavity—'Segmentation cavity' or 'Blastocœl'. The body itself is variously called 'Blastula' or 'Blastosphere'. *Ibid.* ii. 50 Segmentation..of Sponges..results in the formation of a hollow blastula. **1889** *Cent. Dict.*, Blastulation. **1893** TUCKEY *Hatschek's Amphioxus* 43 An equal segmentation leading to a blastula without any well-defined main axis. **1924** E. W. MACBRIDE *Stud. Heredity* iii. 70 When the [sea-urchin's] egg has divided into about 1000 cells these form a little hollow balloon or vesicle known as the blastula. **1931** J. NEEDHAM *Chem. Embryol.* II. III. iv. 642 Vles concluded that blastulation involves a change of some kind in the metabolism of the embryo. **1962** D. NICHOLS *Echinoderms* x. 120 The resulting blastula is oval, hollow and ciliated all over.

blastule ('blæstjuːl). [dim. (on L. type) f. Gr. βλαστ-ός.] A small germ; a blastosphere.

1882 C. K. PAUL in *19th Cent.* Oct. 515 We may trace their development from the first organic blastules.

blasty ('blɑːstɪ, -æ-), *a.* [f. BLAST *sb.*¹ + -Y¹.]

1. Characterized by blasts of wind; gusty.

1583 STANYHURST *Æneis* III. (Arb.) 84 On a suddeyn thee doors winds blastye doe batter. **1870** HAWTHORNE *Eng. Note-Bks.* (1879) II. 160 This bleak and blasty shore. **1872** *Mem. R. Paul* ix. 98 An unsteady blasty wind.

†**2.** Causing blight; blasting vegetation. *Obs.*

1667 BEALE in *Phil. Trans.* II. 424 [Giving] notice of a blasty Noon (it being then a Sultry weather), and within a day or two shewing the proof upon the Cherry-blossom.

blasyn, blasynge, obs. ff. BLAZE, -ING.

blat, *v.* orig. and chiefly *U.S.* Also blatt. [Imitative.] **1.** *intr.* To bleat, or make similar sounds. Also *fig.*, to talk noisily or impulsively. Hence **'blatting** *ppl. a.*

1846 in W. K. NORTHALL *Recoll. Yankee Hill* (1850) 102 Your fellow-countrymen..are not allowed to emigrate north of the Columbia River, on account of a raging he-calf who is of bla-ting on the other side. **1884** 'MARK TWAIN' *Huck. Finn* xxv. 248 He blatted along, and managed to inquire about pretty much everybody. **1888** *San Francisco News Let.* 4 Feb. (Farmer), One of these insects of an hour rears up and blatts. **1890** L. C. D'OYLE *Notches* 34 The poor 'blatting' creatures were dragged over to the fire. **1902** KIPLING *Traffics & Discoveries* (1904) 22 He'd wipe his long thin moustache..and blat off into a long 'a-aah'. **1932** W. FAULKNER *Light in Aug.* (1933) xiii. 271 Others came out from town in racing and blatting cars. **1951** L. HOBSON *Celebrity* (1953) iv. 46 She has more self-control... I'd have blatted to the first customer. **1959** I. JEFFERIES *13 Days* x. 151, I blatted up to the little shed [on a motor-bicycle].

2. *trans.* To blurt *out*; to emit (a shrill noise).

1879 HOWELLS *Lady of Aroostook* I. v. 50 If I have anything on my mind, I have to blat it right out. **1931** F. D. DAVISON *Man-Shy* (1932) xiii. 136 Calves blatted their shrill fear. **1942** R. CHANDLER *High Window* (1943) viii. 66 The radio..was still blatting the baseball game.

blat, *sb.*¹ orig. *U.S.* [Imitative.] A bleating or shrill sound.

1904 M. E. WALLER *Wood-carver* 71 Not a sound outside except..the thin blat of a sheep beneath the barn. **1925** *Glasgow Herald* 8 Sept. 6 A bold spirit fired off his gun, and the 'blat' of the shot betrayed the cheat.

blat, *sb.*[2] *slang* (orig. *U.S.*). Also **blatt**. [ad. G. *blatt* leaf, newspaper.] A newspaper. Cf. BLADDER *sb.* 6 d.

1932 D. RUNYON in *Collier's* 21 Aug. 32/2 In fact, there is some mention of it in the blats. **1965** I. FLEMING *Man with Golden Gun* x. 130, I saw it reprinted in the American blatts. **1969** J. FREDMAN *Fourth Agency* xii. 120 Once the blats get hold of the story you're a ruined man. **1986** *Times* 29 Apr. 16/5 An otherwise bald and unconvincing interview on the telly or column in the blats.

† **blat**. *Obs.* An adaptation of L. BLATTA.

ˈ**blatancy**. [f. BLATANT, after forms from L. sbs. in *-antia*: see -ANCY.] Blatant quality.

1610 FOLKINGHAM *Art of Survey* To Rdr. 3 Who can be secured from base carping Blatancie? **1884** *Punch* 1 Nov. 213 Birmingham blatancy.

blatant (ˈbleɪtənt), *a.* (and *sb.*) Also 6–7 **blattant**. [Apparently invented by Spenser, and used by him as an epithet of the thousand-tongued monster begotten of Cerberus and Chimæra, the 'blatant' or 'blattant beast', by which he symbolized calumny. It has been suggested that he intended it as an archaic form of *bleating* (of which the 16th c. Sc. was *blaitand*), but this seems rather remote from the sense in which he used it. The L. *blatīre* to babble, may also be compared. (The *a* was probably short with Spenser: it is now always made long.)]

1. In the phrase 'blat(t)ant beast', taken from Spenser (cf. *F.Q.* v. xii. 37, 41; vi. i. 7, iii. 24, ix. 2, x. 1, xii. *advt.*, xii. 2): see above.

1596 SPENSER *F.Q.* v. xii. 37 Unto themselves they [Envie and Detraction] gotten had A monster which the blatant beast men call, A dreadful feend of gods and men ydrad. —— vi. i. 7 'The blattant beast,' quoth he, 'I doe pursew.' **1602** *Return fr. Parnass.* v. iv. (Arb.) 69 The Ile of Dogges, where the blattant beast doth rule and raigne. **1636** FITZ-GEFFREY *Bless. Birthd.* (1881) 128 That blatant beast So belched forth from his blaspheaming brest. *a* **1658** CLEVELAND *Gen. Poems* (1677) 60 Cub of the Blatant Beast. **1768** TUCKER *Lt. Nat.* I. 596 The blatant beast..with his unbridled tongue. **1812** BYRON *Ch. Har.* I. xxvi. (Orig. MS.), Then burst the blatant beast [*note*, a figure for the mob], and roar'd, and raged. **1856** MISS MULOCH *J. Halifax* (ed. 17) 340 He was one of the most 'blatant-beasts' of the Reign of Terror.

2. *fig.* **a.** Of persons or their words: Noisy; offensively or vulgarly clamorous; bellowing.

1656 BLOUNT *Glossogr.*, *Blatant*, babling, twatling. **1674** MARVELL *Reh. Transp.* II. 371 You are a Blatant Writer and a Labrant. **1821** SOUTHEY *Vis. Judgem.* x. Wks. X. 223 Maledictions, and blatant tongues, and viperous hisses. **1872** BAGEHOT *Physics & Pol.* (1876) 92 Up rose a blatant Radical. **1874** H. REYNOLDS *John Bapt.* viii. 515 A blatant, insolent materialism threatens to engulf moral distinctions.

b. Clamorous, making itself heard.

1790 COWPER *Odyss.* VII. 267 Not the less Hear I the blatant appetite demand Due sustenance. **1863** GEO. ELIOT *Romola* (1880) I. II. xxix. 359 An orator who tickled the ears of the people blatant for some unknown good. **1866** WHIPPLE *Char. & Charac. Men* 166 All agree in a common contempt blatant or latent. **1867** J. MACGREGOR *Voy. Alone* 65 A mass of human being whose want..misery, and filth are..patent to the eye, and blatant to the ear.

c. In recent usage: obtrusive to the eye (rather than to the ear as in orig. senses); glaringly or defiantly conspicuous; palpably prominent or obvious.

1889 W. S. GILBERT *Gondoliers* II, I write letters blatant On medicines patent. **1903** G. GISSING *Private Papers H. Ryecroft* 274 The blatant upstart who builds a church, lays out his money in that way not merely to win social consideration. **1912** G. B. SHAW *Let.* 19 Aug. in *Shaw & Mrs. P. Campbell* (1952) 38 You don't loathe the scenery for being prosy and mediocre in spite of its blatant picturesqueness as you do in Switzerland. **1930** SAYERS & EUSTACE *Documents in Case* li. 246 The blatant way in which he had marked his trail..[etc.] were actions entirely inconsistent with the carelessness of an innocent man. **1937** H. NICOLSON *Helen's Tower* ix. 191 If they were kept in the Museum..their blatant lack of human interest had caused me to pass them by. **1942** *New Statesman* 11 July 26/1 Mankind, he said, is led by half-truths or blatant lies. **1957** A. E. COPPARD *It's Me, O Lord!* v. 55 The colonel..clad in a suit of blatant check, spats, and a monocle. **1957** *Times* 19 Dec. 4/3 A blatant piece of late tackling.

3. a. Bleating, bellowing (or merely, loud-voiced).

1791 COWPER *Iliad* XXIII 39 Many a sheep and blatant goat. **1866** J. ROSE *Ecl. & Georg. Virg.* 69 Rooks rejoicing, and the blatant herds.

b. Noisily resonant, loud.

1816 SCOTT *Old Mort.* xiv, A blatant noise which rose behind them. **1867** *Cornh. Mag.* Jan. 30 The vibrating and blatant powers of a hundred instruments.

† **B.** as *sb.* One who has a blatant tongue. *Obs.*

1610 FOLKINGHAM *Art of Survey* Introd. Poem, Couch rabid Blatants, silence Surquedry.

blatantly (ˈbleɪtəntlɪ), *adv.* [f. prec. + -LY[2].] **1.** In a blatant manner.

1851 R. BURTON *Goa* 292 Sated with the joys of the eye and mouth, you..inquire blatantly what amusement it has to offer you.

2. Obtrusively, unashamedly, defiantly; as an obvious untruth. (Cf. prec.)

1878 MISS BRADDON *Open Verd.* vi. 47 A stone sun-dial with a blatantly false inscription to the effect that it recorded only happy hours. **1911** E. WALLACE *Sanders of River* viii. 160 Sanders was blatantly unrepentant. **1928** A. WAUGH *Nor Many Waters* ii. 70 His features were delicate, but not blatantly aristocratic. **1941** H. G. WELLS *You can't be too Careful* v. i. 237 The professional Jewish 'champions' set themselves..to ignore as blatantly as possible the common need for a world settlement. **1959** *Sunday Times* 22 Mar. 9 The Turkish-Cypriot leader..has announced that his T.M.T. organisation has no arms to surrender—rather blatantly, considering the number of Greek Cypriots who were fired upon by Turkish Cypriots. **1959** *Observer* 14 June 17/6 'No waiting' signs are often habitually and blatantly ignored by the motorist.

† **blatch**. *Obs.* Forms: 5 **blacche**, 6 **blatche**, **blache**. [ME. *blacche*, answering to an OE. **blæcce*, not found, but pointing to an OTeut. **blakkjo-* or **blakkjâ-*, f. **blakkó-* 'black': see BLACK *a.*, and cf. BLACK *sb.*, BLEACH *sb.*[2], BLECK, and BLETCH.] Blacking. Hence **blatch-pot**, **blacche-pot**.

a **1500** *Metr. Voc.* in Wr.-Wülcker 628 *Attramentorium* (blacchepot), *sunt attromenta* (blacche), *sed atrum* (blacke). **1519** HORMAN *Vulg.* 81 b, Wrytters ynke shulde be fyner than blatche [*lectius esset sutorio*]. **1552** HULOET, *Blache* that shomakers vse *Atramentum sutorium*.

† **blatch**, *v. Obs.* [f. prec.: cf. BLACK *v.*, BLEACH *v.*[2], BLETCH *v.*] *trans.* To smear with blacking or other black substance.

[*c* **1205** LAY. 17700, Iblæcched he hæfede his licame swulc ismitte of cole.] **1587** J. HARMAR tr. *Beza's Serm.* 195 (R.) No man can like to be smutted and blatched in his face. **1607** *Schol. Disc. agst. Antichr.* II. ix. 110 It is with the enimies crosse that we are blatched.

blate (bleɪt, *dial.* bleːt, blɪət), *a. Sc.* and *north. dial.* Also 6 **blait**, 7 **bleat(e**, **bleit**. [Found in Sc. late in 15th c. It answers phonetically to OE. *blát* livid, pale, ghastly; but the connexion of meaning, though possible, is not attested by the evidence. The general sense since 16th c. is 'blunt,' 'not sharp or ready' in feeling, courage, discernment, manner, action, etc. (Connexion with OE. *bléat* miserable, wretched, is not justified: still less with *bléað* soft, weak, timid. These words gave *blete*, *blethe*, in ME.)]

† **1.** Pale, ghastly. (In OE. In the second quotation the sense is quite uncertain: cf. sense 3.)

c **1000** in *Cod. Vercell.* I. (1843) 63 Hungres on wenum blates beodgæstes. *c* **1450** HENRYSON *Mor. Fabl.* 34 The fauour of thy face, For thy defence is foule and disfigurate, Brought to the light, blased, blunt, and blate.

† **2.** Void of feeling, physically insensible, feelingless. (Perhaps, like a dead body). *Obs.*

1513 DOUGLAS *Æneis* I. viii. 129 The Phenitianis nane sa blait breistis hes. *a* **1548** *Thrie Priests Peblis* in *Pinkerton* (1792) I. 29 (JAM.) In sa far as the saull is forthy Far worthier than the blait body.

† **3.** Void of spirits, abashed, having the courage blunted or daunted, spiritless, timid. *Obs.*

1535 STEWART *Cron. Scot.* II. 632 Als blait and basit as ane scheip. *Ibid.* 639 So blunt, so blait, berand himself so law. *a* **1560** ROLLAND *Crt. Venus* Prol. 55 Soft, blait, and blunt, of curagon.

4. Not 'sharp' in discernment, stupid.

[**1513** see BLATELY.] **1581** N. BURNE *Disput.* 96 b (JAM.) As the Italianis had bene sa blait, that they culd nocht discerne betuix ane man and ane woman. **1811** *Statist. Acc. Nairn & Moray* (JAM.) *Blate*, easily deceived.

† **5.** Blunt in manner, curt. *Obs.*

1663 in Spalding *Troub. Chas. I.* (1792) I. 143 (JAM.) They got a bleat answer, and so tint their travel.

6. Bashful, backward, *esp.* from natural diffidence or awkwardness; slow to come forward or assert oneself; diffident, sheepish, shamefaced.

c **1600** *Rob. Hood* (Ritson) I. iii. 40 If they have supt e'er I come in, I will look wondrous blate. **1674** RAY *N.C. Wds.* Coll., A toom purse makes a bleit Merchant. *Scot. Prov.* **1725** RAMSAY *Gent. Sheph.* I. i, Be nae blate, Push bauldly on and win the day. **1787** BURNS *Ep. Mrs. Scott* I When I was beardless, young, and blate. **1808** *Cumbr. Ballads* xxix. 67 I' God's neame step forret; nay, dunnet be bleate. **1823** SCOTT *Quentin D.* II. xiv. You are not blate—you will never lose fair lady for faint heart. **1865** *Cornh. Mag.* Mar. 328 He's 'no blate,' as they used to say in Scotland, and made himself quite at home to-night.

† **7.** Of a fight, a market: Dull, slow. *Obs.*

1597–1605 MONTGOMERIE *Poems* (1821) 46 But ȝit his batill will be blate, Gif he our forss refuse. **1768** ROSS *Helenore* 55 (JAM.) Gang hame again? Na, na, That were my hogs to a blate fair to ca'.

Hence ˈ**blately** *adv.*, ˈ**blateness**.

1513 DOUGLAS *Æneis* Prol. 251 The last sax buikis of Virgill..Caxtoun sa blaitlie lettis ourslip. **1823** GALT *Entail* III. iii. 41 It will be ill put-on blateness.

blate (bleɪt), *v. rare.* [A late word, perhaps arising out of BLEAT (sense 2 b), influenced by BLATANT. *Bleat* was formerly pronounced (bleːt), as in *great.*]

trans. and *intr.* To babble, prate, give mouth (about), talk blatantly.

1666 PEPYS *Diary* (1879) IV. 46 He blates to me what has passed between other people and him. **1878** GILDER, *Poet & Master* 38 They peddle their petty schemes, and blate and babble and groan.

blate, var. of BLEAT, cry like a sheep.

† ˈ**blaterate**, *v. Obs.*[−0]. [f. L. *blaterāt-* ppl. stem of *blaterāre* to babble: cf. F. *blatérer* and BLATTER.] 'To babble or talk vainly.' Bullokar 1676.

blateration (blætəˈreɪʃən). Also **blatt-**. [ad. late L. *blaterātiōn-em*, n. of action f. *blaterāre*: see prec. Cf. BLATTER *v.*] Babbling chatter.

1656 BLOUNT *Glossogr.*, *Blateration*, vain-babling, flattering in speech. **1864** R. BURTON *Dahome* II. 260 Heralds proclaimed the royal titles with normal blateration.

† **blateˈroon**. *Obs.* Also **blatt-**. [ad. L. *blatero*, *-ōnem* babbler, f. *blaterāre*.] A babbler.

c **1645** HOWELL *Lett.* (1650) II. 117 I hate such blateroons. **1656** BLOUNT *Glossogr.*, *Blateron*, or *Blatteroon*, a babler, an idle-headed fellow.

† **blathe**, *v. Obs. rare*[−1]. ? To cry out.

1640 J. GOWER *Ovid's Fest.* VI. 127 The poore young child for help and soccour blathed.

ˈ**blather** (ˈblæðə(r)), *v.* orig. *dial.* [Variant of BLETHER *v.*] *intr.* To talk foolishly, talk nonsense. Often in *ppl. a.* Hence ˈ**blatherer**, a foolish talker (1866 in *E.D.D.*).

1825 BROCKETT *Gloss. N. Country Words* 18 He blathers and talks, is a common phrase where much is said to little purpose. A person of this kind is..styled a *blathering hash*. **1891** KIPLING *Light that Failed* iv. 59 If you were only a mass of blathering vanity,..I wouldn't mind. **1892** *Cassell's Fam. Mag.* Dec. 11/1 Hold your tongues, you blathering idiots. **1900** *Century Mag.* Feb. 504/1 Morland had a blathering contempt for nobility and society. **1920** D. H. LAWRENCE *Touch & Go* III. i. 76 They've got a set of loud-mouthed blatherers and agitators among them. **1951** *Essays in Criticism* I. 17, I sympathize with O'Casey's character Who called him 'a tired-out old blatherer'. **1951** 'J. WYNDHAM' *Day of Triffids* i. 15 Gentlemanly tones which blathered about this 'magnificent spectacle' and 'unique phenomenon'.

blather, variant of BLADDER *sb.*

blather, *sb.*: see BLETHER *sb.*

ˈ**blatherskite**. A blustering, talkative fellow (*U.S. colloq.*): see BLETHERSKATE.

ˈ**blathery**, *sb.* and *a. Sc.* Also **bladarie**, **bladdrie**, **bladry**, **blaidry**, **blaithrie**. [Etymological form and history uncertain: perh. a derivative of BLADDER *sb.*, and more properly spelt *bladdery*. It has with less likelihood been referred to BLETHER to speak nonsense.]

A. *sb.* Something unsubstantial, hollow, or deceptive; flummery; phlegm from the bronchial tubes.

1591 R. BRUCE *Serm.* (JAM.) The inward heart is full of bladarie, quhilk bladarie shal..multiply thy torments. *a* **1605** MONTGOMERIE *Poems* (1821) 75 This barme & blaidry buists up all my bees. **1703** D. WILLIAMSON *Serm. bef. Gen. Ass.* 42 It was a fair horse that came into Troy, but there was meikle blathery in his Belly which the Trojans saw not. **1709** M. BRUCE *Soul Confirm.* 23 (JAM.) Nothing..but bladdrie instead of wholesome food. **1721** J. KELLY *Scot. Proverbs* 296 Shame fall the gear and the blad'ry o't.' *a* **1758** RAMSAY *Poems* (1800) I. Life 44 (JAM.) Frae ilka vice and blaidry free.

B. *adj.* Unsubstantial, rotten, trashy.

1708 M. BRUCE *Lect.* 28 (JAM.) A 4th sort of blathrie ware we bring to Christ's grave, is a number of ill-guided complaints. [**1863** ATKINSON *Danby Provinc.*, *Bladdry*, muddy, dirty. **1875** ROBINSON *Whitby Gloss.* (E.D.S.), *Blathery*..'It's blathery walking.']

‖ˈ**blatta**. Also anglicized in 7 **blat**. [L.]

1. By Roman writers and their translators applied to various insects shunning the light: a kind of moth, mite, or beetle. Vaguely and empirically used by 17th c. writers, but at length specialized as the generic name of the Cockroach.

1601 HOLLAND *Pliny* II. 370 Two or three of these flies called Blattæ sodden in oile, make a soueraigne medicine to cure the eares. **1658** ROWLAND *Mouffet's Theat. Ins.* 998 There are three sorts of Blattæ; the soft Moth, the mill Moth, and the unsavoury or stinking Moth. *Ibid.* The worms of the belly some call Blattæ. Cardanus in one place calleth the worms that breed in meal or bran, Blattæ... The Blatta is an Insect flying in the night, like to a Beetle, but wanteth the sheath wings. **1796** STEDMAN *Surinam* (1813) II. xxiii. 179 Destroyed by the blata or cockroaches. **1816** KIRBY & SP. *Entomol.* (1843) I. 222 The all devouring Blatta or cockroach. **1830** LYELL *Princ. Geol.* (1832) II. 148 The devastation of the ants and blattæ.

2. Purple; purple silk.

1658 ROWLAND *Mouffet's Theat. Ins.* 999 Much variety of opinion there is..of the colour of the Blat Moth, or the Blattean colour. For if these Insects..are the Blattæ truly so called, why should not the black be the Blat colour, rather than red purple colours? **1876** ROCK *Text. Fabr.* v. 39 The costly purple-dyed silks called 'blatta.'

† ˈ**blattean**, *a. Obs.* [f. L. *blatte-us* purple + -AN.] Purple.

1658 ROWLAND *Mouffet's Theat. Ins.* 998 The Blattean colour is died with worms which come out of the grain of Cockle, out of whose bloud is produced a..colour, not black, as some think, but a bright purple or scarlet.

blatter (ˈblætə(r)), *v.* Also 6–7 **blotter**. [In sense 1, ad. L. *blaterāre* to talk idly, babble, prate, perhaps partly through F. *blatérer*. But the use

of the word is probably largely influenced by its phonetic suggestiveness of forcible and repeated noise: cf. *batter*, *chatter*, *clatter*, *patter*, and *bl*-words expressing impetus, like *blow*, *blash*, *blast*.]

1. *intr.* To speak or prate volubly. (Also with *it.*)

a **1555** LATIMER *Serm. & Rem.* (1845) 358 Procuring also certain preachers to blatter against me. **1579** FULKE *Heskins' Parl.* 224 Boyes and girles can blatter it against Christes presence in the sacrament. **1603** HOLLAND *Plutarch's Mor.* 193 If peradventure it [the tongue]..will blatter out and not tarrie within, we might bite it. **1656** CROMWELL *Lett. & Sp.* (Carl.) Sp. 17 Sept., It is to be clamoured at, and blottered at. **1865** PUSEY *Eiren.* 375 They blatter..that the Church forms new dogmas at will.

b. *trans.* Often with *out*, *abroad*.

1556 ABP. PARKER *Psalter* xciv. 294 They blatter out euen what they list. **1590** C. S. *Right Relig.* 16 Hee blottereth out his owne traditions. **1615** CHAPMAN *Odyss.* Ep. Ded. 51 What the brazen head Blatters abroad. **1645** G. DANIEL *Poems* Wks. II. 101 Noe matter tho' Ignorance blatter Follie. **1705** HICKERINGILL *Priest-Cr.* II. ii. 21 Be not rash with thy Mouth, to blatter out any thing before God.

2. *intr.* To hurry or rush with clattering noise. (*Sc.*)

1790 A. WILSON *To W. Mitchell* Poet. Wks. (1846) 113 Down the brae, It blatter't wi' a blash I' the burn that day. **1840** HOGG *Tales & Sk.* VI 53 Maxwell's feet blattered down the lowest stair. **1862** J. BROWN *Horæ Subsec.* Ser. III. (1882) 202 The snow blattered in his face.

blatter ('blætə(r)), *sb. Sc.* [f. prec.] A volley of clattering words, or sound of rapid motion.

1816 SCOTT *Antiq.* ix, 'Oot cam sic a blatter o' Latin about his lugs, that poor Rab Tull..was clean overwhelmed.' **1865** LIVINGSTONE *Zambesi* x. 211 Hundreds of turtle doves rise, with great blatter of wing.

blatteration, variant of BLATERATION.

blatterer ('blætərə(r)). [f. BLATTER *v.* + -ER[1].] A voluble prater or babbler; a blusterer.

1627 SCLATER *Expos. 2 Thess.* (1632) 206 Blatterers and bablers in prayer they would make us. **1867** *N. Y. Nation* 3 Jan. 2/2 All the famous blatterers and swindlers.

blattering, *vbl. sb.* [f. as prec. + -ING[1].]

1613 R. C. *Table Alph.* (ed. 3), *Blattering*, vaine babling.

blattering ('blætərɪŋ), *ppl. a. Sc.* [f. as prec. + -ING[2].] That blatters.

1721 RAMSAY *Poet. Wks.* (1848) III. 72 The blatran hailstones. —— *Lyric P., Ode fr. Hor.*, The blattering winds dare nae mair move.

blatteroon, variant of BLATEROON. *Obs.*

'**blatting,** *vbl. sb.* The action of the verb BLAT.

1935 S. LEWIS *It can't happen Here* xxix. 315 The nervous blatting of tremendous traffic. **1946** F. DAVISON *Dusty* vi. 61 There was much bellowing and blatting [of cows]. **1955** M. MILLAR *Beast in View* iii. 46 Anyway, you didn't come here to listen to my blatting.

Blattnerphone ('blætnəfəʊn). Also b-. [Named after the inventor L. *Blattner* (1881–1935) + -PHONE.] An instrument for recording sound on magnetic tape. Also *attrib.*

1931 *Wireless World* 17 June 664/1 A few days ago I was privileged to see and hear the Blattnerphone in operation. **1932** *B.B.C. Techn. Tables & Glossary* 45/2 *Blattnerphone*, a system of recording speech or music on a steel wire or tape by means of variable magnetisation along the length of the wire or tape. **1932** *BBC Year-Bk.* 101 In some ways the most important event of the year has been the adoption by the BBC of the Blattnerphone recording apparatus. **1937** *Brit. Jrnl. Psychol.* Jan. 282 If there are any blattnerphone records..of psychoanalysis they are unlikely to be long or numerous because of their great expense.

blau, obs. form of BLOW.

blaud, variant of BLAD. *Sc.*

blaunc, blaunch(e, -er, blaundish, etc., obs. ff. BLANK, BLANCH, -ER, BLANDISH, etc.

blaunchmer, blaundemere: see BLAUNNER.

† '**blaundrell.** *Obs.* Forms: 5 blawnd(e)relle, blaunderel(le, 6 blaundrelle, (brandrel), 7 blaundrell. [a. OF. *blandurel* the apple now called 'calville blanc.'] A kind of white apple, formerly in much repute.

c **1440** *Promp. Parv.* 38 Blawndrelle, frute [*v.r.* blaunderel], *melonis.* *a* **1483** *Lib. Nig. Edw. IV* in *Househ. Ord.* (1790) 82 Pourveyours of blaunderelles, pepyns, and all other fruytes. **1494** FABYAN *Chron.* VII. 605 Quynces, blaunderellys, peches, and other fruytes. **1611** COTGR., *Blandureau*, the white apple, called in some part of England a blaundrell.

† '**blaundsore.** *Obs.* A dish in cookery. Cf. Warner *Antiq. Culin.* (1790) 55.

1430–50 *Gregory's Chron.* 170 The thyrde course of thys ryalle feste..Quynsys in composte. Blaundsore. *c* **1631** *Turn. Tottenham* 268 in *E.P.P.* (Hazl.) III. 95 Bell clapurs in blawndisare, With a nobull cury.

† '**blaunner.** *Obs.* Forms: 4 blaunner, -ier, 5 blauner; also 5 blaundemere, blaunchmer. [app. *blaun(n)er* was the same as *blaundemere*, which in its turn suggests a Fr. **blanc de mer* 'sea white,' though the application of the name seems to be lost.] A species of (? white) fur used to line hoods, etc.

c **1330** *Syr Degarré* 701 (Halliw.) He ware a cyrcote that was grene; With blaunchmer it was furred, I wene. *c* **1340** *Gaw. & Gr. Knt.* 155 A mere mantile abof..With blyþe blaunner ful bryȝt, & his hod boþe. **1460** *Lybeaus Disc.* 117 in Ritson *Metr. Rom.* II. 6 Sche was clodeth in Tars, Rownie and nodyng skars, Pelured wyth blauner. *Ibid.* 128 in Furniv. *Percy Fol.* II. 420 (Mätz.) Cladd all in greene and ffurred with blaundemere.

blaunsher, obs. form of BLANCHER.

‖ **blauwbok** ('blaʊbɒk). [Du. *blaauwbok*, f. *blaauw* blue + *bok* buck, he-goat.] A name given by the Dutch settlers to a large Antelope (*A. leucophæa*) in South Africa, on account of the effect produced by its black hide showing through its ashy-grey hair.

1786 tr. *Sparrman's Voy.* II. 219 The blaauw-bok is also one of the large species of gazel. **1832** *Penny Cycl.* II. 88/1 The Blauwbok..is six feet in length.

† '**blaver,** *v. Obs. rare.* A variant of BLABBER.

1461 *Paston Lett.* 402 II. 28 He and hys wyfe and other have blaveryd here of my kynred.

blaw, north. and Sc. form of BLOW.

blawnche, blawnsher, obs. ff. BLANCH, -ER.

'**blawort.** *Sc.* [f. *bla*, BLAE + *wort* herb, plant.] The name in Scotland of two plants: the Harebell (*Campanula rotundifolia*), and the Corn Bluebottle (*Centaurea Cyanus*). Cf. BLEWART.

1728 RAMSAY *Poet. Wks.* (1848) III. 137 Of colour like a blawart blue. *a* **1774** FERGUSSON *Poems* (1845) 35 Een as blue's a blawort Wi' straiks. **1824** SCOTT *St. Ronan's* II. 165 (JAM.) His poor wizened houghs as blue as a blawart.

blaxploitation (blæksplɔɪ'teɪʃən). *U.S. colloq.* Also **blacksploitation.** [Blend of BLACK *sb.* and EXPLOITATION, after SEXPLOITATION.] The exploitation of Blacks, esp. as actors in films of historical or other interest to Blacks. Chiefly *attrib.*

1972 *New York* 12 June 16/1 This blaxploitation picture's about a pre-Civil War slave. **1974** *Collier's Year Bk. 1973* 368/1 At the most violent end of the spectrum were the kung fu and blacksploitation pictures. **1977** *Time Out* 28 Jan. 12/3 An interesting failure of a film that marks the midway stage in the development of black consciousness/blaxploitation films out of the racial-tension/liberal films of the Fifties and early Sixties. **1978** *Sat. Rev.* (U.S.) Dec. 35 The black glistening giants of blacksploitation films. **1983** *Washington Post* 10 July K5/2 That whole rash of blaxploitation films was, for the most part, unrealistic, degrading.

blay, bley (bleɪ), *sb.* Also 7 (*rare*) blea. [OE. *blǽȝe* (wk. fem.) is cogn. w. Ger. *blei(h)e*, MDu. *bleie*, mod.Du. *blei*:—OTeut. **blaijôn*. Franck thinks it may be derived from the same root as Ger. *blei* lead, and OE. *bléo*, BLEE, complexion.] The name of a small fish, the bleak.

c **1000** ÆLFRIC *Gloss.* in Wr.-Wülcker *Voc.* 180 *Gobio*, blæȝe. **1611** COTGR., *Able*, a blay, or bleake, fish. **1720** *Stow's Surv.* (ed. Strype 1754) II. v. xxvii. 479/2 No such person shall within the said bounds or limits fleet with any Blay net. **1787** BEST *Angling* (ed. 2) 4 Alburnus, the Bleak or Bley. **1822** IMISON *Sc. & Art* II. 336 The blay, or bleak fish which is very common in the rivers near London. **1849** *Sidonia Sorc.* II. 47 We have taken bley: the nets are all loaded.

blay (bleɪ), *a.* [Variant of BLAE *a.*] = BLAE *a.* 5 ('unbleached'). Frequent in Irish use.

1785 *Ann. Reg. 1783* (Useful Projects) 85/1 When I mention white flax, I do it in opposition to that, which..has the appellation of blay. **1861** O'CURRY *MS. Materials* 38 Some with..green or blay or white cloaks. **1869** *Dublin Gen. Advert.* 24 Dec., Twilled and plain white calico sheets..blay ditto. **1913** 'G. A. BIRMINGHAM' *Gen. John Regan* xvii, They draped it..in a large sheet of blay calico of a light yellowish colour.

blay, variant of BLEA *v.* to bleat.

blay, -berry, dial. variant of BLAE, -BERRY.

'**blaying, bleying,** *vbl. sb.* [See BLEA.] The bleating of lambs or kids; crying of children.

† **blayk(e,** *a. Obs.* Also 3–4 bleik(e, 5 bleyke. [ME. *bleik*, a. ON. *bleikr* shining, pale, cogn. w. OE. *blác*, OS. *blêc* (MDu. *bleec*, Du. *bleek*), OHG. *bleih* (MHG. and mod.G. *bleich*):—OTeut. **blaiko-z*, f. the stem of *blîkan*, pa. t. *blaik*, to shine. Cf. the synonyms BLAKE, BLEAK, BLOKE.]

a. Pale. **b.** Yellow.

a **1300** *Havelok* 470 That weren for hunger grene and bleike. *a* **1325** *E.E. Allit. P.* A. 27 Blomez blayke & blwe & rede. **1440** *Promp. Parv.* 39 Bleyke of coloure, *pallidus.* **1570** LEVINS *Manip.* 198 Blayke, *flauus.*

blayle, obs. variant of BRAIL.

1622 R. HAWKINS *Voy. S. Sea* (1847) 188 His sayles..prevented with martnets blayles and caskettes.

blayn(e, obs. form of BLAIN.

blaze (bleɪz), *sb.*[1] Forms: 1 blæse, 1–7 blase, 3 blass, 6– blaze; *north.* and *Sc.* 3–6 bles(e, 4 blose, 6 bleis(e, bleiss, 7– bleeze. [OE. *blase*, *blæse*, wk. fem., chiefly in sense of 'torch' (OTeut. type **blasôn*-), is cogn. w. MHG. *blas* neut., a torch, with OHG. *blass*, mod.G. *blass* 'pale, whitish' (originally 'shining'), and with BLAZE *sb.*[2] The northern forms with *ē* probably originated in a lengthening of the vowel of OE. *blæse*.]

† **1.** A torch, firebrand. *Obs.*

c **1000** ÆLFRIC *Gloss.* in Wr.-Wülcker 126 *Lampas*, blase. *c* **1000** *Ags. Gosp.* John xviii. 3 Iudas..com þyder mid leohtfatum & mid blasum. **1160** *Hatton G.* ibid. Blesen, *v.r.* bleosum. **1513** DOUGLAS *Æneis* IV. x. 87 The feirfull brandis and blesis of hait fyre, Reddy to birne thi schippis. **1535** STEWART *Cron. Scot.* I. 332 Sa mony bleises into the tyme hes brint Of pik and tar.

2. a. A bright glowing flame or fire. ***in a blaze*** (***on blaze*** obs.): on fire, in flames.

a **1000** *Guthlac* (Gr.) 648 In bælblæsan. *c* **1205** LAY. 2859 In þere temple he lette beornen enne blase of fure. *a* **1300** *Cursor M.* 8877 Vte o þat tre it brast a blese (*other MSS.* blass, blase) þat brent þam al wit-in a rese. **1377** LANGL. *P. Pl.* B. XVII. 212 A torche, The blase þere-of yblowe out. **1393** GOWER *Conf.* II. 244 They setten all on blase. **1513** DOUGLAS *Æneis* VI. ix. 129 A fell bleiss of thundir. **1612** T. TAYLOR *Comm. Titus* ii. 12 It is as fire in straw, a blase and away. **1725** DE FOE *Voy. round World* (1840) 331 A few withered dry sticks, with which they made a blaze. **1857** WILLMOTT *Pleas. Lit.* xi. 46 The strongest blaze soon goes out when a man always blows and never feeds it.

b. (slang.) ***blazes***: pl. referring to the flames of hell, used in several forcible expressions, as ***blue blazes***, ***the blazes!*** ***like blazes***: furiously, impetuously. ***to (the) blazes***: to perdition, 'to the deuce'; used in imprecations.

1818 A. BURTON *Johnny Newcome* 41 They thought he must be mad as blazes. **1818** M. L. WEEMS *Drunkard's Looking Glass* (ed. 6) 49 Ye steep down gulphs of liquid fire! Ye blue blazes of damnation! **1837** DICKENS *Pickw.* liv. 587 How the blazes you can stand the head-work you do, is a mystery to me. **1838** —— *O. Twist* 91 What the blazes is in the wind now? **1845** DISRAELI *Sybil* (Rtldg.) 284 She sets her face against gals working in mills like blazes. **1853** DE QUINCEY *Sp. Nun* Wks. 1862 III. 84 The horse..went like blazes. **1853** DICKENS in *Househ. Words* 5 Feb. 483/2 Letting the teeth go (to Blazes, he observed indefinitely). **1858** S. A. HAMMETT *Piney Woods Tavern* 37 And the two Jacobs swore like blue blazes agin him. **1861** DICKENS *Gt. Expect.* I. x. 160 What the Blue Blazes is he? **1924** G. L. MALLORY *Let.* 7 May in E. F. Norton *Fight for Everest* (1925) 231 The *moral* of A party had gone to blazes. **1925** W. DEEPING *Sorrell & Son* xiii. § 1. 119 When you have found out what you want to do—then go at it like blazes. **1948** C. DAY LEWIS *Otterbury Incident* ix. 121 What the blue blazes is all this?

† **c.** A 'flash' (of lightning), a moment. *Obs.*

1590 GREENE *Never too late* (1600) 71 Lightning, that beautifies the heauen for a blaze.

3. *fig.* A sudden kindling up of passion as of a fire; a violent outburst.

[*a* **1240** *Ureisun* in *Lamb. Hom.* 185 Ontend me wiþ þe blase of þi leitende loue.] **1593** SHAKS. *Rich. II*, II. i. 33 His rash fierce blaze of Ryot cannot last. **1606** —— *Tr. & Cr.* IV. v. 105 Hector in his blaze of wrath subscribes To tender obiects. **1646** BUCK *Rich. III*, I. 15 The Blaze of Ambition. **1758** JOHNSON *Idler* No. 4 ⁋10 There is danger lest the blaze of charity..should die away. **1874** STOUGHTON *Ch. of Rev.* xii. 279 Which fanned the Lower House into a blaze of resentment.

4. Brilliant light, brightness, brilliancy; a glow of bright colour.

1564 HARRINGTON *To Isabella Markham* 4 Eyes that mock the diamonds blaze. **1586** M. ROYDON *Elegy* 169 in *Spenser's Wks.* (1842) V. 283 The blaze whereof when Mars beheld. **1671** MILTON *Samson* 80 O dark, dark, dark, amid the blaze of noon. **1801** SOUTHEY *Thalaba* x. xiv, The rich geranium's scarlet blaze. **1848** MACAULAY *Hist. Eng.* II. 587 The theatres were..one blaze of orange ribands.

5. *fig.* **a.** = BLAZING STAR 2, cynosure.

1579 LYLY *Euphues* (Arb.) 102 Thy beautie hath made thee the blaze of Italy.

b. Glory, splendour, brilliant display.

1579 LYLY *Euphues* 180 'Beauty, where is thy blaze?' **1712** ADDISON *Spect.* No. 369 ⁋8 A most glorious Blaze of Poetical Images. **1850** TENNYSON *In Mem.* xcviii, Sadness flings Her shadow on the blaze of kings. **1875** JOWETT *Plato* (ed. 2) II. 169 Enveloping in a blaze of jests the most serious matters.

c. Clear or full light, as of noon.

1748 RICHARDSON *Clarissa* (1811) I. i. 3 Now to your regret, pushed into blaze, as I may say. **1869** LECKY *Europ. Mor.* II. i. 64 The blaze of publicity. **1879** FARRAR *St. Paul* (1883) 150 In the full blaze of contemporary knowledge.

6. *Physiol.* An electric current passing along living tissue in response to mechanical stimulus. Also *attrib.* in ***blaze current***. Hence ***blaze reaction***, ***response***, reaction or response so obtained.

1902 *Nature* 18 Sept. 491/2 The blaze reaction..requires short strong currents for its manifestation. **1903** *Ibid.* 9 July 238 This 'blaze' response is the algebraic sum of post-anodic and post-kathodic currents. **1903** *Jrnl. R. Microsc. Soc.* Oct. 599 A crystalline lens is a good object upon which to study the nature of blaze-currents.

7. In poker: (see quot.). *U.S.*

1880 'TRUMPS' *Amer. Hoyle* (ed. 13) 197 *Blaze.* This hand consists of five court cards, and, when it is played, beats two pairs.

8. *Comb.*, as ***blaze-trailing***.

1809 J. BARLOW *Columb.* VII. 231 Blaze-trailing fuses vault the night's dim round.

blaze (bleɪz), *sb.*[2] [Appears first in 17th c.; no corresponding form occurs in OE. or ME. But

clearly identical with ON. *blesi* 'white star on a horse's forehead,' MDu. *blesse*, Du. *bles*, mod.G. *blässe*, *blesse*, all in same sense, from stem *blas-*, *blaz-* shining, white; cf. OHG. *blass* whitish, MHG. *blas* bald, mod.G. *blasz* pale. It is possible that the ON. word was adopted in north. dial., and thence passed at a later date into general use; but the Du. or LG. form may also have been introduced as a technical term *c* 1600.

(In either case the spelling has to be explained: the regular repr. of ON. *blesi* would have been *blese*, *bleeze*; if this occurred in north dial., it would be identical with the northern form of BLAZE¹, and might, like it, be made *blaze* in the literary language; if adopted from Du. or LG., *blaze* must be a phonetic spelling.)]

1. A white spot on the face of a horse or ox. Also of other animals.

1639 De Grey *Compl. Horsem.* 23 If the blaze be not too broad. **1650** Fuller *Pisgah* iv. vii. 128 A black bull..with a fair square blaze in his forehead. **1685** *Lond. Gaz.* No. 2030/4 A black Mare about 12 or 13 hands high, having a Blaze in her right Eye. **1850** Cumming *S. Afr.* ix. 53/1 The blesbok..is one of the true antelopes... A broad white band, or 'blaze', adorns the entire length of its face. **1858** Hughes *Scour. White Horse* 17 If it wasn't for the blaze in her face, and the white feet. **1884** *Blackw. Mag.* Aug. 170/2 Herefords with great 'blazes' of white on their honest faces. **1952** C. L. B. Hubbard *Pembrokeshire Corgi Handbk.* x. 108 *Blaze*, a white (usually bulbous) marking running up the centre of the head.

2. *tranf.* A white mark made on a tree, generally by chipping off a slice of bark, to indicate a path or boundary in a forest; also a track indicated by a line of such marks. (First in U.S.) Also *attrib.* in ***blaze-mark***.

1662 in *Groton Rec.* (1880) 7 The meetinge house shall be set..by a small whit oak marked at the souwest side with two notches and a blaze. **1737** Wesley *Wks.* (1872) I. 68 We then found another blaze and pursued it. **1813** Mrs. Schimmelpennick tr. *C. Lancelot's Tour* (1816) I. 123 A little blaze here and there, on particular trees, is the only direction. **1820** Southey *Wesley* I. 123. **1822** De Quincey *Confess.* (1862) 243 A blaze of white paint upon a certain elite of the trees marked out by the forester as ripe for the axe. **1830** Galt *Lawrie T.* viii. iii. (1849) 365 We had come to the sixth mile blaize, a boundary mark on a pine. **1885** *Pall Mall G.* 7 May 4/2 Tracked by the land surveyor's blazes on the huge trunks. **1885** Mrs. C. Praed *Head Station* xlvi, Here were new blaze-marks; and here, upon a bottle-tree,—the bark unhealed—that old trace of Durnford's tomahawk.

blaze (bleɪz), *v.*¹ Forms: 3 blas-ie(n, 4-5 blas-en, 5 -yn, 4-6 blase, 5-7 blaise, -ze, 6- blaze; *Sc.* 5-6 blese, 6-7 bleise, 8- bleeze. *Pa. t.* and *pple.* blazed. [f. BLAZE *sb.*¹: no corresp. vb. in OE., or in any other Teut. lang.]

1. a. *intr.* To burn with a bright fervent flame. Often with *away*, *forth*, *out*. ***to blaze up***: to burst or flash into a blaze.

a **1225** *Ancr. R.* 296 Al þet hus blasie uorð er me lest wene. **1393** Langl. *P. Pl.* C. xx. 185 A kyx oþer a candele þat cauht haþ fuyr, and blaseþ. **1393** Gower *Conf.* I. 258 The sparke ..blaseth out on every side. **1513** Douglas *Æneis* xii. iv. 30 The altar blesand of hayt fyre. **1570** Levins *Manip.* 36 Blase, *efflammare*. **1718** Pope *Iliad* ii. 369 We raised Our verdant altars, and the victims blazed. **1790** Burns *Tam O'Shant.*, Fast by an ingle bleezing finely. **1813** Scott *Rokeby* ii. xx, When that spark blazed forth to flame. **1860** Tyndall *Glac.* i. §16. 106 In one of these [clefts] a pine-fire was soon blazing briskly.

b. *transf.* Said of the place lighted by the blaze.

1876 Green *Short Hist.* vii. §6 (1882) 408 The streets of London blazed with bonfires.

2. *trans.* To cause to blaze, to give to the flames. *rare.* ***to blaze up***: to set a-blaze.

c **1485** *Digby Myst.* (1882) iii. 745 They be blasyd both body and hals. *c* **1525** Skelton *Replyc.* 294 Doutlesse ye shall be blased And be brent at a stake. **1865** *Sat. Rev.* 16 Dec. 754 If some new Guy Faux were to succeed in blazing up the Houses of Lords and Commons.

3. *intr.* To burn with the fervour of devotion, excitement, or passion: said of persons and their feelings. ***to blaze up***: to 'fire up' in wrath.

a **1225** *Ancr. R.* 426 Luue is Jesu Cristes fur þet he wule þet blasie in vre heorte. **1393** Langl. *P. Pl.* C. xx. 188 Til þe holy gost by-gynne to glowen and blase. **1593** Shaks. *3 Hen. VI*, v. iv. 71, I need not adde more fuell to your fire, For well I wot, ye blaze to burne them out. **1841** D'Israeli *Amen. Lit.* (1867) 306 His anger too easily blazed forth. **1878** Seeley *Stein.* III. 528 Stein..blazed up, and there was an exchange of hot words.

4. ***to blaze out*** (trans.): to cause to flare away, to exhaust in a blaze of passion or excess (*arch.*); (*intr.*) to go out with a flare, subside from its blaze.

1779 Johnson *Rochester, L.P.* (1816) 179 He..blazed out his youth and his health in lavish voluptuousness. **1824** Dibdin *Libr. Comp.* 718 He blazed out his life. **1884** *L'pool. Daily Post* 27 June 5 The temporary excitement..had blazed out, and numbers were leaving the House.

5. a. *intr.* To shine like flame or fire; to shine brightly, glitter, be resplendent. Also with *forth*.

1393 Langl. *P. Pl.* C. xxi. 243 Tho þis barn was ybore þer blased a sterre. **1398** Trevisa *Barth. De P.R.* xvi. iv. (1495) 553 It is kyndly that shynynge of metall blase the more yf they be shynyd wyth other lyght. **1667** Milton *P.L.* i. 194 Eyes That sparkling blaz'd. **1718** Pope *Iliad* ii. 527 The dreadful aegis..Blazed on her arm. **1831** Carlyle *Sart. Res.* ii. ix, But Half-men, in whom that divine handwriting has never blazed forth. **1835** Lytton *Rienzi* ix. i. 371 Robed in scarlet that literally blazed with gold. **1877** A. B. Edwards *Up Nile* xxi. 608 The sun blazing over head.

b. *trans.* with cognate object.

1667 Milton *P.L.* x. 65 The Father..on the Son Blaz'd forth unclouded Deitie. **1697** Congreve *Mourn. Bride* i. iii, All conspired to blaze promiscuous light.

6. *intr.* To shine or be conspicuous with brilliancy of character, splendour of position or talents, grandeur, renown. Also with *out*.

1387 Trevisa *Higden* Rolls Ser. I. 5 Blaseþ and schineþ clerliche þe riȝt rule of þewes. **1639** Fuller *Holy War* ii. xxx. (1840) 89 The less his fame blazed, the more his devotion burned. **1756** Burke *Subl. & B.* Wks. I. 170 In this description..the terrible and sublime blaze out together. **1859** Helps *Friends in C.* Ser. ii. I. i. 20 To blaze out into a successful marriage. **1865** Carlyle *Fredk. Gt.* I. iii. iv. 158 Cardinal Albert Kur-Mainz..blazes widely abroad, in the busy reign of Karl V.

†**7.** *trans.* ? To dazzle or daze with light; *fig.* to blind. *Obs.*

c **1450** Henryson *Moral Fables* 34 The fauour of thy face, For thy defence is foule and disfigurate, Brought to the light, blased, blunt and blate. **1570** *Piththy Note Papists* (Collier) 15 As thogh Ye would the People blase, And make them think I did not wel: this said he without maze.

8. intr. ***to blaze away***: to fire continuously with guns or artillery; *fig.* to work at anything with enthusiastic vigour (*colloq.*). Cf. *fire away*. Also ***to blaze*** (***out***) ***at***.

1776 *Battle of Brooklyn* (1873) ii. p. i, We bid them stand and blazed away like brave boys. **1826** *Sheridaniana* 331 Sheridan blazed away, right and left. **1843** Dickens in *Life* 141 I went at it again, and..blazed away till 9 last night. **1857** Livingstone vii. 140 We..blazed away at the lions. **1883** 'Mark Twain' *Life on Mississippi* lix. 531 The elements..banged and blazed away in the most blind and frantic manner. **1909** T. E. Lawrence *Lett.* (1938) 76 He had just bought a Mauser, and blazed at everything with it. **1914** *Ibid.* 173 They all grabbed rifles & revolvers, & through the windows blazed out at everyone they saw.

9. *trans.* ***to blaze*** (***off***): to cause (the grease) to flash in the operation of tempering steel; also, of the grease, to flash; to temper (steel) by this process. Hence **'blazing (off)** *vbl. sb.*

1823 *New Monthly Mag.* IX. 121 The cast steel articles.. may be quenched in this composition, in order to harden them; and then be blazed off. **1860** Tomlinson *Useful Arts & Manuf.* Ser. ii. 36 Large saws..are moved backwards and forwards over the fire till the unctuous matter adhering to the surface of the saw begins to ignite or 'blaze-off'. *Ibid.* 37 During this 'blazing off', the saw is removed from the furnace and allowed to cool. **1885** *Spons' Mech. Own Bk.* 66 They are then heated..till the grease inflames. This is called being 'blazed'.

blaze (bleɪz), *v.*² Forms: 4-5 blas-en, 5 blasin, -yn, 6-7 blase, 6- blaze. *Pa. t.* and *pple.* blazed (*pa. pple.* once in 6 blasen; cf. Ger. *geblasen*, Du. *geblazen* blown). [In sense 1 apparently the same word as ON. *blása* to blow (as the wind, with the mouth, bellows, a trumpet), OHG. *blâsan* (MHG. and mod.G. *blâsen*), MDu. and Du. *blâzen*, Goth. *-blêsan* (in *uf-blêsan* to blow up, puff up):—OTeut. **blǣs-an*, f. root **blǣ-* (Aryan **bhlē-*, L. *flā-re*: see BLOW) with suffixal *-s-* (perhaps from the present stem) taken into the root. The verb (**blǣs-an*) was not preserved in OE., where it was represented only by the derivative sb. *blǣs-t*, BLAST 'blowing.' The ME. vb. was prob. a. ON. *blása* (unless direct connexion with LG. or Du. *blâsen*, *blâzen*, can be traced). Its later history is confused with that of BLAZON, evidently through associating the infinitive *blas-en* with the pre-existing sb. *blason*, BLAZON 'shield, heraldic shield.' The proper senses of *blaze* and *blazon*, acted and reacted upon each other in the 16th c.: see senses 3-6, and BLAZON *v.* 4-6. In later uses of sense 2, there may also be often traced an association with BLAZE *v.*¹, as if to 'blaze abroad,' were to 'expose to the full blaze of publicity.']

†**1.** To blow (e.g. with a musical instrument); to puff. Also with *out*. *Obs.*

c **1384** Chaucer *H. Fame* (1866) With his blake clarioun He gan to blasen [*v.r.* -yn, -in] out a soun As lowde as beloweth wynde in helle. **1481** Caxton *Reynard* (Arb.) 78 They [beer and wulf] conne wel huylen and blasen, stele and robbe. **1535** [cf. BLAZING *ppl. a.*²]

2. *trans.* To proclaim (as with a trumpet), to publish, divulge, make known.

c **1450** [see BLAZER².] **1541** Barnes *Wks.* (1573) 198 Then were you first of all, assoyled of your allegyance, and that absolucion was blasen and blowen, preached, and taught, throughout all the world. **1548** Udall, etc. *Erasm. Par.* Pref. 11 In blasyng the Antichristian decrees. **1580** Sidney *Arcadia* ii. 227 What ayles this ardour To blase my onely secrets? **1588** Greene *Pandosto* (1843) 14 This proclamation being once blased through the country. **1613** Heywood *Silv. Age* iii. i. Wks. 1874 III. 139 Through all our Ebbes and Tides my Trump hath blaz'd her. **1753** Foote *Eng. in Paris* ii. (1763) 26 The Secret might soon be blaz'd. **1823** Scott *Peveril* (1865) 37 What I have to tell you is widely blazed. **1859** Tennyson *Vivien* 593.

b. with *abroad* (*forth*, *about*). The prevalent use.

1552 Huloet, Blase abrode, *publico*. **1564** *Brief Exam.* **iij, Rather to be lamented..then to be blased abrode in wordes. **1601** Shaks. *Jul. C.* ii. ii. 31 The Heauens themselues blaze forth the death of Princes. **1611** Bible *Mark* i. 45 He went out, and beganne to publish it much, and to blase abroad the matter. **1622** Wither in Farr's *S.P.* (1848) 220 I know..his worth To be the same which I have blazed forth. **1791** Boswell *Johnson* (1816) II. 346 *note*, Fearing..that I should blaze it abroad in his lifetime. **1824** W. Irving *T. Trav.* I. 335 The affair was blazed about next morning.

†**c.** with *clause*: To spread the report *that*. *Obs.*

1553-87 Foxe *A. & M.* (1684) II. 47/1 They falsely accuse him, which blaze, that he began with plausible matter. **1578** T. N. tr. *Conq. W. India* 90 Fame flew abroade, blazing that Mutezuma feared the Christians.

†**d.** To decry, defame, hold up to infamy. *Obs.*

1580 North *Plutarch* (1676) 6 Minos was alwayes blazed and disgraced throughout all the Theaters of Athens.

†**3.** To describe heraldically, to BLAZON. *Obs.*

c **1440** *Promp. Parv.* 38 Blasyn or dyscry armys, *describo*. **1530** Palsgr. 456 He can blase armes as well as any herault. **1572** Bossewell *Armorie* ii. 24 His Armes are thus to be blazed..He beareth a Shielde Argente, etc. **1605** Verstegan *Dec. Intell.* v. (1628) 120 Our mixed manner of blasing armes in broken French and English put together. *a* **1628** F. Greville *Sidney* (1652) 44 What Herald [can] blaze their Arms without a blemish?

†**b.** *absol.* *Obs.*

1586 Ferne *Blaz. Gentrie* 163 Able to blaze by all those waies..whereby Armes were euer blazoned.

†**c.** (*fig.*). ***to blaze one's arms***, was used in sense 2 = to publish, celebrate, describe. *Obs.*

1573 G. Harvey *Letter-bk.* (1884) 17 A veri frend..hath dun mi arrand and blasd mi arms abrode. **1579** Tomson *Calvin's Serm. Tim.* 735/2 Let their armes bee blased, that euery man may detest them.

4. With mixture of senses 2 and 3.

†**a.** To describe, set forth with éclat, celebrate.

[**1553** Douglas *Æneis* xiii. Prol. 165 And forthirmore, to blasin [*MSS. read* blason] this new day, Quhay micht discryue the birdis blisful bay?] **1566** T. Stapleton *Ret. Untr. Jewell* iii. 131 Haue you..blased out the Apostle of that people, with these Charitable Titles: Hypocrite, etc.? **1574** tr. *Marlorat's Apocalips* 15 This title agreeth to god only, according as he blazeth himselfe by it saying: I am God almighty. *a* **1635** Corbet *Poems* (1807) 65 He..that would write And blaze thee thoroughly, may at once say all, Here lies the anchor our admiral.

†**b.** To describe pictorially, depict, portray. *Obs.*

1579 E. K. in *Spenser's Sheph. Cal.* Ep. Ded. §1 They use to blaze and portraict..the..lineaments. **1642** R. Carpenter *Exper.* vi. vii. 169 In blazing the Transfiguration of Christ, they put it off without any blazing figure, without a transfiguration of words.

†**5.** To paint or adorn with armorial bearings or heraldic devices: to BLAZON. *Obs.*

1620 *Unton Inv.* 18 One hanginge table blazed wth armes.

†**6.** To emblazon. *poet. rare.* (in quot. *fig.*)

1813 Scott *Rokeby* iv. xvi, High was Redmond's youthful name Blazed in the roll of martial fame.

blaze, *v.*³ [f. BLAZE *sb.*²] *trans.* To mark (trees) with white by chipping off a piece of bark. Also to indicate (a spot or path) by such marks. Also *transf.* and *fig.*, esp. in phr. ***to blaze the way*** (***trail***, etc.).

1750 T. Walker *Jrnl. Exploration* 30 Apr. (1888) 50, I Blazed a way from our House to the River. *Ibid.* 23 May 56, I Blazed several Trees in the fork. **1812** J. Henry *Camp. agst. Quebec* 24 A path tolerably distinct, which we made more so by blazing the trees. *Ibid.* Blazing every carrying-place. **1841** in Thornton *Amer. Gloss.* (1912) i. 70, I desire to new blaze landmarks which..have divided Federal and Democratic parties. **1850** *Fraser's Mag.* XLI. 22 The settlers..blazed roads through the woods, by chipping the bark off the trees. **1850** *Southern Quarterly Rev.* XVIII. 418 Champollion..having done little more than 'blaze out' the road to be travelled by others. **1859** Holland *Gold F.* iii. 42 Plunge into the eternal forest that sleeps in front, and blaze the trees. **1878** H. M. Stanley *Dark Cont.* II. xiii. 366 We 'blazed' very many of the largest with our hatchets. **1902** L. Mead *World-Coinage* vi, Professor Bréal has blazed the way for future explorers in the wilderness of philology. **1904** *Daily Chron.* 29 Nov. 4/4 So intricate a maze that an old warder of long standing used to 'blaze' his way through the corridors with the help of a piece of chalk. **1937** *Discovery* Sept. p. lxxiii (Advt.), Dufaycolor blazes a new trail!

blazed, *ppl. a.*¹ *rare.* [f. BLAZE *v.*¹] Set in flames; *fig.* inflamed.

1631 R. H. *Arraignm. Whole Creat.* xi. §1. 97 Or Orall and Vocall [Organs], bleared and blazed from the Hell-inflamed tongue.

blazed, *ppl. a.*² [f. BLAZE *v.*²] Published, made famous.

1590 Spenser *Muiopotmos* 266 Her blazed fame. **1671** Milton *Samson* 528 The sons of Anak, famous now and blazed.

blazed (bleɪzd), *ppl. a.*³ [f. BLAZE *sb.*² and *v.*³]

1. Having a blaze or white mark on the face.

1685 *Lond. Gaz.* No. 2030/4 A Brown bay Gelding.. blaz'd down his Face. **1727** Bradley *Fam. Dict.* s.v. *Horse*, He is prized far That is Cole-black, and blazed with a Star. **1787** Washington *Diaries* (1925) III. 155 A sorrel mare, blazed face, off hind foot white. **1869** *Overland Monthly* III. 126, I had seen..an old gray mare, considerably flea-bitten, with a blazed face and a docked tail.

2. *U.S.* Of trees: Marked with white by cutting off a patch of the bark. Of a path or boundary line: Indicated by blazed trees.

1737 Wesley *Wks.* (1872) I. 68 A line of blazed trees, (that is, marked by cutting off part of the bark). **1822** J. Flint *Lett. Amer.* 154 To follow the blazed lines marked out by the

surveyor. **1883** Bret Harte *Carquinez* viii. 176 At right angles with the 'blazed' tree.

ˈblazeless, *a.* Without blaze or flame.
1820 *Blackw. Mag.* VII. 176 A bright but blazeless fire.

†**ˈblazen,** *v. Obs.* A by-form of BLAZE *v.*[1]
1716 M. Davies *Athen. Brit.* II. 74 Had not the Representation..prov'd abortive, and expir'd like a blazening Star.

blazer[1] (ˈbleɪzə(r)). [f. BLAZE *v.*[1] + -ER[1].]
1. a. Anything which blazes or shines; as a comet (*obs.*), or (*familiarly*) a very bright day.
a **1635** Corbet *Poems* (1807) Thus we leave the blazers coming over. **1875** Miss Braddon *Hostages Fort.* I. iii. 88 The day..a blazer, cloudless blue.
b. A light jacket of bright colour worn at cricket or other sports. Now usu. an unlined jacket of lightweight material (often flannel), freq. with coloured stripes, decorated edges, or a badge on the breast-pocket, worn esp. with sports clothes or as part of a school uniform.
1880 *Times* 19 June, Men in spotless flannel, and club 'blazers.' **1885** *Durham Univ. Jrnl.* 21 Feb. 91 The latest novelty..for the river is flannels, a blazer, and spats. **1889** *Daily News* 22 Aug. 6/6 In your article of to-day..you speak of 'a striped red and black blazer', 'the blazer', also of 'the pale toned' ones... A blazer is the red flannel boating jacket worn by the Lady Margaret, St. John's College, Cambridge, Boat Club. When I was at Cambridge it meant that and nothing else. It seems from your article that a blazer now means a coloured flannel jacket, whether for cricket, tennis, boating, or seaside wear. **1892** Kipling *Lett. Travel* (1920) 93 More does he wonder still at the city clerk in a blazer. **1963** *Times* 23 Jan. 12/4 A simple short blazer-type jacket. **1964** *Which?* Mar. 94/2 More navy blue blazers are sold than any other colour. *Ibid.* 96/1 Blazer cloth was not originally intended for hard daily wear, but for more occasional use—sitting in a cricket pavilion, for instance.
2. Someone or something that attracts attention. Chiefly *U.S.*
1845 Mrs. Kirkland *Western Clearings* (1846) 127 T'other gal is likely enough, but the mother's a blazer! **1892** 'H. Lawson' in *Penguin Bk. Austral. Ballads* (1964) 154 You must prove that you're a blazer—you must prove that you have grit. **1903** A. Adams *Log Cowboy* vi. 81 Are you sure you wasn't running a blazer yourself? **1906** *Springfield Weekly Republ.* 19 Apr. 1 The Kaiser's telegram..recalls some of his blazers in the past.
3. A small cooking apparatus. *N. Amer.*
1889 in *Cent. Dict.* **1895** *Harper's Mag.* May 885/1 Delicacies which Tom prided himself on being able to prepare on a blazer. **1967** *Canadian Antiques Collector* Apr. 17/1 Cooking can be done in the blazer pan over a direct flame.
4. A sheet of metal placed against the bars of a grate to create a draught and cause the fire to blaze; a blower. *north.*
1892 Heslop *Northumb. Words, Bleezer,* a hood to blow up a fire. 'Put the bleezer up, and let's hev a lowe.' *a* **1922** T. Burt *Autobiogr.* (1924) 177 Women and children.. armed with 'blazers' and tin-cans..used as cymbals.

ˈblazer[2]. Also 4 blasour, 5 -eyr, 5-6 -er. [f. BLAZE *v.*[2] + -ER[1].]
1. One who proclaims or publishes; a 'trumpeter.'
c **1450** *Test. Love* I. (1560) 280 b/1 Tho loveden blasours, tho curreiden glosours, the welcomeden flatterers. **1552** Huloet, Blaser of bruite or fame. **1617** Hieron *Wks.* (1620) II. 354 A blazer of that worth & excellencie which is in God. *a* **1618** Raleigh *Maxims St.* in *Rem.* (1661) 74 To have their blazers abroad to set out their virtues.
†**2.** A blazoner. *Obs.*
1486 *Bk. St. Albans* B iv b, The blaseyr shall..blase the colowre sentri. **1587** Golding *De Mornay* iii. (1617) 37 The first blazer of their Pedegrees.

ˈblazered, *a.* [f. BLAZER[1] 1 b + -ED[2].] Wearing a blazer.
1931 *Times Lit. Suppl.* 14 May 386/4 When his blazered team play the village. **1959** *Times* 12 June 13/7 The blazered cheer-leader swings a vast dial on the wall chart.

ˈblazery. [f. BLAZE *sb.*[1] or *v.*[1] + -ERY; cf. *finery.*] Splendour, adornment; jewellery.
1883 *Harper's Mag.* Mar. 520/2 Buy..the biggest diamond ring..and wear such blazery wherever you go.

blazing (ˈbleɪzɪŋ), *vbl. sb.*[1] Also 5 blasynge. [f. BLAZE *v.*[1] + -ING[1].]
a. A flaming, burning. **b.** Shining, splendour.
c **1440** *Promp. Parv.* 38 Blasynge or flamynge of fyre, *flammacio.* **1563** *Homilies* II. *Excess. Appar.* (1859) 316 The more thou garnish thy selfe with these outward blazings. **1639** Fuller *Holy War* I. ii. (1840) 2 A fading comet, whose blazing portended the ruin of that nation. **1859** G. Wilson *E. Forbes* iv. 99 No needless blazings of phosphorus.

ˈblazing, *vbl. sb.*[2] [f. BLAZE *v.*[2] + -ING[1].]
1. a. Proclaiming or 'trumpeting.' **b.** Boasting.
1563 *Homilies* II. *Idolatry* (1859) 237 Blasphemous bold blasing of manifest Idolatry. **1589** Nashe *Anat. Absurd.* 7 The blazing of Womens slender praises. **1628** Feltham *Resolves* I. lxxx. (1647) 248 The blazings of the proud will goe out in a stench and smoke.
†**2.** = BLAZONING. *Obs.*
c **1440** *Promp. Parv.* 38 Blasynge of armys, *descripcio.* **1486** *Bk. St. Albans, Her.* A j, Folowyth the Blasyng of all maner armys. **1530** Palsgr. 165 *Blason,* a blasyng or discryvyng of ons armes. **1583** Golding *Calvin on Deut.* x. 56 Some painted picture or blasing of armes.

ˈblazing, *vbl. sb.*[3] [f. BLAZE *v.*[3]] The marking of trees by chipping off a patch of the bark.
1818 Cobbett *Resid. U.S.* (1822) 273 We soon lost all appearance of the track..and of the '*blazing*' of the trees.

ˈblazing, *ppl. a.*[1] In northern ME. blesand; for other forms see the vb. [f. BLAZE *v.*[1] + -ING[2].]
1. Flaming with force.
c **1400** *Rom. Rose* 3706 Of brennynge fyre a blasyng bronde. **1513** Douglas *Æneis* XIII. ix. 103 The blesand torchys schayn. **1667** Milton *P.L.* I. 728 Blazing Cressets fed With Naphtha and Asphaltus. **1855** Macaulay *Hist. Eng.* III. 340 The sight of the blazing dwellings.
fig. **1850** Mrs. Stowe *Uncle Tom* xxxiii. 299 She..fixed a glance blazing with rage and scorn on the driver.
2. a. Shining vehemently; bright-coloured, glaring.
1387 Trevisa *Higden* Rolls Ser. VI. 297 Gay blasynge cloþes. **1425** *Ord. Whittington's Alms-ho.* in Entick *London* IV. 354 That the overcloathing..be dark and brown of colour, and not staring ne blaising. **1848** Thackeray *Van. Fair* i, Horses in blazing harness. **1855** Dickens *Dorrit* i, A blazing sun upon a fierce August day.
b. *fig.*
1576 Lambarde *Peramb. Kent* (1826) 134 The fame thereof is..above all other most blasing and glorious. **1596** Spenser *F.Q.* I. iv. 8 Her bright blazing beautie.
3. *Venery.* Of scent: Very strong; as opposed to a *cold scent, i.e.* a weak one.
1875 'Stonehenge' *Brit. Sports* I. II. i. §2. 142 They..can hunt a cold scent, and yet with a blazing one they run breast high.
4. Used as a substitute for a profane epithet.
1888 Kipling *Plain Tales fr. Hills* (1890) 19 Once I said, 'What's the blazing hurry, Major?' **1916** 'Boyd Cable' *Action Front* 66 You have the blazing cheek to keep me lying here in the filthy muck.

ˈblazing, *ppl. a.*[2] [f. BLAZE *v.*[2] + -ING[2].]
†**1.** Blowing. *Obs.*
1535 Coverdale *Wisdom* xvii. 18 Whether it were a blasynge wynde, or a swete song of yᵉ byrdes.
†**b.** Boastful (? 'blowing their own trumpet').
1533 Tindale *Answ. to More's Dial.* Wks. III. 107 The blasing hypocrites. **1549** Coverdale *Erasm. Par. 2 Cor.* xii. 12 Let them never so muche with their blasyng wordes boaste themselves.

blazingly (ˈbleɪzɪŋlɪ), *adv.* [f. BLAZING *ppl. a*[1]. + -LY[2].] In a blazing manner.
1830 *Fraser's Mag.* II. 434 The interior..was blazingly illuminated. **1874** Masson *Three Devils* 313 The lesson.. may be enforced, less blazingly perhaps, but still clearly.

blazing star.
†**1.** A comet. *Obs.*
1502 Arnolde *Chron.* (1811) 36 This yere..a blasing Sterre. **1587** Fleming *Cont. Holinshed* III. 344/1 In the moneth of Maie..a blasing starre appeared, descending in the north-west, the beard whereof streamed into the south-east. **1601** Shaks. *All's Well* I. iii. 91 And wee might haue a good woman borne but ore euerie blazing starre, or at an earthquake, 'twould mend the Lotterie well. **1640-1** Ld. J. Digby *Sp. in Ho. Com.* 9 Feb. 7 I looked upon it..with terrour, as upon a Commet, a blasing starre. **1711** Addison *Spect.* No. 127 ¶5 The same Prognostication as the Tail of a Blazing Star. **1762** Falconer *Shipwr.* III. 563 Advances to the sun some blazing star.
2. *fig.* The brilliant centre of admiration; 'cynosure,' 'star.' *arch.*
1460 *Pol. Rel. & L. Poems* (1866) 54 Heyle blasyng starre withowte peere! I beseche the as thou art moder of mercy. **1559** *Mirr. Mag., Mowbray's Ban.* xiii, Proud I that would alone be blasyng sterre. **1611** Barksted *Hiren* (1876) 106 Her beauty like a blazing starre admired. **1634** S. R. *Noble Soldier* III. i. in Bullen *O. Pl.* (1882) I. 291 But that I must be held Spaines blazing Starre. **1818** Scott *Hrt. Midl.* xlviii, She has been the ruling belle—the blazing star—the universal toast of the winter.
†**3.** = BLAZE *sb.*[2] 1.
1705 *Lond. Gaz.* No. 4183/4 A bay Gelding..3 white Feet, a Blazing Star.
4. The popular name of three different North American plants: *Aletris farinosa, Chamælirium luteum,* and *Liatris squarrosa.* Also used of other plants with star-shaped flowers.
1789 *Trans. Amer. Philos. Soc.* III. p. xx, The root of *Aletris farinosa*..is called star-root, blazing star, devil's bit. **1822** A. Eaton *Man. Bot.* (ed. 3) 303 Blazing star; false unicorn root. **1836** A. H. Lincoln *Fam. Lect. Bot.* (ed. 5) App. 110 *Liatris scariosa,* blue blazing star. **1947** *Desert Mag.* May 28/3 Visitors will find..blazing star..in the Valley of Fire and other rocky areas.

blazon (ˈbleɪz(ə)n), *sb.* Forms: 4 blasoun, blasen, 4-7 blason, 5 *Sc.* blasowne, 6- blazon. [a. F. *blason* (found in other Romanic langs., as Sp. *blason,* Pg. *brasão,* It. *blasone,* Pr. *blezo, blizo*). By Diez and Littré referred to a Teut. word identical either with Eng. BLAZE *sb.*[1] flame, with BLAZE *sb.*[2] a conspicuous mark, or with Ger. *blasen* to blow (BLAZE *v.*[2]), OHG. *blâsô* a trumpeter. But the original meaning of OF. *blason* was not, as these conjectures assume, 'glory' or 'proclamation,' or even 'armorial shield,' but simply 'shield' in the literal sense. This is proved by the earliest quotations in Fr. and Eng., and by the derived OF. sense of 'shoulder-blade.']
I. Proper senses.
†**1.** A shield used in war. *Obs.*
c **1340** *Gaw. & Gr. Knt.* 828 His bronde & his blasoun boþe þay token. ? *a* **1400** *Morte Arth.* 1860 Blasons blode and blankes they hewene. *c* **1425** Wyntoun *Cron.* VIII. xxxiii. 21 Willame of Spens percit a Blasowne. [see also 2.]
2. *Her.* A shield in heraldry; armorial bearings, coat of arms; a banner bearing the arms. (The first 3 quotations connect this with sense 1.)
c **1325** *Coer de L.* 5727 In his blasoun, verrayment, Was i-paynted a serpent. *c* **1350** *Will. Palerne* 3572 Bereth in his blasoun · of a brit hewe a wel huge werwolf · wonderli depeinted. **1377** Langl. *P. Pl.* B. XVI. 179 A ful bolde bacheler · I knewe hym by his blasen.
1575 Turberv. *Venery* iii. 7 The authour of that booke which amongst other things gaue this blason to the hounds of that Lords kennel. **1605** Camden *Rem.* (1637) 228 The first Christians used no other blazon in their shields then the name of Christ and a crosse. **1720** Welton *Suff. Son of God* I. vii. 138 To stamp their Escutcheon with a Blazon of the most high Descent to future ages. **1814** Scott *Ld. of Isles* III. xx, With St. George's blazon red. **1832** Macaulay *Armada* 20 Slow upon the labouring wind the royal blazon swells.
fig. **1601** Shaks. *Twel. N.* I. v. 312 Thy tongue, thy face, thy limbes, actions, and spirit, Do giue thee fiue-fold blazon.
b. *Sc. Law.* The badge of office worn by a king's messenger on his arm. (Jamieson.)
1773 Erskine *Inst. Law Scot.* IV. iv. §33 (Jam.) The libel will be cast, if it do not expressly mention that the messenger ..displayed his blazon.
3. Description or representation, according to the rules of Heraldry, of armorial bearings.
1610 Guillim *Heraldry* I. ii. (1660) 13 Blazon is taken.. strictly for an explication of Armes in apt and significant terms. **1667** E. Chamberlayne *St. Gt. Brit.* I. II. ii. (1743) 53 The blazon of the Arms of Great Britain..is as follows. **1722** A. Nisbet (*title*) A System of Heraldry..With the True Art of Blazon, according to the most approved Heralds in Europe. **1864** Boutell *Heraldry Hist. & Pop.* xix. 300 The earliest blazon of a Royal Banner..occurs in the Roll of Caerlaverock.
II. The following show more or less influence of BLAZE *v.*[2]
4. *transf.* A description or record of any kind; *esp.* a record of virtues or excellencies.
1577 Hellowes *Gueuara's Fam. Ep.* 60 It doth not seeme to me a man may haue better blason in his house, than to be, & also descended of, a bloud vnspotted. *c* **1600** Shaks. *Sonn.* cvi, In the blazon of sweet beauties best. **1631** B. Jonson *New Inn* I. iii, Fair mien, discourses, civil exercise, And all the blazon of a gentleman. **1748** Thomson *Cast. Indol.* II. lxiii, Beyond the blazon of my mortal pen. **1854** Patmore *Angel in Ho.* II. II. iv, Their many gentle virtues miss Proud virtue's blazon.
5. 'Show, divulgation, publication' (Johnson); = BLAZING *vbl. sb.*[2] 1.
1602 Shaks. *Ham.* I. v. 21 But this eternall blason must not be To eares of flesh and bloud. *a* **1734** North *Examen* I. ii. ¶141 If the facts are not true..the adverse Party soon make a Blazon of them abroad.
¶ ? Cf. prec. quot. from *Hamlet,* and BLAZE *sb.*[1] 4.
1857 Sears *Athan.* vi. 56 The prophet could not bear the sudden blazon, and fell as one dead beneath the too ardent effulgence.

blazon (ˈbleɪzən), *v.* [f. prec. sb., or directly from F. *blasonner* (similarly f. F. *blason*) in use in 15th c. As shewn under BLAZE *v.*[2], that vb. was in earlier use in this sense; and in the 16th c. the two words acted and reacted on each other: cf. 4-6 below, and senses 3-6 of BLAZE *v.*[2] Indeed so far as the evidence goes, the non-heraldic senses are the earlier, though the heraldic use of *blasyn* (BLAZE *v.*[2] sense 3) in the *Promp. Parv.* makes it likely that *blazon* in sense 1 may go back to *c* 1500.]
I. Heraldic, and extensions.
1. *trans.* To describe in proper heraldic language. Also *absol.*
1586 Ferne *Blaz. Gentrie* 202 If this following be blazoned by you. **1610** Guillim *Heraldry* I. i. 5 To blazon is to expresse what the shapes, kinds, and colour of things born in Armes are together with their apt significations. **1775** T. Warton *Hist. Eng. Poetry* I. 455 They pretend to blazon the arms painted in the glass windows. **1815** *Scribbleomania* 303 In the same book we find the exact arms properly blazoned of Semiramis, Queen of Babylon.
2. To depict or paint (armorial bearings) according to the rules of heraldry.
1570 *Sempill Ballates* (1872) 65 With Guldis and Rukis, blasnit equallie Is the auld armes of the Hammiltounis. **1593** *Rites & Mon. Ch. Durh.* (1842), Having his armes verie excellentlie blasoned in fine coulored glasse. **1864** Skeat tr. *Uhland's Poems* 381 In colours bright and fair, Each warrior's name and scutcheon is duly blazoned there. **1875** Furnivall in *Thynne's Animadv.* 98 The arms of the Chancellor are blazond at the back of the title.
b. *transf.* and *fig.* To paint or depict in colours; to illuminate, set off or set out with fine colouring.
1699 Garth *Dispens.* I. 15 She blazons in dread Smiles her hideous form. **1772** Fletcher *Logica Genev.* 41 The Christian virtues which blazon his character. **1812** Byron *Ch. Har.* I. iii, Nor all that heralds rake from coffined clay Can blazon evil deeds, or consecrate a crime. **1851** Ruskin *Mod. Paint.* II. III. I. v. §5 Their effect is oftentimes deeper when their lines are dim, than when they are blazoned with crimson and pale gold. **1871** R. Ellis *Catullus* lxiv. 51 A broidery..whose curious art did blazon valour of heroes.
3. To inscribe (anything) *with* arms, paintings, names of distinction, set forth in colours, or in

some ornamental way; to adorn as with blazonry.

1813 SCOTT *Trierm.* III. xix, A hall, whose walls so wide Were blazon'd all with feats of pride. **1827** —— *Surg. Dau.* i. 24 The door itself was blazoned with the name of Gideon Grey, M.A. Surgeon, &c. &c. **1862** MRS. BROWNING *Forced Recruit* viii, And blazon the brass with their names. **1866** MOTLEY *Dutch Rep.* II. iii. 166 The blood-red flag of the 'Sacred office'.. blazoned upon either side with the portraits of Alexander and of Ferdinand.

b. *fig.* To adorn or give lustre to (as great names fittingly illuminated adorn a genealogical roll or record).

1815 *Scribbleomania* 130 *note*, One more individual shall blazon my page. *Ibid.* 197 One of the greatest men that ever blazoned the annals of painting.

II. Related also to BLAZE *v.*²

4. To describe fitly, set forth honourably in words; = BLAZE *v.*² 4.

1513 DOUGLAS *Æneis* I. Prol. 329 By him perfitlie blasonis he All wirschep, manheid and nobilite. **1592** SHAKS. *Rom. & Jul.* II. vi. 26 If the measure of thy ioy Be heapt like mine, and that thy skill be more To blason it. **1824** CAMPBELL *Theodric* 90 Glowing pages, blazoning forth The fancied image of his leader's worth. **1863** MRS. C. CLARKE *Shaks. Char.* xv. 384 No herald more eloquently blazons the kingly attributes and virtues.

5. To publish vauntingly or boastfully, boast of. (Cf. BLAZING *vbl. sb.*², *ppl. a.*²)

1534 LD. BERNERS *Gold. Bk. M. Aurel.* (1546) Q iij, I wold neuer blasen loue with my tongue. *Ibid.* I i vij, And there we blason and boste. **1549** *Compl. Scot.* 14 Ther is diuerse men that can blason the veyris in the tauerne, or at the fyir syde, amang the vulgar ignorant pepil. **1807** W. IRVING *Salmag.* (1824) 124 My friend Launcelot is not a man to blazon any thing. **1812** SOUTHEY *Essays* (1832) I. 133.

6. To proclaim, make public, 'trumpet'; = BLAZE *v.*² 2. Also with *forth, out.* Often in a bad sense.

1577 HANMER *Anc. Eccl. Hist.* (1619) 215 To be silent, and not to blason at all so hainous an offence. **1591** SPENSER *Teares Muses* 102 To blazon out their blames. **1681** BAXTER *Apol. Nonconf. Min.* 18 To blazon and aggravate our sufferings. **1731** FIELDING *Mod. Husb.* IV. i, A common trick .. to blazon out the reputation of women whose virtue you have destroyed. **1845** LD. CAMPBELL *Chancellors* (1857) II. xxxiv. 106 That the Queen's shame .. might not be blazoned on the journals. **1863** KINGLAKE *Crimea* II. ix. 94 To have it blazoned out to the world.

b. with *compl.*

a **1619** FOTHERBY *Atheom.* I. xiii. §3 (1622) 138 He, whom you blazoned to be immortall.

blazoned ('bleɪzənd), *ppl. a.* [f. prec. + -ED¹.]

1. Painted with a heraldic device.

1830 PRAED *Poems* (1865) I. 176 Far from me is the gazing throng, The blazoned shield, and the nodding plume.

2. *transf.* and *fig.* Conspicuously or brilliantly displayed; proclaimed, celebrated, 'trumpeted.'

1762 FALCONER *Shipwr.* I. 132 Blazon'd glories spread from zone to zone. **1855** TENNYSON *Ode Wellington* 56 Bright let it be with his blazon'd deeds. **1870** DISRAELI *Lothair* xxviii. 126 There would be a blazoned paragraph in the journals.

blazoner ('bleɪzənə(r)), [f. as prec. + -ER¹.]

1. One who blazons arms; a herald.

1586 FERNE *Blaz. Gentrie* Ded., Our new conceited Blazonners, which haue borrowed onely their lights at the lamps of two late English Armorists. **1610** GUILLIM *Heraldry* II. vi. 62. **1611** COTGR., *Vair* .. the grayish colour of some eyes; also, that which our Blasonners call Verry. **1728** S. KENT *Banner Displ.* II. 764 Some Blazoners hold .. that then such Bearing is more aptly termed *Parted per Cross.* **1815** *Encycl. Brit.* (ed. 5) X. 399/1 There is a sort which blazoners call assumptive arms.

2. *transf.* One who records or sets forth with commendation: one who proclaims or 'trumpets.'

1603 FLORIO *Montaigne* I. xxv. (1632) 86 If I were a great blazoner of mine owne actions. **1796** BURKE *Let. Noble Ld.* Wks. VIII. 37 These historians, recorders, and blazoners of virtues and arms.

blazoning ('bleɪzənɪŋ), *vbl. sb.* [f. as prec. + -ING¹.]

1. The art of describing heraldic devices.

1610 GUILLIM *Heraldry* I. ii. 6 In Blazoning you must vse an aduised deliberation before you enter therunto. *a* **1586** CAMPION *Hist. Irel.* (1633) x. 32 His skill in blasoning of armes.

2. The painting of heraldic devices; *concr.* a heraldic device.

a **1649** DRUMM. OF HAWTH. *Consid. to Parl.* Wks. (1711) 185 Without the bar in the blazoning of his arms. **1828** TYTLER *Hist. Scot.* (1864) I. 321 On the shield of Prince Henry .. there is no appearance of any heraldic blazoning. **1852** MISS YONGE *Cameos* (1877) II. xxxi. 327 Subtleties, representing Catherine's patron Saint, blazonings, or her motto and Henry's.

b. = 'Illuminating.'

1843 LYTTON *Last. Bar.* I. v. 68 The blazoning of missals.

3. The action of proclaiming or publishing.

1533 BELLENDEN *Livy* II. 202 The blasoning and predicacioun of his luffing. **1642** R. CARPENTER *Exper.* v. vii. 243 Be not so large in the blazoning of your due Obedience.

'blazoning, *ppl. a.* [f. as prec. + -ING².] That paints or describes heraldic devices.

1864 BURTON *Scot. Abr.* II. 814 Man is a blazoning animal.

†**'blazonize,** *v. Obs.* [see -IZE.] To celebrate.

1614 *Sco. Venus* (1876) 22 Whose loue may .. blazonize thy wanton sports.

'blazonment. [f. as prec. + -MENT.]

1. Blazoning, setting forth in bright colours.

1883 *Gd. Words* 238 The .. chapel, with its lovely reredos and its blazonment of colour.

2. The action of proclaiming or publishing.

1876 GEO. ELIOT *Dan. Der.* v. xxxvi. 332 A blazonment of herself as the infelicitous wife who had produced nothing but daughters.

blazonry ('bleɪzənrɪ). [f. as prec. + -RY.]

1. The description or depicting of heraldic devices.

1622 PEACHAM *Compl. Gentl.* xv. (1634) 158, I purpose not heere to enter into a large field and absolute discourse of Blazonry. **1829** SCOTT *Demonol.* iii. 98 Those who practise the art of blazonry.

2. A heraldic device, or collection of heraldic devices; armorial bearings.

a **1649** DRUMM. OF HAWTH. *Disc. Impresas* Wks. (1711) 228 The old impresa or arms, blazonry of the house and family. **1805** SOUTHEY *Madoc in W.* x, Madoc approach'd, and saw the blazonry. **1845** CARLYLE *Cromwell's Lett. & Sp.* (1873) I. 19 The Cromwell blazonry .. has given place to Montague blazonry.

b. *fig.*

1850 BLACKIE *Æschylus* II. 273 Broidered vestments torn in many a shred, Grief's blazonry. **1877** FARRAR *My Youth* xxxiv. 342 To make you .. read on your souls the heraldic blazonry of their high origin from God.

3. *fig.* Display by brilliant colouring, setting forth with artistic skill.

1814 SOUTHEY *Roderick* III. 14 That vision floated still Before his sight with all her blazonry. **1816** J. SCOTT *Vis. Paris* (ed. 5) 173 The blazonry, in stone or canvass, of the exploits that have wasted their blood and treasure. **1878** MRS. STOWE *Poganuc P.* iii. 19 No pageants, no sights, no shows, except the eternal blazonry of nature.

†**'blazure.** *Obs.* = BLAZON *sb.* 3, BLAZONRY.

1523 LD. BERNERS *Froiss.* I. cclxxxi. 421 The blasure of his armes was goules, two fesses sable, a border sable.

blazy ('bleɪzɪ), *a.* [f. BLAZE *sb.*¹ + -Y.] Full of blaze, blazing.

1838 P. PARLEY *Tales ab. Christm.* xxxii. 293 A great blazy fire. **1850** CLOUGH *Remains* (1869) I. 167 In the grimy or the blazy period, in the imprisonment or deliverance of the gases.

ble, obs. f. BLEA *sb.*; var. BLEE, *Obs.*, colour, etc.

-ble, a. OF. *-ble*:—L. *-bilem*, nom. *-bili-s*, suffix forming verbal adjs., with the sense 'given to, tending to, like to, fit to, able to'; as in *sta-bili-* 'like, fit to stand.' After consonant stems, *-ibili-*, as *vend-i-bili-, vinc-i-bili-*; after stems ending in *a, e, i, o, u, -ābili-, -ēbili-, -ībili-, -ōbili-, -ūbili-*, as *honōrā-bili-, delē-bili-, sepelī-bili-, nō-bili-, volū-bili-*. Some of these L. words lived on into OFr., e.g. *noble, amable, fleble, meuble*; later, these became models for the extensive adoption of others from the Latin of literature. Many of both sorts were from 12th to 15th c. adopted in Eng. from Fr., and here served as models for the direct adoption or formation of others from Latin, a process which has gone on to the present day. By far the most numerous of the *-ble* words are those in *-able*. In L., *-ābili-* adjs. arose only from verbs in *-āre*; but, in Fr., all pres. pples. in *-ant* may give rise to an adj. in *-able*, and as *-ant* is now the universal form of pres. pple., *-able* is the universal form of the adj. suffix as a living element; *-ible* being only a fossil survival in words from L. like *horrible, possible, visible*, not directly attached to a living Fr. verb. When the verb lives in Fr., a modern adj. in *-able* has always taken the place of the earlier *-ible* form, as in *vendable, croyable, préférable*, for L. *vendibilis, credibilis, *præferibilis*. But in Eng. there is a prevalent feeling for retaining *-ible* wherever there was or might be a L. *-ibilis*; while *-able* is used for words of distinctly Fr. or Eng. origin, as *conceivable, movable, speakable*. Hence, where there is a verb in French and English, as well as in Latin, English usage is distracted by conflicting and irreconcileable analogies. Thus in the compounds of *-fer*, L. *fero*, Latin analogy requires *preferible, referible* (Walker, *Rhym. Dict.*), *sufferible*; French example gives *preferable, referable*; Fr. and Eng. analogy *sufferable* (cf. *suffering*); Eng. analogy (cf. *refer-ring*) gives *referrable* (Bailey), *conferrable, deferrable*; there is also a mongrel spelling *referrible*, sanctioned by Dr. Johnson, but defensible on no analogy. So with the variant spellings *admittable, -ible, tractable, contractible, partable, -ible*. These discrepancies no mere etymological grounds can settle; though their number might be lessened by following French precedent, and extending *-able* to all words having a verb (with the same accent) in Eng., thus *admittable, contractable, corruptable, exhaustable, vendable*, etc., leaving *-ible* in *credible, intelligible, legible, possible*, etc. See -ABLE, -IBLE. The omission or retention of a final *e* mute before *-able* is also to a certain extent optional. In words directly from L. it is etymologically absent, as in *excusable, declinable*; in words from Eng. (beside cases where it *must* be orthographically retained after *c, g*, as *peaceable, changeable, chargeable*, the latter also in Fr.), there is a prevalent feeling for retaining the *e* in monosyllables, as *tameable, nameable, saleable*, which otherwise would have their meaning obscured (e.g. *tamable, namable, salable*). This produces ambiguity of form in such words as *blamable* (F. *blâmable*,) *blameable, movable, moveable, lovable, loveable, sizable, sizeable*, etc. As much reason can be given and as much authority cited for one spelling as for the other, and until a reform of Eng. spelling is made, the double form of these words must continue. In words of English formation, a final consonant is usually doubled before *-able*, when doubled in the pres. pple., as *clubbable, biddable, deferrable*. As to the meaning, Palsgrave (1530) says (p. 302):

'Of every adjectyve partyciple .. in *ant* may be formed an adjectyve by chaungynge of *ant* into *able*, as of *muant, muable*; *honorant, honorable*; .. whose signifycacion may serve bothe actyvely and passively, as *muable*, apte or mete or able to chaunge, or .. to be chaunged; *honorable* apte or mete or able to honour or .. to be honoured .. In this thyng the french tonge is moche more parfyte than our tonge is, for where as they may forme of every partyciple in their tonge an adjectyve endyng in *ble*, in our tonge we have none suche, but must nedes use circumlocution by .. apte, mete, or able, and our infinityve mode; save that we have admitted as well adjectyves of the frenche tonge endyng in *able* and *ible*, as *commendable, visible*,' etc.

As here stated, adjs. in *-bili-, -ble*, were originally active (and neuter) as well as passive. Many of the former exist in Eng., e.g. *capable, comfortable, suitable, agreeable, conformable, companionable, durable, equable*; but the majority have become obsolete or remain only with a passive force, as in *credible, audible, flexible*, which is also the only use of *-able* as a living formative, e.g. *bearable, eatable, likeable, preferable, insufferable, saleable*. (For exhaustive treatment of these words see F. Hall *Eng. Adjectives in* -able; London 1877.)

blea (bliː), *sb. rare.* Also 8 ble(e. [Perh. from *blea*, BLAE *a.* in sense of 'livid, pale.'] The young wood of a tree under the bark; the alburnum or white wood.

1730–6 BAILEY (*fol.*) *Ble, Blea, Blee* (in Chirurgery), the inward Bark of a Tree, or that Part of the wood, which was last form'd. **1753** CHAMBERS *Cycl. Suppl.* s.v., While the blea remains yet soft .. it may maintain a feeble vegetation. **1830** J. G. STRUTT *Sylva Brit.* 20 The blea and the inner bark.

†**blea,** *v. Obs.* exc. *dial.* Also 6 **blay,** 7 **bley, blee;** 8–9 *Sc.* **blae.** [Prob. imitative of the sound; perhaps with associations of *bleat, blab, blabber*, etc. Jamieson compares F. *bêler*, L. *balāre*: cf. OSlav. *blejati* to bleat, also Gr. βληχάομαι I bleat, βληχή bleating, with the same initial sound. Variously pronounced in dialects (bleː, blɪə, bliː).]

intr. To bleat as a lamb or kid; to cry piteously as a child. Hence **'blaying, 'bleying** *vbl. sb.*

1568 *Jacob & Esau* IV. vi. in Hazl. *Dodsley* II. 237 Methinketh I hear a young kid blea! **1581** SIDNEY *Astr. & Stella* ix, Tell her in your piteous blaying Her poor slaves unjust decaying. **1601** HOLLAND *Pliny* I. 242 In their sleepe, they seeme to low or blea, and thereupon they be called Sea-calues. **1617** F. MORYSON *Itin.* III. I. i. 10 The bleying of Sheepe. **1623** J. TAYLOR (Water P.) *Merry Wh.* (1885) 15 Cocks did crow, and lambs did bleat and blee.

blea, -berry, obs. form of BLAY, BLAE, -BERRY.

bleach (bliːtʃ), *sb.*¹ Also in 4 bleche. [Sense 1 is perh. the same as OE. *blǽco* paleness, f. *blác, blǽc*, shining, pale. Sense 3 is directly from the vb.: cf. 'a wash.']

†**1.** Whiteness, paleness. *Obs.*

c **1050** *Cott. Cleop. Gloss.* in Wr.-Wülcker *Voc.* 465 *Pallor*, blæco. **1400** *Pol. Rel. & L. Poems* (1866) 255 Brest & hert was bete to bleche.

†**2.** A disease of the skin. Cf. OE. *blǽce* leprosy.

1601 HOLLAND *Pliny* I. 391 A certaine gum that is passing good for the bleach, scabs and scals in little children.

3. An act of bleaching; as 'a thorough bleach in the sun.' A bleaching process; also, a bleached condition.

1887 *Sci. Amer.* 16 Apr. 249/3 What is known as 'the three-quarter bleach' with flax. **1920** *Discovery* Mar. 86/2 A perfect bleach is almost impossible to secure.

4. A bleaching liquor or powder.

1898 *Daily News* 15 Dec. 6/5 A quantity of bleach escaped from a tank at one of the paper mills. **1910** *Daily Chron.* 23

Apr. 7/3 There are several good nail bleaches that are safe to use. **1970** _Which?_ May 149/1 All the scouring powders contained some bleach.

5. _Comb._ (See BLEACH _v._ 1) as _**bleach-croft**_, _**-field**_, _**-green**_, _**-grounds**_, _**-works**_, _**-yard**_. Cf. BLEACHING.

1852 TOMLINSON _Encycl._ I. 133/2 Across the *bleach croft. **1753** _Scots Mag._ Sept. 468/2 Indicted for stealing.. some stockings from a *bleachfield. **1806** _Gaz. Scotl._ 339/2 The excellence of its water for bleaching processes has induced many to establish extensive printfields and bleachfields on its banks. **1957** R. WATSON-WATT _Three Steps Victory_ v. 33 A polychromatic stream which served.. as a carrier of bleachfield effluents. **1724** _Chron._ in _Ann. Reg._ 114/1 The workmen employed at a neighbouring *bleach-green. **1815** _Encycl. Brit._ (ed. 5) III. 678 Who has large *bleach-grounds at Glasgow. **1818** COBBETT _Resid. U.S._ (1822) 296 Some oil of vitriol works near to my *bleach-works. _a_ **1788** MRS. DELANY _Life & Corr._ (1861) III. 515 This place is.. much enriched with *bleach yards.

† **bleach**, _sb._[2] _Obs._ Also [5 blek(e), 5-6 bleche, bleeche, bletche. [A derivative of BLACK, but the etymological formation is obscure. ME. _bleche_ looks like the southern form of _blek_, _bleke_ in same sense, prob. identical with Icel. _blek_, Sw. _bläk_, Da. _blæk_ blacking, ink: see BLECK. But it may go back to an OE. _blęce_ or _blæce_: see BLACK. _Bleech_, _bleach_ are later spellings of _bleche_. But _bletche_ implies a ME. _blecche_, OE. *_blęcce_, parallel to BLATCH, ME. _blacche_, OE. *_blæcce_, on the OTeut. types *_blakjo-_ and *_blakkjo-_: see BLACK.]

1. Any substance used for blacking; e.g. ink, soot, lamp-black, and esp. shoemakers' or curriers' black used for leather.

[_c_ **1440** _Promp. Parv._ 39 Bleke, _atramentum_. _c_ **1483** _Cath. Angl._ 34 Blek.] _a_ **1500** in Wr.-Wülcker _Voc._ 566 _Atramentum, anglice_, bleche. **1530** PALSGR. 199/1 Bleche for souters, _attrament_. **1576** BAKER _Gesner's Jewell of Health_ 101 b, Shoemakers yncke or bleeche. **1580** BARET _Alv._ B 794 Courriors bleach.. _atramentum sutorium_. **1611** COTGR., _Attrament_, inke; or bleach for Shoomakers. —— _Suye_, soot of a chimney; any bleach.

†**2.** Hence, in the old 'Compaynys of beestys [etc.]' the term for, A company of sutors. _Obs._

1486 _Bk. St. Albans_ F vj b, A Bleche of sowteris, a Smere of Coryouris, a Clustre of Grapys.

† **bleach**, _a._ _Obs._ Also 4-5 bleche. [ME. _bleche_ was prob. the continuation of OE. _blǽc_, variant form of _blác_ shining, white, pale (usually explained as:—OTeut. *_blaiki-z_ and *_blaiko-z_ respectively).]

1. Pale = BLEAK _a._ 1.

1340 _Ayenb._ 53 Al huet þou art bleche and lhene. **1393** GOWER _Conf._ II. 210 She is pale and bleche.

2. = BLEAK _a._ 2.

1598 FLORIO, _Piaggioso_, medowie, large, bleach, fieldie. **1655** FULLER _Ch. Hist._ I. vi. §4 A bleach barren place.

bleach (bliːtʃ), _v._[1] Forms: 1 blǽcan, 2-5 blechen, 6 bleche, bleache, 8 bleech, 6- bleach. See also the (northern) form BLEAK. _Pa. t._ and _pple._ bleached (bliːtʃt): in ME. _blaȝte_, _blaȝt_, _bleyȝt_: cf. _teach_, _taȝt_, _teiȝht_, now _taught_. [Com. Teut.: OE. _blǽc(e)an_ wk. vb. = ON. _bleikja_, OHG. _bleichên_:—OTeut. *_blaikjan_ to bleach, f. *_blaiko-z_, _blaiki-z_ white: see prec. and BLAKE _a._]

1. a. _trans._ To whiten (linen, etc.) by washing and exposure to sunlight, or by chemical processes.

_c_ **1200** _Trin. Coll. Hom._ 57 Sume bereð clene cloð to watere to blechen. _a_ **1225** _Ancr. R._ 324 Wule a weob beon, et one cherre, mid one watere wel ibleched. _c_ **1440** _Promp. Parv._ 39 Blechen clothe [_v.r._ blekyn], _candido_. **1588** SHAKS. _L.L.L._ v. ii. 916 When.. Maidens bleach their summer smockes. **1632** MASSINGER _City Mad._ IV. iv, Some chandlers daughters, Bleaching linen in Moorfields. **1727** POPE, etc. _Art Sinking_ 108 Say that his linen was finely spun, and bleached on the happy plains. **1832** BABBAGE _Econ. Manuf._ vi. (ed. 3) 41 Bleaching linen in the open air.

b. _fig._ To free from stain, purify, sanctify. _rare._

1868 HEAVYSEGE _Saul_ 428 She may still live, be bleached with pious sighs, And showers of tears.

2. a. _gen._ To blanch or make white, to deprive of colour, _esp._ by exposure.

1583 STANYHURST _Æneis_ II. (Arb.) 58 [The adder] his slougth vncasing, hym self now youthfulye bleacheth. **1662** DRYDEN _Wild Gall._ v. i. (1725) 156 'To have me Face bleach'd like a Tiffany with thy Brimstone.' **1791** BURNS _Lament Earl Glencairne_ ii, His locks were bleachèd white with time. **1810** SCOTT _Lady of L._ III. v, The bones of men.. bleached by drifting wind and rain. **1837** CARLYLE _Fr. Rev._ (1872) I. v. ix. 179 His old head which seventy-four years have bleached.

b. To make pale with fear, etc.

_c_ **1760** SMOLLETT _Ode to Indep._ 8 Immortal Liberty, whose look sublime Hath bleached the tyrant's cheek.

c. _Photogr._ To remove the silver image from (a negative or print) after development; _**bleach-out process**_: a system of colour printing, now disused, whereby dyes are decolourized by being exposed through transparencies.

1889 R. MELDOLA _Chem. of Photogr._ vi. 209 A solution of potassium iodide also bleaches the darkened product of photo-decomposition under the influence of light. **1889** C. F. TOWNSEND _Chem. for Photographers_ (ed. 2) vi. 84 The image is first bleached with mercuric chloride, which converts the black silver image into a white double silver-mercurous chloride. **1911** B. E. JONES _Cassell's Cycl. Photogr._ 305/1 The negative is bleached in an acidified solution of bichromate salt, and then re-developed. **1914** G. L. JOHNSON _Photogr. in Colours_ (ed. 2) xi. 169 The difficulty of reproducing colour transparencies.. has at length been more or less overcome by the Bleach-out Process of colour printing. **1925** F. J. MORTIMER _Wall's Dict. Photogr._ (ed. 11) 101 The print may be bleached after the final wash. **1936** J. DESCHIN _New Ways in Photogr._ xvii. 244 A photograph may be converted into a drawing by.. the bleach-out process.

3. a. _intr._ To become white, whiten; to become pale, pallid, or colourless.

1611 SHAKS. _Wint. T._ IV. iii. 5 The white sheete bleaching on the hedge. **1709** ADDISON _Tatler_ No. 154 ¶11 Virgil.. describes some Spirits as bleaching in the Winds. **1853** KANE _Grinnell Exp._ xxxi. (1856) 266 To see the faces around him bleaching into waxen paleness. _c_ **1865** LETHEBY in _Circ. Sc._ I. 98/1 Different kinds of wax bleach with different degrees of facility. **1865** MISS BRADDON _Sir Jasper_ i. I. 22, Bones of travellers bleaching amongst the yellow sand.

b. _fig._ To become free from stain, be purified.

1799 SOUTHEY Wks. III. 63 The poor souls that bleach.. In that great Purgatory crucible. **1823** LAMB _Elia_ Ser. I. xxi. (1865) 167 Where does the taint stop? Do you bleach in three or four generations?

† **bleach**, _v._[2] _Obs._ [f. BLEACH _sb._[2], or perhaps cogn. with it, and repr. an OE. *_blæcean_. Cf. BLETCH _v._] _trans._ To blacken, make black.

1611 COTGR., _Poislé_.. smeered, bleached, begrymed with soote. —— _Noircir_, to blacke, blacken; bleach, darken.

bleach, _v._[3] (? misprint) for _bealch_ = BELCH.

1557 NORTH _Gueuara's Diall Pr._ (1582) 102 b, To bleache and breake wind after his surfette.

bleached (bliːtʃt), _ppl. a._ Also 4-5 blaȝt, bleyȝt; see the vb. [f. BLEACH _v._[1] + -ED.] Whitened (_esp._ by exposure to light and air), blanched; pale.

_c_ **1325** _E.E. Allit. P._ A. 212 Her ble more blaȝt þen whallez bon. **1384** CHAUCER _Former Age_ 45 No down of fetheres ne no bleched shete Was kyd to hem. **1398** TREVISA _Barth. De P.R._ XVII. xcvii, Than þe þred is sode, bleyȝt, and boukid. _a_ **1400** _Alexander_ (Stev.) 54 As blaȝt ere thaire wedis As any snyppand snaw. **1601** WEEVER _Mirr. Mart._ F j b, Vnto my bleached cindars she might come. **1845** DARWIN _Voy. Nat._ iv. (1879) 68 Bleached bones of horses. **1853** KANE _Grinnell Exp._ xxix. (1856) 240 The bleached faces of my mess-mates. **1859** GEO. ELIOT _A. Bede_ 87 Her little store of bleached linen.

bleacher (ˈbliːtʃə(r)). [f. as prec. + -ER[1]:]

1. One who bleaches.

1550 COVERDALE _Spir. Perle_ vi. (1588) 75 The dier, blecher, or the laundresse. **1703** VAN LEUWENHOEK in _Phil. Trans._ XXIV. 1526 A Bleecher cast Water with his Scoop. **1850** MRS. JAMESON _Leg. Monast. Ord._ (1863) 382 Woolcombers, bleachers, and fullers. **1863** J. MURPHY _Comm. Gen._ i. 26.

2. A vessel used in bleaching.

1883 _Century Mag._ XXVI. 812 Poured into the bleachers—boxes with perforated bottoms.

3. One of a roofless set of benches for spectators at outdoor events such as baseball and football games; also, an occupant of these benches. Usu. in _pl._ Also _attrib._ orig. and chiefly _U.S._ Hence **ˈbleacherite** _U.S._, a frequenter of bleachers; **ˈbleachery** _U.S._, an open-air stand for spectators.

1889 _Chicago Tribune_ 18 May 6/1 The grand stand and bleachers were well filled with something over 2,000 spectators. **1896** _Ibid._ 3 July 9/3 The money for it is being subscribed by the bleacherites. **1909** _Cent. Dict._ Suppl., Bleacherite, Bleachery. **1917** MATHEWSON _Sec. Base Sloan_ xviii. 237 The two boys settled themselves in their places on the bleachers. _Ibid._ 238 More than half of the bleacher seats were empty. _Ibid._ 239 'Sailor' was a grand favourite with the bleacherites. **1964** _Sun-Herald_ (Brisbane) 21 June 136/5 Those empty bleachers at the Beatles' concerts on Thursday and Friday. **1968** _Listener_ 29 Feb. 261/2 The many innocent spectators on the south-east bleachers.

4. _Photogr._ An agent for bleaching a negative or print (see BLEACH _v._[1] 2 c).

1911 B. E. JONES _Cassell's Cycl. Photogr._ 196/1 Any reducer or bleacher may be used. **1912** F. J. MORTIMER _Wall's Dict. Photogr._ (ed. 9) 113 If the print is a big one it is generally as well to wet it.. before placing it in the bleacher.

bleachery (ˈbliːtʃərɪ). [f. as prec. + -ERY.] A place where bleaching is done.

1714 _Fr. Bk. Rates_ 191 No Bleechers shall receive into their Bleecheries any Linens which are not so mark'd. **1816** W. PHILLIPS _Mineral._ (1823) Pref. 49 Chloride of lime consumed in the bleacheries of Britain.

bleach-ferm, erron. form of _blench-farm_: see BLANCH _a._ 3.

bleaching (bliːtʃɪŋ), _vbl. sb._[1] [f. BLEACH _v._[1]]

1. The art or process of whitening or cleansing by washing and exposure, or by chemical agents.

1552 HULOET, Bleachynge, _insolatio_. **1598** SHAKS. _Merry W._ IV. ii. 126 Behold what honest cloathes you send forth to bleaching. **1878** HUXLEY _Physiogr._ 109 It is this oxygen.. which is the really active agent in bleaching.

†**2.** A bleachery. _Obs._

1677 YARRANTON _Engl. Improv._ 135 There are.. by the River Avon side, convenient places to make Bleachings.

3. _Attrib._ and _Comb._, as _**bleaching-croft**_, _**-field**_, _**-fluid**_, _**-ground**_, _**-liquor**_, _**powder**_; **bleaching-clay** (see quot.).

1818 SCOTT _Rob Roy_ xxi, The large open meadow which.. serves at once as a bleaching-field and pleasure-walk for the inhabitants. **1822** IMISON _Sc. & Art_ II. 161 The rationale of the bleaching processes. **1833** HT. MARTINEAU _Vanderput & S._ v. 85 In yonder bleaching ground. **1854** J. SCOFFERN in _Orr's Circ. Sc._ Chem. 422 Commercial bleaching-powder, or so-called chloride of lime. **1865** _Athenæum_ No. 1957. 584/1 The bleaching-crofts of Lancashire. **1881** RAYMOND _Mining Gloss._, _Bleaching-clay_, Kaolin, used with size, to whiten.. cotton goods.

† **ˈbleaching**, (_vbl._) _sb._[2] _Obs._ [f. BLEACH _v._[2]] (Shoemakers') blacking.

_c_ **1500** _Cocke Lorelles B._ 1 The currier and cobler.. offred Cocke a blechynge pot.

ˈbleaching, _ppl. a._ [f. BLEACH _v._[1] + -ING[2].]

a. That bleaches or whitens: _fig._ cleansing, purifying. **b.** Becoming white from exposure.

1884 J. COLBORNE _With Hicks Pasha_ 204 The ground.. was strewn with the bleaching bones of the slain.

bleachy (ˈbliːtʃɪ), _a._[1] _dial._ [f. BLEACH _sb._[1] or _v._[1] + -Y[1].] Bleached, pale.

1821 CLARE _Vill. Minstrel_ II. 194 Nodding lands of wheat in bleachy brown. **1835** —— _Rural Muse_ 106 The mowers swept the bleachy corn.

bleachy (ˈbliːtʃɪ), _a._[2] _dial._ Brackish.

1825 JENNINGS _Observ. Dial. W. Eng._ **1879** HARDY _Wessex T._ (1888) II. 148 It makes the stuff [_sc._ rum] taste bleachy.

† **blead.** _Obs._ [OE. _blǽd_ str. masc. = OHG. _blât_:—WGer. *_blâd_:—OTeut. *_blǣdu-z_, f. stem _blǣ-_ BLOW: cf. L. _flātu-s_.] Blowing, breath, inspiration.

_c_ **890** K. ÆLFRED _Bæda_ IV. iii, Mare blæd windes. _a_ **1000** CYNEWULF _Phœnix_ 549 (Gr.) þurh gæstes blæd. _c_ **1175** _Lamb. Hom._ 97 He mid his bleade on-ealde eorðlichen monnan heortan.

blead, obs. form of BLEED.

bleak (bliːk), _sb._ Forms: 5 bleke, 7 bleake, 7- bleak. [The 15th c. _bleke_ points to an unrecorded OE. *_blǽce_ weak fem. = ON. _bleikja_, OHG. _bleicha_:—OTeut. *_blaikjôn-_ f. *_blaiko-_ white, shining: see next word. But the only known OE. name is _blǽge_, BLAY _sb._, which is not directly connected with _bleak_; and it is possible that _bleke_ was from ON., although _bleyke_, _blayke_ would then have been the expected form.] A small river-fish, called also the Blay (_Leuciscus alburnus_); and scientifically the genus to which it belongs; also an allied sea-fish.

1496 _Bk. St. Albans, Fysshynge_ 32 The bleke is but a feble fysshe, yet he is holsom. **1597** BRETON _Wit's Trenchm._ (1876) 7 Little fishes, as Bleakes, Roches. **1653** WALTON _Angler_ 205 There is also a Bleak, a fish that is ever in motion. **1655** MOUFFET & BENN. _Health's Improv._ (1746) 237 Bleaks of the Sea, or Sea-Bleaks.. are as.. wholesome, as any Carp. _Ibid._ 269 Bleys or Bleaks are soft flesh'd, but never fat. **1787** BEST _Angling_ 59 The bleak, on account of its eagerness to catch flies, is called by some, the river swallow. **1880** GÜNTHER _Fishes_ 604 'Bleak' are numerous in Europe and Western Asia, fifteen species being known, the common Bleak is found north of the Alps only.

bleak (bliːk), _a._ Forms: 6 (bleke in _bleke-ly_) bleeke, 6-7 bleake, 7- bleak. [A form (not found before the 16th c.) parallel to the synonymous _bleche_ (_bleach_), _bleyke_ (_blayke_), _blake_, _bloke_, in earlier, and partly in contemporary use. Its exact relation to these normal forms is not easily determined. _Bleke_, _bleak_ may have been the northern form of _bleche_, BLEACH _a._; cf. BLEAK _v._ = BLEACH _v._; but there is no evidence of its having originated in the north. It is also possible that it was a 16th c. spelling of _bleyke_, _blayke_, from ON., or even of the northern dial. _blake_; or that it resulted from a blending of _bleach_, with _bleyke_ or _blake_. Cf. BLAKE, BLEACH, BLEYKE _a._]

†**1.** Pale, pallid, wan; deficient in colour, esp. deficient in the ruddy bloom of health, or the full green of vegetation; of a sickly hue: also used like _pale_ to modify other colours (see b). Still _dial._

1566 PAINTER _Pal. Pleas._ I. 198 b, [She] began to recoloure her bleake and pale face with a vermilion teinte and roseall rudde. **1578** LYTE _Dodoens_ I. xlviii. 69 The floures be.. more pale or bleaker. **1597** GERARD _Herbal_ I. xxxv. § 1. 48 This Iris hath his flower of a bleake white colour. **1625** HART _Anat. Ur._ I. iv. 43 She was of a whitish bleake colour, and of a cachecticall disposition. **1633** G. HERBERT _Church-rents_ ii. in _Temple_, Calamities Turned your ruddie into pale and bleak. **1840** FORBY _Norf. & Suff. Wds._, _Bleek_ is still used in Norfolk to signify pale and sickly.

b. **1578** LYTE _Dodoens_ I. lxxix. 117 Small pale or bleake yellow floures. _Ibid._ II. xxvi. 277 Sometimes a bleeke or faynt yellow. **1629** J. PARKINSON _Parad. in Sole_ xc. 388 Of a faire bleake blew Colour, and in others pure white. **1665-76** RAY _Flora_ 78 The flowers are of a bleak ash colour.

2. Bare of vegetation; exposed: now often with some mixture of sense 3, wind-swept.

1538 [see BLEAKLY]. **1574** R. SCOT _Hop Gard._ (1578) 3 Many.. lay their Gardens very open and bleake to the South. **1608** SHAKS. _Per._ III. ii. 14 Our lodgings, standing bleak upon the sea. **1697** DRYDEN _Virg. Georg._ III. 543 The bleak Meotian Strand. **1750** JOHNSON _Rambl._ No. 80 ¶5 Bleak hills and leafless woods. **1783-94** BLAKE _Songs Exp._,

Holy Thursd. 10 Their fields are bleak and bare. **1824** W. IRVING *T. Trav.* I. 44 On a bleak height in full view.

b. In transferred use. *rare.*

1764 GOLDSM. *Trav.* 167 Where the bleak Swiss their stormy mansion tread. **1862** MRS. BROWNING *Musical Ins.* iii. in *Last Poems* 55 With his hard bleak steel.

3. Cold, chilly; usually of wind or weather.

1595 SHAKS. *John* v. vii. 40 To make his bleake windes kisse my parched lips. **1671** MILTON *P.R.* II. 72 Scarce a shed..to shelter him or me From the bleak air. **1795** SOUTHEY *Joan of Arc* II. 267 The cold wintry wind Blew bleak. **1814** WORDSW. *Excurs.* I. 888 In bleak December, I retraced this way. **1858** HAWTHORNE *Fr. & Ital. Jrnls.* I. 3 The wind was bleak.

4. *fig.* Cheerless, dreary.

a **1719** ADDISON (J.) Bleak and barren prospects. **1834** H. MILLER *Scenes & Leg.* xiv. (1857) 212 His course..lying barely beyond the bleak edge of poverty. **1846** KEBLE *Lyra Innoc.* (1873) 126 Firmest in the bleakest hour.

5. quasi-*adv.*

1596 SPENSER *F.Q.* I. ii. 33 Where Boreas doth blow full bitter bleake.

† **bleak** (bliːk), *v. Obs.* Forms: 5 blek-yn, bleke, 6– bleak. [Strictly we have here 2 or even 3 formations. In sense 1, *bleak* is the normal northern form of BLEACH *v.*[1]; in 3 it is treated as a direct derivative of BLEAK *a.*; sense 4 is a variant of BLEACH *v.*[2], ME. *blecche* to blacken.]

I. 1. To make white or pale by exposure to light; = BLEACH, *v.*[1] 1, 2.

1398 TREVISA *Barth. De P.R.* XVII. cxvii, þe þred is sode, bleyȝt [**1495** blekyd, **1535** bleked] and boukid. *c* **1440** *Promp. Parv.* 39 Bleyk cloþe or qwysters [*v.r.* blechen clothe, blekyn], *candido.* **1612** WOODALL *Surg. Mate* Wks. (1653) 215 As white wax is made of yellow wax, by the bleaking it in the ayr.

2. *intr.* To grow pale; to pale; = BLEACH, *v.*[1] 3.

1606 SYLVESTER *Du Bartas* (1641) 108/2 The Bedlam Bacchanalian froes, Who..Bleaking and blushing, panting, shreeking, swouning. —— *Trophies* 1272 Blushing and bleaking, betwixt shame and fear.

II. 3. *trans.* To chill or ? make livid with cold.

1605 HEYWOOD *Know not me* Wks. 1874 I. 291 Tis better to be bleakt by winters breath, Then to be stifled vp with summers heat.

III. 4. To blacken, darken; = BLEACH *v.*[2]

1611 COTGR., *Haler*..to bleak, or make swart, a thing, by displaying it in a hot Sunne.

† **bleaked,** *ppl. a. Obs.* [f. BLEAK *v.* 1. + -ED.] Made pale, bleached.

1548 UDALL, etc. *Erasm. Par. Rev.* vi. 8 (R.) Pale and bleaked for very sorrow and heuynes.

† **'bleaker.** *Obs.* [f. BLEAK *v.* 4.] (See quot.)

1611 COTGR., *Ternisseur*, bleaker, blemisher, discolourer.

† **'bleaking,** *vbl. sb. Obs.* [f. BLEAK *v.* 1.] Bleaching. Also *attrib.*, as in *bleaking-house.*

a **1627** MIDDLETON *No Wit, etc.* IV. ii, Left at Shoreditch, as a pledge For rosa solis, in a bleaking house.

bleakish ('bliːkɪʃ), *a.* [f. BLEAK *a.* + -ISH[1].]

† **1.** Rather pale. *Obs.*

1579 STUDLEY *Seneca's Hippol.* (1581) 67 A faynting fallow pale his bleakish cheekes disgrace.

2. Rather bleak or exposed.

1862 *Times* 18 Feb. 9/2 Kingsdown and Lansdown—two bleakish heaths in the West of England.

bleakly ('bliːklɪ), *adv.* [f. as prec. + -LY[2].]

† **1.** Palely. *Obs.*

1611 COTGR., *Pallement*, palely, bleakly, wanly.

2. In a bleak or exposed situation.

1538 LELAND *Itin.* V. 99 Standing veri blekely and object to all Wynddes. **1798** PENNANT *Hindoostan* II. 353 The lake is..situated bleakly. **1857** MRS. GASKELL *C. Brontë* I. iv. 61 The moors, stretching bleakly and barely far up from the dwelling.

3. Coldly, chilly.

1795 COLERIDGE *Soldier's Wife* in Southey *Lyr. P.* II. 140 Bleakly the blinding snow beats in thy hagged face.

4. Cheerlessly.

1938 E. WAUGH *Scoop* II. iv. 203 The Minister..smiled bleakly, the wry smile of one heroically resisting an emotion of almost overwhelming repulsion. **1941** *New Review* 28 Aug. 5/3 The treasury bleakly announced that no extra allowance or increases would be granted to Army Officers.

bleakness ('bliːknɪs). [f. as prec. + -NESS.] The quality of being bleak; chilly bareness.

1600 F. WALKER tr. *Span. Mandeville* 136 a, The bleeknes [*printed* bleetenes] of this wind..is cause that..the Rivers, ponds, and Lakes are all frozen. **1695** WOODWARD *Nat. Hist. Earth* II. (1723) 81 The great Bleakness and Cold of those Countryies. **1851** NICHOL *Archit. Heav.* 27 The awful bleakness of space.

bleaky ('bliːkɪ), *a.* [f. BLEAK *a.*; cf. *chilly, whity, blacky, goody*, and similar forms.] Inclining to BLEAK (in senses 2 and 3).

1687 DRYDEN *Hind & P.* III. 612 Bleaky plains, and bare unhospitable ground. **1695** BLACKMORE *Pr. Arth.* IV. 203 Bleaky Continents and frozen Isles. *a* **1701** SEDLEY *Virgil's Past.* Wks. 1722 I. 313 Ye bleaky Winds! your wonted Rigour spare. **1797** BURNS *Death R. Dundas*, Lone on the bleaky hills.

blear (blɪə(r)), *a.* Forms: 5–6 blere, 6–7 bleare, 7 bleer(e, 7– blear. [ME. *blere*, an epithet of the eyes: this and the cognate verb are of uncertain origin. There are no corresponding words in OE., and the only cognates in other Teutonic langs. are the mod.G. *blerr* soreness of the eyes, LG. *blarr-oged, bleer-oged* blear-eyed. Sw. *plira*, Da. *plire* to blink, leer, can hardly be connected. Though the vb. appears in our quotations before the adj., the form of the words and general analogies make it probable that the vb. was formed on the adj.]

1. Of the eyes or sight: Dim from water or other superficial affection.

1398 TREVISA *Barth. De P.R.* VIII. xxi. (1495) 333 The syghte of a candyll is seen wythout lette of an eye that is hole, but of a blere eye it is nat seen wythout lykenesse and shape of a manere rayne bowe. **1547** BOORDE *Brev. Health* ccv. 70 b, Blere eyes which is when the under lyd of the eye is subverted. **1561** DAUS tr. *Bullinger on Apoc.* (1573) 60 A medicine..to lay to sore and blere eyes. **1621** BURTON *Anat. Mel.* I. ii. II. i. (1651) 71 It causeth bleer eyes. **1840** THACKERAY *Paris Sk.-Bk.* (1872) 49 Her eyes grew watery and blear. **1843** AINSWORTH *Tower Lond.* (1864) 47 His eyes were blear and glassy.

fig. **1641** MILTON *Ch. Discip.* I. (1851) 30 If our understanding..be blear with gazing on other false glisterings.

2. *transf.* Dim, misty, indistinct in outline.

1634 MILTON *Comus* 153 To cheat the eye with blear illusion. **1809** J. BARLOW *Columb.* I. 596 The blear ice..sheds a dazzling glare. **1830** AIRD in *Blackw. Mag.* XXVIII. 813 On the blear autumn eves, When small birds shriek adown the wind.

Hence BLEAR-EYED *a.* q.v.; **blear-witted,** having the mental faculties dimmed.

1599 B. JONSON *Ev. Man out of Hum.* v. ii, They were very blear-witted, i' faith, that could not discern the gentleman in him.

blear, *sb. rare.* [? f. the adj. or vb.] Blearing, blearness; in *pl.* bleareness of eyes, bleared eyes.

1603 *Philotus* vi, I think ane man sir, of ȝour ȝeiris, Sould not be blyndit with the bleiris. **1868** BUSHNELL *Serm. Living Subj.* 125 The blear of our sin.

blear (blɪə(r)), *v.*[1] Forms: 3 bleri, 4–6 blere, 6 bler (blirre), 6–7 bleer(e, bleare, 6– blear. [The ME. forms point to an OE. **blerian* or **blierian* intr. in sense 1, f. the adj.; but no such form is known: see BLEAR *a.* Cf. also BLUR.]

† **1.** *intr.* To have watery or inflamed eyes, to be blear-eyed. (Said also of an albino.) *Obs.*

a **1300** *Old Age* in *E.E.P.* (1862) 149, I stunt i stomere, I stomble . i blind, i bleri. **1430** LYDG. *Chron. Troy* I. x, For she..Unwarely can do blere a mannes eye. **1483** *Cath. Angl.* 34 To Blere, *lippire, lippiscere.* *a* **1560** ROLLAND *Crt. Venus* IV. 667 Quhat may ȝone fell freik be, [that] With the quhite berd and scarlat ene dois bleir? **1570** LEVINS *Manip.* 209 To Bleare, *lippire.*

b. with complemental object.

1649 G. DANIEL *Trinarch., Hen. V*, clxxxvii, The new-raised morne (like Eyes ill-wak't) Blears through the Deaw faint Raies.

2. *trans.* To dim (the eyes) with tears, rheum, or inflammation; to dim the vision of.

1340–1525 [see BLEARED]. **1528** MORE *Heresyes* III. Wks. 206/2 The brightnesse blered myne eye. **1530** PALSGR. 457/2 His eyes be so bleared with drinkyng that they be as reed as a fyrret. **1606** SYLVESTER *Du Bartas* (1641) 2/2 The Suns bright beams do blear the sight Of such as fix'dly gaze against his light. **1728** T. SHERIDAN *Persius* iii. (1739) 45, I used to find out Ointments to blear my Eyes. **1851** LONGF. *Gold. Leg.* I. lviii, He..bleared his eyes with books.

b. To blur (the countenance) as with tears.

c **1400** *Destr. Troy* 9132 The teris..blaknet with bleryng all hir ble qwite. **1837** CARLYLE *Fr. Rev.* II. III. i. vii. 170 The Earth smiles not on us, nor the Heaven; but weeps and blears itself, in sour rain. **1861** TEMPLE & TREVOR *Tannhäuser* 8 That tremendous Doom..Shatter'd the superstitious dome that blear'd Heaven's face to man.

3. (*fig.*) *to blear the eyes*: to deceive, blind, 'hoodwink,' 'throw dust in the eyes.' Very common in 16th c.

c **1325** *Coer de L.* 3708 So queyntyly to blere myn eye. *c* **1386** CHAUCER *Maunc. T.* 148 For al thy waytyng, blered is thin ye. *a* **1400** *Octouian* 1387 For to blere the Soudanes ye Queynte lesynges he gan to lye. **1537** T. CROMWELL in Froude *Hist. Eng.* III. 229 You have bleared my eyes once. Your credit shall never more serve you so far to deceive me the second time. **1596** SHAKS. *Tam. Shr.* v. i. 120 While counterfeit supposes bleer'd thine eine. **1714** ELLWOOD *Autobiog.* 220 To blear Mens Eyes with Fopperies. **1815** SCOTT *Guy M.* xxxix, 'I want nane o' your siller..to make ye think I am blearing your ee.' **1860** MOTLEY *Netherl.* (1868) I. iii. 91 Henry III was seeking to blear the eyes of the world.

† **b.** In the same sense the simple vb. was used.

1530 PALSGR. 457/2 I bleare, I begyle by dissymulacyon. [**1570** LEVINS *Manip.* 142 To blirre, *fallere.*] **1613** SIR E. HOBY *Counter-sn.* 14 Blearing his Reader, that these are but worme-eaten sayings. **1642** T. TAYLOR *God's Judgem.* I. I. xvii. 54 He was so besotted and bleared with them.

† **blear,** *v.*[2] *Obs.* Forms: 4–7 blere, 5 bleere, 6 bleare, 6– blear. [app. distinct from the prec.: perhaps onomatopœic, but naming a gesture rather than a sound, though some inarticulate sound may have originally been implied. Cf. BLARE *v.*] *intr.* To protrude the tongue in mockery. Also *to blear with the tongue*. *trans. to blear (out) the tongue* (at, against, upon).

a **1340** HAMPOLE *Pr. Consc.* 2226 And grymly gryn on hym and blere. *c* **1430** *Hymns Virg.* (1867) 60 While þou art a child, With þi tunge on folk þou bleere. **1481** CAXTON *Reynard* (Arb.) 86 The asse..bleryd, grennyd and songe. **1530** PALSGR. 457/2, I bleare with the tonge. *Ibid.* The knave bleareth his tonge at me. **1535** COVERDALE *Isa.* lvii. 4 Vpon whom gape ye with youre mouth, & bleare out youre tonge? **1550** —— *Spir. Perle* xxix. (1588) 279 Not once to blear or to open their mouths against it. **1605** BP. ANDREWES *Serm.* ii. 173 Wagging their heads, writhing their mouths, yea blearing out their tongues.

¶ Cf. the following, and BLARE *v.*

1616 T. SCOTT *Christ's Polit.* 7 All that the silly sheep can do, is only to bleare and bleate a little with his tongue.

bleared (blɪəd), *ppl. a.* Forms: 4 bleried, 4–5 blerid, 4–6 blered, 5 bleryd, bleryed, (*Sc.*) bleirit, 6 blerde, bleered, 6–7 bleard, 8 (*Sc.*) bleerit, 6– bleared. [f. BLEAR *v.*[1] + -ED.]

1. Of the eyes: Dimmed with tears, morbid matter, or inflammation. Also *fig.*; see BLEAR *v.*[1] 3.

c **1340** *Gaw. & Gr. Knt.* 962 þe tweyne yȝen were..sellyly blered. **1362** LANGL. *P. Pl.* A v. 109 Bitel-brouwed with twei blered [*v.r.* blerid(e) eiȝen. **1382** WYCLIF *Gen.* xxix. 17 Lya was with blerid eyen. **1525** LD. BERNERS *Froiss.* II. x. 21 Kyng Robert of Scotlande..with a payre of reed blered eyen. **1579** GOSSON *Sch. Abuse* (Arb.) 27 Searching for moats with a pair bluearde eies. **1792** BURNS *Duncan Gray*, Duncan..Grat his een baith bleer't and blin'. **1848** LYTTON *Harold* i. 307 The witch..looking into her face with bleared and rheumy eyes.

2. Said of the face or person: Blurred with running from the eyes; blear-eyed.

1500 *Ort. Voc.* in *Promp. Parv.* 39 *note, Lippus* dicitur.. blered of the eye. **1596** SHAKS. *Merch. V.*, III. ii. 59 With bleared visages come forth to view The issue of th' exploit. **1793** BURNS *Meg o' the Mill* ii, The Laird was a widdiefu', bleerit knurl. **1863** KINGSLEY *Water Bab.* viii. (1878) 369 Mr. Grimes so sooty and bleared and ugly.

† **3.** *fig.* Mentally blinded, deceived. *Obs.*

1549 CHEKE *Hurt. Sedit.* (1641) 31 So much blered, that you did think impossible things.

blearedness ('blɪədnɪs). [f. prec. + -NESS.]

1. Bleared condition.

1398 TREVISA *Barth. De P.R.* XVII. clxxxv. (1495) 726 The dronklew mannes..eyen ben full of whelkes and pymples and of bleryednesse. *c* **1475** *Found. St. Barthol. Hosp.* II. i. (1886) 81 This man putte a syde bleriednes of yen. **1563** T. GALE *Antidot.* II. 36 It amendeth the blearednes, and consumeth the teares.

transf. **1881** W. RUSSELL *Ocean Free L.* I. v. 195 There was a haziness about the azure, a blearedness resembling the film on a sick man's eyes.

2. *fig.* Affection of the mental or moral vision.

1678 R. BARCLAY *Apol. Quakers* v. §21. 165 The Blearedness of the Eyes of our Minds. **1851** S. JUDD *Margaret* III. (1871) 401 Will unkindness, traducement, insinuation, blearedness never cease?

blear-eyed ('blɪər'aɪd), *a.* [f. *blear eye* + -ED.]

1. *lit.* Having blear eyes.

1382 WYCLIF *Lev.* xxi. 20 If crokid-rigge or bleereyed [**1388** blereiȝed]. **1393** LANGL. *P. Pl.* C. xx. 306 þorw smoke and smorþre..Til he be bler-eyed oþer blynde. **1526** *Pilgr. Perf.* (W. de W. 1531) 153 b, Lya was blere-eyed, & myght not se clerely. **1562** TURNER *Herbal* II. 133 The iuice [of Aygrene]..is good for them that are blare eyed. **1642** T. TAYLOR *God's Judgem.* I. I. ii. 3 Those who..being bleare eyed and tender sighted are rather dazled and dimmed by the Sunnes beames. **1787** WOLCOTT (P. Pindar) Wks. 1812 I. 458 The wrinkled blear-eyed, good old Granny. **1798** [see *collier-woman* s.v. COLLIER III]. **1935** W. S. MAUGHAM *Don Fernando* xi. 232 You have painted me ugly and blear-eyed.

2. *fig.* Having the mental vision dimmed; dull of perception, short-sighted.

1561 T. NORTON *Calvin's Inst.* III. xvii. (1634) 395 The judgement of God farre surmounteth the bleare-eyed sight of men. **1581** J. BELL *Haddon's Answ. Osor.* 221 Their bleare eyed dulnes. **1663** J. SPENCER *Prodigies* (1665) 340 Men quickly hated this blear-ey'd Religion. **1687** DRYDEN *Hind & Panther* II. 61 That ev'n the blear-ey'd sects may find her out. **1927** YEATS *October Blast* 15 Nor blear-eyed wisdom out of midnight oil.

Hence **blear-'eyedness.**

c **1440** *Promp. Parv.* 39 Blerydnesse [**1499** blere iyednesse], *lippitudo.* **1611** COTGR., *Chacie*, bleare-eyednesse; a running, or waterishnesse of the eyes. **1653** GAUDEN *Hierasp.* 96 That darkness and bleareyednesse, which prejudice and perverseness carry with them. **1877** WRAXELL *V. Hugo's Miserables* I. Contemporary admiration is blear-eyedness.

blearily ('blɪərɪlɪ), *adv.* [f. BLEARY *a.*] In a bleary manner.

a **1918** W. OWEN *Coll. Poems* (1963) 72 He..Just blinked at my revolver, blearily. **1922** *Blackw. Mag.* Mar. 274/1 Thomas Owen looked up blearily from his task.

bleariness ('blɪərɪnɪs). [f. BLEARY + -NESS.] = BLEAREDNESS.

1398 TREVISA *Barth. De P.R.* VI. xxi. (1495) 211 Wyne.. dooth awaye webbes and blerines of eyen. **1468** *Medulla Gram.* in *Cath. Angl.* 34 *Lippitudo*, blerynes off the eye. **1832** *Blackw. Mag.* XXXI. 118 The small bleariness of their opaque optics.

blearing ('blɪərɪŋ), *vbl. sb.*[1] [f. BLEAR *v.*[1]]

1. The condition of being bleared, blearedness.

1542 UDALL *Erasm. Apoph.* 59 a, Lippitudo Atticae, that is, the bleryng of Attica.

2. The action of making blear; *fig.* deception.

c **1386** CHAUCER *Reeves T.* 11 Ful wel coude I the quyte With bleryng of a prowd mylleres ye. *c* **1400** *Destr. Troy* 9134 The teris þat trickilt on her tryet chekes..blaknet with bleryng all hir ble qwite.

3. *transf.* The guttering of a candle; as resembling the rheum which blears the eyes.

1705 BERKELEY in Fraser *Life* (1871) 509, I know not what more fitly to compare it to than to the blearings of a candle.

†**blearing**, *vbl. sb.*^{2} *Obs.* [f. BLEAR *v.*^{2} + -ING^1.] The protruding of the tongue or making of mouths in mockery.

c **1440** *Promp. Parv.* 39 Blerynge or mowynge wythe the mowthe, *valgia*.

ˈ**blearness.** *arch.* or *Obs.* [f. BLEAR *a.* + -NESS.] Blearedness (of the eyes).

1543 TRAHERON *Vigo's Chirurg.* II. ii. 50 Blerenes of the eyelyddes. **1585** LLOYD *Treas. Health* A j, There shal many be troubled with blernesse. **1748** *Vegetius' Distemp. Horses* 157 A great Blearness of the Eyes.

bleary (ˈblɪərɪ), *a.* [f. BLEAR *a.* (or ? *sb.*) + -Y^1. In the 14th c. quot. all MSS. save one read *blered, -id, -yd*: so that *blery* is of slight authority; but cf. BLEARINESS.] **a.** More or less blear of the eyes.

1393 LANGL. *P. Pl.* C. VII. 198 He was bytelbrowed and baberlupped · with two blery eyen. **1655** *Francion* 24 The glutinous quality of that bleārie humour. **1770** ARMSTRONG *Imitat.* (1859) 82 He with bleary eye Blazons his own disgrace. **1810** TANNAHILL *Poems* (1846) 117 The comers were cheery, the gangers were blearie. **1830** *Blackw. Mag.* XXVII. 436 His little red bleary eyes.

b. *Comb.*, as **bleary-eyed** *a.*, = BLEAR-EYED *a.* I.

1927 *New Republic* 9 Mar. 71. **1930** 'SAPPER' *Finger of Fate* 261 An unshaven, bleary-eyed man. **1957** R. CAMPBELL *Portugal* 33 The weirdest lot of bleary-eyed thugs.

bleary (ˈblɪərɪ), *sb. rare*$^{-1}$. (See quot.)

1812 J. HENRY *Camp. agst. Quebec* 65 Boiling a bleary, which was no other than flour and water.

bleat (bliːt), *v.* Forms: 1 **blǣtan**, 3 *Orm.* **blætenn**, 4–5 **blete**, 6 *Sc.* **blait**, 6–7 **bleate**, (**blate**), 7 **bleet**, 7– **bleat**. [Com. WGer.: OE. *blǣtan* = OHG., MHG. *blâzen*, mod.Du. *blaten*:—WGer. *blâtan*, of imitative origin: cf. mod.G. *blöken*; also OSlav. *blejat*ı to bleat, and see BLEA.]

1. *intr.* To cry, as a sheep, goat, or calf.

a **1000** *Riddles* (Gr.) xxv. 2 Ic..blǽte swá gát. *c* **1000** ÆLFRIC *Gram.* xxii. 129 Scēp blǽt. *c* **1200** ORMIN 1315 Itt [lamb] cann cnawenn swiþe wel Hiss moderr þær 3ho blæteþþ. *a* **1300** *E.E. Psalter* lxiv. 14 Schepe þat blete. **1549** *Compl. Scot.* vi. 39 The scheip began to blait. **1611** SHAKS. *Wint. T.* I. ii. 68 We were as twyn'd Lambs, that did..bleat the one at th' other. **1735** SOMERVILLE *Chase* III. 30 The mournful Ewe Wanders perplex'd, and darkling bleats in vain. **1859** GEO. ELIOT *A. Bede* 60 Our friends the calves are bleating from the home croft.

b. *trans.* (with cognate object.) Also *to bleat out*: to give forth with a bleat.

1719 D'URFEY *Pills* (1872) IV. 337 The tender Flocks their Pasture mourn, and bleat a sadder Moan. **1864** SWINBURNE *Atalanta* 936 Let her..stretch her throat for a knife, Bleat out her spirit and die. **1871** B. TAYLOR *Faust* I. v. (Chandos) 61 An old he-goat..Should his good-night in lustful gallop bleat her.

2. *transf.* Used contemptuously of the human voice.

a **1563** BECON *Jewel of Joy* Wks. (1844) 429 Nourishing many idle singing-men to bleat in their chapels. **1569** E. HAKE *Newes Powles Churchy.* F vj, Thus bleate the Popish Balamites. **1869** HEAVYSEGE *Saul* 312 If she bleats now, Why, 'tis her nature, and the gift of women.

b. *trans.* To give mouth to, babble, prate. Cf. BLATE.

1692 WASHINGTON tr. *Milton's Def. Pop.* vi. (1851) 165 You, who bleat what you know nothing of [Lat. *qui ea blatis*].

c. Used of sounds likened to the cry of a sheep.

1880 HOWELLS *Undisc. Country* viii. 123 Their bells were bleating everywhere.

bleat (bliːt), *sb.* Also 4 **blet**, 6 *Sc.* **bleit**, 8 **blate**. [f. prec. vb.] **a.** The cry of a sheep, goat, or calf.

[**1382** WYCLIF *Ps.* lxxvii[i]. 70 Fro the aftir berende blet he toc hym [**1388** fro bihynde scheep with lambren; Vulg. *de post fœtantes accepit eum*].]

1590 SHAKS. *Much Ado* V. iv. 51 A Calfe..Much like to you, for you haue iust his bleat. **1697** DRYDEN *Virg. Georg.* III. 826 The Rivers, and their Banks, and Hills around, With Lowings, and with dying Bleats resound. **1795** SOUTHEY *Occas. Pieces* iii, His barkings loud and quick Amid their tremulous bleat. **1842** TENNYSON *Ode Memory* v, The live-long bleat Of the thick-fleeced sheep.

b. *transf.* Any similar cry; *spec.* that of a snipe.

1863 KINGSLEY *Water-Bab.* 131 The owl's hoot and the snipe's bleat and the fox's bark.

c. A similar sound made by the human voice.

c **1505** DUNBAR *Flyting* 204 Thay bickerit the with mony bae and bleit. **1799** *Month. Rev.* XXIX. 142 The inarticulate vulgarity, the calf's blate of those speakers.

d. A (feeble) complaint. *colloq.*

1916 'TAFFRAIL' in *Royal Mag.* Dec. 99/2 'Got a bleat, 'ave yer?' growled an unsympathetic Petty Officer. **1948** N. SHUTE *No Highway* 107 He had heard nothing..in reply to his signal stating Mr. Honey's bleat.

bleat(e, obs. form of BLATE *Sc.*

bleater (ˈbliːtə(r)). [f. BLEAT *v.* + -ER^1.]

1. An animal that bleats, as a sheep, calf, etc.

1567 MORTON *Gt. Bull* in *Harl. Misc.* (1811) VII. 536 Some calves with blacke faces, as blacke soule and hys fellowes common bleaters. **1755** *Gentl. Mag.* XXV. 568 Swift o'er the lawns the little bleaters bound. **1808** JAMIESON, *Bleater*, the cock snipe, *Ettr. For.*; denominated from its bleating sound. **1855** SINGLETON *Virgil* I. 87 Plunge the flock of bleaters in the healthful stream.

†**2.** *Thieves' slang*: (see quot.) *Obs.*

1609 DEKKER *Lanthorne* Wks. 1884–5 III. 290 They that are Cheated by Iacke in a Boxe, are called *Bleaters*.

bleating (ˈbliːtɪŋ), *vbl. sb.* [f. as prec. + -ING^1.] The crying of a sheep, goat, or calf; also *contemptuously* said of human utterances.

1398 TREVISA *Barth. De P.R.* XVII. xlvi. (1495) 807 A kydde..knowyth and sekyth his moder wyth bletyng. **1578** *Gude & Godlie Ballates* (1868) 163 Sing on guk, guk, the blating of zour queir. **1611** BIBLE *Judges* v. 16 To heare the bleatings of the flocks. **1781** COWPER *Convers.* 588 Known by thy bleating, Ignorance thy name. **1828** SCOTT *F.M. Perth* III. 343 The brute beasts in their lowing and bleating.

b. *attrib.* (passing into the *ppl. a.*)

1773 G. WHITE *Selborne* xxxix, In breeding time the cock-snipes make a bleating noise. **1834** J. FORBES *Laennec's Dis. Chest* 429 The voice, having the bleating character strongly marked.

bleating, *ppl. a.* [f. as prec. + -ING^2.] That bleats; also *fig.*

c **1380** WYCLIF *Serm.* Sel. Wks. I. 139 Bletyng sheep. **1595** SPENSER *Col. Clout* 955 To draw their bleating flocks to rest. **1651** CALDERWOOD *Hist. Kirk* (1843) II. 157 The queene..and her bleeting preests. **1884** BLACK *Jud. Shaks.* xxxi, Lambs, with bleating oratory, craved the dams' comfort.

bleaty (ˈbliːtɪ), *a.* [f. BLEAT *sb.* + -Y^1.] Having a sound like the bleat of a beast.

1925 W. G. WHITTAKER *Class-Singing* 77 'A' (as in 'axe') is..apt to be 'bleaty'.

†**bleaunt.** *Obs.* Forms: 4 **blihant**, **-and**, **blehand**, **bleaunt**, **bleeaunt**. [ad. OF. *bliaut*, *-aud*, *bliat*, earlier *blialt*; found also in other Romanic langs., Pr. *blial*, *bliau*, *bliaut*, *blizaut*, Sp., Pg. *brial*, medL. *blialdus*, *bliaudus*, *blisaudus*, an article of dress, a tunic worn both by men and women often richly embroidered; also in MLG. *bliant*, *blyant*, MHG. *blîalt*, *blîat* a silk gold-stuff for clothes, bed-covers, etc. Of uncertain origin: see Diez and Mahn. The appearance of the *n* in the English and MLG. is unaccounted for. *Bleaunt* for **bliant*, may be compared with ME. *geaunt* = *giant*.]

A kind of tunic or upper garment; also a rich stuff or fabric used for this garment.

c **1314** *Guy Warw.* (Turnb.) 208 His blihant he curf, his schert also. *c* **1320** *Sir Tristr.* I. xxxviii, In o robe Tristrem was boun..Was of a blihand broun The richest that was wrought. *Ibid.* I. xli, In blehand was he cledde. *c* **1325** *E.E. Allit. P.* A. 163 A mayden..Blysnande whyt watz hyr bleaunt. *c* **1340** *Gaw. & Gr. Knt.* 879 A mere mantyle..Of a broun bleeaunt enbrouded ful ryche. *a* **1400** *Alexander* (Stev.) 167 A blewe bleaunt obove brade him all over.

bleb (blɛb), *sb.* Also 7 **blebb**. [app. like BLOB and BLUBBER, from the action of making a bubble with the lips. In relation to *blob*, *bleb* expresses a smaller swelling; cf. *top*, *tip*, etc.]

1. A blister or small swelling on the skin; also a similar swelling on plants.

1607 TOPSELL *Four-f. Beasts* 319 Wingals..be little swellings like blebs or bladders, on either side the joynt. **1677** PLOT *Oxfordsh.* 174 The blebs or blisters we find on the leaves of many Trees and Shrubs. **1876** DUHRING *Dis. Skin* 228 Blebs may occur in the place of vesicles.

fig. **1651** MORE *Enthus. Triumph* (1656) 180 You blebs of venery, you bags of filth!

2. A bubble of air in water, glass, or other substance at some time fluid.

1647 H. MORE *Song of Soul* Notes 165/2 Dancing blebs and bubbles in the water. **1716** DESAGULIERS in *Phil. Trans.* XXIX. 447 The Lens ought to be..without Veins or Blebs. **1861** FURNIVALL *San Graal* (Roxb.) Pref. 8 A..green vessel ..showing by a bleb in it that it was of glass.

3. A vesicular body.

1775 ELLIS in *Phil. Trans.* LXVI. 15 *note*, The cell-like divisions..are only a row of single blebs of pith. —— CLAYTON *ibid.* 105 From the surface oozes out a gum in round blebs. **1880** J. E. BURTON *Handbk. Midwives* §38. 25 The ovum, or egg, is at first a little bladder, or bleb.

4. *Cytology.* A protuberance on the surface of a cell.

1962 *Lab. Investigation* XI. 1012/1 Lysis of membranes, bleb formation, and disappearance of villi. **1977** *Sci. Amer.* May 63/1 (*caption*) Death of a cancer cell is indicated by the blebs, or deep folds, that have appeared on its surface membrane. **1981** *Ibid.* Mar. 67/2 Many animal cells are capable of amoeboid motion. They flatten out and retract; they develop transitory bumps or bubbles called blebs. **1983** *Environmental Res.* XXXI. 343 These blebs contained cell organelles, such as mitochondria, vesicles, and ribosomes.

bleb, *v.* [f. prec. sb.] **1.** *trans.* To furnish with blebs.

1821 CLARE *Vill. Minstr.* II. 84 While big drops..bleb the withering hay with pearly gems.

2. *intr.* Of a cell: to develop a bleb or blebs. Of paint: to blister.

[**1934** WEBSTER, *Bleb, v.t.* & *i.*, to cover with blebs or bubbles; bubble. *Dial.*] **1973** A. K. HARRIS in *Locomotion of Tissue Cells* (Ciba Found. Symp. No. 14) 9 As cells respread after being detached, their margins first bleb, until ruffling gradually takes over. **1976** *Nature* 3 June 413/1 One of the cells did not bleb while the other seven initiated a new bleb every 30 s. **1977** *Evening Post* (Nottingham) 24 Jan. 9/2 His Lada car was still under guarantee when he notified the suppliers that the paint was 'blebbing'. **1983** *Jrnl. Fish Dis.* VI. 33 The membrane facing the PV was smooth and blebbed into the PV.

Hence **blebbed** *ppl. a.*; ˈ**blebbing** *vbl. sb.*, the formation of a bleb; a bleb; also as *ppl. a.*

1960 *Sci. Amer.* Jan. 134/1 Membrane-blebbing and related phenomena. **1961** WEBSTER, Blebbed. **1966** *Exper. Cell Res.* XLI. 624 In the glutaraldehyde fixed eggs..a large number of membranous outpocketings, membrane blebbings and blister-like elevations can be observed. *Ibid.* 628 Doubts..that the blebbing membranes are present all the time. **1973** A. K. HARRIS in *Locomotion of Tissue Cells* (Ciba Found. Symp. No. 14) 253 In the life of a given culture the majority of cells are isolated..and display vigorous blebbing activity. **1980** *Jrnl. Protozool.* XXVII. 270/1 The numerous pellicular blebs over these inflated cisternae suggest that their contents may be released by blebbing. **1982** *Exper. Cell Res.* CXXXIX. 275 Actively dividing cells retained a high proportion of rounded, ruffled and blebbed cells during all phases of the cell cycle.

blebby (ˈblɛbɪ), *a.* Full of blebs or bubbles.

1754 LEWIS in *Phil. Trans.* XLVIII. 687 The mass, when cold..appeared very porous, blebby, of a dull grey colour. **1880** DANA *Mineral.* 431 [It] fuses to a white blebby glass.

bleberry, obs. form of BLAEBERRY.

blec(c)en, obs. f. BLESS *v.*^{1}

blecere, var. form of BLECHURE.

†**bleche**, *v.* *Obs.* [a. north.F. *blechier* = OF. *blecier* (mod. *blesser*, whence the later BLESS *v.*^{2}) to wound.] *trans.* To wound, hurt, injure.

1340 *Ayenb.* 40 Sacrilege is huanne me brecþ, oþer blecheþ,..þe holy þinges. *Ibid.* 147 Huanne me smit þane uot: þe mouþ zayþ, þou me blechest.

bleche, -er, obs. forms of BLEACH, -ER.

†**blechure.** *Obs.* Also 5 **blecere**. [a. ONF. *blecheüre*, OF. *bleceüre*, (modF. *blessure*), wound, from *blechier*, *blecier*, *blesser* to wound: see BLECHE.] A wound.

1483 CAXTON *Gold. Leg.* 109/4 Thys hurte and blechure of thys peple. *Ibid.* 303/4 In al oure hurtes, blechures and sores. *c* **1500** *Partenay* 3572 Without hurt or blecere any.

bleck, *sb.* *Obs.* exc. *dial.* Also **blek(e**, **blecke**. [The OE. *blæc* looks like the adj. *blæc*, BLACK, used subst. If so, ME. *blek(e* must be unrepresented in OE., and correspond to ON. *blek* ink (Sw. *bläck*, Da. *blæk* ink), OTeut. type **blakjo(m*, f. **blak-* BLACK.]

1. Black fluid substance; *spec.* ink (*obs.*); a preparation used by curriers and shoemakers for blacking leather (also called *bletch*, *blatch*, *bleach*) (*obs.*); black grease round an axle or other revolving part. *north. dial.*

[*c* **970** K. EADGAR *Canons* (*Anc. Laws* II. 244) We lærað þæt hi..habban blæc and bocfell to heora ȝerædnessum. *a* **1000** ÆLFRIC *Gloss.* Wr.-Wülcker *Voc.* 164 *Incaustum vel atramentum*, blæc.] *c* **1440** *Promp. Parv.* 39 Bleke [**1499** blecke], *atramentum*. **1483** *Cath. Angl.* 34 Blek, *attramen*, *attramentum*. *c* **1505** DUNBAR '*This Nycht in my Sleip*' vii, 'Fy,' quod the Feynd, 'thou [sowttar] sairis of blek, Go clenge the clene, and cum to me.' **1570** LEVINS *Manip.* 47 Blecke, bleche, *atramentum*. **1855** *Whitby Gloss.*, *Bleck*, the dirty-looking oil or grease at the axle of a cart-wheel. **1876** in *Mid. Yorksh. Gloss.* **1877** in *Holderness Gloss.*, etc.

2. Soot or smut, a particle of soot. (Still *Sc.*)

c **1590** A. HUME *Ep. G. Moncrief*, The Censor is impropre to correck, That in himself has ony kinde of bleck.

3. a. A blackamoor. **b.** A blackguard. *mod.Sc.*

4. *Comb.*, as †**bleck-fat** (= *vat*), **blek-pot**, a vessel for holding 'bleck.'

1468 *Medulla Gram.* in *Cath. Angl.* 34 *Atramentarium*, an ynkhorne or a blek pot. **1483** *Cath. Angl.* 34 Blek potte, *attramentorium*. **1562** *Richmond. Wills* (1853) 156 In a litill house, stocks of a bedde and bleckfatts.

bleck, *v.* *Obs.* exc. *dial.* Also 5 **blekkyn**, 5–6 **blek**. *Pa. t.* 6 *Sc.* **blekkit**. [App. f. *blek* BLECK *sb.*: but cf. the parallel BLETCH *v.*, of which this may be the northern form, going back to an OE. **blęccan*:—OTeut. **blakjan*, f. **blako-* BLACK.]

1. *trans.* To make black; *esp.* to blacken with ink, soot, tar, or the like. Still in *north. dial.*

1382 WYCLIF *Job* xxx. 30 My skin is bleckid up on me. *c* **1440** *Promp. Parv.* 39 Blekkyn wythe bleke [**1499** blackyn with blecke], *atramento*. **1570** LEVINS *Manip.* 47 To blecke, bletch, *nigrare*. **1646** ROW *Hist. Kirk* (1842) 440 It was his comfort on his death-bed that he never blecked nor disfigured the well-favoured face of the Kirk of Scotland. *Mod. Sc.* How hae ye blekkit yeir face?

2. To enter or inscribe with ink; to write.

c **1460** *Towneley Myst.* 311 Thus told I youre tax, thus ar my bokys blekyt. *c* **1570** *Leg. Bp. St. Andrews* in *Scot. Poems 16th C.* II. 340 Not all the paper of this towne, And blek[k]it baith vnder and abone, May had the half that he hes done.

3. *fig.* To blacken morally, to make or declare guilty; to defile. (Still *dial.*)

c **1380** WYCLIF *Sel. Wks.* III. 211 Boþe partis ben bleckid with þis synne. **1535** STEWART *Cron. Scot.* II. 715 Quhither or nocht he wes thairof to blek. **1552** ABP. HAMILTON *Catech.* (1884) 139 Syn..that fylis and blekkis our saulis.

¶**4.** Here perhaps representing ON. *blekkja* 'to impose upon, deceive,' = OE. *blęncan* to BLENCH.

1573 *Sege Edinb. Cast.* in *Scot. Poems 16th C.* II. 307 Sen ye are wairned, I wald not ye were blekkit.

†ˈ**bleckert.** *Obs.* [Evidently containing BLECK *sb.*: cf. *bleck-fatt, bleck-pot.*]

1562 *Richmond. Wills* (1853) 152 A bleckert vjs. viijd. iij coldrons and a kettill xxxiijs. iiijd. **1588** *Inv. T. Atkinson, Kendal*, Itm a bleckart iiijs.

bled (blɛd), *ppl. a.* [f. BLEED *v.*] **1.** Drained of blood or sap.

1894 *Pop. Sci. Monthly* June 284 A series of tests and examinations of bled and unbled timber has been carried on.

2. Of a page, illustration, etc.: see BLEED *v.* 13.

1940 GRAVES & HODGE *Long Week-end* xxv. 434 'Bled' photographs..printed to cover the whole of the page, without a margin. **1942** H. A. MADDOX *Dict. Stationery* 15 Bled-off pictures cause a larger size of paper to be used to accommodate the protruding blocks. **1959** *Camb. Rev.* 21 Nov. 187/2 Its front cover is..a 'bled on' photograph of Great St. Mary's.

‖**bled** (blɛd), *sb.* [Fr., f. colloq. Arab. *bled*, representing (depending on context) *balad* vast stretch of country or *bilād* land, country.] In parts of North Africa formerly under French rule: an uncultivated wasteland; the hinterland behind a fertile, populated area. Also, in extended use: a rolling plain or other open stretch of land.

[**1927** H. MCLAURIN *What about N. Afr.?* xxxiii. 282 This part of the country called the *Bled El Djerid*, or 'land of dates', was known to the Romans.] **1930** H. L. FOSTER *Vagabond in Barbary* iii. 21 This *bled*, or rolling prairie, was not the wasteland it appeared to be. **1946** G. MILLAR *Horned Pigeon* xx. 337 It's the *bled* all right. A wilderness of rain and mud and discomfort. **1960** *Times* 23 Feb. 10/6 As a result of these pressures, the *bled* is now dotted with camps. **1971** F. FORSYTH *Day of Jackal* I. i. 20 When he got his lieutenant-colonelcy Marc Rodin moved out of the bled and into the cities. **1985** S. STEVENS *Anvil Chorus* ii. 31 Laffage had led much of the early secret war against the FLN, first in the Algerian *bled* and later in the cities.

bled, bledd(e, blede: see BLEED.

bledder(e, obs. form of BLADDER *sb.*

†**blede.** *Obs.* [OE. *blóed, bléd* (*blǽd*) str. fem. 'flower, blossom, fruit' = OHG. *bluot*, MHG. *bluot* pl. *blüete*, Ger. *blüte*:—OTeut. **blôdi-z* fem. root *blō̆-* in BLOW, BLOOM, etc.; cogn. with OIr. *blá-th*, L. *flō-s.*] A flower, blossom; fruit.

c **975** *Rushw. Gosp.* Matt. vii. 17 Yfel þonne treow yfle westmas *vel* blæd bereþ. *c* **1000** *Sax. Leechd.* II. 228 ȝenim þreo croppan laures bleda. *c* **1205** LAY. 28832 þa bleden [*c* **1250** bledes] uorð comen. *a* **1250** *Owl & Night.* 1042 He is wod þat soweþ his sed þar never gras ne springþ ne bled. *a* **1300** *Hymn Virg.* in *Trin. Coll. Hom.* 256 Of þe sprong þeô edi blede þe holi gost hire on þe seuȝ.

bledsed, -sung, obs. forms of BLESSED, -ING.

blee (bliː). *arch.* Forms: 1 blío, blíoh, bléo(h, 1–4 bleo, (3 blo), 3–9 ble, 4–7, 9 blee, (6 bleye). [OE. *bléo* (*bléoh*, after *féoh*) str. neut. = OS. *blî*, OFris. *blî, blie*, north.Fris. *bläy*:—OTeut. **blîjo-*(*m* colour, hue. (Not connected with BLAE, BLUE.) A purely poetical word in ME., which gradually became obs. in the course of the 16th or early in the 17th c. (not in Shakspere); but being frequent in ballads and metrical romances, it has been used by one or two modern poets. Cf. dial. BLY, thought by some to be a survival of *ble.*]

1. Colour, hue. *arch.*

c **888** K. ÆLFRED *Boeth.* xv, Ne seolocenra hræȝla mid mistlicum bleowum hi ne ȝimdon. *a* **1000** *Metr. Boeth.* xxxi. 7 Habbað blioh and fær bu ungelice. *c* **1000** ÆLFRIC *Numb.* xi. 7 Hwites bleos swa cristalla. *c* **1250** *Gen. & Ex.* 749 A water of loðlic ble. *c* **1325** *E.E. Allit. P.* A. 76 As blwe as ble of ynde. **1460** *Lybeaus Disc.* 458 In armes bryght of ble. **1623** LISLE *Ælfric on O. & N.T.* Ded. 9 Greene, Red, Yellow, Blew, Of sundry blee; more sad, or light, in graine. **1850** MRS. BROWNING *Poems* II. 57 The captain, young Lord Leigh, with his eyes so grey of blee.

2. Colour of the face, complexion; visage. *arch.*

a **1225** *St. Marher.* 9 Hire bleo bigon to blakien. *c* **1240** *Wohunge* 269 ȝif hit to þi blisfule bleo mihte beo euenet. *c* **1325** *E.E. Allit. P.* A. 212 Her ble more blaȝt þen whallezbon. *c* **1440** *York Myst.* xxviii. 259, I will no more be abasshed For blenke of thy blee. *a* **1500** (*MS. 16th c.*) *Chester Pl.* II. 187 Wher is my bleye that was so brighte? **1557** *Tottell's Misc.* (Arb.) 100 Who nothing loues in woman, but her blee. **1615** T. ADAMS *Spirit. Navig.* 42 Of a fresher blee than Daniel. ?*a* **1700** *Lovers' Quarrel* 2 in Hazl. *E.P.P.* II. 253 Ladies that been so bright of blee. **1834** *Blackw. Mag.* XXXV. 715 His daughter bright of blee.

†**3.** *transf.* Appearance, form. *Obs.*

a **1000** *Salomon & Sat.* (1848) 144 Hu moniȝes bleos bið ðæt deofol. *c* **1330** *Arth. & Merl.* 1988 Where that Merlin dede him se In o day in thre ble.

bleea, -berry, dial. var. of BLAE, -BERRY.

bleeaunt, variant of BLEAUNT, *Obs.*, a tunic.

bleeche, -er, etc., obs. forms of BLEACH, -ER.

bleed (bliːd), *v.* Pa. t. and pple. bled. Forms: 1 blédan, 3–5 blede (6 *Sc.* bleid, blead, bleth), 7 bleede, 6– bleed. *Pa. t.* 1 blédde, 2–5 bledde, 3 blede, 3–5 bledd, 7 bleeded, 3– bled. *Pa. pple.* 1–4 bléded, 7–8 bleeded, 5– bled. [OE. *blédan*:—OTeut. **blôdjan* to bleed (whence also ON. *blǽða*, mod.G. *bluten*), f. OTeut. **blôdo*(*m* BLOOD.]

I. *intr.*

1. a. To emit, discharge, or 'lose' blood; to drop, or run with, blood. Said of a person or animal, a part of the body, a wound, etc.

a **1000** *Salomon & Sat.* 144 Blédaþ ædran. *c* **1205** LAY. 7523 þat hæfed [hæfde, **1250** heued] bledde. *c* **1300** *K. Alisaunder* 5845 His woundes bledden. **1460** CAPGRAVE *Chron.* (1858) 162 Thei..founde the Prince bledying, and the Sarasine ded. **1596** SHAKS. *Merch. V.* IV. i. 258 To stop his wounds, least he should bleede to death. **1607** DEKKER *Wh. Babylon* Wks. 1873 II. 264 They are no common droppes when Princes bleede. **1658** A. FOX *Wurtz' Surg.* v. 353 The wound bleeded vehemently. **1715** BURNET *Own Time* (1766) II. 217 He fell a bleeding at the nose. **1828** SCOTT *Tales Grandf.* Ser. II. xxxvii. 153/1 Bleeding to death from the loss of his right hand.

b. The body of a murdered man was supposed to bleed afresh when the murderer approached, and thus to reveal his guilt: hence, of a crime: *to bleed* = to come to light (*obs.*).

[**1591** *Murder Ld. Bourgh* (Collier) 10 Wherunto he was no sooner approched..but his wounds bled more freshlie then when they were first giuen; whereby the people in the house..made foorth to search, for sure lie they supposed the murtherer was not farre off. **1628** EARLE *Microcosm.* v. 13 His fear is, lest the carkass should bleed.] *c* **1645** HOWELL *Lett.* (1650) I. 31 The murdering of her Marquis of Ancre will yet bleed, as some fear.

c. ***the heart bleeds***, used *fig.* to express great anguish, sorrow, or pity. So ***to bleed inwardly.***

c **1374** CHAUCER *Troylus* IV. Prol. 12 For whiche myn herte now right gynneth to blede. **1607** SHAKS. *Timon* I. ii. 211, I bleed inwardly for my Lord. **1610** —— *Temp.* I. ii. 63 O my heart bleedes To thinke oth' teene that I haue turn'd you to. **1792** BURKE *Corr.* (1844) IV. 24 My heart bleeds for the poor emigrants, whose case is truly deplorable. **1860** KINGSLEY *Misc.* II. 349 What heart would not bleed for a beautiful woman in trouble.

2. a. To lose blood from severe or fatal wounds; to be severely wounded in battle, or the like; to shed one's blood or die by bloodshed.

a **1300** *Havelok* 2403 Crist þat wolde on rode blede. **1377** LANGL. *P. Pl.* B. XIX. 103 So comsed ihesu, Tyl he had alle hem þat he fore bledde. *a* **1400** *Sir Isumb.* 621 Wel a sevene score garte he blede. *c* **1400** *Destr. Troy* 14044 He..þat bled for our Syn. **1601** SHAKS. *Jul. C.* II. i. 171 Cæsar must bleed for it. **1732** POPE *Ess. Man* I. 81 The Lamb thy riot dooms to bleed to day. **1787** J. BARLOW *Oration 4th July* 10 Those who bled in so glorious a field. **1839** THIRLWALL *Greece* II. 349 Those who had fought and bled in the cause.

fig. **1665** PEPYS *Diary* 1 Apr., The King's service in the meantime lies a-bleeding.

b. *transf.* Of a dye: to 'run' or become diffused when wetted.

1862 C. O'NEILL *Dict. Cal. Printing & Dyeing* 34/1 Woollen articles [are] worked in it until saturated with colour, then washed well..until the colour begins to 'bleed', that is until the washing water begins to remove the blue and become tinged with it. **1893** E. KNECHT et al. *Man. Dyeing* 724 Fastness to washing and to bleeding or running should be determined with water alone and with soap. *Ibid.* 725 Most of the direct cotton colours bleed very much when dyed on cotton.

c. 'To leak; especially, to leak an iron-stained liquid, as the seams of a boiler' (*Funk's Standard Dict.* 1893).

1888 *Lockwood's Dict. Terms Mech. Engin.*, *Bleeding*, the red streaks of rust which weep through the scale adherent to the insides of boilers, and which reveal the presence of corrosion in the plates underneath.

3. Of plants: To emit sap when wounded.

1674 GREW *Anat. Trunks* II. i. §12 The Trunk or Branch of any Plant being cut, it always bleeds at both ends. *a* **1711** KEN *Blondina* Wks. 1721 IV. 526 The Trees..When in their Stems a wound is made, In od'rous Balsam bleed away. **1796** C. MARSHALL *Gardening* xii. (1813) 160 Cutting branches or shoots in summer is apt to make them bleed as it is called. **1874** *Rep. Vermont Board Agric.* II. 289 If pruned later the trees will often 'bleed', though it is stated that a perfectly healthy tree will not bleed if pruned at any season. **1965** BELL & COOMBE tr. *Strasburger's Textbk. Bot.* II. 237 Many plants bleed only in the spring and at a certain stage of development, in others bleeding can occur at almost any time.

†**4.** 'To lose blood medicinally' (J.). *Obs.* (now, *To be bled.*)

1625 HART *Anat. Ur.* II. iv. 73, I caused him bleed oftner then once. **1697** J. D. in Tutchin *Search Honesty* A ij, Goe Bleed, use Hellebore, and shave thy head.

5. *fig.* **a.** Of corn, etc. ***to bleed well***: to give a large yield. *dial.*

1641 BEST *Farm. Bks.* (1856) 143 Att such times when corne bleedes not well. **1691** RAY *N.C. Wds.* 8 Corn Bleeds well; when upon threshing it yields well. **1786** *Har'st Rig* in Chambers *Pop. Sc. Poets* 51 It should bleed weel, and mak prime food Frae 'neath the flails. **1808** in JAMIESON.

b. Of persons: To lose or part with money to an extent that is felt; to have money drawn or extorted; to 'pay through the nose' *for. colloq.*

1668 DRYDEN *Even. Love* IV. i, He is vehement, and bleeds on to fourscore or an hundred. **1680** COTTON in Singer *Hist. Cards* 337 They will purposely lose some small sum at first, that they may engage him the more freely to bleed (as they call it). **1751** SMOLLETT *Per. Pic.* lxvi, To whom he was particularly agreeable, on account of his..bleeding freely at play. **1848** THACKERAY *Van. Fair* xiv, A City man, immensely rich, they say. Hang those City fellows, they must bleed. **1885** *Manchest. Even. News* 23 June 2/2 Men who give bills have to bleed for the accommodation.

6. a. Said of blood, etc.: To drop, flow, ooze forth.

c **1305** *Song Mercy* in *E.E.P.* (1862) 120 Myn herte blood for þe gan blede. **1713** POPE *Windsor For.* 393 For me the balm shall bleed, and amber flow.

b. with *away, into*: To pass by bleeding.

1595 SHAKS. *John* V. iv. 24 Retaining but a quantity of life, Which bleeds away, euen as a forme of waxe Resolueth from his figure 'gainst the fire. **1650** FULLER *Pisgah* 401 This wound, whence so much precious wealth did bleed forth. **1865** BUSHNELL *Vicar. Sacr.* IV. ii. 517 If the good that is in him will get into men's bosoms, it must bleed into them.

7. a. With cognate obj.: To emit as blood.

a **1300** *Cursor M.* 16775 For þe mikel blod he bled. **1377** LANGL. *P. Pl.* B. XIX. 320 Of his blode þat he bledde on Rode. **1483** CAXTON *Gold. Leg.* 233/3 Hys hede was al to brused and bledde moche blood. **1697** DRYDEN *Virg. Georg.* III. 759 Roapy Gore, he from his Nostrils bleeds.

b. *transf.* of other liquids.

1611 SHAKS. *Wint. T.* V. ii. 96 Shee did (with an Alas) I would faine say, bleed Teares; for I am sure, my heart wept blood. **1667** MILTON *P.L.* VI. 331 Nectarous humour..such as Celestial Spirits may bleed. **1763** CHURCHILL *Proph. Famine* Poems I. 119 And the grape bleed a nectar yet unknown. **1850** B. TAYLOR *On Leav. Californ.* (1866) 273 Thy tawny hills shall bleed their purple wine.

8. *fig.* To appear bleeding, to be as red as blood.

1833 BROWNING *Pauline* 17 Her..lips which bleed Like a mountain berry.

II. *trans.*

9. To draw or let blood from, *esp.* surgically.

c **1430** *Syr Tryam.* 686 For at the justyng wolde y bene.. My body for to blede. *c* **1500** *Spirit. Remed.* in Halliw. *Nugæ P.* 67 For us thou letteste thy breste be bled. **1674** R. GODFREY *Inj. & Ab. Physic* 102 Her Husband was Bleeded by an Apothecaries order. **1737** POPE *Hor. Epist.* II. ii. 197 That, from a patriot..Have bled and purg'd me to a simple vote. **1804** ABERNETHY *Surg. Observ.* 177 As he was perfectly well he was but slightly bled.

10. To draw or extort money from. ***to bleed white***: see WHITE *a.* 5 b. *colloq.* Cf. 5 b.

1680 COTTON in Singer *Hist. Cards* 343 When they intend to bleed a coll to some purpose..they always fix half a score packs of cards before. **1849** THACKERAY *Pendennis* lxviii, By Jove, sir, you've bled that poor woman enough.

11. Naut. ***to bleed the buoys***: to let the water out.

1833 MARRYAT *P. Simple* vi, 'And, Mr. Chucks, recollect this afternoon that you bleed all the buoys.' Bleed the boys! thought I, what can that be for?

†**12.** To make bloody, to smear with blood.

1634 *Malory's Arthur* (1816) I. 309 Sir Tristram he bled both the upper sheet, and the nether sheet, and pillows.

13. *Bookbinding* and *Printing.* To cut into the print of (a book) in trimming the margin; to print (an illustration) so that it reaches beyond the normal margin to the edge of the page. Also *intr.* (see quots.). So ***to bleed off*** or ***on.***

1835 'J. A. ARNETT' *Bibliopegia* 203 A work is said to bleed, if cut into the print. **1876** *Daily Tel.* 9 June 2/1 (Farmer), The pages bleed in many places—*i.e.* the binder's knife when cutting the edges has also cut away portions of the printed matter. *a* **1877** KNIGHT *Dict. Mech.* I. 297/2 *Bleeding*, cutting into the printed matter of a book when cutting the edges. **1917** GRESS *Typography* (ed. 2) 126 This plate can then be printed in color on gummed paper and the paper trimmed so as to 'bleed' the edges of the printed background. **1942** H. A. MADDOX *Dict. Stationery* 14 If a guillotine operator slightly cuts into the type of a printed forme when trimming the edges, he is said to have bled the edges. The term Bleed-off is a modern adaptation applied to the style of..magazine pages in which illustrations are actually run right off the edge of the paper. The term employed by some printers is..'cut to bleed'. **1948** *Words into Type* (*Appleton-Century-Crofts Inc., N.Y.*) 533 Printing is said to bleed when the margins are overcut in trimming and the printing mutilated. **1962** *Listener* 26 July 142/3 It looks brilliant to place a detail from one Cézanne beneath the whole of another and to make the detail 'bleed' off.

14. To allow (liquid) to drain away or (gas) to escape through a cock, valve, or the like. Also with *off.* Cf. BLEEDING *vbl. sb.* 3.

1889 *Cent. Dict.* s.v., *To bleed the brakes*, in a locomotive, to relieve the pressure on the air-brakes by opening the bleeding-valve or release-cock of the brake-cylinder. **1959** *Motor Manual* (ed. 36) iii. 61 A very rich mixture of fuel, and a little air bled in by the air bleed at the top of the well. **1962** A. SHEPARD in *Into Orbit* 104 The technicians found they were able to bleed off the excess pressure by turning some of the valves by remote control. **1962** *Which? Car Suppl.* Oct. 138/1 The sponginess of the brake system could not be entirely overcome by bleeding the hydraulic system.

bleed, *sb.* [f. the vb.] **1.** = BLEEDING *vbl. sb.* 1 a.

a **1585** A. MONTGOMERY *Flyting between Montgomerie & Polwart* 309 The bleid[s] and bellithrow. **1852–6, 1890** [see NOSE-BLEED 2] . **1922** T. HARDY *Late Lyrics* 26 The silent bleed of a world decaying.

2. The action of BLEED *v.* 13; a page or illustration that is printed or trimmed so as to leave no margin. Also *attrib.*

1939 in WEBSTER Add. **1948** *Words into Type* (*Appleton-Century-Crofts Inc., N.Y.*) 533 Illustrations which extend to the edges of the page when printed are called bleed cuts. **1967** KARCH & BUBER *Offset Processes* 531 *Bleed*, a printed image area, an illustration, extending beyond any one or more edges of a sheet.

3. = BLEEDING *vbl. sb.* 3; also, the cock, valve, or the like through which bleeding occurs. Freq. *attrib.* So *bleed-off.*

1949 *Gloss. Aeronaut. Terms* (*B.S.I.*) II. 21 *Bleed*, to eliminate air from a hydraulic system; e.g., by undoing bleed screws. **1958** *Times Rev. Industry* July 26/1 The..range comprises turbo-jet, air-bleed, free turbine, and shaft-drive units. **1959** [see BLEED *v.* 14]. **1962** *New Scientist* 19 July 139

An opacity-measuring instrument..controls a continuous bleed-off of dirty water.

bleeder ('bliːdə(r)). [f. BLEED *v.* + -ER[1].]

1. a. One who draws blood.

1788 H. WATSON in *Med. Commun.* II. 276 These accidents..seldom hurt the reputation of the bleeder. **1823** LAMB *Elia* (1860) 226 Submits to the scythe of the gentle bleeder Time. **1848** THACKERAY *Van. Fair* lxi, The bleeders and cuppers came.

b. One who extorts money. *U.S.*

1846 *Swell's Night Guide* 114/1 *Bleeder*, a sponger. **1894** *Columbus* (Ohio) *Dispatch* 5 Oct. The police of New York were not the only bleeders.

2. *Med.* A person subject to hæmophilia, i.e. disposed by natural constitution to bleed.

1803 OTTO *Med. Repos.* VI. 3 Some persons..suppose they can distinguish the bleeders..even in infancy. **1884** *Brit. Med. Jrnl.* in *Standard* 4 Apr. 3/5 Free blood in the knee-joints of a bleeder.

3. *low slang.* A very stupid, unpleasant, or contemptible person; also *transf.*; also used inoffensively, preceded by *little*, *poor*, etc., = DEVIL *sb.* 4 c.

1887 *Sessions Paper* 26 Apr. 16 Look out, Carry; don't let the bleeder take me. **1889** BARRÈRE & LELAND *Dict. Slang* 134/2 (University), a 'regular *bleeder*' signifies a superlative duffer. **1902** J. H. M. ABBOTT *T. Cornstalk* xi. 188 'Bleeder'..seemed to be a pet name for a typical low-class Londoner—a slum-dragger. **1913** D. H. LAWRENCE *Sons & Lovers* xiii. 343 'What'll you have?'..'Nowt wi' a bleeder like you!' **1936** J. CURTIS *Gilt Kid* xxiv. 241 Give me the damn groin, you robbing bleeder. **1938** L. MACNEICE *Earth Compels* 59 His brother caught three hundred cran... Threw the bleeders back in the sea. **1952** A. BARON *With Hope, Farewell* 44 She'll kill the poor little bleeder.

4. a. A pipe, valve, or the like used for 'bleeding' (see BLEEDING *vbl. sb.* 3). Also *attrib.*

1893 *Funk's Stand. Dict.*, *Bleeder*..a pipe fitted on engines by which steam may be passed directly from the main steam-pipe to the condenser. Called also *bleeder-pipe*. **1910** *Hawkins's Electr. Dict.* 38/2 *Bleeder*, a small cock or valve to draw off water of condensation from a range of piping.

b. *Electr.* A resistor, permanently connected across a voltage source to improve voltage regulation. In full, ***bleeder resistance*** or ***resistor***. Also *attrib.*

1935 NILSON & HORNUNG *Pract. Radio Communication* xiii. 609 The value of the bleeder resistance in transmitting circuits depends on conditions in the circuit. A value of bleeder current equal to 25 or 30 per cent of the total drain on the rectifier unit is used in many installations. **1953** *Electronic Engin.* XXV. 202/1 The voltage across a small part of a..bleeder resistor.

bleeding ('bliːdɪŋ), *vbl. sb.* [f. BLEED + -ING[1].]

1. a. The flowing or dropping of blood (from a wound, etc.); hæmorrhage.

c **1385** CHAUCER *L.G.W.* 849 Thou shalt feele as well the blood of me As thou hast felt the bleding of Tisbe. **1398** TREVISA *Barth. De P.R.* XVII. cxxxvi. (1495) 693 Powder of drye roses staunchyth bledynge at the nose. **1617** HIERON *Wks.* II. 309 Bleeding of the person slaine, at the presence of the murtherer. **1828** SCOTT *F.M. Perth* (1860) Pref. 15 He ..applied some lint to stop the bleeding.

b. Of plants: The emission of sap (from a wound). Also *attrib.*, as in ***bleeding-season***.

1674 GREW *Anat. Trunks.* II. i. §8 The Bleeding of Plants ..properly enough expresses, The eruption of the Sap out of any Vessels. **1712** tr. *Pomet's Hist. Drugs* I. 161 The Bleeding of the Vine. **1882** VINES *Sachs' Bot.* 677 The phenomenon known as the 'bleeding' of wood cut in the winter.

2. Drawing or 'letting' of blood. Also *attrib.*, as ***bleeding-bowl*** (see quot. 1916), ***-knife***.

c **1440** *Promp. Parv.* 38 Bledynge, *sanguinacio*, *fleobotomia*. *Ibid.* 39 Bledynge yryn, *fleobotomium*. **1541** R. COPLAND *Guydon's Quest. Chirurg.* Mj, What is bledyng or blode lettynge. **1670** COTTON *Espernon* III. XII. 647 His Physician resolv'd upon a Bleeding. *c* **1783** W. STARK in *Med. Commun.* I. 383 Bleeding is the appropriated remedy for a cough. **1837** HOGG *Ettr. Shep. Tales* III. 35 The butcher came up with his bleeding-knife. **1911** C. J. JACKSON *Hist. Eng. Plate* I. I. ix. 264 Surgeon's bleeding-bowl, with pierced handle. **1916** *Connoisseur* Dec. 229/2 The so-called Bleeding Bowl, or Cupping Dish... Such bowls were used by surgeons when bleeding their patients.

fig. **1796** SOUTHEY *Lett. Spain & Port.* 427 This bleeding is more dreadful, because the Holy Office is the bleeder. **1850** ALISON *Hist. Europe* II. viii. §54 In the language of the times..a new bleeding was required for the state.

3. The draining of liquid, gas, etc., through a cock, valve, or the like (see BLEED *v.* 14). Also *attrib.*

1889 [see BLEED *v.* 14]. **1928** *Daily Tel.* 17 Jan. 5 Where turbine 'bleeding' is resorted to for feed heating. **1959** *Engineering* 2 Jan. 26/3 The bleeding of air from the compressor to cool the blades. *Ibid.* 27 Feb. 263/3 The hydraulic system is..provided with bleeding screws to allow the escape of air enclosures.

4. a. Of a dye: see BLEED *v.* 2 b.

1893 [see BLEED *v.* 2 b]. **1959** *Which?* Oct. 129/2 The washed samples [of carpet] were then examined for any changes in colour and in particular for any bleeding of colours in the patterned sample.

b. The penetration of a coat of paint or the like by colour or other substance from an underlying surface.

1888 [see BLEED *v.* 2 c]. **1926** *Paint, Oil & Chem. Rev.* 25 Nov. 14/1 *Bleeding*, a defect of pigments by which they slowly soak into or penetrate an overlying coat, or the dissolving of a pigment in the vehicle. **1951** R. MAYER *Artist's Hand-Bk.* ii. 91 An obstacle in the way of the adoption of coal tar colours of really superior permanence to light, is that most of them have the property of bleeding or striking through when used with oil or oily mediums.

c. (See quots.)

1914 H. P. BOULNOIS *Gloss. Road Terms* 14 *Bleeding*, the exudation of pitch or bitumen from the road surface or from the prepared material. **1954** *Highway Engin. Terms* (*B.S.I.*) 30 *Bleeding*, a road condition in which free binder exudes in liquid form from the surface of a bituminous..road in hot weather. *Ibid.* 36 *Bleeding*, the formation of a thin layer of water on the exposed surface of concrete during the finishing processes.

bleeding, *ppl. a.* [f. BLEED + -ING[2].]

1. a. Losing or emitting blood, or *transf.* sap.

a **1225** *Ancr. R.* 118 Bledinde mon is grislich. **1398** TREVISA *Barth. De P.R.* V. xxii. (1495) 129 A bledynge wounde. **1703** ROWE *Ulysses* IV. i. 1706 That poor bleeding King. **1787** WINTER *Syst. Husb.* 45 Thistles..cut close to the ground, are destroyed by scattering soaper's ashes over the bleeding stumps.

b. Running or suffused with blood.

c **1305** *Leg. Rood* (1871) 133 Bounden . in bledyng bondes. **1595** SHAKS. *John* II. i. 304 Whose sonnes lye scattered on the bleeding ground.

2. *fig.* **a.** Full of anguish from suffering, deep pity, or compassion.

1596 SPENSER *F.Q.* I. vii. 38 These bleeding words she gan to say. **1597** HOOKER *Eccl. Pol.* V. xlii. §2 With bleeding hearts. **1628** FELTHAM *Resolves* I. lxi. (1647) 189 Calamities that challenge a bleeding eye. **1687** N. N. *Old Popery*, Compassionate and Bleeding Thoughts. **1713** *Guardian* No. 31 (1756) I. 134 All those good-natured offices that could have been expected from the most bleeding pity.

b. *metaphor. Obs.*

1597 SHAKS. *Lover's Compl.* 153 Experience for me many bulwarkes builded Of proofs new bleeding. *a* **1674** CLARENDON *Hist. Reb.* I. v. 387 Cruelty..of which they every day received fresh and bleeding evidence.

3. *fig.* and *transf.* Said of nations devastated by war or the like, etc. Also, as in BLEED 5 b.

1668 DRYDEN *Even. Love* IV. i, This is the Folly of a bleeding Gamester. *a* **1674** CLARENDON *Hist. Reb.* I. v. 537 The relief of bleeding and miserable Ireland. **1689** LUTTRELL *Brief Rel.* (1857) I. 503 The bleeding condition of Ireland. **1863** MARY HOWITT tr. *F. Bremer's Greece* I. i. 9 Greece herself, bleeding and exhausted after her efforts in the War of Liberation.

4. quasi-*adv.* (Cf. 2 b.)

1607 SHAKS. *Timon* I. ii. 80 So they were bleeding new my Lord, there's no meet like 'em.

5. *Comb.* **bleeding heart**, (*a*) the popular name for several plants; *e.g.* the Wallflower (*Cheiranthus Cheiri*), the *Aristotelia peduncularis*, *Colocasia esculenta* of the Sandwich Islands, *Dicentra formosa*, and a variety of Cherry (Miller); (*b*) *fig.* an excessively soft-hearted or sympathetic person (*colloq.*); also *attrib.*; **bleeding root** = BLOOD-ROOT; **bleeding tooth**, the shell of a gastropod mollusc, *Nerita peloronta*, which has a red mark on the columella tooth.

1691 EVELYN *Kal. Hort.* (ed. 8) 171 Cherries... Bleeding Heart. **1803** [see HEART *sb.* 30]. **1825** BRITTON *Beauties of Wilts.* III. 371 *Bleeding-heart*, the wall-flower. **1887** *Cent. Mag.* July 325 The white-hearts (related to the bleeding-hearts of the gardens, and absurdly called 'Dutchman's breeches'). **1916** D. H. LAWRENCE *Amores* 130 The tender, mild Flowers of the bleeding-heart. **1958** J. BINGHAM *Murder Plan Six* iii. 74 You want to think straight, Victor. You want to control this bleeding-heart trouble of yours. **1960** 'I. T. Ross' *Murder out of School* vi. 68 A lot of bleeding-hearts got the idea they knew about everything. **1714** *Phil. Trans.* XXIX. 64 The root call'd the Bleeding Root, curing the Jaundies. **1863** PRIOR *Plant-n.* 24. **1881** *Jrnl. Conchology* III. 165, I did not find the 'Bleeding Tooth' very common at Key West. **1954** R. T. ABBOTT *Amer. Seashells* 128 *Nerita peloronta* Linné. Bleeding Tooth. Southeast Florida, Bermuda and the West Indies.

6. A substitute for BLOODY *a.* 10 (and *adv.* 2). *low slang.*

1858 FURNIVALL in *Athenæum* 24 July 118 Costermongers have lately substituted the participle 'bleeding' for the adjective ['bloody']. 'My bleeding barrow' is the latest phrase in vogue. **1876** BESANT & RICE *Son of Vulcan* II. xxiii, When he isn't up to one dodge he is up to another. You make no bleeding error. **1884** *Sessions Paper* 8 Jan. 325 If you don't bleeding well let me go. **1896** A. MORRISON *Child of Jago* i. 4 This is a bleed'n' unsocial sort o' evenin' party. **1922** [see BLIMEY *int.*]. **1967** *Times* 17 Nov. 8/4 Why don't you bleeding do something about it? *Ibid.*, He wants to take bleeding care that light duty work is continuous.

bleȝ, obs. pa. t. of BLOW *v.*[1]

bleep (bliːp), *sb.* [Echoic.] **1. a.** A thin, high-pitched blipping sound, *spec.* one made by electronic equipment.

1953 *N.Y. Herald-Tribune* 2 Aug. II. 5 The bleeps of Geiger counters make 'penny stocks' on the country's exchanges palpitate into investors' bonanzas. **1957** *Daily Mail* 7 Oct. 1/1 From now on we shall be living in a different world, for science 'fiction' has become fact. Those eerie 'bleeps' from outer space tell us that. *Ibid.* 1/2 Instead of the quick bleep-bleep sound it [*sc.* the Russian earth satellite] made on the first 24 hours of its journey, New York radio stations reported a long, continuous B-L-E-E-P as it crossed the United States. **1958** *Times* 29 July 10/7 The driver honked his horn. 'Bleep, bo-o-oop, parp.' **1966** *New Scientist* 497/2 The slow pattern of bleeps from the loudspeaker..suddenly changes.

b. The sound made by a bleeper or paging device; a radio signal used to communicate with someone carrying a bleeper. **c.** = BLEEPER.

1975 *Courier-Mail* (Brisbane) 22 Apr. 1/7 If a Member is required urgently a switchboard operator will give him..a 'bleep' and relay any messages. **1982** *Sci. Amer.* Nov. 11 Thanks to the national radio paging system, a doctor can be alerted to an emergency by a 'bleep', carried about his person. **1985** *Medical Woman* Spring 15 We share a bleep. **1986** *Daily Tel.* 19 May 26/8 A bleep to a maintenance man working away from his van..can provide the signal to call base via PMR.

2. a. A bleeping sound edited over and replacing a taboo-word or undesirable expression used during a recorded interview, etc. Cf. BLIP *sb.* **b.** The word (written or spoken) used to replace such an expression.

1968 *Life* 12 Apr. 18/4 The Rowan and Martin staff, they say, is so free-wheeling that a fulltime censor has been assigned... Over in Smothersville, similar ballyhoo is made over every insignificant bleep. **1975** *Pix* (Austral.) 27 Nov. 2/2, I fail to see why bleeps are used in radio and television interviews to cover up 'unsavoury' words and expressions. As soon as the bleep is heard the listeners immediately think —Oh, a four-letter word. **1978** *Detroit Free Press* 5 Mar. B10/3, I..stand up there with my coffee or cola or ginger ale and (bleep) away on an emotional high. His talk is full of idiom requiring bleeps for family readers. **1978** *Rugby World* Apr. 36/2 When that particular sequence.. eventually appeared on BBC 2.., it miraculously contained only two bleeps. **1981** *Gossip* (Holiday Special) 50/3 I've never believed off-Broadway and that kind of theatre is only for friends and 'we're better than the others' stuff. I've always believed it is great horse (bleep). **1983** *N.Y. Times* 22 May II. 1/1 It looks like the same old (bleep) to me. **1984** *Ibid.* 8 Jan. 2A 3/1 On Tuesday night at 8, ABC will present 'Foul Ups, Bleeps and Blunders'.

bleep, *v.* [f. the sb.] **1.** *intr.* To make a thin, high-pitched blipping sound or 'bleep'.

1957 *Times* 11 Oct. 11/6 There is a Soviet satellite bleeping round the earth. **1958** *Daily Mail* 15 Aug. 2/5 Every dinghy was fitted with a radio which bleeps out S O S at the touch of a simple switch.

2. *trans.* To replace (a taboo expression used in a recorded interview, etc.) with a bleep; to censor. Freq. with *out*.

[**1968** *N.Y. Times* 29 Apr. 86 Some of his nightly quips are 'blipped' from tape before air time.] **1973** *Houston* (Texas) *Chron. Texas Mag.* 14 Oct. 2/3 It offends me to have to 'bleep' most of it, because that detracts from our goal of telling it like it is. **1976** *TV Times* (Brisbane) 12 June 13/3 Unfortunately..somebody forgot to bleep the words out. **1981** *Daily Tel.* 24 Sept. 19/3 One swearword..would be muted... Four others would be 'bleeped'. **1983** *Financial Times* 7 Apr. 11/2 Radio stations broadcasting Parliament should use a panic button to bleep out defamatory comments in live broadcasts.

3. a. To summon or alert (someone carrying a bleeper), to 'page'.

1976 *Telegraph* (Brisbane) 14 Feb. 2/6 The Federal Government is to spend more than $60,000 so that Members of Parliament can be 'bleeped' to notify them of telephone calls when they are out of their offices. **1980** *Daily Tel.* 9 Apr. 19/5 People carrying them [*sc.* bleepers] can be 'bleeped' by dialling a ten-figure number. **1983** *Listener* 4 Aug. 34/3 It will even bleep the investor strolling round the golf course.

b. To transmit (information) by electronic means, esp. between computer terminals. Of an electronic device: to signal (a message).

1978 *Washington Post* 5 Mar. M3 That is the increasingly clear message being bleeped to major U.S. companies. **1983** *Ibid.* 16 June A18/3 At the wheel was a black Memphis businessman, his 'fuzzbuster' radar speed trap detector bleeping caution.

Hence **'bleeping** *ppl. a.*, that bleeps; also (*slang*) = BLEEDING *ppl. a.*; also as *vbl. sb.*; **bleeped** (bliːpt) *ppl. a.*, alerted by bleeper.

1957 *Observer* 13 Oct. 12/3 The suggestion has been that most of the weight comes from batteries to power the bleeping radio transmitters. **1966** *New Scientist* 24 Feb. 497/1 The noctule gives a strong response..with a slow and rather deliberate liquid 'bleeping' note. **1968** B. NORMAN *Hounds of Sparta* xvii. 187 The bleeping grew fainter or stronger depending on his position. **1982** *Financial Times* 1 Nov. 16/2 The systems could..tell the selectively 'bleeped' pager-wearer to..call the Pabx operator. **1983** *Washington Post Mag.* 6 Feb. 37/1 The whole bleeping menagerie of cathode critters.

bleeper ('bliːpə(r)). [f. BLEEP *v.* + -ER[1].] A miniature radio receiver that emits a bleeping sound when activated (usu. by telephone), used to contact the person carrying it; = *radio pager* s.v. RADIO *sb.* 7.

1964 J. R. L. ANDERSON *Greatest Race in World* iv. 59 After I had finally got off early in the morning, my bleeper —the ship's radio alarm—woke me up. **1968** A. DIMENT *Gt. Spy Race* ii. 17 These bleepers are little radio receivers which give off a faint cheeping from one's pocket. **1973** *Physics Bull.* Mar. 181/3 This new service, radio paging, is the first in the UK in which a simple telephone call over the ordinary public network will activate pocket 'bleepers'. **1986** B. FORBES *Endless Game* I. vi. 74 When or if he rings, be sure and get word to me on the bleeper.

bleer(e, bleet, obs. forms of BLEAR, BLITE.

bleeze, Sc. form of BLAZE *sb.* and *v.*[1], used in all their senses. The verb is also used (by Scott) in a sense which appears to be influenced by BLAZE *v.*[2]: To declaim, talk loudly.

1816 SCOTT *Old Mort.* xxxv, Ye're bleezing awa about marriage. **1818** —— *Rob Roy* xxvii, Ye're no to be bleezing and blasting about your master's name and mine.

bleeze, *v.*[2] *Sc. trans.* To turn (milk) a little sour, to 'blink.' Also *intr.* Jamieson.

bleezy ('bli:zɪ), *a. Sc.* [cf. prec.] Affected in the eyes, as by alcoholic excitement. Jamieson has also *Bleezed*, explained as 'a little flustered.'
1830 GALT *Lawrie T.* VII. vii. (1849) 282 A red face and bleezy eyes. **1833** *Fraser's Mag.* VII. 622 Their faces grew red, and their eyes bleezy.

blefede, bleft(e, pa. t. and pple. of BELEAVE *v. Obs.*, to remain.

bleflum, obs. form of BLAFLUM. *Sc.*

blehand, var. of BLEAUNT, *Obs.*, a tunic.

bleib, bleid, obs. forms of BLEB, BLEED.

bleike, *a.* and *v.*: see BLEYKE.

bleine, obs. form of BLAIN.

bleinerite ('blaɪnəraɪt). *Min.* = BINDHEIMITE.

†**bleise**. *Obs. rare*⁻¹. ? A blay or bleak.
1598 FLORIO, *Pescherello*, a fish called a bleise.

bleise, bleit, obs. ff. BLAZE, BLATE, BLITE.

blek, bleke, blekk, var. BLECK. *Obs.* or *dial.*

blek(e, obs. form of BLEAK *a.* and *v.*

'blellum. *Sc.* A blab or blabber.
1790 BURNS *Tam o' Shanter* 20 A bletherin, blusterin, drunken blellum.

†**'blely**, *adv. Obs. rare.* [A worn down form of BLETHELY.] Willingly, cheerfully.
c **1380** WYCLIF *Wks.* (1880) 417 An-oþer fend þat wole blely robbe pore men. *c* **1440** *Partonope* 771 He wole not blely aspyed be.

blemish ('blɛmɪʃ), *v.* Forms: 4 **blemyss, -iss, -ess, -ysch, -ysh,** 4–5 **blensch, blench,** 5 **blemissh, -esh, -ysch,** 5–6 **blemyssh(e,** 6– **blemish.** *Pa. t.* and *pple.* **blemished,** in 4 **blemest(e, -yst,** 5 **blemschyd,** 6– **blemisht.** [a. OF. *blemiss-*, extended stem of *blemir* (also *blesmir, blaismir*, in Pr. *blasmar, blesmar*) to render livid or pale, f. *blaisme, blesme, blême* 'livid, pale,' of uncertain origin: see Diez, Littré. The syncopated forms *blemschyd, blensch*, caused partial confusion with BLENCH: see senses 2, 5.]

†**1.** To hurt, damage, do physical damage or injury to, deface. *Obs.*
c **1325** *E.E. Allit. P.* B. 1421 Wine..Breyþed vppe in to his brayn & blemyst his mynde. *c* **1350** *Will. Palerne* 2471 Bihuld aboute on his bodi ȝif it blenched were. ? *a* **1400** *Morte Arth.* 2578 He þet es blemeste with þis brade brande. **1494** FABYAN *Chron.* VII. ccxxiii. 249 Such holdes and castellys, as the Scottis by theyr warrys had blemysshed and apayred. *Ibid.* VII. 386 The towne of Boston was greatly blemysshed with fyre. **1571** DIGGES *Pantom.* I. xxxv. L iij, Blemishing all the..lines..drawen with black lead or such like, that you mayе easely put oute or rase awaye. **1607** TOPSELL *Four-f. Beasts* 129 He cut off his tail..Being demanded why he so blemished his beast, etc.

†**2.** To dim or darken (the eye-sight). *Obs.*
1440 *Promp. Parv.* 39 Blenschyn [**1499** blemysshen], *obfusco.* **1496** *Dives & Paup.* (W. de W.) IV. x. 173 They blemysshe theyr eye in lokynge ayenst the sonne. **1526** *Pilg. Perf.* (W. de W. 1531) 297 My corporal eye..shall be blemysshed or derked by the reason of the lyght. ?**1677** *Lover's Quar.* 82 The salt tears blemished his eye.

3. To mar, spoil, or injure the working of.
c **1430** LYDG. *Min. Poems* (1840) 14 Pité blemeshithe the swerd of rightewisnes. *a* **1555** LATIMER *Serm. & Rem.* (1845) 261 Ye do blemish the annunciation of the Lords death till he come. **1625** SIR H. FINCH *Law* (1636) 338 That the people be not..troubled..nor the peace blemished. **1635** WENTWORTH in Ellis *Orig. Lett.* II. 276 III. 282 To overthrowe or at least to blemishe the proceedings. **1856** FROUDE *Hist. Eng.* (1858) I. iii. 253 An expedient, which though blemished in the execution, was itself reasonable and prudent.

†**b.** To disconcert, put out. Cf. BLENCH *v.*¹ 5.
1544 BALE *Chron. Sir J. Oldcastell* in *Harl. Misc.* (Malh.) I. 264 At this, the archbishopp and hys companye were not a lytle blemyshed.

4. To impair or mar the beauty, soundness, or perfection of; to damage.
c **1460** *Towneley Myst.* 223 Alle blemyshed is thi ble. **1530** PALSGR. 457/1, I blemysshe, I hynder or hurte the beautye of a person. **1594** SHAKS. *Rich. III*, I. ii. 128 These eyes could not endure yᵗ beauties wrack, You should not blemish it, if I stood by. *c* **1746** HERVEY *Medit. & Contempl.* I. 183 Without blemishing their Beauty, or altering their Nature.

b. To impair morally or ideally; to sully, stain, spoil.
c **1380** WYCLIF *Serm.* Sel. Wks. I. 178 Coveitise of wickede preestis blemyshiþ hem. **1593** HOOKER *Eccl. Pol.* Pref. i. §3 Let not the faith..be blemished with partialities. **1660** BOYLE *Seraph. Love* 2 That the extraction of your freedom may no ways blemish it. **1735** OLDYS *Raleigh* Wks. 1829 I. 270 Nothing..that might blemish reputation. **1866** HOWELLS *Venet. Life* (1883) II. xx. 163 The admixture of ruffianism which blemishes most loafers.

c. To cast a slur upon, asperse, defame, discredit, disable. *Obs.* exc. in *Law.*
1414 BRAMPTON *Penit. Ps.* xlvii. 18 Ne with here tungys blemysch my name. **1593** BILSON *Govt. Christ's Ch.* 394 To blemish and reproch so many. **1649** MRS. HUTCHINSON *Mem. Col. Hutchinson* (1846) 341 Blemish not a man that is innocent. **1699** DRYDEN *To J. Driden* 31 Not that my verse would blemish all the fair. **1715** BURNET *Own Time* II. 331 Anything that would..blemish the management of the treasury. **1768** BLACKSTONE *Comm.* II. 291 Whether a man should be permitted to blemish himself, by pleading his own insanity.

†**5.** *intr.* To turn pale, change colour, blench. (Cf. mod.F. *blêmir.*) *Obs. rare.* Cf. BLENCH *v*².
1530 PALSGR. 457/1, I blemysshe, I chaunge colour.. Sawe you nat howe he blemysshed at it.

6. A hunting term: see quot. and cf. BLEMISH *sb.* 4.
1575 TURBERV. *Venery* 104 Blemishing against or over the slot or viewe of the deare. **1792** W. OSBALDISTON *Brit. Sportsm.*, *Blemish*, a hunting term, used when the hounds or beagles, finding where the chase has been, make a proffer to enter but return.

blemish ('blɛmɪʃ), *sb.* Also 6 **blemysh, bleamish(e.** [f. the vb.]

1. Physical defect or disfigurement; a stain. (Used *spec.* of the mark of injury to a horse, as the scar of a broken knee.)
1535 COVERDALE *Tob.* xi. 13 Then beganne the blemysh to go out of his eyes, like as it had bene the whyte szkynne of an egg. —— *Lev.* ix. 3 A calf and a shepe, both..without blemysh [WYCLIF, wemme, wem; **1611** blemish]. **1579** LANGHAM *Gard. Health* (1633) 97 Face spots, or blemishes, anoint with the iuice of the roots. **1597** SHAKS. *2 Hen. IV*, II. iii. 34 Speaking thicke (which Nature made his blemish). **1718** *Freethinker* No. 37. 270 One never sees the least Blemish of ink upon his Nails. **1827** HARE *Guesses* Ser. II. (1873) 500 Nothing hides a blemish so completely as cloth of gold.

2. *transf.* A defect, imperfection, flaw, in any object, matter, condition, or work.
1555 *Fardle Facions* I. i. 23 A moste blessed life without bleamishe of wo. **1611** BIBLE *Pref.* 8 Some imperfections and blemishes may be noted in the setting foorth of it. **1771** *Junius Lett.* xlv. 244 The minor critic..hunts for blemishes. **1863** H. ROGERS *J. Howe* (ed. 2) Pref. 5 The work has now received a careful revision, and it is hoped that..such blemishes are removed. **1869** J. MARTINEAU *Ess.* II. 222 The divine light is without blemish.

3. *fig.* A moral defect or stain; a flaw, fault, blot, slur.
1526 *Pilgr. Perf.* (W. de W. 1531) 64 A blemysshe, which semeth to disteyne all his vertues. **1580** BARET *Alv.* B 796 A bleamishe in ones good name. **1598** BARRET *Theor. Warres* II. i. 27 No blemish vnto any Gentleman to serue as a common souldier in the Captaines squadron. **1611** SHAKS. *Wint. T.* I. ii. 341 Ile giue no blemish to her Honor, none. **1656** BRAMHALL *Replic.* i. 51 Some abuses are..rather blemishes than sinnes. **1859** TENNYSON *Vivien* 681 If they find Some stain or blemish in a name of note.

†**4.** *Venery.* (See quot.) *Obs.*
1575 TURBERV. *Venery* 94 The same huntsman shall go backe to his blemishes immediately. *Ibid.* 114 Blemishes.. are the markes which are left to knowe where a deare hath gone in or out. **1627** TAYLOR (Water P.) *Wks.* (1630) I. 93/1 Blemishes, Sewelling, Auant-laye, Allaye, Relaye..and a thousand more such Vtopian fragments of confused Gibberish. **1656** in BLOUNT *Glossogr.* **1721–90** in BAILEY.

blemished ('blɛmɪʃt), *ppl. a.* Also 6– **blemisht.** [f. BLEMISH *v.* + -ED.] Damaged or disfigured; marred by defect, flaw, or stain; spoiled.
c **1440** *Promp. Parv.* 39 Blemschyde [**1499** blemysshed], *obfuscatus.* *a* **1450** *Knt. de la Tour* (1868) 25 She might not for shame shewe her visage, it was so foule blemisshed. **1594** SHAKS. *Rich. III*, III. vii. 122 The corruption of a blemisht Stock. **1612** T. TAYLOR *Comm. Titus* i. 8 No blind or blemished person might come. **1865** M. ARNOLD *Ess. Crit.* v. (1875) 222 He died and has left a blemished name.

blemisher ('blɛmɪʃə(r)). [f. as prec. + -ER¹.] He who or that which blemishes.
1423 JAMES I *King's Q.* cxl, He that suld of hir gude fame Be blamischere. **1594** GREENE *Look. Glasse* (1861) 124 Nocturnal cares, ye blemishers of bliss. **1630** BRATHWAIT *Eng. Gentl.* (1641) 5 A great darkener and blemisher of the internal glory and beauty of the mind.

blemishing ('blɛmɪʃɪŋ), *vbl. sb.* [f. as prec. + -ING¹.] The action of the verb BLEMISH; physical or moral impairment.
1413 LYDG. *Pylgr. Sowle* v. xiv. (1483) 109 Withouten blemysshynge. **1447** BOKENHAM *Seyntys* (1835) 120 Wyth out blemyssyng of my virgynyte. **1645** TOMBES *Anthropol.* 2 Evill..tending to the..blemishing of the Christian profession. **1727–51** CHAMBERS *Cycl.* s.v. *Abatement*, [In heraldry] Diminution, is the blemishing any part by adding a stain or mark of diminution.

'blemishing, *ppl. a.* That blemishes.
1603 FLORIO *Montaigne* (1634) 502 Blemishing deformities. **1868** GEO. ELIOT *Sp. Gypsy* I. 89 Fedalma's soul Was free from blemishing purpose.

blemishless ('blɛmɪʃlɪs), *a.* [f. BLEMISH + -LESS.] Without blemish.
1583 BABINGTON *Commandm.* 429 Our blemishlesse God. **1850** NEALE *Med. Hymns* 154 Spotless, blemishless, eternal.

blemishment ('blɛmɪʃmənt). [f. BLEMISH + -MENT.] Damage, injury; flaw; impairment.
1596 SPENSER *F.Q.* IV. II. 36 For dread of blame and honours blemishment. **1640–4** in Rushw. *Hist. Coll.* III. (1692) I. 96 To the great dishonour of this Kingdom, and blemishment to the Government thereof. **1884** *Law Times* I Mar. 322/2 That a man should allege..he was not of sane memory in blemishment of himself.

blemmatrope ('blɛmətrəʊp). [f. Gr. βλέμμα look, glance, f. βλέπειν to look + τρόπος turning, f. τρέπειν to turn.] 'An apparatus for illustrating the various positions of the eye' (*Catal. Sci. Appar. S. Kensington*, 1876).

†**'blemmere**. *Obs. rare.* ? A plumber.
c **1420** *Chron. Vilod.* 3644 Mony werkemen he sette to amende þat chirche..& masonus & carpenters & blemmeres also.

blemya ('blɛmɪə). Usu. in pl. **blemyae.** [L. *Blem(m)yae*, f. Gr. Βλέμυες, an Ethiopian people, 'acc. to the fable (Mel. 8), without head and eyes, and with the mouth in the breast' (Lewis and Short).] A type of mediæval carved image (see quot. 1915).
1915 G. C. DRUCE in *Archaeological Jrnl.* LXXII. 138 A pair of Blemyae are carved as wing-subjects upon one of the misericords in Norwich cathedral church... Each of them is represented as a headless man with his face upon his breast. **1955** M. D. ANDERSON *Imagery Brit. Churches* III. xiii. 182 The Blemyae, whose faces are in their stomachs, are carved upon misericords at Ripon and in Norwich Cathedral.

†**blench**, *sb. Obs.* Also (in sense 1) 3–4 **blenk, blenc.** [f. BLENCH *v.*¹ Cf. BLENK *sb.*²]

1. A trick, stratagem. *to do* or *make a blenk* or *blench*: to play a trick.
a **1250** *Owl & Night.* 378 He [the fox] haveþ mid him blenches ȝarewe. *a* **1300** *Havelok* 307 Hope maketh fol man ofte blenkes. *c* **1325** *E.E. Allit. P.* B. 1201 Þe kyng..a counsayl hym takes..A blench for to make. **1330** R. BRUNNE *Chron.* 274 Þe Scottis now þei þenk of gile..How þei mot do a blenk tille Edward & hise. **1340** *Ayenb.* 130 And uerliche makeþ his blench.

2. A turning of the eyes aside, a side glance. *rare.*
c **1600** SHAKS. *Sonn.* cx, Most true it is, that I haue lookt on truth Asconce and strangely: But by all aboue, These blenches gaue my heart an other youth.

blench, *a.*, Sc. form of BLANCH *a.*, where see *blench-farm*, etc.

blench (blɛnʃ), *v.*¹ Forms: 2–3 **blenchen,** 3 **(blinche),** 3–5 **blenche,** 4– **blench.** *Pa. t.* 3–4 **bleinte,** 4 **bleynte, blynchid,** 4–5 **blent.** [A word or series of words of very obscure history. Sense 1 is evidently:—OE. *blęncan* to deceive, cheat = ON. *blekkja* (:—*blenkja*) to impose upon, which point to an OTeut. type **blankjan*, assumed to be the causal of a strong **blinkan* to BLINK; but, as no trace of the latter occurs in early times, the origin of *blęncan* is thus left uncertain. The northern form was BLENK, q.v. The sense-development is involved, from confusion of *blenk* and *blink*, of *blench* and *blanch*, prob. also of the pa. t. *blent* with *blent* pa. t. of BLEND *v.*¹, and other causes: little can be done at present except to exhibit the senses actually found in use.] To cheat, elude, turn aside. Related to BLENK and BLINK.

†**1.** *trans.* To deceive, cheat. *Obs.*
a **1000** *Be monna môde* 33 (Gr.) Wrenceð he and blenceð. *c* **1175** *Lamb. Hom.* 55 Abuten us he is for to blenchen. [*c* **1400** *Destr. Troy* VI. 2483 Let no blyndnes you blenke.]

2. *intr.* To start aside, so as to elude anything; to swerve, 'shy'; to flinch, shrink, give way.
c **1205** LAY. 1460 Corineus bleinte. *a* **1225** *Ancr. R.* 242 Þe horse þet is scheouh, & blencheð uor one scheadewe. *a* **1250** *Owl & Night.* 170 Ich am war, and can well blenche. *c* **1386** CHAUCER *Knt's T.* 226 Ther with al he bleynte and cride A! **1398** TREVISA *Barth. De P.R.* III. xvii, [Rays that] passeth not alwey forþe ryȝte, but blencheþ [**1582** swarue] sum wheþer of þe streite wey. *c* **1500** *Partenay* 4268 Apart Gaffray..Somwhat blent, the stroke..passing by With hym noght mette. **1553** BALE *Gardiner's Obed.* C vij. He obeyeth truly, which..blenchet not out of the waye of Goddes commaundementes. **1603** SHAKS. *Meas. for M.* IV. v. 5 Hold you euer to our speciall drift, Though sometimes you doe blench from this to that As cause doth minister. *a* **1625** FLETCHER *False One* IV. iv, Art thou so proper to blench at what thou hast done? **1808** SCOTT *Marm.* VI. xii, Foul fall him that blenches first. **1876** EMERSON *Ess.* Ser. I. xi. 262, I blench and withdraw on this side and on that.

†**b.** Of a ship: To turn or heel over. *Obs.*
a **1300** *K. Horn* 1411 Þe schup bigan to blenche.

3. *trans.* To elude, avoid, shirk; to flinch from; to blink. [The first quot. perhaps in form belongs rather to BLINK.]
[*c* **1300** *Beket* 2184 He nas noȝt the man that wolde: his heved enes withdrawe, Ne fonde for to blinche a strok.] **1663** EVELYN *Mem.* (1857) III. 142 He now blenched what before..he affirmed to me. **1822** HAZLITT *Table-t.* I. v. 100 Will not suffer me to blench his merits.

†**4.** *trans.* To turn aside or away (the eyes). *Obs.*
c **1400** *Roland* 402 He kest up his browes & blenchid his eye. [*c* **1400** *Melayne* 570.] See BLENK *v.* 3.

†**5.** *trans.* To disconcert, foil, put out, turn aside. Cf. BLENK *v.* 4. *Obs.*
[*a* **1400.** See BLENK *v.* 4.] **1485** CAXTON *Trevisa's Higden* IV. xxxiii. (1527) 181 The enemyes were blente thrugh goddes myghte. **1577** STANYHURST *Descr. Irel.* in *Holinshed* VI. 16 Heere perchanse M. Cope may blench me, in replieing that *Anguis* may be construed generallie. **1602** CAREW *Cornwall*, Carrying vp great trusses of hay before them to blench the defendants sight & dead their shot. *a* **1640** JACKSON *Wks.* (1844) VIII. 122 Being blenched in his right course by the shadow.

6. *intr.* Of the eyes: To lose firmness of glance, to flinch, quail. [The first quot. may belong to 2.]
[*c* **1430** LYDG. *Min. Poems* (1840) 215 This royal bridde.. Blenchithe never for al the cliere light.] **1775** BURKE *Amer.*

Tax. Wks. II. 404 That glaring and dazzling influence at which the eyes of eagles have blenched. **1837** HOWITT *Rur. Life* II. v. (1862) 150 His eyes seemed to blench before her still fixed gaze.

blench, *v.*[2] [A variant of BLANCH *v.*[1] (The confusion is partly phonetic, as in BLANCH, BLENCH *a.*; partly of sense, since, with fear, the cheeks *blanch*, the eyes *blench*.)]

1. *intr.* To become pale.

1813 HOGG *Queen's Wake* 26 Where the vexed rubies blench in death, Beneath yon lips and balmy breath. **1840** BARHAM *Ingol. Leg.* 286 That little foot page he blenched with fear.

2. *trans.* To whiten, make pale. *rare.*

1839 BAILEY *Festus* (ed. 3) 16/1 The northern tribes Whom ceaseless snows and starry winters blench.

blench, *v.*[3], obs. variant of BLEMISH q.v.

blencher (ˈblɛnʃə(r)). [f. BLENCH *v.*[1] + -ER[1].]

†**1.** A person or thing employed to turn or frighten away, *e.g.* a scarecrow: in *Hunting*, one placed to turn the deer from going in particular directions. Cf. BLANCHER[2]. *Obs.*

1531 ELYOT *Gov.* I. xxiii. (1883) 247 The good husbande ..settethe up cloughtes or thredes, whiche some call.. blenchars..to feare away birdes. **1575** TURBERV. *Venery* 192 To set up bleinchers or sewels (which are white papers). *a***1625** FLETCHER *Love's Pilgr.* II. i. 8/2 Hurt those That stand but by as blenchers.

2. One who blenches or flinches.

1873 MORRIS *Love is enough* 55 No blencher in battle.

blenching (ˈblɛnʃɪŋ), *vbl. sb.* [f. as prec. + -ING[1].] The action of the verb BLENCH: †**a.** Turning to one side, swerving, shying; †**b.** turning away of the eyes (? blinking, winking); **c.** flinching, quailing, loss of courage.

1393 GOWER *Conf.* III. 8, I stonde still, withoute blenching of min eye. **1398** TREVISA *Barth. De P.R.* II. v. (1495) 32 Angels..beholde streyght..in god..wythout blenchynge of theyr eyen. *Ibid.* XII. xxxix. (1495) 436 The reremous fleeth in the eue tyde wyth brekynge and blenchynge and swyfte meuynge. **1868** DORAN *Saints & Sin.* II. 186 He saw without blenching the rope by which he was to be strangled.

ˈblenching, *ppl. a.* [f. as prec. + -ING[2].] Causing the eyes to turn away or flinch.

1833 MRS. BROWNING *Prometh. Bound* Poems (1850) I. 186 Let him now hurl his blenching lightnings down. —— *Grief* ibid. I. 326 Under the blenching, vertical eye-glare Of the absolute Heavens.

ˈblenchingly *adv.* = *blanchingly*: see BLENCH *v.*[2]

1850 MRS. BROWNING *Poems* II. 476 This mask of me (Against which, years have beat thus blenchingly With their rains!)

blencorn, var. of BLEND-CORN: see BLEND *sb.* 2.

†**blend**, *v.*[1] *Obs.* Forms: 1 blendan, 2–4 blenden, 3–5 blende, 4–6 blend. *Pa. t.* 1–3 blende, 4 blent(e. *Pa. pple.* 1–4 blend, 3–4 i-blend, 4 blende, 4–5 i-blent, blente, 5 i-blende, blended, 3–7 blent, 6–7 *arch.* y-blent. [Com. WGer.: OE. *blęndan* = OFris. *blenda*, OS. **blendan* (MDu. *blenden*), OHG. *blentan* (MHG., mod.G. *blenden*):—OTeut. type **blandjan* 'to make blind,' a factitive verb apparently formed with ablaut upon the adj. *blind-*, since no trace is found of a strong vb. *blindan.* See BLIND. (The pa. t. *blent* coincided with that of *blench*; whence some confusion in sense 1 b.)]

1. *trans.* To make blind: **a.** permanently.

?*a***1100** *O.E. Chron.* an. 1036 Man hine blende, and hine swa blindne brohte to ðam munecon. *a***1225** *Juliana* 48 Ich habbe i-blend men. *c***1386** CHAUCER *Milleres T.* 622 With that strook he was almost i-blent.

b. temporarily, *e.g.* with bright light: To dazzle.

*c***888** K. ÆLFRED *Boeth.* xxxviii. v, Se dæᵹ blent..hiora eaᵹan. **1297** R. GLOUC. 407 þe smoke..him ssolde boþe stenche and blende. **1377** LANGL. *P. Pl.* B. v. 502 And thorw the liȝte..lucifer was blent. *a***1529** SKELTON *Image Hypocr.* Wks. III. 236 A virgin ffayre and gent That hath our yees blent. **1596** SPENSER *F.Q.* IV. iii. 35 The swownd which him did blend. **1600** FAIRFAX *Tasso* XII. lxxxvi, What hath thy eiesight blent?

2. *fig.* To blind the understanding, judgement, or moral sense; to 'throw dust in the eyes' of.

*c***1200** ORMIN 4525 Grediȝnesse..blendeþþ manness heorrte. *a***1300** *Cursor M.* 819 (Gött.) þe feind had adam blent. *c***1386** CHAUCER *Pers. T.* ¶603 Envye blendith the hert of a man. **1450** MYRC 370 Thus wyth the fende he ys I-blende. **1579** SPENSER *Sheph. Cal.* Apr. 155 Ah foolish boy, that is with loue yblent. **1591** —— *Virgil's Gnat.* xxxix, Feare and yre Had blent so much his sense.

3. To put out of sight, hide, conceal.

1430 LYDG. *Chron. Troy* I. ii, Under coloure was the treason blente.

blend (blɛnd), *v.*[2] Forms: 3–4 blend-en, 5–7 blende, 4– blend, (5 blynde, 5–6 blenne, 6 blynne, blente). *Pa. t.* 3–5 blend(e, 5– blent, blended. *Pa. pple.* 3–5 blend, 4 blende, blente, 4– blent, 6– blended, (8 *arch.* yblent). [ME. *blend-en* wk. vb., appears *c* 1300, at first in northern writers. Evidently akin to BLAND *sb.* mixture, and the OE. strong vb. *bland-an*, ON. *blanda* (Sw. *blanda*, Da. *blande*) to mix: see BLAND *v.* But the ME. vb. (however the change of vowel may be explained) can hardly have been a continuation of the OE. *blandan*, since this was all but obsolete already in OE., while *blenden* was a common word from the 14th c. More probably the latter was an adoption of the ON. *blanda* (which though originally strong, had subsequently weak inflexions); the change of vowel may also have been due to the ON. sing. present *blend*, *blendr*: whether any association with BLEND *v.*[1] (with which it entirely coincides in forms) or other extraneous influence contributed, does not appear. But later identification with BLEND *v.*[1] is shown by the occasional use of *blynde* for this verb also. The 16th c. *blenne* was either phonetic, like the converse *len*, *lend*, or deduced from the pa. pple. *blend.*]

I. *trans.*

1. To mix, to mingle: **a.** things material; **b.** things immaterial. *Obs.* exc. as in **d**, or with some colouring from the other senses (esp. 4).

a. *a***1300** *Cursor M.* 16768 Vinegre & gall þe jews blend. *Ibid.* 18019 (Gött.) Aisel haue i blend wid gall. *c***1400** *Destr. Troy* 3492 To se..the blode..blent with the erthe. *c***1420** *Liber Cocorum* (1862) 50 Grynde tansy, þo iuse owte wrynge, To blynde with þo egges. **1530** PALSGR. 457/2 Wyll you blenne wyne and ale togyther? **1585** LLOYD *Treas. Health* B vij, Putte therin..whyte Lead and Common Salt, and blynne them well together. **1601** HOLLAND *Pliny* II. 394 These beeing dried in the Sun..they vse to blend with bean floure. **1733** CHEYNE *Eng. Malady* II. ix. §3 (1734) 208 Opiates..blended with small proportion of..Aromatick Medicines.

b. *c***1400** *Pes may stond* (Turnb. 1843) 155 Were luf and charite with hus blend. *c***1430** *Hymns Virg.* (1867) 108 þat blaberyng are wiþ oþes blent.

†**c.** To mingle with a company or crowd. *Obs.*

*c***1325** *E.E. Allit. P.* A. 385 In blysse I se þe blyþely blent. **1579** TOMSON *Calvin's Serm. Tim.* 1010/1 These backe-sliders yt haue beene blended amongest vs. **1713** STEELE *Englishm.* No. 6. 39 We are blended with the Nobility.

d. To mix (sorts of spirits, tea, wines, etc.), so as to produce a certain quality.

?*a***1400** *Chester Pl.* II. (1847) 82 All mashers, minglers of wyne in the nighte Brewinge so blendinge againste daye lighte. **1583** STUBBES *Anat. Abus.* II. 25 [Vintners] make of one hogshead almost two..by mixing and blenting one with another, and infusing other liquor. *Ibid.* 28 To intermix and blente the good and naughtie wooll togither. **1884** *Pall Mall G.* 5 Sept. 6/2 A number of brands (varied by the blending of the tobaccos).

†**2.** To mix or stir up (a liquid); hence sometimes, to render turbid, pollute, spoil, destroy; sometimes, to agitate, trouble: to disturb (joy, peace, beauty, weather).

*a***1300** *Cursor M.* 13767 þar-in was won for to descend Angels þe water for to blend. **1384** CHAUCER *Truth* 4 Prees hathe envye and wele is blent over al. *c***1593** SPENSER *Sonn.* lxii, These stormes, which now his beauty blend, Shall turn to calmes. **1594** GREENE *Look. Glasse* (1874) 137 When mildest wind is loth to blend the peace. *Ibid.* (1861) 124 My Hesperus by cloudy death is blent. **1596** LODGE *Marg. Amer.* 65 Thy sap by course of time is blent.

†**b.** Applied (according to ancient physiology) to disturbance or agitation of the blood (from its supposed normal state of rest): *pass.* and *intr.* To rush, flow; also *active*, To shed. *Obs.*

*a***1300** *Cursor M.* 17333 Pilate was þar, his blod was blend, Quen he wessen had his hend. *c***1340** *Gaw. & Gr. Knt.* 2371 Alle þe blode of his brest blende in his face. *c***1460** *Towneley Myst.* 225 To be in payn thus broght, Thi blessid blode to blende.

3. To mingle intimately or closely *with.*

1591 SPENSER *M. Hubberd* 1330 Thy throne royall [is] with dishonour blent. **1788** J. POWELL *Devises* (1827) II. 95 If a testator has blended his real with his personal fund. **1800** WORDSW. *Hart-leap Well* II. xxi, Never to blend our pleasure or our pride With sorrow of the meanest thing that feels. **1863** GEO. ELIOT *Romola* lii. (1868) 405 It blent itself as an exalting memory with all her daily labours.

4. a. To mix (components) intimately or harmoniously so that their individuality is obscured in the product; *esp.* of qualities, properties, effects, etc.; now the most frequent *trans.* use.

1601 SHAKS. *Twel. N.* I. v. 257 Tis beauty truly blent, whose red and white, Natures owne..hand laid on. **1662** FULLER *Worthies* (1840) II. 261 Providence hath so wisely blended the benefits of this county, that..it is defective in nothing. **1711** ADDISON *Spect.* No. 128 ¶11 Their Virtues are blended in their Children. **1816** BYRON *Ch. Har.* III. xxix, Rider and horse,—friend, foe,—in one red burial blent. **1835** LYTTON *Rienzi* I. iii. 13 In one of those wide spaces in which Modern and Ancient Rome seemed blent together. **1848** —— *Harold* I. i. 4 In that beauty were blended two expressions. **1876** GREEN *Short Hist.* ix. §2. 610 A common persecution soon blended the Nonconformists into one.

b. Also (chiefly *Cookery*), to mix *in* (a component).

1936 I. S. ROMBAUER *Joy of Cooking* 247/2 Blend in: 2 tablespoons flour. **1956** C. SPRY *Cookery Bk.* vi. 173 Cashew nut or almond sauce... Draw aside, blend in the flour, add the stock, and stir till boiling. **1963** R. CARRIER *Gt. Dishes of World* 99/2 Crush garlic to a smooth paste in a mortar with a little salt; blend in egg yolks until the mixture is a smooth homogeneous mass.

†**5.** To mix up in the mind, regard as the same, confound *with. Obs. rare.*

1780 COXE *Russ. Discov.* 74 Six islands..to the North West of the Fox Islands..must not be blended with them.

II. *intr.*

6. To mix, mingle; *esp.* to unite intimately, so as to form a uniform or harmonious mixture.

*c***1325** *E.E. Allit. P.* B. 1788 Boþe his blod & his brayn blende on þe cloþes. *c***1340** *Cursor M.* 5690 Moses sagh þai dide ham wrange & sone he blende ham a-mange. *c***1400** *Destr. of Troy* XXIV. 9642 The bloberond blode blend with the rayn. **1713** YOUNG *Last Day* III. 251 Cities and desarts in one ruin blend. **1792** WORDSW. *Descr. Sk.* Poet. Wks. I. 83 All motions, sounds, and voices..Blend in a music of tranquillity. **1871** R. ELLIS tr. *Catullus* lxviii. 18 She whose honey delights blend with a bitter annoy.

7. To pass imperceptibly into each other by assimilation or confusion of contiguous parts, esp. in reference to colour. ***to blend away***: to pass away by blending.

1812 J. WILSON *Isle of Palms* I. 111 Oh! ne'er did sky and water blend In such a holy sleep. **1820** IRVING *Sketch Bk.* I. 9 In Europe, the features and population of one country blend almost imperceptibly with those of another. **1860** TYNDALL *Glac.* I. §27. 196 The distant peaks gradually blended with the white atmosphere above them. **1862** DARWIN *Fertil. Orchids* v. 159 The division between them, in this their leading character, blends away.

blend, *sb.* [f. prec. vb.] **1. a.** A blending; a mixture formed by blending various sorts or qualities (e.g. of spirits, wines, tea, tobacco, etc.).

1883 *Academy* 14 Apr. 253/2 It resembles a blend made by imitating the later style of Lever and the earlier style of Lord Beaconsfield. **1885** *Pall Mall G.* 28 Sept. 2/1 Public-houses, with flaming bills in their windows announcing..the sale of American Blend.

b. *spec.* A mixture of different kinds of woollen or other fibres (see also quot. 1959).

1884 W. S. B. MCLAREN *Spinning* ix. 184 The quantity used varies very much, but for blends half wool and half shoddy 10 lb. of oil per 100 lb. of wool is a common allowance. *Ibid.*, After this operation the blend is again spread on the floor. **1888** R. BEAUMONT *Woollen & Worsted Cloth Manuf.* ii. 47 A layer of teazed cotton is, in such blends, first spread for a foundation, then lighters of wool and cotton alternately. **1898** *Eng. Dial. Dict.* s.v., A blend varies in size and weight from 1 pack upwards. **1911** *Encycl. Brit.* XXVIII. 810/2 A blending of various materials..to obtain a cheap blend which may be spun into a satisfactory warp or weft yarn. **1959** *Chambers's Encycl.* XIV. 661/1 If a mixture yarn is required, the necessary proportions of dyed and undyed wool are built up in layers in a stack (usually known as the 'blend') and passed into a machine which.. mixes the materials.

2. *Philol.* A word or phrase formed by blending (see BLENDING *vbl. sb.* 2); so ***blend-word.***

1909 *Cent. Dict.* Suppl., Blend-word. **1911** *Mod. Philol.* IX. 197 All the so-called 'streckformen' may not be blends. **1914** L. POUND *Blends: Their Relation to Eng. Word Formation* i. 1 Blend-words, amalgams, or fusions may be defined as two or more words, often of cognate sense, telescoped as it were into one. **1935** A. C. BAUGH *Hist. Eng. Lang.* x. 377 Words of the type of *electrocute*..are often called *portmanteau* words, or better, *blends.*

3. *transf.* A combination or mixture of different abstract or personal qualities.

1931 H. CRANE *Let.* 12 Dec. (1965) 391 The figure of the Virgin of Guadalupe..is a typical Mexican product, a strange blend of Christian and pagan strains. **1951** J. HAWKES *Land* i. 9, I lie looking at the stars with that blend of wonder and familiarity they alone can suggest. **1958** I. MURDOCH *Bell* vi. 89 He had found Paul's blend of aestheticism and snobbery thoroughly distasteful. **1984** *Church Times* 6 Jan. 2/3 Attitudes which, in their unhealthy blend of the throwaway mentality..and of supposedly early Christian primitivism, attempt to provide a rationale for the destruction of church buildings.

†**blend(e**, *pa. pple.* and *ppl. a.* Also bland. Obs. pa. pple. of BLEND *v.*[2] Also used as *adj.* = BLENDED.

1300 [see BLEND *v.*[2] 2 b.] **1571** *Wills & Inv. N.C.* (1835) 352, Xxxti boles of maid malt being halff bland. **1616** SURFL. & MARKH. *Countr. Farm* 93 Take two parts straw, and one part hay, and mix it together, which is called blend fodder. **1679** PLOT *Staffordsh.* (1686) 161 The third sort of Iron.. they call blend-metall.

2. *esp.* in **blend corn, blencorn**, wheat and rye sown and grown together; **blend-water**, a urinary disease of cattle (Chambers *Cycl. Supp.* 1753).

1523 FITZHERB. *Husb.* §34 Vppon that ground sowe blend corne, that is both wheate and rye. **1583** *Wills & Inv. N.C.* II. (1860) 78 In bygge 8*l.* In ottes 40*j.* In blandcorne 40*j.* **1616** SURFL. & MARKH. *Countr. Farm* 550 You shall not lead your blend-corne so soone as you doe your cleane Wheat, or your cleane Rie. **1798** W. HUTTON *Autobiog.* 11 A sixpenny loaf of coarse blencorn bread. **1855** *Whitby Gloss.*

blende (blɛnd). *Min.* Also 8 blend. [a. Ger. *blende*, from *blenden* to deceive: so called 'because while often resembling galena, it yielded no lead' (Dana); = *blendendes erz* 'deceiving ore' (Grimm). Hence also called *pseudogalena*, and *sphalerite* from σφαλερός deceitful.] Sulphide of zinc occurring as a native crystalline mineral.

1683 [cf. BLENDY]. **1753** CHAMBERS *Cycl. Supp.*, *Blende*.. called by some mock-lead. **1780** *Specif. M. Sanderson's Patent* No. 1243. 3 Decomposed or calcined blend. **1812** SIR

H. DAVY *Chem. Philos.* 373 Zinc is procured from blende by a similar operation. *Ibid.* 377 In the blendes or supposed sulphurets of zinc. **1869** ROSCOE *Elem. Chem.* 230 The chief ores of zinc are the sulphide or blende, etc.

b. ? Formerly used of other metallic sulphides, or worthless ores. (Cf. HORNBLENDE.)

1781 J. DILLON *Trav. Spain* 231 There is no doubt but that it is cobalt, of which that state is the blend.

'blended, *ppl. a.* [f. BLEND *v.*[2] + -ED.] Mingled, intermixed.

1621 H. KING *Sermon* 26 A blended mixture of the qualities. **1656** MILTON *State Lett.* Wks. (1851) 375 The confus'd and blended havock of Fire and Sword. **1796** BURKE *Regic. Peace* iii. Wks. VIII. 370 Flowing in one blended stream. **1869** J. MARTINEAU *Ess.* II. 175 The blended hymn of past, present, and future.

blender ('blɛndə(r)). **a.** One who or that which blends; an implement for blending pigments.

1872 C. KING *Sierra Nev.* x. 208 He neatly rubbed up the white and sienna with his 'blender.' **1884** *Pall Mall G.* 5 Sept. 6/2 A blender [of tobaccos] is born not made.

b. *Cookery.* An electric food processor, used to blend (purée, etc.) ingredients; = LIQUIDIZER.

1948 *Amer. Home* June 117/2 Relax with a blender at your elbow... Start out with the recipes in your blender book. **1950** [see LIQUIDIZER]. **1955** M. MCCARTHY *Charmed Life* ii. 32 Vitamin soups made in the blender with nine raw vegetables. **1965** 'L. EGAN' *Detective's Due* ii. 18 A good many gadgets..electric can opener, blender, ice crusher mounted on the wall. **1976** *Whig-Standard* (Kingston, Ontario) 4 May 6/6 At our house..the blender is used only to fashion the occasional daiquiri. **1984** *N.Y. Times* 22 Jan. VI. 48/3 Cut the remaining salmon into small cubes and put them in the container of a food processor or electric blender.

blending ('blɛndɪŋ), *vbl. sb.* [f. as prec. + -ING[1].] **1. a.** The process of mixing intimately; the resulting state; a harmonious mixture.

1795 *Act. Geo. III*, civ. §25 in *Oxf. & Camb. Enactm.* 109 The blending of money belonging to different Colleges. **1816** BYRON *Ch. Har.* III. xlvi, A blending of all beauties. **1855** *Whitby Gloss.*, *Blendings*, a minglement of beans and peas. **1876** GREEN *Short Hist.* ii. §6 (1882) 88 This blending of the two races.

b. *spec.* The action or process of mixing materials used in woollen manufacture.

1884 W. S. B. MCLAREN *Spinning* ix. 184 Blending..is one of the most important operations in the whole manufacture... Blending may mean many things. It may be different colours of dyed wool, or wool and shoddy, mungo or flocks, or wool and cotton, or wool and silk, or all these together.

2. *Philol.* = CONTAMINATION 1 d.

1892 H. SWEET *New Eng. Gram.* 48 Grammatical and logical anomalies often arise through the blending of two different constructions... The plural *themselves* may be regarded as a blending of *himself* and *ourselves*. **1894** JESPERSEN *Progress in Lang.* vii. 188 Contaminations or blendings of two constructions between which the speaker is wavering occur in all languages. *Ibid.* 190 The blending was due to the fact that what was grammatically the object of one verb was logically the subject of another verb. **1906** G. A. BERGSTRÖM (*title*) Blendings of Synonymous or Cognate Expressions in English. **1960** H. MARCHAND *Categories Present-day Eng. Word-Formation* x. 367 Blending can be considered relevant to word-formation only insofar as it is an intentional process of word-coining. We shall use the term here to designate the method of merging parts of words into one new word, as when *sm/oke* and *f/og* derive *smog*.

'blending, *ppl. a.* That blends.

1642 W. PRICE *Sermon* 41 The Text may be meant of a blending mixture in Religion. **1812** *Examiner* 30 Nov. 763/2 Gradations..soft and blending. **1873** TRISTRAM *Moab* iii. 50 Parted..without any blending belt of..scrub.

blendous ('blɛndəs), *a.* *Min.* [f. BLENDE + -OUS.] Pertaining to or containing blende.

1847 in CRAIG.

blendure ('blɛndjʊə(r)). *rare.* Blending, mixture.

1701 *Answ. P. Hurly's Vind.* 6 The blendure and conjunction of things at some distance from each other. **1806–31** A. KNOX *Rem.* (1844) I. 55 The aristocratic character has been injured by a neutralizing blendure.

blendy ('blɛndɪ), *a.* [f. BLENDE + -Y.] Containing blende.

1683 PETTUS *Fleta Min.* I. (1686) 290 Lead oars..taken from flinty, blendy, or mountainous places.

† **blenge,** *v. Obs. rare*[−1]. [cf. *blend* and *menge* to mingle.] *trans.* To mingle, mix up.

1573 TUSSER *Husb.* (1878) 190 Backbiting talk that flattering blabs know wily how to blenge.

Blenheim ('blɛnɪm, -ɪm). Name of the Duke of Marlborough's house, near Woodstock, Oxfordshire; used to distinguish, **a.** A breed of spaniels; **b.** *Blenheim Orange*, a golden-coloured apple. *Blenheim Pippin.* Also *ellipt.*

(*a*) **1839** C. SINCLAIR *Holiday House* xv. 332 She..had taken into the berth beside her a little Blenheim spaniel. *c* **1845** C. BRONTË *Professor* (1857) I. xiv. 238 To lead in a ribbon her Blenheim spaniel or Italian greyhound. **1851** MAYHEW *Lond. Lab.* II. 62 (Hoppe) A good fancy breed of 'King Charleses' or 'Blenheims.' **1957** *Encycl. Brit.* VII. 497B/2 *English Toy Spaniel*... There are several varieties of this breed, including the Prince Charles,..Ruby and Blenheim, the main variations being in colour.

(*b*) **1862** R. HOGG *Fruit Man.* (ed. 2) [7] Blenheim Pippin (Woodstock Pippin; Northwick Pippin). **1877** E. S. DALLAS *Kettner's Bk. of Table* 34 Dessert Apples... Blenheim Pippin. **1879** JEFFERIES *Wild Life S. County* 173 In the fork of a great apple tree—a Blenheim orange—the missel-thrush has built her nest. **1882** *Garden* 13 May 321/1 The Blenheim Orange is not a good bearer when young. **1925** BLUNDEN *Eng. Poems* 17 And the sweet smell of Blenheims lapped in straw.

† **blenk,** *v. Obs.* Forms: 4 blenken, 4–7 **blenk.** *Pa. t.* 4 **bleynte, blenkede, blenkyt, -it, blenknyt,** 4–6 **blenked.** *Pa. pple.* 5 **blent.** [Partly the northern equivalent of BLENCH *v.*, partly the earlier equivalent of modern BLINK, presenting the etymological difficulties of both words.]

I. = BLENCH.

1. *trans.* To blind, deceive, cheat; = BLENCH 1.

a **1000** Blenceð [see BLENCH 1]. *c* **1400** *Destr. Troy* 2483 Let no blyndnes you blenke.

2. *intr.* To start aside, so as to elude anything; to flinch, swerve; = BLENCH *v.*[1] 2.

c **1300** *Cursor M.* 7668 [Saul] þan hent a sper scarp to stair him þoru vnto þe wau, bot dauid sagh and blenked lau [*v.r.* blenkid, blenched *bis*]. **1330** R. BRUNNE *Chron.* 115 For þise ne salle ȝe blenk, bot hold vp þer honoure. *a* **1330** *Otuel* 460 He wolde haue smiten otuwel, & he blenkte swiþe wel, And roulond smot þe stede broun.

3. *trans.* To turn aside, raise (the eyes, eyebrows); = BLENCH *v.*[1] 4.

c **1400** MELAYNE 570 He wolde noghte say 'good mornynge,' ne ones his browes blenke.

4. To cheat, disappoint, disconcert, bilk; or ? to turn aside or away. *rare.*

? *a* **1400** *Morte Arth.* 2858 We salle blenke theire boste, for alle theire bold profire.

5. *trans.* To make pale, to blanch. Cf. BLENCH *v.*[2]

c **1400** *Melayne* 1359 A newe tydynge That blenkede all his blee. *a* **1600** *Felon Sowe Rokeby*, The Sewe..rudely rushéd at the freer That blynkéd all his blee.

II. = the later BLINK.

6. *intr.* To shine, glitter, gleam.

1303 R. BRUNNE *Handl. Synne* 428 A nyȝt whan þou slepys..Before þy yȝen hyt blenkys. *c* **1340** *Gaw. & Gr. Knt.* 799 Vp on bastel-rouez, þat blenked ful quyte. **1375** BARBOUR *Bruce* VIII. 217 The sone..That blenknyt on the scheldis braid. **1535** STEWART *Cron. Scot.* I. 349 Bemes bricht blenkand on euerilk bench. **1605** in *Foxe's A. & M.* (1684) III. 942 The Sun blenks often hottest to foretel a following showr.

7. To glance, cast a glance, give a look; to look *up* (from sleep); = BLINK 3, 4 a.

c **1350** *Will. Palerne* 3111 þei lokede a boute & bleynte bi hinde þe busch & seiȝen. **1375** BARBOUR *Bruce* VI. 633 The King..blenkit hym by And saw the twa-some. *Ibid.* VII. 203 The kyng blenkit vp hastely, And saw his men slepand him by. *c* **1450** HENRYSON *Mor. Fab.* 83 The Wolfe was ware, and blenked him behind. **1501** DOUGLAS *Pal. Hon.* I. 326 Backwert he blent to give them knawledging. *a* **1625** JAS. I. in D'Israeli *Cur. Lit.* (1866) 174/1 Scarslie, but at stolen moments, having the leisure to blenk upon any paper.

blenk, *sb.*[1] north. f. BLENCH, trick, stratagem.

† **blenk,** *sb.*[2] *north. Obs.* [f. BLENK *v.*; now, like the vb., represented by BLINK.]

1. A sudden gleam of light.

c **1340** *Cursor M.* 19648 (Fairf.) Noȝt a blenke muȝt he se. **1513** DOUGLAS *Æneis* VII. ix. 113 The bricht mettell..Quharon the son blenkis betis clere.

2. A glance of the eye; usually, a bright, cheerful glance.

c **1440** *York Myst.* xxviii. 259, I will no more be abasshed for blenke of thy blee. *c* **1450** *Wisd. Sol.* in *Ratis Rav.* 21 Na wys men suld behald the bewte of women that thai be nocht tan with thar suet blenkis. **1535** STEWART *Cron. Scot.* I. 31 The ȝoung virgeins with blenkis amorus.

† **'blenking,** *vbl. sb. Obs.* [f. BLENK *v.* + -ING.[1]] Glancing, blinking.

c **1450** HENRYSON *Test. Creseide*, The swete visage and amorous blenking.

blenne, obs. form of BLEND *v.*[2]

blennioid ('blɛnɪɔɪd), *a.* and *sb.* **A.** *adj.* Allied to the BLENNY. **B.** *sb.* A fish of this kind.

1865 *Reader* No. 110. 143/2 Fishes which resemble at first Gadoïds or Blennioïds.

blenno-, blenn-, a. Gr. βλέννο-ς, βλέννα, mucus, in which sense it is extensively used in combination in *Pathology*; as in **blenno'genic, ble'nnogenous** *a.*, generating or producing mucus. **'blennoid** *a.*, resembling mucus. **blenno'rrhagia, blenno'rrhœa** (-'riːə), discharge of mucus; hence **blenno'rrhagic** (-'rædʒɪk), **blenno'rrhoic** *a.*

1859 TODD *Cycl. Anat. & Phys.* V. 617/2 Catarrh or blennorrhœa of the mucous membrane. **1861** BUMSTEAD *Ven. Dis.* (1879) 142 Five of these cases were not blennorrhagic.

blenny ('blɛnɪ). [ad. L. *blennius* (in Pliny), f. Gr. βλέννος; so called from βλέννος slime, in reference to the mucous coating of its scales.]

A genus of small spiny-finned fishes, of which several species frequent the British coasts.

[**1753** CHAMBERS *Cycl. Supp.* s.v., The common Blennius of authors. **1769** PENNANT *Zool.* III. 173.] **1774** GOLDSM. *Nat. Hist.* (1862) II. III. i. 295 The Blennius or Blenny. **1863** H. PENNELL *Angler-nat.* 394 Viviparous fishes, such as the Sharks, Blennies, etc.

blensch, obs. form of BLENCH, BLEMISH.

blent, *ppl. a.* [f. BLEND *v.*[2]] Mingled.

1872 GEO. ELIOT *Middlem.* xliii, The habits of the different ranks were less blent than now. **1876** —— *Dan. Der.* VIII. lxiii. 566 That blent transmission must go on.

blent, obs. form of BLEND *v.*[2] (Perhaps sense 2 is meant by the following:)

1530 PALSGR. 457/2, I blente, I lette or I hynder..This terme is to moche northerne.

† **blent(e,** obs. pa. t. and pple. of BLENCH, BLEND, BLENK, *v.*

bleo, bleoman: see BLEE, BLOMAN.

blepharo- ('blɛfərəʊ), a. Gr. βλέφαρο-ν eyelid; used in numerous terms of *Pathology*, etc.: as **blepha'ritis,** inflammation of the eyelids. **'blepharo,plasty,** the operation of supplying any deficiency caused by wound or lesion of the eyelid; hence **,blepharo'plastic** *a.* **'blepharospasm,** spasm of the orbicular muscle of the eyelids. **'blepharostat,** an instrument for fixing the eyelid during operations in the eye. (*Syd. Soc. Lex.*)

1872 F. THOMAS *Dis. Women* 137 The same relation which blepharospasm [bears] to the lids. **1875** H. WALTON *Dis. Eye* 332 Blepharospasm, by which the eyelids are violently and persistently closed.

,blepharoconjuncti'vitis. *Path.* [mod.L., f. BLEPHARO- + CONJUNCTIVITIS.] Inflammation of the eyelids and conjunctiva.

1890 in BILLINGS *Med. Dict.* I. 171/2. **1962** *Lancet* 28 Apr. 877/1 He presented..a typical picture of primary ocular vaccinial blepharoconjunctivitis.

blepharoplast ('blɛfərəʊplɑːst, -æ-). *Biol.* [f. BLEPHARO- + -PLAST.] **a.** A centrosome-like protoplasmic body found in the sperm-cells of certain plants. **b.** In protozoans, a minute granule at the base of each flagellum.

1897 H. J. WEBBER in *Bot. Gaz.* Oct. 233, I would..suggest the name *blepharoplast* to distinguish them from other organs of the cell. **1908** *Practitioner* Feb. 227 Flagellated forms [possess] a nucleus and blepharoplast. **1964** M. HYNES *Med. Bacteriol.* (ed. 8) xxviii. 433 In the anterior half of the cell (Trichomonas vaginalis) are the nucleus and the blepharoplast from which arises a cluster of four flagella of equal length.

,blepharop'tosis. *Path.* [mod.L., f. BLEPHARO- + PTOSIS.] = PTOSIS a.

1807 MORRIS & KENDRICK *Edinb. Med. & Phys. Dict.* I, *Blepharoptosis*, a prolapsion, or falling down of the upper eyelid, so as to cover the cornea. **1846** BRITTAN tr. *Malgaigne's Man. Opt. Surg.* 279 Blepharoptosis may arise from two principal causes. **1961** *Brit. Med. Dict.* 204/1 Blepharoptosis.

blere, obs. form of BLEAR.

blerry ('blɛrɪ), *a.* *S. Afr. slang.* Also **blerrie, blirry.** [S. Afr. corruption of BLOODY *a.*] = BLOODY *a.* 10. Cf. PLURRY *a.* and *adv.*

1920 R. Y. STORMBERG *Mrs. Pieter de Bruyn* 10 What's the meaning of 'blirry domkop'? **1949** O. WALKER *Wanton City* 61 Where's our blerry scoff, eh? **1959** *Encounter* Dec. 17/2 That's what every blerry visitor thinks. **1964** L. NKOSI *Rhythm of Violence* 4 It's the blerry English and their City Council! If this was a Boer town nothing like this would ever happen! **1973** *Argus* (Cape Town) *Mag. Suppl.* 24 Feb., The blerrie police was here this afternoon checking our typewriters. **1986** C. LASSALLE *Breaking Rules* 183 Do you boys call this blerry muck breakfast?

bles, obs. form of BLAZE *sb.*

‖ **bles-bok** ('blɛsbɒk). Also **bless bok, 'bless-buck.** [Du., f. *bles* blaze on forehead + *bok* goat.] A South African antelope, the *Gazella albifrons.*

1824 BURCHELL *Trav.* II. 335 The Blesbok is so called from having a white mark on its forehead. **1869** E. GRAY *Guide Brit. Museum* 2 The Blessbok, Hartebeest, and Sassaybe of South Africa. **1879** ATCHERLEY *Boërland* 73 The bless-buck, a larger antelope than the [spring-buck].

blesce, obs. form of BLESS *v.*[1]

† **'blesche,** *v. Obs.* Also 3 **blessen, blissen.** [ME. *bleschen, blessen*, identical with MDu. *blesschen* (mod.Du., and LG. *blusschen*) to extinguish or quench, taken to represent an OTeut. **bilaskjan*, f. *bi-*, BE- + *laskjan*, OHG. *leskên* to quench, extinguish (MHG., MLG. and late MDu. *lesschen*, mod.G. *löschen*), causal of OHG. *leskan* (MHG. *leschen*, mod.Ger. also *löschen*) to 'go out' as fire. How it came into ME. does not appear.]

trans. To quench, extinguish; *fig.* to put a stop to, blot out.

c **1250** *Gen. & Ex.* 553 So cam on werlde wreche and wrake for to blissen swilc sinnes same. *Ibid.* 3653 Fier is on hem bisiden liȝt..Moyses it blessede wið his bede. *c* **1440** *Promp. Parv.* 39/2 Bleschyn, or qwenchyn [**1499** blesshyn], *extinguo.*

Hence **blesching** *vbl. sb.*

c **1440** *Promp. Parv.*, Bleschynge, or qwenchynge of fyre.

blese, obs. f. BLAZE *sb.*[1] and BLESS *v.*[1]

† **ble'siloquent**, *a. Obs. rare*$^{-0}$. [ad. L. **blæsi-loquent-em*, f. *blæsus* lisping, stammering + *loquent-em* speaking.] 'Broad-spoken, or that speaks stammeringly.' Blount *Glossogr.* 1656.
Thence in PHILLIPS and BAILEY.

blesome, obs. form of BLISSOM.

bless (blɛs), *v.*[1] Forms: 1 blóedsian, blédsian, blétsian, 2 bletsien, bletcæn, blecen, bleccen, 2–3 bledsen, bletsen, (*Orm.*) blettcenn, blettsenn, 2–4 blescen, 2–5 blessen, 3 bletseiȝen, blesci, blicen, 3–4 blixen, blissen, 4 blisce, blis, blist, 3–7 blesse, bliss(e, 5 blysch(e, blyssh(e, 5–6 blysse, 7– bless. *Pa. t.* and *pple.* blessed, blest (*arch.* and *poet.*); in 1 blédsod, blétsod, 2–3 bledsed, 2–5 bletsed, blecced, blesced, blisced, 2– blessed, 5– blest. [OE. *blóedsian, blédsian, blétsian*: not found elsewhere in Teutonic, but formed on the OTeut. type **blôdisôjan*, f. **blôdo-m* (OE. *blód*) blood: cf. OE. *mildsian, miltsian*, ME. MILCE, to be *mild*, show pity; also, for the formation, OE. *rícsian* to rule = OHG. *rîchisôn*:—OTeut. **rîkisôjan*, f. **rîk-s*, Goth. *reiks* ruler, king. (An equally satisfactory derivation of *blétsian*, if it were the original form, would be from *blót* sacrifice, on OTeut. type **blôtisôjan*; but besides that *blóedsian* actually occurs earlier, the change of *ds* to *ts* is phonetically natural, while the reverse is not.) The etymological meaning was thus 'to mark (or affect in some way) with blood (or sacrifice); to consecrate'. But the sense-development of the word was greatly influenced by its having been chosen at the Eng. conversion to render L. *benedīcere*, and Gr. εὐλογεῖν, which started from a primitive sense of 'speak well of or to, eulogize, praise,' but were themselves influenced by being chosen to translate Heb. *brk*, primarily 'to bend,' hence 'to bend the knee, worship, praise, bless God, invoke blessings on, bless as a deity.' Hence, a long and varied series of associations, heathen, Jewish, and Christian, blend in the Eng. uses of *bless* and *blessing*. Senses 4–6 arise mainly from *benedīcere*, εὐλογεῖν. At a very early date the popular etymological consciousness began to associate this verb with the sb. BLISS 'benignity, blitheness, joy, happiness,' which affected the use of both words (see esp. senses 7, 8), and led to occasional ME. spelling of the vb. with *i*, *y*.
The *pa. t.* and *pple.* are now generally spelt *blessed*, though always pronounced (blɛst) in modern prose; the pple. may be pronounced ('blɛsɪd) in verse, or liturgical reading. As an adj. *blessed* ('blɛsɪd) is now the regular prose form, but the archaic *blest* is frequent in verse, and traditional phrases as e.g. 'the Isles of the Blest.']

Orig. meaning (prob.), To make 'sacred' or 'holy' with blood; to consecrate by some sacrificial rite which was held to render a thing inviolable from profane use of men and evil influence of men or demons. (The streaking of the lintel and doorposts with blood, *Exod.* xii. 23, to mark them as holy to the Lord and inviolable by the destroying angel, was apparently the kind of idea expressed by *blóedsian* in pre-christian times. Cf. also the history of the Latin words *consecrāre* and *sacrificium*.) Hence, in historical use:

I. To make sacred, consecrate, hallow.

1. *trans.* To consecrate (a thing) by a religious rite, the utterance of a formula or charm; in later times by a prayer committing it to God for his patronage, defence, and prospering care, as in *to bless food*, to ask God's blessing on it (cf. 5).

c **1000** *Ags. Gosp.* Matt. xxvi. 26 Se Hælend nam hlaf and hyne bletsode and bræc. *c* **1200** ORMIN 17193 þatt waterr þatt iss att te funnt Blettcedd wiþþ Godes wordess. **1377** LANGL. *P. Pl.* B. XI. 229 Tyl he blessed and brak þe bred þat þei eten. *c* **1400** *Apol. Loll.* 30 If þe prest sacre Crist wan he blessiþ þe sacrament of God in þe auter. *a* **1593** H. SMITH *Serm.* (1637) 376 Before thou hast blessed it with prayer, thou hast no promise it shall prosper. **1596** SHAKS. *Merch. V.* III. ii. 79. **1637** GILLESPIE *Eng. Pop. Cerem.* IV. iv. 20 It was behoofefull for their cause, distinctly and severally to blisse those Elements. **1649** MILTON *Eikon.* Wks. 1738 I. 427 Where the Master is too resty, or too rich to.. bless his own Table. **1798** SOUTHEY *Bp. Bruno* Wks. VI. 149 And now the bishop had blest the meat.

† **b.** To consecrate (a person) to a sacred office.
1154 *O.E. Chron.* (Laud MS.) Þa was he [Henry II] to king bletcæd in Lundene. *c* **1420** *Chron. Vilod.* 563 And was blessud Abbas in þ^t^ same place. *Ibid.* 1168 Þen was Alfyne y blessud Abbas of þ^t^ plase.

2. *spec.* To sanctify or hallow by making the sign of the cross; usually as a defence against evil agencies. esp. *refl.* and *absol.* To cross oneself. *arch.*

c **950** *Lindisf. Gosp.* John viii. 48 Ahne bloedsade ue usic *vel* sæȝnade [*mistransl. of* nonne bene dicimus nos?] *a* **1225** *Ancr. R.* 290 Breid up þene rode stef, & sweng him aȝean a uour halue—þene helle dogge. Þet nis nout elles bute blesce þe al abuten mid te eadie rode tocne. *c* **1500** *Yng. Children's Bk.* in *Babees Bk.* (1868) 17 Aryse be tyme oute of thi bedde, And blysse þi brest & thi forhede. **1562** J. HEYWOOD *Prov. & Epigr.* (1867) 91, I nother nod for sleepe.. nor blisse for spirites. **1577** HOLINSHED *Chron.* I. 157/2 Blesse your eies with the signe of the crosse, and trie whether you can see that I see. **1653** URQUHART *Rabelais* I. xxxv, When they heard these words, some.. blest themselves with both hands, thinking.. that he had been a devil disguised. **1719** LADY M. W. MONTAGUE *Lett.* II. xlvii. 47, I fancy I see you bless yourself at this terrible relation.

b. *to bless oneself from*: see 3 b.

† **c.** *to bless into, out*: to change into, cast out, by making the sign of the cross. *Obs.*

1534 MORE *Passion* Wks. (1557) 1273/1 When the dyuell fyrste casteth any proude vayne thoughte into our mynd.. let vs forthwith make a crosse on our breast, and blesse it oute. **1589** NASHE *Pasquils Ret.* Wks. 1885 I. 93 One Pope or other.. blest me into a stone to stoppe my mouth.

d. *not to have a penny to bless oneself with*: in allusion to the cross on the silver penny (cf. Ger. *Kreuzer*), or to the practice of crossing the palm with a piece of silver.

1557 NORTH *Gueuara's Diall Pr.* (1619) 625/2 The pestilence of penny.. he hath in his purse to blesse himself with. **1562** J. HEYWOOD *Prov. & Epigr.* (1867) 73 He had not.. one peny to blisse him. **1861** GEO. ELIOT *Silas M.*, I have not a shilling to bless myself with.

† **e.** *humorously* (with allusion to holy water.)
1609 *Man in the Moone* 11 Bless his beard with a bazen of water, least he burne it.

† **3.** To protect or guard, save, keep *from* (evil): said of God, supernatural influence, a charm or prayer; also loosely of other things. *Obs.*

c **1175** *Lamb. Hom.* 59 From alle . uuele he scal blecen us. **1543** BECON *New Y. Gift* Wks. (1843) 315 With such I love not to meddle. God bless me from them! **1594** NASHE *Unfort. Trav.* 43 Kisse the ground as holy ground which she vouchsafed to blesse from barrennes by her steppes. **1594** SHAKS. *Rich. III*, III. iii. 5 God blesse the Prince from all the Pack of you. **1596** SPENSER *F.Q.* I. ii. 18 Glauncing down his shield from blame him fairly blest. **1632** MILTON *Penseroso* 83 Or the bellmans drowsy charm To bless the doors from nightly harm. **1646** FULLER *Wounded Consc.* (1841) 349 God bless you and yours from fire. **1650** BP. HALL *Cases Consc.* 181 Doubtlesse, the Devill is a most skilfull Artist.. but God blesse us from imploying him. **1855** KINGSLEY *Westw. Ho!* ii. (*Traditional Spell*)'Matthew, Mark, Luke, and John, Bless the bed that I lie on.'

† **b.** *refl.* To guard oneself (with God's help) *from*, keep out of the way of, give a wide berth to, shun, eschew. (Sometimes, probably, by crossing oneself, as in sense 2.) *Obs.*

c **1449** PECOCK *Repr.* III. xix. 411 If thilk doctor.. hadde blessid him silf fro this.. perel. **1530** PALSGR. 458/1, I wyll never medle with hym, if I may blesse me from hym. **1549** CHALONER *Erasm. Moriæ Enc.* E iv b, Whiche of you woulde not lothe and blisse you from the company of suche maner a man. **1618** RALEIGH *Rem.* (1644) 97 From Suretieship, as from a Man-slayer, or Enchanter, blesse thy self. **1622** FLETCHER *Span. Curate* I. i. 27 Blesse yourselves from the thought of him and her. **1651** MORE *Enthus. Triumph.* (1656) 172 Bless thee from madness, Tom, and all will be well. **1753** SMOLLETT *Ct. Fathom* (1784) 137/2 He blessed himself from such customers.

II. To hold or call holy; to extol as holy (see Isa. vi. 3, Rev. iv. 8), divine, gracious.

4. To call holy; to extol, praise, or adore (God) as holy, worthy of reverence.

a **1000** *Cædmon's Daniel* 400 (Gr.) We ðec bletsiað, Fæder ælmihtiȝ. *c* **1000** *Ags. Psalter* xcv[i]. 2 Singað nu drihtne and his soðne naman bealde bletsiað. *c* **1175** *Lamb. Hom.* 57 Þi nome beo iblecced. *c* **1305** *Deo Gratias* in *E.E.P.* (1862) 125 To þonke and blesse hym we be bounde. **1382** WYCLIF *Jas* iii. 9 In it we blessen God the fadir, and in it we cursen men. **1593** HOOKER *Eccl. Pol.* I. iii. §4 The Creator.. alone to be blessed, adored and honoured of all for ever. **1651** HOBBES *Leviath.* II. xxxi. 189 The subject of Magnifying and Blessing, being Power. **1825** J. MONTGOMERY *Hymn 'Stand up and bless'* 6 Stand up and bless the Lord, The Lord your God adore.

5. *esp.* with an added notion of thanksgiving or acknowledgement of gracious beneficence or goodness: To praise or extol with grateful heart; 'to glorify for benefits received' (J.)

a. *orig.* God or his attributes.

c **1000** *Ags. Gosp.* Luke i. 68 Gebletsod [*Lindisf.* ȝebloedsad] si drihten israhela god, forþam þe he ȝeneosode. **1382** WYCLIF *ibid.* Blessid be the Lord God of Israel for ..[CRANMER, Praysed be]. *c* **1440** *York Myst.* xii. 217 Blest be þou ay, For þe grace þou has me lente. **1526** *Pilgr. Perf.* (W. de W. 1531) 251 To laude and blesse god for his goodnes. **1596** SHAKS. *Tam. Shr.* IV. v. 18 Then God be blesst, it is the blessed Sunne. **1795** SOUTHEY *Joan of Arc* II. 309, I.. blest my God I was not such as he. **1843** NEALE *Hymns for Sick* 44 But Thy Love—Oh give me grace to bless It every hour!

b. other influences, e.g. one's stars, one's fortune or luck, the day of one's birth, etc. Now generally in a more or less ludicrous sense: To thank, attribute one's good fortune to.

c **1440** *Ywaine & Gaw.* 3344 Folk.. blissed the time that he was born. *a* **1845** HOOD *Pauper's Christmas Carol* iii, Ought not I to bless my stars? **1846** *Punch* IX. 13 Let me bless my prudence.

c. persons: see 6 b, which sometimes passes into 'praise or extol with grateful regard.'

III. To declare to be supernaturally favoured; to pronounce or make happy.

6. To pronounce words that confer (or are held to confer) supernatural favour and well-being.

a. Said of a superior, i.e. of one entitled to speak in God's name, a priest or sacred person (e.g. Balaam, Moses), an aged or dying parent (e.g. Isaac, Jacob); also of God himself. When said of men, the sense has passed into that of officially or paternally commending to divine protection and favour.

c **1000** ÆLFRIC *Gen.* xxvii. 4 Bring me þæt ic ete, and ic þe bletsiȝe ær þam þe ic swelte. *c* **1000** *Ags. Gosp.* Mark x. 16 Ða beclypte he hí, and his handa ofer hi settende bletsode [*Lindisf.* ȝebledsade, *Rushw.* ȝibletsade, *Hatton* bletsede] hi. *c* **1205** LAY. 32157 Me and mine wiue: he scal bletseiȝen & scriue. *a* **1300** *Cursor M.* 637 God ham blesset and bad ham brede, and multiply. *c* **1383** WYCLIF *Sel. Wks.* III. 323 Þei cursen hem þat God blisseþ. **1388** —— *Numb.* xxiii. 11 What is this that thou doist? Y clepide thee that thou schuldist curse myn enemyes, and aȝenward thou blessist hem [**1382** blessest to hem]. *c* **1410** LOVE *Bonavent. Mirr.* xv. 38 (Gibbs MS.), After he hadde i blessed hem wente vppe aȝayne to heuene. **1549** *Bk. Com. Prayer, Confirm.*, Then shal the Busshop blisse the children, thus saying. **1810** SCOTT *Lady of L.* III. vii, Stood prompt to bless or ban.

b. Of one not a superior: Piously to invoke God's blessing upon, to commend gratefully and affectionately to God's favour, to load with one's devout good wishes; to speak well of and wish well to.

1330 R. BRUNNE *Chron.* (1810) 97, I blisse Anselme þerfore. *c* **1330** *Amis & Amil.* 344 Men blisted him, bothe bon and blod, That euer him gat and bare. **1613** SHAKS. *Hen. VIII*, III. i. 54 To taint that honor euery good Tongue blesses. **1667** MILTON *P.L.* x. 821 So disinherited how would ye bless Me now your Curse! **1712** STEELE *Spect.* No. 264 ⁋1 The Fatherless.. and the Stranger bless his unseen Hand in their Prayers. **1742** W. COLLINS *Ode* vi, By all their country's wishes blest. **1850** TENNYSON *In Mem.* cxix, I.. think of early days and thee, And bless thee.

7. To confer well-being upon; 'to make happy; to prosper, make successful' (J.): *orig.* said of God; in later use also of men and things, but generally with an implication of their conferring instrumentally a divine blessing. (Here the association of *bless* with *bliss* becomes apparent.)

a **1000** *Cædmon's Gen.* 2357 (Gr.) Ic Ismael estum wille bletsian. *a* **1300** *Hymn to God* 16 in *Trin. Coll. Hom.* App. 258 Louerd þu vs blesce. **1388** WYCLIF *Gen.* xxxix. 5 And the Lord blesside the hows [**1382** to the hows] of Egipcian for Joseph. **1549** *Bk. Com. Prayer, Matrim.*, Look, O Lord, mercifully upon them from heaven, and bless them. **1578** *Gude & Godlie Ballates* (1868) 65 Blis, blissit God, thir giftes gude Quhilk thow hes geuin to be our fude. **1596** SHAKS. *Merch. V.* IV. i. 186 It [mercy] is twice blest, It blesseth him that giues, and him that takes. **1597** —— *2 Hen. IV*, I. ii. 248 Heauen blesse your Expedition. **1697** DRYDEN *Virg. Georg.* IV. 729 But she return'd no more, to bless his longing Eyes. **1718** POPE *Iliad* I. 144 When first her blooming beauties bless'd my arms. **1813** BYRON *Giaour* 1115, I have possess'd, And come what may, I have been blest. **1848** THACKERAY *Van. Fair* xxxi,'God bless the meat,' said the Major's wife, solemnly. **1850** LYNCH *Theo. Trin.* v. 88 To say that good gives pleasure seems poor expression of the truth that it blesses us.

b. To make happy *with* some gift: *orig.* of God as the giver; also of persons or things. (In the first example, *blitsian* may be really = *bliðsian*, BLISS.)

[*a* **831** *Charter of Oswulf* (Sweet *O.E.T.* 444) Ðaette ȝe sien ȝeblitsude mid ðem weorldcundum godum.] **1598** B. JONSON *Ev. Man out of Hum.* II. iii, Shee was blest with no more copie of wit. **1602** *Return fr. Parnass.* II. v. (Arb.) 30, I will blesse your eares with a very pretty story. **1610** SHAKS. *Temp.* II. i. 124 You may thank your selfe.. That would not blesse our Europe with your daughter. **1650** BAXTER *Saint's R.* III. (1654) 4 Return him hearty thanks upon my knees, that ever he blessed his Word in my mouth with such.. success. **1712** ARBUTHNOT *John Bull* (1755) 30 Mrs. Bull.. blessed John with three daughters. **1767** FORDYCE *Serm. Yng. Wom.* I. i. 14 Are you.. blest with parents? **1839** BAILEY *Festus* i, To bless him with salvation.

8. *refl.* To account or call oneself supremely happy; to congratulate or felicitate oneself, *with*, *in*, *that*.

1611 BIBLE *Jer.* iv. 2 The nations shall blesse themselues in him, and in him shall they glorie. **1674** N. FAIRFAX *Bulk & Selv.* To Rdr., I.. blisst my self that I was there. **1684** BUNYAN *Pilgr.* II. (1879) 246 Old men have blessed themselves with this mistake. **1839** BAILEY *Festus* iv, To.. bask, and bless myself, Upon the broad bright bosom.

¶ In ME., and above all by Wyclif, *bless* was construed with *to*, app. in imitation of *benedicere alicui* of the Vulgate.

a **1300** *Cursor M.* 17890 To oure lord iesu crist ȝe blisse. *c* **1380** WYCLIF *Serm.* Sel. Wks. II. 249 Cristene men shulden blesse to oþer þat pursuen hem here. **1382** —— *Gen.* i. 21 And God.. blisside to hem, seiynge, Growith, etc. *Ibid.* xii. 3, I shal blis to thoo that blissen thee.

IV. Exclamatory, elliptical and ironical uses.

9. In exclamatory invocations and ejaculations of surprise; **a.** in sense 3, as ***God bless me!*** elliptically ***bless me! bless*** (also ***save***) ***the mark!*** (see MARK). **b.** in sense 7, as ***(God) bless you!***

a. 1590 SHAKS. *Mids. N.* IV. ii. 14 A Paramour is (God blesse vs) a thing of nought. **1646** MILTON *Sonn.* xi. 5 Cries the stall-reader, 'Bless us! what a word on A title-page is this!' **1709** STEELE *Tatler* No. 25 ⁋10 Bless me! Sir, there's no Room for a Question. **1752** MRS. LENNOX *Fem. Quix.* I. III. v. 161 'Lord bless me, madam!' said Lucy, excessively astonished. **1844** DICKENS *Mart. Chuz.* v. 50 'Bless my life!' said Mr. Pecksniff, looking up. **1849** —— *Dav. Copp.* xii. 138 'Bless and save the man'.. 'how he talks!' **1851** RUSKIN *King Gold. Riv.* i. (1856) 12 'Bless my soul!' said Schwartz when he opened the door.

b. 1588 SHAKS. *L.L.L.* II. i. 77 God blesse my Ladies, are they all in loue? **1732** FIELDING *Miser* v. i. (1775) 67 Bless her heart! good lady! **1840** MARRYAT *Poor Jack* xxix, Bless

you, my child, bless you! **1872** Ruskin *Fors Clav.* II. xx. 8 The Colonel might have said 'Bless you, my children,' in the tenderest tones.

10. Hence, *to bless oneself*: to ejaculate 'God bless me!' or other exclamation of surprise, vexation, or mortification.

1615 T. Adams *Black Dev.* 71 He..would blesse himselfe to think that so little a thing could extend itself to such a capacity. **1665** Pepys *Diary* 1 Apr., How my Lord Treasurer did bless himself, crying he could do no more, etc.

¶ **11.** In many senses (esp. 5 b, 7, 8, 9, 10) *bless* is used euphemistically or ironically for a word of opposite meaning, 'curse, damn,' etc.

1812 Miss Austen *Mansf. P.* xviii, Could Sir Thomas look in upon us just now, he would bless himself. **1838** Dickens *O. Twist* xiii, An emphatic and earnest desire to be 'blessed' if she would. **1878** H. Smart *Play or Pay* viii. (ed. 3) 156 Fuming, blessing himself, dashing himself.

V. *Comb.*, as †*bless-beggar*, a thing to bless a beggar with. (*ironical.*)

1589 R. Harvey *Pl. Perc.* (1860) 33 My quarter staffe, is it not a blesse-begger thinke you?

†**bless**, *v.*² *Obs.* Also 4-6 blyss(e, bliss. [a. F. *blesse-r*:—OF. *blecier* to injure, wound: cf. BLECHE. Often associated with BLESS *v.*¹, either humorously or in ignorance. (The sense of the second quotation is doubtful: cf. BLESS *v.*³)] To wound, hurt; to beat, thrash, drub.

[*c* **1325** *Coer de L.* 546 Whenne I hym had a strok i-fet, And wolde have blyssyd hym bet. *c* **1350** *Will. Palerne* 1192 [He] blessed so wiþ his briȝt bront · aboute in eche side þat, what rink so he rauȝt · he ros neuer after.] **1526** Skelton *Magnyf.* 1641, I have hym coryed, beten and blyst. **1545** Ascham *Toxoph.* (Arb.) 145 As thoughe they woulde tourne about and blysse all the feelde. **1575** J. Still *Gamm. Gurton* III. iii, Tarry, thou knave..I shall make these hands bless thee. **1577** Hellowes *Gueuara's Fam. Ep.* 237 When he did leuell to shoote, he blessed himselfe with his peece, and killed them with the pellat. **1612** Shelton *Quix.* I. iii. 173 That of the Battle..when they bless'd your Worship's Cheek Teeth.

†**bless**, *v.*³ *Obs.* Also 6 blesse, bliss. [Much affected by Spenser: perhaps taken from such a use as that quoted from *William of Palerne* under BLESS *v.*²; perhaps, as others think, 'to flourish as in making the sign of the cross': cf. BLESS *v.*¹ 2 (quot. 1225), also 3 (quot. 1596). In any case it can hardly be an independent word.] *trans.* and *absol.* To wave about, brandish; also *trans.* to brandish round (an object *with* a weapon).

1596 Spenser *F.Q.* I. v. 6 They..burning blades about their heades doe blesse. *Ibid.* I. viii. 22 His sparkling blade about his head he blest. *Ibid.* VI. viii. 13 And with his club him all about so blist, That he which way to turne him scarcely wist. **1600** Fairfax *Tasso* IX. lxvii, His armed head with his sharpe blade he blest.

†**bless**, *sb.* *Obs.* [f. BLESS *v.*¹; but perhaps confused with BLISS *sb.*] A blessing.

1526 *Pilgr. Perf.* (W. de W. 1531) 45 The viii beatitudes, otherwyse called the viii blesses. **1725** Pope *Odyss.* xv. 202 This promised bless.

bless, obs. form of BLISS.

blessbok, -buck, var. of BLES-BOK, antelope.

blessed, blest (ˈblɛsɪd, blɛst), *ppl. a.* [f. BLESS *v.*¹ + -ED. For the forms and pronunciation see note under BLESS *v.*]

1. Consecrated, hallowed, holy; consecrated by a religious rite or ceremony.

c **1200** *Trin. Coll. Hom.* 25 Bledsed be þi name on us, *sanctificetur nomen tuum.* *a* **1300** *Cursor M.* 21677 Þat blisced lambs blod. **1504** *Will* in *Ripon Ch. Acts* 295 Afore the blissed rode. **1556** *Chron. Gr. Friars* (1852) 95 A proclamacion for the blyssyd sacrament. **1578** *Gude & Godlie Ballates* (1868) 177 Mariage is ane blessit band. **1688** Stradling *Serm.* 195 Who receive him worthily in the Blessed Sacrament. **1839** Marryat *Phant. Ship* i, I..dipped my finger in the blessed water. **1855** Browning *Holy Cross Day*, Blessedest Thursday's the fat of the week.

2. That is the object of adoring reverence, adorable, worthy to be blessed by men.

c **1230** *Hali Meid.* 47 Ihesu crist leue þe þurh his blescede nome. *a* **1240** *Lofsong* in *Cott. Hom.* 209 Þurh þine eadi flesche and þine iblescede blode. *c* **1380** Wyclif *Serm.* (Sel. Wks.) I. 131 Crist..in his blessid passioun. *a* **1400** *Relig. Pieces fr. Thornton MS.* (1867) 39 In his Godhede so blyschede. **1493** *Petronylla* 32 Oure blessyd lorde Iesu. **1556** *Will* in *Ripon Ch. Acts* 361 Our blessed lady saunte Mary. **1656** H. More *Antid. Ath.* III. x. (1662) 119 Crying out, 'Blessed God, what's here to do.' **1868** Bp. Wordsworth *Hymn*, '*Hark, the sound of Holy voices*,' In the Beatific Vision Of the Blessed Trinity.

3. a. Enjoying supreme felicity; happy, fortunate.

c **1175** *Lamb. Hom.* 47 Ædie and blessede beon alle þeo þe ihereð. *a* **1300** *Cursor M.* 16655 þe baraigne blisced sal man call. *c* **1400** *Ave Regina* (Turnb. 1843) 145 Heyle be tho bleste that euer bare chylde. *c* **1410** Occleve *Mother of God* 24 Among all wommen blessed thow be. **1592** Shaks. *Ven. & Ad.* 466 Blessed bankrupt, that by love so thriveth. **1640** Howell *Dodona's Gr.* (1645) 69 The blessedst of mortal Wights. **1790** Burns *Tam o' Shanter*, Kings may be blest, but Tam was glorious. **1875** Jowett *Plato* (ed. 2) I. 14 If to beauty is added temperance, then blessed art thou.

b. Enjoying the bliss of heaven, beatified (cf. 5).

1475 *Bk. Noblesse* 3 Men..whiche as verray trew martirs and blissid souls have taken theire last ende by werre. **1572** R. H. *Lavaterus' Ghostes* (1596) 102 Cælum Empireum.. which they say is the seate ordeined for the blissed sort. **1591** Shaks. *Two Gent.* II. vii. 38 And there Ile rest, as after much turmoile A blessed soule doth in Elizium. **1667** Milton *P.L.* III. 136 The blessed Spirits elect.

c. *absol.* The beatified saints; those in paradise.

c **1200** *Trin. Coll. Hom.* 173 Cumeð ibledsede and underfoð eche lif. **1551** Robinson tr. *More's Utop.* (1869) 148 It were an vnconvenient thinge that the blessed shoulde not be at libertie to goo whether they woulde. **1675** Dryden *Aurengz.* I. i. 144 T' augment the number of the Bliss'd above. **1810** Southey *Kehama* XII. i, The joys which Heaven hath destin'd for the blest. **1863** Tennyson *Wages* 8 She desires no isles of the blest, no quiet seats of the just.

4. a. Bringing, or accompanied by, blessing or happiness; pleasurable, joyful, blissful.

1458 *MS. Christ's Hosp. Abingdon* in *Dom. Archit.* III. 41 Another blissed besines is brigges to make. **1526** *Pilgr. Perf.* (W. de W. 1531) 150 There foloweth the moost blessed effecte. **1660** Pepys *Diary* 23 May, The Royalle company by themselves [dined] in the coach, which was a blessed sight to see. **1679** Burnet *Hist. Ref.* Ep. Ded., The short, but blessed reign of king Edward. **1719** Young *Busiris* IV. i. (1757) 72, I have thought..thirst and toil Blest objects of ambition. **1863** Fr. Kemble *Resid. Georgia* 10 The blessed unconsciousness and ignorance of childhood.

b. Of plants and herbs: Endowed with healing virtues; hence in plant names (= Lat. *benedictus*), as **blessed rose**, ? the peony; **blessed thistle**, *Carduus benedictus*; (erroneously) *C. Marianus*.

1563 Hyll *Art Garden.* (1593) 102 The stalk..beareth big and reddish flours, of some named the blessed Rose. **1578** Lyte *Dodoens* IV. lxx. 532 This Blessed Thistell is sowen in gardens. **1602** *Metamorph. Tobacco* (Collier) 44 The blessed Thistle and Herbe-grace Had lost their names, and been accounted base. **1608** Shaks. *Per.* III. ii. 35 The blest infusions That dwell in vegetives. **1863** Prior *Plant-n.* 24 Blessed thistle..from the milk of the Virgin having fallen upon its leaves, as she nursed the infant Jesus.

c. *blessed word*: (applied to) a long and high-sounding word, erroneously or ironically taken to be of great significance. Cf. MESOPOTAMIA 2.

1910 *N. & Q.* 9th Ser. I. 458/2 That blessed word Mesopotamia. **1919** G. B. Shaw in *Irish Statesman* 25 Oct. 427/2 There is at first sight something to be said for the blessed word Devolution. **1928** D. L. Sayers *Unpleasantness at Bellona Club* x. 119 Complexes explain so much, like the blessed word hippopotamus.

5. Euphemistically or ironically used for 'cursed' or the like.

[cf. **1526** Bp. J. Clerk *Let.* 13 Sept. in Brewer *Lett. & Pa.* IV. 1109 Circa istud benedictum divortium.] **1806** Windham *Let.* in *Speeches* (1812) I. 77 As one of the happy consequences of our blessed system of printing debates, I am described to-day..as having talked a language directly the reverse of that which I did talk. **1865** tr. *Spohr's Autobiog.* I. 221 The whole of the members..must attend every blessed evening in the theatre.

6. quasi-*advb.* Blessedly.

c **1600** Shaks. *Sonn.* xcii, Whats so blessed faire that feares no blot.

7. *Comb.* as *blessed-making*.

1657 R. Carpenter *Astrology Proved Harmless* 36 The benign and blessed-making Aspect of God.

†ˈ**blessedful**, *a.* *Obs.* Also blestful. [f. prec. + -FUL: an unusual formation.] Full of blessing, either as imparting it or as enjoying it.

a **1300** *Cursor M.* 11234 (Gött.) Þat bl[i]ssidful birth in betheleem. *c* **1400** *Lay-Folks Mass-Bk.* App. iii. 123 Þis hooly and blessydful sacramente. *c* **1400** *Epiph.* (Turnb. 1843) 123 Unto the..we clepe and call, Thou blestful quene. **1556** Veron *Godly Sayings* (1846) 153 That blessedful and everlastynge lyfe. *a* **1618** Raleigh *Pilgr.* (1651) 136 That happy blestfull day.

Hence ˈ**blessedfully** *adv.*, ˈ**blessedfulness**.

a **1500** in Wright's *Songs & Carols* (1847) 22 (Mätz.) The braunch so blessedfully sprong. **1526** Tindale *Rom.* iv. 6 David desscribeth the blessedfulnes of a man. [So in **1557**.]

†ˈ**blessedhede.** *Obs.* [f. BLESSED + *-hede*, -HEAD.] Blessedness, beatitude.

a **1300** *Cursor M.* 6852 A land of blissed-hede. *Ibid.* 23372 Fourten blisced hedes. **1340** *Ayenb.* 97 Virtue of zoþe blyssedhede.

blessedly (ˈblɛsɪdlɪ), *adv.* Also blestly. In a blessed manner; fortunately, happily.

1388 Wyclif *Gen.* xxx. 10 Lya seide, Blessidly. *c* **1420** *Chron. Vilod.* 2711 Blessedlocurre..he ladde hurre lyff. **1561** T. Norton *Calvin's Inst.* II. i. (1634) 104 To make him live well and blessedly. **1610** Shaks. *Temp.* I. i. 63 Blessedly holpe hither. **1640** Fuller *Abel Rediv.* (1867) I. 35 By John Huss Jerome was blestly aided. **1741** Richardson *Pamela* I. liii. 383 All blessedly met once more! **1870** Spurgeon *Treas. Dav.* Ps. xl. 10 Blessedly blended in the gospel.

blessedness (ˈblɛsɪdnɪs). [f. as prec. + -NESS.] The state of being blessed, *esp.* with Divine favour; felicity; beatitude. Also *concr.*

a **1300** *Cursor M.* 17080 Qua mai tel þe teind part þe blisced-nes o þe! *c* **1400** *Epiph.* (Turnb. 1843) 124 We may not haue full the blessednes Of thi vysage nor of thi presence. *a* **1520** *Myrr. Our Ladye* 73 Delyuered from the seuen dedly synnes . and so to come vnto the seuen blessednesses. **1613** Shaks. *Hen. VIII*, IV. ii. 66 He..found the Blessednesse of being little. *c* **1746** Hervey *Medit.* (1753) II. 18 An Ante-past of eternal Blessedness. **1823** Lamb *Elia* (1860) 305, I have a quiet homefeeling of the blessedness of my condition.

b. *single blessedness*: used by Shaks. to express 'divine blessing accorded to a life of celibacy'; hence (more or less jocularly), the unmarried state.

1590 Shaks. *Mids. N.* I. i. 78 Earthlier happie is the Rose distil'd, Then that which withering on the virgin thorne, Growes, liues, and dies, in single blessednesse. **1823** Lamb *Elia* (1860) 109 She was one whom single blessedness had soured. **1836** Dickens *Sk. Boz* (1850) 265/1 Single blessedness, as bachelors say, or single cursedness, as spinsters think.

c. Used as a title of honour. Cf. *holiness*.

1670 G. H. *Hist. Cardinals* I. III. 94 The Popes began to usurp the Titles of Holiness, and Blessedness. **1848** Kingsley *Saint's Trag.* II. iii. 78 The Landgrave Lewis With humble greetings prays his blessedness To make, etc.

blesser (ˈblɛsə(r)). One who blesses.

1577 Vautroullier *Luther's Ep. Gal.* 120 Abraham had him for hys blesser and Sauiour. **1651** Jer. Taylor *Holy Living* (1727) 87 The..blesser of the action.

blessful, etc., obs. or improper f. BLISSFUL, etc.

blessing (ˈblɛsɪŋ), *vbl. sb.* Forms: 1 bledsung, bletsung, -unge, 2 blescunge, blessunge, 3 (*Orm.*) blettcing, bliscing, blesing, blising, 3–4 blessyng, 4 blissinge, bluseing, blys(s)yng, blisteing, 3–6 blessinge, blissing, 4–6 blissyng, blyssinge, blessynge, 6 blyssynge, 4– blessing. [f. BLESS *v.*¹ + -ING¹.]

†**1. a.** Hallowing, consecration. *Obs.*

1070 *O.E. Chron.* (Parker MS.) Swa Thomas to þam timan aȝean ferde buton bletsunga. *c* **1205** Lay. 13261 Na man..þat mihte blessinge don in [**1250** vppe] þan kinge.

†**b.** The making the sign of the cross; crossing oneself. *Obs.*

1562 J. Heywood *Prov. & Epigr.* (1867) 91 This busy blissing and noddyng. **1563** Foxe in Latimer's *Serm. & Rem.* (1845) Introd. 23 The fashion of their mass..with such..kissing, blissing, crouching, becking, crossing, knocking.

2. a. Authoritative declaration of divine favour and countenance, by God or one speaking in his name; benediction; passing into **b.** Invocation of divine favour by any one. **c.** The form of words used in this declaration or invocation.

a **855** *O.E. Chron.* an. 813 (Parker MS.) Mid bledsunge [*Laud MS.* bletsunge] ðæs papan. *a* **1131** *Ibid.* an. 1123 Se papa..sende him ham ða mid his bletsunge. *c* **1250** *Gen. & Ex.* 1568 Fader dere, bidde ic ðe, ðat sum bliscing gif ðu me. **1297** R. Glouc. 421 He ȝaf hym hys blessyng, & al hys tresour þerto. *c* **1315** Shoreham 57 The signe hys of thys sacrement The bisschopes blessynge. *c* **1380** Wyclif *Sel. Wks.* III. 453 Blyssyngs of bischopis, it is a feyned þing. **1549** *Bk. Com. Prayer, Commun.* Rubr., The Priest..shall let them depart with this blessing. **1610** Shaks. *Temp.* v. i. 179 All the blessings Of a glad father, compasse thee about. **1678** N. Wanley *Wonders* VI. xxvii. 613/2 Having taken a blessing from the Priest, he enters the house. **1837** *Ann. Reg.* 9 July 77 The dean now read the collect and the blessing. **1838** T. Jackson *Early Methodists* (1846) I. 380 He gave them his dying blessing.

†**d.** *pl.* The beatitudes pronounced by Christ.

c **1400** Maundev. viii. 96 There..our Lord sat, whan he preched the 8 Blessynges. **1588** A. King *Canisius' Catech.* 186 These quhilk S. Ambrose callis our Lords beatitudes and blissings.

†**e.** A charm, spell, incantation. *Obs.*

1572 R. H. *Lauaterus' Ghostes* (1596) He that is superstitious vseth some blessing (as they call it) to heale his Horsses disease.

3. a. The bestowal of divine favour and prospering influence; favour and prospering influence of God.

c **825** *Vesp. Psalter* iii. 9 Dryhtnes is haelu, & ofer folc ðin bledsung ðin. **971** *Blickl. Hom.* 51 He us sendeþ ufan his bletsunga. *c* **1200** Ormin 4019 Drihhtin haffde ȝifenn himm Swillc blettcing. *c* **1380** Wyclif *Wks.* (1880) 41 Wiþ þe blissyng of god. **1562** J. Heywood *Prov. & Epigr.* (1867) 55 Out of gods blessing into the warme sunne. **1601** Shaks. *All's Well* II. iii. 97 Blessing vpon your vowes. **1789** Burns *John Anderson* i, But blessings on your frosty pow. **1881** Flor. Nightingale *Nursing* ii. 25 'With God's Blessing he will recover,' is a common form of parlance.

b. In this sense we now say 'to ask a blessing' on food; though 'to say a blessing' or 'the blessing of meat' originally belonged to 2.

1738 Wesley *Wks.* (1872) I. 87 Mr. Kinchin told them.. that gentleman would ask a blessing for them. **1838** T. Jackson *Early Methodists* (1846) I. 387 At breakfast, dinner, etc., he never asked a blessing sitting. **1884** *Harper's Mag.* Mar. 562/2 The child said blessing.

4. a. A beneficent gift of God, nature, etc.; anything that makes happy or prosperous; a boon.

1340 *Ayenb.* 97 Þise zeue þinges touore yzed byeþ ycleped blyssinges, uor hy makeþ man yblyssed ine þise wordle.. and more yblyssed ine þe oþre. **1413** Lydg. *Pylgr. Sowle* IV. xx. (1483) 65 My blissing in to payne retourned is. **1613** Shaks. *Hen. VIII*, II. iii. 30 Eminence, Wealth, Soueraignty; Which to say sooth, are Blessings. **1634** Milton *Comus* 772 Nature's full blessings would be well-dispensed. **1709** Addison *Tatler* No. 100 ⁋1 Wealth, Honour, and all other Blessings of Life. **1752** Johnson *Rambl.* No. 204 ⁋2 Wilt thou not partake the blessings thou bestowest? **1844** Ld. Brougham *Brit. Const.* iii. (1862) 52 The blessings of a regular and tranquil government. **1875** Jowett *Plato* (ed. 2) V. 165 Aged relatives are a blessing to the good. *Mod. Colloq.* What a blessing to be rid of them all!

†**b.** A gift or favour bestowed, a present. (A Hebraism of Bible translation.) *Obs.*

1382 Wyclif *1 Sam.* xxv. 27 Wherfor tak this blessynge [**1611** blessing] that thin hoond womman hath brouȝt to thee. **1611** Bible *2 Kings* v. 15, I pray thee, take a blessing of thy seruant.

c. Phr. ***a blessing in disguise***: an apparent misfortune that works to the eventual good of the recipient.

1746 HERVEY *Refl. Flower-Garden* 76 Ev'n Crosses from his sov'reign Hand Are Blessings in Disguise. **1873** *Cassell's Mag.* VI. 296/2 Like many similar disasters, this great calamity was in truth only a blessing in disguise. **1900** *Jrnl. Soc. Arts* 15 June 595 We find that the Pacific cable scheme has really been a blessing in disguise to those who dreaded it most. **1907** *Westm. Gaz.* 3 May 2/1 Religion would gain greatly if the clergy would make a more sparing use of the blessing-in-disguise argument.

5. The rendering of grateful adoration. Now chiefly gerundial, as 'in praising and blessing God.'

1382 WYCLIF *Rev.* v. 12 The lomb that is slayn is worthi for to take..honour and glory and blessing. **1393** GOWER *Conf.* I. 271 All was thanking, all was blessing. *a* **1586** SYDNEY in Farr's *S.P.* (1848) I. 60 When from their lippes most blessing flows.

6. A euphemism for: A curse.

1878 H. SMART *Play or Pay* iv. (ed. 3) 68 Richardson's name rose once to his lips, coupled with a blessing of dubious import.

blessing, *ppl. a.* [f. -ING^2.] That blesses.

1659 HAMMOND *On Ps.* xiii. 1 The blessing beames of thy countenance. **1870** MORRIS *Earthly Par.* III. IV. 429 With his small blessing voice the hushed air thrilled.

'blessingly, *adv.* In a way that blesses.

1836 MRS. BROWNING *Poems* (1850) I. 257 While you pardon me, all blessingly, The woe mine Adam sent.

blessum, obs. form of BLISSOM.

blest, pa. t. and pple. of BLESS *v.*^{1}

blester, obs. form of BLISTER.

blestly, obs. form of BLESSEDLY.

blet (blɛt), *v.* [Adopted by Lindley from F. *blett-ir* 'devenir blet,' f. *blet, blette* 'sleepy' as an over-ripe pear.] *intr.* To become 'sleepy,' as an over-ripe pear, a special form of decay to which fleshy fruits are subject. Hence **'bletting** *vbl. sb.*

1835 LINDLEY *Introd. Bot.* (1848) II. 257 After the period ..of ripeness, most fleshy fruits undergo a new kind of alteration; their flesh either rots or blets. *Ibid.* Bletting is.. a special alteration. **1864** *Reader* 21 May 653 The decomposition..of the pericarp begins with fermentation, and, after having passed through the intermediate stage of bletting [to use Dr. Lindley's word], ends in the total obliteration of the cellular structure.

blet, *sb.* [f. prec.: in Webster (where the only authority cited is Lindley's use of the verb). But this would not give 'A decayed spot on fruits,' as erroneously stated, but, That form of decay which is commonly called 'sleepiness' (in which there are *no external spots* to indicate the change).]

blet, obs. form of BLEAT *sb.*

†**bletch(e,** *sb. Obs. rare.* [*Bletche*, 16th c., implies a ME. **blecche*, OE. **blęcce*, OTeut. **blakjo-*, from **blako-* BLACK: cf. BLATCH and BLEACH *sb*^{2}. in same sense. (It may also be the southern form of northern *blek, bleck.*)] Shoemaker's blacking.

1570 LEVINS *Manip.* 88 Bletche, *atramentum.*

†**bletch,** *v. Obs. rare*$^{-1}$. [f. BLETCH *sb.*, or repr. a ME. **blecchen*, OE. **blęcc(e)an*, OTeut. type **blakjan*: cf. BLATCH and BLACK.] To BLACK.

1570 LEVINS *Manip.* 47 To Blecke, bletch, *nigrare.*

†**'bletchy,** *a. Obs.* [f. prec. sb. + -Y.] Smutted with 'bletch'; inky, sooty, dirty.

1520 WHITTINTON *Vulg.* (1527) 25 Thou blurrest and blottest them as thou wert a bletchy sowter [*atramentosi sarctoris*]. **1633** J. CLARK *Two-f. Praxis* 43.

†**blete,** *a. Obs.* In 1 bléat, 3 blete. [Com. Teut.: OE. *bléat* ? miserable, ? naked, = OFris. *blât* miserable, MDu., Du. *bloot* naked, poor, OHG., MHG. *bloȝ*, mod.G. *blosz* naked.] Naked, bare.

a **1000** *Guthlac* 963 (Gr.) Đone bleatan drync deopan deaþweȝes. *a* **1250** *Owl & Night.* 57 Bare, And..blete. *Ibid.* 616 Treon wel grete, Mid þicke boȝe no þing blete.

blete, var. of BLITE.

†**blethe,** *a. Obs.* In 1 bleað, 3 bleð(e. [Com. Teut.: OE. *bléað* weak, gentle, timid = OS. *blôði* (MDu. *blôde, bloot*, Du. *blood*), OHG. *blôdi* (MHG. *blœde*, mod.G. *blöde* weak), ON. *blauðr* soft, weak, Goth. **blauþs* (in *blauþjan* to make of no force):—OTeut. **blauþi-s* without force, weak.] Spiritless, timid.

a **1000** *Riddles* xli. 15 (Gr.) Ic eom to ðon bleað ðæt mec mæg grima abreȝan. *c* **1205** LAY. 23620 And moni ænne gode wifmon iwhorht to bleðere widewe. *c* **1250** *Gen. & Ex.* 3907 Friȝti nam forð ðis folc and bleð.

†**'blethely,** *adv. Obs.* [ME. *blethli*, in form a deriv. of BLETHE, but apparently associated, in later use at least, with BLITHE.] **a.** Gently, kindly, graciously, benevolently. **b.** Blithely, gladly, fain.

a **1300** *Cursor M.* 11958 Iesus wel blethli wald þai warn. *c* **1300** *Vox & Wolf* 171 in *E.P.P.* (1864) 63 Tho he herde speken of mete, He wolde bletheliche ben thare. *a* **1340** HAMPOLE *Pr. Consc.* 184 Many has lykyng trofels to here, And vanites wille blethly lere. *c* **1380** WYCLIF *Serm.* Sel. Wks. I. 107 Jesus bleþeli dide mercy whan he was clepid David sone. *a* **1430** *How Wif taught D.* 11 in *E.P.P.* (1864) 180 Blethely ȝeue thi tythys..The pore men at thi dore ..ȝeue hem blethely of thi good.

blether, blather ('blɛðə(r), 'blæðə(r)), *v. Sc.* and *north. dial.* Also (?) 6 **blother.** [ME. *blather*, a. ON. *blaðra* to talk stupidly, f. *blaðr* nonsense. *Blather* is the etymological form, *blether* being Sc. and north. Eng. (like *gether* = *gather* etc.). But in mod.Eng., the word is generally accepted as Scotch (from Burns, Scott, Carlyle, etc.) and in the Scotch form. In U.S. *blather* appears to be more frequent.]

1. *intr.* To talk nonsense loquaciously.

1524 A. SCOTT *Vision* xix, And limpand Vulcan blethers. [**1526** SKELTON *Magnyf.* 1049, I blunder, I bluster, I blowe and I blother.] **1787** BURNS *Holy Fair* viii, Some are busy blethrin Right loud that day. **1867** E. WAUGH *Owd Bl.* iv. 89 in *Lanc. Gloss.*, He blether't abeawt religion. **1884** *Punch* 1 Mar. 102 Fluent folly may maunder and blether.

b. *trans.* To babble.

1810 TANNAHILL *Poems* (1846) 145 She blethered it round.

2. *intr.* To cry loudly, to blubber. *dial.*

1863 MRS. TOOGOOD *Yorksh. Dial.* s.v., What's thou blethering at? child. **1855** *Whitby Gloss.*, *Blether*, to blubber, to weep aloud.

blether, blather ('blɛðə(r), 'blæðə(r)), *sb.* [f. prec., or a. ON. *blaðr* nonsense.] Voluble talk void of sense.

1787 BURNS *Vision* iv, Stringin blethers up in rhyme, For fools to sing. **1843** MRS. CARLYLE in *Lett.* I. 257 Untormented by his blether. **1863** *Tyneside Songs* 36 'Mang the noise and the blether. **1865** *Richmond* (*U.S.*) *Exam.* in *Morn. Star* 3 Feb., All the eloquence and all the blather in the world will not alter the facts.

blethering ('blɛðərɪŋ), *vbl. sb.* [f. BLETHER *v.* + -ING^1.] Voluble senseless talking; = prec.

a **1834** COLERIDGE *Cholera cured* Wks. 1847 II. 143 So without further blethring, Dear Mudlarks! my brethren!

'blethering, *ppl. a.* [f. as prec. + -ING^2.] **1.** Volubly and foolishly talkative.

1759 *Fordun Scotichron.* II. 376 (JAM.) Blyth and bletherand. **1790** BURNS *Tam o' Shanter* 20 A bletherin, blusterin, drunken blellum. **1816** SCOTT *Old Mort.* xiv, Listening to twa blethering auld wives. **1864** ATKINSON *Whitby Gloss.* s.v. *Blethering*, A coarse blethering fellow.

2. = BLINKING *ppl. a.* 4. Cf. BLITHERING *ppl. a. colloq.*

1915 A. KINROSS in *Times Red Cross Story Bk.* 148 If my boy ever gets married on the quiet and plays the fool, I'll break his blethering neck for him.

'bletherskate, 'blatherskite, *dial.* and *U.S. colloq.* [f. BLETHER *v.* + SKATE in Sc. used contemptuously. The Scotch song *Maggie Lauder*, in which this word occurs, was a favourite ditty in the American Camp during the War of Independence (J. Grant Wilson, *Poets and Poetry of Scotl.* I. 82); from this, *bletherskate* or, as more commonly used, *blatherskite*, became a familiar colloquialism in U.S.] **a.** A noisy talkative fellow; a talker of blatant nonsense. Hence also a *vbl. sb.* **blatherskiting; bletherumskite** (Ir. *dial.*) = BLETHER *sb.*

c **1650** F. SEMPILL *Maggie Lauder* i, Jog on your gait, ye bletherskate [*v.r.* bladderskate]. **1848–60** BARTLETT *Americanisms* 35 *Blatherskite*, a blustering, noisy, talkative fellow. **1864** WEBSTER, *Blatherskite* ('Local U.S.'). **1864** *Spectator* No. 1884. 906 A muddle-headed 'bletherskite' called Colorado Jewett. **1880** *Echo* 28 Dec. 3/5 What is expressed by the slang word 'blatherskiting,' consumed three of the five days.

b. Foolish talk; nonsense.

1825 C. CROKER *Tradit. S. Ireland* 170 He was, as usual, getting on with his bletherumskite about the fairies. **1861** *N.Y. Tribune* 28 Dec., To wit, our proving, not by verbal blatherskyte, but by facts, that the C.S.A. is dependent on us. **1892** J. BARLOW *Bog-land* 82 Wid your little black book full o' blatheremskyte. **1894** *Daily News* 29 May 5/1 It is still six hundred pages of sheer blood and blatherumskite. **1907** G. B. SHAW *John Bull's Other Is.* 111, There's too much blatherumskite in Irish politics. **1956** C. WILSON *Outsider* ix. 272 For Nietzsche..there is no such thing as abstract knowledge; there is only useful knowledge and unprofitable blatherskite.

blethery ('blɛðərɪ), *a.* [f. BLETHER *sb.* + -Y^1.] Characterized by blether.

1889 G. M. HOPKINS *Let.* 29 Apr. (1935) 304 *Rot* about babies, a blethery bathos.

'Bletonism. (See quot.) Hence **'Bletonist.**

1821 *Month. Mag.* LI. 315 Bletonism is a faculty of perceiving and indicating subterraneous springs and currents by sensation; the term is modern, and derived from a Mr. Bleton, who for some years past has excited universal attention by his possessing the above faculty.

bletsien, blettcen, -sen, obs. ff. BLESS.

‖**bleu** (blø), *sb.* and *a.* [Fr., see BLUE *a.*] **A.** *sb.* **1.** Used in the names of various French cheeses with veins of blue mould; **bleu cheese** [part-tr. Fr. *fromage bleu*] = *blue cheese* (see BLUE *a.* 13).

1918 *U.S. Dept. Agric. Bull.* 608 6 The names Pâté Bleu and Fromage Bleu are applied to several kinds of hard, rennet cheese made from cows' milk in imitation of Roquefort cheese. *Ibid.*, Several more or less distinct kinds ..designated Bleu d'Auvergne, Cantal..and St. Flour. **1952** W. PLOMER *Museum Pieces* xiv. 117 His favourite cheese—*bleu d'Auvergne.* **1957** O. NASH *You can't get there from Here* 86 Every time the menu lists *bleu* cheese I want to order *fromage* blue.

2. *Canad. Pol.* (Also with capital initial.) A Quebec Conservative or 'Blue' (BLUE *sb.* 8).

1885 *Weekly Manitoba Liberal* 25 Dec. 4/4 The *Mail* is frantic over the defection of the rank and file of the Bleus in Quebec. **1946** A. R. M. LOWER *Colony to Nation* 302 Among the French, the word 'Bleu' did not necessarily mean 'Conservative'. **1963** *Globe & Mail* (Toronto) 26 Mar. 7/7 The real tug of war no longer is between the rouges and the bleus—the Liberals and the Tories—but between the 'old' and the 'new' parties. **1966** *Economist* 11 June 1178/1 The diehard *bleus* whose instinct is to pull the province [*sc.* Quebec] back into antique isolation. **1978** *Globe & Mail* (Toronto) 5 Oct. 8/7 'Joe Clark is not exactly my man, but we have to take whatever they give us' said Paul Paris, a lifetime 'bleu'.

B. *adj.* Of or pertaining to the conservative party in Quebec or its policies. Cf. sense 2 of the sb.

[**1876** in R. M. Hamilton *Canad. Quotations* (1965) 68/1 It is not for me, mes enfants, to tell you for which party you should vote, but I would have you remember that the place on high..is *bleu*, while the other..is *rouge*.] **1900** *Canad. Mag.* Sept. 548/2 There are strong Conservatives who would place the maximum Bleu victories at fifteen. **1963** *Kingston* (Ont.) *Whig-Standard* 9 Mar. 13/3 In the rural ridings..the very low income segment of the population tends to be more bleu than rouge.

‖**bleu-de-roi** (blø də rwa). *Ceramics.* Also **-du-**. [Fr., = king's blue.] The ultramarine blue of Sèvres porcelain; also called *bleu de Sèvres*. Also *attrib.*

1848 H. R. FORSTER *Stowe Catal.* 38 A coffee-cup and saucer—bleu du Roi. **1868** SALA *Notes & Sk. Paris Exhib.* xiii. 153 A Sèvres vase, *bleu-de-roi.* **1902** *Connoisseur* Jan. 70/1 Sèvres bleu du roi china. **1959** G. SAVAGE *Antique Coll. Handbk.* 63 A rich blue enamel ground, the *bleu de Roi*, was introduced in 1749.

bleve, var. of BELEAVE *v. Obs.* to remain.

'blevindeliche, *adv. Obs.* [f. *blevinde*, pr. pple. of *bleven*, BELEAVE, to remain, continue + -LY^2.] Perseveringly.

1340 *Ayenb.* 141 Wiþ guode wille and bleuindeliche. *Ibid.* 208 Diligentliche and..bleuindeliche.

†**'bleving(e,** *vbl. sb. Obs.* [see BELEAVING.] **a.** Remaining. **b.** Persevering.

blew, bleu, pa. t. of BLOW *v.*

blew(e, obs. form of BLUE.

blew, var. BLUE *v.*^{2}

'blewart. *Sc. rare.* [prob. = *blaewort*, f. BLAE *a.* + WORT: cf. BLAWORT.] The Germander Speedwell (*Veronica chamædrys*). Britten and Holland.

1821 HOGG *When Kye comes Hame*, When the blewart bears a pearl, And the daisy turns a pea.

blewits ('bl(j)uːɪts). [prob. f. BLUE, in reference to the colour: cf. F. *bluet*, applied to various flowers.] A kind of edible mushroom.

1830 WITHERING *Brit. Plants* (ed. 7) IV. 192 *note*, This species [*Agaricus violaceus*]..is sold in Covent-Garden market under the name of Blewits, for making catsup. **1871** M. COOKE *Fungi* (1874) 91 *Lepista personata* used to be sold in Covent Garden Market under the name of blewits. **1883** *Gd. Words* 589/2 Chantarelles, and morells, and blewitts.

†**'blexter.** *Obs.*$^{-0}$ [for *blekster*, f. BLECK *v.*] One who blackens.

c **1440** *Promp. Parv.* 39 Blextere, *obfuscator.*

bley, var. of BLAY, BLEE.

bleyȝt, obs. form of BLEACHED.

†**bleyke, bleike,** *a. Obs.* [ME. *bleik*, a. ON. *bleikr* shining, white. See BLAYK(E.] Pale.

a **1300** *Havelok* 470 For hunger grene and bleike. *c* **1440** *Promp. Parv.* 39 Bleyke of colour, *pallidus.*

†**bleyke, bleike,** *v. Obs.* [f. prec. adj.; cf. the analogy of BLAKE *a.* and *v.* But ON. had *bleikja* to whiten, bleach, f. *bleikr* pale.]

intr. To become pale; = BLAKE *v.* 1.

c **1327** *Poem Times of Edw. II.* in *Pol. Songs* 397 Thanne gan bleiken here ble. *a* **1475** *Play Sacram.* 477 Now am I bold with batayle him to bleyke [*rime-wd.* stryke].

†**'bleykster.** *Obs.* [f. prec.] A bleacher.

c **1440** *Promp. Parv.* 39 Bleystare or wytstare [*K.* bleyster, *H.* bleyestare or qwytstare; **1499** bleykester or whytster], *candidarius.* **1499** —— 525 (Pynson), Whytstar or blykstar.

† **bleymes.** *Obs.* [a. F. *bleime* (*blaime* in Cotgr.), of same meaning, identified by Littré, etc., with *blême* adj. pale: see BLEMISH.] (See quot.)

1725 BRADLEY *Fam. Dict., Bleymes*, an Inflammation between the Sole and Bone of the Foot of a Horse towards the Heel. *Ibid.* This sort of Bleymes may be prevented by keeping his Feet clean and moist, etc.

bleyn(e, obs. form of BLAIN.

bleynt(e, obs. pa. t. of BLENCH *v.*

† **'blichening**, *sb. Obs. rare*$^{-1}$. [perh. vbl. sb. from *blichen, a southern form of *blikne*, BLIKEN, to become pale. Cf. BLIGHT.]

Mildew, rust, or blight in corn.

c **1420** *Pallad. on Husb.* I. 827 For blichenyng [*rubigine*] and myst take chaf and raf, And ley it on thi lande.

blick (blɪk). [a. Ger. *blick* shining, sheen.] 'The brightening or iridescence appearing on silver or gold at the end of the cupelling or refining process.' Raymond *Mining Gloss.* 1881.

bliessom, obs. form of BLISSOM.

blife, var. of BELIVE.

bligh, bliht, obs. forms of BLITHE.

blight (blaɪt), *sb.* Also 7–8 **blite.** [A word of unknown origin; which entered literature, apparently from the speech of farmers or gardeners, in the 17th c.; literary men were at first doubtful as to its proper spelling, and seem to have thought of the plant BLITE.

(Among suggestions as to its origin are: that it is somehow related to BLICHENING above; that it may possibly represent an ON. *bleht-r, the antecedent of Icel. *blettr* stain, spot, blot; that it is a derivative of the verb *blike*, or of the stem *black* or *bleyke*, *bleach*, *bleak*; or onomatopœic, with a feeling for *blow*, *blast*, and kindred *bl-* words.)]

1. *gen.* Any baleful influence of atmospheric or invisible origin, that suddenly blasts, nips, or destroys plants, affects them with disease, arrests their growth, or prevents their blossom from 'setting'; a diseased state of plants of unknown or assumed atmospheric origin.

1669 WORLIDGE *Syst. Agric.* viii. §3 (1681) 159 Spoiled by the various mutations of the Air, or by Blights, Mildews, etc. **1697** DRYDEN *Virg. Georg.* IV. 468 With Blites destroy my Corn. —— *Palamon & Arc.* II. 59 So may thy tender Blossoms fear no blite. **1699** GARTH *Dispens.* VI. 78 Their blissful Plains no Blites, nor Mildews fear. *a* **1700** TEMPLE *Miscell., Gardening* Wks. 1720 I. 188 [not in ed. 1690] A Soot or Smuttiness upon the Leaves [of Wall fruit]..I complained to the oldest and best Gardeners, who.. esteemed it some Blight of the Spring. **1720** GAY *Poems* (1745) II. 87 Fade not with sudden blights or winter's wind. **1737** MILLER *Gard. Dict.* (R.) Blights are often caused by a continued easterly wind. **1812** J. WILSON *Isle of Palms* IV. 762 Flowers.. Unharm'd by frost or blight.

2. Specifically applied to: **a.** Diseases in plants caused by fungoid parasites, as mildew, rust, or smut, in corn. (App. the earliest use.)

1611 COTGR., *Brulure*, blight, brancorne; (an hearbe). **1671** SKINNER *Etymol., Blight*, idem quod *milldew*.. quæ fruges corrumpit. **1807** VANCOUVER *Agric. Devon* (1813) 434 Wheat.. very much smitten with the bligh[t], or rust, as it is generally called in this neighbourhood. **1830** LINDLEY *Nat. Syst. Bot.* 337 The blight in corn, occasioned by *Puccinia graminis*. **1859** W. COLEMAN *Woodlands* (1866) 75 If a tuft of this blight as it is called be closely examined.

b. A species of aphis, destructive to fruit-trees.

[Cf. **1727** BRADLEY *Fam. Dict.* s.v., The common People ..are well satisfy'd that Blights are brought by the East Wind, which brings or hatches the Caterpillar.] **1802** PALEY *Nat. Theol.* xxvi. (1819) 423 What we call blights are oftentimes legions of animated beings. **1882** *Garden* 11 Feb. 99/2 The worst insect enemy to the attacks of which the Apple is liable is what is termed the American blight. **1885** *Contemp. Rev.* Oct. 561 It thinks there are some 'blight' among the blossoms at the top, and if there are it will eat them.

c. A close hazy overcast state of the atmosphere, which sometimes prevails in summer or autumn.

1848 LYTTON *Harold* iv. 194 In that smoke as in a blight the wings withered up.

3. Applied to affections of the face or skin: **a.** An eruption on the human skin consisting of minute reddish pimples, 'a form of Lichen urticatus.'

1864 in WEBSTER. **1880** in *Syd. Soc. Lex.*

b. Facial palsy arising from cold. *Syd. Soc. Lex.*

c. *blight in the eye*: extravasation of blood under the conjunctive membrane.

4. *transf.* and *fig.* **a.** Any malignant influence of obscure or mysterious origin; anything which withers hopes or prospects, or checks prosperity.

a **1661** HOLYDAY *Juvenal* 246 Let Isis with her timbrel strike me blind (not properly with the sistrum it self, but with its invisible power, with a blite). **1797** GODWIN *Enquirer* I. v. 35 Genius.. may.. suffer an untimely blight. **1873** BURTON *Hist. Scot.* VI. lxx. 212 A strange mysterious punishment, which seemed like a blight or judgement of a higher power. **1884** *Fortn. Rev.* Jan. 79 The withering blight of Turkish rule.

b. *spec.* An unsightly urban area (cf. BLIGHTED *ppl. a.* 1 b).

1938 L. MUMFORD *Culture of Cities* 8 We.. face the accumulated physical and social results of that disruption: ravaged landscapes, disorderly urban districts,.. patches of blight, mile upon mile of standardized slums. **1952** M. LOCK et al. *Bedford by River* i. 23/1 Blight clearance will affect another 4,100 people who will be displaced from the main clearance areas. *Ibid.* 23/2 Isolated pockets of blight.

5. *Comb.*, as ***blight-beetle***. **blight-bird** *Austral.* and *N.Z.*, an early settlers' name for a bird belonging to the Australian genus *Zosterops*.

1852 T. HARRIS *Insects New Eng.* 79 This insect, which may be called the blight-beetle, from the injury it occasions, attacks also apple, apricot, and plum trees. **1870** R. TAYLOR *Maori & Eng. Dict.* 17/2 Kanohimowhiti, or Tauhau, *white eye* or blight bird (*Zosterops lateralis*) was first observed July, 1856 in the South, and about Auckland. **1882** T. H. POTTS *Out in Open* 130 The white-eye or blight-bird.. clears away multitudes of small insect pests. **1888** NEWTON in *Encycl. Brit.* XXIV. 824/1 In 1856 it was noticed.. as occurring in the South Island of New Zealand, when it became known.. to the English settlers as the 'Blight-bird'. **1965** *Austral. Encycl.* VIII. 129/2 Silvereyes.. do much good by destroying scale-insects and other pests, and have thereby earned the name of blight-birds.

blight (blaɪt), *v.* [f. the sb.]

1. *trans.* To affect with BLIGHT (see the sb., sense 1).

1695 J. WOODWARD *Nat. Hist. Earth* IV. 212 It then blasts Vegetables,.. blights Corn and Fruits, and is sometimes injurious even to Men. **1727** BRADLEY *Fam. Dict.* s.v. *Blight*, Some do conjecture, that it is the East Wind of itself that Blights. **1803** R. ANDERSON *Cumberld. Ballads* 79 She bleets the cworn wi' her bad e'e. **1834** PRINGLE *Afr. Sk.* iv. 186 A sharp frost.. blighted all our early potatoes. **1842** TENNYSON *Poet's Mind* 18 There is frost in your breath Which would blight the plants.

b. *transf.* of parts of the body.

1811 SCOTT *Roderick* v. li, Blighted be the tongue That names thy name without the honour due.

2. *fig.* To exert a baleful influence on; to destroy the brightness, beauty, or promise of; to nip in the bud, mar, frustrate.

1712 ADDISON *Spect.* No. 457 ¶3 It [Lady Blast's whisper] blights like an easterly wind. **1735** OLDYS *Life Raleigh* Wks. 1829 I. 357 Yet could [they].. blite them [brave and active spirits] from advancing to any fruitful or profitable conclusions. **1832** LEWIS *Use & Ab. Pol. Terms* iii. 34 Deprivation of rank.. which blights so many prospects. **1863** GEO. ELIOT *Romola* II. iv. (1880) II. 44 The delusion which had blighted her young years.

blighted ('blaɪtɪd), *ppl. a.* [f. prec. + -ED.]

1. a. Affected with blight; blasted.

1664 *Phil. Trans.* I. 28 Vegetables growing on blighted Leaves. **1674** RAY *S.E. Co. Wds.* 59 *Blighted corn*, blasted corn. *Sussex.* **1750** JOHNSON *Rambl.* No. 5 ¶17 A blighted spring makes a barren year. **1855** MACAULAY *Hist. Eng.* III. 380 The blighted prospects of the orphan children. **1857** S. OSBORN *Quedah* iv. 56 The aged trunk of a blighted tree.

b. Applied to an urban area (see quot. 1951).

1938 L. MUMFORD *Culture of Cities* iv. 283 The unbearable municipal burden of blighted areas. **1951** B. J. COLLINS *Development Plans Explained* 42 *Blighted area*, an area characterized by conditions of bad layout or obsolete development. **1952** M. LOCK et al. *Bedford by River* vi. 95/1 The primary object of the housing survey was to find out how many dwellings could be considered 'blighted' i.e. at or near the end of their economic life, or for some other reason requiring to be demolished.

2. Used as a mild substitute for BLASTED *ppl. a.* 3. *slang.*

1915 LOCKE *Jaffery* xxi. 271, I think he's a blighted malingerer. **1946** WODEHOUSE *Joy in Morning* ii. 15, I wished I hadn't been caught in the act of apparently buying this blighted *Spindrift*.

blightening, *ppl. a.* [f. assumed vb. *blighten.]

1743 MAXWELL *Impr. Agric.* 266 (JAM.) Blightning winds.

blighter ('blaɪtə(r)). **1.** Anything that blights.

1822 DE QUINCEY *Confess* (1886) 16 Old age.. is a miserable corrupter and blighter to the genial charities of the human heart. *a* **1845** HOOD *Spring* ii, The Spring!.. I find her breath a bitter blighter!

2. *slang.* A contemptible or unpleasant person; often merely as an extravagant substitute for 'fellow'. Also *transf.*

1896 *Idler* Mar. 282/1 'Larry,' says they, 'you ain't going to let that blighter throw you.' **1900** *Westm. Gaz.* 28 Mar. 9/3 Down with the dirty blighters who will not remove their hats. **1904** KIPLING in *Windsor Mag.* Jan. 226/2 'There's an accommodatin' blighter for you!' said Pyecroft. **1920** LOCKE *House of Baltazar* xviii. 218 He could buy up this old blighter of a lord twice over. **1922** *Daily Mail* 3 Nov. 15, I never dreamt the little blighter would go off in such a hurry. **1952** R. FINLAYSON *Schooner came to Atia* 101 Chapham suddenly became aware of the loud chatter of mina birds. 'Noisy blighters' he said. **1957** J. I. M. STEWART *Use of Riches* 16 'What we have to contrive,' he said, 'is fair shares —or something near it—for each of the little blighters.'

blighting ('blaɪtɪŋ), *vbl. sb.* The action of the vb. BLIGHT; the fact of being blighted.

1669 WORLIDGE *Syst. Agric.* (1681) 214 Very much differing from Mil-dews is the blighting of Corn, the Mil-dews.. happening only in dry Summers, when on the contrary Blighting happens in wet. **1693** EVELYN *De la Quint. Compl. Gard.* Dict., *Bligh[t]ing* is said of Flowers or Blossoms, that shed or fall without knitting for Fruit.

'blighting, *ppl. a.* [f. as prec. + -ING^{2}.]

1. That blights; blasting, withering.

1796 COLERIDGE *'Pang more sharp'* 50 One pang more blighting-keen than hope betrayed. **1805** SOUTHEY *Madoc in W.* ix, Cold winds.. and blighting seasons. **1850** PRESCOTT *Peru* II. 351 Pining.. under the blighting malaria.

2. = BLIGHTED *ppl. a.* 2. *slang.*

1916 'BOYD CABLE' *Action Front* 187 There's that blighting maxim again. **1934** T. S. ELIOT *Rock* i. 32 'E showed up the 'ole blightin' swindle.

blightingly ('blaɪtɪŋlɪ), *adv.* [f. prec. + -LY^{2}.] In a blighting manner; with blighting influence.

blighty ('blaɪtɪ), *a.* [f. BLIGHT *sb.* + -Y^{1}.]

† **a.** = BLIGHTING *ppl. a. Obs.*

1731 SWITZER *Pract. Fruit-Gard.* (ed. 2) 287 Those blighty Airs rise, and by Elasticity are driven in Columns against Fruit-Trees.

b. Affected with blight; blighted.

1900 *Standard* 9 Nov., The acorn crop is an abundant one, the fruit being rather blighty and undersized.

Blighty, blighty ('blaɪtɪ), *sb. Army slang.* [Contracted form, originating in the Indian army, of Hind. *bilāyati* = *wilāyatī* foreign, and esp. European, f. *wilāyat* prop. Arabic, inhabited country, dominion, district, VILAYET, in Hind. esp. foreign country (cf. Arab. *walī* governor of a province, VALI, WALI).

Cf. *Bilayutee pawnee*, *Bilâtee panee*. The adject. *bilāyatī* ..is applied specifically to a variety of exotic articles,.. and most especially *bilāyatī pānī*, 'European water', the usual name of soda-water in Anglo-India (Yule & Burnell, *Hobson-Jobson*).]

England, home. (Used by soldiers on foreign service.)

[**1886** KIPLING *From Sea to Sea* (1899) II. 358 Let the town hear of the wonders which I have seen in Belait.] **1915** *Times* (weekly ed.) 8 Oct. 852 The only thing they looked forward to was getting back to 'Blighty' again. **1916** *N. & Q.* 19 Feb. 151/1 One poem I have recently seen begins:—Oh, send me back to Blighty. **1917** P. MACGILL *Gt. Push* xix. 238 I'll send out the money and fags when I go back to blighty. **1968** J. R. ACKERLEY *My Father & Myself* vii. 60, I was not happy in Blighty.

b. *attrib.* or *adj.* 'Home', as distinguished from 'foreign'.

1918 *Aussie* Aug. 9/2 The C.O. endeavours to persuade Private Hardcase to accept Blighty Leave. **1926** *Morn. Post* 8 Dec., An Exhibition and Sale of Blighty Industries.

c. In the war of 1914–18 applied to a wound that secured return to England. Also *attrib.*

1916 *N. & Q.* 4 Mar. 194/2 I believe that 'B.B.' is the regular, though unofficial description of any non-fatal wound serious enough to send its victim back to a base hospital—Blighty Boy. **1916** *Daily Mail* 1 Nov. 4/4 So-and-so stopped some shrapnel and is back at the base in hospital, ..he wasn't lucky enough to get a blighty. **1917** 'CONTACT' *Airman's Outings* 29 A Blighty bullet sent him back to England and gave him a mention in the casualty list. **1918** LOCKE *Rough Road* xix, Mo says he's blistering glad you're out of it and safe in your perishing bed with a Blighty one. **1927** *Daily Express* 18 Oct. 1/1 Soldiers are visiting the battlefields.. in the hope of finding trenches, dug-outs, or the exact spot where they received their 'blighties'. **1934** V. M. YEATES *Winged Victory* I. xii. 104 Marsden.. had had his left arm damaged by a bullet and had gone to hospital very pleased with himself for having picked out of the dip the ideal Blighty.

blihand, -ant, var. of BLEAUNT, *Obs.*, a tunic.

† **blik, blike**, *v. Obs.* In 1 **blícan**; 3 **blikien, blykyen**, 4 **bliken, blikken**. [Here there appear to be two or more cognate forms: (1) OE. *blícan* to shine, gleam, a com. Teut. str. vb. = OS. *blîkan* (MDu. *blîken*, Du. *blijken* to look, appear), OHG. (in comp.) *-blîhhan* (MHG. *blîchen*, mod.G. *-bleichen*), ON. *blîkja* str. vb:—OTeut. *blîk-an 'to shine, gleam,' pointing to Aryan *bhlig-: cf. OSlav. *bli-sk-atⁱ* to sparkle, Gr. φλέγειν to burn, L. *fulgēre* to shine. (2) The cognate ON. *blika* (wk. v.) found beside the str. *blíkja* to shine, glitter: cf. Sw. *blicka*, also MDu. and mod.G. *blicken* to glance, Du. *blikken* to twinkle, turn pale. The early ME. *blikien* points back to an OE. *blician wk. vb., answering to ON. *blika*.]

intr. To shine, glisten, glitter.

a **1000** *Sol. & Sat.* 235 (Gr.) Ðu.. ȝesihst Hierusalem weallas blican. *c* **1205** LAY. 27360 Iseȝen.. sceldes blikien. *a* **1225** *St. Marher.* 9 His lockkes ant his longe berd blikede al o gold. *c* **1300** Wright's *Lyric P.* xvi. (1842) 52 Hire bleo blykyeth so bryht. *c* **1325** *E.E. Allit. P.* B. 603 Bryȝt blykked þe bem of þe brode heuen. **1340** *Alex. & Dind.* 411 Hur face to enoine, For to bliken of hur ble.

blik (blɪk), *sb. Philos.* [Arbitrary formation.

'Some commentators on my ideas have tried to find a connexion with the German word *Blick*, and have attributed to me an intention to suggest something like 'outlook' or even 'Weltanschauung'. But I had no such conscious intention, and was merely looking for a pronounceable monosyllable that had no meaning hitherto. I could as well have chosen 'plik', and perhaps it is a pity that I did not.' (R. M. Hare, private letter to ed., 18 July 1985.).]

R. M. Hare's word for a behavioural or affective tendency which influences one's interpretation of experience, a personal slant (on something); a conviction, esp. a religious one.

1950 R. M. HARE in Flew & Macintyre *New Ess. Philos. Theol.* (1955) 100 Let us call that in which we differ from this lunatic, our respective *bliks*. He has an insane *blik* about dons; we have a sane one. **1972** D. A. PAILIN in Cox & Dyson

20th-Cent. Mind III. iv. 135 Hare calls these structures 'bliks' and, probably unfortunately, describes them in terms of a lunatic's conviction that 'all dons want to murder him'. **1976** J. HICK *Death & Eternal Life* 30 A 'ptolemaic' faith can have the triumphant invulnerability of what R. M. Hare has called a *blik*, a comprehensive interpretation which no evidence is allowed to threaten because it interprets all the evidence from its own standpoint. **1976** P. DONOVAN *Religious Lang.* iii. 25 R. M. Hare agreed with Flew that religious statements were factually empty as statements, but then offered an account of their meaningfulness as what he called *bliks*, i.e. as principles by which one lives and in accordance with which one interprets experience. *Ibid.* 28 There may be..factual assumptions behind the adoption of a blik, even though the blik itself is not an assertion of fact. **1976** *Theology* July 194 The possibility of varied interpretations..does not confer a licence on the theologian to adopt that kind of interpretation to which he is drawn by his particular *blik* on the New Testament.

†**'bliken, -ne**, *v. Obs.* [ME. *blykne(n*, a. ON. *blikna* to become pale, inchoative deriv. of vb. stem *blik-*: see BLIK, BLIKE *v.*]

1. *intr.* To turn pale.

c **1325** *E.E. Allit. P.* B. 1759 þenne blykned þe ble of þe bryȝt skwes. *a* **1400** *Pol. Rel. & L. Poems* 224 His lippes shulle bliken.

2. To shine; = BLIK, BLIKE *v.*

c **1325** *E.E. Allit. P.* B. 1467 For alle þe blomes of þe boȝes were blyknande perles.

blimbi(ng, variant of BILIMBI.

blimey ('blaɪmɪ), *int.* Also **bli' me, blime, blymy.** Vulgar corruption of the imprecation *blind me!* or *blame me!* (BLAME *v.* 7 a). (Cf. GORBLIMEY.)

1889 in BARRÈRE & LELAND *Dict. Slang.* **1894** *Punch* 27 Oct. 193/1 Blymy, you're a knockout! **1897** W. S. MAUGHAM *Liza of Lambeth* ix. 153 Bli' me if I know wot yer all talkin' abaht. **1922** JOYCE *Ulysses* 305 God blimey if she aint a clinker... Blimey it makes me kind of bleeding cry. **1932** *Punch Almanack 1933* 7 Nov. [18/1] 'Your mentality is erroneous and—er—soggy. Blime! *what* a cod!' he concluded. **1954** 'R. CROMPTON' *William & Moon Rocket* viii. 235 'Blimey!' said Charlemagne. 'Pardon him, dear,' said Miss Milton in a shaking voice. 'He doesn't often use bad language.'

blimp (blɪmp). [Of uncertain origin. Said to have been coined by the aviator Horace Shortt (see quot. 1918) or by Lieut. A. D. Cunningham (1951 *Aeroplane* 5 Oct.), and to have been based on the adj. LIMP.]

1. A small non-rigid airship orig. consisting of a gas-bag with the fuselage of an aeroplane slung underneath; in the war of 1939–45 the name was sometimes applied to a barrage balloon.

1916 ROSHER *In R.N.A.S.* 11 Feb. 146 Visited the Blimps ..this afternoon at Capel. **1918** *Illustr. Lond. News* 27 July 96 Nobody in the R.N.A.S. ever called them anything but 'Blimps', an onomatopœic name invented by that genius for apposite nomenclature, the late Horace Shortt. **1926** J. R. R. TOLKIEN in *Year's Wk. Eng. Stud. 1924* 52 It is perhaps more in accordance with their looks, history, and the way in which words are built out of the suggestions of others in the mind, if we guess that *blimp* was the progeny of *blister* + *lump*, and that the vowel *i* not *u* was chosen because of its diminutive significance—typical of war-humour. **1928** GAMBLE *North Sea Air Station* x. 149 The Submarine Scout non-rigid type. The name was abbreviated to S.S. airships, but they were generally known as 'Blimps'. **1934** *Discovery* Jan. 14/2 Excellent photographs..could probably be secured next summer from a small 'blimp' carrying a pilot and a photographer and directed by wireless telephony. **1939** *War Illustr.* 29 Dec. 538/1 The term 'blimp' originated in the last war, when British lighter-than-air aircraft were divided into A-rigid, and B-limp (i.e. without rigid internal framework). The modern barrage balloon may therefore be classed as a blimp. **1940** HARRISSON & MADGE *War begins at Home* v. 125 The [barrage] balloons, so suitably called blimps, became a major symbol in the first three months of the war.

b. *Cinematogr.* A sound-proof covering for a ciné camera. *colloq.*

1936 C. B. DE MILLE in *Words* Oct. 6/1 A 'blimp' in studio jargon is..a soundproof covering for the camera. **1959** *John o' London's* 3 Dec. 287/2 If I asked you to fetch me a 'blimp' ..you might toss over..a light cover to deaden the sound of a ..cine camera, so that its whirring didn't get recorded on the sound track.

2. (Colonel) Blimp, a character invented by David Low (1891–1963), cartoonist and caricaturist, pictured as a rotund pompous ex-officer voicing a rooted hatred of new ideas. Hence **blimp**, a person of this type; also *attrib.* Also **'blimpery, 'blimpishness, 'blimpism,** behaviour or speech characteristic of a blimp; **'blimpian, 'blimpish** *adjs.*, typical of a blimp.

1934 *Evening Standard* 28 May 10 Prime Minister Blimp: 'Gad, sir, the Air League is right. We must oppose all proposals for the abolition of military aviation.' **1935** *Ibid.* 2 Sept. 15 Blimpian 'statesmanship'—'Gad, madam, you can't lock up the explosives! That's a warlike act!' **1937** 'G. ORWELL' *Road to Wigan Pier* x. 197 Easy to laugh at..the Old School Tie and Colonel Blimp. **1937** F. P. CROZIER *Men I Killed* 13 Blimp still reigns, unfortunately, in places of greater responsibility where he can make a fool of himself more easily. *Ibid.* vii. 137 Our new system of rearmament is at least serving the purpose of encouraging our Colonel Blimps to hide their heads..in the sand. **1937** *New Statesman* 18 Dec. 1055/1 All to the good if people would be careful to send the full context and not send other people's ironical remarks or conscious jokes as if they were Blimpisms. **1938** *Ibid.* 5 Nov. 715/2 The modern clothes *Hamlet* at the Old Vic has excited a lot of Blimpish indignation. **1941** 'G. ORWELL' *Lion and Unicorn* 44 Thirty years ago the Blimp class was already losing its vitality. **1941** N. MARSH *Surfeit of Lampreys* viii. 115 [He's] very nice... Sort of old-world without any Blimpishness. **1942** *Times* 26 Feb. 8/3 The essence of blimpery is a refusal to entertain new ideas, and a determination to keep the bottom dog permanently in his place. **1943** C. BEATON *Near East* ii. 29 Blimpism, plus the Cairene climate, are two of Hitler's strongest weapons. **1944** H. G. WELLS *'42 to '44* 147 The more Blimp-like officers began to exclude this 'dangerous' topic. **1958** *Times* 15 Oct. 8/7 His innate Blimpishness suddenly arrests itself and he sings a jolly nostalgic song about the cricket fields of Harrow. **1968** *Daily Tel.* 13 Dec. 16/4 His usual comic character of pub pundit or cockney blimp.

†**blin, blinn**, *v. Obs.* Forms: 1 blinn-an, 3 blinnen, (bline, 4–5 bilynne, bylynne, blym, 6 blinn, blene), 3–6 blinne, (4–6 blyne, blyn, 3–7 blynne), 3–8 blin. *Pa. t.* 1 blann, 2–3 blann, 4–5 blan(e, 4–8 blanne, 6 blinned. *Pa. pple.* blunnen, blun (*rare*). [OE. *blinn-an* str. vb., syncopated from **bi-linnan* = OHG. *bilinnan* to cease, leave off, f. *bi-* BE- *pref.* + OE. and com. Teut. *linnan* to cease (found in Goth. in *af-linnan* to depart, and in ON. *linna* wk. vb., to leave off, cease, stop), ME. *linnen*: see LINN *v.* In the 14–15th c. the resolved form *bi-*, *by-lynne* (not preserved in OE.) frequently occurs.]

1. *intr.* To cease, leave off, desist.

[*c* **950** *Lindisf. Gosp.* Matt. xiv. 32 Geblann þæt wind.] *c* **1250** *Gen. & Ex.* 1963 Nile he blinnen. *c* **1325** *E.E. Allit.* P.A. 728 þer is þe blys þat cannot blynne. **1330** R. BRUNNE *Chron.* 48 Neuer he blanne. *c* **1386** CHAUCER *Chan. Yem. Prol. & T.* 618 Til he had torned him, couthe he nought blynne. *c* **1430** *Hymns Virg.* (1867) 60 His childhode blynnes Whanne he is fourtene ȝeer olde. **1557** *Mylner of Abingt.* 258 in Hazl. *E.P.P.* III. 110 My litell brother blinned nought, Ere their horse was home brought. **1642** H. MORE *Song of Soul* I. III. vi, The heavy hammers never blin. **1729** *Old Song* in Ramsay *Tea-t. Misc.* 18 The Minstrels they did never blin. *a* **1765** in Child *Ballads* III. (1885) 53/1 Till he had oretaken King Estmere, I wis he never blanne.

b. Const. *of* (*about*, *on*, *from*), *infin.* with *to*.

a **1000** *Cod. Vercell.* I. (1843) 80 þær þu..wuldres blunne. *c* **1200** ORMIN 14564 Ne blann itt nohht to reȝȝnenn. *a* **1300** *Cursor M.* 265 Nou of þis prologe wil we bline. *Ibid.* 14089 (Fairf.) A-boute seruise dide ho neuer blyn. *a* **1460** *Towneley Myst.* 255 Of shynyng blan bothe son and moyne. **1567** TURBERV. *Poems* in Chalmers *Eng. Poets* II. 589/1 And from their battaile blin. **1587** —— *Trag. T.* (1837) 199 Her teares did never blin To issue from her cristall eyes. *a* **1765** *Ballad 'Glasgerion'* iii. in Child *Ballads* III. (1885) 138/1 Strike on, Glasgerrion, Of thy striking doe not blinne.

2. *trans.* To cease from, stop; put a stop to.

c **1314** *Guy Warw.* (1840) 255 Of alle night he no blan rideinge. *c* **1460** *Towneley Myst.* 133 This chyld..Alle baylle may blyn. **1596** SPENSER *F.Q.* III. v. 22 Nathemore.. Did th' other two their cruell vengeaunce blin. **1601** *Death Earl Huntingt.* v. ii. in Hazl. *Dodsl.* VIII. 320 She never would blin telling, how his grace Sav'd, etc.

3. *intr.* To delay, tarry, stay.

a **1300** *Cursor M.* 20204 Langer bline nu i ne may. **1590** GREENE *Poems* (1861) 303 When in the Balance Daphnes leman blins.

4. To cease speaking, keep silence.

a **1300** *E.E. Psalter* xxvii[i]. 1 Mi God, ne blinne fra me. —— xxxi[i]. 3 For I blan [Vulg. *tacui*].

†**blin**, *sb.*[1] *Obs.*[f. prec. vb.] Cessation, end; delay, fail. (In phr. ***without(en blin.)***

a **1300** *Cursor M.* 881 Sco me bedd, wit-outen blin. *Ibid.* 1897 [þe doue] come again, wit-outen blin. [**1863** SALA *Capt. Dang.* I. i. 8 Of sins likewise without blin, and grievous ones.]

blin (blɪn), *sb.*[2] Pl. **blini, bliny** ('blɪnɪ), **'blinis.** [Russ., pancake.] (See quots.)

1889 *Harper's Mag.* LXXVIII. 854/1 The terrible Russian General absorbs before his soup a dozen *blinies*—which are heavy pancakes stuffed with caviare and seasoned with hot melted butter. **1892** T. F. GARRETT *Encycl. Pract. Cookery* II. 157/2 *Blinis*, small meal cakes which are eaten in Russia during Lent. **1920** M. W. DAVIS *Open Gates to Russia* xvi. 247 *Bliny*, the crisp Russian pancakes. **1943** E. M. ALMEDINGEN *Frossia* x. 376 They remembered *bliny*, those famous Carnival pancakes, thin and golden, eaten sometimes with sour cream, and oftener with caviare. **1945** E. WAUGH *Brideshead Revisited* I. vi. 152 The maitre d'hotel was turning the blinis over in the pan.

blinche, obs. form of BLENCH *v.* (or BLINK *v.*).

blind (blaɪnd), *a.* (and *adv.*) Forms: 1– blind, (4 blynt, 4–6 blynd(e, 4–7 blinde, 8– *Sc.* blin'). [A com. Teut. adj.: OE. *blind* = OS. *blind* (MDu. *blint(d)*, Du. *blind*), ON. *blindr* (Da., Sw. *blind*), OHG. *blint*, (MHG. *blint(d)*, mod.G. *blind*), Goth. *blinds*:—OTeut. **blindo-z*, of which the Aryan form would be **bhlendh-*: cf. Lith. *blę́ndza-s* blind, *blę́sti* to become dark, Lettish *blendu* I do not see clearly, OSlav. *blědŭ* pale, dim, pointing perhaps to an earlier sense 'become dim or dark' (Franck).]

I. Literal.

1. a. Destitute of the sense of sight, whether by natural defect or by deprivation. In comparisons, as ***blind as a bat*** or †***brickbat***; also ***blind as a beetle, mole, stone*** (see the sbs.); ***to turn a blind eye***: see EYE *sb.*[1] 5 e.

c **1000** *Ags. Gosp.* Mark x. 46 Bartimeus sæt blind wið þone weȝ wædla. *c* **1200** ORMIN 1859 He wass æness wurrþenn blind. *c* **1365** CHAUCER *A.B.C.* 105 O verrey light of eyen that ben blynde. *c* **1420** *Chron. Vilod.* 3632 As bleynde as a betulle. **1562** J. HEYWOOD *Prov. & Epigr.* (1867) 60 Blinde men should iudge no colours. **1571** GOLDING *Calvin on Ps.* xvi. 5 Blynd folke runne gadding hither and thither like mad Bedlems. **1588** J. HARVEY *Disc. Probl.* 40 As blinde, as moules, or bats. **1618** LATHAM *2nd Bk. Falconry* (1633) 50 After the old Prouerbe, Who so blinde, as he that will not see? **1639** J. CLARKE *Parœm.* 52 As blind as a bat at noone. **1705** HICKERINGILL *Priest-cr.* IV. (1721) 238 Hittee Missee, happy go lucky, as the blind Man kill'd the Crow. **1712** ADDISON *Spect.* No. 464 ¶5 Jupiter..left him to strole about the World in the blind Condition wherein Chremylus beheld him. **1840** in *Amer. Speech* (1965) XL. 127 For blind as a bat he was. **1850** DICKENS *Dav. Copp.* xlii, The old Scholar..is as blind as a brickbat. **1859** MASSON *Milton* I. 737 Galileo, frail and blind. **1925** W. DEEPING *Sorrell & Son* xviii. §2, I was blind as a bat. Pushed into a job by my people. **1943** E. CALDWELL *Georgia Boy* iii. 50 I've done gone and got as blind as a bat. I can't see nothing at all.

b. Temporarily deprived of sight, as when dazzled with a bright light.

1483 CAXTON *Cato* F ij, Lyke hym whyche is blynde of the rayes of the sonne.

c. Used punningly of a needle: Eyeless.

a **1800** COWPER *Manual more anc. Art of Poetry*, The smaller sort, which matrons use, Not quite so blind as they.

d. *absol.* A blind person, esp. as *pl.* Those who are blind, as a section of the community.

c **1000** *Ags. Gosp.* Matt. xx. 30 And þa sæton tweȝen blinde wið þone weȝ. *a* **1300** *Cursor M.* 13527 Wit þis blind þar can he mete. *Ibid.* 14370 Crepels gan, þe blind haf sight. **1611** BIBLE *Matt.* xv. 14 If the blinde lead the blinde, both shall fall into the ditch. *Mod.* The Royal Asylum for the Blind.

e. (*attrib.* of prec.) Of, pertaining to, or for the use of the blind as a class: as ***blind asylum.***

1881 *Durham Univ. Jrnl.* 12 Nov., The question of blind education. **1882** *Pall Mall G.* 8 June 7/2 The requirements for the blind scholarships are similar.

f. (See quot.)

1879 *Encycl. Brit.* IX. 292/2 The side [of a flat-fish] which is turned towards the bottom..is generally colourless, and called 'blind', from the absence of an eye on this side.

g. Short for *blind drunk* (see 15).

1630 J. TAYLOR *Water-Cormorant* in *Wks.* III. 5/1 For though he be as drunke as any Rat, He hath but catcht a Foxe, or Whipt the Cat. Or some say hee's bewitcht, or scratcht, or blinde, Which are the fittest tearmes that I can finde. **1845** A. M. HALL *Whiteboy* v. 49 They'll be all *blind* by the time they get home from G. F.'s wedding. **1903** 'A. MCNEILL' *Egreg. Eng.* 145 The artisan..improves the shining hours, by 'getting blind', to use his own elegant phrase. **1930** W. S. MAUGHAM *Gent. in Parlour* xliii. 263 On the night he arrived in London he would get blind, he hadn't been drunk for twenty years.

h. In Poker, *to go blind*: to put up a blind (see BLIND *sb.* 8); hence *to go* (a specified stake) ***blind.*** Hence applied to forms of Poker in which this is done; so ***blind hand.***

1872 [see i below]. **1882** *Poker* 88 For some reasons players never give the blind hand credit for a good or even an average hand. **1885** *Encycl. Brit.* XIX. 283/2 The age is sometimes allowed to *go blind*, i.e., to raise the ante before he sees his cards. **1885** [see STRADDLE *v.* 7].

i. fig. ***to go it blind***: to act without previous investigation of the circumstances; to plunge without regard to the risks involved. Also ***to go blind*** (***on*** ——). orig. *U.S.*

1840 *Spirit of Times* (N.Y.) 14 Mar. 18 Don't think of 'going it blind', but according to Walker! **1846** *Congress. Globe* App. 120 All I ask of him is that he will not 'go it blind' upon Oregon. **1848** LOWELL *Biglow P.* Ser. I. viii. 155 It gives a Party Platform, tu, jest level with the mind..Of.. honest folks thet mean to go it blind. **1872** SCHELE DE VERE *Americanisms* 328 Poker, when played by betting before looking at one's hand, is called *Blind Poker*, and this has given rise to the very common phrase, to *go it blind*, used whenever an enterprise is undertaken without previous enquiry. **1875** GEN. SHERMAN *Mem.* I. 342, I know that in Washington I am incomprehensible, because at the outset of the war I would not go it blind. **1892** KIPLING *Barrack-r. Ballads* 63 And faith he went the pace and went it blind. **1909** *Daily Chron.* 8 Feb. 4/4 If that be true, shall we be quite wise to 'go blind' on Dreadnoughts alone? **1924** GALSWORTHY *White Monkey* III. viii, Yes; they go it blind; it's the only logical way now.

j. *Aeronaut.* Applied to flying and aerial bombing executed by means of instruments without direct observation. Also as *adv.* Hence ***blind-bombing, -flying, -landing*** attrib.; **blind approach** (see 16).

1919 *Aviation* 1 Feb. 22 Flying in fog, clouds or darkness —which may be called 'blind flying'—involves difficulties not encountered in clear air. **1928** A. KLEMIN *If you want to Fly* 54 We have all sorts of instruments to tell us whether the plane is flying over an even keel, but it seems almost impossible to fly 'blind'. **1930** *Techn. News Bull., Bureau of Standards* June 61/1 Various combinations of the three elements making up the blind-landing system have been tried. **1936** *Nature* 23 May 863/2 His development of blind-flying instruments employing gyroscopic principles. **1937** *Times* 16 Oct. 11/5 A machine which..can be landed 'blind' from any height. **1940** W. S. CHURCHILL *Into Battle* (1941) 284 The diminution of the damage done by blind bombing. **1944** *Times* 31 Jan. 4/6 Frankfurt was covered by cloud and 'blind bombing' methods were used. **1958** *Times* 17 Oct. 3/4 The blind landing experimental unit have now shown that it is possible to complete the landing automatically without the pilot touching the controls or even seeing the ground.

k. ***a blind***: used *colloq.* with a following sb. to mean 'a single ——', 'the least or slightest ——'.

1938 J. CURTIS *They drive by Night* xvii. 193, I don't want a blind word out of either of you. **1941** *Penguin New Writing* II. 87 There's not a blind thing you can do about it. **1966** 'L. LANE' *ABZ of Scouse* 9 'E wooden take a blind bit er notice of me. *Ibid.*, Nobody could get a blind bit er sense outer 'im.

l. *to swear blind*: to affirm emphatically and without qualification. *colloq.*

1963 J. FOWLES *Collector* II. 138 He swears blind that he sent the CND cheque, but I don't know. **1975** *Economist* 25 Jan. 72/3 The state is now to control over two-thirds of British Petroleum—but swears blind it won't behave as if it did. **1985** *Byte* Feb. 190/3 You can swear blind it's solving a partial differential equation and they would be hard put to prove it is not.

II. *fig.* Without perception.

2. a. Of persons, their faculties, etc.; also *transf.* of things: Lacking in mental perception, discernment, or foresight; destitute of intellectual, moral, or spiritual light.

c **1000** *Ags. Gosp.* Matt. xxiii. 17 Ealá ȝe dysegan and blindan. *c* **1200** ORMIN 16954 Unnwis mann iss blunnt and blind. *a* **1340** HAMPOLE *Pr. Consc.* 240 Four thynges..þat mase a mans wytt blynd. *c* **1385** WYCLIF *Serm.* Sel. Wks. II. 230 Blynde jugement of men. **1594** T. B. *La Primaud. Fr. Acad.* II. 2 They are called blind in holy scripture, that haue not the true knowledge of God. **1645** MILTON *Tetrach.* Wks. (1851) 273 The blindest and corruptest times of Popedom. **1775** SHERIDAN *Duenna* II. ii. 201 How blind some parents are! **1877** MOZLEY *Univ. Serm.* i. 8 That would be a blind and mistaken inference.

b. Const. *to* (*in* obs.).

1662 GERBIER *Brief Disc.* (1665) 8 Surveyours who..are blind in the faults which their Workmen commit. **1759** FRANKLIN *Ess.* Wks. 1840 III. 368 The assembly chose..to be blind to the artificial part of his speech. **1856** TREVELYAN in *Life Macaulay* II. xiv. 460 To be blind to the merits of a great author.

c. ***blind side***: the unguarded, weak or assailable side of a person or thing, weakness; also, formerly, the unsightly or unpresentable side. Also, the side on which the view is obstructed from sight. In *Rugby Football*, the side of a scrum opposite to that on which the main line of the opponents' backs is ranged.

1606 CHAPMAN *Gentleman Usher* I. i, For that, we'll follow the blind side of him. **1655** GURNALL *Chr. in Arm.* (1845) 27 The imperfect knowledge Saints have here is Satan's advantage against them: he often takes them on the blind side. **1711** SWIFT *Lett.* (1767) III. 147 This is the blindside of my lodging out of town; I must expect such inconveniencies. **1884** *Chr. World* 4 Sept. 657/1 The forts which they were enabled..to approach on their blind side. **1917** 'CONTACT' *Airman's Outings* 212 An instinct for the 'blind side' of whatever Hun machine he had in view, made him a master in the art of approaching unobserved. **1959** *Times* 30 Nov. 3/6 Cambridge were in peril now, but they came again, worked the blind side.

3. a. Undiscriminating, for which no reason can be given; inconsiderate, heedless, reckless.

c **1340** *Cursor M.* 4116 (Trin.) To haue her wille blynde *c* **1450** *Crt. of Love* cliii, Blind apetite of lust. **1615** BEDWELL *Moham. Imp.* II. §65 The Disciples..became blind and fearelesse. **1753** HOGARTH *Anal. Beauty* xi. 91 The blind veneration that generally is paid to antiquity. **1822** HAZLITT *Table-t.* I. xi. 254 Self-will and blind prejudice. **1854** DICKENS *Hard T.* v. 14 Who came round the corner with such blind speed. *a* **1859** MACAULAY *Hist. Eng.* V. 254 His enemies struck at him with blind fury.

b. Purposeless; fortuitous, random.

1873 BROWNING *Red Cott. Night-C.* 177 Service that's blind and objectless—A servant toiling for no master's good.

4. Not possessing intelligence or consciousness; acting without discernment.

1692 BENTLEY *Boyle Lect.* vi. 198 It is the Product not of blind Mechanism or blinder Chance. **1853** MAURICE *Proph. & Kings* ix. 152 It is Will and not a blind necessity which rules in the armies of heaven. **1865** MOZLEY *Mirac.* vii. 292 *note*, Throughout the whole realm of nature blind agents or physical laws have been discovered.

†**5.** That blinds or misleads: false, deceitful. *Obs.*

1393 GOWER *Conf.* I. 73 He..with blinde tales so her ladde That all his will of her he hadde. **1526** *Pilgr. Perf.* 34 His blynde prophecyes and deceytfull myracles. **1559** *Mirr. Mag., Jack Cade* v. 3 Iustly called false and blynde.

III. Transferred.

6. a. Enveloped in darkness; dark, obscure. *arch.*

a **1000** *Be Domes Dæge* 230 Sauwle on liȝe On blindum scræfe byrnað & yrnað. *a* **1300** *Cursor M.* 3463 Bituix vnborn a batel blind. **1571** tr. *Buchanan's Detect. Mary* in H. Campbell's *Love-lett. Mary* (1824) 152 Go hide yourself in a blind hole. **1606** HOLLAND *Sueton.* 237 Meeting noe bodie [they] searched..everie blind corner. **1650** R. STAPYLTON *Strada's Low-C. Warres* VIII. 11 The blind and darksome night. **1666** PEPYS *Diary* (1879) IV. 94 The little blind bed-chamber. **1809** J. BARLOW *Columb.* III. 251 Dark fiend, that hides his blind abode.

†**b.** Not lighted, having its light extinguished or cut off. ***blind lantern***: a dark lantern.

1393 LANGL. *P. Pl.* C. xx. 228 3e brenneþ, ac 3e blaseþ nat · and þat is a blynde bekne. **1581** B. RICHE *Farewell Mil. Profession* (1846) 168 One of these little Lanters, that thei call blinde Lanterns (because thei tourne them, and hide their light when they liste). **1591** in DE FOE *Hist. Ch. Scot.* Addend. 56 Two Candlesticks with Two Blind Candles. **1705** HICKERINGILL *Priest-Cr.* II. v. 55 They adore the bare Altar, and blind Candles.

7. a. Dim, as opposed to *bright* or *clear*; dim, like faded writing; indistinct, obscure. Now mostly *fig.*

c **1325** *E.E. Allit. P.* A. 83 Þe sunnes bemez bot blo & blynde. **1398** TREVISA *Barth. De P.R.* XVI. xlvii. (1495) 569 We vse to call al manere of precyous stones, that ben not precyous and shynynge, blynde. **1536** BELLENDEN *Cron. Scot.* (1821) I. 254 Auld bukis..writtin craftly on rude and hard parchement; bot thay wer sa blind, we micht nocht reid ilk tent wourd. **1552** HULOET, Blynde letters or wrytynges, *caducæ literæ.* **1852** HAWTHORNE *Grandf. Chair* II. iv. 20 Written in such a queer, blind..hand.

b. of a road or path: (see quot.)

1815 SCOTT *Guy M.* xxii, Let him look along that blind road, by which I mean the track so slightly marked by the passengers' footsteps, that it can but be traced by a slight shade of verdure from the darker heath around it, and being only visible to the eye when at some distance, ceases to be distinguished while the foot is actually treading it. **1820** —— *Monast.* xxiii. **1854** H. MILLER *Sch. & Schm.* i. 1 A blind pathway..winding through the stunted heath.

c. Used of a letter indistinctly or imperfectly addressed. ***blind man***, ***officer***, ***reader***, a post-office employé who deals with such letters.

1864 W. LEWINS *Her Maj. Mails* 204 The 'blind Letter Office' is the receptacle for all illegible, misspelt, and misdirected or insufficiently addressed letters or packets. **1883** *Pall Mall G.* 20 Aug. A few specimen letters which have recently racked the brains of the 'blind readers' at the Post Office. **1885** *Pall Mall G.* 13 May 5 The ingenuity of the 'blind' men of the Post Office.

d. *Bookbinding.* Ungilt; cf. *blind-blocking*, *-tooling* in 16, BLIND *v.* 8.

1835 'J. A. ARNETT' *Bibliopegia* 125 Graining may be properly considered as a blind ornament. **1846** DODD *Brit. Manuf.* VI. 105 The block..imprints the device; whether it be gilt or 'blind'.

8. a. Out of sight, out of the way, secret, obscure, privy. Cf. BLIND ALLEY.

c **1386** CHAUCER *Chan. Yem. Prol. & T.* 105 Lurkynge in hernes and in lanes blynde. **1557** NORTH *Gueuara's Diall Pr.* (1582) 409a, Feasting..their secret friends in gardeins and blind tauerns. **1583** [see BLIND ALLEY]. **1660** BLOUNT *Boscobel* II. (1680) 13 To a blind Inn in Charmouth. **1661** PEPYS *Diary* 15 Oct. To St. Paul's Churchyard to a blind place where Mr. Goldsborough was to meet me. **1814** SCOTT *Wav.* xliii, Bailie Macwheeble having retired to..some blind change-house.

b. Of a way or path: the notion of 'secret, obscure,' is often mixed up with those of 'difficult to trace, confused or confusing, intricate, uncertain.'

a **1593** H. SMITH *Wks.* (1866–7) I. 218 Like a mark of knowledge in the turnings that lead unto blind by-ways. **1603** KNOLLES *Hist. Turks* (1621) 316 He..went by certaine blind wayes through the mountains and woods. **1634** MILTON *Comus* 181 In the blind mazes of this tangled wood. **1719** DE FOE *Crusoe* (1858) 357 Inaccessible, except by such windings, and blind ways, as they themselves only who made them could find. **1870** MORRIS *Earthly Par.* II. III. 76 Through blind ways of the wood he went.

9. a. Covered or concealed from sight.

1513 DOUGLAS *Æneis* III. x. 100 Blynd rolkis of Libie. **1555** EDEN *Decades W. Ind.* I. I. (Arb.) 66 The keele..ranne vpon a blynde rocke couered with water. **1614** MARKHAM *Cheap. Husb.* To Rdr., By evry high-way side or blinde ditch. **1650** R. STAPYLTON *Strada's Low-C. Warres* 47 The place was full of blind Pits covered over with Rubbish. **1796** MORSE *Amer. Geog.* II. 631 Surrounded with blind rocks, sunk a few feet below the water. **1882** *Standard* 16 Nov. 3/5 The ditches, overgrown with long grass and trailing brambles, were very 'blind.'

b. Applied to a corner or other feature where the road or course ahead is concealed from view.

1927 W. E. COLLINSON *Contemp. Eng.* 34 A further safety first proposal..is to eliminate the blind corners, i.e. corners where oncoming traffic cannot be seen. **1954** WODEHOUSE *Jeeves & Feudal Spirit* xvi. 161 No speeding? No passing on blind corners? **1957** S. MOSS *In Track of Speed* xii. 148 We could keep at 170 over blind hillbrows.

c. Applied to (the conduct of) a test or experiment in which information about the test that might lead to bias in the results is concealed from the tester or the subject (or both) until after the test is made, esp. as ***blind testing***, ***test***. Of a person: taking part in such a test. Also as *adv.* Cf. DOUBLE(-)BLIND *a.*

1937, etc. [see DOUBLE(-)BLIND *a.*]. **1962** *Lancet* 28 Apr. 874/1 The observer was reading the vaccine takes 'blind'. **1971** *Daily Tel.* 25 Nov. 3 The place: The King's Lynn Festival... The purpose: a 'blind' test between a fine and a good red wine. **1971** *Ibid.* 20 Dec. 11/1, 20 wines will have to be identified, some of them down to their vintage. Apart from the 'blind' tasting there will be a short written paper. **1977** *Lancet* 5 Nov. 952/2 The performance was scored by two professional musicians... They were 'blind' not only to the drug therapy but also to the medical assessments and to each other's scoring. **1980** *San Francisco Bay Guardian* 16–23 Oct. 16/2, I participated in a blind tasting designed to compare leading examples of *methode Champenoise* sparkling wines from several countries.

10. Having no openings or passages for light.

a. *Arch.* Of walls, etc.: Without windows or openings; (a window or door) walled up.

1603 KNOLLES *Hist. Turks* (1621) 516 The Cloister..shut in on everie side with high and blind wals. **1736** CARTE *Ormonde* I. 273 Some of the inhabitants who let the rebels into the place through an old blind door that was broke open for them. **1820** L. HUNT *Indicator* No. 38 (1822) I. 297 This tower..seemed as blind as it was strong. **1870** F. WILSON *Ch. Lindisf.* 41 The north walls of both nave and vestry were blind. **1874** PARKER *Illustr. Goth. Archit.* I. iii. 61 In..Christ Church Cathedral, Oxford..the clerestory window has a smaller blind arch on each side of it.

b. Of hedges and the like: Too thick or leafy to be seen through.

1718 POPE *Iliad* XI. 595 Some huntsman..From the blind thicket wounds a stately deer. **1863** *Spring & Sum. Lapland* 54 The hedges were getting too blind for hunting.

c. Of an alphabetic letter: written or printed with the loop closed or filled in: *spec.* in *Typogr.* defining the paragraph mark with a closed loop.

1820 KEATS *Lett.* (1958) II. 262 The fault is in the Quill: I have mended it and still it is very much inclin'd to make blind es. **1888** JACOBI *Printers' Vocab.*, *Blind P.* A paragraph mark ¶ so called from the loop of the P being closed. **1905** F. H. COLLINS *Author & Printer* 34 Blind ¶, paragraph mark.

d. *Cookery.* Applied to a pastry case baked before the filling is added (see quots.). Also as *adv.*

1943 A. SIMON *Concise Encycl. Gastronomy* IV. 92/2 Bake 'blind' till golden... 'Blind' means pricking paste well and filling with tissue paper and beans to stop crust rising. **1952** B. NILSON *Penguin Cookery Book* 313 If the flan is to be baked without a filling (i.e. 'blind'), prick the bottom well. **1958** *Woman* 4 Oct. 23/1 'Baking blind', simply means lining the pastry with a round of greaseproof paper, then weighting this down with rice or beans to prevent it rising during cooking.

11. a. Closed at one end. Cf. BLIND ALLEY.

1662 [see BLIND ALLEY]. **1668** CULPEPPER & COLE *Barthol. Anat.* i. 303 Yet could I not..find the Anastomoses of Vena Cava and Vena Porta open, but all blind. **1678** SALMON *New Lond. Dispens.* 818 They are of use in the blind Alembick. **1724** [see BLIND ALLEY]. **1847–9** TODD *Cycl. Anat. & Phys.* IV. 736 The cæcum towards its blind termination. **1878** JEFFERIES *Gamekpr. at H.* 116 Cross-passages, 'blind' holes and 'pop' holes.

b. ***blind holes*** in *Mechanics*: holes not coincident in plates to be riveted together.

1869 SIR E. REED *Shipbuild.* x. 194 The greater number of what are termed blind, or half-blind, holes are found in the edges.

c. Applied to a geographical feature, as a spur, reef, or valley, that terminates abruptly.

1848 C. J. PHARAZYN *Jrnl.* 15 Jan. (MS.) 97 Teddy and W. to lambs to drive them to pen, smother'd 10 in a blind gully. **1861** J. VON HAAST *Rep. Topogr. & Geol. Expl. Nelson Prov.* i. 8 We had selected a so-called blind spur, which fell abruptly into a deep gully. **1882** W. D. HAY *Brighter Britain* II. viii. 299 Eventually it proved that the find was but a 'blind reef', a 'pocket', a mere isolated dribble from the main continuous vein we had at first supposed we had struck. **1898** J. GEIKIE *Earth Sculpture* xiii. 217 Not less characteristic features of the karst-lands are the so-called blind-valleys and dry-valleys. Through the former a river flows to disappear into a tunnel at the closed or blind end. **1942** O. D. VON ENGELN *Geomorphology* xxii. 578 Blind valleys differ from pocket valleys in that the latter develop where underground water emerges in greater or less volume.

d. Of a baggage-car on a train: see quot. 1901. *U.S.*

1893 *Daily Ardmoreite* (Oklahoma) 8 Nov. 1/4 They didn't even have an opportunity to fire a tramp off the blind baggage. **1901** *Scribner's Mag.* XXIX. 429/1 The train's got a blind baggage-car on... That's a car that ain't got no door in the end that's next the engine. **1926** J. BLACK *You can't Win* ix. 120 With much caution I made my way..till I got near enough to the depot to get aboard the blind end of a baggage car.

12. Of plants: Without buds or eyes, or without a terminal flower. ***blind bud***, one that bears no bloom or fruit, an abortive bud.

1884 J. E. TAYLOR *Sagac. & Mor. Plants* 70 Should such flowers fail to be crossed, no fruit is borne, and the flowers are then blind. *Mod.* These asters have turned out 'blind.'

13. ***blind story***, one without point.

1699 BENTLEY *Phal.* Pref. 64 He insinuates a blind Story about something and somebody. **1762–71** H. WALPOLE *Vertue's Anecd. Paint.* (1786) II. 75 This story which in truth is but a blind one.

†**14.** *transf.* from sight to sound. *Obs.*

1398 TREVISA *Barth. De P.R.* XIX. cxxxi. (1495) 942 The blynde voyc stynteth soone · and is stuffyd and dureth not longe: as the sowne of erthen vessell.

IV. Combinations.

15. General, as ***blind-born***, ***-drunk*** (Sc. ***blin'-fou***), so intoxicated as to see no better than a blind man, ***-eyed***, ***-hearted***, ***-weary***.

c **975** *Rushw. Gosp.* John ix. 32 Eȝo ðæs blinda-borones. *a* **1225** *Ancr. R.* 178 Þu ert blind iheorted, & ne isihst nout hwu þu ert poure & naked of holinesse. *a* **1300** *Cursor M.* 13601 3e sai þat blind-born man was he. **1720** WELTON *Suff. Son of God* II. xxii. 610 The poor, Blind-Born Man. *c* **1775** *Sandman's Wedding*: *A Cantata*, She being blind drunk Sir, Joe drove her away in his Cart. **1827** W. CLARKE *Every Night Book* 191 Whenever I've been tipsy in your company, you have always been blind drunk. **1845** DISRAELI *Sybil* III. iv. x. 132 Hang me if I wasn't blind drunk at the end of it. **1887** MORRIS *Odyssey* x. 493 Tiresias..The blind-eyed, the foreseer. **1902** *Daily Chron.* 18 Feb. 3/2 Are we to suppose, then, that Goethe..was a blind-eyed fool? **1923** D. H. LAWRENCE *Birds, Beasts & Flowers* 107 [The bat] flying slower, Seeming to stumble, to fall in air. Blind-weary. **1935** *Mind* XLIV. 434 Blind-born persons, such as Helen Keller, talk *intelligently* about colours. **1953** E. O'NEILL *Moon for Misbegotten* IV. 140 Sure, I got so blind drunk at the Inn I forgot all about our scheme.

16. Special comb., as **blind advertisement**, also **blind ad.** *U.S.* (see quot. 1948); **blind approach** *Aeronaut.*, an approach made without direct observation (see 1 j); applied *attrib.* to a radio navigation system controlling such an approach; **blind area** (*Arch.*), a clear space around the basement wall of a house; **blind-axle**, one that turns but does not move any other part of the mechanism, = *dead-axle*; **blind back**, applied *attrib.* to a type of house that has no back door; **blind-ball**, the Puff-ball (*Lycoperdon bovista*), a fungus containing dust which is supposed to blind the eyes; **blind-beetle**, a popular name for beetles which are apt to fly against people, esp. by night; hence ***blind-beetledness***; also, a small beetle found in rice; **blind-blocking**, **-tooling** (*Bookbinding*),

ornamental impressions on book-covers produced by heated blocks, or tools, without goldleaf; **blind booking**, the booking of films by cinema proprietors without previous selection on their merits; **blind creek** (see quot.); **blind date** [DATE *sb.*[2] 2 c] orig. and chiefly *U.S. colloq.* (see quot. 1929); also, the person with whom such a 'date' is arranged; **blind-fish**, the *Amblyopsis spelæus*, a fish without eyes found in the Mammoth Cave of Kentucky; **blind-gallery** (see BLIND *a.* 10); **blind-harry** (*Sc.*), blind-man's-buff; **blind hazard**, (*a*) a game at cards; (*b*) *Golf* (see quot.); **blind-hob**, some game unknown; **blind hole** *Golf* (see quots.); **blind-hookey**, a game at cards; **blind ink** (see quot.); **blind-level** (see quot.); †**blind-mouse**, the mole; also the water shrew-mouse; **blind-pig** *U.S. colloq.*, a place where liquor is illicitly sold; hence *blind-pigger*, *-pigging*; **blind poker** *U.S.* (see 1 h); **blind printing** (see quots.); **blind roller** [ROLLER *sb.*[1] 15] (see quot. 1948); **blind-seed disease**, a fungal disease of rye grass in which the seed fails to germinate; so *blind-seed fungus*; **blind-shaft**, a winze; **blind-shell** (*Artillery*), a shell containing no powder, also one that fails to explode when fired; **blind spot**, (*a*) the spot on the retina which is insensible to light; (*b*) *Cricket*, that spot of ground in front of a batsman where a ball pitched by the bowler leaves the batsman in doubt whether to play forward or back; (*c*) *Radio* (see quot. 1923); (*d*) *transf.* and *fig.*; **blind staggers** (see STAGGER *sb.*[1] 2); **blind-stamping** = *blind-blocking*; hence *blind-stamped* ppl. a.; **blind stitch**, a stitch taken on one side of the material so as to be invisible on the other; hence as *v. trans.*, to sew or fasten with blind stitch; **blind-story** (*Arch.*), a triforium or series of arches below the clerestory of a cathedral, admitting no light; **blind tiger** *U.S.* = *blind-pig*; **blind tooling** = *blind-blocking*; **blind trust** *N. Amer.*, a trust that administers the private business interests of a person in public office in order to prevent any possibility of conflict between these and the public interest; **blind-window**, ? a window that admits no light; an arch of the blind-story. Also BLIND -COAL, -GUT, -HEAD, -NETTLE, -WORM, q.v.

1948 MENCKEN *Amer. Lang.* Suppl. II. xi. 731 **Blind ad.*, an unsigned newspaper or magazine advertisement. **1962** 'A. A. FAIR' *Stop at Red Light* ii. 25 The insurance company have been running a blind ad.. offering one hundred dollars for any witness.. to an accident.. at Seventh and Main Streets. **1842** *Ainsworth's Mag.* II. 43 The Puff Preliminary is known to..'printer's devils', by the less euphonious title of 'a *blind advertisement'. **1936** C. B. ALLEN *Wonder Book of Air* 300 To aid him in this, the present set-up in the radio '*blind approach' system.. includes the use of a string of powerful and distinctive lights. **1947** R. A. SMITH *Radio Aids to Navig.* xi. 88 It is generally felt now that some form of glide path is preferable to an altimeter for blind approach. **1937** 'G. ORWELL' *Road to Wigan Pier* iv. 53 House in Wallgate quarter. *Blind back type. One up, one down. *Ibid.* 56 Houses of what is called the 'blind back' type.. in which the builder has omitted to put in a back door. **1649** LIGHTFOOT *Battle w. Wasp's N.* (1825) 389 If you must shame any body for *blind beetledness. **1927** *Glasgow Herald* 20 Jan. 7 '*Blind-booking' was responsible for a very large percentage of the machine-made pictures which came from America to this country. **1927** *Daily Tel.* 15 Mar. 9/2 The Labour-Socialists.. are in favour of the proposals for the abolition of blind booking and restrictions on advance booking. **1886** J. W. ANDERSON *Prospector's Handbk.* 115 *Blind Creek, a creek, dry, except during wet weather. **1925** *Lit. Digest* 14 Mar. 65/1 No, got a *blind date on to-night. **1929** *Amer. Speech* IV. 420 *A blind date*, a date with someone whom the datee does not know but which is arranged by a third person. **1947** *Chicago Tribune* 14 June 18/8 In describing your blind date, I would say she has a wonderful personality. **1880** GÜNTHER *Fishes* 618 The famous *Blind Fish of the Mammoth Cave in Kentucky.. is destitute of external eyes. **1816** SINGER *Hist. Cards* 263 We are informed the modern name of this game [Bankrout] is *Blind Hazard. **1900** A. E. T. WATSON *Yng. Sportsman* 315 A Blind hazard is also a hazard which is hidden from his view. *a* **1845** MRS. BRAY *Warleigh* xvii. (1884) 135 In the servants' hall, playing at *blind hob and hot cockles. **1900** A. E. T. WATSON *Yng. Sportsman* 315 A *Blind hole is one of which the putting-green is not visible to the player as he plays his shot. **1862** THACKERAY *Philip* II. 100 Victimized by his own uncle.. at a game called '*blind hookey.' *a* **1884** KNIGHT *Dict. Mech.* Suppl., **Blind Ink.* Invented by Edison. An ink which.. swells up into relief on the paper. **1881** RAYMOND *Mining Gloss.*, **Blind level*, 1. A level not yet connected with other workings. 2. A level for drainage, having a shaft at either end, and acting as an inverted siphon. **1607** TOPSELL *Four-f. Beasts* 563 It hunteth Moles or *blinde Mice. **1770** PENNANT *Zool.* IV. 83 It [the water shrewmouse] is called, from the smallness of its eyes, the blind mouse. **1887** *Minnesota Gen. Statutes Suppl.* (1888) 248 Whoever shall attempt to evade or violate any of the laws of this state.. by means of the artifice or contrivance known as the '*Blind Pig' or 'Hole in the Wall'.. shall.. be punished. **1903** *N.Y. Even. Post* 23 Sept., But a 'blind pig' is at best but a sordid institution. **1961** *Spectator* 28 July 135 Blind pigs—establishments with anonymous blank facades entered by a basement front door with a peep-hole. **1894** *Voice* (N.Y.) 6 Dec. 1/5 Headed by one of the *blind-piggers who was under arrest. **1918** WEBSTER Add., **Blind-pigging*, n. **1927** *Blackw. Mag.* June 833/1 Amongst the common herd two crimes ranked as serious—'blind-pigging' and 'high-grading'. **1904** E. F. STRANGE *Japanese Colour Prints* xi. 110 In addition to the blocks for various colours, an effect of *blind printing (*gauffrage*) was often secured by the use of an additional printing from a clean block. **1926** H. HUBBARD *How to distinguish Prints* 21 Charpentier and others.. experimented with 'blind printing', that is, the use of an uninked relief block that merely embossed the paper with its engraved design. **1888** G. O. PRESHAW *Banking under Difficulties* xxv. 155 '*Blind rollers' often rising and swamping a boat. **1948** R. DE KERCHOVE *Internat. Maritime Dict.*, *Blind rollers*, relatively heavy and often dangerous ocean swell caused by water in motion meeting lesser depth as it passes over shoals or approaches land. **1939** J. C. NEILL & E. O. C. HYDE in *N.Z. Jrnl. Sci. & Technol.* Feb. 283A, Low-germination trouble of otherwise apparently sound, well-harvested crops [of rye-grass] is caused by a pathogenic fungus... So unnoticeable are the symptoms that it has not yet even received a common name... It is proposed that it be called **Blind-seed Disease*. *Ibid.* 288A, The blind-seed fungus appears to be allied to *Helotium herbarum* Fries. **1956** *Nature* 10 Mar. 466/1 Blind seed disease of ryegrass caused by *Phialea temulenta*. **1864** *Daily Tel.* 4 May, The day was closed with.. *blind shells for the purpose of completing the tables of ranges. **1864** *Baily's Monthly Mag.* Sept. 301 Now the great difficulty of slows, besides being (as they ought all to be) 'in the *blind spot', consists in the elevation.. of a dropping ball. **1872** HUXLEY *Phys.* ix. 219 So long as the image.. rests upon the entrance of the optic nerve, it is not perceived, and hence this region of the retina is called the blind spot. **1891** GRACE *Cricket* iii. 73 Too often would come a ball on the blind spot. **1907** G. B. SHAW *John Bull's Other Is.* Pref. p. xli, You find that there is a blind spot on their moral retina, and that this blind spot is the military spot. **1910** GALSWORTHY *Justice* I. 19 No doing anything with them... They've got a blind spot. **1923** *Daily Mail* 13 Feb. 7 Wireless blind spots, where distant broadcasting is heard more clearly than that nearer at hand. **1932** E. V. LUCAS *Reading, Writing & Remembering* viii. 150 He was too full of prejudices and had too many blind spots, to be the perfect critic. **1784** J. LEWIS *Diary* 4 Mar. in *New Jersey Hist. Soc. Proc.* (1941) LIX. 169 We discovered that my horse had a distemper called the *blind staggers. **1874** *Rep. Vermont Board Agric.* II. 341 The disease is frequently called 'blind staggers'. **1931** *Library* XI. 395 Long after *blind-stamped pictorial panels had gone out of use in Paris. *Ibid.* 425 Business in the Gothic blind-stamped bindings. **1910** *Encycl. Brit.* IV. 217/1 English binders excelled in this art of '*blind' stamping, that is, without the use of gold leaf. *a* **1884** KNIGHT *Dict. Mech.* Suppl., **Blind Stitch.* (Harness)... A stitch that is shown on one side only of the leather. **1909** *Daily Chron.* 14 Jan. 7/5 Facings should be blind-stitched into place. *c* **1520** MYLN *Vitæ Dunkeld. Episcop.* in Parker *Gloss. Goth. Arch.* I. 57 Construxit usque secundos arcus, vulgariter le *blyndstorys. **1848** RICKMAN *Goth. Archit.* Introd. 18, There is a passage in the thickness of the wall of the clerestory as well as in the triforium or blind-story. **1857** *Spirit of Times* 23 May 182/1, I sees a kinder pigeon-hole cut in the side of a house, and over the hole, in big writin', 'Blind Tiger, ten cents a sight.'.. That '*blind tiger' was an arrangement to evade the law, which won't let 'em sell licker there, except by the gallon. **1884** *Arkansas Digest Laws 1883* 493 Any person.. who shall sell .. any alcohol.. by such device as is known as 'the blind tiger',.. shall be deemed guilty of a misdemeanor. **1818** *Art Bk.-binding* 31 In addition to the gilt back, rolled plain, that is, *blind-tooling, on the inside of the board. **1847** L. HUNT *Men, Women, & Bks.* II. vi. 78 The charms of.. tall copies, and blind tooling. **1969** *Sunday Times* 23 Mar. 34 David Packard has put his $300 million worth of Hewlett Packard stock into a so-called *blind trust. **1972** *Fortune* Jan. 110/1 He resigned all of his other posts and put his holdings into a blind trust before taking the job. **1979** *N.Y. Times* 18 Jan. A1 The day he became President, Mr. Carter's 62 percent interest in the business was transferred to a 'blind trust' administered by.. an Atlanta lawyer. **1506** *Bury Wills* (1850) 107, I byqueth toward the makyng of ij *blynde wyndowes in the seid monasterij.. *xli.*

blind (blaɪnd), *v.* Also 4–5 blynd(e. *Pa. t.* and *pple.* blinded: pple. in 4 blind, iblind, (5 blynyd). [f. BLIND *a.*, first in ME.: taking the place of the earlier equivalent BLEND *v.*[1]; or rather perhaps to be viewed as a phonetic variation of the latter, caused by assimilation to the adjective.]

1. *trans.* To make blind, deprive of sight: **a.** permanently.

a **1300** *Cursor M.* 7246 Þai blinded him and prisund bath. *c* **1440** *Promp. Parv.* 40 Blyndyn, or make blynde, *exceco.* *a* **1450** *Syr Eglam.* 318 To the yeant he gafe a sowe And blyndyd hym in that tyde! **1753** HANWAY *Trav.* I. v. lxxvi. 347 Ali was taken prisoner and blinded. **1875** MAINE *Hist. Inst.* ii. 37 He had been accidentally blinded of one eye.

b. temporarily, *e.g.* by dazzling with a bright light, or by bandaging the eyes: To render insensible to light or colour.

1388 WYCLIF *Ecclus.* xliii. 4 The sunne blyndith iȝen. **1530** PALSGR. 458/1 This great light blyndeth my syght. **1632** MASSINGER & FIELD *Fatal Dow.* IV. iv, Fear nothing, I will only blind your eyes. **1827** HOOD *Hero & L.* xlv, His eyes are blinded with the sleety brine. **1860** TYNDALL *Glac.* I. §5. 38 The effect.. upon the eye is to blind it in some degree to the perception of red.

c. Used in vulgar imprecations, as *blind me!* Cf. BLIMEY *int.*

1890 FARMER *Slang* I. 230/1 *Blimey*, a corruption of 'blind me!'; an expression little enough understood by those who constantly have it in their mouths. **1923** E. O'NEILL *Hairy Ape* v. 47 There's a 'ole mob of 'em like 'er, Gawd blind 'em! *a* **1953** — *In Zone* (1955) 523 'E ain't arf a sly one wiv 'is talk of submarines, gawd blind 'im.

2. *fig.* **a.** To close the eyes of the understanding or moral perception; to deceive, 'throw dust in the eyes' of (persons and their faculties). Also, to render (mentally) blind or oblivious *to. refl.*, to shut one's (mental) eyes *to.*

a **1300** *Cursor M.* 17452 To man þat couaitis has blind. **1382** WYCLIF *Ex.* xxiii. 8 Ȝiftes, that also blynden wise men. **1538** BALE *Thre Lawes* 979 To blynde the rulers and deceyve the commynalte. **1611** BIBLE *2 Cor.* iii. 14 But their mindes were blinded. **1720** OZELL tr. *Vertot's Rom. Rep.* II. IX. 92 A great Presumption blinded him from seeing his own Incapacity. **1729** BUTLER *Serm.* Wks. 1874 II. 123 Good-will to another may.. blind our judgement. **1775** SHERIDAN *Duenna* III. vi. 224 How jealousy blinds people! **1856** FROUDE *Hist. Eng.* I. ii. 98 Wolsey could not blind himself to the true condition of the church. **1908** E. F. BENSON *Climber* x. 148 Even Edgar's invariable neatness did not blind her to the fact that he, too, was genuine. **1935** I. COMPTON-BURNETT *A House & its Head* i. 6, I hope that my allowing you to treat the occasion as a festival, has not blinded you to its significance. **1944** W. S. MAUGHAM *Razor's Edge* i. 10 The glamour of their resounding titles blinded him to their faults. **1979** T. BENN *Arguments for Socialism* i. 29 We should.. not allow the horrors of persecution committed at various times in history by societies proclaiming themselves to be Christian to blind us to the true teachings of Christ.

b. *intr.* To go blindly or heedlessly; to drive very fast. Also *fig. slang.*

1923 *Daily Mail* 21 June 12 Motor-cyclists who blind along the road. **1928** *Daily Express* 19 May 10/6 By recreation I do not mean blinding along the Brighton road at fifty miles an hour. **1935** *Punch* 21 Aug. 198/1 It is far better to get a little work done which is perfectly planned and organised than to let people go blinding on without anyone in authority knowing what they are doing. **1937** M. ALLINGHAM *Dancers in Mourning* iv. 58, I was blinding... Didn't see her until I was over her. **1954** C. FRY *Dark is Light Enough* II. 71 A trap, they've set for us. Who's got our pistols? Gone blinding into it.

3. a. To put out of sight, hide, conceal; make difficult to see or trace.

c **1340** *Cursor M.* 21357 (Fairf.) Þe iewes hid hit efter-sone fra cristen men hit to blinde. **1709** C. PLACE in *Bibl. Topogr. Brit.* III. 106 The way [is] cunningly blinded by diversions. **1813** SCOTT *Rokeby* II. iv, Oft doubling back in mazy train, To blind the trace the dews retain. **1821** KEATS *Lamia* 373 Wherefore did you blind Yourself from his quick eyes.

†**b.** To hide from the understanding, to obscure; to represent as obscure. *Obs.*

1622 HEYLIN *Cosmogr.* III. (1682) 166 Those desarts which Ptolomy blindeth under the name Terra Incognita. *a* **1700** STILLINGFL. (J.) The state of the controversy.. he endeavoured with all his art to blind and confound.

†**4.** To come in the way of; to intercept. *Obs.*

1303 R. BRUNNE *Handl. Synne* 12152 Oure shryfte þe deuyl blyndep. *c* **1450** LONELICH *Grail* lvi. 174 From here schepis we scholen hem blynde.

5. a. To deprive (things) of light; to darken.

a **1643** W. CARTWRIGHT *Lady Errant* I. iii. (1651) 10 They have laid aside their Jewels, and so Blinded their garments. *a* **1700** DRYDEN (J.) Such darkness blinds the sky. **1847** J. WILSON *Chr. North* (1857) I. 146 Let the honeysuckle.. blind unchecked a corner of the kitchen-window.

b. To dim by excess of light; to eclipse.

1633 P. FLETCHER *Pisc. Eclog.* vi. (L.) Her beauty all the rest did blind. **1842** TENNYSON *Tithonus* 38 Thy [Aurora's] sweet eyes.. blind the stars.

6. *Gunnery.* To provide with blindages.

1850 ALISON *Hist. Europe* XIV. lxxxvii. §4 Extraordinary precautions.. to render nugatory the effects of a bombardment, by blinding the ships.. with turf, wet blankets, and.. other articles. **1870** *Standard* 12 Dec., Guns blinded with iron mantelets.

7. *intr.* To be or become blind or dim. *arch.*

c **1305** *Old Age* ix. in *E.E.P.* (1862) 149, I blind, I bleri. *c* **1325** *E.E. Allit. P.* B. 1126 Ho blyndes of ble. **1822** BEDDOES *Bride's Trag.* II. iv, Thy bright eye would blind at sights like this!

8. *trans.* In *Bookbinding*, to stamp *in* (a pattern) without gilding.

1901 COCKERELL *Bookbinding* 212 The pattern is blinded in through the leather.

9. To cover the surface of (a newly made road) with fine material. Cf. BLINDING *vbl. sb.* 4.

1812 J. SINCLAIR *Syst. Husb. Scot.* I. 66 No large stones to be employed.. nor sand, earth or other matter, on pretence of *blinding* [the road]. **1880** W. H. PATTERSON *Gloss. Antrim & Down* s.v., To 'blind a road' = to spread small stones or cinders so as to cover up the large stones, with which a new road has been 'pitched', and to fill the interstices.

blind (blaɪnd), *sb.* Also 4 blynde, 6 blynd, 6–7 blinde. [f. BLIND *v.* (? or *adj.*)]

1. Anything which obstructs the light or sight.

1702 C. MATHER *Magn. Chr.* VII. iv. (1852) 522 Blinds to keep.. light from entring into the souls of men. **1768** BLACKSTONE *Comm.* II. 402 If I have an antient window overlooking my neighbour's ground, he may not erect any blind to obstruct the light. **1815** BYRON *Parisina* xvii, To bind Those eyes which would not brook such blind.

2. *spec.* A screen for a window, made of woven material mounted on a roller, of wire gauze, etc.; used to prevent the entrance of too much light, or to keep people from seeing in. ***Venetian blinds***: those made of light laths fixed on strips of webbing.

1730 Window-Blind [see WINDOW *sb.* 5 a]. **1771** J. S. COPLEY in *Copley-Pelham Lett.* (1914) 142 Those Windows having new fassioned Blinds such as you see in Mr Clarke's Keeping room. **1786** tr. *Beckford's Vathek* (1868) 19 The women.. flew to their blinds to discover the cause. **1788** LD. AUCKLAND *Corr.* (1861) II. 67 The making visits.. is done in a carriage with blinds. **1855** DICKENS *Dorrit* i, Blinds, shutters, curtains, awnings were all closed and drawn.

3. A blinker for a horse; cf. 11.

1828 WEBSTER s.v., A blind.. for a horse. **1848** *Congress. Globe* 30 June, App. 820/1 [Mr. Polk] was worked into the Presidency with Oregon and Texas on either side, as a horse is worked with blinds. **1901** *Munsey's Mag.* XXV. 739/1 A halter has a soft leather covered bit, and is without blinds.

4. *Fortification.* A blindage.

1644 in Rushw. *Hist. Coll.* III. II. 739 Massey caused a blind to be made across the street. **1710** *Lond. Gaz.* No. 4692/1 We had thrown up some Blinds to cover our Men. **1802** C. JAMES *Mil. Dict.* s.v.

5. Any means or place of concealment. *spec.* a hiding-place in which a hunter conceals himself from the game. (*U.S.*).

1646 SHIRLEY *On Death of C. Dalby*, So will they..sleep Till the last trumpet wake 'em, and then creep Into some blind. **1697** DRYDEN *Virg.* (1806) III. 52 The watchful shepherd, from the blind, Wounds with a random shaft the careless hind. **1818** *Niles' Reg.* XV. 64/2 Col. Boon rode to a deer lick, seated himself within a blind raised to conceal him from the game. **1869** *Game Laws* (*Penn.*) in *Fur, Fin & Feather* (1872) 94 No person shall..build blinds for the purpose of killing..any wild turkey. **1874** J. W. LONG *Wild-Fowl Shooting* 45 Ingenuity in the providing of proper ambush, or blind, as all such hiding places are generally termed by wild-fowlers. **1894** *Outing* (U.S.) XXIV. 73/2 A glance..discloses the fact that no time should be wasted in getting started for the blinds.

6. *fig.* Any thing or action intended to conceal one's real design; a pretence, a pretext. *spec.* (see quot. 1929).

1664-94 SOUTH *12 Serm.* II. 208 A Practice, which duly seen into, and stript of its Hypocritical Blinds, could not, etc. **1713** STEELE *Guardian* No. 150 (1756) II. 263 Her constant care of me was only a blind. **1732** SWIFT *Wks.* (1841) II. 127 These verses were only a blind to conceal the most dangerous designs of the party. **1833** COLERIDGE *Table-t.* 14 May, There is one sonnet [of Shakspeare's] which, from its incongruity, I take to be a purposed blind. **1929** *Amer. Speech* IV. 338 *Blind*, a legitimate business used to conceal an illegitimate one. **1938** F. D. SHARPE *Sharpe of Flying Squad* viii. 107 Another man..used to trade dogs as a blind.

†**7.** *Naut.* A spritsail [= Du. *blinde*]. *Obs.*

1535 STEWART *Cron. Scot.* (1858) I. 20 With fuksaill, topsaill, manesall, musall, and blynd.

8. In Poker, a stake put up by a player before seeing his cards (see quots.); cf. BLIND *a.* 1 h. Also *attrib.* in *blind-money*. Also *fig.*

1857 *Hoyle's Games* (Amer. ed.) 289 Should a party see fit to call the blind, [he] must put twice the number in the pool. **1872** 'MARK TWAIN' *Innoc. at Home* (1882) ii. 268 Now you talk! You see my blind and straddle it like a man. **1882** *Poker* 49 The straddle is nothing more than a double blind. *Ibid.* 91 It is an error on the part of the Age to fill the Blind simply because he has already invested the Blind-money. **1885** *Encycl. Brit.* XIX. 283/2 The next player [to the age] may *double the blind*, i.e., raise to double what the age staked; the next may *straddle the blind*, i.e. double again,..and so on. Only the age can start a blind. **1888** FARMER *Americanisms*, *Blind* (in poker), the ante deposited by the age previous to the deal... To make a blind good costs double the amount of the ante, and to make a straddle good costs four times the amount of the blind. **1894** *Congress. Rec.* May 4408/2 Put up your blind. It's my deal.

9. A blind baggage car on a train (see BLIND *a.* 11 d). *U.S.*

1893 *Chicago Record* 14 July 11/3 In hobo language 'beating the blinds' means to steal a ride on the mail car next to the engine. **1895** *Dialect Notes.* I. 390 *Jump the blind*, to steal a ride on platform of baggage-car. **1948** *Sat. Even. Post* 31 July 89/1 If there were any hobos on the blind, they would step off into my arms.

10. [f. BLIND *a.* 1 g.] A drunken bout or orgy; a binge.

1917 A. WAUGH *Loom of Youth* I. iii. 37 For six weeks we'll train like Hades, and then, when we've got the cup, we'll have a blind. **1936** G. GREENE *Journey Without Maps* II. iv. 189 It became more and more like a blind in Paris..in the Montparnasse bar. **1943** J. B. PRIESTLEY *Daylight on Sat.* x. 67 I'm not off on a blind, if that's what you're worrying about. **1943** *Mind* LII. 280 How much of my reaction against a 'blind' on a Saturday night is due to my puritanical upbringing?

11. *Comb.* chiefly attrib., as (in sense 2) ***blind-cord***, ***-maker***, ***-pulley***, ***-roller***, etc.; (in sense 3) ***blind-halter***, ***-winkers***; **blind-bridle**, a bridle with blinkers.

1711 *Lond. Gaz.* No. 4875/4 Galled on both sides of her Head with a blind Halter. **1833** J. HALL *Harpe's Head* 30 Some rode with blind-bridles. **1837** N. WHITTOCK *Bk. Trades* 488 Blind (Venetian)..maker. **1866** YOUATT *Horse* v. (1872) 113 Last of all, the blind winkers. **1881** *Mechanic* §714 How to make a blind-roller. **1883** CABLE *Dr. Sevier* vi, A quarter circle of iron-work set like a blind-bride. **1894** *Daily News* 12 Nov. 7/2 William Wilshaw.., a blindmaker, was sentenced to death.

blindage. [f. prec. + -AGE.] A screen or other structure used in fortification, sieges, etc. to protect from the enemy's firing; a mantelet. = BLIND *sb.* 4.

1812 WELLINGTON in Gurw. *Disp.* IX. 196 Troops are well protected from the effects even of the heaviest fire of shells, by what are called blindages. **1882** E. O'DONOVAN *Merv Oasis* II. xxxiii. 69 The Turcomans having constructed blindages in connection with their huts.

blind alley. †**a.** An out-of-the-way or secret alley. *Obs.* **b.** An alley closed at one end (see BLIND *a.* 11); a cul-de-sac; also *fig.*, a course of action that fails to effect its purpose or from which there is no resultant benefit.

1583 STANYHURST *Æneis* II. (Arb.) 66 Through crosse blynd allye we iumble. **1662** DRYDEN *Wild Gall.* II. i. (1725) 113 He must meet me in a blind Alley. **1681** —— *Spanish Fryar* I. 7 I'll e'en go lose my self in some blind Alley; and try if any courteous Damsel will think me worth the finding. **1724** SWIFT *Irish Manuf.* Wks. 1755 V. II. 7 A hedge-press in some blind-alley about Little-Britain. **1854** BAYLE ST. JOHN *Purple Tints Paris* II. 2 When..he..is compelled to become one of the blind-alleys of the species. **1882** P. H. FITZGERALD *Recreat. Literary Man* I. ii. 12 A familiarity with all the blind alleys..and passages of letters. **1898** E. GREY in *Westm. Gaz.* 6 June 2/3 Many of Lord Salisbury's concessions were blind alleys which led to nowhere. **1925** W. DEEPING *Sorrell & Son* iii. §2 No blind alleys, or office stools.

c. *attrib.* and *fig.*, applied to something that 'leads nowhere', esp. employment that offers no opportunities for promotion or advancement.

1902 *Westm. Gaz.* 10 June 2/1 The second act, with its long 'blind alley' episode of Paolo's wife, lets down the piece severely. **1909** *Ibid.* 27 Oct. 2/1 'Blind alley' employments. **1910** *Ibid.* 6 Jan. 3/3 The number of lads between the age of fifteen and twenty who are engaged in what have come to be known as 'blind-alley occupations'. **1937** 'G. ORWELL' *Road to Wigan Pier* v. 88 The youth who leaves school at fourteen and gets a blind-alley job is out of work at twenty. **1957** J. S. HUXLEY *Relig. without Revel.* (new ed.) ix. 215 Through this radiating fan of restricted improvements and blind-alley specialisations there runs a trend towards major advance.

†**blin'dation.** *Obs.* [f. BLIND *sb.* + -ATION: cf. *starvation.*] = BLINDING, BLIND *sb.* 4–6.

1588 J. HARVEY *Discoursive Probl.* 52 The pretended cloke of Incubus, or such like glozing blindation. **1617** COLLINS *Def. Bp. Ely* II. vii. 260 That's the blindation. *a* **1734** NORTH *Exam.* I. iii. ¶106. 196 These Authors..build up Blindations before one of the foulest Knots of Inquiry that ever defiled the Sun's Light.

blind-coal. Non-bituminous coal, or anthracite, which burns without flame.

1802 PLAYFAIR *Illustr. Hutton. The.* 148 Coal may exist without bitumen as in the instance of blind-coal. **1831** J. HOLLAND *Manuf. Metals* I. 129 Blind-coal is used in the smelting establishments in the South of Wales with great advantage. **1849** J. JACKSON *Minerals* xxii, Anthracite..called in Staffordshire, Stone coal, in Scotland Blind coal.

blinded ('blaɪndɪd), *ppl. a.* [f. BLIND *v.* and *sb.* + -ED[1].]

1. Made blind, deprived of sight or light.

1596 SPENSER *Astroph.*, *Thest.* 134 The blinded archer-boy. **1821** CLARE *Vill. Minstr.* I. 198 Each eye..In blinded slumber closes.

2. *fig.* Having the understanding darkened; deluded; deceived, benighted, foolish.

1535 COVERDALE *Numb.* xiv. 44 They were blynded to go vp to the toppe of the mountaine. **1558** KNOX *First Blast* (Arb.) 49 The approbation and consent of a blinded multitude. **1660** BAXTER *Call Unconv.* Pref., Thou art a blinded Atheist. **1826** SCOTT *Woodst.* (1832) 178 The blinded Papists.

3. With the window-blinds drawn down.

1709 ADDISON *Tatler* No. 120 ¶5, I found the Windows were blinded. **1876** MISS YONGE *Womank.* xxx. 267 The drawing-room is left blinded and tenantless.

4. Provided with blindages.

1877 *Daily News* 22 Oct. 6/1 Its summit was surrounded with breastworks, ditches, rifle-pits, and blinded batteries. **1884** GEN. GORDON *Let. 24 Aug.* in *Standard* 24 Feb. (1885) 5/7 Our steamers are blinded and bullet-proof.

blinder ('blaɪndə(r)), *sb.* [f. BLIND *v.* + -ER[1].]

1. a. He who or that which blinds. Also *fig.*

1587 GOLDING *De Mornay* ii. (1617) 22 The same Sunne is the lightner of our eyes..and..the blinder of them. **1829** CARLYLE in Froude *Life* (1882) II. 75 To the bodily eye Self is a perpetual blinder.

b. Something 'dazzlingly' good or difficult, esp. an excellent piece of play in Rugby Football or Cricket. *colloq.*

1950 W. HAMMOND *Cricketers' School* iii. 35 Striking out at an innocent-looking ball, I've sent a blinder—dead into the fieldsman's hands. **1960** D. STOREY *This Sporting Life* I. ii. 17 You played a blinder... It was the best game I ever saw. **1963** *Times* 16 Feb. 3/3 They dropped one easy catch and caught three blinders.

2. A blinker for a horse. Also *fig.*, an obstacle to clear judgement or perception. Usu. *pl.* (Chiefly in U.S.)

1809 J. BARLOW *Columb.* x. 414 Shake off their manacles, their blinders cast. **1856** EMERSON *Eng. Traits* v. 92 In common, the horse works best with blinders. **1860** TRISTRAM *Gt. Sahara* ii. 39 The blinders, worn for show and not for use, as none of them reached forward as far as the horse's eyes. **1934** in WEBSTER. **1965** 'MALCOLM X' *Autobiogr.* (1968) xii. 308 He had returned to his work in 1946, to remove the blinders from the eyes of the black man in the wilderness of North America. **1971** A. HAILEY *Wheels* xx. 296 Cars turn us on. But it doesn't mean that any one of us is headed for Detroit wearing blinders. **1979** *Arizona Daily Star* 5 Aug. J4/4 We can't go through life with blinders on. **1986** *Jrnl.* (Fairfax Co., Va.) 27 May A7 The bill will remove the blinders which we have had on for too long.

blindfold ('blaɪndfəʊld), *v.* Forms: 3 blindfellen, 4 blyndfelle(n, blynfelle, 5 blyndfellyn, -feyld, blynfelde, 6 blyndfell, -felde, blindfield, blyndfold, 6– blindfold. *Pa. pple.* 3 iblindfelled, 4 blindfelled, -feld, blynd-folde, blynfeld, yblyndfalled, 5 blynd(e)fellyd, -fylde, 5–6 blynd(e)felde, 6 blind-filded, -fielded, 6– blindfolded. [ME. *blindfelle(n* to strike blind, f. *fellen* to strike, FELL; occurring mostly in the pa. pple. *blindfelled*, *-feld*, *-fuld*, *-fylde*, whence the *-d* was, in the 15th c., erroneously admitted into the stem of the vb. Hence the 16th c. perversion *blindfold*, associated with the notion of *folding* something round the eyes, which had come to be the common use of the word.]

†**1.** *trans.* To strike blind; to blind. *Obs.*

a **1300** *Cursor M.* 19615 Blinfeld [*v.r.* blenfelled, blindfeld, blyndfolde] he was als he sua lai. *c* **1320** R. BRUNNE *Chron.* 54 He suore..þat neuer Alfred his broþer þorgh him was dede No blynfeld, no slayn. *c* **1440** *Promp. Parv.* 40 Blyndyn, or make blynde. Blyndfellen, *idem est.*

2. To cover the eyes, *esp.* with a bandage.

a **1225** *Ancr. R.* 106 He þolede..þet me hine blindfellede ..þauh þu þin eien..blindfellie on eorðe. **1388** WYCLIF *Luke* xxii. 64 And thei blynfelden hym, and smyten his face. **1483** *Cath. Angl.* 35 To Blyndfeyld [blyndfelle], *velare.* **1494** FABYAN VI. ccx. 225 She was blyndefelde & lad vnto the place. *c* **1510** BARCLAY *Mirr. Good Mann.* (1570) C iv, Here eyne blindfielded. **1526** TINDALE *Luke* xxii. 64 And blyndfolded hym. **1526** *Pilgr. Perf.* (W. de W. 1531) 259 Y[e] cloth with y[e] whiche our Sauyour was blyndfelde. **1530** PALSGR. 458, I blyndefelde one, I cover his sight. **1599** *Life Sir T. More* in Wordsw. *Eccl. Biog.* (1853) II. 17 He tooke a napkin..wherewith he blindfolded his own eies. **1727** SWIFT *Wonder of Wond.* Wks. 1755 II. II. 58 He..gives any person leave to blindfold him. **1835** ANSTER *Faust* 314 They bind and blindfold me.

3. *fig.* To darken the understanding or judgement.

1581 MARBECK *Bk. Notes* 1037 They are blindfolded, they are snared. **1674** ALLEN *Dang. Enthus.* 60 If Prejudice do not blindfold you. **1790** BURKE *Fr. Rev.* 344 They..blindfold themselves, like bulls that shut their eyes when they push. **1879** H. GEORGE *Progr. & Pov.* II. iv. (1881) 125 Men ignore facts when blindfolded by a pre-accepted theory.

'blindfold, *a.* Forms: see prec. (in pa. pple.): also 5–6 blynfeld(e, blyndfeld(e, (blindfield(e, blyndefielde), blyndefolde, 6 blyndfild, 7 blindefold, 6– blindfold.

1. a. Having the eyes bandaged so as to prevent vision. (Rarely *attrib.*; often *advb.*)

1483 CAXTON *Gold. Leg.* 88/1 He fonde them on theyr knees and blyndfeld. **1553** T. WILSON *Rhet.* 115b, Shall some gentilman playe blyndefolde at the chesse. **1555** EDEN *Decades W. Ind.* (Arb.) 347 They can in maner go thyther blyndfielde. **1768** TUCKER *Lt. Nat.* II. 606 He that follows another blindfold. **1792** S. ROGERS *Pleas. Mem.* I. 36 And turned the blindfold hero round and round.

b. *transf.*

1593 SHAKS. *Rich. II*, I. iii. 224 My inch of Taper will be burnt and done, And blindfold death not let me see my sonne.

c. Of a match at chess: conducted by a player without seeing the board but not necessarily blindfolded; hence ***blindfold player***.

1790 'MR. PHILIDOR' (*title*) Analysis of the Game of Chess ..to which is added several Parties, Played Blindfold, against three adversaries. **1850** BROWNING *Christm.-Eve* 90 Playing pawns at blindfold chess. **1900** *Westm. Gaz.* 31 May 2/1 In almost all these blindfold games I have the move... Occasionally I overlook something..in a blindfold match... The blindfold player..cannot see so far ahead as if he were looking at the board.

2. *fig.* With the mind blinded; without perception; without forethought, heedless, reckless. Cf. BLIND *a.* 3.

c **1450** *De Deguileville's Pilgr.* in *Cath. Angl.* 35 Of þaim that er blynfelde and er as blynde. **1570** B. GOOGE *Pop. Kingd.* I. 3, But blyndefielde every man must take, whatsoeuer he settes out. **1592** SHAKS. *Ven. & Ad.* 554 With blindfold fury she begins to forage. **1687** DRYDEN *Hind & P.* I. 324 The blind-fold blows of ignorance. **1878** MORLEY *Crit. Misc.* Ser. I. 158 Sailing blindfold and haphazard.

†**3.** Dark. Cf. BLIND *a.* 6. *Obs.*

1601 YARINGTON *Two Traj.* Prol. 7 in Bullen *O. Pl.* IV, Each stately streete, And blinde-fold turning.

'blindfold, *sb.* [f. the adj.: in sense 2 leaning upon FOLD *sb.*]

†**1.** That which is blindfold. *Obs.*

1643 *Myst. Iniq.* 14 Where blindfold is the onely play.

2. A bandage over the eyes; *fig.* anything which takes away perception or judgement.

1880 L. WALLACE *Ben-Hur* II. v. 106 To the excellences of other peoples the egotism of a Roman is a blindfold.

'blindfolded, *ppl. a.* [f. BLINDFOLD *v.* + -ED[1].] = BLINDFOLD *a.*

1579 E. K. in *Spenser's Sheph. Cal.* Mar. 89 *Gloss.*, He is described..to be blindfolded. **1661** BURNEY *Κέρδ. Δῶρον* 131 Blindfolded Iudges. **1730** A. GORDON *Maffei's Amphit.* 250 Those who did any thing in a blindfolded manner. *c* **1860** C. S. BROOKS *Marullo* in *Casquet Lit.* (1877) I. 390/2 To tell his story to the blindfolded girl.

'blindfoldedness. Blindfolded condition.

1863 SALA *Capt. Dang.* I. x. 295 That Blindfoldedness of Ignorance.

'blindfolder. [f. BLINDFOLD *v.* + -ER[1].] One who blindfolds or hoodwinks.

a **1649** DRUMM. OF HAWTH. *Speech* Wks. (1711) 219 The malicious blind-folders. **1861** GEN. P. THOMPSON *Audi Alt.* P. III. clxiii. 180 The political blindfolders.

'blindfolding, *vbl. sb.* In 3 -fellunge, fallunge. [f. as prec. + -ING[1].] The action of covering up the eyes; hoodwinking; the apparatus used in the action; the state produced.

a **1225** *Ancr. R.* 96 Uor hore blindfallunge. *Ibid.* 188 Godes pinen..buffetes, spotlunge, blindfellunge. **1583** GOLDING *Calvin on Deut.* xvi. 94 Lustes and likings..bee as blindfoldings to keepe vs from seeing God. **1793** T. BEDDOES *Math. Evid.* 65 Actual blind-folding and muffling.

'blindfoldly, *adv. rare.* [f. BLINDFOLD *a.* + -LY.[2]] In a blindfold manner, blindly.

1642 J. EATON *Honey-combe* 218 The matter, which they daily, like Parrots, doe blindefoldly prattle of.

†'**blindful**, *a. Obs. rare.* Blind, blinded.
1621 SYLVESTER *Mottoes* 74 Man..brute and blindefull.

blind gut. [See BLIND *a.* 11.] One of the intestines closed at the lower end; the *cæcum.*
1594 T. B. *La Primaud. Fr. Acad.* II. 350 The first of these great ones is called the blinde gut, because..it hath but one way, both to receive in, and to let out the matter received. **1758** J. S. *Le Dran's Observ. Surg.* (1771) B b 2 b, The blind Gut, so called from being perforated at one End only.

†'**blind-head.** *Obs.* A cover for an alembic or retort; a retort with such a cover.
1662 R. MATHEW *Unl. Alch.* §108. 176 Put on a blind head, and let it stand in ashes, or Balneo Maria. **1667** BOYLE *Orig. Formes & Qual.*, A Glasse Body, with a blind head luted to it. **1736** BAILEY *Housh. Dict.* 129 Clap on a blind-head, lute it well. **1743** *Lond. & Country Brew.* IV. 305 Hops that have been..stewed on Purpose in a blind Head.

†'**blindhead, -hood.** *Obs.* [f. BLIND *a.* + -HEAD, -HOOD.] Blindness.
a **1340** HAMPOLE *Psalter* xcvi. 2 Til ill men, cloudy & myrke in syn, for thaire blynhede, he semys myrk.

blinding ('blaɪndɪŋ), *vbl. sb.* [f. BLIND *v.*]
1. The action of making blind.
1868 FREEMAN *Norm. Conq.* (1876) II. vii. 79 So striking an event as the blinding of an Emperor.
2. *fig.* Darkening of the mental or moral sense.
c **1380** WYCLIF *De Dot. Eccl.* Sel. Wks. III. 439 Love of God is quenched bi blyndyng of þe world. *c* **1449** PECOCK *Repr.* v. xv. 563 Pointis of wicchecraft and blindingis. **1705** STANHOPE *Paraphr.* I. 37 The blinding of Passion.
3. = BLINDAGE.
1829 *Sun* 17 Sept. 1/5 It was proposed..to cover the low batteries with a strong blinding.
4. The process of covering the surface of a newly made road with fine material to fill up the spaces between the stones; also, the material used for this purpose. Cf. BLIND *v.* 9.
1843 *Civil Engin. & Arch. Jrnl.* VI. 274/1 The stoning and blinding is conducted in the same manner as in ordinary roads. *a* **1877** KNIGHT *Dict. Mech.* **1926** *Missionary Rec. United Free Ch. Scotl.* May 224/1 The fierce wind tore the blinding from the hard clay roads.

'**blinding**, *ppl. a.* [f. as prec. + -ING².] That blinds. (See the vb.)
1784 BURNS *Winter* i, The blinding sleet and snaw. **1860** GOSSE *Rom. Nat. Hist.* 42 A dense fog of blinding sand.

'**blindingly**, *adv.* [f. prec. + -LY².] In a blinding manner; so as to blind.
1849 HARE *Par. Serm.* II. 153 The darkness which lay blindingly on the hearts and souls of mankind. *Mod. Newspaper*, The snow flying blindingly.

blindish ('blaɪndɪʃ), *a.* [f. BLIND *a.* + -ISH¹.] Somewhat blind.
1611 FLORIO, *Cecutiente*, blindish, dimme of sight. **1636** *Ariana* 230 'Tis a passion something blindish. **1855** BROWNING *Men & Wom.* I. 179 An old dog, bald and blindish.

†**blindled**, *ppl. a. nonce-wd.* Darkened.
1606 SYLVESTER *Du Bartas* I. i. (1641) 5/2 Or whether else some other Lamp he kindled Upon the Heap (yet all with Waters blindled).

'**blindless**, *a.* [f. BLIND *sb.* + -LESS.] Of a window: Having no blind.
1853 C. BRONTË *Villette* xx. (D.) The high blindless windows. **1859** TENNYSON *Enid* 71 The blindless casement.

'**blindling**, *sb.* [f. BLIND *a.* + -LING: cf. *weakling.*] A blind person.
1549 J. PONET *Def. Marr. Priests* 44 God..hathe scattred those blyndlynges to their vtter confusion. **1563–87** FOXE *A. & M.* II. 310 A sort of blindlings.

'**blindling, -lings**, *adv. north. dial.* Forms: 3 blindlunge, 6 -lingis, -lings, -ling, -lynge, 9 *Sc.* blin(d)lins. [f. BLIND *a.* + -LING(S *advb. suffix.*] Blind-wise, blindly, heedlessly.
a **1225** *St. Marher.* 15 Ich habbe ablend ham þat ha blindlunge gað. **1513** DOUGLAS *Æneis* II. vii. [vi.] 74 Quhen blindlingis in the battell fey thai fycht. **1544** BALE *Chron. Sir J. Oldcastell* in *Harl. Misc.* I. 275 They will..leade you blindelynge into hell with themselues. **1858** M. PORTEOUS *Souter Johnny* 31 Blinlins did the carline speak it.

blindly ('blaɪndlɪ), *adv.* [f. BLIND *a.* + -LY².]
1. In a blind way; after the manner of the blind; *fig.* without foresight or reason, deludedly.
c **893** K. ÆLFRED *Oros.* I. x. §6 Hu blindlice moneȝe þeoda sprecað ymb þone cristendom. *c* **1380** WYCLIF *Antecrist & Meynee* 152 If þe puple..folowe hem blyndly. **1594** SHAKS. *Rich. III*, v. v. 24 The Brother blindely shed the Brothers blood. **1697** DRYDEN *Virg. Eclog.* vi. 52 How Seas, and Earth, and Air and active Flame..Were blindly gather'd in this goodly Ball. **1832** CARLYLE in *Fraser's Mag.* V. 399 Whigs struggling blindly forward, Tories holding blindly back. **1855** LONGF. *Hiaw.* Introd. 96 Groping blindly in the darkness.
†**2.** Dimly, indistinctly. *Obs.* Cf. BLIND *a.* 7.
1686 *Lond. Gaz.* No. 2168/4 A Dun Gelding..R.B. blindly upon the same Leg.
3. Without an opening. Cf. BLIND *a.* 11.
1872 HUXLEY *Phys.* viii. 202 The scala media..at its opposite end terminates blindly.

†**blindman.** Now written as two words.
c **1325** *Chron. Eng.* 769 in Ritson's *Metr. Rom.* II. 302 Ant a blindmon hede sihte. **1599** SHAKS. *Much Ado* II. i. 205 You strike like the blindman.
Hence **blind man's ball**, a local name of the Puff-ball fungus, or Blind-ball; see BLIND *a.* 16.
1812 WITHERING *Brit. Plants* (1830) IV. 349.

blind-man-buff, *v. nonce-wd.* [f. next, in its earlier form.] *trans.* To blindfold, hoodwink.
1705 HICKERINGILL *Priest-cr.* IV. (1721) 209 The best Engine that ever Priest-craft invented, to Blind-man-buff the silly Laiety.

blind-man's-buff (ˌblaɪnd mænz 'bʌf). Also 6–7 blindman-buff(e, (-buffet, -bough, -bluff,) 7–9 **blindman's-buff**. [f. BLIND-MAN + BUFF = buffet, blow, stroke.]
1. A game in which one player is blindfolded, and tries to catch and identify any one of the others, who, on their part, push him about, and make sport with him.
1600 ROWLANDS *Let. Humours Blood* iv. 64 At hot-cockles, leape-frogge, or blindman-buffe. **1628** GAULE *Pract. The.* (1629) 231 Others make him [Christ] no better then their Pastime, at no more discreet a Sport then Childs, or Fooles Blind-man-Buffet: *Prophecie vnto us, who is he that smote thee?* **1634** J. TAYLOR (Water-P.) *Gt. Eater Kent*, Gregorie Dawson, an English-man, devised the unmatchable mystery of Blind-man-buffe. **1696** *Month. Mercury* VII. 55 They oblig'd him to play with 'em at Blindman-Buff. **1766** GOLDSM. *Vic. W.* xi, Mr. Burchell..set the boys and girls to blindman's buff. **1866** R. CHAMBERS *Ess.* Ser. I. 186 The whole parlour put into disorder by blind man's buff.
2. *fig.*
1590 *Three Lords Lond.*, Ile to my stall; Love, Lucre, Conscience, blindman buffe to you all. **1643** BRAMHALL *Serpent Salve* §1 We desire to see what they have done, before we go to blindman's buffet one with another. **1648** C. WALKER *Hist. Indep.* I. 55 Me thinks..we are compelled to play at blind-man-bough for our lives. **1837** CARLYLE *Fr. Rev.* I. VI. iii. 278 Government by Blind-man's-buff.

blind man's holiday. A humorous phrase for the time just before candles are lighted, when it is too dark to work, and one is obliged to rest or 'take a holiday'; formerly used more widely.
1599 NASHE *Lent. Stuffe* in *Harl. Misc.* VI. 167 (D.) What will not blind Cupid doe in the night, which is his blindmans holiday. **1611** in FLORIO. **1796** PEGGE *Anonym.* iii. §18 The twilight, or rather the hour between the time when one can no longer see to read and the lighting of the candle, is commonly called blindman's holiday. **1866** *Aunt Judy's Mag.* Oct. 358 At meal-times, or in blindman's holiday, when no work was to be done.

blindness ('blaɪndnɪs). [f. BLIND *a.* + -NESS.]
1. Blind condition; want of sight.
c **1000** ÆLFRIC *Deut.* xxviii. 28 Sende þe Drihten on..blindnysse, þæt þu gropie on midne dæȝ. *a* **1300** *Cursor M.* 20957 A jugelur wit blindnes he [Paul] smat. **1398** TREVISA *Barth. De P.R.* VI. xxiv. (1495) 213 Blyndenesse is pryuacyon of syghte. *c* **1440** *Promp. Parv.* 40 Blyndnesse, *cecitas.* **1611** BIBLE *Deut.* xxviii. 28 The Lord shall smite thee with madnesse and blindnesse. **1671** MILTON *Samson* 196 That which was the worst now least afflicts me, Blindness. **1859** MASSON *Milton* I. 717 Galileo's blindness had become total.
2. *fig.* Want of intellectual or moral perception; delusion, ignorance; folly, recklessness.
971 *Blickl. Hom.* 23 þæt we onȝyton þa blindnesse ure ælþeodiȝnesse. *a* **1340** HAMPOLE *Prose Tr.* (1866) 19 A nakede mynde..of Ihesu..withowtten lyghte of knawynge in resoune, es bot a blyndnes. **1526** *Pilgr. Perf.* (W. de W. 1531) 243 b, Tempestes of desperacyon or blyndnes of mynde. **1611** BIBLE *Rom.* xi. 25 Blindnesse in part is happened to Israel. **1796** BP. WATSON *Apol. Bible* 209 The blindness of your rage. **1837** DICKENS *Pickw.* (1847) Pref. 11 A host of petty jealousies, blindnesses, and prejudices.
†**3.** *transf.* Concealment. *Obs. rare.*
1590 SHAKS. *Com. Err.* III. ii. 8 Muffle your false loue with some shew of blindnesse.
4. Of a plant: abortiveness.
1921 *Times Lit. Suppl.* 24 Feb. 130/3 The Frit Fly, which produces blindness in oats.

'**blind-nettle.** *Herb.* [f. BLIND *a.* 12; from its wanting the characteristic stinging quality of nettles proper.] The Dead-nettle; also the Hemp-nettle and Hedge Nettle or Wood Woundwort.
c **1000** ÆLFRIC *Gram.* 311 *Archangelica*, blindnetle. **1398** TREVISA *Barth. De P.R.* XVII. cxciii. (1495) 730 The deed nettyll or the blynde nettyl. **1578** LYTE *Dodoens* I. lxxxviii. 131 At this present time it is called..in English Blinde Nettel. **1736** BAILEY *Househ. Dict.* 113 Blind Nettle..is of a heating, drying, digestive and incisive quality. **1878** BRITTEN & HOLLAND *Plant-n.*

†**blinds.** *Obs.* (See quot.)
1674 RAY *Smelting Silv.* 118 There is a white Fluor about the vein which they call Spar and a black which they call *Blinds.* This last covers the vein of Oare, and when it appears they are sure to find Oare.

blind(-)side, *v. N. Amer.* [f. the phr. *blind side* s.v BLIND *a.* 2c.] *trans.* In sport, to attack or strike (an opponent) on the blind side. Chiefly *fig.*, to take advantage of a weakness in (another), to take unawares.
1968 H. HIGDON *Pro Football, USA* 305 Usually it is the quarterback who gets blind-sided as he is about to pass. **1972** *Atlantic Monthly* Mar. 28 That great sportsman..took the cheapest shot of all time when he slammed into (blindsided, as these brave gladiators say) an overexuberant spectator who ran onto the field in a Baltimore-Miami game. **1973** *Newsweek* 3 Dec. 33 Tom McCall asked..whether those Republicans who stand with the President were going to be 'blindsided by any more bombs'. **1974** *Whig-Standard* (Kingston, Ontario) 17 Oct. 9/3 His committee has been accused of 'blind-siding' those who are opposed to the proposal. **1983** *Fortune* 21 Feb. 54/1 Some companies will find themselves blind-sided by competitors they never imagined existed.

†**blindwharved**, *pple. Obs.* In 4 blyntwharuet, blynwherued. [f. BLIND *a.* + *wherven, wharven* to turn.] Blinded, blindfolded.
c **1320** *Cast. Love* 1146 His eȝen weore blynt-wharuet bo.

blind-worm ('blaɪndwɜːm). *Zool.* [Cf. Da. *blindorm*: so called from the smallness of its eyes.] A reptile (*Anguis fragilis*) also called Slow-worm. (Formerly applied also to the Adder.)
c **1450** *Gloss.* in Wr.-Wülcker *Voc.* 706 *Hec scutula*, a blyndworme. *c* **1480** *Ibid.* 766 *Idrus, idra, matrix*, a blynd-wurme. **1590** SHAKS. *Mids. N.* II. ii. 11 Newts and blinde wormes do no wrong. **1712** H. SLOANE in *Phil. Trans.* XXVII. 491 We caused a Whelp to be bit..by a Blind-Worm. **1763** *Brit. Mag.* IV. 352 He was stung by a blind-worm, for so they call them here. **1772** PENNANT *Tours Scotl.* (1774) 240 Any kind of serpent except the harmless blind worm. **1810** SCOTT *Lady of L.* III. v, There the slow blind-worm left his slime.

blini: see BLIN.

blink (blɪŋk), *v.* Forms: (4 blynke), 6–7 **blinke**, 7 **blynck**, 7– **blink**. [In ME., only as an occasional variant of BLENK, esp. in Robert of Brunne; and perh. in the form *blinche* (once, in *Beket*), also in a sense of *blench.* Otherwise exclusively mod.English (since *c* 1575). It coincides in its late appearance, as well as in form and sense, with MDu. and mod.Du. *blinken*, mod.Ger. *blinken*, the origin of which is equally obscure. They are conjecturally regarded as nasalized forms of the stem *blik-* to shine (see BLIK), but no satisfactory account can be given of their late appearance. In ME., *blenke* was used regularly where *blink* now takes its place: see BLENCH, BLENK.]
I. To deceive, elude, turn away.
†**1.** *trans.* To deceive. *Obs. rare.* [For ME. BLENCH *v.*¹ 1, BLENK *v.* 1.]
1303 R. BRUNNE *Handl. Synne* 4169 We Englys men þeron shulde þynke þat enuye us nat blynke.
2. †**a.** *intr.* To start out of the way, so as to elude anything; = BLENCH *v.*¹ 2, BLENK 2. *Obs. rare.*
a **1300** *Cursor M.* 7626 (Gött.) þoru he had his bodi born Ne had he blinked him biforn [*v.r.* blenked (2), blenched].
b. *trans.* (*Coursing.*) To elude (the dogs) temporarily.
1876 *Coursing Calendar* 197 The hare blinked Grace at the fence. *Ibid.* 252 Hylactor and Blue Sea ran very evenly for some distance, but, as puss blinked them in a hollow, Hylactor was so well placed that he made a few weak points before effecting the death.
¶ *trans.* To avoid, flinch from.
Cf. *blinche c* **1300** in BLENCH *v.*¹ 3.
II. To move the eyelids, twinkle, peep, wink.
†**3.** *intr.* To look, look up from sleep, open the eyes. [Only in this author; otherwise BLENK *v.* 6.]
1303 R. BRUNNE *Handl. Synne* 5675 Pers of hys slepe gan blynke, And gretely on hys dreme gan þynke.
4. To twinkle with the eye or eye-lids. In various shades of meaning which run into one another: in the earlier, the notion of 'glancing' predominates; in the later, that of 'winking.'
a. To glance, cast or let fall a glance, have a peep; to look with glances (and not steadily).
1590 SHAKS. *Mids. N.* v. i. 178 Sweet and louely vvall, Shew me thy chinke, to blinke through vvith mine eine. **1592** JAS. VI. in Ellis *Orig. Lett.* II. 236. III. 163 Turne your eyes a littell..to blinke upon the necessaire cace of youre Friend. *c* **1650** *Ld. of Learne* 428 in Furniv. *Percy Folio* I. 197 Rather..then all the gold that ere I blinket on with mine eye. **1729** in Ramsay's *Tea-t. Misc.* 16 On him she did na gloom, But blinkit bonnilie.
b. To look with twinkling eye-lids, as one half-awake or dazzled with light.
1600 J. LANE *Tom Tel-troth* 132 It blinds the sight, it makes men bleare-eyd blinke. **1806** COLERIDGE *Christabel* II. xxii, A snake's small eye blinks dull and shy. **1850** MRS. STOWE *Uncle Tom* ix. 77 Holding the candle aloft, and blinking on our travellers with a dismal and mystified expression. **1861** MRS. NORTON *Lady La G.* IV. 176 The babe..with tender eyes Blinks at the world a little while, and dies. **1863** MISS BRADDON *J. Marchmont* III. i. 2 A brown setter..lay upon the hearth-rug..blinking at the blaze.
c. To shut the eyelids momentarily and involuntarily; to wink for an instant.
1858 M. PORTEOUS *Souter Johnny* 30 Or silly mortal blinks an ee. **1865** DICKENS *Mut. Fr.* 269 London was blinking, wheezing and choking. **1876** FOSTER *Phys.* III. v. (1879) 544 When we stimulate one of our eyelids with a sharp electrical shock, both eyelids blink.

d. *trans. to* **blink** (tears) *away* or *back*: to send (tears) away, to avoid shedding (tears), by blinking.

1905 E. GLYN *Viciss. Evang.* 215 Tears kept rising in my eyes, and I did not even worry to blink them away. **1919** F. HURST *Humoresque* 146 She blinked back the ever-recurring tears. **1924** ROSE MACAULAY *Orphan Island* xxi. §1 Rosamond blinked away tears, with the salt Pacific, from her eyes. **1945** 'BRAHMS' & SIMON *Six Curtains for Stroganova* xx. 162 Above her flowers Dourakova bowed, smiled, and blinked back her tears.

5. To cast a sudden or momentary gleam of light; to twinkle as a star; to shine with flickering light, or with a faint peep of light; to shine unsteadily or dimly.

1786 BURNS *Ep. J. Smith* ii, Ev'ry star that blinks aboon. **1807** CRABBE *Par. Reg.* I. 378 Where blinks through paper'd panes the setting sun. **1821** CLARE *Vill. Minstr.* I. 76 As stars blink out from clouds at night. **1828** SCOTT *F.M. Perth* II. v. 164 The very tapers are blinking, as if tired of our conference. **1872** BLACK *Adv. Phaeton* xxx. 398 The sun was ..blinking on the windows.

6. a. *trans.* To shut the eyes to; to evade, shirk, pass by, ignore: *orig.* a sporting phrase.

1742 FIELDING *J. Andrews* I. xvi. (1815) 39 There's a bitch ..she never blinked a bird in her life. **1811** BYRON *Hints fr. Hor.* 555 Dogs blink their coveys. **1823** DE QUINCEY *Lett. Educ.* i. (1860) 20 Children, however, are incidents that will occur in this life, and must not be blinked. **1859** GEO. ELIOT *A. Bede* 114 It was no use blinking the fact.

b. With *at* (improperly).

1857 SEARS *Athan.* vi. 43 Why have these passages..been blinked at and ignored?

7. a. *trans.* To turn (milk, beer, etc.) slightly sour. [The origin of this use has been sought in the glance of an evil eye, the 'blinking' of milk being formerly ascribed to witchcraft; also in the effect of lightning, since thunder generally 'blinks' milk.]

1616 SURFL. & MARKH. *Countr. Farm* 589 Bottle ale.. must not only be coold sufficiently, but also blynckt a little to giue it a quick & sharp tast. **1689** *Gazophyl. Anglic.* s.v. To blink beer; a word frequently used in Lincolnshire. **1713** *Lond. & Countr. Brew.* IV. (1743) 263 They are apt to blink or give a little sourish Taste to their Drink.

b. *intr.* To turn slightly sour.

a **1648** DIGBY *Closet Open.* (1677) 91 There let the wort.. stand till it begin to blink and grow long like thin syrup. **1769** MRS. RAFFALD *Eng. Housekpr.* (1778) 317 Wine..if you let it stand too long before you get it cold..summer-beams and blinks in the tub.

¶ **8.** *trans.* To cause one to blink; to blindfold. [A pseudo-archaism in Landor.]

1846 LANDOR *Exam. Shaks.* II. 278 He who blinketh the eyes of the poor wretch about to die doeth it out of mercy. **1853** KANE *Grinnell Exp.* xli. (1856) 376 With the sun.. blinking my eyes.

¶ **9.** See BLENK *v.* 6–7.

10. To look upon with the evil eye, to bewitch. *Sc.* and *Irish*. Cf. 7 a.

1880 W. H. PATTERSON *Gloss. Antrim & Down* 9 Cow's milk is said to be *blinked* when it does not produce butter, in consequence of some supposed charm having been worked. **1886** *Folk-Lore Jrnl.* IV. 255 Cattle can be fairy-struck or bewitched..the first is called 'sheetin' and the second 'blinked'. **1892** *Ballymena Observer* (E.D.D.), *Blink*, to bewitch cattle and cause them to have little or no milk and butter. **1926** *Blackw. Mag.* Apr. 479/1 Perhaps we are bewitched or blinked, as Shamus Byrne would say. **1927** *Scots Observer* 15 Oct. 2/5 Mrs. Hazelton..had indeed blinked William Blair's cows. *Ibid.*, He had set fire to the wisp of straw and had put it under a blinked cow's nose.

† **blink**, *sb.*[1] *Obs.* [f. BLINK *v.* 1, and like it in ME. only in Robert of Brunne, for the BLENK, BLENCH of his contemporaries.]

1. A trick, stratagem; = BLENCH, BLENK, *sb.* 1.

1303 R. BRUNNE *Handl. Synne* 4185 He shal þynke or to do þe a wykkede blynke.

2. *pl.* Boughs thrown to turn aside deer from their course; also, feathers, etc. on a thread to scare birds. Cf. BLENCHER.

1611 COTGR., *Brisees*, boughes..left in the view of a deere, or cast ouerthwart the way to hinder his running..Our wood-men call them, *Blinkes*. **1611** MARKHAM *Countr. Content.* I. xi. (1668) 59 They are like blinks, which will ever chase your game from you. **1625** —— *Farew. Husb.* 96 The nearer that these Blinkes..come to the ground..the better it is, lest the fowle finding a way to creep vnder them, begin not to respect them.

blink (blɪŋk), *sb.*[2] Forms: 4 blynke, 6 blinck, 7 blinke, 7– blink. [f. BLINK *v.* 3–4; like which it is found in ME. in Robert of Brunne, where contemporaries used BLENK.]

1. a. A sudden or momentary gleam of light from the sun, a fire, etc.; a slight flash; a peep of light; a twinkling gleam, as of the stars; a gleam of sunshine between showers: also *poet.* 'glimmer.'

1717 *Protest. Mercury* 5 July 6 A terrible Fire..caus'd.. by a Blink of Fire that issued from some adjoining Chimney, and lodg'd in the Thatch. **1818** SCOTT *Hrt. Midl.* xi, Creep out of their holes like blue-bottle flies in a blink of sunshine. **1833** WORDSW. *Sonn.* vii, Not a blink Of light was there. **1834** R. MUDIE *Brit. Birds* (1841) I. 323 The blink of reddish orange displayed by the flirt of the tail. **1855** BROWNING *Statue & Bust*, In a bed-chamber by a taper's blink.

b. *fig.* A 'glimmer' or 'spark' of anything good.

c. A brief gleam of mental sunshine.

1303 R. BRUNNE *Handl. Synne* 4449 þe leste þoghte..þat of godenesse hadde any blynke. **1730** T. BOSTON *Mem.* vi. 132, I sometimes have blinks of great joy. *a* **1752** R. ERSKINE in Spurgeon *Treas. Dav.* Ps. ci, I will sing of my blinks and of my showers. **1833** M. SCOTT *Tom Cringle* xix. (1859) 542, I shall always bless heaven for my fair Blinks.

d. *on the blink*: on the point of becoming extinguished; in a bad state, out of order. *slang* (orig. *U.S.*).

1901 'H. MCHUGH' *John Henry* 83 A stranglehold line of business that will put Looey Harrison on the blink. **1904** 'O. HENRY' *Cabbages & Kings* iii. 51 This café looks on the blink, but I guess it can set out something wet. **1912** WODEHOUSE *Prince & Betty* xiii. 176 That punt-pole's on the blink. I tried it yesterday, and it creaked. **1934** —— *Right Ho, Jeeves* xi. 136 All those years he spent in making millions in the Far East put his digestion on the blink. **1960** J. ASHFORD *Counsel for Defence* vi. 68 No good, David. The 'frig. is on the blink again.

2. a. A glance (usually, a bright, cheerful glance); a glimpse. (Chiefly *Sc.*)

1594 CAREW *Tasso* (1881) 7 Lookes downe, and in one blinck, and in one vew, Comprizeth all what so the world can shew. *Ibid.* 95 Her eyes Sweet blinck. **1715** *Let.* in *Wodrow Corr.* (1843) II. 66 We have had a sweet blink at the sacrament last Sabbath. **1790** BURNS *Tam O'Shanter*, For ae blink o' the bonnie burdies. **1816** SCOTT *Old Mort.* xxxvii, I wish my master were living to get a blink o't. **1839** BAILEY *Festus* xviii. (1848) 185 By the blink of thine eye.

b. The action or an act of blinking.

1924 GALSWORTHY *White Monkey* I. xii, He did not miss the shift and blink in the manager's eyes.

3. *transf.* The time taken by a glance; an instant, the twinkling of an eye; = Ger. *Augenblick*. (Chiefly *Sc.*)

a **1813** A. WILSON *Hogmenae*, The liquor was brought in a blink. **1827** SCOTT *Two Drovers*, Stay Robin—bide a blink. **1864** HAWKER *Quest Sangraal* 24 Whole Ages glided in that Blink of Time.

4. = ICE-BLINK: a shining whiteness about the horizon produced by reflection from distant masses of ice. Also, loosely, a large mass or field of ice, an iceberg.

1772–84 COOK *Voy.* (1790) V. 1854 A brightness in the northern horizon, like that reflected from ice, usually called the blink. **1818** *Edin. Rev.* XXX. 17 The blink from packs of ice, appears of a pure white. **1837** MACDOUGALL tr. *Graah's Greenland* 80 During the three hours we took to pass this blink, it calved about twenty times. **1856** KANE *Arct. Exp.* I. v. 49, I ascended to the crow's-nest, and saw..the ominous blink of ice ahead.

5. blink microscope [G. *blinkmikroskop*], an instrument for viewing two photographs of the same section of the sky alternately in rapid succession. Also called **blink comparator**.

[**1910** C. PULFRICH in *Zeitschr. f. Instrumentenkunde* XXX. 1 Die Anwendung des Blinkmikroskops.] **1911** C. PULFRICH in *Encycl. Brit.* XXV. 900/2 Since 1904 binocular observation of stellar plates..has been gradually discarded for the method devised by Pulfrich, which consists in the monocular observation of the two plates..with the assistance of the so-called 'blink' microscope. **1930** *Discovery* Aug. 252/2 It [*sc.* the planet Pluto] was identified from its motion past the numerous fixed stars as revealed on plates of the same star field while being compared under the blink comparator.

blink, *sb.*[3] *U.S.* A fisherman's name for the mackerel when about a year old.

1856 [see TINKER *sb.* 3]. **1888** ATWOOD in Goode *Amer. Fishes* 174 Fish of this size are sometimes called 'Spikes'... The next year I think they are the 'Blinks', being one year old.

blink (blɪŋk), *a.* Also 7 blinck. [Cf. BLINKED.]

1. Of the eyes: Habitually blinking. Hence **blink-eyed** *a.* Also *fig.*

1575 GASCOIGNE *Hearbes* 152 Remembre Batte the foolish blink eyed boye. *c* **1590** MARLOWE *2nd Pt. Tamburl.* I. i, The blink-ey'd burghers heads. *a* **1695** WOOD *Life* (1848) 220 A blinkeyed bookseller in Cheapside. **1695** *Lond. Gaz.* No. 3041/4 Blink Ey'd, high Nos'd. **1823** THACHER *Jrnl. Amer. Rev.* 320 It was the doctor's misfortune to have one blink eye. **1846** DICKENS *Pictures from Italy* 9 Blink-eyed little casements. **1929** J. B. PRIESTLEY *Good Compan.* III. i, A piebald blink-eyed, ..little pierrot show.

2. Of milk, etc.: Slightly sour. Cf. BLINK *v.* 7.

1883 C. F. SMITH *Southernisms* in *Trans. Amer. Philol. Soc.* 45 *Blink milk*, 'milk somewhat soured.' *West Virginia*.

blinkard ('blɪŋkəd). Also 6 blincarde, blinkarde, blenkard. [f. BLINK *v.* + -ARD.]

1. A reproachful name for one who habitually blinks or winks; one who has imperfect sight.

c **1510** BARCLAY *Mirr. Good Mann.* (1570) B j, An one eyed blincarde. **1580** BARET *Alv.* B 819 A Blinkarde, he that hath such eies that the liddes couer a great part of the apple. **1665** *Char. Holland* in *Harl. Misc.* (1745) V. 575 Among the Blind, the one-ey'd Blinkard reigns. **1688** R. HOLME *Armoury* II. xvii. 427 *Blinkard* or *Blinking*, is to have the Eye-lids ever moving: so that there is no perfect sight. **1786** WOLCOTT (P. Pindar) *Ode to R.A.'s* xi. Wks. 1812 I. 157 Yes Blinkards: and with Lustre shine.

b. *transf.* A star that shines dimly.

1627 HAKEWILL *Apol.* III. vii. §2 In some parts wee see many glorious..starres..in some none but blinkards and obscure ones.

2. *fig.* One who lacks intellectual perception.

1523 SKELTON *Garl. Laurel* I. 610 Brainles blenkards that blow at the cole. **1855** KINGSLEY *Westw. Ho!* (1861) 180 Calling himself an ass and a blinkard. **1882** BLACKIE in *Gd. Words* Oct. 640 A race of blinkards, who peruse the case And shell of life, but feel no soul behind.

†**3.** One who 'shuts his eyes' to what is happening, who blinks facts. *Obs.*

1583 GOLDING *Calvin on Deut.* xiv. 82 So as God should play the blinkard or shut his Eyes.

4. *attrib.* or *adj.*, usually *fig.*

a **1529** SKELTON *Balettes* 24 Thou blinkerd blowboll; thou wakest to late. **1652** URQUHART *Jewel* Wks. (1834) 254 Look out with both their eyes, and have no blinkard minds. **1837** CARLYLE *Misc.* (1857) IV. 92 A blinkard precipitancy.

blinked, *ppl. a.* [f. BLINK *v.* + -ED.] Affected with a blink or blinking.

1596 SPENSER *F.Q.* III. ix. 5 And keepe continuall spy Upon her with his other blincked eye.

blinker ('blɪŋkə(r)). [f. as prec. + -ER[1].]

1. a. One who blinks; a blinking or purblind person.

1636 ABP. J. WILLIAMS *Holy Table* (1637) 219 He was but a blinker, and saw..but with half an eye. *a* **1704** T. BROWN *Cupid turn'd T.* Wks. 1730 I. 113 What does our sly graceless blinker? **1835** BROWNING *Paracel.* I. 20 As earnest blinkers do Whom radiance ne'er distracted.

b. One who casts blinks or sly glances. *Sc.*

1786 BURNS *Ep. to Mayor Logan* x, The witching, cursed, delicious blinkers Hae put me hyte.

2. a. *pl.* A kind of spectacles for directing the sight in one direction only, so as to cure squinting, or for protecting the eyes from cold, dust, etc.; = GOGGLES.

1732 M. GREEN *Grotto* 10 (R.) Bigots who but one way see Through blinkers of authority. **1803** BRISTED *Pedest. Tour* I. 38 A little fellow, with blinkers over his eyes. **1851** THACKERAY *Eng. Hum.* iv. (1858) 205 Who only dare to look up at life through blinkers.

b. Leather screens attached to a horse's bridle on each side, to prevent his seeing in any direction except straight ahead.

1789 W. GILPIN *Tour Lakes* II. 154 (R.) On being pressed by her friends..to go to court; 'By no means,' said she, 'unless I may be allowed to wear blinkers.' **1861** MUSGRAVE *By-Roads* 174 An old female hostler, who gave us neither cruppers, blinkers, or breeching.

3. The eye. (*slang.*)

1816 'QUIZ' *Grand Master* I. 11 A patent pair of goggle winkers, Conceal'd from public view his blinkers.

4. A sporting dog that refuses to see and mark the position of game. Cf. BLINKING *vbl. sb.* 3.

1814 W. DOBSON *Kunopædia* 98 We shall, I fear, be compelled to class him along with the blinker of a very different nature, the brute of perverse..yet snivelling disposition. **1845** YOUATT *Dog* iii. 91 The chastisement.. would make the setter disgusted..and leave him a mere *blinker*. **1848** W. N. HUTCHINSON *Dog Breaking* 94 Excess of punishment has made many a dog of good promise a confirmed blinker.

5. An intermittent flash-light. In full, *blinker light*. *U.S.*

1923 R. D. PAINE *Comr. Rolling Ocean* xvi. 285 Take this bug-light [*sc.* an electric torch] and use it as a blinker. You learned the Morse code at Camp Stuart. **1943** J. STEINBECK *Once there was a War* (1959) I. 52 The second in command takes up the blinker and signals. **1959** N. MAILER *Advts. for Myself* (1961) 432 Motels, blinker lights, salt-eroded billboards. **1964** 'M. E. CHABER' *Six who Ran* (1965) i. 17 Three passenger cars were stolen... One of them was converted into a State Police car with the aid of a blinker light.

Hence **'blinkerless** *a.* (sense 2 b.)

1872 *Daily News* 23 Oct., Fleet blinkerless horses.

'blinker, *v.* [f. prec. sb.] *trans.* To put blinkers on; *fig.* to blind, hoodwink, deceive.

1865 W. PALGRAVE *Arabia* I. 140 But Telal was not so easily to be blinkered, and kept to his first judgment.

blinkered ('blɪŋkəd), *ppl. a.* [f. BLINKER *sb.* or *v.* + -ED.] Of a horse: provided with blinkers. Also *fig.*, having a limited range of outlook.

1867 HARDY *Time's Laughingstocks* (1909) 53 A century which..Will show..A scope above this blinkered time. **1897** *Daily News* 19 June 9/1 The colt..could not quite withstand the rush of the blinkered El Diablo. **1898** *Westm. Gaz.* 27 Aug. 1/3 The padded, blinkered life of her spinster sister. **1962** *Daily Tel.* 8 May 14/2 This is merely a case of legal procedure grinding along on its blinkered way.

blinking ('blɪŋkɪŋ), *vbl. sb.* [f. BLINK *v.*]

1. The action of the vb. BLINK in its various senses.

1875 JOWETT *Plato* (ed. 2) III. 84 Something they are able to behold without blinking. **1878** MORLEY *Crit. Misc.* Ser. I. 248 There is no blinking of the eyes to the part which.. sordid or foul circumstances play in life.

2. *spec.* in *Brewing*: The operation of giving a sharp taste to beer by letting the wort stand for some time. Also of beer: Turning sour during fermentation. (Cf. BLINK *v.* 7 a. and 7 b.)

1713 *Lond. & Countr. Brew.* IV. (1743) 271 Souring of the Grains, or what some call Blinking or Charing, is prevented. **1727** BRADLEY *Fam. Dict.* s.v. *Brewing*, In the North of England..they let their first Wort stand in their Receivers till it is very clear..which they call Blinking.

3. The faulty action, in a sporting dog, of refusing to see and mark the position of game. Cf. BLINKER 4.

1814 W. DOBSON *Kunopædia* 89 (*heading*) On Blinking. Defect in blood, a suspected cause. **1848** W. N. HUTCHINSON *Dog Breaking* 10 The unreasonableness of not always giving initiatory Lessons. Causes Blinking. **1865** *Ibid.* (ed. 4) 202 Some argue that blinking arises from a defective nose, not from punishment. **1897** H. DALZIEL *Brit. Dogs* (ed. 2) III. 336 Blinking..is caused..by undue

severity or punishment administered for chasing game or poultry.

'blinking, *ppl. a.* [f. as prec. + -ING².]

1. a. Looking with twinkling or half-open eyelids; winking; weak-eyed.

1568 T. HOWELL *Arb. Amitie* (1879) 29 A Furious God: an Archer blincking boy. **1596** SHAKS. *Merch. V.* II. ix. 54 The portrait of a blinking idiot. **1718** POPE *Iliad* II. 264 One eye was blinking, and one leg was lame. **1870** MORRIS *Earthly Par.* III. IV. 39 Stood with blinking gaze Before a fire's unsteady blaze.

b. *Sc.* Glancing pleasantly.

1724 RAMSAY *Tea-t. Misc.* (1733) I. 90 Blinkin daft Barbara M'Leg. *Ibid.* II. 119 His blinkan eye and gate sae free. **1822** SCOTT *Nigel* xvii, Guided by one of these blinking Ganymedes.

2. Shining dimly or intermittently, twinkling, flickering.

1681 COTTON *Poet. Wks.* (1765) 327 By a blinking and promiscuous light. **1785** BURNS *Cotter's Sat. Nt.* iii, His wee bit ingle, blinkin bonilie. **1820** W. IRVING *Sketch Bk.* I. 233 A solitary lamp to throw its blinking rays athwart his effigy.

3. ***blinking chickweed***; = BLINKS 2.

1775 LIGHTFOOT *Flora Scot.* (1789) 110.

4. Used as a substitute for a strong expletive. *slang.*

1914 *Scotsman* 12 Oct. 7/5 One.. Guardsman.. declared .. that His Majesty seemed to carry the 'blinking Army List in his 'ead'. **1927** *Observer* 21 Aug. 17/5 The type of golfer who.. hurls the bag of clubs after it, accompanied by the remark, 'Go on, have the blinking lot'.

'blinkingly, *adv.* With blinking eyes.

1876 MISS BRADDON *J. Haggard* II. 15 The sisters.. regarded him blinkingly, like owls in a zoological collection.

blinks (blɪŋks). [f. BLINK *sb.*]

1. A nickname for one who blinks.

1616 HOLYDAY *Persius* 298 And winks At him, whose sight is bad, calling him blinks.

2. *Herb.* The Water Chickweed, or Blinking Chickweed, *Montia fontana.*

1835 HOOKER *Brit. Flora* 59 Water Blinks. **1863** PRIOR *Plant-n.* 25 *Blinks* or *blinking-chickweed*, from its half-closed little white flowers peering from the axils of the upper leaves, as if afraid of the light.

blinky ('blɪŋkɪ), *a.* Inclined to blink.

1861 RUSSELL in *Times* 11 June (L.) One's eyes became quite blinky watching for the flash.

blintze (blɪnts), and variants. [Yiddish *blintse*, f. Russ. *blinets*, dim. of BLIN.] = BLIN.

1903 *Jewish Encycl.* IV. 256/1 The *kasha* and *blintzes* of the Russian Jews.. are dishes adopted by the Jews from their Gentile neighbors. **1932** L. GOLDING *Magnolia St.* I. ii. 32 Wouldn't it be nice to make a few *blintsies* for Mr. Emmanuel. **1958** W. BICKEL tr. *Hering's Dict. Class. & Mod. Cookery* 10 *Cheese blinzes*.., crêpes au fromage á la juive. **1961** *Woman* 21 Jan. 16/3 Blintzes are cheese-filled pancakes served with jam.

bliny: see BLIN.

blip (blɪp), *v.* [Echoic.] **1. a.** *trans.* To strike with a brisk rap or tap. **b.** *intr.* To make a quick popping sound. Hence **'blipping** *ppl. a.*

1924 A. A. MILNE *When we were Very Young* 93 They pulled him out and dried him, and they blipped him on the head. **1946** K. TENNANT *Lost Haven* (1968) xviii. 311 A big moth flopped into the room and blipped about. **1952** 'C. BRAND' *London Particular* vi. 64 Some horrible burglar.. blipped him on the head and killed him. **1955** W. GOLDING *Inheritors* iii. 60 Little bubbles bulged out of the scum, wandered and blipped out. **1957** 'C. E. MAINE' *High Vacuum* xiii. 108 The signal blipped hollowly from the speaker, fading and sporadic. **1963** P. MCCUTCHAN *Man from Moscow* xx. 205 The only noise was that of the blipping tyres.

2. *slang.* To switch an aeroplane engine on and off. Also *trans.* and *intr.*, to open and close (the throttle of an aeroplane, car, etc.); to rev (an engine) momentarily with the clutch disengaged. Hence as *sb.* Also **'blipping** *vbl. sb.*

1925 FRASER & GIBBONS *Soldier & Sailor Words* 26 *To blip*, to switch an aeroplane engine on and off. **1931** *Vanity Fair* Nov. 78/2 *Blipping* is the flippant term for nonchalantly and rapidly switching the ignition off and on while in flight. **1946** F. HAMANN *Air Words* 9 *Blip*, rapidly opening and closing the engine throttle... Also to clean possible ice out of the carburetor. **1958** 'N. SHUTE' *Rainbow & Rose* iii. 79 They brought back memories of slow-revving engines blipping on the switch. *Ibid.* 84, I.. flew her over to the hangar in little blips of engine on the switch. **1972** *Drive* Summer 106/2 If the car has a synchromesh gearbox.. blipping the throttle in the middle of a gearchange is a waste of petrol. **1979** *Daily Mail* 7 June 31/1 Riders who 'blip' the throttle while waiting at traffic lights are wasting petrol.

blip (blɪp), *sb.* [Echoic.] **1.** Any sudden brisk blow or twitch; a quick popping sound.

1894 'MARK TWAIN' in *St. Nicholas* Apr. 540/1 We took him a blip in the back and knocked him off. **1927** A. A. MILNE *Now we are Six* 23 It wasn't that he did not care For blips and buffetings and such. **1932** AUDEN *Orators* II. 56 Three warnings of enemy attack—depression in the mornings—rheumatic twinges—blips on the face. **1947** CROWTHER & WHIDDINGTON *Science at War* 16 A 'blip' or 'break' which marks the moment of emission of the pulse. **1958** *Times* 29 July 10/6 A series of preliminary blips [of a motor-horn]. **1962** A. NISBETT *Technique Sound Studio* vii. 130 A burst of applause lasting, say, ten seconds is very difficult to cut down to five without a slight 'blip' at the join.

2. A small elongated mark projected on a radar screen.

1945 *Electronic Engin.* XVII. 716 Note the calibration scales, in this case formed of small and larger 'blips', not bright dots. **1957** *Times* 11 Oct. 10/2 The first 'blip' appeared on a blue trace which was crossing the screen of an ex-military radar set.

†**blirre,** *sb. Obs. rare.* [Origin uncertain: prob. a variant of BLEAR *v.*¹] A deception.

1570 LEVINS *Manip.* 142 A Blirre, *deceptio.*

†**blirre,** *v. Obs.* [see prec.] To deceive.

1570 LEVINS *Manip.* 142 To Blirre, *fallere.*

blirt (blɜːt). *v. north. dial.* [prob. an onomatopœic word nearly identical with BLURT: with the *bl-*, cf. *blow, blast, blash*, etc.; with the rest, cf. *spirt, squirt*, expressing the forcible emission of liquid.] To burst into tears, weep violently; disfigure with tears.

1721 in Kelly *Sc. Prov.* 397 (JAM.) 'Ill gar you blirt with both your een.' **1879** JAMIESON *Sc. Dict.*, 'She's a' blirted wi' greeting.' *Fife.*

blirt, *sb.* [f. prec.]

1. An outburst of tears, a sudden fit of weeping. (*Sc.*)

a **1796** BURNS *Braw Lads of Gala W.* iii, The lassie lost a silken snood, That cost her mony a blirt and bleary.

2. A short dash of rain coming with a gust of wind. (*Sc.* and *Naut.*)

1810 [see BLIRTY.] **1867** SMYTH *Sailor's Word-Bk.*, *Blirt*, a gust of wind and rain.

'blirty, blirtie, *a. north.* [f. prec. + -Y.⁴] Characterized by blirts or gusts of wind and rain.

1810 TANNAHILL *Poems* (1846) 16 O poortith is a wintry day! Cheerless, blirtie, cauld, and blae.

blisce(n, obs. form of BLESS *v.*¹

bliss (blɪs), *sb.* Forms: 1 **blíðs, blíds, bliss, blis;** 3–7 **blisse,** 4–6 **blysse, blis,** 6– **bliss;** *occas.* 4–7 **blesse, bless.** [OE. *blíðs* (acc. *blíðse*) str. fem. = OS. *blîdsea, blîtzea, blîzza*:—OTeut. type **blîþsjâ-* f. **blîþi-s*, Goth. *bleiþs*, OS. *blîthi*, OE. *blíðe* blithe, joyous + suffix *-sjâ-*, standing, after dentals, for original *-tjâ* (cf. L. *lætitia*). Goth. has, instead, the parallel form *bleiþ-ei*:—OTeut. **blîþ-în-*. In later OE. by assimilation and vowel-shortening *bliðs* became *bliss, blis*, ME. *blisse*: cf. OE. *milds, milts* (:—OTeut. **mild-sjâ-* = **mild-tjâ-*) mildness, clemency, ME. *milze, milce, milse*. The meaning of *bliss* and that of *bless* have mutually influenced each other since an early period; cf. BLESS *v.*¹; confusion of spelling is frequent from the time of Wyclif to the 17th c. Hence the gradual tendency to withdraw *bliss* from earthly 'blitheness' to the beatitude of the blessed in heaven, or that which is likened to it.]

†**1.** Blitheness of aspect toward others, kindness of manner; 'light of one's countenance,' 'smile.' (Only in OE.)

a **1000** *Metr. Bœth.* ii. 30 Hi me towendon heora bacu bitere and heora blisse from.

2. Blitheness; gladness; joy, delight, enjoyment: **a.** physical, social, mundane: passing at length into **b.**

971 *Blickl. Hom.* 3 Maria cende þone Drihten on blisse. *a* **1000** *Cotton Psalm* l. 99 (Gr.) Sæle nu blidse me, bilewit dryhten. *c* **1200** *Trin. Coll. Hom.* 115 Hie weren swo bliðe þat hie ne mihten mid worde here blisse tellen. *c* **1340** *Cursor M.* 1013 (Trin.) Mony oþere blisses elles, Floures þat ful swete smelles. *c* **1380** WYCLIF *Serm.* Sel. Wks. II. 234 Two blessis ben,—blesse of þe soule and blisse of þe bodi. *c* **1386** CHAUCER *Man Law's T.* 1021 This glade folk to dyner they hem sette; In ioye and blisse at mete I lete hem dwelle. *a* **1450** *Knt. de la Tour* (1868) 55 She lost alle worshipe, richesse, ese, and blysse. **1535** STEWART *Cron. Scot.* III. 268 Tha rouch rillingis, of blis that war full bair. **1593** SHAKS. *2 Hen. VI*, I. ii. 31 And all that Poets faine of Blisse and Ioy. **1667** MILTON *P.L.* IV. 508 These two Imparadis't in one anothers arms.. shall enjoy thir fill Of bliss on bliss. **1806** WORDSW. *Ode Immortality* 86 Behold the Child among his new-born blisses. **1841** L. HUNT *Seer* (1864) 54 He does not sufficiently sympathise with our towns and our blisses of Society.

b. Mental, ethereal, spiritual: perfect joy or felicity, supreme delight; blessedness. (Early instances difficult to separate from prec.)

c **1175** *Lamb. Hom.* 15 Blisse and lisse ic sende. *a* **1300** *Cursor M.* 605 A land o lijf, o beld, and blis, þe quilk man clepes paradis. *c* **1380** WYCLIF *Serm.* Sel. Wks. I. 142 To lyve evere in blis wiþouten peyne. **1483** CAXTON *G. de la Tour* F iij, The grete reame of blysse and glory. **1591** SHAKS. *1 Hen. VI*, V. v. 64 The contrarie bringeth blisse, And is a patterne of Celestiall peace. **1597** HOOKER *Eccl. Pol.* V. xxii. §13 To them whose delight.. is in the Law.. that happiness and bliss belongeth. *a* **1649** DRUMM. OF HAWTH. *Cypr. Grove* Wks. 31 O only blest, and Author of all bliss. *Ibid.* 26 All bless returning with the Lord of bliss. **1667** MILTON *P.L.* VIII. 522 The sum of earthly bliss Which I enjoy. **1747** GRAY *Ode Eton Coll.*, Where ignorance is bliss, 'Tis folly to be wise. **1764** GOLDSM. *Trav.* 62 May gather bliss, to see my fellows blest. **1875** B. TAYLOR *Faust* I. xii. 141 The purest bliss was surely then thy dower.

c. *esp.* The perfect joy of heaven; the beatitude of departed souls. Hence, the place of bliss, paradise, heaven.

971 *Blickl. Hom.* 25 We maȝon.. éce blisse ȝeearnian. *a* **1225** *Juliana* 21 Ich schal bliðe bicumen to endelese blissen. *a* **1300** *Cursor M.* 17972 Fro helle to paradys þat blis. *c* **1384** WYCLIF *Sel. Wks.* III. 344 He [the pope] is not blessid in þis lif, for blis falliþ to the toþir lyf. **1509** HAWES *Examp. Virt.* i. 12, I wyll.. brynge thy soule to blesse eterne. **1593** SHAKS. *3 Hen. VI*, III. iii. 182 By the hope I haue of heauenly blisse. **1607** WALKINGTON *Opt. Glass* 65 The soul is.. wrapt up into an Elysium and paradise of blesse. **1667** MILTON *P.L.* I. 607 Far other once beheld in bliss. **1781** COWPER *Truth* 301 The path to bliss abounds with many a snare. **1871** MORLEY *Voltaire* (1886) 255 Any one who accepted them in the concrete and literal form prescribed by the church, would share infinite bliss.

d. *concr.* A cause of happiness, joy, or delight.

a **1000** *Ags. Ps.* (Spelm.) xxxi. 9 (Bosw.) Ðú eart blis mín. *c* **1386** CHAUCER *Nonnes Pr. T.* 346 Womman is mannes Ioye and al his blis. **1850** TENNYSON *In Mem.* xcvii. 26 A wither'd violet is her bliss.

†**3.** Glory. (Translating *gloria* and *κλέος*.) *Obs.*

c **1200** *Trin. Coll. Hom.* 115 *Quis est iste rex glorie?* hwat is þis blissene king. *a* **1300** *Cursor M.* 8100 þe king o blis. **1387** TREVISA *Higden* II. 363 Hercules is i-seide of *heros* þat is a man, and of *cleos* þat is blisse; as þey Hercules were to menynge a blisful man and glorious.

†**4.** ***a bliss of birds***: a blithe singing, a 'choir.'

c **1430** LYDG. *Min. Poems* 228 A blysse of bryddes me bad abyde, For cause there song mo then one.

5. *Comb.* **a.** objective, as ***bliss-giving, bliss-making*** adjs.; **b.** adverbial, as ***bliss-bright.***

1610 HEALEY *St. Aug. Citie of God* 309 This blesse-affording good. **1645** BP. HALL *Content.* 103 The blisse-making vision of God. **1839** BAILEY *Festus* xiv. (1848) 147 The bliss-bright stars. **1876** GEO. ELIOT *Dan. Der.* II. xxvii. 184 The bliss-giving 'yes.'

bliss, *v.* Forms: 1 **blíðsian, blissian, -iȝan,** 2 **blissien,** 3 **bliscen, (blescien),** *Orm.* **blissenn,** 3–4 **bliss(en,** 4 **blesse.** [OE. *blíðsian, blissian* = OS. *blîdsean, blizzen*, f. *blíðs, bliss* sb. Now blended in the verb BLESS.]

1. *Obs. intr.* To be blithe or glad, to rejoice.

c **897** K. ÆLFRED *Gregory's Past.* xlix. 385 Bliðsa, cniht, on ðinum ȝioȝuðhade. *c* **1000** *Ags. Gosp.* Luke xv. 9 Blyssiað mid me. *a* **1225** *Ancr. R.* 360 Gif we þolieð mid him, we schulen bliscen mid him. **1377** LANGL. *P. Pl.* B. xii. 187 Wel may þe barne blisse [C. *text* blesse] þat hym to boke sette.

b. *refl.*

c **1175** *Lamb. Hom.* 33 Ne mei nan man.. blissien him mid þisse wordle. [*a* **1225** *Ancr. R.* 358 Blescieð ou & gledieð.]

2. *trans.* To give joy or gladness to (orig. with *dative*); to gladden, make happy. (In 16–17th c. blended with *bless.*) *Obs.*

a **1000** *Hymns* vii. 34 (Gr.) Ðu engla God eallum blissast. *c* **1200** *Trin. Coll. Hom.* To gladien, and to blissen us. *a* **1300** *Cursor M.* 12779 (Gött.) To blissen þaim vte of þair wa. **1594** CONSTABLE *Diana* VI. x, She stands wotlesse whom so much she blisseth. **1636** FITZ-GEFFRAY *Holy Transport.* (1881) 189 To thee, who com'st from heauen to blisse the earth.

3. ***to bliss out*** (U.S. slang) [after *to freak out* s.v. FREAK *v.* 3], to reach a state of ecstasy. Chiefly **blissed out** (blɪst) *pa. pple.* and *ppl. a.*, in such a state; **'blissing out** *vbl. sb.*

1973 *National Observer* (U.S.) 3 Nov. 1 A 'soul rush' of blissed-out young pilgrims is heading for the Western mecca of The Most Important Movement in the History of Mankind. **1973** *Newsweek* 19 Nov. 157 Initiates learn to see a dazzling white light, hear celestial music, feel ecstatic vibrations... The process is called 'blissing out'. **1974** *New Yorker* 8 Apr. 32 The nonstop, glowing smile and the glazed eyes of one who is 'blissed out'. **1977** *Rolling Stone* 7 Apr. 23/3 Gold albums share the walls with photographs of blissed-out holy men. **1983** *Atlantic Monthly* July 104/2 Toward the end,.. Harvey is too blissed out to do much more than bask in Rinpoche's gaze. **1986** *New Yorker* 22 Sept. 84/3 Long-haired Westerners.. blissing out or freaking out in the streets.

Hence (sense 3) **blissout**, a state of ecstasy.

1974 *Time* 26 Aug. 66/1 The beach bliss-out was a response the profession can ill afford. **1976** *New Yorker* 20 Dec. 117 This blissout is the movie every actress must.. have dreamed of making. **1982** *Guardian* 30 Dec. 1/2 A 'blissout', derived from religious cults, is a state of intense happiness.

bliss(e, obs. form of BLESS *v.*¹

blissen, var. of BLESCHE *v. Obs.* to quench.

blissful ('blɪsfʊl), *a.* Forms: 2–4 **blisful(le,** 4 **-uolle, blysfol,** 4–6 **-ful, blesful(l, blesseful(l,** 6 **blisseful(l, blisfull,** 7 **blissfull, blessful,** 3– **blissful.** [f. BLISS *sb.* + -FUL.]

1. Of persons: Full of bliss, joyful; happy or joyous in the highest degree.

a **1240** *Sawles Warde* in *Lamb. Hom.* 259 Hu he sit blisful on his fader riht half. *c* **1386** CHAUCER *Frankel. T.* 362 O blisful artow now thou Dorigen, That hast thy lusty housbonde in thyne Armes. **1388** WYCLIF *Eccles.* iv. 3 Y demyde hym, that was not borun ȝit.. to be blisfulere than euer eithir. **1646** CRASHAW *Steps Temp.* 65 Let the blessful heart hold fast Her heavenly armful. **1863** TENNYSON *Welc. Alexandra* 27 Blissful bride of a blissful heir.

2. Of things: Full of or fraught with bliss.

c **1175** *Lamb. Hom.* 77 þe engel hire brohte þe blisfulle tidinge. *c* **1385** CHAUCER *L.G.W.* 682 From that blisful our. **1589** GREENE *Menaph.* (1616) 47 To turne my blissefull sweet to balefull sowre. **1667** MILTON *P.L.* I. 5 Till one greater Man Restore us, and regain the blissful Seat. **1776** GIBBON *Decl. & F.* I. 205 To live with Ormusd in a blissful eternity. **1881** MORLEY *Cobden* I. 14 All blessed by nature with a kind of blissful mercurial simplicity.

†**3.** Blessed, beatified; sacred, holy. *Obs.*

a **1225** *St. Marher.* 21 Beo þu a iblescet and ti blisfule sune iesu crist. *a* **1300** *Cursor M.* 8906 þe lauerd of hele, þat blisful king. **1340** *Ayenb.* 186 þe blisuolle blode of Iesu Crist. **1496** *Dives & Paup.* I. (W. de W.) iii. 93/2 Marye Magdaleyn anoynted the blysful fete of our lorde Ihesu. **1534** LD. BERNERS *Gold. Bk. M. Aurel.* (1546) M iij b, It is ordeyned by the holy senate, by consente of blisfull men.

†**4.** Glorified, transfigured; cf. BLISS *sb.* 3. *Obs.*

1387 [see BLISS *sb.* 3]. **1398** TREVISA *Barth. De P.R.* VIII. xl, A bodi þat is blisful [L. *glorificatus*]. *Ibid.* XIV. xliv, In toppe of þis mounte oure Lorde schewid him selfe blysful.

†**5.** Having power to bless. *Obs.*

1598 FLORIO *Dict.* Ep. Ded. 4 Laie then your blisse-full handes on his head (right Honorable).

†**'blissfulhed, blisfulhede.** *Obs.* [f. prec. + *-hede*, -HEAD.] Blissful condition, joy, beatitude.

a **1340** HAMPOLE *Psalter* i. 1 *Beatus vir*.. Hightand blisfulhed til rightwise men. *c* **1340** *Cursor M.* 6852 (Trin.) A londe of blisfulhede. **1413** LYDG. *Pylgr. Sowle* II. xli. (1859) 46 Al bounte, beaute, joye and blysfulhede.

blissfully ('blɪsfʊlɪ), *adv.* [f. as prec. + -LY².] In a blissful manner, happily, joyously.

a **1225** *Ancr. R.* 360 ȝif we wulleð a domesdei blissfuliche arisen. *a* **1300** *Cursor M.* 9117 A quile regnd king salamon Blisfulli ouer al þat land. **1489** CAXTON *Faytes of A.* IV. vii. 246 The sowles ben blysfully in paradise. *a* **1711** KEN *Anodynes* Poet. Wks. 1721 III. 462 Wrapt Blissfully with God below. **1820** KEATS *St. Agnes* xxvii, Blissfully haven'd both from joy and pain. **1884** *Harper's Mag.* Sept. 648/1 Blissfully ignorant.

blissfulness ('blɪsfʊlnɪs). [f. as prec. + -NESS.] The quality or state of being blissful; joyfulness, happiness.

c **1374** CHAUCER *Boeth.* IV. ii. 113 Blisfulnesse is þilke same goode þat men requeren. **1382** WYCLIF *Gen.* xxx. 13 Lya seide, That for my blisfulnes. **1548** UDALL, etc. *Erasm. Par. Mark* iii. 35 To be rewarded with euerlasting blissfulnesse. **1580** SIDNEY *Arcadia* (1622) 3 It is not for me to attend so high a blissefulnesse. **1633** FORD *Broken H.* I. iii. (R.) My better stars, that offer'd me the grace Of so much blissfulness. **1858** NEALE *Bernard de M.* 19 In blissfulness and mirth. **1871** PALGRAVE *Lyr. Poems* 71 A peace more deep disclosed its blissfulness.

blissing, obs. f. BLESSING.

'blissless, *a.* [f. BLISS *sb.* + -LESS.] Without bliss; hapless, miserable.

1580 SIDNEY *Arcadia* III. 352 So many have come to my blissless lot. **1591** KYD *Span. Trag.* IV. in Hazl. *Dodsley* V. 155 Barren the earth, and blissless whosoever Imagines not to keep it unmanur'd! **1952** *Antiquity* XXVI. 95 In our present blissless ignorance.

blissom ('blɪsəm), *a.* [a. ON. *blœsma* adj. (a ewe or goat) in heat; ODu. *blesme* (Kolkar).] Of a ewe: In heat. (See quot.)

1668 WILKINS *Real Char.* II. ix. §2. 234 Carnal, fleshly, blissom, clicket, proud. **1727** BRADLEY *Fam. Dict.* s.v. *Ewe*, Ewe is Bliessom, a Term peculiar to Sheepherds, signifying that the Ewe has taken Tup.

'blissom, *v.* [f. as prec.]

1. *trans.* Of a ram: To couple with a ewe; to tup. In *pass.* said of the ewe.

1432-50 tr. *Higden* Rolls Ser. II. 303 Iacob putte the roddes.. afore the siȝhte of schepe when thei scholde be blissomede. **1483** *Cath. Angl.* 34 To Blessum, *arietare.* **1523** FITZHERB. *Husb.* §37. **1616** SURFL. & MARKH. *Countr. Farm* I. xxv. 111 One Ramme will serue to blesome fiftie Ewes. **1656** in BLOUNT *Glossogr.*; **1721** in BAILEY, and in later Dicts.

2. *intr.* 'To caterwaul, to be lustful.' J.

Hence **'blissoming** *vbl. sb.*, **'blissomed** *ppl. a.*

a **1300** *E.E. Psalter* lxxvii[i]. 70 Of after-blismed, [Vulg. *de post fœtantes*], him name he. **1721** BAILEY, *Blissoming*, the Act of generation between a Ram and a Ewe. **1766** RIDER *Dict.* s.v., To go a blissoming is to desire the Ram.

blist, var. of *blyschit* (see BLUSH *v.*); obs. form of BLEST, of BLESS *v.*¹, and BLISS *sb.*; obs. Sc. form of BLAST.

blisteing, obs. form of BLESSING.

blister ('blɪstə(r)), *sb.* Also 3 blester, 6 bluster, blyster. [ME. *blester*, *blister*, perh. a. OF. *blestre* ('tumeur, bouton,' Godef.), also *blostre*: the double form may be explained as an adoption of ON. *blástr*, dat. *blæstri* 'swelling,' also 'a blast, blowing,' f. *blása* to blow (whence also mod.Sw. *blåsa*, Ger. *blase*, blister). The 16th c. variant *bluster* suggests the MDu. or Flemish *bluyster* (Kilian), which points to earlier **blûstra*, from same root (cf. ON. *blístra* to whistle). An OE. *blǽster*, *bléster* or *blýster*, cogn. with the ON. or Du., might have been expected, but is not found.]

1. A thin vesicle on the skin, containing serum, caused by friction, a burn, or other injury, or the action of a vesicatory.

a **1300** *Cursor M.* 6011 (Gött.) Bile and blester [*v.r.* blister], bolnand sare. ?*a* **1500** *Flower & Leaf* lix, For blisters of the Sunne brenninge, Very good.. ointmentes. **1523** FITZHERB. *Husb.* § 61 There is a blyster rysen vnder the tounge. **1561** HOLLYBUSH *Hom. Apoth.* 22 b, Good.. agaynst blusters or reed pustuls. **1664** DRYDEN *Riv. Ladies* III. i. (1725) 216 This Hand would rise in Blisters shouldst thou touch it. **1810** HENRY *Elem. Chem.* II. 371 Acetic acid, thus prepared.. raises a blister when applied to the skin. **1884** W. C. SMITH *Kildrostan* 88 Your wet ropes And clumsy oars.. give blisters first And then a horny hand.

2. a. A similar swelling, containing fluid or (more usually) air, on the surface of a plant, on metal after cooling, a painted surface, and the like.

1597 GERARD *Herbal* III. cxvi. (1633) 1480 On these leaves .. grow blisters or small bladders. **1671** RAY *Philos. Lett.* (1718) 97, I had thought that the Kermes-berry had been a Blister of the Bark of the Oak. **1678** *Ripley Reviv'd* 155 Our compound in this heat riseth in blisters. **1799** G. SMITH *Laborat.* I. 148 The paste would be cloudy and full of blisters. **1885** *Athenæum* 30 May 704/2 Nor is this cracking all the mischief which has lately befallen this picture.. there is rather a large blister.

b. A disease incident to peach-trees, caused by the fungus *Exoascus deformans*, which produces a distortion of the leaves.

1864 *Ohio Agric. Rep.* XVIII. 460 For some years, in this country, the disease which produces the 'Blister and Curl' in the peach leaf, and decay in the peach fruit, has.. produced extensive ravages. **1919** *Board Agric. & Fisheries Leaflet* No. 120 'Curl' or 'leaf blister' proves very injurious to peaches and nectarines during certain seasons.

c. *Naut. colloq.* An outer covering fitted to a vessel to provide protection against torpedoes and mines or to improve stability. Hence, a ship so protected. Also *attrib.*

1919 *Chambers's Jrnl.* 26 July 543/1 Immunity from the evil effects of torpedoes and mines is sought by the provision of a swelling, commonly called a 'bulge' or a 'blister', below the water-line on each side. **1921** *Flight* XIII. 584/1 By suitable methods of 'blister' construction of ships, however, this mining effect could be reduced to something as negligible as the direct hit. **1923** W. S. CHURCHILL *World Crisis* II. i. 23 When at last Monitors, 'Blisters' and Tanks had been devised and built. **1948** R. DE KERCHOVE *Internat. Maritime Dict.* 64/1 Blisters which communicate with the open sea, are fitted on some ships as an anti-rolling device.

d. A rounded compartment protruding from the body of an aeroplane. Also *attrib.*

1939 *Meccano Mag.* Sept. 517/2 There are five machine gun positions, one in the fuselage nose, and four others in the form of streamlined 'blisters' on the top, bottom, and sides of the fuselage. **1941** *Illustr. London News* CXCVIII. 516 An air-gunner in one of the carefully stream-lined blister gun turrets of a 'Catalina'. **1943** 'T. DUDLEY-GORDON' *Coastal Command at War* xv. 140 Two big gun blisters, with sliding, rounded panels of perspex, in which two gunners are always on watch.

3. *Med.* Anything applied to raise a blister; a vesicatory.

1541 R. COPLAND *Guydon's Quest. Chirurg.*, And the blysters potencyall cauteres be applyed. **1758** WHYTT in *Phil. Trans.* L. 570, I advised a blister to be applied. **1875** H. WOOD *Therap.* (1879) 561 Blisters are especially useful in inflammations of serous membranes.

4. A derogatory term for a person, esp. an annoying one. *slang.*

1806 J. BERESFORD *Miseries* I. vii. 145 A perpetual blister; — alias, a sociable next-door-neighbour, who has taken a violent affection for *you.* **1880** W. H. PATTERSON *Gloss. Antrim & Down* 9 *Blister*, an annoying person. **1914** 'I HAY' *Lighter Side School Life* iii. 81 Mr. Wellings' reputation throughout the school.. was that of a 'chronic blister'. **1930** WODEHOUSE *Very Good, Jeeves!* xi. 308 Women are a wash-out. I see no future for the sex, Bertie. Blisters, all of them.

5. A summons. *slang.*

1903 *Sessions Paper* 17 Nov. 33, I was served with four *blisters* yesterday. **1906** *Daily Chron.* 20 Mar. 5/6 'Have you never had a "blister"?'.. The solicitor explained to the Court that a 'blister' was a summons for 'scorching'. **1947** F. SARGESON in *Penguin New Writing* XXIX. 62 He'd been paying off a few bob every time he had a few to spare.... And then he gets a blister!

6. *Comb.*, as **blister-beetle, -fly**, an insect used for raising blisters, *spec.* the Spanish fly (*Cantharis vesicatoria*); **blister blight**, a disease of the tea-plant caused by the fungus *Exobasidium vexans*, which produces blisters on the leaves; **blister-copper**, copper having a blistered surface, obtained during smelting just before the final operation; hence attrib. ***blister-copper ore***; **blister furnace**, a furnace for the conversion of copper regulus or matte into blister-copper; **blister gas**, a poison gas which causes blisters on or intense irritation of the skin; **blister pack** *sb.*, a pack consisting of a piece of usu. transparent plastic moulded over an article and sealed to a flat card; so **blister-pack** *v. trans.*, to package in this way; **blister-packed** *ppl. a.*, **-packing** *vbl. sb.*; **blister package** = *blister pack* sb. above; **blister packaging** *vbl. sb.*, packaging in blister packs; **blister pearl**, a pearly excrescence of irregular shape found on the shell of a pearl oyster; **blister-plant**, a name for different species of *Ranunculus*, esp. *R. acris*, *R. sceleratus*; **blister-plaster**, a plaster for raising a blister; **blister-steel**, steel having a blistered surface, obtained during the process of converting iron into shear-steel or cast-steel; attrib. ***blister-steel furnace***.

1816 KIRBY & SP. *Entomol.* (1843) I. 31 If the apothecary cannot distinguish a.. *blister-beetle from a Carabus. **1877** S. BAILDON *Tea in Assam* 45, I do not know whether it has been really ascertained what causes '*Blister blight'. A leaf gets a small speck upon it at first, which, as it enlarges, assumes the appearance of a blister. **1949** *Ann. Reg. 1948* 144 Tea bushes were attacked by blister blight. **1861** J. PERCY *Metall.* I. 325 The *blister-copper is tapped into sand-moulds. **1875** URE *Dict. Arts* (ed. 7) I. 398 *Blister Copper-ore*, a botryoidal variety of copper-pyrites. **1585** *Blister fly [see WHELK² 1 (*Comb.*)]. **1842** Blister-fly [see SPANISH *a.* 8 b]. **1862** COLEMAN *Woodlands* 23 The brilliant Blister-fly.. is only very sparingly met with in this country. **1902** *Encycl. Brit.* XXVII. 237/1 The multiple system anodes are sometimes cast directly from the *blister furnace or the converter. **1936** *Current Hist.* July 61/2 In Class D come the *vesicants* or *blister gases. **1938** *Encycl. Brit. Bk. of Year 1938* 144/1 The blister gases.. penetrate nearly every material except glass, porcelain, and unglazed metals. **1964** *Drug & Cosmetic Industry* July 54/1 (*heading*) *Blister-pack. **1969** L. S. MOUNTS in W. R. R. Park *Plastics Film Technol.* v. 116 Blister packs are usually rigid. **1971** *Islander* (Victoria, B.C.) 30 May 6/4 Sophisticated machinery to blister pack articles for protection during shipment. **1977** *Times* 22 Oct. 12/7 The cheapest bangers [*sc.* fireworks] are now sold in blister-packs of six at 21p each. **1983** *N.Y. Times* 13 Aug. 14/1 Tamper-resistant packages, such as blister packs. **1954** *Mod. Plastics* May 89/3 *Very* small and simple pieces, such as dome-like '*blister' packages. **1964** *Drug & Cosmetic Industry* July 54/2 Cardboard and plastic may be combined in several different ways to yield the desired blister package. **1954** *Mod. Plastics* May 97/1 Master Rule Mfg. Co., Middletown, N.Y., has.. opened a new phase in '*blister' packaging by encasing a steel tape measuring rule in the package during the vacuum forming operation. **1976** *Oxf. Consumer* Mar. 7/2 The shopkeepers' opinions are divided on the blister packaging... Once the shopkeeper has broken the blister.. the article is no use for further sale. **1976** *CB Mag.* June 22/1 (Advt.), Attractively *blister packed. **1976** *Lancet* 4 Dec. 1239/1 The use of *blister-packing.. could lead to important savings of drugs discarded each year in English hospitals. **1885** *Encycl. Brit.* XVIII. 446/2 The mollusc.. depositing nacreous matter.., thus forming a hollow body of irregular shape known as a '*blister pearl'. **1910** *Daily Chron.* 4 Apr. 4/5 Overdress of gauze encrusted with blister pearls. **1796** WOLCOTT (P. Pindar) *Sat.* Wks. 1812 III. 390 He Gilead's Balm; but you a *Blister-plaster. **1831** J. HOLLAND *Manuf. Metals* I. 230 When the iron has absorbed a quantity of carbon in the *blister steel furnace. **1837** BREWSTER *Magnet.* 319 Needles of shear steel received a greater magnetic force than those of blister steel. **1880** C. M. MASON *Forty Spires* 65 When the bars are removed from the furnace they are in a blistered state; they are known as blister-steel.

blister ('blɪstə(r)), *v.* [f. prec.]

1. *trans.* To raise blisters on. Also *absol.*

1541 R. COPLAND *Guydon's Quest. Chirurg.*, Those that blyster make no scarre. **1610** SHAKS. *Temp.* I. ii. 324 A south-west blow on yee and blister you all ore. **1624** CAPT. SMITH *Virginia* III. vii. 69 The Axes.. blistered their tender fingers. **1776** WITHERING *Bot. Arrangem.* (1801) III. 496 It is very acrid, and easily blisters the skin. **1822** SCOTT *Nigel* xxiii, Patients might be bled, cupped, or blistered. **1842** S. LOVER *Handy Andy* ii. 18 I'll slap at him.. I'll blister him. **1866** J. H. NEWMAN *Gerontius* iv. 33 Ice which blisters may be said to burn.

fig. **1603** SHAKS. *Meas. for M.* II. iii. 12 Who, falling in the flaws of her own youth, hath blistered her report. **1605** —— *Macb.* IV. iii. 12 This tyrant whose sole name blisters our tongue. **1884** BROWNING *Ferishtah* (1885) 33 Abominable words which blister tongue.

2. *transf.* To raise blisters on (iron bars, etc.) in the process of conversion into steel.

3. *intr.* To be or become covered with blisters.

1496 *Bk. St. Albans, Fysshynge* 3 He blowyth tyll his lyppes blyster. **1611** SHAKS. *Wint. T.* II. ii. 33 If I proue hony-mouth'd, let my tongue blister. **1734** ATWELL in *Phil. Trans.* XXXIX. 399 The Wound has blister'd. **1799** J. ROBERTSON *Agric. Perth* 168 The bark blisters and rises from the reed. **1821** *Cook's Oracle* (ed. 3) 92 Otherwise it [roast sucking-pig] will be apt to blister.

†**4.** To rise in or as a blister. *Obs.*

1644-7 CLEVELAND *Char. Lond. Diurn.* (1677) 102 Our Modern Noble Men; those Wens of Greatness, the Body Politick's most peccant Humours, Blistred into Lords.

5. *trans.* Used as an imprecation. *slang.*

1840 COCKTON *Val. Vox* xxvi, Blister 'em! Where can the scoundrels be got to? **1964** WODEHOUSE *Frozen Assets* iii. 46 Why didn't they send it up before, blister their insides? I've been in agonies of suspense.

6. Of a policeman: to record a person's name for an alleged offence; esp. in *pass.*, to have one's name recorded in this way; to be summoned or punished for an offence (cf. BLISTER *sb.* 5). *slang.*

1909 WARE *Passing Eng.* 34/2 *To blister*.. Used chiefly by cabmen in relation to magisterial fines, *e.g.*, 'I was blistered at Bow Street to-day for twenty hog.' **1938** F. D. SHARPE *Sharpe of Flying Squad* 329 *Blistered*, served with a summons. **1939** H. HODGE *Cab, Sir?* xvi. 225 When the policeman puts his notebook away again, we've usually been 'blistered'. During recent years, policemen have been blistering us over three thousand times in a twelvemonth.

blistered ('blɪstəd), *ppl. a.* [f. prec. + -ED.]

1. a. Affected with blisters, covered with vesicles.

1563 HYLL *Art Garden.* (1593) 116 This hearb.. healeth the blistred lungs. **1886** STEVENSON *Dr. Jekyll* i. 4 The door .. was blistered and distained.

b. Of steel, etc.: cf. BLISTER *sb.* 6. orig. *U.S.*

1744 in *Maryland Hist. Mag.* (1926) XXI. 243, 3 ffaggotts Blistered Steel. **1750** FRANKLIN *Wks.* (1840) 225 Sometimes the surface.. of the needle.. appears blistered. **1770** *Carroll Papers* in *Maryland Hist. Mag.* (1918) XIII. 65 My Smiths say the Bristol or Blister'd steel sent to us is very bad. **1821** R. TURNER *Abridgm. Arts & Sc.* 227 The iron combines with a quantity of carbon, and is converted into blistered steel. **1870** *Eng. Mech.* 18 Feb. 547/3 'Blistered'copper is recognised by.. being covered with scales of the oxide.

c. Provided with a 'blister' (see BLISTER *sb.* 2 c).

1923 W. S. CHURCHILL *World Crisis* II. i. 23 The Monitor and the 'bulged' or 'blistered ship' were the beginning of the torpedo-proof fleet. **1928** *Daily Express* 21 Nov. 1/1 The methods of defence employed by surface craft consist of

anti-aircraft guns..; of reinforced or 'blistered' bottoms..; and of manœuvre.

2. Ornamented with puffs, puffed.

1592 NASHE *P. Penilesse* Wks. 1884 II. 391 His back.. blisterd with light sarcenet bastings. **1613** SHAKS. *Hen. VIII*, I. iii. 31 Short blistred Breeches.

blistering ('blɪstərɪŋ), *vbl. sb.* [f. as prec. + -ING¹.] The action or result of the vb. BLISTER.

1563 HYLL *Art Garden.* (1593) 95 The same water helpeth ..the blistering of the mouth. **1660** BP. HALL *Rem. Wks.* 188 Not a scorching and blistering but..full torrefaction. **1711** ADDISON *Spect.* No. 195 ¶2 Blistering, Cupping, Bleeding are seldom of use. **1842** S. LOVER *Handy Andy* ii, You'll get such a blistering from me. **1863** KINGSLEY *Water Bab.* iv. 172 Bullyings, Bumpings, Blisterings, Bleedings.

'blistering, *ppl. a.* [f. as prec. + -ING².] **1.** That causes blisters. Hence **'blisteringly** *adv.*

1562 TURNER *Herbal* II. D iij a, Wythout blystringe mustarde plasters. *Ibid.* T vj a, Byting and very blystring. **1859** TENNYSON *Enid* 1364 Till she..Had bared her forehead to the blistering sun. **1877** SPURGEON *Treas. David* Ps. cxxx. 1 In the chamber of despair, the floor of which is blisteringly hot.

2. Used as a substitute for a strong expletive. *slang.*

1900 *Daily News* 30 July 6/4 One blistering young woman actually unstraps her kodak and begins operations upon the great white mountain.

blistery ('blɪstərɪ), *a.* [f. BLISTER *sb.* + -Y¹.] Characterized by blisters.

1743 *Lond. & Country Brew.* IV. 329 When such frothy black blistery Head is first..put into the small Beer. **1843** CARLYLE *Past & Pr.* (1858) 98 A little blistery friction on the back! **1845** NEWBOLD in *Jrnl. Asiat. Soc. Bengal* XIV. 283 Lined with blistery and stalactitic hematite.

blite (blaɪt, ? also blɪt). *Herb.* Also 6 **blete, bleit, blyte, blittes,** 6–7 **bleet,** (8–9 **blight**), 7–9 **blit.** [ad. L. *blitum* orache, spinach, a. Gr. *βλίτον* 'perh. strawberry blite, or amaranth blite'.] Book-name for various plants of the N.O. *Chenopodiaceæ*: esp. Wild Spinach (*C. Bonus-Henricus*), *Amaranthus blitum*, various species of *Atriplex*, and the genus *Blitum* (STRAWBERRY BLITE). Formerly also for Garden Spinach.

c **1420** *Pallad. on Husb.* IV. 291 Iche erthe ywrought nowe blite wol multiplie. **1551** TURNER *Herbal* (1568) I. F vi b, It may be called in englyshe a blyte or a blete. **1586** COGAN *Haven Health* lxxxiv. (1636) 87 Bleet is used for a Pot-hearbe among others. **1601** HOLLAND *Pliny* II. 76 Bleets seeme to be dull, vnsauorie and foolish Woorts, hauing no tast nor quicknesse at all. **1727** BRADLEY *Fam. Dict.* s.v. *Abscess*, Give 'em Lettice or Blites chopped small. **1796** C. MARSHALL *Garden.* xix. (1813) 350 Mulberry blight, or more properly blite..whose fruit resembles a red unripe mulberry. **1853** SOYER *Pantroph.* 68 Blit was eaten boiled, when nothing better was to be had.

blite, obs. form of BLIGHT.

blithe (blaɪð), *a.* (*sb.* and *adv.*) Forms: 1–3 **blíðe,** (3 **bliht, bligh**), 4 **bliþ(e, blyþe, (bliȝe,** 5 **blyde),** 3–7 **blith,** 3–8 **blyth,** 4–9 **blythe,** 3– **blithe.** [Com. Teut.: OE. *bliðe* = OS. *blîdi* (MDu. *blîde*, Du. *blijde, blij*, LG. *blide, blyde*), OHG. *blîdi* (MHG. *blîde*), ON. *bliðr* mild, gentle, kind, (Sw., Da. *blid*), Goth. *bleiþs* kind, merciful:—OTeut. **blîþi-z*; possibly f. verbal stem **blî-* to shine, but no cognates are known outside Teutonic. The earlier application was to the outward expression of kindly feeling, sympathy, affection to others, as in Gothic and ON.; but in OE. the word had come more usually to be applied to the external manifestation of one's own pleased or happy frame of mind, and hence even to the state itself.]

A. *adj.*

†1. Exhibiting kindly feeling to others; kind, friendly, clement, gentle. *Obs.*

a **1000** *Elene* 1317 (Gr.) Him biþ engla weard milde and bliðe. *c* **1340** *Alex. & Dind.* 624 God is spedeful in speche Boþ blessed & blyþe. *c* **1400** *Destr. Troy* 2342 Your biddyng to obey, as my blithe fader. **1570** LEVINS *Manip.* 151/46 Blythe, *blandus*.

†**b.** *fig.* (Of the waves.) *Obs.*

c **1000** *Ags. Psalter* cvi[i]. 28 þa yða swyȝiað, bliðe weorþaþ.

2. Exhibiting gladness: jocund, merry, sprightly, gay, mirthful. In ballads frequently coupled with *gay*. Rare in mod.Eng. prose or speech.

a **1000** *Cædmon's Poems, Christ* 739 (Gr.) Hleahtre bliðe. *a* **1300** *Cursor M.* 7255 Quils þai war blithest at þat fest. *Ibid.* 11066 When John was borne also swyþe His frendes was ful gladd and bliþe. *c* **1470** HENRY *Wallace* II. 222 Yhe birds, blyth as bellis. **1616** BULLOKAR, *Blith*, merry, frolicke, joyfull. **1632** MILTON *Allegro* 24 So buxom, blithe, and debonair. **1725** POPE *Odyss.* xx. 199 Magnificent, and blithe, the suitors come. **1754** RICHARDSON *Grandison* (1766) V. 277 Emily; good girl! quite recovered, and blyth as a bird. **1796** *Campaigns* 1793–4 II. viii. 53 Forth we instantly sallied, so blythe and so gay. **1807** CRABBE *Par. Reg.* III. 957 Thus brides again and bridegrooms blithe shall kneel.

b. *transf.* of things. (More common.)

a **1300** *Cursor M.* 828 Alle blurded þat was for-wit bliþe. *c* **1340** *Gaw. & Gr. Knt.* 155 With blyþe blaunner ful bryȝt. **1621** BEAUM. & FL. *Thierry & Theod.* v. i, A bonny countenance and a blithe. **1808** SCOTT *Marm.* I. x, A blithe salute The minstrels well might sound. **1855** PRESCOTT *Philip II*, I. I. iv. 50 Blithe sounds of festal music. **1857** H. REED *Lect. Eng. Poets* xiii. II. 136 The rightful gayety of those blithe early years.

3. Of men, their heart, spirit, etc.: Joyous, gladsome, cheerful; glad, happy, well pleased. Rare in Eng. prose or colloquial use since 16th c., but frequent in poetry; still in spoken use in Scotland.

971 *Blickl. Hom.* 7 Bliþe mode heo sang. *c* **1000** ÆLFRIC *Ex.* xviii. 9 þa wæs Iethro bliðe for eallum ðam þingum ðe Drihten dyde Israhela folce. *c* **1205** LAY. 1636 He was swiðe bliðe for his muchele biȝate. *c* **1386** CHAUCER *Knts. T.* 1020 With good hope and herte blithe. *c* **1440** *York Myst.* xv. 86 Breder, bees all blythe and glad. **1599** SHAKS. *Hen. V*, II. iii. 4 Bardolph, be blythe. **1663** in Spalding *Troub. Chas. I*, (1829) 25 Blyth to win away with his life. **1667** MILTON *P.L.* IX. 625 To whom the wilie Adder, blithe and glad. **1715** ROWE *Lady J. Gray* IV. (1746) 217, I trust that we shall meet on blither terms. **1816** SCOTT *Old Mort.* 114 'I'm blythe to hear ye say sae,' answered Cuddie. **1871** MORLEY *Voltaire* (1886) 49 His spirit was blithe and its fire unquenchable. **1871** R. ELLIS *Catullus* ix. 11 Know ye happier any, any blither?

†4. Yielding milk. *Obs.* or ? *dial.*

1656 BLOUNT *Glossogr.*, *Blith* (Brit.), that yeelds milk, milky. **1669** WORLIDGE *Syst. Agric.* 322 Blith, yielding Milk.

5. Heedless, careless. Freq. used to intensify following *sb.* describing a negative quality.

1922 D. H. LAWRENCE *England my England* 23 From mother and nurse it was a guerilla gunfire of commands, and blithe, quicksilver disobedience from the three blonde, never-still little girls. **1977** *Time* May 194/1 The era of cheap fuels led to a blithe disregard of second-law fundamentals. **1979** A. MCCOWEN *Young Gemini* 31 The thing that puzzled me most was their complacency, and their blithe intolerance of most of the outside world. **1984** *Washington Post* 2 Sept. 6 Constant Defender sidesteps these charges—but with such blithe indifference..that it may well prove an antidote to the anxiety.

B. *sb.*

†1. A blithe one: cf. *fair*. *Obs.*

a **1548** *Song, Murning Maidin* xvii, Into my armes swythe Embrasit I that blythe.

†2. **a.** Compassion, mercy, good-will; **b.** Gladness, mirth, pleasure, delight. *Obs.*

c **1325** *E.E. Allit. P.* A. 354, & sech hys blyþe ful swefte & swyþe. *c* **1400** *Destr. Troy* 2196 Ger hom bowe as a berslet & þi blithe seche. *c* **1420** *Liber Cocorum* 36 Coloure hit with safrone, so have þou blythe. *c* **1450** *Bk. Curtasye* 47 in *Babees Bk.* (1868) 300 Loke thy naylys ben clene, in blythe. **1585** *Will A. Robinson, Kendal* (Somerset Ho.) To William Pott wyfe for hir greate blythe of drinke.

C. *adv.* [OE. *bliðe*.] †**a.** Kindly, benignantly. *Obs.* **b.** Blithely, cheerfully.

c **1000** *Ags. Ps.* liv. [lv.] 17 þu me milde and bliðe.. ahluttra. *a* **1300** *Cursor M.* 11635 Iesus loked on hir blith. *c* **1435** *Torr. Portugal* 338 The chyldyr namys I wolle telle blythe. **1486** *Bk. St. Albans* E vij b, The man to his mayster spekyth full blyth. **1785** COWPER *Faithf. Bird* 7 They sang, as blithe as finches sing.

D. *Comb.*, as ***blithe-hearted***, †***blithelike***, ***blithe-looking*** adjs.

1570 *Sempill Ballates* (1872) 77 Ze plesand Paun & Papingaw Cast of zour blyithlyke cullour. **1848** LYTTON *Harold* xi. vii, Leofwine, still gay and blithe-hearted. **1848** DICKENS *Dombey* (C.D. ed.) 47 A blithe-looking boy.

†**blithe,** *v. Obs.* [f. the adj.: a later formation, instead of OE. *bliðsian, blissian*, BLISS.]

1. *intr.* To rejoice, to be merry; = BLISS *v.* 1.

a **1300** *Cursor M.* 17870 (Gött.) Adam..bigan þan forto blith [*v.r.* to glade] in hast. **1563** SACKVILLE *Compl. Dk. Buckhm.* 108 Take hede by me that blithd in balefull blisse.

2. *trans.* To make blithe, gladden, delight; = BLISS *v.* 2 and BLITHEN.

c **1400** *Destr. Troy* 2554 Hit blithet all the buernes þat aboute stode. *c* **1440** *Promp. Parv.* 40 Blythyn or welle cheryn, *exhillero*. **1627** FELTHAM *Resolves* I. lxxxi. Wks. (1677) 124 Hope flatters Life..She blythes the Farmer.

blitheful ('blaɪðfʊl), *a.* [f. BLITHE *sb.* or ? *a.* + -FUL; cf. *blissful*.]

†1. Kindly, friendly. Cf. BLITHE *a.* 1. *Obs.*

a **1300** *Cursor M.* 4078 Ne wald þai apon him sei..with blithful ei. *Ibid.* 8547 And..spak wit blithful [*v.r.* blisful] chere. *a* **1300** *E.E. Psalter* cxi[i]. 5 Blithefull man he es for-þi.

2. Joyous, joyful; = BLITHE *a.* 2, 3.

1530 LYNDESAY *Papyngo* 627 Edinburgh..Within quhose boundis rycht blythfull haue I bene. **1648** HERRICK *Poems* (1869) I. 245 Live here blithefull, while ye may. **1837** *Blackw. Mag.* XLII. 552 That blitheful noise.

'blithefully, *adv.* Joyously, cheerfully.

1864 SALA in *Daily Tel.* 26 Feb., He sallies out more or less blithefully.

blithely ('blaɪðlɪ), *adv.* Forms: 1 **blíðelíce,** 2 **blyðelice,** 2–3 **bluþeliche, bliðeliche,** 3 **bliðe-like, blithlik, -li,** 3–4 **blythly, blitheliche,** 4 **bly-, bliþely,** 4–5 **blithly,** 6 *Sc.* **blyithlye, -lyke,** 6–8 **blythely,** 6– **blithely.** [f. BLITHE *a.* + -LY².]

†1. With kindness, benignantly. *Obs.*

c **1000** *Ags. Gosp.* Luke xix. 6 Ða efste he and hine bliþelice onfengc. *c* **1400** *Destr. Troy* XXII. 9109 There the body of the bold blithly was set, Of honerable Ector, as I ere said. **1592** GREENE *Poems* 137 Astraea..'Gan blythely comfort me.

2. In a blithe manner; joyfully, joyously, merrily; gladly.

c **1175** *Lamb. Hom.* 23 þu gast to chirche bluþeliche. *c* **1230** *Hali Meid.* 3 þat..heo him ase fader þe bliðeluker lustni. *a* **1300** *Cursor M.* 3243 Blithli, sir, it sal be don. **1375** BARBOUR *Bruce* VIII. 457 He vald ysche fer the blithlyer. **1513** DOUGLAS *Æneis* III. iii. 40 Tell thi awne fadir blythlie Thir tithingis. **1791** BURNS *Craigieburn Wood* i, And blythely awaukens the morrow. **1794** SOUTHEY *Lyric P., To Hymen*, Returning blithely home. **1820** SCOTT *Monast.* x, I listened blithely enough.

3. Heedlessly, carelessly; taking no account of the consequences. Freq. used to intensify following *adj.* with negative connotation.

1921 E. O'NEILL *Diff'rent* II., in *Emperor Jones* 265 His eyes cannot conceal..a wounded look of bewildered hurt. *Emma.* (Blithely indifferent to this—pleasantly.) **1978** *Economist* 22 July 26/1 Mr Carter himself often seems blithely unconcerned with his political 'image'. **1986** *N.Y. Times* 18 Aug. A17/1 Andrew Wyeth is an anachronism insofar as he is blithely unconcerned with any of these things.

'blithemeat. ? *Obs. Sc.* An entertainment provided upon the birth of a child; the dainties then partaken of.

1681 in R. Law *Mem.* (1818) 191 (JAM.) Sabbath days feastings, blythemeats, banquetings. **1823** GALT *Entail* I. xxxiii. 295, I hope, poor thing, she'll hae an easy time o't, and that we'll hae blithes-meat before the sun gangs doun.

†**'blithemod,** *a. Obs.* [OE. *blíðemód*, f. *blíðe* BLITHE + *mód* disposition, MOOD.] Of blithe mood; of cheerful disposition.

1065 *O.E. Chron.* (Cott. MS.) Wæs á bliðe mod bealuleas kyng. *c* **1205** LAY. 29701 þa wes he ful bliðemod.

blithen ('blaɪð(ə)n), *v.* [mod.f. BLITHE *a.* + -EN²: cf. *gladden*.] *trans.* To make blithe.

1824 GALT *Rothelan* II. v. ix. 255 To blithen the morning with cheerful reveillies. **1830** —— *Lawrie T.* III. xv. (1849) 134 Glimpses of merriment..which blithen the fire-side.

blitheness ('blaɪðnɪs). [OE. *blíðnes, -nys*: f. *bliðe*, BLITHE + *-nes*: see -NESS.] The state of being blithe; joyousness, cheeriness, merriness, happiness. (*Orig.* a synonym of *bliss*.)

c **1000** *Sax. Leechd.* III. 212 Wineard wyrcen bliðnysse líf ȝetacnað. *a* **1275** *Prov. Alfred* in *O.E. Misc.* 105 He is one blisse ouer alle bliþnesse. *c* **1374** CHAUCER *Boeth.* II. iii. 37 Vnder the blyþenesse of people. **1578** *Gude & Godlie Ballates* (1868) 109 Giue me the blyithnes & the blis Of my sweit Sauiour. **1647** W. BROWNE *Polex.* II. 177 Give over your teares, and put on againe your former blithenesse. **1725** RAMSAY *Gent. Sheph.* v. iii. What double blytheness wakens up this day. **1874** HARDY *Madding Crowd* II. i. 14 Troy's blitheness might become aggressive.

†**'blither,** *sb.*¹ *Obs. rare.* [f. BLITHE *v.* + -ER¹.] One who makes blithe; a gladdener.

a **1455** *Houlate* xxiv, Hail, blyther of the Bapteist.

blither ('blɪðə(r)), *sb.*² (*dial.* or) *colloq.* [var. BLETHER *sb.*] Nonsense. Cf. BLETHER *sb.*

1866 *Banffshire Jrnl.* 27 Mar. 3 Some lightly [*i.e.* belittle] Scotland their auld mither An' ca' her tongue a vulgar blither. **1901** *Daily Chron.* 10 Aug. 4/7 We have heard a lot of blither (and, perhaps, a little sense). **1911** E. FERBER *Dawn O'Hara* v. 68 'What utter blither!' I scoffed.

blither ('blɪðə(r)), *v.* (*dial.* or) *colloq.* [var. BLETHER *v.*] *intr.* To talk nonsense; = BLETHER *v.* 1. Hence **'blitherer,** one who blithers; **'blithering** *vbl. sb.*

1868 VERNEY *Stone Edge* i, What did the imp come blitherin' and botherin' there for? **1902** W. RALEIGH *Let.* 6 Jan. (1926) I. 237 A 'Civic Society' of earnest burgesses and blitherers. **1903** J. K. JEROME *Tea-Table Talk* i. 20 If he was to blither, it was only fair that she should bleat back. **1916** W. OWEN *Let.* Aug. (1967) 402 One old blitherer let his bullet off by accident. **1921** *Blackw. Mag.* Oct. 455/1 The inevitable pasty-faced babu waddled up, blithering about the delay. **1925** *Public Opinion* 13 Mar. 258/2 He ignores all their blithering.

blithering ('blɪðərɪŋ), *ppl. a. colloq.* [f. BLITHER *v.* + -ING².] Senselessly discursive or talkative, babbling; esp. of a person, used chiefly as an intensive adjective, with the meaning 'consummate' (freq. in ***blithering idiot***); also more widely = despicable, contemptible.

1889 *Punch* 9 Feb. 65 I'll state pretty clearly that his son is a blithering idiot. **1895** *Ibid.* 30 Mar. 153, I had thought that you..would have had a soul above blithering detail. **1903** 'A. MCNEILL' *Egreg. Eng.* 179 These songs..are of the most blithering and bathotic nature. **1923** *Blackw. Mag.* Jan. 70/2, I was cursing myself for the blitheringest ass that ever was born. **1926** G. FRANKAU *Masterson* xxix, I was a blithering idiot to get in—knowing you as well as I do. **1928** 'REBECCA WEST' *Strange Necessity* 310 The blithering incompetence of English statesmen during the War of Independence.

blithesome ('blaɪðsəm), *a.* [f. BLITHE *a.* + -SOME: cf. *gladsome*.] Cheery.

1724 RAMSAY *Tea-t. Misc.* (1733) I. 89 The blythsome Bridal. **1794** SOUTHEY *Botany-B. Eclog.* ii, Blithesome as the lark. **1862** LYTTON *Str. Story* II. 176 The solitudes of that blithesome and hardy Nature.

'blithesomely, *adv.* [f. BLITHESOME *a.* + -LY².] In a blithesome manner; cheerily. So **'blithesomeness.**

1858 WHITTIER *Pipes at Lucknow* in *Writings* (1888) I. 185 Full tenderly and blithesomely The pipes of rescue blew! **1886** *New Princeton Rev.* II. 78 A glad blithesomeness belonged to her, potent to conquer even ill health and suffering. **1888** A. S. SWAN *Doris Cheyne* xvii, 'I should scold you.., but I am so glad to see you that I have not the heart,' she said blithesomely.

blitter, dial. f. BITTERN: cf. BOG-BLUTTER.
1788 BURNS *My Hoggie* ii, But the howlet cry'd frae the castle wa' The blitter frae the boggie.

blitz (blɪts), *sb.* [Short for BLITZKRIEG.] An attack or offensive launched suddenly with great violence with the object of reducing the defences immediately; *spec.* an air-raid or a series of them conducted in this way, esp. the series of air-raids made on London in 1940. Also *attrib.*
1940 *Daily Express* 9 Sept. 1 Blitz bombing of London goes on all night. *Ibid.* 10 Sept. 1/1 In his three-day blitz on London Goering has now lost 140 planes. **1940** *Daily Sketch* 21 Sept. 8/3 Neighbourhood Theatre braved the blitz and yesterday presented a new play. **1941** *New Statesman* 15 Feb. 160/3 The Home Guard of young architects who spent the night of the City 'blitz' battering out Hitler's incendiaries. **1944** *Ourselves in Wartime* viii. 177 All under five, many born since the beginning of the war, 'blitz' babies knew instinctively that the ground floor was safest. **1958** *New Statesman* 22 Feb. 223/3 Depopulation..began even before the war and the blitz.
b. *transf.* and *fig.*
1940 *Topeka Jrnl.* 19 Apr. 4/4 Setting the stage for a 'blitz' comeback. **1941** WYNDHAM LEWIS *Let.* 16 Apr. (1963) 288 At the time I was going through a minor economic Blitz of my own. **1960** *Guardian* 30 Dec. 10/5 The women did only the bare essentials of housework during the week, with a 'blitz' at weekends.
c. *N. Amer. Football.* A charge by one or more defensive backs into the offensive backfield, esp. to prevent or disrupt a passing play.
1963 S. HUFF *Defensive Football* viii. 98 Red-dogging answers to many names: storm, blitz, shooting, stunting. **1966** ROTE & WINTER *Lang. Pro Football* III. 104 *Blitz*, surprise defensive maneuver where one or more linebackers and/or defensive backfield men charge across line of scrimmage after ball carrier. **1970** *Washington Post* 30 Sept. D3/4 Left linebacker Bobby Bell pulled a blitz and first Colt he touched was Unitas. **1976** *Webster's Sports Dict.* 44/2 A blitz is sometimes successful in stopping a running play when an extra defensive player suddenly appears in the offensive backfield. **1984** *Washington Post* 22 Jan. B7 Send the corners on an all-out blitz.

blitz (blɪts), *v.* [f. prec.] **a.** To attack with a blitz; to hit, blast, destroy, etc., by an air-raid.
1939 in *Amer. Speech* (1940) XV. 110/2 Formal committee chairmen must have known how the poor Poles felt when the German blitzkrieg suddenly started 'blitzing' around their ears yesterday noon. **1940** *Daily Sketch* 2 Sept. 7 We 'blitz' hun planes in week-end raids. **1942** *Ann. Reg. 1941* 100, 70,000 meals had to be provided by the Emergency kitchens for people 'blitzed' out of their homes. **1945** 'G. ORWELL' in *Contemp. Jewish Record* VIII. 165 The Jewish quarter of Whitechapel was one of the first areas to be heavily blitzed.
b. *N. Amer. Football. intr.* To mount a blitz or blitzes (sense c); to charge the offensive backfield.
1965 *Sports Illustr.* 4 Jan. 11/2 The Browns, a team that seldom blitzes, blitzed more often in this game. **1968** *Globe & Mail* (Toronto) 15 Jan. 17/3 Lombardi said Oakland played generally as he expected 'although they did blitz a little more than we anticipated'. **1984** *Washington Post* 30 Jan. C1 Pro Bowl rules do not allow defenses to blitz. 'Without blitzing,' said Martin, 'it was his kind of day.'
So **blitzed** (blɪtst) *ppl. a.*, attacked or destroyed by a blitz; **ˈblitzing** *vbl. sb.* and *ppl. a.*; **ˈblitzer**, a defensive back who blitzes.
1940 *Daily Express* 6 Dec. 1/6 A south coast town felt the heaviest weight of last night's Nazi blitzing. **1941** *War Illustr.* 30 Dec. 377 For the past few months demolition squads have been working on this heavily blitzed site. **1955** *Times* 25 Aug. 5/4 Local authorities..decided to recondition 30,000 sub-standard houses in 'blitzed or blighted' areas. **1960** *Sports Illustr.* 4 Jan. 14/3 The Giants might have chased Unitas out of this formation by blitzing — sending the linebacker in after him to get him before he could throw. **1963** R. SMITH *Pro Football* xiii. 166 Conerly of the Giants dodged and ducked the blitzing Colts. **1968** *N.Y. Times* 6 Sept. 51 He's blocked well, picked up blitzers, caught the ball and has been a very quick runner with a good cut. **1968** H. HIGDON *Pro Football* v. 159 Chuck Drulis, our defensive coach, was the innovator of the safety blitz with Larry Wilson doing the blitzing. **1977** *Chicago Tribune* 2 Oct. III. 12/2 Fullback Russell Davis, bursting up the middle against swarming blitzers, led Michigan's ground game with 110 yards in 19 tries. **1984** *N.Y. Times* 16 Jan. C7/2 The Redskins are not a big blitzing team.

‖**Blitzkrieg, blitzkrieg** (ˈblɪtskriːg, -kriːk). [G., f. *blitz* lightning + *krieg* war.] (See BLITZ *sb.*)
1939 *War Illustr.* 7 Oct. 108/1 In the opening stage of the war all eyes were turned on Poland, where the German military machine was engaged in *Blitz-Krieg*—lightning war—with a view to ending as soon as possible. *Ibid.* 9 Dec. 386/3 Everything was ready for the opening of the 'Blitzkrieg' on the West. **1940** *Ann. Reg. 1939* 217 The complete failure of the Soviet *Blitzkrieg* [on Finland]. *Ibid.* 225 Germany's 'Blitzkrieg' methods had proved only too effective [in Poland]. **1940** *New Statesman* 19 Oct. 371/2 Since the Blitzkrieg started and people went underground. **1955** *Times* 25 June 6/2 It opened with the new type of blitzkrieg. Widespread 'atomic attacks' were made on major targets.
b. *transf.* and *fig.*
1939 *N.Y. Daily News* 19 Oct., Now that that blitzkrieg of puns is over. **1941** H. G. WELLS *You can't be too Careful* I. vi. 41 She had brought herself down to a vulnerability that gave any old germs a fair chance with her. Their blitzkrieg was swift and successful. **1963** *Times* 23 Feb. 9/6 Hours elapsed before the spate came jostling down the valley. Today it is a blitzkrieg.

bliue, obs. form of BELIVE *adv.* quickly.

blivit, blivet (ˈblɪvɪt). *U.S. slang.* (chiefly *joc.*). [Etym. unkn.; cf. BLIP *sb.*, WIDGET, and phonosymbolic force of *bl-* with repeated minimal vowel to indicate inconsequence, rejection, etc.] A pseudo-term for something useless, unnecessary, annoying, etc.; hence, = THINGAMAJIG (see quots.).
1967 WENTWORTH & FLEXNER *Dict. Amer. Slang* Suppl. 673/2 *Blivit*, n., anything unnecessary, confused, or annoying. Lit. defined as '10 pounds of shit in a 5-pound bag'. Orig. W.W. II Army use. The word is seldom heard except when the speaker uses it in order to define it; hence the word is actually a joke. **1980** *Aviation Week & Space Technol.* 15 Sept. 61 Refueling of helicopters..surfaced as an alternative to air dropping fuel blivits. **1981** *N.Y. Times* 27 Mar. C25/1 The main ingredient of this charm is a facility for saying it before you can, for calling 'Palm Sunday' a 'blivet' before you can call it a piece of junk. **1981** *Sci. Amer.* Dec. 28/2 This little book for grade school psychologists and philosophers presents a few dozen of these interesting but less familiar illusions, along with the arrow lengths, outline cubes, Eschers and three-pronged blivits of the standard optical-illusion list. **1982** *Industr. Robots Internat.* 22 Mar. 8 'Single station machines for assembly', he says, 'are blivets. Anybody who wants a definition can call me up.' **1983** *Washington Post* 26 Aug. D1 For such tasks, you obviously need a magic tool that lets you get 10 pounds into a five-pound bag. Such a heaven-sent, makeshift magic part is called a 'blivit'.

blizzard (ˈblɪzəd). [A modern word, prob. more or less onomatopœic; suggestive words are *blow, blast, blister, bluster*: the Fr. *blesser* to wound, has also been conjectured, but there is nothing to indicate a French origin. As applied to a 'snow-squall,' the word became general in the American newspapers during the severe winter of 1880-81; but according to the *Milwaukee Republican* 4 Mar. 1881, it had been so applied in the *Northern Vindicator* (Estherville, Iowa) between 1860 and 1870. It was apparently in colloquial use in the West much earlier; but whether Col. Crockett's use of it in 1834 (sense 1) was *fig.*, taken from the stifling blast, or was the earlier sense, and subseq. transferred to the blast, is not determined.]
1. A sharp blow or knock; a shot. Also *fig. U.S.*
1829 *Virginia Lit. Museum* 16 Dec. 418 *Blizzard*, a violent blow. **1834** CROCKETT *Tour down East* 16 (Bartlett) A gentleman at dinner asked me for a toast; and supposing he meant to have some fun at my expense, I concluded to go ahead, and give him and his likes a blizzard. **1856** *Sacramento City* (Cal.) *Item* (Th.), When some true archer, from the upper tier, Gave him a 'blizzard' on the nearest ear. **1872** SCHELE DE VERE *Americanisms* 443 *Blizzard*..means in the West a stunning blow or an overwhelming argument.
2. A furious blast of frost-wind and blinding snow, in which man and beast frequently perish; a 'snow-squall'. Also *attrib.* and *Comb.* orig. *U.S.*
1859 L. B. WOLF *Diary* 1 Dec. in *Kansas Hist. Q.* (1932) I. 205 A blizzard had come upon us about midnight... Shot 7 horses that were so chilled could not get up. **1876** *Monthly Weather Rev.* Dec. 424 The very severe storms known in local parlance as 'blizzards' were reported on the 8th as prevailing in Iowa and Wisconsin. **1880** *Let.* 29 Dec., fr. Chicago in *Manch. Even. News*, 24 Jan. 1881 The thermometer was 17 degrees below zero last night, and it was blowing a blizzard all the time. **1881** *Standard* 22 Jan. 5/1 The region [Manitoba] is swept by those fearful blasts known as 'blizzards' which send the 'poudre', or dry snow, whirling in icy clouds. **1881** *N.Y. Nation* 184 The hard weather has called into use a word which promises to become a national Americanism, namely 'blizzard'. It designates a storm (of snow and wind) which men cannot resist away from shelter. **1882** *Contemp. Rev.* Sept. 350 Those bitter 'blizzards' so justly dreaded by all who have to do with live stock. **1888** T. WATTS in *Athenæum* 18 Aug. 224/2 By Ferrol Bay those galleys stoop To blasts more dire than breath of Orkney blizzard. **1902** R. F. SCOTT *Jrnl.* 12 Aug. in *Voyage of 'Discovery'* (1905) I. ix. 383 Another blizzard, so thick that one cannot see one's hand before one's face. **1903** *Ibid.* 12 Dec. II. xviii. 276 Our long stay in the blizzard camp. **1912** —— *Jrnl.* Mar. in *Scott's Last Expedition* (1913) I. xx. 592 It was blowing a blizzard. He [*sc.* Captain Oates] said, 'I am just going outside and may be some time.' He went out into the blizzard and we have not seen him since. **1963** D. W. & E. E. HUMPHRIES tr. *Termier's Erosion & Sedimentation* i. 8 The coldest, blizzard-swept regions of the world. **1969** *Times* 8 Feb. 1/2 Blizzards and icy winds swept across Britain yesterday.
Hence **ˈblizzarded** *pa. pple.*, a more emphatic form of 'blowed' (BLOW *v.*[1] 29); **ˈblizzardy** *a.*, characterized by, or resembling, a blizzard or blizzards; **ˈblizzardly, ˈblizzardous** *a.*
1883 *Let.* in *Advance* 1 Mar., Driving snow, with very blizzardly tendencies. **1888** *San Francisco News Let.* (Farmer), I should like to have seen the Colonel's face when he got that very cold blizzardy letter. **1892** GUNTER *Miss Dividends* I. vi. 67 Then he suddenly ejaculates 'Well I'm blizzarded!' **1946** *Chicago Daily News* 5 Mar. 8/4 [It] would ruin the disposition of the throngs..especially on blizzardy nights.

†**blo**, *a. Obs.* Also bloe, bloo, blow(e. [The midland and southern form of the word still preserved in north.Eng. and Sc. as *blae, blea*:—ON. *blá* livid. *Blo* died out in literary Eng. during the 16th or 17th c.: for the etymology and senses, see BLAE.] Blackish blue, livid, leaden-coloured. (In early writers sometimes = BLUE.)
c **1250** *Gen. & Ex.* 637 Rein-bowe, men cleped reed and blo. *c* **1314** *Guy Warw.* (A.) 341 Tristor he hete wiþ þe berd blowe. *c* **1325** *E.E. Allit. P.* C. 221 In bluber of þe blo flod. **1377** LANGL. *P. Pl.* B. III. 97 Al to blo [C. IV. 125 blewe] askes. *c* **1430** *Pol. Rel. & L. Poems* (1866) 206 Nowe ligiȝt he ded boþe blok and blo. *c* **1440** *Promp. Parv.* 40 Blo erþe, *argilla.* **1526** SKELTON *Magnyf.* 2080, I wax bothe wanne and bloo. **1530** PALSGR. 306/2 Blo, blewe and grene coloured, as ones body is after a drie stroke. **1565** GOLDING *Ovid's Met.* III. (1593) 56 Licking with his blo and blasting toong their sorie wounds. **1652** RIPLEY *Comp. Alch.* in Ashmole 188 The Crowys byll bloe as lede. **1788** W. MARSHALL *Yorksh.* (1796) II. 65 The blue, blow, or lead-coloured flax.
Hence **blo-wipe**, a blow or stroke causing a bruise.
1622 R. CALLIS *Stat. Sewers* (1647) 169 If one be presented in a Leet Court for a Blowipe or any other personal wrong.

†**bloached**, *ppl. a. Obs.* [? a corruption or modification of BLOTCHED.] Blotched with yellow or white, variegated; hence ***bloached-leaved*** adj.
1725 BRADLEY *Fam. Dict.* s.v. *Phyllyrea*, The plain Phyllyrea, and the bloach'd leav'd one, are very quick Growers. **1769** H. T. CROKER *Dict. Arts & Sc.* III. s.v. *Variegation*, Those leaves whose middles are variegated with yellow or white, in spots, are called bloached.

bloak, variant of BLOKE, *slang*, man.

bloamon, var. of BLOMAN, *Obs.*, a blackamoor.

bloat (bləʊt), *sb.* [f. BLOAT *a.*[2]]
1. a. Bloatedness.
1905 G. B. SHAW *Irrational Knot* xi. 226 He..had noted with aversion a certain unhealthy bloat in her face. **1911** F. H. BURNETT *Secret Garden* xxvii. 300 If he took his food natural sir, you'd think he was putting on flesh—but we're afraid it may be a sort of bloat.
b. *spec.* in *Veterinary Path.* A disease of livestock characterized by an accumulation of gases in the stomach; = HOOVE.
1878 G. H. DADD *Amer. Cattle Doctor* iii. 65 *Tympanites rumenites* signifies distension of the rumen in the bovine species—the ox and cow—and, in the phraseology of the grazier, is known as bloat or hoven. **1962** R. SEIDEN *Livestock Health Encycl.* (ed. 2) 65/2 *Bloat*, hoven, tympanites, or tympany in livestock (especially in cattle, sheep and goats)..is primarily caused by vigorous fermentation in the rumen.
2. A conceited or contemptible person (see also quot. 1888). *U.S. slang.*
1860 in *Amer. Speech* (1947) XXII. 299/1, I considered such an old bloat not worth minding. **1871** *Congress. Globe* Feb., App. 129/1 Wife whippers, penitentiary birds, street vagabonds, beastly bloats, and convicted felons. **1888** FARMER *Americanisms* 64/1 *Bloat* (cant), a drowned body; also a drunkard.
3. 'A hammer swelled at the eye.' Raymond *Mining Gloss.* 1881.

bloat (bləʊt), *a.*[1] Also 3-6 blote, 7 bloate. [The spelling *bloat* occurs in this sense earlier than in that of next word, with which this is often identified, though in the present state of our knowledge it is safer to keep them distinct. The ME. *blote* is perhaps identical with ON. *blaut-r* in the sense 'soft with moisture, soaked, wet'; or from a parallel form **blót-*: cf. the ME. vb. *blotne*, ON. *blotna* to soften, moisten (see BLOTEN), also Sw. *blöt* soft, moist, yielding. But it would also answer in form to OE. *blát* 'livid, pale', though this sense is less likely. Sense 2 recalls ON. *blautr fiskr*, i.e. 'soft fish', applied to 'fresh' fish, but in Sw. *blöt fisk*, to 'soaked' fish (Vigf.). Though evidence of actual connexion is wanting, it is conjectured that the Eng. 'bloat herring' is, in some way, identical with these, and means, etymologically, either 'soft (moist) herring', in opposition to 'dried', or else 'soaked, steeped herring', in reference to part of the process of curing the herrings so termed. In *Act 18 Chas. II.* ii. 'bloated' is opposed to 'dried', and it is explained by Blount as 'half-dried'; but most of the quotations give it as meaning (in actual use) 'smoked', (smoking being an important part of the process). One at least (1613 below) appears to identify it with 'puffed up', and thus with sense 2 of the next word, whereas Sylvester, in 1616, says 'Herrings shrink in bloating'; but moist herrings are naturally plumper than those more thoroughly dried. See also next word, and BLOAT *v.*[1]]
†**1.** ? Soft with moisture (or ? livid, pale). *Obs.*
c **1300** *Of Men Lif* xiii. in *E.E.P.* (1862) 154 ȝe sutters [? *suters* = sutors]..wiþ ȝour blote hides of selcuþ bestis.
2. ***bloat herring***: a smoked half-dried herring, cured by the process described in BLOAT *v.*[1]; a bloated herring, a bloater. Also a term of contempt for a human being. ? *Obs.*
a **1586** SIDNEY *Remed. for Love* 65 (Grosart II. 176) Her compound, or electuary, Made of olde linge or caviarie,

Blote herringe, cheese. **1602** DEKKER *Satirom.* 245 Bloate herring dost heere? *a***1613** OVERBURY *A Wife* (1638) 177 He'l bee puft up to your hand like a bloat Herring. **1621** B. JONSON *Masque Augurs*, You stink like so many bloat-herrings newly taken out of the chimney! **1661** PEPYS 5 Oct., To the Dolphin, and there eat some bloat herrings.

bloat (bləʊt), *a.*² Forms: 4 bloute, 6–7 blowt(e, 7– bloat. [Apparently distinct at first (as an Eng. word) from the prec., since the earlier form of that was *blote*, but of this *blout*; though of parallel origin, and, since the 17th c., identified in form, and often associated in meaning. ME. *blout, blowt*, was the regular adopted form of ON. *blautr-* soft (as a baby's limbs, a bed, silk; see Vigf.); cf. Sw. *blöt* 'soft, yielding, pulpous, pulpy'. The later form *bloat* does not answer phonetically to *blout, blowt*, yet its modern use is largely owing to the 'blowt king' of Hamlet having been printed 'bloat' by editors since Warburton, 1747; G. Daniel had also spelt the word in this way *c* 1640–50. Possibly BLOAT *a.*¹ in 'bloat herrings' (found as early as 1602) was in the 17th c. a much better known word than this, and being, rightly or wrongly, identified with it, influenced its form. It is to be noted that BLOAT *v.*, and its derivatives BLOATED, BLOATING, are all of earlier use as applied to the herring, than in senses connected with this word. Sense 2 is a natural enough extension of 1; but it may have been influenced by association with *blow, blown*; the mutual influence of this and the prec. since 1600, cannot be settled without more definite knowledge of the exact notion at first attached to 'bloat herring'.]

†**1.** *Blowte, bloute*: ? Soft, soft-bodied, flabby, pulpy; passing into 'puffy, puffed, swollen'. *Obs.*

c **1300** *Havelok* 1910 He leyden on . . [blows] . . He maden here backes al so bloute Als he[re] wombes, and made hem rowte Als he weren kradel-barnes. **1602** SHAKS. *Ham.* III. iv. 182 Let the blowt king tempt you againe to bed. [So all the Quartos, exc. Q 1, where wanting; the Folios read *blunt*.] **1603** H. CROSSE *Vertues Commw.* (1878) 145 The body I say is subiect to so much pestilence . . the face blowte, puft vp, and stuft with the flockes of strong beere.

2. *Bloat*: Puffed, swollen, inflated, esp. with self-indulgence. Hence ***bloat-faced*** adj. (In modern writers an echo of Shakspere's word since that has been written *bloat*. BLOATED occurs in the same sense from 1664.)

1638–48 G. DANIEL *Eclog.* iii. 83 The foolish rites Of bloatfac'd Bacchus. **1649** —— *Trinarch., Hen. V*, ccxcii, The Bloat Face of Rusticitie, Smuggs, looking in A Mirrour. **1747** [WARBURTON printed *bloat* for *blowt* and *blunt* in Hamlet.] **1832** *Blackw. Mag.* XXXII. 661 The bloat and ugly villain. **1857** HEAVYSEGE *Saul* (1869) 332 To fetch a calf or sheep, That its bloat master may it stick and slay? **1861** TEMPLE & TREVOR *Tannhäuser* 11 From foul embrace Of that bloat Queen.

b. *transf.*

[**1635** QUARLES *Embl.* I. Invoc., Scorn, scorn to feed on thy old bloat desires. (? cf. *bloat herring*.)] **1646** G. DANIEL *Poems* Wks. 1878 I. 89 What I loose or win To bloat opinion, that below my fate I ever value.

bloat, *v.*¹ Also 7 blote. [App. f. BLOAT *a.*¹, with the sense 'to make bloat'.]

trans. To cure (herrings) by a process which leaves them soft and only half-dried. This is now done by leaving them in dry salt on a floor for 24 hours, washing in fresh water, spitting, and smoking them over an oak fire for a period varying from 24 hours to 3 or 4 days, according to the time they are to be kept before being eaten. (Earlier authorities speak of their being *steeped* for a time in brine before smoking; which has to be remembered in discussing the original meaning of *bloat*.)

Bloated herrings are opposed to *dried* or *red* herrings, which are left in 10 days, and smoked for 14 days, whence their deep colour and shrivelled dryness.

1611 COTGR., *Fumer*, to . . bloat, besmoake, hang, or drie in the smoake. **1618** FLETCHER *Isl. P'cess* II. i. 102, I have more smoke in my mouth then would Blote a hundred herrings. **1682** J. COLLINS *Salt & Fishery* 109 Of Bloated and Dryed Fish. These the Fishmongers say are bloated as followeth, to wit, they sink them 3 or 4 hours in a Brine . . and then hang them up a drying in Chimnies.

bloat, *v.*² [app. f. BLOAT *a.*²: its identity with or distinctness from the prec. depends of course upon the relation of the two adjectives.]

1. a. *trans.* To blow out, inflate, swell, make turgid. Also *absol.*

1677 DRYDEN *Circe* Prol. 25 Encourage him, and bloat him up with praise, That he may get more bulk before he dies. **1711** ADDISON *Spect.* No. 127 ¶6 To see so many well-shaped innocent Virgins bloated up, and waddling up and down like big-bellied Women. **1727–51** CHAMBERS *Cycl.* s.v. *Epispastic*, Of epispasticks, there are some which . . swell and bloat the skin. **1748** CHESTERF. *Lett.* II. clviii. 64 All malt-liquors fatten, or at least bloat. **1815** *Encycl. Brit.* III. 549 Butchers have a kind of blast or bellows . . by which they bloat or blow up their meat when killed. **1834** H. MILLER *Scenes & Leg.* xvi. (1857) 240 Dead bodies . . bloated by the water. *a* **1878** STIRLING-MAXWELL in *Edin. Rev.* No. 323. 19 Excess, both in eating and drinking . . had bloated his cheek.

b. *fig.*

1896 J. A. HOBSON *Probl. Unempl.* 1 Well-meaning . . social reformers stretch the term ['unemployment'] and bloat it out to gigantic proportions.

2. *intr.* To swell, become swollen or turgid.

a **1735** ARBUTHNOT (J.) If a person of a firm constitution begins to bloat. **1813** T. JEFFERSON *Corr.* (1830) 221 No man knows what his property is worth, because it is bloating while he is calculating. **1839** *Fraser's Mag.* XIX. 94 Who shut me up In darkness . . to fatten, swell, and bloat.

bloated ('bləʊtɪd), *ppl. a.*¹ [f. BLOAT *v.*¹ + -ED.] Of fish: Cured by the process described in BLOAT *v.*¹; half-dried in smoke.

1648 HERRICK *Oberon's F.* Poems (1869) I. 127 A newt's stew'd thigh, A bloated earwig. **1666** *Act 18 Chas. II*, ii, Any Ling, Herring, Cod or Pilchard, fresh or salt, dried or bloated. **1670** BLOUNT *Law Dict.*, *Bloated Fish* or Herring . . are those which are half-dried. **1753** CHAMBERS *Cycl. Supp.* s.v., Bloated herrings are made by steeping them in a peculiar brine, and then hanging them in a chimney to dry. **1830** M. DONOVAN *Dom. Econ.* II. 239 A new flavor . . in which that of a bloated herring is sometimes distinguishable.

'bloated, *ppl. a.*² [f. BLOAT *v.*² + -ED.]

1. Of the body, face, etc.: Swollen, puffed up, turgid; *esp.* as describing the effect of gluttony and self-indulgence.

1664 H. MORE *Myst. Iniq.* 475 Disguised in some uncouth habit with circumcised crowns, and moaped or bloated looks. **1711** F. FULLER *Med. Gymn.* 56 A Bloated Habit of Body. **1713** *Guardian* No. 17 (1756) I. 79 The tender fool has wept till her eyes are swelled and bloated. **1782** COWPER *Prog. Err.* 495 Bloated spiders. **1820** KEATS *St. Agnes* xxxix, The bloated wassailers will never heed.

2. *transf.* and *fig.* **a.** Of things: Swollen, inflated, crammed; overgrown, of excessive size.

1711 *Werenfelsius' Meteors of Stile* 235 He affected the Eloquence of bloated and high-sounding Words. **1785** COWPER *Task* I. 739 His overgorged and bloated purse. **1846** PRESCOTT *Ferd. & Is.* III. xvi. 194 The bloated magnificence of succeeding monarchs. **1862** DISRAELI in *Hansard* Ser. III. CLXVI. 1426 Those bloated armaments which naturally involve states in financial embarassments. **1879** GEO. ELIOT *Theo. Such* ii. 47 Its bloated, idle charities.

b. Of persons or their attributes: Swollen with pride of rank or wealth; puffed up, pampered.

1731 SWIFT *To Gay* Wks. 1755 IV. I. 169 A statesman . . A bloated minister. **1863** STANLEY *Jew. Ch.* xiii. 311 The bloated pluralists of the mediæval Church. **1868** J. H. BLUNT *Ref. Ch. Eng.* I. 355 The 'bloated aristocracy' of a republican ideal.

3. *Comb.*, as ***bloated-bellied*** adj.

1875 B. TAYLOR *Faust* I. xxi. 180 Is't the salamander pushes Bloated-bellied through the bushes?

bloatedness ('bləʊtɪdnɪs). [f. prec. + -NESS.] Bloated quality or state.

1660 H. MORE *Myst. Godl.* x. xiv. 538 Unsound blotedness and ventosity of Spirit. **1732** ARBUTHNOT *On Diet* ii. (R.) Bloatedness, scorbutical spots. *c* **1875** BESANT & RICE *Harp & Cr.* xx. 209 To paint the bloatedness of our prelates.

bloater ('bləʊtə(r)). [f. BLOAT *a.*¹ + -ER: app. like the vulgar *deader, liver, four-wheeler.*] A 'bloat' or bloated herring: see BLOAT *a.*¹, *v.*¹

1832 S. TYMMS *Family Topogr.* III. 142 Herrings, at Yarmouth where the method of curing is unrivalled, called 'Yarmouth bloaters.' **1871** M. COLLINS *Mrq. & Merch.* II. iv. 97 He had been breakfasting on a bloater. **1882** BUCKLAND *Notes Anim. Life* 202 Real Yarmouth bloaters are herrings very slightly salted, and smoked for three or four hours only.

bloating ('bləʊtɪŋ), *vbl. sb.*¹ [f. BLOAT *v.*¹ + -ING¹.] The process of curing (fish) by smoking for a short time; the preparation of bloaters.

1616 SYLVESTER *Tobacco Batt.* 499 Herrings, in the Sea, are large and full, But shrink in bloating, and together pull.

'bloating, *vbl. sb.*² [f. BLOAT *v.*² + -ING¹.] 'A puffing up or inflation of the exterior habit of the body, lodged chiefly in the adipose cells.' Chambers *Cycl. Supp.* 1753.

'bloating, *ppl. a.* That bloats or (?) blotches.

1759 W. WILKIE *Epigon.* v. (1769) 106 His crooked form he reared With horror pale, with bloating clay besmeared.

†**'bloaty**, *a. Obs. rare.* [In this and the prec. it looks as if *bloat* were confounded with *blot*, and 'bloated' taken as 'disfigured with blotches'.]

1705 HICKERINGILL *Priest-Cr.* II. viii. 76 Dashing out those bloody and bloaty Colours, wherewith Superstition has pourtrayed and arayed him [the Creator].

blob (blɒb), *sb.*¹ Also 9 *Sc.* blab. [The vb. appears in 15th, the sb. in 16th c. Like BLEB, expressing the action of the lips in producing a bubble. Some feeling of association with BLOW may have helped the formation or perpetuation of the word. Cf. BLAB, BLOBBER, BLUBBER.]

1. A bubble. *Obs.* exc. *north. dial.*

1536 BELLENDEN *Cron. Scot.* (1821) I. p. xliii, Gif thay be handillit, thay melt away like ane blob of watter. **1570** LEVINS *Manip.* 154 Blob on the water, *bulla.* **1863** MRS. TOOGOOD *Yorksh. Dial.*, *Watter-blobs*, bubbles of soap and water made with a pipe by children. **1875** *Whitby Gloss.* (E.D.S.) *Bleb* or *Blob*, a bubble.

2. A pimple, pustule. *north. dial.* Also *fig.*

1597 LOWE *Chirurg.* (1634) 82 Little blobs upon the skin, produced of an ebulition of the bloud. **1614** *Sco. Venus* (1876) 32 O filthy blob and staine.

3. a. A drop or globule of liquid or viscid substance. Also *fig.*

1725 RAMSAY *Gentle Sheph.* II. ii, Her een the clearest blob o' dew outshines. **1823** GALT *Entail* I. xxiii. 201 Haud it [a humble bee] till I take out the honey blob. **1857** HUGHES *Tom Brown* iii, The letter was . . stuck down with a blob of ink. **1866** ARGYLL *Reign of Law* ii. (ed. 4) 120 Animals which are mere blobs of jelly. **1905** W. RALEIGH *Lett.* (1926) II. 286 Christianity caught on by its very rumness; all the loose floating blobs of superstition ran to it.

b. Applied to a soft round fruit, as a gooseberry; also *dial.* to globular or drop-like flowers, as the Globe-flower, Foxglove, etc.

c **1750** LD. BALMERINO in Ramsay *Remin.* (ed. 18) 254 Gie me a ha'porth of honey blobs [yellow gooseberries]. **1868** HOLME LEE *B. Godfrey* xlix. 275 The scarlet blobs [= cherries] that they . . loved.

c. Someone of no account, a 'cipher' or fool. *colloq.* and *slang* (chiefly *Austral.*).

1916 J. B. COOPER *Coo-oo-ee* ii. 26 How do I know he loves me if he does not tell me so? . . There's half a dozen 'blobs' here who would do so if I gave them the chance. **1917** W. OWEN *Let.* 2 Sept. (1967) 490 They had to mind their babies . . unmannerly blobs of one to three years. **1920** B. CRONIN *Timber Wolves* x. 185 Maybe they're all right, but it don't do to run risks. Tell some of them blobs they'll need to walk to Green Valley next time they get a thirst up, if they don't act reasonable. **1936** M. FRANKLIN *All that Swagger* li. 472 Adrienne was no blob or woop-woop. **1945** BAKER *Austral. Lang.* vi. 130 Fools of one kind and another . . *Billy Muggins, blob*, boofhead, [etc.]. **1983** *Listener* 3 Feb. 19/3 If you could only see what a pathetic blob you look in your leotard and tights you'd never do another class.

4. a. A small rounded mass of colour.

1863 *Reader* 31 Oct. 502 In the design one of the wrestlers [is] destitute of eyebrows . . but adorned with compensating blobs of hair upon the forehead. **1872** BLACK *Adv. Phaeton* v. 54 A little blob of strong colour. **1880** BIRDWOOD *Ind. Art* II. 9 Worthless gems which have no value as precious stones, but only as barbaric blobs of colour.

b. *Cricket colloq.* A batsman's score of no runs, so called from the zero placed against his name in the score-sheet; = DUCK'S EGG b. Hence *fig.* generally, 'nought'; also, a senseless error, a blunder.

1889 *Cricket* 18 Apr. 60/2 St. Leonard's were all out for 25 . . Seven 'blobs' was the total. **1903** *Punch* 27 May 366 To come home and be treated as if I'd made a brace of blobs. **1912** J. B. HOBBS *Recov. Ashes* 19 Mr. Foster . . taking the first wicket of the tour by bowling Mr. E. R. Mayne for a 'blob'. **1952** M. ALLINGHAM *Tiger in Smoke* i. 17 Crooks can be . . wanting in the top storey, but I've never heard of one who'd make a blob like that. **1958** B. HAMILTON *Too Much of Water* vi. 134 A cricketer . . may make a string of blobs, and then hit a couple of hundreds. **1960** L. COOPER *Accomplices* II. ii. 86 He'd been in trouble with us before and he knew that another blob would about finish him.

5. A solid oval mass of iron forming the base of one of the iron beams or posts which support the deck of a ship.

1863 *Times* 19 Mar. 14/2 The tee, the beam, and the blob were made separately in lengths, and then welded together.

6. a. *fig.* A pouting lower lip.

1762 COLLINS *Misc.* 122 (Halliw.) Wit hung her blob, ev'n Humour seem'd to mourn.

b. *slang phrase. on the blob*: by word of mouth. Cf. BLAB.

1851 MAYHEW *Lond. Lab.* I. 311 Those [professional beggars] who 'do it on the blob' (by word of mouth) and those who do it by 'screwing', that is, by petitions and letters.

7. *Comb.*, as ***blob-cheeked***, ***-headed*** adjs.

1552 HULOET, Blobbe cheked, *buccones.* **1553** T. WILSON *Rhet.* 78 b, A man with a bottell nose, blobb cheaked. **1865** *Morn. Star* 8 May, A blob-headed man with mauve-coloured hair.

blob, *sb.*² *local.* A bait used in fishing for eels, consisting of a worm strung on a worsted thread. (Cf. BOB *sb.*¹ 7.)

1874 E. PEACOCK *J. Markenfield* vii, Along o' my runnin' away wi' her crewell ball, and makin' a blobb for eels wi' it. **1905** *Westm. Gaz.* 28 Apr. 3/1 Your plan is now, when the eel is thus grabbing the worm, to lift the 'blob' very gently.

blob, *v.* Chiefly *north.* Also 6 blab. [cf. BLOB *sb.*¹]

1. *trans.* To mark with a blob of ink or colour; to blot or blur.

1429 *Sc. Acts. Jas. I*, II. 17/2 Swa þat þai halde þe forme of the breif . . & be nocht rasit na blobit in suspect place. **1599** PORTER *Angry Wom. Abingd.* (1841) 91 She will not haue one of those pearled starres To blab her sable metamorphosis. **1609** SKENE *Reg. Maj.* 114 Gif the libell or summons is blobbed, or rased in suspect places.

2. *intr.* To rise in a bubble or bubbles.

1855 *Whitby Gloss.*, *Blob*, to boil or bubble up like water, when anything acts upon it by plunging or otherwise.

3. *intr.* ? To produce blobs or bubbles; to 'flop' in the water.

1875 *Whitby Gloss.* (E.D.S.) *Blob*, to plunge into the water. **1884** *Blackw. Mag.* Mar. 346/1 The wretched trout . . blobbing and jumping on the stream.

4. *intr.* To make a 'blob' (see BLOB *sb.*¹ 4 b); to score no runs. *Cricket colloq.*

1905 N. GALE *More Cricket Songs* 34 I've tasted Sweet and bitter supplied by Luck, . . Whether I blobbed or whether I stuck.

blobbed, *ppl. a.* [f. BLOB *sb.*[1] + -ED[2].] Affected with pimples or swellings.

1486 *Bk. St. Albans* C vj b, When thou seeth thy hauke vppon his mouth and his chekis blobbed.

blobber ('blɒbə(r)), *a.* [A variant of BLABBER, perh. influenced by BLOB.]

Of the lips: Thick, swollen, protruding. Hence **blobber-lipped** *a.* Cf. BLUBBER *a.*

1593 *Pass. Morrice* 83 She was monstrous blobber lipt. **1674** GREW (J.) A blobber-lipped shell seemeth to be a kind of mussel. **1685** DRYDEN *Lucretius* Misc. Wks. (1760) II. 457 Hanging blobber lips but pout for Kisses. **1692** R. L'ESTRANGE *Fables* i. (1714) 1 Some will have his Person deformed..Blobber-Lipp'd. **1818** *Blackw. Mag.* III. 282 Lazy streams of delight from their blobber lips falling.

blobber, obs. and dial. f. BLUBBER *sb.* and *v.*

blobbing ('blɒbɪŋ), *vbl. sb. local.* [f. BLOB *sb.*[2]] The method of fishing with a bob for eels (cf. BOBBING *vbl. sb.* 3).

1877 E. PEACOCK *Gloss. Manley, Blobbing*, a method of catching eels by means of worms strung on a worsted thread. **1905** *Westm. Gaz.* 28 Apr. 3/1 That is 'blobbing'.

blobby ('blɒbɪ), *a.* [f. BLOB *sb.*[1] + -Y[1].] Characterized by blobs; resembling a blob.

1882 *Garden* 10 June 399/3 A delicious bunch of Pinks.. fringed petals—blobby flowers. **1884** *American* VII. 253 Flat and blobby fragments.

blober, -ure, -yr, obs. forms of BLUBBER.

†'**blob-tale.** *Obs.* [f. *blob*, var. of BLAB + TALE. Cf. the combs. in BLAB *v.*[1] 5.] A tell-tale.

a **1670** HACKET *Abp. Williams* II. (1692) 67 These blob-tales, when they could find no other news to keep their tongues in motion, laid open our Bishop for a malignant.

‖**bloc** (blɒk). [Fr., = BLOCK *sb.*] In Continental politics, a combination of divergent political parties which supports the government in power. Also *transf.*, a combination of persons, groups, parties, or nations formed to foster a particular interest. Also *attrib.*, as in *bloc vote* = *block vote* s.v. BLOCK *sb.* 24.

1903 *Ann. Reg. 1902* 272 The Government remained in the hands of the *bloc*; and the Radical-Socialist party was free to proceed with the enforcement of the law with regard to the Congregations. **1905** *Spectator* 14 Jan. 38/1 It is more probable..that when the votes are open the members of the 'Bloc' will shrink from turning out M. Combes. **1907** *Westm. Gaz.* 5 Dec. 5/1 Prince Bülow..summoned the leaders of the 'bloc' parties to a meeting. **1908** *Daily Chron.* 9 Oct. 4/6 Clémenceau, who was..the man of the Bloc, who had invented the name. **1921** *Nation* 21 Sept. 308/2 The formation of the agricultural bloc which came close to holding the balance of power in the Senate. **1923** *Daily Mail* 29 Mar. 6 France also can stand apart from Great Britain. She can join a Continental *bloc* with Italy and the Little Entente and Belgium. **1946** *Times* 22 May 5/5 The Soviet Union has been..forming a compact and well-organized political and economic *bloc*, stretching from the Baltic to the Black Sea. **1957** *Observer* 29 Dec. 1/4 Military circles in Jakarta have indicated that they believe in the superiority of American to Soviet bloc weapons. **1969** *Latin Amer.* 28 Feb. 72/2 It looks as if previous support for Brazilian UN resolutions from the African bloc vote is likely to diminish. **1985** *Washington Post* 12 July A8/5 The bloc vote, taken in a fast-emptying chamber as senators headed home after a grueling week, will allow several key nominees to take office.

bloc, variant of BLOKE *a. Obs.* pale; black.

†'**bloccuz.** *Obs.* [a. 16th c. F. *blocus*, now *blockhaus*, BLOCKHOUSE *sb.*] A fortification, a bulwark.

1600 HOLLAND *Livy* VIII. xxv. 299 e By certaine skonces and bloccuzes [*munimentis*] betweene the enemies fortes and forces, one part was cut from the other.

block (blɒk), *sb.* Forms: 4–5 blok, 5 blokke, 5–7 blocke, 6 block. [In sense 1, app. a ME. adoption of F. *bloc*, of same meaning; but in senses 17–20 taken directly from BLOCK *v.* OF. *bloc* is, according to Diez and Littré, a. OHG. *bloh* (MHG. *bloch*, mod.Ger. *block*) in same sense (MDu. *bloc*, Du. *blok*, MLG. *block*, Sw. *block*, Da. *blok*), the origin of which is uncertain. Grimm and others identify it with MHG. *bloch*, OHG. *biloh* (MDu. *beloc, beloke*) 'closure, obstruction, shut place,' referred to *bi-lûkan*, f. *lûkan* to close, shut. Kluge considers it a distinct word, and possibly related farther back to *balk* BALK.]

I. A solid piece of wood.

1. A log of wood; part of the trunk of a tree, a stump.

c **1305** *Leg. Rood* (1871) 141 Whon crist was knit with corde on a stok His bodi bledde a-ȝein þat blok. **1393** GOWER *Conf.* I. 314 This king..made..Of grete shides and of blockes Great fire. **1481** CAXTON *Reynard* (Arb.) 27 They.. drewe hym ouer stones and ouer blockes wythout the village. **1552** HULOET, Blocke, *truncus.* **1594** T. B. *La Primaud. Fr. Acad.* II. 131 [No] more motion or feeling then is in a blocke or stone. **1830** DISRAELI *Home Lett.* x. 84, I looked at the wood fire and thought of the blazing blocks in the hall at Bradenham. **1884** FROUDE *Carlyle* II. xxiii. 176 Sitting patient on a big block—huge stump of a tree-root.

b. Often used in similes as a type of inertia, senselessness, stupidity. Cf. sense 15: also POST.

c **1410** *Sir Cleges* 440 He yaffe the styward sech a stroke, That he fell dovn as a bloke. **1678** *Ripley Reviv'd* 383 They are as stupid as Blocks. **1718** POPE *Auth. Successio* 10 When you like Orpheus, strike the warbling lyre, Attentive blocks stand round you and admire. **1875** BUCKLAND *Log-Bk.* 68 As deaf as a block.

†**c.** *contemptuously.* An idol, a 'stock'.

1563–87 FOXE *A. & M.* (1596) 1340/1 His great God was not exalted..ouer the aultar, nor his blocke almighty set seemely in the roode loft.

†**d.** Contrasted with 'straw' in some obsolete proverbial phrases. Cf. sense 11: also BEAM and MOTE. *Obs.*

1526 *Pilgr. Perf.* (W. de W. 1531) 93 Lest of a strawe we make a blocke. **1551** CRANMER *Answ. Bp. Gardiner* 201 (T.) You can spy a little mote in another mans eye, that cannot see a great block in your own. **1562** J. HEYWOOD *Prov. & Epigr.* (1867) 76 Ye stumbled at a strawe, and lept ouer a blocke.

†**2.** The stump or trunk of a figure without the limbs.

1535 COVERDALE 1 *Sam.* v. 5 The block laie there onely.

3. A large solid piece of wood, of which the top or surface is used for various operations:

a. A piece of wood on which a butcher chops his meat, or on which firewood is cut, or which is used for beetling or hammering on, or otherwise in various mechanical crafts. ***between the beetle and the block***: see BEETLE[1] 1 c.

c **1485** *Digby Myst.* (1882) i. 157 If I fynde a yong child I shall choppe it on a blokke. **1766** ENTICK *London* IV. 65 Stalls for butchers, with..blocks. **1849** DICKENS *Dav. Copp.* xix, He looked such a very obdurate butcher as he stood scraping the great block.

b. The piece of wood on which the condemned were beheaded or mutilated.

1541 *Act 33 Hen. VIII*, xii. §18 The serieant..shal bring to the said place of execucion a blocke with a betill a staple& cordes to binde the saide hande vpon the blocke. **1597** SHAKS. *2 Hen. IV*, IV. ii. 122 Some guard these Traitors to the Block of Death. *a* **1674** CLARENDON *Hist. Reb.* (1704) III. XIV. 384 He laid down his head upon the Block. **1829** H. NEELE *Lit. Rem.* 25 The sovereign who sent Raleigh to the block. **1876** GREEN *Short Hist.* vii. §1 (1882) 341 It was by bills of attainder..that the great nobles were brought to the block.

c. A stump by which to mount, or dismount from, a horse. Also *fig.*

1614 MARKHAM *Cheap Husb.* I. ii. (1668) 12 Observing to mount and dismount at the block only. *a* **1659** OSBORN *Observ. Turks* iii. (1673) 265 The promoters of Sedition, are seldom found to take Horse at any other block than what they perceive the People aptest to stumble at. **1841** ORDERSON *Creol.* viii. 76 [He] rode dashingly up to the block.

d. The stump on which a slave stood when being sold by auction.

1853 *Chamb. Jrnl.* Oct. 39 Boy mounts the block..the auctioneer kindly lends him a hand. **1866** BRYANT *Death Slavery* vii, There shall the grim block remain, At which the slave was sold.

e. A falcon's perch.

1844 *Proc. Berw. Nat. Club.* II. 97 The hawk..was soon receiving..a good meal of beef upon her block.

4. A piece of wood or other substance on which something is moulded, shaped, or fashioned: *spec.*

a. A mould for a hat.

1575 GASCOIGNE *Hearbes, Weedes, etc.* Wks. (1587) 154 A coptanke hat made on a Flemish block. **1604** DEKKER *Honest Wh.* I. xiii. Wks. 1873 II. 79 We have blockes for all heads. *a* **1680** BUTLER *Rem.* (1759) II. 217 His Head is, like his Hat, fashioned upon a Block. **1858** HAWTHORNE *Fr. & It. Jrnls.* I. 81 Wolsey's hat..might have been made on the same block.

b. *fig.* Shape, style, fashion (of hat).

1580 LYLY *Euphues* (Arb.) 323 A hat of the..best block in al Italy. **1599** SHAKS. *Much Ado* I. i. 77 He weares his faith but as the fashion of his hat, it euer changes with yᵉ next block. **1612** ROWLANDS *More Knaues Yet* 6 Hats of newest block. **1820** SCOTT *Abbot* xxv, A beaver hat of the newest block.

c. ***barber's block***: a wooden head for a wig.

1688 R. HOLME *Armoury* II. xviii. 464 A *Finishing Block* is a Wooden head set on a Stand, on which the rounds of hair are sowed on the Cawl. **1754** *Connoisseur* No. 36 Their heads..have worn as many different kinds of wigs as the block at their barber's. *a* **1843** SOUTHEY *Ep. A. Cunningham* Wks. III. 318 From such a barber..was that portrait made, I think, or per adventure from his block.

d. *transf.* A head, esp. in *to knock one's block off.* So ***off one's block***: angry, insane. Also *to lose* or *do* (*in*) *one's block* (chiefly Austral. and N.Z.), to become angry, excited, or anxious. (*slang.*)

1635 SHIRLEY *Lady of Pleas.* II. i, Buy a beaver For thy own block. **1862** H. KINGSLEY *Ravenshoe* II. ix. 86, I cleaned a groom's boots on Toosday, and he punched my block because I blacked the tops. **1913** A. J. REES *Merry Marauders* ii. 23 When I seen that 'earse of yours comin' a-plungin' down straight towards me..I admit I fair lost me block. **1916** J. B. COOPER *Coo-oo-ee!* i. 19 Mrs. Muller went on no end! Did in her block, thinking of the night's ride Nipper had given her. *Ibid.* xiv. 211 Sandy Pilkins..always lost his block at the local football match. **1916** C. J. DENNIS *Songs Sentimental Bloke* 118 *To lose* or *do in the block*, to become flustered; excited; angry; to lose confidence. *To keep the block*, to remain calm, dispassionate. **1918** *N.Z.E.F. Chrons.* 21 June 22/1 If you can keep your block, while those about you are losing theirs. **1925** FRASER & GIBBONS *Soldier & Sailor Words* 26 *Block*, head, face. 'Off his block', angry, off his head. **1928** T. E. LAWRENCE *Lett.* (1938) 572 If I had any side, they would knock off what they call my 'block'. **1931** V. PALMER *Separate Lives* 220 There was a sheelah back in Salisbury who did her block on me. **1933** *Bulletin* (Sydney) 15 Nov. 33/1 The Cossack done his block again —slapped Plato on the cheek. **1939** H. G. WELLS *Holy Terror* I. i. 12 Many suggestions were made, from 'Knock his little block off', to 'Give him more love'. **1939** A. UPFIELD *Myst. Swordfish Reef* (1943) vi. 52 Some will lose their blocks, get excited, and then something has to go west. **1956** E. GRIERSON *Second Man* vii. 144, I did my block—panicked, I reckon you'd say. **1966** 'L. LANE' *ABZ of Scouse* 10 *I done me block*; I went off my head; I lost my temper.

e. *generally.* A substratum or core.

1691 RAY *Creation* I. (1704) 119 To serve as a Form or Block to sustain the succeeding annual Coat.

5. *Mechanics.* A pulley or system of pulleys mounted in a case, used to increase the mechanical power of the ropes running through them; employed esp. for the rigging of ships, and in lifting great weights. They take various names from their shape, position, or use, as ***fiddle block, sister block***, etc.

1622 MALYNES *Anc. Law-Merch.* 143 Damages sustained by bad Hookes, Ropes, Blockes, or Lines. **1627** CAPT. SMITH *Seaman's Gram.* v. 19 Blocks or Pullies are thick peeces of wood hauing shiuers in them. **1752** SMEATON *Tackle* in *Phil. Trans.* XLVII. 494 An inconvenience arises, if above 3 pullies are framed in one block. **1762** FALCONER *Shipwr.* II. 58 Thro' rattling blocks the clue-lines swiftly run. **1824** W. IRVING *T. Trav.* II. 236 The stump of a mast, with a few ropes and blocks swinging about.

b. Naut. phrase. ***block and block*** (see quot.).

1627 CAPT. SMITH *Seaman's Gram.* v. 19 When we hale any Tackle or Haleyard to which two blocks doe belong, when they meet, we call that blocke and blocke. **1769** FALCONER *Dict. Marine* (1789) *Block and block*, the situation of a tackle when the two opposite blocks are drawn close together, so that the..power becomes destroyed.

c. ***block and tackle***, = TACKLE *sb.* 3; also *fig.*

1838 *Knickerbocker* XII. 373 The diver began to don his submarine habiliments, which were swung inward from the vessel's side..by means of a block-and-tackle. **1864** O. W. NORTON *Army Lett.* (1903) 221 General Birney seems to consider the Eighth as..block and tackle by which to hoist his favorites into place and power. **1910** *Hawkins' Electr. Dict.* 39/1 *Block and Tackle*, a term including the block and the rope wove through it, for hoisting or obtaining a purchase. **1936** *Discovery* Aug. 238/1 The camera is lowered on its mount by means of special block and tackle installation fixed to the cabin roof.

6. A piece of wood which acts as a support:

a. *Carpentry.* A square piece of wood glued into the angle at a joint to strengthen it; = BLOCKING 3.

b. A piece of scantling for elevating cannon; called a ***whole, half***, or ***quarter block***, according to its thickness.

c. A frame to support the end of a log in a saw-mill.

d. *Carriage-making* (see quot.).

1801 FELTON *Carriages* I. 120 Those platforms, raisers, or blocks, are added to a carriage, either as matter of necessity or appearance..their use is to elevate and support the budget, boot, hind foot-board, and springs.

e. A shaped piece of wood forming part of a shoeblack's equipment, on which a customer places his foot.

1872 *Cassell's Mag.* V. 84/1 The boys are provided with their uniforms, their block, blacking, and brushes by the society.

f. *Drapery.* A roll of material wound on a board: now called *piece.*

1905 H. G. WELLS *Kipps* I. vi. §4 Being subsequently engaged in serving cretonnes, and desiring to push a number of rejected blocks up the counter. **1934** —— *Exper. in Autobiogr.* I. iv. 149 Wrappered blocks labelled incomprehensibly Hard Book or Turkey Twill.

7. A piece of wood on which lines, letters, or figures are engraved, in order to be printed from it in ink or colours on paper, calico, etc., or to be stamped by pressure on any yielding surface.

1732 S. PALMER *Hist. Printing* vi. (*title*), An enquiry into the first books printed on blocks of wood. **1727–51** CHAMBERS *Cycl.* s.v. *Cutting*, The cutters in wood begin by preparing a plank or block. **1780** R. BURROW *Comp. Ladies Diary* 6 Engraving wooden blocks for printing pictures with the letter-press. **1837** WHITTOCK *Bk. Trades* (1842) 94 [*Calico-printer*] They have from the earliest period used blocks and stencils to produce the pattern. **1880** *Print. Trades Jrnl.* xxx. 10 Printed in four colors, from engraved blocks.

8. Various solid pieces of wood about a ship: see quots.

c **1850** *Rudim. Navig.* (Weale) 97 *Block*, the large piece of elm out of which the figure is carved at the head of the ship. *Blocks* for building the ship are those solid pieces of oak timber fixed under the ship's keel, upon the groundways. *Blocks* for transporting the ship are two solid pieces of oak or elm, one fixed on each side of the stern above the taffrail, and a snatch with a large score cut each way in the middle. *a* **1856** LONGF. *Build. Ship* 95 Thus, said he, we will build this ship! Lay square the blocks upon the slip.

†**9.** The peg or 'hob' aimed at in throwing quoits; the 'Jack' at bowls. *Obs.*

1598 FLORIO, *Buttiro*, a maister or mistres of boules or coites, whereat the plaiers cast or play: some call it the blocke.

II. A bulky piece of any substance.

10. a. *gen.* Any solid or compact mass of matter with an extended surface.

1530 PALSGR. 199/1 Blocke of tynne, *savmon destain.* **1577** HARRISON *Descr. Brit.* v. 12 These huge blocks were ordeined and created of God. **1670** J. CLARIDGE *Sheph. Banbury's Rules* (1744) 38 A block of this kind of stone as big as a large rolling stone. **1758** BORLASE *Nat. Hist. Cornwall*

xv. §18. 182 The metal when hardened is called a block of tin. **1799** KIRWAN *Geol. Ess.* 166 Granite is most commonly found in huge blocks. **1813** *Gentl. Mag.* LXXXIII. I. 609/2 A square block of masonry has been raised to support the stone. **1860** TYNDALL *Glac.* I. §2. 17 The more solid blocks of ice shoot forward in advance of the lighter débris.

b. A large quantity of anything dealt with at once. Hence ***in block***: in the mass, as a whole, 'wholesale'; = Fr. *en bloc.*

1870 MEDBERY *Men & Myst. Wall St.* 134 Block. A number of shares, say 5,000 or 10,000, massed together, and sold or bought in a lump. **1876** HOLLAND *Sev. Oaks* xxiv. 331 The combination began by selling large blocks of the Stock for future delivery. **1876** GLADSTONE in *Contemp. Rev.* June 3 Puritans.. who rejected in block the authority of creeds. **1901** MERWIN & WEBSTER *Calumet 'K'* iii. 40 A big block of treasury stock.

c. = PAD *sb.*[3] 4. Also *attrib.*, as ***block calendar.***

1865 G. M. HOPKINS *Note-Bks. & Papers* (1937) 54 Shewing a sketching-block, he asked if there would be any objection to his sketching there. **1893** Sketch-block [see SKETCH *sb.* 7]. **1908** Scribbling-block [see SCRIBBLING *vbl. sb.*[1] 4]. **1910** *Brit. Empire Paper Trades' Jrnl.* Feb. 66/2 Blotting pads, books, etc., note books, note blocks, address books, etc. *Ibid.* May 186 Portrait and Figure Studies, with Daily Tear-off Block and Quotations for every day in the year. *Ibid.* 187/1 A new series of larger size shilling block calendars. **1940** H. G. WELLS *Babes in Darkling Wood* II. i. 128 He pushed the paper-block back and began writing on the blotting-paper before him.

d. The carcass of a bullock; also *attrib.*, as ***block test***, ascertainment of the dead weight of a beast when on the butcher's block for cutting up.

1893 *Westm. Gaz.* 8 Mar. 9/1 The 'block test'.. used by Mr. McJannet, of Stirling... A set of tables by which, when the weight of the live bullock is ascertained, the weight of the 'block' as it hangs up in the flesher's shop for sale can be established within about a couple of pounds. **1902** *Encycl. Brit.* XXV. 188/1 In 1895 the Smithfield Club instituted a carcase competition... The cattle and sheep entered for this competition are shown alive on the first day, at the close of which they are slaughtered and the carcases hung up for exhibition, with details of live and dead weights. The competition thus constitutes what is termed a 'block test'.

e. = BLOC.

1925 M. EASTMAN *Since Lenin Died* ii. 19 To perfect and solidify the block which they had already formed against him among the leaders of the party. **1940** *Manch. Guardian Weekly* 12 July 25 Working for the entry of France into a vast Continental block with Germany and Italy as the chief partners. **1957** *Economist* 7 Sept. 744/1 The extent to which the Soviet block is believed to have settled down again.

f. *Computers.* A set of data or instructions: (i) a group of successive locations in a memory and the data they contain; (ii) a group of words treated as a single unit in a program or by a computer.

1948 *Math. Tables & other Aids to Computation* III. 11 Characterizing a block of data on a table tape by a single block number. *Ibid.* 71 If a block has been called for, the machine.. automatically transfers the first number in this block into the table register. **1958** GOTLIEB & HUME *High-Speed Data Processing* ix. 179 A block is an integral number of words stored in a single register and transferred as a whole from one part of the machine to another. **1964** A. LYTEL *Fund. Data Processing* iv. 202 A block is a series of declarations and statements enclosed between the words *begin* and *end.* **1964** *Ann. N.Y. Acad. Sci.* CXV. 663 Reels of ¾ inch-wide tape which contain 512 consecutively numbered blocks, each capable of storing 256 12-bit numbers. **1968** LEHMAN & BAILEY *Digital Computing* x. 200/2 The common area of memory may be divided into any number of separate regions, or blocks.

11. a. A lump of wood, stone, or other matter, that obstructs one's way; a bar; *fig.* an obstacle or obstruction. Now only in ***stumbling-block.***

a **1500** *Songs & Carols 15th C.* (Wright) 81 (Mätz.) Ale mak many a mane to stombyle at the blokkes. **1573** G. HARVEY *Lett.-Bk.* (1884) 32, I tould him there was a certain block in the wai. **1597** J. PAYNE *Royal Exch.* 38 At which common block many weakelings do stumble. **1649** SELDEN *Laws Eng.* I. xv. (1739) 29 This was.. a block in the way of Prelacy, and a clog to keep it down. *a* **1718** PENN *Life* Wks. 1726 I. 2 A Block in the Way to Preferment. **1845** S. AUSTIN *Ranke's Hist. Ref.* I. 531 By maintaining these passages he laid a stumbling block in his own path.

b. A piece of wood or other material placed in front of a wheel of an aeroplane to prevent it from moving forward; a chock. Also *attrib.*, as ***block time*** (see quot. 1950), etc.

[**1918** W. G. MCMINNIES *Pract. Flying* 228 *Chocks*, wooden blocks placed in front of the wheels of a machine to prevent it moving when the engine is started.] **1930** P. WHITE *How to fly an Airplane* xiii. 189 You must remove the blocks from under the wheels. **1936** *Jrnl. R. Aeronaut. Soc.* XL. 852 On short ferry services the time occupied at each end in taking off and landing had a curiously levelling effect, so that the block-to-block speed was much the same as for high or low speed aircraft. **1948** *Ibid.* LII. 624/2 This method of arriving at stage distance—by taking a block time and by relating that time to the distance which would be covered at the block speed in the wind conditions. **1950** *Gloss. Aeronaut. Terms (B.S.I.)* I. 11 *Block time*, the period from the time the chocks are withdrawn, brakes released or moorings dropped, to the time of return to rest, or taking up of moorings after flight.

12. *spec.* **a.** A mass or lump of rock or stone in its natural or unhewn state. ***erratic block***, a boulder transported by physical agencies far from its native site.

1847 TENNYSON *Princ.* vii, All her labour was but as a block Left in the quarry. **1851** RUSKIN *Stones Ven.* (1874) I. i. 19 The glacier stream[s] of the Lombards and.. Normans left their erratic blocks wherever they had flowed. **1872** JENKINSON *Guide Eng. Lakes* (1879) 149 The Bowder Crag from which the immense block has fallen, is directly above.

b. A solid piece of stone, etc., prepared for building purposes; *also* the 'bricks' with which children build toy-houses.

c **1854** LONGF. *Builders* iii, Our to-days and yesterdays Are the blocks with which we build. **1885** R. L. STEVENSON *Child's Garden* 63 *Block City*, What are you able to build with your blocks, Castles and palaces, temples and docks?

c. *Archit.* Each of the squared pieces above and sometimes below the columns of a chimney-piece.

1775 J. WEDGWOOD *Let.* 14 Jan. in E. Meteyard *Life* (1866) II. 321, I.. stand in need of your directions relative to the blocks & ovals to the Tablets. **1875** E. METEYARD *Wedgwood Handbk.* Gloss. s.v., The more ordinary chimney-pieces had only a tablet and blocks... Occasionally the base of the columns had blocks also.

†**13.** A whetstone. *Obs.*

1592 GREENE *Groatsw. Wit* (1617) 28 He serued but for a blocke to whet Robertoes wit on.

14. a. A compact or connected mass of houses or buildings, with no intervening spaces; (esp. in U.S. and Canada) the quadrangular mass of buildings included between four streets, or two 'avenues' and two streets at right angles to them. **b.** A portion of a town or space of ground so bounded, whether occupied by buildings or not. orig. *U.S.*

1796 *Aurora* (Philad.) 13 Dec. (Th.), The whole block of buildings included between that slip, Front Street, and the Fly Market. **1817** S. R. BROWN *Western Gaz.* 101 Each block of lots has the advantage of two 16 feet alleys. **1837** *Knickerbocker* IX. 72 Paved thoroughfares and manufacturing or commercial blocks. **1843** DICKENS *Mart. Chuz.* xvi. 203 A neighbouring bar-room, which.. was 'only in the next block'. **1851** *Househ. Narrative* Mar. 69 The blocks.. are rapidly filling up by the erection upon them of large houses. **1855** *Act* 18–19 *Vict.* cxx. §74 A group or block of contiguous houses.. may be drained more economically .. in combination. **1882** FREEMAN in *Longm. Mag.* I. 89 American towns are built in blocks. **1884** *Boston (Mass.) Journal* 12 Sept., When the matinee between brother and sister had closed Blossum was about two blocks away. **1963** J. T. STORY *Something for Nothing* vi. 214 Outside the office there was nowhere to park... She cruised round the block twice, then finally double-parked and hurried into the building.

c. A fashionable promenade outside a particular block of buildings and shops in some Australian cities; hence ***on the block***, on the promenade; ***to do the block***, to lounge or saunter on the fashionable promenade.

1869 M. CLARKE *Peripatetic Philosopher* 13 (Morris), If our Victorian youth showed their appreciation for domestic virtues, Victorian womanhood would 'do the Block' less frequently. **1872** 'RESIDENT' *Glimpses of Life in Victoria* 349 A certain portion of Collins Street, lined by the best drapers' and jewellers' shops.. is known as 'The Block'. **1896** *Argus* 17 July 4/7 (Morris), Just as the busy man, who generally walks quickly, has to go slowly in the crowd on the Block. **1902** *Daily Chron.* 20 Oct. 5/2 Sundowners.. who once enjoyed fat berths in Melbourne, 'doing the block' every afternoon in Collins street. **1906** E. DYSON *Fact'ry 'Ands* viii. 96 Man 'n' woman ud come jiggin' erlong in their block clobber. **1916** J. B. COOPER *Coo-oo-ee!* i. 14 When I go to town I'm crowded on the Block, I can't breathe.

d. Each of the large lots into which land is divided for settlement and development; any (fairly) large area of land; also (*Austral.*), a building section or lot. See also BACK BLOCKS. *Austral.* and *N.Z.* (For N. Amer. examples see *D.A.*)

1840 in *Hist. Rec. Austral.* (1924) 1st Ser. XX. 744 If a Person should pay at once for 5,120 Acres or 8 Square Miles, We propose to allow him the privilege of demanding a Survey of that Quantity in one Block in any part of the Colony he may choose. **1841** W. DEANS *Let.* 25 Mar. (1937) 31 We are insured our land, but are bound.. to take the 110,000 acres for the principal settlement in one continuous block, round Port Nicholson... The boundaries of the block are now pretty well defined. **1858** SIMMONDS *Dict. Trade*, *Block*,.. in colonial parlance a piece of land. **1866–7** *Acts S. Australia* 30 *Vict.* No. 21 §6 No.. lease shall be granted at a lower yearly rent than at the rate of Ten Shillings for every block or Section, and no such block or Section shall exceed one square mile of land therein comprised. **1872** *Ibid.* 35 & 36 *Vict.* No. 18 §24 No person shall hold.. more than three separate and detached blocks of land; and such area shall.. be comprised in one block. **1909** B. R. WISE *Commw. Australia* 100 Some far-seeing men.. would have set aside defined blocks for agricultural settlement. *Ibid.* 113, 27,000 acres, in forty-acre blocks. *Ibid.* 127 There has.. been some 'dummying', but the majority of the block-holders are *bonâ-fide* occupiers. **1933** *Bulletin* (Sydney) 11 Jan. 25 My block of 200 acres had previously been sub-divided for cropping. **1950** *N.Z. Jrnl. Agric.* Oct. 293/2 Old fences were removed.. and new ones erected to subdivide the run into blocks of convenient size. **1969** *Advertiser* (Adelaide) 8 Feb. 42/1 (Advt.), Older Style Marino Home and 2 established adjoining building blocks, corner position, all blocks enjoy magnificent coastal views. **1969** *Age* (Melbourne) 24 May 4/4 Mrs. Smith said that the Normanton Aborigines had a reserve of 82 blocks on a hill overlooking the town, separated by a salt pan. **1969** *Northern Territory News* 11 July 4/3 (Advt.), Freehold Residential Holiday Sites. N.T. Real Estate Pty. Ltd. have great pleasure in introducing the sale of these excellent freehold blocks.

†**e.** A blockhouse. *U.S. Obs.*

1829 J. F. COOPER *Wish-ton-wish* vii. 108 He that is wise, however, will take but little of the latter, until his head be safely housed within some such building as yon block. **1845** W. G. SIMMS *Wigwam & Cabin* Ser. I. 57 As it was only a short mile and a half from the block, and we could hear of no Indians.

f. A large single building, esp. one containing a number of flats or offices; ***block dweller, dwellings***: see 23.

1849 in MRS. F. L. ADAMS *Pioneer Hist. Ingham County* (1923) 149 A little old 'corner grocer' building occupied the corner where Pratt & Millsapugh's block now stands. **1903** G. GISSING *Private Papers H. Ryecroft* 256 The sixth floor of a 'block' in Shoreditch. **1915** J. BUCHAN *39 Steps* i. 13 My flat was the first floor in a new block behind Langham Place. **1933** *Discovery* Aug. 254/1 The designers of large blocks of flats. **1969** *Times* 20 Oct. 9/5 Like the great bulk of Glasgow's nineteenth century housing Bernard Street consists of four-storey tenement blocks.

III. Figurative senses.

15. A person resembling a block or log of wood:

a. in unintelligence: A blockhead. **b.** in want of feeling: A hard-hearted person.

a **1553** UDALL *Royster D.* III. iii. Ye are suche a calfe, suche an asse, such a blocke. **1601** SHAKS. *Jul. C.* I. i. 40 You Blockes, you stones, you worse than senslesse things. **1682** N. O. tr. *Boileau's Lutrin* II. 16 See how the Stupid Block stands mute, and moping! **1803** BRISTED *Pedest. Tour* II. 661 In vain we endeavoured to move the compassion of these two blocks in female shape. **1810** TANNAHILL *Poems* (1846) 88 The greatest dunce, the biggest block.

16. Phrases. ***a chip of the*** (***same*** or) ***old block***: a piece of the same stuff; a descendant reproducing the qualities of a parent or ancestor. ***as deaf*** (etc.) ***as a block***: (see 1 b.) ***to cut blocks with a razor***: (a metaphor describing absurdly incongruous and futile application of abilities or means: 13).

1627 SANDERSON *Serm.* I. 283 Am not I a child of the same Adam, a vessel of the same clay, a chip of the same block, with him? **1655** LESTRANGE *Chas. I*, 126 Episcopacy, which they thought but a great chip of the old block Popery. **1774** GOLDSM. *Retal.* 42 'Twas his fate unemployed or in place, sir, To eat mutton cold and cut blocks with a razor.

IV. Senses from BLOCK *v.*

†**17.** 'A scheme, contrivance; generally used in a bad sense.' (Jamieson.) *Sc. Obs.*

1513 DOUGLAS *Æneis* v. xi. 12 Rolling in mynd full mony cankarit bloik.

†**18.** A bargain, bartering, exchange. *Sc. Obs.*

1568 *Sempill Ballates* (1872) 232 Abydand on sum merchand blok. **1637** RUTHERFORD *Lett.* cxx. (1862) I. 300 What a sweet block was it by way of buying and selling, to give and tell down a ransome.. for grace and glory to dyvours! *a* **1800** *Ballad 'Fair Isabell'* xvi. in Child's *Ballads* III. (1885) 216/2 So many blocks have we two made, And ay the worst was mine.

19. A blocking up. **a.** An obstruction or stoppage of traffic or progress. **b.** The obstruction of the free passage of a bill through the House of Commons: see quot.

1860 W. CLARK *Vac. Tour* 19 Naples is the only continental capital which is liable to blocks. **1863** *Cornh. Mag.* Feb. *Life Man-of-War*, It is after you have become lieutenant, that the 'block' makes itself felt. **1882** *Pall Mall G.* 14 July 2/2 What is the practical effect of the notice that a bill will be opposed—which is what is known as a block? Simply this, that it prevents any stage of a bill being taken during (1) the last ten minutes of a morning sitting, or (2) the last fifteen minutes of a Wednesday afternoon sitting, or (3) after half-past twelve o'clock at any other sitting.

c. block system (on *Railways*): a system by which the line is divided into short sections, having at the end of each a signal, and a connexion with the electric telegraph, so worked that no train is allowed to pass into any section till it is wholly clear; thus securing an absolute interval of space between successive trains. So ***block signal, block signalling, block instrument***, etc.

1864 *Realm* 29 June 1 The only remedy for the danger is the adoption of what is technically called the 'block system.' **1865** *Lond. Rev.* 18 Mar. 309 Mr. William Henry Preece.. recommends the adoption, in connection with the electric telegraph, of the 'block system' of ensuring the safety of railway trains. **1882** *Oracle* 20 May 313 The method of working electric block-signals.. Mr. Tyer produced his first block-signalling instrument in 1852. *Ibid.* A modification of the single needle as a block instrument.

d. *Neurol.* Obstruction of the passage of a nervous or muscular impulse; an instance of this. Cf. BLOCK *v.* 4 b and *heart-block* (HEART *sb.* 56).

1882 W. H. GASKELL in *Phil. Trans.* CLXXIII. 1031 If the section is severe the block will be complete; no contractions will pass. **1883** —— in *Jrnl. Physiology* IV. 66 The contraction wave is unable to pass, then the 'block' is complete... Romanes.. has.. made use of the term 'block' to express any artificial hindrance to the passage of the contraction. I therefore make use of the same term in speaking of the results of experiments on the cardiac muscle which are very similar to those which he performed on the muscle of the Medusa. **1905** *Amer. Jrnl. Physiology* XIII. p. xxvii, A condition of partial 'block' in which the rhythm of the auricle is to the rhythm of the ventricle as 3 is to 1. **1957** *Encycl. Brit.* I. 864/2 When the local anaesthetic agent is injected so that it blocks the nerve supply, the method is known as 'block' or 'conduction' anaesthesia. *Ibid.*, Spinal anaesthesia is a special form of block anaesthesia in which the local anaesthetic agent is deposited in the spinal fluid. **1963** G. B. CARTER et al. *Dict. Midwifery* 404/2 *P[udendal] block*, infiltration of the pudendal nerve with a local anaesthetic.. preparatory to forceps delivery or to repair of perineal rupture.

e. *Psychol.*, spec. = BLOCKING *vbl. sb.* 1 f.

1931 A. G. BILLS in *Amer. Jrnl. Psychol.* XLIII. 230 The term 'block'.. refers to those periods, experienced by

mental workers, when they seem unable to respond and cannot, even by an effort, continue until a short time has elapsed. **1946** W. S. KNICKERBOCKER *20th Cent. Eng.* 187 Some 'block' in his mental make-up. **1949** *Brit. Jrnl. Psychol.* Sept. 38 Occasional breakdowns of response, or 'blocks' occurred. **1969** *Times* (Sat. Rev.) 15 Nov. p. iv/3 Henry James.. freeing himself from emotional and work blocks.

f. *Amer. Football.* The obstruction of an opponent by interposing one's body. Cf. BLOCK *v.* 4e.

1931 *Collier's Mag.* 17 Oct. 61/3 In the 'Indian block', as it came to be called, a man left the ground entirely, half turning as he leaped so as to hit an opponent just above the knees with his hip. **1955** *Sports Illustr.* 7 Nov. 44/3 Brown ..has what I like to term 'second reaction' — the ability to absorb the initial shock of a block and still make the tackle. **1966** ROTE & WINTER *Lang. Pro Football* III. 104 *Block*, act of obstructing an opponent by making legal body contact. **1976** *Honolulu Star-Bull.* 21 Dec. H-1/2 Charley Hannah tipped it and it came right to me. I got a couple of blocks, one I know from Charley. **1984** *N.Y. Times* 2 Jan. 29/1 He ..threw a block when Kenny King scored on a 9-yard run.

20. *Cricket.* The position in which a batsman blocks balls; that in which he holds his bat in front of the wicket before striking, otherwise called the *centre*; hence ***block-hole*** (or shortly *block*), a mark made in the ground to indicate this position. Also, a stroke of the bat to block a ball.

1825 *New Monthly Mag.* XIII. 498, I..admired the dexterity of the block at hand, which frustrated the perilous three-quarter ball. **1837** D. WALKER *Games & Sports* 215 The popping crease.. having in its middle.. a hole called the block hole. **1845** WANOSTROCHT *Felix on Bat.* I. ii. 12, I next recommended him to take the block for the middle stump, about five inches behind the popping crease. **1851** [see WORK *sb.* 2b]. **1866** 'CAPTAIN CRAWLEY' *Cricket* 8 The block is the spot where the batsman grounds his bat when prepared to play. **1956** N. CARDUS *Close of Play* 11 After he had taken guard and marked his block-hole, he would pat the crease neatly.

V. *Attrib.* and *Comb.*

21. *attrib.* or *adj.* Taken in the block, aggregate, lump.

1864 LD. LYTTELTON in *Morn. Star* 22 Jan. 3/6 The first cost requires a block sum, which.. is just what the working classes cannot command.

22. General comb., chiefly attrib., as ***block-coal***, ***-ice***, ***-shot***, ***-stone***; (sense 5) ***block-maker***, ***-pulley***, ***-sheave***, ***-strop***; ***block-faced***, ***-like*** adjs.

1751 SMOLLETT *Per. Pic.* (1779) I. v. 37 A squinting, *block-faced, chattering piss-kitchen. **1881** *Chicago Times* 4 June, *Block ice is never created in the river rapids to clog or impede machinery. **1561** J. HEYWOOD *Seneca's Hercules* (1581) 16 Her head from *blocklyke body gone Is quight. **1861** L. NOBLE *Icebergs* 85 Numbers of block-like bergs. *a* **1687** PETTY *Pol. Arith.* (1690) 78 Many Artisans.. are employed upon Shipping: viz. Painters, *Block-makers, Rope-makers. **1793** SMEATON *Edystone L.* §122 *note*, An ingenious blockmaker at Plymouth. **1884** *Harper's Mag.* Jan. 220/2 The block-maker and sail-maker each a sixteenth. **1864** CHAMBERS *Bk. of Days* II. 684 [Brunel's] plan for making *block-pulleys for ships by machinery. **1883** *Fisheries Exhib. Cat.* 42 Projectile Anchors, Cone *Block Shot to throw Rove Rope or Messenger Line. **1879** SIR G. SCOTT *Lect. Archit.* I. 270 If he used *blockstone.. he studied to use [it] so as to look well. **1769** FALCONER *Dict. Marine* (1789) E iij, It is bound with a sort of rope-ring.. which is called a *block strop.

23. Special comb. **block ball** *Baseball*, a ball, either hit or thrown, which is handled or stopped by a non-player; **block-battery** (see quot.); **block-board**, a plywood board having a core of thin wooden strips with the grain at right angles to the adjacent veneers; **block bond** *Bricklaying* (see quots. and BOND *sb.*[1] 13a); **block-brush**, a bunch of BUTCHER'S-BROOM, used by butchers to clean the blocks, and borne in the insignia of their Company; **block-buster**, an aerial bomb capable of destroying a whole block of buildings; also *transf.* and *fig.*; **block-busting** *a.*, of the nature of a block-buster (*fig.*); also as *vbl. sb.* and *attrib.*, *U.S. colloq.* (see quot. 1959); **block capital**, a capital letter written or printed without serifs; **block chain**, an endless chain composed of alternate blocks and links; **block-chopper**, a workman who trims a block of stone; **block coal**, coal that splits easily into blocks; *spec.* an American bituminous furnace coal; also, coal in large lumps; **block coefficient** *Naval Archit.* (see quot.); **block-cutter**, an artificer who cuts in relief the blocks used in printing or engraving (see sense 7); **block diagram**, (*a*) a type of relief model (see quot. 1924); (*b*) a diagram in which squares and other conventional symbols show the order and arrangement of parts of an apparatus; **block dwellings** *pl.*, dwellings consisting of flats for working-class families in large barrack-like buildings several storeys high; hence *block dweller*; **block-faulting** *Geol.*, faulting which divides a region into blocks; **block-flute** (see quot.); **block-furnace** = BLOOMERY; **block lava** *Geol.*, a lava field composed of angular blocks; = AA[2]; **block letter**, (*a*) in *pl.*, printing-types of large size cut out of wooden blocks; (*b*) = *block capital*; **block-machine**, a machine for making the 'blocks' associated with 'tackle' in ships; so **block-machinery**; **block model** *Shipbuilding*, a model of a ship shaped from a block made up of flat pieces of wood fastened together, the lines of junction showing, on a reduced scale, the water-lines of the vessel to be built; **block mountain**, a mountain formed by faulting of the earth's crust; **block-ornament** (*slang*) = BLOCKER 3; **block-pate** = BLOCKHEAD; **block plan**, an outline plan or sketch, esp. of a building-site; **block plane** (see quots.); **block-printing**, printing from wooden blocks, instead of movable types, as in the BLOCK-BOOKS, now also used for printing calico, paper-hangings, etc.; so **block-printed** *a.*; **block-ship**, a ship moored to block the entrance to a harbour, an old man of war used as a store-ship, etc.; **block test** (see sense 10d); **block-tin**, see TIN; **block train**, a railway train of which the component parts are kept permanently made up; **block universe** *Philos.*, the universe conceived as being like a block, as a unitary closed system of interlocking parts in which there is neither genuine plurality nor room for alternative possibilities; **block welding** (see quot. 1952); †**block-wheat**, buckwheat; **block working**, the working of railway traffic on the block system (see BLOCK *sb.* 19c).

1891 N. CRANE *Baseball* 79 **Block ball*, a batted or thrown ball handled by an outsider. **1802** C. JAMES *Mil. Dict.* (1816) 54/1 **Block-battery*, in gunnery, a wooden battery for two or more small pieces mounted on wheels, and moveable from place to place. **1932** A. MORA *Plywood* 86 (*caption*) Method of cross cutting core pieces for *block boards. **1936** *Archit. Rev.* LXXIX. 76/1 The only structural difference between a sheet of three-ply and a laminated board or blockboard is that in both the latter the core is of composite vertical formation instead of being a single or continuous horizontal sheet of veneer. **1939** *Ibid.* LXXXVI. 129/4 Blockboard plywood, i.e., plywood with an interior composed of strips of solid timber, was first industrially produced by Kümmel's at Rehfelde near Berlin about 1902. **1865** WEBSTER s.v. *Bond*, English or *block bond. **1901** STURGIS *Dict. Archit.* s.v. *Bond*, Block Bond. Same as Flemish Bond. **1942** *Time* 14 Sept. 29/1 Inside a sturdy observation tower a mile from the exploding *block busters which the Army is now testing. **1943** *Times* 22 Dec. 4/5 Bombs were falling ..many 8,000 lb. and 4,000 lb. 'block-busters' among them. **1957** G. SMITH *Friends* vi a. 114 One day I had what seemed to me like a block-buster of an idea for a musical play. **1967** *Spectator* 6 Oct. 394/2 The 'block-buster' is a figure in American urban life who has yet to emerge in this country. He is a property dealer who by subterfuge introduces black residents into all-white neighbourhoods. **1943** *New Statesman* 20 Nov. 332/3 Those English Labour M.P.s who in their speeches show only a *blockbusting contempt for Ulster. **1959** *Economist* 31 Jan. 415/2 Once a single negro moves into a block.. the houses on both sides of the street from corner to corner are bound to become.. Negro... Such 'block-busting' [etc.]. **1961** *Nation* 7 Oct. 223/2 The block-busting real-estate men show homes in integrated districts.. only to prospective Negro buyers. **1902** *Combined Training* (War Office) 61 Names of places and persons will be written in *block capitals. **1924** *Contemp. Rev.* Apr. 482, I published an article in the *Novoie Vremya* under the title 'Bread', which appeared in large block capitals. **1896** A. SHARP *Bicycles & Tricycles* xxvi. 431 The 'Roller' has the advantage over the 'Humber', or *block chain, that its rubbing surface is very much larger. **1904** GOODCHILD & TWENEY *Technol. & Sci. Dict.*, Block Chain (*Cycles*). **1883** *Stonemason* Jan., It is then trimmed (or scalped) into shape by men called '*block-choppers', who adroitly wield heavy axes. **1871** *Amer. Naturalist* V. 177 A visit will be made to the celebrated *Block-coal field (iron smelting coal). **1874** *Amer. Cycl.* IV. 726/1 We shall herein denote the prominent varieties as.. non-caking or block coal, and caking or coking coals. **1883** GRESLEY *Gloss. Coal-m.*, Block coal. **1901** *Feilden's Mag.* IV. 421/1 In every case it is advisable also to calculate the value of the '*block coefficient' or so-called coefficient of fineness. **1902** *Encycl. Brit.* XXXII. 551/1 The block coefficient is the ratio of the volume of the immersed portion of the ship to the volume of the parallelopipedon. **1859** CHADWICK in Smiles *Workmen's Earnings* (1861) 21 *Block-cutters and printers in calico-printing. **1924** A. K. LOBECK *Block Diagrams* I. i. 1 A *block diagram presents the relationship between the surface of the ground and the underground structure by representing an imaginary block cut out from the earth's crust. **1944** *Electronic Engin.* June 24/3 Fig. 2 shows a block diagram of the circuit technique used. **1962** *Gloss. Terms Autom. Data Proc.* (*B.S.I.*) 59 *Block diagram*, a conventional drawing of a system, instrument, computer or program in which all portions are represented by annotated boxes. **1902** C. F. G. MASTERMAN *From Abyss* iii. 37 No.. dreams of impossible millennium will haunt the *block dweller of the future. **1899** *Daily News* 17 Jan. 3/2 The slums are sickening,.. and the *block dwellings often more like warehouses than homes. **1902** *Encycl. Brit.* XXXII. 673/2 Slum dwellings have been cleared under Cross's Acts 1875–82, and the Housing of the Working Classes Act, 1890; and.. block dwellings have been erected. **1921** A. W. GRABAU *Textbk. Geol.* I. xxi. 689 *Block faulting, the dropping down or raising of circumscribed blocks, is not uncommon. **1940** E. S. HILLS *Structural Geol.* 63 Regions which are divided by faults into a number of differentially elevated or depressed blocks are said to exhibit *block faulting*. **1965** G. J. WILLIAMS *Econ. Geol. N.Z.* v. 42/1 The schist.. must have been steeply tilted by block-faulting in some places. **1852** SEIDEL *Organ* 91 **Block-flute*.. is a flue-register sometimes open, sometimes stopped, and.. imitates the tone of a flute. **1914** R. A. DALY *Igneous Rocks* xiii. 291 The vesiculation of pahoehoe or ropy lava was found to be more evenly developed than in the aa or *block lava. **1920** A. HOLMES *Nomencl. Petrology* 47 *Block-lava*, a term applied to lava flows which occur as a tumultous assemblage of angular blocks having extremely rough surfaces due to the abundant development of large vesicles; = *aa*-lava or *aphrolithic* lava. **1908** *Installation News* II. 115/2 The cost of current for a large *block-letter sign is frequently six or seven pounds a week. **1929** *Humorist* 5 Jan. 682 Name and address should be written here in plain block letters. **1901** *Feilden's Mag.* IV. 426/1 The angle of entrance ..may either be measured from the *block-model or calculated. **1896** J. W. GREGORY *Great Rift Valley* xii. 221 (*caption*) Section across a '*Block Mountain'. **1901** C. R. DRYER *Lessons Physical Geogr.* xiv. 181 *Block Mountains*, probably the simplest mountains in existence are those of southern Oregon and northern California and Nevada. **1929** L. J. WILLS *Physiogr. Evolution Brit.* I. ii. 11 Differential elevation of a block relative to its surroundings may produce a *plateau* or a *block-mountain*. **1851** MAYHEW *Lond. Labour* I. 52 They buy *block-ornaments.. as they call the small dark-coloured pieces of meat exposed on the ..butchers' blocks. **1598** R. BERNARD *Terence* (1607) 251 To be called a *blockpate, a dulhead, an asse, a lumpish sot. **1909** WEBSTER, *Block plan. **1941** *City of Oxford Building Byelaws* No. 134 A person who intends to erect a building.. shall send or deliver to the clerk or surveyor.. a block plan of the building. *a* **1884** KNIGHT *Dict. Mech.* Suppl., **Block Plane*, a plane, the bit of which is set at a very acute angle to the working surface, to enable it to plane across the grain of the wood. **1966** A. W. LEWIS *Gloss. Woodworking Terms* 66 *Block plane*, small low-angled (20°) plane, not more than 8 in long, used for cleaning up mitres and end grain. **1816** SINGER *Hist. Cards* 75 *note*, The Portuguese Missionaries on their first visit to Japan, in 1549, found the art of *block printing in use there. **1883** *Standard* 26 Jan. 3/2 Mere block-printed papers. **1801** *Hist. Europe* in *Ann. Reg.* 113/1 There was not on board their *Block ships a single surgeon. **1902** *Encycl. Brit.* XXXII. 154/2 In *block-trains, where the component coaches are permanently coupled together, one dynamo sometimes lights all the carriages. **1963** *Times* 18 Feb. 6/5 Instead of its being carried in mixed freight trains, the block trains will carry nothing but coal. **1881** T. DAVIDSON *Let.* 24 Dec. in R. B. Perry *Tht. & Char. W. James* (1935) I. 736 That last remnant of mythology and scholasticism, *viz.*, theism and a *block-universe. **1884** W. JAMES *Will to Believe* (1897) 181 Is not the notion of eternity being given at a stroke to omniscience only just another way of whacking upon us the block-universe? *a* **1910** —— *Some Probl. Philos.* (1911) xii. 191 It is the famous 'principle of causality' which, when combined with the next two principles, is supposed to establish the block universe, and to render the pluralistic hypothesis absurd. **1943** W. G. JOHN in *Electr. Welding in Shipbuilding* (*H.M.S.O.*) 187 *Block welding should be used for thicknesses above ⅝", the blocks starting from the centre of a seam and alternate block welds made from the centre outwards. **1952** *Gloss. Welding & Cutting of Metals* (*B.S.I.*) 41 *Block welding*, welding in which increments of the weld are made by superimposing a number of runs up to the full section before proceeding with the next increment. **1611** COTGR., *Dragee aux chevaux*, *blocke-wheat or bolimong. **1904** *Westm. Gaz.* 19 Jan. 10/2 With *block working, only about 25,000 miles.. are at present worked in America on the block-system.

24. *attrib.* and *Comb.*, with the meaning 'in a block or mass', 'inclusive', 'solid', etc.: **block-booking**, (*a*) (see quot. 1925); hence *block-booker*; (*b*) the booking of a block of reservations; **block closure**, the legislative closure of the clauses of a measure in a block or in blocks; **block grant**, a fixed inclusive grant of money made by the Exchequer to a local authority, esp. for education; also *attrib.* and *transf.*; **block heater**, see *block-storage heater*; **block rate**, a uniform rate charged in a given area, etc.; **block release**, used esp. *attrib.* of a system whereby a person is released from his work for a stated period in order to pursue a course of study; **block (-storage) heater**, a heating unit which accumulates warmth during the night and gives it off during the day; so *block-storage heating*; **block vote**, (*a*) the vote of a considerable number of people used for a particular end; (*b*) a method of voting at a congress, conference, or the like, whereby a delegate's vote has the value of the number of members he represents; such a vote; so *block voting*.

1927 *Daily Express* 25 July 6 The Wicked 'Block-booker'. **1925** *Weekly Westm.* 29 Aug. 444/3 Block-booking is the system whereby American producers refuse to let the English exhibitors have one important film unless they take also a 'block' of others, which they may never have seen. **1926** *Manch. Guardian Weekly* Mar. 221/3 The Government are prepared to remove the block-booking grievance by legislation if necessary. **1939** J. PHILLIPS in T. Harrisson & C. Madge *War begins at Home* (1940) ix. 237 The B.B.C. gradually took back the bands. They started off with block bookings. **1960** *Guardian* 17 Mar. 9/1 Sorting out a 'double' block booking in the dress circle. **1963** *Ibid.* 23 Jan. 7/7 Among the first block bookings [on a car ferry] was one for a party of 1,300 French Boy Scouts. **1901** *Daily Chron.* 14 Aug. 3/6 There was a block closure to which the Government could resort. **1900** *Westm. Gaz.* 24 Mar. 2/2 Schools earning the very highest grants will suffer because their block grant will be less than the old variable grant. **1901** *Daily Mail Year Bk.* 226/2 The Code for 1900 created a revolution in the method by which grants had been paid to schools... This is called the 'block grant system'. **1928** Block grant [see PERCENTAGE]. **1966** *Rep. Comm. Inquiry Univ. Oxf.* I. 424 The total block grant for libraries should be allocated between the libraries by the General Board. **1958** *Engineering* 4 July 32/3 The houses will be equipped.. with block heaters in the living room. **1909** *Westm. Gaz.* 1 Mar. 10/3 The insurance offices are reducing the block rate of £1 per cent. that has been charged in the fire-zone of the City. **1958** *Engineering* 28 Feb. 279/3 The theoretical side of apprentice training can best be covered by block-release courses instead of by part-time day releases. **1963** *Higher*

Educ. (*Cmnd. 2154*) 318 Students who are released by their firms to take a series of short periods of full-time study..are counted..as part-time day students. Their courses are known as *block releases.* **1960** *Engineering* 17 June 810/2 Block storage heaters are growing in popularity in the United Kingdom. **1962** *Ibid.* 5 Oct. 460/2 Block storage heating is being installed in many offices. The principle is simple: a large block of refractory material is heated by an element during the night and gives off heat to the surroundings during the day. **1901** *Daily Chron.* 15 July 7/3 Welsh miners, who, by the block vote, were enabled to return a Welshman to the Victorian Parliament. **1955** *Times* 12 July 9/3 Resolutions from the branches are critical of the way in which the block vote of the union is used at the Trades Union Congress and Labour Party conferences. **1928** *Daily Sketch* 10 Aug. 2/1 Glasgow Corporation, through block voting by Labour members, had to refuse a civic welcome to the officers.

b. *Mus.* Applied to a succession of chords in which all the parts change in the same rhythm.

1934 WEBSTER, *Block chords.* **1942** E. BLOM *Mus. in Engl.* i. 17 It may have..made use of its harmony vertically, in block chords. *Ibid.* v. 81 The choruses that often move impressively in solid block harmony. **1948** *Down Beat* 19 May 14 The final chorus is git [*sc.* guitar] and block chords. **1955** G. ABRAHAM in H. van Thal *Fanfare for E. Newman* 15 Block changes of harmony at each half-bar are now avoided. *Ibid.* 22 Chromatic and diatonic passing-notes..are used to break up some of the earlier block-chords. **1967** *Listener* 2 Mar. 288/2 In the glee, one voice had the tune, and the others accompanied it, mainly in block chords.

block (blɒk), *v.* [a. F. *bloque-r* (15th c. in Littré), of same meaning, f. *bloc* BLOCK *sb.*, the orig. sense being apparently to put 'blocks' in a way; but in later senses, 8–11, directly from BLOCK *sb.*]

1. a. *trans.* To obstruct or close with obstacles (a passage). Predicated either of the personal agent, or of the obstructions. Also *fig.*

[*c* **1425** WYNTOUN *Cron.* VII. Prol. 21 Swa my wan-wyt.. A matere gud suld block or spyle.] **1645** QUARLES *Sol. Recant.* v. 24 All his ways Are blokt with troubles. **1862** STANLEY *Jew. Ch.* (1877) I. xi. 208 The mouth of the cave was blocked by huge stones. **1881** *Chicago Times* 12 Mar., The Illinois Central Road is again blocked.

b. with *up.*

1580 NORTH *Plutarch* (1656) 926 They shut and blocked up all the ways from the one sea to the other, with mighty great pieces of timber across. **1719** DE FOE *Crusoe* (1840) I. iv. 65 I blocked up the door..with some boards. **1833** HT. MARTINEAU *Br. Creek* iv. 91 Were the avenues of the temple blocked up?

2. To shut *up* or *in* by obstructing ingress and egress, to prevent access to or exit from. Predicated of the agent or the obstruction, as in 1.

1630 PRYNNE *God No Impostor* 9 Blocking vp their hearts against the Lord. **1631** GOUGE *God's Arrows* ii. §22. 160 Blocking up people within narrow compasses. **1733** *Swift's Lett.* (1766) II. 187 We are throwing down a parcel of walls, that blocked us up every way. **1853** KANE *Grinnell Exp.* xxii. (1856) 178 Our little harbor was completely blocked in by heavy masses [of ice].

3. *spec.* **a.** To blockade, invest. [So F. *bloquer.*]

1591 UNTON *Corr.* 30 All Poictou is reduced..excepte Poictiers, by the Prince Conty, who hath also blocked that. **1796** NELSON in Nicolas *Disp.* (1845) II. 228, I ought not to have less than four Vessels to block the Port. **1871** BROWNING *Balaust.* 103 Back must you, though ten pirates blocked the bay!

b. usually with *up.*

1639 MASSINGER *Unnat. Combat* I. i, Our navy should be blocked up. **1709** STEELE *Tatler* No. 40 ¶ 10 The Blockade of Olivenza was continued..it is at present so closely blocked up that, etc. **1790** BEATSON *Nav. & Mil. Mem.* I. 334 The British fleet..bombarded and blocked it up by sea. **1839** THIRLWALL *Greece* II. 303 The danger of being defeated and blocked up in Salamis.

c. *Draughts.* To force (one's opponent's men) into such a position that they cannot move.

1850 H. G. BOHN *Handbk. Games* 408 The game is won by him who can first succeed in capturing, or blocking up, all his adversary's men. **1877** *Encycl. Brit.* VII. 445/2 The game [*sc.* draughts] proceeds until one of the players has all his men and kings taken, or has all those left on the board blocked.

d. *Cards.* (See quots.)

1884 W. B. DICK *Dick's Games of Patience* 7 *Available cards.*—Those which are not 'covered' or 'blocked' by other cards; that is, not forbidden by the particular rules of each game to be used. **1885** 'CAVENDISH' *Whist Devel.* Pref. p. x, All good players know that it is disadvantageous to block their partner's long suit. *Ibid.* 57 If the lead was from ace, queen, knave, ten only, B would block his own suit. **1898** MELROSE *Scientific Whist* 24 The retaining of a high card against a partner's command is termed 'blocking' or 'obstructing' his suit. **1901** 'TARBART' *Games of Patience* I A Patience is said to be *blocked* when, before completion, no further card is playable.

4. a. To obstruct the way or course of.

1844 G. W. KENDALL *Santa Fé Exped.* II. xiii. 260 Soon after [he] ordered his own men to leave the gambling cot of the leper, and by this means 'blocked the game'. **1865** BUSHNELL *Vicar. Sacr.* III. iii. 238 One [attribute in God] totally blocking another, and refusing to allow a step of movement till it has gotten its complete satisfaction. **1875** J. HEATH *Croquet-player* 16 A ball is blocked when another ball lies in the way. **1884** *Boston* (*Mass.*) *Jrnl.* 20 Dec. 2/2 Their little game was blocked.

b. *Neurol.* To obstruct the passage of a nervous or muscular impulse. Cf. BLOCK *sb.* 19 d.

1876 *Proc. R. Soc.* XXIV. 148 At whatever point in a contractile strip that is being progressively elongated by section the contractile wave becomes blocked, the blocking is sure to take place completely and exclusively at that point. **1877** *Ibid.* XXV. 483 Anæsthetics block spasmodic waves [in *Medusæ*]. **1906** [see *heart-block*, HEART *sb.* 56]. **1957** [see BLOCK *sb.* 19 d].

c. *to block off*: to stop, to head off. *U.S. colloq.*

1893 W. K. POST *Harvard Stories* 86 The two opposing crowds..swept across the diamond 'blocking off' the owners of the two dogs. **1899** A. H. QUINN *Pennsylv. Stories* 190, I tried to fix up two or three things with Miss Fitzgerald and she blocked me off each time, very nicely, it is true, but still she blocked me off.

d. To restrict the use or conversion of currency or other assets. Cf. FREEZE *v.* 5 e.

1932 *Economist* 30 Jan. 221/2 Unsecured cash advances may be converted into 'blocked' investments in Germany. **1937** E. AMBLER *Uncommon Danger* i. 30 At that time all German bonds were 'blocked' and not negotiable abroad. **1959** *Chambers's Encycl.* VII. 689/1 This is the 'blocked' currency. This method exerts pressure on the foreigner to buy goods from the blocking country which he would not otherwise wish to take at the price.

e. *Amer. Football.* To obstruct (an opponent, esp. a defensive player) by interposing one's body. Also *absol.* or *intr.*

1889 in *Cent. Dict.* **1891** W. CAMP *Amer. Football* 64 They [*sc.* guards] must be taught to block securely until the ball is on its way to the runner or kicker. **1896** CAMP & DELAUD *Football* v. 108 It is wise to get as close as possible to the man you wish to block. **1957** *Encycl. Brit.* IX. 479/1 Most young football players are decidedly upset if they have been taught to block a given defender on a given play and then suddenly discover that the foe is not there to be blocked. **1976** *Webster's Sports Dict.* 44/2 Offensive players block defensive players to prevent their reaching the ballcarrier or the passer or in order to drive the defensive player out of position to create a hole for the ballcarrier. **1984** *Daily Tel.* 10 Mar. 14/4 Certain players can have wonderful seasons.., yet never get their hands on the ball. This is the likelihood for the men on the line who block and protect.

5. *Cricket.* To stop (a ball) with the bat, so as merely to protect the wicket, without attempting to hit so as to score runs; also *absol.* and with wicket as obj.

1772 in H. T. Waghorn *Dawn of Cricket* (1906) 35 As the lame man could only block his wicket. **1773** *Gentl. Mag.* Nov. 568 The modern way of blocking every ball at play. **1827** E. NEALE *Living & Dead* 165 I've heard of him. Blocked well—best long stop in England. **1837** DICKENS *Pickw.* (1847) 55/1 He blocked the doubtful balls, missed the bad ones, took the good ones. **1879** W. G. GRACE in *Cricketer's Ann.* 32 When you hit, hit hard; when you block, do not be deterred from using vigour even in this movement.

6. *Parliament.* To prevent or postpone the passage of a bill; *spec.* to give notice of opposition to a bill in the House of Commons, which prevents it from being taken after half past twelve (midnight). (See BLOCK *sb.* 19 b.)

1884 MR. SPEAKER in *Times* 4 Apr. 6 The term 'blocking' is a colloquial expression recognized in this House. **1884** DK. ST. ALBANS in *Contemp. Rev.* Aug. 171 The House of Lords, by blocking the Bill, has denied to two million persons the right of having votes.

7. *intr.* To bargain. *Sc.*

c **1570** *Leg. Bp. St. Andrews* in *Scot. Poems 16th C.* II. 334 Eftir that he had lang tyme blockit, With grit difficultie he tuik thame. **1637** RUTHERFORD *Lett.* cvi. (1862) I. 269 God forbid that there were buying and selling and blocking for as good again, betwixt Christ and us.

8. a. *trans.* To shape on a block: see BLOCK *sb.* 4.

1622 ROWLANDS *Gd. Newes & Bad* 33 His hat new block'd. [**1637** HEYWOOD *Roy. King* III. iii, The haberdasher will sooner call us blockheads than block us.]

b. To hammer smooth or into a particular shape on a block.

1831 J. HOLLAND *Manuf. Metals* I. 338 The saw is once more submitted to the hammer..but it is now termed blocking. **1884** *Law Times Rep.* LI. 274/2 The hammering carried on in the process of tin blocking. *Mod.* Blocking-down, in silver manufacture, is the first process when the article has to be made from a flat piece of metal.

c. To emboss the covers of books by pressure with a device from a block.

1869 G. DODD *Dict. Manuf.* 38 In blocking, the tools are fixed into a frame to form a device for the whole cover of a book; it receives the name of gold blocking or blind blocking according as gold is or is not used.

9. a. To sketch out, mark out roughly (work to be finished afterwards); to lay out, plan. Now usually with *out*; also *in.*

1585 JAMES I. *Ess. Poesie* (Arb.) 55, I tuke earnist and willing panis to blok it [this short treatise]. **1652** URQUHART *Jewel* Wks. (1834) 264 Which designe, though intended, essayed, and blocked by many others. **1753** WASHINGTON *Diaries* (1925) I. 59 They..told 50 [canoes]..besides many others which were blocked-out, in Readiness to make. **1829** *Massachusetts Spy* 16 Dec. (Th.), There are portions [of the message] which bear the marks of having been 'blocked out' by General Jackson. **1837** LOCKHART *Scott* (1839) III. 15 The latter Cantos having..been merely blocked out when the first went to press. **1881** *Academy* 8 June 33/2 The head ..seems scarcely to belong to the rather rudely blocked limbs; but it is a nice little picture. **1884** LADY MAJENDIE *Out of Element* I. viii. 111 Pictures blocked in roughly. **1911** H. S. HARRISON *Queed* iv. 49, I wish you would block out a series of articles..designed to prepare the public mind for a thorough-going reform.

b. *Theatr.* (See quots. 1961.) Also without *out.*

1961 A. BERKMAN *Singers' Gloss. Show Bus. Jargon* 9 In a stage play the director *blocks* the scene when he designates the position and action of each of the players, as well as the location on stage of all the props. **1961** BOWMAN & BALL *Theatre Lang.* 32 *Block out*, to work out the principal business, positions and movements of actors, including their entrances and exits, during rehearsals. **1967** P. MCGERR *Murder is Absurd* vi. 73 Wednesday Warren finished blocking the first act. **1967** *Listener* 24 Aug. 240/1 At the first rehearsal..we were blocking out the moves.

10. a. To cut *out* or make into blocks.

1863 SMILES *Indust. Biog.* 305 Making wooden wedges used in pitwork, and blocking out segments of solid oak required for walling the sides of the mine. *Mod.* Coal is always blocked from the bottom of the seam.

b. *Drapery.* To make into a block (BLOCK *sb.* 6 f).

1905 H. G. WELLS *Kipps* I. iii. §2 With hands much exercised in rolling and blocking. *Ibid.* III. iii, One whole piece most exquisitely blocked of every possible width of tape.

11. a. To support or fit with blocks of wood.

1881 *Mechanic* §765 When the top of any table of this kind is a fixture, it is generally blocked, that is to say rectangular blocks of wood..are glued at short intervals into the angle formed by the meeting, etc.

b. To pave (a street) with blocks.

1891 *Argus* (Melbourne) 25 Nov. 7/8 Only those streets in which the most traffic takes place will be blocked.

blockade (blɒˈkeɪd), *sb.* [f. BLOCK *v.*, on the pattern of words in -ADE from Fr. The Fr. equivalent *blocus* dates to 16th c. *Blockade* sb. must have been used before 1684, when the vb. appears.]

1. a. The shutting up of a place, blocking of a harbour, line of coast, frontier, etc., by hostile forces or ships, so as to stop ingress and egress, and prevent the entrance of provisions and ammunition, in order to compel a surrender from hunger or want, without a regular attack. ***paper blockade***: one that is declared by a belligerent party to exist, but is not effective.

1693 *Mem. Ct. Teckely* III. 55 This Blockade was turn'd into a formal Siege in the beginning of March. **1775** R. MONTGOMERY in Sparks *Corr. Amer. Rev.* (1853) I. 485 Were a blockade alone to be the measure adopted. **1836** MACGILLIVRAY tr. *Humboldt's Trav.* iii. 42 On account of the blockade by the English. **1863** LD. RUSSELL *Let. Mr. Mason* (Bernard 293) The Declaration of Paris was in truth directed against what were once termed 'paper blockades', that is, blockades not sustained by any actual force, or sustained by a notoriously inadequate naval force. **1880** W. E. HALL *Internat. Law* (1884) 339 What is called *pacific blockade* has been used as a means of constraint short of war. **1885** *Times* 20 Feb. 5/1 The coast is really only patrolled at intervals. The use of the word 'blockade' is, therefore, an abuse of the term.

b. ***to raise a blockade***: to withdraw the investing forces, or to compel them to withdraw. ***to break a blockade***: to enter a blockaded port by force. ***to run a blockade***: to enter or leave a blockaded port by eluding the blockading force, esp. for the purpose of conveying supplies, or carrying on trade.

1810 WELLINGTON in Gurw. *Disp.* VI. 349 To induce him to raise the blockade of La Puebla. **1869** *Overland Monthly* 47 (*title*) How we ran the blockade.

2. *transf.* A blockading force; a party of blockade-men.

1882 FLEET *Glimpses Ancestors* Ser. I. 84 The chief boatman of the Blockade was killed.

3. a. *transf.* and *fig. spec.* in U.S., a stoppage or block on a railway by snow or some accident.

1742 POPE *Dunciad* IV. 191 Broad hats and hoods, and caps, a sable shoal; Thick and more thick the black blockade extends. **1833** MACAULAY *Walpole's Lett., Ess.* (1854) I. 269 The blockades laid by the Duke of A. to the hearts of the Marquise de B. and the Comtesse de C. **1835** T. HOOK *G. Gurney* I. iii. (L.) This was a blockade which even the ingenuity of the wit could not evade. **1856** *N.Y. Herald* 8 Jan. 1/4 The railroads are being slowly relieved from the blockade of snow. **1873** J. H. BEADLE *Undevel. West* xix. 350 With the snow sheds since constructed, and other precautions, we may reasonably expect no more blockades. **1881** *Chicago Times* 12 Mar., The snow blockade told more severely in the produce trade. **1881** *Ibid.* 16 Apr. [A railway accident] causing a blockade of the road for several hours. **1910** *N.Y. Even. Post* 13 Dec. 3 When a drawbar on the middle car of a third Avenue elevated train broke..a long blockade began.

b. A barrier on a river. *U.S.*

1871 *Game Laws* (*N.C.*) in *Fur, Fin & Feather* (1872) 153 It shall not be lawful for any person to draw a seine.. between the blockade near Hill's Point..and the falls at Wm. S. Battle's factory.

4. *Attrib.* and *Comb.*, as ***blockade force***; **blockade-man**, a member of the force employed to prevent smuggling; a coastguardsman; **blockade-run, -running**, the action of running a blockade; **blockade-runner**, a vessel which runs or attempts to run into a blockaded port; the owner, master, or one of the crew of such a vessel. (These words obtained special notoriety during the American War of Secession, when many British ships were engaged in running the blockade of Richmond and other southern ports.)

1882 FLEET *Glimpses Ancestors* Ser. I. 83 A *Blockade force of 40 men. *Ibid.* 82 Constant conflicts between the *blockade-men and the smugglers. **1836** DICKENS *Sk. Boz* (1850) 214 Blockade-man after blockade-man had passed the spot, wending his way towards his solitary post. **1863** *St. James's Mag.* VIII. 346 My first and last *blockade run. **1863** *Rep. Secr. of Navy* (*U.S.*) p. v, Not a single *blockade-runner has succeeded in reaching the city [of Charleston] for months. **1878** *N. Amer. Rev.* CXXVII. 381 The English blockade-runners passed through the American blockading

squadron. **1879** *Cassell's Techn. Educ.* IV. 371/2 Steel was.. used extensively in 'blockade-runners' built during the American civil war. **1864** *Rep. Secr. of Navy* (*U.S.*) p. xvii, This species of illicit traffic and *blockade running.

blo'ckade, *v.* [f. prec. sb.]

1. *trans.* To subject to a blockade as an incident of war; to beset by a hostile force, so as to prevent ingress or egress.

c **1680** in Somers *Tracts* I. 471 Those who were set to blockade the Castle. **1684** *Scanderbeg Rediv.* v. 95 To quarter round about Caminiec, and strictly Blockade that place. **1781** T. JEFFERSON *Corr.* Wks. 1859 I. 299 The enemy are.. blockaded by land. **1836** MACGILLIVRAY tr. *Humboldt's Trav.* xx. 294 The port was.. strictly blockaded. **1880** MCCARTHY *Own Time* III. xliii. 289 A state cannot blockade its own ports.

2. *transf.* and *fig.* To block up, obstruct. *spec.* in U.S., to block (a road or railway, etc.). Cf. BLOCKADE *sb.* 3.

1732 POPE *Ep. Bathurst* 57 Huge bales of British cloth blockade the door. **1814** SCOTT *Wav.* xxxvii, All precautions to blockade his view were.. abandoned. **1816** *Niles' Reg.* X. 216/2 In consequence of the vast body of ice with which it [*sc.* the harbour] is yet *blockaded*, they were unable to get in. **1846** PRESCOTT *Ferd. & Is.* II. xix. 185 Every avenue to the hall was blockaded. **1872** *Rep. Vermont Board Agric.* I. 24 An exceedingly severe snow storm.. completely blockaded many of the roads.

blo'ckaded, *ppl. a.* [f. prec. + -ED.] Invested with a blockade; completely beset, blocked up.

1846 ARNOLD *Hist. Rome* II. xxviii. 114 *note*, A besieged or blockaded army. **1850** ALISON *Hist. Europe* V. xxxiii. §9. 487 A blockaded port is to be understood only when such a force is stationed at its entrance as makes it dangerous to enter.

blo'ckader. [f. as prec. + -ER[1].] One who blockades; a blockading vessel.

1849 GROTE *Greece* II. l. VI. 317 To repel with spears and darts all approach of the blockaders. **1863** *Glasgow Her.* 8 Sept., All the blockaders are hung up for want of coal.

blo'ckading, *ppl. a.* [f. as prec. + -ING[2].] That blockades; besetting.

1708 *Chron.* in *Ann. Reg.* 85/2 The general of a blockading army. **1844** THIRLWALL *Greece* VIII. lxiv. 284 The blockading squadron.

blockage ('blɒkɪdʒ). [f. BLOCK *sb.* + -AGE: cf. F. *blocage.*] A blocked (up) state; obstruction.

1874 GLADSTONE in *Contemp. Rev.* Oct. 669 The mutilations and blockages of the fabrics. **1883** *Pall Mall G.* There was a blockage in the traffic.

'block-book. [f. BLOCK *sb.*] †**a.** A book of wooden tablets. *Obs.* **b.** A book printed from engraved wooden blocks.

1727-51 CHAMBERS *Cycl.* s.v. *Book*, Block Books.. those written on wooden planks or tablets, smoothed for that purpose with an ascia, and a plane. **1816** SINGER *Hist. Cards* 109 These Block books excited the idea of the invention of moveable characters. **1859** *Encycl. Brit.* (ed. 8) XVIII. 522 The design and execution are very superior to those of the St. Christopher and the block-books.

blocked (blɒkt), *ppl. a.* [f. BLOCK *v.* + -ED.] Shut up by obstructions, blockaded, obstructed, stopped in a course; shaped on or with a block, roughly shaped; furnished with blocks.

1856 KANE *Arct. Exp.* I. xxx. 408 A square, blocked-out aspect. [see BLOCK *v.*]

blocker ('blɒkə(r)). [f. BLOCK *v.* + -ER[1].] **1.** One who blocks. *spec.* in *Shoemaking* and *Bookbinding.* Also in *Hat-making* (cf. BLOCK *sb.* 4 a, *v.* 8).

1609 SKENE *Reg. Maj.* Table 69, Fishers, Forestallers, Regraters, Sutours, Kemesters, Bloccers. **1866** *Lond. Rev.* 27 Oct. 459/2 There are various epithets for shoemakers.. there are welters.. clickers, blockers, runners, &c. **1884** *Pall Mall G.* 4 Jan. 10/1 A blocker, in the employ of Messrs. ——, bookbinders. **1884** *Manch. Exam.* 8 Aug. 5/7 The inveterate blocker. **1894** *Daily News* 26 Apr. 2/5 A straw hat blocker. **1898** *Daily Chron.* 14 Oct. 10/5 Blocker.. for felt and straw hats.

2. A tool for blocking.

1407 *Test. Ebor.* I. 347 Lego Petro apprenticio meo j. chipax.. j. blokker, j. twybyll.

3. *colloq.* A small piece of meat placed for sale on the butcher's block, as opposed to the 'joints' hung on hooks.

1848 *Fraser's Mag.* XXXVII. 396 Forced to substitute a 'blocker' of meat, with its cheap accompaniment of bread and vegetables.. for poultry and rump-steaks.

4. a. A cricketer who habitually blocks the bowling. (Cf. BLOCK *v.* 5.)

1851 J. PYCROFT *Cricket Field* vii. 14 One of the most awkward, poking, vexatious blockers that ever produced a counterfeit of cricket defied Bayley and Cobbett at Oxford in 1836,—three hours, and made five and thirty runs.

b. *Amer. Football.* An offensive player whose task is to obstruct an opponent with his own body. Also *fig.*

1935 *Collier's Mag.* 21 Dec. 12/4 Riley Smith of Alabama was the year's finest blocker. **1945** L. H. BAKER *Football* xiv. 13 Much of the success of a team depends on the efficiency of its blockers. **1957** *Encycl. Brit.* IX. 479/1 These lines.. further aided the defensive team by confusing the offensive team's blockers on their assignments. **1973** *Black Panther* 22 Sept. 10/1 After futilely awaiting some sign from the sidelines that they were not mere blockers, to be used and trod upon in their football loving president's game plan to power, the four have decided to talk. **1984** *N.Y. Times* 2 Jan. 31/1 Mark Schellen,.. fullback, fills the twin roles of blocker and rusher.

5. *slang.* A bowler hat.

1934 J. BROPHY *Waterfront* xi. 204 He'd worn one at the wedding, the first 'blocker' he'd ever had. **1966** F. SHAW et al. *Lern Yerself Scouse* 58 Foremen traditionally wore bowler-hats, or 'blockers'.

blockhead ('blɒkhɛd). [f. BLOCK *sb.* + HEAD.]

†**1.** A wooden head, a wooden block for hats or wigs; *hence*, a head with no more intelligence in it than one of these, a blockish head. *Obs.* (This would now be written *block head* or *block-head.*)

1549 [implied in BLOCKHEADED]. **1589** *Hay any Work* B, The ofspringes of your owne blockheads. **1607** SHAKS. *Cor.* II. iii. 31 Your wit.. 'tis strongly wadg'd vp in a blocke-head. *a* **1680** BUTLER *Rem.* (1759) I. 217 To maintain their own Hypotheses, Broke one another's Blockheads, and the Peace. **1698** VANBRUGH *Prov. Wife* v. v, How long would my blockhead have been a-producing this!

2. Hence, One whose head is blockish or 'wooden'; an utterly stupid fellow.

1549 COVERDALE *Erasm. Par. 1 Cor.* xi. 14 A blockheade that hathe loste the judgemente of nature. **1593** NASHE *Christs T.* 69 b, Bee he the veriest block-head vnder heauen. **1668** CULPEPPER & COLE *Barthol. Anat.* I. xxiv. 59 Block-heads and dull-pated Asses. **1712** BUDGELL *Spect.* No. 307 ¶12 Being dismissed as an hopeless Block-head. **1875** JOWETT *Plato* (ed. 2) I. 222 He might think me a blockhead, and refuse to take me.

†**B.** *adj.* Blockheaded, stupid. *Obs.*

1606 in Bullen *O. Pl.* (1884) III. 32 The block-head heart of a woman. **1705** HICKERINGILL *Priest-cr.* IV. 239 Oh! the Block-head World we live in! **1719** D'URFEY *Pills* (1872) IV. 2 All such Blockhead fools.

Hence **'blockheadess.** *nonce-wd.* [see -ESS.] A female blockhead.

1827 LADY MORGAN *O'Briens & O'Fl.* IV. 361 All the blockheads and blockheadesses think themselves printable.

blockheaded ('blɒk,hɛdɪd), *a.* [f. BLOCK-HEAD (sense 1) + -ED[2].] Having a 'block-head'; obtuse of intellect, dull, stupid. Of persons (rarely their productions). Hence **,block'headedness.**

1549 OLDE *Erasm. Par. Ephes.* Prol. C iij, Blockeheaded asses.. doublefaced frendes. **1594** CAREW *Huarte's Exam. Wits* xiii. (1596) 233 He is block-headed and dull. **1657** FLATMAN *Cordial* 1/2 See, how the block headed Multitude wonders! **1702** *Eng. Theophrast.* 377 Old men are only great block-headed boys with beards. **1860** MISS YONGE *Stokesley Secr.* viii. (1880) 252 My father said I was too block-headed to beat navigation into.

1716 M. DAVIES in *Ath. Brit.* II. 168 The loudest piece of blockheadedness, and the last shift of Dunces.

blockheadish ('blɒk,hɛdɪʃ), *a.* [see -ISH.] Of the nature of a blockhead; stupid, obtuse. Hence **,block'headishness.**

1833 *Fraser's Mag.* VIII. 741 A dull, proud, prosy, block-headish person. **1863** CARLYLE in Froude *Life* II. xxvi. 280, I feel myself to have become foul and blockheadish. **1656** EARL MONM. *Advt. fr. Parnass.* 405 By their supine blockheadishness.

blockheadism ('blɒkhɛdɪzm). [see -ISM.] The characteristic action, conduct, or condition of a blockhead; stupidity.

1753 SMART *Notes to Hilliad* (R.) Though now reduced to that state of blockheadism. **1823** *Blackw. Mag.* XIV. 698 One of the most delightful pieces of self-satisfied blockheadism. **1843** CARLYLE *Past & Pr.* 46 They set no quackeries and blockheadisms anywhere to rule over us.

†**'blockheadly**, *a. Obs.* [f. as prec. + -LY[1].] Of or pertaining to, or like a blockhead; stupid.

1612 CHAPMAN *Widdowes T.* Dram. Wks. 1873 III. 18 Your blockheadly tradesman. **1693** SHADWELL *Volunteers* IV. Plays 1720 IV. 467 This is made up by some blockheadly Fellow! **1694** ECHARD *Plautus* 4 What a blockheadly question.. for a Deity to ask?

blockhouse ('blɒkhaʊs), *sb.* [Common since *c* 1500: of uncertain history. The Ger. equivalent *blochhaus* ('einen steinen Blochhaus') is quoted by Grimm 1557 and 1602; the Du. *blokhuis* is in Kilian 1599; Fr. *blocus*, generally considered to be the same word, and orig. in same sense, is quoted by Littré in the 16th c. (cf. BLOCCUZ). So far as evidence goes, the Eng. is thus the earliest; but we should expect it to be of Du. or Ger. origin. In any case the sense was not originally (as in modern notion) a house composed of blocks of wood, but one which blocks or obstructs a passage. The history and age of the Ger. *blockhaus* and F. *blocus* require more investigation.]

1. a. *orig.* A detached fort blocking or covering the access to a landing, a narrow channel, a mountain pass, a bridge, or other strategical point. **b.** In later use: An edifice of one or (formerly) more storeys, constructed chiefly of timber, loop-holed and embrasured for firing.

1512 *Act 4 Hen. VIII*, i. §1 Nother pile blokhouse ne Bulwork is made to greve or annoye theym at theyr landyng. **1538** LELAND *Itin.* III. 21 There is a Blok House and a fair Pere in the Est side of the Peninsula. **1550** LEVER *Serm.* 94 Block houses and bulwarkes, made and kepte.. for the saue garde of thys realm. **1577** HOLINSHED *Chron.* III. 946/2 All the havens to be fensed with bulworks, and blockehouses. **1597** GERARD *Herbal* xli. §4. 257 It.. groweth by the blockhouse of Tilberie. **1615** G. SANDYS *Trav.* 210 At the end of the peir stands a paltry blockhouse furnished with suitable artillery. **1712** *Lond. Gaz.* No. 5014/1 The Highway between Highgate Gatehouse.. and Barnet Blockhouse. **1813** WELLINGTON *Disp.* X. 502 A strong stone block house which served as a head to the bridge. **1816** C. JAMES *Mil. Dict.* 54/1 *Block-house*.. a kind of wooden fort or fortification, sometimes mounted on rollers, or on a flat-bottomed vessel, serving either on the lakes or rivers, or in counterscarps or counter-approaches. **1859** TURNER *Dom. Archit.* III. II. vii. 322 Calshot Castle is one of the block-houses erected by Henry VIII. to defend the coast. **1878** BLACK *Green Past.* xliv. 356 A curious little inn which had originally been a blockhouse against the Indians.

c. *slang.* A prison.

[cf. **1624** CAPT. SMITH *Virginia* III. xi. 85 To stop the disorders of our disorderly Theeues.. built a Blockhouse.] **1796** GROSE *Dict. Vulgar Tongue*, *Block Houses*, prisons, houses of correction, &c.

d. A house of squared logs of timber.

1857 *Penny Mag.* VI. 437 Block-houses, which are built of blocks, or squared logs of timber. **1878** LADY HERBERT tr. *Hübner's Ramble* I. ii. 18 The Backwoodsman who begins by building a blockhouse.

e. A reinforced concrete shelter used as an observation point, etc.

1953 *Monsanto Mag.* July 4 This blockhouse is as close as anyone gets to a missile at take off. **1962** A. SHEPARD in *Into Orbit* 104 All the training we had gone through with the blockhouse crew and booster crew was really paying off.

2. *transf.* and *fig.*

1559 *Mirr. Mag.*, *Rudacke* i. 7 Bloudshead a blockehouse to beat away ill. **1615** *Curry-c. for Cox-c.* v. 230 The Scripture is a sufficient shelter against Atheisme, were the Blockhouses of your Miracles battered to the ground. **1856** KANE *Arct. Exp.* I. xxix. 385 Flour, beans, and dried apples make a quadrangular blockhouse on the floe.

3. blockhouse system, the system of separating the theatre of war by chains of blockhouses, devised by Lord Kitchener in the later stages of the South African war, 1899–1902, and also used elsewhere.

1901 *Daily Chron.* 4 Sept. 5/3 The section of the line south of Pienaars River.. is not yet fully protected by blockhouses, the blockhouse system having been first applied to those sections most requiring such protection. **1946** *Ann. Reg.* *1945* 270 The Communists were.. moving freely through the gaps in the Japanese block-house system.

blockhouse ('blɒkhaʊs), *v.* [f. the sb.] *trans.* To cut off from occupation or attack by a line of blockhouses under the ***blockhouse system***.

1901 *Daily Chron.* 4 Sept. 5/3 Two thousand miles of railway are already 'blockhoused'. *Ibid.* 27 Dec. 4/5 General De Wet.. is doing his best to prevent the 'block-housing' of the north-eastern angle of the Orange River Colony.

'blocking, *vbl. sb.* [f. BLOCK *v.* or *sb.* + -ING[1].]

1. a. The action of the vb. BLOCK.

1637 [see BLOCK *v.* 7]. **1659** in Rushw. *Hist. Coll.* I. 69 The besieging of Manheim, and the blocking of Frankendale. **1706** *Lond. Gaz.* No. 4242/1 Orders.. for the close blocking up of that Place. **1850** 'BAT' *Cricket Manual* 31 It was totally useless for blocking. **1864** *Times* 13 Oct., Detained by the blocking up of the line. **1870** *Daily News* 6 Sept. 5 The blocking of Bazaine at Metz.

attrib. **1836** *New Sporting Mag.* Oct. 360 Mr. Massey.. in his anxiety to preserve his wicket, has carried the blocking system too far. **1867** G. H. SELKIRK *Guide to Cricket-Ground* vii. 120 Some men adopt what they call a blocking game, never hitting at a ball unless it is decidedly wide of the wicket. **1884** *Pall Mall G.* 7 Apr. 3/1 Mr. Warton.. has returned to his blocking habits.

b. Signalling by the 'block system' (see BLOCK *sb.* 19 c). Also *attrib.*, as ***blocking inspector***.

1903 *Westm. Gaz.* 26 Oct. 13/1 Blocking inspector between Eastwood and Bradford. **1908** TRATMAN *Railway Track* (ed. 3) 266 In some cases a third position [of the semaphore arm] is introduced for permissive blocking. **1908** W. G. RAYMOND *Railroad Engin.* 121 The foregoing description introduces no distant signals, and in early automatic blocking there were none. **1909** H. R. WILSON *Safety Brit. Railways* 59 The signalman must give what is known as the blocking-back signal.

c. *Bookbinding.* The action of the verb (sense 8 c); also *attrib.*, as ***blocking-machine***, ***-press***, ***-shop***.

1846 DODD *Brit. Manuf.* VI. 103 This is.. effected.. by means of a small blocking-press. *Ibid.* 105 The punches or small devices.. are fixed.. to a metallic plate, and thus impressed on the book at one blow by a press. This is then called 'blocking'. In the 'blocking-shop' are [etc.]. **1902** *Encycl. Brit.* XXVI. 302/2 Blocking Machine... A blocking press is now, in consequence of the size of many of the blocks, a large and cumbersome machine.

d. *Hat-making.* The shaping of a hat on the block (see BLOCK *sb.* 4 a); also *attrib.*, as ***blocking-kettle***, ***-machine*** (hence ***-machinist***).

1845 DODD *Brit. Manuf.* V. 170 The shaping of hats, from the first rough 'blocking' to the production of a flat and smooth-edged brim. *a* **1877** KNIGHT *Dict. Mech.*, *Blocking-kettle*, a hot bath in which hats are softened in the process of manufacture, so as to be drawn over blocks. *a* **1884** *Ibid.* Suppl., *Blocking machine*, a machine in which the crude cone-shaped hat-body is brought to shape. **1921** *Dict. Occupational Terms* (1927) §409 *Blocking machinist*: (i) (felt hats) pulls felt hood by hand on to block [etc.]; (ii) (straw hats) presses hat.. in a gas-heated machine [etc.].

e. *Bootmaking.* (See quot. *a* 1877.)

a **1877** KNIGHT *Dict. Mech.*, *Blocking*,.. the process of bending leather for boot-fronts to the required shapes. **1889** G. B. SHAW *Fabian Ess. Socialism* 67 A visitor to a shoe factory to-day will see the following machines.. for blocking.

f. *Psychol.* The inhibition of a train of thought or association, etc.

1890 W. JAMES *Princ. Psychol.* II. xxvi. 527 We shall study anon the blocking and its release. Our higher thought is full of it. **1930** *Psychol. Abstr.* IV. 120/2 Concerning the question of associative blockings. **1943** *Mind* LII. 364 Köhler believes that there may be 'blocking' processes of an electro-chemical character.

g. *Amer. Football*: see BLOCK *v.* 4 e.

1891 W. CAMP *Amer. Football* 50 When a drop is to be attempted, the blocking on both sides must be close and long. **1957** *Encycl. Brit.* IX. 479/1 Coaches met this situation by drilling their players in two sets of blocking assignments, one for the five-man line and one for the six-man defense. **1970** *Washington Post* 30 Sept. D4/8 Blocking has been the hardest thing for the kids to learn,..and the offensive line play is usually the last thing that comes around.

h. *Theatr.* The action of the verb (sense 9 b).

1961 A. BERKMAN *Singers' Gloss. Show Bus. Jargon* 9 *Blocking*, the act of planning the stage action of a play. **1967** P. McGERR *Murder is Absurd* vii. 92 On Friday the blocking was completed and Mark was beginning to feel secure in his movements and the handling of his props.

2. The product of this action; the thing blocked.

1585 JAMES I. *Ess. Poesie* (Arb.) 21, I haue put in, the French on the one side of the leif, and my blocking on the other. **1853** KANE *Grinnell Exp.* xvii. (1856) 130 The square blocking of the rugged precipices.

3. *Carpentry*, etc. (see quots. and cf. BLOCK *v.* 11.)

1823 P. NICHOLSON *Pract. Build.* 192 With blockings glued in the internal angles. **1876** GWILT *Encycl. Archit.*, Gloss., *Blockings*, small pieces of wood fitted in and glued to the interior angle of two boards or other pieces, for the purpose of giving additional strength to the joint. **1883** *Harper's Mag.* 937/2 The blocking is knocked away.

4. blocking-course or **blocking**: 'the plain course of stone which surmounts the cornice at the top of a Greek or Roman building: also a course of stone or brick forming a projecting line without mouldings at the base of a building.' *Gloss. Goth. Archit.* 1845.

1760 RAPER in *Phil. Trans.* LI. 815 The height of the blocking was probably intended for 2 Roman feet. **1859** *Encycl. Brit.* III. 508 *Blocking course*, a deep but slightly projecting course in an elevation, to act as cornice to an arcade, or to separate a basement from a superior story.

5. Blocks collectively.

1901 *Daily Chron.* 3 Sept. 7/4 Karri blocking.

blockish ('blɒkɪʃ), *a.* [f. BLOCK *sb.* + -ISH.]

1. Of the nature of a block.

1565 CALFHILL *Answ. Treat. Crosse* (1846) 20 The blockish Images, the dead Crosses. **1869** LOWELL *Cathedral* Poet. Wks. (1879) 446 Fear, That makes a fetish and misnames it God (Blockish or metaphysic, matters not).

2. Like a senseless block in the want of apprehension; excessively dull, stupid, obtuse.

a. of persons.

1548 UDALL, etc. *Erasm. Par. Luke* iii. 7 The grosse and blockishe ignoraunte multitude. **1587** GOLDING *De Mornay* ix. 136 With the allowance euen of the blockishest. **1680** HICKERINGILL *Meroz* 38 To Gull the Blockish English. **1756** WESLEY *Wks.* (1872) X. 489 We see..dull, heavy, blockish Ministers. **1868** NETTLESHIP *Browning* i. 23 While the other seems morose and blockish, this man is kindly.

b. of personal qualities, productions, etc.

a **1555** RIDLEY *Wks.* 225, I will make it evident how blockish and gross your answer is. **1670** MILTON *Hist. Eng.* IV. Wks. (1851) 172 Left only to obscure and blockish Chronicles. **1741** OLDYS *Eng. Stage* v. 63 Blockish Stupidity, as in Rusticks. **1835** BROWNING *Paracels.* 101 Whose innate blockish dullness.

3. Blocklike in form; roughly blocked out, rude, clumsy.

1880 SWINBURNE *Stud. Shaks.* ii. (ed. 2) 100 Such a blockish model as this. **1880** GRANT WHITE *Every-Day Eng.* 295 Our speech would be clumsy, the forms of our thought blockish.

'blockishly, *adv.* [f. prec. + -LY².] In a blockish manner; stupidly, dully.

1553 GRIMALDE *Cicero's Offices* I. (1558) 57 That.. nothing blockishly or carterly wee do. **1590** C. S. *Right Relig.* 9 So blockishly blind. **1650** A. B. *Mutat. Polemo* 14 Blockishly impudent. **1734** A. WELWOOD *Glimpse Glory* 167 What Sweetness before I experienced blockishly and in Part.

'blockishness. [f. as prec. + -NESS.] The quality of being blockish; gross stupidity or dullness.

1561 T. NORTON *Calvin's Inst.* I. v. 9 Such is our grosse blockisshenesse. **1610** HOLLAND *Camden's Brit.* I. 109 O desperate dulnesse, and blind blockishnesse of mind. **1651** FULLER *Abel Rediv., Melancthon* 235 Wonder at the insulsitie and blockishnesse of the man. **1702** C. MATHER *Magn. Chr.* IV. ii. 42 Extreme blindness and blockishness.

† **'blockman¹.** *Obs.* A watcher, a coast-guard.

1570 LEVINS *Manip.* 20 Blockman, *spiculator.*

blockman² ('blɒkmən). [f. BLOCK *sb.*] An assistant in a butcher's or fishmonger's shop employed chiefly at the block in cutting up meat, filleting fish, etc.

1903 *Daily Chron.* 16 Sept. 8/5 Fishmongers.—Good blockman wanted.

block tin: see TIN.

† **'blockwood.** Obs. name of LOGWOOD.

1581 *Act 23 Eliz.* ix. §1 Stuff called Logwood, *alias* Blockwood. **1619** DALTON *Countrey Just.* xviii. (1630) 48 Concerning the using of Logwood alias blockwood in dying. **1667** *Lond. Gaz.* No. 133/4 Two small Vessels, one..of 40. Tuns, with Block-wood and Iron.

blocky ('blɒkɪ), *a.* [f. BLOCK *sb.* + -Y¹.] **1.** Of the nature of or resembling a block, *esp.* **a.** Of a person or animal: of solid build, stocky. **b.** Defining a commercial grade of shellac.

1879 G. F. JACKSON *Shropsh. Word-bk., Blocky*.., short and stout. **1895** *Daily News* 4 Sept. 7/5 Shellac... Ordinary to good second orange cakey and blocky 115s. to 119s. **1900** *Westm. Gaz.* 11 Dec. 7/3 A most shapely beast [*sc.* a heifer], ..being grandly filled up, and of a most blocky type throughout. **1904** *N.Y. Tribune* 15 May, A blocky pair of forty-seven inch ponies. **1958** *Times* 1 July ii/5 The level blocky beef animal, which delighted the farmer's eye in the past. **1968** H. HARMAR *Chihuahua Guide* 232 *Blocky*,..used to describe a head which is cube-shaped, as in the Boston Terrier.

2. *Photogr.* Having the appearance of being printed in blocks, from an unequal distribution of light and shade.

1889 in *Cent. Dict.*

blodge (blɒdʒ). [Imitative; cf. BLOTCH, SPLODGE *sb.*] = SPLOTCH *sb.*

1930 'R. CROMPTON' *William's Happy Days* viii. 192 Sixpennoth of cream blodges, please. Big 'uns. **1951** S. SPENDER *World within World* 153 The pink blodges, small black dots, lines like brackets, characteristic of this style of decoration.

† **blok.** *Obs.* [Cf. OHG. *biloh*, MHG. *bloch* an enclosure (Mätz.).] An enclosed space.

c **1325** *E.E. Allit. P.* C. 272 Til he blunt in a blok as brod as a halle.

† **blok(e, bloc,** *a. Obs.* [The normal ME. repr. of OE. *blác*:—OTeut. **blaiko-z*, f. the stem of *blîkan, blaik* to shine. But the OE. *blæc*, BLACK had also a long-vowel form *blǣc-*, which would also give ME. *bloke*; and in the few known instances it is difficult to say which is the sense. Cf. BLAKE.]

Pale; also (by confusion of forms) black, dark.

c **1200** *Trin. Coll. Hom.* 171 þe unbileffule men bicumeð in þe fure swo bloke and swo eiseliche and swo ateliche, þat bi hundredfealde [ben] grisluker þan ani niht þeoster. *a* **1225** *Ancr. R.* 332 Te soule þet was bloc, & nefde bute dead heou, haueð ikeiht cwic heou, & is iruded feire. *c* **1430** *Pol. Rel. & L. Poems* 206 Nowe ligiȝt he ded boþe blok & blo.

bloke (bləʊk), *sb. slang.* Also bloak. [Origin unknown: Ogilvie compares 'Gypsy and Hind. *loke* a man.'] **a.** Man, fellow.

1851 MAYHEW *Lond. Labour* III. 397 (Hoppe) If we met an old bloke we propped him. **1862** KINGSLEY in *Macm. Mag.* Dec. 96 Little better than blokes and boodles after all. **1865** MISS BRADDON in *Temple Bar* XIII. 483 The society of the aged bloke is apt to pall upon the youthful intellect.

b. *Naval slang.* The ship's commander.

1914 'WATCH-KEEPER' *Five Minutes to One Bell* 7 Also the sailor will come to say of you, 'Oh! once you're taken before '*Im*, you're safe to see "The Bloke" in the morning.' **1919** W. LANG *Sea Lawyer's Log* I. vi. 69 If you gets noisy and boisterous-like you sees the Bloke in the morning. **1946** J. IRVING *Royal Navalese* 33 *Bloke*..the traditional Lower-Deck name for a warship's Commander and Executive Officer.

† **bloke,** *v. Obs.* In 3 blokien. [Obs. southern form of BLAKE *v.*, OE. *blácian*, f. *blác* pale: see BLOK(E, BLOC *a.*] *intr.* To turn pale.

c **1250** LAY. 19799 His neb bi-gan to blokie [**1205** his neb bigon to blakien]. *c* **1275** *Signs Death* in *O.E. Misc.* 101 [H]wenne þin heou blokeþ And þi strengþe wokeþ.

† **'blokne(n,** *v. Obs.* [ME. southern form of *blaknen*, BLAKE: cf. BLAIKEN.] = prec.

c **1315** SHOREHAM 4 Thi body arise schel, Of deithe nammore to blokne.

blom(e, obs. form of BLOOM.

† **'bloman.** *Obs.* Also 3 bleo-, bloa-, blamon, 4–6 blooman. [f. BLO *a.* + MAN: corresp. to and perh. ad. ON. *blámaðr* in same sense. The northern form was *blamon*, a later literary Eng. form BLUEMAN. Hence mod. Welsh *blowmon, blewmon* negro.] A black man, negro; a blackamoor.

c **1205** LAY. 25380 Of Ethiope he brohte þa bleomen. *a* **1225** *Ancr. R.* 236 Blac as a bloamon. *a* **1225** *St. Marher.* (1862) 10 Muchele del blaccre then euer eni blamon. *a* **1300** *Cursor M.* 2118 (Gött.) Indie..lijs mast into þe south þar þe blomen [*v.r.* blamen] mast er couth. **1398** TREVISA *Barth. De P.R.* III. xxiv. (1495) 73 Ethyopia, bloo men londe. *Ibid.* VIII. xxii, þe londe of blo men [**1535** bloo men; **1582** bliew men]. *a* **1400** *Octouian* 1406 The stede was broght out of stable: The bloman hym ladde with a cable.

blomange, obs. form of BLANCMANGE.

blomary, -ie, obs. forms of BLOOMERY.

† **'blommer.** *Obs. rare*⁻¹. ? Uproar, confusion.

a **1529** SKELTON *Elynour Rum.* 407 Amonge all the blommer, Another brought a skommer.

blond, obs. variant of BLAND *v.*

blonde, blond (blɒnd), *a.* and *sb.* Forms: 5 blounde, 7– blonde, 8– blond. [a. F. *blond, blonde* yellow-haired, 'a colour midway between golden and light chestnut' (Littré), = Sp. *blondo*, It. *biondo*:—med.L. *blondus, blundus* yellow (explained in a passage quoted by Du Cange '*flavus* qui vulgo dicitur *blondus*'). Origin uncertain: see Diez and Littré. In English used by Caxton (in form *blounde*); reintroduced from mod.Fr. in 17th c., and still sometimes treated as French, as to be written without final *e* when applied to a man, esp. substantively, *a blonde*; in N. Amer. commonly written *blond* like the Fr. masculine, but in Britain the form *blonde* is now preferred in all senses.

Cf. OE. *blanden-feax, blonden-feax* having mixed or grizzly hair, grey-haired, old; also *beblonden*, given in Bosworth as 'dyed', both from *blondan* to mix, BLAND *v.* Hence Du Cange, s.v. *Blundus*, conjectures the original sense to be 'dyed', the ancient Germans being accustomed to dye the hair yellow.]

A. *adj.* **a.** Properly (of the hair): Of a light golden brown, light auburn; but commonly used in sense of light-coloured, 'fair', as opposed to 'dark', or 'brunette', and extended to the complexion of those who have hair of this colour.

1481 CAXTON *Myrr.* II. xvii. 103 The rayes of the sonne make the heer of a man abourne or blounde. **1484** —— *Ryall Bk.* O v, They arraye theyr heer lyke wymmen and force it to be yelowe, and yf they be blacke, they by crafte make them blounde and abourne. **1683** EVELYN *Mem.* (1857) II. 192 Prince George of Denmark..had the Danish countenance, *blonde*. **1798** *Life Cath. II.* (ed. 2) I. iv. 426 A fine blond head of hair. **1834** CAMPBELL *Life Mrs. Siddons* II. ii. 55 A delicate and blonde beauty. **1860** GEO. ELIOT *Mill on Fl.* v. iv. 306 If the blond girl were forsaken.

b. of flowers. *poet.*

c **1865** M. ARNOLD *Thyrsis* xiii, Red loosestrife and blond meadow-sweet.

c. *blond(e lace*: see B 2.

1771 SMOLLETT *Humph. Cl.* (1815) 84, I missed three quarters of blond lace. *c* **1840** LADY BLESSINGTON *Sk. & Fragm.* in *Casquet Lit.* (1877) I. 216/2 Wore my new Parisian robe of blonde lace.

d. *Comb.*, as **blonde-complexioned, -locked,** adjs.; **blond(e) beast** [tr. G. *blonde bestie*], a man of the Nordic type; **blond-metal,** a variety of clay ironstone of the coal measures.

1831 J. HOLLAND *Manuf. Metals* I. 33 In the neighbourhood of Wednesbury is dug that peculiar species of iron ore called blond metal. **1837** CARLYLE *Fr. Rev.* II. I. xi. 73 That little blonde-locked too hasty Dauphin. *c* **1880** GRANT ALLEN *Anglo-Sax. Brit.* 56 We know that the pure Anglo-Saxons were a..blonde-complexioned race. [**1887** F. W. NIETZSCHE *Zur Genealogie der Moral* I. 21 Das Raubthier, die prachtvolle nach Beute und Sieg lüstern schweifende blonde Bestie.] **1907** G. B. SHAW *Maj. Barbara* Pref. 151 Nietzsche..is the victim in England of a single much quoted..phrase 'big blonde beast'. **1911** G. K. CHESTERTON *Innoc. Father Brown* x. 266 The man..was a magnificent creature... In structure he was the blonde beast of Nietzsche. **1949** G. B. SHAW *16 Self Sketches* xiv. 105 My auburn hair was never really Highland red like my sister Agnes's. But I was a 'blonde beast' of Danish type unmistakably. **1967** M. PROCTER *Exercise Hoodwink* x. 73 If he did not throw in his lot with this big blond beast he would go to prison anyway.

B. *sb.*

1. A person with blond hair; one with light or 'fair' hair and the corresponding complexion; *esp.* a woman, in which case spelt *blonde*.

1822 *Edin. Rev.* 199 Brenda, the laughing blue-eyed blonde. **1833** *Penny Cycl.* s.v. *Albinos*, The blonds of the European race. **1858** O. W. HOLMES *Aut. Breakf.-t.* 212 Negative or washed blondes, arrested by Nature on the way to become albinesses.

2. a. (More fully *blonde lace*): A silk lace of two threads, twisted and formed in hexagonal meshes; orig. of the colour of raw silk, but now white or black: see quot. 1882. Now usually written *blonde*, (as always in Fr. (sc. *dentelle*).

c **1755** MRS. DELANY in *Harper's Mag.* (1884) July 260/1 A French cap..of blond. **1760** *Lond. Mag.* XXIX. 389 Raving about gauze, Blon, Brussels, and ruffles. **1766** ANSTEY *Bath Guide* iii. 87 Fringes, Blonds, and Mignionets. **1828** MOORE *Prop. Gynæocr.* Wks. (1862) 549 Burdetts in blonde, and Broughams in bustles. **1882** BECK *Draper's Dict.* s.v., Blonde laces were first made in 1745, and being produced from unbleached silk, were known as 'Nankins' or 'Blondes'.

b. *attrib.* Of blonde.

1816 SCOTT *Antiq.* vi, Triple blond ruffles. **1837** CARLYLE *Fr. Rev.* III. I. viii. 78 Beautifullest blonde-dresses and broadcloth coats.

blonder, -dre, obs. ff. of BLUNDER.

blonder, -ding, var. of BLANDER, -DING. *Obs.*

Blondin, blondin ('blɒndɪn). [F. *blondin* cable-way, f. the name of '*Blondin*' (J. F. Gravelet, 1824–97), a French tight-rope walker.] A tight-rope, a cable-way. Also *fig.*, a tight-rope walker. Also *attrib.*

1863 DICKENS *Uncommercial Trav.* in *All Year Round* 15 Aug. 588/2 An appalling accident happened at the People's Park near Birmingham..the enterprising Directors.. hanging the Blondin rope as high as they possibly could hang it. **1906** *Westm. Gaz.* 27 Mar. 5/2 Scores of cranes, blondin and other transporters..are continually at work. **1934** *Discovery* Oct. 299/2 A hair-raising trip in the 'Blondin' carrier down to the quarry face. **1934** *Essays & Stud.* XIX. 123 The tight-rope of serio-comic wit from which so many literary Blondins have been ignominiously precipitated. **1937** *Nature* 21 Aug. 312/2 The crossings of the Tigris and the Euphrates had to be made by 'Blondins'

(overhead cable ways). **1958** *Times* 3 Dec. 20/2 Hoppers of concrete being carried by blondin cables to each section [of a dam] in turn.

blondine, *a.* *rare*⁻¹. [a. F. *blondin*, *-e*, It. *biondino*.] Diminutive of BLOND.

1866 CARLYLE *Remin.*, *E. Irving* 265 The milky, smaller blondine figure..was Emerson [Tennent].

blondine (blɒn'di:n). *U.S.* [f. BLOND *a.* + -INE⁴.] **a.** A bleach for the hair. **b.** A woman with hair made blonde by bleaching. Also *attrib.* Hence as *vb.*, to bleach the hair with blondine; also **blondining** *vbl. sb.*, **blondined** *ppl. a.*

1888 in *Amer. Speech* (1960) XXXV. 267 *Blondine*, a preparation for dying the hair a blond color. *Blondining*, dyeing the hair by the application of blondine. **1890** S. J. DUNCAN *Social Departure* xxxvii. 349 A fair woman, *passée*, blondined, in widow's weeds, with red eyes. **1894** in G. Langford *Alias O. Henry* (1957) 256 She [*sc.* the New Woman] wears shirts and ties, and either cuts her hair short or blondines it. **1908** S. FORD *Side-Stepping with Shorty* vi. 95 'There, now!' says the blondine. **1909** F. CALHOUN *Miss Minerva* 73 Jimmy..returned with a big bottle of a powerful 'blondine' in one hand. **1920** S. LEWIS *Main Street* xxv. 312 Swell dame with blondine hair? **1957** V. KEHOE *Technique Film & T.V. Make-Up* vi. 85 Hair should be darkened or blondeened if gray is present.

blondinette (blɒndɪ'nɛt). [Fr., lit. 'little blonde girl', f. BLOND + -INE² + -ETTE.] A breed of oriental frilled pigeons.

1879 L. WRIGHT *Pract. Pigeon Keeper* 177 Blondinettes.. are..peak-crested and plain-headed. **1881** J. C. LYELL *Fancy Pigeons* 234 The blondinette has been produced in recent years, according to Mr. Caridia.. The blondinettes bear the same relation to the satinettes, in their several varieties, as the *schietti* or whole-coloured Triganicas do to the *gazzi* or pied ones. *Ibid.*, The blondinettes are grouse-legged and generally peak crested.

blondish ('blɒndɪʃ), *a.* [See -ISH.] Somewhat blonde; rather light-coloured.

1961 in WEBSTER. **1968** 'R. MACDONALD' *Instant Enemy* ii. 15 'What colour is his hair?' 'Blondish.'

blondism ('blɒndɪz(ə)m). [f. BLOND, BLOND *a.* and *sb.* + -ISM.] The state of being blonde; blondness.

1939 C. S. COON *Races of Europe* iv. 98 The blondism of Hetep-Heres II apparently belonged to the Delta. **1965** COON & HUNT *Living Races of Man* i. 8 Blondism in Europe may be less than 10,000 years old.

'blondness. [f. BLOND *a.* + -NESS.] Blond quality; lightness of complexion or hair.

1872 GEO. ELIOT *Middlem.* xvi. (D.) With this infantine blondness.

†**'bloness.** *Obs.* [f. BLO *a.* + -NESS.] Blackish blue quality; lividness; also, a wound of that colour made by a blow: see also BLAENESS.

1382 WYCLIF *Ex.* xxi. 25 Wounde for wounde, blones for blones.

†**blonk.** *Obs.* Forms: 1 blanca, 3 blank, 3–6 blonk. [OE. *blanca*, *blǫnca*, def. form of **blanc* = OHG. *blanch* white (cf. OHG. *blanc ros* white horse, and the neut. adj. *planchaz*, *planchiz*, used subst. in same sense), meaning properly '*white* horse', but used as a poetic synonym for 'horse' generally. Cf. ON. *blakkr* poet. for a horse (Vigf.).] Poetic word for 'horse'; steed.

a **1000** *Beowulf* 1716 Beornas on blancum. *c* **1205** LAY. 5862 Lihteð of eowre blanken [**1250** hors]. *Ibid.* 13512 Fortiger hæhte his sweines sadeli his blonken [**1250** stedes]. *c* **1350** *Will. Palerne* 3326 Þe nobul blonk þat him bar. *c* **1440** *Gaw. & Gologr.* ii. 19 (JAM.) Bery broune wes the blonk. **1535** STEWART *Cron. Scot.* II. 478 Mony bald man of his blonk wes borne.

blonket, variant of BLUNKET.

bloo, var. of BLO *Obs.*, blackish-blue.

blood (blʌd), *sb.* Forms: 1 blód, 2–5 blod (o:), 4–6 blode, 4– blood. Also 4 blodde, 5 bloode, 6–7 bloude, 6–8 bloud, 6 bludde, blud; *Sc.* 4–6 blud, 5–8 blude, 8–9 bluid, *Sc. n.e. dial.* bleid, bleed. [Com. Teut.: OE. *blód* = OFris., OS. *blôd* (LG. *blôd*, Du. *bloed*), OHG. *blôt*, *bluot* (mod.Ger. *blut*), ON. *blóð* (Sw., Da. *blod*), Goth. *blôþ*:—OTeut. **blôdo(m*, answering to an Aryan type **bhlātóm*, not found with a suitable sense outside Teutonic, there being no general Aryan name for 'blood'; doubtfully referred to verbal root *blŏ-* 'blow, bloom', which suits the form, but is less certain as to the sense. Like some other words in OE. long *ó*, *blood* has undergone more than the normal phonetic change; this would have left it (blu:d), riming with *food*, *wooed*; early in 16th c. the vowel was shortened (blud, blʊd), as in *good*, *wood*, and this subsequently changed to (ʌ) (blʌd), as in *flood* and Sc. *wud* = *wood*, etc.]

I. Literally.

1. a. *prop.* The red liquid circulating in the arteries and veins of man and the higher animals, by which the tissues are constantly nourished and renewed; also (by later extension) the corresponding liquid, coloured or colourless, in animals of lower organization.

c **1000** *Ags. Gosp.* John vi. 55 Min blod is drinc. *a* **1100** *O.E. Chron.* an. 1012 His haliȝe blod on ða eorðan feoll. *c* **1175** *Lamb. Hom.* 187 Þi blod isched on þe rode. *a* **1300** *Cursor M.* 9999 It es rede als ani blod. *c* **1360** *Song Mercy* in *E.E.P.* (1862) 120 Myn herte blood 'ran from me doun. *c* **1440** *Promp. Parv.* 40 Blode. **1483** *Cath. Angl.* 35 Blude. **1538** WRIOTHESLEY *Chron.* (1875) I. 90 Yt was no bloude. **1563** *Homilies* II. *Rebellion* I. (1859) 558 No shedder of our bloods. **1580** BARET *Alv.* B 840 Bludde, *sanguis*. **1595** SHAKS. *John* II. i. 48 We shall repent each drop of bloud. **1611** BIBLE *Lev.* xvii. 14 Ye shall not eat the blood of no maner of flesh: for the life of all flesh is the blood thereof. **1654** TRAPP *Comm. Ps.* iv. 3 The bloud of a Swine might not be offered in Sacrifices. **1711** *Lond. Gaz.* No. 4793/1 On the 16th the Blood of St. Januarius was exposed as usually. **1786** BURNS *Wks.* III. 21 But feels his heart's bluid rising hot. **1861** HULME tr. *Moquin-Tandon* II. I. 38 The blood, or nutrient fluid, is a liquid of a more or less intense red..at other times it is almost colourless, as in most of the invertebrated animals.

b. *flesh and blood*: the distinctive characteristics of the animal body; hence = 'humanity' as opposed to 'deity or disembodied spirit'. See FLESH.

†**c.** *to the blood*: through the outer skin, 'to the quick', till the blood flows; also *fig.* *Obs.*

a **1300** *Cursor M.* 16230, I rede men..bete him to þe blod. **1662** PEPYS *Diary* 10 Oct., I could not get on my boots, which vexed me to the blood.

†**d.** *to let blood* (in Surgery): to open a vein so as to let blood flow from the body; to bleed; also *transf.* to shed the blood of, to put to death. With *indirect passive*, 'he was let blood'. *arch.*

c **1000** *Sax. Leechd.* III. 184 Mona se ðridda..nis na god mona blod lætan. **1483** *Cath. Angl.* 35 To latt Blude, *fleobotomare*. **1526** *Pilgr. Perf.* (W. de W. 1531) 107 b, Spared not to suffer hym selfe to be let blode. **1588** SHAKS. *L.L.L.* II. i. 186 Is the soule sicke?.. Alacke, let it bloud. **1594** —— *Rich. III*, III. i. 180 His ancient Knot of dangerous Aduersaries To morrow are let blood at Pomfret Castle. **1614** MARKHAM *Cheap Husb.* I. i. (1668) 7 It is good whilst a horse is in youth..to let him blood twice in the year. **1679** *Jesuites Ghostly Ways* 7 She was the next morning early to be let blood. **1725** BRADLEY *Fam. Dict.* s.v. *Garden*, Let them Blood in the Neck-Vein. *c* **1819** KEATS *Ode to Fanny* 1 Physician Nature! let my spirit blood! O ease my heart of verse and let me rest.

e. Formerly used in oaths and forcible ejaculations, as *God's blood! Christ's blood! 'S blood!* and *Blood!* (cf. *'s wounds*, ZOUNDS.)

a **1541** WYATT *Defence* Wks. (1861) Pref. 39 God's blood, the King set me in the Tower. *c* **1590** MARLOWE *Faust* (2nd vers.) 1028 Blood, he speaks terribly! **1599** SHAKS. *Hen. V*, IV. viii. 10 'Sblud, an arrant Traytor as any es in the Vniuersall World. **1607** HEYWOOD *Wom. Kilde* Wks. 1874 II. 119 Sblood sir I loue you. **1762** STERNE *Tr. Shandy* V. xxi. 89 Blood an 'ounds, shouted the corporal. **1822** BYRON *Juan* VIII. i, Oh blood and thunder! and oh blood and wounds! These are but vulgar oaths.

f. Phrase. (*you cannot get*) *blood out of* (or *from*) *a stone* or *turnip*: (you cannot achieve) the impossible, esp. pity from the hard-hearted, or money from the avaricious.

1662 G. TORRIANO *Second Alphabet* 148/1 To go about to fetch bloud out of stones, *viz.* to attempt what is impossible. *Ibid.* 165/1 To go about to fetch bloud out of a turnip, *viz.* to attempt impossibilities. **1836** F. MARRYAT *Japhet* I. iv. 41 There's no getting blood out of a turnip. **1849** DICKENS *Dav. Copp.* xi. 114 Blood cannot be obtained from a stone, neither can anything on account be obtained at present..from Mr. Micawber. **1889** STEVENSON & OSBOURNE *Wrong Box* 8 'You cannot get blood from a stone,' observed the lawyer. **1929** *Observer* 21 July 15 This Court has no machinery that I know of for extracting blood from stones. **1938** R. D. FINLAYSON *Brown Man's Burden* 27 You may as well try to get blood out of a stone as evidence out of a native! **1940** A. E. HERTZLER *Doctors & Patients* (1941) x. 261 The age old difficulty of getting blood out of a turnip.

2. *fig.* and *transf.* Applied, always with conscious reference to prec., to liquids or juices in some way resembling or suggesting it, as **a.** to a blood-like juice; **b.** *poet.* to the water of a river personified; **c.** by partially scientific analogy, to the sap of plants.

1382 WYCLIF *Gen.* xlix. 11 He shal wasshe..in blood of a grape his mantil. **1607** SHAKS. *Timon* IV. iii. 432 Go, sucke the subtle blood o' th' Grape. **1807** J. E. SMITH *Phys. Bot.* 45 It [the sap] is really the blood of the plant, by which its whole body is nourished. **1842** C. JOHNSON *Farmer's Cycl.* s.v. *Aortal*, The elaborated juice or blood of plants. **1854** B. TAYLOR *Poems Orient* (1866) 138, I from the flood Of his own brown blood Will drink to the glory of ancient Nilus! *Ibid.* 162 Golden blood of Lebanon.

3. a. Blood shed; hence, bloodshed, shedding of blood; taking of life, manslaughter, murder, death.

c **1000** ÆLFRIC *Gen.* iv. 10 Ðines broðor blod clypað up to me of eorðan. **1382** WYCLIF *Isa.* i. 15 Ȝoure hondis ben ful of blod. **1593** HOOKER *Eccl. Pol.* Pref. ii. §5 Either my blood or banishment shall sign it. *a* **1604** HANMER *Chron. Irel.* (1633) 122 Bent to blood and villany. **1609** BIBLE (Douay) *Nahum* iii. 1 Wo to thee ô citie of blouds. *a* **1639** W. WHATELEY *Prototypes* II. xxix. (1640) 144 Beware of Blouds. **1648** *Resol. Officers of Parl. Army*, That it is our duty..to call Charles Stuart, that man of blood, to an account for that blood he has shed..in these poor nations. **1711** ADDISON *Spect.* No. 99 ¶7 An Affront that nothing but Blood can expiate. **1866** FELTON *Anc. & Mod. Gr.* I. xi. 205 Then blood doth blood Demand. **1878** MORLEY *Crit. Misc.* (1886) I. 107 The true inquisitor is a creature of policy, not a man of blood by taste.

b. Often used in the Bible and theological language for blood shed in sacrifice; *esp.* the atoning sacrifice of Christ.

c **1000** ÆLFRIC *Exod.* xxiv. 8 Þis ys þære treowðe blod þe Drihten eow behet be eallon þison spræcon. **1382** WYCLIF *Ex.* xxiv. 8 This is the blood of the boond of pees, that the Lord couenauntide with ȝow [**1611** the blood of the Couenant]. **1382** —— *Ephes.* ii. 13 Ȝe that weren sum tyme ferr, ben maad nyȝ in the blood of Crist [**1611** by the blood of Christ]. **1644** *Direct. Publ. Worship* 26 The new Testament in the bloud of Christ. **1842** CHALMERS *Lect. Romans* lxxix, The sin..now washed away by the blood of a satisfying expiation.

c. The guilt or responsibility of bloodshed.

c **1000** *Ags. Gosp.* Matt. xxvii. 25 Sy hys blod ofer us, and ofer ure bearn. **1382** WYCLIF *Lev.* xx. 11 Thurȝ deth dien thei bothe; the blood of hem be vpon hem. **1611** BIBLE *Matt.* xxvii. 25 His blood be on vs, and on our children! *Ibid.* *Josh.* ii. 19 His blood shalbe vpon his head, and we will bee guiltlesse.

d. *blood and thunder*, bloodshed and violence; used *attrib.* in *blood-and-thunder book*, *tale*, etc., one describing the murderous exploits of desperadoes. (orig. *U.S.*) Also shortened to *blood* (esp. in *pl.*), as in *blood books*, (*penny*) *bloods*.

1852 *Lantern* (N.Y.) II. 67/2 Most, however, of these 'blood, thunder, and whiskey articles', are written by raw lads. **1857** *Quinland* II. 76 Mrs. Bill, left to herself, resumed reading a blood and thunder romance. **1894** *Daily News* 29 May 6/4 'Blood and thunder books';..'blood books'—brief and brutal—is the expression in general use. **1897** W. J. LOCKE *Derelicts* iii, A writer of 'penny bloods'. **1925** W. DE LA MARE *Two Tales* 32 The penny blood concealed in his 'Arithmetic'. **1935** *Discovery* Nov. 346/2 As exciting reading as any blood-and-thunder novelette.

e. *blood and iron* [G. *blut und eisen*], military force as distinguished from diplomacy, esp. in *the man of blood and iron*, Prince Bismarck, who advocated the use of this as his policy.

1869 *Porcupine* 18 Sept. 235/1, I don't wonder at that man of 'blood and iron'—Bismarck—openly expressing himself an admirer of *La* good-looking Lucca. **1872** *New Dominion Monthly* Oct. 195/1 You will find him indeed a man of 'blood and iron'. **1889** H. P. HUGHES *Social Chr.* v. 74 'There,' they are saying, 'nothing succeeds like a blood-and-iron policy.' **1898** A. J. BUTLER tr. *Bismarck's Refl. & Remin.* I. 310 We should be unable to avoid a serious contest, a contest which could only be settled by blood and iron. **1922** C. E. MONTAGUE *Disenchantment* v. 69 In the whole blood-and-iron province of talk he would..outshine any actual combatant.

f. *blood and soil* [G. *blut und boden*], a Nazi catch-phrase, used *attrib.* to denote Nazi members or ideology.

1940 AUDEN *I Believe* 22 The success of Fascist blood-and-soil ideology. **1957** M. K. JOSEPH *I'll soldier no More* (1958) xii. 223 There was a pile of stuff..put out by some kind of East-Prussian patriotic blood-and-soil gang.

II. Properties, attributes, and states of body or feeling connoted by *blood*. (Often derived from earlier superficial or erroneous notions of its character and action.)

†**4. a.** The vital fluid; *hence*, the vital principle, that upon which life depends; life. †**b.** *for the blood of him*: for the life of him, though his life were involved. *Obs.*

a **1300** *Cursor M.* 21462 His blod to sell. **1535** COVERDALE *Ps.* lxxi. [lxxii.] 14 Deare shal their bloude be in his sight. **1592** SHAKS. *Rom. & Jul.* III. i. 188 He slew Mercutio, Who now the price of his deare blood doth owe. **1679** *Trial Wakeman* 83 These mens Bloods are at stake. **1694** R. LESTRANGE *Fables* 12 A Royston Crow..could not for his blood break the shell. **1734** tr. *Rollin's Anc. Hist.* (1827) VI. xv. §18. 299 This silver was no other than the blood of nations. **1740** *Christmas Entertainm.* v. (1884) 51 He could not get over the Stile for the Blood of him.

5. The supposed seat of emotion, passion; as in 'it stirs the blood', 'it makes the blood creep' or 'run cold', 'his blood is up', 'my blood boils'; whence, Passion, temper, mood, disposition; *emphatically*, high temper, mettle; anger. Very frequent in Shakspere: now chiefly in certain phrases, as *to breed bad* or *ill blood*: to stir up strife, cause ill-feeling. *in cold blood*: not in the heat of passion, deliberately.

a **1300** *Cursor M.* 5054 Quen þe tan þe toþer sei Na wight moght þair blodes lei. *a* **1330** *Otuel* 70 Tydinges..þat a-moeuede al here blod. **1526** *Pilgr. Perf.* (W. de W. 1531) 37 b, Theyr blode and imaginacyon is sore troubled. **1596** SHAKS. *Merch. V.* I. ii. 20 The braine may deuise lawes for the blood, but a hot temper leapes ore a colde decree. **1597** —— *2 Hen. IV*, IV. iv. 38 When you perceiue his blood enclin'd to mirth. **1605** —— *Lear* IV. ii. 64 Were't my fitness To let these hands obey my blood. **1626** MASSINGER *Rom. Actor* IV. ii., Carry her to her chamber..till in cooler blood I shall determine of her. **1646** BUCK *Rich. III*, II. 61 High in bloud and anger. **1704** SWIFT *Batt. Bks.* (1711) 232 Hot words passed..and ill Blood was plentifully bred. **1727** [see RUN *v.* 20 c]. **1787** T. JEFFERSON *Corr.* (1830) 273 It would not excite ill blood in me. **1818** *Edin. Rev.* XXX. 238 Her whole appearance, gestures, voice and dress, made De Courcy's blood run cold within him. **1823** LAMB *Elia*, *Poor Relat.*, Bad blood [was] bred. **1829** G. GRIFFIN *Collegians* II. xviii. 55 To use a vulgar but forcible expression, the blood of Hardress was now completely up. **1852** STOWE *Uncle Tom* i. 4 It kinder makes my blood run cold to think on't. **1868** FREEMAN *Norm. Conq.* (1876) II. viii. 271 The taking away of human life in cold blood. **1879** FROUDE *Cæsar* vii. 65 The blood of the people was up.

6. The supposed seat of animal or sensual appetite; hence, the fleshly nature of man.

1597 SHAKS. *Lover's Compl.* 162 Nor gives it satisfaction to our blood, That we must curb it upon others proof. **1610** —— *Temp.* IV. i. 53 The strongest oathes, are straw To th' fire ith' blood.

7. Hunting phrase, ***in blood***: in full vigour, full of life. ***out of blood***: not vigorous, lifeless. (As applied to hounds the expression refers perhaps to the tasting of blood.)

1588 SHAKS. *L.L.L.* IV. ii. 3 The Deare was.. sanguis in blood, ripe as a Pomwater. **1596** —— *1 Hen. IV*, IV. ii. 48 If we be English Deere, be then in blood. **1781** P. BECKFORD *Hunting* (1802) 308 When hounds are out of blood, there is a kind of evil genius attending all that they do.. while a pack of fox-hounds well in blood, like troops flushed with conquest, are not easily withstood.

III. Race and kindred as connoted by *blood*.

8. Blood is popularly treated as the typical part of the body which children inherit from their parents and ancestors; hence that of parents and children, and of the members of a family or race, is spoken of as identical, and as being distinct from that of other families or races.

blue blood: that which flows in the veins of old and aristocratic families, a transl. of the Spanish *sangre azul* attributed to some of the oldest and proudest families of Castile, who claimed never to have been contaminated by Moorish, Jewish, or other foreign admixture; the expression probably originated in the blueness of the veins of people of fair complexion as compared with those of dark skin; also, a person with blue blood; an aristocrat. ***fresh blood***: the introduction in breeding of a new strain or stock not related by blood to the family; *fig.* new members or elements, with new ideas and experiences, admitted to a society or organization. ***new blood*** = ***fresh blood***.

1377 LANGL. *P. Pl.* B. XI. 193 For alle are we crystes creatures.. And bretheren as of o blode. *c* **1440** *Gesta Rom.* I. xlii. 141 The othir too bethe bastardes, and not of his blode. **1543** EARL OF ANGUS *Let.* in Tytler *Hist. Scot.* (1864) III. 8 *note*, Considering the proximite of blude that was betwix us. **1608** *Yorksh. Trag.* I. ii. 199 You are a gentleman by many bloods. **1611** BIBLE *Acts* xvii. 26 [God] hath made of one blood all nations of men. *a* **1631** DONNE *Poems* (1658) 1 And in this flea our two blouds mingled be. **1734** POPE *Ess. Man* IV. 201 Your antient but ignoble blood Has crept thro' Scoundrels ever since the Flood. **1768** BLACKSTONE *Comm.* II. 203 So many different bloods is a man said to contain in his veins, as he hath lineal ancestors. **1776** GIBBON *Decl. & F.* I. 34 The pure blood of the ancient citizens. **1834** MAR. EDGEWORTH *Helen* xv. (D.) One [officer].. from Spain, of high rank and birth, of the *sangre azul*, the *blue blood*. **1838** ARNOLD *Hist. Rome* I. ii. 25 A mixed race in which other blood was largely mixed with that of the Latins. **1853** LYTTON *My Novel* II. v. ii. 9 Long may the new blood circulate through the veins of the mighty giantess [*sc.* England]. **1879** FROUDE *Cæsar* xi. 120 A young nobleman of the bluest blood. **1880** *Baily's Mag.* Oct. 149 There was a good deal of change in the judicial bench... New blood was infused through Colonel —, Mr. —, and Major —. *a* **1887** *Mod.* You want some fresh blood to give new life and activity to your society. **1894** *Daily News* 16 Apr. 3/6 Many an aristocratic blue-blood.. was glad to marry a rich burgher's daughter. **1920** GALSWORTHY *In Chancery* II. i. 128 Round Crum were still gathered a forlorn hope of blue-bloods with a plutocratic following.

9. a. Hence, Blood-relationship, and *esp.* parentage, lineage, descent; *also* in a wider sense: Family, kin, race, stock, nationality. ***blood royal*** or ***the blood***: royal race or family.

whole blood: race or relationship by both father and mother, as distinguished from that of ***half blood***, relationship by one parent only. Hence concr. ***half-blood***: one whose blood is half that of one race and half that of another, *e.g.* the offspring of a European and an Indian.

c **1250** *Gen. & Ex.* 1451 He was bigeten of kinde blod. *c* **1400** *Destr. Troy* 6226 His brother of blud. *c* **1430** *Syr Tryam.* 430 Sche was of gentylle blode. **1513** MORE *Edw. V.* (1641) 5 The Queene or the Nobles of her Bloud. **1602** WARNER *Alb. Eng.* XI. lxvii. (1612) 284 This Ladie also of the blood, and heire vn to her Father, A mightie Prince. **1605** VERSTEGAN *Dec. Intell.* Ded., Your Maiestie is descended of the chiefest bloud Royall of our antient English-Saxon Kings. **1650** R. STAPYLTON *Strada's Low-C. Wars* III. 6 Anthony of Bourbon.. being the first Prince of the bloud. **1697** POTTER *Antiq. Greece* I. viii. (1715) 40 The distinction .. between those of the whole, and those of the half Blood of Athens. **1798** Bay *Amer. Law Rep.* (1809) I. 109 Covenant to stand seised cannot be supported except by consideration of blood. **1807** CRABBE *Par. Reg.* III. 528 They proved the blood, but were refused the land. **1810** COLEBROOKE *Hindu Law Inherit.* 180 The distinction regarding the whole and the half blood is contradicted, etc. **1820** SCOTT *Monast.* xiii, The old proverb.. 'Gentle deed Makes gentle bleid' (with play on sense 1).

b. Proverb. ***blood is thicker than water***: the tie of relationship is strong.

1815 SCOTT *Guy Mannering* II. xxxviii. 318 Weel—blood's thicker than water—she's welcome to the cheeses. **1867** TROLLOPE *Chron. Barset* xxxii. 271 'I am aware that there is a family tie, or I should not have ventured to trouble you.' 'Blood is thicker than water, isn't it?' **1920** A. HUXLEY *Leda* 35 For Blood, as all men know, than Water's thicker, But Water's wider, thank the Lord, than Blood.

10. *concr.* **a.** Persons of any specified 'blood' or family collectively; blood-relations, kindred, family, race.

1382 WYCLIF *Sel. Wks.* III. 515 Alle lordis and ladies and here blod and affinite. **1413** LYDG. *Pylgr. Sowle* IV. xxxi. (1483) 80 His kynrede that is the royal blood of the reame. **1475** *Bk. Noblesse* 2 Arthur, king of the Breton bloode. **1595** SHAKS. *John* III. i. 301 *Daul.* Father, to Armes! *Blanch.* Vpon thy wedding day? Against the blood that thou hast married? *a* **1649** DRUMM. OF HAWTH. *Hist. Scot.* (1655) 2 He being now matched with the Royall Blood of England in Marriage. **1681** DRYDEN *Abs. & Achit.* 641 By that one Deed Enobles all his Blood. **1838** ARNOLD *Hist. Rome* I. 107 He [Brutus] had loved justice more than his own blood. **1884** W. C. SMITH *Kildrostan* 66 Your ancestors were.. mated with the best blood of the land.

†**b.** A family descended from a common ancestor; a clan or sept. *Obs.*

1612 DAVIES *Why Ireland* (1787) 79 Five principal bloods, or septs, of the Irish, were by special grace enfranchised.

c. ***to run in the*** (formerly ***a***) ***blood***: i.e. in a family or race.

1621 SANDERSON *Serm.* I. 178 Tempers of the mind and affections become hereditary, and (as we say) run in a blood. **1641** MILTON *Ch. Govt.* iv. Wks. (1851) 112 Unlesse we shall choose our Prelats only out of the Nobility, and let them runne in a blood. *a* **1703** BURKITT *On N.T.* Matt. xiv. 5 Cruelty runs in a blood. **1774** SHERIDAN *Rivals* IV. ii, Tell her 'tis all our ways—it runs in the blood of our family.

11. a. More particularly: Offspring, child, near relative, one dear as one's own offspring. Formerly in sing., with pl. *bloods*.

c **1374** CHAUCER *Troylus* II. 545 Now beth nought wroth, my blode, my nece. **1525** LD. BERNERS *Froiss.* II. ccxlii. [ccxxxviii.] 748 To se suche difference within yᵉ realme, and bytwene his nephues and blode. **1682** DRYDEN *Mac Fl.* 166 Thou art my blood where Jonson has no part. **1741** H. WALPOLE *Corr.* I. 99 I have so many cousins, and uncles, and aunts and bloods that grow in Norfolk.

b. ***(own) flesh and blood***: near kindred, children, brothers and sisters. See FLESH.

12. Blood worth mention, good blood; good parentage or stock. (Cf. BIRTH *sb.*[1] 5 b.) **a.** Of human beings: Noble or gentle birth, good family.

1393 GOWER *Conf.* III. 330 They be worthy men of blood. **1526** *Pilgr. Perf.* (W. de W. 1531) 92 Bostynge hym selfe of his auncestres and kynrede, or of his rychesse or blode. **1642** FULLER *Holy & Prof. St.* v. xix. 436 Others were upstarts, men of no bloud. **1789** MRS. PIOZZI *Journ. France & It.* I. 97 Blood enjoys a thousand exclusive privileges. **1855** MACAULAY *Hist. Eng.* III. 209 The highest pride of blood. **1860** EMERSON *Cond. Life* v. (1861) 104 The obstinate prejudice in favour of blood, which lies at the base of the feudal and monarchical fabrics of the old world.

b. Of bred animals: Good breed or pedigree. Also with a qualifying word. Cf. *bit of blood* (BIT *sb.*[2] 4 h).

1792 *Sporting Mag.* I. 101/1 The Wold dogs beat the blood of the Norfolks, as some of the best bred of the late Lord Orford were completely worsted. **1793** *Ibid.* II. 334/1 That famous horse *Eclipse*, whose excellence in speed, blood, pedigree, and progeny, will be, perhaps, transmitted to the end of time. **1817** J. SCOTT *Paris Revisit.* (ed. 4) 188 That quality which may be termed the nobility of animal nature; which is called blood, and game, in the inferior creatures. **1846** EG.-WARBURTON *Hunt. Songs, Gros-Veneur*, In horses and hounds there is nothing like blood. **1859** *Blackw. Mag.* Sept. 269/1 The limbs.. of a cleanness and beauty of outline enough alone to stamp blood on their possessor. **1895** C. B. LOWE *Breeding Racehorses* 180 He will always do best with a strong return to his stout Blacklock, Bird-catcher, and Glencoe blood. **1902** *Encycl. Brit.* XXV. 190/2 When Shorthorn breeders of to-day talk of 'Booth blood', or of 'Bates blood', they refer to animals descended from the respective herds of Thomas Booth and Thomas Bates.

c. *attrib.*, esp. in BLOOD-HORSE (q.v.). Also ellipt. *blood* = blood-horse.

1794 *Sporting Mag.* IV. 31/1 He [*sc.* a race-horse] is now a stallion.. at 3 gs a mare, and 5s. the groom, blood mares. **1818** SCOTT *Rob Roy* vii. A bit of a broken-down blood-tit condemned to drag an over-loaded cart. **1824** W. IRVING *T. Trav.* I. 228 A politely spoken highwayman on a blood mare. *c* **1865** R. SULLIVAN *Lady Betty's Pocket-bk.*, A spark of quality, who drove four bloods.

13. ***to restore in*** or ***to blood***: to readmit to forfeited privileges of birth and rank those who by attainder of themselves or their ancestors lie under sentence of 'corruption of blood'; see ATTAINDER.

1591 SHAKS. *1 Hen. VI*, III. i. 159 Our pleasure is, That Richard be restored to his Blood. **1633** T. STAFFORD *Pac. Hib.* iii. (1821) 47 His Vncle Sir Edmond is not restored in blood. **1752** JOHNSON *Rambl.* No. 192 ¶7 A kind of restoration to blood after the attainder of trade.

IV. A person.

†**14.** [from 1.] One in whom blood flows, a living being. *Obs.*

c **1250** *Gen. & Ex.* 1192 A ðhusant plates of siluer god Gaf he sarra ðat faire blod. *a* **1300** *Cursor M.* 1055 þis abel was a blissed blod. *c* **1314** *Guy Warw.* (1840) 154 Thou fel treytour, unkinde blod. **1382** WYCLIF *Deut.* xxvii. 26 That he smyte the soule of the innocent blood.

15. a. 'A hot spark, a man of fire' J.; a 'buck', a 'fast' or foppish man, rake, roisterer. [Generally appearing to arise out of sense 5, but in many cases associated with sense 12 as if = aristocratic rowdy.] Obs. in Great Britain except as a reminiscence of last century.

1562 BULLEYN *Sicke Men, &c.* 73 a, A lustie blood, or a pleasaunte brave young roister. **1595** SHAKS. *John* II. i. 278 As many and as well-borne bloods as those. **1622** BACON *Hen. VII*, 49 The Newes.. put diuers Young Bloods into such a furie. **1749** H. WALPOLE *Corr.* (1837) I. 140 Anecdotes of the doctor's drinking, who, as the man told us, had been a blood. **1763** *Brit. Mag.* IV. 261 The buck and blood [suppose wisdom to consist] in breaking windows and knocking down watch-men. **1774** GOLDSM. *Author's Bed-Ch.* 4 The drabs and bloods of Drury-lane. **1824** W. IRVING *T. Trav.* I. 341 I now.. became a blood upon town. **1848** THACKERAY *Van. Fair* x, A perfect and celebrated 'blood' or dandy about town. **1882** *Harper's Mag.* Mar. 490 The [privateers] were commanded and manned by the bloods of the city [of New York].

b. ***'young blood'*** no longer implies a rake or 'fast' man, but simply a youthful member of a party, who brings to it youthful freshness and vigour; cf. 8.

1862 *Sat. Rev.* 8 Feb. 159 To give the young bloods of the present day a notion of what the Northern Circuit was in the year 1825. **1885** *Manch. Exam.* 13 July 5/6 The younger bloods in the Irish party are looking forward with eager delight to the occurrence of a scene.

c. At public schools and universities applied to those who are regarded as setting the fashion in habits and dress; also, a youthful member of a party, etc.

1892 *Pall Mall Gaz.* 8 Mar. 7/1 The result was that the new party won by 127 to 103... A great triumph for the Bloods—as we are accustomed to call them—who mustered in great force to defeat Mr. Childers. **1893** *Granta* 9 June 374/2 A Committee, consisting of a blood, a Girtonian, and a resident married M.A., shall supervise all flirtations. **1896** *Ibid.* 16 May 310/1 Mifflin and 'is friends talked.. an' said 'ow much better Cambridge'd be if there wasn't no 'bloods' to spoil things. **1955** *Times* 25 Aug. 11/5 The rugger match dinner at the Trocadero with a select club of 'bloods'.

d. A passenger on a ship. *Ship's stewards' slang.*

1929 BOWEN *Sea Slang* 14 *Bloods*, the modern steward's name for the passengers—used only when they are regarded kindly. **1962** *Harper's Bazaar* Dec. 74/3 Stewards will help you... Behind your back they will call you a 'blood'—.. they themselves being 'wingers'—and wonder how much 'rent' you will pay them at the end of the voyage.

V. Technical senses.

†**16.** A disease in sheep and in swine. *Obs.*

1523 FITZHERB. *Husb.* §48 There is a sicknes among shepe ..called the bloude. **1741** *Compl. Fam.-Piece* III. 495 The Blood in Sheep.. we take to be a sort of Measles or Pox. *Ibid.* 501 The Blood in Swine, or the Gargut, as some call it. **1787** WINTER *Syst. Husb.* 223 A disorder [in swine] generally called (in this part of the country) *the blood*.

17. A commercial name for Red Coral.

1861 HULME tr. *Moquin-Tandon* II. III. ii. 88 Five varieties of Coral are known in commerce.. 1, the Froth of Blood; 2nd the Flower of Blood; 3rd, 4th, and 5th, Blood of the first, second, and third quality.

18. *ellipt.* = *blood orange* (see 19).

1907 N. MUNRO *Daft Days* i. 6 Oranges! Oranges!—rale New Year oranges, three a penny; bloods, a bawbee each!

19. A tribe of North American Indians belonging to the Blackfoot confederacy; a member of this tribe. Also *attrib.*

1794 *Mass. Hist. Soc. Coll.* (1810) 1st Ser. III. 24 The tribes of Indians which he passed through, were called.. Blood Indians, the Blackfeet tribe.. and several others. **1863** *Trans. Amer. Phil. Soc.* XII. 249 The Blackfeet inhabit a portion of country farther north than the Bloods. **1957** *Encycl. Canadiana* I. 403/1 Together with the Piegan and the Blood, they [*sc.* the Blackfoot] covered an enormous area of the western prairies and lower foothills of the Rockies.

VI. *Comb.* and *Attrib.*

20. General combinations (These being formed at will, only a few samples are given): **a.** attributive, as (sense 1) ***blood-beat, -circulation, -clot, -corpuscle, -disease, -drop, -flow, -freezer, -gout, -mark, -spoor, -spot, -stream, -supply, -system***; (senses 3, 4) ***blood-compensation, -field, -revenge, -rite, -sacrifice, -spirit, -trade, -value, -vengeance***; (sense 5) ***blood-curdler***; (senses 8, 9) ***blood-affinity, -bond, -brother, -brotherhood, -covenant, -descendants, -feud, -friend, -kin, -kinship, -name, -tie***; **b.** objective, with pres. pple., n. of agent or action, as (sense 1) ***blood-circulating, -freezing, -spiller, -spilling, -sprinkling, -sweating***; (senses 3–4) ***blood-loving, -monger, -offering, -seller, -wreaker***; (sense 5) as ***blood-curdling, -stirring*** (hence ***-stirringness***) adjs.; **c.** instrumental and locative, as (sense 1) ***blood-bedabbled, -besprinkled, -bubbling, -dabbled, -discoloured, -drenched, -dyed, -filled, -flecked, -frozen, -gushing, -masked, -plashed, -soaked, -sodden, -tinctured*** adjs.; (senses 3, 4) ***blood-bought, -cemented, -defiled, -fired, -polluted*** adjs.; **d.** parasynthetic and similative, as ***blood-black, -coloured, -dark, -faced, -hued***, etc. (Such combs. are especially common in the writings of D. H. Lawrence, as, ***blood-being, -bondage, -consciousness***, (also ***-conscious***), , ***-desire, -knowing, -knowledge, -passion, -pride, -soul***.)

1865 TYLOR *Early Hist. Man.* x. 278 The seventh degree of *blood-affinity is the limit. **1947** E. SITWELL *Shadow of Cain* 11 The *blood-beat of the Bird. **1621** QUARLES *Argalus & P.* (1678) 119 She prostrate lay Before their *blood-bedabled feet. **1895** YEATS *Poems* 22 Along the blood-bedabbled plains. **1915** D. H. LAWRENCE *Let.* 8 Dec. (1962) 394 All living things, even plants, have a *blood-being. If a lizard falls on the breast of a pregnant woman, then the blood-being of the lizard passes with a shock into the blood-being of the woman, and is transferred to the foetus... We have a blood-being, a blood-consciousness, a blood-soul, complete and apart from the mental and nerve consciousness. **1593** SHAKS. *2 Hen. VI*, v. i. 117 O *blood-bespotted Neopolitan. **1601** YARRINGTON *Two Lament. Traj.* II. v. in Bullen *O. Pl.* IV, His dissevered *blood-besprinkled lims. *a* **1918** W. OWEN *Poems* (1963) 69 Sunlight seems a blood-smear; night comes *blood-black. **1645** RUTHERFORD *Tryal & Tr. Faith* (1845) 178 *Blood-bonds, nature-relations are mighty. **1926** D. H. LAWRENCE *Plumed Serpent* ix. 154 And there was a thin little thread of *blood-bondage between them. **1779** COWPER *Hymn*, '*There is a Fountain*', A *blood-bought free reward. **1879** TODD *Cycl. Anat. & Phys.* IV. 668/1 In which [apartment] are

located the *blood-circulating organs. **1818** CARLYLE *Sart. Res.* III. vii, A *blood-circulation, visible to the eye. **1859** TODD *Cycl. Anat. & Phys.* V. 562/2 The *blood-clot.. generally found contained within the ruptured airsac. **1762–71** H. WALPOLE *Vertue's Anecd. Paint.* (1786) V. 97 A *blood-coloured ribband with Death's head, swords, &c. **1958** MIDDLETON & TAIT *Tribes without Rulers* 27 Such features are..chiefship, *blood-compensation and non-empirical, religious sanctions. **1923** D. H. LAWRENCE *Stud. Class. Amer. Lit.* vii. 126 They [*sc.* Americans] *admire* the *blood-conscious spontaneity. **1593** SHAKS. *2 Hen. VI*, III. ii. 61 Might..*blood-consuming sighes recall his Life. **1845** *Blood-corpuscle [see CORPUSCLE 2]. **1886** *Encycl. Brit.* XXI. 137/2 The sacramental rites of mystical sacrifice are a form of *blood-covenant. **1889** BARRÈRE & LELAND *Dict. Slang* s.v., It will contain..a *blood-curdler, by the murder-man. **1906** E. DYSON *Fact'ry 'Ands* xv. 197 That one yowl was er blood-curdler. **1934** *Essays & Stud.* XIX. 13 The *blood-curdling nature of the cry. **1904** W. H. HUDSON *Green Mansions* xxi. 306 Cla-cla's wrinkled dead face and white, *blood-dabbled locks. **1885** YEATS in *Dublin Univ. Rev.* July, A star-lit rapier, half *blood-dark. **1958** R. S. THOMAS *Poetry for Supper* 38 You were born on a blood-dark tide. **1930** D. H. LAWRENCE *A Propos of Lady Chatterley's Lover* 46 The two blood-streams are brought into contact, in man and woman, just the same as in the urge of blood-passion and *blood-desire. **1875** B. TAYLOR *Faust* II. III. 171 With *blood-discolored eyes. **1902** *Encycl. Brit.* XXXI. 557/1 Anaemia is often used as a generic term for all *blood diseases. *c* **1390**, *a* **1400** *Blood-drop [in *M.E.D.*] **1823** BYRON *Island* III. iv, Blood-drops, sprinkled o'er his yellow hair. **1923** D. H. LAWRENCE *Birds, Beasts & Flowers* 91 Away with a pæan of derision You winged blood-drop. **1873** SYMONDS *Grk. Poets* vii. 227 Hound not Those *blood-faced, snake-encircled women on me. **1858** FROUDE *Hist. Eng.* IV. xviii. 8 A *blood-feud, deep and ineffaceable divided the Douglases and the Hamiltons. **1535** COVERDALE *Matt.* xxvii. 8 Wherfore the same felde is called the *bloudfelde vnto this daye. **1645** G. DANIEL *Poems* Wks. 1878 II. 9 Though the *blood-fir'd Ruffian, rageing come. **1873** T. H. GREEN *Introd. Path.* (ed. 2) 329 Thrombosis from Retardation of the *Blood-flow. **1886** H. BAUMANN *Londinismen* 12/1 **Blood-freezer*..Schauerroman. **1902** W. JAMES *Varieties Relig. Exp.* vi. 162 The grisly *blood-freezing heart-palsying sensation of it [*sc.* evil] close upon one. **1596** SPENSER *F.Q.* I. ix. 25 Yet nathëmore..Could his *blood-frozen heart emboldned bee. **1800** *Bloud-gout [see GOUT *sb.*[1] 5 a]. **1952** R. CAMPBELL tr. *Poems of Baudelaire* 45 Sabres bleak With crimson blood-gouts lit the air above. *a* **1711** KEN *Hy. Evang.* Poet. Wks. 1721 I. 57 *Blood-gushing Veins. *a* **1849** MANGAN *Poems* (1859) 121 That lone flower, *blood-hued at heart. **1535** COVERDALE *Mark* v. 25 There was a woman which has a *bloudeyssue twelue yeares. **1880** 'MARK TWAIN' *Tramp Abroad* 173 The seven hundred inhabitants are all *blood-kin to each other. **1937** R. H. LOWIE *Hist. Ethnol. Theory* vi. 65 The classification of kin survives from a period in which the closest blood-kin regularly cohabited. **1883** A. LANG in *Contemp. Rev.* Sept. 410 Exogamy is the prohibition of marriage within the supposed *blood-kinship, as denoted by the family name. **1915** D. H. LAWRENCE *Let.* 8 Dec. (1962) I. 394 When I take a woman, then the blood-percept is supreme, my *blood-knowing is overwhelming. *Ibid.*, Some tribes no doubt really *were* kangaroos; they contained the *blood-knowledge of the kangaroo. **1827** BYRON *Sardan.* I. ii. 238 That *blood-loving beldame, My martial grandam, chaste Semiramis. **1928** BLUNDEN *Undertones of War* 5 Others lay near him, also *bloodmasked. **1858** GLADSTONE *Homer* I. 163 In the fourth and fifth of the divisions in the Trojan Catalogue Homer specifies no *blood-name or name of race whatever. **1725** POPE *Odyss.* I. 40 A *blood-polluted Ghost. **1923** D. H. LAWRENCE *Kangaroo* xvii. 367 The brave, silent *blood-pride. **1932** W. FAULKNER *Light in August* (1933) i. 4 The bleak heritage of his bloodpride. **1855** R. MARTINEAU tr. *Gregorovius's Corsica* I. x. 144 Many a case is known of one bandit having..slain another..for *blood-revenge. **1877** *Gentl. Mag.* Apr. 478 The vendetta or duty of blood-revenge. **1602** WARNER *Alb. Eng.* XI. lxv. 279 Not of the Samoeds..*blood-Rites wil we tarry. **1591** SHAKES. *1 Hen. VI* v. iii. 20 Cannot my body, nor *blood-sacrifice, Intreate you to your wonted furtherance? **1866** SWINBURNE *Poems & Ballads* 70 With offering and blood-sacrifice of tears. **1801** MOORE *Ring* lvi. 221 He saw the *blood-scrawled name. **1905** *Daily Chron.* 16 Jan. 3/4 A staggering, *blood-soaked figure. **1929** YEATS *Winding Stair* 11 The heart in his *blood-sodden breast. *a* **1674** CLARENDON *Hist. Reb.* III. XI. 204 They had..terrified the People with *Blood-Spectacles. **1818** SCOTT *Rob Roy* xxvi, Honour is a homicide and a *blood-spiller. **1585** ABP. SANDYS *Serm.* (1841) 257 We shall behold nothing but rape, spoil, *blood-spilling. **1861** GEN. P. THOMPSON *Audi Alt.* III. cxliv. 128 Keeping down the *blood-spirit unhappily inherent in all mankind. **1863** W. C. BALDWIN *Afr. Hunting* v. 129 The *blood-spoor of one of the wounded koodoos. **1860** G. H. K. *Vac. Tour* 118 There is many a broad *blood-spot in your country. **1880** SAINTSBURY in *Academy* 4 Dec. 397 This same quality of *blood-stirringness. *c* **1205** LAY. 28359 Ȝurren þa stanes mid þan *blod-stremes. **1884** J. L. CORNING *Brain Exhaustion* ii. 45 The demands of an abnormally developed muscular system upon an already insufficient *blood-supply. **1962** *Lancet* 2 June 1166/2 The blood-supply to the central nervous system. *c* **1240** *Lofsong* in *Lamb. Hom.* 207 In his *blodswetunge. **1912** J. S. HUXLEY *Indiv. in Animal Kingdom* ii. 63 Cyclosis..performs the same general functions for the organism as does a *blood-system. **1876** J. F. MCLENNAN *Stud. Anc. Hist.* II. ii. 373 The system of *blood-ties and the system of addresses would begin to grow up together. **1965** G. MCINNES *Road to Gundagai* xvi. 282 The call of the Anglo-Saxon or Anglo-Celtic bloodties. **1860** GEN. P. THOMPSON *Audi Alt.* III. ci. 2 It is all the same where the war is, so the *blood-trade flourishes. **1880** BROWNING *Muleykeh* 9 Ten thousand camels the due, *Blood-value paid perforce for a murder done of old. **1893** *Funk's Standard Dict.*, *Blood-vengeance. **1926** A. MØLLER tr. *Pedersen's Israel* I. II. 269 Blood-vengeance, which in its old form is one of the most pronounced outcomes of the solidarity of the family. **1382** WYCLIF *Josh.* XX. 5 Whanne the *bloodwreker hym pursue.

21. Special comb.: **blood agar** *Bacteriol.*, a culture medium containing blood and nutrient agar; **blood-alley** [ALLY *sb.*[2]], a boy's white marble marked with red spiral lines; †**blood-band**, a bandage for stopping bleeding; **blood-bank**, a place where a supply of blood for transfusion is stored (cf. BANK *sb.*[3] 7 f); also, a reserve of blood so stored; **blood-baptism**, in reference to the early Christians, the martyrdom of converts who had not been baptized; **blood-bath**, 'a bath in warm blood ... supposed to be a very powerful tonic in great debility from long-continued diseases, etc.' (*Syd. Soc. Lex.* s.v. *Bath*); also (as in Ger., Du., Da., Sw.) a wholesale slaughter, a massacre; **blood-bay** *a.*, a reddish bay (colour); **blood-beet**, the red beet-root; **blood-boat** (see quot. 1914); also *attrib.*; †**blood-boltered** *ppl. a.*, clotted or clogged with blood, *esp.* having the hair matted with blood; [see BALTER]; **blood-brother**, (*a*) a brother by birth; (*b*) one who has been bound to another in solemn friendship by a ceremonial mingling of blood; so ***blood-brotherhood***; also *fig.*; †**blood-bulk** (cf. BULK); **blood cell**, any of the cells or cell-types that circulate in the blood; **blood chit** *colloq.* (see quots.); **blood count**, (the determination of) the number of blood cells contained in a given volume of blood; †**blood-craft**, murderous plot; **blood culture** [CULTURE *sb.* 3 c] *Bacteriol.*, a culture of a sample of blood to detect micro-organisms in it; **blood disc**, a red blood-corpuscle; also = *blood-plaque*; **blood donor**, one who gives blood for transfusion; **blood-drinker**, a primitive savage who killed and feasted on his 'kill'; *fig.* one who has a lust for blood; **blood-drinking** *a.*, that drinks blood; also *fig.*; **blood dust**, a collective name for the minute refractive bodies found floating free in the blood plasma; **blood-eagle** [ON. *blóð-ǫrn*], a Viking method of killing someone, usually the slayer of a man's father, by cutting out the ribs in the shape of an eagle; †**blood-eyes**, blood-shot eyes; **blood film**, a thin smear of blood (cf. SMEAR *sb.* 3 b); **blood-fine**, a fine paid as whole or part compensation for murder; **blood-flower** (*Bot.*), *Hæmanthus*; **blood fluke** [FLUKE *sb.*[1] 2], = SCHISTOSOME; **blood-frenzy**, a frenzy for shedding blood, homicidal mania; **blood-gas**, the gas or gases present in the blood; also *attrib.*; **blood-groove**, a groove cut in the head or the shaft of an arrow or spear, supposed to increase the flow of blood from the wound made by the weapon; **blood group**, one of the genetically determined types into which human blood may be divided on the basis of its compatibility with the blood of other individuals; *esp.* one of the four original red cell groups; **blood grouping**, the determination of the blood group of a person or of a sample of blood; also = *blood group*; **blood-hot**, excited for bloodshed; †**blood-hunter**, one who tracks the authors of crimes of blood, one who tracks criminals; **blood-knot**, a knot tied in a rope to draw blood when it is used as a whip; **blood line** = LINE *sb.*[2] 24, 25; (see also quot. 1909); **blood-lust**, lust for the shedding of blood; **blood meal** [G. *blutmehl*], dried blood used for feeding animals and as a fertilizer; '**blood-mobile** [formed after AUTOMOBILE *sb.*] *U.S.* (see quot. 1961); **blood orange**, a variety of orange having the pulp streaked with red; earlier *blood-red orange*; **blood pheasant**, a species of pheasant (see quot. 1864) marked with red on the throat and breast; **blood picture**, (*a*) (see quot. 1881) *disused*; (*b*) the condition of the blood as determined by chemical or microscopical analysis; **blood plaque, plate, platelet**, a minute disc-shaped body found in large numbers in mammalian blood; **blood plasma**, the fluid part of the blood in which the cells and platelets are suspended (Billings 1890); **blood plum**: see PLUM *sb.* 3 b; **blood-poisoning**, a morbid condition of the blood formerly thought to be caused by the absorption of putrefying matter but now recognized as being due to infection; *spec.*, septicæmia or pyæmia; **blood pressure**, the pressure of circulating blood on the walls of the blood-vessels, esp. the systemic arteries; **blood pudding**, a black-pudding; also *transf.*; **blood-pump**, (*a*) see quot. 1902; (*b*) *Pugilistic slang*, the heart; **blood purge**, one that is achieved by bloodshed; also *fig.*; **blood-rain**, rain which has acquired a red colour; also an appearance produced by the rapid growth of a minute plant which has been referred to the Algæ, *Palmella prodigiosa* (Treas. Bot.); **blood-raw** *a.*, (of meat) so lightly cooked that the blood remains red and liquid; **blood-red orange** = *blood orange*; **blood-ripe** *a.*, (of fruit) so ripe that the juice has become blood-coloured, hence **blood-ripeness**; †**blood-run** *a.*, bloodshot; **blood-sausage**, a black-pudding; †**blood-shrunk** *a.*, having the blood or vital principle dried up, withered; **blood-sister**, a woman bound to another in the same manner as blood-brothers (see also quot. 1933); so ***blood-sisterhood***; **blood sports** *sb. pl.*, sports involving the killing of animals, esp. sports of the chase; **blood-stick** (see quot.); **blood-stream**, the stream of blood circulating through the human or animal system; **blood-striking**, a disease incident to cattle (see STRIKING *vbl. sb.* 2 b); **blood sugar**, glucose contained in the blood; **blood-tax** *fig.*, a tax paid by bloodshed; *spec.* a derogatory term for military conscription; **blood test**, a test performed on blood for some specific purpose; also *fig.*; hence ***blood-tested*** adj.; **blood transfusion** = TRANSFUSION 2; also *attrib.* and *fig.*; **blood-tree** (*Bot.*), *Croton gossypiifolium*; **blood-tub** *slang*, †(*a*), a rough or rowdy (*U.S. obs.*); (*b*) a theatre presenting lurid melodrama; **blood type** = *blood group*; hence ***blood-typing*** vbl. sb. and *attrib.*; **blood-urea**, the concentration of urea in the blood; **blood-vein**, a kind of moth (*Bradyepetes amataria*); **blood wagon** *slang*, an ambulance (see also quot. 1969); **blood-wealth** *Anthrop.*, money or goods given as compensation for a murder; †**blood-weed** (*Bot.*), a species of *Polygonum*; †**blood-wipe**, a wound, also a kind of small club or truncheon; **blood-wood**; a name applied to several foreign trees, e.g. in Jamaica *Gordonia hæmatoxylon*, in Norfolk Island *Baloghia lucida*, in Australia various species of *Eucalyptus*, in India *Lagerstrœmia reginæ*; **blood-worthy** *a.*, sufficient to warrant bloodshed; **blood-wound**, a wound from which blood flows, as distinguished from one in which the skin is not broken.

1899 T. BOWHILL *Man. Bacteriol. Technique* II. 54 (*heading*) *Blood Agar. **1927** R. A. KELSER *Man. Vet. Bacteriol.* v. 57 *Blood Agar.* Add 10 per cent of sterile defibrinated horse, sheep or rabbit blood to a definite amount of sterile nutrient agar..which has been completely melted and allowed to cool to 45° C. **1854** A. E. BAKER *Gloss. Northampt. Words* 10 *Blood alleys. **1881** A. B. EVANS *Leic. Words* 91 If streaked with red veins it is called a 'blood alley'. **1963** COMPTON MACKENZIE *Life & Times* II. 49 A blood alley was a pinkish stone with some deeper pink markings. *a* **1225** *Ancr. R.* 420 Ne *blod-bendes of seolke. *a* **1400** *Morte Arth.* 2576 Us bus have a blodebande. **1938** *N.Y. Post Digest* April 23/1 Bellevue and Kings County Hospitals in New York have now followed the lead of Chicago and Philadelphia hospitals in the establishment of '*blood banks'. **1942** *Times of India* 2 May 6/2 The appeal..for blood donors to come forward and contribute to the blood bank which has been opened in the city. **1837** CARLYLE *Fr. Rev.* I. VI. iii. 277 A Great Personage worn out by debauchery was believed to be in want of *Blood-baths. **1867** FREEMAN *Norm. Conq.* I. vi. 454 The marriages of Emma would seem to have required a blood-bath as their necessary attendant. **1709** *Lond. Gaz.* No. 4521/4 Stoln..a *blood-bay Mare. **1829** *Free Press* (Tarboro, N.C.) 20 Feb., *Blood Beets. **1831** PECK *Guide for Emigrants* II. 141 The blood beet [is] less deeply colored. **1889** BARRÈRE & LELAND *Dict. Slang*, **Blood boat* (naval). **1899** BULLEN *Log Sea-Waif* 230 Half the crew..looked as if all the ways of 'Western Ocean blood-boats' were familiar to them. **1914** LD. CHAS. BERESFORD *Mem.* I. i. 2, I was only the 'blood-boat' (the jolly-boat bringing beef to the ship) midshipman of a man-of-war. **1605** SHAKS. *Macb.* IV. i. 123 Now I see 'tis true, For the *Blood-bolter'd Banquo smiles vpon me. **1848** MILLER *First Impr.* ii. (1857) 23 The old blood-boltered barons. **1890** LD. LUGARD *Diary* 7 Oct. (1959) I. 314 His camp.. where Dualla had *blood brothers. **1933** E. E. EVANS-PRITCHARD in *Africa* VI. 370 If you exchange blood with a member of the Akowe clan all other members of this clan rank as your blood-brothers. **1885** H. M. STANLEY *Congo Free State* II. xxvi. 23 The next day we made *blood brotherhood. The fetish-man pricked each of our right arms, pressed the blood out..and the black and white arms were mutually rubbed together. **1909** *Daily Chron.* 11 Sept. 4/6 His Majesty..will doubtless..drink a toast or two with especial reference to that blood-brotherhood between the two nations. **1937** E. SNOW *Red Star over China* v. 195 They swore blood brotherhood in the tribal manner. **1563–87** FOXE *A. & M.* (1596) 711/1 His *bloudbulke was broken by reason they had so vily beaten him and brused him. **1575** TURBERV. *Bk. Venerie* 129 Up to the mydryffe betweene the Bloudboulke and the sides. **1846** T. W. JONES in *Philos. Trans. R. Soc.* CXXXVI. 65 The red oval corpuscle of the blood of the Skate under consideration, I propose to name nucleated blood-cell, in contradistinction to the granule-cell, which..in consequence of its being filled with granules is otherwise well designated granule *blood-cell. **1866** AITKEN *Pract. Med.* (ed. 4) II. 57 Salts..in which the blood-cells ultimately become deficient. **1878** F. J. BELL tr. *Gegenbaur's Comp. Anat.* 172 In many Nemertina the blood-cells have a red colour. **1943** C. H. WARD-JACKSON *Piece of Cake* 15 **Blood chit*, any written authorisation supplied to an individual to 'cover' him; or, more originally, a ransom note supplied to pilots over possibly hostile territory in the East. **1954** *Neuphilologische Mitteilungen* LV. 47 *Blood-chit*, 'document, signed by a non-R.A.F. passenger before a flight, which exonerates the R.A.F. in the event that they damage or destroy him'. **1900** DORLAND *Med. Dict.*, *Blood-count. **1907** *Practitioner* Dec. 852 A blood-count, made two years ago, showed: Red cells, 5,000,000 [etc.]. **1947** *Mind* LVI. 246 Healthy children with a normal red blood count. **1561** DAUS tr. *Bullinger on Apoc.* (1573) 225 b, Fornications, wonderful surfetting, *bloudcraftes and

counselles. **1899** *Jrnl. Exper. Med.* IV. 429 *Blood cultures made in cases of pneumonia..indicate..a general blood invasion. **1963** *Lancet* 5 Jan. 55/2 Blood-cultures were negative. **1840** *Philos. Trans. R. Soc.* CXXX. 596 Whether the globules into which the *blood-disc resolves itself, are the foundations of new corpuscles of the blood, I do not know. **1845** TODD & BOWMAN *Phys. Anat.* I. 60 Certain particles, the blood-discs, which float in it [*sc.* the blood] in great numbers. **1879** *Jrnl. Anat. & Physiol.* XIV. 295 All cells..from which red blood-discs may spring. **1921** *Lancet* 26 Nov. 1123/1 In a recent number of the *Guy's Hospital Gazette* the editor protests against the too free use of students as *blood-donors. **1958** *Times* 7 July xxi/4 The unselfish help of many thousands of voluntary blood donors. **1968** *Brit. Med. Bull.* XXIV. 210/2 Histograms of readings of serum chloride and urea taken from 1,000 blood donors are shown. **1898** MEREDITH *Odes Fr. Hist.* 16 The *blood-drinker's madness fast upon her. **1899** *Daily News* 28 June 8/4 The primitive 'food group' of hunters, who, like the beasts they killed, were 'blood-drinkers'. **1588** SHAKS. *Tit. A.* II. iii. 224 In this detested, darke, *blood-drinking pit. **1591** —— *1 Hen. VI* II. iv. 108 My blood-drinking hate. **1903** *Edin. Rev.* Oct. 307 Blood-drinking savages. **1900** DORLAND *Med. Dict.* s.v. *Blood*, *Blood-dust, or hemoconiæ. **1839** G. STEPHENS tr. *Tegnér's Frithiof's Saga* XVI. 158 *Blood-eagle lines on Thy foe shall be flowing. **1922** *Cambr. Med. Hist.* III. xiii. 329 Cutting the blood-eagle in the back of the fallen foe is well known from the vengeance for their father taken by the sons of Ragnarr Loðbrók. **1964** G. TURVILLE-PETRE *Myth & Religion of North* xiii. 254 A peculiarly revolting form of human sacrifice was that of cutting the 'blood-eagle' (*blóðørn rista*). The ribs were cut from the back and the lungs drawn out. **1607** TOPSELL *Serpents* 695 An Eye-salve against the whitenesse and *bloud-eyes. **1904** *Blood film [see SMEAR *sb.* 3 b]. **1961** *Lancet* 5 Aug. 315/1 To stain a blood-film the solution is added drop by drop till it entirely covers it. **1851** SIR F. PALGRAVE *Norm. & Eng.* I. 489 The Were or *bloodfine for every Dane who had been killed. **1872** *Brit. Med. Jrnl.* 27 July 89/1 She was suffering from the effects of an invasion by the African *blood-fluke, a parasite now generally recognized by the generic and specific title of *Bilharzia hæmatobia*. **1962** *New Scientist* 6 Sept. 490/3 The disease known as bilharziasis, caused by three species of bloodflukes or schistosomes, is carried by various types of water snail. **1880** BURTON *Reign Q. Anne* III. xv. 80 The *blood-frenzy called in the East running amuck. **1908** J. BARCROFT in *Jrnl. Physiol.* XXXVII. 12 (*title*) Differential Method in *Blood-Gas Analysis. **1922** J. S. HALDANE *Respiration* i. 11 Careful blood-gas determinations showed that when apnoea had been produced by forced ventilation of the lungs the arterial blood contained..more oxygen. **1966** *Lancet* 24 Dec. 1394/2 The hypothetical absorption of significant amounts of oxygen from the skin or upper respiratory tract has never been substantiated by arterial blood-gas measurements. **1897** *Geogr. Jrnl.* X. 156 Arrowheads and spears, many of them curiously barbed and twisted, and some showing a knowledge of the value of the '*blood-groove'. **1916** W. V. BREM in *Jrnl. Amer. Med. Assoc.* LXVII. 190/2 Isohemolysins cannot be used, therefore, in determining *blood groups. **1917** *Brit. Med. Jrnl.* 24 Nov. 696 The selection of an ideal donor—that is, one belonging to the same blood group as the patient—may be made. **1935** HUXLEY & HADDON *We Europ.* iv. 127 We plot the distribution of the three blood-group genes on a map. **1958** *Listener* 28 Aug. 320/2 It is now thought to be possible to discover the blood groups of ancient peoples from their bones. **1916** W. V. BREM in *Jrnl. Amer. Med. Assoc.* LXVII. 190/2 We have been able to modify the technic of *blood grouping so that it can be done easily and accurately within a few moments' time. **1962** *Lancet* 15 Dec. 1279/2 In 16·6% of myoadenoma patients and 11·0% of the carcinoma patients the blood-grouping was not recorded. **1865** KINGSLEY *Herew.* xviii. 227 He would not allow his men to enter the city while they were *bloodhot. **1794** GODWIN *Cal. Williams* 262 The sordid and mechanical occupation of a *blood-hunter. **1901** 'L. MALET' *Hist. Sir R. Calmady* III. viii. 233 *Blood-knots in the whip-lash. **1910** J. MASEFIELD *Lost Endeavour* I. iv. 45 A 'teaser', or blood-knot of hard, tarred spunyarn. **1968** E. FRANKLIN *Dict. Knots* 9 *Blood knot*, a multiple Overhand Knot tied in the end of a rope...used as a weapon or for inflicting punishment. **1909** *Cent. Dict.* Suppl., **Blood line*, a particular transmissible character in an animal, or, analogically, in a plant. **1927** *Daily Tel.* 6 Dec. 9/1 [The steer] reflected his excellent bloodline descent in his shapely contour. **1948** C. L. B. HUBBARD *Dogs in Britain* 31 He [*sc.* the breeder] will doubtless endeavour to improve or alter his blood-lines as the necessities arise. **1848** LYTTON *Harold* I. III. ii. 175 Hear me, thou with the vulture's *blood-lust. **1942** WYNDHAM LEWIS *Let.* 25 Oct. (1963) 338 He [a soldier] would be disgusted and amazed to find us all foaming at the mouth, our eyes full of bloodlust. **1887** F. H. STORER *Agric. Rel. with Chem.* I. xiv. 399 Nitrate of soda and horn-meal did well, and fermented *blood-meal also. *Ibid.* 383 Fresh blood is made to separate into liquid serum..and into a solid clot, which, when dried and ground, is the substance used as a fertilizer and known as dried blood or blood-meal. **1956** GILLESPIE & HATHWAY *Textbk. Gen. Agric.* xvii. 225 Blood-meal, another residue from the slaughterhouse, is a favourite ingredient of rations for pigs and poultry. **1948** *Sci. News Let.* 10 July 26 (*caption*) Red Cross *Bloodmobile. **1961** *Guardian* 28 Jan. 12/7 'An automobile equipped for collecting blood from volunteer donors'..bloodmobile. **1855** E. ACTON *Mod. Cookery* xxviii. 571 Tangerine Oranges... There is another variety of this fruit known commonly as the **blood-orange*. **1862** HEREMAN *Vine & Fruit Tree Cultiv.* 43 Maltese Blood Oranges. **1892** *Granta* 14 May 321/1 The piles of blood oranges were diminishing rapidly. **1864** JERDON *Birds India* III. 522 *Ithaginis cruentus* ..the Green *Blood-Pheasant. **1884** *Encycl. Brit.* XVII. 341/1 Among the birds [of Nepal] are..the blood pheasant (*Ithaginis cruentus*),..&c. **1964** E. P. GEE *Wild Life India* xiv. 117 All along that magnificent country in Sikkim, Bhutan and N.E.F.A... Marvellous birds, including horned, monal and blood pheasants, live up there. **1881** *Syd. Soc. Lex.* I, **Blood pictures*, the network formed by the adhesion of the red corpuscles to each other on a slide under the microscope, and supposed to be of a different pattern in human blood to that formed in the blood of other animals. **1908** *Practitioner* Feb. 234 The blood-picture of pernicious anaemia is presented. **1961** *Lancet* 16 Sept. 617/1 The blood-picture returned gradually to normal in seven days. **1889** *Buck's Handbk. Med. Sci.* VIII. 626/2 *Blood-plaques, methods of studying. **1907** *Practitioner* Aug. 195 The alkalinity of the inorganic constituents of the *blood-plasma is increased in cancer. **1945** *Daily Tel.* 3 July, Administering penicillin and blood plasma. **1885** *Buck's Handbk. Med. Sci.* I. 554/1 The *blood-plates are not products of the degeneration of white corpuscles. **1898** W. S. L. BARLOW *Gen. Pathol.* 153 The number of *blood-platelets in normal blood has been variously estimated from 180,000 to 500,000 per cubic millimetre. **1962** *Lancet* 22 Dec. 1316/1 The part that blood-platelets play in stopping bleeding from an injured blood-vessel is now well established. **1863** *Illustr. Times* 17 Oct. 243 The alleged cases of '*blood-poisoning' in Bethnal Green. **1886** *Encycl. Brit.* XXI. 666/2 After a wound..blood-poisoning may occur. **1874** GARROD *Mat. Med.* (ed. 4) 123 Small doses raise the *blood-pressure. **1888** *Encycl. Brit.* XXIV. 97/2 The blood-pressure gradually diminishes from the heart to the periphery. **1919** WODEHOUSE *Damsel in Distress* iv, His blood-pressure at a far higher figure than his doctor would have approved of. **1583** PLAT *Divers new Exper.* (1594) 13 Boile this bloud..until it come to the nature and shape of a *bloudpudding. **1741** RICHARDSON *Pamela* I. 94, I hope to make my hands as red as a Blood-pudden. **1916** D. H. LAWRENCE *Lett.* (1962) I. 492 We have read the 'Cavalleria Rusticana': a veritable blood-pudding of *passion*! **1898** *Daily News* 15 Nov. 8/4 Ryan [i.e. a boxer] kept to work at his little target over the *blood-pump. **1902** *Encycl. Brit.* XXX. 379/1 For the purpose of his researches on the gases in the blood, he [*sc.* C. F. W. Ludwig] designed the mercurial blood-pump. **1935** *Mind* XLIV. 438 This *blood-purge in philosphy must rest..with the logical positivists. **1959** *Encounter* July 78/1 The murderous days of the blood-purges. **1866** BERKELEY in *Treas. Bot.* I. 150 One curious point about the fungous *Bloodrain..when cultivated on rice paste. **1882** GEIKIE *Text-bk. Geol.* III. II. i. §2. 326 Rain falling through such a dust-cloud mixes with it, and..is popularly called blood-rain. *c* **1590** MARLOWE *Faust.* iv. 9 He would give his soul to the devil for a shoulder of mutton though it were *blood-raw. **1838** LOUDON *Arbor. et Fruticetum Brit.* I. 396 The kinds are, the common, Seville, and *blood-red orange. **1871** M. COLLINS *Mrq. & Merch.* III. xi. 249 An aged mulberry-tree..overladen with *blood-ripe fruit. **1826** E. IRVING *Babylon* II. 325 The vine of the earth, which hath brought her grapes to *blood-ripeness. *a* **1674** CLARENDON *Hist. Reb.* II. VII. 342 When the eyes of the mind, no more *blood-run with passion, did discern things right. **1868** W. JAMES *Let.* 4 Mar. (1920) I. 136 The sausages (liver sausages, *blood sausages, and more). **1965** *House & Garden* Jan. 60 Some blood sausages are cooked and cured and ready to eat; others must be grilled. **1634** FORD *Perkin Warb.* I. i. (1839) 99 Sending to this *blood-shrunk commonwealth A new soul. **1933** E. E. EVANS-PRITCHARD in *Africa* VI. 370 The term *nakurëmi*, my *blood-sister, is occasionally used for the wife of a blood-brother. **1957** V. W. TURNER *Schism & Continuity* x. 307 A special form of friendship similar to blood-brotherhood and *blood-sisterhood. **1895** *Humanity* Oct. 58 If a poll could be taken, we believe that *blood sports would be condemned by a larger number of persons than could be mustered on any other humanitarian issue. **1937** *Discovery* July 226/1 He has tended to limit his blood-sports. **1872** YOUATT *Horse* xxii. 458 A *blood-stick—a piece of hard wood loaded at one end with lead—is used to strike the fleam into the vein. **1873** T. H. GREEN *Introd. Pathol.* (ed. 2) 109 The reproduction of the malignant growth in distant tissues is..owing to the entry of its elements into the *blood-stream. **1913** *Field* 30 Aug. 493/3 Infection does not impair the health of the cow. .. The responsible organism gets into the blood stream both by the alimentary and genital tracts. **1928** *Daily Express* 6 June 5/3 Alkaline citrates, which are changed into alkaline carbonates in the blood stream. **1834** YOUATT *Cattle* xi. 356 Inflammatory fever..is termed..*blood-striking, shewt of blood, &c. **1861** Blood-striking [see STRIKING *vbl. sb.* 2 b]. **1927** HALDANE & HUXLEY *Anim. Biol.* vii. 156 A dose of 100 grams will make the *blood-sugar rise above 0.17 per cent. **1961** *Times* 22 Dec. 5/7 Insulin reduces the blood-sugar level. **1890** H. P. HUGHES *Philanthropy of God* v. 75 France is the mother of Conscription. What has she gained by that *blood-tax? **1901** SHEE *Briton's 1st Duty* 250, I appeal to the working men of Great Britain..not to be misled by catch-phrases about 'the liberty of the subject' and the ridiculous cant about a 'Blood Tax'! **1910** W. JAMES *Mem. & Stud.* (1911) xi. 291 They would have paid their blood-tax, done their own part in the immemorial human warfare against nature. **1912** KIPLING *As Easy as ABC* 4 Democracy is Disease. I've proved it by the *blood-test, every time. **1969** *Times* 27 Jan. 10/8 Blood tests will be required from all except fully credited herds. **1960** *Farmer & Stock-breeder* 2 Feb. 132/1 All our chicks are bred from 100% *blood-tested breeding stock. **1879** E. A. SCHÄFER in *Med. Times & Gaz.* 702 (*title*) Report..to determine..by what methods the operation of *blood-transfusion may best be performed. **1916** *Lancet* 2 Sept. 429/2 (*title*) Employment of blood transfusion in war surgery. **1943** *Ann. Reg. 1942* 354 The blood transfusion service revealed interesting differences in the blood grouping of people of various localities. **1958** *Times* 1 July vii/3 British agriculture has long benefited by money earned in industry being reinvested in the form of capital equipment for farm land. It may be that forestry will benefit..by a similar blood transfusion. **1885** LADY BRASSEY *The Trades* 112 The *blood-tree..when wounded, sends forth a juice like blood. **1861** in F. Moore *Rebellion Rec.* (1862) I. III. 73/1 '*Blood-tubs' and 'Plug-Uglies', and others galore, Are sick for a thrashing in sweet Baltimore. **1910** A. BENNETT *Clayhanger* II. ii. §1, The Bulgarian Atrocities had served to give new life to all penny gaffs and blood-tubs. **1963** *Times* 25 Apr. 16/2 In its 145 years of life ..making successive come-backs as a burlesque house, a home of melodrama, a notorious blood-tub, and a centre of moral uplift. **1932** *Jrnl. Amer. Med. Assoc.* XCIX. 2129/1 There are particular features in the distribution of the *blood types among athletes. **1928** *Jrnl. Laboratory & Clin. Med.* XIII. 774 (*caption*) *Blood-typing plate. *Ibid.* 774 The macroscopic slide agglutination method of blood typing is considered. **1960** *Farmer & Stockbreeder* 8 Mar. 101/1 Blood typing, protein typing and the use of genetic markers may revolutionize sire selection in the seventies. **1915** *Jrnl. Exper. Med.* XXII. 213 When the *blood urea remains constant the rate times the square root of the concentration in the urine remains constant. *Ibid.* 231 A comparison of the chloride results with the blood urea figures. **1966** *Lancet* 24 Dec. 1384/2 Blood-urea 55 mg. per 100 ml. **1802** J. RENNIE *Butterflies and M.* 115 The *Blood Vein..appears at the end of June. **1922** *Flight* XIV. 34/2 'The old *blood wagon', as the air ambulance..was generally called. **1957** STIRLING MOSS *In Track of Speed* vi. 82 Out came the 'blood wagon' and back to the ambulance station in the paddock I went. **1969** R. PETRIE *Despatch of Dove* III. 152 A full-length stretcher sledge. A blood-wagon, as the laconic skiers dub it. **1951** E. E. EVANS-PRITCHARD *Kinship among Nuer* iii. 98 *Blood-wealth, the payment of cattle in compensation for homicide. **1611** COTGR., *Playe*, a wound, *bloudwipe, sore cut. **1661** RAY *Itin.* (1760) 144 A small Mace for the Water-Bailiff; also another little one called the Blood-wipe, which they use in parting of Frays. **1724** in F. Moore *Trav. Inner Afr.* (1738) 267, I shall now describe the *Pau de Sangue*, or *Bloodwood, so call'd from a Red Gum which issues from it. **1880** SILVER *Handbk. Australia* 275 Blood-wood and turpentine both hard and durable. **1828** SOUTHEY in *Q. Rev.* XXXVIII. 575 In their opinion, the differences between the Roman Catholic and the Protestant are what they call *bloodworthy. **1841** TYTLER *Hist. Scot.* (1864) III. 238 The bodies of both..were unscathed by fire or powder, and..no

blood (blʌd), *v.* [f. prec.]

1. a. *trans.* To cause blood to flow from; *esp.* in *Surg.*, to 'let blood', to BLEED (which is more common).

1633 P. FLETCHER *Purple Isl.* VII. lxx, His horse he bloods, & pricks a trembling vein. **1746** W. THOMPSON *R.N. Advoc.* (1757) 41 They [slaughtered oxen] are neither sufficiently blooded, nor dressed in any tolerable manner. **1780** JOHNSON *Lett.* II. ccxliv. 158 Yesterday I fasted and was blooded, and to day took physick and dined. **1840** DICKENS *Barn. Rudge* lxxxii, Being promptly blooded..he rallied. **1857** LIVINGSTONE *Trav.* xii. 223 They had scruples about eating an animal not blooded in their own way.

†**b.** *transf.* To let sap flow from (trees). *Obs.*

1623 *Althorp MS.* in Simpkinson *Washingtons* Pref. 50 Nov. 22 To Dunkley for..one daie blouding trees £00 01s.

2. To wet or smear with blood. ? *Obs.* or *dial.*

c **1593** SPENSER *Sonn.* xx, Let none ever say, That ye were blooded in a yeelded pray. **1691** SHADWELL *Scowrers* IV. i. 359 She has scratched and blooded me all over. *a* **1700** DRYDEN *Fables* (J.) Reach out their spears afar, And blood their points. **1749** FIELDING *Tom Jones* VII. xii, Having blooded his waistcoat. **1862** BORROW *Wild Wales* II. 31 One of the hardest battles which ever blooded English soil.

3. *Venery.* **a.** To give a hound its first taste, or sight and smell of the blood of the game it is to hunt. Also *fig.*

1781 P. BECKFORD *Hunting* (1802) 97 Here they are blooded to fox. **1848** MACAULAY *Hist. Eng.* II. 513 It was most important..that his troops should be blooded.

b. To smear the face of (a novice at hunting) with the blood of a fox, etc., after the kill. Also *transf.* and *fig.*

1908 L. C. R. CAMERON *Otters & Otter-Hunting* xvi. 198 *Blooding*,..marking a boy or girl on the brow and cheeks with a small piece of Otter's flesh to 'enter' him or her to the sport. **1922** M. ARLEN *'Piracy'* I. iv. §4. 55 He rolled and wallowed in it, he let life 'blood' him. **1926** J. FAIRFAX-BLAKEBOROUGH *Hunting & Sporting Reminisc. H. W. S. Lowndes* ii. 8 Harry Lowndes was blooded to hounds at the early age of four and a half..by Tom Whitmore, the celebrated Oakley huntsman. **1927** W. E. COLLINSON *Contemp. Eng.* 37 A year or so ago..I met the word blooding in an illustrated weekly, depicting the ceremony of smearing with the fox's blood a girl taking part in her first hunt. **1929** J. MASEFIELD *Hawbucks* 93 Carrie had had the brush and been blooded. **1955** *Times* 24 May 15/5 These largely mining areas are of little use to Conservatism save as battle courses for blooding new candidates. **1959** *20th Cent.* Dec. 484 Lee is, of course, blooded—'he criss-crossed her cheek thoroughly'. Blooding is an invariable feature of pony books.

†**4.** To raise the blood of, i.e. to make eager for combat or bloodshed, to exasperate; *esp.* soldiers at the beginning of a fight. *Obs.*

1622 BACON *Hen. VII.* (J.) The auxiliary forces of French and English were much blooded one against another. **1677** *Govt. Venice* 61 The consideration of a Sequin..for every Turks head they bring in has..blooded them against those Infidels.

5. To apply a coat of blood to (leather) in leather-colouring, in order to obtain a good black.

190. *Mod. Amer. Tanning* 110 (Cent. Dict. Suppl.).

6. *intr.* with *it*: to play the 'blood' (see BLOOD *sb.* 15 c).

1922 JOAD *Highbrows* v. 179 When I wasn't 'blooding' it with the second-year men..your scout..used to bring your lunch down into my rooms.

blooded (ˈblʌdɪd), *a.* [f. BLOOD *v.* or *sb.* + -ED.]

†**1.** Stained with blood. *Obs.*

c **1250** LAY. 26811 Blodede feldes, falewede nebbes. **1637** EARL MONMOUTH *Romvlvs & Tarqvin* 155 Rather to haue his hands blouded than his head crowned.

2. Having (*hot, cold,* or other) blood.

1805 W. SAUNDERS *Min. Waters* 14 Greater..in the warm, than in the cold blooded animals. **1835** MARRYAT *Olla Podr.* xiv, Being..all cold-blooded animals.

3. Of horses: Of good breed.

1858 GEN. P. THOMPSON *Audi Alt.* I. lxii. 241 A few thoroughly-blooded [horses] of the English breed. **1858** O. W. HOLMES *Aut. Breakf.-t.* (1865) 14 Let me beg you..not to speak of a 'thorough-bred' as a 'blooded' horse, unless he has been recently phlebotomised. **1883** A. S. HARDY *But yet Wom.* 118 He had in his stables..blooded animals of the purest race.

†ˈ**blooder.** *Obs.* [f. BLOOD *v.* + -ER[1].] He who or that which draws or lets blood.

1398 TREVISA *Barth. De P.R.* VII. xxix. (1495) 244 *Sanguissuga* is a bloder other a leche.

'blood-guilt. [f. BLOOD + GUILT, after next.] The guilt of unrighteous bloodshed.
1882 F. HARRISON *Crisis in Egypt* 9 It would be blood-guilt in this country to enforce these guarantees at the cost of war.

'blood-guilty, *a.* [f. as prec. + GUILTY.] Guilty of bloodshed; responsible for the murder or death of any one.
1597 DRAYTON *Mortimer.* 34 Murthered by her owne blood-guiltie hands. **1795** SOUTHEY *Joan of Arc* IX. 24 That proud prelate, that blood-guilty man. **1858** GEN. P. THOMPSON *Audi Alt.* I. lvi. 221 Look at Spain..and see whether no solemn lesson has been read to the blood-guilty.
Hence **blood-'guiltiness**, blood-guilt. So also **blood-'guiltless** *a.*, guiltless or innocent of bloodshed or murder.
1535 COVERDALE *Ps.* l. [li.] 14 Delyuer me from bloudgyltynesse o God. **1649** MILTON *Eikon.* xix. Wks. (1851) 478 Hee hath confess'd..the bloodguiltinesse of all this Warr to lie upon his own head. **1753** H. WALPOLE *Lett. H. Mann* (1833) III. 40 (D.) I am glad you have got rid of your duel blood-guiltless. **1884** *Weekly Times* 10 Oct. 3/3 It would be blood-guiltiness.

'blood-,heat. The ordinary heat of blood in the healthy human body, commonly marked in thermometers at 98.6° Fahr., though really rising in the interior of the body to 100°. Also *fig.*
1812 L. HUNT in *Examiner* 25 May 322/2 It has a knack..of being at blood-heat. **1849** TODD *Cycl. Anat. & Phys.* IV. 115/1 Fibrin..subjected to a blood-heat, begins to change into matter, such as that now described.
attrib. **1868** *Lessons Mid. Age* 48 The opinions we held so feverishly..in the blood-heat season of youth.

'blood-horse. Chiefly *U.S.* [BLOOD *sb.* 12 b.] A thoroughbred or pedigree horse.
1794 *Sporting Mag.* IV. 35/2 The various judicious crosses that have brought the breed of blood horses into such a state of unprecedented perfection. **1800** A. CARLYLE *Autobiog.* iii. (1860) 146 A couple of grooms leading four fine blood-horses. **1841** H. S. FOOTE *Texas & Texans* II. 383 They [*sc.* wild horses]..are..inferior to the American blood-horse in volume of muscle. **1856** MRS. STOWE *Dred* II. 145 The fleet blood-horse was whirling Harry and Lizette past bush and tree. **1860** O. W. HOLMES *Prof. Breakf.-t.* iii. 65 Admiral Sir Issac Coffin sent out two fine blood-horses.

'bloodhound, *sb.*
1. A large, very keen-scented dog (*Canis sanguinarius*), formerly much used for tracking large game, stolen cattle, and human fugitives. There are three important breeds, the English, Cuban, and African.
c **1350** *Will. Palerne* 2183 Seiȝe blod-houndes bolde. *c* **1440** *Promp. Parv.* 40 Bloode howndе, *molosus.* **1483** *Cath. Angl.* 35 A Blude hunde. **1548** HALL *Chron. Rich. III*, an. 3. 26/1 Pleiyng the parte of a good blood hunde. **1624** CAPT. SMITH *Virginia* II. 32 They follow him like bloud-hounds. **1774** GOLDSM. *Nat. Hist.* II. 166 The bloodhound was a dog of great use & high esteem among our ancestors. **1820** KEATS *St. Agnes* xli, The wakeful bloodhound rose, and shook his hide.
2. *fig.* applied to men: A hunter for blood.
a **1400** *Morte Arth.* 3641 And gere theme brotheliche blenke, alle ȝone blod-hondes. **1550** COVERDALE *Spir. Perle* xi. Wks. 1844 I. 128 Manasses..was a very bloodhound and a tyrant. **1818** SCOTT *Hrt. Midl.* xxxiii, The blood-hounds of the law were so close after me.
3. *attrib.*
1820 BYRON *Mar. Fal.* IV. ii. 248 To have set The bloodhound mob on their patrician prey. **1864** *Times* 17 Nov., Possessing an almost bloodhound instinct in following up the very faintest tracks.

'bloodhound, *v. rare.* [f. the sb.] *trans.* To pursue ruthlessly.
1935 G. BARKER *Janus* i. 15, I am by blood bloodhounded out of doors. **1961** *Guardian* 25 May 10/4 Naïvely imagining that MI 5 was only bloodhounding those with supposed Cliveden or Mosley ideas.

bloodied ('blʌdɪd), *ppl. a.* [f. BLOODY *v.* + -ED¹.] Made bloody; smeared with blood.
1597 SHAKS. *2 Hen. IV*, I. i. 38 A Gentleman..That stopp'd by me, to breath his bloodied horse. **1631** HEYLIN *Hist. St. George* 256 Raging with bloudied swords. **1814** SCOTT *Ld. of Isles* VI. xxxv, Broken plate and bloodied mail. **1871** ROSSETTI *Staff & Scrip* xxxii, His bloodied banner crossed his mouth.

†**'bloodierly,** *adv. Obs.* [cf. *former-ly.*] A rare and obsolete formation for: More bloodily.
1602 WARNER *Alb. Eng.* IX. li. (1612) 230 A bloodier Law vsde bloodierly was never heard or shed.

†**'bloodiful,** *a. nonce-wd.* Full of blood, bloody.
1583 STANYHURST *Æneis* I. (Arb.) 29 Bluddyful altars.

bloodily ('blʌdɪlɪ), *adv.* [f. BLOODY *a.* + -LY².] In a bloody manner (see senses of the adj.); with blood (shed); as blood (*obs.*); bloody-.
1565 JEWEL *Repl. Harding* (1611) 248 Christs Blood is not Really or Bloodily Present. **1594** SHAKS. *Rich. III*, III. iv. 92 Mine Enemies To day at Pomfret bloodily were butcher'd. **1649** BP. HALL *Cases Consc.* (1650) 95 This false and bloodily uncharitable ground. **1654** GATAKER *Disc. Apol.* 69 All of that Religion ar bloodilie minded. **1749** FIELDING *Tom Jones* XI. ix, 'You are always so bloodily wise,' quoth the husband. **1780** BURKE *Spch. Bristol* Wks. III. 384 Bloody executions (often bloodily returned). **1830** G. S. FABER *Diff. Romanism* 386 Christ..who once, upon the altar of the cross, offered himself bloodily. **1861** PEARSON *Early & M. Ages Eng.* 170 The Welsh were bloodily beaten back.

bloodiness ('blʌdɪnɪs). [f. as prec. + -NESS.]
1. Bloody state or condition.
1591 PERCIVALL *Sp. Dict., Ensangrentamiento*, bluddines. *a* **1617** HIERON *Wks.* (1620) II. 472 The brine..to be purged from the bloudinesse it hath sucked out of the flesh. **1617** MARKHAM *Caval.* VI. 9 And bloodines of sides [of a horse].
2. Sanguinary quality, tendency to bloodshed.
1610 HEALEY *St. Aug. Citie of God* 784 What goodnesse they changed into bloudinesse. *a* **1674** CLARENDON *Hist. Reb.* III. XI. 156 War..carried on..with some circumstances of bloodiness. **1685** BAXTER *Paraphr. N.T.* Acts xv. 29 Do nothing that..savoureth of cruelty and bloodiness.

blooding ('blʌdɪŋ), *vbl. sb.* [f. BLOOD *v.*]
1. The letting of blood, bleeding; wounding with loss of blood.
1597 LOWE *Chyrurg.* (1634) 369 Blouding, which the Greekes call *Phlebotomia.* **1651** WITTIE tr. *Primrose's Pop. Err.* IV. 255 Bloodding is never good for a Flegmatick man. **1741** MONRO *Anat.* (ed. 3) 68 Surgeons..trust to the Blooding. **1852** JAMES *Pequinillo* I. 97 The young baronet..received, himself, a far more severe blooding.
attrib. **1685** *Lond. Gaz.* No. 2079/4 A Chesnut Mare..with a swelling on her neck, about her blooding place.
2. The action of giving hounds a first taste of and appetite for blood (see BLOOD *v.* 3).
1875 'STONEHENGE' *Brit. Sports* I. II. iv. §5. 175 The necessity for blooding the hounds is the..most immediate object of cub-hunting. **1876** WHYTE-MELVILLE *Katerfelto* xxv. 273 The honour of blooding a pack of hounds.

†**'blooding,** *sb. Obs.* [f. BLOOD *sb.*, app. after *pudding*; cf. BLACKING, LIVERING.] A black-pudding.
c **1460** *Towneley Myst.* 89 Oure mete now begyns..Two blodynges, I trow, a liveryng betwene. **1562** *Apol. Priv. Masse* (1850) 10 Will ye inhibit the folks to eat bloodings, or pigeons, or capons, such as are killed by stifling? **1639** HORN & ROBOTHAM *Gate Lang. Unl.* xxxvi, The pudding-maker..maketh puddings and sawsages..chitterlings, liverings, bluddings. **1783** AINSWORTH *Lat. Dict.* (Morell) I, A blooding, or blood pudding, *apexabo.*

†**'blood-,iron.** *Obs.* [f. BLOOD *sb.* + IRON *sb.*] An instrument for letting blood; a lancet.
c **1440** *Promp. Parv.* 40 Bloodeyryn, bledynge yryn. **1451** *Invent.* in *Test. Ebor.* III. 118 De blode yrens et launcettes in j case. **1523** FITZHERB. *Husb.* §58 Take a bloud yren..and smyte hym bloudde on bothe sydes.

†**'bloodish,** *a. Obs.* [f. BLOOD + -ISH.] Of the nature or appearance of blood.
1530 PALSGR. 306/2 Blodisshe, *sanguinolent.* **1547** BOORDE *Brev. Health* lxxiii. 23 Yf the blode do come frome the lyver the urine is clere blouddyshe.

†**'blood-,les,** *sb. Obs.* In 1 blódlǽs(s, 4 blodles; [OE. f. *blód* blood + *lǽss* letting:—OTeut. *lǣs-si-z, for *lǣt-ti-z, f. *lǣtan* to let. Cf. OE. *blód-lǣtan* to let blood.] Letting of blood.
c **1000** *Sax. Leechd.* II. 146 Blodlæs is to forganne fiftyne nihtum ær hlafmæsse. **1387** TREVISA *Higden* Rolls Ser. VI. 115 þe nynþe day after his blodles [*post phlebotomiam*].

bloodless ('blʌdlɪs), *a.* [f. BLOOD *sb.* + -LESS.]
1. Without blood; *hence*, lifeless; also *fig.*
a **1225** *St. Marher.* 18 Blodles ant banles, dumbe ant deaue. **1552** HULOET, Bloudles, or wythout bloude. **1594** SHAKS. *Rich. III*, I. ii. 7 Thou bloodlesse Remnant of that Royall Blood. **1658** A. FOX *Wurtz' Surg.* III. xiii. 256 These things..do befall wounds, exiccated by the Suns heat..insomuch that they are left bloudless. **1881** *Internat. Rev.* XI. 76 A slave to a dry and bloodless system.
b. Pale from a diminished supply of blood to the surface of the body; pallid.
1592 SHAKS. *Ven. & Ad.* 1037 Overcome by doubt and bloodless fear. **1593** —— *2 Hen. VI*, III. ii. 162 A timely-parted Ghost, Of ashy semblance, meager, pale and bloodlesse. **1718** POPE *Iliad* XIII. 365 He stands..a bloodless image of despair. **1871** PALGRAVE *Lyr. Poems* 45 She knotted her hands behind her In a knot of bloodless gray.
2. Not attended with bloodshed.
1601 SHAKS. *Twel. N.* II. v. 117 Silence like a Lucresse knife: With bloodlesse stroke my heart doth gore. **1604** HIERON *Wks.* I. 569 How can a masse a pardon bring, Sith 'tis a bloud-lesse offering? **1858** FROUDE *Hist. Eng.* III. xiii. 119 A bloodless victory.
Hence **'bloodlessly** *adv.*, **'bloodlessness**.
1820 BYRON *Mar. Fal.* V. iii. 48 She..Shall..bloodlessly and basely yield Unto a bastard Attila. **1863** LE FANU *House by Churchy.* (ed. 2) III. 174 Glaring bloodlessly at the justice. **1883** MISS BRADDON *Gold. Calf* xxviii. 329 Hands almost transparent in their bloodlessness.

†**blood-let,** *ppl. a. Obs.* In 3 blod-leten [from the phrase *to let blood*: see BLOOD *sb.* 1 d.] Bled (surgically).
a **1225** *Ancr. R.* 260 Two maner men habbeð neode uorte eten wel, & drinken wel—swinkinde men, & blod-letene.

blood-letter ('blʌd,lɛtə(r)). [OE. *blód lǣtere* (see prec.).] He who or that which lets blood.
c **1000** ÆLFRIC *Voc.* in Wr.-Wülcker *Voc.* 117 *Flebotomarius*, blodlætere. *c* **1440** *Promp. Parv.* 40 Bloode latare. **1612** WOODALL *Surg. Mate* Wks. (1653) 19, I have seen the like once done by an ignorant blood letter. **1840** HOOD *Up Rhine* 10 It's a self-acting blood-letter.

blood-letting ('blʌd,lɛtɪŋ). [see prec.] The action or process of letting blood; phlebotomy.
a **1225** *Ancr. R.* 14 þe uttre riwle..of ower werkes, & of ower blod letunge. *c* **1400** *Poem Blood-lett.* in *Rel. Ant.* I. 189 Maystris that uthyth blode letyng. **1623** COCKERAM, *Phlebotomie*, bloud-letting. **1651** WITTIE tr. *Primrose's Pop. Err.* IV. 236 There are many that..use purging and bloud-letting every yeare. **1866** A. FLINT *Princ. Med.* (1880) 134 The evils of bloodletting arise from its spoliative effect.
b. *fig.*
1883 *Scotsman* 6 Sept. 5/3 Exacting the fines incurred..a form of bloodletting which would be at once wholesome and effective.

blood-like ('blʌdlaɪk), *a.* [f. BLOOD *sb.* + LIKE.]
1. Resembling blood.
c **1425** WYNTOUN *Cron.* VII. v. 184 þe Mone all rede wes sene Blwd lyk. **1855** BROWNING *Serenade at Villa*, Blood-like, some few drops of rain.
2. Like one of good blood; like a blood (horse).
1885 *Bell's Life* 15 June 1/3 A brown horse..with immense bone and muscular development, and fine blood-like style.

†**'bloodling.** *Obs.* [f. as prec. + -LING.] A black-pudding or blood-pudding.
1598 FLORIO, *Insanguinacci*, bloodlings, or blood-puddings.

†**'bloodly,** *a. Obs. rare.* [+ -LY¹.] = BLOODY.
1575 *Brieff Disc. Troubl. Franckford* (1846) 45 This bloudly, cruell and outragious attempt. **1591** HORSEY *Trav.* (1857) 257 The race of that bloudly generacion.

'blood-,money. [f. as prec. + MONEY.]
Money paid as the price of blood: **a.** A reward for bringing about the death of another; money paid to a witness who gives evidence leading to the conviction of a person upon a capital charge. **b.** Money paid to the next of kin as compensation for the slaughter of a relative.
1535 COVERDALE *Matt.* xxvii. 6 It is not laufull to put them in to the Gods chest for it is bloudmoney. **1818** COBBETT *Resid. U.S.* (1822) 228 Spies and blood-money bands. **1862** H. MARRYAT *Year in Sweden* I. 160 [She] received a thousand marks of pure silver as blood-money for the massacre of her husband and her two sons. **1862** R. PATTERSON *Ess. Hist. & Art* 186 The village benefited by the blood-money that was brought home; the Zemindar, or headman, was paid a tribute or hush-money. **1862** MARY E. ROGERS *Dom. Life Palestine* 295 He was..condemned to pay a certain sum, as '*blood-money*,' to the heirs of the deceased.

blood-red ('blʌd,rɛd), *a.* Red like blood.
1297 R. GLOUC. 313 An robe..of blodrede scarlet. *c* **1440** *Sir Gowther* 452 in Utterson *E.P.* I. 180 God sent Sir Gowghter..A blode rede stede, and armour bryght. **1657** N. BILLINGSLY *Brachy-Martyr.* xxvi. 94 A blood-red comet with a flaming beard. **1827** HEBER *Hymn St. Stephen's Day*, His blood red banner streams afar. **1855** KINGSLEY *Heroes* v. 61 Drinking the blood-red wine.

'blood-re'lation. [see RELATION.] A person related (to another) by birth or consanguinity; a kinsman. Hence **blood-re'lationship**, consanguinity, kinship; also *fig.*
1709 W. STEUART *Coll. conc. Govt. Church Scotl.* II. iv. §8, Those of our Houshold and Blood-Relations, as Husband with Wife, and Father with Children or the like. **1846** GROTE *Greece* I. xx. II. 113 Cousins, and the more distant blood-relations. **1837** MARRYAT *Olla Podr.* xxxiv, Blood relationship has nothing to do with it. **1878** BELL tr. *Gegenbauer's Comp. Anat.* 5 The Blood-relationship of Organisms or Phylogeny.

'blood-'relative. = prec.
1863 HAWTHORNE *Our Home* I. 26 They..announced themselves as blood-relatives of Queen Victoria.

'blood-root. A popular name of several plants: *esp.* the Tormentil (*Potentilla Tormentilla*); Crimson Crane's Bill (*Geranium sanguineum*), and Red Puccoon (*Sanguinaria canadensis*) of N. America.
1578 LYTE *Dodoens* 48 The sixth [kind of Geranium] is called Sanguine roote, or Bloud roote. **1722** DUDLEY in *Phil. Trans.* 295 Remedies for the sting of a Rattle-snake; among others..is a Root they call Blood-root. **1865** PARKMAN *Champlain* ix. (1875) 307 The white stars of the bloodroot gleamed among dank, fallen leaves.

bloodshed ('blʌdʃɛd), *sb.* (*a.*) [f. the phrase *to shed blood.*]
1. The spilling or shedding of blood; slaughter.
1536-40 *Pilgrim's T.* 396 in Thynne *Animadv.* App. 88 For by bloud-shed thy hop to be kepyd in stall. **1541** *Act 33 Hen. VIII*, xii. (*title*), An acte for murder and malicious bloudshed within the courte. **1711** STEELE *Spect.* No. 139 ¶7 He took the French Lines without Bloodshed. **1876** GREEN *Short Hist.* VI. §3 (1882) 295 The accession of Henry the Seventh ended the long bloodshed of the Civil Wars.
†**2.** A single act of bloodshedding, a slaughter, a murder. (With *plural.*) *Obs.*
1594 HOOKER *Eccl. Pol.* IV. (1617) 167 Mutuall combustions, bloud-sheds and wastes. **1620** J. WILKINSON *Coroners & Sherifes* 67 A sherife may inquire of blood-sheddes in his turne. **1677** HALE *Prim. Orig. Man.* II. x. 226 The violent bloodsheds of the Papists upon the Protestants.
†**3.** The shedding or parting with one's own blood; *orig.* said of the death of Christ, who in voluntarily submitting to death is said to have 'shed his blood' for the salvation of men. ? *Obs.*
? *a* **1500** *Chester Pl.* I. (1843) 6 His scourginge, his whippinge, his bloude shedd and passion. **1587** GOLDING *De Mornay* xxxii. 513 The countries are conquered to Jesus Christ by those fewe Disciples preaching his bloudshed and shedding their owne. **1869** BLACKMORE *Lorna D.* ii. (ed. 12)

10 He came up to me—with a piece of spongious coralline to ease me of my bloodshed.

†**4.** = BLOOD-SHOT *sb.* and *adj. Obs.*

1684 tr. *Bonet's Merc. Compit.* III. 68 Who..hath not suffered the least Taraxis (or Bloud-shed) in his Eye. **1702** *Lond. Gaz.* No. 3853/4 Had a little Bloodshed in the inside Corner of his right Eye.

1658 A. FOX *Wurtz' Surg.* II. ix. 82, I undertake to heal.. wounded Eyes and eye-lids, though they be never so much bloudshed. **1697** *Lond. Gaz.* No. 3254/4 Light grey Eyes often Bloodshed.

bloodshedder (ˈblʌdʃɛdə(r)). One who sheds blood, one who commits slaughter; a murderer.

1530 TINDALE *Pract. Prelates* Wks. II. 264 A cruel and unrighteous bloodshedder. **1611** BIBLE *Ecclus.* xxxiv. 22 Hee that defraudeth the labourer of his hire, is a bloodshedder. **1862** MAYHEW *Crim. Prisons* 145 The bloodshedder who was passing the prison yard moodily.

bloodshedding (ˈblʌdʃɛdɪŋ), *vbl. sb.*

1. The shedding of blood, slaughter.

a **1225** *Ancr. R.* 50 Mid hore blodshedunge irudded & ireaded, ase þe martirs weren. **1297** R. GLOUC. 548 þerafter com muche blodssedinge. **1494** FABYAN V. lxxxvi. 64 The Kynge whiche is cruell and full of blode shedynge. **1593** SHAKS. *2 Hen. VI*, IV. vii. 108 These hands are free from guiltlesse bloodshedding. **1868** GLADSTONE *Juv. Mundi* x. (1870) 384 With respect to blood-shedding, the morality of the Greeks of Homer was extremely loose.

†**b.** The shedding of one's own blood; submission to a bloody death. Cf. BLOODSHED 3. *Obs.*

a **1533** FRITH *Disput. Purgat.* (1829) 136 Jesus Christ.. hath delivered us through his blood-shedding. **1583** STUBBES *Anat. Abus.* II. 116 Ye precious death, passion, blood-shedding, and obedience of Christe Jesus.

ˈblood'shedding, *ppl. a. rare.* That sheds blood, that causes death by bloodshed.

1633 *Costlie Whore* IV. iii. in Bullen *O. Pl.*, The halter, poyson, or bloodshedding blade. **1826** E. IRVING *Babylon* II. VII. 183 To deliver them with a blood-shedding vengeance.

bloodshot (ˈblʌdʃɒt), *a.* and *sb.* [Shorter form of BLOOD-SHOTTEN (*shot* being the later form of the pa. pple.).] **A.** *adj.*

1. Of the eye: Over-shot or suffused with blood; having the exposed part of the eyeball more or less tinged with blood from inflammation of the blood-vessels of the conjunctiva.

[**1552** HULOET, Bloudeshot in the eye.] *a* **1618** RALEIGH *Rem.* (1664) 124 Those whose Eyes are blood-shot. *a* **1679** T. GOODWIN *Wks.* (1865) X. 149 As we say of the eye that it is blood-shot, so we may of the heart that it is sin-shot. **1720** GAY *Poems* (1745) I. 44 Pale cheeks and blood-shot eyes her grief express. **1824** W. IRVING *T. Trav.* I. 110 His eyes were bloodshot; his cheeks pale and livid.

2. *fig.* and *transf.*

Cf. BLOODSHOT *v.* quot. 1593.

1851 THACKERAY *Eng. Hum.* i. (1858) 43 What fever was boiling in him, that he should see all the world blood-shot? **1879** *Q. Rev.* Apr. 412 The papal scare assumed a novel and a bloodshot hue.

†**B.** *sb.* [The adj. used absolutely.] *Obs.*

†**1.** An effusion of blood, resulting from inflammation of the conjunctiva of the eye.

1607 TOPSELL *Four-f. Beasts* 582 Very profitable for the bleardness or bloud-shot of the eyes. **1671** SALMON *Syn. Med.* I. lii. 128 Ophtalmia, Inflamation of the Eyes, is that which is called by some Blood-shot.

†**2.** An effusion of blood in any other part. *Obs.*

1611 COTGR., *Engeleure*, a chilblane; or, the bloud-shot which cold settles, and congeales, vpon the fingers.

†**blood-shot** (ˈblʌdʃɒt), *v. Obs.* Also 7 blood-shoote. [App. the original form was *blood-shot*, from the adj. without analysis (cf. *to blind*); *blood-shoot* being a later 'rational' alteration founded on analysis, as we might from *panic-stricken* deduce a verb to *panic-strike*.] To make blood-shot.

1578 [cf. BLOOD-SHOTTING]. **1593** NASHE *Christ's T.* (1613) 69, I will bloud-shot mine eies, that all may seeme sanguine they looke on. **1632** HEYWOOD *Iron Age* II. v. i. Wks. 1874 III. 423 This sad spectacle, Which bloud-shootes both mine eyes. **1643** *Answ. Ld. Digby's Apol.* 22 All that might bloud-shot other mens eys.

blood-shotten (ˈblʌdʃɒt(ə)n), *a.* (*sb.*) *arch.* [An instrumental combination like *panic-stricken*, *blood-stained*, f. *shotten*, pa. pple. of SHOOT *v.*; thus meaning 'shot' or suffused with blood.]

A. *adj.* Earlier form of BLOOD-SHOT: now *arch.*

? **1507** *Communyc.* (W. de W.) Bij, My ghoostly eyen.. ben blodeshotten with fleshly luste. **1544** PHAËR *Regim. Lyfe* (1546) C vj, A wete cloute thereof.. healeth blood-shotten eies. **1641** LD. J. DIGBY *Sp. in Ho. Com.* 21 Apr. 11 Let us take heed of a blood-shotten eye of Judgement. **1850** B. TAYLOR *Eldorado* xliii. (1862) 431 My eyes.. were strongly blood-shotten.

†**B.** *sb.* = BLOOD-SHOT *sb. Obs.*

1578 LYTE *Dodoens* II. xxvi. 279 It is good against the webbe and bloudshotten of the eyes.

Hence †**ˈblood-ˌshottenness.**

1659 GAUDEN *Tears Ch.* (1659) 60 Bring down such a Rheume and blood-shottennesse into mens eyes. **1684** tr. *Bonet's Merc. Compit.* XIII. 391 Pain of the eyes, Inflammation, Bloudshottenness.

†**ˈblood-ˌshotting,** *vbl. sb. Obs.* Also 6 -shoting, 6–7 -shooting. [f. BLOOD-SHOT *v.*, and similarly varied in form.] = BLOODSHOT *sb.* 1.

1578 LYTE *Dodoens*, Good agaynst the bloodshoting of the eyes. **1579** LANGHAM *Gard. Health* (1633) 568 Apply it to the eyes.. to stop the flux of bloud of the same, or blood-shooting. **1601** HOLLAND *Pliny* II. 42 To cure.. the bloudshotting or red streaks, in the white [of the eies].

blood-spavin: see SPAVIN.

blood-stain (ˈblʌdsteɪn), *sb.* [An attrib. comb. of BLOOD and STAIN *sb.*; cf. *blood-stained*.] A stain or discolouring mark made by blood.

1820 SHELLEY *Prometheus Unbound*, etc. 194 Hide the blood-stains now. **1838** DICKENS *O. Twist* (1850) 257/2 Whether it is a wine-stain, fruit-stain.. or blood-stain. **1864** *Derby Mercury* 14 Dec., Species of plants and animals which put on the appearance of blood stains.

So **blood-stain,** *v.* [A poetic formation, deduced from *blood-stained*.] To stain with blood.

1816 BYRON *Siege Cor.* xxii, Your fellows.. in a fiery mass, Bloodstain the breach through which they pass.

blood-stained (ˈblʌdsteɪnd), *a.* [An instrumental comb.: see BLOOD *sb.* VI, and STAINED.] Stained with blood. *lit.* and *fig.*

1596 SHAKS. *1 Hen. IV*, I. iii. 107 Swift Seuernes flood.. Blood-stained with these Valiant Combatants. **1725** POPE *Odyss.* xv. 301 The blood-stain'd exile, ever doom'd to roam. **1870** BRYANT *Iliad* x. I. 303 O'er his shoulders threw the blood-stained hide.

bloodstock (ˈblʌdstɒk). [f. BLOOD *sb.* 12 c + STOCK *sb.*[1] 54.] Thoroughbred or pedigree horses collectively. Also *attrib.*

1830 *Sporting Mag.* 2nd Ser. I. 333/2 We cannot trace the pedigrees of a large proportion of our blood stock up to foreign mares. **1888** W. DAY *Horse* 9 Those engaged in breeding blood-stock only. **1909** *Westm. Gaz.* 15 July 12/2 Messrs. Tattersall's bloodstock sales at Newmarket. **1912** (*title*) The bloodstock breeder's review.

blood-stone (ˈblʌdstəʊn).

1. A name applied to certain precious stones spotted or streaked with red, supposed in former times to have the power of staunching bleeding, when worn as amulets; particularly the modern HELIOTROPE, a green variety of jasper or quartz, with small spots of red jasper looking like drops of blood; also the *heliotrope* of Pliny, 'a leek-green stone (prase or plasma) veined with blood-red (jasper), the latter so abundant as to give a general red reflection to the whole when it was put in water in the face of the sun.' Dana.

1551 T. WILSON *Logike* 43 The bloodstone stoppeth blood. **1587** in Wadley *Bristol Wills* (1886) 251 To the said Thomas my bloode stone. **1685** *Lond. Gaz.* No. 2040/4 Lost .. a Necklace of Green Blood-stones. **1747** DINGLEY *Gems* in *Phil. Trans.* XLIV. 505 The Blood-Stone, is green, veined or spotted with red and white. **1874** WESTROPP *Prec. Stones* 51, 113. **1879** *Cassell's Techn. Educ.* IV. 309/2 The opaque [stones], white and coloured, such as the opal, the sardonyx, the agate, the onyx, the blood-stone.

2. Hematite, a red iron-ore. (Perhaps only in Dicts., as a verbal rendering of *hæmatites*, applied by Pliny also to the gem: see HEMATITE).

1864 in WEBSTER. **1880** LEWIS & SHORT *Lat. Dict.*, *Hæmatites*, bloodstone, a kind of red iron-ore.

ˈblood-strange. *Herb.* [Skinner suggested 'as if = *blood-stringe*, from its checking bleeding (*a stringendo sanguinem*)'; and Parkinson speaks of its use as a styptic: but *-strange*, *-stringe*, can hardly have been taken, for the nonce, from L. *stringĕre*. It may possibly be a corruption of ME. *streng* 'string, tie'; hardly of early ME. *strenge* 'strength, force', or of *staunch*. The word looks rather like an Eng. adaptation of a German or Dutch name: cf. Ger. *harnstrenge* morbid retention of urine, dysury, to which **blutstrenge* would be analogous, though no evidence of its use has been found.] An obsolete name of the Mousetail (*Myosurus minimus*). Found in the Herbals since Lyte, but apparently never in popular use.

1578 LYTE *Dodoens* I. lxv. 96 It is called in English Mouse tayle and Bloud strange. **1597** GERARD *Herbal* xcv. §4. 346 Mousetaile is called.. in English Bloodstrange. **1640** PARKINSON *Theat. Bot.* 501 *Blood-strange*, I think corruptly from blood-staying. **1863** PRIOR *Plant-n.* 25.

†**ˈblood-suck,** *v. Obs.* [f. BLOOD *sb.* + SUCK *v.*] *trans.* To suck blood from; said of leeches. Also *fig.* To extort money from, rob by extortion.

1541 R. COPLAND *Guydon's Quest. Chirurg.*, Howe ought he to be ruled that hath ben blode sucked. **1592** GREENE *Upst. Courtier* in *Harl. Misc.* (Malh.) II. 245 Thus blood-sucketh he the poore for his owne priuate profite.

blood-sucker (ˈblʌdˌsʌkə(r)). [f. BLOOD *sb.* + SUCKER: cf. prec.]

1. *spec.* **a.** An animal which sucks blood; *esp.* the leech.

1387 TREVISA *Higden* Rolls Ser. IV. 243 Virgill þrewe a goldene blood soukere in to þe botme of a pitte. **1533** ELYOT *Cast. Helth* (1541) 61 Evacuation by wormes founde in waters called bloudde suckers, or leeches. **1579** LANGHAM *Gard. Health* (1633) 66 If one haue drunke a Horse-leech, or Bloudsucker. **1698** VAN LEEUWENHOEK in *Phil. Trans.* XX. 174 A small Gnat, of that sort that.. are no Blood-Suckers.

b. *spec.* A lizard belonging to the species *Lacerta cristata*, the individuals of which change their colour, especially about the neck, from grey to dark red.

1819 J. MORTON *Poet. Rem. J. Leyden* p. xc, A large lizard, termed a blood-sucker. **1840** E. NAPIER *Scenes & Sp. For. Lands* I. Pref. 32 The blood-sucker, a large kind of lizard, though perfectly harmless, is so called from his ferocious appearance and bloodstained countenance. **1882** *Encycl. Brit.* XIV. 736/2 *Calotes* is another genus of agamoids peculiar to the East Indies; it comprises numerous species well known in India by the name of 'blood-suckers'.

c. A lizard of the genus *Amphibolurus* (*Grammatophora*), esp. of the species *A. muricata*.

1852 L. A. MEREDITH *My Home in Tasmania* II. 37 Another description of lizard is here vulgarly called the 'blood-sucker'. **1886** F. MCCOY *Zool. Victoria* II. XII. 47 Grammatophora muricata... The Blood-sucker.

†**2.** One who draws or sheds the blood of another; a blood-thirsty or blood-guilty person. *Obs.*

1561 DAUS tr. *Bullinger on Apoc.* (1573) 92 He hath reserued this time to hymself, when he will reward the bloud suckers. **1577** tr. *Bullinger's Decades* (1592) 315 The seuenth bloud-sucker after beastlie Nero, was Decius. *a* **1659** CLEVELAND *On O.P. Sick* in Craik II. 31 Fall Thou subtle bloodsucker, thou cannibal!

3. *fig.* One who extorts or preys upon another's money or substance; an extortioner; a sponger.

1668 R. LESTRANGE *Vis. Quev.* (1708) 13, I.. cast my Eye upon a certain Tax-gatherer.. ask'd the Devil, whether they had not of that sort of Blood-suckers among the rest, in their Dominions. **1724** SWIFT *Wks.* (1841) II. 3 While there is a silver sixpence left, these blood-suckers will never be quiet. **1857** S. OSBORN *Quedah* xx. 276 A floating population.. of pirates and those bloodsuckers who lived upon them.

ˈblood-ˌsucking, *vbl. sb.* and *ppl. a.* [cf. prec.]

1593 SHAKS. *3 Hen. VI*, IV. iv. 22 The rising of blood-sucking sighes. **1601** YARRINGTON *Two Lament. Traj.* II. ii. in Bullen *O. Pl.* IV, Blood-sucking Avarice. **1648** *Hunting of Fox* 17 Cannibals.. compar'd with the Blood-sucking Sectaries, lose the style of cruelty. **1683** *Addr. fr. Boston* in *Lond. Gaz.* No. 1857/3 Not contented with the Blood-sucking of a Monarch so matchless Merciful. **1836–9** TODD *Cycl. Anat. & Phys.* II. 907/2 The mouth is formed.. as in the blood-sucking Diptera.

†**ˈblood-ˌsupper.** *Obs.* [f. BLOOD *sb.* + SUP *v.*] A blood-thirsty person. (Frequent in 16th c.)

1524 S. FISH *Supplic. Begg.* (1529) 5 A cruell, deuelisshe bloudsupper. *a* **1563** BALE *Sel. Wks.* (1849) 324 Killed by these unsaciate blood-soupers for his truths sake.

blood-thirst (ˈblʌdθɜːst). Thirst for blood, eagerness for bloodshed.

1587 *Mirr. Mag.*, *Malin* xii, Bloudthirst cryes for vengeaunce, at his hand. **1610** HEALEY *St. Aug. Citie of God* (1620) 91 Sylla's.. intollerable pride and bloud-thirst. **1882** L. BRACE *Gesta Chr.* 273 It could control.. the passions and hate and blood-thirst of men.

†**ˈblood-ˌthirster.** *Obs.* One who thirsts for blood; a bloodthirsty man.

1560 DAUS tr. *Sleidane's Comm.* 251 b, The cruell counselles of bludthirsters. **1564** HAWARD *Eutropius* 95 He demeaned hymselfe wyth great cruelty, and as a bloudthyrster.

So †**ˈblood-ˌthirsting** *ppl. a.* = next.

a **1617** HIERON *Wks.* I. 20 The malicious and bloud-thirsting humour of Cain. **1642** S. ASH *Best Refuge* 7 Blood-thirsting Saul. **1763** CHURCHILL *Duellist* III. 68 (D.) Assassination, her whole mind Blood-thirsting, on her arm reclin'd.

bloodthirsty (ˈblʌdˌθɜːstɪ), *a.* [see THIRSTY *a.*] Thirsting for blood, eager for bloodshed.

1535 COVERDALE *Ps.* xxv. 9 O destroye not my soule with the synners, ner my life with the bloudthurstie. **1581** MARBECK *Bk. of Notes* 753 God will abhorre those bloudthirstie and deceiptfull men. **1639** G. DANIEL *Ecclus.* xxii. 86 Some busines for blood-thirsty Swords. **1809** SYD. SMITH *Wks.* (1867) I. 160 The rage of an insane and bloodthirsty faction.

Hence **ˈblood,thirstily, ˈblood,thirstiness.**

1880 J. HAWTHORNE *E. Quentin, etc.* II. 12 Gentlemen.. wore long swords with basket hilts, and were bloodthirstily polite in using the same. **1649** BP. REYNOLDS *Serm. Hosea* iii. 9 The bloudthirstinesse of the Leech. **1862** SHIRLEY *Nugæ Crit.* §5. 209 Even the bloodthirstiness of Alva could not rival his master's.

blood-vessel (ˈblʌdˌvɛsəl). One of the flexible tubes (veins or arteries) in the bodies of animals which convey the blood throughout the system.

1694 SALMON *Iatrica* I. v. 244/2 Some of the Blood-vessels, chiefly the Arteries.. must be broken. **1718** J. CHAMBERLAYNE *Relig. Philos.* (1830) I. iv. §3 A Tunicle full of Blood-Vessels; that is of Veins and Arteries. **1836** DICKENS *Sk. Boz* v. 19/1 She burst a bloodvessel one mornin', and died.

ˈblood-warm, *a.* As warm as blood; of the normal temperature of blood in the body.

1577 B. GOOGE *Heresbach's Husb.* (1586) 130 b, Seeth them together.. and give it him bludwarme in the morning. **1719** HAUKSBEE *Phys.-Mech. Exper.* Supp. 255, I caus'd some Water to be heated about Blood-warm.

b. *fig.*

1837 EMERSON *Misc.* (1855) 94 This writing is blood-warm.

blood-wite ('blʌdwaɪt). Also (incorrectly) **-wit.** [OE. *blódwíte*, f. *blód* blood + *wíte* punishment, penalty, fine.]

1. A penalty for bloodshed: **a.** in *Old English Law*, A fine for shedding blood, to be paid to the aldorman or king, in addition to the *weregild*, or legal value of the life destroyed, paid to the family of the person killed.

[*a* **1000** *Lamb. Ps.* xv. 4 (Bosw.) Of blodum oððe of blodwitum.] **1228** *Mem. Ripon* (1882) I. 52 Blodewyt. *c* **1250** *Gloss. Law Terms* in *Rel. Ant.* I. 33 Blodwite, quite de sanc espondu. **1609** SKENE *Reg. Maj.* 67 Bludeweit hes na place within burgh. **1614** SELDEN *Titles Hon.* 263 *Wite*..is a Punishment or Mulct, as in our words occurring in old monuments, *Blodwite, Frithwite*, and the like. **1754** ERSKINE *Princ. Sc. Law* (1809) 45 He might, by our later practice, have judged..in riots and bloodwits. **1814** SCOTT *Wav.* xlviii, The bloodwit was made up to your ain satisfaction by assythment. **1876** GREEN *Short Hist.* i. 2 The blood-wite or compensation in money for personal wrong.

b. *generally*. A penalty for murder.

1881 CLOUSTON *Arab. Poetry* Introd. 27 In the Sunnat.. the amount of the bloodwit was increased to one hundred camels. **1882** J. PAYNE *1001 Nights* II. 202 That my son's head be paid with the bloodwit of Sherkan's head only.

2. *contextually*. **a.** The right of levying the foregoing fine. **b.** The privilege of exemption from it.

a **1067** *Chart. Eadweard* in *Cod. Dipl.* IV. 216 Ic an heom ðerofer sace and socne..and blodwite and werdwite. **1641** *Termes de la Ley* 42 Bloodwit, that is, to bee quit of amerciaments for blood-shedding.

blood-worm ('blʌdwɜːm). **a.** A small bright-red earth-worm used by anglers. **b.** The scarlet larva of a genus of crane-flies (*Chironomus*) found in rain-water cisterns and pools.

1741 *Compl. Fam.-Piece* II. ii. 350 They will bite freely at the small Red-worm called the Blood-worm. **1799** G. SMITH *Laboratory* II. 280 In the winterseason, the fittest baits for the New River are bloodworms. **1833** J. RENNIE *Angling* 37, I mean here water blood-worms, and not the smaller bright red earth-worms sometimes so named in books on angling. **1840** BROWNING *Sordello* II. 289 Circling blood-worms, minnow, newt, or loach.

blood-wort ('blʌdwɜːt). [f. as prec. + WORT.] A name applied to various plants having red roots or leaves, or popularly supposed to stanch blood or to draw blood. Among these are the Bloody Dock (*Rumex sanguineus*), the Dwarf Elder or Danewort (*Sambucus Ebulus*); also Burnet (*Sanguisorba officinalis*), the American Blood-root (*Sanguinaria canadensis*), and genus *Hæmodorum*.

c **1250** *Gloss.* in Wright *Voc.* 140 *Bursa pastoris*, sanguinarie, blodwurt. **1538** LELAND *Itin.* V. 4 A certen Bloodeworth growith ther wher the Bloode was shedde. **1552** HULOET, Bludwort herb, or that which stoppeth bloud. **1578** LYTE *Dodoens* III. xlv. 380 This herbe is called..in Englishe Walwort, Danewort, and Bloodwort. **1671** SALMON *Syn. Med.* III. xxii. 405 *Lapathum Sanguineum*.. Bloodwort, cleanses the blood much. **1812** WITHERING *Bot. Arrangem.* (1830) II. iv. 235 *Sanguisorba officinalis*, Wild Burnet, Bloodwort. **1872** ROSSETTI *Ho. of Life* (1882) li, With tear-spurge wan, with blood-wort burning red.

bloody ('blʌdɪ), *a.* and *adv.* Forms: 1 blódiȝ, 3–4 blodi, 3–7 blody, (4 blode, bloide), 6 blouddie, bluddie, -y, 6–7 bloudie, -y, bloodie, 6– bloody. *Sc.* 5 bludy, 6 bludie, 8–9 bluidie, -y. [Com. Teut.: OE. *blódiȝ* = OFris. *blodich*, OS. *blôdag*, *-ig* (Du. *bloedig*), OHG. *bluotag* (MHG. *bluotec*, mod.Ger. *blutig*), ON. *blóðug-r*, *-ig-r*:—OTeut. **blôdago-z*: see BLOOD and -Y.]

A. *adj.*

1. a. Of the nature of, composed of, or like blood.

a **1000** ÆLFRIC *Gloss.* in Wr.-Wülcker *Voc.* 113 *Dissenteria*, blodiȝ utsiht. *a* **1240** *Lofsong* in *Lamb. Hom.* 207 Bi his blodie swote..Bi his blodi Rune þet ron inne monie studen. *c* **1440** *Promp. Parv.* 40 Blody, *sanguinolentus*. **1526** *Pilgr. Perf.* (W. de W. 1531) 260 In great agony he swet blody droppes. **1815** *Encycl. Brit.* (ed. 5) III. 461 Some authors speak of bloody baths..prepared especially of the blood of infants. **1818** BYRON *Ch. Har.* IV. cxlii, Here, where Murder breathed her bloody steam. **1875** B. RICHARDSON *Dis. Mod. Life* 15 The phenomenon called, in early times, 'bloody sweat,' has been disputed.

b. Pertaining or relating to the blood.

1716 M. DAVIES *Dissert. Physick* 4 in *Athen. Brit.* III, Cæsalpinus had a proper Opportunity to speak at large of that Bloody discovery [*i.e.* of the circulation of the blood].

2. a. Covered, smeared, stained, with blood; bleeding.

a **1117** *O.E. Chron.*, Wearð se mona lange nihtes swylce he eall blodiȝ wære. **1297** R. GLOUC. 311 Here ys þat knyf al blody. *a* **1400** *Relig. Pieces fr. Thornton MS.* 85 His bludy woundes was reuthe to see. **1530–1** *Act 22 Hen. VIII*, xii, To be beten with whippes..tyll his body be blody. **1593** SHAKS. *3 Hen. VI*, II. v. 71 My Teares shall wipe away these bloody markes. **1656** H. MORE *Antid. Ath.* III. ix. (1662) 117 Dirty bloody spots. **1757** GRAY *Bard* I. iii. 48 Weave with bloody hands the tissue of thy line. **1800** WINDHAM *Sp. Parl.* (1812) I. 336 That scuffle, amongst Englishmen, would have terminated in a black eye or a bloody nose.

b. *bloody grave*: the grave of one who has died by bloodshed. † *bloody hand*, in *Forest-law* (see quot.; cf. RED-HAND(ED); in *Heraldry*, the armorial device of Ulster, derived from the O'Neils; hence borne by baronets.

1800 SCOTT *Eve St. John* xli, By Eildon tree, for long nights three, In bloody grave have I lain. **1885** *Sat. Rev.* 25 Apr. 525/2 Gordon sleeps in his bloody grave.

1598 MANWOOD *Lawes Forest* xviii. §9 Bloudy hand is, where a man is found coursing in the Forest..and is any manner of way imbrewed with bloud, or, that is found imbrewed with bloud..in the Forest, although he be not found Hunting or coursing there. **1727–51** CHAMBERS *Cycl.*, *Bloody Hand*, one of the four kinds of trespasses in the king's forest. **1835** MARRYAT *Pacha* i, The bloody hand in the dexter chief of a baronet. **1852** *Househ. Wds.* V. 8 One sunbeam, coming through a grimed window, and illuminating a bloody hand. There had been a murder done there. **1874** *Student's Hume* xx. 367 Hence baronets bear on their shields the arms of Ulster, a bloody hand.

3. Of animals, or parts of their bodies: Having blood in the veins; containing blood. *arch.* or *Obs.*

1398 TREVISA *Barth. De P.R.* XVIII. cviii. (1495) 850 In all beestes that haue blody lounges is a bledder. **1595** SHAKS. *John* IV. ii. 210 Slaues, that take [Kings] humors for a warrant, To breake within the bloody house of life. **1607** TOPSELL *Serpents* 597 A Serpent [is]..a Bloody Beast without feet. **1818** *Art Preserv. Feet* 53 The bloody corn.. is apt to yield blood on the first touch of the knife.

4. a. Accompanied by or involving the flowing or spilling of blood.

c **1385** CHAUCER *L.G.W.* 1388 Or hadde in armys manye a blodi box. **1530** PALSGR. 199/1 Blody mensyn sickenesse. **1605** SHAKS. *Macb.* II. iv. 23 Is't known who did this more then bloody deed? *c* **1620** Z. BOYD *Zion's Flowers* (1855) 155 Our bloody blowes assuredly he feeles. **1828** CARLYLE *Misc.* (1857) I. 94 Their bloody idolatry, and stormful untutored energy. **1853** KINGSLEY *Hypatia* xxi, I have offered for years the unbloody sacrifice to Him who will perhaps require of me a bloody one.

b. *esp.* Attended with much bloodshed and slaughter; sanguinary.

1593 BILSON *Govt. Christ's Ch.* 306 The bloudie stormes of tyrants. **1597** HOOKER *Eccl. Pol.* V. xlviii. §10 A bitter and a bloody conflict. **1678** N. WANLEY *Wonders* v. i. §102 That long and bloody War in the Empire of Germany. **1711** ADDISON *Spect.* No. 70 ¶4 The Poet..describes a bloody Battle and dreadful Scene of Death. **1848** MACAULAY *Hist. Eng.* I. 227 The most bloody day of the whole war.

5. Of thoughts, words, etc.: Concerned with, portending, decreeing bloodshed.

a **1225** *Ancr. R.* 288 Ruben, þu read þeof, þu blodi delit. *c* **1300** *Beket* 537 Alto blodi was that word: and deore it was i-bouȝt. *c* **1384** CHAUCER *H. Fame* 1239 That maken blody soun In trumpe, beme, and claryoun. **1561** T. NORTON *Calvin's Inst.* Pref., Without hearyng the cause bloody sentences are pronounced against it. **1610** SHAKS. *Temp.* IV. i. 220, I do begin to haue bloody thoughts. **1766** PORNY *Heraldry* iii. (1777) 23 A print of the bloody Warrant for the execution of K. Charles I.

6. Addicted to bloodshed, blood-thirsty, cruel; tainted with crimes of blood, blood-guilty.

1563 BP. BONNER in Foxe *A. & M.* 1254/2 They reporte me to seek bloud, and call me bloudye Boner. *c* **1577** NORTHBROOKE *Dicing* (1843) 179 Howe the blouddie Papistes murther and slaughter in all places rounde aboute vs our poore brethren. **1611** BIBLE *Ps.* v. 6 The Lord will abhorre the bloodie and deceitfull man. **1681** *Addr. fr. Radnor* in *Lond. Gaz.* No. 1671/4 The Factious Schismaticks, and Bloody Romanists. **1795** WINDHAM *Speeches Parl.* (1812) I. 278 The administration of the bloody Robespierre. **1853** DICKENS *Child's Hist. Eng.* xxx, As Bloody Queen Mary, this woman has become famous, and as Bloody Queen Mary, she will ever be remembered with horror and detestation. **1862** *Sat. Rev.* 8 Feb. 154 Our native bloody villains.

7. Of the colour of blood, blood-red.

1591 SHAKS. *1 Hen. VI*, II. iv, 61 *Yorke.* Now Somerset, where is your argument? *Som.* Here in my Scabbard..that Shall dye your white Rose in a bloody red. **1671** *Lond. Gaz.* No. 627/4 A Bloody Bay Gelding,..was stollen out of Stamford Fields. **1755** *Gentl. Mag.* XXV. 280 Near the spot where this accident happened, an anchor was immediately dropped, and a red buoy (called the bloody buoy) fixed to it. **1798** COLERIDGE *Anc. Mar.* II. vii, The bloody sun at noon, Right up above the mast did stand. **1823** LOCKHART *Sp. Ballads, Moor Cal.* iv, His banner..Whereon revealed his bloody field its pale and crescent moon.

†**8.** Allied by blood. (In Langland, with fig. reference to the blood of Christ.) *Obs.*

1362 LANGL. *P. Pl.* A. VII. 196 Heo beoþ my blodi breþeren, for god bouȝte vs all. [Also B. VI. 10; XI. 195; C. IX. 17.]

9. *dial.* Of good blood, well descended.

1877 PEACOCK *Linc. Gloss.* (E.D.S.), He comes of a bloody stock; that's why he's good to poor folks.

10. a. In foul language, a vague epithet expressing anger, resentment, detestation; but often a mere intensive, *esp.* with a negative, as 'not a bloody *one*'. [Prob. from the adv. use in its later phase.]

1785 *Fifth Session Old Bailey* May 722/1 The prisoner Fennell swore an oath, if he had a knife he would cut his bloody fingers off. **1840** R. DANA *Bef. Mast* ii. 2 You'll find me a bloody rascal. *Ibid.* xx. 61 They've got a man for a mate of that ship, and not a bloody sheep about decks! **1880** RUSKIN *Fiction Fair & F.* §29 The use of the word 'bloody' in modern low English is a deeper corruption, not altering the form of the word, but defiling the thought in it. **1950** *Landfall* IV. 23 You mind your own bloody business. **1950** G. WILSON *Brave Company* v. 83 Thrilling? Hell's bloody bells!

b. Bad, unpleasant, deplorable; perverse. Cf. BLOODY-MINDED *a.* 2. Hence as *sb.*, an unpleasant person.

1934 *Neuphilologische Mitteilungen* XXXV. 129 Modern slang (e.g. *bloody* as in *Jones is bloody* 'Jones is objectionable', [etc.]). **1936** R. LEHMANN *Weather in Streets* ii. 48 He developed my nastiness from a mere seed into a great jungle. He made me so mean and bloody... Well, I just am a bloody character, I suppose. **1939** R. W. CHAMBERS *Man's Unconquerable Mind* xii. 391 'It's bloody,' I said. 'To call it bloody, ' Ker replied, slowly and sadly, 'is fulsome flattery.' **1954** A. HECKSTALL-SMITH *Eighteen Months* xiii. 164 Why go out of your way to be bloody about Archie when I'm trying to help him? **1960** D. POTTER *Glittering Coffin* vii. 106 A few bloodys were provoked into their usual braying. **1960** *20th Cent.* Nov. 492 The new generation of college bloodies out on the cobbles.

B. *adv.* †**1.** Bloodily; with blood. *Obs.*

c **1400** *Destr. Troy* 10424 Buernes on þe bent blody beronen.

2. As an intensive: Very....and no mistake, exceedingly; abominably, desperately. In general colloquial use from the Restoration to *c* 1750; now constantly in the mouths of the lowest classes, but by respectable people considered 'a horrid word', on a par with obscene or profane language, and usually printed in the newspapers (in police reports, etc.) 'b——y'. Also in tmesis.

[The origin is not quite certain; but there is good reason to think that it was at first a reference to the habits of the 'bloods' or aristocratic rowdies of the end of the 17th and beginning of the 18th c. The phrase 'bloody drunk' was apparently = 'as drunk as a blood' (cf. 'as drunk as a lord'); thence it was extended to kindred expressions, and at length to others; probably, in later times, its associations with bloodshed and murder (cf. a bloody battle, a bloody butcher) have recommended it to the rough classes as a word that appeals to their imagination. We may compare the prevalent craving for impressive or graphic intensives, seen in the use of *jolly, awfully, terribly, devilish, deuced, damned, ripping, rattling, thumping, stunning, thundering*, etc. There is no ground for the notion that 'bloody', offensive as from associations it now is to ears polite, contains any profane allusion or has connexion with the oath ''s blood!']

1676 ETHEREDGE *Man of Mode* I. i. (1684) 9 Not without he will promise to be bloody drunk. **1684** DRYDEN *Prol. Southerne's Disappointm.* 59 The doughty Bullies enter bloody drunk. **1693** SOUTHERNE *Maid's last Pr.* II. ii. 31 Faith and troth, you were bloody angry. *Ibid.* III. i. 38 She took it bloody ill of him. **1727** SWIFT *Poison. E. Curll* Wks. 1755 III. I. 149 His wife..said, 'Are you not sick, my dear?' He replied 'Bloody sick.' **1742** RICHARDSON *Pamela* III. 405 He is bloody passionate. I saw that at the Hall. **1743** FIELDING *Wed. Day* III. vi, This is a bloody positive old fellow. **1753** FOOTE *Eng. in Paris* II. (1763) 29 She's a bloody fine Girl. **1801** M. EDGEWORTH *Belinda* I. vii. 208 Sir Philip writes a *bloody* bad hand. **1914** SHAW *Pygmalion* III, *Liza.* Walk! Not bloody likely. (*Sensation*). I am going in a taxi. **1923** MANCHON *Le Slang* 65 Half bloody dead...stoney bloody broke..like any-bloody-thing..a handi-bloody-cap ..hoorah! hoo-bloody-rah! **1935** Abso-bloody-lutely [see ABSOLUTELY *adv.*¶]. **1937** 'J. BELL' *Murder in Hospital* viii. 156 I've always thought her a bloody awful great brute. **1951** E. TAYLOR *Game of Hide-and-Seek* I. iii. 61 Serve them bloody right. **1953** —— *Sleeping Beauty* ix. 156 You bloody know you didn't. **1963** L. MEYNELL *Virgin Luck* v. 101 Remember the *News Chronicle*?.. On sale one day. Amalga-bloody-mated the next.

C. In combination.

1. Obvious combinations, as ***bloody-black***; chiefly parasynthetic, as ***bloody-backed, -eyed, -faced, -handed, -hearted, -sceptred***, BLOODY-MINDED, with their derivatives, as BLOODY-MINDEDNESS; also others somewhat analogous, as ***bloody-intended*** having bloody intentions; or adverbial, as † ***bloody-crying*** (crying for blood); † ***bloody-hunting*** (hunting for blood).

1824 SCOTT *Redgauntlet* ch. xv, They have the *bloody-backed dragoons..with them. **1772** CULLUM in *Phil. Trans.* LXII. 466 Half a pint of a *bloody-black water in the thorax. *a* **1617** HIERON *Wks.* II. 317 They are all *bloudy-crying-sinnes, and such as to which belongs an especiall wo. **1597** SHAKS. *2 Hen. IV*, I. iii. 22 In a Theame so *bloody fac'd, as this. **1821** BYRON *Sardan.* IV. i. 115 A..bloody-eyed, And *bloody-handed, ghastly, ghostly thing. **1654** GATAKER *Disc. Apol.* 91 How poor a curb..to keep men from being *bloodie-hearted, and bloodie-handed. **1599** SHAKS. *Hen. V*, III. iii. 41 Herods *bloody-hunting slaughter-men. **1606** *Bk. Com. Prayer, Prayer 5th Nov.*, The most traiterous and *bloody-intended Massacre by Gun-powder. **1605** SHAKS. *Macb.* IV. iii. 104 O Nation miserable! With an untitled Tyrant, *bloody Sceptred.

2. a. Special combinations: **bloody back** *U.S. slang*, a contemptuous name for a British soldier (*Obs.* exc. *Hist.*); cf. BLOODY-*backed*, LOBSTER[1] 3 a, REDCOAT 1 a; † **bloody fall**, an ailment of the feet similar to chilblains; † **bloody flux** (formerly *flix*), dysentery; hence **bloody-fluxed** *a.*; **Bloody Mary**, a drink containing vodka and tomato juice; **bloody nose beetle**, the popular name of *Timarcha* (see quot.); also **bloody-nosed beetle**; † **bloody-water**, a disease, *hæmaturia*.

1770 *Mass. Gazette Extraord.* 21 June 2/2 You Rascals, you *bloody Backs, you Lobster Scoundrels; fire if you dare. **1962** *Times* 24 Apr. 12/7 We dislike hearing the Mall echo to the notes that 'bloodybacks' heard. **1601** HOLLAND *Pliny* II. 76 The angry chilblanes and *bloudy-fals that trouble the feet in the night season. **1473** WARKW. *Chron.* (1839) 23 Unyversalle feveres, axes, and the *blody flyx. **1579** LANGHAM *Gard. Health* (1633) 441 Bloudy fluxe. **1611** BIBLE *Acts* xxviii. 8 The father of Publius lay sicke of a feuer and of a bloody-flixe. **1706** tr. *Lemery's Treat. Foods* II. vi. 161 They make use of its [the sheep's] suet inwardly taken to stop the Bloody-flux. **1615** BP. HALL *Contempl. N.T.* IV. iii, It was free and safe for the leper and *bloody-fluxed to touch thee. **1956** *Punch* 15 Aug. 191/1 Those two..are eating raw steaks and drinking *Bloody Marys. **1961** *House & Garden* Apr. 93/2 Vodka is..mixed with tomato juice ('Bloody Mary'). **1826** KIRBY & SP. *Entomol.* III. 142 In that of the *bloody-nose beetle that segment is bifid. **1847** CARPENTER *Zool.* §660 The *Timarcha lævigata*..emits a

reddish yellow fluid from the joints when disturbed; from which circumstance it is commonly known by the name of the Bloody-nose Beetle. **1880** *Encycl. Brit.* XIII. 150/1 *Timarcha* (the *Bloody-nosed Beetle). **1959** E. F. LINSSEN *Beetles Brit. Isles* II. 89 A species..which owing to its method of 'bleeding' is called the Bloody-nosed Beetle. **1734** ARBUTHNOT in *Swift's Lett.* (1766) II. 205, I had forborn [to ride] for some years, because of *bloody water.

b. In popular names of plants, as **bloody cardinal** = CARDINAL-FLOWER; **bloody finger**, the Foxglove; **bloody man's finger**, the same; also the Arum or Wake-Robin; **bloody rain** = Blood rain (see BLOOD *sb.* 21); **bloody dock** (*Rumex sanguineus*); **bloody twig**, the Dogwood (*Cornus sanguinea*); **bloody warrior**, a dark Wall-flower. (See Prior, Britten and Holland.)

1758 BORLASE *Nat. Hist. Cornwall* xix. §9. 235 The bloody sea-dock. **1838** *Econ. Vegetation* 156 The 'gory dew,' *Palmella cruenta*, and 'bloody rain,' *Lepraria kermesina*..are referrible to these humble and harmless tribes of vegetation. **1851** D. G. MITCHELL *Dream Life* (1852) 199 The bloody cardinal of the swamp-lands. **1861** MISS PRATT *Flower. Pl.* III. 108 The branches were so red, so like twigs of coral, that ..its name of Bloody Twig..seemed appropriate.

bloody ('blʌdɪ), *v.* [f. the adj. Not etymologically identical with OE. (*ȝe*)*blodegian*, *-blodgian* (in 3rd c. *blodeke*, with suffix *-eg-*, *-ek-*) which preceded in the same sense.]

1. *trans.* To make bloody by causing to bleed or by smearing with blood.

[*a* **1000** *Beowulf* 5378 He ȝeblodegod wearð sawul-driore. *a* **1225** *Ancr. R.* 418 Ne mid breres ne ne biblodge [*T.* blodeke] hire sulf.] **1530** PALSGR. 458/1 This parker blodyeth his clothes. **1633** T. STAFFORD *Pac. Hib.* xxi. (1821) 421 No man did bloody his sword more than his Lordship did that day. **1814** CARY *Dante* (Chandos) 122 There came I, Pierc'd in the heart..And bloodying the plain. **1820** SOUTHEY in *Life & Corr.* (1849) I. 4 The sword which was drawn (not bloodied, I hope) in this unlucky quarrel.

b. *trans.* and *fig.* To make blood-red; to stain with bloodshed.

1647 W. BROWNE *Polex.* I. 197 His shield was black in many places, and the rest bloodied with the long tresse of a Comet. **1655** J. JENNINGS *Elise* 12 Nor the only instrument of these tragick businesses, the which bloodies the course of this History.

†**2.** To exasperate; = BLOOD *v.* 4. *Obs.*

1633 T. ADAMS *Exp. 2 Peter* i. 14 Saul, being so bloodied against David..became as unmerciful to himself.

bloody-bones ('blʌdɪˌbəʊnz). Formerly **-bone**. A phrase used, generally in conjunction with *Rawhead*, as the name of a bug-bear to terrify children; also *fig.* 'bug-bear, terror.' (Possibly associated with the apparition of a murdered man supposed to haunt the scene of his murder.)

c **1550** *Wyll of Deuyll* (Collier) 13 Our faythfull Secretaryes, Hobgoblyn and Blooddybone. **1598** FLORIO, *Mani*..imagined spirits that nurces fraie their babes withall to make them leaue crying, as we say bug-beare, or els rawe head and bloodie bone. **1622** FLETCHER *Prophetess* IV. v, But now I look Like Bloody-Bone and Raw-head, to frighten children. *a* **1680** BUTLER *Rem.* (1759) I. 77 To terrify those mighty Champions, As we do children now with Bloody-bones. **1817** T. JEFFERSON *Corr.* (1830) 301 Hancock and the Adamses were the raw-head and bloody bones of Tories and traitors. **1830** T. HAMILTON *C. Thornton* (1845) 393 As if he had come back from the wars a mere raw-head and bloody-bones.

ˌbloody-ˈminded, *a.* [BLOODY *a.* C. 1.]

1. Inclined to bloodshed; bloodthirsty, cruel.

1584 R. GREENE *Gwydonius* f. 57ᵛ, I will neither bee so bloudie minded as to breede thy bane. **1593** SHAKS. *2 Hen. VI*, IV. i. 36 Yet let not this make thee be bloody-minded. **1647** BEAUMONT & FLETCHER *Lawes of Candy* v. 67/2 She is bloudy minded, And turnes the justice of the Law to rigor. **1739** HUME *Hum. Nat.* II. ii. §iii, He is bloody-minded, and takes a pleasure in death and destruction. **1845** DARWIN *Voy. Nat.* vii. (1873) 140 When the old bloody-minded tyrant is gone to his long account. **1920** R. MACAULAY *Potterism* II. i. 58 To make out that all our combatants were full of sweet reasonableness..and all our non-combatants bloody-minded savages.

2. Perverse, tiresome, cantankerous; stubbornly intransigent or obstructive.

1935 J. AGATE in *Sunday Times* 17 Mar. 6/2 A man says to a presumed lady, 'What a bloody-minded woman you are!' **1944** 'N. SHUTE' *Pastoral* vii. 148 They'll lose this fishing, and they'll all get bloody-minded about that. **1959** *Spectator* 1 May 604/1 The building unions..have never been as bloody-minded about demarcation as the shipbuilders and others.

ˌbloody-ˈmindedness. [f. prec. + -NESS.]

1. Inclination to bloodshed; bloodthirstiness, cruelty.

1789 G. VASSA *Life* I. v. 218 By the 329th Act, page 125, of the Assembly of Barbadoes, it is enacted 'That..if any man shall out of wantonness, or only of bloody-mindedness ..wilfully kill a negro..he shall pay into the public treasury fifteen pounds sterling'. **1822** CARLYLE *Let.* July (1886) II. 108 The persecution of the Albigenses has little to distinguish it from other persecutions..except a darker tinge of bloody-mindedness. **1870** LOWELL *Study Wind.* 214 What a difference between the straight-forward bloody-mindedness of Orestes and the metaphysical punctiliousness of the Dane.

2. Perversity, contrariness, cantankerousness.

1910 *Daily Chron.* 15 Mar. 6/7 Sparrows..do not eat the flowerets of the larch, but merely peck them off out of sheer devilry and 'bloodymindedness'. **1953** R. LEHMANN *Echoing Grove* 69 They all agreed, too monstrous, your bloody-mindedness, insufferable rudeness to me. **1959** *Spectator* 19 June 875/1 We can only hope that the intransigence so far shown by both sides [in the printing dispute] will not develop into bloody-mindedness, as such disputes sometimes do.

blooey ('blu:ɪ), *a.* *U.S. slang.* Also **blooie**. [Etym. unknown.] Awry, amiss; usu. in *to go blooey*. Also as *int.*

1920 G. ADE *Hand-made Fables* iii. 30 The Orders stopped coming. Collections went blooey. **1926** WHITEMAN & MCBRIDE *Jazz* ii. 32, I spilled the salt. It rained. At rehearsal my fiddle went blooey. **1928** [see G. III. f]. **1929** *Collier's* 5 Jan. 40/4 But in 1920 I weakened. As a result, my bank roll went blooie. **1948** J. BLISH in D. Knight *Dark Side* (1966) 40 One minute I was..all set to shoot him and get my wife out of there; and then blooey! **1961** J. UPDIKE *Rabbit, Run* 142 A clear image suddenly in the water wavering like a blooey television set.

bloom (blu:m), *sb.*[1] Forms: 3-4 blom, 3-6 blome, 4-6 *Sc.* blwme, 6 bloume, *Sc.* blume, 6-7 bloome, 7- bloom. [ME. *blom*, *blome*, only northern (or north. midl.); a. ON. *blóm* neut. 'a flower, bloom, blossom', and *blómi* masc. 'bloom, prosperity', *pl.* 'flowers, blossoms', the latter = OS. *blômo* masc. (MDu. *bloeme*, Du. *bloem* fem.), OHG. *bluomo* masc., *bluoma* fem. (MHG. *bluome* masc. and fem., mod.G. *blume* fem.), Goth. *blôma* m.:—OTeut. **blômon-* m., from the vb. stem **blō̆-* 'blow', with the suffix *-mon-* of nouns of action. The OE. *blôma* (masc.), in form the same word, had only the sense of BLOOM *sb.*[2], the sense 'flower' being expressed by *blóstm*, *blóstma*, *blósma*, BLOSSOM.]

1. a. The blossom or flower of a plant. (Not extended like 'flower' to a whole 'flowering plant', and expressing a more delicate notion than 'blossom', which is more commonly florescence bearing promise of fruit, while 'bloom' is florescence thought of as the culminating beauty of the plant. Cherry trees are said to be in *blossom*, hyacinths in *bloom*.)

c **1200** ORMIN 10773 Nazaræþ bitacneþþ uss Onn Ennglissh brodd and blome. *c* **1325** *E.E. Allit. P.* B. 1467 Alle þe blomes of þe boȝes were blyknande perles. **1375** BARBOUR *Bruce* v. 10 The treis begouth to ma Burg-conys and brycht blwmys alsua. *c* **1440** *Promp. Parv.* 40 Blome flowre, *flos*. **1526** *Pilgr. Perf.* (W. de W. 1531) 296 The fruytes of the holy goost..be more lyke..to be called blomes and floures than fruytes. **1570** *Sempill Ballates* (1872) 77 Thou grene Roismary hyde thy heid, Schaw not thy fair blew blumis. **1667** MILTON *P.L.* v. 25 How the Bee Sits on the Bloom extracting liquid sweet. **1697** DRYDEN *Virg. Georg.* I. 273 If od'rous Blooms the bearing Branches load. **1770** GOLDSM. *Des. Vill.* 4 Parting summer's ling'ring blooms. **1882** *Bazaar* 15 Feb. 173 To preserve cut blooms for some length of time.

†**b.** (fig.) *to bear the bloom*: to flourish. *Obs.*

1330 R. BRUNNE *Chron.* 322 Þei were born in Rome alle þe Columpneis, þat kynde bare þe blome, riche men & curteis.

c. *collect.* Blossom, flowers, florescence.

a **1300** *Cursor M.* 9328 Þe wand bar lef and frut and blom. *a* **1400** *Sir Isumb.* 176 Playe the with the blome. **1667** MILTON *P.L.* III. 43 Not to me returns Day, or the sweet approach of Ev'n or Morn, Or sight of vernal bloom. **1821** SHELLEY *Prometh. Unb.* I. 840 The yellow bees in the ivy-bloom. **1878** GILDER *Poet & Master* 14 Not yet the orchard lifted Its cloudy bloom to the sky.

d. *in bloom*: in flower, flowering, blossoming.

1644 FARY *God's Severity* (1645) 8 Blossomes that be all in a bloome, as we say. **1735** OLDYS *Life Ralegh* Wks. 1829 I. 383 Like some flowers which are sweeter in their fall than others in their bloom. **1820** W. IRVING *Sketch Bk.* I. 182 It was the month of May, when every thing was in bloom. **1864** TENNYSON *Islet* 32 For the bud ever breaks into bloom on the tree.

e. *transf.* of persons. Cf. 'flower'.

a **1300** *Havelok* 63 He was Engelondes blome. *c* **1460** *Towneley Myst.* 81 Welcom, Mary, blyssed blome. *c* **1750** SHENSTONE *Elegies* iv. 32 The frailty of so fair a bloom. **1871** R. ELLIS *Catullus* lxiv. 4 A chosen array, rare bloom of valorous Argos.

2. *fig.* State of greatest beauty or loveliness, most flourishing condition or season, prime, perfection.

c **1325** *E.E. Allit. P.* A. 577 More haf I of ioye & blysse here-inne, Of ladyschyp gret & lyuez blom. **1599** SHAKS. *Much Ado* v. i. 76 Despight..His Maie of youth, and bloome of lustihood. **1711** ADDISON *Spect.* No. 164 ¶3 While her Beauty was yet in all its Height and Bloom. **1742** POPE *Dunciad* IV. 513 Poor W., nipp'd in folly's broadest bloom, Who praises now? **1850** LEITCH tr. *Müller's Anc. Art* §159 The real bloom of this art was past when the Romans conquered the East. **1875** HAMERTON *Intell. Life* VI. i. (1876) 195 The bloom of perfect manhood.

3. a. The crimson tint of the cheek; flush, glow. Also *fig.*

1752 FIELDING *Amelia* Wks. 1775 X. 136 Miss Bath had not only recovered her health but her bloom. **1793** T. BEDDOES *Consumption* 117 That vermilion bloom, which..is the harbinger or attendant of an incurable disease. **1847** TENNYSON *Princ.* IV. 364 Over brow And cheek and bosom brake the wrathful bloom. **1879** FARRAR *St. Paul* (1883) 332 Those simple, faithful natures which combine the glow of courage with the bloom of modesty.

b. *gen.* Suffusion of glowing colour over a surface.

1832 L. HUNT *Sir R. Esher* (1850) 142 The colours of the awnings over head struck down a bloom over the whole scene.

4. a. The delicate powdery deposit on fruits like the grape, plum, etc., when fresh-gathered, and on certain plant-leaves. (So called perh. from prec.)

Cf. *Song.* Meet me in the evening When the bloom is on the rye.

a **1639** [see BLOOMY *a.*[1] 3.] **1678** [see *bloom-coloured* in 7]. **1755** JOHNSON, *Bloom*, the blue colour upon plums and grapes newly gathered. **1860** DELAMER *Kitch. Gard.* (1861) 156 Tying grapes in muslin bags assists their ripening..The pity is, that the taking them off spoils the bloom. **1882** VINES *Sachs' Bot.* 99 Very frequently the wax extends..over the cuticle..constituting the so-called 'bloom' on fruits and some leaves. **1883** P. FITZGERALD *Recreat. Lit. Man* 170 And before the end of those weary hours the bloom is off the rye —he is stale and stupid.

b. *fig.* Freshness, delicate charm or beauty. *to take the bloom off* (a thing): to deprive it of its first freshness or beauty.

1777 JOHNSON in *Boswell* (1831) I. 159 It [the Plan of Dictionary] would have come out with more bloom if it had not been seen before by any body. **1859** HELPS *Friends in C.* Ser. II. I. 182 The bloom of his regard would be rubbed off.

c. In various spec. senses, e.g. The yellowish deposit on well-tanned leather, the powdery appearance on newly-struck coins, the fluorescence exhibited by petroleum, etc. Also, the cloudy appearance on a varnished surface. Cf. BLOOMING *vbl. sb.*[1] 2.

1842 *Penny Cycl.* XXIV. 38/2 This bloom [on leather] consists of the finer portion of the gelatin from the interior of the skin. **1882** *Pharmaceut. Jrnl.* 343 Petroleum having a bloom or fluorescence. **1884** *Times* 1 Mar., The 'bloom' on the wall..around the actual spot of the explosion, was sufficient to show that the material used was not gunpowder. **1885** *Eng. Mech.* 20 Feb. 532 Until the bud is covered with 'bloom', or the so-called ellagic acid. **1885** *Cornh. Mag.* Mar. 281 That coating of indigo and gypsum which imparts [to tea leaves] the bloom so highly prized in the European market. **1886** in OGILVIE *Imperial Dict.* **1953** *Gloss. Paint Terms* (*B.S.I.*) 6 *Bloom*, a thin film which sometimes forms on glossy paint or varnish films, thereby dimming their lustre or veiling their depth of colour.

d. (See quots.)

1908 *Animal Managem.* 134 In no case should..the work [be] so hard, that the colt's 'bloom', *i.e.*, his round and glossy sleekness, disappears. **1952** C. L. B. HUBBARD *Pembrokeshire Corgi Handbook* 108 *Bloom*, glossiness or good sheen of coat.

e. = WATER-BLOOM.

1939 B. M. GRIFFITHS in *Proc. Linn. Soc.* CLI. 13 In 1838 Drummond gave a description of the greenish bloom on Glaslough, Co. Monaghan. **1948** *Hydrobiologia* I. 1 About 65 species [of algae] are known to cause 'blooms' in lakes. **1957** *Penguin New Biol.* XXIII. 87 At least two early chroniclers have recorded that the occurrence of a red bloom ..forewarned of the untimely death of William Rufus. **1969** *Daily Colonist* (Victoria, B.C.) 16 May 32/1 Dr. Parsons said that although the deep Pacific was uneconomical, similar plankton blooms had been found at the juncture of the Fraser River and the sea.

5. A fine variety of raisin.

1841 *Penny Cycl.* XIX. 274/1 Different kinds of raisins are distinguished..as muscatels, blooms, sultanas. **1875** URE *Dict. Arts* III. 692 These are muscatels or blooms.

6. Used attributively to denote a certain appearance or state assumed by sugar in the process of clarifying and refining.

1825 S. & S. ADAMS *Compl. Servant* 113 It may then be boiled to any degree you please, as smooth, bloom, feathered, crackled, and caramel.

7. The perfume exhaled from wine, bouquet.

1888 *Encycl. Brit.* XXIV. 602/2 The smell common to all wines (which remains in an empty wine cask after the bloom proper has gone).

8. *Comb.* and *Attrib.*, as *bloom-colour*, *-flinder*, *-hour*, *-stem*; *bloom-bright*, *-coloured*, etc., adjs. Also **bloom-fell**, a plant; according to Britten and Holland, *Lotus corniculatus*.

1833 TENNYSON *Hesperides*, A slope That ran *bloom-bright into the Atlantic blue. **1797-1804** BEWICK *Brit. Birds* I. 112 The breast, belly and sides are of a fine pale rose or *bloom colour. **1678** *Lond. Gaz.* No. 1273/4 The Hood lined with *bloom-coloured Silk. **1799-1824** *Prize Ess. in Highl. Soc. Trans.* III. 524 (JAM.) Ling, deer-hair, and *bloom-fell, are also scarce. **1840** BROWNING *Sordello* III. 345 Her ivory limbs are smothered by a fall, *Bloom-flinders, and fruit-sparkles, and leaf-dust. **1850** LYNCH *Theo. Trin.* xi. 208 The maiden..in the *bloom-hour of her life.

bloom (blu:m), *sb.*[2] [:—OE. *blóma* in same sense; identical in form with the word for 'flower' in the other Teut. langs. (OS. *blômo*, etc.: see BLOOM *sb.*[1]), but the history of the sense is not ascertained. No examples of the word have been found between OE. times and the end of 16th c.]

1. 'A mass of iron after having undergone the first hammering.' Weale. *spec.* An ingot of iron or steel, or a pile of puddled bars, which has been brought, by passing through one set of 'rolls', into the form of a thick bar, and left for further rolling when required for use.

a **1000** In Wr.-Wülcker *Voc.* 141/36 *Massa*, dað, *uel* bloma. **1584** [cf. BLOOMERY]. **1674** RAY *Iron Work* 127 At the Finery by the working of the hammer they bring it into Blooms and Anconies. **1679** PLOT *Staffordsh.* (1686) 163 They work it into a bloom, which is a square barr in the middle, and two square knobs at the ends, one much less then the other, the smaller being call'd the Ancony end, and the greater the Mocket head. **1719** *Glossogr. Nova*, *Bloom*, in the Iron-Works, is a four-square Mass of Iron about two

Foot long. **1845** *New Statist. Acc. Scotl.* VI. 79 An extensive forge for the manufacture of blooms was erected. **1862** *Times* 12 Aug., Lord Dudley presents numerous specimens of fractured blooms and bars. **1881** *Academy* 6 Nov. 350 It may possibly be a 'bloom' from a prehistoric foundry. **1882** *Engineer* 24 Feb. 133/1 The blooms from the hammer are then heated and rolled down to make puddled bar.

¶**2.** Sometimes improperly applied to the 'ball' or mass of iron from the puddling furnace which is to be hammered or shingled into a bloom.

1865 *Derby Merc.* 15 Feb., An immense bloom of iron, looking like a huge egg, and weighing 5 cwt., showing the state of the iron as delivered by the furnace. **1875** URE *Dict. Arts* II. 1013 The bloom or rough ball from the puddle-furnace. **1879** *Cassell's Techn. Educ.* I. 410 After pig-iron has been puddled, the 'blooms', as the masses of iron are termed, while still white-hot from the puddling furnace, are dragged to the helve.

3. *Comb.*, as ***bloom-shearing***; **bloom-hook**, an implement used for handling heated blooms; so **bloom-tongs**; **bloom-smithy**, a forge or smithy where blooms are made.

1601 HOLLAND *Pliny* I. 459 This kind of charcole serueth only the Bloom-smithies and furnaces. **1831** J. HOLLAND *Manuf. Metals* I. 18 At the suppression of the bloomaries (or iron smithies) the tenants charged themselves with the payment of this rent, which is called Bloom Smithy, or Wood rent. **1884** *Imp. & Mach. Rev.* 1 Dec. 6719/2 A large bloom-shearing machine, capable of cutting steel blooms.

†**bloom**, *sb.*^{3} *Obs. rare*$^{-1}$. [App. connected with BLOW *v.*^{1}; cf. BLOOMY *a.*^{2}] A hot wind.

1699 DAMPIER *Voy.* I. 529 I have always observed the Sea-winds to be warmer than Land-winds; unless it be when a bloom, as we call it, or hot blast blow from thence.

bloom (bluːm), *v.*^{1} Forms: 3–5 **blome(n**, (4 *Sc.* **bleume**), 5 **blomyn, blume**, 5–6 **blome, bloume**, 6 **bloome**, (7 **blowm**, 8 *Sc.* **blume**), 7– **bloom**. [ME. *blomen*, f. BLOOM *sb.*^{1}]

1. *intr.* To bear flowers; to be in flower, come into flower; to blossom.

c **1250** *Gen. & Ex.* 2061 Orest it blomede, and siðen bar ðe beries ripe. *a* **1300** *Cursor M.* 10743 þat his wand suld blome. **1398** TREVISA *Barth. De P.R.* XVII. lxiv. (1495) 641 In Thessalia feildes that beenes growe in ben eerid whan the beenys bloume. *c* **1440** *Promp. Parv.* 40 Blomyn, *floreo, floescor.* **1523** FITZHERB. *Husb.* §24 Hasell..begynneth to blome as soon as the lefe is fallen. **1667** MILTON *P.L.* III. 355 A Flour which once In Paradise, fast by the Tree of Life Began to bloom. **1727** BRADLEY *Fam. Dict.* s.v. *Coriander*, This Plant..blooms in July and August. **1821** SHELLEY *Prometh. Unb.* I. 170 Blue thistles bloomed in cities.

2. *fig.* and *transf.* To come into full beauty; to be in fresh beauty and vigour; to flourish.

c **1200** ORMIN 3636 Godess þeowwess blomenn ȝȝ Inn alle gode þæwess. *c* **1425** *Festivals Ch.* 245 in *Leg. Rood* 218 A childe þat choisly chees In maydenes blode to blome. **1513** DOUGLAS *Æneis* XI. xii. 103 Forgane the speris so bustuus blomyt he. **1590** GREENE *Fr. Bacon* (1830) 42 For fancie bloomes not at the first assault. **1738** GLOVER *Leonidas* I. 224 With all my honours blooming round my head. **1759** JOHNSON *Rasselas* xxviii. (1787) 81 The daughter begins to bloom before the mother can be content to fade. **1831** CARLYLE *Sart. Res.* II. vi, Life bloomed up with happiness and hope. **1875** JOWETT *Plato* (ed. 2) II. 486 Your beauty is fading away, just as your true self is beginning to bloom. **1878** H. H. GIBBS *Ombre* 2 Quadrille also has faded away, or blooms only in some old-fashioned nooks of England.

3. *trans.* To bring into bloom; to cause to flourish. Chiefly *fig. Obs.* or *arch.*

1592 GREENE *Poems* 108 Each fair thing that summer bloomed. **1597** HOOKER *Eccl. Pol.* v. iii. §4 Rites & customs ..in their first original beginnings when the strength of virtuous, devout, or charitable affection bloomed them. **1611** BIBLE *Numb.* xvii. 8 The rod of Aaron..brought forth buds, and bloomed blossomes. **1667** MILTON *P.L.* IV. 219 The Tree of Life..blooming Ambrosial Fruit Of vegetable Gold. **1742** YOUNG *Nt. Th.* IX. 385 Tenderness divine.. That planted Eden, and high bloom'd for man A fairer Eden.

4. *intr.* To glow with warm colour.

1860 TYNDALL *Glac.* I. §11. 75 Heaps of snow..as the day advanced, bloomed with a rosy light. **1884** *Christm. Graphic* 4/2 A little salon, in which a circular iron stove bloomed red-hot all round.

5. *trans.* To give a bloom to; to colour with a soft warm tint or glow.

a **1821** KEATS *Autumn* 25 While barred clouds bloom the soft-dying day. **1844** TUPPER *Prov. Philos.* (1852) 179 The eye is bright with trust, the cheek bloomed over with affection.

6. *techn.* To cloud a varnished surface. (See quot., and cf. BLOOMING *vbl. sb.*^{1} 2.)

1859 GULLICK & TIMBS *Paint.* 214 Whatever varnish may be employed..a current of cold or damp air, which 'chills' or 'blooms' them [paintings] should be avoided.

bloom, *v.*^{2} [f. BLOOM *sb.*^{2}] To hammer or squeeze the ball or lump of iron from the puddle-furnace into a 'bloom'; to shingle.

1875 URE *Dict. Arts* II. 1012 To prepare the puddle balls for the rolling mills, they have to undergo the process of 'shingling' or 'blooming;' this is effected either by the hammer or by the squeezer: the latter has almost entirely superseded the former.

bloomage ('bluːmɪdʒ). [f. BLOOM *sb.*^{1} + -AGE I; cf. *leafage*.] Blooms or blossoms in the mass.

c **1872** J. ADDIS *Elizab. Echoes* (1879) 66 Rushing through lavish bloomage of the brake.

bloomary, variant of BLOOMERY^{1}.

bloomed (bluːmd, *poet.* -ɪd), (*ppl.*) *a.* [f. BLOOM *sb.* and *v.* + -ED.] **1.** Covered with, bearing, or having bloom; in bloom. Also *fig.*

c **1505** DUNBAR *Gold. Targe* 55 Hard on burd vnto the blomyt medis..Arrivit sche. **1523** FITZHERB. *Surv.* xxxvi. (1539) 54 Whan it is full bloomed. **1646** CRASHAW *Steps to Temp.* 29 A mouth, whose full-bloom'd lips..are roses. **1830** TENNYSON *Recoll. Arab. Nts.* ii, Rustling thro' The low and bloomed foliage.

2. Of a photographic lens: covered with a 'bloom'; see BLOOMING *vbl. sb.*^{1} 4.

1945 A. COX *Optics* (ed. 4) 224 This latter [*sc.* straining] gives not a bloomed effect to the surface of the lens but a *frosted* effect. **1957** AMOS & BIRKINSHAW *Television Engin.* I. ix. 190 One way of reducing the reflection at lens surfaces is by coating them with a very thin film of silica or evaporated fluorite... Lenses treated in this way are termed *coated* or *bloomed* and have a characteristic blue appearance.

bloomer^{1} ('bluːmə(r)). [f. BLOOM *v.*^{1} + -ER^{1}.]

1. a. A plant that blooms (in some way).

1730–6 BAILEY *Bloomers*, blooming buds. **1882** *Garden* 7 Jan. 8/2 Those that have a tendency to be shy bloomers are placed in the lightest part of the house. **1885** *Harper's Mag.* Apr. 710/2 A New England white rose, a perennial bloomer.

b. [Perh. a different word.] A large white crusty loaf resembling the Vienna roll, with a rounded diagonally slashed top, and baked on the oven bottom. Also *attrib.*, as ***bloomer loaf***.

1937 W. T. BANFIELD in *Brit. Baker* 12 Mar. 20/1 This bloomer loaf is also the easiest loaf to cut into slices... The loaf is glazed by setting the dough into a suitably humid oven... A genuine bloomer is enriched with milk, sugar, lard or butter. **1958** *Times* 21 Nov. 7/2 Rye loaves, wheatmeal loaves, baton-shaped loaves called 'Bloomers', Scottish baps, all had a place. **1969** M. WIGGIN *Cottage Idyll* iv. 114, I bought my bread, saying clearly and distinctly, 'Two small bloomer loaves, please.'

2. [for *blooming letter*: see BLOOMING *ppl. a.* 6.] A floriated initial letter of the alphabet.

1899 MACKAIL *W. Morris* II. 256 The large floriated initials, or 'bloomers', in the slang of the press. **1901** *Sunday Times* 21 Apr., This book will be in the new type, with a fresh set of 'bloomers' specially designed for it.

3. *slang.* [See quot. 1889.] A very great mistake: chiefly in phr. ***to make a bloomer***.

1889 BARRÈRE & LELAND *Dict. Slang*, *Bloomer* (Australian), prison slang for a mistake. Abbreviated from the expression 'a blooming error'. **1902** *Westm. Gaz.* 25 Nov. 8/1 The defendant replied, 'You have made a bloomer, old chap; you never made a greater mistake in your life.' **1928** *Daily Express* 19 Apr. 15 His mount, Clearmount, made a terrible bloomer at the last fence. **1959** *Economist* 6 June 920/1 'The Times'..has this week made a bloomer about a minister.

4. *Comb.* **bloomer-pit**, a tan-pit or large vat in which hides are treated with a strong infusion of tanning liquor or ooze; a 'layer.'

'**bloomer**^{2}. [After Mrs. Bloomer, an American lady who introduced the costume; in earlier and historical uses often with capital initial.]

1. a. (More fully ***Bloomer costume, dress***): A style of female attire consisting of a short skirt and long loose trousers gathered closely round the ankles. So attrib. ***Bloomer principles, movement***.

1851 *Boston Transcript* 27 May 2/3 (Th.), The *Bee* says the daughter of Dr. Hanson, of this city, appeared in the Bloomer suit..last week. **1851** *Ibid.* 29 May 2/4 (Th.), The first 'Bloomer' made its appearance in our city yesterday. *Ibid.*, Quite a large number of young ladies in that city have made arrangements to attend church tomorrow in the Bloomer costume. **1853** 'OLD ETONIAN' *Alphabet Annotated* 61 Until they all the Bloomer dress assume. **1855** *Kansas Tribune* (Th.), Perhaps Lawrence [Kansas] is the only city in America where the majority of the ladies wear Bloomers. **1868** READE *True Love* II. iv. 154 At sight of Miss Courtenay in a Bloomer he was ravished. **1875** MISS BIRD *Sandw. Isl.* (1880) 85 Deborah looked very piquante in a bloomer dress of dark blue.

b. Regularly in *pl.* Loose trousers reaching to the knee or knickerbockers worn by women for bicycling, gymnasium practice, etc.; called also 'rational dress'. Also, a woman's knee-length undergarment (the usual sense in later usage).

In quots. 1862, 1863, man's attire.

1862 DICKENS *Somebody's Luggage* in *All Year Round* (Christmas) 9/1 A corporal of his country's army, in..the line of his waist, the broadest line of his Bloomer trousers, and their narrowest line at the calf of his leg. **1863** *Miss Jemima's Swiss Jrnl.* (1963) i. 7 Soldiers in many uniforms, some of them most laughable, their capacious bloomer costume reaching to the centre of the calf of the leg. **1895** *Westm. Gaz.* 25 July 8/1 Female teachers who have been riding bicycles in male attire, commonly called bloomers. **1906** GALSWORTHY *Man of Property* III. i. 289 She could tell you..what they were doing in Paris about wearing bloomers. **1909** *Daily Chron.* 5 Aug. 7/3 [The hockey girl] in her short skirts, bloomers, flannel blouse, and cloth cap. **1967** *Observer* 30 Apr. 29/3 The tireless search for something else has paused for a moment to put matching bloomers or shorts under the skirt.

2. A woman who wears bloomer costume.

1851 *Punch* 30 Aug. 103/2 If women assume the dress of men, let them undertake men's duties; hence, every Bloomer shall be liable to be drawn for the militia, without benefit of substitute. **1853** R. S. SURTEES *Mr. Sponge's Sporting Tour* xliii. 238 (*heading*) A Literary Bloomer. *Ibid.* 239 Lucy,—a young lady of a certain age—say liberal thirty —an ardent Bloomer. **1868** READE *True Love* II. ii. 153 She then burst out crying, which was an unfair advantage the Bloomer took over poor Reginald.

3. A kind of hat with a broad brim worn by ladies.

1883 *Life Mrs. Prentiss* vi. 177 A small shawl and my bloomer on.

Hence '**bloomered** *a.*, wearing bloomer costume; '**bloomerism**, the principles of Mrs. Bloomer as to female costume; '**bloomerize** *v. trans.*, to dress in bloomers; also *fig.*

1851 (*title*) 'Bloomerism', or The New Female Costume of 1851. **1857** C. READE *Course True Love* II. ii. 134 She was pretty far gone in bloomerism. **1882** LADY HARBERTON *Dress Reform* in *Macm. Mag.* XLV. 456 'Bloomerism' still lurks in many a memory. **1885** MRS. LYNN LINTON *Chr. Kirkland* III. i. 18 Doubtful whether they were girls Bloomerized or boys in feminine tunics. **1895** *Advance* (Chicago) 6 June 1287 The 'new woman',..though not necessarily of the bloomered type, is marching..to victory in Wisconsin. **1897** *Daily News* 3 Feb. 6/4 The New Woman..has fairly bloomerised journalism in the United States. **1900** *Daily News* 4 Dec. 6/5 In these days of Lady Wranglers and bloomered 'sportswomen'. **1907** *Westm. Gaz.* 2 Oct. 1/3 The outer lines were marked by companies of..bloomered Tirailleurs. **1960** *Times* 27 Sept. 13/6 A bloomered girl in the foreground.

bloomery^{1}, **-ary** ('bluːmərɪ). Forms: 6–7 **blomarie**, 7–8 **blomary**, 7– **bloomery, -ary**. [f. BLOOM *sb.*^{2} + -ERY, -ARY.] The first forge in an iron-works through which the metal passes after having been melted from the ore, and in which it is made into blooms.

1584–5 *Act 27 Eliz.* xix, Any maner of Yron Milles, Furnaces, Hammer, Finarie, Forge or Blomarie. **1672** PETTY *Pol. Anat.* 374 There are in Ireland..above twenty forges and bloomeries. **1693** LISTER in *Phil. Trans.* XVII. 866 Those Bars which are wrought out of a Loop, taken up out of the Finnery Harth, or second Forge, are much better Iron than those which are made in the Bloomary or first Harth. **1762** ELIOT *ibid.* LIII. 56 It is wrought or smelted in a common bloomary. **1851** TURNER *Dom. Archit.* II. Introd. 30 The bloomeries of Furness..were in full operation in the thirteenth century. **1866** JEVONS *Coal Quest.* (ed. 2) 217 When the charcoal bloomary and forge gave place to the coke blast furnace.

bloomery^{2}. *nonce-wd.* [f. BLOOM *sb.*^{1} + -ERY.] A collection or place full of blooms.

1832 J. WILSON in *Blackw. Mag.* XXXI. 864 Leading you sometimes into a greenery of glade, and sometimes into a bloomery of sweet-briars.

Bloomfieldian (ˌbluːm'fiːldɪən), *sb.* and *a.* [f. the name of Leonard *Bloomfield* (1887–1949), American linguist + -IAN.] **A.** *sb.* An adherent of the linguistic theories of Bloomfield. **B.** *adj.* Of, pertaining to, or characteristic of Bloomfield or his theories. Cf. POST-BLOOMFIELDIAN *a.* and *sb.*

1946 G. L. TRAGER in *Studies in Philol.* XLIII. 461 Bloomfield's contributions to all kinds of linguistics have been so great that all of us linguists are basically Bloomfieldians. **1947** C. F. HOCKETT in *Language* XXIII. 275 *Blackbird*..by the Bloomfieldian test is a minimum free form. **1953** A. MARTINET in A. L. Kroeber *Anthropol. Today* 577/1 The Bloomfieldians' main concern with analysis contrasts with the constant emphasis placed by other schools on the structural nature of language. **1963** J. T. WATERMAN *Perspectives in Linguistics* 95 Some people maintain that the 'Bloomfieldians' deny the importance of meaning. **1975** *Amer. Speech 1972* XLVII. 244 There is a logic that claims the ancient Chinese philologists were gulity of 'underanalysis'—that is, settling for recurrent pieces that were too large. If the logic is correct, then exactly the same logic applies to Bloomfieldian phonemes. **1977** *Word 1972* XXVIII. 288 For a Bloomfieldian, the model must be general. **1980** *Amer. Speech 1976* LI. 255 The reader must have a thorough familiarity with a number of models of linguistic structure, including Bloomfieldian and neo-Bloomfieldian structuralism.

'**bloomful**, *a.* [f. BLOOM *sb.*^{1}] Rich in bloom.

1890 *Lippincott's Mag.* Mar. 392 Bloomful maidens. **1913** MRS. G. S. PORTER *Laddie* xv, Then she leant toward me all wavery, and shining eyed, and bloomful.

bloominess ('bluːmɪnɪs). [f. BLOOMY *a.*^{1} + -NESS.] The condition of being covered with bloom or having a bloom-like surface.

1889 'THEO GIFT' *Not for Night-time* 75 A canary-coloured gown, with a white bloominess on the edges of it. **1895** *Westm. Gaz.* 22 Apr. 3/1 In the lanes where the woodbine leaves are showing the brown bloominess on the backs of their unfolding leaves.

blooming ('bluːmɪŋ), *vbl. sb.*^{1} [f. BLOOM *v.*^{1}]

1. a. The action or state of coming into or being in bloom. Also *fig.*

1398 TREVISA *Barth. De P.R.* XVII. xcvi. (1495) 663 All codware louyth water tofore the blossom and drinesse after the blowmynge. *c* **1630** DRUMM. OF HAWTH. *Wks.* (1711) 12 A virgin in the blooming of her prime. **1684** *Scanderbeg Rediv.* i. 2 To know the first Bloomings of a Tree which has yielded such happy Fruit. **1709** POPE *Ess. Crit.* 501 Like some fair flow'r..That gayly blooms, but ev'n in blooming dies.

†**b.** *concr.* A blossom, inflorescence. *Obs.*

1622 WITHER *Mistr. Philar.* (1633) 590 Low Sallowes on whose bloomings Bees doe fall. **1657** W. COLES *Adam in Eden* lx, Small heads..which are the Bloomings or Flowers.

c. *attrib.*, as in ***blooming-time***.

1398 TREVISA *Barth. De P.R.* XVII. clxxvii. (1495) 718 Vynes haue a specyall euyll whan they ben spronge wyth euyll dewe or reyne in blowmyng tyme. **1883** C. MONKHOUSE in *Academy* No. 577. 358/3 A true, if not a complete, view of English song-writing in its blooming-time.

2. *Painting.* A cloudy appearance on a varnished surface, *esp.* of a picture. Cf. BLOOM *v.* 6.

1859 GULLICK & TIMBS *Paint.* 204 The vehicles of the oil painter subject him to innumerable perplexities by their bad drying, change of colour, cracking, and blooming. **1879** *Cassell's Techn. Educ.* IV. 222/2 Spotting, blooming, pinholing.

3. *Television.* (See quots.)

1940 D. G. FINK *Princ. Telev. Engin.* iii. 72 The brightness contrast is limited by halation and saturation of the luminescent screen and by the defocusing effect ('blooming') associated with the electron gun when large signals are impressed upon it. **1945** N. M. COOKE *Electronics Dict.* 37/2 *Blooming*, a fuzzy effect in a reproduced television picture.

4. *Photogr.* Coating with a 'bloom'; the process of coating a photographic lens with a metallic fluoride in order to reduce surface reflection.

1943 A. COX *Optics* 267 In the cases of some older lenses which had acquired a *bloom* on their surfaces with the passing of time the amount of reflection was cut down at each of these surfaces. But the blooming could not be produced regularly as a practical proposition. **1944** *Photogr. Jrnl.* LXXXIII. 225/2 It is on account of this colour that the process is often called 'blooming'. **1957** T. L. J. BENTLEY *Man. Miniat. Camera* (ed. 5) v. 59 The 'blooming' treatment gives to the surface of new lenses an even purple coating by deposition of magnesium fluoride, to a minute and finely adjusted thickness.

'blooming, *vbl. sb.*[2] [f. BLOOM *v.*[2] + -ING[1].] The reducing of cast- or pig-iron into 'blooms.' Also *attrib.*, as ***blooming mill***; **blooming machine, blooming rolls** (see quots.).

1812 SIR H. DAVY *Chem. Philos.* 392 In the process for reducing cast iron into malleable iron called blooming. **1869** *Spons' Dict. Engin.* I. 367 The blooming machine, invented by Jeremiah Brown..consists of three large eccentric rolls ..placed horizontally in the strong holsters.., the centres of the rolls being arranged in a triangular position, and the bottom roll..being nearly central between the two top rolls. **1871** *Trans. Amer. Inst. Mining Eng.* I. 203 This first reduction or blooming is usually done in this country in a 30-inch 3-high rolling mill. **1884** *Imp. & Mach. Rev.* 1 Dec. 6719/2 Adjacent to this..the roughing mill, together with a ..blooming mill. **1888** *Lockwood's Dict. Terms Mech. Engin.*, *Blooming Rolls*, see Puddling Rolls... *Puddling Rolls*, or *Forge Train*, the first set of rolls through which a shingled bloom is passed.

'blooming, *ppl. a.* [f. BLOOM *v.*[1] + -ING[2].]

1. That blooms, or is in flower.

1664 EVELYN *Kal. Hort.* (1729) 219 Old unthriving, or over-hastily blooming Trees. **1728** THOMSON *Spring* 10 When Nature all Is blooming and benevolent. **1866** GEO. ELIOT *F. Holt* 3 Pots full of blooming balsams or geraniums.

2. *fig.* **a.** In the bloom of health and beauty, in the prime of youth; flourishing.

1675 DRYDEN *Aurengz.* I. i. 77 That Character..Of Valour, which in blooming youth he gain'd. **1774** T. BLACKLOCK *Graham* II. xiv, His blooming bride. **1855** MACAULAY *Hist. Eng.* IV. 329 Again England was given over; and again the strange patient persisted in becoming stronger and more blooming.

b. Of things: Flourishing, full of fair promise.

c **1375** ? BARBOUR *St. Adrian* 232 His hart wes ful of bleumand blis. *a* **1674** CLARENDON *Hist. Reb.* III. XI. 155 Their blooming hopes. **1684** *Scanderberg Rediv.* i. 6 [He] gave in early Youth all the blooming Presages of a growing Hero.

c. Bright, shining.

1513 DOUGLAS *Æneis* XI. xv. 12 In broone sangwane weill dycht Abuf hys onkouth armour blomand brycht. **1830** CUNNINGHAM *Brit. Paint.* I. 285 Who purchased blooming works, which were destined to fade in their possession. **1847** TENNYSON *Princ.* VI. 129 Wan was her cheek With hollow watch, her blooming mantle torn.

†**d.** Of style: Florid, flowery. *Obs.*

1685 F. SPENCE *House Medici* 360 Machiavell..whose stile is so blooming and correct that it's tax'd with being too finical and tawdry.

†**3.** That produces blooms or blossoms. *rare.*

1587 TURBERV. *Trag. T.* (1837) 284 By meanes of heate mixt with the blooming raine.

¶**4.** *slang.* Full-blown; often euphemistic for BLOODY (sense 10) or the like. Cf. BLESSED (5).

1882 *Macm. Mag.* XLVI. 441 Oh, you blooming idiot! **1885** *Scotsman* 20 Aug. 5/4 You asks me no bloomin' imper'int questions, an' I tells yer no bloomin' lies.

5. ***blooming sally*** [i.e. *sallow*], a Willow-herb (*Epilobium angustifolium*, rarely *E. hirsutum*).

6. ***blooming*** (***initial***) ***letter***: a floriated initial letter of the alphabet; = BLOOMER[1] 2.

1713 JAS. WATSON in *Hist. Printing* Pref. 9 Curiously cut Head-Pieces, Finis's, Blooming-Letters [etc.]. **1785** W. HERBERT *Typogr. Antiq.* 527 The chronicle of each reign begins with a blooming letter. **1902** SAYLE *Init. Lett. Early Eng. Printed Bks.* in *Trans. Bibliogr. Soc.* VII. 18 The bloomers or blooming initials as Herbert calls them.

Hence **'bloomingly** *adv.*, **'bloomingness.**

1831 *Blackw. Mag.* XXIX. 809 As bloomingly beautiful as at the time of her marriage. **1859** G. MEREDITH *Song of Courtesy* in *Once a Wk.* 9 July I. 30 'Shall I live bloomingly?' Said she. **1847** CRAIG, *Bloomingness.*

bloomless ('bluːmlɪs), *a.* [f. BLOOM *sb.*[1] + -LESS.] Without bloom or blossom; flowerless.

1593 G. FLETCHER *Licia* (1876) 14 Like bloomelesse buds, too base to make compare. **1622** WITHER *Prayer Habak.*, Bloomlesse shall the fig-tree bee. **1860** C. PATMORE *Faithf. for Ever*, Among the bloomless aftermath.

Bloomsburian (bluːmz'bjʊərɪən, -bərɪən). [f. *Bloomsbury* (see below) + -AN.] A dweller in Bloomsbury, London; *spec.* = BLOOMSBURYITE.

1902 *Daily Chron.* 24 Nov. 4/4 The flippant playwright who made one of his characters say that 'the Bloomsburians live mainly on a dish called "smoked 'addick"'. **1927** *Weekly Dispatch* 23 Oct. 11/2 A horde of minor Bloomsburians. **1967** *Guardian* 4 Oct. 7/2 A Jacques like some last of the Bloomsburians in a faded white alpaca suit.

Bloomsbury ('bluːmzbərɪ). **1.** A set of writers, artists, and intellectuals living in or associated with Bloomsbury (see prec.) in the early 20th century; a member of this set. Also *attrib.*, associated with, or having similar intellectual pretensions to, the Bloomsbury set. So ***Bloomsbury group, set***, the above-mentioned set of writers, etc. Also ***Bloomsbury gang***, a political party that appeared in July 1765, led by the 4th Duke of Bedford, and otherwise known as 'the Bedford party'.

1910 *Encycl. Brit.* III. 619/1 Bloomsbury gang. **1914** J. M. KEYNES *Let.* 2 July in R. F. Harrod *Life* (1951) iv. 171 She..is asking no one but a few of my so-called 'Bloomsbury set'! **1920** D. H. LAWRENCE *Let.* 7 May (1962) I. 628 Nothing will happen to the world: Bloomsbury will go on enjoying itself in Paris and elsewhere. **1928** A. P. HERBERT *Trials of Topsy* 8 My dear *too* Bloomsbury for anything, and such *forests* of hair both of them. **1931** R. CAMPBELL *Georgiad* i. 12 It was a voice of 1930 model And in a Bloomsbury accent it could yodel. **1951** R. F. HARROD *Life of J. M. Keynes* v. 184 The Bloomsbury voice was a distinct contribution. It was based on Lytton Strachey's, consisting not so much in a special pronunciation of words as in the cadences of sentences. **1954** J. K. JOHNSTONE (*title*) The Bloomsbury Group.

2. A member of the Bloomsbury group. Chiefly in *pl.* and humorously respelt **Bloomsberries** (see quot. 1956).

1917 J. M. MURRY *Let.* 15 Sept. in A. Alpers *Katherine Mansfield* (1980) 253, I think these rumours that are put into motion, whether by Clive or the other Bloomsburies, too preposterous to be taken seriously. **1948** WYNDHAM LEWIS *Let.* 9 Oct. (1963) 460 It was written by Raymond Mortimer—an old Bloomsbury. **1956** C. BELL *Old Friends* viii. 129 The name [*sc.* Bloomsbury] was first applied to a set of friends by Lady MacCarthy—Mrs. Desmond MacCarthy as she then was—in a letter: she calls them 'the Bloomsberries'. The term, as she used it, had a purely topographical import; and the letter, which doubtless could be found at the bottom of one of five or six tin boxes, must have been written in 1910 or 1911. **1967** E. B. C. LUCAS in M. Holroyd *Lytton Strachey* I. ix. 409 Like all 'Bloomsberries', he [*sc.* Lytton Strachey] disliked pretension and silliness. **1981** *Sunday Times* 1 Feb. 43/1 To the Bloomsberries she boldly attributes a liberating power over her young life.

Hence **'Bloomsburyite.**

1933 *Times Lit. Suppl.* 2 Mar. 148/4 The descriptions..of young earnest and well-meaning Bloomsburyites..could not be bettered.

bloomy ('bluːmɪ), *a.*[1] [f. BLOOM *sb.* 1 + -Y[1].]

1. Full of blooms or blossoms, flowery. *poet.*

1593 DRAYTON *Eclog.* iv. Wks. (1793) 594/1 The bloomy brier. *c* **1640** MILTON *Sonn.* i, O Nightingale that on yon bloomy spray Warblest at eve. **1710** PHILIPS *Pastorals* vi. 24 The bloomy Season of the Year is nigh. **1828** STERLING *Ess. & Tales* (1848) ii. 199 Over meadow and bloomy bank.

2. *fig.* Blooming, in the beauty or flower of youth.

1651 DAVENANT *Gondibert* III. iii, Thou who..thy bloomy bride Lead'st to some temple. **1725** POPE *Odyss.* x. 331 On his bloomy face Youth smil'd celestial. **1807** CRABBE *Par. Reg.* II. 356 What if, in both, life's bloomy flush was lost.

†**b.** Of language: Flowery, florid. *Obs.*

1685 F. SPENCE *House Medici* 282 He top'd him..by strewing his discourse with bloomy, flourishing expressions.

3. Covered with bloom, as a plum; of the colour of this bloom.

a **1639** T. CAREW *Inquiry* iii, In bloomy peach, in rosy bud, There wave the streamers of her blood. **1700** DRYDEN *Flower & L.* 343 Florence satin, flowered with white and green, And for a shade betwixt the bloomy gridelin. **1844** HOOD *Haunted H.* xxii, Showers of bloomy plums. **1860** T. MARTIN *Horace* 267 Rush-bound cucumbers..with their sides of bloomy green. **1881** MRS. H. HUNT *Childr. Jerus.* 40 A soft bloomy colour, like corroded old copper.

4. *Comb.* **bloomy-down,** Sweet William (*Dianthus barbatus*), Britten and Holland.

†**'bloomy,** *a.*[2] *Obs.* [app. f. BLOOM *sb.*[3] + -Y[1].] Of the nature of a bloom (*sb.*[3]): Hot, close.

1620 VENNER *Via Recta* Introd. 5 The north winde might in the Summer passe in, to coole the bloomie aire. **1681** GLANVILL *Sadducismus* II. 99 The room was presently filled with a bloomy noisome smell, and was very hot.

b. quasi-*adv.* After the manner of a bloom.

1620 VENNER *Via Recta* (1650) 225 You must beware that the room be not bloomie hot.

bloones: see BLAENESS, BLONESS.

bloop (bluːp), *sb.* [Echoic.] **1. a.** A plopping sound; a howling sound. **b.** A blooping patch that prevents such a sound (see next).

1931 L. COWAN *Recording Sound for Motion Pictures* 360 *Bloop*, dull thud emitted in sound reproduction, due to a poorly made Blooping Patch. **1953** K. REISZ *Technique Film Editing* 278 *Bloop*, small opaque patch over a splice in a positive sound-track designed to smother any intrusive noise which the splice might otherwise produce. **1962** A. NISBETT *Technique Sound Studio* xii. 219 Sounding like a series of pips, beeps, and bloops.

2. *Baseball.* Used *attrib.* of a ball lobbed over the infield so as to come down just beyond their reach, or of a run or runs scored by hitting such a ball (as ***bloop single***, etc.). Cf. BLOOP *v.* 2 and BLOOPER 3.

1947 *San Francisco Examiner* 5 July 13/2 His swing enabled Garriott to steal second, from where he scored after bloop singles by Sauer and Barton. **1970** *Washington Post* 30 Sept. D2/4 The latter gave up a bloop two-bagger to Reichardt. **1978** *Detroit Free Press* 2 Apr. 4E/3 Babe McBride's ninth-inning bloop double to left scored two runs to give the Philadelphia Phillies a 9–8 exhibition victory over the St. Louis Cardinals Saturday. **1985** *Globe & Mail* (Toronto) 10 Oct. C2/1 The Dodgers scored one run in the fourth innings on an error, a stolen base and a bloop single by Pedro Guerrero.

bloop (bluːp), *v.* [Echoic.] **1. a.** *intr.* To make a howling noise; to operate a radio set in such a way that it emits such a noise. **b.** *trans.* To cover a splice on a sound-track with a blooping patch (see quot. 1931[2]). So **'blooping** *vbl. sb.*, the process of covering such a splice.

1926 *Radio Rev.* Jan. 23 That neighbor who constantly 'bloops' and sends out his cat-calls just at the time all ears are focussed on the umpth symphony of Rubenthoven. **1927** *People's Pop. Monthly* Mar. 281 You can make any type of receiver regenerate or 'bloop' to more or less extent. **1931** L. COWAN *Recording Sound for Motion Pictures* 360 *Bloop*, to prepare a Blooping Patch. *Ibid.*, *Blooping Patch*, triangular or oval black section introduced over a splice in the positive sound track, to prevent the noise which the splice would otherwise cause. **1934** [see BLOOPER 1]. **1936** *Words* Oct. 6/1 Blooping is dying a film splice with ink sprayed from an airgun so that the splice will run through the projectors without making unnecessary noise. **1959** W. S. SHARPS *Dict. Cinematogr.* 80/2 *Blooping ink*, the ink used to paint a sound track in blooping. **1960** O. SKILBECK *Film & TV Working Terms* 19 Dubbing Tracks printed from an Edited sound negative are often electrically blooped by the Labs. with a device which automatically brings a special fogging light up and then down at joins.

2. *Baseball.* To score (a run or runs) by hitting the ball just beyond the reach of the infield. Cf. BLOOP *sb.* 2 and BLOOPER 3.

1970 *Globe & Mail* (Toronto) 26 Sept. 39/5 Rookie Steve Brye drove in Minnesota's only run, blooping a two-out double to right centre field. **1974** *Spartanburg* (S. Carolina) *Herald* 21 Apr. B3/7 The Giants came within a run in the seventh when Dave Rader blooped a double down the left field line. **1979** *Arizona Daily Star* 5 Aug. C2/2 Stearns' eighth homer of the season..came after Willie Montanez had blooped a leadoff single to left.

blooper ('bluːpə(r)). *colloq.* [f. BLOOP *v.*] **1.** (See quots.)

1926 *Dairy Farmer* (Des Moines, Iowa) 15 May 12 It is this type of set which is commonly criticized for causing interference and when improperly operated soon becomes known as a 'blooper'. **1934** WEBSTER, *Blooper*, a radio receiving set which generates current of radio frequency, thus causing radiation from the receiving antenna. This radiation, under certain circumstances, causes near-by sets to bloop or howl.

2. A blunder or howler, esp. of a public or politically embarrassing kind; = BLOOMER[1] 3.

1947 *Partisan Rev.* XIV. 550/2 Why does Farrell write so badly? Why in his latest book such bloopers as 'art.. presents *imaginary images* of life'. **1951** in WENTWORTH & FLEXNER *Dict. Amer. Slang* (1960) 44/2 But on one subject —'security'—he may have felt he pulled a political blooper. **1956** *Amer. Speech* XXXI. 252 In radio and television broadcasting, where the spoken word is of utmost interest and importance, lapses are known as *bloopers*, *fluffs*, *slips* and *boners*. **1961** *Daily Tel.* 28 Jan. 11/5 The Administration had made a 'blooper' over the custom of allowing members of Congress to provide constituents with guided tours of the White House.

3. *Baseball.* A ball lobbed over the infield so as to come down just beyond their reach; a ball pitched high by the pitcher. Also *attrib.* Cf. BLOOP *sb.* 2 and *v.* 2 and *Texas leaguer* s.v. TEXAS 2.

1937 *N.Y. Times* 8 Oct. 29/6 A 'blooper' is a soggy fly to an unoccupied spot behind the backs of the infield. **1946** *San Francisco Examiner* 10 July 19/1 'Rip' Sewell..made the mistake of tossing one of his blooper balls to Williams with two on base. **1948** *Chicago Tribune* 27 June II. 4/8 His homer on one of Rip Sewell's famous blooper pitches was the only one ever knocked against the Pittsburgh veteran's specialty. **1967** C. POTOK *Chosen* i. 35, I went into a long, elaborate windup and sent him a slow, curving blooper, the kind a batter always hits and always misses. **1977** *Rolling Stone* 5 May 47/4 Fidrych pitches five innings, slow-pitch, blooper-balls, tossed underhand without any great effect. **1985** *Globe & Mail* (Toronto) 10 Oct. C3/4 Centre fielder Lloyd Moseby may have caught Frank White's blooper, although only Moseby knows for certain.

bloosme, obs. form of BLOSSOM *sb.*

blooth, variant of BLOWTH, bloom.

bloother, dial. variant of BLUBBER.

blore (blɔə(r)), *sb. arch.* [app. related to *blow*, *blast*; but the form does not seem capable of etymological explanation; perhaps it is partly onomatopœic (an 'expressive word,' Johnson). The last quot. is of course an echo of Chapman, who was exceedingly addicted to the word.]

A violent blowing, a blast or gust; also *fig.* stormy breath, bluster.

c **1440** *York Myst.* xxvi. 188 Byde me here bewchere Or more blore be blowen. **1559** *Mirr. Mag.* 838 Hurried headlong with the south-west blore. **1598** CHAPMAN *Iliad* IX. 5 The west wind and the north..join in a sudden blore. **1616** —— *Musæus* 306 Take heed that no ungentle blore The torch extinguish. **1755** JOHNSON, *Blore*, act of blowing; blast; an expressive word, but not used. **1872** BLACKIE *Lays Highl.* 9 A cloud came darkling From the west with gusty blore.

b. *transf.* The air. [L. *aura*.]

c **1614** CHAPMAN *Odyss.* IV. 1138 She, through the key-hole of the door, Vanish'd again into the open blore.

blore, *v.* *Obs.* exc. *dial.* [A variant or parallel form of BLARE.] *intr.* To cry, cry out, weep; of animals, to bleat, bray, bellow.

c **1440** *Promp. Parv.* 40 Bloryyn or wepyn, *ploro, fleo.* **1865** *Cornh. Mag.* July 38 [The peasant] possesses a series of imitative sounds for the cries of various animals..Cattle are said to 'blore,' and sheep 'rout.' **1877** PEACOCK *Lincoln. Gloss.*, *Blore*, to bellow as oxen do; to cry loudly: commonly used with regard to children.

blosme, blosmy, obs. forms of BLOSSOM, -Y.

blossom ('blɒsəm), *sb.* Forms: 1 **blostm, blostma,** 1–2 **blosma,** 2–4 **blostme,** 2–5 **blosme,** 3 **blossem,** *Orm.* **blosstme,** 4–5 **blossum,** 4–8 **blossome,** (5 **blosle**), 6 **blossome, blossum(m,** 7 **blosom,** 4– **blossom.** [OE. *blóstm* str. masc., *blóstma, blósma* wk. masc., cognate w. MDu. and Du. *bloesem*, MLG. *blosem, blossem*; cf. also ON. *blómst-r* masc. Generally referred to the same root as BLOOM (*blō̆-*); some consider *blos-* an extended stem = L. *flos, flor-*; others with greater probability take the *-st* as well as *-m* as a suffix.]

1. 'The flower that grows on any plant, previous to the seed or fruit. We generally call those flowers *blossoms*, which are not much regarded in themselves, but as a token of some following production.' (J.)

Blostma, blosme was the OE. word for 'flower', previous to the adoption of ON. *blóm* (BLOOM), and OF. *flor, flur* (FLOWER). See BLOOM *sb.*[1]

a. An individual flower (with *plural*).

971 *Blickl. Hom.* 7 Mid eallum missenlicum afeddum blostmum sy se Cristes brydbur ȝefrætwod. *c* **1000** *Sax. Leechd.* I. 236 Genim þysse ylcan wyrte blostman. *c* **1175** *Lamb. Hom.* 109 Iliche þan treo þe bereð lef and blosman. and nane westmas ne bereð. *a* **1225** *Ancr. R.* 276 Breres bereð, rosen, & berien, & blostmen. *c* **1385** CHAUCER *L.G.W.* 143 The braunches ful of blosmes softe. **1600** SHAKS. *A.Y.L.* II. iii. 64 Thou prun'st a rotten tree, That cannot so much as a blossome yeelde. **1667** MILTON *P.L.* IV. 148 Blossoms and Fruits at once of golden hue Appeerd. **1756** BURKE *Subl. & B.* Wks. I. 209 An orange-tree, flourishing at once with its leaves, its blossoms, and its fruit. **1822** BYRON *Heav. & Earth* I. iii. 730 Yet quivers every leaf, and drops each blossom.

b. *collectively.* The mass of flowers on a fruit-tree, etc. (Cf. BLOOM *sb.*[1] 1 c.) Hence *in blossom*. Also said of grain, grass, etc.

a **1300** *Cursor M.* 8256 Was neuer tre suilk blossem bare. *a* **1400** *Morte Arth.* 6 (Roxb.) Hyr rode was rede as blossom on brere. *c* **1440** *Promp. Parv.* 41 Blosme, or blossum, *frons.* **1769** WASHINGTON *Diaries* (1925) I. 327 The head [of the wheat] was shot out, and in many places in Blossom. **1789** MRS. PIOZZI *Journ. France* I. 120 One plum tree have I seen in blossom. **1869** *Rep. U.S. Commissioner Agric. 1868* 423 F. V. Stewart..states that his practice has been to commence cutting the grass when in the 'second blossom'. **1878** B. TAYLOR *Deukalion* III. i. 107, I go with the flying blossom, as I came with the flying seed.

c. *fig.* (by *simile*.)

1789–94 BLAKE *Songs Exp.*, *Lit. Girl Lost* 34 O the dismal care That shakes the blossoms of my hoary hair. **1842** TENNYSON *Œnone* 76 He prest the blossom of his lips to mine. **1860** TYNDALL *Glac.* I. §18. 130 Nature..showered down upon us those lovely blossoms of the frost [snow-crystals].

2. *fig.* **a.** An attribute, product, or token, compared in its character to the preceding.

c **1230** *Hali. Meid.* 11 Meidenhad is te blosme þat beo ha eanes fulliche forcoruen ne spruteð ha neauer eft. **1596** SPENSER *F.Q.* VI. Introd. iv, Amongst them all growes not a fairer flowre Then is the bloosme of comely courtesie. **1692** DRYDEN *St. Euremont's Ess.* 259 Which takes away all the Blossom of the good they do us. **1775** SHERIDAN *Duenna* I. iii. 192 The rich blossoms of my daughter's beauty. **1843** PRESCOTT *Mexico* II. i. (1864) 67 The first blossoms of that literature which was to ripen into so rich a harvest.

b. One lovely and full of promise.

c **1440** *York Myst.* xxxvi. 138 Allas! þat þis blossome so bright Vntrewly is tugged to þis tree. **1588** SHAKS. *Tit.* IV. ii. 72 Sweet blowse, you are a beautious blossome sure. **1591** —— *1 Hen. VI*, IV. vii. 16 There di'de My Icarus, my Blossome, in his pride. **1847** TENNYSON *Princ.* v. 79 My babe, my blossom, ah, my child.

c. A stage of development which answers to that of blossom. Cf. *flower, bloom.*

a **1225** *Ancr. R.* 192 Ine blostme of ower ȝuweðe. **1602** SHAKS. *Ham.* I. v. 76 Thus was I..Cut off euen in the Blossomes of my Sinne. *a* **1656** BP. HALL *Rem. Wks.* (1660) 8 Mine hopes nipt in the blossome. **1662** J. BARGRAVE *Pope Alex. VII.* (1867) In the blossom of his popedom, he did one of the worthiest actions of his life.

3. *techn.* **a.** *Mining.* 'The oxidized or decomposed outcrop of a vein or coal-bed, more frequently the latter.' (Raymond *Mining Gloss.*) Also, radiated quartz (*U.S.*). **b.** The colour of a horse whose hairs are white interspersed with sorrel or bay, peach-colour; a horse so coloured.

1819 H. R. SCHOOLCRAFT *View of Lead Mines of Missouri* 71 This variety of quartz has acquired the popular name of blossom of lead, or mineral blossom. *Ibid.* 91 In searching for ore, the soil, the slope of the hills, spar, blossom, trees, etc., are taken as guides. **1882** J. H. BEADLE *Western Wilds* (ed. 2) xxxiv. 560 We are certainly near the outcrop from which the 'blossom' was broken.

4. *Comb.* and *Attrib.*, as ***blossom-ball, -bough, -time***; ***blossom-bearing, -bordered, -bruising, -laden*** adjs.; **blossom-faced** *a.*, having a red bloated face; so **blossom-nosed**; **blossom-headed** *a.*, (of a parrot) having a rose-coloured head; **blossom-rock** *U.S.* (see sense 3 a).

1864 TENNYSON *Aylmer's F.* 87 He..Had..to pleasure Edith..Made *blossom-ball or daisy-chain. **1847** —— *Princ.* v. 353 Above the garden's glowing *blossom-belts. **1839** BAILEY *Festus* xix. (1848) 197 *Blossom-bordered, silvery paths. *a* **1845** HOOD *Depart. Summ.*, Under the hawthorn's *blossom-bough. **1784** COWPER *Task* v. 141 *Blossom-bruising hail. **1859** TENNYSON *Vivien* 131 Foot-gilt with all the *blossom-dust of those Deep meadows. **1865** DICKENS *Mut. Fr.* IV. ix. Half a dozen *blossom-faced men. **1867** JEAN INGELOW *Dreams came true* l, The *blossom-laden trees. **1871** *Colorado Gaz.* 156 The '*blossom rock' (quartz stained with metallic oxides), which indicates the proximity of mineral deposits, differs but little in gold and silver lodes. **1878** J. H. BEADLE *Western Wilds* xxx. 479 Men were let down from above to 'prospect', a crevice was found with blossom rock. **1713** *Lond. & Countr. Br.* III. (1743) 166 *Blossom-time is accounted dangerous for brewing. **1860** J. KENNEDY *Horse Shoe R.* vii. 89 Up to the blossom-time of life.

blossom ('blɒsəm), *v.* [OE. *blóstmian*, ME. *blosme(n*, f. prec. sb. Cf. Du. *bloesemen*, and BLOOM *v.*, FLOWER *v.*]

1. *intr.* To put forth blossoms, bloom, flower.

c **890** K. ÆLFRED *Bæda* v. xii, (Bosw.) Ðæs blostmiendan feldes. *c* **1386** CHAUCER *Merch. T.* 218 Though I be hoor I fare as dooth a tree That blosmeth er þat fruyt ywoxen bee. *c* **1440** *Promp. Parv.* 40 Blomyn, or blosmyn. **1527** ANDREW *Brunswyke's Distyll. Waters* A ij b, Whan it begynneth to blossome. **1604** SHAKS. *Oth.* II. iv. 383 Fruites that blossome first, will first be ripe. **1704** POPE *Spring* 42 Now hawthorns blossom, now the daisies spring. **1864** TENNYSON *En. Ard.* 587 Huge trees that branch'd And blossom'd in the zenith. **1882** VINES *Sachs' Bot.* 935 Parasites and saprophytes..which vegetate below and blossom above ground.

2. *transf.* and *fig.*

1377 LANGL. *P. Pl.* B. v. 140 Sithen þei blosmed obrode in boure to here shriftes. **1388** WYCLIF *Ps.* lxxi[i]. 16 Thei schulen blosme [**1382** floure] fro the citee, as the hey of erthe doith. **1613** SHAKS. *Hen. VIII*, III. ii. 353 This is the state of Man; to day he puts forth The tender Leaues of hopes, to morrow Blossomes, And beares his blushing Honors thicke vpon him. **1664** BUTLER *Hud.* II. i. 458 'Tis Beauty always in the Flowre That buds and blossoms at fourscore. **1847** LONGF. *Ev.* I. iii, One by one..Blossomed the lovely stars, the forget-me-nots of the angels.

b. Const. *into.*

1852 LONGF. *Gold. Leg.* I. 28 They make the dark and dreary hours Open and blossom into flowers. **1884** *Manch. Exam.* 27 Oct. 5/3 The historic craft of the barber..has blossomed into an art.

c. Const. *out.*

1894 G. DU MAURIER *Trilby* I. II. 162 He..blossomed out into beautiful and costly clothes..so that people would turn round and stare at him. **1929** J. B. PRIESTLEY *Good Compan.* II. vii. 447 Very shortly, you'll see, I shall be Blossoming Out—and then I shall expect a cable from S. Africa. **1947** AUDEN *Age of Anxiety* (1948) ii. 39 Black umbrellas blossom out.

'blossomed, *ppl. a.* [f. BLOSSOM *sb.* and *v.* + -ED.] Full or covered with blossoms; in full bloom, opened into flower.

c **1374** CHAUCER *Parl. Foules* (MS. Ff.) 183 A garden saw I full of blossummede bowes. **1503** HAWES *Examp. Virt.* iii. 32 A royall tre With buddys blossomed of grete beaute. **1593** BARNES *Elegies* in Arb. *Garner* V. 455 The blossomed Hawthorn, white as chalk. **1824** MISS MITFORD *Village* Ser. I. (1863) 79 Bright tufts of blossomed broom. **1830** TENNYSON *Circumstance* 2 Two graves..Wash'd with still rains and daisy-blossomed.

fig. **1645** QUARLES *Sol. Recant.* ii. 20 Thus fool'd with vain pursuit Of blossom'd happinesse that bears no fruit. **1862** B. TAYLOR *Poet's Jrnl.* (1866) 67 The fragrance of a blossomed heart.

blossoming ('blɒsəmɪŋ), *vbl. sb.* [f. as prec. + -ING[1].] The putting forth of blossoms, coming into flower; blooming, flowering.

c **1440** *Promp. Parv.* 41 Blosmynge, or blossummynge, *frondositas.* *a* **1821** KEATS *To Moon* 34 In the summer tide of blossoming. **1860** RUSKIN *Mod. Paint.* V. 327 Colour is..especially connected with the blossoming of the earth.

fig. **1602** FULBECKE *1st Pt. Paral.* 18, I desire greatly to knowe the originall and first blossoming of other seignories.

attrib. **1603** SHAKS. *Meas. for M.* I. iv. 41 Blossoming Time That from the seednes the bare fallow brings To teeming foyson.

'blossoming, *ppl. a.* [f. as prec. + -ING[2].] That blossoms or puts forth flowers; flowering, blooming; also *fig.*

1430 LYDG. *Chron. Troy* I viii, When euery bushe is freshe and blosomynge. **1579** SPENSER *Sheph. Cal.* May 8 Bushes with bloosming Buds. **1606** SHAKS. *Ant. & Cl.* IV. xii. 23 [They] melt their sweets On blossoming Cæsar. **1828** SCOTT *F.M. Perth* III. 109 Confidence in the blossoming virtues of his successor.

blossomless ('blɒsəmlɪs), *a.* [f. BLOSSOM *sb.* + -LESS.] Without blossoms.

1837 *New Month. Mag.* LI. 115 Budless, and blossomless. **1845** T. COOPER *Purgat. Suicides* (1877) 16 Weeds huge and dank, And blossomless as stones.

blossomry ('blɒsəmrɪ). [f. BLOSSOM *sb.* + -RY.] Blossoms collectively.

1901 ABP. OF ARMAGH in *Westm. Gaz.* 3 Jan. 8/2 Such souls predestined have not one high range, One climate's blossomry alone.

blossomy ('blɒsəmɪ), *a.* Also *poet.* **blosmy.** [f. BLOSSOM *sb.* + -Y[1].] Covered or adorned with blossoms; flowery.

c **1374** CHAUCER *Troylus* II. 772 With blosmy bowis grene. *c* **1386** —— *Merch. T.* 219 And blosmy tree nys neither drye ne deed. **1798** COLERIDGE *Nightingale* 79 On blosmy twig still swinging from the breeze. **1824** MISS MITFORD *Village* Ser. I. (1863) 31 That bit of grassy and blossomy earth..is very dear to me. **1831** ALFORD in *Life* (1873) 68 The blos'my groves of paradise.

fig. **1858** CARLYLE *Fredk. Gt.* II. x. i. 570 Leafy, blossomy Forest of Literature. **1877** BLACKIE *Wise Men Gr.* 93 What he knew he sung With blossomy phrase.

blot (blɒt), *sb.*[1] Also 4–6 **blotte,** 5–7 **blott,** 6 **blote.** [Appears first in 14th c.: no corresponding form is known outside English, and the word may be really connected with PLOT, or may unite a notion of *spot* with some words in *bl-*. It has been compared with ON. *blettr* blot, stain, plot, spot of ground, Da. *plet* spot, blot, stain; and with Ger. *bletz*, Goth. *plats* patch of cloth: but no normal phonetic relation to these words can be affirmed.]

1. a. A spot or stain of ink, mud, or other discolouring matter; a disfiguring spot or mark.

c **1325** [see 2]. *c* **1440** *Promp. Parv.* 41 Blotte vpon a boke, *oblitum.* **1530** PALSGR. 158 *Vne paste*, a blotte made with ynke. **1593** SHAKS. *Rich. II*, II. i. 64 Inky blottes and rotten Parchment bonds. **1714** GAY *Trivia* II. 172 Whose dashing Hoofs..mark, with muddy Blots, the gazing 'Squire. **1866** R. M. BALLANTYNE *Shift. Winds* xi. (1872) 110 A globule of ink, which fell on the paper..making a blot as large as a sixpence. **1876** E. JENKINS *Blot Queen's Head* 31 The ruthless hand had painted in an ugly black crown, which..only looked like a great blot.

b. An obliteration by way of correction.

1704 SWIFT *T. Tub* Author's Apol., Which he could have easily corrected with a very few Blots. **1788** BURNS *Let.* clxvii. Wks. (Globe) 437 Glance over the foregoing verses and let me have your blots.

c. *transf.* Any black or dark patch, especially as contrasted with light surroundings; also, anything that sullies or mars a fair surface, a blemish or disfigurement. Esp. in phr. ***a blot (up)on the landscape***; also *fig.*

1578 LYTE *Dodoens* III. cxiii. 306 It taketh away the hawe or webbe in the eye & al spottes or blottes in the same. **1595** SHAKS. *John* III. i. 45 If thou..wert grim, Full of vnpleasing blots, and sightlesse staines. **1634** MILTON *Comus* 133 When the dragon womb Of Stygian darkness..makes one blot of all the air. **1730** THOMSON *Autumn* 1143 Distinction lost; and gay variety One universal blot. **1823** LAMB *Elia* Ser. i. xxii. (1865) 169, I have a kindly yearning towards these poor blots [little sweeps]. **1853** KANE *Grinnell Exp.* xix. (1856) 148 There are the black hills, blots upon rolling snow. **1872** BLACK *Adv. Phaeton* xix. 262 That plain gilt cross..is rather a blot, is it not? **1912** T. E. LAWRENCE *Let.* 20 Feb. (1938) 137 His two Kufti people..will be rather a blot on the landscape. **1960** WODEHOUSE *Jeeves in Offing* i. 8 'And a rousing toodle-oo to you, you young blot on the landscape,' she replied cordially. **1962** *Listener* 11 Jan. 90/2 Charabancs and monstrous hordes of hikers are blots upon the landscape.

d. *spec.* A set of ink-blots made on a piece of paper as a basis for the composition of an imaginary landscape, according to the technique invented by Alex. Cozens (d. 1786). (Cf. RORSCHACH.) Also *attrib.*

a **1786** A. COZENS *New Method in Drawing Landscape* 7 A blot is an assemblage of dark shapes or masses made with ink upon a piece of paper. All the shapes are rude and unmeaning, as they are formed with the swiftest hand. But at the same time there appears a general disposition of these masses, producing one comprehensive form. **1931** *Times* 24 Mar. 19/6 Examples of Cozens's 'blots' have long been known. But it was only the other day that five blots accompanied by the five drawings made from them, were discovered. **1962** *Listener* 19 July 95/2 The manipulation of accident in the blot landscapes of Alexander Cozens.

e. *Painting.* (See quot.)

1910 *Edin. Rev.* Apr. 371 Painters are accustomed to speak of the 'Blot' of a picture, meaning its immediate appearance as colour, line, massing, or flat space.

2. *fig.* **a.** A moral stain; a disgrace, fault, blemish. Also in extended use: a person who is a disgrace (Webster, 1909).

c **1325** *E.E. Allit. P.* A. 781 Vnblemyst I am wyth-outen blot. *c* **1386** CHAUCER *Parson's T.* 936 But lat no blotte be bihynde, lat no synne been vntoold. **1583** STARKEY *England* 193 Thys..ys a grete blot in our pollycy. **1671** MILTON *Samson* 411 O indignity, O blot To honour and religion! **1790** BURKE *Fr. Rev.* Wks. V. 61 Do these theorists..mean..to stain the throne of England with the blot of a continual usurpation? **1876** GREEN *Short Hist.* iv. §3 (1882) 186 The execution of Wallace was the one blot on Edward's clemency. **1938** E. BOWEN *Death of Heart* I. iii. 60 Those four chaps were a blot. **1961** M. KELLY *Spoilt Kill* ii. 116 The silly blot forgot to switch on.

b. Imputation of disgrace; defamation.

1587 *Mirr. Mag., Forrex* iv. 7 Without the blots of everlasting blame. **1605** *Tryall Chev.* IV. i. in Bullen *O. Pl.* III. 324 Of all that ever liv'd deserv'd she not The worlds reproch and times perpetuall blot. **1728** YOUNG *Love Fame* v. (1757) 139 If on your fame our sex a blot has thrown, 'Twill ever stick, thro' malice of your own.

3. *Comb.*, as *blot-headed* adj.; **blot-book** (*Sc.*) = blotting-book; **blot-sheet** (*Sc.*), a sheet of blotting-paper.

1857 MRS. CARLYLE *Lett.* (1883) II. 313 She will find Mrs. Cook's bill in my blot-book. **1866** R. M. BALLANTYNE *Shift. Winds.* xi. (1872) 106 The Bu'ster stood by with the blot-sheet, looking eager, as if he rather wished for blots.

blot, *sb.*[2] [Origin conjectural: the sense suggests Da. *blot*, Sw. *blott* bare, naked, uncovered, Du. *bloot* naked, exposed (cf. *blootstellen* to expose), if the history of backgammon should support such an origin. (The word is not used as a sb., nor app. in this special sense in any of these langs.)]

In *Backgammon*: An exposed piece or 'man' liable to be taken or forfeited; also, the action of so exposing a piece. ***to hit a blot***: to 'take' the piece so exposed.

1598 FLORIO, *Caccia*, a hunting, a chasing.. Also.. a blot at tables. **1599** PORTER *Angry Wom. Abing.* (1841) 12 You neuer vse to misse a blot, Especially when it stands so faire to hit. **1672** WYCHERLEY *Love in Wood* v. v, Tho' I made a blot, your oversight has lost the game. **1880** *Boy's own Bk.* 620 The frequent occurrence of this taking of a blot gives an adversary a great advantage.

b. *fig.* An exposed or weak point in one's procedure; a fault or failing; also, a mark, butt.

1649 G. DANIEL *Trinarch., Hen. IV*, 367 Vpon termes gave over in the Sett, For Orleance, had the Dice, to save his Blott. **1698** DRYDEN *Æneid* Ded. (J.) He is too great a master of his art, to make a blot which may so easily be hit. **1734** *Pol. Ballads* (1860) II. 248 Its faults.. have taught him the wit, The blots of his neighbours the better to hit. **1781** COWPER *Hope* 558 The very butt of slander, and the blot For every dart that malice ever shot. *Mod.* Here the critic has undoubtedly hit a blot.

blot (blɒt), *v.*[1] [f. BLOT *sb.*[1]]

1. *trans.* To spot or stain with ink or other discolouring liquid or matter; to blur.

*c*1440 *Promp. Parv.* 41 Blottyn bokys, *oblitero.* **1530** PALSGR. 458, I blotte as a writer dothe with an yvele penne, *je barbouille.* **1698** DRYDEN *Æneid* II. 293 His holy Fillets the blue Venom blots. *c*1750 SHENSTONE *Elegies* iii. 8 And blots the mournful numbers with a tear. **1837** DICKENS *Pickw.* x, His note-book, blotted with the tears of sympathising humanity, lies open before us.

b. *absol.* To make blots.

1447 BOKENHAM *Seyntys* (1835) 27 Evene as he [my pen] goth he doth blot. **1570** ASCHAM *Scholem.* (Arb.) 116 Like pennes ouer full of incke, which will soner blotte, than make any faire letter at all. **1612** BRINSLEY *Lud. Lit.* 29 Inke.. which wil not run abroad, nor blot.

c. *intr.* To become blotted, contract a blot.

1860 TRENCH *Serm. Westm. Abb.* xiii. 144 The soul in this resembling paper which, where it has been blotted once, however careful the erasure of the blot may have been, there more easily blots and runs anew than elsewhere.

d. *trans.* To write with blots or blottesquely.

1870 LOWELL *Among my Bks.* Ser. i. (1873) 242 Trammels and pot-hooks which the little Shearjashubs and Elkanahs blotted and blubbered across their copy-books.

2. To cover (paper) with worthless writing; to disfigure. *arch.* or *Obs.*

1494 FABYAN VII. 592 Whose oppinyons, for the heryng of them shuld be tedious & vnfrutefull, I therfore wyll nat w[t] them blot my booke. **1596** SHAKS. *Merch. V.* III. ii. 253 Heere are a few of the vnpleasant'st words That euer blotted paper. **1607** TOPSELL *Four-f. Beasts* 367, I spare to blot much paper with the recital of those things. *a*1652 J. SMITH *Sel. Disc.* i. 14 They are not always the best men that blot most paper.

b. To paint coarsely, to daub. (Cf. BLOTTESQUE.)

1844 RUSKIN *Mod. Paint.* Pref. 67 Cattermole.. began his career with finished and studied pictures, which never paid him; he now prostitutes his fine talent.. and blots his way to emolument and oblivion.

3. *fig.* **a.** To cast a blot upon (good qualities or reputation); to tarnish, stain, sully. *arch.* or *Obs.*

1566 T. STAPLETON *Ret. Untr. Jewel* Ep., And Blotted yourselfe so much, intending to Blemish your Adversarie. **1596** SHAKS. *Tam. Shr.* v. ii. 139 Vnknit that thretaning vnkinde brow.. It blots thy beautie. **1644** MILTON *Judgm. Bucer* Wks. (1851) 301 To do me honour in that very thing, wherein these men thought to have blotted me. *a*1718 ROWE (J.) Blot not thy innocence with guiltless blood.

absol. **1588** SHAKS. *L.L.L.* IV. iii. 241 She passes prayse, then prayse too short doth blot.

†**b.** To stigmatize, calumniate, throw dirt at.

1581 E. CAMPION in *Confer.* (1584) A a ij, Neyther doeth Paul blotte the holy Ghost when he saide that he was *rudis sermone.* **1595** SHAKS. *John* II. i. 132 Theres a good mother, boy, that blots thy father! **1611** BIBLE *Pref.* 2 He hath been blotted by some to bee an Epitomiste.

4. To make a blot over (writing) so as to make it illegible; to obliterate, efface. (Usually with *out.*)

1530 PALSGR. 458/2 Who hath blotted out this worde. **1542-3** *Act 34 & 35 Hen. VIII*, i, Persons, havinge anie bibles.. with anie suche annotacions or preambles shall.. cutte out or blotte the same, in such wise, as they cannot be perceiued nor red. **1593** SHAKS. *Rich. II*, I. iii. 202 My name be blotted from the booke of Life. **1709** STEELE & ADD. *Tatler* No. 75 ¶8 By Culture, as skilful Gardiners blot a Colour out of a Tulip that hurts its Beauty. *a*1784 JOHNSON in *Boswell* (1831) I. 307 He submitted that work to my castigation; and I remember I blotted a great many lines. **1859** TENNYSON *Vivien* 328, I took his brush and blotted out the bird.

absol. **1737** POPE *Hor. Epist.* II. i. 281 The last and greatest art, the art to blot.

5. *fig.* To efface, wipe out of existence, sight, or memory; to annihilate, destroy. (Usually with *out.*)

1561 T. NORTON *Calvin's Inst.* I. 19 Vtterly to blot and deface it out of mennes remembrance. **1611** BIBLE *Acts* iii. 19 Repent yee therefore.. that your sins may be blotted out. **1667** MILTON *P.L.* XI. 891 Not to blot out mankind. **1856** FROUDE *Hist. Eng.* (1858) I. ii. 178 One, the tragedy of whose fate has blotted the remembrance of her sins. **1875** BRYCE *Holy Rom. Emp.* vii. (ed. 5) 113 As the Persian monarchy had been blotted out by Alexander.

b. To put out of sight, obscure, eclipse; also *fig.*

1592 SHAKS. *Ven. & Ad.* 184 Like misty vapours when they blot the sky. **1718** ROWE *Lucan's Pharsalia* I. (R.) The moon.. Was blotted by the earth's approaching shade. **1780** COWPER *Table T.* 270 No shades of superstition blot the day. **1862** WISE *New Forest*, Neither sea nor sky is seen—nothing but a dense haze blotting everything.

6. To dry with blotting-paper.

1854 W. COLLINS *Hide & Seek* I. 214 (Hoppe) Here Mr. Thorpe carefully blotted the first page of the letter.

blotch (blɒtʃ), *sb.* [A comparatively recent word, with no cognates outside Eng. App. an onomatopœic modification of BLOT, for which it is commonly used dialectally: the sound seems to express a broader spreading *blot*, of the nature of a *patch*. But in sense 1 there may have been association with the earlier BOTCH. The suggestion that it is a variant of BLATCH 'blacking', finds no support in the history of either word.]

1. a. An inflamed eruption, or discoloured patch, on the skin; a pustule, boil, or botch.

1604 [see BLOTCHED]. **1669** W. SIMPSON *Hydrol. Chym.* 72 In its road it leaves its character of Spots, Stains, Blotches, Buboes, Ulcers, &c. in.. the skin. **1711** ADDISON *Spect.* No. 16 ¶2 Healing those Blotches and Tumours which break out in the Body. **1740** CHEYNE *Regimen* Pref. 34 The Diseases of Infancy are generally Scabs, Blotches and Blains over the Face, etc. **1866** ROGERS *Agric. & Prices* I. xv. 293 Dark blotches appear on the skin.

fig. **1882** FARRAR *Early Chr.* II. 199 Which showed that they regarded Gentiles as worthless, and even Proselytes as little better than a blotch on the health of Israel.

b. *spec.* A disease in dogs.

1824 *Annals Sporting* VI. 265, I found his haunches exhibited appearances of a disease.. termed the 'blotch'.

c. A disease of fruit or leaves, characterized by the formation of spots; ***sooty blotch***, a disease of the apple.

1909 *Cent. Dict.* Suppl.

2. a. A large irregular spot or blot of ink, colour, etc.; a dab or patch.

1768 TUCKER *Lt. Nat.* II. 396 To brush off the soil.. and not suffer it to gather in pitchy blotches upon the surface. **1807** SIR R. WILSON in *Life* II. vii. 83 The snow fell in large blotches. **1870** H. MACMILLAN *Bible Teach.* x. 201 Its leaves are covered with brown unsightly blotches. **1873** MOGGRIDGE *Ants & Spiders* II. 76 Four blotches of paler colour.

b. *fig.* = BLOT 2.

1860 HAWTHORNE *Marble Faun* (1879) II. xii. 122 Ignoring all moral blotches.

c. *transf.* A rude clumsy daub.

1860 SMILES *Self-help* iv. 71 The artist.. attempting to produce a brilliant effect at a dash, will only produce a blotch.

d. A shapeless object.

1872 BROWNING *Fifine* lxxix. 17 Catch the puniest.. And, as you nip the blotch 'twixt thumb and fingernail, etc.

3. = BLOT (of ink). (North of Eng. and Scotl.)

Cf. BLOTCHING, BLOTCHY.

1863 ATKINSON *Provinc. Danby*, *Blotch*, a blot, in a copy-book, or on a clean piece of paper. *Blotch paper*, blotting paper.

blotch (blɒtʃ), *v.* [f. prec. sb.]

1. *trans.* To mark or cover with blotches.

1604 [see BLOTCHED]. **1774** GOLDSM. *Hist. Earth* v. 79 The tail is.. irregularly barred and blotched with an obscure ash colour. **1853** KANE *Grinnell Exp.* xxxii. (1856) 281 A great plain, blotched by dark, jagged shadows. **1865** BARING-GOULD *Werewolves* vi. 75 Its walls were blotched with lichen.

2. = BLOT *v.*[1] (Common in Scotl. and north of Eng., as 'He has blotched two pages of his book.') Cf. BLOTCHING, BLOTCHY.

blotched (blɒtʃt), *ppl. a.* [f. prec. vb. + -ED.] Marked, discoloured, or covered with blotches.

1604 DRAYTON *Moses* II. 328 To giue their bloch'd and blister'd bodies ease. **1785** BURNS *Ep. J. M'Math* xii, Tho' blotch't and foul wi' mony a stain. **1870** HOOKER *Stud. Flora* 252 *Pulmonaria officinalis*, Leaves.. always blotched with pale green.

'blotching, *vbl. sb.* [f. as prec. + -ING[1].] The action of marking with blotches; discolouring.

1767 *Specif. T. Long's Patent* No. 869 A machine for the blotching, printing.. colours on.. calicoes, etc. **1872** DANA *Corals* ii. 137 A blotching of the rock with various shades of pink and purple.

b. *concr.* Botch, disfigurement, smudging.

1865 CARLYLE *Fredk. Gt.* IX. xx. i. 6 Read him with a Map; and divine for yourself what the real names are, out of the inhuman blotchings made of them.

'blotching, *ppl. a.* That makes blotches.

1865 RUSKIN *Sesame* 32 Owing to the spread of a shallow, blotching, blundering, infectious 'information' everywhere, and to the teaching of catechisms and phrases at schools.

blotchy ('blɒtʃɪ), *a.* [f. BLOTCH *sb.* + -Y[1].] Characterized by blotches or blotching.

1824-9 LANDOR *Wks.* (1853) II. 107 Slim, straddling, blotchy writers. **1860** *All Y. Round* 545 The vaults themselves have.. got blotchy and bepimpled.

†**blote, blot.** *Obs.* [? Connected with *blow* in *blow-fly, fly-blown.* (The sense can hardly be explained from OE. *blát* 'livid, pale', to which the form answers.)]

The egg or larva of flies and other insects.

1657 S. PURCHAS *Pol. Flying-Ins.* 44 The Kings [i.e. queen-bees] do at certain seasons cast forth worms in multitudes as flies their flye blotes. *Ibid.* 48 As the blotes of the flyes are nourished by the flesh wherein they are blown. *Ibid.* II. 314 If the Bees be few, [Moths] will breed their blots in their combes.

blote, obs. form of BLOAT, BLOT.

†**bloten, blotne**, *v. Obs. rare.* [a. ON. *blotna* to become soft or moist: see BLOAT.] *trans.* To soften or moisten; to anoint.

*c*1325 *Metr. Hom.* (1862) 17 Scho wiped his feet wit her hare.. And blotned thaim wit smersles suete.

blother, obs. form of BLUTHER.

blotless ('blɒtlɪs), *a.* [f. BLOT *sb.*[1] + -LESS.] Without blot or stain; pure, immaculate.

? *a*1400 *Chester Pl.* I. (1843) 202 Cleaner than ever was any one, Blottles of blude and bone. **1664** *Floddon F.* v. 45 Knowing his blotless blood unblam'd. **1885** *Manch. Guard.* 28 Aug. 5 Clean and blotless pages.

blotted ('blɒtɪd), *ppl. a.* [f. BLOT *v.* + -ED.] Spotted or stained with ink, etc.; blurred.

1499 *Promp. Parv.* 41 Blottyd, *oblitteratus.* **1597** THYNNE *Names & Arms* in *Animadv.* (1865) Introd. 100 And for.. the blotted and rude wrytinge, I craue your Lordship also to passe yt ouer. **1751** JOHNSON *Rambl.* No. 169 ¶11 The blotted manuscripts of Milton now remaining. **1876** BLACKIE *Songs Relig. & Life* 201 Gorgeous Nature's pictured show Is now a blotted book.

b. *fig.* Soiled, tarnished, stained.

1596 SPENSER *F.Q.* II. I. 20 Now therefore Ladie.. see the saluing of your blotted name. **1817** JAS. MILL *Brit. Ind.* II. IV. ix. 304 Consideration of his services, blotted by offences, yet splendid and great.

blotter ('blɒtə(r)). [f. as prec. + -ER[1].]

1. One who, or that which, blots.

a. A scribbler, a sorry writer; **b.** One who stains or defiles; **c.** ***blotter out***: a quencher, extinguisher, annihilator.

1601 CORNWALLYES *Ess.* xv, These blotters of paper. *a*1631 HARSNET *Serm.* in *Stuart's Serm.* (1656) 131 (L.) Thou tookest the blotting of Thine image in Paradise as a blemish to Thyself; and Thou saidst to the blotter, Because thou hast done it, on thy belly shalt thou creep. **1827** HOOD *Hero & L.* lxxxiv, Blank Oblivion—Blotter-out of light.

2. A thing used for drying wet ink-marks, as a piece of blotting-paper or a blotting-pad.

1591 PERCIVALL *Sp. Dict.*, *Borrador*, a blotter, a blotting paper. **1859** R. BURTON *Centr. Afr.* in *Jrnl. Geogr. Soc.* XXIX. 78 Paper—soft and soppy by the loss of glazing—acts as a blotter. **1884** *Boston Lit. World* 19 Apr. 132/2 His pen spluttered.. and he used no blotter.

3. 'A term applied in counting-houses to a waste-book' (Craig 1847); also to a rough copy of a letter.

4. A record of arrests and charges in a police office; a charge-sheet; also *gen.* a record-book or list. *U.S.*

1887 *Harper's Mag.* Mar. 500/2 Every item of police duty, and of civil or criminal occurrence, is inscribed on the 'blotter'. **1906** *Atlantic Monthly* Feb. 264 It was necessary.. to examine the day-book or blotter in the chief clerk's office [at the Patent Office]. **1910** *Washington Times* 14 Dec. 1 Three more additions were made yesterday to the hospital blotters. **1926** J. BLACK *You can't Win* xix. 299, I never put his name, which is my name, on a police blotter or a prison register while he was alive. **1965** 'R. L. PIKE' (*title*) Police blotter.

blotter, obs. form of BLATTER *v.*

blottesque (blɒ'tɛsk), *a.* [f. BLOT *v.* + -ESQUE, after *grotesque, picturesque*, etc.] **a.** Of painting: Characterized by blotted touches heavily laid on. *fig.* of descriptive writing. (It belongs to the phraseology of Art-Criticism.)

1856 RUSKIN *Mod. Paint.* IV. v. v. Pl. 27, Modern, or, Blottesque. *Ibid.* 80, I have given, Fig. 1., a Durereseque, and Fig. 3. a Blottesque, version of the intermediate wall. **1866** SWINBURNE *Lett.* (1959) I. 165 'Guy Deverell' I think too hasty—too blurred and 'blottesque'. **1880** *Daily News* 3 Jan. 2/2 The Landscape.. is powerful in the unaffected blottesque manner. **1885** *Spectator* 24 Jan. 119/1 The fashionable blottesque school, wherewith modern painters smear their way to 'emolument and oblivion.' **1886** *Athenæum* 19 June 808/3 The manner of relation [of the novel] might not inaptly be described as blottesque. **1934** H. G. WELLS *Exper. in Autobiogr.* I. vi. 345 My notes and comments were sometimes more blottesque than edifying. *Ibid.* II. vii. 424, I sat down.. to my blottesque red corrections again.

b. quasi-*sb.* A roughly-executed picture, a daub.

1882 F. G. Fleay in *Jrnl. Educ.* May 146 To produce showy blottesques for framing in drawing-rooms.

Hence **blo'ttesquely** *adv.*, with blottesque effect.

1886 Ruskin in *Pall Mall G.* 19 Jan. 2/1 Putting my pen lightly through the needless, and blottesquely through the rubbish.

blotting ('blɒtɪŋ), *vbl. sb.* [f. blot *v.* + -ing[1].]

1. The action of the verb blot; *concr.* a blot, smear, obliteration.

c **1440** *Promp. Parv.* 41 Blottynge, *oblitteracio.* **1542-3** *Act 34-35 Hen. VIII*, i, The blotting or cutting out of anie quotacion. **1656** *Artif. Handsomeness* (1662) 47 The most accurate pencils were but blottings which presumed to mend Zeuxis or Apelles works. **1791** Boswell *Johnson* (1831) I. 350 Blottings, interlineations, and corrections. **1842** Browning *Waring* iii, There were certain jottings, Stray-leaves, fragments, blurrs and blottings.

2. *blotting out*: obliteration of writing, etc.; also, effacement, destruction, annihilation.

1808 Syd. Smith *Plymley's Lett.* Wks. 1859 II. 159/2 [No] one of his conquered countries the blotting out of which would be as beneficial to him. **1861** Mill *Repr. Govt.* 137 The virtual blotting out of the minority is no necessary or natural consequence of freedom. **1879** Calderwood *Mind & Brain* 306 A blotting out of impressions.

3. *techn.* Material for blotting-paper; also, the finished article.

1872 *Eng. Mech.* 15 Nov. 228/3 [To] give to used..or dry ..blotting its original absorbent power. **1880** J. Dunbar *Pract. Papermaker* 72 For pink blottings furnish two thirds of white cottons and one third of turkey reds. *Ibid.*, In this way the author has made blotting which was considered a good article. **1920** *Printers' & Stat. Yr. Bk.* 13 Calf Papers, Blottings. Enamelled Blottings.

4. *Comb.*, as **blotting-book**, a book consisting of leaves of blotting-paper for drying the ink of letters and the like; also, a rough note-book in which entries of transactions are made as they occur, a waste-book; **blotting-case**, a case or cover enclosing blotting-paper; **blotting-pad**, a pad consisting of a number of sheets of blotting-paper joined at the edges, used for the same purpose as a *blotting-book*. Also blotting-paper.

1598 Florio *Worlde of Wordes* 39/3 *Bastardolo*, a blotting booke, a daie booke, a house booke to write in euery thing. **1848** H. R. Forster *Stowe Catalogue* 28, Item 453 A blotting book. **1857** W. Collins *Dead Secret* (1861) 21 She signed these lines with her name,—pressed them hurriedly over the blotting-pad. **1874** H. H. Cole *Catal. Ind. Art S. Kens. Mus.* 321 A blotting-book cover.

'blotting, *ppl. a.* [f. as prec. + -ing[2].] That blots or smears.

1828 Lamb *Corr.* ccxviii. 522 The blotting pen.

Hence **'blottingly** *adv.*

1653 Gauden *Hierasp.* 248 That pen, which now writes blottingly.

'blotting-ˌpaper. A bibulous paper made without size, used to absorb superfluous ink. Also *attrib.*

1519 Horman *Vulg.* 80 b, Blottynge papyr serueth to drye weete wryttynge lest there be made blottis or blurris. **1612** Brinsley *Lud. Lit.* 29 Each to haue a blotting paper to keep their books from soyling, or marring vnder their hands. **1755** Mauduit in *Phil. Trans.* XLIX. 207 It is less bibulous than the common blotting paper. **1853** Mrs. Gaskell *Cranford* ix. 163 The same confused sort of way in which written words run together on blotting-paper. **1894** H. Nisbet *Bush Girl's Rom.* vii. 68 Acid with the soup, salt and warmth with the fish to intensify its brain-feeding and blotting-paper qualities. **1904** *Daily Chron.* 6 Feb. 9/1 Blotting-paper pink and turtle-dove drab. **1937** E. J. Labarre *Dict. Paper* 26/1 *Blotting paper*..is, peculiarly enough, produced from the same materials as the most expensive papers, viz: rags... It is now also largely made from chemical wood pulp, esparto, etc. **1967** E. Short *Embroidery & Fabric Collage* iv. 108 Once the work is complete it should be stretched face upwards over damp blotting paper.

blotto ('blɒtəʊ), *a. slang.* [Obscurely f. blot.] Fuddled with liquor, intoxicated.

1917 W. Muir *Observations of Orderly* xiv. 230 The words for drunkenness are innumerable—'jingled', 'oiled', 'tanked to the wide', 'well sprung', 'up the pole', 'blotto', etc. **1919** *Winter's Pie* Pl. 17. **1921** *Blackw. Mag.* Feb. 157/1 The evening's potations left him, by bed-time, in a state somewhere between 'blotto' and 'blithero-blotto'. **1923** *Daily Mail* 13 June 12, I got properly 'blotto' and don't know what I did. **1951** Wodehouse *Old Reliable* xiii. 149 Did you ever see a blotto butler before?

blotty ('blɒtɪ), *a.* [f. blot *sb.*[1] + -y[1].] Disfigured with blots; dauby.

1856 *Sat. Rev.* II. 125/2 [Those pictures] blotty and hasty as they all are.

blou(e, obs. form of blow, blue.

bloubred, obs. form of blubbered.

blough, variant of bluff *a.*

† **blought**, *a. Obs.*—[0] [Deriv. and meaning uncertain: see quot. Cf. bloat *a.*[2]] ? Swollen, plump.

1611 Cotgr. s.v. *Glas*, *Bled glas*, blought wheat. **1632** Sherwood s.v. *Wheat*, Blought wheate, *bledglas*, *touzelle*, *tozelle*. [**1611** Cotgr., *Touzelle*, fine wheat, white winter wheat; a head of smooth wheat, which hath an vpright stalke, and a very white graine.]

† **'bloughty**, *a. Obs. rare*—[1]. [var. of prec.] Swollen, bulky.

1620 Bp. Hall *Hon. Mar. Clerg.* i. §2 One dash of a penne might thus iustly answer the most part of his bloughtie volume.

bloume, obs. form of bloom.

blounchet, obs. form of blanched.

bloure, var. of blure *Obs.* blister.

blouse (blaʊz), *sb.* [a. mod.F. *blouse* (pron. bluz) of obscure etymology: see Littré and Scheler.]

1. a. A light loose upper garment of linen or cotton, resembling a shirt or smock-frock; properly applied (as an alien term) to the well-known blue blouse of the French workman, but in England sometimes used loosely to designate more or less similar garments.

1828 *Engl. in France* II. 100 (Stanford), Neither wearers of plaid, nor devourers of porridge, but *blousses* and *soupe maigre* well supplied the want. [**1834** Planché *Brit. Costume* 89 A garment called *bliaut* or *bliaus*, which appears to have been only another name for the surcoat or super-tunic..In this *bliaus* we may discover the modern French *blouse*, a tunic or smock-frock.] **1840** Thackeray *Paris Sketch Bk.* (1872) 6 Another has a shooting dress, a third has a blouse. **1875** J. Curtis *Hist. Eng.* 153 The lower classes wore a blouse or kind of small frock, made of canvas or fustian. **1879** Kingston *Australian Abr.* ii. 11 A blue blouse, tied with a sash around the waist.

b. (*a*) *U.S.*, a waist-length dress or undress military coat; (*b*) the upper part of a soldier's or airman's battledress.

1861 *Chicago Tribune* 26 May 1/3 Cassinet pants are supplied the volunteers... They cost the State $5, and blouses made of shoddy, with pants, $10. **1939** *Jrnl. R. United Service Instit.* Nov. 858 Commanders of formations only will wear a scarlet cord boss at each point of the collar of the battle dress blouse. **1943** *Sun* (Baltimore) 16 June 8/6 For retreat formations the battalion turns out in dress blouses with buttons shining. **1948** A. Baron *From City, from Plough* v. 41 Alfie sweated, trembled inside his battleblouse.

2. *transf.* A French workman.

1865 G. Berkeley *Life* II. 281 No wealth of gold would tempt a blouse to risk a charge from an old boar at such close quarters. **1872** Lytton *Parisians* xi. xi. (1878) II. 223 De Mauléon came on a group of blouses.

3. A loosely-fitting bodice worn by women and girls, usually tucked inside the skirt at the waist. Also, formerly called ***blouse-bodice*** (cf. blousée, *shirt-blouse*).

1870 *Young Ladies' Jrnl.* 1 Oct. 626/1 A costume for a young lady... A blouse, or tunic, of white and pink-striped silk. **1887** *Cassell's Fam. Mag.* Sept. 631/1 Frenchwomen show just the same favour to the blouse bodices as their sisters across the Channel. **1899** *Daily News* 14 Jan. 2/4 The fashionable blouse, or 'blouse-bodice'. **1909** *Westm. Gaz.* 15 Feb. 5/2 Blouses will be more in evidence this season than ever, for the mere strap that forms the bodice of the newest gowns, and the high waists, and bretelles, all demand the finishing touch of a blouse.

4. *attrib.* and *Comb.*, as ***blouse-maker***, ***-making*** (also *attrib.*), ***panier***; ***blouse-clad***, ***-like*** adjs.; **blouse coat**, a blouse to be worn outside the skirt at the waist; **blouse length**, a piece of material sufficient for the making of a blouse, cut off for sale; **blouse slip** (see slip *sb.*[3] 4 c); **blouse suit**, a blouse and skirt finished complete, and ready to wear.

1892 *Daily News* 2 July 6/7 A comparison between the blouse-clad ladies and those who wear habit-bodices. **1898** *Westm. Gaz.* 16 June 3/2 Blouses and blouse coats of Irish lace. **1910** *Westm. Gaz.* 29 Jan. 3/3 Who..would venture to buy a blouse-length with the fate of the Budget hanging in the balance? **1874** Boutell *Arms & Arm.* 107 The body armour is..a long, narrow, blouse-like garment. **1905** *Daily Chron.* 18 Oct. 3/5 A wife who was employed at a blouse-maker's. **1905** *Pearson's Mag.* July 105/1 The blouse-making industry. **1908** *Westm. Gaz.* 21 Aug. 8/2 Working at blouse-making. **1883** *Myra's Jrnl.* Aug., Narrow box-pleated blouse paniers. **1907** *Westm. Gaz.* 21 Feb. 8/2 How to make a Blouse-Slip. **1909** *Daily Chron.* 22 Feb. 7/5 With these cashmere gowns, blouse-slips of various kinds can be worn. **1905** *Daily Chron.* 20 Oct. 8/5 Blouse-Suits in Velveteens, Silks, and Various Cloths.

blouse (blaʊz), *v.* [f. the sb.] **1.** *intr.* To assume a blouse-like form (Webster, 1909).

1938 J. Rice *Somers Inheritance* iv. vii. 270 Her hat fell off and her hair bloused about her ears.

2. *trans.* To make (the bodice of a garment) full, like a blouse.

1934 *Times* 12 Nov. 17/5 She blouses the bodices.

blouse, variant of blowze.

bloused (blaʊzd), *ppl. a.* [f. blouse *sb.* + -ed[2].]

1. Wearing a blouse, dressed in a blouse.

1850 Kingsley *Alt. Locke* xxxiii. (D.) There was a bloused and bearded Frenchman or two. **1860** *All Y. Round* No. 54. 79, I have seen baby London short-coated, and frocked, and breeched, and jacketed, and bloused.

2. Of a bodice: made full, like a blouse.

1935 *Times* 11 Feb. 15/6 The bloused bodice is shirred into shape in front and at the back. **1958** *Vogue* May 122 Lanvin-Castillo's spare little dress, the top lightly bloused and buttoned behind.

blousée ('bluːzeɪ), *a.* [f. blouse + Fr. *-ée*.] In ***blousée bodice*** = blouse *sb.* 3.

1899 *Westm. Gaz.* 24 Aug. 3/2 The simple blouse, or I might say *blousée* bodice, which will probably be the favourite for indoor wear. **1903** *Ibid.* 19 Feb. 4/2 The becoming *blousée* bodice for gowns.

‖ **blouson** (bluzɔ̃). [Fr.] A short jacket shaped like a blouse. Also *attrib.*

1904 *Westm. Gaz.* 27 Oct. 4/2 No doubt there will be many fur coats quite short in the bolero blouseon build and in the sac species. **1958** *Woman's Own* 6 Aug. 20/1 Crisply fresh at the office in a white drip-dry cotton 'blouson'. **1959** *Ibid.* 20 June 12/2 Drip dry poplin hooded blouson with drawstring waist. **1960** *Guardian* 22 July 8/4 The line leaves the shoulders in a blouson effect to end smoothly at hip-line. **1970** *Ibid.* 23 July 9/4 Suits with raglan *blouson* tops.

blousy, var. blowzy *a.*

blout (blaʊt), *sb. Sc.* [App. onomatopœic: cf. *blow*, *blast*, *blash*, etc.]

1. The sudden breaking of a storm; a sudden downpour of rain, hail, etc., accompanied by wind.

1786 *Harvest Rig* in Chambers *Hum. Sc. Poems* (1862) 52 For 'tis a blout will soon be laid, And we may hap us in our plaid, Till it blaws ower. **1804** Tarras *Poems* 63 (Jam.) Vernal win's, wi' bitter blout, Out owre our chimlas blaw.

2. Cf. *gouts* (of blood).

1827 J. Wilson *Noct. Ambr.* Wks. 1855 I. 338 Wringing her hauns as if washin them in the cleansin dews frae the bluots o' blood.

† **blout**, *a. Sc. Obs.* Also blowt. [Cf. Du. *bloot* naked, bare, ON. *blaut-r* soft, wet. The ON. accounts best for the form, but the Du. agrees in sense.] Naked, bare, desolate.

1513 Douglas *Æneis* vii. Prol. 65 Woddis, forestis, wyth nakyt bewis blout, Stud strypyt of thair weyd in every hout. *Ibid.* xi. xvii. 8 The baneris left all blowt and desolait. *Ibid.* xiii. vi. 227 Planys..blowt of bestis; and of treis bayr.

blout(e, obs. form of bloat.

'blouter. *Sc.* [f. blout *sb.*] A blast of wind.

1804 Tarras *Poems* 129 (Jam.) An' blew a maikless blouter.

blouth, *sb.* [? Cf. blowth.]

1643 Lightfoot *Gleanings* (1648) 10 He had hazzarded their lives..both of them [mother and new-born child] being in their blouth and blood.

blouze, obs. form of blowze.

blow (bləʊ), *v.*[1] Pa. t. blew. Pa. pple. blown (also in sense 29 blowed). Forms: 1 bláwan, 2-3 blawen, (2 blauwen), blouwen, 3 bloawen, 5 blowen, blowyn, 3-7 blowe, 5- blow; (*north.*) 3-4 blau, 4-6 blawe, 3- blaw. *Pa. t.* 1 bleów, bléw, 2-3 bleu, 4 blwe, blee3, ble3, 3-5 blu, 5 blue, 4-6 blewe, 4- blew. Also 4 blowide, 7 blowd, blowede, 6- blowed. *Pa. pple.* 1 bláwen, blouen, 4-7 blowen, 6-7 blowne, 7- blown; also 4 y-blowe, blowun, blowe, 4-6 i-blowe, 7 bloun; *north.* 3 blaun, 4 blawun, 4-5 blawen, 6 blawne, blawin, blauen, blaw, 6- blawn. Also 6- blowed. [OE. *bláwan*, pa. t. *bléow*, pple. *bláwen*, elsewhere as a strong vb. only in OHG. *blâ(h)an* (pa. pple. *blâhan*, *blân*):—Goth. type **blaian*, **baiblô*, OTeut. ? **blǣjan*, cogn. w. L. *flā-re* to blow. (In OHG. this, like other verbs with *ai* in Gothic, passed into the weak conj. *blâen*, *blâhen*, *blâjen*, *blâwen*, *blân*, MHG. *blæjen*, *blæwen*, *blæn*, Ger. *blähen*.) In OE. only in a few senses: see 1, 2, 14; but an immense development of sense and constructions has taken place in middle and modern Eng., and in later times distinct senses have influenced each other, or run together, in a manner difficult to exhibit in a linear series.]

I. *properly.* To produce a current of air; to set in motion with a current of air.

* *intransitively.*

1. a. *intr.* The proper verb naming the motion or action of the wind, or of an aerial current. Sometimes with subject *it*, as 'it blows hard', and often with complement, as 'it blew a gale, a hurricane'. ***to blow great guns***: to blow a violent gale. ***to blow up***: to rise, increase in force of blowing.

c **1000** *Ags. Gosp.* Luke xii. 55 þonne ʒe ʒeseoð suðan blawan. *c* **1175** *Lamb. Hom.* 167 Lutel he hit scaweð..hu biter wind þer blaweð. *a* **1225** *Ancr. R.* 124 ȝif a wind bloweð a lutel touward us. *a* **1300** *Cursor M.* 532 Wynd þat blaws o loft. **1382** Wyclif *Ecclus.* xliii. 22 The cold northerne wind bleeȝ [**1388** blew]. **1530** Palsgr. 130 *Il uente*, it bloweth. **1580** Baret *Alv.* B 829, I turne sayle that way as the winde bloweth. **1653** Walton *Angler* 208 Heark how it rains and blows. **1697** Dryden *Virg. Georg.* iii. 549 All the Weste Allies of stormy Boreas blow. **1785** Burns *Cotter's Sat. Nt.* ii, November chill blaws loud wi' angry sugh. **1793** Smeaton *Edystone L.* §313 It blowed very hard, especially on the night of lighting. **1802** Gouv. Morris in Sparks *Life & Writ.* (1832) III. 166 Straws and feathers..show which way the wind blows. **1840** Marryat *Poor Jack* x, The gale had blown up again. **1854** H. Miller *Sch. & Schm.* (1858) 14 It soon began to blow great guns.

b. Phr. ***blow high, blow low***: whatever may happen. *U.S.*

1774 P. V. FITHIAN *Jrnl.* (1900) 235 Ben is in a wonderful Fluster lest he shall have no company to-morrow at the Dance—But blow high, blow low, he need not be afraid; Virginians.. will dance or die! [**1776** C. DIBDIN *Seraglio* I. 11 Blow high, blow low, let tempests tear The mainmast by the board.] *a* **1861** T. WINTHROP *John Brent* (1883) vi. 52 I've booked Brother John fur Paradise; Brother Joseph's got a white robe fur him, blow high, blow low! **1923** R. D. PAINE *Comr. Rolling Ocean* x. 171 There were three musketeers.. who were blithely resolved to stand by each other through thick and thin, blow high, blow low.

2. a. To send from the mouth a current of air (stronger than that produced by ordinary breathing); to produce a current of air in any way, *e.g.* said of bellows. (Cf. sense 7.)

c **1000** *Ags. Gosp.* John xx. 22 þa bleow he on hi and cwæð to him under-foð haline gast. *a* **1300** *Cursor M.* 12540 He.. hent his hand and bleu þar-in. **1382** WYCLIF *Ezek.* xxi. 31 In fier of my wodnes Y shal blowe in thee. **1526** *Pilgr. Perf.* (W. de W. 1531) 263b, She waueth with her wynges and so bloweth, that by her mouynge she engendreth an hete in them. **1572** GASCOIGNE *Wks.* (1587) 1 My lights and lungs like bellows blow. *a* **1620** J. DYKE *Sel. Serm.* (1640) 63 When the word is preached, then the Bellowes blowes to kindle the fire. **1646** SIR T. BROWNE *Pseud. Ep.* 176 Serrous or jarring motion like that which happeneth while we blow on the teeth of a combe through paper. **1715** DESAGULIERS *Fires Impr.* 42, I blowed upon the Thermometer. *a* **1856** LONGF. *Vill. Blacksmith* 14 You can hear his bellows blow.

b. ***to blow hot and cold***: (*fig.*) to be or to do one thing at one time, another at another; to be inconsistent or vacillating. (In reference to one of Æsop's Fables.)

1577 tr. *Bullinger's Decades* (1592) 176 One which out of one mouth, doeth blowe both hoat and colde. **1638** CHILLINGW. *Relig. Prot.* I. ii. §113. 95 These men can blow hot and cold out of the same mouth to serve severall purposes. **1690** W. WALKER *Idiom. Anglo-Lat.* 61 With the same breath to blow hot and cold. [**1694** R. LESTRANGE *Fables* (J.) Says the satyr, 'If you have gotten a trick of blowing hot and cold out of the same mouth, I've e'en done with ye.] **1866** MOTLEY *Dutch Rep.* v. v. 750 Being constantly ordered 'to blow hot and cold with the same breath.'

†**3.** To make a blowing sound; to hiss, whistle.

1340 *Ayenb.* 32 Þe childe þet ne dar guo his way vor þe guos þet blauþ. *c* **1420** *Avow. Arth.* 64 Alle wrothe wex that sqwyne, Blu, and brayd vppe his bryne. **1535** COVERDALE *Zech.* x. 8, I wil blowe [**1611** hisse] for them & gather them together.

4. a. To breathe hard, pant, puff. ***to blow out***: to be winded. (Cf. sense 8.)

c **1440** *Erle Tolous* 442 in Ritson *Met. Rom.* III. 111 The thrydd fledd, and blewe owt faste, The erle ovyrtoke hym at the laste. **1513** DOUGLAS *Æneis* XII. xii. 234 At sic debait that bayth thai pant and blaw. **1530** PALSGR. 458/2 He bloweth lyke a horse that came newe from galoppyng. **1608** ARMIN *Nest Ninn.* (1842) 23 They puft and they blowede, they ran as swifte as a pudding would creepe. **1718** POPE *Iliad* II. 465 Each spent courser at the chariot blow. **1847** TENNYSON *Princ.* v. 20 The huge bush-bearded Barons heaved and blew.

b. To breathe; to take breath. *dial.* ***to blow short***: (of a horse) to be broken-winded.

c **1440** *York Myst.* xxxi. 142 Nowe gois a-bakke both, and late þe boy blowe. **1523** FITZHERB. *Husb.* §84 Pursy is a disease in an horses bodye, and maketh hym to blowe shorte. **1647** WARD *Simp. Cobler* 36 They gave him such straynes as made him blow short ever since. **1786** BURNS *To Auld Mare* Thou never lap, and sten't an' breastit, Then stood to blaw. **1860** HOLLAND *Miss Gilbert* ii. 29 I'll sit here and blow, till he comes around.

5. Of whales, etc: To eject water and air from the 'blow-holes', before taking in fresh air; to spout.

1725 DUDLEY in *Phil. Trans.* XXXIII. 261 Once in a Quarter of an Hour.. they are observed to rise and blow, spouting out Water and Wind, and to draw in fresh Air. **1779** FORREST *Voy. N. Guinea* 128 Many porpoises blowing near us. **1851** H. MELVILLE *Whale* xlvii. 239 The Sperm Whale blows as a clock ticks.

6. To utter loud or noisy breath, to bluster: **a.** To boast, brag (chiefly *regional*). **b.** To fume, storm, speak angrily (chiefly *colloq.*).

c **1400** *Apol. Loll.* 97 Blouing veynly wiþ fleschli wit. *c* **1420** *Avow. Arth.* xxiii, I, Kay, that thou knawes, That owte of tyme bostus and blawus. **1519** *Four Elements* in Hazl. *Dodsley* I. 41 Why, man, what aileth thee so to blow? **1789** BURNS *Tam Glen* iii, He brags and he blaws o' his siller. **1863** MRS. C. CLARKE *Shaks. Char.* x. (1876) 270 He has been blowing and storming about this drum. **1873** TROLLOPE *Australia* xxv, In the colonies.. when a gentleman sounds his own trumpet he 'blows.' **1873** LADY BARKER *Station Amusements in N.Z.* xiv. 237, I.. mention this, not out of any desire to 'blow' about our sheep. **1878** *Cornh. Mag.* June 680 'My sister ain't the best,' the child declared, 'she's always blowing at me.' **1885** MRS. PRAED *Austral. Life* ii. 45 He was famous for 'blowing', in Australian parlance,.. of his exploits. **1896** H. A. BRYDEN *Tales S. Afr.* iii. 68 You know I don't 'blow', Jim, or spout tall yarns. **1917** *N.Z.E.F. Chrons.* 5 Sept. 35/2, I don't care about blowin' about it.

¶ *dial.* To smoke a pipe: see 9b.

** *causal uses of the preceding.*

7. a. Beside the expressions ***to blow with bellows***, and ***the bellows blow*** (see 2), one is said ***to blow the bellows***, i.e. to work them so as to make them blow.

c **1440** *Leg. Rood* (1871) 85 Scho blew þe belise ferly fast. **1509** HAWES *Past. Pleas.* XXXVI. xxiii, Afrycus Auster made surreccion, Blowyng his bellowes by great occasion. **1577** NORTHBROOKE *Dicing* (1843) 81 Many which lacke armes may worke with their feete, to blowe smithes bellowes. **1880** GROVE *Dict. Mus.* II. 577 The four bellows are blown in a manner which we here meet with for the first time.

†**b.** fig. ***to blow the bellows***: to stir up passion, strife, etc. *Obs.* (Cf. *to blow the coals*, 17b.)

1596 SPENSER *F.Q.* II. iii. 9 He cast for to.. blow the bellowes to his swelling vanity. *a* **1657** SIR J. BALFOUR *Ann. Scotl.* (1825) II. 263 The bischopes blouing the bellowes, and still craying fyre and suord.

8. (causal of 4.) To cause to pant, to put out of breath: usually of horses.

1651 DAVENANT *Gondibert* II. xliii, From thence, well blown, he [i.e. Stag] comes to the Relay. **1760** *Hist. Europe* in *Ann. Reg.* 24/1 They came up five miles on a full trot without being blown. **1771** P. PARSONS *Newmarket* I. 108 How much water, given to a horse before he starts, will blow him. **1816** SCOTT *Old Mort.* xii, Move steadily, and do not let the men blow the horses. **1859** *Blackw. Mag.* Mar. 306/1 The Russians.. were.. pretty well blown in the pursuit.

*** *trans.* (with *the air, breath*, etc., as obj.)

9. a. *trans.* To breathe out, emit, produce (a current of air, breath, etc.) with the mouth; to give forth by breathing; also to force or cause to pass (a current of air) *through, into, upon*, by other means. Also *fig.*

c **1175** *Lamb. Hom.* 75 Þan deþliche atter · þet þe alde deouel blou on adam. *Ibid.* 99 [Crist ableow þana halȝa gast ofer þa apostlas]. *c* **1375** WYCLIF *Antecrist* (Todd) 148 Þei blowen on hem a stynkand breþe. **1382** —— *Wisd.* xv. 11 That bleȝ [**1388** blowide] in to hym a lifli spirit. **1509** HAWES *Past. Pleas.* XXXVI. iii, A fende.. Blowyng out fyre. **1591** SPENSER *Bellay's Ruines Rome* xxvi, Where colde Boreas blowes his bitter stormes. **1651** HOBBES *Leviath.* VI. I. ii, Good thoughts are blown into a man by God. **1784** J. ADAMS *Diary* Wks. 1851 III. 388 If inflammable air were blown through the pipe. **1842** LONGF. *Wreck Hesp.* 19 He blew a whiff from his pipe. **1866** HUXLEY *Phys.* iv. (1869) 96 If a pipe be now fitted into the bronchus, and air blown through it.

b. To smoke (tobacco); also *intr.* (*dial.*) But ***to blow a cloud*** is a common figurative expression for to smoke a pipe. See also CLOUD *sb.* 5b.

1808 in JAMIESON, To blaw Tobacco; to blaw. **1848** *Sessions* Mar. 847, I could sit down and *blow* my *'bacco.* *c* **1855** HAWTHORNE *Mother Rigby's Pipe* i, Smoke, puff, blow thy cloud. **1856** MAYHEW *Great World of London* 5 Smoke a *pipe* of *baccer*.. blow your yard of *tripe* of *nosey-me-knacker*.

c. To lay out or get through (money) in a lavish manner; to squander; = BLUE *v.*[2] 1. *slang.* Also *refl.* (U.S. dial.): see quot. 1896.

1874 HOTTEN *Slang Dict.*, *Blew, or blow*,.. to lose or spend money. **1892** *Daily News* 5 Sept. 6/3 Sometimes you'll blow a little money.. but another week you may make a lot. **1896** *Dialect Notes* I. 412 'To blow oneself', to spend money freely. **1904** W. H. SMITH *Promoters* v. 100 The Church people in England were the folks that had the money to blow. **1932** H. SIMPSON *Boomerang* x. 244 A thousand pounds, which she proposed.. to blow in a couple of months' high living. **1957** *Economist* 21 Dec. 1030/1 He will probably feel able to blow with a clear conscience the £2,000.

d. ***to blow in***: to spend, squander. Also *absol. slang* (chiefly *U.S.*).

1886 in *Amer. Speech* (1950) XXV. 30/2 When Davis has a dollar he's dead bent on blowing it all in. **1887** F. FRANCIS Jr. *Saddle & Mocassin* 144 'Sam went off on a bend.' 'To blow in?' Jake laughed assent. **1903** *Outlook* 7 Nov. 586 He had blown in all his earnings in a grand frolic. **1934** J. T. FARRELL *Young Manhood* (1936) i. 163 Last winter I got sixty bucks from him for tuition and books and blew it in. **1938** R. D. FINLAYSON *Brown Man's Burden* 24 After breakfast I'll borrow Henare's car and we'll blow in the cash. **1946** F. SARGESON *That Summer* 35 Then he'd go to town and blow his money in, usually at the races.

e. To lose or bungle (an opportunity, etc.); to mishandle (a situation); to ruin, spoil. Freq. with *it*. *slang* (orig. *U.S.*).

1943 W. R. BURNETT *Nobody lives Forever* I. x. 60 He'll probably blow it. He's beginning to look old. **1950** H. E. GOLDIN *Dict. Amer. Underworld Lingo* 30/1 *Blow*, v... 3. To lose; to bungle. 'Don't blow that piece (revolver); it cost me a double sawbuck (twenty dollars).' **1967** *Boston Herald* 1 Apr. 16/4 There wasn't anyone in the Boston contingent who could recall him ever blowing three layups in a game before. **1971** *It* 9–23 Sept. 19/1 This could have been a wonderful record but they blew it. **1977** *Tennis World* Sept. 17/1 If a player is nervous he 'muffs', 'flubs' or 'blows' his shots. **1983** *Times* 22 Jan. 1/2 Let's go in June, and win, rather than blow it in March, 1984.

10. ***to blow off***: (*trans.*) to allow (steam or the like) to escape forcibly with a blowing noise; also *fig.* to get rid of (superfluous energy, emotion, etc.) in a noisy way; *intr.* (for *refl.*) of steam, gas, etc.: to escape forcibly.

1837 MARRYAT *Dog-Fiend* xi, The widow.. sat.. fuming and blowing off her steam. **1865** JEVONS *Coal Quest.* (ed. 2) 65 Carburetted gas.. is liable to blow off and endanger the lives of hundreds of persons. **1884** *Chr. Commonw.* 24 Jan. 348/1 Blowing off their superfluous energy in singing and shouting.

†**11.** To utter: also with *out*. Most frequently in a bad sense: To utter boastfully, angrily, etc. ***to blow into one's ear***: to whisper privily. *Obs.*

1375 BARBOUR *Bruce* IV. 122 The gret bost that it [pryde] blawis. *c* **1380** WYCLIF *Three Tracts* i. 69 Censuris þat þe fend bloweþ (as ben suspendis and interdicyngis). *c* **1380** *Sir Ferumb.* 5421 Þan wax þe Amyral glad.. & gan to blowe bost. *c* **1440** HYLTON *Scala Perf.* (W. de W. 1494) II. xlii, Blowynge psalmes & louynges to Jhesu. **1549** *Compl. Scot.* vi. 38 That samyn sound as thay beystis hed blauen. *a* **1563** BECON *New Catech.* Wks. (1844) 344 He blowed out many furious and unseemly words. **1642** T. TAYLOR *God's Judgem.* I. I. xii. 35 Threats were blowne out on every side against the Faithful. **1652** COTTERELL *Cassandra* (1676) IV. 61 These things which malitious Roxana blew into Statira's ears.

**** *trans. To drive or transport by blowing.*

12. a. *trans.* To drive or carry (things) by means of a current of air; also *fig.* Const. *simply*, or with preps. or adverbs of direction, as *away, down, from, off, to*, etc.

a **1300** *Cursor M.* 22922 Þof his bodi al war brint, And blaun ouer al þe puder tint. *c* **1300** *K. Alis.* 5630 The wynde you may theder blawen, In lesse than in twenty dawen. **1382** WYCLIF *Mal.* i. 13 Ȝe han blowe it awey. *c* **1400** *Destr. Troy* 1982 [Þai] were blouen to þe brode se in a bir swithe. **1577** HANMER *Anc. Eccles. Hist.* (1619) 174 The heate of persecution was blowne against vs. **1593** SHAKS. *3 Hen. VI*, III. i. 84 Looke, as I blow this Feather from my Face, And as the Ayre blowes it to me againe. **1597** —— *2 Hen. IV*, v. iii. 90 *Fal.* What winde blew you hither, Pistoll? *Pist.* Not the ill winde which blowes none to good. **1697** DRYDEN *Virg. Georg.* III. 217 Winnow'd Chaff by Western Winds is blown. **1712** ADDISON *Spect.* No. 269 ¶7 The Wind.. blew down the End of one of his Barns. **1865** TYLOR *Early Hist. Man.* iii. 38 What children call 'blowing a kiss.' **1870** F. WILSON *Ch. Lindisf.* 68 The roof was blown off.

b. *intr.* (for *refl.*) To be driven or carried by the wind; to move before the wind. Same const. Also (*U.S. colloq.*), to move as if carried or impelled by the wind.

1842 TENNYSON *Goose* 51 Her cap blew off, her gown blew up. **1842** —— *Day-Dream* 141 The hedge broke in, the banner blew. **1844** *Knickerbocker* XXIII. 51, I was half awake.. when Bob came in, blew about the room for a while, and cried out. **1868** S. HALE *Lett.* (1919) 42 She is a picturesque looking creature... Why she blows up and down the Nile year in and year out,.. I dunno.

c. ***to blow over*** (formerly in perf. ***to be blown over***): (of storms or storm-clouds) to pass over a place without descending upon it; to pass away, come to an end; also *fig.* of misfortune, danger, etc. Also ***to blow off*** in same sense.

1617 J. FOSBROKE *Englands Warn.* (1633) 25 When the storm is blown over, they return to their old bias again. **1641** SMECTYMNUUS *Vind. Answ.* §13. 131 This cloud will soone blow over. **1692** SOUTH *12 Serm.* (1697) I. 564 Do they think that.. this dreadfull Sentence [shall] blow off without Execution? **1794** GOUV. MORRIS in Sparks *Life & Writ.* (1832) II. 399 The affair is blown over. **1850** ALISON *Hist. Europe* VIII. liv.§18 The danger had blown over.

d. ***to blow in***: to appear or turn up unexpectedly; to drop in. *colloq.* (orig. *U.S.*).

1895 F. REMINGTON *Pony Tracks* 104 We were all very busy when William 'blew in' with a great sputtering. **1904** G. H. LORIMER *Old Gorgon Graham* 47 Yesterday our old college friend, Clarence, blew in from Monte Carlo. **1913** R. BROOKE *Let.* 6 Sept. (1968) 505, I 'blew in' here yesterday, & found about nine letters from you. **1940** *War Illustr.* 16 Feb. ii/3 He just blew in out of the black-out and asked if he might use the telephone.

e. To go away, to leave hurriedly. *slang* (orig. *U.S.*).

[**1902** *B. Burgundy's Lett.* 50 Then we had another and blew the joint.] **1912** ADE *Knocking the Neighbors* 93 She.. tied up the Geranium and took the unfinished Tatting and Blew. **1936** J. CURTIS *Gilt Kid* 130 Sorry and all that, but I'm afraid I must blow now. **1937** E. LINKLATER *Juan in China* xxv. 315 'And what's happened to Rocco?'.. 'He's blown. He's gone up north.' **1961** J. I. M. STEWART *Man who won Pools* iii. 38 All I want is that all these people should blow.

f. To depart (esp. suddenly) from; to vacate or quit. *U.S. slang.*

1902 [see BLOW *v.*[1] 12e]. **1926** *Flynn's* 16 Jan. 640/1 Knock-'em Loose, the Bull, was on the razee an' I got trun out, so I blew de joint. **1949** in Wentworth & Flexner *Dict. Amer. Slang* (1960) 45/2 Alive, you're ready to blow town. **1971** 'R. MACDONALD' *Underground Man* iv. 28 I'm blowing this town tonight and taking the money with me. **1984** J. DAVIS *Garfield: Who's Talking?* 75 'Let's blow this joint, Garfield.' 'Hang on!'

13. *trans.* (*fig.*) To proclaim, publish, blaze, spread *abroad, about*, (*out* obs.), etc.

c **1205** LAY. 27021 Þæ king of Peytouwe, har[d] mon iblowen. *c* **1384** CHAUCER *H. Fame* 1139 And her fames wide yblowe. **1513** DOUGLAS *Æneis* (ad fin.) Direction 129 Thy fame is blaw, thy prowes and renoun Dyvulgat ar. **1541** *Act 33 Hen. VIII*, xxi, They shal not openly blow it abrode. **1603** KNOLLES *Hist. Turks* (1621) 429 These news.. being blown out of the campe into the citie. **1819** SCOTT *Ivanhoe* II. xi. 199 As soon as Richard's return is blown abroad. **1859** TENNYSON *Guinevere* 151 A rumour wildly blown about.

II. To act upon an object, by blowing air into, upon, or at it.

* *To blow a musical instrument.*

14. a. *trans.* To make (a wind-instrument) sound. (Formerly also with *up, out.*) ***to blow one's own trumpet***: (*fig.*) to sound one's own praises, to brag. **b.** To sound (a note or blast) *on* or *with* an instrument. **c.** To sound the signal of (an alarm, advance, retreat, etc.) *on* an instrument. **d.** Predicated of the instrument.

c **1000** *Ags. Gosp.* Matt. vi. 2 Ne blawe man byman beforan þe. *c* **1200** *Trin. Coll. Hom.* 115 Þe bemene drem þe þe engles blewen. *c* **1384** CHAUCER *H. Fame* 774 Whan a pipe is blowen sharpe The aire ys twyst with violence. *c* **1450** LYDG. *Mer. Missæ* 171 Pryd gothe beforen And schame comythe aftyr, and blawythe the horne. **1490** CAXTON *Eneydos* xlvi. 139 They.. blew vp their trompettes for to gyue a sharpe sawte. **1535** COVERDALE *1 Macc.* iii. 54 They blewe out the trompettes. **1611** BIBLE *Psalm* lxxxi. 3 Blow vp the trumpet in the new Moone. *Ibid. Hosea* v. 8 Blow yee the cornet in Gibeah. **1842** TENNYSON *Pal. of Art* 63 The belted hunter blew His wreathed bugle-horn.

b. *c* **1340** *Gaw. & Gr. Knt.* 1141 Blwe bygly in bugler þre bare mote. **1486** *Bk. St. Albans* E v b, Iij. motis shall ye blaw

booth lowde and shill. c **1600** *Rob. Hood* (Ritson) II. ix. 60 Let me have my beugle horn, And blow but blasts three. **1793** Burns *Soldier's Ret.* i, When wild war's deadly blast was blawn. **1843** Caroline Fox *Jrnls.* II. 12 Though he has blown so loud a blast.

c. c **1320** *Sir Tristr.* I. xlviii, Þe tokening when þai blewe. c **1420** *Anturs of Arthure* v. 10 The king blue a rechase. **1552** Huloet, Blowe the Retreate in battayle. **1561** Daus tr. *Bullinger on Apoc.* (1573) Pref. 5 The Deuill..bloweth the onset. **1634** *Malory's Arthur* (1816) I. 112 Then king Arthur blew the prize, and dight the hart there. **1621** Bp. Mountagu *Diatribæ* 398 Wee must goe blow the Seeke, and cast about againe. a **1641** —— *Acts & Mon.* (1642) 385 He tels they were Grecians born..where, when, upon what termes, you must, if you will, goe blow the seek. **1805** Southey *Madoc in Azt.* xviii, Ye blow the fall too soon!

d. **1593** Shaks. *2 Hen. VI*, v. ii. 43 Let the generall Trumpet blow his blast. **1667** Milton *P.L.* I. 540 Sonorous mettal blowing Martial sounds. **1761** Beattie *Ode to Peace* ii. 3 The hoarse alarms Her trump terrific blows.

e. To play jazz on (any instrument). Also *intr. colloq.* (orig. *U.S.*).

1949 L. Feather *Inside Be-Bop* II. 72 Nobody ever gave Diz or Bird a lesson in the art of blowing a jazz chorus. **1962** *John o' London's* 3 May 433/1 A blowin' session is a general term used to describe that form of jazz where men get together for the pleasure of making free and spontaneous music. **1962** *Radio Times* 17 May 43/3 A jazz musician never *plays* an instrument—he *blows* it, whether it be drums, piano, bass, or horn. Should he 'blow' with feeling, or great excitement ('like wild') he is either 'way out' or 'wailing'. **1966** *Crescendo* Sept. 27/1 The not-so-advanced suffered from insufficient outlet, and opportunity to blow and to improve. **1966** *Melody Maker* 15 Oct. 6 Dave Gelly is a school librarian who also blows jazz tenor with the New Jazz Orchestra. **1968** *Jazz Monthly* Apr. 23/2 His style was hard to fit into the standards of hard bop blowing sessions.

15. *intr.* **a.** Of a wind-instrument: To give forth a sound by being blown. Also with *up* (obs.).

a **1225** *Ancr. R.* 210 Þe englene bemen..þet schulen..biuoren þe grureful dome grisliche bloawen. a **1340** Hampole *Pr. Consc.* 4677 Þe beme þat blaw sal on domsday. c **1430** *Syr Tryam.* 1092 The kyng..herde a bewgulle blowe! **1535** Stewart *Cron. Scot.* II. 181 All the trumpettis blawand vp in tune. **1606** Shaks. *Tr. & Cr.* I. iii. 256 Trumpet, blow loud, Send thy Brasse voyce through all these lazie Tents. **1647** Fanshawe *Pastor Fido* (1676) 52 But list a little, doth not a Horn blow? **1875** O. W. Holmes *Old Camb.* Poems (1884) 306 Our trumpets needs must blow.

b. Of the blower: To sound a blast. ***to blow up***: to sound a whistle (as a signal).

c **1205** Lay. 8054 Þe king lette blawen & bonnien his ferden. **1375** Barbour *Bruce* III. 484 Quhen he hard sa blaw and cry. c **1400** *Destr. Troy* 1308 Þe kyng..henttes his horne and hastily blawes. **1523** Ld. Berners *Froiss.* 410 At the houre of ix. theyr mynstrels blewe vp on highe. **1530** Palsgr. 459/1 He bloweth in a trompet. **1602** *Return fr. Parnass.* II. v. (Arb.) 29 There is an excellent skill in blowing for the terriers. **1611** Bible *Judg.* vii. 18, I blow with a trumpet. a **1882** Longf. *M. Angelo*, Blow, ye bright angels, on your golden trumpets. **1889** Barrère & Leland *Dict. Slang* 135/2 To *blow up* (*i.e.*, to sound the whistle), is to call the men to work; used by foremen and ga[n]gers. **1954** J. B. G. Thomas *On Tour* vi. 65 The referee blew up to see who was actually lying on the ball.

c. Of the blast or note: To sound.

1599 Shaks. *Hen. V*, III. i. 5 When the blast of Warre blowes in our eares. **1852** Tennyson *Ode Wellington* iii, Let the mournful martial music blow.

** *To blow a fire, and the like.*

16. *trans.* To direct a current of air against (anything) so as to cool, warm, or dry it. Sometimes with complemental words expressing the effect of the action, as *to blow* (something) ***dry***.

1398 Trevisa *Barth. De P.R.* XV. cxxxviii. (1495) 539 Stones ben dygged and ben strongly blowen wyth fyre and torne to brasse and metall. **1566** Drant *Horace Sat.* ix. E iij, All the reaste might blow their nayles. **1592** Shaks. *Ven. & Ad.* 52 To fan and blow them dry again she seeks. a **1659** Cleveland *News fr. Newcastle* 120 And in embroidered Buck-skins blows his Nails. **1841** Marryat *Poacher* xxiv. The winter was cold..and he blew his fingers. **1850** Tennyson *In Mem.* lxxii, Blasts that blow the poplar white.

17. a. *esp.* To direct a current of air into (a fire), in order to make it burn more brightly. Also with *up*.

a **1300** *Havelok* 913 Y wile..The fir blowe, an ful wele maken. **1530** Palsgr. 458/2 Where be the bellowes, I praye the, blowe the fyre. **1611** Bible *Isa.* liv. 16 The smith that bloweth the coales in the fire. **1631** Gouge *God's Arrows* IV. xiii. 391 Yet were..the sparkes of that fire so blowne up, as dazled the eyes. **1677** Moxon *Mech. Exerc.* (1703) 7 The Phrase Smiths use..is, Blow up the Fire, or sometimes, Blow up the Coals. **1781** Hayley *Tri. Temper* I. 374 Chemic fires, that patient labour blows. **1830** tr. *Aristophanes' Acharn.* 29 The sparks, blowed with a favourable puff of the bellows, leap aloft.

b. fig. ***to blow the coals*** or ***the fire***: to stir up or promote strife; to fan the flame of discord.

1581 *Let.* in Tytler *Hist. Scot.* (1864) IV. 41 After every effort to 'blow the coals,' as he [Bowes] expressed it. **1670** Cotton *Espernon* II. VII. 309 The Chancellor..had also help'd to blow the fire. **1725** Ramsay *Gent. Sheph.* IV. i, To thole An ethercap like him to blaw the coal.

c. ***to blow out***: (*a*) *trans.* to extinguish (a flame) by a current of air; (*b*) *intr.* to be extinguished by a current of air.

1377 Langl. *P. Plow.* B. XVII. 212 As þow seest some tyme sodeynliche a torche, The blase þere-of yblowe out. **1596** Shaks. *Tam. Shr.* II. i. 136 Though little fire growes great with little winde, yet extreme gusts will blow out fire. **1617** P. Bayne in Spurgeon *Treas. David* Ps. cxix. 29 As candles new bloun out are soon bloun in again. **1665** Boyle *Occas. Refl.* (1675) 353 A Candle..inclos'd in a Lanthorn..is in less danger to be blown out. **1839** Dickens *Nich. Nick.* viii, Squeers..opened the shutters and blew the candle out. **1842** Tennyson *Goose* 49 The glass blew in, the fire blew out.

†**18.** *fig.* To excite, inflame, arouse, fan (feeling, passion, discord, etc.; *rarely*, a person *to* some feeling or action). Usually with *up. Obs.*

a **1225** *Ancr. R.* 256 Ȝif þe ueond bloweð bitweonen ou eni wreððe. **1654** G. Goddard in Burton *Diary* (1828) I. 93 These two interests..being constantly blown up by the enemies beyond the seas. **1677** Yarranton *Engl. Improv.* To Rdr., They..blow up a War betwixt England and Holland. **1720** Ozell *Vertot's Rom. Rep.* I. II. 118 Finding the People were blown up again to their former Animosity. **1776** Gibbon *Decl. & F.* I. vi. 127 Some trifling accident blew up their discontent into a furious mutiny.

19. a. In *Metallurgy*. ***to blow in***: (*trans.*) to put a blast furnace in operation. ***to blow out***: to put a blast furnace out of blast, by ceasing to charge it with fresh materials, and by continuing the blast, until all the contents have been smelted. Also said *intr.* of the furnace.

1864 *Daily Tel.* 26 Oct., It was a question..of allowing half the furnaces in the district to blow out. **1881** *Sat. Rev.* 1 May 565, 127 new furnaces have now been blown in. **1885** *Law Times* LXXIX. 188/2 A few workmen only were kept on until the furnaces could be blown out.

b. ***to blow on***: (*trans.*) to solder on by means of the blow-lamp.

1893 *Spons' Mechanics' Own Bk.* (ed. 4) 641 Lead the pipe away to the main supply, and 'blow' it on by means of a union suited to the case.

c. *Electr.* (*intr.*) Of a fuse: to melt under an abnormally high electric current; to fuse. Also with *out*. Also *trans.*, to cause (a fuse) to melt. Hence *fig.* (*colloq.*).

1902 in Webster Suppl. **1908** *Installation News* II. 86/1 A fuse has blown owing to a fault on the circuit. **1925** Wodehouse *Carry On, Jeeves!* viii. 188 However firmly and confidently he started off, somewhere around the third bar a fuse would blow out. **1949** S. J. Perelman *Listen to Mocking Bird* x. 120 Relax..or you'll blow a fuse. **1962** A. Battersby *Guide to Stock Control* ix. 81 If a fuse blows at home, the effect is immediate—the lights go out. **1969** *Woman's Own* 1 Nov. 15/1 This means plugging all three appliances into one 13 amp. socket. Are you likely to blow a fuse?

†**20.** *trans.* To cast (of molten metal). *Obs.*

a **1300** *Cursor M.* 6503 A goldin calf þar-of þai blu. **1483** Caxton *Gold. Leg.* 61/3 They haue made to them a Calf blowen and haue worshyped it.

*** *To clear* (*a pipe, etc.*) *by blowing.*

21. *trans.* To clear from mucus or other adherent matter by sending a current of air through; as, ***to blow the nose***, ***to blow eggs***, ***gas*** or ***water pipes***.

c **1532** Dewes in Palsgr. 906 To blowe the nose, *le moucher*. a **1613** Overbury *Char.* Wks. (1856) 129 He hath learnt to cough and spit, and blow his nose. **1795** Wolcott (P. Pindar) *Pindar*. Wks. 1812 IV. 209 He blows his mean pug-nose. **1828** W. Sewell *Oxf. Prize Ess.* 80 Socrates..had done what he rarely did, washed, put on a pair of shoes, and blown his nose. **1880** Wood in *Boy's Own Paper* 24 Apr., Do not worry yourself about blowing the eggs at the time. *Mod.* The plumber will try whether the obstruction can be removed by blowing the pipe.

**** *To inflate by blowing.*

22. a. *trans.* To swell (*up* or *out*) by sending a current of air into; to inflate, puff up.

c **1420** *Liber Cocorum* (1862) 26 Þe skyn þou opon..blaw hym with penne; þenne ryses þo skyn before. c **1425** *Seven Sag.* (P.) 1523 Hys body was al to-blaw. c **1550** Balfour *Practicks* 379 Challenge of Fleshouris..That they blaw the flesh, and cause it seme fat and fair. **1674** Ray *N.C. Wds.* 48 *Tharm*..guts prepared, cleansed and blown up for to receive puddings. **1770** A. Young *Tour N. Eng.* I. 65 Boys blowing bladders. **1875** Jowett *Plato* (ed. 2) III. 38 Because a man has blown himself out like a bladder.

b. To form or shape by means of inflation, as ***to blow bubbles***, ***glass***. Const. *simply*, or *up*, *out*.

1589 *Pappe w. Hatchet* D iij, Not like to glasse mettal, to be blowne in..fashion of euerie mans breath. **1660** Boyle *New Exp. Phys.-Mech.* ii. 40 Glass bubles, such as are wont to be blown at the flame of a Lamp. **1869** Tyndall *Light* ii. (1873) 66 Spending his days in blowing soap-bubbles. **1875** Ure *Dict. Arts* II. 659 The bulb of glass being put into the mould, and blown while very hot.

c. *Veterinary Path.* To cause (the stomach of an animal) to swell. (Cf. blowing *vbl. sb.*[1] 2 d.) Also *refl.*

1778 W. H. Marshall *Minutes Agric.* 16 Jan., sig. Z2 *verso*, Perhaps it was the core of a cabbage which blowed the cow. **1893** Dartnell & Goddard *Gloss. Wilts.* 14 Sheep and cattle 'blow' themselves, or get 'blowed', from overeating when turned out into very heavy grass or clover, the fermentation of which often kills them on the spot, their bodies becoming terribly inflated with wind.

23. † **a.** *fig.* To inflate or puff *up* (a person) with pride or vanity. Also *absol. Obs.*

1388 Wyclif *1 Cor.* iv. 19 The word of hem that ben blowun with pride. —— viii. 1 Kunnynge blowith, charite edifieth. c **1430** *Hymns Virg.* (1867) 115 Charite..Ne blowen is with pride. **1594** T. B. *La Primaud. Fr. Acad.* 147 Crœsus..he perceived to be blowen and puft up with pride. **1651** Hobbes *Leviath.* II. xxv. 135 When they blow one another with Orations. **1715** Burnet *Own Time* (1766) II. 78 Blown vp with popularity. **1718** Hickes & Nelson *J. Kettlewell* III. §110. 462 Never Capable of Blowing up his Mind with the least Vanity.

† **b.** *fig.* To inflate, enlarge, magnify; to make (a thing) appear greater or grander than it really is. Also, To invent a report of. Usually with *up. Obs.*

1536 Starkey *Let.* in *England* (1871) Life 37 Blowyng vp that authoryte wyth such arrogancy. **1666** Pepys *Diary* (1879) IV. 198 That we at Court do blow up a design of invading us. **1699** Bentley *Phal.* Pref. 6, I had no apprehension..that the Business could have been blown to this Hight. **1711** Addison *Spect.* No. 39 ¶6 A vulgar [sentiment] that is blown up with all the sound and energy of expression.

c. In *Photogr.*, ***to blow up***: to enlarge (a photograph, etc.). *colloq.*

1930 *Popular Sci.* Jan. 27/3 The little sixteen-millimeter film of such cameras is too small for projection..and when it is 'blown up' to standard size, the images often blur. **1959** *Punch* 21 Oct. 337/3, I blew up the two faces on an epidiascope. **1961** G. Millerson *Telev. Production* iii. 29 Reducing the lens angle 'blows up' a proportionately smaller area of the centre of the shot, to fill the whole screen.

***** *To explode by blowing.*

24. a. *trans.* To shatter, destroy, or otherwise act upon by means of explosion. Const. with various adverbs of direction, esp. *up*; also with such phrases as *to atoms* and *to bits*; in technical use often simply *to blow*, like 'to blast'.

1599 Sandys *Europæ Spec.* (1632) 76 They may..blow uppe the mines of their adversaries. **1602** Shaks. *Ham.* III. iv. 209, I will delve one yard below their mines And blow them at the moon. **1605** *Act 3 Jas. I*, iv, That more than barbarous and horrible attempt to have blowuen up with Gunpowder the Kinge Queene Prince Lordes and Commons. **1679–88** *Secr. Serv. Moneys Chas. & Jas.* (1851) 50 To Thomas Silver, Gunner, for a reward..in blowing up several buildings, and suppressing the late fire. **1709** Steele *Tatler* No. 80 ¶9 One of our Bombs fell into a Magazine..and blew it up. **1799** J. Robertson *Agric. Perth* 366 The small expence of blowing a few yards of rock. **1801** Wellington in Gurw. *Disp.* I. 361 After blowing open the gates. **1802** *Monthly Mag.* XIV. 31/1 [Robert Fulton] proposes to blow men of war to atoms. c **1880** Grant *Hist. India* I. lxxv. 399/1 The breaching guns..were blown in the touch-hole. **1936** *Discovery* July 229/1 The old..story that Fulton was the father of the steamboat, blown to bits in favour of the cruelly forgotten John Fitch.

b. ***to blow any one's brains out***: to shoot him through the head (with fire-arms). Cf. brain *sb.* 1 b.

1816 Scott *Old Mort.* xiv, If they attempt an escape, blow their brains out.

c. ***to blow from*** (***the mouth of***) ***a gun***, etc.: to execute summary justice on (a traitor, etc.) by binding him to the muzzle of a gun and firing the piece.

[**1776** *Monthly Rev.* LV. 276, I ordered..the artillery officers to prepare to blow them away.] **1857** *Blackw. Mag.* Sept. 389/1 That if there be 10,000 who refuse to use them, they are to be blown away from cannon. **1885** *Century Mag.* Jan. 411/2 That Black Idol..Was..Blown hellward from the cannon's mouth. **1893** W. S. Gilbert *Rosencrantz & Guild.* 11, The Bench of Bishops seize you..And blow you from a gun.

d. *Sporting.* To shatter (a game bird) in shooting; more explicitly ***to blow to pieces***. So (U.S. slang) ***to blow apart***.

1892 W. W. Greener *Breech-Loader* 275, I defy any one, after a day's shooting, to point out a single bird that has been 'blown'. My experience has proved beyond doubt that the choke-bore does not blow pheasants or any other game to pieces at 20 yards. **1920** Mulford *J. Nelson* iv. 45 'Squint,' said his captor in a hard, level voice, 'if you give me th' least excuse I'll blow you apart.'

e. To remove by the force of an explosion; with advbs. *away*, *back*, *off*.

1899 *Westm. Gaz.* 13 July 7/2 Cartridges in which the caps have been blown back when the rifle was discharged.

f. ***to blow the lid off*** (fig.): to expose (a state of affairs). orig. *U.S.*

1928 *Daily Tel.* 1 May 9/5 He 'blew the lid' off a notorious national condition of affairs.

g. ***to blow out***: (of a cock, valve, etc.) to be driven out by the expansive force of gas or vapour.

1909 in Webster.

h. To produce by blowing or shooting.

1871 Bret Harte *East & West: Poems* 18 Walker of Murphy's blew a hole through Peters For telling him that he lied. **1891** C. Roberts *Adrift Amer.* 153 If you talk to me like that I'll blow a hole through you.

i. ***to blow one's top*** (less commonly ***topper***): to lose control of oneself through anger, excitement, etc. (see also quot. 1938).

1928 R. J. Tasker *Grimhaven* iii. 28 Unless you say 'blew his top' or 'blow his topper'; then it means to go crazy. **1938** *New Yorker* 12 Mar. 47/2 If he smokes to excess, he blows his top; that is, he gets sick. **1941** *Amer. Speech* XVI. 163/2 *To blow your top*: vocal loss of temper. **1947** Steinbeck *Wayward Bus* 90 He blew his top and lost his job and came bellyaching to Loraine. **1958** *Economist* 1 Nov. 387/2 This was not just a newly retired officer blowing his top after years of enforced silence.

j. ***to blow*** (a person's) ***mind***, to induce hallucinatory experiences (in a person) by means of drugs, esp. LSD; hence *transf.*, to produce (in a person) a pleasurable (or shocking) sensation.

[**1966** *San Francisco Examiner & Chron.* 12 June 33/3 The Barry Goldberg Blues Band..does an LP called 'Blowin' My Mind'.] **1967** *San Francisco Examiner* 12 Sept. 26/3 On a hip acid (LSD) trip you can blow your mind sky-high. **1967** *San Francisco Chron.* 2 Oct. 49/3 Because when the Red Sox rallied to beat the Minneapolis Twins..Boston fans blew their minds. **1968** J. D. MacDonald *Pale Grey*

for Guilt (1969) xii. 152 They had some new short acid from the Coast that never gives you a down trip and blows your mind for an hour only. **1970** *Rolling Stone* 30 Jan. 1/2 Blue blazer, grey flannel pants, shirt and a beautiful scarf with a chunky Mexican turquoise/silver bracelet and ring which blew the white-shirted jury's minds.

25. fig. ***to blow up***: †**a.** to destroy, put an end to; to ruin. *Obs.*

1660 Sir H. Finch in Cobbett *Parl. Hist.* (1808) IV. 146 He could not think any thing more dangerous than the writing this Book..it blew up this parliament totally, and damned the Act of Oblivion. **1746** Chesterf. *Lett.* II. cciii. 270 A despatch with less than half these faults would blow you up for ever. **1791** J. Hampson *Mem. Wesley* I. 105 It was reported, that the college censors were going to blow up the Godly Club.

b. To scold, rail at. *colloq.*

1710 Duchess of Marlborough *Let.* in A. T. Thomson *Mem.* (1839) II. viii. 173 This plainly showed that the cabal had been blowing her up, but that she could not, however, contradict her own order. **1807** Geo. Colman *Let.* 10 Dec. in J. C. Young *Mem. C. M. Young* (1871) I. ii. 47 Now for this I will blow you up! **1827** Lytton *Pelham* lv. (L.) Lord Gravelton..was blowing up the waiters. **1882** B. Ramsay *Recoll. Mil. Serv.* I. iii. 55 He began to blow me up for not having provided quarters for his men and horses.

c. To go to pieces, give out, fail. Chiefly *U.S. slang.*

1934 in Webster. **1957** N. Frye *Anat. Criticism* iii. 178 An epilogue in Plautus informs us that the slave-actor who has blown up in his lines will now be flogged.

26. a. *intr.* To undergo explosion; to go to pieces by explosion; to erupt. Usually with *up*. †**b.** *transf.* To give way, collapse.

1694 *Lond. Gaz.* No. 2994/3 Two Magazines blew up. **1783** Page in *Phil. Trans.* LXXIV. 13 The work..from the weight upon one part only, might have blown. **1863** Kingsley *Water-bab.* vi. 242 The mountain had blown up like a barrel of gunpowder.

c. ***to blow out*** (see quot.). Said also of veins of metals; and *fig.*

1857 *Trans. Ill. Agric. Soc.* II. 364 Quantities of the public lands were entered to cover the supposed copper mines. It has all blown out. **1873** J. H. Beadle *Undevel. West* xviii. 333 The fluid turned aside to existing crevices, or 'blew out' through hollow chambers. **1881** Raymond *Mining Gloss.*, *Blow-out*..a shot or blast is said to *blow out* when it goes off like a gun and does not shatter the rock.

d. With *up*. To lose one's temper; to 'explode'. Cf. sense 24 i. *colloq.*

1871 'Mark Twain' *Lett.* (1917) I. x. 189 Redpath tells me to blow up. Here goes! **1935** A. J. Cronin *Stars look Down* III. iii. 497 'Good God, Harry,' Joe blew up dramatically... 'D'you mean to say it was as bad as that?' **1979** N. Mailer *Executioner's Song* (1980) II. x. 652 At this point, Gary blew up, 'Those sons of bitches, those sons of bitches,' he kept saying.

III. Senses of doubtful position.

27. a. *trans.* To expose, betray, inform upon. (Formerly sometimes ***blow up***.) Now *slang.* Cf. 30. Also ***to blow the gab*** or ***gaff*** (see gab *sb.*[2] 2, gaff *sb.*[2] 2).

1575 *Appius & Virg.* in Hazl. *Dodsley* IV. 136 Was all well agreed? did nobody blow ye? **1702** Vanbrugh *False Fr.* IV. ii, So! she's here!..Now we are blown up! **1742** Richardson *Pamela* IV. 275 Thou deservest to be blown up, and to have thy Plot spoiled. **1770** Langhorne *Plutarch* (1879) II. 1035/1 So near was the great secret being blown. *c* **1805** Mar. Edgeworth *Wks.* (Rtldg.) I. 185 He was afraid that the mulatto woman should recollect either his face or voice, and should blow him. **1821** Lockhart *Valerino* I. xi. 202 The time is not yet come to blow his private doings. **1833** Marryat *P. Simple* xliii, I wasn't going to blow the gaff [= let out the secret]. **1925** E. Wallace *Mind of Mr. J. G. Reeder* v. 165 This officer 'blew' the raid to Tommy. **1958** G. Greene *Our Man in Havana* II. 99 We can't risk blowing him now. *Ibid.* III. i. 111 They're anxious you should take no risk of being blown. It doesn't matter so much if I'm blown. **1961** 'B. Wells' *Day Earth caught Fire* vii. 114 You can't go on blaming him for blowing the story you gave him.

b. *absol.* To tell tales, 'peach'. (See also 30.)

1848 E. Judson *Mysteries N.Y.* II. 48 To 'blow' would be to tell of some of my stealing. *a* **1859** L. Hunt *Country Lodging* in *Casquet Lit.* (1877) I. 42/1 D——n me, if I don't blow..I'll tell Tom Neville. **1928** E. Wallace *Gunner* xxxiii. 281 If..Mr. Morell..has blown— has told the story of Taffany's, every boat will be watched. **1967** C. Drummond *Death at Furlong Post* xii. 154 If Ada blows she gets life, they don't like Crown Evidence these days.

28. Said of flies and other insects: To deposit their eggs. [This sense is apparently connected with old notions of natural history. It has nothing to do with the notion of blowing or inflating meat.]

†**a.** *trans.* (with 'blotes' or eggs as obj.) *Obs.*

1607 Topsell *Four-f. Beasts* 49 Worms..which are not bigger then such as flyes blow in rotten flesh. **1657** S. Purchas *Pol. Flying-Ins.* 44 They [bees] then blow in it [a cell of the comb] a thing less then, or as little as a flye-blote.

†**b.** *absol.* or *intr. Obs.*

1604 Shaks. *Oth.* iv. ii. 67 As Sommer Flyes..that quicken euen with blowing. **1657** S. Purchas *Pol. Flying-Ins.* 44 The matter in which they [bees] blow or breed is something that they gather of the flowers. **1692** T. Wagstaffe *Vind. Chas. I*, xii. 83 It is the Nature of Flies to be ever buzzing, and blowing upon any thing that is raw. **1771** Gullet in *Phil. Trans.* LXII. 350 This blows in the ear of the corn, and produces a worm.

c. *trans.* To deposit eggs on or in (a place); to fill with eggs. Cf. fly-blown.

1588 Shaks. *L.L.L.* v. ii. 409 These summer flies Haue blowne me full of maggot ostentation. **1610** —— *Temp.* III. i. 63 To suffer The flesh-flie blow my mouth. **1650** B. *Discollim.* 50 When Eagles are deplum'd, the flyes will blow their breech.

†**d.** with *up*. *rare. Obs.*

1650 Fuller *Pisgah* II. viii. 172 No wonder if Worms quickly devoured him [Herod], whom those flesh-flies had blown up before. [A word-play on sense 23.]

29. Used in imprecations: To curse, 'confound', 'hang'. *vulgar.* (The pa. pple. is *blowed*.) Also with the implication of ignoring or disregarding; ***blow!***: used *absol.* as an exclamation of anger or vexation; ***blow me tight!*** (cf. sense 22).

1781 G. Parker *View of Society* I. 48 Blow me up (says he) if I have had a fellow with such *rum toggys* cross my company these many a day. **1819** T. Moore *Tom Crib's Mem. to Congress* 46 Says Bill, 'there's nothing like a Bull: And *blow me tight*.' **1821** P. Egan *Life in London* iii. 225 Blow me tight if ever I saw such a thing in my life before. **1827** J. Wight *More Mornings at Bow St.* 55 *Blow me* if I do! **1835** Marryat *Olla Podr.*, If I do, blow me! **1836** Dickens *Sk. Boz.* in *Morning Chron.* 11 Oct. 3/4 The said Thomas Sludberry repeated the aforesaid expression, 'You be blowed!' **1859** —— *T. Two Cities* II. i. 36 One blowed thing and another. **1865** —— *Mut. Fr.* II. iv. xv. 287 Blowed if I shouldn't have left out lakes. **1871** *Blackw. Mag.* May 551/2 Oh, blow it, governor. **1881** *Daily Tel.* 28 Jan., 'Isn't it rather risky?' I asked. 'Blow risks,' he answered. **1882** *Three in Norway* xxiv. 207 Retributive justice be blowed! **1922** F. Hamilton *P.J., Secret Service Boy* ii. 70 I'm absolutely blowed if I know what to do. *Ibid.* 84 Oh, blow! And I go back to school in ten days. **1933** P. MacDonald *Myst. Dead Police* i. 6 'Blow me *tight*!' said Sergeant Guilfoil. For things were certainly happening in Farnley. **1957** I. Cross *God Boy* (1958) xv. 124 Then blow me if Dr Hutchinson..didn't come padding round the post office corner. **1963** *Listener* 28 Mar. 540/1 It is no longer proper to use as our second national motto in education 'Blow you, Jack, our top five per cent. are absolutely splendid'.

30. to blow up(on) (a person or thing) has been used in various senses (see a); among others: To take the bloom off; to make stale or hackneyed; to bring into discredit, defame; also, to tell tales of, inform upon, expose (cf. 27). With indirect passive, ***to be blown upon*** (see b). In this latter sense the simple *blow* also occurs *trans.* (see c).

a. ? *a* **1400** *Morte Arth.* (1819) 47 A monge hem all be fore the dese He bloweth oute vppon the quene, To haue hys ryght. **1470–85** (ed. 1634) Malory *Arthur* (1816) II. 438 Then Sir Gawaine made many men to blow upon Sir Launcelot, and all at once they called him 'False recreant Knight!' **1808** Jamieson *Dict.* s.v. *Blaw*, To Blaw out on one, formally to denounce one as a rebel by three blasts of the king's horn at the market-cross of the head-borough of the shire; an old forensic phrase. **1844** *Spirit of Times* 20 Jan. 557/2 Go! Get off; I'll not blow on you. **1876** J. Weiss *Wit, Hum. Shaks.* ii. 51 Why..does she not blow upon the doctor? **1877** J. Greenwood *Dick Temple* II. i. 10 She ain't got nobody but me to keep a secret for her, and I've been and blowed on her. **1916** E. Wallace *Clue Twisted Candle* (1918) xvii. 197, I'm not going to blow on it, if it's going to get me into trouble, but if you'll promise me that it won't, I'll tell you the whole story. **1960** W. Haggard *Closed Circuit* viii. 94 There could be only one explanation: Menderez had blown on him.

b. *c* **1645** Howell *Lett.* I. §6 (1726) 277, I thank you for the good opinion you..have of my fancy of Trees: It is a maiden one, and not blown upon by any one yet. **1678** Norris *Misc.* (1699) 325, I wave these, and fix upon another account less Blown upon. **1679** Penn *Addr. Prot.* App. 246 A Man of Wisdom, Sobriety and Ability..if a Dissenter, must be blown upon for a Phanatick. **1708** Mrs. Centlivre *Busie Body* II. ii. (1749) 36 If I can but keep my Daughter from being blown upon 'till Signior Babinetto arrives. **1711** Addison *Spect.* No. 105 ¶5 He will..whisper an Intrigue that is not yet blown upon by common Fame. **1712** *Ibid.* No. 464 ¶1, I am wonderfully pleased when I meet with any Passage in an old Greek or Latin Author, that is not blown upon. **1749** Fielding *Tom Jones* x. ii, The reputation of her house, which was never blown upon before, was utterly destroyed. **1845** Ford *Handbk. Spain* i. 7 If once blown upon, no one would employ them. **1848** Macaulay *Hist. Eng.* II. 48 The credit of the false witnesses had been blown upon. **1877** A. M. Sullivan *New Ireland* xxiii. 276 They had got word that the plot was 'blown upon' by some traitor.

c. **1864** Dk. Manchester *Crt. & Soc. Eliz.* to *Anne* I. 80 Puebla's character had been somewhat blown.

†**31.** ***to blow a bowl*** or ***in a bowl***: to tipple, to be a habitual drunkard. *Obs.*

c **1500** *Blowbol's Test.* in Halliw. *Nugæ P.* 1 Many a throw Of good ale bolys that he had i-blowe. **1515** Barclay *Eglog.* i. (1570) A iv/3 To blowe in a bowle, and for to pill a platter.

32. To treat (someone) *to*. *U.S. slang.* Also *refl.* (See also quot. 1889.)

1889 Barrère & Leland *Dict. Slang* I. 134/1 *To blow off*, to treat to drinks. **1896** Ade *Artie* xvii. 155 'I noticed that you'd been talking bicycle lately, but I didn't know you were going to get one.' '..I'm goin' to do the sucker act and blow myself.' **1903** C. L. Burnham *Jewel* 97 Father took me to the horse show... He told mother he was going to blow me to it. **1949** A. Miller *Death of Salesman* 11, Tell Dad, we want to blow him to a good meal.

33. *coarse slang.* To fellate. Also *intr.*, to practise fellatio.

1933 *Brevities* 12 Oct. 1 (*heading*) Sexy sailors blow! Bawdy boys run riot on high seas as fags stir emotions of rollicking rovers. **1941** G. Legman in G. W. Henry *Sex Variants* II. 1158 *Blow*, to fellate or cunnilingue, the object being the person, and not the genital organ. **1959** W. Burroughs *Naked Lunch* 86 'Darling, I want to blow you,' she whispers. **1968** J. Updike *Couples* ii. 148 The bitch won't blow unless she's really looped. What did the Bard say? To fuck is human; to be blown, divine. **1969** P. Roth *Portnoy's Complaint* 191 'I want you to come in my mouth,' and so she blew me. **1978** M. Puzo *Fools Die* vi. 82 There was a whole regiment of floozy Nightingales passing through his hotel room, washing him, feeding him and, as they tucked him in, blowing him to make sure he was relaxed enough to get a good night's sleep.

☛*Phrase-key.* *b* abroad, about 13; *b* away 12, 24 e; *b* back 24 e; *b* bellows 7; *b* brains out 24 b; *b* bowl 31; *b* bubbles 22 b; *b* coals 17; *b* down 12; *b* eggs 21; *b* fire 17; *b* flies' eggs 28; *b* from 12; *b* from (mouth of) guns 24 c; *b* gab, gaff 27; *b* glass 22 b; *b* great guns 1; *b* high, low 1 b; *b* hot and cold 2 b; *b* in 9 d, 12 d, (furnace) 19; *b* into 9; *b* into one's ear 11; *b* lid off 24 f; *b* me tight 29; *b* mind 24 j; *b* nose 21; *b* off 10, 12, 12 c, 24 e; *b* on 19 b, 30; *b* one's top(per) 24 i; *b* out 4, 11, 13, 14, 17 c (= extinguish), 19 (furnace), 19 c, 22 (= inflate), 24 g, 26 c; *b* over 12 c; *b* short 4 b; *b* through 9; *b* to 12, 32; *b* to atoms 24; *b* to bits 24 a; *b* to pieces 24 d; *b* trumpet 14; *b* up 1, 14, 15, 18, 22–3 (= inflate, enlarge), 24–6 (= explode), 25 b (= scold), 27, 28 d; *b* upon 9, 30.

blow- in *combinations* as *blow-tube*, *blow-bowl*, *blow-coal*, etc.: see after blow *sb.*[2]

blow (bləʊ), *v.*[2] Pa. t. **blew** (bl(j)uː). Pa. pple. **blown** (bləʊn). Forms: 1 **blówan**, 2–5 **blowen**, 3–7 **blowe**, 6– **blow**. *Pa. t.* 1 **bléow**, 3 **bleou**, (**bloude**). *Pa. pple.* 1 (**ȝe**)**blówen**, (3–4 **blowe**), 6– **blown**. [OE. *blówan*, 3rd sing. *bléwþ*, pa. t. *bléow*, pa. pple. *blówen*, represented in the other W.Ger. langs. by weak vbs., OS. *blôjan* (MDu. and Du. *bloeien*), OHG. *bluojan* (MHG. *blüejen*, *blüen*, mod.G. *blühen*), pointing to an OTeut. str. vb. **blôjan*, from root *blō̆-*, cogn. with L. *flōs*, *flōrem* flower, *flōrēre* to bloom; cf. bloom, blossom, blade, blede. Already in OE. the pa. t. coincided with that of *bláwan*, blow *v.*[1], and in ME. the two verbs ran together in form.]

1. *intr.* To burst into flower; to blossom, bloom.

c **1000** *Sax. Leechd.* I. 98 Ðonne heo grewð & blewð. *c* **1200** *Trin. Coll. Hom.* 177 Trewes growen, blouwen and bereð blostmen. *c* **1205** Lay. 2013 Bi-heold he þene wode hu he bleou [**1250** bloude]. *c* **1400** in *Househ. Ord.* (1790) 472 April, May, and June, while that trees blowen. **1578** Lyte *Dodoens* v. xxi. 578. **1590** Shaks. *Mids. N.* II. i. 249, I know a banke where the wilde time blows. **1667** Milton *P.L.* vii. 319 These scarce blown, Forth flourish't thick the clustring Vine. **1697** Dryden *Virg. Past.* III. 83 The Blossoms blow; the Birds on Bushes sing. **1855** Tennyson *Daisy* 16 Here and there..A milky-bell'd amaryllis blew.

b. *transf.*

c **1430** *Hymns Virg.* (1867) 69 Now seiþ he, he loued me to longe, For myn heer bigynneþ to blowe.

2. *fig.* To flourish, bloom; to attain perfection.

1610 Guillim *Heraldry* III. ix. 110 Our flowry youth..It growes, it blowes, it spreds—it sheds her beauty in one day. **1675** Dryden *Aurengz.* Prol. 33 Wit in Northern Climates will not blow. **1830** Tennyson *Talk. Oak* 76 In these latter springs I saw Your own Olivia blow.

3. *trans.* To cause to blossom. *lit.* or *fig.* ? *Obs.*

a **1645** Habington *Elegie* viii, The enamour'd Spring by kissing blows Soft blushes on her [the rose's] cheek. **1745–6** Mrs. Delany *Autobiog.* (1861) II. 417 Houses built up for blowing auriculas. **1801** Mar. Edgeworth *Early Less.*, *Rosamond* (1827) 158 Directions for blowing bulbous-rooted flowers.

blow (bləʊ), *sb.*[1] Forms: 5 *Sc.* and *north.* **blaw**, 6 **bloe**, 6–7 **blowe**, 6– **blow**. [First found in 15th c., the earliest instances being Sc. and north. Eng. with form *blaw*. Origin doubtful.

(The etymology of *blow* has been naturally sought in the stem of the OTeut. vb. **bleuwan*, Goth. *bliggwan* to beat (which is not related to L. *flīgĕre*), in OHG. *bliuwan*, MHG. *bliuwen*, mod.G. *bläuen* 'to beetle, batter, beat, drub' (whence *bläuel* a beetle), MDu. and mod.Du. *blouwen* 'to beat, thrash, drub', now esp. 'to brake or swingle flax or hemp' (whence *blouwel* a brake for flax). The OE. cognate would have been **bléowan*, but of this no trace is found, and it is not easy on any theory to understand its giving rise to a substantive in the 15th c. without ever appearing itself. It is still less likely that an English substantive could be formed from the Du. *blouwen* or its Ger. equivalent, when there is no such substantive in these langs. ('Du. *blowe*' in J. is a figment.)

Another suggestion which suits the form and accounts also for the early Sc. and north. English variant *blaw*, is that this is the same word as blow *sb.*[2], or at least, like it, derived from blow *v.*[1] The difficulty is, that, as to the sense, early uses of the word do not indicate any such origin, while historically, blow *sb.*[2] (in its own undoubted senses) is of later appearance. The analogy of Fr. *soufflet*, also, in which a word for 'a blow with the flat of the hand' arises out of the vb. *souffler* 'to blow wind', though striking at first sight, proves on examination of the history of *soufflet* to be merely superficial.)]

1. a. A stroke, esp. a firm stroke; a violent application of the fist or of any instrument to an object.

c **1460** *Towneley Myst.* 195 Bot I gif hym a blaw my hart wille brist. *c* **1470** Henry *Wallace* I. 348 He gat a blaw, thocht he war lad or lord, That proferryt hym ony lychtlynes. **1509** Hawes *Past. Pleas.* xxxiii. xviii, Upon the side I gave him such a blow That I right nere did him overthrow. **1555** *Fardle Facions* II. xii. 279 The Bishoppe [in confirming]..giueth hym a blowe on the lefte chieke. **1590** Shaks. *Com. Err.* III. i. 56 Well strooke, there was blow for blow. **1611** Bible *Ps.* xxxix. 10, I am consumed by the blowe of thine hand. **1643** Burroughes *Exp. Hosea* iv. (1652) 66 It is not the last blow of the axe that fells the oak. **1754** Richardson *Grandison* IV. iv. 28 Before hard blows are struck, that will leave marks. **1860** Tyndall *Glac.* II. §17. 317 A loud dull sound, like that produced by a heavy blow. **1866** Kingsley *Herew.* xiii. 178 He felled him with one blow.

b. *fig.* Cf. 'stroke'.

1605 Shaks. *Lear* IV. vi. 225 A most poore man, made tame to Fortunes blows. **1609** *Ev. Wom. in Hum.* II. i. in Bullen *O. Pl.* IV, Yᵉ are a wag, Flavia, but talk and you must needes have a parting blowe. **1791** Boswell *Johnson* 97 The hard blows which the great man had given me. **1883** Froude

Short Stud. IV. I. ix. 100 A direct blow at the authority of the young king.

c. A stroke of the shears in shearing sheep. *Austral.* and *N.Z.*

1878 'IRONBARK' *Southerly Busters* 180 If coves would let me 'open out', And take a bigger 'blow'. **1890** *Melbourne Argus* 20 Sept. 13/7 The shearers must make their clip clean and thorough. If..a 'second blow' is needed, the fleece is hacked. **1956** G. BOWEN *Wool Away!* (ed. 2) iii. 23 The first blow starts at the top of the brisket. **1959** H. P. TRITTON *Time means Tucker* 26/1 Bill would shear to the whipping side, then pass the sheep to me, and..seven or eight blows would complete the job.

d. An outcrop of mineral. *Austral.* and *N.Z.*

1879 W. J. BARRY *Up & Down* xxii. 224, I then came to the conclusion that the lode was not a permanent one, but only what is called a 'blow' of quartz. **1922** *Chambers's Jrnl.* Nov. 704/1 Silver-lead (galena) outcrops standing out in great 'blows'. **1934** *Geogr. Jrnl.* LXXXIV. 504 Quartz blows and ironstone reefs were noted. **1965** G. J. WILLIAMS *Econ. Geol. N.Z.* iii. 29/2 A large blow of quartz was found on the surface of the Rainy Creek property in 1872.

2. *fig.* A severe disaster, a sudden and painful calamity; especially as sustained or felt by the sufferer, a sudden and severe shock.

1678 N. WANLEY *Wonders* v. i. §94. 467/2 The Hungarians ..received from the Turks that terrible blow. **1841** MACAULAY in Trevelyan *Life* II. ix. 130 His death will be a terrible blow. **1847** L. HUNT *Jar Honey* (1848) Pref. 10 They have never recovered the blow given them by the invidious heaviness of the Puritans.

3. 'An act of hostility.' (J.) Usually in pl. *blows* = 'combat, fighting, war', in the phrases ***to be at blows, come*** (or ***go***), ***fall to blows, exchange blows***.

1593 SHAKS. *2 Hen. VI*, II. iii. 81 Come, leaue your drinking, and fall to blowes. **1606** —— *Ant. & Cl.* II. vi. 44 When Caesar and your Brother were at blowes. **1647** W. BROWNE *Polex.* II. 226 Wee..wished for nothing else then to be at blowes with our enemies. **1651** HOBBES *Leviath.* I. v. 19 Their controversie must either come to blowes, or be undecided. **1848** MACAULAY *Hist. Eng.* I. 322 Too young to have themselves exchanged blows with the cuirassiers of the Parliament. *Ibid.* 556 There was reason to fear that the two parties would come to blows.

4. Phrases.

a. ***at a blow***, or ***at one blow***: by one stroke; *fig.* by one vigorous act; suddenly; at once.

1593 SHAKS. *3 Hen. VI*, v. i. 50, I had rather chop this Hand off at a blow. **1697** DRYDEN *Virg. Georg.* III. 365 To redeem his Honour at a Blow. **1837** DICKENS *Pickw.* xi, What it is at one blow to be deserted by a lovely and fascinating creature. **1859** TENNYSON *Elaine* 42 Each had slain his brother at a blow.

b. fig. ***to strike a blow***: to make an attack, take vigorous action. So, ***to strike the first blow***. ***without striking a blow***: without a struggle.

1790 BEATSON *Nav. & Mil. Mem.* II. 211 A good blow might be struck here. **1812** BYRON *Ch. Har.* II. lxxvi, Who would be free, themselves must strike the blow. **1848** MACAULAY *Hist. Eng.* I. 261 But neither side dared to strike the first blow. *Ibid.* 542 Deputies, without whose consent no great blow could be struck.

5. *Comb.*, as *blow-giver, -reach, -striking*. **blow-by-blow** (orig. *U.S.*), used *attrib.* to designate a detailed account of the sequence of punches given in a boxing match; freq. *transf.*

1548 UDALL, etc. *Erasm. Par. John* xviii. (R.) Our Lord Jesus might..haue letted this blowgeuer. **1586** T. B. *La Primaud. Fr. Acad.* 54 To submit themselves willinglie.. without blowe-striking. **1871** *Member for Paris* II. 17 [He] was within blow-reach of them. **1933** *Amer. Speech* Oct. 34/2 Radio announcers..describe the struggle as they see it, give the blow by blow account of its progress. **1939** *Time* 23 Jan. 30/3 Joe Louis v. John Henry Lewis... Blow-by-blow report by Clem McCarthy and Edwin C. Hill. **1948** H. LAWRENCE *Death of Doll* ix. 225 Maybe we'd better get together. Blow by blow description. **1962** *Times* 7 June 17/3 Blow-by-blow descriptions of Jonson-Jones masques.

¶ This may have some association with BLOW *sb.*[2]

1596 SHAKS. *Tam. Shr.* I. ii. 209 A womans tongue, That giues not halfe so great a blow to heare, As wil a Chessenut in a Farmers fire.

blow (bləʊ), *sb.*[2] [f. BLOW *v.*[1] Not certainly found bef. 17th c., which separates it from BLOW *sb.*[1]]

1. A blowing; a blast.

a. of the wind. Also, a breath of fresh air; a 'breather' (sense 3); ***to get a blow***: to expose oneself to the action of a fresh breeze (*colloq.*).

1660 STANLEY *Hist. Philos.* (1701) 8/1 The Etesian (yearly) winds..beginning the blow from the North. **1777** W. DALRYMPLE *Trav. Sp. & Port.* xliv, Rain or blow. **1840** R. DANA *Bef. Mast* iv. 8 The first blow that I had seen which could really be called a gale. **1849** *Theatrical Programme* 9 July 48/2 A 'blow' upon the river. **1856** DICKENS *Out of Season* in *Househ. Words* 28 June 554/1, I really ought to go out and take a walk in the wind... I was under a moral obligation to have a blow. **1857** R. TOMES *Amer. in Japan* i. 31 The 'Mississippi', in doubling the Cape of Good Hope.. escaped any very heavy blow, altho' hardly a week passes without a gale from some quarter. *a* **1887** *Mod. colloq.* Went down to Gravesend by the steamer to get a blow. **1888** C. M. YONGE *Beechcroft at Rockstone* II. xv. 40 'You must be tired out!'..'Oh no, Aunt Ada! Quite freshened by that blow on the common.' **1936** R. LEHMANN *Weather in Streets* IV. i. 386 Been for a blow?.. It freshens you up.

b. of whales.

a **1851** F. COOPER in *Casquet Lit.* (1877) V. 211/1 There is the blow of a whale. **1853** KANE *Grinnell Exp.* xxxix. (1856) 359 It had more of voice mingled with its sibilant 'blow' than I had ever heard.

c. of a wind-instrument or other musical instrument; a musical session. Also, of the nose. Cf. BLOW *v.*[1] 14 e.

1723 STEELE *Consc. Lovers* I. i. (1735) 16 You went to dinner..when the great Blow was given in the Hall at the Pantry-door. **1835** MARRYAT *Jac. Faithf.* iii, The astonishing effects of a blow from Domine Dobiensis's sonorous and peace-restoring nose. **1849** DICKENS *Dav. Copp.* v, 'Have a blow at it [a flute]', said the old woman coaxingly. **1962** *Sunday Times* (Suppl.) 10 June 3 He is now rarely heard having a relaxed blow in the clubs. **1965** G. MELLY *Owning-Up* vii. 75 We played three one-hour sessions and relied on musicians who wanted a blow to fill in the gaps. **1966** *Crescendo* Oct. 31/3 Ernie Garside scoured the city for a set of vibes, but he was unlucky! So Gary didn't get to have a 'blow'. **1968** *Ibid.* May 31/1 He told me that he was drastically curtailing the activities of his big band. The musicians might come together now and again for a blow, but to all intents and purposes it's finished as a regular aggregation.

†**d.** of gunpowder, or other explosive. *Obs.*

1694 *Lond. Gaz.* No. 2994/3 Hearing some guns go off first, and presently after several Blows. **1720** *Stow's Surv.* (ed. Strype 1754) I. II. iii. 375/2 This Church was..ruined by a lamentable Blow of 27 Barrels of Gunpowder.

2. *fig.* **a.** A boast; vaunting, boastfulness.

1684 *Roxb. Bal.* (1885) V. 464 They followed their blows, In Musick and Gaming, and acting of Shows. **1883** *19th Cent.* Nov. 848 Colonial blow, bounce, and impudence.

b. A boaster, a blow-hard. *U.S. dial.*

1904 J. C. LINCOLN *Cap'n Eri* xviii. 329 'Cap'n Jonadab Wixon used to swear that his grandfather told him 'bout a gale that blew the hair all off a dog, and then the wind changed of a sudden, and blew it all on again.' Elsie laughed. 'That must have been a blow,' she said. 'Yes. Cap'n Jonadab's something of a blow himself, so he ought to be a good jedge.' **1915** *Dialect Notes* IV. 181 That feller is nothing but a big blow. **1968** E. KELLNER *Devil & Aunt Serena* 105 Willadene, whose father was the biggest Blow in Henry County.

3. The oviposition of flesh-flies or other insects.

Cf. FLY-BLOW *sb.*

1611 CHAPMAN *Iliad* XIX. 24, I much fear lest with the blows of flies His brass-inflicted wounds are fil'd. **1875** HOUGHTON *Sk. Brit. Insects* 114 By depositing its eggs (fly-blows).

4. *Metallurgy.* 'A single *heat* or operation of the Bessemer converter' (Raymond *Mining Gloss.* 1881); also the quantity of metal dealt with at a single operation.

1883 *Daily News* 20 Sept. 2/1 Instead of blows of three or four tons, we have now to deal with twelve to fifteen tons.

blow- in *comb.*

For convenience of reference all the combinations are treated here, although those under 3, certainly, and 2, apparently, are formed from the verb.

1. With adverbs, denoting actions; as **blow-away** *a.* (cf. BLOW *v.*[1] 12 a), susceptible to the influence of a current of air, hence fragile; also *fig.*; **blow-back**, the act or process of blowing back; spec. (*a*) the back-pressure in a boiler or internal-combustion engine; (*b*) in fire-arms (cf. BLOW *v.*[1] 24 e); **blow-by** (see quot. 1959); also *attrib.*; **blow-down**, a gust of wind and smoke down a chimney; **blow-off**, (*a*) the action or operation of ridding a boiler of water or sediment by the force of steam; also *attrib.*; (*b*) *fig.* an outburst; **blow-over** *Glass-making*, the surplus glass forced out of the mould in blowing (Knight *Dict. Mech.*, *a*1877); **blow-through**, (*a*) the process of blowing steam through the cylinder of an engine, etc., to clear it of air; used *attrib.* in ***blow-through cock, valve***; (*b*) defining a jet or lamp for the blowing of oxygen through a flame against lime or magnesium to produce a brilliant light; **blow-up**, an explosion; *fig.* a disturbance, a quarrel. See also BLOW-OUT, BLOW-UP.

1858 *Jrnl. R. Agric. Soc.* XIX. 257 It is represented as being at that time a *blow-away sand. **1908** *Daily Chron.* 22 June 3/4 The Commissioners got little of the right sort of evidence.., and were dealing..with 'a mass of blow-away stuff'. **1938** F. SCOTT FITZGERALD *Let.* 18 Nov. (1964) 42 You unveiled the story of the blow-away pink slip. **1958** *Vogue* July 86 The blowaway prettiness of an Empire dress. **1883** J. D. FULTON *Sam Hobart* 224 The flames originated from the '**blow back*' on the engine. **1899** *Westm. Gaz.* 13 July 7/2 Foul barrels were the cause of ineffectual shots and 'blow-back' caps. **1905** *Kynoch Jrnl.* Jan.–Mar. 10 The cracks..will at once develop into fissures when the cartridge is fired, cause 'blow-backs', and seriously reduce the velocity of the projectile. **1929** *Evening News* 18 Nov. 14/3 He received his injuries as the result of a blow-back in one of the boilers when pulverised fuel was being lit. **1940** *Chambers's Techn. Dict.* 98/2 *Blow back*, the return, at low speeds, of some of the induced mixture through the carburettor of a petrol-engine; due to late closing of the inlet valve during compression. **1933** STREETER & LICHTY *Internal Combustion Engines* (ed. 4) xv. 432 The oil film is blown out by the high-pressure gases, and *blow-by occurs. **1959** *N.Y. Times* 6 Dec. 67/5 The gasoline vapors, called 'blowby' by automotive engineers, are hydrocarbons forced between the cylinder wall and the piston during the compression stroke. **1961** *Times* 19 Dec. 2/6 A method of making the engine consume its own 'blowby' vapours. **1884** *Health Exhib. Catal.* 52/1 Chimney Can for curing a *blow-down. **1842** *Civil Engin. & Archit. Jrnl.* V. 367/2 *Blow-off cocks. **1859** RANKINE *Steam Engine* §305, The blow-off apparatus consists, in fresh-water boilers, simply of a large cock at the bottom of the boiler. *a* **1877** KNIGHT *Dict. Mech.*, Blow-off Pipe. **1898** S. M. FERGUSSON in '*House' on Sport* I. 174 A blow-off in this wise [*i.e.* swearing at golf] does one good now and then. **1899** *Daily News* 9 Mar. 5/3 The blow-off pipes into the sea being broken, the chief engineer..had to let the water run out of the boilers into the hold. **1934** J. M. CAIN *Postman always rings Twice* xii. 93 What we had the big blow-off over was the beer licence. *a* **1877** KNIGHT *Dict. Mech.*, *Blow-through valve. **1892** *Photogr. Ann.* II. 231 Blow-through jet. **1906** *Westm. Gaz.* 24 Nov. 14/2 A blow-through lamp.

2. With sb., qualified by *blow-* (the verb-stem) in sense of 'blowing', or 'that blows' or 'is blown', as **blow-ball**, the globular seeding head of the dandelion and allied plants; also *fig.*; **blow-cock**, a cock or tap by which to blow off steam; **blow-fish**, a popular name for any of several fishes which inflate their bodies when stimulated by fear, etc.; **blow-george** (see quot.); **blow-gun** = BLOW-PIPE 2; **blow job** *slang* (orig. *U.S.*), (the act of performing) cunnilingus or fellatio; cf. BLOW *v.*[1] 33; **blow-lamp**, a lamp designed to give a condensed hot flame, directed by air-pressure or gas on the spot to be heated; **blow-line** (*Angling*), a fishing line of the lightest floss silk, used with the living fly, so web-like as to allow the wind to blow it out over the stream; **blow-post**, a system of conveying letters and parcels by pneumatic tubes; **blow-room** = *blowing-room*: see BLOWING *vbl. sb.*[1] 5; **blow-torch** = *blow-lamp*; **blow-tube** = BLOW-PIPE 2; also a tube used in glass-blowing; **blow-valve**, the snifting valve of a condensing engine; **blow-well** (see quot.) Also BLOW-HOLE, BLOW-PIPE.

1578 LYTE *Dodoens* v. xvi. 568 Condrilla hath..double flowers; the whiche past, they turne into rounde *blowballes, like to fine downe or cotton. **1640** SHIRLEY *Impost.* IV. ii, I'm your blow-ball, Your breath dissolves my being. *a* **1670** HACKET *Abp. Williams* II. (1692) 90 Shake him from his stalk, like a downy blow-ball. **1885** *Standard* 28 May 6/3 Joint of *blowcock of boiler gave way. **1893** *Funk's Standard Dict.*, **Blowfish*, the wall-eyed pike-perch. **1933** A. DAVENPORT *Country Holiday* viii. 240 'Theer'll be hundreds o' great fish followin' every shoal—blow-fish, porpoise, [etc.]. **1934** *Bulletin* (Sydney) 1 Aug. 21/4 North Australian waters contain..the blowfish... When it is hooked it inflates itself to many times its normal size. Among its *aliases* are balloon-fish, puffball and windbag. **1871** *Trans. Amer. Inst. Mining Eng.* I. 303 Ventilated in the driving by a '*blow george' (hand-fan). **1864** *Athenæum* No. 1929. 504/2 The *blow-gun, thro' which short poisoned arrows are propelled by the breath. **1961** A. HECHT in *Hudson Rev.* XIV. 371 59 And you can get a *blow-job Where other men have pissed. **1969** *Oz* May 14 No, I don't want a blow job—I'm a girl. **1976** T. SHARPE *Wilt* iv. 35 'You want a blow job, is that it? You want for me to give you a blow job?' She got off the bed and came towards him. **1986** P. BOOTH *Palm Beach* vii. 139 Turning the other cheek was for girls who hadn't had to give blow jobs to tramps in exchange for a few pieces of candy. **1896** J. W. HART *External Plumbing Wk.* 259 The tinning can be done best by means of a *blow-lamp of some kind. **1909** *Westm. Gaz.* 27 Apr. 12/4 He was filling a blow lamp with motor spirit when it exploded. **1857** KINGSLEY *Two Y. Ago* Introd. (D.) Great anglers..who could do many things besides handling a *blow-line. **1867** F. FRANCIS *Angling* (1876) 260 Having baited the hook as in blow-line fishing. **1881** *Daily News* 8 Nov. 5/5 A writer..advocates the extension of the '*blow-post.' **1885** *Pall Mall G.* 5 Mar. 4/1 In Paris the blow post is being steadily developed. **1908** *Daily Chron.* 5 Aug. 1/6 The card and *blow room hands. **1909** *Century Dict.* Suppl., *Blow-torch. **1921** R. D. PAINE *Comr. Rolling Ocean* xvi. 274 Down to the engine-room went Briscoe and returned with..a blow-torch. **1963** J. OSBORNE *Dental Mechanics* (ed. 5) xv. 340 The face of the blowtorch nozzle. **1871** TYLOR *Prim. Cult.* i. 60 Nearly the same may be said of the *blow-tube. **1799** A. YOUNG *Agric. Linc.* i. 15 In the parishes of Tetney, Fulstow, and that vicinity, *blow-wells, which are deep flowing pits of clear water, which flow in considerable streams. **1854** *N. & Q.* Ser. I. IX. 283/1 Natural springs in the northern slope of the Chalk in Lincolnshire..called blow-wells, which may be considered as naturally Artesian. **1924** KENDALL & WROOT *Geol. Yorks.* I. xlvii. 626 On the warp-lands of Holderness and the Humber estuary there bubble up with great vigour a series of springs known as 'blow-wells'... A 'blow-well' is a natural artesian discharge.

3. With sb., which is the object after *blow* (in the sense of 'one who blows'), as **blow-bottle**, **blow-bowl**, a habitual drinker, tippler, sot (cf. BLOW *v.*[1] 31); † **blow-coal** (*fig.*), one who stirs up or promotes strife (cf. BLOW *v.*[1] 17 b); † **blow-point**, a game (see quot. 1801).

1580 BARET *Alv.* A 270 A common haunter of alehouses.. an aleknight: a tipler..a *blowbottell. **1530** PALSGR. 199/1 *Blowbole, *yuroigne*. **1622** H. SYDENHAM *Serm. Sol. Occ.* (1637) 262 These are..the common *blow-coales in Ecclesiastick tumults. **1580** SIDNEY *Arcadia* II. 224 How shepheards spend their days At *blow-point, hot cockles, or else at keeles. **1640** SHIRLEY *Hum. Courtier* v. iii, Do not trust the Archduke: he cozened me at blow-point. **1801** STRUTT *Sports & Past.* IV. iv. (1876) 513 Blow-point was probably blowing an arrow through a trunk at certain numbers by way of lottery.

4. With *vb.* or derivative form, as **blow-dry** *v. trans.*, to style and dry (hair) with a brush or comb and hand-held hair-dryer; also as *sb.*; hence **blow-dried** *ppl. a.*, **blow-drying** *vbl. sb.*; **blow-dryer**, a kind of hair-dryer used in blow-drying.

1976 *Morecambe Guardian* 7 Dec. 31/3 Tailored Curl by Wella the body perm for *blow dried hair. **1981** W. SAFIRE in *N.Y. Times Mag.* 29 Mar. 9/1 David A. Stockman,..a blow-dried Grim Reaper. **1966** J. S. COX *Illustr. Dict. Hairdressing* 21/2 *Blow waving*, the setting of waves in the hair by means of a comb and a hair dryer with a flattened nozzle by which the wave is shaped and *blow-dried into position. **1968** *Guardian* 7 Oct. 7/1 Gregory will shampoo, cut and blow-dry a man's hair (like a woman's) for roughly £2 2s. **1975** A. BEEVOR *Violent Brink* v. 115 They blow dried what was left of his hair. **1977** *Oxf. Consumer* June 6/2 Prices..varied enormously, from £1.25 to £4.50 for a trim and blow-dry. **1977** C. MCFADDEN *Serial* (1978) xxii. 51/2, I didn't use the *blow-dryer. **1977** *Cork Examiner* 8 June 6/3 *Blow-drying is easy, but a little know-how will give much better results.

blow (bləʊ), *sb.*³ [f. BLOW *v.*²: of recent origin.]

1. a. A state of blossoming; bloom; chiefly in phrases ***in blow***, ***in full blow***, etc.

1744 in *Amer. Speech* (1940) XV. 226/2 The aple trees are full in the blow. **1759** B. STILLINGFL. in *Misc. Tracts* (1762) 149 The wood-anemone was in blow. **1799** J. ROBERTSON *Agric. Perth* 216 When the plants are in full blow, and before their flowers begin to fade. *a* **1845** HOOD *Two Peacocks of B.* viii, I were sorely vext To..cut short the blow Of the last lily I may live to grow. **1866** M. ARNOLD *Thyrsis* in *New Poems* (1867) 76 And stocks in fragrant blow. **1895** MEREDITH *Amazing Marr.* I. iv. 45 Purple crocuses in bud and blow.

b. *fig.*

1753 RICHARDSON *Grandison* (1781) I. ii. 4 Her beauty hardly yet in its full blow. **1770** LANGHORNE *Plutarch* (1879) II. 1031/1 This amour was in full blow about the time. **1834** MAR. EDGEWORTH *Helen* 236 She is not out of blow yet, only too full blown rather for some tastes.

2. A display of blossoms; *fig.* a display of anything brilliant.

1710 ADDISON *Tatler* No. 218 ¶4 Such a blow of tulips, as was not to be matched. **1857** H. MILLER *Test. Rocks* i. 49 It exhibits no rich blow of colour.

3. Manner, style, or time of blossoming. Also *fig.*

1748 RICHARDSON *Clarissa* (1811) V. 285, I have..added to it all the flowers of the same blow. **1857** H. MILLER *Test. Rocks* xi. 500 Flowers of richer colour and blow.

4. Blossom.

1797 DOWNING *Disord. Horned Cattle* 31 Take Fox-glove blows. **1866** *Morn. Star* 2 Oct., The blow of the cotton-wood borne by the winds of spring.

blowe, variant of BLO *a. Obs.* livid, blue.

blowed, occasional *pa. t.* and *pple.* of BLOW *v.*¹

'blowen. *slang.* Also blowing. A wench, trull.

1812 J. H. VAUX *Flash Dict.*, *Blowen*, a prostitute; a woman who cohabits with a man without marriage. **1823** BYRON *Juan* XI. xix, With black-eyed Sal (his blowing). **1851** KINGSLEY *Yeast* xi, A short simple service..that might catch the ears of the roughs and the blowens.

blowen, obs. pa. pple. of BLOW *v.*¹

blower¹ (ˈbləʊə(r)). [OE. *bláwere*, f. *bláwan* to BLOW¹: see -ER¹.]

1. *gen.* One who, or that which, blows. Usually followed by *of* (the object blown).

c **897** K. ÆLFRED *Gregory's Past.* xxxvii. 268 Idel wæs se blawere. *c* **1320** *Sir Tristr.* I. xlix, The best blower of horn. **1545** *Ludlow Churchw. Accts.* (1869) 21 To the blower of the organs. **1775** *Phil. Trans.* LXV. 67 An expert blower of the German flute. **1872** TENNYSON *Last Tourn.* 540 O hunter, and O blower of the horn.

2. *spec.* A marine animal which 'blows' (see BLOW *v.*¹ 5); *e.g.* a whale.

1854 BUSHNAN in *Circ. Sc.* I. 140 The common cetaceans, popularly known as blowers.

3. a. A mechanical contrivance for producing a current of air; *e.g.* a plate or sheet of metal fixed before a fire to increase the draught.

1795 *Specif. Crook & German's Patent* No. 2032 The blower was let down close to the top of the grate, so that no air could pass otherwise than through the grate. **1869** *Eng. Mech.* 24 Dec. 344/1 It can..be hung in front of the fire to act as a blower. **1881** RAYMOND *Mining Gloss.*, *Blower*, a fan or other apparatus for forcing air into a furnace or mine. **1885** *Manch. Exam.* 21 July 8/1 The sweepings [were]..put through the blower instead of the winnower.

b. *esp.* An apparatus for creating an artificial current of air by pressure, used as a ventilator, dryer, etc., and to produce a blast of air in a furnace, etc. Also *attrib.*, as ***blower-engine***, ***-fan***, ***-pipe***.

1858 SIMMONDS *Dict. Trade*, *Blower*,..a fan used on board American river steam-boats, to increase the current of air. **1875** *Encycl. Brit.* III. 552/2 The rotary blower, invented by Messrs. Root of Connersville, Ind., is one which has of late years found extensive use both in America and Europe. **1900** *Everybody's Mag.* III. 528 The waves, breaking over the blower-pipes, poured through in such quantities as to dampen the belts of the blower-engine. **1903** *Daily Chron.* 9 Dec. 6/3 The air is first filtered... Afterwards it passes through a blower-fan. **1958** *Times* 19 Aug. 11/7 The car..was fitted with a heater..and had a plastic knob for the blower. **1959** *Listener* 22 Jan. 159/2 Blowers which blast the snow into banks at the roadside.

c. A blowing-machine: (*a*) for cleansing and 'opening' the fibres of cotton or wool; (*b*) for cleansing and separating rabbit fur.

1867 *Chambers's Encycl.* IX. 46/2 The cotton or wool..is ..taken to the 'blower' or 'opener', and being put into a shaft, is there acted upon by a stream of air..which blows it forward, removes extraneous matters, [etc.]. *a* **1877** KNIGHT *Dict. Mech.*, *Blower*, a machine for separating the hair from the fur fibres [in hat-making].

d. In an aeroplane engine, esp. a supercharger.

1920 *Flight* XII. 1004/2 A blower driven off the Renault engine was provided. **1922** *Advisory Comm. Aeronaut. Techn. Rep. 1918–19* 50 In connection with high altitude flying a large number of experiments have been carried out on different forms of blowers for aircraft engines. **1933** *Jrnl. R. Aeronaut. Soc.* XXXVII. 86 Further developments in scavenging and supercharging by auxiliary blowers. **1946** B. SUTTON *Jungle Pilot* xiii. 66 At this height I found I could climb appreciably faster than the Tomahawks. This was due to my two-speed 'blower'.

e. A speaking-tube or telephone. *colloq.*

1922 E. WALLACE *Flying Fifty-Five* xxx. 182 The club enjoyed a 'blower service'. The 'blower' is difficult for the outsider to understand. **1926** —— *More Educ. Evans* v. 121, I heard it on the telephone... They got that price from the blower round at the Arts Club. **1945** PARTRIDGE *Dict. R.A.F. Slang*, *Blower*, from the Naval sense, 'telephone' or, rather, the speaking-tube connecting Bridge and Engine-Room. **1951** 'N. SHUTE' *Round the Bend* vii. 217 'Somebody must have got on the blower from Bahrein.'.. He meant the radio telephone that connects the aerodromes all down the eastern route. **1957** 'J. WYNDHAM' *Midwich Cuckoos* iii. 24 I'd of said the old girl was *always* listenin' when there was anyone on the blower.

4. An escape of inflammable gas through a fissure in a coal-mine; the fissure itself; a similar current of air escaping through a fissure in a glacier.

1822 IMISON *Sc. & Art* II. 59 It is disengaged from fissures in the strata..called by the miners *blowers*. **1860** TYNDALL *Glac.* 87 While cutting away the surface further, I stopped the little 'blower'. **1862** SMILES *Engineers* III. 111 The explosive gas was issuing through a blower in the roof of the mine with a loud hissing noise. **1866** *Reader* 21 July 671 'Blowers' as they are called in the north of England.. streams of inflammable gas issuing from the ground.

5. *fig.* A boaster. *dial.* and in *U.S.* and *colonies.*

1863 MANHATTAN in *Even. Standard* 10 Dec., General Grant..is not one of the 'blower' generals. **1864** *Spectator* 22 Oct. 1202 1 Notorious among our bar and the public as a 'blower'.

6. *Comb.* with various adverbs (cf. BLOW *v.*¹), as ***blower forth***, ***in***, ***up***.

1550 J. COKE *Debate Her. Eng. & Fr.* (1877) 121 Blowers forth of fayned fables. **1601** SHAKS. *All's Well* I. i. 132 Blesse our poore Virginity from vnderminers and blowers vp. **1635** SWAN *Spec. M.* v. §2. 176 The winds..the blowers in of rain.

'blower². [f. BLOW *v.*² + -ER¹.] A plant which blows or blooms. (Cf. *bloomer.*)

1796 C. MARSHALL *Garden.* xx. (1813) 402 Biennials and perennials, if late blowers, may yet be transplanted.

blowess, variant of BLOWZE *sb.*

blow-fly (ˈbləʊflaɪ). [f. BLOW *v.*¹ 28 + FLY.] **a.** A recent popular name of the Flesh-fly.

1821 T. NUTTALL *Trav. Arkansa* xiv. 201 The green blow-flies, attracted by the meat brought to our camp, exceeded everything that can be conceived. **1852** T. HARRIS *Insects New Eng.* 490 Various kinds of flesh-flies, blow-flies, house-flies. **1858** *Sat. Rev.* 20 Nov. 500/2 Linnæus said.. that a blowfly would consume the carcase of a horse faster than a lion. [According to Kirby and Spence, L. said 'three flesh-flies and their progeny'.]

b. ***blow-fly strike***: a disease affecting sheep. (Cf. STRIKE *v.* 45 d.)

1933 *Council Sci. & Ind. Res.* Pamphlet No. 37 ii. 17 Though death following blowfly strike is not uncommon, its actual causation has never been thoroughly investigated. **1955** J. H. WELLINGTON *Southern Africa* II. I. v. 74 Other points of superiority in the new strain [of sheep] include.. a low liability to blowfly strike.

blow-hard, *a.* and *sb.* *colloq.* (orig. *U.S.*). [BLOW *v.*¹ 6.]

A. *adj.* Boastful, blustering.

1855 *Oregon Weekly Times* 21 July (Th.), The *Oregonian* ..has a blowhard article on the subject. **1921** R. D. PAINE *Comr. Rolling Ocean* vi. 105 He don't get by with his blow-hard stuff, but I'll have to say he is entertaining. **1946** K. TENNANT *Lost Haven* (1947) xvi. 248 He's a blow-hard bugger.

B. *sb.* A blustering person; a braggart.

1857 DUFFERIN *Lett. High Lat.* 161 He is a fine old grey-headed blow-hard of fifty odd. **1880** HARDY *Trumpet-Major* xxxi, Bob's temper began to rise. 'Don't you talk so large, about your pinioning, my man...' 'Now or never, young blow-hard,' interrupted his informant. **1964** *Punch* 8 Apr. 514/2 'Old *John Bull*' might be a blabbermouth and blowhard.

blow-hole (ˈbləʊhəʊl). [See BLOW *v.*¹ 5.]

1. Each of the two holes (constituting the nostrils) at the top of the head in whales and other cetaceans, through which they breathe or 'blow'.

1787 HUNTER in *Phil. Trans.* LXXVII. 380 The blow-holes are two in number in many, in others only one. **1822** I. PLATTS *Bk. Curios.* 205 A double opening, called the spout-holes, or blow-holes. **1861** J. LAMONT *Seahorses* v. 75 They give one spout from their blow-holes, take one breath of fresh air..and then they are all down.

2. = AIR-HOLE 2.

1691 T. H[ALE] *Acc. New Invent.* 96 Certain defects in Cast-lead..called by the Plumber Blow-holes. **1878** *Ure's Dict. Arts* IV. 835 The following experiments were made in order to prepare solid steel without blow-holes by the crucible process. **1906** *Westm. Gaz.* 29 Aug. 2/1 The way to prevent steel rusting..is to have no blow-holes. **1960** *Jrnl. Iron & Steel Inst.* CXCV. 223/2 (*title*) Blowholes in castings, and methods of preventing their occurrence.

3. A hole through which air or gas escapes (see quots.); *spec.* for the escape of foul air from underground passages, of steam from railway tunnels, etc. Also = *puffing-hole.*

1858 JOHN SHAW *Gallop to Antipodes* vii. 131 That is a blowhole. Don't you see the water forced into the air, like a whale spouting?.. You will see the water first and afterwards you will hear the report. **1872** [see PUFFING *vbl. sb.* 5]. **1875** MISS BIRD *Sandwich Isl.* (1880) 56 An intermittent jet of lava..kept cooling round what was possibly a blow-hole. **1883** *Pall Mall G.* 1 June, The erection of the blow-holes on the Embankment. **1884** *Ibid.* 15 Mar. 2/2 Can no doubt 'construct' the Parks Railway without blowholes. **1891** R. WALLACE *Rural Econ. Austral. & N.Z.* i. 24 Here also the cavernous condition of the subjacent rocks extended, and every here and there was a large pit or depression like a deserted quarry which had fallen in. From some of these so-called 'blow-holes' water could be pumped for the stock in dry seasons. **1938** *Times* 7 Sept. 9/1 He..crawled in through the 'blow-hole' [of a barrage-balloon] to look for leaks and examine the pressure valve. **1958** ARMSTRONG & ROBERTS *Illustr. Ice Gloss.* II. 91 *Blow-hole*, opening through a snow bridge into a crevasse or system of crevasses which are otherwise sealed by snow bridges. **1961** J. CHALLINOR *Dict. Geol.* 24/1 *Blow-hole*, a natural chimney, on a coast, reaching from the inner end of a cave to the surface of the ground above. **1962** *Listener* 11 Jan. 57/2 The whole thermal area of the North Island [of New Zealand], with its hot pools and geysers and blowholes.

4. A hole in the ice to which whales and seals come to breathe.

blowing (ˈbləʊɪŋ), *vbl. sb.*¹ [f. BLOW *v.*¹ + -ING¹.]

1. a. *gen.* The action expressed by the vb. to BLOW.

c **1000** ÆLFRIC *Judges* vii. 16 (Bosw.) Heora byman him to ðære blawunge. **1398** TREVISA *Barth. De P.R.* XVII. clvii. (1495) 708 Wyth blowynge of wynde. *a* **1422** *Le Venery de Twety* in *Rel. Ant.* I. 153 Ye shul change your speche and blowyng booth too. **1621** SIR R. BOYLE in *Lismore Pap.* (1886) II. 17 My 2 new ffurnaces..had ffier to begin theer blowing put into them. **1710** PALMER *Proverbs* 178 This impious blowing upon other people's reputations. **1799** J. ROBERTSON *Agric. Perth* 279 Saving..boring and powder.. avoiding the trouble and danger of blowing.

b. *Cotton-manuf.* The cleansing of cotton. Cf. BLOWER¹ 3 c (a).

1844 [see SCUTCHING *vbl. sb.*² 1]. **1875** *Ure's Dict. Arts* I. 955 The willowing, scutching, or blowing, an operation which removes the seeds and dirt, and prepares the material in the form of a continuous lap.

c. The shattering (of a bird) in shooting. (Cf. BLOW *v.*¹ 24 d.)

1892 W. W. GREENER *Breech-Loader* 271 No one could detect the 'blowing' of a single bird.

d. (See quot.)

1881 R. HUNTER et al. *Encycl. Dict.*, *Blowing of Firearms* (Gunnery), the art or operation of constructing firearms in such a way that the vent or touch-hole is run or 'gullied', and becomes wide, allowing the powder to blaze out.

e. ***blowing off***: the action or process of firing (a rifle) to cleanse the barrel.

1893 *Daily News* 2 Feb. 2/6 The ammunition..was issued in packets of ten, thus allowing for blowing off and for one compulsory sighting shot.

f. *fig.* Boasting, bragging. *U.S.*, *Austral.*, etc. Cf. BLOW *v.*¹ 6 a.

1840 *Congress. Globe* App., 9 Jan. 50/1 [I advise them] to treat with contempt and scorn, all the blasting, blowing, blustering, and bullying displays that they may see. **1873** TROLLOPE *Australia & N.Z.* I. 387 A fine art much cultivated in the colonies, for which the colonial phrase of 'blowing' has been created. **1878** J. H. BEADLE *Western Wilds* ix. 134 Its bright and saucy editorials excelled all specimens extant of Kansas blowing.

2. a. Breathing; hard breathing; esp. of animals.

c **1175** *Lamb. Hom.* 75 Hore loking, hore blawing, hore smelling, heore feling. **1398** TREVISA *Barth. De P.R.* XVIII. ciii. (1495) 847 Brockes holdeth in the brethe and blowynge. **1523** FITZHERB. *Husb.* §87 Broken wynded, and pursyfnes, is but shorte blowynge. **1591** PERCIVALL *Sp. Dict.*, *Bufido*, the puffing and blowing of a horse. **1815** SCOTT *Guy M.* xlv, Listening for the blowing of an otter. **1883** G. DAVIES *Norfolk Broads* xix. (1884) 143 Until they see the 'blowing' of an eel, as the bubbles issuing from the mud are termed.

†b. Swelling, tumefaction. *Obs.*

1398 TREVISA *Barth. De P.R.* XVI. lxxxvi. (1495) 582 The saphire hath singuler vertue to swage blowynge.

c. The formation of bubbles or blisters in the texture of a manufactured article.

1872 *Spons' Dict. Engin.* v. 1547 As the pressure is kept on the metal until it is well set and solid, such a thing as blowing will never, or very seldom take place.

d. = BLOAT *sb.* 1 b. (Cf. BLOW *v.*¹ 22 c.)

1891 R. WALLACE *Rural Econ. Austral. & N.Z.* xxii. 301 Cattle not accustomed to an abundant supply of green food are liable to suffer from 'hoven' or 'blowing' after eating it.

e. Of a tin of food (see quot.).

1950 J. G. DAVIS *Dict. Dairying* 43 *'Blowing' of condensed milk*, the bulging or bursting of tins of condensed milk usually due to the production of carbon dioxide by fermentation of the sugar by micro-organisms, usually yeasts.

3. a. The oviposition of flesh-flies, and formerly of other insects. **†b.** *concr.* The 'blote' or egg of a flesh-fly or other insect (*obs.*).

1558 BP. WATSON *Sev. Sacr.* xxiv. 153 A fleshe flye..wyll leaue fylthy blowinges in the fleshe. **1577** HOLINSHED *Chron.* III. vi. 229 Beyond the seas..they stampe and streine their combs, bees, and young blowings altogither into the stuffe. **1616** SURFL. & MARKH. *Countr. Farm* 320 Bees are bred of Bees, either of their blowings, or some other matter of their generation. **1677** HALE *Prim. Orig. Man.* II. ix. 209 The blowings of Flies, and almost all kind of Insects.

4. ***blowing up***, an explosion; *colloq.* a scolding.

1772 *Phil. Trans.* LXIII. 44 The blowing up of a magazine of gun-powder. 1820 G. SIMPSON *Jrnl.* 18 Aug. in *Hudson's Bay Record Soc. Publication* (1938) I. 17 Mr. Clarke gave him what is vulgarly called 'a good blowing up'. 1839 HALIBURTON *Letter-bag Gt. West* iv. 42, I would give him a good blowing-up. 1874 MRS. WOOD *J. Ludlow* Ser. I. xxv. 448, I..received a good blowing up from Mr. Brandon for my pains.

5. a. *Comb.*, as **blowing-cone**, a volcanic cone by which vapours escape from a subterranean molten lake; **blowing-cylinder**, the air-cylinder of a blast-engine; **blowing-engine** (= *blowing-machine*); **blowing-furnace**, a blast furnace used in glass-working; †**blowing-house**, a tin-smelting house; **blowing-iron, -pipe, -tube** (*Glass-working*), an iron tube used in blowing glass; **blowing-machine**, (*a*) any mechanical contrivance for producing a blast of air; (*b*) a machine for cleansing and separating fur in hat-manufacture; (*c*) an apparatus forming part of the machine for cleansing the cotton in cotton-manufacture; (*d*) an apparatus for blowing glass-ware (*Cent. Dict.*, 1889); **blowing-pot**, a vessel containing clay paste which the workman 'throws' on pottery by blowing; **blowing-room**, a room in which the cleansing or separating of materials is done, esp. in a cotton factory; also *attrib.*, as (*card and*) *blowing-room hand, machinery, operative*.

1895 DANA *Man. Geol.* (ed. 4) 279 In cases, outside of the lava-lakes, where the bubbles are bursting beneath an opening in the bottom of the crater, the vapors and lava driblets escape from the aperture with a rush and a roar. The driblet-cone, thus made, is sometimes called a blowing-cone. 1845 DODD *Brit. Manuf.* V. 159 Blowing-Engine. 1875 URE *Dict. Arts* II. 654 A blowing furnace for blowing the pear-shaped balls..into large globes. 1674 RAY *Prepar. Tin* Coll. 120 The black Tin is smelted at the blowing house with Charcoal. 1875 URE *Dict. Arts* III. 1005 Formerly in Cornwall nearly all the tin was smelted in blast-furnaces; these works were called blowing-houses. 1855 tr. *Labarte's Arts Mid. Ages* ix. 352 Gathers with the blowing-iron a small quantity of white glass. 1835 URE *Philos. Manuf.* II. ii. 111 The blowing machine for thoroughly opening out the cotton into clean individual fibres. 1839 —— *Dict. Arts* I. 345 Batting (*beating*), scutching, and blowing machines. 1845 DODD *Brit. Manuf.* V. 158 The 'blowing-machines'.. act as follows. 1868 F. H. JOYNSON *Metals* i. 18 The blast from the blowing machine is conducted into the furnace by means of the tuyers. 1940 *Chambers's Techn. Dict.* 99/1 *Blowing machines*, machines for forming molten glass into articles by the use of air under pressure. 1875 *Ure's Dict. Arts* III. 622 Common earthenware is coloured by means of ..the blowing-pot. 1845 DODD *Brit. Manuf.* V. 158 The fur ..is conveyed to the blowing-room, finally to effect the separation [of the coarse from the fine fur]. 1887 J. E. HOLME *Cotton Spinning* Introd., The blowing-room machinery should be kept well oiled. 1892 *Daily News* 14 Apr. 3/4 The card and blowing-room hands. 1898 *Westm. Gaz.* 23 Dec. 7/3 The Card and Blowing-room Operatives Society.

b. With advs.: **blowing-in, -out**: the action or process of putting a blast furnace into or out of action (see BLOW *v.* 19); **blowing-off, -through** = *blow-off, -through* (see BLOW-).

1925 *Jrnl. Iron & Steel Inst.* CXII. 409 The methods pursued..in the blowing in, in damping down, and blowing out of blast furnaces. 1944 *Ibid.* CL. 378P From blowing-in to blowing-out furnace operation is handicapped, because we do not know what is going on inside the furnace. 1863 ATKINSON tr. *Ganot's Physics* vi. 328 Blowing off taps, for use when the pistons are in motion. *a* 1877 KNIGHT *Dict. Mech.*, Blowing-off... Blowing-through.

'blowing, *vbl. sb.*[2] [f. BLOW *v.*[2] + -ING[1].] The action of blossoming or blooming. †**b.** A bloom or blossom: also *fig.* (*obs.*).

c 1380 WYCLIF *Serm.* Sel. Wks. I. 220 þe blowinge of þes fruitys must faile. 1578 LYTE *Dodoens* 692 Clustering togither lyke the cattes tayles or blowinges of the Nut tree. 1609 C. BUTLER *Fem. Mon.* (1634) 58 At the blowing of Palm ..they [wasps] fly abroad for food. 1660 E. WATERHOUSE *Arms & Arm.* 184 These budds and blowings of Nobility and Gentry. 1797 HOLCROFT *Stolberg's Trav.* (ed. 2) III. lxix. 58 Flowers..whose periodical blowing is advertised in our newspapers.

'blowing, *ppl. a.*[1] [f. BLOW *v.*[1] + -ING[2].] That blows (see the vb.); *esp.* windy.

blowing adder, snake, a snake of Virginia, remarkable for inflating and extending the surface of its head before it bites.

c 1175 *Lamb. Hom.* 87 Eislic swei . and blawende beman. 1604 *Friar Bacon's Proph.* 290 in Hazl. *E.P.P.* IV. 278 No butcher now can keepe His flesh from blowing flies. 1678 *Lond. Gaz.* No. 1365/1 His Majesties Ships..are kept in this Harbor by the blowing weather. 1688 J. CLAYTON in *Phil. Trans.* XVIII. 134 The Blowing-Snake, an absolute Species of a Viper. 1794 NELSON in Nicolas *Disp.* (1845) I. 411 It had the appearance of blowing weather. 1845 *Gard. Chron.* 107 Blowing-Sands..or hills of moveable sand which are accumulated by the winds. 1870 SWINBURNE *Ess. & Stud.* (1875) 347 With rounded mouth and blowing hair. 1884 *Public Opinion* 5 Sept. 305/1 The blowing adder was formerly common in..Orange County, New York.

'blowing, *ppl. a.*[2] [f. BLOW *v.*[2] + -ING[2].] Blossoming, in bloom.

917 *Blickl. Hom.* 57 Fæȝerness..swylc þes blowenda wudu. 1667 MILTON *P.L.* IX. 629 One small Thicket..Of blowing Myrrh and Balme. 1835 WORDSW. *Death C. Lamb*, Green, untrodden turf, and blowing flowers.

blowing, variant of BLOWEN *sb.*

blo-wipe, a blow causing a bruise: see BLO.

blowm, obs. form of BLOOM *v.*

blown (bləʊn), *ppl. a.*[1] [pa. pple. of BLOW *v.*[1]]

1. Fanned, driven or tossed by the wind.

1552 ABP. HAMILTON *Catech.* 286 Saiffit, swa as be ane blawin fyre. 1746 COLLINS *Ode Liberty* 70 To the blown Baltic. 1862 ANSTED *Channel Isl.* IV. xx. (ed. 2) 462 Blown sea-sand covers the soil.

2. Out of breath.

1674 MARVELL *Reh. Transp.* II. 33 And chase the blown Deer out of their Heard. 1735 SOMERVILLE *Chase* III. 461 Now the blown Stag..Has measur'd half the Forest. 1873 BLACK *Pr. Thule* x. 162 Too blown to speak.

†**3.** Stale, flat, that has lost its freshness; tainted.

1600 ROWLANDS *Let. Humours Blood* vi. 75 Blowne drinke is odious, what man can disiest it? 1640 BP. HALL *Episc.* II. x. 139 Some blowne ware out of the pack of his Recognitions.

4. Breathed out, whispered, hinted.

1604 SHAKS. *Oth.* III. iii. 182 When I shall turne..To such exufflicate, and blown [*Fol.* blow'd] Surmises.

5. a. Inflated; swollen; formed by inflation. Also ***blown-up***. Applied spec. to glassware formed by forcing air into molten glass.

c 1425 *Seven Sag.* (P.) 2181 Grete blowen bladdyrs he brake. 1596 SHAKS. *1 Hen. IV*, IV. ii. 53 How now blowne lack? how now Quilt? 1618 BOLTON *Florus* III. v. 183 Floting on a blowne Bladder. 1830 M. DONOVAN *Dom. Econ.* I. 93 Too quick a heat of the kiln expels the water from the malt in a state of steam, with such force as to burst the grain. This is called blown malt. 1831 BREWSTER *Optics* xii. 100 The thinnest films of blown glass. 1870 SWINBURNE *Ess. & Stud.* (1875) 347 A boyish torch-bearer with blown cheeks. 1961 *Listener* 26 Oct. 674/1 Not many people are even aware of the difference between blown glass and pressed glass. 1962 *Gloss. Terms Glass Ind.* (*B.S.I.*) 36 *Blown glassware*, glassware formed by air pressure produced by mouth or by a machine.

b. *fig.* Inflated with pride or the like (*arch.*); more recently, 'exaggerated'.

1483 CAXTON *Gold. Leg.* 154/3 Ambrose can not be so blowen and [s]wollen as thou arte. 1605 SHAKS. *Lear* IV. iv. 26 No blowne Ambition doth our Armes incite. 1866 KINGSLEY *Herew.* i. 37 More of a blown-up ass than thou art already. 1958 A. J. P. TAYLOR in *New Statesman* 15 Nov. 664/1 The talk about homosexuals corrupting young boys is blown-up nonsense, a perverted wish-fulfilment. 1961 *Listener* 23 Nov. 887/1 The sorrows of a blown-up 'pop singer' became moving.

c. *Veterinary Path.* (See BLOW *v.*[1] 22 c.)

1833 YOUATT *Compl. Grazier* (ed. 6) VI. i. 316 No distemper is of more frequent occurrence among cattle than that of being swollen, *blown*, or *hoven*. 1898 in *E.D.D.* 1950 *N.Z. Jrnl. Agric.* Feb. 167/2 The combination of them causes fermentation, with disastrous results—blown cows and digestive disorders.

d. Filled with bubbles or the like. (Cf. BLOWING *vbl. sb.*[1] 2 c.)

1872 *Spons' Dict. Engin.* V. 1548 The..result is what moulders term a *blown* casting; that is, its surface becomes filled with bubbles of air, rendering its texture porous and weak.

e. Of a tin of food: swollen or inflated (see BLOWING *vbl. sb.*[1] 2 e).

1899 *Daily News* 16 Jan. 3/3 The sanitary inspector explained that the contents of a 'blown' tin would 'not taste so bad after the gas had come out'. 1955 J. G. DAVIS *Dict. Dairying* (ed. 2) 79 Blown cans of evaporated milk and canned cream.

f. *colloq.* = SUPERCHARGED *ppl. a.* (Cf. BLOWER[1] 3 d.)

1934 *Neuphilologische Mitteilungen* XXXV. 131 Motoring ..a blown model 'model fitted with a supercharger'. 1940 *Chambers's Techn. Dict.* 99/1 *Blown*, a colloquial term applied to a supercharged petrol-engine. 1959 *Motor* 2 Sept. 92/2 Sears'..blown 4½-litre model. *Ibid.* 11 Nov. 532/3 Won the..Handicap at 125 m.p.h. in a blown Bugatti.

g. ***blown oil***: oil that has had air blown through it in order to increase its viscosity.

1887 *Analyst* xii. 33 Blown or thickened oils are prepared from various seed oils, by heating the oil in a suitable tank to 70° C., and then blowing air into them through a perforated tube. 1951 R. MAYER *Artist's Hand-bk. Mat. & Techniques* iii. 109 Heavy, viscous blown oils are prepared commercially in large quantities.

6. a. *Plumbing.* Of a joint: made with a blow-pipe. **b.** *Electr.* Of a fuse (see BLOW *v.*[1] 19 c).

1904 GOODCHILD & TWENEY *Technol. & Sci. Dict.*, Blown Joint. 1909 *Installation News* III. 137 We will allow 33⅓ per cent. of the nett price for all 'blown' cartridge fuses of our manufacture.

7. With advs., as ***blown-back, -down, -up***. For *blown in* and *out* see BLOW *v.*[1] 19.

1864 TROLLOPE *Small Ho. at Allington* II. xvi. 165 The clerks in this room would not infrequently be blown up.. and..the blown-up young man would refer Mr. Kissing to his enemy. 1866 Blown-up [see sense 5 b]. 1878 W. MORRIS in J. W. Mackail *Life* (1899) I. 360 The blown-down tree was a fine branchy tree. 1905 *Westm. Gaz.* 13 Sept. 6/3 The blown-up steamer. 1926 E. BOWEN *Ann Lee's* 196 Her forehead and blown-back hair.

blown, *ppl. a.*[2] [see BLOW *v.*[2]] In bloom; that has blossomed. Cf. FULL-BLOWN.

c 1000 *Sax. Leechd.* II. 146 Geblowenne wyrta. *a* 1250 *Owl & Night.* 1636 þe nihtegale..hupte uppon on blowe ris. 1606 SHAKS. *Ant. & Cl.* III. xiii. 39 The blowne Rose. 1842 TENNYSON *Lotos-Eaters* 47 Petals from blown roses on the grass. 1865 SWINBURNE *Poems & Ballads, Match* 5 Blown fields and flowerful closes.

blow-out. [BLOW- I.] **1.** An outbreak of anger; a quarrel, disturbance, row. *dial.* and *U.S.*

1825 J. K. PAULDING *John Bull in Amer.* 137 We had a *blow out* here last Sunday, and half a dozen troublesome fellows ..were done for by the brave *rowdies*. 1826 SCOTT in *Lockhart* (1839) IX. 44 At dinner we had a little *blow-out on Sophia's part. 1842 *Spirit of Times* (Philad.) 15 Feb. (Th.), I've had five breezes, seven blow-outs, nine shindies, and a dozen ructions on this $1 Relief note.

2. A dinner, supper, or other entertainment for which an abundant supply of food and drink is provided or at which it is consumed; a 'feast' or 'feed'. *colloq.*

1824 SCOTT *St. Ronan's* xxxiii, 'She sent me a card for her blow-out,' said Mowbray, 'and so I am resolved to go.' 1840 R. DANA *Bef. Mast* xxvi. 87 They had a grand blow-out, and ..drank in the forecastle, a barrel of gin. 1856 F. PAGET *Owlet of Owlst.* 174 Such a jolly blow-out as there was when the Bishop was here. 1930 R. LEHMANN *Note in Music* vii. 264 Have a nice blowout and a good sleep afterwards. 1966 'J. HACKSTON' *Father clears Out* 172 Saint's menu in between such blood-building blowouts was rabbit, with pollard as a savoury.

3. a. *Mining.* A portion of a lode where the mineral appears to have been dislodged by some eruptive force. Also *fig. U.S.*

1873 J. H. BEADLE *Undevel. West* xviii. 333 All the strange terms in mining parlance: 'true lodes,..blow-outs'. 1901 S. E. WHITE *Westerners* xxiii. 214 He saw that..a third [claim] ..gave indications of being nothing but a blow-out.

b. A butte, the top of which has been blown out by the wind until it resembles the crater of a volcano; a hollow in an area of shifting sand, or light soil, caused by the action of the wind. orig. *U.S.* Also *spec.* a water-hole (see quot. 1935).

1893 SMITH & POUND in *Bot. Surv. Nebraska* II. 8 If a spot on a dry hill becomes bare, the loose sand is blown away, a small hollow is made... Such blow outs were seen 100 surrounding meters in diameter and 15..meters deep. 1895 P. A. RYDBERG in *U.S. Nat. Herb. Contributions* III. 135 It sometimes happens that settlers [in the sand-hill region] a few years after breaking their land find a field transformed into a big blowout. 1897 POUND & CLEMENTS *Phytogeogr. Nebraska* (1898) 248 A small number of these grasses are especially adapted to these localities and are uniformly to be found in such blow outs... These grasses mark a second formation, which may be called the blow out formation. *Ibid.*, The blow out grasses..bind the sand together with their roots. 1911 F. O. BOWER *Plant Life* ix. 151 Close by an effete Dune with its grasses weakened in growth is being attacked by the wind, and eroded into hollows or 'Blow-outs'. 1935 *Discovery* Dec. 359/2 'Blow outs', i.e. dried up water holes, from which the wind has eroded the sands.

4. A burst in a pneumatic rubber tyre caused by air-pressure from the inside. Also *fig.*

1908 *Westm. Gaz.* 7 Jan. 4/1 Miraculum will not seal a blow-out. 1915 *Lit. Digest* (N.Y.) 21 Aug. 387/1 The Goodyear Cord Tires, without a blow-out, took the car back to Detroit. *Ibid.* 4 Sept. 482/1 (Advt.), No domestic punctures or blow-outs—just easy running over smooth roads to Health and Happiness. 1967 I. HAMILTON *Man with Brown Paper Face* vii. 94 This road..safe enough if you don't have a blow-out.

5. *Electr.* The suppression of an arc in an electric circuit; a device for producing this. Also *attrib.*

1902 *Encycl. Brit.* XXVIII. 97/2 A magnetic blow-out is simply a small magnet so arranged that the arc caused by breaking the circuit takes place in the magnetic field. 1916 *Standardization Rules of Amer. Inst. Electr. Engin.* 28 June §731 Fuses of the magnetic blow-out type. 1930 *Engineering* 7 Feb. 173/3 Anything which tends to produce sudden speed-changes, such as..magnetic blow outs.

6. A rapid, uncontrolled uprush of fluid from an oil well. Freq. *attrib.* in **blow-out preventer**, a heavy valve or assembly ('stack') of valves usu. fitted at the top of a hole during drilling and closed in the event of a blow-out to control the flow.

1916 A. B. THOMPSON *Oil-Field Devel.* vii. 367 An apparatus which is largely employed with rotaries is what is called a 'Blow-out Preventer'. *Ibid.* x. 457 Heavy mud mixtures are an additional safeguard against 'blow-outs'. 1932 *Amer. Speech* VII. 264 *Blow-out*, the violent and uncontrolled outburst of gas under high pressure, or of such gas accompanied by oil. 1966 *Petroleum Handbk.* (Shell Internat. Petroleum Co.) (ed. 5) 38/1 A system of control equipment..installed at the well head..termed the 'blow-out preventer stack' can close off the annulus between drill pipe and casing within 15 seconds..and can hold pressure up to 5000 lb/in². 1968 *Daily Tel.* 16 Nov. 1 Lifeboats saved 47 men from the gale-lashed North Sea after a 'blow out' on a gas-drilling platform. *Ibid.* 22/5 'The well blew out.'..A blow-out happens when gas rushes up the bore-hole at about 4,000 lb a square inch making it uncontrollable. 1984 A. C. & A. DUXBURY *Introd. World's Oceans* xi. 365 This transport process exposes the world's coasts and estuaries to the hazard of oil spills... The drilling of offshore wells exposes these areas to the risks of blowouts. 1986 *New Yorker* 27 Jan. 69/2 The disaster occurred in the space of five minutes, between the removal of the Christmas tree and the repositioning of the blowout preventer.

blow-pipe, blowpipe. [f. BLOW *v.*[1] + PIPE.]

1. a. A tube through which a current of air (or other gas) is blown into a flame to increase the heat, for the purpose of fusing metals, etc.; especially employed in chemical experiments, analysis, etc. (Hence, often *attrib.*, as in *blowpipe analysis, character, flame.*) **b.** *Glass-blowing.* A tube by means of which the molten glass is blown into the required shape.

1685 BOYLE *Effects of Motion* iv. 36 A small crooked pipe of metal or glass, such as Tradesmen..call a Blow-pipe. **1765** DOUGLAS in *Phil. Trans.* LVIII. 185 The flame of a candle was directed to it by means of a blow-pipe. **1830** HERSCHEL *Stud. Nat. Phil.* II. vi. (1851) 162 These great masses are made up of watch-glassfuls, and blowpipe-beads. *c* **1865** J. WYLDE in *Circ. Sc.* I. 396/2 Much art is required in using the blow-pipe. **1868** DANA *Min.* Introd. 20 Physical and Blowpipe characters. **1879** WATTS *Dict. Chem.* I. 616 A blowpipe flame of great power.

2. A long tube through which American Indians and other races propel arrows or darts by force of the breath.

1825 WATERTON *Wand. S. Amer.* I. i. 89 They will..send the poisoned dart from the blow-pipe true to its destination. **1840** MARRYAT *Olla Podr.* (Rtldg.) 291 Like an arrow from the blow-pipe of a South American Indian.

blowre, variant of BLURE, *Obs.*

blowse, -sed, -sy: see BLOWZE, BLOWZED, -Y.

blowser ('blaʊzə(r)). *local.* Also **blouser**. A landsman who assists in working the seine nets at pilchard-fishing time. Also **'blowsing** *sb.*

1816 PARIS *Mount's Bay* 91 It [*sc.* the net] is moored, or where the shore is sandy and shelving, as in Saint Ives Bay, drawn into shallow water, by a number of men, who are called *Blowsers.* **1877** *Fraser's Mag.* XV. 220 The whole is warped nearer to the shore by blousers, who are landsmen.. employed on land during the pilchard season for general purposes. **1879** *Encycl. Brit.* IX. 254/2 Landing and carrying the fish to the curing houses is done by men termed 'blowsers'. **1880** M. A. COURTNEY *W. Cornw. Gloss.*, *Blowsing*, working in seine boats.

blowt, var. of BLOUT. *Obs.*, naked.

blowt(e, obs. form of BLOAT *a.*[2]

†**'blowter**, *v. Obs.* [Cf. BLUTHER, BLOUTER, BLUTTER.] *intr.* To blubber; to weep effusively.

AGN. STRICKLAND *Queens Scot.* (1851) II. 257 Derided the tears, which he [Duke of Norfolk, 1560] elegantly terms the blowtering, of Mary of Lorraine.

†**blowth**. *Obs.* exc. *dial.* Also 7 **blouth**, 7- (s.w. dial.) **blooth**. [f. BLOW *v.*[2] + -TH[1]: cf. *growth.*] Blowing or blossoming; blossom, bloom.

1602 CAREW *Cornwall* in Wither *Prosop. Brit.*, The tree Which forth this blooth hath brought. **1614** RALEIGH *Hist. World* I. 155 The seeds and effects..were as yet but potentiall, and in the blowth and bud. **1769** *Month. Rev.* XLII. 185 The thorn's first blowth. **1859** CAPERN *Ball. & Songs* 129 The furze-blooth on the hill. **1862** BARNES *Rhymes Dorset Dial.* II. 95 A zummer hedge in blooth.

blow-up. [BLOW- I.]

1. = BLOW-OUT I.

1809 W. GELL *Let.* 22 Jan. in C. K. Sharpe *Lett.* (1888) I. 355 There won't be any quarrel, so you need not fear. The only chance is Keppel making a blow up when she abuses me. **1813** LD. CASTLEREAGH *Let.* in Sir R. Wilson *Diary* (1861) II. 201 W. and he must not have any connexion together or there will be a blow up. **1834** J. WILSON *Noct. Ambr.* (1864) IV. 133 O'Connell and Littleton had a blow-up and abused each other like pickpockets. **1846** SOL. SMITH *Theatrical Apprent.* 132 When we had got their jealousy and hatred excited to a proper pitch, it was agreed that a regular 'blow up' between the two should end the joke. **1900** H. LAWSON *Over Sliprails* 46 Some others were making a night of it..as they'd been doing pretty often lately—and went on doing till there was a blow-up about it. **1947** STEINBECK *Wayward Bus* 56 After the initial blow-up the subject had never verbally come up again, but her mother disapproved with her face.

b. An explosion.

1807 W. IRVING et al. *Salmagundi* (1811) xiii. 58 Our citizens did not refuse the invitation of the society to the *blow up.* **1852** DICKENS *Bleak Ho.* xxvi. 260 It was after the case-filling blow-up, when I first see you. **1867** M. ARNOLD *Let.* 14 Dec. (1895) I. 376 Every one is full of the Clerkenwell blow-up.

2. *Sugar-manuf.* The place where the raw sugar is dissolved; also *attrib.*, as ***blow-up cistern, pan***, a vessel used in dissolving raw sugar by 'blowing' or forcing steam through it.

1833 B. SILLIMAN *Man. Sugar Cane* 77 The vats, or blow-ups, as they are called, containing the sugar,..are heated by steam tubes passing through them. **1845** DODD *Brit. Manuf.* V. 108 A steam-pipe, in communication with a boiler, is enclosed within the 'blow-up cistern' [for dissolving sugar]; and..steam is forced or 'blown' by its own pressure into the solution. *a* **1877** KNIGHT *Dict. Mech.*, Blow-up Pan. (*Sugar-Machinery.*) **1886** *Harper's Mag.* June 82/2 These 'mixers' or 'blow-ups' are really great stew-pans set in the ground. **1935** *Discovery* Dec. 363/2 The resultant mixture..becomes a syrup known as 'blow-up thick juice'.

3. A photographic enlargement (cf. BLOW *v.*[1] 23 c). *colloq.* (orig. *U.S.*).

1945 *Life* 9 July 100/2 (*caption*) The wall behind bar has blowups of the arm insignia of every U.S. division in Europe. **1946** *Electronics* Sept. 157 (*caption*) Big Blow-up... Electronics and Photography work together to produce records like this 47,500-diameter magnification. **1957** *New Yorker* 5 Oct. 34/2 Gigantic photographic blowups of the more important candidates.

blowy ('bləʊɪ), *a.* [f. BLOW *v.*[1] + -Y[1].] Characterized by blowing.

1830 MISS MITFORD *Village* Ser. IV. (1863) 269 It was a raw blowy March evening. **1840** WILLIS *Loiterings* III. 239 A very cold, blowy and rough night. **1864** LD. PALMERSTON in *Daily Tel.* 26 Aug., I had at one time nearly 1,000 acres of blowy sand where no blade of grass grew.

blowze (blaʊz). Also 6 **blowesse**, 6-7 **blowse**, 7 **blouze**, 8 **blowz**, 6- **blouse**. [Of unknown origin: cf. various Du. and LG. words with the sense of 'red' or 'flushed' under BLUSH; but some of the uses appear to be influenced by BLOW *v.*[1] Perhaps originally a cant term. Cf. BLOWEN.]

†**1.** A beggar's trull, a beggar wench; a wench.

1573 TUSSER *Husb.* (1878) 43 Whiles Gillet, his blouse, is a milking thy cow, Sir Hew is a rigging thy gate or the plow. **1621** BURTON *Anat. Mel.* III. iii. IV. ii. (1651) 628, I had rather marry a fair one, and put it to the hazard, than be troubled with a blowze. **1631** BRAITHWAIT *Whimzies* 144 His bonny blouze or dainty doxie, being commonly a collapsed tinker's wife or some highway commoditie taken up upon trust. **1639** FORD *Lady's Trial* III. i. 266 Wench is your trull, your blowze, your dowdie. **1648** HERRICK *Hesper.* (1869) 278 Yet he'll be thought or seen, So good as George-a-Green; And calls his blowze, his queene. **1709** *Rambl. Fuddle-Cups* 8. **1719** D'URFEY *Pills* (1872) I. 5 That keeps a blowz And beats his spouse.

2. 'A fat, red-faced, bloted wench, or one whose head is dressed like a slattern.' Bailey 1731; 'a ruddy fat-faced wench.' J. **b.** Hence ***blowze-like*** adj.

1588 SHAKS. *Tit. A.* IV. ii. 72 Sweet blowse, you are a beautious blossome sure. **1600** HEYWOOD *1 Edw. IV*, Wks. 1874 I. 60 My Besse is fair, And Shores wife but a blowze, compared to her. **1628** WITHER *Brit. Rememb.* VI. 644 Their flaring curles about their shag shorne browes Doe, of the fairest Lady, make a blouse. **1632** HEYWOOD *Iron Age* II. I. i. Wks. III. 364 As fayre a blowse As you, sweete Lady. **1647** *Let.* in Harrington *Nugæ Ant.* 126 The woman, bravest prized, now blouze-like woud appear.

blowzed (blaʊzd), *a.* Also **blowsed**. [It has the form of a pa. pple. of a vb. *to blowze*, in the sense of 'to make blowzy': cf. prec.]

1. Rendered blowzy in the face; excited; disordered in dress or hair; dishevelled, frowzy.

1766 GOLDSM. *Vic. W.* x, I don't like to see my daughters trudging up to their pew all blowzed and red with walking. *Ibid.* xi, My eldest daughter was hemmed in and thumped about, all blowzed in spirits, and bawling for fairplay. **1847** TENNYSON *Princ.* IV. 260 Huge women blowzed with health and wind and rain And labour. **1884** *Longm. Mag.* June 175 The cook came out with tolerably 'blowsed' hair.

†**2.** ***blowzed off*** (see quot.). *Obs.*

1748 RICHARDSON *Clarissa* (1811) VIII. xli. 156 The paint lying in streaky seams not half blowzed off, discovering coarse wrinkled skins.

blowzily ('blaʊzɪlɪ), *adv.* Also **blowsily**. [f. BLOWZY *a.* + -LY[2].] In a blowzy way, coarsely. So **'blowziness, 'blowsiness.**

1866 M. E. BRADDON *Lady's Mile* xxii, She was a very handsome lady..in spite of a little blowsiness. **1905** *Daily Chron.* 5 Apr. 4/7 Daintiness would certainly pay better than the present blowziness [of the flower-seller]. **1914** W. J. LOCKE *Fortunate Youth* i, Once blowsily good-looking. **1933** *Times Lit. Suppl.* 28 Sept. 653/3 The much-emphasized charm of the slatternly Kate is perhaps less convincing than her equally emphasized blowsiness. **1959** *Times* 23 Feb. 12/3 Drawings of..blowsily ample girls undressing.

†**'blowzing**, *a. Obs.* [In form a pr. pple. of a vb. *to blowze*: cf. BLOWZED *a.*] Tending to be blowzy.

1753 RICHARDSON *Grandison* (1781) V. ix. 48 Aunt Nell, who has naturally a good blowzing north-country complexion, turned as pale as ashes. *a* **1851** JOANNA BAILLIE (O). That blowzing wig of his.

blowzy ('blaʊzɪ), *a.* Also **blousy**, **blowsy**. [f. BLOWZE + -Y[1].]

1. Like a blowze; having a bloated face; red and coarse-complexioned; flushed-looking.

1778 MAD. D'ARBLAY *Diary & Lett.* I. 149 Thinking herself too ruddy and blowzy, it was her custom to bleed herself three or four times against the Rugby races. **1787** WOLCOTT (P. Pindar) *To Laureate* Wks. 1812 I. 476 Large-red-poll'd, blowzy hard two-handed jades. **1880** *Blackw. Mag.* Feb. 221 Like a common-place blowzy dairymaid. *fig.* **1922** *Blackw. Mag.* Mar. 353 That frousy, blousy, lousy tug.

2. Of hair, dress: Dishevelled, frowzy, slatternly.

c **1770** T. ERSKINE *The Barber* in *Poet. Regr.* (1810) 328 Long his beard, and blouzy hair. **1854** THACKERAY *Newcomes* I. 137 Smiled at him from under her blowsy curl-papers. **1931** S. BENSON *Tobit Transplanted* iii. 33 His mother's large blousy bun of hair was always coming down.

3. Coarse, rustic.

1851 HELPS *Comp. Solit.* v. (1874) 64, I cannot fancy the blowsy wisdom of the country.

†**bloysterous**, *a.* (Cf. *boisterous, blusterous.*)

1568 T. HOWELL *Newe Sonets* (1879) 144 Do bloysterous blastes that blow, compell to hoyse thy sayle.

blu(e, obs. pa. t. of BLOW *v.*[1]

blub, *v.* [A variant or parallel form of BLOB *v.*]

†**I. 1.** *trans.* To swell, puff out with weeping or otherwise. *Obs.*

1559 *Mirr. Mag.* 112 My face was blown and blub'd with dropsy wan.

†**2.** *intr.* To swell, protrude. *Obs.*

1684 SOUTHERNE *Disappointm.* II. i. Wks. (1721) 101 Her eyes and lips, see how they blubb and pout.

II. 3. Short for BLUBBER *v.* in sense 4. (*colloq.*)

1804 TARRAS *Poems* 124 (JAM.) Your cheeks are sae bleer't, and sae blubbit adown?

4. Short for BLUBBER *v.* in sense 3, to weep, cry. *colloq.*

1866 A. DOBSON in *Beeton's Annual* 211 Bob privately confessed to me that he always felt inclined to 'blub' over those whipper-tunes. **1884** BLACKMORE *T. Upmore* vi, Keep up your spirits, young fellow, and don't blub. **1899** KIPLING *Stalky* 48 Stalky..pretended to blub... Then I blubbed, too. **1928** TEMPLE THURSTON *Portrait of Spy, Paris* §1 He was blubbing in her arms.

†**blub**, *a. Obs.* An attrib. use of BLUB *v.*, chiefly used in combination (cf. *knock-knee'd*) with sense 'Swollen, puffed, protruding', as in ***blub-cheeks, -lips***; whence in comb. ***blub-cheeked, blub-faced***, etc.

1603 KNOLLES *Hist. Turkes* (1621) 775 Blub cheeked, and exceeding red faced. **1620** SHELTON *Quix.* III. x. 64 A Country Wench..blub-fac'd, and flat-nosed. **1679** SHADWELL *True Widow* II. Wks. 1720 III. 147 You have a pretty pouting about the mouth..and fine little blub-lips.

blub (blʌb), *sb.* [f. BLUB *v.* 4.] A fit or spell of weeping.

1894 G. DU MAURIER *Trilby* II. 255 It would do him good once more to have a good blub. **1968** *Listener* 11 July 38/3, I had a good blub down the first five miles of the dual carriageway.

blubber ('blʌbə(r)), *sb.*[1] Also 4 **bluber**, 4-6 **blober**, 5 **blobure**, **blobyr**, **blubbir**, 7 **blobber**, (**bloother**). [ME. *blober*, *bluber* sb., *blubren*, *blober* vb. are both found in 14th c.: it is uncertain which was of prior formation; perhaps the verb. Being so much earlier than *blob*, *blub*, they cannot be extensions of the latter; but are prob. onomatopœic, from the action of the lips in making a bubble, or imitating various bubbling sounds or motions of liquids. Cf. the parallel BLABBER. There is also a dial. Ger. *blubbern*, said of water casting up bubbles, and a LG. *blubbern* in *herût blubbern* to babble or 'blether'. See other analogous forms in Wedgwood. The relation to *bubble* is seen also in the fact that in north. dial. 'bubble' is used for the vb. in senses 3, 4, as Sc. 'to bubble an' greit' = to blubber and weep.]

†**1.** The foaming or boiling of the sea. *Obs.*

c **1325** *E.E. Allit. P.* C. 221 In bluber of þe blo flod bursten her ores. *Ibid.* C. 266 How fro þe bot in-to þe blober watz with a best lachched.

†**2.** A bubble of foam or air upon water. *Obs.* exc. *dial.*

c **1440** *Promp. Parv.* 40 Blobure [**1499** blobyr], *burbulium.* *c* **1450** HENRYSON *Test. Cres.* 192 And at his mouth a blubbir stode of fome. **1530** PALSGR. 199/1 Blober upon water, *bouteillis.* *a* **1808** *State, Leslie of Powis* 136 (Jam.) s.v., That he has seen blubbers upon the water..that by blubbers he means air-bubbles. **1830** FORBY *East. Angl. Gloss.*, *Blubber*, a bubble.

3. A jelly-fish or Medusa, also called sea-nettle.

1602 CAREW *Cornwall* 34 b, There Swimmeth also in the Sea, a round slymie substance, called a Blobber, reputed noysome to the fish. **1775** DALRYMPLE in *Phil. Trans.* LXVIII. 393 There were many blubbers in the ship's wake, which made a very luminous appearance. **1835** MARRYAT *Jac. Faithf.* xxxi, The sailors call them blubbers, because they are composed of a sort of transparent jelly.

4. The fat of whales and other cetaceans, from which train oil is obtained.

1664 *Phil. Trans.* I. 12 The Oyl of the Blubber is as clear and fair as any Whey. **1666** *Lond. Gaz.* No. 47/1 She..had in her about twelve hundred weight of Bloother for Oyl. **1671** RAY in *Phil. Trans.* VI. 2275 The fat, which..our Seamen call the Blubber. **1746** W. THOMPSON *R.N. Advoc.* (1757) 43 Not properly Flesh, but Slush, or Blubber, like Whales Blubber. **1870** YEATS *Hist. Comm.* 281 In a large whale the blubber will weigh thirty tons.

5. The action of blubbering or weeping.

1825 *Bro. Jonathan* I. 85 Jotham..whose every breath was a hoarse blubber. **1865** CARLYLE *Fredk. Gt.* III. IX. xi. 180 All in a blubber of tears.

6. *Comb.* and *Attrib.* (chiefly in sense 4), as ***blubber-boat, -cask, -chopper, -fork, -hook, -knife, -oil, -room, -ship; blubber-fed*** adj.; also, **blubber-boiler** *slang*, a whaling ship; **blubber-guy**, a large rope, or 'guy', suspended between the fore and main masts of a whaler, to assist in securing and supporting the carcase of a whale; **blubber-lamp**, a lamp which burns blubber-oil; **blubber-spade**, a spade-like knife used by whalers.

1820 SCORESBY *Acc. Arctic Reg.* II. 299 The harpooners.. divide the fat into oblong pieces or 'slips', by means of 'blubber-spades', and 'blubber-knives'. **1835** SIR J. ROSS *N.-W. Pass.* vi. 83 We passed a blubber cask. **1849-52** TODD *Cycl. Anat. & Phys.* IV. 1316/1 The fat, blubber-fed.. Esquimaux. **1851** H. MELVILLE *Moby Dick* II. xi. 75 They ..repeat gamesome stuff about 'spouters' and 'blubber-boilers'. *Ibid.* II. xxx. 204 The blubber-hook was inserted into the original hole. **1856** KANE *Arct. Exp.* II. ii. 29, I carried in our blubber-lamp. **1884** *Gd. Words* Jan. 40/2 A wooden jetty, a blubber-boat, and a pile of casks.

'blubber, *sb.*[2] One who blubs.

1832 CARLYLE in *Fraser's Mag.* V. 393 The purfly sand-blind lubber and blubber, with his open mouth, and face of bruised honeycomb.

'blubber, *a.* [Altered from the earlier BLABBER, BLOBBER, probably under the influence of *blub* and *blubber* sb.] Swollen, protruding; esp. said of the lips. (Often with hyphen.)

Hence **blubber-lipped, -cheeked** *a.*

1667 DAVENANT & DRYDEN *Tempest* III. iii, My dear Blubber-lips; this observe my Chuck. **1677** *Lond. Gaz.* No. 1211/4 Henry Blomfield..of a ruddy complexion, having full blubber lips very remarkable. **1690** *Ibid.* No. 2550/4 George Crockeford..with short black Hair..and Blubber-Lipped. **1711** J. GREENWOOD *Eng. Gram.* 178 Blubber-cheek't. **1825** SCOTT *Talism.* (1863) 196 A Negro, is he not ..with black skin..a flat nose, and blubber lips? *a* **1845** HOOD *Doves & Crows* iii, Stretch ev'ry blubber-mouth from ear to ear.

blubber ('blʌbə(r)), *v.* [For forms and etymology see the sb.]

†**1.** *intr.* To bubble, bubble up; to give forth a bubbling sound, as a spring, boiling water. *Obs.*

c **1325** *E.E. Allit. P.* B. 1017 Blo, blubrande, & blak, vnblyþe to neȝe. *c* **1340** *Gaw. & Gr. Knt.* 2174 Þe borne [= rivulet] blubred þerinne, as hit boyled hade. **1750** R. PULTOCK *Life P. Wilkins* xii. (1883) 38/2 My kettle..had been boiling, till hearing it blubber very loud..I whipped it off the fire.

2. *trans.* †**a.** To allow (tears) to bubble *forth*, to give copious vent to (tears). *Obs.* **b.** To utter or cry *out* with copious tears and sobs.

1583 STUBBES *Anat. Abus.* (1877) 108 Blubbering foorth seas of teares. **1590** GREENE *Never too late* (1600) 26 The teares trickled down the vermilion of her cheeks, and shee blubbred out this passion. **1720** GAY *Poems* (1745) II. 63 She thus begins, And sobbing, blubbers forth her sins. **1749** FIELDING *Tom Jones* XVII. iii, Western, whose eyes were full of tears..blubbered out 'Don't be chicken-hearted'.

3. *intr.* To weep effusively; to weep and sob unrestrainedly and noisily. (Generally used contemptuously and in ridicule for 'weep'.)

c **1400** *Test. Love* II. (1560) 283/1 Han women none other wrech..but blober and wepe till hem list stint. **1530** PALSGR. 458/1, I blober, I wepe, *je pleure.* *a* **1553** UDALL *Royster D.* III. iv, What, weep? Fie for shame! And blubber? **1562** PHAËR *Æneid* IX. B b iv b, Shee blobbryng still, and kindlyng further greif. **1605** B. JONSON *Volpone* II. vii. Wks. (1616) 477 What, blubbering? Come, drie those teares. **1748** SMOLLETT *Rod. Rand.* xliv. (1804) 292 He blubbered like a great school-boy who had been whipt. **1826** SCOTT *Woodst.* iv, Phœbe Mayflower blubbered heartily for company. **1857** HUGHES *Tom Brown* viii. (1871) 179.

4. *trans.* To wet profusely or disfigure (the face) with weeping; to beweep. Also *fig.* (The notion of 'swell with weeping' is later, and influenced by BLUBBER *a.*)

1584 GREENE *Card of Fancy* Wks. 1882 IV. 164 Whome he found all blubbered with tears. **1596** SPENSER *F.Q.* II. i. 13 Her face with teares was fowly blubbered. *a* **1631** DONNE *Serm.* lv. 553 God sees Teares in the heart of a man before they Blubber his face. **1638** SUCKLING *Aglaura* V. i. (1646) 56 The pretty flowers blubber'd with dew.

b. *transf.*

1870 LOWELL *Among my Bks.* Ser. I. (1873) 242 Trammels and pot-hooks which the little..Elkanahs blotted and blubbered across their copy-books.

blubbe'ration. = BLUBBERING: see -ATION.

1812 H. & J. SMITH *Rej. Addr.* (1833) 155 They sung a quartetto in grand blubberation.

'blubbered, *ppl. a.* Also 6 bloubred. [f. BLUBBER *v.* + -ED.] Flooded with tears; said of the eyes, cheeks, face; in later usage also, swollen and disfigured with weeping.

c **1575** *Cambyses* in Hazl. *Dodsley* IV. 208 With blubb'red eyes into my arms I will thee take. **1591** SPENSER *Daphn.* 551 Did rend his haire, and beat his blubbred face. *c* **1630** DRUMM. OF HAWTH. *Wks.* 51 A blubber'd band Of weeping virgins. **1718** PRIOR *Poems* 96 Dear Cloe, how blubber'd is that pretty Face? **1860** HAWTHORNE *Marb. Faun* (1878) I. vii. 86 Representing the poor girl with blubbered eyes.

†**2.** Loosely used for BLUBBER *a.*: Swollen; **a.** said of thick protruding lips. *Obs.*

1634 SIR T. HERBERT *Trav.* 14, I omit their flat noses, and blubberd lips, bigge enough without addition. **1697** DRYDEN *Virg. Eclog.* III. 35. **1714** GAY *Sheph. Week* III. 39 Her blubber'd Lip by smutty Pipes is worn.

†**b.** *fig.* Inflated like a bubble. *Obs. rare.*

1699 POMFRET *Poems* (1724) 72 Swell'd with Success and blubber'd up with Pride.

blubberer ('blʌbərə(r)). [f. as prec. + -ER[1].] One who blubbers or weeps violently.

1786 tr. *Beckford's Vathek* (1868) 29 Without the counsels of that blubberer. *a* **1848** MARRYAT *R. Reefer* xxxi, The blubberer in the smock-frock.

'blubbering, *vbl. sb.* [f. as prec. + -ING[1].] The action of weeping profusely and noisily.

1580 NORTH *Plutarch* (1676) 172 Lamentations made at the funerals of the dead, with blubbering and beating themselues. **1741** RICHARDSON *Pamela* (1824) I. xi. 22 He was angry, and said..Cease your blubbering. **1872** DARWIN *Emotions* vi. 156 Paroxysms of violent crying or blubbering.

'blubbering, *ppl. a.* Also 4–5 bloberond. [f. as prec. + -ING[2].]

†**1.** Bubbling, gurgling (like a spring). *Obs.*

c **1400** *Destr. Troy* 9642 Till the bloberond blode blend with the rayn. **1646** CRASHAW *Steps to Temp.* 33 At my feet the blubb'ring mountain, Weeping, melts into a fountain. **1863** BARING-GOULD *Iceland* xxi. 363 The bottom of this is also full of little blubbering springs.

2. Shedding tears profusely (*obs.*); weeping and sobbing noisily and unrestrainedly. A contemptuous expression for 'weeping'.

1581 NEWTON *Seneca's Thebais* 49 b, My trickling teares, my blubbring Eyes, may put you out of doubt. **1753** JANE COLLIER *Art Torment.* 46 Begone out of my sight, you blubbering fool. **1862** *Sat. Rev.* 13 Sept. 301 The somewhat scornful astonishment which is aroused in the undeveloped English mind when it is first called upon to sympathize with the blubbering demigods of Ilium.

Hence **'blubberingly** *adv.*

1835 BECKFORD *Recoll.* 116 Donna Inez was called..and embraced by his right reverence most blubberingly. **1844** TUPPER *Crock of G.* xxv. 202 She..kept calling blubberingly for 'Simon,—poor dear Simon'.

'blubberous, *a.* = BLUBBER *a.*

1863 SALA *Capt. Dang.* II. ii. 65 They went Raving Mad, gnawing their Tongues and poor blubberous Lips to pieces.

blubbery ('blʌbərɪ), *a.* [f. BLUBBER *sb.* + -Y[1].] Of the nature of (whale's) blubber. Also *fig.*

1791 E. DARWIN *Bot. Gard.* I. 44 Spears and javelins pierce his blubbery sides. **1853** LANDOR *Last Fruit* (1853) 345 Democracy is the blubbery spawn begotten by the drunkenness of aristocracy. **1880** *Daily Tel.* 20 Sept., The gelatinous and blubbery surface of the whale's body.

'blucher. [Named after the Prussian commander Field-Marshal von Blücher (blʏçər), but commonly mispronounced ('bluːtʃə(r)) or ('bluːkə(r)).]

1. A strong leather half-boot or high shoe, the actual pattern varying with the fashion.

1831 CARLYLE *Sart. Res.* I. iii. (1838) 25 Ink-bottles alternated with..tobacco-boxes, Periodical Literature, and Blücher Boots. **1854** THACKERAY *Newcomes* I. 130 My own bootmaker wouldn't have allowed poor F. B. to appear in Bluchers. **1859** *Sat. Rev.* 19 Feb. 220/2 If they [ladies] will trample on us with a hobnailed blucher.

2. (See quots.)

1864 *Soc. Sc. Rev.* I. 406 The railway companies recognize two other classes of cabs, called the 'privileged'.. and the 'Bluchers' named after the Prussian Field Marshal who arrived on the field of Waterloo only to do the work that chanced to be undone. **1870** *Athenæum* 5 Mar. 328 Non-privileged cabs, which are admitted to stations after all the privileged have been hired, are known as Bluchers.

†**'bludder,** *v. Obs.* Perhaps = To blunder; perh. To talk stuff; cf. BLETHER, BLUTHER. (Much used by Bale.) Hence **'bluddering** *ppl. a.*

1553 BALE *Vocacyon* in *Harl. Misc.* (Malh.) I. 359 The blinde bludderinge papistes. **1554** —— *Declar. Bonner's Articles* xxxvi. (D.) This bussard, this beast, and this bluddering papiste.

bludder, variant of BLUTHER *v.*

blude, Sc. and north. dial. form of BLOOD.

†**blude-black.** *Obs. rare*[−1]. (See quot.)

1647 LILLY *Chr. Astrol.* viii. 60 The Bat or Blude-black, Crow, Lapwing. [? for *blinde b[l]ack.*]

bludge (blʌdʒ), *v. slang.* [Back-formation from BLUDGER.] *intr.* **a.** To act as a prostitute's pimp. **b.** *Austral.* and *N.Z.* To shirk responsibility or hard work; to impose *on*. Also *trans.*, to cadge or scrounge.

1919 DOWNING *Digger Dial.* 12 *Bludge on the flag*, to fail to justify one's existence as a soldier. **1931** V. PALMER *Separate Lives* 264 I've stood you too long already, loafing around here, and bludging on your mother. **1937** L. MANN *Murder in Sydney* 222 A bludger is a ruffian living on the earnings of an immoral woman. Britannia may be..an immoral woman, but there's no need for Australia to bludge on her. **1939** K. TENNANT *Foveaux* II. iv. 176 Everybody bludges and robs. **1941** —— *Battlers* iii. 26 You..bludging little mongrel! **1944** J. H. FULLARTON *Troop Target* xxvi. 186 You were one of the 95 per cent who bludged at base in Enzed or England or Yankee-land. **1944** L. GLASSOP *We were Rats* xxv. 147 Probably a Free Frenchman bludging a lift. **1945** *Southern Cross* (London) 15 Dec. 4/1 Place seemed to be full of..sisters and cousins, all staying with the blokes Herbert had aimed to bludge on. **1945** E. G. WEBBER *Johnny Enzed in Middle East* 43 Those oysters you bludged from me. **1967** I. HAMILTON *Man with Brown Paper Face* vi. 73 He bludged three cigarettes off me. **1967** *Southerly* XXVII. 199 The bludging, dirty mong to whom she had..entrusted heart and hand.

Hence as *sb.*, an easy job or assignment; a period of loafing.

1945 Baker *Austral. Lang.* viii. 156 *Bludge*, a soft job. **1949** J. CLEARY *Long Shadow* 195 He was happy in his job, it was a good bludge. **1969** *West Australian* 16 Jan. 13/3 Prime Minister Gorton..quoted..as saying..he was coming to.. the Commonwealth Prime Ministers' conference 'on a bit of a bludge'.

bludgeon ('blʌdʒən), *sb.* [Not found before the 18th c.: origin unknown.

Blogon (with *g* = *j*) is quoted by Dr. Whitley Stokes from the Cornish drama *Origo Mundi* (? 14th c.), but its relation to the English is uncertain. Other Celtic etymologies sometimes proposed are on many grounds untenable. A Du. vb. *bludsen* to bruise, has also been compared; and it has been suggested that the word is of cant origin, connected with *blood.*]

A short stout stick or club, with one end loaded or thicker and heavier than the other, used as a weapon.

1730 BAILEY, *Bludgeon*, an oaken stick or club. **1755** *Gentl. Mag.* XXV. 135 These villains..knocked him down with a bludgeon. **1798** in *Ld. Auckland's Corr.* (1862) III. 413 They were attacked by nine men..armed with swords and short bludgeons. **1818** SCOTT *Hrt. Midl.* (1873) 59 Scarce any weapons but staves and bludgeons had been yet seen among them. **1875** STUBBS *Const. Hist.* III. xviii. 103 Called by the annalists the parliament of bats or bludgeons.

b. *Comb.* **bludgeon-man,** one armed with a bludgeon; **bludgeon-work,** fighting with bludgeons, hand-to-hand fighting.

1797 W. TAYLOR in *Month. Rev.* XXII. 528 Assisted by the bludgeon-men of some powerful faction. **1813** WELLINGTON *Let.* 5 Aug. in Gurw. *Disp.* X. 602 The battle of the 28th was fair bludgeon work.

'bludgeon, *v.* [f. prec. sb.] **a.** *trans.* To strike or fell with a bludgeon or similar weapon.

1868 DORAN *Saints & Sin.* I. 295 Such a preacher.. would be bludgeoned into a mummy. **1884** *Pall Mall G.* 15 Oct. 3/1 To bludgeon an opponent who has a sharp tongue.

b. *fig.* To strike heavily, as with a bludgeon. Const. *in:* to drive in as with a bludgeon. Hence **'bludgeoning** *vbl. sb.* and *ppl. a.*

1888 W. E. HENLEY *Bk. of Verses* 56 Under the bludgeonings of chance My head is bloody, but unbowed. **1892** STEVENSON & OSBOURNE *Wrecker* xviii. 273 Repentance bludgeoned me. **1894** *Athenæum* 14 July 55/1 It is not..the artful bludgeoning that gets the praise. **1906** R. WHITEING *Ring in New* 238 The militant knifing and bludgeoning men. **1928** E. BLOM *Limit. Music* 37 A truth that has no need of literal bludgeoning-in.

'bludgeoned, *a.* [f. BLUDGEON *sb.* + -ED[2].] Armed with a bludgeon, or with bludgeons.

1780 *Hist. Europe* in *Ann. Reg.* 194/2 They had a bludgeoned mob waiting for them in the street. **1831** *Fraser's Mag.* IV. 505 The bludgeoned fury of the rabble.

'bludgeoned, *ppl. a.* [f. BLUDGEON *v.* + -ED[1].] Struck down or wounded with or as with a bludgeon.

1887 STEVENSON *Misadv. J. Nicholson* vi, Next bludgeoned vanity raised its head again, with twenty mortal gashes.

'bludgeoner, -'eer. [f. as BLUDGEONED *a.* + -ER[1], -EER[1].] One who uses, or is armed with, a bludgeon.

1842 R. OASTLER *Fleet Papers* II. 8 They have set their hired bludgeoners at me. **1852** *Blackw. Mag.* 224 Those brutal bludgeoneers..go out..in gangs to poach. **1855** TROLLOPE *Warden* xiv. 144 Old St. Dunstan with its smiting bludgeoners has been removed.

bludgeonist ('blʌdʒənɪst). [f. BLUDGEON *sb.* + -IST.] One who strikes with or as with a bludgeon.

1811 *Ann. Reg.* *1809* 680 No hired bludgeonists astound him. **1903** *Daily Chron.* 25 May 3/3 Critic is a mild word to use. Bludgeonist would suit the case better.

bludger ('blʌdʒə(r)). *slang.* [Shortened from BLUDGEONER.] **1.** = BLUDGEONER; *spec.* a prostitute's pimp.

1856 [see *stick-slinger*, STICK *sb.*[1] 17]. **1898** *Bulletin* (Sydney) 17 Dec. Red Page/2 A *bludger* is about the lowest grade of human thing, and is a brothel bully. **1936** 'R. HYDE' *Passport to Hell* vi. 103 The male defenders of the prostitutes' quarters, known to the dictionary as *souteneurs*, and to the troops as bludgers. **1937** [see BLUDGE *v.*]. **1960** *Observer* 28 Aug. 28/2 They are strikingly different to the white prostitutes who ply their trade for coloured bludgers.

2. A parasite or hanger-on; a loafer. Now often in weakened sense. *Austral.* and *N.Z.*

1939 X. HERBERT *Capricornia* (1949) 81 All the men here are loafers and bludgers. **1941** BAKER *Dict. Austral. Slang* 11 *Bludger*, a loafer, idler, ne'er-do-well; one who imposes on others. **1942** *2 N.Z.E.F. Times* 21 Dec. 17/4 Some bludger's got my tin hat. **1953** R. BRADDON in I. Bevan *Sunburnt Country* 130 A *bludger* is a shirker. **1969** *Courier-Mail* (Brisbane) 12 June 2/5 Surely if one is willing to give a good day's work for a good day's pay one should be given a chance to earn. I'm no bludger.

blue (bluː, bljuː), *a.* Forms: 3 bleu, 3–8 blew, 4 blu(e, bluw(e, 4–5 blwe, 4–6 blewe, 7– blue. [ME. *blew*, a. OF. *bleu*, a Common Romanic word (= Pr. *blau*, *blava*, OSp. *blavo*, It. dial. *biavo*, med.L. *blāvus*), ad. OHG. or OLG. *blâw-*:—OTeut. *blǣwo-z* blue, whence also ON. *blá-*, likewise adopted in ME. as *bla*, *blo*, now BLAE. The corresponding OE. form *bláw* (or **blǣw*) is known only in *Erfurt Gloss.* 1152, 'blata, pigmentum: *haui-blauum*', and the derivative *blǣwen* (:—*blâwîno-*) 'perseus'. But neither of these survived into ME., where their place was supplied by the adoption of ON. *blá*, in sense of '*lividus*', and of F. *bleu* in sense of '*cæruleus*'. The OTeut. *blǣwo-* was perh. cognate with L. *flāvus* yellow (though *blôwo-z* would be the expected Teutonic form), the names of colours having often undergone change in their application; thus OSp. *blavo* was 'yellowish-grey'. (The guess that *blǣwo-* was derived from the stem **bliuwan*, Goth. *bliggwan* to beat, as 'the colour caused by a blow' is not tenable.) The present spelling *blue* is very rare in ME., and hardly known in 16–17th c.; it became common under French influence only

after 1700. In pronunciation, nearly all the dictionaries *c* 1887 still recognized (blju:), but the more easily pronounced (blu:) was already general in educated speech.]

I. Properly.

1. a. The name of one of the colours of the spectrum; of the colour of the sky and the deep sea; cerulean.

a **1300** [see BLUE *sb.* 1]. *c* **1325** *E.E. Allit. P.* A. 423 Art þou þe quene of heuenez blwe. **1366** *Test. Ebor.* (1836) I. 81 Unam robam blue. **1394** *Ibid.* I. 198 Un drape de blew saye. **1382** WYCLIF *Ex.* xxvi. 14 Another couertour of blew skynnes. *c* **1386** CHAUCER *Sqrs. T.* 636 And by hire beddes heed she made a mewe, And couered it with veluettes blewe [*v.r.* blue, bluwe]. **1486** *Bk. St. Albans* A ij b, It hade need to be died other green or blwe. **1570** LEVINS *Manip.* 94 Blewe, *ceruleus.* **1596** SPENSER *Astroph.* 185 The gods.. Transformed them.. Into one flowre that is both red and blew. **1669** BOYLE *Contn. New Exp.* I. xliv. (1682) 153 Between blew and green. **1718** POPE *Iliad* xv. 195 And to blue Neptune thus the goddess calls. **1797** COLERIDGE *Christabel* I. Concl., The blue sky bends over all. **1855** DICKENS *Dorrit* i, A sea too intensely blue to be looked at. **1884** W. SHARP *Earth's Voices, etc.* 142 Bluer than bluest summer air.

b. Said of the colour of smoke, vapour, distant hills, steel, thin milk. *Magnetism*, defining the south pole of a magnet (of a steel-blue colour) as distinguished from the north (red) pole; also, the magnetism of this pole.

1602 SHAKS. *Ham.* v. i. 277 The skyish head Of blew Olympus. **1728** POPE *Dunciad* III. 3 Him close she curtain'd round with vapours blue. **1809** J. BARLOW *Columb.* VII. 400 His blue blade waved forward. **1831** LYTTON *Godolph.* xxxiv, That chain of hills.. stretched behind.. their blue and dim summits melting into the skies. *a* **1859** DE QUINCEY *Wks.* (1863) II. 14 Skimmed or blue milk being only one half-penny a quart—in Grasmere. **1860** DICKENS *Uncomm. Trav.* xi. 107 Sails of ships in the blue distance. **1893** SLOANE *Electr. Dict.* 345 A two-fluid theory of magnetism has been evolved... It assumes a north fluid or 'red magnetism' and a south fluid or 'blue magnetism'.

c. Said of a pale flame or flash without red glare (as of lightning, etc.); e.g. in phr. ***to burn blue***, which a candle is said to do as an omen of death, or as indicating the presence of ghosts or of the Devil (perh. referring to the blue flame of brimstone: see De Foe, *Hist. Devil* ch. x.).

1594 SHAKS. *Rich. III*, v. iii. 180 The Lights burne blew! It is now dead midnight. **1601** —— *Jul. C.* I. iii. 50 The crosse blew Lightning. **1611** BEAUM. & FL. *Knt. Burn. Pestle*, Ribands black and candles blue For him that was of men most true. **1649** BP. REYNOLDS *Serm. Hosea* i. 54 In a mine, if a damp come, it is in vaine to trust to your lights, they will burn blew, and dimme, and at last vanish. **1726** DE FOE *Hist. Devil* x, That most wise and solid suggestion, that when the candles burn blue the Devil is in the room. **1824** BYRON *Juan* XVI. xxvi, His taper Burnt, and not *blue*, as modest tapers use.. Receiving sprites.

d. Said of the veins as they show through the skin. Cf. *blue blood* (see BLOOD 8).

1606 SHAKS. *Ant. & Cl.* II. v. 29 There is Gold, and heere My blewest vaines to kisse: a hand that Kings haue lipt. **1845** BROWNING *Bishop orders Tomb*, Some lump.. of lapis lazuli.. Blue as a vein o'er the Madonna's breast. **1885** MRS. OLIPHANT *Madam* II. xxvi. 50 Blue veins showing distinctly through the delicate tissue of his skin.

e. Often taken as the colour of constancy or unchangingness (? with regard to the blue of the sky, or to some specially fast dye). Hence ***true blue*** (*fig.*): faithful, staunch and unwavering (in one's faith, principles, etc.): sterling, genuine, real. See also 6 b.

a **1500** *Balade agst. Women Unconst.* in Stow's *Chaucer* (1561) 340 To newe thinges your lust is euer kene. In stede of blew, thus may ye were al grene. **1672** WALKER *Parœm.* 30 in Hazl. *Eng. Prov.*, True blue will never stain. **1674** N. FAIRFAX *Bulk & Selv.* 171 It being true blew Gotham or Hobbes ingrain'd, one of the two. **1705** HICKERINGILL *Priest-Craft* II. viii. 86 The Old Beau is True-Blew, to the Highflown Principles [of] King Edward's First Protestant Church. **1783** AINSWORTH *Lat. Dict.* I. s.v. *Blue.*

f. The particular shade is expressed by words prefixed, as *clear, dark, deep, intense, light*; *azure, indigo, lavender, plum, sky, slate, ultramarine, violet*; also by arbitrary words, as *Prussian, Berlin, royal, navy*. See also BLUE *sb.* 2, GREY-BLUE, POWDER-BLUE 2, *smalt-blue* (SMALT *sb.* 4), STONE-BLUE 2.

1415 *Test. Ebor.* (1836) I. 382 Lectum de worstede de light blewe et sadde blewe. ?*c* **1475** *Sqr. lowe Degre* in *Dom. Archit.* II. 140 Damaske whyte and asure blewe. **1509** HAWES *Past. Pleas.* XVIII. xii, Velvet, al of Indy blewe. **1611** COTGR., *Couleur perse*, skie-colour, azure colour.. light blue. **1622** PEACHAM *Compl. Gentl.* I. xxiii. (1634) 78 That which we call skye colour or heavens-blew. **1882** *Garden* 18 Mar. 183/3 Rich azure blue, dark blue.. violet blue, rich blue.

g. Defining a quality of sheep's wool (see quot.).

1888 *Encycl. Brit.* XXIV. 656/2 In the worsted trade the classification [of wool] goes.. in descending series, from fine, blue, neat, brown, breech, downright, seconds, to abb. .. The greater proportion of good English long wool will be classified as blue, neat, and brown.

h. Applied to animals with fur of a bluish-grey colour. So *blue hare* (see 12 a).

1863, 1884 [see *blue fox*, sense 12 a]. **1887** P. M. RULE *Cat* v. 66 *Blue or Silver Tabby*.. The ground-colour is a silver grey, with the stripes of a darker shade. **1909** *Daily Chron.* 15 Dec. 3/5 Cats of all colours, from 'blue' (which stands for smoke-grey in the cat-world) to 'cream'. **1968** H. HARMAR *Chihuahua Guide* 232 *Blue*, a blue-gray, such color as might be seen in the whippet or Bedlington.

i. blue and white *a.*, having a surface diversified with blue and white; *spec.* of china. Hence *ellipt.* as *sb.*

1719 LADY FERMANAGH *Let.* 19 Mar. in M. M. Verney *Verney Lett. 18th Cent.* (1930) II. II. xxiii. 60, I shall want a dozen of blew and white china plates. **1753** *Aris's Birmingham Gaz.* Nov. in E. Meteyard *Life of J. Wedgwood* (1865) I. 243 This is to give notice to all painters in the blue and white potting way, and enamellers on china ware, that [etc.]. **1830** P. NEILSON *Recoll. Six Years' Residence in U.S.* 320 Trowsers and frocks made of common drugget, (or blue and white as it is called). **1848** H. R. FORSTER *Stowe Catal.* 1 Twelve fruit dishes, of old blue and white. *Ibid.* 215 A blue-and-white bowl and covers. **1856** C. M. YONGE *Daisy Chain* I. i. 2 The fire-place.. was ornamented with blue and white Dutch tiles bearing marvellous representations of Scripture history. **1875** *Cornh. Mag.* XXXI. 538 The blue-and-white porcelain of Nankin. **1941** E. BOWEN *Look at all those Roses* 236 Blue-and-white plates, in metal clamps, hung in lines up the walls. **1968** K. WEATHERLY *Roo Shooter* 120 The blue-and-white roo had chosen.. a day camp.

j. *blue china.* Cf. BLUE *sb.* 4.

1833 LAMB *Old China* in *Last Ess.* 218 A set of extraordinary old blue china. **1881** TROLLOPE *Ayala's Angel* i, A few little dinner parties to show off his blue china. **1937** V. WOOLF *Years* 9 A Dutch cabinet with blue china on the shelves.

2. a. Livid, leaden-coloured, as the skin becomes after a blow, from severe cold, from alarm, etc.; = obs. BLO, and dial. BLAE. ***black and blue***: see BLACK *a.* 13, BLAE 1 b. Cf. also BLUE EYE.

1393 LANGL. *P. Pl.* C. IV. 125 Þat fur shal falle and forbrenne al to blewe [**1377** blo] askes The houses and þe homes of hem þat taken ȝyftes. *c* **1485** *Digby Myst.* (1882) I. 340, I shuld bete you bak and side tyll it were blewe. **1598** SHAKS. *Merry W.* v. v. 49 There pinch the Maids as blew as Bill-berry. **1634** MILTON *Comus* 434 Blue meagre hag, or stubborn unlaid ghost. **1748** SMOLLETT *Rod. Rand.* II. 23 My fingers cramped and my nose.. blue. **1814** SCOTT *Ld. of Isles* v. xxvi, His trembling lips are livid blue.

b. Phr. ***blue (in the face)***: livid with effort, excitement, etc. Used hyperbolically.

1864 TROLLOPE *Small Ho. at Allington* II. xvii. 175 You may talk to her till you're both blue in the face, if you please. **1917** 'H. H. RICHARDSON' *Fortunes R. Mahoney* II. viii. 175 He alone must argue himself blue in the face over it. **1928** N. COWARD *C. B. Cochran's 1928 Revue* I. v. 10 Beckon and coo Till you are blue, Mermaids have got no dam chance at all. **1934** F. BALDWIN *Innoc. Byst.* (1935) xi. 212 I've talked myself blue in the face to him. **1959** 'P. QUENTIN' *Shadow of Guilt* x. 89 Swear till you're blue in the face that Chuck was with you all day. **1968** *Observer* 3 Nov. 3/3 I've been looking into.. cases of dealers' rings.. until I'm blue in the face.

3. *fig.* a. Affected with fear, discomfort, anxiety, etc.; dismayed, perturbed, discomfited; depressed, miserable, low-spirited; esp. in phr. ***to look blue. blue funk*** (slang): extreme nervousness, tremulous dread; also ***blue-funk school***, a jocular perversion of 'blue-water school'; ***blue fear***, a variant of *blue funk*.

a **1550** *Peblis to Play* ii. 6 Than answerit Meg full blew. *c* **1600** *Rob. Hood* (Ritson) II. xxxvi. 84 It made the sunne looke blue. **1682** N. O. *Boileau's Lutrin* I. 316 But when he came to't, the poor Lad look't Blew. **1783** AINSWORTH *Lat. Dict.* (Morell) I. s.v. *Blue*, He looked very blue upon it, *valde perturbatus fuit.* **1840** DISRAELI *Corr. w. Sister* (1886) 15 Great panic exists here, and even the knowing ones.. look very pale and blue. **1861** *Sat. Rev.* 23 Nov. 534 We encounter.. the miserable Dr. Blandling in what is called.. a blue funk. **1871** MAXWELL in *Life* (1882) xii. 382 Certainly χλωρὸν δέος is the Homeric for a blue funk. **1883** *Harper's Mag.* Mar. 600/1 I'm not a bit blue over the prospect. **1883** STEVENSON in *Longm. Mag.* Apr. 683 The very name of Paris put her in a blue fear. **1908** *Daily Chron.* 24 Feb. 4/6 The identification by Mr. Harvey, M.P., of the 'blue-water school' with the 'blue funk school'. *Ibid.* 20 July 4/3 The Jingo.. is a nobler being than the disciples of our 'blue-funk' school.

b. Intoxicated. *slang* (chiefly *U.S.*).

1818 M. L. WEEMS *Drunkard's Looking Glass* (ed. 6) 4 The patient goes by a variety of nicknames.. such as boozy—groggy—blue—damp. **1860** [see sense 10]. **1945** BAKER *Austral. Lang.* ix. 166 A man who is drunk is said to be ..*blue*.

c. Of affairs, circumstances, prospects: dismal, unpromising, depressing. Chiefly in ***a blue look-out, to look blue.***

1833 *Mirror of Lit.* 25 May 350 'Why it's a blue look out, Master,' said he. **1857** TROLLOPE *Three Clerks* xxix, Charley replied that neither had he any money at home. 'That's blue,' said the man. **1879** HARTIGAN & WALKER *Stray Leaves* Ser. II. xv. 257 If our present officers are like them.., it's a blue look-out for the Afghans! **1888** 'R. BOLDREWOOD' *Robb. under Arms* II. xvii. 258 It seemed a rather blue look-out. **1966** WODEHOUSE *Plum Pie* iii. 84 You don't want Freddie's whole future to turn blue at the edges.., do you?

d. Of, pertaining to, or characteristic of the singing or playing of the BLUES. So ***blue note***: a minor interval occurring where a major would be expected; an off-pitch note; also *transf.* and *fig.*

1919 *Dancing Times* Aug. 482/2 From the clarionet began to flow the weirdest blue notes ever heard. **1928** *Melody Maker* Oct. 1093/1 Gramophone enthusiasts will be able to determine.. the class of rhythm of the rendering, i.e. Blue, slow, or fast Fox-trot. **1930** E. RICE *Voy. Purilia* x. 134 In the jazz symphony of life, there are many blue notes. **1945** V. THOMSON *Musical Scene* i. 30 The greatest master of 'blue', or off-pitch, notes. **1955** H. KURNITZ *Invasion of Privacy* (1956) vi. 49 Her voice trailed off in a forlorn blue-note fashion. **1969** C. BOOKER *Neophiliacs* iii. 68 The 'blue notes' and 'flattened chords'.. which provide sensations in jazz.

†**4.** Of the colour of blood; ? purple. *Obs.*

1483 *Cath. Angl.* 35 Blew [A. blowe], *blodius.*

II. *transf.* and *fig.*

5. a. Dressed in blue; wearing a blue badge.

1598 B. JONSON *Ev. man in Hum.* II. iv, We that are Bluewaiters. **1605** ARMIN *Foole upon F.* (1880) 42 Blew John, that giues Food to feede wormes. **1647** MAY *Hist. Parl.* III. vi. 112 The blew auxiliary Regiment. **1709** *Lond. Gaz.* No. 4508/2 Two Battalions of the blue Foot-Guards. **1883** READE *Tit for Tat* i, Gainsborough's blue boy.

b. ***Blue Squadron***: one of the three divisions made of the English Fleet in the 17th c.

1665 *Lond. Gaz.* No. 3/3, 17 or 18 sail of English Men of War (of the Blew Squadron). **1689** *Ibid.* No. 2467/4 This day Mr. *Edward Russell*, Admiral of the Blue Squadron, sailed from *St. Helens.* **1703** *Ibid.* No. 3896/3 *John Leake*, Esq. [is advanced] from Rear-Admiral of the Blue, to be Vice-Admiral of the same Squadron. **1840** *Penny Cycl.* XVI. 160 Admirals of the red, white, blue, squadrons.. bear a square flag of the colour of their squadron at the main.. top gallant mast.

c. Blue was formerly the distinctive colour for the dress of servants, tradesmen, etc., also of paupers, charity-school boys, almsmen, and in Scotland of the king's almoners or licensed beggars; cf. *blue apron* (see 13), BLUE-BOTTLE, BLUE-COAT, BLUE-GOWN.

1609 B. JONSON *Case Altered* I. ii. (N.) [*A serving-man*] Ever since I was of the blue order.

d. See BLUE *sb.* 9.

6. a. Belonging to the political party which, in any particular district, has chosen blue for its distinctive colour. (In most parts of England the Conservative party.)

1835 DISRAELI *Corr. w. Sister* (1886) 35, I.. have gained the show of hands, which no blue candidate ever did before. **1868** HOLME LEE *B. Godfrey* li. 292 She had not won his promise to vote *blue*. *Ibid.* lii. 297 This was a blue demonstration, a gathering of the Conservative clans.

b. *true blue*: (see above 1 e) specifically applied to the Scottish Presbyterian or Whig party in the 17th c. (the Covenanters having adopted *blue* as their colour in contradistinction to the royal *red*); but also with any use of *blue*, as in quot. 1860 where it = 'staunchly Tory'.

1663 BUTLER *Hud.* I. I. 191 For his Religion it was fit To match his Learning and his Wit; 'Twas Presbyterian true Blew. **1785** BURNS *Author's Earn. Cry* xiii, Dempster, a true blue Scot I'se warran. **1818** SCOTT *Hrt. Midl.* (1873) 75 A tough true-blue Presbyterian, called Deans. **1860** TROLLOPE *Framley P.* i. 10 There was no portion of the county more decidedly true blue.

7. Of women: Learned, pedantic. See BLUE-STOCKING. (Usually ***contemptuous.***)

1788 MAD. D'ARBLAY *Diary* (1842) IV. 219 Nobody would have thought it more odd or more blue. **1813** MAR. EDGEWORTH *Patron.* II. xxvi. 117 They are all so wise, and so learned, so *blue*. **1834** SOUTHEY *Doctor* xv. (1862) 37 A Lady.. bluer than ever one of her naked, woad-stained ancestors appeared. **1842** DICKENS *Amer. Notes* (1850) 38/2 Blue ladies there are, in Boston. **1864** *Spectator* No. 1875. 660 A clever, sensible woman, rather blue.

8. *fig.* Often made the colour of plagues and things hurtful. ***blue murder***, used in intensive phrases: see MURDER *sb.* 3. Cf. senses 1 c., 3 b., and BLUE DEVIL.

1742 YOUNG *Nt. Th.* v. 157 Riot, pride, perfidy, blue vapours breathe. **1742** R. BLAIR *Grave* 628 Racking pains, And bluest plagues, are thine. **1783** AINSWORTH *Lat. Dict.* (Morell) I. s.v. *Blue*, It was a blue bout to him, *istud illi fatale fuit.* **1847** BARHAM *Ingol. Leg., Black Mousquet.* II. xv, Those mischievous Imps, whom the world.. Has strangely agreed to denominate 'Blue.' **1856** BRYANT *On Revisit. Country* v, The mountain wind.. Sweeps the blue streams of pestilence away.

9. *colloq.* a. Indecent, obscene. Cf. BLUE *sb.* 14 and BLUENESS 4.

1864 HOTTEN *Slang Dict.* 78 *Blue*, said of talk that is smutty or indecent. **1935** *Economist* 16 Mar. 584/2 The songs sounded not vulgar exactly, but.. 'a bit on the blue side'. **1959** *Spectator* 14 Aug. 180/1 It meant that the theatre-going public were deprived of.. outstanding contemporary plays, yet allowed to visit 'blue' variety shows. **1965** *Punch* 2 June 799/1 He also wanted to see a blue movie.

b. (See quot. 1890.)

1890 FARMER *Slang* I. 256/1 *To make the air blue*, to curse; to swear; to use profane language. **1924** 'R. CROMPTON' *William—the Fourth* iv. 72 A man in his shirt-sleeves whose language is turning the air blue for miles around.

10. Phrases (*colloq.*). ***till all is blue***: said of the effect of drinking on the eyesight. ***by all that's blue***: cf. Fr. ***parbleu*** (euphem. for ***pardieu.***)

1616 R. C. *Times' Whis.* v. 1835 They drink.. Vntill their adle heads doe make the ground Seeme blew vnto them. **1838** *Fraser's Mag.* XVII. 313 Cracking jokes and bottles, until all is blue. **1840** MARRYAT *Poor Jack* xxiii, 'The black cat, by all that's blue!' cried the captain. **1860** BARTLETT *Dict. Amer.*, *Blue*.. a synonym in the tippler's vocabulary for 'drunk'. To drink 'till all's blue' is to get exceedingly tipsy. **1867** SMYTH *Sailor's Word-bk.* s.v., *Till all's Blue*: carried to the utmost—a phrase borrowed from the idea of a vessel making out of port, and getting into blue water.

III. *Comb.*

11. General combinations: **a.** qualifying the names of other colours, as ***blue-green, -grey, -lilac, -purple, -roan, -violet, -white***; also BLUE-BLACK.

1855 SINGLETON *Virgil* I. 211 His eyeballs, flashing with a *blue-green glare. **1859** GEO. ELIOT *A. Bede* 61 The keen glance of her *blue-grey eye. **1882** *Garden* 2 Dec. 481/2 The colour varies from a deep *blue-purple to a bright violet-purple. **1687** *Lond. Gaz.* No. 2224/4 A Mare of a *blue roan colour. **1881** *Daily News* 24 Feb. 3/1 A blue roan..which won at Oxford last summer. **1879** ROOD *Chromatics* ix. 122 The three fundamental colours..red, green, and *blue-violet. **1909** *Westm. Gaz.* 1 May 2/3 With half-mad eyes and *blue-white quivering lips.

b. parasynthetic and instrumental, as ***blue-aproned*** [f. *blue apron* + -ED[2]], ***-backed, -bleak, -blooded, -bloused, -brilliant, -cheeked, -chequed, -clad, -coloured, -faced, -flowered, -haired, -hearted, -laid*** [see LAID], ***-lined, -mantled, -nailed, -shirted, -stained, -suited, -throated, -ticked, -washed, -winged***; ***blue-glancing, -glimmering***.

1640 BP. HALL *Chr. Moder.* 33/1 A separatist, a *blue-aproned man, that never knew any better school than his shop-board. **1651** CLEVELAND *Poems* 51 *On J. W.* 17 A fair blew-apron'd Priest. **1845** *Proc. Berw. Nat. Club* II. 174 A *blue-backed gull, and a curlew. **1877** G. M. HOPKINS *Poems* (1918) 29 And *blue-bleak embers..Fall, gall themselves. **1853** MRS. GASKELL *Cranford* vii. 128 The old *blue-blooded inhabitants of Cranford. **1863** KINGSLEY *Water Bab.* iii. 129 Like an old blue-blooded hidalgo of Spain. **1885** WARREN & CLEVERLY *Wand. of Beetle* i. 3 The women..attended *by blue-bloused admirers. **1949** BLUNDEN *After Bombing* 48 And blue-bloused workmen in the yards at meals. **1923** D. H. LAWRENCE *Birds, Beasts & Flowers* 143 The peacock..struts *blue-brilliant out of the far East. **1815** SCOTT *Guy M.* xxxix, The Dominie, taking his *blue-checqued handkerchief from his eyes. **1787** LATHAM *Synopsis of Birds* Suppl. 93 *Blue-cheeked C[urucui]. **1956** *Nature* 3 Mar. 404/2 The blue-cheeked bee-eater, added to the British list only in June 1951. **1871** WHITMAN *Passage to India* 91 Disperse, ye *blue-clad soldiers! **1858** W. ELLIS *Visits Madagasc.* xi. 280 The little ..*blue-flowered lobelia appeared in great abundance. **1647** H. MORE *Song of Soul* II. III. I. xxii, The Sun, the Moon, the Earth, *blew-glimmering Hel. **1634** MILTON *Comus* 29 This isle..He quarters to his *blue-haired deities. **1855** KINGSLEY *Heroes* v. 167 Poseidon the blue-haired king of the seas. **1956** R. FULLER *Image of Society* vii. 178 Rose conferred with a blue-haired saleswoman. **1894** *Geol. Mag.* Oct. 463 A *blue-hearted limestone. *c* **1865** J. WYLDE in *Circ. Sc.* I. 153/1 Cream and *blue-laid paper. **1658** MAY *Old Couple* I. i. in *Dodsley* (1780) X. 448 The blushing rose, *blue-mantled violet. **1920** T. S. ELIOT *Ara Vus Prec* 15 A meagre, *blue-nailed, phthisic hand. **1907** *Westm. Gaz.* 6 May 7/1 The voiceless millions of *blue-shirted fellaheen. **1934** *Times* 19 Feb. 17/3 General O'Duffy was met by 2,000 blue-shirted men and women yesterday. **1925** BLUNDEN *English Poems* 87 *Blue-suited Labour's hoeing By Labour's graves. **1961** *Guardian* 12 June 7/1 Blue-suited young organisation men. **1862** ANSTED *Channel Isl.* II. ix. (ed. 2) 205 *note*, The *blue-throated warbler (*Sylvia suecica*) may be named as a rare visitor. **1908** *Daily Chron.* 29 Aug. 7/4 The *blue-ticked dog. **1637** MORTON *New Canaan* II. iv, Teales there are of two sorts, green winged and *blew winged. **1732** Blue-wing'd [see SHOVELLER[2] 2]. **1789** MORSE *Amer. Geogr.* 59 The Blue winged Teal. *Ibid.*, The Blue winged shoveller. **1878** GEO. ELIOT *Coll. Breakf.* 60 A blue-winged butterfly. **1931** *Hardy's Anglers' Guide* 60 Dry Flies ..Blue Winged Olive, Male.

12. Used more or less descriptively and distinctively, in forming the names of natural objects: **a.** *Animals*, as **blue-bill** *U.S.* and *dial.*, = SCAUPDUCK; **blue-breast**, the Blue-throated Redstart or Warbler; **blue bull**, the Nyl-gau or Nhilgai of India; **blue cat**, a Siberian cat valued for its fur; also a North American species of cat-fish; **blue cocks**, the *Salmo albus*; **blue fly**, a blue-bottle fly; **blue fox**, a variety of the Arctic fox, and its fur; **blue-grey** (see quot. 1902); **blue hare**, the varying hare (see VARYING *ppl. a.* 3); **blue hawk**, (*a*) the Peregrine Falcon (*F. peregrinus*); (*b*) the Ring-tailed Harrier (*Circus cyaneus*), also called *blue glede* and *blue kite*; **blue-head**, a worm used as bait; **blue heeler**, an Australian cattle-dog with a dark blue speckled body; **blue ling**, popular name of a kind of ling, *Molva byrkelange* (earlier called *lesser ling*); **blue pointer**, the popular name of a shark of either of two species found esp. in Australasian waters (see quot. 1953); **blue poker**, a kind of duck, the Pochard; **blue-poll**, the *Salmo albus* (= blue cocks); **blue-rock**, a kind of pigeon; **bluetail**, (*a*) *dial.* the fieldfare; (*b*) ***red-flanked bluetail***: an Asian bird, *Tarsiger cyanurus*; **blue-throat**, any of various birds esp. of the genus *Cyanecula* or *Cyanosylvia* (see quots.); **blue tit**, the Blue Titmouse; = BLUE CAP 4; **blue whale**, a bluish-grey rorqual, *Sibbaldus musculus*; **blue-wing**, name of a genus of ducks; *spec.* an American variety of teal. Also ***blue goose, jay, linnet, shark***, etc.; and in the names of many artificial angling flies, as ***blue dun, blue gnat, blue jay***, etc. Also BLUE-BIRD, BLUE-BOTTLE, BLUE-CAP, BLUE-FISH.

1813 WILSON *Ornith.* VIII. 84 Scaup Duck..better known among us by the name of the *Blue Bill. **1890** J. WATSON *Nature & Woodcraft* vii. 83 The fishermen hereabout call them [*sc.* scaups] 'dowkers' and 'bluebills'. **1909** R. W. CHAMBERS *Firing Line* x, The little blue-bill ducks came swimming in scores. **1965** *Jrnl. Lancs. Dial. Soc.* Jan. 13 *Scaup* (bluebill, cockleduck: Morecambe Bay, 1892). **1835** J. MARTIN *Descr. Virginia* 347 Fine fish, particularly the mud and *blue cat. **1877** R. I. DODGE *Hunting Grounds Gt. West* 250 The blue cat is also common in all the plain streams, attaining sometimes a weight of fifteen to twenty-five pounds. **1759** GOLDSM. *Bee* No. 4 ¶30 A large *blue fly fell into the snare. **1856** STOWE *Dred* 160 He just puts me in mind of one of these blue-flies. **1910** W. DE LA MARE *Three Mulla-Mulgars* xi. 151 That howl brings half the forest against me, like blue-flies to meat. **1863** BARING-GOULD *Iceland* 324 We disturbed a *blue Arctic fox. **1884** *Daily News* 27 Oct. 2/1 Costly fur, such as sable, blue fox, otter, or beaver. **1902** *Encycl. Brit.* XXV. 191/2 The cross between the Shorthorn and the Aberdeen-Angus [breed of cattle], known as the '*Blue Grey'. **1960** *Times* 25 Jan. 19/1 The original Galloways were put to a Shorthorn bull. This gave us a Bluegrey cow. **1895** R. LYDEKKER *Handbk. Brit. Mammalia* 226 The geographical distribution of the Mountain, Alpine, *Blue, Irish, or Polar, Hare, as the animal is variously called, is very extensive. **1962** M. BURTON *Dict. Mammals of World* 92 Varying Hare..also known as Blue Hare, Scottish Hare or Alpine Hare..has bluish tinge in spring and autumn, at change of coat. **1875** 'STONEHENGE' *Brit. Sports* I. v. xi. 6 §3.312 The Marsh-worm or *Blue-head is found in moist..localities. **1946** F. D. DAVISON *Dusty* (1947) xvii. 196 One of the dogs was a *blue heeler, a cattle dog. **1530** PALSGR. 911 The *blewe kyte, *faulz perdrier*. **1916** A. MEEK *Migrations of Fish* xviii. 237 Genus Molva..*M. byrkelange*. *Blue or lesser ling. *Ibid.* 238 The blue ling is occasionally landed at our ports from boats which have been fishing in deep water to the north. **1882** J. E. TENISON-WOODS *Fish of N.S.W.* 95 (Morris), On the appearance of a '*blue pointer' among boats fishing for schnapper outside, the general cry is raised, 'Look out for the blue pointer'. **1917** *Chambers's Jrnl.* Sept. 588/1 Those that the Sydney fisherman knows best,..and destroy human life, are the tiger shark, the blue pointer [etc.]. **1953** J. L. B. SMITH *Sea Fishes S. Afr.* 49 *Carcharodon carcharis*..Blue-Pointer (Durban)... This swift and voracious shark is a terror to all who venture on or in the water. *Ibid.* 50 *Isurus glaucus*..Blue Pointer, Mako Shark... A famous angling fish, abundant in Australasian waters, very swift and powerful. **1780** G. WHITE *Selborne* xliv. 111, I readily concur with you in supposing that house-doves are derived from the small *blue rock pigeon. **1863** H. KINGSLEY *A. Elliot*, A cage containing five-and-twenty 'blue-rocks'. **1866** J. BOWRING in *Trans. Devonshire Assoc. Advancem. Sci.* I. v. 18 The **blue-tail*..and many more will probably fly away. **1878** H. E. DRESSER *Hist. Birds of Europe* II. LXVII. 2 Nemura Cyanura (Red-flanked Bluetail)..this richly coloured Asiatic bird is found throughout Asia. **1885** SWAINSON *Prov. Names Birds* 5 *Fieldfare*..From the predominant bluish tinge of its upper plumage are derived:—Blue tail (Midlands; West Riding), [etc.]. **1948** S. BRUCE in *Scottish Naturalist* LX. 6 (*title*) The Red-Flanked Bluetail in Shetland. *Ibid.*, The bluetail will henceforward appear on the British list... The bluetail is related to the redstarts, bluethroats, robins, and chats. **1873** W. YARRELL *Hist. Brit. Birds* (ed. 4) I. 321 The *Bluethroat *Phœnicura Suecica*. *Ibid.* 323 The majority of Bluethroats which come to the rest of Continental Europe..were..first distinguished by Brehm as *Cyanecula leucocyana*. **1954** BANNERMAN *Birds Brit. Isles* III. 307 Bluethroat, *Cyanosylvia svecica*... Red-spotted Bluethroat, *Cyanosylvia svecica svecica*... White-spotted Bluethroat, *Cyanosylvia svecica cyanecula*. **1845** *Gard. Chron.* 86 The robin..seems to fear the *blue-tit. **1851** H. MELVILLE *Moby Dick* I. xxxi. 229 There are a rabble of uncertain, fugitive, half-fabulous whales..the Iceberg Whale..the *Blue Whale; &c. **1888** *Encycl. Brit.* XXIV. 524/2 The 'blue whale', the largest of all known animals, attains a length of 80 or even sometimes 85 feet. **1937** *Discovery* Nov. 357/2 The largest animal known, the blue whale or Sibbald's rorqual. **1709** LAWSON *Carolina* 148 The Blue-Wings are less than a Duck, but fine Meat. **1754** [see TEAL 2]. **1768** WASHINGTON *Diaries* (1925) I. 294 Went into the Neck and up the Creek after Blew Wings. **1874** J. W. LONG *Amer. Wild-fowl Shooting* xv. 192 They are a trifle smaller than the blue-wings. **1895** *Outing* (U.S.) Oct. XXVII. 43/1 A bunch of blue-wing teal rose from the ice-pond.

b. *Plants*, as **blue ash** *U.S.*, a North American variety of ash; **blue-berry**, the name of various species of *Vaccinium*, especially the American *V. corymbosum*; **blue-blaw, blue-cup**, *Centaurea cyanus*: = BLUEBOTTLE 1; **blue-bush**, a popular name of any of several varieties of shrub, esp. the Australian *Kochia pyramidata*; **blue chamomile** or **blue daisy**, the Sea Starwort, and other blue composite flowers; **blue-gage**, a kind of plum; **blue gum (tree)**, the *Eucalyptus globulus* of Australia; **blue-hearts**, *Buchnera americana*; †**blue-pipe**, the Lilac; †**blue poppy** (*dial.*), BLUEBOTTLE 1; **blue rocket**, *Aconitum pyramidale*; **blue star** (see quot.); **blue tangles**, *Vaccinium frondosum*; **blue-weed**, Viper's Bugloss, *Echium vulgare*. Also in numberless specific names, as *blue crane's-bill*, etc. See also BLUEBELL, BLUEBONNET, BLUEBOTTLE.

1783 W. FLEMING in N. D. Mereness *Trav. Amer. Col.* (1916) 667 *Blue Ash a spieces of the White Ash and called so from the bark tinging water of that colour. **1819** D. THOMAS *Trav.* 93 The blue ash..is a fine stately tree of two or three feet diameter, generally of a straight grain, and may be easily split into rails. **1832** D. J. BROWNE *Sylva Amer.* 156 The Blue Ash is unknown to the Atlantic parts of the United States. **1772–84** COOK *Voy.* (1790) VI. 2181 *Blue-berries, black-berries, cran-berries, and crow-berries. **1883** *Harper's Mag.* Mar. 603/2 We are feasting now upon blue-berries. **1578** LYTE *Dodoens* II. xiii. 161 This floure is called ..of Turner Blew bottell, and *Blewblaw. **1601** HOLLAND *Pliny* II. 92 No sooner hath the Rose plaied his part, but the blew-blaw entereth the stage. **1611** COTGR., *Blaveoles*, Blew bottles, Blew blawes, Corne-flowers. **1876** W. HARCUS *South Australia* 124 (Morris), Thickly grassed with short fine grass, salt and *blue bush, and geranium and other herbs. **1933** *Bulletin* (Sydney) 7 June 25/2 Blue bush is far-famed among cattlemen—a stout shrub of 2ft. or 3ft. high, with short thick leaves. **1934** *Ibid.* 5 Dec. 20/2 Sandalwood-tree..grows over the whole s.-w. of Queensland, though not always in commercial quantities, and is generally known as 'plum' or 'bluebush'. **1936** F. CLUNE *Roaming round Darling* xviii. 177 All about this country grows a bluebush shrub (actually more green than blue), with closely assembled leaves, very good for sheep. **1958** L. VAN DER POST *Lost World of Kalahari* i. 24 A cleft over-grown and purple with the shadow of blue-bush. **1597** GERARD *Herbal* lxxxviii. 334 Women that dwell by the sea side, call it..*blew Daisies, or *blew Camomill. **1881** MISS BRADDON *Asph.* II. 95 The purple bloom of grapes and *blue-gages. **1808** HOME in *Phil. Trans.* XCVIII. 305 The tender shoots of the *blue gum tree. **1845** DARWIN *Voy. Nat.* xix. (1873) 435 The trees with the exception of some of the Blue-gums. **1884** *19th Cent.* Feb. 321 The *Eucalyptus globulus* or Blue Gum tree of Australia, has a special power of antagonising the spread of malaria. **1697** J. PETIVER in *Phil. Trans.* XIX. 679 The Common Lilac or *Blew Pipe Tree. **1886** *Encycl. Brit.* XX. 174/1 The *blue star [grass, of Queensland], *Chloris ventricosa*.

c. *Minerals*, as **blue asbestos** = CROCIDOLITE; **blue-billy** (see quots.); **blue clay**, a clay of this colour, esp. (*a*) that used in pottery manufacture (see quot. 1957); (*b*) = *blue ground* (see sense 13); **blue copper, blue malachite**, = AZURITE; see also COPPER *sb.* 1 b; **blue copperas, blue vitriol**, sulphate of copper (see VITRIOL); **blue felspar, blue spar**, = LAZULITE; **blue iron** = VIVIANITE; **blue lead** (see quots.); **blue metal**, name given by the workmen to a sulphide of copper obtained during the process of copper-smelting; also, argillaceous shale of a bluish colour, used esp. in road-making; **blue slipper**, local name of the Gault clay. Also ***blue verditer***, etc. See also BLUE-JOHN, BLUESTONE.

c **1865** LETHEBY in *Circ. Sc.* I. 118/1 Carbonic acid, cyanogen, and sulphuretted hydrogen, are extracted from the gas; these combine with the lime, and produce a.. compound, which is technically termed **blue-billy*. **1881** RAYMOND *Mining Gloss.*, *Blue-billy*, the residuum of cupreous pyrites after roasting with salt. **1733** ELLIS *Chiltern & Vale Farming* 17 Black or *Blue Clays—I am now come to touch on the very best of all Clays. **1784** R. KIRWAN *Elem. Min.* viii. 78 Blue clays. These sometimes lose their colour and become white when heated. **1886** G. A. FARINI *Through Kalahari Desert* iii. 31 Two, three, four blasts followed..and some tons of hard blue clay were loosened ready to be carried to the 'floors'. **1938** *Thorpe's Dict. Appl. Chem.* II. 309/1 Diamonds occur sparingly in river beds or embedded in 'blue clay'. **1957** *Encycl. Brit.* VII. 842/2 *Ball Clay*. This is found principally in Devon and in Dorsetshire, and is sometimes known as blue clay, owing to its greyish-blue colour, which is due to organic matter. When fired..it becomes white. **1875** URE *Dict. Arts* I. 407 *Blue Lead, a name used sometimes by the miners to distinguish galena from the carbonate, or white lead. **1881** RAYMOND *Mining Gloss.*, *Blue-lead* (pronounced like the verb *to lead*), the bluish auriferous gravel and cement deposit found in the ancient river-channels of California. **1808** *Blue metal [see METAL *sb.* 10]. *a* **1835** J. PHILLIPS *Geol.* in *Encycl. Metrop.* (1845) VI. 628/2 The least fragment of jet or morsel of bituminous shale, especially if accompanied by 'blue metal' is enough to make a credulous proprietor listen to an ignorant collier. **1892** R. O. HESLOP *Northumberland Words* 69 *Blue metal*, indurated argillaceous shale, of a bluish purple colour, resembling that of blue slates. **1909** A. H. DAVIS *On our Selection* (1953) vi. 30 We had been accustomed to pelt her with potatoes and blue-metal. **1966** 'J. HACKSTON' *Father clears Out* 102 They came close enough into the college to send messages to the teacher by showering blue metal on the roof of their Alma Mater. **1881** *Daily News*, A great deal of the most charming scenery of the Undercliff..is due to the freaks of what is locally called the '*blue slipper.' **1770** WATSON in *Phil. Trans.* LX. 332 *Blue vitriol, corrosive sublimate. **1856** *Farmer's Mag.* Jan. 90 The qualities of blue vitriol used for soaking wheat.

13. Special combinations or phrases. †**blue apron**, one who wears a blue apron, a tradesman; **blue baby**, an infant suffering from congenital cyanosis; **blue bag**, a barrister's (orig. a solicitor's) brief-bag of blue stuff; hence, one carrying such a bag; so (*nonce*) ***to forget the blue bag***, to ignore (the indications of) one's rank; **blue band**, a band of glacier ice of a blue colour due to the absence of air-bubbles; **blue beat** [f. the name of the record label on which it was principally distributed in Britain], used chiefly *attrib.* of a style of popular music of Jamaican origin characterized by a strong off-beat; a British development of SKA; **blue blanket**, the banner of the Edinburgh craftsmen; *fig.* the sky; **blue blood** (see BLOOD 8); **blue boy** *slang*, a policeman (usu. in *pl.*): cf. *boys in blue* s.v. BLUE *sb.* 3 b; so **Blue Force**; **blue brick** (see quot. 1889); **blue brittleness**, the brittleness of steel at blue heat; **blue butter** = *blue ointment*; **blue cheese**, a cheese marked with veins of blue mould (cf. BLEU); **blue-collar** *attrib.* (chiefly *U.S.*), designating a manual or industrial worker, as distinct from a 'white-collar' worker; so *blue-collared* adj.; **blue comb (disease)**, a disease affecting young pullets in which there is cyanosis of the comb; **blue dahlia**, an expression for anything rare or unheard of; **blue disease**, a popular name for *Cyanosis*; **blue-domer** *colloq.*, one who does not go to church, preferring to worship beneath the 'blue dome' of heaven; hence **blue-domeism**, this attitude to worship, **blue-domeist**, one who has such an attitude;

blue earth = *blue ground*; **blue fire**, a blue light used on the stage for weird effect; hence *attrib.* sensational (cf. sense 1 c); **blue flint** (see quot.); **Blue Force** (see *blue boy*); **blue gas** (see quot.); **blue ground**, the dark soil, normally greyish-blue, in which diamonds are found; **Blue Guide** [cf. F. *Guide Bleu*], one of a series of popular guide-books with blue covers; **blue heat**, a temperature of about 550° Fahr., at which ironwork assumes a bluish tint; **blue jacket**, a sailor (from the colour of his jacket); *esp.* used to distinguish the seamen from the marines; **blue jaundice** (= *blue disease*); **blue-jean** *attrib.*, made of blue jean; as *sb. pl.*, trousers made of blue jean; also *transf.*; hence *blue-jeaned* adj.; **blue laws**, severe Puritanic laws said to have been enacted last century at New Haven, Connecticut, U.S.; hence *fig.*; **blue light**, a pyrotechnical composition which burns with a blue flame, used also at sea as a night-signal; **blue line** (in *Tennis*), the service-line (so coloured); **blue mantle**, the dress, and the title, of one of the four pursuivants of the English College of Arms; **blue measure** (see quot.) *Obs.*; **Blue Monday**, (*a*) the Monday before Lent; (*b*) a Monday spent in dissipation by workmen (cf. Ger. *der blaue Montag*); **blue moon** (*colloq.*), a rarely recurring period; **blue-mould**, the mould of this colour produced upon cheese, consisting of a fungus, *Aspergillus glaucus*; hence **blue-moulded, -moulding** *a.*; **blue-mouldy** *a.*, covered with blue mould; also *fig.*; **Blue Mountain (coffee)**, a type of Jamaican coffee; **blue mud**, a marine deposit coloured by organic matter and iron sulphide; **Blue Nun** = CONCEPTIONIST 2; **blue oil** (see quot.); **blue ointment** mercurial ointment (see MERCURIAL *a.* 5); **blue pencil**, a blue 'lead' pencil used chiefly in marking corrections, obliterations, and the like; **blue-pencil** *v. trans.*, to mark, score through, or obliterate with a blue pencil; hence, to make 'cuts' in; to censor; also used euphemistically (cf. BLANK *sb.* 12 b); hence **blue-pencilling** *vbl. sb.*; **Blue Peter**, (*a*) a blue flag with a white square in the centre, hoisted as the signal of immediate sailing; hence, in *Whist*, the playing a higher card than is needed, as a signal or 'call' for trumps; (*b*) *U.S.* (see quots.); **blue pigeon** *slang*, †(*a*) (the act of stealing) lead, esp. that used for roofing; also *attrib.*; hence ***to fly the blue pigeon***: to steal lead; (*b*) *Naut.* the sounding lead; see PIGEON *sb.* 4 b; **blue pill**, (*a*) a mercurial pill of antibilious operation; (*b*) *U.S. slang*, a bullet; hence **blue-pilled** *a.*; **blue-plate**, *U.S.* (see quot. 1961); **blue point** (see POINT); **blue pot**, a pot made of a mixture of clay and graphite, a black-lead crucible; **blue process** (see quot.); **blue (process) paper**, a sensitized paper used for copying maps and plans, made by saturating the paper with potassium ferrocyanide; **blue ruin** (*slang*), gin, usually of bad quality; **Blue Shirt, Blueshirt**, one who wears a blue shirt as a sign of allegiance to or membership of a particular group, party, etc.; **blue streak** *colloq.* (orig. *U.S.*), (*a*) something resembling a flash of lightning in speed, vividness, etc.; (*b*) a constant stream of words; esp. in phr. *to talk a blue streak*; **Blue Train** [cf. F. *Train Bleu*] (see quot. 1951); **blue-vinnied** *a. dial.* [cf. FINNY, VINNY *a.*[2]], having a blue mould; hence **blue-vinn(e)y**, a blue-mould cheese made in Dorsetshire; **blue-washed** *a.*, (*a*) washed by the blue sea; (*b*) covered with a blue wash; **blue water**, the open sea; **blue water-gas** = *blue gas*; **blue-water school**, a collective term applied to politicians or political thinkers who regard a strong navy and the command of the sea as essential to the security of the country, or as the chief or the only sufficient defence. See also BLUE-BEARD, BLUE-BOOK, etc.

1726 AMHERST *Terræ Fil.* xliii. 230 For, if any saucy *blue apron dares to affront any venerable person.. all scholars are immediately forbid to have any dealings or commerce with him. **1903** R. H. BABCOCK *Dis. Heart* xxix. 692 The little patient had been a **blue baby* from birth. **1964** M. MCLUHAN *Understanding Media* II. xxviii. 282 Watching a blue-baby heart operation on TV. **1809** MALKIN tr. *Le Sage's Gil Blas* II. v. i. 343 Said I to myself, every now and then, when they forgot the *blue-bag: this is the way of the world! Every one fancies himself to be..superior to his neighbour. **1817** *Black Dwarf* 31 Dec. 814 Black legs, blue-bags, learned wig-blocks. **1837** DICKENS *Pickw.* xxxiii, Mr. Pickwick..followed Mr. Perker and the blue bag out of court. **1852** —— *Bleak Ho.* i, A battery of blue bags is loaded with heavy charges of papers and carried off by clerks. **1910** Blue bag [see BRIEF *sb.* 11]. **1895** DANA *Man. Geol.* (ed. 4) 243 Lamellar or straticulate structure of glacier-ice modified by..the '*blue bands', or 'veined structure'. **1937** *Discovery* Feb. 36/1 There are 'blue bands' or layers of a very much harder ice, containing small bubbles of air. **1968** *Listener* 29 Feb. 284/3 Surprising..to see his group of pugnacious London 13 to 14-year-olds acting out a kind of ballet about cowboys to their own selection of *blue-beat music. **1971** [see ROCKSTEADY]. **1974** A. ALI *Westindians in Gt. Brit.* 96 He..cherishes the memories of 'the Blue Beat era'. **1980** *Oxford Times* 18 Jan. 15/1 The name most commonly applied to the Specials' style is 'ska' or 'bluebeat', which means that it harks back to the pre-reggae sound of West Indian music. **1599** JAS. I. *Basil. Doron* (1603) 51 If they in any thing be controlled, up goeth the *blew-blanket. **1726** DE FOE *Hist. Devil* I. v, We must be content till we come 'tother side the Blue-blanket, and then we shall know. **1780** (*title*) Historical Account of the Blue Blanket or Craftsmen Banner, with the Prerogatives of the Crafts of Edinburgh. **1828–41** TYTLER *Hist. Scotl.* (1864) II. 224 Calling out the trained bands and armed citizens beneath a banner presented to them on this occasion [1482] and denominated the Blue Blanket. **1883** JAS. GREENWOOD *Odd People in Odd Places* 68 The instrumental '*blue boys' belonging to several metropolitan divisions. **1912** A. S. M. HUTCHINSON *Happy Warrior* v. vii. §2 The Blue Boys from the police-station.. scoured the country. **1850** R. PROSSER in E. Dobson *Manuf. Bricks & Tiles* I. iv. 99 An ordinary *blue brick weighs, wet from the mould, 12 lbs. 4 oz. **1889** E. J. BURRELL *Elem. Building Construction* xiv. 218 *Staffordshire blue bricks.* These are composed of clay containing a large percentage of oxide of iron, which is converted into the black oxide by intense heat, giving a characteristic dark-blue colour to the bricks. **1940** *Chambers's Techn. Dict.* 99/1 *Blue bricks*, ..(made chiefly in Staffordshire and North Wales)..form the best quality engineering bricks. **1919** *Jrnl. Iron & Steel Inst.* C. 521 Fettweis..explains the phenomenon of '*blue-brittleness and the aging of steel. **1959** *Ibid.* CXCI. 100/2 It was found that the best heat treatment for reducing blue brittleness in 0·55% C steel was subcritical annealing at 550° C. **1874** HOTTEN *Slang Dict.*, **Blue Butter*, mercurial ointment used for the destruction of parasites. **1925** L. J. LORD *Pract. Butter & Cheese Making* xxvi. 145 This kind [*sc.* Stilton] and that next described are full-milk *blue cheeses. **1950** *Tuscaloosa News* 25 Nov. 1/5 '*Blue collar' workers also include helpers, laborers, and supervisors. **1958** *Listener* 23 Oct. 631/1 The blue-collar people, the machine operators. **1959** *Observer* 1 Nov. 8/2 The split is no longer between white- and blue-collar workers, but between those with and those without the college diplomas. **1967** *Boston Herald* 1 Apr. 5/8 He thought his main appeal would be to the 'little business men', clerks, auto workers, building and trade workers and similar blue collar groups. **1959** V. PACKARD *Status Seekers* (1960) ii. 25 The recent great gain of white-collared workers over *blue-collared ones. **1967** *Guardian* 16 May 2/4 The traditional 'iron curtain' between white and blue collared civil servants. **1941** *Amer. Jrnl. Vet. Res.* II. 261/2 Depression is marked and the comb may be wilted and cyanotic, hence the popular name '*blue comb'. **1950** *N.Z. Jrnl. Agric.* May 442/1 The condition of poultry known as pullet disease, blue-comb disease, new wheat disease, or X disease has been known in Great Britain and America for several years. [**1820** SHELLEY *Cloud* vi, And the winds and sunbeams with their convex gleams, Build up the blue dome of air.] **1945** A. HUXLEY *Time must have a Stop* xxx. 289 Those of us who..have found that humanism and *blue-domeism are not enough. **1952** J. MASEFIELD *So Long to Learn* II. 100 There were..Celtic Fringers,..Blue Domeists, [etc.]. **1961** PARTRIDGE *Dict. Slang* (ed. 5) 1005/1 *Blue-domer*, an officer that absents himself from church parade. **1962** *Times Lit. Suppl.* 3 Aug. 554/4 'Blue-domer' parents in whose eyes the most damnable thing was to be 'pi'. **1897** *Westm. Gaz.* 22 May 3/2 The well-known '*blue earth' of the diamond mines. **1875** C. L. KENNEY *Mem. Balfe* 131 The same theatre..set up a formidable opposition..in the shape of a *blue fire melodrama. **1861** J. SHEPPARD *Fall Rome* vi. 309 Many persons living can recollect that their English auxiliaries were termed *Blue Flints by the peasants of Vendée, from the unusual colour of the flints in their musket-locks. **1927** *Daily Express* 27 Dec. 1 The '*Blue Force',—that is, the uniform branch of the police. **1902** *Encycl. Brit.* XXVIII. 602/1 Water gas in its original state is called '*blue gas', because it burns with a blue, non-luminous flame. **1886** J. NOBLE *Handbk. Cape Good Hope* 192 The '*blue ground'..far from being barren of diamonds ..yielded even better returns than the upper layers of 'yellow ground'. **1911** *Daily Chron.* 25 Mar. 3/2 Of very great rarity is a piece of 'blue ground' with a diamond embedded in it... The 'blue ground'..is..not uncommonly black or brown. **1918** (*title*) The *Blue Guides: London & its Environs. **1935** *Discovery* June 156/2 The Blue Guides..bear the mark of an original and scholarly mind. **1793** SMEATON *Edystone L.* §328 The iron came to about, or rather above, a *blue heat. **1879** *Cassells Techn. Educ.* IV. 400/1 A temperature known as a blue or black heat. **1830** MARRYAT *King's Own* ii, Every '*blue jacket' would walk over. **1859** L. OLIPHANT *Elgin's Miss. China* I. 128 The ladders..were soon swarming with marines and blue-jackets. **1855** H. MELVILLE *Israel Potter* xx. 216 Across the otherwise *blue-jean career of Israel, Paul Jones flits and re-flits like a crimson thread. **1932** F. L. WRIGHT *Autobiogr.* I. 16 Blue-jean overalls with blue cotton suspenders. **1957** Blue jeans [see JEAN]. **1960** *20th Cent.* Dec. 557 A simple provincial gaucheness, a corny blue-jeans innocence. **1956** J. POTTS *Diehard* viii. 138 She..swung her *blue-jeaned legs. **1781** S. PETERS *Hist. Connecticut* (1877) 44 Even the religious fanatics of Boston and the mad zealots of Hertford..christened them the '*Blue Laws'. **1842** DICKENS *Amer. Notes* I. v. 175 The local legislature of Connecticut, which sage body enacted..the renowned code of 'Blue Laws'. **1876** EMERSON *Ess.* Ser. I. viii. 204 Simple hearts..play their own game in innocent defiance of the Blue-laws of the world. **1805** NELSON *Disp.* (1846) VII. 57, I had rather that all the Ships burnt a *blue-light. **1833** MARRYAT *P. Simple* (1863) 51 Blue lights and Catharine wheels..all firing away. **1616** BULLOKER, **Blewmantle*, the name of an office of one of the Pursueants at armes. **1766** ENTICK *London* IV. 27 The four pursuivants..are Rougecroix, Bluemantle, Rougedragon, and Portcullis. **1814** SCOTT *Wav.* ii, A tie which Sir Everard held as sacred as either Garter or Blue-Mantle. **1891** *Daily News* 27 Apr. 3/2 The '*Blue' Measure... A measure called the blue (which contained two-thirds of a pint, and was universally used in Wales). **1801** W. RENDER *Tour through Germany* I. 100 Germany is indebted to this wise emperor [*sc.* Joseph II], among many other abolitions, to the two following in particular; namely, *Der blaue Montag*, 'the *blue Monday', and the 'infamy of certain trades'. **1840** *Boston Transcript* 2 Mar. 2/2 This was blue Monday in the House. **1844** W. HOWITT tr. *Holthaus's Wand. Journeyman Tailor* ix. 109, I did not omit on Sundays, and sometimes too on blue Mondays, to go about and observe the life and manners of this great city [*sc.* Constantinople]. **1885** *Harper's Mag.* 873/1 The workman getting sober after his usual 'blue Monday'. **1821** P. EGAN *Real Life in London* I. xiv. 249 'How's Harry and Ben?—haven't seen you this **blue moon.*' [*Footnote*] *Blue Moon*—This is usually intended to imply a long time. **1869** E. YATES *Wrecked in Port* xxii. 242 That indefinite period known as a 'blue moon'. **1876** MISS BRADDON *J. Haggard's Dau.* xxiv. 246 A fruit pasty once in a blue moon. **1664** *Phil. Trans.* I. 28 *Blew mould and Mushromes. **1863** *Cornh. Mag., Roundab. Papers* xxvii, Carps..with great humps of blue mould on their old backs. **1864** C. O'DOWD *Men & Wom.* 7 The Austrians, as Paddy says, are *blue-moulded for want of a beatin. [The expression is usually 'blue-mouldy for want of a bāting'.] **1876** *Daily News* 3 Nov. 5/5 If this [bad weather] continues there is a danger of us all getting blue-moulded. **1874** HARDY *Madding Crowd* II. iii. 39 Stales [*sc.* cakes], that are all but *blue-mouldy, but not quite. **1900** *Daily News* 3 Apr. 2/5, I was 'blue-mouldy for want of a batin',' as they say in certain parts of the Empire. **1922** JOYCE *Ulysses* 293, I was blue mouldy for the want of that pint. **1922** W. H. UKERS *All about Coffee* xxiv. 350 Jamaica produces two distinct types of coffee, the highland and the lowland growths. Among the first named is the celebrated *Blue Mountain coffee, which has a well developed pale blue-green bean that makes..a pleasantly aromatic cup. **1963** L. DEIGHTON *Horse under Water* xxxiii. 130, I was drinking a second cup of Blue Mountain. **1876** J. MURRAY in *Proc. R. Soc.* XXIV. 499 A *blue mud containing:—A great many pelagic Foraminifera and some Pteropod shells. **1882** GEIKIE *Text-Bk. Geol.* III. ii. 438 The deposits were found to consist of blue and green muds derived from the degradation of older crystalline rocks. **1885** Blue mud [see MUD *sb.*[1] 1 c]. *a* **1700** in *Harleian Misc.* (1744) I. 425/2 A Monastery of Visitation-Nuns, otherwise **Blue Nuns*. *a* **1848** E. PETRE *Notices of Eng. Colleges* (1849) p. v, Nuns of the Conception, *or Blue Nuns*, at Paris. **1931** *N. & Q.* 22 Aug. 143/2 The most prominent of them is Elizabeth Anne, who helped to establish the Blue Nuns in Paris, and became their Abbess. **1885** *Encycl. Brit.* XVIII. 242/2 The oil from which hard and soft paraffin are separated..exhibits a blue fluorescence, and is hence called *blue oil. **1839** *R. Hooper's Lex. Med.* (ed. 7) 268/1 **Blue ointment*, the mercurial ointment. **1888** *N.Y. Herald* 29 July (Farmer), The editor of the *Century Magazine* *blue pencils magazine articles by the bushel. **1893** KIPLING *Many Invent.* 167 The blue pencil plunged remorselessly through the slips. **1899** *Daily News* 17 Feb., The actor will have a better chance after the blue pencil has eliminated the unnecessary verbiage in the dialogue. **1904** S. E. WHITE *Blazed Trail Stories* iii. 48 One log had not been blue-pencilled across the end. **1914** G. CANNAN *Old Mole* 39 He blue-pencilled false quantities in Latin verse. **1925** *Mus. Assoc. Proc.* 60 He would blue-pencil an unprepared chord of the seventh in a motet in the style of Palestrina. **1940** *New Statesman* 13 Apr. 491/2 They certainly are blue-pencil unpopular with a lot of people in wartime. **1904** A. BENNETT *Great Man* xxviii. 331 The *blue-pencilling of the play proceeded. **1709** LAWSON *Carolina* 151 *Blue-Peters, the same as you call Water-Hens in England, are here very numerous. **1823** BYRON *Juan* XI. lxxxiii, It is time that I should hoist my '*blue Peter', And sail for a new theme. **1862** MAYHEW *Crim. Prisons* 23 At the foremast head..the 'blue Peter' was flying as a summons to the hands on shore to come aboard. *c* **1875** Beeton's *Handy Bk. Games* 358 Since the introduction of Blue Peter, the necessity of leading through your adversary's hand has become less and less. **1917** *Birds of Amer.* I. 214 Coot. *Fulica americana*... Other names.—American Coot..Blue Peter. **1732** *Select Trials Old-Bailey* (1735) II. 468/1 We could find no better Business than stealing Lead—We call it the **Blue Pigeon*, or the *Buff-Lay*. **1781** G. PARKER *View of Society* II. i. 63 *Blue Pigeon-Flyer.* These are Journeymen Plumbers and Glaziers who repair houses, and Running Dustmen. To *fly the Blue Pigeon* is cutting off lead from what they call a Prayer Book up to a Bible. **1789** —— *Life's Painter* xv. 165 *Blue pigeon flying.* Fellows who steal lead off houses, or cut pipes away. **1856** *Harper's Mag.* XIII. 589/1 The speed [of the ship] was slackened, and the 'blue pigeon' kept constantly moving. **1887** *Judy* 27 Apr. 200 A burglar whose particular 'lay' was flying the blue pigeon, i.e., stealing lead. **1897** Blue pigeon [see PIGEON *sb.* 4 b]. **1794–1824** D'ISRAELI *Cur. Lit., Med. & Mor.*, The most artificial logic..may be swallowed with the *blue pill, or any other in vogue. **1834** 'J. DOWNING' *Andrew Jackson* 111 They saw no hopes from fitin, they wern't fond of blue pills. **1861** E. MAYHEW *Dogs* 102 A few years ago..blue-pill with black draught literally became a part of the national diet. **1871** PLANCHÉ *K. Christmas*, There are blue devils which defy blue pills. **1945** S. LEWIS *C. Timberlane* (1946) xix. 112 They were taking the *Blue Plate Dinner. **1952** AUDEN *Nones* 27 Having finished the Blue-plate Special And reached the coffee stage. **1961** WEBSTER *Blue Plate.* 1. A restaurant dinner plate divided into compartments for serving several kinds of food as a single order. 2. A main course (as of meat and vegetable) served as a single menu item. **1827** FARADAY *Chem. Manip.* iv. 85 The..crucibles for this purpose are known by the name of *blue-pots. *a* **1884** KNIGHT *Dict. Mech.* Suppl., **Blue Process for Copying*, a mode of copying tracings in lieu of re-tracing them. **1819** MOORE *Epist. fr. T. Cribb* 15 One swig of *Blue Ruin is worth the whole lot! **1831** CARLYLE *Sart. Res.* III. x. 334 This latter [Potheen] I have tasted, as well as the English Blue-Ruin, and the Scotch Whisky. **1933** YEATS *Let.* 13 July in *New Statesman* (1965) 19 Mar. 441/2 Our chosen colour is blue and *Blueshirts are marching about all over the country. **1937** E. SNOW *Red Star over China* i. 30 Chiang Kai-shek's own Blueshirt gendarmes. *Ibid.*, Over 300 Communists were imprisoned..and the Blueshirts were hunting for more. **1938** *Ann. Reg. 1937* 274 He also demanded that the Blueshirts, a sort of private army of the Wafd, should be dissolved. **1965** C. D. EBY *Siege of Alcázar* (1966) ii. 48 Moscardó discovered the sixty Falangists hiding in the photography laboratory... Vela argued that if fighting broke out, the Blue Shirts would be useful to the Alcázar. **1830** *Kentuckian* 14 May, To pass.. with such rapidity as not even to leave a '*blue streak' behind him. **1847** *Knickerbocker* XXX. 178 Interspersing his vehement comments with a 'blue streak' of oaths. **1895** S. HALE *Lett.* (1919) 289, I..drove in her sort of..carryall

..talking a blue streak two miles to her house. **1937** RUNYON *More than Somewhat* iii. 64 She hears..a guy cussing a blue streak. **1949** *Landfall* III. 236 Sid was talking a blue streak to Jean. **1968** 'R. RAINE' *Night of Hawk* xxii. 109, I was talking a blue streak, my expression like thunder. **1928** A. CHRISTIE *Mystery of *Blue Train* ix. 65 *The* best train is what they call 'The Blue Train'. You avoid the tiresome Customs business at Calais. **1951** *Oxf. Jun. Encycl.* IV. 46/2 *Blue Train.* This train, named from the colour of its cars, was originally the Calais–Mediterranean express, which carried passengers to and from the sea-side towns of the French Riviera. More recently, however, the main Blue Train has worked between Paris and Mentone..though sleeping cars run through from Calais to Mentone without a change. **1893** DARTNELL & GODDARD *Wiltshire Gloss.* 14 **Blue-vinnied,* covered with blue mould. **1863** *Blue vinny [see FINNY *a.*[2]]. **1886** W. BARNES *Gloss. Dorset Dial.* 50 *Blue-vinny, or vinnied, cheese,* blue mouldy. **1895** 'C. HARE' *Down Village Street* 231 Us do want..a pen'orth o' blue-vinny cheese. **1955** J. G. DAVIS *Dict. Dairying* (ed. 2) 190 Dorset Blue cheese (also known as Blue Vinney)..is a skimmed-milk cheese. **1905** *Westm. Gaz.* 18 Nov. 6/3 A small stone city, set round a *blue-washed bay. **1906** *Ibid.* 13 Jan. 4/3 Out in the blue-washed bay. *Ibid.* 14 Nov. 2/1 From the blue-washed wall an unshaded lamp shone brilliantly. **1833** MARRYAT *P. Simple* (1863) 202 When we once are fairly out of harbour, and find ourselves in *blue water. **1921** *Flight* XIII. 387/2 There is also a hydrogen plant, of the blue water gas type, having a capacity of 200,000 cu. ft. per day of hydrogen at not less than 99·2 per cent. purity. **1944** *Gloss. Terms Gas Industry* (*B.S.I.*) 20 *Blue water-gas* (*B.W.G.*), gas consisting almost exclusively of carbon monoxide and hydrogen in nearly equal proportions. **1902** *Westm. Gaz.* 13 Jan. 3/2 Mr. Roosevelt is revealed..as convinced a member of the *blue-water school as Mr. Clowes in England. **1908** [see sense 3]. **1966** *New Statesman* 25 Feb. 247/1 The differences between the Powellites and the Blue Water school on China, Vietnam, Aden [etc.].

blue, *sb.* [the adj. used absol. or elliptically.]

1. Blue colour. (It may have a plural.)

a **1300** *Cursor M.* 9920 þe toiþer..Es al o bleu, men cals Ind. *c* **1500** *Maid & Magpie* in Halliw. *Nugæ P.* 43 His love was as a paynted blewe. **1599** GREENE *George a Gr.* (1861) 258 Right Coventry blue. *a* **1656** BP. HALL *Occas. Medit.* (1851) 59, I do not like these reds and blues. **1810** HENRY *Elem. Chem.* (1826) I. 224 Its solution..first reddens, and then destroys, vegetable blues. **1821** CRAIG *Lect. Drawing* v. 270 Begin with the blue of the sky. **1846** RUSKIN *Mod. Paint.* I. II. I. vii. §21 The blue of distance, however intense, is not the blue of a bright blue flower.

2. a. A pigment of a blue colour: usually with some defining word prefixed, as *Prussian, French, cobalt, smalt, ultramarine, royal.* See also BLUE *a.* 1 f.

1724, etc. [see PRUSSIAN *a.* 2 a]. **1835** [see COBALT 2 a]. **1862** *Handbk. Water-Col.* (Winsor & Newton) 19 French blue or Imitative Ultramarine. **1862** *Lond. Rev.* 26 July 87 Another highly valued and brilliant variety of Prussian blue, commercially known as Turnbull's blue.

b. *spec.* A blue powder used by laundresses.

1618 ROWLANDS *Nt. Raven* (1620) 34 Set her to starch a band, (I vow tis true) She euer spoyles the same with too much blew. **1800** *New Ann. Direct.* 231 Walton & Mitchel, Blue-makers, 10 Silver-street. **1822** KITCHINER *Cook's Oracle* 500 As much powder Blue as will lie on a sixpence.

c. A cake or ball of blue powder for laundry use; also *attrib.* in **blue bag**, a bag containing one of these for such use (see also quot. 1869). See also POWDER-BLUE 1, STONE-BLUE 1. Hence ***blue-bagged*** adj.

1836 *Mag. Dom. Econ.* I. 6 Make also a proper flannel 'blue-bag'. **1869** MRS. BEETON *Bk. Househ. Managem.* 1098 To remove a Bee Sting, pull the sting out at once..wipe the place, suck it, and then apply the blue-bag. **1904** H. G. WELLS *Food of Gods* I. ii. §5 She 'athen't even got a Blue Bag, Thir. **1928** *Daily Express* 9 Aug. 3/3 The blue bag—that truly rural remedy for wasp stings. **1953** DYLAN THOMAS *Under Milk Wood* (1954) 72 She sees in the still middle of the bluebagged bay Nogood Boyo fishing from the Zanzibar. **1961** *Coast to Coast 1959–60* 128 Knobs of blue.

3. a. Blue clothing or dress; esp. of blue uniform, e.g. of policemen, wounded soldiers in hospital, (*U.S.*) the Northern or Union soldiers (contrasted with the Southern or Confederate grey), *spec.* a kind of stuff.

1482 CAXTON *Chron. Eng.* ccli. 321 The kyng..clad in blewe. **1527** *MS. Invent. T. Cromwell,* A rydyng cote of browne blewe weltyd with tawney vellet. **1611** BIBLE *Ezek.* xxiii. 6 The Assyrians..Which were clothed with blew. **1721** C. KING *Brit. Merch.* II. 96 Plunkets, Violets, and Blues, formerly made in Suffolk. **1759** B. MARTIN *Nat. Hist. Eng.* II. 53 Needham..which had a good trade once for Blues and Broad Cloths. **1831** *The Olio* June 341/2 A young off'sir—a likely youngster he would have been in blue, 'stead o' red. **1867** F. M. FINCH in *Atlantic Monthly* XX. 369 (*title*) The Blue and the Grey. **1879** TOURGÉE *Fool's Err.* xxv. 153 He wore the blue. **1884** *Eng. Illustr. Mag.* Dec. 167 Answered the warder, 'He's in blue, so he's in his last year.' **1893** *Cassell's Fam. Mag.* Apr. 338/2 My little friend in blue [i.e. messenger boy]. **1918** *Reveille* Aug. 94 The discharged men..no longer cut the handsome gaudy figure of the man in blue. **1930** T. E. LAWRENCE *Let.* 8 Jan. (1938) 677, I haven't drawn my blue yet! **1952** R. SHERBROOKE-WALKER *Khaki & Blue* i. 9 Why 'Khaki' found so much to criticise in 'Blue'. *Ibid.* ii. 15 From these early 'soldiers in blue'.. there was ultimately evolved..the R.A.F. Regiment.

b. ***the men*** (***gentlemen*** or ***boys***) ***in blue***: (*a*) policemen; (*b*) sailors; (*c*) American Federal troops.

1851 F. STARR *Twenty Yrs. Trav. Life* xxxii. 317, I was not long managing my exit..whilst the 'gentleman in blue' was busy examining other tickets. **1857** H. LAWRENCE in W. Brock *Biogr. Sk. Sir H. Havelock* (1858) viii. 125 The gentlemen in blue—the sailors. **1866** L. P. BROCKETT *Camp, Battle Field,* etc. II. 264 Tread lightly, oh! loyal-hearted, the boys in blue are lying there. **1866** *Congress. Globe* 27 Jan. 460/1 The brave 'boys in blue' fought manfully and through their efforts the Union has been preserved. **1868** *Cassell's Mag.* 8 Aug. 240/1 The man in fustian lies under certain obligations to the man in blue. **1882** BESANT *All Sorts* xliii, You must now begin to think seriously about handcuffs and prison, and men in blue. **1943** WYNDHAM LEWIS *Let.* 26 Jan. (1963) 344 He will choose..*The Navy.* He will plump for the boys-in-blue every time.

4. a. Elliptically, for blue species or varieties of animals, objects, or substances, the nature of which is explained by the context, *e.g.* one of the blue butterflies (*Polyommatus*); a blue artificial fly used in angling; a blue potato, etc.; blue china, etc. Also applied to police and sailors.

1787 BEST *Angling* (ed. 2) 115 The sky-coloured blue..is a neat, curious, and beautiful fly. **1838** DICKENS *Mem. Grimaldi* ii. 22 Capturing no fewer than four dozen Dartford Blues. **1844** HOOD *Whimsicalities* II. 186 Whether this here mobbing..Will grow to such a riot that the Oxford Blues [*i.e.* policemen] must quell it. **1845** *Morn. Chron.* 22 Nov. 5/2 The potatoes were salmons and blues. **1860** GOSSE *Rom. Nat. Hist.* 5 On the..open downs the lovely little 'blues' are frisking in animated play. **1860** HOTTEN *Dict. Slang* (ed. 2), *Blue,* a policeman. **1877** W. H. THOMSON *Five Years' Penal Servitude* iv. 257 'Bilking the blues,'—evading the police. **1884** GOSSE *Rom. Nat. Hist.* Nov. 833/2 Bits of old Nankin 'blue'. **1898** KIPLING *Fleet in Being* iii. 40 Next time you see the 'blue' ashore you do not stare unintelligently. **1903** F. SIMPSON *Bk. Cat* xi. 126/2 As tiny kittens blues frequently exhibit tabby markings. **1968** K. WEATHERLY *Roo Shooter* 62 The last one [*sc.* kangaroo] was a tremendous blue.

b. A blueberry or bilberry. *U.S.*

1587 R. HAKLUYT tr. *Laudonnière's Notable Hist.* 2[r], There are Raspisses, and a little bearie which we call among us Blues, which are very good to eate. **1709** J. LAWSON *New Voy. Carolina* 104 The Hurts, Huckle-Berries, or Blues of this Country are four sorts... The first sort is the same Blue or Bilberry, that grows plentifully in the North of England.

c. A 'blue chip' in the game of poker. *U.S.*

1890 BIFF HALL *Turnover Club* 206 When turned to faro, You sometimes caused 'a stack of blues' to win. **1920** MULFORD *J. Nelson* xxi. 228 'Two pairs... Well I'll see it an' add a blue.' 'Any time you raise a blue, you got two pairs, all right!'

5. a. The sky. Phrases: ***out of the blue***, 'out of a clear sky' (cf. SKY *sb.*[1]), without warning, unexpectedly; ***a bolt from*** (or ***out of***) ***the blue***, something unexpected, a complete surprise. **b.** The sea.

1647 H. MORE *Song of Soul* II. App. lxxxvii. 99 Ne any footsteps in the empty Blew. **1738** WESLEY *Psalms* cxlvii. iv, Thro' the etherial blue. **1821** BYRON *Cain* II. i. 144 Oh, how we cleave the blue! **1837** CARLYLE *Fr. Rev.* III. VI. i. 347 Arrestment, sudden really as a bolt out of the Blue, has hit strange victims. **1850** TENNYSON *In Mem.* cxiv, Drown'd in yonder living blue The lark becomes a sightless song. **1861** L. NOBLE *Icebergs* 63 Far out upon the blue were many sails. **1876** GEO. ELIOT *Dan. Der.* IV. liv. 102 Where one may float between blue and blue. **1910** O. W. HOLMES *Let.* 19 Dec. (1964) 58, I got an encouragement out of the blue..in the form of an honorary degree from Berlin. **1911** W. F. BUTLER *Autobiogr.* xxi. 380 Like a bolt from the blue came the news of the Jameson raid. **1919** W. T. GRENFELL *Labrador Doctor* (1920) xx. 334 Nothing in my life ever came more 'out of the blue' than my marriage. **1925** 'SAPPER' *Out of the Blue* i. 10 Suddenly—out of the blue—comes one disconnected event. **1930** W. S. CHURCHILL *My Early Life* xiii. 178 Spontaneously and 'out of the blue', he formed a wish to make the acquaintance of its author. **1933** *Mind* XLII. 289, I do not state it out of the blue, with no reason at all. **1953** X. FIELDING *Stronghold* III. i. 175 Then, suddenly, out of the blue, the leading question. **1970** *Times* 30 Apr. 5/8 Out of the blue comes a request for information about the work of the Estimates Committee.

6. = *Blue Squadron* (see BLUE *a.* 5 b).

1703 [see BLUE *a.* 5 b]. **1727–41** CHAMBERS *Cycl.* s.v. *Admiral,* Thus we say the Admiral of the red, the Admiral of the blue. **1806** A. DUNCAN *Nelson* 72 Sir Horatio Nelson, as rear-admiral of the blue, carried the blue flag at the mizen.

7. *pl.* Applied to various companies of troops, distinguished by wearing blue. **a.** The Royal Horse Guards, in 1690 distinguished from b as the 'Oxford Blues', from their commander, the Earl of Oxford. **b.** Dutch troops of William III. **c.** The troops of the French Republic of 1792.

1766 WESLEY *Jrnl.* 16 July, A whole troop of the Oxford Blues..kept them in awe. **1812** *Examiner* 12 Oct. 652/2 The Blues are about to embark for Spain. **1813** WELLINGTON *Let.* in Gurw. *Disp.* X. 69, I have been appointed Colonel of the Blues. **1848** MACAULAY *Hist. Eng.* xvi, While vainly endeavouring to prevail on their soldiers to look the Dutch Blues in the face. *Ibid.* I. 294 Another body of household cavalry distinguished by blue coats and cloaks, and still called the Blues, was..quartered in the neighbourhood of the capital. **1878** TRIMEN *Regiments Brit. Army* 12 It was also known as the 'Blue Guards' during the campaign in Flanders 1742–45, and is now commonly called 'The Blues'.

8. As the colour worn by a party or faction (identified with different principles at different times and places); hence, *transf.* an adherent of such party. Also ***true blue***: see BLUE *a.* 1 e, 6.

1755 *Gentl. Mag.* XXV. 339 The blues being in the old interest, and the yellows in the new. **1762** *Ibid.* 442 Honest true blues, a staunch, firm, chosen band. **1790** BURNS *Election Ballad* ix, As Queensberry blue and buff unfurl'd. **1835** DISRAELI *Corr. w. Sister* (1886) 35 Labouchere has picked up many blues (my colour). **1881** MORLEY *Cobden* I. 91 Making citizenship into something loftier and more generous than the old strife of Blues and Yellows.

9. Light blue and dark blue have become the distinctive colours of the representatives both of Eton and Harrow Schools, and of Cambridge and Oxford Universities, in their rival athletic contests. So the 'Dark Blues' denote Oxford men or Harrow boys; 'to win his blue', or 'to be a Blue', is to be chosen to represent his University or School in rowing, cricket, etc.; 'an old Blue' is one who has rowed or played in an inter-University contest.

1879 *Daily News* 7 Apr. 3/2 At the Creek..the Light Blues were all but clear of their opponents. **1882** —— 18 Jan. 2/2 Ainslie, of Oriel..may be successful in winning his blue. **1883** *Standard* 8 May 3/7 There are five 'Old Blues' playing. *Ibid.* 19 June 3/8 He has..received his 'blue'. **1884** *Q. Rev.* No. 316. 485 What [Eton] boy who has 'won his blue', etc.

10. A 'Blue-coat boy'; a scholar of Christ's Hospital.

1834 W. TROLLOPE (*title*) Christ's Hospital, with Account of the Plan of Education..and Memoirs of Eminent Blues.

11. a. Short for 'blue-stocking'.

1781 F. BURNEY *Diary* 12 June (1904) I. 498 A whole tribe of *blues,* with Mrs Montagu at their head. **1788** MAD. D'ARBLAY *Diary* (1842) IV. 219 His literary preference of reading to a blue. **1813** BYRON *Br. Abydos* II. v. *note,* Perhaps some of our own '*blues*' might not be worse for bleaching. **1824** W. IRVING *T. Trav.* I. 203 The company of village literati and village blues. **1832** DISRAELI *Corr. w. Sister* (1886) 6 There were a great many dames there of distinction, and no blues. **1849** MISS MULOCH *Ogilvies* ii. (1875) 12 Every one talked of her as a 'clever woman'— 'a blue'.

b. *transf.* Female learning or pedantry.

1824 BYRON *Juan* XVI. xlvii, She also had a twilight tinge of '*Blue*'.

12. ***the blues*** (for '*blue devils*'): depression of spirits, despondency. *colloq.*

1741 D. GARRICK *Let.* 11 July (1963) I. 26, I am far from being quite well, tho not troubled wth y[e] Blews as I have been. **1807** W. IRVING *Salmag.* (1824) 96 In a fit of the blues. **1856** WHYTE MELVILLE *K. Coventry* viii. 89 The moat alone is enough to give one the 'blues'. **1883** *Harper's Mag.* Dec. 55 Come to me when you have the blues. **1887** 'J. S. WINTER' *That Imp* ii. 11, I wonder you and Betty don't die of the blues. **1960** *New Statesman* 27 Feb. 274/2 The post-election blues are beginning.

13. *Archery.* (The second ring from the centre of the target is coloured blue.)

1882 *Standard* 31 Aug. 6/4 The prize for the lady making the most blues..was won by Mrs. E., who made eight blues. *Ibid.* The Lady Paramount's prize for most blues.

14. = BLUENESS 4. Cf. BLUE *a.* 9.

1824 MACTAGGART *Gallov. Encycl.* 446 *Thread o' Blue,* any little smutty touch in song-singing, chatting, or piece of writing. **1889** BARRÈRE & LELAND *Dict. Slang* I. 145/2 'A bit of *blue*', an obscene or libidinous anecdote.

15. *U.S.* The style or mood of the BLUES. Cf. BLUE *a.* 3 d.

1924 G. GERSHWIN (*title of music*) Rhapsody in blue.

16. *Army slang.* **a.** (See quot.)

1925 FRASER & GIBBONS *Soldier & Sailor Words* 28 *In the blue,* failure. Something gone wrong. An attack that broke down, or troops who got out of touch, would be said to be 'in the blue'.

b. ***the blue***: the desert, *spec.* in N. Africa in the 1939–45 war.

1944 *Return to Attack* (*Army Board, N.Z.*) 9/1 Although their business address was the Western Desert, the New Zealanders were not yet ready for action. They trained hard. At intervals they disappeared 'into the blue' for a few days. **1958** L. VAN DER POST *Lost World of Kalahari* v. 83 You ought to have letters from us to our people in the blue just in case of need. **1963** *Times* 26 Jan. 9/6 In the 20 years since the tide of battle finally receded, 'up the blue', as the Desert Rats called it, has been tidied of war debris.

17. *Austral.* and *N.Z. slang.* **a.** A summons (cf. BLUEY *sb.* 4). **b.** An argument; a fight or brawl. **c.** A mistake or blunder. Cf. BLACK *sb.* 12.

1941 in BAKER *Dict. Austral. Slang* II.

1944 in L. GLASSOP *We were Rats* (Partridge *Slang* Suppl.). **1946** J. MORRISON in *Coast to Coast* 156 There's a bit of a blue on, and he can hear nearly every word they say. **1953** K. TENNANT *Joyful Condemned* iv. 37 Every time Rene comes round there's some kind of a blue. **1957** 'N. CULOTTA' *They're Weird Mob* (1958) iv. 54 When you get into a blue do yer pull knives?

1941 BAKER *Dict. Austral. Slang* 11 *Blue,* an error or mistake; a loss. **1957** 'N. SHUTE' *On Beach* i. 23, I put up a blue right away by ordering a pink gin. **1961** B. CRUMP *Hang on a Minute, Mate* 17 Trouble with you blokes is you won't admit when you've made a blue.

blue, *v.*[1] [f. the adj.]

1. *trans.* To make blue; *spec.* to heat (metal) so as to make it blue.

1606 SYLVESTER *Du Bartas* (1621) 466 Plaid the painter, when hee did so gild The turning globes, blew'd seas, and green'd the field. **1727** MATHER *Yng. Man's Comp.* 309 To Blew Skins. **1816** W. TAYLOR in *Month. Mag.* XLI. 330 He rivets coats of mail, Or the bright sword-blade in his oven blues. **1855** BROWNING *Statue & Bust,* The blood that blues the inside arm. **1881** GREENER *Gun* 253 Any amateur may blue by placing the pan of charcoal upon a fire, and burying the work to be blued in it.

2. To treat (linen) with blue (see BLUE *sb.* 2 b).

1862 *Lond. Rev.* 16 Aug. 154 The articles of dress..being well starched, blued, and rough dried.

†**3.** To cause to look blue, (or ? to blush). *Obs.*

1719 OZELL tr. *Misson's Trav. Eng.* 170 (D.) This action set many of the company a laughing, which very much blew'd the Countess.

†**4.** *intr.* To blush. (*slang.*) *Obs.*

1709 STEELE & SWIFT *Tatler* No. 71 ¶8 If a Virgin blushes, we no longer cry she Blues.

blue (blu:), *v.*[2] *slang.* Also blew. **1.** *trans.* To spend or get through (money) lavishly or extravagantly; = BLOW *v.*[1] 9c.

1846 *Swell's Night Guide* 76 The coves..vot we blues a bob or a tanner to see. **1859** HOTTEN *Dict. Slang.* s.v. *Blewed*, 'I blewed all my blunt last night', I spent all my money. **1867** T. W. ROBERTSON *Caste* 111, 'So Papa Eccles had the money?' 'And blued it!' **1884** *Daily Tel.* 28 May 5/1 He took to horses, and blewed the blooming lot [i.e. £1,700] in eighteen months. **1888** FARJEON *Miser Farebrother* III. i. 5 You brought down two thousand pounds with you, and you blued it. **1930** W. DE LA MARE *On Edge* 228 She had taken a holiday and just blued some of her savings. **1959** *Observer* 17 May 8/5 Men in cotton shirts and corduroys met there to 'blue' their cheques on supplies and on fiery colonial rum.

2. To make a mess of, spoil, ruin.

1880 *Punch's Almanack* 2 This top coat would blue it.

blueback ('blu:bæk). [f. BLUE *a.* + BACK *sb.*[1]]

1. A species of fish, or bird, having a bluish back. Also *attrib.*

c **1532** in PALSGR. 912 The blewe back and redbrest, *la pioue.* **1812** W. BENTLEY *Diary* 22 Oct. (1914) IV. 125 Mr Osgood..had taken great numbers of the Herrings called Bluebacks..this season. **1843** J. E. DEKAY *Zool.* in *Nat. Hist. N.Y.* v. 24 There is a variety of the Lobster, termed Bluebacks, on account of their dark bluish colour. **1871** *Game Laws* in *Fur, Fin, & Feather* (1872) 158 This section shall not apply to the taking of blue back trout in Franklin and Oxford counties. **1881** *Amer. Naturalist* XV. 178 Of these species, the blue-back predominates in Frazer's river. *Ibid.* 180 Little blue-backs [*sc.* salmon] of every size down to six inches are also found in the Upper Columbia in the fall. **1883** *Century Mag.* Sept. 684/1 The blue-back's nest was scarcely a foot from the ground. **1965** *Jrnl. Lancs. Dial. Soc.* Jan. 9 *Fieldfare*,..blueback: 'Fylde',..Warrington, Liverpool.

2. A legal-tender note issued by the Confederacy during the Civil War. *U.S.*

1869 in MATHEWS *Beginnings Amer. English* (1931) 156 The Rebels had their 'bluebacks' for money. **1872** SCHELE DE VERE *Americanisms* 47 During the Civil War..the original Blue Backs of the Confederacy (so-called in opposition to the Green Backs of the Union) soon became known as Shucks.

3. Chiefly *pl.* Paper money issued by the Transvaal Government in 1865. *S. Afr.*

1878 TROLLOPE *South Africa* II. 225 The blue-backs as they were called were printed. **1900** *Daily News* 17 Sept. 5/2 President Kruger has deserted them, taking all the gold, and leaving them only 'blue-backs'.

blue bag: see BLUE *a.* 13, and *sb.* 2c.

Bluebeard ('blu:bɪəd). A personage of popular mythology, so called from the colour of his beard. References are frequent in literature to the locked turret-chamber, in which hung the bodies of his murdered wives.

1822 DE QUINCEY *Confess.*, That room was to her the Blue-beard room of the house. **18..** CARLYLE (in *Brewer*) The Bluebeard chamber of his mind, into which no eye but his own must look. **1854** BADHAM *Halieut.* 29 About half a mile from the town [Naples], are certain Bluebeard-looking towers..erected for the purpose of snaring wood-pigeons.

†**blue-beat**, *v. Obs. rare*$^{-1}$. To beat black and blue (cf. BLUE *a.* 2).

a **1626** W. SCLATER *Three Serm.* (1629) 9 Therefore S. Paul kept his body in subiection, and, that he might keepe it vnder, blue-beate it.

blue bell, 'blue-bell. [see BELL *sb.*[1] 4.] The popular name of two widely different flowers.

1. A species of Campanula (*C. rotundifolia*) which grows on open downs, hills, and dry places, and flowers in summer and autumn, with a loose panicle of delicate blue bell-shaped flowers on slender peduncles. This is the 'blue bell of Scotland', and of the north of England, and of the Elizabethan herbalists. (Usually blu:'bɛl or as two words.)

1578 LYTE *Dodoens* II. xxiii. 174 Blew Belles [with a figure of *Campanula*] whan their plante beginneth first to spring up ..haue small rounde leaues. **1783** AINSWORTH *Lat. Dict.* (Morell) 1, Blue bells, or bell flowers, *Campanula flore cæruleo.* **1795** BURNS *Their Groves o' sweet Myrtle* ii, Where the blue-bell and gowan lurk. **1837** LOCKHART *Scott* (1839) VII. 178 He had scrambled to gather blue bells and heath flowers. *a* **1872** W. MILLER *The Blue Bell* in *Poets & Poetry of Scotl.* 1877 II. 340 For glaumorie is round the sweet blue bell.

2. In the south of Eng. generally and in many modern Eng. poets: ('blu:bɛl) a bulbous-rooted plant, *Scilla nutans* (*Hyacinthus non-scriptus* Linn.), growing in moist woods and among grass, and flowering in spring, with a nodding raceme of drooping narrow bell-like flowers.

(Those who call this 'blue-bell' or 'bluebell', generally call the other 'hair-bell' or 'hare-bell'.)

1794 MARTYN *Rousseau's Bot.* xviii. 250 The Wild Hyacinth or Blue-Bells of the European woods. **1802** SOUTHEY *Thalaba* IV. xxiii, Amid the growing grass The blue-bell bends, the golden king-cup shines, And the sweet cowslip scents the genial air. **1846** KEBLE *Lyra Innoc.* IV. vii. 121 Forest bluebells in a row Stoop to the first May wind. **1851** MARY HOWITT *Sk. Nat. Hist.* 83 The nodding Blue-bell's graceful flowers, The Hyacinth of this land of ours.

'blue-bird.

1. a. A small perching bird allied to the Warblers (*Motacilla sialis* Linn., *Sylvia sialis* Wilson, *Erythaca Wilsonii* Swainson), common in the United States, where it appears in early spring, taking its departure in the autumn. Its upper part is sky-blue; breast and throat reddish-chestnut.

1688 J. CLAYTON in *Phil. Trans.* XVII. 996 A Bird they call a Blew-bird, of a curious azure colour, about the bigness of a Chafinch. *a* **1813** A. WILSON (*title*) The American Blue-Bird. **1846** LONGF. *Not always May* i, The blue-bird prophesying spring. **1881** J. HAWTHORNE *Fort. Fool* I. xxxiii, Blue-birds, with a flash of sky on their backs.

b. *fig.* Happiness (in allusion to the title of a play, *L'Oiseau bleu* by Maurice Maeterlinck).

1909 A. T. DE MATTOS tr. *Maeterlinck's Blue Bird* III. ii. 131 You are looking for the Blue Bird, that is to say, the great secret of things and of happiness. **1909** M. BEERBOHM *L'Oiseau Bleu* in *Yet Again* 300 All these ladies..have tried to catch this same Blue Bird. **1968** K. O'HARA *Bird-Cage* vi. 46 A little blue dickey-bird. A bluebird of happiness, a love-bird of happiness.

2. ? A species of albatross (*Diomedea fuliginosa* 'albatross of China,' *Penny Cycl.*).

1731 MEDLEY *Kolben's Cape G. Hope* II. 152 The description..of the Cape Blue-bird.

blue-black, *a.* and *sb.*

A. *adj.* Black or dark with a tinge of blue.

1853 *Q. Rev.* Mar. 309 The coarse blue-black locks of the North American squaw. **1871** M. COLLINS *Mrq. & Merch.* II. i. 11 Face closely shaven, chin blue-black where the beard was..repressed.

B. *sb.* A pigment of this colour.

1823 P. NICHOLSON *Pract. Build.* 416 Blue-Black is the coal of some kind of wood burnt in a close heat. **1857** RUSKIN *Elem. Drawing* 41 Take cakes of lake, of gamboge, of sepia, of blue-black, of cobalt.

Hence **blue-blackness.**

1880 L. WALLACE *Ben-Hur* II. iv. 96 A bank of blue-blackness over in the west which they knew to be mountains.

blue bonnet, -'bonnet. [cf. BLUE-CAP.]

1. *spec.* A broad round horizontally flattened bonnet or cap of blue woollen material, formerly in general use in Scotland. Hence **blue-'bonneted** *a.*

1682 *2nd Plea Nonconf.* 4 In a Jesuit's long Robes, and a Scotish blew Bonnet. **1859** MASSON *Milton* I. 667 The blue-bonneted and plaided peasantry of the shires.

2. *transf.* A blue-bonneted peasant, or soldier.

1818 SCOTT *Rob Roy* xxvi, Rob soon gathered an unco band o' blue-bonnets at his back. **1820** —— *Monast.* xxv, When the Blue Bonnets came over the Border.

3. A Scotch name of species of *Centaurea*, as the Bluebottle; also of species of Scabious and other round-headed blue flowers.

1863 MARG. PLUES *Rambl. Wild Fl.* 168 The corn blue bottle..Its brilliant colour entitles it to its Scotch appellation of Blue bonnet. The French call it *bluet.*

4. Dial. name of the Blue Tit-mouse; = BLUE-CAP.

'blue book, 'blue-book. a. A book bound in blue; *spec.* one of the official reports of Parliament and the Privy Council, which are issued in a dark blue paper cover; also in extended use.

1633 S. GOFFE *Let.* 7 Nov. in *Cal. State Papers* (1863) 279 Dr. Ames's death has put them in hope that they shall not be troubled so much with blue books as heretofore. **1715** ASHMOLE *Hist. Ord. Garter* vi. 155 The second of these Books is called the Blue Book; so called, being bound in Blue velvet; it begins with the first year of Queen Mary, and ends at the 18th of King Jac. i. **1793** *Gent. Mag.* LXIII. 59/2 A work which, among the Roman Catholicks, is known by the name of 'The Third Blue Book'. **1824** (*title*) The Royal Blue Book [published by T. Gardiner & Son, Princes St.]. **1845** DISRAELI *Sybil* (1863) 185 On another table were arranged his parliamentary papers, and piles of blue books. **1848** (*title*) The Blue Book of the British Manufacturers. **1909** B. WARD *Dawn Cath. Revival* I. i. 2 It is described in the Third Blue Book as follows. *Note*, The Blue Books were the official publications of the Catholic Committee. **1912** CONAN DOYLE *Lost World* vi. 89, I was the flail of the Lord up in those parts, I may tell you, though you won't find it in any Blue-book. **1928** *Daily Tel.* 5 May 7/6 The 'Blue Book', the directory..of the electrical engineering and allied trades. **1967** *Listener* 10 Aug. 173/3 What was new was the copious Blue Book documentation that Marx gave.

fig. **1881** SEELEY in *Macm. Mag.* XLV. 51/1 History..is the great Blue-book of the statesman.

b. *U.S.* 'A printed book containing the names of all persons holding office under the government of the United States, with their place of birth, amount of salary, etc.' Bartlett *Dict. Amer.* (1860).

1836 BENTON in *Deb. Congress* June 1719 An array of names more numerous..than was to be found in the 'Blue Book'. **1904** *Brooklyn Eagle* 7 Sept. 5 The bulky Blue Book of the present day..is in two volumes, and..of more than 1000 pages.

Hence **blue-booky** *a.*, **blue-bookiness.**

1894 *Speaker* 9 June 649/1 A dry, blue-booky article. **1909** *Fabian News* XX. 76/1 His volume is..readable, notwithstanding the complete blue bookiness of its contents.

'bluebottle.

1. a. The common name for the Blue Corn-flower (*Centaurea cyanus*).

1551 TURNER *Herbal* I. N iv, Blewbottel groweth in the corne. **1611** FLORIO, *Battisegola*, the weed blewbottle, Corneflower, or hurtsickle. **1672** T. JORDAN *Lond. Tri.* in Heath *Grocers' Comp.* (1869) 494 Grain..intermingled with yellow flowers, Blew-bottles and erratick Poppies. **1794** MARTYN *Rousseau's Bot.* xxvi. 402 Blue Bottle..whose beautiful blue colour would have attracted regard, had it been rare. **1863** PRIOR *Plant-n.* 26.

b. Applied vaguely to other blue flowers.

1656 RIDGLEY *Pract. Physic* 118 Made of the flowers of Succory or Blew-bottles. **1884** W. MILLER *Plant-n.* 15 Blue Bottle, *Scilla nutans, Centaurea cyanus*, and various other blue flowers.

2. A nickname for a man in a dark blue uniform, as a beadle or policeman. Also *attrib.*

1597 SHAKS. *2 Hen. IV*, v. iv. 22 [*Addressing a beadle*] I will haue you as soundly swindg'd for this, you blue-bottle [*1st Fol.* blew Bottel'd] Rogue. **1607** *Miseries Enforced Marr.* in Hazl. *Dodsley* IX. 471 How now, blue-bottle, are you of the house? **1846** G. W. M. REYNOLDS *Myst. London* I. ii. 5/2 Them chaps in..the House of Commons gets on their legs and praises the bluebottles up to the skies as the most acutest police in the world. **1864** SALA in *Daily Tel.* 13 Sept., Caught in his own toils by the bluebottles of Scotland-yard. **1946** WODEHOUSE *Joy in Morning* xi. 87 'Stilton turns out to be the village bluebottle.'.. 'A policeman, sir?'

3. *bluebottle fly*: a fly (*Musca vomitoria*) with a large bluish body; the Meat-fly or Blow-fly.

c **1720** PRIOR *Flies* Poems (1741) 158 A Fly upon the Chariot-Pole Cries out 'What Blue-bottle alive Did ever with such fury drive?' **1817** BYRON *Beppo* lxxiv, Humming like flies around the newest blaze, The bluest of bluebottles you e'er saw. **1822** W. IRVING *Braceb. Hall* II. 199 The buzzing of a stout blue-bottle fly.

4. A Portuguese man-o'-war (MAN-OF-WAR 4). *Austral.* and *S. Afr.*

1933 *Bulletin* (Sydney) 29 Nov. 21/3 The stings of the pestilent 'bluebottle', or Portuguese man-o'-war. **1947** L. G. GREEN *Tavern of Seas* xv. 143 A seashore strewn with physalia, better known as blue-bottles or Portuguese men-o'-war, is no place for bare feet. **1956** S. HOPE *Diggers' Paradise* 164 The risk to swimmers and surfers in the southern seas is mainly from..the Portuguese man-o'-war which the Aussies call a 'bluebottle'. **1964** *Cape Times* (Week-End Mag.) 11 Jan. 4/3 The Portuguese Man o' War is small... The common name is bluebottle.

blue buck. Also **bluebuck. 1.** Transl. the Dutch name BLAUWBOK.

1834 *Penny Cycl.* II. 88/2.

2. A small South African antelope of the genus *Cephalophus.*

1835 J. W. D. MOODIE *Ten Years S. Africa* II. 139 The woods also abound with..an elegant little antelope,..called the '*blaawe bock*' or blue buck. **1893** J. NOBLE *Handbk. Cape & S. Afr.* 62 The diminutive bluebuck, not bigger than a rabbit.

'blue-cap. [Cf. BLUE-BONNET.]

1. A cap of blue material; formerly worn by servants and tradesmen (see BLUE *a.* 5c.); the 'blue bonnet' of Scotchmen. Also *attrib.*

1674 FLATMAN *Belly God* 114 The Kentish Pippin's best, I dare be bold, That ever blew-cap Costard monger sold.

2. *transf.* One who wears this head-dress; †a Scotchman, a BLUE-BONNET (*obs.*).

1596 SHAKS. *1 Hen. IV*, II. iv. 392 Well, hee is there too, and one Mordake, and a thousand blew-Cappes more. **1627** E. F. *Hist. Edw. II* (1680) 39 (D.) A rabble multitude of despised Blue-caps encounter, rout, and break the flower of England. **1663** in *Select. Harl. Misc.* (1793) 367 The precipitate blue-cap..would needs fall upon them at Dunbar.

3. *dial.* A salmon in its first year, a grilse; so called because it has a blue spot on its head.

1677 in *Ray's Corr.* (1848) 127 These [salmon] have a broad blue spot on their heads, and are therefore called Blue-caps. **1865** COUCH *Brit. Fishes* IV. 220 In the west of the Kingdom the name of Blue cap is applied by some fishermen to the Salmon in the first year of its growth.

4. The Blue Titmouse (*Parus cæruleus*).

1804 WORDSW. *Kitten & Falling L.* 64 Where is he that giddy sprite, Blue-cap with his colours bright, Who was blest as bird could be. **1837** MACGILLIVRAY *Hist. Brit. Birds* II. 431 Blue Titmouse..Blue-cap, Blue bonnet, etc.

5. The Blue Corn-flower; = BLUE BONNET 3.

1821 CLARE *Vill. Minstr.* II. 131 Till summer's blue-caps blossom mid the corn.

6. A kind of ale.

1822 KITCHINER *Cook's Oracle* 60 The Irishman loves Usquebaugh, the Scot loves Ale called Blue-Cap.

†**7.** A kind of stone. *Obs.*

1679 PLOT *Staffordsh.* (1686) 158 A sort of stone from its colour call'd blew-cap, good for nothing.

8. (See CAP *sb.*[1] 11c.)

blue chip. orig. *U.S.* [BLUE *a.* + CHIP *sb.*[1] 2d.] A blue counter used in Poker, usu. of high value. Also *transf.*, spec. *Stock-Exchange*, a share considered to be a fairly reliable investment, though less secure than gilt-edged; hence any reliable enterprise, etc. Also *attrib.* or quasi-*adj.* Cf. BLUE *sb.* 4c.

1904 S. E. WHITE *Blazed Trail Stories* viii. 146, I reckon I don't stack up very high in th' blue chips. **1929** *Sun* (Baltimore) 30 Oct. 12/2 Agriculture still has too much to reclaim..to become a 'blue chip' in the near future. **1932** *Ibid.* 16 Apr. 15/8 Investors do not see as much intrinsic value in lower-priced issues as they do in the so-called 'blue chips'. **1935** *Economist* 17 Aug. 339/1 The result is not a 'blue-chip' boom. **1954** *Ibid.* 20 Feb. 568/2 Tobacco equities seem rather more vulnerable than other industrial 'blue-chips'. **1957** R. POWELL *Philadelphian* 185 One of the gilt-edged prep schools..or even the blue-chip ones. **1958** *Times* 2 Jan. 12/2 Demand was again concentrated on the 'blue chip' issues and a comparatively few store..and chemical shares. **1967** *Listener* 5 Oct. 423 (Advt.), M & G General Trust Fund is a very big Fund..with a portfolio

largely of British 'blue chips', plus a number of overseas stocks.

blue coat, 'blue-coat.

1. a. Formerly the dress of servants and the lower orders; hence of almoners and charity children.

?*c* **1600** *Distr. Emperor* I. i. in Bullen *O. Pl.* III. 169 Thou that has worne thy selfe and a blewe coate To equall thryddbareness. **1628** EARLE *Microcosm.* liv. 117 His antient beginning was a blue coat, since a livery.

b. A bluish colour of the coat in deer at a certain period.

1870 *Amer. Naturalist* IV. 190 The spike-horn was shot just as deer were attaining the 'blue coat'.

2. a. One who wears a blue coat; *e.g.* an almsman, a beadle; a blue-coated soldier or sailor; a policeman.

1593 SHAKS. *1 Hen. VI*, I. iii. 47 Draw men..Blew Coats to Tawny Coats. **1598** E. GILPIN *Skial.* (1878) 52 A..swaggering blew-coate at an ale-house doore. **1608** DEKKER *Belman Lond.* Wks. 1885 III. 149 This counterfeit Blew-coate, running in all haste for his masters cloake-bag. **1699** BENTLEY *Phal.* 222 That the fame..could so soon reach Phalaris's ear in his Castle through his Guard of Blue-coats. *a* **1852** MAYHEW *Lond. Labour* (1861) II. 369/1, I thinks them Chartists are a weak-minded set..a hundred o' them would run away from one blue-coat. **1862** *Sat. Rev.* 8 Feb. 159 The admiral..became..gracious and condescending to his brother bluecoats. **1875** *Chicago Tribune* 29 Aug. 5/4 One of the blue coats would attempt to put back the crowd. **1932** J. FARRELL *Young Lonigan* (1936) iv. §2. 74 No cop could think that he was going to get away with pushing his son. And he told the damn bluecoat that..he'd punch him all over the corner.

b. *attrib.* (for quot. 1821 cf. BLUE-STOCKING.)

a **1653** G. DANIEL *Idyll* v. 115 In Blue-Coat Philosophy. *a* **1704** T. BROWN *Pleas. Ep.* Wks. 1730 I. 110 The blue coat infantry. **1821** BYRON *Juan* IV. cix, The blue-coat misses of a coterie.

c. A soldier in the Federal army during the Civil War. *U.S.*

1865 G. W. NICHOLS *Story Gt. March* xxiii. 154 So we jogged on for awhile, and then..we descried a blue coat and a white-eared mule approaching. **1879** TOURGÉE *Fool's Err.* xxi. 122 But only wait until the States are restored and the 'Blue Coats' are out of the way.

3. (More fully *Blue-coat boy, girl*): A scholar of a charity school wearing the almoner's blue coat. Of these schools there are many in England; the most noted being Christ's Hospital in London, whose uniform is a long dark blue gown fastened at the waist with a belt, and bright yellow stockings. So *attrib.*, as in ***Blue-coat Hall, Hospital***.

1665 PEPYS *Diary* 1 June, We..saw all the funeral; which was with the blue-coat boys and old men, all the Aldermen, and Lord Mayor. **1691** WOOD *Ath. Oxon.* I. /164 Among the blew coats in Ch. Ch. Hospital. **1695** PEPYS *Let.* 20 Sept. (1926) I. 110 Two wealthy citizens are lately dead, and left their estates, one to a *Blewcoat-Boy* and the other to a *Blew-Coat-Girl* in Christ's Hospital. **1701** DE FOE *True-born Eng.* I. (1703) 13 From Blewcoat Hospitals. **1711** *Lond. Gaz.* No. 4920/3 A General Meeting..will be held at Blue-coat-Hall in Christ's-Hospital. **1861** NICHOLSON *Annals of Kendal* 195 The Blue Coat School and Hospital..The advancement of the Charity and maintenance of the blue-coat boys. **1894** *Daily News* 30 Mar. 5/1 To many..the notion of a Bluecoat 'girl' will be somewhat strange. It appears, nevertheless, that the Hertford establishment now shelters no fewer than 112 scholars of that sex.

'blue-coated, *a.* Wearing a blue coat.

1691 WOOD *Ath. Oxon.* II. /591 He..became Teacher of the Blew-coated-children in Ch. Ch. Hospital. **1820** SCOTT *Abbot* xxi, A pair or two of blue-coated serving-men.

blue devil.

1. A baleful demon (cf. BLUE *a.* 3, 8).

1616 R. C. *Times' Whistle* vii. 3443 Alston, whose life hath been accounted evill, And therfore calde by many the blew devill. **1870** LOWELL *Among my Bks.* Ser. I. (1873) 364 He ..keeps a pet sorrow, a blue-devil familiar, that goes with him everywhere.

2. *fig.* in pl. ***blue devils***: **a.** Despondency, depression of spirits, hypochondriac melancholy.

1781 F. BURNEY *Diary* 2 July (1904) II. 17 Thinking..that generous wine will destroy even the blue devils. **1787** [see *blue devilism* below]. **1798** G. COLMAN (*title*) Blue Devils, a Farce. **1800** W. RHODES *Bom. Fur.* i. (1836) 8 Do the blue devils your repose annoy? **1810** T. JEFFERSON *Writ.* (1830) IV. 144 We have something of the blue devils at times. **1823** BYRON *Juan* x. xxxviii, Though six days smoothly run, The seventh will bring blue devils or a dun. **1880** *Weekly Dispatch* 8 Feb. 12/2 He got discontented and had fits of blue devils.

b. The apparitions seen in *delirium tremens*.

1822 COBBETT *Resid. U.S.* 42 Just the weather to give drunkards the 'blue devils'. **1830** SCOTT *Demonol.* i. 18 They, by a continued series of intoxication, become subject to what is popularly called the Blue Devils.

Hence **blue-'devil** *v. trans.*, to affect with the 'blue devils'; **blue-'devilage, blue-'devilism; blue-'devilled** *ppl. a.*; **blue-'devilish, blue-'devilly** *adjs.*

1787 BURNS *Lett.* lxviii. Wks. (1875) 355 In my bitter hours of blue-devilism. **1816** ELPHINSTONE in *Edin. Rev.* (1884) July, He styles Childe Harold exquisite blue-devilage. **1817** T. L. PEACOCK *Melincourt* I. iii. 32 When Mr. Hippy was blue-devilled, old Harry was vapourish. **1824** *New Monthly Mag.* XI. 427 Our blue-devilish and hypochondriacal countrymen. **1832** WHEWELL *Let.* 1 July in Todhunter *W.W.* (1876) II. 143 Do not wait till I become blue-devilled with hard work. **1836** in *Jrnl. Southern Hist.* (1935) I. 364 To be hemmed up in a strange place without ..anything to interest you,..is enough to Blue Devil one. **1871** L. W. L. LOCKHART *Fair to See* I. viii. 208 The pine-trees loomed through stagnant mists with a dejected, blue-devilly aspect.

blue eye.

†**a.** = BLACK EYE 2 (cf. BLUE *a.* 3). †**b.** A blueness or dark circle round the eye, from weeping or other cause. **c.** An eye of which the iris is blue.

1552 HULOET, When a wife hathe a blewe eye, she sayth she hath stombled on hir good man his fyste, *suggillatio, liuor.* **1600** SHAKS. *A.Y.L.* III. ii. 393 A leane cheeke..a blew eie and sunken. *a* **1639** S. WARD *Serm.* 150 (D.) To whom are wounds, broken heads, blue eyes, maimed limbs? **1735** POPE *Mor. Ess.* II. 284 When those blue eyes first open'd on the sphere. **1820** SCOTT *Ivanhoe* iii, His face was broad, with large blue eyes.

d. An Australian species of honey-eater (see quots.).

1848 J. GOULD *Birds Australia* IV. pl. 68 *Entomyza cyanotis*, Swains. Blue-faced Entomyza. Blue-eye of the Colonists. **1861** *Chambers's Encycl.* II. 171/1 Blue-eye (*Entomyza cyanotis*), a beautiful little bird, abundant..in New South Wales.

blue-eyed, *a.* [See BLUE EYE.] **1. a.** Having a blue eye or eyes (now in sense c).

1610 SHAKS. *Temp.* I. ii. 269 This blew ey'd hag, was hither brought. **1656** COWLEY *Pind. Odes* (1669) 2 The blew-eyed Nereides. **1736** THOMSON *Liberty* IV. 670 Strong And yellow-hair'd, the blue-ey'd Saxon came. **1868** WOOD *Homes without H.* xxviii. 531 The pretty Blue-eyed Yellow Warbler.

b. *fig.* Innocent, ingenuous; favoured, esp. in phr. ***blue-eyed boy***.

1924 WODEHOUSE *Bill the Conqueror* xix. 278 If ever there was a blue-eyed boy, you will be it. **1935** AUDEN & ISHERWOOD *Dog beneath Skin* I. ii, You can keep that blue-eyed stuff for the others. **1959** *Manch. Guardian* 4 Aug. 4/6 The blue-eyed enthusiasm of a writer. **1963** *Times* 5 Mar. 7/1 During this period, farmers were 'blue-eyed boys'.

2. ***blue-eyed grass***: *Sisyrinchium Bermudianum. U.S.*

1784 CUTLER in *Mem. Amer. Acad. Arts & Sci.* I. 487 *Sisyrinchium*. Blue-Eyed Grass. Blossoms blue. **1884** W. MILLER *Plant-n.*

'blue-fish. [f. BLUE *a.* + FISH.]

a. A fish, a species of *Coryphæna*, found about the Bahamas and on the coast of Cuba. **b.** (See quot.)

1734 MORTIMER in *Phil. Trans.* XXXVIII. 318. **1782** P. H. BRUCE *Mem.* XII. 424 The sea hereabouts [Bahamas] abounds with fish unknown to us in Europe..parrot-fish, blue-fish, sucking-fish. **1848–60** BARTLETT *Dict. Amer.*, *Blue-Fish* (Temnodon saltator), a salt-water fish of the mackerel order, but larger in size. **1873** *Echo* 11 Mar. 2/2 Large quantities of halibut, bass, blue fish, flounders, and weak fish are also caught. **1880** GÜNTHER *Fishes* 447.

blue gown, 'blue-gown. [cf. BLUE-COAT.]

†**1.** A blue gown was: a. 'The dress of ignominy for a harlot in the house of correction' (Nares); **b.** The dress of an almoner, in Scotland of a king's bedesman or licensed beggar. *Obs.*

1604 DEKKER *Honest Wh.* Wks. 1873 II. 165 Your Puritanicall Honest Whore sits in a blue gowne. **1787** BURNS *Ep. J. Rankine* iv, It's just the blue-gown badge an' claithing O' saunts.

2. One who wears this dress: in Scotland, a king's bedesman or licensed beggar, who wore the dress as a badge. Also *attrib.*

1816 SCOTT *Antiq.* xxiv, 'Edie Ochiltree, nae maister—your puir bedesman and the king's', answered the Blue-Gown. *Ibid.* xxxvii, Here has been an old Blue-Gown committing robbery!

blue grass, blue-grass. Chiefly *U.S.* [BLUE *a.* 12 b.]

1. a. A field-grass (*Poa compressa* or *pratensis*), characteristic especially of Kentucky and Virginia. (See also quot. 1903.)

1751 C. GIST *Jrnls.* (1893) 47 It is..full of beautiful natural Meadows covered with wild Rye, blue Grass and Clover. **1879** SIR G. CAMPBELL *Black & Wh.* 14 The *blue-grass of Kentucky is famous; though it is not blue at all, but green, and very like our common natural grass. **1883** *Harper's Mag.* Oct. 719/2 The blue-grass..is not blue at all ..It is 'blue limestone grass' properly. **1889** *Harper's Mag.* Jan. 259/1 The blue-grass..blooms toward the middle of June in a bluish, almost a peacock blue, blossom, which gives to the fields an exquisite hue. **1903** CLAPIN *Dict. Amer.* 60 In Maryland the term *blue grass* is applied to a species of grass very injurious to wheat and clover, and hard to eradicate.

b. The region of the blue grass; *spec.* the State of Kentucky.

1872 SCHELE DE VERE *Americanisms* 407 Both the region where it grows naturally, and the settlers there are known as Blue Grass simply, and hence the State of Kentucky especially is often thus designated. **1887** *Harper's Mag.* June 48/2 To that pleasant land of the Kentuckian, the 'Blue-grass'.

c. A type of American folk-music. Also *attrib.*

1958 in *Amer. Speech* (1960) XXXV. 223. **1960** *20th Cent.* Dec. 559 A new compromise simulacrum, the bluegrass band..five-string banjo, mandolin, guitar, bass, fiddle and a holler-vocalist. **1969** *Rolling Stone* 28 June 11/3 Hillman has watched the rock scene change over the years (as a bluegrass mandolin player, then one of the original Byrds).

d. *attrib.* So **Blue Grass State**, Kentucky.

1772 *Pennsylvania Gaz.* 16 Apr. 4/3 Timothy and blue grass hay to be sold. **1863** E. DICEY *Six Months in Federal States* II. 64 What is called the Blue Grass region of Kentucky. **1883** *Harper's Mag.* Oct. 715/1 The blue-grass country is reached by traversing central Virginia and Kentucky. **1886** *Chicago Wkly. News* 29 Apr. 4/3 Kentucky ..is also called the Blue Grass state.

e. *ellipt.* as *adj.* Belonging to or characteristic of the blue-grass country.

1889 *Harper's Mag.* Aug. 459/2 Bud rode into the yard on Mollie.. 'Blue-grass all over. I wonder how he came by her.' **1913** G. STRATTON-PORTER *Laddie* x. 274 There's a strain of Arab in the father,..and the mother is bluegrass.

2. Applied to other grasses.

1811 W. AITON *Gen. View Agric. Ayr* 305 Carices, sedge-grasses..are, by the Ayrshire farmers, called blue, sour, one-pointed grasses. **1845** *New Statist. Acc. Scot.* VII. 518 We have but very little of the blue or star-grass (*carex panicea*). **1902** *Encycl. Brit.* XXXII. 108/2 On the extensive plains [of Queensland]..may be seen..'Blue grass' (*Andropogon sericeus, A. pertusus, A. refractus,* and *A. erianthoides*).

Blue Hen. *U.S.* The state of Delaware; chiefly in ***Blue Hen's chickens*** (see quot. 1840), ***Blue Hen State***.

1830 MRS. ROYALL *Lett. fr. Alabama* 69 He told one of our party he was 'One of the blue hen's chickens'. **1840** *Niles' Reg.* 9 May 154/3 In the revolutionary war..Captain Caldwell [of Delaware] had a company called by the rest 'Caldwell's game cocks', and the regiment after a time in Carolina was nicknamed from this, 'the blue hen's chickens' and the 'blue chickens'... But after they had been distinguished in the south the name of the *Blue Hen* was applied to the state. **1864** *Congress. Globe* June 2968/2, I remember the early history of the Blue Hen's Chickens and it is a proud one. **1867** *Trübner's Amer. Lit. Rec.* 1 Aug., [Delaware] is popularly known..as The Blue Hen or Diamond State. **1897** *Congress. Rec.* Mar., App. 68/2, [I thank] the gentleman from the 'Blue Hen State' for his suggestion.

blueing, bluing ('blu:ɪŋ), *vbl. sb.* [f. BLUE *v.*[1]]

1. A making blue; *spec.* the process of giving a blue colour to metals. Also *attrib.*, as ***blueing-pan***.

1766 CROKER, etc. *Dict. Arts & Sc.* (1768) I., *Blueing* of Metals is performed by heating them in the fire, till they assume a blue colour. **1851** *Art Jrnl. Catal. Gt. Exhib.* 63/3 The [sword-] blade..combines embossing with engraving, blueing, and gilding. **1884** F. BRITTEN *Watch & Clockm.* 34 The articles to be blued are placed in a blueing pan.

2. A substance that gives a blue tint, laundresses' blue.

1669 SIR THOMAS BROWNE *Let.* 28 Apr. (1946) 51 Enquire after smalt, a stone wherof they make bleweing for paynting & starch. **1889** *Cent. Dict.*, *Bluing*..The indigo, soluble Prussian blue, or other material, used in the laundry to give a bluish tint to linen. **1895** *Cal. Univ. Nebraska* 1895–6 174 Soaps, washing powders, polishing powders, bluing, etc. **1897** *Star* 17 Sept. 4/7 Dust the glass with powdered bluing done up in a bit of cheese cloth.

blueism ('blu:ɪz(ə)m). Also **bluism.** [f. BLUE *a.* + -ISM.] The characteristics of a 'blue' or 'blue-stocking'; feminine learning or pedantry.

1822 *Blackw. Mag.* XII. 589 What was heroism with our Chatham, was but blueism and cant in De Staël. *a* **1841** T. HOOK *Man of Many Fr.* (D.) He had..fallen a victim to her beauty and blueism. **1848** *Fraser's Mag.* XXXIX. 542 She had prejudiced him against bluism in women.

'Blue-John.

†**1.** = AFTER-WORT. Hence *fig. Obs.*

1672 MARVELL *Reh. Transp.* I. 82 His Defence was but the blew-John of his Ecclesiastical Policy, and this Preface the Tap-droppings of his Defence. **1683** SALMON *Doron Med.* I. 242 Brewers Afterworts, or Wash, called 'Blew-John'.

2. A local name of the blue Fluor-spar found in Derbyshire.

1772 GILPIN *Lakes Cumberland* (1788) II. 217 It..is known in London by the name of the Derbyshire drop. But on the spot it is called Blue John, from the beautiful blue veins which overspread the finest parts of it. **1840** HUMBLE *Dict. Geol. & Min.* (1843) s.v., The blue-john or fluor spar mine near Castleton in Derbyshire.

'bluely, *adv.* [f. BLUE *a.* + -LY[2].]

1. With a blue colour or tinge.

1647 H. MORE *Song of Soul* II. App. xciv, Then blewly pale, then duller still, till perfect dead. **1818** KEATS *Endym.* I. 605 Her hovering feet, More bluely vein'd..Than those of sea-born Venus. **1844** HOOD *Haunted Ho.* lxiii, The taper burning bluely. **1852** D. MOIR *Graves of Dead* i.

†**2.** Badly, with bad success; only in phrase ***to come off bluely***. *Obs.*

c **1650** *2nd Narrat. late Parl.* in *Select. Harl. Misc.* (1793) 425 Yet [he]..came off bluely in the end. **1653** URQUHART *Rabelais* IV. xxxv, He still came off but bluely by reason of the Care and Vigilance of the Chitterlings. **1710** T. WARD *Eng. Ref.* I. 67 (D.) We shall come off but blewly here. **1783** AINSWORTH *Lat. Dict.* (Morell) I, Bluely [badly], *male.* He came off but bluely, *malè res successit.*

†**'blueman.** *Obs.* [A late form of BLOMAN, due to the original identity of *blo*, BLAE, and BLUE.] A negro; = BLOMAN.

1387 TREVISA *Higden* Rolls Ser. I. 157 Þe men of þe lond [Ethiopia] þat beþ blewe men. *Ibid.* VI. 379 Þe Blewman chaungeþ nouȝt liȝtliche his skyn. **1468** *Mann. & Househ. Exp.* 578 Richard Fyrthyng, a blewmane.

blueness (ˈbluːnɪs). Forms: 5 blunesse, 5–7 blewnes, 6–7 blewnesse, 8– blueness. [f. BLUE *a.* + -NESS.]

1. The state or quality of being blue, blue colour.

1600 FAIRFAX *Tasso* VI. xc, His azure robe the orient blewnesse lost. **1742** RICHARDSON *Pamela* IV. 35 The..fine thin Blueness given to the first Milk. **1882** HOWELLS in *Longm. Mag.* I. 51 A..sky..of more than Italian blueness.

2. The quality or state of being livid, as a bruise; the mark of a bruise.

?**1491** CAXTON 15 *Oes* in Blades *Caxton* 353 The blewnes of thy woundes. **1577** tr. *Bullinger's Decades* (1592) 47 And with the blewnesse of his stripes are we healed. **1678** OTWAY *Friendship in Fash.* 14 Ay, and then that blewness under the eyes.

3. *fig.* The quality of a blue-stocking; feminine learning or pedantry.

1881 M. A. LEWIS *Two Pretty G.* III. 37 They might go in for some other line—fastness, or blueness, or music.

4. Indelicacy, indecency. (Cf. BLUE *a.* 9.)

1840 CARLYLE *Diderot, Ess.* 240 (L.) The occasional blueness of both [writings] shall not altogether affright us. **1891** *Sat. Rev.* 8 Aug. 168/2 That tinge of 'blueness' which repels English propriety.

5. a. A state of depression or melancholy.

1867 W. JAMES *Let.* 7 Nov. (1920) I. 120, I am in a mood of indigestion and blueness. **1911** J. C. LINCOLN *Cap'n Warren's Wards* ix. 147 Before evening his blueness had disappeared.

b. The fact or quality of music being 'blue' (see BLUE *a.* 3 d). orig. *U.S.*

1949 R. BLESH *Shining Trumpets* II. viii. 193 The beautiful, unveiled tone that on other occasions could transmit a blueness difficult to imagine. **1959** W. RUSSELL in M. T. Williams *Art of Jazz* (1960) 36 Those devices that gave a feeling of blueness to his harmony.

ˈblue-nose. (Chiefly in U.S.)

1. A purplish potato grown in Nova Scotia.

1837–40 HALIBURTON *Clockm.* **1861** *Illustr. Lond. News* 15 Jan. 564.

2. a. A nick-name for a native of Nova Scotia.

1837–40 HALIBURTON *Clockm.* (1862) Pref. 7 When blue-nose hears that, he thinks he's got a bargain. **1842** *United Serv. Mag.* II. 328 Of the nation of Bluenoses.

b. A Canadian, esp. Nova Scotian, ship.

1889 in *Cent. Dict.* **1899** *Daily News* 2 Dec. 6/4 For sheer brutality commend me to the life on board a 'Bluenose', as we call the Canadian whalers. **1949** LAWSON & SWEET *Our New Brunswick Story* 229 In those old days all the ships of the Maritime Provinces were known among sailors the world over as Bluenoses.

3. A kind of clam shell-fish.

1883 *Leisure Hour* 252/1 The coarsest is the mud clam, or blue nose.

4. A person who is excessively puritanical. Also *attrib.* *U.S.*

1927 H. C. BROWN *In Golden Nineties* v. 187 With a lot of blue noses on the Board,..this concession was not secured without great diplomacy. **1929** *Variety* 3 Apr. 11/4 That this picture may aggravate blue nose censors is not beyond the bounds of possibility. **1945** *Chicago Daily News* 2 Aug. 10/7 Our bluenoses are doing a grave injury to the men serving overseas, who have got the impression that married women are running wild.

blue-nosed, *a.* [BLUE *a.* 1.] Having a blue nose; also (chiefly *U.S.*) *transf.* and *fig.*, esp. as a term of disparagement or contempt; *spec.* priggish, puritanical (cf. BLUE-NOSE 4).

1809 W. IRVING *Knickerb.* III. ii, A goodly, blue-nosed, skim'd milk, New-England cheese. **1866** C. H. SMITH *Bill Arp* 87 The blue-nosed Yankees were to pollute our sacred soil the next morning. **1890** *Amer. N. & Q.* V. 6 Can you tell me why Presbyterians are sometimes called 'blue-nosed'? **1959** F. BOWERS *Textual & Lit. Crit.* iii. 112 It is an ignorant view..that bibliography acts as a blue-nosed and puritanical censor to take all the joy out of the textual critic's life. **1959** P. H. JOHNSON *Humbler Creation* xxxv. 235 Let's not be blue-nosed, but..he's doing it under the rose.

blue point, bluepoint. *U.S.* [The name of a headland near Great South Bay, Long Island.] Used *attrib.* or *ellipt.* to designate a small oyster from the south shore of Long Island; orig. one from a bed off Blue Point.

1789 in *Mass. Hist. Soc. Proc.* (1869) XI. 24 Judge Hobart ..treated us with Blue Point oysters from the shell. **1868** G. ROSE *Great Country* 25 [Oysters] are called by many names; 'saddle rocks', 'blue points', and 'Shrewsburys', being the most popular. **1897** *Daily News* 19 Nov. 5/2 The menu will include such national dishes as..blue points, and pumpkin pie. **1909** 'O. HENRY' *Roads of Destiny* xx. 343 He got along fine with the olives and celery and the bluepoints. **1951** *Good Housek. Home Encycl.* 578/1 The large American Blue Points (now cultivated in the British Isles)..are bought for cooking.

blue-print, blueprint, *sb.* Also blue print. [BLUE *a.* 1.]

1. (A process for making) a photographic print composed of white lines on a blue ground or of blue lines on a white ground, used chiefly in copying plans, machine-drawings, etc.; also, a blue-toned photograph.

1886 *Electrician* XVI. 466/2 The Western Edison Light Company of Chicago..have adopted an arrangement for taking blue print by electric light. **1887** *U.S. Postal Laws & Reg.* §364. 152 'Blue prints' reproduced only as copies of the original. **1892** *Photogr. Ann.* II. 102 Blue Prints can be obtained on albumenised paper. **1936** *Economist* 15 Feb. 351/2 Blue-prints were drawn for 'mastodon' capital ships of 60,000 tons, and for cruisers of 20,000 tons. **1943** J. S. HUXLEY *TVA* 141 Specifications for TVA Demountable Defense Houses (pp. v + 42, illus. and blueprints).

b. *attrib.*

1895 *Montgomery Ward Catal.* 211/2 Blue print paper. **1909** *Cent. Dict.* Suppl. I. 147/2 *Electric blue-print machine*, a machine in which the sensitized paper is exposed behind tracings to a series of electric lights instead of to sunlight. **1923** H. A. MADDOX *Dict. Stationery* 14 *Blueprint paper*, a type of photographic paper used for taking rapid duplicates from machine plans, etc., the lines of the drawing developing out in white relief against a solid blue background or *vice versa*.

2. *fig.* A (detailed) plan or scheme; a pattern.

1926 *Spectator* 11 Sept. 385/1 Surely he can complete his life by giving us the blue-prints of the millennium. **1939** *Times Lit. Suppl.* 11 Feb. 87/2 Blue-prints of a new society come with better grace from Mr. Wells than from any other contemporary novelist. **1942** J. S. HUXLEY in *Fortune* Dec. 152/2 To nail some elaborate blue-print of international organization to our masthead.

blue-printing, *vbl. sb.* **a.** (The process of) printing in blue beneath the glaze on china, as distinguished from 'black-printing'. **b.** The action or method of making a photographic blue-print (*Cent. Dict.*, 1889). So **blue-printer**. Also (as a back-formation or f. *blue-print* sb.) **blue-print, blueprint** *v.*, lit. and fig. (see prec.).

1825 J. NICHOLSON *Operat. Mechanic* 470 *Blue-printing* is the impressions taken from engraved copper-plates by means of a rolling-press. *Ibid.*, The blue-printer lays the plate upon a stove. *Ibid.* 482 The *blue-printed pottery* is a very popular kind. **1865** L. JEWITT *Wedgwoods* 391 Blue Printing was introduced at Etruria at an early date, and has, of course, with black, etc., been continued to the present day. **1939** J. B. PRIESTLEY *Let People Sing* ix. 215 Though these girls kept away, thousands of others were only too eager to be blue-printed, numbered and air-conditioned. **1942** H. A. WALLACE *Cent. Common Man* 28 Dec. (1944) 36 We cannot now blueprint all the details, but we can begin now to think about some of the guiding principles of this world-wide new democracy. **1948** A. O'RAHILLY *Soc. Principles* viii. 55 The tidy bureaucratic minds of planners and blue-printers. **1960** AUDEN *Homage to Clio* I. p. 24 Do-it-yourself America Prophetically blue-printed this Palace kitchen. **1966** R. JEFFRIES *Death in Coverts* ix. 97 The first death might or might not have been part of a pattern, but the second death blueprinted that pattern.

ˈbluer. [f. BLUE *v.*[1]] One who blues metal.

1747 *Gentl. Mag.* XVII. 101 The gun-makers' business.. is divided into 21 different branches..viz. barrel-forger, brich-forger..bluer [*printed* bleur].

blue ˈribbon, riband.

1. A ribbon of blue silk worn as a badge of honour; *esp.* the broad dark blue ribbon worn by members of the order of the Garter.

1651 *Let. fr. France* in *Proc. in Parl.* No. 116. 1800 The Queen [of France] hath sent to the Count of Doignion.. promising him the staffe of the Marshall of France, and of a blew Ribbon. **1690** TEMPLE *Ess. Health* Wks. 1731 I. 274 A White Staff will not help gouty Feet..nor a Blue Ribband bind up a Wound so well as a Fillet. **1867** MORLEY *Burke* 56 Rising to thunderous denunciations of 'the noble lord in the blue ribbon.'

2. The greatest distinction, the most distinguished place, the first prize.

1848 DISRAELI in *Harper's Mag.* Aug. (1883) 340/2 'You do not know what the Derby is!' 'Yes, I do. It is the Blue Ribbon of the Turf.' **1875** POSTE *Gaius* I. §7. 37 The blue ribbon of the profession should never be conferred on any lawyer who had antiquarian notions of constitutional law. **1883** *Standard* 21 May 2/1 The Blue Riband of the Turf is destined to go to Heath House.

3. A small strip of blue ribbon worn by certain abstainers from alcoholic beverages, as a means of mutual recognition, and as a public indication of their principles; hence ***to take the blue ribbon***. ***Blue Ribbon Army***: the association of such Total Abstainers. Hence **blue-ribboner, blue-ribbonism, blue-ribbonist, blue-ribbonite.**

1878 *Christian* 16 May (*heading*) Gospel-Temperance in Hoxton—A 'Blue Ribbon Army.' **1882** *Society* 11 Nov. 22/2 He has joined..the Blue Ribboners. *Ibid.* 30 Dec. 20/1 [It] would make even a blue-ribbon man think kindlily of spirits. **1884** *Graphic* 9 Aug. 134/2 At an hotel it might be supposed that most people have taken the Blue Ribbon. **1885** *Athenæum* 31 Oct. 567/3 Such forms of extravagance as ritualism and blue-ribbonism. **1885** C. LOWE *Life Bismarck* II. 488 Not his the heart that could be cheered by blue-ribbon liquors.

blue rinse. [RINSE *sb.* 2 c.] **a.** *Hairdressing.* A solution or cream used as a rinse on grey or white hair so as to give it a temporary blue tint. Also *attrib.*

1944 M. LASKI *Love on Supertax* x. 93, I think I'll have a blue rinse to-day. **1949** N. MITFORD *Love in Cold Climate* 221 A blue rinse for her grey hair. **1959** *Spectator* 24 Sept. 394/3 Women..with bitter-sweet smiles and blue-rinse bobs. **1981** *N.Y. Times Mag.* 22 Feb. VI. 82/1 Another French shampoo..acts as a blue rinse on the hair. **1985** *Amer. Banker* 6 Nov. 24 She is elderly, her wealth is inherited, she favors a blue rinse for her hair.

b. *fig.* Used *attrib.* to refer to the group of middle-class elderly ladies who favour a blue rinse, or to elderly women in general.

1964 *Punch* 28 Oct. 633/2 The blue-rinse vote went down the drain, and..the Northern liberals and the coons went with 'em. **1977** *New Yorker* 3 Jan. 46/3 The Sydney Green Bans..originated in an unlikely coalition of affluent communities, led by embattled suburban matrons known as 'the blue rinse set'. **1982** *Financial Times* 14 Apr. II. 17/1 The Liberal Party: that great grey mass of middle-class small businessmen, shopkeepers,..blue-rinse ladies, widows, [etc.]. **1986** *Los Angeles Times* 16 Aug. v. 9/3 During his 16-year tenure with the Los Angeles Philharmonic, Mehta was at once a matinee idol of the blue-rinse brigade and a favorite target of critical barbs.

Hence **blue-rinsed** *ppl. a.*; **blue-rinse** *v. trans.*, to apply a blue rinse to (the hair).

1958 J. CANNAN *And be a Villain* ii. 47 He thought with satisfaction of his own blue-rinsed little-black-frocked mother-in-law. **1962** J. BRAINE *Life at Top* xiii. 170 Tom was..very proud of his mane of white hair... There were some people in Dufton who said that he blue rinsed it a little. **1968** *Listener* 31 Oct. 565/3 'Is this what you call an education?' said a blue-rinsed Manhattan matron.

blues (bluːz). orig. *U.S.* [A use of the pl. *blues* (see BLUE *sb.* 12), treated as either sing. or pl.] A melody of a mournful and haunting character, originating among the Negroes of the Southern U.S., freq. in a twelve-bar sequence using many 'blue' notes. Also *attrib.*

1912 W. C. HANDY (*tune-title*) Memphis Blues. **1917** *Lit. Digest* 25 Aug. 29/2 'Must I Hesitate?', 'The Blues', 'Franky and Johnny', and other classics of the levee underworld. **1921** *Outward Bound* May 58/2 These 'labour songs',..like the 'blues' of to-day, were rather humorous. **1923** *Daily Mail* 28 July 7 Noisy 'jazz' music..is being driven out..by the soft pulsing of muffled melody in new tunes known as 'Blues'. *Ibid.*, A special 'Blues Trot' has been devised for dancing with the tunes, which are slower than [those of] a fox-trot. **1927** *Melody Maker* Sept. 865/2 The Yale..is danced to 'blues' tempo. **1928** *Oxf. Mag.* 1 Nov. 84/2 The use of a blues for the slow movement is interesting. **1949** R. BLESH *Shining Trumpets* I. v. 107 The blues scale..enters into and colors all singing and playing by American Negroes. *Ibid.* II. xi. 247 The blues-shouting trombone. **1956** MORGAN & HORRICKS *Modern Jazz* 16 The twelve-bar blues, long a source of expression for the outpouring of emotion, underwent a startling change with the introduction of the riff in jazz.

blue sky, blue-sky. [BLUE *a.* 1.]

1. *attrib.* Having the pleasant appearance of a blue sky; by extension, with difficulties ignored, unrealistic; spec. ***blue-sky book*** (orig. *U.S.*): see quot. 1956. Also, fanciful, hypothetical; not practical or profitable in the current state of knowledge or technological development (also **blue skies**).

1895 *Daily News* 2 Nov. 6/3 Paintings of Venice..which may be described as a blue sky series, so cheerful and gay is the aspect under which this artist generally views the picturesque city. **1920** W. HARD *Raymond Robins' Own Story* iii. 136 Lenin and Trotzky never gave me any blue-sky talk. They never promised unless they had the will and the *power* to deliver. **1956** *Observer* 15 Jan., Blue Sky Books are those literary works which, without any specific technique or expert knowledge, tell us their authors' views on the nature and purpose and proper conduct of human life. **1957** H. CROOME *Forgotten Place* iv. 55 The manuscript in this case is a blue-sky book, about to regenerate family life. **1967** *Economist* 18 Nov. 766/2 'The possible development, necessarily long-term, of the vast reserves of oil locked in non-conventional sources such as the Western Hemisphere oilsands and shales.' This is blue-sky stuff, the real security is now seen to lie in boosting oil stocks. **1977** *Time* 21 Feb. 48/2 The first is to put faith in blue-sky technologies, such as development of solar and geothermal power. **1985** *Times* 19 Apr. 13/4 If..the cutting edge of blue skies research becomes somewhat blunted, [etc.].

2. Used *attrib.* to denote dealing in doubtful or worthless securities, or legislation relating to this. (The allusion is supposed to be to one ready to sell the 'blue sky' to a credulous buyer.)

1906 C. R. WOOLDRIDGE *Grafters of Amer.* 48 They were what I would term 'blue sky and hot air' securities. **1912** *N.Y. Even. Post* 13 Jan., Financ. Suppl. 3 The 'Blue Sky' law of Kansas prohibits the sale..of stock or bonds of any company chartered outside the State, unless [etc.]. **1921** *Springfield Weekly Republ.* 3 Mar. 1 The origin of 'blue sky law'—legislation providing for State regulation of the sale of corporate securities—is middle western. **1948** MENCKEN *Amer. Lang.* Suppl. II. vii. 149 Carruth..suggested that *blue-sky*, to indicate a bad investment, might be from the German *blauer dunst*.

blue-stocking (ˈbluːˌstɒkɪŋ), *sb.* Also Blue-stocking, etc. [As an attributive phrase, with the sense of 'wearing blue stockings', this is found as early as the 17th c. (see 1 a.); in its transferred sense it originated in connexion with re-unions held in London about 1750, at the houses of Mrs. Montague, Mrs. Vesey, and Mrs. Ord, who exerted themselves to substitute for the card-playing, which then formed the chief recreation at evening parties, more intellectual modes of spending the time, including conversation on literary subjects, in which eminent men of letters often took part. Many of those who attended eschewed 'full dress'; one of these was Mr. Benjamin Stillingfleet, who habitually wore grey or 'blue' worsted, instead of black silk stockings. In reference to this, Admiral Boscawen is said (Sir W. Forbes *Life of Beattie* (1806) I. 210 *note*) to have derisively dubbed the coterie 'the Blue Stocking Society' (as not constituting a dressed assembly). The ladies who supported the reform were at first called *Blue Stockingers*, *Blue Stocking Ladies*, and at length, about 1790, when the actual

origin of the term was remembered by few, *Blue Stockings*, in later slang abbreviated to *Blues*.]

1. *attrib.* Wearing blue worsted (instead of black silk) stockings; *hence*, not in full dress, in homely dress. (*contemptuous.*)

a. Applied to the 'Little Parliament' of 1653, with reference to the puritanically plain or mean attire of its members.

a **1683** *Autobiog. Sir J. Bramston* (1845) 89 That Blew-stocking Parliament, Barebone Parliament, a companie of fellowes called togeather by Cromwell, the armie and councell thereof pickt out for the purpose.

b. Applied depreciatively to the assemblies that met at Montagu House, and those who frequented them or imitated them.

[**1757** MRS. MONTAGUE *Let.* in Doran *Lady of Last C.* (1873) He [Mr. Stillingfleet] has left off his old friends and his blue stockings. **1780** MAD. D'ARBLAY *Diary* (1842) I. 326 Who would not be a blue stockinger at this rate?] **1791** BOSWELL *Johnson* viii. 86 These societies were denominated *Blue-stocking Clubs.* **1885** F. CUSS *E. Barnet* 113 A member of the..Blue Stocking coterie.

c. Hence, Of women: Having or affecting literary tastes; literary, learned.

1804 *Edin. Rev.* IV. 219 To hear blue-stocking ladies jingle their rhymes. **1824** MACAULAY *Misc. Writ.* (1860) I. 127 The travelled nobles and the blue stocking matrons of Rome.

2. = *Blue Stocking lady*: *orig.* one who frequented Mrs. Montague's 'Blue Stocking' assemblies; thence transferred sneeringly to any woman showing a taste for learning, a literary lady. (Much used by reviewers of the first quarter of the 19th c.; but now, from the general change of opinion on the education of women, nearly abandoned.)

1790 WOLCOTT (P. Pindar) *To Apollo* Wks. 1812 II. 277, I see the band of Blue Stockings arise, Historic, critic, and poetic Dames. **1807** *Edin. Rev.* X. 192 This would scarcely go down..even among the blue stockings of Montagu house. **1822** HAZLITT *Table-t.* II. vii. 168, I have an utter aversion to *blue-stockings.* I do not care a fig for any woman that knows even what *an author* means. **1858** DE QUINCEY *Autobiog. Sk.* Wks. 1862 I. xiii. 353 *note*, The order of ladies called Bluestockings, by way of reproach, has become totally extinct amongst us.

b. *attrib.*

1832 *Edin. Rev.* LV. 521 A blue-stocking contempt for household cares. *a* **1859** DE QUINCEY *Wks.* (1863) II. 133 A blue-stocking loquacity.

3. 'The American Avocet (*Recurvirostra americana*). A common bird in the Northern states.' Bartlett *Dict. Amer.*

Hence (from sense 2) **blue-stocking** *v.* (*nonce-wd.*), **blue-stocking'd** *a.*, † **blue-stockinger** (see above in 1 b), **blue-stockingish** *a.*, **blue-stockingism, blue-stockingship.**

1784 H. WALPOLE *Corr.* (1833) IV. 381 [To Hannah More] When will you blue-stocking yourself, and come amongst us? **1818** *Blackw. Mag.* III. 286 The tawdry blue-stockingship of a young lady from the manufacturing district. **1820** *Ibid.* VIII. 99 Blue-stockingism was in its cerulean altitude. *c* **1822** J. WILSON in *Byron's Wks.* (1846) 232/2 *note*, The women..are blue-stockingish. **1824** SCOTT *St. Ronan's* xxxii, That d——d, vindictive, blue-stocking'd wild cat. **1858** DE QUINCEY *Autobiog. Sk.* Wks. 1862 II. v. 316 The utter want of pretension, and of all that looks like Bluestockingism, in the style of her habitual conversation.

bluestone, blue stone. [BLUE *a.* 12 c.]

1. a. Copper sulphate.

1651 BIGGS *New Disp.* 27 That divine blew stone, is but Roman vitriol, that is to be had at every Druggist and Apothecaries shops. **1883** *Knowledge* 1 June 323/2 Crystals of pure bluestone (sulphate of copper, $CuSO_4$). **1932** R. F. FORTUNE *Sorcerers of Dobu* 46, I doctored a leg-sore with bluestone.

b. Gin or whisky of so poor a quality as to be comparable with vitriol (sense 4). *slang.* Cf. *blue ruin* s.v. BLUE *a.* 13.

1880 *Blackw. Mag.* June 786 The effects of the mixture of spirits of wine, bluestone, and tobacco-juice. **1882** *N. & Q.* V. 348 'It wasn't whiskey,' he said, 'it was nothing but bluestone.'

2. a. A building or paving stone of a bluish grey colour; spec. *U.S.*, a bluish argillaceous sandstone quarried near the Hudson river. Also *attrib.*

1709 LAWSON *Carolina* 50 This [river]..affords as good blue Stone for Mill-Stones, as that from Cologn. **1852** A. CARY *Clovernook* 106 A little puddle of water had..soiled the bluestone hearth. **1895** DANA *Man. Geol.* (ed. 4) 593 The thicker layers [of flagstones] are called bluestone, from the bluish gray color. **1906** CHAMBERLIN & SALISBURY *Geol.* II. 559 Bluestone formation... Purple shale and thin red sandstone, with calcareous beds.

b. A basalt used for building and other industrial purposes. *Austral.* and *N.Z.*

1850 *Australasian* Oct. 138 A stone not unlike the trap or bluestone around Melbourne. **1886** J. HECTOR *Handbk. N.Z.* (ed. 4) 58 Basalts, locally called 'blue-stones', occur of a quality useful for road-metal, house-blocks, and ordinary rubble masonry. **1961** *Coast to Coast 1959–60* 36 He built the bluestone house near that little chapel you can see from here. **1969** *Melbourne Truth* 12 July 2/3 The hotel..has been renovated by putting brick veneer over the original bluestone.

c. Term applied to the stones, geologically foreign to the site, forming the inner circle and inner horseshoe of Stonehenge; later identified as spotted dolerite from the Prescelly Hills in Pembrokeshire. Also *attrib.*

1812 R. C. HOARE *Anc. Hist. S. Wilts.* v. 127 One of the blue stones of Stonehenge. **1865** J. LUBBOCK *Pre-historic Times* ii. 52 Fragments, not only of Sarcen stones, but also of the blue stones which form the inner circle at Stonehenge. **1926** *Man* XXVI. 42 Stonehenge—the supposed blue stone trilithon. **1957** CHILDE *Dawn Europ. Civilization* (ed. 6) xviii. 331 From the Presely Mountains in South-West Wales huge blocks of spotted dolerite (Bluestone) were transported to Salisbury Plain.

bluesy ('bluːzɪ), *a.* [f. BLUES + -Y[1].] Of music: resembling or characteristic of the blues; using 'blue notes' or having some other feature in common with the blues.

1958 J. SILVERMAN *Folk Blues* (1968) 22 Guitarists, particularly, will recognize these two chords... Aesthetically, they sound bluesy. **1961** *Sunday Mercury* (Birmingham) 8 Jan. 16/6 This slow, almost haunting, bluesy piece. **1967** *Melody Maker* 29 Apr. 10/4 As a soloist he is hardly a jazz giant, but these are pleasing, jumping, bluesy tracks which should appeal to the jazz fringe audience in particular. **1968** *Listener* 8 Aug. 186/1, I heard something Hebraic rather than bluesy in the crushed chord-clusters of all 12 semitones. **1977** *Rolling Stone* 24 Mar. 65/1 Willie Smith's drumming is recorded up front, his cymbal socks sounding inscrutably bluesy. **1984** *Listener* 19 Apr. 34/4 A bluesy score..and some relentlessly grim pans of the bed-sit and the dank staircase leading to it, underline what is a lonely, cheerless existence. **1986** *City Limits* 10 Apr. 39 A voice that is more bluesy than churchy.

bluet, -ett. Also 3 blouet. [Strictly two words: 1. a. F. *bluette*, fem. dim. of *bleu, bleue*, '*bluette du Rhin*, basse laine d'Allemagne' (Boiste), in med.L. *bluetum, bluettum*; 2. a. F. *bleuet, bluet*, in same sense, masc. dim. of *bleu.*]

† **1.** A kind of woollen cloth of bluish colour. *Obs.*

[*a* **1300** *Chron. de Mailros* in Gale *Rer. Angl. Script. Vet.* (1684) I. 236 Inter suos domesticos contentus erat amictu rosseti, inter majores terræ raro Scarleti, frequenter vero bloueti vel burneti amiciebatur indumento.] **1437** *Bury Wills* (1850) 10 Item lego Gilberto Skut xxs. et togam meam de bluett furr'. [**1866** ROGERS *Agric. & Prices* I. xxii. 575 Bluett is quoted by the yard, and by the pannus or piece.]

2. The Corn Bluebottle (*Centaurea Cyanus*). Also applied to other blue flowers, as in U.S. to *Oldenlandia cærulea*, 'a delicate little herb producing in spring a profusion of light blue flowers fading to white, with a yellowish eye' (Gray), and to a species of Bilberry (*Vaccinium angustifolium*).

1727 BRADLEY *Fam. Dict., Blue-Bottle*, or Bluet..grows amongst Wheat and other Corn.

blueth. *nonce-wd.* Blueness.

1754 H. WALPOLE *Corr.* (1820) I. 347 (D.) Now in the height of its greenth, blueth, gloomth.

blue tongue, blue-tongue.

1. [Afrikaans *bloutong.*] A virus disease affecting horses and sheep, in which the tongue becomes swollen and blue. orig. *S. Afr.*

1863 J. S. DOBIE *S. Afr. Jrnl.* 19 Apr. (1945) 86 Blue tongue here also (which is a swelling of the tongue and lips which prevents the poor beast from eating). **1887** RIDER HAGGARD *Jess* viii, It's a beautiful veldt..no horse sickness, no blue-tongue. **1905** *Nature* 4 Sept. 502/2 Catarrhal Fever of Sheep: Blue Tongue. **1963** *Times* 22 Apr. 2/6 Blue tongue, though it exists no nearer to the United Kingdom than Spain and Portugal, is so feared in Australia that it has led to a ban on all livestock imports from Britain. **1966** *New Scientist* 3 Nov. 250/3 The most serious potential threat is probably from the bluetongue virus to which Merinos are highly susceptible.

2. An Australian lizard of the genus *Tiliqua*, belonging to the family Scincidæ.

1883 F. MCCOY *Zool. Victoria* I. VIII. 15 These Lizards are very sluggish, so that the popular name 'Sleepy Lizard' as well as 'Blue-tongue' comes to be applied to both. **1904** *Daily Chron.* 28 Jan. 6/2 The 'Australian Blue-Tongue' is a ..lizard, with a curious habit of thrusting forth a long tongue as bright as turquoise blue. **1963** E. WORRELL *Reptiles of Australia* 34 The best-known lizards are the Bluetongue group (*Tiliqua*).

b. = ROUSTABOUT 2. *Austral. slang.*

1943 in BAKER *Austral. Slang* (ed. 3) 12. **1955** G. BOWEN *Wool Away!* 157 The poor old rouseabout... Australians sometimes call this hand a 'blue tongue'.

Hence **blue-tongued** *a.*, having a blue tongue; ***blue-tongued lizard*** = 2 above.

1883 F. MCCOY *Zool. Victoria* I. VIII. 13 Cyclodus Gigas. .. The Northern Blue-tongued Lizard. **1887** *Ibid.* II. 120 'Blue-tongued Lizard' or 'Sleepy Lizard'.

bluette (bluːˈɛt). A breed of oriental frilled pigeons having a white body and blue or silver wings.

1879 L. WRIGHT *Pigeon Keeper* 180 This is almost exactly the marking of the Bluette. **1891** R. WOODS *Pigeon-Culture* 138 Brunettes, Bluettes and Silverettes are..subvarieties of the Satinette, differing only in colour and markings.

blue-veined, *a.* [BLUE *a.* 11 b.]

a. Having blue veins.

1593 SHAKS *Ven. & Ad.* 125 These blue-veined violets, whereon we lean. **1797** COLERIDGE *Christabel* I. ix, Her blue-veined feet unsandal'd were. **1953** R. GRAVES *Poems* 10 In the warm blue-veined nook Of your elbow crook.

b. spec. ***blue-veined cheese*** = *blue cheese* (see BLUE *a.* 13); so ***blue vein, blue veiny*** (***cheese***). (Cf. *blue-vinnied* adj.)

1892 I. BEETON *Househ. Managem.* xli. 894 Dorsetshire yields us a very good cheese called *Blue veiny*, from its blue-veined appearance. **1950** J. G. DAVIS *Dict. Dairying* 43 *Blue-veined cheese*, a term applied to Stilton, Wensleydale, Roquefort, and Gorgonzola cheese, in which the blue-green mould, *Penicillium roqueforti*, grows in cracks and is an important ripening agent. **1959** MCLINTOCK *Descr. Atlas N.Z.* 58 The main kind of cheese produced [in N.Z.] is 'cheddar', with one factory at Eltham producing 'blue vein' cheese.

bluey ('bluːɪ), *a.* and *sb.* [f. BLUE *a.* + -Y[1].]

A. *adj.* Inclined to blue; more or less blue; also as *adv.* Also *Comb.*

1802 SOUTHEY *Thalaba* II. v, The lips were bluey pale. **1830** *Blackw. Mag.* XXVIII. 26 Pale bluey bodies. **1889** *Pall Mall Gaz.* 1 May 3/1 An exquisite effect in bluey grey. **1900** *Daily News* 11 May 5/2 A bluey green colour. **1908** *Westm. Gaz.* 6 Feb. 4/3 There are few furs so eminently satisfactory..as the pretty, soft, bluey-grey squirrel.

B. *sb.* **1.** (in Australia): A bushman's bundle, the outside wrapper of which is generally a blue blanket. Esp. (of tramps or hikers) in the phr. *to **hump** bluey*, to travel with a swag, to hit the trail.

1890 *Melbourne Argus* 16 Aug. 13/2 'We shall have to hump "bluey" again,' said Tom... Early November saw us again on the track. **1891** R. WALLACE *Rural Econ. Austral. & N.Z.* 73 'Humping bluey' is for a workman to walk in search of work. **1896** C. J. O'REGAN *Poems* 29 You can fancy, old mate, how I'm longing..To flee with a 'billy' and 'bluey'. **1903** H. B. KING *Bill's Philos.* 28 It ain't for bluey-humpers To travel on *his* road. **1911** E. M. CLOWES *On Wallaby* xi. 278 An expression used for what in England we call 'tramping', is 'going on the wallaby', otherwise 'humping the swag', or 'the bluey', or 'sundowning'. **1966** G. MCINNES (*title*) Humping my Bluey. **1968** K. WEATHERLY *Roo Shooter* 43 The shooter walked fifteen or twenty miles carrying his swag, had a few at the pub, then found somewhere to roll his bluey.

2. Lead. (Cf. BLUE *a.* 12 c.) See also quot. 1897. *slang.*

a **1852** MAYHEW *Lond. Labour* Extra vol. (1862) 26 'Bluey-hunters', or those who purloin lead from the tops of houses. **1859** HOTTEN *Dict. Slang* 9 *Bluey*, lead. **1897** R. H. SHERARD *White Slaves of Eng.* v. 188 When the lead is cold, it is carried by the blue-bed women to the stack-house... They are called blue-bed women because after the molten lead has cooled in the moulds it assumes a bluish hue. The blueys can sometimes earn two shillings a day.

3. A rough outer garment, or the material of which such a coat is made. *Austral.*

1891 W. TILLEY *Wild West Tasmania* 29 (Morris), Miners, with their swags, surveyors in their 'blueys'. **1898** MORRIS *Austral Eng.* 39/2 *Bluey.* In the wet wildernesses of Western Tasmania a rough shirt or blouse..worn over the coat like an English smock-frock. Sailors and fishermen in England call it a 'Baltic shirt'. **1934** T. WOOD *Cobbers* 86 A seamless coat of 'Tasmanian bluey', cut low round the neck and under the arms.

4. A summons. Also *transf.* (Cf. BLUE *sb.* 17.) *Austral.* and *N.Z. colloq.*

1909 T. H. THOMPSON *Ballads about Business* 13 I'll show you walls papered with blueys. *Ibid.* 49 How they served the 'blueys'. **1941** in BAKER *Dict. Austral. Slang* 11. **1942** *2 N.Z.E.F. Times* 16 Mar. 6/5 That speed cop, who gave me my last bluey on point duty. **1945** O. BURTON *In Prison* i. 9 A summons, vulgarly known as a 'bluey'. **1951** J. FRAME *Lagoon* 122 The headmaster sent Mum a bluey saying action will be taken unless [etc.]. **1965** G. MCINNES *Road to Gundagai* xiii. 242 A uniformed John Hop..handed me the dreaded 'bluey', the summons for riding a bike without lights.

5. A blue Australian cattle-dog. *colloq.*

1933 *Bulletin* (Sydney) 13 Sept. 21/1 The third [dog] was a common little bluey I bought..as a pup. **1945** BAKER *Austral. Lang.* iii. 73 The *bluey* is a type of cattle dog: originally a cross of the smooth-haired Scotch sheep dog and the dingo.

bluff (blʌf), *a.* Also 7 *rarely* blough. [A nautical word of uncertain origin: it has been compared with an obsolete Du. *blaf* (given by Kilian 1599, in *blaf aensicht* broad flat face, *blaf van vorhoofd*, rendered by L. *fronto* 'having a broad forehead'). This appears to be identical in sense with the Eng. word; but, outside Kilian, nothing is known of it.]

1. Presenting a broad flattened front; *esp.*

a. Of a ship: Opposed to *sharp* or *projecting*, having little 'rake' or inclination, nearly vertical in the bows.

1627 CAPT. SMITH *Seaman's Gram.* ii. 4 If her stem [*printed* sterne] be vpright as it were, she is called Bluffe, or Bluffe-headed. *Ibid.* xi. 55 If shee haue but a small Rake, she is so bluffe that the Seas meet her..suddenly. **1674** PETTY *Disc. bef. R. Soc.* 29 The chief cause, why short, bluff, undermasted Vessels sail cheaper than others. **1769** FALCONER *Dict. Marine* (1789) G iij, The former of these is called by seamen a *lean*, and the latter a *bluff* bow. **1861** G. BERKELEY *Sportsm. W. Prairies* ix. 149 The steamer brings her bluff bows alongside. **1867** SMYTH *Sailor's Word-bk.*, *Lean*, used in the same sense as *clean* or *sharp*; the reverse of *full* or *bluff* in the form of a ship. **1873** *Brit. Q. Rev.* Jan., Shorter and bluffer, but handier ships.

b. Of a shore or coast-line: 'Presenting a bold and almost perpendicular front, rather rounded than cliffy in outline.' Smyth *Sailor's Word-bk.*

1658 R. FRANCK *North. Mem.* (1821) 165 The pleasant banks of Ilay..where..the water runs most on a level, and

the banks very blough. **1769** FALCONER *Dict. Marine* (1789) G iij, *Côte en écore*, a bluff or bold shore. **1772-84** COOK *Voy.* (1790) V. 1823 An elevated bluff point, which we called Rock Point. **1791** COWPER *Odyss.* v. 486 The rude coast a headland bluff Presented. **1849** MURCHISON *Siluria* vii. 129 This rock frequently forms bluff cliffs. **1872** DANA *Corals* ii. 144 Every variety of slope, from the gradually inclined bed of corals to the bluff declivity.

†**c.** Of a broad face or forehead of men or animals. *Obs.*

1664 *Phil. Trans.* I. 12 The head pretty bluff, and full of bumps on both sides. **1687** DRYDEN *Hind & P.* III. 1144 A son of Anak for his height..Black-browed and bluff, like Homer's Jupiter. [Cf. sense 2.]

†**d.** *transf.* ***to stand bluff***: to stand firm or stiff. ? *Obs.*

1777 SHERIDAN *Sch. Scand.* II. iii. 255 That he should have stood bluff to old bachelor so long, and sink into a husband at last.

e. Of other objects: see quots.

?**1637** *Trav. P. Mundy* (MS. Rawl. A. 315), Peeces of wood..bluffe or blunt att both ends. **1920** *Discovery* Mar. 78/1 The streamline form for a kite balloon is rather bluff.. and short compared with an airship. **1949** O. G. SUTTON *Science of Flight* ii. 48 Bodies which have sharply truncated tails (such as a shell) leave behind them a large disorderly wake and have large form drag. Such shapes are called *bluff bodies*.

2. *fig.* Of persons and their manner, actions, etc.:

a. in an unfavourable sense: 'Big, surly, blustering' (J.); toned down in later use into 'rough, abrupt, blunt', and so into b.

1705 MRS. CENTLIVRE *Gamester* I. 141 As bluff as a midnight constable. **1742** *Pol. Ballads* (1860) II. 278 Cock your great hat, strut, bounce, and look bluff. *a* **1745** SWIFT *Dan Jackson's Reply* Wks. 1755 IV. I. 259, I maul'd you, when you look'd so bluff. **1762** H. WALPOLE *Vertue's Anecd. Paint.* (1786) I. 136 That capital picture..of Henry VIII.. The character of his majesty's bluff haughtiness is well represented. **1788** —— *Reminisc.* vii. 55 A bluff Westphalian accent. **1829** I. TAYLOR *Enthus.* ix. 241 Martial arrogance..fanatical zeal, and..bluff devotion. **1848** LYTTON *Harold* vii. 156 Finally wound up with a bluff 'Go, or let alone.'

b. Good-naturedly blunt, frank, or plain-spoken; rough and hearty; usually giving the notion of personal power or energy exhibiting itself in an abrupt but good-natured way. (Perhaps the shifting of sense is due to the notion attached to the designation 'Bluff King Hal': cf. 1762 in a.)

1808 SCOTT *Marm.* VI. xxxviii, That bluff King Hal the curtain drew. **1819** —— *Ivanhoe* xxxii, I greatly misdoubt the safety of the bluff priest. **1820** W. IRVING *Sketch Bk.* II. 370 A bluff but not unpleasant countenance. **1827** LYTTON *Pelham* xxxvi, A bluff, hearty, radical, wine merchant. **1863** KINGLAKE *Crimea* (1877) II. xiv. 240 The potentate dealt with England in a bluff, kingly, Tudor-like way. **1865** *Sat. Rev.* 5 Aug. 181/1 Typical of bluff downright honesty.

3. *Comb.*, as ***bluff-bowed, -browed, -chested, -headed*** (see sense 1 a); **bluff-head**, a bluff headland, the top of a bluff; also *fig.* as a term of contempt (cf. *blockhead*).

1699 DAMPIER *Voy.* III. 137 When we came abreast of the Bluff-head..we had but 7 Fathom. **1794** J. O'KEEFE *Wild Oats* I. i, How dare you sit in my presence, you bluff-head? **1823** BYRON *Island* II. xxi, From the bluff-head..I saw her in the doldrums. **1833** T. HOOK *Parson's Dau.* III. vii. 423 As short and as bluff-bowed as a collier, or as sharp and as choppy as a wedge. **1851** MELVILLE *Moby Dick* I. xli. 304 When Adam walked..bluff-browed and fearless. *Ibid.* 303 Milk-white charger..small-headed, bluff-chested. **1867** SMYTH *Sailor's Word-bk.*, *Bluff-headed*, when a ship has but a small rake forward on, being built with her stem too straight up.

bluff (blʌf), *sb.*¹ [f. BLUFF *a.*] **1. a.** A cliff or headland with a broad precipitous face. (First used in N. America, and still mostly of American landscapes.)

1687 in *S. Carol. Hist. & Gen. Mag.* (July 1929) 131 We landed on a Bluffe where some shads were. **1707** *S. Carol. Warrants for Lands* (1915) 206 One hundred acres of land on the uppermost bluff. **1737** WESLEY *Wks.* (1830) I. 63 Savannah stands on a flat bluff, so they term any high land hanging over a creek or river. **1776** L. MCINTOSH in Sparks *Corr. Amer. Rev.* (1853) I. 150 A bluff or sandhill thirty feet high or more above the water. **1830** LYELL *Princ. Geol.* xv. (1850) 211 The..boundaries of the alluvial region..consist of cliffs or bluffs, which on the east side of the Mississippi are very abrupt, and are undermined by the river at many points. **1837** W. IRVING *Capt. Bonneville* (1849) 45 The wild and picturesque bluffs in the neighborhood of his lonely grave. **1842** TENNYSON *Gold. Year* 76, I heard..the great echo flap And buffet round the hills from bluff to bluff. **1865** GEIKIE *Scen. & Geol. Scot.* vii. 188 Bold bluffs, that mark the limits of an ancient shore.

b. *attrib.*

1666 in *S. Carol. Hist. Soc. Coll.* V. 62 The North East side is a bluffe land, rounding from the River. **1768** J. LEES *Jrnl.* (1911) 33 With rather blowing Weather went round that large Bluff point. **1880** DANA *Man. Geol.* (ed. 3) 549 The loess... In the Mississippi valley, it covers the 'Orange sand', forming with it the 'Bluff formation'—so called because standing in bluffs in Missouri. **1882** *Encycl. Brit.* XIV. 42/2 (Kentucky) A homogeneous buff-coloured silicious loam known as the 'bluff' or loess formation. **1884** *Ibid.* XVII. 309/2 (Nebraska) These so-called 'bluff lands', composed of loess materials.

2. *Canada.* A grove or clump of trees.

c **1752** W. COATS *Geogr. Hudson's Bay* (1852) 52 Near the same latitude, on the west main, is a bluff of wood, caled Point Mourning, from buriing one of Captain James men there. **1895** *Times* 13 Sept. 12/3 [Manitoba.] Level or rolling prairie with scattered 'bluffs' (small patches of wood) in some districts. **1912** N. L. MCCLUNG *Black Creek Stopping-House* 209 The Fourth came in a glorious day..with birds singing in every poplar bluff. **1959** *Country Guide* (Winnipeg) Apr. 71/1 The cabin still stood in the bluff above the pass.

bluff, *sb.*² [Belongs to BLUFF *v.*¹: analogically with *bridle, bit, blind, cover*, either the verb or the sb. might come first and give rise to the other; here the accessible evidence is in favour of the priority of the verb, though, in the obscurity of the etymology, certainty is not at present possible.]

1. A blinker for a horse. *Obs.* or *dial.*

1777 DARWIN *Squinting* in *Phil. Trans.* LXVIII. 88 Bluffs used on coach-horses. **1881** EVANS *Leicestersh. Gloss.* (E.D.S.) *Bluft*, anything used to cover the eyes, such as a blinker for a horse, a board fastened in front of the eyes of a bull or cow to prevent its running, the handkerchief used to bandage the eyes in blind-man's-buff, etc.

2. *slang.* 'An excuse.' Mayhew *Lond. Labour* I. 217 (in a list of slang words). ? A false excuse intended to blindfold or hoodwink, a 'blind'.

3. a. The action of bluffing at cards, in the game of *poker*; see BLUFF *v.*¹ and cf. BRAG; also = POKER *sb.*⁴ *Hence*, challenging or boastful language or demeanour, not intended to be carried out, but merely 'tried on' with the design of frightening or influencing an opponent who allows himself to be imposed upon by it. (First used in U.S.) So ***to call one's*** (or ***the***) ***bluff*** (orig. *U.S.*); *fig.* to make a person show his 'hand'; so, to accept a challenge or invite a showdown; cf. CALL *v.* 1 e (*b*); ***to run a bluff on*** (U.S.): to use bluff against or practise deception on (someone).

1846 S. SMITH *Theatr. Apprent.* 148 The game of 'bluff' or 'poker', as it is more generally called. **1848-60** BARTLETT *Dict. Amer.*, *Bluff*, a game of cards. So in WEBSTER **1864**. **1866** *Harvard Mem. Biographies* I. 400 It is a very magnificent game of Bluff that we are playing. **1876** BRET HARTE *Two Men of Sandy Bar* 17 But suppose that he sees that little bluff, and calls ye. **1883** *L'pool Daily Post* 22 Jan., The whole is a bluff to influence the..election next week. **1883** *Pall Mall G.* 3 Nov. 1/1 A bold bit of play in the game of bluff..between St. Petersburg and Sophia. **1884** *Boston (U.S.) Jrnl.* 25 Sept., The offer was only a bluff. **1887** F. FRANCIS Jr. *Saddle & Mocassin* 130 'You got the stock, though?' 'Oh,—yes! I run a bluff on 'em.' **1891** *Chambers's Jrnl.* 26 Sept. 618/2 A man may have a big name as a fighting man and yet not be able always to run a bluff on people so easily. **1896** *Congress. Rec.* 26 Mar. 3248 Where shall we be when the bluff is called? **1898** *Times* 4 Nov. 3/6 The policy of the Russian Foreign Office..has been a series of prodigious bluffs. Some of these Lord Salisbury has seen fit to 'call'; others he has refrained from 'calling'. **1933** *Discovery* Sept. 282/2 The childish questioner will very quickly call our bluff.

b. *attrib.* as ***bluff game***.

1846 J. J. HOOPER *Adv. Simon Suggs* x. 129 'No!' said Simon.., 'the bluff game ain't played here!' **1888** *St. Louis Globe Democrat* 29 Apr. (Farmer), They..thought he could outnumber them. It was a bluff game, and he won.

4. A bluffer. *U.S.*

1904 S. E. WHITE *Blazed Trail Stories* ii. 27 'You're a bluff!' said he, insultingly.

bluff, *v.*¹ [Immediately related to BLUFF *sb.*² 'a blinker for a horse', which, as it appears later than the verb, was presumably named from it, though the reverse is also possible. The etymology is quite unknown: the meaning 'blindfold, hoodwink' does not appear to have any possible connexion with BLUFF *a.* or *sb.*¹; the word is probably one of the numerous cant terms (see BAM, BAMBOOZLE) which arose between the Restoration and the reign of Queen Anne. Sense 2 had certainly originally the same meaning; but it looks as if recent users imagined a connexion with BLUFF *a.* or *sb.*¹, and made it mean 'to blindfold or hoodwink by assuming a fictitious bold front'.]

1. *trans.* 'To blind-fold or hood-wink'. Bailey.

1674-91 RAY *N.C. Wds.*, *Bluff*, to blind-fold. **1706** in PHILLIPS. **1721** in BAILEY: [so in all edd. to **1800**. Not in JOHNSON, nor in ASH.] **1881** EVANS *Leicestersh. Gloss.* (E.D.S.) s.v. *Bluft*, 'Ah'm glad yew'n got that theer bull o' yourn blufted.'

2. In the game of *poker*: To impose upon (an opponent) as to the value of one's hand of cards, by betting heavily upon it, speaking or gesticulating or otherwise acting in such a way as to make believe that it is stronger than it is, so as to induce him to 'throw up' his cards and lose his stake, rather than run the risk of betting against the bluffer. (Of U.S. origin.) Hence, *transf.* of other wagering, political tactics, international diplomacy, etc. ***to bluff off***: to frighten off or deter (an opponent) by thus imposing upon him as to one's resources and determination.

1846 S. SMITH *Theatr. Apprent.* 149 Inasmuch as I believe you only trying to bluff me off, I go two hundred. *a* **1859** *N.Y. Spirit of Times* (Bartlett), 'I goes you five dollars this time,' says Jim... 'I..goes you ten better,' said Bill; 'you ain't agoin' to bluff dis child.' **1864** SALA in *Daily Tel.* 29 Sept., How can you hope to 'bluff' those who are such consummate masters of the game of brag? **1871** *Daily News* 4 Jan., The great point..is the shutting in of Paris, and the 'bluffing off' of France. **1885** *N. York Weekly Sun* 13 May 2/7 He went his whole heart, soul, and pocket on three aces and was bluffed by his opponent with a pair of trays.

3. *intr.* To practise or attempt the imposition described in 2; to assume a bold, big, or boastful demeanour, in order to inspire an opponent with an exaggerated notion of one's strength, determination to fight, etc.

1854 *Congress. Globe* 3 May 1070 We both know how that game [of brag] is played. I thought I would bluff back on him. **1882** *Sat. Rev.* 1 July 4 Nor is a Government always to be reproached because when it bluffs it fails. Sometimes a great country is entitled to take the benefit of ancient policy of courage, and to see what effect it can produce by the mere terror of its name. **1883** *Longm. Mag.* Sept. 498 By sheer bluffing—in other words, by lying. **1884** *St. James's Gaz.* 12 Jan. 4/1 There seems little reason for one party to keep on 'bluffing' when the other party has 'called'.

Hence **ˈbluffable** *a.*, capable of being imposed upon or influenced by bluffing.

1885 *Sat. Rev.* 30 May, The whole thing is..a game of bluff against a player who is known to be bluffable.

bluff, *v.*² *Obs.* or *dial.* [? Onomatopœic, associated with *blow, puff*. According to Halliwell, 'A tin tube through which boys blow peas is in Suffolk called a "bluff".' Cf. BLOUGHT, BLOUGHTY.] *intr.* To swell out, become distended.

a **1722** LISLE *Husb.* (1757) 483 Pigs would bluff & swell much with their feeding the first six or seven days.

bluff, *v.*³ *rare.* [f. BLUFF *a.*]

trans. To make bluff, raise bluffly.

1809 J. BARLOW *Columb.* I. 643 Where dread Niagara bluffs high his brow.

ˈbluffer. [f. prec. verbs.]

†**1.** 'An Host or Landlord. *Country word.*' Bailey 1721-1800; Ash 1775; Halliwell 1878.

2. One who bluffs at *poker*, etc. orig. *U.S.*

1888 *Detroit Free Press* 5 May (Farmer), Is Uncle Sam a bluffer? **1891** 'L. HOFFMANN' *Cycl. Card & Table Games* 197 (*Poker*) Unless E has the reputation (a very undesirable one) of a habitual bluffer, B will probably begin to feel alarmed. **1894** *Westm. Gaz.* 24 Sept. 2/1 The 'bluffer', she who trades on the gilded European's illusion that all American girls are heiresses, and catches him under this false pretence, only to discover that she has fallen into the hands of a male 'bluffer' whose pretensions are equally baseless. **1946** *Sci. News Let.* 23 Mar. 188/1 The *puff adder*..is one of the world's biggest bluffers.

ˈbluffing, *vbl. sb.* [f. BLUFF *v.*¹ 2 and 3.] The action of using bluff; also *attrib.* or as *ppl. a.*

1850 *Congress. Globe* 14 May, App. 606/1, I cannot look upon the effort of Texas in any other light than a bluffing, brow-beating game. *c* **1850** *Southern Sketches* 137 (Bartlett 1859), Jim..tried the bluffing system. **1871** [see BLUFF *v.*¹ 2]. **1948** *Redbook* (U.S.) Mar. 23/1 Andy was a blustering, bluffing, not too straitlaced fellow.

bluffly (ˈblʌflɪ), *adv.* [f. BLUFF *a.* + -LY².]

1. With a bluff or bold face, abruptly.

1870 *Daily News* 28 Dec., The lofty summit of Noisy.. standing bluffly up against the horizon.

2. Abruptly, bluntly, offhandedly.

1794 WOLCOTT (P. Pindar) *Rowl. for Oliver* Wks. II. 427 Turns bluffly from the charms that taste adores. **1852** HAWTHORNE *Blithed. Rom.* I. x. 190 'You shall do no such thing'..said Hollingsworth, bluffly. **1883** *Standard* 18 May 3/2 Both canvases present us with bluffly picturesque figures.

bluffness (ˈblʌfnɪs). [f. as prec. + -NESS.] Abruptness; bluntness of manner, offhandedness.

1863 MRS. C. CLARKE *Shaks. Char.* xvii. 419 His soldierly bluffness. **1865** *Fraser's Mag.* Oct. 434 He told his story with all the bluffness of a sailor.

bluffy (ˈblʌfɪ), *a.* [f. BLUFF *sb.*¹ + -Y.]

1. Full of bluffs, precipitous.

1872 BLACKIE *Lays Highl.* 7 Cliff, and bay, and bluffy foreland. **1882** *Century Mag.* Sept. 707 The Penobscot winds around the bluffy headlands.

2. Rather bluff, inclining to bluffness.

1844 TUPPER *Crock of G.* xxii. 176 A fat, sturdy, bluffy old woman.

bluggy (ˈblʌgɪ), *a.* Pretended infantile pronunciation of BLOODY (see quot. 1876), used subsequently as a euphemistic pronunciation of 'bloody', esp. to define literature of the blood-and-thunder type (see BLOOD *sb.* 3 d).

1876 J. HABBERTON *Helen's Babies* 68 Bliaff's head was all bluggy, an' David's sword was all bluggy—bluggy as everyfing. **1890** *Scott. Leader* 17 July 4 The shriek with which Mr. Hall Caine greeted Mr. Grant Allen's protest against bluggy novels. **1921** *19th Cent.* May 770 East End ambuscades where the air is thick with the smell of fried fish and Yiddish and bluggy rhetoric. **1966** 'K. NICHOLSON' *Hook, Line & Sinker* vi. 74 Bluggy Joan of Arc, with her messages.

Hence **ˈblugginess**.

1894 *Punch* 30 June 305 It is not poesy, culture, wisdom, wit, that make the literary world go round. Much 'blugginess' has more to do with it. **1901** *Academy* 2 Nov. 404 In the close it falls sheer into rant and 'blugginess'.

bluish ('bluːɪʃ), *a.* Forms: 5 **blewyssh**, 6 **-isshe**, 6–8 **-ish**, 6– **bluish**, 8– **blueish**. [f. BLUE *a.* + -ISH[1].] Somewhat blue.

1398 TREVISA *Barth. De P.R.* XIX. xix. (1495) 875 The colour is blewe or blewyssh. **1586** WARNER *Alb. Eng.* IV. (R.) Her snowish necke with blewish vaines. **1712** tr. *Pomet's Hist. Drugs* I, Tending to a little blewish Colour. **1713** ROWE *J. Shore* v. Wks. 1792 II. 180 A waving flood of blueish fire. **1860** TYNDALL *Glac.* II. §7. 261 Thin milk, when poured upon a black surface, appears bluish.

b. *Comb.* modifying other colours, as ***bluish-brown, -green, -purple, -red, -white***, etc.; also ***bluish-coloured***.

1769 SIR J. HILL *Fam. Herbal* (1812) 1 The leaves are of a bluish green. **1792** *Gentl. Mag.* LXII. I. 113 The capitulum is..bluish brown. **1836** TODD *Cycl. Anat. & Phys.* I. 443/2 A bone..exhibits a bluish-grey colour. **1858** W. ELLIS *Visits Madagasc.* viii. 199 The dark bluish-coloured original limestone.

Hence also **'bluishly** *adv.*, **'bluishness**.

1611 COTGR., *Lividité*, roannesse, bleakenesse, palenesse, blewishnesse. **1790** WEDGWOOD in *Phil. Trans.* LXXX. 313 The usual bluishness, arising from the iron always found in the common acids. **1875** HOWELLS *Foregone Concl.* 4 That transparent blueishness, which comes from much shaving of a heavy black beard.

bluism, var. of BLUEISM.

blumbering, *vbl. sb.* [? Onomatopœic.] Rumbling, lumbering noise.

1556 J. HEYWOOD *Spider & F.* iii. 13 What is this buzzynge, blumberinge, trow we: thunder?

blume, obs. form of BLOOM.

†**blund**, *v. Obs. rare*[−1]. [cf. ON. *blunda* to doze.] *intr.* ? To stagger, to flounder.

c **1325** *E.E. Allit. P.* C. 272 Til he blunt in a blok as brod as a halle.

blunder ('blʌndə(r)), *v.* Forms: 4–5 **blondren, blundren**, 5 **blundir, -yr**, 5–6 **blondre, -er, blounder, blundre**, 7– **blunder**. [ME. *blondren*; of uncertain origin: a good deal depends upon whether the ME. *-on-* here, as often (cf. *wonder, sunder*), stands merely graphically for *-un-*, or is etymological. In the latter case an explanation of *blonder* as a frequentative of *blond*, BLAND *v.*, to mix, would well account for the transitive senses. The suggestion that it is a frequentative from Icel. *blonda* to doze (Sw. *blunda* to shut the eyes), suits the intransitive senses, but is otherwise doubtful; cf. however BLUND. Perhaps there are really two distinct verbs, with their later senses affected by each other.]

I. To confuse, confound.

†**1. a.** *trans.* To mix up or mingle confusedly; to confuse, disturb; to make (water) turbid. *Obs.*

c **1440** *York Myst.* xvi. 4 Blonderand þer blastis, to blaw when I bidde. **1530** PALSGR. 458/2 I blonder, *Je perturbe*..Who hat blondred these thynges on this facyon? **1586** FERNE *Blaz. Gentrie* Ded., The whole..frame of this earth seemeth blundered and confounded with the innumerable Catalogues of Interpreters. **1638** BAKER tr. *Balzac's Lett.* III. vi. (1654) 75, I blunder the water of all Rivers I cross.

†**b.** To confound, distract (in understanding).

? *a* **1400** *Morte Arth.* 3976 'Blyve,' sais thies bolde mene 'Thow blondirs þi selfene.' **1740** DITTON *On Resurrect.* 63 (R.) So as by any means whatsoever to blunder an adversary.

†**c.** To put out of order, derange, injure. *Obs.*

1440 J. SHIRLEY *Dethe K. Jas.* (1818) 15 The lokes ver so blundrid, that thay nethir couth ne myght shut hit [a door].

2. To confound (in one's mind) stupidly.

a **1699** STILLINGFL. (J.) He blunders and confounds all these together. **1842** S. R. MAITLAND *Remarks* 9 That ingenious writer also blunders him with Arnold of Brescia.

II. To move, act, or perform, blindly or stupidly.

3. a. *intr.* To move blindly or stupidly; to flounder, stumble. Often with *on*; also ***to blunder one's way along***; and in senses partaking of 7, as ***to blunder into, against***.

c **1386** CHAUCER *Chan. Yem. Prol. & T.* 861 Bayard the blynde, That blundreth [*v.r.* blondreth] forth, and peril casteth noon. **1520** WHITTINTON *Vulg.* (1527) 2 Wandre bloundryng as a blynde man. *a* **1700** DRYDEN *Pal. & Arc.* I. 435 The sot..blunders on and staggers every pace. **1766** *New Bath Guide* i. 67 To see them blund'ring by my side. **1858** HAWTHORNE *Fr. & It. Jrnls.* I. 79 We had blundered into the carriage-entrance. **1869** PARKMAN *Disc. Gt. West* v. (1875) 55 A large fish..blundered against Marquette's canoe. **1869** FREEMAN *Norm. Conq.* (1876) III. xii. 175 They..blundered on hopelessly through the unknown..country. **1880** MISS BIRD *Japan* II. 143 The horses had to blunder their way along a bright, rushing river.

b. *fig.* To flounder, stumble.

1641 MILTON *Ch. Discip.* I. Wks. (1851) 30 Blundring upon the dangerous and suspectfull translations of the Apostat Aquila. **1728** YOUNG *Love Fame* v. (1757) 132 Puzzled learning blunders far behind. **1735** POPE *Prol. Sat.* 186 He who now to sense, now nonsense leaning, Means not, but blunders round about a meaning. **1817** BYRON *Beppo* xxvii, He had somehow blunder'd into debt. **1871** LOWELL *Study Wind.*, A tempest is blundering round the house.

c. ***to blunder upon***: to come upon by a blunder or 'fluke'.

1710 H. BEDFORD *Vind. Ch. Eng.* 78 Our Discoverer has..happen'd to blunder upon the truth. **1798** WOLCOTT (P. Pindar) *Tales Hoy* Wks. 1812 IV. 418 Who never so much as blundered on a bon-mot.

d. *trans.* ***to blunder out***: to produce by mere blundering or blind action.

1678 CUDWORTH *Intell. Syst.* I. v. 679 The things of the world..not..made by the previous counsel, contrivance, and intention of any understanding Deity..blunder'd out themselves, one after another, according to the train or sequel of the fortuitous motions of matter.

†**4.** *intr.* To deal blindly and stupidly. *Obs.*

c **1386** CHAUCER *Chan. Yem. Prol. & T.* 117 We blondren [*v.r.* blondern, bloundren, blundren, blundere] euere, and pouren in the fuyr. **1471** RIPLEY *Comp. Alch.* v. xli. in Ashm. (1652) 157 These Phylosophers..Medlyth and blondryth wyth many a thyng.

5. *trans.* To utter thoughtlessly, stupidly, or by a blunder, to blurt out. Usually with *out*.

1483 *Cath. Angl.* 35 To Blundir, [*A.* blundyr, *blandior*]. **1570–87** HOLLINSHED *Scot. Chron.* (1806) II. 81 The same began to be blundered from one to another of the train. **1587** *Censure loy. Subiect* (Collier) 28 He blundered forth his prognostication. **1701** SWIFT *Mrs. Harris' Petit.* Wks. 1755 III. II. 61 Before I was aware, out I blunder'd; 'Parson,' said I. **1755** SMOLLETT *Quix.* (1803) II. 33 Sancho blundered out—'Then, in good faith, Mr. Licentiate,' etc.

6. *refl.* (in sense of 3 or 7.)

a **1652** J. SMITH *Sel. Disc.* iii. 51 Herein all the Epicureans..do miserably blunder themselves.

7. a. *intr.* To make a stupid and gross mistake in doing anything. ***to blunder away*** (trans.): to throw away, lose by blundering: cf. *to fool away*.

1711 SWIFT *Lett.* (1767) III. 101 See how I blundered, and left two lines short. **1792** *Anecd. W. Pitt* I. ii. 36 The wretch that, after having seen the consequences of a thousand errors, continues still to blunder. **1801** W. TAYLOR in *Month. Mag.* XII. 588 Mr. Fox has never blundered away the interests of his country. **1855** TENNYSON *Charge Lt. Brigade* 12 The soldier knew Some one had blunder'd.

b. *trans.* To bring or cause to fall *into* a state by clumsy or inept behaviour; to use blunderingly.

1901 *Westm. Gaz.* 27 June 4/3 They believe that Mr. Chamberlain has blundered the country into war. **1912** A. S. M. HUTCHINSON *Happy Warrior* v. x. §1. 347 He..hated to have blundered all his dullness on so rare and exquisite a thing.

8. *trans.* To mismanage, make a blunder in.

1805 WELLINGTON in Owen *Disp.* 789 They must have blundered that siege terribly. **1816** SCOTT *Antiq.* vi, The banker's clerk, who was directed to sum my cash-account, blundered it three times. **1876** HUMPHREY *Coin Coll. Man.* xxvi. 391 Inscriptions blundered by the die engraver.

¶COCKERAM (1623) has '*Blunder*, to bestir ones selfe.'

blunder ('blʌndə(r)), *sb.* Forms: 4 **blondyre**, 5 **blondre, blonder, blundur**, 6 **blounder**, 4– **blunder**. [app. f. the vb.: though extant instances of the sb. are earlier.]

†**1.** Confusion, bewilderment, trouble, disturbance, clamour. *Obs.* (The early quotations are vague in sense: the latest shade off into 2.)

c **1340** *Gaw. & Gr. Knt.* 18 Oft boþe blysse and blunder Ful skete hatz skyfted. *c* **1375** ? BARBOUR *St. Theodora* 542 þat wald bring me in sik blondyre. *c* **1440** *York Myst.* xxxiii. 94 With his blure he bredis mekill blondre. *c* **1450** *Agst. Friars* in *Rel. Ant.* I. 322 Amonges men of holy chirch, thai maken mochel blonder. *c* **1460** *Towneley Myst.* 30 I shalle make ye stille as stone, begynnar of blunder. **1519** HORMAN *Vulg.* 270 Hoste that is out of araye and in a blounder scatered. **1600** HOLLAND *Livy* x. xlii. 383 He heard a confused crie and blunder [*clamorem*] in the citie. *Ibid.* xlii. 1124 The bruite was also blowne to Rome, and blunder there was of the death of Eumenes. **1774** GOLDSMITH *Retal.* 21 Then, with chaos & blunders encircling my head, Let me ponder.

2. A gross mistake; an error due to stupidity or carelessness.

The words of Talleyrand as to the murder of the Duc d'Enghien—'ces paroles stoïquement politiques, "C'est plus qu'un crime, c'est une faute"' (Lucien Bonaparte *Mem.* an. 1804 (1882) I. 432) have been englished, 'It is worse than a crime, it is a blunder,' and are often quoted or alluded to.

1706 PHILLIPS, *Blunder*, a mistake, fault, or oversight. **1711** SWIFT *Lett.* (1767) III. 209 The twenty pounds I lend you is not to be included; so make no blunder. **1726** DE FOE *Hist. Devil* I. v. (1840) 63 Another mistake, not to call it a blunder. **1848** MACAULAY *Hist. Eng.* I. 239 The numerous crimes and blunders of the last eighteen years. **1865** EARL DERBY in *Parl.* 3 May, If the Confederate authorities had directly or indirectly sanctioned this assassination..it would be on their part worse than a crime, it would be a blunder. *a* **1867** BUCKLE *Misc. Wks.* (1872) I. 25 Ingratitude aggravated by cruelty must..be a blunder as well as a crime.

¶ **1729** WOOLSTON *Disc. Miracles* 28 Now-a-days, dull and foolish and absurd stuff we call Bulls, Fatlings, and Blunders.

blunderbuss ('blʌndəbʌs). Also 7 **blunderbush**, 7–8 **-bus**. [ad. Du. *donderbus* with same meaning, f. *donder* thunder + *bus* gun (orig. box, tube); perverted in form after *blunder* (perhaps with some allusion to its blind or random firing).]

1. A short gun with a large bore, firing many balls or slugs, and capable of doing execution within a limited range without exact aim. (Now superseded, in civilized countries, by other fire-arms.)

1654 GAYTON *Fest. Notes* IV. xi. 244 In the antient wars, before these Bomards, Blunderbushes, Peters. **1657** COLVIL *Whigs Supplic.* (1751) 25 A blunderbush hang'd at his back, Of terrible report and crack. **1682** LUTTRELL *Brief Rel.* (1857) I. 164 Two of which fired two blunderbusses at him, charg'd with severall shott. **1774** MRS. DELANY *Life & Corr.* Ser. II. (1862) II. 60 Lord Berkeley..attacked by a Highwayman..shot him with a blunderbuss. **1808** SYD. SMITH *Plymley's Lett.* x, A tithe procter in Ireland collects his tithes with a blunderbuss. **1863** KINGSLEY *Water-Bab.* viii. 329 A tremendous old brass blunderbuss charged up to the muzzle with slugs.

2. *transf.* †**a.** A blustering noisy talker (*obs.*). **b.** A blundering fellow, a blunderhead.

1685 *Answ. Dk. Buckhm. on Lib. Consc.* 23 Securing the Person of his Prince, and the Peace of his Country from Religious Rumbalds, and Conventicling Blunderbusses. **1692** WASHINGTON tr. *Milton's Def. Pop.* Pref. (1851) 18 Not such a hair-brain'd Blunderbuss as you. **1706** *Refl. on Ridicule* 129 Those blunderbusses that talk loud and long. **1768** TUCKER *Lt. Nat.* I. 475 He must be a numskull, not to say a beetle, nor yet a blunderbuss.

†**3.** ? A blunder; trouble. *Obs. rare.*

1726 AMHERST *Terræ Fil.* xlviii. 259 More horrors still! Yea, verily! & a new blunderbuss into the bargain.

4. *attrib.*

1864 R. BURTON *Dahome* II. 76 The Agbary or blunderbuss-women are the biggest and strongest of the force.

'blunderbuss, *v.* To shoot with a blunderbuss.

1870 *Daily News* 4 June, The risk of being pistolled or blunderbussed by a patriot.

'blunderbussed, *a.* [f. prec. sb. + -ED[2].] Armed with a blunderbuss.

1851 H. D. WOLFF *Pict. Sp. Life* (1853) 30 The blunder-bussed guard.

blunderbussier (ˌblʌndəbʌ'sɪə(r)). *rare.* [see -IER.] A man armed with a blunderbuss.

a **1734** NORTH *Exam.* 302 (D.) Some of the blunderbussiers of the Rye.

'blundered, *ppl. a.* [f. BLUNDER *v.* + -ED[1].]

†**1.** Mixed, muddled, turbid. *Obs.* exc. *dial.*

1855 *Whitby Gloss.*, *Blunder'd*, render'd thick and muddy as liquids appear when the sediment is shaken up.

2. Done or made wrong by blundering; bungled.

1880 H. N. HENFREY in *Antiquary* No. I. 20/1 Pennies of this type with blundered legends..I have noted eight different blundered reverses. **1884** *Athenæum* 26 Jan. 123/3 A Saxon or Dano-Saxon penny with a blundered legend.

blunderer ('blʌndərə(r)). [f. as prec. + -ER[1].]

†**1.** One who flounders about blindly in his work; a blind or stupid worker. *Obs.*

c **1440** *Promp. Parv.* 41 Blunderer or blunt warkere, *hebefactor, hebeficus*. **1523** *Garl. Laurel* (R.) What blundrer is yonder that playeth diddil? **1678** CUDWORTH *Intell. Syst.* 853 Meer Blunderers in that Atomick Physiology.

2. One who makes gross mistakes by incompetence or negligence.

1741 H. WALPOLE *Lett. H. Mann* (1834) I. xiii. 41 'Take care you don't get my old name.' 'What's that?' 'Blunderer.' **1782** COWPER *Progr. Err.* 539 Your blund'rer is as sturdy as a rock. **1855** MACAULAY *Hist. Eng.* IV. 87 At best a blunderer, and too probably a traitor.

'blunderful, *a.* [f. BLUNDER *sb.*; cf. *wonderful*.] Full of blunders.

1881 *Academy* No. 502. 449 As to spoken English, everybody knows how slovenly and blunderful that is.

blunderhead ('blʌndəhɛd). [f. BLUNDER *sb.* or *v.* + HEAD: probably an alteration of the earlier *dunderhead*, as *blunderbuss* represents *donderbus*.] A blundering muddle-headed fellow.

1697 VANBRUGH *Relapse* IV. i. (1730) 72 My Fellow's a Blunderhead. *a* **1704** LESTRANGE (J.) This thick-skulled blunderhead. **1884** *Academy* 22 Mar. 199 That order of good-natured blunderheads wherein certain lady novelists..delight.

Hence **'blunderˌheaded** *a.*, blundering, stupid, muddle-headed; **'blunderˌheadedness**.

1763 *Brit. Mag.* IV. 418 The blunder-headed fellow had laid the white-stone plates. **1835** SIR J. ROSS *N.-W. Pass.* lvi. 720 With the blunderheadedness of men on such occasions, he assured me that I had been dead two years.

'blundering, *vbl. sb.* [f. BLUNDER *v.* + -ING[1].]

†**1.** Bungling or stupid action. *Obs.*

c **1440** *Promp. Parv.* 41 Blunderynge or blunt warkynge, *hebefaccio*.

†**2.** Confusion, disturbance. *Obs.*

c **1526** SKELTON *Magnyf.* 406 I hate this blunderyng thou dost make.

3. The making of gross mistakes.

1857 TOULM. SMITH *Parish* 169 There is no check on carelessness or blundering.

'blundering, *ppl. a.* [f. as prec. + -ING[2].] †**a.** Blindly staggering. **b.** Making or characterized by gross mistakes.

1367 TREVISA *Higden* Rolls Ser. II. 169 þe men beeþ to fore þe dede blondrynge [L. *importuna*] and hasty. **1710** H. BEDFORD *Vind. Ch. Eng.* 184 His blundering account of it. **1828** SCOTT *F.M. Perth* III. 175 A piece of blundering valiancy. **1861** WRIGHT *Ess. Archæol.* II. xxii. 226 Blundering citations and erroneous interpretations.

'blunderingly, *adv.* [f. prec. + -LY[2].] In a blundering manner.

1807 G. CHALMERS *Caledonia* I. II. ii. 248 This king..is mentioned, blunderingly, by Langhorn. **1838–9** HALLAM *Hist. Lit.* I. I. ii. §30 A calendar..blunderingly ascribed to Roger Bacon. **1879** G. MEREDITH *Egoist* II. iii. 46 She perceived how blunderingly she had acted.

† **'blunderkin.** *Obs. rare.* [f. BLUNDER, taken in sense of 'blunderer' + -KIN.] A blundering fellow, a muddlepate.

1596 NASHE *Saffron Walden* Ded., Two blunderkins having their braines stuft with nought but balderdash.

† **'blunderly,** *a. Obs. rare.* [f. BLUNDER *sb.* + -LY[1].] Clumsily or badly made.

1746 in *Leisure Hour* (1880) 23 The front window..was a great blunderly thing.

'blundersome, *a.* [f. BLUNDER *sb.* + -SOME.] Of the nature of, or tending to, blunders.

1837-40 HALIBURTON *Clockm.* (1862) 225 You should know all about fixin' the sails the right way for the wind—if you don't, it's blundersome.

blunesse, obs. form of BLUENESS.

blunge (blʌndʒ), *v. Pottery.* [app. onomatopœic: with a feeling for *plunge*, and perhaps for *blend*, *bludgeon*, *blow*, or other *bl-* words.] *trans.* To mix (clay, powdered flint, etc.) up with water. Hence **'blunging** *vbl. sb.*

c **1830** *Potter's Art*, First we blunge (amalgamate and blend) the liquid flint And moisten'd clay..With wielded paddle-staff (a blunger call'd) Until the blended matter, all afloat, Thin slip becomes. **1832** G. PORTER *Porcelain* 36 The mixing of the clay, which is called blunging, is effected in a trough. **1879** *Cassell's Techn. Educ.* XII. 346 For pottery.. the clay is what is termed 'blunged'—that is—beaten up in tanks of water by means of powerful revolving arms or cutters.

blunger ('blʌndʒə(r)). [f. prec. + -ER[1].] An appliance for blunging; formerly 'A long, flat, wooden instrument, with a cross handle at the top' (Halliwell); now an apparatus driven by power.

c **1830** [see BLUNGE]. **1879** J. YOUNG *Ceram. Art* 67 The ingredients are mixed in a 'blunger'. **1883** BINN *Worcester Porcelain Wks.* 17 Several vats, containing blungers, which are worked by machinery.

blunk, *sb. Sc.* [Cf. BLUNKET.] In *pl.* 'Linen or cotton cloths which are wrought for being printed; calicoes' (Jamieson).

1830 *Chamb. Jrnl.* (1836) 31 Dec. 392 That Catrine blunks wad hae a chance To tak the lead; Nocht like them can be got frae France Sae cheap an' guid.

blunk, *v. Obs.* or *dial.* [app. a corruption of BLENK or BLINK.]

† **1.** *intr.* To turn aside, blench, flinch, shrink. *Obs.*

1655 GURNALL *Chr. in Arm.* ix. §2 (1669) 56/1 The presumptuous sinner..goes on & never blunks. **1680** HICKERINGILL *Meroz* 27 That can swallow Oath upon Oath ..and still their Consciences blunk no more than a piece of Brass?

2. (*trans.*) *Sc.* 'To spoil a thing, to mismanage any business' (Jamieson).

blunk, variant of BLONK, *Obs.*, steed.

blunker ('blʌŋkə(r)). *Sc.* [f. BLUNK *sb.* or ? *v.*] 'One who prints cloths' (Jamieson).

1815 SCOTT *Guy M.* iii, Dunboy is nae mair a gentleman than the blunker that's biggit the bonnie house down in the town.

† **'blunket,** *a.* and *sb. Obs.* Forms: 5-7 **blanket,** 6 **bluncket, blancket, bloncket, bloncat,** 7 **blonket,** 5-8 **blunket.** [It is uncertain whether the adj. sense gave its name to the fabric, or whether the name of the fabric was transferred to its colour. The original form of the word is also doubtful, though *blunket* is both the earliest and by far the most frequent. This makes it doubtful whether it can have been an adoption of OF. *blanquet*, var. of *blanchet*, dim. of *blanc* white (and thus originally the same as BLANKET), a derivation which would to some extent suit the sense.]

A. *adj.* Grey, greyish blue, light blue.

1488 *Lord High. Treas. Accts.* (JAM.) For x elne and j quarter of blanket caresay to be hos. *c* **1534** *Pol. Verg. Eng. Hist.* (1846) I. 74 Thei weare called Pictes..ether of their bluncket heres, ether of certaine marckes made with whot irons. *a* **1552** LELAND *Brit. Coll.* III. 138 Cæsius, gray of colour, or blunket. **1552** HULOET, Blancket coloure, *cæsius.* **1579** SPENSER *Sheph. Cal.* May 5 Our bloncket liueryes [*gloss.* gray coates] bene all to sadde. **1611** COTGR., *Couleur perse*, skie colour, Azure colour, a Blunket, or light blue. **1622** PEACHAM *Compl. Gentl.* (1661) 155 Blanket colour, i.e. a light watchet. **1657** W. COLES *Adam in Eden* cxxxv, Gilloflowers of such variable colours..Horseflesh, blunket, purple, and white. **1783** AINSWORTH *Lat. Dict.*, *Cæsius*, gray, sky-coloured, with specks of gray blunket.

B. *sb.* A fabric presumably of light grey or blue colour; possibly the same as BLANKET *sb.* I.

c **1420** *Anturs Arth.* xxix, Here belle [= cloak] was of blunket. *c* **1440** *Gaw. & Galar.* ii. 3 (JAM.) Here belte was of blunket. **1541** *Aberd. Reg.* (JAM.) Three elln of bloncat. **1600** *Queen's Wardrobe* in Nichols *Progr. Q. Eliz.* III. 506 One rounde kirtle of white clothe of silver chevernd, with blunket, with lace of golde.

blunt (blʌnt), *a.* and *sb.* Also 3 *Orm.* **blunnt,** 5-6 **blont.** [Etymology unknown: found in Ormin *c* 1200, in a sense which has suggested some connexion with ON. *blunda* to doze, *blunda augum* to shut the eyes, *blundr* dozing, sleep (Vigfusson). It has been proposed to explain the form as a contracted pa. pple. for *blunded, blund*, ON. *blundað, blundat*; but pa. pples. in *-nt* from *-nd* are not found so early as 1200; Ormin has none. And this would hardly give the required sense, since *blunda* was intransitive in ON., and the pple. could hardly exist there. Other suggestions are that *blunt* might be some kind of side-form of *blind*, or a nasalized deriv. of an OTeut. root **blut-*, whence ON. *blaut* soft, weak, mod.G. *blosz* naked, Fris. *blat, bleat* naked, OE. *bléat* wretched. But in the present state of the question these are mere conjectures, having no contact with the history of the word.]

A. *adj.*

1. Dull, insensitive, stupid, obtuse: said, it appears, originally of the sight, whence of the perceptions generally, and the intellect. (Now generally with some antithesis to *sharp*, as in sense 2.)

c **1200** ORMIN 16954 Unnwis mann iss blunnt, & blind Off herrtess eȝhe sihhþe. *c* **1325** *E.E. Allit. P.* A. 176 Such a burre myȝt make myn herte blunt. *c* **1386** CHAUCER *Pers. T.* ¶649 Undevocioun thurgh which a man is so blunt, and.. hath such a langour in soule, that he may neyther rede ne synge in holy chirche. *c* **1440** *Promp. Parv.* 41 Blunt of wytte, *hebes.* **1594** CAREW *Huarte's Exam. Wits* (1616) 319 Others, who of ordinarie are borne blunt and void of iudgement. **1596** SPENSER *F.Q.* I. x. 47 All were his earthly eien both blunt and bad And through great age had lost their kindly sight. **1597** SHAKS. *2 Hen. IV*, Induct. 18 The blunt Monster, with vncounted heads, The still discordant, wauering Multitude. **1766** JOHNSTONE in *Phil. Trans.* LVII. 125 The feelings are by no means acute, but blunt and confused. **1824** CAMPBELL *Love & Madn.* 30 Ill can your blunter feelings guess the pain. **1846** RUSKIN *Mod. Paint.* I. II. III. i. §3 They are but the blunt and the low faculties of our nature.

2. a. Of an angle, edge, or point: Not sharp, obtuse. Of a tool or weapon: Without edge or point. spec. *blunt instrument*, a loose term covering any large, heavy object that might be used as a murder weapon; *transf.*, a crude threat.

For this notion *blunt* is now the proper word; and this is also now the leading literal sense, which tends to influence the other senses.

1398 TREVISA *Barth. De P.R.* XII. xviii. (1495) 426 The capon is more cowarde of herte..his spores ben made blonte. *c* **1440** *Promp. Parv.* 41 Blunt of edge. **1530** PALSGR. 306/2 Blont nat sharpe, *rabatu, agasse.* **1562** TURNER *Herbal* II. Mij a The poyntes of the leues wer blunter. **1594** BLUNDEVIL *Exerc.* II. (ed. 7) 119 The middle letter doth alwayes signifie the angle propounded, bee it right, sharpe, or blunt. **1611** BIBLE *Eccles.* x. 10 If the yron be blunt. **1753** *Scots Mag.* June 280/1 A blunt pencil. **1885** *Where Chineses Drive* 140 The hatchet was too blunt to be of any service. **1923** D. L. SAYERS *Whose Body?* vi. 147 The blow..had been made with a heavy, blunt instrument. **1966** *Observer* 13 Nov. 6/7 He chided the Government for using words like 'freeze' as blunt instruments.

b. *transf.* to the effect.

1656 COWLEY *Davideis* IV. 144 Its least and bluntest stroke.

c. *fig.*

1562 J. HEYWOOD *Prov. & Epigr.* (1867) 210 Great diffrence betweene blounte woordes and sharp swoordes. **1635** QUARLES *Embl.* v. (1718) 311 Lord, whet my dull, my blunt belief. **1831** HEIDIGER *Didon.* IX. 270 Invention's blade is made sharper, and not blunter, by much use.

† **3.** Barren, bare. *Obs.*

1553 DOUGLAS *Æneis* (ed. 1710) XIII. vi. 227 The large plains..Stude blunt [*MSS. & ed.* 1874, blowt] of beistis and of treis bare. **1596** SPENSER *F.Q.* VI. xi. 9 Merchants.. Arrived in this isle though bare & blunt T' inquire for slaves. **1599** PORTER *Angry Wom. Abingd.* (1841) 22 Our blunt soyle offords none such.

† **4. a.** Rude, unpolished, rough, without refinement. *Obs.* or *arch.*

1477 NORTON *Ord. Alch.* vii. in Ashm. (1652) 106 In English blunt and rude. **1513** DOUGLAS *Æneis* I. Prol. 314 Thocht myne be blunt his [Vergil's] text is maist perfyte. **1530** PALSGR. 306/2 Blont in maners or rude—*rude.* **1655** FULLER *Hist. Camb.* (1840) 152 This blunt preaching was in those dark days admirably effectual. **1702** POPE *Jan. & May* 742 Tho' not in phrase refin'd; Tho' blunt my tale. *c* **1760** SMOLLETT *Ode Indep.* 57 He steel'd the blunt Batavian's arms. **1826** SCOTT *Woodst.* viii, His demeanour was so blunt as sometimes might be termed clownish.

† **b.** Rough, harsh; unfeeling, unsparing. *Obs.*

1592 SHAKS. *Ven. & Ad.* 884 The blunt boar, rough bear or lion proud. **1593** —— *3 Hen. VI*, v. i. 86 Trowest thou.. that Clarence is so harsh, so blunt, vnnaturall?

5. Abrupt of speech or manner; plain-spoken; curt; without delicacy; unceremonious.

1590 GREENE *Neuer too late* (1600) 51 One blunt fellow amongst the rest that was plaine and without falshood, told her the whole cause. **1599** SHAKS. *Hen. V*, IV. vii. 185 By his blunt bearing he will keepe his word. **1635** K. LONG *Barclay's Argenis* (1636) B iv a, A rude and blunt people, wont to call a Figge a Figge, and a Boat a Boat. **1704** POPE *Ess. Crit.* 577 Blunt truths more mischief than nice falsehoods do. **1797** MRS. RADCLIFFE *Italian* xiii. (1824) 606 Be pretty blunt with them if they want to come in here. **1865** TROLLOPE *Belton Est.* iii. 27 He was blunt in his bearing, saying things which her father would have called indelicate and heartless. **1871** DIXON *Tower* III. xxviii. 312 The blunt and earnest speaker..was Cromwell.

6. *Comb.*, chiefly parasynthetic, as ***blunt-angled, -edged, -ended, -featured, -fingered, -headed, -hearted, -nosed, -pointed, -sighted, -topped, -witted***; adverbial, as ***blunt-spoken***; **blunt-file,** a file with very little taper; **blunt head,** a snake belonging to the family Amblycephalidæ; **blunt-hook,** a surgical instrument used in midwifery; **blunt-point,** a tool used in aquatinting; **blunt-sharp** *a.*, sharp but not pointed with malice; † **blunt-worker,** a blunderer; † **blunt-working,** blundering.

1551 RECORDE *Pathw. Knowl.* II. xiii, A *blunte angeled triangle. **1836** TODD *Cycl. Anat. & Phys.* I. 312/2 *Blunt-edged bills. **1916** JOYCE *Portrait of Artist* v. 232 MacCann's flushed *bluntfeatured face. **1858** A. IRVINE *Handbk. Brit. Plants* 440 *Veronica triphyllos.* *Blunt-fingered Speedwell. **1869** GILLMORE tr. *Figuier's Reptiles & Birds* (1870) 51 The *Amblycephalidæ*, or *Blunt Heads comprise a few species of moderate or small size. **1845** DISRAELI *Sybil* (1863) 61 A selfish husband, at once sharp-witted and *blunt-hearted. **1772** FORSTER in *Phil. Trans.* LXIII. 151 The common *blunt-nosed Sturgeon of Germany. **1834** *Penny Cycl.* II. 203/2 Every line of the design is..gone over with an instrument called a *blunt point. **1881** *Trans. Obstetr. Soc.* XXII. 37 A curved, *blunt-pointed bistoury. **1937** *Discovery* Jan. 13/2 A straight-rooted, blunt-pointed tooth. **1613** HAYWARD *Norm. Kings* 150 Colomannus the eldest, who was lame, bunch-backed, crab-faced, *blunt-sighted. **1662** FULLER *Worthies* (1840) II. 464 Excellent at *blunt-sharp jests, and perchance sometimes too tart in true ones. **1878** BLACK *Green Past.* iv. 34 Something more than *blunt-spoken..a trifle too anxious to tread on people's corns. **1908** E. STEP *Wayside Ferns* 108 *Blunt-topped Horsetail. *Equisetum pratense.* **1963** *Times* 25 May 9/6 The hills are old and blunt-topped. **1593** SHAKS. *2 Hen. VI*, III. ii. 210 *Blunt-witted Lord, ignoble in demeanor. *c* **1440** *Promp. Parv.* 41 Blunderer or *blunt warkere, *hebefactor. Ibid.* Blunderynge, or *blunt warkynge, *hebefaccio.*

B. *sb.*

† **1.** A blunt sword for fencing, a foil. *Obs.*

1611 COTGR. s.v. *Fer. Batre le fer*, to play at blunt, or at foyles. **1694** SIR W. HOPE *Swordsm. Vade Mec.* 25 The only Safe and Secure Play, with either Blunts or Sharpes.

2. A size or make of needle.

1833 J. HOLLAND *Manuf. Metals* II. 360 The latter [needles with broken points] are generally repointed as blunts. **1862** MORRALL *Needle Making* 39 The Blunts are half a size thicker and a size shorter than Betweens, and have still stronger points, being suited for the heaviest work, such as bed-ticks, shoe-binding, stay-making, etc.

3. *slang.* Ready money.

1812 J. H. VAUX *Flash Dict.*, *Blunt*, money. **1823** SCOTT in *Lockhart* (1839) VII. 99, I will remit the blunt immediately. **1838** DICKENS *O. Twist* 202/1, I must have some blunt from you to-night. *a* **1845** HOOD *Tale Trump.* xx, You must fork out the blunt.

blunt, *v.* Also 4-5 blont. [f. BLUNT *a.*]

1. *trans.* To dull, or make less sharp (an edge or point).

1398 TREVISA *Barth. De P.R.* XVI. xliv. (1495) 568 Whan the egge of yren is dulled and blonted. **1580** HOLLYBAND *Treas. Fr. Tong* s.v. *Reboucher*, To blunte the edge or point of a thing. **1596** DRAYTON *Legends* i. 610 That Blade..Was too much blunted. **1713** SWIFT *Cadenus & V.* Wks. 1755 III. II. 3 Cupid now..blunts the point of ev'ry dart. *a* **1860** G. P. MORRIS *Poems* (ed. 15) 61 Let us by this gentle river Blunt the axe and break the quiver.

b. To weaken the sharpness of (anything acid or corrosive); to neutralize partially; to dilute.

1732 ARBUTHNOT *Rules of Diet* 257 They operate by blunting the Acrimony of the Salts. **1771** J. S. *Le Dran's Observ. Surg.* (ed. 4) 48 To touch it with the mercurial Solution..blunted with common Water. **1787** WINTER *Syst. Husb.* 333 It did not effervesce in, nor blunt the acidity of vinegar.

c. *intr.* To become dull of edge or point.

1684 BUNYAN *Pilgr.* II. 174 Its edges will never blunt. **1805** SOUTHEY *Madoc in W.* VII, The flint-edge [will] blunt and break.

2. *trans.* To make dull (the feelings or faculties).

1597 SHAKS. *2 Hen. IV*, IV. iv. 27 Blunt not his Loue..By seeming cold, or carelesse of his will. **1683** BURNET tr. *More's Utopia* 49 Necessity and Poverty blunts them, makes them patient, and bears them down. **1835** SIR J. ROSS *N.-W. Pass.* xvi. 270 Our long conviction of the inevitable event had blunted those feelings. **1866** GEO. ELIOT *Felix Holt* (1868) 20 The mother's love is at first an absorbing delight, blunting all other sensibilities.

† **3.** *to blunt out* or *forth*; to utter bluntly or abruptly. *Obs.* Cf. BLURT.

a **1535** MORE *Wks.* (1557) 76/1 It were paradventure good rather to keepe a good silence thyself than blunt forth rudely.

'blunted, *ppl. a.* [f. prec. + -ED[1].] Made blunt; having point or edge dulled; also *fig.*

1677 MOXON *Mech. Exerc.* (1703) 349 With the blunted point of a Needle. **1697** DRYDEN *Virg.* (1806) III. 249 Part New grind the blunted axe. **1853** F. HALL in *Leslie's Misc.* II. 176 A man whose moral judgment has become altogether blunted. **1871** PALGRAVE *Lyr. Poems* 14 The blunted souls by lust defiled.

† **'blunten,** *v. Obs. rare.* [f. BLUNT *a.* Cf. *sharpen.*] *trans.* To blunt, take off the edge of.

1615 J. STEPHENS *Ess. & Char.* in Halliw. *Charact.-Bks.* 171 Good for nothing but to blunten a Cheaters pollicy.

'blunter. [f. BLUNT *v.* + -ER[1].] One who blunts or dulls.

1609 W. M. *Man in Moone* in Halliw. *Charact.-Bks.* (1857) 87 He is his owne beauties blemisher, his wittes blunter.

'blunting, *vbl. sb.* [f. BLUNT *v.* + -ING¹.] The action of making or of becoming blunt; anything in which this action is realized.

1611 COTGR., *Espointement*, an vnpointing; a blunting; a breaking the point of. **1656** *Artif. Handsomeness* 72 Not impediments or bluntings, but rather as Whetstones, to set an edge on our desires. **1870** *Eng. Mech.* 7 Jan. 397/2 We.. remarked this blunting of the.. horn.

'bluntish ('blʌntɪʃ), *a.* [f. BLUNT *a.* + -ISH.] Rather blunt, somewhat blunt.

1578 T. PROCTER *Gorg. Gallery* in *Heliconia* I. 182 To Bluntish blocks I see I doo complayne. **1713** DERHAM *Phys. Theol.* To Rdr. 5 He hath represented it as tubular, or bluntish at the Top. **1880** WATSON in *Jrnl. Linn. Soc.* XV. 99 Apex bluntish, and a little obliquely rounded.

Hence **'bluntishness.**

1691 WOOD *Ath. Oxon.* (1815) II. 582 An honest bluntishness, far from court insinuation.

bluntly ('blʌntlɪ), *adv.* [f. BLUNT *a.* + -LY².]

†**1.** Stupidly; with dulled perception; without quickness of wit. Cf. BLUNT *a.* 1. *Obs.*

1557 Tottell's *Misc.* (Arb.) 136 For he that blontly runnes, may light among the breers. **1583** STANYHURST *Æneis* II. (Arb.) 45 Al our senses weare.. bluntlye benummed. **1711** C. M. *Lett. to Curat* 75 You may guess how bluntly I look'd, upon being taken up so sharp.

2. Without a sharp point or edge; obtusely.

1578 LYTE *Dodoens* II. ciiii. 290 Leaues bluntly iagged rounde about the edges. **1768** PARSONS in *Phil. Trans.* LVIII. 193 Bluntly serrated. **1821** HOOKER *Flora Scot.* II. 22 Pileus deep buff, bluntly conical.

3. Rudely; without ceremony or delicacy; abruptly, curtly.

1579 TOMSON *Calvin's Serm. Tim.* 796/2 Because we come bluntly to it. **1605** SHAKS. *Lear* I. iv. 36, I can.. deliuer a plaine message bluntly. **1617** HIERON *Wks.* (1620) II. 415 Neuer fall bluntly to any religious dutie which God requires. **1741** H. WALPOLE *Lett. H. Mann* (1834) I. x. 32 They bluntly refused to go. **1873** BLACK *Pr. Thule* xvii. 269 Ingram had come prepared to state harsh truths bluntly.

'bluntness. [f. BLUNT *a.* + -NESS.]

†**1.** Dullness of wit, stupidity. *Obs.*

1483 *Cath. Angl.* 35 A Bluntnes, *ebitudo*. **1623** COCKERAM, *Hebetude*, bluntnesse, dulnesse.

2. Obtuseness or dullness of point or edge.

1530 PALSGR. 199/1 Bluntnesse of any edged toole. **1655** GURNALL *Chr. in Arm.* xiii. (1669) 92/2 His worldly employments do not turn the edge of his affections, & leave a bluntness upon his spirit. **1794** G. ADAMS *Nat. & Exp. Philos.* III. xxxi. 243 Rounded with a fine bone.. which causes a sufficient bluntness or rolling edge.

3. Rudeness, absence of delicacy or refinement; abruptness of manner or address, curtness.

1605 SHAKS. *Lear* II. ii. 102 Who hauing beene prais'd for bluntnesse, doth affect A saucy roughnes. *a* **1674** CLARENDON *Hist. Reb.* III. x. 36 The bluntness and positiveness of the few words he spoke. **1751** FIELDING *Amelia* Wks. 1775 X. 124 Bluntness, or rather rudeness, as it commonly deserves to be called, is not always so much a mark of honesty as it is taken to be. **1833** MARRYAT *P. Simple* (1863) 237 The bluntness with which he used to contradict and assert his disbelief of Captain Kearney's narratives.

'blunty, -ie, *a. Obs.* or *dial.* [f. BLUNT *a.*]

1. Of blunt nature or tendency.

1598 YONG *Diana* 206 Thou that art of bluntie lead, Strike thou some womans hart so dead In cruell hate, that she shall neuer feele The sense of loue.

2. as *sb.* A stupid fellow; one not sharp of wits.

1768 ROSS *Helenore* 36 (JAM.) I.. like blunty sat. **1794** BURNS *O for ane an' twenty* ii, They snool me sair, and haud me down, And gar me look like bluntie, Tam.

blur (blɜː(r)), *sb.* Forms: 6–7 blurre, 7– blurr, blur. [*Blur* sb. and vb. appear about the middle of the 16th c.: their mutual relation is doubtful, and the origin of both unknown: they have been conjecturally viewed as a variant of BLEAR, and may perhaps be onomatopœic, combining the effect of *blear* and *blot*. The mod. Sc. is *blore.*]

1. A smear which partially obscures, made with ink or other colouring matter, or by brushing the surface of writing while still wet.

1601 HOLLAND *Pliny* II. 306 With it a man may wash away any blots or blurs of ink. **1640** QUARLES *Enchirid.* III. xiii, He that clenses a blot with blotted fingers makes a greater blurre. **1665** PEPYS *Diary* (1879) III. 151, I minded it so little as to sleep in the middle of my letter to him, and committed forty blotts and blurrs. **1705** in Perry *Hist. Coll. Amer. Col. Ch.* I. 178 The Blots, Blurs, and Defacements of many of the Pages. **1871** BROWNING *Pr. Hohenst.* 392 Why keep each fool's bequeathment, scratch and blurr Which overscrawl and underscore the piece?

2. *fig.* A stain which bedims moral or ideal purity, a blemish; an aspersion on character.

1548 UDALL, etc. *Erasm. Par. Luke* xviii. 144 Sette a great blurre on myne honestie. **1593** SHAKS. *Lucr.* 222 This blur to youth. **1641** MILTON *Ch. Discip.* I. Wks. (1851) 21 These blurs are too apparent in his life. **1866** *Cornh. Mag.* May 557 The place from a distance, compared with the surrounding country, was a blur and a blemish as it were. **1883** *Contemp. Rev.* June 784 Many a blur of human error.

3. An effect like that of blurred writing or painting; an indistinct blurred appearance; indistinctness, confused dimness.

1860 EMERSON *Cond. Life* (1868) 281 The fine star-dust and nebulous blur of Orion. **1870** LOWELL *Study Wind.* 39 The vast blur of a north-northeast snow-storm. **1873** BROWNING *Red Cott. Night-c.* 878 The face, to me One blurr of blank.

blur (blɜː(r)), *v.* [See prec.]

1. *trans.* To obscure or sully (what has been fair) by smearing with ink or other colouring liquid.

1592 LYLY *Midas* IV. ii, To blurre his diademe with blood. **1612** R. CARPENTER *Soules Sent.* 54 His.. black booke, blurde and blotted with the register of sin. **1650** FULLER *Pisgah* IV. ii. 20 A full paper blurred over with falsehoods. **1884** BROWNING *Ferishtah* 117 Blacks blur thy white?

b. *intr.* To make blurs in writing.

1622 MABBE *Aleman's Guzman D'Alf.* II. 134 My pen did so blur, that I did despaire, to come off cleanly with it. **1689** EVELYN *Mem.* (1857) III. 314, I see how I have blurred: but tis not worth the writing fairer. **1878** BROWNING *Poets Croisic* xxxvii, Over the neat crowquill calligraph His pen goes blotting, blurring.

2. *fig.* To stain, sully, blot, or blemish the purity, beauty, or truth of (anything); to disfigure, befoul, defile, asperse.

1593 SHAKS. *2 Hen. VI*, IV. i. 39 Neuer yet did base dishonour blurre our name, But with our sword we wip'd away the blot. **1602** —— *Ham.* III. iv. 41 Such an Act That blurres the grace and blush of Modestie. **1663** BUTLER *Hud.* I. iii. 876 Sarcasms may eclipse thine own But cannot blur my lost renown. **1674** FLATMAN *To Orinda* 3 A weeping evening blurs a smiling day. **1794** SULLIVAN *View Nat.* V. 28 Irish history, blurred.. with extravagancy and fable. **1825** COLERIDGE *Lett., Convers. etc.* II. 237 The human face divine is blurred and transfigured by being made the impress of the mean and selfish. **1885** W. C. SMITH *Kildrostan* 74 To blur a father's memory.

3. *to blur out*: to efface (writing, etc.) by blurring it. *to blur over*: to put out of sight, or obscure by a blur. Mostly *fig.*

1581 J. BELL *Haddon's Answ. Osor.* 13 If the lively authoritie of the holy scriptures have so utterly quasshed and blurred out this bald ceremonie. **1621** QUARLES *Esther* (1638) 123 And from remembrance blurre his Generation. **1642** MILTON *Apol. Smect.* Wks. 1738 I. 121 To blur over, rather than to mention that public triumph. **1663** SIR G. MACKENZIE *Relig. Stoic* vii. (1685) 54 Blur the names.. out of the Book of Life. **1690** LOCKE *Hum. Und.* I. iii. (1695) 25 Concerning innate Principles, I desire these Men to say, whether they can, or cannot.. be blurr'd and blotted out. **1863** ALCOCK *Capit. Tycoon* I. 159 A constant tendency to blur out distinctions.

4. To make indistinct and dim, as writing is by being blurred. Also *fig.*

1611 SHAKS. *Cymb.* IV. ii. 104 Time hath nothing blurr'd those lines of Fauour Which then he wore. **1681** *Ess. Peace & Truth Ch.* 2 The Blurring these Impressions. **1859** TENNYSON *Guinevere* 5 One low light.. Blurr'd by the creeping mist. **1871** ROSSETTI *Stream's Secr.* viii, Thine eddy's rippling race Would blur the perfect image of his face.

5. *transf.* **a.** To dim (the sight or other senses, the perception, or judgement), so that they no longer receive or form distinct impressions.

c **1620** Z. BOYD *Zion's Flowers* (1855) 112 Feare.. blurres your senses. **1791** COWPER *Iliad* xx. 392 With shadows dim he blurr'd the sight Of Peleus' son. **1871** ROSSETTI *Staff & Scrip* xxvii, Our sense is blurr'd With all the chants gone by. **1878** MORLEY *Crit. Misc.* Ser. I. 264 Social equity in which charity is not allowed to blur judgment.

b. *intr.* To become blurred (to one's perceptions).

1856 E. B. BROWNING *Aurora Leigh* VII. 290 But presently the winding Rhone Washed out the moonlight large along his banks.. shadow of town and castle blurred Upon the hurrying river. **1888** MRS. H. WARD *R. Elsmere* I. viii. 234 The calm, simple outlines of things are blurring before her eyes; the great placid deeps of the soul are breaking up. **1950** E. HEMINGWAY *Across River & into Trees* iii. 15 They were on a straight stretch of road now and were making time so that one farm blended, almost blurred, into another farm and you could only see what was far ahead and moving towards you. **1964** J. DIDION *Run, River* ix. 80 She watched the street lights blur through the blown branches. **1985** *Globe & Mail* (Toronto) 10 Oct. B25/3 Roles in the information world are blurring.

6. *Comb.*, as †**blur-paper**, a writer who merely blurs paper; a scribbler.

1603 FLORIO *Montaigne* II. xxxii. (1632) 404 Scriblers and blur-papers which now adayes stuffe Stationers shops.

¶ Cf. BLARE, BLORE *v.*

1611 COTGR., *Grailler*, to winde a Horne hollowly; to blurre a Trumpet.

blurb (blɜːb). *slang* (orig. *U.S.*). [See note below.] A brief descriptive paragraph or note of the contents or character of a book, printed as a commendatory advertisement, on the jacket or wrapper of a newly published book. Hence in extended use: a descriptive or commendatory paragraph. Also *Comb.*

Said to have been originated in 1907 by Gelett Burgess in a comic book jacket embellished with a drawing of a pulchritudinous young lady whom he facetiously dubbed Miss Blinda Blurb. (D.A.) See Mencken *Amer. Lang.* Suppl. I. 329.

1914 G. BURGESS *Burgess Unabridged* 7 *Blurb*, 1. A flamboyant advertisement; an inspired testimonial. 2. Fulsome praise; a sound like a publisher... On the 'jacket' of the 'latest' fiction, we find the blurb; abounding in agile adjectives and adverbs, attesting that this book is the 'sensation of the year'. **1918** *Wine, Women & War* (1926) 106 Americans, despite blurb in home press, [have] not yet succeeded in revolutionizing art of war. **1923** *Nation* 1 Aug. 121/2 The publishers.. clapped on a jacket containing a blurb. **1924** *Spectator* 27 Sept. 426 The note of vanity is ominously accentuated by the publisher's blurb on the dust-cover, as silly and vulgar as the present writer has ever seen. **1926** *Times Lit. Suppl.* 21 Oct. 710/2 The paragraph briefly setting forth the merits of the book (known in 'the trade' as a 'blurb'). **1934** A. HUXLEY *Beyond Mexique Bay* 2 The blurb-writers promise to take you into the very heart of all these variegated delights. **1947** *Penguin Music Mag.* Sept. 60 The cast, the 'blurb' tells us, includes the pick of the younger generation of Italian operatic singers. **1948** *Ibid.* Oct. 22 Her name appeared recently [in concert advertisements] mixed up with a blurb about 'the greatest living exponent' and so on. **1955** *Times* 4 Aug. 9/5 For why must publishers prefix to novels of this school a blurb in which much of the substance of the thriller is already revealed?

†**blure, bloure, blowre,** *sb. Obs.* [App. from root of BLOW *v.*: cf. BLADDER *sb.*] = BLADDER *sb.* 2; blister, swelling.

c **1440** *York Myst.* xi. 294 Grete loppis ouere all þis lande þei flye, That with bytyng makis mekill blure [*Towneley Myst.* viii. 294 Where thay byte thay make grete blowre]. *c* **1460** *Towneley Myst.* 310 So many Thus broght I on blure. *a* **1499** GARLANDIA *Equiv.* in *Promp. Parv.* 43 *Bulla, tumor, laticum*, i.e. *aquarum*, a bollynge or a bloure.

†**blurre.** *Obs.* ? = prec.; cf. also BLUR, BLOW, BLORE.

1526 SKELTON *Magnyf.* 1194 Mary, as thou sayst, he gaue me a blurre.

blurred (blɜːd), *ppl. a.* [f. BLUR *v.* + -ED¹.]

1. Smeared with or as with ink, as when wet writing is rubbed or brushed.

1553 DK. NORTHUMB. in *Four C. Eng. Lett.* 22 To whom I have also sent my blurred letters. **1660** W. SECKER *Nonsuch Prof.* 189 There is no removing of blots from the paper by laying upon it a blurred finger. **1790** BURKE *Fr. Rev.* Wks. 1842 V. 167 Paltry blurred shreds of paper about the rights of man. **1875** STUBBS *Const. Hist.* II. xvii. 625 The writing of the fourteenth century is coarse and blurred.

2. Stained, sullied, befouled.

1708 MOTTEUX *Rabelais* IV. xii, A Country all blurr'd and blotted. **1856** MRS. BROWNING *Aur. Leigh* VIII. 362 His cheeks all blurred with tears and naughtiness.

3. Made indistinct and dim like blurred writing.

1701 *Lond. Gaz.* No. 3746/4 The W. a little blurr'd. **1842** DICKENS *Amer. Notes* (1850) 132/2 A blurred lithograph of Washington. **1878** BLACK *Green Past.* vii. 54, I don't know .. what blurred image or idol he had in his mind.

Hence **blurredness** ('blɜːdnɪs).

1864 FURNIVALL in *Reader* 22 Oct. 511/2 The frequent blurredness [of the type] and missing of dots and strokes in this reduction.

blurrer ('blɜːrə(r)). [f. BLUR *v.* + -ER.] He who or that which blurs.

1681 RYCAUT *Critick* 117 Their tongues [turned to] blurrers of fame.

blurriness ('blɜːrɪnɪs). [f. BLURRY *a.* + -NESS.] The quality of being blurry; blurredness.

1937 *Burlington Mag.* Jan. p. xiv/2 The days of romantic blurriness are finished, and with them the indeterminate, fuzzy attitude towards art. **1958** *Listener* 6 Nov. 730/1 The increasing redness and blurriness of their later paintings.

blurring ('blɜːrɪŋ), *vbl. sb.* [f. BLUR *v.* + -ING¹.] The action of the vb. BLUR.

1601 HOLLAND *Pliny* I. 393 [The Paper] would not hold inke.. and was euermore in danger of blurring and blotting. *a* **1638** MEDE *Wks.* IV. xxix. 784 Everlasting mending, blurring, and pausing at every sentence to alter it. **1864** SIR F. PALGRAVE *Norm. & Eng.* III. 440 The blurring of the lime, on the greensward.

'blurring, *ppl. a.* [see -ING².] That blurs.

1851 MRS. BROWNING *Casa Guidi Wind.* 88 For men to spit at with scorn's blurring brine.

blurry ('blɜːrɪ), *a.* [f. BLUR *sb.* + -Y¹.] Full of blurs; faultily indistinct in features.

1884 *Leeds Mercury* Wkly. Supp. 15 Nov. 1/6 The tutti music was wanting in tone.. and the execution was frequently very blurry.

blurt (blɜːt), *v.* [app. a modern onomatopœia, expressive of a discharge of breath or fluid from the mouth after an effort to retain it; with the *bl*-element, cf. *blow, blast, blash*, etc.; with the rest cf. *spurt, spirt, squirt*, etc.: see also BLIRT.]

1. *intr.* To emit the breath eruptively from the mouth; to snort in sleep. Also *trans.* with *out*. Now *dial.*

1611 COTGR., *Souffler les choux en dormant*, to puffe, or blurt out puffes, in sleeping. *a* **1825** *MS. Poem* (JAM.) He blortit an' startit.

†**2.** To make a contemptuous puffing gesture with the lips, to puff in scorn, to 'pooh'. *Obs.*

a. *intr.* Also with indirect pass. *to be blurted at.*

1596 *Edw. III*, IV. vi. (N.) All the world will blurt and scorn at us. **1601** SHAKS. *Per.* IV. iii. 34 None would look on her But cast their gazes on Marinas face; Whilst ours was blurted at. **1611** FLORIO, *Boccheggiare*.. to make mouths or blurt with ones lips. **1654** GAYTON *Fest. Notes* IV. xvii. 259 The other part.. sneeze and blurt.. make mouths, and flowt in Spanish postures.

b. *trans.* To treat contemptuously.

1621 FLETCHER *Wild-G. Chase* II. ii, I never was so blurted, Nor ever so abused. *a* **1663** SANDERSON *Serm.* (1681) 92 Baffled and Blurted by every lewd companion.

3. *trans.* (commonly with *out*): To utter abruptly, and as if by a sudden impulse; to ejaculate impulsively; to burst out with.

1573 G. Harvey *Letter-bk.* (1884) 9 Blurting out sutch iests as he had gottin togither for the nons. **1656** H. More *Enthus. Tri.* (1712) 35 Blurting out any garish foolery that comes into their mind. **1768** Tucker *Lt. Nat.* II. 566 Sometimes people will blurt out things inadvertently, which if judgment had been awake it would have suppressed. **1772** Goldsm. *Stoops to Conq.* II. i, To blurt out the broad staring question of, Madam will you marry me. **1848** Macaulay *Hist. Eng.* II. 180 They are fortunate if they possess an indiscreet friend who blurts out the whole truth. **1854** Mrs. Gaskell *North & S.* v, 'Papa is going to leave Helstone!' she blurted forth. **1876** Blackie *Songs Relig. & Life* 147 To blurt a dash of broad-cast Scottish truth, Athwart his lisping lips.

fig. **1611** Tourneur *Ath. Trag.* IV. iv. 124, I should ha' done't slily without discouery, and now I am blurted upon 'em before I was aware.

b. *absol.*

1641 Milton *Animadv.* Wks. (1851) 189 To blurt upon the eares of a judicious Parliament with such a..Proem.

4. *transf.* To thrust out abruptly.

1818 *Religio Clerici* 52 Fled is the genuine Muse, and in her place A brisk pretender blurts her shameless face.

5. To burst out into weeping. (Cf. BLIRT.)

1843 W. Carleton *Traits* I. 139 Able-bodied spalpeens blurting, like overgrown children, on seeing their own blood.

blurt (blɜːt), *sb.* [f. the vb.: see also BLIRT.]

†**1.** An eruptive emission of breath from the mouth, esp. as expressive of contempt. *Obs.*

1580 North *Plutarch* (1676) 633 Meaning to give Cassander a slampant and blurt. **1611** Florio, *Chicchere*, a ..blurt with ones mouth in scorne or derision.

2. An abrupt impulsive utterance or outburst.

1865 Carlyle *Fredk. Gt.* VI. xvi. ix. 245 This blurt of La Mettrie's goes through him like a shot of electricity.

blurt, *adv.* and *int.* [The verb-stem used without const., as in 'to go bang', 'to cut bang off'.]

A. *adv.* Blurting, with a blurt.

1698 Vanbrugh *Prov. Wife* III. iii, When they come blurt out with a nasty thing in a play.

†**B.** *interj.* An exclamation of contempt: 'pooh!' 'a fig for!' See BLURT *v.* 2. *Obs.*

1592 Lyly *Midas* II. ii. 21 Blirt to you both. **1602** Middleton (*title*) (N.) Blurt, Master Constable. **1604** Dekker *Honest Wh.* Wks. 1873 II. 22 Blurt on your sentences. **1606** in *N. Riding Records* (1883) I. 37 Will. Forde fined for using evill speaches to the Constable saying 'Blirt, Mr. Constable'.

'blurting, *vbl. sb.* [f. BLURT *v.* + -ING[1].]

†**a.** The contemptuous abrupt emission of breath from the lips (*obs.*). **b.** The uttering of words abruptly and heedlessly.

1598 Florio, *Smorfia*, a mowing, a mocking, or pish with ones mouth..a blurting.

blurting, *ppl. a.* [f. as prec. + -ING[2].]

a. Bursting forth in short sudden puffs. **b.** Making abrupt unexpected utterances; impulsively communicative.

1850 Mrs. Browning *Drama Exile* Poems I. 87 Shall the horse's nostrils steam the blurting breath. **1863** Geo. Eliot *Romola* III. xiv. (1880) II. 156 He would be suddenly blurting and affectionate. **1872** —— *Middlem.* v. 187 The blurting, rallying tone with which he spoke.

blush (blʌʃ), *v.*[1] Pa. t. and pple. **blushed, blusht** (blʌʃt). Forms: 4–6 **blusche, blusshe,** 4 **blosche,** 4–5 **blysche,** 5 **blushe,** 6 **bluss,** 6– **blush.** (Rare pa. t. in 5 **blist** = **blyscht**). [Evidently related to a series of words found in Old Norse and Low German, but not known in OHG. or Gothic, pointing back to a stem **blŭsi-* from verbal root **blŭs-* in sense of 'burn, glow, be red'. Cf. OE. **blysian* in *ablisian* to blush, *ablysung*, *ablysȝung* 'redness of confusion, shame', with MDu. *blōzen*, *blōzen* (from earlier *bleuzen*), Du. *blozen* to blush, *blos* (formerly *bleus*) blush, MLG. *blosen*, *bloschen*; also OE. *blysa* wk. masc., *blysiȝe* wk. fem., ON. *blys* neut. 'torch' (Sw. *bloss* torch, *blossa* to blaze, Da. *blus* torch, *blusse* to blaze, to blush), LG. *blüse* flame, *blüsen* to set on fire, *bleusteren* to inflame, glow, become red. The nearest relatives of ME. *blusche*, *blosche*, *blysche*, are app. MLG. *bloschen*, LG. *blüsken* (*Brem. Wb.* I. 105): and its antecedent form is perhaps to be found in OE. *blyscan*, *bliscan* 'rutilare' (in the *Aldhelm Glosses*, Mone *Q. und F.* 355): but its comparatively late appearance in ME., apparently first in the north, its various vowel-forms, and the doubtful relations of the senses, esp. sense 2, all combine to leave the history of the word very obscure. OE. *blyscan*, *bliscan*, has also been conjectured to be for **blicsian*, from root **blik-* to shine, in which case it would not be related to the *blŭsi-* words, nor to ME. *blusche*. (The Da. deponent *blues* to blush, may also be compared.)]

(The order of the senses is uncertain; with 1 and 2 cf. BLINK.)

†**1.** *intr.* To shine forth. (in allit. poetry.) *Obs.*

c **1340** *Gaw. & Gr. Knt.* 1817 Þat bere blusschande bemez, as þe bryȝt sunne. *c* **1400** *Destr. Troy* 4665 The bremnes abatid; blusshit the sun.

†**2.** To cast a glance, glance with the eye, give a look. (in allit. poetry.) *Obs.*

c **1325** *E.E. Allit. P.* B. 998 Ho blusched hir bihynde, þaȝ hir forboden were. *Ibid.* C. 343 Þe bonk þat he blosched to, & bode hym bisyde. ? *a* **1400** *Morte Arth.* 116 The kynge blyschit one the beryne with his brode eghne. *c* **1400** *Ywaine & Gaw.* 3163 The lioun bremely on tham blist. *c* **1400** *Destr. Troy* 1316 He blusshed ouer backeward to þe brode see. *c* **1450** *Merlin* xvi. 259 [Thei] ne wiste no worde till sodeinly thei blusshed vpon a grete parte of saisnes.

b. *to blush to the earth*: to glance to the earth, *i.e.* to fall face downwards.

c **1450** *Merlin* vii. 120 The stroke descended on the horse ..and ydiers and his horse blusshet to the erthe. *Ibid.* 137 Thei smot so v of the first that thei metten that thei blushit to the erthe.

c. *to blush on*: to approach in look or appearance. Cf. BLUSH *sb.* 3.

c **1530** Ld. Berners *Arth. Lyt. Bryt.* (1814) 381 A lyghte kyrtell of chaungeable vyolet tartorne, somewhat blusshynge on a red coloure.

3. *intr.* To become red in the face, (usually) from shame or modesty; to 'colour up'. Often with compl. *to blush red*, etc., also with cogn. object.

c **1450** *Crt. Love* clxxii, Shamefastnes was there..That blushed red, and durst not ben aknow She lover was. **1514** Barclay *Cyt. & Uplondyshm.* (1847) 11 Anone she blusshed, revolvynge in her mynde..That it was token of to great carnall lust. *c* **1532** Ld. Berners *Huon* 550 She changed coloure and blussyd as rudy as a rose. *Ibid.* 286 He blusshed in the face for the gret yre that he was in. **1588** Shaks. *Tit. A.* v. i. 122, What canst thou say all this and neuer blush? **1611** Bible *Jer.* vi. 15. **1667** Milton *P.L.* VIII. 511 To the Nuptial Bowre I led her blushing like the Morn. **1709** Pope *Ess. Crit.* 545 And virgins smiled at what they blushed before. **1769** *Junius Lett.* xxxv. 153 That prince.. used..to blush for his..ignorance. **1828** Scott *F.M. Perth* III. 53 Catharine blushes a blush of anger. **1872** Darwin *Emotions* xiii. 311 The young blush much more freely than the old. Women blush much more than men..The tendency to blush is inherited. **1882** Besant *All Sorts* 137 She blushed a pretty rose red.

fig. **1750** Gray *Elegy* xiv, Full many a flower is born to blush unseen.

†**b.** To look *on* with a blush. *Obs.*

1593 Shaks. *Lucr.* 1339 Blushing on her.

c. *trans.* With extended force: To express, exhibit, make known by blushing. Chiefly *poetic.*

1592 Warner *Alb. Eng.* VIII. xli. 201 She blush't out beauty. **1611** Shaks. *Wint. T.* IV. iv. 595 Ile blush you Thanks. **1651** Fuller *Abel Rediv.* 224 Many unworthy Schollars..whose scarlet Gowns might seeme to blush the wearers Ignorance. **1800** Moore *Anacreon* lxiii. 4 The boy, who breathes and blushes flowers! **1855** Tennyson *Maud* xvii. 16 Pass the happy news, Blush it through the West.

d. To make or turn *into*, *out of*, by blushing.

1636 R. Durham in *Ann. Dubrensia* (1877) 55 Whom chast Diana blusht into a beast. **1660** Fuller *Mixt Contempl.* (1841) 188 They will blush themselves out of their former follies. *a* **1848** Marryat *R. Reefer* xx, *I* should blush myself black in the face.

4. *fig.* To be ashamed. Const. *inf.*, *at* or *for*.

1530 Palsgr. 459/1, I blusshe, I waxe ashamed. **1583** Stubbes *Anat. Abus.* II. 33, I blush to tell you. **1593** Shaks. *2 Hen. VI*, II. iv. 48 Be thou milde, and blush not at my shame. **1692** Bentley *Boyle Lect.* vii. 241 So monstrous an Absurdity, as even They will blush to be charged with. **1734** Bolingbr. in *Swift's Lett.* (1766) II. 199, I do not blush to own, that I am out of fashion. **1791** Burke *Corr.* (1844) III. 332 As one of the people, I blush for what has followed. **1871** Freeman *Hist. Ess.* Ser. I. iii. 76.

5. *transf.* To become or be red, or roseate.

1679 *Est. Test.* 38 If our streets..should blush with the blood of Massacred Protestants. **1697** Dryden *Virg. Georg.* II. 601 Trees of Nature..with red Berries blush. **1791–1824** D'Israeli *Cur. Lit.* (1866) 523/1 Hills..blushing with vines. **1866** B. Taylor *Thro' Baltimore* Poems 402 The streets..Blushed with their children's gore. **1866** Alger *Solit. Nat. & Man* I. 19 Whole orchards of apple-blossoms blush in correspondence.

6. *trans.* To make red.

1593 Shaks. *2 Hen. VI*, III. ii. 167 Ne're returneth, To blush and beautifie the Cheeke againe. **1747** T. Gibbons *Elegy* xiii. in Doddridge *Col. Gardiner* App. ii. 216 A Robe of spotless White, But where the Saviour's flowing Vein Had blush'd it with a sanguine Stain. **1820** Keats *St. Agnes* xxiv, A shielded scutcheon blushed with blood of queens and kings.

blush (blʌʃ), *sb.* (*a.*) [f. the vb.: cf. Du. *blos.*]

A. *sb.* †**1.** A gleam, a blink. *Obs.*

c **1340** *Gaw. & Gr. Knt.* 520 A blysful blusch of þe bryȝt sunne. **1661** Burney *Κέρδ. Δῶρον* 4 Their Prerogative, which is not a blush from the people, but 'tis a beam resultant from Gods Majestie, and reflects upon the people for their good.

2. A glance, glimpse, blink, look. *Obs.* exc. in phr. *at, on*, etc. (*the*) *first blush*: at the first glance.

a **1375** *Joseph Arim.* 657 Aftur þe furste blusch we ne miȝte him biholden. *c* **1530** Ld. Berners *Arth. Lyt. Bryt.* (1814) 494 As the emperour loked in at a windowe..he had a blushe of Florence. *a* **1563** Bale *Sel. Wks.* (1849) 572 The two horns are like the lambs horns at a blush. **1583** Stubbes *Anat. Abus.* II. 7 Hir Grace is..able at the first blush to discearne truth from falsehood. **1611** Bp. Andrewes *Serm. Nativity* vi. Wks. 1841 I. 94 Vidimus. And that not..'at a blush', passing by; but had a full sight. **1624** Bedell *Lett.* v. 82 This discourse hath a prettie shew at the first blush. **1629** Quarles *Argalus & P.* i. 33 And at first blush, she seemes, as if it were Some curious statue on a Sepulchre. *a* **1641** Bp. Mountagu *Acts & Mon.* 402 Looking pale, wan, and meagre, that men might say of them, at the blush, This man fasts to day. **1838** G. S. Faber *Inquiry* 308 The very vagueness of the allegation..may well, even on the first blush, induce a full presumption that, etc. **1844** Disraeli *Coningsby* II. i. 58 At the first blush, it would seem that little difficulties could be experienced. **1886** *Bibliotheca Sacra* XLIII. 618 This sounds, at first blush, very neat, if not even very profound. **1955** *Times* 11 May 18/1 It may, at first blush, seem invidious to single out anyone in particular for special comment.

†**3.** A look, appearance, resemblance. *Obs.* exc. *dial.* In *Bk. St. Albans* a 'company' of boys.

[**1486** *Bk. St. Albans* F vi b, A blush of boyes.] **1620** N. Brent *Hist. Counc. Trent* (1676) 204 Which followed.. without any blush of absurdity. **1640** Fuller *Joseph's Coat* (1867) 13 Reports relish of their relators, and have a blush and a smack of their partial dispositions. [**1824** *Craven Dialect* 15 Shoe wod a hed a feaful blush of her mother.]

4. a. The reddening of the face caused by shame, modesty, or other emotion.

1593 Shaks. *3 Hen. VI*, III. iii. 97 Bewray thy Treason with a Blush. **1599** —— *Hen. V*, v. ii. 253 Put off your Maiden Blushes. **1718** Pope *Iliad* IV. 403 The hero's warmth o'erspread His cheek with blushes. **1828** Wordsw. *Triad*, But her blushes are joy-flushes. **1876** Geo. Eliot *Dan. Der.* III. xxxv. 37 A blush is no language: only a dubious flag-signal which may mean either of two contradictories.

b. *to put to the blush*: to cause to blush, put to shame.

1649 Selden *Laws Eng.* I. iv. (1739) 10 They do it with that solemn reverence as may put all the Christian world to the blush. **1711** J. Distaff *Char. Don Sacheverellio* 7 It has put to the blush..the best Performances of an Apelles. **1858** Hawthorne *Fr. & It. Jrnls.* (1872) I. 11 Puts London to the blush, if a blush could be seen on its dingy face.

5. *transf.* A rosy colour or glow, as that of the dawn; in wider sense, a flush of light or of colour.

1590 Greene *Arcadia* (1616) 70 Pleusidippus..seeing Samela come foorth like the blush in the morning. **1618** Dekker *Owles Alman.*, And the Vintners latisses must haue a new blush. **1667** Milton *P.L.* XI. 184 Aire suddenly eclips'd, After short blush of Morn. *a* **1773** Lyttelton *Uncertainty* i. (R.) And light's last blushes ting'd the distant hills. **1850** Mrs. Jameson *Leg. Monast. Ord.* (1863) 313 The little cemetery..all one blush of roses.

B. *adj.* (or the *sb.* used *attrib.*) Of the colour of a blush.

1633 *Gerard's Herbal* II. lxviii. 357 A pale purple tending to a blush colour. **1665–76** Ray *Flora* 82 Flowers..white, a little inclining to blush. **1699** Wafer in *Phil. Trans.* LV. 51 Some tincture of a blush or sanguine complexion. **1882** *Garden* 1 Apr. 223/2 Blossoms of a delicate blush tint.

C. *Comb.*, as ***blush-pink***, ***-white***; ***blush-coloured***, ***-compelling***, ***-making***, ***-tinted*** adjs.; **blush-rose**, a variety of rose of a very delicate pink; also *attrib.* or as *adj.*

1626 Bacon *Sylva* §513 Blossomes Blush-Coloured. **1713** J. Petiver in *Phil. Trans.* XXVIII. 37 Beautiful Blush-coloured Flowers. **1924** *Spectator* 12 Apr. 604/1 Otherwise we should have been spared those blush-making passages. **1944** T. Rattigan *While Sun Shines* III. i, Some idiotic, blushmaking, sentimental slush. **1629** Parkinson *Parad.* cix. 420 The flowers are small single blush Roses, of little or no sent at all. **1707** Mortimer *Husb.* xviii. 478 The *Blush Rose*, that differs in nothing from the other [*sc.* White Rose], but in the Colour of the Flowers. **1811** W. Spencer *Poems* 71 Pillow'd on her blush-rose bed. **1888** W. D. Hay *Blood* xi. 47 Soft dimpling blush-rose cheeks. **1818** Keats *Endym.* I. 619 Blush-tinted cheeks, half smiles, and faintest sighs. **1882** *Garden* 18 Nov. 451/3 Large, broad-sepaled flowers, blush-white.

blusher ('blʌʃə(r)). [f. BLUSH *v.* + -ER[1].] **1.** One who blushes or exhibits a sense of shame; a thing which blushes, i.e. is red or roseate.

1665 Boyle *Occas. Refl.* v. vii. (1675) 320, I envy not Arabia's Odours, whil'st that of this fresh Blusher [a Nosegay] charms my sense. **1872** Darwin *Emotions* 315 A lady, who is a great blusher.

2. The popular name for the mushroom *Amanita rubescens.*

1887 W. D. Hay *Elem. Text-bk. Brit. Fungi* vii. 50 The Blusher is first-rate eating, perfectly wholesome, and makes a remarkably good ketchup. **1921** *Nature* 25 Aug. 822/2 Mr. Britten has watched them [*sc.* squirrels] feeding on the Blusher (*Amanita rubescens*). **1966** F. H. Brightman *Oxf. Bk. Flowerless Plants* 130/2 Amanita rubescens ('Blusher') is found commonly in all kinds of woodland.

3. A cosmetic used to give an artificial colour to the face.

1965 *Vogue* 1 Apr. 27 (Advt.), 'Ultima II' blushing creme. .. You can do no wrong with this 'transparesscent' blusher —it is so blendable, so edgeless, so *atmospheric* in texture. **1969** *Woman* 11 Jan. (Make-up Booklet) 8 Blushers and shaders are large-size block rouges in variety of shades to add colour and shape. **1969** *Guardian* 9 Sept. 7/2 The famous Roman Glow cream blusher..an unusual terracotta colour that is blended on chin and forehead as well as on cheekbones.

†**'blushet.** *Obs.* [f. BLUSH *sb.* + dim. -ET[1] (app. confined to B. Jonson).] Little blusher; modest girl.

1625 B. Jonson *Stapl. News* II. i, Though mistress Baud would speak, Or little blushet Wax be ne'er so easy. *a* **1637** —— *Wks.* (1692) 319 Go to, little Blushet, for this, anan, You steal forth a Laugh in the shade of your Fan.

blushful ('blʌʃfʊl), *a.* [f. BLUSH *sb.* + -FUL.]

1. Full of blushes, apt to blush, modest, bashful.

1611 Cotgr., *Vergongneux*..shamefull, shame-fac'd, bashfull, blushfull. **1794** Wolcott (P. Pindar) *Rowl. for Oliver* Wks. II. 154 Thou sly and blushful maid. **1871** M. Collins *Mrq. & Merch.* II. 130 Amy's shy, quiet, blushful face.

†**2.** Calling for a blush, shameful. *Obs.*

1656 TRAPP *Comm. Matt.* xvi. 11 Ignorance under means is a blushful sin.

3. *transf.* Blush-coloured, rosy, ruddy.

1804 WOLCOTT (P. Pindar) in *Beauties Eng. Poetry* I. 135 The berry..hides beneath a leaf its blushful hue. **1877** BLACKIE *Wise Men* 66 The blushful peach.

Hence **'blushfully** *adv.*, **'blushfulness.**

1873 M. COLLINS *Sqr. Silchester's* I. xii. 167 Silvia's bosom was blushfully buttoned. **1613** HEYWOOD *Braz. Age* II. ii. Wks. 1874 III. 185 Let me in your face Reade blushfullnesse and feare.

blushiness ('blʌʃɪnɪs). [f. BLUSHY + -NESS.] The quality of being given to blushing.

1865 S. PHILIP *New York,* The peculiar blushiness of pretty servants when they have a message to deliver to nice gentlemen.

blushing ('blʌʃɪŋ), *vbl. sb.* [f. BLUSH *v.* + -ING[1].] The action of the vb. BLUSH.

1581 R. GOADE in *Confer.* II. (1584) L iij b, Worthy of hissing, and of blusshing too. **1648** JENKYN *Blind Guide* i. 6 Even the sectaries read it with blushing. **1663** J. SPENCER *Prodigies* (1665) 146 As the blushings of the Evening. **1872** DARWIN *Emotions* xiii. 310 Blushing is the most peculiar, and the most human of all expressions.

'blushing, *ppl. a.* [f. as prec. + -ING[2].]

1. a. That blushes; modest. Also used, often somewhat facetiously, with *bride.*

1613 R. C. *Table Alph.* (ed. 3) *Bashfull,* blushing, or shamefast. **1764** GOLDSM. *Trav.* 408 The modest matron, and the blushing maid. **1803** JANE PORTER *Thaddeus* xlvii. 428 Her blushing eyes were shedding tears of delight. **1858** [see BRIDE *sb.*[1] 1]. **1955** D. LESSING *Proper Marriage* I. i. 25 Martha remarked irritably that Dr. Stern was something of an old woman, 'sitting all wrapped up behind his desk like a parcel in white tissue paper, being tactful to a blushing bride'.

b. *blushing bride*: the S. African proteaceous plant *Serruria florida*; also its flower.

1917 R. MARLOTH *Flora S. Afr.* 13 *Blushing bride. Serruria florida*..from one of the valleys of the upper Berg-river (Franschhoek). Flowering in winter. **1955** K. A. THOMPSON *Great House* vii. 213 The small, frail-looking pink protea called the Blushing Bride..was supposed to be extinct when he found it flowering in a tiny kloof in the Fransch Hoek Mountains.

2. Ruddy; roseate.

1593 SHAKS. *Rich. II,* III. iii. 63 The blushing discontented sun. **1648** HERRICK *Hesper., To Phillis,* The blushing apple, bashful pear. *a* **1721** PRIOR *Garland* (R.) The dappled pink and blushing rose. **1805** SOUTHEY *Madoc in W.* xiv, Antic trees Shone with their blushing blossoms.

3. Causing blushes, shameful. *Obs.*, exc. in *blushing honours*, in sense 'causing blushes', in imitation of Shakespeare.

1613 [see HONOUR *sb.* 6 b]. **1625** BACON *Ess. Friendsh.* (Arb.) 181 Things..Gracefull in a Frends Mouth, which are Blushing in a Mans Owne. **1806** M. EDGEWORTH *Leonora* II. xlii. 7 To be handed into her own coach with all the blushing honours of a bride. **1857** TROLLOPE *Three Clerks* I. xiii. 275 Alaric, with his blushing honours thick upon him, was left alone.

'blushingly, *adv.* [f. prec. + -LY[2].] With blushing; modestly; as if ashamed.

1598 FLORIO *Dict.* Ep. Ded. 3 Made me blushinglie confesse my ignorance. **1692** VILLIERS (Dk. Buckhm.) *Chances* Wks. (1714) 171, I must blushingly beg leave to say, etc. **1884** *Harper's Mag.* Nov. 914/2 Blushingly conscious of the admiring eyes that followed her.

blushless ('blʌʃlɪs), *a.* [f. BLUSH *sb.* + -LESS.] Without a blush, unblushing; impudent, shameless.

1566 PAINTER *Pal. Pleas.* I. 60 With blushles face and vnstaied penne. **1608** TOURNEUR *Rev. Trag.* III. v. 80 Some darken'd blushlesse Angle. **1635** QUARLES *Embl.* I. viii. (1718) 34 But bold-fac'd mortals in our blushless times Can sing and smile, and make a sport of crimes. *a* **1743** SAVAGE *Wks.* II. 123 (Jod.) Not blushless Henley less abash'd appears. **1886** BLACKIE *What does Hist. Teach* 31 Aristocratic Poland did this in a much more blushless way than democratic Greece.

Hence **'blushlessly** *adv.*

1604 MARSTON *Malcont.* I. i, Contested blushlessly he loved you but for a spurt or so.

blushy ('blʌʃɪ), *a.* [f. BLUSH *sb.* + -Y[1].]

a. Blush-coloured; **b.** Suffused with blushes.

1626 BACON *Sylva* §507 Blossomes..of Apples, Crabbs, Almonds, and Peaches, are Blushy, and Smell sweet. **1666** G. HARVEY *Consump.* (J.) A blushy colour in his face. **1742** A. ASTON *Brief Suppl. Colley Cibber* 9 Black sparkling eyes, and a fresh blushy complexion. **1865** S. PHILIP *New York* 140 She answered..with a very pleasant blushy smile.

blusne, var. of BLYSNE *v. Obs.* to shine.

bluster ('blʌstə(r)), *v.* Also 4–5 **blostre,** 4–6 **blustre,** 6 **blaster.** [It is very doubtful whether the obsolete ME. sense 1 has any connexion with the later word in the other senses. With the former Mätzner compares the LG. *blustern, blistern* 'to flutter or flap the wings in alarm like a frightened dove, etc.', which perhaps may be a parallel onomatopœia. The 16th c. word has evident relations both in form and sense with the verbs BLOW, BLAZE *v.*[2], and BLAST: cf. especially ON. *blástr* sb. 'blast, breath, blowing, hissing' with the form *blasterand* in G. Douglas (= BLUSTERING *ppl. a.*). Prof. Skeat also compares an East Frisian *blüstern* to bluster, from *blüssen* to blow, akin to *blasen*; and it is worthy of note that the Sc. pronunciation is (blystə(r)). But evidence is wanting as to the actual introduction of the word about 1500.]

I. The ME. verb.

†**1.** *intr.* To wander or stray (or ? to rush) blindly or aimlessly. *Obs.* Cf. BLUNDER *v.* 3.

c **1325** *E.E. Allit. P.* B. 886 þay blustered as blynde as bayard watz euer. **1377** LANGL. *P. Pl.* B. v. 521 Ac þere was wyȝte non so wys þe wey þider couthe, But blustreden [**1393** blostrede] forth as bestes ouer bankes and hilles.

II. The modern verb.

2. a. *intr.* Of the wind: To blow boisterously or with stormy violence. Also said of water agitated by wind or flood.

1530 PALSGR. 459/1 This wynde blustereth a pace. **1579** GOSSON *Apol. Sch. Abuse* (Arb.) 65 The wynde blustereth about the hilles yet can not remove them from their place. **1621–31** LAUD *Serm.* (1847) 207 If God provide not a fence for this light of justice against the winds of temptation that bluster about it. **1725** POPE *Odyss.* XII. 342 Loud winds arise, Lash the wild surge, and bluster in the skies. **1842** TENNYSON *Dream Fair Wom.* 38 When to land Bluster the winds and tides the self-same way. **1863** BARING-GOULD *Iceland* 118 The winter storms began to bluster up the glen.

b. *fig.* of the storm or tempest of the passions.

1549 COVERDALE *Erasm. Par. James* 25 Whan the storme of sorowes cometh blustreing in. **1645** BP. HALL *Content.* 109 The..passions which daily bluster within us.

c. *trans.* To blow about, disarray, dishevel. *rare.* †*to bluster down*: to blow down with violence (*obs.*).

16.. *Seasonable Serm.* 26 (T.) Doth the devil, by a tempestuous gust, bluster down the house? **1876** G. MEREDITH *Beauch. Career* II. iii. 42 A south-western autumnal gale..made threads of Cecilia's shorter locks.. blustering the curls that streamed..from the silken band.

†**3. a.** *intr.* Of persons: To blow, breathe hard.

1530 PALSGR. 459/1 He blustereth as thoughe he had laboured sore.

†**b.** Of a wind-instrument: To blow or blast boisterously. *Obs.*

a **1590** RANDOLPH in M'Crie *Life Knox* II. 41 Six hundred trumpets continually blustering in our ears.

4. *trans.* To utter with a blast, or with stormy violence and noise. Usually with *out* or *forth.*

a **1535** MORE *Wks.* 374 He bloweth and blustereth out at last his abhominable blasphemy. **1548** CRANMER *Catech.* 23 These more then deuylish swerers..do blowe & bluster oute of theyr vngodly mouthes such blasphemies. **1604** T. WRIGHT *Passions* IV. i. 110 Foolish mouths..bluster foorth follies. **1891** C. GRAVES *Field of Tares* 181 He blustered out another oath as he looked at her. **1913** W. OWEN *Let.* 2 Nov. (1967) 205 She blustered 'it was now too late to go out!' **1955** A. CLARKE *Later Poems* (1961) 48 A child of clay Had blustered it away.

5. a. *intr.* Of persons: To storm or rage boisterously; to talk with inflated violence; to utter loud empty menaces or protests, to hector, play the bully.

a **1494–1631** [see BLUSTERING *vbl. sb.*[1] 2]. **1633** T. ADAMS *Exp. 2 Peter* i. 18 There stalks pride, blustering through the streets. *a* **1688** VILLIERS (Dk. Buckhm.) *Milit. Couple* Wks. (1775) 128 Sir John..swore and bluster'd like a hero in one of our modern tragedies. *a* **1690** BP. HOPKINS *Wks.* 739 (R.) When they storm and bluster at the difficulties of salvation. **1773** JOHNSON *Lett.* 79 (1788) I. 136 Boswell blustered, but nothing could be got. **1835** MARRYAT *Jac. Faithf.* xxix, Monsieur Tagliabue stormed and blustered. **1866** FELTON *Anc. & Mod. Gr.* II. ix. 154 He [Cleon] could talk and bluster on the bema.

b. *trans.* To force, or drive, by blustering.

a **1661** FULLER (Webster), He meant to bluster all princes into a perfect obedience. **1753** RICHARDSON *Grandison* (1781) I. ii. 5 We have..blustered away between us half a score more of her admirers. **1867** E. YATES *Forl. Hope* xxviii, The one point on which he could neither satisfy himself by a feeling of pity, nor bluster himself into a fit of indignation.

bluster ('blʌstə(r)), *sb.* [f. prec. vb.]

1. Boisterous blowing; a rough and stormy blast.

1583 STANYHURST *Æneis* I. (Arb.) 21 Thee northen bluster aproching Thee sayls tears tag rag. **1611** SHAKS. *Wint. T.* III. iii. 4 The skies looke grimly, And threaten present blusters. **1667** MILTON *P.L.* x. 665 To the Winds they set Thir corners, when with bluster to confound Sea, Aire, and Shoar. **1748** RICHARDSON *Clarissa* (1811) II. 139 Could we but direct the bluster, and bid it roar when..we pleased.

†**b.** *fig.* Tempest of wrath, blast of envy, etc.

1607 SHAKS. *Timon* v. iv. 41 The bluster of thy wrath. **1665** MANLEY *Grotius' Low-C. Warres* Ep. Ded., Able to bear up against the Malevolent Blusters of Envy

c. *fig.* A noisy and stormy commotion; a violent disturbance.

1656 H. MORE *Antid. Ath.* (1712) Pref. 11 The laying or preventing the usual blusters of Christendom. **1773** CRADOCK in Goldsm. *Stoops to Conq.* Epil., In town I'll fix my station And try to make a bluster in the nation. **1876** BLACKMORE *Cripps* v. (1877) 26 The footman..ran in a bluster of rage and terror.

2. The boisterous blast of a wind instrument, or any similar sound.

1724 SWIFT *Prometh.* Wks. 1755 III. II. 151 The brazen trumpets' bluster. **1868** HAWTHORNE *Amer. Note-Bks.* (1879) II. 156 The locomotive..making a great bluster.

3. Boisterous inflated talk, violent or angry self-assertion, noisy and empty menace, swaggering.

a **1704** LESTRANGE (J.) A coward makes a great deal more bluster than a man of honour. **1728** MORGAN *Algiers* I. Pref. 1 In spite of all the Blusters of the..Ignorant. **1840** CARLYLE *Heroes* v. 301 Mirabeau has much more of bluster; a noisy, forward, unresting man. **1868** M. PATTISON *Academ. Org.* §1. 7 A great deal of foolish bluster was talked about interference with private property.

4. *Comb.*, as †**bluster-master,** a great blusterer.

a **1670** HACKET *Abp. Williams* II. (1692) 99 A book publish'd by a bluster-master..call'd, A Coal from the Altar.

bluster, obs. form of BLISTER.

bluste'ration. *dial.* and *colloq.* [f. BLUSTER *v.* + -ATION.] A blustering, bluster.

1803 R. ANDERSON *Cumbrld. Ballads* 73 He..talks o' stocks and Charley Fox, And makes a blusteration. **1864** WEBSTER says '*colloq.* U.S.'

†**'blustered,** *ppl. a. Obs.* (See the vb.)

a **1662** R. BAILLIE *Lett.* I. 125 (JAM.), I read to them out of my blustered papers that which I sent you of Arminianism.

blusterer ('blʌstərə(r)). [f. BLUSTER *v.* + -ER[1].] One who or that which blusters.

a. One who utters loud empty boasts or menaces; a loud or violent inflated talker, a braggart.

1597 SHAKS. *Lover's Compl.* 58 A reverend man.. Sometime a blusterer, that the ruffle knew of court, of city. **1624** GATAKER *Transubst.* 68 You see what substantiall proofes this great Blusterer hath brought. **1712** STEELE *Spect.* No. 484 ⁋5 We live in an age wherein a few empty blusterers carry away the praise of speaking. **1833** LAMB *Elia* (1860) 401 Milton has made him at once a blusterer, a giant, and a dastard. **1836** *Fraser's Mag.* XIII. 195 A mixture of the blusterer and the sneak.

b. A blustering wind.

1877 BRYANT *Among Trees* 18 When he, The exhausted Blusterer, flies beyond the hills?

'blustering, *vbl. sb.*[1] [f. as prec. + -ING[1].]

1. Boisterous blowing of the wind; tempest.

1530 PALSGR. 199/1 Blustryng of wyndes, *behovrdis.* **1577** tr. *Bullinger's Decades* (1592) 414 Then sodeinly came a whirlwind with a wonderfull storme and blustering.

2. *fig.* Of a person: Raging, storming; violent or turbulent speech; noisy and windy talk; loud swaggering insolence.

a **1494** HYLTON *Scala Perf.* (ed. W. de W.) II. xlv, The soule dredeth no more the blustrynge of the fende, than þe stirynge of a mows. **1562** COOPER *Answ. Def. Truth* (1850) Quietly and calmly, without storming or tempestuous blustering at you. **1628** EARLE *Microcosm.* lxiii. 135 His labour is meer blustering and fury. **1631** R. H. *Arraignm. Whole Creat.* xviii. 326 These tossings, tumblings, blusterings, bickerings..of the unruly passions. **1711** ADDISON *Spect.* No. 40 ⁋5 Their Swelling and Blustring upon the Stage. **1837** CARLYLE *Fr. Rev.* I. I. vi. v. 184 That thick murk of Journalism, with its dull blustering.

†**blustering,** *vbl. sb.*[2] *Obs.*

1400–1560 *Test. Love* I. (1560) 273 b, Truly in the blustering of her look she yave gladnesse and comfort suddainly to all my wits.

'blustering, *ppl. a.* [f. as prec. + -ING[2].]

1. Blowing boisterously; stormy, tempestuous.

1513 DOUGLAS *Æneis* I. iii. 15 Ane blusterand [ed. **1553** blasterand] bub, out fra the northt braying. **1579** SPENSER *Sheph. Cal.* Dec. 132 His blustring blast eche coste doth scoure. **1633** G. HERBERT *Temple* 90 While blustring windes destroy the wanton bowres. **1747** HERVEY *Medit. & Contempl.* (1818) 134 If the..flowers should presume to come abroad in the blustering months. **1878** BLACK *Green Past.* xviii. 143 These moist and blustering November days.

2. *fig.* Tempestuous, stormy; turbulent.

1587 BRYSKETT *Mourn. Muse Thestylis* 78 Whose blustring sighes at first their sorrow did declare. **1633** BP. HALL *Hard Texts* 503 The blustring and unsteady state of all these earthly Kingdoms. *a* **1656** —— *Rem. Wks.* (1660) 149 Gods Spirit leads not in a blustring and hurrying violence.

3. Violent in speech and demeanour; loud-talking, self-assertive, hectoring, boastful, swaggering.

1652 WHARTON *Rothmann's Chirom.* Ded. 2 The Blustring noise of an Empty Title. **1770** *Junius Lett.* xxxviii. 187 Such..were the blustering promises. **1884** *Sat. Rev.* 14 June 766/2 A turbulent and blustering diplomatist.

'blusteringly, *adv.* [f. prec. + -LY[2].] In a blustering manner.

1552 HULOET, Blowe vehementlye or blusteringelye. *a* **1714** M. HENRY *Wks.* (1835) I. 145 To do it blusteringly. **1835** *Fraser's Mag.* XII. 269 Silently, not blusteringly and boisterously, or with threats.

blusterous ('blʌstərəs). *a.* Also 6 **blusterus, bloustreous,** 7 **blustrous.** [f. BLUSTER *sb.* + -OUS.]

1. Boisterous, rough, stormy.

1548 UDALL, etc. *Erasm. Par. Luke* vi. 48 (R.) Agaynste any bloustreous storme or tempeste. **1608** SHAKS. *Per.* III. i. 28 Mild may be thy life! For a more blustrous birth had never babe. **1841** MARRYAT *Poacher* i, A blusterous windy night.

2. *fig.* Violent, truculent; given to blustering.

1663 BUTLER *Hud.* I. III. 880 Benigne, and not blustrous Against a vanquisht Foe. **1866** *Sat. Rev.* 21 Apr. 473 His rude and blusterous wrath. **1877** MOTLEY *Barneveld* II. xvii. 232 A certain blusterous gentleman.

Hence **'blusterously** *adv.*

1548 UDALL, etc. *Erasm. Par. Luke* xxiv. 37 If lyke perill had bloustreously come upon theim. **1576** NEWTON tr. *Lemnie's Complex.* (1633) 149 Northerne blasts (which sometime blusterously blow in the Summer season). **1905** G. R. GISSING *Will Warburton* xl. 273 'The counter; *my* counter!'..shouted Will blusterously.

blustery ('blʌstərɪ), *a.* Also blustry. [f. BLUSTER *sb.* + -Y[1].]

1. Boisterously blowing.

1774 P. V. FITHIAN *Jrnl.* (1900) 105 The day very blustry & cold. **1804** JAGO *Beauties Eng. Poetry* I. 120 The blustry tempest and the chilling snow. **1874** ALDRICH *Prud. Palfr.* xvii, It was a blustery, frosty morning.

2. *fig.* Stormy, noisily self-assertive, swaggering.

1739 G. OGLE *Gualth. & Gris.* L'Envoy l. 2468 Why, to his blustry Oath, such Def'rence paid? **1850** CARLYLE *Latt.-day P.* v. 41. **1858** —— *Fredk. Gt.* III. xii. I. 211 He seems to have been of a headlong, blustery, uncertain disposition. *Ibid.* XII. x. IV. 236 The once very haughty, blustery, and now much-humiliated man.

†**'bluter**, *a. Obs.* 'Dirty' (Halliwell).

c **1550** *Rob. Hood* (Ritson) I. iii. 171 That we two can be dung With any bluter base beggar, That has nought but a rung. [cf. **1724** RAMSAY *Tea-t. Misc.* (1733) I. 89 And there will be Tam the blutter With Andrew the Tinkler, I trow.]

bluther ('blʌðə(r)), *v. Sc.* and *north. dial.* Also blother, bludder. [An onomatopœic word, of similar formation to BLUBBER, with which it is often synonymous, though perhaps expressing more specifically the sound of air and liquid in the mouth, nose, and throat: cf. also BLETHER, and esp. its form *blother* in Skelton. Wedgwood compares, as of similar formation, LG. *plodern* to sound like water gushing, Bavarian *pludern* to guggle like water gushing out of a narrow opening (cf. MHG. *blôdern* to rush, rustle); also mod.Ger. *plaudern*, Bav. *blodern*, *plodern*, LG. *plûdern* to gabble, jabber, chatter. See also *bloother* as a variant of BLUBBER (of the whale).]

1. *intr.* 'To raise wind-bells in water', Jamieson. (Rather the bubbling sound made in doing so.)

2. *intr.* To cry with a voice smothered with tears and sobs; to blubber. *to bluther out* (trans.): to weep out.

1697 W. CLELAND *Poems* 35 (JAM.) Heraclitus, if he had seen, He would have bluther'd out his een.

3. *trans.* To make wet, mucous, and foul with weeping, etc.

1637 RUTHERFORD *Lett.* cv. (1862) I. 267 Christ..hath wiped a bluthered face which was foul with weeping. **1768** Ross *Helenore* 28 (JAM.) His een..bluddert now with strypes of tears and sweat. **1790** A. SHIRREF *Poems* 42 (JAM.) And drunken chapins bluther a' his face.

4. To blur and disfigure (writing, etc.) with wetting (Jamieson); also *fig.*

1727 P. WALKER *Remark. Passages* 57 (JAM.) That his faithful contendings for..reformation, should be blotted and bluthered with these right-hand extreams, and left-hand defections.

Hence **'bluthered** *ppl. a.* (see above), **'blutherment** *dial.* (in *Whitby Gloss.*).

†**'blutter**, *v. Obs.* [Of onomatopœic origin, with association of *blurt* and other *bl-* words; and perh. of *utter*, *mutter*, etc. Cf. also *blatter*, *splutter*, *sputter*.]

trans. To give hasty utterance to, to blurt out.

1680 BAXTER *Cath. Commun.* (1684) 12 If the Minister should blutter out any Errour or Undecency. **1705** HICKERINGILL *Priest-cr.* IV. (1721) 227 Let not thine Heart ..blutter any thing before God.

‖**blutwurst** ('bluːtvʊrst). orig. *U.S.* [G.] = BLOOD-*sausage*.

1856 *Spirit of Age* (Sacramento, Calif.) 27 Mar. 3/1 'What is the German diet?' 'Sourkrout, pretzels, plutworst, and lager beer.' **1911** *Cosmopolitan* Feb. 314/1 See that I have blutwurst, brattwurst, and mettwurst every day for breakfast. **1951** M. LOWRY *Let.* Feb. (1967) 233 Or is perhaps Daseinsaussage his translation of my *boudin*—a sort of cousin to blutwurst? **1969** *Coast to Coast 1967–8* 189 She bought leber-wurst and long thin met-wursts and big hunks of blut-wurst speckled with rice, delicious when they were fried.

blw-, see BLU-, BLOO-.

†**bly.** *Obs.* exc. *dial.* Also 7 blye. [Still common in eastern and S.E. dial.: perh. a variant of *blee*; though the phonetic relation is not clear.] 'Likeness, resemblance' (Halliw.), look, aspect, species, character.

1615 W. HULL *Mirr. Maiestie* 81 The indignities which the tumultuous Iewes wrought against our Lord were of this blye. **1847–78** in HALLIWELL (as *Eastern*). **1875** PARRISH *Sussex Dial.* 19, I see a bly of your father about you.

bly- in numerous words; see BLI-.

blykstar: see BLEYKSTER.

†**blym**, *v. Obs.* Also blyym. [prob. error for *blyyin* - *blyþin*: see BLITHE *v.*] To gladden.

c **1440** *Promp. Parv.* 40 Blym, or gladde, or make glad [*K.* blyym or glathyn in herte, **1499** blithen or gladen].

blymy, see BLIMEY *int.*

blype. *Sc.* [Of unknown etymology: cf. FLYPE.] A pellicle, shred.

1787 BURNS *Halloween* xxiii, 'Till skin in blypes cam haurlin' Aff's nieves that night.

†**blysne**, *v. Obs.* Also 4 blusne. [ME. *blysn-en*, an inceptive deriv. of verb-stem *blys-* to shine; see BLUSH.] *intr.* To shine, to gleam.

c **1325** *E.E. Allit. P.* A. 163 Blysnande whyt watz hyr bleaunt. *Ibid.* 1047 þurȝ hym blysned þe borȝ al bryȝt. *Ibid.* B. 1404 Brode baneres þer-bi blusnande of gold.

blyve, var. of BELIVE *adv.* and *v.*

BMX (biːɛm'ɛks). [Abbrev. of *b*icycle *moto-cross*.] Organized bicycle-racing on a dirt-track, esp. for youngsters. Also, a bicycle used for this or similar activities, esp. one which is robust and highly-manœuvrable. Freq. *attrib.*

1978 *Washington Post* 9 Nov. (Maryland Weekly Suppl.) 3/2 When police began chasing the teens off their makeshift race courses, a parents' group known as the Rockville BMX Association was organized to help teenagers find a site for a permanent race course. **1979** *Telegraph* (Brisbane) 25 Oct. 27/1 That infernal BMX—you know, that dragster-cross bicycle with the technicolor wheels. *Ibid.* 27/5 Barry was responsible for turning an unused council dump at The Gap into one of Brisbane's best BMX courses. **1981** *Sunday Mail Mag.* (Brisbane) 8 Feb. 3/1 In the two weeks before Christmas one Brisbane suburban bike shop delivered more than 200 BMX machines to its customers. **1983** *Sounds* 3 Dec. 6/3 Danny and the Mongoose Team promote the 'fastest growing youth sport in the country'—BMX bike racing—with a single called 'BMX Boys'. **1985** *Trade Marks Jrnl.* 15 May 1144/2 *Team BMX*...Registration of this Trade Mark shall give no right to the exclusive use of the letters 'BMX'...Pedal cycles adapted for bicycle motocross.

†**bo**, *a.* (*pron.*) *Obs.* Forms: *Nom.* and *Acc. masc.* 1 beȝen, 2–3 *Orm.* beȝȝen, 3 bæien, beien(e, beine, beie, beye, 4 baye, bayne, beyne; *fem.*, in ME. *common* and *neuter*, 1 bá, 2–3 ba, 3 boa, 3–4 bo, 5 boo; *neuter*, 1 bu; *Genitive.* 1 beȝ(r)a, 2 beira, 2–4 beire, 3 beyre, 4 beyer; *Dative.* 1 bám, bǽm, 3 ba. [OE. *beȝen*, *ba*, *bu*, answer to Goth. nom. masc. *bai*, neut. *ba*, acc. masc. *bans*, dat. *baim*, the stem being a Gothic *ba-*, OTeut. *bo-*, which occurs also with a prefixed element in Skr. *u-bha-*, Gr. ἀμ-φο-, L. *am-bo-*, OSlav. *o-bo-*, both. In the other Teutonic langs. (exc. for the ON. gen. pl. *beggja*) this simple form is replaced by one with a suffixal extension: see BOTH.] The earlier word for BOTH.

a. as simple adjective.

c **1000** *Sax. Leechd.* II. 258 Micel sar on bam sidum. *c* **1205** LAY. 9804, A ba [*c* **1275** boþe] halue. *c* **1275** *Ibid.* 22588 His sones beine. *a* **1250** *Owl & Night.* 990 þat ut berste bo þin(e) eȝe. *a* **1330** *Syr Degarré* 2 Maken him lesen hise stiropes bayne.

b. in concord or apposition with a pronoun.

c **1000** *Ags. Gosp.* Matt. xv. 14 Hiȝ feallað beȝen on ænne pytt. *c* **1175** *Lamb. Hom.* 103 Hi ba habbeð unafillendliche gredinesse. *c* **1200** ORMIN 15091 þatt Hallȝhe Frofre Gast þatt cumeþþ off hemm beȝȝenn. *c* **1205** LAY. 14811 Hali men heo weoren bæien [*c* **1275** beiene]. **1297** R. GLOUC. 284 Seyn Edward and Aeldred, þat kynges were beye. *a* **1300** *Floriz & Bl.* 730 Ȝe schulle deie togadere bo. *c* **1325** *Chron. Eng.* 348 in Ritson *Met. Rom.* II. 284 Hy were beyne yfond. *c* **1330** *Arth. & Merl.* 1529 Ther thai gun to rest baye. **1387** TREVISA *Higden* (1865) I. 419 There were Merlyns tweyne And prophecied alle beyne. **1450** MYRC 3 In to þe dyche þey fallen boo.

c. gen. pl. *oure*, *ȝure*, *here beyre*: of us, you, them both. Cf. *ure ealra*, *oure aller*, etc. in ALL D 4.

c **1175** *Lamb. Hom.* 99 þe feder, and his sune and heore beira gast. *a* **1250** *Owl & Night.* 1582 On thare beire nede. *c* **1300** *Beket* 2455 Bi here beire rede. **1393** LANGL. *P. Pl.* C. XXI. 36 And deme here beyer ryght.

d. *absol.*

a **1000** *Elene* 889 (Gr.) Gador bu samod lic and sawl. *c* **1205** LAY. 281 þæt boa sculde fallen: fader & his moder. *Ibid.* 17952 þu scalt beien [*c* **1275** beiene] slæ þer Passent and Gillomar. *a* **1225** *Ancr. R.* 60 Bo beoð heaued sunne. *c* **1230** *Hali Meid.* 7 Godes brude & his freo dohter, for ba to gederes ha is.

e. Frequently strengthened by the addition of *two*: OE. *bá twá*, *butu*, ME. *bo two*, of all genders. [Cf. It. *ambidue*.]

a **1000** *Cædmon's Gen.* 765 (Gr.) Sorgedon bá twá, Adam and Eue. *a* **1100** *O.E. Chron.* an. 871 (Laud MS.) Æðered and Ælfred his broðor..hi butu ȝeflymdon. *c* **1205** LAY. 2399 Mid childe heo weren ba twa [*c* **1275** boþe two]. *a* **1225** *Ancr. R.* 212 Heo sleateð adun boa two hore earen.

†**bo**, *conj. Obs.* In 1–3 ba. [The neuter or common form of prec. used with *and*. The transition to the conjunctional use is seen in BO *a.* d. quots. 1000 and 1205, and in 1225 here. See BOTH.] The earlier word for BOTH.

a **1225** *Ancr. R.* 22 Siggeð Pater Noster & Ave Maria, bo biuoren & efter. *a* **1225** *Leg. Kath.* 50 Poure ba & riche comen þer. *a* **1240** *Sawles Warde* in *Lamb. Hom.* 247 Ba wið eie ant wið luue. *c* **1300** in Wright *Lyric P.* xviii. 58 Thin werkes bueth bo suete ant gode.

bo, boh (bəʊ), *int.* Also 6–7 boe, 7 bough. [A combination of consonant and vowel especially fitted to produce a loud and startling sound: cf. L. *bo-āre*, Gr. βοά-ειν to cry aloud, roar, shout.] An exclamation intended to surprise or frighten.

c **1430** LYDG. *Smyth & Dame* 407 in Hazl. *E.P.P.* III. 216 Speake now...And say ones, bo. **1575** CHURCHYARD *Chippes* (1817) 153 Beyond the reach of common peoples boe. **1672** R. WILD *Poet. Licent.* 26 The Pope's Raw-head-and-bloody-bones cry Boh Behind the door! **1829** SCOTT *Demonol.* vi. 178 We start and are afraid when we hear one cry Boh! **1855** BROWNING *Holy-Cr. Day*, Boh, here's Barnabas!

b. Proverbial phr. *to say* or *cry 'bo' to a goose*, (also occas.) *a battledore*: to open one's mouth, speak.

1588 *Marprel. Ep.* (Arb.) 43 He is not able to say bo to a goose. **1621** BP. MOUNTAGU *Diatribæ* 118 The clergy of this time were..not able to say bo to a battledore. **1624** —— *Gagg* To Rdr. 8, I could say..not so much as bough to a goose. **1748** SMOLLETT *Rod. Rand.* liv, I could not say Bo to a goose. **1864** MISS YONGE *C'tess Kate* vii. 125 Dear me, Mary, can't you say bo to a goose! **1866** BLACKMORE *Cradock N.* xxx. (1883) 166 Bob could never say 'bo' to a gosling of the feminine gender.

†**bo**, *v. Obs. rare.* [? f. prec.] *intr.* To cry 'bo'; *hence*, to shout (*at*, *against*, *on*).

?*c* **1505** DUNBAR *Tua Mariit Wem.* 276 Weil couth I.. with a bukky in my cheik bo on him behind.

bo (bəʊ), *sb. slang.* Chiefly *U.S.* [Cf. HOBO and BOZO, but since it is recorded earlier *bo* is perh. more likely to have been orig. a shortening of *boy*.] A familiar form of address.

1825 W. N. GLASCOCK *Naval Sketch-Bk.* (1826) I. 148 Small helm bo—steady—ey-a. **1874** M. CLARKE *His Natural Life* I. v. 74 Half a gallon a day, bo', and no more. **1879** *Punch* 24 May 239/2 *Traveller*..'Which is the—quickest Way—for me to get to the Station?' *Street Arab.* 'Wh' run bo'!' **1893** *Chicago Record* 14 July 11/3 An' den w'en ye meets one uv yer own kind ye feels like old pals, 'cause he calls ye 'Ho' an' ye calls him 'Bo'. See? **1916** *Lincoln Even. News* 1 Jan. in *Dialect Notes* IV. 272 The swaggerest rag you can put on, bo, is one of the non-skid, full-dress shirt bosoms. **1919** *Judge* (ibid.), The man who tells the bootblack 'Keep the change, bo'.

boa ('bəʊə). Also 5 boua, 5–6 boas, 6 boath. Pl. boas (occas. in Lat. form boæ). [a. L. *boa* (Pliny *N.H.* VIII. xiv), of unknown origin: Pliny and St. Jerome derived it from *bos* an ox, for different reasons.]

1. *Zool.* A genus of serpents native to the tropical parts of S. America, distinguished for their large size and immense muscular strength. They are destitute of poison fangs, and kill their prey by constriction or compression. Popularly the name is extended to all the large serpents of similar habits, including the Pythons of the Old World.

1398 TREVISA *Barth. De P.R.* XVIII. ix. (1495) 759 Enidris that is a water adder..many men call it Boua, for the dyrte of an oxe is remedy therfore. *Ibid.* 761 Boas..hath that name Boas of Bos: an oxe..and settyth hymselfe gylefully to the vdders of the beestys that ben full of mylke and suckyth and sleeth them. **1623** COCKERAM III, *Boa*, a Serpent of that bignesse, that being found dead, there was a childe found whole in his belly. **1804** *Phil. Trans.* XCIV. 71, I was shown ..in the Hunterian Museum, two colubers, and three boæ. **1815** MOORE *Lalla R.*, *Veiled Proph.* III, Not the gaunt lion's hug, nor boa's clasp. **1836** *Penny Cycl.* V. 20/2 The Boæ have a spur on each side of the vent. **1860** GOSSE *Rom. Nat. Hist.* 123 The American species belonging to the genus *Boa*, and those of Africa and Asia to *Python*.

fig. **1822** W. IRVING *Braceb. Hall* (1849) 93 It was the lion of trees perishing in the embraces of a vegetable boa.

†**2.** *Her.* The representation of a serpent used as a device or portion of a 'charge'. *Obs.*

1572 BOSSEWELL *Armorie* II. 63 P. beareth, Gold, a Boath, Sable, betwene two barres Gemewes Azure. 'Boas' is a Snake in Italie, great of bodye.

3. A snake-like coil of fur worn by ladies as a wrapper for the throat.

1836 DICKENS *Sk. Boz* (1850) 225/1 Ladies' boas, from one shilling and a penny half-penny. **1837** HAWTHORNE *Twice-told T.* (1851) II. xii. 190 Red cheeks set off by quilted hoods, boas, and sable capes. **1870** YEATS *Nat. Hist. Comm.* 276 The tail is used in the manufacture of boas.

4. *Comb.*, as **boa-form** *a.*, of the shape of a boa.

1849 MRS. SOMERVILLE *Phys. Geog.* (1862) 459 Known species of serpents..Fresh-water 33, Boaform 15.

Hence **boa'd** *ppl. a.*, provided with, or wearing a lady's boa.

1831 *Blackw. Mag.* XXX. 967 Furred, muffed, and boa'd, Mrs. Gentle adventures abroad.

boa-constrictor ('bəʊə kən'strɪktə(r)). [f. BOA + L. *constrictor*, one who squeezes or draws together.]

1. The specific name of a large Brazilian serpent of the genus *Boa*, of which it was supposed by Linnæus to be the largest species; though this is not the case, the name (partly no doubt from its meaning) has taken hold of the popular fancy as that of the largest and most terrible of the serpents, and is commonly applied to any great crushing snake, whether a Boa or Python.

[**1788** LINNÆUS *Syst. Nat.* I. III. 1083 Boa, (β) constrictor, *rex serpentum*.] **1809** GEN. P. THOMPSON *Let. fr. Sierra Leone* 26 Jan., The Boa Constrictor is described by the Natives and our Colonists with evident marks of the magnifying power of fear. **1811** L. SIMOND *Tour & Resid. Gt. Brit.* (1817) II. 252 The boa Constrictor is a gigantic Snake. **1836** *Penny Cycl.* V. 27/1 The name of Anaconda, like that of Boa Constrictor, has been popularly applied to all the larger and more powerful snakes. **1872** BAKER *Nile Tribut.* x. 161 We came upon a fine boa-constrictor (python).

2. *fig.*

1826 DISRAELI *Viv. Grey* IV. i. 138 [His letters] are.. perfect epistolary Boa Constrictors.. I myself have suffered under their voluminous windings. **1848** H. ROGERS *Ess.* (1874) I. vi. 320 He feels himself within the coils of a great logical boa constrictor.

Hence **boa-con'strictorish**, **-con'strictorlike** *a.*

1835 CLOUGH *Poems & Prose Rem.* (1869) I. 58 All the physic which has lengthened the doctor's bill to a most boa-constrictor-like size. **1881** *Blackw. Mag.* July 123 Many a boa-constrictorish adventurer.. victualling himself for many days to come.

boad, obs. f. BODE *v.*, and pa. t. of BIDE.

boak, obs. and dial. f. BOLK, BOKE, BULK.

boal(e, obs. form of BOLE and BOWL.

boaling, variant of BOLING. *Obs.*

boan, boand, obs. ff. BONE, BONED.

1592 NASHE *P. Penilesse* (1842) 69 To dig a pit.. right in the way where this big boand gentleman should passe.

‖**Boanerges** (bəʊə'nɜːdʒiːz), *proper name*. Also 4 **Boenarges, Boonerges**, 6 **Bonarges.** [a. Gr. βοανεργές (*Mark* iii. 17), probably representing Heb. *b'nēy regesh* (or its Aramaic equivalent), explained as 'sons of thunder'.] The name given by Christ to the two sons of Zebedee. Hence, often as a sing. (pl. *-es, -esses*), a loud vociferous preacher or orator.

1382 WYCLIF *Mark* iii. 17 He putte to hem names Boonerges [**1388** Boenarges, COVERD. Bonarges, **1611** Boanerges]. *a* **1617** HIERON *Wks.* II. 465 The crying out of some Boanerges, some sonne of thunder. **1650** B. *Discolliminium* 26 So wise.. as to chuse no more *Boanerges*, but such as are right and true *Heliastæ*. **1667** H. MORE *Div. Dial.* v. v. (1713) 416 Thunderstruck by the powerful Boanergesses of the Gospel under the last Vial. **1680** —— *Apocal. Apoc.* **1869** R. S. HAWKER *Cornish Ballads* 28 Loud laughed the listening surges.. You might call them Boanerges From the thunder of their wave.

comb. **1881** MORLEY *Cobden* II. 371 The politicians who most disliked what one of them called Boanerges-Liberalism.

Hence **Boa'nergism**, †**Boa'nergy** [see -ISM, -Y³], loud oratory, vociferous denunciation.

1861 SALA in *Temple Bar* III. 25 He turned away from cant, and howling Boanergism. **1778** *Saints* 18 Boanergy on Mobs to make Impression.

boanthropy (bəʊ'ænθrəpɪ). [f. Gr. βοάνθρωπ-ος (f. βοῦς ox + ἄνθρωπος man) + -Y³; cf. *misanthropy*.] A form of madness in which a man believes himself to be an ox (see *Daniel* iv. 33).

1864 PUSEY *Lect. Daniel* vii. 427 The exact form of the disease, which would be Boanthropy, I have not found any notice of. **1866** *Athenæum* No. 2004. 393/2 The traditions of kunanthropy and boanthropy.

boar (bɔə(r)), *sb.* Forms: 1-3 **bár**, 3-7 **bor**, 4-7 **boor, boore, bore**, 5-7 **boare**, 7- **boar.** Also 3 *Lay.* **bær, ber**; *north.* 4 **bar**, 4-6 **bare**, 6 **baire, bayre.** [Known only in W.Ger.: OE. *bár* = OS. *bêr* (*-swîn*), MDu. and Du. *beer*; OHG., MHG. *bêr*, mod.G. *bär*, on OTeut. type **bairo-z*. Ulterior etymology unknown; cf. Russ. *borovŭ* boar.]

1. The male of the swine, whether wild or tame (but uncastrated).

c **1000** ÆLFRIC *Gram.* viii. 27 *Aper*, bar. *a* **1121** *O.E. Chron.* an. 1086 He forbead þa heortas swylce eac þa baras. *a* **1300** *Havelok* 1989 Was neuere bor þat so fauht so he fauht þanne. *c* **1325** *E.E. Allit. P.* B. 55 For my boles & my borez arn bayted & slayne. **1377** LANGL. *P. Pl.* B. xv. 294 Noyther bere, ne bor ne other best wilde. **1398** TREVISA *Barth. De P.R.* XVIII. lxxxvii. (1495) 836 The wylde male swyne ben callyd Boores. **1513** DOUGLAS *Æneis* XIII. iii. 21 As quhen that the fomy bayr hes bet With his thunderand awfull tuskis gret. **1523** FITZHERB. *Husb.* §121 Let them be bores and sowes all, and no hogges. **1607** SHAKS. *Timon* v. i. 168 Who like a Bore too sauage, doth root vp His Countries peace. **1697** DRYDEN *Virg. Georg.* III. 625 The bristled Rage Of Boars. **1820** W. IRVING *Sketch-Bk.* II. 114 The old ceremony of serving up the boar's head on Christmas day.

b. The flesh of the animal.

c **1460** J. RUSSELL *Bk. Nurture* 489 in *Babees Bk.* (1868) 147 Venesoun bake, of boor or othur venure. **1878** MORLEY *Diderot* II. 9 Savoury morsels of venison or boar.

c. *spec.* **wild boar**: usual name of the wild species (*Sus Scrofa*) found in the forests of Europe, Asia, and Africa.

c **1205** LAY. 16094 þat beoð a wilde bar [*c* **1275** bor]. *a* **1225** *Ancr. R.* 280 þe wilde bor ne mei nout buwen him. *c* **1400** *Destr. Troy* 6523 As wode as a wild bore. **1595** DUNCAN *Append. Etymol.* (E.D.S.) *Verres, porcus non castratus*, a baire; *aper*, a wilde baire. **1671** MILTON *Samson* 1138 Bristles.. that ridge the back Of chaf'd wild boars. **1863** LYELL *Antiq. Man* 23 The tame pig.. had replaced the wild boar as a common article of food.

d. *fig.* (or *heraldically*) applied to persons.

1297 R. GLOUC. 133 Cornewailes bor.. þat was Kyng Arthure. **1594** SHAKS. *Rich. III*, IV. v. 2 In the stye of the most deadly Bore, My Sonne George Stanley is frankt vp in hold. **1651** *Proc. in Parl.* No. 122 The Wild Boare of Antichristianity.

2. *Comb.*, as *boar-dog, -hound, -hunt, -hunting, -pig, -skin*; †**boar-cat**, a male cat, a tom-cat; **boar's-ears** (a corruption of *bear's ears*), a plant = AURICULA 3; **boar's-foot**, a plant, *Helleborus viridis* (cf. *bear's-foot*); †**boar-frank** (see quot.); **boar-seg** (*dial.*) = *boar-stag*; **boar-spear**, a spear used in boar-hunting; †**boar-staff** (= *boar-spear*); **boar-stag** (*dial.*), a castrated boar; **boar-thistle**, (?) a corruption of *bur thistle*, common name of *Carduus lanceolatus*, the Spear Thistle, also of *C. arvensis*.

1607 TOPSELL *Four-f. Beasts* 87 The males will kill the young ones, if they come at them like as the *Bore cats. **1797** BRYDGES *Homer Travestie* II. 293 Scratch and bite and tear and kick Like two *boar-cats hung 'cross a stick. **1792** OSBALDISTONE *Brit. Sportsm.* 431 All dogs whatsoever, even from the terrible *Boar-dog to the little Flora, are all one in the first creation. **1880** HARTING *Ext. Brit. Anim.* I. 96 In olden times the enclosure in which the Boars used to be fattened was termed a '*Boar-frank.' **1884** LADY BRASSEY in *Gd. Words* May 316/1 Close by her was an enormous *boarhound. **1843** MRS. H. GRAY *Tour Sepul. Etruria* iv. 193 There are friezes representing *boar-hunts. **1768** HAMILTON in *Phil. Trans.* LIX. 20 His Sicilian Majesty takes the diversion of *boar-hunting. **1597** SHAKS. *2 Hen. IV*, II. iv. 250 Thou whorson little tydie Bartholmew *Bore-pigge. **1747** *Scheme Equip. Men of War* 36 A strong, fat, well-grown *Boar Pig. **1686** *Lond. Gaz.* No. 2114/4 A large black *Boar Skin, lined with new Canvas. **1465** MARG. PASTON *Lett.* 503 II. 189 Imprimis, a peyr briggandyrs, a salet, a *boresper. **1600** HOLLAND *Livy* XXV. ix. 552k, Nicomenes thrust him through with his borespeare [*venabulo*]. **1816** SCOTT *Antiq.* xviii. 123 Snatching his boar-spear from the wall.. Martin Waldeck set forth. **1579** NORTH *Plutarch* 400 Perswading them to use the pyke and shielde, in steade of their litle target, speare, or *borestaffe. **1714** *Let.* in *Phil. Trans.* XXIX. 64 A Thistle call'd the *Boar-Thistle; very short and prickly.

†**boar**, *v.* *Obs.* [f. prec. sb.] Of swine: To copulate, to be in heat. *trans.* and *intr.*

1528 PAYNELL *Salerne Regim.* G ij, Hogges.. that hath nat boorred a sowe. **1607** TOPSELL *Four-f. Beasts* 523 In years that will prove moist, they will ever be boring. *Ibid.* 519 We in English call it 'Boaring'.

boar, obs. f. BORE, BOOR.

board (bɔəd), *sb.* Forms: 1-7 **bord**, (4-6 **borde**), 4-7 **boord**, (5-6 **boorde, bourde**, 6-7 **bourd**, 6 **boarde**), 6- **board**; *north.* 4-8 **burd**, 4-7 **burde**, 4 *Sc.* **buird**, 6- *Sc.* **brod**: cf. BRED. [A word or agglomeration of words of complicated history, representing two originally distinct sbs., already blended in OE., and subsequently reinforced in ME. by French uses of one of them, and possibly by Scandinavian uses of one or both. (1) OE. had *bord*¹ neut. 'board, plank, shield, ? table', a Common Teut. str. neut. sb., = OFris. and OS. *bord* (MDu. *bort, -de*, Du. *boord* 'board', *bord* 'shelf, plate, trencher'), MHG. and mod.G. *bort* 'board', Goth. *baurd* in *fotubaurd* 'foot-stool', ON. *borð* 'board, plank, table, maintenance at table' (Sw. and Da. *bord* table):—OTeut. **bord-o(m*, repr. an Aryan **bhṛdhom*, Skr. **bṛdham*: see BRED *sb.* (2) OE. had *bord*² 'border, rim, side, ship's side', esp. in phrases *innan, utan bordes*, also a Common Teut. sb., orig. str. masc. but often also (by confusion with *bord*¹) neuter: cf. OS. *bord* masc. (? neut.), MDu. *bort, boort -de*, Du. *boord* masc., 'border, edge, ship's side', OHG., MHG. *bort* masc., mod.G. *bord* masc. (and neut.) 'margin, border, ship-board', ON. *borð* neut. 'margin, shore, ship-board' (Sw., Da. *bord* 'ship-board'):—OTeut. **bord-oz* side, border, rim. (3) Relationship between these two words is uncertain: Franck suggests that *bord*² is a ppl. form from vbl. root *ber-* to raise, representing an Aryan **bhṛtós* 'raised, made projecting'. But the two were associated and confused at an early date: in most of the Teutonic langs., some of the senses of the masc. word, in ON. and perh. in OE. all of them, have gone over to the neuter. It is certain that the sense 'side or board of a ship' belongs to *bord*²; so prob. did that of 'shield', the original sense being 'rim, limb, or border of the shield'; the sense 'table' is doubtful. (4) The WGer. *bord*² masc. 'border, edge, coast, side, ship's side' was adopted in Romanic, giving med.L. *bordus*, It., Sp., Pg. *bordo*, F. *bord*. In the ME. period, and subsequently, the French use of the word has in return greatly influenced the Eng., so that certain modern uses and phrases of *board* are really from French. It is also possible that the development in ME. was in some points (see branch II.) due to Scandinavian uses.]

I. A board of wood or other substance. [OE. *bord*¹:—OTeut. *bordo(m*.]

1. a. A piece of timber sawn thin, and having considerable extent of surface; usually a rectangular piece of much greater length than breadth; a thin plank. Rarely used without the article, as in *made of board*, i.e. of thin wood.

Technically, *board* is distinguished from *plank* by its thinness: it ought to be more than 4 inches in width, and not more than 2½ in thickness, but is generally much thinner.

c **1000** ÆLFRIC *Gen.* vi. 14 Wirc ðe nu ænne arc of aheawenum bordum. *c* **1300** *K. Alis.* 6415 Al so hit weore an oken bord. **1375** BARBOUR *Bruce* IV. 126 Fyre all cleir Soyn throu the thik burd can appeir. **1393** LANGL. *P. Pl.* C. XII. 239 He shop þe ship of shides and of bordes. *c* **1440** *York Myst.* viii. 97 To hewe þis burde I wyll begynne. **1535** COVERDALE *Zeph.* ii. 14 Bordes of Cedre. **1596** SHAKS. *Merch. V.* I. iii. 32 Ships are but boords. **1611** BIBLE *Acts* xxvii. 44 Some on boords, and some on broken pieces of the ship. **1661** S. PARTRIDGE *Double Scale Proport.* 36 A plain Superficies, as a Board or Plank. **1716-8** LADY M. W. MONTAGUE *Lett.* I. xxxviii. 149 Covered.. with boards to keep out the rain. **1798** SOUTHEY *Ballads, Cross Roads* 25 They carried her upon a board In the clothes in which she died. **1826** J. WILSON *Noct. Ambr.* Wks. 1855 I. 122 The cheeks never muve, nae mair than gin they were brods. **1881** *Mechanic* 50. §146 Floor boards are, or ought to be, an inch in thickness. Boards are generally distinguished as 'half-inch board', 'three-quarter board', etc.

b. A flat slab of wood fitted for various purposes, indicated either contextually, or by some word prefixed, as *ironing-board, knife-board*, etc., the *backing, burnishing, cutting, gilding boards*, used by bookbinders, etc., the *bare boards* (of a floor). Also *spec.* = *surf-board*, esp. in *attrib.* uses. So BACK-BOARD, etc.

1552 HULOET, Bourde or shelf whervpon pottes are sette. **1779** J. KING *Jrnl.* Mar. in *Cook's Voy.* (1785) III. v. vii. 145 Twenty or thirty of the natives [of the Sandwich Islands], taking each a long narrow board, rounded at the ends, set out together from the shore. *Ibid.* 146 As soon as they have gained.. the smooth water beyond the surf, they lay themselves at length on their board, and.. place themselves on the summit of the largest surge, by which they are driven along with amazing rapidity toward the shore. *a* **1837** GR. KENNEDY *Anna Ross* 144 Lying on a board to keep her figure straight. **1845** ELIZA ACTON *Mod. Cookery* xvi. (1852) 336 Dust a little flour over the board and paste-roller. **1864** TENNYSON *Grandmoth.* 79 Pattering over the boards, she comes and goes at her will. **1866** HOLME LEE *Silver Age* 128 Laces fresh from the ironing-board. **1898** [see *surf-riding*, SURF *sb.* 3]. **1962** *Austral. Women's Weekly* Suppl. 24 Oct. 3/1 Special sections of most beaches are now reserved for board-riders. **1963** *Observer* 13 Oct. 15/6, I hate to think of the next kid that gets stoked on board riding.. and wins a world championship and nobody even knows him. **1966** *Weekly News* (N.Z.) 19 Jan. 10/4 Lyall Bay.. has a regular and well-shaped wave suitable for both swimmer and board rider.

c. *spec.* in *pl.* The stage of a theatre; hence in various phrases. Cf. STAGE and TREAD *v.* 1 b.

1768 A. MURPHY *Let.* 14 Mar. in *Private Corr. Garrick* (1831) I. 291 Mrs. Yates would have died on the boards sooner than have served me in that manner. *a* **1779** GARRICK in Boswell *Johnson* (1848) 490/1 The most vulgar ruffian that ever went upon boards. **1815** *Scribbleomania* 120 To gain a footing upon the theatrical boards. **1838** DICKENS *Mem. Grimaldi* i, He was brought out by his father on the boards of Old Drury. **1883** *Fortn. Rev.* 470 One of the most honest actors that ever trod the boards. **1948** W. S. MAUGHAM *Catalina* xxxii. 220 Nor must you think that you demean yourself by treading the boards.

2. a. A tablet or extended surface of wood, whether formed of a single wide board, or of several united at the edges.

Used *e.g.* for educational purposes (*black board*), for stretching paper on in drawing, for moulding, for modelling, for kneading or making pastry on (*bake-board, paste-board*), for arithmetical calculations (see ABACUS), for reflecting or reinforcing sound (*sounding-board*), for standing on (*foot-board*), for springing or diving from (*spring-board, diving-board*), for temporarily closing an aperture, chimney-place, window, etc., etc. Also extended to tablets of other material, *e.g.* papier-maché, similarly used.

b. *esp.* (= *notice-board.*) A tablet upon which public notices and intimations are written, or to which they are affixed.

to keep one's name on the boards: to remain a member of a college (at Cambridge).

c **1340** *Cursor M.* 16684 Abovyn his hed.. a borde was made fast There-on was the tytle wretyn. *c* **1400** *Ywaine & Gaw.* 186 A burde hung us biforn.. nowther of yren, ne of tre. **1566** KNOX *Hist. Ref.* Wks. 1846 I. 227 Compelled to kyss a paynted brod (which thei called 'Nostre Dame'). **1626** BACON *Sylva* §145 The strings of a Lute.. do give a far greater Sound, by reason of the Knot and Board, and Concave underneath. **1692** WASHINGTON tr. *Milton's Def. Pop.* vii. Wks. (1851) 179 Go on, why do you take away the Board [*abacum*]? Do you not understand Progression in Arithmetick? **1847** TENNYSON *Princ.* II. 60 Which [statutes] hastily subscribed, We enter'd on the boards. **1870** F. WILSON *Ch. Lindisf.* 100 On a board amidst the firs.. is a second notification. **1883** *Daily Tel.* 15 May 2/7 This hit [at cricket] caused three figures to appear on the board. **1885** *Free Ch. Coll. Calendar* 21 The matriculation takes place in the Senate Hall at times indicated on the Board at the gate.

c. *spec.* The tablet or frame on which some games are played, as *chess-board, draught-board, bagatelle-board, backgammon-board*; the frame used for scoring at cribbage. Also, the target in the game of darts. Often *fig.*

1474 CAXTON *Chesse* 6 The maner of the table, of the chesse borde. **1647** WARD *Simp. Cobler* 67 They will play away King, Queene.. Pawnes, and all, before they will turn up the board. *a* **1674** CLARENDON *Hist. Reb.* (1704) III. xv. 497 There is scarce any thing but pawns left upon the board. **1824** MISS MITFORD *Village* Ser. I. (1863) 217, I cannot help suspecting that, board for board, we cribbage-players are as well amused as they [chess-players]. **1880** DISRAELI *Endym.* viii. 35 The Tories.. were swept off the board. **1936** R. CROFT-COOKE *Darts* ii. 10 However boards may vary in size, in the arrangement of double spaces, the numbers are always placed in the same order. **1940** N. MARSH *Death at Bar* ii. 28

Cubitt hurled his last dart at the board. *Ibid.* 31 If you'll stretch your hand out flat on the board I'll outline it with darts. **1969** *Punch* 25 Nov. 808/2, I am the man who gets a double 20 with his opening dart, then never again even reaches the board.

d. *Austral.* and *N.Z.* (See quots. 1890 and 1941.)

[**1857** R. B. Paul *Lett. fr. Canterbury* vi. 90 A tarpaulin or a few boards to shear on.] **1878** 'R. Boldrewood' *Ups & Downs* vii. 74 Next year I hope we shall have fifty thousand to shear, and.. I don't see why there shouldn't be a hundred thousand on the board before you sell out. **1890** *Chambers's Jrnl.* 17 May 310/2 Down each side [of the Australian woolshed] is a clear space some ten feet in width, technically known as 'the board'. Here the shearers work. **1925** R. Rees *Lake of Enchantment* viii. 113 The shed hands with brooms [swept] the 'board' clear. **1941** Baker *Dict. Austral. Slang* 11 *Board*, the floor of a shearing shed; the whole number of shearers employed in a single shearing shed. **1956** G. Bowen *Wool Away!* (ed. 2) vii. 96 If a 'sheepo' wants to stay popular with the board of shearers he will be fair at all times.

e. ***across the board***: see ACROSS B. 2 c.

3. a. A kind of thick stiff paper; a substance formed by pasting or squeezing layers of paper together; usually in combinations, as *pasteboard*, *cardboard*, *mill-board*, *Bristol board*, *perforated board*.

1660 *Act 12 Chas. II*, iv. Sched., Boards vocat. Pastboards for bookes.

b. In *pl.*, playing-cards. *slang.*

1923 S. T. Felstead *Underworld of London* i. 11 The.. steward [at the Cardsharpers' Club] is a well-known criminal famous for his skill with the 'boards'. **1927** E. Wallace *Mixer* i. 7 The greatest and most amazingly clever card-sharp that ever handled the 'boards'.

4. *Bookbinding.* Rectangular pieces of strong pasteboard used for the covers of books. A book ***in boards*** has these only covered with paper; if they are covered with cloth it is ***in cloth boards***; if with leather, parchment, or the like, the book is *bound*. Formerly (still occas.) the boards were of thin wood, as 'an ancient tome in oaken boards'.

1533 More *Apol.* iv. Wks. 850/2, I wil be bounden to eate it, though the booke be bounden in boardes. **1533–4** *Act 25 Hen. VIII*, xv. §1 Printed bookes..bounde in bourdes, some in lether, and some in parchement. **1549** *Bk. Com. Prayer* (Colophon), [To] sell this present booke.. bounde in paste or in boordes. **1790** Scott in *Lockhart* (1839) I. 233 The bookseller..had not one in boards. **1832** *Athenæum* No. 241. 375 Published in a neat pocket volume, cloth boards. **1852** *Househ. Wds.* VI. 290 A little drab volume in boards. **1883** *Fortn. Rev.* Apr. 495 In the case of really good books, 'boards' should always be regarded as temporary inadequate coverings.

II. A table. [A doubtful sense of OE. *bord*; but common already in 12th c. Cf. ON. *borð*, used also as in sense 7, Sw., Da. *bord*.]

†**5. a.** *gen.* A table. *Obs.* (exc. in specific senses.)

a **1000** *Ags. Ps.* (Spelm.) lxviii[ix]. 23 (Bosw.) Geweorþe bord oððe mese [*mensa*] heora beforan him. *a* **1300** *Cursor M.* 14733 [Iesus] þair bordes ouerkest, þair penis spilt. *c* **1400** *Apol. Loll.* 57 þe auteris of Crist are maad þe bordis of chaungis. *c* **1400** *Destr. Troy* 1657 There were bordis full bright.. of Sedur tre fyn. *c* **1470** Henry *Wallace* II. 279 Sche gart graith up a burd.. With carpetts cled. **1771** P. Parsons *Newmarket* II. 24 That board of green cloth, the billiard-table.

(With the following cf. also sense 2 c.)

b. ***above board***: open, openly, in the sight of all the company; see ABOVE-BOARD. Similarly †***under board***: secretly, deceptively (*obs.*).

1603 Sir C. Heydon *Jud. Astrol.* ii. 67 After the fashion of iugglers, to occupie the minde of the spectatour, while in the meane time he plaies vnder board. **1620** R. Carpenter *Conscionable Chr.* (1623) 118 All his dealings are square and above the boord. **1686** W. de Britaine *Hum. Prud.* xvi. 74 Keep formality above board, but Prudence and Wisdom under Deck. **1841** L. Hunt *Seer* II. (1864) 61 All.. was open and above-board.

c. ***to sweep the board*** (at cards): to take all the cards, to pocket all the stakes. Also often *transf.* and *fig.*, to carry off all the stakes or prizes; hence, to carry off all the honours.

1680 Cotton in Singer *Hist. Cards* (1816) 346 He who hath five cards of a suit..sweeps the board. **1711** Pope *Rape Lock* III. 50 Spadillio first.. Led off two captive trumps, and swept the board. **1822** Scott *Nigel* xxi, 'Tis the sitting gamester sweeps the board. **1882** H. Smart in *Li-quor Christmas Ann.* II. 7/1 We have swept the board so far [in racing]. **1884** *Livestock Jrnl.* 25 July 83/3 Mr. Parry Thomas swept the board in Any Variety Sheep-dogs with his Sir Guy and Welsh Boy. **1905** Hornung *Thief in Night* 256 The bloated Guillemard usually sweeps the board with his fancy flyers [*sc.* horses].

6. *spec.* **a.** A table used for meals; now, always, a table spread for a repast. Chiefly *poetical*, exc. in certain phrases, esp. in association with *bed* to denote domestic relations; see BED 1 c. †***God's board***: an old name of the Lord's table, or Communion table in a church. †***to begin the board***: to take precedence at table.

a **1200** *Moral Ode* 307 in *Lamb. Hom.* 179 Be-fore godes borde. *c* **1200** *Trin. Coll. Hom.* 93 Mi bord is maked. Cumeð to borde. *a* **1225** *Ancr. R.* 324 Hwon gredie hundes stondeð biuoren þe borde. **1340** *Ayenb.* 235 Hi serueþ at godes borde. *c* **1386** Chaucer *Prol.* 52 Fful ofte tyme he hadde the bord bigonne. *c* **1440** *Gesta Rom.* (1879) 259 Afor mete, whenne the bordes er sette and made redye. *c* **1450** *Sir Beues* (1887) 1957 Palmer, thou semest best to me.. Begyn the borde, I the pray. **1484** *Ripon Ch. Acts* (Surtees Soc.) 162 Here I take the, Margaret, to my hanfest wif, to hold and to have, at bed and at burd. **1526** *Pilgr. Perf.* (W. de W. 1531) 10 With humble & reuerent loue go to the borde of god. **1553** *Primer* in *Liturgies Edw. VI.* (1844) 375 Pray we to God the Almighty Lord.. To send his blessing on this board. **1561** Hollybush *Hom. Apoth.* 27 a, And when thou wilt ryse from the borde or supper. **1606** Holland *Sueton.* 38 Inviting a friend to his bourd. **1636** Featly *Clavis Myst.* 340 To present ourselves at the Lord's board. **1815** Scott *Ld. of Isles* II. xvii, Gleaming o'er the social board. **1862** Trollope *Orley F.* viii. (ed. 4) 56 He looked at the banquet which was spread upon his board. **1869** Freeman *Norm. Conq.* (1876) III. xi. 12 The wife whom he had once driven away from his hearth and board.

b. ? A wooden tray. (Cf. sense 2.)

?*c* **1475** *Sqr. lowe Degre* 464 There he them warned.. To take up the bordes everychone.. Full lowe he set hym on his kne, And voyded his borde full gentely.

7. *transf.* **a.** Food served at the table; daily meals provided in a lodging or boarding-house according to stipulation; the supply of daily provisions; entertainment. Often joined with *bed* or *lodging*.

[Cf. ON. *vera á borði með* to be at board with.]

c **1386** Chaucer *Chan. Yem. Prol. & T.* 464 Sche wolde suffre him no thing for to pay For bord ne clothing. **1465** Marg. Paston *Lett.* 505 II. 193 He payth for hys borde wykely xx*d.* **1466** *Mann. & Househ. Exp.* 211 For v. mennes bord.. ij*s.* x*d.* **1575** *Brieff Disc. Troub. Franckford* (1846) 145 In a great deale off dett.. for their necessary bourde. **1636–46** Row *Hist. Kirk* (1842) Pref. 26 Till I suld see how his burd suld be payit. **1856** Olmsted *Slave States* 47 Let them find their own board.

b. The condition of boarding at another's house.

a **1658** Cleveland *Gen. Poems* (1677) 29 Or break up House, like an expensive Lord, That gives his Purse a Sob, and lives at Board. **1632** Field & Mass. *Fatal Dow.* IV. i, Young ladies appear as if they came from board last week out of the country.

8. a. A table at which a council is held; *hence*, a meeting of such a council round the table.

1575–6 *Lansdowne MS.* 21 in Thynne *Animadv.* (1865) Introd. 53 Called before the highe boorde of thee counsell. *a* **1674** Clarendon (L.) Better acquainted with affairs than any other who sat then at that board. **1702** *Lond. Gaz.* No. 3840/1 One of the Clerks of Her Majesty's Board of Green-Cloth. **1828** Scott *F.M. Perth* II. 5 Taking a place at the council board. **1848** Macaulay *Hist. Eng.* I. 443 The new King..took his place at the head of the board. *Ibid.* II. 75 His gloomy looks showed how little he was pleased with what had passed at the board.

b. Hence: The company of persons who meet at a council-table; the recognized word for a body of persons officially constituted for the transaction or superintendence of some particular business, indicated by the full title, as ***Board of Control***, ***B. of Trade***, ***B. of Commissioners***, ***B. of Directors***, ***B. of Guardians***, ***Local (Government) Board***, ***Sanitary Board***, ***School Board***.

1613 Shaks. *Hen. VIII*, I. i. 79 The Honourable Boord of Councell. **1635** Naunton *Fragm. Reg.* in *Phœnix* (1707) I. 190 In the ordinary course of the Board. **1712** Steele *Spect.* No. 478 ¶14, I would propose that there be a board of directors. **1780** Burke *Sp. Econ. Reform* Wks. 1842 I. 249 We want no instructions from boards of trade, or from any other board. **1796** (*title*) Report of the Board of Health, at the first annual Meeting, May 27. **1804** Hansard's *Parl. Deb.* I. 1168 By command of the Master General and Board of Ordnance. **1838** Dickens *O. Twist* ii, 'Bow to the board,' said Bumble. Oliver..seeing no board but the table, fortunately bowed to that. **1848** Macaulay *Hist. Eng.* II. 195 The treasurer had been succeeded by a board, of which a Papist was the head. **1863** H. Cox *Instit.* III. ix. 732 It is carried into execution by local Boards.

c. *U.S.* (*a*) The stock exchange; also *attrib.*; ***big board*** (colloq.), *spec.* the New York Stock Exchange or a quotation board for securities listed there; (*b*) (See quot. 1909.)

1837 *Hennepin* (Illinois) *Jrnl.* 26 Oct. 1/4 The sales of specie to-day, at the Board, were $1,700 in American gold. **1905** *Daily Chron.* 28 Apr. 4/4 None of the 'board members'—as the Stock Exchange men are called—ever appears on the kerb... While fortunes are made and lost on the kerb, it does not seem so serious a business as 'on the board'. **1909** *Ibid.* 3 May 4/6 A 'board' appears to be a 'committee' in the United States, while their word committee is applied to what we should call a board. **1929** *Times* 30 Oct. 14/1 Just before the close of the market on the 'big board'. **1969** *Daily Tel.* 6 Feb. 3/6 The New York Stock Exchange, known as the 'big board', does about twice the amount of business, but is less speculative than the American Stock Exchange.

9. Any piece of furniture resembling a table; with various defining words, as *dressing board* a dresser, *sideboard* a side table; also, the platform on which tailors sit while sewing, etc.

1400 *Test. Ebor.* (1836) I. 260 Unum platyngborde.. vj. brade bordes beste in domo. **1601** F. Tate *Househ. Ord. Edw. II.* (1876) 68 Every messe that commeth from the dressing bourd. **1807** Crabbe *Par. Reg.* II. 162 By trade a tailor.. again he'd mount the board.

III. A shield. [OE. *bord²*: if orig. 'border' or 'rim'.]

†**10.** A shield. *Obs.*

a **1000** *Elene* 114 (Gr.) þær wæs borda ȝebrec. *c* **1205** Lay. 9283 His gold ileired bord. *c* **1400** *Destr. Troy* 5827 He hit hym so hetturly.. on the shild, þat he breke þurgh the burd. **1535** Stewart *Cron. Scot.* III. 457 Content he wes.. On fit to fecht withoutin ony hors, Doublet alane, withoutin ony bourd.

IV. A border, side, coast. [OE. *bord²*; lost in ME. and replaced by F. *bord*.]

11. The border or side of anything; a hem; an edge; a coast. *Obs.* exc. in *seaboard*, sea-coast.

c **897** K. Ælfred *Gregory's Past.* Pref. 2 (Sw.) Hu hi.. sibbe innan bordes ȝehioldon.. and hu mon utan bordes.. lare hider on lond sohte. *c* **1340** *Gaw. & Gr. Knt.* 159 Spures vnder, Of bryȝt golde vpon silk bordes. *c* **1420** *Pallad. on Husb.* IV. 149 In other place a borde of hem [plants] let make. **1513** Douglas *Æneis* XI. ii. 36 Twa robbis.. Of rich purpour and styf burd of gold. **1535** Stewart *Cron. Scot.* I. 369 Out of Denmark be se burd mony myle. **1600** Dymmok *Ireland* (1843) 34 The approaches..should be..carryed to the board of the counterscarp. **1874** Mahaffy *Soc. Life Greece* viii. 243 To venture down from the hill forts to the sea board.

V. A ship's side. [OE. *bord²*: reinforced by OF. *bord*, and perh. by ON. *borð*, Da. *bord*.]

12. *Naut.* **a.** The side of a ship. (See ABOARD.) Now only in phrases, as ***within board***, ***without board***; ***over (the) board***, over the ship's side, out of the ship, into the sea; ***weather-board*** (see quot.). (See also the following, and cf. LARBOARD, STARBOARD, etc.)

a **1000** *Cædmon's Gen.* 1354 (Gr.) Ða be-utan beoþ earce bordum. *c* **1205** Lay. 1518 Ne cume ȝe neauer wiðuten scipes bord. *c* **1325** *E.E. Allit. P.* C. 211 Berez me [Jonah] to þe borde & baþeþes me þer-oute. ?*a* **1400** *Morte Arth.* 1699 Broghte us..to Bretayne..with-in [s]chippe-burdez. *c* **1420** *Chron. Vilod.* 867 Fast by þe shippus bord. *c* **1430** *Syr Gener.* 364 Shuld cast hem ouer the ship bord. **1470–85** Malory *Arthur* (1816) II. 328 They came within board. **1513** Douglas *Æneis* III. x. 21 And within burd hes brocht That faithfull Greik. *c* **1532** Ld. Berners *Huon* 478 Huon.. stode lenynge ouer the shyppe bord beholding the see. **1630** Wadsworth *Sp. Pilgr.* v. 38 They..brought vs from the Prow to the board of the Gally to helpe them in rowing. **1650** T. Froysell *Gale of Opport.* (1652) 31 The Marriners they cast him over Ship-board. **1829** Marryat *F. Mildmay* x, I ..kept..my anger within board. *c* **1850** *Rudim. Navig.* (Weale) 160 *Without-board*, without the ship. *Within-board*, within the ship. **1867** Smyth *Sailor's Word-bk.*, *Weather-board*, that side of the ship which is to windward.

b. ***by the board***: (down) by the ship's side, overboard, as ***to slip by the board***: 'to slip down a ship's side' (Smyth *Sailor's Word-bk.*). ***to come, go,*** etc. ***by the board***: to fall overboard, to go for good and all, to be 'carried away'. ***to try by the board***: to try boarding. Also *fig.*

1630 J. Taylor (Water P.) *Wks.* III. 40/1 In this fight their Reare-Admirals Maine Mast was shot by the boord. **1666** *Lond. Gaz.* No. 60/3 Our Main-stay, and our Main Top-Mast..came all by the board. **1666** Pepys *Diary* 11 Feb., The storms..have driven back three or four of them with their masts by the board. **1705** *Lond. Gaz.* No. 4098/3 All her Masts came by the board. **1836** Marryat *Midsh. Easy* (1863) 210 Captain Wilson, therefore, resolved to try her by the board. **1856** Longf. *Wreck Hesp.* xix, Her rattling shrouds, all sheathed in ice, With the masts, went by the board. **1859** *Autobiog. Beggar Boy* 14 Every instinct and feeling of humanity goes by the board. **1875** Whitney *Life Lang.* vi. 103 A class of grammatical distinctions which have gone by the board.

c. ***on board***: on one side, close alongside (*of* a ship or shore); also as *prep.*, short for ***on board of***. (See also 14.) ***to lay (a ship) on board***: to place one's own ship alongside of (it) for the purpose of fighting. ***to run on board (of)***, ***to fall on board (of)***: *lit.* to run against, fall foul *of* (a ship); *fig.* to make an attack, fall, *upon* (a person or thing). ***on even board with***: exactly alongside with; *fig.* on even terms with, 'square' with.

c **1505** Dunbar *Gold. Targe* 55 Hard on burd vnto the blomyt medis.. Aryvit scho. **1630** Brathwait *Eng. Gentl.* (1641) 351 Hee hath kept himselfe on even boord with all the world. **1655** Gurnall *Chr. in Arm.* i. (1669) 2/1 His hungry soul for want of better food, falls on board upon the Devil's chear. **1677** *Lond. Gaz.* No. 1202/3 The *Glorieux*.. laid the *Arms of Leyden* on Board, which took Fire, and was burnt. **1707** *Ibid.* No. 4380/3 We saw.. a cluster of 5 or 6 Ships on board each other. **1720** De Foe *Capt. Singleton* iii. 40 Keeping the coast close on board. **1797** Nelson in A. Duncan *Life* (1806) 41 The San Nicholas luffing up, the San Josef fell on board her. **1829** Marryat *F. Mildmay* iii, A large..frigate ran on board of us. **1860** *Merc. Mar. Mag.* VII. 172 It is better to keep the land on board as far as Solitary Isle.

d. ***board on board***, (corruptly) ***board and board***, ***board by board***: side by side, close alongside of each other. [= Fr. *bord à bord* 14th c. in Littré, also ON. *borð við borð*.]

c **1450** Lonelich *Grail* xxxix. 370 It [a shipe] aproched so ny, Tyl bord on bord they weren. **1614** Raleigh *Hist. World* v. i. §6 When they were (as we call it) boord and boord, that is when they brought the Gallies sides together. **1634** W. Wood *New Eng. Prosp.* I. i, Roome for 3 Ships to come in board and board. **1697** *Lond. Gaz.* No. 3278/3 A Fight of several hours Board by Board. **1761** *Chron.* in *Ann. Reg.* 64/2 The Ships were board and board three different times, which occasioned great slaughter on both sides.

e. ***board and board***: (sailing) by a succession of close tacks.

1926 R. Clements *Stately Southerner* 156 She met with a severe hammering off the Horn, but clawed her way to windward, and, after a week of board and board, managed to slip round.

†**13.** (*poetically* in OE.) A ship. *Obs.*

a **1000** *Elene* 238 (Gr.) Bord oft onfeng..yða swengas. *a* **1000** *Gnomica* 188 (Gr.) He..druȝað his ar on borde. *c* **1325** *E.E. Allit. P.* B. 470 Bryngez þat bryȝt vpon borde.

14. a. ***on board*** (beside the technical sense in 12 c) has now, in common use, the meaning: On or in a ship, boat, etc.; into or on to a ship. That this expression is elliptical, is witnessed by the

fuller form *on ship-board* (cf. ME. 'within schippe burdez' in 12), and the construction 'on board of the ship', or 'on board the ship' (where it is perhaps often supposed that 'board' means the *deck*). Hence ***board-ship*** used attrib. or as adj.

On board appears to be a later expansion (cf. *afoot, on foot*) of ABOARD, *a-bord*, and this to have been taken directly from Fr. *à bord*, as in *aller ou monter à bord, être à bord*, short for *au bord du vaisseau*, in which *bord* 'ship's side' comes contextually to be equal to 'ship' itself. Similar phrases are used in other modern Teut. langs., as Du. *aan boord*, Ger. *an bord*, Sw., Da. *om skibsbord*. Although *on borde* occurs poetically in OE., and *vpon borde* in ME., in sense of 'in, upon ship', these appear to have no historical connexion with the later *a-board*, which begins about 1500, and *on board*, which appears late in the 17th c.

1688 LUTTRELL *Brief Rel.* (1857) I. 450 Sir John Narborough..died on ship board. **1705** ADDISON *Italy* 6 A Capuchin who was on Board with us. **1768** TUCKER *Lt. Nat.* II. 528 The common sailor will not return on board. *c* **1800** P. HOARE *Song*, On board of the Arethusa. **1835** MARRYAT *Jac. Faithf.* i, He went on shore for my mother, and came on board again. **1840** —— *Poor Jack* xxiii, The captain..had his grog on board. **1852** *Life in Bombay* 216 The board-ship habit of taking brandy and water at night. **1894** M. DYAN *Man's Keeping* II. iii. 62 The liberal allowance of 'board-ship' flirtation. **1924** *Blackw. Mag.* June 743/2 In the curiously intimate routine of a board-ship life..we became very friendly.

b. *on board* is used as prep. for *on board of*.

1693 *Lond. Gaz.* No. 2847/3 They..put on board her 10 French Men. **1711** *Ibid.* No. 4887/3 From on Board Sir Edw. Whittaker, off the Lizard. **1720** DE FOE *Capt. Singleton* xvi. 270 Nor would we let any of our men go on board them, or suffer any of their men to come on board us. **1847** GROTE *Greece* II. xlvii. IV. 189 They were placed on board a fleet. **1875** JOWETT *Plato* (ed. 2) I. 74 This man Stesilaus has been seen by him on board ship.

c. *transf.* (orig. U.S.). In or into a railway train, tram-car, omnibus, etc. Also, in or into an aircraft.

1872 MARK TWAIN *Innoc. Abr.* xii. 79 Once on board, the train will not start till your ticket has been examined. **1881** *Daily News* 7 Sept. 5/4 (*U.S. Corresp.*) The train started at 6.30, having on board Mrs. Garfield and her daughter. **1883** *Harper's Mag.* 847/1 She..found herself..on board the other train. **1915** *Sphere* 6 Feb. 151 The forward end of the front gondola of a Zeppelin is screened to protect the pilot. .. Searchlights..are carried on board to be used when necessary. **1969** *Times* 28 Nov. 1/4 A four-jet B.O.A.C. VC 10 airliner with 69 people on board.

d. Of drink: having been consumed (by a person). *slang.*

1800 R. LOWTH *Billesdon Coplow* 2 Well sous'd by their dip, on they brush'd o'er the bottom, With liquor on board enough to besot 'em. **1840** MARRYAT *Poor Jack* xxiii. 164 The captain..had his grog on board, and was as brave as brass. **1940** N. MARSH *Death at Bar* iv. 72 With a brandy like this on board, I'd face the devil himself.

e. *to take on board* (fig.), to drink or consume; to swallow; also, to accept (an idea, etc.), to grasp.

1908 K. GRAHAME *Wind in Willows* x. 234 When Toad had taken as much stew on board as he thought he could possibly hold, he got up and said good-bye to the gipsy. **1979** *Management Today* Nov. 17/1 (*heading*) TV interviews can lose fears if Peter Fairley's techniques are taken on board. **1983** *Listener* 16 June 32/4 Someone who has previously given hardly any thought to nuclear weapons suddenly takes on board the full realisation of what they mean in terms of destruction. **1985** M. GEE *Light Years* xxxix. 257 She did love me once. You might find that hard to take on board. **1986** *Theology* July 304 ARCIC's failure to take on board what the critical study of religion has to tell us about how religious communities..really work.

15. *Naut.* Sideward direction (in reference to the ship's course); the course of a ship when tacking. *to make boards*: to tack. *to make short boards*: to tack frequently. Also in some *fig.* phrases, as † *to sail on another board*: to take another course of conduct. Cf. TACK.

[Of Fr. origin: cf. Fr. *virer de bord* to turn the ship's side in another direction; *courir des bords* to tack. Cf. STARBOARD and LARBOARD used as directions in reference to a ship's course.]

1533 BELLENDEN *Livy* I. (1822) 73 Seing her husband wes dede, scho began to sail on ane uthir burde. **1535** STEWART *Cron. Scotland* (1858) I. 17 Thai salit..Ay be ane burd fyve dais and fyve nycht. **1596** SIR F. VERE *Comm.* 30 Making still toward them upon one board. **1685** COTTON *Montaigne* III. 456 To this and that side I make tacks and bords. **1772–84** COOK *Voy.* (1790) IV. 1404 We passed the night in making short boards. **1837** MARRYAT *Dog-Fiend* xlii, Standing in..to make a long board upon the next tack. **1862** *Harper's Mag.* (1884) Jan. 229/1 The tendency was to give her a stern board [*i.e.* to sail her stern first]. **1875** 'STONEHENGE' *Brit. Sports* II. VIII. i. §5 The vessel will do it in two boards if there be room in the channel.

VI. In *Coal-mining.*

16. The name given in some colliery districts to each cutting or excavation in the direction of the working in the method called 'board-and-pillar', or 'post-and-stall' work; 'a passage driven across the fibres or grain of the coal'. *Newcastle Mining Terms.*

[Found in beginning of 18th c.: the coal was then dragged from the 'face' in sledges over wooden boards or deals laid down as 'ways'. It is suggested that *board* thus came to mean 'way', 'passage.' Cf. *Boardways Course* in 18.]

1708 *Compleat Collier*, A yard and quarter wide for a headways..and out of this it is we turn off the boards or other workings for every particular hewer. **1839** *Penny Cycl.* XV. 247 A series of broad parallel passages or bords about eight yards apart, communicating with each other by narrower passages or 'headways'. **1854** *North of England Inst. Mining Engineers* II. 252 It is the practice here..to arrange board and pillar workings so that the goaf may lay on the dip of the face of the work. **1860** FORDYCE *Coal, etc.* 32 The hewers working at the face of the bords or the pillar workings. **1875** URE *Dict. Arts* III. 326 Working with pillars and rooms or boards, styled post and stall. (There are 'narrow-boards', 'travelling-boards', 'stow-boards', the ' mother's gate or common going board', etc.—R. Oliver Heslop, Corbridge.) **1877** *Encycl. Brit.* VI. 64/1 In the former [*sc.* pillar work], which is also known as..'bord and pillar' in the north of England,..the field is divided into strips. **1960** *Times Rev. Industry* Oct. 34/3 Bord-and-pillar working.

VII. *Comb.* and *Attrib.*

17. General comb., chiefly attrib., as (sense 1) ***board-lining, -work***; ***board-built*** adj.; (sense 6) ***board-end, -head, -knife***; (sense 8) ***board-house, -minister, -officer, -room*** (also *transf.*, the members of a board).

1837 HAWTHORNE *Amer. Note-Bks.* (1871) I. 46 *Board-built and turf-buttressed hovels. *a* **1652** BROME *Damoiselle* IV. i. A *Boordsend-King, a pay-all in a Tavern. **1820** SCOTT *Abbot* xxiii, Take thy place at the board-end, and refresh thyself after thy journey. **1637** RUTHERFORD *Lett.* civ. (1862) I. 264, I wonder what He meaneth to put such a slave at the *board-head. *a* **1758** RAMSAY *Poems* (1844) 82 Sat up at the boord-head. **1772** WILSON in *Phil. Trans.* LXIII. 62 The *Board-house, which is a large building for the use of the *board-officers. *c* **1440** *Promp. Parv.* 44 *Boordeknyfe, *mensacula*. **1530** PALSGR. 200/1 Borde knyfe, *couteav de escuier*. **1879** JEFFERIES *Wild Life in S. County* 159 The same *board-lining of the window. **1801** HUNTINGTON *Bank of Faith* 30 They were *board-ministers, or ministers belonging to the board. **1836** DICKENS *Sk. Boz* i, A miserable looking woman is called into the *board-room. **1935** G. GREENE *England made Me* ii. 47 The monogram had been designed by Sweden's leading artist..E.K. in the board-room; E.K. in the restaurants. **1959** *Times* 5 Oct. 2/6 The work involves..convincing the boardroom, management and operatives. **1825** *Bro. Jonathan* I. 8 The snow..driving thro' every nook and crevice of the *board-work.

18. Special comb. **board-and-bat, -batten,** applied *attrib.*, esp. to a building constructed from wide boards, normally in conjunction with narrow battens; **board-bill** orig. *U.S.*, the charge made for board (sense 7); **board coal**, a kind of coal resembling wood in its markings; **board-fellow**, a companion at table, a messmate; **board-fence** *U.S.*, a close fence made with boards; so ***board-fencing***; **board foot**, the volume of wood in a piece of timber 1 ft. square and 1 in. thick; †**board-form**, a trapezium; **board-game**, a game played on a board (sense 2c); †**board-land** (see BORD-LAND); **board-man**, a man who carries advertisement boards, a 'sandwich man'; **board-measure**, superficial measure applied to boards; **board-money** = BOARD-WAGES; **board-nail**, a spike or large brad; **Board of Trade unit**, the commercial unit of electrical energy, equivalent to one kilowatt-hour of current; abbrev. B.T.U.; **board-rule**, a scale for finding the superficial area of a board without calculation; †**boardstock**, a piece of timber to be sawn into boards; **boardway's course**, 'the direction perpendicular to the cleavage of the coal' (*Coal-trade Terms, Northld. & Durh.*, 1851); **board-work, -worker** (see quots.). Also BOARD-CLOTH, -SCHOOL, -WAGES.

1902 G. ELLIS *Mod. Pract. Joinery* xxiii. 350 **Board and batten*, a method of forming the walls of wooden houses with a thick and thin board placed alternately. **1918** H. A. VACHELL *Some Happenings* x. 157 A collection of the worst-looking board-and-batten shacks between Shasta and San Diego. **1939** STEINBECK *Grapes of Wrath* xv. 182 Board-and-bat shacks. **1833** E. T. COKE *Subaltern's Furlough* ii, He has gone away without paying..his *board bill. **1952** KOESTLER *Arrow in Blue* xv. 129 My board-bill in the Pension Glaser was often overdue for several weeks. **1760** MILLES in *Phil. Trans.* LI. 537 That which they call the wood coal, or *board coal, from the resemblance which the pieces have to the grain of deal boards. **1811** J. PINKERTON *Petral.* I. 596 Straight flat pieces, three or four feet in length, which are called board-coal. **1382** WYCLIF *Judg.* xiv. 11 Thei ȝouen to him *bordfelawis thretti. **1741** RICHARDSON *Pamela* (1824) I. 102 Be you once more bed-fellows and board-fellows. **1718** in *Records Early Hist. Boston* XIII. 48 They..shall..maintain a substanciall *board fence..from the Barn to three rods distant southerly from the dwelling house. **1860** O. W. HOLMES *Prof. Breakf.-t.* xi. 331 When the boys used to make pictures of me with chalk on the board-fences. **1917** MATHEWSON *Sec. Base Sloan* xi. 143 It had a board fence around it. **1870** *Trans. Ill. Agric. Soc.* VIII. 232 By means of hedging and movable *board fencing, keep up a great deal of pasturage. **1896** *Vermont Board of Agric. Rep.* XV. 83 About 24 cubic feet per acre is added.. annually—this means about 150 board feet. **1551** RECORDE *Pathw. Knowl.* I. *Def.*, Called of the Grekes trapezia..may be called in englishe *borde formes. **1934** *Discovery* Oct. 287/2 Among Vikings as well as Celts *board-games of this type are widely known. **1884** *Cassell's Fam. Mag.* Dec. 32 The announcements were borne by a gang of unhappy *board-men. **1656** H. PHILLIPS *Purch. Patt.* (1676) 142 Draw the like line for *Board measure. **1809** R. LANGFORD *Introd. Trade* 62 *Board Money, and Small Charges. **1866** ROGERS *Agric. & Prices* I. xx. 498 The spike or *board-nails of the records. **1913** *Metal Industry Handbk.* 41/1 The *Board of Trade Unit is the commercial standard for purposes of public supply, and is measured by the product at the rate of doing work into the hours divided by 1,000: hence 1 B.T.U. = 1,000 Watt hours. **1619** SIR R. BOYLE in *Lismore Papers* (1886) I. 217, 240 tymber trees..wherof most is squared and reserved for *boordstocks. **1623** E. WYNNE in Whitbourne *Newfoundland* 105 Wee got home as many boordstocks, as afforded vs aboue two hundred boords. **1887** CREER (*title*) *Board work, or the Art of Wig making. *Ibid.* Introd., Board-work, in the fullest extent of its signification, means all that which is done by clever hairdressers and wig-makers in the workshop and at the work table. **1927** *Daily Express* 5 July 5/4 Students are taught the general principles of dressing hair and the technique of board-work, or preparation of hair for making transformations, wigs, and curls. **1921** *Dict. Occup. Terms* (1927) §428 **Board worker*; hairdresser's model maker, perruquier, postiche worker, posticheur, wig-maker; general terms for all workers engaged in..making wigs [etc.].

board (bɔəd), *v.* Forms: 4–6 borde, 5–7 bord, 6–7 boord, bourd, 6 boarde, *Sc.* burd, 6– board. [f. prec. sb.: cf. F. *border*; in senses 4 to 9 influenced by F. *aborder*. Cf. ABORD.]

I. Related to *board* = side of a ship, coast.

1. *trans.* **a.** To come close up to or alongside (a ship), usually for the purpose of attacking; to lay on board, or fall on board of. **b.** In later use, To go on board of or enter (a ship), usually in a hostile manner.

1494 FABYAN VII. 450 So cruelly assaylyd y^t they were borded or they myght be rescowyd. **1530** PALSGR. 460/1, I borde a shyppe..*Jaborde vne nauire.* **1601** SHAKS. *Twel. N.* v. i, 65 This is he that did the *Tiger* boord. **1672** *Lond. Gaz.* No. 700/4 The Cambridge boarded one of the biggest of them, having beaten all her Men from the Decks, but..did not venture to let any of her Men enter her. **1706** *Ibid.* No. 4204/3 A..Privateer came up with her..boarded her, and lash'd her fast, in which manner they fought two hours. **1797** NELSON in A. Duncan *Life* (1806) 43 In boarding the San Nicholas..we lost about seven killed. **1882** HAMLEY *Traseaden Hall* II. 251 The English vessel had..grappled the enemy and finally boarded her, the boarding party being led by the captain.

fig. **1580** LYLY *Euphues* 333 Ladyes pretende a great skyrmishe at the first, yet are boorded willinglye at the last.

†**c.** intr. *to board with* (in sense a.) *Obs.*

c **1460** FORTESCUE *Abs. & Lim. Mon.* (1714) 45 All the Kyngs Navye schall not suffice to bord with Caryks, and other grete Schippis. **1622** R. HAWKINS *Voy. S. Sea* (1847) 102 We had taken the Vice-Admirall, the first time shee bourded with us.

d. *absol.* (in sense b.)

1753 HANWAY *Trav.* (1762) I. II. xvi. 70 Their general practice is to board immediately. **1803** in Nicolas *Disp. Nelson* V. 186 *note*, Lieutenant Jones, in boarding, was mortally wounded. **1846** ARNOLD *Hist. Rome* II. xl. 575 To enable their men..to decide the battle by boarding.

2. *trans.* **a.** To go on board of, embark on.

1597 WARNER *Alb. Eng.*, *Æneidos* 325 Hee boording his Shippes..left Carthage. **1883** H. M. KENNEDY tr. *Ten Brink's E.E. Lit.* 232 The fisherman prepares a ship, which he boards with his wife and children.

b. *transf.* To enter (a vehicle, railway train, aircraft, etc.). Also *absol.* orig. *U.S.*

1848 J. BURNS *Notes of Tour in U.S. & Canada* vi. 108 We ..then *boarded*, to use a Yankeeism, the stage for Cleveland. **1879** *Good Words* Jan. 50 The tramps had boarded a train 50 miles away. **1935** *Discovery* Feb. 58/2 London bus-conductors..are having a busy time dissuading would-be passengers from trying to board their buses. **1959** I. FLEMING *Goldfinger* xii. 164 Going to ask both to board the plane before the car. **1968** A. HAILEY *Airport* II. iv. 184 A would-be stowaway merely boarded an aeroplane..and sat quietly, waiting for departure. *Ibid.* III. viii. 399 The gate agent who had been in charge at gate forty-seven when Flight Two left..did not remember Guerrero boarding.

†**3.** *trans.* To put or take on board ship. *Obs.*

1542 in *Harl. Misc.* (Malh.) I. 243 A great nombre of the Spanyardes beyng caryed and borded. **1593** P. NICHOLS *Drake Revived* in Arb. *Garner* V. 558 Boarding and stowing our provisions.

4. *fig.* To approach, 'make up to', accost, address, 'assail'; to make advances to. Cf. ACCOST.

a **1547** EARL SURREY *Æneid* IV. 395 At length her self bordeth Aeneas thus. **1580** LYLY *Euphues* (Arb.) 332 Philautus..began to boord hir in this manner. **1596** SPENSER *F.Q.* II. ii. 5 Whom thus at gaze the palmer gan to bord With goodly reason. **1600** FAIRFAX *Tasso* XIX. lxxvii, With some courtly tearmes the wench he bords. **1642** R. CARPENTER *Experience* I. Med. III. 56 When the body is.. borded by a sicknesse. *a* **1726** VANBRUGH *False Fr.* I. i. 97 What..do you expect from boarding a woman..already heart and soul engag'd to another?

5. *intr.* Of a ship: To tack; to sail athwart the wind on alternate sides, so that the general course is against the wind. Also *to board to and again, to board it, to board it up.*

1627 CAPT. SMITH *Seaman's Gram.* ix. 39 This we call boording or beating it vp vpon a tacke in the winds eye. *a* **1631** DONNE *Serm.* (1839) IV. 307 It is well..if we can beat out a Storm at Sea with Boarding-to-and-again. **1682** WHELER *Journ. Greece* III. 286 They resolved..to board it till Morning. **1692** in *Capt. Smith's Seaman's Gram.* I. xvi, *To make a board*, or *board it up*, is to turn to Windward.

†**6.** *trans.* To border on, approach; *intr.* to lie close *by*, border *upon.*

1596 SPENSER *F.Q.* IV. xi. 43 The stubborne Newre [Nore], whose waters gray By faire Kilkenny and Rosseponte boord. **1610** P. HOLLAND *Camden's Brit.* I. 242. **1636** FAMES *Iter Lanc.* 4 In a wan fainte paleness boarding death.

II. Related to *board* = thin wood, etc.

7. a. *trans.* To cover or furnish with boards. ***to board over***: to cover with boarding. ***to board up***: to close with boarding.

1530 Palsgr. 460/1 Let your parlour be boorded. **1677** Moxon *Mech. Exerc.* (1703) 153 The Floors being Boarded. **1885** Howells *S. Lapham* I. iii. 77 Many of the house-holders had boarded up their front doors. *Ibid.* iv. 89 The floors were roughly boarded over.

†**b.** To put in a coffin; to bury. *Sc. Obs.*

1535 Stewart *Cron. Scot.* II. 687 Syne in Tynmouth.. Tha burdit him thair richt solempnitly.

c. *Bookbinding.* To bind (a book) in boards.

1813 Scott *Let.* in *Lockhart* (1839) IV. 51 The demand for these continuing faster than they can be boarded. **1857** Buckle in A. Huth *Life* I. 132, I should prefer having the whole impression boarded at once.

d. To treat (leather) with a graining-board.

1860 Ure *Dict. Arts* (ed. 5) 691 The stiffer parts being boarded both on the grain and flesh sides. **1882** *Encycl. Brit.* XIV. 387/1 When dry enough for the purpose, the skin is boarded,..the effect of which is to bring up the grain,..and also to make it supple. **1968** J. Ironside *Fashion Alphabet* 237 *Box leather*: This is the result of 'boarding' the leather (i.e. breaking up the natural grain surface by close parallel creases) and is a process used on high-grade smooth leathers.

III. Related to *board* = table, regular meals.

8. a. *trans.* To provide (a lodger, etc.) with daily meals; now generally to supply with both food and lodging at a fixed rate. See also boarding *vbl. sb.* 7.

1599 Shaks. *Hen. V*, ii. i. 35 We cannot lodge and board a dozen or fourteene Gentlewomen. **1662** Fuller *Worthies* (1840) III. 308 In his own house he boarded and kept full four and twenty scholars. **1724** *Lond. Gaz.* No. 6265/4 At Mrs. Grandmaison's School..young Gentlewomen are Boarded.

b. To put up and feed (an animal). orig. *U.S.*

1875 *Cincinnati Daily Times* 1 July 2/8 Metropolitan Livery, Boarding and Sale Stables..Special attention given monthly and day boarding horses. **1880** W. D. Howells *Undiscovered Country* 261 The mare..was consequently boarded out of town a good deal. **1905** *N.Y. Even. Post* 24 Feb. 1 The owner of a large stable..said that..he had recently had some seventy horses to board. **1969** *Times* 14 Nov. 20/6 (Advt.), Two adorable scottie pups... Will board 4s. per day till Christmas.

9. a. *intr.* To have stated meals as a lodger at another person's house; to be supplied with food and lodging at a fixed rate; to live with a family as one of its members for a stipulated charge.

1556 J. Heywood *Spider & F.* lxiii. 48 To paie for boord, where euer this flock boords. **1667** Pepys *Diary* (1879) IV. 332 My boy's time, when I boarded at Kingsland. **1712** Steele *Spect.* No. 296 ¶6 Gentlemen and Ladies, who board in the same House. **1850** W. Irving *Goldsmith* xxxiv. 324 He had engaged to board with the family.

b. ***to board round*** or ***around***: to board in succession in different houses. *U.S.*

1828 *Ladies' Mag.* (Boston) I. 215, I boarded *round*, as they termed it, that is, I boarded with every family in proportion to the number of scholars they sent. **1831** *Ibid.* IV. 557 [There was] a custom..that the instructor should 'board around' as it is called. That is board a short period in each family who sent children to the school—the length of time regulated by the number of scholars sent. **1833** *Niles' Reg.* XLIV. 347/1 Our schoolmasters are..'boarded round', so as to save the drawing the pay of the schoolmaster's board from the school fund. **1869** [see around *adv.* 5 a, b]. **1871** C. M. Yonge *Pioneers & Founders* vi. 165 The system was that of 'boarding round'—*i.e.* the young mistress had to live a week alternately at each house, and went from thence to her school.

10. *causal.* To place at board. So ***to board out***.

1655 *Francion* 69 He..boorded me with the Master of the College at Lysieux. **1876** Lowell *Among my Bks.* Ser. ii. 203 The boys were boarded among the dames of the village. *Mod.* Many workhouse children are now boarded out with cottagers.

11. To call before a selection board, medical board, or the like. Usu. in *pass.*

1917 W. Owen *Let.* 25 Sept. (1967) 496, I am to be boarded today, and am waiting to be called in at any moment. **1917** G. S. Gordon *Let.* 1 Dec. (1943) 82 He has never been boarded. **1964** *New Society* 16 Apr. 13/1 Of the 715 candidates boarded, 104 were selected.

boardable ('bɔədəb(ə)l), *a.* [f. prec. + -able.] That can be boarded, as a ship; *fig.* that can be approached or accosted; approachable, affable.

1611 Cotgr., *Abordable*, affable, abbordable, approachable, boordable. [In mod. Dicts.]

boardage, obs. form of bordage.

†**'board-cloth.** *Obs.* or *north dial.* Also 5 borclothe. A cloth used to cover a table, a table cloth.

c **1200** *Trin. Coll. Hom.* 163 Hire bord cloðes ben makede wite. **1411** *E.E. Wills* (1882) 19 A boorde cloþe with .ij. towelles of deuaunt. *c* **1505** Dunbar *Flyting* 206 Thy burd claith neidis no spredding. **1552** Huloet, Bourde cloth, or carpet. **1839** *Cumberld. & Westmoreld. Dialogues* 13 Spin tow for bord claiths en sheets.

'boarded, *ppl. a.* [f. board *v.* + -ed[1].]

1. Made of or furnished with boards or planks. ***boarded up***: see board *v.* 7.

1444 *Test. Ebor.* (1855) II. 100 Lego eidem optimum bordetbed in le withdrawyng-chaumbre cum curtens pendentibus circa idem. **1557** Boorde *Sleep* in *Babees Bk.* (1868) 248 Nor lye in no lowe Chambre, excepte it be boorded. **1662** Gerbier *Princ.* (1665) 29 The first Stories ought rather to be vaulted than boarded. **1769** Priestley in *Phil. Trans.* LIX. 65 A dry boarded floor. **1806** A. Duncan *Nelson's Fun.* 13 A boarded partition..was erected. **1890** *Harper's Mag.* Dec. 102/2 It was not long before the dismal little, boarded-up, spidery coquina house was as clean as a whistle. **1905** *Daily Chron.* 26 Jan. 5/1 The boarded-up shop fronts and broken windows. **1961** K. Reisz *Technique Film Editing* (ed. 9) ii. 199 People standing in front of boarded-up shops.

2. Bound in boards.

1842 *Penny Mag.* XI. 381 A boarded book is attached to its covers..by the boards being pasted to the blank leaves.

3. Provided with board (i.e. stated meals) as a lodger at another person's house. Also ***boarded-out*** (see board *v.* 10).

1884 H. M. Stanley in *Pall Mall G.* 8 Aug. 1/2 Boarded justice would soon become mockery. **1897** *Daily News* 4 Apr. 3/1 Amongst boarded-out children ophthalmia is almost unknown.

†**'boarden,** *a. Obs.* [f. board *sb.* + -en[1].] Made of boards.

1454 *Test. Ebor.* (1855) II. 173 Ye borden bed that I lye in. *c* **1470** Henry *Wallace* iv. 509 Burdyn durs and loks. **1485** *Inv.* in *Ripon Ch. Acts* 365 Borden bedde.

†**'boarden,** *v. Obs.* [f. as prec. + -en[2].] *trans.* To floor or lay with boards.

1552 Huloet, Bourden, or make of bourdes. **1641** Best *Farm. Bks.* (1856) 24 The roome wheare the wooll lyeth shoulde allwayes bee bordened under foote.

boarder ('bɔədə(r)). Forms: 6–7 boorder, 6 bourder, *Sc.* buirdir, 7 border, 7– boarder. [f. board *v.* + -er[1].]

1. a. One who boards, or has his food, or food and lodging, at the house of another for compensation; one who lives in a boarding-house or with a family as one of its members, at a fixed rate. *Spec.* a boy who boards and lodges at a school, as distinguished from the *day-boy* who comes and goes daily, and the *day-boarder* who remains at school for dinner, but goes home at night.

1530 Palsgr. 199/2 Boorder that gothe to borde, *commensal.* **1576** Newton tr. *Lemnie's Complex.* (1633) 43 Some Schoole-masters..pinch their poore Pupils and Boorders by the belly. **1620** R. Seton *Hist. M. & S. Rep. Eglinton Papers* (1885) No. 128. 45 Hes preceis price of his buirdirs sitting at tabill is tuo hunder merk. **1740** J. Clarke *Educ. Youth* 190 A Boarding-school, where none but Boarders are received. **1882** J. Hawthorne *Fort. Fool* i. xiv, This..woman..did not pretend to know who those boarders of hers really were.

b. A horse that is put up and fed. (Cf. board *v.* 8 b.)

1806 Sir W. Scott *Let.* 11 Aug. (1932) I. 314, I wish I could promise to add to your convenience by accommodating the boarder, but our grass has been so scanty that we could not do him justice. **1903** *N.Y. Tribune* 20 Sept., (Advt.), Boarders wanted at Rochville Boarding Stable.

2. One who boards (an enemy's) ship.

1769 Falconer *Dict. Marine* (1789) F iij b, If the boarder is repulsed. **1797** Nelson in A. Duncan *Life* (1806) 41 Calling for the boarders, [I] ordered them to board. **1862** Thornbury *Turner* I. 337 The French..closing their lowerdeck port, for fear of the boarders.

3. One who puts the boards on books.

1882 *Daily News* 28 Dec. 5/2 'Boarders', or they who 'board' books, stitchers, and other toilers.

boarder, var. of bourder *Obs.* a jouster.

'boarding, *vbl. sb.* [f. board *v.* + -ing[1].]

1. *Naut.* The action of coming close up to, or of entering (a ship), usually in a hostile manner.

1591 Raleigh *Last Fight Rev.* 21 The voleis, bourdings, and entrings. **1691** *Lond. Gaz.* No. 2719/3 He thrice repulsed the Enemy, who boarded him, but at the fourth boarding was taken. **1801** Nelson in A. Duncan *Life* (1806) 196, I directed the attack to be made by four divisions of boats, for boarding.

†**2.** The action of approaching or accosting.

1546 *St. Papers Hen. VIII*, XI. 49 The bordyng of th-Emperour soo playnly in the matier of the warre. **1636** Healey *Theophrast.* 49 A troublesome bourding and assaulting of those, with whom we have to doe.

†**3.** *Naut.* The action of tacking. *Obs.*

a **1618** Raleigh *Royal Navy* 10 That shee stay well, when bourding and turning on a wind is required.

4. The act of covering or furnishing with boards; the mass of boards so used, a structure of boards.

1552 Huloet, Bourdinge, or ioynynge of bourdes together. **1663** Gerbier *Counsel* 22 The bording..is much subject to rott. **1847** Grote *Greece* (1862) III. xli. 460 The wooden palisades and boarding..took fire.

5. *Currying.* The treatment of leather with a graining-board. (See Ure *Dict. Arts* III. 97.)

1870 *Eng. Mech.* 11 Feb. 534/3 When dry, repeat the boarding, and you will have a good Memel grain. **1885** *Harper's Mag.* Jan. 278/1 The 'boarding' makes them [hides] very pliable.

6. The supplying of stated meals; the obtaining of food, or food and lodging, at another person's house for a stipulated charge.

1531 *Dial. Laws Eng.* ii. xxiv. (1638) 102 To pay for the chamber and boording a certain summe, etc. *a* **1667** Cowley *College* Wks. 1710 II. 621 For the lodging and boarding of young scholars. **1861** *Rebel War Clerk's Diary* (1866) 255 The boarding of my family comes to more than my salary.

7. *Comb.*, as (sense 1) ***boarding-brand, -bridge, -card, knife, -netting*** (a netting put round the ship to hinder the enemy's attacks), ***party, pass, -pike, ticket***; (sense 4) ***boarding-shop***; (sense 6) ***boarding-kennel***; **boarding-book,** a register for recording particulars of every ship boarded (Smyth *Sailor's Word-bk.*); **boarding-car** *U.S.*, a railway carriage fitted with sleeping, cooking, and dining accommodation; **boarding foreman** (see quot.); **boarding-house,** a house in which persons board; **boarding-master,** a keeper of a boarding-house for seamen; **boarding officer** = *boarding foreman*; **boarding-out,** the obtaining of stated meals at another person's house; the placing of destitute children in families where they are treated as members; **boarding-place** *U.S.*, a boarding-house; **boarding-stable** *U.S.*, a livery stable. Also boarding-school.

1875 Bedford *Sailor's Pocket-bk.* vi. (ed. 2) 223 When boarding foreign men-of-war the *boarding book should not be taken on board. **1814** Byron *Corsair* i. vii, Be the edge sharpen'd of my *boarding-brand. **1878** Bosw. Smith *Carthage* 105 Had they been less afraid of the *boarding-bridges, [the left wing] must ere this have been victorious. **1867** *Commerc. & Financ. Chron.* (U.S.) 8 June 726 The equipment of the road consists of..4 *boarding and 8 wrecking cars. **1891** C. Roberts *Adrift Amer.* 87 The boarding cars had to be fitted up, the cooking appliances put in order, &c. **1958** *Spectator* 22 Aug. 251/3 It is now necessary, when travelling abroad by air, to carry passports, travel tickets, embarkation cards, *boarding cards, luggage vouchers, bus tickets and airport passes. **1962** L. Deighton *Ipcress File* v. 30 A steward took my..boarding card. **1921** *Dict. Occup. Terms* (1927) §731 **Boarding foreman, boarding officer*, is responsible to harbour or dock authority for seeing that ship's papers, etc., are in order before allowing her to enter dock or harbour. **1728** A. Rogers *Let.* 16 Aug. in *Mem. of Royal Chaplain* (1905) 110 Mr. Gill has a Daughter..who ..has for many Years last past kept a *Boarding-House at Yarmouth. **1823** Bentham *Not Paul* 355 The priests, in whose boarding-house he was. **1837** Hawthorne *Amer. Note-Bks.* (1871) I. 71 A nice, comfortable, boarding-house tavern without a bar. **1883** *Harper's Mag.* Jan. 235/1, I was calling on a..friend in a high and narrow city boarding-house. **1969** R. Rendell *Best Man to Die* ii. 17 The dog had awakened him..with long-drawn howls... 'This isn't a boarding kennels, you know,' he said. **1807** in *Maryland Hist. Mag.* (1910) V. 176 She proved to be a small Pilot Boat .., with 50 Muskets ready loaded, about 18 *Boarding knives, &c. **1869** *Porcupine* 217/2 The moment a sailor is shipped he obtains his advance-note..and the cupidity of the *boarding-master is called into action. **1904** *Daily Chron.* 31 Mar. 7/6 A Greek boarding-master boarded a vessel in the Roath Dock with sailors. **1833** Marryat *P. Simple* (1863) 252 The *boarding nettings..were tied up to the yard-arms, and presented a formidable obstacle to our success. **1881** *Instr. Census Clerks* (1885) 36 *Boarding Officer. **1863** Fawcett *Pol. Econ.* iv. vi. (1876) 608 The *boarding-out system has lately been engrafted on our poor-law. **1886** *Pall Mall G.* 1 Jan. 4/1 Boarding-out..means the placing in select homes, and with select foster-parents, destitute healthy children under the age of twelve years. **1882** *Boarding party [see board *v.* 1]. **1946** C. S. Forester *Lord Hornblower* vi. 55 Have the boarding-party secured as they come on board. **1969** *Daily Express* 17 Nov. 13/7 She had to stop to have her *boarding pass checked. **1970** *Sunday Times* 18 Jan. 13/6 He gave me the boarding pass which got me aboard one of the last relief planes. **1801** *Hist. Europe* in *Ann. Reg.* 269/1 Our men were provided with *Boarding-pikes, tomahawks and cutlasses only. **1835** Marryat *Pacha* v, We received them with..boarding-pikes. **1854** M. J. Holmes *Tempest & Sunshine* iv. 21 Mr. Middleton set off for Frankfort to find 'as smart a *boarding-place for his gals as anybody had'. **1911** H. S. Harrison *Queed* iii. 28 She runs this boarding-place, and people of various kinds come to her. **1842** *Penny Mag.* XI. 378 The *'boarding-shop'..wherein all the operations are conducted for binding books in cloth boards. **1903** *Boarding stable [see boarder 1 b]. **1967** M. Drabble *Jerusalem the Golden* viii. 206 Clara..obtained her boarding ticket, and went and sat down on a plastic covered seat to await..the announcement of her flight.

'boarding, *ppl. a.* [f. as prec. + -ing[2].]

1. That boards (a ship).

1797 Holcroft *Stolberg's Trav.* (ed. 2) IV. xci. 163 The boarding Romans. **1829** Marryat *F. Mildmay* v, He had not been of the boarding party.

2. That boards in another person's house.

c **1860** Mrs. Spofford *Pilot's Wife* in *Casquet Lit.* (1877) IV. 7/2 She despised these boarding people.

'boarding-school. A school in which scholars are boarded as well as taught. Also *attrib.*

1677 *Lond. Gaz.* No. 1180/4 In Oxford there is set up a Boarding School for young Gentlewomen (by John Waver, Master in the Art of Dancing). **1713** Swift *Cadenus and V.* 767 A blockhead with melodious voice In boarding-schools can have his choice. **1812** *Examiner* 28 Dec. 827/1 Every.. boarding-school miss. **1884** *Pall Mall G.* 30 Aug. 5/1 History treated from the boarding-school point of view.

'boardless, *a.* [f. board *sb.* + -less.] Without a board or table.

1377 Langl. *P. Pl.* B. xii. 201 But sitte as a begger bordeless [*C.* bordles] bi my-self on þe grounde.

boardly, anglicized spelling of buirdly *a. Sc.*

c **1817** Hogg *Tales & Sk.* VI. 105 Interposing his boardly frame between the combatants. **1881** *Autobiog. J. Younger* xi. 116 A crying Shame to talk of hanging a boardly Man.

boardsailing ('bɔədseɪlɪŋ). *Sport.* Also **board sailing, board-sailing.** [f. board *sb.* + sailing *vbl. sb.*[1]] An official name for windsurfing (s.v.

WINDSURF *v.*); cf. *sailboarding* s.v. SAIL *sb.*[1] 11. Also *attrib.*

1980 *Washington Post* 18 July D4 Other events added for Los Angeles were board sailing (also known as 'wind-surfing'), [etc.]. *Ibid.* 16 Dec. D5/3 Winner tried twice before to set new board-sailing distance records. **1981** J. HEATH (*title*) Boardsailing. **1983** *Times* 13 Jan. 17 A few years ago the Royal Yachting Association decreed that.. henceforth the sport in Britain would be called boardsailing. **1984** *USA Today* 6 Apr. 1C/3 They are members of the.. eight-man, three-woman USA boardsailing team training here together. **1984** *Sunday Times* (Colour Suppl.) 28 Oct. 26/2 This year board sailing was made an Olympic event for the first time. **1986** *Expression!* July 43/1 Or perhaps you'd like to try something a little more daring, like boardsailing — or even a parachute jump?

Hence **'boardsailer, boardsailor,** one who takes part in boardsailing.

1980 *N.Y. Times* 23 June C10/1 For the advanced board sailor, there is now a sailboard..designed for use only in winds of more than 15 knots. **1981** *Daily Mail* 9 Apr. 39/2 A more contentious point is whether HRH and his fellow enthusiasts are wind surfers, sailboarders, boardsailers or simply bored sailors. **1984** *Times* 25 Aug. 11/3 Boardsailors have crossed the Channel.

'board-school. [f. BOARD *sb.* + SCHOOL.]

†**1.** A boarding-school. *Obs.*

1740 J. CLARKE *Educ. Youth* (ed. 3) 204 To have a Board-school in his House.

2. A school under the management of a School-board, as established by the Elementary Education Act of 1870. Also *attrib.*, as in ***board-school mistress, education,*** etc.

1873 FAWCETT in *Hansard* 17 July, I would far sooner that the child were attending the Board school. **1882** BESANT *All Sorts* i. (1884) 15 In Well-close Square, next to the Board Schools.

'board-'wages, board wages. Wages allowed to servants to keep themselves in victual.

1539 *Househ. Ord.* (1790) 211 Bills of allowance..for Wages and Boardwages. **1557** *Order of Hospitals* Fvj. **1692** SOUTHERNE *Wives Exc.* I. i. Dram. Wks. (1721) 270 Starve under the tyranny of a Housekeeper, and never know the comfort of boardwages again. **1695** CONGREVE *Love for L.* I. i. 12 If you please, I had rather be at Board-wages. **1875** JOWETT *Plato* (ed. 2) III. 46 They are on board wages.

board-walk. orig. *U.S.* [BOARD *sb.* I.] A footway or walking-path constructed of boarding.

1872 F. M. A. ROE *Army Lett.* (1909) 53 We reached a narrow board-walk that was supposed to run along by her side fence. **1895** C. KING *Fort Frayne* vii. 98 The back gate stood open..and the board walk leading from it to the rear door was visible for half its length. **1906** *Harper's Mag.* June 61 A few days later, on the board-walk at the sea-shore, she came face to face with Hugh Wilberding. **1951** *Archit. Rev.* CX. 100 This board-walk has a row of tables along its outer edge and thus combines the functions of open-air café and river promenade.

boardy ('bɔədɪ), *a.* [f. BOARD *sb.* + -Y[1].]

1. (See quot.)

1893 JACOBI in *Trans. Bibliogr. Soc.* I. 197 Thickness has to be studied—a stout paper being clumsy, and handling very 'boardy'—an expression applied to cardboards.

2. Of the wire teeth of card-clothing when worn down: stiff, not pliable.

1909 in *Cent. Dict.* Suppl.

boar-fish ('bɔəfɪʃ). A fish (*Capros aper, Zeus aper*) akin to the Mackerel; so called from the shape of its snout, which is turned up.

1836 *Penny Cycl.* VI. 274/2 The boar-fish..may be distinguished by its mouth being more attenuated and protractile. **1861** BLIGHT *Week Land's End* 130 Off the Runnel Stone, the boar fish, *Zeus Aper*, though an exceedingly rare British fish, is abundant.

boarish ('bɔərɪʃ), *a.* [f. BOAR *sb.* + -ISH[1].] Of or pertaining to a boar; resembling a boar; sensual; cruel. (As *borish* was a former spelling of both *boarish* and *boorish*, the two were often confounded; and it is hard to say to which word many passages ought to be referred.)

1550 BALE *Apol.* 65 Ye beastlye boryshe buggerers. **1593** NASHE *Christ's T.* 57a, Therefore we call a leatcherous person, a boarish companion. **1643** MILTON *Divorce* ix. Wks. (1851) 45 A grosse and borish opinion. **1645** *Sacred Decretal* 21 His Boarish Tusks, his huge great Iron fangs. *a***1718** PENN *Life* Wks. 1726 I. 33 To have expected this Boarish Fierceness from the Mayor of London. **1834** J. WILSON in *Black. Mag.* XXXV. 1003 Boarish bristle and leonine hair.

Hence **'boarishly** *adv.*, **'boarishness.** (Formerly often confused with *boorishly, -ness.*)

*a***1563** BECON *Cast. Comfort* Wks. (1844) 558 The wicked papists, which so boarishly sweat to maintain their usurped power. **1682** H. MORE *Annot. Glanvill's Lux O.* 55 The roughness and boarishness of his style.

boarship (bɔːrʃɪp). *humorous.* [see -SHIP.] The personality of a boar.

1796 SOUTHEY *Lett. Spain & Port.* (1799) 140 His boarship remained unhurt, and was suffered to go to his den.

boar-spright, obs. variant of BOWSPRIT.

boart, variant of BORT.

boas, obs. form of BOA.

boast (bəʊst), *sb.*[1] Forms: 3-7 bost, 4-6 boste, 4-5 boost, 6 *Sc.* boist, 6- boast. [ME. *bōst* sb., *bōsten* vb. are both found before 1300: their mutual relation and origin are unknown. (The Celtic words, Welsh *bostio*, Gael. *bòsd*, etc., which have been hastily assumed as the source, appear to be merely adopted from English.) Various conjectures and comparisons may be seen in Wedgwood, and E. Müller, but nothing to purpose.

The phonetic history of *boast*, showing ME. long *ō* surviving as mod.Eng. long *ō* (*oa*) in north. as well as standard Eng., shows that *boast* is not:—OE. **bāst*, which would have given north. ME. *bast*, mod. *baist* (cf. *ghaist, maist*, Sc. for *ghost, most*); nor:—OE. **bóst*, which would have given mod. *boost*, north. *buist*; nor:—OE. **bost*, which would have retained short *o* (cf. *frost*); but from a word of later (foreign) introduction. Its phonetic analogues are the Romanic words in *-ost*, with the *o* lengthened in later Eng., *coast, roast, toast, hōst, pōst*, which would lead us to expect an OF. **boster*; but of this no trace has been found.]

†**1.** Loud noise of the voice, outcry, clamour.

*c***1300** *K. Alis.* 5290 Now ariseth cry and boost Among Alisaunders oost Of scorpiouns and addres. *c***1330** *Arth. & Merl.* 3147 Vp thai sterten with gret bost, Euerich king with al his ost. **1377** LANGL. *P. Pl.* B. XIV. 247 And whether be liȝter to breke? lasse boste it maketh, A beggeres bagge þan an yren-bounde coffre! *c***1385** CHAUCER *L.G.W.* 887 Tesbe rist vppe withouten noyse or booste. *c***1430** *Life St. Kath.* (Halliw.) 8 Maxent then with grete boste, Made hur to be bownde to a poste. **1813** WHITAKER *P. Plowm.* XVII. 89 *note*, *Boost*, a noise; a provincial word still familiar in the midland counties.

†**2.** Speaking big, threatening, menace. *north.*

1375 BARBOUR *Bruce* IX. 231 Thair bost has maid me haill and fer. *c***1460** *Towneley Myst.* 178 For his bost be not abast. *c***1470** HENRY *Wallace* XI. 389 Scho wald nocht tell, for bost, nor ȝeit reward. **1578** *Gude & Godlie Ballates* (1868) 91 Ȝour bludie boist na syith can satisfie. **1600** J. MELVILL *Diary* (1842) 54 He could nocht be broken be bost. **1637** RUTHERFORD *Lett.* ci. (1862) I. 258 Slip not from it [the truth of Christ] for any bosts or fear of men.

3. Proud or vain-glorious speech; 'tall talk'; vaunt, brag; the expression of ostentation.

*c***1300** *Song* 92 in *E.E.P.* (1862) 132 Vr bost vr brag is some ouerbide. *c***1462** in Ellis *Orig. Lett.* I. I. 15 The King maketh right grete bostes of you for the truest and the feithfullest man that any Christen Prince may have. **1611** SHAKS. *Cymb.* V. v. 162 The swell'd boast Of him that best could speake. **1709** STEELE & ADD. *Tatler* No. 93 ¶2 One of the Gentlemen..told me by Way of Boast, That there were now seven Wooden Legs in his Family. **1871** FREEMAN *Norm. Conq.* (1876) IV. xviii. 266 They soon found such a boast was vain indeed. **1884** CHILD *E.S. Ballads* II. 282/1 If they cannot make good their boasts.

†**b.** Ostentation, pomp, vain-glory. *Obs.*

1297 R. GLOUC. 258 þe kyng..bynome al ys bost. *a***1300** *Cursor M.* 6224 Quen [pharaon] had mad al bun his ost, He went wit mikel prid and bost. *c***1325** *E.E. Allit. P.* B. 179 As for bobaunce & bost & bolnande priyde. **1387** TREVISA *Higden* (Rolls Ser.) VI. 167 Guthlacus þe confessour forsook armes and þe boost and pompe of þis world. *c***1440** *Gesta Rom.* (1879) 119 When thow forsakist the devil, & al his bostys, & pompis.

c. 'A cause of boasting, an occasion of pride, the thing boasted.' J.

1593 SHAKS. *Lucr.* 1193 My resolution, love, shall be thy boast. **1737** POPE *Hor. Epist.* II. i. 7 Edward and Henry, now the boast of fame. **1792** *Anecd. W. Pitt* II. xxix. 125 It is my boast, that I was the first Minister who looked for it [merit]. **1848** MACAULAY *Hist. Eng.* I. 332 Those divines who were the boast of the universities and the delight of the capital.

4. Phrases. †***to blow*** **(*a*)** ***boast***: to boast, brag (cf. BLOW, BLAST, BLAZE). ***to make*** **(*one's*)** ***boast***: to boast *of*, to glory *in*; also *absol.*; so †***to shake boast***: cf. L. *jactari*.

1375 BARBOUR *Bruce* IV. 122 The gret bost that it [pryde] blawis. *c***1385** CHAUCER *L.G.W.* 267 Mak of ȝoure trouthe in loue no bost ne soun. **1509** BARCLAY *Shyp of Folys* (1570) 45 He shaketh boast and oft doth him auaunte Of fortunes fauour. **1550** LYNDESAY *Meldrum* 266 Thair was into the Inglis oist Ane campioun that blew greit boist. *a***1560** ROLLAND *Crt. Venus* III. 341 Blaw furth ȝour boist busteous. **1611** BIBLE *Ps.* xxxiv. 2 My soule shall make her boast in the Lord. **1850** TENNYSON *In Mem.* xl. vii, How often shall.. she..bring her babe, and make her boast.

boast (bəʊst), *v.*[1] Forms: 4 bost(en, 4-5 boost(e, 5 boaste, 5-6 boste, 6 *Sc.* boist, 6-7 bost, 6- boast. [See the sb.] The primary sense was prob. 'to lift up one's voice', 'speak with a loud voice'.

I. To threaten.

†**1.** *intr.* To utter a threat, to threaten. Also with *cogn. object* of the thing threatened. *Obs.*

*c***1300** *K. Alis.* 2597 They bostodyn..Alisaundres hed of to smyte. **1513** DOUGLAS *Æneis* II. xi. (x.) 119 The tree branglis, bosting to the fall. **1552** ABP. HAMILTON *Catech.* 28 Punitions..that God in haly scripture bostis and schoris aganis all the brekaris of his commandis. *c***1610** SIR J. MELVIL *Mem.* (1683) 70 She boasted to marry the Arch-duke Charles.

†**2.** *trans.* To threaten; to bully, terrify. *Sc.*

1513 DOUGLAS *Æneis* X. xiv. 122 Quhat wenys thou so to effray and bost me? **1533** BELLENDEN *Livy* I. (1822) 101 And sum time begun to boist hir with deith. **1582-8** *Hist. James VI.* (1804) 137 He was boistit with toirtour unles he should tell. **1645** RUTHERFORD *Tryal & Tri. Faith* (1845) 371 Yonder standeth our Creator boasting us, and therefore we will obey. **1756** MRS. CALDERWOOD *Jrnl.* v. (1884) 147 Some others near him boasted him for it.

II. To speak ostentatiously.

3. *intr.* To speak vaingloriously, extol oneself; to vaunt, brag; to brag *of, about*, glory *in*. (So ***to boast it***: to practise boasting.)

*c***1340** *Cursor M.* 22289 (Trin.) þat anticrist..he sal men do of him to boost Ouer alle oþere to preise moost. **1377** LANGL. *P. Pl.* B. II. 80 To bakbite and to bosten · and bere fals witnesse. *c***1420** *Avow. Arth.* xxiii, I, Kay, that thou knawes That owte of tyme bostus and blawus. **1587** *Mirr. Mag., Stater* v. 5, I neede not of honour or dignitie boast. **1591** SHAKS. *1 Hen. VI*, III. iii. 23 Nor should that Nation boast it so with vs. **1611** BIBLE *Ps.* xliv. 8 In God we boast all the day long. **1655** *Theophania* 80, I can never consent that [he] should boast in any favor of mine. **1711** ADDISON *Spect.* No. 73 ¶2 He has not much to boast of. **1844** LD. BROUGHAM *Brit. Const.* x. (1862) 131 To boast of the honours enjoyed by their remote ancestors.

4. *refl.* in same sense. [Cf. Fr. *se vanter*.]

*a***1300** *Cursor M.* 17983 Iesu..þat boost him goddes sone to be. *c***1400** *Apol. Loll.* 92 þat he boost him silf in his dede. **1477** EARL RIVERS (Caxton) *Dictes* 86 To preyse and boste him self of his goode dedis. **1526** *Pilgr. Perf.* (W. de W. 1531) 92 Whan he bosteth hymselfe to haue y[t] whiche he hath not. **1535** COVERDALE *Ps.* li. 1 Why boastest thou thy self..that thou canst do myschefe? **1611** BIBLE *Prov.* xxvii. 1 Boast not thy selfe of to morrow. —— *Ps.* lii. 1 Why boastest thou thyselfe in mischiefe, O mightie man? **1755** JOHNSON in *Boswell* (1816) I. 242 That dream of hope, in which I once boasted myself. **1876** GREEN *Short Hist.* ii. §6 (1882) 88 The descendants of the victors at Senlac boasted themselves to be Englishmen.

5. *trans.* To extol; to speak of with pride or ostentation; to brag of, vaunt.

a. with *obj. clause*, usually with *that*. (? *orig. intrans.*)

*c***1380** WYCLIF *Sel. Wks.* III. 53 To booste not þat we ben of holy chirche. *c***1600** SHAKS. *Sonn.* cxxiii, No! Time, thou shalt not bost that I doe change. **1718** POPE *Iliad* II. 577 We ..guess by rumour, and but boast we know. **1873** MORLEY *Rousseau* I. 234 Voltaire boasted that if he shook his wig, the powder flew over the whole of the tiny republic.

b. with *simple object*.

1543 GRAFTON *Contn. Harding* 524 When the duke beganne fyrste to prayse and boaste the Kyng. **1603** B. JONSON *Sejanus* V. xxiv. 63 Forbeare, you things..To boast your slippery height. **1671** MILTON *P.R.* I. 409 Who boast'st release from hell. **1734** tr. *Rollin's Anc. Hist.* (1827) II. II. §2. 11 He boasted his having vanquished the enemy.

6. To display vaingloriously or proudly. *arch.*

1590 GREENE *Orl. Fur.* (1599) 23 Kinde Flora boast thy pride. **1681** DRYDEN *Abs. & Achit.* 162 Would steer too nigh the Sands, to boast his Wit. **1703** MAUNDRELL *Journ. Jerus.* (1732) 126 A short Chain cut in Stone; of what use I know not, unless to boast the Skill of the Artificer. **1777** SIR W. JONES *Pal. Fortune* 28 In vain, ye flowers, you boast your vernal bloom.

7. *fig.* To possess as a thing to be proud of, to have to show.

1697 DRYDEN *Virg. Eclog.* VIII. 10 Whatever Land or Sea thy Presence boast. **1795** SOUTHEY *Joan of Arc* IV. 463 A humble villager, who only boasts The treasure of the heart. **1810** SCOTT *Lady of L.* I. xxvi, The clematis, the favoured flower, Which boasts the name of virgin-bower. **1871** R. ELLIS *Catullus* xiii. 8 He boasts but a pouch of empty cobwebs.

boast, *v.*[2] Also bost. [Of uncertain etymology: F. *bosse* swelling, relief, as in *ronde bosse* 'full relief', has been suggested; but with little apparent fitness.]

1. *Masonry.* To pare stone irregularly with a broad chisel and mallet.

1823 [see BOASTING *vbl. sb.*[2]]. **1876** SIR E. BECKETT *Building* 167 More trouble is taken to work the stone with small chisels..than it would take to 'boast' (as they call it) into a fairly level surface.

2. *Sculpture.* To shape (a block) roughly before putting in details.

3. *Wood-carving.* To model roughly the details of (the design). So with *in* or *out*. See BOASTING *vbl. sb.*[2]

1867 G. A. ROGERS *Wood Carving* 11 When the stalk and leaves have been bosted into the agreeable curves they assume in nature. **1875** T. SEATON *Fret Cutting* 36 Every piece of work of any importance must go through the three stages—blocked out, bosted, finished. *Ibid.* 97 The leaf having been bosted it must now be finished, so let my readers take pencil in hand, and..let them sketch on the bosted mass each leaflet, division, and part. **1890** C. G. LELAND *Wood Carving* 50 The three stages of blocking out, bosting, and finishing. *Ibid.* 56 In commencing or bosting out this pattern. **1907** E. ROWE *Pract. Wood-Carving* vi. 68 The next step is to *bost in* the ornament. **1970** H. BRAUN *Parish Churches* vii. 90 The mason would leave a rough lump called a 'boasting' as a basis for the intended carving.

boast (bəʊst), *v.*[3] and *sb.*[2] *Tennis* and *Rackets.* [?f. F. *bosse* the place where the ball hits the wall. (Cf. BOAST *v.*[2])] *trans.* To hit (the ball) so that it strikes either of the side-walls before it strikes the end-wall; also to make (a stroke of this kind), and *intr.* Also *sb.* = the stroke. So **'boasted** *ppl. a.*, **'boasting** *vbl. sb.*

1878 J. MARSHALL *Ann. Tennis* 156 This stroke is called *a boast*, or *boasted stroke*. *Ibid.* 176 What is called *boasting* the ball. *Ibid.*, We..call them all *boasts* or *boasted* balls indifferently, whether struck from one or the other side of the net. **1898** KENNEDY & COHEN *Tennis* in '*House' on Sport* I. 421 The service was boasted under the winning gallery wall. **1902** E. MILES *Racquets*, etc. 194 This is called 'boasting', and it gives the ball a powerful twist. *Ibid.* 231 The Boasted Volley, the Volley hit direct onto the Side-wall. **1959** *Times* 4 Mar. 4/5 A liberal use of the boasted stroke. **1963** *Ibid.* 8 Jan. 3/5 This Binns did with his usual touch strokes, boasting with precision. *Ibid.*, This reaching and

turning repeatedly for boasts is the most tiring way to be forced to run.

boasted ('bəʊstɪd), *ppl. a.*[1] [f. BOAST *v.*[1] + -ED[1].] Vaunted, bragged of.

1667 MILTON *P.L.* I. 510 Heav'n and Earth Thir boasted Parents. **1871** FREEMAN *Norm. Conq.* (1876) IV. xvii. 43 As illustrating the boasted clemency of William.

'boasted, *ppl. a.*[2] [f. BOAST *v.*[2] + -ED[1].] Rough-hewn with a broad chisel.

1884 *Congregational Year Bk.* 400 The best white Holmfirth ashlar and wallstones, clean boasted.

boaster[1] ('bəʊstə(r)). Forms: 4 **bostere, booster, bostour, boosteere,** 4–6 **boster,** 5 **boister, bostare, bostoure,** 5–6 **boastar,** 6 **bostar,** 6– **boaster.** [f. BOAST *v.*[1] + -ER[1].] One who boasts: †**a.** a loud talker (*obs.*); **b.** one who threatens (*obs.*); **c.** one who extols his own deeds or excellences, a braggart, vaunter, arrogant person.

c **1325** *E.E. Allit. P.* B. 1499 Now a boster on benche bibbes þer-of. *c* **1375** WYCLIF *Antecrist*, in *Three Treat.* (Todd) 131 þei chesen to hem boosters sotil men & slyȝe, riche, proude, & Japers. ? *a* **1400** *Chester Pl.* 106, I wotte, by this boisters beare That tribute I muste paye. **1580** BARET *Alv.* B 964 A craker, a boster, a glorious personne. **1747** LADY M. W. MONTAGUE *Lett.* xxxviii. III. 63 Complainers are seldom pitied, and boasters are seldom believed. **1758** JOHNSON *Idler* No. 14 ¶9 The boaster.. blusters only to be praised. **1870** SPURGEON *Treas. Dav.* Ps. ix. 6 He plucks the boaster's song out of his mouth.

'boaster[2] ('bəʊstə(r)). [f. BOAST *v.*[2] + -ER[1].] A broad-faced chisel used by masons in making the surface of a stone nearly smooth.

1876 in GWILT.

boastful ('bəʊstfʊl), *a.* [f. BOAST *sb.*[1] + -FUL.]

1. Of words or actions: Full of boasting.

c **1325** *Coer de L.* 3827 Bostful wurdes for to crake. *c* **1440** *Bone Flor.* 270 My doghtur gete ye noght, For all yowre bostefull fare. **1599** SHAKS. *Hen. V*, IV. Cho., Steed threatens Steed, in high and boastfull Neighs. **1867** EMERSON *Lett. & Soc. Aims* vii. (1875) 171 We have had enough of these boastful recitals.

2. Of persons, or things personified: Given to boasting, ostentatious, self-praising. Const. *in*, *of*.

c **1380** WYCLIF *Sel. Wks.* I. 2 þis riche man was boostful in speche. **1486** *Bk. St. Albans, Her.* A v a, That he be not to bostfull of his manhod. **1779** JOHNSON *L.P.* Wks. 1816 X. 20 Boastful of his own knowledge. **1859** W. WHITMORE *G. Marlowe* 10 Time wears to dust the boastful monuments.

†**3.** ? Menacing. *Obs.*

1382 WYCLIF *2 Sam.* xii. 31 [David] sawede the puple of it, and ladde about upon hem boostful yren carris.

'boastfully, *adv.* [f. prec. + -LY[2].] In a boastful manner; vauntingly.

c **1430** *Life St. Kath.* (Gibbs MS.) 55 Wher yn bostfully she enhaunceth hir self. **1845** LD. CAMPBELL *Chancellors* (1857) III. li. 4 Observing boastfully, 'We inherit all our genius from our mother'.

'boastfulness. [f. as prec. + -NESS.] The quality of being boastful.

1810 COLERIDGE *Friend* (1865) 168 With all the boastfulness of national prepossession. **1879** FARRAR *St. Paul* I. 8 Driven.. to an appearance of boastfulness of which the very notion was abhorrent to him.

boasting ('bəʊstɪŋ), *vbl. sb.*[1] [f. BOAST *v.*[1] + -ING[1].]

1. Ostentatious or vainglorious speaking.

c **1380** WYCLIF *Serm.* Sel. Wks. I. 408 þe gospel tellip of bosting of a proude man. **1526** *Pilgr. Perf.* (W. de W. 1531) 90 b, Iactaunce or bostynge, ypocrisy or fayned holynes. **1607** SHAKS. *Cor.* II. i. 23 Topping all others in boasting. **1830** TENNYSON *Poems* 32 Is not my human pride brought low? The boastings of my spirit still?

†**2.** Threatening, menacing language. *Obs.*

1600 J. MELVILL *Diary* (1842) 68 He braks out in coler & bosting.

Hence †**'boastingful** *a.*

1552 in HULOET.

'boasting, *vbl. sb.*[2] [f. BOAST *v.*[2] + -ING[1].]

1823 P. NICHOLSON *Pract. Build.* 581 Boasting; in stone-cutting, paring the stone irregularly with a broad chisel and mallet; in carving, the rough cutting of the outline, before the minuter parts.

'boasting, *ppl. a.* [f. BOAST *v.*[1] + -ING[2].]

1. That boasts or brags.

1552 HULOET, Boastynge or that doth boast, *gloriosus.* **1602** N. BRETON *Mothers Bless.* xiv, A boasting tongue is like a heard-mans horne. **1769** BURKE *Pres. St. Nat.* Wks. II. 117 After all the boasting speeches.. of his faction.

†**2.** Threatening. *Sc. Obs.*

1646 ROW *Hist. Kirk* (1842) 324 Whilk occasioned the King to writ doune a verie sharp and boasting letter. **1820** SCOTT *Abbot* Note L, Lindesay was arrived in a boasting, that is, threatening humour.

'boastingly. [f. BOASTING *ppl. a.* + -LY[2].] In a boasting or bragging manner, boastfully.

1552 HULOET, Boastynglye, *gloriose.* **1561** NORTON *Calvin's Inst.* Pref. [They] doo boastyngly sett oute to sale their owne woorke. **1785** BURKE *Sp. Nab. Arcot's Debts* Wks. IV. 272 He boastingly tells you, that he has seen, read, digested, compared every thing. **1862** TROLLOPE *N. Amer.* I. 73, I do not say this boastingly or with pride.

†**'boastive,** *a. Obs. rare.* [f. BOAST *v.*[1] + -IVE.] Given to boasting, boastful.

a **1763** SHENSTONE *Wks. & Lett.* (1768) I. 278 How must his fellow streams Deride the tinklings of the boastive rill.

'boastless, *a. rare.* [f. BOAST *sb.*[1] + -LESS.] Without boasting.

1632 QUARLES *Div. Fanc.* IV. xciv. (1660) 170 A boastlesse hand; A Charitable purse. **1727** THOMSON *Summer* 1644 Diffusing kind beneficence around, Boastless.

boaston, var. of BOSTON, a card-game.

†**'boasty,** *a. Obs.* ? Clamorous; boastful.

a **1300** in Wright's *Pop. Treat. Sc.* 138 Hynder and bosti y-nouȝ, hardi and wel he.

boat (bəʊt), *sb.* Forms: 1–3 **bát,** 4 **bot,** 4–5 **boot,** (4–6 **boote**), 4–7 **bote,** 6–7 **boate,** (6 **botte, boitt,** 7 *Sc. pl.* **bottes**), 6– **boat;** *north.* 4–6 **bate,** 5–6 **bait, bayt,** (5 *pl.* **bat(t)is**). [OE. *bát*: the subsequent phonetic history in Eng. is perfectly normal; but the origin of the OE. word, and its relation to forms in other languages presents difficulties.

OE. *bát* (unless onomatopœic) must have been either the regular representative of an OTeut. **baito-*, (*-u-*), or an adoption of a word *bāt* from some other language. (1) The chief relevant fact in Teutonic is that ON. had also *bát-r* in the sense 'small boat', whence regularly Sw. *båt*, Da. *baad* 'boat'. But the OE. and ON. words were not cognate, since the ON. form corresponding to OE. *bát* would have been **beit-r*, while the OE. form corresp. to ON. *bát-r* (= OTeut. **bǣto-*) would have been **bǣt*, **bēt*, giving mod.Eng. **beet*. In one of the two langs., therefore, *bát-* must have been adopted from the other: the accessible evidence is on the whole in favour of its priority in OE. This is further favoured by the actual occurrence in ON. of a neuter sb. *beit* 'boat' (*Hávamál* st. 90, etc.), which, exc. in gender, is the required form corresponding to OE. *bát*, from OTeut. **baito-*. It is therefore highly probable that the OE. *bát* is original, and *bátr* an ON. adoption of it. (2) In any case the absence of the word from continental West Germanic is remarkable: here an OTeut. **baito-* would have given OS. *bêt*, Du. *beet*, OHG. *beiȝ*, Ger. *beisz*; an OTeut. **bǣto-* would have given OS. *bât*, Du. *baat*, OHG. *bâz*, mod.G. *basz*. No such forms exist; on the contrary, mod.Du., LG. and mod.G. have actually *boot*: of these the Ger. word is a recent adoption from LG. or Du. *boot*, found in early MDu. *c* 1250, the *ō* of which can be accounted for only by its adoption from early ME., or from Scand., at a date when the *á* of these langs. had already become (ɔː). (3) A stem *bāt-* or *batt-* must have had an early diffusion in Romanic: cf. F. *bateau*, OF. *batel*, Pr. *batelh*, Cat. *batell*, Sp. *batel*, It. *batello* (Florio), now *battello*, diminutives from a primitive **bāto*, *batto* (the latter actually used in It. in sense of 'small sea-vessel'), OF. *bat* 'small boat' found in 12th c.; med.L. had also *bātus*, *battus*, the former app. only in English documents, the latter (as well as *batellus*) continental. But no etymology of these is found in Romanic; on the contrary Diez can only refer them back to OE. *bát*: this is extremely improbable; and the difficulties are only a little lessened by substituting ON. *bátr* as the presumed source. Moreover this derivation requires **bātus* as the original type, while the form really indicated by OF., med.L., and It. is **battus*. Unless the latter could be a *neben-form* of *bātus* (cf. It. *tutto*, beside L. *tōtus*, Sp. *todo* etc.), it could hardly have any etymological connexion with English-Norse *bát-*. A Celtic source has been frequently attributed to both the OE. and Romanic words; but Celtic scholars now know that the cited OWelsh *bat*, Welsh *bad*, is merely an adoption of the OE. word. (4) Franck points out that, in MDu., *boot* fem. meant 'cask', as in mod.Sc. *meal-boat* = 'cask, barrel, tub', prob. identical with F. *botte*, Pr. and Sp. *bota*, It. *botte*, med. Lat. *bota*, *butta*, BUTT; and suggests that this may bear at least upon the Du. and LG. *boot*: it is true that words of general sense like 'vessel', *vaisseau*, and specific words like 'tub', have been applied to ships and boats; but besides that no vestige of any such sense as 'cask, tub', etc. appears either in ON. or OE. *bát*, these last could in no way be connected in form with *bota*, *botta*, or *butta*. (5) The conclusions at present tenable are, therefore, that apparently there was an OTeut. **baito-*, preserved only in ON. *beit* and OE. *bát*; that the latter was also adopted in ON. as *bát-r*, and that either from Eng. or Norse the word was adopted in Low Ger. and Dutch, as *bôt*, *boot*. But that the Romanic *batto*, *bāto*, and its family, arose out of the English-Norse word is very doubtful.]

1. a. A small open vessel in which to traverse the surface of water, usually propelled by oars, though sometimes by a sail.

891 *O.E. Chron.* (Parker MS.) þrie Scottas cuomon to Ælfrede cyninge on anum bate. *Ibid.* 1046 (Laud MS.) His sciperes wurpon hine on þone bat, and.. reowan to scipe. *a* **1225** *Juliana* 60 Buten brugge ant bat. **1330** R. BRUNNE *Chron.* 156 Philip.. To boote mad him bone. *c* **1340** *Cursor M.* 13280 (Fairf.) Petre & Andrew.. laft þaire batis [*Cott.* scipps, *Gött.* schippis] twin. **1375** BARBOUR *Bruce* III. 408 Na bait fand thai. **1423** JAS. I *King's Q.* xvii, My feble bote full fast to stere and rowe. **1513** DOUGLAS *Æneis* IV. xi. 8 Othir schip or bait. **1552** LYNDESAY *Monarche* II. 3039 Twoo thousand boittis with hir scho careis. **1591** SHAKS. *1 Hen. VI*, IV. vi. 33 To hazard all our liues in one small Boat. **1616** R. C. *Times' Whis.* v. 2266 Being olde, One foote already within Charons bote. **1798** COLERIDGE *Anc. Mar.* VII. vii, The boat came close beneath the ship. **1850** TENNYSON *In Mem.* cxxi. iv, The market boat is on the stream.

b. Extended to various vessels either smaller than, or in some way differing from, a 'ship'; esp. small sailing vessels employed in fishing, or in carrying mails and packets, and small steamers. (Sometimes applied to large ocean steamers, though these are more properly 'steam ships'.)

1571 HANMER *Chron. Irel.* (1633) 140 Some thirteene botes out of Waterford. **1703** *Lond. Gaz.* No. 3888/4 Boats to Convoy Letters and Pacquets between England and the Islands of Barbadoes, Antego, etc. **1764** TUCKER in *Phil. Trans.* LIV. 83 At King-Road.. the officers observed the king's boat to float suddenly. **1861** SALA *Tw. round Clock* 14 Boats from Hartlepool, Whitstable, Harwich, Great Grimsby, and other English seaports.. They are all called 'boats', though many are of a size that would render the term 'ship'.. far more applicable. **1880** *Whitaker's Alman.* Advts. 22 White Star Line.. the Boats are uniform and vary very little in point of speed. *Mod.* To take the boat to Gravesend. Waiting at Margate Pier for the 'husbands' boat' on Saturday afternoon.

c. With qualifications: as COCK-BOAT, FERRYBOAT, GUNBOAT, STEAMBOAT, etc., q.v.

d. Phrases. ***to take boat***: to embark in a boat. ***to have an oar in another's boat, in every boat***, etc. (fig.): to meddle with other people's affairs, to be a busybody. ***to be in the same boat*** (fig.): to be in the same position or circumstances. ***to sail in the same boat*** (fig.): to pursue the same course, act together. ***to miss the boat*** (see MISS *v.*[1]). ***to rock the boat*** (fig.): to disturb the equilibrium (of a situation, etc.).

1548 HALL *Chron.* (1809) 279 Duke Charles of Burgoyne.. would nedes have an Ower in the Erle of Warwickes boate. **1576** LAMBARDE *Peramb. Kent* (1826) 179 Thomas Becket secretly tooke boate at Rumney. **1577** HOLINSHED *Chron.* II. 173 The pope must have his ore in everie mans bote, his spoone in everie mans dish. **1584** HUDSON *Judith* iii. 352 (D.) Haue ye pain? so likewise pain haue we; For in one boat we both imbarked be. **1668** R. LESTRANGE *Vis. Quev.* (1708) 30 Medlers.. that will have an Oar in every Boat. **1845** DICKENS *Cricket on Hearth* i. 40 You'll come to the wedding? We're in the same boat. **1857** HUGHES *Tom Brown* 131 'But my face is all muddy', argued Tom. 'Oh, we're all in one boat for that matter.' **1921** H. CRANE *Let.* 17 Oct. (1965) 68 He.. made me feel myself, as a poet, as being 'in the same boat' with him. **1931** F. L. ALLEN *Only Yesterday* vi. 156 Unfortunate publicity had a tendency to rock the boat. **1944** AUDEN *For Time Being* (1945) iii. 33 Some stranger vision of the large loud liberty violently rocking yet never, he is persuaded, finally upsetting the jolly crowded boat. **1958** *Punch* 15 Jan. 111/1 The trouble with these people who nail their colours to the mast—they always rock the boat.

e. Short for *boat-race* b, rhyming slang for 'face'.

1958 F. NORMAN *Bang to Rights* 35 As soon as he had stripped this crank down the boat. **1962** R. COOK *Crust on its Uppers* i. 26 We've seen the new boat of the proletariat, all gleaming eyes.

2. A vessel or utensil resembling a boat in shape: **a.** A dish used to serve sauces, etc. in.

1684 *Lond. Gaz.* No. 1990/4 A Silver Tankard.. and a silver Boat and silver Spoons. **1796** MRS. GLASSE *Cookery* iii. 18 Make some good apple-sauce, and send up in a boat. **1834** D. FOX *Pregnancy* 102 The child should be obliged to receive its food in this manner, instead of from a spoon or boat. **1875** *Chamb. Jrnl.* No. 133. 13 There being some sauce in the boat.

b. 'The vessel that holds the incense before it is put into the censer.' Lee *Direct. Angl.* 352.

3. *Comb.*, chiefly attrib., as ***boat-bedding, -builder, -building, -hand*** [HAND *sb.* 8], ***-head, -hire, -keeper, -load, -pole, -race, -racing, -rowing, -shop, -side, -song, -work***; ***boat-green, -less, -like, -shaped*** adjs.; ***boat-fashion, -wise*** advs.; also **boat-axe** *Archæol.* [Sw. *båtyx*], a boat-shaped battle-axe of the neolithic period in Scandinavia, applied *attrib.* to the culture characterized by these axes and to the people of this culture; **boat-bearer,** a man or boy who carries the incense-boat, in attendance on the thurifer; **boat-bone,** a bone of the carpus and tarsus, *os naviculare*; **boat-boy,** (*a*) a boy engaged to help to manage a boat; (*b*) a boy who carries an incense-boat; **boat-bridge,** a bridge of boats; **boat-car,** (*a*) a wheeled car used for launching or beaching a boat; (*b*) an airship-car built like a boat; **boat-chain,** a chain by which a boat is moored; **boat-cloak,** a large cloak worn by officers on duty at sea; **boat-cradle** [CRADLE *sb.* 9], a cradle for holding a boat; **boat-deck,** the deck of a ship from which lifeboats are launched; **boat-drill,** practice by a ship's crew and passengers in the launching and manning of lifeboats; **boat-express,** an express train timed to meet a boat; **boat-hat** = BOATER 2; †**boat-haw** (see quot.); **boat-hook,** an iron hook and spike fixed at the end of a long pole, by means of which a boat is pulled towards, or pushed off from, any fixed object; **boat-house,** a house communicating with the water, in which boats are kept; **boat-insect,** the BOAT-FLY; **boat-launch,** a place or contrivance for launching a boat; **boatlift** chiefly *U.S.* [after AIR-LIFT 2], a transportation of persons, etc., by boat, esp. during an emergency; *spec.* applied to the transportation of refugees in small boats from Cuba to the U.S. in the early 1980s; cf. *sea-lift* s.v. SEA *sb.* 23 a; also as *v. trans.*, to transport by boat; **boat-master,** the captain of a boat; **boat neck(-line)** = *bateau (neck-)line*; cf. *boat-shaped*; **boat people** *sb. pl.*, (*a*) (any of) a number of peoples of S. and E. China and of S.E. Asia who live in boats; (*b*) a colloq. name for refugees (*esp.*

from Vietnam and S.E. Asia) who fled their country by putting out to sea in small boats; **boat-plug**, a plug in the bottom of a boat to let water out when on shore; **boat-quarters**, the quarters occupied by members of the crew detailed to man the boats; **boat-race**, (*a*) a race between rowing crews; *spec.* a race between crews of the universities of Oxford and Cambridge, rowed annually over a course from Putney to Mortlake; also *attrib.*; (*b*) *rhyming slang* for 'face'; **boat-rope** (see quot.); **boat-setter**, a steersman; **boat-shaped** *a.*, shaped like a boat; esp. applied to a wide neck-line curving downwards from the shoulders; **boat-shell**, the genus *Cymba* of molluscs; **boat-slide**, a double inclined plane (with rollers), over which a boat may be drawn, instead of passing through a lock; **boat-slip** = *boat-launch*; **boat-sponge**, a fine sponge of the Bahamas and Florida (see quot.); **boat-steerer** (see quot. 1845); **boat-stretcher** = STRETCHER *sb.* 7; **boat-tail**, a genus of birds (see quot.); **boat-train**, a railway train timed to meet a boat, a tidal train; †**boat-ward**, a boat-keeper; **boat-wright**, a boat-builder; **boat-yard** (orig. *U.S.*), a yard in which boats are built and stored. Also BOAT-BILL, BOAT-FLY, BOATFUL, BOATSWAIN, BOAT-WOMAN, q.v.

1919 *Jrnl. R. Anthrop. Inst.* XLIX. 197 Almgren has shown...that Scandinavian culture of a type which he calls *båtyx* or *boat-axe culture, which is found in the passage-graves of Sweden, had reached the coastal areas of Finland before the close of the Neolithic Period. **1957** CHILDE *Dawn Europ. Civilization* (ed. 6) ix. 162 The distribution of these graves..leaves no doubt that the Boat-axe folk were intruders. **1899** P. DEARMER *Parson's Handbk.* 128 The thurifer and *boat-bearer enter with the censer and boat. **1918** A. FORTESCUE *Cerem. Rom. Rite* 25 *note*, The boat-bearer will stand or kneel at the thurifer's left. **1615** CROOKE *Body of Man* 1007 The outside of this *Boatebone is large, round and sinuated..It..endeth into an internall narrow processe [Fig. 10], resembling the prow of a ship. **1889** GRETTON *Memory's Harkback* 78 One day I set out with a *boat-boy to sail and row to Ely. **1902** P. DEARMER *Parson's Handbk.* (ed. 4) 245 There is no English authority for a 'boat-boy' to accompany the thurifer. **1794** J. B. S. MORRITT *Let.* 22 May (1914) ii. 29 The Danube..which we crossed on one of the *ponts volants* or *boat bridges you have heard me mention as on the Rhine. **1959** E. POUND *Thrones* xcvi. 9 By the boat-bridge over Euphrates. **1679** BEDLOE *Popish Plot* 19 A Fire.. which began..in a *Boat-Builders-yard. **1708** SEWALL *Diary* (1879) II. 236 A smith's shop.. and a Boat-builder's Shed. **1878** *Harper's Mag.* Feb. 324/2 The inhabitants are fishermen, farmers, and boat-builders. **1963** *Times* 24 Apr. 17/3 The film tells the story of a firm of family boatbuilders. **1780** in *Virginia State P.* (1875) I. 391 It is absolutely necessary that the '*Boat-building business' be pushed. **1863** FAWCETT *Pol. Econ.* I. v. (1876) 57 Boat-building has not hitherto required any great division of labour. **1907** *Westm. Gaz.* 11 Sept. 8/3 A dozen soldiers hung on by the *boat-car..to keep it down. **1909** *Daily Chron.* 1 June 1/2 The two boat-cars which carry the engines. **1948** R. DE KERCHOVE *Internat. Maritime Dict.* 69/1 *Boat cradle.* **1773** *Gentl. Mag.* XLIII. 144 All hid in a captain's *boat-cloak. **1821** SHELLEY *Fugitives*, One *boat-cloak did cover The loved and the lover. **1960** *Guardian* 19 Sept. 2/4 For sailing families, *boat-cradle, mast support, and long tow-bar can be bought as extras [to caravans]. **1927** G. BRADFORD *Gloss. Sea Terms* 17/1 **Boat Deck*, that upon which the lifeboats are secured. **1938** *British Birds* XXXII. 113 Two adult starlings with one young one..settled on the boat-deck. **1906** *Act 6 Edward VII* xlviii. §9 The Master of every British ship shall enter..a statement..of every occasion on which *boat drill is practised on board the ship. **1943** H. PEARSON *Conan Doyle* x. 139 Unfortunately [on the *Titanic*] there had been neither boat-muster nor boat-drill. **1910** *Daily Chron.* 9 Apr. 1/4 A *boat-express passenger. **1911** FLETCHER & KIPLING *School Hist. England* xii. 247 The boat-express is waiting your command! **1821** *Deb. Congress* I. 46 This admiralty jurisdiction had done much to ruin those who were engaged in..[steamboat] navigation, by making the *boat-hands unfaithful. **1936** *Discovery* Dec. 380/1 There had been a great demand for boat-hands. **1889** GRETTON *Memory's Harkback* 310 The dandy of that time in Anglesea *boat hat, blue coat with brass buttons, high velvet collar, and swallow-tails. **1766** ENTICK *London* IV. 365 The church..took its..name from a **boat-haw*, or *boat-builder's-yard.* **1832** TENNYSON *L. Shallott* IV. 24 As the *boat-head wound along, The willowy hills and fields among. *c* **1440** *Promp. Parv.* 45 *Boothyr, *potomium.* **1675** HOBBES *Odyss.* (1677) 188 Somewhat else boat-hire to pay. **1611** COTGR., *Havet*..a *boat-hooke, a pole hauing a hooke at th' ende. **1840** R. DANA *Bef. Mast.* xxiii. 71 The bow-man had charge of the boat-hook and painter. **1722** SWIFT *Let.* 22 Dec. (1963) II. 440 Is this a Time to build *Boat-Houses, or pay for Carriage? **1801** D. WORDSWORTH *Grasmere Jrnl.* 8 Dec. in *Jrnls.* (1941) I. 89 Mary and William walked to the boat house at Rydale. **1824** MISS MITFORD *Village* Ser. I. (1863) 90 A point of view presenting the boat-house, the water, the poplars. **1925** DREISER *Amer. Tragedy* (1926) III. xix. 230 And next to him, the boathouse-keeper who had rented him the boat. **1769** FALCONER *Dict. Marine* (1789) **Boat-Keeper*, one of the rowers, who remains..to take care of any boat. **1792** *Gentl. Mag.* LXII. I. 270 The natives..stole away the cutter one night, murdered the boat-keeper who was in her. **1872** TAUNT *Sh. Guide Thames* 41 There is a *boat-launch here..It consists of a series of rollers down an incline. **1884** *St. Nicholas* II. 373 Left *boatless on a desert-isle. **1980** *Washington Post* 25 Apr. 1/5 The refugee *boatlift from Castro's Cuba continued to wash into this tropical port [*sc.* Key West, Florida] today. **1983** *Christian Science Monitor* 4 Nov. B6 A murderer boatlifted from Cuba..drives a Trans-Am and works as a male stripper. **1985** *N.Y. Times* 28 May A19/2 Although there is a warning system..there are no bridges or boatlifts to carry them to safety on the mainland. **1630** DRAYTON *Noah's Flood* (R.) His [the swan's] *boat-like breast. **1680** in *New Castle* (Pennsylvania) *Court Rec.* (1904) 442 Wee have sent away a *boat load. **1745** J. MACSPARRAN *Letter Book* (1899) 27 In the last Boat-load..I lost my dear Servant. **1807** R. SOUTHEY *Lett. from England* (1951) 480 Here they are selling the sublime and beautiful by the boat-load! **1956** K. CLARK *Nude* iii. 76 Boat-loads of tourists. [**1932** R. LEHMANN *Invit. Waltz* I. iii. 50 What about the bodice, now? V, rounded, boat, or square?] **1960** *Times* 18 Jan. 15/5 There are sweaters with V necks, and wide *boat necks. **1968** *Woman* 14 Dec. 8/2 *Cuddly popover*..has a wide boat neckline. **1848** *Boat-people [see TANKA]. **1878** J. H. GRAY *China* II. xxix. 282 The boat people of Canton. **1935** *Nankai Social & Econ. Q.* VIII. 250 The boat people of the Grand Canal between Tung Hsien of Hopei and Hangchow of Chekiang..have lived in boats for a considerable period, though not as long as the *Tanka.* **1977** *Chicago Tribune* 2 Oct. II. 6 Repressive rule in the south has created a new classification of refugees, 'the boat people'. These are the thousands of families of Vietnamese..who push off in leaky boats and rafts into the South China Sea. **1979** *Cuisine* Oct. 60/3 Hire a boatman and row out to explore the life of the Tanka boat people. **1980** *Time* 9 June 47 Some 55,000 Haitian 'boat people' have made the 800-mile crossing to Florida, most of them as illegal immigrants. **1986** *Sydney Morning Herald* 5 June 11/5 It was not possible to authenticate the boat people's stories, but members of the group spoke spontaneously and emotionally. **1836–9** TODD *Cycl. Anat. & Phys.* II. 73/2 A person having a heavy *boat-pole in his hands. **1904** *Westm. Gaz.* 29 Dec. 8/2 The crew were kept at *boat-quarters in readiness for immediate launching. **1791** H. WALPOLE *Let.* 23 Aug. (1944) XI. 341 On Monday was the *boat-race. I was in the great room.. to see the boats start. **1834** *Bell's Life in London* 25 May 2/5 We are sorry to state that the proposed boat race between the two Universities will not take place. **1861** HUGHES *Tom Brown Oxf.* I. xiii. 244 To get a man into training for a boat-race now-a-days. **1882** BLACK *Shandon Bells* xxiii, At the Bell Inn at Henley, when all the confusion of the boat-races was about. **1889** E. DOWSON *Let.* 24 Mar. (1967) 54, I am sick of 'varsity men & shall leave on Friday for Brighton & so escape whiskey & whores on boat race night. **1914** G. B. SHAW *Fanny's First Play* 11, Everyone said it was a bit of English fun, and talked about last year's boat-race night when it had been a great deal worse. **1958** F. NORMAN *Bang to Rights* 36 A big bandage round his thumb and a big smile on his boat race. **1959** I. & P. OPIE *Lore & Lang. Schoolchildren* xvi. 349 Until the last war the event which most excited children's loyalties was the Boat Race. **1831** DISRAELI *Yng. Duke*, There was no end to *boat-racing. **1627** CAPT. SMITH *Seaman's Gram.* vi. 28 The *Boat rope is that which the ship doth tow her Boat by, at her sterne. **1840** MARRYAT *Poor Jack* vi, The *boatsetter dodged him. **1871** ALABASTER *Wheel of Law* 269 *Boat shops..moored in close lines on one of the smaller canals. **1882** TAUNT *Sh. Guide Thames* 4 Iffley Lock..a new *boat slide on the mill stream ..saves waste of time for small boats. **1886** *Act 49 Vict.* xvii. 7 The Commission may construct..any pier, quay, *boat-slip, or landing-place. **1818** SCOTT *Hrt. Midl.* xlvi, The.. melancholy *boat-song of the rowers, coming on the ear with softened and sweeter sound. **1785** *Daily Universal Register* 1 Jan. 3/2 *Boat-shaped snuffer pans. **1855** C. KINGSLEY *Glaucus* 159 That wondrous bug the Notonecta, ..rowing about his boat-shaped body. **1883** S. KENT in A. J. Adderley *Fisheries Bahamas* 47 The so-called Velvet, Abacco-velvet, or *Boat-sponge (*Spongia equina*, var. *meandriniformis*). **1937** E. V. GORDON tr. *Shetelig & Falk's Scandinavian Archaeol.* v. 68 The boat-shaped battle-axe, which appears in the later part of the passage-grave period. **1959** *Times* 24 Aug. 6/6 The dresses, with boat-shaped necks and bell-shaped skirts. *Ibid.* 26 Sept. 8/3 A gown of white grosgrain with a boat-shaped neckline. **1845** E. J. WAKEFIELD *Adv. N.Z.* I. xi. 317 The **boat-steerer* pulls the oar nearest the bow of the boat, fastens to the whale with the harpoon, and takes his name from having to steer the boat under the headsman's directions while the latter kills the whale. **1851** MELVILLE *Moby Dick* I. xxvi. 188 His boat-steerer or harpooner. **1888** CHURCHWARD *Blackbirding* xii. 220 If they tried to shirk rowing, the chap in the bows or stern would fetch them a crack with the *boat-stretcher. **1868** WOOD *Homes without H.* xxv. 473 A group of birds.. scientifically known as *Quiscalinae.* They are also called **Boat-tails* because their tail-feathers are formed so as to take the shape of a canoe. **1884** *Pall Mall G.* 3 Apr. 8/1 He proceeded at once to Victoria by *boat train. *c* **1425** WYNTOUN *Cron.* VI. xvi. 63 Scho a *Batward eftyr þat Tyl hyr spowsyd Husband gat. **1697** DAMPIER *Voy.* (1729) I. 29 Canoes..are nothing but the tree it self made hollow *Boat wise. **1767** W. LEWIS *Statius' Thebaid* VI. (R.) Vessels boat-wise form'd. *c* **1440** *Promp. Parv.* 45 *Botwryhte [**1499** botewright], *navicularius.* **1606** *Wily Beguiled* in Hazl. *Dodsley* IX. 308, I am a boat-wrights son of Hull. **1847** L. COLLINS *Hist. Sketches Kentucky* (1850) 335 *West Point* is situated at the mouth of Salt river..and recently there has been an extensive **boat yard* established. **1960** DELMAR-MORGAN *Cruising Yacht Equipment* vii. 83 Stores in boatyards..are only comparatively dry.

boat (bəʊt), *v.* [f. prec. sb.]

1. *trans.* To place in a boat; to carry in a boat. ***to boat the oars***: see quot.; cf. *to ship oars.*

1613 SHERLEY *Trav. Persia* 19 [They] left me not vntill I was boated. **1681** *Discourse of Tanger*, 22 The Horses..were boated ashore. **1810** J. T. in *Risdon's Surv. Devon* Introd. 33 The rubble boated out of the tunnel. **1849** *Blackw. Mag.* LXVI. 697, I was going to be boated off to a transport. *c* **1860** H. STUART *Seaman's Catech.* 6 To..toss their oars and boat them. **1867** SMYTH *Sailor's Word-bk.*, *To boat the oars*, is to cease rowing and lay the oars in the boat.

†**2.** *intr.* To take boat: to embark. *Obs.*

1610 J. MELVILL *Diary* (1842) 670 No small concourse of people to sie thame boat.

3. *intr.* To go in a boat, to row; to conduct a freight-boat (*U.S.*).

1673 RAY *Journ. Low C.* 19 We boated to Antwerp. **1842** TENNYSON *E. Morris* 108 The friendly mist of morn Clung to the lake. I boated over, ran My craft aground. **1861** *Sat. Rev.* 14 Dec. 612 There is a large mass who..well managed, go on reading, and who form friendships and boat, and ride, and enjoy the sweet spring of their life. **1871** M. COLLINS *Mrq. & Merch.* III. xiii. 301 They..boated on the river.

b. ***to boat it*** (in same sense).

1687 *Addr. Thanks* 10 [They] would Boat it over to Lambeth. **1813** SOUTHEY *Life Nelson* II. 110 Nelson himself saw the soundings made..boating it upon this exhausting service, day and night, till it was effected. **1853** KANE *Grinnell Exp.* vi. (1856) 45 They boat or sledge it from post to post.

4. To go in a boat upon, sail upon, navigate.

1740–99 [see BOATED]. **1850** CARLYLE *Latter-day Pamph.* V. 32 Said river..can be waded, boated, swum, etc.

boatable (ˈbəʊtəb(ə)l), *a.* [f. BOAT *v.* or *sb.* + -ABLE: app. first in U.S.] Navigable by boat.

1683 PENN *Descr. Pennsylv.* Wks. 1782 IV. 315 The Schuylkill being an hundred miles boatable above the Jules. **1796** MORSE *Amer. Geog.* I. 536 The boatable waters of the Allegany. **1807** VANCOUVER *Agric. Devon* (1813) 383 Where the tidal waters flow, and are always boatable. **1864** MARSH *Man & Nat.* 420 A boatable channel.

boatage (ˈbəʊtɪdʒ). [f. as prec. + -AGE.]

1. Carriage by boat; a charge or customs paid on such carriage.

1611 COTGR., *Droict de Rivage*, shorage, or boatage; the custome, or toll for wine, or other wares, put vpon, or brought from, the water, by boats. **1810** J. T. in *Risdon's Surv. Devon* Introd. 31 Sixpence a ton per mile, even if we include the boatage. **1861** OLMSTED *Cotton Kingd.* I. 17 Longhaulage and boatage to market.

†**2.** Boats and similar craft collectively. *Obs.*

1662 FULLER *Worthies* (1840) III. 304 He cut a passage.. in the river Petteril, for the conveyance of boatage into the Irish Sea.

ˈ**boat-bill.** [f. BOAT *sb.* + BILL *sb.*[2]] A genus of birds (*Cancroma*) belonging to the Heron tribe; esp. the species *C. cochlearia* of South America, so called from the shape of its bill.

1776 P. BROWN *Illustr. Zool.* 92 The Boat-Bill. **1836** *Penny Cycl.* V. 28/2 The common boat-bill is about the size of a domestic hen. **1862** WOOD *Nat. Hist. Birds* 678 The very remarkable Boat-bill Heron inhabits Southern America.

boated (ˈbəʊtɪd), *ppl. a.* [f. BOAT *sb.* + -ED.] Furnished with boats; navigated by boats.

1740 H. WALPOLE *Corr.* (1820) I. 50 Our little Arno is not boated and swelling like the Thames. **1799** W. TAYLOR in Robberds *Mem.* I. 268 To bepraise the boated lake.

boatel, var. BOTEL.

ˈ**boater.** [f. BOAT *v.* + -ER[1].] **1.** One who rows or manages a boat: **a.** a canal-boat man; **b.** one who goes a boating for pleasure. *rare.*

1605 *Ayr Session Records* 14 Jan., Johne Boyd, boater and his wyfe. **1883** *Athenæum* 22 Dec. 822/1 A Thames-side subject, with boaters loitering at the bank. **1884** G. SMITH in *Pall Mall G.* 8 Apr. 11/2 Interfering with the boaters and their earnings.

2. A stiff straw hat with a flat crown and brim, originally one suitable to wear when boating. Also ***boater straw.***

1896 *River* 8 Aug. 5/1 The news has gone forth from one end of Wood-street to the other that the Prince of Wales has purchased a 'boater', and will wear it..for the rest of the summer. **1905** *Daily Chron.* 2 June 4/7 In a shop on Ludgate-hill, there are placards announcing 'straw boaters'. **1910** H. G. WELLS *Mr. Polly* vii. 151 Boater straws, imitation Panamas, [etc.]. **1926** *Blackw. Mag.* June 735/1 That horrible and obsolete form of head gear..known as a 'boater'. **1963** C. MACKENZIE *My Life & Times* II. 120 The word 'boater' was never used, and did not exist outside the catalogue of a firm like Ponting's... 'Boater' was intended to suggest to maidservants that they were as familiar with Maidenhead as Gaiety girls.

boatewe, obs. form of BOTEW, a kind of boot.

ˈ**boat-fly.** [f. BOAT *sb.*] A species of water-bug (*Notonecta glauca*), whose body resembles a boat.

1753 CHAMBERS *Cycl. Supp.*, *Boat-fly*, a water-insect..he swims, says Moufet, on his back. **1860** GOSSE *Rom. Nat. Hist.* 15 The merry little boatflies are frisking about, backs downwards, using their oar-like hind feet as paddles.

boatful (ˈbəʊtfʊl). Pl. boatfuls, formerly boatsful. [f. BOAT *sb.* + -FUL.] The quantity or number which fills a boat.

1652 *Season Exp. Netherl.* 9 Loaden by Boats full. **1873** SYMONDS *Grk. Poets* ix. 289 A boatful of careless persons. **1883** *Contemp. Rev.* June 851 Whole boatfuls of women.

boath, obs. form of BOA, BOTH.

boating (ˈbəʊtɪŋ), *vbl. sb.* [f. BOAT *sb.* and *v.*]

†**1.** Boats, in a collective sense. Cf. *shipping.* *Obs.*

1610 J. MELVILL *Diary* (1842) 707 Taking the first convenient boiteing com by watter to Westminster. *Ibid.* 711 We tuik boitting the 2 of July.

2. The action of going by boat, or of rowing; now *esp.* rowing as an amusement.

1788 FALCONBRIDGE *Afr. Slave Tr.* 18 Another mode of procuring slaves..by what they term boating..The sailors ..go in boats up the rivers, seeking for negroes. **1856** KANE *Arct. Exp.* I. ix. 92 We came to the end of our boating. **1874** BLACKIE *Self-Cult.* 45 Boating..is a manly and characteristically British exercise.

b. *attrib.*

1835 MARRYAT *Olla Podr.* v, We were on a boating expedition. **1881** W. E. NORRIS *Matrim.* I. 290 To change his boating flannels.

†**3.** A punishment in ancient Persia, in which the offender was tied down in a boat, and left to perish, or be eaten by vermin.
1753 CHAMBERS *Cycl. Supp.*

ˈboating, *ppl. a.* [f. as prec. + -ING^{2}.] Addicted to boating.
1884 J. HATTON in *Harper's Mag.* July 229/2 Celebrated as boating men.

†**boation** (bəʊˈeɪʃən). *Obs.* [n. of action f. L. *boāre* to bellow: see -ATION.] Bellowing, roaring.
1646 SIR T. BROWNE *Pseud. Ep.* III. xxvii. 142 Whether the large perforations.. may not much assist this mugiency or boation. **1713** DERHAM *Phys.-Theol.* (1727) 133 To send their Minds at great Distances, in a Short Time, in loud Boations.

boatman (ˈbəʊtmən). [f. BOAT *sb.* + MAN.]
1. A man who manages a boat.
1513 DOUGLAS *Æneis* VI. v. 41 This sorofull boitman. **1514** FITZHERB. *Just. Peas* (1538) 39 Enquere of botemen, and bargemen. **1600** C. SUTTON *Disce Mori* xxix. (1838) 297 Do not as boatmen are wont, who row one way but look another. **1855** SINGLETON *Virgil* II. 105 The boatman from the Stygian wave. **1871** MORLEY *Voltaire* (1886) 78 Meeting a boatman one day on the Thames.
2. = BOAT-FLY.
1841 E. NEWMAN *Hist. Insects* 106 The boatman dives under the water, occasionally coming to the surface for a supply of air. *Ibid.* 267 Water-boatmen or Notonectites.

†**ˈboatmanage.** *Obs.* [f. prec. + -AGE.] The occupation of a boatman; charge for his services.
1720 *Stow's Surv.* (Strype 1754) II. v. xxii. 421/2 Any boatman.. that taketh more for Boatmanage.. than is ordained.

ˈboatmanship. [f. as prec. + -SHIP.] The art of, or skill in, managing a boat.
1812 J. HENRY *Camp. agst. Quebec* 56 What skill in boatmanship! **1865** G. MACDONALD *A. Forbes* xli. 184 They greatly improved his boatmanship.

†**ˈboatsman.** *Obs.*
1. A boatswain.
1549 *Compl. Scot.* vi. 40 The master of the galiasse gart the botis man pas vp to the top. **1622** MALYNES *Anc. Law Merch.* 135 The persons that are in a Ship may bee thus in order.. The Master of the Ship, the Pilot, the Masters mate, the Ship-wright or Carpenter, the Boats-man, the Purser, the Chirurgeon, the Cooke, and the Ships boy.
2. = BOATMAN I.
1598 W. PHILLIP *Linschoten's Trav.* in Arb. *Garner* III. 30 Some of the boatsmen were Indians. **1684** DRYDEN *Ovids Met.* xv. *Fables* (1700) 520 Boatsmen, through the Water, show To wond'ring Passengers the Walls below.

boatswain (ˈbəʊtsweɪn, usually ˈbəʊs(ə)n). Forms: 5 **botswayne**, 6 **boteswayne**, **-son**, **boateswayne**, 6–7 **boteswaine**, **boatswaine**, 7 **boteswan**, **boateswaine**, **-son**, **batsuein**, **boatswayne**, **-son(ne**, 7–8 **boson**, 7– **boatswain**. [Late OE. *bátswegen* (Earle's *Land Charters* 254), f. *bát* BOAT *sb.* + **swegen*, a. ON. *sveinn* SWAIN; see BOSUN, BO'SUN.]
1. An officer in a ship who has charge of the sails, rigging, etc., and whose duty it is to summon the men to their duties with a whistle.
c **1450** *Pilgrim's Sea-Voy.* 21 in *Stacions Rome* (1867) 38 Bestowe the boote, bote-swayne, anon. **1463** *Mann. & Househ. Exp.* 191 To the botswayne of the Mary Talbot a jaket. *c* **1500** *Cocke Lorell's B.* (1843) 14 The bote swayne blewe his whystell full shryll. **1610** SHAKS. *Temp.* I. i. 10 Good Boteswaine haue care: where's the Master? **1635** BRERETON *Trav.* (1844) 165 Boatswain, corruptly called boseon. **1635** J. HAYWARD *Banish'd Virg.* 172 Obeying the boatsonne. **1685** DRYDEN *Albion & Alb.* II. Wks. 1725 V. 396 The merry Boson from his Side His whistle takes. **1762–9** FALCONER *Shipwr.* I. 694 Thrice with shrill note the boatswain's whistle rung. **1864** TENNYSON *En. Ard.* 123 His vessel China-bound, And wanting yet a boatswain.
2. The Arctic Skua (*Cataractes parasiticus*).
1835 SIR J. ROSS *N.-W. Pass.* iii. 40 We also saw.. many of the birds called boatswains. **1876** DAVIS *Polaris Exp.* xvi. 378 On the 14th, Joe shot a bird called a boatswain.
3. *Comb.* **boatswain-bird** (see quot.); **boatswain's chair**, **cradle**, a board on which a sailor (or other workman) sits when at work aloft; **boatswain's-mate**, a boatswain's deputy or assistant.
1652 *Proc. in Parl.* No. 170 A Boatswains mate *il.* 15*s.* **1829** MARRYAT *F. Mildmay* xi, Among our killed, was a Dutch boatswain's mate. **1867** SMYTH *Sailor's Word-bk.*, Boatswain-bird, *Phaeton æthereus*, a tropical bird, so called from its sort of whistle. It is distinguished by two long feathers in the tail, called the marling-spike. **1894** Bo'suns chair [see BOSUN]. **1928** *Daily Express* 19 Nov. 11/7 When you have been sitting up in a bo'sun's cradle playing hell with a pneumatic riveter.

ˈboat-woman. [f. BOAT *sb.* + WOMAN.] A woman who manages a boat.
a **1843** SOUTHEY *Com.-Pl. Bk.* Ser. II. 316 Perhaps Spenser remembered the portrait of Idilnesse when he so beautifully painted the wanton boatwoman. **1883** *Harper's Mag.* Oct. 674/2 The most famous boatwomen are the girls of the parish of Rättvik.

boaty (ˈbəʊtɪ), *a. colloq.* [f. BOAT *sb.* + -Y^{1}: cf. *horsey*.] Fond of or given to boating.
1886 *Mehalah* 66 Mehalah is quite of another kind.. She is more boaty than you are.

bob (bɒb), *sb.*^{1} [Of unknown origin: Ir. *baban* tassel, cluster, Gael. *baban*, *babag*, have been compared. Some of the senses are from BOB *v.*^{1}]
I. 1. A bunch or cluster (of leaves, flowers, fruit, etc.). *north.* Still in Scotland the name for a bunch, nosegay, or small bouquet of flowers.
c **1340** *Gaw. & Gr. Knt.* 206 In his on honde he hadde a holyn bobbe. *c* **1400** *MS. Lincoln* A. i. 17. f. 42 (Halliw.) With wondere grete bobbis of grapes, for a mane myȝte unnethez bere ane of them. *c* **1460** *Towneley Myst.* 118 A bob of cherys. **1483** *Cath. Angl.* 36 A Bob of grapys, *botrus.* *a* **1548** *Thrie Priests Peblis* 21 (JAM.) The King the bob of birkis can wave. **1570** LEVINS *Manip.*, A bobbe of leaves, *frondetum.* A bob of flowers, *floretum.* **1807** HOGG *Mount. Bard* 198 (JAM.) The rose an' hawthorn sweet I'll twine, To make a bobb for thee. *Mod. Sc.* To gather a bob of primroses.
†**2. a.** A rounded mass or lump at the end of a rod or the like; a knob. *Obs.* in general sense.
1601 HOLLAND *Pliny* I. 252 [Lobsters'] hornes.. haue a round point or bob at the end. **1627** CAPT. SMITH *Seaman's Gram.* xiv. 66 A Rammer is a bob of wood at the other end to ramme home the Powder. *a* **1659** OSBORN *Misc.* (1673) 589 Instead of an unsightly Bob, to form a sharp comely Bone.
b. *spec.* The weight at the end of a pendulum.
1752 *Phil. Trans.* XLVII. 519 A pendulum.. at the end of which is the bob or weight. **1828** HUTTON *Course Math.* II. 222 A portable pendulum, made of painted tape with a brass bob at the end. **1862** H. SPENCER *First Princ.* II. xvii. §139 A pendulum.. though unaffected in its movements by a change in the weight of the bob, alters its rate of oscillation when taken to the equator.
c. The plummet or weight on a plumb-line; the shifting weight on the graduated arm of a steelyard (*dial.*); a beam or other oscillating part in a pumping engine (*dial.*).
1832 MRS. OPIE in *Life* (1854) 288 There is here the largest steam engine, perhaps, in Europe; when I entered the room, I went up to see the immense beam or bob. **1867** DENISON *Astron. without Math.* 16 Seeing how much the plumb bob is pulled aside by the attraction of a mountain. **1881** RAYMOND *Mining Gloss.*, *Bob* (Cornwall), a triangular frame, by means of which the horizontal motion imparted from an engine is transformed into a vertical motion of the pump-rods in a shaft.
d. A short sleigh-runner. *N. Amer.*
1857 *Knickerbocker* XLIX. 67 The 'stage' consisted of a rickety pair of bobs [etc.]. **1888** FARMER *Americanisms*, *Bob* or *Bob Sled* or *Bob Sleigh*, a sleigh used in the West for conveying large timber, its special characteristic being two pairs of *bobs* or short runners. **1927** *Atlantic Monthly* Mar. 335 We sat on some boards nailed on the front bob of his old bobsled. **1964** *Canad. Geogr. Jrnl.* Mar. 86/2 Many carriages could have their wheels and sled runners or 'bobs' bolted on to replace them in winter.
e. Abbrev. of BOB-SLED, -SLEIGH; also *attrib.*, as ***bob-run.*** orig. *U.S.*
1856 M. Y. JACKSON *Diary* 27 Jan. in *Minn. Farmers' Diaries* (1939) 145 Went to Kinnik-kinnik yesterday with the bobs. Had to stay over night & return to day with part of a load of lumber. **1887** *Harper's Mag.* Dec. 113/2 The Captain's sleigh went townward toward evening, and the butcher's 'bob' tore an ugly groove along the lower edge. **1888** *Ibid.* May 973/1 Telling the little ones how they might have been mangled by one of the swift 'bobs'. **1897** *Sears, Roebuck Catal.* 63/2 Bob Woods.. Bob Runners.. Bob Sleigh gearing.. Bob Beams. **1906** *Daily Colonist* (Victoria, B.C.) 13 Jan. 2/3 Robertson's bob crashed with terrific momentum into a horse and cutter. **1906** *N.Y. Even. Post* 19 May 9 The same spruce and hemlock logs drawn on bobs. **1927** *Observer* 18 Dec. 9/4 Long and well-made bob-runs. **1963** *Times* 1 Feb. 4/3 The No. 2 British bob was the first to crash. *Ibid.* 7 Feb. 3/7 The fastest time ever recorded on the St. Moritz bob run.
f. In plural form = prec. sense. *U.S.*
1911 S. E. WHITE *Bobby Orde* (1916) xvii. 194 At last Bobby saw.. a magnificent bobs that had not before appeared. *Ibid.* 195 If the bobs upset, or the horse went too fast.
†**3.** An ornamental pendant; an ear-drop. *Obs.*
1648 GAGE *West Ind.* xii. (1655) 57 Their bare.. brests are covered with bobs hanging from their chaines of pearls. **1733** FIELDING *Quixote in Eng.* I. iv, Two bobs that my wife wears in her ears. **1734** MRS. DELANY *Life & Corr.* I. 432 A green diamond to hang as a bob to her necklace. **1773** GOLDSM. *Stoops to Conq.* III. i, My cousin Con's necklaces, bobs, and all.
4. A knot or bunch of hair such as that in which women sometimes do up their back hair; also, a short bunch or tassel-like curl: cf. *bob-curl*. Hence (*b*) **bob-peruke**, **-periwig**, **-wig**, a wig having the bottom locks turned up into 'bobs' or short curls, as opposed to a 'full-bottomed wig'; often (*c*) abbreviated to *bob*.
1688 R. HOLME *Armoury* II. xviii. §118. 463 A Peruque.. with a Curled Foretop, and Bobs. This is a kind of Travelling Wig, having the side or bottom locks turned up into Bobs or Knots, tied up with Ribbons. *Ibid.* A Campaign Wig, hath Knots or Bobs (or a Dildo on each side) with a Curled Forehead. *Mod.* The old lady has her hair twisted up in a bob.
b. 1685 *Lond. Gaz.* No. 2076/4 John Rixon.. wears a light bob Wigg. **1686** *Ibid.* No. 2175/4 A light coloured close Coat and a brownish Bob-Periwig. **1688** SHADWELL *Sqr. Alsatia* II. i. 36 Bob peruke. **1753** *Scots Mag.* Oct. 490/2, I.. procured a brown bob perriwig. **1840** DICKENS *Barn. Rudge* 12/1 His three-cornered hat and bob-wig.
c. 1688 R. HOLME *Armoury* 463 A short Bobb, a Head of Hair, is a Wig that hath short locks, and a hairy Crown. **1704** STEELE *Lying Lover* IV. (1747) 56 What shall I do for Powder for this smart Bob? **1752** FOOTE *Taste* I. i. 17 Let your Bob be bushy, and your Bow low. **1815** MAR. EDGEWORTH *Patron.* (1832) I. xx. 339 A decent powdered doctor's bob.

5. a. A horse's tail docked short; a short knob-like tail.
1711 *Lond. Gaz.* No. 4934/4 A high bob unusual in Horses. **1721** DUDLEY *Moose-Deer* in *Phil. Trans.* XXXI. 166 He has a very short Bob for a Tail.
b. A style of cutting women's hair short and even all round. (See BOB *v.*^{5} 2.) Also, hair cut in this way.
1926 GALSWORTHY *Silver Spoon* III. xi. 312 Her hair, again in its more natural 'bob', gleamed lustrously under the light. **1940** M. DICKENS *Mariana* v. 141 'Haven't you cut it rather short?'.. 'Oh no, 's a lovely bob.'
6. A knob, knot, or bunch of coloured yarn, ribbons or the like; a weight on the tail of a kite.
1761 STERNE *Tr. Shandy* III. xxix. 142 An old.. chair.. fringed around with.. worsted bobs. **1837** HOGG *Ettrick Sheph. T.* III. 265 Capering with her bobbs of crimson ribbons. **1849** LOWELL *Biglow P.* Wks. (1879) 165 To delay attaching the bobs until the second attempt at flying the kite. **1861** RAMSAY *Remin.* II. 121 A broad Scottish blue bonnet, with a red 'bob' on the top.
7. A bunch of lob-worms threaded on pieces of worsted, somewhat like a small mop, used to catch eels. Called in East Anglia a *bab* or *clod*. Also *U.S.* (See quot. 1883.) Cf. BOBBING *vbl. sb.*^{1} 3.
1660 HEXHAM *Du. Dict.*, *Peuren*, to take Eeles in the night with a bob of wormes. **1669** WORLIDGE *Syst. Agric.* (1681) 260 When you perceive by moving of your Bob, that the Eels do tug at it. **1874** A. BATHGATE *Colonial Experiences* xvii. 243 The eels bolt the 'bob', and are readily pulled out of the water, the same bait serving again and again. **1882** *Blackw. Mag.* Jan. 99 It is only occasionally it takes the 'bab', the bunch of worms strung on worsted with which the eel-babber works. **1883** G. C. DAVIES *Norfolk Broads* xxxi. (1884) 243 The babber sits in his boat through the night, with a short rod in each hand, and every now and then lifts the bab a little. **1883** *Century Mag.* July 383/1 The 'bob', which is formed by tying three hooks together, back to back, and covering their shanks with a portion of a deer's tail.
8. A small roundish or knob-like body: †**a.** A seed vessel of flax or other plants (*obs.*). **b.** A lump or nodule of clay used by potters.
1615 MARKHAM *Eng. Housew.* II. v. (1668) 132 The round bells or bobs which contain the seed [of flax]. **1679** PLOT *Staffordsh.* (1686) 124 Pieces of clay called Bobbs for the ware to stand on, to keep it from sticking to the Shragers. **1725** BRADLEY *Fam. Dict.* s.v. *Hemp*, Breaking off from the stalks, the round bells or Bobbs that contain the seed. **1866** HOWELLS *Venet. Life* iii. 35 A small pot of glazed earthen-ware having an earthen bob.
†**9.** An insect: **a.** The grub or larva of a beetle used as bait for fish. **b.** A beetle: chiefly in comb., as ***black-bob***, ***blind-bob*** (also *fig.*). *Obs.* or *dial.*
1589 *Pasquil's Ret.* D iiij, It is neither losse of liuing nor life, nor so blind a bob as Blind Asse, that will scare a Caualiero. *a* **1613** J. DENNYS *Angling* in Arb. *Garner* I. 176 Yellow bobs turned up before the plough are chiefest baits. **1653** WALTON *Angler* 62 A Bob which you will find [under cow-dung].. and in time will be a beetle. **1713** *Lond. & Country Brew.* IV. (1743) 259 A further Account of the Wevil.. At Winchester, they call this Insect, Pope, Black-bob, or Creeper. **1787** BEST *Angling* (ed. 2) 19 Bobs.. are worms as big as two maggots, have red heads. **1790** G. WHITE *Selborne* (*Blatta orientalis*), Her house was overrun with a kind of black beetle, or as she expressed herself with a kind of black-bob [cockroach]. **1792** OSBALDISTONE *Brit. Sportsm.* 662 All sorts of worms are better for being kept, except earth-bobs.
10. *Comb.*, as **bob-curl**, ? a short curl like a tassel; **bob-jerom**, a bobwig; **bob-pendulum**, **-balance**, a pendulum or balance with a bob or bobs; **bob-periwig**, **-peruke**, **-wig**: see 4. See also BOB-TAIL.
1685 *Lond. Gaz.* No. 2017/8 A large Gold Watch.. with a Steel Chain and a Bob Pendulum. **1701** *Ibid.* No. 3710/4 Stolen.. 2 Silver Minute bob Pendulum Watches. **1701** *Ibid.* No. 3717/4 Lost.. a Silver Pendulum Minute Watch.. with a Bob Ballance. **1782** MISS BURNEY *Cecilia* IX. i. (D.) To suppose a young lady of fortune would marry a man with a bob jerom. **1867** MISS BROUGHTON *Cometh up as Fl.* xi. 106 Mamma in a sad coloured gown, with bob curls.
II. 11. a. The refrain or burden of a song (? as if a pendant to each stanza). ***to bear a bob***: to take up the refrain, join in the chorus.
1606 *Choice, Chance, etc.* (1881) 69 Can beare the Bob, while other play and sing. **1692** L'ESTRANGE *Fables* 283 (1708) I. 299 To Bed, to Bed will be the Bob of the Song. **1752** FIELDING *Amelia* Wks. 1775 XI. 121 We'll sing it next Sunday at St. James's Church, and I'll bear a bob. **1788** *Lond. Mag.* 398 The real ass.. bore a-bob in the chorus.
b. (In modern writers) The short line (often of 2 syllables only) at the end of the stanza in some old forms of versification; sometimes it introduces riming lines in a distinct measure, called the WHEEL.
1838 GUEST *Eng. Rhythms* (1882) 573 The bob is a very short and abrupt wheel or burthen. —— 620 Of all the wheels known to our language, the most important are those fashioned on the *bob*, that is on the short and abrupt wheel, which came into fashion during the 12th and 13th centuries. —— 621 The simplest kind of *bob-wheel* consists of the *bob*, and a long verse following, and riming with it. **1842** ROBSON *Three Metr. Romances* Introd. 19.

†**bob**, *sb.*^{2} *Obs.* [f. BOB *v.*^{1}, to befool, cheat, make sport of; possibly a. OF. *bobe* deception, mocking (*faire la bobe* = *faire la moue*, Godef.), f. OF. *bober*, the source of BOB *v.*^{1}] A trick,

deception, befoolment. *to give (any one) the bob*: to mock, make a fool of, impose upon.

a **1528** SKELTON *Image Hypocr.* iv. Wks. II. 444 To blinde us by bobbes. **1589** *Pappe w. Hatchet* (1844) 14 The vile boy hath manie bobbes, and a whole fardle of fallacies. **1589** GREENE *Menaph.* (Arb.) 85 He smiled in his sleeve to see howe kindely hee had given her the bobbe. **1682** *New News fr. Bedlam* 39 When the Pope and his Party shall give him the bobb.

2. This runs together with the fig. use of BOB *sb.*[3] in the sense of 'taunt, bitter jest, scoff'.

bob (bɒb), *sb.*[3] [f. BOB *v.*[2]]

†**1.** A blow with the fist; a firm rap. ***dry bob***: a blow that does not break the skin. *Obs.*

1571 ASCHAM *Scholem.* (Arb.) 47 So cruellie threatened, yea presentlie some tymes with pinches, nippes, and bobbes, and other waies. **1589** *Pappe w. Hatchet* (1844) 21 Giue thee as many bobs on the eare, as thou hast eaten morsels. *a* **1604** CHURCHYARD in Nichols *Progr. Q. Eliz.* III. 437 They feel fowl bobs that for their bucklars strives. **1616** SURFL. & MARKH. *Countr. Farm* 711 Give him many a drie bob. *a* **1626** BP. ANDREWES *Serm.* (1856) I. 261 They..then gave Him a bob blindfold. **1721** CIBBER *Rival Fools* III. ad fin., I only find Bobs, Blows and Noise In my poor Wooing.

†**2.** *fig.* A 'rap' with the tongue, a sharp rebuke, a 'rap over the knuckles'; often (by uniting with the sense of BOB *sb.*[2]), a taunt, bitter jest or jibe, scoff. (Also *dry bob* as in 1.) *Obs.*

1571 *Damon & P.* in Dodsley (1874) IV. 81 You are like to bear the bob, for we will give it. **1580** LODGE *Answ. Gosson* 19 Here is the greatest bob I can gather out of your booke. **1600** SHAKS. *A.Y.L.* II. vii. 55 Hee, that a Foole doth very wisely hit, Doth very foolishly, although he smart, Seeme senselesse of the bob. **1606** *Sir G. Goosecappe* v. i. in Bullen *O. Pl.* III. 75 Marry him, sweet Lady, to answere his bitter bob. **1611** COTGR., *Ruade seiche*, a drie bob, jeast, or nip. **1709** *Rambl. Fuddle-Cups* 7 Keep your Flirts to your self, and your merry dry Bobs. **1731** BAILEY, *Dry Bob*, a Taunt or Scoff. *a* **1734** NORTH *Exam.* II. v. ¶ 164 So here is a Bob for the Court, and they deserve it.

3. A light or elastic blow as with anything rebounding; a tap. (Influenced by next word.)

1611 COTGR., *Mantonniere*, a chocke, or bob vnder the chinne.

¶ Hence perh. *blind-bob*, an old name of *blind-man's-buff*: cf. BOB *v.*[1] 3.

1783 AINSWORTH *Lat. Dict.* s.v. *Myinda*, Bond-man-blind, blind-bob.

bob (bɒb), *sb.*[4] [f. BOB *v.*[3]]

1. An act of bobbing, or suddenly jerking up and down; a light rebounding movement.

2. A Scotch name applied to some dances.

c **1550** WEDDERBURN *Godly Ballates, Popische Mes*, Dustifit and Bob-at-evin Do sa incres. **1727** RAMSAY *Wks.* II. 252 If ye'll go dance the Bob of Dunblane. **1818** SCOTT *Hrt. Midl.* xl.

3. A curtsy.

1825 *Bro. Jonathan* I. 138 With a bow, or a bob. *Mod.* The village girls made a 'charity bob' as they passed.

bob (bɒb), *sb.*[5] *Bell-ringing.* [perh. connected with BOB *sb.*[4]] 'A term used by change-ringers to denote certain changes in the working of the methods by which long peals of changes are produced.' ***treble bob*** is a method in which the bells, and more especially the 'Treble', have a dodging course. A ***bob minor*** is rung upon 6 bells, a ***bob triple*** upon 7, a ***bob major*** upon 8, a ***bob royal*** upon 10, a ***bob maximus*** upon 12. (Grove *Dict. Music* s.v. *Change*.)

1671 *Tintinnalogia* Pref. Verses (*title*) Upon the Presentation of Grandsire Bob To the Colledge-youths By the Author of that Peal. *Ibid.* 102. **1677** F. S[TEDMAN] *Campanologia* 82 Upon six bells there are also single and double Courses, viz. twelve changes in every single Course, as in Grandsire Bob, etc. and twenty four changes in every double Course, as in Colledg Bob, etc. **1702** *Campanologia Impr.* 26 The word Extream we must confess is the most proper Signification, in regard to the Change, but there is now and for some time has been a word call'd Bob, instead of Extream, upon what account the word was chang'd, we know not. **1807** W. IRVING *Salmag.* (1824) 197 A great hand at ringing bob-majors. **1822** BYRON *Juan* VII. lxxxv, The next shall ring a peal to shake all people, Like a bob-major from a village steeple. **1837** CARLYLE *Fr. Rev.* II. VI. iii. 336 A distracted empty-sounding world; of bob-minors and bob-majors, of triumph and terror. **1872** ELLACOMBE *Bells of Ch.* iii. 43 Perhaps the most remarkable is one of 12,000 Treble bob royal which was rung in 1784.

Hence **bob-'majoring**. *nonce-wd.*

1865 CARLYLE *Fredk. Gt.* (1873) V. 139 Huge huzzahing, herald-trumpeting, bob-majoring bursts forth from all Prussian towns.

bob (bɒb), *sb.*[6] An apparatus for polishing silver, plated goods, or other burnished metal surfaces, consisting of a disc or discs of leather or cloth, or a wooden disc with a tuyère of buff leather, revolving rapidly on a spindle, and used with or without emery-powder, sand, etc., according to the class of work in hand.

1879 *Cassell's Techn. Educ.* IV. 414/1 They will first be 'bobbed'..the finishing 'bobs' are made of a number of loose discs of cloth placed close together and threaded on the spindle like an old fashioned mop, the spoon is pressed against the soft pad, dressed with grease and fine powder. **1881** GREENER *Gun* 252 The bobs and laps should be driven by steam power, as is the case in Birmingham.

Bob (bɒb), *sb.*[7] Also bob. A pet form of the name *Robert*.

1. Hence, perhaps, the use of the word, in various combinations, denoting persons: as **dry-bob**, a boy (at Eton) who devotes himself to land-sports, as cricket, football, etc.; **wet-bob**, one who devotes himself to boating; **light-bob**, a soldier of the light infantry, or of a light company.

1721 MRS. CENTLIVRE *Platon. Lady* Epil., Some Cheapside-Bobbs too trudge it to our play. **1844** DISRAELI *Coningsby* I. ix. 102 'The match to-morrow shall be between Aquatics and Drybobs,' said a senior boy. **1844** W. H. MAXWELL *Sports & Adv. Scotl.* xxxv. (1855) 282 Me, that never..listened to a light-bob. **1848** THACKERAY *Van. Fair* xxiv. (1853) 102 Mr. Stubble, as may be supposed from his size and slenderness, was of the Light Bobs. **1865** W. L. C. *Etoniana* xi. 172 Of course a 'dry-bob' boats occasionally, and a 'wet-bob' plays cricket. **1886** *Sat. Rev.* 27 Mar. '*Reformed Eton*,' We are not even informed whether he is a wet bob or a dry bob.

2. Short for BOB-WHITE.

1883 *Century Mag.* Aug. 483/2 The European partridge.. weighs twice as much as Bob White, but he has not Bob's sturdy, rapid..flight. **1902** SANDYS & VAN DYKE *Upland Game Birds* 9 Then brave, brown Bob..enters Love's fateful lists.

3. Slang phr. ***Bob's (bob's) your uncle***: everything is all right.

1937 in PARTRIDGE *Dict. Slang* (ed. 2) 981/2. **1946** S. SPENDER *Europ. Witness* 143 He mixes up phrases such as 'Oh boy, oh boy', with cockney such as 'Bob's-your-uncle'. **1949** 'N. BLAKE' *Head of Traveller* iv. 60 Three curves and a twiddle, label it 'Object', and bob's your uncle.

bob (bɒb), *sb.*[8] *slang.* [Origin unknown; in OF. *bobe* was a coin, apparently about $1\frac{1}{2}$ pence (deniers) of the 14th c.: see Godef. But its survival in English slang is very unlikely.]

1. A shilling.

1789 *Sessions' Papers* June 550/1 *Bulls* and *half bulls* are crowns and half crowns, in coiner's language, and a *bob* is a shilling. **1812** J. H. VAUX *Flash Dict.*, *Bob*, or *Bobstick*, a shilling. **1837** DICKENS *Pickw.* (1847) 351/2 Will you take three bob? **1840** T. HOOK *Fitzherbert* II. vi. 150, I haven't a bob to pay for the hire of these skates. **1864** *Athenæum* 558/3 'Bob' is thought to have first distinguished the shilling in Sir Robert Walpole's time. **1915** 'BARTIMEUS' *Tall Ship* iv. 73 Have I got time to borrow five bob from the messman before the boat shoves off?

2. Phrases. ***bob a job***: the slogan of the Boy Scout organization in an annual effort to raise money for funds by doing jobs, orig. at a shilling a time; also (with hyphens) as attrib. phr.; ***bob a nob*** [NOB *sb.*[2]] *colloq.*: a payment of a shilling a head; also *attrib.*; ***bob in*** (*Austral.* and *N.Z. colloq.*): a subscription of a shilling to a common fund.

1823 'JON BEE' *Dict.* 13 *A bob a nob*, a shilling a head. **1851** MAYHEW *London Lab.* I. 313/2 These he would engage at 'a bob a nob' (one shilling each). **1889** W. DAVIDSON *Stories N.Z. Life* 5 From tricks at cards, the fun changed to 'a bob in' the winner shouting. **1933** *Bulletin* (Sydney) 28 June 36/3 What say we rig a few bob-ins for the poor cow? **1944** *Times* 19 May 2/3 Among the younger boys the effort is already known as the 'Bob-a-Job' or ' Bob-a-Nob' Day. **1945** BAKER *Austral. Lang.* ix. 172 Just as the *shout* is an institution in this part of the world so are the *bob in, two bob in*, [etc.]..all of which concern the creation of a jack-pot, usually with the object of buying drinks. **1954** 'N. BLAKE' *Whisper in Gloom* I. iii. 41 Clean your car, sir? Bob a job. Kensington Scouts. **1958** 'R. CROMPTON' *William's Telev. Show* vi. 162 William took his 'Bob-a-Job' book from his pocket and studied it complacently. **1959** *Daily Tel.* 28 July 12/4 A shilling-a-head subscription, popularly known as the 'bob-a-nob', for some form of testimonial was launched to-day. **1966** J. HACKSTON *Father clears Out* 113 The Red Range Federal Capital Site Committee (bob in and the winner shout) met on a Sunday.

bob, *sb.*[9], var. of BUB, *Obs.*, storm, gust.

bob (bɒb), *sb.*[10] Altered form of GOD, used in oaths and exclamatory phrases.

1823 'JON BEE' *Dict.* 13 'So help me *bob*,' is an oath to deceive the hearer, doubly; for a *bob* is but a shilling, and not a fit thing to swear by. **1842** [see S'ELP]. **1905** W. RALEIGH *Let.* 17 Nov. (1926) II. 284 It's all very well Jesus Christ being imagination, but when it comes to nothing but menageries of howling giants—s'welp me Bob! I can't show it up, I don't know enough.

bob, *a.* [In sense app. due to taking *bob* in *bobtail* as an adj.: cf. BOBBISH.]

1. Cut short (as a horse's tail); bobbed.

1709 *Lond. Gaz.* No. 4571/4 A Mare..with a grisled Mane and Tail full bob.

2. *slang.* ? Lively, 'nice'. Cf. BOBBISH.

1721 CIBBER *Refusal* I. sp. 109 Yesterday, at Marybone, they had me all Bob as a Robin. **1864** MISS YONGE *Trial* I. 113 'That's a nice girl'..'Bobber than bobtail'.

†**bob**, *v.*[1] *Obs.* [ME. *bobben*, 14th c., a. OF. *bobe-r* to befool, mock, deceive; cf. Sp *bobo* fool.]

1. *trans.* To make a fool of, deceive, cheat.

c **1320** *Seuyn Sages* (W.) 2246 Tha bobbed the pie bi night. *c* **1380** WYCLIF *Dominion* Wks. (1880) 291 þe fend may hide mennes wittis & bobbe hem in here resoun. *c* **1430** LYDG. *Min. Poems* 261 Bete and eek bobbid by fals illusioun. **1567** TURBERV. *Pretie Epigr.* (R.) To play her prancks, and bob the foole the shrowish wife begon. **1612** *Pasquil's Night-Cap* (1877) 70 I'le not be bob'd with such a slight excuse. *a* **1716** SOUTH *12 Serm.* III. 100 The Devil stands Bobbing and Tantalizing Men's Gaping hopes with Some Preferment in Church, or State. **1725** SWIFT *Wood's Petit.* Wks. 1755 IV. I. 285 And so you may daintily bob him.

b. *to bob of, out of*: to cheat (out) of. *to bob off*: to get rid of by fraud.

1605 *Tryall Chev.* I. i. in Bullen *O. Pl.* III. 273, I had rather dye in a ditch than be bobd of my fayre Thomasin. **1606** SHAKS. *Tr. & Cr.* III. i. 75 You shall not bob vs out of our melody. *a* **1652** BROME *City Wit* III. iv, If you could bob me off with such payment. **1676** *Packet Adv. Men of Shaftesbury* 8 Had I been bobb'd out of All.

c. To take by deception, to filch.

1604 SHAKS. *Oth.* v. i. 16 Gold, and Iewels, that I bob'd from him.

2. To make sport of, mock, flout. Also *intr.* with *to*.

1382 WYCLIF *1 Esdr.* i. 51 Thei weren bobbende his profetus. —— *Jer.* xxxviii. 19 Thei bobbe to me [**1388** thei scorn me].

3. *Comb.* †**bob-fool**, †**bob-her**, †**bob and hit**, names of games or forms of diversion; ***to play bob-fool with***, to make a fool of, to befool. (But these may belong to BOB *v.*[2])

1599 GREENE *Alphonsus* Wks. 1831 II. 49 Do they think to play bobfool with me? **1611** COTGR., *Savate*..the play called Bob and Hit, or Hodman Blind. **1631** *Celestina* xv. 162 Thou hast plai'd bob-foole with mee, by thy vaine and idle offers. **1702** *Burlesque of R. Lestrange's Vis. Quevedo* 269 Useful and skilful Knight at Bob-her.

bob (bɒb), *v.*[2] [ME. *boben, bobben*, found in the 13th c.; of uncertain origin; perhaps onomatopœic, expressing the effect of a smart, but not very weighty blow. In its frequent early application to the buffeting of Christ, there may have been association with BOB *v.*[1] sense 2.]

†**1.** To strike with the fist, to pommel, buffet. *Obs.*

c **1280** *Fall & Pass.* 59 in *E.E.P.* (1862) 14 He was ibobid an i-smitte . an hi spette in is face. **1432–1450** tr. *Higden* Rolls Ser. I. 241 [The slave in the triumphal car] scholde bobbe besily the victor. **1493** *Festivall* (W. de W. 1515) 172 Our moost benygne savyour..was bobbed, buffeted and spytte upon. **1531** ELYOT *Gov.* I. vii. (1557) 20 If anye man hapned..to shewe hymselfe to be wery, he was sodeynly bobbed on the face by the seruantes of Nero. **1578** *Chr. Prayers* in *Priv. Prayers* (1851) 508 Thou wast..buffeted, blindfolded, bobbed with fists. **1605** ARMIN *Foole upon F.* (1880) 23 The fellowe..got the fooles head vnder his arme, and bobd his nose.

†**2.** To strike with any thing rounded or knobbed.

c **1400** *Destr. Troy* 7316 With the bit of his blade he bobbit hym so. **1589** NASHE *Martins Months M.* 2, I haue..bobde them with their owne bable. [Still in dialect use.]

3. To rap or tap with a slight (usually elastic) blow.

a **1745** SWIFT *Wks.* (1841) II. 361 When you carry a glass of liquor to any person..do not bob him on the shoulder. *Mod.* (Parlour Game) 'Brother, I am bobbed'.

4. To cause (anything) to rap or bounce *against, at*, etc. This sense blends gradually with BOB *v.*[3]

1612 SHELTON *Quix.* I. Pref. 13 There is nothing else to be done, but to bob into it some Latin Sentences. **1748** RICHARDSON *Clarissa* (1811) V. 377 An unfledged Kite.. wanting to swallow a chicken, bobbed at its mouth by its marauding dam. **1840** W. IRVING *Wolfert's R.* (1855) 185 Bobbing their cups together, as if they were hob-or-nobbing. *Mod.* Wasps bobbing their heads against the window pane.

bob (bɒb), *v.*[3] [Used since the 16th (? 14th) c. Apparently onomatopœic, expressing short jerking or rebounding motion. There is an obvious association with certain senses of BOB *sb.*[1], esp. those of the ball of a pendulum, plummet, tassel, pendant, all of which 'bob' when moved; but it is doubtful whether this is original or subsequent. There is also contact with the senses of BOB *v.*[2]]

1. *intr.* To move up and down like a buoyant body in water, or an elastic body on land; *hence*, to dance; to move to and fro with a similar motion, esp. said of hanging things rebounding from objects lightly struck by them.

[**1386** CHAUCER *Manciples Prol.* 2 A litel toun, which that ycleped is Bobbe up and down Vnder the Blee in Caunterbury weye.] *a* **1550** *Christis Kirke Gr.* vi, Platefute he bobit up with bendis, For Mald he made requiest. **1611** CORYAT *Crudities* 64 Many tassels bobbing about. **1623** COCKERAM III, *Tantalus*..hath Apples bobbing at his nose. **1719** D'URFEY *Pills* (1872) II. 271 The fruit was bobbing at his chin. **1794** HERSCHEL in *Phil. Trans.* LXXXV. 54 Solid bodies bobbing up and down in a fiery liquid. **1830** *Gentl. Mag.* Jan. 49/2 With what consummate craft he bobbed in and out, as to office. **1858** HAWTHORNE *Fr. & It. Jrnls.* (1872) II. 164 A postilion..bobbing up and down on the offhorse. **1872** BLACK *Adv. Phaeton* ix, A bottle bobbing about in the sea.

b. ***to bob for apples, cherries***, etc.: to snatch with the mouth at apples, or other fruit, floating on water, or dangling from a string, the fruit in either case generally eluding the mouth of the would-be captor.

1823 LAMB *Lett.* xviii. 175, No. 92 may bob it as she likes but she catches no cherry of me. **1858** *Sat. Rev.* 31 July 98 Like a schoolboy who fruitlessly bobs in the tub of water after the apple.

c. *to bob on*: to await anxiously (the turn of events). *slang.*

1925 FRASER & GIBBONS *Soldier & Sailor Words* 29 *Bobbing on*, anticipating or expecting something..with the sense of looking forward to something unpleasant. *a* **1935** T. E. LAWRENCE *Mint* (1955) I. xxiv. 85 I'm bobbing on not getting that intelligent job from him.

2. a. *intr.* To move up or down with a bob or slight jerk; *spec.* curtsy. Also, with cognate obj., *to bob a curtsy*.

a **1794** *Old Song*, When she cam ben she bobbit. **1848** THACKERAY *Van. Fair* i, Bobbing, and curtseying and smiling. **1873** BLACK *Pr. Thule* x. 156 The servant..bobbed a curtsey to her. *Mod.* He bobbed down, and the stone missed him. The end of the pole bobbed up and struck me.

b. To come or go *in, into, up*, etc.

Quot. 1835 may belong to sense 2 a.

1835 DICKENS in *Sk. Boz* (1836) ser. I. II. 27 'Please, Sir, missis has made tea,' said a middle-aged female servant, bobbing into the room. **1890** *Texas Siftings* 8 Nov. 7/1 The straws man bobs up serenely at the regular time every four years. **1924** GALSWORTHY *White Monkey* I. viii, Thanks, old man, awfully good of you—will you bob in, then? **1928** *Public Opinion* 19 Oct. 371/1 Everything but the kitchen stove, as our idiom has it, is likely to bob up for notice.

c. In phr. *to bob and weave*, of a boxer: to move the head and body constantly up and down and from side to side as an evasive tactic. Also *to weave and bob fig.*, to move erratically or evasively, to move rapidly and unpredictably in one direction after another.

1928 J. O'BRIEN *Boxing* vii. 59 The mighty Sullivan might have ruined Corbett, but he couldn't reach or land on the bobbing, weaving, and left-hooking 'Gentleman Jim'. *Ibid.* 65 Keep weaving and bobbing at a comfortable pace. **1932** E. EAGER *Fighting for Fun* v. 70 Before me a rhythmic tiger, with human face, was weaving and bobbing. **1950** [see WEAVER¹ 2 b]. **1951** *Sport* 30 Mar.–5 Apr. 11/3 When the bell went Kelly came bobbing and weaving into the centre of the ring. **1956** [see GLITTERATI *sb. pl.*]. **1969** T. WILLIAMS *My Turn at Bat* III. 151 Nobody will be a greater heavyweight than Joe Louis... They said, 'He couldn't take a punch.'.. What they *didn't* say was that he was moving in all the time, not bobbing and weaving and flashing or running around. **1975** *Business Week* 4 Aug. 12/3 Production bobs and weaves from week to week. **1979** *Washington Post* 23 Mar. E8/1 He's gotta bob and weave. He's gotta crowd Holmes, throw punches underneath. **1984** S. NAIPAUL *Beyond Dragon's Mouth* x. 215 She bobbed and weaved; she brandished her pale arms; she rotated her hips. **1986** *Los Angeles Times* 6 Oct. III. 13/3 Red Sox coaches used fungo bats to aim baseballs at the pitcher, forcing him to bob and weave.

3. *trans.* To move (a thing) up or down with a bob or slight jerk. Cf. BOB *v.*² 4.

1685 *Abridgm. Eng. Mil. Discip.* 67 Take care not to bob up the Spear of your Pike. **1818** KEATS *Endym.* I. 291 Dolphins bob their noses through the brine. **1845** DARWIN *Voy. Nat.* iii. (1879) 56 The Carrancha takes little notice, except by bobbing its head.

4. *Comb.*, as **bob-a-cherry** *transf. attrib.* (cf. *bob-cherry*); **bob-apple**, a game in which children bob for apples, either floating in water, or suspended; **bob-cherry**, a game in which the player tries to catch with his teeth a cherry suspended at the end of a string; † **bob-chin**, one who bobs his chin; **bob-fly**, in angling, a second artificial fly that bobs on the surface of the water, to indicate the position of the end-fly; **bob-up** *attrib.*, that bobs up; † **bob-wood**, a bob or float used with a harpoon.

1899 T. S. MOORE *Vinedresser*, etc. 19 'Kisses sadly blown across the sea..*Bob-a-cherry kisses 'neath a tree—'O, give me one.' **1926** MASEFIELD *Odtaa* ii. 22 They're bobacherry birds. You always see them working their lower jaws as though to get the cherry in. **1681** *Reply Mischief of Imposit.* 2 To see their Children play at *Bob-apple. **1940** F. KITCHEN *Brother to Ox* i. 15 We children..played snapdragon and bob-apple. **1959** I. & P. OPIE *Lore & Lang. Schoolchildren* xii. 271 In Liverpool Hallowe'en is known as 'Duck Apple'..in Pontypool 'Bob Apple' or 'Crab Apple Night'. *Ibid.* 272 *Bob Apple* is also known as 'Snap Apple' or 'Apple on the Line'. **1714** ARBUTHNOT, etc. *Martinus Scribl.* v. (1756) 24 *Bob-cherry..teaches at once two noble virtues, patience and constancy. **1885** *Pall Mall G.* 15 July 10 Lord Robert Montagu..described Government, upon the question of Reform, as 'playing at bob-cherry with the nation'. **1614** B. JONSON *Barth. Fair*, Keepe it during the Fayre, *Bobchin. **1832** E. JESSE *Gleanings Nat. Hist.* Ser. I. 300 You can easily find the *bob-fly on the top of the water, and thus be sure that the end-fly is not far off. **1883** *Century Mag.* 378 He looped on for dropper, or bob-fly, a 'Lord Baltimore'. **1935** *Discovery* Jan. 10/1 This type of mechanism has come to be known as the '*bob-up' type. **1697** DAMPIER *New Voy.* (1699) I. 35 At the other end of his staff [for a Harpoon] there is a light piece of wood called *Bob-wood, with a hole in it, through which the small end of the staff comes.

bob (bɒb), *v.*⁴ Also 9 *dial.* bab. [f. BOB *sb.*¹ 7.] *intr.* To fish (*for* eels) with a bob. (Hence *humorously*, 'to bob for whales'.)

1614 MARKHAM *Cheap Husb.* (1623) 178 Other wayes..to take Eeles, as..with bobbing for them with great wormes. **1672** DAVENANT *Vac. in Lond.* Wks. (1673) 290 All day on Thames to bob for Grig. **1766** H. WALPOLE *Acct. Giants* Wks. 1798 II. 94 These giants..seldom come down to the coast; and then I suppose only to bob for whales. **1833** *Fraser's Mag.* VII. 54 He..bobs and dibbles till he hooks his prey. **1883** G. C. DAVIES *Norfolk Broads* iii. (1884) 22 The eel is the support of numbers of fishermen, who 'bob' for it with bundles of worms threaded on worsted.

b. *fig.* To seek to capture or obtain by artifice; to 'fish for'.

1672 DAVENANT *Wits* Wks. (1673) 183 He lies not there To bob for Griggs, but to bob for the People. **1840** E. NAPIER *Scenes & Sp. For. Lands* II. v. 163 Even captains are not catchable every day; she bobs away at them for a couple of years.

bob (bɒb), *v.*⁵ [f. BOB *sb.*¹ (sense 5). Cf. BOB *a.* 1 and BOBBED *a.*]

1. To dock, cut short (a horse's tail, etc.). Also with *off*. ? *U.S.*

1822 J. FOWLER *Jrnl.* (1898) 112 Two of them [*sc.* wild horses] must have been in Hands, as their tails were Bobed short. **1889** *Cent. Dict.*, *Bob*¹ v. 2. To cut short; dock: often with *off*: as, to *bob* or *bob off* a horse's tail.

2. To cut (the hair of a woman or girl) short and even all round.

1918 *Punch* 25 Sept. 193 Alarming spread of bobbing. **1919** *Home Notes* 8 Feb. 130, I went to a hairdresser's... He bobbed my hair. **1920** R. MACAULAY *Potterism* I. i, When the time came to bob the hair, she bobbed it. **1940** M. DICKENS *Mariana* v. 140, I want to have my hair bobbed, please.

bob (bɒb), *v.*⁶ [f. BOB *sb.*⁶] *trans.* To polish (metal) with a bob (see BOB *sb.*⁶).

1879 *Cassell's Techn. Educ.* IV. 414/1 Our spoons..will be first 'bobbed' with fine sand on an ordinary buff-covered polishing wheel.

bob, *v.*⁷ [See BOB *sb.*¹ 2 e.] **a.** *trans.* To carry on a bob-sleigh. **b.** *intr.* To ride on a bob-sleigh.

1880 *Wisconsin Rep.* 254 Injuries suffered..by collision with persons 'bobbing' or 'coasting' on such street. **1909** *Cent. Dict.* Suppl., *Bob*, v.t. To transport (a load, as of logs) on a bob or sled.

bob (bɒb), *adv.* The verb stem of BOB *v.*² or *v.*³, used to denote sudden action.

1673 MARVELL *Reh. Transp.* II. 253 Turne but over the Leaf and you meet full bob; 'Reverendissimo in Christo Patri et Domino.' **1872** BAKER *Nile Tribut.* ii. 32 Bob! and away it went.

‖**bobac** ('bəʊbæk). Also **boback, bobak.** [Pol. *bobak.*] A burrowing-squirrel found in Poland and adjoining countries, called also Polish Marmot.

1697 LOCKE *Let. to Bp. of Worcester* 195 Three *Bobaques* are all true and real *Bobaques*, supposing the Name of that Species of Animals belongs to them. **1774** GOLDSM. *Nat. Hist.* II. 261 This animal [marmot] is found in Poland under the denomination of the boback. **1802** BINGLEY *Anim. Biog.* (1813) I. 387 The burrows which the Bobacs form in the ground, are constructed obliquely. **1901** *Westm. Gaz.* 31 Dec. 5/3 The bobac, the still living marmot of the Siberian steppes. **1968** F. KERTESZ *Lang. Nuclear Sci.* 12 The underground nuclear tests at Los Alamos were designated first by burrowing mammals such as..Bobac.

bobachee ('bɒbədʒiː). *Anglo-Ind.* Also **babachy, bobarchee, bobba-, bobberjee,** etc. [Corruption of Hindi *bāwarchī.*] A male cook.

1810 T. WILLIAMSON *E. Ind. Vade-Mecum* I. 238 It being in the power of the *babachy* to baste any part with great precision. **1863** G. O. TREVELYAN *Dawk Bungalow* 18 And every night and morning The Bobarchee he shall kill The sempiternal Moorghye, And we'll all have a grill. **1883** E. H. AITKEN *Tribes on Frontier* 35 He was only a *maistry*, or more vulgarly a *bobberjee*. **1920** *Outward Bound* Nov. 67/1 Here, you, bobbajee, khansammeh, send up a sack of potatoes. **1958** *Manch. Guardian* 11 June 3/2 Sergeant Frederick McManus, who joined the army in 1937, said, '..I miss the cooks—bobajees we used to call them.'

'Bobadil. Name of a thrasonical character in Ben Jonson's *Every Man in Hum.*, used to designate a blustering braggart who pretends to prowess. Hence **Boba'dilian, 'Boba,dilish** *adjs.* **'Boba,dilism.**

1771 P. PARSONS *Newmarket* I. 82 Stay, stay, my good Bobadil, I have not done with you yet. *c* **1778** *Conquerors* 34 Such valiant Bobadils are caress'd and knighted. **1830** *Blackw. Mag.* XXVII. 735 This bluster and braggadocio, these burly Bobadilisms. **1832** *Fraser's Mag.* V. 163 A Bobadilish bulletin. **1837** CARLYLE *Fr. Rev.* II. III. iii. 145 That Bobadilian method of contest.

† **bo'ban(t.** *Obs.* [a. OF. *boban, bobant*, in same sense: see prec.] Pride, boasting; = BOBANCE.

c **1314** *Guy Warw.* (A.) 2816 þe riche soudan, So prout he is, & of so gret boban. *a* **1450** *Knt. de la Tour* (1868) 38 Not hauing her herte to the bobant of the worlde. *c* **1489** CAXTON *Sonnes of Aymon* viii. 193 By this boban, Roulande and Olyver ben mounted in to so grete bobe(n)t.

† **bo'bance.** *Obs.* Also 4–5 **bob(b)aunce.** [a. OF. *bobance* (also *boban, -ant*) arrogance, pomp: cf. Pr. *bobansa* of same meaning. See Diez.]

Boasting, pride, pomp.

c **1325** *E.E. Allit. P.* B. 179 Bobaunce & bost & bolnande priyde. *c* **1380** *Sir Ferumb.* 383 Y..am y-come wyþ þe to fiȝt: for al þy grete bobbaunce. *c* **1386** CHAUCER *Wifes Prol.* 569 Certeinly I sey for no bobance, Yet was I neuere withouten purueiance Of mariage. **1523** LD. BERNERS *Froiss.* I. cccxcix. 693 For all the great pride and bobance that they were of before. **1534** —— *Gold. Bk. M. Aurel.* (1546) A v j b, How often we trust the bobance of this world.

b. *concr.* in *pl.* 'Pomps and vanities.'

1475 *Bk. Noblesse* 80 Escheweng alle costius arraiementis of clothing, garmentis, and bobaunces.

† **bobbed,** *ppl. a. Obs.* [f. BOB *v.*- + -ED¹.] Struck with the fist; ? swollen with blows.

1573 TUSSER *Husb.* (1878) 206 What bobbed lips, what ierks, what nips! [but ? *blobbed.*]

bobbed (bɒbd), *a.* [f. BOB *sb.*¹ + -ED².]

a. Furnished with a BOB (in various senses); formed into a bob; cut short (as a horse's tail).

1658 J. ROBINSON *Eudoxa* III. 130 Frogs..are.. metamorphosed into another shape..from tailed to bobbed. **1675** *Lond. Gaz.* No. 999/4 A white Mane shorn, white Tail bob'd. **1696** *Ibid.* No. 3201/4 A Bright Bay Nag..with..a shorn Main and bob'd Tail. **1768** WASHINGTON *Diaries* (1925) I. 256 Hunting again, and catchd a fox with a bobd Tail and cut Ears. **1894** *Outing* (U.S.) XXIV. 193/1 There is nothing more hideous than a bobbed jib. **1897** *Ibid.* XXIX. 464/2 Small boys strutting about in tall beavers with bobbed-off coats, looking..like tailless sparrows.

b. Of a woman's or girl's hair: cut short and even all round (see BOB *v.*⁵ 2). Hence **bobbed-hair, -haired** *a.*, with bobbed hair.

1918 *Home Chat* 3 Aug. 106/1 There is quite a craze for 'bobbed' hair, for big and little girls alike. **1924** GALSWORTHY *White Monkey* I. viii. 63 Her bobbed black hair, crinkly towards the ends. **1928** *Punch* 30 May 589/3 The new bobbed-haired lady cat-burglar. **1952** S. KAUFFMANN *Philanderer* (1953) ix. 141 She was a young, bright, snub-nosed, bobbed-hair cartoon character.

† **'bobber**¹. *Obs.* [f. BOB *v.*¹, ² + -ER¹.]

1. A deceiver.

1542 UDALL *Erasm. Apoph.* 6 a, Those persones he pronounced woorthie to be accounpted deceytful, bobbers of menne, whiche by fraude dyd make eche manne beleue, etc.

2. A mocker, one who taunts.

1576 NEWTON tr. *Lemnie's Complex.* (1633) 160 The Cholericke are bitter taunters, dry bobbers, nipping gibers, and scornefull mockers of others.

bobber² ('bɒbə(r)). [(Two or more words) f. BOB *v.*³,⁴ + -ER¹.]

1. He who or that which bobs up and down or in and out; *spec.* a float used in angling, also the bob-fly (see BOB *v.*³ 4).

1837 LOCKHART *Life Scott* (1839) IX. 247 To catch one trout..with the fly and another with the bobber. **1881** *Harper's Mag.* Oct. 654 You can see the bobber dance upon the ripples.

2. One who bobs for eels. (In East Anglia called *babber.*)

1882 *Blackw. Mag.* Jan. 99 The bunch of worms strung on worsted with which the eel-babber works. **1883** G. C. DAVIES *Norfolk Broads* [see BOB *sb.*¹ 7].

3. *dial.* and *slang.* A fellow-workman, mate, or 'chum'. Cf. BOB *sb.*⁷

1860 W. WHITE *Round Wrekin* 34 Bobber being the equivalent of chum. **1871** *Daily News* 19 May, As he sells these, the buyers or their 'bobbers' carry them off.

bobber³ ('bɒbə(r)). [f. BOB *v.*⁶] One who polishes articles on a bob or polishing-disc.

1881 *Instr. Census Clerks* (1885) 53 Locksmith, Bellhanger. Bobber and Grinder. **1906** *Daily Chron.* 23 Apr. 10/6 Good emery bobber: must be used to cycle work. **1921** *Dict. Occup. Terms* (1927) §237 Emery bobber (foundry). *Ibid.* 238 Bobber and polisher.

bobber⁴ ('bɒbə(r)). [f. BOB *v.*⁷] One who rides on a bob-sleigh.

1904 *Windsor Mag.* Jan. 248/2 Thus spoiling many a race and importing many a risk to the bobber. **1906** *Tribune* 16 Jan. 3/7 Curlers and skaters have been enjoying themselves, but skiers and bobbers..are grumbling.

bobber⁵ ('bɒbə(r)). [perh. f. BOB *sb.*⁸ (see quot. 1921).] In full *fish bobber*: a workman who unloads fish from trawlers and drifters to the quay. So **'bobbing** *vbl. sb.*³, working as a 'bobber'.

1921 *Dict. Occup. Terms* (1927) §745 *Bobber, fish bobber* (East Coast term which originated when fish porters were paid 1s. per hour). **1934** 'TAFFRAIL' *Seventy North* ix. §1. 185 Men called 'bobbers', hired by the owners, unloaded all the fish in baskets. **1959** *Times* 20 Jan. 6/3 The fish bobbers —men who unload trawlers. *Ibid.*, The bobbers are members of the General and Municipal Workers' Union. **1962** J. TUNSTALL *Fishermen* iii. 81 Bobbing..can easily be done by men in their fifties.

bobbery ('bɒbəri), *sb. slang.* [According to Col. Yule, and others, an Anglo-Indian representation of Hindī *Bāp re!* O father!, a common exclamation of surprise or grief. Forby has it in 1830 as East Anglian dialect; and it has been plausibly (as to the form) referred to Sp. *boberia* folly; but the evidence for its origination in India is decisive.] Noise, noisy disturbance, 'row'.

1816 'QUIZ' *Grand Master* (*Adventures in Hindostan*) XI. 48 The muse now blushes to disclose The bobbery that here arose. **1833** MARRYAT *P. Simple* xxvii, There'll be a bobbery in the pig-sty before long. **1867** SMYTH *Sailor's Word-bk.*, *Bobbery*, a disturbance, row, or squabble; a term much used in the East Indies and China. **1879** *Punch* 17 May 227, I might in quiet hold my own, And not go kicking up a bobbery.

bobbery ('bɒbəri), *a.* Chiefly *Anglo-Ind.* Also bobberee. [? f. BOBBERY *sb.*] Of a pack of hounds: miscellaneous in breed or quality. Also more widely: poor, of indifferent quality, 'scratch'. See also quot. 1934.

1873 'A. CHEEM' *Lays of Ind.* 2nd Ser. 86 Other servants bobbery pack, Drinking up what master leave, sir. **1878** *Life in the Mofussil* I. 142 On the mornings when the 'bobberee' pack went out. **1894** M. DYAN *Man's Keeping* i, The daily drills and the hunts with the bobbery packs. **1901** 'LINESMAN' *Words by Eyewitness* (1902) 234 A mounted officer pushing forward here, another there trying to turn his 'bobbery' horse to get back. **1934** *S.P.E. Tract* XLI. 20 The

word [bobbery] is scarcely used by Anglo-India, except in the phrase 'bobbery pack', where *bobbery* is an adjective, bearing the derived meaning 'mixed', 'mongrel', i.e. not composed of fox-hounds, &c.; also, occasionally (= fidgety), of a horse or infant. **1968** 'J. WELCOME' *Hell is where you find It* xi. 146 And what the hell do I do.. besides breaking my neck in a bobbery second-class steeplechase?

bobbin ('bɒbɪn), *sb.*[1] Forms: 6 bobbyn, 6–8 bobin, 7– bobbin. [a. F. *bobine* 'a quil for a spinning wheele; also a skane or hank of gold or silver thread' (Cotgr. 1611); origin unknown: see guesses in Littré and Diez.]

1. An article round which thread or yarn is wound, in order to be wound off again with facility, and as required, in weaving, sewing, etc.

a. 'A small pin of wood, with a notch, to wind the thread about when women weave lace.' J. (A cylinder 3 or 4 in. long, like a thickish pencil.)

b. A wooden or metal cylinder, perforated so as to revolve on a spindle, having a flange or 'head' at one or both ends (according to the purpose for which it is adapted), used to receive thread or yarn, and give it off by unwinding, in the processes of spinning, warping, weaving, frame-work knitting, etc.

c. A small spool for receiving the thread, placed within the shuttle, in some sewing machines.

d. In many parts of England: An ordinary 'reel' or 'spool', on which sewing cotton, silk, etc. are wound for sale and use, having the form of a small wooden cylinder, with a broad edge or rim at both ends.

1530 PALSGR. 199/1 Bobbyn for a sylke woman, *bobin.* **1603** HOLLAND *Plutarch's Mor.* 1220 Turned in maner of spindles or bobins, as folke spin or twist therewith. **1662** FULLER *Worthies* I. 246 Bone-lace it is named, because first made with bone (since wooden) bobbins. **1729** PULLEIN in *Phil. Trans.* LI. 23 The old method of reeling the silk over a bobin. **1736** SHERIDAN in *Swift's Lett.* (1768) IV. 165 If my skin were dry, my bones would rattle like a bag of bobbins. **1869** PALLISER *Lace* vii. 110 The oftener the bobbins are twisted the clearer and more esteemed is the Valenciennes. **1876** J. WATTS *Brit. Manuf.* III. 136 It draws out the cotton, twists it, and winds it upon a bobbin.

e. A reel round which wire is coiled in electrical instruments.

1870 R. FERGUSON *Electr.* 41 The thread..is wound round a slender movable bobbin. **1871** TYNDALL *Fragm. Sc.* (ed. 6) II. xvi. 441 The bobbins, in which the currents are induced.

2. 'A fine cord in haberdashery' (Beck *Draper's Dict.*); 'round tape' (Webster).

1578 [BECK *Draper's Dict.* s.v., In 1578 we find 'Skotish bobin sylke', and 'bobbing' appearing in an inventory of that date in conjunction with twine and thread]. **1641** MILTON *Animadv.* Wks. (1851) 191 To rumple her laces, her frizzles, and her bobins. **1843** LYTTON *Last Bar.* II. i, Tied with bobbins of gold thread. **1866** BLACKMORE *Cradock N.* xlvi. 305 A leathern bag..wash leather tied with bobbin.

†**3.** *Sc.* The seed-pod of the birch. (Jamieson.)

c **1562** A. SCOTT *Month of May*, To bring in bowis and birkin bobbynis.

4. A rounded piece of wood attached to a string, which passes through a door, and is fastened to the latch, so as to raise it. Hence ***bobbin-latch.***

Little Red Riding-hood (ed. 1820) 'Pull the bobbin and the latch will go up'. Little Red Riding-hood pulled the bobbin, and the door opened.

5. *Comb.*, as ***bobbin-boy, bobbin-mill, -turner***; **bobbin-lace**, lace made on a pillow with bobbins; **bobbin-stand**, a frame for holding the bobbins of a weaving- or spinning-machine; **bobbin-winder**, a contrivance for winding thread, etc. on a bobbin; †**bobbin-work**, 'work woven with bobbins'. J. See also BOBBIN-NET.

1681 GREW *Museum* (J.) Not netted nor woven with warp and woof, but after the manner of bobbinwork. **1857** MRS. GASKELL *C. Brontë* I. 68 A bobbin-mill..where wooden reels were made. **1871** J. R. LOWELL *My Study Windows* 45 Not everybody has the genius to be a Bobbin-Boy! **1876** *Pall Mall G.* 23 Aug. 4/2 Born at Troutbeck..he served his time to the trade of bobbin-turner. **1921** *Dict. Occup. Terms* (1927) §399, *Bobbin boy* (jute)..*bobbin boy* (rope and twine).

bobbin, *sb.*[2] *dial.* [Cf. BABBIN: but can it be the same as prec.?] A small bundle or fagot of fire wood.

Kent. dial. Buying wood, making it up into bobbins, and then selling it for fire-lighting.

bobbin ('bɒbɪn), *sb.*[3] [Etym. obscure.] Applied *attrib.* to the payment made to a fish porter at Billingsgate market.

1936 J. L. HODSON *Our Two Englands* xii. 239 The carrying prices, or bobbin rates, are all fixed in the trade. **1953** *Times* 3 Jan. 3/2 They heard of 'bobbin charges', paid by the customer to the porter for carrying the fish from the merchant.

'bobbin, *v.* [f. BOBBIN *sb.*[1]] To wind on bobbins. Hence **'bobbining** *vbl. sb.*

1883 *Glasgow Weekly Her.* 5 May 8/5 Rope yarn bobbining machine wanted, 4, 6 or 8 spindles.

bobbinet, var. of BOBBIN-NET.

'bobbing, *vbl. sb.*[1] Also (in sense 3) babbing. [Several words, f. BOB *v.* in various senses.]

1. Beating, striking; also *fig.* the giving of a sharp 'rap' in speech. (See BOB *sb.*[3] 2.) Hence ***bobbing-block.***

1526 *Pilgr. Perf.* (W. de W. 1531) 250 b, With spyttynges, bobbynges, and other turmentes many and dyuerse. **1558** PHAËR *Æneid* v. N iij, Loude their brests w[t] bobbings rings. **1575** GASCOIGNE *Wks.* (1587) 296 A bobbing blocke, a beating stocke, an owle. **1692** *Poems in Burlesque* 4 To leave off Stumming for dry Bobbing.

2. Movement up and down; dancing, curtsying, etc. (See BOB *v.*[3]).

a **1776** in Herd *Coll. Sc. Songs* II. 114 (JAM.) Wi' bobbing Willie's shanks are sair. **1832** HT. MARTINEAU *Each and All* v. 62 There was plenty of bobbing from the girls. **1865** *Englishman's Mag.* Oct. 310 Bees..making a ceaseless bobbing in the flowers.

3. Fishing for eels with a bob. (In East Anglia *babbing*, which also signifies a method of catching crabs; see quot. 1867.) Also *U.S.* (see BOB *sb.*[1] 7).

1653 W. LAUSON *Secr. Angling* in Arb. *Garner* I. 195 There is a third usual way to catch Eels, called 'Bobbing'. **1673** MARVELL *Reh. Transp.* II. 105 This grave and ponderous creature may like Eeles be taken and pull'd up only with bobbing. **1815** S. L. MITCHILL in *Trans. Lit. & Philos. Soc. N.Y.* I. 360 The eel..is also taken..by a bunch of tough bait, after a manner called *bobbing.* **1867** SMYTH *Sailor's Word-bk.*, *Babbing*, an east-country method of catching crabs, by enticing them to the surface of the water with baited lines and then taking them with a landing net. **1874** A. BATHGATE *Colonial Experiences* xvii. 243 The manner most frequently adopted for catching eels, called 'bobbing', is primitive enough, and is by means of a line formed of narrow stripes of flax leaves, to the end of which is tied a bundle of earth worms. **1883** *Century Mag.* July 383/1 Bobbing has been practiced in Florida for more than a century, and is a very simple but remarkably 'killing' method of fishing. **1888** GOODE *Amer. Fishes* 62 Trolling with the rod, 'skittering', and 'bobbing' are other modes of local popularity.

'bobbing, *vbl. sb.*[2] [f. BOB *sb.*[1] 2 e.] The action or pastime of riding on bob-sleighs. Also *attrib.*

1888 *Troy Daily Times* 31 Jan. (Farmer), All the village bobbing clubs will participate in the carnival at Albany tomorrow... There are seventy-eight entries for the bobbing parade. **1888** *Harper's Mag.* May 973/1 Ruby and Ned displeased their mother by joining a 'bobbing' party on a neighbouring 'hill' street. **1904** *Windsor Mag.* Jan. 245/1 Bobbing can be practised on any high-road having a sufficient length of suitable slope. **1928** *Evening Standard* 5 Jan. 6/2 Bobbing is carried out either on bobs (five passengers) or boblets (three passengers). **1942** A. KOROLEFF *Efficiency in Skidding Wood* 5/2 Other methods in which log carriers of some kind are used (such as 'bobbing', 'draying', 'boganning', etc.).

bobbing, *vbl. sb.*[3]: see BOBBER[5].

'bobbing, *ppl. a.* [Several words, f. BOB *v.* in various senses.]

†**1.** Mocking, flouting, satirical. *Obs.*

1605 CAMDEN *Rem.* 22 With these bobbing rimes.

†**2.** Striking. *Obs.*

1567 STUDLEY *Seneca's Hippolytus* (1581) 65 Dash out on mee thy bobbing bolt.

3. That bobs up and down or from side to side; dancing; curtsying.

a **1700** DRYDEN (J.) Jewels, rings, and bobbing pearls, Pluck'd from Moors' ears. **1821** CLARE *Vill. Minstr.* I. 72 Bobbing rabbits, wild and shy. **1868** *Gd. Words* July 445 He took off his hat to bobbing apple-women.

b. *Bobbing Joan*: an old dance-tune. ***Bobbing John***: a nickname of the Earl of Mar in 1715, referring to his behaviour to successive dynasties.

1756 *Hop Garland* (N.) Strike up Bobbing Joan, Or I'll break your fiddle. **1840** BARHAM *Ingol. Leg.*, *Nell Cook* Moral, Don't let your Niece sing 'Bobbing Joan'!

bobbin-net, bobbinet ('bɒbɪn,nɛt, 'bɒbɪnɛt). [f. BOBBIN + NET.] A kind of machine-made cotton net, originally imitating the lace made with bobbins on a pillow. Also *attrib.*

1814 JANE AUSTEN *Let.* 22 Nov. (1952) 413 Mrs. Clement walks about in a new Black velvet Pelisse..& a white Bobbin-net-veil. **1819** H. BUSK *Vestriad* III. 85 Ye kerchief'd damsels, who encushion'd fret,..your stiffen'd bobinet. **1824** M. WILMOT *Let.* 19 Jan. (1935) 204 The finest bobbinett dresses sprigged to imitate brussels lace. **1832** BABBAGE *Econ. Manuf.* xxxiii. (ed. 3) 350 The bobbin-net machine occupies little space. **1836** *Scenes of Commerce* 217 The frame net lace, or bobbinet, is a recent invention, manufactured by machinery. **1884** *Stubbs' Mercant. Circular* 19 Mar. 270/2 The increasing supersession of pillow-made lace by lace bobbinet made by machine power.

bobbish ('bɒbɪʃ), *a. dial.* and *slang.* [Cf. BOB *a.*, BOB *v.*[3]] Well; in good health and spirits.

1780 R. TOMLINSON *Slang Pastoral* 3, I was so good-natur'd, so bobbish and gay. **1813** [cf. BOBBISHLY]. **1819** SCOTT in *Lockhart* xliv. (1842) 394, I trust you will find me pretty bobbish. **1839** DICKENS *Nich. Nick.* lvii, 'The cows is well, and the boys is bobbish.' **1851** DE QUINCEY *Ld. Carlisle on Pope* Wks. XIII. 5 Finding himself 'pretty bobbish' on the morning after the memorable night in the Black Hole of Calcutta. **1862** TROLLOPE *Rachel Ray* II. xiii. 268 Pretty bobbish, thankee, Mr. Rowan; and how's yourself? **1928** GALSWORTHY *Swan Song* III. vi. 28 He did not feel so 'bobbish' before this third encounter with that fellow.

Hence **'bobbishly** *adv.* Well, fairly, briskly.

1813 SCOTT in *Lockhart* x. (Chandos) 223 The book has gone off here very bobbishly. **1819** —— *ibid.* xlv. IV. 285 You will find me looking pretty bobbishly. **1936** WODEHOUSE *Laughing Gas* xxix. 304 'Oh, so you know about that, too?' She laughed, though not too bobbishly.

'bobble ('bɒb(ə)l), *v. colloq.* [frequentative of BOB *v.*[3] (see -LE), helped by onomatopœic suggestiveness: cf. also BOBLE, BABBLE, BUBBLE.] *intr.* To move with continual bobbing. Also *transf.* and *refl.* So **'bobbling** *ppl. a.*

1812 W. TENNANT *Anster F.* I. xxxvi, Hobbling, bobbling round, and straining hard for Mag. **1836** T. HOOK *G. Gurney* III. vi. 316 The..Ship..was comfortably bobbling herself about at Spithead. **1892** *Daily News* 20 Sept. 6/4 If they must shoot something, let them pop away at bottles.. in a bobbling sea. **1896** W. PARK *Game of Golf* x. 202 It is absolutely essential that a putting-green be firm and smooth, and the turf close and short, so that the ball will roll on it and not 'bobble' or jump, as it certainly will if the turf be brushy and uneven. **1942** W. FAULKNER *Go Down, Moses* 18 He never even bobbled; he knocked Uncle Buck down and then caught him..without even stopping. **1960** I. CROSS *Backward Sex* iii. 79 The stretch and wriggle of her shoulders bobbled her body.

'bobble, *sb.*[1] [f. prec. vb.] The movement of agitated water.

1880 BESANT & RICE *Seamy Side* xxviii. 236 Outside Swanage Bay there is always what the jocose captain of the Heather Bell calls a 'bit of a bobble'. **1884** *St. James's Gaz.* 22 Mar. 6/2 There'll be a pretty bobble up across tide afore we get under the land.

bobble ('bɒb(ə)l), *sb.*[2] [dimin. of BOB *sb.*[1]: see -LE 1.] A small woolly ball used as an ornament or trimming. Also *attrib.*

1923 *Daily Mail* 13 Feb. 1 Knitted Wool Jumpers, finished cord and bobbles. *Ibid.* 17 Apr. 1 Trimmed with bobbles of own material arranged in sets. **1927** RUSSELL THORNDIKE *Slype* vi, A black gaberdine with bobbles on it. **1938** G. GREENE *Brighton Rock* II. i. 76 A stand lamp in a red silk shade with a bobble fringe. **1948** M. SHARP *Flowering Thorn* II. i. 55 There's a lot of stuff I think must be rep—it's got bobbles all round the edge. **1968** *Guardian* 20 Sept. 1/6 A man in an orange bobble hat walked across the hill.

bobbled ('bɒb(ə)ld), *a.* [f. BOBBLE *sb.*[2] + -ED[2].] Ornamented with bobbles.

1955 E. BOWEN *World of Love* iv. 76 The bobbled edge of the curtain. **1960** L. R. BANKS *L-Shaped Room* vi. 90 There was a bookshelf, garnished with a bobbled fringe.

bobbly ('bɒblɪ), *a. colloq.* [f. BOBBLE *v.* + -Y[1].] Jumpy, uneven; knobbly.

1909 *Westm. Gaz.* 1 Feb. 12/2 The hard ground, the bobbly putting, and all the other horrors of golf in frosty weather. **1921** *Chambers's Jrnl.* Jan. 3/1 The fully-opened door revealed the white coat and bobbly trousers of a veritable bed-room steward. **1969** P. DICKINSON *Pride of Heroes* 51 The first-floor windows mirrored one bobbly cloudlet.

bobby ('bɒbɪ), *sb.*

1. (With capital initial.) Pet form of *Bob*, familiar perversion of *Robert.*

2. [Hence probably in allusion to the name of Mr. (afterwards Sir) Robert Peel, who was Home Secretary when the new Metropolitan Police Act was passed in 1828.] A slang nickname for a policeman. See also PEELER.

1844 *Sessions' Paper* June 341, I heard her say..'a *bobby*'..it was a signal to let them know a policeman was coming. **1851** MAYHEW *Lond. Labour* 16 (Hoppe) He could muzzle half a dozen bobbies before breakfast. **1877** BESANT & RICE *Son of Vulc.* II. xxiii. 367 [He] might have been killed only that the bobbies interfered. **1884** L. J. JENNINGS in *Croker Papers* II. xiv. 17 Frequently when the constables made their appearance..they were hooted and insulted, mobs following them crying out 'crusher', 'raw lobster', 'Bobbies', and 'Peelers'.

3. ***bobby wren*** (*dial.*): see quot.

1885 SWAINSON *Prov. Names Birds* 35 *Wren*..From its short bob-tail it has the names of Cutty or Cut..Bobby wren (Norfolk), [etc.].

4. In full ***bobby calf***, an unweaned calf slaughtered soon after birth. Cf. BOB-VEAL.

1927 *Meat Trades Jrnl.* 16 June 1209/7 Central Meat Market..*Veal*: Moderate supply of fat calves..bobbies very short and dear. **1928** *Auckland Weekly News* 26 July 58/3, 30,000 bobby calves, mostly from the Waikato, were exported..last season as boneless veal. **1929** *Daily Express* 7 Nov. 15/5 Veal..specials 8s.–9s., bobbies 4s.–5s. **1938** *N.Z. Statutory Regulations* 334 'Bobby calf' means a calf which is intended for slaughter for human consumption as boneless veal. **1960** *Farmer & Stockbreeder* 16 Feb. 11/1 Scotch bobbies, 1s. 4d. to 1s. 6d. **1965** *Economist* 2 Oct. 70/2 In the past, the calf of a pure dairy cow, unless she was a heifer and so a potential milk-factory, was classed as a useless 'bobby' calf fit only for veal.

'bobby, *v. Obs. rare.* ? = BOB *v.*[1] 2, or BOB *v.*[2] 1.

14.. *MS. Addit.* 11748 f. 145 (Halliw.) The clooth byfore þi eyen to, To bobby þe [Christ] þay knit hit so.

bobby-dazzler ('bɒbɪ 'dæzlə(r)). orig. and chiefly *dial.* [DAZZLER.] Something striking or excellent; a strikingly-dressed person. Hence **bobby-dazzling** *sb.* and *a.*

1866 *N. & Q.* X. 290/2 *Morgan-rattlers*... In Cornwall the word is frequently applied to..things that are particularly striking or excellent of their kind. What a Lancashire man would sometimes call a 'regular bobby-dazzler', a Cornishman would call a 'regular morgan-rattler'. **1891** J. BARON *Blegburn Dickshonary* 15 *Bobby-dazzler* (a grand one). A lass is a bobby-dazzler when hoo's

getten a new frock on. **1913** J. L. Waugh *Robbie Doo* (1914) ii. 22 And, at last, wi' a perfect bobby-dazzler, he landed trampie yin below the jaw that made him spin like a peerie. **1913** D. H. Lawrence *Sons & Lovers* i. vi. 122 She had got a new cotton blouse on... 'Oh, my stars!' he exclaimed. 'What a bobby-dazzler!'.. 'It's not a bobby-dazzler at all!' she replied. 'It's very quiet.' *Ibid.* xii. 334 There isn't room in *this* house for two such bobby-dazzlers. **1915** —— *Rainbow* ix. 237 That's a bobby-dazzlin' posy you've brought! **1931** V. Palmer *Separate Lives* 177 There's a filly. .. She'd be good to win a race or two with—a real bobby-dazzler, she might turn out to be. **1944** *Gen* 1 Jan. 19/2 Matthews' bobby-dazzling wouldn't be wanted in a line containing authentic inside forwards. **1949** E. de Mauny *Huntsman in Career* 155 A real bobbydazzler of a morning. **1959** J. Braine *Vodi* xviii. 215 By God, you're what my old Nanny used to call a bobby-dazzler in that dress.

ˈbobby pin. *U.S.* [Etym. uncertain, but cf. bob *v.*⁵ and bobby sock.] A kind of sprung hair-pin or small clip, orig. for use with bobbed hair.

1936 J. Lawrence *If I have Four Apples* iv. vii. 201 She wondered whether she had lost all the bobby-pins from her marcelled hair. **1939** C. Morley *Kitty Foyle* viii. 81 How patient he was picking up bobby pins and the caps of coke bottles. **1952** M. McCarthy *Groves of Academe* (1953) iii. 32 Her dark, straight, glossy hair was worn short and loose, without so much as a bobby-pin. **1956** R. Heinlein *Double Star* (1958) v. 87 Penny girl, got a bobby pin?

ˈbobby sock. orig. *U.S.* [Etym. uncertain, but cf. bob *v.*⁵ to cut short.] (Usu. in pl., **bobby socks, sox**), socks reaching just above the ankle, esp. those worn by girls in their teens; also *attrib.* Hence **ˈbobby-socker,** (more commonly) **-soxer,** an adolescent girl, esp. one in her early teens, wearing bobby socks.

1943 *Time* 5 July 26/1 Hundreds of.. girls in bobby socks sat transfixed. **1944** *Newsweek* 6 Mar. 88 In New York City last week, the 'Bobby-sox Brigade' had swelled to such alarming proportions.. that police imposed an unofficial curfew. **1944** *Birmingham* (U.S.) *News-Age-Herald* 19 Nov. 11 A/4 About 6,000 bobby soxers attended the concert. **1944** *Life* 27 Nov. 76/2 When bobby-socker squeals, sound is carried to loudspeaker. **1945** Sinclair Lewis *C. Timberlane* (1946) xlvii. 333 Small white wool socks, 'bobby socks' they were called, to be worn with bare legs that were made-up to look tanned. **1945** *This Week* (U.S.) 15 Apr. 21/2 Comments on teen-age bobby-sock girls afflicted with dementia-Sinatra. **1946** *Jazz Writings* 22/1 George Webb's Dixielanders.. had the satisfaction of laying a mainly bobby-sox audience flat in the aisles. **1948** *Observer* 8 Feb. 3/2 His air of smiling tolerance could deceive none but a bobby-soxer. **1958** *Times Lit. Suppl.* 10 Oct. 573/2 The recent spate of elopement scandals and bobby-sox novelists.

bobcat. *N. Amer.* [bob *sb.*¹ 5, in allusion to the short tail.] The bay lynx, *Lynx rufus*, a small North American lynx with a spotted reddish-brown coat. Also *transf.*

1888 T. Roosevelt in *Century Mag.* Mar. 656 We also keep hens, which, in spite of the damaging inroads of hawks, bob-cats, and foxes, supply us with eggs. **1906** *Springfield Weekly Republ.* 20 June 2 The creation of this new commonwealth on virgin soil, where for centuries the wolves, bob-cats and Indians had leisurely roamed. **1911** O. Wister *Members of Family* vii. 250, I came for a box of matches, y'u bawlin' bobcat.

bob-cherry: see bob *v.*³ 4.

†**bobet,** *sb. Obs.* [f. bob *sb.*³ or *v.*²; with the suffix cf. *buffet.*] A blow with the fist, a cuff.

c **1340** *Cursor M.* 16623 (Trin.) Siþen in his honde þei sett: a muchel greet rede And to him pleiden a bobet: & bad him say in dede Whiche of hem ȝaf þe stroke. *c* **1440** *Promp. Parv.* 41 Bobet, *collafa, collafus.* **1530** Palsgr. 199/1 Bobet on the heed, *covp de poing.*

†**bobet,** *v. Obs.* [f. prec.] *trans.* To strike with the fist; to cuff. Hence **bobetting,** *vbl. sb.*

c **1440** *Promp. Parv.* 41 Bobettyn, *collaphizo.* —— Bobetynge, *collafizacio.*

bob-fool, bob-her: see bob *v.*¹ 4.

bob-haired, *a.* [See bob *a.* 1 and bob *v.*⁵ 2.] Of a woman or girl: having the hair cut short all round.

1923 C. Sidgwick *None-Go-By* xvii, The bob-haired female gazed at him as if she wished to probe into his soul. **1925** *Daily News* 7 Sept. 5/4 A bob-haired brunette.

bobinet, var. of bobbin-net.

†**ˈboble,** *v. Obs.* To babble. [But cf. also bobble, bubble.] Hence **ˈbobling** *ppl. a.*

c **1530** Barclay *Behaving in Church,* These fooles.. Are chatting and bobling as it were in a fayre. **1566** Studley *Seneca's Agamemnon* (1581) 156 There the head doth lye, With wallowing, bobling, mumbling tongue.

boblet (ˈbɒblɪt). [f. bob *sb.*¹ 2 e + -let.] A bob-sleigh for two persons. Also *attrib.*

1914 *Winter Sports Ann.* 15 (*caption*) Boblet.. Race on Schatzalp, at Davos, 1913. **1923** *Daily Mail* 11 Jan. 9 Boblet Races Results. **1958** *Times* 27 Dec. 3/5 Lord Kimberley arrived here [*sc.* at St. Moritz] to-day to start training for the world two-man boblet championships.

bobolink (ˈbɒbəlɪŋk). *U.S.* Also **bob-a-link, bob-a-linkum; boblincoln, -lincon, boblink, bob-o'-linck,** (**bob-o-lincoln, bob-o-linkhorn,** Audubon). [app. at first *Bob Lincoln,* or *Bob o' Lincoln,* a free rendering of the note or call of the bird.] A North American singing-bird (*Dolichonyx oryzivorus*), which appears in the northern states in spring, and returns southwards at the end of summer. Called also *Reed-bird* and *Rice-bird.*

1774 J. Adams *Diary* 24 Oct. in *Wks.* (1865) II. 401 Young Ned Rutledge is a perfect Bob-o-Lincoln. **1783** [see Conquedle]. **1796** Morse *Amer. Geog.* I. 210 Boblincoln. **1809** W. Irving *Knickerb.* (1861) 75 In the merry month of June.. [when] the luxurious little boblincon revels among the clover blossoms of the meadows. **1826** T. Flint *Recoll.* 243 Those merry and chattering birds, that we call bob-a-link, or French blackbird. **1840** W. Irving *Wolfert's R.* (1855) 20 The happiest bird of our spring.. is the Boblincon, or Boblink, as he is commonly called. **1840** C. F. Hoffman *Greyslaer* III. i. 104 There he goes.. singing for all the world like a Bob-a-linkum on the wing. **1847** *Tom Pepper* I. 145 (Th.), I heard her voice, which was sweeter than a bob-o'-linck's. **1849** T. Parker *Wks.* VII. 243 Who listen to the whippoorwill and the bobolink. **1855** in *Life W. Irving* IV. 163 The history of the boblink, or bob-o-lincoln. **1879** Lowell *Poet Wks.* 372 The bobolink has come.

†**bobolyne.** *Obs. rare.* [Cf. bob *v.*¹, also Sp. *bobo* fool.] A fool, a gaby.

a **1528** Skelton *Image Hypocr.* iv. Wks. II. 445 Be we not bobolynes Sutch lesings to beleve.

‖**bobotie** (bɒˈbəʊtɪ). *S. Afr.* Also **babotie** and variants. [Afrikaans, prob. of Malay or Javanese origin.] A dish of curried minced meat with a variety of ingredients.

1870 *Cape Monthly Mag.* Oct. 224 '*Babootie*' and '*frickadel*' and '*potatoe-pie*' are great improvements upon the minced meats of England. **1883** O. Schreiner *Afr. Farm* i. viii. 133 Till there is not one bone left in your old body that is not broken as fine as bobootie-meat, you old beggar. **1919** M. Higham *Household Cookery in S. Afr.* (ed. 2) 90 Bobotee. 1 lb. beef or mutton.. Mince the meat; chop onions finely. *a* **1920** O. Schreiner *From Man to Man* (1926) ii. ix. 318 For dinner and supper she made sosatie and bobotie. **1950** *Cape Times* 6 June 16/2 Something typically South African like babotie. **1950** L. G. Green *Land of Afternoon* iv. 61 Mrs. Dykman made her bobotie from minced meat.. bread, butter, onion, pounded almonds, lemon juice, eggs, curry powder and a small bunch of orange leaves. The mixture was baked and served with boiled rice.

Bob's-a-dying. *dial.* Also in contracted form bobsy-die (quots. are N.Z.). A great fuss; pandemonium.

1829 W. N. Glascock *Sailors & Saints* II. iv. 80 Nothing but dining, and dancing, and Bob's-a-dying on deck from daylight till dark. **1872** Hardy *Greenw. Tree* I. ii. vi. 204 She used to kick up Bob's-a-dying at the least thing in the world. **1876** —— *Ethelberta* Sequel II. 309 She threatened to run away from him, and kicked up Bob's-a-dying, and I don't know what all. **1892** R. O. Heslop *Northumb. Words* I. 72 'What a *Bob's-a-dying* they made!' means 'What a row they kicked up'. **1940** N. Marsh *Surfeit of Lampreys* (1941) xvi. 251 If she's right.. it plays Bobs-a-dying with the whole blooming case. **1952** *Here & Now* (N.Z.) II. iv. 25 Or Dido kicked up quite such bobsy-die If she had had a squint in her left eye. **1960** T. McLean *Kings of Rugby* vii. 50 By generally kicking up bobsy-die.

bob-sled, bob-sleigh. orig. *U.S.* A sled or sleigh, made of two short sleds or sleighs coupled together; used in drawing logs from the forest to a river or public road, and for various other purposes. Also **bob-sleighing** *vbl. sb.*, the sport of riding on a bob-sleigh.

1839 in *Amer. Speech* (1948) XXIII. 44/1 Then there would be wear and tear of bob-sled. **1848–60** in Bartlett. **1888** [see bob *sb.*¹ 2 d]. **1892** *Eng. Illustr. Mag.* Sept. 882 The logs are loaded on bob-sleds and taken to the mills. **1894** H. Gibson *Tobogganing* 163 Bobsleighing is another amusing form of tobogganing which has become very popular during the last few years. *Ibid.*, A Bobsleigh consists of two machines.. connected together endways by a board, upon which the crew sit or lie. *Ibid.*, The Bobsleigh, Bobsled, or double-ripper. **1910** *Daily Chron.* 12 Jan. 7/2 An English bobsleigh team.. dashed down the bobsleigh run and route above Grindelwald at a great speed. **1959** *Maclean's Mag.* 9 May 82/4 A winded horse, his sleighbells jingling, struggled to pull a real bobsled up the icy slope. **1968** *Listener* 12 Sept. 335/2 The night that we first transmitted our £60,000 production of *Hamlet at Elsinore*, they gave the front cover to the world bob-sleigh finalists.

bobstay. [f. bob (uncertain in what sense) + stay *sb.*] 'A rope used to confine the bowsprit of a ship downward to the stem... [Its use] is to draw down the bowsprit and keep it steady; and to counteract the force of the stays of the fore-mast, which draw it upwards.' Falconer *Dict. Marine* (1769).

1758 *Chron.* in *Ann. Reg.* 78/1 They.. passed the end of the mizen top sail sheet through the enemy's bobstay. **1840** R. Dana *Bef. Mast* xxx. 111 New and strong bobstays [were] fitted in the place of the chain ones. **1875** 'Stonehenge' *Brit. Sports* ii. viii. i. §5 Heave down the bobstay, and then haul the topmast forward again.

b. *attrib.*, as in *bobstay-collar, -hole, -plate.*

1867 Smyth *Sailor's Word-bk., Bobstay-collars*.. are almost entirely superseded by iron bands. *Ibid., Bobstay-holes,* those cut through the fore-part of the knee of the head, between the cheeks, for the admission of the bobstay; they are not much used now, as chain bobstays are almost universal, which are secured to plates by shackles.

bob-tail. [f. bob *sb.*¹ + tail.]

A. Properly two words (ˈbɒb ˈteɪl): The tail (of a horse) cut short.

[Must be earlier than 1577: when the vb. occurs.] **1667** *Lond. Gaz.* No. 211/4 A fine light Bay Stone-horse.. with his Mayne shorn, and a bob tail. **1720** *Ibid.* No. 5818/4 A brown Nag.. with a Bob Tail.

B. *attrib.* (ˈbɒbteɪl). Having a bob tail. **bobtail car** *U.S.* (see quot. 1888); **bobtail discharge** *U.S.* (see quot.); **bobtail plough** (see quot. 1743).

1605 Shaks. *Lear* iii. vi. 73 Hound or Spaniell, Brache, or Lym: Or Bobtaile tight [tike] or Troudle [*Qq.* trundle] taile. **1829** Marryat *F. Mildmay* xxiii, The bob-tail Cur. **1848** Lowell *Biglow P.* i, Trainin' round in bobtail coats. **1875** *Chicago Tribune* 8 Sept. 8/2 The bobtail cars ought to be taken off the streets right away, or conductors put on them. **1883** *Philadelph. Even. Star* 13 Feb. 3/4 Bob-tail Courtesies.. The old familiar bob-tail cars. **1888** Farmer *Americanisms, Bobtail car,* the popular name for a small tram-car horsed by a single animal, and on which the only official is a driver, whose office it is to collect fares and generally perform the duties of conductor in addition to his own. **1886** *Outing* (U.S.) Dec. 227/2 Upon the expiration of his first enlistment, he was given what is called a *bobtail* discharge, a discharge without character. **1733** Ellis *Chiltern & Vale Farm.* xxxviii. 319 Either the Swing, Bobtail, or Foot Plough. **1743** —— *Mod. Husb.* May i. 6 The Creeper or Bobtail Plough, is a two-Wheel Plough, differing but very little from the Fallow Wheel Plough.

C. *sb.* (ˈbɒbteɪl).

1. a. A horse or dog with its tail cut short.

1676 *Lond. Gaz.* No. 1115/4 A white Mare, and a black Nag.. both Bob-tails. *a* **1843** Southey *Ep. A. Cunningham* Wks. III. 309 Mongrel and cur and bob-tail, let them yelp.

†**b.** A kind of arrow: see quot.

1544 Ascham *Toxoph.* (Arb.) 126 Those that be lytle brested and big toward the hede called by theyr lykenesse taper fashion.. and of some merrye fellowes bobtayles.

c. = *bobtail discharge. U.S.*

1915 *Recruiters' Bulletin* (U.S.) June 8/1 (*title*) Bobtails. **1926** R. A. Bennet *Boss of Diamond A* viii. 72 My discharge is in that trunk of mine. I'll show you it's no bobtail! **1937** *Amer. Speech* XII. 75/1 *Bobtail,* (yellow-colored) dishonorable discharge.

†**2.** *transf.* A contemptible fellow, a cur. *Obs.*

1619 Fletcher *M. Thomas* ii. ii. 390 I'le not be bob'd i' th' nose with every bobtail.

†**3.** (See quot.) *Obs.*

1583 Higins *Junius' Nomenclator* 533 (D.) Cousins by mariage, or kinred (as they commonly terme it) by bobtaile.

4. *collectively.* [Perh. referring to 2 and 3.] *tag-rag and bob-tail,* or *tag, rag, and bob-tail*: the common herd, the rabble. Also *pl.* See tag.

1659–60 Pepys *Diary* 6 Mar., The dining-room.. was full of tag, rag, and bobtail, dancing, singing, and drinking. **1785** Wolcott (P. Pindar) *Ode to R. A's* ii. Wks. 1812 I. 80 Tagrags and Bobtails of the sacred Brush. **1800** Colquhoun *Comm. Thames* ii. 75 That lowest class of the community who are vulgarly denominated the Tag-Rag and Bobtail. *c* **1817** Hogg *Tales & Sk.* V. 255 The tag-rag and bob-tail part of the citizens of Edinburgh. **1820** Byron *Blues* ii. 23 The rag, tag, and bobtail of those they call 'Blues'. **1840** Dickens *Barn. Rudge* xxxv, 'We don't take in no tagrag and bobtail at our house.' **1926** J. Black *You can't Win* xiii. 180 She poured liquor into the bums, beggars, ragtags and bobtails that hung around the saloons.

5. In full ***bobtail flush, straight.*** A four-card flush or straight in the game of poker. *U.S.*

1875 *Cincinnati Enquirer* 2 July 2/3 The gentlemen.. can not 'bluff' to any success on their 'bob-tail flush'. **1887** *Courier Jrnl.* 20 Jan. 4/1 The Confederates would.. bet away the Washington monument on a 'bob-tail flush'. **1901** R. F. Foster *Poker* 26 The value of the 'bobtail', as a four-card flush is called, is nothing unless it can be improved in the draw.

bobtail (ˈbɒbteɪl), *v.* [f. prec.] *trans.* To dock the tail of; *fig.* to cut short, shorten, curtail.

1577 Stanyhurst *Descr. Irel.* in *Holinshed* VI. 28 A noble man, having a surpassing good horse.. did bobtaile him, least anie of his friends.. should craue him. *a* **1680** Butler *Rem.* (1759) II. 168 He is very just to the first Syllables of Words, but always bobtails the last. *a* **1700** *Songs Costume* (1849) 179 This Cloak.. bobtayl'd the gown, Put prelacy down, And trod on the mitre to reach at the crown.

Hence **bob-tailed** *a.* [f. vb. or sb.], with tail cut short; short-tailed. spec. U.S. ***bobtailed flush, straight*** = bob-tail C. 5; ***bobtailed car*** = *bobtail car* (see above).

1640 *King & North. Man* 62 in Hazl. *E.P.P.* IV. 295 His bob-tailed dog he out did call. **1702** *Lond. Gaz.* No. 3850/4 A clubbed bob-tail'd black Mare. **1863** Hawthorne *Our Home* I. 19 The bob-tailed coat and mixed trousers constituted a very odd-looking court-dress. **1873** *Winfield* (Kansas) *Courier* 15 Feb. 1/5 Well up in all the mysteries of a 'pair' or a 'bobtailed flush'. **1875** *Chicago Tribune* 16 Oct. 11/3 In regard to public feeling being against bobtailed cars. **1901** S. E. White *Westerners* i. 4 He owned.. a light, two-wheeled wagon of the bob-tailed type. **1944** *Amer. N. & Q.* Sept. 85/1 Bobtailed Straight or Flush.

bob-veal. *U.S.* [bob *sb.*¹; cf. *staggering bob* (staggering *ppl. a.* 1 d).] The veal of a very young calf. Cf. bobby 4.

1855 in De Voe *Market Assistant* (1867) 421 Butchers call this *bob-veal.* **1888** *San Francisco Weekly Exam.* 22 Mar. (Farmer), It is time this traffic in.. bob-veal was stopped. **1911** *N.Y. Even. Post* 13 Oct. 1 A former butcher was sentenced.. for.. shipping.. the carcasses of five bob veal calves to this city.

bob-white (ˈbɒbhwaɪt). [So called from its note.] A popular name of the common partridge of North America (*Odontophorus Virginianus*).

[**1812** Wilson *Amer. Ornith.* VI. 25 The quail.. will sometimes sit, repeating, at short intervals, 'Bob White', for half an hour at a time.] **1819** J. F. Stephens in *Shaw's Gen. Zool.* XI. ii. 380 By the natives of New England they [*sc.* Northern Colins] are called *bob-white.* **1883** *Century Mag.* Aug. 483/1 Of all the game birds of America, none is better

appreciated by the sportsman than little Bob-white. **1907** *Westm. Gaz.* 24 Aug. 16/1 The Virginian quail is more familiarly known by the name of 'Bob White', being the nearest rendering of the clear and loud call of the male bird. **1936** T. S. ELIOT *Coll. Poems 1909–35* 152 The bob-white Dodging by bay-bush.

bob-wig: see BOB *sb.*[1] 4.

bob-wire. *U.S.* colloq. alteration of *barb wire* (see WIRE *sb.* 1 e).

1929 J. F. DOBIE *Vaquero of Brush Country* 116 Chaos demanded order, and the means of order were to be barbed wire—'bob-wire', most people used to call it. **1939** STEINBECK *Grapes of Wrath* iv. 26 Some sisters took to beatin' theirselves with a three-foot shag of bobwire. **1940** C. MCCULLERS *Heart is Lonely Hunter* (1943) II. xi. 233 We got to climb the bob-wire fence.

boc, boc-land, etc.: see BOOK *sb.*

boc, obs. pa. t. of BAKE *v.*

‖**bocage.** [mod.F. *bocage* (bɔkaʒ) wood:—OF. *boscage.*] **1.** Woodland: a by-form of BOSCAGE.

1644 EVELYN *Mem.* (1857) I. 68 Whole fields, meadows, bocages. **1869** FREEMAN *Norm. Conq.* (1876) III. xii. 147 The men of the bocage and the men of the plain.

2. The representation of silvan scenery in ceramics. Also *attrib.*

1902 W. BURTON *Hist. & Descr. Eng. Porcelain* v. 49 Little figures were produced with wreaths of flowers and foliage, and, finally, the fully developed boscage, or bocage pieces. *Ibid.* vii. 73 Little figures on stands, with *bocages*, and nozzles for candlesticks, were also produced at Bow. **1950** *Antiquity* XXIV. 111 The 19th century ushers in John Walton, with his well-known 'bocage', which has been described as 'the art of the pastry-cook'. **1961** *Connoisseur New Guide to Antique Eng. Pott., Porc. & Glass* 66 Ralph Salt of Hanley specialised in the rather more costly *bocage* pieces, sporting dogs, and sheep with hand-raised wool. **1961** *Times* 8 Apr. 11/6 The leafy arbour of *bocage* groups associated with exquisite porcelain.

‖**bocal** (bɔkal, ˈbəʊkəl). [mod.F. and Sp. *bocal*, related to late L. *baucale*, ad. Gr. βαύκαλις vessel for cooling liquids in, βαυκάλιον narrow-necked vessel. Cf. It. *boccale*, and Ger. *pokal.*] A glass bottle or jar with a short wide neck.

[**1756** *Gentl. Mag.* XXVI. 8 There are now fourteen French ships in our mole, the greatest part of which are laden with bocalas.] **1847** in CRAIG; and in mod. Dicts.

‖**boˈcane.** *Obs.* [Fr., f. the name of the inventor, *Bocan*, dancing master to Queen Anne of Austria.] 'A stately figure-dance, much esteemed in the 17th cent.' Littré.

a **1701** SEDLEY *Grumbler* III. i. Wks. (1766) 225 You would have a grave, serious dance, perhaps?..the courante, the bocane, the sarabande?

†**ˈbocardizing**, *ppl. a. nonce-wd.* [f. next: see -IZE.] Forming awkward or bad syllogisms; reasoning awkwardly.

1652 *Woman's Univ.* in Watson *Sc. Poems* III. 103 Her bocardising Captions are, From ποῦ, or else from πότε.

bocardo, bokardo (bəʊˈkɑːdəʊ). [In med.L. the logical term goes back to the 12th or 13th c. On the question of its relation to senses 2, 3, there appears to be no evidence: the conjecture has been offered that the prison may have been named in jocular reference to the impossibility of directly reducing this mood to the First Figure, or because it was considered an awkward form of the syllogism to get out of. The mutual relation of senses 2 and 3 is also uncertain: so far as the evidence goes, 2 may be a specific use of 3, or 3 a generalized application of 2. If the prison was named from the scholastic term, there would be an appropriateness in the name being first given in Oxford.]

1. *Logic.* A mnemonic word, representing by its vowels the fifth mood of the third figure of syllogisms, in which the premisses are a particular negative and a universal affirmative, and the conclusion a particular negative, the middle term being the subject of both premisses: thus some M is not P; all M is S; some S is not P.

1509 BARCLAY *Shyppe of Folys* (1874) I. 144 Another comyth in with bocardo and pheryson. **1838** SIR W. HAMILTON *Logic* xxii. I. 443 Bocardo, which..was the opprobrium of the scholastic system of reduction. **1870** BOWEN *Logic* 204 Baroko and Bocardo have been stumbling-blocks to the logicians.

†**2.** The name of the prison in the old North Gate of the city of Oxford, pulled down in 1771.

1535 R. LAYTON in Strype *Eccl. Mem.* I. I. 210 Wee haue set Dunce [Duns Scotus] in Bocardo, and haue utterly banished him Oxford for ever, with all his blynd glosses. **1555** LATIMER *Let.* ibid. III. II. App. xxxvi. 99 An epistle sent by Mr. Latimer to all the unfayned lovers of Godds trewthe owte of a prison in Oxenford, called Bocardo. **1694** STRYPE *Abp. Cranmer* III. xi. 341 And so Cranmer was returned to Bocardo, and the other two [Ridley and Latimer] to other Places. **1772** WHARTON *Newman's Verses*, Rare tidings for the wretch whose ling'ring score Remains unpaid, bocardo is no more. **1874** M. BURROWS *Worthies All Souls* iii. 37 His brother, who was confined in Bocardo, the famous old prison-gateway which formerly stood at the top of Cornmarket Street. **1875** M. PATTISON *Casaubon* 415.

†**3.** A prison, dungeon. In phr. *in, into* (*to*) *Bocardo.*

1535 [The quot. of this date in 2, may possibly have the general sense of 'in prison'.] **1550** LATIMER *Serm. bef. Edw. VI*, 232 Elias had preached Gods word..Was not this a seditious fellow? was not this fellows preaching a cause of all the trouble in Israel? Was he not worthy to be cast into bocardo or little ease? **1583** STUBBES *Anat. Abus.* K vij b, If he haue not to satisfie aswel the one as th'other then to Bocardo goeth he as round as a ball, where he shalbe sure to lye untill he rotte. **1653** ROB. BAILIE *The Dissuasive..vindicated* (1655) 62 For myself, I care the less to be cast in these Bocardo's. **1709** *Let. to Ld M[ayor]* 6 Your Lordship cou'd..not put him in Bocardo.

bocare, obs. f. BOOKER, scribe.

bocasin (ˈbɒkəsɪn). Also 5 **bokesy**, 6–7 **boccasin(e.** [a. Sp. *bocací* cotton stuff used for lining, (also of its Fr. form *boccasin* (Cotgr.), now *boucassin*), a. Turk. *bōhāsī* or *bōghāsī* cotton cloth (Kieffer el Bianchi).] 'A kind of fine Buckeram, that hath a resemblance of taffata, and is much used for lining.' Cotgr.

1485 *Inv.* in *Ripon Ch. Acts* 366, viij ulnæ de blakke bokesye . una toga lyned cum bokesy. **1611** COTGR., *Boccasin*, Boccasin. **1714** *French Bk. Rates* 36 Boucasin-stuff per Piece of 12 Ells. **1721** BAILEY, *Boccasine*, fine Buckram, a sort of Linen Cloth. **1755** JOHNSON, *Bocasine* [as in BAILEY]; and in later Dicts.

‖**bocca** (ˈbokka, ˈbɒkə). [It.; = 'mouth'.]

1. A circular opening in a glass-furnace, through which the melting-pots are inserted and withdrawn.

1799 G. SMITH *Laborat.* I. 167 The mouth of a glass furnace is called the bocca. **1832** G. PORTER *Porcelain* 159 The openings..serving for the introduction of the materials and for the removal of the melted glass, are called boccas.

2. (See quot.)

1881 *Pop. Sci. Monthly* XIX. 51 The active bocca or mouth of Vesuvius.

‖**boccarella** (bokkaˈrɛlla, bɒkəˈrɛlə). [It., dim. of prec.] A smaller opening on either side of the 'bocca' in a glass-furnace.

1799 G. SMITH *Laborat.* I. 167 On each side of the bocca, is a smaller hole, or boccarella. **1832** G. PORTER *Porcelain* 158 Sometimes called a boccarella, but more generally by the familiar name of nose-hole.

boccaro (ˈbɒkərəʊ). Also **bucaro, buccaro.** [Prob. ad. Pg. *búcaro* clay cup:—L. *poculum* cup.] A scented red earthenware brought originally by the Portuguese from Mexico and similar earthenware made in Portugal and Spain from the 16th to the 18th century; the name is also applied to unglazed Yi-hsing ware of China.

1872 J. F. RIANO *Catal. Art Objects of Spanish Production in S. Kens. Mus.* p. xxix, This author [*sc.* Mme D'Aulnoy] also mentions the red earthen pottery, bucaros of Toledo. **1898** M. L. SOLON *Pottery Worship* 13 Guadalaxara, in Mexico, sent over the most highly-scented Buccaros. *Ibid.* 17 In 1568 Buccaros were made at Talavera, in Spain, as the imitation of those..imported from Portugal. *Ibid.* 30 True Buccaros never came from China..and..must not be looked for out of the pottery sent over from Central America, or the Portuguese imitations. **1910** *Encycl. Brit.* V. 741/2 From the 16th to the 18th century a special kind of unglazed pottery vessels known as *buccaros* were extensively made both in Spain and Portugal... The vessels were delicately scented, like a ware imported from Mexico. **1945** W. B. HONEY *Ceramic Art of China* II. 136 The Yi-hsing ware..made of various brown, buff and reddish clays,..is unglazed... In Europe, from their similarity to a Spanish-American ware they were sometimes called '*boccaro*' (or '*buccaro*') ware.

bocche, boccher, obs. ff. BOTCH, BUTCHER.

bocconia (bɒˈkəʊnɪə). [mod.L.; named after the Sicilian botanist, Paolo Boccone (1633–1704).] A tall herbaceous plant or shrub of the papaveraceous genus of the name, with large lobed leaves and panicles of flowers. The favourite species is *B. cordata*, with cream-coloured flowers growing on tall stems.

1867 K. PROSPER in *Floral World* Apr. 107, I have had the honour to introduce the Bocconia to cultivation on the continent... This plant is of most quick growth, the great leaves are deeply notched, and with much of whitish colour. The flowers are like poppies..and the colour rose, or pink, or white. **1902** W. P. WRIGHT *Cassell's Dict. Gard.* I. 128 The herbaceous Bocconias like a rich, heavy soil. **1961** *Times* 2 Dec. 11/4 Herbaceous plants such as..bocconias.

†**boce**[1]. *Obs. Ichthyol.* [ad. L. *bōx*, pl. *bōces*, the name of a fish in Pliny (*N.H.* XXXII. xi.); cf. Fr. *bocque* a 'great-eyed Cackerell fish' (Cotgr.).] An acanthopterygian fish (*Box* or *Boöps vulgaris*), also called Bogue (family *Sparidæ*), found in the Mediterranean, and rarely on the British coast.

1617 RIDER *Dict.*, Boces, small fishes so called, *Leucomænides.* **1753** CHAMBERS *Cycl. Supp.*, *Boce*, the name given by Aristotle, and many other of the antient Greek writers to the fish commonly called by authors *boops.*

†**boce**[2]. *Obs.* [a. OF. *bos* wood, bush.] A by-form of BUSH.

1482 *Monk of Evesham* (Arb.) 40 A full depe valeye and a derke set with bocis and brackys on euery syde.

boce, obs. form of BOOSE, BOSS, BOTCH.

bochchare, obs. f. BOTCHER.

Boche (bɒʃ). Also *erron.* **Bosch(e.** [Fr. slang, = rascal, German, said to be shortened from *caboche* head, or from *Alboche*, modification of *Allemand* German.] The (French) soldiers' name for a German. Also *attrib.* or *adj.*, German.

[**1887** A. BARRÈRE *Argot & Slang, Boche*..rake... *Tete de boche*, German.] **1914** *Daily Express* 30 Sept. 4/2 Monsieur had better come under cover. The 'Bosches' are still firing this way. **1915** *National Rev.* Mar. 21 Easter passed without the promised bonne-bouche for the Bosches. **1917** G. S. GORDON *Let.* 12 Mar. (1943) 72 Our Archibalds are peppering a Boche aeroplane. **1919** 'BOYD CABLE' *Old Contemptibles* viii. 130 A Boche..proceeded to drop bombs all over the place. **1920** *Punch* 20 Oct. 305/1 Bosch aeroplane observers. **1940** W. S. CHURCHILL *Into Battle* (1941) 296 All Europe, if he [*sc.* Hitler] has his way, will be reduced to one uniform Boche-land. **1952** E. F. DAVIES *Illyrian Venture* ii. 43 If the Boche wanted a rough-house he could rely on Pickering to give it to him.

bocher, -or, bochsar, etc., obs. ff. BUTCHER.

bocht, obs. form of BOUGHT.

†**ˈbocion.** *Obs. rare.* [irreg. f. mod.L. *bocium*, f. F. *boce*: cf. BOSS *sb.*[1], BOTCH *sb.*[1]] A glandular swelling in the neck.

1547 BOORDE *Breu. Health* xlv. 22 Bocium or Nauta be the latin wordes. In English it is a swelling the which doth grow in the throte and in the necke..naturall bocions commonly chyldren hath..accidental bocions commeth to age or by myschaunce.

bock (bɒk). [Fr., a. G. *bock*, in full *bockbier*, shortened f. *Eimbockbier*, now *Einbecker bier*, f. *Einbeck*, *Eimbeck*, a town in Hanover.] In full *bock beer.* A strong dark-coloured variety of German beer. Also, a glass of this or any other beer.

1856 *Ill. State Reg.* 26 June 4/3 There is a Bavarian lager beer which is called 'bock'. **1867** SIMMONDS *Dict. Trade* Suppl., *Bock-beer*, a favourite Bavarian double strong malt beverage, of the best lager description. **1879** SALA *Paris Herself Again* I. 183 A 'bock', or glass of light and frothy beer. *Ibid.* 186 Allsopp at fifty centimes the 'bock'. **1899** WILDE *Lett.* (1962) 784, I go there on foot daily and have a *bock.* **1917** T. S. ELIOT *Prufrock* 19 Let us..sit for half an hour and drink our bocks.

bock, bock-land, etc.: see BOOK *sb.*

bock, var. of BUCK and BOLK *v.* to belch.

bockeler(e, bocler, obs. ff. BUCKLER.

†**ˈbockerel, ˈbockeret.** *Obs.* [Origin unknown: cf. BAWREL, BAWRET.] Names said to be given to the male and female, respectively, of a kind of long-winged hawk.

1653 WALTON *Angler* 12 The Gerfalcon and Jerkin..the Bockerel and Bockeret. **1672** RAY *Philos. Lett.* (1718) 113 There are, besides..a Boccarell, and a Boccaret. They are the Names of the Male and Female. **1721–1800** in BAILEY.

bocket, obs. form of BUCKET.

bockey (ˈbɒkɪ). [Bartlett compares Du. *bokaal* (see BOCAL), of which it may be diminutive form.] 'A bowl or vessel made from a gourd. A term peculiar to the city of New York and its vicinity.' Bartlett *Dict. Amer.* (1860).

bocking (ˈbɒkɪŋ). [f. the village *Bocking* in Essex.] A kind of coarse woollen drugget or baize.

1759 B. MARTIN *Nat. Hist. Eng.* II. *Essex* 23 Bays, of which this Village has a peculiar Sort, called Bockings. **1848–60** BARTLETT *Dict. Amer.*, *Bocking*, a kind of baize or woollen cloth..used to cover floor or to protect carpets.

bocle, bocull(e, obs. forms of BUCKLE.

†**ˈboc-leden.** *Obs.* [OE. *bóc* book + *léden*, *læden*, Latin, hence, literary language: see LEDEN.] Book-Latin, the Latin language; afterwards book-language.

a **1000** *O.E. Chron.* Introd., Her sind on þis iȝlande fif ȝepeode, Englisc, and Brittisc and Wilsc, and Scyttisc, and Pyhtisc, and Boc Leden. *c* **1175** *Lamb. Hom.* 117 Episcopus is gerkisc noma þet is on boc leden speculator. *c* **1200** *Trin. Coll. Hom.* 151 Iacob on boc leden is icleped under-plantere.

bocsom, -um, obs. forms of BUXOM.

†**ˈbocspell.** *Obs.* [OE. *boc* book + OE. *spell* story.] A history or narrative.

c **1205** LAY. 17487. *Ibid.* 19423 Nu ich þe wulle tellen a þissen boc-spællen [*c* **1275** þisse boc-spelle].

†**ˈbocstaff, -stave.** *Obs.* [OE. *bócstæf* corresp. to OS. *bôcstab* (MDu. *boekstaf*), OHG. *buohstab* (MHG. *buochstap*, mod.G. *buchstabe*), ON. *bókstafr* (Sw. *bokstaf*, Da. *bogstav*). Cf. Goth. **bôkastafs*, 'letter (of the alphabet)', f. *bôk* writing-tablet, book + *staf-* staff, letter; according to some, orig. 'beech-staff', but see BOOK. This interesting old word, still in full use in continental languages, survived in English

only to the 13th c., when it was superseded by *letter*. Its modern form would have been *bookstaff* or *buckstaff*, as a connexion with *book* was or was not explicitly retained.] A letter (of the alphabet).

a **1000** *Elene* 91 (Gr.) Se blaca beam bocstafum awriten. *c* **1200** ORMIN 4305 Writenn o Grickisshe boc Rihht wiþþ bocstafess sexe. *c* **1205** LAY. 7637 Feole cunne boc-staven æ ðere hilte wes igrauen [not in later text].

bod (bɒd). Slang abbrev. of BODY *sb.* in various senses; esp. a person. (In Sc. quots. 1788 and 1813, perh. abbrev. of BODACH.)

1788 J. MACAULAY *Poems* 143 While aulder bods were babees birling, We took our slide. **1813** E. PICKEN *Poems* II. 131 Sae he made a long blaw about graces, an' gods, Like Vulcan, an' Bachus, an' ither sic bods. **1933** R. STRACHEY *Many Happy Returns* I. 33 The Red, the White and the Blue is unfurled and covers the dead bod, the corpse of a grocer given for England. **1953** 'N. SHUTE' *In Wet* vi. 187 The rest go to the camp with the R.A.A.F. bods. **1954** C. P. SNOW *New Men* xxii. 151 'Bods' meant bodies, people, any kind of staff: scientists were bods, so were floor cleaners. **1955** P. SHARP in Chambers & Landreth *Called Up* iii. 73 To join a station you have to get these cards signed by odd bods all over the place. **1966** *Crescendo* Aug. 8/1 The show-tune formula is quite simple—I know dozens of bods who make a living using it.

bodach ('bodəx). *Ir.* Also **-agh, 8 buddough.** [Gaelic and Ir. *bodach*.] A peasant, churl; also (*Sc.*) a spectre.

1732 SWIFT *Irish Eloquence* His Neighbor Squire Doll is a meer Buddough. **1814** SCOTT *Wav.* III. xii. 157, I have seen the Bodach Glas [*i.e.*, the Grey Spectre]. **1827** —— *Highl. Widow* i, Oh! then the mystery is out. There is a bogle or a brownie,..a bodach or a fairy, in the case? **1830** W. CARLETON *Traits Irish Peasantry* I. 28 Hut! he's none iv yer proud, stingy, upsthart *bodaghs*. **1865** *Dublin Rev.* July 73 It admits of no doubt that the Gaelic is withering away... The coarse Bodach almost alone retains it as the language of common life. **1903** *Westm. Gaz.* 18 May 4/3 Father Dinneen's play 'The Enchanted Well' dealt with a rivalry in love between a rich 'bodach' and a poor poet. **1903** W. B. YEATS *Hour-Glass* 13, I met a bodach on the road yesterday.

bodacious (bə'deɪʃəs), *a. U.S. dial.* Also **bow-**. [Perh. a variant of Eng. dial. *boldacious*, a combination of *bold* and *audacious*.] Complete, thorough, arrant. Also as *adv.*

1845 W. T. THOMPSON *Chron. Pineville* 178 She's so bowdacious unreasonable when she's raised. **1887** 'C. E. CRADDOCK' *Keedon Bluffs* 153 Air ye turned a bodacious idjit, Skimp? **1941** *Time* 17 Mar. 23/2 The bodacious blurt did him no good with his brother Navy men.

bo'daciously, *adv.* *U.S. dial.* Also **bodyaciously.** [See prec.] Completely, thoroughly.

a. **1837** A. SHERWOOD *Gaz. Georgia* (ed. 3) 69 *Bodaciously*, wholly. **1840** *Congress. Globe* 20 July 545 (Th.), [It has been proclaimed abroad] that the Administration is bodaciously used up. **1843** 'CARLTON' *New Purchase* 143 It was now snowing so bodaciously fast. **1887** 'C. E. CRADDOCK' *Keedon Bluffs* 104 He drug two needles bodaciously out an spiled fower rows. **1904** HARBEN *Georgians* vii. 69 You was ruinin' yoreselves bodaciously.

β. **1833** J. HALL *Leg. West* 82 It seems like it would jist use me up bodyaciously. **1833** *Sk. D. Crockett* Pref. p. v, A constant repetition of the terms bodyaciously, teetotaciously, obflisticated, &c.

bodd- see BOD-.

bodder, boddom, obs. f. BOTHER, BOTTOM.

boddle, variant of BUDDLE, corn marigold.

bode (bəʊd), *sb.*¹ [Com. Teut.: OE. *boda* = OFris. *boda*, OS. *bodo* (MDu. and Du. *bode*), OHG. *boto* (MHG. and mod.G. *bote*), ON. *boði*:—OTeut. **bodon-*, f. *bod-* stem of *beud-an*: see next.]

One who makes an announcement; a herald, a messenger. *Obs.* from 12th c., but recently affected by some writers on OE. history.

c **888** K. ÆLFRED *Boeth.* xxxvi. i, þu þe eart boda and forrynel ðæs soþan leohter. *c* **1175** *Cott. Hom.* 219 *Angeli* (boden), *archangeli* (hahboden). **1613** R. C. *Table Alph.* (ed. 3), *Bode*, a messenger. **1848** LYTTON *Harold* III. i. 49 Fast.. went the bodes and riders of the Earl. **1872** E. ROBERTSON *Hist. Ess.* 114 The Beadle..the Bode or messenger of the Court. **1880** *Blackw. Mag.* Mar. 344 Their bodes brought the news of the landing at Pevensey.

bode (bəʊd), *sb.*² Also 1–4 **bod, 6 boad.** [Com. Teut.: OE. *bod* (chiefly northern for *ȝebod*; cf. *bebod*), neuter = OFris. *bod*, OS. *gibod* (Du. *gebod*), OHG. *gabot*, (mod.G. *gebot*, *bot*), ON. *boð* (Sw., Da. *bud*):—OTeut. **gabodo(m*, f. *bod*-pa. ppl. stem of *beudan* to offer, etc., see BID *v.*]

†**1.** Command, order, behest. *Obs.*

a **1000** *Hymns* vii. 109 (Gr.) We..þine bodu bræcon. *c* **1205** LAY. 30121 þat bod wes ihalden. *c* **1340** *Gaw. & Gr. Knt.* 852 þere were boun at his bode burnez in-noȝe.

†**2.** Message, tidings. *Obs.*

c **1205** LAY. 27999 He brohte boden swiðe gode. *c* **1330** *Arth. & Merl.* 2046 A bod com fram the sarrazin. *c* **1450** LONELICH *Grail* xliv. 340 Thanne cam he to þe messengers ..and of here bode ȝaf hem answeryng. **1637** RUTHERFORD *Lett.* clxxvii. (1862) I. 419 His bode is ever welcome to me, be what it will.

†**3.** Premonition, omen, augury. *Obs.*

c **1374** CHAUCER *Parl. Foules* 343 The owl eke, that of death the bode ybringeth. **1613** PURCHAS *Pilgr.* I. iii. xvii. 285 It was a good bode and happie presage. **1632** SHIRLEY *Love in Maze* Epil., If no fate Have an unlucky bode.

4. Presentiment, foreboding. *arch.*

1587 FLEMING *Contn. Holinshed* III. 1338/1 With better boad of lucke and lot, receive thou now the same. **1857** HEAVYSEGE *Saul* (1869) 214 Down black bodes, false flies.

5. An offer of a price, a bid. Still in north. dial.

c **1200** *Trin. Coll. Hom.* 213 þe beggere [= buyer] ecneð his bode. **1394** *P. Pl. Crede* 716 [Friars] bene at lone and at bode As burgeses vsithe. **1790** BURNS *Lett.* 62, I refused fifty-five shillings for her, which was the highest bode I could squeeze. **1816** SCOTT *Antiq.* xxxix, 'Ye should never tak a fish-wife's first bode.' **1853** READE *C. Johnstone* 63 Half-a-crown was his first bode.

†**6.** ? Prayer, petition. *Obs.* cf. BEDE.

c **1175** *Lamb. Hom.* 65 Wenne scal þos bode [*v.r.* beode] us god don.

†**bode,** *sb.*³ *Obs.* Forms: 3–4 **bod,** 4–6 **bode;** *north.* 4–5 **bad,** 4–6 **bade,** (4 **baide,** 6 **beed**). [Not found in OE., and either formed at a later time on BIDE, on the analogy of *abide, abode*, or an aphetic form of ABODE itself. In later use chiefly Sc., in form *bade, baid*.] Biding, tarrying, waiting, delay. ***but bode***: without delay.

a **1300** *Cursor M.* 2485 An auter [abram] raised wit-outen bad. *Ibid.* 2535 Wit-outen baide. *c* **1350** *Will. Palerne* 149 Boute bod he braydes to þe quene. **1375** BARBOUR *Bruce* VI. 403 [He] gert arme his men..forouten baid. *c* **1440** *Bone Flor.* 1018 Than was there no lenger bode. **1535** STEWART *Cron. Scot.* I. 213 He dressit him..But ony baid. **1593** PEELE *Chron. Edw. I.* (1874) 384 Make thou thy bode In resolution to revenge these wrongs.

†**bode,** *sb.*⁴ *Obs.* [Origin and standing uncertain: see note in *Cath. Angl.*] A pole or perch.

1483 *Cath. Angl.* 36 A Bode; *pola*.

Bode ('bəʊdə), *sb.*⁵ *Astr.* [The name of Johann Elert *Bode* (1747–1826), German astronomer.] ***Bode's law***: see LAW *sb.*¹ 17 c.

1833 [see LAW *sb.*¹ 17 c]. **1959** *Listener* 30 July 171/1 During the eighteenth century a German named Titius worked out a numerical relationship in connection with the distances of the various planets; in 1772 this relationship was discussed by another German, Bode, and is generally, though rather unfairly, known as Bode's Law.

bode (bəʊd), *v.*¹ Forms: 1 **bodiȝ(e)an,** 1–2 **bodian,** 2–4 **bodien,** 4, 7 **boden,** 6–7 **boad(e,** 4– **bode.** [OE. *bodian*, f. *boda* messenger; cf. ON. *boða* of same meaning.]

†**1.** *trans.* To announce, proclaim, preach. *Obs.*

a **1000** *Hymns* x. 23 (Gr.) Bododon englas, þæt acenned wæs Crist on eorðan. *c* **1000** *Ags. Gosp.* Matt. xxiv. 14 þis godspel byð bodod [*c* **1160** *Hatton G.* boded] ofer ealle eorðan. *a* **1225** *Leg. Kath.* 1480 Men schal beoden & bodien hit ouer al.

†**b.** *absol.* To preach (the gospel). *Obs.*

c **1000** *Ags. Gosp.* Matt. iv. 17 Syððan ongan se Hæland bodian, and cweðan, Doð dæd-bote. *Ibid.* Mark v. 20 He ongan bodiȝean [*c* **1160** *Hatton G.* bodiȝen] on decapolim. *c* **1175** *Lamb. Hom.* 93 [Hi] bodeden mid ane speche.

†**2.** To proclaim authoritatively, decree, order, bid, command (a person) *that*. *Obs.*

c **1205** LAY. 23730 Leteð blawen bemen and bodien mine monnen þat æuer ælc god mon to niht wakien. *a* **1225** *St. Marher.* 17, I bidde ant bodie þat tu wurche mi wil.

3. To announce beforehand, foretell, predict, prognosticate, presage. *arch.*

a **1000** *Elene* 1141 (Gr.) þæt wæs oft bodod feor ær beforan fram fruman worulde. *c* **1175** *Cott. Hom.* 235 Hi..bodeden ures hlafordes tocyme. *a* **1250** *Owl & Night.* 1155 Other thu bodes huses brune..Other thu bodes cualm of orve. **1676** BULLOKER, *Bode*, to foretel, or prognosticate. **1715** POPE *Iliad* I. 132 Prophet of plagues, for ever boding ill! **1771** FRANKLIN *Autobiog.* Wks. 1840 I. 79 There are croakers in every country, always boding its ruin.

4. Of things: To give promise of, be indicative of, betoken, portend.

1387 TREVISA *Higden* (1865) II. 293 It bodid grete merite and vertue. **1483** *Cath. Angl.* 36 To Bode, *portendere*. **1602** SHAKS. *Ham.* I. i. 69 This boades some strange eruption to our State. **1650** R. STAPYLTON *Strada's Low-C. Warres* III. 60 All things seemed to boad a Civill warre. **1822** BYRON *Werner* II. i. 248 So much haste bodes Right little speed. **1860** TYNDALL *Glac.* I. § 5. 37 That lingering rosy hue which bodes good weather.

b. *esp.* (with *well* or *ill*) To give *good* or *bad* promise, to augur *well* or *ill*.

a **1700** DRYDEN (J.), Whatever now The omen proved, it boded well to you. **1832** WHATELY *Let.* in *Life* (1866) I. 159, I can see nothing that bodes well to the Church Establishment: I fear its days are numbered. **1870** DISRAELI *Lothair* lxxxiv. 454 Some think this bodes ill for the Church.

†**c.** To signify, typify. *Obs.*

1387 TREVISA *Higden* Rolls Ser. III. 13 Solomon's temple, bodede holy chirche [*in figura præsentis ecclesiæ*].

5. To have a presentiment of; to forebode (generally *evil*).

1740 RICHARDSON *Pamela* (1824) I. 80 My presaging mind bodes horrid mischiefs. **1850** BLACKIE *Æschylus* II. 229 And my soul, dark-stirred with the prophet's mood, Bodes nothing good.

bode, *v.*² *Sc.* [prob. f. BODE *sb.*² 5 = to make a 'bode'.] *trans.* To bid for, make an offer for.

Scotch Adage, Bode a robe and wear it, Bode a poke and bear it.

bode, early var. of *boðe*, BOOTH, and of BODEN.

bode = behoved, pa. t. of BUS *v.*

bodeful ('bəʊdfʊl), *a.* [f. BODE *sb.*² + -FUL. A modern formation (not in Todd, Richardson, or Craig 1847) very frequent in modern poets and essayists.] Full of presage, boding, ominous.

1813 SCOTT *Rokeby* VI. xxi, Over Redesdale it came, As bodeful as their beacon-flame. **1832** *Fraser's Mag.* VI. 392 The pause was bodeful. **1837** CARLYLE *Fr. Rev.* I. I. III. iii. 55 A sign and wonder; visible to the whole world; bodeful of much. **1870** LOWELL *Among my Bks.* Ser. I. (1873) 186 The voice of the bodeful bird.

‖**bodega** (bo'dega). [Sp.; = wine-shop:—L. *apothēca*, a Gr. ἀποθήκη dépôt, store.] A wine-shop in Spain; recently adopted as a specific name for a cellar or shop for the sale of wines only.

1846 R. FORD *Gatherings fr. Spain* xiii. 148 The best vineyards and *bodegas* or cellars are those which did belong to Don Carlos. **1872** LADY C. SCHREIBER *Jrnl.* (1911) I. 144 He took us..on foot, to the bodega of Messrs. Gonzalez.. where we were asked to taste a number of different wines. **1876** *Vineyard to Decanter* 18 The bodega..unlike the English idea of a wine cellar, is a large building above ground. **1879** ESCOTT *England* I. 162 Wine-shades, bodegas, and saloons abound both above and under ground [in Liverpool]. **1885** *Manch. Examiner* 14 July 5/3 An enterprising firm of wine merchants have popularised their specialities by the multiplication of bodegas.

‖**bodegon** (bode'gon). Pl. **-ones** (-'ones). [Sp., f. *bodega* BODEGA.] Properly, a Spanish tavern-piece; hence, any Spanish picture representing still-life or a *genre* subject.

[**1748** H. JOHNSON tr. *Lozano's Earthquake at Lima* (ed. 2) 317 Those who keep the Bodegones, (a Sort of Taverns, which are no better than a Chandler's-shop; for besides Wine, they sell Candles, Fish, Salt, Cheese and Bacon).] **1843** *Penny Cycl.* XXVI. 189/1 Beginning with subjects of still-life..such as meat, vegetables, and kitchen utensils: hence the generic name *Bodegones*, by which they are still known. **1848** W. STIRLING-MAXWELL *Artists of Spain* II. 580 These 'bodegones' of his early days are worthy of the best pencils of Flanders. **1896** W. ARMSTRONG *Life Velazquez* 12 His earliest independent works were *bodegones* —kitchen and tavern scenes.

bodekyn(ne, obs. form of BODKIN.

bodel, bodelich, obs. form of BODLE, BODILY.

bodement ('bəʊdmənt). [f. BODE *v.*¹ + -MENT (Romanic suffix).]

1. An omen, augury, presage.

1605 SHAKS. *Macb.* IV. i. 96 Who can impresse the Forrest, bid the Tree Vnfixe his earth-bound Root? Sweet boadments, good. **1613** BP. HALL *Holy Panegyr.* 61 It was a iust bodement of his future greatnesse.

2. Foreboding, presentiment.

1642 *Life G. Villiers* in *Harl. Misc.* (Malh.) V. 321 Whether he had never any secret bodements in his mind? **1820** H. COLERIDGE *Poems* II. 303 Bodements sweet of immortality.

†**3.** Signification. *Obs. rare.*

1658 W. BURTON *Itin. Anton.* 200 Faustinus in the Latine ..having the bodement or signification of felicity, or favour.

4. Prophecy, prediction, prognostication.

1826 MISS MITFORD *Village* Ser. II. (1863) 368 The blessed sun himself may have been rash enough to contradict her bodements. **1833** COLERIDGE *Poems* II. 367 Her deep prophetic bodements.

†'**boden,** *v. Obs.* [Extended form of BODE *v.*¹: see -EN. Much used by P. Holland.] = BODE *v.*¹

1561 DAUS tr. *Bullinger on Apoc.* (1573) 19 b, Any euill or fearful spirit, bodening any misfortune. **1600** HOLLAND *Livy* VII. 270, I dread to boden what it may import. *Ibid.* XXIX. 736 As if they bodened and foretokened by their arrival that they were come for a new pillage.

'**boden,** *ppl. a. Sc.* Forms: 5–9 **bodin,** 6 **-yn, boidin,** 7 **boddin,** 9 **boden.** [*Boden* occurs in the Scottish Acts from 1429 in the sense of 'accoutred, armed'. The form is that of the pa. pple. of BID, and it has been conjectured that in the formula 'all boden in feir of weir' it meant originally either 'offered' or 'summoned by proclamation'; but if this was so, it is difficult to account for the change in the use of the word. (The sense suggests some connexion with *boun*, BOUND, 'ready, prepared'.) See FEIR.]

†**1.** Provided with arms, accoutred, armed. *Obs.*

[cf. **1375** BARBOUR *Bruce* viii. 103, I trow he suld be hard to sla, And he war bodyn all evynly.] **1429** *Scot. Acts Jas. I.* (1597) § 122 Ilk Barronne..sall see and ordaine his men to be bodin, as is before written. And gif he dois not this..the Schireffe sall raise of ilk ȝeaman then not bodin, as is foresaid, a wedder. *Ibid.* § 123 Burgesses of twentie pundes in guds salbe bodin with hat, doublet, or habirgeon. *c* **1505** DUNBAR *Daunce* 36 Bostaris, braggaris and barganeris..All bodin in feir of weir. **1513** DOUGLAS *Æneis* VII. xii. 126 For thai wald be lycht bodyne ay to ryn. **1535** STEWART *Cron. Scot.* II. 644 Weill boidin with bow, buklar and brand. **1639** *His Majesty's Procl. Scotl.* 6 Great troups and bands of men, all boddin in fear of war, with guns and pistolets. [**1820** SCOTT *Monast.* xxxiii, Bodin in all that effeirs to war. **1828** —— *F.M. Perth* I. 20 Bodin in effeir of war.]

2. Provided, furnished, fitted out, prepared; dressed. Usually with *well* or *ill*.

c **1425** WYNTOUN *Cron.* VII. ix. 213 The Byschapys, and the gret Prelatis..thai war better bodyn to pay. *a* **1774** FERGUSSON *Election Poems* (1845) 40 'Where's Johnny gaun, That he's sae gaily bodin?' **1776** RAMSAY *Sc. Prov.* 32 (JAM.) He's well boden there ben, that will neither borrow nor lend. **1806** in R. Jamieson *Pop. Ballads* I. 293 (JAM.) His pantrie was never ill-boden.

boden, obs. pa. pple. of *bede*, BID, and BIDE.

boder ('bəʊdə(r)). [f. BODE *v.*¹ + -ER.¹] One who or that which bodes.

c **975** *Rushw. Gosp.* Luke ix. 33 Bodere [*Lindisf.* bodare = *Vulg.* praeceptor], god is us her to wosane. **1692** E. WALKER *Epictetus' Mor.* xxiii, You should suppose This Boder could Futurity disclose. **1846** LANDOR *Hellenics* Wks. II. 485 The sunny circles..boders of a storm.

boder, obs. form of BOTHER.

† '**bodeword.** *Obs.* exc. *dial.* [f. BODE *sb.*² + WORD. Only northern.]

†**1.** Commandment, behest. *Obs.*

c **1200** ORMIN 4377 þa tene bodewordess. *c* **1250** *Gen. & Ex.* 361 For ðhu min bodeword haues broken. *a* **1300** *E.E. Psalter* ii. 6 (Mätz.) Spelland his bodeworde.

†**2.** Message, announcement. *Obs.*

c **1250** *Gen. & Ex.* 2880 Godes bode-wurd bringe ic. *c* **1325** *Metr. Hom.* 44 Hou sain Jon bodword broht bald. He was ryt Cristes messager. **1375** BARBOUR *Bruce* XV. 423 Of this avow soyne bodword was Brocht till schir Iames of douglass. *c* **1460** *Towneley Myst.* 58 Gladly they wold me greyf, If I syche bodworde broght. **1513** DOUGLAS *Æneis* VII. vi. 4 Of peax and concord bodword brocht agane. *a* **1700** *Ballad 'Batt. Harlaw'* Sent nae bodword back again.

3. Premonition, presage.

1832–53 *Whistle-binkie* (Sc. Songs) Ser. III. 84 Sae braw a mornin' gae a bodeword fell, That some wanchance was no that far awa.

†**bodge**, *sb.*¹ *Obs.* or *dial.* [f. BODGE *v.*: cf. BOTCH *sb.*²]. A clumsy patch; a botched piece of work.

1589 *Pappe w. Hatchet* (1844) 20 You shall blush at your owne bodges. **1598** FLORIO, *Sbozzi*, bodges, or bunger-like workes. **1877** PEACOCK *North Lincolnsh. Gl.*, *Bodge*, a botch, a clumsy patch.

†**bodge**, *sb.*² *Obs.* Also 6 bogge. A measure used in selling oats, etc.; app. about half a peck.

1520 *MS. Acc. St. John's Hosp., Canterb.*, iij busshellis & iij bogges of benys. **1631** B. JONSON *New Inn* I. v. Wks. (1692) 726 To the last Bodge of Oats, and Bottle of Hay. **1683** *Rob. Conscience* in *Harl. Misc.* I. 50 Their bodges, which for half-pecks go, They vowed at my head to throw.

†**bodge**, *v.* *Obs.* or *dial.* [An altered form of BOTCH *v.*; cf. *grudge* from *grutch*.]

1. *trans.* To patch or mend clumsily.

1552 HULOET, Bodge or botche olde clothes. **1570** LEVINS *Manip.* 156 To Bodge, *sarcire.* **1870** —— [in *Leicestersh., Nth. Lincolnsh., Shropsh.*, and other dial. Glossaries].

2. *to bodge up*: to put together clumsily; to botch up, to do or make up in a clumsy fashion.

1578 T. WHITE *Serm. St. Paules Cross* 33 To bodge up a house which will never abide the trial. *Ibid.* 47 A disease is but bodged or patched up that is not cured in the cause. **1593** NASHE *Christ's T.* 55 b, They..that bungle and bodge vppe wicked verses. **1881** *Daily News* 31 Aug. 2/2 Gaps bodged up by the rudest of post and pole barriers.

bodge, obs. or dial. f. BADGE *v.*², BUDGE.

†**bodged**, *ppl. a.* *Obs.* or *dial.* [f. BODGE *v.* + -ED¹.] Made up clumsily, botched.

1519 HORMAN *Vulgaria* in *Promp. Parv.* 42 Thou hast but bodchyd and countrefeat Latten, *imaginarie umbratilisque figure.* **1569** J. SANFORD *Agrippa's Van. Artes* 12 b, With bodged verses to delite the eares of fooles.

bodger, *sb.*¹ *Obs.* or *dial.* [f. BODGE *v.* + -ER¹.] One who 'bodges'; a botcher.

1552 HULOET, Bodger, botcher, mender, or patcher of olde garmentes. **1567** HARDING in Jewell *Def. Apol.* (1611) 500 Be they..Tinkers or Tapsters, coblers or Bodgers. [In modern dialects.]

'**bodger**, *sb.*² *Obs.* or *dial.* [? = BADGER *sb.*¹] ? A travelling dealer, a pedlar.

1736 W. ELLIS *New Exper. Husb.* 49 (E.D.S.) The sheep-bodgers or dealers. **1810** CRABBE *Borough* v. Wks. 1834 III. 108 The warmest burgess wears a bodger's coat.

bodger ('bɒdʒə(r)), *sb.*³ *dial.* In full *chair bodger.* A local name in Buckinghamshire for a chair-leg turner. Hence (*chair-*)*bodgering*, the action or process of chair-leg turning.

1911 G. ELAND *Chilterns & Vale* vi. 136 The men who thus work in the woods are called 'chair-bodgers'. *Ibid.* 137 The purchaser then employs the 'bodger' to turn it [*sc.* a 'fall' of beech] into chair-legs. **1921** K. S. WOODS *Rural Industries round Oxford* II. i. 102 Most village turners or 'chair bodgers' confine themselves to the making of legs which they sell to the factories, mainly at Wycombe. **1939** D. HARTLEY *Made in England* i. 23 The shed for bodgering jobs may be left standing the whole year.

bodger ('bɒdʒə(r)), *a.* *Austral. slang.* Inferior, worthless; (of names) false, assumed.

1945 BAKER *Austral. Lang.* viii. 156 *Bodger*, worthless, second-rate. (This term is apparently related to English dialect in which *bodge* means to botch or work clumsily.) **1950** F. J. HARDY *Power without Glory* 383 This entailed the addition of as many more 'bodger' votes as possible. **1954** —— in *Coast to Coast 1953–4* 76 We stuck together all through the war—we was in under bodger names.

† '**bodgery.** *Obs.* Botched work, bungling.

1592 NASHE *Strange News* B iv b, Doe you know your owne misbegotten bodgery?

bodgie ('bɒdʒɪ). *Austral.* and *N.Z.* [Perh. f. BODGER *a.* + -IE.] A teenage boy who conforms to certain fashions in dress, etc. (see quots. 1952); the Australasian counterpart of a TEDDY-BOY. Hence '**bodgieism**, the state or condition of being a 'bodgie'.

1952 *Sunday Chron.* 6 Jan. 4/8 *Bodgie*, boy with crew-cut and zoot-suit, playing juke-box in milk-bar. **1952** H. BOYLE in Wentworth & Flexner *Dict. Amer. Slang* (1960) 49/1 A bodgie is a jitterbug-crazy boy 'who wears his hair curled and long and a sport coat too big for him'. **1958** A. E. MANNING *The Bodgie* vii. 89/2 These 'Bodgies' and 'Widgies' are not *bad* however repellent their conduct may appear. **1958** *N.Z. Listener* 3 Oct. 10/3 Every psychologist who has talked with bodgies will know that fear of an uncertain future is one of the factors in youthful misconduct. **1958** *N.Z. Herald* 5 Nov. 14/7 Some of New Zealand's suggested cures for 'bodgieism' were not only 'wide of the mark' but surprisingly 'vindictive', says Dr. D. P. Ausubel.

† '**bodging**, *vbl. sb.*¹ *Obs.* Also 6 and 9 *dial.* bogging. [f. BODGE *v.* + -ING¹.]

1. The action of patching clumsily.

1633 SANDERSON *Serm. ad Aul.* iii. (1681) II. 36 The Bodging in of a course Shred into a fine garment.

2. Botching, bungling.

1612 BRINSLEY *Lud. Lit.* 107 To turne the prose of the Poets into the Poets owne verse, without any bodging.

'**bodging**, *vbl. sb.*² (*dial.*) = *bodgering*; see BODGER³.

1953 A. JOBSON *Househ. & Country Crafts* xx. 178 Of all the woodland crafts, that of chair-bodging seems the most rural. **1957** *Times* 2 July (Agric. Suppl.) p. viii/7 The demonstration of chair leg bodging.

‖**Bodhisattva** (bɒdɪ'sætvə). *Buddhism.* Also Bodhisat, Bodhisatta, Bodhisatwa. [Skr., 'one whose essence is perfect knowledge', f. *bodhi* perfect knowledge (*budh* to know: see BUDDHA) + *sattvá* being, reality.] One destined to become a Buddha; a Buddhist saint who, having only one birth to undergo before attaining Nirvana, consents to be reborn for the sake of suffering mankind; a superhuman being of infinite wisdom and compassion. Hence **bodhi'sattvahood, -ship, -'satship**, the state of a Bodhisattva.

1828 *Asiatic Res.* XVI. 422 The form of the works..is that of a lecture, or lesson, delivered by a Buddha to his Bodhisatwas, or disciples. **1850** R. SPENCE HARDY *Eastern Monachism* xviii. 170 The Játakan, containing an account of 550 births of the Bódhisat who afterwards became Gótama Budha. **1889** M. MONIER-WILLIAMS *Buddhism* v. 98 He [*sc.* Buddha] gave to every being destined to become a Buddha the title Bodhi-sattva (Bodhi-satta), 'one having knowledge derived from *self-enlightening intellect* for his essence'. *Ibid.* 181 He had transferred the Bodhi-sattvaship to Maitreya. **1895** L. A. WADDELL *Buddhism of Tibet* vi. 138 The Arhats being dead cannot be active, the Bodhisattvas as living beings can. **1926** *Encycl. Brit.* XVI. 96/2 The leaders of the Great Vehicle urged their followers to seek to attain, not so much to Arahatship, which would involve only their own salvation, but to Bodhisatship. **1927** A. HUXLEY *Proper Studies* 181 Buddhism became an entirely new religion, with a pantheon of Bodhisattvas. **1951** H. ZIMMER *Philos. India* 510 His [*sc.* Fa Hian's, c. 400 A.D.] account of the cities further west reveals that at Mathurā the Bodhisattvas Mañjuśrī and Avalokiteśvara received worship as divinities —which is a Mahāyāna feature. *Ibid.* 553 Within the hearts of all creatures compassion is present as the sign of their potential Bodhisattvahood. **1957** B. J. GOULD *Jewel in Lotus* 210 The Dalai Lamas are Bodhisattvas in whom is incarnate Chenrezi, the God of Mercy.

bodice ('bɒdɪs). Forms: 6–7 bodies, 8–9 boddice, 7– bodice. [A variant of *bodies* (see BODY *sb.* 6), retaining the earlier sound of final *-s*, the original phrase being 'a pair of bodies'; even with the spelling *bodice* the word was formerly (like *pence, mice, dice, truce*) treated as a plural.]

1. *Formerly.* **a.** An inner garment for the upper part of the body, quilted and strengthened with whalebone (worn chiefly by women, but also by men); a corset, stays; freq. called *a pair of bodies* (*bodice*) = '*a pair of stays*'.

1618 FLETCHER *Loyal Subj.* II. i. 31 If the bones want setting In her old bodies. *a* **1637** B. JONSON *Elegie* lx. (1854) 829 The whale-bone man That quilts those bodies I have leave to span. **1674** GREW *Anat. Plants* v. §3 A Flower without its Empalement, would hang as uncouth and taudry, as a Lady without her Bodies. **1679** LUTTRELL *Brief Rel.* (1857) I. 23 Mowbray..having a pair of bodice on, and falling down as if really dead, the assassinate fled. **1706** *Lond. Gaz.* No. 4196/4 A pair of new blewish Bodice. **1779** JOHNSON *Pope, L.P.* (1787) IV. 91 [Pope] was invested in boddice made of stiff canvass, being scarce able to hold himself erect till they were laced.

b. *fig.*

1732 FIELDING *Covent Gard. Jrnl.* No. 55 His sentiment, when let loose from that stiff boddice in which it is laced. **1855** MACAULAY *Hist. Eng.* xviii. (1872) III. 303/1 It was never..found politic to put trade into straitlaced bodices.

2. The upper part of a woman's dress, a tight-fitting outer vest or waistcoat, either made in a piece with the skirt or separate (cf. BODY *sb.*); formerly also, an inner vest worn immediately over the stays.

1566–7 *Prec. Treas.* in Chalmers *Mary* (1818) I. 207 Of ormaise taffatis to lyne the bodies and sclevis of the goune and vellicote. **1625** FLETCHER *Fair Maid* II. ii. 35 Nothing but her vpper bodies. **1682** WHELER *Journ. Greece* I. 64 They wear a Bodies of Red or Green Velvet. **1712** STEELE *Spect.* No. 276 ¶3 He keeps me in a pair of Slippers, neat Bodice, warm Petticoats. **1873** BLACK *Pr. of Thule* vii. 98 She wore a tight-fitting bodice of cream-white flannel.

3. *Comb.* and *Attrib.*, as *bodice hand, -maker, -seller.*

1672 R. WILD *Declar. Lib. Consc.* 2 A neighbouring Bodies-maker, that whistles a Psalm-tune. **1684** *Lond. Gaz.* No. 1980/4 Mr. John Nichols Bodice seller at the Falcon on London Bridge. **1701** *Ibid.* No. 3758/8 At Mr. Cade's, a Bodice-seller. **1758** JOHNSON *Idler* No. 40 ¶12 The taylors and boddice-makers of the present age.

bodied ('bɒdɪd), *ppl. a.* [f. BODY *sb.* + -ED.]

1. Having a body or trunk; usually with an adjective, forming a parasynthetic comb., as *big-bodied*, ABLE-BODIED, etc.

a **1547** SURREY *Æneid* IV. 582 Like to the aged boysteous bodied oke. **1590** SHAKS. *Com. Err.* IV. ii. 20 He is deformed ..Ill-fac'd, worse bodied, shapelesse euery where. **1625** PURCHAS *Pilgrims* II. 1421 The women in Camienitz goe with their Coates close bodied. **1662** FULLER *Worthies* (1840) II. 339 He [unicorn] is commonly pictured, bodied like a buck. **1729** T. COOKE *Tales, Propos. etc.* 121 Light body'd Cranes. **1875** BLACKMORE *C. Vaughan* xv. 49 Of moderate stature, gauntly bodied, and loosely built.

b. Having substance, strength, consistency, etc.

1611 SPEED *Theat. Gt. Brit.* x. (1614) 19/1 Springs.. gathering stil strength with more branches, lastly grow bodyed able to beare ships into the land. *c* **1645** HOWELL *Lett.* (1650) I. 372 The most firm, the best bodied, and lastingest wine. **1666** EVELYN *Diary* (1827) II. 260 Drebbell, inventor of yᵉ boedied scarlet.

2. Endowed with material form or being; made corporeal or material; embodied.

1646 J. HALL *Poems* 39 Ne're a body'd nothing shall perceive How we unite, how we together cleave. **1840** CARLYLE *Heroes* iii. 140 Bodied or bodiless, it is the one fact important for all men:—but to Dante, in that age, it was bodied in fixed certainty of scientific shape. **1855** BROWNING *One Word More*, in *Men & Wom.* II. 240 Like the bodied heaven in clearness Shone the stone.

†**'bodify**, *v.* *Obs.* [f. BODY *sb.* + -FY.] To embody.

1685 *Roxb. Ballads* (1885) V. 541 Arch-Angels sure, leaving their glorious Sphere, Once more themselves have Bodified and here Resolve as English Nobles to appear.

† '**bodiȝlich.** *Obs. rare.* [A compound used by Ormin; f. *bodiȝ*, BODY *sb.* + LICH, body; also used by him separately as synonymous terms.] = BODY *sb.*

c **1200** ORMIN 16294 Cristess hallȝhe bodiȝlich. *Ibid.* 16340 Adam..Off whamm I toc mi bodiȝlich.

† '**bodikin, bodikie.** *Obs.* Also bodkin. [dim. of BODY *sb.*: see -KIN², -KIE.]

1. A diminutive body; a corpuscle, an atom.

1668 CULPEPPER & COLE *Barthol. Anat.* II. vi. 106 Small Boddikies or indivisible Particles of the Blood..If any reliques of the said Bodikies did remain. **1721–1800** BAILEY, *Bodykin*, a little body. *Obs.*

2. (*God's, ods*) *bodikins! bodkins!* (*bodlikins!*) God's dear body!: an oath. Cf. BODY *sb.*4.

1598 SHAKS. *Merry W.* II. iii. 46 Body-kins M. Page. **1602** —— *Ham.* II. ii. 554 Gods bodykins [*Qq.* Bodkin] man, better. **1733** FIELDING *Quix. in Eng.* II. viii, Odsbodlikins.. you have a strange sort of a taste. **1753** SMOLLETT *Ct. Fathom* (1784) 63/1 As for the matter of dress, bodlikins!

bodiless ('bɒdɪlɪs), *a.* [f. BODY *sb.* + -LESS.]

1. Having no body, no material form or being; incorporeal; without substance, unsubstantial.

1398 TREVISA *Barth. De P.R.* II. ii. (1495) 27 Angel is substancia intellectuall alway mouable . free and bodylesse. **1561** T. NORTON *Calvin's Inst.* III. 266 A vain bodylesse shew of fayth doth not iustifie. **1602** SHAKS. *Ham.* III. iv. 138 This is the very coynage of your Braine, This Bodilesse Creation extasie Is very cunning in. **1610** W. FOLKINGHAM *Art Survey* II. vi. 58 Gum-water, very thinne and bodilesse. **1733** SWIFT *Legion Club* Wks. 1755 IV. I. 203 Phantoms bodiless and vain. **1868** ROBERTSON *Serm.* Ser. IV. xxix. 221 Man becomes for ever a bodiless spirit.

2. Wanting the trunk; trunkless.

1587 *Censure loyall Subj.* (Collier) 9 My eies saw their traiterous harts burned, and bodilesse heads aduanced to view. **1810** SOUTHEY *Kehama* XI. viii, Two winged Hands came in, Armless and bodyless. **1831** *Blackw. Mag.* XXIX. 219 The bodiless cherubs on our churchyard stones.

Hence '**bodilessness.**

1847 J. C. & A. W. HARE *Guesses at Truth* (series 1, ed. 3) 55 The living energy and definiteness and bodiliness of Homer's characters. **1869** R. WALLIS *Delitzsch's Bibl. Pyschol.* 513 In contradiction to..bodilessness.

'**bodilize**, *v.* *nonce-wd.* [suggested by *spiritualize.*] *trans.* To make corporeal or material.

1843 SOUTHEY *Doctor* clxxxiv. (D.) Unless we endeavour to spiritualise ourselves..age bodilises us more and more.

bodily ('bɒdɪlɪ), *a.* Also 3–5 bodili, 4 bodi-, bodylich(e, 4–6 bodely, 4 bodeli, 6 bodelie, bodyly(e, 7 bodilie. [f. BODY *sb.* + -LY¹.]

†**1.** Of the nature of body, corporeal, material, physical; as opposed to *spiritual.* *Obs.*

a **1300** *Cursor M.* 428 Wit angel þat es gastli, And with man þat es bodili. *a* **1340** HAMPOLE *Pr. Consc.* 3129 Som clerkes, þat spekes of purgatory Says þat þe fire þare is bodily, And noght gastly als þe saule es. *c* **1449** PECOCK *Repr.* II. xvi. 243 The bodili heuen and hise seid bodili parties. **1528** MORE *Heresyes* I. Wks. 152/2 That any bodily thyng should drawe an other without touching. **1633** EARL MANCH. *Al Mondo* 178 There are three bodily Inhabitants already gone to heaven. **1674** N. FAIRFAX *Bulk & Selv.* 198 The World..that bulk of bodily beings we see.

2. Of or belonging to the body or physical nature of man. ***bodily fear***: alarm for one's personal safety, apprehension of physical harm.

a **1300** *Cursor M.* 12929 (Gött.) Bodili fode. *c* **1325** *E.E. Allit. P.* A. 477 With bodyly bale hym blysse to byye. *c* **1380** WYCLIF *De Pseudo-Freris* Wks. (1880) 305 Bodiliche chastite is ofte broken. **1454** *E.E. Wills* (1882) 132 Beyng in good bodely helth. **1494** FABYAN VI. clxxxi. 179 The bysshop..myght departe thens without bodely harme. **1651** HOBBES *Leviath.* II. xxvii. 155 The fear..of corporeall hurt, which we call Bodily Fear. **1711** BUDGELL *Spect.* No. 161 ¶5 Fatigues of bodily Labour. **1785** REID *Int. Powers* 276 My memory is not limited by any bodily organ. **1837** DICKENS *Pickw.* xl, 'I'm in bodily fear.' **1838** —— *Nich. Nick.* xxi, Bodily illness is more easy to bear than mental.

†**b.** Real; actual; physically carried out. *Obs.*

1607 SHAKS. *Cor.* I. ii. 5 What euer [counsels] haue bin thought one in this State That could be brought to bodily act, ere Rome Had circumuention.

†**c.** ***bodily oath***: = CORPORAL OATH. Perhaps, originally, an oath taken on the consecrated host or 'body' of Christ; but used also of oaths taken with a 'bodily touch' of other sacred things. *Obs.*

c **1470** HENRY *Wallace* IV. 190 The bodelye ayth thai maid him with gud will. **1639** *Council Rec.* in *Inverness Courier* (1884) 25 Oct. 3/4 The said A. B. has givine his great and bodielie aith.

†**3.** Solid; of or pertaining to a solid. *Obs.*

1557 RECORDE *Whetst.* C iij b, Thereof be thei named bodily nombers, or sound nombers. The leaste of them all is commonly called a Cube. **1570** BILLINGSLEY *Euclid* XI. Introd. 312 In these bookes following he entreateth of..bodely figures: as of Cubes. **1601** HOLLAND *Pliny I.* 20 That they [clouds] be thicke, grosse, and of a bodily consistence.

Hence †'**bodili͜hede**, '**bodili͜ness**, corporeality; '**bodily-wise** *adv.*, corporeally, in the body.

c **1440** HYLTON *Scala Perf.* (W. de W. 1494) II. xxxiii, The kynde of god that is..ferrest fro bodily hede. **1587** GOLDING *De Mornay* xiv. 205 It behoueth the same [Soule] to be altogether bodylesse it selfe: for had it any bodylinesse at all, it could not receiue any body into it. **1869** LYNCH *Church & St.* 24 We cannot be in the country and in the town at the same time bodily-wise.

bodily ('bɒdɪlɪ), *adv.* [f. as prec. + -LY².]

†**1.** In the manner of, or with regard to, the body; corporeally (often = 'unspiritually'). *Obs.*

c **1370** *Lay-Folks Mass-Bk.* App. iv. 630 God þat diȝed vppon þe tre, þat þe prest receyuede bodile. **1394** *P. Pl. Crede* 619 All þo blissed beþ þat bodyliche hungreþ. *c* **1440** LONELICH *Grail* (Roxb.) I. 450 Of man that in this world lyveth bodily. **1579** FULKE *Heskin's Parl.* 323 It fedde the faithfull, not onely bodily, but also spiritually. **1685** BAXTER *Paraph. N.T.* Mark vi. 53 That we could as bodily believe and trust him for our..Souls.

2. In or with the body; in the flesh; in person.

c **1440** *Three Kings* (1885) 26 þe tyme was to-come þat he schulde þer appere bodelich. **1578** THYNNE *Let.* in *Animadv.* Introd. (1865) 59 Since I ame..barred bodely to approche your presence. **1640** SIR E. DERING *Prop. Sacr.* (1644) 45 Christ..bodily present. **1803** SOUTHEY *Wks.* VI. 173 This is our father Francisco, Among us bodily.

3. *transf.* With the whole body or bulk, 'body and all'; all together, in one mass, as a whole.

1793 SMEATON *Edystone L.* §322 The seas came in bodily over the Barbican wall. **1850** MRS. BROWNING *Poems* II. 4 As if that, over brake and lea, Bodily the wind did carry The great altar of St. Mary. **1877** A. B. EDWARDS *Up Nile* xviii. 520 A full-length portrait of Seti I., cut out bodily from the walls of his sepulchre.

bodiment ('bɒdɪmənt). *rare.* [f. BODY *sb.* + -MENT.] Giving of form or body; embodiment.

1873 G. C. DAVIES *Mount. & Mere* iv. 25 No alive and outward bodiment.

bodin, var. of BODEN *ppl. a. Sc.* provided.

†'**bodiness.** *Obs. rare.* [f. BODY *sb.* + -NESS.] The state or quality of having bodily form; corporeity, material condition.

1398 TREVISA *Barth. De P.R.* VIII. xl, In what maner wise þey beþ medlid togederes, askes and water, þe water abideþ in his bodiness [**1535** corporalnesse]. **1674** N. FAIRFAX *Bulk & Selv.* 100 A least bitling is made as much for cleaving, if it had but a wherewith to be cloven; its leastness, not its bodiness forbidding it.

boding ('bəʊdɪŋ), *vbl. sb.* [f. BODE *v.*¹ + -ING¹.]

†**1.** Annunciation, proclamation, preaching. *Obs.*

c **1000** *Ags. Gosp.* Matt. xii. 41 Hiȝ dydon dædbote on Ionas bodunge. *c* **1160** *Hatton G.* ibid., Bodiunge. *c* **1175** *Lamb. Hom.* 89 Godspelles bodunge.

2. Premonition, presentiment; *concr.* prognostic, omen, portent.

1297 R. GLOUC. 428 þe taylede sterre, þat gret bodynge ys. **1398** TREVISA *Barth. De P.R.* XVIII. i. (1495) 737 Beestes haue redynesse of wytte in bodynge of chaungynge of tyme and wedders. **1555** HARPSFIELD *Divorce Hen. VIII.* (1878) 280 A sorrowful boding of the..mischief that..did afterward chance. **1768** GOLDSM. *Good Nat. Man.* v. i, I have had some boding of it these ten days. **1810** WORDSW. *Scenery Lakes* (1823) 115 A Shepherd accustomed to watch all mountain bodings.

3. Prediction, prophecy (generally of evil).

1668 TEMPLE *Let.* Wks. 1731 II. 169 Too much entertained with ill Bodings and Complaints. **1817** COLERIDGE *Sibyl. Leaves* (1862) 188 Better fate be thine And mock my boding! **1833** HT. MARTINEAU *Brooke F.* iv. 54 Norton..would listen to no evil bodings.

boding ('bəʊdɪŋ), *ppl. a.* [f. BODE *v*¹ + -ING².] That bodes; presaging, portending, ominous.

1593 SHAKS. *Ven. & Ad.* 647 My boding heart pants, beats, and takes no rest. **1594** —— *Rich. III*, v. iii. 228 The sweetest sleepe, And fairest boading Dreames. **1702** ROWE *Amb. Step-Moth.* I. i. 434 Spight of my boding fears. *a* **1771** GRAY *Poems* (1775) 53 No boding Maid of skill divine Art thou. **1785** COWPER *Task* I. 205 The boding owl That hails the rising moon. **1824** W. IRVING *T. Trav.* II. 257 Listening to the boding cry of the tree toad.

Hence '**bodingly** *adv.*

1811 SHELLEY *St. Irvyne* i, They bodingly presag'd destruction and woe. **1839** LOWELL *Summ. Storm* Poet. Wks. (1879) 81 All is so bodingly still. **1866** MOTLEY *Dutch Rep.* IV. iv. 619 Sorrowfully and bodingly Mansfeld withdrew to consult again.

†'**bodiship.** *Obs. rare.* [f. BODY *sb.* + -SHIP.] Corporeality, material substance or condition.

1674 N. FAIRFAX *Bulk & Selv.* 53 All bodiship, with those its belongers which make it sensible unto us.

bodken, -kin, variants of BAUDEKIN, *Obs.*, cloth.

bodkin ('bɒdkɪn). Forms: 4 **boidekyn, boytekyn, bode-, boydekynne,** 4–5 **boyde-, bodekyn,** 5 **boddekyn,** 6 **boddkynne, botken, -kin, bodkyn, bodkine,** 7 (**boidkene**), 5– **bodkin.** [Of unknown etymology: the orig. form in Eng. was *boydekin, boidekyn*, in 3 syllables. The form naturally suggests a dim. in *-kin*: but no primitive of the required form appears in Eng. or other related language. The phonetic history is also difficult.

(In default of finding it elsewhere, the derivation has been sought in Celtic. The Welsh *bi'dogyn* 'little dagger', fixed on by some, must be discarded, both because it is accented on the penult, and because the ME. word was itself adopted in Welsh as *bwytkin*; but some still think it possible that *boydekin* may have originated in some kind of corruption of Ir. *bideog*, Gael. *biodag*, Welsh *bidog* dagger.)]

†**1.** A short pointed weapon; a dagger, poniard, stiletto, lancet. *Obs.*

1386 CHAUCER *Reeves T.* 40 Slayn of Symkyn With panade or with knyf or boidekyn [*v.r.* boydekyn, boytekyn, Boydekynne]. *c* **1430** LYDG. *Bochas* VI. xii. (*title*), Victorious Julius Cæsar..was murdred with bodkins. **1477** EARL RIVERS (Caxton) *Dictes* 49 One of his disciples tooke a boddekyn & prikked him in his feete. **1535** COVERDALE *1 Kings* xviii. 28 They..prouoked them selues with knyues & botkens [**1611** lancets]. **1547** SALESBURY *Dict. Eng. & Welsh*, *Bwytkin*, a bodkyn. **1580** SIDNEY *Arcadia* 276, I..doe defie thee, in a mortall affray from the bodkin to the pike vpward. **1602** SHAKS. *Ham.* III. i. 76 When he himselfe might his Quietus make With a bare Bodkin. **1657** TRAPP *Comm. Esther* iv. 3 This was now a bodkin at their hearts. [**1850** MRS. JAMESON *Leg. Monast. Ord.* (1863) 137 The long bodkin with which those wicked Jews pierced his side.]

2. A small pointed instrument, of bone, ivory, or steel, used for piercing holes in cloth, etc.

c **1440** *Promp. Parv.* 42 Boydekyn or bodekyn, *subucula, perforatorium.* **1555** *Fardle Facions* II. x. 212 About the poincte of the chinne thei haue a feawe heares as it ware pricked in with Bodkins. **1589** *Pappe w. Hatchet* (1844) 28 Wee challenge him at all weapons from the taylors bodkin to the watchmans browne bil. **1602** PLAT *Delightes for Ladies* III. xxx, Make little holes in the Cowcumber first with a wodden or bone bodkin. **1609** A. CRAIG *Poet. Recreat.* 4 Who according to the antient custome hath bored his eare with a boidkene. **1785** REID *Int. Powers* II. xix. 325 A spire at a very great distance seems like a point of a bodkin.

3. A long pin or pin-shaped ornament used by women to fasten up the hair.

1580 BARET *Alv.* B 875 A bodkine or big needle to crest the heares, *discriminale.* **1635** J. TAYLOR (Water P.) in *Harl. Misc.* IV. 218 Women's masks, busks, muffs, fans, perriwigs, and bodkins. **1714** POPE *Rape Lock* v. 95 Then in a bodkin grac'd her mother's hairs. **1716** LADY M. W. MONTAGUE *Lett.* x. I. 32 Their hair is..set out with three or four rows of bodkins (wonderfully large, that stick out two or three inches from their hair). **1820** SCOTT *Monast.* xvii, She undid from her locks a silver bodkin around which they were twisted. **1851** D. WILSON *Preh. Ann.* II. III. iv. 118 A rude bodkin of bone..employed in fastening the dress. **1864** LONGF. *King Olaf* VIII. viii, 'Tis the bodkin that I wear When at night I bind my hair.

†**b.** A frizzling-iron. *Obs.*

1580 BARET *Alv.* B 874 A bodkine or fine instrument that women curle their heare withall..a friseling iron.

4. A needle-like instrument with a blunt knobbed point, having a large (as well as a small) eye, for drawing tape or cord through a hem, loops, etc.

1714 POPE *Rape Lock* II. 128 Wedg'd whole ages in a bodkin's eye.

5. *Printing.* An awl-like tool used to pick out letters in correcting set-up type.

1846 *Print. Apparatus Amateurs* 17 The bodkin is used to pick out such of the types as are misplaced.

6. *transf.* (*colloq.*) A person wedged in between two others where there is proper room for two only; esp. in phr. *to ride* or *sit bodkin.*

[**1638** FORD *Fancies* IV. i. (1811) 186 Where but two lie in a bed, you must be—bodkin, bitch-baby—must ye?] **1798** *Loves of the Triangles* 182 (L.) While the pressed bodkin, punched and squeezed to death, Sweats in the midmost place. **1848** THACKERAY *Van. Fair* II. 241 (Hoppe), He's too big to travel bodkin between you and me. **1872** FLOR. MONTGOMERY *Thrown Together* ii. 62 The three called a hansom outside, and Cecily..sat bodkin.

7. *Comb.* and *Attrib.*, as ***bodkin-case, bodkin-work***; ***bodkin-wise*** adv.; **bodkin-beard,** a pointed, dagger-shaped beard.

a **1529** SKELTON *Elynour R.* Prol. 82 Scarfes, feathers, and swerds, And thin bodkin beards. **1591** LYLY *Endym.* III. iii. 36 Whether I shall frame the bodkin beard or the bush. **1565** GOLDING *Ovid's Met.* IV. (1593) 97 Both his shankes do grow In one round spindle bodkin-wise with sharpned point below. **1828** SCOTT *F.M. Perth* I. 41, I will have no more close hugs—no more bodkin work.

'**bodkin,** *v.* [f. prec.] *trans.* To make a bodkin of, squeeze in as a bodkin; cf. BODKIN *sb.* 6.

1791 GIBBON *Let.* 31 May in *Mem.* (1839) 354 If you can bodkin the sweet creature into the coach.

bodkin, (*Ods bodkins!*) var. of BODIKIN.

bodkin, bodkin-work, variant of BAUDEKIN.

'**bodkinize,** *v.* = BODKIN *v.*

1833 HOOK *Parson's Dau.* II. v. 202 Seat him in the carriage 'bodkinized' between the two fair ladies.

bodle¹ ('bɒd(ə)l, -ɔː-). *Sc.* Also 7 **bodel, bawdle,** 8 **boadle,** 8–9 **bodde.** [Reputed to be from the name of a mint-master *Bothwell*; but no documentary evidence is cited.] A Scotch copper coin of the value of two pennies Scots, or (*c* 1600) one sixth of an English penny; the smallest coin; hence, like *farthing*, etc., in the phrase ***not to care a bodle.***

1650 A. B. *Mutat. Polemo* 12 Whom they valued not really at the estimation of 200000 Scotch bawdles. **1688** R. HOLME *Armoury* III. ii. 29/2 A Bodel, three of them makes an half penny English. *c* **1730** BURT *Lett. N. Scotl.* (1818) I. 42 The bridge is..maintained by a toll of a bodle. **1820** SCOTT *Abbot* vi, It was not that I cared a brass bodle for his benison or malison either. **1834** H. MILLER *Scenes & Leg.* xix. (1857) 279 All the placks and boddles of the party.

bodle², obs. f. BUDDLE, corn-marigold.

1557 TUSSER *100 Points Husb.* lxxx, Bodle for barley, no weede there is such.

Bodleian (bɒd'liːən, 'bɒdlɪən). [f. the name of Sir T. Bodley, who in 1597 restored and refounded the Library of the University of Oxford.]

a. *adj.* Of or pertaining to Sir T. Bodley or the Library bearing his name; hence **b.** quasi-*sb.* The Oxford University Library; also colloquially called **Bodley. c.** *fig.* and *transf.*

1663 COWLEY *Verses & Ess.* (1669) 7 The mysterious Library, The Beatifick Bodley of the Deity. **1710** H. BEDFORD *Vind. Ch. Eng.* 45 The Bodleian Copies of the Articles. **1862** WHYTE MELVILLE *Ins. Bar.* vi. (ed. 12) 297 The richest mental food the Bodleian itself can afford. **1884** SPURGEON *Clew of Maze* 33 It is a million-times magnified Bodleian of teaching.

bodom, -ery, obs. form of BOTTOM, -RY.

Bodoni (bəʊ'dəʊnɪ). A book produced by the celebrated Italian printer Giambattista Bodoni (1740–1813); a modern type based on that of Bodoni. Also *attrib.* in ***Bodoni type.***

1880 [see ALDINE *a.* and *sb.*]. **1922** D. B. UPDIKE *Printing Types* II. 235 The 'Bodoni' type of commerce is a composite picture of many of Bodoni's fonts, rather than a reproduction of any one of them. **1928** *Scholartis Press Catal.* June, Printed by the Glasgow University Press in Bodoni type. **1967** E. CHAMBERS *Photolitho-offset* ii. 12 Some families have dozens of different type faces (Caslon, Bodoni, Baskerville, Plantin, etc.).

†'**bodrag(e.** *Obs.* Also **bodrak(e, bordrag(e.** [prob. a corruption of some Ir. word: cf. *buaidhreadh* molestation, disturbance (O'Reilly), *buadre*, tumult (Stokes).] A hostile incursion, a raid. Hence, in same sense, **bo(r)draging.**

1537 *St. Papers Hen. VIII*, II. 480 The castelles be not for our defence agaynst ther stelthe and bodrakes. **1586** J. HOOKER *Girald. Irel.* II. 172/2 Nothing liking the outrages, bodrages, and villanies dailie practised by Barrie, Condon, and others. **1595** SPENSER *Col. Clout* 315 No nightly bodrags, nor no hue and cries. **1596** —— *F.Q.* II. x. 63 Yet oft annoyd with sondry bordragings.

bod-stick, var. *bott-stick*: see BOTT 2.

1883 T. D. WEST *Amer. Foundry Pract.* (ed. 2) 331 The melter..runs the bod-stick without any clay on it into the running iron. **1900** [see BOTT 2].

bodword, var. of BODEWORD *Obs.*

body ('bɒdɪ), *sb.* Forms: 1 **bodiȝ,** 3 **bodiȝ,** 3–4 **bodi, bode,** 3–7 **bodie,** 4–6 **bodye,** 6 **bodey,** 3– **body.** [OE. *bodiȝ* neut., elsewhere in Teut. only in OHG. *potah, botah*, MHG. *botich, -ech, potih* str. masc. 'body'; cf. mod.Bav. dial. *bottech* the 'body' of a chemise, Grimm. The word has died out of Ger., its place being taken by *leib*, orig. 'life', and *körper* from Lat.: but, in Eng., *body* remains as a great and important word.

Since Ger. *botah, potah*, with final *h*, is not the exact phonetic equivalent of OE. *bodiȝ*, there is ground for supposing that the word has been adopted in English from some foreign source. E. Müller connects *botah* with *botahha* fem., mod.G. *bottich* masc. 'cask, tub, vat', identified by

Wackernagel with med.L. *butica* = Gr. ἀποθήκη. But there does not appear to be any clear way of connecting the two words. (Fick's conjectural derivation from *bhadh* 'to bind' is out of the question. Gaelic *bodhaig* is from Eng.)]

I. The material frame of man (and animals).

1. a. The physical or material frame or structure of man or of any animal: the whole material organism viewed as an organic entity. (In *Biol.* sometimes also used of plants.)

c **890** K. ÆLFRED *Bæda* III. xiv. (Bosw.) Wæs Oswine se cyning on bodiȝe heah. *c* **1200** ORMIN 4773 Hiss bodiȝ.. All samenn, brest, and wambe, and þes, and cnes, and fet, and shannkess, etc. *a* **1300** *Cursor M.* 869 Our bodis ar now al bare. **1480** CAXTON *Chron. Eng.* lxxviii. 64 He shold come fyght with hym body for body. **1523** LD. BERNERS *Froiss.* I. clv. 186 To fight body to body, or power to power. **1557** F. SEAGER *Sch. Vertue* 676 in *Babees Bk.* (1868) 347 Thy bodie vprighte, Thy fete iuste to-gether. **1665–9** BOYLE *Occas. Refl.* IV. xi. (1675) 174 A Lark.. lighted among some clods of Earth.. of the colour of her Body. **1752** JOHNSON *Rambl.* No. 208 ¶10 A body languishing with disease. **1847** CARPENTER *Zool.* §870 The common Oyster.. always appears inclined to adapt its shell to the form of the body. **1881** HUXLEY in *Nature* XXIV. 346 The body is a machine of the nature of an army, not of that of a watch, or of a hydraulic apparatus. Of this army each cell is a soldier, each organ a brigade.

1875 DAWSON *Dawn of Life* viii. 214 Their bodies like those of plants.. show tendencies to spiral modes of growth. **1878** HUXLEY *Physiogr.* 222 The individual cells of which the body of the plant is made up.

(In early use almost always applied to that of man: hence)

b. often contrasted with the *soul*.

a **1240** *Lofsong* in *Cott. Hom.* 205 þauh þet werc nere i þe bodie þe wil was in þe heorte. **1398** TREVISA *Barth. De P.R.* IX. i. (1495) 345 The body meuyth as the soule woll. *c* **1450** LONELICH *Grail* xlii. 112 Bothe body & sowle distroyed ȝe be. **1651** *Let.* in *Proc. Parliament* No. 81. 1241 A great comfort to the godly, both to their soules and bodies. **1732** POPE *Ess. Man* I. 268 All are but parts of one stupendous whole, Whose body Nature is, and God the soul. **1864** TENNYSON *Aylmer's Field* 377 The foul adulteries That saturate soul with body. *Mod.* 'A hard struggle to keep body and soul together.'

c. The corporeal or material nature or state of man, the material body and its properties.

c **1200** ORMIN 15124 To clennsenn þeȝȝre bodiȝ swa Off all þe bodiȝ sinne. **1382** WYCLIF *2 Cor.* xii. 2 Wher in body, wher out of body, I woot not, God woot. **1580** NORTH *Plutarch* (1676) 4 This Phœa was a woman robber.. and naught of her body. **1611** BIBLE *2 Cor.* xii. 2 Whether in the body, I cannot tell, whether out of the body, I cannot tell. **1816** SCOTT *Old Mort.* vi, While we are yet in the body. **1869** GOULBOURN *Purs. Holiness* ix. 78 By 'the body' is to be understood the mass of matter which we carry about with us, with all the various animal properties that belong to it.

d. (Usu. hyperbolic.) Phr. ***over my*** (etc.) ***dead body***.

1833 SEBA SMITH *Life & Writings J. Downing* (1834) 137 You don't go through this door to-night, without you pass over the dead body of Jack Downing. **1936** H. BRIGHOUSE *New Leisure* in *Best One-Act Plays 1936* 81 Elsie Dixon doing confidential secretary! Over my dead body. **1963** *Times* 27 May 6/2 If the number of distinguished gentlemen who cry 'Over my dead body' really mean what they say, this will be a fairly lethal summer in Whitehall.

2. Short (or euphemistic) for 'dead body', corpse.

c **1280** *Fall & Pass.* 76 in *E.E.P.* (1862) 14 Iosep of arimathie.. nem þat swet bodi adun, an biriid hir in a fair plas. *a* **1300** *Cursor M.* 14309 And quar haf yee his bode laid? *c* **1400** *Destr. Troy* 7150 þai.. brent vp the bodies vnto bare askis. **1535** COVERDALE *1 Kings* xiii. 24 The lyon stode by the body [**1382** WYCLIF careyn, **1388** deed bodi]. **1595** SHAKS. *John* v. vii. 99 At Worster must his bodie be interr'd. **1619** CROOKE *Body of Man* 19 Choose a bodie that is sound and vntainted, and either hanged, smothered, or drowned. **1835** HOOD *Dead Robbery* ii, To steal a body. **1855** TENNYSON *Maud.* I. i. 5 In the ghastly pit long since a body was found.

3. Applied symbolically or mystically to the bread in the sacrament of the Lord's Supper.

[**1357** *Seven Sacr.* in *Lay-Folks Mass-Bk.* 118 The sacrement of the auter, cristes owen bodi in likeness of brede.] **1382** WYCLIF *Matt.* xxvi. 26 Take ȝee, and ete; this is my bodi. **1549** *Bk. Com. Prayer, Commun.* Exhort., The holy communion of the body and blood of our Saviour Christ. **1562** *39 Articles* xxviii, The Body of Christ is given, taken, and eaten in the Supper, only after an heavenly and spiritual manner. **1579** FULKE *Heskins' Parl.* 82 He caried the Lords body in a wicker basket. *c* **1880** J. CANDLISH *Sacraments* 98 All who believe in Him receive that one body that was broken for all.

†**4.** Used in oaths and forcible ejaculations, as ***body of me!***, ***body of our Lord!***, ***God's body!***, ***by cocks body!***, etc. *Obs.* Cf. BODIKIN.

c **1530** REDFORDE *Play Wit & Sc.* (1848) 7 Oh the bodye of me! What kaytyves be those. **1573** *New Custom* II. ii. in Hazl. *Dodsley* III. 32 Body of our Lord, is he come into the Country? **1596** SHAKS. *1 Hen. IV*, II. i. 29 Gods body! the turkeys in my pannier are quite starved. **1613** —— *Hen. VIII*, v. ii. 22 Body a me: where is it? **1695** CONGREVE *Love for L.* II. v. 35 Body o' me, I have a Shoulder of an Egyptian King, that I purloin'd from one of the Pyramids. **1828** SCOTT *F.M. Perth* (1860) 9 'Body of me' exclaimed Simon, 'I should know that voice!'

II. The main portion; the trunk.

5. a. The main portion of the animal frame, to which the extremities, etc. are attached; the trunk. Opposed to the members or limbs; also to the head, esp. as the seat of intelligence and guidance.

a **800** *Epinal & Erf. Gloss.* 947 (O.E. Texts) *Spina*, bodei. —— *Corpus Gl.* 1891 *Spina*, bodeȝ. *c* **1000** *Ags. Voc.* in Wr.-Wülcker *Voc.* 265 *Truncus*, bodiȝ. *c* **1000** ÆLFRIC *Minster Hom.* 203 a in *Sax. Leechd.* III. 355 He næfdon þæt heafod to þam bodiȝe. **1382** WYCLIF *Ephes.* iv. 16 Crist the heed; of whom al the body sett to-gidere, and boundyn to gidere by ech ioynture of vndirseruyng. **1593** SHAKS. *3 Hen. VI*, IV. vii. 26 When the Fox hath once got in his Nose, Hee'le soone finde meanes to make the Body follow. *c* **1600** C'TESS SOUTHAMPTON in *Shaks. C. Praise* 40 All heade and veri litel body. **1840** THIRLWALL *Greece* VII. lv. 86 A body without a head, unable either to act or to deliberate. **1867** F. FRANCIS *Angling* x. (1880) 364 Body, orange-yellow, merging into.. burnt sienna at the shoulder.

b. The main stem, trunk, stock, of a plant or tree.

1523 FITZHERB. *Husb.* §133 Cut the boughe on bothe sydes a fote or two foote from the bodye of the tree. **1609** C. BUTLER *Fem. Mon.* ii. (1623) E j, Boughes hanging out alone from the bodies. **1697** DRYDEN *Virg. Georg.* IV. 183 Cucumers.. With crooked Bodies, and with Bellies deep.

†**c.** The wood under the bark. L. *corpus*. *Obs.*

1603 R. JOHNSON *Kingd. & Commw.* 167 The black rinde of a certaine tree.. betweene the bodie and the barke.

d. *fig.* In biblical or theol. language, ***the body of Christ***: the Church of which Christ is the head.

c **1200** ORMIN 1555 Swa þatt teȝȝ shulen alle ben An bodiȝ and an sawle And Jesu Crist himm sellf shall ben Uppo þatt bodiȝ hæfedd. **1382** WYCLIF *Ephes.* iv. 12 And he ȝaf summe sotheli apostlis, summe forsoth prophetis.. into the work of mynisterie, into edificacioun of Cristis body. **1535** COVERDALE *Col.* i. 18 And he is the heade of the body, namely, of the congregacion. **1611** BIBLE *1 Cor.* xii. 27 Now yee are the body of Christ, and members in particular.

6. The part of a dress which covers the body, as distinct from the arms; also the part of a woman's dress above the waist, as distinguished from the loose skirt. ***a pair of bodies***: see BODICE.

1585 *Wills & Inv. N.C.* (1860) II. 114 One petticote of house-wyfe clothe.. An upper bodye of durance. **1611** in Heath *Grocers' Comp.* (1869) 92 That none should wear.. any body or sleeves of wire, whalebone or with any other stiffing. **1696** J. F. *Merchant's Wareho.* 38 Cut of Ell ½ off of one of the half bredths.. which take for the body of your Shifts. **1698** LASSELS *Voy. Italy* II. 288 Twelve breast and back pieces (like womens close bodies). **1868** Q. VICTORIA *Life in Highlands* 124, I and the girls [were] in royal Stewart skirts and shawls over black velvet bodies.

7. a. The main, central, or principal part, as distinguished from parts subordinate or less important; the part round which the others are grouped, or to which they are attached as appendages, etc.

c **1000** *Sax. Leechd.* I. 402 Nim þonne þæt sæd sete on þæs sules bodiȝ. **1595** SHAKS. *John* IV. ii. 112 Neuer such a powre.. Was leuied in the body of a land. **1670** COTTON *Espernon* I. I. 35 The body of the Emblem was a figure of the Duke himself. **1719** DE FOE *Crusoe* (1840) I. xx. 355 He got into the body of the tree. **1790** BURKE *Fr. Rev.* 234 The body of all true religion consists.. in obedience to the will of the Sovereign of the world. **1863** H. COX *Instit.* II. x. 562 Crimes committed at sea, or on the coast out of the body of any County. **1874** BOUTELL *Arms & Arm.* ix. 173 The body of the blade.

b. The foundation of a felt or silk hat. Also Comb. ***body-maker***.

1845 DODD *Brit. Manuf.* V. 159 The 'body', or 'foundation', of a good beaver hat is.. made of eight parts rabbits' fur [etc.]. **1880** *Encycl. Brit.* XI. 519/2 A silk hat consists of a light stiff body covered with a plush of silk. **1881** *Instr. Census Clerks* (1885) 74 Silk Hat Making: Body Maker. Finisher. Shaper. **1906** WATSON SMITH *Chem. Hat Manuf.* 65 The stiffening and proofing of hat forms or 'bodies'. **1921** *Dict. Occup. Terms* (1927) §409 Body-maker [of hats].

8. *spec.* **a.** The middle aisle, or the whole nave, of a church. **b.** In *Fortification* (see quot. 1862). **c.** The shaft of a pillar. **d.** The resonance box of a musical instrument. **e.** In *Anat.* The main portion of a bone, esp. of one of the vertebræ. **f.** The main portion of a document, as distinguished from the introduction or preamble, and esp. from an appendix, a codicil, or other supplementary matter.

1418 *E.E. Wills* (1882) 30 To the werkis of the body of the Parisshe Chirche. **1552** *Bk. Com. Prayer, Commun.* Rubric, The Table.. shall stand in the body of the church. **1559** ABP. HETHE in Strype *Ann. Ref.* I. II. App. vi. 7 The body of this acte touchinge the supremacy. **1580** BARET *Alv.* B 871 The bodie of a pillour, betweene the chapitre and the base. **1661** BRAMHALL *Just Vind.* iv. 80 The incroachments.. mentioned in the body of that law. **1712** PRIDEAUX *Direct. Ch.-wardens* (ed. 4) 24 In the City of London.. the Parishioners repair the Chancel as well as the Body of the Church. **1736** KING in *Swift's Lett.* (1768) IV. 179 The tracts.. may be printed by way of appendix. This will be indeed less trouble than the interweaving them in the body of the history. **1831** R. KNOX *Cloquet's Anat.* 17 In every vertebra, there are distinguished a body, seven processes, four notches, and a hole. **1862** TROLLOPE *Orley F.* i. (ed. 4) 2 The body of the will was in the handwriting of the widow, as was also the codicil. **1862** F. GRIFFITHS *Artil. Man.* (ed. 9) 262 *The Body of the place*, (or *Enceinte*) consists of the work next to, and surrounding the town, in the form of a polygon, whether regular, or irregular. **1878** H. H. GIBBS *Ombre* Pref. 7 Bringing the supplementary Chapter into the body of the Book.

g. (*a*) The part of a vehicle fitted to receive the load; (*b*) used for the corresponding part in a motor-car and in an aeroplane; (*c*) *attrib.* and *Comb.*

(*a*) **1523** FITZHERB. *Husb.* §5 The bodye of the wayne of oke. **1666** PEPYS *Diary* (1879) VI. 68 There I do find a great many ladies sitting in the body of a coach. **1761**, **1794** [see CARRIAGE 28]. **1881** J. W. BURGESS *Coach-building* 42 The body is a species of box, fitted with doors and windows, and lined and wadded for the purpose of comfort. **1897** J. PHILIPSON *Coachbuilding* 2 The body is the most essential part of the carriage.

(*b*) **1896** *Horseless Age* May 20 Width of body [of motorcar] 32 inches; length of body 8 feet 6 inches. **1906** *Motors* 52 The Tonneau body was till lately most popular. **1909** A. BERGET *Conquest of Air* 166 The body.. is the space designed to carry the motor, propeller, and the aviator. **1920** JONES & FRIER *Aeroplane Design* 109 The main function of the body or fuselage is to provide accommodation for cargo, pilot, passengers, flying instruments, and a reliable bearing for the power unit.

(*c*) **1611** [see *body-maker*, sense 29 below]. **1802** *Sporting Mag.* XIX. 205/1 In the first shop [of a coach manufactory] the body-makers are employed. **1846** DODD *Brit. Manuf.* VI. 113 'Body-makers' [are] employed principally on delicate framework and panelling. **1884** [see BODY 29]. **1891** *Daily News* 29 Dec. 6/4 The body-making and harness departments. **1908** *Westm. Gaz.* 19 Mar. 4/1 A large number of chassis.. fitted with every class of bodywork. **1909** *Ibid.* 17 June 4/1 The body-painting, smithy, and upholstery shops. **1914** C. W. TERRY *Motor Body-building* 58 Materials used by body-builders. **1920** JONES & FRIER *Aeroplane Design* 99 The outer, inner, and body struts. **1963** *Times* 14 May 7/3 The bodywork is virtually as good as new after years of operation. **1967** *Autocar* 28 Dec. 2/1 The Hillman Super Minx, with which the previous Vogue had shared a common body-shell.

h. *Naut.* The hull of a ship; the section of this as viewed from different positions.

1691 T. H[ALE] *Acc. New Invent.* 22 The whole Bodies of their Ships under Water. **1769** FALCONER *Dict. Marine* (1789) D ij b, The fore-body of the ship, i.e. before the midship-frame. *c* **1850** *Rudim. Navig.* (Weale) 99 The figure of a ship, abstractedly considered, is supposed to be divided into different parts,.. to each of which is given the appellation of *Body*. Hence we have the terms *Fore Body*, *After Body*, *Cant Bodies*, and *Square Body*. Thus the *Fore Body* is the figure, or imaginary figure, of that part of the ship afore the midships or dead-flat, as seen from ahead... The *Square Body* comprehends all the timbers whose areas or planes are perpendicular to the keel and square with the middle line of the ship; which is all that portion of a ship between the cant bodies.

9. The main portion of a collection or company; the majority; the larger part, the bulk of anything.

1599 SHAKS. *Much Ado* I. i. 287 The body of your discourse is sometime guarded with fragments. **1603** KNOLLES *Hist. Turkes* (1621) 1359 The bodie of the Turkes armie followed bihinde. **1678** N. WANLEY *Wonders* v. ii. §64. 471/2 The main body of the Empire. **1732** NEAL *Hist. Purit.* I. 19 The Body of the inferiour Clergy were disguised Papists. **1848** MACAULAY *Hist. Eng.* I. 166 The great body of the people leaned to the royalists. **1856** FROUDE *Hist. Eng.* (1858) I. i. 66 Under Henry [VIII] the body of the people were prosperous.

†**10.** The vessel in which a substance to be distilled is placed; a retort. (There appears to have been a reference here to *spirit*.) ? *Obs.*

1559 MORWYNG *Evonym.* I Moist thinges put into a body (for so do they cal the bigger vessel from whence the vapour is lifted up) by the force of heate are extenuated into a vapour. **1594** PLATT *Jewell-ho.* II. 3 Put them into your pot, or body. **1641** FRENCH *Distill.* i. (1651) 28 Put this bread into a Glass-body, and distill it in *Balneo*. **1721–1800** BAILEY, *Body* (in Chymistry) is the Vessel which holds the Matter in distilling the Spirits of Vegetables.

11. *Type founding.* The breadth of the shank of the type, which is the same throughout the fount, while the thickness varies with the letter (e.g. I and W); hence, size of type.

1824 J. JOHNSON *Typogr.* II. ii. 11 The several bodies to which printing letters are cast.. are nineteen in number.

III. Personal being, individual.

12. a. The material being of man, as the sign and tangible part of his individuality, taken for the whole; the person. Chiefly in legal phrases.

1393 GOWER *Conf.* III. 208 She hath her owne body feigned, For fere as though she wolde flee Out of her londe. **1549** *Bk. Com. Prayer, Matrimony*, With this Ring I thee wed.. with my body I thee worship. **1603** KNOLLES *Hist. Turkes* (1621) 870 An armie.. consisting of most choice bodies. **1652** *Proc. Parliament* No. 135. 2100 A Warrant in the nature of a Habeas Corpus.. to bring without delay the body of the same prisoner. **1710** *Lond. Gaz.* No. 4695/3 A barbarous Murder was committed on the Body of Mr. Henry Widdrington. **1753** CHAMBERS *Cycl. Supp.* s.v., A man is said to be bound or held in Body and goods; that is, he is liable to remain in prison; in default of payment. **1822** SCOTT *Nigel* xxvii, Two pages of the body.

b. ***heir of the body***: an heir who is a direct descendant.

a **1626** BACON *Max. & Uses Com. Law* 51 The heires males of his body. **1732** NEAL *Hist. Purit.* (1822) I. 12 An act of Parliament for settling the crown upon the heirs of her body. **1768** BLACKSTONE *Comm.* II. 114 As the word *heirs* is necessary to create a fee, so, in farther imitation of the strictness of the feodal donation, the word *body*, or some other words of procreation, are necessary to make it a fee-tail. **1788** J. POWELL *Devises* (1827) II. 469 You here find a child described as an heir of the body.

13. A human being of either sex, an individual. Formerly, as still dialectally, and in the combinations ANY-, EVERY-, NO-, SOME-BODY, etc., exactly equivalent to the current 'person'; but now only as a term of familiarity, with a tinge of compassion, and generally with adjectives implying this.

1297 R. GLOUC. 489 The beste bodi of the world in bendes was ibrouȝt. *c* **1340** *Cursor M.* 3360 (Fairf.) A better body drank neuer wine. **1377** LANGL. *P. Pl.* B. x. 258 Ac blame þow neuere body and þow be blame-worthy. **1475** CAXTON *Jason* 90 Euery noble body ought soner chese deth thene to

do..thing that sholde be ayenst their honour. **1535** COVERDALE *Ps.* xiii[i]. 1 The foolish bodyes saye in their hertes: Tush, there is no God. **1539** *Bury Wills* 137, I will that my executors gyve..in breade to iiij poore bodies j *d.* **1598** SHAKS. *Merry W.* I. iv. 105 'Tis a great charge to come vnder one bodies hand. **1653** WALTON *Angler* 56 It shall be given away to some poor body. **1693** LOCKE *Educ.* §143. iv, One angry body discomposes the whole Company. **1771** SMOLLETT *Humph. Cl.* (1815) 201 The countess was a good sort of a body. **1777** SHERIDAN *Trip Scarb.* III. iv. Wks. 505 What do you din a body's ears for? **1833** HT. MARTINEAU *Loom and Lugg.* I. ii. 17 His wife was a more tidy body.

IV. A corporate body, aggregate of individuals, collective mass.

14. a. *Law.* An artificial 'person' created by legal authority for certain ends; a corporation; commonly a corporation aggregate, but also applied to a corporation sole (cf. quots. 1641, 1642). Always with defining adj. ***body corporate, body politic.***

1461 *Act 1 Edw. IV*, i. §4 Any Fraternitie, Guild, Companie, or Fellowship, or other bodie corporate. **1528** PERKINS *Prof. Bk.* i. §64 (1642) 30 A bodie politique, as a Maior and Comminaltie. **1641** *Termes de la Ley*, Bodies Politique are Bishops, Abbots, Priors, Deanes, Parsons of Churches, and such like, which have succession in one person onely. **1642** MILTON *Argt. conc. Militia* 27 The King is a body politick, for that a body politique never dieth. **1768** BLACKSTONE *Comm.* I. 467 These artificial persons are called bodies politic, bodies corporate, or corporations. **1837** *Penny Cycl.* VIII. 46/2 For the purpose of maintaining and perpetuating the uninterrupted enjoyment of certain powers, rights, property, or privileges, it has been found convenient to create a sort of artificial person, or body-politic, not liable to the ordinary casualties which affect the transmission of private rights, but capable, by its constitution, of independently continuing its own existence. This artificial person is in our law called an incorporation, corporation, or body-corporate.

b. ***body politic*** has also the wider sense of 'organized society'.

1634 CANNE *Necess. Separ.* (1849) 185 To knit themselves together in a spiritual outward society or body politic. **1702** C. MATHER *Magn. Chr.* I. vi. (1852) 82 With mutual consent they became a body-politick, and framed a body of necessary laws and orders. **1839** YEOWELL *Anc. Brit. Ch.* viii. 77 Associations and bodies politic within the church.

c. *spec.* **the body politic**: the nation in its corporate character; the state. (Orig. there appears to have been, in this use of *body*, a reference to the *headship* of the sovereign.)

1532–3 *Act 24 Henry VIII*, xii, This Realm of England is an Empire..governed by one supreme Head and King.. unto whom a Body politick, compact of all Sorts and Degrees of People..been bounden and owen to bear a natural and humble Obedience. **1593** HOOKER *Eccl. Pol.* (Pref.) v. §2 A law is the deed of the whole body politic. **1636** HEALEY *Epictetus' Man.* xxxi. 40 But what place shall I hold then..in the body politicke? **1782** V. KNOX *Ess.* (1819) I. xii. 69 All conduct extensively injurious to individuals, is injurious to the body politic. **1874** REYNOLDS *John Bapt.* ii. 116 Radical changes in the body-politic.

d. (Cf. L. *totum corpus reipublicæ*.)

1570 *Act 13 Eliz.* xviii. Pream., Beneficial Causes..to insue to the Body of this Common Wealth. **1625** BURGES *Pers. Tithes* 20 The Lawes..enacted by the King and the whole Body of the Kingdome.

15. A number of persons taken collectively, usually as united and organized in a common cause or for common action, as for deliberation, government, business; a society, association, league, fraternity.

1689 BURNET *Tracts* I. 71 There are three different Bodies or Leagues. **1732** LEDIARD *Sethos* II. IX. 271 The Governor ..had not time to form a defensive body. **1848** MACAULAY *Hist. Eng.* I. 165 It is seldom that a man inrolls himself in a proscribed body from any but conscientious motives. **1852** BRIGHT *Let.* in *Speeches* (1876) 552 Grants of public money to any public body. **1866** LIDDON *Bampt. Lect.* i. (1875) 10 That little Body the disciples of Christ, and nucleus of His future Church. **1880** *Chr. Leader* 588/3 A preacher of the U.P. body.

16. An organized collection of fighting men acting together; a force. (The most general term that can be so applied.)

1597 SHAKS. *2 Hen. IV*, I. iii. 66, I thinke we are a Body strong enough (Euen as we are) to equall with the King. **1651** *Proc. Parliament* No. 84. 1278 Leaving moving bodies behind to prevent their designes. **1693** *Mem. Ct. Teckely* II. 151 Some pierced even to the Body of Reserve. **1769** ROBERTSON *Chas. V*, V. IV. 390 Escorted by a body of horse. **1839** THIRLWALL *Greece* III. 117 The Athenians..sent a body of troops to garrison it. **1849** MACAULAY *Hist. Eng.* II. 4 The bodies now designated as the first six regiments of dragoon guards, etc.

17. (more loosely) An assemblage of units characterized by some common attribute, and thus regarded as a whole; a collective mass: **a.** of persons.

1598 GRENEWEY *Tacitus' Descr. Germ.* vi. 269 The Semnones..by their great body, they take themselues to be the head of the Sueuians. **1663** GERBIER *Counsel* 10 A whole Body (consisting of number of Persons). **1677** C. HATTON in *Corr.* (1878) 152 The clergy did not goe in a body. **1755** JOHNSON in *Boswell* (1831) I. 275 We might go and drink tea with Mr. Wise in a body. **1832** HT. MARTINEAU *Life in Wilds* viii. 100 All formed in a body to go and meet the new arrivals.

b. of things.

1593 HOOKER *Eccl. Pol.* I. xiv. §4 The entire body of the Scripture. **1796** BURKE *Let. noble Ld.* Wks. 1842 II. 259 Since the total body of my services..have obtained the acceptance of my sovereign. **1874** MAHAFFY *Soc. Life Greece* x. 309 This large and respectable body of opinion. **1875** WHITNEY *Life Lang.* x. 181 The High-German body of dialects.

18. A comprehensive and systematic collection of the details of any subject; an arranged whole of information; *hence*, a pandect (cf. L. *corpus juris*); a text-book.

[Cf. **1593** in prec.] **1647** COWLEY *Mistr.*, *The Soul* iii, If she do near thy Body prize Her Bodies of Philosophies. **1652** NEEDHAM tr. *Selden's Mare Cl.* 169 Whether they comment upon the bodie of Justinian. **1659** MILTON *Hirelings* 92 Som wholesom bodie of divinitie as they call it. **1699** BENTLEY *Phal.* 361 A Body of Laws. **1711** ADDISON *Spect.* No. 121 ¶8, I could wish our Royal Society would compile a Body of Natural History. **1830** HERSCHEL *Nat. Phil.* III. vi. (1851) 352 Digests and bodies of science. **1860** ABP. THOMSON *Laws Th.* Introd. 10 Science is a body of principles and deductions, Art is a body of precepts.

V. Transferred from the material part of man to matter generally as opposed to the immaterial.

19. A separate portion of matter, large or small, a material thing; something that has physical existence and extension in space: **a.** in common language and *Physics*.

heavenly bodies: (in modern use) the masses of matter that exist away from the earth, the sun, moon, planets, comets, meteors, stars, etc.; *orig.* a phrase of the astro-alchemists, applied to the seven 'bodies celestial': see 22 a.

c **1380** WYCLIF *De Dot. Eccl.* Sel. Wks. III. 437 þe bemes of þe sonne..þat shyneþ freliche in bodyes. *c* **1391** CHAUCER *Astrol.* 15 To knowe the altitude of the sonne or of othre celestial bodies. *a* **1568** COVERDALE *Hope Faithf.* xiv. (1574) 91 A wal is a body. **1586** T. B. *La Primaud. Fr. Acad.* 19 A bodie is a masse or lump, which, as much as lieth in it, resisteth touching, and occupieth a place. **1642** ROGERS *Naaman* 348 Cannot the Lord..restraine the influence of the upper bodies from the lower at his pleasure? **1678** CUDWORTH *Intell. Syst.* Pref., The onely Principles of Bodies, are Magnitude, Figure, Site, Motion, and Rest. **1752** JOHNSON *Rambl.* No. 207 ¶9 All attraction is increased by the approach of the attracting body. **1754** SHERLOCK *Disc.* (1759) I. iv. 159 The Magnitudes and Distances of the heavenly Bodies. **1841** *Liebig's Lett. Chem.* vi, The ultimate particles of bodies, or atoms, must occupy a certain space.

b. viewed metaphysically.

1656 tr. *Hobbes' Elem. Philos.* (1839) 102 A body is that, which having no dependance upon our thought, is coincident or coextended with some part of space. **1785** REID *Int. Powers* 186 What we call a body, is only a bundle of sensations. **1846** MILL *Logic* I. iii. §7 A body..may be defined, the external cause to which we ascribe our sensations.

c. *spec.* In *Physiol.* often forming the base of nomenclature, as ***pituitary body, pacchionian body.***

1866 HUXLEY *Phys.* (1869) 143 Nothing certain is known of the functions of any of these bodies [the ductless glands]. *Ibid.* The spheroidal bodies called *corpuscles of the spleen*,.. consist of a solid aggregation of minute bodies.

†**20.** *Geom.* A figure of three dimensions; a solid. ***regular body***: one of the five Regular Solids. *Obs.* in modern Geometry.

1570 DEE *Math. Pref.* 3 A thicke Magnitude we call a Solide, or a Body. **1570** BILLINGSLEY *Euclid* I. def. xvi. 3 A superficies being moued maketh a solide or bodie. **1635** J. BABINGTON *Geometry* 42 The cube..is accounted one of the five regular bodies. **1796** HUTTON *Math. Dict.* I. 215 The five Regular Bodies..These bodies were called *platonic*, because they were said to have been invented, or first treated of, by Plato. *a* **1864** tr. *Weisbach* (W.) The path of a moving point is a line, that of a geometric body is another body.

21. a. A compact quantity or mass; amount; bulk; quantity.

1650 FULLER *Pisgah* 388 Ezekiels Temple had not the same body with Solomons, but greater. **1663** GERBIER *Counsel* 38 A proportionable Body to the..weight it is to bear. **1772** *Town & Country Mag.* 161 A large body of land, extending thirty miles up the Coofaw river. **1828** HUTTON *Course Math.* II. 139 Body is the mass, or quantity of matter, in any material substance. **1849** MURCHISON *Siluria* vi. (1867) 108 Another body of igneous rock lies subjacent. **1855** BAIN *Senses & Int.* II. ii. §1 (1864) 224 A large body of light. **1878** HUXLEY *Physiogr.* 40 A body of cold air.

b. *spec.* A mass or deposit of metalliferous ore.

1909 *Westm. Gaz.* 9 Feb. 11/4 The opening of an entirely new body carrying on an average 3 per cent. copper and 15 ounces of silver to the ton. **1929** *Times* 25 Jan. 12/3 A number of areas [in Great Britain] are worth prospecting in the hope of discovering new ore bodies.

22. A distinct form or kind of matter:

†**a.** *Alchemy* and *Astrol.* The ***seven bodies terrestrial***: the seven ancient metals answering to the seven 'heavenly bodies' (the sun, moon, and five old planets). *Obs.*

c **1386** CHAUCER *Chan. Yem. Prol. & T.* 267 The foure spirites and the bodies seuene. The bodies seuene eek loo hem here anoon, Sol gold is, and luna siluer, we threpe, Mars yren, Mercurie quik siluer we clepe, Saturnus leed, and Iupiter is tyn, And venus copir, by my fader kyn. **1393** GOWER *Conf.* II. 84 The bodies, whiche I speke of here, Of the planettes ben begonne.

b. *Chem.* and *Min.* Any kind of 'substance', simple or compound, solid, liquid, or gaseous. ***simple bodies***: the chemical elements; ***compound bodies***: the substances formed by their combination.

1594 PLAT *Jewell-ho.* I. 13 Niter, and other Aromaticall bodies. *a* **1682** SIR T. BROWNE *Tracts* 12 A gummous body and dissoluble in water. **1695** WOODWARD *Nat. Hist. Earth* (1723) 7 The said Metallick and Mineral Bodies. **1724** WATTS *Logic* 16 They supposed the heavens to be a quintessence, or a fifth sort of body. **1831** BREWSTER *Optics* xxiii. 204 Crystallised bodies, such as nitre and arragonite. **1841** *Liebig's Lett. Chem.* iv. (1844) 63 The employment of symbols enables the chemist to express..the constitution of every compound body.

c. The paste or clay (of a particular kind) used in the manufacture of porcelain.

1774 J. WEDGWOOD *Let.* 21 July (1965) 163 At one time the body is white and fine as it should be, the next we make ..is a Cinamon color. **1839** Mortar body [see MORTAR *sb.*[1] 5 b]. **1893** E. A. BARBER *Pott. & Porc. U.S.* 127 The proportion of phosphate of lime..being..a very much smaller percentage than in the English bone body. **1902** A. BENNETT *Anna of Five Towns* viii. 169 The four sorts of clay used in a common 'body'—ball clay, China clay, flint clay and stone clay.

23. *abstractly* (in *Metaphysics*, formerly also in *Physics*). That which has sensible qualities, or is perceptible by the senses; matter; 'substance'.

1668 WILKINS *Real Char.* 413 Spirit. The Opposite to which..is Body. **1678** CUDWORTH *Intell. Syst.* 49 He that will undertake to prove that there is something else in the World besides Body, must first determine what Body is, for otherwise he will go about to prove that there is something besides He-knows-not-what. **1690** LOCKE *Hum. Und.* II. xxiii. (1695) 164 The primary Ideas we have peculiar to Body, as contradistinguished to Spirit, are the Cohesion of solid, and consequently separable parts, and a power of communicating Motion by impulse. **1762** KAMES *Elem. Crit.* (1833) 475 Every substratum of tangible qualities is called body. **1794** J. HUTTON *Philos. Light, &c.* 288 Body in the abstract..must be inert. **1870** BOWEN *Logic* iii. 55 We cannot think of body without extension.

†**24.** Substance, as opposed to representation, shadow, etc.; reality. *Obs.* or *arch.*

1382 WYCLIF *Col.* ii. 17 Whiche ben schadowe of thingis to come; forsoth the body is of Christ. *c* **1386** CHAUCER *Merch. T.* 552 Parfourned hath the sonne his Ark diurne No lenger may the body of hym soiurne On thorisonte. **1602** SHAKS. Ham. III. ii. 26 To shew Vertue her owne Feature.. and the verie Age and Bodie of the Time, his forme and pressure. **1702** *Eng. Theophrast.* 327 Men suffer themselves to be enchanted with the shadow and appearance of a thing whose real body does not so much as affect them.

25. 'Substance' or substantial quality, as opposed to insubstantiality, thinness, weakness, flimsiness, or transparency: said of colours, wine, paper, textile fabrics, etc.

c **1645** HOWELL *Lett.* (1650) I. 371 In Greece there are no wines that have bodies enough to bear the sea for long voyages. **1735** *Dict. Polygraph.* s.v., *To bear a body*, a term us'd of painting colours..capable of being ground so fine, and mixing with the oil so intirely, as to seem only a very thick oil of the same colour. **1784** J. BARRY *Lect. Art* vi. (1848) 216 Those colours without body which are more immediately considered as transparent. **1851** H. MAYO *Philos. Living* i. 66 The vintages, differ in fulness of body and lusciousness. **1859** GULLICK & TIMBS *Paint.* 10 Less liable to be affected by damp than colouring with more body or substance. **1862** *Times* 12 Aug., Staffordshire cannot produce fine-grained iron equal to theirs in body, i.e. in its power of standing the fire.

fig. **1824–8** LANDOR *Imag. Conv.* (1846) 80, I hate both poetry and wine without body. **1884** *Spectator* 4 Oct. 1304/1 Metaphor and language..meant to conceal the want of body in the thought and emotion beneath.

26. Main substance; fundamental constituent.

1787 WINTER *Syst. Husb.* 109 Every soil must contain as sufficient a body for those manures to act upon. **1875** FORTNUM *Maiolica* i. 3 The characteristics of the soft wares are a paste or body which may be scratched with a knife.

†**27.** *Metaph.* An entity, a thing which has real existence; an agent or cause of phenomena. *Obs.*

1587 GOLDING *De Mornay* ii. 21 To drawe some peculiar good..out of another bodies workes..as out of Poyson, health..from the night, rest. **1660** STANLEY *Hist. Philos.* (1701) 326/1 The Soul is a Body, because it maketh us to be living Creatures. *Ibid.* 326/2 Night and Day are Bodies. Voice is a Body, for it maketh that which is heard; in a word, whatsoever is, is a Body and a Subject.

VI. *Comb.* and *Attrib.*

28. *simple attrib.* Of body, physical, material.

c **1200** [see 1 c]. **1674** N. FAIRFAX *Bulk & Selv.* 112 A fresh train of hangers on in the body kind.

29. General combinations: **a.** objective with pr. pple., vbl. sb., or agent-noun, as ***body-bending, -breaking, -curer, -killing, -maker, -making, -wearing***; **b.** attributive: (*a*) pertaining to the human body, as ***body-armour, -being, -blow*** (also *fig.*), ***-build, -ease, -garment, -medicine, -odour, -play, -plague, -sin, -swing, -weight***; (*b*) reserved for personal attendance or use, as ***body-carriage, -chariot, -coach, -coachman, -physician, -servant, -slave, -valet,*** also BODY-GUARD; (*c*) in various senses of body, as ***body-bolt, -girth, -lining, -scent, -wall; body-wise*** adv.

1828–41 TYTLER *Hist. Scot.* (1864) I. 322 A breastplate and back-piece, etc...formed..the *body-armour. *a* **1652** J. SMITH *Sel. Disc.* iv. 105 If all *body-being in the world were destroyed. **1792** *Sporting Mag.* I. 43/2 After sparring some time..Stanyard put in a *body blow. **1857** HUGHES *Tom Brown* ii, That body-blow left Joe's head unguarded. **1908** *Daily Chron.* 24 Aug. 5/5 Its latest action is a body-blow to the growers. **1950** DEMPSEY *Champ. Fighting* 39 Face-punches and body-blows. **1958** *Times* 22 Apr. 6/7 It is a body blow. I am carrying the can for somebody else. **1886** *Ripon Chron.* 4 Sept. 3/5 The *body bolt of the phaeton suddenly gave way, and the occupants were thrown out. **1533** FRITH *Answ. More* (1829) 443 They believe not in his *body-breaking and blood-shedding. **1923** C. B. DAVENPORT (*title*) *Body-build and its inheritance. **1961** *Lancet* 12 Aug. 341/2 On admission her weight was 129 lb., which was proportional to her height and body-build. **1766**

ENTICK *London* IV. 54 Wheels of *body carriages. **1704** *Lond. Gaz.* No. 4052/1 Her Majesty's *Body Chariot. **1702** *Ibid.* No. 3862/1 Then Her Majesty, habited in Purple..in her *Body Coach drawn by 8 Horses. **1735** *Swift's Lett.* (1768) IV. 135 Were his majesty inclined to-morrow to declare his *body-coachman his first minister. **1598** SHAKS. *Merry W.* III. i. 100 Soule-Curer, and *Body-Curer. **1546** BALE *Eng. Votaries* II. (1550) iv b, Fournished the Clery there with such possessions and *body-ease. **1870** EMERSON *Soc. & Solit.* i. 14 Dressed in arts and institutions as well as in *body-garments. **1725** DE FOE *Voy. round World* (1840) 135 Wrapped round her very tight, like a *body-girt to a horse. **1761** STERNE *Tr. Shandy* III. iv. 14 Your jerkin..and the *body-lining to it. **1611** RICH *Honest. Age* (1844) 37 Then haue we those that be called *Body-makers. **1884** *Birmingham Daily Post* 24 Jan. 3/3 Coachmakers—Wanted, an experienced Bodymaker, for first-class work. **1544** LATIMER *Wks.* 1845 II. 481 The popish consecration, which hath been called Gods *body-making. **1933** D. L. SAYERS *Murder must Advertise* iv. 69 Do you ever ask yourself about *Body-Odour? **1881** *Gentl. Mag.* CCL. 163 Ready equally for mind-play or *body-play. **1875** 'STONEHENGE' *Brit. Sports* I. I. vii. §8 Few retrievers can hit off the *body-scent of a dead cock. **1760** STERNE *Tr. Shandy* (ed. 2) II. v. 34 Besides what he gained..as a *body-servant. *a* **1240** *Ureisun* in *Lamb. Hom.* 189 Wasche mine fif wittes of alle *bodi sunnen. **1896** *Daily News* 13 Mar. 8/4 The form of the men at the slow stroke was admirable, *body-swing and feather alike being capital. **1950** W. HAMMOND *Cricketers' School* v. 54 Thus gaining the sort of body-swing that won Maurice Tate his wickets. **1847** LD. LINDSAY *Chr. Art* I. 25 The *body-wall bulging out and lopping over. **1873** C. H. RALFE *Physiol. Chem.* 81 Men excrete little more urea in proportion to their *body weight than women. **1907** *Westm. Gaz.* 23 Aug. 4/2 He [*sc.* the batsman] throws his body-weight on the left, the forward foot. **1966** *Lancet* 24 Dec. 1380/1 No patient was preselected on the basis of serum-lipid level or body-weight. **1884** *Homiletic Monthly* Apr. 409 If..man were *body-wise related by descent to the brute creation.

30. Special comb.: **body-bag**, a bag to sleep in; **body belt**, a belt worn close to the body; **body-box**, a brood-box, brood-chamber; **body-builder**, (*a*) one who practises body-building to develop muscular fitness; (*b*) a manufacturer of vehicle bodies; **body-building**, the feeding and strengthening of the human frame by diet and exercise; also *attrib.* or *adj.*; **body carpet, carpeting**, carpeting manufactured in strips that are joined together to form the required size; also *body* ellipt.; **body-cavity** *Zool.*, the cœlom; **body cell** *Biol.*, a somatic cell; **body-centred** *a.*, applied to a type of crystal structure in which an atom or ion occurs at each corner and in the centre of a cubic unit cell; **body-chamber**, the outer and largest chamber of a shell occupied by the body of the animal; **body-check**, a movement in lacrosse (see quot. 1892); also, a similar movement in ice-hockey; hence as *v.*; so **'body-,checking** *vbl. sb.*; **body clock**, the biological clock of the human body; cf. *biological clock* s.v. BIOLOGICAL *a.*; **body-cloth**, a cloth, or rug, to cover horses or other animals; **body-clothes, -clothing**, clothes for the body; **body-coat**, a coat fitting more or less closely to the body, †a dress-coat; **body-colour**, a colour that has consistency, or body, in distinction from a tint or wash (cf. 25); a colour rendered opaque by the addition of white; **body count**: in the war in Vietnam, the count of enemy soldiers killed by U.S. and allied troops in combat (see quot. 1968); also *transf.*; **body drop**, a throw in ju-jitsu; **body-face** = *body-type*; **body-hoop**, a hoop securing the arris pieces of a made mast; **body-horse** (still *dial.*), a shaft-horse; **body-image** *Psychol.*, the subjective picture or mental image of one's own body; **body language** *Psychol.*, the gestures and movements by which a person unconsciously or indirectly conveys meaning; also *transf.*; **body-lifter** = *body-snatcher*; **body-line bowling**, fast bowling delivered persistently on the leg side so as to be likely to strike the batsman's body; also in other collocations; **body-louse**, a species of louse, *Pediculus corporis*, which infests the body of the uncleanly; **body-mark, stroke** *Printing*, the stem or 'thick-stroke' of the face of a type-letter; **body-mind** *Philos.* (see quots.); **body-plan**, in *Shipbuilding*, an end elevation of a ship, showing the breadth, contour of the sides, timbers, etc.; **body-popping** *vbl. sb.* orig. *U.S.*, a style of (street-)dancing popular among teenagers, esp. in urban areas, and characterized by robotic, jerking movements; hence as *ppl. a.* and **body-pop** *v. intr.*, **body-popper**; **body-rope** *Naut.* (see quots.); **body scanner** [SCANNER 3 a], a scanning X-ray machine which with the aid of a computer can produce tomograms of the whole body; **body-schema** = *body-image*; **body-snatcher**, one who secretly disinters dead bodies in churchyards for the purpose of dissection, a 'resurrectionist'; so **body-snatching, -stealing**; **body-soul**, body and soul regarded as a unified whole; also *attrib.* or *adj.*; †**body-stead**, the nave of a church; †**body-spirit** = *esprit de corps*; **body stocking** (see quot. 1968); **body strike** [STRIKE *sb.*]: see quot. 1957; **body-tube**, the main tube forming the body of an organ-pipe; **body-type**, the type used for printing the text of a book; **body-urge**, sexual passion; **body-wall** *Zool.*, the general envelope of an animal body; the cell-wall of a lower organism; **body-whorl**, the last and largest whorl of a shell, containing the body of the mollusc; **bodywork** (see sense 8 b (c)).

1885 *Harper's Mag.* Apr. 820/1 A fur over-coat and *body-bag. **1911** *Alfred Weeks's Sales Catal.* All Wool *Body Belts..to clear 6¾d. **1962** T. C. H. JACOBS *Red Net* xviii. 178 A wide body-belt which Carlo had worn next to his skin... Two rows of tiny pockets ran its entire length. **1881** T. W. COWAN *Bee-keeper's Guide Bk.* 37 A second hive, having eight frames the same size as those used in the *body-box, is provided for use on the top of the other. **1895** *Modern Bee-Keeping* (ed. 8) 22 The body-box or brood-chamber. **1890** *Boston Herald* 21 Dec. 18/5 Prof. Robert J. Roberts, the noted *body builder now connected with the gymnasium of the Young Men's Christian Association of this city. **1928** *Daily Express* 5 Oct. 2/1 In Paris body-builders are making use of a new base material with which the car is covered. **1970** *Times* 4 Mar. 13/5 A girl torn between a brainy weed and a manic body-builder. **1983** *Truck & Bus Transportation* Oct. 48/2 The Interbus is bound to intensify competition among bus bodybuilders. **1986** *Strength Athlete* June/July 32/2 Back in the old days, people may have flocked to see the 'freaks'—nowadays, bodybuilders are regarded as exemplary fitness aficionados to be emulated. **1904** *Daily Chron.* 4 May 4/3 Proteid, or the *body-building element. **1904** E. SANDOW (*title*) Body Building, or Man in the Making. **1962** *Times* 14 Nov. 3/7 The swimming club has 45 minutes on body-building. **1946** *Carpet Rev.* Oct. 15/2 A large quantity of special heavy Wilton *body carpet..was also made by the firm for the cabin class. **1947** *Ibid.* May 23/1 As for piece goods, there is quite a demand for ¾ stair and runners, but one often sells body goods to fill the want, as stair carpets are in short supply. A good deal of plain body is sold. **1947** J. F. C. BRINTON *Carpets* v. 37 Originally, carpeting was only made in body or filling 27 in. wide, and border 22½ or 18 in. wide. **1957** *Times* 14 Oct. 13/5 For close-carpeting it is more economical to buy 'body' carpeting for alcoves, fireplaces and other odd corners. **1963** *Which?* Mar. 71/1 This.. carpet..is made on a broad loom (6 ft. wide or more) instead of the usual 'body' carpet which is in rolls 18–54 in. wide. **1875** HUXLEY & MARTIN *Elem. Biol.* 100 The *body-cavity [in *Hydra*]. **1888** ROLLESTON & JACKSON *Anim. Life* Introd. p. xxix, The cavity, or series of cavities, known as body cavities or coelome. **1927** HALDANE & HUXLEY *Anim. Biol.* i. 10 The stomach and intestine lie in a space, the general body-cavity or coelom. **1896** E. B. WILSON *Cell in Devel. & Inherit.* ix. 329 Whether these variations first arise in the idioplasm of the germ-cells..or whether they may arise in the *body-cells and then be reflected back upon the idioplasm. **1926** J. S. HUXLEY *Essays Pop. Sci.* i. 7 The nucleus of an ordinary body-cell. **1921** *Physical Rev.* XVII. 574 The calculated spacings are those of a *body centered cubic lattice, the side of the cube being 2·895 Å., and the distance between nearest atoms 2·508 Å. **1925** *Jrnl. Iron & Steel Inst.* CXII. 502 There are only two polymorphous phases..a cubic body-centred modification..and a cubic face-centred modification. **1944** *Electronic Engin.* XVII. 142 In the case of iron the atoms form a regular cubic pattern known as 'body-centred' in which, if we consider an elemental cube of the crystal or unit cell, there will be an atom at each corner of the cube and another at the centre. **1854** WOODWARD *Mollusca* (1856) 79 The *body-chamber is always very capacious. **1892** *Lacrosse: Laws* 6 **Body-check* is the placing one's body in the way of an approaching opponent, so that the latter is simply impeded. No checker shall use force in the body-check. **1901** *Encycl. Sport* I. 608/1 When a player is dodging, no notice should be taken of his crosse, the *Checker* simply taking care to place his body in the way of the dodger. This is known as the *body check*, and no force may be imparted to it, or it becomes a charge, which is forbidden. Body checking is of most use out of the field. **1909** *Westm. Gaz.* 17 Dec. 12/2 It might be a hint to Forster to body check more efficiently [in lacrosse]. **1962** *Amer. Speech* XXXVII. 126 Bodychecks and unpermitted blows occurred [in ice-hockey]. **1936** *Times Lit. Suppl.* 14 Mar. 227/2 It [ice hockey] offers to the eye the clash of bodies (for all the rules about *body-checking). **1960** *Times* 29 Nov. 17/5 Oxford and Cambridge completed their lacrosse programmes for the term... Cambridge started slowly. Their defence was open, there was little body-checking. **1968** G. HOUSEHOLD *Dance of Dwarfs* 163 How long did this take from the time the beast looked over the neck and saw me?.. One's own *body clock is speeded up so fast that it is impossible to tell. **1986** *Today* 8 Dec. 3 (*caption*) He admitted to photographers: My body clock is still on 4 am and I haven't had a chance to shave yet. **1685** *Lond. Gaz.* No. 2021/4 Occasioned by the hindermost Buckles of a *Body-Cloth. **1706** *Ibid.* No. 4212/4 A white Streak down the Side, occasioned by *Body-Clothes. **1753** HANWAY *Trav.* (1762) II. I. ix. 46 They cover their cows with *body-cloths. **1828** SCOTT *F.M. Perth* v, God-a-mercy, wench, it were hard to deny thee time to busk thy body-clothes. **1856** KANE *Arct. Exp.* II. xvi. 168 Blankets were served out as the material for *body-clothing. **1820** T. MITCHELL *Aristoph.* I. Introd. 62 His ring, his seal, his *body-coat, his perfume-box, his upper and under mantle. **1784** J. BARRY *Lect. Art* vi. (1848) 215 Employing stiff *body colour on a white ground. **1859** GULLICK & TIMBS *Painting* 107 The difficulty of calculating when 'wet' the difference of tone the body-colour will assume when dry. **1968** *Economist* 29 June 25/2 The Americans have largely abandoned the '*body count' system, according to which a Vietcong was supposed to be reported dead only if his body was actually seen and counted. **1970** *N.Y. Times* 11 Sept. 40 State and Federal aid programs that are based on live body counts will provide less support to the cities and increase their support to the suburbs. **1984** *Listener* 22 Mar. 6/1 Since then, according to the body-count kept by the American Embassy, the rate of killings has dropped to around 100 a month. **1948** G. KOIZUMI *Twelve Judo Throws* 26 *Body-drop (Taiotoshi)..is one of the hand throws. **1960** *Oxf. Mail* 10 Mar. 8/3 Buley scored a point with a body drop throw, but Garnett scored points with hip and body drop throws. **1898** J. SOUTHWARD *Mod. Printing* I. 134 *Body or text faces. *c* **1430** LYDG. *Min. Poems* 201 A belfry for the *bodyfaunt. **1597** BACON *Coulers Good & Evill* x. (Arb.) 154 The *body-horse in the Cart, that draweth more then the forehorse. **1934** P. SCHILDER in *Proc. Assoc. Res. Nerv. Ment. Dis.* XIII. 466 (*title*) Localization of the *body image. **1935** —— *Image & Appearance of Human Body* 11 The body schema is the tri-dimensional image everybody has about himself. We may call it 'body-image'. **1950** *Lancet* 25 Feb. 335/1 The expression body-image..refers to the mental idea which an individual possesses as to his own body and its physical and æsthetic attributes. [**1941** D. EFRON *Gesture & Environment* I. 5 The bodily language of the Mediterranean is a 'swinging, and dancing of gestures'.] **1966** *Psychol. Abstr.* XL. 1252/2 Langage corporel et théorie de l'information (*Body-language and information theory). **1967** P. L. WACHTEL in *Psychotherapy* IV. III. 97 (*heading*) An approach to the study of body language in Psychotherapy. **1970** [see KINESICS]. **1972** T. MCHUGH *Time of Buffalo* xiii. 152 Buffalo also express themselves in 'body language', assuming certain positions or moving in a particular way. **1983** *Chem. Engin.* 7 Feb. 90 Various types of 'body language'—such as shuffling feet, yawns, glances at watches..and so on—may signal that it's time to call for a break. **1832** SOUTHEY in *Q. Rev.* XLVII. 517 Not coming from a professional *body-lifter. **1861** RAMSAY *Remin.* Ser. II. 133. **1933** *Times* 19 Jan. 12/6 The Australian Cricket Board of Control has sent the following telegram to the M.C.C.: '*Body-line bowling has assumed such proportions as to menace the best interests of the game, making the protection of his body by a batsman his main consideration [etc.].' **1955** I. PEEBLES *Ashes 1954–55* ix. 93 Voce did so [*sc.* took ten wickets], aided by a wet wicket, and Larwood by a bodyline field. **1575** J. STILL *Gamm. Gurton* II. iv, She went as brag as it had ben a *bodelouce. *a* **1652** BROME *Crt. Beggar* Epil., As briske as a Body-lowse in a new Pasture. **1861** HULME tr. *Moquin-Tandon* II. VI. i. 294 The Body (or Clothes) Louse..was for a long time confounded with the former [the Head Louse]. **1896** DE VINNE *Moxon's Mech. Exerc., Printing* 414 Stem is the thick-stroke of a letter, sometimes called by type-founders the *body-mark. **1877** G. H. LEWES *Physical Basis of Mind* III. iii. 350 We know ourselves as *Body-Mind; we do not know ourselves as Body *and* Mind, if by that be meant two coexistent independent Existents. **1945** *Mind* LIV. 58 The defenders of this view have recently been making quite a point of speaking not of 'a mind' and 'a body' but of a 'body-mind', seeking to emphasize by the hyphen in this compound word the monistic identity or inseparableness of the mental and bodily components. *c* **1850** *Rudim. Navig.* (Weale) 137 The *plan of projection*, commonly called the *body plan, which exhibits the outline of the principal timbers, and the greatest heights and breadths of the same. **1984** *Times* 13 July 10/8 Dwellers on Planet Rock..are often to be seen on pavements, *body-popping. **1986** J. SAVARIN *Naja* ii. 35 The black disc-jockey body-popped with unbelievable athleticism. **1984** *N.Y. Times* 15 Apr. x. 51/2 The girls wanted to go back to Covent Garden to watch the punks and *body-poppers. **1984** *Financial Times* 26 Mar. 11 A mute, *body-popping robot. **1984** *Dance Theatre Jrnl.* May 14/3 It's a very strong statement from the streets..that whole movement—breaking, *body-popping. **1985** *Times* 2 Feb. 9/4 The mechanical movements of body popping can be traced to mime and to robotic disco dancing. **1883** *Man. Seamanship Boys' Training Ships* 41 The ropes [for royals] are of two sizes only—viz., head rope from earring to earring, and a *body rope on the foot and leeches. *Ibid.* 46 The largest or body rope..and the head rope. **1975** *Globe & Mail* (Toronto) 1 May 1/7 The *body scanner is a refinement of a similar scanner for the brain and skull in use since 1972... The $575,000 body scanner will start clinical trials shortly in a hospital just outside London. **1978** *Lancashire Life* Mar. 115/2 The Pat Seed Appeal Fund for a body-scanner for the Christie Hospital in Manchester (itself a world leader in the treatment of cancer). **1983** *Daily Tel.* 29 Nov. 18/4 There are now plenty of consultants who are disappointed with the usefulness of the body scanner. **1935** *Body-schema [see *body-image*]. **1942** *Brit. Jrnl. Psychol.* Apr. 280 The notion of the 'body schema' (or 'body image') has come to enjoy something of a vogue in contemporary neuropsychiatry. **1962** HOENIG & HAMILTON tr. *Jaspers' Gen. Psychopathol.* i. 89 The car I drive, if I am a good driver, becomes part of my body-schema or image and is like an extended body which I invest fully with my own senses. **1834** SIR F. HEAD *Bubbles of Brunnen* 126 Any one of our *body-snatchers would have rubbed his rough hands. **1863** *Reader* 22 Aug., At that time (1827–28) ..*'body-snatching' became a trade. *a* **1897** W. WALLACE *Lect.* (1898) 152 As if we were to say of a human being (and it is what perhaps we dare say of the fewest), that he or she was *body-soul: the body the transparent and perfect temple of the spirit. **1956** E. L. MASCALL *Christ. Theol. & Nat. Sci.* vii. 271 The doctrine that the human soul..is only one part of the twofold body-soul unity of the man. **1958** D. M. BAILLIE *Out of Nazareth* II. i. 150 Man is a body-soul organism. **1623** *Resol. Ch. Cartmell* in *Sat. Rev.* (1884) 5 July 14 The *bodystead of the Church shall be decentlye repaired. **1794** W. TAYLOR in *Month. Rev.* XIII. 39 He endeavoured to inspire the senate with a *body-spirit. **1880** S. WARREN *Grave Doings* in *Casquet Lit.* (1877) V. 185/1 My ..exploit in the way of *body-stealing. **1965** *Vogue* 15 Apr. 93 New *body stocking..body-coloured, body-shaped Lycra, just about invisible. **1968** J. IRONSIDE *Fashion Alphabet* 66 *Body-stocking*, covering for the entire body from neck to feet, sometimes with sleeves; they are the same as a dancer's leotard... They are worn as a single undergarment in place of brassière, pants and stockings. Nowadays body-stockings are often flesh coloured and only opaque over the actual body, to give an impression of nudity under a transparent dress. **1969** P. ROTH *Portnoy's Complaint* 203 Walking into a restaurant with a long-legged *kurveh* on his arm! An easy lay in a body stocking! **1937** BELSCHNER & SEDDON *Stud. Sheep Blowfly Problem* in *Dept. Agric. N.S. Wales Sci. Bulletin* No. 54 (*title*) Observations on Fleece Rot and *Body Strike in Sheep. *Ibid.* 24 Body strike follows the development in the fleece of the condition known as fleece rot. **1957** *New Biol.* XXII. 94 Strike starting on some other part of the body [of sheep] such as the shoulder or over the back, is referred to as body strike. **1959** S. J. BAKER *Drum* 110 Flystrike, infestation of sheep by blowflies... Also, body-strike. **1898** J. SOUTHWARD *Mod. Printing* I. 140 The thick lines..are called the *body strokes.

1854 BUSHNAN in *Circ. Sc.* (1865) I. 283/2 The air.. passes out in undulating movements from the *body-tube. **1898** J. SOUTHWARD 134 *Body or text types, used for plain paragraph matter. **1961** T. LANDAU *Encycl. Librarianship* (ed. 2) 43/2 *Body type*, type suitable for reading matter (8–14 point) as in the text of a book, as distinguished from display type, used in headings, display lines in advertisements, etc. **1930** *Body-urge [see IT *pron.* 1 f]. **1932** S. GIBBONS *Cold Comfort Farm* xvii. 237 Teck's a good kid.. but he's got no body-urge. **1888** ROLLESTON & JACKSON *Anim. Life* 357 The *body wall [in Vertebrata]. **1898** A. SEDGWICK *Zool.* I. 549 The soft part of the body-wall [in Polyzoa], which consists of ectoderm and mesoderm. **1909** *Westm. Gaz.* 28 Aug. 13/2 A special series of muscles in the body-wall. **1959** E. F. LINSSEN *Beetles* I. 14 Another characteristic feature of insects is the hard, horny body-wall consisting of plates.. composed mostly of chitin. **1854** WOODWARD *Mollusca* (1856) 101 The last turn of the shell, or *body-whorl, is usually very capacious.

body (ˈbɒdɪ), *v.* [f. prec.] *trans.*

1. To furnish or provide with a body; to embody.

c **1449** PECOCK *Repr.* 245 We.. holden now oure God to be bodili and to be Bodied in a Maner which no Cristen man kan at the ful comprehend. **1621** BOLTON *Stat. Irel.* 315 (*an. 11 Eliz.*) His head sundred from his bodie.. and.. bodied with a stake. **1634** HABINGTON *Castara* 14 In some faire forme of clay Myself I'de bodied. **1656** COWLEY *Davideis* II. Wks. 1710 I. 353. **1858** SEARS *Athan.* III. x. 335 The state where every man's real and dominant life is.. bodied and robed according to its intrinsic quality.

†**2.** To give body, consistence, or strength to. *lit.* and *fig. Obs.*

1563 T. GALE *Antidot.* II. 41 Boyle them.. vntyll they bee well bodyed and incorporate together. **1657** MAY *Satyr. Puppy* 43 Bodying each word with active emphasis.

†**3.** To draw up or form (troops, etc.) into a body, to form in a body. (Also *intr.* for *refl.*) *Obs.*

1651 *Proc. Parliament* No. 80. 1215 The Earl of Sunderland.. hath bodied above 500 of his tenants, & other people under his jurisdiction. *Ibid.* No. 104. 1603 But we could not hear of any bodying considerably, so that we could onely disperse severall parties. **1653** GAUDEN *Hierasp.* 14 Bodying into small Corporations.

4. *to body forth*: **a.** to represent to oneself as in bodily form; to give mental shape to.

1590 SHAKS. *Mids. N.* v. i. 14 Imagination bodies forth the forms of things Vnknowne. **1820** SCOTT *Monast.* xiii, The *beau-ideal* which Dame Glendinning had been bodying forth in her imagination. **1855** BAIN *Senses & Int.* III. iv. §16 The power of bodying forth or realizing what is described in language, is one of the meanings of Conception.

b. To put (an idea) into outward shape or tangible form, to exhibit in outward reality.

1800–24 CAMPBELL *Chaucer & Windsor* I Long shalt thou flourish, Windsor! bodying forth Chivalric times. **1835** LYTTON *Rienzi* IV. i. 191 Wonderfully did her beauty.. body forth the brightest vision that ever floated before the eyes of Tasso. **1840** CARLYLE *Heroes* iv. (1858) 277 The spiritual will always body itself forth in the temporal history of men.

c. To represent; to symbolize, typify.

1846 KEBLE *Lyra Innoc.* (1873) 54 One bodies forth a Virgin form Holding aloft a Cross of might. **1879** CHURCH *Spenser* iv. (1883) 90 The allegory bodies forth the trials which beset the life of man. **1883** *Spectator* No. 2874. 958 Both as egotist and as patriot M. de Lesseps bodies forth the age.

d. To indicate, betoken.

1831 SCOTT *Kenilw.* xvii, A sharp, lively, conceited expression of countenance, seemed to body forth a vain hair-brained coxcomb.

5. *to body out*: to give body or a body to; to fill out (a skeleton), to clothe (a mind) with bodily form.

1839 BAILEY *Festus* xxii. (1848) 285 If thus they bodied out The immortal mind. **1883** *Academy* 20 Oct., To body-out the meagre accounts of Thucydides.

body-guard (ˈbɒdɪˌgɑːd). [cf. F. *garde du corps*.]

1. A guard for the person (esp. of a sovereign or dignitary); a retinue or escort.

a **1735** ARBUTHNOT *Wks.* II. 107 (JOD.) Several bees go with him, as a bodyguard. **1738** F. MOORE *Trav.* II. 404 (JOD.) Troops.. with increased pay and exclusive privileges under the denomination of bodyguards. **1768** TUCKER *Lt. Nat.* II. 182 That body-guard of Popery the Jesuits. **1820** SCOTT *Abbot* xxi, A page is a formidable addition to my body-guard of females. **1822** BYRON *Werner* I. i. 676 I'll promote you to the ranks In the prince's body-guard. **1847** GROTE *Greece* (1862) III. xlii. 513.

fig. **1858** J. MARTINEAU *Studies Chr.* 72 Defended by a body-guard of passions.

2. A soldier of the body-guard, a guard's-man.

1861 W. SARGENT *André* 390 The.. execution.. of one of the body-guards.

bodyhood (ˈbɒdɪhʊd). [f. BODY *sb.* + -HOOD.] The quality of having a body or of being body.

1674 N. FAIRFAX *Bulk & Selv.* 12 Upon the account of our animalities or beghosted bodyhood. *Ibid.* 46 Not only the things of body are given to things not body, but even bodyhood it self is. **1839** BAILEY *Festus* xx. (1848) 254 Spirit lives: And gloriously falsified are all Earth's caverned prophecies of bodyhood.

bodying (ˈbɒdɪɪŋ), *vbl. sb.* [f. BODY *v.* + -ING[1].] The action of the vb. BODY: embodiment.

1641 FRENCH *Distill.* v. (1651) 163 Vapours of Nitre.. being neer to congelation, and bodying. **1841** MIALL *Nonconf.* I. 401 The bodyings forth of that intelligence which is contained in the public mind.

ˈbodylet. *nonce-wd.* [After *armlet*, etc.: see -LET.] An ornamental ring for the body.

1870 LUBBOCK *Orig. Civiliz.* ii. (1875) 55 The savage also wears necklaces and rings, bracelets and anklets, armlets and leglets—even, if I may say so, bodylets.

ˈbody-like, *a.* and *adv.* Also 6 bodilike. [f. BODY *sb.* + LIKE.]

A. *adj.* Like a body; real, solid.

1570 BILLINGSLEY *Euclid* XI. def. 26. 320 The figure of the parallelipipedon, which appeareth more bodilike.

†**B.** *adv.* In bodily form, bodily. *Obs.*

1663 in Spalding *Troub. Chas. I.* (1829) 33 This monster was seen body-like swimming above the water. **1674** N. FAIRFAX *Bulk & Selv.* 29 It might then be cut a pieces body-like.

bodym, obs. form of BOTTOM *sb.*

†**bodysome,** *a. Obs.* [see -SOME.] Corporeal.

1674 N. FAIRFAX *Bulk & Selv.* 17 We and all body-some Beings.

boe, obs. form of BOUGH, BOW, and BO *int.*

boec, boef, obs. form of BOOK, BEEF.

Boehm (bøːm). The name of Theobald *Böhm* (1794–1881), German musician, applied *attrib.* to the system of keys and fingering which he invented in 1832. Hence applied to a flute which he designed, and to other wood-wind instruments with similar features.

1845 R. CARTE (*title*) A Complete Course of Instructions for the Boehm flute... Preceded by an analysis of the Boehm flute and of the old eight keyed flute. **1889** G. B. SHAW *London Music 1888–89* (1937) 77 In spite of the splendors of the Boehm flute, it is often lost in passages where the old flute used to tell when violins were less numerous. **1905** *Harmsworth Encycl.* IV. 2510/2 Nearly all concert flutes now in use are constructed upon the Boehm system, or modifications of it. **1935** *Chambers's Encycl.* IV. 727/2 The modern cylinder flute.. when combined with the Boehm fingering.. forms a nearly perfect instrument. **1954** *Grove's Dict. Mus.* (ed. 5) II. 324/1 In 1844 H. Klosé.. and A. Buffet devised an entirely new clarinet.. now generally known as the Boehm clarinet.

Bœhmenism (ˈbøːmənɪz(ə)m). Commonly **Behmenism.** The doctrines taught by Jacob Bœhme, a German mystic and theosophist (1575–1624). So **Bœhmenish, Bœhmenistic** *adjs.*; **Bœhmenist** (also **Bœhmist**) *sb.* and *a.*, **Bœhmenite.**

1656 MORE *Euthus. Tri.* (1712) 49 Ranters and Quakers took their original from Behmenism and Familism. **1655** BAXTER *Quaker's Catech.* Pref. C iij b, I could tell you of abundance of Popery that the Quakers and Behmenists maintain. **1731** SWIFT *Let.* 10 Sept. in Pope *Wks.* (1757) IX. 142 A very profound Behmist assures me, the style is poetic. **1739** JOHN WESLEY *Jrnl.* 23 Oct. (1938) II. 297, I read over Mr. Law's book on the New Birth.. Behmenish, void, and vain! **1824** COLERIDGE *Aids Refl.* (ed. 2) 135 By any favouring the errors of the.. Behmenists. **1846** *Byron's Wks.* 668 *note*, [founder of the sect called Behmenites]. **1854** *Encycl. Brit.* IV. 805/1 The sect of Boehmists. **1912** W. C. BRAITHWAITE *Beginnings of Quakerism* ii. 38 We are reminded of the similar Familist and Boehmist teaching with respect to perfectionism. **1919** P. H. OSMOND *Myst. Poets Eng. Church* viii. 258 The Behmenistic view is too much influenced by the thought of the caprice and passion associated with human anger. **1961** W. H. G. ARMYTAGE *Heavens Below* I. iv. 38 Law channelled Behmenist thought into the main current of English mysticism.

boel, obs. form of BOWEL.

Bœotarch (ˈbiːəʊtɑːk). [ad. Gr. βοιωτάρχης, f. βοιωτ-ία Bœotia + -αρχης ruler: cf. F. *Béotarque*.] A chief magistrate of the Bœotian league.

a **1822** SHELLEY *Œdipus Tyr.* Advt., Before the duties.. had been repealed by the Bœotarchs. **1838** THIRLWALL *Greece* V. xxxix. 108 The yearly term for which he held his office of Bœotarch had expired.

Bœotia (biːˈəʊʃ(ɪ)ə). A district of ancient Greece proverbial for the stupidity of its inhabitants: hence *fig.*

1786 WOLCOTT (P. Pindar) *Ep. Boswell* Wks. 1794 I. 313 A dim Bœotia reigns in every skull. **1884** *Harper's Mag.* Nov. 895/2 Essex appears to be looked on as the Bœotia of England.

Hence **ˈBœotize** *v.*, to become or make Bœotian.

1789 PARR *Wks.* (1828) VII. 410, I live quite in Bœotia, and Bœotize daily. **1846** GROTE *Greece* (1854) I. 183 These inhabitants of Orchomenos, before it became bœotised.

Bœotian (biːˈəʊʃ(ɪ)ən), *a.* and *sb.* [f. prec. + -AN.]

A. *adj.* **a.** Of Bœotia. **b.** Dull, stupid.

1598 MARSTON *Pigmal.* ii. 142, I dull-sprighted fat Boetian Boore. **1809** BYRON *Bards & Rev.* 82 To be misled By Jeffrey's heart, or Lambe's Bœotian head. **1831** CARLYLE *Sart. Res.* III. i, The earnestness and Bœotian simplicity.. with which that 'Incident' is here brought forward.

B. *sb.* **a.** A native of Bœotia. **b.** A stupid clown, a 'thick-head'.

1649 G. DANIEL *Trinarch., Hen. V*, lix, These Trencher-Sts.; full-paunch't Boetians, Contemne all Bodies bred in purer Ayre, As Atticke leanness. **1821** LOCKHART *Valerius* II. x. 296 An opportunity.. which I should have been a Bœotian indeed had I neglected. **1839** THIRLWALL *Greece* VIII. 465.

Bœotic (biːˈɒtɪk), *a.* [ad. L. *Bœōticus*, ad. Gr. Βοιωτικός Bœotian.] = prec. adj.

1678 CUDWORTH *Intell. Syst.* 741 The Dull Bœotick Air had too much Effect upon him. **1851** JELF *Greek Gram.* ii. §10. 9 The dialects then are.. The Doric, as spoken by the Dorians, The Bœotic, by the Bœotians. **1869** *Eng. Mech.* 19 Mar. 577/3 A.. man of a very blunt Bœotic dull wit.

Boer (bʊə(r), bəʊə(r), or bɔə(r), Afrikaans buːr)). Formerly **boor.** [a. Du. *boer* 'countryman, peasant, farmer', the same word that in a general sense is spelt BOOR. The latter was formerly used also for the Dutch settlers in South Africa, but in more recent times the Du. spelling *boer* has been appropriated to this sense.]

a. A Dutch colonist in South Africa engaged in agriculture or cattle-breeding. 'In recent newspaper language, the name has been applied especially to those of the Transvaal and other districts beyond the British dominions' (*N.E.D.*, 1887).

See earlier quots. under BOOR 2 b.

1834 PRINGLE *Afr. Sk.* i. 127 Tall Dutch-African boors.. were bawling in Colonial-Dutch. *Ibid.* iv. 182 To begin the world respectably as a *Vei Boer*, or grazier. **1857** LIVINGSTONE *Trav.* ii. 29 The Boers of the Cashan Mountains.. The word *Boer* simply means 'farmer', and is not synonymous with our word *boor*. **1865** TYLOR *Early Hist. Man.* i. 11 Such a story.. would be naturally referred to the Dutch boers.

b. **ˈBoerdom,** the community or state of the Boers.

1884 *Pall Mall G.* 15 Oct. 6/1 Boerdom develops faster than British progress.

2. *S. Afr.* In special *Comb.* signifying made, produced, used by, or typical of Boers; often also ‖**boere-** (ˈbuːrə): ***boerbeskuit, boer biscuit, boermeal, boer(e)musiek, boer-rusk, boer(e)-wors*** (-vɔːs), ***boerwyn*** (-veɪn).

1943 'B. KNIGHT' *Covenant* (1944) IV. xix. 232 There was a good supply of.. *biltong* and Boerbeskuit and a couple of roasted fowls. **1882** MRS. HECKFORD *Lady Trader in Transvaal* xxviii. 309 Hendrik managed to get some Boer biscuits from this man. *a* **1920** O. SCHREINER *From Man to Man* (1926) iii. 111 One morning.. Baby-Bertie was kneeling in the pantry, making Boer biscuits. **1873** F. BOYLE *To the Cape for Diamonds* x. 141 Boer meal (cheap at this moment (42s per *muid* (200 lbs)). [**1878** *Roche's 'On Trek in the Transvaal'* 110 (Pettman), Bread we could not get, only the *Boer's meal*, i.e. the flour of the country.] **1949** *Cape Times* 24 Sept. 8/7 We used to get on farms the boermeal bread made from wheat, and nothing but wheat. **1952** *Ibid.* 27 Sept. 4/4 The music blared forth real *boeremusiek* which sent the whole crowd dancing. **1937** S. CLOETE *Turning Wheels* xxv. 392 Going without food except for the Boer rusks and biltong that he carried. **1944** V. POHL *Adv. Boer Fam.* i. 12 Saddlebags stuffed to bursting with boer-rusks, bread and biltong. **1948** *Cape Times* 18 Sept. 9/6 An expert on *sosaties, boerwors,* and *braaivleis*. **1950** L. G. GREEN *Land of Afternoon* iv. 63 Boerewors is another farm product which some still make in the old way; a sausage in which the meat has been pounded with a wooden stamper rather than minced. Modern boerewors.. is usually a mixture of lean beef with pork fat, seasoned with wine or vinegar. **1947** *Cape Times* 14 May 3/6 Boerwyn—the unfortified wine sold to coloured patrons.

3. Special Comb. **Boer War,** the South African war (1899–1902), between the Boer republics of Transvaal and the Orange Free State, and Great Britain and her colonies; cf. *Anglo-Boer* s.v. ANGLO- 2.

[**1899** G. MEREDITH *Let.* 27 Oct. (1970) III. 1337, I need patience even to speak of this Boer War.] **1900** C. M. YONGE *Let.* 17 July in C. Coleridge *C. M. Yonge* (1903) xii. 345 Aimée tried to explain the rights of the *Boer War. **1914** C. MACKENZIE *Sinister St.* II. III. v. 587 He.. figuratively marched across the road to the Canning.. galvanizing.. the Oxford Tories now wilting under the strain of the Boer war. **1955** G. GREENE *Quiet American* I. iv. 52 Like a panorama of the Boer War in an old *Illustrated London News*. **1981** H. DOMISSE in D. Harrison *White Tribe of Africa* i. 24 This Boer War, was the stupidest war the English ever carried on.

boe-spritte, obs. form of BOWSPRIT.

†**ˌboeˈthetic.** *Obs. rare*[−1]. [ad. Gr. βοηθητικ-ός, f. βοηθέ-ειν to help.] Helpful, curative.

1660 STANLEY *Hist. Philos.* (1701) 164 Medecine is of five kinds; Boethetick, removeth disease.

‖**bœuf** (bœːf). [Fr.] Beef; used with postpositive adj. to designate a beef dish cooked in a particular manner, the adj. indicating either the sauce in which the dish is served, as ***bœuf bordelais***, or the region of supposed origin, as ***bœuf bourguignon***, beef braised with red wine and served with bacon and mushrooms. Similarly used with a proper name, as **bœuf stroganoff**: see STROGANOFF.

[**1907** A. ESCOFFIER *Guide Mod. Cookery* 379 *Piece de Bœuf a la Bourguignonne.* Lard the piece of beef, and marinade it for three hours in brandy and red wine.] **1936** LUCAS & HUME *Au Petit Cordon Bleu* 92 *Ragoût de bœuf bourguignonne.* 2 lb. topside beef. **1942** E. PAUL *Narrow St.* iii. 25 Mary inspected carefully the two portions of *bœuf bordelais*. **1960** E. DAVID *French Provincial Cooking* 335 This is the French method even with what might be termed first-class secondary joints such as topside and the equivalent of our aitchbone, which are used for such delicious dishes as *bœuf mode* and *bœuf bourguignon*. **1965** M.

KENYON *May you die in Ireland* i. 8 He would have liked someone to cook *bœuf bourguignon* for him in the evenings.

boezar, obs. form of BEZOAR.

boff, bofet, boffet, obs. ff. BUFF, BUFFET.

boffin ('bɒfɪn). *slang.* [Etym. unknown. Numerous conjectures have been made about the origin of the word but all lack foundation.]

1. An 'elderly' naval officer.

1941 C. GRAVES *Life Line* 143 Their ages are as youthful as air crews. Thirty-two is considered the maximum... In H.M.S. *Wasps' Nest*, anyone aged thirty-two is officially a 'boffin'. There is even a song about them... 'He glares at us hard and he scowls, For we're the Flotilla Boffins.' **1942** 'SEA-WRACK' *Random Soundings* 71 We were 'Old Boffins', the Pay. and I. He had been in the Bank of England for many years, and in the R.N.R. almost as long... I hadn't been to sea in a professional capacity for some eighteen years.

2. A person engaged in 'back-room' scientific or technical research. Hence **'boffin(e)ry**, boffins collectively; also, the activity of a boffin.

The term seems to have been first applied by members of the Royal Air Force to scientists working on radar.

1945 *Times* 15 Sept. 5/4 A band of scientific men who performed their wartime wonders at Malvern and apparently called themselves 'the boffins'. **1948** 'N. SHUTE' *No Highway* iii. 61 'What's a boffin?' 'The man from Farnborough. Everybody calls them boffins. Didn't you know?'.. 'Why are they called that?'.. 'Because they behave like boffins, I suppose.' **1948** LORD TEDDER in A. P. Rowe *One Story of Radar* p. vii, I was fortunate in having considerable dealings in 1938–40 with the 'Boffins' (as the Royal Air Force affectionately dubbed the scientists). **1952** *Picture Post* 30 Aug. 20/1 Only a backroom boffin out of touch with the classroom could hold this pious belief. **1954** *Economist* 19 June Suppl. 6/3 The graduate from research ——roughly..the boffin of industry. **1957** R. WATSON-WATT *Three Steps to Victory* xxiii. 201 The proud title of Boffin was first conferred on a few radar scientists by Royal Air Force officers with whom they worked in close co-operation..... I am not quite sure about the true origins of this name of Boffin. It certainly has something to do with an obsolete type of aircraft called the Baffin, something to do with that odd bird, the Puffin; I am sure it has nothing at all to do with that first literary Back Room Boy, the claustrophiliac Colonel Boffin. **1958** *Times Lit. Suppl.* 14 Feb. 83/3 In one of those diverting interludes..he writes an anatomy of Boffinry. **1958** *Economist* 25 Oct. 298/1 The unexpected success of the boffins' conference at Geneva.. ending in agreement on the feasibility of controlling a nuclear test suspension. **1960** J. MACLAREN-ROSS *Until Day* viii. 132, I was engaged in some boffinery in a blasted back-room unit.

Bofors ('bəʊfəz). [Site of munition works in Örebro, Sweden.] Used *attrib.* or *ellipt.* of a type of light anti-aircraft gun.

1933 *Jane's Fighting Ships* 406/2 Armament: 5–4·7 inch, 50 cal., Bofors. **1939** *War Illustr.* 25 Nov. 330 A quick-firing two-pounder Bofors anti-aircraft gun of Swedish design, built by licence in Great Britain. Such guns were introduced into the British Army in 1938, but they soon formed the standard equipment of light anti-aircraft units whose job it is to deal with low-flying..aircraft. **1941** W. S. CHURCHILL *Secret Session Speeches* (1946) 31 Already 200 Bofors or their equivalents have been ordered to be made available by A.D.G.B. and the factories.

bog (bɒg), *sb.*[1] Forms: 6–7 bogg, bogge, 7 boghe, 6– bog. [ad. Ir. or Gael. *bogach* a bog, f. *bog* soft, used in composition in the sense of 'bog', as *bog-luachair* bulrush. In Scotland apparently from Gaelic, in England from Irish.]

I. 1. a. A piece of wet spongy ground, consisting chiefly of decayed or decaying moss and other vegetable matter, too soft to bear the weight of any heavy body upon its surface; a morass or moss.

c **1505** DUNBAR *Of James Dog* 15 Chassand cattell through a bog. *a* **1552** LELAND *Brit. Coll.* (1774) II. 545 They.. fledde alle, and levyng theyr Horses, tooke the Marresis, or Bogges. **1599** SHAKS. *Hen. V*, III. vii. 61 They that ride so ....fall into foule Boggs. **1611** SPEED *Theat. Gt. Brit.* (1614) 143/1 Certain places [of Ireland]..which of their softnesse are usually termed Boghes. **1631** *Star Chamb. Cases* (1886) 34 The Country of Ireland is full of boggs on the ground and mists in the aire. **1667** MILTON *P.L.* II. 592 That Serbonian Bog Betwixt Damiata and mount Casius old, Where Armies whole have sunk. **1751** CHAMBERS *Cycl.* s.v., The inconveniences of Bogs are..that they are a great destruction to cattle: they are also a shelter to Tories and Thieves. **1810** SCOTT *Lady of L.* III. xiii, The trembling bog and false morass. **1846** MCCULLOCH *Acc. Brit. Empire* (1854) I. 325 These bogs are included under the general designation of the Bog of Allen.

b. (without *pl.*) Bog-land, boggy soil.

a **1687** PETTY *Pol. Arith.* (1690) 2 Bog may by draining be made Meadow. **1846** MCCULLOCH *Acc. Brit. Empire* (1854) I. 269 A large extent of hill pasture, moor, and bog. **1861** *Times* 29 Aug., Long brown gaps of stagnant-looking bog, where the piles of neatly-cut turf were stacked out in rough black cones.

c. *fig.* (Cf. 'fog'.)

1614 BP. KING *Vitio Palat.* 30 Quagmires and bogges of Romish superstition. **1787** BURNS *To Miss Ferrier* iii, Last day my mind was in a bog. **1840** C. DICKENS *Barn. Rudge* (1849) 331/1 He wandered out again, in a perfect bog of uncertainty. **1878** MORLEY *Diderot* I. 331 The Serbonian bog of dramatic rules.

II. *Attrib.* and *Comb.*

2. General comb., as ***bog-black*** adj. ***bog-bred*** adj.; ***-hay, -peat, -pit, -plant, -stalker, -turf, -water, -way***.

1953 DYLAN THOMAS *Under Milk Wood* (1954) 48 The lickerish *bog-black tea. **1850** MARG. FULLER *Wom. 19th C.* (1862) 324 Because that *bog-bred youth..tells you lies. **1799** J. ROBERTSON *Agric. Perth* 222 In general *bog hay.. is about one third inferior in quality to that from sown grass. **1743** ELLIS *Mod. Husb.* III. I. 113 In a low Meadow..there is a Peat dug called **Bog-peat*. **1958** *New Biol.* XXVI. 91 Peat is of two main types (with intermediates): (1) fen peat ....(2) bog peat formed under acid conditions. **1820** SCOTT *Abbot* xvi, The kelpie must flit from the black *bog-pit. **1854** S. THOMSON *Wild Fl.* III. (1861) 138 Our common *bog-plants. *a* **1758** RAMSAY *Poems* (1800) II. 338 Ill-bred *bog stalker. **1847** E. BRONTË *Wuthering Heights* II. xiv. 280 The **bog-water got into her head, and she would have run home, quite flighty, but I fixed her. **1866** CARLYLE *Remin.* I. 205 A gush of bog-water. **1869** BLACKMORE *Lorna D.* iii. (ed. 12) 12 Before coming to the black *bog-way.

3. In many names of plants growing in bogs: as ***bog asphodel, cinquefoil, pimpernel***, etc.; **bog bean, bog nut, bog trefoil**, also called BUCKBEAN; **bog berry**, the Cranberry; **bog moss**, various species of Sphagnum, by the growth and decay of which bogs are chiefly formed; **bog myrtle**, Sweet Gale (*Myrica Gale*); **bog onion**: see ONION *sb.* 2 b; **bog orchis**, *Malaxis paludosa*; **bog pink**, Lady's Smock (*Cardamine pratensis*); **bog rush**, *Schœnus nigricans*; also *U.S.*, a plant of the genus *Juncus*; **bog violet** = BUTTERWORT (*Pinguicula*).

1881 G. ALLEN in *Academy* 13 Aug. 113/3 A little marsh ....made room for *bog-asphodel. **1794** MARTYN *Rousseau's Bot.* xvi. 176 Marsh Trefoil, Buckbean or *Bogbean will discover itself to you immediately. **1857** HUGHES *Tom Brown* i, What the bog-bean and wood-sage are good for. **1858** ELIZ. TWINING *Lect. Plants* 345 Our marsh Bog-bean which I described to you as an intensely bitter herb. **1760** J. LEE *Introd. Bot.* 297/1 *Bogberries, *Vaccinium*. **1892** J. BARLOW *Irish Idylls* viii. 217 She made a feint of looking for bogberries. **1785** MARTYN tr. *Rousseau's Bot.* xxxii. 493 Sphagnum, or *Bog-moss, has the capsule covered with a lid. **1840** [see SPHAGNUM]. **1959** J. CLEGG *Freshwater Life* (ed. 2) iii. 63 Of the mosses, the most important are the species of Bog Mosses (*Sphagnum*).. which form soft carpets of vegetation in the damp areas. **1884** Q. VICTORIA *More Leaves* 290 Bonnets with a black cock's tail and *bog-myrtle. **1760** J. LEE *Introd. Bot.* 315/1 Rush, Round black-headed, Marsh or *Bog, *Schœnus*. **1843** J. TORREY *N.Y. Nat. Hist. Surv.: Flora* II. 325 *Juncus effusus*..Bog-rush. **1855** Lesser Bog Rush [see RUSH *sb.*[1] 4 a]. **1898** C. M. YONGE *John Keble's Parishes* xvi. 231 Bogrush (*L. campestris*).—Little rush.

4. Special comb.: **bog-blitter, -bluiter, -bumper**, provincial names of the Bittern; **bog-butter**, a fatty hydrocarbon found in the peat-bogs of Ireland; **bog-deal** = *bog-pine*; **bog-down**, Cotton-grass (*Eriophorum*); **bog-earth**, earth composed of, or largely mixed with, peat; **bog fir** = *bog pine*; **bog-garden**, a piece of ground laid out and irrigated to grow plants whose habitat is bog-land and a peaty soil; **bog-hole**, a natural hole with a swampy bottom; **bog iron, bog iron ore**, a brittle, porous variety of brown hæmatite found in bogs; **bog-jumper**, (*local*) the Bittern; **bog-land**, marshy land, a boggy country; *humorously*, Ireland; hence **bog-lander**; **bog Latin**, a spurious form of Latin; cf. *dog-Latin*; also = SHELTA; **bog manganese** (see quot.); †**bog-mine, bog-mine-ore, bog ore** = *bog iron ore*; †**bog-mire**, a quagmire; **bog-mould** = *bog-earth*; **bog oak**, the wood of oak preserved in a black state in peat-bogs, etc.; **bog-pine**, pinewood found buried in peat-bogs; **bog-spavin**, an encysted tumour on the inside of the hock of a horse; **bog-timber, bog-wood**, the trunks of trees found buried in peat-bogs.

1815 SCOTT *Guy M.* i, The deep cry of the *bog-blitter, or bull-of-the bog. **1866** *Inverness Courier* 4 Jan., The bittern of British Zoology; provincially the *bog-bumper and mire-drum. **1863** WATTS *Dict. Chem.* I. 617 *Bog-butter, a fatty substance found in the peat-bogs of Ireland. **1794** G. ADAMS *Nat. & Exp. Philos.* IV. xlvii. 301 Touch the needle with a piece of *bog-down, or a cork ball. **1865** *Pall Mall G.* 24 Oct. 5 Cloth made of bog-down (*Anglice*, cotton grass). **1787–8** *Botan. Mag.* II. 46 Soil, a mixture of loam and *bog earth. **1769** BARRINGTON in *Phil. Trans.* LIX. 33 Why these *bog-firs may be found in places where there is no such tree at present. **1883** W. ROBINSON *Engl. Flower Garden* p. lxiii/1 A more perfect *bog garden is made by forming a basin of brickwork and Portland cement, about one foot in depth. **1908** R. FARRER *Alpines & Bog-plants* 154 The prime.. necessity of the bog-garden is the most perfect drainage. **1788** G. O'NIAL *The Minor* II. III. iii. 14 He and his horse had bounced into a *bog-hole. **1839** 'MRS. M. CLAVERS' *New Home* i. 15 Down came our good horse to the very chin in a bog-hole. **1936** P. FLEMING *News from Tartary* III. vi. 138 Slippery flats, pitted with bog-holes. **1789** MILLS in *Phil. Trans.* LXXX. 89 *Bog iron ore is met with in the mosses. **1690** DRYDEN *Prol.* to *Prophetess* 31 Men without hearts, and women without hose. Each bring his love a *Bogland captive home. **1745** ELLIS *Mod. Husb.* VI. II. 47 A proper Plough to plow Bog lands. **1940** L. MACNEICE *Last Ditch* 9 The night came down upon the bogland. **1730–6** BAILEY *Dict.*, **Bog-Landers*, a nick-name given Irish-men. **1755** W. MOFFAT *Irish Hudib.*, A bunch of three-leaved grass Called by the boglanders shamrogues. **1785** GROSE *Dict. Vulgar T.*, ***Bog latin*, (*Irish*) barbarous latin. **1891** [see SHELTA]. **1927** J. JOYCE *Let.* 20 May (1957) 254 *Dulce et decorum est prope mare sedere*—boglatin for it is a sweet and seemly thing to sit down by the sea. **1875** URE *Dict. Arts* III. 200 Wad, or *Bog Manganese, is the old English name of the hydrated peroxide of manganese. **1590** R. PAYNE *Descr. Irel.* (1841) 6 There is..greate plentie of Iron stone, and one sort more than we have in England, which they call *Bogge myne. **1762** ELIOT in *Phil. Trans.* LIII. 56 Add some bog mine ore, which abounds with cinder. **1624** CAPT. SMITH *Virginia* II. 32 They slew my men, and tooke me prisoner in a *Bogmire. **1834** *Brit. Husb.* I. 414 When brought to the decayed condition of *bog-mould, or rich earth. **1813** M. EDGEWORTH *Let.* 24 Oct. in S. H. Romilly *Romilly-Edgeworth Lett.* (1936) 60 This necklace, and bracelets, are genuine Irish—made of **bog-oak*—that is, of oak found in our bogs. **1857** PARSONS in *Phil. Trans.* L. 398 This is called bog-oak, or bog deal, well known to country people in many places. **1940** L. MACNEICE *Last Ditch* 9 Stumps of hoary bog-oak. **1772** PENNANT *Tours Scotl.* (1774) 219 That species of iron called *bog-ore. **1842** S. LOVER *Handy Andy* xxxv. 336 A torch made of *bog-pine. **1631** BRATHWAIT *Whimzies* 76 His stable is a very shop of all diseases; glanders, yellowes..*bogspavings, with a myriad more. **1802** D. BLAINE *Veterinary Art* (ed. 2) 499 *Bog Spavin.* This is only a bursal enlargement of the mucous capsule on the inner side of the hock. **1807** VANCOUVER *Agric. Devon* (1813) 52 These morasses are found frequently to abound with *bog-timber. **1828** SCOTT *F.M. Perth* III. 107 A piece of lighted *bog-wood which he carried in a lantern. **1883** *Longm. Mag.* III. 48 A generation ago the old art of carving bog-wood was revived in Dublin.

†**bog, bogge**, *sb.*[2] *Obs.* [Possibly a variant of *bugge*, BUG 'terror, bugbear', found in 14th c.: cf. BOGLE, BOGGLE, and BOGGARD.] A bugbear, a source of dread. ***to take bog***: to BOGGLE *v.* 1, 2. Cf. BOGGLE *sb.*[1]

1527 *St. Papers Hen. VIII*, I. 206 Against whom..it shal not a litel conferre, that this man be a bogge. **1656** SANDERSON *Serm.* (1689) 128 Men who make no conscience of a lye, do yet take some bog at an Oath. **1676** ETHEREDGE *Man of Mode* I. i. (1684) 5 Farewel Bogg.

†**bog**, *a.* (*sb.*[3]) *Obs.* exc. *dial.* [Derivation unknown. In Derbyshire, Lincolnshire, etc. the dialectal form is *bug*, pronounced (bug).]

A. *adj.* Blustering, bold, proud, saucy.

1592 WARNER *Alb. Eng.* VII. xxxvii. (1612) 184 The Cuckooe, seeing him so bog, waxt also wondrous wroth. **1642** ROGERS *Naaman* 18 Thy bog and bold heart to be abashed. **1691** RAY *S. & E. Countr. Wds.* 90 *Bogge*, bold, forward, sawcy. So we say, a very bog Fellow. **1693** G. FIRMIN *Daviss' Vind.* iv. 32 A bog fellow, forward to put forth himself.

B. *sb.* Brag, boastfulness. *dial.*

1839 C. CLARK *J. Noakes, &c.* 3 Their bog it nuver ceases.

bog, *sb.*[4] *slang.* = BOG-HOUSE, *latrina.*

a **1789** in J. HOWARD *Lazarettos* (1789) 181 That no dirt.. be thrown out of any window, or down the bogs. **1864** HOTTEN *Slang Dict.* 79 *Bog*, or *bog-house*, a privy as distinguished from a water-closet. **1929** H. WILLIAMSON *Beautiful Years* xxiii. 165 His headquarters are in The Bog, ...where the kids go and hide, locking themselves in when they think those cads are after them. **1959** W. GOLDING *Free Fall* i. 23 Our lodger had our upstairs, use of the stove, our tap and our bog. **1960** *New Left Rev.* May–June 61/1 Toilet paper in the bogs. **1962** P. PURSER *Peregrination 22* xv. 71 Rolls of brown bog paper.

bog (bɒg), *v.*[1] Also 7 bogg, 8 bogue. [f. BOG *sb.*[1]]

1. *trans.* **a.** To sink, submerge, or entangle, in a bog. Also *fig.*

1641 MILTON *Animadv.* Wks. (1851) 238 Whose profession to forsake the world..boggs them deeper into the world. **1730** T. BOSTON *Mem.* ix. 245, I mistook the way and bogued my horse through the moss beyond R. **1865** J. LUDLOW *Epics Mid. Ages* II. 194 He is unskilled..and succeeds in bogging his cart.

b. (passive.) *to be bogged*: to be sunk and entangled in a bog or quagmire; also = sense 2. Also with *down*; chiefly *fig.*

1603 [see BOGGED]. **1743–7** N. TINDAL *Contn. Rapin's Hist.* (1751) I. 136 His horse was bogged on the other side. **1828** SCOTT *F.M. Perth* I. 63 Any other horse and rider must have been instantly bogged up to the saddle-girths. **1841** ARNOLD *Let.* in *Life & Corr.* (1844) II. x. 304, I hope to see some of my boys and girls well bogged in the middle of Bagley Wood. **1928** *Amer. Speech* IV. 132 To be 'bogged down' or 'mired down' is to be mired, generally in the 'wet valleys' in the spring. **1953** A. UPFIELD *Murder must Wait* xii. 108 The investigation stopped when bogged down by official impatience. **1955** *Times* 11 May 10/3 His approach to them would not be bogged down by 'minor points of protocol'.

2. *intr.* (for *refl.*) To sink and stick in a bog. Also with *down* and *fig.*

a **1800** *Trials Sons Rob Roy* (1818) 120 (JAM.) Duncan Graham in Gartmore his horse bogged; that the deponent helped some others to take the horse out of the bogg. **1900** SMITHWICK *Evol. State* 325 The animal had bogged in crossing the little creek. **1903** A. ADAMS *Log Cowboy* xii. 77 Bob Blades attempted to ride out of the river below the crossing, when his horse bogged down. **1928** *Sat. Even. Post* 12 May 184/2 On a clean sheet of paper he wrote the words "We know", and there he bogged down. **1937** *Times* 22 Nov. 12/5 Congress..may bog down and do nothing. **1951** E. TAYLOR *Game Hide-&-Seek* I. iii. 70 'I wish Tiny and Kitty would come,' anxious young hostesses would think when parties bogged down.

†**bog**, *v.*[2] *Obs.* [possibly related to BOG *a.*] *trans.* To provoke.

1546 *St. Papers Henry VIII*, XI. 163 If you had not written to me..we had broken now, the Frenchmen bogged us so often with departing. **1553** GRIMALDE *Cicero's Offices* III. (1558) 164 A frenchman whom he [Manlius Torquatus] slewe, being bogged [*provocatus*] by hym.

bog, *v.*[3] [A low word, scarcely found in literature, however common in coarse colloquial language. Cf. BOGGARD[2] and BOG-HOUSE.] *intr.* To exonerate the bowels; also *trans.* to defile with excrement.

bog, boge, early form of BOUGH, BOW.

boge, boget, obs. form of BUDGE, BUDGET.

bogen, obs. pa. pple. of BOW *v.*

bogey ('bəʊgɪ). *Golf.* Also bogy, bogie. [The following story reproduces the current account of the origin of the term:——

One popular song at least has left its permanent effect on the game of golf. That song is 'The Bogey Man'. In 1890 Dr. Thos. Browne, R.N., the hon. secretary of the Great Yarmouth Club, was playing against a Major Wellman, the match being against the 'ground score', which was the name given to the scratch value of each hole. The system of playing against the 'ground score' was new to Major Wellman, and he exclaimed, thinking of the song of the moment, that his mysterious and well-nigh invincible opponent was a regular 'bogey-man'. The name 'caught on' at Great Yarmouth, and to-day 'Bogey' is one of the most feared opponents on all the courses that acknowledge him (1908 *M.A.P.* 25 July 78/1).]

a. The number of strokes a good player may be reckoned to need for the course or for a hole.

1892 *Field* 2 Jan. 6/1 A novelty was introduced in shape of a Bogey tournament for a prize... Fourteen couples started, but the Bogey defeated all. **1903** *Westm. Gaz.* 21 Feb. 6/2 Jones, with a handicap of 17, receives an allowance against Bogey of 13 strokes. **1910** *Encycl. Brit.* XII. 221/2 There is also a species of competition called 'bogey' play, in which each man plays against a ' bogey' score—a score fixed for each hole in the round before starting.

b. *transf.* and *fig.*

1922 WODEHOUSE *Clicking of Cuthbert* iii. 80 'Weren't you giving yourself rather a large family?'.. 'Was I?' he said, dully. 'I don't know. What's bogey?' **1958** J. A. BARLOW *Elem. Rifle Shooting* (ed. 5) iii. 43 It is a good plan to set oneself a definite score below which one must never fall. In other words, a bogey score for the practice or shoot. **1959** *Listener* 5 Nov. 802/1 Par Contract is a way of playing bridge against bogey.

c. A score of one stroke over par for a hole. *U.S.*

1946 E. C. ACREE et al. *Golf Simplified* 113 *Bogey*, a hole scored in one stroke over par. **1951** *Golf World* 15 June 16/1 Hall had seven birdies, two eagles and one bogie. **1954** R. T. JONES in H. W. Wind *Compl. Golfer* 302/1 One must really see Pine Valley to appreciate it... Thrill with one's pars, be satisfied with a 'bogey', and continue on far from downcast after a 'double bogey'. **1961** J. S. SALAK *Dict. Amer. Sports* 54 *Bogey* (golf), the total score any average player might make on a hole. Not any hole shot in one over par, though this interpretation has at times gained some acceptance. **1974** *Greenville* (S. Carolina) *News* 23 Apr. 8/5 He made bogey from the woods. **1977** *New Yorker* 8 Aug. 56/2 He struggled down in two putts, holing from three and a half feet for his bogey 5 and a four-round total of 278. **1982** S. B. FLEXNER *Listening to Amer.* 266 After the rubber golf ball was invented in America in 1898.., the bogey that had been established for the old gutta-percha ball became too easy and the British lowered their bogies by about one stroke per hole and kept the term, but Americans began to use the word *par* instead, keeping the old British word *bogey* to mean the older, easier expected score of a good player, usually one stroke more than the new par.

bogey ('bəʊgɪ), *v.* *Golf* (orig. *U.S.*). [f. BOGEY *sb.* c.] *trans.* To complete (a hole) in one stroke over par. Also *absol.*

1948 B. HOGAN *Power Golf* v. 57 After he drove into the rough he bogeyed the hole and lost his advantage. **1971** *Rand Daily Mail* 27 Mar. 23/1 Gary Player bogeyed two of the last three holes. **1977** *N.Y. Times* 13 June 43 Player hooked his approach, missed the green and bogeyed. **1984** *News* (Mexico City) 12 Mar. 32/5 But he bogeyed again, catching a bunker on the 15th.

bogey, variant of BOGIE, BOGY[1], BUDGE, fur.

boggard[1], **-art** ('bɒgəd, -ət). Also 6 buggard, 8 bag-. [A word in popular use in Westmoreland, Lancashire, Cheshire, Yorkshire, and the north midlands, and of occasional appearance in literature since *c* 1570. Evidently related to BOGGLE, BOGLE, and BOG *sb.*[2]: if the status of the last-named were more assured, it would be natural to see in *bogg-ard* a derivative with the augmentative suffix -ARD; or if the occasional variant *buggard* could be assumed as the etymological form, it might stand in the same relation to BUG. See BOGLE.]

1. A spectre, goblin, or bogy; in dialectal use, esp. a local goblin or sprite supposed to 'haunt' a particular gloomy spot, or scene of violence.

1570 LEVINS *Manip.* 30 A Boggarde, *spectrum.* *c* **1730** BURT *Lett. N. Scotl.* (1818) I. 227 All that quarter of England is infested with boggarts of all sorts. **1821** MRS. WHEELER *Westmorld. Dial.* 39 Sic a terrable boggart as I beleev nivver onny yan saa befoar. **1855** *Whitby Gloss.*, *Boggle, Boggart*, a fearful object, a hobgoblin. **1857** in Bohn's *Handbk. Proverbs* 152 He thinks every bush a boggard.

b. *fig.* A bugbear, a source of dread.

1575 *Brieff Disc. Troubl. Franckford* (1846) 160 Nor be such buggardes to the poor, yff they may not beare the bagge alone. **1616** *Rollocke's Hist. Passion* 132 (JAM.) Hell is but a boggarde to scarre children.

†**2.** An object real or imaginary at which a horse shies or 'boggles'. *Obs.*

1617 MARKHAM *Caval.* II. xii. 112 How to correct a horse that is skittish, and fearefull and findeth many boggards. **1639** DE GREY *Compl. Horsem.* 28 The horse will.. stare and see boggards in his keepers face. **1725** BRADLEY *Fam. Dict.* II. s.v. *Horses*, It betrays a weak, slight and unnecessary Starting, or finding of Baggards. [**1863** *Standard* 1 Jan., When a horse takes fright at some object unobserved by its master the vulgar opinion is that it has seen the boggart.]

†'**boggard**[2]. *Obs.* [f. BOG *v.*[3]] A privy.

1552 HULOET, Siege, jacques, bogard, or draught, *latrina.* **1628** SHIRLEY *Witty Fair* IV. vi. **1647** WARD *Simp. Cobler* 76 He [the Devil] thought it wisdome to keep the land [Ireland] for a Boggards for his unclean spirits.

'**boggarty**, *a. north. dial.* [f. BOGGART + -Y.] Haunted by boggarts.

1867 *Cornh. Mag.* XV. 744, 'I darena come up the lone moor by night, for 'tis a very boggety bit.'

bogge, variant of BOG, BODGE *sb.*[2]

bogged (bɒgd), *ppl. a.* [f. BOG *v.*[1] + -ED.] Plunged or entangled in a bog; bemired. Also *fig.*

1603 B. JONSON *Sejanus* IV. (1692) 142 Bogg'd in his filthy Lusts. **1854** HOOKER *Himal. Jrnls.* II. xxx. 323 My elephant got bogged in crossing a deep muddy stream.

'**bogger**. *dial.* See quot. So '**bogging** *vbl. sb.*

1858 M. PORTEOUS *Souter Johnny* 18 It was then the custom for the country shoemaker, like the tailor, to go to the house of his employer, and there do his work. This practice was technically called 'bogging', and on such occasions the accommodating bogger would make shoes for the whole family.

†'**boggify**, *v. Obs. rare.* [f. BOGGY *a.* + -FY.] To make boggy.

1649 BLITH *Eng. Improv. Impr.* viii. (1653) 43 Such Mills .. as are kept up, or dammed so high, as that they boggifie all the Lands that lye under their Mill-head.

bogginess ('bɒgɪnɪs). Boggy quality.

1649 BLITHE *Eng. Improv. Impr.* (1653) 37. **1670** SHARROCK *Vegetables* 87 Bogginess.. breeds the rush and other incommodities. **1885** *Standard* 2 Apr. 5/2 The 'haughs' are wet, almost to bogginess.

†'**bogging**, *vbl. sb. Obs.* [perh. an obs. spelling of *bodging*: see BODGER, BADGE *v.*[2]] Peddling, hawking; going up and down as a dealer; also *fig.*

1554 PHILPOT *Exam. & Writ.* (1842) 308, I would they would.. leave bogging of heresies to their own damnation & decaying of many. **1577** HOLINSHED *Chron.* III. 64 The busie bogging of the divell alwaies.

†'**boggish**, *a.*[1] *Obs.* [f. BOG *a.* + -ISH.] ? Inclined to bluster or brag; puffed up; bold. Hence '**boggishly** *adv.*, in a vaunting manner.

c **1440** *Promp. Parv.* 42 Boggyschyn [*K.H.* boggysche. **1499** boggisshe], *tumidus.* *c* **1350** *Will. Palerne* 1707 And bogeysliche as a boye busked to þe kychene. *c* **1440** *Promp. Parv.* 42 Boggyschely, *tumide.*

†'**boggish**, *a.*[2] [f. BOG *sb*[1].] Of boggy nature.

1633 T. STAFFORD *Pac. Hib.* xxi. (1821) 416 On the front a boggish Glyn.

boggle ('bɒg(ə)l), *v.* Also 6 buggell, 7 bogle. [app. f. *boggle*, var. of BOGLE a spectre, (such as horses are reputed to see). In later times there has been a tendency to associate the word with *bungle*, which appears in sense 4, and in the derivatives.]

1. *intr.* To start with fright, to shy as a startled horse; to take alarm, be startled, scared *at.*

1598 CHAPMAN *Iliad* x. 420 They [steeds] should not with affright Boggle, nor snore. **1601** SHAKS. *All's Well* v. iii. 232 You boggle shrewdly, euery feather starts you. **1638** SUCKLING *Brennoralt* IV. i. 35 Thou.. boglest at every thing, foole. **1655** GURNALL *Chr. in Arm.* xiv. 221/1 Balaam.. spurs on his conscience (that boggl'd more than the Asse he rode on). **1678** R. LESTRANGE *Seneca's Mor.* (1702) 426 We Boggle at our own Shadows, and Fright one another. **1769** WESLEY in *Wks.* (1872) III. 373 The shaft-horse then boggled and turned short toward the edge of the precipice. **1865** MISS BRADDON *Doctor's Wife* x. 93 Boggling a little when she turned the corners.

2. To raise scruples, hesitate, demur, stickle (*at*, occas. *about*, *over*, etc., or *to do* a thing).

a **1638** MEDE *Wks.* I. xxxvii. (1672) 202 A Sound and Loyal heart is not that which boggles and scruples at small sins. **1667** PEPYS *Diary* (1877) V. 241, I find the Parliament still bogling about the raising of this money. **1681** CHETHAM *Angler's Vade-m.* xxxix. §13 (1689) 287 They would not bogle to give 1000 sesterces. **1692** R. LESTRANGE *Josephus' Ant.* v. x. (1733) 125 He never shrunk or boggled for the matter. *a* **1734** NORTH *Exam.* II. iv. ¶115 He boggled at first against testifying at all. **1798** MARY WOLLSTONECR. *Posth. Wks.* IV. lxviii. 8 Since you boggle about a mere form. **1868** BROWNING *Ring & Book* IX. 1378 Nor do thou Boggle, oh parent, to return the grace. **1876** GREEN *Short Hist.* vi. §6. 336 One, who was known to have boggled hard at the oath.

3. 'To play fast or loose' J.; to palter, quibble, equivocate.

a **1613** OVERBURY *A Wife* (1638) 219 He doth boggle very often. *a* **1649** DRUMM. OF HAWTH. *Skiamachia* Wks. (1711) 199 Are ye not afraid to boggle thus with God Almighty? *a* **1674** CLARENDON *Hist. Reb.* (1704) III. XI. 206 He boggled so much in his answer, that they would be of opinion that, etc. **1816** HAZLITT *Modern Apost.*, They have never sneaked nor shuffled, botched or boggled in their politics.

4. To fumble, bungle, make a clumsy attempt.

[**1536** LATIMER *Serm. & Rem.* (1845) 373 If I have one there to help me, I shall do the more good; if not I shall buggell myself as well as I can.] **1853** *C. Auchester* II. 9 He boggled at the lock for a minute or two, but at last admitted himself. **1880** L. STEPHEN *Pope* vii. 169 He uses only one epithet, but it is the right one, and never boggles and patches.

†**5.** *trans.* To cause to hesitate, to scare. *rare.*

1663 *Flagellum or O. Cromwell* (1672) 155 This bogled at first three quarters of them.

boggle ('bɒg(ə)l), *sb.* [f. prec. vb.]

1. The act of boggling as a horse. †*to take boggle*: to shy with fright, to take alarm.

1660 G. FLEMING *Stemma Sacr.* 30 They had taken boggle at some State overtures. **1824** *Craven Dial.* 22 His skaddle tit, glentin its ee up at me, took boggle, maad a girt flounder, an ran back.

2. Demur, scruple, objection, difficulty, fuss; chiefly in *to make boggle.* *Obs.* or *arch.*

1667 PEPYS *Diary* (1879) IV. 459 The Dutch do make a further bogle with us about two or three things. **1768** TUCKER *Lt. Nat.* I. 140 The plain man makes no boggle at the ideas of creation, annihilation, or vacuity.

3. A bungle. *boggle-de-botch, boggledy botch* (colloq.): a complete bungle, a 'mess' See BOTCH *v.* and *sb.*

1834 MAR. EDGEWORTH *Helen* xxvi, A fine boggle-de-botch I have made of it. **1841** GRESLEY *C. Lever* 21 What a boggle he did make of it to be sure. **1862** *Sat. Rev.* XIII. 121 Jones of the 43rd, who got into that boggle in Armenia.

boggle, dialectal variant of BOGLE, goblin.

'**boggled**, *ppl. a.* [f. BOGGLE *v.* + -ED.] Clumsily attempted, bungled. Cf. BOGGLE *v.* 4.

1877 LYTTEIL *Landmarks* I. iv. 32 *Camstraddin*.. being clearly a boggled form of *Kempu-stadrin.*

'**boggler**. [f. BOGGLE *v.* + -ER[1].] One who boggles or hesitates; a stickler.

1606 SHAKS. *Ant. & Cl.* III. xiii. 110 You haue beene a boggeler euer.

boggling ('bɒglɪŋ), *vbl. sb.* [f. as prec. + -ING[1].] The action of the vb. BOGGLE.

1640 SHIRLEY *Arcadia* II. i, Leave Your bogling & your trim-tram tricks. **1656** R. ROBINSON *Christ all* 117 He keeps a huge boggling, he doth exceedingly dodge with Jesus Christ. **1834** C. GREVILLE *Mem. Geo. IV*, (1875) III. xxiii. 79 He made a great boggling of reading his petition.

'**boggling**, *ppl. a.* [f. as prec. + -ING[2].] That boggles; starting with fright; stickling; bungling.

1645 W. LITHGOW *Siege Newcastle* (1820) 15 Like unto Calabrian Females with their bogling bushs. *a* **1683** OLDHAM *Sat. Jesuits* Wks. (1686) 10 Nice bogling consciences. **1870** MISS BROUGHTON *Red as Rose* 252, I can mend stockings in a boggling.. sort of way.

bogglingly ('bɒglɪŋlɪ), *adv.* [f. prec. + -LY[2].] In a boggling manner.

1863 *All Y. Round* 422 [He] slowly and bogglingly reads .. what has been written for him to say.

†'**bogglish**, *a. Obs.* [f. BOGGLE *sb.* + -ISH.] Inclined to BOGGLE; skittish.

1656 *Artif. Handsomeness* 172 Nothing is more sly, touchy and boglish.

boggy ('bɒgɪ), *a.* [f. BOG *sb.* + -Y[1].] Of the nature of, or characterized by, bog; swampy.

1586 J. HOOKER *Girald. Irel.* in *Holinshed* II. 168 Passed through the boggie mounteine of Slewlougher into Kerrie. **1652** FRENCH *Yorksh. Spa* ii. 5 Drunk up by some boggie, spongious earth. **1667** MILTON *P.L.* II. 939 Quencht in a Boggie Syrtis, neither Sea Nor good dry Land. **1727** BRADLEY *Fam. Dict.* I. s.v. *Fir tree*, Venice and Amsterdam are built on Piles of this timber driven into boggy Places. **1872** JENKINSON *Guide Eng. Lakes* (1879) 104 Composed of rocky hillocks and boggy hollows.

fig. **1644** QUARLES *Barnabas and B.* 44 Let me drain my boggy soul from those corrupted inbred humours.

b. *transf.* Of a soft, spongy consistency; flabby.

1664 H. POWER *Exp. Philos.* I. 66 Carried with the Bloud ..up into the Brain, and there by that lax and boggy substance are imbibed. **1852** *Fraser's Mag.* XLV. 639 The flesh boggy to the touch.

bogh, boghed, etc.: see BOUGH and BOW *v.*

Boghead, boghead ('bɒghɛd). The name of an estate near Bathgate in West Lothian applied *attrib.* to a deep brown shale found there. See TORBANITE.

1858, 1867 [see TORBANITE]. **1919** *Chambers's Jrnl.* June 390/2 The famous oil-shale of Torbanehill, torbanite or bog-head cannel, is often regarded as a variety of cannel coal. **1937** *Nature* 20 Feb. 340/1 Boghead coal is a comparatively rare and valuable material yielding gas and paraffin on distillation. **1960** *Gloss. Coal Terms* (*B.S.I.*) 6 *Boghead coal, Torbanite*, coal resembling cannel coal in physical appearance and properties, but distinguished microscopically by the presence of the remains of algae.

'**bog-house**. *dial.* and *vulgar.* [see BOGGARD[2].] A privy, 'a house of office' J. So **bog-shop**.

1666 R. HEAD *Eng. Rogue* x. 85 Fearing I should catch cold, they out of pitty covered me warm in a Bogg-house. **1705** HICKERINGILL *Priest-Cr.* II. v. 48 The Jaques, the Bog-house or House of Office. *c* **1714** ARBUTHNOT, etc., *M. Scriblerus* I. xiv, He cast them all into a bog-house near St. James'. **1761** *Brit. Mag.* II. 163 They had found the intrails of a body in the bog-house.

boghsom, obs. form of BUXOM.

boght, obs. pa. t. and pa. pple. of BUY.

bogie ('bəʊgɪ). Also bogy, bogey. [A northern dialect word, which has recently been generally diffused in connexion with railways as applied to the plate-layer's bogie, but especially in sense 2. Of unknown etymology: notwithstanding absurd stories in the newspapers (invented *ad rem*), it has (as the sense might show) nothing to do with BOGY[1], which is not a northern word.]

1. *north. dial.* A low strong truck upon four small wheels, also called *trolly*, *hurly*, etc. 'A kind of cart with low wheels and long shafts, used by masons to remove large stones' (Peacock *Lonsdale Gloss.*); 'a rude contrivance for moving heavy articles, consisting of a simple plank on low wheels' (*Lanc. Gloss.*). *esp.* in Newcastle, A strong low truck (about 1 ft. high) on 4 small wheels, used, since *c* 1817, for transporting a single cask or hogshead from the quay to the town; also a flat board with 4 very small wheels on which lads career down steep banks or roads, as in the Canadian sport of *tobogganing*. Hence, in general use, the low truck used by platelayers on a railway.

c **1817** [Remembered in Newcastle by living witnesses (1887)]. **1835** A. GILCHRIST in Robson *Bards of Tyne* (1863) 416 In Dean Street, when carts or when bogies came down. **1840** T. WILSON *Poems* (1872) 93 A kind o' hearse on bogie wheels. **1869** *N. & Q.* Ser. IV. IV. 570/1 In Scotland in the engineering works they have a small carriage..which they call a 'bogie.'.. I find it has been known by that name for fully 60 years. **1874** *Trans. Amer. Inst. Mining Eng.* II. 82 The slag may be allowed to deposit itself in layers in the truck or bogie, placed underneath the rolls. **1885** *Birmingham Wkly. Post* 26 Sept. 4/7 This work has often had to be done with a plate-layer's bogie, propelled by feet touching the road. (See R. Oliver Heslop, in *Newcastle Daily Journal*, 1 Nov. 1886.)

2. A low truck or frame running on two or more pairs of wheels and supporting the fore-part of a locomotive engine or the ends of a long railway-carriage, to which it is attached by a central pivot, on which it swivels freely in passing curves; a revolving under-carriage.

1844 *Specif. J. Wright's Patent*, No. 10173 Constructing railway carriages by supporting the bodies near the ends on two eight-wheel, six-wheel, and four-wheel bogies or revolving under-carriages. **1865** *Railway News* 2 Dec. 579 The Bissell Bogie..for Locomotive Engines, so much prized on American and foreign Railroads. **1878** F. WILLIAMS *Midl. Railw.* 665 The new Midland passenger carriages..rest on two six-wheeled bogies. **1879** *Cassell's Techn. Educ.* XI. 307 In some engines the front part, instead of being mounted on a single pair of wheels, is supported on a'bogie' or truck with two pairs.

3. *attrib.*, as in **bogie car**, **carriage**, **engine**, **truck**; **bogie-barrow** = sense 1 ('known in Fife for sixty years or more', Prof. W. Wallace).

1843 *Proc. Inst. Civil Eng.* 99 What is termed a 'bogie' engine, having a four-wheeled truck to support one end of the boiler, whilst the other end rests upon the driving wheels. **1851** *Specif. C. Cowper's Patent* No. 13705 Improvements in the fore carriages, or as they are sometimes called 'bogy frames,' of locomotive engines. **1869** *Eng. Mech.* 19 Nov. 236/1 These engines are constructed with a bogie truck. **1880** *Birmingham Wkly. Post* 2 Oct. 1/6 He was in the last compartment of the last bogie carriage.

bogie, variant of BOGY[1].

bogle ('bəʊg(ə)l). Forms: 5–6 bogil(l, 7 bogell, 8– bogle; 7–9 *north. Eng.* boggle. [Of the various names *bogle*, *boggard*, *bogy*, applied to a goblin, *bogle* is the earliest known, being common in Scottish literature since 1500. In the present century its use by Burns, Scott, Hogg, and others has introduced it into English literature; but the special English form seems to be *boggle* (with short *o* as in BOGGARD), found in north. Eng. dialects from Cumberland to Lincolnshire. The derivation of the whole group is uncertain: the primitive may be *bogge*, BOG *sb.*[2], and this may be a variant of *bugge*, BUG; which is not improbably a. Welsh *bwg* (= bug) ghost, bugbear, hobgoblin. The form of *bogle*, *boggle*, would still remain unexplained: it is perhaps worth while to compare Welsh *bwgwl* (= 'bugul) 'terror, terrifying' (whence *bygylu* (bʌ'gʌly) to terrify), and *bygel* (or *bugail*) *nos* a hobgoblin of the night: see BUG. But there are also German words of similar form and meaning, *bögge* and *boggel-mann* 'a bogy, a bogle': so that uncertainty attaches to the source. Cf. BOGGARD.]

1. A phantom causing fright; a goblin, bogy, or spectre of the night; an undefined creature of superstitious dread. (Usually supposed to be black, and to have something of human attributes, though spoken of as *it*.) Also, applied contemptuously to a human being who is 'a fright to behold'.

c **1505** DUNBAR *Tua mariit Wem.* 111 The luif blenkis of that bogill, fra his blerde ene. **1535** STEWART *Cron. Scot.* III. 134 Like ane bogill all of ratland banis. **1646** R. BAILLIE *Anabapt.* (1647) 44 The Devils are nothing but only boggles in the night, to terrifie men. **1752** *Scots Mag.* (1753) Sept. 451/1 There used to be bogles seen. **1790** BURNS *Tam o'Shanter*, Whiles glow'ring round wi' prudent cares, Lest bogles catch him unawares. **1808** *Cumbrian Ball.* iii. 8 A boggle's been seen wi' twee heads. **1814** SCOTT *Wav.* lxxi, I played at bogle about the bush wi' them. **1822** BEWICK *Mem.* 20, I had not..got over a belief in ghosts and boggles. **1824** BYRON *Juan* XI. lxxii, A sort of sentimental bogle, Which sits for ever upon memory's crupper. **1832** SOUTHEY *Lett.* (1856) IV. 281 Boggles and Barguests are the only supernatural beings we hear of in these parts [Keswick]. **1864** TENNYSON *North. Farmer* viii, Theer wur a boggle in it, I often 'eerd un mysen.

2. *fig.* and *transf.* **a.** A bugbear (not a phantom). **b.** A thing unsubstantial, a mere phantom.

1663 LAUDERDALE in *Papers* (1884) I. cvi. 185, I have written so much that I doe feare my hand shall grow a bug-beare, or as we say heir a bogell. **1792** BURNS *Despondency* iii, The sillie bogles, wealth and state, Can never make them eerie.

3. *transf.* A scarecrow. (In common use in north.)

1830 GALT *Lawrie T.* VII. ix. (1849) 343 Bogles made of clouts. **1884** *Gd. Words* May 324/2 Potato bogles or scarecrows..vary in size..and dress, in nearly every parish.

Hence ˌ**bogle-'bo** [see BO.] = BOGLE; '**bogledom**, the realm or domain of bogles.

1603 *Philotus* ii, Quhat reck to tak the Bogill-bo, My bonie burd for anis. **1678** COLES *Lat. Dict.*, *Boggle-bo*..an ugly wide-mouthed picture carried about with May games. **1730–6** BAILEY, *Boggle-boe*, a bugbear to fright Children, a scare crow. ? *a* **1800** *Rhymes* in *Proc. Berw. Nat. Club* I. v. 148 The bogle bo' of Billy Mire Wha kills our bairns a'. **1860** G. H. K. *Vac. Tour* 171 Donald! Donald! keep out of the regions of bogledom.

boglet ('bɒglɪt). [see -LET.] A little bog.

1869 BLACKMORE *Lorna D.* lix. (1872) 399 Tufty flaggy ground, pocked with bogs and boglets.

Bogomil, -mile ('bəʊgəmɪl, bɒ-, -maɪl). *Hist.* [ad. med.Gr. Βογόμιλος, of disputed origin; the first syllable may represent Russ. *Bog* God.] A member of a heretical Bulgarian sect which arose in the 10th or 11th century, whose main tenet was that God the Father had two sons, Satan and Christ. Hence **Bogo'milian** *a.* and *sb.*, '**Bogomilism**, '**Bogomilist**.

[**1574** R. BRISTOW *Plaine Wayes Truthe* To Rdr. *iiij b, In the twelfth hundred [year after Christ], the Bogomili, the Petrobusians, the Apostolikes.] **1841** *Penny Cycl.* XX. 271/1 The sect of the *Bogomiles*, which was well known in the Greek empire. **1852** J. TORREY tr. *Neander's Ch. Hist.* VIII. 356 The Bogomilian view of the Trinity. *a* **1875** FINLAY *Hist. Greece* (1877) III. 69 A Bogomilian who was put to the torture by the imperial officers. **1887** M. GASTER *Greeko-Slavonic Lit.* 17 Bogomilism..ruled Bulgaria for not less than five centuries. *Ibid.* 20 Nikita, the bishop of the Bogomils of Constantinople. *Ibid.* 35, I will here give the version which comes nearest to the original Bogomilist form. **1920** *Q. Rev.* Jan. 71 He invited the Bogomile heretic, Basil, to a private colloquy. **1939** A. J. TOYNBEE *Stud. Hist.* IV. iii. 633 The Bogomil Church is a monument of the successful execution of this project. **1941** 'R. WEST' *Black Lamb & Grey Falcon* I. 172 The Puritan heresy known as Paulicianism or Patarenism or Bogomilism or Catharism.

bogong, var. BUGONG.

bog-shop, vulgar equivalent of BOG-HOUSE.

bogt, obs. pa. t. and pa. pple. of BUY.

'**bog-trot**, *v.* [f. BOG *sb.*[1] + TROT *v.*: app. due to the earlier formation BOG-TROTTER.] *intr.* To trot over bogs; to live among bogs. Hence '**bog-trotting** *vbl. sb.* and *ppl. a.*

a **1734** NORTH *Exam.* II. v. §14 (1740) 323 Better..to bog-trot in Ireland, than to pirk it in Preferment no better dressed. **1762** GOLDSM. *Cit. W.* II. lxviii, Rock advises the world to beware of bogtrotting quacks. **1839** STONEHOUSE *Axholme* 398 It required very great care in stepping from tuft to tuft, which in Ireland, is called bog-trotting.

bog-trotter ('bɒg-ˌtrɒtə(r)). [f. BOG *sb.* + TROTTER.]

†**1.** One accustomed to make his way across bogs, or to run to bogs for refuge. *Obs.*

1700 RYCAUT *Hist. Turks* III. 276 Being very nimble and active, and a kind of Bog-trotter, Achmet escaped over a Marsh. **1755** JOHNSON, *Bog-trotter*, one that lives in a boggy country.

2. *spec.* Applied to the wild Irish in the 17th c.; continued in the 18th c. as a nickname for Irishmen.

1682 *Philanax Misopappas, Tory Plot* II. 18 An idle flam of shabby Irish Bogtrotters. *a* **1733** NORTH *Lives* I. 406 His friends were termed Bog trotters, wild Irish, or, which means the same thing, Tories. **1753** SMOLLETT *Ct. Fathom* (1784) 80/1 A beggarly Scot, and an impudent Irish bog-trotter. **1773** JOHNSON *Lett.* 79. I. 132 Moss in Scotland is bog in Ireland, and moss-trooper is bog-trotter. **1855** MACAULAY *Hist. Eng.* IV. 712 Two Irishmen, or, in the phrase of the newspapers of that day, bogtrotters.

bogue (bəʊg). [Fr. (16 c.), f. OPr. *boga*, f. med.L. *boca*, L. *bōx* (see BOCE[1]), Gr. βῶξ, contraction of βόαξ a grunting fish.] = BOCE[1].

1862 J. COUCH *Fishes Brit. Isl.* I. 225 In some parts of the European side of the Mediterranean the Bogue is a common fish... The first British example we have a record of was caught..at St. Mawes. *Ibid.* 226 The Bogue grows to the length of eight or nine inches. **1880** F. DAY *Fishes Gt. Brit.* I. 28 *Sparidæ*: Box vulgaris..*Bogue*..*Habitat.* From the southern shores of the British isles as far south as Madeira and the Canaries... Common throughout the Mediterranean. **1936** J. T. JENKINS *Fishes Brit. Isl.* (ed. 2) 41 The Bogue (*Box vulgaris*) is also a Mediterranean species [of Sea Bream] which occasionally migrates into British waters.

bogus ('bəʊgəs), (*sb.*[1]) *a.* [A cant word of U.S., about the origin of which many guesses have been made, and 'bogus' derivations circumstantially given.

Dr. S. Willard, of Chicago, in a letter to the editor of this Dictionary, quotes from the *Painesville* (*Ohio*) *Telegraph* of July 6 and Nov. 2, 1827, the word *bogus* as a sb. applied to an apparatus for coining false money. Mr. Eber D. Howe, who was then editor of that paper, describes in his *Autobiography* (1878) the discovery of such a piece of mechanism in the hands of a gang of coiners at Painesville, in May 1827; it was a mysterious-looking object, and some one in the crowd styled it a 'bogus', a designation adopted in the succeeding numbers of the paper. Dr. Willard considers this to have been short for *tantrabogus*, a word familiar to him from his childhood, and which in his father's time was commonly applied in Vermont to any ill-looking object; he points out that *tantarabobs* is given in Halliwell as a Devonshire word for the devil. BOGUS seems thus to be related to BOGY[1], etc.]

†**1.** *sb.* **a.** An apparatus for counterfeit coining. *Obs.*

1827 *Painesville Tel.* (*Ohio*) 6 July, That he never procured the casting of a *Bogus* at one of our furnaces. *Ibid.* 2 Nov. The eight or ten boguses which have been for some time in operation.

b. ***bogus press***, ***machine*** = sense 1 a.

1844 *Spirit of Times* (Philad.) 12 Oct. (Th.), A bogus press for making counterfeit money. **1850** *Frontier Guardian* (ed. O. Hyde) 23 Jan. (Th.), We employed that same Bill Hickman to ferret out a bogus press and a gang of counterfeiters...A part of the bogus machine has been found.

†**c.** Counterfeit coin. Also *Comb.*

1842 *Life in West* 297 They had attempted to pass bogus (base coin). **1844** *Nauvoo Neighbor* 12 June (Th.), To bolster up the interests of blacklegs and bogus-makers. **1854** B. YOUNG in *Jrnl. Discourses* I. 270 The Magicians of Egypt ..produced a very good bogus, but it was not quite the true coin.

2. *adj.* Counterfeit, spurious, fictitious, sham: 'originally applied to counterfeit coin' (Webster).

1839 MRS. KIRKLAND *New Home* xxxii. 212 The boxes.. contained..half-dollars 'principally bogus'. **1852** HUGHES in J. Ludlow *Hist. U.S.* 338 This precious house of representatives—the bogus legislature, as it was at once called. **1857** *Boston Daily Courier* 12 June, The learned Judge took occasion to manifest his abhorrence of the use of slang phrases..by saying that he did not know the meaning of 'bogus transactions'. **1859** 'DOW JR.' *New Patent Sermons* 216 Crocodile tears are bogus. **1866** *Cornh. Mag.* Nov. 582 A mere juggle, or as Americans would say, a 'bogus' parliament. **1874** M. COLLINS *Frances* III. 80 They've got some good money, as well as bogus notes. **1877** R. GIFFEN *Stock Exch. Securities* 65 A bogus Company..instead of paying dividends to its Shareholders, goes into Liquidation. **1878** BLACK *Green Past.* xxv. 202, I am not going to spend a penny in a bogus contest. **1892** G. B. SHAW *Pen Portraits & Rev.* (1932) 243 Mr. Frederic Harrison deliberately talked bogus Shelleyism to the reporters. **1940** N. MITFORD *Pigeon Pie* xvi. 244, I also hoped they would show people here that the whole thing was bogus. **1942** E. WAUGH *Put out more Flags* i. §6. 68 You..haven't got any of those bogus regional connections like the Scots and Irish and Welsh.

bogus ('bəʊgəs), *sb.*[2] *U.S.* [Has been conjectured to be ad. F. *bagasse* sugar-cane refuse; but perhaps is the same word as prec.] 'A liquor made of rum and molasses.' Bartlett *Dict. Amer.*

bogusly ('bəʊgəslɪ), *adv.* orig. *U.S.* [f. BOGUS *a.* + -LY[2].] In a bogus manner; spuriously.

1862 *N.Y. Herald* 2 May, When..the oath was sent to us, we filed it bogously [*sic*], and sent it to Richmond without swearing to it. **1932** AUDEN *Orators* I. i. 19 The bogusly cheerful—the games master. **1941** *Mind* L. 111 To reply ..'By analogy' is very apt to be bogusly soothing and thus misleading. **1964** I. FLEMING *You only live Twice* v. 61 The bogusly important-looking entrance.

bogusness ('bəʊgəsnɪs). [f. BOGUS *a.* + -NESS.] The fact or quality of being bogus.

1921 H. L. MENCKEN *Prejudices* 2nd Ser. I. ix. 79 The old bogusness hangs about them [*sc.* the intelligentsia], as about the fashionable aristocrats of the society columns. *c* **1935** R. SHERIDAN *Let.* in C. Sheridan *To Four Winds* (1957) xxvii. 298 The pettiness, dirtiness, meanness, bogusness of it all. **1953** F. SWINNERTON *Month in Gordon Square* 9 The affectation was part of his general bogusness. **1958** *Times Lit. Suppl.* 24 Jan. 47/3 Produces the same sort of bogusness as do those actors on the stage who cannot represent a member of the rural lower classes without bent knees.

bogy[1], **bogey** ('bəʊgɪ). Also boguey, bogie. Pl. bogies. [Found in literature only recently; old people vouched (1887) for its use in the nursery as early as 1825, but only as proper name (sense 1). Possibly a southern nursery form of *bogle*, *boggle*, and *boggard*, or going back like them to a simpler form which, as mentioned under BOG and BOGLE, may be a variant of *bugge*, BUG 'terror, bugbear, scarecrow'. But in the absence of evidence, positive statements concerning its

relation to these words cannot be made. (That they are connected with the Slavonic *bog* 'god', is a mere fancy from the similarity of form, without any evidence.)]

1. As quasi-proper name: The evil one, the devil.

1836-40 BARHAM *Ingol. Leg.*, *Witches' Frolic*, But hears the words 'Scratch' and 'Old Bogey' and 'Nick'. *Ibid.* (1840) 322 Then Boguey'd have you sure as eggs is eggs. **1840** GEN. P. THOMPSON *Exerc.* (1842) V. 88 To admit to evidence such as avow their credence in 'old Bogie'. **1851** THACKERAY *Eng. Hum.* v. (1858) 239 The people are all naughty and Bogey carries them all off. **1865** E. CLAYTON *Cruel Fort.* III. 85 I'll put out the light and go away, and leave you all by yourself with Bogie. **1879** M. CONWAY *Demonol.* I. I. iii. 16.

2. A bogle or goblin; a person much dreaded.

1857 S. OSBORN *Quedah* ii. 17 Malay pirates.. those bogies of the Archipelago. **1863** KINGSLEY *Water Bab.* (1878) 19 On the top of each gate post a most dreadful bogy. **1863** BARING-GOULD *Iceland* 118 The sheepwalks have got a bad name for bogies.

3. *fig.* An object of terror or dread; a bugbear.

1865 *Daily Tel.* 27 Nov. 2/3 Reform is not a bogy to cheat, but a blessing to recognise and regulate. **1878** *N. Amer. Rev.* 135 Men.. who discover bogies in every measure.

4. *Criminals' slang.* A detective; a policeman.

1924 S. SCOTT *Human Side* i. 23 Men will listen to the vilest epithets, but call them 'bogey', 'brassey', 'copper', or 'policeman', and they will be at your throat. **1931** W. F. BROWN in *Police Jrnl.* Oct. 501 She told a detective (bogey) she knew that Jack was in the brothel (case). **1936** J. CURTIS *Gilt Kid* 17 One of the bogies from Vine Street reckernizes me. **1960** *Observer* 24 Jan. 7/2 Suppose.. a bogy did get it up for a villain now and again by making sure that some gear was found in his flat?

5. A piece of dried nasal mucus. *colloq.*

1937 in PARTRIDGE *Dict. Slang* 853/1 s.v. *sweep*. **1955** K. AMIS *That Uncertain Feeling* xii. 158 'You've got a bogey on your nose. Improves your looks no end.' I was near the mirror... I peeped in and saw the bogey. It was large and vermiform and clung to the wing of my right nostril. *Ibid.* xiii. 176, I felt my nostrils carefully, testing for bogeys. **1967** D. PINNER *Ritual* xv. 148 He.. removed wax from ears, bogeys from nose, blackheads from chin.

6. An unidentified aircraft; an enemy aeroplane. *slang.*

1943 WARD-JACKSON *Piece of Cake* 16 *Bogey*, a friendly aircraft [corrected in ed. 1945 to:] a suspect aircraft. **1944** *Life* 17 July 20 Before supper was over this evening, several 'bogeys'—as unidentified planes are called under such circumstances—were seen approaching from different directions.

7. *attrib.* and *Comb.*, as ***bogy-man***, ***-word***, etc.

1863 KINGSLEY *Water Bab.* iv. 146 The old German bogy-painters. *c* **1890** Bogey man [see note s.v. BOGEY]. **1912** G. B. SHAW in *Christian Globe* 22 Feb. 433/4 It was manlier than clinging to Britannia's skirts for protection against the Bogey Man with the triple tiara. **1919** J. L. GARVIN *Econ. Found. Peace* 112 To confuse or weaken the Allies by using 'Bolshevism' as a bogey-word. **1926** FOWLER *Mod. Eng. Usage* 559/1 Bogy-haunted creatures who for fear of splitting an infinitive abstain from doing something quite different. **1954** J. R. R. TOLKIEN *Fellowship of Ring* I. vi. 121 The old bogy-stories Fatty's nurses used to tell him. **1959** *Listener* 16 Apr. 657/2 Black children were brought up to believe that if they were naughty the white bogy-man would come and gobble them up.

Hence **'bogydom**, the domain of Old Bogy. **'bogyism**, the recognition of bogies. **bogy'phobia**, dread of bogies.

1880 *Daily Tel.* 2 Dec., A sulphurous odour.. suggestive of bogeydom. **1876** *Athenæum* 14 Oct. 495/3 The author seems to be a spiritualist, or, at least, to have a leaning to banshees and bogyism. **1872** LIVINGSTONE in *Daily News* 29 July, I am not liable to fits of bogiephobia.

bogy², **bogey²** ('bəʊgɪ). *Austral. slang.* Also bogie. [App. Aboriginal word.] **a.** A bathe. **b.** A bathing-place, a bath. Also *attrib.* Hence as *v. intr.*, to bathe; so **'bogying** *vbl. sb.*

1849 A. HARRIS *Emigrant Family* viii. 145 'Bogie,' I suppose must be aboriginal also... Its signification is *a bathe*. **1893** K. MACKAY *Out Back* iv. 50, I don't care to bogey in our drinking tank. **1928** 'BRENT OF BIN BIN' *Up Country* (1966) ii. 24 They.. took her for bogeys in the swimming hole. **1934** *Bulletin* (Sydney) 13 June 19/4 Blacks on the tidal creeks and rivers of Queensland prefer to bogey when the tide is on the ebb. **1941** BAKER *Dict. Austral. Slang* 11 *Bogie*, a swim, a bath, or wash. (2) A swimming hole, a bath. Also, 'bogiehole', 'bogiehouse'. **1945** —— *Austral. Lang.* xiii. 223 Then there are the aboriginal words which we have borrowed and extended in meaning, e.g. *bogie* or *bogey*, to bathe, from which we have taken *bogiehole*, a swimming hole, *bogiehouse*, a bathroom, and *bogieing*, bathing. **1946** F. D. DAVISON *Dusty* viii. 82 They went down for a bogey on warm days.

bogy, var. BOGIE, obs. form of BUDGE *sb.*, fur.

bogyll, obs. form of BUCKLE.

boh (bəʊ). *India.* [Burmese *bo.*] A chief or leader of dacoits.

1888 [see DAH]. **1890** KIPLING *Departm. Ditties* (ed. 4) 82 Bohs that were brave departed. **1923** *Chambers's Jrnl.* Oct. 650/2 He would ask which was their Boh, or leader. **1926** *Ibid.* Feb. 85/2 A man, obviously the Boh, or Chief.

boh, variant of BO *int.*, obs. form of BOW.

Bohairic (bəʊ'haɪərɪk), *a.* and *sb.* Also **Bahiric**. [f. *Bohairah*, *Bahirah* (*Boheira*, *Beherah*), the Arabic name of Lower Egypt (Arab. *buhaira* lake).] The designation of the classical or standard form of Coptic spoken in Alexandria and the north-western Delta, and of the version of the Bible (the official version of the Bible of the Coptic Church) written in this language. (= MEMPHITIC.)

1830 H. TATTAM *Gram. Egypt. Lang.* 135 The Coptic, or, as it has been called, the Bahiric, but more properly the Memphitic, was the Dialect of Lower Egypt. **1874** LIGHTFOOT in Scrivener *Crit. N.T.* (ed. 2) 327 The Bahiric or Memphitic Version. **1898** G. W. HORNER (*title*) The Coptic Version of the New Testament in the Northern Dialect otherwise called Memphitic and Bohairic. **1958** F. KENYON *Our Bible* (ed. 5) viii. 234 Originally, however, the dialect in which it is written belonged only to the coast district near Alexandria, and another dialect was in use in Memphis itself; hence it is better to avoid the term Memphitic, and use the more strictly accurate name *Bohairic*.

bohea (bəʊ'hiː), *a.* and *sb.* Also 8 bohee. [ad. Chinese *Wu-i(shan)* the *Wu-i* hills in north of Fuhkien. Morrison gives 'Bohea Tea, *wu i cha*' (*cha* = tea), and Edkins, *Mandarin Gram.* 89, says that the Fuhkien dialect uses *b* for *w* or *v*. By some 18th c. writers accented '*bohea*.]

A. *adj.* Of the Wu-i hills, whence black tea was first brought to England; applied also to tea of similar quality grown elsewhere.

1704 STEELE *Lying Lover* II. (1747) 36 Set Chairs, and the Bohea Tea, and leave us. **1718** QUINCY *Compl. Disp.* 116 Bohee Tea.—This is one of those things which Luxury has introduced into Diet. **1773** *Gentl. Mag.* XLIII. 607 The infusion of the leaves of the same plant, which.. is like common bohea-tea.

B. *sb.*

1. = *Bohea tea.* The name was given in the beginning of the 18th c. to the finest kinds of black tea; but the quality now known as 'Bohea' is the lowest, being the last crop of the season.

1701 J. CUNNINGHAM *Voy. Chusan.* ii. in *Phil. Trans.* XXIII. 1205 The Bohe (or Voiii, so call'd of some Mountains in the Province of Fokien).. is the very first bud gather'd in the beginning of March. **1727-8** MRS. DELANY *Life & Corr.* (1861) I. 172 Tea of all prices—Bohea from thirteen to twenty shillings, and green from twelve to thirty. **1852** MCCULLOCH *Dict. Comm.* 1290 The black teas.. beginning with the lowest qualities: Bohea, Congou, Souchong, and Pekoe.

2. An infusion of this tea taken as a beverage.

1706 ESTCOURT *Fair Examp.* I. i. 10 To dine at my Lord Mayor's, and after Dinner be entertain'd with a Dish of Bohea by my Lady Mayoress. **1714** POPE *Rape Lock* IV. 156 In some lone isle, or distant northern land.. Where none learn ombre, none e'er taste bohea! **1728** YOUNG *Love Fame* vi. (1757) 152 How two red lips affected Zephyrs blow, To cool the Bohea, and inflame the Beau. **1841** L. HUNT *Seer* (1864) 19 Thy unsophisticated cup of bohea. **1851** THACKERAY *Eng. Hum.* v. (1858) 273 Richardson's goddess was.. fed on muffins and bohea.

Bohemia (bəʊ'hiːmɪə).

1. A kingdom of central Europe, forming part of the Austrian empire. (Earlier forms were *Boeme, Beme, Beeme, Bohem, Bohemy.*)

c **1449** PECOCK *Repr.* I. xvi. 86 The hoole rewme of Beeme. **1527** ANDREW *Brunswkye's Distyll. Waters* B ib, Bohemy glas. **1641** 'SMECTYMNUUS' *Answ.* (1653) Post. 91 In Bohem, with the Schisme of the Hussites. **1836** *Penny Cycl.* V. 55/1 The circuit of Bohemia is estimated at about 810 miles.

2. Gipsydom: see BOHEMIAN *sb.* 2.

1871 M. COLLINS *Mrq. & Merch.* I. i. 25 Bohemia wanders, and steals.

3. The community of social 'Bohemians', or the district in which they chiefly live. So F. *la bohème*. [Both in Fr. and Eng. taken from the use of BOHEMIAN *sb.* 3.]

1861 THACKERAY *Adv. Philip* v. in *Cornh. Mag.* Feb. 186 What is now called Bohemia had no name in Philip's young days, though many of us knew the country very well. A pleasant land, not fenced with drab stucco, like Tyburnia or Belgravia, etc.

Bohemian (bəʊ'hiːmɪən), *a.* and *sb.* [f. prec. + -AN. The transferred senses are taken from French, in which *bohême, bohémien*, have been applied to the gipsies, since their first appearance in the 15th c., because they were thought to come from Bohemia, or perhaps actually entered the West through that country. Thence, in modern French, the word has been transferred to 'vagabond, adventurer, person of irregular life or habits', a sense introduced into Eng. by Thackeray.]

A. *sb.*

1. A native of Bohemia.

1603 SHAKS. *Meas. for M.* IV. ii. 134 A Bohemian borne: But here nurst vp & bred. **1845** S. AUSTIN tr. *Ranke's Hist. Ref.* II. 469 He acceded to the demand of the Bohemians.

b. A follower of John Huss, a Bohemian Protestant or Hussite.

1579 FULKE *Heskins' Parl.* 189 The Bohemians vsed this text, to proue the communion in both kindes.

2. A gipsy. [F. *bohême, bohémien.*]

1696 PHILLIPS, *Bohemians*, the same with Gypsies, Vagabonds that strowl about the Country. **1823** SCOTT *Quentin D.* xvi, I am a Zingaro, a Bohemian, an Egyptian, or whatever the Europeans.. may choose to call me; but I have no country. **1841** BORROW *Gipsies of Spain* (1843) I. 38, I arrived at the resting place of 'certain Bohemians' by whom I was received with kindness.

3. A gipsy of society; one who either cuts himself off, or is by his habits cut off, from society for which he is otherwise fitted; especially an artist, literary man, or actor, who leads a free, vagabond, or irregular life, not being particular as to the society he frequents, and despising conventionalities generally. (Used with considerable latitude, with or without reference to morals.)

1848 THACKERAY *Van. Fair* lxiv, She was of a wild, roving nature, inherited from father and mother, who were both Bohemians, by taste and circumstances. **1862** *Westm. Rev.* July & Oct. 32-33 The term 'Bohemian' has come to be very commonly accepted in our day as the description of a certain kind of literary gipsey, no matter in what language he speaks, or what city he inhabits.. A Bohemian is simply an artist or littérateur who, consciously or unconsciously, secedes from conventionality in life and in art. **1865** *Cornh. Mag.* Feb. 241 There are many blackguards who are Bohemians, but it does not at all follow that every Bohemian is a blackguard. **1875** EMERSON *Lett. & Soc. Aims* x. 256 In persons open to the suspicion of irregular and immoral living,—in Bohemians.

4. *Comb.*, as ***Bohemian-like***.

1886 *Cyclists Tour. Club Handbk.* Apr. 5 The Bohemian-like contempt he harbours for all conventionalities.

B. *adj.* **1.** Of or belonging to Bohemia.

2. Of or pertaining to the gipsies.

1848 THACKERAY *Van. Fair* lxv, The band of renowned Bohemian Vaulters and tumblers.

3. Of, or characteristic of, social Bohemians.

1861 THACKERAY *Adv. Philip* v. in *Cornh. Mag.* Feb. 186 Having.. only lately quitted the Bohemian land. **1865** TROLLOPE *Belton Est.* i. 3 The young man commenced Bohemian life in London. **1881** SAINTSBURY *Dryden* 105 Smith, the Bohemian author of Phaedra and Hippolytus.

4. *Comb.*, as **Bohemian chatterer**, or **waxwing**, a bird of passage visiting Great Britain (*Ampelis* or *Bombycilla garrula*); **Bohemian glass**, a fine kind of glass, originally made in Bohemia, in which potash is the alkali used.

1722 BARRINGTON in *Phil. Trans.* LXII. 316, I always conceived the Bohemian chatterer was not observed in Great Britain but at very distant intervals of years. **1841** *Proc. Berw. Nat. Club.* I. 252 That beautiful member of the Ampelidæ, the Bohemian waxwing (*Bombycilla garrula*). **1854** J. SCOFFERN in *Orr's Circ. Sc.* Chem. 433 Potash glass is less subject to crack.. Bohemian glass is of this kind.

Bo'hemianism. [f. prec. + -ISM.] The characteristic conduct of manners of a Bohemian. So **Bo'hemianize** *v. intr.*, to live as a Bohemian; *trans.* to make bohemian in life and habits.

1861 SALA *Tw. round Clock* 180 Auctioneering is the Bohemianism of commerce. **1863** *Temple Bar* July 551 Henry Murger.. the high-priest of Bohemianism avers that it exists and is possible only in Paris. **1868** MISS BRADDON *Dead-Sea Fr.* iv. I. 73 There was even the faintest flavour of Bohemianism about her position, spotless though her reputation might be. **1883** *Punch* 8 Sept. 114/2 Those who want to Bohemianise a bit, and get away.. from our veneered town-life. **1898** WATTS-DUNTON *Aylwin* ii. 52 To run the risk of becoming bohemianised like Cyril Aylwin.

†**Bo'hemic**, *a. Obs.* = BOHEMIAN, Hussite.

1612 BREREWOOD *Lang. & Relig.* Pref. 6 Some embracing the Waldensian, or the Bohemick, others the Augustane, and some the Helvetian Confession.

bohereen, **bohireen**, varr. BOREEN.

bo-ho, **bo-hoo**, variants of BOO-HOO.

‖**bo'hourt.** *Obs. rare.* [OF. *bohourt, behourt* a lance, a jousting.] Jousting, tilting: cf. BOURDIS.

1801 STRUTT *Sports & Past.* IV. iv. 336 The bohourts, the tournaments, and most of the other superior pastimes have been subjected to youthful imitation.

Bohr (bɔə(r)). The name of Niels Henrik David *Bohr* (1885–1962), Danish physicist, used to designate certain theories, measurements, etc., formulated by him; as ***Bohr atom***: the atom as described by the Bohr theory; ***Bohr('s) magneton***: see MAGNETON; ***Bohr model***: a model of the structure of the hydrogen atom; ***Bohr radius***: the radius of the smallest electron orbit in the Bohr model; ***Bohr('s) theory***: a theory of the structure of the hydrogen atom (and hence of other atoms).

1923 KRAMERS & HOLST *The Atom & the Bohr Theory of its Structure* v. 119 The Bohr model of the hydrogen atom in the simplified form. *Ibid.* 120 In the Bohr atom, likewise, the frequency of revolution *ω* of the electron in its stationary orbit has no direct connection with the frequency of the radiation emitted when the electron passes from this orbit. **1923** H. L. BROSE tr. *Sommerfeld's Atomic Structure* iv. 212 The times of revolution in the Bohr circles are proportional to the cubes of the quantum numbers. *Ibid.* 249 We shall call the value (15) the Bohr magneton. **1927** [see MAGNETON]. **1936** *Nature* 1 Feb. 187/2 The Bohr formula for the Rydberg constant is not correct. **1938** R. A. HOUSTOUN *Treat. Light* (ed. 7) xviii. 335 Bohr's Theory of the Hydrogen Spectrum... Bohr supposed that the electron was circling round the proton, and that the centrifugal force was balanced by the electrostatic attraction. **1956** *Nature* 4 Feb. 241/2 *R* is the Bohr radius, 0·529 A. **1958** *Chambers's Techn. Dict.* 101/1 *Bohr theory*, a combination of the Rutherford conception of the atom as a central, positively-charged nucleus surrounded by planetary electrons, with the quantum theory, which restricts the permissible orbits

in which the electrons can revolve. **1968** J. J. C. SMART *Betw. Sci. & Philos.* iii. 74 The Bohr theory of the atom may appeal to us because it somehow reduces the behavior of atoms to the more familiar behavior of the solar system.

bohreen, var. BOREEN.

boht(e, obs. pa. t. and pple. of BUY *v.*

bohu, bohw, obs. forms of BOUGH.

bohunk ('bəʊhʌŋk). *N. Amer. slang.* [App. f. Bo(HEMIAN + *-hunk*, alt. of HUNG(ARIAN.] A derogatory term for a Hungarian; an immigrant from central or south-eastern Europe, esp. one of inferior class; hence, a low rough fellow, a lout. Also *attrib.*

1903 *Cincinnati Enquirer* 9 May 13/1 Bohunk—A Bohemian; a foreigner. **1910** *Butte* (Mont.) *Even. News* 24 July 1 The bohunk miner is a low grade foreigner who buys his job from the foreman and pays him for keeping it. **1914** G. ATHERTON *Perch of Devil* I. 58 The 'Bohunks', or 'dark men', an inferior class of Southern Europeans. **1921** *Chambers's Jrnl.* 848/2 To condemn his girl to a yellow bohunk like Milroy. **1927** *Daily Tel.* 24 May 17/6 A contractor for railroad ties employing hundreds of the roughest of bohunks to hew and carry them for him. **1930** J. DOS PASSOS *42nd Parallel* I. 82 Bohunk and polak kids put stones in their snowballs. **1963** H. GARNER in R. Weaver *Canad. Short Stories* 2nd Ser. (1968) 52 If you and that bohunk partner of yours had checked the gang press as you're supposed to, Colby mightn't have spoiled so many pieces.

boi-, Sc. spelling of *bō-*: see BO-.

†**boie.** *Obs. rare.* [Identical with Walloon *boie*, in OSp. *boya*, It. *boja* executioner: Diez thinks it may be a transf. use of *boja, boia*, OF. *buie, boye* fetter, chain.] An executioner, a hangman.

c **1320** *Seuyn Sag.* 503 'Blethliche!' the boies quathe. *Ibid.* 960 He het mani a wikke boie His son lede toward the hanging.

boier, obs. f. BOWYER and BEVER *sb. Obs.*

†**boiette.** *Obs.* [perh. for 16th c. F. *boëtte, boete*, variant of *boîte* box, chest, cask: cf. BOIST.] A case or casket.

1525 LD. BERNERS *Froiss.* II. xxx. 87 Ther they founde in boiettes a thre M. frankes.

boigh, obs. form of BUOY.

‖**boiguacu.** [in Tupi *boiguaçú*, f. *boi, boya* serpent + *guaçú, goaçu* big.] A native Brazilian name of the Boa Constrictor or other large boa.

1774 GOLDSM. *Nat. Hist.* (1862) I. i. 148 The boiguacu, which is the largest of the serpent kind, is sometimes forty feet in length.

boikin, obs. variant of BODKIN.

boil (bɔɪl), *sb.*[1] Forms: α. 1 býl, (4 bele, biel, byil, 4–5 bule (*ü*), 5 beel, 4–7 byle, 6 byelle), 3–9 bile; β. 6–7 boyle, 7 boile, 7– boil. [OE. *býl*: com. Teut. = OS. *bûlia (MDu. and MLG. *bûle*, Du. *buil*), OHG. *bûlia, bûlla (MHG. *biule*, mod.G. *beule*:—OTeut. *bûljâ-* str. fem., f. root *bŭl-* in Goth. *uf-bauljan* to blow up. A diphthongal form **baul-* is the base of the cognate ON. *beyla* hump, OF. *beil, bel.* The ME. form was regularly *bile* (Kentish *bele*, s.w. *büle*), which still prevails dialectally: it is not clear whether *boil* is due to association with the verb *boil*, or influenced by the Du. or other form. Cf. BEAL.]

1. A hard inflamed suppurating tumour; a furuncle.

Bile or *Byle*, in nearly all the dialect glossaries.

α. *a* **1000** *Gloss.* in Wr.-Wülcker *Voc.* 5 *Furunculus*, byl. *a* **1300** *Cursor M.* 6011 Bile, and blister, bolnand sare. **1340** *Ayenb.* 224 Goutes and beles. **1382** WYCLIF *Deut.* xxviii. 27 Smyit the the Lord with the byil of Egipt. *Ibid.* 35 The moost yuel biel in knees. —— *Luke* xvi. 20 Houndis camen, and..lickiden his bylis. **1393** LANGL. *P. Pl.* C. XXIII. 84 Bules [*v.r.* byles, belis, boilus] and bocches. **1483** CAXTON *Gold. Leg.* 57/2 Ful of botchis, beelis and blaynes. **1562** BULLEYN *Bk. Simples* 39 a, Painfull sores, Biles and pusshes. **1607** SHAKS. *Cor.* I. iv. 31 You Shames of Rome; you Heard of Byles and Plagues Plaister you o're. **1617** MARKHAM *Caval.* VII. 71 They rise betweene his chappes like a huge Byle. **1737** J. HERVEY *Life & Lett.* (1772) 212 Holy Job healed of his biles. **1748** tr. *Vegetius' Distemp. Horses* 62 He will have ..small Biles in his Back.

β. **1529** MORE *Supplic. Soules* Wks. 292/2 One yt hath but a poore boyle vpon hys finger. **1611** BIBLE *2 Kings* xx. 7 They tooke and layd it on the boile, and he recouered. **1755** JOHNSON, *Bile*, this is generally spelt *boil*; but, I think, less properly. **1782** PRIESTLEY *Nat. & Rev. Relig.* II. 37 The boils..are said..to have been upon Pharoah. **1858** CARLYLE *Fredk. Gt.* (1865) II. VII. iv. 285 The maddest boil..does at length burst, and become an abscess.

b. A swelling [= MDu. *bûle*].

1481 CAXTON *Reynard* (Arb.) 86 And with his feet made two grete bules aboute his eris.

c. *transf.* A swelling on a painted surface resembling a boil; a blister.

1840 DICKENS *Barn. Rudge* lxiv. 303 The paint on the houses..crackled up, swelling into boils.

2. *fig.*

1537 *State Papers Hen. VIII*, II. 410 The chief soare bile and hinderance of his obedience. **1579** J. STUBBES *Gaping Gulf* C iij, A politique bile enflaming the peace of a settled and euen state. **1655** FULLER *Ch. Hist.* VII. i. §21 The Rebellion..which from a small pustle might have proved a painfull bile.

boil (bɔɪl), *sb.*[2] [f. BOIL *v.*]

1. An act of boiling. *spec.* in *N.Z.*, the act of making tea in a billy. Cf. BOIL *v.* 4 c and BOIL-UP.

c **1440** *Anc. Cookery* in *Househ. Ord.* 470 Gif hom but a boyle. **1727** BRADLEY *Fam. Dict.* s.v. *Apricock*, Give 'em seven or eight smart Boils. **1845** ELIZA ACTON *Cookery* ii. (1852) 55 Give the sauce a minute's boil. **1875** URE *Dict. Arts* II. 655 The extrication of gas called the boil, which accompanies the fusion of crown-glass. **1940** W. S. GILKISON *Peaks, Packs & Mountain Tracks* 82 The best part of a tramp on the home hills is the mid-day 'boil'. **1953** B. STRONACH *Musterer on Molesworth* iv. 26 We had a boil and then started the ascent.

2. a. The state of boiling or being at boiling point; also *transf.* and *fig.* a state of agitation.

1813 HOGG *Queen's Wake* 302 The next [moment] nor ship nor shadow was there, But a boil that arose from the deep below. **1837** M. DONOVAN *Dom. Econ.* II. 341 As soon as the liquor comes to a boil. **1861** DICKENS *Gt. Expect.* I. 44 The pudding was already on the boil. **1870** *Daily News* 30 Dec., The coffee was near the boil.

b. *boil-off*, the evaporative loss from liquefied natural gases, esp. methane. Also *attrib.*

1956 *Trans. Inst. Gas Engin.* 1955–56 986 Storage tanks for liquid methane... The heat losses from the spherical tanks were found to be lower than anticipated and the measured rate of 'boil off' was equivalent to 0·23 per cent per day of the tank content. *Ibid.* 988 A vapour connexion to carry away the 'boil off' gas. **1960** *Times* 8 Mar. 17/3 It [*sc.* liquid methane] has been kept in special containers, the 'boil-off' being pumped to the board's Romford works.

3. That which is boiled, a boiling preparation.

1755 *Phil. Trans.* XLIX. 159, I put the linen..into a boil of soap.

4. *U.S.* (See quots.)

1805 CLARK in *Lewis & Clark Exped.* (1905) III. 151 In those narrows the water was agitated in..boils, swells, & whorlpools. **1853** *Putnam's Monthly* Aug. 188/2 These 'boils', as the boatmen call them, are immense upheavings of the moving waters [of the Mississippi]. **1883** 'MARK TWAIN' *Life Mississippi* ix. 120 Those tumbling 'boils' show a dissolving bar and a changing channel there.

5. *Angling.* A sudden bold rise of a fish at a fly. (Cf. BOIL *v.* 11.)

1893 *Field* 17 June 894/3 A fish had made a boil at my fly. **1894** *Daily News* 22 Aug. 5/1 The only hopeful sign is when salmon now and then break the surface of the water with a 'boil', a movement like the rise of a trout.

boil (bɔɪl), *v.* Forms: 3–4 boille, boili, boile(n, 4–7 boyle, 5–6 boyll, 6–7 boyl, 7 boile, 6– boil. Also 4 buyle, ? bayl, ? bele, 5 bule, bulle, bylle, byle, 5–6 boll, 6 *Sc.* bull. [ME. *boille-n, boile-n*, a. OF. *boill-ir* (*boill-ant*), mod.F. *bouillir*:—L. *bullī-re* to form bubbles, to boil.]

1. *intr.* **a.** Of a liquid: To bubble up in agitation through the action of heat causing the lowest portions of the liquid to pass into the gaseous form and escape; to roll about under the influence of heat; also said of the vessel containing the liquid. Also with *up* and *fig.*

1612 W. STRACHEY *Travaile into Virginia* (1849) II. 184/2 To boyle up, potopotawh tawh. **1747** H. GLASSE *Art of Cookery* ix. 94 Let it boil up till it is thorough hot. **1818** W. TUCKER *Fam. Dyer & Scourer* (ed. 2) 61 When this has boiled up, cool down your copper. **1871** L. W. M. LOCKHART *Fair to See* (1872) II. xiii. 62 Just as things were boiling up very satisfactorily to a climax, in came Mrs M'Killop..and cleared them off. *Ibid.* III. xxxv. 150 All this time Mrs M'Killop..had been bridling and boiling up on her sofa, waiting for recognition.

b. To reach the boiling point, to turn from the liquid into the gaseous state. *to boil over*: to bubble up so as to run over the side of the vessel; also said of the vessel. Cf. *run over, overflow*, etc.

a **1225** *Juliana* 72 þis maide isei þis led boili. *a* **1225** *St. Marg.* 247 He let hete water oð seopinge: & þo hit boillede faste. *a* **1300** *Cursor M.* 11886 þai fild a lede o pik and oyle, And fast þai did it for to boile. **1393** GOWER *Conf.* III. 32 Which hath ever his pottes hote Of love boilend on the fire. *c* **1440** *Promp. Parv.* 43 Boylyn ouyr, as pottys on þe fyre, *ebullio.* **1611** BIBLE *Isa.* lxiv. 2 The fire causeth the waters to boyle. **1813** *Domestic Cookery* 249 Room (for the liquor) to boil as quick as possible, without boiling over. **1860** TYNDALL *Glac.* II. §24. 356 Water deprived of its air will not boil at 212° Fahr. **1875** JOWETT *Plato* (ed. 2) I. 53 Putting in anything that we like while the pot is boiling.

2. *transf.* **a.** To move with an agitation like that of boiling water; to bubble, to seethe. Also said of that from which something gushes tumultuously: To overflow *with.*

c **1300** *K. Alis.* 2464 Me myghte y-seo..Heorten blede, braynes boyle. **1382** WYCLIF *Job* xli. 22 He shal make the depthe of the se to boilen as a pot. —— *2 Macc.* ix. 9 Wormes buyliden out of the body of the vnpyteous man. **1388** —— *Ex.* xvi. 20 It bigan to buyle with wormes, and it was rotun. **1526** *Pilgr. Perf.* (W. de W. 1531) 291 b, Myghty newe wyne ..boyleth upward, as though it wolde brast the vessell. **1616** R. C. *Times' Whis.* v. 2061 When the poyson boylde In every veine. **1670** COTTON *Espernon* II. VI. 253 His blood boiling in great quantities out of his mouth. **1725** POPE *Odyss.* III. 357 The storm thickens, and the billows boil. **1820** SOUTHEY *Lodore* 93 Recoiling, turmoiling and toiling and boiling.

b. To undulate like a boiling fluid.

1882 *Observatory* V. 355 The Sun's limb was boiling all about it.

3. *fig.* **a.** Said of passions, persons under the influence of passion, their words, etc. Also *to boil over.* Cf. *the blood boils* in 10 b.

c **1386** CHAUCER *Pers. T.* ¶272 The brennyng of lecchery boylid in al his body. **1393** GOWER *Conf.* I. 294 So boilen up the foule sawes. **1548** UDALL, etc. *Erasm. Par. Luke* xii. 58 Whan his herte thus boiled. **1577** HANMER *Anc. Eccl. Hist.* (1619) 499 The people..boiled with anger. **1625** N. R. tr. *Camden's Hist. Eliz.* I. (1635) 88 O'Neal..boyled in hatred against the English. **1667** MILTON *P.L.* IV. 16 His dire attempt, which nigh the birth Now rowling, boiles in his tumultuous brest. **1761–2** HUME *Hist. Eng.* (1806) IV. li. 60 Resentment was boiling in his sullen, unsociable mind. **1875** JOWETT *Plato* (ed. 2) III. 55 He cannot chafe or boil or get into a state of righteous indignation. **1879** FROUDE *Cæsar* xvii. 288 The political frenzy was now boiling over.

b. *trans. to boil forth*: to give forth in a boiling or agitated manner.

1609 BIBLE (Douay) *Prov.* xv. 2 The mouth of fooles boyleth forth follie.

4. a. *trans.* To cause (a liquid) to bubble with heat (see sense 1); to bring to the boiling point: *esp.* said of food, wholly or partly liquid, in the process of cooking; also of the containing vessel.

c **1420** *Liber Cocorum* 11 Boyle hit and sture lest hit brenne. *a* **1500** *E.E. Misc.* (1855) 34 Sume byllyd mettayl. **1692** *Lond. Gaz.* No. 2800/4 The Copper boyls betwixt 15 and 16 Hogsheads at a time. **1831** CARLYLE *Sart. Res.* II. ix, As kind housewives..were boiling their husbands' kettles.

b. *intr.* (for *refl.*) Cf. *to eat, cut*, etc.

1845 E. ACTON *Cookery* xxi. (1852) 493 The fruit should be finely flavoured, and..should boil easily.

c. *to boil up*: *absol.* to boil or wash clothes. *U.S.* and *N.Z. colloq.* Also (*Canad.* and *N.Z.*), to make tea. Also *to boil the billy*, to make tea (*Austral.* and *N.Z. colloq.*).

1839, 1881 [see BILLY[3] 1]. **1891** [see DAMPER 6]. **1902** B. BAYNTON in Murdoch & Drake-Brockman *Austral. Short Stories* (1951) 42 Blest if I evven fergot t' bile th' billy. **1911** W. H. KOEBEL *In Maoriland Bush* x. 150 When you boil the 'billy', you make tea, *voila tout.* **1929** *Amer. Speech* IV. 338 *Boil up*, to wash your clothes. **1933** E. MERRICK *True North* 30 At three we boiled up again. **1947** P. NEWTON *Wayleggo* (1949) iii. 34 Musterers..carry billies..and 'boil-up'.. when circumstances permit.

†**5.** *fig.* To agitate and inflame, to make fervent (persons or their feelings). *Obs.*

1648 *Eikon Basilike* 115 Let no fire of affliction boil over my passion to any impatience. *a* **1661** HOLYDAY *Juvenal* 237 Wrath boils thy breast! *a* **1704** T. BROWN *Dk. Ormond's Recov.* Wks. I. 49 What lust of power, or what nefarious charms, Ferment your blood, or boil you into arms?

6. To act upon (anything) by continued immersion in boiling liquid; to subject to heat in boiling water. **a.** To cook (solid articles) in this way; **b.** To cleanse (clothes, etc.) by immersion in boiling water; **c.** To prepare, make, or produce by boiling. **d.** To put to death by boiling.

c **1325** *Coer de L.* 2831 In watyr we baylyd the blood. *c* **1386** CHAUCER *Prol.* 383 A Cook they hadde..To boille the chiknes with the Marybones..He koude rooste and sethe and boille and frye. **1556** *Chron. Gr. Friars* (1852) 45 The x. day of March was a mayde boyllyd in Smythfelde for poysynyng of dyvers persons. **1611** BIBLE *Ezek.* xlvi. 20 The place where the Priests shall boyle the trespasse offring. **1641** J. JACKSON *True Evang. T.* II. 107 He is..a Kid.. boyled in his Mothers milk. **1696** *Lond. Gaz.* No. 3145/4 A silver-hilted Sword..was lately Boiled, and the Handle gilt. **1697** DRYDEN *Virg. Georg.* I. 380 Some steep their Seed, and some in Cauldrons boil. **1842** *Penny Cycl.* XXIII. 232 The important improvement of boiling sugar in vacuo. **1842** TENNYSON *Stylites* 51 Martyrs..were stoned, or crucified, Or burn'd in fire, or boiled in oil. **1865** TYLOR *Early Hist. Man.* i, Modes of making fire and boiling food.

7. *intr.* To undergo the action produced by immersion in boiling liquid.

1633 P. FLETCHER *Purple Isl.* I. lvii, Boyling in sulphur, and hot-bubbling pitch. **1813** *Dom. Cookery* VIII. 185 Set it [rice] to boil in milk.

8. *to boil away* (intr.): to evaporate in boiling. *to boil down*: to lessen the bulk of (anything)by boiling; *fig.* to condense, epitomize.

1845 E. ACTON *Mod. Cookery* xxi. (1852) 464 For jams and jellies it [fruit] cannot be too soon boiled down. **1880** *Sat. Rev.* No. 1288. 28 It is surprising to see how much research Mr. S. has sometimes contrived to boil down into a single line.

†**9.** *slang.* To betray. *Obs.*

1602 ROWLANDS *Greene's Cony-catchers* 16 His cloyer or follower forthwith boyles him, that is, bewrayes him. **1611** MIDDLETON & DEKKER *Roar. Girle* Wks. 1873 III. 220 Wee are smoakt..Wee are boyl'd, pox on her!

10. Phrases. **a.** *to boil the pot*: to supply one's livelihood. So *to keep the pot boiling*: also = to keep anything going. Cf. POT.

1808 WOLCOTT (P. Pindar) *Peep at R. Acad.* Wks. 1812 V. 352, I think this Piece will help to boil the pot. **1837** MARRYAT *Dog-Fiend* ix, Huzza, my lads! we'll keep the pot boiling.

b. *the blood boils*: phrase expressing strong emotion, esp. of anger or indignation.

1675 OTWAY *Alcibiades* 38, I am impatient, and my blood boyls high. **1848** MACAULAY *Hist. Eng.* I. 230 The thought of such intervention made the blood, even of the Cavaliers, boil in their veins. **1859** JEPHSON *Brittany* xv. 248 A sight which made his blood boil.

11. *Angling.* Of a fish: to rise boldly at a fly.

1898 J. A. GIBBS *Cotswold Village* viii. 164, I see one [*sc.* a trout] boil up just above that mess of weed.

boilable ('bɔɪləb(ə)l), *a.* That can be boiled.

1882 W. M. WILLIAMS *Science in Short Chap.* 23 They boiled everything that was boilable.

boilary, obs. var. of BOILERY.

boiled (bɔɪld), *ppl. a.* [f. BOIL *v.* + -ED.]

1. a. Brought to the state of ebullition; subjected to boiling; cooked, cleansed, etc., by boiling.

¶ In quot. 1611 ***boiled stuff*** = harlots: with allusion to the sweating-tub.

c **1420** *Liber Cocorum* (1862) 43 þenne boylyd blode take þou shalle. **1562** J. HEYWOOD *Prov. & Epigr.* (1867) 37 We went where we had boylde beefe. **1611** SHAKS. *Cymb.* I. vi. 125 Such boyl'd stuffe As well might poyson Poyson. **1676** *Lond. Gaz.* No. 1137/4 One Set of..Plate Buttons newly boyl'd. **1863** KINGSLEY *Water Bab.* v. 185 To cut such capers as you eat with boiled mutton. **1881** MORLEY *Cobden* I. 245 Where men and women subsisted on boiled nettles. *fig.* **1611** SHAKS. *Wint. T.* III. iii. 4 These boylde-braines of nineteene and two and twenty.

b. *ellipt.* Boiled beef or mutton. *colloq.*

1804 M. EDGEWORTH *Pop. Tales* I. v. 277 Mr. Hill commenced a practice..of going..into the kitchen..to take a slice from the roast or the boiled before it went up to table. **1834**, **1856** [see ROAST *sb.* 2]. **1844** DICKENS *Christm. Carol* (Hoppe) A great piece of cold boiled. **1861** [see STEWED *ppl. a.*[1]].

c. Intoxicated. *slang.* Also phr. ***as drunk as a boiled owl.***

[**1885** *Referee* 31 May 3/3 Twiss..had just the boiled-owlish appearance that is gained by working all night in a printing-office.] **1886** J. A. PORTER *Sks. Yale Life* 156 There is a balm for a headache caused by last night's debauch to have it said you were 'slightly cheered' or 'slewed' or 'boiled'. **1892** *Daily Tel.* 12 Dec. 5/4 The expression, 'Intoxicated as a boiled owl', is a gross libel upon a highly respectable teetotal bird. **1922** JOYCE *Ulysses* 300 He brought him home as drunk as a boiled owl. **1928** *Amer. Speech* IV. 102 Expressions synonymous with or circumlocutory for 'drunk'..blotto, boiled. **1940** 'H. PENTECOST' *24th Horse* (1951) v. 45 He's boiled to the ears.

2. Special Combs.: **boiled crow** (see CROW *sb.*[1] 3); **boiled dinner** (orig. *U.S.*), a dinner of meat and vegetables boiled together; **boiled oil**, a preparation of linseed oil used as a drying-oil; **boiled shirt**, (*a*) *U.S.* a white linen shirt (see SHIRT *sb.* 1); (*b*) a man's dress shirt.

1805 *Pocumtuc Housewife* (1906) 9 Directions for a Boiled Dinner may seem unnecessary. **1897** HOWELLS *Landlord Lion's Head* iii. 13 The woman brought in a good boiled dinner of corned beef, potatoes, turnips, and carrots. **1858** SIMMONDS *Dict. Trade* 43/2 *Boiled oil*, a drying oil made by boiling a small quantity of litharge in linseed oil, till it is dissolved. **1887** F. B. GARDNER *Painters' Encycl.* 53 *Boiled oil*,..an oil which has been brought by the action of heat and of oxidising materials into a state of greater activity, in fact—into a state of incipient slow oxidation. **1921** C. WORTH *Yacht Cruising* (ed. 2) 407 Boiled oil is darker and thicker than raw linseed oil and dries more quickly. **1853** in *Amer. Speech* (1954) XXIX. 7 When I get shaved and get a 'boiled shirt' on, which I have not had on since I left home, for we don't boil our shirts here, for we think cold water quite enough in a country where there is no female society. **1854** [see SHIRT *sb.* 1]. **1872** *Dublin Univ. Mag.* Feb. 219 Every man arrays himself in 'store-clothes' and boiled shirts. **1920** 'SAPPER' *Bulldog Drummond* ii. 47 If one goes about..in boiled shirts while pretending merely to be out for the afternoon, people have doubts as to one's intellect. **1928** D. L. SAYERS *Unpleasantness at Bellona Club* xxi. 266 You've sent for a bloke in a boiled shirt to take your place, I suppose?

boiler (ˈbɔɪlə(r)), *sb.* [f. BOIL *v.* + -ER[1].]

1. One who boils (anything).

c **1540** *Househ. Ord.* 236 That the Cookes and Boylers doe dresse the Meate well. *a* **1691** BOYLE (J.) The boilers of saltpetre. **1835** URE *Philos. Manuf.* 204 Wool-sorters.. fullers or millers, boilers, giggers.

2. a. A vessel in which water or any liquid is boiled.

1725 DE FOE *Voy. round World* (1840) 65 They had built several furnaces and boilers. *a* **1728** WOODWARD (J.) Several pots and boilers before the fire. **1815** ELPHINSTONE *Caubul* II. 187 Messes of ten each, who have a tent, a boiler, and a camel between them.

b. *spec.* In a steam-engine, the large vessel, usually of wrought-iron plates riveted together, in which the water is converted into steam; the tank or vessel commonly attached to a kitchen grate; the vessel in which clothes are boiled before washing.

1757 *Phil. Trans.* L. 54 The engine at the York-buildings Water-works, the boiler of which is 15 feet diameter. **1829** R. STUART *Anecd. Steam Eng.* I. 305 Boilers built solely of cast iron. *Mod.* The boiler of a locomotive burst.

c. ***to bu(r)st one's boiler*** (fig.), to come, or bring, to grief. *U.S. colloq.*

1824 in Thornton *Amer. Gloss.* (1912). **1834** CARRUTHERS *Kentuckian in N.Y.* I. 218 That'll make them think somebody's busted their biler. **1847** PAULDING *Madmen All* 189 May my boiler be eternally busted, if there isn't that are lady.

3. What makes anything boil, as in ***pot-boiler***, a piece of work done to *boil the pot*: see BOIL *v.* 10 a.

4. A vegetable, fruit, etc. suited for boiling.

1812 *Examiner* 5 Oct. 634/1 Having but few Peas at Market..fine boilers are 10s. per quarter dearer. **1864** *Times* 24 Dec., Peas in good demand for all descriptions, and boilers rather dearer.

5. In the West Indies and Bermudas, a sunken coral reef into which the sea breaks with foam and spray.

1909 in *Cent. Dict.* Suppl.

6. *Comb.* and *Attrib.* (in sense 2 b) as ***boiler-house, explosion***; **boiler-alarm**, an apparatus for indicating lowness of water in a boiler; **boiler-deck** *U.S.*, the lower deck of a steamer, lying immediately above the boilers; **boiler-feeder**, an apparatus for supplying a boiler with water; **boiler-float**, a float which by its rising or falling turns the feed-water off or on; **boilerful**, the amount of water or steam that will fill a boiler; **boiler-iron**, rolled iron of $\frac{1}{4}$ to $\frac{1}{2}$-inch thickness, used for making steam-boilers, etc.; **boiler-maker**, a maker of boilers for engines; **boiler-man**, a man who attends to a boiler; **boiler plate** (*a*) = *boiler-iron*; (*b*) *transf.* (*U.S.*), stereotyped or formulaic writing; *spec.* syndicated matter issued to the newspaper press; (*c*) *Mountaineering* (see quot. 1957); **boiler-protector**, a coating to prevent the escape of heat from a boiler; **boiler-smith**, a boiler-maker; **boiler suit**, an outer garment combining overalls and shirt, worn to protect clothing; **boiler-tube**, one of the tubes by which heat is diffused through the water in a boiler.

1840 S. A. HOWLAND *Steamboat Disasters* 131 *Boiler-deck,—being that part of the upper deck situated immediately over the boilers. **1877** HABBERTON *Jericho Road* i. 10 The new hand reached the boiler-deck, and reported to the mate. **1885** *Pall Mall G.* 14 Feb. 7/2 A *boiler explosion..occurred at the Mid Kent Brickworks, Beckenham, yesterday. The *boiler-house was completely demolished. **1883** *Knowledge* 1 June 323/2 A *boilerful of steam. **1851** C. CIST *Cincinnati* 213 The yearly products are ..five hundred tons *boiler-iron, heads, etc. **1877** R. W. RAYMOND *Statistics Mines* 29 It [*sc.* the water-jacket] is constructed of the heaviest boiler-iron. **1865** *Derby Mercury* 25 Jan., The principal engineers and *boiler makers in the united kingdom. **1834** M. SCOTT *Cruise Midge* (1859) 390 The cries of the *Boilermen to the fire makers. **1860** W. FORDYCE *Hist. Coal, &c.* 112 Various descriptions of Iron, such as nail-rods, *boiler-plates, hoop and sheet iron. **1875** URE *Dict. Arts* I. 410 The average resistance of boiler plates is reckoned at 20 tons to the square inch. **1893** *Congress. Rec.* Aug. 465/1 The country weeklies have been sent tons of 'boiler plates' accompanied by..letters asking the editors to use the matter as news. **1905** D. G. PHILLIPS *Plum Tree* 190 He attended to the subsidizing of news agencies that supplied thousands of country papers with boiler-plate matter to fill their inside pages. **1924** J. BUCHAN *Three Hostages* xi. 165 Left me to finish my ascent by way of some very loose screes and unpleasant boiler-plates. **1957** R. G. COLLOMB *Dict. Mountaineering* 32 *Boiler Plates*, Overlapping, undercut slabs of rock; convex slabs are usual. **1965** 'E. MCBAIN' *Doll* (1966) viii. 113 The rest of the will was boilerplate. Meyer scanned it quickly. **1969** *Word Study* Apr. 3/2 Other examples of standard slang are *debugging* and *boiler-plate* (used in regard to formula-type language standard for all reports). **1928** *Sunday Express* 28 Oct. 3/7 The students had thoughtfully attired themselves in *boiler suits. **1949** F. MACLEAN *Eastern Approaches* III. ix. 412 The Prime Minister..was wearing a bright blue boiler-suit.

boiler (ˈbɔɪlə(r)), *v. trans.* To furnish (a steamship) with its boiler or boilers. So ˈ**boilering** *vbl. sb.*

1890 *Whitby Times* 3 Jan. 4/4 The steamers built and launched at this port have to go elsewhere to be engined and boilered. **1897** *United Service Mag.* June 226 The special conditions which..govern the boilering of warships.

boilery (ˈbɔɪlərɪ). Also 6 **boillourie, boilary**. [a. F. *bouillerie* in same sense, f. *bouillir* to BOIL: see -ERY.] A place where boiling or evaporation is carried on; a place for boiling anything, *e.g.* salt or sugar. Usually in comb., as ***sugar-boilery***. See also BULLERY.

1628 COKE *On Litt.* 4 b, By the grant of the boillourie of salt, it is said that the soile shall passe, for it is the whole profit of the soile. **1670** BLOUNT *Law Dict.*, *Boilary* or *Bullary of Salt*, a Salt House, or Salt-pit, where Salt is boiled and made. **1838** HOLLOWAY *Dict. Provinc.*, *Boilary*, a place where salt is boiled.

boiling (ˈbɔɪlɪŋ) *vbl. sb.* [f. BOIL *v.* + -ING[1].]

1. a. The action of bubbling up under the influence of heat; ebullition.

c **1380** WYCLIF *Serm.* Sel. Wks. II. 202 þis boylyng wole after quenche. **1398** TREVISA *Barth. De P.R.* VII. xxxvi. (1495) 251 The heete that makyth boyllynge and sethyng. **1552** HULOET, Bollynge or bubblynge vp of water. **1878** HUXLEY *Physiogr.* 40 Evolved rapidly, with formation of bubbles, as in the ordinary process of boiling.

b. With *down*: the process of boiling or heating something to reduce its bulk or to liberate oil or the like. Also *attrib.*

1848 H. W. HAYGARTH *Bush Life in Australia* vi. 71 The process of 'boiling down', or converting the whole carcase into tallow. **1859** F. FULLER *5 Years' Resid. in N.Z.* viii. 166 A boiling-down price for wethers would be reached in a few years. **1903** *Westm. Gaz.* 31 Jan. 8/1 A Grimsby fishing vessel..if properly equipped with boiling down works could gather the oil [from seals].

2. *transf.* and *fig.* **a.** A bubbling like that of boiling water; disturbance, turmoil, raging. **b.** Heating of the body or mind; violent agitation, inflammation, fever, etc.

1382 WYCLIF *Jonah* i. 15 The se stode of his buylyng. **1398** TREVISA *Barth. De P.R.* XVII. xcii. (1495) 660 Letuse kelyth hete and boyllynge of blood. **1580** BARET *Alv.* B 889 The boyling or risinge vp of water out of a spring. *c* **1660** J. GIBBON in Spurgeon *Treas. David* Ps. cxix. 9 A young man all in the heat and boiling of his blood. **1676** HALE *Contempl.* I. 214 Tortures and boylings of mind. **1882** *Observatory* V. 357 It [a comet] shows a turmoil or boiling of the light about the nucleus.

3. a. The action of heating a liquid to boiling point; of subjecting (anything) to the action of a boiling liquid, esp. so as to cook it; of making or obtaining some substance by this process.

1481–90 *Howard Househ. Bks.* (1841) 422 For the dressynge and boylyng of iij. saltes, ijs. **1631** JORDAN *Nat. Bathes* ii. (1669) 13 The boyling of Beans. **1678** N. WANLEY *Wonders* III. xliii. §15. 224/1 The boyling and baking of Sugar as it is now used. **1719** DE FOE *Crusoe* (1840) I. xvi. 288, I set Friday to work to boiling and stewing. **1725** BRADLEY *Fam. Dict.* I. s.v. *Goose*, Give them fourteen or fifteen Boilings. **1845** E. ACTON *Cookery* vii. (1852) 153 The advantages of gentle simmering over the usual fast boiling of meat.

b. With *down*: the process of condensing or abridging literary matter; *concr.* a condensation or epitome. (See BOIL *v.* 8.)

1898 *Daily News* 27 Jan. 8/4 The book is little more than a boiling-down of the vast literature on the subject. But the boiling-down is well done.

4. That which is boiled or being boiled, a decoction; a quantity boiled at one time: hence ***the whole boiling*** (slang): 'the whole lot'.

1674 N. FAIRFAX *Bulk & Selv.* 113 Syrup, steepings, boylings, setlings or extract. **1837** MARRYAT *Dog-Fiend* xiii, [He] may..whip the whole boiling of us off to the Ingies. *c* **1842** LANCE *Cottage Farm.* 13 This liquor is to be boiled until it is a thick syrrup; skim the boiling.

5. *Comb.* and *Attrib.*, as ***boiling-like*** adj.: **boiling-furnace**, a reverberatory furnace sometimes employed in the decarbonization of cast-iron; **boiling-house**, a building for boiling (soap, sugar, etc.), a boilery; **boiling-heat, -point, -temperature**, the temperature at which anything boils, i.e. turns from the liquid to the gaseous state; *spec.* the boiling-point of water (at the sea level 212° Fahr., 100° Cent.); *fig.* a high degree of excitement, indignation, etc.

1875 URE *Dict. Arts* II. 1001 The construction of the '*boiling' furnace does not materially differ from that of the 'puddling' furnace. **1846** *Punch* IX. 206 The maids have subsided from *boiling-heat to simmering. **1647** HAWARD *Crown Rev.* 30 The *Boyling house. Two Yeomen. **1712** *Act 10 Anne* in *Lond. Gaz.* No. 5012/2 All Soap, Oil, Tallow.. in any private Boiling-house. **1835–6** TODD *Cycl. Anat. & Phys.* I. 629/1 The water..was thrown into a *boiling-like motion. **1773** HORSLEY in *Phil. Trans.* LXIV. 227 M. de luc's *boiling point. **1807** HUTTON *Course Math.* II. 243 At the freezing point is set the number 32, and..212 at the boiling point. **1870** EMERSON *Soc. & Solit.* iv. 55 One man is brought to the boiling-point by the excitement of conversation.

ˈ**boiling**, *ppl. a.* [f. as prec. + -ING[2].]

1. a. Bubbling up under the influence of heat; at boiling temperature.

c **1320** *Seuyn Sag.* 2460 A gret boiland cauderoun. **1501** DOUGLAS *Pal. Hon.* 1318 Full of brimstane, pick, and bulling leid. **1788** GIBBON *Decl. & F.* (1827) VIII. lxiv. 34 Cast headlong into the boiling water. **1832** *Athenæum* No. 219. 17 The cook with the boiling kettle in her hand. **1839** THIRLWALL *Greece* III. 229 Two boiling sulphureous springs.

b. Hyperbolically: extremely hot. *colloq.*

1930 R. LEHMANN *Note in Music* 34 He was the sort of boy who would..declare on the coldest day that he was boiling.

2. *transf.* Violently agitated, raging; fiercely hot; heaving with molecular disturbance.

1382 WYCLIF *Isa.* lvii. 21 As the boilinge se, that resten mai not. **1523** LD. BERNERS *Froiss.* I. cccxxii. 501 None coude abyde there, for it was all a quycke boylyng sande. **1697** DRYDEN *Virg. Georg.* I. 443 Rocks the bellowing Voice of boiling Seas rebound. **1868** T. W. WEBB *Celest. Objects* II. (1873) 39 [The comet] is quite hazy, luminous in the centre, and boiling (atmospherically unsteady).

3. *fig.* Inflamed, in a state of passionate agitation, bursting with passion, etc.

1579 TOMSON *Calvin's Serm. Tim.* 238/2 Mens desires are too much boyling. **1600** HOLLAND *Livy* XXI. x. 398 A youth boyling in ambition. **1672** DRYDEN *Conq. Granada* II. (1725) 44 My boiling Passions settle and go down. **1742** YOUNG *Nt. Th.* VIII. 1175 His understanding 'scapes the common cloud Of Fumes, arising from a boiling Breast. **1836** J. C. YOUNG *Mem. C. M. Young* (1871) 236 She found him in a state of boiling indignation. **1878** MORLEY *Diderot* I. 319.

4. quasi-*adv.*, in phrase ***boiling hot.***

1607 TOPSELL *Four-f. Beasts* 312 Hogs grease and bran boiling hot. **1862** *Enquire Within* 83 It should be poured on boiling-hot.

ˈ**boilingly**, *adv.* [-LY[2].] In a boiling manner.

1817 BYRON *Manfred* I. i. 91 The lakes of bitumen Rise boilingly higher.

boilloury, obs. var. of BOILERY.

† **boiˈloun.** *Obs.* [a. OF. *boillon*, mod.F. *bouillon* bubble, f. *bouillir* to boil.] A bubble.

c **1320** *Seuyn Sag.* 2488 Thise boilouns that boilen seuen.

boil-up (ˈbɔɪlʌp). [f. BOIL *sb.*[2] + UP *adv.*[1]] **a.** = BOIL *sb.*[2] 1; the act of boiling or washing clothes, (*Canad.* and *N.Z.*) making tea, etc. Also *attrib.*

1728 E. SMITH *Compleat Housewife* (ed. 2) 24 Strain out some of the liquor..give it a boil up. **1861** MRS. BEETON *Bk. Househ. Managem.* 103 Mix with it the cream and milk. Give one boil up, at the same time adding the tails. **1933** E. MERRICK *True North* 262 Some of the peas we save for..one of the boil-ups during the day. **1934** *Detective Fiction Weekly* 21 Apr. 108/2 The boil-up can is generally an oil can with the top removed. **1938** J. ROBERTSON *With Cameliers in*

Palestine xiii. 113 No opportunity was lost of having a 'boil up'. **1949** *Here & Now* (N.Z.) Oct. 17/3 Once a week or once a fortnight there's a copper boil-up. **1958** *Tararua* XII. 26 The billy brings to our mind the inevitable *boil-up*, the boiling of the billy for a cup of tea.

b. *transf.* and *fig.*

1871 L. W. M. LOCKHART *Fair to See* (1872) III. xxxiii. 85 Americans, filled with envious admiration by the costliness of the spectacle, were reminded of the superior though somewhat similar 'boil-up' of Mrs Thaddeus G. Cass of Boston, U.S. **1941** BAKER *Dict. Austral. Slang* 11 *Boil-up*, a row or argument. **1963** *Listener* 14 Mar. 477/3 The girl.. swings into a symphonic boil-up of a popular number.

'boily, *sb. dial.* [a. F. *bouillie* in same sense, f. *bouillir* to boil.] A decoction of flour and milk; gruel.

1819 ANDERSON *Cumbld. Ballads* 55. **1855** *Whitby Gloss.*

boily ('bɔɪlɪ), *a.* In 6 byly, 7 boylie. [f. BOIL *sb.*[1] + -Y[1].] Full of, or characterized by, boils.

1559 MORWYNG *Evonym.* 289 Certaine outwarde byly diseases. *a* **1603** T. CARTWRIGHT *Confut. Rhem. N.T.* (1618) 166 They would have turned stricken, made boylie, or some such thing.

†**boin**, *v. Obs. rare.* [f. dial. '*boine* a swelling, Essex' (Way and Halliw.), perhaps = OF. *bugne*, *beugne*, mod.F. *bigne* swelling from a blow: see BUNNY, BUNION.] *intr.* To swell.

1565 GOLDING *Ovid's Met.* VIII. (1593) 206 And with exceeding mightie knubs her heels behind boind out.

boin, var. of BOYNE *Sc.*, a tub.

‖**boina** ('bɔina). [Sp.] A flat cap worn in northern Spain.

1904 GALLICHAN *Fishing in Spain* 19 In his blue boina, a cap resembling the tam-o'-shanter, he looked like a 'braw Scot'. **1922** *Chambers's Jrnl.* 15 July 519/2 He wore a hat of soft black felt or else a *Boina* (the Biscayan bonnet). **1937** *Times* 16 Nov. 17/6 All over Spain the traditionalists donned their red *boinas* and rose in the name of Don Carlos to battle with innovation. **1957** R. CAMPBELL *Coll. Poems* II. 153 The scarlet boinas trickled to the plain.

†**'boinard.** *Obs.* Also boyn-. [a. OF. *buisnart*, *buinard* silly fellow.] A fool, simpleton; rogue, scoundrel.

a **1300** *Siriz* 288 (Mätz.) Be stille, boinard. **1399** LANGL. *Rich. Redeless* I. 110 Than wolde oþer boynardis · haue ben abasshyd. *Ibid.* II. 164þe blerneyed boynard · þat his bagg stall.

boing (bɔɪŋ), *int.* Also boing boing. [Echoic.] The noise made when a compressed spring is suddenly released; a reverberating sound.

1952 B. CLEARY *Henry & Beezus* i. 21 'Boi-i-ing!' shouted the two boys together. **1957** MANVELL & HUNTLEY *Technique Film Music* iii. 156 Gerald is the despair of his parents since he cannot talk; he only speaks sound effects of which the most formidable is the familiar 'boing' of the cartoon world, a noise made by a short length of strong wire spring attached to a sounding board. *Ibid.* 157 He didn't talk words. He went 'boing-boing' instead. **1967** I. HAMILTON *Man with Brown Paper Face* iv. 60 He had big coil springs fitted to the heels of his boots and with a merry *boing boing* he would spring out from the night shadows to confront ladies on the street. **1967** A. J. MARSHALL in L. Deighton *London Dossier* 141 The newest and nicest tower block is Centre Point—boing!

†**boiny**, *a. Obs. rare.* [f. *boine* sb. (see BOIN *v.*) + -Y.] Full of swellings, knotty.

1615 W. HULL *Mirr. Maiestie* A 4 b, For Mercury is not earned out of euery boynie block.

bois, boist, obs. Sc. form of BOSS *a.* BOAST.

‖**bois brûlé** (bwa bryle). *N. Amer.* [Fr., 'burnt wood'.] An American Indian half-breed, esp. one of French and Indian extraction.

In popular use corrupted into *bob ruly*.

1805 LEWIS in *Deb. Congress* 1047 The Tetons Bois brûlè killed and took about 60 of them last summer. **1840** C. F. HOFFMAN *Greyslaer* III. 260 Of Guisbert or Guise, as the 'Bois-brulé', or half-blood child was generally called, we have as yet been enabled to gather but few traditions. **1878** J. H. BEADLE *Western Wilds* xxix. 380 Most of the drivers were of the pure Bois Brules stock. **1960** *Press* (Vancouver) Dec. 14 The result of the Bay proclamations was to provoke civil disobedience on the part of the boisbrules and active opposition by the Nor' westers.

‖**bois d'arc** (bwa dark). *N. Amer.* Also bow-dark, ‖bodok. [Fr., 'wood of bow'.] The wood of the osage orange, used by American Indians for making bows.

1805 *Ann. 9th Congr. 2 Sess.* 1138 At this place Mr. Dunbar obtained one or two slips of the '*bois d'arc*'. **1848** BARTLETT *Dict. Amer.*, *Bow-dark tree* (Fr. *bois d'arc*), a western tree, the wood of which is used to make bows with. **1853** R. B. MARCY & MCCLELLAN *Expl. of Red River* 98 (Bartlett), The bows [of the Comanches] are made of the tough and elastic wood of the bois d'arc, or osage orange. **1877** R. I. DODGE *Hunting Grounds Gt. West* 348 The best wood [for bows] is the Osage Orange (*bois d'arc* of the old French trappers, corrupted into 'bow dark' by plains Americans).

‖**boiserie** (bwazəri). [Fr.] Wainscoting, wooden panelling.

1832 S. AUSTIN tr. *Pückler-Muskau's Tour German Prince* III. 196 The walls of the dining room are covered with oaken boiserie. **1833** J. DALLAWAY *Discourses Archit. Eng.* v. 312 The walls of the state-chambers were painted, and sometimes lined with wainscot, of curious carved *boisserie* on the panels. **1909** *Daily Chron.* 20 Mar. 4/5 The ball-room.. is panelled with dark French boiserie work, the wood embellished with gilding. **1940** *Horizon* II. Nov. 263 A shadowy, oval room with gilt boiseries.

†**boist**, *sb. Obs.* Forms: 3–5 boist(e, 4–7 boyste. Also 3 buste, 5 bust; 4, 6 bost, 6–7 boost(e; 4 bouste; 5 buist, buyste, 9 *Sc.* buist. See BOOST, BUIST, BUST. [ME. *boiste*, a. OF. *boiste* 'box', in Pr. *bostia*, repr., through late L. *bossida*, *boxida*, *buxida*, L. *pyxida*, a. Gr. πυξίδα, acc. of πυξίς box (Brachet). The phonetic history of the variant forms in Eng. and Sc. is obscure: but *uy* is prob. an early variant of *oi*, and the forms in *o*, *u*, seem due to simplification of the diphthong, as in 16th c. Sc. *jone* = *join*, etc.]

1. A box, a casket; chiefly used of a box for ointment, a vase or flask for oil, etc. (= BOX *sb.*[2] I.)

a **1225** *Ancr. R.* 226 He haueð so monie bustes [*v.r.* boistes] ful of his letuaries. *a* **1300** *Cursor M.* 14003 (Gött.) A boist of smerles has scho nomin. **1362** LANGL. *P. Pl.* A. XII. 68, I haue a gret boyste At my bak, of broke bred þi bely for to fylle. *c* **1375** ? BARBOUR *St. Nicolaus* 294 Scho has brocht A boyst of oyle. *c* **1400** *Destr. Troy* 883 He anoyntide hym anon with his noble boyste. *c* **1450** LONELICH *Grail* xvii. 131 The awngel took a boist with oynement anon. **1633** *Treas. Hid. Secrets* cxv, Also of the wood of Rosemarie, make a boyst to smell thereto.

b. *bleeding-boist*: a cupping-glass.

c **1440** *Promp. Parv.* 38 Bledynge boyste, *ventosa, guna.*

2. Dialectal name for a rude hut. [? same word.]

1840 *Times* 24 Apr. 3/6 Along the London and Brighton line of Railway there have been erected a great number of rude huts or cabins.. For the use of these places to sleep in, the workmen pay, each 1*s.* or 1*s.* 6*d.* a-week—two and not unfrequently three of them sleeping together in these 'boists'.

†**boist**, *v. Obs. rare.* [f. prec. sb.] *trans.* To cup, to scarify. (Cf. BOIST *sb.* 1 b.)

c **1440** *Promp. Parv.* 42 Boyston, *scaro, ventoso.*

†**'boisterly**, *adv. Obs.* = BOISTEROUSLY.

1520 WHITTINTON *Vulg.* (1527) 41 Boysterly and rudely to anoye hym that sytteth next hym.

boisterous ('bɔɪstərəs), *a.* Forms: 5–8 boistrous, 6–7 boystrous, boysterous, 6 bou-, bowstrous, 6– boisterous. [Used in the same sense as the earlier *boisteous*, *boistuous*, BOISTOUS, of which it appears to be a variant modified by some obscure analogy.]

I. Rough or coarse in quality.

†**1.** Rough, coarse, as *e.g.* food. *Obs.*

1474 CAXTON *Chesse* III. i, The labourer of the erth vseth grete and boistrous metis.

†**2.** Of rough, strong, or stiff texture; stout, stiff, unyielding. *Obs.*

1572 tr. *Buchanan's Detect. Mary* in H. Campbell *Love-lett. Mary* (1824) 135 She could abide at the poop, and.. handle the boisterous cables. **1577** HOLINSHED *Chron.* III. 915/1 Hauing vpon him a great gowne of boisterous veluet. **1586** WARNER *Alb. Eng.* II. viii. (1612) 37 About his boistrous necke full oft their daintie armes they cast. **1594** T. B. *La Primaud. Fr. Acad.* II. 33 Hee hath not made the ligaments.. nor the sinewes of any such boisterous or stiffe matter. **1700** DRYDEN *Sigismonda & G.* 59 The leathern out-side, boistrous as it was, Gave way.

†**3.** Roughly massive, bulky, big and cumbrous.

1596 SPENSER *F.Q.* I. viii. 10 His boystrous club. **1633** J. FOSBROKE *Warre or Conflict* 30 Goliah, notwithstanding.. his huge and boisterous armour, etc. **1641** R. BROOKE *Eng. Episc.* I. x. 59 The Pandects of the Civill Law are too boystrous, and of too great extent for any Civilian to comprehend. **1642** MILTON *Apol. Smect.* Wks. (1851) 292 If the work seeme more triviall or boistrous then for this discourse.

†**4.** Rough to the feelings; painfully rough. *Obs.*

1592 SHAKS. *Rom. & Jul.* I. iv. 26 Is loue a tender thing? it is too rough, Too rude, too boysterous, and it pricks like thorne. **1595** —— *John* IV. i. 95 Feeling what small things are boysterous there [in the eye].

†**5.** Rough in operation; not skilful or delicate.

1609 PAULE *Abp. Whitgift* 28 This bishop was not so boysterous a surgeon.

†**6.** Strong- or coarse-growing, rank. *Obs.*

1622 WITHER *Philar.* in *Juv.* (1633) 590 [The pool] overgrowne with boystrous Sedge. **1671** MILTON *Samson* 1164 As good for nothing else, no better service, With those thy boysterous locks.

II. Acting roughly, violent.

†**7.** Violent in action or properties. *Obs.*

1544 PHAËR *Regim. Lyfe* (1560) N ii b, The saide venime is so swift, so fearce, and so boistrous of itselfe. **1645** MILTON *Colast.* Wks. (1851) 349 A boisterous and bestial strength. **1695** WOODWARD *Nat. Hist. Earth* VI. (1723) 294 The Heat becomes too powerful and boisterous for them.

8. Of wind, weather, waves, etc.: Rough, the opposite of 'calm'.

1576 THYNNE *Ld. Burghley's Crest* in *Animadv.* App. iv. (1865) 113 In calme or boystrous tyde. **1596** DRAYTON *Leg.* iii. 488 The boyst'rous Seas. **1684** *Contempl. State of Man* I. ii. (1699) 20 A boystrous Wind had blown away the Leaves. **1726–7** BOLINGBR. in *Swift's Lett.* (1766) II. lxxiii, This boisterous climate of ours. **1836** MACGILLIVRAY tr. *Humboldt's Trav.* xxi. 299 A boisterous passage of twenty-five days. **1843** PRESCOTT *Mexico* (1850) I. 194 Finding some difficulty in doubling a boisterous headland.

9. Of persons and their actions.

†**a.** Full of rough violence to others, violently fierce, savage, truculent. *Obs.*

1581 MARBECK *Bk. of Notes* 753 Those boysterous Nemrothes, that neuer will be satisfied with the slaughter of Innocents. **1593** SHAKS. *3 Hen. VI*, II. i. 70 Oh.. boyst'rous Clifford, thou hast slaine The flowre of Europe. **1681** E. SCLATER *Serm. Putney* 11 What care boisterous Enemies for what these can do unto them? **1713** POPE *Frenzy J.D.* in *Swift's Wks.* (1755) III. I. 144 By your indecent and boisterous treatment of this man of learning, I perceive you are a violent sort of person. **1791** COWPER *Iliad* v. 370 Distant from the boisterous war.

b. Rough and violent in behaviour and speech, turbulent; too rough or clamorous. (Orig. in a distinctly bad sense, but gradually passing into c.)

1568 T. HOWELL *Newe Sonets* (1879) 139 Feare not his boustrous vantinge worde. **1593** SHAKS. *Rich. II*, I. i. 4 Heere to make good yᵉ boistrous late appeal. **1667** E. CHAMBERLAYNE *St. Gt. Brit.* I. I. iii. (1743) 8 The men are strong and boisterous, great wrestlers, and healthy. **1690** CROWNE *Eng. Frier* I. i. 3 Pox o' this boystrous fool. **1705** OTWAY *Orphan* v. xix. 2296 Stand off thou hot-brain'd boistrous noisy Ruffian. **1853** MARSDEN *Early Purit.* 55 Every form of church government.. had for awhile its boisterous advocates.

c. Abounding in rough but good-natured activity bordering upon excess, such as proceeds from unchecked exuberance of spirits.

a **1683** SIDNEY *Disc. Gov.* iii. §25 (1704) 334 That boisterous humor being gradually temper'd by disciplin. **1709** STEELE *Tatler* No. 45 ¶8 Their boisterous Mirth. **1752** HUME *Ess. & Treat.* (1777) I. 5 It renders the mind incapable of the rougher and more boisterous emotions. **1822** W. IRVING *Braceb. Hall* xix. 167 A rich, boisterous, foxhunting baronet. **1848** MACAULAY *Hist. Eng.* I. 213 Under the outward show of boisterous frankness.

†**10.** quasi-*adv.* Boisterously. *Obs.*

1595 SHAKS. *John* IV. i. 76 Alas, what neede you be so boistrous rough?

boisterously ('bɔɪstərəslɪ), *adv.* [f. prec. + -LY[2].] Roughly; violently; tumultuously; with rough and superabundant energy.

a **1550** *Christis Kirk Gr.* xii, The buff so boisterously abaist him, That he to the eard dusht doun. **1595** SHAKS. *John* III. iv. 136 A Scepter snatch'd with an vnruly hand, Must be as boysterously maintain'd as gain'd. **1670** MILTON *Hist. Eng.* Wks. 1738 II. 118 Godwin and his Sons did many things boistrously and violently. **1845** LD. CAMPBELL *Chancellors* (1857) V. cxi. 201 Respectable politicians have seen reason.. to join those whom they have been accustomed boisterously to assail. **1871** M. COLLINS *Mrq. & Merch.* I. ii. 66 With Big Dog boisterously bounding from side to side.

'boisterousness. [f. as prec. + -NESS.] Boisterous quality; rude strength (*obs.*); violence, tempestuousness; rough behaviour.

1589 WARNER *Alb. Eng.* VI. xxxi. (1612) 153 But checked of my boystrousnesse [I] was balked with a blush. **1618** BOLTON *Florus* III. ii. (1636) 166 The thing which most frighted the Barbarous was the sight of the elephants, as those which matcht themselves in boistrousnesse. **1656** TRAPP *Comm. Thess.* iii. 15 A stoical sourness, or an imperious boisterousness. **1726** *Nat. Hist. Irel.* 28 The Irish sea.. in regard of its boysterousness and.. tempestuousness. **1873** HOLLAND *A. Bonnic.* iv. 71 Boys whose surplus vitality happened to lead them into boisterousness or mischief.

†**'boistly**, *adv. Obs.* = BOISTOUSLY.

c **1400** *Beryn* 104 The Preest & the clerk ful boystly bad me goon. *Ibid.* 163 Then passid they forth boystly, goglyng with hir hedis.

†**boistness, boyste-.** *Obs.* = BOISTOUSNESS.

1398 TREVISA *Barth. De P.R.* XIX. viii. (1495) 866 Some bodyes letteth all passage of syghte, so that no thynge is seen there thurgh, As boystenesse, stones, trees and metall.

†**'boistous**, *a. Obs.* Forms: 3–6 boistous, boystous, buystous(e, (also 4 booistous, boystoyse, 5 boistose, boistoys, boistez, boysteis), buystuous, boystuys, (bostuous, bioustious), 5–6 boystows(e, boi-, boysteous, -ious, 6 buistous, boystuous(e, (bostyous). Also, *North.* 4 bostwys, bustwys, (boustes), 4–5 boustous, 5–6 bustus, *Sc.* bustows(e, boustous, bousteous, -tious, busteous, -ious, -uous, -uus. [Of uncertain etymology. Certainly not connected with *bost*, BOAST (as has been suggested on the ground of the 16th c. Sc. spelling *boist* for *bōst*). The phonology and form suggest French origin, and in form the ME. word exactly answers to OF. *boisteus*, AF. *boistous*, mod.F. *boiteux* lame; but no connexion of sense appears to be traceable, at least if the etymology proposed by Diez for the French word from *boiste* 'box', 'knee-joint' holds good. The essential meaning in Eng. from the first appears to have been 'coarse, rough', but senses 1–4 are all nearly equally early. The later variants *boisteous*, *boystuous*, led to the modern BOISTEROUS.

(The mod. Cornwall dialect has in WCorn. *boist* corpulence, *boustis*, *bustious* stout, overfat, burdensome to oneself; in ECorn. *boostis* fat, well-conditioned: cf. sense 3. This occurrence of a sense so long obs. in literary Eng., and esp. of an apparent radical sb. *boist*, not known at all in literature, is very curious: but there are no similar words known in Celtic Cornish. The Welsh *bwyst* 'wildness' appears to be a figment of Owen Pugh, but *bwystus* 'wild,

ferocious' occurs in the 14th c., and may be a deriv. of an obs. **bwyst*:—L. *bēstia*; or it may be merely the ME. *buystous*.)]

1. Of persons, etc.: Rough, rude; untaught, rustic; coarse, unpolished.

c **1300** *K. Alis.* 5659 It is boystous folk. **1340** *Ayenb.* 103 We þet byeþ greate and boystoyse to spekene of zuo heȝe þinge. **1387** TREVISA *Higden* Rolls Ser. II. 311 Men þat were vnkonnynge and boistous as bestes. **1388** WYCLIF *2 Chron.* xiii. 7 Roboam was buystuouse [Vulg. *rudis*, **1382** rude]. **1494** FABYAN v. cxix. 96 The state of holye Churche in Brytayne was as yet rude and boystyous. **1500** *Ortus Voc.* in *Promp. Parv.* 42 *Rudis, indoctus, inordinatus, quasi ruri datus*, boystous. **1513** DOUGLAS *Æneis* I. Prol. 48 Weill ma I schaw my burell busteous thocht. **1547** BOORDE *Introd. Knowl.* 160 They be rude & rusticall, & very boystous in theyr speche.

2. Full of rude strength and fierce vigour; rough, fierce, savage; powerful, violent in action. (Often an epithet of the *boar* or *bear*.)

c **1325** *E.E. Allit. P.* A. 910 Bustwys as a blose. **1387** TREVISA *Higden* (1865) I. 291 þe men þere of beeþ boistous men of dedes. *Ibid.* Rolls Ser. II. 251 Nemproth the bostuous [*robustus*] oppressor of men. ? *a* **1400** *Morte Arth.* 774 A blake bustous bere. **1483** CAXTON *Gold. Leg.* 56/3 By strong hande he shal late you goo and in a boystous he shal caste you fro his land. **1539** TAVERNER *Erasm. Prov.* (1552) 5 A strong disease requyreth a stronge medecine..A boysteous horse, a boysteous snaffell.

3. Roughly massive; bulky; clumsy.

(Still dial.; see note to Etymology.)

c **1325** *E.E. Allit. P.* A. 813, Brede vpon a bost-wys bem. ? *a* **1400** *Morte Arth.* 2175 The boustous launce þe bewelles attamede. **1485** CAXTON *Chas. Gt.* 29 Of body he was moche ample & boystous of stature. *a* **1547** EARL SURREY *Æneid* IV. 582 Like to the aged boysteous bodied oke. **1567** TURBERV. *Poems* in Chalmers *English Poets* II. 616/2 Time makes the tender twig to bousteous tree to grow.

4. Coarse in texture, gross, rough; thick, stiff.

1388 WYCLIF *Matt.* ix. 16 No man putteth a clout of buystous clothe in to an elde clothing. **1398** TREVISA *Barth. De P.R.* III. xvi, þe laste and þe moste boystous of alle [the senses] is gropynge, for þe kynde þerof is erþi. *c* **1450** *Merlin* xi. 168 Grete boysteis shone of netes leder. **1578** LYTE *Dodoens* I. xxix. 41 Medesweete..hath..leaues..rough, boysteous and harde.

5. Rough, loud or violent in sound.

c **1430** LYDG. *Bochas* VI. xv. (1554) 143 b The boystous thunder. *c* **1450** HENRYSON *Mor. Fab.* 30 Hee heard ane bousteous Bugill blaw. *c* **1460** *Towneley Myst.* 195 Youre wordes ar bustus. **1552** LYNDESAY *Monarche* IV. 5597 That terribyll Trumpat..That boustious blast thay sall obey.

6. Of the wind, sea, weather: Rough and violent, BOISTEROUS.

1470 HARDING *Chron.* clxxxiv. ii, The wind was so boistous..houses and trees Were blow doune. **1548** UDALL, etc. *Erasm. Par. Matt.* xvi. 3 A foule and a boystuouse day. **1553** EDEN *Treat. New Ind.* (Arb.) 33 The sea was very rough, and the wether stormie and boysteous. **1571** GOLDING *Calvin on Ps.* xviii. 8 Boystowse vyolence of wyndes.

† **'boistously**, *adv. Obs.* For forms see prec. [f. prec. + -LY².] With rough violence, roughly, rudely, coarsely, violently, boisterously.

c **1386** CHAUCER *Clerkes T.* 735 He on a day in open audience ffol boistously [*Harl. MS.* boystrously] haþ seyd hire this sentence. **1447** BOKENHAM *Seyntys* (1835) 68 Hys doughtir he smote ful bustously Up on the cheke. **1513** DOUGLAS *Æneis* I. ii. 53 Thai [winds] vmbesett the seis busteously. **1549** CHALONER *Erasm. on Folly* ii, Than cometh Silenus..with Poliphemus boisteously stampyng. **1583** GOLDING *Calvin's Serm. Deut.* xl. 237 If we reproue them boystowsly without any charitable affection.

† **'boistousness.** *Obs.* [f. as prec. + -NESS.]

1. Rudeness, roughness, lack of polish, want of gentleness or courtesy.

? *c* **1450** *Chaucer's Dreme* 64 Of your gentilnesse I you requyre my boistousnesse Ye let passe, as thing rude. **1526** *Pilgr. Perf.* (W. de W.) 110 Ungentylnesse or buystousnesse.

2. Coarseness, grossness, stiffness.

1398 TREVISA *Barth. De P.R.* VI. xxii, þe whiche mete for his þiknesse and boystousnesse may not passe þe narow weyes..wiþ oute helpe of moysture of drynke. **1530** PALSGR. 199/1 Boystuousnesse, *roydevr*.

3. Violence, boisterousness.

1530 PALSGR. 200 Boustuousnesse, *impetuosite*. **1548** UDALL, etc. *Erasm. Par. Matt.* xiv. 30 (R.) The boysteousnes of the winde. **1571** GOLDING *Calvin on Ps.* xxv. 17 Temptacions now and then cast us downe with their boustousnesse.

† **'boisture.** *Obs. rare*⁻¹. Boisterousness.

1667 WATERHOUSE *Fire London* 55 To proportion the fire to its breadth as well as boisture of fury.

boit, obs. Sc. form of BOAT *sb.*

‖**boîte** (bwat). [Fr., lit. 'box'.] A small restaurant or night-club. Also *boîte de nuit*.

1922 W. S. MAUGHAM *Writer's Notebk.* (1949) 188 They'd gone to *boîte* after *boîte* till every penny was spent. **1925** A. HUXLEY *Along Road* I. 6 In a Montmartre *boîte*..sat three young American girls. **1932** J. LAVER *Nymph Errant* v. 101 *Boîtes de nuit* where the sham *apaches* were paid so much a night to impress the gaping visitor. **1942** D. POWELL *Time to be Born* (1943) i. 26 'Jean's', the new little *boite*..with red-checked tablecloths and a sixty-five cent dinner. **1960** *Harper's Bazaar* Aug. 60 The *boîtes* of the Left Bank. **1968** *Times* 13 Nov. 10/4 The opening of this first boite de nuit in the new shopping and entertainment centre of Kalininsky Prospekt.

bok, bokardo, variant of BUCK, BOCARDO.

bok(e, bokere, obs. ff. BOOK, BOOKER.

bokay (bəʊ'keɪ). Repr. a vulgar pronunciation of BOUQUET.

1848 THACKERAY *Van. Fair* xxix. 248 Bedad it's him..and that's the very bokay he bought in the Marshy aux Flures! **1904** E. NESBIT *Phoenix & Carpet* iii. 62 'What! all them lovely bokays for me!' exclaimed the enraptured cook. **1947** N. MARSH *Final Curtain* xvi. 244 She..asked in that ghastly voice for what she called her bokay.

† **boke**, *v. Obs.* exc. *dial.* Also **boak**. [Of uncertain origin, but app. akin to POKE *v.*] *intr.* and *trans.* To thrust or push out; to butt, to poke.

1601 HOLLAND *Pliny* I. 326 Armed with two long hornes boking out before them. **1610** —— *Camden's Brit.* (1637) 99 On the reverse a bull boaking with his hornes. **1649** BAXTER *Saints' R.* III. xvi. §xi. *marg.* (1651) As Hens in a coop alwaies boaking to get out. **1674** RAY *N.C. Wds.* 6 To *Boke* at one, to Point at one. *Chesh.* **1874** E. WAUGH *Chimney C.* in *Lanc. Gloss.*, I boked my finger at his oppen e'e.

boke, obs. pa. t. of BAKE *v.*, north. var. BOLK *v. obs.*, to belch, and obs. f. BUCK.

† **bo-keik.** *Obs. Sc.* [cf. KEIK.] = BO-PEEP.

1535 LYNDESAY *Satyre*, Thay play bo-keik, even as I war a skar. [Now *Keik(a)bo*.]

bokel, bokeler, obs. ff. BUCKLE, BUCKLER.

bokeram, bokram, obs. ff. BUCKRAM.

bokesy(e, early form of BOCASIN.

boket(t, obs. form of BUCKET.

Bokhara (bəʊ'kɑːrə). Also **Bukhara**. The name of a town and district in the Uzbek Soviet Socialist Republic, applied *attrib.* to a rug or carpet made there. Also *absol.*, a rug or carpet of this kind.

1913 T. E. LAWRENCE *Home Lett.* (1954) 246 The little Bokhara you have was a very exceptional find. **1918** W. S. CATHER *My Antonia* (1919) II. xiv. 265 The deep, velvety red that is in Bokhara carpets. **1936** A. CHRISTIE *Cards on Table* xv. 149 He'd got some good rugs. Two Bokharas and three or four really good Persian ones. **1941** L. MACNEICE *Plant & Phantom* 53 Flicking the ash On the Bokhara rug. **1966** *Guardian* 16 June 8/3 We owned also two Bokharas, one white and one red.

‖**bokmakierie** (bɔkma'kiri). *S. Afr.* Also **bac-**, and variants. [Afrikaans, onomatopœic.] The shrike *Telephorus zeylonus* of southern Africa.

1834 *C.G.H. Lit. Gazette* IV. 52 (Pettman), The..cry of the backbacery. **1852** GODLONTON & IRVING *Kaffir War, 1851-2* 247 (Pettman), The cry of the back-my-keerie (whip-poor-will). **1867** E. L. LAYARD *Birds S. Afr.* 161 Its loud call of 'bacbakiri', its imitative powers, and bright plumage, render it one of the most conspicuous birds of the colony. **1949** *Cape Argus* 15 Oct. (Magazine) 2/6 One of the most familiar birdcalls in this country is that of the bokmakierie. The loud, ringing note of this handsome yellow and green shrike may be heard almost anywhere. **1966** E. PALMER *Plains of Camdeboo* xii. 197 Here soon would be shrikes in numbers, the yellow, green and black bokmakierie with its clear, melodious calls, and that shocking little cannibal, the butcher bird or fiscal shrike.

boko ('bəʊkəʊ). *slang.* Also (*U.S.*) **boke**. [Origin unknown.] The nose.

1859 G. W. MATSELL *Vocabulum* 13/2 Boke, the nose. **1874** HOTTEN *Slang Dict.*, *Boko*, the nose. Originally pugilistic slang, but now general. **1879** BESANT & RICE *Seamy Side* (1880) i, 'Conk or boko,' said Nicholas the vulgar. 'It's all the same.' **1901** G. B. SHAW *Admir. Bashville* II. i. 313 Flush on the boko napped your footman's left. **1910** C. E. MONTAGUE *Hind let Loose* i. 12 Brumby got one for his nob... Bellona's other bridegroom took it on the boko.

bokulle, bokyll, obs. ff. BUCKLE.

bol, bolace, obs. ff. BOLE, BULL, BULLACE.

bolar ('bəʊlə(r)), *a.* [f. BOLE *sb.* + -AR¹: cf. F. *bolaire*.] Consisting of, or of the nature of, bole.

1676 *Phil. Trans.* XI. 615 Some are marly..some bolar, some sandy, some talky, some limy. **1791** HAMILTON *Berthollet's Dyeing*, I. Introd. 20 Some of the bolar earths were likewise employed [in washing]. **1852** TH. ROSS tr. *Humboldt's Trav.* II. xxiv. 502 The bolar and sigillated earths of Lemnos, which are clay mingled with oxide of iron.

† **'bolary**, *a. Obs.* [f. as prec. + -ARY.] = prec.

1646 SIR T. BROWNE *Pseud. Ep.* 67 Chiefly consisting of a bolary and clammy substance.

‖**bolas** ('bolas), *sb. pl.* Also used as a sing., with *pl.* bolases. [Sp. (and Pg.): pl. of *bola* ball; used in S. America in sense given.] A missile, used by the Patagonians and other S. American tribes, consisting of two or more balls or stones connected together by strong cord; these are swung round the head and discharged at the animal to be captured, so as to wind round and entangle it.

1843 CARLYLE *Misc.* (1857) IV. 270 Flourishing their nooses and bolases. **1860** GOSSE *Rom. Nat. Hist.* 201 The Guachos are able to entangle them [birds] with the bolas or weighted cord. **1865** LUBBOCK *Preh. Times* 430 The weapons which are most characteristic of the Patagonians..are the bolas. **1874** BOUTELL *Arms & Arm.* vi. 87 The Patagonians of Southern South America have the Bola and the Lasso.

bolas, obs. form of BULLACE.

† **bolbanac, bolbonac.** *Obs. Herb.* The plant 'Honesty' (*Lunaria biennis*).

1578 LYTE *Dodoens* II. vi. 154 The Herboristes..do call this herbe by a certayne barbarous and strange name Bolbonac. **1597** GERARD *Herbal* cxvii. §1 Bolbonac or the Sattin flower. **1640** PARKINSON *Theat. Bot.* 1366 *Viola Lunaria sive* Bulbonach.

† **bold** *sb. Obs.* Also 2-3 **bolde**, 4 **boolde**. [OE. *bold*, dwelling, is, according to Sievers, prob. for **bodl*, **boðl*, **boþl*, which also appears as *botl*, identical with OSax. *bodl-*, ON. *ból* (:—*boðl*):—OTeut. **boþlo-*, from *bu-*, *bo-*, 'dwell' + instrumental suffix *-tlo* = *-tro* (Gr. -τλο-, -τρο-). Parallel examples are OE. *seld* = *setl*, north. *seþel* 'seat, settle', also *nǽld* = *nǽdl*, **nǽþl* 'needle', *áld* = *ádl*, **áþl* 'disease'. It appears that original *þ* before *l* and *m* became in certain circumstances (after short vowel) *t*: cf. *botm* for *boþm*, OHG. *bodam*. The ON. *ból* from *boðl* has many parallels: *mál*:—*maðl*; *stál*:—*staðl*, etc. See BOTTLE *sb.*¹] A dwelling, habitation, building.

a **1000** *Beowulf* 1998 Wæs þæt beorhte bold tobrocen. *c* **1250** *Hymns Virg.* in *Trin. Coll. Hom.* 257 Bring us to þine bolde. *c* **1270** *Earth* in *E.E.P.* 152 Er erþe go to erþe bild þi long bold. **1297** R. GLOUC. 383 þe fayre halle, & oþer bold, þat hys fader let rere. **1387** TREVISA *Higden* Rolls Ser. VI. 169 He made hem bulde meny booldes.

bold (bəʊld), *a.* Forms: 1-4 **bald**, 3- **bold**, 4-7 **bolde**, 4-5 **boold(e**, 6 **bould**, 7 **boulde**. Also, 1 *WSax.* **beald**, 2-4 **beld**, 3 **bæld**; *north.* 3-6 **bald**, 3 **baald**, 4-5 **balde (bowde)**, 5- **bauld**, 6 **bawlde**. [Com. Teut.: OE. *bald* (in WSax. *beald*) = OS., OHG. *bald*, MHG. *balt-des* (whence mod.G. *bald* adv. 'quickly'), MDu. *bout -de*, Du. *boud*, ON. *ball-r*, Goth. **balþs*, only found in derivatives, as *balþei*, *balþjan*:—OTeut. **balþo-z*. No related words appear outside Teutonic.]

1. a. Of persons: Stout-hearted, courageous, daring, fearless; the opposite of 'timid' or 'fearful'. Often, with admiration emphasized = *brave*.

a **1000** *Ags. Ps.* cxviii. [cxix.] 162 Ic blissiȝe bealde mode. *c* **1205** LAY. 16325 þus bælde Hængest..cnihten alre hændest. *Ibid.* 25410 Speke we of Arthur, baldest alre kinge. **1297** R. GLOUC. 465 King Stefne was the boldore. *c* **1314** *Guy Warw.* (A.) 669 Feir & beld to tellen by. *a* **1340** HAMPOLE *Pr. Consc.* 6855 Swa hardy es na man, ne swa balde. *c* **1380** WYCLIF *Serm.* Sel. Wks. II. 36 So myȝten boolde men seie, to þes ordris. *c* **1400** *Destr. Troy* 5952 So bold was no buerne his bir to withstond. *c* **1470** HENRY *Wallace* II. 354 Baulder in battaill. **1593** SHAKS. *Lucr.* 1430 When their brave hope, bold Hector, march'd to field. **1611** BIBLE *Prov.* xxviii. 1, The righteous are bolde as a lyon. **1790** BURNS *Tam O'Shanter*, Inspiring bold John Barleycorn! **1842** TENNYSON *To J.S.* viii, A man more pure and bold and just Was never born. **1863** C. ST. JOHN *Nat. Hist. Moray* vii. 171 The Cormorant..is a bold, confident bird.

fig. **1611** SHAKS *Wint. T.* IV. iv. 125 Pale Prime-roses..bold Oxlips, and the Crowne Imperiall.

b. *absol.* A bold man. Now only pl. *the bold*.

a **1300** *Cursor M.* 16055 He beheilde þa bitter bald. ? *a* **1400** *Morte Arth.* (Roxb.) 81 That many a bolde sythen a bought. *c* **1400** *Destr. Troy* 1210 Lamydon..Bare don mony bolde. *Ibid.* 1405 Mony boldes (?) for þat bright in batell be kylde. **1852** TENNYSON *Ode Wellington* v, There he shall rest for ever Among the wise and the bold.

c. quasi-*adv.* = BOLDLY.

1593 SHAKS. *Rich. II*, I. iii. 3 The Duke of Norfolke, sprightfully and bold, Stayes but the summons of the Appealants Trumpet. **1598-9** *Parismus* II. (1661) 24, I have the boldir presumed to detain you. **1786** BURNS *To Edinb.*, Bold-following where your fathers led!

2. Of words, actions, etc.: Showing or requiring courage; daring, brave.

a **1250** *Owl & Night.* 1715 þurh belde worde. *c* **1320** *Seuyn Sag.* (W.) 2042 A dede queinte and beld. *c* **1340** *Cursor M.* 7033 Of troye & grece þo batailes bolde [*Cott.* bald]. **1597** SHAKS. *2 Hen. IV*, IV. v. 197 All these bold Feares..I haue answered. **1667** MILTON *P.L.* II. 386 The bold design Pleas'd highly those infernal States. **1712** POPE *Rape Lock* I. 11 In tasks so bold can little men engage? **1844** THIRLWALL *Greece* VIII. lxv. 351 [He] ventured on a very bold step. **1875** JOWETT *Plato* (ed. 2) I. 11 My former bold belief in my powers of conversing.

3. Phrases. ***to make (so) bold, to be (so) bold***: to venture, presume so far as, take the liberty (*to do* a thing). † ***to make*** or ***be bold with*** (*obs.*): to take liberties, make free with.

c **1385** CHAUCER *L.G.W.* 879 Ho hath been so bold..to sle myn lyf [i.e. Pyramus]. **1393** GOWER *Conf.* II. 259 Iason..upon Medea made him bolde Of art magique. *a* **1535** MORE *Edw. V.* (1641) Ded., I am bould to crave your patronage herein. **1596** SHAKS. *Tam. Shrew* I. ii. 251 Sir, let me be so bold as aske you. **1598** —— *Merry W.* II. ii. 262, I will first make bold with your money. **1599** —— *Much Ado* III. ii. 8. **1601** —— *Jul. C.* II. i. 86, I thinke we are too bold vpon your Rest. **1613** —— *Hen. VIII*, III. ii. 318 You made bold To carry into Flanders, the Great Seale. **1676** 'A. RIVETUS, JUN.' *Mr. Smirke* K ii b, Because they were all Christians, they thought..they might make the bolder with them, make bolder with Christ, and wound him again. **1699** BENTLEY *Phal.* 216 Whether of these our Author made bold with, I cannot determin. **1852** MCCULLOCH *Taxation* II. ix. 337 We are bold to say that no instance can be found. **1876** GLADSTONE *Homeric Synchr.* 166 Nothing, I make bold to say, can be more improbable.

4. a. In bad sense: Audacious, presumptuous, too forward; the opposite of 'modest'.

c1200 ORMIN 2185 Son se maȝȝdenn wurrþeþþ bald, 3ho wurrþeþþ sone unnþæwedd. c1250 *Gen. & Ex.* 323 'Eue', seide he, ðat neddre bold, 'Quat oȝet nu ðat for-bode o-wold'. 1340 *Ayenb.* 216 Naȝt þe bolde ne þe naȝt ssamueste. c1440 *Promp. Parv.* 43 Bolde, *presumptuosus, effrons.* 1501 DOUGLAS *Pal. Hon.* II. 987 Ane deuill of hell, Is na compair to the iniquitie, Of bald wemen. 1505 *Answ. Secret Instr. Hen. VII resp. Q. Naples,* Not to bolde, but somewhat shamefast womanly. 1605 SHAKS. *Lear* I. iv. 263 Men so disorder'd, so debosh'd, and bold, That this our court.. Shewes like a riotous Inne. 1733 POPE *Hor. Sat.* II. i. 106 The bold front of shameless, guilty men. 1847 TENNYSON *Princ.* III. 233 You are bold indeed: we are not talk'd to thus. *Mod.* A bold young woman.

†**b.** *absol.* An audacious or shameless person. *Obs.*

a1300 *Cursor M.* 8693 Do me bote a-gain þis bald. *Ibid.* 15378 Þat ilk es he, þat baald.

c. quasi-*adv.*

a1300 *Cursor M.* 7131 Vn-to þat birde was biddand bald, Sampson al þe soth hir tald.

5. Strong, mighty, big. (*obs.*) Of grain, etc.: Well-filled, plump. Of fire or wind: Strong, fierce (*Sc.*)

c1300 *K. Alis.* 5004 Wymmen there ben mychel and belde. c1314 *Guy Warw.* (1840) 149 Forestes ful of hertes beld. a1400 *Cov. Myst.* 3 He sent to Noe an Angel bolde. c1505 DUNBAR *'Now cumis Aige'* ii, Trew luvis fyre nevir birnis bauld. 1513 DOUGLAS *Æneis* XIII. iv. 65 The bald flambis and brym blesis stowt. 1724 RAMSAY *Tea-t. Misc.* (1733) I. 114 Boreas with his blasts sae bauld. 1787 WINTER *Syst. Husb.* 186 Being a bolder and better grain, weighed heavier. 1818 SCOTT *Rob Roy* xxix, 'An the brandy hadna been ower bauld for your brain.' 1864 *Times* 8 Dec., Coffee ..sold at 69*s.* to 72*s.* 6*d.*, for good to fine ordinary bold.

†**6.** Confident (*in*), certain, sure (*of*). *Obs.*

a1300 *Cursor M.* 2675 Qua es not sua þai mai be bald, þai sal not o mi folk be tald. c1400 *Ywaine & Gaw.* 169 This ilk Knight, that, be ye balde, Was lord and keper of that halde. c1435 *Torr. Portugal* 2440 We wylle hym kepe and we may, Thereof be ye bold! c1440 *York Myst.* viii. 119 He wille be my beylde, þus am I bowde. 1526 *Pilgr. Perf.* (W. de W. 1531) 17b, We sholde be bolde of his grace. 1588 SHAKS. *Tit. A.* v. i. 13 Be bold in vs, weele follow where thou lead'st. 1609 HOLLAND *Amm. Marcel.* XVIII. iv. 109 Bearing himselfe bold of helpe from those nations. 1611 SHAKS. *Cymb.* II. iv. 2, I would I were so sure To winne the King, as I am bold, her Honour Will remaine her's. 1616 R. C. *Times' Whis.* ii. 703 These he dares be bolde, And more then these.

7. *fig.* Showing daring, vigour, or licence of conception or expression; vigorous, striking.

a1667 COWLEY (J.) The figures are bold even to temerity. a1687 WALLER (J.) Bold tales of gods or monsters. 1737 POPE *Hor. Epist.* II. ii. 165 Mark where a bold expressive phrase occurs. 1763 JOHNSON in *Boswell* xv. (1848) 137/1, I do not think Gray a first-rate poet. He has not a bold imagination.

8. a. 'Standing out to the view; striking to the eye' (J.); firmly marked, 'pronounced'.

1678 J. PHILLIPS *Tavernier's Trav.* II. I. x. 64 Had it been finish'd..it had excell'd all the boldest structures of Asia. 1753 *Scots Mag.* July 318/2 Her pulse easy, bold, and regular. 1775 SHERIDAN *Rivals* III. iv. (1883) 115 I'll write a good bold hand. 1850 MRS. STOWE *Uncle Tom's C.* xxi. 225 His curling hair hung round a high, bold forehead. 1857 H. MILLER *Test. Rocks* iii. 144 Standing out in bold relief. 1867 LADY HERBERT *Cradle L.* vii. 175 The walls are panelled with precious inlaid marbles, in bold patterns.

b. *Typogr.* Of type = BOLD-FACE 2. Also *ellipt.* or as *sb.*

c1871 V. & J. FIGGINS *Types Specimen Bk.*, Pica Bold Italic. Long Primer Bold Italic. Brevier Bold Italic. Nonpareil Bold Italic. 1884 *Type in Use at Messrs. Parker's Printing Office, Oxford* May 25 Pica bold..brevier bold.. nonpareil bold..pearl bold. 1933 D. L. SAYERS *Murder must Advertise* viii. 132 Can you cut away the headline and re-set in Goudy Bold? 1962 *Which? Car Suppl.* Oct. 114/1 Version tested [*sc.* is printed] in **bold**.

9. In *Nautical* lang., applied to a coast rising steeply from deep water; also, to the deep water close to such a shore: also, in ordinary lang., to any broad, steep or projecting face of rock. Of a ship: Broad and bluff in the bows.

1628 DIGBY *Voy. Medit.* (1868) 13 It is a bold shore. 1697 DAMPIER *Voy.* (1729) I. 34 A bold Shore, that is, high land and deep water close home by it. 1787 T. JEFFERSON *Writ.* (1859) I. 96 At Honfleur..they can ride in bold water, in a good bottom. 1793 SMEATON *Edystone L.* §170 Built unusually bold in their Bows. 1810 SCOTT *Lady of L.* I. v. 12 The pine-trees blue On the bold cliffs of Ben-venue. 1860 *Merc. Mar. Mag.* VII. 196 The soundings..show bold water, from 19 to 75 fathoms, close in shore. 1862 ANSTED *Channel Isl.* I. v. (ed. 2) 111 The southern part of St. Ouen's Bay is extremely bold. 1867 SMYTH *Sailor's Word-bk.*, *Bold-shore,* a steep coast where the water, deepening rapidly, admits the near approach of shipping without the danger of grounding. *Ibid.*, *Bold-to,* steep-to.

10. *Comb.*, as *bold-hearted, -spirited;* BOLD-FACE.

1853 DE QUINCEY *Sp. Mil. Nun* Wks. III. 23 Our bold-hearted Kate. 1597 HOOKER *Eccl. Pol.* v. Ded., Confident and bold-spirited men. 1603 KNOLLES *Hist. Turks* (1638) 286 One of the souldiers..a rough bold spirited fellow.

†**bold,** *v. Obs.* Forms: see BOLD *a.* [OE. *bealdian,* = OHG. *baldên,* f. *bald* adj.: see prec.]
1. *intr.* To be, or show oneself, bold; to become bold, grow strong or big.

a1000 *Beowulf* 4360 Swa bealdode beorn Ecgþeowes. a1300 *Cursor M.* 7539 To gar þam wit hope to bald. c1420 *Pallad. on Husb.* XII. 223 And ther is warme eke hugely thai [plum-trees] bold. c1425 *Seven Sag.* (P.) 640 The wenche bygane to bolde. 1534 LD. BERNERS *Gold. Bk. M. Aurel.* (1546) K k vij, Oure hardines soo boldeth. 1706 DE FOE *Jure Div.* IX. 201 No tame Subjection did their Kingdoms yield, But bolding courted Freedom in the Field.

2. *trans.* To make bold, embolden, encourage.

c1205 LAY. 4385 To balden þine leoden [c1275 to boldi]. a1300 *Cursor M.* 10425 Men suld bald þam to be blith. c1300 *K. Alis.* 2468 His Gregeys ful faire he boldith. 1377 LANGL. *P. Pl.* B. III. 198, I batered hem on þe bakke and bolded here hertis. 1535 COVERDALE *Deut.* iii. 28 Geue Iosua his charge, and corage him and Bolde him. c1540 LADY BRIAN in Ellis *Orig. Lett.* II. II. 79 Now et boldethe me to shew yow my powr mynd. 1605 SHAKS. *Lear* v. i. 26 It toucheth us, as France invades our land, Not bolds the king.

b. To make (a fire) strong or fierce. *north. dial.*

a1400 *Sir Perc.* 792 He tase the knyghte bi the swire, Keste hym reghte in the fyre The brandes to balde. *Mod. Sc.* 'To bauld the glead', to kindle the glowing coal, i.e. to make the fire bold, to blow it up. *Roxb.* (Jamieson).

bold, obs. f. BOLT *sb.*[1]

†**bold-beating,** *a. Obs.* App. a confusion of *bold-faced* and *brow-beating.*

1598 SHAKS. *Merry W.* II. ii. 28 You..will en-sconce your red-lattice phrases, and your bold-beating-oathes, vnder the shelter of your honor.

†'**bolden,** *v. Obs.* exc. *dial.* Also 6–7 **boulden.** [f. BOLD *a.* + -EN[2].]
1. *trans.* To make bold, embolden, encourage. *refl.* To take courage, 'make bold' (*to do* a thing).

1526 TINDALE *1 Cor.* viii. 10 Shall not the conscience of hym that is weake be boldened to eate those thynges. 1530 PALSGR. 459/2 It is good to bolden a boye in his youth. 1535 COVERDALE *1 Sam.* xiii. 12, I boldened my selfe, & offred a burntofferynge. 1709 KENNET tr. *Erasm. Praise Folly* 46 These..bolden us likewise and spur us on.

2. *intr.* To take courage, be bold. *dial.*

1864 ATKINSON *Whitby Gloss.*, 'Bowden tiv her man! faint heart never won fair lady.'

Hence '**boldened** *ppl. a.*, '**boldening** *vbl. sb.*

1575 TURBERV. *Bk. Venerie* 182 For the better boldnyng and encouraging of them. 1595 SPENSER *Sonn.* v, Boldned innocence. 1621 BOLTON *Stat. Irel.* 333 [*Act 11 Eliz.*], The boldening and incouraging of many offendours. 1628 FELTHAM *Resolves* I. lviii. Wks. (1677) 90 Vice braves it with a boldned face.

†'**bolden, boldne,** *v.*[2] *Sc. Obs.* Also **bowden.** [var. BOLNE to swell, with *d* generated between *l* and *n.*] *intr.* To swell.

a1510 DOUGLAS *K. Hart* 78 Boldning to ryis the castell to confound. 1513 —— *Æneis* I. viii. 73 The fluide boldnit [ed. 1710 boldynnyt], and stormy Orion..catit ws anon. 1536 BELLENDEN *Cron. Scot.* Excus. Prentar (JAM.) Sum boldin at othir in maist cruel feid. 1597 J. MELVILL *Diary* (1842) 428 Invy and Malice Did bowden in the breist of craftie men.

†'**bolden, -in,** *pa. pple. Sc.* (*obs.*) Also **boulden, bowden, -in.** [var. of BOLLEN: cf. prec.] Swollen.

1536 BELLENDEN *Cron. Scot.* (1821) II. 112 The river.. was be inundation of snawis, boldin above the brayis. 1553 LYNDESAY *Monarche* 3885 They grew so boildin [*MS. E.* boldin], in thare breistis. 1567 *Sempill Ballates* (1872) 30 That bowdin bludy beist. c1590 A. HUME *Thanks Summ. Day,* The birds, with boulden throats. 1768 ROSS *Helenore* 61 (JAM.) Her breast with wae was bowden.

bolder, var. of BOULDER.

bold-face ('bəʊldfeɪs). [f. BOLD *a.* + FACE *sb.*]
1. One who has a bold face; an impudent person; also *attrib.*

1692 R. LESTRANGE *Fables* (1708) I. cclxiii. 279 How now Bold-Face, crys an Old Trot. 1741 RICHARDSON *Pamela* I. 43 If I have been a Sauce-box, and a Bold-face, and Pest, and a Creature, as he calls me. 1793 J. WOLCOTT (P. Pindar) *Apple-dumplings* Wks. I. 100 A ragged, bold-face, ballad-singing crew. 1859 DICKENS *T. Two Cities* III. ii, 'Well, I am sure, Boldface! I hope you are pretty well!'

2. Bold-faced type; also *attrib.*.

1889 *Cent. Dict.*, Bold-face. 1902 DE VINNE *Pract. Typogr., Processes Type-making* (ed. 2) i. 50 A bold-face with hair-lines and serifs too weak. 1905 F. H. COLLINS *Authors' & Printers' Dict., Bold-face type*..indicated in MS. by wavy underlining. 1931 *Boys' Mag.* XLV. 148/1 To use Roman, *italic,* and bold face capitals, and lower case as well as numerals, signs, borders, etc., one needs no fewer than 225 characters.

bold-faced ('bəʊldfeɪst), *ppl. a.* [f. as prec. + -ED.] **1.** Having a bold or confident face or look; usually impudent. Hence '**bold-facedness** *sb.*

1591 SHAKS. *1 Hen. VI,* IV. vi. 12 Prowd desire Of bold-fac't Victorie. 1635 QUARLES *Embl.* I. viii. (1718) 34 Bold-fac'd Mortals in our blushless times Can sing and smile, and make a sport of crimes. 1818 SCOTT *Hrt. Midl.* xxxiii, A fine, gay, bold-faced ruffian. 1832 L. HUNT *Transl.* Poems 264 The least pain to thy bold-facedness.

2. Used to designate type with a thick or 'fat' face, such as 'Clarendon' or 'antique'.

1890 WEBSTER, Bold-faced. 1902 DE VINNE *Pract. Typogr., Processes Type-making* (ed. 2) xii. 331 A bold-faced clarendon with strong bracketed serifs.

†'**boldhede.** *Obs.* [f. BOLD *a.* + *-hede,* -HEAD.] Boldness, audacity.

a1250 *Owl & Night.* 514 I-fallen is al his boldhede. 1330 R. BRUNNE *Chron.* 281 His boldhede did þam wynne.

boldly ('bəʊldlɪ), *adv.* [f. BOLD *a.* + -LY[2].] In a bold manner.
1. Courageously, daringly, fearlessly.

a1000 *Juliana* (Gr.) 492 Sume..ic bealdlice..minum hondum..sloȝ. c1205 LAY. 19923 þer wes Bruttene weored: baldeliche isomned [c1275 boldeliche gadered]. c1305 *St. Christ.* 36 in *E.E.P.* (1862) 60 Cristofre hem mette baldeliche. 1375 BARBOUR *Bruce* III. 14 He bauldly thaim abaid. 1480 *Robt. Devyll* 30 He thought boldlyer for to abyde. 1611 BIBLE *Mark* xv. 43 Ioseph of Arimathea..went in boldly vnto Pilate, and craued the body of Iesus. 1728 YOUNG *Love Fame* iii. (1757) 101 They who boldly dare, Shall triumph o'er the sons of cold despair. 1876 GREEN *Short Hist.* v. §1 (1882) 223 The Prince seized the opportunity to fall boldly on their front.

2. In bad sense: With effrontery, impudently, shamelessly; presumptuously.

1387 TREVISA *Higden* Rolls Ser. IV. 281 His sones.. stryue þe boldloker [*licentius*]. c1400 *Apol. Loll.* 108 Fro hem þat beggun wiþ out nede..or for oþer vndu caus beggen baldly. c1440 *Promp. Parv.* 43 Boldely or malapertly, *effronter, presumptuose.* 1586 THYNNE *Animadv.* Introd. 70, I have like blind baiard boldlie run into this matter. a1656 BP. HALL *Rem. Wks.* (1660) 150 He..that can sin the boldlyest. 1785 T. JEFFERSON *Corr.* (1830) 423 Their principle is to lie boldly that they may not be suspected of lying.

3. Confidently, with assurance; without doubt, without hesitation; assuredly.

c1175 *Lamb. Hom.* 125 Alswa baldeliche mei þe wrecchesta mon clepian drihtan him to federe. a1300 *Cursor M.* 3586 Baldlik þat dar i sai. c1384 CHAUCER *H. Fame* 581 Be ful assured boldely I am thy frende. c1400 *Destr. Troy* 840 Ye shall boldly be blameles. c1420 *Chron. Vilod.* 388 Wherfore y dar wryte and baldelyche say. 1563 *Homilies* II. *Sacrament* (1859) 442 So may we the boldlier have access thither. 1695 LD. PRESTON *Boeth.* II. 48, I dare boldly affirm, that, etc. 1810 COLERIDGE *Friend* (1865) 138 To hope too boldly of human nature.

4. With bold expression or handling; strongly, vigorously, strikingly.

1762 H. WALPOLE *Vertue's Anecd. Paint.* I. 158 Several other figures, boldly painted, but not highly finished. 1828 COLERIDGE *Eolian Harp* 18 Its strings Boldlier swept.

†**boldly,** *a. Obs.* Also 3 **baldli,** 4 **baldeli.** [f. BOLD *a.* + -LY[1]; cf. *goodly.*] Bold-looking.

a1300 *Cursor M.* 16032 (Gött.) Wid a ful baldli chere. *Ibid.* 8541 (Trin.) He was a boldly bachilere. 1819 *Blackw. Mag.* IV. 730 Scan ye near Those boldly lineaments.

boldness ('bəʊldnɪs). [f. BOLD *a.* + -NESS.] The quality of being bold.
1. Courage, daring, fearlessness.

c1400 *Destr. Troy* 226 That the flese..Were brought throw þi boldness into þis big yle. 1489 CAXTON *Faytes of A.* II. xxxv. 151 The rommayns yssued ayenst hym by grete boldnes. 1577 tr. *Bullinger's Decades* (1592) 175 There is demaunded a boldnesse of stomacke to dare to doe the thing. 1597 SHAKS. *2 Hen. IV,* II. i. 134 You call honorable Boldnes, impudent Sawcinesse. 1690 LOCKE *Hum. Und.* II. xxiii. (1695) 156 Boldness is the Power to speak or do what we intend, before others, without fear or disorder. 1876 GREEN *Short Hist.* v. §3 The boldness of his words sprang perhaps from a knowledge that his end was near.

†**b.** *to take* (*a* or *the*) *boldness*: to venture, to take the liberty (*to do* a thing). *Obs.* or *dial.*

1526 *Pilgr. Perf.* (W. de W. 1531) 74b, The serpent toke a boldnesse to tempte the woman. 1650 FULLER *Pisgah* II. x. 211 The Amorites took the boldness to keep possession thereof. c1680 BEVERIDGE *Serm.* (1729) I. 273 Who are we, that we should take the boldness to ask any thing of him? [1864 *dial.* (*Epsom, Surrey*), 'Father's boldness, Ma'am, and he've sent you a few flowers.']

2. Impudence, shamelessness, presumption.

1377 LANGL. *P. Pl.* B. XVIII. 386 þe boldnesse of her synnes. c1440 *Promp. Parv.* 43 Boldenesse or homelynesse, *presumpcio.* 1594 SHAKS. *Rich. III,* I. ii. 42 Vnmanner'd Dogge..Ile strike thee to my Foote, And spurne vpon thee Begger for thy boldnesse. 1601 —— *All's Well* II. i. 174 A strumpets boldnesse. 1602 MANNINGHAM *Diary* (1868) 10 Nov., I told her of her saucy boldness. 1850 TENNYSON *In Mem.* cxiii, Should licensed boldness gather force.

†**3.** Confidence, assurance, security. ***upon boldness of***: in reliance on, on the security of. *Obs.*

1330 R. BRUNNE *Chron.* 40 For boldenes he wild him bynd to som berde in boure. 1447–8 SHILLINGFORD *Lett.* (1871) 91 Upon boldenysse of the said nywe charter. a1535 MORE *Edw. V,* in Southey *Comm.-pl. Bk.* Ser. II. (1849) 91 Unthrifts riot and run in debt upon boldness of these places. 1603 SHAKS. *Meas. for M.* IV. ii. 165 In the boldnes of my cunning, I will lay my selfe in hazard. a1656 BP. HALL *Occas. Medit.* (1851) 28 Perfect righteousness shall give us perfect boldness both of sight and fruition. [1717 DE FOE *Hist. Ch. Scot.* 6, I take upon me with Boldness to assure the World, it is not so.]

4. *transf.* Vigour or freedom of conception or execution; forcibleness.

a1700 DRYDEN (J.) The boldness of the figures is to be hidden, sometimes by the address of the poet. 1777 ROBERTSON *Hist. Amer.* (1783) II. 209 Rivalling the great masters..in boldness of design. 1826 DISRAELI *Viv. Grey* VI. vi. 345 Brilliancy of colouring and boldness of outline. 1856 RUSKIN *Mod. Paint.* III. IV. iii. §20 There is as much difference between the boldness of the true and the false masters, as there is between the courage of a pure woman and the shamelessness of a lost one.

boldo ('bɒldəʊ). Also **boldu.** [Sp., a. the native Chilean word.] An evergreen tree of Chile, *Peumus boldus;* also, a medicinal preparation of the leaves of this tree, formerly used as a tonic.

1717 tr. *Frézier's Voy. to South-Sea* 78 The woods are full of Aromatick Trees, as..*Boldu,* the Leaf whereof smells like Frankincense. 1872 *Pharm. Jrnl. & Trans.* 26 Oct. 323/2 The boldo is a tree indigenous to Chili..and belongs to the order *Monimiaceæ.* 1908 *Practitioner* Aug. 339 Slight cholagogues, such as..boldo. 1924 RECORD & MELL *Timbers Tropical Amer.* II. 172 *Peumus Boldus* Mol...is an aromatic evergreen tree 40 to 60 feet high, growing on the dry sunny hills in Chile, where it is known as the 'boldo' or 'boldu'. 1934 *Brit. Pharm. Codex* 255 Boldo is now used principally in the form of tincture, as a diuretic and supposed liver stimulant. 1934 *Tropical Woods* XXXIX. 20 The leaves of *Peumus* yield a product known under such names as 'Folia

Boldo' and ' Boldo Leaf Oil', from which a stomachic is derived; this was formerly an article of commerce, but by 1900 had apparently become obsolete. **1951** G. H. M. Lawrence *Taxon. Vascular Plants* 512 Chilean boldo wood ..sometimes reaches our markets [in the U.S.A.] as a rarity for cabinet work.

Hence **'boldin** [-IN[1]], a glucoside having hypnotic properties found in the boldo; **'boldine** (also †*boldeine*, †*boldina*) [a. F. *boldine* (Bourgoin & Verne 1872, in *Jrnl. de Pharm. et de Chim.* XVI. 191): see -INE[5]], a bitter, light-sensitive alkaloid, $C_{19}H_{21}O_4N$, found in the boldo and formerly used as a hypnotic; **boldo'glucin** = BOLDIN.

1872 *Pharm. Jrnl. & Trans.* 26 Oct. 323/2 The leaves.. contain an essential oil and an organic alkali, to which the authors propose to give the name of boldine. **1907** *Brit. Pharm. Codex* 167 The leaves also contain a bitter alkaloid, boldine..and a glucoside, boldin or boldoglucin. **1928** Solis-Cohen & Githens *Pharmacotherapeutics* 1189 Boldo ..contains..a glucoside (boldin or boldoglucin), an alkaloid (boldeine or boldine), gum and tannin. **1939** T. A. Henry *Plant Alkaloids* (ed. 3) 324 Boldine, like bulbocapnine, antagonises but does not invert the action of adrenaline in raising blood pressure.

†**'boldship.** *Obs.* [see -SHIP.] Boldness.

c **1275** Lay. 24943 Hire baldsipe [*c* **1205** ræhscīpe] sal ȝam seolue: to moche rouþe teorne.

boldspreet, obs. form of BOWSPRIT.

bole[1] (bəʊl). also 7 **boal(e**, 7–8 **boll.** [a. ON. *bol-r* masc., also written *bulr*, trunk of a tree; cf. MHG. *bole* (fem.), mod.G. *bohle* plank.]

The stem or trunk of a tree.

c **1314** *Guy Warw.* (1840) 260 His nek is greter than a bole. *c* **1325** *E.E. Allit. P.* B. 622 By bole of þis brode tre we byde þe here. **1521** Fisher *Wks.* (1876) 315 The shadowe of the bole of the tree. **1641** Evelyn *Mem.* (1857) I. 32 Five upright and exceeding tall suckers, or bolls. **1677** Plot *Oxfordsh.* 158 Whose boughs shoot from the boal fifteen or sixteen yards. **1727** Bradley *Fam. Dict.* s.v. *Dressing*, Boughs and Suckers, which have made themselves and the Boll knotty. **1848** Lytton *Harold* I. 306 Gnarled boles of pollard oaks and beeches. **1870** Bryant *Iliad* IV. I. 129 A fair, smooth bole, with boughs Only on high.

b. *transf.* Anything of a cylindrical shape like the trunk of a tree, as a roll, a pillar.

1676 *True Gentleman's Delight* (N.) Make it up in little long boles or rowles. **1884** *Pall Mall G.* 11 Jan. 1/2 The sky ..seen between the boles of stone.

c. *Comb.*, as †*bole-fashion* adv., *bole-like* adj.

1578 Lyte *Dodoens* IV. I. 508 Another Holy, whose roote is not bolefashion. **1854** H. Miller *Sch. & Schm.* (1858) 313 The bole-like stems of great plants.

bole[2] (bəʊl). Also 4 **bol**, 5–6 **boole.** [ad. med.L. *bōlus*, a. Gr. βῶλος clod of earth; first used in Eng. in *bole armeniac* or *armoniac*: thence extended to similar substances.]

1. The name of several kinds of fine, compact, earthy, or unctuous clay, usually of a yellow, red, or brown colour due to the presence of iron oxide.

1641 French *Distill.* iii. (1651) 78 Such things as will flow must have bole, or powder of brick mixed with them. **1645** Evelyn *Mem.* (1857) I. 143 A..paper of a red astringent powder, I suppose of bole. **1686** *Phil. Trans.* XVI. 144 It may perhaps be better reckon'd amongst Boles than Stones. **1759** B. Martin *Nat. Hist. Eng.* I. 73 A red Bole, called by the Country People Redding, or Ruddle. **1843** Portlock *Geol.* 152 A soft clayey amygdaloid, decomposing into a rich and deep red bole. **1868** Dana *Min.* 476.

b. *spec.* **bole armeniac**, formerly also *armoniak*, etc.: an astringent earth brought from Armenia, and formerly used as an antidote and styptic.

c **1386** Chaucer *Chan. Yem. Prol. & T.* 238 Bol armoniak [armonyak, -ac, amoniak] verdegres, boras. **1547** Boorde *Brev. Health* liii. 24 Take of Terre sigillate, of boole Armoniake, of eche an unce. **1558** Warde *Alexis' Secr.* (1568) 40b, Take..Bolearmenicke. **1591** Percivall *Sp. Dict.*, *Bolarmenico*, Bolearminack. **1607** Topsell *Four-f. Beasts* 34 Plaister is made thereof with Bole-Armorick. **1610** Markham *Masterp.* II. cxxxii. 435 Take of bolearmony a quarterne. **1626** Bacon *Sylva* §701 Bole-Arminick is the most Cold of them. **1718** Quincy *Compl. Disp.* 107 Bole Armonick..is a natural Earth. **1758** J. S. *Le Dran's Observ. Surg.* (1771) 94 A Defensitive composed of Bole Armenia. **1799** G. Smith *Laborat.* II. 401 Take..bole armenic, parched barley, etc. **1832** *Fraser's Mag.* VI. 714 The best toothpowder in the world is Armenian bole.

†**2.** A large pill, a BOLUS; also *fig. Obs.*

1601 Holland *Pliny* II. 141 Thirty grains of Lentils swallowed down by way of Bole. **1649** Jer. Taylor *Gt. Exemp.* III. xvi. 57 Ignorant..persons, who swallow down the bole and the box that carries it. **1725** Bradley *Fam. Dict.* II. s.v. *Water Germander*, The plant..may..be prescribed in Boles as well as in infusion.

bole[3] (bəʊl). *Sc.* Also **boal.** [Origin unknown.]

a. A small square recess in the wall of a room for holding articles. **b.** An unglazed aperture in the wall of a castle, cottage, stable, etc, for admitting air or light; sometimes closed with a shutter.

1728 Ramsey *Wks.* (1848) III. 167 Bring from yon boal a roasted hen. **1816** Scott *Antiq.* xxxii, Open the bole wi' speed, that I may see if this be the right Lord Geraldin. *c* **1817** Hogg *Tales & Sk.* VI. 97 We have been benighted, and have been drawn hither by the light in your bole. **1834** H. Miller *Scenes & Leg.* xxv. 365 The gold, which you will find in the little bole under the tapestry of my room. **1875** J. Veitch *Tweed* 92 A narrow bole High near the top.

bole[4]. (See quot.)

1670 Pettus *Fodinæ Reg.* Gloss. s.v., *Boles* or *Bolestids* are places, where in ancient time (before Smelting Mills were invented) the Miners did fine their lead. **1785** *Archæologia* VII. 170 (D.) There was a bole..where in ancient times.. miners used to smelt their lead ores.

bole, obs. form of BOLL, BOWL, BULL.

†**'bole-ax.** *Obs.* Also 3 **bulaxe.** [a. ON. *bol-öx*, *bul-öx* 'pole-axe', prob. f. *bolr*, *bulr* bole of a tree + *öx* axe; cf. Sw. *bolyxa* 'great axe'.] A large axe; ? a pole axe.

c **1200** Ormin 9281 Nuȝȝu iss bulaxe sett Rihht to þe treowwess rote. *c* **1308** *Satire* in *Rel. Ant.* II. 176 Hail be ȝe potters with ȝur bole-ax. *a* **1400** *Octouian* 1039 Two bole-axys grete and longe.

bolection (bəʊ'lɛkʃən). *Arch.* Also 9 **ba-, be-, bilection, bolexion.** [Of uncertain form and unknown origin.] A term applied to mouldings which project before the face of the work which they decorate, as a raised moulding round a panel.

1708 [E. Hatton] *New View Lond.* I. 95/1 A Gallery..the front of which is large Bolection, with raised Pannels. **1819** Nicholson *Archit. Dict.* I. 44 Balection mouldings: see *Belection*. **1823** Rutter *Fonthill* 15 Large raised pannels and bolection mouldings. **1845** *Gloss. Goth. Archit.* I. 56 *Bilection Mouldings*. **1876** Gwilt *Archit.* Gloss., *Balection* or *Bolection Mouldings*, mouldings which project beyond the surface of a piece of framing.

†**bo'lectioned,** *a. Obs.* Also 7 **bellexioned,** [f. prec. + -ED.] Having bolection moulding.

1693 *MS. Acc. bk. of Watts' Charity, Preston-next-Wingham, Kent*, The pews were also made uniform with new bellexion'd Deal-boord work.

boled, variant of BOLLED *ppl. a. Obs.*

bolero (bɒ'lɛərəʊ, bə'lɪərəʊ). [Sp.] **1.** A lively Spanish dance; also the air to which it is danced.

1787 J. Townsend *Journ. Spain* (1792) I. 331 The happiness to see Madame Mello dance a volero. **1809** Byron *Ch. Har.* I. lxxxiv. (1st draught) Wks. 1846 14/1 *note*, She mingles in the gay Bolero [*rime-wd.* hero]. *a* **1845** Hood *Drink. Song* iii, The jigs, the boleros, fandangos, and jumps. **1862** *Athenæum* 25 Jan. 111/3 The Fandango and Bolero are only a more decent form of an originally African dance..the Bolero was invented in 1780.

fig. **1869** Ld. Lytton *Orval* 165 The new dance of the Libertines! Freedom's bolero.

2. (Also 'bɒlərəʊ.) A short jacket coming barely to the waist; worn by men in Spain; applied to a similar garment worn by women elsewhere, usually over a blouse or bodice. Also *attrib.*

1892 [see TOREADOR c]. **1893** *Daily News* 1 Apr. 2/4 The Zouave is quite as popular as it was last year... Sometimes it is pure bolero. **1899** *Westm. Gaz.* 6 July 3/2 Robbing the coat of its basque has created..the bolero corsage, really an actual bodice, though appearing a bolero coat and skirt. **1909** 'O. Henry' *Roads of Destiny* ix. 151 He wore a suit of coarse brown ducking, the coat being a sort of rakish bolero. **1924** *Countries of World* 2495/2 Farmers and peasants.. with wide-brimmed black felt hats, boleros, coloured sashes, and tight-fitting trousers. **1941** 'R. West' *Black Lamb* I. 407 The boleros the women wore over their white linen blouses. **1968** J. Ironside *Fashion Alphabet* 35 *Bolero*, a short jacket reaching to the waist, worn open over a blouse ..sleeved or sleeveless..worn by Spanish dancers and bullfighters.

bo'lero, *v. nonce-wd.* To dance a bolero.

1834 Beckford *Italy* II. 364 Thirteen or fourteen couples started, and boleroed and fandangoed away.

bolesprit, obs. form of BOWSPRIT.

†**'boletate.** *Chem. Obs.* [f. next + -ATE[4].]

1810 Henry *Elem. Chem.* (1826) II. 241 With the alkalis and earths, it [boletic acid] unites, and forms a class of salts, which may be called boletates.

†**bo'letic,** *a. Chem. Obs.* [f. next + -IC.] Of or pertaining to *boletus*, as *boletic acid.*

1819 J. Children *Chem. Anal.* 275 Boletic acid was obtained by M. Braconnot from the boletus pseudo igniarius. **1863** Watts *Dict. Chem.* I. 618 *Boletic acid*..since shown by Bolley and Dessaignes to be identical with fumaric acid.

boletus (bəʊ'liːtəs). *Bot.* [a. L. *bōlētus* a mushroom, ad. Gr. βωλίτης of same meaning, perh. f. βῶλος lump.] A large genus of fungi, having the under surface of the pileus full of pores, instead of gills as in *Agaricus.*

1601 Holland *Pliny* II. 133 Glaucias..affirmeth, That the Mushromes Boleti be good for the stomacke. **1832** *Veg. Subst. Food* 336 Many species of fungi are..considered edible..A species of boletus is raised by the Italians. **1862** W. Coleman *Woodlands* 32 On very old trees..a massive fungus as large as a child's head, called the Birch Boletus.

bolge (bɒldʒ). *rare*[−1]. An adaptation of the It. *bolgia* 'gulf-hole' (Florio), applied by Dante to the gulfs of the eighth circle of the Inferno.

1881 *Contemp. Rev.* Dec. 849 The archetype of one bolge of the Inferno.

bolge, obs. form of BULGE.

†**'bolghen, bolȝen,** *ppl. a. Obs.* 1 (**ȝe**)**bolȝen,** 2 (*Orm.*) **bollȝhenn,** 3 **i-bolȝe.** [OE. *bolȝen*, *ȝebolȝen*, pa. pple. of *belȝan* to swell, be proud or angry: see BELL *v.*[1] and BOLLEN.]

a. Swollen with rage, angry, wrathful. **b.** Physically swollen; = BOLLEN.

c **1000** *Ags. Gosp.* Matt. xxvi. 8 And wurdon ȝebolȝene. *c* **1160** *Hatton G.* ibid., And wurðen ȝebolȝen. *c* **1200** Ormin 7145 Herode King Wass gramm and grill and bollȝhenn. *a* **1250** *Owl & Night.* 145 And sat toswolle and ibolȝe.

bolgit, obs. form of BULGED.

bolide ('bɒlaɪd). [a. F. *bolide*, ad. L. *bolid-em* (nom. *bolis*) large meteor, a Gr. βολίς missile, f. stem of βάλλειν to throw.] A large meteor; usually one that explodes and falls in the form of aerolites; a fire-ball.

1852 Th. Ross tr. *Humboldt's Trav.* I. x. 352 Not..a space equal in extent to three diameters of the moon, which was not filled every instant with bolides and falling stars. **1870** Proctor *Other Worlds* ix. 192 Explode into small fragments, as bolides and fireballs have been observed to do. **1884** Jefferies *Life of Fields* 183 It was not for some seconds I thought of looking for the bolide.

bolimong, variant of BULLIMONG, *Obs.*

bolin(e, -ing, obs. forms of BOW-LINE.

†**'boling,** *vbl. sb. Obs.* [f. BOLE *sb.*[1] and assuming a vb.] The formation of the bole of a tree.

1610 Folkingham *Art of Survey* I. iii. 6 The boaling, spreading, arming, timbring and tapering of trees.

bolino, early form of BURIN, for engraving.

bolion, obs. form of BULLION.

bolisme, -mus, obs. forms of BULIMY.

Bolivian (bə'lɪvɪən), *a.* and *sb.* [f. *Bolivia*, a republic in South America, founded in 1825: named after Simon *Bolivar* (1783–1830), South American soldier and statesman.] **A.** *adj.* Of or pertaining to Bolivia. **B.** *sb.* A native or inhabitant of Bolivia.

1835 *Jrnl. R. Geogr. Soc.* V. 71 The great emporium of the foreign trade to the Bolivian provinces. **1854** L. H. de Bonelli *Trav. Bolivia* I. ii. 49 On the following day the two Bolivians started. **1876** *Encycl. Brit.* IV. 16/1 It [*sc.* the constitution] guarantees to the Bolivians civil liberty..and equality of rights. **1934** *Times Lit. Suppl.* 28 June 456/2 The Bolivian poet Ricardo Jaimes Freyre. **1967** *Listener* 10 Aug. 182/3 Régis Debray's..capture the following month by the Bolivian army.

boliviano (bəlɪvɪ'ɑːnəʊ). [Sp.] A monetary unit of Bolivia.

1872 I. S. Homans *Coin Book* 83 *Boliviano*, the new peso or dollar of Bolivia, equal to five francs. **1957** *Encycl. Brit.* III. 820/2 The monetary unit, as accepted by the International Monetary Fund on April 8, 1950, is the gold boliviano, equal to..0·0148112 g. of fine gold. **1962** R. A. G. Carson *Coins* 441 A decimal coinage, introduced in 1863, had as its unit the peso or boliviano in silver... The coinage of 1951 consists of 1, 5 and 10 boliviano pieces. **1964** *Whitaker's Almanack* 828/2 From Jan. 1, 1963, the *Boliviano* is replaced by the *Peso Boliviano* at the rate of Bs. 1,000 = *Peso* 1 ($b. 1).

†**bolk,** *v. Obs.* exc. *dial.* Forms: 4–6 **bolke,** 5 **bulk,** 5–6 **bulke,** 6 **bolk, bolck, balk, balck,** (*Sc.*) **bok;** (*north.*) 6–8 **boke, bock,** 7– **boak, bouk, bowk.** [ME. *bolk-en*, cogn. w. mod.G. *bolken*, *bölken* 'to roar, bawl', and Du. *bulken* 'to bellow'; f. same root as BELCH; pointing to an OTeut. ablaut series *balkan*, *bęlkan*, *bolkan*; though perhaps of later formation.]

1. *intr.* To eructate; = BELCH 1.

1387 Trevisa *Higden* Rolls Ser. II. 195 Somme þat bolked neuere. *c* **1440** *Promp. Parv.* 43 Bolkyn, *ructo, eructo.* **1552** Huloet, Belke, or bolke, or breake wynde vpwarde. **1674** Ray *N.C. Wds.* 6 To *boke*..to Belch. *Lincoln.*

2. *to bolk out* (trans.): to give vent to, ejaculate, vociferate; = BELCH 2.

1382 Wyclif *Ps.* xviii. [xix.] 3 Dai to the dai bolketh [**1388** tellith] out woord. —— *Matt.* xiii. 35, I shal bolke out, *or telle oute*, hid thingus. **1553** Brende *Q. Curtius* VII. 4 Rashenes of wordes bulked out.

3. *trans.* To emit (wind) by belching; = BELCH 3.

a **1535** More *Wks.* 1360 Balk out ye stinking sauor of thy rauenous surfeting. **1616** T. Adams *Soul's Sickn.* Wks. 1861 I. 500 His own commendation rumbles within him, till he hath bulked it out; and the air of it is unsavoury.

4. *intr.* To vomit; to retch, or make efforts as in vomiting. Still *dial.*

1398 Trevisa *Barth. De P.R.* XVII. clxxxv. (1495) 726 The dronklew mannys stomak bolkyth. *c* **1480** *Babees Bk.* (1868) 18 Bulk not as a beene were yn þi throte. **1674** Ray *N.C. Wds.* 6 *Boke*, to Nauseate, to be ready to vomit, also to Belch. **1764** T. Brydges *Homer Travest.* (1797) II. 369 Boaking as if I'd bring my pluck up. **1832** *Blackw. Mag.* XXXII. 647 He began to strain and to bock. **1855** *Whitby Gloss.*, To *Boak*, the effort to vomit, to reach.

b. *trans.* Also with *up. dial.*

1790 A. Wilson *Callamp. Elegy* Poet. Wks. 105 His vera guts he's bockan In blude this day. **1863** Robson *Bards of Tyne* 433 Whey, she had bowk't the sma' beer up.

5. *fig.* and *transf.* To emit as in vomiting, to eject (as a volcano).

1513 DOUGLAS *Æneis* III. viii. 136 It.. will.. Furth bok the bowalis.. of the hill. **1561** STUDLEY *Seneca's Medea* (1581) 128 Ætna bolking stifling flames and dusky vapours up. **1787** BURNS *Winter Nt.*, Burns.. thro' the mining outlet boked, Down headlong hurl.

6. *intr.* To heave or throb like a confined gas or fluid. ***to bolk up***: to 'rise' in the stomach.

1561 HOLLYBUSH *Hom. Apoth.* 37 a, The meate bulketh up agayne. *a* **1679** T. GOODWIN *Wks.* (1861) III. 424 Humours.. may stir and boake in the stomach, when yet they come not up, nor prevail unto vomiting.

7. *intr.* To gush, flow in gulps.

a **1550** *Christis Kirke Gr.* xxi, Blude at breastis out bokkit. **1541** BARNES *Wks.* (1573) 251/2 Theyr plenteous wine presses and their full sellers bolkyng from thys vnto that. *a* **1600** *Rob. Hood* (Ritson) I. iii. 131 At his mouth came bocking out The blood of a good vain.

† **bolk**, *sb. Obs.* Also 7- **bock.** [f. prec. vb.] An eructation, a belch.

1377 LANGL. *P. Pl.* B. v. 397 He bygan *benedicite* with a bolke. **1697** W. CLELAND *Poems* 104 (JAM.) When he return'd he got it ov'r Without a host, a bock, or glour. **1859** *Autobiog. Beggar Boy* 150 To relieve himself of the dry bock.

bolk, obs. form of BULK.

† **'bolken**, *v. Obs. rare.* Also 7 **boaken.** [f. BOLK *v.* + -EN: cf. *light, lighten.*]

1. *intr.* To gush, flow in gulps. = BOLK 7.

a **1300** *E.E. Psalter* cxliii[iv]. 13 Cleves.. Bolkenand fra þat in to yit [? þis; *v.r.* from þis in þat; Vulg. *eructantia ex hoc in illud.*]

2. To throb. = BOLK 6.

1697 *Phil. Trans.* XIX. 379 The tops of my Fingers.. did boaken and ake, as when after extream cold, one has the hot-ach in them.

† **'bolking**, *vbl. sb. Obs.* exc. *dial.* [f. BOLK *v.*]

1. Belching, eructation, retching, vomiting.

1398 TREVISA *Barth. De P.R.* VII. xlviii. (1495) 260 Vnsauery bolkynges. by the whyche bolkinges the pacyente raueth. *c* **1440** *Promp. Parv.* 43 Bolkynge, or bulkynge, *orexis, eructacio.* **1519** HORMAN *Vulg.* 32 b, It is a balkynge of yesterdays meate. **1561** HOLLYBUSH *Hom. Apoth.* 33 b, A bulkinge or breakinge of winde. **1670** LASSELS *Voy. Italy* (1698) II. 174 Stones, which.. Vesuvius.. had vomited up with such a boaking. **1822** GALT *Steamboat* 76 (JAM.) Even between the bockings of the sea-sickness.

2. Heaving, throbbing.

1655 GURNALL *Chr. in Arm.* II. 381 The invenomed head of sin's arrow, that lies burning in conscience, and by its continual boking and throbbing there, keeps the poor sinner out of quiet.

boll (bəʊl), *sb.*[1] Forms: 1 bolla, 2-6 bolle, (6-7 bowle, 7 bol, bole), 7- boll. [A variant of BOWL *sb.*[1]:—OE. *bolla* = MDu. *bolle*, Du. *bol*, ON. *bolli* wk. masc., cognate with OHG. *bolla*, MHG. *bolle* wk. fem. 'bud, globular vessel'; see BOWL. Sense 2 may also be compared with L. *bulla*, It. *bolla*, F. *boule*, *bulle* bubble.]

† **1.** Earlier spelling of BOWL *sb.*[1], q.v.

† **2.** A vesicle or bubble. *Obs.*

a **1300** *Fragm. Pop. Science* (Wr.) 331 As ic seide ȝou er of þreo bollen, if ȝe understode; In þe nyþemeste bolle þer þe lyvre doþ out springe. **1398** TREVISA *Barth. De P.R.* XIX. cxxviii. (1495) 935 The bolle that ryseth on the water that boyleth.. highte bulla.

3. *spec.* A rounded seed-vessel or pod, as that of flax or cotton.

? *a* **1500** *Med. MS. Cathedr. Hereford* 8 (Halliw.) Take the bolle of the popy while it is grene. **1523** FITZHERB. *Husb.* §146 The bolles of flaxe.. made drye with the son to get out the sedes. **1562** TURNER *Herbal* II. (1568) 39 a, These knoppes or heades [of flax] are called in Northumberland bowles. **1601** HOLLAND *Pliny* II. XIX. 30 A second kind of poppie called black, out of the heads or bols whereof a white juice or liquor issueth. **1660** SHARROCK *Vegetables* 22 They thresh it [flax] not out of the boles till March. **1865** LIVINGSTONE *Zambesi* x. 214 They cultivate cotton.. the staple being long and the boll larger than what is usually met with.

† **4.** A round knob on any utensil, piece of furniture, or the like. *Obs.*

? *a* **1600** *Turke & G.* 220 in Furniv. *Percy Folio* I. 98 Gawaines boy to it did leape, & gatt itt by the bowles great. **1660** HOWELL *Dict.* XII, The Bolls, *i pomi, les pommes.*

† **5.** The Adam's apple: see THROAT-BOLL. *Obs.*

6. *Comb.*, as † **boll-roaking** (see quot.); † **boll-weed**, the Greater Knapweed (*Centaurea Scabiosa*); **boll-weevil** (in full ***cotton-boll weevil***), a weevil (*Anthonomus grandis*) destructive to the cotton-plant; also *fig.*; **boll-worm**, an insect which destroys the cotton boll or pod.

1641 BEST *Farm. Bks.* (1856) 59 That [straw] which is layd in the filling overnight to save the stack from wettinge is called boll-roakinge of a stacke. **1895** *Insect Life* Mar. 295 Report on the Mexican Cotton-Boll Weevil in Texas.. by C. H. Tyler Townsend.. [dated] December 20, 1894. **1903** *Westm. Gaz.* 26 Nov. 12/1 The boll weevil.. has caused America a loss of £14,000,000. **1906** *Ibid.* 19 Dec. 1/3 The Mexican cotton boll-weevil. **1906** *Springfield Weekly Republ.* 19 July 16 The 'boll-weevil democrats' is the term of opprobrium which a southern paper applies to democrats who favour Hearst. **1928** *Manch. Guardian Weekly* 31 Aug. 180/1 Reports of boll weevil damage and crop deterioration. **1950** A. LOMAX *Mr. Jelly Roll* (1952) 113 The longshoremen had two parades—one for the union men and one for the boll weevils, the scabs. **1848** *Rep. Secretary U.S. Dept. Agric.* *1847* 171 The destruction caused by the boll worm. **1888** *Congress. Rec.* 12 May 4070 Then comes the 'army worm', and then the 'boll-worm'.

boll (bəʊl), *sb.*[2] Forms: 4-5 bolle, 5- boll, (6 boull, 6-7 boule, 7 bole), also *Sc.* 6- bow. [app. distinct from the preceding, being pronounced (bʌʊ) in modern Scotch, and vernacularly written *bow, bowe*, since 16th c., while *bowl* is pronounced (bol). As it is entirely a northern word, it may possibly be a. ON. *bolli*, Da. *bolle*, the Scandinavian equivalent of OE. *bolla* BOWL.]

A measure of capacity for grain, etc., used in Scotland and the north of England, containing in Scotland generally 6 imperial bushels, but in the north of England varying locally from the 'old boll' of 6 bushels to the 'new boll' of 2 bushels. Also a measure of weight, containing for flour 10 stone (= 140 pounds). (A very full table of its local values is given in *Old Country and Farming Words* (E. Dial. Soc. 1880 p. 168).

c **1375** BARBOUR *Bruce* III. 211 Off Ryngis.. He send thre bollis to Cartage. **1536** BELLENDEN *Cron. Scot.* II. 298 He delt, ilk owlk, iv bowis of quheit. **1570** *Wills & Inv. N.C.* (1835) I. 344 Sex bolls aitis and sex bollis beir. **1590** *Ibid.* (1860) II. 248, Xxij boules of otes there 44*s.* iij boulls of big there 10*s.* **1609** SKENE *Reg. Maj.* 57 The boll.. salbe in the deipnes nine inches.. And in the Roundnes aboue, it sall contein thrie score and twelue inches. **1630** J. TAYLOR (Water P.) *Penniless Pilgr.* Wks. I. 130/2 Euery Bole containes the measure of foure English bushels. **1651** *Proc. Parliament* No. 88. 1353 And [the Scots Forces] seized 20000 Boules of Corne at Leith. **1691** RAY *N.C. Wds., Boll* of salt, i.e. two bushels. **1725** RAMSAY *Gent. Sheph.* II. i. (1844) 18 Yestreen I brew'd a bow o' maut. **1799** J. ROBERTSON *Agric. Perth* 291 In Strathearn it [shell marle] is sold from eight to ten pence the boll, being eight cubical feet. **1820** SCOTT *Abbot* xxvi, You are owing to the Laird four stones of barleymeal and a bow of oats. **1851** *Coal-tr. Terms Northumbld. & Durh.* 8 The coal boll contains 9676·8 cubic inches, or 34·899 imperial gallons. **1875** URE *Dict. Arts* III. 1126 In Northumberland (Alnwick, Morpeth, and Hexham markets) [wheat is sold] per new boll of 16 gallons; in Bedford and Wooller markets by the old boll of 48 gallons. **1883** *Times* 9 Mar., Out of 65 towns selling by measure, only 35 used the Imperial quarter, the others selling by coombs, sacks, loads, bolls, etc.

boll, *sb.*[3] *dial.* [Editors of Lancashire Glossary suggest connexion with BOGLE.] An apparition; a bogle, an object of fear. See BOLLY.

1847-78 in HALLIWELL. **1875** in *Lanc. Gloss.* (E.D.S.) 46.

† **boll**, *v.*[1] *Obs.* Also 5 bolle. [ME. *boll-en* 14th c., found beside the earlier *bolnen*, of which it is prob. a phonetic modification (as in *mill* = *miln*).]

1. *intr.* To swell.

c **1340** *Cursor M.* 6011 (Trin.) Bile & blister bollynge [3 *earlier MSS.* bolnande] sore. **1362** LANGL. *P. Pl.* A. v. 67 His Bodi was Bolled [*other MSS.* bolnid]. **1387** TREVISA *Higden* (1865) I. 298 Bocches vnder þe chyn i-swolle and i-bolled. **1547** BOORDE *Brev. Health* xxxviii. 19 b, The belly wyl boll and swel.

fig. **1388** WYCLIF *1 Cor.* v. 2 ȝe ben bolnyd [*v.r.* bollid] with pride. **1480** CAXTON *Chron. Eng.* ccxxi. 211 Anone for wrath his hert gan bolle.

b. *fig.* To increase.

1580 SIDNEY *Arcadia* 158 Euen while the doubtes most bolled, shee thus nourished them.

† **boll**, *v.*[2] *Obs.* Also 6 bole, bowle. [f. *boll*, BOWL *sb.*] To quaff the bowl; to booze.

1535 COVERDALE *Mich.* ii. 11 They might syt bebbinge and bollynge. **1567** HARMAN *Caveat* 32 They bowle and bowse one to another. **1577** KENDALL *Flowers of Epigr.* (N.) Gull, bib, and bole.. Eche can in Germany. **1586** J. HOOKER *Girald. Irel.* II. 95/1 Parese caused such as kept the ward, to swill and boll.

† **boll**, *v.*[3] *Obs.* [f. BOLL *sb.*[1] (sense 3).] To be or begin to be in boll. Cf. BOLLED *ppl. a.*[2]

1601 HOLLAND *Pliny* XIX. vi. (R.) Garlic indeed should not be suffered to boll and run up to seed.

boll, obs. Sc. spelling of BOW *sb.*[1]

boll-, bolpece, obs. f. *bowl-piece*: see BOWL *sb.*[1]

Bollandist ('bɒləndɪst). [f. *Bolland*, name of a Flemish Jesuit of the 17th c. + -IST.] *pl.* The Jesuit writers who continued the work called *Acta Sanctorum*, begun by John Bolland.

1751 CHAMBERS *Cycl.*, *Bollandists*.. certain Jesuits of Antwerp.. employed in collecting the lives and acts of the saints. *a* **1843** SOUTHEY *Comm.-pl. Bk.* Ser. II. 15 A question which the Bollandists ask in a note. **1883** *Contemp. Rev.* Oct. 518 The history of St. Patrick's purgatory is.. supported by the grave authority of the Bollandists.

bollard ('bɒləd, -ɑːd). *Naut.* [Derivation unknown; possibly f. BOLE *sb.*[1] + -ARD.] **a.** A wooden or iron post, on a ship, a whale-boat, or a quay, for securing ropes to. Also *attrib.*, as in ***bollard-head, -timber*** (see quot.).

1844 A. KEY *Recov. Gorgon* (1847) 67 The threefold block taken close forward to a bollard on the forecastle. **1863** *Times* 19 Mar. 14/2 Like the Warrior she will have on each quarter strong iron towing bollards. **1867** SMYTH *Sailor's Word-bk.* 115 Bollard, a thick piece of wood on the head of a whale-boat, round which the harpooner gives the line a turn, in order to veer it steadily, and check the animal's velocity. **1880** T. HARDY *Trump. Major* in *Gd. Words* Oct. 661 Standing by a bollard a little farther up the quay.

attrib. *c* **1850** *Rudim. Navig.* (Weale) 127 *Knight-heads*, or *Bollard-Timbers*, large oak timbers fayed and bolted to each side of the stem, the heads of which run up sufficiently above the head of the stem to support the bowsprit. **1869** SIR E. REED *Shipbuild.* xv. 291 In iron ships bollard heads and towing bollards are frequently of cast iron.

b. A post on a traffic island.

1948 *Archit. Rev.* CIV. 80 Demarcation of pavement.. is left to discretion of designer. In this drawing a two-foot band of setts is used with bollards at intervals. **1955** *Times* 23 June 6/6 The woman was waiting between the bollards in the middle of the crossing.

bolle, obs. form of BOWL *sb.*[1], also variant of BOLLEN *pa. pple.*

† **bolled**, *ppl. a.*[1] *Obs.* [f. BOLL *v.* + -ED.]

1. Swollen, inflated, gibbous; *fig.* swollen with pride, puffed up.

c **1375** *Homily in Rel. Ant.* I. 39 Poure in spirit, that is, not proud ny bolled. **1578** BANISTER *Hist. Man* I. 29 The seuenth [bone].. hath some sides hollow, others boled, or gibbous. [**1881** EVANS *Leicestersh. Words* s.v., The grains (of wheat) are so bolled, they are ready to jump out of the ear. Cf. BOLD *a.* 5, also BOLLED *ppl. a.*[2]]

† **2.** Embossed; embellished. *Obs.*

c **1325** *E.E. Allit. P.* B. 1464 Al bolled abof with braunches & leues. **1400** *Pol. Rel. & L. Poems* (1866) 14, V. paraffys grete & stoute Bolyd in rose red.

† **bolled**, *ppl. a.*[2] *Obs.* exc. *dial.* [f. BOLL *v.*[3] or *sb.*[1] 3 + -ED. Cf. *seeded, podded.*] Having bolls; *esp.* having seed vessels, in pod, in seed.

1535 COVERDALE *Ex.* ix. 31 Y^e^ flax was boulled. [**1611** The flaxe was bolled; **1382** WYCLIF, The flax now buriownde coddes; **1388** The flax hadde buriounned thanne knoppis]. **1639** HORN & ROBOTHAM *Gate Lang. Unl.* xii. §131 Garlick, onions, leekes.. are bolled [round-headed].

† **'bollen**, *sb. Obs.* Also **bollien, bolline, bolyn.** [Only in Lyte: some kind of erroneous formation on BOLL.] = BOLL *sb.*[1] 3.

1578 LYTE *Dodoens* I. xxxvi. 55 The seede [of Pimpernell] is contayned in small round littell bolliens or knappes. *Ibid.* I. lxxiii. 109 The stalkes.. vpon the toppes whereof groweth small round knappes or bollines. *Ibid.* v. lxxviii. 645 The rounde bollens, or imbossed heades of the right Squilla.

† **'bollen**, *ppl. a. Obs.* Also 4-5 **bollun**, 5 **bolle**; and 6 **boln(e, boalne, bowlne.** [pa. pple. of BELL *v.*[1] *Obs.* to swell; cf. BOLGHEN. In the 16th c. there was a monosyllabic variant *boln*, etc. (see β); also in Sc. a form BOLDEN, mod. *bowden*, with *d* generated between *l* and *n*.]

Swollen; inflated, puffed up.

a **1225** *Ancr. R.* 282 A bleddre ibollen ful of winde. *c* **1340** *Cursor M.* 12685 (Trin.) His knees þerof were bollen so [*v.r.* bolnd, bolned]. **1382** WYCLIF *2 Tim.* iii. 4 Bollun with proude thouȝtis. *c* **1430** LYDG. *Bochas* VIII. xv. (1554) 186 b, Tofore Bochas came Hermenricus.. Inflate and bolle. **1493** *Festyvall* (W. de W. 1515) 99 His knees.. were bollen out lyke a camell. **1593** SHAKS. *Lucr.* 1417 Here one, being thronged, bears back, all bollen and red.

β. boln, bolne, boalne, bowlne. [Cf. *swoln.*]

1509 HAWES *Past. Pleas.* 135 His breste fatte, and bolne in the wast. *a* **1547** SURREY *Æneid* II. 346 Whose feet were bowln With the strait cords. **1566** STUDLEY *Seneca's Medea* (1581) 133 His body boalne big, wrapt in lumpes. **1598** SYLVESTER *Du Bartas* II. iv. III. (1641) 225/1 With foaming fury swoln, With boystrous beasts of angry tempests boln. **1609** HOLLAND *Amm. Marcel.* XXVIII. ix. 341 With a big and bolne necke of his owne.

bollene, obs. form of BOWLINE.

† **'boller.** *Obs.* [f. *bolle*, earlier form of BOWL.]

1. One who continues at the bowl; a tippler, a drunkard. Cf. *bowl-fellow.*

c **1320** R. BRUNNE *Medit.* 477 Both bollers of wyne and eche a gadlyng. *c* **1340** *Alex. & Dind.* 675 Baccus þe boller. **1393** LANGL. *P. Pl.* C. x. 194 Bollers atten ale. **1413** LYDG. *Pylgr. Sowle* III. ix. (1483) 55 Bollers of wyn and ale. **1542** UDALL *Erasm. Apoph.* 33 a, A greate boller of wyne.

2. ? A bowl-maker.

1415 *York Myst.* Introd. 25 Turnours, Hayresters, Bollers.

bollett(e, bolletine, obs. ff. BULLET, BULLETIN.

bolling ('bəʊlɪŋ), *sb.* [app. f. BOLE[1] trunk.] A pollard (tree).

1691 RAY *N.C. Words*, s.v. BOLL, *Bolling* trees is used in all countries for pollard trees, whose heads and branches are cut off, and only the bodies left. **1697** *Surv. Bower Hall, Pentlow, Essex* (*MS.*) Bowlings which ye tenant hath liberty to cropp for fireing. **1776** (June 1) *Boundaries*, Up the road and marked an Elm Bolling.. Marked a Bolling Oak.. Marked an old Bolling against Burnt-field. **1847** in CRAIG; and in mod. Dicts.

† **'bolling**, *vbl. sb.*[1] *Obs.* [f. BOLL *v.*[1] + -ING[1].] Swelling.

c **1340** *Cursor M.* 10463 (Trin.) And of bollyng of hir herte She kest hir wordis ouerþwerte. **1362** LANGL. *P. Pl.* A. VII. 204 For bollyng of heore wombes. **1533** ELYOT *Cast. Helth* IV. iv. (1541) 85 A swellynge or bollynge of the bodye.

† **'bolling**, *vbl. sb.*[2] *Obs.* [f. BOLL *v.*[2] + -ING[1]: the mod. spelling would be *bowling.*] Excessive drinking, boozing.

a **1529** SKELTON *Image Hypocr.* IV. 583 How they iest and iolt, With bowsing and bollinge. **1544** ASCHAM *Toxoph.* (Arb.) 93 Disynge cardyng and boouling. **1570-6** LAMBARDE *Peramb. Kent* (1596) 356 This vicious plant of unmeasurable boalling. **1574** NEWTON *Health Mag.* 59 Superfluous bollinge and beastlie swilling of much wyne. **1583** STANYHURST *Æneis* III. (Arb.) 81 With whip cat bowling they kept a myrry carousing.

† 'bolling, *ppl. a. Obs.* [f. BOLL *v.*[1]] Swelling, protuberant.

1519 HORMAN *Vulg.* 26 b, Bollynge yes out, se but febely. Womens brestis be bollynge out.

‖ bo'llito. ? *Obs.* [It. *bollito* boiled, made to bubble.] (See quot.)

1753 CHAMBERS *Cycl. Supp.*, *Bollito*, in the glass-works, the calcined materials for glass-making. This is commonly called frit. 1799 G. SMITH *Laborat.* I. 170 Take of the crystal frit, called also bollito.

bollix ('bɒlɪks), *v. low slang.* Also bollux. [Alt. of *bollocks*, pl. of BOLLOCK.] *trans.* To bungle, make a mess of, confuse; also with *up*. So **'bollixed** *ppl. a.*

1937 J. WEIDMAN *I can get it for you Wholesale* 36 Watch your script... You're getting your cues all bollixed up. 1945 A. J. LIEBLING in *Best Amer. Short Stories* (1946) 275 He explained that a ratfest was 'a rat race, but all bollixed up'. 1945 A. KOBER *Parm Me* 139 So rather I should tell it and maybe bollix up the whole thing, it's better that it should come from Billie. 1952 STEINBECK *East of Eden* I. 478 He'd made a mess of things. He wondered if he'd bollixed up the breaks. 1953 C. ARMSTRONG *Catch-As-Catch-Can* xxii. 177 That skunk.. bolluxed Pearl's radio.

Also as *sb.*, a mess, confusion.

1935 DYLAN THOMAS *Let.* July (1966) 156 I've been meaning.. to learn about.. the bollix of the old gang. 1936 'G. ORWELL' *Let.* 3 Apr. (1968) I. 215 My novel.. would have been out a month ago if it had not been for all that bollux about libel. 1957 J. BLISH *Fallen Star* v. 62 Some kind of intra-departmental bollix.

bollman ('bəʊmən), *dial.* [f. ON. *ból* an abode (cf. BOLD *sb.*) + MAN.] A cottager (In Orkney and Shetland). See also BOUMAN.

a 1796 *Statist. Acc. Scot.* XV. 415–6 (JAM.) The amount of what a cottager or bollman, and his wife can earn annually. 1866 EDMONDSTON *Shetl. & Orkney Gloss.*, *Bollman*, a cottager, pronounced *bowman*.

bollock ('bɒlək). [var. BALLOCK.] **1.** *pl.* The testicles. Cf. BALLOCK 1.

1744 *School of Venus* in D. Thomas *Long Time Burning* (1969) 362 You.. can now without blushing call prick, stones, bollocks, cunt, tarse and the like names. 1763 WILKES & POTTER *Essay on Woman* (1871) 19 Prick, cunt, and bollocks in convulsions hurl'd. 1874 *Lett. fr. Friend in Paris* II. 158 At the same time handling the noble bollocks. 1968 *Landfall* XXII. 17 Fine specimen of a lad, my Monty. All bollocks and beef.

2. *Naut.* Either of two blocks fastened to the topsail-yard, for the topsail-ties to reeve through.

1889 *Cent. Dict.*, Bollock-block. 1898 ANSTED *Dict. Sea Terms*, *Bollocks*, blocks secured to the middle of the topsail yards in large ships; the topsail ties pass through them, and thereby gain an increase of power in lifting the yards.

3. *pl.* (See quot. 1919); also, a mess, a muddle; nonsense (also as *int.*). As *adj.*, naked. *low slang.* Cf. BALLOCK 2.

1919 DOWNING *Digger Dial.* 12 Bollocks (n. or adj.), absurd; an absurdity. 1950 G. WILSON *Brave Company* (1951) viii. 142 He's stark bollock. *Ibid.* ix. 159 Christ, what a bollocks. 1969 *It* 11–24 Apr. 15/2 Bollocks, nobody at all wants to know. *Ibid.* 15/3 It's really a load of bollocks.

bollocking, etc.: see BALLOCK *v.*

bolluga, obs. variant of BELUGA.

† **'bolly**, *sb. Obs.* or *dial.* Also bolleroy. [dim. of BOLL *sb.*[3]] A bogy, hobgoblin.

1724 *Trial E. Arnold* in Howell's *State Trials* (1812) XVI 737 (*A Witness*).. He came.. raving at the bollies and bolleroys.. and said, The bollies plagued him. *Ibid.* 762 (*Mr. Justice Tracy*) 'He asked.. whether they were plagued with the bollies and bugs, as formerly?'

† **'bolly**, *a. Obs. rare*$^{-1}$. [f. BOLL *sb.*[1] 2 + -Y.] Covered with bubbles.

1582 BATMAN *Barth. De P.R.* XI. ii. 159 The winde maketh the over parte of water bolly and uneuen.

bollyon, obs. form of BULLION.

† **bolm.** *Obs. Sc. rare*$^{-1}$. [Scotch spelling of *bŏm*, a. Flem. or Du. *boom* (used in same sense); independent of the later English adoption of BOOM in other senses.] A pole (for punting, etc.).

1513 DOUGLAS *Æneis* v. iv. 93 With lang bolmis of tre Pikit with irn.

boln, bolne, by-form of BOLLEN *a. Obs.* swollen.

† **bolne**, *v. Obs.* Also 4 bulne, boln, 5 ? bollen, 6 boulne. [ME. *bolne(n*, a. Da. *bolne*:—ON. *bolgna* (Sw. *bulna*) to swell (intr.); inchoative of *belg-*, pa. pple. *bolg-en*, to inflate. (The pa. pple. *bolnun* mixes up *bolned* with BOLLEN.)]

1. *intr.* To swell.

a 1300 *Cursor M.* 6011 Bile and blister, bolnand sare. c 1325 *Metr. Hom.* (1862) 25 The first dai sal al the se Boln and ris. c 1340 *Cursor M.* 12531 (Fairf.) A nedder.. stanged Iam in his riȝt hande.. He bulned grete. 1468 in *Cath. Angl.* 36 *Tumeo*, to bolnyn. 1530 PALSGR. 460/1 Se howe this toode bolneth. 1576 T. NEWTON tr. *Lemnie's Complex.* (1633) 132 Immoderately to bolne, swell, and therewith thorowly to bee cloyed.

2. *fig.* To swell with pride, anger, etc.

c 1375 WYCLIF *Serm.* Sel. Wks. II. 266 þe fifþe condicioun of þis love is þat, it bolneþ not bi pride. 1382 —— *1 Cor.* v. 2 And ȝe ben bolnun with pride. c 1449 PECOCK *Repr.* v. i. 480 Bolned with witt of his fleisch.

3. *trans.* To cause to swell; to inflate; also *fig.*

a 1340 HAMPOLE *Psalter* i. 5 Pride, that heghis & bolnes thaim as wynd dos. c 1380 WYCLIF *Confess.* Wks. (1880) 327 Mannes kunnyng bolniþ hym bi pride.

† **bolned**, *ppl. a. Obs.* Also -et, -it. [f. BOLNE *v.* + -ED.] Swollen; inflated, puffed up.

a 1300 *Cursor M.* 12685 Hes knes war bolnd [*v.r.* bolned]. c 1380 WYCLIF *Sel. Wks.* III. 20 Proude bolnyd maliciouse dampned men and wommen. c 1440 *York Myst.* xlvi. 45 That blissid body blo is & bolned for betyng. 1483 *Cath. Angl.* 36 Bolnyd, *tumidus, tumedulus*.

† **'bolning**, *vbl. sb. Obs.* [f. as prec. + -ING[1].] **1.** Swelling, state of being swollen; *concr.* a swelling, a tumour.

a 1340 HAMPOLE *Psalter* lxxxvii[i]. 17 Grete bolnynge of water. c 1430 LYDG. *Bochas* II. xxviii. (1554) 64 a, Agayn such bolnyng, auaileth no triacle. 1483 *Cath. Angl.* 36 A Bolnynge, *tumor, inflacio*. 1530 PALSGR. 200/2 Boulnyng, swelling. 1610 BARROUGH *Meth. Physick* I. xii. (1639) 15 Distension and bolning in the head.

2. *fig.* (with pride, anger, etc.)

a 1300 *Cursor M.* 12083 þe bolning of his hert. a 1340 HAMPOLE *Psalter* l. 8 It [mekenes] purges him fro bolnynge of pride. a 1400 *Relig. Pieces fr. Thornt. MS.* (1867) 12 Wrethe.. es a wykkede stirrynge or bollenynge of herte.

† **'bolning**, *ppl. a. Obs.* Swelling.

a 1300 *Cursor M.* 6011 Bile & blister bolnand sare. c 1325 *E.E. Allit. P.* B. 179 Bobaunce & bost & bolnande priyde.

bolo[1] ('bəʊləʊ). [Sp.] A kind of cutlass used in the Philippine Islands for agricultural and domestic work and as a fighting weapon. *Comb.*, *bolo-maker*; **bolo-man**, one armed with a bolo.

1901 *Westm. Gaz.* 1 Oct. 10/1, 400 bolomen attacked the garrison of seventy-two Americans. 1901 *Daily Chron.* 11 Oct. 5/7 Insurgents, who were armed only with bolos. 1905 LE ROY *Philippine Life* 85 The local blacksmith and bolo-maker, as he generally is (for the bolo is the chief working implement of the Filipino in the thicket or the field or about the house, as well as being, in another form, his principal weapon). 1906 *Macmillan's Mag.* Oct. 903 We had never visited the place before, and, for all we knew to the contrary, it was full of *bolo*-men.

Bolo[2] ('bəʊləʊ). **1.** One who pursues antipatriotic 'underground' activities like those of Paul Bolo, a French adventurer shot for treason, 17 April 1918; one suspected of engaging in pacifist propaganda in favour of Germany during the war of 1914–18.

1917 *19th Cent.* Dec. 1265 The activity of those whom we might call the British and German Bolos, naturalised or not. *Ibid.* 1266 As far back as 1907 these Bolos were working under the guidance of German agents.

2. Misused for: a Bolshevik. Also *collect. sing.* = the Bolshevists. Also *attrib.*

1919 *Blackw. Mag.* June 742/1 The Bolo was ignorant of the fate of our raft gun. *Ibid.* Nov. 722/1 A party of Bolo prisoners. 1920 *Ibid.* Mar. 396/1 The missing Bolos from Selmenga. 1924 *Ibid.* Sept. 387/2 Bolo and anti-Bolo propaganda. 1937 C. MADGE in C. Day Lewis *Mind in Chains* 158 Attempts have also been made to prove that Broadcasting House is the headquarters of a conspiracy of 'bolos'. 1963 *Spectator* 27 Sept. 377/1 The police, of course, had passed this bolo under the illusion that he was only some simple patriotic goon.

bolo[3] ('bəʊləʊ). *U.S.* Also *bolo punch*. An upper cut in pugilism.

1950 DEMPSEY *Championship Fighting* xvii. 114 A long-range right uppercut called the 'bolo' punch. *Ibid.*, The *bolo* is more showy than explosive. 1954 F. C. AVIS *Boxing Ref. Dict.* 13 *Bolo*, a very powerful upper cut, brought from the rear of the body and taking the full weight of the boxer using it.

Bologna (bə'ləʊnjə, bə'lɒnjə). Also 5 Bonony, 6 Bononye, 8 Bolonia. A town in Italy, anciently called Bononia. Hence **Bolognan, Bononian** *a.*: also **Bologna bottle, flask, phial**, an unannealed bottle (see quot.); **B. phosphorus**, a phosphorescent preparation of Bologna stone and gum; **B. sausage**, a large kind of sausage first made at Bologna; also (U.S.) ellipt.; **B. spar, stone**, native sulphate of baryta found near Bologna, having phosphorescent properties.

1563 GRAFTON *Chron.* 601 To forsake the cytie of Bonony. 1744 *Phil. Trans.* XLIII. 272 A Phænomenon, which is called of the Bologna *Bottle, because it was first discover'd at Bologna. If you let these Bottles fall perpendicularly from some Height upon a Brick-floor, they will not be broken; but if you drop into them some little hard Bodies, they will burst in Pieces. 1875 B. LOEWY tr. *Weinhold's Exp. Physics* 774 Bolognian *flasks are simply small glass bottles which, after being formed, have been suddenly cooled in the air. 1822 IMISON *Sc. & Art* II. 90 Sulphate of barytes.. when calcined.. forms the Bolognian *phosphorus. 1875 URE *Dict. Arts* I. 295 Bologna spar is notable for phosphorescence.. when heated; the so-called '*Bologna Phosphorus*' was made by powdering this stone, and cementing the powder into the form of sticks, by means of gum. 1596 NASHE *Saffron Walden* Wks. 1883–4 III. 162 As big as a Bolognian *sawcedge. 1842 'MEG DODS' *Cook & Housew. Manual* III. i. 267 *note*, Real Bologna sausages labour under the imputation of being made of asses' flesh. 1850 *Knickerbocker* XXXV. 23 Relishing 'Bolognas', will he plead that a jelly-eyed roaster is disgusting? 1916 C. SANDBURG *Chicago Poems* 24 The dago shovelman finishes the dry bread and bologna. 1674 N. FAIRFAX *Bulk & Selv.* 196 Light may otherwise arise than from suns, as may be seen by.. the Bononian *Stone. 1694 *Phil. Trans.* XVIII. 35 Method of Preparing the Bononian Stone or Phosphorus. 1791 E. DARWIN *Bot. Gard.* i. *note*, The Bolognian stone.. has been long celebrated for its phosphorescent quality.

Bolognese (bɒlə'n(j)eɪz, ‖ bolo'ɲeze), *a.* and *sb.* [a. It. *Bolognese*: see BOLOGNA + -ESE.]

A. *adj.* Of or belonging to, made in or obtained from, Bologna in the north of Italy, or its school of painting.

1821 M. WILMOT *Jrnl.* 1 Nov. in *More Lett.* (1935) 138 We saw.. some of the chef d'œuvres of the Bolognese school. 1826 M. KELLY *Reminiscences* (ed. 2) I. 121, I had a letter to deliver to a Bolognese nobleman. 1926 *Glasgow Herald* 8 Apr. 4 Bolognese paper of about 1473, made entirely of linen. 1968 *Listener* 20 June 813/2 During the second half of the 17th century.. the Bolognese composers .. played an important part in.. Italian music.

B. *absol.* or as *sb.* **1.** A native or an inhabitant of Bologna. (Unchanged for *pl.*) **b.** The dialect of Italian used by the Bolognese. **2.** *the Bolognese*: the territory of Bologna. **3.** A type of toy dog.

1756 A. BUTLER *Lives Saints* II. 206 In the Romagna, the marquisate of Ancona, Tuscany, the Bolognese, and the Milanese. 1818 SHELLEY *Let.* 9 Nov. (1964) II. 51 There is another painter here called Franceschini, a Bolognese. 1839 *Dublin Rev.* VI. 3 We can sufficiently understand them.. to put ourselves at ease with the peasants of any district. *Bolognese*, however, is yet too much for us. 1876 *Encycl. Brit.* IV. 19/2 In the Crusades the Bolognese took an active share. 1905 H. DE BYLANDT *Dogs all Nations* II. 729 Bolognese, a ladies' toy dog, somewhat dolent. 1935 *Hutchinson's Dog Encycl.* I. 161 In 1880 the Toy Dog known as the Bolognese was greatly admired in Central Europe.

bolograph ('bəʊləgrɑːf, -æ-). [See BOLOMETER and -GRAPH.] An automatic record of the indications of a bolometer. Hence **bolo'graphic** *a.*, pertaining to this.

1903 S. P. LANGLEY in *Astrophys. Jrnl.* Mar. 93 A study of the yearly variations of the selective absorption of the Earth's atmosphere by the aid of a long series of bolographs. 1903 AGNES M. CLERKE *Probl. Astrophysics* 22 Using a 'bolographic' method, in which the camera registers what the bolometer *feels*.

Boloism ('bəʊləʊɪz(ə)m). [See BOLO[2].] Nefarious anti-patriotic activities resembling those of Paul Bolo; *esp.* the engineering of underground pacifist propaganda in favour of an enemy country. Also *erron.*, Bolshevism.

1917 LLOYD GEORGE in *Times* 23 Oct. 6/2 See what has happened in France.. and look out for Boloism in all its shapes and forms. 1919 *War Slang* in *Athenæum* 11 July 582/2 In his [*sc.* the British soldier's] linguistic haziness he used 'Boloism' as a synonym for 'Bolshevism', and found an etymology for both in 'Bolo', a variant of 'diabolo', the devil.

bolok, obs. form of BULLOCK.

bolometer (bəʊ'lɒmɪtə(r)). [f. Gr. βολή beam of light + μέτρον measure.] An electrical instrument of great sensitiveness for measuring radiant heat. Hence **bolometric** (bɒləʊ'mɛtrɪk), *a.*

1881 *Nature* XXV. 14 An instrument.. capable of indicating a change of temperature as minute as 1-100,000th of a single Centigrade degree.. is termed by its discoverer, Professor S. P. Langley, the *bolometer*, or actinic balance. 1882 *Athenæum* 2 Sept. 310/1 His 'bolometer', or radiation measurer—an instrument some twenty times more sensitive than the thermopile. 1881 C. A. YOUNG *Sun* 306 Shown by the bolometric measures described above.

boloney (bə'ləʊnɪ). Chiefly *U.S.* Also **balony**, bolony. [Cf. BALONEY, BOLONEY.] Alteration of BOLOGNA (*sausage*).

1907 *Dialect Notes* III. 182 *Bolóny*, a thick sausage of mixed cooked meat, sold at groceries. 1935 E. WEEKLEY *Something about Words* 64 *Boloney* must surely be for *Bologna* sausage.., influenced perhaps by the contemptuous sense associated with the German *wurst*. 1936 MENCKEN *Amer. Lang.* (ed. 4) 391 Most English newspapers... still spell bologna (sausage) balony. 1976 *U.S. News & World Rep.* 26 Jan. 40/2 It is painfully obvious to everyone all over the country that you are really asking us to settle for crumbs and boloney when all President Ford would have to do is to sign the Consumer Protection Act.

boloney, var. BALONEY.

bolotade, variant of BALLOTADE.

bolpece: see BOWL *sb.*[1]

bolsh (bɒlʃ), *v. intr.* A jocular back-formation from BOLSHEVIK and derivs.

1921 D. H. LAWRENCE *Let.* 2 Mar. (1962) II. 644, I think Italy will not revolute or bolsh any more. *Ibid.* 645 There will be no definite revolution or bolshing at all. 1924 *British Wkly.* 6 Nov. 134/4 *On Rowdyism.* If people want to 'bolsh' they will 'bolsh', rain or no rain.

Bolshevik ('bɒlʃɪvɪk), *sb.* and *a.* Also rarely -ic. [a. Russ. *bol'shevík*, f. *ból'she* more, f. *bol'shóĭ* big. The Russ. pl. *bol'shevikí* has been used by some English writers.]

A. *sb.* A member of that part of the Russian Social-Democratic Party which took Lenin's side in the split that followed the second

Congress of the party in 1903, seized power in the 'October' Revolution of 1917, and was subsequently renamed the (Russian) Communist Party. Cf. MENSHEVIK.

1917 *19th Cent.* July 141 The Mensheviki or Minimalists (Moderate Socialists)... The Bolsheviki (Extreme Socialists). **1917** *New Europe* 6 Dec. 236 It was from this Conference [of Socialists at Stockholm, 1903] that the cleavage between Bolševiks and Menševiks dates, the former being those who held a 'majority' at the Conference, the latter a 'minority'. **1918** E. J. DILLON *Eclipse of Russia* 10 The Bolsheviks at once outbid the Cadets. *Ibid.* 33 After the triumph of the Bolsheviki. **1918** C. E. RUSSELL *Unchained Russia* 253 The Bolshevic was in Russia the most natural fruitage. *a* **1968** M. RICHLER in R. Weaver *Canad. Short Stories* 2nd Ser. (1968) 196 The crazed man behind him, another old bolshevik, repeats over and over again, 'This could never happen in a socialist country.'

b. *transf.* and *fig.* A person of subversive or revolutionary views; an out-and-out opponent of the existing social order or accepted codes.

1926 W. R. INGE *Lay Thoughts* 29 The cliques of literary Bolsheviks, who seem to be inspired by a destructive hatred ..of civilisation.

B. *adj.* = BOLSHEVIST *a.*

1907 I. ZANGWILL *Ghetto Comedies* 401 Go to the Labour Parties... Not the Bolsheviki faction..but the Mensheviki **1917** *New Europe* 8 Nov. 112 The Bolševik mentality. **1918** C. E. RUSSELL *Unchained Russia* 261 The Bolshevic movement. **1919** J. POLLOCK *Bolshevik Adv.* p. xx, The part played by the Jews in Bolshevik Russia. **1952** *Economist* 25 Oct. 240/1 The party is no longer Bolshevik, even in name. The Politburo has been dropped.

Hence **'Bolshevikism** = BOLSHEVISM; **'Bolshevikize** *v.* = BOLSHEVIZE *v.*

1918 *Nation* (N.Y.) 7 Feb. 135/1 What Germany is resolved upon is that these lands shall not be Bolshevikized economically. **1919** H. S. KING *Russia during War* 49 The rising tide of Bolshevikism.

Bolshevism ('bɒlʃɪvɪz(ə)m). [a. Russ. *bol'shevízm*: see BOLSHEVIK.] The doctrines and practices of the Bolsheviks; the communistic form of government adopted in Russia since the Bolshevik Revolution of October (November), 1917.

1917 *New Europe* 8 Nov. 112 The good sense of Russian democracy threw off the yoke of Bolševism. **1918** THEO. ROOSEVELT in *Metropolitan Mag.* June 9/1 The most powerful indictment of the corrupt and inefficient tyranny of the Romanoffs..is that it produced Bolshevism. *Ibid.* 9/2 Parlor or pink-tea bolshevism dear to the hearts of so many ..who like to think of themselves as intellectuals. **1918** *Times* 7 Dec. 9/6 There must be no Bolshevism in [British] land policy. **1926** W. R. INGE *Lay Thoughts* 159 Bolshevism is no new thing there [*sc.* in Russia]. **1926** D. H. LAWRENCE *Plumed Serpent* ii. 47 Bolshevism only smashed your house or your business or your skull, but Americanism smashes your soul.

Hence **Bolshe'visia** [-IA[1]], **'Bolshevy** [after *Muscovy*], the land of Bolshevism; Russia under the rule of the Bolsheviks.

1919 J. POLLOCK *Bolshevik Adv.* 195 A producer [of stage-plays] in Bolshevisia. **1920** *Chambers's Jrnl.* 514/1 Life in Bolshevisia—such as it was in July 1918. **1921** *Times Lit. Suppl.* 18 Mar., Bolshevy from within. **1922** *Times* 18 Apr. 21/1 The Bondmaid of Bolshevy.

Bolshevist ('bɒlʃɪvɪst). [a. Russ. *bol'shevíst* (now disused) BOLSHEVIK.] A Bolshevik; a supporter of Bolshevism. Also *transf.*, esp. as a term of reproach for an out-and-out revolutionary. Also *attrib.* or as *adj.*

1917 *19th Cent.* Dec. 1106 The reign of Bolshevists and Terrorists. **1920** *Edin. Rev.* July 33 The Government of Styria, which, having a large industrial population of its own, is particularly sensitive to the 'Bolshevist Peril'. **1920** *Chambers's Jrnl.* Aug. 513/1 Packing the meetings with Bolshevist agents. **1922** E. WALLACE *Flying Fifty-Five* xxxiv. 204, I call a horse a Bolshevist when he doesn't run twice alike. **1926** W. J. TODD *Port* v. 83 Cheese (of not too bolshevist a nature) prepares the palate, but cheese is too violent a preparation for a fine old Port. **1940** *Tablet* 4 May 417/1 Under the Bolshevist-Nazi dictatorship, two hundred million human beings are forced to live deprived of the foundations on which Western civilization was built.

Hence **Bolshe'vistic** *a.*, of, pertaining to, or characteristic of, the Bolshevists; **,Bolshe'vistically** *adv.*

1920 *Glasgow Herald* 14 May 9 London has established the alarming precedent of applying such words as 'horrible' and 'Bolshevistic' to the well-intentioned proposals of certain pious Churchmen. **1920** *Punch* 13 Oct. 282/1 In these Bolshevistic days I should have preferred of course to have started off with 'Comrade' or 'Brother'. **1923** D. H. LAWRENCE *Birds, Beasts & Flowers* 69 Never, bolshevistically To be able to stand for all these!

Bolshevize ('bɒlʃɪvaɪz), *v.* [f. BOLSHEV(IK + -IZE.] *trans.* To make Bolshevist in character; to convert (a country) to a Bolshevistic form of government.

1919 *Observer* 23 Mar. 10/5 Unless we want to bolshevise the Boche and the world. **1920** *19th Cent.* Mar. 536 Taking her chance that Germany will be Bolshevised before Russia is Germanised. **1920** *Contemp. Rev.* Aug. 268 Thereby preventing these people from being Bolshevized.

Hence **'Bolshevized** *ppl. a.*; **'Bolshevizing** *vbl. sb.* and *ppl. a.* Also **,Bolshevi'zation**, the process of making, or becoming, Bolshevist.

1920 *19th Cent.* Mar. 536 Great Britain has been accused ..of pursuing a policy aimed at the Balkanisation of the Baltic provinces. It may appear that we have only achieved their Bolshevisation. **1920** *Glasgow Herald* 15 Apr. 7/1 Syndicalists of a Bolshevik or Bolshevising hue. *Ibid.* 2 Oct. 7/2 The withdrawal of the Bolshevised troops from Asia Minor. **1927** *Daily Tel.* 16 Aug. 11/5 With a view to the Bolshevising of the 400,000,000 of Chinese. *Ibid.*, A Bolshevised China would be the world's greatest peril. **1940** *Manch. Guardian Weekly* 22 Mar. 225 Since 1918, when the German Army took some small part in freeing Finland from Bolshevisation.

Bolshy, Bolshie ('bɒlʃɪ), *sb.* and *a.* [-Y[6].] **A.** *sb.* A jocular or contemptuous name for a Bolshevik. Also *transf.* and *fig.*

1920 *John Bull* 28 Aug. 1 We can quite understand the Bolshies' repugnance to labour—except with the jaw. **1920** *Punch* 10 Nov. 373/1 Mr. Stanton could think of no better retort than the stereotyped 'Bolshie!' **1921** HICHENS *Spirit of Time* xii, Those Russians.. breed more princesses than we do..but they seem to be giving them toko over there —the Bolshies, I mean. **1923** D. H. LAWRENCE *Kangaroo* i. 1 A comical-looking bloke! Perhaps a Bolshy. **1940** 'G. ORWELL' in *Horizon* Mar. 187 If the Russian Revolution is anywhere referred to it will be indirectly, in the word 'Bolshy' (meaning a person of violent disagreeable habits).

B. *attrib.* or as *adj.* **a.** = BOLSHEVISTIC *a.* **b.** *transf.* and *fig.* Left-wing; uncooperative, recalcitrant.

1918 D. H. LAWRENCE *Lett.* (1962) I. 565 The railway people, when one travels, seem rather independent and Bolshy. **1922** T. E. LAWRENCE *Lett.* (1939) 382 My nature doesn't second the demands of discipline very well, and unless I keep working at something I get Bolshie! **1930** H. G. WELLS *Autocr. Mr. Parham* III. vi. 208 The young men of science, the clever ones, are all going Bolshy or worse. *Ibid.* IV. iv. 296 Street-corner boys and Bolshie agitators. **1934** G. B. SHAW *On the Rocks* II. 231 Lenin and Stalin and Trotsky and all that Bolshy lot. **1966** *New Statesman* 1 Apr. 473/1 The neglected dullards not unnaturally turn bolshy. **1969** D. CLARK *Nobody's Perfect* v. 156 You can stop looking so bolshie, because I think you've done what you did well enough.

Hence **'bolshiness**, obstructive or recalcitrant behaviour; political or temperamental disinclination to obey authority.

1975 *Economist* 14 June 22/2 Trading off bolshiness on these outstanding issues—and on EEC quotas and prices for New Zealand butter..—against good behaviour on others will be hard. **1985** *Times* 12 Apr. 2/3 Poor production at the three pits has been caused by 'bolshiness' at the end of the miners' strike.

bolson ('bəʊlsən, ‖bol'son). *U.S.* [Sp., augmentative of *bolsa* purse.] In the south-western U.S. and Mexico, a basin-shaped depression surrounded by mountains. Also ***bolson-plain***.

1838 A. GANILH *Mexico v. Texas* 9 A desert known, in the maps [of Mexico], under the name of 'Bolson of Mapimi'. **1847** RUXTON *Adv. Mexico* xiii. 96 The sun was fast sinking behind the rugged crest of the 'Bolson', tinging the serrated ridge..with a golden flood of light. **1904** *Amer. Geol.* Sept. 164 The bolson plains may be considered as sections of an upraised peneplain surface in its earliest infancy, at a stage in which they are as yet untouched by stream-action. **1964** F. O'ROURKE *Mule for Marquesa* 15 It would be..the Bolsón, ten thousand square miles of the high desert, cupped within the waterless mountains.

bolster ('bəʊlstə(r)), *sb.*[1] Forms: 2–5 **bolstre**, 5 **bolstyr**(e, (6 **bolstarre, boylster**), 6–8 **boulster**, 1, 5– **bolster**; *Sc.* 5 **bowstowre**, 6– **bowster**. [Com. Teut.: OE. *bolster* = MDu. and Du. *bolster*, OHG. *bolstar* (MHG. *bolster*, mod.G. *polster*). OE. *bolster* is cogn. w. ON. *bolstr* (Sw. *bolster* 'bed', Da. *bolster* 'bed-ticking'):—OTeut. **bolstro-z*, f. OTeut. root **bŭl* to swell, the causal of which is found in Goth. *ufbauljan* to puff up.]

1. a. A long stuffed pillow or cushion used to support the sleeper's head in a bed; the name is now restricted to the under-pillow, stuffed with something firm, which extends from side to side, and on which the softer and flatter pillows are laid.

a **1000** *Beowulf* 2484 Beddum and bolstrum. *c* **1200** *Trin. Coll. Hom.* 139 He..ches..bare eorðe to bedde . and hard ston to bolstre. *c* **1425** *Leg. Rood* (1871) 210 With hym on bedde, man, þou sat On þe bolstre of heuene blisse. **1444** *Test. Ebor.* (1855) II. 100 Lectum plumarem cum le bolster. **1479** *Will Walt. Paston* in *Lett.* III. 249 Unum pulvinar vocatum le bolstar. **1494** *Act 11 Hen. VII*, xix, Feather-beds, Bolsters, and Pillows. **1535** STEWART *Cron. Scot.* II. 445 But bed or bowster to lig on the stro. **1596** SHAKS. *Tam. Shr.* IV. i. 204 Heere Ile fling the pillow, there the boulster. **1611** BIBLE *1 Sam.* xix. 13 And Michal..put a pillow of goats haire for his bolster. **1640** BRATHWAIT (*title*) Art asleepe Husband? a Boulster Lecture; stored with witty Jests. **1688** *Lond. Gaz.* 22 Oct./2 The said Deponent stood at the Queens Bolster. **1837** HOWITT *Rur. Life* III. iii. (1862) 246 Propped up in bed with bolsters and pillows.

b. A cushion or pad for leaning or sitting upon, etc.

c **1275** *Death* 90 in *O.E. Misc.* 174 Neaver sitten on bolstre ne on benche. **1703** MAUNDRELL *Journ. Jerus.* (1732) 29 Furnished all round with Bolsters for leaning upon.

2. Applied to various things of the nature of a pad, used to obviate friction or chafing, or pad out hollows or deficiencies, etc.

†**a.** A surgical pad or compress to support or protect any injured part of the body. *Obs.*

1541 R. COPLAND *Guydon's Quest. Chirurg.*, Wherfore serueth the bolsters?..To stay and conpryme the places dissolued. **1607** TOPSELL *Four-f. Beasts* 327 Bolster the tent with a bolster of flax. **1758** LAYARD in *Phil. Trans.* L. 749 He applied bolsters dipped in warm red wine and water. **1813** J. THOMSON *Lect. Inflammation* 299 Application of bolsters or pads of lint..to prevent the matter exuding.

†**b.** A pad worn by porters. *Obs.*

1552 HULOET, Bolsters whyche bearers of burdens, as porters do weare for freatynge. **1580** BARET *Alv.* B 905.

†**c.** A ridge of padding on a saddle. *Obs.*

1592 GREENE *Art Conny catch.* II. 5 His saddle..hath cantle and bolsters. **1611** COTGR., *Batte*, the boulster of a Saddle. **1753** CHAMBERS *Cycl. Supp.*, *Bolsters* of a saddle..those parts which are raised on the bows, both before and behind, to rest the rider's thighs..Common saddles have no bolsters behind or even before.

†**d.** A padding in a garment used to fill up or round out some part. *Obs.*

1600 ROWLAND *Lett. Humours Blood* vii. 83 A boulster for their Buttockes, and such stuffe. **1731** SWIFT *Nymph going to Bed* Wks. 1755 IV. I. 147 Off she slips The bolsters, that supply her hips. **1753** CHAMBERS *Cycl. Supp.* s.v., By a constitution, the clergy are forbidden to wear bolsters about their shoulders, in their gowns, coats, or doublets.

e. *Naut.* in *pl.* 'Small cushions or bags of tarred canvas, used to preserve the stays from being chafed by the motion of the masts.' Smyth *Sailor's Word-bk.* Also pieces of timber fixed in various positions to prevent chafing between ropes and other parts of the ship.

1769 FALCONER *Dict. Marine* (1789) *Bolsters*..are used to preserve the stays from being chafed or galled by the motion of the masts. *c* **1850** *Rudim. Navig.* (Weale) 99 Bolsters for the Anchor Lining are solid pieces of oak, bolted to the ship's side..Bolsters for Sheets, Tacks, &c. are small pieces of fir or oak fayed under the gunwale, &c., with the outer surface rounded to prevent the sheets and other rigging from chafing. *c* **1860** H. STUART *Seaman's Catech.* 76 The bolsters are bolted above the trussletrees.

f. A pad or cushion employed to deaden noise in pianofortes.

3. Applied to various parts of mechanism which form a solid support or base, on which other parts rest or exert pressure.

†**a.** Some part of a plough. *Obs.*

1523 FITZHERB. *Husb.* §4 But their most speciall temper is at the bolster, where as the plough beame lyeth. **1733** J. TULL *Horse-hoeing Husb.* xxi. 145 Sometimes we use a Piece of Shoe-Leather instead of an iron bolster.

†**b.** A support for a bee-hive. *Obs.*

1609 C. BUTLER *Fem. Mon.* v. (1623) K ij, Reare the full Hiue with three Bolsters, two on the West side, and one on the East, some foure or fiue inches high. *Ibid.* (1634) 47 Also rear the swarms, that being under-hived do lie forth, with a Skirt or Bolsters of that thickness, that may but let in the Bees.

c. The bearing for a water wheel shaft. *dial.*

1671 *Phil. Trans.* VI. 2108 A great beam, turned by an over-shoot-water-wheel on 2 boulsters.

d. A block of wood fixed on a siege-gun carriage, on which the breech rests during transport.

e. The transverse bar over the axle of a wagon, which supports the bed, and raises it from the axle. Also, the principal cross-beam of a railway truck or carriage body.

1686 HOLME *Armory* III. viii. §49 The Bolster is that on which the fore-wheels with the axle-tree turn in wheeling the waggon on a cross Road. **1834** *Brit. Husb.* I. 158 The shafts of the cart rest on the bolster of the waggon-wheels, to which they are secured; and a long copse, or fore-ladder resting also upon the bolster, projects over the shaft-horse.

f. The part of the pier or abutment on which a truss-bridge rests.

g. The spindle-bearing in the rail of a spinning-frame.

1825 *Specif. of Andrew's Patent* No. 5079 From the top of the spindle to the first bearing, which is denominated a bolster, is about 7 inches. **1873** LEIGH *Cotton Spin.* 219 The theory of the bolster rail lift is very plausible.

h. A horizontal cap-piece laid upon the top of a post or pillar, to shorten the bearing of the beam of a string-piece supported by it.

i. In the centering of an arch, each of the transverse pieces which lie across the ribs and support the voussoirs of the arch.

j. The plate or block in a punching-machine on which the metal to be punched is laid, and which is perforated or excavated to fit the punch.

1677 MOXON *Mech. Exerc.* (1703) 11 Your Punch will print a bunching mark upon the hole of a Bolster, that is, a thick Iron with a hole in it. **1790** *Specif. of Clifford's Patent* No. 1785 The nails are to be cut..by means of a punch.. having a hollow boulster (commonly called a bed) the hollow and aperture of which must also be made to the size and form of the nail. **1856** HOLTZAPFFELL *Turning* II. 929 Punches..used in combination with bolsters.

4. Applied to various things of the nature of a supporting or strengthening ridge.

a. The projecting 'shoulder' of a knife, chisel, etc., where the blade is inserted into the handle.

1827 *Specif. of Smith's Patent* No. 5470 To form the blade and bolster and tang at one and the same operation. **1831** J. HOLLAND *Manuf. Metals* I. 291 The bolster, or that prominent part of a common table knife which abuts upon the handle.

b. The metallic plate on the end of the handle of a pocket-knife.

c. A raised ridge on the wrestplank of a piano to give bearing to the strings by raising them.

5. *Arch.* One of the rolls forming the sides of an Ionic capital; = BALUSTER 5.

1876 GWILT *Archit.* Gloss., *Bolster* or Pillow, the baluster part of the Ionic capital on the return side.

6. *Comb.*, as ***bolster-piece***; ***bolster-shaped*** adj.; **bolster collar**, a bolster-shaped collar of a woman's coat or cloak.

1860 R. S. BURN *Handbk. Mech. Arts* (ed. 2) 197 Where the tie-rods..join the ring at the angles, bolster-pieces are inserted, against which the nuts are screwed hard up. **1900** *Westm. Gaz.* 16 May 2/1 The bolster-shaped kit bag. **1904** *Windsor Mag.* Jan. 238/2 Long bolster-shaped sweets. **1923** *Daily Mail* 19 June 1 New short coat..with smart finely pleated bolster collar.

bolster ('bəʊlstə(r)), *sb.*[2] [? cf. BOASTER[2].] A type of chisel used by bricklayers for cutting bricks.

1908 C. F. MITCHELL *Brickwork & Masonry* (ed. 2) ii. 96 *Brick-Cutting Tools*..The club hammer and bolster, for cutting with greater exactitude than with the trowel. **1924** H. L. BRIGGS *Pract. Bricklaying* iv. 39 For finer work the brick-cutting chisel, or 'set' or 'bolster', as it is usually called, is used. **1936** *Archit. Rev.* LXXIX. 240/4 (*caption*) The bolster, a long-edged, cold chisel used for cutting bricks and also for cleaning joints.

bolster ('bəʊlstə(r)), *v.* Also 6 *Sc.* bowster, 6–8 boulster, 7 bowlster. [f. BOLSTER *sb.*[1]]

1. *trans.* To support with a bolster. (Usually in pa. pple.)

1610 BARROUGH *Meth. Physick* III. ix. (1639) 113 Let your head be bolstered up high. **1791** E. DARWIN *Bot. Gard.* II. 77 Bolster'd with down, amid a thousand wants. **1873** BLACK *Pr. Thule* xx. 328 She was bolstered up in bed.

†**2.** *transf.* To support, prop *up*. *Obs.*

1567 STUDLEY *Seneca's Hippolytus* (1581) 61 Thunderpropping brawny shoulderd sier, That heaued and bolstred up the Welkin throne. **1615** CROOKE *Body of Man* 118 Vnder the beginning of the duodenum is the Pancræas placed..to boulster them vp.

3. *fig.* To prop up, support, uphold. Also with *up*. In later use usually with some approach to c.

1508 FISHER *Wks.* (1876) 175 Suche maner stronge and constaunt people dooth bolster and holde up bothe themselfe and other in crystes chyrche, they be lyke vnto pyllers. **1548** HALL *Chron.* (1809) 432 To upholde, fortefye and bolster the enterpryce. **1591** *Troubl. Raigne K. John* (1611) 46 Arthur thou seest, Fraunce cannot bolster thee. **1664** H. MORE *Myst. Iniq.* 512 Bolstering up one another by reflexion upon their numerosity. **1813** T. JEFFERSON *Corr.* (1830) 185 To bolster themselves up on the revered name of that first of our worthies.

b. To uphold or bear out (evil doers, illegal action, crime, or error); to aid and abet, to countenance. Also with *out* (obs.) and *up*.

1523 [cf. BOLSTERER]. **1549** [cf. BOLSTERING *vbl. sb.*] **1583** FULKE *Defence* ii. 177 You frame your translations to bolster your errors and heresies. **1612** T. JAMES *Jesuits Downef.* 29 They haue bolstred, banded, bearded, and borne out many foule matters. **1821** HONE *Facetiæ* 18 There is..not a public job that he has not bolstered; not a public knave that he has not shielded.

1530 *Proper Dyaloge* (1863) 3 Which..They bolstred out vnder abusyon. **1586** FERNE *Blaz. Gentrie* II. 118 He bolstered out a murtherer in acquiting the murtherer by vnlawful means. **1654** E. JOHNSON *Wond.-wrkg. Provid.* 65 Yet were they boulstered out in this their wicked act by those who set them one worke.

1561 T. NORTON *Calvin's Inst.* IV. viii. (1634) 568 *marg.* To bolster up a most unlawfull power in the Church. **1612** T. TAYLOR *Comm. Titus* ii. 12 (1619) 477 Can bolster vp their friends, children, and seruants in things worthie punishment. **1640** BP. HALL *Episc.* II. xviii. 193 Would in their very offices bolster up the pride of Antichrist. **1830** ARNOLD *Let.* in *Life & Corr.* (1844) I. vi. 285, I want to get up a real Poor Man's Magazine, which should not bolster up abuses and veil iniquities.

c. Now usually (with some mixture of sense 4): To give fictitious support to (a thing unable to stand of itself). Commonly with *up*, rarely *out*.

1581 J. BELL *Haddon's Answ. Osor.* 447 Wherewith they may bolster upp not their credytt, but their false packyng. **1635** SWAN *Spec. M.* i. §3 (1643) 18 These things have.. been boulstered out by Rabbinical traditions. **1641** MILTON *Ch. Discip.* II. Wks. (1851) 38 Bolstering, and supporting their inward rottenes by a carnal and outward strength. **1804** WELLINGTON in Gurw. *Disp.* III. 275, I have done every thing in my power to bolster up the credit of the government. **1868** M. PATTISON *Academ. Org.* §4. 81 What we..teach requires to be bolstered up by bounties to the taught.

4. To pad, furnish, or stuff out with padding; to puff. Also with *out*, *up*.

1530 [cf. BOLSTERING *vbl. sb.* 2]. **1562** J. HEYWOOD *Prov. & Epigr.* (1867) 217 That breeche was bolstred so with such brode barres. **1576** GASCOIGNE *Steele Gl.* Epil., They bumbast, bolster, frisle, and perfume. **1609** *Man in Moone* (1849) 35 A white necke, if it be not plastered; a straight backe, if it be not bolstered. **1710** STEELE *Tatler* No. 245 ¶2 Three Pair of Stays, boulstered below the Left Shoulder. **1847** L. HUNT *Men, Wom. & Bks.* I. xiv. 277 For a lady to look like an hour-glass, or a huge insect, or anything else cut in two, and bolstered out at head and feet.

b. *fig.*

1568 *Sempill Ballates* (1873) 232 Bowstert with pryd. **1616** *Manifest. Abp. Spalato's Motives* 31 Their Reuenues are great, and boulstered out with secular dignities. **1826** SCOTT *Woodst.* iii, Whose sermons were all bolstered up with..Greek and Latin.

†**5.** *spec.* in *Surg.* To furnish with a pad or compress. Also *fig.* *Obs.*

1607 TOPSELL *Four-f. Beasts* 322 It will..not only require more business in bolstering it, but also put the Horse to more pain. **1649** G. DANIEL *Trinarch., Rich. II*, 332 Thus Broken Hearts Are bolstred vp, and none can tell their Smarts. **1766** SHARP *Fractures* in *Phil. Trans.* LVII. 84 With the common wooden splints (properly bolstered).

6. ? *intr.* To lie on the same bolster.

1604 SHAKS. *Oth.* III. iii. 399 If euer mortall eyes do see them boulster, More then their owne.

7. *trans.* (among schoolboys): To belabour with bolsters. Cf. *pillow-fight*.

1871 A. R. HOPE *Schoolboy Friends* (1875) 287 And then they bolstered us.

†**8.** To pervert, abuse, or ? suspend (laws). *Obs.*

1494 FABYAN VII. 646 [They reported] how the lawes be delayed & bolstred by suche as stande in his fauoure. **1538** STARKEY *England* II. iv. §26 Materys are so borne and bolsteryd that justyce can not haue place wyth indyfferency.

bolstered ('bəʊlstəd), *ppl. a.* [f. prec. + -ED.]

1. Propped up, supported.

1566 DRANT *Horace Sat.* iv. C, Mars broke brasen bars, bare boulstred boulwarkes backe.

2. a. Padded, stuffed out.

1656 *Artif. Handsomeness* 44 A bumbast or bolstered garment. **1840** *New Month. Mag.* LVIII. 455 Privilege..in itself but the bolstered title for abuse.

b. With *up* in sense of BOLSTER *v.* 4 b.

1901 *Westm. Gaz.* 17 Sept. 7/3 There is a fearful lot of over-trading and bolstered-up credit..in German industrials.

bolsterer ('bəʊlstərə(r)). [f. as prec. + -ER[1].]

1. One who bolsters up (anything); a supporter, upholder. (Generally in bad sense.)

1523 LD. BERNERS *Froiss.* I. cccl. 561 Who durst begyn suche a ryot..without some bolsterer or comforter in their dede. **1552** LATIMER *Serm. Lincoln* ii. 75 Magistrates ought not to be bolsterers and bearers with wickedness. **1640** A. HARSNET *God's Summons* 224 Enemies would have said that God had beene a Bolsterer and Patron of Sinne.

2. Cf. BOLSTER *v.* 6.

? *a* **1600** *Hye way Spyttel Ho.* 831 in Hazl. *E.P.P.* IV. 60 Incestes, harlots, bawdes and bolsterers.

'bolstering, *vbl. sb.* [f. as prec. + -ING[1].]

1. The action of maintaining or upholding; almost always in bad sense; in modern use, the factitious propping up of what cannot stand of itself.

1549 LATIMER *Serm. bef. Edw. VI* (Arb.) 154 O Lord what bearyng what bolstering of naughtye matters is thys. **1552** —— *Serm. Lord's Prayer* iii. 16 Yea in the place of iustice, there I haue seene bearing and bolstring. **1645** PAGITT *Heresiogr.* (1661) 75 Communicating with known offenders, bolstering of sins, and willing connivences. **1823** LAMB *Elia* (1860) 200 He let the passion or the sentiment do its own work without prop or bolstering.

2. (usually *concr.*): Padding, puffing; in *Surg.* A pad or compress; = BOLSTER *sb.*[1] 2 a.

1530 PALSGR. 199/2 Bolsteryng, stuffyng, *fulsement*. **1562** J. HEYWOOD *Prov. & Epigr.* (1867) 179 The barres of mens breeches haue..Such bolstring, such broydring. **1579** LYLY *Euphues* (1636) F iij, Take from them..their roles, their boulsterings, and thou shalt soon perceiue, that a woman is the least part of her selfe. **1612** WOODALL *Surg. Mate* Wks. (1653) 406 Let him..be provided with..fitting boulstring and convenient bandage. **1828** STEUART *Planter's G.* 269 A strong Bolstering of double Mat, filled with hay or straw.. so that the bark of the stem may not be injured.

3. Fight with bolsters (in school dormitories).

1857 HUGHES *Tom Brown* vii. (1871) 152 Great games of chariot-racing, and cock-fighting, and bolstering.

bolt (bəʊlt), *sb.*[1] [OE. *bolt* (str. masc.) a cross-bow bolt, cogn. with OHG. *bolz*, mod.G. *bolz*, *bolzen* 'cross-bow arrow', also 'bolt for a door', MDu. and Du. *bout*, MLG. *bolte, bolten* bolt, fetter, piece of linen rolled up. The remoter etymology is unknown; but it cannot be referred to the verb stem *bul-* to swell, be round.]

I. A projectile.

1. a. An arrow; especially one of the stouter and shorter kind with blunt or thickened head, called also *quarrel*, discharged from a cross-bow or other engine. Often *fig.*, esp. in the proverbial phrase ***a fool's bolt is soon shot***, so common from the 13th to 18th c. † ***at first bolt***: at the first go off.

a **1000** *Gloss.* in Wr.-Wülcker 508, 372 *Catapultas*, speru, boltas. *a* **1225** *Leg. Kath.* 54 ȝoure bolt is sone ischote. *a* **1275** *Prov. Alfred* 421 in *O.E. Misc.* 129 Sottis bold is sone i-scoten. *c* **1386** CHAUCER *Milleres T.* 78 Long as a Mast, and vprighte as a bolt. *a* **1400** *Cov. Myst.* 136 He that shett the bolt is lyke to be schent. *c* **1475** *Voc.* in Wr.-Wülcker 812 *Hec sagitta*, a harrow; *hoc petulium*, a bolt. *c* **1485** CAXTON *Sonnes of Aymon* (1885) 529 But he made to be cast boltes of wilde fyre in to the galley of the admyrall. **1562** J. HEYWOOD *Prov.* (1867) 75 Than wolde ye mend, as the fletcher mends his bolte. **1612** *Pasquil's Night-Cap* (1877) 15 The grosser foole, the sooner shootes his bolt. **1676** 'A. RIVETUS, JUN.' *Mr. Smirke* 5 At first bolt..he denounces sentence before inquiry. **1748** SMOLLETT *Rod. Rand.* liii, 'Zounds, I have done', said he. 'Your bolt is soon shot, according to the old proverb', said she. **1819** SCOTT *Ivanhoe* II. iv. 70 Look that the cross-bowmen lack not bolts. **1874** BOUTELL *Arms & Arm.* viii. 129 The cross-bow-men had to open the discharge of their bolts while their bow-strings were still wet from a heavy shower.

†**b.** Phrase. ***to make a shaft or a bolt of it***: to risk making something or other out of it; to accept the issue whatever it may be, to run the risk, make the venture. (Cf. *to make a spoon or spoil a horn.*) *Obs.*

1598 SHAKS. *Merry W.* III. iv. 24 Ile make a shaft or a bolt on't, slid, tis but venturing. **1679** *Hist. Jetzer* 17 Without any regard to the Displeasure..of God [they] resolv'd to make a shaft or a bolt of it. **1687** R. L'ESTRANGE *Answ. Dissenter* 46 One might have made a Bolt or a Shaft on't.

2. a. A discharge of lightning, a thunderbolt.

1535 COVERDALE *Ps.* lxxvii[i]. 48 How he smote their.. flockes with hote thonder boltes. **1586** M. ROYDON *Elegie* 178. **1667** MILTON *P.L.* VI. 491 That they shall fear we have disarmd The Thunderer of his only dreaded bolt. **1791** COWPER *Odyss.* XIV. 370 Then, thund'ring oft, he hurl'd into the bark His bolts. **1802** CAMPBELL *Hohenlind.*, And louder than the bolts of heaven Far flashed the red artillery. **1859** TENNYSON *Vivien* ad fin., Scarce had she ceased, when out of heaven a bolt..struck Furrowing a giant oak.

b. *fig.* So in ***bolt from the blue***: see BLUE *sb.* 5.

1577 tr. *Bullinger's Decades* (1592) 601 The hote bolts of that thunder, euen sentences definitiue of excommunication. **1803** JANE PORTER *Thaddeus* viii. (1831) 70 The undistinguishing bolt of carnage. **1884** TENNYSON *Becket* 10 That so the Papal bolt may pass by England.

3. An elongated bullet for a rifled cannon.

1871 TYNDALL *Fragm. Sc.* (ed. 2) i. 17 In artillery practice the heat generated is usually concentrated upon the front of the bolt.

4. A cylindrical jet.

1842 H. MILLER *O.R. Sandst.* x. (ed. 2) 216 A bolt of water ..came rushing after like the jet of a fountain. **1884** *Public Opinion* 11 July 47/1 The blowers skilfully gather the molten bolts of glass from the pots and blow huge cylinders.

II. A stout pin for fastening.

5. a. An appliance for fastening a door, consisting of a cylindrical (or otherwise-shaped) piece of iron, etc., moving longitudinally through staples or guides on the door, so that its end can be shot or pushed into a socket in the door-post or lintel.

b. That part of a lock which springs out and enters the staple or 'keeper' made for its reception.

c **1400** *Destr. Troy* 10463 Þai..Barrit hom full bigly with boltes of yerne. **1463** *Mann. & Househ. Exp.* 155 To bye lokkys and boltys ffor my lorddys schambre. **1570** LEVINS *Manip.* 218 Y[e] Boult of a doore, *pessulus*. **1643** MILTON *Divorce* II. xx. Wks. (1851) 118 Forc't Vertue is as a bolt overshot; it goes neither forward nor backward. **1688** R. HOLME *Armory* III. vii. §8 In a Lock—The Bolt or Shoot.. The Staples, those as holds the Bolt to the Plate. **1753** CHAMBERS *Cycl. Supp.* s.v., Bolt of a lock is the piece of iron which entering the staple, fastens the door. **1815** SCOTT *Ld. of Isles* v. iii, How came it here through bolt and bar.

†**6.** An iron for fastening the leg, a fetter. *Obs.*

1483 CAXTON *Gold. Leg.* 192/1 Delyuerd of theyr irons, as guyues, boltes, and other. **1530** PALSGR. 199/2 Bolte or shacle, *entraue*. **1590** MARLOWE *Edw. II*, I. i. ad fin., He shall to prison, and there die in bolts. **1592** GREENE *Art Conny catch.* II. 31 Clap a strong paire of bolts on his heeles. **1649** JER. TAYLOR *Gt. Exemp.* I. iv. 128 Some wore iron upon their skin and bolts upon their legs. **1688** R. HOLME *Armory* III. vii. §86 Prison-shackles or Prisoners Bolts; they are Irons fastned about the Legs of Prisoners.

7. a. A stout metal pin with a head, used for holding things fast together. It may be permanently fixed, secured by riveting or by a nut, as the bolts of a ship; or movable, passing through a hole, as the bolts of a shutter.

The bolts in ships, gun-carriages, etc. have various names according to their nature, purpose, or position, as ***clinch-bolts***, ***ring-bolts***, ***set-bolts***; ***bed-bolts***, ***eye-bolts***, etc. See CLINCH, RING, etc.

1626 CAPT. SMITH *Accid. Yng. Seamen* 10 Bindings, knees, boults, trunions. **1627** —— *Seaman's Gram.* ii. 5 Set bolts for forcing the workes and plankes together. **1672** *Compl. Gunner* vi. 7 For fear any Bolts should give way or draw. **1769** FALCONER *Dict. Marine* (1789) I. iv. b, Breeching-bolts, with rings, through which the breechings pass. **1792** *Gentl. Mag.* Apr. 344 A machine for driving bolts ..into ships. **1794** W. FELTON *Carriages* (1801) I. 103 The common bolt, which receives a screwed nut at the bottom. **1850** LAYARD *Nineveh* xiii. 344 Holes for bolts exist in many of the slabs.

b. A sliding metal rod in the breech mechanism of a rifle which opens and closes the bore and positions the cartridge.

1859 'STONEHENGE' *Shot-gun & Sporting Rifle* IV. iii. 259 The barrel-maker has to braze on with great care two lumps of iron to the lower sides of the barrels, one of which..forms about three-fifths of the socket in which the circular bolt fixed in the stock revolves. In order to understand the exact form of the bolt, a gun on this principle must be examined, and moreover as scarcely any two makers adopt the same shape, the description of one would not suffice for all. **1881** W. W. GREENER *Gun & its Devel.* 129 The piece is cocked by the thumb, as is the needle-gun; the bolt is then turned one-quarter of a circle to the left, and drawn back: the cartridge is put in and pushed home by the bolt; this bolt is turned back one-quarter of a circle to the right; the piece is then ready for firing. **1930** G. BURRARD *In Gunroom* 122 It is extremely difficult to insert an incorrectly assembled bolt into the action, and this can only be done by a combination of undue force and careful manipulation. **1969** [see *bolt action* in sense 15].

III. Transferred uses.

8. A roll of woven fabric: generally of a definite length; being, in various cases, 30 yards, 28 ells, or 40 feet.

1407 *Will of Wollebergh* (Somerset Ho.), Lego Isabelle Wollebergh..iiij boltes de Worstede. **1592** GREENE *Art Conny catch.* Q. 22 A boult of Saten, veluet, or any such commoditie. *a* **1600** *Custom Duties, Add. MS.* 25097 Poldavies, the bolte, containing xxx yards, xxs. **1638** T. VERNEY in *Verney Papers* 20 May 197 Fouer bolts of canvas to send cotton home in. **1721** BAILEY, *Bolt* of Canvas, a piece containing 28 ells. **1834** M. SCOTT *Cruise Midge* (1863) 18 Stiff and upright like a bolt of canvass on end. *c* **1860** H.

STUART *Seaman's Catech.* 52 Canvas is made in lengths of 40 feet, called bolts. *Mod. Sc.* How many bowts of tape?

9. A bundle (of osiers, etc.) of a certain size; a bundle of reeds, 3 ft. in circumference.

1725 BRADLEY *Fam. Dict.* II. s.v. *Ozier*, Such as are for white work being made up into Bolts as they call them. **1863** MORTON *Cycl. Agric* (E.D.S.) *Bolt*, or *Boult*, of oziers. (*Berks.*), a bundle, measuring 42 inches round, 14 inches from the butts. (*Ess.*), a bundle, of which 80 make a load. (*Hants.*), 42 inches round at the lower band. **1879** *Standard* 17 Apr., To Rod Dealers, Basket Makers..25 scores bolts of fine, well-grown, clean, Green Willow Rods.

10. Wood in special size for cleaving into laths.

1688 R. HOLME *Armory* III. iii. §50 Boults, the sawed pieces into lengths, out of which Laths or Latts are cloven. **1753** CHAMBERS *Cycl. Supp.*, Bolts in carpentry denote pieces of wood cleft with wedges in order to be split into laths.

11. (See quots.)

1875 *Whitby Gloss.* (E.D.S.), *Bolts*, narrow passages or archways between houses; hiding-holes. In our former-day writings, the word applies to trenches or gutters. **1880** *Cornwall Gloss.* (E.D.S.), *Bolt*, a stone-built drain. **1884** *Local Govt. Chron.* 8 Mar. 191 A Local Board found it necessary, for the purpose of taking away the waste water, etc. of a village, to construct a covered bolt across a garden ..The house..stands immediately over this bolt.

12. *Bookbinding.* The fold at the top and front edge of a folded sheet.

1875 URE *Dict. Arts* I. 423 Those leaves which present a double or quadruple fold, technically termed 'the bolt'.

13. An obsolete or local name for some plants. **a.** The Globe-flower, *Trollius* (Gerard *Appendix* 1597), and Marsh Marigold. **b.** Species of Buttercup (Parkinson *Theatr. Bot.* 1640).

IV. *Attrib.* and *Comb.*

14. *attrib.* quasi-*adj.* Bolt-like, bolt-shaped.

1859 TENNENT *Ceylon* II. VIII. v. 368 The smallest had a little bolt head covered with woolly brown hair.

15. *Comb.*, as ***bolt-auger***, ***-extractor***, ***-header***, ***-maker***, ***-making***, etc.; ***bolt-like***, ***-shaped*** adjs.; also **bolt action** (see quot. 1969[1]); also (with hyphen) *attrib.*; also *ellipt.* = a bolt-action gun; †**bolt-bag**, a quiver for bolts; †**bolt-boat**, old term for a boat which makes good weather in a rough sea (Smyth *Sailor's Wd.-bk.*); **bolt-chisel**, a cold chisel for cutting bolts; **bolt-cutter**, one who cuts bolts; a machine for cutting bolts, or threads on bolts; †**bolt-glass**, ? = BOLT-HEAD 2; **bolt-hole**, a hole through which a bolt passes; **bolt-iron**, round bar iron; †**bolt's-shoot**, the distance to which a bolt can be shot (cf. *stone's throw, bow shot*); **bolt-strake** (*Naut.*), certain strakes of plank which the beam fastenings pass through (Smyth *Sailor's Wd.-bk.*); **bolt-threader**, a machine for cutting screw-threads on bolts. BOLT-HEAD, -ROPE. ***bolt-upright***; see BOLT *adv.*

1871 W. W. GREENER *Modern Breech-Loaders* 52 In all cases where they exploded caps with '*bolt' actions, the mark of the striker was found upon the cap. **1896** —— *Gun & its Devel.* (ed. 6) xxx. 702 (*heading*) Bolt-action systems. **1958** R. ARNOLD *Automatic & Repeating Shotguns* ii. 46 In the United States the bolt-action has given excellent results at both Down-the-line and Skeet. **1969** D. C. FORBES *Sporting Gun* 137 *Bolt action*, refers to a gun with a breech which is opened by a bolt being turned and slid back. The cartridge is laid in front of the bolt and the bolt slid forward to push the cartridge into the breech. **1969** *New Yorker* 29 Nov. 150/2 He was carrying a First World War Czech bolt-action rifle. **1562** PHAËR *Æneid* IX. Cciij, Ratling noyse of *boltbag fine. **1883** *Harper's Mag.* Feb. 440/1 The *bolt-bearer of the gods. **1594** PLAT *Jewell-ho.* II. 44 Pour that which you haue..into a *bolt glasse, hauing a long steale. **1691** T. H[ALE] *Acc. New Invent.* 45 To Plugg up the *bolt-holes. **1793** SMEATON *Edystone L.* §147 The *Bolt iron composing the chain had been..five eighths of an inch in diameter. **1677** PLOT *Oxfordsh.* 336 About a *Bolts-shoot off, on the other side the hedge.

bolt (bəʊlt), *sb.*[2] [f. BOLT *v.*[2]] The act of bolting.

1. A sudden spring or start.

1550 LYNDESAY *Sqr. Meldrum* 146 Bot with ane bolt on thame he bendit. **1577** HELLOWES *Gueuara's Chron.* 335 The two Consuls gaue a boylt aloft on their chariots.

2. The act of suddenly breaking away; breaking away from a political party (*U.S. colloq.*).

a **1859** DE QUINCEY *Whiggism* Wks. VI. 64 He suddenly made a bolt to the very opposite party. **1867** F. FRANCIS *Angling* i. (1880) 62 He will make a bolt to his hold. **1884** *Pall Mall G.* 7 July 11/2 It is the 'Blaine bolt' which lends so extraordinary an interest to the Chicago Convention.

3. The act of bolting food.

1835 J. WILSON in *Blackw. Mag.* XXXVII. 133 The difference between a civilized swallow and a barbarous bolt.

4. *Comb.* BOLT-HOLE.

bolt, boult, *sb.*[3] In 5 bult(e, 6 bout, 5–7 boult. [f. BOLT *v.*[1]] **1.** A flour-sieve, a boulter. Hence (or from the verb-stem) †**bolt-cloth**, a cloth for bolting or sifting; a fabric suitable for this; **bolt feeder**, an apparatus for regulating the passage of meal to the flour-bolt; †**bolt-poke**, a bolter or bag for sifting.

c **1425** *Voc.* in Wr.-Wülcker 663 *Hoc pollitridium*, bultclathe. *c* **1440** *Promp. Parv.* 55 Bulte pooke or bulstare ..*politrudum.* **1592** *Wills & Inv. N.C.* (1860) II. 212, xj yards of boutcloth 6*s.* **1611** *Book of Rates* (JAM.) Boultclaith, the eln xs. **1847** CRAIG, *Bolt*, a sieve.

2. A hypothetical law case propounded and argued for practice by students of the Inns of Court. (Cf. BOLTING *vbl. sb.*[1] 2 b.)

1556 *Black Books of Lincoln's Inn* (1897) I. 316 Everi daye (except Sondayes and festifall dayes, when ther is a mote or a bolte). **1570** in R. J. Fletcher *Pension-bk. Gray's Inn* (1901) I. 4 Item it is ordered..that upon the other dayes not appointed for the moting it shalbe lawfull to the utter baristers to keepe bolts. **1593**- in Douthwaite *Gray's Inn* (1886) 83 None shall be called to the barr but such as..have put Cases at Bolts in Term six times. **1880** *Encycl. Brit.* XIII. 89/1 Bolts were of an analogous character, though deemed inferior to moots. Both had fallen into desuetude until lately. **1956** A. L. ROWSE *Early Churchills* ii. 14 The readings, moots and bolts—the public exercises that tested the knowledge acquired by the students from their seniors.

bolt, boult (bəʊlt), *v.*[1] Forms: 2–3 (*Orm.*) bullt, 4–6 bult(e, 6 boulte, bowlt, boolt, 5–8 boult, 6– bolt, *north.* 5–6 bowt, 6 bout. [a. OF. *bulte-r* (now *bluter*):—earlier OF. *buleter*, which (as appears from OF. *buretel* boultel, meal-sieve = mod.F. *bluteau*) is for **bureter* = It. *burattare*; no OF. **buret* is recorded, but It. *buratto* is a meal-sieve, and also 'a fine transparent cloth'. Diez and Littré refer it originally to *bura, bure*, a kind of cloth: see BUREAU, BURRELL. The historical spelling of the word is *boult*: unfortunately the dictionaries have confounded it with BOLT *v.*[2] (see JOHNSON) and authorized the spelling *bolt*: cf. BOULTEL.]

1. *trans.* To sift; to pass through a sieve or bolting-cloth. ***to bolt out***: to separate by sifting.

c **1200** [see BOLTED[1]]. **1398** TREVISA *Barth. De P.R.* XVII. lxvii, The floure of þe mele, whan it is bultid [**1535** boulted] and departid from þe bran. **1562** J. HEYWOOD *Prov. & Epigr.* (1867) 51 Fancy may boult bran, and make ye take it floure. **1617** MARKHAM *Caval.* III. 38 Grinde all these together, and boult them through an ordinarie bolting cloath. **1633** *Gerard's Herbal* II. cccxl. 912 Pouder of the roots..searced or bolted into most fine dust. **1725** POPE *Odyss.* xx. 134 To bolt the bran From the pure flour. **1871** NAPHEYS *Prev. & Cure Dis.* I. ii. 77 Flour has the bran bolted from it.

b. *transf.* and *fig.*

1599 SHAKS. *Hen. V*, II. ii. 137 Such and so finely boulted didst thou seeme. **1611** —— *Wint. T.* IV. iv. 375 The fan'd snow, that's bolted By th' Northerne blasts.

2. *fig.* To examine by sifting; to search and try. ***to bolt out***: to find out, or separate by sifting.

c **1386** CHAUCER *Nonne Prestes T.* 420, I ne kan nat bulte it to the bren. **1544** ASCHAM *Toxoph.* I. 97 You Persians for your great wisdom can soon bolt out what they mean. **1553** Q. MARY in Strype *Eccl. Mem.* III App. xiv. 35 Wherby ye may the better bulte out the malicious. **1576** LAMBARDE *Peramb. Kent* (1826) 375 Neither may I..boult out the whole Etymologie (or reason) of every Townes name. **1640–4** SIR B. RUDYARD in Rushw. *Hist. Coll.* III. (1692) I. 25 Let the matters bolt out the Men; their Actions discover them. **1791** BURKE *Let. Memb. Nat. Assemb.* Wks. VI. 49, I must first bolt myself before I can censure them. [**1868** BROWNING *Ring & Bk.* I. 923 The curious few Who care to sift a business to the bran Nor coarsely bolt it like the simpler sort.]

bolt (bəʊlt), *v.*[2] Forms: 3 bulten, 3–4 bult (3rd sing. pa. t.), 5 bult, 6 bolte, *Sc.* bowt, 6–7 boult, 7 bowlt, 8 *Sc.* bout, 4– bolt. [f. BOLT *sb.*[1] in its two main senses of 'a missile' and 'a fastening': the former has given rise to uses of the most diverse kinds, connected merely by the common notion of sudden or hasty motion or application of force, some of them being directly contrary to others: cf. 'to bolt a dart' 4 a, 'bolt a cony' 4 b, 'bolt a paraphrase' 5, 'bolt an egg', 'bolt the bill' 6, 'bolt the ticket' 7, besides 'bolt the door' 9, 'bolt a ship' 10.]

I. To spring, move suddenly, with its causal.

* *intr. To go off like a bolt.*

†**1.** To start, spring. *Obs.*

†**a.** To spring back, rebound, recoil; to fall violently backward. *Obs.*

a **1225** *Ancr. R.* 366 Hit pulteð up [*v.r.* hit bultes] aȝean o þeo þet þer neih stondeð. *c* **1400** *Destr. Troy* 7476 Both went backward & bult vppon the erthe.

†**b.** To spring or start; esp. with *up*, *upright*. *Obs.* or *arch.*

c **1425** WYNTOUN *Cron.* IX. viii. 162 Suddanly He boltyd up welle nere-hand þame by Wyth twelf displayed Baneris. **1483** *Cath. Angl.* 36 To Bolt up, *emergere.* **1594** PLAT *Jewell-ho.* III. 74 They shall not be able to rise or bolt vp againe. **1621** QUARLES *Esther* (1638) 90 What made..thy haire Bolt up? *a* **1771** SMOLLETT *Humph. Cl.* (1815) 199 The patient, bolting upright in the bed, collared each of these assistants with the grasp of Hercules. **1813** SCOTT *Trierm.* II. x, Screaming with agony and fright, He bolted twenty feet upright.

2. To move or come as with a spring or sudden bound, to dart.

a. To come or spring suddenly *upon* (*obs.*); to enter with a spring or sudden bound *in, into.*

1666 PEPYS *Diary* 20 Feb., Bolting into the dining-room, I there found Captain Ferrers. **1666** BUNYAN *Grace Ab.* ¶143 Suddenly this sentence bolted in upon me. **1709** STEELE *Tatler* No. 91 ¶1 Who came privately in a Chair, and bolted into my Room. **1779** JOHNSON *Lett.* 225 II. 96, I think to bolt upon you at Bath. **1839** DE QUINCEY *Murder* Wks. IV. 72 In therefore he bolted and..turned the key. **1840** GEN. P. THOMPSON *Exerc.* (1842) V. 92 Men were bolting in a hurry out of one religious tyranny, and it was not so wonderful they should bolt into another.

b. To dart *forth, forward, out.* (Often with the idea of start running, as in 3.)

1513 DOUGLAS *Æneis* V. vi. 58 Furth bowtis with a bend Nisus. **1550** LYNDESAY *Sqr. Meldrum* 519 [He] bowtit forward with ane bend. *a* **1680** BUTLER *Rem.* (1759) I. 92 Bolting out of Bushes in the dark. **1697** DRYDEN *Virg. Georg.* Ded. (1721) I. 188 Some bolting out upon the Stage with vast applause. *a* **1779** GARRICK *Lying Valet* I. Wks. 1798 I. 42 Out bolts her husband upon me with a fine taper crab in his hand. **1834** PRINGLE *Afr. Sk.* viii. 259 With..a furious growl, forth he bolted from the bush.

c. *Hawking.* (See quot.)

1855 SALVIN & BRODRICK *Falconry Brit. Isles* Gloss. 149 *Bolt*, to fly straight from the fist at game, as Goshawks and Sparrow-Hawks do.

d. *Horticulture.* To 'run to seed' prematurely.

1889 in *Cent. Dict.* **1961** *Amateur Gardening* 16 Sept. 12/2 In April or early May many of the plants 'bolted'.

3. To dart off or away, make off with himself, take flight, escape; to rush suddenly *off* or *away.*

a. *gen.* of men or beasts. *spec.* of a rabbit, fox, etc.: to escape from its burrow or earth.

1575 TURBERV. *Venerie* 179 Put in a Ferret close musseled, and she will make the Conies bolte out agaîne into your pursenets. *Ibid.*, It will make the Conies bolte out of the earth. **1611** BEAUM. & FL. *Philast.* II. ii, Here's one bolted; I'll hound at her. **1616** FLETCHER *Hum. Lieut.* IV. viii. 142 He will bolt now for certain. **1838** HAWTHORNE *Amer. Note-Bks.* (1871) I. 156 The landlord of the tavern keeping his eye on a man whom he suspected of an intention to bolt. **1851** [see BOLT-HOLE 1]. **1865** DICKENS *Mut. Fr.* iii, At once bolting off in cabs. **1879** F. POLLOK *Sport. Brit. Burmah* II. 94 The rhinoceros bolted, and I got two shots as it crossed an open piece. **1900** A. E. T. WATSON *Young Sportsman* 234 A rabbit will bolt much sooner from a ferret that is free. *Ibid.*, A rabbit will sometimes decline to bolt, and will be killed in the burrow.

b. *spec.* Of a horse: To break away from the rider's control; to make a violent dash out of his course.

1820 SCOTT *Monast.* v, The mule..bounded, bolted, and would soon have thrown Father Philip over her head. **1877** A. B. EDWARDS *Up Nile* xxii. 683 My donkey bolted about every five minutes. **1884** E. L. ANDERSON *Mod. Horsemanship* I. viii. 44 Bolting is the quick, determined movement, usually off the course and often against some obstacle, that a horse makes to break away from restraint.

c. *transf.* To break away from a political party. (*U.S. politics.*) Cf. 7.

1821 in E. S. Brown *Missouri Compromises* (1926) 43 Parker of Virginia, & some others, bolted. **1871** *St. Louis Democrat* 3 Apr. (De Vere), Several of our contemporaries have announced..that Carl Schurz has bolted from the Republican party. **1884** *Boston (Mass.) Jrnl.* 11 July (*heading*) Belief that Butler and Tammany will bolt.

** *trans. To send off like a bolt.*

4. To let off or discharge like a bolt; to shoot.

a **1420** OCCLEVE *De Reg. Princ.* 2226 Disceyte..Bultethe out shame, and causethe grete smertnesse. **1581** J. BELL *Haddon's Answ. Osor.* 439 A frivolous devise boulted out of the forgeshoppe of Lumbarde. **1618** *Barnevelt's Apol.* C, Against your woundless brest he bolts his dart in vaine. **1648** MARKHAM *Housew. Gard.* III. viii. (1668) 71 One of these seeds put into the eye..will..bolt itself forth without hurt to the eye. **1799** KIRWAN *Geol. Ess.* 169 Some may have been bolted off by the shock of an earthquake.

b. To drive out suddenly or forcibly; to expel. *spec.* To cause (a fox, rabbit, otter, etc.) to retreat from its hole or burrow. Also *transf.* and *fig.*

1610 GUILLIM *Heraldry* III. xiv. (1660) 166 You shall say Bowlt the Cony. **1612** BEAUM. & FL. *Cupid's Rev.* Wks. III. 415 This is one of her Ferrets that she bolts business out withall. **1622** FLETCHER *Span. Curate* V. ii. 48 All your devills wee will bolt. **1638** GUILLIM *Heraldry* (ed. 3) III. xiv. 176 You shall say Bowlt the Conie. **1805** WORDSW. *Prel.* III. 77 To have been bolted forth, Thrust out abruptly into Fortune's way. **1863** ATKINSON *Stanton Grange* 201 He intended to dig at his leisure until he bolted him [*sc.* an otter]. **1892** MRS. J. E. H. GORDON *Eunice Anscombe* 176 The terrier..was put into the hole to 'bolt' the otter. **1902** *Daily Chron.* 13 Mar. 8/2 A brace of foxes were next bolted from an artificial earth. **1914** R. CURLE *Life is a Dream* 229 The dogs became wildly excited, pawing at the sand around the hole, bolting the crab, and then biting it. **1922** E. PHILLPOTTS *Grey Room* vii. 172 He'll bolt it [*sc.* the evil spirit] yet,..like a ferret bolts a rat.

c. ***to bolt upright***: to cause to stand on end.

1794 J. WOLCOTT (P. Pindar) *Ep. Bruce* Wks. II. 463 Tales ..That bolt like hedge-hog-quills the hair upright.

5. To utter hastily, ejaculate, blurt *out* or *forth.*

1577 HANMER *Anc. Eccl. Hist.* (1619) 392 He bolted out such rash and vnadvised sayings. **1634** SIR T. HERBERT *Trav.* 123 Mahomet-Ally-Beg undesired, bolted out, that hee knew, etc. **1649** G. DANIEL *Trinarch., Rich. II*, 347 The Rudest Head will bolt a Paraphrase. **1692** R. LESTRANGE *Josephus' Antiq.* XVI. vi. (1733) 431 The Princes..bolted out at a Venture, whatever came at their Tongue's End. **1821** COLERIDGE *Lett., Convers., &c.* XV. I. 161 What we struggle with inwardly, we find..easiest to bolt out.

6. *colloq.* To swallow hastily and without chewing, swallow whole or with a single effort, gulp *down.*

1794 J. WOLCOTT (P. Pindar) *Path. Odes* Wks. III. 401 Bolting his subjects with majestic gobble. **1818** SCOTT *Hrt. Midl.* xxviii, He..bolted the alcohol, to use the learned phrase, and withdrew. **1835** MARRYAT *Pacha* ix, Bolting them down to satisfy the cravings of..hunger. **1859** DARWIN *Orig. Spec.* xi. 362 Some hawks and owls bolt their prey whole. **1882** *Pall Mall G.* 2 June 3/1 It would be much simpler for the House of Commons to bolt the bill whole.

*** *trans.* development of 3, 3 b, c.

7. To break away from (a political party or platform to which one has hitherto docilely adhered); = *bolt from* in sense 3. (*U.S. politics.*)
1813 *Portsmouth* (N.H.) *Oracle* 20 Nov. 2/3 (Th.), Others, ..without sufficient courage to do their duty, bolted the question. **1884** *Boston* (*Mass.*) *Jrnl.* 11 July, It is believed that Butler and Tammany will bolt the ticket. **1884** *U.S. Newspaper*, Several prominent Irishmen had bolted Cleveland. **1885** HOWELLS in *Harper's Mag.* July 262/1 The *Democrat-Republican*..bolted the nomination of a certain politician of its party for Congress.

II. To make fast or confine with a bolt.

†8. *trans.* To fetter, shackle; also *fig. Obs.*
1377 LANGL. *P. Pl.* B. VI. 138 If he be..bolted with yrnes. *a* **1535** MORE *Wks.* (1557) 1246 He bolteth their arms with a paulsy, that they cannot lift their hands to their heads. **1606** SHAKS. *Ant. & Cl.* V. ii. 6 That thing..Which shackles accedents, and bolts vp change.

9. *trans.* To secure (a door, etc.) with a bolt.
1580 BARET *Alv.* B 906 The olde woman bolted the dore. **1611** BIBLE *2 Sam.* xiii. 17 Put now this woman out from mee, and bolt the doore after her. **1663** BP. PATRICK *Parab. Pilgr.* 439 You haue obstinately bolted your heart against all these pious stories. **1720** T. BOSTON *Hum. Nat.* (1794) 142 Labouring to enter into heaven by the door, which Adam's sin..bolted. **1865** TROLLOPE *Belton Est.* xiii. 147 The kitchen door, which he locked and bolted.

b. *to bolt out, in, up*: to exclude, shut in, shut up, by bolting a door, etc. Also *fig.*
c **1620** Z. BOYD *Zion's Flowers* (1855) 32 Yee grace barre out, and vanitie bolt in. **1691** E. TAYLOR *Behmen's Incarn.* 330 The Divine Substantiality did sit bolted up therein. **1839** BAILEY *Festus* v, Where God is bolted out from every house.

c. *absol.* or *intr.*
1847 MARRYAT *Childr. N. Forest* ii, We can bolt and bar.

d. *intr.* for *pass.*
1907 *Smart Set* Feb. 77/1 The door bolts on the inside.

10. To fasten together or furnish with bolts.
1727-38 CHAMBERS *Cycl.* I. s.v. *Keel*, Into this are..the ground-timbers and hooks fastened, and bolted. **1780** BURKE *Sp. Bristol* Wks. III. 419 The..fabrick..is well cramped and bolted together in all its parts. **1787** NELSON in Nicolas *Disp.* (1845) I. 207, I have ordered her [a ship] to be new bolted. **1824** URE *Dict. Chem.* 9 A disc of cast-iron well fitted and firmly bolted to it. **1875** MCLAREN *Serm.* Ser. II. iii. 55 A strong shaft of iron bolting together the two tottering walls of some old building.

III. 11. The vb.-stem in Comb. **bolt-on** *a.*, of an optional addition to a car, machinery, etc.: able to be attached to the original parts by bolts; also *fig.*, (able to be) added on to something when required; cf. ADD-ON *sb.* (and *a.*) and *screw-on* a. s.v. SCREW *v.* 25 a.
1963 *Times* 8 Jan. 11/1 To test the effectiveness of a '*bolt-on' conversion unit during everyday motoring, I had the latest Lockheed diaphragm servo system fitted to a Morris 1100. **1967** *Time* 12 May 88/3 Decked out with bolt-on guns and rocket launchers, the shaking, rattling and rolling choppers are less than perfect for close-in fire support. **1974** *Daily Tel.* 4 Sept. 12/1 Bolt-on aerofoils for your Ford or Austin could be the next motor accessory craze. **1986** *Pract. Gardening* Mar. 12/1 We came up with the idea of a 'bolt-on' garden.

bolt, *adv.* [The sb. (BOLT[1]) and stem of the vb. (BOLT[2]), used to qualify adjectives and verbs.]

1. The sb. is used *similatively* (cf. *snow-white, sand-blind*) = 'as a bolt,' in ***bolt up*** (obs.), ***bolt upright*** (see UPRIGHT); whence **bolt-'uprightness** *sb.*
c **1386** CHAUCER *Reeve's T.* 346. *c* **1420** *Pallad. on Husb.* I. 967 Bere it bolt upright..and ley her downe upright. **1580** NORTH *Plutarch* (1676) 706 His hair stood bolt upright upon his head. **1635** BRATHWAIT *Arcad. Pr.* 158 Epimonos all this while sat bolt-upright in a chaire. **1651** CLEVELAND *Poems* 12 On his knees..With hands bolt up to Heaven. **1824** W. IRVING *T. Trav.* I. 87, I suddenly sprang bolt upright in my chair, and awoke.
1726 AMHERST *Terræ Fil.* xxix. 155 That bolt uprightness of mien. **1850** MRS. STOWE *Uncle Tom's C.* xv. 152 Stiffness and squareness, and bolt-uprightness.

2. The vb. stem is used *advb.* to express a sudden rapid motion; = 'bolting, with one bolt, straight'.
a **1845** HOOD *Not a single Man* vi, Bolt up the stairs they ran. **1877** BLACKIE *Wise Men* 121 A pitchy pillar of thick-volumed smoke Shot bolt to heaven.

bolted, boulted ('bəʊltɪd), *ppl. a.*[1] [f. BOLT *v.*[1] + -ED.] Sifted; *fig.* carefully selected, choice.
c **1200** ORMIN 992 Recles smec, & bulltedd bræd þatt bakenn wass inn ofne. *c* **1440** *Promp. Parv.* 55 Bu[l]tyd, *taratan-tarizatus.* **1607** SHAKS. *Cor.* III. i. 322 He..is ill-school'd In boulted Language.

'bolted, *ppl. a.*[2] [f. BOLT *sb.*[1] and *v.*[2] + -ED.]

1. Closed and fastened with a bolt; also *fig.*
1588 T. L. *To Ch. of Rome* (1651) 19 Those bar'd and bolted hearts of yours. **1687** H. MORE *Death's Vis.* viii. 200 Id'e Storm those Bolted Ears. **1784** COWPER *Task* IV. 304 The bolted shutter. **1828** CARLYLE *Misc.* (1857) I. 143 That bolted towers should encircle her.

2. Formed into or like bolts.
1747 T. GIBBONS *Elegy* vi, His shafted Lightnings, and his bolted Storms. **1860** T. MARTIN *Horace* 79 Bolted lightnings flash.

3. Fastened together with bolts.
1797 *Encycl. Brit.* s.v. *Ship*, They..have the beams, knees, and fore-hooks bolted into them. **1832** DE LA BECHE *Geol. Man.* 75 Blocks..squared and bolted together in the form of piers and jetties.

4. ***bolted arrows***: (app.) arrows with blunt heads, bird-bolts.
1864 *Reader* 24 Dec. 792/3 Shooting, with bolted arrows, partridge or pigeon.

boltel ('bəʊltəl). *Arch.* Also 5 boltell, 5-9 bowtel(l, 6-7 bou(l)tell, boultle, 8 boultine, 9 boutel. [Conjectured to be f. BOLT *sb.*[1] 'from its resemblance to the shaft of an arrow or bolt' (*Gloss. Archit.*): but as *bolt* is a Teutonic word, and *-el* of Fr. origin, the conjecture is hazardous.]

An old name for a plain round moulding; a shaft of a clustered pillar.
1463 *Bury Wills* (1850) 39 To sette here ageyn the bowtell there hire light stant. **1565** COOPER *Thesaurus* s.v. *Stria*, The boltell or thing that riseth up betwene the two chanels. **1677** MOXON *Mech. Exerc.* (1703) 267 Ovolo, or Boltel. **1738** CHAMBERS *Cycl.*, *Boultine* or *Boltel*, in architecture, the workman's term for a convex moulding, whose periphery is just ¼ of a circle. **1848** T. RICKMAN *Archit.* xvii, The mouldings are good Norman, consisting merely of plain rounds, or boutells. **1849** FREEMAN *Archit.* 381 We sometimes find such shafts or bowtels, with bases. **1876** GWILT *Archit.* Gloss., *Bowtel* or *Boltel.*

Hence **'boltelled** *ppl. a.*, moulded with boltels.
1575 LANEHAM *Let.* 50 Each windo..parted from oother ..by flat fayr bolteld columns. **1611** COTGR., *Embouti*, boultled; raised into, wrought with boultles.

bolter[1], **boulter** ('bəʊltə(r)). Forms: 5 bulture, -tar, 5-7 bulter, 6 *north.* bowter, bultre, boultar, 5- boulter, 7- bolter. [f. BOLT *v.*[1] + -ER[1]: or ? a. OF. *buleteor* one who sifts, f. *buleter* to BOLT *v.*[1]]

1. One who sifts meal, etc.
c **1440** *Promp. Parv.* 55 Bulture [**1499** bultar]. *c* **1450** *Voc.* in Wr.-Wülcker 688 *Hic polentradinator*, a bulter. **1481-90** *Howard Househ. Bks.* 27 John Xpofer, a boulter. **1548** UDALL, etc. *Erasm. Par.* Pref. to King 10 a, The boulter tryeth out the branne from the mele.

2. A piece of cloth used for sifting; a sieve, strainer; a bolting-machine. Also *fig.*
1530 PALSGR. 462/1, I boulte meale..in a boulter. **1546** LANGLEY *Pol. Verg. De Invent.* III. i. 64 b, Bultres of lynnen in Spayne. **1564** BAULDWIN *Mor. Philos.* (Palfr.) 169 b, Bee not like the Boulter that casteth out the flower and keepeth in the bran. **1596** SHAKS. *1 Hen. IV*, III. iii. 81, I haue giuen them away to Bakers Wiues, and they haue made Boulters of them. **1616** SURFL. & MARKH. *Countr. Farm* 574 The temze or bolter through which they passe. **1704** SWIFT *T. Tub* vii, By some called the Sieves and boulters of learning. **1880** T. HARDY *Trump.-Major* II. xxii. 123 Bob opened the bolter.. the result being that a dense cloud of flour rolled out.

b. The fabric used for this purpose.
1612 *Naworth Househ. Bks.* 43, Iij yardes of boulter ijs. vjd. **1754** *Stow's Surv.* (ed. Strype) II. v. xviii. 382/2 [Duty on] Bolters and Bewpers the dozen pieces 1*d.*

3. 'A boulter or a racket to play with, *reticulum*.' *Withals Dict.* (1634) 615.

4. *Comb.*, as **bolter-cloth**.
1586 COGAN *Haven Health* (1636) 125 Searsed through lawne, or a fine boulter cloth.

'bolter[2]. [f. BOLT *v.*[2] + -ER[1].]

1. a. One that bolts or runs; *esp.* a horse that bolts.
1840 THACKERAY *Paris Sk. Bk.* (1872) 244 The engine may explode..or be a bolter. **1871** LE FANU *Checkmate* II. xiii. 123 Kickers and roarers, and bolters and jibbers.

b. A fugitive from justice. Now *Austral. hist.*
1699 B. E. *Dict. Cant. Crew*, *Bolter of White Friers*, one that Peeps out, but dares not venture abroad, as a Coney bolts out of the Hole in a Warren, and starts back again. **1737** DYCHE & PARDON *Dict.* (ed. 2), *Bolter*, a Cant Name for one who hides himself in his own House, or some priviledged Place, and dares only peep, but not go out of his Retreat. **1855** *Argus* (Melbourne) 19 Jan. 5/4 The arrest in London of a well-known bolter from Melbourne. **1897** 'P. WARUNG' *Tales Old Régime* 160 One of the 'bolters', advertised by Mr. F. A. Hely, J.P., Principal Superintendent of Convicts, in the *Sydney Gazette*, in the year 1827. **1964** R. WARD *Penguin Bk. Austral. Ballads* 23 Some convicts 'took to the bush' as 'bolters' or bushrangers.

2. One who 'bolts' from his party. (*U.S.*)
1883 *Atl. Monthly* LII. 327 To whom a 'scratcher' or a 'bolter' is more hateful than the Beast. **1884** *American* VIII. 100 To denounce the twenty-seven as bolters from their party.

3. One who swallows (food) hastily or whole.
1825 *New Monthly Mag.* XVI. 178 Pettifogging strainers at gnats and bolters of camels. **1833** T. HAMILTON *Men & Manners in Amer.* I. ii. 44 The most expeditious bolters of dinner.

bolter[3], var. BOUL-, BULTER, a long fishing line.

boltered: see *blood-boltered* (BLOOD *sb.* 21).

†**'boltering, boultering.** *Obs.* [f. BOLTER *sb.*[1] + -ING[1].] The fabric used for bolters or sieves.
1609 C. BUTLER *Fem. Mon.* i. (1623) Cij, For the safeguard of your face..provide a purs-hood made of course boultering. **1634** *Althorp MS.* in Simpkinson *Washingtons* 25 For other boltering and thinne canves.

bolt-head, bolt's-head. Also 7 boult head, boulthed. [f. BOLT *sb.*[1]]

1. The head (*a*) of a bolt, or arrow; (*b*) of a bolt for holding parts together.
c **1475** *Voc.* in Wr.-Wülcker 812 *Hec cuspis*, a bolthed. **1483** *Cath. Angl.* 36 A Bolte hede, *capitellum.* **1691** T. H[ALE] *Acc. New Invent.* 20 The Bolt-heads, etc., being fairly parcelled.

2. *Chem.* A globular flask with a long cylindrical neck, used in distillation.
1610 B. JONSON *Alch.* II. ii, Blushes the bolts-head? *Ibid.* IV. iv, This doctor..Will close you so much gold in a bolt's-head. **1667** BOYLE *Orig. Formes & Qual.*, Having plac'd the mixture in a Bolt-head or Glass-egg with a long neck. **1763** *Brit. Mag.* IV. 63 Put it into a large bolt-head, with a long neck. **1820** SCOTT *Abbot* xxvi, Crucibles, bolt-heads, stoves, and the other furniture of a chemical laboratory. **1877** GRIFFIN *Chem. Handicr.* 146.

†3. A dragon-fly. *Obs.*
1668 WILKINS *Real Char.* II. v. §2. 126 Naked winged Insects. 7 Dragon Fly, Bolts head.

bolt-hole. [BOLT *v.*[2]] 1. = *bolting-hole* (see BOLTING *vbl. sb.*[2] 5).
1851 STERNBERG *Dial. Northampt.*, *Bolt-hole*, the hole from which the rabbit makes its escape; or, in the phraseology of the craft, '*bolts*'. **1877** E. PEACOCK *Gloss. Manley*, *Bolt-hole*, (1) the hole by which a rabbit makes its escape when the ferret pursues it. (2) Any unknown hole by which a person makes his way into or out of a house. **1887** KIPLING *Lett. Marque* v. in *From Sea to Sea* (1900) 49 A figure in saffron came out of a dark arch into the sunlight, almost falling into the arms of one in pink... The pink and saffron figures..disappeared into separate bolt-holes. **1891** *Pall Mall Gaz.* 4 June 6/2 We left them no bolt-hole,..so every man fought till he was killed. **1924** E. MARSH tr. *42 Fables of La Fontaine* 71 [The hare] heard a rustle, And took the hint to bustle Off to his bolt-hole. **1932** H. SIMPSON *Boomerang* xii. 306 A girl who had been jilted might choose any bolt-hole to hide her shame. **1967** *Listener* 30 Nov. 705/3 With all the mental bolt-holes stopped up, a clear look at England around 1930 produced traumatic results.

2. *Coal-mining.* A short connecting heading or opening.
1839 URE *Dict. Arts* 981 Two, three, or even four bolt-holes open into a side of a work, according to its extent. **1860** *Eng. & For. Mining Gloss.* (ed. 2) 69 *Bolt hole*, a passage..from the gate-road into a side of work. **1877** *Encycl. Brit.* VI. 66/1 From the gate road a heading called a bolt-hole is opened. **1963** *Gloss. Mining Terms* (*B.S.I.*) II. 8 *Bolt hole.* 1. A short connecting passage made for ventilation purposes.

†**'bolting**, *sb.* Also boltin, bolton. [f. BOLT *sb.*[1] (9).] A bundle of straw.
1784 TWAMLEY *Dairying* 129 Take a boltin, or bundle of Wheat or Rye-straw. **1886** *Blackw. Mag.* Aug. 224 Twenty boltings or bundles of straw, tied up from the thrashing machine.

bolting, boul- ('bəʊltɪŋ), *vbl. sb.*[1] [f. BOLT *v.*[1]]

1. The act of sifting. ***boltings***: the bran or coarse meal separated by sifting; siftings.
a **1300** W. DE BIBLESWORTH in Wright *Voc.* 155 Per bolenger (*gloss.* bultingge) est ceveré La flur. **1335** in *Mem. Ripon* (1885) II. 115 Unum magnum doleum pro bultynges. **1606** SHAKS. *Tr. & Cr.* I. i. 18, *Troy.* Haue I not tarried? *Pan.* I the grinding; but you must tarry the bolting. **1638** PENKETHMAN *Artach.* A. b. **1877** PEACOCK *Lincolnsh. Gloss.* *Boltings*, the coarse meal separated from the flour.

2. *fig.* Sifting of evidence, etc.; close scrutiny. ***boulting out***: getting at by sifting.
1563-87 FOXE *A. & M.* (1596) 1286/1 The boulting out of the true signification of οὐσία. **1623** SANDERSON *Serm.* (1681) I. 88 Means for the boulting out of the truth. **1771** BURKE *Corr.* (1844) I. 256 Among those in opposition, there has been of late a good deal of boulting.

†b. The private arguing of law cases for practice. *Obs.*
1598 STOW *Surv.* ix. (1603) 79 They frequent readings, meetings, boltinges and other learned exercises. **1670** BLOUNT *Law Dict.*, *Bolting*, at Greys-Inn. The manner is thus; An Ancient, and two Barristers sit as Judges, three Students bring each a Case, and the Judges chuse which of them shall be argued: which done, the Students first argue it, then the Barristers.

3. *Comb.*, as (in sense 1) ***bolting-cloth, -house, -hutch, -machine, -mill, -pipe, -poke, -tub, -tun.***
1452 *Test. Ebor.* III. 137, Ij *bultynge-clothes, iiij*d.* *c* **1500** *Ibid.* IV. 192, Xxix yerdes off bowtyng cloth xl*d.* **1617** MARKHAM *Caval.* III. 38 Boult them through an ordinarie bolting cloath. **1885** *Harper's Mag.* July 256/1 The finest.. silk fabric made is bolting-cloth for the use of millers. **1532** HERVET tr. *Xenophon's Househ.* (1768) 40 The instrumentes that belonge..to the kechin, to the bathe, and to the *boultynge house. **1704** *Lond. Gaz.* No. 4003/4 Wash-house, Boulting-house, Bake-house. **1596** SHAKS. *1 Hen. IV*, II. iv. 495 That *Boulting-Hutch of Beastlinesse. **1641** MILTON *Animadv.* Wks. (1851) 205 Saving this passing fine sophisticall boulting hutch. **1807** VANCOUVER *Agric. Devon* (1813) 122 It has a pair of stones of about four feet in diameter, and a *bolting machine. **1846** G. WRIGHT *Cream Sci. Knowl.* 49 The bolting-machine of a flour-mill..The flour is sifted..through a cloth of a peculiar texture, called a bolting-cloth. Instead of the cloth, a cylinder formed of wire-gauze of different degrees of fineness is sometimes used. **1766** *Chron.* in *Ann. Reg.* 139/1 They took an aversion to all *bolting-mills, and accordingly destroyed 7 or 8. **1534** in *Eng. Ch. Furniture* (1866) 189 A *bultynge pipe coverid with a yarde of canvesse. **1588** *Lanc. Wills* (1857) III. 137 In the backe house and brewe house..a boltinge pype viij*d.* **1552** HULOET, Bultre, or *bultyng poke for fyne meale. **1530** PALSGR. 200/1 *Boultyng tubbe, *husche a bluter.* **1581-2** *Inv.* in Best *Farm Bks.* (1856) 172 In þe bowtinge house..one bowting tube. **1485** *Inv.* in *Ripon Ch. Acts* 371, j *bultington.

'bolting, *vbl. sb.*[2] [f. BOLT *v.*[2] + -ING[1].]

†1. Hasty utterance, sudden blurting out. *Obs.*
1692 R. LESTRANGE *Josephus' Wars* I. xvii. (1733) 588 The Bolting of this Privacy made Herod stark mad.

2. a. A sudden starting off; making off, running away, flight; (in *U.S. politics*) sudden secession from a political party.

1820 SCOTT *Abbot* xvii, These pretty wild-geese..have as many divings, boltings, and volleyings. **1860** G. H. K. *Vacat. Tour.* 169 The bolting of the Caithness men from the Sutherland men. **1884** *N.Y. Times*, This caucus system of ours is a despotism, tempered only by bolting.

b. *Horticulture.* The action of BOLT *v.*² 2 d.

1933 *Discovery* Mar. 76/1 The often troublesome 'bolting' of lettuce may be prevented by short periods of light. **1961** *Amateur Gardening* 16 Sept. 12/2 'Bolting' is a gardening term meaning that the plants throw up seed heads instead of forming the tight hearts we aim at producing.

3. Fastening with bolts.

1856 KANE *Arct. Exp.* I. vii. 74 The pintles torn from their boltings.

4. Hasty swallowing.

1872 MARK TWAIN *Innoc. Abr.* xii. 79 No five-minute boltings of flabby rolls.

5. *Comb.*, as **bolting-hole**, a hole by which to bolt or escape; *fig.* a means of escape.

c **1788** BURKE *Art. W. Hastings* Wks. 1842 XIV. 68 It afforded him two bolting holes, by which he is enabled to resist the authority of the Company. **1881** *Sat. Rev.* No. 1321, 238 A secluded spot in a clearing, where a bank is honeycombed with burrows and bolting-holes.

bolting ('bəʊltɪŋ), *ppl. a.* [f. BOLT *v.*² + -ING².] That bolts or runs to cover.

1907 *Daily Chron.* 28 Nov. 8/1 Some of the bolting escort were returning. **1908** *Westm. Gaz.* 31 Jan. 4/2 The bolting rabbit.

b. *Horticulture.* That is prematurely 'running to seed'. Cf. BOLT *v.*² 2 d.

1961 *Auckland Weekly News* 5 July 41/1 Bolting cabbages and savoys can be restored to normal if the stem is pierced one inch above soil level with a sharp penknife and a small pebble inserted in the slit.

'boltless, *a.* [BOLT *sb.*¹] Without a bolt or bolts (in various senses); not formed into bolts, as 'boltless lightning' (*poet.*).

1832 I. TAYLOR *Saturday Even.* xv. 248 The boltless thunders of the mere man of rhetoric. *c* **1877** THEODORE WATTS in *Westm. Gaz.* (1900) 15 Feb. 10/1 'Mid boltless thunder. **1902** 'MONKSHOOD' & GAMBLE *R. Kipling* 259 The boltless door. **1903** KIPLING *Five Nations* 75 We shall go back by boltless doors, To the life unaltered our childhood knew.

Bolton ('bəʊltən). The name of a county borough in Lancashire used attrib. in: **Bolton bay**, a variety of fowl, gold and silver in colour and minutely marked; **Bolton sheeting**, a twill cotton fabric containing a condenser weft and used for curtains, linings, etc.; **Bolton twill**, a twill cotton fabric manufactured in Bolton.

1854 *Poultry Chron.* II. 295/1 Provincial terms, as Minorcas, Bolton Bays,..Pheasants, Chitteprats. **1861** MRS. BEETON *Bk. Househ. Managem.* 475 *Pencilled Hamburg.* This variety of the Hamburg fowl is..also known, in different parts of the country, as Chitteprats, Creoles, or Corals, Bolton bays and grays. **1880** L. HIGGIN *Handbk. Embroidery* ii. 12 (*heading*) Bolton, or workhouse sheeting, is a coarse twilled cotton fabric, seventy-two inches wide, of a beautiful soft creamy colour. **1938** D. GARNETT in *T. E. Lawrence Lett.* 40 He hung the walls of his study with green Bolton sheeting which made it very quiet. **1967** *J. W. Coates & Co. Catal.* Spring 11/1 Heavy Quality, hemmed Bolton Twill Sheets..39/6 pr.

'boltonite. *Min.* A unisilicate mineral, a variety of Forsterite, found near Bolton, Mass. (Dana *Min.* 255.)

bolt-rope ('bəʊltrəʊp). *Naut.* [f. BOLT *sb.*¹ + ROPE.] 'A rope sewed all round the edge of the sail, to prevent the canvas from tearing.' Smyth *Sailor's Word-bk.*

1626 CAPT. SMITH *Accid. Yng. Seamen* 14. **1627** —— *Seaman's Gram.* vi. 27 The Bolt ropes are those wherein the sailes are sowed. **1762–9** FALCONER *Shipwr.* II. 461 The..mizen..In fluttering fragments from its bolt-rope fled. **1830** I. TAYLOR *The Ship* 154. **1840** R. DANA *Bef. Mast* xxv. 82 The jib was blown to atoms out of the bolt-rope.

boltspreet, -sprit, obs. var. of BOWSPRIT.

bolt upright-ness: see BOLT *adv.*

Boltzmann ('bɒltsmən). The surname of Ludwig *Boltzmann* (1844–1906), an Austrian physicist, used *attrib.* or in the possessive of various laws, phenomena, etc., in *Physics*. **Boltzmann's constant** (see quot. 1959).

1879 *Trans. Cambridge Phil. Soc.* XII. 547 (*title*) On Boltzmann's Theorem on the average distribution of energy in a system of material points. **1910** *Sci. Abstr.* A. XIII. 184 The value of Boltzmann's universal constant is found to be $K = 7{\cdot}5 \times 10^{-17}$. **1915** *Proc. Roy. Soc.* A. XCI. 529 Where ϵ is the charge and m the mass of an electron and k is Boltzmann's constant. **1958** *Chambers's Techn. Dict.* 961/1 *Boltzmann equation*, algebraic equation stating that the entropy of a system of particles depends on the logarithm of the probability of its macroscopic state. **1959** *Chambers's Encycl.* XI. 398/1 The constant k is known as Boltzmann's constant, sometimes called the entropy constant. It represents the gas constant divided by the number of molecules in the gas (gas constant per molecule). **1962** SIMPSON & RICHARDS *Junction Transistors* i. 11 In transistor technology these conditions apply almost invariably so that the Boltzmann distribution is generally used. **1968** P. A. P. MORAN *Introd. Probability Theory* vii. 341 The density of the probability distribution of their potential energies will be proportional to $\exp\left(-\frac{U}{kT}\right)$, where U is the potential energy, k is Boltzmann's constant, and T is the absolute temperature.

bolus ('bəʊləs). Pl. boluses: 7 bolus, 7–8 bolus's, 8–9 bolusses. [a. mod.L. *bōlus*, a. Gr. βῶλος clod, lump of earth.]

1. *Med.* **a.** A medicine of round shape adapted for swallowing, larger than an ordinary pill. (Often used somewhat contemptuously.)

1603 FLORIO *Montaigne* (1634) 554, I will not have a Bolus, or a glister. **1681** tr. *Willis' Rem, Med. Wks.* Voc., *Bolus*, is a medicine made up into a thick substance to be swallow'd not liquid, but taken on a knives point. **1751** SHENSTONE *Wks. & Lett.* III. 178, I have been taking saline draughts and bolus's. **1832** ANNA M. PORTER *Hungar. Bro.* v. 53 Physic him to death with pills and boluses. *fig.* **1637** EARL MONM. *Malvezzi's Romvlvs* 229 Cruell actions are so many bolus, which are never better taken than when wrapt up in gold. **1780** COWPER *Lett.* 3 May, Swallowing such boluses as I send you. **1878** BLACK *Green Past.* iii. 23 Resolved not to swallow your Home Rule bolus.

b. A single dose of a drug, contrast medium, etc., introduced rapidly into a blood-vessel.

1967 *Jrnl. Appl. Physiol.* XXII. 497/2 A single bolus of 1.5–2.5μc ^{84}RbCl was injected rapidly into the superior vena cava. **1977** *Lancet* 20 Aug. 376/1 sGaw [*sc.* specific airways conductance] was measured 5 min after intravenous salbutamol sulphate (25 μg boluses) up to a cumulative dose of 300 μg. **1980** *Brit. Med. Jrnl.* 29 Mar. 922/2 All treatment was stopped and a bolus of 10ml of 10% calcium gluconate given.

2. A small rounded mass of any substance.

1782 A. MONRO *Compar. Anat.* (ed. 3) 23 The bolus would be in danger of falling out of the mouth. **1835** T. HOOK *G. Gurney* (1850) I. i. 3 A round mirror, encircled with gilt boluses. **1867** F. FRANCIS *Angling* i. (1880) 9 A barley-meal bolus is the bait for roach. **1881** *Sat. Rev.* No. 1320, 206 One leaden bolus of the old ounce-of-lead pattern.

3. A kind of clay; = BOLE² 1.

1682 GREW *Anat. Plants* 242 Bolus's are the Beds, or as it were, the Materia prima, both of opacous Stones, and Metals. **1863** BARING-GOULD *Iceland* xii. 210 The soil is composed of soft bolus full of splinters of trachyte.

Hence **bolus-ways, -wise,** *adv.*, as a bolus.

1689 MOYLE *Sea Chyrurg.* Pref., If the Patient cannot take a Medecine in one form (as Bolus-waies).

† **bolwaie.** *Obs.* ? A boil.

1628 P. M[ATHIEU] *Life Seianvs* 88 His face full of pimples and Fistulas, knots and bolwaies.

bolwark, obs. f. BULWARK.

boly, obs. form of BOIL *v.*

† **bolye.** *Obs. rare.* [ad. med.L. *bolis*, a. Gr. βολίς sounding-lead.] (See quot.)

1552 HULOET, Bolye or plummet whyche mariners vse, *bolis.*

bolyen, bolyon, obs. forms of BULLION.

bolyn, var. of BOLLEN *sb.*, and obs. f. BOWLINE.

bolys, obs. form of BULLACE.

‖**bom**¹, **boma.** Also **bomma, aboma.** The native name in Congo, W. Africa, of 'a huge non-poisonous snake swallowing deer, etc.' (see Merolla, *Vocab.*; Proyart; Cavazzi *Congo, Matamba, & Angola*; Magyar *Süd-Afrika*). Apparently carried by the Portuguese from Congo to Brazil (Roquete has *bom bôma* 'serpent d'Angola et du Brésil'), and there applied to the largest boas, in which sense it appears in some English works. (The history has been traced for us by Dr. E. B. Tylor.)

1864 in WEBSTER and in other recent Dicts.

bom² (bɒm). [Of imitative origin.] The sound caused by the discharge of a gun, less deep and sonorous than a 'boom'. Also, the sound of a heavy object falling.

1906 *Westm. Gaz.* 11 June 8/2 A faint distant Bom! and everybody murmurs with one accord, 'First Gun!' **1922** JOYCE *Ulysses* 97 Bom! Upset. A coffin bumped out on to the road.

bom, bomarang, obs. ff. BUM, BOOMERANG *sb.*

boma ('bəʊmə). *E. Afr.* [Swahili.] **a.** An enclosure or stockade used for herding beasts and for defensive purposes. **b.** A police post. **c.** A district commissioner's or magistrates' office; an administrative centre associated with such an office.

1878 STANLEY *Dark Cont.* I. vi. 137 From the staked bomas..there rise to my hearing the bleating of young calves. **1898** *Geogr. Jrnl.* (R.G.S.) XI. 389, I went out on a sandspit into the lake and camped, cutting down the bush and placing it across the shore end of the bank so as to form a boma. **1903** STORDY in *Jrnl. Soc. Arts* 10 July 691/2 The construction of the boma employed fifty hands for the space of nine weeks. **1920** *Blackw. Mag.* Jan. 59/1 It [*sc.* the fort] was a typical Boma, built of bricks and plaster. **1961** *New Scientist* 24 Aug. 451 The innumerable trails that radiate from each cattle boma. **1964** C. WILLOCK *Enormous Zoo* iii. 49 A boma..that would have held a herd of a hundred or more zebra. **1967** L. KAYIRA *Looming Shadow* (1968) v. 60 He did not have the vaguest notion about the implications of the Boma and the law. **1969** N. CARR *White Impala* ii. 20 The hunter was awarded the 'ground' tusk.., while the other was to be handed in to the Boma. *Ibid.*, Nowadays the word 'Boma'..is used to mean a Government administrative centre. But more particularly it means the District Commissioner's office and all the services that go with it—dispensary, post office, agricultural officer's office, and so on.

bomah ('bəʊmə). Also **boomah.** [Cf. Zulu *imboma* aloe-berry.] ***bomah nut***, the fruit of a southern African shrub *Pycnocoma macrophylla*, used in tanning.

1874 LINDLEY & MOORE *Treas. Bot.* II. 943/1 Boomah Nuts. **1887** MOLONEY *Forestry W. Africa* 417 The Bomah Nut..is extensively cultivated by the natives near the Victoria Falls.

bomaree, var. of BUMMAREE.

bomb (bɒm, bʌm), *sb.* Forms: 6 **bome,** 7 **bombe, bombo, boom(b,** 7– **bomb.** [a. F. *bombe*, ad. Sp. *bomba* (see first quot.), prob. f. *bombo* 'a bumming or humming noise':—L. *bombus*. The word is thus ultimately identical with *boom*. Cf. the earliest Eng. instance *bome*, directly from Sp.; also 17th c. *bombo* from Sp. or It. Variously pronounced: see the rimes: in the British army (bʌm) was formerly usual.]

†**1.** Transl. of Sp. *bomba de fuego* 'a ball of wilde-fire,' Minsheu. *Obs.*

1588 R. PARKE *Hist. China* (transl. fr. Span.) 65 They vse ..in their wars..many bomes of fire, full of olde iron, and arrowes made with powder & fire worke, with the which they do much harme and destroy their enimies.

2. a. An explosive projectile consisting of a hollow iron sphere filled with gunpowder or some other charge, and fired by a fuse ignited in the act of discharge from the mortar; a bombshell; now generally called a *shell*. In modern use: a case filled with explosive, inflammable material, poison gas, or smoke, etc., fired from a gun, dropped from aircraft, or thrown or deposited by hand. Also freq. in Comb., as ***atomic, flying, gas, incendiary bomb***, etc. (see under the first elements).

1684 *Lond. Gaz.* No. 1937/2 They shoot their Bombes near two Miles, and they weigh 250 English Pounds a piece. **1687** EVELYN *Mem.* (1857) II. 275, I saw a trial of those devilish murdering, mischief-doing engines called bombs, shot out of the mortar-piece on Blackheath. **1687** RYCAUT *Hist. Turks* II. 196 The Turks threw..quantities of Bomboes and Stink-pots. **1692** *Siege Lymerick* 5, 800 Carts of Ball and Boombs. *Ibid.* 6, 600 Booms. *a* **1721** PRIOR *Alma* III. 369 The longitude uncertain roams, In spite of Whiston and his bombs. *c* **1730** YOUNG *Sea-Piece* Poems (1757) I. 246 A thousand deaths the bursting bomb Hurls from her disembowel'd womb. **1829** SOUTHEY *Yng. Dragon* IV, The hugest brazen mortar That ever yet fired bomb, Could not have check'd this fiendish beast As did that Holy Thumb. **1914** *Times* 9 Oct. 6/5 A German aeroplane flew over the outskirts of Paris early this morning and threw several bombs. **1914** *Whitaker's Almanack 1915* 821/2 Lieut. Marix, who also made an attack on the Dusseldorf shed, and by means of a bomb destroyed it. **1940** *Times* 15 Aug. 4/3 Numerous direct hits with heavy calibre bombs were scored ..and the crew of one aircraft whose bombs fell in a line across the main buildings, reported that one had hit and destroyed the main power house. *Ibid.* 17 Oct. 4/4 Almost as soon as the sirens sounded bombs fell in some districts in the London area. **1943** *Times Weekly* 18 Aug. 18/4 About 10 tons of light demolition bombs, besides incendiary bombs, were scattered over a wide area.

b. **(the) bomb** (also *Bomb*), a pregnant expression for the atomic or hydrogen bomb, as used or to be used by any country as a weapon of war, and regarded as unique because of its utterly destructive effects.

[**1932** H. NICOLSON *Public Faces* I. 23 True it was that their acute distaste for the bomb..did credit to their humanity, to their state of civilisation.] **1945** *Times* 15 Aug. 5/5 (*headline*) Victory and the Bomb. **1959** *Sunday Times* 5 Apr. 19/5 Twenty years ago, I mean: before the war, the Bomb, the satellites, the space-travellers and the nudist paradises. **1966** *Listener* 20 Jan. 83/1 One of the most persistent fallacies of the..debate about nuclear weapons is the proposition that 'the bomb', as it has come to be called almost with affection, has put an end to war.

c. Short for *radium bomb* (RADIUM b).

1930 *Brit. Med. Jrnl.* 8 Feb. 232/2 The apparatus to be described was designed..to meet the problem of making.. use of the 4 grams of national radium that had been lent to the hospital for use as a 'bomb'.

d. A success (esp. in entertainment); also *U.S.*, a failure. So phr. ***like a bomb*** and varr., with great speed; with considerable effectiveness or success. *colloq.*

1954 *Amer. Speech* XXIX. 99 *Like a bomb*,..very fast. **1961** *New Yorker* 28 Oct. 43/2 What had once been called a failure became a 'bomb'. **1962** *Listener* 11 Oct. 581/2 Leslie Crowther, introducing *The Black and White Minstrel Show* ..from the Victoria Palace, remarked, 'We're going like a bomb here.' **1963** *The Beatles* 5 Once, Paul McCartney and I played Reading as the Nurk Twins. Went down a bomb, I recall. **1967** A. DIMENT *Dolly Dolly Spy* ii. 15 His straight-backed 'visitor's' chair, which for pure discomfort would have gone down a bomb with the Gestapo.

e. A large sum of money. *slang.*

1958 F. NORMAN *Bang to Rights* II. 79 There are not many bent screws the reason being that many of them are to honest or to scared to do any trafficing but the ones that do make a bomb. **1963** M. LEVINSON *Taxi!* x. 122 Large original oil paintings..which, in cab-driver's language, looked as though they were 'worth a bomb'. **1969** A. E. LINDOP *Sight Unseen* xxiv. 202 Can I have that instead of the five pounds? I might flog it for a bomb in me old age.

f. A (large) marijuana cigarette; = BOMBER 3 a. *slang.*

1960 *Times Lit. Suppl.* 16 Sept. 589/4 *The Scene* is written by a junkie with a bee for bombs... Mr. Cooper, that is to say, was once a dope addict. **1967** E. WYMARK *As Good as Gold* xiv. 204 First they simply smoke marijuana... They refer to the smokes as sticks or bombs, depending on their size. **1968** J. HUDSON *Case of Need* III. i. 173 Bombs... You know... Speed. Lifts. Jets. Bennies.

†**3.** A mortar, a shell-gun. *Obs. rare*$^{-1}$.

1684 J. PETER *Siege Vienna* 95 The enemy..play'd on us with their Cannon and Bombs.

†**4. a.** A small war-vessel carrying mortars for throwing bombs. Called more fully *bomb-galliot, bomb-ketch, bomb-ship, bomb-vessel*, and *bombard.*

1704 *Lond. Gaz.* No. 4029/3 Portsmouth Bomb. *Ibid.* No. 3992/3 Her Majesty's Ships the *Mortar* and *Terror* Bombs. **1747** J. LIND *Lett. Navy* i. (1757) 21 Those who have the command of sloops, bombs, fireships. **1806** DUNCAN *Nelson* 45 He proceeded with the Thunder bomb..to bombard the town. **1813** *Examiner* 18 Jan. 47/1, 18 sloops—4 bombs.

b. An old car (see also quot. 1953). *Austral.* and *N.Z. slang.*

1953 BAKER *Australia Speaks* iv. 106 *Bomb*, an old car or motor cycle. **1961** *Coast to Coast 1959–60* 120 Get out, buy yourself a car... Do as I did, start with a bomb and keep adding a bit and trading it in till you've got what you want. **1965** M. SHADBOLT *Among Cinders* xviii. 163 The car.. wasn't much more than an old bomb. **1967** F. SARGESON *Hangover* vii. 53 We had a job shoving her into the bomb.

5. (*volcanic*) *bomb*: a roundish mass of lava thrown out of a volcano.

1798, 1833 [see VOLCANIC *a.* 1 c]. **1845** DARWIN *Voy. Nat.* xxi. (1852) 493, I noticed volcanic bombs, that is, masses of lava which have been shot through the air whilst fluid and have consequently assumed a spherical or pear-shape. **1878** HUXLEY *Physiogr.* 193 Sometimes the masses of lava..fall as ..volcanic bombs. **1956** W. EDWARDS in D. L. Linton *Sheffield* 8 Tuffs are especially well seen in the Ashaver anticline,..and are dark green, brown, and purple well-bedded basaltic ashes with 'bombs' of basalt, limestone, and chert. **1969** *Nature* 8 Nov. 557/2 Volcanic activity occurred at several places along this fracture and fresh bombs rest on the ice close to the edge of the chasm.

6. *Comb.*, as *bomb battery, -bed, -cart, -chest, -galliot, -quay, -ship, -vessel*; *bomb-battered* adj.; also in many obvious comb. relating to aerial bombs, as *bomb-aimer, -aiming, -carrier, -carrying, -crater, -damage, -dropper, -dropping, -dump* [DUMP *sb.*⁴ 1 c], *-load, -maker, -raid, -release, -thrower, -throwing*; *bomb-damaged, -pitted, -shattered* adjs.; **bomb alley** *Service slang*, an area repeatedly attacked by bombing; **bomb bay**, a compartment in an aircraft for holding bombs; **bomb calorimeter** (see quot. 1928); **bomb-disposal**, the removal and detonation of unexploded and delayed-action bombs; usu. *attrib.*, esp. in *bomb-disposal squad*; **bomb door**, usu. in *pl.*: the movable covering of a bomb bay; **bomb-happy** *a. colloq.* [-HAPPY], mentally affected by exposure to a bomb or shell explosion at close quarters; shell-shocked; hence *bomb-happiness*; **bomb-lance**, a harpoon with an explosive in its head; **bomb line** (see quot. 1944); **bomb-rack**, a rack (in an aircraft) for holding bombs; **bomb run** (also *bombing run*), the line of flight of bombing aircraft over the target; **bomb sight** (also *bombing sight*), a device for sighting the target in bombing from an aeroplane; so *bomb-sighting* vbl. sb.; **bomb-site**, ground on which buildings, etc., have been destroyed by aerial bombing. See also BOMB-KETCH, BOMB-PROOF, BOMB-SHELL.

1935 *Meccano Mag.* Oct. 577/2 The telegraphist is also acting as *bomb-aimer. **1937** *Jrnl. R. Aeronaut. Soc.* XLI. 423 A stable platform for *bomb-aiming. **1942** W. SIMPSON *One of our Pilots is Safe* ii. 18 We were..given an extra gun —firing downwards and backwards out of the bomb-aiming hatch. **1942** *Hutchinson's Pict. Hist. War* 10 June–1 Sept. 263 The narrow stretch of water between the island of Pantellaria and Sicily, officially known as the Sicilian Channel, but called *Bomb Alley by the Navy and Merchant Service. **1945** *Ann. Reg. 1944* 76 The inhabitants of the so-called 'bomb alley' had also suffered considerably. **1854** J. ABBOTT *Napoleon* (1855) I. xxxiv. 533 Having fled from their *bomb-battered and burning dwellings. **1695** *Lond. Gaz.* No. 3124/2 This day the *Bomb-Battery was begun. **1918** *Aeronaut. Insp. Directorate Data Bk.* (Handley Page V/1500) 3 The *bomb bay is rectangular, and built entirely of spruce. **1934** *Flight* 15 Feb. 156/1 Bombs are internally stowed in a bomb bay closed by doors controlled by the bomber. *c* **1850** *Rudim. Navig.* (Weale) 100 The beams which support the *bomb-bed in bomb-vessels. **1902** *Encycl. Brit.* XXVII. 444/1 The potential energy..is measured by the heat of combustion in the *bomb calorimeter. **1928** A. B. CALLOW *Food & Health* 29 The apparatus used for this laboratory oxidation is a small calorimeter which is known as the bomb calorimeter, because the oxidation takes place inside a thick-walled vessel which in some ways resembles a bomb. **1928** GAMBLE *Story N. Sea Air Station* vii. 109 The only standard *bomb-carriers in service at this period were the single 16-lb bomb and the 20-lb gear for two Hale 20-lb bombs. *Ibid.*, Equipping all the machines with *bomb-carrying and release gear. **1712** *Lond. Gaz.* No. 4970/2 Two *Bomb Carts ..and five Pieces of Ordnance. **1755** *Gentl. Mag.* XXV. 377 Bomb-carts, filled with necessaries for the camp, were likewise sent. **1704** J. HARRIS *Lex. Techn.*, *Bomb-chest, is a kind of chest, which being filled with Gunpowder and Bombs..is placed under Ground to blow it up into the Air, together with those that stand upon it. **1920** *Blackw. Mag.* July 76/1 Ploughed up with *bomb-craters. **1941** *Partisan Rev.* Nov.–Dec. 498, I can see no *bomb damage anywhere, except for a few churches. **1942** *Ann. Reg. 1941* 328 Four galleries..being closed on account of bomb damage. **1945** W. S. CHURCHILL *Victory* (1946) 157 *Bomb-damaged houses in the London area. **1954** R. MACAULAY *Last Lett.* (1962) 150 It was one of the City churches very little bomb-damaged, I think. **1954** 'N. BLAKE' *Whisper in Gloom* I. vi. 77 A row of bomb-damaged houses. **1940** *War Illustr.* 4 Oct. 338 The *Bomb Disposal Sections of the Royal Engineers whose job it is to dig up and destroy the time-bombs. *Ibid.* 6 Dec. 612 The bomb-disposal squads of the Royal Engineers..described..the removal of delayed-action bombs. **1939** *Meccano Mag.* Mar. 150/3 Large *bomb doors cover the bottom of the fuselage. **1928** GAMBLE *Story N. Sea Air Station* vii. 104 The last three machines were classified as 'Gun Machines' and '*Bomb Droppers'. **1910** R. FERRIS *How It Flies* xvii. 372 There have been many contests by aviators in '*bomb-dropping'. **1939** R. CAMPBELL *Flowering Rifle* VI. 148 Keep safe his *bomb-dump while our patience lasts. **1941** *Illustr. London News* CXCVIII. 728/2 Bombing up the 'planes is the work of the armourers, who also have charge of the vast station bomb-dump. **1715** *Lond. Gaz.* No. 5301/2 Some *Bomb Galliots. **1944** J. H. FULLARTON *Troop Target* iii. 29 Now, when '*bomb-happiness' and the 'jitterbugs' threatened to touch the troop with palsied fingers. **1943** *San Francisco Chron.* 1 Dec. 2/2 A barrage so incessant..that many troops of the crack 65th Nazy Division were rendered '*bomb happy' and fell easy prisoners. **1944** A. JACOB *Traveller's War* iv. 68, I was, in fact, slightly 'bomb happy'. **1751** SMOLLETT *Per. Pic.* (1779) II. lxiv. 210 The entertainers landed at the *bomb-keys. **1883** *Fisheries Exhib. Catal.* 199 The *bomb-lance, darting-bomb, and rocket-bomb. **1901** F. T. BULLEN *Sack of Shakings* 18 He took..an extra supply of bomb-lances, in the use of which he was an acknowledged expert. **1917** *Chambers's Jrnl.* Sept. 590/1 This monster..was killed by a bomb-lance from a whale-boat. **1943** G. L. CHESHIRE *Bomber Pilot* i. 9 On the large map on the wall was a red line; they called it the *bomblin[e], and it was supposed to represent the area behind which we could [not] bomb. **1944** *Times* 17 Apr. 3/3 The 'bomb line'—that is, the line ahead of the troops behind which aircraft supporting the ground forces should not drop their bombs. **1961** W. VAUGHAN-THOMAS *Anzio* ii. 23 We could not..pick up any feature we could recognise... We turned tail and flew disconsolately back over the bomb line. **1921** *Aeronaut. Jrnl.* Mar. 166 The *bomb load of the standard..four-engined machines amounted to 3,000 kilograms. **1905** *Westm. Gaz.* 19 June 5/1 The *bomb-makers..were inextricably trapped. **1943** T. HORSLEY *Find, Fix & Strike* 15 Operating from *bomb-pitted aerodromes. **1917** *Advis. Comm. Aeronaut., Rep. & Mem.* No. 378 Tests were made up at the request of the Air Board, who supplied drawings of a *bomb rack to carry two 112-lb. bombs. **1918** *Times* (Engineering Suppl.) 26 Apr. 88/1 The bomb-racks in the covered-in passage..are capable of holding five 25-pounder bombs. **1944** *Times* 23 May 4/2 The Spitfires..saw the German aircraft pass them at high speed with bomb-racks full. **1917** 'CONTACT' *Airman's Outings* 259 A daylight *bomb raid is seldom a complete failure. **1945** W. S. CHURCHILL *Victory* (1946) 29 Bomb-raid damage repairs in London. **1928** GAMBLE *Story N. Sea Air Station* v. 87 Very little work had been done with *bomb releases. *Ibid.* vii. 110 Bomb-release gears. *Ibid.* xiii. 224 Bomb release-slips. **1941** *Science Digest* Nov. 53/1 The pilot controls the '*bomb run', which is the line of flight of the plane. **1944** *Hutchinson's Pict. Hist. War* 12 Apr.–26 Sept. 30/2 The deliberate bomb run through the target flak itself. **1945** H. READ *Coat of Many Colours* lxvi. 319 The *bomb-shattered ruins of human tenderness and faith. **1949** M. LASKI *Little Boy Lost* III. xvi. 209 The emptiness of the bomb-shattered square. **1695** *Lond. Gaz.* No. 3086/2 Having been to view the *Bomb ships in the *Maese*. **1806** DUNCAN *Nelson* 136 The bomb-ship and schooner gun-vessels made their escape. **1917** 'CONTACT' *Airman's Outings* vii. 176 Owing to the difficulty of correct aim, before the advent of modern *bomb-sights, all the early raids were carried out from a low altitude. **1928** GAMBLE *Story N. Sea Air Station* v. 87 Of the available bomb sights, the most practical and successful were those invented by Lieutenant Scott, U.S.N., and Zeiss. **1931** *Air Annual Brit. Empire* 230 The platform is filled with navigation and *bomb-sighting equipment for the observer's use. **1945** *Daily Express* 23 May 3/3 (*caption*) British workmen from a *bomb-site about 100 yards away. **1959** *Times* 8 Dec. 5/6 Many of the bomb-site parks in central London are seldom full. **1891** *Pall Mall Gaz.* 14 Dec. 5/2 The *bomb-thrower, who lost his life in attempting that of Mr. Russell Sage. **1916** 'BOYD CABLE' *Action Front* 24 The bomb-thrower seized the missile quickly,..threw the bomb, and jumped back under cover. **1905** *Westm. Gaz.* 13 May 7/2 The workmen [of St. Petersburg] practised shooting and *bomb-throwing. **1908** *Daily Chron.* 14 Aug. 4/4 The attack from bomb-throwing airships is very little, if any, more alarming than from a gunboat. **1693** *Lond. Gaz.* No. 2893/4 *Bomb vessels lately Launch'd. **1828** SPEARMAN *Brit. Gunner* (article), Bomb-Vessels.

bomb (bɒm, bʌm), *v.* [f. prec.]

1. *trans.* **a.** To fire bombs at; to bombard.

1688 I. CLAYTON in *Phil. Trans.* XVII. 984 The Town could never be Bomb'd by Land. *a* **1704** SEDLEY *Poems* Wks. 1722 I. 78 While you Bomb Towns in France. **1797** NELSON in Nicolas *Disp.* (1846) VII. p. cxlvi, The intention of bombing us still goes on.

b. To attack with an explosive bomb placed or thrown for the purpose of destruction; (of aircraft) to attack with bombs from the air; to drop a bomb or bombs upon. So *to bomb one's way*: to advance by bombing; *to bomb out*: to clear by bombing; esp. in pa. pple. (see *bombed out* s.v. BOMBED *ppl. a.*² 1). Also *transf.*

1909 *Daily Chron.* 25 Feb. 1/6 Attempts had been made.. to bomb trains known to contain Europeans. **1915** *Draconian* Apr. 1683/1 They bombed us periodically during the day and night. **1916** 'BOYD CABLE' *Action Front* 174 He himself had known a line bombed out. *a* **1917** E. A. MACKINTOSH *War, the Liberator* (1918) 97 When we're bombing our way up the streets of Berlin. *Ibid.* 133 He turned to bomb the big dug-out. **1969** *Daily Tel.* 17 Dec. 3/8 Hundreds of pigeons congregated in the area, ruining washing and 'bombing' children.

2. To throw with violence, let fly. *dial.*

3. *to bomb up*: to load (aircraft) with bombs.

1939 *Flight* 28 Sept., (*caption*) 'Bombing up' a squadron of Ju 87s at Kitzingen-on-Main aerodrome. **1940** *Illustr. London News* CXCVII. 308/1 The order has been given to 'bomb up' this hardy squadron of 'Whitley' bombers. **1943** G. L. CHESHIRE *Bomber Pilot* i. 9 When we landed, the armourers were standing by to bomb up.

4. *intr.* To fail. Also const. *out. slang* (orig. *U.S.*).

1963 *Amer. Speech* XXXVIII. 168 To fail to pass an examination: flunk.., flag, blow, bomb. **1966** *Listener* 9 June 838/3 When a machine goes wrong it 'bombs out' and has to be 'debugged'. **1968** *TV Times* (Austral.) 10 Apr. 11/4 Everyone had expected it to be [good], so when it bombed it was a shock.

5. *trans.* To drug or dope (a racehorse). *Austral. slang.*

1950 *Austral. Police Jrnl.* Apr. 110 *To bomb*, to dope. **1959** BAKER *Drum* 92 *Bomb* v., to dope a racehorse.

6. *intr.* To move or travel quickly. With advb. (phr.) *slang.*

1966 R. THORP *Detective* iv. 64 When my parents thought I was at Gloria's house..we were out bombing around town. **1969** N. COHN *Pop from Beginning* xi. 93 At weekends, they bombed up and down the coastline in their hotrods. **1974** H. EVANS et al. *We learned to Ski* 31 Nothing is more demoralizing for a beginner than having all the skiers in the resort bombing past him. **1982** BARR & YORK *Official Sloane Ranger Handbk.* 97/2 Social life revolves around your clique ..and dinner at each other's houses, weekends bombing off somewhere together in your young Sloane motors.

bomb, obs. form of BOOM and BUM.

bombable (ˈbɒməb(ə)l), *a.* [f. BOMB *v.* + -ABLE.] Open to attack by bombing.

1930 *New Statesman* 9 Aug. 570/2 It is very hard to say what part of a nation's wartime industrial organisation is not bombable. **1938** *Ibid.* 24 Sept. 452/1 They [*sc.* the working class] are more numerous, live closer together, and are therefore more bombable, than other classes.

†**ˈbombace, -ase.** *Obs.* Forms: 6 bombage, 6–7 bombase, -bace. [a. OF. *bombace* cotton, cotton wadding:—late L. *bombāce-m*, acc. of *bombax* cotton, a corruption and transferred use of L. *bombyx* silk, a Gr. βόμβυξ silkworm, silk.]

1. The down of the cotton-plant; raw cotton.

1553 EDEN *Treat. New Ind.* (Arb.) 13 This cotton, is otherwyse called *Bombage* or sylke of the trees. *Ibid.* 30 They tie the postes together with ropes of bombage cotton. **1578** LYTE *Dodoens* VI. xvii. 679 Fayre white cotton, or the downe that we call Bombace. **1579** LANGHAM *Gard. Health* (1633) 536 The oile is to be taken away with bombase or cotton dipt in it. **1609** HARINGTON *Schoole Salerne* (1624) 358 To vse garments of Silke or Bombace.

2. Cotton fibre dressed for stuffing or padding garments; cotton-wool, cotton-wadding.

1592 *Wills & Inv. N.C.* (1860) II. 212, xx yds. of course harden 6*s.* 6*d.* v lbs. of bombace 5*s.* **1635** J. HAYWARD *Banish'd Virg.* 149 A body that needed not the common helpes of rectifying its proportion by bombace or the like.

3. *fig.* Padding, stuffing: see BOMBAST *sb.* 2 b, 3.

1662 FULLER *Worthies* (1840) III. 34 A sermon..to the university, the stuff, or rather bombace, whereof we have set down in our 'Ecclesiastical History'.

bombaceous (bɒmˈbeɪʃəs), *a. Bot.* [f. mod.L. *bombax* (f. L. *bombyx* silk) + -ACEOUS.] Of or pertaining to plants of the genus Bombax, or the Silk-cotton family.

1864 BATES *Nat. on Amazon* xvi. 139 The trees the dome-topped giants of the Leguminous and Bombaceous orders.

‖**bombachas** (bɒmˈbɑːtʃəz), *sb. pl.* [S. Amer. Sp., f. *bombacho* loose-fitting, wide.] The characteristic baggy trousers, tied in at the ankles on men and at the knees on boys, worn in some S. American countries, esp. for agricultural and other outdoor work.

1936 H. CHILDS *El Jeminy* i. 32. He was dressed in the usual camp (country) style; bright scarf, baggy bombachas (wide trousers) bound about the waist with a gay hand-woven sash, tied in at the ankles after bloomering out about the legs. **1956** G. DURRELL *Drunken Forest* xi. 207 They were wearing the typical peon's outfit: wrinkled, black half-boots with small spurs; *bombachas*, the baggy trousers that hang down over the top of the boot like plus-fours; [etc.]. **1977** B. CHATWIN *In Patagonia* (1979) lv. 110 A young gaucho in bombachas came in. **1982** *N.Y. Times* 23 Aug. A2/5 José Sergio Scoane stood in his bombachas, the baggy pants of the pampas, sipping tea with lemon through a metal straw.

†**ˈbombal.** *Obs. rare*$^{-1}$. [? Related to BOMB.]

a **1659** CLEVELAND *Sir I. Presbyter* (1677) 6 In Pulpit Fire-works, which the Bombal vents.

†**bombance.** *Obs.* [a. F. *bombance*, variant of *bobance* boastfulness, ostentation: of uncertain deriv.: see Littré.] Ostentation, pride.

c **1325** *Coer de L.* 4494 Come prykand with bombance.

bombard (ˈbɒm-, ˈbʌmbəd), *sb.* Forms: 5–7 bumbard, 6 boumbard, 5–9 bombarde, 6– bombard. [a. OF. *bombarde* 'a murthering-piece' (Cotgr.), in med.L. *bombarda*, originally a

mechanical engine for throwing large stones (see Du Cange); prob. f. L. *bombus* a humming noise + *-arda*, fem. form of Romance suffix -ARD.]

I. 1. a. The earliest kind of cannon, usually throwing a stone ball or a very large shot.

c **1430** LYDG. *Bochas* I. iii. (1544) 6 a, That none engine may thereto attayne, Gonne, nor bumbard by no subtiltie. **1481** CAXTON *Reynard* 77 All them that ben archers, and haue bowes, gonnes, bombardes..to besiege Maleperduys. **1523** LD. BERNERS *Froiss.* I. cxliv. 172 Fortyfied with springalles, bombardes, bowes, and other artillary. **1573** *Sege Edinb. Castel* in *Scot. Poems 16th C.* (1801) II. 290 The bumbard stanis directit fell sa euin. **1623** COCKERAM, *Bombards*, great guns. **1664** *Floddan F.* iii. 22 With Bombard shot the walls he bet. **1874** BOUTELL *Arms & Arm.* 219 Towards the end of the 14th century pieces called *bombardes* were in existence, which threw balls of stone weighing as much as 200 lbs... These heavy bombards proved to be of very little practical use.

†**b.** *transf.* The ball or stone thrown by a bombard. *Obs. rare*⁻¹.

1575 CHURCHYARD *Chippes* (1817) 153 A kind of shot that we great bombards call..And where that huge and mighty stone did fall..it did great wonders breede.

†**c.** Bombarding volley, shot. *Obs. rare*⁻¹

1809 J. BARLOW *Columb.* VII. 228 Then bids the battering floats his labors crown, And pour their bombard on the shuddering town.

2. A bomb-vessel or bomb-ketch; = BOMB *sb.* 4.

1799 NELSON in Nicolas *Disp.* (1845) IV. 65 Buonaparte has passed Corsica in a Bombard, steering for France. **1812** *Examiner* 23 Nov. 740/1 The vessels captured consisted of a bombard, a lugger, 3 feluccas. **1860** EARL DUNDONALD *Autobiog. Seaman* I. v. 99 A French bombard bore up, hoisting the national colours.

†**3. a.** A leather jug or bottle for liquor; a blackjack. Probably from some resemblance to the early cannons. *Obs.* exc. *Hist.*

1596 SHAKS *1 Hen. IV*, II. iv. 497 That huge Bombard of Sacke. **1610** —— *Temp.* II. ii. 20 Like a foule bumbard that would shed his licquor. **1635** HEYWOOD *Philocoth.*, The great black jacks and bombards at the Court, which, when the Frenchmen first saw, they reported..that the Englishmen used to drink out of their bootes.

†**b.** *fig.* A toper. *Obs.* See also BUMBARD.

1617 J. TAYLOR in *Shaks. C. Praise* 126 This bezzeling Bombards longitude, latitude, altitude, and crassitude.

†**II. 4. a.** A deep-toned wooden musical instrument of the bassoon family. *Obs.* Also BOMBARDO.

1393 GOWER *Conf.* III. 358 Suche a soune Of bomharde and of clarioune. ?*c* **1475** *Sqr. lowe Degre* 1072 With pypes, organs and bumbarde. **1878** STATHAM in Grove *Dict. Mus.* I. 151 A class of instruments named bombards, pommers, or brummers..seems to have been the immediate predecessor of the bassoon.

b. [Also in Fr. form.] A foot reed-stop of an organ.

1876 STAINER & BARRETT *Dict. Mus. Terms.* **1884** *Encycl. Brit.* XVII. 833/1, 32 contra trombone, posaune, bombarde, sackbut (reed).

III. 5. *Comb.*, as †*bombard-like* adv.; †**bombard-man**, a servant who carried out liquor to customers, a pot-boy; †**bombard-phrase** (trans. of L. *ampulla*), inflated language, bombast.

1664 *Floddan F.* vi. 53 Bombard like, did boasts discharge. *a* **1616** B. JONSON *Love Restored* 86 A bombard man, that brought bouge for a Countrey Lady or two that fainted. **1640** —— *Horace's Ars Poet.* VII. 173 (N.) They..must throw by Their bombard-phrase, and foot and half-foot words.

bombard (bɒm'bɑːd), *v.* [f. F. *bombarder* (16th c.) 'to discharge a bumbard, to batter or murder with bumbards' (Cotgr.), f. *bombard* sb.: see prec. It has no immediate relation to *bomb*.]

†**1.** *intr.* To fire off bombards or heavy guns. *Obs.* (exc. as absol. use of 2.)

1598 FLORIO, *Sbombardare*, to shoote off peals of guns, to bombard. [**1695** *Lond. Gaz.* No. 3096/3 Colonel Richards, with nine English Bomb Vessels..began to Bombard.]

2. *trans.* **a.** To batter with shot and shell; to assault with ordnance so as to destroy, disable, or reduce to submission.

1686 *Lond. Gaz.* No. 2211/3 General Caraffa is making Preparations to bombard Agria. **1692** *Siege Lymerick* 7 We still continued to Batter and Bombard the Town very furiously. **1813** WELLINGTON *Let.* in Gurw. *Disp.* XI. 33 If the town is to be bombarded, it may as well be done from the sand hills. **1858** FROUDE *Hist. Eng.* IV. 427 The admiral.. thought they might anchor and bombard the town.

b. *fig.* To assail with persistent force or violence.

1765 FALCONER *Demag.* 405 Where fulminating, rumbling eloquence..bombards the sense. **1853** BRIGHT *Admiss. Jews Parl.* in *Sp.* (1876) 527 Go on year after year bombarding the Lords with this Jew bill. *a* **1884** M. PATTISON *Mem.* 332 Milton..bombarding Salmasius with foul epithets.

3. *Cookery.* To stuff (a fillet of veal).

1747 H. GLASSE *Art of Cookery* ii. 28 Bombarded veal. **1769** MRS. RAFFALD *Eng. Housekpr.* (1778) 93 Bombarded Veal. Cut the bone nicely out of a fillet, etc. **1837** DISRAELI *Venetia* I. iv. (1871) 15 The tempting delicacies of bombarded veal.

4. *Physics.* To subject to a stream of ions or sub-atomic particles.

1907 J. J. THOMSON in *Phil. Mag.* XIII. 562 All gums &c. when bombarded by the rays are liable to give off gas. **1913** *Chem. Abstr.* 1442 The most abundant supply of these gases was obtained by the process of bombarding with cathode rays metals and other substances. **1932** *Discovery* May 139/1 The tiny nuclei at the centre of certain light elements were bombarded with the swift massive particles spontaneously ejected by the element polonium. **1941** *Ann. Reg. 1940* 352 Nishing and others..examined the products obtained by bombarding uranium with fast neutrons. **1969** *Times* 11 Feb. 12/4 Elements beyond uranium are not known to occur naturally, although several have been prepared in the laboratory by bombarding heavy nuclei with atomic particles in circumstances that encourage fusion.

bombarder (bɒm'bɑːdə(r)). [f. prec. vb. + -ER¹, or ad. F. *bombardier* (16th c. in Littré).] He who or that which bombards; a bombarding vessel. In early use = BOMBARDIER.

1583 *Exec. Treason* (1675) 29 The Popes Canonists being as his Bombarders, do make his Excommunications.. appear fearful. **1808** WHITBREAD in *Cobbett's Parl. Deb.* (1808) X. 729 The bombarders of Copenhagen. **1866** *Daily Tel.* June, Stopped the bombardment by sinking the bombarder.

†**bom'bardical**, *a. Obs.* [f. BOMBARD *sb.* + -ICAL.] 'Thundering, or roaring like a piece of ordnance.' Blount *Glossogr.* 1656.

c **1645** HOWELL *Lett.* (1650) II. 72 He that entitles himself Most Puissant and Highest Monarch of the Turks..with other such bombardicall titles.

bombardier (bɒm-, bʌmbə'dɪə(r)). [a. F. *bombardier*, f. *bombard*: see BOMBARD and -IER.]

†**1.** A soldier in charge of a bombard, an artilleryman. *Obs.* or *arch.*

1560 WHITEHORNE *Arte Warre* (1573) 82 Smithes, Masons, Ingeners, Bombardiers. **1611** COTGR., *Bombardier*, a bombardier or gunner that vseth to discharge murthering peeces; and, more generally, any gunner. **1691** LUTTRELL *Brief Rel.* (1857) II. 292 Our bombardeers are to practice the throwing bombs on ship board. **1709** *Tatler* No. 88 ¶3 The bombardier tosses his balls into the midst of a city. **1779** G. SMITH *Mil. Dict.* **1836** MARRYAT *Midsh. Easy* xxxix, Her two brothers are lieutenants in the bombardiers.

2. *spec.* †**a.** in 17th and 18th c.: One of the master-gunner's men, employed more especially about the mortars and howitzers. *Obs.*

1688 *List of (Jas. II's) Artillery Train*, Firemaster to Trayne, Chief Bombardier, 12 Bombardiers, Chief Petardier, 4 Petardiers. **1746** *Rep. Cond. Sir J. Cope* 55 He gave the Witness a Bombardeer and four Gunners. **1769** FALCONER *Dict. Marine* (1789) Yyiij b, He has also the command of the gunners, matrosses, and bombardiers. [**1855** SARGENT *Braddock's Exped.* 136 A matross is an artillery soldier of a rank inferior to the bombardier or gunner.]

b. In the British army: A non-commissioned officer in the artillery. Several are attached to each battery of artillery.

1844 *Queen's Regul. Ord. Army* 4, Bombardiers of the Royal Regiment of Artillery rank as Corporals.

c. A bomb-aimer in an aircraft. *U.S.*

1932 in H. I. T. CRESWELL et al. *Dict. Mil. Terms* 55. **1942** *Time* 2 Feb. 35/2 At 30,000 feet, flying 200 m.p.h., a bombardier at best has only about 60 seconds in which to locate his target.

†**3.** A bomb-ship. *Obs.*

1686 *Lond. Gaz.* No. 2142/2, 20 Men of War, 2 Fire-Ships and 3 Bombardiers.

4. *Comb.*, as **bombardier beetle**, a genus of beetles (especially *Brachinus crepitans*) which, when irritated, eject fluid with a sharp report and blue vapour; †**bombardier-galliot**, a kind of bomb-vessel.

1802 BINGLEY *Anim. Biog.* (1813) III. 147 The bombardier, or exploding beetle..When it is touched, we are surprised with a noise resembling the discharge of a musket in miniature, during which a blue smoke may be seen to proceed from its extremity. **1861** HULME tr. *Moquin-Tandon* II. iv. i. 214 The..Bombardier Beetles discharge a still more offensive fluid. **1805** *Chron.* in *Ann. Reg.* 391/2 A large flotilla..of Bomba[r]dier galliots, gun sloops and flat bottomed vessels completely armed.

bombarding (bɒm'bɑːdɪŋ), *vbl. sb.* [f. BOMBARD *v.* + -ING¹.] An assailing with shot and shell; a bombardment.

1687 *Lond. Gaz.* No. 2226/2 The preparations for the Bombarding of Agria. **1756** BURKE *Vind. Nat. Soc.* Wks. I. 31 The present perfection of gunnery, cannoneering, bombarding, mining. **1880** MCCARTHY *Own Times* III. xlv. 357 There were more murders and more bombardings yet.

bombardment (bɒm'bɑːrdmənt). [f. BOMBARD *v.* + -MENT.] **1.** The process of bombarding; continuous attack upon a place with shot and shell.

1702 *Lond. Gaz.* No. 3807/3 Which gives us great Apprehensions of a Bombardment. **1790** BEATSON *Nav. & Mil. Mem.* II. 402 To destroy these vessels..by means of a bombardment. **1813** WELLINGTON *Let.* in Gurw. *Disp.* XI. 33 The Bombardment answered no purpose whatever, excepting to destroy the town.

2. *Physics.* Subjection to a stream of particles (see BOMBARD *v.* 4).

1898 J. J. THOMSON *Discharge Electricity* 191 The thermal effects are readily explained on the corpuscular theory by the heating of the substance by the bombardment with the particles. **1932** *Discovery* May 139/1 From a bombardment of nitrogen, aluminium and other elements in this way, the alchemist's dream of changing one kind of element into another has been undoubtedly effected on an exceedingly minute scale. **1945** *Electronic Engin.* XVII. 669 The use of α-particles as projectiles for nuclear bombardment was responsible for the next great step forward. **1969** *Times* 5 Feb. 13/6 The Xi particles were formed in the bombardment of a tank of liquid hydrogen with very fast particles emitted by the accelerator.

‖**bom'bardo.** [It.: 'a certain wind instrument resembling the oboe.'] = BOMBARD *sb.* 4.

'bombardon, -'one, *Mus.* [a. It. *bombardone*, augmentative form of *bombardo*.] A brass instrument of the trumpet-kind, in tone resembling an ophicleide; also a bass reed-stop on the organ.

1856 MRS. C. CLARKE tr. *Berlioz' Instrument.* 176 The Bombardon..is a low instrument without keys and with three cylinders. **1876** HILES *Catech. Organ* x. (1878) 71 *Bombardone, Bombardon, Bombarde*, a reed-stop of metal or wood. **1880** GROVE *Dict. Mus.* I. 259 *Bombardon, bombard*.. were originally names of the different varieties of the oboe or bassoon family; the bombardon, or largest instrument, reaching to contra F. From these the name was transferred to a bass reed-stop on the organ, with 16-foot tone.

†**bombase**, *v. Obs.* Also 6 bum-, boombas; pa. pple. **bombast**. [f. BOMBACE *sb.*: stress orig. on the last, and afterwards on the first syllable.]

1. *trans.* To stuff with cotton-wool; to pad.

1558 *Will of R. Lee* (Somerset Ho.), My doublett of sacke clothe that is bumbased. **1598** FLORIO, *Imbottire*..to stuffe, to quilt, to bumbase.

b. *fig.* and *transf.* To stuff, pad.

1572 GASCOIGNE *Voy. Holland* in Southey *Comm.-pl. Bk.* Ser. II. (1849) 311 They march bumbast with buttered beer. **1577** B. GOOGE *Heresbach's Husb.*, The camel..is bumbast upon the backe for bearing of burdens.

2. To stop (the ears) as with cotton-wool.

1583 STANYHURST *Æneid* IV. 107 What reason him leadeth to my suite too boombas his hearing?

bombase, variant of BOMBACE *sb.*

bombase, -baze, variants of BUMBAZE.

bom'basic, *a. rare.* [f. BOMBACE (or BOMBASIE) + -IC: perh. referring to the colour of Nankeen cotton, or ? of raw silk.] Of a pale yellow or straw colour; bombycinous.

1825 J. FOSBROOKE *Observ. Pathol. Relat.* 53 Skin of a Bombasic tint. *Ibid.* 62 A fine straw-coloured or bombasic tint.

†**'bombasie.** *Obs.* Also 6 **bombezie**. [variant of BOMBACE or BOMBASINE.]

1. Raw cotton, cotton-wool.

1576 BAKER *Gesner's Jewell Health* 189 b, A feather or fine bombasie wette in the oyle. **1578** LYTE *Dodoens* VI. xlvi. 719 Dip a little Cotton or Bombasie in the sayde milke, and lay it to your tooth.

2. = BOMBASINE 2.

1588 *Record* in Law *Memorials* Pref. 33 *note*, 3 elles of bombezie.

bombasine ('bɒm-, 'bʌmbəziːn). Forms: 6 **bombasyne**, 6–9 **-in**, 7 **bumbazine**, 7–9 **bombazin**, 8 **bumbasine**, 8–9 **bombazeen**, 9 **bombazine**, 7– **bombasine**. [a. F. *bombasin*, ad. late L. *bombasinum*, var. of *bombȳcinum* (Isidore) a silk texture, neuter of *bombȳcinus* silken, f. *bombyx*, *-ȳcem* silk-worm, silk. On the later transfer of *bombyx*, *bombax*, and its derivatives to 'tree-silk' or cotton, *bombasin* was also applied to cotton fabrics, 'fustaine ou bombasin, et toute autre chose faicte de coton, *xylinum*', R. Estienne *Petit Dict.*]

†**1.** Raw cotton; = BOMBACE 1. *Obs.*

1555 EDEN *Decades W. Ind.* I. II. (Arb.) 69 *marg.*, This Cotton the Spaniardes call *Algodon* & the Italians *Bombasine*. **1580** HOLLYBAND *Treas. Fr. Tong*, *Du Bombasyn*, Bombasin, cotton.

2. A twilled or corded dress-material, composed of silk and worsted; sometimes also of cotton and worsted, or of worsted alone. In black the material is much used in mourning.

1572 *Wills & Inv. N.C.* (1835) I. 373 One doblat of white bombasyne. **1611** COTGR., *Bombasin*, the stuffe Bumbazine; or any kind of stuffe that's made of cotton, or of cotton and linnen. **1660** *Act 12 Chas. II*, iv. Sched., Boratoes or Bombasines—narrow the single piece not above 15 yards, vjl. **1747** MRS. DELANY *Autobiog.* (1861) II. 478 Black bombazeen will do very well in a sack. **1789** WOLCOTT (P. Pindar) *Expost. Ode* xv. Wks. 1812 II. 248 In Sorrow's dismal crape or bombazeen. **1820** MISS MITFORD in L'Estrange *Life* (1870) II. iv. 83 Crape and bombazin and broad-hemmed frills. **1831** G. PORTER *Silk Manuf.* 299 Bombasin..a twilled manufacture, having its warp of silk, and its shoot of worsted.

b. *attrib.* and *comb.*

1666 PEPYS *Diary* (1879) III. 494 Putting on my black stuffe bombazin suit. **1766** ANSTEY *Bath Guide* xi. (1804) 94 Who is that bombazine lady so gay, So profuse of her beauties, in sable array? **1819** *P.O. Lond. Directory* 19 Bombazeen Manufacturers. *Ibid.* 144 Bombazeen-dressers.

†**'bombasing**, *sb. Obs.* In 6 bum-. [f. BOMBASE *v.* + -ING¹.]

1. = BOMBASINE 2 (perh. a corruption).

1580 BARET *Alv.* Bumbasing or anything made of cotten.

2. Padding with bombace.

1598 FLORIO, *Imbottitura*..a quilting, a bumbasing.

bombast ('bɒm-, 'bʌmbəst, -bæst), *sb.* Forms: 6 bom-, bumbaste, 6–8 bumbast, 6– bombast. [A

variant of BOMBACE, *bombase* (F. *bombace*), in 16th c. pronounced (bɒm'baːs), the *t* being either simply phonetic (the converse of *bass, bast*) or perhaps influenced by the pa. pple. *bombast* of BOMBASE *v.* Originally accented on second syllable, as still in Byron: but already in Shakspere on the first. Most dictionaries make the first syllable (bʌm-), but contemporary usage favours (bɒm-).]

†**1.** The soft down of the cotton-plant; raw cotton; cotton-wool. *Obs.*

1568 T. HOWELL *Arb. Amitie* (1879) 61 From all meate soft, as wooll and flaxe, bombaste and winds that bloe. **1582** HESTER *Secr. Phiorav.* II. xx. 99 Wet a little Bumbast in our Caustick. **1597** GERARD *Herbal* II. cccxxxv. 901 Called in English & French, Cotton, Bombaste & Bombace. **1615** G. SANDYS *Trav.* 15 The head [of the Cotton plant]..ripening breakes, and is deliuered of a white soft Bombast. **1665** G. HAVERS *P. della Valle's Trav.* 23 Which linnen..is altogether of Bumbast or Cotton, (there being no Flax in India).

†**b.** *attrib.* Cotton. *Obs.*

1599 HAKLUYT *Voy.* II. I. 222 Scarlet, or white Bumbast cloth. **1600** DEKKER *Gentle Craft* 15 You bombast cotten-candle queane. **1653** URQUHART *Rabelais* III. xli. (1737) III. 139 The bumbast and cotton bushes.

†**2.** Cotton-wool used as padding or stuffing for clothes, etc. *Obs.* exc. *Hist.*

1572 GASCOIGNE *B. Withipoll*, To stuff thy doublet full of such bumbaste. **1601** R. J. *Kingd. & Commw.* 140 Iacks quilted with bombast to resist arrowes. **1685** CROWNE *Sir C. Nice* II. 18 For the inside; do you like much bombast, madam? **1849** *Mem. Kirkaldy of Gr.* viii. 77 Their large..trunk-hose, being quilted and stuffed with bombast.

†**b.** *fig.* Padding, stuffing; stopping of the ears.

1575 GASCOIGNE *Wks.* (1587) 83 It hath no bumbast now, but skin and bones. **1588** SHAKS. *L.L.L.* v. ii. 791 As bumbast and as lining to the time. **1631** *Celestina* x. 120 Frame..for your eares the bumbast or stuffing of sufferance and bearing.

3. *fig.* Inflated or turgid language; high-sounding language on a trivial or commonplace subject; 'fustian'; 'tall talk'. [This sense has been erroneously supposed to have originated in the name of Paracelsus (P. A. T. Bombast von Hohenheim).]

1589 NASHE in Greene *Menaphon* (Arb.) Ded. 6 To outbrave better pens with the swelling bumbast of a bragging blanke verse. *a* **1625** FLETCHER *Chances* v. iii, I like his words well; there's no bombast in 'em. **1710** POPE *Lett.* Wks. 1736 V. 107 The ambition of surprising a reader, is the true natural cause of all fustian, or bombast in poetry. **1762** KAMES *Elem. Crit.* iv. (1833) 124 False sublime known by the name of bombast. **1811** BYRON *Hints from Hor.* 44 Another soars, inflated with bombast. **1850** KINGSLEY *Alt. Locke* xxxiii. (1879) 342 Their eloquence is all bombast.

b. *transf.*

1817 COLERIDGE *Biog. Lit.* 221 What might be called mental bombast, as distinguished from verbal. **1821** CRAIG *Lect. Drawing* iv. 213, I have insuperable objections to this sort of bombast in painting.

bombast, *v. arch.* [f. prec. sb., which see for pronunciation: in the vb. the accent is more frequently on the final syllable.]

†**1.** To stuff, pad, or fill out with cotton-wool, or the like. *Obs.*

1565 JEWEL *Repl. Harding* (1611) To Rdr. 2 To couer the smalnesse..of their bodies, [he] had bomebasted, and embossed out their coates. **1576** GASCOIGNE *Steele Gl.* Epil. 82 [They] bumbast, bolster, frisle and perfume. **1650** BULWER *Anthropomet.* xvi. 162 They bumbast their Doublets. **1820** SCOTT *Abbot* xv, My stomach has no room for it; it is..too well bumbasted out with straw and buckram.

2. *fig.* and *transf.* To stuff, swell out, inflate.

1566 STUDLEY *Seneca's Medea* (1581) 136 Her hawty breast bumbasted is wyth pryde. **1599** NASHE *Lent. Stuffe* (1871) 58 The first should have his gut bombasted with beef. **1607** CHAPMAN *Bussy D'Amb.* Plays 1873 II. 43 A great man ..that by his greatnesse Bumbasts his private roofes, with public riches. **1624** T. SCOTT *Vox Dei* 68 A place and people that..bombasted their reputations with the winde of complement. **1633** HEYWOOD *Eng. Trav.* Prol, Not so much ..As Song, Dance, Masque, to bumbaste out a Play. **1822** SOUTHEY in *Q. Rev.* XXVII. 34 The want of incidents..he has endeavoured to supply by invention, and in bombasting the fable with machinery.

b. To swell out, render grandiose (a speech or literary composition) with bombastic language.

1573 R. SCOT *Hop Gard.* (1578) Epist., Not bumbasting the same with the figures and flowers of eloquence. **1599** BP. HALL *Sat.* I. iv. 9 Then strives he to bumbast his feeble lines With farre-fetcht phrase. **1603** FLORIO *Montaigne* I. xxv. (1632) 83 That doth..bumbast his labours with high swelling and heaven-disimbowelling words.

'bombast, *ppl. a.* Also 6–7 **bumbast(e.** [pa. pple. of BOMBASE *v.* to stuff; but in later use hardly separable from the sb. used *attrib.*]

†**1.** Stuffed, padded, puffed out. *Obs.*

1575 GASCOIGNE *Wks.* (1587) 157 Hys bombast hose wyth linings manifold. **1656** *Artif. Handsomeness* 44 A bumbast or bolstered garment.

2. *fig.* Puffed, empty, inflated; over-elaborate. Of language: Turgid, grandiloquent, bombastic.

1604 SHAKS. *Oth.* I. i. 13 A bumbast circumstance, Horribly stufft with Epithites of warre. **1616** *Pasquil & Kath.* IV. 316, I doe hate these bumbaste wits, That are puft vp with arrogant conceit. **1674** R. GODFREY *Inj. & Ab. Physic* 122 He scorns to be frightened at a Bombast word, or Fustian Term. **1781** GIBBON *Decl. & F.* (1802) VI. 134 *note*, Forty bombast lines. **1834** *Fraser's Mag.* X. 435 A frothy, verbose, and bombast writer. **1842** MAITLAND *Notes &c.* II. 26.

bombast(e, variant of BUMBASTE *v. Obs.*

bombasted, *ppl. a.* [f. BOMBAST *v.*, which see for pronunciation.]

†**1.** Stuffed or padded with cotton-wool; puffed out. *Obs.*

1583 STUBBES *Anat. Abus.* (1877) 55 Stuffed, bombasted and sewed. **1611** MARKHAM *Countr. Content.* (1649) 111 Which Hats are soft bumbasted roules of leather. **1626** T. H. *Caussin's Holy Crt.* 224 Your garments playted, bumbasted, loose hanged.

2. Inflated, turgid (language). *arch.*

1589 PUTTENHAM *Eng. Poesie* (Arb.) 266 Vsing such bombasted wordes, as seeme altogether farced full of winde. **1631** R. H. *Arraignm. Whole Creat.* xi. §1. 99 With braggodokean and bumbasted words. **1829** SOUTHEY in *Q. Rev.* XXXIX. 103 The bombasted heroics of Dryden's tragedy.

†**3.** Characterized by bombast. *Obs.*

a **1619** FOTHERBY *Atheom.* II. i. §8. (1622) 190 Leontinus Gorgias, that bombasted Sophister. **1620** MELTON *Astrolog.* 15 The souldiers bumbasted Tongue.

†**bombaster** (see the vb.). *Obs.* [f. as prec. + -ER[1].] One who stuffs or pads.

1611 COTGR., *Embourreur*, a stuffer, bumbaster or puffer up of things with flocks, etc. **1708** MOTTEUX *Rabelais' Pantag. Prognost.* v, Stuffers and Bumbasters of Pack-saddles.

bombastic (bɒm'bæstɪk), *a.* [f. BOMBAST *sb.* + -IC.]

1. Of the nature of bombast; inflated, turgid.

1704 *Key to Rehearsal* Pref. 4 Outdoing them in their Bumbastick Bills. **1756** NUGENT *Montesquieu's Spir. Laws* XXVIII. i, Frivolous in the substance, and bombastic in the style. **1855** MACAULAY *Hist. Eng.* IV. 600. **1861** TULLOCH *Eng. Purit.* ii. 326 His bombastic words signify nothing.

2. Given to the use of bombastic language.

1727 DE FOE *Hist. Appar.* iv. (1840) 30 A certain bombastic Author. **1864** KINGSLEY *Rom. & Teut.* iii. 59 Claudian, the poet, a bombastic panegyrist of Roman scoundrels.

bom'bastical, *a.* [f. as prec. + -ICAL.]

†**1.** Of or pertaining to the padding of garments.

1650 BULWER *Anthropomet.* xix. 195 If they be not corpulent [they] counterfeit [it] by the bombastical dissimulation of their garments.

2. = BOMBASTIC.

1649 BULWER *Pathomyot.* Pref. 7 Barbarismes..fit only for the bombasticall Anatomy of Paracelsus. **1858** HALPIN in *Grosart's Spenser* (1882) III. Introd. 94 He was.. pedantic and bombastical.

bom'bastically, *adv.* [f. prec. + -LY[2].] In a bombastic manner, with bombastic language.

1803 *Edin. Rev.* II. 103 We are bombastically told that all the outcry..arose from the new philosophy. **1853** F. W. NEWMAN *Horace* 31 The strife between the two is bombastically terrific.

†**bombasting,** *vbl. sb. Obs.* [f. BOMBAST *v.* + -ING[1].] Padding.

1603 FLORIO *Montaigne* (1634) 623 The bombasting of my doublet, serves me now for no more use then a stomacher. **1611** COTGR., *Embourrement*, a stuffing, or bumbasting with flockes, haire, etc.

bom'bastious, *a.* ? *Obs. rare.* [f. BOMBAST *sb.* + -IOUS.] Of or pertaining to cotton.

1824 GALT *Rothelan* II. IV. i. 98 The spindle..drawing in the bombastious rowan, and growing thicker and thicker.

†**bombastly,** *adv. Obs.* = BOMBASTICALLY. (In H. Walpole.)

†**'bombastry.** *Obs. rare*$^{-1}$. [f. BOMBAST *sb.* + -RY.] Bombastic composition.

1704 SWIFT *T. Tub* Wks. 1760 I. 27 Bombastry and buffoonry, by nature lofty and light, soar highest of all.

bombax ('bɒmbæks). [Altered from L. *bombyx* raw silk; see BOMBACE.] A genus of tropical trees (N.O. *Sterculiaceæ*), which bear a fruit containing seeds surrounded by a beautiful silky fibre; esp. *B. Ceiba*, the Silk-cotton tree of West Indies.

1834 *Nat. Philos.* III. *Phys. Geog.* (U.K.S.) 46 Humboldt measured..a bombax ceiba more than 120 feet high. **1863** *Wanderings W. Africa* I. 143 Scattered with tall Bentangs or Bombax trees. **1884** *Edin. Rev.* July 159 Stately bombaxes, flecked with the snowy tufts of their bursting seed-pods.

bombax, obs. f. BOMBYX.

Bombay (bɒm'beɪ). The name of a city in India, used attrib. in: **Bombay chair** (cf. *Bombay furniture*); **Bombay duck** (see DUCK *sb.*[1] 10); **Bombay furniture**, a style of furniture combining European forms with Indian ornamentation; **Bombay hemp** (see HEMP 5); **Bombay pearl** (see quot.); **Bombay shell**, the bull's-mouth shell, *Cassis rufa*, used for cutting shell cameos.

1896 *Pall Mall Mag.* Mar. 399 [They] succeeded in installing themselves in two immense Bombay Chairs. **1910** *Encycl. Brit.* IV. 185/2 The workmen who manufacture the most artistic Bombay furniture are a special class with inherited traditions. **1967** M. PEGLER *Dict. Interior Design* 59 *Bombay furniture*, furniture manufactured in India after 1740... The furniture is a conglomeration of French and Portuguese styles and forms which are overlaid with typically elaborate and minute Indian carving. **1885** *Encycl. Brit.* XVIII. 447/1 Most of the products of this fishery [*sc.* in the Persian Gulf] are known as 'Bombay pearls', from the fact that many of the best are sold there. **1858** SIMMONDS *Dict. Trade*, Bombay Shells.

bombazeen, -zin(e, var. of BOMBASINE.

bomb-boat, obs. form of BUMBOAT.

‖**bombe** (bɔ̃b). *Cookery.* [Fr.; see BOMB *sb.*] A conical or cup-shaped confection, freq. frozen. Also *attrib.*

1892 T. F. GARRETT *Encycl. Pract. Cookery* I. 40/2 Apricot Bombe with Maraschino... Set two freezing-pots and a bombe-mould in some pounded ice and bay-salt. **1902** *Daily Chron.* 24 May 5/4 Fish bombes are made with any kind of cooked white fish. *Ibid.*, Turn it out on a hot dish, place four little 'bombes' round it. **1960** J. BETJEMAN *Summoned by Bells* ix. 101 Claret and *tournedos*; a *bombe surprise*.

‖**bombé** (bɔ̃be), *a.* [Fr., pa. pple. of *bomber* to swell out; cf. BOMBED *ppl. a.*[1]] Having an outward swelling curve, esp. of furniture. Also in *Comb.*

1904 R. D. BENN *Style in Furniture* 109 A chest of drawers, or 'commode', and wardrobe, in which the *bombé* form is introduced. **1941** *Burlington Mag.* Feb. 59/2 The shaping of a base of a cabinet or chest of drawers (often termed today *bombé*)..was called in the eighteenth century ' comode shaped'. **1955** *Times* 21 May 5/4 Marquetry cabinet, in the French style, with slightly *bombé* front and curved and splayed sides. **1962** *Times* 1 June 8/5 A pair of eighteenth-century painted bombé-shaped Venetian commodes.

bombed (bɒmd, 'bɒmbɪd), *ppl. a.*[1] *rare.* [ad. F. *bombé* rounded like a bomb.] Rounded, convex.

1872 BROWNING *Fifine* lx. 22 That bombèd brow, that eye, a kindling chrysopras, Beneath its stiff black lash. **1896** A. H. KEANE *Ethnology* I. viii. 185 The small flat concave [nose] is usually correlated with high cheek-bones..; the short with wide nostrils and depressed root, with everted lips and bombed frontal bone (Negro).

bombed, *ppl. a.*[2] [f. BOMB *v.* + -ED[1].] **1.** Having come under attack by explosive bombs; esp. ***bombed out***, driven by bombs out of a building, etc. (Cf. BOMB *v.* 1 b.)

1940 *New Statesman* 19 Oct. 373/1 What..is happening to the host of shopkeepers..driven from their shops..or bombed out of them?.. Our ruined or bombed-out shopkeeper will pay out of his income. **1940** *War Weekly* 25 Oct. 1313 (*heading*) Story of a bombed-out family.

2. *slang.* Drunk; under the influence of drugs. Chiefly *predic.*, esp. in phr. ***to get bombed***. Freq. with *out*. Cf. BOMB *sb.* 2 f, *v.* 5, STONED *ppl. a.* 7 a, b.

1959 N. MAILER *Advts. for Myself* 411 With each week of work, bombed and sapped and charged and stoned with lush, with pot,..I was working live, and tiring into what felt like death. *Ibid.*, I..went home at closing, fell into a leaden bombed-out sleep. **1964** *N.Y. Times Mag.* 23 Aug. 64/2 *Bombed*, a stupor induced by alcohol or narcotics, as in 'He was bombed out of his mind'. **1967** R. J. SERLING *President's Plane is Missing* (1968) x. 190 Some night I'll get bombed with you. **1969** *Time* 5 Dec. 62 Usually, when an editor says he got bombed last night, he means he had too much to drink. **1974** O. MANNING *Rain Forest* iii. 55 'Poor little brat! They'll take her off on the heroin trail and she'll die between here and the Philippines.' 'They're bombed out. Where do they get the stuff?' **1978** *Courier-Mail* (Brisbane) 12 Aug. 8/8 Stewart had been smoking cannabis all day and by nightfall he was 'bombed'. **1984** A. LURIE *Foreign Affairs* iii. 78, I was bombed out—didn't know what I was doing.

bomber ('bɒmə(r)). [f. BOMB *sb.* or *v.* + -ER[1].]

1. One who throws a bomb; *esp.* in military use, one of a bombing party.

1915 J. BUCHAN *Nelson's Hist. War* V. 25 The bombers.. seizing one of these rocket-like bombs from their belts.. hurl them high above the parapet. **1927** *Daily Tel.* 8 Mar. 12/2 A fifth attempt to dynamite the Roman Catholic Church of S. Peter and Paul, San Francisco, ended yesterday in the killing of one bomber.

2. An aircraft equipped with bombs for bombing an enemy, his positions, territory, etc.

1917 'CONTACT' *Airman's Outings* 260 The fighters guard the bombers until the eggs are dropped. **1923** *Daily Mail* 19 Mar. 9 Goods-'planes—all capable of transformation into bombers. **1940** *Times Weekly* 27 Nov. 10/3 Our medium bombers were the first to arrive. **1941** *Ibid.* 30 July 7/1 For 27 hours on end we were subjected to continuous attacks from bombers—high level, dive and torpedo. **1956** A. H. COMPTON *Atomic Quest* 224 American bombers attacked.. the power station.

b. *attrib.* and *Comb.*, as ***bomber aircraft, base, force***; **Bomber Command**, an organization of bomber aircraft forming part of the Royal Air Force.

1935 C. G. BURGE *Complete Bk. Aviation* 193/1 Bomber aircraft. **1959** *Listener* 22 Jan. 156/1 American bomber bases. **1939** *Flight* 7 Dec. 455/1 Bomber Command.. pounces when a worthy objective is in sight. **1945** W. S. CHURCHILL *Victory* (1946) 174 The glorious part..played by Bomber Command in forging the victory. **1940** —— *Into battle* (1941) 231 We have a very large bomber force also.

3. A marijuana cigarette. *U.S. slang.*

1952 *Amer. Speech* XXVII. 24 *Bomber*, giant-size marijuana cigarette. **1957** J. KEROUAC *On Road* (1958) IV. v.

283 Victor proceeded to roll the biggest bomber anybody ever saw.

b. *slang.* A barbiturate drug. Cf. *black bomber.*

1962 K. ORVIS *Damned & Destroyed* xiii. 87 Last year, eighteen tons..of barbiturates were sold in this country. Kids all over are going ga-ga over them. They call them goof-balls and bombers—and they hold bomber parties. **1966** 'K. NICHOLSON' *Hook, Line & Sinker* x. 116, I was planning to go back on bombers today.

bombic ('bɒmbɪk), *a.* [f. L. *bomb-yx* silk-worm (see BOMBYX) + -IC.] Of or pertaining to the silk-worm; as in ***bombic acid***, an acid secreted by the silk-worm, now believed to be nearly pure acetic acid (*Syd. Soc. Lex.*).

1816 MRS. MARCET *Conv. Chem.* (1841) II. 335. **1836** TODD *Cycl. Anat. & Phys.* I. 47/1 There are also certain acids almost peculiar to individual animals, such as the bombic.

†'**bombice.** *Obs. rare.* [var. of BOMBACE, conformed to L. *bombyx, bombȳcem.*] Raw cotton.

1559 MORWYNG *Evonym.* 6 Putting wull of woode, or bombice into the upper hoole of the aludel.

bombilate ('bɒmbɪleɪt), *v. rare*$^{-0}$. [f. reputed L. **bombilāre*, an erroneous reading (commonly accepted in med.L.) of *bombitāre* to hum, buzz, f. *bombus* hum, buzz.] *intr.* To hum, to buzz.
Only in mod. Dicts.

bombilation (bɒmbɪ'leɪʃən). Also 7 **bombulation.** [f. as prec.: see -ATION. The L. word is *bombitātio.*] Humming, buzzing, droning sound.

1646 SIR T. BROWNE *Pseud. Ep.* 89 How to abate the vigour thereof, or silence its bombilation, a way is promised by Porta. **1656** BLOUNT *Glossogr.*, *Bombilation*, a humming as of Bees. *Vul. Err.* **1885** *Pall Mall G.* 17 Feb. 2 A concerto of regurgitations and nasal bombilations.

bombill, bomble, obs. forms of BUMBLE.

‖**bombilla** (bom'biʎa). [Sp., dim. of *bomba.*] A vessel from which maté is drunk in South America.

1866 *Commissioners of Patents Jrnl.* 24 July 1094/1 Patent 1895 [for] apparatus used for imbibing or sucking in liquids, known as 'bombillas'. **1921** *Glasgow Herald* 11 Feb. 9 A bombilla manufactured specially for the South American market. **1921** *Chambers's Jrnl.* June 382/1 *Maté* circulates in a small gourd-shaped vessel, each person taking a pull at the *bombilla*, a kind of spoon-strainer perforated to let the liquid pass.

'**bombinate,** *v.* [f. L. *bombināre* a corrupt or doubtful variant of *bombitāre*, or *bombizāre*; see BOMBILATE.] To buzz, make a buzzing noise.

[RABELAIS II. vii, Questio subtilissima, utrum chimera in vacuo bombinans possit comedere secundas intentiones. (In ridicule of the subtle discussions of the Schoolmen.)] **1880** SWINBURNE *Study Shaks.* iii. 199 (ed. 2) As easy and as profitable a problem to solve the Rabelaisian riddle of the bombinating chimæra. **1880** *Daily News* 21 June The power of a chimæra bombinating in a vacuum to eat second intentions is scarcely less suggestive of a..solution.

bombination (bɒmbɪ'neɪʃən). [vbl. sb. from prec.; cf. BOMBILATION.] Buzzing, humming.

1816 KIRBY & SP. *Entomol.* (1843) II. xxiv. 304 The larger humble-bees, whose bombination, booming, or bombing, may be heard from a considerable distance.

bombing ('bɒmɪŋ, 'bʌmɪŋ), *vbl. sb.* [f. BOMB *v.* + -ING[1].] An attacking with bombs; bombarding; the action or operation of throwing or dropping bombs. Also *transf.*

1691 LUTTRELL *Brief Rel.* (1857) II. 195 The bombing of which had cost them a good summ of money and men. **1719** D'URFEY *Pills* (1872) II. 129 The General would leave Bombing, Of Towns in hot Campaigns. **1915** *Daily Mail* 18 May 6/4 Three Air Raids on Calais. Futile bombing by 3 Zeppelins. **1940** 'GUN BUSTER' *Return via Dunkirk* II. xi. 167 The bombing had been mercilessly thorough. **1953** N. TINBERGEN *Herring Gull's World* iv. 31, I watched Hooded Crows picking up the mussels and dropping them on the road... I could not but conclude that they had concentrated their 'bombing' on the road. **1956** A. H. COMPTON *Atomic Quest* 228 These bombings were reducing Japan's fighting machine to impotence. **1968** LUND & LUDLAM *PQ17* vi. 127 During all this time the bombing had continued, hour after hour.

Also *attrib.*, as ***bombing attack, offensive, party, plane, raid, sight, squad***; **bombing run** = *bomb run.* Also **bombing up**, the loading of aircraft with bombs.

1942 *Times Weekly* 2 Dec. 6/3 While Stukas were occasionally used for level bombing attacks 'they did not carry out one proper dive-bombing attack during the entire campaign'. **1917** 'CONTACT' *Airman's Outings* 171 After a tribute has been paid to the bombing offensives for which the Naval Air Service has always been famous. **1915** *Morning Post* 29 May 8/1 A bombing party presents a weird sight... The men carry 5 or 6 grenades each. **1934** WEBSTER, Bombing plane. **1936** *Discovery* Feb. 33/1 The Air Ministry ..use them as practice ranges for bombing planes. **1917** *Flying* 14 Feb. 89/1 In bombing raids..it is necessary for aeroplanes to fly in a fixed formation. **1941** J. HAMMERTON *ABC of RAF* 23 An aspect of training for night-flying: after a practice 'bombing run' with a camera obscura the pupils check up results. **1946** *News Chron.* 2 Mar. 3/3 Trent completed his bombing run..and dropped his bombs in the target area. **1920** *Flight* XII. 744/2 An invention of bombing sights for aeroplanes. **1944** *Times* 20 Apr. 5/7 One factory turned from making fountain pens and propelling pencils to the production of aircraft bombing sights. **1923** KIPLING *Irish Guards* I. 11. 125 O'Brien started to train fresh bombing-squads with the Mills bomb. **1932** *Flight* 10 June 508/1 *(caption) Bombing up*: Fixing a 550-lb. bomb in its rack. **1939** *Times* 3 Nov. 8/5 In another hangar the King watched a demonstration of 'bombing up'. On low trucks bombs were run under the body of the aeroplane and there by mechanical means loaded into the machine.

bombing, obs. form of BOOMING.

†'**bomb-ketch.** *Obs.* [See BOMB and KETCH.] A small ketch-rigged vessel, carrying one or two mortars for bombarding.

1693 *Lond. Gaz.* No. 2862/2 Several Bomb-ketches, Fire-ships, etc. **1762** *Gentl. Mag.* 341 Four French men of War and a bomb-ketch, entered the bay. **1830** I. TAYLOR *The Ship* 105 The bomb-ketch is contrived to carry one mortar, but is yet enough of a ship to bear the sea. **1875** Johnson's *New Univ. Cycl.* (New York) I. 548/1 *Bomb-ketch*, an obsolete form of mortar-vessel..nearly seventy feet long and drew eight or nine feet of water. It..carried two mortars.

bomblet ('bɒmlɪt). [f. BOMB *sb.* + -LET.] A small bomb; any of many explosive devices forming part of a larger, complex weapon. Also *fig.*

1937 G. FRANKAU *More of Us* ii. 30 What, readers few, ah, what were Sophie's feelings, When burst that bomblet at her shell-like ear? **1950** J. D. GREENWAY *Fish, Fowl & Foreign Lands* vii. 80 In a safe in an outbuilding was a case of tear-gas bomblets which had been left behind by some unknown former mission and were presumably used for de-ratting purposes. **1968** *New Scientist* 29 Feb. 465/2 Chemicals are also packed into missile warheads. There may be several hundred bomblets in each. **1972** *Courier-Mail* (Brisbane) 30 Mar. 1/4 Devices such as people sniffers, spider mines, and silent button bomblets. **1977** *New Scientist* 24 Feb. 443/1 FAE bombs carry a number of canisters or bomblets containing a volatile and highly inflammable fuel. **1986** *Daily Tel.* 4 Mar. 5/6 The idea is to ground-launch or air-launch rockets containing dozens or even hundreds of bomblets.

bombo, bomboat, var. of BUMBO[1], BUMBOAT.

bombora (bɒm'bɔərə). *Austral.* (and *N.Z.*). Also **bomboora.** [Aboriginal.] A dangerous stretch of water where the waves break over a submerged reef of rocks.

1933 *Bulletin* (Sydney) 24 May 27/1 'Bombora' is an aboriginal word applied to the high-crested wave which breaks, even on windless days, over submerged rocks near the coastline and in some cases at entrances to coastal harbors and inlets. **1945** BAKER *Austral. Lang.* xiii. 224 *Bomboora* to describe a dangerous reef of rocks usually found at the foot of cliffs. This is naturally confined to coastal regions. **1966** *Weekly News* (N.Z.) 19 Jan. 6/5 Surf sizes range from small 'hotdogging' waves with excellent shapes to 'bombora' surf. **1968** W. WARWICK *Surfriding in N.Z.* 34/1 Two left and right bomboras (large reef breaks), best at high tide.

bombous ('bɒmbəs, 'bʌmbəs), *a.* [In sense 1, f. L. *bombus*, a. Gr. βόμβος boom, hum + -OUS: in sense 2 f. BOMB *sb.*]

†**1.** Booming, humming. *Obs.*

1715 tr. *Pancirollus' Rerum Mem.* I. IV. xii. 202 The Indians..beating..Drums..made an horrible Noise, and a Bombous kind of Sound. *Ibid.* II. xviii. 383 Call'd Bombardæ, from the bombous kind of Noise they make.

2. Convexly rounded; having the shape of a fragment of a bomb or sphere.

1878 BELL *Gegenbauer's Anat.* 423 In some parts as, for example, on the head, they often have a bombous surface, and are set irregularly. **1882** in *Jrnl. Linn. Soc.* XVI. 195 Dorsal profile rather high and bombous over the disk.

'**bomb-proof,** *a.* and *sb.* [see PROOF.]

A. *adj.* **a.** Strong enough to resist bombs or shells. Also *transf.* and *fig.*

1702 T. MARWOOD in *Cath. Rec. Soc. Publ.* VII. 124 Walls & Vaults all Bombe proof [of Fort]. **1734** A. WILLIAMSON *Diary* (1912) 85 So that it is bomb proof as I believe all the arched cellers in the Towers are. **1755** *Gentl. Mag.* XXV. 390 There is no magazine bomb-proof. **1858** BEVERIDGE *Hist. India* III. VIII. viii. 518 The grand mosque, which was supposed to be bomb-proof. **1862** F. GRIFFITHS *Artil. Man.* (ed. 9) 248 Casemates..are made bomb-proof. **1915** G. B. SHAW in *New Statesman* 13 Mar. 559/2 In Dunkirk, Düsseldorf, Freiburg and other towns where the women and children, being foreign, are conventionally assumed by us to be naturally bomb-proof. **1918** *Flying* 6 Feb. 90/1 A bomb penetrated the building..in what was regarded as a more or less bomb-proof shelter. **1940** N. MARSH *Surfeit of Lampreys* (1941) vii. 104 Each locked up inside his mental bomb-proof shelter.

b. Not exposed to the dangers of war. *U.S.*

1867 *Harper's Wkly.* 6 Apr. 211/1 The 'bomb-proof' editors will probably continue to repeat the heroics of the war. **1868** *Putnam's Mag.* I. 715/1 During the late war the Simminses did their share of the fighting, for..none of them had influence to get 'bomb-proof' places, and keep in the rear. **1928** S. V. BENÉT *John Brown's Body* 155 Muddy Washington..full of..'Bombproof' officers, veterans back on leave.

B. *sb.* **a.** Bomb-proof shelter or structure.

1755 J. THOMAS *Diary* in F. Parkman *Montcalm & Wolfe* (1898) I. 260 One of our large shells fell through what they called their bomb-proof. **1780** W. HEATH *Let.* 2 Feb. in *Coll. Mass. Hist. Soc.* (1905) V. 28 The bunks and lineing of the bomb proof were taken out. **1809** J. BARLOW *Columb.* VII. 618 And housed in bomb-proof all the host she bore. **1811** WELLINGTON *Let.* in Gurw. *Disp.* VII. 262, I do not think bomb proof absolutely necessary. **1861** RUSSELL in *Times* 11 June, We entered a lofty bomb-proof, which was the bed-room of the commanding officer. **1870** *Daily News* 12 Nov., In the rear of the bomb-proofs..were the earthworks..for batteries of field guns. **1918** E. M. ROBERTS *Flying Fighter* iii. 26, I was obliged to find shelter in a bomb-proof.

b. One who avoids exposure to the dangers of war. Also '***bomb-proofer.*** orig. *U.S.*

1869 *Overland Monthly* III. 128 In the cis-Mississippi States they were generally dubbed 'bomb-proofs'. **1872** SCHELE DE VERE *Americanisms* 281 Officials who were not expected to expose themselves to the fire of the enemy, like quartermasters, commissaries, etc. were nicknamed *bomb-proofs.* **1925** FRASER & GIBBONS *Soldier & Sailor Words* 32 *Bomb-proofer*, a man given to scheming methods of evading duty on dangerous occasions. **1936** M. MITCHELL *Gone with Wind* xviii. 314 Things must be in a desperate pass if this rabble of bombproofers, old men and little boys were being called out! **1950** R. CHANDLER *Let.* 18 May (1962) 88 Doesn't he [*sc.* Partridge] overlook some of the most commonly used words of soldier-slang? E.g. 'bomb-proofer', 'cushy job', 'bivvy'.

bomb-shell ('bʌm-, 'bɒmʃɛl). = BOMB 2. Often *fig.* (or in fig. phr.). A shattering or devastating act, event, etc. Phr. ***blonde bomb-shell***, a fair-haired person, esp. a woman, of startling vitality or physique.

1708 *Lond. Gaz.* No. 4467/3 Kill'd..by a piece of Bomb-Shell. **1860** MOTLEY *Netherl.* (1868) II. xiv. 206 The famous ..letter, which descended like a bombshell, in the midst of the decorous council-chamber. **1926** MAY SUTHERLAND *One o' the Herd* vii, Do you think it was kind to let her think she had plenty and then drop down on her like this? It's a regular bomb-shell. **1928** *Manch. Guardian Weekly* 26 Oct. 337/1 The letters do not drop any historical bombshells. **1942** BERREY & VAN DEN BARK §184/14 Blonde Bombshell (as a nickname). **1949** A. HYND *Public Enemies* 41 (Wentworth & Flexner), Bonnie Parker was a rootin', tootin', whisky-drinking blonde bombshell. **1951** E. COXHEAD *One Green Bottle* iii. 86 Cathy..now had standing and a soubriquet. She became the Merseyside Menace, or, alternatively, the Birkenhead Bombshell. **1955** M. HASTINGS *Cork & Serpent* ii. 29 'What was she like?'..'A blonde bombshell I should call her, sir.' **1965** *Times Lit. Suppl.* 25 Nov. 1072/3 The bombshell effects..of the intellectual and social crises of late antiquity.

‖**bombus** ('bɒmbəs). [L. *bombus* boom, hum.]

1. *Med.* A humming or buzzing noise in the intestines, ears, etc.

1753 CHAMBERS *Cycl. Supp.* s.v. **1880** *Syd. Soc. Lex.*, *Bombus*, a ringing noise in the ears. Also a sonorous movement of flatus in the intestines.

†**2.** 'In music, an artificial motion with the hands, imitating, in cadence and harmony, the buzzing of bees.' Chambers *Cycl. Supp.* 1753. *Obs.*

3. *Entomol.* The genus of insects containing the humble-bees.

†**bombycine** ('bɒmbɪsɪn), *a. Obs.* [ad. L. *bombȳcinus*, f. *bombyx* silk-worm, silk.]

1. Silken, silk; also as *sb.*, a silk fabric.

1599 HAKLUYT *Voy.* II. II. 90 Let vs proceed vnto the Silke or Bombycine fleece, whereof there is great plentie in China. **1730–6** BAILEY, *Bombycine*, Silk Yarn or silken Cloth, silken.

2. Of cotton, of paper made of cotton.

1886 W. M. LINDSAY in *Acad.* 4 Dec. 382/1 In No. 973 we have the oldest dated bombycine (*i.e.* cotton paper) MS... No. 1196, a cotton-paper MS., with leaves enlarged by linen-paper borders.

†**bombycinous** (bɒm'bɪsɪnəs), *a. Obs.* [f. L. *bombycin-us* silken + -OUS.]

1. Made of silk, silken.

1656 in BLOUNT *Glossogr.* **1721** in BAILEY.

2. Of a pale yellow colour, like the silk-worm before it spins.

1794–6 E. DARWIN *Zoon.* (1801) II. 5 What is peculiar to this disease..is the bombycinous colour of the skin, which like that of full-grown silkworms, has a degree of transparency with a yellow tint. *c* **1820** T. SANDWITH *Venous Congest.* 10 That pale sickly hue which Darwin calls bombycinous.

bombykol ('bɒmbɪkɒl). *Entom.* Also (*rare*) **-col.** [a. G. *Bombykol* (loc. cit., quot. 1961), f. L. BOMBYX, *bombȳc-* + -OL.] A sex pheromone of the female of the silkworm moth, *Bombyx mori.*

1961 A. BUTENANDT et al. in *Zeitschr. f. physiol. Chem.* CCCXXIV. 83 The isolation and purification of bombykol, the sex-attractant of the female silk worm moth..is described. **1974** *Nature* 4 Jan. 3/3 The antennae of the male silkworm rapidly degrade the sex pheromone bombycol following stimulation. **1974** L. THOMAS *Lives of Cell* (1975) 18 'At home, 4 p.m. today,' says the female moth, and releases a brief explosion of bombykol. **1978** *Nature* 12 Jan. 157/1 Since the isolation of the first insect sex pheromone, bombykol,..and its full identification by synthesis as (10*E*,12*Z*)-10,12-hexadecadienol, the number of characterised pheromones has increased dramatically.

†**bom'bylious,** *a. Obs.* [f. L. *bombylius*, a. Gr. βομβυλιός a humble-bee or other buzzing insect (f. βόμβος boom, hum), now made the generic name of a dipterous insect, the Humble-bee Fly.] Buzzing, humming, like a large bee.

1713 DERHAM *Phys. Theol.* IV. xiv. 249 The Horse Fly.. is vexatious to horses—not by stinging them, but only by their bombylious noise. [mispr. *bombylicus*; *bombilious* is an error of recent Dicts.]

‖**bombyx** (ˈbɒmbɪks). Also 5 **bombax.** [L. *bombyx* (in med.L. *bombax*), a Gr. βόμβυξ the silkworm, silk.]

1. The silkworm.

1398 TREVISA *Barth. De P.R.* XVIII. xviii. (1495) 777 The Bombax fyrste cometh forth as a worme..that gnawyth caul leuys and vyne leuys..and weuyth webbes as spynners doo. **1753** CHAMBERS *Cycl. Supp., Bombyx* is..a name given to the silk-worm. **1837-40** HALIBURTON *Clockm.* (1862) 47.

†**2.** Raw silk. *Obs.*

1398 TREVISA *Barth. De P.R.* XV. xciii. (1495) 524 In Mauritanea growen wonder hie trees..as it were wyth heere or wyth wulle. and therof ben clothes made by crafte: as it were bombax.

3. *Ent.* A genus of moths, of which the most important is the silkworm moth (*Bombyx mori*). Sometimes any moth of the sub-order *Bombycina.*

1847 CARPENTER *Zool.* §710 The genus Bombyx is one of great interest and importance. **1857** J. GREENE *Pupa Digging* 21 The collector in want of any particular tree-feeding Bombyx or Noctua.

†**4.** (See quot.) *Obs.*

1658 ROWLAND *Mouffet's Theat. Ins.* 930 The Bombyx..is a creature resembling the Wasp, of a black hue, having a sting like as the Wasp hath. **1753** CHAMBERS *Cycl. Supp.* s.v.

bome, bomme, obs. forms of BOMB, BOOM.

bomerang, obs. form of BOOMERANG *sb.*

bomespar (ˈbəʊmspɑː(r)). Also 8 **bomspare.** [f. Du. *boom* tree, pole + *spar* spar.] 'A spar of a larger kind.' Smyth *Sailor's Word-bk.* 1867.

1660 *Act 12 Chas. II*, iv. Sched., Bomespars the hundred, containing 120. **1727** W. MATHER *Yng. Man's Comp.* 410 For which they import..Bomspares.

bominable, aphetic form of ABOMINABLE.

†**bomination,** *a. Obs.* [Aphetic form of ABOMINATION, used attrib.] Abominable.

1589 *Hay any Work* (1844) 10 By reason of his bomination learning. **1599** CHAPMAN *Hum. Dayes Myrth* Plays 1873 I. 106 O bommination Idole, Ile none of them.

bommeree, variant of BUMMAREE.

‖**bon** (bɔ̃), *a.* The French word for 'good'; adopted in ME. from OF., in the form *bon, bone,* BOON, q.v.; also used in certain French phrases.

a. bon-accord (ˈbɒnəˈkɔrd). *Sc.* Agreement, good-will, good-fellowship; an expression of good will.

a **1670** SPALDING *Troub. Chas. I*, I. 214 (JAM.) Articles of Bonaccord to be condescended upon by the magistrates of Aberdeen. *Ibid.* 216 A peremptory or present answer of bon-accord or mal-accord. *Ibid.* II. 57 During the time he was in Aberdeen, he got no bon-accord drunken to him. *Mod.* (Aberdeen is sometimes called 'the city of *Bon-accord*': the word is also frequent in the titles of Scottish charitable and convivial societies.)

b. bon appétit (bɔn apeti). [Fr. = 'good appetite']. A salutation before eating.

1860 MRS. GASKELL *Let.* Aug. (1966) 626 We wandered about in the Park, being bitten by gnats..& there was no need to wish them 'Bon Appetit!' **1965** I. FLEMING *Man with Golden Gun* xiii. 170 The circling buzzard had found its offal... Bond wished it 'bon appétit'. **1984** *Washington Post* 12 Feb. H7/2 Take it as a challenge to redirect your cooking skills by preserving the pleasures of dining out and at the same time protecting your health. Bon appetit!

c. bon-chrétien (bɔ̃kretjɛ̃). Also 6-7 **-chrestien, -crestien.** [Fr. = 'good Christian'.] A name given to one or two kinds of pears.

c **1575** *Arte of Planting* 39 Specially the Peare called bon Chrestien. **1664** EVELYN *Kal. Hort.* (1729) 191 Winter Bergamot, Winter Bon-crestien. **1673** —— *Rapin's Garden.* (1795) 312 In Amiterna's rule the Sabine boors Added Bon-cretiens to their former stores. **1708** MOTTEUX *Rabelais* IV. liv, I'll call them bon-christian or good-christian pears. **1859** LOUDON *Encycl. Gardening, Kitchen Pears* 60 Spanish bon Chrétien, long known in France, probably from Spain.

d. bon enfant (bɔn ɑ̃fɑ̃). lit. 'good child'; an agreeable or jolly companion.

1836 H. GREVILLE *Leaves fr. Diary* (1883) 105 He is very merry and *bon enfant*, and quickly enters into conversation. **1848** THACKERAY *Van. Fair* lxiv, Look, Madame Crawley, you were always *bon enfant*, and I have an interest in you, *parole d'honneur.* **1883** *Sat. Rev.* 6 Jan. 3/1 He was always and to every one *bon enfant.*

e. bon gré mal gré *adv. phr.*, willingly or unwillingly. (See BONGRE.)

1818 E. BLAQUIÈRE tr. *Panánti's Narr. Residence in Algiers* xii. 233 The mother is constantly in attendance, to enforce their being devoured *bon gré malgré.* **1818** LADY MORGAN *Fl. Macarthy* I. iii. 153 And now, you may depend upon it, bon gré, malgré, we shall be fated to stop at this Lis—something. **1825** H. WILSON *Mem.* I. 172 Your sister Amy..drove me, bongré malgré, to her house, and then insisted on my walking up stairs, and supping with her. **1848** TROLLOPE *Kellys & O'Kellys* II. xi. 249 They were going to drag him into the box *bongré malgré.* **1870** C. M. YONGE *Caged Lion* x. 177 She must submit, *bon gré, mal gré*, to become the wife of the Scottish prince.

f. bon jour (bɔ̃ ʒur). lit. 'good day'; a form of salutation on meeting in the daytime; hence, a civil greeting.

a **1577** GASCOIGNE *Fable of Ieronimi* in *Wks.* (1587) 260 Who after theyr Boniure dyd all seeme to lament the sicknesse of Ferdinando. **1588** SHAKES. *Tit. A.* I. i. 494 Tomorrow..With horne and Hound, Weele giue your Grace *Bon iour.* **1595** GOODWINE *Blanchardine* K2, After Sadony had royally presented himselfe to the veiw of all, giuing a princely boniure to the Lordes. **1823** SCOTT *Quentin D.* iii, The landlord entered,—answered Maitre Pierre's *bon jour* with a reverence. **1853** THACKERAY *Newcomes* I. v. 50 The sea being recommended to him Mrs. Newcome..transferred him to his maternal aunt at Brighton. Then it was *bonjour.*

g. bon mot (bɔ̃ mo), *pl.* (moz). [Fr. = 'good saying'.] A clever or witty saying; a witticism, repartee.

1735 KING in *Swift's Lett.* (1768) IV. 115 What is he doing with his bons mots? **1781** COWPER *Truth* 307 The Scripture was his jest-book, whence he drew Bon mots to gall the Christian and the Jew. **1824** BYRON *Juan* XIII. xcvii, What unexpected woes Await those who have studied their bon mots. **1826** DISRAELI *Viv. Grey* IV. iv. 151 Come! a bon-mot. **1875** EMERSON *Lett. & Soc. Aims* vi. 146 The bon-mots that circulate in Society.

h. bon-ton (bɔ̃tɔ̃). *arch.* Good style, good breeding; polite or fashionable society; the fashionable world. Also *attrib.*

1747 CHESTERFIELD *Let.* 1 Dec. in *Wks.* (1777) III. 173 Leipsig is not the place to give him that *bon ton*, which I know he wants. **1771** SMOLLETT *Humph. Cl.* (1815) 120 She lives in the bon ton..and is visited by persons of the first fashion. **1807** W. IRVING *Salmag.* (1824) 356 To harangue the bon-ton reader. **1865** *Pall Mall G.* 1 Aug. 10/2 There was a word, or rather a phrase, in common use among them a century or so gone by which has fallen into desuetude with us. No one now speaks of *bon ton.*

i. bon-vivant (bɔ̃vivɑ̃); *fem.* **bonne vivante** (bɔn vivɑ̃t). One fond of good living; a gourmand.

a **1695** HALIFAX *Works* (1912) 164 The truth is, the habit of such *Bons vivants*, which is the fashionable word, maketh a suspicion so likely. **1798** MAR. & R. L. EDGEWORTH *Pract. Educ.* (1822) I. 357 The sympathy of bon vivants is..very lively and sincere towards each other. **1824** BYRON *Juan* XV. lxiv, But though a 'bonne vivante'..Her stomach's not her peccant part. **1862** *Fraser's Mag.* July, 46 He was also a *bon-vivant*, a diner-out, and a story-teller.

j. bon viveur (bɔ̃ vivœr). [F. *viveur* a living person.] A pseudo-French substitute for BON VIVANT.

1865 'OUIDA' *Strathmore* I. xx. 297 A cosy bachelor-villa that had been long inhabited by an old English *bon viveur.* **1888** *Athenæum* 11 Feb. 171/3 Mr. Rogers has said and eaten as many good things as those excellent *bons viveurs.*

k. bon voyage (bɔ̃ vwajaʒ): see BOON *a.* 2. 'Pleasant journey': used esp. as an expression of farewell to a traveller.

1680 R. L'ESTRANGE tr. *Erasmus sel. Colloq.* iii. 51 After this, a swinging Glass was put about, to the *Bon Voyage.* **1825** H. WILSON *Mem.* II. 149, I coolly wished him un bon voyage, and..jumped into the carriage. **1848** THACKERAY *Van. Fair* xxxii, *Bon voyage* as they say. **1936** *Times Lit. Suppl.* 20 June 512/4 The reader will wish her *bon voyage*, many adventures..and a safe return. **1954** W. STEVENS *Let.* 6 Apr. (1967) 824 Good luck and bon voyage!

See BONAIR, BONALLY, BON-BON, BONCHIEF, BONGRACE, BONGRE, BONHOMIE, BONHOMME; cf. BONNE.

bon, obs. f. *boun*, BOUND, ready, and BOON.

†**bonable,** *a. Obs. rare*⁻¹. ? A corruption of *bominable, abominable.* (Also conjecturally referred to BAN to curse, BONE, and F. *bon* good.)

1575 J. STILL *Gamm. Gurton* III. ii, Diccon! it is a vengeable knave, gammer, 'tis a bonable whoreson.

bonace bark. The bark of a Thymelaceous shrub (*Daphnopsis tinifolia*) found in Jamaica.

1756 P. BROWNE *Jamaica* 372 Bonace-bark Tree. The bark makes very good ropes.

‖**bona fide,** *adv.* and *adj.* [L. *bonā fidē* = 'with good faith'. Commonly anglicized in pronunciation as (ˈbəʊnə ˈfaɪdɪ), though classical scholars sometimes preserve the Latin quantity of the vowels, with or without the Latin vowel sounds.]

A. *adv.* In good faith, with sincerity; genuinely.

1542-3 *Act 34 & 35 Hen. VIII*, iv, The same to procede bona fide, without fraude. **1600** HOLLAND *Livy* XXXII. xxxiii. 830 He dealeth not soundly and bona fide [*neque cum fide agit*] in treaties of peace. **1722** *Lond. Gaz.* No. 6082/3 A Horse..that is not Bona Fide his own. **1793** SMEATON *Edystone L.* §177 Our men were really and bonâ fide employed in the Edystone service.

B. *adj.* (orig. used with agent nouns, or those involving some quality, as in 'bona fide purchaser', 'bona fide poverty', 'bona fide traveller'.) Acting or done in good faith; sincere, genuine.

1788 J. POWELL *Devises* (1827) II. 17 Act not to extend to bonâ fide purchasers for a valuable consideration. **1865** *Sat. Rev.* 5 Aug. 170/2 Interfering with the bonâ fide character of the proceeding. **1882** *Med. Temp. Jrnl.* No. 50. 83 The bona fide poor are benefited.

Hence ˌ**bonaˈfidically,** *adv. nonce-wd.*

1822 SOUTHEY *Lett.* (1856) III. 314 Two men who love nonsense so cordially, and naturally, and bonâfidically.

‖**bona fides** (ˈbəʊnə ˈfaɪdiːz). *Law.* [L. *bona fidēs* good faith.]

1. Good faith, freedom from intent to deceive.

1845 *Penny Cycl.* Supp. I. 214/1 Bona Fides is therefore opposed to fraud, and is a necessary ingredient in contracts. **1885** *Law Reports* XXIX. Chanc. Div. 468 It was said that this shewed bona fides on their part.

¶**2.** Erroneously treated as pl. form of *bona fide* (assumed to be *sb. sing.*): guarantees of good faith.

1944 *N. & Q.* CLXXXVI. 246/1, I notice in one of our best sellers the remark, 'If Mina's *bona fides* are once questioned'. **1962** B. E. WALLACE *Device* xxvii. 195 All strangers whose bona fides..are not completely verified must be immediately reported to your superior officer.

†ˈ**bonage.** *Sc. Obs.* Also **bonnage.** [app. variant of BOONAGE, perh. confused with *bondage.*] Services rendered by a tenant to his landlord as part of rent.

1791 *Statist. Acc. Scotl.* I. 433 Bonnage is an obligation on the part of the tenant to cut down the proprietor's corn. This duty he must perform when called on. **1794** DONALDSON *Agric. Surv. Kincard.* 213 (JAM.) Another set of payments consisted in services, emphatically called Bonage (from bondage). These were exacted in seed-time, in ploughing and harrowing the proprietor's land..in harvest, in cutting down his crop. **1861** C. INNES *Sk. Scotch Hist.* iii. 384 A lease of a half-merk land of Port Loch Tay, with steelbow and 'bonage', according to custom.

†**bonagh.** *Obs.* Also **bonogh, bonough, bownogh.** [Irish: O'Reilly has *buana* a billeted soldier, also *buanadh* a soldier; Keting in O'Curry II. 379 *buanadh* 'permanent soldiers of the Kings of Erinn'.] A permanent soldier.

1600 DYMMOK Ireland (1843) 51 [Tyrone's] wealthe..wilbe in shorte tyme exhausted, by the maynteyninge of his Bonaghs. **1633** T. STAFFORD *Pac. Hib.* iii. (1821) 43 Three hundred were Bonoughes, the best furnished men for the warre.

†**bonaght.** *Obs.* Also 6-7 **bonnaght, bonoghty,** 7 **bonaught, bonnoght.** [Irish: O'Reilly has *buanacht* subsidy, quartering of soldiers; O'Donovan *buanacht* military service.]

A tax or tribute formerly levied by Irish chiefs for the maintenance of soldiers.

1568 in Dymmok *Ireland* App. (1843) 88 Bonaghtes due to the Queens Majestie for her Galloglasses. **1586** J. HOOKER *Girald. Irel.* in *Holinshed* II. 78/2 The Irish impositions of quinio and liverie, cartings, carriages..bonnaght and such like. **1633** T. STAFFORD *Pac. Hib.* v. (1821) 69 Large promises, for increasing his Bonnoght. **1827** HALLAM *Const. Hist.* (1876) III. xviii. 357 The barbarous practices of coshering and bonaght..borrowed from those native chieftains.

†**bonair(e,** *a. Obs.* Forms: 4-5 **bonure,** 4-6 **boner(e, -aire,** 5 **-our, -ayr, -eyre,** 6 **bonnair,** 6-7 **bonayre,** 4-7 **bonair.** [a. OF. *bonnaire* gentle, courteous, affable, shortened from *debonnaire.* The accent shifted in ME.]

1. Well-bred, gentle, courteous, kind, complaisant.

c **1300** *K. Alis.* 6732 With wordes bonere, Heom answerith swithe faire. *c* **1325** *E.E. Allit. P.* B 733 Blessed be þow..so boner & þewed. *c* **1430** *How Gd. Wijf tau3te Dau.* 103 in *Babees Bk.* (1868) 41 To bitter ne to bonour with hem þat þou ne be. **1460** *Lybeaus Disc.* 1727 Sche ys meke and boneyre. **1542** *Sarum Manual* 64 To be bonere and buxum in bedde and at the borde. **1600** HOLLAND *Livy* IV. ii. 446 To have been..made more bonair and gratious. **1623** COCKERAM I, *Bonayre*, gentle, milde. **1696** PHILLIPS *Bonair*, see Debonair.

2. quasi-*adv.* = BONAIRLY.

c **1320** *Sir Tristr.* I. xxix, The mariner spac bonair. *c* **1350** *Will. Palerne* 332 Bere þe boxumly & bonure.

†**bonairly,** *adv. Obs.* [f. prec. + -LY²: cf. F. *bonnairement* (Cotgr.)] Courteously; meekly.

c **1340** *Cursor M.* 23872 (Fairf.) He þat can mare þen anoþer bonerli [*other MSS.* debonerli] to teyche his broþer. **1340** *Ayenb.* 265 Lybbe we sobrelyche..an bonayrelyche. **1522** *World & Child* in Hazl. *Dodsley* I. 243 Look ye bow bonerly to my bidding.

†**bonairness.** *Obs.* [f. as prec. + -NESS: cf. next.] Gentleness, mildness, courtesy.

c **1375** WYCLIF *Serm.* Sel. Wks. II. 357 Bonernesse, þat is a vertue of mekenesse, whanne men done as þei ben conseilid. **1382** WYCLIF *1 Cor.* iv. 21 Schal I come to 3ou..in spirit of bonernesse, *or myldenesse*?

†**bonairty.** *Obs.* Forms: 4 **boneryte, -erte, -airete.** [a. OF. *bonerte*, later *bon(n)aireté* (Cotgr.); see BONAIR.] = prec.

1303 R. BRUNNE *Handl. Synne* 1927 Twey wymmen..Of so moche boneryte. *c* **1325** *E.E. Allit. P.* A. 761 He calde me to hys bonerte. *c* **1386** CHAUCER *Melibeus* ¶656 By pité and by bonairete. **1656** BLOUNT *Glossogr., Bonairite.*

†**bonally, bonaillie** (bəʊˈnælɪ, -ˈeɪlɪ). *Sc.* Also 5 (*pl.*) **bonalais,** 8 **bonnaille, bonnaillie,** 9 **bonnail.** [ad. F. *bon* good + *aller* to go, going.] Good-speed, fare-well; as in 'to drink one's bonallie': cf. *boon voyage*, BOON *a.* 2.

c **1470** HENRY *Wallace* IX. 45 Bonalais drank rycht glaidly in a morow, Syn leiff thai tuk. **17..** *Trial for Witchcr.* in *Statist. Acc. Scotl.* XVIII. 557 (JAM.) His son sailed..and gave not his father his bonnaillie. **1811** SCOTT *Biogr. Mem. Leyden* in *Edin. Ann. Reg.* IV, A party of his friends had met..to drink, in Scottish phrase, his Bonallie. **1830** —— *Farew. Mackenzie* 4, I drank his bonnail And farewell to Mackenzie, High Chief of Kintail.

bonano, obs. form of BANANA.

bonanza (bə(ʊ)ˈnænzə, bəʊˈnænsə). *U.S. colloq.* [Sp.; = fair weather, prosperity, f. L. *bon-us* good.]

1. (See quot. 1881. The *bonanza* mines *par excellence* were the great silver ones on the Comstock lode. See *Sat. Rev.* 31 July 1866.) Also *fig.*

[**1842** 'A. T. MYRTHE' *Ambrosio de Letinez* II. 127 This was what Mexicans term a *bonanza*.] **1844** J. GREGG *Commerce of Prairies* I. 170 When the Placer was in its greatest *bonanza*—yielding very large profits to those engaged in the business. **1847** RUXTON *Adv. Mexico* xi. 79 The..famous black vein of Sombrerete yielded the greatest *bonanzas* of any mine on the continent of America. **1875** *Scribner's Mag.* July 272 But a bonanza with 'millions in it' is not struck every week. **1878** *N. Amer. Rev.* CXXVII. 12 The 'boss', the 'railroad king', and the bonanza Crœsus. **1881** RAYMOND *Mining Gloss.*, *Bonanza*, in miners' phrase, good luck, or a body of rich ore. A mine is *in bonanza* when it is profitably producing ore. **1892** STEVENSON & OSBOURNE *Wrecker* ix. 139 It's not a bonanza, but there's boodle in it; we'll try it on. **1955** *Bull. Atomic Sci.* Mar. 88/2 At the time Steen's diamond-core drill struck the bonanza, he was financially hard-pressed. **1963** *Listener* 10 Jan. 98/3 The show is still, as topical entertainment, a real bonanza.

fig. **1878** R. TAYLOR in *N. Amer. Rev.* CXXVI. 239 If silence be golden, he was a 'bonanza'. **1883** *Harper's Mag.* Nov. 940/1 This..company..proved..a bonanza to its stockholders.

2. *attrib.*, as in **bonanza farm**, a farm which is a 'mine of wealth'; one on a large scale with all modern scientific appliances; so **bonanza farmer**.

1883 *Fisheries Exhib. Catal.* 79 The bonanza farms of America, where every kind of agricultural process is accomplished by steam. **1884** *Lisbon (Dakota) Star* 27 June, One of Ransom county's bonanza farmers.

Bonapartism (ˈbəʊnəpɑːˌtɪz(ə)m). [see -ISM.] Attachment to the government and dynasty founded in France by Napoleon Bonaparte.

1815 T. JEFFERSON *Writ.* (1830) IV. 247 Disgraced by an association in opposition with the remains of Bonaparteism. **1831** ARNOLD *Let.* in *Life & Corr.* (1844) I. vi. 290 Nothing can be more opposite than Liberalism and Bonapartism. **1870** *Pall Mall G.* 17 Sept. 7 Germany will not move a finger in the cause of Bonapartism.

Bonapartist (ˈbəʊnəpɑːtɪst), *sb.* and *a.* Also Buonapartist. [see -IST.]

A. *sb.* An adherent of the government and dynasty of the Bonapartes in France.

1815 J. W. CROKER in *Papers* (1884) I. iii. 61 We drove into Abbeville, where the garrison were savage Buonapartists. **1873** *Daily News* 12 Sept. 4/4 A blank denial of the national sovereignty, hitherto a first article in the faith alike of Orleanists, Republicans, and Bonapartists.

B. *adj.* Adhering to Bonaparte or Bonapartism.

1869 *Pall Mall G.* 1 Sept. 2 A new Bonapartist pillar of Imperialism.

bonarets, bonarate. Erroneous adaptations of the Russian *Baranetz*, the Scythian Lamb, a fabulous plant. See BAROMETZ.

1598 SYLVESTER *Du Bartas* II. i. I. (1641) 86/1 True Beasts, fast in the ground still sticking, Feeding on grass..Such as those Bonarets in Scythia bred Of slender seeds, and with green fodder fed. **1621** LODGE *Summ. Du Bartas* II. 33 Bonarate, which is as much to say as a little Lambe.

Bonarges, obs. form of BOANERGES.

‖**ˈbona-ˈroba.** *Obs.* [a. It. *buonaroba* 'as we say good stuffe, that is a good wholesome plum-cheeked wench' (Florio), f. *buona* good, *roba* robe, dress, stuff, gear.] A wench; 'a showy wanton' J.

1597 SHAKS. *2 Hen. IV*, III. ii. 26 Wee knew where the Bona-Roba's were. **1680** DRYDEN *Kind Kpr.* I. i, Such food for Concupiscence, such Bona-Roba's. **1822** SCOTT *Nigel* xvi, Your lordship is for a frolic into Alsatia?..there are bona-robas to be found there.

‖**Boˈnasus, boˈnassus.** *Zool.* Also 6 bonasius, bonaze. [a. L. *bonasus*, a. Gr. *βόνασος* bison.] A genus (or species) of the ox family (*Bovidæ*): the BISON. See also AUROCHS.

1572 BOSSEWELL *Armorie* 56b, The fielde is of yᵉ Diamond, a Bonaze Perle..Bonasius is a Beaste in fourme like a Bull. **1774** GOLDSM. *Nat. Hist.* (1862) I. xiv. 234 The Cow kind, comprehending the Urus, the Buffalo, the Bison, and the Bonassus. **1790** BEWICK *Quadrupeds* (1824) 45 Whether it be the wild or the tame Ox, the Bonasus or the Urus.

‖**bona vacantia** (ˈbəʊnə vəˈkæntɪə). [L., ownerless goods (*vacāre* to be ownerless).] Goods without any apparent owner.

1756 W. BLACKSTONE *Comm. Laws Engl.* I. viii. 288 Besides the particular reasons before given why the King should have the several revenues of royal fish, shipwrecks, treasure-trove, waifs, and estrays, there is also one general reason which holds for them all; and that is, because they are *bona vacantia*, or goods in which no one else can claim a property. **1927** F. A. ENEVER *Bona Vacantia* i. 13 Bona vacantia are chattels real and personal which not being previously Crown property become through lack of other ownership the property of the Crown. **1959** *Listener* 23 Apr. 709/2 What is known as *bona vacantia*, that is to say, goods without an owner.

†**bonaˈventure.** *Obs.* [app. ad. It. *buonaventura* good luck; in quot. 1592 the name of a ship; of the generic use no explanation appears.]

1. A kind of boat or ship.

1592 BRETON *Pilgr. Paradise* Wks. 1875–9 I. 15 The pilgrime must imbarke, Within a shippe the Buonaventure named. **1614** *Way to Wealth* in *Harl. Misc.* (Malh.) III. 235 Busses, bonadventures, or fisher-ships.

2. 'The old outer mizen, long disused,' Smyth, *Sailor's Word-bk.*

c **1500** *Cocke Lorelles B.* (1843) 12 Some pulled up the bonauenture, Some to howes the tope sayle dyde entre. **1626** CAPT. SMITH *Accid. Yng. Seamen* (Arb.) 13. **1704** J. HARRIS *Lex. Techn.* s.v. *Missen-Mast*, Some great Ships require two [missens]; then that next the Main-mast is the Main-missen; and that next the Poop, the Bonaventure-missen.

3. ? An adventurer; cf. BONEVENTOR.

1598 CHAPMAN *Blinde Begg.* Plays 1873 I. 14 Oh sir, you are but bonaventure, not right spanish I perceave.

bonavist (ˈbɒnəvɪst). Also 8 bonny-vis. [ad. It. *buona vista* good sight.] A species of tropical pulse (? *Lablab vulgaris*).

1700 W. KING *Transactioneer*, The Dr. resolves many Doubts and Difficulties..relating to..the Bonavists, and the Dildoe. **1750** G. HUGHES *Barbados* 216 The Buona Vista commonly called Bonny-vis. **1883** *Caval. & Roundh. in Barbados*, Bonavists are a species of kidney beans.

‖**bon-bon** (ˈbɒnˌbɒn). [Fr.; = good-good; a name originating in the nursery; cf. *goody*.]

1. A lozenge or other confection made of sugar. Also *attrib.*

1796 MADAME D'ARBLAY *Camilla* III. vi. iii. 171 Clarendel, lounging upon a chair in the middle of the shop, sat eating *bon bons*. **1818** MOORE *Fudge Fam. Paris* v, The land of Cocaigne..Where for hail they have bon-bons, and claret for rain. **1819** M. WILMOT *Let.* 26 Nov. (1935) 32 The pretty papers with which the bon bon plates are covered. **1831** DISRAELI *Yng. Duke* 3 Lady Fitz-Pompey called twice a week..with a supply of pine-apples or bon-bons. **1886** A. T. RICHIE *Let.* 1 Jan. (1924) x. 192 The bonbon tongs had an immense success. **1911** *Daily Colonist* (Victoria, B.C.) 29 Apr. 4/4 (Advt.), Cut Glass..Handled Bon Bon Dishes £3.00. **1964** M. LASKI in S. Nowell-Smith *Edwardian England* iv. 195 Innumerable bon-bon dishes and table napkins.

transf. and *fig.*

1856 *Farmer's Mag.* Nov. 426 A good thing, quite a bon-bon. **1955** *Times* 30 Aug. 5/4 They opened this morning with a programme of French bon-bons.

†**2.** A dainty, a delicacy. *Obs.*

1821 *Cook's Oracle* (ed. 3) 330 [In a] Catalogue of Persian 'Bons Bons', there is a list of 28 differently flavoured Mustards. **1842** 'MEG DODS' *Cook & Housew. Man.* II. v. 125 *note*, They [onions] used to form the favourable bon-bons of the Highlander.

3. In full *cracker bon-bon*: see CRACKER 6b. Also *attrib.*

1846 DICKENS *Pictures from Italy* 170 What with this green, and the intolerable reds and crimsons, and gold borders..the whole concern looked like a stupendous Bon-bon. **1894** H. NISBET *Bush Girl's Rom.* 287 Gilt paper and coloured bon-bon stuff. **1901** *Daily Chron.* 10 Aug. 10/3 Frieze suits in the loveliest bon-bon shades of blue and red.

‖**bonbonnière** (bɔ̃bɔnjɛr). [Fr., f. *bon-bon*.] A small fancy box to hold sweets.

1818 LADY MORGAN *Autobiogr.* (1859) 176, I have sent you several letters and shabby little trifles:—a scarf, books, music, shoes, workboxes, bonbonnières. **1862** *Cornh. Mag.* V. 441 A bonbonnière full of sweetmeats. **1883** *Harper's Mag.* 899/1 A huge floral offering..had innumerable pretty bonbonnières floating at its long ribbon.

bonc, obs. form of BANK *sb.*[1]

bonce (bɒns). [Origin unknown; ? related to BOUNCE.]

1. a. A large marble for playing with. **b.** A game played with such marbles.

1862 *Yng. England* I. 141 Bonce is played with very large marbles. One boy pitches his bonce, and another tries to strike it, each throwing by turns. **1865** FURNIVALL in *Reader* No. 146. 420/3 Little boys playing at bonce.

2. The head. *slang.*

1889 in BARRÈRE & LELAND *Dict. Slang* 158/1. **1909** J. R. WARE *Passing English* 42/1 Look out, or I'll fetch you a whack across the bonse. **1959** I. & P. OPIE *Lore & Lang. Schoolchildren* ix. 155 Children go in for short sharp words, as..'bonce', 'block', and 'dome' for head. **1962** L. DEIGHTON *Ipcress File* xv. 91 This threat..[is] going to be forever hanging over your bonce like Damocles' chopper.

bonche, obs. form of BUNCH.

†**bonchief.** *Obs.* Forms: 4 bonchef, -chif, boonchief, 5 boncheff, -cheef, -chyef, -chief, bonechief, bonnecheve. [f. F. *bon* good + *chef* 'head', hence 'end, issue' (see CHIEF); opposed to, and perhaps formed an analogy of, MISCHIEF.] Good fortune, prosperity, easy circumstances.

c **1340** *Gaw. & Gr. Knt.* 1764 Al watz blis & bonchef. **1387** TREVISA *Higden* Rolls Ser. I. i. xii. 87 Good happes and boonchief, as wel as yuel happes and meschief. **1563** FOXE *A. & M.* I. 603/2 If I consented to do here after your will, for bonchief or mischief that may befal unto me in this life.

bond (bɒnd), *sb.*[1] Also 4–5 boond, 5–7 bonde, 6 bound. [ME. *bond*, a phonetic var. of BAND *sb.*[1] (cf. *land lond*, *stand stond*, etc.), used interchangeably with it in early senses; but *bond* preserved more distinctly the connexion with *bind*, *bound*, and is now the leading or exclusive form in branch II.]

I. *lit.* That with or by which a thing is bound.

1. a. Anything with which one's body or limbs are bound in restraint of personal liberty; a shackle, chain, fetter, manacle. *arch.* (and only in *pl.*).

c **1250** *Gen. & Ex.* 2230 Bondes ben leid on Symeon. *c* **1340** *Cursor M.* 7202 (Trin.) Alle his bondes he brake in two [*other MSS.* bandes, -is]. **1382** WYCLIF *Acts* xvi. 26 The bondis of alle ben vnbounden. **1570** LEVINS *Manip.* 166 Bonde, *vinculum*. **1611** BIBLE *Acts* xxvi. 29 Altogether such as I am, except these bonds. **1785** COWPER *Task* II. 36 I had much rather be myself the slave, And wear the bonds, than fasten them on him.

fig. **1802** BINGLEY *Anim. Zool.* (1813) I. 44 As soon as the parts of the animal, within the shell of the chrysalis, have acquired strength sufficient to break the bonds that surround it.

b. *abstr.* Confinement, imprisonment, custody. (In later times only in *plural*.) *arch.*

a **1225** *St. Marher.* 13 þu..þᵗ haldes me in bondes. *c* **1250** *Gen. & Ex.* 2075 Ic am..holden in bond. **1330** R. BRUNNE *Chron.* 123 Arnulf..was taken als thefe, & abrouht in bond. *c* **1400** *Gamelyn* 401 Lese me out of bond. *c* **1430** *Hymns Virg.* (1867) 6 Let me neuere falle in boondis of þe queed! **1595** SHAKS. *John* III. iv. 74, I..will againe commit them to their bonds. **1667** MILTON *P.L.* II. 207 To endure Exile, or ignominy, or bonds, or pain. **1722** SEWEL *Hist. Quakers* (1795) I. 61 Drunkards, and fighters, and swearers, have their liberty without bonds. **1884** TENNYSON *Becket* 190 Prate not of bonds.

†**c.** *Our Lady's bonds*: pregnancy; confinement at child-birth, accouchement. *Obs.*

1504 *Will of W. Pryor* App., I Alys beyng in the bondis of owr lady. **1558** BP. WHITE in Strype *Eccl. Mem.* III. II. lxxxi. 286 To dye in the bond, as they call it, of our Lady, and travail of child.

2. a. That with which a thing is bound or tied down, or together, so as to keep it in its position or collective form: formerly including metal hoops girding anything; still the regular name for the withe which ties up a fagot, and in various technical senses. Cf. also 13.

c **1340** *Cursor M.* 1671 (Trin.) Bynde [þe tymber] furste wiþ balke & bonde. **1420** *E.E. Wills* (1882) 46, I bord mausure with a bond of seluer. **1542–3** *Act 34 & 35 Hen. VIII*, iii, The bonde of euery whiche faggotte to conteine three quarters of a yarde. **1690** LOCKE *Hum. Und.* II. xxiii, What conceivable Hoops, what Bond he can imagine to hold this mass of Matter. **1879** JEFFERIES *Wild Life S. County* 123 Binding [the thatch] down with a crosswork of bonds, to prevent the gales..unroofing the rick.

†**b.** Formerly more generally, 'string, band, tie'.

1388 WYCLIF *Judges* xvi. 13 If thou plattist seuene heeris of myn heed with a strong boond. *c* **1450** *Merlin* xxiii. 425 Bounden to the sadell with two bondes. *a* **1550** *Kyng & Hermit* 466 in Hazl. *E.P.P.* 31 The frere gaff him bow in hond, Iake, he seyd, draw up the bond. **1674** *Pardon of Rome* in Staveley *Rom. Horseleach* (1769) 55 In the Chirch of St. Crucis..there is a Bond that Chryst was led with to his Crucifyeing.

fig. *c* **1250** *Gen. & Ex.* 2113 Non so wis..Ðe kuðe undon ðis dremes bond.

†**3.** A bandage. *Obs.*

1382 WYCLIF *John* xi. 44 And anoon he that was deed, cam forth, bounden the hondis and feet with bondis [**1611** graue-clothes]. **1541** R. COPLAND *Guydon's Quest. Chirurg.*, What quantite of length and brede ought the bondes to be? **1670** EACHARD *Cont. Clergy* in Arb. *Garner* VII. 259 To make a bond or give a glyster.

†**4.** A quantity bound together; bunch, bundle.

c **1462** *Wright's Chaste Wife* 226 Sche toke hym a bonde[of hemp]..And bade hym fast on to bete. **1483** CAXTON *Gold. Leg.* 67/1 Abygail toke..C bondes of grapes dreyde.

II. *fig.* A restraining or uniting force.

5. (*fig.* from 1) Any circumstance that trammels or takes away freedom of action; a force which enslaves the mind through the affections or passion; in *pl.* trammels, shackles.

c **1250** *Gen. & Ex.* 2716 Moyses..hente ðe cherl wið hise wond, And he fel dun in dedes bond. **1398** TREVISA *Barth. De P.R.* III. xiii. (1495) 57 The soule..muste suffre for the bonde of the body that he is joyned to. *c* **1440** *Gesta Rom.* ii. 7 Helde in the bond of seruitute of synne. **1526** *Pilgr. Perf.* (W. de W. 1531) 57 Thou must cutte away all outwarde bondes whiche..sholde be let or hynderaunce to perfeccyon. **1832** LANDER *Exped. Niger* II. vi. 129 Nor does the marriage ceremony break the bonds of the woman's slavery. **1871** MORLEY *Voltaire* (1886) 25 Hindered by the tight bonds of an old order.

6. a. A constraining force or tie acting upon the mind, and recognised by it as obligatory.

1330 R. BRUNNE *Chron.* 260 þe bondes of homage & feaute. **1592** WEST *Symbol* I. I. §2 Therefore it is termed the bond of right or law. **1651** HOBBES *Leviath.* I. xiv. 65 The Bonds, by which men are bound, and obliged. **1769** *Junius Lett.* i. 9 Justice is, perhaps, the firmest bond to secure a cheerful submission of the people. *a* **1876** J. H. NEWMAN *Hist. Sk.* (1876) I. I. iv. 172 What serves as a bond to-day will be equally serviceable to-morrow.

†**b.** Obligation, duty. *Obs.*

c **1449** PECOCK *Repr.* III. vii. 316 The ensaumple..makith no boond that preestis..lyue withoute endewing of vnmouable possessions. **1526** *Pilgr. Perf.* (W. de W. 1531) 160b, Prayers of bonde or duty. **1535** BP. GARDINER in Strype *Eccl. Mem.* I. II. App. lx. 148, I know my duty and bond to your highnes. **1643** BURROUGHES *Exp. Hosea* v. (1652) 231 There is no such bond upon conscience..as this, etc.

7. a. A uniting or cementing force or influence by which a union of any kind is maintained.

1382 Wyclif Ephes. iv. 3 Besy for to kepe vnite of spirit in the bond of pees. 1549 Bk. Com. Prayer, Quinquag. Sunday Collect, Charitie, the verie bonde of peace and all vertue. 1690 Locke Hum. Und. iii. xi, Speech being the great Bond that holds Society together. 1789 Belsham Ess. I. viii. 163 An urgent and obvious want of some common bond of union. 1820 W. Irving Sk. Bk. I. 43 The only bond that can keep hearts together—unreserved community of thought and feeling.

b. Senses 6, 7, and 8 seem to be present in ***the bond(s of wedlock*** or ***matrimony***.

1552 Huloet, Bonde of matrimonye or wedlocke. 1601 Shaks. Jul. C. ii. i. 280 Within the Bond of Marriage. 1645 Milton Tetrach. Wks. 1738 I. 241 That divorce which finally dissolves the bond, and frees both parties to a second Marriage. 1712 Hughes Spect. No. 525 ¶1 He is ready to enter into the bonds of matrimony. 1859 Tennyson Elaine 1200 Our bond is not the bond of man and wife.

8. a. An agreement or engagement binding on him who makes it. **b.** A covenant between two or more persons.

1330 R. Brunne Chron. 311 If þe Kyng..had mad þat bond, & drawen it. c1386 Chaucer Frankl. T. 806, I yow relesse..euery surement and euery bond That ye han maad to me. c1500 Lancelot 1673 O kingis word shuld be a kingis bonde. 1535 Coverdale Josh. ix. 11 We are youre seruauntes, therfore make now a bonde with vs. a1564 Becon Demands Holy Script. in Prayers, &c. (1844) 618 This confirmation is as it were a discharge of the godfathers bounds. c1610 Sir J. Melvil Mem. (1735) 12 A Bond offensive and defensive. 1759 Robertson Hist. Scot. I. vii. 496 To unite the party a bond of confederacy was formed. 1810 Coleridge Friend (1865) 171 The whole treaty of Amiens is little more than a perplexed bond of compromise respecting Malta. 1833 Marryat P. Simple (1863) 145 My word's as good as my bond. 1851 Coal-tr. Terms Northumbrld. & Durh. 8 Bond, the agreement to hire between coal owners and pitmen.

†**c.** ***to enter bonds***: to give a bond, pledge oneself (*obs.*). ***to put under bonds***: see quot.

1563-87 Foxe A. & M. III. 353 If I shall enter bonds, covenant, and promise to appear. 1809 Kendall Trav. III. lxxxii. 253 To put a prisoner under bonds is to order him to find bail.

III. Legal and technical senses.

9. a. *Eng. Law.* A deed, by which A (known as the *obligor*) binds himself, his heirs, executors, or assigns to pay a certain sum of money to B (known as the *obligee*), or his heirs, etc.

A may bind himself to this payment absolutely and unconditionally, in which case the deed is known as a ***single*** or ***simple bond*** (*simplex obligatio*): bonds in this form are obsolete. Or a condition may be attached that the deed shall be made void by the payment, by a certain date, of money, rent, etc. due from A to B, or by some other performance or observance, the sum named being only a penalty to enforce the performance of the condition, in which case the deed is termed a ***penal bond***.

1592 West Symbol. Bij. § 31 For a written Bond, is a Contract whereby any man confesseth himselfe by his writing orderly made, sealed, and deliuered to owe any thing unto him with whom he contracteth. 1596 Shaks. Merch. V. i. iii. 146 Goe with me to a Notarie, seale me there Your single bond. a1656 Bp. Hall Rem. Wks. (1660) 282 One cares to make his mony sure by good bonds. 1805 J. Poole Reply R. Gardiner 2 Devaux..having lost the original bons ..importuned him until he signed a fresh set. 1809 R. Langford Introd. Trade 105 A bond, for money lent..is a deed in writing, whereby one person binds himself to another, to pay a sum of money, or perform some other act. 1844 H. H. Wilson Brit. India I. 495 The Company petitioned the House of Commons for permission to raise two millions upon bond.

b. *Scotch Law.* A mortgage.

1862 Burton Bk.-hunter ii. 131 We [Scotch] speak of a bond instead of a mortgage.

10. A document of this nature (but not necessarily or usually in the form of an ordinary bond) issued by a government or public company borrowing money: in modern use synonymous with *debenture*.

1651 Proc. Parliament No. 123. 1902 Large sums of Loan Money, Borrowed money on the Publick bonds. 1788 J. Powell Devises (1827) II. 25 Bonds of turnpike commissioners, and navigation shares. 1873 Law Rep. 8 Q.B. 179 The bond numbered B. 499 was drawn as one of those to be paid off..according to the conditions printed on the back of the debenture. 1881 Morley Cobden II. 221 Friends..recommended him only to hold bonds or paid-up shares.

11. a. Surety; one who becomes bail.

1632 Star Chamb. Cases (1886) 278 Some of them appeared by bond. 1667 Pepys Diary (1879) IV. 266 The King of England shall be bond for him.

b. *U.S. Law.* = ***bail-bond*** s.v. BAIL *sb.*¹ 7.

c. = BAIL *sb.*¹ 5 a, esp. in phr. ***on bond***.

1886 Pacific Reporter IX. 935 A bond, or as it is commonly called, a bail-bond, is..an obligation..under seal, signed by the party giving the same, with one or more sureties, under a penalty, conditioned to do some particular act. 1970 Globe & Mail (Toronto) 25 Sept. 9/2 He was taken before U.S. Commissioner Ed Swan, who set bond at $500,000. 1974 Aiken (S. Carolina) Standard 22 Apr. 4-B/1 Five white men accused of killing a black youth from Fairfax, S.C., four years ago were released on bond Saturday after spending the night in jail. 1979 Tucson (Arizona) Daily Citizen 20 Sept. 7c/3 O'Brien has remained free on bond during the appeals process.

12. ***in bond***: (goods liable to customs-duty) stored in special warehouses (known as *bonded* or *bonding warehouses* or *stores*) under charge of custom-house officers, till it is convenient to the importer to pay the customs-duty and take possession. The importer on entering the goods pledges himself by bond to redeem them by paying the duty. So ***to take out of bond***, ***release from bond***.

1851 Ht. Martineau Hist. Peace v. xiv, More foreign corn was let out of bond. 1852 McCulloch Taxation ii. x. 350 Taking the price of bohea and low congou in bond in London at 1s. per lb. 1863 Fawcett Pol. Econ. ii. iii. (1876) 552 A merchant may not wish to sell immediately the goods he imports, he is therefore permitted to place them in bond.

13. Technical uses: **a.** *Bricklaying and Masonry.* The connexion or union of the bricks or stones in a wall or structure by making them overlap and hold together; a method of disposing the bricks in a wall by which the whole is bound into one compact mass: as in ***English bond***, that in which the bricks are placed in alternate courses of 'headers' (bricks laid with their ends towards the face of the wall or structure) and 'stretchers' (bricks laid longitudinally); also ***English cross bond*** (see quots.); ***Flemish bond***, that in which each course consists of alternate 'headers' and 'stretchers'; ***garden bond***, etc.; also a brick or stone placed lengthways through a wall to bind and strengthen it, a binder, bond stone. **b.** *Carpentry.* The jointing or fastening of two or more pieces of timber together; also in *pl.* the timbers used for strengthening the walls of a building. **c.** *Slating.* The distance which the lower edge of one roofing-slate or tile extends beyond the nail of the one below it.

1677 Moxon Mech. Exerc. (1703) 157 When Workmen say make good Bond, they mean fasten the two or more pieces of Timber well together. Ibid. 259 Do not work any Wall above 3 foot high before you work up the next adjoining Wall, that so you may..make good Bond in the Work. 1793 Smeaton Edystone L. §82 The tail of the header was made to have an adequate bond with the interior parts. 1823 P. Nicholson Pract. Build. 347 Bricks are laid in a varied, but regular, form of connection, or Bond. Ibid. 352 You will have proper bond; and the key-bond in the middle of the arches. 1825 G. A. Smeaton Builder's Pocket Man. i. iv. 100 The principal methods of brick-laying are known under the appellation of English bond and Flemish bond. Ibid., The English bond is composed of alternate courses of headers and stretchers. 1842 N. Whittock et al. Bk. Trades 75 The disposition of bricks in a building where there are alternate courses of headers and stretchers, is called English bond. 1869 Phillips Vesuv. ii. 34 York bond being made of broad bricks laid in several courses among squared small stone. 1872 Yeats Techn. Hist. Comm. 87 They used large thin bricks or wall-tiles as a bond for their rubble construction. 1876 Encycl. Brit. IV. 461/1 English bond should have preference when the greatest degree of strength and compactness is considered. 1888 C. F. Mitchell Building Constr. & Drawing ii. 37 English Cross Bond, a class of English bond. Every other stretching course has a header placed next the quoin stretcher, and the heading course has closers placed in the usual manner. 1909 Webster 251/3 English cross bond, called also cross bond, is a modification of English bond in which the stretcher courses break joints with each other. 1936 Archit. Rev. LXXIX. 242/3 English Cross bond is a slight deviation from pure English bond, and has a header laid, as second brick from the angle, in each alternate stretcher course; the stretchers therefore 'break-joint', and there is a little more play in the pattern of the bond. 1964 C. Dent Quantity Surveying by Computer v. 52 One brick wall in Flettons in English bond in cement mortar.

d. *Electr.* A metallic connection between conductors forming part of an electric circuit, as between the abutting or adjoining rails of an electric railway line.

1903 [see BONDER¹ 3]. 1904 Westm. Gaz. 14 Dec. 10/2 To provide electric continuity [both] are connected together by flexible strips of copper called 'bonds'.

e. *Chem.* = LINKAGE. Also *attrib.*

1884 Frankland & Japp Inorg. Chem. viii. 58 Each unit of atom-fixing power will be named a bond,—a term which involves no hypothesis as to the nature of the connexion. 1936 Discovery Nov. 339/1 It is convenient in chemistry to show the linking between any two atoms by means of a line or lines, commonly called bonds. 1938 Ann. Reg. 1937 346 The view [was] advanced that spontaneous mutations are mono-molecular reactions produced by thermal agitation when this oversteps the energy threshold of the chemical bonds. 1962 S. Glasstone Textbk. Physical Chem. (ed. 2) viii. 588 The bond energy..is the average amount of energy required to dissociate bonds of the same type in 1 mole of a given compound.

IV. 14. *Comb.*, as (sense 1) ***bond-led***, ***-stript*** (stripped of bonds) adjs.; (sense 7) ***bond-friend***; (sense 9) ***bond-creditor***, ***-debt***; (sense 10) ***bond-salesman***; (sense 13) ***bond-piece***; **bond paper**, a paper of superior manufacture used for bonds and other documents; also simply *bond* in some trade-names of writing paper; **bond-stone** = BONDER; **bond-timber** (see quot.); **bond washing** (see quots.); hence *bond washer*. Also BOND-HOLDER. For ***bail-bond***, ***bond of caution***, ***corroboration***, ***manrent***, ***presentation***, ***relief***, ***settlement***, etc., see under BAIL *sb.*¹ 7, CAUTION, CORROBORATION, etc;

1710 Lond. Gaz. No. 4701/3 The *Bond Creditors of Philip, late Earl of Pembroke..are desired..to bring their Bonds. 1768 Blackstone Comm. III. 397 In order to strengthen a bond-creditor's security. 1707 Lond. Gaz. No. 4343/8 The Bond-Creditors..are desired to meet the Administrator..to certifie their said *Bond Debts. 1858 Ld. St. Leonards Handy Bk. Prop. Law xxiv. 186 Where an estate of a deceased debtor is liable to a bond debt, which binds the heir. 1860 Rawlinson Herodotus vii. ccxxxvii. IV. 195, Speaking ill of Demaratus, who is my *bond-friend. a1618 Sylvester Du Bartas, Maidens Blush (1621) 843 The Father makes the Pile: Hereon he layes His *bond-led, blind-led Son. a1877 Knight Dict. Mech., *Bond-paper. 1909 Buckeye Informer IX. 214/2 A small quantity of Japan dryer added to heavy black inks will accelerate their drying on linen and bond papers. 1952 A. Christie Mrs. McGinty's Dead vii. 48 She stretched up to a top shelf for notepaper and envelopes... 'Here you are, sir, that's a nice blue Bond, and envelopes to match.' 1862 Smiles Engineers II. 29 The long pieces or stretchers were retained between the two headers or *bond-pieces. 1925 F. Scott Fitzgerald Great Gatsby (1926) iii. 68, I knew the other clerks and young *bond-salesmen by their first names. 1879 Cassell's Techn. Educ. I. 98 *Bond-stones are stones placed with their greatest length going through the thickness of the wall. 1855 Singleton Virgil I. 274 The other..Uplifted to the stars his *bond-stript hands. 1823 P. Nicholson Pract. Build. 219 *Bond-timbers, horizontal pieces, built in stone or brick walls, for strengthening them. 1785 Burke Nab. Arcot's Debts Wks. IV. 233 So known and established a *bond-vendor, as the nabob of Arcot, one who keeps himself the largest bond warehouse in the world. 1959 Times 8 Apr. 17/2 The *bond-washer would buy shares, notably gilt-edged bonds, cum dividend and sell them ex-dividend with the gross investor reclaiming the tax. 1937 Economist 24 Apr. 220/1 The Chancellor proposes to abolish '*bondwashing'—a term used to describe operations by which the owner of securities sells them at a price which covers accrued dividend, and repurchases them ex dividend. 1966 Ibid. 29 Jan. 439/2 Bond-washing also refers to the conversion of (taxable) dividend income into (tax-free) capital gains.

bond (bɒnd), *sb.*² and *a.* Forms: 3-6 **bonde**, (5 **bounde**, 6 **band(e**, **bund**), 3- **bond**. [Early ME. *bonde*:—OE. *bonda*, *bunda* husbandman, householder, husband, a. ON. *bónde(-i)*, contr. of *bóande*, *búande* 'occupier and tiller of the soil, peasant, husbandman; husband', ppl. sb. from *búa*, *bóa* to dwell, L. *colĕre*, and thus equivalent in sense and etymology to Ger. *bauer*. In Iceland the *bónde* was a peasant proprietor 'including all owners of land from the petty freeholder to the franklin. In the more despotic Norway and Denmark, *bóndi* became a word of contempt, denoting the common low people; and in mod.Da. *bönder* means *plebs*. In the Icelandic Commonwealth the word has a good sense, and is often used of the foremost men.. this notion of the word (a franklin) still prevails in the mind of Icelanders' (Vigf.). In OE., *bonda*, *bunda* appears first in the Laws of Cnut, apparently in the same sense as in ON., and nearly, if not entirely, = OE. *ceorl*. When, through the effects of the Norman Conquest, the *ceorl* sank from the position of a free-man tilling his own land to that of a tenant bound to certain services to a lord (see Freeman *Norm. Conq.* V. 477), *bonde* became equivalent to 'villain', and so at length to 'serf, slave' (sense 3), and was thenceforth evidently associated with BOND *sb.*¹ and BOUND. Hence the occas. variant *bande*: but *bounde* may represent the OE. variant *bunda*.]

A. *sb. Obs.*

†**1.** Householder, master of the house; husband. (Only in OE.)

c1025 Laws of Cnut pol. 8 (Bosw.) Swa ymbe friðes bote, swa ðam bondan [v.r. bundan] si selost. Ibid. pol. 70 And ʒif se bonda [bunda] beclypod wære. Ibid. pol. 74 Ne mæʒ nan wif hire bondan [bundan] forbeodan, ðæt he ne móte, etc. [the Latin versions have bonda i.e. paterfamilias.]

†**2.** Peasant, churl. Often used as a designation of rank or condition below *burgess* (and then also put collectively, or (?) as adjective).

c1205 Lay. 15291 Þer wes of Salesburi an oht bonde [c1275 Þar was a bond] icumen. c1275 Passion of our Lord in O.E. Misc. 56 Heo..fullede kinges, eorles & bondes. c1350 Will. Palerne 2128 Barouns, burgeys & bonde & alle oþer burnes. 1393 Langl. P. Pl. C. iv. 201 Trewe burgeis and bonde to naught hue bringeþ ofte. ?a1450 Chester Pl. II. 187 When I soughte silver..Of baron, burges, or of bande.

†**3.** Base vassal, serf [transl. med.L. *nativus*]; one in bondage to a superior; a slave; also *fig.* (In late examples blending with the adjective use.)

c1320 Sir Tristr. 971 To long ichaue ben hir bond. c1340 Cursor M. 4188 Sel him forþ to yone chapmen..to be þair bonde [earlier MSS. thral] for euer-lastande. 1393 Langl. P. Pl. C. xi. 263 A bastarde, a bounde, a begeneldes douhter. c1440 Promp. Parv. 43 Bonde as a man or woman, servus serva. 1526 Pilgr. Perf. (W. de W. 1531) 83 A mayde seruaunt, thrall and bonde. 1535 Stewart Cron. Scot. II. 499 Tha war maid to be bondis and thrall. 1583 T. Watson Poems (1870) 76, I liue her bond, which neither is my foe, Nor frend. 1618 Bolton Florus (1636) 131 A very base fellow, unknown whether a free man, or a bond.

B. *adj.*

1. In a state of serfdom or slavery; not free; in bondage (*to*). Also *fig. arch.*

1330 R. Brunne Chron. 171 Lered men & lay, fre & bond of toune. c1440 Partonope 1497 The bonde kynred I made free. 1483 Cath. Angl. 36 Bonde, natiuus, serulis. 1526

TINDALE *John* viii. 33 And were never bonde to eny man. **1551-6** ROBINSON tr. *More's Utop.* 125 He restoreth the bonde persone from seruitude to libertie. **1571** ASCHAM *Scholem.* (1863) 70 Makyng them selves bonde to vanitie and vice. **1611** BIBLE *1 Cor.* xii. 13 Whether wee bee Iewes or Gentiles, whether wee bee bond or free. *a* **1625** BOYS *Wks.* (1630) 115 Christ was made bond vnto the law, to redeeme them that were bound vnto the law. **1866** FERRIER *Grk. Philos.* I. x. 240 Sensation..is bond, not free.

†**2.** Of or pertaining to slaves; servile, slavish.

1398 TREVISA *Barth. De P.R.* VI. xi. (1495) 195 A seruyng woman of bonde condycion. **1526** *Pilgr. Perf.* (W. de W.) 73 This feare is called the seruyle feare, or the bonde feare. *a* **1567** COVERDALE *Bk. Death* II. ii. 223 Is it not a bonde, gredy and voluptuous thinge to spoyle the deade coarse.

‖**bond**, *sb.*³ [Du. *bond* league, confederation (= Ger. *bund*), f. *binden* to bind.] In reference to the Dutch-speaking population of South Africa: A league or confederation. Hence **bondsmen**.

1884 *Times* 6 Mar. 7/6 The Afrikander Bond..was sending petitions that the Basutos should be handed back to the British Government. *Ibid.* The views of many members returned to parliament as Bondsmen. **1886** *Pall Mall G.* 22 Apr. 3/1 Whether the continued affiliation of the Bond beyond the boundary of the colony was advisable.

bond (bɒnd), *v.* [f. BOND *sb.*¹]

1. *trans.* **a.** in *Building*: To bind or connect together (bricks, stones, or different parts of a structure) by making one overlap and hold to another, so as to give solidity to the whole; to hold or bind together by bond-stones, clamps, etc.

1677 MOXON *Mech. Exerc.* (1703) 260 Other Work adjoining, that should be bonded or worked up together with them. **1793** SMEATON *Edystone L.* §82 The blocks of stone could be bonded to the rock, and to one another. **1858** NEALE *Bernard de M.* 27 Thine ageless walls are bonded With amethyst unpriced. **1862** SMILES *Engineers* II. 29 The best mode of bonding the blocks of stone to the rock.

b. To build up (coals, etc.) in a stack.

1865 *Times* 30 May, Instructions..that the coals were to be 'bonded'—*i.e.* built up by themselves.

2. *intr.* To hold together so as to give solidity.

1836 *Scenes Comm. by Land & S.* 288 In building, the bricklayer takes care to lay the bricks in a certain manner, to make them bond.

3. *trans.* To encumber with bonded debt; to mortgage.

1883 *Harper's Mag.* Nov. 938/1 They said the road..was too heavily bonded.

4. To put into bond (see BOND *sb.*¹ 12).

[See BONDED *ppl. a.* 2.]

5. To subject to bondage.

1835 MARRYAT *Olla Podr.* xxiv, His wife..will be bonded in the same manner.

6. *Electr.* To connect with an electrical bond. (See BOND *sb.*¹ 13 d.)

1904 *Jrnl. Franklin Inst.* Apr. 287 My experience in bonding rails is that [etc.]. **1908** *Installation News* II. 103/2 Care should be taken to maintain the continuity of the run ..by means of bonding round the block with a piece of copper wire.

bond(e, obs. form of BOUND; obs. pa. t. BIND *v.*

bondage ('bɒndɪdʒ). Also 5 bondeage, 6-7 boundage. [ME. *bondage*, a. AF. *bondage*, or ad. Anglo-L. *bondagium*, f. BOND *sb.*² (in AF. *bond*, *bonde*, in Anglo-L. *bondus*) + -AGE. The natural English formation was BONDEHEDE, or *bondescipe*, BONDSHIP. In later times associated in thought with BOND *sb.*¹, as of a man 'in bonds', or constrained by a bond: see *esp.* senses 2 c, 3.]

†**1.** The tenure of a *bonde* or BOND after the Norman Conquest; tenure in villenage; the service rendered by a *bonde*. *Obs.*

[? *a* **1300** *Leges Baron. Scot.* lvi. 3 Si autem nativi domino suo negent nativitatem suam sive Bondagium, tunc attachiabuntur per Ministros Domini Regis. **1381** *Charter of Rich. II.* in Walsingham 254 (Du Cange) Et eorum quemlibet ab omni bondagio exuimus, et quietos facimus. *Ibid.* 270 Quod nulla acra terræ quae in Bondagio vel servitio tenebit, altius quam ad 4 denarios haberetur.] **1651** *Proc. Parliament* No. 126. 1951 Set free from their former dependencies and bondage services & shall be admitted as Tenants, Freeholders.

b. *Sc.* 'Services due by a tenant to the proprietor, or by a cottager [rather cotter] to the farmer.' Jam. **c.** *esp.* The service of the BONDAGER.

(These are relics of sense 1 surviving to modern times in Scotland and adjacent parts of England.)

1818 *Edin. Mag.* Aug. 126-7 (JAM.) The farmer..holds his farm from the landlord..for payment of a certain sum of money;—a certain number of days' work with his horses, carts, and men..The very name that this service gets here, bondage, indicates the light in which it is viewed by the tenantry. **1845** *New Statist. Acc. Scotl.* XII. 1004 What was termed bondages to the heritor, which embraced the labour of man and beast, long and short carriages, and the yearly payment of poultry, and in some cases of sheep, butter and tallow, are now abolished.

c. **1872** E. ROBERTSON *Hist. Ess.* 99 The bondage-system, entailing..the necessity of finding extra labour in field work. **1872** J. THOMSON *Peter Plough* 8 The bothy system there, like our bondage system here, is not as it should be. *Mod.* The hind's daughter does the bondage work for the house.

†**d.** Arbitrary or tyrannical impost. *Obs.*

c **1650** *2nd Narr. late Parl.* in *Select. Harl. Misc.* (1793) 416 Appearing and standing..for right and freedom, against the bondages, which, contrary to engagements, covenants and promises, were put upon the good people of this land.

2. The position or condition of a serf or slave; servitude, serfdom, slavery.

1330 R. BRUNNE *Chron.* 71 In þat bondage, þat brouht was ouer þe se, Now ere þei in seruage fulle fele þat or was fre. **1398** *Barth. De P.R.* VI. xv. (1495) 199 Some seruauntes ben bonde, and bore in bondage. **1460** CAPGRAVE *Chron.* 30 That wretchid bondage of the Hebrew puple in Egipt. **1593** SHAKS. *Rich. II*, I. iii. 89 Neuer did Captiue with a freer heart, Cast off his chaines of bondage. **1671** MILTON *Samson* 270 What more oft in Nations grown corrupt, And by their vices brought to servitude, Than to love Bondage more than Liberty. **1830** MACKINTOSH *Eth. Philos.* Wks. 1846 I. 52 Those who purchased them, nor those who hold them in bondage.

†**b.** Applied to the condition of being bound apprentice. (Cf. *service, servitude.*) *Obs.*

a **1577** SIR T. SMITH *Commw. Eng.* III. x. (1609) 129 Another kind of seruitude or bondage is vsed in England.. which is called apprenticehood.

c. *transf.* The condition of being bound or tied up; that which binds. *poet.*

1597 SHAKS. *Lover's Compl.* 34 Some [hair] in her threaden fillet still did bide, And true to bondage would not break from thence. **1611** —— *Cymb.* V. v. 306 *Cym.* Binde the Offender..*Bel.* Let his Armes alone, They were not borne for bondage. **1728** THOMSON *Spring* 649 The callow young Warmed and expanded into perfect life, Their brittle bondage break.

d. Sado-masochism of a sexual nature involving the binding of one partner with rope, handcuffs, or the like. Also *attrib.*

1966 *Guardian* 24 Mar. 14/2 'Spankers' and 'bondage' books, the cognoscenti's terms for books devoted to sexual sadism and masochism. **1976** *Toronto Star* 15 May A1/4 A police spokesman said the seized magazines showed explicit pictures of whipping, bondage and other acts of sexual violence. **1980** J. O'FAOLAIN *No Country for Young Men* vii. 156 Cards in London tobacconist's windows..: discipline and bondage: severe Swedish lessons. **1985** *Listener* 28 Feb. 26/3 She frequented sex shows, public baths, rough gay bars, doss-houses, bondage houses.

e. *Fashion.* Used *attrib.* to designate a style of clothing favoured by punks or punk rockers (see PUNK *sb.*³ 4 d, PUNK ROCK), in which much use is made of black leather, shackled or trimmed with chains, thongs, etc.

1980 *Daily Mirror* 9 Apr. 17/1 They think if you put on a pair of bondage trousers you're a Punk. **1984** J. NUNN *Fashion in Costume 1200-1980* 212 The pop music scene continued to stimulate..the punk style, a deliberately anarchic and ill-assorted assemblage of garments.. including bondage trousers (the legs linked by straps across the back), fake leopardskin..and safety pins. **1986** *Times* 13 Feb. 15/2 Kevin, a Mohican-haired under-caretaker, clonking keys along with his bondage gear. **1986** *City Limits* 10 Apr. 14 What about Blue's fetishistic, super-realist paintings of Candy, in leather bondage gear?

3. *fig.* Subjection to some bond, binding power, influence, or obligation.

a **1450** *Knt. de la Tour* (1868) 55 One synne puttithe her.. into this seruage and bondage. **1540** COVERDALE *Old Faith* Prol. (1844) 4 The bondage of sin and vice. **1651** CALDERWOOD *Hist. Kirk* (1843) II. 21 Subject to death, and to the boundage of the same. *a* **1716** SOUTH (J.) To be brought under the bondage of observing oaths. **1866** ARGYLL *Reign Law* vii. (ed. 4) 362 The bondage under which all true Science lies to fact.

†**b.** Binding force, obligation. *Obs.*

1611 SHAKS. *Cymb.* II. iv. 111 The Vowes of Women, Of no more bondage be, to where they are made, Then they are to their Vertues.

bondage ('bɒndɪdʒ), *v.* *Obs.* or *arch.* [f. prec. sb.] *trans.* To reduce to bondage, to enslave.

1611 HEYWOOD *Gold. Age* IV. i. Wks. 1874 III. 59 To bondage me that am a princesse free. **1803** J. BRISTED *Pedest. Tour* I. 354 Shackling and bondaging the better sex.

bondaged ('bɒndɪdʒd), *ppl. a. arch.* [f. prec. + -ED¹.] Reduced to bondage, enslaved.

1790 A. WILSON *Fly & Leech*, Mean, ugly lump of bondaged sloth. **1852** D. MOIR *Cast. Time* viii, Life forfeited, and bondaged land. **1853** LYNCH *Self-Improv.* vi. 150 [Christianity] presupposes the bondaged insufficiency of men.

bondager ('bɒndɪdʒə(r)). *Sc.* [f. BONDAGE *sb.* 1 c + -ER.] One who performs bondage-service; *spec.* in recent times, in the south of Scotland and Northumberland, a female out-worker, whom the occupier of a cot-house on a farm, and generally also each 'hind' or married farm-worker occupying a 'hind's house', undertakes, as a condition of his tenancy, to supply from his own family, or else to engage, board, and lodge, to do regular field-labour on the farm.

[Not in JAMIESON 1808-25.] **1837** HOWITT *Rur. Life* II. iv. (1862) 119 These female bands in the fields.. I heard these women called Bondagers. **1844** H. STEPHENS *Bk. Farm* II. 386 The first class of ploughmen were each bound to supply a field-worker for the farm during the year..these latter have long been designated by the odious name of bondagers. **1853** JOHNSTON *Nat. Hist. E. Bord.* I. 106 The row of bondagers on the haugh with the light rattle of their hoes. **1855** A. SOMERVILLE *Autobiog.* 6 When we lived in Springfield, the house rent was paid by finding one shearer for the harvest..also an outfield worker winter and summer for the farmer..[The latter] called the 'bondager' was paid ten-pence per day. **1869** *Pall Mall G.* 3 Aug. 12.

bonded ('bɒndɪd), *ppl. a.* [f. BOND *sb.*¹ + -ED.]

1. Held, pledged, or confirmed by bond.

1597 SHAKS. *Lover's Compl.* 279 That strong bonded oth. **1844** TUPPER *Proverb. Philos.* (1852) 384 Death..hath seized his bonded debtor.

2. Put into bond (see BOND *sb.*¹ 12). Hence **bonded store, warehouse**, a store or warehouse in charge of Custom-house officials, in which goods may be kept in bond.

1809 R. LANGFORD *Introd. Trade* 130 *Bonded goods*, goods deposited in a warehouse till the duty is paid. **1846** C. DICKENS *Pict. from Italy* 56 Goods brought in from foreign countries pay no duty until they are sold and taken out, as in a bonded warehouse in England. **1851** HT. MARTINEAU *Hist. Peace* IV. xiv, The bonded stores connected with the Dublin custom-house. **1868** ROGERS *Pol. Econ.* xxii. (ed. 3) 289 Bonded warehouses, in which duty-paying goods, whether liable to customs or excise, are stored till they are needed for sale. **1884** *Pall Mall G.* 15 Aug. 5/2 Wholesale and bonded supplies of the article.

†'**bondehede.** *Obs. rare.* [f. ME. *bonde*, BOND *sb*² + *-hede*, -HEAD.] The condition of a bond or vassal; vassalage; bondage.

c **1340** *Cursor M.* 5405 (Fairf.) Atte þou vs take in þi bondehede [*v.r.* thainhede, bundhede], In bondehede [*v.r.* thainhed, thraldam, þraldome] take our landes alle.

bondel(l, obs. form of BUNDLE.

bonder¹ ('bɒndə(r)). [f. BOND *v.* + -ER.]

1. *Building.* A binding stone or brick; (see quot.)

1845 *Gloss. Goth. Archit.* I. 57 *Bonders, bond-stones, binding-stones*..reach a considerable distance into, or entirely through a wall for the purpose of binding it together.

2. A person who puts goods into bond, or owns goods in bond.

3. One who fixes or adjusts the metallic bonds of an electric circuit. (Cf. BOND *sb.*¹ 13 d and *v.* 6.)

1903 *Westm. Gaz.* 20 Jan. 9/2 The bonders being told off to attend to the copper bonds which make the electrical connexion between each of the three rails.

‖**bonder**² ('bɒndə(r)). [A wrong formation from Norweg. *bonde*, pl. *bönder.*] A Norwegian peasant farmer or petty freeholder. **bonderman**.

1848 *Fraser's Mag.* XXXVIII. 182 On the white-scoured deal floors of the bonder's house. **1856** EMERSON *Eng. Traits* iv. 63 The 'Heimskringla'..is the Iliad and Odyssey of English history..The actors are bonders or landholders, every one of whom is named. **1870** MORRIS *Earthly Par.* II. III. 81 Knight, or fair lord..If thou mayst share a bonder's feast, Sit by me. **1804** *N. Brit. Rev.* No. 80. 425 So the Norwegian Olaf..forced his lendermen and bondermen.. to overthrow the temples.

Bonderized ('bɒndəraɪzd), *a.* Also **bonderized**. [Trade-mark.] Of metal: coated with a patented solution that acts as a surface protection and primer. '**Bonderizing** ('**bonderizing**) *vbl. sb.*, the process of coating with such a solution. Hence (as back-formation) '**bonderize** *v.*

1932 A. R. PAGE in *Metal Ind.* XL. 369/1 The new processes are known as Parkerizing and Bonderizing. **1932** —— *Ibid.* 369/2 The..insoluble basic phosphates..are chemically combined with the ferrous surface. The Parkerized or Bonderized surface, therefore, cannot be removed by peeling off. **1938** *Steel* 22 Aug. 42 Bonderizes automatically..Once the assembled windows..are put on the conveyor system, no hand touches them until after they have been washed, bonderized [etc.]. **1956** *Archit. Rev.* CXX. 348/1 The cabinets are bonderized aluminium. **1959** *Engineering* 13 Feb. 210/2 The steel is either bonderised or electro-zinc-coated on the reverse side.

†'**bondhold.** *Obs.* exc. *hist.* [f. BOND *sb.*² + HOLD: cf. *copyhold, freehold.*] Tenure in bond service, tenure of bond-land; a distinct sort of *copyhold*. Also *attrib.*

1611 *Anct. Customs Knaresboro' & Scriven* (1844) 4 If any bondholder there die seized of six acres of bondhold land.

†'**bondholder**¹. *Obs.* exc. Hist. [f. prec. + -ER; or f. BOND *sb.*² + HOLDER.] A tenant in bond service, or of bond-land.

1539 *Will T. Everard of Sizewell, Suffolk* (Somerset Ho.) [Witnesses described as Bond-holders]. **1611** [see prec.]

bondholder² ('bɒnd,həʊldə(r)). [f. BOND *sb.*¹ 9 + HOLDER.] A person who holds a bond or bonds granted by a private person or by a public company or government, as ***Egyptian bondholder***, a holder of Egyptian government bonds.

So '**bondholding** *a.*

1823 *Drama* IV. 403 The next claim to be reduced was that of the bond-holders, to the amount of £24,416. **1844** *N. Amer. Rev.* Jan., A contract made by the State and the Banks with every bondholder. **1865** *Railw. News* Dec., A committee of preference bondholders. **1868** *Morning Star* 2 June, The Eastern *bondholding wing of the Democracy. **1880** LORD HATHERLY *Law Rep.* 5 App. Cases 189 On behalf of the bondholders, who advanced their money upon the bonds of the company.

‖**bondieuserie** (bɔ̃djøzəri). [Fr., f. *bon* good + *Dieu* God.] A collective term for church ornaments or devotional objects, esp. those of

little artistic merit; an ornament or object of this kind.

1941 'R. West' *Black Lamb* I. 164 It is defaced by hideous bondieuseries of the modern Roman Catholic church. **1958** *Times* 22 May 13/2 The touched-up photographs..the sugary smiles on the plaster statues, all this *bondieuserie* has obscured the strength and simplicity of Thérèse Martin's character and doctrine. **1961** *Encounter* XVII. 32 The saccharine *bondieuseries* which desecrate almost every religious building one enters.

bonding ('bɒndɪŋ), *vbl. sb.* [f. BOND *v.* + -ING¹.]

1. a. *Building.* The binding or connecting together (bricks, stones, or parts of a structure) by making them overlap and hold together; *also*, binding or strengthening by means of bonders. Also *gen.*, the binding or connecting together of any substances esp. by adhesion. Hence *concr.*, a material or substance used for bonding.

1677 Moxon *Mech. Exerc.* (1703) 257 The well-working and bonding of Brick-walls conduces very much to their strength. **1879** Sir G. Scott *Lect. Archit.* II. 36 The bonding of [pilaster strips] by alternate vertical & horizontal stones. **1958** *Spectator* 30 May 691/2 Its special undercoating provides a bonding of immense strength.

b. *attrib.*

1852 Wright *Celt, Rom. & Sax.* v. 158 The Roman bricks or tiles..were built in as bonding courses. **1864** *Even. Standard* Oct., A [Roman] wall..consisting of regular ashlar, alternating with rows of bonding tiles. **1884** *Health Exhib. Catal.* 93/2 Bonding Bricks for hollow walls. **1917** *Machinery's Encycl.* V. 318/2 Bonding or junction coatings can be freely applied to brick, metal, or porcelain connections with the metal spray. **1962** A. Nisbett *Technique Sound Studio* iv. 84 The iron oxide is distributed throughout the bonding material. *Ibid.* 244 The two ends [of the magnetic tape] are overlapped and fixed together by an adhesive or bonding agent.

c. *Electr.* The connecting of metal parts with an electrical bond (cf. BOND *sb.*¹ 13 d); spec. in aircraft (see quot. 1940).

1910 A. Hay *Electr. Distributing Networks* xv. 206 A third form of bonding device..consists of a tinned copper strip soldered to the lead sheathing and screwed to the side of the sealing chamber of the joint-box. **1911** *Whittaker's Electr. Engin. Pocket-bk.* (ed. 3) 527 *Bonding* may have some minor advantages, but it is better for all systems of armoured cables to be split up into sections, the metallic sheathing of each section being isolated. **1922** *Flight* XIV. 519/2 *Electrical Bonding* (in the case of aircraft fitted with *Wireless Apparatus*).—Methods of jointing—Points where bonding is necessary and position of same. **1940** *Chambers's Techn. Dict.* 102/2 *Bonding*, electrical connexion of all available metal on an aircraft, in order to give earth-capacity for wireless purposes.

2. The action of pledging under bond to the repayment of money borrowed.

1877 Burroughs *Taxation* 407 The assent..of the taxpayers to the bonding of the town.

3. The storing of goods in bond; hence **bonding-house, -warehouse**.

1865 Draper *Intell. Dev. Europe* iv. 96 This implied an extensive system of depôts and bonding. **1863** Fawcett *Pol. Econ.* iv. iii. (1876) 552 Bonding-houses offer great.. advantages to those who import taxed commodities.

bond-land. [OE. *bondeland*, f. *bonda*, BOND *sb.*² + LAND.] Land held by bondage tenure; an early form of copyhold land.

[*c*1120 *O.E. Chron.* (Laud MS.) an. 777 Þa let he Cuðbriht ealdorma[n] x bonde-land [*terram x manentium*] æt Swines heafde.] **1861** Pearson *Early & Mid. Ages Eng.* 200 It is probable that the freemen upon bond-land were in the first instance Britons who retained their holding on condition of paying tribute. **1882** C. Elton *Orig. Eng. Hist.* 192 In some places..there are two kinds of copyhold land, the one called 'Bond-land' and the other 'Soke-land'.

bondless ('bɒndlɪs), *a.* [f. BOND *sb.*¹ + -LESS.] Free from bonds; unfettered, unrestrained.

1839 Bailey *Festus* iv. (1848) 33 Such as my bondless brain hath oft-times drawn.

†'**bondling.** *Obs. rare*⁻¹. [f. BOND *sb.*² + -LING.] A slave; a slave-child.

1587 Golding *De Mornay* xxiii. (1617) 379 They sacrificed none but their..Changelings, Bastards and Bondlings.

†'**bondly,** *adv. Obs.* [f. BOND *sb.* + -LY².]

1. ? By bondhold.

1465 Marg. Paston *Lett.* 504 II. 191 They wold put hem owte of such londs as they huld bondly of the Lordshyp.

2. Servilely; as a slave or slaves.

1553 W. Turner in Strype *Eccl. Mem.* III. i. iv. 49 If ye saw them [the bishops] how slavely and bondly they handle the rest of the Clergy.

'**bondmaid, -maiden.** [BOND *a.*] A slave girl. So '**bondservant, -service.**

1526 Tindale *Gal.* iv. 22 Abraham had two sonnes, the one by a bonde mayde, the other by a fre woman. **1535** Coverdale *Lev.* xxv. 44 Yf thou wylt haue bonde seruauntes and maydens. **1552** Abp. Hamilton *Catech.* 193 Behald the boundmaidin of our Lord. **1591** Spenser *Virg. Gnat* 489 Th'one was rauisht of his owne bondmaide. **1596** Shaks. *Tam. Shr.* ii. i. 2 To make a bondmaide and a slaue of mee. **1611** Bible *1 Kings* ix. 21 A tribute of bond-seruice. **1815** Scott *Lord of Isles* ii. xxv, Like a..bond-maid at her master's gate.

bondman ('bɒndmən). *arch.* [f. BOND *sb.*² + MAN: cf. *husband, husbandman*; but in later times evidently connected in thought with senses of BOND *sb.*¹] Cf. BONDSMAN.

1. = BOND *sb.*² 2. *Obs.* exc. *Hist.*

*c*1250 *Owl & Night.* 1577 Moni chapmon and moni cniht ..And swa deþ moni bondeman. *a*1300 *Havelok* 32 Hym louede..Knict, bondeman, and swain. **1503-4** *Act 19 Hen. VII*, xv. §4 Yf eny bondeman purches eny landes..in fee symple. [**1809** Bawden *Domesday Bk.* 289 The King has there sixteen villanes & two bordars & one bondman having four ploughs.]

2. A man in bondage; a villein; a serf, slave.

*a*1340 Hampole *Pr. Consc.* 1155 Whar-to serves man þe world þan, And mas hym þe worldes bondman. **1477** Earl Rivers (Caxton) *Dictes* 25 To be solde as a prysonner or a Bondeman. **1580** Baret *Alv.* B 920 A prysonner taken in warre, a bondeman, a captiue. **1605** Camden *Rem.* 181 That no Christian should be bondman to a Jew. **1645** Milton *Tetrach.* Wks. (1851) 150 Instead of freeing us..make us bondmen. **1866** Bryant *Death of Slavery* ii, Fields where the bondman's toil No more shall trench the soil.

3. ***bond-man-blind***: old name of *blind-man's buff*.

1783 Ainsworth *Lat. Dict.* (Morell) v, *Myinda*..The play called bond-man-blind, blind-bob, or blind-man-buff.

'**bondmanship.** [f. prec. + -SHIP.] The state or condition of a bondman; serfdom, slavery.

1611 Cotgr., *Esclavage*, slauerie, bondmanship; villenage. **1880** McCarthy *Own Times* IV. xlviii. 6 He consented to put himself into the comfortable bondmanship of subordinate office.

bondon (bɔ̃dɔ̃). [Fr., = bung.] A soft Neufchâtel cheese made to resemble a bung in shape.

1894 G. du Maurier *Trilby* I. i. 58 A little cylindrical cheese called 'bondon de Neufchâtel'. **1902** *Encycl. Brit.* XXVII. 355/2 The Neufchâtel, Gervais, and Bondon cheeses are soft varieties intended to be eaten quite fresh, like cream cheese. **1951** *Good Housek. Home Encycl.* 359/2 *Bondon*, a small, soft, whole-milk cheese made in France, shaped in the form of a bun[g].

'**bondship.** *Obs.* or *dial.* [f. BOND *sb.*² + -SHIP.] †**a.** The condition of a 'bond'; serfdom, bondage (*obs.*). **b.** Suretyship. (*dial.*)

*c*1440 *Promp. Parv.* 43 Bondschepe, *nativitas*. **1477** Earl Rivers (Caxton) *Dictes* 20 Trust is in maner of a bondeship, and mystrust is a liberte. **1542** Udall *Erasm. Apoph.* 59 a, Phryne, who, this other daye, Out of hir bondeship did remoue. **1808** R. Anderson *Cumberld. Ballads* (1819) 50 His fadder hed yence heaps ov money, But bonship throws monie fwok wrang.

bondslave ('bɒndsleɪv). [f. BOND *a.* + SLAVE.] A more emphatic term for slave or bondman.

1561 Daus tr. *Bullinger on Apoc.* (1573) 79 We were..very bondesslaues of the deuill. **1577** tr. *Bullinger's Decades* (1592) 440 Now they, whome the Lorde deliuereth, are bonslaues. **1611** Bible *1 Macc.* ii. 11 Of a free-woman shee is become a bondslaue. **1671** Milton *Samson* 38 Put to the labour of a beast, debased Lower than bondslave! **1848** Kingsley *Saint's Trag.* ii. vi. 97 We are sold for bondslaves.

Hence **bond slavery**.

1835 Marryat *Olla Podr.* xxiv, So are his children given in bond slavery to his debtor.

bondsman ('bɒndzmən). [f. BOND *sb.*¹ + -MAN, the *'s* being in sense 1 genitival; sense 2 is treated as a variant of BONDMAN, which in later times had come to be associated with BOND sb.¹: cf. the plural *bonds*.]

1. One who becomes surety by bond.

1754 Richardson *Grandison* IV. iv. 26 Being the bondsman for the duty of Mr. Beauchamp. **1828** E. Irving *Last Days* 189 The disappointed creditors, the broken faith of bondsmen. **1871** *Standard* 20 Jan., Three of the leading men seized as security. The Mayor paid the sum..and the 'bonds' men were released.

2. A man in bondage; a villein; a serf, slave.

*a*1735 Derham (J.) Carnal greedy people, without such a precept, would have no mercy upon their poor bondsmen and beasts. **1815** Scott *Ld. of Isles* i. viii. From chieftain's tower to bondsman's cot. **1851** Mrs. Browning *Casa Guidi Wind.* 54 A bondsman shivering at a Jesuit's foot.

fig. **1850** Tennyson *In Mem.* iv. 2 To Sleep I give my powers away; My will is bondsman to the dark.

'**bondswoman.** *rare.* Variant of BONDWOMAN.

1611 B. Jonson *Catiline* ii. ad fin., My lords, the senators Are sold for slaves, and their wives for bondswomen.

‖**bonduc** ('bɒndʌk). [a. F. *bonduc*, a. Arab. *bunduq*, now meaning 'hazel-nut', but formerly a foreign nut of some kind; prob. from Persian: OPers. had *pendak, fendak* (mod.Pers. *finduq, funduq*, the latter also Arab.), perh. = Skr. *pindaka*, dim. of *pinda* 'ball, lump' (J. Platts).] A tropical leguminous shrub of two species (*Guilandina Bonduc* and *G. Bonducella*) bearing respectively yellow and lead-coloured seeds, hard and beautifully polished, also called Nicker nuts.

1696 Ray *Philos. Lett.* (1718) 292, I have received..the Bean called the Ash Coloured Nickar or Bonduch. **1838** *Econ. Vegetation* 79 The bonduc, or nicker-tree. **1866** *Treas. Bot.* 556 The seeds are very hard and beautifully polished, and are called Nicker nuts or Bonduc nuts.

bondwoman ('bɒndwʊmən). [Orig. two words: see BOND *a.*] A female slave.

1387 Trevisa *Higden* (1865) II. 97 (Mätzn.) Leyre wite, amendes for liggynge by a bondwommen. **1526** Tindale *Gal.* iv. 30 Put awaye the bonde woman. **1671** Milton *P.R.* ii. 308 The fugitive bondwoman, with her son, Outcast Nebaioth. **1782** Burke *Reform Ho. Comm.* Wks. X. 102 Yorkshire, like the child of the bond-woman, is turned out to the desert. **1872** Yeats *Techn. Hist. Comm.* 143 The most exalted lady was no more exempt than the lowliest bondwoman.

bone (bəʊn), *sb.* Forms: 1 bán, baan, 2–3 ban, 3–5 bon, (4 boen, buon), 4–5 boon, (boone, 5 bonne), 3– bone; *north.* 3–9 bane, 5 baan, bayne; (9 *dial.* bowne, byen). [Com. Teut.: OE. *bán* corresp. to OFris. and OS. *bên* (MDu., Du., LG. *been*), OHG. (MHG. and mod.G.) *bein*, ON. *bein* (Sw. *ben*, Da. *been*):—OTeut. **baino(m)*, not appearing in Gothic, and (unlike names of parts of the body generally) not related to any words for 'bone' outside Teutonic. The ON., OHG., MHG., and Du., have, beside the general sense 'bone', the specific sense 'shank (of the leg)', which is the ordinary sense in mod.Ger. Hence it has been suggested that the original meaning was 'long bone'; and that the word may have connexion with the ON. adj. *bein-*, nom. masc. *beinn*, 'straight'. But this is a bare conjecture; the standing of the ON. adj. being itself obscure. In English there has never been any tendency to the specific sense, for which OE. had *sceanca* SHANK.]

I. Properly.

1. a. The general name for each of the distinct parts which unitedly make up the skeleton or hard framework of the body of vertebrate animals.

They are distinguished, according to shape, as *long, short, flat*, and *irregular bones*; the long bones have an internal channel containing marrow. They are also named from their position, nature, form, etc., e.g. *ankle-, arm-, back-, blade-, breast-, collar-, jaw-, splint-, thigh-bone*, etc.

*c*1000 *Ags. Gosp.* John xix. 36 Ne for-bræce ȝe nan ban on him. *a*1300 *Cursor M.* 9405 He wroght a felau of his ban. **1340** *Ayenb.* 148 Ase þe buones bereþ þe tendre uless. **1382** Wyclif *Ezek.* xxxvii. 27 Bones wenten to boones, eche to his ioynture. **1398** Trevisa *Barth. De P.R.* v. i. (1495) 99 The bones of the breste defende the herte. **1483** *Cath. Angl.* 20/1 From bane to bane, *ossim*. **1549** *Compl. Scot.* 152 The corrupit flesche is consumit fra the banis. **1592** Shaks. *Rom. & Jul.* ii. v. 27 Fie how my bones ake. **1681** E. Sclater *Serm. Putney* 11 Weapons, that to be sure, draw no Blood, nor break any Bones. **1872** Huxley *Phys.* i. 10 The bones.. are masses either of cartilage, or of connective tissue hardened by being impregnated with phosphate and carbonate of lime. **1873** Mivart *Elem. Anat.* ii. 23 In the earlier stages of existence there are no bones at all. *Prov.* Hard words break no bones.

b. *pl.* as material for agricultural or industrial processes.

1814 Sir H. Davy *Agric. Chem.* 289 Bones are much used as a manure. **1834** *Brit. Husb.* I. xix. 396 Turnips.. manured with bones. **1870** Yeats *Nat. Hist. Comm.* 307 Bones are extensively employed by the cutler, comb and brush maker, chemist, confectioner, and agriculturist.

†**c.** Applied *spec.* to the fingers in the asseveration ***by these ten bones***. *Obs.*

*c*1485 *Digby Myst.* (1882) 4 *note*, By thes bonys ten thei be to you vntrue. **1589** *Pappe w. Hatchet* C iij b, Martin sweares by his ten bones. **1593** Shaks. *2 Hen. VI*, i. iii. 193 By these tenne bones..hee did speake them to me.

d. Proverb. expression: ***hard,*** or ***dry, as a bone***.

1833 Marryat *P. Simple* i, It's as dry as a bone. **1837** R. Nicoll *Poems* (1843) 83 Dubs were hard as ony bane.

e. *spec.* One used by Australian Aborigines when pronouncing certain spells intended to cause sickness or death; cf. BONE *v.*¹ 5.

1904 *Daily Chron.* 16 July 3/3 From one of two causes, either the abduction of a woman or the 'giving of a bone', the members of two groups will be at enmity. **1934** A. Russell *Tramp-Royal* x. 78 'Milbuka point bone at Boss Tuck's bruder,' she muttered stealthily to Tuck in her native English. **1962** *John o' London's* 22 Mar. 266/1 An aborigine stockboy..is found to have been the victim of 'bone-pointing'.

2. *pl.* **a.** The whole bones of the body collectively, the skeleton; also, by extension, the bodily frame, body, person (with pathetically humorous force). Phr. ***to*** (***live to***) ***make old bones***: (*a*) with negative: not to live to an old age; (*b*) to seem or feel old.

1398 Trevisa *Barth. De P.R.* v. lvii. (1495) 172 The bones ben the sadnesse of the body. *a*1400 *Sir Perc.* 267 Nothyng ..That he myȝte inne his bones hyde, Bot a gaytes skynne. *c*1489 Caxton *Sonnes of Aymon* iii. 108 Alarde..beganne to deffende well hys bones. **1563-87** Foxe *A. & M.* III. x. 92/1 He [Latimer] ran as fast as his old bones would carry him. **1601** Shaks. *Jul. C.* v. v. 41 Night hangs vpon mine eyes, my Bones would rest. **1605** *Chron. K. Leir*, What, breedes young bones already! **1694** Lestrange *Æsop's Fab.* (J.) Puss had a month's mind to be upon the bones of him. **1709** J. Stevens *Quevedo's Wks.* 305 Feeding on me Day and Night, which has brought me to the very Bones. **1740** *Christmas Entertainm.* 16 Now (says she) take care of your bones between this and home. **1872** C. Reade *Wandering Heir* (1905) ix. 175 She..will ne'er make old bones. **1873** M. F. S. *Lily Merton's Summer* 28 Poor, pale, pretty little dear.. she'll never live to make old bones. **1886** M. E. Braddon *One Thing Needful* i, Lord Lashmar would never make old bones. **1924** R. H. Mottram *Spanish Farm* i. 75 Poor old father, he's making old bones; it's the boys he misses. **1953** 'N. Shute' *In Wet* viii. 259 Edward the Seventh and George the Fifth—they neither of them made old bones.

†**b.** Exclamation: ***bones of me! of you!***

1588 *Marprel. Ep.* (Arb.) 44 The puritanes will be O the bones of you too badd for this kind of arguing. **1592** Chettle *Kind-harts Dr.* (1841) 70 Bones a me!

c. The bones being the most permanent parts of the dead body, 'bones' is put for 'mortal remains'.

c **1000** ÆLFRIC *Gen.* I. 25 And he cwæþ Lædeþ mine ban of þison lande. *c* **1205** LAY. 32202 His ban beoð iloken faste i guldene cheste. **1362** LANGL. *P. Pl.* A. VII. 84 Þe Chirche schal haue my Careyne And kepe mi Bones. **1592** NASHE in *Shaks. C. Praise* 5 Have his bones newe embalmed. **1616** *Inscr. over Shakspere's Grave*, Bleste be yᵉ man yᵗ spares thes stones, And cvrst be he yᵗ moves my bones. **1651** *Proc. Parliament* No. 82. 1255 He will reduce the place, or leave his bones before it. **1750** GRAY *Elegy* xx, These bones from insult to protect Some frail memorial still erected nigh. **1880** TENNYSON *Columbus*, Then some one standing by my grave will say, 'Behold the bones of Christopher Colon'.

3. a. The bony structure or substance considered as one of the components of the body; esp in the expressions, ***blood and bone, flesh and bone, skin and bone, bred in the bone***, etc. (Used as *collect. sing.*)

c **1000** ÆLFRIC *Gen.* ii. 23 Adam ða cwæð ðis is nu ban of minum banum. *a* **1300** *Cursor M.* 194 (Gött.) Iesu him raysed in fless and ban. *c* **1430** *Hymns Virg.* (1867) 25 Loue byndiþ boþe blood & baan. **1562** J. HEYWOOD *Prov. & Epigr.* (1867) 72 It will not out of the fleshe that is bred in the bone. **1606** SHAKS. *Tr. & Cr.* III. iii. 172 High birth, vigor of bone, desert in seruice. **1611** BIBLE 2 *Sam.* xix. 13 Art thou not of my bone, and of my flesh? **1719** DE FOE *Crusoe* (1840) II. i. 1 What is bred in the bone will not go out of the flesh. **1837** DICKENS *Pickw.* v, An immense brown horse displaying great symmetry of bone.

b. ***to the bone***: through the flesh, so as to touch the bone; *hence*, to the inmost part, to the core. (Cf. *backbone.*) Also similarly ***in the bone***. ***to feel*** (etc.) ***in one's bones***: to have a sure intuition of (something); ***to work one's fingers*** (or ***oneself***) ***to the bone***: to work extremely hard; ***near*** (occas. ***close to***) ***the bone***: (*a*) miserly, niggardly; (*b*) hard up, destitute; also ***on one's bones***, (N.Z.) ***on the bone***; (*c*) 'near the knuckle' (see KNUCKLE *sb.*).

a **1300** *Cursor M.* 15788 Ilk dint þat þai him gaf it reked to þe ban. *c* **1400** *Rom. Rose* 1059 They prile & poynten The folk right to the bare boon. **1709–10** *Tatler* (J.), There was lately a young gentleman bit to the bone. **1841** DICKENS *Barnaby Rudge* liii. 242, I seem to hear it, Muster Gashford, in my wery bones. **1844** in T. W. Barnes *Mem. Thurlow Weed* (1883) 123 It was in my bones all summer. **1850** MRS. STOWE *Uncle Tom's C.* iv. 17 A cook she certainly was, in the very bone and centre of her soul. **1853** [see WORK *v.* 19 b]. **1853** LYTTON *My Novel* V. xviii. 80 I'll work my fingers to the bone till I pay back the other five. **1855** M. THOMSON *Doesticks* xvi. 130 For I know that I am charitable; I feel it in my bones, like rheumatism. **1858** CARLYLE *Fredk. Gt.* (1865) I. III. xx. 267 He being Calvinist..she Lutheran..and strict to the bone. **1901** *Aberdeen Wkly. Free Press* 30 Mar. (E.D.D.), I hate yer near the bane wyes. **1912** MULFORD & CLAY *Buck Peters* iii. 57 Son, there's a big time due in these parts; I feel it in my bones. **1922** GALSWORTHY *Loyalties* I. i. 13 Ronny Dancy's on his bones again, I'm afraid. **1923** WODEHOUSE *Inimit. Jeeves* x. 100 That poor, misguided pinhead worked himself to the bone over it. **1933** in *Sc. Nat. Dict.* s.v. *bane*, He's awfu' near the bane. **1935** 'J. GUTHRIE' *Little Country* x. 178 Mr. Winks, who had no other living but politics, had 'been on the bone'.., scratching an existence from commission work. **1941** A. L. ROWSE *Tudor Cornwall* xiii. 337 Charging him..with having 'two harlots begotten with child in his own house'... This was getting pretty near the bone. **1947** N. CARDUS *Autobiogr.* 9 He declined, in a family which was always living close to the bone, to take on any job. **1950** A. L. ROWSE *Engl. of Eliz.* v. 162 One sees how much nearer the bone they were in medieval circumstances.

c. *fig.*

1573 R. SCOT *Hop Gard.* Epist., Greedy to tast of the marrowe of gaines and loth to breake the bone of labour. **1874** BLACKIE *Self-Cult.* 84 The real blood and bone of human heroism. **1884** *Harper's Mag.* Mar. 517/1 The..bone and sinew of the country.

4. a. The material or substance of the bones (in prec. senses), which consists of animal matter, *ossein*, and salts of carbonate and phosphate of lime in varying proportions.

1471 RIPLEY *Comp. Alch.* I. in Ashm. (1652) 129 Dry as askys of Tre or Bone. **1597** SHAKS. *Lover's Compl.* 45 Many a ring of poised gold and bone. **1814** SIR H. DAVY *Agric. Chem.* 290 The basis of bone is constituted by earthy salts. **1855** OWEN *Skel. & Teeth* 165 The primitive basis, or 'blastema,' of bone is a subtransparent glairy matter. **1874** BOUTELL *Arms & Arm.* vi. 83 Implements and weapons formed exclusively of wood and bone and stone.

b. Applied to other animal substances more or less akin to bone; as the dentine of the teeth, the ivory of the tusks of the elephant, walrus, etc. (See WHALEBONE.)

a **700** *Erfurt Gloss.* 351 (*O.E.T.*) *Ebor*, elpendes ban. *c* **725** *Corpus Gl.* 712 *Ebor*, elpendbaan. *c* **1205** LAY. 23778 Ane sielde gode he wes al clane of olifantes bane. *a* **1450** *Sir Eglam.* 1083 Crystyabelle, yowre doghtur bryght, As whyte as bone of whalle. **1588** SHAKS. *L.L.L.* v. ii. 332 His teeth as white as Whales bone. **1616** W. BROWNE *Brit. Past.* II. 67 (N.) An ivory dart she held of good command; White was the bone. **1843** *Penny Cycl.* XXVII. 295 There are upwards of three hundred of these plates of whalebone on each side of the jaw. **1870** NICHOLSON *Zool.* 462 The so-called 'bone' of the skeleton of Fishes is only occasionally true osseous tissue.

5. Applied to various articles, originally or usually manufactured of bone, ivory, whalebone, etc.

a. *pl.* Dice.

c **1386** etc. [see BICCHED b]. *a* **1529** SKELTON *Wks.* (ed. Dyce) I. 52 On the borde he whyrled a payre of bones. **1624** FLETCHER *Rule a Wife* I. Wks. 1778 III. 433 Thou won'st my money too, with a pair of base bones. **1724** SWIFT *Wood's Exec.* Wks. 1755 V. II. 157 *Gamester.* I'll make his bones rattle. **1822** SCOTT *Nigel* xii, If thine ears have heard the clatter of the devil's bones. **1848** THACKERAY *Van. Fair* lxvii. No, no, Becky..We must have the bones in.

b. *pl.* Pieces of bone struck or rattled, to make rude music; *esp.* two pieces of bone or ivory held between the fingers of each hand and rattled together as an accompaniment to the banjo or other instrument; chiefly used by 'nigger minstrels'. Also *humorously* used as a name for the player. (Cf. also MARROWBONE.)

1590 SHAKS. *Mids. N.* IV. i. 33 Wilt thou heare some musicke..Let vs haue the tongs and the bones. **1846** R. FORD *Gatherings from Spain* xxiii. 325 Many a performer, dusky as a Moor, rivals Ethiopian 'Bones' himself. **1851** *Househ. Words* III. 245 Now, the Ethiopians..play old banjoes and bones. **1865** *Times* 17 July, Amateur negro melodists..thumbed the banjo and rattled the bones. **1884** *Sat. Rev.* 7 June 740/1 A single row of negro minstrels seated on chairs..while at the end are Bones and Sambo.

c. *pl.* 'A sort of bobbins, made of trotter bones, for weaving bonelace.' J.

1601 SHAKS. *Twel. N.* II. iv. 46 The free maides that weaue their thred with bones. **1691** RAY *N.C. Wds* 9 *Bones*, bobbins, because probably made at first of small Bones. Hence *Bone-lace.*

d. A strip of whalebone used to stiffen stays, etc.; also attrib., as in ***bone-casing***.

1595 GOSSON *Pleas. Quippes* in Hazl. *E.P.P.* IV. 256 These privie coates, by art made strong With bones. **1884** *Dress Cutting Assoc. Circular* ii, All the seams should be opened, the edges neatly over-handed, and bone casings put on. *Mod.* She had the misfortune to break one of the bones of her stays.

e. Also in various comb. as *guile bones, ten-bones, Napier's bones*, etc., q.v. † ***St. Hugh's bones***: see quot.

1600 DEKKER *Gentle Craft* iv. (1862) 15 Skoomaker, have you all your tools..your hand-and thumb-leathers and good Saint-Hughs bones to smooth up your work.

f. *Golf.* (See quot.)

1900 A. E. T. WATSON *Young Sportsman* 315 *Bone*, the piece of horn, vulcanite, or other material let into the sole of wooden clubs to protect the lower edge of the face.

6. a. A bone (or part of one) 'with as much flesh as adheres to it, a fragment of meat' (J.). Often in comb. as *aitch-, knuckle-, marrow-bone*, etc.

c **1386** CHAUCER *Knights T.* 319 We stryuen as dide the houndes for the boon. *c* **1420** *Proverb* in *Rel. Ant.* I. 233 Two dogges and one bone Maye never accorde in one. **1816** SCOTT *Antiq.* xxvii. 193 'I'll gie ye something better than that beef bane, man'. **1837** DISRAELI *Corr. w. Sister* (1886) 76, I..supped..with a large party off oysters, Guiness, and broiled bones.

b. *bones* (fig.): something relished.

1884 TUPPER *Heart* vii. 61 'Now, that's what I call bones.' It was a currish image, suggestive of the choicest satisfaction.

c. ***a bone to pick*** or ***gnaw***: something to occupy one as a bone does a dog; a difficulty to solve, a 'nut to crack'. ***to have a bone to pick with one***: to have a matter of dispute, or something disagreeable or needing explanation, to settle with a person.

1565 COLFHILL *Answ. Treat. Cron.* (1846) 277 A bone for you to pick on. **1579** GOSSON *Sch. Abuse* (Arb.) 30 Some Archplayer..will cast me a bone or ii to pick. **1602** FULBECKE *Pandectes* 69 He..gaue them a bone to gnawe, Date quod est Cæsaris Cæsari, and quod Dei Deo. **1783** AINSWORTH *Lat. Dict.* (Morell) I. s.v. *Pick*, To give one a bone to pick, *scrupulum alicui injicĕre*. **1850** H. ROGERS *Ess.* II. II. (1874) 103 Many a 'bone' in these lectures which a keen metaphysician would be disposed to 'pick' with the author.

7. ***bone of contention, discord***, etc.: something that causes contention, discord, etc.; formerly also simply *bone* in phrase ***to cast a bone between***: in allusion to the strife which a bone causes between dogs.

a **1562** J. HEYWOOD *Prov. & Epigr.* (1867) 47 The diuell hath cast a bone to set stryfe Betweene you. **1576** LAMBARDE *Peramb. Kent* (1826) 425 This became such a bone of dissention between these deere friends. **1660** *Trial Regic.* 79 But you cast in Bones here to make some difference. **1692** R. LESTRANGE *Josephus' Antiq.* XVI. xi. (1733) 439 By this Means she..cast in a Bone betwixt the Wife and the Husband. **1711** C. M. *Lett. to Curat* 33 The Liturgie, since it was first Hatched, has been the Bone of Contention in England. **1803** WELLINGTON in Gurw. *Disp.* I. 517 A great bone of contention between Scindiah & Holkar.

8. ***to make bones of*** or ***about*** (***at, in, to do*** obs.): to make objections or scruples about, find difficulty in, have hesitation in or about. So ***without more bones***. Formerly also ***to find bones in***, and similar phrases, referring to the occurrence of bones in soup, etc., as an obstacle to its being easily swallowed. Now usu. with negative.

1459 *Paston Lett.* 331 I. 444 And fond that tyme no bonys in the matere. *a* **1529** SKELTON *Elynour Rum.* 381 Supped it up at once; She founde therein no bones. **1548** UDALL etc. *Erasm. Par. Luke* i. 28 He made no manier bones ne stickyng, but went in hande to offer up his only son Isaac. **1571** GOLDING *Calvin on Ps.* lxxxiii. 9 As for mans hand, they make no bones at it. **1581** MARBECK *Bk. of Notes* 325 What matter soever is intreated of, they never make bones in it. **1589** NASHE *Almond for P.* 12 b, A boule of Beere, which ..you tooke..and trilled it off without anie more bones. **1598** SYLVESTER *Du Bartas* II. iv. IV. (1641) 227/1 Hee..makes no bone To swear by God (for, hee beleeves there's none). **1642** ROGERS *Naaman* 579 Who make no bones of the Lords promises, but devoure them all. **1670** G. H. *Hist. Cardinals* I. II. 40 The Pope makes no bones to break..the Decrees. **1850** THACKERAY *Pendennis* lxiv. (1884) 635 Do you think that the Government or the Opposition would make any bones about accepting the seat if he offered it to them? **1878** SIMPSON *Sch. Shaks.* I. 51 Elizabeth was thus making huge bones of sending some £7000 over for the general purposes of the government in Ireland. **1885** W. E. NORRIS *Adrian Vidal* III. xxxiv. 117, I didn't quite like to draw out my money so long as Pilkington held on; but I shall make no bones about it with this fellow. **1955** *Bull. Atomic Sci.* Sept. 256/1 On the other hand, Dr. Libby makes no bones about the catastrophe of a nuclear war.

9. ***to put a bone in any one's hood***: an obs. humorous expression for To break (or ? cut off) his head; ***to have a bone in one's leg, throat***, etc.: as a feigned objection to the use of one's legs, etc.

1542 UDALL *Erasm. Apoph.* 337 b, He refused to speake, allegeyng that he had a bone in his throte, & could not speake. **1560** *Nice Wanton* in Hazl. *Dodsl.* II. 170 Then, by the rood, A bone in your hood I shall put, ere it be long. *a* **1738** SWIFT *Pol. Conv.* iii. (D.), I can't go, for I have a bone in my leg.

II. Transferred and fig. senses.

†**10.** The stone of stone-fruit (transl. L. *os*). *Obs.*

1382 WYCLIF *Baruch* vi. 42 Wymmen..sitten in weyes, brennynge boonys of olyues [Vulg. *succendentes ossa olivarum*]. *c* **1420** *Pallad. on Husb.* II. 394 Nowe sette in peches boon.

11. A callous growth in different parts of the legs of horses, becoming as hard as bone; as in *bone-spavin* (see 17), *ring-bone*, etc.

12. a. The hard framework or 'skeleton' of anything, e.g. of a ship.

1634 SIR T. HERBERT *Trav.* 209 The shipwracke of a Dutch Ship cald the Mauritias that laid her bones here. **1854** THACKERAY *Newcomes* I. 89 Curtains were taken down, mattresses explored, every bone in bed dislocated and washed. **1868** BAKER *Cast up by Sea* iii. 46 Steer straight between the fires..she'll break her bones if she follows. **1878** *N. Amer. Rev.* CXXVI. 106 The bones of the language gradually were weakened.

b. Usu. *pl.* The 'skeleton' of a novel, play, or other literary work; basis of literary style; ***the bare bones***: the mere essentials.

1888 *Sat. Rev.* 15 Dec. 714/2 There are 'the bones of' something like a novel of some merit in *The Jewel Reputation.* **1905** *Westm. Gaz.* 23 Mar. 7/3 Counsel did not allege that Mr. Tanner had copied plaintiff's dialogue, but the 'bone' was the same. **1915** J. BUCHAN *39 Steps* iv. 81 The bare bones of the tale were all that was in the book. **1928** *Publishers' Weekly* 9 June 2373 My own bed-book is Mrs. Gaskell's 'Cranford', and as I read it again that night I could find no bones in it at all. **1962** A. NISBETT *Technique Sound Studio* xiii. 233 He will need time..to present the bare bones of the argument.

c. A hardness of the ground due to frost.

1906 *Westm. Gaz.* 23 Feb. 5/1 The night's frost had left a great deal of 'bone' in the ground. **1927** *Observer* 18 Dec. 25/2 The ground had been protected by straw, but there seemed to be a good deal of bone in it.

13. *Min.* 'The slaty matter intercalated in coal-seams.' Raymond *Mining Gloss.* 1880.

14. †**a.** ***to carry the bone***, i.e. one half of the stake, at the game of BONE-ACE. *Obs.* [Perhaps a distinct word connected with F. *bon, bonne*, good.]

1680 COTTON *Compl. Gamester* in Singer *Hist. Cards* (1816) 342 He that hath the biggest card carries the bone, that is one half of the stake.

b. *Naut.* ***to carry a bone in the mouth*** or ***teeth***: said of a ship, when she makes the water foam before her.

1627 CAPT. SMITH *Seaman's Gram.* ii. 10 If the Bow be too broad, she will seldome carry a Bone in her mouth or cut a feather, that is, to make a fome before her. **1851** LONGF. *Gold. Leg.* v, See how she leaps..and speeds away with a bone in her mouth.

c. A dollar. *N. Amer. slang.*

1896 ADE *Artie* ii. 10, I guess I saw as much as two bones change hands. **1921** *Daily Colonist* (Victoria, B.C.) 6 Apr. 4/3 Tory and Grit, Tom Uphill too, Declared that they were speaking true, Two thousand bones to each was due, Or else they would be scabbing.

III. *Comb.* and *Attrib.*

15. *simple attrib.* (or *adj.*). Of bone.

1488 *Inv. Jas. III.* in Tytler *Hist. Scot.* (1864) II. 393 Item a bane coffre, and in it a grete cors of gold. **1875** URE *Dict. Arts* I. 419 A bone or ivory folding stick. **1879** LUBBOCK *Sci. Lect.* v. 150 These cavemen were very ingenious, and excellent workers in flint..their bone pins, etc. are beautifully polished.

16. General relations: **a.** attrib. (consisting of, pertaining to, made of, or obtained from bones) as ***bone-cartilage, -cell, -gelatine, -glue, -knife, -knowledge, -pus, -salt, -snacks, -tissue, -yard***. **b.** objective with pr. pple., vbl. sb., or agent-noun, as ***bone-boiling, -breaking, -crushing, -gnawer, -grinding, -piercing, -rotting***; **c.** similative, as ***bone-like, -dry, -white***, adjs.

1896 KIPLING *Seven Seas* 73 *Bone-bleached my decks. *c* **1865** LETHEBY in *Circ. Sc.* I. 96/2 Refuse grease from glue-making and *bone-boiling. **1808** BENTHAM *Sc. Reform* 50 The bone setting and *bone breaking hundred-mile road. **1839–47** TODD *Cycl. Anat. & Phys.* III. 856/2 *Bone-cells appear in the ossified intercellular tissue. **1920** R. GRAVES *Country Sentiment* 51 Honest men..with glaring eyes, *Bone-chilled. **1951** S. SPENDER *World within World* 229 A

full moon..exposing walls of *bone-coloured palaces. **1676** W. Row *Contn. Blair's Autobiog.* x. (1848) 168 The burden of that congregation very ponderous and only not *bone-crushing. *a* **1825** R. Forby *Vocab. E. Anglia* (1830) I. II. 32 **Bone-dry*, adj. perfectly dry; as dry as a bone long bleached in the weather. **1919** 'Boyd Cable' *Old Contemptibles* xvi. 268 They was like a good long drink to a bone-dry man. **1969** *Jane's Freight Containers 1968–69* 530/2 At one container exhibition, York light-heartedly moored a standard container at sea for a week. It was found to be bone-dry inside when retrieved. *c* **1865** *Circ. Sc.* I. 332/2 *Bone-gelatine is obtained by boiling bones in water. **1884** *Athenæum* 6 Dec. 727/1 The..*bone-gnawer of 'Kent's Cavern'. **1936** L. B. Lyon *Bright Feather Fading* 24 One *bone-grey sun-ray between dreamer and dreamer! **1924** A. J. Small *Frozen Gold* i. 23 The *bone-hard stamp of starvation. **1959** *Listener* 19 Mar. 516/3 The bone-hard ground. **1839** H. Rogers *Essays* (1874) II. iii. 143 Nothing would be gained but ridicule if we were to substitute '*bone-knowledge' for 'osteology'. **1849–52** Todd *Cycl. Anat. & Phys.* IV. 930/2 Covered with the *bone-like substance. **1599** Marston *Sco. Villanie* I. iii. 183 A thrice-turn'd, *bone-pick't subject gnaw. *a* **1639** W. Whateley *Prototypes* II. xxxii. (1640) 127 The *bone-rotting vice of envy. **1849–52** Todd *Cycl. Anat. & Phys.* IV. 930 The cells.. receiving into their interior the *bone-salts. **1926** J. S. Huxley *Ess. Pop. Sci.* xviii. 278 A *bone-structure in the foot which is still more or less adapted to an arboreal life. **1939** D. Cecil *Young Melbourne* vi. 171 Ghastly pale, *bone-thin..she looked insane. **1954** J. R. R. Tolkien *Two Towers* IV. iii. 253 Arms and legs almost bone-white and bone-thin. **1855** Holden *Hum. Osteol.* (1878) 16 This mixture of earthy granules and animal matter we call '*bone-tissue'. **1856** C. Bindley *Pract. Horsemanship* (ed. 2) Introd. 13 She [a mare] is the 'milk-white'. Now there is a breed of '*bone-whites', of a bluish tinge, with blackish muzzles. **1883** *Century Mag.* XXVII. 3 Torture them [horses] in their last hours on the way to the *bone-yard.

d. Used adverbially, 'to the bone'; used as an intensive, usu. with adjs., as ***bone-idle***, ***-lazy*** (so ***-laziness***), ***-tired***, etc.

a **1825** R. Forby *Vocab. E. Anglia* (1830) I. II. 32 *Bone-lazy, bone-sore, bone-tired*, adj. so lazy, sore, or tired, that the laziness, the soreness, or the fatigue, seem to have penetrated the very bones. **1836** Carlyle *New Lett.* (1904) I. 8 For the last three weeks I have been going what you call bone-idle. **1849** G. E. Jewsbury *Let.* 29 Mar. in *Sel. Lett. to J. W. Carlyle* (1892) 287, I am 'bone lazy', as my nurse used to phrase it. **1891** Kipling *Light that Failed* vi. 98 Bone-idle, is he? Careless, and touched in the temper? **1899** C. J. Cutcliffe Hyne *Further Adv. Capt. Kettle* vii. 136 This the bone-weary crew were but feebly competent to give. **1912** A. S. M. Hutchinson *Happy Warrior* I. i. §3 Egbert was bone-tired. **1925** M. Wiltshire *Thursday's Child* iii. 72 It's nothing in the world but bone-laziness that makes you shy at it. **1939** G. Greene *Confid. Agent* I. ii. 78 That doesn't mean a thing to me... I'm bone-ignorant. **1942** 'R. West' *Black Lamb* II. 478 Lazy, bone-lazy, they wish to believe that life is lived simply by living. **1965** G. McInnes *Road to Gundagai* x. 178 The Baas..strode up and down the line of bone-tired scouts.

17. Special comb.: **bone-ache**, **-ague**, pain in the bones; *spec.* venereal disease; **bone-ash**, the mineral residue of bones burnt in contact with air, a white, porous, and friable substance, composed chiefly of phosphate of lime; †**bone-baster** (see quot.); **bone-bed**, a geological stratum abounding with bones of animals; **bone-black**, the product of the carbonization of bones, extensively used as a decolorizing and deodorizing agent, as a pigment, etc.; **bone-boiler**, a workman who performs the operation of boiling or steaming bones used in the manufacture of glue, bone meal, etc.; **bone-breaker**, he who or that which breaks bones; a name of the Osprey (L. *ossifraga*, Ger. *Beinbrecher*); also attrib.; **bone-breccia**, breccia containing many fragments of bones: **bone-brown**, a pigment obtained from bones or ivory by roasting till rendered uniformly brown; **bone-cave**, a cave in which are found bones of extinct or recent animals; **bone-cell**, **-corpuscle**, an osteoblast; **bone-charcoal** = *bone-black*; **bone china**, china-ware made of clay mixed with bone-dust or phosphate of lime; **bone-dog**, a kind of Dog-fish; **bone-dust**, bones ground for manuring purposes; **bone-earth** = *bone-ash*; **bone-fat**, marrow; fatty matter extracted from fresh bones for use in the manufacture of soap, etc.; **bone-fever**, 'phlegmonous inflammation of the hand and arm, often seen in workers in bone' (*Syd. Soc. Lex.*); **bone-flour**, a flour obtained by sifting ground bones, used as a fertilizer; **bone-flower**, dial. name of the daisy (J. Hutton *Tour Caves* Gloss.); **bone-forceps**, a pair of short strong shears for cutting bone during surgical procedures; **bone-grease**, or *Sc.* **bane-grease**, 'the oily substance produced from bones, bruised and stewed on a slow fire' (Jamieson); **bone-grubber** = *bone-picker*; **bone-head** *slang* (orig. *U.S.*), a block-head; also *attrib.* or as *adj.*; **bone-headed** *a. slang* (orig. *U.S.*), thick-headed, stupid; hence **bone-headedness**; **bone-heap**, a heap of bones; *spec.* in *Archæol.*, a refuse pile of bones, etc., of a prehistoric village (*Funk's Standard Dict.* 1893); also *fig.*; **bone-house**, a charnel-house; a coffin; the human body; **bone-manure**, a manure prepared from bones; **bone (manure) man** (see quot. 1921); **bone-marrow** = MARROW *sb.*[1] 1; **bone-meal** (orig. *U.S.*), the coarser siftings of ground bones, used as a fertilizer; **bone-mill**, a mill for grinding or crushing bones or bone-black; **bone-nippers** (*Surgery*), 'cutting forceps, used in the removal of bone' (*Syd. Soc. Lex.*); **bone-oil**, a fetid, blackish-brown, thick oil obtained by the dry distillation of bones, and in the preparation of bone-black; **bone phosphate**, a commercial name for tricalcium phosphate, the phosphate that forms bone-tissue; **bone-picker**, one who lives by collecting bones from heaps of refuse, etc.; **bone-pit** *U.S.* (see quot.); **bone-polisher** (*slang*), the cat-o'-nine tails, or the man who wields it; **bone porcelain** = *bone china*; **bone powder**, powdered bone, used as a fertilizer; **bone-saw**, a surgical saw for cutting bone; **bone-seed** (see quot.); **bone-seeking** *a. Med.*, tending to be deposited in the bones following entry into the animal body; hence **bone-seeker**; **bone-shaker**, a humorous name given to the bicycle as it existed before the introduction of india-rubber tires and other improvements; **bone-shark**, the basking-shark; **bone-spavin**, a bony excrescence or hard swelling on the inside of a hock of a horse's leg; **bone-spirit**, a crude ammoniacal liquor obtained from bone; **bone-throwing** *vbl. sb.*, the throwing of bones; *spec.* that practised by some primitive peoples as a means of divination; hence as *ppl. a.*; so **bone-thrower**; **bone turquoise** (see TURQUOISE 4); †**bone-work**, work done with bone bobbins (applied to bone-lace). Also BONE-FISH, -LACE, -SET, -SETTER, -SHAW, -WORT.

1398 Trevisa tr. *Bartholomeus Anglicus's De Propr. Rerum* 63 a (M.E.D.), Þe *boneache is I rotid. **15..** Becon *Jewel of Joy* in *Catechism*, etc. (1844) 464 Grieved with bone-ache. *c* **1520** Skelton *Magnyfycence* 1907 To cry out of the bone ake. **1606** Shaks. *Tr. & Cr.* II. iii. 20 The vengeance on the whole Camp, or, rather the bone-ach. **1900** *Daily News* 15 Nov. 6/5 He was attacked with headache, bone-ache, lassitude, [etc.]. **1659** Clobery *Div. Glimpses* 35 (Halliw.) They a *bone-ague get to plague their crimes. **1622** Malynes *Anc. Law-Merch.* 284 The Assay-master tooke foure copples or teasts, which are made of *Bone-ashes. **1822** J. Platts *Bk. Curiosities* lxxiv. 719 The..cupel, which was composed of bone-ash. **1600** Rowlands *Let. Humours Blood* iv. 64 And lets him see *Bone-baster; thats his staffe. **1841** Lyell *Elem. Geol.* (ed. 2) II. xxii. 82 There intervenes ..a dark-coloured stratum, well known by the name of the '*bone-bed'. **1880** Gunther *Fishes* 194 In the upper Silurian Rocks, in a bone-bed of the Downton sandstone. **1815** *Specif. J. Taylor's Patent* No. 3929 Bones converted either into ivory or *bone black, animal charcoal, or into white bone ash. **1861** Hulme tr. *Moquin-Tandon* II. III. 160 Known as animal charcoal, or bone black. **1843** *Civil Eng. & Arch. Jrnl.* VI. 216/2 Any trade or business such as ..*bone-boiler. **1906** *Daily Chron.* 26 May 2/7 Bone boilers and tallow melters. **1598** Florio, *Ossifraga*, a kind of hauke or eagle called a *bone-breaker. **1721–1800** Bailey, *Bone-breaker*, a kind of Eagle. **1865** Lubbock *Preh. Times* 249 In a *bone-breccia of this nature the flint-implements would be relatively more abundant. **1895** *Montgomery Ward Catal.* 252/3 Artists Tube Oil Colors..Blue Black—*Bone Brown —Brown Pink. **1865** Lubbock *Preh. Times* 63 Our knowledge of this ancient period is derived principally from ..the *Bone-Caves. **1878** A. Ramsay *Phys. Geog.* xxviii. 459 Bone-caves..always occur in limestone strata. *a* **1847** *Todd's Cycl. Anat.* III. 856/1 The *bone-cells..form the outer layer of cells in the Haversian system. **1903** L. M. E. Solon *Old Eng. Porcelain* 220 Josiah Spode..composed a new china body which..from the nature of its chief constituent..received the vulgar name of '*Bone China'. *Ibid.*, This evergreen 'bone china' has remained unaltered ever since the first pieces of it came out of Spode's oven. **1965** Finer & Savage in *J. Wedgwood's Lett.* 179 It abandoned true porcelain for a bone-china body. **1875** *Encycl. Brit.* I. 854/1 The lacunæ look like solid, black bodies, and..were erroneously called by the earlier observers *bone-corpuscles. **1859** Yarrell *Brit. Fishes* (ed. 3) II. 519 The Picked Dog-fish..along the south-eastern coast..is almost universally called the *Bone-Dog. **1834** *Brit. Husb.* I. 397 Effects of *bone-dust and bones. **1848** *Gard. Chron.* 437 The clergyman had..put a handful of bone-dust under every tree and shrub. **1851** *Fraser's Mag.* Feb. 246/2 They have a cheap substitute in superphosphate of lime, a soluble form of *bone-earth. **1886** A. H. Church *Eng. Porcelain* iii. 29 There can be no difficulty in identifying the earth produced by the calcination of certain animal and vegetable matters with bone-earth, that is, calcined bones which consist mainly of phosphate of lime. **1873** Spon *Workshop Rec.* Ser. I. 373/2 For purifying *bone fat, melt the fat and a small quantity of saltpetre together. **1887** *Jrnl. Soc. Chem. Industry* VI. 825/1 Loss of Nitrogen in the Manufacture of Bone-fat and the Analysis of Bone-fat. **1888** *Jrnl. Soc. Chem. Industry* VII. 81/2 The bones..are first broken up more or less finely, and go to produce what are known as—½ inch bones. ¼ inch bones. Crushed bones. Bonedust. Bonemeal. *Bone flour. **1879** *St. George's Hosp. Rep.* IX. 259 One of these presented a bony growth..the end of which was cut off with *bone-forceps. **1862** Mayhew *Crim. Prisons* 40 A black-chinned and lanthorn-jawed *bone-grubber. **1908** C. Dryden in *Chicago Daily Trib.* 24 Sept. 12/1 Then came the *bone-head finish which left the bugs puzzled and wondering. **1909** R. Beach *Silver Horde* xx. 271 What's the use?.. That bone-head wouldn't understand! **1915** J. London *Let.* 5 Nov. (1966) 463 Now, why be serious with this bone-head world? **1917** Conan Doyle *His Last Bow* viii. 292 James was a bonehead —I give you that. **1958** J. & W. Hawkins *Death Watch* (1959) iii. 82 The best of us have made a bonehead mistake or two. **1903** *Smart Set* IX. 96 You talk like a *bone-headed fool! **1915** Wodehouse *Something Fresh* v. 149 You blanked bone-headed boob! **1923** —— *Adv. Sally* xiii. 212 The wilful bone-headedness of our fellows. **1940** 'G. Orwell' *Inside Whale* 142 The ancient *boneheap of Europe, where every grain of soil has passed through innumerable human bodies. **1799** *Chron.* in *Ann. Reg.* 3/2 The *bone-house in the Church yard. **1846** Walbran *Guide Ripon*, The celebrated 'Bone-house' no longer exists. **1870** Emerson *Soc. & Sol.* vi. 119 This wonderful bone-house which is called man. **1899** *Daily News* 21 July 5/2 Defendant gave instructions for the *bone man to take away the bad meat. **1921** *Dict. Occup. Terms* (1927) §149 *Bone manure man*, general term for any unskilled worker, other than a maintenance man, employed in a bone manure factory. **1908** W. E. C. Dickson (*title*) The *Bone-Marrow. **1927** Haldane & Huxley *Anim. Biol.* ix. 189 An extra production of red blood-corpuscles by the bone-marrow. **1850** *New Engl. Farmer* II. 44 On Mr. Preston's farm..they began to use *bone-meal. **1933** *Jrnl. R. Hort. Soc.* LVIII. 119 Prepared soil..may consist of equal parts of loam and leaf-soil to which has been added some bone-meal. **1849** Craig, *Bone-phosphate. **1871** Roscoe *Elem. Chem.* 219 Calcium phosphate, or bone phosphate. **1861** Mayhew *Lond. Labour* Extra vol. (1862) 314/2 The people who usually lodge here are crossing-sweepers, *bonepickers, and shoeblacks. **1872** Schele de Vere *Americanisms* i. 25 In the State of New York and in Canada there are..many places.. where the Indians buried their dead, and these are known as **bonepits*. *a* **1848** Marryat *R. Reefer* lvii, Master at arms, brush up the *bone-polishers. **1857** *Old Commodore* II. 192 He became body servant and bone-polisher to No. 2. *a* **1884** Knight *Dict. Mech.* Suppl., **Bone Porcelain*, a ware into the composition of which enters phosphate of lime in the form of bone dust. **1888** *Jrnl. Soc. Chem. Industry* VII. 133/1 The *bone-powders of commerce are not always products of manufacture solely derived from the grinding of bones. *a* **1884** Knight *Dict. Mech.* Suppl., *Bone Saw. **1908** Hardy *Dynasts* III. vii. v, A surgeon's horse..laden with bone-saws,..and other surgical instruments. **1866** Lindley & Moore *Treas. Bot.*, **Bone-seed*, the common name for *Osteospermum*. **1948** M. Heller in W. Bloom *Histopathol. of Irrad.* 101 In young rats treated with strontium 89 (and probably also other '*bone seekers') an initial cessation of growth was followed by a period of growth resumption. **1955** *Sci. Amer.* Aug. 37/1 Most fission products are known as 'bone-seekers': they tend to concentrate in the skeleton. **1947** *Radiology* XLIX. 347/1 In the case of rats, the effect of the *bone-seeking isotopes is a bit different. **1874** A. Howard *Bicycle* 10 In 1870 and 1871 the low, long '*bone-shaker' began to fall in public esteem. **1883** C. Spenser in *Echo* 1 Sept. 1/6 The bicycle of the present day differs [greatly] from the 'bone-shaker' I introduced into England in 1868. **1802** in *Mass. Hist. Soc. Coll.* VIII. 199 There is a large shark in the harbour, named the *bone-shark, and similar in shape to the man-eating shark, but harmless. **1917** *Chambers's Jrnl.* Sept. 590/1 The tiger shark of the Indian Ocean and the 'bone shark'. **1607** Topsell *Four-f. Beasts* 316 The dry spaven..is a great hard knob..in the inside of the hough..called of some the *bone-spaven. **1953** P. Abrahams *Return to Goli* v. 180 In desperation she went to a '*bone-thrower'. **1927** E. V. Gordon *Introd. Old Norse* 185 The Danish practice of *bone-throwing is heard of in actual history. **1931** J. Mockford *Khama* xxxiii. 236 First he had found it necessary to fight with his bone-throwing father. **1577** Holinshed *Chron.* III. 1099/2 A faire hat of veluet, with a broad *bone-worke lace about it.

bone, *a. Thieves' cant.* [app. f. F. *bon* good; or a retention of ME. *bon*, *boon*: see BOON.] Good.

1851 Mayhew *Lond. Labour* I. 364 A mark..placed on the door post of such as are bone or gammy in order to inform the rest of the school where to call.

bone (bəʊn), *v.*[1] [f. BONE *sb.*]

†**1.** *intr.* ? To throw out spicules of bone. *Obs.*

1664 in Pepys *Diary* (1879) III. 96 [*Charm against a thorn*] Jesus..Was pricked both with nail and thorn; It neither wealed, nor belled, rankled nor boned.

2. *trans.* To deprive of the bone; to take out the bones, e.g. from meat, fish, etc.; also *fig.*

1494 *Act 11 Hen. VII*, xxiii, Fish..not boned or splatted. **1552** Huloet, Bonen, or plucke oute bones, *exosso*. **1674** tr. *Scheffer's Lapland* xviii. 92 Having boiled the fish they first bone them. **1853** Soyer *Pantroph.* 139 Cook a ham..then bone it. **1880** Ruskin *Deucalion* No. 7 You give it [a book] to a reviewer, first to skin it, and then to bone it, and then to chew it, and then to lick it, and then to give it you down your throat like a handful of pilau.

3. To furnish with bones, as **a.** to manure with bones; **b.** to stiffen (stays) with whalebone.

1871 *Figure-Training* 49 Having my stays very fully boned and fitted with shoulder-straps. **1873** R. Caldecott in *Pall Mall G.* 11 June (1886) 4/1 A fine grass field..well boned last winter.

4. *intr.* To study hard; to apply oneself diligently or determinedly. Freq. with *down*, *in*, and esp. *up* (*on*). *slang* (orig. and chiefly *U.S.*).

1841 Greeley in W. M. Griswold *Corr. R. W. Griswold* (1898) 53 Webb..has been round boring every big-bug in the State to bone for him. *a* **1861** T. Winthrop *Life in open Air* etc. (1863) 148 We was about sick of putty-heads and sneaks that..didn't dare to make us stand round and bone in. **1883** H. A. Beers in *Century Mag.* June 273/2 I'm going to bone right down to it. **1887** E. B. Custer *Tenting on Plains* (1889) ix. 286, I have known the General to 'bone-up', as his West Point phrase expressed it, on the smallest details of some question at issue. **1959** *Punch* 14 Oct. 309/1 The Wrens..boned up on Russian to be ahead for the next war. **1968** *Daily Tel.* (Colour Suppl.) 29 Nov. 67/4 Mr Robert Powell,..who is on the set as technical adviser but who wastes no opportunity to bone up on his hobby—Romanesque architecture.

5. *trans.* To point a bone at (someone) as part of a spell or curse; cf. BONE *sb.* 1 e.

1904 *Daily Chron.* 16 July 3/3 They will be 'boned' by men of the moiety of the tribe. **1934** A. Russell *Tramp-*

Royal x. 80 One of their number 'boned' him; that is, pointed the magic bone at him. Eight weeks later he was dead. **1936** M. FRANKLIN *All that Swagger* 384 The whole world is paralysed by the mumbo-jumbo of banking jargon, like a binghi 'boned' by a medicine man.

bone (bəʊn), *v.*² *slang.* [Origin unknown: it has been conjectured to be a sense of prec., 'to seize as a dog does a bone'; also referred to BONE *a.*]

trans. To take into custody, apprehend; to lay hold of; to seize and take possession of, steal.

1819 J. H. VAUX *Mem.* II. 157 Tell us how you was boned, signifies, tell us the story of your apprehension. **1846** *Comic Jack Giant Killer* II. i. (ed. 3) 6 For not the slightest 'bones' made he Of 'boning' people's 'grub'. **1879** F. POLLOK *Sport Brit. Burmah* II. 22, I wounded a tusker .. but the Karens .. found it dead and boned the tusks.

bone, *v.*³ See BONING *vbl. sb.*²

bone obs. form of BANE, BOON, BOUN.

†**bone-ace.** *Obs.* [see BONE *sb.* 14.] A game at cards in which the third card dealt to each player is turned up, and the player who has the highest obtains the 'bone' or half the stake; also the name of the ace of diamonds, which is the highest card in this game.

1611 FLORIO, *Trentuno*, a game at cards called one and thirtie, or bone-ace. **1617** *Machivell's Dogge* (Halliw.) What shall bee our game? Primero? Gleeke? Or one and thirty, bone-ace, or new-cut? **1680** COTTON *Compl. Gamester* in Singer *Hist. Cards* (1816) 342 The ace of diamonds is Bone-Ace, and wins all other cards whatever. *a* **1726** VANBRUGH *Prov. Husb.* II. Plays (1730) 305 You, and I, and sister .. may play at one and thirty Bone-ace purely.

boned (bəʊnd), *ppl. a.* [f. BONE + -ED.]

1. Having bones. Chiefly in composition, as *big-, high-, strong-boned*, etc.

1297 R. GLOUC. 414 þycke man he was ynou .. wel yboned & strong. **1413** LYDG. *Pylgr. Sowle* IV. xxxii. (1483) 81 Wel ioynted and myghtely boned. **1588** SHAKS. *Tit. A.* IV. iii. 46 No big-bon'd-men fram'd of the Cyclops size. **1871** NAPHEYS *Prev. & Cure Dis.* I. iii. 95 Families raised on this water are larger boned than others.

fig. **1645** RUTHERFORD *Tryal & Tri. Faith* (1845) 165 Faith is sinewed and boned with spiritual courage.

2. Furnished with bone or bones; as **a.** manured with bone; **b.** stiffened with whalebone.

1834 *Brit. Husb.* I. xix. 394 Land of similar quality, but not boned. **1871** *Figure-Training* 58 A nicely-fitting and well-boned corset.

3. Deprived of the bones; esp. in *Cookery*.

1725 BRADLEY *Fam. Dict.* s.v. *Soles*, The flesh of Bon'd Soles. **1864** *Daily Tel.* 9 Feb., Boned turkey, ham, salad.

boneen (bəˈniːn). *Irish.* Also bonyeen. [ad. Ir. *bainbhín* sucking-pig, f. *banbh* pig + *-in* dim. suffix.] A young pig.

1841 LEVER *C. O'Malley* lxxxv, What's that you have dragging there behind you? A boneen, sir. **1855** MUNDY *Antipodes* (ed. 3) xviii. 438 The wretched shieling of poor Paddy, with his dudeen, his caubeen, his boneen. **1892** EMILY LAWLESS *Grania* I. iv. 22 The relative number of cows, turkeys, feather-beds, boneens, black pots and the like. **1892** YEATS *C'tess Kathleen* iii. 47, I in image of a nine-monthed bonyeen. **1949** E. POUND *Pisan Cantos* lxxx. 106 A sow with nine boneen.

bone-fish. Chiefly *U.S.* [BONE *sb.*] A name applied to various fishes (see quots.).

1734 MORTIMER in *Phil. Trans.* XXXVIII. 317 *Mormyrus, ex cinereo nigricans*, the Bone-Fish. **1809** KENDALL *Trav.* II. lii. 204 The species of whale taken was .. the bone-fish .. valued for the article called in commerce whale-bone. **1884** GOODE *Nat. Hist. Aquatic Anim.* 279 The 'Bone-fish' of Key West, according to Stearns, belongs to this [sturgeon] family and genus. *Ibid.* 612 With us it [sc. *Albula vulpes*] is usually called the 'Lady-fish'; in the Bermudas the 'Bone-fish', or Grubber. *Ibid.* 674 In Southern New England this fish [*sc.* dogfish] is called the 'Bone-fish'. **1897** *Outing* (U.S.) XXIX. 331/1 The bone-fish somewhat resembles a whiting in shape, with the mouth of a sucker and no teeth.

bone-lace. [f. BONE *sb.* 5 c + LACE.]

1. Lace, usually of linen thread, made by knitting upon a pattern marked by pins, with bobbins originally made of bone; formerly called *bone-work lace*; now largely superseded by bobbin-net.

1574 HELLOWES *Gueuara's Ep.* (1577) 316 To see her .. take her cushin for bone lace, or her rocke to spinne. **1666** *Lond. Gaz.* No. 94/3 Our Manufactures .. of Points and Bone-laces. **1709** STEELE *Tatler* No. 61 ⁋4 [They] should be sent to knit, or sit down to Bobbins or Bone-lace. **1807** VANCOUVER *Agric. Devon* (1813) 4 Its chief manufactures are the different kinds of woollen cloths, as also of bone-lace.

2. *attrib.* and in *comb.*, as *bone-lace-edging, -maker.*

1634 *Simp. Reasons* in *Harl. Misc.* (Malh.) IV. 178 Davison a bonelace-maker. **1883** *Daily News* 26 June 5/7 An Innish-macsaint body-trimming and a bone-lace edging.

ˈ**bone-laced,** *ppl. a.* [f. prec. + -ED².] Trimmed with bone-lace.

1762 STERNE *Tr. Shandy* V. vii. 43 Her bone-laced caps.

boneless (ˈbəʊnlɪs), *a.* [OE. *bánléas*, f. *ban*, BONE + *léas*, -LESS.]

Without bones; destitute of bone.

c **1000** *Riddles* xlvi. 3 (Gr.) þæt banlease bryd. *a* **1225** *St. Marher.* 18 Blodles ant banles, dumbe ant deaue. **1605** SHAKS. *Macb.* I. vii. 5, I would .. Haue pluckt my Nipple from his Bonelesse Gummes. **1618** CHAPMAN *Hesiod* II. 25 The bonelesse fish [octopus] doth eat his feet for colde. **1854** BADHAM *Halieut.* 439 The boneless eel of Archestratus was no doubt the lamprey.

b. *fig.* Wanting 'backbone'; without 'stamina'; 'invertebrate'.

1882 A. B. HOPE *Brandreths* III. l. 280 The Lord Chancellor read a Queen's Speech jubilant with more boneless promises of gigantic reform. **1884** *Contemp. Rev.* May 630 Those boneless beings who repeat idiotically all they hear.

bonelessness (ˈbəʊnlɪsnɪs). [f. BONELESS *a.* + -NESS.] Boneless condition. Also *transf.* and *fig.*

1885 *Spectator* 20 June 805 They weary of the besetting defect of modern English statesmen, bonelessness. **1895** *Athenæum* 2 Mar. 289/1 The partial bonelessness .. is [perhaps] due to them. **1928** *Daily Express* 9 Nov. 15/1 The softness of this chair! .. And its bonelessness and bendability!

bonelet (ˈbəʊnlɪt). [see -LET.] A small bone.

1854 H. MILLER *Footpr. Creat.* v. (1874) 93 The carpal bonelets of the pectoral fins.

boner (ˈbəʊnə(r)). *slang* (orig. *U.S.*). [f. BONE *sb.* + -ER; cf. *bone-head.*] A mistake, a blunder.

1912 *Amer. Mag.* June 200/1 Boner—a stupid play; a blunder in the science of the game. **1913** *Ibid.* Sept. 94/3 Got his signals mixed and pulled a boner. **1933** *Passing Show* 9 Dec. 9/3 Poor Carol ... She made a boner to-night ... Ronnie was simply livid. **1960** *Spectator* 7 Oct. 509 This Government has made about every boner possible.

boner(e, -eyre, variants of BONAIR *a. Obs.*

boneset (ˈbəʊnˌsɛt). [prob. f. BONE + SET *v.*¹, in allusion to reputed medicinal virtues.] †**a.** The common Comfrey, *Symphytum officinale. Obs. rare.* **b.** The popular name of a North American plant, *Eupatorium perfoliatum*, valued for its medicinal properties; thorough-wort. Also *attrib.*

1670 RAY *Catal. Plant. Angliæ* in Britten *Plant-n.* s.v., Fracturas ossium consolidat, unde et Anglicè à nonnullis *Boneset* dicitur. **1830** LINDLEY *Nat. Syst. Bot.* 199 *Eupatorium perfoliatum* is known in North America under the name of Boneset. **1866** MRS. STOWE *Lit. Foxes* 51 Go into the kitchen and make yourself some good boneset tea.

bone-setter (ˈbəʊnˌsɛtə(r)). One who sets dislocated or broken bones; a surgeon; now applied *spec.* to one who makes a distinct calling of treating fractures, without being a certified surgeon.

c **1470** *Play Sacram.* 539 He ys allso a boone setter. *c* **1510** BARCLAY *Mirr. Good Mann.* (1570) D vj, A bone setter he hyreth. **1622** PEACHAM *Compl. Gentl.* xi. (1634) 99 Accounted the best Bone-setter in the Country. **1706** HEARN *Rem. & Coll.* (1885) I. 226 An Eminent Bone-setter and a good Surgeon. **1884** *Pall Mall G.* 24 Sept. 5/1 A bone-setter is a sort of amateur surgeon, who has learnt the art of curing dislocations empirically, and who practises that particular branch of surgery in an informal, irregular manner .. Of late .. the art of the bone-setter has risen into some repute with the regular profession.

So **bone-setting** *vbl. sb.* and *ppl. a.*

1591 PERCIVALL *Sp. Dict.*, *Algebra*, bone-setting. **1676** WISEMAN *Surg.* (J.) A fractured leg set in the country by one pretending to bonesetting. **1808** BENTHAM *Sc. Reform* 50 The bone setting or bone breaking hundred-mile road.

†ˈ**boneshaw.** *Obs.* Forms: 4 boon-, 4–5 bon-, 5 bane-, baynschawe, boneshawe, 7 boneshaw, 8 boneshave. [f. BONE *sb.* 1; but the meaning of *shaw* does not appear: the Exmoor *-shave* appears to be due to popular etymology.]

1. Sciatica or hip-gout.

c **1350** J. ARDERNE *Chirurg.* in *Promp. Parv.* 44 *note*, Ad guttam in osse que dicitur bonschawe, multum valet oleum de vitellis ovorum, si inde ungatur. *c* **1400** *Sloan MS.* 100 f. 7 in *Promp. Parv.* 44 *note*, A good medicyn for boon-schawe. *c* **1440** *Promp. Parv.* 44 Bonschawe, sekenesse .. *tessedo, sciasis.* **1483** *Cath. Angl.* 20/1 þe Bane schawe, *ossedo.* **1579** LANGHAM *Gard. Health* (1633) 93 For the boneshaw and gout, seethe the flowers with wine. *a* **1600** MONTGOMERIE in Watson *Coll. Sc. Poems* III. 13 With Bockblood and Benshaw. *a* **1778** *Chorus* in *Exmoor Scolding* note, As the water runs by the stave Good for bone-shave.

2. = *bone-spavin*: see BONE sb. 17. (? An error.)

1790 GROSE *Prov. E. Dict.*, *Boneshave*, a bony or horny excrescence or tumor growing out of horses heels.

bonet(e, -tt(e, obs. forms of BONNET.

bonetta, variant of BONITO.

†**bone'ventor.** *Obs. rare.* [? Can the name have arisen in some way from Fr. *bonne aventure* or It. *buonaventura* good luck, as if 'happy-go-lucky fellows, adventurers'.] See quot. Cf. BONAVENTURE 3.

1643 *Five Years K. Jas. etc.* in *Harl. Misc.* (Malh.) V 351 Divers sects of vicious persons .. as the sect of roaring-boys, boneventors, bravado's, quarterers, and such like, being persons prodigal .. having run themselves in debt.

†ˈ**bone-wort.** *Obs.* Forms: 1 banwyrt, 3 bonwurt, 5 banworte, 6 banwort, banwurt, banwoort, 7–8 bonewort. [OE. *bánwyrt*, f. *bán*, BONE + *wyrt*, WORT.]

A name given, on account of their supposed bone-healing properties, to several different plants, as the common Daisy, Golden-Rod, Centaury (*Erythræa*), Yellow Mountain Pansy, *Consolida minor*, and Osmund Royal or Flowering Fern.

c **1000** *Ags. Voc.* in Wr.-Wülcker 300 *Uiola aurosa et uiola purpurea*, banwyrt. *c* **1000** *Sax. Leechd.* I. 294 Ðeos wyrt þe man violam, & oðrum naman banwyrt nemneð, ys ðreora cynna. *c* **1265** *Voc.* in Wr.-Wülcker 556 *Osmunda*, osmunde, bonwurt. *c* **1400** *Roy. MS.* 18 A vi. f. 72 b in *Promp. Parv.* 52 *note*, Bryse-wort or bon-wort or daysye. **1483** *Cath. Angl.* 20/1 Banworte, *consolidum.* **1513** DOUGLAS *Æneis* XII. Prol. 115 In battill gyrs burgionys the banwort wyld. **1565–73** COOPER *Thesaur.*, *Bellis*, the whyte daysy, called of some the margarite, in the North banwoort. **1736** BAILEY *Househ. Dict.* 2 Take adder's spear, alehoof .. bone-wort.

bone-yard, boneyard. orig. *U.S.* [BONE *sb.*] **a.** A yard or place where the bones of dead animals are collected for subsequent use; **b.** (see quot. 1903); **c.** a cemetery (*slang*).

1854 J. R. PLANCHÉ *Once upon Time* I. i in *Extravag.* (1879) 331 Or in a bone-yard with some knacker dwell. **1866** 'MARK TWAIN' *Lett. fr. Hawaii* (1967) 277 It's one of them infernal old ancient graveyards ... Yes, likely. I suppose you didn't know that bone yard was there. **1902** W. J. LONG *Beasts of Field* 70, I have met men .. who speak of 'bone yards' which they have discovered ... They say that the caribou go there to die. **1903** *N.Y. Even. Post* 7 Oct. 7 A dilapidated horse saved from the bone-yard. **1945** R. FINLAYSON in F. Sargeson *Speaking for Ourselves* 17 He wouldn't have gone home late at night past the old bone-yard.

†**bonfacion,** *a. Obs.* [? f. F. *bonne* good + *façon* fashion.] ? In fashion, fashionable.

1584 *Three Ladies Lond.* I. in Hazl. *Dodsl.* VI. 254 And art thou gotten so bonfacion and brave?

bonfire (ˈbɒnfaɪə(r)), *sb.* Forms: *Sc.* 5- bane-, 6 bain-, 5–8 bone-, 6- bonfire; also 6 bonne, boane-, boun-, bond-, 7 boon(e, 8 burnfire; *north.* and *Sc.* 5–9 bane-, 6 bainfire. [f. BONE *sb.* 1 + FIRE = fire of bones. The etymological spelling *bone-fire*, Sc. *bane-fire*, was common down to 1760, though *bonfire* was also in use from the 16th c., and became more common as the original sense was forgotten. Johnson in 1755 decided for *bonfire*, 'from *bon* good, (Fr.) and *fire*'. But the shortening of the vowel was natural, from its position; cf. *knowledge, Monday, collier*, etc. In Scotland with the form *bane-fire*, the memory of the original sense was retained longer; for the annual midsummer 'banefire' or 'bonfire' in the burgh of Hawick, old bones were regularly collected and stored up, down to *c.* 1800.]

†**1.** A fire of bones; a great fire in which bones were burnt in the open air. *Obs.*

(The 17th c. quotations are chiefly allusive, implying a knowledge that *bon(e)fires* ought to burn bones.)

1483 *Cath. Angl.* 20/1 A banefyre, *ignis ossium.* **1493** *Festyvall* (W. de W. 1515) 105 In worshyppe of saynte Johan the people waked at home, & made iij maner of fyres. One was clene bones and noo woode, and that is called a bone fyre. *a* **1552** in Leland *Brit. Coll.* I. p. lxxvi, In some parts of Lincolnshire .. on some peculiar nights, they make great fires in the public streets of their Towns with bones of oxen, sheep, &c. which are heaped together before. I am apt to believe .. that from hence came the original of Bonefires. **1586** MARLOWE *1st Pt. Tamburl.* III. iii, Making bonfires for my overthrow. But, ere I die, those foul idolaters Shall make me bonfires with their filthy bones. **1684** DINELEY *Dk. Beaufort's Progr. Wales* 154 A fire of joy .. called a Bonfire .. being part wood and part bones. [**1655** FULLER *Ch. Hist.* IX. 52 Both parties .. would in a bonefire of their generall joy, have burnt this unhappy bone of dissention cast betwixt them. **1674** W. STANLEY *Rom. Horseleech* 82 (Skeat) Causing all the bones of Becket to be burnt .. and how his arms should escape that bonefire is very strange.]

†**2.** A fire in which to consume corpses, a funeral pile, a pyre. (The ordinary transl. of L. *pyra, rogus* in 16–17th c.) *Obs.*

1552 HULOET, Bonefyre .. *pyra.* **1565** GOLDING *Ovid's Met.* VII. Or els without solemnitie were burnt in bone-fires hie. **1583** STANYHURST *Æneid* IV. (Arb.) 119 Madlye she [Dido] scaleth Thee top of her banefyer. **1639** HORN & ROBOTHAM *Gate Lang. Unl.* xcvii. §961 The dead corps is buried: they of old made a bone-fire, and therein burnt it. **1658** SIR T. BROWNE *Hydriot.* ii. 22 Burning [was] perhaps not fully disused till Christianity fully established gave the finall extinction to these sepulchrall Bonefires.

3. A fire for immolation; a fire in which heretics, bibles, or proscribed books were burnt. Still familiarly applied to a great fire for burning up thorns, brushwood, or rubbish, though, as *the purpose* is not now specifically considered as constituting a bonfire, not distinguished from sense 4 b.

1581 J. BELL *Haddon's Answ. Osor.* 483/2 You would have made boanefiers with yᵉ blood of many good Preachers. **1611** SPEED *Hist. Gt. Brit.* VI. ix. (1632) 79 Their holy Bibles cast into Bone-fires. **1638** SHIRLEY *Mart. Soldier* IV. ii. in Bullen *O. Pl.* (1882) I. 228 Methinks Christians make the bravest Bonefires of any people in the Universe. **1640** BROME *Sparagus Gard.* I. v. 132 Making a Bon-fire in Smithfield. **1653** A. WILSON *Jas. I*, 47 He [James I] thanks them for the Bonefire they made of certain Papers. **1678** BUTLER *Hud.* III. II. 1543. **1711** ADDISON *Spect.* No. 98 ⁋3

Many of the Women threw down their Head-dresses in the Middle of his Sermon, and made a Bonfire of them. **1845** S. AUSTIN *Ranke's Hist. Ref.* II. 9 Luther's writings were collected and publicly burned; but the emperor might be seen to smile ironically as he passed these bonfires.

†**b.** (*Ireland*) An incendiary fire. *Obs.*

1633 T. STAFFORD *Pac. Hib.* ii. (1821) 231 That..the County of Clare might be freed from bonfires. *Ibid.* xvii. 183 They departed, before they had made any Bonfiers in Mounster.

4. A large fire kindled in the open air for a celebration, display, or amusement:

a. (orig.) on certain anniversaries, *esp.* on the eves of St. John and St. Peter (cf. Fr. *feu de la Saint-Jean*, Ger. *Johannisfeuer*, and BALE-FIRE). These were originally *bone-fires* in sense 1 (where cf. quot. 1493), and appear to have come down from heathen times.

1493 *Privy Purse Exp. Hen. VII*, in Brand *Pop. Ant.* (1870) I. 174 To the makyng of the bonefuyr on Middesomer Eve, 10*s.* **1570** B. GOOGE *Pop. Kingd.* IV. 54 b, Then doth the ioyfull feast of John the Baptist take his turne, When bonfiers great with loftie flame, in every towne doe burne. **1575** *Ord. Cooks Newcastle* in Brand *Pop. Ant.* (1870) I. 178 The said Felloship of Cookes shall yearelie.. mainteigne and keep the Bone-fires..that is to say, one Bone-fire on the Even of the Feast of the Nativitie of St. John Baptist..and the other on the Even of the Feast of St. Peter the Apostle. **1581** *Sc. Acts Jas. VI.* (1597) §104 Setteris out of Bane-fyers, singers of Carrales..and of sik vthers superstitious and Papisticall rites. **1600** ROWLANDS *Let. Humours Blood* iv. 65 At leaping ore a Midsommer bonfier. **1867** in Brand *Pop. Ant.* (1870) I. 177 Bonfires are still made on Midsummer Eve, in the northern parts of England and in Wales.

b. (In general modern use) in celebration of some event of public or local interest, or on some festive occasion, as a victory, jubilee, the birth or marriage of the heir to an estate, etc.; but also applied to any great blazing fire made for amusement, or combining amusement with the burning of rubbish, thorns, weeds, etc. (Cf. sense 3.)

(The Fifth of November bonfires combined various senses of the word.)

1530 PALSGR. 199/2 Bonne fyre, *feu de behovrdis.* **1556** *Chron. Gr. Friars* (1852) 32 Commandement..that there shulde be a gret bonfyer at Powlles churche dore..for the good tydynges. **1558** MAITLAND *Quenis Maryage*, All burrows townis..To maik bainfyres, fairseis and clerk-playis. **1582** NORTH *Gueuara's Diall Pr.* 73 b Great bond-fires. **1591** RALEIGH *Last Fight Rev.* 17 Celebrate the victorie with bonefiers in euerie town. **1603** DRAYTON *Bar. Warres* IV. xxiii, With Bells and Bone-fires welcomes her ashore. **1660** BOYLE *New Exp. Phys. Mech.* xxxvii. 309 The People..testified their Joy by numerous Bon-fires. **1710** ADDISON *Whig-Exam.* No. 2 ⁋9 The mob has huzza'd round bonefires. **1736** BYROM *Rem.* (1856) II. I. 35 You have had burnfires and bells and shooting and drinking. **1772** PRIESTLEY *Inst. Relig.* (1782) I. 384 Our custom..of making bonfires on the fifth of November. **1836** W. IRVING *Astoria* (1849) 365 They built a great bonfire..and men and women danced round it. **1848** MACAULAY *Hist. Eng.* I. 631.

c. *attrib.* or *comb.*

1596 SHAKS. *1 Hen. IV*, III. iii. 47 Thou art a perpetuall Triumph, an euerlasting Bone-fire-Light. **1690** *Hist. Wars Ireland* 111 Bonfire-Works..were no sooner lighted, but the Allarm-Signal was given.

bonfire (ˈbɒnfaɪə(r)), *v. rare.* [f. prec.]

1. *trans.* To illuminate with bonfires.

1605 ROWLANDS *Hell's broke Loose* 35 Boone-fier the streets; set Bells a worke to ring. *a* **1797** H. WALPOLE in J. Doran *Hanover Queens* The streets were illuminated & bonfired.

2. *intr.* To make bonfires. Hence **ˈbonfiring.**

1865 CARLYLE *Fredk. Gt.* VI. xv. xii. 96 That was the Old Dessauer's bonfiring for the Victory of Sohr.

bong (bɒŋ), *sb.*[1] *U.S.* [Imitative.] 'A deep resonant sound as of a bell' (Webster 1934). Hence as *v.*, to emit such a sound.

1924 in *Dial. Notes* V. 263. **1936** STEINBECK *In Dubious Battle* vi. 94 The pump bonged with a deep, throaty voice. **1960** V. NABOKOV *Invit. Beheading* iv. 43 The merciless bong of the clock. **1961** STEINBECK *Winter of Discontent* 181 The clock bell of the firehouse began bonging.

bong (bɒŋ), *sb.*[2] *Mountaineering* (orig. *U.S.*). [? Echoic or var. of BUNG *sb.*[1]] A variety of large angle piton (see quots.). Also redupl. as *bong-bong*.

1965 *Mountaineering* (ed. 2) xi. 171 Sizes [of pitons] vary from the tiny '*crack-tack*' or '*rurp*'..to giant '*bong-bong*' angle pitons... Bong-bongs up to 6 inches in width can be used in cracks too small for stemming. **1965** A. BLACKSHAW *Mountaineering* (1968) ix. 252 Recently, hard steel hollow wedges ('bongs') have become available from America; these are more robust than wooden wedges, and are becoming generally used. **1968** P. CREW *Encycl. Dict. Mountaineering* 27/1 *Bong-bong*, an American chrome-molybdenum piton, made with a U-shaped blade,.. intended for use in wide cracks of 2" and over. The name comes from the sound made by the bongs when knocked together. **1973** C. BONINGTON *Next Horizon* xvi. 224 Rusty took six hours to lead the pitch, clearing away the loose sand, hammering in his bongs. **1976** [see RURP]. **1979** CLARKE & PRICE *Rock Climbing* v. 81 When an angle piton is wider than 1½ in (37 mm) it is usually called a 'bong' and is available up to a width of 6 in (150 mm)... Bongs are quite often drilled out to reduce weight.

bong (bɒŋ), *sb.*[3] Chiefly *U.S.* [ad. Thai *baung*, lit. 'cylindrical wooden tube'.] A kind of water-pipe used for smoking marijuana.

1971 *Marijuana Rev.* Jan.-June 18 Many thanks to Scott Bennett..for the beautiful special bong he made for my pipe collection. **1975** *High Times* Dec. 11/1 One hit of this weed produces creeping nirvana when smoked in a bong. **1977** *Rolling Stone* 24 Mar. 81/2 (Advt.), Genuine bamboo bongs with removable bamboo bowls are wax lined and come in two sizes; the one-foot bong..and the two-foot bong. **1978** *N.Y. Times* 30 Mar. B2/2 Bongs, looking like pot-bellied vases.., give the most concentrated 'drag' possible by channeling smoke and preventing its escape into the air. **1979** *Christian Science Monitor* (Eastern ed.) 21 Nov. B1/1 Bongs, roach clips, coke spoons are as familiar as blue jeans to kids in the US today.

bong, bongle, obs. forms of BUNG, BUNGLE, *v.*

bong, var. BUNG *a.*[2]

bongo[1] (ˈbɒŋgəʊ). [Cf. Bangi *mbangani*, Lingala *mongu*.] An antelope, *Boocercus eurycerus*, found in central Africa, from Sierra Leone to Kenya.

1861 P. B. DU CHAILLU *Equat. Afr.* xvi. facing p. 306 (*caption*) The Bongo Antelope... The chief features of the animal are the stripes on each side. **1902** O. THOMAS in *Ann. & Mag. Nat. Hist.* X. 309 No evidence as yet exists as to whether the true western Bongo has horns in the female. **1910** *Westm. Gaz.* 1 Mar. 11/1 Next come nine white rhinoceroses and a couple of bongos, a specimen of the latter animal never before having fallen to the gun of a white man. **1911** ROOSEVELT in Ld. Charnwood *T. Roosevelt* (1923) 243 He had killed a bongo, a bull. **1958** E. S. WARNER *Silk-Cotton Tree* xvii. 175 The chiefs..were announced..with great blasts blown on bongo horns. **1964** E. P. WALKER et al. *Mammals of World* II. 1418/1 Bongos live in the densest, most tangled parts of the forest.

bongo[2] (ˈbɒŋgəʊ). orig. *U.S.* Pl. bongo(e)s. [Amer. Sp. *bongó*.] One of a pair of small (Cuban) drums, usu. held between the knees and played with the fingers; in full *bongo drum*.

1920 J. HERGESHEIMER *San Cristóbal de la Habana* 232 My head filled with the resonant bos and bongos of ñañiguismo. **1928** *Vanity Fair* Nov. 72 A fashionable evening event along the Havana water-front is a concert by black boys with their primitive instruments, the bongó..and claves. **1934** S. R. NELSON *All about Jazz* 167 Then we have the Bongos, which are a kind of tom-tom, used in pairs. **1952** *New Yorker* 1 Nov. 6/2 Candido, whose peculiar fancy is bongo drums. **1956** *Ibid.* 11 Feb. 92/2 She's been doing her calypso act —with bongo accompaniment—since 1941.

†**ˈbongrace.** *Obs.* Also 6 bun-, 6–7 bone-, boone-, 7 bond-, boun-grace. [a. F. *bonne-grace* 'th' vppermost flap of the down-hanging taile of a French-hood (whence belike our *Boon-grace*)' Cotgr.; f. *bonne* good, *grace* grace.]

1. A shade or curtain formerly worn on the front of women's bonnets or caps to protect the complexion from the sun; a sunshade. (See quot. 1617; the later one may consequently belong to 2.)

1530 PALSGR. 907 The bone grace, *le moufflet.* **1533** *Pardoner & Fr.* in Hazl. *Dodsl.* I. 203 Her bongrace which she ware, with her French hood, When she went out always for sun-burning. **1595** R. WILSON *Pedlar's Proph.* Bij, Fillets and bungraces. **1604** DEKKER *King's Entert.* 311 This boon-grace hee made of purpose to keepe his face from heate. **1617** MORYSON *Itin.* III. IV. i. 170 A French shadow of veluet to defend them from the Sunne, which our Gentle-women of old borrowed from the French, and called them Bonegraces, now altogether out of vse with us. **1636** DAVENANT *Platon. Lovers* Wks. (1673) 411 Had she been but old enough to wear a Bongrace.

fig. **1609** HEYWOOD *Brit. Troy* VI. civ. 137 A Grove through which the lake doth run, Making his bowes a Bon-grace from the Sun.

2. A broad-brimmed hat fitted to shade the face. *arch.* or *Obs.*

1606 HOLLAND *Sueton.* 75 A broad brim'd Hat [*marg.* or Bond-grace = *petasatus*] upon his head. **1638** *Songs Costume* (1849) 140 Straw hats shall be no more bongraces, From the bright sun to hide your faces. **1719** D'URFEY *Pills* (1872) IV. 107 Her Bongrace of wended Straw. **1815** SCOTT *Guy M.* iii, An old-fashioned bonnet called a *bon-grace*.

3. 'Junk-fenders; for booming off obstacles from a ship's sides or bows'. Smyth *Sailor's Word-bk.*

†**bongre**, *adv.* and *prep. Obs.* [a. F. *bon gré* (for *de bon gré* of good will), in advb. phr. *bon gré mal gré* willingly or unwillingly: cf. *maugre*.]

A. *adv.* With good will, agreeably. **B.** *prep.* Agreeably to.

c **1325** *E.E. Allit. P.* C. 56 Þe had bowed to his bode, bongre my hyure. **1598** TOFTE *Alba, The Months Minde* (1880) 30 His seruice is not tooke boun gree.

bonham. *Irish.* [dial. var. (in Ulster and Connaught) of Ir. *banbh* pig.] A sucking-pig. Cf. BONEEN.

1880 W. H. PATTERSON *Gloss. Antrim & Down* 11 Bonham. **1938** J. CARY *Castle Corner* v. 279 She's as fat as a bonham.

‖**bonheur du jour** (bɔnœr dy ʒur). [Fr.] A small writing-table or desk, sometimes fitted to hold toilet accessories.

1878 B. PALLISER tr. *Jacquemart's Hist. Furnit.* I. iii. 66 In small objects for ladies, such as 'bonheurs-du-jour' étagères, work-tables, nothing more elegant can be seen. **1902** *Provisional Catal. Furnit. etc. in Wallace Coll.* 283 Small Bureau of the 'Bonheur du Jour' type, in marqueterie of various natural and stained woods. **1926** H. SCHMITZ *Encycl. Furnit.* xxii. 53 The writing-table for ladies, known as the *bonheur du jour*, receives a rectangular upper part, the panels of which imitate book backs. **1955** *Times* 21 May 5/4 A magnificent Louis XVI black lacquer *bonheur-du-jour*, on slightly square, curved and tapering legs. **1967** *Times* 7 Mar. 21/5 (Advt.), A Hepplewhite bonheur du jour.

‖**bonhomie** (bɔnɔmi, ˈbɒnəmɪ). Also **bonhommie.** [mod.F. *bonhomie*, formerly *bonhommie*, f. *bonhomme*.] Good nature; the quality of being a good fellow.

1803 MAR. EDGEWORTH *Belinda* (1832) I. iii. 48 My lord swallowed the remedy..with a bonhommie which it did me good to behold. **1815** SCOTT *Guy M.* xxxix, The *bonhommie* of his character. **1850** W. IRVING *Goldsm.* xiv. 174 That bonhommie which won the hearts of all who knew him. **1878** MORLEY *Diderot* II. 259 Diderot's candour, simplicity, happy bonhomie, and sincerity.

‖**Bonhomme** (bɔnɔm). Also 6–7 bon-, bonehome. [Fr.; = good man.]

†**1.** A member of an order of begging friars who came over to England in the 13th c.

c **1526** PYNSON (*title*) The Extirpacion of Ignorancy. By Sir Paule Bussle preest and Bonhome of Edyndon. **1530** PALSGR. 199/2 Bonhom a religious man, *bonhomme.* **1610** HOLLAND *Camden's Brit.* I. 244 William de Edindon.. erected a Colledge *Bonis hominibus*, Bon-homes, as they called them, that is for good men. **1655** FULLER *Ch. Hist.* VI. III. 278. *a* **1697** AUBREY *Wilts Coll.* in *Sat. Rev.* (1864) XVIII. 462/1 This Country was very full of Religious Howses; a man could not have travelled but he must have mett Monkes, Fryars, Bonhommes..in their severall habits.

†**b.** A member of a reformed order of Franciscan friars, said by Littré to owe their name to the appellation *Bonhomme* given by Louis XI. to St. Francis de Paule, their founder; a friar minim.

1656 BLOUNT *Glossogr.*, *Bonhomes*, a religious order of Fryers entituled by Saint Francis de Paulo. **1678** PHILLIPS, *Bon-hommes*..were also called Fryer Minims, or Minorites.

†**2.** A name given to the Albigenses. *Obs.*

1751 CHAMBERS *Cycl.* s.v. *Albigenses*, They were also known by various other names; as..Bons-hommes, Passagers, etc.

‖**3.** A peasant. ***Jacques Bonhomme***: the French peasant.

1851 SIR F. PALGRAVE *Norm. & Eng.* (1864) III. 2 The bon-homme Sperling..and house-folk, and the Duke and his circle each kept themselves to themselves.

bonhomous (ˈbɒnəməs), *a.* Also (*rare*) bonhomm(i)ous. [f. BONHOM(IE + -OUS.] Full of bonhomie or good-fellowship. Hence **ˈbonhomously** *adv.*

1905 *Spectator* 18 Feb. 257/2 A delightful bonhommious person. **1914** C. MACKENZIE *Sinister Street* II. III. v. 593 'He's not a very bonhomous lad,' said Lonsdale. **1927** *Observer* 10 July 6 The hearty and bonhomous J. D. Marstock. **1928** E. WAUGH *Decline & Fall* x. 109 Lady C.'s hardly what you might call bonhommous. **1960** *Spectator* 5 Feb. 185 An air of bonhomous candour. **1965** *Economist* 5 June 1126/1 The American Secretary of Defence departs.. waving bonhomously.

bonibel, variant of BONNIBEL.

Boniface (ˈbɒnɪfeɪs). [Proper name.] The name of the jovial innkeeper in Farquhar's *Beaux' Stratagem* 1707; whence taken as the generic proper name of innkeepers; 'mine host', or 'the landlord' of the inn.

[Not in BAILEY, JOHNSON or TODD.] **1803** BRISTED *Pedest. Tour* I. 120 To give the characteristic features and to stamp the peculiar traits of honest Boniface. **1829** SCOTT *Wav.* Note 5, The devolution of the whole actual business..of the Inn upon the poor gude wife was very common among the Scottish Bonifaces. **1861** EMERSON *Cond. Life* ii. 42, I knew a burly Boniface who for many years kept a public-house in one of our rural capitals.

Hence (*humorously*) **boniˈfacial** *a.*

1859 SALA *Gaslight & D.* viii. 99 There is the landlord, in ..his bonifacial apron.

†**ˈbonifate**, *a. Obs.*$^{-0}$ [ad. late L. *bonifātus* (= Gr. εὔμοιρος), f. *bonum* good, *fātum* fate.] Lucky, fortunate, well-fated.

1656 BLOUNT *Glossogr.*, *Bonifate*, that hath good fortune.

bonification (bɒnɪfɪˈkeɪʃən). [a. F. *bonification*, n. of action f. *bonifier*: see BONIFY.]

†**1.** Amelioration, bettering; augmentation of the produce of a tax, etc. *Obs.*

1789 T. JEFFERSON *Corr.* (1830) 460 He showed that this could be made up without a new tax, by economies and bonifications which he specified.

2. The paying of a bonus.

1876 GOSCHEN in *Daily News* 4 Oct. 6/3 The bonification of 25 per cent. to the holders of the floating debt.

boniform (ˈbɒnɪfɔːm), *a.* [ad. mod.L. *boniformis* (f. *bonum* good + *-formis* having the form of), used by H. More (*Enchir. Ethic.* I. ii.) to translate Plato's ἀγαθοειδής.] Having the form of good; akin to the Good. Used by H. More to denote a faculty by which moral goodness is appreciated.

1677 GALE *Crt. Gentiles* II. IV. 254 The divine effulgence and operation is one essence, both simple, and impartible,

and boniforme. **1678** CUDWORTH *Intell. Syst.* 204 Knowledge and Truth, may..be said to be Boniform things, and of Kin to the Chief Good. **1691** NORRIS *Pract. Disc.* 186 The Moral Tast and Relish, that which the Platonists call Ἀγαθοειδὲς the Boniform faculty of the Soul. **1793** T. TAYLOR *Orat. Julian* 21 The heavens are replenished from the sun with boniform powers. **1830** MACKINTOSH *Eth. Philos.* Wks. 1846 I. 93 Dr. Henry More ..seems to have given the first intimations of a distinct moral faculty, which he calls 'the Boniform Faculty'.

bonify ('bɒnɪfaɪ), *v.* [ad. F. *bonifie-r* (in Cotgr.), f. L. *bonus* good + *-fier*:—L. *-ficāre* to make.]

†**1.** *trans.* To do good to, benefit. *Obs.*

1603 FLORIO *Montaigne* (1634) 493 To bonifie or benefit.

2. To make good, turn into good.

1678 CUDWORTH *Intell. Syst.* 221 To be able to Bonifie Evils, or Tincture them with Good. *Ibid.* 876 The Divine Art..appeareth, in Bonifying these Evils. **1880** *Minerva* Aug. 177 The Romans did..bonify the air and soil of their city by filling up marshes and constructing sewers.

boniness ('bəʊnɪnɪs). Bony quality.

1884 ANNIE THOMAS in *West. Morn. News* 26 Aug. 6/4 The..extra boniness..of bullocks.

boning ('bəʊnɪŋ), *vbl. sb.*^{1} [f. BONE *v.* + -ING^{1}.]

1. The removing of bones from meat, fish, etc.

1495 *Act 11 Hen. VII*, xxiii, For bonyng napyng and packing of a barell fisshe, jd. **1884** *Girl's Own Paper* June 491/3 Boning meat and poultry.

2. The applying of bones to land as manure.

1875 *Agric. Holdings Act* xcii. §5 An improvement comprised in following..Boning of land with undissolved bones.

boning ('bəʊnɪŋ), *vbl. sb.*^{2} *Surveying, Building*, etc. The process of levelling or of judging of the straightness of a surface or line by the eye, as by looking along the tops of two straight edges or along a line of poles placed some distance apart; also *attrib.*, as in ***boning rod, stick, telescope***.

1785 ROY *Survey.* in *Phil. Trans.* LXXV. 411 Twenty-four boning rods had been originally provided. **1795** *Trigon. Surv.* ibid. LXXXV. 477 Using the transit as a boning telescope. **1823** P. NICHOLSON *Pract. Build.* 581 Joiners try up their work by boning with two straight-edges, which determine whether..the surface be twisted or a plane. **1877** PEACOCK *N.W. Linc. Gloss.* (E.D.S.) *Boning-stick*, a simple instrument used for setting out the depth of drains or other cuttings in the soil. **1886** *Blackw. Mag.* Sept. 326/1 Spirit level, boning rod and telescope.

†'**bonish**, *a. Obs. rare.* [f. BONE *sb.* + -ISH.] Having large or prominent bones.

1530 PALSGR. 306/2 Bonysshe, that hath great bones, *ossu.*

bonism ('bɒnɪz(ə)m). [f. L. *bonus* good + -ISM.] The doctrine that the world is good, but not the best possible. So '**bonist**, one who favours this doctrine; hence **bo'nistic** *a.*

1882 J. W. BARLOW *Ultim. Pessimism* 5 So we see that Optimist and Pessimist are no longer suitable names..; and the positive forms Bonist and Malist would certainly be more appropriate. **1893** MYERS *Sci. & Future Life* 10 The view of the universe loosely styled optimism, but which some now term *bonism*, with no greater barbarism in the form of the word, and more accuracy in its meaning. **1895** TOLLEMACHE *Jowett* 91 Jowett's optimism verges on pessimism, or, let us say, his *bonism* verges on *malism*. *Ibid.* 95 After putting side by side the bonistic and malistic sayings of Jowett.

bonitarian (bɒnɪ'tɛərɪən), *a. Rom. Law.* [f. late L. *bonitāri-us* (cited only in Greek spelling, δεσπότης βονιτάριος, Theophilus I. 5. 4), f. L. *bonus* good, or *bonitas* good quality, in reference to the classical *in bonis esse, in bonis habere.*] = next.

1861 MAINE *Anc. Law* viii. (1876) 295 The Roman distribution of rights over property into *Quiritarian* or legal, and (to use a word of late origin) *Bonitarian*, or equitable. **1876** DIGBY *Real Prop.* vi. 281 Beneficial, or, as it was barbarously called by the commentators, *bonitarian* ownership. **1880** MUIRHEAD *Gaius* 458.

bonitary ('bɒnɪtərɪ), *a.* [see prec.] Beneficial; having possession with all its benefits, but without a legal 'title'.

1833 J. KENRICK in *Philol. Museum* II. 634 They were compelled to concede to the revolted plebeians at first only the bonitary dominion of their lands, i.e. the power of using them liable to perpetual revocation. **1875** POSTE *Gaius* II. com. 188 He [Theophilus] also calls bonitary dominion natural dominion, as opposed to statutory, civil, or quiritary dominion.

‖**bonito** (bo'nito). Forms: 7 **bonuto**, 7–9 **-eto**, 8 **bineto, boneeto, -ite, -ata**, 8–9 **-eta, -ita, -etta**, 6– **bonito**. [a. Sp. *bonito*, of doubtful origin: *bonito* adj. 'pretty good, pretty' is a native Sp. word; but the Sp. Academy derive the name of the fish from an Arabic *baiṉīth*, which looks like an adaptation of the Spanish.]

The striped tunny; a fish growing to the length of three feet, common in tropical seas, living chiefly on the flying-fish. The name is also given to one or two other similar fish.

1599 HAKLUYT *Voy.* II. II. 105 Bonitos and flying fishes. **1622** R. HAWKINS *Voy. S. Sea* (1847) 67 The bonito, or Spanish makerell, is altogether like unto a makerell, but that it is somewhat more growne. **1713** *Phil. Trans.* XXVIII. 234 We took..a Fish which some thought was a Boneta. **1773** COOK *1st Voy.* I. 98 The heaviest and most vigorous fish, such as bonettas and albicores. **1829** SOUTHEY *O. Newman* I. Wks. X. 275 Gay bonitos in their beauty glide. **1833** MARRYAT *P. Simple* (1863) 217 The bonetas and dolphins.. chased the flying fish. **1845** DARWIN *Voy. Nat.* viii.

†'**bonity**. *Obs.* [ad. L. *bonitas* 'goodness', which it has been formed to represent in the original sense, no longer present in the living representative F. *bonté*, Eng. BOUNTY.] Goodness.

1585 R. PARSONS *Chr. Exerc.* II. iii. 295 Bonitie, in hurting no man. *a* **1619** FOTHERBY *Atheom.* II. x. §3 (1622) 304 He is ..a Super-good..as surpassing all other Bonitie. *a* **1670** HACKET *Cent. Serm.* 797 The inherent bonity which is in our works. **1790** B. MARTIN *Bibl. Techn.* xi. 194 Goodness or Bonity is defined to be the Convenience or Agreement of things with the Law and Standard of their Nature.

bonk (bɒŋk), *v.* [Echoic; cf. BANG *v.*, BUMP *v.*^{1}, CONK *v.*^{1}, etc.] **1.** *colloq.* **a.** *trans.* To hit (a solid surface or bony part of the body) resoundingly with or against something hard and unyielding. (See also quot. 1931.)

1931 BROPHY & PARTRIDGE *Songs & Slang 1914-18* (ed. 3) 286 *To bonk*, to shell; generally in the passive. **1937** N. HUNTER *Professor Branestawm's Treasure Hunt* i. 13 The carrier men..bonked and rattled and squerked the package through the almost too small doorway and set it down with a thump. **1938** PARTRIDGE *Dict. Slang* (ed. 2) Add. 981/2 *Bonk*,..to hit (v.t.) resoundingly: mostly Public Schools': from 1919. **1963** *Observer* 10 Nov. 1/1 Each time a golfer wearing it raises his head while making a shot the pendulum bonks him in the face. **1975** *Verbatim* Sept. 1/2 Similar is *bonk* (*bang* + *conk*) in 'A door nearly bonked her in the face'. **1984** *N.Y. Times* 26 Feb. 55/1 This snake came out. My grandfather pulled this wrench out of the plower and he bonked it on the head.

b. *intr.* To bang or bump; to make an abrupt thudding noise (see BONK *sb.* 1).

1960 K. AMIS *Take Girl like You* iv. 49 The heavy door creaked and bonked shut. **1967** *Time* 19 May 109/1 Skelton got a concussion bonking into a 'break-away' door. **1986** *Washington Post* 25 May H2/5 The dreaded saber-toothed tiger..came prowling by, bonking into things.

2. *trans.* and *intr.* To have sexual intercourse (with). *slang.*

1975 *Foul* Mar. 9/4 (*caption*) Rita is currently being bonked by the entire Aston Villains defence! **1984** McCONVILLE & SHEARLAW *Slanguage of Sex* 34/2 'They're not even bonking any more.'.. Entirely cross-sexual, with women being just as likely to say they bonk as are men. **1985** *Venue* 26 Apr. 29 He goes home early, only to find his wife merrily bonking with another bloke. **1986** *Look Now* Oct. 88/2 It was rather a surprise..to learn that he had booked us on a singles holiday with the express intention of bonking his way back to happiness. **1986** *Daily Tel.* 29 Oct. 14/8 Fiona ..has become so frustrated that she has been bonking the chairman of the neighbouring constituency's Conservative association. **1987** *Sun* 21 Feb. 20/6 Fans who were at the concert..were still convinced that Carol *had* 'bonked' the virgin — and one of the band. *Ibid.* 20/7 It certainly looked like she and the boy were bonking.

Hence '**bonking** *vbl. sb.*, (*a*) = BONK *sb.* 1; (*b*) *slang*, sexual intercourse.

1958 *New Scientist* 20 Nov. 1324/3 A simple, mass-produced car..must be expected to give up the ghost to a procession of rattlings and bonkings soon after it has travelled 50,000 miles. **1985** *Venue* 26 Apr. 30 Some midnight assignations, a bit of bonking and a good deal of philosophising are obviously par for the course. **1986** *Guardian* 11 Nov. 26/3 A witty, blurred focus shot of a beaten-up 2CV in a romantic landscape, rocking with the steamy bonking of its occupants.

bonk (bɒŋk), *sb.* [Echoic: see the vb.] **1.** An abrupt, heavy sound, as when a solid object strikes a hard surface or bony part of the body; a bump or blow. Also as *int. colloq.*

1938 N. HUNTER *Larky Legends* iv. 47 The third [arrow] struck the dummy dragon bonk right on the boot-box. **1941** *Dandy Comic* 20 Sept. 15/2 (*in figure*) Bonk... Yow! What's hit me? **1948** [see BONKERS]. **1957** MANVELL & HUNTLEY *Film Music* iii. 168 Sketches of cogs, gears, belt-drives, looms and engines..are shown to an orchestration of clangs, clicks, whirrs and 'bonks'. **1977** *Washington Post* 4 June C2/1 One girl guarded her resonating bells from bypassers who thought they might as well go bonk-bonk as they strolled past. **1985** *Times* 15 Jan. 13/5 No matter what the axle weight, three axles give rise to six bonks instead of four and it is the bonks and not the axle weight that do the damage to our historic houses. **1986** *Guardian* 27 Dec. 30/7 This geezer come at me — 38 stone tub of lard in a loincloth — and, bonk! It's all over.

2. *Sport.* (A sudden attack of) fatigue or light-headedness sometimes experienced by racing cyclists and other athletes (see quot. 1983). *slang.*

1952 *Daily Mail* 14 Apr. 2/8 He hoped to ward off that sinking feeling which comes after prolonged effort and which athletes call 'bonk'. **1978** WATSON & GRAY *Penguin Bk. Bicycle* vi. 255 The British call this attack of nauseous weakness the 'Bonk'. **1983** *Times* 1 July 12/2 'You've got to watch out for the bonk.'.. 'The bonk' is a sudden collapse of the blood sugar level, instantly bringing on delirium and delusion.

3. An act of sexual intercourse. *slang.*

1984 McCONVILLE & SHEARLAW *Slanguage of Sex* 34/2 *Bonk*, sexual intercourse. As in 'Did you have a good bonk last night?' **1986** *Private Eye* 13 June 8/1 Competition to guess the meaning of the letters 'GB'...Suggestions.. include 'Great Bonk', 'Ginger Bush', 'Geoff Barnard' and 'Georgie Best'. **1986** *Today* 22 Dec. 11/4 Mistakes are referred to as boobs — which seems fair enough. What is a little surprising is that even the programme's adult representatives claim they don't quite know what a bonk might be.

4. Special Comb.: **bonk bag** *Cycling slang*, a small bag for carrying light food that can be nibbled while racing so as to prevent 'the bonk' (sense 2 above).

1978 WATSON & GRAY *Penguin Bk. Bicycle* ii. 65 *Musettes* or bonk-bags..avoid the problems caused by heavier paraphernalia. **1983** *Times* 1 July 12/2 The cyclists may use up to 6,000 calories during a race; to stave off 'the bonk' they nibble constantly from small snacks in the 'bonk-bags' they all wear.

bonk(e, obs. form of BANK *sb.*^{1}

bonkers ('bɒŋkəz), *a. slang.* [Origin unknown.] **a.** (See quot. 1948). **b.** (The usual current sense.) Mad, 'crackers'.

1948 PARTRIDGE *Dict. Forces' Slang* 23 *Bonkers*, light in the head; slightly drunk. (Navy.) Perhaps from *bonk*, a blow or punch on the *bonce* or head. **1957** J. OSBORNE *Entertainer* v. 37 One Catholic poet who went bonkers. **1961** SIMPSON & GALTON *Four Hancock Scripts* 60/2 By half-past three he'll be raving bonkers. **1967** *Spectator* 4 Aug. 130/3 I think you're bonkers 'cos your attitude's all wrong. You're more than bonkers. You're sick.

†**bonket**. *Obs. rare.* (See quot.)

1611 COTGR., *Astragale*, a huckle-bone or bonket; the first bone of th' instup; the Game thats played with huckle-bones.

bon mot: see BON.

bonnack, -ock, variants of BANNOCK.

c **1730** BURT *Lett. N. Scotl.* (1818) I. 246 The bonnack.. baked on a plate over the fire. **1786** BURNS *Earnest Cry* xx, Twa mashlum bonnocks.

bonnage, variant of BONAGE.

bonnaght, variant of BONAGHT. *Obs.*

bonnaille, variant of BONALLY. *Sc.*

Bonnaz ('bɒnæz). [Name of J. *Bonnaz*, of Lyons, inventor (1863) of a chain-stitch embroidery machine.] A kind of machine-made embroidery.

1881 *Instr. Census Clerks* (1885) 75 Bonnaz Machinist. **1903** *Daily Chron.* 2 Mar. 9/6 (Advt.), Bonnaz Machinists. .. Bonnaz Braiding Machines. **1921** *Dict. Occup. Terms* (1927) §278 Bonnaz hook maker.

‖**bonne** (bɔn), *a.* and *sb.* [F. *bonne*, fem. of *bon* good; also sb. a nurse, i.e. 'good woman'.]

†**A.** *adj.* Good. *Obs.*

a **1529** SKELTON *Magnyf.* 1003 Her fethers donne, Well-faueryd, bonne.

B. *sb.* †**1.** A good girl; ? a novice. *Obs.*

a **1529** SKELTON *Image Hypocr.* IV. 133 Systers and nonnes And littel pretty bonnes.

2. A (French) nursemaid.

1771 WILKES *Corr.* (1805) IV. 85 Do not forget me to your *bonne*. **1837** CARLYLE *Fr. Rev.* III. I. ii. 22 Old ladies..rang for their Bonnes and cordial-drops. **1848** THACKERAY *Van. Fair* xxxvi, Her French *bonne* with her, the child by her side.

C. In certain French phrases, now or formerly in English use:

bonne-bouche (bɔn buʃ). *Pl.* **bonnes bouches**. [F. *bonne* good, *bouche* mouth.] In French 'A pleasing taste in the mouth' (Littré): but in English taken for 'dainty mouthful or morsel' (in French 'morceau qui fait ou donne bonne bouche').

1762 SYMMER in Ellis *Orig. Lett.* II. 495 IV. 455, I must give you a piece of good news by way of a *bonne bouche*. **1822** KITCHINER *Cook's Orac.* 343 Its high rank on the list of savoury *Bonnes Bouches*. **1870** *Eng. Mech.* 21 Jan. 449/1 Some early bird, to which a caterpillar is a *bonne bouche*.

bonne femme (bɔn fam). [F. *bonne* good, *femme* wife.] Also ***à la bonne femme***. In the manner of a good housewife: applied esp. postpositively to food prepared in various ways.

1824 BYRON *Don Juan* xv. lxiii. 36 There was a goodly 'soupe à la *bonne femme*'. **1869** M. JEWRY *Warne's Model Cookery* 35/2 Eggs a la Bonne Femme. **1959** R. POSTGATE *Good Food Guide* 148 Sole bonne femme.

bonne fortune (bɔn fɔrtyn). [Fr.] A lady's favours, as a thing to boast of or pride oneself on; also *transf.*

1823 BYRON *Don Juan* XIV. lxiv. 149 'Tis best to pause, and think..If that a '*bonne fortune*' be really '*bonne*'. **1825** H. WILSON *Memoirs* I. 314 Beauclerc was, in due time, tired of his bonne fortune. *Ibid.* II. 86 She flattered their vanity with the idea, that her acquaintance was an unusual bonne fortune. **1939** *Times Lit. Suppl.* 4 Nov. 637/1 London drawing-rooms, whose *bonnes fortunes* were many and gratifying even by Regency standards.

†**bonne mine** (bɔn min). *Obs.* Good appearance, good show. ***to make a bonne-mine*** (Mil.): to display oneself in force, to show a bold front.

1644 SIR G. DUDLEY *To Prince Rupert* 3 (D.) We expected they would have disputed our passage over the river Dun, but they only made a bon-mine there and left us the Toune. **1660** BLOUNT *Boscobel* 9 Sultan Oliver appear'd..on Redhill ..where he made a Bonne-mine but attempted nothing.

bonne, obs. form of BUN and BOON *a.*

bonner ('bɒnə(r)). *University slang.* [f. BONFIRE + -ER[6].] A bonfire. *Obsolescent.*

1898 *Oxford Mag.* 19 May, While the Bonner burns, make haste to pass The Revellers firework-scattered on the Grass. **1898** *Westm. Gaz.* 6 Dec. 10/1 The authorities of a certain college gave permission for the turf of the quadrangle to be taken up in order to make better provision for the 'bonner'. **1927** *Daily Tel.* 15 Mar. 10/4 We should be rightly apprehensive if we were to hear of no more 'rags' or 'bonners'.

†**'Bonnering,** *vbl. sb. Obs.* [f. name of *Bonner*, bishop of London during the Marian persecution.] Burning for heresy.

1613 W. BROWNE *Brit. Past.* I. v. 382 The sacred Trine did bring Us out of bonds, from bloody Bonnering. **1627** BP. HALL *Holy Panegyr.* 482 No Bonnering or butchering of Gods saints.

bonnet ('bɒnɪt), *sb.* Forms: 4-7 bonet, (4 bonat, 4-6 bonette), 6- bonnet, (5-6 bonett, 5 bonyte, *Sc.* bannate, 6 bonnette, bonete, bonnit, bunnet, 6-8 bonnett, *Sc.* bannet). [ME. *bonet*, a. OF. *bonet, bounet, bonnet*, in same sense, short for *chapel de bonet* (of which see instances in Godef.), 'hat or cap of *bonet*', a material mentioned in med.L. documents, as *bon(n)etus, bon(n)etum*: see Du Cange. Ulterior history unknown.]

1. An article of apparel for the head; 'a covering for the head, a hat, a cap'. (J.)

a. A head-dress of men and boys; usually soft, and distinguished from the *hat* by want of a brim. In England, superseded in common use (app. before 1700) by *cap*, but retained in Scotland; hence sometimes treated as = 'Scotch cap'. ***to vail*** (or ***vale***) ***the bonnet***: to take it off in respect.

1375 BARBOUR *Bruce* IX. 506 He gert ay ber about Apon a sper ane red bonat. **1483** CAXTON *Gold. Leg.* 262/3 And couerd his hede with a bonet. *c* **1530** LD. BERNERS *Arth. Lyt. Bryt.* (1814) 342 Than Arthur.. wente to the Kynge, and dyde of hys bonet. **1532-3** *Act 24 Hen. VIII*, xiii, No man ..[shall] weare..anye wollen clothe made out of this realme ..except in bonnettes only. **1593** SHAKS. *Rich. II*, I. iv. 31 Off goes his bonnet to an Oyster-wench. **1673** R. LEIGH *Transposer Reh.* 19 Many a Scotch Kirkman [loses] his Blue Bonnet. **1700** RYCAUT *Hist. Turks* III. 317 Having on his Head his Ducal Bonnet. **1704** in *Blackw. Mag.* (1818) Feb. 521/2 Most of the men..wear thrumb caps in Scotland, which they call bonnetts. **1785** BURNS *Cotter's Sat. Night* xii, His bonnet rev'rently is laid aside. **1814** SCOTT *Wav.* xviii, The martial air of the bonnet, with a single eagle's feather as a distinction. **1850** MRS. JAMESON *Leg. Monast. Ord.* (1863) 333 Wearing the lawyer's bonnet.

1562 COOPER *Answ.* (1850) 213 All to whom they be shewed, do vail their bonnets. *a* **1618** RALEIGH *Rem.* (1644) 204 It would make all Nations to vail the Bonnet to England. **1641** R. BROOKE *Eng. Episc.* 85 All Officers vaile bonnet, when the party giving them power is present. **1682** BUNYAN *Holy War* 204 To see men veil their Bonnets to that set, that have officed them. **1830** T. HAMILTON *C. Thornton* (1845) 73 The shepherd vailed his bonnet.

†**b.** A cap of mail, a kind of helmet. *Obs.*

c **1505** DUNBAR *Sev. Deadly Sins* 37 Iakkis, and stryppis and bonettis of steill.

†**c.** A night-cap. *Obs.* (F. *bonnet de nuit.*)

1513 *Bk. Keruynge* in *Babees Bk.* (1868) 283 Put on..his kercher and his bonet.

d. A head-dress of women out of doors; distinguished from a *hat* (at present) mainly by the want of a brim, and by its covering no part of the forehead.

1499 *Acct.* in *Comm.-place Bk. 15th C.* (1886) 167 It. for a bonet of welwete bowte for hyr at Norweche. *c* **1505** DUNBAR *Sev. Deadly Sins* 17 Pryd, With bair wyld bak and bonet on syd. **1530** *Papers Earls of Cumbld.* in Whitaker *Hist. Craven* 305 Three black velvet bonnetts for women. **1716** *S. Masters' Patent* No. 403 A new way of working and staining in straw and..adorning hatts and bonnetts. **1786** *Lounger* No. 79 The progress of bonnets from the quaker to the Shepherdess and Kitty Fisher, and thence to the Werter, the Lunardi, and Parachute. **1836** DICKENS *Pickw.* x, You Rachael..get on your bonnet and come back. **1881** GRANT WHITE *Eng. Without & W.* ii. 55 A bonnet has strings, I believe, and a hat has not.

e. *Her.* The velvet cap within a coronet.

f. ***bonnet rouge*** (Fr.): the red cap of the French sans-culottes of 1793, taken as a type of the revolutionary spirit.

1815 *Scribbleomania* 213 Gallia's red bonnet de nuit. **1835** MARRYAT *Olla Podr.* xix, The province..was among the first to receive..the *bonnet rouge*.

2. *Naut.* An additional piece of canvas laced to the foot of a sail to catch more wind. (It appears to have been formerly laced to the top of the sail, or to have been itself a top-sail.) Hence ***to vale*** (or ***vail***) ***a bonnet***: cf. 1 a.

1399 LANGL. *Rich. Redeless* IV. 72 They bente on a bonet, and bare a topte saile Affor þe wynde ffresshely to make a good ffare. ? *a* **1400** *Morte Arth.* 3657 They..trussene upe sailes, Bot bonettez one brede. **1483** *Cath. Angl.* 36 A Bonet of a saille; *superus*. **1513** DOUGLAS *Æneis* V. xiv. 4 Fessyn bonettis beneth the mane saile doun. **1613** PURCHAS *Pilgr.* VIII. iii. 740. *a* **1618** RALEIGH *Invent. Shipping* 16 We have lately added the Bonnett, and the Drabler. **1627** CAPT. SMITH *Seaman's Gram.* vii. 31 We say, lash on the bonet to the course, because it is made fast with Latchets into the eylot holes of the saile, as the Drabler is to it, and vsed as the wind permits. **1769** FALCONER *Dict. Marine* (1789). **1840** R. DANA *Bef. Mast* xxv. 84 A storm-jib with the bonnet off. **1867** SMYTH *Sailor's Wd.-bk.* s.v., Bonnets have lately been introduced to secure the foot of an upper topsail to a lower-topsail yard. **1884** G. C. DAVIES *Norfolk Broads* iv. 29.

1509 HAWES *Past. Pleas.* xxxvi. xvi, Her bonet she vayled, and gan to stryke sayle. *a* **1529** SKELTON *Agst. Venom. Tongues* Wks. I. 133 Then let them vale a bonet of their proud sayle.

3. *Fortification.* A portion of the works at any salient angle, raised 2 or 3 feet in height on the parapet between the guns. It assists in protecting from enfilade fire and ricochet.

1700 RYCAUT *Hist. Turks* III. 322 The Turks had formed a mine under the Bonnet. **1755** JOHNSON, *Bonnet*, a kind of little ravelin, without any ditch, having a parapet three feet high, anciently placed before the points of the saliant angles of the glacis. **1877** KINGLAKE *Crimea* III. v. 364 Three out of the four remaining angles of the octagon were furnished with small bonnettes and barbettes.

4. The second stomach of ruminants.

1782 A. MONRO *Compar. Anat.* (ed. 3) 39 The second stomach..is called κεκρύφαλος *reticulum*, the bonnet, or king's-hood. **1836-9** TODD *Cycl. Anat. & Phys.* II. 11/1 The second stomach..has received the appellation of..bonnet.

†**5.** A weel or snare for fish. *Obs.*

1715 tr. *Pancirollus' Rerum Mem.* I. I. i. 5 They cast abundance of them [Shell-fish] into the Sea, in Weels or Bonnets for that purpose.

6. Applied to a protective covering or defence in various technical uses:

a. The cowl at the top of a lighthouse, chimney, ventilating shaft, etc.; **b.** A wire covering over the chimney of a locomotive engine or steamer to prevent the escape of sparks (chiefly in U.S. where wood is largely burnt for fuel); **c.** A covering over the cage in mines for protection against objects falling down the shaft; **d.** A protecting cap for a safety lamp; **e.** An iron plate covering the openings in the valve-chambers of a pump; **f.** A hinged cover over the engine (in some makes over the luggage compartment) at the front of a motor vehicle.

1862 J. BLIGHT *Wk. Land's End* 93 The bonnet or corvel which crowns the structure [a lighthouse]. **1880** *Print. Times* 59/2 It is advisable to have a large cover or 'bonnet' for the [melting] pot. **1881** RAYMOND *Mining Gloss.* **1883** *Harper's Mag.* Jan. 198/2 The wire bonnet of the smoke-stack is worn on one side. **1884** *Athenæum* 25 Oct. 533/2 Safety lamps..fitted with 'bonnets' or protectors. **1902** HARMSWORTH *Motors & Motor-Driving* 181 If you have a flare-up,..take off bonnet to save the paint, and smother the flames. **1904** YOUNG *Compl. Motorist* 111 The engine, instead of being placed vertically under a bonnet in front of the car, lies horizontally immediately in front of the dash-board. **1955** *Times* 21 June 5/4 The forward view from the driving seat is better than the rather high bonnet would suggest.

7. A plant; = BLUE-BONNET.

1883 *Century Mag.* 383 Saw-grass water-lettuce, bonnets, or other aquatic plants.

8. A thing or person used to conceal or put a good face upon underhand proceedings; a pretended player at a gaming-table, or bidder at an auction, secretly in league with the proprietor or auctioneer to lure others to play or buy; a thimble-rigger's accomplice; a decoy. Also *fig.*

[**1812** J. H. VAUX *Flash Dict.*, *Bonnet*, a concealment, pretext, or pretence; an ostensible manner of accounting for what you really mean to conceal.] **1833** *Fraser's Mag.* VIII. 342 His look and bearing are positively those of a bonnet at a fashionable hell. **1860** *All Y. Round* No. 41. 341 A sly smile, such as a thimble-rig man greets his 'bonnet' with. **1877** BESANT & RICE *Son of Vulc.* I. vii. 80 He [schoolmaster] is looking out for more boys. Ah, Myles! what a lovely bonnet that child of yours would make! **1884** SIR S. NORTHCOTE in *Parl.* (*Times* 2 Apr. 8/5), My noble friend [Ld. R. Churchill] is very adroit and agile in the positions he has taken up, but this is the first time I have seen him perform the part of 'bonnet' to the Government. **1885** *Morn. Post* 5 Sept. 7/3 There was no distinct evidence to connect him with a conspiracy to defraud..He might have been used as a sort of 'bonnet' to conceal the utter worthlessness of propositions made by the others.

9. Phrases. ***to have a bee in one's bonnet***: see BEE[1] 5. ***to fill a person's bonnet***: to fill his place, equal him in any respect. ***to rive the bonnet of***: to excel (Jamieson). ***to have a green bonnet***: to have failed in business (Ogilvie).

1726 *Poems Comp. Archers* 33 (JAM.) May every archer strive to fill His bonnet..And praise like him deserve. **1816** SCOTT *Old Mort.* xvii, 'He's but a daidling coward body. He'll never fill Rumbleberry's bonnet'.

10. *Comb.*, as ***bonnet-basket, -box, -folder, -lining, -maker, -sewing, -string***; **bonnet-cap**, a cap worn inside a bonnet; **bonnet-fluke** *Sc.*, a fish, the Brill; **bonnet-headed** *a.* (*Arch.*), of a window in which the outside of the arch is more splayed than the jambs; †**bonnet-laird** *Sc.*, a petty proprietor in Scotland, wearing a bonnet like the humbler classes; **bonnet-limpet**, the genus *Pileopsis* of gasteropodous molluscs, so called from the shape of the shell; **bonnet-macaque, bonnet-monkey**, a kind of monkey (*Macacus Sinicus*), so called from the arrangement of the hairs on its head; **bonnet-man**, the wearer of a bonnet, a Highlander; **bonnet-pepper**, a kind of Capsicum, with fruit shaped like a Scotch bonnet; **bonnet-piece**, a gold coin of James V. of Scotland, on which the effigy of the sovereign is represented wearing a bonnet; **bonnet-shape**, the frame-work of a bonnet.

1834 DICKENS *Sk. Boz* (1836) I Ser. I. 152 Trunks, *bonnet-boxes, muff-boxes. **1871** *Memb. for Paris* I. 259 Papers, which had lain hidden in one of her bonnet-boxes. **1835** DICKENS *Sk. Boz* (1836) I Ser. I. 318 The derangement of their curls and *bonnet-caps. **1872** GEO. ELIOT *Middlem.* VIII. lxxiv. 212 She brushed her hair down and put on a plain bonnet-cap, which made her look suddenly like an early Methodist. **1879** SIR G. SCOTT *Lect. Archit.* I. 278 The *bonnet-headed window may be seen at Holy Trinity Church, Colchester. **1816** SCOTT *Antiq.* iv, It belonged to auld Johnnie Howie, a *bonnet-laird hard by. **1844** W. H. MAXWELL *Sports & Adv. Scotl.* i. (1855) 23 The humbler pinnace of a 'bonnet-laird'. **1876** WALLACE *Distrib. Anim.* II. 511 The..*Bonnet-limpets, are found on the coasts of all seas from Norway to Chili and Australia. **1826** MISS MITFORD *Village* Ser. III. (1863) 523 A blush that makes her *bonnet-lining pale. **1530** PALSGR. 199/2 *Bonnet maker, *bonnettier*. **1811** C. JAMES *Mil. Dict.* (1816) 57/1 *Bonnet* worn by the Highlanders, hence called *Bonnet-men. **1702** BP. NICOLSON *Sc. Hist. Libr.* 300 (JAM.) The common gold coins of this reign well known by the name of *Bonnet Pieces. *c* **1817** HOGG *Tales & Sk.* VI. 284, I will halve this bonnet-piece of gold between us. **1837** DICKENS *Sk. Boz* (1850) 38/1 One [shop] was a *bonnet-shape maker's. **1848** —— *Dombey* vi, Do untie your *bonnet-strings and make yourself at home.

bonnet ('bɒnɪt), *v.* [f. prec. sb.]

†**1.** *intr.* ? To take off the bonnet in token of respect; to 'vail the bonnet'. *Obs.*

1607 SHAKS. *Cor.* II. ii. 30 Those, who hauing beene supple and courteous to the People, Bonnetted, without any further deed, to haue them at all into their estimation.

2. *trans.* To put a bonnet on.

1858 GEO. ELIOT *Scenes Cler. Life* 239 She was duly bonneted and pinafored.

3. To crush down a person's hat over his eyes.

1837 DICKENS *Sk. Boz* (1850) 239/1 Two young men.. varied their amusements by 'bonneting' the proprietor of this itinerant coffee-house. **1882** *Sat. Rev.* LIV. 629 The Students hustled and 'bonnetted' a new Professor.

4. To provide (a safety lamp) with an iron bonnet or shield.

1901 *Jrnl. Inst. Elect. Engin.* XXX. 834 In appearance it is a bonneted Mueseler lamp.

'bonneted, *ppl. a.* [f. BONNET *sb.* or *v.* + -ED.] Wearing a bonnet; having a bonnet.

1824 MISS MITFORD *Village* Ser. I. (1863) 15 Hooded, veiled, and bonneted as she is. **1860** J. KENNEDY *Rob of Bowl* ii. 14 Buildings..of which several were bonneted like hay cocks. **1868** MISS BRADDON *Run to Earth* xiii. II. 281 Bonneted and cloaked for the journey.

'bonneting, *vbl. sb.* [f. BONNET *v.* + -ING[1].]

a. The action of putting on a bonnet. **b.** The act of crushing a person's hat over his eyes.

1826 MISS MITFORD *Village* Ser. II. (1863) 277 Oh, the lacing, the bracing, the bonneting, the veiling, the gloving. **1867** MRS. WOOD *Orville Coll.* (1879) 426 He had not enjoyed his bonneting.

bonnetless ('bɒnɪtlɪs), *a.* [f. BONNET *sb.* + -LESS.] Without a bonnet: in various senses.

1847 E. BRONTË *Wuthering H.* ix, Standing bonnetless and shawlless. **1848** CLOUGH *Bothie* II, A capless, bonnetless maiden.

bonnibel ('bɒnɪˌbɛl). *arch.* Also 6 bonibell, 7 bonnie-bell, 6 and 9 bonnibell, 8 bonibel, 9 bonny belle. [app. f. BONNY *a.* + BELLE *a.* and *sb.*; but possibly f. F. *bonne et belle* good and fair: cf. the equivalent BELLIBONE.] Fair maid, bonny lass.

1579 SPENSER *Sheph. Cal.* Aug. 62, I saw the bouncing, Bellibone; Hey ho Bonibell. *Ibid.* Apr. 92 Gloss., A bellibone, or a Bonibell, homely spoken for a fair mayde, or Bonilasse. **1600** LODGE *Engl. Helicon* P b, She simpred smooth like bonnie-bell. **1823** LOCKHART *Sp. Ballads, Vow Reduan* ii, But bid a long farewell..To bower and bonni-bell, thy feasting and thy wooing!

†**'bonnilass(e.** *Obs.* Also bonilass. Now written as two words: bonny lass.

1546 BALE *Eng. Votaries* I. (R.) And so become byshoppes bonilasses. **1579** SPENSER *Sheph. Cal.* Aug. (L.) As the bonnilasse passed by. *Ibid.* Aug. 78 Hey ho bonilasse.

bonnily ('bɒnɪlɪ), *adv.* Now *Sc.* [f. BONNY *a.* + -LY[2].] In a bonny manner; beautifully, finely, pleasantly.

1595 DUNCAN *Append. Etymol.* (E.D.S.) *Scite*, eleganter, pretilie, bonnilie. **1673** DRYDEN *Assign.* I. i. Wks. 1725 III. 295, I am glad to see you look so bonily to-day. **1680** *Spir. Popery* 29 The work of Reformation went Bonnily on. **1785** BURNS *Cotter's Sat. Nt.* iii, His wee bit ingle blinkin bonilie. **1818** SCOTT *Hrt. Midl.* xlii, It was a goodly and pleasant land, and sloped bonnily to the western sun.

bonniness ('bɒnɪnɪs). [f. as prec. + -NESS.] The quality of being bonny; beauty; healthy plumpness.

1603 *Philotus* i, Your bonyness, your bewtie bricht. **1882** ANNIE THOMAS *Allerton T.* II. i. 6 Ethel seems to have lost the bonnieness and roundness of youth.

bonnoght, variant of BONAGHT. *Obs.*

bonny ('bɒnɪ; see below), *a.* Forms: 6 bony(e, 8 -ie, 6- bonny, bonnie. [Of uncertain origin: presumably to be referred in some way to OF. *bon, bone* 'good', or its ME. naturalized form *bon, bone, boone* (see BOON *a.*); but no satisfactory

account of the formation can be offered. In Sc. the pronunciation is often *bōnie* ('bɒnɪ, 'boːnɪ), in Border Counties even ('bʊnɪ).

A notable coincidence in form and sense is presented by the Sp. *bonito* 'pretty, bonny', dim. of *bueno* 'good'; but there is no corresponding form in OF. to which ME. *bonie* might be referred. And analogy does not much favour the possibility of a derivative form from ME. *bon, bone*, good.]

1. Pleasing to the sight, comely, beautiful, expressing homely beauty. Now in common use only in Scotland and north or midland counties of England; occasionally employed, with local or lyrical effect, by English writers, but not a word of ordinary English prose.

1552 ABP. HAMILTON *Catech.* (1884) 53 The ymage of our lady..beirand in her arme the bony ymage of hir sone.. representis to us the blissit Incarnatioun..of our salviour. **1570** LEVINS *Manip.* 102 Bonye, *scitus, facetus.* **1589** GREENE *Menaph.* (Arb.) 43, I saw a little one, A bonny prety one. **1593** SHAKS. *2 Hen. VI*, v. ii. 12 The bonnie beast he loued so well. **1602** —— *Ham.* IV. v. 187 For bonny sweet Robin is all my joy. **1674** PLAYFORD *Skill Mus.* I. 64 Merry lads are playing Each with his bonny lass. **1790** BURNS *Tam O'Shanter*, Auld Ayr, wham ne'er a town surpasses For honest men and bonny lasses. *c* **1820** SCOTT *Bonny Dundee*, For it's up with the bonnets of bonny Dundee. **1856** LONGF. *Bird & Ship* iii, I greet thee, bonny boat. **1859** GEO. ELIOT *A. Bede* 23 Here Dinah turned to Bessy Cranage, whose bonny youth and evident vanity had touched her with pity.

b. Sometimes as a term of fondness or coaxing, as in 'my bonnie bairn'.

a **1540** *Peblis to Play* 13 My bonny heart, how says the sang?

†**2. a.** In earlier Eng. it appears to have often had the sense: Of fine size, big (as a good quality). *Obs.*

a **1600** HOOKER *Serm.* vii. III. 878 Issachar though bonny & strong enough unto any labours, doth couch. **1600** SHAKS. *A.Y.L.* II. iii. 8 The bonnie priser of the humorous Duke.

b. In mod. dialect, and to a certain extent colloquially, it has the sense of 'looking well (in health)', often connoting healthy plumpness: 'It seems to be generally used in conversation for *plump*' (J.).

1749 FIELDING *Tom Jones* XI. ix, The bonny housemaid begins to repair the disordered drum-room. **1877** *Holderness Gloss.* (E.D.S.) s.v., Hoo's thy wife? Oh, she's bonny. **1877** E. PEACOCK *Lincolnsh. Gloss., Bonny*, well in health.

†**3.** Pleasant-looking, smiling, gladsome, 'bright'.

1599 SHAKS. *Much Ado* II. iii. 69 Then sigh not so, but let them goe And be you blithe and bonnie. **1616** BEAUM. & FL. *Scornf. Lady* III. ii, Be blithe and bonny, steward. **1681** JORDAN *London's Joy* in Heath *Grocer's Comp.* (1869) 547 From torments or troubles of Body or Mind, Your Bonny Brisk Planters are free as the wind. **1682** BUNYAN *Holy War* 242 It will make you bonny and blith. **1820** SCOTT *Ivanhoe* v, Report speaks you a bonny monk.

4. *Sc.* and *Eng. dial.* A general epithet of eulogy or appreciation, answering nearly to 'fine' in its vaguest sense: like 'fine' also often ironical. Sometimes also = 'considerable in extent or amount'. ***to pay a bonny penny for***: to give a long or heavy price for. ***a bonny row***: a 'jolly' uproar. ***bonny and***: = 'fine and', 'nice and', considerably.

a **1548** *Thrie Priests Peblis* 9 (JAM.), Quhilk..of many smals couth mak This bonie pedder ane gude fute pak. **1752** WALPOLE *Lett. H. Mann* (1834) III. 6 Mr. Chute cannot bear it; says it..looks bonny & Irish. **1823** LOCKHART *Reg. Dalton* VII. v. (1842) 425 Glenstroan..is a gay bonnie bit addendum. **1827** J. WILSON *Noct. Ambr.* xi. Wks. (1855) 283 You're a bonny fellow to ask that question. **1863** MRS. TOOGOOD *Yorksh. Dial.*, It will mak a bonny country-side talk. **1864** ATKINSON *Whitby Gloss* s.v., A bonny building, and a bonny size—handsome and spacious. **1881** EVANS *Leicestersh. Wds. Bonny*, good, jolly, pretty, etc., an almost universally applicable epithet of eulogy.

†**B.** *absol.* or quasi-*sb.* A bonny one. *Obs.*

a **1529** SKELTON *Elynour Rum.* 227 Wyth 'Bas, my pretty bonny'.

C. quasi-*adv.* Finely, beautifully.

c **1826** A. CUNNINGHAM '*The sun rises bright*,' My hamely hearth burn't bonnie.

†**bonny**, *sb. Obs. Mining.* Also **bonney**. [? Cf. BUNNY, a swelling.] (See quots.)

1671 *Phil. Trans.* No. 69. 2098 *Squatts* are certain distinct places in the earth, not running in veins, differing from *Bonnys*..in this only that *Squatts* are flat, Bonnys are roundish. **1721** BAILEY *Bonny*, (with miners) is a distinct bed of Oar, that communicates with no Vein. [Hence in later Dicts.]

†**bonny, bony**, variants of BONAGH. *Obs.*

1600 SIR E. CAREW in *Carew MSS.* (1869) 387 Strengthened with 1000 bonies. *a* **1604** HANMER *Chron. Irel.* (1633) 28 Their bonnys were..active and venturous souldiers.

bonny, var. BONY, and of BUNNY, *Obs.*, a swelling.

bonny-clabber ('bɒnɪ'klæbə(r)). *Anglo-Irish.* Forms: 7 bonneyclabber, bon(n)iclabber, bonny-clabbore, bony-clabo, 7–8 bonny clabber, 8 bonnaclaber, 7–9 bonniclapper, bonnyclabber. [a. Irish *bainne* milk, *claba* thick. (O'Reilly).]

Milk naturally clotted or coagulated on souring; called in Scotland *loppert* or *lappert* milk.

1631 B. JONSON *New Inn* I. i, To drink such balderdash, or bonny-clabber. **1631** R. H. *Arraignm. Whole Creat.* v. 36 They would eate the sowrest Bonniclapper. **1635** STRAFFORD *Lett.* (1739) I. 441 All the comfort I have is a little Bonneyclabber..it is the bravest, freshest drink you ever tasted. **1691** TRYON *Wisd. Dictates* 152 Bonniclabber is nothing else but Milk that has stood till it is sower, and become of a thick slippery substance. **1716** T. WARD *Engl. Ref.* 234 Curds, Cream, and Hatted-Bonnaclaber, Wou'd make a hungry Parson Caper. **1730** SWIFT *Answ. Craftsman* ad fin., The people live with comfort on potatoes and bonny-clabber. **1883** *Harper's Mag.* Mar. 603/2, I had so much bonny-clabber, or curdled milk.

attrib. **1689** G. HARVEY *Cur. Dis. Expect.* vi. 38 These Bonny-Clabber Physicians are deservedly censured Criminal.

'bonnyish, *a. dial.* Rather bonny, pretty fair.

1864 ATKINSON *Whitby Gloss.* s.v., They're a bonnyish lot.

bonny-vis, variant of BONAVIST.

bonobo ('bɒnəʊbəʊ). [Native name for the animal.] The pygmy chimpanzee, *Pan paniscus*, found south of the Congo river.

1954 *Zool. Record* XVIII. 101/2 (*summary of German paper*) Generic separation of *P[an] t[roglodytes] paniscus* as *Bonobo* not justified. **1962** *Internat. Zoo Yearbk.* IV. 77/1 The bonobo comes exclusively from south of the great curve of the Congo. **1966** R. & D. MORRIS *Men & Apes* viii. 255 The strange bonobo, or pygmy chimpanzee..was originally described in 1929 as a small, black-faced race of the common chimpanzee.

bonogh, variant of BONAGH. *Obs.*

‖**bonsai** ('bɒnsaɪ, 'bəʊnsaɪ). [Jap.] A Japanese potted plant or small tree, intentionally dwarfed; the method of cultivating such a plant. Also *attrib.*

1950 N. KOBAYASHI (*title*) Bonsai—miniature potted trees. **1960** KOESTLER *Lotus & Robot* II. vii. 191 The cultivation of bon-sai, that is, trees planted in pots..and made to grow into genuine dwarfs. **1960** *Times* 4 Jan. 13/4 Sales of bonsai plants. **1963** *Times* 6 Feb. 12/3 *Bonsai* is now attracting many admirers in Britain.

bonsense ('bɒnsəns). [f. BON *a.* + SENSE *sb.*, after *nonsense.*] Good sense.

1681 S. COLVIL *Whiggs Supplication* II. 38 A *Cerberus* with three-heads: Neither of which barks any bon-sence. **1714** CRAIG in R. Smith *Poems of Controversy* 11 As to thy Poetry its nonsense, and therein not a word of bonsense. **1900** H. HARLAND *Cardinal's Snuffbox* xxi, Nonsense or bonsense, that is the sober truth.

bonspiel ('bɒnspiːl, -spɪl). *Sc.* Forms: 6 bonspeill, 8 -speel, 9 -spel, -speil, -spiel. [Of uncertain origin and history: many conjectures may be seen in Jamieson and elsewhere; perhaps it represents a Du. **bondspel* f. *bond* = *verbond* 'covenant, alliance, compact', and *spel* 'play'. The word prob. entered Scotch as a whole, *spiel, spel*, having never been in common use for 'play'.]

†**1.** A set match at some game. *Obs.*

c **1565** R. LINDSAY *Cron. Scotl.* 348 (JAM.) The kingis mother..tuik ane waigeour of archerie vpoun the Inglishmanis handis, contrair the king hir sone..The king, heiring of this bonspeill of his mother, was weill content.

2. *spec.* A 'grand curling-match' between two distinct clubs or districts.

(The *spiels*, and definition of them, in quot. 1831, are constructed by the writer from his own etymological fancies.)

a **1772** J. GRÆME in Anderson *Poets* XI. 447 (JAM.) Some hoary hero..tedious talks..of many a bonspeel gain'd Against opposing parishes. **1815** SCOTT *Guy M.* xxxii, He never..gave another glance at the bonspiel, though there was the finest fun amang the curlers ever was seen. **1831** *Blackw. Mag.* XXX. 972 Bonspiels or bonspels in contradistinction to spiels, which may be defined to imply a game or match between members of the same society, or of a limited number of adversaries, are matches between rival parishes or districts. **1865** *Times* 22 Feb. *Quebec*, The grand 'bonspiel' of the Curling Club comes off tomorrow.

bontay, -é, -ie, obs. ff. BOUNTY.

‖**bontebok** ('bɒntəbɒk). Also **bontbok** ('bɒntbɒk). [Du. *bontebok*: f. *bont* pied + *bok* buck, goat.] A South African antelope (*Damalis Pygarga*, Gray) also called Pied Antelope, and Nunni: closely allied to the Blesbok, and having a similar blaze on the face, so that both animals were formerly confused under the appellation *blesbok* and specific name *Pygarga*.

1786 tr. *Sparrman's Voy.* II. 219 The bonte-bok, the painted or pied goat..somewhat less than the harte-beest. **1834** *Penny Cycl.* II. 85/1 The Blessbok (*A. Pygarga*)..this splendid animal, which is likewise called *bontebok* or painted goat. **1869** E. GRAY *Guide Brit. Mus.* 3 The Bonte-bok, with its inscribed sides. **1959** *Cape Argus* 22 Aug. 8/8 Moving the ..herd of bontbok to its new pasture. **1960** *Times* 30 Mar. 9/4 The well-known Bredasdorp Bontbok herd.

bon-ton: see BON.

bont tick. Also 9 bonte tick. [Afrikaans, f. Du. *bont* variegated + TICK *sb.*[1]] A South African tick, *Amblyomma hebræum*, parasitic on cattle, ostriches, and man.

1881 DOUGLASS *Ostrich Farming* 17 The large Bonte tick that..produces terrible sores on all animals. **1900** C. P. LOUNSBURY in *Proc. Assoc. Econ. Ent.* 41 (Cent. Dict. Suppl.), The tick of greatest importance, because of its injuries to stock, is *Amblyomma hebræum* Koch, commonly known as the bont tick. **1952** *Cape Times* 20 Feb. 2/6 The dreaded 'heartwater' disease which was caused by the bont tick.

bonus ('bəʊnəs). [An ignorant or jocular application of L. *bonus* 'good (man)', probably intended to signify a boon, 'a good thing' (*bonum*). Prob. originally Stock Exchange slang.] A boon or gift over and above what is normally due as remuneration to the receiver, and which is therefore something wholly 'to the good'.

a. (*a*) Money or its equivalent, given as a premium, or as an extra or irregular remuneration, in consideration of offices performed, or to encourage their performance; sometimes merely a euphemism for *douceur, bribe.* Hence ***bonus-fed*** adj.

1773 MACKLIN *Man of World* III. i, Got my share of the clothing..the contracts, the lottery tickets, and aw the political bonuses. **1802** *Edin. Rev.* I. 104 The bonus of one half per cent. interest will not mend the matter. **1852** MCCULLOCH *Taxation* I. i. §2. 68 Except their owners, none would occupy them [costly edifices] unless tempted by the offer of a considerable bonus. *Ibid.* III. i. 435 There have.. been large deductions from the loans for prompt payment, and bonuses of various descriptions. **1886** *Pall Mall G.* 23 Feb. 2/2 Bring a bonus-fed production from the West into competition with it.

(*b*) *fig.*; cf. 'premium'.

1813 *Examiner* 17 May 319/1 As a bonus..the old gentleman engaged to pay off my debts. **1813** SYD. SMITH *Wks.* (1867) I. 220 A bonus is given to one set of religious opinions. **1840** CARLYLE *Misc.* (1857) I. 291 A sort of bait and bonus to Satan.

b. An extra dividend paid to shareholders in a joint-stock company from surplus profits; a portion of the profits of an insurance company distributed, 'pro rata', to the policy-holders.

1808 SCOTT in *Lockhart* (1839) III. 134 The Editor.. makes a point of every contributor receiving this Bonus. **1855** MACAULAY *Hist. Eng.* IV. 133 Every proprietor received as a bonus a quantity of stock equal to that which he held. **1861** *Sat. Rev.* 30 Nov. 553 To share, in the shape of interest and bonuses, in the profits realized.

c. A gratuity paid to workmen, masters of vessels, etc., over and above their stated salary.

1863 FAWCETT *Pol. Econ.* II. ix. 254 One half of the surplus profits are distributed amongst the labourers as a bonus.

d. *attrib.* or quasi-*adj.*, as ***bonus share, year***, etc.

1883 SIR G. JESSEL *Law Times Rep.* XLIX. 149/1 He had accepted certain bonus shares, as they are called—that is, shares which were given him free from calls.

bonus ('bəʊnəs), *v.* [f. prec.] *trans.* To give a bonus to; to assist or promote by bonuses.

1886 *Pall Mall G.* 23 Feb. 2 To stimulate American exports by bonusing production. *Ibid.* Railroads have been so bonused by State money and land grants.

bon-vivant: see BON.

bonxie ('bɒŋksɪ). The name given in Shetland to the skua gull (*Lestris catarractes*).

1802 G. MONTAGU *Ornith. Dict.* (1833) 49 *Bonxie*, a name for the Skua. **1822** SCOTT *Pirate* iv, The very sheerwaters and bonxies are making to the cliffs for shelter.

bony ('bəʊnɪ), *a.* [f. BONE *sb.* + -Y[1].]

1. Of, pertaining to, of the nature of bone or bones; consisting or made of bones.

a **1535** MORE *Wks.* (1557) 77 Yᵉ lothely figure of our dead bony bodies biten away yᵉ flesh. **1607** TOPSELL *Four-f. Beasts* 91 A certain bony substance. **1804** ABERNETHY *Surg. Observ.* 103 Bony matter was deposited. **1842** PRICHARD *Nat. Hist. Man* 116 The bony structure of the head.

2. a. Abounding in bones; having large or prominent bones; big-boned.

1598 SYLVESTER *Du Bartas* (1621) 227 A lean, bare, bonny face [of a horse]. **1726** THOMSON *Winter* 394 Bony, and gaunt, and grim. **1836** DICKENS *Pickw.* v, A tall bony woman —straight all the way down. *Mod.* Neck of mutton is a very bony joint.

b. Of coal: containing a considerable amount of slate or shale. *U.S.*

1857 *Harper's Mag.* Sept. 463/1 Much of the slate and 'bony coal' that occurs in the vein is separated.

3. *Comb.*, as ***bony-skeletoned***; also **bony-fish** *U.S.*, the menhaden or moss-bunker (*Brevoortia tyrannus*); **bony-hoof** (see quot.); **bony-pike**, a ganoid fish inhabiting rivers and lakes in America.

1768 CROKER, etc. *Dict. Arts & Sc.* II, Bony Hoof is a round bony swelling, growing on the very top of a horse's hoof, which is always caused by some blow or bruise. **1815** *Trans. Lit. & Philos. Soc. N.Y.* I. 453 Bony-fish, Hard-heads, or Marsbankers. **1848** CARPENTER *Zool.* §572 The Lepidosteus or Bony Pike..has many of the characters of the Pike, with the structure of the head of the Herring. **1871** HARTWIG *Subterr. W.* ii. 13 Any bony-skeletoned fish of our days. **1871** *Game Laws N.Y.* in *Fur, Fin & Feather* (1872) 21 Bony fish, or moss bunkers..are exempted from the operation of this section. **1884** L. F. ALLEN *New Amer. Farm Bk.* 80 The moss-bonker, or bony-fish [etc.]..are caught in seines, and sold to the farmers by the wagon load.

bony, *v. nonce-wd.* [f. prec.] *trans.* To make bony; to harden.

1684 *Gt. Frost* p. xxix, [*Thames says*] Father Frost and Sister Snow have bonyed my borders.

bony ('bəʊnɪ), *sb. U.S. mining.* [f. the adj.] = BONE *sb.* 13.

1874 RAYMOND *Statist. Mines & Mining* 39 It [*sc.* the coal] is interstratified with sand-rock and shale. In some of the mines the roof consists of a mixture of the two, called by the men 'bony'. *Ibid.* 41 The Black Diamond vein has for roof and floor shale, slate, and 'bony'.

bony, var. BONNY, and BUNNY, *Obs.*, a swelling.

bonze (bɒnz). Forms: 6 bonso, 7 boze, *pl.* bosses, 7–8 **bonzee**, 7– **bonze**. [prob. a. F. *bonze*, ad. Pg. *bonzo* (early mod.L. *bonzus, bonzius*); according to Col. Yule prob. ad. Japanese *bonzô* or *bonzi*, ad. Chinese *fan seng* 'religious person', or of Jap. *bo-zi*, ad. Ch. *fă-sze* 'teacher of the law'. Some of the earlier Eng. forms appear to represent the Japanese word directly.]

A term applied by Europeans to the Buddhist clergy of Japan, and sometimes of China, and adjacent countries.

[**1552** XAVIER *Epist.* V. xvii. (1667) (Y.) Erubescunt enim et confunduntur Bonzii.] **1588** PARKE *Hist. China* 379 (Y.) They haue amongst them [in Japan] many priests of their Idols whom they do call Bonsos, of the which there be great couents. *a* **1590** *Exct. Treat. China* in Hakluyt II. 580 In China called Cen, but with us at Japon are named Bonzi. **1618** COCKS *Diary* II. 75 (Y.) There is 300 boze (or pagon pristes). *Ibid.* I. 143 Bosses. **1688** *New Hist. China* 46 In these Temples..Bonzes have their Habitations. **1713** *Guardian* No. 3 (1756) I. 20 The Bonzes of China have books written by the disciples of Fo-he. **1756** BURKE *Vind. Nat. Soc.* Wks. I. 60 The absurd tricks, or destructive bigotry of the bonzees [of China]. **1878** LADY HERBERT tr. *Hubner's Ramble* II. ii. 249 A bonze appears on the threshold of the temple.

bonzer ('bɒnzə(r)), *a. Austral.* (and *N.Z.*) *slang.* Also **bonza**, **bonser**, etc. [Perhaps alteration of BONANZA.] Excellent, extremely good. Also *absol.* as *sb. Obsolescent.*

1904 *Bulletin* (Sydney) 14 Apr. 29 A bonser or bonster is comparatively superior to a bons. **1906** E. DYSON *Fact'ry 'Ands* xiv. 182 What's er bonzer like you doin' spreadin' sour paste fer yer daily? *Ibid.* xviii. 246 'E had er bonzer nose. He'd fair run t' nose. **1915** C. J. DENNIS *Sentimental Bloke* 18 An' on the air a sad, sweet music breaves A bonzer song. **1922** *Glasgow Herald* 8 Nov. 8, I have..heard Australians described as 'Bonzers', probably owing to the way they have of overworking that strange compound. It is used in the various States in place of the adjectives good, great, and splendid, as, for example, 'Massenger is a bonzer player; he scored a bonzer try.' **1927** FRANCIS BRETT YOUNG *Portrait of Clare* 653 She came from Toowoomba, in Queensland, a bonza spot. **1936** F. CLUNE *Roaming round Darling* xxiv. 244 It's bonzer in the water. Aren't you coming in? **1947** D. M. DAVIN *Gorse blooms Pale* 200 An Iti bint..with bonzer black eyes. **1949** F. SARGESON *I saw in Dream* viii. 60 A bonser afternoon. **1969** *Advertiser* (Adelaide) 30 Dec. 1/3 (*heading*) 1970? She'll be bonzer.

bonzery ('bɒnzərɪ). *rare.* [f. BONZE + -ERY, or a. F. *bonzerie.*] A Buddhist monastery.

1788 PRIESTLEY *Lect. Hist.* v. lvii. 453 There are more than six thousand bonzeries in the city and district of Peking.

bonzess (bɒn'zɛs). *rare.* [f. F. *bonzesse*, fem. of *bonze*, 18th c. in Littré.] A female bonze.

1860 *All Y. Round* No. 64. 322 Buddhism and Lamaism ..permit women..to escape from the sorrows of social life by making a religious and monastic profession, under the title of Bonzesses.

Bonzo ('bɒnzəʊ). [Arbitrarily formed by Capt. Bruce S. Ingram, editor of 'The Sketch'.] The figure of a comically-shaped puppy which came into vogue through a series of drawings by G. E. Studdy (the first of which appeared in 'The Sketch' 8 Nov. 1922), and is used in various forms, as toys, etc. Hence (*trivial*) '**Bonzoid** *a.*

1927 *Bulletin* 11 Oct. 5/4 The craze for vanity bags in the form of Teddy Bears, Bonzos, and other zoological specimens. **1928** GALSWORTHY *Swan Song* II. vi. 152 You're 'for it', as they say in this Bonzoid age. **1934** 'G. ORWELL' *Burmese Days* ii. 22 For ornament there were a number of 'Bonzo' pictures. **1949** A. WILSON *Wrong Set* 40 A side table ..embellished with china models of Bonzo and Felix the cat.

bonzoline ('bɒnzəliːn). A composition used as a substitute for ivory in the manufacture of billiard balls.

1896 *Daily News* 18 Apr. 6/1 During the last two or three years the balls have been made of a new composition called bonzoline. **1899** *Westm. Gaz.* 10 Nov. 5/2 Bonzoline billiard balls.

boo, booh (buː). *int.* (and *sb.*[1]) A sound imitating the lowing of oxen; also used to express contempt, disapprobation, aversion. Used *subst.* as a name for itself, *esp.* as the sound of hooting. Cf. BO, BOOHOO.

1801 R. GILL in Chambers *Hum. Sc. Poems* (1862) 176 He heard a boo ahint a hedge. **1855** THACKERAY *Rose & Ring* viii. (1866) 48 He..fell asleep and snored horridly. Booh, the nasty pig! **1884** *Chr. World* 25 Sept. 717/1 The sibilant hiss and the contemptuous 'boo'. **1885** *Pall Mall G.* 6 Oct. 2/1 When the names of the agents..came out, you should have heard the roar of savage 'boos'.

boo (buː), *sb.*[2] *slang* (orig. *U.S.*). [Origin uncertain.] = MARIJUANA.

[**1959** J. E. SCHMIDT *Narcotics Lingo & Lore* 19 *Bo-bo jockey*, a capnophilist who smokes marijuana cigarettes. Noted in 1947.] **1959** *Esquire* Nov. 70H *Boo*, marijuana. Also, Gage, Greens, Head, [etc.]. **1965** *Harper's Mag.* Aug. 49/2 The story, sounding as if it originated with somebody full of Mexican boo smoke, came to prominence in *The Independent American.* **1967** [see MARY JANE 2]. **1975** *New Yorker* 26 May 33/2 The old Portagee is cheerful, healthy as a pippin apple,..smokes a little boo, has a whole string of foxy chicks who keep him up most of the night. **1979** *High Times* Mar. 18/2 There was 'boo'—very popular in late-'50s/early-hipster New York City. Why boo? From 'taboo', perhaps. **1985** *Playboy* XXXII. 119/2 Where's the fun in.. inhaling carbon-monoxide fumes, when you could be toking refreshing essence of boo smoke.

boo (buː), *v.* [f. prec.] **1.** *intr.* **a.** To low as a cow; to make a similar noise. **b.** To utter 'boo!'; to hoot. Hence '**booing** *ppl. a.* and *vbl. sb.*

1816 'QUIZ' *Grand Master* VII. 188 At the Presidency, Some people boo with complaisancy. **1852** *Q. Rev.* Dec. 212 The poor neighbours..were wont to exclaim, 'There he [Wordsworth] is; we are glad to hear him booing about again'. **1882** JEFFERIES *Bevis* II. 77 The booing of distant cows. **1884** *Rept. Ld. Salisbury's Sp.* in *Times* 23 July 10/1 'We have been informed by Mr. Gladstone' (Great booing and cheering). **1884** *Gd. Words* May 324/2 A voice booing and hulloing.

2. *trans.* To assail with cries of 'boo!' as an expression of dissatisfaction or disapproval; to condemn by booing. Hence '**booer**.

1893 *Daily News* 27 Jan. 5/1 It was not a booing that booed the piece to immediate perdition. **1904** *Daily Chron.* 19 Nov. 4/6 The 'booer', she argues, does not make himself heard at the opening of all new hotels, banks, and public buildings. What indeed would be thought of the man who 'booed' his dinner at the Carlton because his appetite failed? **1923** *Daily Mail* 28 Sept. 6/3 Then..the booer will learn to give vent to his feelings in a more civilised way. **1955** *Times* 4 Aug. 10/4 Some of the audience booed the performance on the first night. **1967** *Listener* 12 Jan. 45/2 François Mauriac ..tried to boo the singer off the stage.

boo, variant form of BO *a. Obs.* both.

boo-ay ('buːaɪ). *N.Z.* and *Austral. colloq.* Also **boo-ai, booeye, boohai**. [? f. place-name *Puhoi*, N. Auckland.] Remote rural districts. Phr. ***up the boo-ay***, completely astray, altogether wrong.

The word is much older but has not been found in printed sources earlier than 1955.

1955 D. NILAND *Shiralee* 67 He could have been out there in the boo-eye, thrusting his body into the wind and rain. **1959** G. SLATTER *Gun in Hand* viii. 86 Slingin' off at me he was. You're up the boo-ay he told me. **1963** R. CASEY *As Short Spring* xxi. 244 You fancy them up here in the boo-eye, mortgaged up to their necks for the rest of their lives.

boob (buːb), *sb. slang* (orig. *U.S.*). [Shortened f. BOOBY *sb.*]

1. = BOOBY *sb.* 1 e.

1908 J. M. SULLIVAN *Crim. Slang* 4 *Boob*, the lockup, station house, or city prison. **1911** G. BRONSON-HOWARD *Enemy to Society* v. 159 Stooling for the coppers and swearing many a right guy into the boob. **1923** E. WALLACE *Missing Million* xiii. 108, I thought you were in 'boob'. **1941** *Coast to Coast 1941* 232 Seeing Don get chucked out of the Ballarat and carted off to the boob. **1958** M. PUGH *Wilderness of Monkeys* xiv. 177 'Got six months in jail,' May added. 'Half a stretch in the boob,' Maguire said.

2. = BOOBY *sb.* 1 a.

1909 *Sat. Even. Post* 27 Mar. 7/3, I had to tell her the boob had gone for the day. **1915** [see BONE-*headed a.*]. **1920** *Chambers's Jrnl.* May 282/1 Of course war is wrong—any boob knows that. **1923** W. DEEPING *Secret Sanctuary* xvi. 160 And not a soul to speak to but that boob of a boy once in the day. **1930** G. B. SHAW *Apple Cart* I. 26 You gave it away, like the boobs you are, to the Pentland Forth Syndicate. **1961** [see BOO-BOO].

3. A foolish mistake or blunder. Also *attrib.*, foolish, inane.

1934 R. STOUT *Fer-de-Lance* (1935) i. 8 A boob thing to say. **1959** 'O. MILLS' *Stairway to Murder* xvi. 167 Boob Number Two... The prison service isn't quite like the Army, Colonel Clive. **1966** P. MOLONEY *Plea for Mersey* 55 Newspapers have I read in every town And many a boob and misprint have I seen. **1969** *Daily Tel.* (Colour Suppl.) 10 Jan. 7 (U.S.A.) A factory hand released by technology into ever greater leisure may be content to watch the 'boob toob' (TV) or go fishing.

4. [prob. shortening of BOOBY *sb.*[2]] *pl.* The breasts. *slang.* (orig. *U.S.*)

1949 H. MILLER *Sexus* (1969) xiii. 305, I felt her sloshy boobs joggling me but I was too intent on pursuing the ramifications of Coleridge's amazing mind to let her vegetable appendages disturb me. **1955** T. WILLIAMS *Cat on Hot Tin Roof* (1956) I. 7 He always drops his eyes down my body when I'm talkin' to him, drops his eyes to my boobs an' licks his old chops! **1968** *Daily Mirror* 27 Aug. 7/5 If people insist on talking about her boobs, she would rather they called them boobs, which is a way-out word,..rather than breasts.

boob (buːb), *v. slang.* [cf. sense 3 of prec.] *intr.* To make a foolish mistake or blunder. Also *trans.* (see quot. 1941).

1935 T. E. LAWRENCE *Lett.* (1938) 851 The camera seems wholly in place as journalism: but when it tries to re-create it boobs. **1941** *Amer. Speech* XVI. 76/1 Slang of the R.A.F. ..*He boobed it*, he made a mess of it. **1951** 'N. SHUTE' *Round Bend* v. 132 If I boob on this one it'll mean the finish of the business.

†'**boobily**, *a. Obs.* [f. BOOBY + -LY[1].] Boobyish, booby-like.

1714 MANDEVILLE *Fab. Bees* (1725) I. 346 Raw ignorant country wenches and boobily fellows that can do, & are good for, nothing. **1740** CIBBER *Apol.* (1756) I. 115 The boobily heaviness of Lolpoop in the 'Squire of Alsatia'.

booboisie (buːbwa'ziː). *U.S. slang.* [Jocular formation f. BOOB *sb.* 2 + *-oisie*, after *bourgeoisie.*] 'Boobs' as a class.

1922 in MENCKEN *Amer. Lang.* (ed. 4, 1946) xi. 560. **1927** ST. JOHN ERVINE in *Observer* 24 Apr. 15/1, I would not for the world rob the booboisie of their entertainments. Let them have their footling stories..on the screen. **1959** J. THURBER *Years with Ross* iv. 61 Those well-known..objects of..scorn and ridicule, the booboisie. **1961** *20th Cent.* Jan. 72 They wanted to be as eccentric as they pleased..and.. could not do that among the *booboisie* of America.

boo-boo ('buːbuː). *slang* (orig. *U.S.*). [Prob. redupl. of BOOB *sb.*] = BOOB *sb.* 3.

1954 *Los Angeles Times* 17 Oct. II. 1 Defense Secretary Wilson, whose recent boo-boo..threatens to become historic. **1957** *Harper's* Aug. 51/1 The original boo-boo that started all this confusion. **1961** *Guardian* 2 Nov. 7/6 Mr Melvin Lasky, though certainly no boob..has made a booboo. **1967** 'O. MILLS' *Death enters Lists* iv. 33 My fault, I'm afraid. I've just made what the Yanks call a boo-boo.

boobook ('buːbʊk, 'buːbuːk). Also '**buckbuck**. [Imitative of the bird's note.] The name given in Australia to a medium-sized brown spotted owl, *Ninox novæ-seelandiæ boobook*; the mopoke. In full, **boobook owl**.

1801 LATHAM *Gen. Synop. Birds* Suppl. II. 64 *Boobook O[wl]*, size of the Brown Owl, and at first sight somewhat resembles it, especially on the upper parts. This inhabits New Holland, where it is known by the name of *Boobook.* **1826** *Trans. Linnean Soc.* XV. 188 The native name of this bird, as Mr. Caley informs us, is Buck'buck. **1916** J. B. COOPER *Coo-oo-ee* ii. 31 A boo-book owl calling 'Mopoke!' **1934** A. RUSSELL *Tramp-Royal* 11 The insistent 'morepork' of the boobook owl. **1936** M. FRANKLIN *All that Swagger* vii. 66 At night there were the unfailing boobooks and dingoes to augment the curlews' concert. **1968** V. SERVENTY *Wildlife Austral.* 79 The best known of Australian owls is the boobook, named after its call.

booby ('buːbɪ), *sb.*[1] Also 8 boobee, 9 boobie. [probably ad. Sp. *bobo*, used both in the sense of 'fool' and 'booby' (the bird), of doubtful origin. (The Ger. *bube*, MHG. *buobe*, is used frequently in the sense of 'fool, lubber'; but connexion with it is hardly possible: its LG. form is *boeve, boef.*)]

1. a. 'A dull, heavy, stupid fellow: a lubber' (J.); a clown, a nincompoop. Also, *spec.* a cry-baby (*dial.* or *children's colloq.*).

1599–1603 *Patient Grissil* 48 [*Welshman loq.*] Then, mage a pooby fool of Sir Owen. God's plude, shall! **1616** FLETCHER *Cust. Country* I. ii, Cry, you great booby. **1687** T. BROWN *Saints in Upr.* Wks. 1730 I. 74 Such a booby as thou art, pretend to dispute the precedence? **1711** STEELE *Spect.* No. 113 ¶3, I bowed like a great surprised Booby. **1776** JOHNSON in *Boswell* (1831) III. 352 We work with our heads, and make the boobies of Birmingham work for us with their hands. **1824** W. IRVING *T. Trav.* I. 260, I was so awkward a booby that I dared scarcely speak to her. **1891** R. P. CHOPE *Dial. Hartland, Dev.* 29 *Booby*, a big child given to crying. **1945** E. WAUGH *Brideshead Revisited* I. viii. 189 'Poor simple monk,' I thought, 'poor booby.' **1959** I. & P. OPIE *Lore & Lang. Schoolchildren* x. 186 Gloucestershire children comment: you babby, big baby,..booby, [etc.].

b. *spec.* The last boy in a school class, the dunce.

1825 LD. COCKBURN *Mem.* i. 4, I never got a single prize, and once sat boobie at the annual public examination. **1849** C. BRONTË *Shirley* III. iv. 75 He was the booby of.. grammar school.

c. *attrib.*

1728 YOUNG *Love Fame* II. (1757) 95 The booby father craves a booby son. **1748** RICHARDSON *Clarissa* xxxi. I. 205 Never was there booby squire that more wanted it [improvement]. **1818** SCOTT *Hrt. Midl.* iv, There is not a boy on the booby form but should have been scourged for such a solecism in grammar.

d. *to beat the booby*: see BEAT *v.*[1] 41.

e. Shortened f. *booby-hutch*: a lock-up or cell. *slang.*

1938 F. D. SHARPE *Sharpe of Flying Squad* 329 Booby or *Booby Hutch*, the cell.

2. A name for different species of gannet, esp. *Sula fusca.*

1634 SIR T. HERBERT *Trav.* 10 One of the Saylers espying a Bird fitly called a Booby, hee mounted to the top-mast and tooke her. The quality of which Bird is to sit still, not valuing danger. **1707** SLOANE *Jamaica* I. 31 Boobies..so called of Seamen because they do not stir from you, but suffer themselves to be catch'd by the hand. **1819** BYRON *Juan* II. lxxxii, At length they caught two boobies, and a noddy. **1860** GOSSE *Rom. Nat. Hist.* 83 The booby and the noddy sit on the bare rock in startling tameness.

3. *Comb.*, as **booby-hack** *U.S.* = *booby-hut*; **booby hatch** (*a*) (*Naut.*), a smaller kind of companion which lifts off in one piece, in use for merchantmen's half-decks; (*b*) a lock-up or gaol (*U.S. slang*); (*c*) a home for the insane (*U.S. slang*); **booby-hut**, a hooded sleigh used in New England; **booby-hutch**, a small clumsy cart or carriage used in some parts of England; see also quot. 1881; also, a lock-up or cell; a police station; **booby-prize**, a prize awarded in ridicule or fun to the player with the lowest score;

booby-trap, a kind of practical joke in vogue among schoolboys and others (see quots.); also *Mil. colloq.*, a harmless-looking object concealing an explosive charge, designed to go off if the object is disturbed; hence as *v. trans.*, to set with a booby-trap; so ***booby-trapped*** ppl. adj.

1888 *Boston Daily Globe* (Farmer), They collided with Crowley's *booby hack, knocking the horse down and demolishing the front of the vehicle. **1840** R. DANA *Bef. Mast* xxxiv. 130 The sky-light and *booby-hatch [are] put on. **1859** G. W. MATSELL *Vocabulum* 13/2 *Booby-hatch*, station-house. **1883** *Chamb. Jrnl.* 141 The after or booby-hatch was covered with a network of lashings. **1897** ADE *Pink Marsh* 3 They'd have him in the booby-hatch in about two hours. **1923** *Time* 10 Mar. 15/3 Liane,.. whose specialty is driving lover after lover to ruin, death, or the booby-hatch. **1931** G. IRWIN *Amer. Tramp & Underworld Slang* 33 *Booby Hatch*, a police station or village gaol. **1936** WODEHOUSE *Laughing Gas* xi. 111 What, tell people you're me and I'm you. Sure we could, if you don't mind being put in the booby-hatch. **1720** *Weekly Jrnl.* 4 June 1623/2 Not a Raw bon'd Jade, or a *Booby-Hutch in City and Suburbs but will be hacked out to City Apprentices. **1818** HAN. MORE *Hist. Mr. Fanton* Stories (1830) I. 10 All that multitude of coaches, chariots, chaises, vis-a-vis, booby-hutches, sulkies, etc. **1881** EVANS *Leicestersh. Gloss.* (E.D.S.), *Booby-hutch*, a hand-barrow; a small deep cart; a sentry-box; any movable 'coop' or 'hutch' of any kind intended for the use of a single human occupant. The carts drawn by dogs before the passing of Martin's Act were often so called. **1889** BARRÈRE & LELAND *Dict. Slang* I. 161/1 *Booby-hutch* (thieves), the police-station. **1938** Booby hutch [see sense 1 e]. **1889** *Puck* (U.S.) 17 July 378/1 Into infinitesimal shreds he tears A beautiful *Booby Prize. **1900** E. T. FOWLER *Farringdons* iii. 55 Your prize would have been no better than a booby-prize. **1929** G. STOWELL *Hist. Button Hill* I. 64 The incorrigible Mr. Denworthy presented as a booby-prize a small sample bottle of Worcester sauce. **1850** F. E. SMEDLEY *Frank Fairlegh* iii. 28 The construction of what he called a '*booby-trap'. **1868** *Chamb. Jrnl.*, A 'booby-trap'.. it consists.. of books, boots, etc., balanced on the top of a door, which was left ajar, so that the first incomer got a solid shower-bath. **1882** *Sat. Rev.* 4 Nov. 600 Perpetually on the alert for booby-traps. **1917** E. F. WOOD *Note-Bk. Intelligence Officer* xix. 271 'Booby' traps were sprinkled about the country in the form of bombs. **1918** P. GIBBS *From Bapaume to Passchendaele* 4 The enemy left .. 'booby-traps' to blow a man to bits or blind him for life if he touched a harmless-looking stick or opened the lid of a box. **1943** *Illustr. London News* 1 May 483 Doors and windows are easily booby-trapped. **1959** 'M. DERBY' *Tigress* iii. 130 The ugly foreground, mined and booby-trapped and ambushed.

booby ('bu:bɪ), *sb.*[2] = BUBBY[1]. *slang* (orig. *U.S.*).

1934 H. MILLER *Tropic of Cancer* 315 She was lying on the divan with her boobies in her hands. **1968** *Guardian* 2 Sept. 4/6 The characters were constantly referring to her large bosom (even descending to calling them 'big boobies').

'booby, *v. rare*[−1]. [f. BOOBY *sb.*[1]] In *to booby about*: to go about like a booby.

1807 W. IRVING *Salmag.* (1824) 53 Those brainless pert bloods.. Who lounge and who loot, and who booby about.

boobyalla (bu:bɪ'ælə). *Austral.* Also boobialla. [Native name.] **1.** The native name in Australia for the Australian wattle. **2.** Any of various shrubs or trees of the genus *Myoporum*, having clusters of small white flowers.

1835 *Hobart Town Almanack* 63 *Acacia sophora*, Sophora podded Acacia or Booby-aloe. **1843** J. BACKHOUSE *Narr. Visit to Austral. Colonies* 59 The sandbanks at the mouth of Macquarie Harbour are covered with Boobialla, a species of *Acacia*. **1861** L. A. MEREDITH *Over Straits* ii. 62 Boobyalla bushes lay within the dash of the ceaseless spray. **1934** *Antiquity* VIII. 182 Sand dunes clothed with boobyallas and other indigenous shrubs.

boobyish ('bu:bɪɪʃ), *a.* [f. BOOBY *sb.*[1] + -ISH[1].] Savouring of the booby, awkwardly silly.

1778 MISS BURNEY *Evelina* (1794) I. 185 Till the violence of this boobyish humour is abated. **1839** HALLAM *Hist. Lit.* III. III. vi. §38. 305 Awkward and boobyish among civil people, but at home in rude sports.

boobyism ('bu:bɪɪz(ə)m). [f. as prec. + -ISM.] The character or characteristic action of a booby.

1833 *Fraser's Mag.* VII. 112 The boobyisms of Bulwer. **1836** DICKENS *Sk. Boz* (1850) 72/1 To exhibit their ignorance and boobyism on the stage of a private theatre.

booc(e, obs. f. BOSS, and of BOOSE, cattle-stall.

bood, obs. pa. t. BIDE; also = *behoved*: see BUS *v.*; also var. BOUD, a weevil; obs. f. BUD.

†**boodge.** *Obs.* [App. a variant of BOUGE *sb.*[1]] A prominence from the back of the body of a carriage to carry parcels in; the 'sword-case'. Felton.

1801 FELTON *Carriages* I. 15 The sword-case, so called from its length and convenience for carrying swords or sticks, is sometimes called a boodge; the ends are made of thick boards.

boodge, obs. form of BUDGE.

Boodh, Booddha, -ism, etc.: see BUDDHA, etc.

boodie ('bu:dɪ). *Sc.* [perh. ad. Gael. *bodach* ghost. But cf. BOLLY.] A spectre, a hobgoblin.

?*a***1700** *Ballad, Baroune o' Gairtly* in Smith *Hist. Aberdeensh.* (1875) I. 650 Nae gruesome gaist, nor black boodie Cud fleg that bold Baroune. **1785** *Jrnl. fr. Lond.* 6 in *Poems Buchan Dial.* (JAM.) About the time o' night that the boodies begin to gang. **1868** G. MACDONALD *R. Falconer* I. 12 He rins as gin I war a boodie.

boodie-rat ('bu:dɪræt). *local* (S.W.) *Austral.* Also boodee, boody-rat. [Native name.] A species of rat-kangaroo. Also called boodie.

[**1863** J. GOULD *Mammals of Australia* II. 74 Hypsiprymnus (Bettongia) Lesueuri.. *Boor-dee*... The Boor-dee is exclusively a nocturnal feeder, and.. one of the most destructive animals to the garden of the settler in Western Australia.] **1910** G. C. SHORTRIDGE in *Proc. Zool. Soc. 1909* 823 Bettongia Lesueuri.. kangaroo-rats.. Boodee Rat of Colonists. 'Boodee' of natives (S.W.). **1924** D. H. LAWRENCE & SKINNER *Boy in Bush* vii. 96 Little hunts of wallabies or bandicoots or bungarras, or boody-rats. **1963** *New Scientist* 3 Jan. 12 Boodies apparently emit a series of grunts and chuckles when chased.

boodle[1] ('bu:d(ə)l). [Origin and history obscure; but the mod. U.S. *boodle*, in sense 1, must be the same as Markham's *buddle*: sense 2 (also only in U.S.) may be a different word; it suggests Du. *boedel* 'estate, possession, inheritance, stock', which it is not so easy to connect with sense 1.]

1. Crowd, pack, lot: as in the contemptuous 'the whole boodle'. Cf. CABOODLE.

1833 J. NEAL *Down-Easters* I. 61, I know a feller 'twould whip the whool boodle of 'em an' give 'em six. **1847** D. P. THOMPSON *Locke Amsden* 76 [He] stumped all the rest to come on, one at a time, and there wasn't a soul of the whole boodle that dared do it. **1858** O. W. HOLMES *Autocrat* 139 He would like to have the whole boodle of them (I remonstrated against this word, but the professor said it was a diabolish good word..) with their wives and children shipwrecked on a remote island. **1895** [see KIT *sb.*[1] 3].

2. a. Counterfeit money. *U.S. slang.*

1858 *Harper's Weekly* 3 Apr. (Th.), Boodle is a flash term used by counterfeiters... The leaders [of the gang] were the manufacturers and bankers of the boodle. **1884** *Boston (Mass.) Globe* 7 Oct., 'Sinews of war'.. 'soap' and other synonymes for campaign boodle are familiar.

b. Money acquired or spent illegally or improperly, esp. in connection with the obtaining or holding of public offices; the material means or gains of bribery and corruption; also, money in general. *slang* (orig. *U.S.*).

1883 *Judge* (U.S.) 3 Mar. 7/1 As long as the people pay, As long as there's 'boodle' to capture. **1884** *Mag. Amer. Hist.* XII. 566/2 *Boodle*.. has come to mean a large roll of bills such as political managers are supposed to divide among their retainers. **1887** *Nation* (N.Y.) 14 Apr. 307/3 New York is better known all over the.. world for boodle Aldermen and municipal rings than for anything else. **1888** *St. Louis Globe Democrat* (Farmer), She presented a draft for 2000 dols. drawn upon a Detroit bank, and received the cash. Immediately after that she left for the East with the boodle. **1892** STEVENSON & OSBOURNE *Wrecker* ix. 138 It took my fancy; it was so romantic, and then I saw there was boodle in the thing. **1917** CONAN DOYLE *His Last Bow* viii. 294 'What about the dough?' he asked... 'The boodle. The reward. The £500.' **1922** JOYCE *Ulysses* 600 Ready to decamp with whatever boodle they could.

Hence **'boodle** *v. trans.*, to bribe; *intr.*, to practise bribery; **'boodler**, one who practises boodling; **'boodling** *vbl. sb.*, bribery, bribing.

1872 G. P. BURNHAM *Mem. U.S. Secret Service* 347 He ventured to collar Wightman, knowing him.. to be grand Sachem among these 'boodlers' or confidence men. **1888** in *Amer. Speech* (1960) XXXV. 267 *Boodling*, taking money unlawfully by way of bribe or otherwise. **1894** *Congress. Rec.* Aug., App. 1229/1 What we call the government of the people.. has become a government of boodlers. **1903** *N.Y. Even. Post* 31 Aug., We fancy that the people of Missouri will conclude to diminish boodling rather by taking from than adding to the powers of the dominant machine. **1904** W. H. SMITH *Promoters* iv. 86 If you're going to boodle you've got to do it on a party basis. If I wanted to boodle an Illinois legislature, [etc.]. **1909** C. F. G. MASTERMAN *Condition of England* iv. 153 The average citizen.. is not yet convinced that its [*sc.* Socialism's] adherents will make a better job of it than the 'boodlers' and 'blood suckers'.

boodle[2] ('bu:d(ə)l). *slang.* A stupid noodle.

1862 KINGSLEY in *Macm. Mag.* Dec. 96 A good many people.. have seen all the world, and yet remain little better than blokes and boodles after all.

boodle[3], var. of BUDDLE, corn-marigold.

boody ('bu:dɪ), *v. rare.* [app. ad. F. *bouder* to pout, sulk.] *intr.* To sulk, mope, be sullen.

1857 TROLLOPE *Barchester T.* xxvii, Don't boody with me; don't be angry because I speak out some home truths. **1877** —— *Prime Min.* lxxvi. (D.) Left to boody over everything by himself, till he becomes a sort of political hermit.

booget, obs. form of BUDGET *sb.*

boogie[1] ('bu:gɪ). *U.S. slang.* [Perh. alteration of BOGY.] A derogatory term for a Negro.

1923 *Confessions of Bank Burglar* vii. 40 Three coons came into the barn.. the three of them took a drink and then put the bottle in the hay... At noon the 'boogies' came in for another shot. **1925** *Flynn's* 1 Aug. 572/1 One of the cops.. caught two boogies. We picked up the two hard-lookin' young negroes. *Ibid.*, The boogie jus' got up and grinned. **1937** HEMINGWAY *To have & have Not* III. xiv. 205, I seen that big boogie there mopping it up.

boogie ('bu:gɪ), *sb.*[2] orig. *U.S.* [Origin uncertain.] **a.** A party, *esp.* a rent party.

1917 (*jazz-music title*) Boogie rag. **1929** in B. Rust *Jazz Records 1897–1942* (1978) 516 We're gonna pitch a boogie right here. **1960** P. OLIVER *Blues fell this Morning* 163 He re-christened the [boogie-woogie] style after the 'boogies' or parties on the South Side. **1976** G. OAKLEY *Devil's Music* 163 When rent day was due, you 'pitched a boogie', inviting the neighbours round and charging an entrance fee of perhaps a quarter and a jug of gin.

b. A style of blues (orig. piano) music popular at rent parties; = BOOGIE-WOOGIE. The term was adopted by rock groups in the late 1960s for music whose rhythm derived from repeated sequences of blues chords played on guitars. Also *occas.* dancing to this music.

1941 *Brunswick Records Catal.* 6 (*title*) Scrub me, Mama with a Boogie Beat. **1956** G. P. KURATH in A. Dundes *Mother Wit* (1973) 107/1 Jitterbugging.. during the Boogie-Woogie musical period.. was known as Boogie. **1960** *20th Cent.* Dec. 560 Negro boogie pianists. **1976** *Gramophone* Sept. 493/1 Among the newer exponents of southern white 'boogie'.. the Amazing Rhythm Aces and the Atlantic Rhythm Section stand out. **1983** W. MELLERS *Beethoven & Voice of God* II. iv. 261 The syncopated chords hold the breath against the upward-thrusting and downward-quivering arpeggios, which incorporate acridly sharp leading notes into their boogie rhythm.

boogie ('bu:gɪ), *v.* orig. *U.S.* [f. BOOGIE *sb.*[2]] *intr.* To dance to boogie-woogie music.

Pres. pple. *boogieing, boogeying.*

1955 BROONZY & BRUYNOGHE *Big Bill Blues* 30 Oh let's boogie, children, because Joe Turner's sure good to us. **1974** *Time* 24 June 83 They are up on the seats boogieing and running around the hall. **1978** *Daily Mirror* 12 Jan. 1/2 Night after night she flirts and boogies the hours away. **1980** D. NORDEN in Muir & Norden *Oh, my Word!* 113 Frank was now boogeying with a neighbour. **1985** S. BOOTH *True Adventures Rolling Stones* xvi. 150 There was no feeling of violence, only the desire to get close and boogie.

boogie-woogie ('bu:gɪ'wu:gɪ). orig. *U.S.* [Redupl. f. BOOGIE *sb.*[2].] A style of playing blues (usu. on the piano) marked by a persistent bass rhythm.

1928 (*title*) Pinetop's Boogie Woogie. **1935** *Swing Music* Aug. 153 This side [of the record] might be an instruction disc in Swedish Drill.. only it's a lesson in Boogie Woogie. **1938** *Manchester Guardian Wkly.* 2 Sept. 188/3 Sometimes they play 'boogie-woogie' (on the heavy brass instruments). **1940** *Time* 4 Mar. 48/2 Boogie-woogie is a kind of blues piano playing in which the left hand drones a set bass phrase over and over, while the right hand goes to town with whatever variations the player can think up. **1941** *N.Y. Times* x. 7/3 The twelve-bar structure which is the basis of almost all boogie-woogie music is also one of the mainstays of hot jazz as a whole. **1950** S. MORTON *Unfamiliar Name* v. 76 They wanted the jive and boogie-woogie boys. **1966** *Crescendo* Nov. 14/3 I'd listen to a lot of boogie woogie records and copy them off by ear. This led to me making up my own boogie woogies.

boohoo (bu:'hu:), *int.* and *sb.* A word imitative of the sound of noisy weeping or laughter; also an expression of contempt (*Sc.*).

c **1525** SKELTON *Replyc.* 75 Wytlesse wandring to and fro! With, Te he, ta ha, bo ho, bo ho! **1850** THACKERAY *Pendennis* II. 148 Warrington fairly burst out into a boo-hoo of laughter. **1808–79** JAMIESON *Roxb.*, I wouldna gi' a boo-hoo for you. **1884** *Graphic* 11 Oct. 387/2 Shrill and dolorous boo-hoo's.

boo'hoo, *v.* Also bohoo. [f. prec.] *intr.* **a.** To weep noisily; **b.** to bellow, roar, shout, hoot.

1837–40 HALIBURTON *Clockm.* (1862) 49 The wenches they fell to a cryin, wringin their hands, and boo-hooin like mad. **1884** *Punch* 1 Nov. 216/1 Irish Members boo-hoo.. and use shillelaghs. **1884** *Harper's Mag.* Oct. 697/1, I.. boo-hooed like a baby.

booit, dial. f. of BOWET, lantern.

boojery, var. BUDGEREE *a.*

boojum ('bu:dʒəm). [Invented by 'Lewis Carroll' (C. L. Dodgson) in *The Hunting of the Snark* (1876).] An imaginary animal, a particularly dangerous kind of 'snark'.

1904 B'NESS VON HUTTEN *Pam* III. vi. 146 We shall see a good deal of each other. I am a boojum, and I know. **1922** *Edin. Rev.* Oct. 241 Both these beautiful abstractions are in reality boojums. **1925** *Blackw. Mag.* Mar. 345/1 A solitary Boojum-like person. **1950** AUDEN *Enchafèd Flood* (1951) i. 42 The dreadful Boojum of Nothingness.

book (bʊk), *sb.* Forms: 1 bóc, booc, 2–4 boc, 3–5 bok, 4–6 boke, 4–7 booke, 4– book; (also 4–6 bock, 7 boock; *north.* 4 buk, 4–8 buke, *Sc.* 6–8 buick, 6– buik). Pl. books; in 1 béc, béc. [A com. Teut. word, differing however in gender and other points in the various langs. With OE. *bóc* monosyllabic fem. (pl. *béc*) cf. OFris. and OS. *bôk* (pl. *bôk*) fem. and neut. (MDu. *boek* neut. and often masc., Du. *boek* masc.), OHG. *buoh* (pl. *buoh*) neut., also masc. and fem. (MHG. *buoch*, mod.G. *buch* neut.), ON. *bók* (pl. *bœkr*) fem. (Sw. *bok*, Da. *bog*), all in sense of 'written document, book'. These forms indicate an OTeut. **bôk-s* str. fem., the plural of which was

in OHG. and elsewhere sometimes made neuter (after the analogy of neuter monosyllabic plurals), and this gender extended to the sing. The original meaning was evidently 'writing-tablet, leaf, or sheet': cf. Venantius Fortunatus *Carm.* vii. 18, 19 'barbara fraxineis pingatur runa tabellis', also OS. *thia bôk* the writing-tablet, '*pugillaris*' Luke i. 63 (in *Heliand* 232, 235), OE. *bóc* charter: in pl. tablets, written sheets, hence 'book,' a sense subseq. extended to the singular. Gothic does not show ***bôks***, but an apparently derivative form *bôka* str. fem., in sense of 'letter' of the alphabet, pl. *bôkôs litteræ*, *γράμματα*, writing, document, book.

Generally thought to be etymologically connected with the name of the beech-tree, OE. *bóc*, *béce*, ON. *bók*:—(see BEECH), the suggestion being that inscriptions were first made on beechen tablets, or cut in the bark of beechtrees; but there are great difficulties in reconciling the early forms of the two words, seeing that *bôk-s* 'writing-tablet' is the most primitive of all.]

I. †**1.** A writing; a written document; *esp.* a charter or deed by which land (hence called *bócland*) was conveyed. *Obs.*

872-915 in Thorpe *Diplomat.* 168 (Bosw.) Ic him sealde ðæt lond on ece erfe and ða bec. **886-899** *Ibid.* 137 Heo cyðaþ on ðisse bec. **938** *Ibid.* 187 Ðis is seo boc ðe Æðelstan cing ȝebocode. *c* **1000** *Ags. Gosp.* Matt. v. 31 Swa hwylc swa his wif forlæt, he sylle hyre hyra hiwȝedales boc [*Rushw.* bec]. **1382** WYCLIF *Isa.* l. 1 What is this boc of forsaking of ȝoure moder. **1417** *E.E. Wills* (1882) 27 Excepte ham þat I haue ynemned in þis bok to-for. **1483** *Cath. Angl.* 36 A Boke, *carta, cartula, codex, codicillus, liber, libellus*, etc. **1553** EDW. VI. *Will* in Strype *Eccl. Mem.* II. II. xxii. 431 All such as have paid their monies upon any bargain for lands, to have their books and bargains performed. **1596** SHAKS. *1 Hen. IV*, III. i. 224 By that time will our Booke, I thinke, be drawne. **1611** BIBLE *Jer.* xxxii. 12 The witnesses, that subscribed the booke [**1885** *R.V.* deed] of the purchase. [**1818** HALLAM *Mid. Ages* (1872) II. 294 Might be conveyed by boc or written grant. **1876** DIGBY *Real Prop.* i. 12 The grants were effected by the king..by means usually of a 'book' or charter.]

†**2.** A (written) narrative or account, record, list, register. *Obs.* (In the Bible only a following of Greek and Latin precedents, in their rendering by *βίβλος*, *liber*, the Heb. *sēpher*, *kᵉthāb* 'writing, written account'.)

a **1000** ÆLFRIC *Gen.* v. 1 Ðis is seo boc Adames mæȝrace. **1535** COVERDALE *Matt.* i. 1 The boke of the generacion of Jesus Christ. **1582-8** *Hist. James VI.* (1804) 123 The clerks and writters to the Lords of Sessioun compellit to rander the buicks of parliament unto thame. **1611** BIBLE *Gen.* v. 1 This is the booke of the generations of Adam. **1681** BURNET *Hist. Ref.* II. 14 He intended to create some new peers; and ordered him to write a book of such as he thought meetest.

3. *gen.* A written or printed treatise or series of treatises, occupying several sheets of paper or other substance fastened together so as to compose a material whole.

In this wide sense, referring to all ages and countries, a *book* comprehends a treatise written on any material (skin, parchment, papyrus, paper, cotton, silk, palm leaves, bark, tablets of wood, ivory, slate, metal, etc.), put together in any portable form, e.g. that of a long roll, or of separate leaves, hinged, strung, stitched, or pasted together.

a. *spec.* (In reference to modern things.) Such a treatise occupying numerous sheets or leaves fastened together at one edge called the *back*, so as to be opened at any particular place, the whole being protected by binding or covers of some kind. But, since either the form of the book or its subject may be mainly or exclusively the object of attention, this passes on either side into

b. The material article so made up, without regard to the nature of its contents, even though its pages are occupied otherwise than with writing or printing, or are entirely blank (cf. 10): e.g. 'a handsome book', i.e. a trophy of the binder's art, 'a tiny book,' one that may be put in the waistcoat pocket.

c. A literary composition such as would occupy one or more volumes, without regard to the material form or forms in which it actually exists; 'an intellectual composition, in prose or verse, at least of sufficient extent to make one volume' (Littré s.v. *livre*). In this sense Carlyle described himself as 'a writer of books'.

It is not now usual to call a (modern) literary composition in manuscript a 'book', unless we think of its printing as a thing to follow in due course. In sense b every volume is a 'book'; whilst in sense c one 'book' may occupy several volumes; and on the other hand one large volume may contain several 'books,' i.e. literary works originally published as distinct books. No absolute definition of a 'book' in this sense can be given: in general, a short literary composition (especially if ephemeral in character, and therefore also in form) receives some other name, as *tract*, *pamphlet*, *sketch*, *essay*, etc.

c **897** K. ÆLFRED *Gregory's Past.* inscr. on Hatton MS., Ðeos boc sceal to Wioȝora ceastre. *Ibid.* (Sweet) 8 Ond ic bibiode..þæt nan mon ðone æstel from þære bec ne doe, ne þa boc from þæm mynstre. *c* **1000** *Ags. Gosp.* John xxi. 25 Ealle þa bec. *c* **1175** *Lamb. Hom.* 101 Swa swa us seggeð bec. *c* **1205** LAY. 7263 For mine bæc [*c* **1275** bokes] hit me suggeð. *a* **1300** *Cursor M.* 1470 Enoch..was þe first þat letters fand And wrot sum bokes wit his hand. *a* **1340** HAMPOLE *Pr. Consc.* 348 Þis buk..I seuen partis divised es. **1377** LANGL. *P. Pl.* B. XI. 135 Baw for bokes! *c* **1425** WYNTOUN *Cron.* v. xii. 278 Sum man may fall þis Buk to rede. **1513** MORE *Edw. V.* (1641) Ded., There comming..into my hand a booke long since printed. **1519** HORMAN *Vulg.* 84 A volume is lesse than a boke, and a boke lesse than a coucher [L. *codice*]. **1534** LD. BERNERS *Gold. Bk. M. Aurel.* (1546) B iv b, I wyll intitle this boke the Golden boke. **1558** *Act 1 Eliz.* ii, Set forth in one book entituled, The Booke of Common-prayer. **1600** *Register Stationers' Co.* 4 Aug., As you Like yt, a booke. **1611** BIBLE *Jer.* xxxvi. 2 Take thee a roule of a booke, and write therein. **1637** *Decree Star Chamb.* in *Milton's Areop.* (Arb.) 9 Seditious, scismaticall, or offensive Bookes or Pamphlets. *a* **1649** DRUMM. OF HAWTH. *Biblioth. Edinb. Lect.* Wks. (1711) 222 Books have that strange quality, that, being of the frailest and tenderest matter, they out-last brass, iron, and marble. **1710** *Act 8 Anne* in *Lond. Gaz.* No. 4686/3 Nine Copies of each Book..that from..the 10th of April, 1710, shall be printed..or re-printed with Additions, shall by the Printers thereof be delivered to the Warehouse-keeper of the..Company of Stationers. **1743** TINDAL tr. *Rapin's Hist. Eng.* II. XVII. 118 Books, as well printed as in Manuscript. **1865** RUSKIN *Sesame* 19 A book is essentially not a talked thing, but a written thing; and written, not with the view of mere communication, but of permanence. **1876** GREEN *Short Hist.* viii. §1 (1882) 447 England became the people of a book, and that book was the Bible. **1884** J. A. H. MURRAY in *13th Addr. Philol. Soc.* 22. I do not know what a book is..Was Shakspere the author of one book or of forty-four books? **1886** *Boston Literary World* 1 May 150/1 The first matter was to settle the seemingly easy but really difficult question, What is a book? This they solved by defining it as 'a literary work substantial in amount and homogeneous in character'.

fig. **1592** SHAKS. *Rom. & Jul.* I. iii. 87 This precious Booke of Loue, this vnbound Louer. **1595** —— *John* II. 485 This booke of beautie. **1847** TENNYSON *Princ.* v. 136 Not ever would she love; but brooding turn The book of scorn.

d. *transf.* Of things composed of 'leaves' or 'plates'.

1840 R. H. DANA *Bef. Mast* (1841) xxix. 85/1 A large 'book' was made of some twenty-five to fifty hides, doubled at the backs, and put into one another, like the leaves of a book. **1859** C. TOMLINSON *Illustr. Useful Arts* 21 *(caption)* Book of Silk from China. **1885** J. S. KINGSLEY in *Q. Jrnl. Microsc. Sci.* Oct. 538 The primary stigma formed by the insinking of the respiratory book is not the functional one of the adult. **1892** *Photogr. Ann.* II. 327 To put the book in camera, the camera is tilted front up. *Ibid.* 328 The book of plate-holders. **1910** *Sessions' Paper* 17 Nov. 21, I..pulled out my cigarette book to make a cigarette. **1937** *Popular Sci.* Nov. 68/2 *(caption)* Match Books Get Foolproof Cover. **1962** J. BRAINE *Life at Top* v. 88 One of the books of matches I'd taken away from the Savoy.

e. An angler's pocket-book for fishing-tackle.

1824 *Sporting Mag.* XV. N.S. 147/1 The fisherman, who has got a book full of good ready-made flies. **1847** STODDART *Angler's Comp.* 61 Angler's trouting book.

f. A magazine. Now *colloq.* and *vulg.*

1800 H. MORE *Let.* 11 Sept. (1925) 177 The Anti-Jacobin Magazine, which is spreading more mischief over the land than almost any other book. **1873** *Young Englishwoman* Aug. 416/2 She has taken in *The Young Englishwoman* for four years, and thinks it is the best of books for young ladies. **1937** A. THIRKELL *Summer Half* ix. 254 Rose was reduced to reading a book, by which..she meant an illustrated weekly. **1942** A. P. JEPHCOTT *Girls Growing Up* v. 98 With..working-class girls, you can create a common interest..by offering..some 'girls' books'. These ' books' are what one would ordinarily call papers or magazines. **1959** I. & P. OPIE *Lore & Lang. Schoolchildren* ix. 161 A good 'book' (i.e. a magazine) is said to be 'smashin''.

4. *fig.* **a.** That in which we may read, and find instruction or lessons.

c **1449** PECOCK *Repr.* I. v. 25 The book of mannis soule. **1532** MORE *Confut. Tindale* Wks. 408/2 To call the ymages of holye payntes..and the figure of Chrystes crosse, the boke of his bitter passion. **1600** SHAKS. *A.Y.L.* II. i. 16 And this our life..Findes tongues in trees, bookes in the running brookes, Sermons in stones. **1605** BACON *Adv. Learn.* I. vi. 16 Laying before us two Books or Volumes to study if we will be secured from error; first the scriptures, revealing the will of God, and then the creatures expressing his power. **1667** MILTON *P.L.* III. 47 For the Book of knowledg fair Presented with a Universal blanc. **1815** SCOTT *Guy M.* xix. **1830** J. G. STRUTT *Sylva Brit.* 2 That great poet to whom the book of Nature and of the human heart seemed alike laid open. **1876** HAMERTON *Intell. Life* x. 371 The infinite book of the world, and life.

b. An example taken as = book of precepts.

c **1380** WYCLIF *Wks.* (1880) 61 Þe lif of prelatis is bok & ensaumple of sugetis. *Ibid.* 92 Þei techen to þe comunes bi here owen wickid lif þat is a bok to here sugetis.

c. (with allusive reference to various real or reputed books, records, etc., and in uses suggested by these.)

1593 SHAKS. *Rich. II*, IV. i. 236 Mark'd with a Blot, damn'd in the Booke of Heauen. —— *2 Hen. VI*, I. i. 100 Blotting your names from Bookes of Memory. **1597** —— *2 Hen. IV*, III. i. 45 Oh Heauen, that one might read the Book of Fate. **1611** —— *Wint. T.* IV. iii. 131 My name put in the booke of Vertue. **1732** POPE *Ess. Man* I. 77 Heav'n from all creatures hides the book of fate.

5. Elliptically or contextually:

a. The Bible, sometimes as the 'divine book' or 'book of books'; frequently with reference to its use in the administration of oaths.

[*c* **1200** *Trin. Coll. Hom.* 11 We radeð on boc þet elch man haueð to fere on engel of heuene. *c* **1250** *Passion Our Lord* 131 in *OE. Misc.* 41 Hit is write in þe bok.] **1297** R. GLOUC. 472 Suerie vpe the bok. *a* **1300** *Cursor M.* 2042 A mantil..he toke, And ȝede bacward, als sais þe bock. **1389** in *Eng. Gilds* (1870) 3 Eche of hem had sworen on þe bok to perfourme þe pointz. *c* **1430** LYDG. *Bochas* II. vii. (1554) 49 a, A sonne he had..Called Abia, the boke doth specifie. *c* **1450** *Why I can't be a Nun* 20 in *E.E.P.* (1862) 138 On a boke I dare well swere In gode feythe and on womanhode. **1598** SHAKS. *Merry W.* I. iv. 156 Ile be sworne on a booke shee loues you. **1678** *Trials of Ireland, &c.* 3 Clerk of Crown..'Sir Philip Matthews to the Book'. **1821** CLARE *Vill. Minstr.* I. 175 As the day closes on its peace and rest, The godly man sits down and takes 'the book.' **1860** W. M. THOMSON *(title)* The Land and the Book. **1864** TENNYSON *En. Ard.* 843 'Swear', added Enoch sternly, 'on the book', And on the book, half-frighted, Miriam swore.

†**b.** The Book of Common Prayer; also the Mass-book, in the phrase ***by bell, book, and candle*** see BELL *sb.*¹ 8. *Obs.*

c **1340** *Cursor M.* 25038 (Fairf.) Pilate..be-takenis feinde of helle, cursed he is wiþ boke and belle. **1556** *Chron. Gr. Friars* (1852) 27 Sir Edmonde de la Poole was pronuncyd acursed opynly wyth boke, belle, and candell, at Powlles crose at the sermonde before none [1502]. **1588** *Marprel. Epist.* (Arb.) 41 Whosoeuer will or haue subscribed vnto the booke and Articles.

c. *Law. pl.* The Year Books; any books reputed of authority in the law of England.

1628 COKE *On Litt.* 1 b, So we commonly say it is holden in our bookes. **1826** KENT *Comm.* I. 476 It will be a bad example to the barristers and students at law, and they will not give any credit to the books or have any faith in them. **1886** SIR N. LINDLEY *Law Rep. 32 Chanc. Div.* 29 There are other cases in the books illustrating the same principle.

d. A telephone directory.

1925 A. CHRISTIE *Secret of Chimneys* iv. 30 You might ring up a number for me now. Look it up in the book. **1960** K. AMIS *Take a Girl* vi. 87 Let's just hypothesise that I give you a ring, shall we? You're in the book, eh?

†**6.** 'Benefit of clergy': from the fact that a person claiming this had to read from a book handed to him, to show his scholarship. *Obs.*

1601 YARINGTON *Two Lament. Traj.* IV. ix. in Bullen *O. Pl.* IV, Williams and Rachell likewise are convict For their concealment; Williams craves his Booke And so receives a brond of infamie. *a* **1626** BACON *Max. & Uses Com. Law* (1635) 17 Some prisoners have their bookes, and be burned in the hand and so delivered..This having their bookes is called their clergy. **1643** HERLE *Answ. Ferne* 5 Flat blasphemy without booke. **1710** *Lond. Gaz.* No. 4739/1 An Act for taking away the Benefit of Clergy in certain Cases, and for taking away the Book in all Cases.

†**7.** Book-learning, scholarship, study, lessons, reading. In later use only *pl.* and passing into 3 c.

1297 R. GLOUC. 420 Vor þat he ȝongost was, to boc hys fader hym drou, þat he was..god clerc ynou. **1377** LANGL. *P. Pl.* B. XII. 187 Wel may þe barne blisse þat hym to boke sette. **1598** SHAKS. *Merry W.* IV. i. 15 My sonne profits nothing in the world at his Booke. **1680** P. HENRY *Diaries & Lett.* (1882) 282 Children at Book again, under Mr. Sam. Lewis. **1767** FORDYCE *Serm. Yng. Wom.* II. viii. 7 An early love of books prevented this languor. **1864** TENNYSON *Aylmer's F.* 460 His rushings to and fro, After his books, to flush his blood with air.

8. A main subdivision of a large treatise; being such as either (*a*) originally constituted a complete treatise of itself, or (*b*) occupied a separate roll or volume, when the whole treatise was for convenience written on several.

a. Each of the separate documents collected in the Sacred Scriptures, as the *Book of Genesis*, *Book of Psalms*.

c **1200** ORMIN 5810 Þatt writenn..Goddspell o fowwre bokess. *c* **1250** *Gen. & Ex.* 2522 Ðe boc ðe is hoten genesis. **1533** FRITH *Answ. More* (1829) 156 Let it [the Church] read these two books..(Sapience & Ecclesiasticus) unto the edifying of the people. **1599** SHAKS. *Hen. V*, I. ii. 98 In the Booke of Numbers is it writ. **1782** PRIESTLEY *Corrupt. Chr.* I. Pref. 23, I have almost always quoted the Book, & Chapter. **1863** STANLEY *Jew. Ch.* Introd. 33 The Books of Moses, Joshua, and Samuel.

b. A main division of the subject-matter of a prose treatise, or of a poem; now usually in prose only when further subdivided into chapters, or portions otherwise distinguished; but formerly used freely, where *chapter* would now be used. So Gr. *βιβλίον* little book, L. *liber*; as in the nine books of Herodotus, the twelve books of Vergil's *Æneid*.

a **1225** *Ancr. R.* Pref. 23 This an Boc is todealet in eahte lesse Boke. **1526** *Pilgr. Perf.* (W. de W. 1531) 1 This treatyse..is distincte and diuyded in to thre bokes, in the honour of the Trinite. **1555** EDEN *Decades W. Ind.* (Arb.) 278 To wryte particularly..of these regions it wolde requyre rather a hole volume then a booke. **1593** HOOKER *Eccl. Pol.* Pref. viii. §2 The last book of this treatise. **1635** J. BABINGTON *Geometry* 36 By the thirteenth of the sixth booke of Euclide. **1713** STEELE *Englishm.* No. 29. 186 The Poem consists of Three Books. **1818** BYRON *Juan* I. cc, My poem..is meant to be Divided in twelve books. **1866** *Reader* 2 June 545 We find the twenty books (or chapters as we should now call them) relate to the following subjects.

9. a. The copy of words to which music is set; the libretto of an opera, oratorio, etc.

1768 STERNE *Sent. Journ.* I. 180 A small pamphlet, it might be the book of the opera. **1882** *Daily News* 18 July 2/2 Tuneful gems of a work which deserved a stronger book.

b. The script of a play.

1598 FLORIO *Worlde of Wordes* 51/3 Buriasso,..a prompter, or one that keepes the book for plaiers. **1879** D. K. T. RANOUS *Diary* 5 Sept. in *Diary of Daly Déb.* (1910) 6 Old Mr. Moore held the book of the play, and the actors moved slowly about the stage with manuscript copies of their *rôles* in their hands. **1895** G. B. SHAW in *Sat. Rev.* 2 Feb. 151/2 The play was..pulled to pieces in order that some bad scenery..might destroy all the illusion which the simple stage directions in the book create. **1923** T. E. LAWRENCE *Lett.* (1938) 442 Your people has no technique, no arts and graces, to put between their 'book' and us. **1933** P. GODFREY *Back-Stage* vi. 82 By the time that the

principals are rehearsing regularly again the company are working without their books.

c. The repertoire or sheet music of an orchestra or musician.

1939 *New Republic* 17 May 47 If the road man wanted to pack Ziggy's book half an hour before the show broke he would say yeah, yeah, yeah. **1958** *New Statesman* 23 Aug. 221/1 There he could learn..how to handle a large 'book' (repertoire) and difficult arrangements.

10. A number of sheets of blank writing-paper bound together to form a volume in which to keep records of commercial transactions, minutes of meetings, etc. Also a volume containing such records. ***a merchant's books***: his account-books. Hence with numerous qualifications: as *bill-*, *cash-*, *day-*, *exercise-*, *minute-*, *note-book*, etc.; see BILL, CASH, DAY, etc.

1498–9 *Old City Acc. Bk.* (*Archæol. Jrnl.* XLIII.) Itm pd to Ric Magson for entryng of the Juells and goods belongyng to the Crafte into this Boke viijd. **1557** *Order of Hospitalls* F iv b, You shall kepe.. the Booke of Children, Which booke shall contayne th' admission of any childe into this Howse. **1580** BARET *Alv.* B 923 A reckening booke, *codex accepti & expensi*. **1605** SHAKS. *Lear* III. iv. 101 Keepe..thy pen from Lenders Bookes. *a* **1612** SIR T. BODLEY in D'Israeli *Cur. Lit.* (1866) 254 Let all these riches be treasured up..in good writings and books of account. **1639** CADE *Serm. for these Times* 60 He keeps his books evenest.. that every night books all his receits and expenses. **1690** W. WALKER *Idiomat. Anglo-Lat.* 65 He was hughly in your books. **1753** *Scots Mag.* Apr. 165/1 To cause their books to be balanced. **1802** MAR. EDGEWORTH *Moral T.* (1816) I. xix. 154 If you received the note from us, it must be entered in our books. **1881** MORLEY *Cobden.* I. 117 The books show that the nett profits of the firm had exceeded £23,000 for the year.

b. *fig.* (= *note-book.*)

1382 WYCLIF *Ps.* cxxxviii [ix]. 16 In thi boc alle shul be writen. **1611** *Ibid.* In thy booke all my members were written..when as yet there was none of them. **1786** BURNS *Invent.* 71 Sae dinna put me in your buke.

c. *West Africa.* (See quots.)

1863 *Fraser's Mag.* LXVII. 146/1 It was resolved..to renew his 'book'. **1897** M. KINGSLEY *W. Africa* x. 203 In order to..simplify this goods traffic, a written piece of paper is employed—practically a cheque, which is called a 'bou' or 'book' and these 'bous' are cashed—i.e. gooded, at the store. *Ibid.* xii. 286, I would give the creditor a book on Hatton and Cookson for the coat.

d. The total of charges that can be made against an accused person. Phr. ***to throw the book at*** (a person): to accuse of all the possible crimes; to award the maximum penalty. So ***to get*** or ***do the book*** (*U.S. slang*), to suffer the maximum penalty.

[**1926** G. H. MAINES *Wise-Crack Dict.* 5/2 *Book*, crook's term for a stretch of life in the penitentiary.] **1928** R. J. TASKER *Grimhaven* (1929) i. 11 I'm doing one life jolt, and two one-to-fiftys..—yes sir, doing the book. **1932** *Flynn's* 6 Feb. 125/1 The prosecuting attorney..determined to try to get the trial judge to 'throw the book' at him, (which means give him the limit). **1961** J. HELLER *Catch-22* (1962) viii. 74 He was formally charged with 'breaking ranks while in formation, felonious assault, indiscriminate behaviour, mopery, high treason, provoking, being a smart guy, listening to classical music, and so on'. In short, they threw the book at him. **1962** 'B. GRAEME' *Undetective* iv. 45 They'll dig out some old act that hasn't been repealed..and then they'll throw the book at him.

11. *Betting.* **a.** A betting-book; a record of a number of bets made with different people, generally kept in a memorandum book.

1812 *Sporting Mag.* XL. 70/1 This is the exact statement of my bets, as my book left with Mr. Smith, Clerk of the Subscription-Betting-Room, at Tattersall's, for the inspection of the public, will prove. **1836** DISRAELI *Henrietta Temple* III. xv. 196 Go and take all the odds you can get upon Goshawk. Come, now, tomorrow you will tell me you have a very pretty book. **1856** LEVER *Martins of Cro' M.* 490 You haven't skill enough to make what is called a 'good book', and you'll always be a sufferer. **1843** —— *J. Hinton* xviii. 125, I have gone on adding wager to wager, until at last I find myself with a book of some eight hundred pounds.

b. = BOOK-MAKER 3 (cf. BOOKIE[2]). *Austral.* and *N.Z. colloq.*

1900 J. SCOTT *Tales Colonial Turf* 134 If the 'books' did not see the horse was doing good work, they would not bite. **1915** C. J. DENNIS *Songs Sentim. Bloke* (1916) 118 *Book*, a bookie.

12. *Whist.* The first six tricks taken by either party.

13. A packet of gold-leaf, containing 25 leaves, which are put up between leaves of soft paper.

II. Phrases.

14. ***Book of the Dead*** [tr. G. *totenbuch*], in *Egyptology* (see quot. 1906); ***book of the*** (or ***a***) ***film***: the reproduction in book form of the script or story of a cinema film; also, the book upon which a film is based; ***Book of God***: God's book, the Bible; ***book of lading*** (see quot.); ***book of life*** (†***livers, the living***): in biblical language the record of the names of those who shall inherit eternal life (cf. *Phil.* iv. 3: *Rev.* xx. 12); ***book of the month***: a book chosen as the most outstanding during a particular month; also as *attrib. phr.*; ***book of rates*** (see quot.); ***book of reference***: a book referred to for information, rather than read continuously; ***book of (the) words***: (*a*) libretto of an opera, etc. (cf. 9); (*b*) *colloq.*, any written or printed record or set of rules; also in extended uses.

971 *Blickl. Hom.* 21 Hwæt awriten is on Godes bocum. *a* **1300** *E.E. Psalter* lxviii[ix]. 28 Of boke of livand be þai done awai. *a* **1340** HAMPOLE *Psalter* cxlvi. 4 All þaire namys ere writen in þe boke of life. **1382** WYCLIF *Ps.* lxviii[ix]. 28 Fro the boc of lyueres. **1548** LATIMER *Ploughers* (1868) 17 All thinges that are written in Goddes boke. **1611** BIBLE *Rev.* iii. 5, I will not blot out his name out of the booke of life. **1651** *Proc. Parliament* No. 119. 1850 According to the price of corn, and Book of Rates. **1809** R. LANGFORD *Introd. Trade* 130 *Book of lading*, book kept by the master of a vessel, containing particulars of the cargo. *Ibid.* *Book of rates*, books specifying the customary duties on all goods payable at the Custom-House. **1837** LOCKHART *Scott* (1839) VII. 407 Shelves filled with books of reference. **1853** L. & J. B. HORNER tr. *Lepsius's Introd. Chronol. Egyptians* 392, I can as little agree with the opinion that the great Book of the Dead of the Egyptians was one of the ten books of the Stolistes. **1885** G. B. SHAW *How to become Musical Critic* (1960) 108 A gentleman who carries a bundle of white pamphlets, and cries incessantly 'Book of the words! Program! Book of the words!' **1906** J. H. BREASTED *Hist. Egypt* xiii. 249 The magical formulæ by which the dead are to triumph in the hereafter become more and more numerous, so that it is no longer possible to record them on the inside of the coffin, but they must be written on papyrus and the roll placed in the tomb. As the selection of the most important of these texts came to be more and more uniform, the 'Book of the Dead' began to take form. **1929** J. B. PRIESTLEY *Good Companions* II. ii. 288 Don't say these things. Think 'em but don't put 'em in the book of words. **1929** H. G. WELLS *King who was King* (*sub-title*) The Book of a Film. **1930** E. GEORGE *Down Our Street* 1, There was nothink ag'inst me, but I was known to frequent bad comp'ny. That's 'ow they put it in the book of words. *a* **1932** in Q. D. Leavis *Fiction & Reading Public* I. i. 16 The filmgoer wishes also to read the book of the film, and the reader to see the picture. **1933** F. R. LEAVIS & THOMPSON *Culture & Environment* 42 The Committee select their 'books of the month'. **1940** GRAVES & HODGE *Long Weekend* iv. 52 The mezzo-brow 'Book of the Month' choice of the dailies. **1946** WODEHOUSE *Money in Bank* iii. 28 There's nothing in the book of the words to prevent Mrs. Cork having the bozo..stowed away in the cooler, if he's a thief. **1947** *Horizon* XVI. Oct. 4 Book-of-the-month clubs. **1955** *Times Lit. Suppl.* 23 Sept. 560/3 Those who would give us the great classics of Greece and Rome in the 'rude language' shorn of all 'superflue' of some rewritten book-of-the-film.

15. ***by (the) book***: formally, in set phrase; also, according to the rules; ***in a person's (good) books***: in favour with him, in his good opinion; ***in a person's bad books, out of a person's books***: in disfavour with him (see also BLACK BOOK 4 b); ***in*** (one's) ***book***: in the opinion of, according to the judgement of (a person); †***out of one's book***: out of one's reckoning, mistaken; ***in the book(s)***, recorded, in existence (*colloq.*); ***without (†one's) book***: without authority; also *lit.* without the aid of a book, from memory, by rote; ***like a book***: see LIKE *adv.*

1509 *Parl. Deuylles* xlvii, He is out of our bokes, and we out of his. **1549** LATIMER *Serm. bef. Edw. VI.* (Arb.) 68 If you folowe theym, you are oute of youre boke. *a* **1569** KINGESMYLL *Man's Est.* xii. (1580) 88 Sainct Paule.. speaketh not without booke, but of experience. **1592** SHAKS. *Rom. & Jul.* I. v. 112 You kisse by th' booke. **1601** —— *Twel. N.* I. iii. 28 He..speaks three or four languages word for word without booke. **1615** W. HULL *Mirr. Maiestie* 24 But, in so saying, he spake without his booke. *a* **1624** BP. M. SMYTH *Serm.* (1632) 4 Why he should be so odious to him, and so farre out of his bookes. *a* **1659** CLEVELAND *Vit. Uxoris* xii, She..To scold by Book will take upon her, Rhetorically chide him. **1692** LOCKE *Toleration* ii. Wks. 1727 II. 272 To shew you that I do not speak wholly without Book. *a* **1707** BP. PATRICK *Autobiogr.* (1839) 87 The very prayers of the Liturgy, which I said without book. **1839** DICKENS *Nickleby* xxxi. 304 If you want to keep in the good books in that quarter, you had better not call her the old lady. **1841** POE *Murders in Rue Morgue* in *Tales* (1845) 118 To have a retentive memory, and to proceed by 'the book', are points commonly regarded as the sum total of good playing. **1861** W. PERRY *Hist. Ch. Eng.* I. xii. 403 The Arminians, who at that time were in his bad books. **1870** LOWELL *Study W.* 257 To speak loosely and without book. **1958** J. KEROUAC *On Road* vi. 148 That night Marylou took everything [i.e. every drink] in the books. **1959** *Listener* 31 Dec. 1172/3 Every human evil in the book was thrown at us—cancer, paralysis, famine, gas-chambers. **1960** J. WAIN *Nuncle* 49 They'll soak me for defamation of character and everything else in the book. **1964** W. MARKFIELD *To Early Grave* (1965) vii. 130 In my book, you're still *putz*. **1966** S. JACKMAN *Davidson Affair* ii. 13 In his book the function of television was to edify, not to entertain. **1968** A. DIMENT *Gt. Spy Race* I. iii. 32 They keep rigidly to the book down here.

16. ***to be upon the books*** (of an institution, etc.): to have one's name entered in the official list of members, patients, etc.; hence ***to take one's name off the books***. †***to drive to book***: to cause (a person) to give evidence on oath. ***to bring to book***: to bring to account, cause to show authority (for statements, etc.); to examine the evidence for (a statement, etc.), investigate. ***to close the books*** (of a business concern): to make no further entries (for a time). ***to shut the books***: to suspend business operations. ***to speak like a book***: i.e. accurately, with full or precise information. ***to suit*** (a person's) ***book*** (orig. a bookmaker's phrase: see sense 11): to fall in with his plans or answer his requirements; to be agreeable to. ***to take a leaf out of*** (a person's) ***book***: to take pattern from him, follow his example.

c **1460** *Launfal* 788 To say the soth, wythout les, Twelve knyghtes wer dryve to boke. **1788** H. WATSON in *Med. Commun.* II. 258 She..continued on the books as an out-patient. **1804** *Sporting Mag.* XXIII. 265/2 'Tis not my business to examine your accounts, Sir—but should I bring you to book..there is something in that sly countenance that tells me you have *sometimes* staked your credit at too great a venture. **1809** [see LEAF *sb.*[1] 7 b]. **1851** R. I. MURCHISON *Let.* 14 Apr. in Lady Prestwich *Life Sir J. Prestwich* (1899) 83 Would it suit your book to make a run of a day or two to the other side of the Weald? **1852** F. E. SMEDLEY *Lewis Arundel* vi, By which time he expects to be so hard up that he must marry somebody, and as there will be plenty of the needful she will suit his book as well as any other. **1858** *Times* in *Merc. Mar. Mag.* V. 46 The oldest merchants are 'shutting their books', as they express it. **1861** HUGHES *Tom Brown Oxf.* I. ii. 32 It is a great pity that some of our instructors in more important matters..will not take a leaf out of the same book. **1865** DICKENS *Mut. Fr.* II. III. xv. 131 I'll bring this young man to book. **1868** HOLME LEE *B. Godfrey* xxxiv. 118 The young scapegrace took his name off the college books. **1868** L. M. ALCOTT *Lit. Women* (1872) II. vii. 292 I'll take a leaf out of her book. **1870** MISS BRIDGMAN *R. Lynne* II. v. 104 We'll bring Sherborne to book. **1879** *Cassell's Techn. Educ.* IV. 215/1 By means of these figures we bring the matter, as it were, to book, and eliminate tangible results. **1955** *Times* 30 Aug. 6/1 Plainly the strikes suit the Communists' book.

III. *attrib.* and *Comb.*

17. *simple attrib.* Of or pertaining to books; entered in books; according to books; bookish. (Often written with hyphen as in 18, 19, but properly all cases where there are two distinct accents belong here.)

1865 *Boston* (*U.S.*) *Commonw.* 11 Mar., These lectures will..be published in book form.

18. General combinations: **a.** attributive, as ***book-astronomer, -auction, -auctioneer, -birth, -box, -cover, -desk, -education, -fair, -jacket, -knowledge, -label, -language, -list, -load, -mania, -market, -package, -prayer, -prop, -prophecy, -quarrel, -rack, -rest, -room, -sale, -shelf, -shop, -speech, -stall, -stock, -teaching, -title, -trade, -unit, -war, -word, -wrapper***, etc.

1837 WHEWELL *Hist. Induct. Sc.* (1857) I. 115 Euclid was merely a *book-astronomer, who had never observed the heavens. **1790** *Pennsylv. Packet* 31 Dec. 3/4 *Book-auction will continue during the season. **1809** KNOX & JEBB *Corr.* I. 532, I was at a book auction of a deceased priest. **1903** (*title*) Book-Auction Records. **1781** *Salem Gaz.* 19 June, The *Book-Auctionier intends also to exhibit a Collection of Books by Auction. **1880** J. L. WARREN *Book-plates* Pref. 3 The large book-auctioneers. **1597** *Gerard's Herbal* To Rdr., This *bookebirth thus brought foorth by Gerard. **1885** C. M. YONGE *Two Sides of Shield* I. i. 7 Dolores, who had in her mother's time been allowed a pretty free range of '*book-box'. **1900** —— *Mod. Broods* iv. 35 Agatha was struggling with the straps of a book box. **1961** T. LANDAU *Encycl. Librarianship* (ed. 2) 45/1 *Book boxes*, boxes, usually of standard sizes, in which books are transported between libraries, often made in plywood for lightness. **1845** POE *Purloined Let.* in *Tales* 206 We also measured the thickness of every *book-*cover*. **1864** MRS. JAMESON, etc. *Hist. Our Lord, &c.* I. 22 The sculptured tablets applied as book-covers to the Sacred Volumes. **1679** PLOT *Staffordsh.* (1686) 383 The most difficult piece of wood work..was a *Book-desk. **1883** *Harper's Mag.* Nov. 903/2 The *book-education they had while boys. **1863** W. WATERSTON *Cycl. Commerce* s.v. *Book*, Two great *book-fairs..held annually at Easter and Michaelmas. **1928** *Publishers' Weekly* 9 June 2359 Several specimens of modern trade *book jackets. **1665** NEEDHAM *Med. Medicinæ* vii. 253 A *Book-knowledge of Hippocrates, Galen, and the rest that are counted Classick. **1833** MILL in *Tait's Edin. Mag.* III. 348 Great natural powers..have supplied the place of a more extensive book-knowledge. **1844** SIR F. PALGRAVE *Truths & Fictions Mid. Ages* (ed. 2) 118 An ounce of mother wit, improved by observation, is worth a stone of book-knowledge. **1880** J. L. WARREN *Book-plates* i. 8 Another view of a *book-label may now be taken..a precaution against..loss or theft. *c* **1645** HOWELL *Lett.* (1650) I. 394 The same fortune that the Greek and Latin tongues had, to become only school and *book-languages. **1937** *Discovery* June 192/2 (*heading*) A Scientific and Technical *Book List. **1907** *Daily Chron.* 19 Dec. 3/5 The heroine, who is the best of the *book-load. **1824** DIBDIN *Libr. Comp.* 39 The turnings and windings of the *Book-mania. **1836** J. S. MILL *Ess. Politics & Culture* (1962) 72 The bulk of the purchasers in the *book-market. **1862** BURTON *Bk.-hunter* I. 55 Auctioneers were surprised at the gradual change coming over the book-market. **1647** SALTMARSH *Sparkl. Glory* (1847) 66 Those forms, as of Common-Prayer, *Book-prayers, outward rules of worship. **1862** LYTTON *Str. Story* I. 214 The sofa..with *book-prop and candlestick screwed to its back. *a* **1679** T. GOODWIN *Wks.* (1861) III. 213 The *book-prophesy..hath this prologue or preface unto it. **1620** SANDERSON *Serm.* (1681) I. 44 Multiplying unnecessary *book-quarrels. **1885** *Harper's Mag.* Mar. 543/1, I had made up my mind to nothing but a *book-rack. **1866** *Direct. Angl.* (ed. 3) 3 The Service Book placed on the *bookrest. **1788** WESLEY *Wks.* (1872) IV. 439, I appointed a Committee for.. superintending the business of the *Book-room. **1871** M. COLLINS *Mrq. & Merch.* III. viii. 212 Away from his own beloved bookroom and laboratory. **1797** W. B. STEVENS *Jrnl.* 11 Apr. (1965) v. 421 To Ashby for a *book sale. **1952** R. CAMPBELL *Lorca* 7 Sincerity is so often subordinated to book-sales. **1818** BYRON *To Mr. Murray*, Along thy sprucest *bookshelves shine The works thou deemest most divine. **1840** CARLYLE *Heroes* vi. 312 We will leave the Polemic stuff of a dead century to lie quiet on its book-shelves. **1862** BURTON *Bk.-hunter* I. 54 Works of ordinary literature to be found in every *book-shop. *a* **1652** J. SMITH *Sel. Disc.* viii. 378 Some who may arrive at that *book-skill and learning in divine mysteries. **1871** EARLE *Philol. Eng. Tong.* §23 The Angles first produced a cultivated *book-speech. **1800** *Ann. Reg.* 319/2, I one day happened at a *book-stall to see a small dictionary. **1913** 'A. R. HOPE' *Half & Half Tragedy* 70, I had something to get at the railway

bookstall. **1957** *BBC Handbook* 102 At the Monitoring Service Centre the *bookstock's accent is on politics and biography. **1874** J. Heath *Croquet Player* 11 *Book-teaching..cannot equal in efficiency practical lessons given by a good player on the lawn itself. **1864** Burton *Scot Abr.* I. iv. 230 Accurate transcripts of *book-titles. **1833** in *N. & Q.* (1942) CLXXXII. 143/2 Times are now so altered in the *book trade, that we can no longer venture on such a work single handed. **1863** W. Waterston *Cycl. Commerce* s.v. *Book*, The modern book-trade dates from the discovery of the art of printing. **1933** *Discovery* Aug. 254/2 Along one wall [are] two plywood *book units. **1670** Walton *Life Hooker* 33 Mr. Hooker became at last, but most unwillingly, to be engaged in a *book-war. **1851** Kingsley *Yeast* xi. 198 Those fine *book-words and long sentences. **1932** *Book-Collector's Q.* Apr.–June 10 The *book-wrapper is relatively and absolutely an upstart, and a good number of people have not yet decided whether they wish to encourage it or not.

b. objective or obj. genitive, as ***book-borrower***, ***-breeder***, ***-buyer***, ***-buying***, ***-collecting***, ***-collector***, ***-cutter***, ***-dealer***, ***-devouring***, ***-fancier***, ***-fancying***, ***-folding***, ***-hawker***, ***-hawking***, ***-hunter***, ***-hunting***, ***-lover***, ***-manufacture***, ***-merchant***, ***-mindedness***, ***-monger***, ***-notice*** [notice *sb.* 8 a], ***-ownership***, ***-preservation***, ***-printer***, ***-printing***, ***-protecting***, ***-purger*** (= *expurgator*), ***-reading***, ***-review***, ***-reviewer***, ***-reviewing***, ***rights***, ***-vender***, ***-worship***, ***-writer***, ***writing***, etc.

1880 J. L. Warren *Book-plates* ix. 96 In the case of the *book-borrowers there is no such Nemesis. **1605** Camden *Rem.* (1637) 288 Sir Thomas Moore..and other *Book-breeders. **1693** Locke *Let.* 2 Jan. in B. Rand *Locke & Clarke* (1927) 366, I wish you would have some care of *book-buyers as well as all of booksellers. **1838** Dickens *Let.* 16 Nov. (1965) I. 455 Not book-buyers I am sorry to say. **1862** Burton *Bk.-hunter* i. 47 Book-buyers among whom his great critical works are forgotten. **1832** Mill in *Tait's Edin. Mag.* II. 343 The wisdom of the *book-buying public. **1853** in *N. & Q.* (1962) CCVII. 84/2 Free Trade has been also a great hinderance to my bookbuying. **1862** Burton *Bk.-hunter* i. 59 The freaks of *book-collecting. **1791–1824** D'Israeli *Cur. Lit.* (1839) III. 342 The most magnificent of *book-collectors, the Duke de la Vallière. **1863** Holme Lee *A. Warleigh* II. 311 Alice paused with a slender pearl *book-cutter in her hand. **1876** Geo. Eliot *Dan. Der.* IV. lviii. 172 The *book-devouring Isabel. **1810** *Irish Mag.* Mar. 127/1 The valuable collection made by this *book-fancier. **1862** Burton *Bk.-hunter* i. 69 The curious blunder which made one of them worth the notice of the book-fanciers. **1870** Emerson *Soc. & Solit.* viii. 168 The annals of bibliography afford many examples of the delirious extent to which *book-fancying can go. **1791–1824** D'Israeli *Cur. Lit.* (1839) III. 342 To what hard hunting these *book-hunters voluntarily doom themselves. **1862** Burton (*title*) The Book-hunter. **1863** Grosart *Small Sins* 78 A book-worm—the pest of *book-lovers—has pierced.. right through it. **1711** Shaftesb. *Charac.* (1737) III. 15 *Book-merchants..undoubtedly receive no small advantage from a right improvement of a learned scuffle. **1805** Wordsworth *Prelude* iii. 395 Antiquity and stedfast truth And strong *book-mindedness. **1903** J. Morley *Life of Gladstone* I. ii. ii. 117 His bookmindedness is unabated. **1662** Fuller *Worthies* iii. 168 He was a great *Book-monger. **1868** W. James *Let.* 24 May in R. B. Perry *Thought & Char. W. J.* (1935) I. 277, I have written a few *book notices lately. **1938** *Times Lit. Suppl.* 17 Sept. 591/1 The majority of the book-notices..were unpaid until the 'fifties. *c* **1500** *Cocke Lorelles B.* (1843) 9 *Boke prynters, peynters, bowers. **1863** J. G. Nichols *Herald & Geneal.* II. 158 Our historical *book-printing societies. **1606** W. Crashaw *Rom. Forg.* I. 147 Instructions, giuen by the Pope..to all *Book-purgers. **1832** *Times* 6 Jan. [3]/3 To be sure, the *book-reading lovers of antiquity would cry 'horrible'. **1910** A. Bennett *Clayhanger* iii. i. 325 A new series of sixpenny reprints which had considerably excited the book-selling and book-reading worlds. **1861** A. J. Graham *Phonographic Odds & Ends* 71 (*heading*) *Book-Review. **1904** W. James *Mem. & Stud.* (1911) iv. 66 His contributions to literature were all anonymous, book-reviews chiefly. **1965** *Times Lit. Suppl.* 25 Nov. 1035/2 The President could not have read all those..book-reviews he was said to. **1898** M. Beerbohm in *Variety of Things* (1928) 224 Even the *book-reviewers could no longer assert that he did not know how to draw. **1873** H. James *Let.* 31 May in R. B. Perry *Thought & Char. W. J.* (1935) I. 348, I am struggling through long delay to get at something better than *book reviewing. **1956** *N. & Q.* CCI. 190/2 Here is the true dawn of book-reviewing in England. **1904** A. Bennett *Let.* 26 Nov. (1966) I. 58 You have also the six short stories, & the *book rights on these. **1915** J. Joyce *Let.* 1 Apr. (1966) II. 338 That [agreement] for my novel should be conditional on Mr Grant Richards' refusal of the book rights. **1701** H. Wanley in *Phil. Trans.* XXV. 1998 The Librarii or *Book-writers were..a particular company of men, and their Business a Trade. *Ibid.* *Book-writing was their profession. **1820** Scott *Monast.* Introd. 32 The *irritabile genus* comprehends the bookselling as well as the book-writing species.

c. instrumental, as ***book-fed***, ***-filled***, ***-formed***, ***-lined***, ***-sworn***, ***-taught***, ***-walled***, etc., adjs.

1932 V. Woolf *Let. to Young Poet* 24 As if they had neither ears nor eyes..but only honest enterprising *book-fed brains. **1965** F. Sargeson *Memoirs of Peon* ii. 32 The back *book-filled room. *a* **1851** Joanna Baillie (Ogilvie), Every table-wit and *book-formed sage. **1897** *Daily News* 18 June 8/4 Warm and cosy, with *book-lined walls. **1947** Auden *Age of Anxiety* (1948) iii. 75 But in book-lined rooms at the back Committees meet. **1558** *Inv. A. Nycholson, Kendal* (Somerset Ho.), Bodely *Buke sworne. **1642** Cudworth *Serm. 1 John* ii. 3 (1676) 40 Not he that is only *book-taught but he that is God-taught. **1760** Goldsm. *Cit. W.* II. lxvii, Our *book-taught philosopher. **1904** W. de la Mare *Henry Brocken* i. 2 Half my youthful days passed in that low, *book-walled chamber.

19. Special comb.: **book account** *U.S.*, a statement of accounts recorded in a book; **book agent** *U.S.*, one who promotes the sale of books; †**book-answerer**, a critic; **book-bearer**, one who carries a book, also a prompter (*obs.*), = *book-holder*; **book-board**, a book-shelf in a pew, pulpit, etc.; **book-bosomed** *a.*, (used by Scott for) having a book in the bosom; **book-bound** *a.*, set round with books; **book-boy**, a boy employed to fetch books for readers in a library; **book-burning**, the destruction of writings regarded as harmful or subversive; so *book-burner*; **book canvasser**, one who canvasses schools, public offices, etc., for the sale of books, esp. on the subscription system; **book-cloth**, a cloth manufactured for the bindings of books; **book-club**, (*a*) a subscription library, also a club in which the subscriptions are expended in the purchase or borrowing of books for the common use of the members; (*b*) a society which produces books for its members, such as the Warton Club, the Roxburghe Club, the First Edition Club; **book concern** *U.S.*, an establishment engaged in the printing and sale of books; **book-crab** = *book-scorpion*; **book-credit**, an amount credited to a person's account in a ledger; **book-debt**, an amount debited to a person's account in a ledger, a debt owing to a tradesman as recorded in his account-books; **book-edge gilder**, **marbler**, a bookbinder's workman who gilds or marbles the edges of books; **book end**, one of a pair of (ornamental) book props (see below), used to keep a row of unshelved books in an upright position; **booketeria** (ˌbʊkəˈtɪərɪə) *U.S.* [after caf)eteria], a self-service book-store or library; **book-farmer**, one who farms with knowledge acquired from books; so **book-farming**; **book-folder**, (*a*) a printer's, bookbinder's, or stationer's employee who folds the paper sheets into page-size; (*b*) the paper wrapper of a newly published book; **book-form**, in advb. phrase *in book form* (see sense 17); also *attrib.*; **book-ghoul** (see quot.); **book-gill** = *gill-book* (s.v. gill sb.[1] 5 b); **book hand**, the hand or writing used by the official transcribers of books before the invention of printing; **book-holder**, one who or that which holds a book, †*spec.* a theatrical prompter, = *book-bearer*; †**book-house**, a library; **book-hunt** *v. intr.*, to follow the pursuit of a book-hunter or searcher of old and rare volumes; **book-label**, a label bearing the title and author's name, the owner's name, etc., affixed to the cover of a book; **book-law**, written law; †**book-leiger**, one who confines his study to book-learning (cf. leiger); **book-length** *attrib.*, of the length of a book; **book-louse**, a minute neuropterous insect (*Psocus pulsatorius*) destructive to books; **book-lung**, the lamellate respiratory organs of a scorpion; **book-mark**, a mark or label placed in or upon a book to indicate ownership; also a piece of ribbon, paper, etc., inserted between the leaves of a book to mark a place; in this sense often called a **book-marker**; **book match**, one of a set of tear-off matches, sold in packets hinged at one end like a book (cf. sense 3 d above); **book-mate**, school-fellow, fellow-student; †**book-matter**, a matter the adequate treatment of which would fill a book; **book mite** (see quot.); **bookmobile** (ˈbʊkməˌbiːl) *U.S.* [after auto)mobile *sb.*], see quot. 1941; †**book-money**, surplice-fees; **book-muslin**, a fine kind of muslin owing its name to the book-like manner in which it is folded when sold in the piece, also *ellipt.* a dress made of such muslin; **book name**, a name of a plant or animal, other than the scientific name, used only in books; also *transf.*; **book-number**, 'in library-cataloguing, a particular number (or a number and a letter) designating the book in its proper sequence in the smallest division to which it belongs' (Cent. Dict. Suppl. 1909); **book-oath**, an oath sworn on the 'book'; **book-packet**, a packet which may be sent through the book-post; **book-page**, (*a*) a page of a book; (*b*) in a newspaper or journal: a page that is devoted to reviews and notices of books; **book piles**, a type of book-plate in which piles of books are used as the design; **book pocket** (see quot. 1955); **book-post**, the system and regulations under which books and printed matter may be sent through the post-office; **book-postage**, the price charged for carriage by book-post; also **book-rate**; **book-press**, a book-case; **book prop**, **support**, an angular support for the end of a row of books, esp. in a partly-filled shelf; **book-scorpion**, an arachnid insect (*Chelifer cancroides*) resembling a scorpion, often found in old books; **book-shy** *a.*, reluctant or unwilling to read books; **book-slide**, an expanding holder or stand for books; **book-society** = *book-club* (*a*); also (in modern use) = *book-club* (*b*); **book-stack**, see stack *sb.*; **book-stamp**, a stamp for embossing the covers of books; **book-stand**, a stand or case for books; **book-table**, a table intended solely or mainly for books; **book token**, a voucher exchangeable at a bookseller's for a book or books; **book-tray**, a tray for carrying books; **book-trough** (see quot. 1961); **book type** (see quot.); **book value** *Book-keeping*, the value of a commodity as shown by a firm's books, as distinguished from its market value; **book-work**, (*a*) work at books, study of text-books; (*b*) the printing of books or similar matter, as opposed to job-work (job *sb.*[2] 1 c); **book-world**, the world of literature; the affairs of life as described in literature; **book-wright**, a maker or author of books. Also book-binder, -case, -craft, -fell, -keeper, etc.

1672 *Mass. Col. Laws* (1887) 39 Inconveniences..through want of seasonable examination..of *Book accompts. **1741** *New Hamp. Probate Rec.* III. 86 My book accompt standing against James Ried. **1883** C. F. Wilder *Sister Ridnour* 232 The treasurer..keeps a correct book-account of all moneys taken and expended. **1830** *Williams's N.-Y. Ann. Reg. 1830* 299 John Emory and Beverly Waugh, *Book Agents, New-York. **1886** *Harper's Mag.* Dec. 162/1 They may both be glad to invoke the aid of the despised book agent, who carries literature from door to door. **1910** Mulford *Hopalong Cassidy* vii. 50 Was you ever an auctioneer..or a book agent? **1760** Goldsm. *Cit. W.* xiii. (1837) 48 If he has much money, he may buy reputation from your *book-answerers. **1530** Palsgr. 199/2 *Boke bearer in a ploye, *prothocolle.* **1636** Prynne *Unbish. Tim.* (1661) 7 Timothy..being so much at Pauls beck, as to be..his Cloack-carrier, and Book-bearer. **1847** C. M. Yonge *Scenes & Char.* ix. 110 She put her arm on the *book board, while rising from kneeling. **1861** Ramsay *Remin.* ii. (ed. 18) 42 A nail on the seat or book-board. **1805** Scott *Last Minstr.* iii. viii, A *book-bosom'd priest. **1863** Jeaffreson *Sir Everard's D.* xiii. 224 His little *book-bound parlour. **1903** *Daily Chron.* 13 Feb. 5/1 His first situation was as *book-boy in the library of the Bristol Law Society. **1899** *Book-Lover* 86/2 The virtuous Romans appear to have been greater *book-burners than the Greeks. **1951** I. Shaw *Troubled Air* xxii. 389 The censors and book-burners. **1892** J. A. Farrer *Books condemned to be Burnt* 170 The custom of *book-burning, never formally abolished, died out at last from a gradual decline of public belief in its efficacy. **1954** *Ann. Reg. 1953* 169 The destruction of many of these [Communist] books provoked a general outcry against 'book-burning'. **1848** *Philadelphia Almanac* 2 (Advt.), *Book canvassers and agents wanted. **1921** *Dict. Occup. Terms* (1927) §774 *Book canvasser*, canvasses schools, public offices, etc., for sale of technical or other books on subscription system. **1891** *Pall Mall Gaz.* 30 Nov. 7/1 Makers of *book-cloth. **1792** A. Young *Trav. France* 90 A *chamber de lecture*, or what we should call a *book-club, that does not divide its books, but forms a library. **1804** W. Taylor in Robberds *Mem.* I. 485 People..wait till it comes to the library or the book-club. **1905** *Times* 20 Sept. 5/5 The privileges of *The Times* Book Club are offered to those only who subscribe to *The Times* for a year. **1929** H. Williams (*title*) Book Clubs and Printing Societies of Great Britain and Ireland..published by the First Edition Club. *Ibid.* 7 The prototype of the book club, the Roxburghe. **1937** V. Gollancz in 'G. Orwell' *Road to Wigan Pier* p. xi, The three selectors of the Left Book Club Choices. **1968** *Listener* 6 June 725/3 There are plenty of people who belong to book clubs but otherwise buy almost no books. **1786** F. Asbury *Jrnl.* 26 Apr. (1852) I. 511 Arrived in Baltimore, and was occupied..in collecting money for the books, and inspecting the accounts of the *Book-Concern. **1872** *Congress. Globe* May 3909/3 Every book published by the Methodist Book Concern..is published on sized paper. **1835** Kirby *Hab. & Inst. Anim.* II. xvi. 90 In the scorpion and the *book-crab..the mandibles..have a moveable joint. **1844** Mill in *Westm. Rev.* XLI. 592 In almost all other transactions between dealers, bank notes are already superseded by cheques, or *book credits. **1863** Fawcett *Pol. Econ.* ii. x. (1876) 261 Tradesmen fail in business, in consequence of their money becoming locked up in book-credits. **1689** *Lond. Gaz.* No. 2480/4 The Creditors..are desired to bring in an Account of their several Debts, whether on Judgements, Bond, or *Book-Debts. **1809** R. Langford *Introd. Trade* 12 Book Debts, if not legally demanded within the space of six years, cannot be recovered by law. **1858** Simmonds *Dict. Trade*, **Book and card-edge gilder and marbler*, a workman who ornaments and finishes off the edges of books, etc. **1898** *Daily Chron.* 24 Sept. 10/6 Book-edge gilders wanted. **1921** *Dict. Occup. Terms* (1927) §548 Book-edge marbler. **1907** *Yesterday's Shopping* (1969) 368/3 **Book ends.* Mahogany, inlaid Marqueterie, heavily weighted, for keeping books in position, pair 23/0. **1932** E. Bowen *To North* xxi. 228 'What did she sell?'..'Oh, paraphernalia—lampshades, book-ends.' **1961** *Lebende Sprachen* VI. 39/2 *Book ends*, die bücher-stützen. **1945** in *Amer. Speech* (1946) XXI. 66/2 Pasadena Junior College has a *booketeria. **1947** *Ibid.* XXII. 306/1 The first *Booketeria*..is located in a popular grocery... Borrowers choose their own reading matter. They select and charge books and the store cashiers record the charges. **1825** Loudon *Encycl. Agric.* iv. 1133/1 **Book farmers*..are those who know agriculture only by reading about it. **1920** R. Frost *Let.* 21 Mar. (1964) 102 'Amatoor!' all the leaves began to murmur. 'Book-farmer!' **1823** R. B. Thomas *Farmer's Almanack 1824* 18–24 Dec., Be not stubborn and unreasonable in your prejudices against what is called **book-farming.* **1923** D. H. Lawrence *Stud. Classic Amer. Lit.* viii. 154 And that's why the idealists left off brook-farming, and took to book-farming. **1872** C. L. Brace *Dangerous Classes N.Y.* 166 She went to be a *book-folder downtown. **1903** *Daily Chron.* 24 Feb. 8/5 (Advt.), Book-folder. Apply..Printing Dept. **1925** *Public Opinion* 5 June 538/3 Blurbs, those interesting little paragraphs which appeared on bookfolders. **1849** Rossetti *Let.* 18 Oct. (1965) I. 82 They will be bound..that they may go in the *book-form. **1856** *Chambers's Jrnl.* V. 322/2 M.

Dumas had previously published it in the book-form. **1893** *Photogr. Ann.* 333 A light camera, with .. book-form double dark slides. **1902** 'MONKSHOOD' & GAMBLE *Kipling* 161 This story passed from 'Lippincott's Magazine' to the pomp and pride of a book-form Edition. **1964** P. F. ANSON *Bishops at Large* vi. 196 They appeared in book-form in 1913. **1881** A. LANG *Library* 56 The *Book-Ghoul is he who combines the larceny of the biblioklept with the abominable wickedness of breaking up and mutilating the volumes from which he steals. **1897** PARKER & HASWELL *Textbk. Zool.* I. xi. 621 External appendages or gills (*book-gills). **1885** *Encycl. Brit.* XVIII. 143/2 Down to the time of the introduction of printing, writing ran in two lines—the set *book-hand and the cursive. **1893** E. M. THOMPSON *Handbk. Gk. & Lat. Palaeogr.* xix. 301 We find it convenient to treat the cursive or charter hand as a separate branch of mediaeval English writing apart from the literary or book hand. **1928** *Daily Tel.* 19 July 15/5 A fifteenth century English manuscript .. with others written in a vernacular book-hand. **1585** HIGINS *Junius' Nomenclator* 501 (Halliw.) He that telleth the players their part when they are out and have forgotten, the prompter or *booke-holder. **1880** LANG *XXII Ballades in Blue China* 23 He *book-hunts, though December freeze. *a* **1000** ÆLFRIC *Voc.* in Wr.-Wülcker 185 *Librarium*, *bochus. **1340** *Ayenb.*, This boc is dan Michelis of Northgate, ywrite in .. the bochouse of Saynt Austines of Canterbury. **1675** MARVELL *Corr.* ccxlix. Wks. 1872-5 II. 466 A new Popish test for Book-Houses. **1905** *Daily Chron.* 19 Dec. 6/2 An interesting copy of the works of Horace, having John Kemble's leather *book-label on both covers. **1837** CARLYLE *Fr. Rev.* II. vi. vi. 357 A court of Law, not *Book-Law but primeval Club-Law. **1672** T. VENN *Mil. & Marit. Discip.* xxii. 169 What can such who are mere *Book-leidgers do? **1938** *Times Lit. Suppl.* 3 Dec. vi/2 His new work is a *book-length lyric in prose. **1953** *Encounter* Nov. 49/1 Vigolo .. has prefaced his edition with a book-length essay. **1867** *Amer. Naturalist* I. 312 The little wingless *book-louse (*Atropos*) scampering irreverently over the musty pages of his *Systema Naturae*. **1897** PARKER & HASWELL *Zool.* I. 604 The organs of respiration are sometimes tracheæ, similar to those of Insects, sometimes *book-lungs or sacs containing numerous book-leaf-like plates. **1862** GEO. ELIOT *Let.* 24 Dec. in J. W. Cross *Life* (1886) II. 295, I have been discontented with the Coventry *book-marks. **1880** J. L. WARREN *Book-plates* ii. 14 *Insigne librorum* .. means simply the book-mark. **1883** *Harper's Mag.* Oct. 806/1 He would .. insert a book-mark at the page he had last finished. **1838** C. M. YONGE *Let.* 6 Aug. in C. Coleridge *C. M. Yonge* (1903) iv. 135 Your W.H.W.B.W. *bookmarker. **1858** *Brit. Postal Guide* 39 Together with Bookmarkers .. or other articles usually appertaining to any such Book. **1939** E. AUGUST *Black-Out Book* 30/1 Hold two '*book' matches side by side between your finger and thumb. **1588** SHAKS. *L.L.L.* IV. i. 102 The Prince and his *Booke-mates. **1548** HOOPER *Ten Commandm.* iv, There be many other causes .. it were a *book-matter to rehearse them. **1883** *Encycl. Brit.* XVI. 528/2 *Cheyletidæ*, the so-called *book mites, .. quite unconnected with books. **1937** *Amer. Speech* XII. 30 State newspapers of Friday, September 4, 1936, made announcement that the Nebraska public library commission had purchased a half-ton panel truck to be used as a **bookmobile*. **1941** *Ibid.* XVI. 311/1 A bookmobile is an automobile fitted with shelves and other necessary equipment for serving rural districts and patrons who cannot visit a library. **1969** *Telegraph* (Brisbane) 30 May 4/1 This year the long-awaited bookmobile service would serve some outlying areas. **1692** SPRAT *Relat. Young's Contriv.* in *Harl. Misc.* VI. 219 (D.) He had all the *book-money, that is, the fees for marriages, burials, and christenings. **1759** *Newport Mercury* 10 Apr. 4/2 *Book Muslin, Cambricks, silk Ferrets. *c* **1793** JANE AUSTEN *Volume the First* (1954) 72 She lies wrapped in a book muslin bedgown. **1836** *Scenes Comm. by Land & S.* 214 Book muslin .. is the clearest and finest of all the muslins. **1839** DICKENS *Nich. Nick.* xiv, A low book-muslin dress and short kid gloves. **1884** *19th Cent.* Mar. 406 Think of a widow insisting on being provided with a book muslin. **1878** BRITTEN & HOLLAND *Dict. Eng. Plant-n.*, *Aconite*, a common *book-name for *Aconitum Napellus*. **1885** *Lisbon* (Dakota) *Star* 27 Mar. 5 A Chinaman .. gets a book-name when he goes to school. **1530** PALSGR. 199/2 *Boke othe, *jvrement de droict*. **1575** J. STILL *Gamm. Gurton* IV. ii, Else ich durst take a book-oath .. My gammer had been slain. *a* **1613** OVERBURY *A Wife, &c.* (1638) 174 Should he be brought upon his Book-oath. **1886** *Post Office Guide* 3 A *book-packet may contain any number of separate books. **1930** WYNDHAM LEWIS *Lett.* (1963) 197 The literary editors of the London *book-pages. **1932** *N. & Q.* CLXII. 84/1 In recent years the same thing was done with photostat prints, in copying book-pages. **1969** *Daily Tel.* 11 Aug. 18 Book page turners for people who have lost the use of their hands. **1902** *Encycl. Brit.* XXVI. 305/1 '*Book-piles', exemplified by the *ex-libris* of W. Hewer (Samuel Pepys's secretary). **1922** JOYCE *Ulysses* 430 Bloom pats with parcelled hands .. *bookpocket. **1955** J. E. LIBERTY *Pract. Tailoring* v. 64 The Hare Pocket .. is like a long welt pocket and is sometimes called a book pocket. It is made in the lining, with the welt 1½ in. wide, lined with linen, and with a hole and button. **1861** ROSSETTI *Let.* 18 Jan. (1965) II. 389, I will send it you by *book-post. **1868** GEO. ELIOT *Let.* 31 Mar. (1955) IV. 426, I send by book post all the printed sheets of the poem. **1870** MISS BRIDGMAN *R. Lynne* II. x. 208 The .. fool .. sent .. a bundle of tracts by the book-post. **1858** *Brit. Postal Guide* 9 A packet .. is forwarded, charged with the deficient *book-postage. **1611** COTGR., *Armoire* .. cupboord; box; little *booke-presse. **1934** H. G. WELLS *Exper. Autobiogr.* I. v. 286 Like so many people who have had the benefit of a simple English education she was *book-shy. **1941** V. WOOLF *Between Acts* 26 Book-shy she was .. and gun-shy too. **1812** SOUTHEY *Ess.* (1832) I. 150 Not subjects to be sent into circulating libraries and *book-societies. **1929** *Times* 27 May 12/2 The Book Society's choice for May is Valentin Kataev's 'The Embezzlers'. **1938** *Times* 5 Jan. 12/3 He was not conscious of any bad effect on his own business of book clubs and book societies. **1967** E. GRIERSON *Crime of One's Own* i. 16 'Sold over five thousand and a Book Society Recommend,' its creator declared with pride. **1900** *Library Jrnl.* Nov. 679/2 Convenient elevators for passengers and freight are provided in the *book-stacks. **1968** *Bodl. Libr. Rec.* VIII. 60 Mobile shelving in the bookstack. **1893** *Funk's Standard Dict.*, *Bookstamp. **1909** CYRIL DAVENPORT (*title*) English Heraldic Bookstamps. **1807** W. SCOTT *Let.* 13 Jan. (1932) I. 346 The great genius who invented the gilded inlaid or Japan *bookstands for boudoirs & drawing rooms. **1891** KIPLING *Light that Failed* xiv. 303 A bookstand that supported a pile of sketch-books. **1895** G. STIKEMAN *Adjustable Book Shelving* 4 *Book supports, for partially filled shelves. **1829** M. HARE *Let.* 12 Sept. in A. J. C. Hare *Mem. Quiet Life* (1872) I. vi. 275, I ordered a *book table according to my own fancy, having two shelves above, a bureau part, and shelves below, with a cupboard at each end. **1905** *Daily Chron.* 23 May 4/6 A lovely inlaid book-table. **1932** *Book Tokens* (Nat. Book Council) 5 In order to give readers some idea of the appearance of the *Book Token this leaflet has been made similar in size and format. **1938** *Times* 5 Jan. 12/3 They had a 7s. 6d. book token which they exchanged for one 5s. book and five 6d. books. **1875** T. SEATON *Fret Cutting* iv. 42 It is a *book-tray end; the full size is six inches by five. **1916** E. F. BENSON *David Blaize* vii. 132, I love looking through old book-trays. **1907** *Yesterday's Shopping* (1969) 131/1 **Book Troughs* .. Fumed oak, length 16 in. ... with repoussé plates .. 4/3. **1929** E. BOWEN *Last Sept.* I. ii. 17 She glanced intently along the books in the book-trough. **1961** T. LANDAU *Encycl. Librarianship* (ed. 2) 52/1 *Book trough*, a V-shaped wooden shelf or rack placed on library tables for the display of books in such a manner that the titles are clearly visible. **1888** *Encycl. Brit.* XXIII. 699/1 Types are divided into two classes—*book type, including Roman and Italic, and job type. **1899** *Westm. Gaz.* 14 June 6/1 Eight years ago the *book value of the *Stella* was £60,000. **1952** *Economist* 6 Sept. 575 The five main companies have fixed assets totalling more than £6 million in book value, but worth probably four times that at replacement values. **1848** CLOUGH *Bothie* VIII. 72 He'll think me .. Neither better nor worse for my gentlemanship and *bookwork. **1881** FITCH *Lect. Teaching* 150 Book-work for lessons has obvious advantages. **1889** *Cent. Dict.*, Book-work. **1926** W. H. SLATER *What a Compositor should Know* III. 1 The work of the composing department .. is divided roughly into two sections: 'Bookwork' and 'Jobwork'. **1858** BAGEHOT *Coll. Wks.* (1965) I. 332 In the *book-world they [*sc.* the Liberal party] enjoyed a domination. **1906** *Daily Chron.* 7 May 3/5 The book-world, which is the edited reflection of life, brings the great facts of contrast into added prominence. **1841** D'ISRAELI *Amen. Lit.* (1867) 88 An unskilful compilation .. made by .. a noted *book-wright in the reign of Elizabeth.

20. Combinations of the type *common-place-book*, *Domesday Book*, *pass-book*, *pocket-book*, *statute-book* will be found under their first element.

book (bʊk), *v.* Forms: 1 bócian, 3-4 boke(n, 4-7 booke, 4- book. [OE. *bócian*, corresp. to OFris. *bôkia*, ON. *bóka*: from the sb.: see prec.]

†**1.** *trans.* To grant or assign (land) by charter: see BOOK *sb.* 1. *Obs.* (exc. *Hist.*)

966 in *Cod. Dipl.* 531 Oswald biscop bocaþ Wihthelme his þegne. **1844** LINGARD *Anglo-Sax. Ch.* (1858) I. App. 374 Ethelwulf, king of Wessex, books the lands of twenty families, not to a subject, but to himself. **1876** DIGBY *Real Prop.* i. 12 Land thus granted was said to be 'booked' to the grantee, and was called bocland or bookland.

2. a. To enter in a book; to record, register.

a **1225** *Ancr. R.* 158 þauh þe engel Gabriel hefde his burde ibocked. **1393** GOWER *Conf.* I. 3 Some newe thing I shulde boke. **1594** NASHE *Unfort. Trav.* 9, I haue done a thousand better iests, if they had been bookt. **1610** HOLLAND *Camden's Brit.* I. 4 The Bardi .. thought it not lawfull to write and booke anything. **1710** *Lond. Gaz.* No. 4677/4 They .. saw him [a horse] book'd in the Market Book. **1854** HOOKER *Himal. Jrnls.* I. x. 247 To seize and book every object worth noticing. **1883** *Manch. Exam.* 26 Nov. 4/2 Not eager to book fresh orders.

b. *fig.*

1575 SIR N. BRETON in Farr *S.P.* (1845) i, How in your heart you may for euer booke it. *a* **1656** BP. HALL *Rem. Wks.* (1660) 183 The Almighty .. books their number for an everlasting remembrance.

c. To make an entry of or against a person's name; *esp.* to enter (a name) in a police register for an alleged offence; see also quot. 1846.

1841 *Fistiana* 58 The names of individuals of distinction were 'booked' for indictment, should the prosecution of the principal .. end in a conviction. **1846** SNOWDEN *Magistrate's Assistant* 344 Caught, taken, or disposed of: *booked*. **1902** WODEHOUSE *Pothunters* iii. 49 If he books a chap out of bounds it keeps him happy for a week. **1935** STEINBECK *Tortilla Flat* viii. 122 The police sergeant said he hadn't booked them for a long time. **1961** P. BARRY *Unwillingly to School* xv. 204 If you hadn't been a learner driver .. I'd have booked you for that!

d. To put (tackle) in a fishing-book.

1892 *Field* 18 June 922/3 We therefore book our cast, and wind up for the day.

3. a. To enter in a list, to enrol, enlist.

1548 UDALL, etc. *Erasm. Par. Acts* v. 14 Which had not yet .. booked themselues as souldiers. **1607** HIERON *Wks.* I. 284 Enrouled and booked among Christians. **1612** J. DAVIES *Why Ireland, &c.* (1787) 176 He caused the marchers to book their men.

b. To enter (the arrival or departure of an employee, hotel guest, etc.) in a book; so *to book in, out.* Also intr. *to book off*, to sign an attendance book on going off duty.

1902 *Daily Chron.* 13 May 10/5 Baker's .. Bookkeeper.—Young lady required, with good experience, to book men and keep books. *Ibid.*, Wanted young lady, .. one able to book in. *Ibid.*, Shopwoman wanted, capable of booking out men. **1928** *Observer* 3 Feb. 12/7 To-night he drives his engine for the last time. To-morrow he 'books off' .. and the Line knows him no more. **1958** *Spectator* 22 Aug. 251/1 Booking in immediately before the flight. **1958** *Times* 3 Sept. 13/4 O'Brien-Greer booked in at the hotel on August 20.

4. a. To engage for oneself by payment (a seat or place in a travelling conveyance or in a theatre or other place of entertainment). Also *absol.*

1826 DISRAELI *Viv. Grey* III. iv. 99, I will give them orders to book an inside place for the poodle. **1837** DICKENS *Pickw.* xxxv, Sam Weller booked for them all. **1878** F. WILLIAMS *Midl. Railw.* 628 When railways were first opened for passenger traffic .. the traveller had to give his name .. his seat was 'booked'. *a* **1887** *Theatrical Advt.* Seats can be booked one month in advance.

b. To enter (the name of a passenger, etc.) for a seat or place; to issue railway tickets to; *refl.* to obtain a railway ticket for oneself. Also intr. *to book through*: to obtain a ticket to cover a whole journey.

1841 MARRYAT *Poacher* xli, He booked himself for the following day's coach. **1844** DICKENS *Mart. Chuz.* li. 592 The other [man], seating himself on the steps of the coach, remained in conversation with Slyme... 'He's booked,' observed the man. 'Through,' said Slyme. **1858** *Penny Cycl.* 2nd Suppl. 565/2 A man may now 'book through' from London to so many continental cities. **1859** JEPHSON *Brittany* ii. 8, I booked myself at the Waterloo Station for Jersey. **1884** *Gt. West. Railw. Time Table* July 53 Passengers are booked through from Warwick.

c. To enter and pay for the transmission of (goods, etc.) by any conveyance.

1807 LAMB *Let.* 29 Jan. (1868) I. 251 Dear Wordsworth—We have book'd off from Swan and Two Necks, Lad Lane, this day (per coach) the Tales from Shakspear. **1829** LAMB in *Select. Bernard Barton* (1849) 139 The parcel is booked for you this 25th March. **1849** DE QUINCEY *Eng. Mail Coach* Wks. IV. 297 [It was] not in the way-bill and therefore could not have been booked. **1885** *Law Times* LXXX. 45/1 His drover .. booked them [cattle] to the Nantwich station.

5. *transf.* To engage (a person) as a guest or the like. Also with *up. colloq.* Cf. BOOKED 3.

1872 *Proc. Amer. Philol. Soc.* 18 It seems singular to the American to hear an Englishman speak of 'booking' his friend for dinner. *a* **1887** *Mod.* I shall book you for that evening. **1906** *Daily Chron.* 20 Oct. 7/2 The defendant .. wrote: 'Thanks for calling. I am pleased to book you for four—or it may be five Sundays.' .. Mr. —— .. said he was engaged at £2. 2. 0 a day. **1923** WODEHOUSE *Inimit. Jeeves* iii. 35 Before I went I had been booked up to take brother and the girl for a nice drive that afternoon.

book, obs. pa. t. of BAKE; obs. f. BUCK, BULK.

bookable ('bʊkəb(ə)l), *a.* [f. BOOK *v.* + -ABLE.] That may be booked.

1903 *Daily Chron.* 30 Mar. 6/6, I think some [seats] should be bookable, and some should be unreserved. **1926** *Music & Letters* Apr. 102 The house .. would be designed .. to accommodate the largest possible audience .. with all seats bookable.

'bookbinder ('bʊkbaɪndə(r)). One who binds books.

1389 in *Eng. Gilds* (1870) 12 Noveritis nos .. hoc presenti scripto nostro confirmasse Stephano Vant Bookbynder .. totum predictum tenementum. *c* **1400** *Destr. Troy* 1589 Belmakers bokebynders, brasiers fyn. **1544** ASCHAM *Toxoph.* (Arb.) 83 On whom I loked on by chaunce in the booke bynders shope. **1666** PEPYS *Diary* 13 Aug., To treat with a bookbinder to come and gild the backs of all my books. **1855** MACAULAY *Hist. Eng.* IV. 361 Petitions .. from booksellers, bookbinders and printers.

So **'bookbindery** (*U.S.*), a bookbinding establishment [cf. BINDERY]; **bookbinding** *vbl. sb.*

1771 B. FRANKLIN *Autobiogr.* in *Life & Writings* (1905) I. 290 Meredith was to work at press, Potts at book-binding. **1787** *Europ. Mag.* XII. 78 He tanned goat-skins .. for bookbinding. **1815** *Niles' Reg.* VIII. 141/2 There are [*sc.* in Pittsburgh] .. 4 book binderies. **1842** [see BAKERY 2]. **1854** CAR. THOMAS *Formingdale* 258 There was but one bookbindery in the town. **1864** KNIGHT *Pass. Working Life* II. 162 Bookbinding is now one of the large manufactures of London. **1884** *Manch. Exam.* 29 Dec. 6/4 A large bookbindery in New York.

bookcase[1] ('bʊkkeɪs). A case or cupboard for books; a set of bookshelves shut in by doors, glazed or otherwise. Hence **'bookcased** *ppl. a.*, **bookcase-maker.**

1726 in *N. & Q.* (1942) CLXXXII. 47/1 [A London shop-sign] Desk & Bookcase. James Field, cabinet-maker. **1742** YOUNG *Nt. Th.* v. 257 This book-case, with dark booty almost burst. **1849** W. IRVING *Crayon Misc.* 225 On each side of the cabinet were book-cases, well stored with works of romantic fiction. **1861** *Our Eng. Home* 132 During the fifteenth century the introduction of bookcases, as articles of domestic furniture.

†**book-case**[2]. *Obs.* A law case found in the books or on record, a precedent. (Cf. BOOK 5 c.)

1552 HULOET *s.v. Preiudice* .. It may be as the ruled cases and matters of the lawe be called bokecases. **1640-4** in Rushw. *Hist. Coll.* III. (1692) I. 597 Book-Cases and Precedents, which without doubt they would have cited. **1726** AYLIFFE *Parerg.* 204, I have not met with any Book-Case, that expressly warrants this opinion.

'book 'case[3]. A case or pair of boards covered with cloth or fancy paper, for binding a volume, or the periodical numbers or parts of a work; also a case for holding unbound serials, music, etc.

1885 C. MACKESON *Brit. Alm. Comp.* 94 In some parts of the country identical titles are very differently applied. Among the double meanings .. [is] Book Case Maker for a Cabinet-maker or Bookbinder.

ˈbook-craft. *Obs.* or *arch.* Book-learning, literary skill, literature: book-making, authorship.

c888 K. ÆLFRED *Boeth.* i, Boeþius..wæs in boccræftum ..se rihtwisesta. **1621** B. JONSON *Gipsies Metamorph.*, Some book-craft you have, and are pretty well spoken. **1831** SCOTT *Ct. Robt.* 17 The technical language of book-craft.

booked (bʊkt), *ppl. a.* [f. BOOK *sb.* and *v.*]

†**1.** Instructed in books. *Obs.*

1393 GOWER *Conf.* III. 319 She was wel taught, she was wel boked.

2. Entered in a book; registered; conveyed by charter.

1842 POE *M. Roget* Wks. 1864 I. 236 The recognized and booked principles. **1875** MAINE *Hist. Inst.* iv. 115 Over his own domain and 'booked' land.

3. *colloq.* Engaged, destined, bound; certain.

1840 HOOD *Up Rhine* 6, I am booked for a much longer journey. **1841** DE QUINCEY *Homer & H.* Wks. VI. 339 He, at least, is booked for the doctor. **1849** R. LEVINGE *C. Doolan* II. ix. 186 [He] declared that 'they were booked to have fine weather'.

4. Entered in an official book or list; scheduled.

1892 *Daily News* 3 June 5/4 That the Board of Trade shall have compulsory powers..to order a railway company to revise the booked time of the men. **1898** *Ibid.* 15 Dec. 7/4 Certain booked trains will be discontinued.

5. Having (a specified amount of) orders or engagements in one's book or books. Also with *up*; and in transf. sense: having engagements, engaged (cf. 3).

1905 *Westm. Gaz.* 3 Oct. 9/1 The iron, steel, and allied trades are heavily booked. **1911** JOHN VINCENT in *Rep. Labour & Social Cond. Germany* III. Nos. vi and vii. 52 We found..the trades were busy and well booked up with orders. **1952** GRANVILLE *Dict. Theatr. Terms* 30 *Booked up*, all seats reserved for a performance.

bookeler, obs. form of BUCKLER.

booker (ˈbʊkə(r)). Forms: 1-2 **bócere**, 2 **bokere**, 3 **bocare**, 9 **booker**. [OE. *bócere*, corresp. to OHG. *buohhâri*, Goth. *bôkareis*, :—OTeut. **bôkârjo-z*, f. *bok-* book; but in the modern senses formed anew on BOOK *v.*]

†**1.** A writer of books, a scribe. *Obs.*

c1000 *Ags. Gosp.* Matt. viii. 19 Ða ȝenealæhte him an bocere, and cwæð. c1175 *Cott. Hom.* 245 þa sunder halȝan and þa boceras. c1205 LAY. 32125 Alle þa bocares wise.

2. One who enters in a book; a book-keeper; **b.** *spec.* (see quot. 1863.)

1863 *All Y. Round* 11 July 472/2 Persons technically known as 'bookers', who were, in fact, spies, travelling in the omnibus, and yielding to the company as account of every passenger. **1881** WHITEHEAD *Hops* 62 The number of bushels..is entered in a book by a booker. **1883** J. Y. STRATTON *Hops & Hop-p.* 31 All being carefully entered in the account kept by the booker.

3. *techn.*

1864 H. BRUCE in *Parlt.* 14 June, With regard to the finishers and bookers..representation had been made to the Government.

bookery. [f. BOOK *sb.* + -ERY.]

†**1.** Study of books. *Obs.*

1599 BP. HALL *Sat.* II. ii. 28 Let them alone for me Busie their braines with deeper bookerie.

2. A collection of books, a library.

1812 MAD. D'ARBLAY *Diary* VI. 346 The abbé..has a bookery in such elegant order that people beg to go and see it. **1870** *Pall Mall G.* 4 Oct. 5 If these bookeries were not saved in time..the town authorities have reason to be ashamed.

†**ˈbook-fell.** *Obs.* (exc. *Hist.*) A skin prepared for writing upon, a sheet of vellum or parchment; a parchment or vellum manuscript.

a1000 in Thorpe *Laws* II. 244 (Bosw.) Ðæt hi habban blæc and bocfel. a1225 *St. Marher.* 23 þat ich hit write on boc-felle. **1863** FURNIVALL in *Reader* 28 Feb. 214 Those who love tall folios and book-fells. **1868** G. STEPHENS *Runic Mon.* I. ix, Our ancient bookfells.

bookful (ˈbʊkfʊl), *sb.* [see -FUL.] As much as fills a book; the entire contents of a book.

1599 SHAKS. *Much Ado* v. ii. 32 A whole booke full of these quondam carpet-mongers. **1879** BAIN *Higher Eng. Gram.* 80 A bookful of problems.

bookful, *a. rare.* †**1.** Full of knowledge gathered from books. *Obs.*

1709 POPE *Ess. Crit.* 616 The bookful blockhead, ignorantly read, With loads of learned lumber in his head.

2. Full or stored with books.

1896 *Literary World* 7 Aug. 115/2 Coleridge, in this bookful age, is..getting to be more and more *nominis umbra*. **1904** *Daily Chron.* 3 Oct. 3/4 In bookful loneliness.

†**ˈbook-hoard.** *Obs.* [OE. *bóc*, BOOK, + *hord*, HOARD.] A repository for books or documents. (An exclusively OE. word which was treated by Blount, and thence included in later Dicts.)

a1000 *Ags. Voc.* in Wr.-Wülcker 194 *Bibliotheca*.. bochord. [1670 BLOUNT *Law Dict.*, *Boc-hord* (Sax.), a place where Books, Evidences, Writings, or other like Monuments are kept, as the Rolls. So PHILLIPS, BAILEY, etc.]

bookhood (ˈbʊkhʊd). [see -HOOD.] †**a.** Knowledge of books, scholarship (*obs.*). **b.** The estate of dignity of a book.

1772 H. WALPOLE *Corr.* (1837) III. 46 Who has a better opinion of my bookhood than I deserve. **1881** *Southern Law Rev.* (*St. Louis*) VII. 289 This book dares to assert its bookhood independent of dress.

ˈbookie[1]. *Sc.* **buikie, bukie** (y). A small book.

1860 RAMSAY *Remin.* Ser. I. (ed. 7) 110 Before ye dee, ye should burn a' your wee bukies.

bookie[2] (ˈbʊkɪ). Also **booky.** Colloquial modification [see -Y[6]] of BOOK-MAKER 3.

1885 *Eng. Illustr. Mag. Apr.* 509/2 No rowdy ring, but a few quiet and well-known 'bookies', who were ready enough to lay the odds to a modest fiver. **1887** *Pall Mall Gaz.* 15 Sept. 5/1 Both played their parts so well that they collared both the 'bookies' without any trouble at all. **1934** SAROYAN *Daring Young Man* (1935) 219 Red, the bookie-clerk..had been stabbed by a crazy Russian who had lost twenty dollars on the ponies. **1949** N. ALGREN in *Penguin New Writing* XXXVI. 95 A tavern with a bookie in the back. **1968** *Times* 15 Nov. 16/2 One of his thirties-style bookie check suits.

ˈbookiness. *rare.* [f. BOOKY *a.*] Bookishness.

1883 DIX in *Standard* 21 Mar. 6/3 Worship of pedantic bookiness.

booking (ˈbʊkɪŋ), *vbl. sb.* [f. BOOK *v.* + -ING[1].]

†**1.** The action of making into a book. *Obs.*

1643 HERLE *Answ. Ferne* 1 What hath bin all this while a booking.

2. The action of entering in a book, *esp.* in order to engage a seat or place; also the issuing of tickets, entitling to the same.

1884 *Pall Mall G.* 5 Aug. 7/2 The number of bookings was much larger than..last year. **1884** *Daily News* 9 Apr. 5/3 The old second-class fares were retained..for first-class bookings.

3. *Sc. Law.* A tenure peculiar to the burgh of Paisley, whereby the proprietors held their lands under the magistrates, the conveyance being entered or 'booked' in the Burgh Register. (Abolished by 'The Conveyancing (Scotland) Act, 1874').

1868 *Act 31-2 Vict.* ci. §152 Lands in the burgh of Paisley, held by the peculiar tenure of booking.

4. *Comb.* **booking-clerk**, the clerk or official who books passengers or goods for a conveyance, or who sells tickets at a booking-office; **booking-office**, an office where places may be booked for a coach or other conveyance, or where goods may be booked for transit; also the place where tickets are sold at a railway or steam-boat station; the place where tickets are sold for a theatre or other place of entertainment (1889 *Cent. Dict.*).

1836-7 DICKENS *Sk. Boz* (1850) 79/2 Sally forth to the booking-office to secure your place. *Ibid.* 80/1 You wonder what on earth the booking-office clerks can have been before they were booking-office clerks. **1881** R. GRANT WHITE *Eng. Within & W.* iii. 60 At the 'booking-office' no booking is done..But as there were booking offices for the stagecoaches which used to run between all the towns..of England, the term had become fixed in the minds, and upon the lips of this nation of travellers. **1948** MENCKEN *Amer. Lang.* Suppl. I. 453 *Punch's* theatre article used to be headed 'Our *Booking Office*'. Today everybody speaks and writes of the *box-office* of a theatre. Only a railway ticket-office is a *booking-office*. **1952** GRANVILLE *Dict. Theatr. Terms* 30 *Booking office*, a theatre-booking agency in the city. Patrons are able to book seats through the agency, which communicates with the theatre concerned.

bookish (ˈbʊkɪʃ), *a.* [f. BOOK *sb.* + -ISH.]

1. Of or belonging to a book or books; literary.

1567 DRANT *Hor. Epist.* xiii. E iij, Thou must retaine thy bookish charge. **1594** *Ord. of Prayer* in *Liturg. Serv. Q. Eliz.* (1847) 657 Did not Saunders second his bookish treasons.. by commotion in Ireland? **1816** *Q. Rev.* XVI. 1 A phenomenon, in these days of bookish luxury. **1817** COLERIDGE *Biog. Lit.* 10 Natural Language, neither bookish nor vulgar. **1878** S. COX *Salv. Mundi* (ed. 3) Pref. 8 To recast these Lectures into a more bookish form.

2. Addicted to the reading of books; studious.

1570 LEVINS *Manip.* 144 Bookish, *studiosus.* **1611** SHAKS. *Wint. T.* III. iii. 73 Though I am not bookish, yet I can reade Waiting-Gentlewoman in the scape. **1665** D. LLOYD *State Worthies* (1670) 672 [Raleigh] An accomplished Gallant, and yet a bookish man. **1775** T. SHERIDAN *Art Reading* 330 Bookish men are remarkable for taciturnity. **1874** MAURICE *Friendship Bks.* i. 12 In this bookish time of James I.

b. Disparagingly: Acquainted with books only.

1593 SHAKS. *2 Hen. VI*, I. i. 259 Whose bookish Rule, hath pull'd faire England downe. **1680** CROWNE *Misery Civ. War* II. 16 Under the reign of this tame bookish Henry. **1712** ADDISON *Spect.* No. 482 ¶2 A bookish man, who has no knowledge of the world. **1864** BURTON *Scot Abr.* II. i. 68 A monkish, bookish person, who meddles with nothing but literature.

3. quasi-*adv.* = next.

1591 FLORIO *2nd Frutes* A iv. b, To..speake bookish.

bookishly (ˈbʊkɪʃlɪ), *adv.* [f. prec. + -LY[2].] In a bookish way, studiously.

a1668 J. THURLOW *St. Papers* II. 104 While she..was more bookishly given. **1840** MRS. TROLLOPE in *New Month. Mag.* LIX. 481 Whether bookishly disposed or not.

bookishness (ˈbʊkɪʃnɪs). [see -NESS.] Bookish quality; fondness for books or study; learning. (Often somewhat contemptuous.)

a1586 SIDNEY *Apol. Poetrie* (1622) 521 A chain-shot against all learning or bookishnesse, as they commonly term it. **1685** BAXTER *Paraphr. Acts* xxvi. 24 Much Learning or Bookishness hath distracted thee. **1878** MORLEY *Diderot* I. 210 Diderot despised mere bookishness.

bookism. *rare.* [see -ISM.] = prec.

1788 MAD. D'ARBLAY *Diary* (1842) IV. 176 A character for bookism and pedantry.

ˈbook-keep, *v. intr.* [Back-formation f. BOOK-KEEPING.] To do book-keeping, keep books.

1886 G. B. SHAW *Cashel Byron's Profession* Prologue 12, I could book-keep by double entry. **1917** *Dialect Notes* 408 *Book-keep*, to act as bookkeeper. 'He book-kept for the camp.'

book-keeper (ˈbʊkkiːpə(r)).

1. A person who keeps the accounts of a mercantile concern, public office, etc.

1555 *Act 2-3 Phil. & M.* vii. §4 The parties to the bargaine..shall come to the open place appointed for the toll taker, or for the booke keeper..and there enter..their names..in the toll takers book. **1842** DICKENS *Amer. Notes* (1850) 109/2 Melancholy ghosts of departed book-keepers, who had fallen dead at the desk.

2. One who hoards books; a book-miser. *rare.*

1884 *Harper's Mag.* Nov. 828/1 The old-fashioned book-keeper, who fears his precious books will be hurt by using.

book-keeping (ˈbʊkkiːpɪŋ). The art of keeping a merchant's or tradesman's books or accounts.

1689 *Lond. Gaz.* No. 2480/4 Merchants..who desire to be accomplish'd with the Famous Art of Book-keeping. **1817** J. SCOTT *Paris Revisit.* 82 What is poetry to one, may be book-keeping to another. **1849** J. FREESE *Comm. Class-bk.* III. 95 An introduction to book-keeping by single and double entry.

†**bookland.** *Obs.* exc. *Hist.* Forms: 1 **bócland**; *Antiq.* 7 **bock-**, 8-9 **boc-**, 9 **bok-**, **bookland.** The Old English name for land taken from the *folcland* or common land, and granted by *bóc* or written charter to a private owner; thus, at length, applied to all land that was not *folcland.* (Hence the common place-name *Buckland.*)

a1000 *Laws of Edgar* i. 2 (Bosw.) Ðe on his boclande cyricean hæbbe. **1641** *Termes de la Ley* 42 Bockland, in the Saxons time..was by that name distinguished from Folkland. **1670** BLOUNT *Law Dict.*, Bocland. **1768** BLACKSTONE *Comm.* II. 90 Book-land, or charter-land. **1860** C. INNES *Scotl. Mid. Ages* ii. 54 Bocland or Charterland was such as was severed by an act of the government, that is, by the King with the consent of his parliament, from the public land. **1875** STUBBS *Const. Hist.* I. v. 76 As the primitive allotments gradually lost their historical character..the ethel is lost sight of in the bookland. **1876** FREEMAN *Norm. Conq.* V. xxiv. 368 The man who received a grant of book-land on such terms as made it practically as much his own as a primitive eðel.

book-lare, -lear, Sc. forms of BOOK-LORE.

book-latin: see BOC-LEDEN.

book-learned (ˈbʊk,lɜːnɪd), *a.* Learned in books or the knowledge acquired from them. (Now generally in disparaging sense). Hence **book-learnedness.**

c1420 *Anturs Arth.* lv, Boke-lornut byrnus, and bischoppus of the beste. **1601** DENT *Pathw. Heauen* 328, I am somewhat ignorant, I am not book-learned. **1697** COLLIER *Ess. Mor. Subj.* I. (1709) 79 Your old Heroes in Homer (for want of being Book-Learned), were none of the Gentilest-Men. a1700 DRYDEN (J.) Whate'er these booklearn'd blockheads say. **1837** EMERSON *Misc.* 77 The book-learned class, who value books as such.

1661 K. W. *Conf. Charac.* (1860) 37 He hath obtained to so high a measure of book-learnednes.

So **ˈbook-ˌlearning,** learning derived from books (merely), knowledge of books.

1589 *Hay any Work* 2 In my book learning, the one was some popish Trull. c1645 HOWELL *Lett.* (1650) III. 14 The extravagant humour of our Countrey is not to be altogether commended, that all men should aspire to booke learning. **1838** HAWTHORNE *Amer. Note-bks.* (1871) I. 157 Intelligent as respects book-learning, but much deficient in worldly tact. **1855** MACAULAY *Hist. Eng.* III. 308 He had as little book-learning as the most stupid ploughboys of England.

†**ˈbook-lered.** *Obs.* [see LERE *v.* to teach.] = BOOK-LEARNED.

c1205 LAY. 25624 Biscopes þis iherden & bocilærede men. a1275 *Prov. Alfred* 4 in *O.E. Misc.* 103. c1325 *Allit. P.* B. 1551 He bede his burnes boȝ to þat were bok lered.

bookless (ˈbʊklɪs), *a.* [see -LESS.]

1. Ignorant of books, unscholarly. *poet.*

1735 SOMERVILLE *Chase* I. 395 How mean, how low, The bookless saunt'ring Youth. a1763 SHENSTONE *Wks.* (1764) I. 293 Why, with the cit, Or bookless churl..deign'st thou to reside? **1847** TENNYSON *Princess* II. 42.

2. Destitute of books.

1788 COWPER *Lett.* (1824) II. 123 Inform a bookless student in what region..his long-lost volumes may be found. **1865** *Pall Mall G.* 7 Oct. 11 The dusty tourist, lounging in the deserted streets of bookless Caceres, or Alcantara.

booklet (ˈbʊklɪt). [see -LET.] A tiny book.

1859 *Sat. Rev.* 19 Feb. 220/1 The infant booklet, deprecating rigid criticism and modestly pleading the advice

of friends. **1885** *Illust. Lond. News* 19 Sept. 290/1 Booklets that we can carry in the pocket.

booklike ('bʊklaɪk), *a.* and *adv.* Like a book.
1839 BAILEY *Festus* xii, It holds the starry transcript of the skies Booklike, within its bosom.

bookling ('bʊklɪŋ). [see -LING.] A little book.
1803 SOUTHEY *Life* (1850) II. 230 The twelfth of the booklings [i.e. cantos] into which it [Madoc] is now divided. **1822** *Blackw. Mag.* XII. 656 The dainty booklings of our poetesses. **1881** *Athenæum* 26 Mar. 425/3 The curious booklings which Eliot saw through the press during his lifetime.

'book-lore. [An OE. and early ME. comb. used again in our own day, with other combinations of LORE. In mod. use first in Sc., where perhaps it may have come down from early times.] Book-learning, knowledge gained from books.
a **1000** *Canons of Ælfric* 23 (Bosw.) Blind biþ se lareow, ȝif he ða boclare ne cann. *c* **1200** *Trin. Coll. Hom.* 155 Oðre lorðeawes þe cunnen holie boc-lore. **1808** JAMIESON *Dict.* s.v., 'I gat nae buik-lare'. **1818** SCOTT *Leg. Montrose* ii, My legs and arms stood me in more stead than either my gentle kin or my book-lear. **1863** GILCHRIST *Life Blake* I. 38 Education—as to book-lore neglected.

book-maker ('bʊkmeɪkə(r)).
†**1.** One who makes a book (as a material product); a printer and book-binder. *Obs.*
1515 in Glasscock *Rec. St. Michaels, Bp. Stortford* 34 Item pd. to th bokemaker and his servaunt..xxxiijs. iiijd. **1711** (*title*) J. DISTAFF *Character of Don Sacheverellio*, Printed and Sold by Francis Higgins, Bookmaker.
2. One who composes or compiles a book; often disparagingly, one who makes a trade of this.
1533 MORE *Apol.* I. Wks. 928/2 For of newe booke makers there are now moe then ynough. **1841** EMERSON *Man the Reformer* Wks. 1875 II. 241 Better that the book should not be quite so good, and the bookmaker abler and better. **1849** EARL LONSDALE in *Croker Papers* (1884) III. xxvi. 202 He [Arthur Young] was spoilt by the success of his early works, and became a bookmaker. **1878** MORLEY *Diderot* I. 218 Cases in which he reproduced, as any mere bookmaker might have done, the thought of his authority.
3. A professional betting man. Cf. BOOK *sb.* 11.
1862 *Lond. Rev.* 30 Aug. 188 Betting there seemed to be none..we could not perceive a single book or book-maker. **1880** W. DAY *Racehorse in Train.* xxiv. 245 Bookmakers pursue a legitimate and lucrative trade by laying against all horses as they appear in the market.

book-making ('bʊkˌmeɪkɪŋ).
†**1.** The manufacture of books (as material articles). *Obs.*
1487 *Ch.-warden's Acc. St. Dunstan's, Canterb.*, John Casse hathe delyueryd..to the booke makyng iijs. iiijd. **1899** T. VEBLEN *Theory of Leisure Class* vi. 162 Artistic book-making. **1930** *Publishers' Weekly* 5 Apr. 1892/1 The increasing attention that the book-trade is giving to the art of book-making.
2. The compilation of books. (Now usually contemptuous: see prec. word.) Also *attrib.*
1589 *Marprel. Epit.* (1843) 8 Note here a new founde manner of bookemaking. **1615** LATHAM *Falconry* Ded., I am not so well experienced in the art of bookemaking. **1794** MATHIAS *Pursuits Lit.* (1798) 384 It is mere book-making, beneath the character of so learned a gentleman as Dr. Warton. **1807** *Cabinet* I. 113 This is a fine *book-making* age. *a* **1856** in K. H. DIGBY *Lover's Seat* (1856) II. xviii. 222 Of all the books in this book-making world the philosophical books are the least intelligible. **1865** *Englishm. Mag.* 220 Bookmaking now has got a bad name, or at any rate the term is used in a bad sense.
3. The making of a betting-book.
1824 *Sporting Mag.* XV. N.S. 51/2 Betting at present proceeds but slowly..what is done consists merely in book-making and speculation. **1836** R. S. SURTEES in Mrs. Mathews *Mem. C. Mathews* (1839) IV. ix. 184 He entered into the spirit and excitement of the thing with the true ardour of a turfite, without any knowledge however of the science of book-making. **1886** *Boston* (*Mass.*) *Herald* 16 July, In England, book-making is rigidly prohibited elsewhere, but on the race tracks it is allowed.
Hence (as back-formation) **'book-make** *v. intr.* (*rare*).
1819 BYRON *Let.* 6 Apr. (1900) IV. xvii. 284, I could have spun the thoughts of the four cantos of that poem into twenty, had I wanted to book-make. **1845** R. BROWNING *Let.* 16 Apr. (1899) 48 Mrs Norton has gone and book-made at a great rate about the Prince of Wales.

bookman ('bʊkmən). A scholar, a student.
1583 *Exec. for Treason* (1675) 42 Scholars, or Book-men. **1588** SHAKS. *L.L.L.* IV. ii. 35 You two are book-men: Can you tell by your wit, etc. **1621** BP. MOUNTAGUE *Diatribæ* 403 You, so great a booke-man, know well enough, etc. **1817** MAR. EDGEWORTH *Ormond* v. (1832) 51 Did you ever hear of the Stoics that the book-men talk of? **1859** GEN. P. THOMPSON *Audi Alt.* II. lxxxiii. 45 A certain Hermann, whom the book-men call Arminius. **1871** MORLEY *Crit. Misc.* (1886) I. 75 He figured as the philosopher and bookman of the party.

†**'book-pad,** *v. Obs.* [f. BOOK + PAD, after *foot-pad.*] *trans.* & *intr.* To steal matter from (a book), to plagiarize. Hence **book-padding** *vbl. sb.*, (perh. confused with the other sense of padding.)
1685 F. SPENCE *House Medici* 281 He book-padded the ancient panegyricks of the noblest thoughts that suited with his subject. **1723** S. MATHER *Vind. Bible* Pref. 3 He charges Dr. Lightfoot with book-padding out of Aynsworth.

book-plate ('bʊkpleɪt). A label, usually pasted inside the front cover of a book, bearing the name or crest of the owner, or other device indicating ownership, position in a library, etc.
1791 J. IRELAND *Hogarth Illustr.* I. Introd. 22 The works of..Callot were probably his first models; and shop-bills and book-plates his first performances. **1850** *N. & Q.* I. 212 The book-plate with the following device—an eagle or vulture feeding with a snake another bird, nearly as large as herself. **1880** WARREN *Book-plates* i. 2 The word book-plate in its technical sense of exact equivalence to *ex-libris.*

'book-ˌread, *ppl. a.* Well read in books, skilled in book-learning.
1591 SPENSER *M. Hubberd* 358 They forg'd another, as for Clerkes booke redd. **1876** EMERSON *Ess.* Ser. II. viii. 187 Rich, ignorant, book-read, conventional, proud men.

bookseller ('bʊkˌsɛlə(r)). A vender of books.
1527 *Higden's Polycron.* (*title*), Imprented..at ye expences of John Reynes bokeseller. **1542–3** *Act 34–35 Hen. VIII*, i, Ani printer, bokebinder, bokeseller, or anie other person. **1615** CROOKE *Body of Man* 420 He dissected a Bookseller, and found his heart more then halfe rotted away. **1788** *Walpoliana* clxix. 77 One of those booksellers in Paternoster-row who publish things in numbers. **1816** J. GILCHRIST *Philos. Etym.* Introd. 4 He only glanced over it for a short time in a bookseller's shop.
Hence **'bookˌsellerish** *a.*, **'bookˌsellerism.**
1778 R. POTTER in *Parr's Wks.* (1828) VIII. 228 The common complaint against authorism and booksellerism. **1815** SOUTHEY *Lett.* (1856) II. 414 It is impossible that any compositions can be more booksellerish.

bookselling ('bʊkˌsɛlɪŋ), *vbl. sb.* The trade of a bookseller.
1530 *Royal Priv.* in Palsgr. p. xi, Medlyng with the faite of printyng or bokesellyng. **1788** *Walpoliana* xxxiii. 17 The manœuvres of bookselling are now equal in number to the stratagems of war. **1839** HALLAM *Hist. Lit.* I. ciii. §145 The trade of bookselling seems to have been established at Paris and at Bologna in the twelfth century.
2. *attrib.* or *adj.* That sells books; pertaining to the selling of books.
1824 DIBDIN *Libr. Comp.* Introd. 17 The several great bookselling houses. **1839** LOCKHART *Ballantyne-humbug* 6 Scott lost a fortune by the bookselling speculation. *Ibid.* 25 The early period prior to the bookselling adventure. **1884** *Athenæum* 12 Jan. 54/1 The bookselling fraternity.

bookspell, -staff, -stave: see BOCSPELL, etc.

book-store. Chiefly *U.S.* [BOOK *sb.* 18 a.] A bookshop.
1763 *Boston Even. Post* 3/3. **1785** A. ELLICOTT in C. V. Mathews *Life & Lett.* (1908) 51 Examined several Book stores. **1810** *Edin. Rev.* XVII. 121 Booksellers' shops passing under the name of '*Book Stores'. **1884** *Harper's Mag.* Feb. 420/2 His bookstore in Boston. **1959** *Times Lit. Suppl.* 6 Nov. p. xx/1 The paperback revolution is at work everywhere, but especially in college towns and in college bookstores.

booksy ('bʊksɪ), *a. colloq.* [f. *books* pl. of BOOK *sb.* + -Y[1].] Having literary or bookish pretensions; usu. in jocular or derisory use.
1934 A. WOOLLCOTT *While Rome Burns* III. iv. 185 The library of this booksy Aspasia. **1945** 'M. INNES' *Appleby's End* ii. 11 In Mr. Raven's presence everything turned booksy. **1958** *Woman's Own* 3 Sept. 55/1 I'm going to borrow Jack and snitch him away from your booksy conversations.

'bookwards, *adv.* [see -WARDS.] In the direction of books, in print.
1850 L. HUNT *Autobiog.* II. xvi. 217 He..never modified or withheld any opinion (in private or bookwards) except in consideration of what he thought they..might not like.

'book-ways, 'bookwise, *adv.* In the manner or form of a book.
1696 *Lond. Gaz.* No. 3228/2 Act allowing Securities, etc., to be written Book-ways.

book-wise ('bʊkˌwaɪz), *a.* Book-learned.
1616 SURFL. & MARKH. *Country Farm* 24 Your Farmer..need not to be Booke-wise. **1885** *Cassell's Fam. Mag.* Jan. 83 Wishing she had had more schooling, and that Peter might grow up 'book-wise'.

book-worm ('bʊkwɜːm).
1. *lit.* A kind of maggot which destroys books by eating its way through the leaves.
1855 MRS. GATTY *Parables fr. Nat.* Ser. XVIII. (1809) 66 The bookworm..had just eaten his way through the back of Lord Bacon's Advancement of Learning. **1886** *Bookseller* 6 Nov. 1180 A living specimen of a bookworm..Book-worms are the larvæ of a small beetle (*anobium.*)..I discovered that many of the volumes contained living bookworms.
2. *fig.* One who seems to find his chief sustenance in reading, one who is always poring over books.
1599 B. JONSON *Cynthia's Rev.* III. ii, Perverted and spoiled by a whoreson book-worm. *a* **1736** POPE *Lett.* Wks. 1736 V. 141, I wanted but a black gown and a salary, to be as meer a bookworm as any there. **1865** MERIVALE *Rom. Emp.* VIII. lxvii. 278 No sophist, no schoolman, no mere dreaming bookworm.

booky ('bʊkɪ), *a. colloq.* Characterized by or derived from books; given to books; bookish.
1832 PAULDING *Westward Ho!* I. xiii. 194 You're one of the booky fellers, that think on one thing while they are talking about another. **1880** MARK TWAIN *Tramp Abr.* II. 202 Lessons in morals..which come not of booky teaching, but of experience. **1884** GRANT ALLEN *Str. Stories* 105 Gladys was clever too, though not booky. **1941** MASEFIELD *Gautama the Enlightened* 13 Basil Blackwell's shop..within whose booky house Half England's scholars nibble books or browse.

booky. Slang representation of BOUQUET. Cf. BOKAY.
1848 THACKERAY *Van. Fair* i. 2 'We have made her a bow-pot.' 'Say a bouquet, sister Jemima, 'tis more genteel.' 'Well, a booky as big almost as a hay-stack.'

bool, mod.Sc. form of BOUL, curvature, round, handle, and of *boule*, BOWL, ball, bowl, marble.
1826 J. WILSON *Noct. Ambr.* Wks. 1855 I. 170 Frae the size o' a peppercorn to that o' a boy's bools.

bool, obs. form of BAWL *v.*

boold(e, obs. form of BOLD.

boole, obs. f. BOLE *sb.*[2], BOWL *sb.*[1] and BULL.

Boolean ('buːlɪən), *a.* Also **Boolian.** [f. the proper name *Boole* (see below) + -AN, -IAN.] Of or pertaining to the work of George Boole (1815–64), English mathematician and logician; ***Boolean algebra***, an abstract system of postulates and symbols applicable to problems in logic and the manipulation of sets; a Boolean ring; ***Boolean expansion***, an expansion of a Boolean expression involving 'or' in terms of a logically equivalent series of expressions each involving only 'and'; ***Boolean operation*** (see quot. 1962); ***Boolean ring***, a ring with unity in which every element is idempotent.
1851 *Cambr. & Dublin Math. Jrnl.* VI. 192 The Hessian, or as it ought to be termed, the first Boolian Determinant. **1889** *Cent. Dict.*, Boolian algebra. **1913** *Trans. Amer. Math. Soc.* XIV. 481 A set of five independent postulates for Boolean algebras. **1924** *Ibid.* XXVI. 175 A commutative boolean operation which always has an inverse is also associative. **1936** M. H. STONE in *Ibid.* XL. 38 We shall..take as the central theme of this paper not merely Boolean algebras, but, more generally, rings in which every element is idempotent, designating the latter systems as Boolean rings or generalized Boolean algebras. **1948** AMBROSE & LAZEROWITZ *Fund. Symbolic Logic* v. 78 Such a listing of the conjunctive conditions for the truth of a disjunction will be called a Boolean expansion, because it expands a function into a form which exhibits all the conjunctive possibilities for its being true. **1955** J. L. AUSTIN *How to do Things with Words* (1962) ii. 17 Despite the name, you do not when bigamous marry twice. (In short, the algebra of marriage is *Boolean.*) **1962** *Gloss. Autom. Data Processing* (*B.S.I.*) 29 *Boolean operation*, an operation depending on the application of the rules of Boolean algebra. By extension, any operation in which the operands and results take either one of two values or states, i.e. any logical operation on single binary digits. **1964** *Language* XL. 266 The designatum of the whole expression is a Boolean sum of the designata of the members.

boolie, var. of BOWLY *Sc.*, crooked.

†**booly.** *Obs.* Also 6 **bolye.** [ad. Irish *buaile* cattle-fold, or its deriv. *buailidh*; deriv. of *bo* cow, or ad. L. *bovīle.*] A temporary fold or enclosure used by the Irish who wandered about with their herds in summer; a company of people and their cattle thus wandering about. Hence Spenser has **booling** for the practice.
1596 SPENSER *State Irel.* (1809) 82 All the Tartarians and ..Scythians, live in hordes; being the very same that the Irish boolies are, driving their cattle with them, and feeding only on their milk and white meats. *Ibid.* 494 By this custom of booling there grow in the meantime many great enormities unto that commonwealth. **1610** FOLKINGHAM *Art of Survey* I. x. 25 In the North of Ireland, they do with much conuenience, by kreating [= creaghting] & shifting their Boolies from seed-fur til haruest bee inned, both depasture & soile their grounds. **1846** W. H. MAXWELL *Capt. Blake* I. vii, The tenants of the lonely *bouillie.* (*Bouillies*, are summer bivouacs, used by shepherds when depasturing their flocks in the mountains.)

boom (buːm), *sb.*[1] Also 6–7 **bomb(e.** [f. BOOM *v.*[1]] **1.** A loud, deep sound with much resonance or humming effect, as of a distant cannon, a large bell, etc.: also the usual word for the cry of the bittern.
? *a* **1500** *Frere & Boye* 176 in Ritson *A.P.P.* 41 Tempre thy bombe, he sayd, for shame. **1626** BACON *Sylva* §151 A Pillar of Iron..which, if you had struck, it would make a little flat noise in the Room where it was struck; but a great bomb in the Chamber beneath. **1795** SOUTHEY *Vis. Maid Orleans* I. xv, The bittern's boom was heard; hoarse, heavy, deep. **1816** KIRBY & SP. *Entomol.* (1843) II. 301 This evening boom of beetles; this nocturnal buz of gnats. **1843** LEVER *J. Hinton* liv. 341 The loud boom of a gun struck upon my ear. **1846** RUSKIN *Mod. Paint.* (1848) I. II. II. i. §21. 151 The dull boom of the disturbed sea. **1858** HAWTHORNE *Fr. & It. Jrnls.* I. 232 The great bell of St. Peter's tolled with a deep boom.
2. Special Comb. **boom box** *slang* (orig. *U.S.*) = *ghetto blaster* s.v. GHETTO *sb.* 3 b.
[**1978** *Time* 23 July 60/1 Their ears are tuned constantly to what they call the box... For a mere £55 a box-toter can get a General Electric tape model... It is called Loudmouth.] **1981** *N.Y. Times* 5 June D5/4 The portable stereo craze actually started three or four years ago with the so-called *boom boxes. **1985** *Washington Post* 26 June C10 How about a law against playing 'boom boxes' in public places?

boom (buːm), *sb.*[2] *Naut.* Also (in sense 3) 8 **bomb.** [a. Du. *boom* 'tree, beam, pole', corresp.

to OHG., MHG. *boum*, mod.G. *baum*, also to OE. *béam*, and mod. BEAM: taken from Du. in senses in which the Eng. *beam* was not used.]

1. a. 'A long spar run out from different places in the ship, to extend or boom out the foot of a particular sail; as jib-boom, flying jib-boom, studding-sail booms.' Smyth *Sailor's Word-bk.* 1867.

1662 in Birch *Hist. Royal Soc.* (1756) I. 91 The violence of it snapt off their boom by the board. **1692** in *Capt. Smith's Seaman's Gram.* xvi. 76 A *Boom*, a long Pole used to spread out the Clew of the Studding-sail, etc. **1719** DE FOE *Crusoe* I. ii. 20 She sail'd with . . a Shoulder of Mutton Sail; and the Boom gib'd over the Top of the Cabin. **1742** ANSON *Voy.* III. v. 341 The mast, yard, boom, and outriggers, are all made of bamboo. **1850** BLACKIE *Æschylus* II. 252 With broken booms and fragments of the wreck.

b. *pl.* That part of a ship's deck where the spare spars are stowed.

1762-9 FALCONER *Shipwr.* II. 262 The yards secure along the booms were laid. **1803** NELSON in Nicolas *Disp.* (1845) V. 205 Hardy [is] rigging the main-yard on the booms. **1833** MARRYAT *P. Simple* (1863) 92 Mr. Chucks then sat down upon the fore-end of the booms by the funnel. **1867** SMYTH *Sailor's Word-bk.*, *Booms*, a space where the spare spars are stowed; the launch being generally stowed between them.

c. *Aeronaut.* (See quot.)

1916 H. BARBER *Aeroplane Speaks* 135 *Boom*, a term usually applied to the long spars joining the tail of a 'pusher' aeroplane to its main lifting surface.

d. A movable bar supporting a microphone or camera. Also *attrib.*

1931 [see MICROPHONE 3]. **1932** *Wireless World* 10 Feb. 146/1 A microphone suspended on a boom. **1958** *Manchester Guardian* 10 June 6/2 The narrative swings as if on a studio boom-arm from character to character. **1959** *Viewpoint* July 34 The boom operator has found his first boom, or microphone, shadow.

†**2.** A pole set up to mark the course of the channel or deep water. ? *Obs.*

1705 HARRIS *Lexicon Techn.* s.v. *Boom* . . The Poles with Bushes or Baskets on the Top, which are placed to direct how to steer into a Channel are called Booms, and by some Beacons. **1755** in JOHNSON; and in mod. Dicts. [Not in SMYTH *Sailor's Word-bk.*]

3. a. A bar or barrier consisting of a strong chain or line of connected spars, pieces of timber bound together, etc., stretched across a river or the mouth of a harbour to obstruct navigation.

c **1645** HOWELL *Lett.* (1650) I. 215 The sea-works and booms were traced out by Marquis Spinola. **1655** LESTRANGE *Chas. I*, 93 Before his coming the Cardinal had finisht his prodigious Boom and Barricado [at Rochelle] through which it was impossible to break. **1689** LUTTRELL *Brief Rel.* I. 549 The Irish had laid a great chain with a boom acrosse the river. **1702** W. J. *Bruyn's Voy. Levant* x. 37 Anciently a Chain or Bomb lay across from Castle to Castle, to prevent the passing of Ships. **1769** FALCONER *Dict. Marine* (1789). **1855** MACAULAY *Hist. Eng.* III. xii, Large pieces of fir wood strongly bound together, formed a boom which was more than a quarter of a mile in length.

b. *pl.* The floating timbers placed between portions of the lines of piles marking the regatta course at Henley-on-Thames, to prevent the encroachment of boats during a race.

1899 *Daily News* 5 July 4/7 It will be impossible to pronounce definitely on the success of the booms until the regatta is in full swing. **1902** *Encycl. Brit.* XXXII. 306/2.

4. a. In the American lumber-trade: A line of floating timber stretched across a river or round an area of water to retain floating logs.

1702 C. MATHER *Magn. Chr.* VII. (1852) App. 592 She stole along by the river side, until she came to a boom, where she passed over. **1829** D. CONWAY *Norway, &c.* 190 The booms that are placed across the stream nearer its mouth. **1848** THOREAU *Maine W.* i. (1864) 32 Showing no traces of man but some low boom in a distant cove reserved for spring use. **1865** —— *Cape Cod.* vi. 105 The inhabitants visit the beach to see what they have caught as regularly as . . a lumberer his boom. **1884** S. E. DAWSON *Hand-bk. Canada* 20.

b. ***fender***, ***glancing***, or ***sheer boom***, a boom erected to guide logs in the desired direction. *U.S.*

1896 *U.S. Monthly Weather Rev.* Nov. 407 (Cent. Dict. Suppl.), The driving of piles . . to hold a sheer boom for the purpose of running the logs.

5. *Comb.*, as ***boom boat***, ***-chain***, ***fence***, ***log***, ***-man***, ***-stick***, ***timber***, etc. (sense 4); **boom-boat**, a boat stowed on the booms (see 1 b); **boom-brace pendant**, 'a rope attached to the extremity of a studding-sail boom, used to counteract the pressure of the sail upon the boom' (Smyth); **boom-cover**, a cover for the spars when stowed on deck; **boom end** *v. trans.*, to run out a boom or spar at the end of a yard so as to extend the foot of a sail; **boom-ended** *a.*, having the studding-sail booms rigged in, so that their ends do not project beyond the yard-arms; **boom-iron**, an iron ring fitted on the yard-arm, through which the studding-sail boom slides when rigged out or in; a similar ring by which the flying jib-boom is secured to the jib-boom, or this to the bowsprit; **boom-jigger**, a tackle for rigging the top-mast studding-sail booms out or in; **boom mat** (cf. MAT *sb.*[1] 4); **boom net**, a fishing-net connected with a boom; **boom-sail**, a sail (foresail or mainsail) which is set to a boom instead of to a yard (opposed to *square foresail* or *mainsail*); **boom-sheet**, a sheet fastened to a boom; **boom-spar**, see BOMESPAR.

1966 *Canad. Geogr. Jrnl.* June 214/3 Log booms, loose logs, and *boom boats were swept out of the bay. **1969** *Islander* (Victoria, B.C.) 7 Sept. 10/2 Mainland Prince had been en route up coast to pick up a tow, with a boom boat tied astern. **1883** J. FRASER *Shanty, Forest, & River Life* 281 The first business of the drive is to . . confine them there by long half-square logs called 'boom timber', fastened at the ends by '*boom chains'. **1969** *Islander* (Victoria, B.C.) 31 Aug. 16/3 He was an excellent swimmer but was carrying boom chains around his shoulders as he went out on the booms. **1890** CLARK RUSSELL *Ocean Trag.* I. viii. 164 Then *boom-ending her fore-topmast studdingsail she backed her main topsail. **1840** R. DANA *Bef. Mast.* xxvii. 90 The studding-sail halyards were let go, and the yards *boom-ended. **1848** THOREAU *Maine Woods* (1864) 42 Surrounded by a *boom fence of floating logs. **1881** *Daily Tel.* 28 Jan., The propeller is fast taking the place of the old *boom-foresail. **1769** FALCONER *Dict. Marine* (1789) **Boom-iron* . . is employed to connect two cylindrical pieces of wood together, when the one is used as a continuation of the other. **1829** MARRYAT *F. Mildmay* viii, A tail block was attached to the boom-iron, at the outer extremity of each fore-yard-arm. **1945** *Reader's Digest* Aug. 86 He and Dad are looking for *boom logs. **1829** MARRYAT *F. Mildway* xx, She had a square mainsail, *boom mainsail, and jib. **1908** M. A. GRAINGER *Woodsmen of West* 28 The work for a practised *boom-man, was now to take a long, light pole, and jumping upon a floating log, to stand upon the log and pole it into the boom-stick enclosure. **1883** *Man. Seamanship Boys' Training Ships* 182 In making a heavy *boom mat a fiddle is used instead of a loom. **1925** *Glasgow Herald* 25 Aug. 5 The relationships of the young year classes caught by *boom-net and seine-net to the mature herring in the drift-net fishery. **1769** FALCONER *Dict. Marine* (1789) *Chandeliers* . . the crutches fixed on the stern or quarter of a *boom-sail vessel. **1836** MARRYAT *Pirate* viii, Ease off the *boom sheet. **1850** S. JUDD *R. Edney* xvi. 207 They found Chuk in trouble; his guys had parted, and his *boom-sticks were broken. **1879** *Lumberman's Gaz.* 18 June 6 It shall be unlawful for any person other than the owner thereof . . to take possession of . . any log, spar, boomstick, etc. . . in any waters in this State [Michigan]. **1883** *Boom timber [see *boom chain* above].

boom (buːm), *sb.*[3] orig. *U.S.* [This and its verb (BOOM *v.*[3]) have arisen recently in U.S.: it is not clear whether the vb. is from the sb., or conversely. The actual origin is also a matter of conjecture; probably, it consisted in a particular application of BOOM *sb.*[1] and its vb., with reference not so much to the sound, as to the suddenness and rush, with which it is accompanied. Cf. esp. BOOM *v.*[1] 1 c., and 2. But association, original or subsequent, with other senses of BOOM, is also possible, and the actual use of the word has not been regulated by any distinct etymological feeling, so that no derivation will account for all its applications.]

1. a. A start of commercial activity, as when a new book, the shares of a commercial undertaking, or the like 'go off' with a 'boom'; a rapid advance in prices; a sudden bound of activity in any business or speculation.

1879 *Lumberman's Gaz.* 19 Dec., There has not been the boom upon lumber experienced in many other articles of merchandise. **1880** *World* 3 Nov. 5 The election of the American President is expected to be followed by a 'boom' that will take up prices. **1884** *St. James's G.* 26 Jan. 4/1 With the revival of prosperity in the United States the great boom in railway properties set in. **1884** *Times* 28 Nov. 4 Building 'Boom' in the United States. —— MARSTON *Frank's Ranche* 36 One railroad spoils a town, two bring it to par again, and three make a 'boom'. **1911** E. M. CLOWES *On Wallaby* ii. 31 The Land Boom—'the Boom', as it is always called . . had a most potentially humanizing effect on the people. **1936** M. PLOWMAN *Faith called Pacifism* 28 The people of this country were enjoying a post-war boom. **1955** *Bull. Atomic Sci.* Mar. 88/2 Thus the uranium boom began. **1966** *Economist* 19 Nov. 778 The country is in boom and therefore deficit.

b. Phr. ***boom and*** (***or***) ***bust***: a period of great prosperity followed by a severe depression. orig. *U.S.*

1943 H. S. CANBY *Walt Whitman* iii. 18 The building trade, as usual, suffered from boom-and-bust. **1947** D. RIESMAN in *Yale Law Jrnl.* Dec. 194 The luxury market would be . . entitled . . to its privilege of boom and bust. **1962** *Times Lit. Suppl.* 13 July 502/1 Cataclysmic alternatives—destruction or utopia, boom or bust.

2. The effective launching of anything with éclat upon the market, or upon public attention; an impetus given to any movement, or enterprise; the vigorous 'running' or writing-up of a candidate for an election; a vigorously worked movement in favour of a candidate or 'cause'.

1879 SALA in *Daily Tel.* 26 Dec., The Grant 'Boom' may be succeeded by the Sherman 'Boom'. **1884** *Reading Morn. Herald* 15 Apr., Blaine's book was issued . . just at the critical moment in his boom for the Presidency. **1884** *Lisbon* (*Dakota*) *Star* 10 Oct., How Electioneering Booms are Worked Up by the Faithful.

3. *attrib.*, as **boom city**, **town**, one that owes its origin, growth, or prosperity to a boom in a particular trade, mining, etc.

1886 *Leslie's Pop. Monthly* XXI. 306/1 Cities . . whose inhabitants had yet to be gathered in from the four corners of the earth by boom magic. **1891** *Anthony's Photogr. Bull.* IV. 23 The old town of San Juan Capistrano I found had been divided in the 'boom' times. **1896** *Chautauquan* XXIII. 219/1 Who first began to talk about . . 'boom' towns? **1904** *Philad. Public Ledger* 14 June 6 No 'boom city' of the West can boast such a record of amazing . . growth. **1944** J. S. HUXLEY *On Living in Revol.* xiii. 138 The boom period in 1928. **1955** *Times* 20 May 14/1 Some call Wolverhampton a 'boom town'. There are full employment, high wages, and no industrial unrest. **1969** *Scotsman* 25 Apr. 9/3 The country's two boom areas—the South-east of England and West Midlands.

boom (buːm), *v.*[1] Forms: 5 **bombon**, **bummyn**, **bumbyn**, **bome**, 6 **bomme**, 7– **bomb**, (9 **bome**), 8– **boom**. [Of imitative origin; whether original in Eng. it is impossible to determine; cf. Ger. *bummen*, Du. *bommen*, of similar meaning, ODu. *bom* a drum; also BOMB, which in its origin is closely allied. The development of sense 2 is not quite clear; it may be a different word.

But in Sc., the equivalent 'bum' is used both of the hum of bees, etc., of the *sound* of a passing shot or stone, and of the rushing *motion* of a stone or the like, as 'to *bum* stones at any one', to kick an object and 'send it *bumming* (i.e. spinning) away'.]

1. *intr.* To hum or buzz, as a bee or beetle; to make a loud, deep sound with much resonance, as a cannon, a large bell, the waves of the sea, etc.; also the usual word to express the cry of the bittern.

c **1440** *Promp. Parv.* 55 Bombon as been [K., H., **1499** bummyn or bumbyn], *bombizo*. **1653** PALSGR. 460/1 This waspe bommeth about myne eare. **1713** YOUNG *Last Day* I. 27 Booming o'er his head The billows close. **1815** HOGG *Pilgrims of Sun* II. Poems (1822) II. 48 Swift as the wild-bee's note, that on the wing Bombs like unbodied voice along the gale. **1840** BARHAM *Ingol. Leg.* 407 Unless I get home, Ere the curfew bome. **1865** MISS BRADDON *Only a Clod* xxxvii. 303 All the machinery in London seemed buzzing and booming in her ears. **1879** FARRAR *St. Paul* II. 44 The bittern booms amid its pestilent and stagnant marshes.

b. *trans.* Usually with *out*. To give forth or utter with a booming sound.

1837 CARLYLE *Fr. Rev.* II. VI. vi. 354 Saint-Antoine booming out eloquent tocsin, of its own accord. **1870** MISS BRIDGMAN *R. Lynne* I. xvii. 303 The . . clock boomed out twelve.

c. In *Curling*, etc.: To move rapidly onward with booming sound. Cf. BUM *v. Sc.*

a **1835** HOGG in *Whistle-binkie* (Sc. Songs) Ser. III. 34 We'd boom across the Milky Way, One tee should be the Northern Wain, Another bright Orion's ray, A comet for a Channel Stane!

2. *intr.* 'To rush with violence; as a ship is said to come booming, when she makes all the sail she can' (Phillips 1706, whence in J. etc.).

? **1617** *Fight at Sea* in Arb. *Garner* II. 200 The first of them booming by himself before the wind. **1706** PHILLIPS. **1876** C. D. WARNER *Winter on Nile* x. 130 We are booming along all night. **1879** *Lumberman's Gaz.* 19 Dec., The three drives . . with plenty of water come booming along at a most lively rate.

boom (buːm), *v.*[2] [f. BOOM *sb.*[2]; in sense 1 b app. directly from Du. *boomen* 'to push with a pole', as the sb. appears not to be used in this sense. Cf. BOLM.]

1. *Naut.* (*trans.*) **a.** ***to boom out***: to extend (the foot of a sail) with a boom. **b.** ***to boom off***: to push (a vessel) off with a pole.

1627 CAPT. SMITH *Seaman's Gram.* ix. 41 With a Boome boome it out. **1840** MARRYAT *Poor Jack* xxxv, We boomed her off from the Wharf. **1857** S. OSBORN *Quedah* vi. 72 Our sails being at the time boomed out.

2. a. To furnish (a river or piece of water) with a boom to retain floating timber; to collect (logs or timber) in a boom. *N. Amer.* See BOOM *sb.*[2] 4.

1879 *Lumberman's Gaz.* 1 Oct., Numerous lakes communicating with the main Slough have been boomed.

b. To protect (a regatta course) from encroachment by pleasure boats during a race, by placing floating booms (BOOM *sb.*[2] 3 b) between the piles. Also with *off*.

1899 *Daily News* 29 Apr. 7/3 It is proposed to 'boom' the whole length of the course along the Bucks side and for some distance on the Berks side. **1902** *Encycl. Brit.* XXXII. 306/2 This proposal to boom off the [regatta] course was very severely criticized.

3. Cf. BOOMING *vbl. sb.* 2.

boom (buːm), *v.*[3] orig. *U.S.* [see BOOM *sb.*[3]]

1. *intr.* to 'go off' with a 'boom'; to burst into sudden activity or briskness; to make rapid (commercial) progress, to advance vigorously.

1871 'MARK TWAIN' *Lett. to Publishers* (1967) 55 My popularity is booming, now. **1875** *Scribner's Mag.* July 272 Stocks may 'boom' to-day, but droop to-morrow. **1879** *Lumberman's Gaz.* 15 Oct., Every one says business is booming. **1882** *Century Mag.* XXV. 101 The gay, storm-beleaguered camp, in the words of its exhibitory press, began to boom. **1883** *Leis. Ho.* 283/2 This metropolis . . has boomed into something highly commonplace and respectable.

2. *trans.* To give a 'boom' to; to push, puff, force upon public attention, 'write up'. Also *absol.* To work up a 'boom'.

1879 *Indianapolis Jrnl.* 23 Apr., The rest are in varying degrees positive, if not 'all "booming" for U. S. Grant'. **1882** *Century Mag.* XXIV. 506 To 'boom' a town in Dakota is an art requiring . . no end of push and cheek . . Fargo is said to be the best-boomed town in Dakota. **1884** *Boston* (*Mass.*) *Jrnl.* 22 Nov. 2/4 The *World* is booming Mr. Conkling for United States Senator. **1891** *Confectioners' Union* 15 Aug.

451/1 Messrs. J. S. Fry..are booming their manufactures in a novel way. **1894** *Country Gentlemen's Catal.* 15/1 If..cider [were] properly 'boomed', the consumption of it might be vastly increased. **1901** *Daily Colonist* (Victoria, B.C.) 27 Oct. 10/1 He says the country was boomed out of all reason, and is now suffering from an inevitable reaction. **1915** W. Owen *Let.* 5 Mar. (1967) 325 My prime object is not..to boom a monster business. **1926** *Spectator* 30 Oct. 752/2 Dreyer's 'diaplytes', most deplorably boomed here, with official support. **1966** *New Statesman* 25 Mar. 414/2 One minor political figure in Alabama, a certain Shorty Price, decided to boom his own wife for governor.

boom, boomb, obs. forms of BOMB.

boomage ('buːmɪdʒ). [f. BOOM *sb.*² + -AGE.] **a.** 'A duty levied to compound for harbour dues, anchorage, and soundage' (Smyth *Sailor's Word-bk.*). **b.** A toll levied by the owner of a boom on its use for storing logs.

1862 *Stat. Pennsylv.* 396 To prevent collecting boomage upon non-marked lumber.

boombas, variant of BOMBASE *v. Obs.*

boom-boat. (Also **bomboat.**) [BOOM *sb.*²] Any of the boats stowed in the booms of a vessel.

1867 Smyth *Sailor's Word-bk.* **1874** Bedford *Sailor's Pocket Bk.* vii. 226 By placing boats inside her present boom boats. **1893** *Daily News* 3 July 5/6 Seeing the critical condition of the Victoria,..boats were immediately prepared and boom boats got ready to be hoisted out.

boomed, *ppl. a. Naut.* [f. BOOM *sb.*² or *v.*² + -ED.] Furnished with or set to a boom.

1628 Digby *Voy. Medit.* (1868) 81 Then wee all chaced with all the sayle we could make (and we added seuerall boomed sayles).

boomer¹ ('buːmə(r)). [f. BOOM *v.*³ 2.] One who 'booms' or pushes an enterprise. *U.S. slang.*

1883 *Times* 26 Sept. 8 [He] is a North-Western 'boomer' of great earnestness. **1885** *Boston* (*Mass.*) *Jrnl.* 19 Aug. 2/4 The Oklahoma boomers.

'boomer². Also formerly **boomah**. **a.** A name given in Australia to the male of the largest species of kangaroo.

1830 Ross *Hobart Town Almanack* 110 (Morris), Snapped the boomah's haunches, and he turned round to offer battle. **1852** Mrs. Meredith *My Home in Tasmania* I. 244 (Morris), The oldest and heaviest male of the herd was called a 'Boomer'. **1881** *Times* 28 Jan. 3/4 The marsupial with a body which surpassed in bulk that of the 'boomer'. **1925** H. Graham *Last of Biffins* ii. 28 A man whom even the older kangaroos ('boomers' as they are locally called) looked up to. **1967** *Sunday Mail Mag.* (Brisbane) 16 Apr. 2 Catching boomers isn't easy because they are big kangaroos.

b. *transf.* Something very large or notable of its kind. *Austral. slang.*

1885 *Australasian Printers' Keepsake* 76 (Morris), When the shades of evening come, I choose a boomer of a gum. **1928** 'Brent of Bin Bin' *Up Country* xiii. 135 Old Healey is always telling some boomer of a scandal behind people's backs. **1941** Baker *Dict. Austral. Slang* 12 *Boomer*, a particularly ambitious lie. Used loosely to denote anything large or noteworthy. **1962** *Austral. Women's Wkly.* Suppl. 24 Oct. 3/1 *Boomer*, big wave.

boomerang ('buːməræŋ), *sb.* Also 8–9 **bomarang, bomerang, boomering.** [Adoption or modification of the native name in a lang. of the aborigines of N. S. Wales.

Collins (Judge Advocate of the colony when founded in 1788) collected a short vocabulary of Port Jackson words, in which *wo-mur-rāng* occurs among 'names of clubs'. (He has also *wo-mer-ra* the throwing stick, which some later writers erroneously identify with the boomerang.) In a short vocabulary of the extinct language of George's River, Botany Bay, printed by Ridley, *Kámilarói* 103, are *womrā* 'throwing stick for spear', *būmarin* 'boomerang'. *Boomerang* was given as 'the Port Jackson term' by Capt. King in 1827; its exact relation to *wo-mur-rāng* and *būmarin*, and the relations of these to each other can perhaps not now be determined. A very graphic account of the use of the weapon (described as 'a bent, edged waddy resembling slightly a Turkish scimitar') is in the *Sydney Gazette* of 23 Dec. 1804: the name *boomerang* has not been found in that paper up to 1823.]

1. An Australian missile weapon: a curved piece of hard wood from two to three feet long, with a sharp edge along the convexity of the curve. It is so made as to describe complex curves in its flight, and can be thrown so as to hit an object in a different direction from that of projection, or so as to return to or beyond the starting-point.

[**1798** Collins *Acct. N. S. Wales*, Vocab. 'names of Spears and other instruments', *Can-ni-cull, Car-ru-wāng, Wom-ur-rāng*, names of clubs.] **1827** Capt. King *Narr. Surv. Coasts Austral.* I. 355 Boomerang is the Port Jackson term for this weapon, and may be retained for want of a more descriptive name. **1830** *Mechanic's Mag.* XIII. 430 Captain Cook, when at Botany Bay, having seen the bomarang, concluded that it was a wooden sword. **1830** *Proc. R. Geog. Soc.* I. 27 The curl or boomering is seldom used as a weapon [in W. Australia]. **1834** L. E. Threlkeld *Austral. Gram.*, *Vocab. Hunter Riv. Tur-ru-ma*, an instrument of war, called by Europeans *Boomering* of a half-moon shape, which, when thrown..returns forming a circle in its orbit from and to the thrower. **1834** G. Bennett *Wand. N. S. Wales, &c.* 116 The males were armed with spears, clubs, and the 'womera' or 'bomerang'. **1838** S. Ferguson in *Trans. R. Irish Acad.* XIX. 22 (*paper*), On the Antiquity of the Kiliee or Boomerang. **1871** Tylor *Prim. Cult.* I. 60 The Australian boomerang has been claimed as derived from some hypothetical high culture.

fig. **1845** Holmes *Modest Req.* Poems (1884) 42 Like the strange missile which the Australian throws, Your verbal boomerang slaps you on the nose. **1870** Lowell *Among my Bks.* Ser. I. (1873) 219 The boomerang of argument, which one throws in the opposite direction of what he means to hit.

2. *attrib.* and *Comb.*; esp. *fig.* (with reference to its action in returning to the thrower).

1892 *Daily News* 30 June 5/5 It is..quite a boomerang business. Tories built the fort in anticipation of the battle of 1880, and to-day the Liberals hold it. **1898** *Ibid.* 21 Apr. 5/2 Rawson, the Australian boomerang thrower, will take part. **1949** C. Fry *Lady's not for Burning* II. 58 Boomerang rages and lunacies. **1955** *Times* 20 May 10/6 The..agitation.. may ultimately have a boomerang effect on the party itself. **1968** *Daily Tel.* 16 Dec. 1/8 Russia's unmanned Zond 5 and 6 made successful 'boomerang' flights round the moon.

boomerang ('buːməræŋ), *v.* [f. the sb.] *intr.* To throw a boomerang; to fly back to the starting-point, after the manner of a boomerang when thrown; also *fig.* Also with advbs. *off, on.* So **'boomeranging** *vbl. sb.*

1880 J. B. Stephens *Misc. Poems* 26 War shouts and universal boomeranging. **1899** *Longman's Mag.* XXXIII. 475 Boomeranging is dangerous for on-lookers, till the thrower is a perfect master of his weapon. **1900** H. Lawson *On Track* 59 The horse..boomeranged off again and broke away through the scrub. **1936** *Discovery* Apr. 125/2 It is easily possible for a deflecting wind to cause a shot to boomerang. **1943** H. Pearson *Conan Doyle* iii. 39 If your magnet is so strong as all that, you would have your own broadside boomeranging back upon you. **1965** *Listener* 24 June 928/1 But the psychologically dangerous stratagem soon boomeranged.

booming ('buːmɪŋ), *vbl. sb.* [f. BOOM *v.*¹,²,³.]

1. The emitting of a deep, resonant sound.

1774 Goldsm. *Nat. Hist.* III. 214 Of all sounds there is none so dismally hollow as the booming of a bittern. **1855** Macaulay *Hist. Eng.* IV. 535 The distant booming of cannon was heard..from the batteries of the Tower. **1878** Black *Green Past.* xxviii. 226 The booming of the fog-horn at night is one of the most horrid sounds in the world.

2. 'The accumulation and sudden discharge of a quantity of water (in placer mining, where water is scarce).' Raymond *Mining Gloss.* 1881.

1880 *Toronto Globe*, Miners in the Far West have a practice of conducting explorations by a means which they call 'booming'. It consists in damming up some gorge on a mountain side and allowing the water from melting snow to accumulate till an immense reservoir has been formed. When the pond is full an outlet is made, and the water rushes down with irresistible force, overwhelming everything in its path..Rich veins and deposits of ore are often uncovered by this process.

3. See BOOM *sb.*³, BOOM *v.*³

1881 *Chicago Times* 1 June, The Texas market is also advised as active, and in some cases excited, but..this 'booming' tendency is at least a little premature.

4. See BOOM *v.*² 2 b.

1900 *Daily News* 6 July 7/4 Owing to the booming of the course, the expenses of the regatta are much heavier.

'booming, *ppl. a.* [f. as prec. + -ING².]

1. Making a deep hollow reverberating sound.

1626 B. Jonson *Masques* Wks. 1692. 647 Bombing sighs. **1762–9** Falconer *Shipwr.* II. 552 O'er The sea-beat ship the booming waters roar. **1853** Kane *Grinnell Exp.* xxxii. (1856) 279 One wild, booming, agonized note, made up of a thousand discords.

2. Of business, etc.: Flourishing, advancing on a tide of prosperity. (See BOOM *v.*³) orig. *U.S.*

1879 *Lumberman's Gaz.* 29 Oct., Salt is 'booming', as it has been all the season. *Ibid.* 12 Nov., New life and energy has been infused into all channels of business—things are booming. **1883** *Leis. Ho.* 283/1 Pueblo is the very centre of South Colorado traffic, and certainly booming. **1896** J. A. Hobson *Probl. of Unempl.* 50 Where improvements of machinery occur during periods of 'booming' trade they do not occasion any large quantity of unemployment or distress. **1964** *Sun-Herald* (Sydney) 21 June 136/4 The railways have been doing booming business this year. **1968** *Times* 9 Dec. 7/2 The booming new science of infra-red astronomy.

'boomingly, *adv.* With a booming noise.

1839 *Fraser's Mag.* XX. 63 The billows of fire rolling boomingly past.

boomkin: see BUMKIN.

boomlet ('buːmlɪt). orig. *U.S.* [f. BOOM *sb.*³ + -LET.] A small boom, esp. on the Stock Exchange.

1880 *Puck* (U.S.) 21 Apr. 106/3 All the other booms and alleged boomlets. **1897** H. Bottomley in J. R. Ware *Passing Eng.* (1909) s.v., I may mention that during the recent West Australian boom—or, as some of my Stock Exchange friends prefer to call it, 'boomlet'—we succeeded in realising, etc. **1898** *Westm. Gaz.* 23 Apr. 9/2 A very favourable feature has been a recovery in Westralian stocks. Something like a boomlet prevailed at first. **1900** *London Stock Market Rep.* 18 Aug. 5 What may be called a Republican boomlet has been started in the Yankee corner. **1961** *New Statesman* 27 Oct. 626/2 The boomlet in shipping shares collapsed at once. **1966** *Economist* 5 Mar. 919/1 A little boomlet in consumer demand towards the end of last year.

‖**boomslang** ('buːmslæŋ, 'boːmslaŋ). *S.* and *E. Afr.* [Afrikaans, f. *boom* tree + *slang* snake.] The tree-snake *Dispholidus typus.*

1793 tr. *Thunberg's Trav.* I. 156 A serpent..was found here, called the *Boomslang*, or (tree serpent) on account of its being frequently found in trees. **1849** Andrew Smith *Illustr. Zool. S. Afr.*, *Reptilia* Plate xiii, The natives of South Africa regard the *Boom-slange* as poisonous; but in their opinion we cannot concur. The *Boom-slange* [*Bucephalus capensis*] is generally found upon trees. **1912** Fitzsimons *Snakes S. Afr.* 136. **1952** *Cape Argus* 7 June 2/7 Cobras, puff-adders, boomslangs and other deadly snakes. **1970** *Cape Times* 22 Jan. 6/3 The ban applies to black mambas as well as green..and also to cobras, rinkhalse, boomslange.. and the..harmless mole snake.

'boomster. *U.S. slang.* = BOOMER¹; one who works up a 'boom'; a speculator.

1879 *Nation* 9 Oct. 236 The trickery and usurpation..of the leading boomster. **1884** S. E. Dawson *Hand-bk. Canada* 331 The speculators, called, in vivid Western parlance, boomsters.

boomy ('buːmɪ), *a.*¹ [f. BOOM *sb.*¹ + -Y¹.] Having the noise or quality of a boom; = BOOMING *ppl. a.* 1.

1909 *Westm. Gaz.* 31 Mar. 2/3 The motor-omnibus..was too bulky, boomy, bumpy. **1939** *Amat. Radio Handbk.* viii. 116 If the speaker is too close to the microphone the quality will tend to be 'boomy'. **1956** E. Delaney in S. Traill *Play that Music* 55 Tune it properly: side-drum crisp, bass-drum nice and deep—not boomy but thick.

boomy ('buːmɪ), *a.*² *colloq.* [f. BOOM *sb.*³ + -Y¹.] Of, pertaining to, or characteristic of an economic, financial, or manufacturing boom; prosperous.

1888 *Manch. Even. News* 7 Sept. 2/3 Yesterday afternoon there was a boomy feeling in the mining market. **1967** *Economist* 12 Aug. 556/1 On balance, therefore, the prospect of British exporters will certainly be brighter if the boom gets boomier but not all that much so if this particularly import-restraining tax goes through. **1977** *Time* 31 Jan. 40/1 The 3% growth figure for the fourth quarter would have been about 8%—the highest since the boomy 9.2% of early 1976.

boon (buːn), *sb.*¹ Forms: 2–7 **bone**, 3–4 **bon**, (2, 5 **bune**, 3 **bun**, 3, 6 **boun**, 4 **boyn**, 5 **boyne**), 4–8 **boone**, (6 **bowne**, **bound**), 5– **boon**. [a. ON. *bón*, the etymological correspondent of OE. *bén*, ME. BENE, prayer. Through such phrases as 'ask a boon', 'have one's boon', 'grant a boon', taken without analysis, the sense easily passed, by insensible transitions, from 'prayer', to 'favour asked', 'favour conferred', 'free gift', 'good thing received'. The adj. *boon* 'good' probably aided in this development.]

†**1.** A prayer, petition, entreaty, request. *Obs.*

a. A prayer to God, Christ, etc.

c **1175** *Lamb. Hom.* 63 Ah lauerd god, her ure bone. *a* **1225** *Ancr. R.* 28 Þe seoue bonen iþe Paternoster. *a* **1300** *Cursor M.* 3690 Godd..has herd mi bon. *Ibid.* 25306 Hu wath it es to bid þis bun. *c* **1380** *Sir Ferumb.* 3948 To ihesu þanne he bad a bone. *c* **1460** *Towneley Myst.* 12 Lord of heven, thou here my boyne [*rime* done]. **1513** Douglas *Æneis* x. v. 90 Ene..can pray and maid hys bone.

b. A request addressed to a human being; *esp.* the asking of a favour.

c **1205** Lay. 14912 Þe king uor his fader bone ȝette hire hir bone [? bene]. *c* **1385** Chaucer *L.G.W.* 1592 The kyng assentede to his bone [*v.r.* boone]. *c* **1440** *Gesta Rom.* (1879) 153 He grauntid, that the trespassour shulde aske iij. bonys or he deyde. **1530** Palsgr. 199/2 Bone, a request, *requeste.* *a* **1581** Campion *Hist. Irel.* II. vii. (1633) 94 Her husband assented, and accomplished her boone effectually. **1623** Cockeram, *Boone*, a request.

†**2.** A request made with authority; a command or order couched in the form of a request. *Obs.*

c **1300** *St. Brandan* 631 Ich aros to don his holi bone. *c* **1325** *E.E. Allit. P.* B. 826 Agayne þe bone of þe burne þat hit forboden hade. *a* **1400** *Cov. Myst.* (1841) 28 Why hast thou synnyd so sone, Thus hastyly to breke my bone. *c* **1400** *Destr. Troy* 505 Sho obeit his bone. **1593** Shaks. *3 Hen. VI*, III. ii. 46 *Wid.* What you command, that rests in me to doe. *King.* But you will take exceptions to my Boone.

3. *transf.* The matter prayed for or asked; *esp.* in ***to have one's boon, to grant one his boon.*** (Cf. use of *prayer, request.*) *Obs.* or *arch.*

c **1175** *Lamb. Hom.* 37 Ȝif þu wult habben bone to drihten. *a* **1300** *Cursor M.* 8414 He yatte hir freli al hir bone. *c* **1385** Chaucer *L.G.W.* 2337 God..sende the thyn bone. *c* **1386** —— *Knts. T.* 1811 Mars hat his wille, his knyght hath al his boone. *c* **1440** *Promp. Parv.* 43 Bone, or graunte of prayer. **1488** Caxton *Chast. Goddes Chyld.* 95 Thou shalt haue thy askynge and thy boone. **1513** More *Rich. III*, Wks. 59/1 God loued her better, then to graunt her her boone. **1645** Milton *Tetrach.* Wks. 1738 I. 245 If the Law come down ..to grant lust his boon. **1823** Scott *Peveril* I. vi. 106 Cousin, you must grant me my boon.

b. A thing asked as a favour; a favour (asked for). *arch.*

c **1200** Ormin 7606 Drihhtin haffde ȝatedd himm þatt bone þatt he ȝeorrnde. *c* **1305** *Pilate* 229 in *E.E.P.* (1862) 117 Grante me ane bone, ȝif me an appel to ete. *c* **1400** *Ywaine & Gaw.* 2790 The yonger mayden than alsone Of the King askes this bone. *c* **1440** *York Myst.* xviii. 36 Þis bone of þe I crave. **1483** Caxton *G. de la Tour* C ij, I pray yow alle..to graunte me a bone and a yefte. **1575** *Appius & Virg.* in Hazl. *Dodsl.* IV. 143 Then tender your child that craveth this bound. **1588** Shaks. *Tit. A.* II. iii. 289 Vpon my feeble knee, I beg this boone, with teares, not lightly shed. *c* **1650** *Rob. Hood & Fryer* 116 A boone, a boone, said the curtall fryer..Give me leave to set my fist to my mouth. **1862** Trench *Mirac.* xxiii. 343 She has a boon to ask for her daughter.

†**c.** *to pray* (*one*) *of a boon. Obs.*

1393 Gower *Conf.* I. 207 He..praid him of a bone, To se this Custe. *c* **1440** *Gesta Rom.* (1879) 411, I pray the,..of a bone, that thou wilte herborow me this nyght. **1481** Caxton

Reynard (Arb.) 34, I pray you of a bone, that I may to fore you alle make my confession.

4. A favour, a gift, a thing freely or graciously bestowed: **a.** in response to asking. *arch.*

c **1460** *Towneley Myst.* 282 Send us, lord, this blissid bone. *c* **1520** *Adam Bel* 509 in Hazl. *E.P.P.* II. 160 Madame, ye myght have asked a bowne, That shuld have ben worth them all three. **1630** PRYNNE *God No Impostor* 30 We deserue no boone, no fauor at his hands. **1712** ARBUTHNOT *John Bull* (1727) 71 What art thou asking of them, after all? Some mighty boon? **1839** THIRLWALL *Greece* VI. 319 A boon like that which Aristotle had obtained from Philip.

b. without the notion of asking. In 17th c. applied to a largess, gratuity or present; but now only *fig.* and *arch.*

1662 FULLER *Worthies* (1840) II. 508 The Queen..seldom gave boons, and never forgave due debts. **1677** MARVELL *Season. Argument* Wks. 1776 II. 558 He..has got by boones, at several times..3000*l.* *Ibid.* 579 A boon given him in the excise which he sold for 13500*l.* **1679** PEPYS *Diary* VI. 130, I have never..done it to the obtaining sixpence from the Crown by any boon extraordinary. **1738** GLOVER *Leonidas* I. 144 The choicest boons of fate. **1830** D'ISRAELI *Chas. I*, III. viii. 161 The Earl..had accepted with difficulty, the boon of his freedom. **1845–6** TRENCH *Huls. Lect.* Ser. II. viii. 269 The gods had no better boon for him than an early death.

†**c.** Grace, favour. *rare.*

1820 KEATS *St. Agnes* xxiv, Down she knelt for heaven's grace and boon. **1821** —— *Isabel* xix, Of thee we now should ask forgiving boon.

5. A gift considered with reference to its value to the receiver; a benefit enjoyed, blessing, advantage, a thing to be thankful for: sometimes without even the notion of giving, but always with that of something that one has no claim to, or that might have been absent. (The usual current sense.)

1767 T. HUTCHINSON *Hist. Prov. Mass. Bay* i, The charter of Massachusets was not so great a boon. **1820** KEATS *St. Agnes* xxxix, An elfin storm from faery land, Of haggard seeming, but a boon indeed. **1855** MAURY *Phys. Geog. Sea* iii. (1860) §185 The presence of the warm waters of the Gulf Stream..is a great boon to navigation. **1856** SIR B. BRODIE *Psychol. Inq.* I. App. 270 The inestimable boon of articulate language. **1876** GREEN *Short Hist.* iii. §3 (1882) 124 The boon of free and unbought justice was a boon for all.

6. An unpaid service due by a tenant to his lord. Cf. 'benevolence'. *Obs.* exc. *dial.*

1634 SANDERSON *Serm.* II. 294 Racking their rents, taking in their commons, overthrowing their tenures, diminishing their wages, encreasing their boons. **1703** BP. T. WILSON in Keble *Life* v. (1863) 194 To leave all such carriages, Boones and services on the same foot as already provided for by Law. **1855** *Whitby Gloss.*, *Boon*, a stated service rendered to the landlord by the tenant.

b. Hence ***boon-day***, ***-loaf*** (a loaf allowed to a tenant when working on a boon-day), ***-man***, ***-work***; also **c. boon-ploughing**, **-shearing**, a day's ploughing or shearing given gratuitously to a farmer by his neighbours on a special occasion.

1679 BLOUNT *Anc. Tenures* 153 The custom was here for the Natives and Cottagers to plow and harrow for the Lord, and to work one *boon-day for him every week in Harvest. **1788** MARSHALL *Rur. Econ. Yorksh.* (1796) I. 41 Tenant agrees..to perform the customary leadings, or boondays. **1863** ATKINSON *Provinc. Danby, &c.* s.v. *Boon-days.* **1679** BLOUNT *Anc. Tenures* 143 Every plow was to be allowed four *boon-loaves. **1727** BP. T. WILSON in Keble *Life* xx. (1863) 680 The *boon-men i.e. they who owe him rent in the way of work. **1886** *Carlisle Jrnl.* 23 Feb. 2/4 *Boon Ploughing at Burgh. **1875** *Lanc. Gloss.* (E.D.S.) **Boon-shearin* (N. Lanc.), a quantity of shearing given as in the case of a boon-ploo [= boon-ploughing]. **1883** SEEBOHM *Eng. Vill. Community* 78, *Precariæ* or *boon-work, i.e. special work at request.

¶ Occasionally *boon* appears to have the sense of 'good', but in the earlier instances at least the sense of 'favour asked' or 'conferred', is more or less apparent. Modern archaists complete the confusion with BOON *a.*

c **1325** *E.E. Allit. P.* B. 1089 Hade bodyly burne abiden þat bone..His lyf wer loste. *c* **1650** *Came you not, &c.* 12 in Furniv. *Percy Folio* I. 254, I haue Land att durham will feitch my hart to boone. **1874** HOLLAND *Mistr. Manse* xxi. 83 The steps were scaled for boon or bale. **1884** SKRINE *Und. Two Queens* II. 34 Boon we mingle and bane.

boon, *sb.*[2] Forms: 4 bon(e, 5–6 bunne, 9 boon: see also BUN. [Of unknown etymology: see BUN.] The stalk of flax or hemp after the fibre has been removed; the stalks of cow-parsnip and other umbelliferous plants.

1388 WYCLIF *Isa.* i. 31 Ȝoure strengthe schal be as a deed sparcle of bonys [*v.r.* stobil], *ether of herdis of flex.* *c* **1440** *Promp. Parv.* 277 Kyx, or bunne, or drye weed. **1615** MARKHAM *Eng. Housew.* (1649) 182 All the loose buns and shivers that hang in the hemp or flaxe. **1838** *Penny Cycl.* X. 305 The flax plants are passed between these cylinders..and the stalk, or boon, as it is technically called, is by this means completely broken without injuring the fibres.

boon (buːn), *a.* (and *adv.*) Forms: 4–9 bon, 4–7 bone, 4–5 bonne, (6 boun), 6–7 boone, (7 boune), 4– boon. [a. OF. *bon*, *bone* good: used esp. in what were orig. French phrases (e.g. *bone chere*, *bon sire*, *bone order*, *bon voiage*, *bone fortune*, etc.), but to some extent in general Eng. use from 14th to 17th c.; after 1600 it seems to have been consciously recognized as French, and gradually dropped, exc. in senses 3 and 4. In sense 3 it was probably associated with the Eng. sb. BOON[1], in its later sense of 'favour, benefaction, good gift'.]

A. *adj.*

†**1.** Good, goodly. *Obs.* (in 17th c.)

c **1325** *E.E. Allit. P.* A. 28 He schal loke on oure lorde with a bone chere. *c* **1325** *Coer de L.* 1540 They come to cyte boon. *c* **1384** CHAUCER *H. Fame* 1022 Seint Iulian! lo, bon hostelle! *c* **1425** *Seven Sages* (P.) 1013 Maugré have thow, bone sire. *c* **1435** *Torr. Portugal* 2143 Of speche he is fulle bone. **1523** LD. BERNERS *Froiss.* I. cccxcix. 692 Euery man drewe in bone order into the feldes. **1537** LATIMER *2nd Serm. bef. Convoc.*, Let vs all make bon chere [ed. **1635** good cheer]. **1617** J. TAYLOR (Water P.) *Trav.* Wks. (1630) III. 78/1 Four pots of boone beere as yellow as gold. *a* **1641** BP. MOUNTAGU *Acts & Mon.* (1642) 302 Nicolaus Damascenus; a great Orator and boon pleader. **1686** W. DE BRITAINE *Hum. Prudence* xviii. (ed. 3) 83, I am of that boon Courage.

†**2.** Advantageous, fortunate, favourable, prosperous: *esp.* in the once universal phrase ***boon voyage*** prosperous journey, also *fig.* good success. Hence, ***to drink upon*** or ***in boon voyage***. *Obs.*

1494 FABYAN VI. ccx. 225 One broughte forthe a bolle full of mede..to drynke vpon bon vyage. **1563–87** FOXE *A. & M.* I. 384/2 Drinking one to another in boun voyage of the spoil of them whom they would take as their prisoners. **1590** GREENE *Never too Late* Wks. 1882 VIII. 20, I may wish boone fortune to thy iourney. **1631** HEYWOOD *Maid of West* IV. Wks. 1874 II. 311 Quaffe unto the health of our boone voyage. *c* **1645** HOWELL *Lett.* I. i. iv. (1726) 21. **1657** S. PURCHAS *Pol. Flying Ins.* 329 These cunning Philosophers..can..with Judas embrace a man with a courtly boone-congee, and at parting cut a mans throat. [**1680–**: cf. *bon voyage* s.v. BON *a.* k].

3. Gracious, bounteous, benign; = L. *almus*, *alma*. *poetic.*

a **1612** HARINGTON *Epigr.* II. (1633) 50 Our boon God did benignly heare. **1667** MILTON *P.L.* IV. 242 Flours..which..Nature boon Powrd forth profuse. *c* **1800** K. WHITE *Poems* (1837) 146 But may all nature smile with aspect boon. **1814** CARY *Dante* (Chandos) 301 Its boon influence. **1841** EMERSON *Method Nat.* Wks. 1875 II. 224 This wasteful hospitality with which boon nature turns off new firmaments. **1869** M. ARNOLD *Switzerl.* III. *Farewell* xxi, How sweet to feel, on the boon air, All our unquiet pulses cease!

4. In ***boon companion***, lit. 'good-fellow', used in a jovial bacchanalian sense, transferred to other phrases, and occas. predicatively: Jolly, convivial.

1566 DRANT *Med. Morall* A v, He is my bone companion, its he that cheares up me. **1604** *Meet. of Gallants at Ord.* 21 A boone companion lighted amongst good fellowes, as they call good fellowes now a dayes, which are those that can drink best. **1622** DEKKER & MASSINGER *Virg. Martyr* II. i, Bacchus..this boon Bacchannalian skinker. **1667** MILTON *P.L.* IX. 793 Hight'nd as with Wine, jocond and boon. **1712** ARBUTHNOT *John Bull* (1755) 6 A boon companion, loving his bottle and his diversion. **1827** LYTTON *Pelham* xiv, He was also the boonest of companions. **1853** KANE *Grinnell Exp.* xxxi. (1856) 268 The effort of each man to..be very boon and jolly. **1884** TENNYSON *Becket* 61 My comrade, boon companion, my co-reveller.

b. Hence **boon companionship**; **boonfellow** (treated as a single word).

1844 DISRAELI *Coningsby* I. v. 23 All the resources of boon companionship. **1876** G. MEREDITH *Beauch. Career* II. ix. 171 A good friend and not a bad boonfellow.

†**B.** *adv.* Well, gently, favourably.

Old Song, '*Oh! firm as Oak*', While boon the wind blows, And smooth the tide flows.

boon, *v.* *Obs.* or *dial.* Also 7 beun. [f. BOON *sb.*[1]]

†**1.** To pray for, ask as a boon. *Obs.*

c **1200** ORMIN 694 þatt Zacariass Godess preost..O Drihhten haffde bonedd. *Ibid.* 5223 Lef faderr, icc þe bone, ȝiff me nu þatt twifalde gast.

2. *trans.* ***to boon away***: to give away in boons.

c **1661** in *Harl. Misc.* (1746) VIII. 27/1 What was got by Oppression, will be booned away by the King's Liberality.

†**3.** *intr.* To do boon-work: see BOON *sb.*[1] 6.

1691 RAY *N.C. Wds.* 9 *To Boon* or *Beun*, to do Service to another as a Landlord.

†**4.** *trans.* To repair (public roads). *dial.* Perhaps as one of the chief forms of *boon-work*: but there may be influence of BOON *sb.*[1] or *a.* in other senses.

1783 AINSWORTH *Lat. Dict.* (Morell) I To boon [repair the roads], *vias hyeme corruptas æstate reparare.* **1877** E. PEACOCK *N.W. Linc. Gloss.*, *Boon*, to repair a highway, 'I'd hev' all cheches pull'd doon to boon th' roads wi'.'

boon(e, **boond(e**, dial. or obs. ff. of BOUND.

†**'boonage.** *Obs.* [f. BOON *sb.*[1] + -AGE. Cf. BONAGE.] = BOON *sb.* 6; boon-work.

1610 FOLKINGHAM *Art of Survey* IV. iv. 84 Boonage, Fines, Heriots, Reliefes.

boondock ('buːndɒk). *U.S. slang.* [ad. Tagalog *bundok* mountain.] Rough country; jungle; an isolated or wild region. Usu. in *pl.* Also *attrib.*

1944 C. WYNN in C. Metcalf *Marine Corps Reader* III. 139 The sand and boondocks of Paris Island. **1950** H. L. MILLER in *Word Study* Oct. 7/1 Today Marines use boondock clothes and boondock shoes for hikes and maneuvers. **1951** *N.Y. Times Mag.* 10 June 39/1 Sculthorpe is known to its temporary guests as 'the boondocks', as much for its isolation as anything else. **1965** *Spectator* 12 Mar. 317/1 Those who have been feeling the public pulse out in the boondocks report a good deal of unrest.

Hence **'boondockers**, shoes suitable for rough outdoor use.

1953 L. M. URIS *Battle Cry* II. iii. 127 Andy Hookans was dumping a can of footpowder into his boondockers. **1957** *New Yorker* 16 Nov. 193/1 My hacking jacket and pair of old Marine Corps boondockers.

boondoggle ('buːndɒg(ə)l), *sb.* and *v.* *U.S. slang.* [Origin unknown.] **A.** *sb.* **a.** (See quots. 1935.) **b.** A trivial, useless, or unnecessary undertaking; wasteful expenditure. **B.** *v. intr.* To engage in trifling or frivolous work. Hence **'boondoggler**, **'boondoggling**.

1935 R. MARSHALL in *N.Y. Times* 4 Apr. 2 'Boon doggles' is simply a term applied back in the pioneer days to what we call gadgets today. **1935** *Word Study* Sept. 2 *Boondoggle* was coined for another purpose by Robert H. Link of Rochester. Through his connection with scouting the word later came into general use as a name given to the braided leather lanyard made and worn by Boy Scouts. **1935** *Chicago Tribune* 4 Oct., To the cowboy it meant the making of saddle trappings out of odds and ends of leather, and they boondoggled when there was nothing else to do on the ranch. **1935** H. L. ICKES *Secret Diary* (1953) I. 435, I am for substantial, worth-while, and socially desirable public works, while Hopkins is for what has come to be known as boondoggling. **1937** *Amer. Speech* XII. 6 [In the 1936 American election] *boondoggling* became the current term for describing the waste assertedly evident in..government agencies and bureaus. Administrators of relief became *boondogglers* to the Republican press and orators. **1947** *Chicago Tribune* 8 June I. 22/2 The cost of this boondoggle has been estimated at perhaps 50 million dollars. **1949** R. K. MERTON *Social Theory* (1951) vi. 178 This eliminates the very rationale of the intellectual's work and dissipates his interest in his work, leading to the 'boon doggling neurosis'. **1969** *N.Y. Rev. Books* 2 Jan. 5 (*heading*) Nixon and the arms race: the bomber boondoggle.

boonfellow, boon companion; see BOON *a.* 4.

boong (buːŋ). *Austral. slang.* Also **boang**. [Aboriginal word.] An (Australian) Aboriginal; a native of New Guinea; also, any coloured person.

1941 K. TENNANT *Battlers* ix. 110 Those boangs are all too matey with the police. **1943** BAKER *Dict. Austral. Slang* (ed. 3) 13 *Boong*, an aboriginal; a native of New Guinea. **1945** R. J. OAKES in *Coast to Coast 1944* 99 He had six wounded men ..and four boongs to help him. **1950** 'N. SHUTE' *Town like Alice* 75 'I thought you were a lot of boongs,' he said. 'You say you're English.' **1962** *Economist* 10 Nov. 577/1 In Australian eyes, Indonesia was a nation of poor struggling 'boongs' (a slang word which in its narrowest sense is applied to the natives of New Guinea). **1969** *Times* 1 Apr. p. ii/5 He is trying to lead Australians away from what he calls the 'poor old bloody boong' mentality.

boong, obs. form of BUNG.

boongary (buːn'gɛərɪ). [Native name: *bangaray* in the Port Jackson dialect.] The tree-kangaroo of North Queensland, *Dendrolagus lumholtzii.*

1889 R. B. ANDERSON tr. *Lumholtz's Among Cannibals* xviii. 227 Upon the whole, the boongary is the most beautiful mammal I have seen in Australia. **1965** E. TROUGHTON *Furred Animals Austral.* (ed. 8) 175 The blacks concluded the Boongary never drank.

booning ('buːnɪŋ) *vbl. sb.* [f. BOON *v.* + -ING.[1]] Doing of boon-work; repairing of public roads.

1862 *Life Among Colliers* 29 The tenants took it in turn to lead our coals, which custom was known as booning. **1863** MORTON *Cycl. Agric.* II. Gloss., *Booning* (Linc.), carting material for repairing the highways.

'booning, *ppl. a.* [f. BOON *v.* + -ING[2]: prob. involving confusion with BOON *a.*] Giving boons.

1821 CLARE *Vill. Minstr.* I. 134 As labour strength regains, From ale's booning bounty given.

boonk. A local name of the Little Bittern (*Botaurus minutus*).

1862 in G. MONTAGU *Ornith. Dict.* (1833) 49.

boonless ('buːnlɪs), *a.* [f. BOON *sb.* + -LESS.] Without a boon. (In *boonless boon* (imitating Gr. ἄδωρον δῶρον) 'a gift that is no gift.)

1863 P. S. WORSLEY *Phaethon, Poems & Transl.* 6 Thou hast asked a boonless boon. *Ibid.* 13 How boonless were the boon, if this were all.

boopic (bəʊ'ɒpɪk), *a.* *rare*[−1]. [f. Gr. βοώπις (f. βοῦς, βο- ox + ὤψ eye).] Ox-eyed.

1854 BADHAM *Halieut.* 66 A collyrium for the eyes of horses and bo-opic patients.

boor (bʊə(r)). Forms: (5 boueer), 6–7 boore, bour, (7 bore, boar), 7– boor (9 bauer). [A word of involved history in and out of English, though the ultimate etymology is clear enough. The 16th c. *bour*, *boore*, may possibly have been native Eng., repr. an earlier **búr*, short for OE. *ȝebúr* 'dweller, husbandman, farmer, countryman' (Bosw.), a deriv. of *búr* 'dwelling, house, cottage, BOWER', f. the verb root, *bū* to dwell: cf. the compound *neighbour*:—ME. *neȝebur*:—OE. *néahȝebúr* 'nigh-dweller', also modern East Anglian BOR 'neighbour' as a form of address. But on the whole, in its literary use, the word is more likely to have been adopted from LG. *bûr*, Du. *boer*: see the quots. under

sense 2, and BOER. These words are themselves etymological equivalents (or nearly so) of OE. *gebúr*; the OHG. form being *gibûr*, *gibûro*, MHG. *gebûr*, *gebûre*, MLG. *gebûr*, and *bûr* (occurring 1365), mod.LG. *buur* (made *bauer* in mod.HG.), MDu. *ghebure*, *ghebuer*, and *buer*; also (late) *geboer*, which was not properly a Du. form, but probably, according to Cosijn, adopted from Frisian, or, according to Franck, from the LG. on the eastern frontier of the Netherlands. This last is in mod.Du. *boer*. The original sense of WGer. *gibûr*, *gibûro*, was 'inmate of a *bûr* or BOWER, fellow-occupier of a dwelling, farm, or village; neighbour, mate'. Partly from being preserved mainly in rural use, but largely from association with the vb. *bûan* (MHG., MDu. *bûwen*, Ger. *bauen*, Du. *bouwen*) to inhabit, cultivate, till (of which, as we have seen, it was not a derivative, though a cognate word from same root *bŭ-*), its original connexion with *bûr*, BOWER, was lost, and the sense more and more confined to that of 'peasant, rustic', and thence 'clown'.

While mod.Ger. has merged the word in form with *bauer*, agent-noun from *bauen* 'to cultivate, to build', mod.Du., on the contrary, makes a distinction in use between the native *buur* (MDu. *ghebure*, *ghebuer*) 'neighbour', and the adopted *boer* (MDu. *geboer*) 'peasant, husbandman, farmer, clown, knave at cards', and keeps both distinct from *bouwer* 'tiller, builder' (though in MDu. the latter was used in senses subsequently taken up by *geboer*, *boer*.]

1. A husbandman, peasant, countryman. *Obs.*, exc. as in sense 3, into which it passes in later use.

[**1430**: see BOWER *sb.*[5]] **1551** TURNER *Herbal* (1568) A iiij b, *Absinthium rusticum*, that is bouris or pesantes wormwode. **1592** R. JOHNSON *9 Worthies* B iv, A countrie Boore, a goodlie proper swayne. **1611** SHAKS. *Wint. T.* v. ii. 173 Not swear it?.. Let Boores and Francklins say it, Ile sweare it. **1762** HUME *Hist. Eng.* (1806) III. App. iii. 633 Some remains of the ancient slavery of the boors and peasants. **1798** MALTHUS *Popul.* (1878) 326 While the land is cultivated by boors. [**1820** SCOTT *Monast.* xxxvii, Times of action make princes into peasants, and boors into barons. **1850** MRS. BROWNING *Vis. Poets*, Poems I. 204 The boor who ploughs the daisy down.]

2. Particularly, a Dutch or German peasant. (For the latter more definitely *bauer* occurs.)

1581 J. BELL *Haddon's Answ. Osor.* 254 To accuse Luther for the uproares raysed by the countrey Boores in Germany. **1612** WOODALL *Surg. Mate* Wks. (1653) 58 My self chanced in Holland into the house of a Bore (as they term him) to lodge. **1642** FULLER *Holy & Prof. St.* II. xviii. 116 Germany hath her Boores, like our Yeomen. **1645** PAGITT *Heresiogr.* (1662) 3 Upon this his preaching, about 40000 Bores and Trades-men rose up in Suevia. **1675** *Lond. Gaz.* No. 977/3 The Bores, assisted with 800 Spanish Soldiers. **1756** NUGENT *Gr. Tour, Netherl.* I. 41 The people of Holland may be divided into five classes. 1. The boors or husbandmen. **1800** COLERIDGE *Piccolom.* I. ii, The Boors Can answer fresh demands already [= der Bauer kann Schon wieder geben]. **1860** MOTLEY *Netherl.* (1868) II. ix. 11 Guarded by fifty men mostly boors of the country. [**1879** BARING-GOULD *Germany* I. 50 Lands were divided and sub-divided till the owners sank from being nobles to bauers.]

b. A Dutch colonist in Guiana, South Africa, etc. (For the latter BOER is now employed.)

1824 BURCHELL *Trav.* I. 13 The Boors must be heard, the Hottentots must be heard. **1832** HT. MARTINEAU *Demerara* ii. 23 The state of a boor as to health, comfort and security of property. **1834** PRINGLE *Afr. Sk.* iv. 184 Few but the very poorest boors.

c. Extended to foreign peasants generally.

1687 CLEVELAND *Rustick Ramp.* 488 What Boars of other Countrys could have compared with the Riches of our Peasants. **1764** GOLDSM. *Trav.* 3 The rude Carinthian boor. **1798** CANNING in *Anti-Jacobin* 12 Mar., Russian boors that daily kick. **1798** MALTHUS *Popul.* II. iii. (1806) I. 368 The fortune of a Russian nobleman is measured by the number of boors that he possesses.

3. A peasant, a rustic, with lack of refinement implied; a country clown.

1598 MARSTON *Pygmal.* ii. 142, I dull-sprighted fat Boetian Boore. *c* **1610** ROWLANDS *Terrible Batt.* 38 A paltry rusticke peasant boore. **1750** WESLEY *Wks.* (1872) II. 207 Three or four boors would have been rude, if they durst. **1871** R. ELLIS *Catullus* xxii. 14 A dunce more boorish e'en than hedge-born boor. **1874** SAYCE *Compar. Philol.* viii. 336 The country boor is blind to the beauties of nature.

b. *fig.* Any rude, ill-bred fellow; a 'clown'.

1598 FLORIO, *Grossolano*, a lubber, a clowne, a boore, a rude fellow. **1723** DE FOE *Col. Jack* (1840) 4 He was as to manners a mere boor or clown. **1849** MISS MULOCH *Ogilvies* i. (1875) 4 Hugh Ogilvie is a common-place, stupid boor. **1872** BLACK *Adv. Phaeton* xiii. 177 An ill-conditioned boor, not fit for the society of well-bred ladies.

4. boor's mustard. [ad. early mod.Ger. *baurensenfe* peasant's mustard.] A name given by herbalists (since Turner) to *Thlaspi arvense*, a British wild plant; by Gerard to *Lepidium ruderale*.

1548 TURNER *Names of Herbes*, *Thlaspi*..is called in duche Baurensenfe..It may be named in englishe dysh-mustard, or triacle Mustard, or Boures Mustard. **1578** LYTE *Dodoens* 628 Turner calleth Thlaspi..Bowers mustarde. **1597** GERARD *Herbal* 204/5 Bowiers or Bowyers mustard. **1878** BRITTEN & HOLL. *Plant-N.*, Boor's mustard.

boor(e, obs. form of BOAR, BOWER.

boord(e, obs. var. of BOARD, BORD(E, BOURD.

boordly, variant of BUIRDLY *a. Sc.*

boorelie, -lye, obs. forms of BURLY.

†**boorinn.** *Obs. rare*[−1]. [?ad. Du. *boerin* countrywoman, fem. of *boer*, BOOR.] A peasant woman, a female boor.

1649 LOVELACE *Poems* 93 And th' blood in each veine doth appeare Part thick Booreinn, part Lady Cleare.

boorish ('bʊərɪʃ), *a.* For forms see BOOR. [f. BOOR + -ISH[1].] Of or pertaining to boors; rustic, clownish, uncultured, rude, coarse, ill-mannered.

1562 TURNER *Herbal* II. 51 Horehounde..groweth..in suche places as the bourishe wormwod groweth. *c* **1620** [FLETCH. & MASS.] *Trag. Barnavelt.* I. i. in Bullen *O. Pl.* (1883) II. 210 With a boorish patience suffer The harvest that I labourd for to be Anothers spoile. **1660** PEPYS *Diary* 19 May, Many Dutch boors eating of fish in a boorish manner. **1697** DRYDEN *Virg.* Ded., The Boorish Dialect of Theocritus has a secret Charm in it. **1726** AMHERST *Terræ Fil.* xlvi. 245 You are the first..that ever call'd Oxford a boorish, uncivilized place. **1866** MRS. STOWE *Lit. Foxes* 105 Comparing..a polished rascal with a boorish good man.

†**b.** quasi-*sb.* ***the boorish***: the vernacular of a boor; rude, illiterate speech. *humorous. Obs.*

1600 SHAKS. *A.Y.L.* v. i. 54 You Clowne..leaue the societie: which in the boorish, is companie, of this female.

boorishly ('bʊərɪʃlɪ), *adv.* [f. prec. + -LY[2]]. In a boorish manner.

1605 VERSTEGAN *Dec. Intell.* x. (1628) 330 A house bourishly built without carpentrie. **1826** SCOTT *Rev. Kemble's Life* (1849) 242 A young man..boorishly educated and home-bred. **1862** MISS BRADDON *Lady Audley* iii. 24 'Are you glad to see me?' 'Of course I'm glad, lass', he answered, boorishly.

boorishness ('bʊərɪʃnɪs). [f. as prec. + -NESS.] The quality of being boorish; rusticity, rudeness.

1794 GODWIN *Cal. Williams* 247 The boorishness of his rank in society. **1866** *Sat. Rev.* 13 Jan. 37/1 The curious mixture of feudal arrogance and clumsy boorishness.. surviving among Prussian aristocrats.

boorka, var. BURKA[1,2].

†**boorn.** *Obs.* [cf. 'Exmoor *bourn* yeast' (Halliw.).] 'Wort, or boiled liquor.' (Fuller.)

1609 C. BUTLER *Fem. Mon.* x, The end of boiling is thoroughly to incorporate the Boorne and the Honie. **1662** FULLER *Worthies* IV. 6 [in a receipt for metheglin] Take.. one Gallon of the finest Honey, and put it into the Boorn.

boorn(e, obs. form of BOURN, a brook.

boor-tree, var. of BOUR-TREE *Sc.*, elder.

boos, obs. form of BOSS.

boosa, var. of BOZA, an oriental drink.

boose (buːz), *sb. north.* Forms: 5 **booc, boce, buse,** 5, 9 **boos, bose,** 5–9 **boose,** 9 **bouse, boost.** [First found in 15th c., but pointing to an OE. **bós* (whence *bósig*, BOOSY, cow-stall), corresp. to ON. *bás-s*:—OTeut. **banso-z*: cf. Ger. *banse*, Gothic *bansts* barn. (The phonetic forms in mod. dialects, Eng. and Sc. cannot be derived from the ON. word, but require an OE. form with *ó*.)] A stall for a cow or (less usually) a horse; *esp.* the upper part of the stall, where the fodder is placed. See also BOOSY.

c **1440** *Promp. Parv.* 41 Booc or boos, netystalle [*K.* boce, *H.*, **1499** bose]. **1483** *Cath. Angl.* 49 A Buse for a noxe, *bocetum*. **1570** LEVINS *Manip.* 222 Boose, stall, *bouile*. **1781** J. HUTTON *Tour Caves* Gloss. (E.D.S.) *Boose*, a stall for a cow or horse. **1808** JAMIESON, *Buse, Buise, Boose*, a cow's stall, a crib. **1875** *Lanc. Gloss.*, *Boose, Boost*, a cattle stall. Often used for the upper part of the stall where the fodder is placed: as 'Yo'll find it in th' cow's bose.'

boose, variant of BOOZE.

boosome, obs. f. BOSOM; obs. Sc. f. BESOM.

†**boost**, *sb.*[1] *Obs.* Also 4–6 *north.* **bost.** A var. of BOIST, box, pyx. Cf. the forms BOUSTE, BUIST.

a **1300** *Cursor M.* 14003 A bost [*v.r.* boist] sco has o smerles nummen. **1535** STEWART *Cron. Scot.* III. 351 Tua bostis of gude wyne. **1570** LEVINS *Manip.* 222 A Booste, boxe, *pixis*. **1651** CALDERWOOD *Hist. Kirk* (1843) II. 33 Adoratioun..and keeping of bread in boxes or boostes.

boost (buːst), *sb.*[2] *colloq.* (orig. *U.S.*) **1.** A lift, a shove up; help, encouragement (by means of publicity, etc.), increase (in value, reputation, etc.). Also, the action of BOOST *v.* 2.

1825 J. NEAL *Bro. Jonathan* II. 101 (Th.), Shall I give him a boost? or no? **1830** SEBA SMITH *Major Jack Downing* (1860) 114 (Th.), I got a pretty good boost in Boston, by the editors giving me recommendations. **1858** DOW *Serm.* (Bartlett) Office-seekers ask you to give them a boost into the tree of office. **1879** LOWELL *Poet Wks.* 417 Bacchus that now is scarce induced To give Eld's lagging blood a boost. **1883** *Harper's Mag.* Nov. 943/1 Nor has its completion given that 'boost' to California..so fondly dreamed of. **1919** WODEHOUSE *My Man Jeeves* 24 You see. A boost for the uncle right away. **1958** *Spectator* 6 June 722/2 After this initial boost, recruiting will fall off again. **1964** *Daily Tel.* (Colour Suppl.) 2 Oct. 7/1 A piece of national prestige-building and a boost to exports too. **1967** *Listener* 6 Apr. 473/3 The recording needs treble boost, but is otherwise excellent. **1969** *Gramophone* Apr. 1502/3 A small amount of bass boost gives a well balanced performance. **1969** *Scotsman* 26 Apr. 6/6 [Scottish manufacturers] have expressed the opinion that they are doing all right..with their exports and need no additional boosts.

2. In an internal-combustion or jet engine: = SUPERCHARGING *vbl. sb.*; supercharger pressure. Also, = BOOSTER 2 c. Hence *attrib.* and *Comb.*

1931 *Air Ann. Brit. Empire* 88 It has been necessary to evolve a practical automatic boost-controlling mechanism. **1931** *Handbk. Aeronaut.* viii. 500 Boost Gauge, Mark II A. **1934** *Aircraft Engin.* Apr. 110/3 Boost pressure is the difference between induction pipe pressure and 760 mm. of mercury. **1941** P. RICHEY *Fighter Pilot* 57, I immediately started clambering after them, with my 'plug' (boost-override) pulled. **1943** L. CHESHIRE *Bomber Pilot* i. 13 He tested..the airscrew pitch controls and the boost. **1950** *Jrnl. Brit. Interplanet. Soc.* IX. 174 The thrust of the boost motors. **1962** F. I. ORDWAY et al. *Basic Astronautics* ix. 385 The boost phase of flight.

boost (buːst), *v.* **1.** *trans.* To hoist; 'to lift or push from behind (one endeavoring to climb); to push up. (*Low*)' Webster. Also *fig.* To assist over obstacles, to advance the progress of; to support, encourage; to increase (in value, reputation, etc.); to praise *up*, to extol; also *absol.* orig. *U.S. colloq.*

1815 D. HUMPHREYS *Yankey in England* 103 *Boost*, raise up, lift up, exalt. **1834** SEBA SMITH *Major Jack Downing* 139 You..give me a lift into public life, and you've been a boosting me along ever since. **1845** *Yale Lit. Mag.* XI. 34 (Th.), There is one poor fellow getting his comrade to boost him, while he hangs to the skirts of the one above. **1848–60** BARTLETT *Dict. Amer.* s.v., Boost me up this tree, and I'll hook you some apples. *a* **1860** *N.Y. Herald* (Bartlett) Lord Palmerston was boosted into power by the agricultural interest of England. **1884** *Harper's Mag.* Aug. 484/1 To boost a jurist of so much helpless avoirdupois in through the carriage door. **1887** F. FRANCIS Jr. *Saddle & Mocassin* 121 If you think that I'm trying to boost the place up because it belongs to us. **1909** *Daily Chron.* 21 Oct. 3/5 In times like these, when trade and other factors are bad, it is the duty of the Press to 'boost' in the interests of the nation, for when trade is good it will 'boost' itself. **1923** WODEHOUSE *Inimit. Jeeves* ii. 22 Young Bingo must have boosted me to some purpose. **1926** *Publishers' Weekly* 16 Jan. 147 Perhaps advertising might help boost their sales.

2. *Electr.* To increase or otherwise regulate the electromotive force in (a circuit, battery, etc.).

1906 A. RUSSELL *Theory Altern. Currents* II. x. 282 The pressure can be boosted positively or negatively. **1911** *Engineer* 10 Mar. 237/2 It is far more profitable to boost the pressure at the generating station. **1959** H. BURSTEIN *Stereo, How it Works* ii. 43 With stereo program material it is no longer necessary to boost the intensity *above* live concert level to hear fine details.

3. To steal, esp. to shoplift; to rob. Also *absol.* Cf. BOOSTER 3. *slang* (orig. *U.S.*).

1912 [implied at BOOSTER 3]. **1915** W. HEALY *Individual Delinquent* xviii. 548 He was a booster himself, he had already stolen. He says 'You come on, I know a place where we can boost.' **1933** *Amer. Speech* VIII. 24/2 *Boost*, steal, especially by shoplifting. **1951** *Life* 11 June 126/3 Boys turn to picking pockets, car 'boosting' and other forms of thievery. **1962** 'K. ORVIS' *Damned & Destroyed* xi. 73 Fay blows in. Loaded to the teeth with a bankroll she got for a tray of watches she boosted. **1971** W. BURROUGHS *Speed* iii. 65, I boosted a guy that was only in a coma. **1978** C. WHITE *They do it All with Mirrors* iii. 27 The route to socks took us through jewelry, past a display of rhinestoned smile face pens, two of which she boosted.

Hence **'boosting** *vbl. sb.* and *ppl. a.*

1906 A. RUSSELL *Theory Altern. Currents* II. x. 282 When a transformer is used in this fashion it is called an auto-transformer or a boosting transformer, or simply a booster. **1911** A. B. SMITH *Mod. Amer. Telephony* v. 76 When the current is too small for effective transmission of signaling the necessity of 'boosting'..arises. **1912** *Baltimore Amer.* 5 Nov., The quiet citizen who has not indulged in boosting will decide the result. **1920** *Chambers's Jrnl.* Aug. 557/2 These arrangements are supplemented by 'boosting' fans at intervals of about 2000 feet. **1962** NISBETT *Technique Sound Studio* i. 17 Switching centres, boosting amplifiers and frequency correction networks on landlines.

boost, by-form of BOOSE; obs. f. BOAST.

booster ('buːstə(r)). *colloq.* (orig. *U.S.*). [f. BOOST *v.* + -ER[1].]

1. One who boosts.

1890 *Stock Grower* 1 Feb. 3/2 The..company, of which Col. Partial Smyth is chief booster, seems to be worried. **1920** *Glasgow Herald* 23 Aug. 7 It is not suggested that we should become 'blatant-boosters'. **1928** *Observer* 1 July 11/2 President Coolidge, a true 'booster' of his country. **1937** G. B. SHAW in *Malvern Fest. Bk.* 8, I am a booster of festivals because they are markets for my plays. **1968** *Globe & Mail* (Toronto) 17 Feb. 1/5 An ardent Trudeau booster.

2. *Electr.* A machine interposed in a circuit for the purpose of increasing or otherwise regulating the electromotive force acting in the circuit.

1894 *Jrnl. Inst. Electr. Engin.* 25 Jan. 79, I found in use in Chicago a system of raising the voltage on the feeders when the pressure falls, owing to the increase of load, by switching in motor dynamos. They have given the name 'boosters' to these instruments. **1902** *Encycl. Brit.* XXV. 34/1 Taking the current from the mains to the battery through a 'booster', that is, a dynamo arranged so that its E.M.F. is added to that of the mains. **1905** R. E. B. CROMPTON *Unsolved Problems in Electr. Engin.* 16 We have obtained regulation by means of automatic motor-generators, to which the name of 'boosters' has been generally given. **1906** *Times* (Engineering Suppl.) 22 Aug. 267/3 The use either of a large full-voltage battery for regulating purposes, a set of cells as

back E.M.F.'s for the near feeders, or as a third alternative, the provision of extra boosters. **1911** *Engineer* 10 Mar. 237/3 A booster in use for boosting the pressure of an overhead conductor of an electric tramway system. **1911** A. B. SMITH *Mod. Amer. Telephony* v. 77 Each line must be provided with its own booster battery. **1924** ROGET *Dict. Electr. Terms* 24/2 *Booster Transformer* (or Boosting Transformer), a transformer with its secondary in series with the line to compensate for line drop on an A.C. feeder.

b. A radio-frequency amplifier for intensifying signals.

1935 NILSON & HORNUNG *Pract. Radio Communic.* viii. 383 If the lines are long, it is necessary to insert *booster amplifiers*... For high-quality transmission such boosters should be inserted every 10 to 20 or more miles. **1954** *Times* 10 Nov. 2/6 The Truleigh Hill booster, installed to improve Sussex reception. **1959** *Economist* 7 Mar. 878/2 Hundreds of remote communities have owed their television fare to 'booster' stations that are built on high places and that relay and amplify the original broadcast signal.

c. *Aeronaut.* An auxiliary engine or rocket, esp. one used to give initial speed to a rocket or missile which is afterwards left to continue under its own power.

1944 A. L. MURPHY *Rockets* 72 Some being catapulted by booster rockets, while other craft will take off as rockets. **1950** *Jrnl. Brit. Interplanet. Soc.* IX. 175 A single annular-shaped tank, the bottom of which is attached to the booster motors. **1961** *Spectator* 21 Apr. 546 The huge boosters that launched Major Gagarin's capsule. **1968** *Times* 16 Dec. 7/4 To begin with, Apollo 8, still attached to the third stage of the Saturn 5 booster, will be parked in a 119-mile earth orbit.

d. *Med.* A dose or injection of a substance that increases or prolongs the effectiveness of an earlier dose or injection. Also *attrib.* and *fig.*

1950 in WEBSTER Add. **1953** FISHBEIN *Med. Progress* 66 The use of 'booster doses' will usually bring the process back under control. **1956** *Collier's Year Bk.* 563/1 The effect of the vaccine, once a child has had both primary shots and a booster, seven or more months later, will last for a long time. **1957** I. ASIMOV *Earth is Room Enough* (1960) 13 Additional work as a postdoctorate teaching fellow acted as a booster shot. **1957** *Times* 9 Dec. 11/5 In the case of diphtheria inoculations, it is usually considered necessary to give what is technically known as a 'booster' injection when the child starts school.

e. Other *techn.* uses.

1917 A. MARSHALL *Explosives* (ed. 2) II. xxxi. 527 Recently brass tubes 4 inches long containing a charge of trinitro-toluene have been introduced under the name of renforts or boosters. **1927** *Engineering* 11 Nov. 631 (*caption*) Booster pumps and compression tank. **1938** FULLER & SNOW *Air Conditioning* v. 196 One of the standard types of booster heaters. **1945** *Reader's Digest* Apr. 97/2 The 74 booster stations in France's long-distance telephone system. **1958** *Observer* 15 June 10/2 Manufacturers [of shampoos] can meet these difficulties by..adding a foam booster.

3. A shoplifter. *U.S. slang.*

1912 A. H. LEWIS *Apaches of N.Y.* (Partridge, *Dict. Underworld*), A gifted booster..of the feminine gender. **1925** *Collier's Mag.* 8 Aug. 30/1 The lowest type of thief is the 'booster'.

4. Special Comb.: **booster chair, seat** orig. *N. Amer.*, a kind of raised seat for a young child, designed to fit on an ordinary chair or car seat.

1960 *Sears Catal.* Fall-Winter 489/3 Padded *Booster chair... Use on adult chair to put your child at adult table height. **1967** *Ibid.* Spring-Summer 297/1 *Booster seat. Chrome-plated tubular steel. **1979** *Chatelaine* Jan. 60/3 There was no high chair, but when I asked for a booster seat, I got it and sat Eric next to the window. **1986** *New Yorker* 23 June 29/2 Elizabeth picked Charlie up off the booster seat.

boosterism ('buːstərɪz(ə)m). *colloq.* (orig. *U.S.*). [f. BOOSTER + -ISM.] A tendency to 'boost' or seek to raise the estimation of (oneself, one's town, product, etc.) by praise; the expression of chauvinism.

1926 *Sat. Even. Post* 30 Jan. 16/3 Those who are possessed of the ambition to become liberal..wince when accused of being orthodox or of failing to comply with the ready-made regulations of the cult; and so they straightway quit thinking for themselves and blush at the imputation of boosterism. **1935** M. M. ATWATER *Crime in Corn-Weather* x. 70 He kissed his wife, grabbed his Panama, and went off downtown, feeling the springs of boosterism and ballyhoo renewed within him. **1948** *Daily Ardmoreite* (Ardmore, Okla.) 8 Apr. 12/2 'Boosterism' will be out when a new Maryland Department of Information begins to warm up the typewriters this year. **1966** *English Studies* XLVII. 207 No reader of Whitman..can gainsay..his attitudes of unrelieved bluffness, heartiness, boosterism, boasting, [etc.]. **1973** *Times* 21 Mar. 21/5 A blending of German thoroughness and American small town boosterism. **1977** *Rolling Stone* 19 May 32/2 The Exposition was, in all, boggling—a nonstop blend of the crassest kind of trade-show boosterism and the fresh-scrubbed naiveté of a high-school science fair. **1985** *Times* 14 Sep. 8/3 Official resentment of this Soviet boosterism was beginning to show.

'**boosy** ('buːzɪ). Chiefly *dial.* Forms: 1 **bósiȝ, bósih,** 7 **bousie, bowzey, boosey.** [OE. *bósiȝ, bósih*: see BOOSE *sb.*] An ox- or cow-stall, a crib; = BOOSE. Also *attrib.*, as **boosey close,** the close in which the cow-sheds stand; **boosey** or **boozy pasture,** pasture land lying near the cowsheds.

c **950** *Lindisf. Gosp.* Luke xiii. 15 An eȝhuelc iuer on symbel-doeȝ ne unbindeð [he] woxo his oððe assald of bósih. *c* **975** *Rushw. G.* ibid., Oxo his oððe easald of bosȝe. **1601** HOLLAND *Pliny* I. 612 *Præsepia* [i. a Crib, Cratch, Bowzey, or Manger]. *Ibid.* II. 285 They must be tied vp sure vnto their bousies. **1688** R. HOLME *Armory* II. ix. §9, *Boosey*, the place where the Cow is tyed. **1777** BRAND *Pop. Antiq.* (1849) I. 30 What is termed the boosy. **1794** T. BROWN *Gen. View Agric. Derby* 45 A specified close, which the way-going tenant has for foddering his cattle in, under the name of a Boosey pasture. **1844** *Jrnl. R. Agric. Soc.* V. I. 86 Tenancy commences..on the 2nd of February as to all the other lands, except the boosey pasture. **1847** G. SOANE *New Curios. Lit.* (1849) 19 Boosy..in the northern counties..is more generally applied to the upper part of the stall where the fodder lies. **1862** *Catal. Internat. Exhib.* II. x. 27 Boosey or manger bricks. **1905** *Oswestry & Border Counties Advertizer* (Advt.), 6 acres of Boozy Pasture. **1922** S. J. WEYMAN *Ovington's Bank* xxxvi. 423 A countryman, whom the news had only just reached in his boosey-close or his rickyard.

boot (buːt), *sb.*[1] Forms: 1–5 **bót,** 3–6 **bote,** 4–7 **boote,** 5– **boot.** Also 4 **bott, bout(e,** 5 **both;** *north.* 4–6 **but(e,** 5 **boyte, buyt,** 6 **buit.** [Com. Teut.: OE. *bót* fem., corresponds to OFris. *bôte*, OS. *bôta* (MDu. and Du. *boete*, LG. *bote*), OHG. *buoza* (MHG. *buoze*, mod.G. *busze*), ON. *bót* (Sw. *bot*, Da. *bod*), Goth. *bôta* 'boot, advantage, good':—OTeut. **bôtâ*- (Aryan type **bhādā*-), prob. a derivative of root *bat*- (Aryan **bhad*-) 'good, useful': see BETTER. Hence the vb. BEET, to make good or better.]

I. Good, advantage, profit, use.

1. Good: in phrase ***to boot***: 'to the good', to advantage, into the bargain, in addition; besides, moreover.

c **1000** *Daniel* 200 (Gr.) Cuð ȝedydon, þæt hie..noldon; oft hie to bote bealde ȝecwædon. **1330** R. BRUNNE *Chron.* (1825) 163 (Mätz), A hundreth knyghtes mo..and four hundreth to bote, squieres of gode aray. **1377** LANGL. *P. Pl.* xiv. 268 Bi assent of sondry partyes and syluer to bote. **1543** J. WILLOUGHBY in Strype *Cranmer* (1694) App. 66 Mr. Gardiner to sign for himself, and Serles to boot. **1652** EARL MONMOUTH *Hist. Relations* 171 To boot that he had received many distastes from the French. *Ibid.* 9 To boot with the Councel of the States General, the United Provinces have three Councels apart. **1653** tr. *Carmeni's Nissena* 42 To boot that it was commonly whispered about, etc. **1660** PEPYS *Diary* 13 Feb., For two books that I had and 6*s.* 6*d.* to boot I had my great book of songs. *a* **1679** T. GOODWIN *Wks.* (1861) I. 88 He shall have all things into boot. *a* **1711** KEN *Damonet* Poet Wks. 1721 IV. 505 Would you give yours, and your whole Flock to boot. **1867** FREEMAN *Norm. Conq.* (1876) I. iv. 222 One who held all Gaul and all Britain, with seemingly Germany to boot.

b. In Sc. ***to the boot, into the boot*** (***buit***).

1645 RUTHERFORD *Lett.* 357 Some..who would exchange afflictions, and give you to the boot. **1814** SCOTT *Wav.* xviii, Alice, who..was, to the boot of all that, the best dancer of a strathspey in the whole strath.

†**2.** That which is 'thrown in', or given in addition, to make up a deficiency of value; a premium, compensation, odds. *Obs.* exc. *Sc. dial.*

1483 *Cath. Angl.* 49 Bute [*v.r.* Buyt], *auctorium, augmentum.* **1593** G. FLETCHER *Licia* (1876) 9 Were all the world offered to make a change, yet the boote were too small. **1597** SKENE *Expl. diffic. Wds.* s.v. *Bote* (JAM.), The aine partie that gettes the better, giues ane bote, or compensation to the vther. **1600** HEYWOOD *1 Edw. IV*, III. i. Wks. 1874 I. 44 If I were so mad to score, what boote wouldst thou giue me? *a* **1652** BROME *Queen* IV. iv, *Doct.* Too many a man.. will change with thee And give good Boot. **1726** CAVALLIER *Mem.* IV. 313 Now I am convinced that my Religion is better than yours since you give me so much Boot.

†**3.** Advantage; profit; avail, use. Chiefly in interrog. or negative phrases or their equivalent, as ***It is no boot***: it avails not, it is no use. ***to make boot of***, to make profit of, gain by; to gain.

a **1300** *Cursor M.* 89 Quat bote is to sette traueil On thyng þat may not auail. *c* **1400** *Destr. Troy* 448 Agayne þe wyles of wemen to wer is no bote. *c* **1420** *Anturs of Arth.* xvi, I bare the of my body, quat bote is to layne? **1535** LYNDESAY *Satyre* 1082 But cum scho to the Kings presence, Thair is na buit for vs to byde. **1596** SPENSER *F.Q.* III. xi. 19 O spare thy happy daies, and them apply To better boot. **1598** SYLVESTER *Du Bartas* I. v. (1641) 42/2 Then loose they all the sheats, but to no boot. **1606** SHAKS. *Ant. & Cl.* IV. i. 9 Giue him no breath, but now Make boote of his distraction. **1606** G. W[OODCOCKE] *Hist. Ivstine* 22 a, They..lost all that before they had made boot of. **1681** R. KNOX *Hist. Ceylon* (1781) 333 We thought it no boot to sit longer..and so took up our bags, and fled. **1693** W. ROBERTSON *Phraseol. Gen.* 272 To no boot, *frustra.*

†**4.** *loosely*, Well-being, weal. *Obs.*

a **1300** *Cursor M.* 1008 (Gött.) Paradis hit is a..lond of lif of roo & rest Wid bliss and bote broidin best. *c* **1430** *Hymns Virg.* (1867) 12 Ihesu! þou brouȝtist man to boote.

II. The making good or mending of anything; the means of doing so; repair; remedy, relief.

†**5.** The repair of decaying structures, *e.g.* bridges; also, a contribution levied for keeping these in repair. Only in OE. (in such combs. as *burhbót, brycgbót*, etc) exc. in late writers on legal antiquities.

a **1000** Thorpe's *Laws* I. 380 (Bosw.) Brycgbota aginne man ȝeorne. *c* **1250** *Gloss. Law Terms* in *Rel. Ant.* I. 33 Briggebote, refere punz à passer. **1670** BLOUNT *Law Dict.*, *Burgbote.* **1839** KEIGHTLEY *Hist. Eng.* I. 83 The 'Bricg-bote'.

†**b.** The right of a tenant to take timber, etc. for repairs, firing, and other necessary purposes, from off the landlord's estate; common of estovers. In comb., as ***fire-bote, house-bote, hedge-bote***, etc.

1528 PERKINS *Prof. Bk.* i. §116 If a stranger grant all manner of Estouers unto me..by this grant I shall have Housbote, Plowbote, and Haybote. **1553** *Procl.* in Strype *Eccl. Mem.* III. I. iii. 30 All other lands, tenements..&c., with reasonable fire-boot, cart-boot, plow-boot, hedge-boot, within the woods of the said manor. **1604** in *Eng. Gilds* (1870) 437 To deliver to the sayd tenants house boot and high boot. **1669** WORLIDGE *Syst. Agric.* (1681) 322 *Boot*, necessary Timber or Wood for necessary uses; as Plough-boot, House-boot, Fire-boot. **1765–8** BLACKSTONE *Comm.* II. 25 The Saxon word, *bote*, is of the same signification with the French *Estover.* **1844** TUPPER *Crock of Gold* vii. 56 No allowances of hedgebote, or housebote.

†**6.** *esp.* A medicinal cure or remedy. *Obs.*

a **1000** CYNEWULF *Elene* 299 (Gr.) þe eow eaȝena leoht fram blindnesse bote ȝefremede. *a* **1225** *Ancr. R.* 120 Monie kunnes remedies..& misliche boten. *c* **1305** *St. Kath.* 304 in *E.E.P.* (1862) 98 Noble relik hit is: sike men to habbe of bote. *c* **1386** CHAUCER *Prol.* 424 Anon he yaf the sike man his boote. *c* **1440** *Promp. Parv.* 45 Bote of [**1499** or] helthe, *salus.* **1548** UDALL, etc. *Erasm. Par. Mark* v. 27 She wente unto another for boote that put her in more assuraunce of healthe.

†**7.** Help or deliverance from evil or peril; assistance, relief, remedy, rescue. Often in phr. ***boot of bale***; cf. BALE *sb.*[1] 6. *concr.* A means or agent of help, relief, or remedy; also, a personal agent, a helper. *Obs.* (or *arch.*)

a **1000** CYNEWULF *Andreas* 949 (Gr.) Him sceal bot hraðe weorðan in worulde. *c* **1000** *Sax. Leechd.* I. 398 Her ys seo bot hu ðu meaht þine æceras betan. **1297** R. GLOUC. 408 Our Lorde..bote þerof him sende. **1377** LANGL. *P. Pl.* B. VI. 196 For þat was bake for bayarde · was bote for many hungry. *c* **1386** CHAUCER *Chan. Yem. Prol. & T.* 928 God sende euery trewe man boote of his bale. *c* **1420** *Sir Amadace* xvii, God, that is bote of alle bale, Dame, Cumford the. *c* **1430** LYDG. *Bochas* I. iv. (1554) 8 a, The poore not wist where to find bote. **1513** DOUGLAS *Æneis* II. vii. [vi.] 106 To vencust folkis is a confort and bute. **1557** *Primer, Praier bef. Sacrament*, I come as a wretche to thee my Lord..to thee my boote. **1591** GREENE *Maidens Dreame* li. 'Virgin', quoth she, 'no boot by tears is had'. **1867** G. MACDONALD *Poems* 144 Laid his sword where he had found Boot for every bale.

†**b.** ***to do*** (***one***) ***boot***: to render help or remedy to; to be of service, advantage, or profit to; to do good to.

a **1225** *Ancr. R.* 88 (*MSS.* T.C.) Ne halp hit me nout to don her one bote. *c* **1386** CHAUCER *Sqrs. T.* 146 And euery gras that groweth vp on roote She shal eek knowe and whom it wol do boote. *c* **1420** *Pallad. on Husb.* IV. 110 Two basketfull of bene chaf doth boote..to grettest treen. **1557** Tottell's *Misc.* (Arb.) 177 As moules that want the earth to do them bote. **1609** F. GREVILLE *Mustapha* v. Cho. i. (1633) 96 Meat, drinke, and drugges alike doe little boot.

c. In apprecatory phrases: as ***Saint George to boot! grace to boot!*** i.e. to our help.

1594 SHAKS. *Rich. III*, V. iii. 301 This, and Saint George to boote. **1611** —— *Wint. T.* I. ii. 80 Grace to boot: Of this make no conclusion, least you say Your Queene and I are Deuils. **1599** GREENE *George a Gr.* (1861) 257 Saint Andrew be my boot, But I'll raze thy castle to the very ground.

d. In various proverbial phrases: as, ***when bale is hext boot is next***: see BALE *sb.*[1] 7. ***boot or bield***: see BIELD *sb.* 3. ***boot of beam***: see BEAM *sb.*[2]; later ***boot in beam*** and ***booty beam*** (? i.e. ***boot i' beam***).

1642 ROGERS *Naaman* 136 Which should..put boote in beame (as we say) securing her of a good and safe issue of her labour. *Ibid.* 257 What a stay, what boot in beame it is? **1674** N. FAIRFAX *Bulk & Selv.* 111 As it had not the latter by it self, so neither had it the former in booty beme, or a power in seed.

†**8.** A way of mending matters, help out of a difficulty; a better way, a resource, alternative, choice. ***ther nis no bote***: there is no help for it. ***none other boot***: no other resource, no alternative.

a **1225** *St. Marher.* 15 Nis ther bote nan: bute fleon thenne. *c* **1385** CHAUCER *L.G.W.* 1992 Ffor If he may this monstre overcome Thanne were he quyt; ther is non other bote. *c* **1410** *Sir Cleges* 355 Sir Cleges sey non othyr bote, But his askyng graunte he most. **1480** CAXTON *Chron. Eng.* ccxxiii. 220 Ther is no bote but deth. *c* **1505** DUNBAR *Tua Mariit Wemen* 309, I gert the buthman obey, ther wes no bute ellis. **1523** LD. BERNERS *Froiss.* I. cccxcii. 674 There was none other boote for hym but to arme him. **1578** T. PROCTOR *Gorg. Gallery* I. 82 For though I serve untill I sterve, I see none other Boote.

III. The making amends for mischief or wrong done; amends made.

†**9.** Compensation paid, according to Old English usage, for injury or wrong-doing; reparation, amends; satisfaction made. (Only in OE., except in late writers on legal antiquities, who usually retain the OE. form *bót* or ME. *bote.*) In many combinations, as ***man-bote, kin-bote, thief-bote***, etc.

a **1000** *Beowulf* 567 Bealuwa bisiȝum bot eft-cuman. *a* **1000** Thorpe's *Laws* I. 12 ȝif feaxfang ȝeweorþ, L scætta to bote. *a* **1450** *Sc. Acts, 1 Robt. I*, ix, Alsua it is ordainyt þat nane tak meyd of a theyff [or thyft bute]. *a* **1609** SKENE *Reg. Maj.* Index (JAM.) The Wergelt, or Theiftbote of ane theife, is threttie kye. [**1845** STEPHEN *Laws Eng.* in *Edin. Rev.* (1884) Apr. 339 'If the great toe be struck off, let twenty shillings be paid him as bot.' **1854** SIR G. NICHOLLS *Eng. Poor Law* I. 13 'That he [the kinsman] make 'bot' for him.' **1872** E. ROBERTSON *Hist. Ess.* 178 Bot or personal compensation was paid to an ealderman, a bishop or an archbishop, by the man who fought, or drew his weapon in their presence.]

†**10.** Expiation of sin, an offering by way of atonement; sin-offering; repentance by act; penance. Cf. DEDBOTE. *Obs.* (exc. as the OE. form may be cited by ecclesiastical antiquaries.)

971 *Blickl. Hom.* 35 Don we urum Drihtne soþe hreowe & bote. *c* **1000** ÆLFRIC *Lev.* iv. 28 And his gylt underȝit, bring ane gat to bote to þam temple. *c* **1175** *Lamb. Hom.* 15 Gif we nulleð gan to bote..hit is riht þet me us nede. *c* **1200** *Trin. Coll. Hom.* 69 þe wile here bot dai laste..Ure bot dai is nu

and lasteð þe wile þe god wile. *a* **1240** *Ureisun* 133 in *Cott. Hom.* 197 Þu ne uorsakest nenne mon..ȝif he is to bote ȝeruh and bit þe uorȝiuenesse. [**1844** LINGARD *Anglo-Sax. Ch.* (1858) I. iii. 102 The fines arising from these ecclesiastical crimes were paid into the treasury of the bishop under the name of 'bots'.]

† **boot**, *sb.*² *Obs.* Also 6-7 **boote**. [App. an application of the prec., influenced by the already-existing BOOTY; perhaps due to the phrase *to make boot of*, 'to make profit of' (cf. BOOT *sb.*¹ 3, quot. 1606), being taken as 'to make booty of'.]

Booty; spoil; plunder.

1598 CHAPMAN *Iliad* XI. 585 We foraged, as proclaimed foes, a wondrous wealthy boot..our prey was rich and great. *a* **1618** SYLVESTER *Job Triumph.* III. 119 Rising be-times for Boot like Free-booters. **1623** BINGHAM *Xenophon* 119 It was decreed, that..all boot taken in priuate should be deliuered vp to the vse of the generalitie.

b. *esp.* in phr. ***to make boot.***

1593 SHAKS. *2 Hen. VI*, IV. i. 13 Thou that art his Mate, make boote of this. **1599** —— *Hen. V*, I. ii. 194 Others [Bees] like Souldiers..Make boote vpon the Summers Veluet buddes: Which pillage, they..bring home. **1596** SPENSER *F.Q.* VII. vii. 38 Harvests riches, which he made his boot. **1641** HEYWOOD *Reader, Here you'l, &c.* 5 They make Boote Of every thing we wear from head to foote. **1885** CHILD *Ballads* III. §61. 57/2 Stopping only long enough to make boot of Hjelmer's gold.

boot (buːt), *sb.*³ Forms: 4-6 **bote**, 4-7 **boote**, 7- **boot**. (Also 4-7 *north.* **bute**, 5 **but**, 6 **botte**, **bowtt**, 6-7 *Sc.* **buitt**.) [ME. *bote*, a. OF. *bote* (mod.F. *botte*), corresp. to Pr., Sp., Pg. *bota*, med.L. *botta*, *bota*, of uncertain origin.

Identified by Diez, Littré, etc. with F. *boute* (also, in mod.F., *botte*) butt, cask, leathern vessel; but 'the phonology of the two words in OF. shows that they are quite distinct' (P. Meyer). In med.L. also *butta* 'butt' and *botta* 'boot' are never confounded, though *bota* is frequent as a by-form of both, which has probably misled etymologists.]

1. a. A covering for the foot and lower part of the leg, usually of leather. (Distinguished from a SHOE by extending above the ankle. In earlier times used only by riders: see quot. from Johnson.)

c **1325** *Poem temp. Edw. II*, 26 Felted botys. *Ibid.* 55 Tho his botes be all totore. *c* **1386** CHAUCER *Prol.* 273 His bootes [*v.r.* botis, -es] clasped faire and fetisly. **1483** *Cath. Angl.* 49 A Bute [*v.r.* Buyt] of ledir or wandis. **1597** SHAKS. *2 Hen. IV*, V. iii. 140 Get on thy Boots, wee'l ride all night. **1746** *Rep. Cond. Sir J. Cope* 116 This Morning Lord President call'd upon me in his Boots on his way Northward. **1755** JOHNSON *Dict.*, *Boot*..a covering for the leg, used by horsemen. **1832** *Tour Germ. Prince* II. iii. 38 A plain farmer, in marsh-boots and waterproof cloak. **1835** *Gentl. Mag.* Nov. 491 My little kid-boots were sadly stain'd. **1860** TYNDALL *Glac.* I. §18. 131 It is more difficult to fix the heel of the boot than the toe securely in the ice.

b. Phrases. † ***to make one boot serve for either leg*** (see quot.); ***the boot is on the other leg***: the case is altered, the responsibility is on the other party; ***the boot (is) on the wrong leg*** or ***foot***; ***to have (wish*** obs.) ***one's heart in one's boots***: to be in a state of extreme fear (a ludicrous extension of 'the heart sinks'); † ***over shoes, over boots***: expressing reckless continuance in a course already begun; ***boot and saddle*** [perversion of F. *boute-selle* 'place saddle'; see BOUTE-SELLE], the signal to cavalry for mounting; ***like old boots*** (slang): vigorously, thoroughgoingly; also ***to put*** (or ***sink***) ***in the boot*** or ***to put the boot in*** (esp. Austral. and N.Z.): to kick (in a brutal manner); also *fig.*; ***boots and all*** (Austral. and N.Z. colloq.): with no holds barred, wholeheartedly; also *attrib.*

1533 MORE *Debell. Salem* Wks. 980/2 That their wordes should haue twoo senses, and one boote serue for either legge. **1642** *Lords' Jrnls.* in Rushw. IV. 559 b, Edward Sanderford..said..that the Earl of Warwick was a Traytor, and wished his Heart in his Boots. **1648** SANDERSON *Serm.* (1681) II. 248 Over shoes, over boots; I know God will never forgive me, and therefore I will never trouble my self to seek His favour..this is properly the sin of despair. **1662** H. FOULIS *Hist. Wicked Plots* (1674) 67 Which so much incensed the Commons that they (over Boots, over Shoes) fell to draw up another. **1697** VANBRUGH *Æsop* I I, To boot and saddle again they sound. **1709** STEELE *Tatler* No. 51 ¶ 1 The Sound was chang'd to Boots and Saddle. **1834** CARRUTHERS *Kentuckian in N.Y.* I. 97 He's got the boot on the wrong leg. **1854** WHYTE-MELVILLE *Gen. Bounce* (1855) II. xvi. 47 The young woman as owns that house has got *the boot on the other leg*. **1856** J. GRANT *Black Drag.* xii, Our trumpets blew 'Boot-and-saddle' in the streets. **1861** 'F. G. TRAFFORD' *City & Suburb* 385 That's what I call putting the boot on the other leg with a vengeance. **1863** (*title*) The Boot on the Other Leg; or, Loyalty above Party. **1865** MISS BRADDON *Sir Jasper* xxvii. 282 I'll stick to you like old boots. **1866** F. MOORE *Women of War* 173 'Ah,' replied the jolly rebel, 'the boot is on the other foot now.' **1870** MISS BRIDGMAN *R. Lynne* I. xiii. 213 She's as tough as old boots. **1883** *Harper's Mag.* Sept. 592/2 [He] felt his courage oozing out at the seams of his boots. **1899** [see LEG *sb.* 2 a]. **1916** C. J. DENNIS *Songs Sentim. Bloke* 42 Plunks Tyball through the gizzard wiv 'is sword, 'Ow I ongcored! 'Put in the boot!' I sez. 'Put in the boot.' *c* **1926** *Transport Workers' Songbook* (N.Z.) 107 All of them helping the worker down, by putting in the 'boot'. **1936** G. B. SHAW *Simpleton* iii. 29, I should say ..that the boot is on the other leg. **1942** V. PALMER in *Coast to Coast* 26 Wait till he gets his opening, Charlie will, and then sink in the boot. **1947** D. M. DAVIN *Rest of our Lives* xix. 96 The next thing he'll do is counter-attack, boots and all. **1949** *Economist* 10 Sept. 566 [N.Z. correspondent] Longer political experience, a greater tactical sense and a 'boots-and-all' ruthlessness. **1955** *Times* 13 Aug. 7/2 When the boot was on the other foot and his own Democratic Party was in opposition the People's Party, then in power, deplored their rivals' use of the boycott weapon. **1955** V. PALMER *Let Birds Fly* 128 This could be no light affair for either of them. 'It's boots and all... Boots and all for both of us.' **1964** *Guardian* 2 Mar. 7/6 When he's lying there some cow in the front row puts the boot in.

c. ***to give*** (a person) ***the boot*** or ***the order of the boot***: to 'kick out', dismiss, 'sack'. So ***to get the boot.***

1888 RIDER HAGGARD *Col. Quaritch* xii. 215 There'll be the money to take over the Moat Farm and give that varmint Janter the boot. **1904** *Minister's Gaz. Fashion* Dec. 219/2 His vivacious accounts of 'padding the hoof', getting the 'boot', [etc.]. **1917** 'TAFFRAIL' *Sub* ii. 62 An habitual slacker ..generally got the Order of the Boot at the end of his third term. **1927** R. A. FREEMAN *Certain Dr. Thorndyke* I. ii. 22 If you hadn't come I should have got the order of the boot to a certainty.

d. *U.S. slang.* A recruit at a boot camp (see sense 8).

1915 *Recruiter's Bull.* (U.S.) Apr. 11/1 One of the 'boots' transferred to the Recruit Depot recently. **1944** [see sense 8 below]. **1963** *Amer. Speech* XXVIII. 78 It is taught to the 'boot' before he leaves boot camp.

e. *slang.* A Negro.

1957 C. MACINNES *City of Spades* I. iii. 17 In England some foolish man may call me sambo, darkie, boot or munt or nigger. **1962** H. SIMMONS *Man walking on Eggshells* II. xxii. 162 A lot of paddy studs still didn't know that boots were human.

f. An act of kicking (a person, ball, etc.); a kick. Cf. BOOT *v.*³ 4 a. *colloq.*

1942 BERREY & VAN DEN BARK *Amer. Thes. Slang* §689/2 *Kick*, boot. *Spec. balloon*, a lofty kick. **1967** *Boston Sunday Herald* 14 May II. 3/1 Joe bounced along the sidelines moaning about his team's mistakes until he finally found some one to agree with him. Then all was calm until the next boot. **1973** T. PYNCHON *Gravity's Rainbow* I. 98 That one impromptu boot so impossibly high, so perfectly parabolic, the ball soaring miles.

† **2.** A piece of armour for the legs, a greave.

1388 WYCLIF *1 Sam.* xvii. 6 He hadde bootis of bras in the hipis [**1382** stelyn legharneis]. **1483** CAXTON *Gold. Leg.* 65/4 He had botes of brasse in his cartes. **1609** BIBLE (Douay) *1 Sam.* xvii. 6 He had brassen bootes on his thighes [**1611** He had greaues of brasse vpon his legs].

3. An instrument of torture formerly used in Scotland to extort confessions from prisoners.

1513-75 *Diurnal Occurrents* (1833) 262 Ane Minister.. quha wes extramelie pynnit in the beittis lang of befoir. **1580-1** RANDOLPH in Tytler *Hist. Scot.* (1864) IV. 324 Being neither offered the boots, nor other kind of torment. **1618** FIELD *Amends for L.* I. i, The rack, strapado, or the boiling boot. **1663** SPALDING *Troub. Chas. I.* (1829) 7 She is..put into the boots, and cruelly tortured, yet confesses nothing. *c* **1706** VANBRUGH *Mistake* I. i, Shall I draw him on a Scotch pair of boots, Master, and make him tell all? **1715** BURNET *Own Time* (1766) I. 333 They put a pair of iron boots close on the leg, and drive wedges between these and the leg. **1816** SCOTT *Old Mort.* xxxvi. **1865** LECKY *Ration.* (1878) II. 41 The bones of their legs were shattered in the boots.

4. Part of a coach. † **a.** The fixed external step of a coach (cf. Fr. *botte* 5 in Littré); **b.** An uncovered space on or by the steps on each side, where attendants sat, facing sideways; later, a low outside compartment before or behind the body of the vehicle. *Obs.*

1608 ARMIN *Nest Ninn.* 27 Shee sets in the boote and rides on. **1609** DEKKER *Gull's Horn-bk.* I. (1862) 7 In the boots of which coach Lechery and Sloth sit like the waiting-maid. **1618** J. TAYLOR (Water P.) in Knight *Once upon Time* I. 152 Drawn sideways, as they are when they sit in the boot of the coach. **1626** BACON *Sylva* §202 If in a Coach, one side of the Boot be down, and the other up. *c* **1645** HOWELL *Lett.* I. iii. 15. **1669** *Lond. Gaz.* No. 421/2, 5 or 6 persons..opening the boot of his Coach discharged on him their Pistoll. *a* **1670** HACKET *Abp. Williams* (1693) I. 196 (D.) He received his son into the coach, and found a slight errand to leave Buckingham behind, as he was putting his foot in the boot. **1714** ELLWOOD *Autobiog.* 10 My Father, opening the Boot, step't out, and I followed. **1716** T. WARD *Eng. Ref.* 400 Rogues to sally out And charge the Coach at either Boot. **1816** SCOTT *Old Mort.* ii, A chaplain stuffed into a sort of lateral recess, formed by a projection at the door of the vehicle, and called, from its appearance, the boot.

c. The receptacle for luggage or parcels under the seats of the guard and coachman. (This appears to have been the fore and hind boot of sense b, covered in as a box, ? about the middle of the 18th c.) Now the ordinary name for the luggage compartment usu. at the rear of a motor vehicle. Also *attrib.*

1781 *Westm. Mag.* IX. 13, I begged protection of the coachman, who advised me to get into the boot of the coach. **1807** *Antidote Miseries Hum. Life* 27 'Mind that sword-case in the boot', cries the captain. **1838** DICKENS *Nich. Nick.* iv, From the door of the hind boot of all the red coaches. **1868** W. E. WATERS *Life among Mormons* 41 The mail is carried in the boots of stage-coaches. **1886** *Leslie's Pop. Monthly* XXI. 66/1 The great boot was securely strapped down over the baggage. **1933** *Boy's Mag.* XLVII. 35/1 The spare wheel is carried in an enclosed luggage boot at the rear. **1955** *Times* 29 June 12/6 The tailboard formed by the lowered boot-door.

d. *U.S.* (See quots.)

1828-32 WEBSTER, *Boot.* 3... An apron or leathern cover for a gig or chair, to defend persons from rain and mud. *This ..application is local and improper.* **1911** J. C. LINCOLN *Cap'n Warren's Wards* i. 9 The 'boot' was a rubber curtain buttoned across the front of the buggy, extending from the dashboard to just below the level of the driver's eyes.

5. A protective covering for the foot and part of the leg of a horse.

1812 *Specif. Purden's Patent* No. 3542 (*title*) An improved Horse boot. **1884** *Longm. Mag.* Apr. 610 The bright chestnut, on which the trainer himself has mounted—after seeing him carefully fitted with 'boots', lest he should cut or overreach.

6. In various technical uses: **a.** *Organ-building* (see quot.). **b.** *Metallurgy* (see quot.). **c.** In bottling liquor: A leathern case in which to put a filled bottle while corking it (cf. *bottle-boot*). † **d.** A (leather) case for a fiddle.

1594 LYLY *M. Bombie* v. iii, A bots on the shoomaker that made this boote for my fiddle, 'tis too straight. **1881** C. A. EDWARDS *Organs* 139 The boot..encloses and supports the block.. The boot also conveys the wind to the speaking part or reed. **1881** RAYMOND *Mining Gloss.*, *Boot*, a leather or tin joint connecting the blast-main with the tuyère or nozzle in a bloomary.

e. The feathered legs of some varieties of pigeons and poultry.

1855 *Poultry Chron.* III. 348/2 The boots, or as Shanghai fanciers would style it, the vulture hock, must be white. **1875** *Contemp. Rev.* XXVI. 949 Instances..in which the feet of pigeons or fowls are abnormally feathered, or, as it is termed, furnished with 'boots'.

f. *Ornith.* An entire tarsal envelope characteristic of the legs of some birds.

1864 E. COUES in *Proc. Philad. Acad. Nat. Sci.* 82 The very long tarsi present the remarkable feature of having their anterior and lateral aspects covered with one smooth unbroken podotheca or 'boot'.

g. Short for *Denver boot* s.v. DENVER. *U.S.*

1968 *Amer. City* Apr. 146/1 The boot is a device that slips over the rim of a car's wheel so that it cannot be moved away. **1977** *U.S. News & World Rep.* 21 Mar. 80/3 One Washington resident recently received her second boot and had to pay $400 for 26 tickets accumulated over seven months.

7. *Comb.*, chiefly in attrib. and objective relations: as ***boot-binder***, ***-cleaning***, ***-edge***, ***-finisher***, ***-garter***, ***-heel***, ***-holder***, ***-lace***, ***-maker***, ***-making***, ***-nail***, ***-pattern***, ***-seam***, ***-sole***, ***-sponge***, ***-spur***, ***-upper*** (UPPER *sb.*¹ 1).

1862 *Macm. Mag.* May 67 One poor old woman, a *boot-binder. **1838** DICKENS *O. Twist* xviii, Went on with his *boot-cleaning. **1824** SCOTT *Redg.* I. 326 (D.) A handsome and flourishing pair of *boot-garters. **1870** 'MARK TWAIN' *Sk. New & Old* (1875) 99 The rims of his *boot-heels. **1891** KIPLING *Light that Failed* vii. 117 You're a work-woman, darling, to your boot-heels. **1920** D. H. LAWRENCE *Lost Girl* vii. 139 Striking a match on his boot-heel. **1630** in Fairholt *Costume* (1846) 453 To a *bootmaker for one pair of boots, white and red, 14*s.* **1871** *Member for Paris* I. 279 They would have taken to *boot-making. *a* **1661** HOLYDAY *Juvenal* 42 A soldier leaves his *boot-nail in my hand. **1612** T. TAYLOR *Comm. Titus* ii. I. (1619) 336 Though the ground in comparison be not better then a *bootshanke, as we vse to say. **1863** DICKENS *Mrs. Lirriper's Lodgings* in *All Year Round* (Christmas no.) 6/1 My *boot-sponge was in my hand. **1848** THACKERAY *Van. Fair* xxii, Clinking his *bootspurs, swaggering prodigiously. *a* **1877** *Boot-upper [see *boot-crimp* in 8 below]. **1879** *Birmingham Weekly Post* 21 June 5/3 Charged with..stealing a quantity of boot-uppers. **1906** *Times* 13 Dec. 4/2 The [stolen] boot uppers were found at the shop.

8. Special comb.: as **boot-black**, a person who blacks boots, a shoe-black (chiefly *U.S.*); **boot-blacking**, (*a*) the polishing of boots and shoes; also *attrib.*; (*b*) blacking for polishing boots and shoes; **boot-boy**, (*a*) a boy employed to clean boots and shoes; (*b*) a violent or rowdy youth of a type characterized by assembling in gangs in search of trouble, wearing short-cropped hair and heavy boots; = *bovver boy* s.v. BOVVER; **boot camp** *U.S. slang*, a centre for the initial training of American naval or Marine recruits; † **boot-catch**, **boot-catcher**, a servant at an inn who pulled off the guests' boots; **boot-clamp**, **-crimp** (see quots.); **boot-closer**, one who sews together the upper leathers of boots; **boot-eater**, **-eating** (see quot.); **boot-faced** *a. colloq.* [f. phr. *to have a sea boot face*, see quot. 1925], grim-faced, sad-faced; with an expressionless face; **boot-grain**, a cowhide leather used for heavy boots; **boot-gusset**, elastic sides inserted in boots; **Boot Hill** *U.S.*, a graveyard or cemetery (orig. *joc.* of a frontier cemetery, in allusion to its occupants' dying with their boots on); freq. *attrib.*; **boot-hole**, the place where boots are cleaned in a large establishment; **boot-hook**, a hook for pulling on boots; **boot-hose** = *boot-stocking*; **boot-housing** (see quot. and HOUSING); **boot-jack**, a contrivance for pulling off boots; † **boot-ketch** = *boot-catcher*; also = *boot-jack*; **boot-last** = *boot-tree*; **boot-laster**, ? one who makes boot-lasts; **boot-lick**, *v.* to toady; *sb.* a toady (*U.S. slang*); **boot machine operator**, **boot machinist**, any person engaged in any machine operation in the manufacture of boots; **bootman**, a dealer in boots and shoes; **boot powder**, a powder, as of soapstone, used for dusting the inside of a boot or shoe; **boot-rack**, a rack or stand for holding boots; **boot-shank**, the piece of leather placed between the outer and the inner sole in the waist of a boot; † **boot-**

sleeve, a wide kind of coat-sleeve; **boot-stocking**, an over-stocking which covers the leg like a jack-boot; **boot-stretcher**, **-tree**, a shaped block inserted into a boot to stretch it or keep it in shape. Also BOOT-TOP, BOOT-TOPPING.

1817 in *Essex Inst. Hist. Coll.* VIII. 246 They had a *boot-black and barber. **1864** SALA in *Daily Tel.* 25 Feb., That negro boot-black on the street corner. **1883** *Harper's Mag.* July 817/1 The San Francisco boot-blacks seem quite a model to their class. **1866** J. C. GREGG *Life in Army* 139 Here are..*boot-blacking establishments. **1948** C. DAY LEWIS *Otterbury Incident* iv. 45 Ted had smears of boot-blacking on his face and hands. **1860** TROLLOPE *Tales of all Countries* 58 'He, he, he,' laughed the *boot boy as he turned them up for me to look at. **1925** W. DEEPING *Sorrell & Son* ix. 84, I don't share out,—with the boot-boy. **1977** *Chainsaw* Sept./Oct. 7/2 And now we're getting fights down the King's Road at weekends between punks, teds and boot boys. **1984** *Daily Tel.* 25 Feb. 36/4 Mr John Cartwright, the SDP whip whose party has taken the brunt of the abuse said: 'We are not going to be silenced by this sort of boot-boy tactics more suited to football hooligans than MPs.' **1944** G. P. BAILEY *Boot; a Marine in the Making* Foreword, Marine inductees are called 'Boots' and it is Marine Corps custom to send them all through a grim process called '*boot camp'. **1955** C. S. FORESTER *Good Shepherd* 45 That boy was one of the new draft, fresh out of boot-camp. **1775** CAMPBELL *Diary Visit Eng.* 221 The number of churches I could not learn from our *boot catch guide. **1745** SWIFT *Direct. Servants* (J.) The ostler and the *boot-catcher ought to partake. **1761** COLMAN *Jealous Wife* IV. ii, There's master, and John ostler, and bootcatcher, all gone after 'em. *a* **1877** KNIGHT *Dict. Mech.*, **Boot-clamp*, a device for holding a boot while being sewed. **1824** J. CONSTABLE *Let.* 12 July (1964) II. 360 Mary is married to her cousin..a *boot closer. *a* **1877** KNIGHT *Dict. Mech.*, **Boot-crimp*, a tool or a machine for giving the shape to the pieces of leather designed for boot uppers. **1880** *Pall Mall G.* 30 Dec. 11/1 A historic juror.. is said to have given final..proof of his resolution to acquit a State defendant..by declaring that he would eat his boots before he would find the man guilty. A '*boot-eater' now designates a particular species of juror. Rumour says there are at least nine boot-eaters in the Parnell jury. [**1925** FRASER & GIBBONS *Soldier & Sailor Words* 253 *To have a sea boot face*, to look gloomy. **1942** M. DICKENS *One Pair of Feet* viii. 180 Everyone wore a face like a boot.] **1958** A. GRAHAM *Foreign Affair* ix. 111 Laughing nervously at the *boot-faced British. **1961** *Bookseller* 12 Aug. 1080/3 Commenting on this remarkable achievement..the *Times* is nicely bootfaced. **1965** J. PORTER *Dover Two* ix. 108 He came down to breakfast more boot-faced than ever and lost no time in burying himself in the morning paper. **1882** *Daily News* 4 Mar., A decline in the trade in *boot gussets in the elastic web manufacture. [**1886** *Outing* Jan. 398/2 Within the rail fence of 'Boot-heel Cemetery', at Flagstaff, my stopping-place, there were fourteen graves.] **1901** *Everybody's Mag.* June 582/2 Occasionally his six-shooter brought order and a new grave or two in *Boot Hill cemetery. **1930** E. FERBER *Cimarron* 160 The body..was interred in Boot Hill, with only the prowling jackals to mourn him. **1935** A. J. POLLOCK *Underworld Speaks* 11/2 *Boot hill*, prison cemetery. **1948** *Southern Sierran* (Los Angeles) May 2/3 The rest of us took Wednesday for an auto trip..through Tombstone of the one and only Boothill Cemetery. **1962** *Times* 12 Apr. 7/3 There's an old saying that every boothill is 'full of fellers that pulled their triggers before aimin''. **1971** J. H. GRAY *Red Lights on Prairies* i. 2 A poor town that could not boast of its local bad men or boothill cemetery. **1902** *Little Folks* II. 162/2 It was Grandmother who happened to discover him sitting in the *boot-hole under the stairs. **1808** 'A CONNOISSEUR' *Fashionable Biogr.* 83 Whether the Romans used *boot-hooks, and of what kind and shape, I have not been able to ascertain. **1588** *Lanc. & Ch. Wills* III. 139 One paire of tawny stockes wth toppes of *boothose of the same. **1611** BEAUM. & FL. *Knt. Burn. Pestle* IV. ii. (D.) The maid That wash'd my boot-hose. **1815** SCOTT *Guy M.* vii, The women spun mittens for the lady, and knitted boot-hose for the laird. **1792** OSBALDISTONE *Brit. Sportsman* 432 *Houzing*, is either *boot-houzing or shoe-houzing; the former is a piece of stuff made fast to the hinder part of the saddle. *a* **1841** T. HOOK *Ramsbottom Pap.* in *Casquet Lit.* 1877 I. 117/1 Tall men are doubled up like *boot-jacks. **1785** MACKENZIE *Lounger* No. 54 ¶8 Sent the *boot-ketch to Hart's for a pair of Spanish boots. **1814** SCOTT *Wav.* xlix, I wish..I had recommended him to attend the circle this evening with a boot-ketch under his arm. **1611** COTGR., *Embouchoir*, a *Boot last, or Boot tree. **1891** *Daily News* 30 Dec. 3/2 *Boot machinist. **1927** *Daily Express* 27 May 6/1 [Obtainable] from all *Bootmen. Fixing Extra. **1837** DICKENS *Pickw.* xlix. 538 A *boot-rack and boot-jack. **1907** *Yesterday's Shopping* (1969) 277/2 Boot Racks..18 in—1/7½. **1732** FIELDING *Miser* I. vi, These *boot-sleeves were certainly intended to be receivers of stolen goods. *a* **1807** BOWLES Note to *Banwell Hill* (D.) In a pair of worsted *boot-stockings, which my father observed would keep my under-stockings from the dirt. **1834** SOUTHEY *Doctor* lvii. (1862) 126 You will not observe his boot-stockings coming high above the knees. **1766** CROKER, etc. *Dict. Arts*, **Boot-Tree*, or *Boot-Last*, is a wooden cylinder slit into two parts, between which, when it is put into the boot, they drive..a wedge. **1855** THACKERAY *Newcomes* xi, Pretty boots, trimly stretched on boot-trees.

boot (buːt), *sb.*[4] *Computing.* [Shortened f. BOOT-STRAP, BOOTSTRAP *sb.*] **a.** The operation or procedure of booting a computer or an operating system. **b.** A bootstrap routine. See BOOT *v.*[1]

1975 ECKHOUSE & MORRIS *Minicomputer Systems* vi. 169 The boot overlay code will overlay the first two instructions of the loader. **1983** W. S. DAVIS *Operating Systems* (ed. 2) xii. 234 The boot contains a small amount of program logic—just enough to read a sector or two from the system disk drive. **1983** [see BOOT *v.*[4] 2]. **1984** PHILLIPS & SCELLATO *Apple //c User Guide* iv. 40 Insert the *Apple at Play* disk into the disk drive. The computer is still turned on, so you can try a procedure called a 'cold boot' that makes the Apple //c think it has just been turned on.

boot (buːt), *v.*[1] Forms: 4–6 bote(n, 5–6 boote, 6– boot; also *north.* 5 buten, buytt, 5–6 bute. [ME. *bōten* f. *bōt*, BOOT *sb.*[1], taking the place of *beten* (see BEET), which was scarcely used in the south after the 14th c. Cf. BOTEN.]

†**1.** *trans.* To make better; to cure, relieve, heal; to remedy. *Obs.*

c **1330** *Amis & Amil.* 2340 Jesu that is heuen king, Schal bote the of thi bale. *a* **1450** *Syr Eglam.* 187 He was botyd of mekylle care. **1481** CAXTON *Reynard* (Arb.) 83 The sauour of hym boteth alle syknessis.

†**2.** *trans.* To make good (a deficiency), to make up (what is deficient); to add by way of equalizing the value of things exchanged; to give 'into the boot'. *Obs.*

1393 LANGL. *P. Pl.* C. VII. 382 Ther were chapmen y-chose þe chaffare to preise; þat he þat hadde þe hod sholde nat habbe þe cloke. Þe betere þyng; by arbytours sholde bote þe werse. *c* **1440** *Promp. Parv.* 45 Botyn, or ȝeue more overe in barganynge, *licitor, in precio superaddo.* **1530** PALSGR. 461/1 What will you boote bytwene my horse and yours?

3. To do good; to be of use or value; to profit, avail, help. (Only used in 3rd pers.)

a. *impers.* (or with *it*): chiefly negative and interrogative. (Usually followed by the real subject, as an infinitive phrase, or subst. clause.)

c **1400** *Roland* 499 It botes not to abide. *a* **1450** *Knt. de la Tour* (1868) 66 The pore soule cried..but it boted not. **1564** GRINDAL *Serm.* Wks. (1843) 25 It needeth not or booteth not, as the old proverb goeth. **1591** SPENSER *Teares of Muses* 445 What bootes it then to come from glorious Fore-fathers? **1656** COWLEY *Pind. Odes, Destinie* iv, With Fate what boots it to contend? **1828** ARNOLD in *Life & Corr.* (1844) I. ii. 88 It boots not to look backwards. **1855** BROWNING *Cleon* in *Men & Wom.* II. 184 What boots To know she might spout oceans if she could?

b. with dative object (or with *to.*) *arch.*

c **1400** *Destr. Troy* 3391 Me botis not barly your biddyng with stonde. **1596** SPENSER *F.Q.* I. iii. 20 Him booteth not resist, nor succour call. **1612** T. TAYLOR *Comm. Titus* i. 8. (1619) 175 It shall not boote a man to say in the day of iudgement, Lord, Lord. **1690** W. WALKER *Idiom. Anglo-Lat.* 65 It will not boot you to say so. **1851** THACKERAY *Eng. Hum.* i. (1858) 45 Boots it to you now, that the whole world loves and deplores you?

c. with sense 'it matters'.

1752 YOUNG *Brothers* III. i, What boots it which prevails? **1760** STERNE *Tr. Shandy* I. xix. 25 Little boots it to the subtle speculatist to stand single in his opinions.

d. with sb. (sing. or pl.) as subject.

1562 J. HEYWOOD *Prov. & Epigr.* (1867) 47 Braulyng booted not. **1596** DRAYTON *Legends* iv. 30 Little, I feare, my labour Me will boot. *a* **1717** PARNELL *Poet. Wks.* (1833) 64 What boots his hand, his heart, his head? **1795** SOUTHEY *Poems* 32 What boot to thee the blessings fortune gave? What boots thy wealth? **1884** BROWNING *Ferishtah* 18 Little boots Our sympathy with fiction!

†**4.** *trans.* To benefit, increase, enrich. *Obs. rare.*

1606 SHAKS. *Ant. & Cl.* II. v. 71 And I will boot thee with what guift beside Thy modestie can begge.

†**boot**, *v.*[2] *Obs. rare*[−1]. [cf. BOOT *sb.*[2], also MLG. *bûten* (Du. *buiten*) to make booty, to seize.]

intr. ? To share as booty.

1554 LYDG. *Bochas* IV. xxiii. 120 b, His desire and his entencion Was to be boting [*ed.* **1494** *has* boty] with them of such pillage As goddes had in their possession.

boot (buːt), *v.*[3] Forms: 5 bote(n, -yn, (bute), 7 boote, 6– boot. [f. BOOT *sb.*[3]]

1. a. *trans.* To put boots on (another or oneself).

1468 *Medulla Gram.* in *Cath. Angl.* 49 *note*, *Ocreo*, to botyn. **1483** *Cath. Angl.* 49 To Bute [Buyyt], *ocreare.* **1600** HEYWOOD *1 Edw. IV*, II. Wks. 1874 I. 33 Let me entreate you would go boote yourselues. **1693** W. ROBERTSON *Phraseol. Gen.* 272 To Boot, *ocreas induere. Ballad 'Young Redin'* x. in Allingham *Ballad Bk.* (1865) 285 They've booted him and spurred him.

b. *intr.* (for *refl.*) To put on one's boots.

1597 SHAKS. *2 Hen. IV*, V. iii. 140 Get on thy Boots.. Boote, boote, Master Shallow. **1813** SIR R. WILSON *Diary* II. 272 Many persons booting..for a journey to Paris. **1855** KINGSLEY *Westw. Ho* (1861) 95 Help me to boot and gird.

2. *trans.* To torture with the BOOT (*sb.*[3] 3).

1580–1 RANDOLPH in Tytler *Hist. Scot.* (1864) IV. 324 He hath been sore booted. **1818** SCOTT *Let.* in *Lockhart* (1839) V. 282 Tradition says..Granger and his wife were booted.

3. *Mil. slang.* To beat, formerly with a long jack-boot, now with a leather surcingle or waist-belt: an irregular conventional punishment inflicted by soldiers on a comrade guilty of dishonesty or shirking duty.

1802 C. JAMES *Mil. Dict.* (1816) 84/2 Scabbarding a soldier, as in the infantry of the line, or booting him, as in the cavalry.

4. a. To kick (a person).

1877 BARTLETT *Dict. Amer.* (ed. 4) 59 To 'boot a man' is to kick him. **1883** D. C. MURRAY *By Gate of Sea* II. ix. 43, I have felt..an electric sensation in the right foot, indicative ..of a desire to boot a noble swell or two who hover in her train. **1891** *Daily News* 11 Feb. 7/3 At him, lads! Boot and kick him! Kill him! **1892** STEVENSON & OSBOURNE *Wrecker* xii. 195, I saw a big hulking beast of a Dutchman booting the ship's boy. **1913** 'IAN HAY' *Happy-go-Lucky* i, You will be booted for that afterwards, my lad.

b. To eject (a person); = KICK *v.*[1] 8 a. Also with *out*. Also *fig.*

1880 *Harper's Mag.* Dec. 160/2 He angrily bade the bore to leave..and never show his face there again; if he did, he would be booted out. **1902** *Westm. Gaz.* 13 Nov. 2/2 Who flocked together in the House of Lords..to 'boot' the Home Rule Bill. **1907** *Daily Chron.* 5 Nov. 10/4 That German scrub wants me to boot [him]. **1909** *Westm. Gaz.* 1 Oct. 7/2 Burgess literally booted him out of his office. **1941** 'R. WEST' *Black Lamb* I. 317 Were not the Turks booted out of here in 1878? **1966** B. KIMENYE *Kalasanda Revisited* 45 Though he led the ladies with charming politeness into his office, his baser instincts were at the same time urging him to boot the whole lot of them down the steps.

5. To kick (the ball) with more than the usual vigour. *Football colloq.*

1914 *Morning Post* 2 Mar. 4/1 The ball was booted too hard and the defence got the touch down. **1932** A. J. WORRALL *English Idioms* 14 The right-back booted the ball far up the field.

boot (buːt), *v.*[4] *Computing.* [f. BOOT *sb.*[4]]

1. *trans.* To prepare (a computer) for operation by causing an operating system to be loaded into its memory from a disc or tape, esp. by a bootstrap routine; to cause (an operating system or a program) to be loaded in this way; to load the program on (a disc) into a computer's memory. Also *to boot up*.

1980 M. E. SLOAN *Introd. Minicomputers & Microcomputers* vi. 158 We turn the power knob to ON, and depress the CONTROL and BOOT switches. We call this procedure booting the system...The computer is now in the machine language mode, in which machine language programs can be entered and run. **1982** FLORES & TERRY *Microcomputer Systems* ii. 40 Upon turn-on, control immediately goes to the ROM monitor or to BASIC, which issues a prompt. The operator then types in a monitor (or BASIC) command to boot the disk operating system. **1984** HITCHING & STONE *Understanding Accounting!* i. 1 The data processing manager is rushing around making sure..that they have all remembered to 'boot' their disks before settling down with their micros! **1985** *Personal Computer World* Feb. 137/3 Booting up GEM is an interesting experience. **1985** *Pract. Computing* May 82/1 When you first boot Deskmate it comes up in monochrome. **1986** *Courier-Mail* (Brisbane) 30 Oct. 29/1 If you boot up your system without the keyboard being plugged in, you will see an error message.

b. *absol.* with *up*.

1983 *Byte* July 219/3 Once you get the two beeps, boot up with a scratch copy BASIC disk. **1986** *What Micro?* Apr. 30/1 Once you boot up and run the new Mac one difference is immediately apparent.

2. *intr.* To undergo booting; *spec.* (of an operating system) to be loaded into a computer's memory; (of a computer) to have an operating system loaded into it.

1983 *Austral. Microcomputer Mag.* Aug. 23/1 Programs that use their own loaders may or may not boot depending on the environment that happens to be established by the boot code. Pascal disks appear to boot without any problems. **1984** *Computerworld* 16 July 93/4 He inserted one IBM Personal Computer program and found it would not boot. **1985** *Personal Computer World* Feb. 146/3 When PCP/M has booted it provides the facility to autorun a program. **1986** *Micro Decision* Oct. 34/3 One of its purposes is to hold MS-DOS so that it can be loaded quickly to workstations when they boot up.

Hence **'booting** *vbl. sb.*[4] (also with *up*), the action of booting a computer, etc.

1982 *380Z Disc System User Guide* App. B. 2 *Booting*,.. the process of loading system software from storage (usually cassette or disc) into computer memory. Firstly, a small part of the software..is loaded into memory, and is in turn used to pull in the rest of the system. **1984** J. HILTON *Choosing & using your Home Computer* III. 80/1 This process of switching the computer on, then waiting for the DOS to take over, is called 'booting-up'. **1985** *Computing Equipment* Sept. 6/1 System booting can be done directly from the hard disk.

boot = *behoved*: see BUS *v.*

bootakin, var. of BOOTIKIN.

†**boot-carouse.** (Cf. BOMBARD *sb.* 3.)

1598 MARSTON *Pygmal.* ii. 147 What brought'st thou els beside..From Belgia what? but their deep bezeling, Their boote-carouse, and their Beere-buttering?

booted ('buːtɪd), *ppl. a.* [f. BOOT *v.*[3] + -ED[1].]

1. a. Wearing boots, having boots on; formerly usually in the sense 'equipped for riding'.

1552 HULOET, Booted, *ocreatus.* **1563–87** FOXE *A. & M.* (1596) 1892/1 Master Leauer was ready booted to..cary it to London. **1690** CROWNE *Eng. Frier* IV. 32 How now, booted Gentlemen, whither are you going? **1835** BECKFORD *Recoll.* 193 Two special couriers..magnificently badged and booted. **1877** BESANT & RICE *Son of Vulc.* I. ii. 32 Who correct their wives with booted feet.

b. esp. in phrase ***booted and spurred***. Also *fig.*

1678 *Gunpowder-Treas.* 19 He..found Faux..booted and spurr'd. **1762** GOLDSM. *Nash* 39 Punch came in booted and spurred. **1833** EG.-WARBURTON *Hunt. Songs* iv. (1883) 12 Come then to Tarporley booted and spurr'd.

2. *transf.* **a.** Clothed or covered as to the legs.

1601 HOLLAND *Pliny* I. 166 Booted..with a pair of buskins or greiues about his legges. **1740** SOMERVILLE *Hobbinol* iii. 179 Her Legs unclean Booted with Grime. *a* **1774** GOLDSM. *Scarron's Comic Rom.* (1775) II. 1 He saw little Ragotin, just arriving, booted up to the waist.

b. Of fowls: Having feathered legs. Also applied to other birds.

1781 LATHAM *Gen. Synop. Birds* I. I. 75 Falcon..Booted F... legs feathered to the toes. **1814** LEWIS & CLARKE *Exped. to Sources of Missouri* II. 182 The large black and white pheasant..is also booted to the toes. **1885** *Bazaar* 30 Mar. 1265/3 Black booted cockerel..Coloured booted bantams. **1954** R. PETERSON et al. *Field Guide to Birds* 72 Booted eagle. *Hieraëtus pennatus*..Tarsi heavily feathered. **1959** VAN TYNE & BERGER *Fund. Ornith.* ii. 48 Several types

of passerine tarsal scutellation have been described.. Booted ('ocreate'): Scutella fused into a single smooth sheath or 'boot', except in some cases, at the very lower end.

bootee (buːˈtiː). [A kind of diminutive of *boot*: see -EE.] A trade name for: **a.** a kind of high-low boot for ladies; **b.** an infant's wool boot.

1799 *Aurora* (Philad.) 15 Nov. (Th.), For sale, 180 pairs of bootees. **1801** *Spirit of Farmer's Museum* 262 He is, literally, made up of marechal powder, cravat, and bootees. **1844** *Congress. Globe* 11 Mar. 361/3 Men's boots or bootees of leather,.. women's boots or bootees,.. children's boots, bootees, and shoes. **1848** BARTLETT *Dict. Amer.*, *Bootee*, dimin. of boot, a boot without a top, or a shoe made like a boot without a leg. **1848** BOAG *Eng. Dict.* 155/1 *Bootee*, a word sometimes used for a half or short boot. **1861** *Revised Regulations U.S. Army* 238 Mounted men may receive one pair of 'boots' and two pair of 'bootees', instead of four pair of bootees. **1929** *Sears Catal.* Fall 76 These bootees make a warm and cozy place to tuck little feet.

booten, rare var. of BOTEN *v. Obs.* to amend.

†ˈ**booter.** *Obs.* [prob. ad. Du. *buiter* plunderer, freebooter.] Spoiler; robber. Found only in comb. FREEBOOTER.

1716 PRIDEAUX *Connect. O. & N. Test.* II. VII. IV. 648 The Country was filled with Thieves and free Booters.

bootery (ˈbuːtərɪ). *U.S.* [f. BOOT *sb.*^{3} + -ERY.] A shop where boots and shoes are sold.

1920 *N.Y. Times* 25 Jan., [In San Francisco] You can buy your groceries in grocerterias.. and your shoes in booteries. **1945** STEINBECK *Cannery Row* xi. 47 The final climax came with the front of Holman's bootery broken out and the party trying on shoes in the display window.

‖**Boötes** (bəʊˈəʊtiːz). *Astron.* [L., a. Gr. βοώτης ploughman, wagoner; also the constellation.] A northern constellation, the Wagoner, situated at the tail of the Great Bear and containing the bright star Arcturus.

1656 BLOUNT *Glossogr.*, *Boötes*, a slow working Star in the North Pole, near to Charls wain, which it follows. **1703** POPE *Thebais* 520 When clouds conceal Boötes' golden wain. **1831** CARLYLE *Sart. Res.* I. iii, What thinks Boötes of them, as he leads his Hunting Dogs over the Zenith?

bootful (ˈbuːtfʊl), *sb.* [f. BOOT *sb.*^{3}] As much as a boot will hold or carry.

1772 PENNANT *Tours Scotl.* (1790) III. 116 Bringing a bootful of earth from different estates.

†ˈ**bootful**, *a. Obs. rare*$^{-1}$. [f. BOOT *sb.*^{1} + -FUL.] Of service; useful, advantageous, profitable.

1594 CAREW *Tasso* (1881) 93 His aduice bootfull and good they call.

booth (buːð), *sb.* Forms: 2–5 boþe, 3–6 bothe, 6–7 boothe, 6– booth. Also *north.* 5–6 buth(e, 6 bouthe, bowthe, *Sc.* boithe, 6– *Sc.* buith. [ME. *bōþe*, *bōthe*, prob. a. ODa. **bóð* (mod.Da. and Sw. *bod* booth, stall, shop = OIcel. *búð* fem. dwelling, f. East Norse *bóa* = Icel. *búa* to dwell. Cf. MHG. *buode* 'hut, tent', mod.G. *bude* 'booth, stall': perh. also from East Norse. Some think the Teutonic word to be adopted from Slavonic: cf. Boh. *bouda*, Pol. *buda*, which are at least cognate.]

1. a. A temporary dwelling covered with boughs of trees or other slight materials. *arch.* in gen. sense.

c **1200** *Trin. Coll. Hom.* 185 Ðar haueð elch patriarche, and prophete, and apostles.. maked faier bode [*for* boðe] inne to wunien. *c* **1325** *E.E. Allit. P.* C. 441 He bowed vnder his lyttel boþe. *a* **1536** TINDALE *Brief Declar. Sacr.* Wks. 1848 I. 376 He had made booths, or houses of boughs for his beasts. **1580** BARET *Alv.* B 930 A Boothe or place couered where men sitte to talke for recreation. **1655** H. VAUGHAN *Silex Scint.* II. 179 Every bush is something's booth. **1703** MAUNDRELL *Journ. Jerus.* (1732) 40 At the North end they led into Booths, and Summer-houses. **1725** DE FOE *Voy. round World* (1840) 178 We cut down branches of trees, and built us two large booths. **1871** MACDUFF *Mem. Patmos* xiii. 174 Temporary booths, made of intertwisted palm, olive.. and willows from the brook.

b. *esp.* A temporary structure covered with canvas, or the like; a tent. Now chiefly as in 2.

1535 COVERDALE *2 Kings* vii. 10 We came to the tentes of the Sirians, and beholde, there is no man there.. but.. the bothes as they stonde. **1674** *Scheffer's Lapland* xiv. 71 That certain boothes and sheds be provided. **1762** GOLDSM. *Nash* 30 Obliged to assemble in a booth to drink tea and chocolate. **1775** R. CHANDLER *Trav. Asia M.* (1825) I. 137 A wild country covered.. with the black booths of the Turcomans. **1838** HAWTHORNE *Amer. Note-bks.* (1871) I. 109.

c. *polling-booth*: a temporary structure for voting purposes at a parliamentary or other election.

1846 MᶜCULLOCH *Acc. Brit. Empire* 1854 II. 111 The booths are erected at the joint expense of the candidates.. the cost of a booth erected for a county election shall not exceed 45*l.*

2. *spec.* **a.** A covered stall at a market; a tent at a fair, or the like, for the sale of wares or refreshments, exhibition of the feats of jugglers, etc. See also TOLL-BOOTH.

c **1200** ORMIN 15573 Ne birrþ ȝuw nohht min Faderr hus Till chepinngboþe turrnenn. *c* **1300** *K. Alis.* 3457 They.. brenten townes, and bothes. *c* **1440** *Promp. Parv.* 46 Boþe, chapmannys schoppe. **1483** *Cath. Angl.* 49 A Buthe, *emptorium.* **1535** LYNDESAY *Satyre* 1015 Ane laidlie lurdan loun, Cumde to break buithis. **1580** BARET *Alv.* B 1038 A bouthe or tente that any occupier maketh in a faire or other places. **1581** J. BELL *Haddon's Answ. Osor.* 271 A denne of Theeves? a Bowthe of brothells? *c* **1610** SIR J. MELVILLE *Mem.* (1735) 227 Unruly Servants broke up the Merchants' Booths. **1723** DE FOE *Col. Jack* (1840) 13 To pay at going into a booth to see a show. **1808** JAMIESON s.v., The Luckenbooths of Edinburgh, wooden shops [which formerly stood in the High Street]. **1848** MACAULAY *Hist. Eng.* I. 350 The booths where goods were exposed to sale projected far into the streets.

b. = *telephone booth.*

1930 *Bell System Techn. Jrnl.* IX. I. 12 A form of booth furnished by the telephone companies, provided with a seat and with lighting. **1952** A. BARON *With Hope, Farewell* 95 He stood in the booth, fumbling with his notebook to find the telephone number.

3. *Comb.*, as ***booth-cloth***, ***-keeper***, †***-mail*** (= boothage).

1552 HULOET, Boothclothes, wherwith boothes or tentes ben couered. *c* **1570** LD. SEMPILL *3 Taverners*, To pay my buith-mail and my stand. **1838** HAWTHORNE *Amer. Note-bks.* (1871) I. 109 Booth-keepers knocking down the temporary structures.

booth, *v. rare.* [f. prec. sb.] *trans.* To provide or shelter with a booth.

1594 *Zepheria* xxxi. in Arb. *Garner* V. 81 She booths her fair with shade of broad-branched trees.

†ˈ**boothage.** *Obs.* [f. BOOTH *sb.* + -AGE.] Dues paid for leave to erect a booth in a market.

1695 KENNETT *Par. Antiq.* (1818) II. 409 A market.. in which the picage, stallage, boothage, tollage, assize of bread and beer.. were granted to the King.

†**boot-hale**, *v. Obs.* [f. BOOT *sb.*^{2} booty + HALE *v.* to haul.]

1. *intr.* To carry off booty or spoil; to practise plundering, marauding or pilfering.

1598 [see BOOT-HALING *vbl. sb.*] **1609** HEYWOOD *Sallust* 33 Some made merchandize of fugitives and others went boot-haling into the confederate countries. **1611** COTGR., *Butiner*, to prey, get bootie.. to bootehale it. **1658** W. BURTON *Itin. Anton.* 150 A people forward to Boot-hale, and consume, but backward to the duties of War. *a* **1670** HACKET *Abp. Williams* II. (1692) 182.

2. *trans.* To spoil; to pillage; to plunder.

1610 HEALEY *St. Aug. Citie of God* 145 Boote-hal'd all the Coast unto Caieta. **1625** LISLE *Du Bartas* 133 No Hircan Tygers flight boot-hailes thy vaulted hills.

†**boot-haler.** *Obs.* Also 7 -hayler. [f. prec. + -ER^1.] A marauder, a marauding or foraging soldier; a freebooter; a highwayman, brigand.

1600 HOLLAND *Livy* XXII. xli. 458 g, To stop and impeach the forragers and boothalers [*prædatoribus*] of Anniball. **1609** C. BUTLER *Fem. Mon.* (1634) 139 The very Boot-halers, or Highway-robbers, are more worthy favour than such. **1621** BP. MOUNTAGU *Diatribæ* 182 A common Boote-hayler. **1686** tr. *Chardin's Trav.*, *Coron. Solyman* 145 Those Boot-halers the Cosaques.

†**boot-haling**, *vbl. sb. Obs.* [as prec. + -ING^1.]

1. The carrying away of booty, plundering of an enemy; marauding, freebooting, brigandage.

1598 FLORIO, *Gualda*, a bootehaling [**1611** bootie-haling], a freebooting. **1603** —— *Montaigne* II. xxxi. (1632) 401 Returning from forage or boot-haling. **1657** TRAPP *Comm. Ps.* lxxxvi. 1 What I can get by boot-haling from the Lords enemies. **1686** tr. *Chardin's Trav.* 92 The wars of the Ningrelians.. are.. meer Incursions and Boots Halings.

2. The proceeds of marauding; booty.

1622 F. MARKHAM *Decades Warre* I. v. §2 His Conscience must tie him, not Spoyle, or Boot-haling.

†**boot-haling**, *ppl. a. Obs.* [f. as prec. + -ING^2.] Pillaging, marauding, freebooting.

1621 MOLLE *Camerar. Liv. Libr.* I. v. 12 These boot-haling fellowes. **1658** W. BURTON *Itin. Anton.* 164 The stragling and boot-haling Companies of such as had lately plundered London.

boothall, booth-hall. [? f. BOOTH + HALL.] A name given to a town-hall, as in the city of Gloucester.

1712 ATKYNS *Gloucestersh.* 89 The Booth-hall or Town-hall is.. subject to the Jurisdiction both of the Out-county and of the City. **1713** *Lond. Gaz.* No. 5112/4 The Boothall in the City of Gloucester.

boothed (buːðd), *a.* [f. BOOTH *sb.* + -ED^2.] Furnished with booths; tented.

1870 *Daily News* 4 June, This thickly-boothed region.

†**boother** (ˈbuːðə(r)). *Obs.* exc. *dial.* A variant of BOULDER; belonging chiefly to the midland counties of England.

c **1680** DINGLEY *Hist. fr. Marble* (1868) 359 Leek Town. This Town wanting some stones, or (as vulgarly call'd in this county) boothers, to pave the street. **1826** *Pennsylv. Hist. Soc. Mem.* I. 285 Different kinds of stone by continual rolling and wearing have become smooth and round; and are called boothers. **1864** RAMSBOTTOM *Lanc. Rhymes* 66 For every cheer [= chair] a boother-stone.

bootikin, bootakin (ˈbuːtɪkɪn, -əkɪn). Also 8 booterkin, 9 bootakin. [dim. of BOOT *sb.*^{3}: see -KIN. Cf. *mannikin.*]

1. A soft boot or mitten made of wool and oiled silk, worn as a cure for the gout.

1767 H. WALPOLE in *N. & Q.* I. I. 232/1 One day's gout, which I cured with the bootikins. **1775** —— *Private Corr.* 11 Apr. IV. 8 My biennial visitant the gout, has yielded to the bootikins. **1794–6** E. DARWIN *Zoon.* (1801) IV. 221 Booterkins made with oiled Silk, as they confine the perspirable matter, keep the part moist and supple.

2. A small kind of boot; a knitted legging or gaiter with feet, worn out of doors by infants.

1844 W. H. MAXWELL *Sports & Adv. Scotl.* xiii. (1855) 122 That species of bootakin, known.. by the title of 'high-lows'. **1885** *Civ. Serv. Store Price List* 160 Infantees, Bootakins, Gaiters, Wool Boots.

3. An instrument of torture; = BOOT *sb.*^{3} 3.

1727 P. WALKER *A. Peden* 26 (JAM.) There will neither thumbikin nor bootikin come here. **1834** M. NAPIER *Mem. Napier of Merchiston* iv. 159 It was proposed to put him in the bootikins, an infernal instrument of torture.

†ˈ**booting**, *sb. Obs. Sc.* In 6 boting. [f. BOOT *sb.*^{3}] 'A half-boot or leathern spatterdash' (Jamieson); perh. collective for *boots.*

c **1505** DUNBAR *Flyting* 212 Thow bringis the Carrik clay to Edinburgh Corse, Upoun thy botingis.

†ˈ**booting**, *vbl. sb.*^{1} *Obs.* [f. BOOT *v.*^{1} + -ING^1.]

1. Relieving, curing, healing, helping; payment to the good; service, avail.

c **1300** *K. Alis.* 5711 The kyng.. Yaf al his folk betyng [*v.r.* botyng]. **1426** AUDELAY *Poems* 15 Our Kyng.. That mai us salve of oure sore, oure botyng to us bryng? *c* **1440** *Promp. Parv.* 45 Botynge or encrese yn byynge, *licitamentum, liciarium.* **1591** HARINGTON *Epigr.* II. (1633) 98 But let alone, Lynus, it is no booting.

2. *Comb.* †**booting-corn.** See quot.

1670 BLOUNT *Law Dict.* s.v., The Tenants.. paid Booting Corn to the Prior of Rochester.. Perhaps it was so called, as being paid.. by way of Bote.. or compensation to the Lord, for his making them Leases, etc.

†ˈ**booting**, *vbl. sb.*^{2} *Obs.* Also *Sc.* 6 buting, butting. [f. BOOT *sb.*^{2} or *v.*^{2} + -ING^1: but sense 1 seems to have begun as a misunderstanding of BUTIN 'booty', mistaken for a vbl. sb. in -ING.]

1. Booty, plunder; = BUTIN.

a **1572** KNOX *Hist. Ref.* Wks. 1846 I. 79 Small butting thei caryed away. **1597** MONTGOMERIE *Cherrie & Slae* xv, Quhair flew ye, quhom slew ye, or quha brings hame the buting? *c* **1600** *Rob. Hood* (Ritson) I. iii. 3 I'll tell you of a brave booting That befell Robin Hood.

2. Taking of booty, plundering: cf. *freebooting.*

1651 HOBBES *Govt. & Soc.* xiii. §14. 203 Under the notion of Booting or taking prey.

booting (ˈbuːtɪŋ), *vbl. sb.*^{3} [f. BOOT *v.*^{3}] **a.** Torture with the boot (see BOOT *sb.*^{3} 3). **b.** Punishment of being beaten with a boot (see BOOT *v.*^{3} 3).

1678 PHILLIPS (App.) *Booting*, a sort of torture among the Scots. **1805** SIR R. WILSON *Diary* 30 Dec., I directed the most culpable to receive a booting from their comrades.

boot-lace (ˈbuːtleɪs). [BOOT *sb.*^{3} 7.] **a.** A lace for fastening a boot or shoe (see LACE *sb.* 3 a). **b.** (See quot. 1934.) Hence as *v. N.Z.* and *Austral.*

1934 *Press* (Christchurch, N.Z.) 13 Jan. 13/7 *Boot laces*, narrow strips of skin cut off by rough shearers, generally when opening up the neck. Hence the verb, to *b.l.* **1955** G. BOWEN *Wool Away!* iii. 41 You are much more likely to bootlace the sheep—i.e. cut the wrinkles off in long thin strips of skin. **1965** J. S. GUNN *Terminol. Shearing Industry* I. 9 Good shearers could easily 'bootlace' wrinkly sheep so it is not the same as 'tomahawking'.

c. A piece of liquorice made in the shape of a boot-lace.

1935 W. DE LA MARE *Early One Morning* xviii. 230 Such casual bounties as brandy balls, pink sherbet, roast sparrow, 'boot laces', [etc.].

boot-leg, bootleg (ˈbuːtlɛg). [BOOT *sb.*^{3} 7.]

1. The leg of a tall boot, or the leather, etc., cut out for this (see also quot. 1875).

1634 *Churchw. Accts. Youlgrave, Derby* in *Reliquary* Jan. (1864) 190 For a payre of Boot-legges needfull to be used about yᵉ bells. **1843** *Knickerbocker* XXI. 523 A pair of linsey-woolsey breeches plunged into his boot-legs. **1855** M. M. THOMSON *Doesticks* xxi. 181 The man who would.. hopefully essay the concoction of a satisfactory stew from jack-knife-handles and bootlegs. **1875** W. D. PARISH *Dict. Sussex Dial.* 20 Boot-legs, short gaiters, not reaching to the knee. **1889** 'C. E. CRADDOCK' *Broomsedge Cove* iv. 65 He.. paused only to slip into his long boot-leg a 'shootin' iron'.

2. *attrib.* **a.** With reference to illicit trading in liquor. Also *ellipt.* Cf. BOOT-LEGGER. orig. *U.S.*

a **1889** *Omaha Herald* (Barrère & Leland), There is as much whisky consumed in Iowa now as there was before, .. 'for medical purposes only', and on the boot-leg plan. **1921** W. D. NEWTON in *Chambers's Jrnl.* Mar. 154/2 Joe left him apparently sleeping the solid sleep of 'bootleg' whisky in his shack. **1928** H. CRANE *Let.* 31 Jan. (1965) 315 Gradually I'm becoming acquainted with all the brands of bootleg that the Westcoast offers. **1929** *Morn. Post* 7 June 11/2 Alleged bootleg ring. **1931** E. LINKLATER *Juan in America* II. ii. 70 She'll get nothing but bootleg rye and bath-tub gin.. after this.

b. Of other commodities, persons, etc.

1928 *Daily Express* 5 Mar. 11/6 Bootleg [*i.e.* smuggled] baby. **1929** *Variety* 10 Apr. 1/2 There is almost as big a market for bootleg disk records as there is for bootlegged books. **1931** *Daily Express* 15 Oct. 11/2 A 'bootleg' house is one which has been erected in defiance of the Building Act. **1944** M. LASKI *Love on Supertax* vii. 72 The occasional bootleg lemon. *Ibid.* ix. 84, I can't eat, said Clarissa, pushing away her bootleg egg.

Hence ˈ**boot-legger**, one who carries liquor in his boot-legs; hence, an illicit trader in liquor; ˈ**boot-legging**, illicit trade in liquor; also *attrib.* and *ppl. a.*; whence ˈ**bootleg** *v.*, to traffic illicitly in (liquor); ˈ**bootlegged** *ppl. a.*, illicit, smuggled; also *transf.*

1889 SANGER *Rep.* in J. B. Thoburn *Hist. Oklahoma* (1916) I. 223 Liquor dealers (or as they are called here 'boot-leggers'). **1890** *Voice* (N.Y.) July 17 The 'boot-legger' is a grim spectre to the anti-Prohibitionist... He is a man who wears boots in whose tops are concealed a flask or two of liquor. **1903** *Cincinnati Enquirer* 3 Jan. 1/3 In the pulpit was a minister when arrested for 'boot-legging'. **1906** in *Dialect Notes* III. 127 William Castell, charged with bootlegging whiskey, was tried.. this morning. **1919** T. K. HOLMES *Man fr. Tall Timber* vi. 59 Who's got the forty-rod, Steve?.. There's a bootlegging place somewhere, I'll be bound. **1922** S. LEWIS *Babbitt* v. 66 The bright lights and the bootlegged cocktails. **1927** 'SAX ROHMER' *Moon of Madness* 14 A deck load of Dagos.. that would have frightened a Chicago bootlegger. **1928** *Observer* 5 Feb. 18/2 Negroes who carried bootlegged liquor. *Ibid.*, The result is that books are bootlegged in Boston as liquor is bootlegged in other cities. **1928** *Daily Express* 5 Mar. 11/6 She 'bootlegged' a baby into her home and.. pretended to her husband that it was hers. **1936** WODEHOUSE *Laughing Gas* vii. 76 Somebody is bootlegging it [*sc.* candy] to him, and I mean to find out who it is. **1948** *Chicago Tribune* 28 Nov. 41/5 The sale of liquor is banned here on the Sabbath, and that's when the bootlegger bootlegs. **1958** *Manch. Guardian Weekly* 1 May 6/1 Customs officers.. regarded it as no business of theirs to prevent the 'boot-legging' of the long-play records imported privately in thousands.

bootless ('bu:tlɪs), *a.*[1] [OE. *bótléas*, f. *bót*, BOOT *sb.*[1]: see -LESS.]

†**1.** Not to be expiated or recompensed by a 'bote'; see BOOT *sb.*[1] 9. (Only in OE. law.)

a **1000** in Thorpe's *Laws* I. 385 (Bosw.) Donne sȝ ðæt botleas. *Ibid.* I. 410 Husbryce is botleas. [**1714** FORTESCUE-ALAND *Fortescue's Abs. & Lim. Mon.* Pref. 62 Boteless, that is, unexpiable. **1839** KEIGHTLEY *Hist. Eng.* I. 79 Of the crimes.. some were 'botelos' or inexpiable, and were to be punished with death: such were treason, murder.]

†**2.** Without help or remedy; incurable, remediless, helpless.

1228 in *Mem. Ripon* (1882) I. 52 In pœna quæ vocatur boteles. *c* **1350** *Will. Palerne* 3984 It is a botles bale.. to willne after a wif þat is a waywarde euere. **1567** DRANT *Horace Sat.* ii. (R.), That were a bootlesse case. **1659** SPRAT *Plague Athens* (R.), They saw the city open lay, An easy and a bootless prey.

3. Void of boot or profit; to no purpose, without success; unavailing, useless, unprofitable.

1559 *Myrr. Mag., Clifford* ii, All care is bootles in a cureles case. **1596** SHAKS. *Merch. V.* III. iii. 20 Ile follow him no more with bootlesse prayers. **1641** J. JACKSON *True Evang. T.* I. 77 Bootlesse problemes. **1736** THOMSON *Liberty* IV. 644. **1782** COWPER *Gilpin* 189 Ah luckless speech, and bootless boast! **1869** FREEMAN *Norm. C.* (1876) III. xii. 255 A few bootless attempts at negociation.

4. quasi-*adv.* = BOOTLESSLY.

1423 JAS. I. *King's Q.* lxx, As Tantalus I trauaile ay butles. **1588** SHAKS. *Tit. A.* III. i. 36, I tell my sorrowes bootles to the stones. **1813** SCOTT *Trierm.* III. i, Of wasted fields.. The Borderers bootless may complain.

bootless ('bu:tlɪs), *a.*[2] [f. BOOT *sb.*[3] + -LESS.] Without boots.

1377 LANGL. *P. Pl.* B. XVIII. 11 One.. Barfote on an asse bakke botelees cam pryk[y]e, Wyth-oute spores other spere. [**1596** SHAKS. *1 Hen. IV*, III. i. 66 Thrice.. haue I hent him Bootlesse home.. *Hotsp.* Home without Bootes, And in foule Weather too, How scapes he Agues in the Deuils name?] **1880** *Harper's Mag.* LX. 676 Hatless, bootless, and trouserless.

'**bootlessly**, *adv.* [f. BOOTLESS *a.*[1] + -LY[2].] Without success or advantage; unsuccessfully; unprofitably; uselessly.

1612 T. TAYLOR *Comm. Titus* i. 15 (1619) 309 Bootlessly to employ all their paines in keeping themselues from outward pollution. **1863** *Pilgrim. over Prairies* II. 264 The hunters, returning bootlessly and sullenly from a large 'cast'.

'**bootlessness.** [f. as prec. + -NESS.] Uselessness; unprofitableness.

1830 *Blackw. Mag.* XXVII. 472 Which beguile the weariness of the journey, and make us sometimes forget its bootlessness.

boot-lick, bootlick ('bu:tlɪk), *v.* and *sb. slang.* [f. BOOT *sb.*[3] + LICK *v.*] **A.** *v. trans.* and *intr.* To curry favour (with); to toady to). **B.** *sb.* A toady, a sycophant; one who curries favour; also *attrib. U.S.*

1846 J. J. HOOPER *Adv. Simon Suggs* (1851) v. 58 A young man who was inclined to boot-lick any body suspected of having money. **1849** *Yale Banger* 6 Nov. 6 When Boot-lick hypocrites upraised their might. **1850** *Yale Battery* 14 Feb., Then he arose, and offered himself as a '*boot lick*', to the Faculty. **1885** *Milnor* (Dakota) *Teller* 1 May 2/3 They must drink, truckle, and bootlick to keep their greatness uppermost. **1932** J. FARRELL *Young Lonigan* (1936) ii. 46 He boot-licked around until he became a ward committeeman.

Hence '**boot-licker,** = sense B above; '**boot-licking** *vbl. sb.* and *ppl. a.* orig. *U.S.*

1846–47 MRS. WHITCHER *Widow Bedott P.* (1856) xxvii. 331 Sweezer's very intimit with the squire's folks—a kind o' bootlicker tew 'em. **1849** *Gallinipper* Dec., Those crouching, fawning, boot-licking hypocrites. **1851** HALL *College Words* 24 Some [students are].. very apt to linger after recitation to get a clearer knowledge of some passage. They are *Bootlicks*, and that is known as *Bootlicking*. **1890** FARMER *Slang, Bootlick, subs.* (American), a flunkey, hanger-on... In England such a one is called a 'bootlicker'. *Verb.* To toady; to hang on; to undertake 'dirty' work. **1894** *Current Hist.* (Buffalo, N.Y.) IV. 472 Working his way by scheming and bootlicking into the good graces of.. a young idiot of a lord. **1906** *Westm. Gaz.* 27 June 2/1 If boot-licking became permanently fashionable, we should in course of time have various grades of boot-lickers. **1938** 'G. ORWELL' *Homage to Catalonia* viii. 140 No privilege and no boot-licking. **1961** L. MUMFORD *City in History* v. 154 The Greek eventually turned the citizen into.. the cadger and bootlicker. **1964** *Daily Mail* 4 Aug. 3/8 That reverential boot-licking tone which we reserve for the heights of human achievement.

boots[1] (bu:ts). [pl. of BOOT *sb.*[3], used as sing.]

1. A name for the servant in hotels who cleans the boots; formerly called *boot-catcher* and *-catch.*

a **1798** O'KEEFE *Fontainebleau* III. i. (L.) Your honour will remember the waiter.. Your honour won't forget Jack Boots. **1836–7** DICKENS *Sk. Boz* (1850) 250/1 'I'm the boots as b'longs to the house.' **1856** W. COLLINS *After Dark* I. 109, I waited in the pantry till Boots had brushed the clothes.

2. (*slang.*) An appellation given to the youngest officer in a regiment, junior member of a club, etc.

1806 SIR R. WILSON in *Life* (1862) I. ii. 60 My chief resistance to discipline was at mess where I could not brook the duties of Boots.

3. In various comb. (humorous or colloq.) = 'Fellow, person': as ***clumsy-, lazy-boots***; see also SLY-BOOTS, SMOOTH-BOOTS.

1623 PERCIVALE *Sp. Dict.*, *Lisongero*, a flatterer, a smooth boots. **1865** DICKENS *Mut. Fr.* IV. xi, You are the most creasing and tumbling Clumsy-Boots of a packer. **1832** LYTTON *Eugene A.* ii, 'Why don't you rise, Mr. Lazyboots?'

†**boots**[2]. *Obs.* or *dial.* [prob. a dial. form of *bouts*, *bolts*, applied to the same plant.] A local English name of marsh marigold (*Caltha palustris*) or meadow bouts.

1597 GERARD *Herbal* cclxxx. §3. 671 Marsh Marigoldes, in Cheshire and those parts it is called Bootes. **1721** BAILEY, *Boots*, the Plant Marshmallows [An error].

boot-strap, bootstrap ('bu:tstræp), *sb.* [f. BOOT *sb.*[3] + STRAP *sb.*] **1.** A strap sewn on to a boot to help in pulling it on or looped round a boot to hold down the skirt of a lady's riding habit; a boot-lace.

1891 R. P. CHOPE *Dial. of Hartland, Devonsh.* 29 *Boot-strap*, a boot-lace. **1908** *Daily Chron.* 11 Sept. 7/5 He put her up, adjusted boot-strap and skirt.

2. Colloq. phr. ***to pull*** (***lift, raise***, etc.) ***oneself*** (***up***) ***by one's*** (***own***) ***boot-straps***: to raise or better oneself by one's own unaided efforts; hence *allusively*.

1922 JOYCE *Ulysses* 630 There were.. others who had forced their way to the top from the lowest rung by the aid of their bootstraps. **1936** KUNITZ & HAYCRAFT *Brit. Authors 19th Cent.* 213/1 A poet who lifted himself by his own boot-straps from an obscure versifier to the ranks of real poetry. **1937** V. D. SCUDDER *On Journey* III. ii. 306 Humanity could never pull itself up by its own bootstraps. **1960** D. LESSING *In Pursuit of English* 35, I had no money, I could have got some by writing to my family, of course, but it had to be the bootstraps or nothing. **1962** *Listener* 23 Aug. 271/2 A rather naïve faith in humanity's ability to pull itself up by its own bootstraps.

3. *Computing.* The procedure of using a fixed sequence of instructions to initiate the loading of further instructions and ultimately of a complete program (esp. the operating system); the initial fixed sequence of instructions used for this. Freq. *attrib.*

1953 *Proc. IRE* XLI. 1273/1 A technique sometimes called the 'bootstrap technique'... Pushing the load button.. causes one full word to be loaded into a memory address previously set up.. on the operator's panel, after which the program control is directed to that memory address and the computer starts automatically. **1962** *Gloss. Terms Automatic Data Processing* (*B.S.I.*) 42 *Bootstrap*, 1. A form of program input in which simple preset computer operations are used to read in initial instructions which in turn cause further instructions to be read until the complete program is assembled. 2. The process of using parts of a compiler to construct the remainder of the same compiler. **1965** K. NICOL *Elem. Programming* iii. 11 When the computer was constructed, a small set of basic instructions were permanently wired into the store and the control unit is made to obey the first of these by pressing an external button. They constitute a small program (known as the 'bootstrap' or 'initial input' routine) whose task is to read characters from the paper tape reader and place them in successive storage locations. **1975** R. H. ECKHOUSE *Minicomputer Systems* vi. 167 The software bootstrap for the PDP-11 is a sequence of instructions for loading user programs... The bootstrap loader source program is shown in Fig. 6-4. **1980** C. S. FRENCH *Computer Sci.* xxiv. 183 Bootstraps or Bootstrap loaders are very simple loaders which are either placed in memory manually by use of the console or placed in memory by a special piece of hardware. **1984** J. HILTON *Choosing & using your Home Computer* 79/2 The bootstrap's job is simply to find the main DOS on the disk, and transfer it byte by byte into RAM, whereupon that DOS can take over and perform some far more sophisticated functions.

4. Chiefly *attrib.* in various technical usages (see quots.).

1946 *Jrnl. Inst. Electr. Engin.* XCIII. III A. 308/1 The 'Bootstrap' Circuit.. is much used for generating a linear rise of voltage with time, for time-base and other purposes. .. It is called a 'bootstrap' circuit because the potential at A is apparently being 'pulled up by its own bootstraps'. **1949** *Electronic Engin.* XXI. 198 The bootstrap valve may be anode loaded to obtain the push-pull output. **1949** R. KELNER in B. Chance et al. *Electronic Time Measurements* v. 125 (*heading*) Bootstrap Triangle Generator with Diode Comparator. **1962, 1965** [see sense 3 above].

bootstrap (bu:tstræp), *v.* [f. BOOT-STRAP, BOOTSTRAP *sb.*] **1.** *trans.* To make use of existing resources or capabilities to raise (oneself) to a new situation or state; to modify or improve by making use of what is already present. More recently, as *transf.* use of sense 2. Usu. *refl.* (Chiefly in technical contexts.)

1958 *Communications Assoc. Computing Machinery* I. 22 Some interesting techniques have been developed whereby it would be possible for a new computer group to 'bootstrap' itself into a position of automatic programming capability upon receiving a new machine. **1960** *Ibid.* III. 607/1 In December, 1958, a hand-coded version of NELIAC.. compiled its first rudimentary code for the Remington Rand Univac COUNTESS. By May 1959 it.. was being used to 'bootstrap' itself, i.e., an improved version is written in NELIAC language.. and then recompiled by itself. **1983** *Sci. Amer.* May 107/2 The prospect of bootstrapping the entire process of data analysis offers hope that an extremely difficult problem will begin to yield. **1983** *Fortune* 30 May 59/2 Using American Jet's earnings for that year as collateral, Paulson bootstrapped his way into bank loans to buy.. the then-unprofitable corporate-jet subsidiary of Grumman Corp. **1983** *New Scientist* 23 June 873/2 This profound question of a self-creating Universe which somehow bootstraps itself into existence using quantum indeterminism as the straps.

2. *Computing.* = BOOT *v.*[4] 1.

1962 [implied at BOOTSTRAPPING *vbl. sb.*] **1978** *Pract. Computing* July–Aug. 42/3 The system is boot-strapped as soon as the power is turned on. **1984** SIMON & MATTHEWS *Mastering Electron* vii. 148 If such a system crashes it has to be 'bootstrapped' from the disc to start it again.

Hence '**bootstrapping** *vbl. sb.*

1960 *Aeroplane* XCVIII. 147/2 The particular process is not, strictly speaking, 'bootstrapping', which in rocket parlance merely means that the engine runs as a self-contained unit, using its own propellents in one way or another to drive its pumps. **1962** SIMPSON & RICHARDS *Junction Transistors* xiii. 317 The process of multiplying the apparent value of a resistance by applying nearly equal signal voltages to each end is known as 'bootstrapping'.

'**boot-top.**

1. The upper part of a boot; esp. of top-boots.

1768 WALES in *Phil. Trans.* LX. 109, I saw one woman with a child in each boot top. **1825** S. ADAMS *Compl. Servant* 384 Liquid for cleansing Boot Tops, etc. **1827** LYTTON *Pelham*, The autocrat of the great world of fashion.. fed the pampered appetite of his boot-tops on champagne.

2. *Naut.* **a.** In phrase 'to give a ship boot-tops': see quot.; **b.** = BOOT-TOPPING b.

1768 CROKER, etc. *Dict. Arts* s.v., It is usual to make her heel, or incline first to one side and then to the other.. having scrubbed off the ooze, shells.. with brushes and brooms, they cover it with a mixture of tallow, sulphur, etc., and this is called giving her boot-tops. **1842** F. COOPER *Jack O' Lant.* I. 126 Every vessel that isn't coppered shows her boot-top.

c. = BOOT-TOPPING c. Also *attrib.*

1788 EARL DUNDONALD *Direct. for using Coal Tar* 24 Painting vessels boot-tops with white lead and oil, has been discontinued.. in the Navy. **1937** H. A. CALAHAN *Ship's Husband* xviii. 229 Between the topsides and the bottom, it is frequently customary to paint a boot-top. The boot-top.. separates the topsides from the bottom. **1949** P. HEATON *Sailing* 247 When painting.. mark in the boot top with tacks. **1958** *Times* 22 Sept. 14/1 The red boot-top line on the yacht's hull was more clearly visible forward than aft.

So as *v.*, to subject (a vessel) to 'boot-topping'.

1724 C. JOHNSON *Gen. Hist. of Pyrates* (ed. 2) xi. 211 Here they watered, boot-topp'd their Ship, and made ready for the designed Cruise. **1768** JAMES COOK *Jrnl.* 15 Nov. (1893) i. 19 Got all the Empty Casks on shore, and set the Coopers to Work to repair them; Heeld and Boot Topt the Starboard side. **1908** *Chambers's Jrnl.* Nov. 829/1 The system is in operation upon the Clyde with great success, boot-topping the fast pleasure-craft plying on the river.

'**boot-ˌtopping.** *Naut.* **a.** (see quot.)

1767 FALCONER *Dict. Marine* (1789), *Boot-topping*, the act of cleaning the upper part of a ship's bottom, and daubing it over with a coat or mixture of tallow, sulphur, resin, etc. Boot-topping is chiefly performed where there is no dock.. or when.. hurry.. renders it inconvenient to have the whole bottom.. cleansed.

b. '*Boot-topping*.. is now applied to sheathing a vessel with planking over felt.' Smyth *Sailor's Word-bk.* 1867.

c. (See quot. 1894.)

1788 EARL DUNDONALD *Direct. for using Coal Tar* Proofs, p. 22 The worm *had not touched* the bottom lower than the boot-topping. **1894** H. PAASCH *From Keel to Truck* (ed. 2) 46/1 *Boot-topping*, is the term applied to that portion of the outside-plating or planking of a vessel between the light-water-line and the load-line. The coating (also the wood-sheathing of wooden vessels) on this part of a ship is likewise so named. **1927** BRADFORD *Gloss. Sea Terms* 18/2 *Boot-topping*, a band of paint at the water-line; usually red; the particular kind of paint used is called boot-topping. **1961** *Times* 2 Aug. 4/1 The paint of the boot-toppings gleamed in the fitful sun.

booty ('bu:tɪ), *sb.* Forms: 5–6 **botye, buty,** 6 **boty, bootye, bootie,** (7 *Sc.* **bouty**), 6– **booty.** [The mod. as well as the early forms, point to a ME. long *ō*, and thus to connexion with *bŏt*, BOOT *sb.*[1] advantage, and *v.*[1] to profit. But there is no accounting for such a formation from *bŏt, boot* directly; and it is generally held that the English word is due to an adaptation of some word cognate with Ger. *beute*, F. *butin* (or the latter itself) influenced in form by association with *bŏt, boot.* The Teutonic words in question are ON.

býti 'exchange, barter', connected with *býta* 'to exchange'; also 'to deal out, distribute'; MDu. and MLG. *büte* (MG. *bûte*, MHG. *biute*, mod.G. *beute*, mod.Du. *buit*), all with the sense 'booty'. *Butin*, from French, was used side by side with *boty*, *booty* during the 16th c., and it is curious that the first known instances of both occur in Caxton's *Chesse*, within a few lines of each other: see BUTIN. Caxton has also *buty* (see 1491), and in 17th c. we find an instance of *bootyn* for *butin*: but on the whole the contact of the two forms appears to be slight. The shorter form BOOT (*sb.*²), and the related BOOT *v.*² BOOTER (*freebooter*), BOOTING, are all later.

(An early but dubiously genuine use appears under BOOTY *a.*, which, if really used by Lydgate *c* 1430, would carry the question farther back, but leave it still more obscure.)]

1. *orig.* Plunder, gain, or profit acquired in common and destined to be divided among the winners.

a. That which is taken from an enemy in war; the collective plunder or spoil. (No plural.)

1474 CAXTON *Chesse* 39 So shold the dispoyle and botye be comune vnto them. **1491** —— *Four Sons Aymon* (1885) 143 The kyng made the buty to be dealed, Wherof the most part he made to be gyven to reynawde & his brethern. **1530** PALSGR. 200/1 Boty that men of warre take, *butin*. **1579** DIGGES *Stratiot.* 129 The Bootie shall be divided, according to the auncient lawes of the warres. **1611** BIBLE *Numb.* xxxi. 32. **1732** LEDIARD *Sethos* II. IX. 287 They were too happy to give them a share of the booty. **1814** WELLINGTON in Gurw. *Disp.* XII. 7 What ought to be considered as booty to the army.

b. That which is captured by robbers or thieves.

1567 HARMAN *Caveat* (1869) 33 When they haue a greatter booty then they maye carye quickly. **1596** SHAKS. *1 Hen IV*, I. ii. 184 When they haue the booty, if you and I do not rob them.

†**2.** A thing taken by force; a prize. (With *pl.*)

1542 UDALL *Erasm. Apoph.* 186 b, His souldyers had conspired..to conuerte all the booties that they shoulde geat, to their owne priuate vse. **1568** *Like will to Like* in Hazl. *Dodsl.* III. 334 Art thou not agreed These two booties equally to divide? **1591** HORSEY *Trav.* (1857) 161 To lose a great deall of his artillerie, buties, and baggage. **1652** NEEDHAM tr. *Selden's Mare Cl.* 481 To..take prizes or booties. **1823** BYRON *Juan* x. lxix, Packets, all whose passengers are booties To those who upon land or water dwell.

3. *loosely.* Plunder, spoil, gain; a prize; without reference to its being common property.

1580 BARET *Alv.* B 932 The Bootie or spoyle that a man hath gotten of his enemies. **1599** R. GREENHAM *Wks.* (ed. 2) 49 A flatterer comming to haue some bootie. **1611** SHAKS. *Wint. T.* IV. iv. 862 Fortune..drops Booties in my mouth. **1662** MORE *Antid. Ath.* II. x. (1712) 71 That she might not be too easie a Booty for him. **1722** DE FOE *Moll Fl.* (1840) 328 He robbed the best Chester coaches and got a very great booty. **1743** FIELDING *Jon. Wild* II. ii, Bagshot..had carried off a pretty considerable booty from their engagements at dice. **1839** THIRLWALL *Greece* I. 329 The ingenious and successful pilferer gained applause with his booty. **1866** KINGSLEY *Herew.* v. 115 He got very little booty there.

4. *to play booty*: To join with confederates in order to 'spoil' or victimize another player; to play into the hands of confederates in order to share the 'plunder' with them; hence to play or act falsely so as to gain a desired object; *esp.* to play badly intentionally in order to lose the game. So (obs.) ***to bowl, cast, perjure, talk, write booty.***

1561 AWDELAY *Frat. Vacab.* 9 And consent as though they will play booty against him. **1592** GREENE *Art Conny catch.* II. 8 The bowlers cast euer booty and doth win or loose as the bet of the gripe leadeth them. **1622** MABBE tr. *Aleman's Guzman d' Alf.* I. 222 Wee are three of vs, let vs all play booty, and joyne together to coozen the Cardinall. **1650** WELDON *Crt. Jas. I*, 99 Some of them played booty, and in truth, the Game was not plaid above board. **1676** ETHEREDGE *Man of Mode* III. i. (1684) 30 What think you of playing it on booty? *Har.* What do you mean? *T. Bell.* Pretend to be in love with one another. **1678** BUTLER *Hud., Lady's Answ.* 180 Can own the same thing, and disown; And perjure Booty, Pro and Con. **1711** ADDISON *Spect.* No. 60 ¶9 Would not one be apt to believe that the Author played booty, and did not make his List of Rhymes till he had finished his Poem? **1771** P. PARSONS *Newmarket* I. 108 Bribing the rider to play booty, to lose the race. **1813** *Examiner* 17 May 319/1, I gave a jockey a handsome premium to play booty. **1831** DISRAELI *Yng. Duke* (L.), One thing remained to be lost—what he called his honour, which was already on the scent to play booty.

b. Hence: *Booty* = playing booty.

1608 DEKKER *Belman Lond.* Wks. 1884–5 III. 135–6 Many other practises there are in bowling tending to cozenage, but yᵉ greatest and grossest is Booty: in which yᵉ deceipt is so open and palpable that I haue seene men stone-blind offer to lay Betts franckely..only by hearing who played, and how the old Grypes had made their layes. **1738** WARBURTON *Div. Legat.* II. 145 A Riddle was frequently the Stratagem for a Booty.

5. *Comb.* †**booty-fellow**: one who shares booty with others; a confederate in plundering, swindling, etc. (cf. sense 4).

1530 PALSGR. 200/1 Botyfelowe, *parsonnier*. **1532** *Dice-Play* (1850) 43 As when one man lost an hundred pound land at shooting, by occasion that some that shot with him on his side were booty fellows against him.

†**'booty**, *sb.*² *Obs.* Erroneously used for BOOT *sb.*¹ A remedy; advantage.

1577 HOLINSHED *Chron.* III. 284 It was no bootie to advise him to the contrarie of that his concluded purpose. **1581** W. STAFFORD *Exam. Compl.* I. (1876) 18 Neede (as yee knowe) hath no booty.

†**'booty**, *a.* *Obs.* [See BOOTY *sb.*¹: but could this be orig. from BOOT *sb.*¹ in sense of 'profit'?] Sharing, participating.

c **1430** LYDG. *Bochas* IV. (1494) Q iv a, His desyre and his entencion Was to be boty [*ed.* **1554** booting] with theym of suche pillage. **1570** LEVINS *Manip.* 111 Bootye, *particeps*.

†**'booty**, *v.* *Obs. intr.* To collect booty.

1580 HOLLYBAND *Treas. Fr. T.*, *Butiner*, to bootie, or pray.

†**'booty-hale**, *v.* *Obs.* [app. an alteration of BOOT-HALE *v.*, assimilated to BOOTY.] = BOOT-HALE. Also **'booty-haling** *vbl. sb.*

1610 HEALEY *St. Aug. Citie of God* III. xvii. 131 Having booty-haled all the whole Cittie. **1611** FLORIO, *Gualda*, a bootie-haling [**1598** boote-], a freebooting.

'bootyless, *a.* [see -LESS.] Void of booty.

1866 *Standard* 27 Feb., The disappointed O'Mahoneyites consoled themselves after this bootyless expedition.

†**'bootyn.** *Obs. rare.* A mixed form combining BOOTY and BUTIN.

1635 HAYWARD *Banish'd Virg.* 196 These folkes had scowr'd the field..got good store of bootyn.

boow(e, obs. form of BOW.

booza, var. of BOZA, an oriental drink.

booze, boose (buːz), *sb. colloq.* Also 8 booz. [f. BOOZE *v.*; = BOUSE *sb.*]

1. a. Drink; a draught.

1732 MRS. PENDARVES *Lett.* 30 Mar. in *Mrs. Delany's Corr.* I. 346 We..had a profusion of 'peck & booz' (terms for meat & drink).

b. Alcoholic drink, chiefly beer; *U.S.* esp. spirits.

1859 HOTTEN *Dict. Slang.* **1895** *Daily Tel.* 2 Dec. 5/1 She heard some men shout that they wanted some more booze. Mr. Justice Wright: 'What?' Mr. Willis: 'Booze, my lord, drink.' Mr. Justice Wright: 'Ah!' **1896** *Voice* (N.Y.) 16 July 1/6 The Duckworth club..consumed large quantities of booze. **1900** *Daily News* 8 Dec. 6/2 On his way home he drops into a pub, and gets some 'booze'. **1932** T. S. ELIOT *Sweeney Agonistes* 30 We're gona sit here and drink this booze.

c. *attrib.* and *Comb.*

1895 *Voice* (N.Y.) 9 May 5/4 Lost souls—lost through the booze traffic. **1922** H. L. FOSTER *Adv. Trop. Tramp* v. 60 After that the police had a private booze-party of their own on the proceeds. **1934, 1941** [see ARTIST 10].

2. a. Drinking, a drinking bout.

1864 BURTON *Scot. Abr.* II. ii. 198 An occasional hard boose, and its consequent headache. **1877** BARING-GOULD *Myst. Suffering* 51 A booze of bad ale. **1884** *St. James's Gaz.* 19 Dec. 4/1 There was a great 'booze' on board.

b. Phr. ***on the booze***: having a spell of hard drinking.

1850 H. HALSE *Let.* 26 Nov. in *McLean Papers* (MS., Wellington, N.Z.) VIII. 271 The sawyers who were to have got the board out of the bush, had been on the booze. **1888** E. W. PAYTON *Round about N.Z.* xxiii. 306 The man..often does not know..how long he has been 'on the booze'. **1889** 'R. BOLDREWOOD' *Robbery under Arms* I. ii. 20 Poor old Mr. Howard wasn't always on the booze. **1892** HESLOP *Northumberland Words* I. 82 'He's on the booze'—that is, he has a drinking fit. **1946** F. SARGESON *That Summer* 31 He was a bit of a one for going on the booze, Bill was. **1959** J. CARY *Captive & Free* 96 If I didn't you'd go on the booze and say it was all my fault.

c. booze-hound, a drunkard; **booze-up**, a drinking bout. *slang.*

1926 WOOD & GODDARD *Dict. Amer. Slang* 23 *Hound* (as in booze-hound, smut-hound, etc.), one fond of a thing. **1947** K. TENNANT *Lost Haven* i. 19 This ruddy old booze-hound. **1897** *Session Paper* 26 Oct. 860 We..had a *booze up* together. **1939** I. BROWN *Down on Farm* in *Best One-Act Plays of 1939* 131 We're celebrating... So we're going to have what the vulgar call..a bit of a booze-up. **1957** J. BRAINE *Room at Top* x. 91 The traditional lunchtime booze-up.

booze, boose (buːz), *v.* [A variant of BOUSE, retaining the pronunciation of ME. *bouse, bowse*, and spelt phonetically; perhaps really a dialectal form: cf. the Sc. and north. Eng. *rooze* (ruːz) = literary Eng. *rouse*, etc. See BOUSE.]

intr. To drink deeply, or for the sake of enjoyment or goodfellowship; to tipple, guzzle, bezzle.

[*c* **1300** *E.E. Poems* (1862) 154 Depe can ȝe bouse. **1616** *Pasquil & Kath.* i. 213 You must needs bouze.] **1768** WALPOLE *Lett. H. Mann*, To booze ale. **1777** COLMAN *Epil. Sch. Scandal* (1883) 76 While good Sir Peter boozes with the squire. **1823** BYRON *Juan* XI. xix. Who..like Tom..could Booze in the ken? **1854** THACKERAY *Newcomes* I. 39, I won't sit in the kitchen and boose in the servants' hall. **1870** LOWELL *Study Wind.* 30 With few resources but to boose around the fire.

boozed (buːzd), *ppl. a.* [f. BOOZE *v.* + -ED.] Intoxicated, drunk, fuddled. Also with *up*. Also *transf.*

1850 P. CROOK *War of Hats* 50 Booz'd in their tavern dens, The scurril press drive all their dirty pens. **1886** *Lantern* (New Orleans) 22 Sept. 3/3 This fortune teller gets boozed up. **1897** W. S. MAUGHAM *Liza of Lambeth* v. 77, I believe I'm boozed. **1936** C. DAY LEWIS *Friendly Tree* xiv. 209 One looks like that when one is a bit boozed up. **1954** *Encounter* May 19/1 *Camino Real*..depends too much on boozed writing and aureate diction. **1969** *Daily Tel.* 12 Nov. 13/4 A boozed and dilapidated Don.

boozer ('buːzə(r)). **1.** One who boozes; a tippler. See BOUSER.

a **1819** WOLCOTT (P. Pindar) *Wks.* (1831) 303 (D.), This land-lord was a boozer stout. **1835** MARRYAT *Jac. Faithf.* xxvi, Don't you think so, my old boozer?

2. A public house. *slang.*

1895 *Daily News* 4 Jan. 3/7 (E.D.D.), I pops around [stays] at the boozer. **1929** 'H. GREEN' *Living* iii. 29 He'd be glad when he was dead: 'glad, more'n glad, I'll go straight into the boozer and 'ave one'. **1966** P. MOLONEY *Plea for Mersey* 38 The boozer on the corner.

boozeroo (ˌbuːzəˈruː). *N.Z. slang.* [f. BOOZ(E *sb.* + -EROO.] A drinking spree.

1943 J. A. W. BENNETT in *Amer. Speech* XVIII. 89 A 'good spree' would be described as a 'proper old boozeroo', this word being of the same pattern as various American words in *-eroo*. **1952** *Landfall* VI. 224 The Saturday night boozeroo in the Sydenham side-street with the keg in the kitchen-sink. **1963** N. HILLIARD *Piece of Land* 28 He played Beethoven at boozeroos. **1970** *N.Z. Listener* 12 Oct. 12/2 It's going to be a real boozeroo.

'boozify, *v.* *nonce-wd. intr.* To take part in a boozing party, to booze.

1824 *Blackw. Mag.* 635 Never boozify a second time with the man whom you have seen misbehave himself in his cups.

boozily ('buːzɪlɪ), *adv.* [f. BOOZY *a.*¹ + -LY².] In a boozy or intoxicated manner.

1893 in *Funk's Standard Dict.* **1912** *English Review* Feb. 493 To claim that women would vote more..'boozily' than men do is mere blarney. **1957** V. PALMER *Seedtime* 140 'Conscience!' repeated Donovan a little boozily.

boozing ('buːzɪŋ), *vbl. sb.* [f. BOOZE *v.* + -ING¹.] Deep drinking, toping.

a **1529** [see BOUSING *vbl. sb.*] **1851** THACKERAY *Eng. Hum.* iv. (1858) 207 That club and coffee-house boozing. **1868** GEO. ELIOT *F. Holt* 119 Extension of the suffrage can never mean anything for them but extension of boozing.

b. *attrib.* and in *comb.* (Cf. BOUSING.)

1824–9 LANDOR *Imag. Conv.* (1846) I. 45 In a boozing-bout, such as some country gentlemen I could mention do hold after dinner. **1873** C. READE *Simpleton* xxviii, Down a filthy close into some boozing ken—I beg pardon, some thieves' public-house.

'boozing, *ppl. a.* [f. as prec. + -ING².] That drinks deeply, addicted to drinking.

1569 [see BOUSING *ppl. a.*] **1770** *Month. Rev.* 73 The boozing companions of old Sir John. **1880** J. C. WATT *Gt. Novelists* 30 Those 'boosing' coteries. **1882** L. STEPHEN *Swift* ii. 26 The boozing fox-hunting squires.

boozy ('buːzɪ), *a.*¹ [f. BOOZE *sb.* + -Y¹.]

1. Showing the effects of boozing or intoxication; influenced or affected by much drinking.

a **1529** [see BOUSY]. **1719** D'URFEY *Pills* (1872) II. 297 All flustered and boozy, the drunken Old Sot. **1829** SOUTHEY *Ep. Annivers.* 18 Leaving behind it in the boozy eyes A swoln and red suffusion, glazed and dim. **1857** KINGSLEY *Two Y. Ago* II. 237 Helplessly boozy from the first.

2. Addicted or given up to boozing; drunken.

1592 [see BOUSY]. **1801** GOUV. MORRIS in Sparks *Life & Writ.* (1832) III. 145 A tedious morning, a great dinner, a boozy afternoon, and dull evening. **1865** *Sat. Rev.* 4 Feb. 145/1 A boozy opium-eating Afghan.

Hence **'booziness.**

1863 HAWTHORNE *Old Home* II. 63 Poor Bozzy's booziness would appear to have become hereditary in his ancient line.

boozy, var. of BOUZY, *a.* bulky, corpulent.

bop (bɒp), *sb.*¹ *colloq.* [Echoic.] = POP *sb.*¹ 2 a.

1937 HEMINGWAY *To Have & Have Not* III. x. 149 Harry ..heard the bop-bop-bop-bop, small and hollow sounding in the wail of the siren. **1942** 'B. J. ELLAN' *Spitfire!* xv. 82 Shells seemed to be exploding very close to us although the familiar 'BOP' was inaudible.

bop (bɒp), *sb.*² orig. *U.S.* **1.** = BEBOP. Also *attrib.* Hence **'bopper, 'bopster** = BEBOPPER.

1948 *Language* Mar. 132 People in Chicago use *rebop* and *bop* for the same kind of music. **1948, 1955** [see BEBOP]. **1948** *Sat. Rev.* 25 Dec. 48/2 It is, in the words of bop hepsters, real crazy. **1950** J. VEDEY *Band Leaders* p. xi, The BBC has not been lacking in fostering its development, even to the point of broadcasting Bop—most advanced of all jazz forms. *Ibid.* 27 He [Harry Roy] is an acknowledged past master at the art of Bop-Scat singing. **1951** M. L. WOLF *Dict. Arts* 573/1 Be-bop and bop, its adherents..are known as bopsters. **1957** *New Yorker* 26 Oct. 174/2 One of the leaders of an increasingly fashionable school of modern jazz called ..'hard bop' or 'funky' is Horace Silver. *Ibid.*, The hard-boppers employ a heavy or sharply accented beat, a florid, staccato attack, and a hardness of timbre that is in direct contrast to the soft, inky sounds of the cool school. **1962** *Radio Times* 10 May 42 *Hard bop*, aggressive, neurotic brand of bop, with a delinquent, flick-knife cutting edge. **1965** G. MELLY *Owning-Up* vi. 66 A whole row of the audience raised, during Bruce Turner's first alto chorus, a long banner reading '*go home dirty bopper*'.

2. A dance to pop music; a party or other occasion for this style of dancing. *colloq.*

1956 G. P. KURATH in A. Dundes *Mother Wit* (1973) 107/1 Jitterbugging..after the forties..took the name of Bop, no matter what music was used. **1970** H. E. ROBERTS *Third Ear* 4/2 *Bop*, a dance. **1982** BARR & YORK *Official*

Sloane Ranger Handbk. 97/1 Couples meet at bops or know each other from London.

bop (bɒp), *v.*[1] [Echoic; cf. BOP *sb.*[1]] **1.** *trans.* **a.** (See quot.) *dial.*

1887 PARISH & SHAW *Dict. Kentish Dial.* 16 *Bop*, to throw anything down with a resounding noise.

b. *colloq.* To hit, strike, punch. orig. *U.S.*

1931 D. RUNYON *Guys & Dolls* (1932) vi. 117 Dave the Dude reaches across the table and bops One-eyed Solly right in the mouth. **1937** 'E. QUEEN' *Door Between* III. xv. 158 If the doc hadn't been on a ship.. when she was bopped, I'd say he did it himself. **1938** WODEHOUSE *Summer Moonshine* xv. 181 I'll bop you over the head with this chair. **1948** C. DAY LEWIS *Otterbury Incid.* 8, I can use it [*sc.* a football] to bop them on the head.

2. *intr.* To fight. So **'bopping** *vbl. sb.* and *ppl. a.* *U.S. slang.*

1958 *Daily Tel.* 8 Apr., *Bop*, to fight. *Bopping club*, a fighting gang. **1958** *Life* 28 Apr. 78 You gotta go on bopping (gang fighting) and hanging around street corners all your life? **1959** *Listener* 29 Jan. 201/2 The 'turf' of a well-known 'bopping club'—and that means the small area of pavement and street called their own by a well-known fighting gang. **1959** H. SALISBURY *Shook-up Generation* iii. 49 Arms and armament.. are not a problem for bopping gangs.

bop (bɒp), *v.*[2] *colloq.* [f. BOP *sb.*[2]] *intr.* **a.** To play bop music, or in the style of this. **b.** To dance to pop music.

1947 in R. S. Gold *Jazz Lexicon* (1964) 33 [Dizzy Gillespie Orchestra] He beeped when he shoulda bopped. **1962** *Down Beat* 6 Dec. 23 We all started bopping. **1976** *New Musical Express* 17 Apr. 12/3, 27 year old Alan Longmuir now feels he is '*too old*' to bop. **1979** J. COOPER *Class* (1980) vi. 145 The conference gang, on the other hand, bop until their thatched hair nearly falls off. **1983** *Daily Tel.* 31 May 28/5 A pumpkin-shaped female bopped furiously.

bo-peep (ˌbəʊ'piːp). Forms: 6 boo-peep, -pepe, -pipe, bo-pepe, -pipe, 6–7 bo-, boe-peepe, 7 boa-peep, boh-peepe, 7– bo-peep. [f. BO *int.* + PEEP *v.*; cf. Sc. *bo-keek, keek-a-boo.*]

1. a. A nursery play with a young child, who is kept in excitement by the nurse or play-mate alternately concealing herself (or her face), and peeping out for a moment at an unexpected place, to withdraw again with equal suddenness. Johnson says 'The act of looking out and then drawing back as if frighted, or with the purpose to fright some other'. Hence ***to play (at) bo-peep (with)***; also *fig.*, in many obvious applications.

1528 TINDALE *Doctr. Treat.* (1848) 214 Mark how he playeth bo-peep with the scripture. **1535** JOYE *Apol. Tindale* (Arb.) 7 Yf Tindal wyll.. playe boo pepe withe the tencis. *c* **1620** [FLETCH. & MASS.] *Trag. Barnavelt* II. i. in Bullen *O.Pl.* (1883) II. 248 This blinded State that plaies a boa-peep with us. **1648** HERRICK *Hesper., Upon her Feet*, Her pretty feet Like snailes did creep A little out, and then, As if they started at Bo-Peep, Did soon draw in agen. **1658** OSBORN *Jas. I.* (1673) 526 Forced to.. die in a Prison, or play at Bo-peep all the remainder of their days with their Creditors. **1701** *Interest of England* 34 Men.. That.. do nothing but play at Bo-peep with God Almighty. *a* **1849** H. COLERIDGE *Poems* (1850) II. 217 What fancy so pretty is playing bo-peep With the innocent's thoughts in the fields of sleep?

b. as *interjection.*

c **1550** *Pride & Abuse Wom.* in Hazl. *E.P.P.* IV. 231 Bo pepe! what have I spyed? A bug, devysing of proud knacks.

c. *attrib.*

1663 COWLEY *Cutter Coleman St.* III. v, There will be a good Bo-peep Love. **1692** VILLIERS (Dk. Buckhm.) *Chances* (1714) 115 Were these your bo-peep Prayers? **1863** W. PHILLIPS *Speeches* xxiv. 547 For the President, in bo-peep secrecy to hide himself in the White House.

2. A look; = PEEP *sb.*[2] 1 a. *Austral.* and *N.Z. colloq.*

1941 *Coast to Coast 1941* 67 'I'll 'ave a bo-peep,' he said. 'You gotter watch 'er. We don't want no dead pups.' **1944** L. GLASSOP *We were Rats* II. xiii. 79 Let's take a bo-peep at what they got in the canteen. **1946** F. SARGESON *That Summer* 61 A smart-looking piece of goods.. having a bo-peep out of the bathroom window. **1961** B. CRUMP *Hang on a Minute, Mate* (1963) 91 Have a bo-peep at this little lot. **1969** *Landfall* XXIII. 323 Take a bo-peep at old Lionel.

bo-'peep, *v. rare. intr.* To play bo-peep.

1606 WARNER *Alb. Eng.* XVI. ci. (1612) 400 Why should faces faire indeed bo-peepe behind a Fanne? **1840** BARHAM *Ingol. Leg., Wedding Day* 26 The National School, Bo-peeping 'midst 'many a mouldering heap'.

†**bo-peeper.** *Obs. rare.* [f. prec. + -ER[1].] That behind which one plays bo-peep; a mask.

1609 *Ev. Wom. in Hum.* v. i. in Bullen *O.Pl.* IV, Wele pull of his bopeeper.

boquet, obs. form of BOUQUET.

bor (bɔː(r)), *sb. dial.* Also 7 bore, 9 borh, boh, bo'. [? :—OE. (*ʒe*)*búr* as in NEIGHBOUR. Cf. the similar use of Du. *buur*: see BOOR.] An East Anglian form of address = Neighbour, gossip, etc.

1677 YARRANTON *Engl. Improv.* 105 Bores, this is the best News that ever I heard. **1830** FORBY *Norf. & Suffolk Voc.* s.v. *Borh, Bor*, 'Co' bor, let's go a sticking in the 'Squire's plantations'. 'Aye, bor, so we will'. **1874** J. WHINBUSH *Tim Digwell* 5 Tim, bor, what d'yow think?

bor, obs. f. BEER, BOAR, BOWER.

bor-, *Chem.*, short for BORON, forming names of compounds of this with the alcohol radicals; e.g. **bor-ethyl** $3(C_2H_5)B$, **bor-methyl** $3(CH_3)B$, obtained by acting on ethyl borate with zinc ethyl and methyl respectively.

1869 ROSCOE *Elem. Chem.* 342 Borethyl is a colourless liquid, possesses a very powerful acrid smell, and takes fire on exposure to the air, burning with a green flame. **1881** ROSCOE *Chem.* III. 244 Bormethyl is a colourless gas.

‖**bora**[1] ('bɔərə). [According to Diez, Venetian, Milanese form of It. *borea* north wind:—L. *Boreas.* But cf. Illyrian (Servia, Dalmatia, etc.) *bura* 'storm, tempest' (Bulg. *bura*, Russ. and OSlav. *burya*), which may have been confounded with the Ital. in the Adriatic.] A severe north wind which blows in the Upper Adriatic.

1864 V'TESS STRANGFORD *E. Shores Adriatic* 263 A violent wind began to blow. 'The Bora! the Bora!' resounded on all sides, in tones of terror and dismay. **1883** *Athenæum* 6 Jan. 11/1 Capt. Burton left Trieste.. too happy to exchange its ferocious bora and distressing sirocco for the.. West African coast.

Bora[2] (bɒ'rɑː). Also bor(r)ah. [Hindi *bohrā.*] A Muslim trader. Also *attrib.*

1698 FRYER *Acc. E. India & P.* 93 Schisms they have made, as *Bilhim, Jemottee*, and the lowest of all is *Borrah.* **1812** M. GRAHAM *Jrnl. Res. India* 33 The inside of a Borah's box is like that of an English country shop. **1863** G. P. BADGER in J. W. Jones tr. *Varthema's Travels* p. xlix, A considerable trade is still carried on, chiefly by Borah merchants of Guzerat and Cutch. **1876** *Encycl. Brit.* IV. 537/1 Borás, a class of commercial Mahometans.

bora[3] ('bɔərə). Also **borah**. [Aboriginal Australian.] A rite amongst the Aborigines of eastern Australia, constituting the admission of a young person to the rights of manhood.

1866 W. RIDLEY *Kamilaroi* 17 Kubura, young man who has attended a bora. **1883** J. FRASER *Aborigines of N.S. Wales* 12 This assembly—the most solemn and unique in the tribal life—is called the Bora and sometimes the Kobbora. *Ibid.* 17 The inner Bora customs. **1885** MRS. C. PRAED *Austral. Life* 24 The great mystery of the Blacks is the Bora—a ceremony at which the young men found worthy receive the rank of warriors. **1948** V. PALMER *Golconda* xiii. 104 The white-haired maker of corroborees.. holding forth to the young men about the need to bring back the borah and all the ancient rites of the tribe. **1953** J. MCLAREN in I. Bevan *Sunburnt Country* II. ii. 72 The 'Bora' ceremonies of initiation are held in some secluded part of the bush, and have rarely been seen by whites.

borable ('bɔərəb(ə)l), *a. rare*—[0]. Also boreable. [f. BORE *v.* + -ABLE.] That may be bored.

1755 in JOHNSON; and in mod. Dicts.

borace, obs. form of BORAX.

‖**bo'rachio.** *Obs.* Forms: 6 bourrachoe, 7 bor-, borracho(e, boraccio, -accia, borracio, burracho, 8 borrachio, borad-, 6–8 borachio. [Adopted from Sp. or It.: cf. Sp. *borracha* leathern bag for wine, with *borracho* drunkard, masc. of *borracho* drunken; also It. *boraccia*, (*borracio* Baretti) 'a boracho, or bottle made of a goates skin, such as they vse in Spaine' (Florio).]

1. A large leather bottle or bag used in Spain for wine or other liquors.

1583 STANYHURST *Æneis* III. (Arb.) 91 With chuffe chaffe wynesops lyke a gourd bourrachoe replennisht. **1594** GREENE *Look. Glasse* Wks. (1861) 133 A borachio of kisses. **1615** tr. *De Montfart's Surv. E. Indies* 5 They make their prouison of water in great Borachoes, made of whole goat-skins. **1616** B. JONSON *Devil an Ass* II. i. (1631) 113 Leather .. like your Borachio Of Spaine, Sir. **1629** CAPT. SMITH *Trav. & Adv.* xiii. 25 The milke they keepe in great skinnes like Burracho's. **1658** USSHER *Ann.* 104 Camels loden with borachoes or lethren baggs full of water. **1736** BAILEY *Househ. Dict.* 260 Such [wines] as have the Borachio or hogskin flavour. **1775** *Phil. Trans.* LXVI. 258 An elastic gum bottle, otherwise called boradchio or caoutchouc.

2. A drunkard, a mere 'wine-bag'.

[**1599** SHAKS. *Much Ado* IV. ii. 11 What is your name, friend? *Bor.* Borachio.] *a* **1627** MIDDLETON *Span. Gipsy* I. i, I am no borachio. *a* **1729** CONGREVE (J.) How you stink of wine! .. you're an absolute borachio.

boracic (bɒ'ræsɪk), *a.* [f. BORAX + -IC.]

1. *Chem.* Of the nature of, pertaining to, or derived from borax. ***boracic acid*** is now in systematic nomenclature *boric acid.*

1801 HATCHETT in *Phil. Trans.* XCII. 58 A white glittering salt.. resembling the concrete boracic acid. **1869** ROSCOE *Elem. Chem.* 152 Boracic or Boric Acid. **1880** MACCORMAC *Antisept. Surg.* 149 Boracic lint, or some similar application.

2. Rhyming slang (in full ***boracic lint***) for 'skint', penniless.

1959 H. HOBSON *Mission House Murder* viii. 56 'You boracic?' she asked.—She meant boracic lint—skint. **1974** P. WRIGHT *Lang. Brit. Industry* x. 87 Current now.. especially round London, is *I'm boracic* from *boracic lint* = *skint* (penniless), a shortening unknown a few years ago. **1984** D. RAYMOND *He died with his Eyes Open* xix. 97 'He's boracic,' said someone. 'He's out grafting.'

boracite ('bɒrəsaɪt). *Min.* [f. prec. + -ITE.] Native borate of magnesia.

1810 HENRY *Elem. Chem.* (1826) I. 619 A natural compound of boracic acid and magnesia.. found near Luneburg in Germany, and known by the name of boracite. **1811** PINKERTON *Petral.* I. 487 [Gypsum] contains.. in rare instances arragonite and boracite.

†**bo'racium.** *Obs. Chem.* [f. BORAX: cf. *sodium, potassium*, etc.] The name at first given to BORON, when it was supposed to be a metal.

1808 SIR H. DAVY in *Phil. Trans.* XCIX. 85 There is strong reason to consider the boracic basis as metallic.. and I venture to propose for it the name of *boracium.* **1812** —— *Chem. Philos.* 245 The bodies.. are six, hydrogene, azote, sulphur, phosphorus, carbon, and boracium or boron.

borage ('bʌrɪdʒ). Forms: 5– borage, 6 bourage, 7 bourrage, 6–8 burrage, 7–8 borrage, 8 burridge. [from med.L. *borrāgo*, or one of the Romanic forms: cf. F. *bourrache* (also OF. *bourrace*), Pr. *borrage*, It. *borraggine, borrace*, Sp. *borraja*, Pg. *borragom*; in mod.L. *borāgo*; prob., according to Diez, f. *borra, burra* 'rough hair, short wool' (cf. late L. *burra* 'a shaggy garment'), in reference to the roughness of the foliage.]

1. A genus of plants, giving its name to a natural order (*Boraginaceæ*). *spec.* The common British species (*Borago officinalis*), which has bright blue flowers, and stem and leaves covered with prickly hairs; it was formerly much esteemed as a cordial, and is still largely used in making *cool tankard*, claret cup, etc.

[*c* **1265** *Anglo-Norm. Voc.* Wr.-Wülcker 557 *Borago*, burage.] *c* **1420** *Liber Cocorum* 47 Take most of cole, borage, persyl. *c* **1500** *To serve a Lord* in *Babees Bk.* (1868) 370 Sawse hym with mustard, burage, suger. **1530** PALSGR. 202/1 Burrage (bourage) herbe, *bovrache.* **1533** ELYOT *Cast. Helth* (1541) 29 Bourage comforteth the harte, and maketh one merye. **1603** HOLLAND *Plutarch's Mor.* 644 Some there be, who put leaves of burrage into their wine. **1619** *Pasquil's Palin.* (1877) 155 No fiery red-fac'd Claret attended with his Borrage. **1709** STEELE *Tatler* No. 31 ¶8 The same Effect as Burridge in the Glass when a Man is drinking. **1710** SALMON *Househ. Comp.* 45 Borrage is one of the four cordial flowers. **1842** SIR W. HOOKER *Brit. Flora* 225 Hence the old Adage—'I Borage always bring Courage'.

2. *Comb.* and *attrib.*, as ***borage-seed, -water***; **borage-wort**, any boraginaceous plant.

1626 BACON *Sylva* §441 Sow here and there some Borrage-seed. **1620** VENNER *Via Recta* vii. 125 Eaten with.. Borage-water and Sugar. **1882** *Garden* 22 July 60/1 A morbid craze for Borage-worts.

boraginaceous (bɒˌrædʒɪ'neɪʃəs), *a. Bot.* [f. mod.L. *borāgo, -āgin-* BORAGE + -ACEOUS.] Of or pertaining to the order *Boraginaceæ*: see prec.

boragineous (bɒrə'dʒɪnɪəs), *a. Bot.* [f. as prec. + -EOUS.] Of or pertaining to a tribe of the *Boraginaceæ*, called *Borangineæ*, containing the typical genus *Borago*; also, loosely, = prec.

borak ('bɔəræk). *Austral.* and *N.Z. slang.* Also borac(k), borax. [Aboriginal Australian. Cf. BARRACK *v.*[2]] Nonsense, humbug; chaff, banter; esp. in ***to poke (the) borak***, to make or poke fun.

1845 T. MCCOMBIE *Arabin* 273 Borack, gammon, nonsense. **1882** *Bulletin* (Sydney) 9 Sept. 9 A smart fellow was 'poking borak' at them, and asked, 'Is the snow in Japan the same as it is in Tasmania?' **1898** in M. Davitt *Life & Progr. Australasia* xxxv. 192 A jest is 'poking borac'. **1904** *Blackw. Mag.* June 832/1 One of the crowd was poking borak and said something pretty bad to him at the beginning. **1916** J. B. COOPER *Coo-oo-ee* ix. 113 At the same time he wondered whether Nipper was not 'pokin' borak' at him. **1944** J. H. FULLARTON *Troop Target* iv. 34 You wouldn't be poking the borax, would you?

boral, var. of BOREL *Sc.*, an auger.

Boran (bə'rɑːn). [Native name.] A breed of cattle native to drier parts of East Africa.

1935 *East Afr. Agric. Jrnl.* I. III. 251/2 Two types of cattle are employed, namely, Boran and Masai. The Boran native type were obtained from a European farmer under whose care a certain amount of selection had taken place. **1953** FAULKNER & BROWN *Improvement of Cattle in Brit. Colonial Territories in Africa* 3 The Boran and Nandi in Kenya have shown conclusively what can be achieved by the selection of pure indigenous stock. **1959** R. B. KELLEY *Native & Adapted Cattle* iii. 35 The second kind of cattle from the desert-grass area are known as Boran, after the nomadic tribes that own them in the Lake Rudolf region. **1969** *Times* (Somali Republic Suppl.) 16 Sept. p. vi/3 Somali cattle (Boran variety) were driven 200 miles out of the republic.

borane ('bɔəreɪn). *Chem.* [ad. G. *boran* (A. Stock 1916, in *Ber. d. Deut. Chem. Ges.* XLIX. 111), f. BOR(ON + -ANE (after *methane*, etc.).] The systematic name for a boron hydride; *spec.* the (hypothetical) compound BH_3; also, any substituted derivative of a boron hydride.

1916 *Jrnl. Chem. Soc. Abstr.* CX. II. 319 BH_4 (unknown) .. would be described as borane. **1923** *Chem. Abstr.* XVII 2242 All attempts to obtain a mono- and a triborane failed. **1933** A. STOCK *Hydrides of Boron & Silicon* i. 17 Our present knowledge of the chemistry of boron leads us now to recommend.. that.. the stable, so to say normal, hydrides.. be called 'boranes'. The less stable hydrides.. should be called 'hydroboranes'. **1965** *New Scientist* 4 Nov. 341 Thought towards solution of the fuel problem was aimed at substituting hydrogen-boron compounds (the boranes) for the hydrocarbon constituents of the classical fuels.

boras, obs. form of BORAX.

‖**bo'rasco, -'asque.** Also bo'rasca, borrasque, burrasca. [Fr. *bourrasque*, and Sp., Pg., Cat. *borrasca*, ad. It. *burasca* (Florio), *burrasca* (Baretti), according to Diez, augmentative of BORA¹.] A violent squall of wind.

1686 GOAD *Celest. Bodies* II. vii. 242 Whirlwinds, Hurricanes, Borasques, Tornado, Tuffon. 1692 SIR T. BLOUNT *Ess.* 143 You may see Vulcano's, Hurricans and Borasco's in him. 1849 J. A. ST. JOHN in *Tait's Mag.* XVI. 733 A borasco overtook them. 1850 *Ibid.* XVII. 28 The burrascas of the Mediterranean are often of short continuance. 1854 BADHAM *Halieut.* 97 A mighty change.. might wind up the evening with a sudden borrasque. 1867 SMYTH *Sailor's Word-bk.*, *Borasca*, a storm, with thunder and lightning.

‖**borassus** (bɒ'ræsəs). *Bot.* [mod.L., ad. Gr. βόρασσος palm-fruit.] A genus of palms, including two species, of which *B. flabelliformis* the Palmyra Palm, yields palm-wine and palm-sugar.

1798 S. WILCOCKE *Stavorinus' Voy.* in Southey *Comm.-pl. Bk.* Ser. II. (1849) 517 At Ceylon.. the leaves of the borassus palm tree.. are used instead of paper. 1878 H. M. STANLEY *Dark Cont.* I. vi. 131 A forest of borassus palms.

borate ('bɔəreɪt). *Chem.* [f. BOR-ON + -ATE.] A salt of boric or boracic acid.

1816 ACCUM *Chem. Tests* (1818) 179 Borate of lead. 1863–72 WATTS *Dict. Chem.* I. 636 *Borax*, the acid borate of sodium which exists in the water of certain lakes in central Asia.

‖**bo'rato.** *Obs.* Also 6 boratta. [app. a. It. *buratto* 'sort of thin transparent cloth'.] A thin fabric: cf. BOLT *v.*¹, also BOLTER *vbl. sb.*¹, BOLTING *sb.*

1578 *Richmond. Wills* (1853) 276, ix yeards of borato at ijs. vjd. a yeard. 1594 BLUNDEVIL *Exerc.* v. iii. (ed. 7) 533 Taffaties, Borattas, Grogaines. 1660 *Act 12 Chas. II*, iv. Sched., Boratoes or Bombasines—narrow, the single piece not above 15 yards. 1720 *Stow's Surv.* (1754) II. v. ix. 266/2 Borratose, wrought with silk containing under twenty yards.

borax ('bɔəræks). Forms: 4–7 boras, 5–6 borace, 6 borras, 7 baurac(h, boraxe, 6– borax; *pl.* (*Obs. rare*) boraces. [ME. *bo'ras*, a OF. *boras* (*borras*, *bourras*), ad. med.L. *baurach*, *borac*, *boracum*, and *borax*, *borac-em*, a. Arab. variously pronounced *bauraq*, *būraq*, *bōraq*, prop. 'natron', but also 'borax': referred by the lexicons to the Arab. *bwrq* to glisten, but prob. ad. Pers. *būrah* borax. According to Léman introduced into the Romanic langs. about the 9th c. Cf. Sp. *borrax* (now written *borraj*), mod.F. *borax*, It. *borrace*.]

1. A native salt; the acid borate of sodium, or biborate of soda ($Na_2B_4O_7$): having, when pure, the form of a transparent or whitish crystal, or white powder, but also imported as crude borax or tincal, a greenish mass greasy to the touch.

*c*1386 CHAUCER *Prol.* 630 Ther nas quyksilver, litarge, ne brimstone, Boras, ceruce, ne oille of tartre noon. 1483 *Cath. Angl.* 37 Borace, *Borax*. 1543 TRAHERON *Vigo's Chirurg.* (1586) 433 Boras, others write it Borax, and Plinie saith, that it is a liquor in pits. 1623 COCKERAM, *Boras*, a white substance like salt-peeter wherewith goldsmiths solder gold and siluer. 1678 R. R[USSELL] *Geber* I. iii. 9 Glass and boraces. 1684 *Phil. Trans.* XIV. 610 The other species [of Nitre] they term Baurac, which they used in seasoning their meat. 1810 HENRY *Elem. Chem.* (1826) I. 566 Tincal, which, when purified, becomes the refined borax of the shops. 1876 HARLEY *Mat. Med.* 157 Borax is supposed to have been the Chrysocolla of Pliny.

2. **borax beads**, beads made of borax, used in blowpipe analysis to distinguish the metallic oxides, and test minerals by the characteristic colours which they give in the oxidizing and the reducing flame.

3. **borax carmine** (see quot. 1890).

1887 *Amer. Naturalist* XXI. 596 For staining, borax-carmine was used. 1890 BILLINGS *Med. Dict.*, *Borax carmine*, an aqueous solution of borax and carmine... A pure and intense nuclear stain if bleached with an acid.

4. Cheap, inferior, or ostentatious goods, esp. furniture; inferior and tasteless design, 'so called fr. the reputed custom of a producer of borax soap of giving cheap furniture as a coupon premium' (Webster 1961). Also *attrib.* orig. *U.S.*

1942 R. CHANDLER *High Window* (1943) xxv. 171 A standing lamp from the basement of some borax emporium. 1948 *Archit. Rev.* CIV. 92 (*title*) Borax, or the chromium-plated calf. *Ibid.* 314/2 'Borax'.. is generally restricted to consumer goods where obviously heavy forms and elaborate jazzy ornament are used in order to add spurious eye-appeal. The term originated in the furniture industry and by analogy is sometimes applied to kitchen appliances and more rarely to automobile design. 1963 *Times* 11 Feb. 13/3 There.. appears to be far too much unnecessary design or 'borax', as useless embellishment has come to be known in financial and trade circles.

borax, var. BORAK.

borazon ('bɔərəzɒn). [f. BOR(ON + AZ(O- + -ON.] A crystalline form of boron nitride, extremely hard and resistant to oxidation at high temperatures.

1957 R. H. WENTORF in *Jrnl. Chem. Physics* XXVI. 956/2 The name 'Borazon' is proposed for this cubic form of boron nitride. 1960 N. KNEALE *Quatermass & Pit* III. 78 We could try borazon. That's several times harder still [than diamond]. Can you get hold of a drill with a borazon bit?

borbecu, obs. form of BARBECUE.

†'**Borborite.** *Obs.* [ad. L. *Borboritæ*, Gr. βορβορῖται, f. Gr. βόρβορ-ος filth.] One of the names, or nick-names, given to certain Ophitic Gnostics, referring, according to Epiphanius, to their unclean living (but various other explanations are offered); in 16–17th c. used as a term of reproach in the sense of 'One who holds filthy or immoral doctrines', and specifically applied to a branch of the Mennonites.

1659 GAUDEN *Tears of Ch.* 572 (D.) The whole Reformed Church of England.. torne and bespattered by those Borborites, those uncleane Spirits. 1685 BAXTER *Paraphr. James* v. 19 Borborites or Gnosticks are not the less such for .. being call'd Bishops. 1882–3 SCHAFF tr. *Herzog's Encycl. Rel. Knowl.* I. 313 Borborites or Borborians.

†**borbo'rology.** *Obs. rare.* [f. as prec. + -λογία discoursing: see -LOGY.] Filthy talk.

1649 TRAPP *Comm. Epist.* 224 Shunne obscene borborology, and filthy speeches.

'**borborygm.** ? Also in Lat. form. borborygmus. *Med.* [ultimately ad. Gr. βορβορυγμός, f. βορβορύζ-ειν to have a rumbling in the bowels. In 16th c. F. *borborygme* (Cotgr. *-igme*).] Also *fig.* Hence **borbo'rygmic** *a.*, characterized by borborygms or rumblings.

1719 *Glossogr. Nova*, *Borborygm*, a rumbling Noise in the Guts. 1794–6 E. DARWIN *Zoon.* (1801) II. 530 Hence the borborigmi, or rumbling of the bowels. 1880 BEALE *Slight Ailm.* 97 Borborygmi.. are a serious annoyance. 1927 H. G. WELLS in *Sunday Express* 1 May 12/4 Elephant hunters say that they can tell the proximity of a herd by the borborygmic (see dictionary) noises the poor brutes emit. 1928 A. HUXLEY *Point Counter Point* xi. 170 The stertorous borborygms of the dyspeptic Carlyle! 1938 *Times* 24 Nov. 12/3 The borborygmic note of the Arabian camel. 1959 E. FENWICK *Long Way Down* vii. 54 The room was very quiet, except for its borborygmic old radiator.

borch(e, obs. Sc. var. of BORROW, a pledge, etc.

borclothe, variant of BOARD-CLOTH, *Obs.*

bord, var. of BOARD, *obs.* exc. in ***bord-and-pillar*** (see BOARD *sb.* 16).

†**bord(e.** *Obs. Thieves' cant.* [? a transf. use of *bord*, BOARD 'shield'.] A shilling.

1567 HARMAN *Caveat* 85 Bouse there a bord, drinke there a shyllinge. 1611 DEKKER *Roar. Girle* Wks. 1873 III. 219 My Lord Noland.. bestowes vpon you two, two boordes and a halfe. 1688 R. HOLME *Armory* III. iii. §68 (Cant Voc.) *Borde*, a shilling. *Half a Borde*, six-pence.

bordage¹ ('bɔːdɪdʒ). *Feudal System.* [a. OF. *bordage* (still in local use in France), = med.L. *bordāgium*, f. OF. *borde*, med.L. *borda* cot + -AGE: see BORDAR. (Erroneously connected in Eng. dictionaries, from Manley and Blount downwards, with *bord* 'table', but clearly explained and illustrated by Du Cange, and in French use by Godefroy.)]

The tenure by which a bordar held his cot at the will of his lord; the services due from a bordar. (As an Eng. word only in modern historians.)

*a*1300 *Coust. de Norm.* I. iii. 15 (Du Cange) Tenure par bordage, si est comme aucune borde [*later edd. add* loge ou maison] est baillie à aucun pour fere les vils services son Seignor: ne poet lomme cel fiement ne vendre, ne engagier ne donner, et de ç'en n'est pas homage fet. 1664 SPELMAN *Gloss.* s.v. *Bordarii*, Bordage. 1771 *Antiq. Sarisb.* 29 From the Grand Customer of Normandy we learn, that Bordage was a base tenure, where such a house or cottage was obliged to thresh, draw water, grind corn, and do such other servile work.

bordage² ('bɔːdɪdʒ). [a. F. *bordage*, f. *bord* side, *border* to border.]

1. *Naut.* 'The planking on a ship's side.' *Mod. Dicts.*

2. That which forms the border of anything.

1860 SIR W. LOGAN in Borthwick *Brit. Amer. Reader* 149 When forced into a narrow part of the channel, the lateral pressure it [the ice] there exerts drives the bordage up the banks, where it sometimes accumulates to the height of from forty to fifty feet.

†**bord alexander.** *Obs.* Also 4–5 burd, boord(e, borde. A kind of striped silk: see ALEXANDER.

1392 in Beck *Draper's Dict.* s.v. *Alexander*, In 1392 Richard Beardsall left as a legacy a piece of burd Alysaunder. 1440 in *Eng. Ch. Furniture* (1866) 184, Vj autere towells of lynen Clothe.. the vth with a frountere of boorde Alisandre. 1482 MARG. PASTON *Will* in *Lett.* III. 286 The hole bedde of borde alisaundre. 1503 *Will of Gaynesford* (Somerset Ho.), Wᵗ celer & tester of borde alisaundre.

bordall, bordalour, Sc. var. of BORDEL, -ER.

†**bord-and-cord.** *Obs.* [perh. f. *bord*, BOARD 'side, border', and CORD.] An obsolete game played with a ball by five on each side.

1591 in Nichols *Progr. Q. Eliz.* III. 117 In this square they (stript out of their dubletts) played, five to five, with the hand ball, at bord and cord (as they tearme it).

bordar ('bɔːdə(r)). *Feudal System.* Also 9 border. [mod. ad. med.L. *bordārius* cottager, f. med.L. *borda* (Pr., Cat. *borda*, F. *borde*) hut, cottage, referred by Diez to Teut. *bord* (neuter) 'wooden board', etc. (The OF. was *bordier*.)

(The actual history of the sense which *borda* has taken in Romanic, and of its fem. gender, is still wanting; one might conjecture a neuter plural *borda* 'thing of boards' taken as a feminine sing.)]

A villein of the lowest rank, who held a cottage at his lord's pleasure, for which he rendered menial service; a cottier. (As an English word, found only in modern historians: the L. *bordarii* is a regular term of Domesday Book.)

[1087 *Domesday Bk., Middlesex, St. Petrus Stanes*, Et xxxvi bordarii de iii hidis, et iv bordarii de xl acris, . et xii servi. 1670 BLOUNT *Law Dict.*, *Bordarii* seu *Bordmanni*, often occur in Domesday; by some esteemed to be Bores, Husbandmen, or Cotagers; which are there always put after Villains.] 1776 STRUTT *Horda Angel-Cyn.* III. 16 The military tenants and socmen had their labourers and dependants, as bordars. 1809 BAWDEN tr. *Domesday Bk.* 11 The King has now there five villanes and three bordars with two ploughs. 1861 PEARSON *Early & Mid. Ages Eng.* 268 Of these [the semi-servile], villeins, borders, or cottiers, make up the mass, about 200,000 in all. 1876 GREEN *Short Hist.* v. §4. 238 The cottar, the bordar, and the labourer were bound to aid in the work of the home-farm.

borde, obs. f. BOARD, and var. of BOURD, *Obs.*

Bordeaux (bɔː'dəʊ). Also 6– **Burdeux**, *Sc.* **Burdeous**, 7 **Burdeaux**, 7–8 **Bourdeaux**. **1.** A city in the south of France; hence, the wine made there, claret. †***Bordeaux hammer*** (humorous): a vinous headache.

[1483 *Cath. Angl.* 48 Burdus [Burdeus], *ciuitas est, burdigallus.*] *c*1570 *Leg. Bp. St. Andrews* in *Scot. Poems 16th C.* (1801) II. 342 His contagious stomack Was sa owersett with Burdeous drummake. 1576 NEWTON tr. *Lemnie's Complex.* (1633) 94 A Burdeaux hammer beating in his head. 1597 SHAKS. *2 Hen. IV*, II. iv. 69 There's a whole Marchants Venture of Burdeux-Stuffe in him. 1714 MANDEVILLE *Fab. Bees* (1725) I. 260 He could content himself with plain Bourdeaux, if it had a good body. 1836 MARRYAT *Three Cutt.* iii, Don't go abroad to drink sour wine, because they call it Bordeaux.

2. A shade of red produced by any of several red azo-dyes derived from beta naphthol.

1904 *Westm. Gaz.* 10 Mar. 4/2 Bordeaux-coloured straw. 1909 *Ibid.* 11 Jan. 5/2 The various shades of violet, blue, and what we have called Bordeaux.

3. ***Bordeaux mixture***: a mixture composed of blue vitriol, lime, and water, used for the destruction of fungi.

1892 *Prev. Potato Dis.* (R. Veitch & Son) 4 The Bordeaux Mixture, or 'Bouillie Bordelaise'. 1921 *Discovery* May 130/1 Bordelaise, or Bordeaux mixture.. was first used to cover grapes growing alongside paths and roads to prevent 'finger blight'. 1959 *Sci. News* LI. 30 The latter causes pod rot and can be dealt with by spraying with Bordeaux mixture.

†'**bordel.** *Obs.* Forms: 4–9 bordel, (4 ? bordeal), 5–7 bordell, 5 bordele, bourdel(l, bordyl(le, burdell, 6 *Sc.* bo(i)rdall, 8 bourdel. [a. OF. *bordel* 'cabin, hut, brothel', corresp. to Pr. *bordel*, Sp. *burdel*, It. *bordello*, med.L. *bordellus*, *-um*, dim. of late L. *borda* (? or of **bordum*): see BORDAR. (Now superseded by *brothel*, which has no etymological connexion with it.)]

1. A house of prostitution, a brothel.

*c*1305 *St. Lucy* 92 in *E.E.P.* (1862) 104 Oþer to comun bordel beo ilad oþer ibore. *c*1386 CHAUCER *Pers. T.* ¶811 Harlottis, that haunten bordels of these foule wommen. 1483 CAXTON *Gold. Leg.* 84/2, I wente to the bourdel. 1535 STEWART *Cron. Scot.* III. 276 Semdill in the kirk and richt oft in the bordell. *c*1620 Z. BOYD *Zion's Flowers* (1855) 79 To make a Bordell of my Masters house. *a*1722 MRS. CENTLIVRE *Marplot* III. i. 153 Egad, maybe it is some private Bourdel. 1828 SCOTT *F.M. Perth* viii, As if they were in a bordel at Paris. 1850 CARLYLE *Latt.-day Pamph.* viii, That this universe.. was a Cookery-shop and Bordel.

b. Prostitution, fornication. [Cf. OF. *faire bordel de.*]

1382 WYCLIF *Lev.* xix. 29 Ne putt thow thi douȝter to bordel. 1393 GOWER *Conf.* II. 162 All his rent In wine and bordel he despent. *c*1440 *Gesta Rom.* (1879) 220.

2. A worthless fellow, a good-for-nothing. (Erroneously used for BROTHEL 1, as on the other hand *brothel* has taken the place of BORDEL in sense 1.)

1474 CAXTON *Chesse* 104 He drof and chased out of the hoost moo than two thousand bourdellys.

3. *attrib.* and *Comb.*, as ***bordel woman, house.***

1382 WYCLIF *Baruch* vi. 11 Of it thei ȝeuen to pute in bordel house, and ournen hooris. *c*1386 CHAUCER *Pers. T.* ¶902 Commune bordeal womman. 1480 CAXTON *Chron. Eng.* cxcvii. 175 Holy chirche tho had no more reuerence than it had ben a bordelhows. 1541 ELYOT *Image Govt.* (1549) 6 In common baines and bordell houses.

¶ Chatterton (misled by Kersey: cf. Phillips 1706) took *bordel* in the OF. sense of 'cot'.

a **1780** CHATTERTON *Wks.* (ed. Skeat) I. 203 Would'st thou ken Nature in her better part? Goe, searche the logges and bordels of the hynde.

† **'bordeler.** *Obs.* Also 4 bordiller, *Sc.* bordalour(e, 6 *Sc.* bordellar. [a. AF. *bordeler* = OF. *bordelier*, f. *bordel*: see prec.] A brothel-keeper; ? a frequenter of brothels.

c **1375** ? BARBOUR *St. Cristofore* 456 þai ware bordalouris parfyt. **1393** GOWER *Conf.* III 322 He..to the bordeler her solde. *c* **1400** *Rom. Rose* 7036 Other bawdes or bordillers. **1536** BELLENDEN *Cron. Scot.* (1821) I. 165 Fidlaris, bordellaris, makerellis..and siclike men of vile estimatioun.

bor'dello. Also 6–8 burdello. [a. It. *bordello*: see BORDEL.] = BORDEL.

1598 B. JONSON *Ev. Man in Hum.* I. ii, From the Burdello, it might come as well. **1642** MILTON *Apol. Smect.* Wks. 1738 I. 109 Proceed now to the afternoon; in Playhouses, he says, and the Bordelloes. **1719** D'URFEY *Pills* (1872) IV. 23. **1794** MATTHIAS *Purs. Lit.* (1798) 69 The stews and bordellos of Grecian and Roman antiquity. **1930** E. POUND *XXX Cantos* xxviii. 130 And was lodged in a bordello (promptly). **1961** J. HELLER *Catch-22* (1962) xxiii. 236 The distant recesses of the strange and marvellous bordello.

† **'bordelry.** *Obs. rare.* [see -RY.] = BORDEL.

c **1440** WYCLIF *Numb.* xxv. 8 (*MSS.* I, S.) He entride aftir the man of Israel in to the bordelrie [**1388** hoore hows; Vulg. *lupanar*].

border ('bɔːdə(r)), *sb.* Forms: 4–7 bordure, 5 bordur, (bordeure), 5– border. Also 5 bourder, -ur, bordore, bowerdur, bordeure, 6 bordde; *Sc.* bordour, -ar. [ME. *bordure*, a. OF. *bordure*, earlier *bordeüre*, corresp. to Pr., Sp., Pg. *bordadura*, It. and late L. *bordatura* 'edging', f. **bordāre* (It., Sp. *bordar*, F. *border*) to edge or border, f. *bordus* (It., Sp. *bordo*, Fr. *bord*) 'side, edge, border', a. Teut. *bord* 'side': see BOARD *sb.* As in some other words the ME. termination *-ure* has been weakened through *-ur* to *-er*, thus disguising the etymology: the earlier BORDURE (in Caxton *bordeure*) is retained in Heraldry.]

1. A side, edge, brink, or margin; a limit, or boundary; the part of anything lying along its boundary or outline.

c **1391** CHAUCER *Astrol.* I. 4 A lyne, that cometh..down to the nethereste bordure. *c* **1400** *Destr. Troy* 1598 Bigget in bourders of the stretes. *c* **1430** *Syr Gener.* 4076 With riche stoones in the bourdure. **1563** HYLL *Art Garden.* (1593) 14 The borders or edges of beddes. **1570** BILLINGSLEY *Euclid* I. vi. 2 The endes, limites, or borders of a lyne, are pointes. **1580** BARET *Alv.* B 943 The borders and endes of ones heare of his head. **1611** BIBLE *Ex.* xix. 12 That ye goe not vp into the mount, or touch the border of it. *a* **1819** HOGG *Hawick Common-riding Song* ix, Down by Teviot's flowery border. **1860** TYNDALL *Glac.* II. §8. 263 The glacier is..loaded along its borders with the ruins of the mountains.

2. a. The district lying along the edge of a country or territory, a frontier; *pl.* the marches, the border districts.

c **1400** *Destr. Troy* 12861 There come..ffro the bowerdurs aboute..Pilours and plodders. **1489** CAXTON *Faytes of A.* I. xii. 31 See..that the frontyers and borders be wel garnysshed. **1494** FABYAN VI. clxxiii. 169 An host of the men of Mercya, and the border there aboute. **1580** *Jrnls. Ho. Commons* I. 125 A Bill touching the Fortifying of the Borders towards Scotland. **1667** MILTON *P.L.* II. 361 Though Heav'n be shut..this place may lye expos'd The utmost border of his kingdom. **1805** SOUTHEY *Madoc in W.* x, Wolves of war, They kept their border well. **1844** H. H. WILSON *Brit. India* II. 80 The Gorkhas ravaged the borders almost in sight of them.

b. The boundary line which separates one country from another, the frontier line. *on the border*: on or close to this line, on either side; hence, in the border district. *on the borders of* (Wales): close to, the frontier of (Wales). *over the border*: across the frontier line.

1535 COVERDALE *Josh.* xv. 6 The border northwarde, is from the see coast..and goeth vp vnto Beth Hagla. **1552** LYNDESAY *Monarche* IV. 5904 Thay sall dwell on the bordour Off Hell. **1665–9** BOYLE *Occas. Refl.* IV. vii. (1675) 211 Upon the Borders of two Hostile Nations. **1703** KIRKTON *Life Welsh* (1845) 1 He joined the thieves on the English Border. **1732** DE FOE, etc., *Tour Gt. Brit.* (1769) III. 254, I am now on the Borders of Scotland. **1815** *Encycl. Brit.* (ed. 3) III. 588 Berwick-upon-Tweed, is a town on the border of England and Scotland, and a county of itself. **1867** BAKER *Nile Tribut.* viii. 181 He takes refuge over the border. **1876** GREEN *Short Hist.* v. (1884) 79 Their inhabitants slain or driven over the Scotch border.

c. With various prepositions, e.g. *within*, *in*, *out of*, and in other connexions, *borders* is equivalent to 'territories, dominions, limits'. (L. *fines*.)

c **1425** WYNTOUN *Cron.* VIII. x. 131 Wyth-in þe Bordwrys of Ingland. **1535** COVERDALE *Ex.* xxxiv. 24 Whan I shal..enlarge thy borders. **1552** ABP. HAMILTON *Catech.* 35, I sall gif peace to all your bordouris [*in finibus vestris*]. **1563–87** FOXE *A. & M.* I. 251 He refused to meet us in the borders of the King. **1607** TOPSELL *Four-f. Beasts* 140 A beggerly Beast brought out of barbarous borders. **1611** BIBLE *Deut.* xii. 20 When the Lord thy God shall enlarge thy border [COVERD. bordes]. **1833** HT. MARTINEAU *Tale of Tyne* iii. 60 No man in our borders is rich enough. **1837** WREFORD *Hymn*, '*Lord, while for all*', O guard our shores from every foe, With peace our borders bless.

3. *spec.* **a.** (Eng. and Sc. Hist.) *the Border*, *the Borders*: the boundary between England and Scotland; the district adjoining this boundary on both sides; the English and Scottish borderland. (The term appears to have been first established in Scotland, where the English border, being the only one it has, was emphatically *the border*.)

1535 STEWART *Cron. Scot.* II. 471 Gif thift or reif wes maid vpon the bordour. *c* **1536** LYNDESAY *Compl.* 384 Baith throw the heland and the bordour. **1601** *Act 43 Eliz.* xiii, Pream., To pay..Black-mail unto divers and sundry inhabiting upon or near the Borders. **1663** LAMONT *Diary* (1810) 207 A student of philosophie in St. Andrews, went away with one Agnes Allane..to the border, to be married at the halfe marke church. **1732** DE FOE, etc., *Tour Gt. Brit.* (1769) IV. ii. 61 Laws relating to the Borders. **1773** MRS. GRANT *Lett. fr. Mountains* (1809) I. 89 Mr. Gray is a native of the border. **1808** SCOTT *Marm.* v. xii, Through all the wide Border his steed was the best. **1864** BURTON *Scot Abr.* I. i. 14 All the way from the border to the Highland line. **1881** J. RUSSELL *Haigs* v. 104 Like his neighbour chiefs on the Borders.

b. *attrib.* Of or pertaining to the Border.

1599 JAS. I. Βασιλ. Δωρον in Chambers *Life Jas. I.* (1830) I. viii. 232 Any Hieland or Border thieves. **1799** WORDSW. *Fountain* iii, Some old border-song or catch. **1805** SCOTT *Last Minstr.* Introd. 8 The last of all the Bards was he Who sung of Border chivalry. *Ibid.* III. iv. *note*, An emphatic Border motto, Thou shalt want ere I want. **1869** BUCKLE *Civilis.* III. iii. 117 He summoned..the border barons. **1881** J. RUSSELL *Haigs* v. 105 With the true old Border instinct, bringing off whatever was transportable on its own four feet.

c. In *U.S.*: The line or frontier between the occupied and unoccupied parts of the country, the frontier of civilization. Also *attrib.*

1827 F. COOPER *Prairie* I. ii. 33 The indirect manner so much in use by the border inhabitants. **1863** W. PHILLIPS *Speeches* xvii. 372 He put a guard at every Border-ruffian's door. **1863** *Times* 10 Apr., The Border ruffianism of Kansas. **1870** R. PUMPELLY *Across Amer. & Asia* i. 1 A border bully, armed with revolver, knife, and rifle.

4. A strip of ground in a garden, forming a fringe to the general area, often reserved for flowers; distinguished from *beds*, or flower-plots formed in the area. Also *attrib.*, as in *a hardy border plant*, *useful border annuals*.

c **1400** *Destr. Troy* 329 [The bourderis about abasshet with leuys]. **1590** SPENSER *Muiopot.* 170 He..doth flie, From bed to bed, from one to other border. **1632** G. HERBERT *Temple, Sunday* iv, The fruitfull beds & borders In Gods rich garden. **1709** ADDISON *Tatler* No. 161 ¶2 A wonderful Profusion of Flowers..without being disposed into regular Borders and Parterres. **1796** C. MARSHALL *Garden.* xx. (1813) 409 Annuals, tender sorts, pot & plant out into the borders. **1866** *Treas. Bot.* s.v. *Campanula*, All the species..are well adapted for decorating flower-borders.

5. a. A defined edging, of distinct material, colour, shape, pattern, or ornamentation, made or fixed along the margin of anything. (With many specific applications in arts and manufactures.)

c **1400** *Destr. Troy* 1652 The windowes..worthely wroght..The bases & bourdurs all of bright perle. *c* **1420** *Anturs of Arth.* xxx, With a bordur aboute alle of brent gold. **1474** CAXTON *Chesse* IV. i, The bordeure about is hygher than the squarenes of the poyntes. **1611** BIBLE *Ex.* xxv. 25 Thou shalt make vnto it a border of an hand bredth round about. **1659** LEAK *Water-Wks.* 22 There must be also the border PQ Soldered upon the Vessel. **1854** OWEN in *Circ. Sc.* (*c.* 1865) II. 66/2 The thickened external border..perforated for the lodgment of the teeth, is the 'alveolar border'. **1876** GWILT *Archit.* Gloss., *Border*, a piece of wood put round the upper edges of anything, either for use or ornament. Such are the three pieces of wood..which are mitred together round the slab of a chimney. *Mod.* This carpet would look better with a border. The newspapers appeared with black borders in sign of mourning.

b. *spec.* A piece of ornamental work round the edge of a garment, cap, etc.

c **1374** CHAUCER *Boeth.* I. i. 6 In þe neþerest[e] hem or bordure of þese cloþes. **1632** MASSINGER *City Mad.* IV. iv, You wore..A velvet hood, rich borders, & sometimes A dainty miniver cap. **1837** DICKENS *Pickw.* xii, Up to the very border of her cap. **1854** MRS. GASKELL *North & S.* i, Indian shawls. Delhi? with the lovely little borders?

c. The upper edge of a basket.

1907 T. OKEY in *Jrnl. Soc. Arts* 11 Jan. 190/2 Besides common borders, many other forms, such as plaited, roped, tracked borders, are used [in basket-making]. **1960** E. LEGG *Country Baskets* 27 At the top, the side stakes are turned down to form the *border*..thus completing the basket.

†**6.** A plait or braid of hair (natural or otherwise) worn round the forehead or temples. *Obs.*

1601 HOLLAND *Pliny* I. 559 Corne..beareth the graines arranged spikewise, and as if they were plaited and braided like a border of haire. **1656** *Artif. Handsomeness* 59 [They] admit not onely borders of forain haire, but full and fair peruques. **1663** PEPYS *Diary* 9 May, I did try two or three borders & perriwigs, meaning to wear one. **1865** *Art Jrnl.* No. 321. 91/2 The old lady's 'borders' and ribbons.

7. *Bot.* The expanded portion at the top of a tubular flower.

1861 MISS PRATT *Flower. Pl.* I. 6 The Primrose, the flat portion of which is called the border.

8. Usu. *pl.* (See quot. 1957.)

1824 J. DECASTRO *Memoirs* 16 It is that [part] of the scenic department from whence the borders of chambers or clouds drop. **1831** J. BOADEN in *Corresp. Garrick* I. p. xlviii, A splendid show for his theatre; where a temperate sky always hangs from the borders. **1881** L. WAGNER *Pantomimes* 57 The flymen, whose..business it is to draw up, and lower the scenes and borders. **1957** *Oxf. Compan. Theatre* (ed. 2) 88/2 *Border*, a narrow strip of painted cloth, battened at the top edge only, used to mask-in, or hide, the top of the stage as seen from the auditorium.

9. *Hydraulic Engineering.* (See quot.)

1847 J. DWYER *Hydraulic Engineer.* 29 The Border of a river, canal, etc. is the sum of the sides and bottom, or it is the perimeter in contact with the water.

10. *fig.* A limit, boundary, 'verge'. (Transferred from place to time and abstract things.)

1728 YOUNG *Love Fame* v. (1757) 137 On the borders of threescore. **1747** HERVEY *Medit. & Contempl.* (1818) 211 A person who walks on the borders of eternity. *a* **1783** H. WALPOLE *Mem. Geo. III.* (1845) I. iv. 52 He affected an impartiality that by turns led him to the borders of insincerity and contradiction. **1866** J. MARTINEAU *Ess.* I. 72 Beyond the rigid border of the science.

11. *attrib.* and *Comb.*, as ***border-country***, ***-flower***, ***-ground***, ***-mark***, ***-plant***, ***-state***, ***-stone***, ***-war***, ***-world***. (See also sense 3 b.)

c **1885** in *Westm. Gaz.* (1904) 24 Sept. 3/1 In the gay *border-country of youth. **1945** E. STEP *Wayside & Woodland Ferns* (ed. 2) 76 In the Border country it is known as Dead-man's Hands. **1851** GLENNY *Handbk. Fl.-Gard.* 12 It is only the mass of flowers..that makes it tolerable as a *border-flower. **1875** JOWETT *Plato* (ed. 2) I. 191 A *border-ground between philosophy and politics. **1613** M. RIDLEY *Magn. Bodies* 28 That divideth the North-part..from the South part, as by a *border-marke. **1842** J. STURGE *Visit to U.S.* 166 Many planters, with their slaves, have emigrated thither [*sc.* to Texas] to escape their creditors from the *border States. **1850** MRS. BROWNING *Poems* II. 18 The grey *border-stone that is wist To dilate and assume a wild shape in the mist. **1809** 'D. KNICKERBOCKER' *Hist. N.Y.* (1820) v. ii. 301 Heart-rending cruelties that disgraced these *border wars. **1965** *New Statesman* 30 Apr. 671/1 Ayub Khan..describes this border war as 'a useless quarrel'. **1878** GEO. ELIOT *Coll. Breakf. P.* 833 That *border-world Of dozing ere the sense is fully locked.

12. Special comb.: **border ballad** = *riding ballad* (see RIDING *vbl. sb.* 5 d); **border-house**, a Border tower, a peel; **Border Leicester**, a variety of sheep originating from the cross-breeding of Cheviot and Leicester sheep; **border-man**, one who dwells on the border of a country, = BORDERER; **border marriage**, see MARRIAGE; **border-pile** (*Hydr. Engineering*), an exterior pile of a coffer-dam; **Border-pricker**, **-rider**, a mounted freebooter or 'thief' living on the Border of England and Scotland; **border-service**, military service in defending a frontier; **Border-side**, the district about the Border (cf. *country-side*); **border-stone**, (*a*) a stone marking a boundary; (*b*) a curbstone; **Border terrier**, a small rough-haired terrier originating in the Cheviot Hills; **Border-warden**, Warden of the Marches (of England and Scotland); **Border-warrant**, a writ issued on one side of the Scottish Border for the apprehension of a person on the other side.

c **1863** E. DICKINSON *Poems* (1955) II. 569 Better entertain Than could *Border Ballad—or Biscayan Hymn. **1941** L. MACNEICE *Poetry of Yeats* iv. 79 The beat and glitter of Housman's verse, partly derived from Heine and the Border ballads. **1792** PENNANT *Tours Scotl.* (1790) 90 The castle is no more than a square tower or *border-house. **1873** *Country Gentleman's Mag.* X. 206/1 The distinguishing features of the Yorkshire and *Border Leicesters, though sprung from the same source, have diverged. **1874** W. C. SPOONER *Hist. of Sheep* (ed. 3) I. 70 The sheep which prevail mostly in the lowlands of Scotland and the good land of the Border Counties are called the Border Leicesters. **1620** W. SCOT *Apol. Narr.* (1846) 82 The wyld *bordermen stood in..awe of the Presbyteries excommunication. **1827** F. COOPER *Prairie* I. ii. 29 A border man..is seldom deficient in the virtue of hospitality. **1865** GROTE *Plato* I. xix. 557 The border-men between philosophy and politics. **1820** SCOTT *Monast.* xvi, With two *Border-prickers, as they are called, for my guides. —— *Abbot* ii, I have no home..it was burnt by your *Border-riders. **1707** *Addr. fr. Cumberland* in *Lond. Gaz.* No. 4334/2 There is, now..no Black Mail to be paid..no *Border-Service. *a* **1700** *Ballad* 'Johnie Armstrang' xiv, Lang mayst thou dwell on the *Border-Syde. **1805** SCOTT *Last Minstr.* IV. xxiv, And burn and spoil the Border-side. **1894** R. B. LEE *Mod. Dogs* (*Terriers*) i. 21 The '*Border terriers'..have been for a long time indigenous to the Border counties, and..so far south as Westmorland, Lancashire, and Yorkshire. **1928** F. T. BARTON *Kennel Encycl.* 51 Border terriers are very hardy and the puppies easy to rear as a rule. **1820** SCOTT *Monast.* xxxiv, A *Border-warden, he will be eager to ride in Scotland. **1816** —— *Antiq.* xxxix, There's *Border-warrants too in the south country, unco rash uncanny things.

border ('bɔːdə(r)), *v.* Also 6 boorder, *Sc.* bordor, -dour. See also BORDURE *v.* [f. prec. sb.]

1. *trans.* To put a border or edging to. Also *fig.*

c **1400** MAUNDEV. xxvii. 276 His throne..bordured with Gold. *c* **1400** *Destr. Troy* 1666 A tabill..Bourdurt about all with bright Aumbur. **1530** PALSGR. 460/2, I wyll border my kote with blacke velvet. **1731** SWIFT *Strephon & C.* Wks. 1755 IV. I. 152 His night-cap border'd round with lace. *a* **1813** A. WILSON *Amer. Blue-Bird*, Your walks border up, sow and plant at your leisure.

2. To form a border or boundary to; to bound.

1570 BILLINGSLEY *Euclid* XI. def. xvi. 317 A Pyramis is ternated and bordered with diuers superficieces. **1590** GREENE *Orl. Fur.* (1599) 21 Those trees that border in those walkes. *c* **1750** SHENSTONE *Elegies* xv. 63 Those wholesome sweets that border Virtue's way. **1807** SIR R. WILSON in *Life* (1862) II. viii. 333 The fields are bordered by large forests. **1859** REEVE *Brittany* 293 A low granite wall borders the road.

†**b.** *fig.* To keep within bounds, confine, limit.

1605 SHAKS. *Lear* IV. ii. 33 That nature, which contemns its origin, Cannot be border'd certain in itself.

3. To lie on the borders of, lie next, adjoin.

1649 SELDEN *Laws Eng.* I. xxviii. (1739) 45 The most ancient that bordered the Britons. **1830** LYELL *Princ. Geol.* (1875) II. III. xli. 420 Lands bordering the Mediterranean. **1837** LYTTON *Athens* II. 120 [They] wore the same armour as the Indians whom they bordered. **1853** KANE *Grinnell Exp.* iv. (1856) 29 The great counter-current, which.. borders the Gulf Stream.

4. *intr.* To lie on the border, be contiguous *on*, *upon*, (*with*, *by*, *unto*, obs.).

1535 COVERDALE *Josh.* xv. 8 The mount.. that borderth on the edge of the valley of Raphaim. **1563** *Homilies* II. *Rogation Wk.* IV. Our neighbours bordering about us. **1604** T. WRIGHT *Passions* III. ii. 82 Euery moderat passion bordureth betwixt two extreames. **1605** VERSTEGAN *Dec. Intell.* v. (1628) 152 The Gaules did anciently border all along on the west side of the Germans. **1645** RUTHERFORD *Tryal & Tri. Faith* (1845) 62 It is good to border with Christ, & to be near-hand to him. **1786** W. THOMSON *Watson's Philip III.* (1839) 311 An island bordering upon Istria. **1841** ELPHINSTONE *Hist. Ind.* I. 361 Hill tribes, bordering on cultivated countries.

5. fig. *to border on* or *upon*: to approach closely in character, resemble closely, verge on.

a **1694** TILLOTSON Wks. 1728 I. 33 Wit which borders upon profaneness. **1771** *Junius Lett.* l. 261 A kind of predilection which borders upon loyalty. **1793** BURKE *Rem. Policy Allies* Wks. VII. 122 A degree of indigence at times bordering on beggary. **1839** H. L. ANDERSON *Haileyb. Observer* i. 18 This borders on the common-place.

†**6.** To broider, to braid. (Cf. *broder*, BROIDER, also BORDER *sb.* 6.) *Obs.*

1585 ABP. SANDYS *Serm.* (1841) 310 The hair.. had been coloured, pleated, and bordered.

†**7.** *trans.* To cut up (a pasty). *Obs.*

1513 *Bk. Keruynge* in *Babees Bk.* (1868) 265 Termes of a Kerver, Border that pasty. **1864** AINSWORTH *Tower of Lond.* 412 In the old terms of his art, he.. bordered the venison pasty, tranched the sturgeon.

border, variant of BORDAR, and BOURDER, *Obs.*

‖**bordereau** (bɔrdəro). Pl. -eaux. [Fr., dim. of *bord* (see BOARD *sb.*).] A memorandum, detailed statement, schedule; *spec.* that which Capt. A. Dreyfus was accused of transmitting (cf. DREYFUSARD).

1897 *Daily News* 2 Dec. 7/5 General de Pellieux.. went on to say 'The bordereau is no business of mine... The court martial has ruled that Dreyfus wrote the 'bordereau'.' **1928** D. H. LAWRENCE *Let.* 28 July (1962) II. 1069 Your letter with two *bordereaux*. **1931** *Times Lit. Suppl.* 26 Feb. 143/3 The famous *bordereau* contained gross technical errors and turns of phrase. **1957** *Encycl. Brit.* VII. 661/1 The *bordereau*, wrongly attributed to Dreyfus, was in Esterhazy's hand-writing.

bordered (ˈbɔːdəd), *ppl. a.* [f. BORDER *v.* and *sb.* + -ED[1].] Having a border, edged, fringed, etc.

c **1400** *Destr. Troy* 3039 Hir ene.. Serklyt with heris.. borduret full clene. **1509** HAWES *Past. Pleas.* XXII. ii, A pavilyon.. Of grene sarcenet bordered with golde. **1608** JAS. I. *Let.* in Chambers *Life* (1830) II. vi. 179 A new jerkin well bordered. **1860** DICKENS *Uncomm. Trav.* ii. 11 Papers, all bordered with black. **1870** HOOKER *Stud. Flora* 214 Beak as long as the bordered fruit. **1882** VINES *Sachs' Bot.* 23 One form of internal thickening.. common in wood-cells and vessels, viz. the formation of Bordered Pits.

borderer (ˈbɔːdərə(r)). Also 6 (bortherer), *Sc.* borderar, bourdurer, 7 bordurer, -drer. [f. BORDER *v.* and *sb.* + -ER[1]: with sense cf. *Londoner.*]

1. One who dwells near the border of a country or district; *spec.* one who dwells near the border of England and Scotland.

1494 FABYAN VII. ccxxxvi. 274 A great parte of Northumberlonde, the whiche he hadde wonne from the borderers. **1513** BP. RUTHALL to *Wolsey* in *Nat. MSS.* II. 8 [They] dare not trust the borderers which be falser than Scottes, and have doon mor harme at this tyme to our folkes. **1599** SHAKS. *Hen. V*, I. ii. 142 A Wall sufficient to defend Our in-land from the pilfering Borderers. **1805** SCOTT *Last Minstr.* III. vi, Stern was the dint the Borderer lent. **1839** STONEHOUSE *Axholme* 63 Inhabitants of the Isle, or Borderers, as they are termed in the Inquisition of 1607. **1884** *Manch. Exam.* 10 Dec. 5/1 Before the Bill passed, these borderers belonged to the county and had no votes.

2. One who dwells in a district bordering upon another; one who borders *on* or dwells close *to* or *by* (a region or its inhabitants); a next neighbour. Formerly also said of a country.

1538 LELAND *Itin.* IV. 57 One Inon a Walsch man, Borderer vnto Hym. **1579** FENTON *Guicciard.* Ep. Ded., Al your neighbours and borderers. **1632** J. HAYWARD tr. *Biondi's Eromena* 113 The former [Corsica] being so neere a borderer to the latter [Sardegna], as they almost joyne. **1649** SELDEN *Laws Eng.* I. iv. (1739) 9 Borderers upon the Roman world. **1776** GIBBON *Decl. & F.* I. 224 The borderers of the Rhine and Danube. *c* **1854** STANLEY *Sinai & Pal.* iii. (1858) 164 Nabal.. was a borderer on the wilderness.

b. *fig.*

a **1637** B. JONSON *Discov.* (L.) The poet is the nearest borderer upon the orator. **1748** RICHARDSON *Clarissa* (1811) II. xlvi. 344 Pride and meanness.. are.. close borderers on each other. **1820** HAZLITT *Lect. Dram. Lit.* 31 Borderers on the savage state. **1858** GLADSTONE *Homer* III. 283 We keep the Phæacians.. as borderers between the world of Greek experience, and the world of fable.

3. One who makes borders or bordering. *black-borderer*: one who makes black-edged paper.

1880 *Daily Tel.* 9 Jan. Advt., Black Borderer wanted. **1881** *Glasgow Trades Direct.* 806/1 Black Borderers.

4. = BORDAR.

1771 *Antiq. Sarisb.* 29 A hide and half of land, and the land of one borderer, in the same Town.

bordering (ˈbɔːdərɪŋ), *vbl. sb.* [f. BORDER *v.*]

1. a. The state of being on the border of, or close to, anything. **b.** The action of making a border to; an edging; = BORDER.

1530 PALSGR. 200/1 Bordering of a garment, *brodevre.* **1580** HOLLYBAND *Treas. Fr. Tong, Abordement*, an arriuing or bordering. **1851** RUSKIN *Stones Ven.* I. xxi. §27, The figurings and chasings and borderings of a dress. **1862** M. HOPKINS *Hawaii* 71 A kerb or bordering of stones.

2. *attrib.* and in *comb.*, as **bordering-wax**, a composition used to form a border to keep in the acid employed to bite into a plate for engraving.

1878 SALA in *Gentl. Mag.* May 561 Bordering-wax is softened in warm water until it is thoroughly ductile.

ˈ**bordering**, *ppl. a.* [f. as prec. + -ING[2].]

1. That borders upon; adjoining, neighbouring, on the border; also *fig.*

1530 PALSGR. 306/2 Bordring to the seesyde, *maritain.* **1590** GREENE *Orl. Fur.* (1599) 35 Daughter I am vnto a bordering Swaine, That tend my flockes within these groues. **1631** GOUGE *God's Arrows* I. §70. 117 A plague.. fell upon Bizantium and the bordering places. **1848** MACAULAY *Hist. Eng.* I. 42 The bordering states must imitate the example.

2. That borders, forms a border, or encloses.

1677 HALE *Prim. Orig. Man.* II. iv. 163 The bordering Mountains of China. **1711** GAY *Rural Sports* I. i. 259 The bord'ring reeds O'erlook the muddy stream. **1861** GEO. ELIOT *Silas M.* 12 A man could cross the bordering heights.

3. Of or pertaining to a border district.

1612 DAVIES *Why Ireland* (1747) 41 They made only a bordering war upon the Irish. **1617** MORYSON *Itin.* III. III. iv. 155 Sent from the governor of Berwick about bordering affairs. **1724** RAMSAY *Ever-Green, Johnie Armstrong* note, Taking much Plunder in the bordering Parts.

ˈ**Borderism.** *rare.* [f. BORDER *sb.* + -ISM.] Words or behaviour characteristic of the Border.

1839 LOCKHART *Scott* x. 227 The burst of genuine Borderism.

ˈ**border-ˌland.** (Also as one and as two words.)

1. A land or district on or near the border between two countries or districts; particularly the border district between England and Scotland.

1813 HOGG *Queen's Wake*, Leyden came from Border land. **1849** GROTE *Greece* II. lv, A neutral strip of borderland. **1876** GREEN *Short Hist.* iv. §1 (1882) 158 Offa tore from Wales the border land between the Severn and the Wye.

2. *fig.*

1823 LAMB *Elia* Ser. I. xi. (1865) 88 Between the affirmative and the negative there is no border-land with him. **1863** LONGF. *Wayside Inn* Prel. 132 The twilight that surrounds The border-land of old romance. **1878** BOSW. SMITH *Carthage* 370 That borderland between fact and fiction.

b. *attrib.*, esp. in the senses (*a*) of or pertaining to the 'land' between this world and the next; (*b*) = BORDER-LINE 2.

1894 F. PODMORE *Apparitions & Thought-Transference* xi. 249 The voice in this case awoke the percipient,.. but it was of the 'borderland' type. *Ibid.* 257 The hallucination should be classed as a 'borderland' case. **1896** *Brit. Med. Jrnl.* 25 Jan. 61/1 Mental or Borderland case. **1898** *Daily News* 30 July 5/5 One thing about the deceased deputy may interest 'Borderland' readers. **1904** E. G. YOUNGER *Insanity in Every-Day Pract.* 99 Borderland states.. are cases of nervous weakness which do not quite fit in with any of the recognised forms of insanity. *Ibid.* 101 Dr. Walsh has told me of a borderland case under his care which benefited greatly under his treatment. **1904** *Westm. Gaz.* 1 Dec. 6/3 He regarded the deceased's as a 'borderland' case. **1909** *Times Lit. Suppl.* 14 Jan. 9/1 It is a vague, borderland word.

borderless (ˈbɔːdəlɪs), *a.* [f. BORDER + -LESS.] Without a border.

1611 COTGR., *Interminant*, boundlesse, borderlesse, vncertaine. **1859** GEO. ELIOT *A. Bede* II. 377 Her white borderless cap. **1872** *Fortn. Rev.* Mar. 281 On the pitiless waves of a borderless sea.

border-line. [BORDER *sb.*] **1.** The strip of land along the border between two countries or districts; a frontier-line; often *fig.*, the boundary between areas, classes, etc.

1869 *Cassell's Mag.* Dec. 31/1 On the very border-line of the Black Country. **1889** KIPLING *Barrack-r. Ball.* (1892) 81 Thou must harry thy father's hold for the peace of the Border-line. **1890** W. JAMES *Princ. Psychol.* II. xvii. 22 Simultaneous contrast is always strongest at the border-line of the two fields. **1917** 'CONTACT' *Airman's Outings* 143 Weather conditions place such duties near the border-line of possible accomplishment. **1965** M. SPARK *Mandelbaum Gate* vii. 313 The armed border patrol.. returned along the border-line.

2. *attrib.* or as *adj.* Occupying a border-line; esp. in phr. ***border-line case***; spec. (*a*) verging on the indecent or obscene; (*b*) verging on insanity.

1907 F. J. POYNTON in *Edin. Med. Jrnl.* Sept. 232 There are border-line cases which are well worthy of consideration by those who are interested in this form of arthritis. **1913** R. H. COLE *Mental Dis.* 223 Many come within the range of the so-called 'Border-line' cases. **1917** E. F. BALLARD *Epit. Mental Dis.* 10 Therapeutic suggestive conversation with these early or border-line types of disorder is never wasted. **1928** *Sunday Express* 29 Apr. 3/4 Men are fond of 'thrillers'. Girls prefer rather shocking 'border-line' books. **1928** *Daily Tel.* 11 May 7 [He] described the cases.. as border-line cases, and bound them over under probation for two years. **1937** *Mind* XLVI. 478 This clear central nucleus is surrounded by a penumbra of borderline cases, such as the credibility of witnesses. **1956** J. E. FLOUD *Social Class* iv. 54 To aid the assessment of borderline candidates, a Composition test was administered. **1965** F. G. CASSIDY in Bessinger & Creed *Medieval & Linguistic Stud.* 78 This has left uncertain the status of the 'borderline cases'.

Hence **border-liner**, a border-line case.

1953 E. PARTRIDGE *'Shaggy Dog' Story* ii. 48, I finally reduced the candidates to five that can fairly be adjudged eligible for the description 'border-liners'.

[**bord-halfpenny:** see BURGHALPENNY.]

bordiller, variant of BORDELER, *Obs.*

bordis, variant of BOURDISE, *Obs.*, tilting.

†**bord-land.** *Obs. Feudal Syst.* [Explained in the 13th c. as f. OE. *bord* a table + LAND: but prob. really land held by a BORDAR in *bordage* tenure.]

c **1250** BRACTON iv. 19 (ed. Twiss) Est autem dominicum quod quis habet ad mensam suam et proprie, sicut sunt Bordlandes Anglice. **1610** FOLKINGHAM *Art of Survey* III. v. 73 These Demesnes were called of the Saxons.. Inlandt (and by Bracton.. Bord-lands). **1664** SPELMAN *Gloss.*, Bordlands *terrae dominicales.* [So in BLOUNT; and in later Dicts.]

†**bord-lode.** *Obs. Feudal Syst.* [Explained by Du Cange as f. *bord* BOARD + LODE leading, conveyance: but prob. some service due by the BORDAR.] 'A Service required of the Tenants, to carry Timber out of the Woods of the Lord to his House.' Bailey 1721. (From Du Cange, who cites it from *Chron. Will. Thorn.* anno 1364.)

†ˈ**bordman.** *Obs. Feudal Syst.* [Found in early times, only in the latinized form *bordmannus*, *bordimannus*, as a synonym of *bordārius*, see BORDAR.] A bordar, or tenant in bordage, a cottier.

1087 *Domesday* (in Du Cange) In dominio est una carucata, et xxv villani, et xxxiii bordmanni, cum iv carucatus. —— *Rental of Havering atte Bowre* (Spelm.) Bordimanni, qui omnes tunc fuerunt bassæ tenuræ. [In mod. Dicts. (erroneously explained).]

bordon, -un, obs. f. BURDEN *sb.*; var. of BOURDON.

bordour, bordre, obs. forms of BORDER.

bordrage, var. BODRAGE, *Obs.*, hostile incursion.

†**bordrie.** *Obs.* prob. = F. *broderie*, *broderie de soie* silken embroidery or embroidered work. (It can hardly be = *bawdry*, BALDRIC.)

1696 AUBREY *Misc.* 216 (D.) The meeting of the gentry.. in the fields or forests, with their hawks and hounds, with their bugle-horns, in silken bordries.

bordure (ˈbɔːdjʊə(r)). [The earlier form of BORDER, F. *bordure*, OF. *bordeure.*]

1. *Her.* 'A Bearing that goes all round, and parallel to the boundary of the Escutcheon, in form of a hem, and always contains a fifth part of the Field in breadth.' Porny *Elem. Her.* 1787.

1460 *Lybeaus Disc.* 858 He bar the scheld of goules.. Of gold was the bordure. **1592** WYRLEY *Armorie* 86 Three rundels.. In sable bordure deepely ingreled. **1610** GUILLIM *Heraldry* I. v. (1660) 30 This term *Entoyre* is proper to all bordures charged with dead things. **1763** *Brit. Mag.* IV. 527 Sable, an eagle displayed, ermine, within a bordure, argent. **1864** BOUTELL *Heraldry, Hist. & Pop.* xiv. 163 The bordure of Holland is blazoned without any dimidiation.

2. = BORDER. (An occasional variant.)

1664 EVELYN *Kal. Hort.* (1729) 199 In such Bordures.. plant neither Herbs nor Flowers. **1693** —— *De la Quint. Compl. Gard.* Gloss., *Bordures* or *Borders* is a term likewise used for Herbs commonly planted in Borders. *a* **1695** WOOD *Life* (1848) 295 *note*, I have here printed my epistle with a bordure and picture in it. **1830** TENNYSON *Poems* 85 In the bordure of her robe was writ *Wisdom.*

ˈ**bordured**, *ppl. a. Her.* Having a bordure.

1610 GUILLIM *Heraldry* vi. 255/1 If a coat armour that is bordured bee borne sole of itself, then shall the bordure enuiron the coat round.

ˈ**borduring**, *vbl. sb. Her.* The application of a bordure; bordures collectively.

1610 GUILLIM *Heraldry* I. v. 21 One example more of Borderings.

†**bordyl(le**, var. of BORDEL *Obs.*, brothel.

bore (bɔə(r)), *sb.*[1] Also 6 *Sc.* boir, 7 boar(e. [Partly f. BORE *v.*[1]; but in senses 1–4 it may be partly adoption of, or cogn. w., ON. *bora* wk. fem. 'bore-hole':—OTeut. *borôn- (the corresp. form *bore is not recorded in OE.; the equivalent OHG. *bora*, Du. *boor* fem., agree in meaning

with 5); and in sense 5:—OE. *bor* 'borer, gimlet' = ON. *bor-r*:—OTeut. **boro-z*: see BORE *v.*[1]]

I. That which is bored.

1. a. A hole made by boring, a perforation; an aperture (irrespective of shape), a chink, crevice, or cranny; in later use chiefly an auger hole, or other cylindrical perforation. *Obs.* or *arch.*

c **1320** *Seuyn Sag.* 1156 Water hi can stop That hit ne mai nowt bi bores drop. *a* **1400** *Cov. Myst.* 319 We xal se Yf the borys be for hym meet. **1430** LYDG. *Chron. Troy* II. xx, That cowardise ne entre at no bore. **1523** FITZHERB. *Husb.* §3 A pynne put throughe, set in the plough-beame, in an augurs bore. **1535** STEWART *Cron. Scot.* II. 515 Out throw ane boir quhair he mycht rycht weill see. **1654** TRAPP *Comm. Job* xxxiii. 16 He openeth the ears of men, He maketh the bore bigger. **1718** ARBUTHNOT in *Swift's Lett.* II. 2 He has shortened his stirrups three bores. **1785** BURNS *Jolly Begg.* 52 Frighted rattons..seek the benmost bore.

b. ***blue bore***: an opening in the clouds showing the blue sky. *Sc.* Also *fig.*

1775 BAILLIE *Lett.* I. 171 (JAM.) This style pleased us well. It was the first blue bore that did appear in our cloudy sky. *c* **1817** HOGG *Tales & Sk.* III. 241 All at once a lovely 'blue bore'..opened in the cloud behind.

†**c.** Applied to the wounds of Christ. ***'S bores***, a profane oath = *God's wounds*, ZOUNDS. *Obs.*

1640 BROME *Sparagus Gard.* IV. iii. Wks. 1873 III. 179 No, no, no not I; s'bores I bit my tongue too hard.

d. *Sc.* '***to wick a bore*** in curling and cricket is to drive a stone or ball dexterously through an opening between two guards.' Jamieson s.v. *Wick.*

1786 BURNS *Tam Samson's E.* v, He was the king o' a' the core, To guard, or draw, or wick a bore.

2. a. *spec.* The cylindrical perforation or cavity of a tube, gun, etc. Also attrib., preceded by a defining word, as *smooth-bore*, *taper-bore*, CHOKE-BORE, q.v. (In quot. 1730 used of a semi-cylindrical groove.)

1572 GASCOIGNE *Weedes*, Wks. (1587) 183 The bravest peece for breech and bore that ever yet was bought. **1611** COTGR., *Ame*..the mould that is within the bore of Artillerie when tis cast. **1635** J. BABINGTON *Pyrotechn.* 1, I take for the sayd length six diameters of the bore, which maketh six inches. **1678** N. WANLEY *Wonders* III. xliv. §28. 227/2 Muskets..to shoot Bullets without Powder, or anything else but Wind or Air compressed in the bore of it. **1730** A. GORDON *Maffei's Amphit.* 349 Several small Bores made hollow by the continued Friction of the Ropes. *a* **1793** G. WHITE *Selborne* (1853) 4 Might plant the mortar with wide threat'ning bore. **1808** J. BARLOW *Columb.* v. 628 Marksmen, skill'd to pour Their slugs unerring from the twisted bore. **1871** B. STEWART *Heat* §16 Part of this mercury will be driven up the bore into the bulb.

b. Hence, the interior measurement or diameter of a tube; the calibre of a gun; also *fig.* and *transf.*

1583 PLAT *Divers new Exper.* (1594) 23 Beeing of petronell bore, or a bore higher. **1602** SHAKS. *Ham.* IV. vi. 27 Yet are they much too light for the bore of the Matter. **1635** J. BABINGTON *Pyrotechn.* xxiii. 27 Holes..which shall be halfe an inch asunder, and likewise half an inch boare. **1672** MARVELL *Reh. Transp.* I. 93 Whose eares are of a just bore for his fable. **1796** MORSE *Amer. Geog.* II. 403 Nearly three hundred pieces of cannon of different bores. **1822** IMISON *Sc. & Art* I. 112 The smaller the bore of the pipe is, the easier he will be able to raise himself. **1845** DARWIN *Voy. Nat.* iii. (1873) 60 The measure or bore of the lightning, if such a term may be used. **1881** *Metal World* ix. 139 An article on measuring the bores of cylinders.

3. a. A deep vertical hole of small diameter, bored into the earth to ascertain the nature of the underlying strata, or to obtain water. In Australia used esp. in sense 'water-hole for cattle'.

1674 N. FAIRFAX *Bulk & Selv.* 185 What we do find at our utmost depths or bores..quarries of stone, Mines of metal, or layers and veins of barren earths. **1875** *Encycl. Brit.* I. 646 A bore of 3 inches was carried to a depth of 2086 feet. **1906** J. W. GREGORY *Dead Heart of Australia* IV. 331 Geysers... With regard to the bore at Westland..there were great pulsations in the evolution of firedamp. **1933** *Bulletin* (Sydney) 23 Aug. 35/2 He crawled more than a mile to a bore-drain. **1936** I. L. IDRIESS *Cattle King* xxxviii. 328 The bore-drain carrying the water from the bore-head would meander for many miles. **1936** F. GERALD *Millionaire in Memories* iii. 73 'Good,' I thought. 'I have time to..bathe in the "bore"'—the Government had bored for water at Barcaldine, and..had struck an inexhaustible supply. **1955** J. CLEARY *Justin Bayard* xix. 285 That night they camped by a bore. The cattle took their fill of the mineral-tasting water. **1963** V. B. CRANLEY *27,000 Miles through Australia* x. 62 We ..filled our water reserves at the bores along the way... Lilly Vale Bore... Wild Dog Bore... Tickalara Bore, and others.

b. *transf.* The tubular outlet of a geyser.

1863 BARING-GOULD *Iceland* 196 The first of the great springs has two bores.

4. A piece of iron bored with holes of various sizes to receive the shanks of nails, while the head is brought to shape by the hammer.

1831 J. HOLLAND *Manuf. Metals* I. 195 This bore is a piece of strong iron, ten or twelve inches in length.

II. That which bores.

†**5.** An instrument for boring. *Obs.*

[*a* **800** *Corpus Gloss.* in Wr.-Wülcker *Voc.* 45 *Scalpellum*, bor.] **1677** MOXON *Mech. Exerc.* (1693) 48 The Square-bore is a square Steel Point..fitted into a square Socket in an Iron Wimble.

III. 6. *Comb.* (in sense 3; some of these might be referred to BORE *v.*[1]): **bore-bit**, a chisel used in boring through rocks; **bore-hole**, a more usual synonym of BORE *sb.*[1] 3; **bore-log**, a perforated block of wood through which the bore-rod passes; **bore-meal**, the débris brought up by boring; **bore-rod**, an iron rod used for making bore-holes.

1869 *Spon's Dict. Engineering* I. 499 The *bore-bit is a simple, flat chisel. **1708** J. C. *Compl. Collier* (1845) 13 About 3 Inches Diameter for a *Bore-hole (or Boreing) is sufficient. **1883** *Athenæum* 7 Apr. 447 [They] sank a bore-hole down to the salt at Saltholme, on the north side of the Tees. **1869** *Spon's Dict. Engineering* I. 501 The mouth of the well.. ought to be secured by the *bore-log. *Ibid.* Each day ..a part of the *bore-meal, or the coarsest débris [should be] saved for future examination. **1851** *Coal-tr. Terms Northumbld. & Durh.* 8 To ascertain the nature of strata, by means of *bore-rods.

bore (bɔə(r)), *sb.*[2] [This, and its vb. BORE[2] arose after 1750; etymology unknown.

(Usually supposed to be f. BORE *v.*[2], which is then regarded as a fig. use of BORE *v.*[1], with the notion of 'persistent annoyance' (cf. Ger. *drillen*). But it seems impossible in this way to account for sense 1 of the sb., which is apparently the source of the other senses, and of the verb itself. If related at all to BORE *v.*[1] or *sb.*[1], the connexion must be much more indirect; possibly there is an allusion to some now forgotten anecdote. The phrase 'French bore' naturally suggests that the word is of French origin; *bourre* padding, hence (in 18th c.) triviality, *bourrer* to stuff, to satiate, might be thought of; but without assuming some intermediate link these words do not quite yield the required sense.)]

†**1.** The malady of *ennui*, supposed to be specifically 'French', as 'the spleen' was supposed to be English; a fit of ennui or sulks; a dull time.

1766 EARL OF MARCH *Let.* in Jesse *G. Selwyn* II. 88 [date misprinted 1776] Augustus Hervey and Lord Cadogan are in a long *bore*. —— G. J. WILLIAMS *Let.* 9 Dec. *Ibid.* 108 He sits every night next to Lord Temple, and has a complete *bore* of it for two hours. —— *Let.* 30 Dec. *Ibid.* 121 Your last letter was the most cheerful that I have received from you, and..without that d—d French *bore*. **1767** LD. CARLISLE *Let.* 8 Mar. *Ibid.* 150, I enclose you a packet of letters, which if they are French, the Lord deliver you from the *bore*.

†**b.** One who suffers from 'bore' or ennui, or affects lack of interest in anything.

1766 G. J. WILLIAMS *Let.* 25 Nov. in Jesse *G. Selwyn* II. 86 You are..such a French *bore*, and all against your poor country, that I believe you imagine your letters are opened at the post-office.

2. A thing which bores or causes ennui; an annoyance, a nuisance.

1778 *Refutation* 16 Advice is well enough—reproof's a bore. **1807** *Antid. Miseries Hum. Life* 27 Conversation is a bore, as 'tis generally managed. **1831** WHATELY in *Life* (1866) I. 111 A formal dinner-party even at Oxford is a bore. **1858** HAWTHORNE *Fr. & It. Jrnls.* I. 190 It is as great a bore as to hear a poet read his own verses.

3. A tiresome or uncongenial person; one who wearies or worries. ***blue bore*** (quot. 1837): in punning allusion to the tavern sign of the Blue Boar.

1812 *Edin. Rev.* XX. 74 A king is in these tribes really regarded as a sort of..bore. **1826** DISRAELI *Viv. Grey* V. vi. 192 The true bore is that man who thinks the world is only interested in one subject, because he himself can only comprehend one. **1837** DICKENS *Pickw.* li, 'Ungrammatical twaddler, was it, sir?' 'Yes, sir, it was..and *blue-bore*, sir, if you like that better. **1848** THACKERAY *Van. Fair* xi, He says the country girls are bores; indeed, I don't think he is far wrong. **1858** O. W. HOLMES *Aut. Breakf. T.* i. 3 'Madam, all men are bores, except when we want them.'

bore (bɔə(r)), *sb.*[3] Also 4 bare, 7–9 boar, 8 boer. [In sense 1, app. a. ON. *bára* wave, billow: it is doubtful whether sense 2 is the same word, since no examples even of its local use in early times have been found.]

†**1.** ? Wave, billow. *Obs. rare.*

c **1320** *Sir Tristr.* 356 Hye seyden: ȝond is þe lond, and here schaltow to bare.

2. A tide-wave of extraordinary height, caused either by the meeting of two tides, or by the rushing of the tide up a narrowing estuary. Cf. EAGRE. Also in *comb.*, as † ***bore-loden*** (= *-laden*), swollen by a tidal wave.

1601 WEEVER *Mirr. Mart.* B ivb, No bridge vpon her bore-lod'n bosome bore. **1613** *Voy. Guiana* in *Harl. Misc.* (Malh.) III. 197 A boar, as the seamen term it, and violent encounter of two tides coming in. **1668** *Phil. Trans.* III. 816 All Vessels that lye in the way of the..Boar, are commonly overset. **1738** *Ibid.* XL. 432 He..suspects, that Spouts and Boars may derive their Origin from the same Cause. **1796** BURKE *Regic. Peace* Wks. 1842 II. 383 The victorious tenth wave shall ride, like the bore, over all the rest. **1830** LYELL *Princ. Geol.* I. 292 The Bristol Channel is very subject to the Bore.

bore (bɔə(r)), *v.*[1] Forms: *Inf.* 1 borian, 2 boren, borien, 5 boryn, boore, 6–7 boar(e, 2– bore. *Pa. pple.* 5 boryn, 7 boared, 2– bored. [Com. Teut.: OE. *borian* wk. v. is cogn. w. OHG. *borôn* (MHG. *born*, mod.G. *bohren*), Du. *boren*, ON. *bora*:—OTeut. **borôn* to bore, f. OTeut. **boro-z*, whence OE., ON. *bor* str. masc., an auger, gimlet (see BORE *sb.*[1]); f. Aryan root meaning to cut, pierce, whence Lat. *forāre* to bore, Gr. φάρος a plough, etc. The orig. short *o* is lengthened by position in ME. and mod.E., as in mod.Ger. and Du. (Some of the latter senses are difficult to account for: 6 may really be a different word.)]

1. *trans.* To pierce, perforate, make a hole in or through; in mod. use *esp.* to pierce by means of a rotatory movement like that of an auger or gimlet. Also with adv. *through.*

c **1000** ÆLFRIC *Gloss.* in Wr.-Wülcker *Voc.* 121 *Termes vel teredo*, wyrm þe borað treow. *c* **1150** *Gloss.* ibid. 550 *Terebro*, ic bore. **1398** TREVISA *Barth. De P.R.* XVII. iii. (1495) 605 Yf almonde trees ben boryd wyth naylles gumme cometh out of them. *c* **1435** *Torr. Portugal* 2238 Ffulle of holis it was boryn. **1594** T. B. *La Primaud. Fr. Acad.* II., To Rdr., Who hath..boared the skin through with infinit pores for evacuation. **1664** POWER *Exp. Philos.* I. 59 Curiously can nature weave the Vessels of the Body; nay, and bore them too. **1780** COXE *Russ. Disc.* 334 All the worm-eaten roots are rejected; the remainder are bored through. **1814** SCOTT *Ld. of Isles* VI. xxiv, The Bruce's care Had bored the ground with many a pit. *Mod.* The wood is apt to split; bore it first for the nails.

†**b.** To pierce, stab, run through with a weapon; to wound. *Obs.*

a **1400** *Leg. Rood* (1871) 201 His breest is bored with deepis armes. **1685** F. SPENCE *Ho. Medici* 133 He first boar'd Giuliano de Medici with a poigniard.

†**c.** Phr. ***to bore (any one's) ears*** (in allusion to Exod. xxi. 6): to consign to perpetual slavery. *Obs.*

[**1535** COVERDALE *Ex.* xxi. 6 Let his master bore [WYCLIF **1382** thrail, **1388** perse] him thorow the eare with a botkin.] **1641** MILTON *Church Govt.* II. (1851) 176 By their corrupt and servile doctrines boring our eares to an everlasting slavery. **1692** SOUTH *12 Serm.* (1697) I. 13 Can any man, that would be faithful to his Reason, yield his Ear to be bored through by his domineering appetites.

¶ Applied in sense 'to insist upon a hearing', 'to force one to listen'; possibly with reference to Psalm xl. 6 in the Heb.; cf. BORE *v.*[2]

a **1617** P. BAYNE *Ephes.* 140 (1658) God by afflictions is said to boar the ear. **1622** H. SYDENHAM *Serm. Sol. Occ.* I. (1637) 76 This is enough for an understanding eare without farther boring it. **1642** SIR E. DERING *Sp. on Relig.* 95 One of them who jog our elbowes, and boar our..ears with *Babylon.*

†**d.** *transf.* To penetrate, make one's way through (a crowd); *fig.* to gain entrance into (the mind).

1622 H. SYDENHAM *Serm. Sol. Occ.* II. (1637) 115 Riddles of eternal generation which can never bore a human intellect. *a* **1732** GAY (J.) Consider what bustling crouds I bor'd.

e. ***to bore out***, to put or force out (*e.g.* the eyes) by boring. *Obs.* or *dial.*

c **1400** *Test. Love* I, Every teare of mine eyen for greatnesse semed they boren out the ball of my sight. **1660** FULLER *Mixt. Contemp.* (1841) 239 Petrus de Vineis..whose eyes he had caused to be bored out for some misdemeanour. **1712** STEELE *Spect.* No. 324 ¶1 Tipping the Lion..is performed by..boring out the Eyes with their Fingers.

2. *trans.* To pierce with a cylindrical aperture or cavity; to hollow out evenly (a cylinder, gun, etc.)

1753 CHAMBERS *Cycl. Supp.* s.v. *Boring*, The method of boring alder poles for water-pipes. **1875** URE *Dict. Arts* II. 381 After the barrel is bored, and rendered truly cylindrical.

3. *absol.* and *intr.* To make a hole (mod. use limited as in 1). Often with *through*, *into*, *under*, or other prep. In *Mining*, to sink a bore-hole (see BORE *sb.*[1] 3 and 6), as ***to bore for coal, for water.***

a **1225** *Leg. Kath.* 1924 Swa þat te pikes and te irnene preones se scharpe and se starke borien þurh. *c* **1430** *Hymns Virg.* (1867) 52 A spere þoruȝ myn herte gan boore. **1535** COVERDALE *Judith* vi. 26 Cut of his heade and pearsed and bored thorow his temples. **1593** SHAKS. *Rich. II*, III. ii. 170 And with a little Pinne Bores through his Castle Walls. **1853** KANE *Grinnell Exp.* x. (1856) 72 By cutting and boring [we] succeeded in penetrating it [the ice]. **1864** TENNYSON *Aylmer's F.* 850 The hedgehog underneath the plantain bores. **1875** URE *Dict. Arts* I. 445 The Chinese method of boring with ropes instead of rigid rods.

fig. **1607** SHAKS. *Timon* IV. iii. 116 Those Milke pappes That through the window Barne [*edd.* bars] bore at mens eyes.

†**b.** To obtain entrance by boring. *Obs.*

1375 *Leg. Rood* (1871) 139 Men miȝte better ha crepet ..þen bored into heuene blis.

c. To advance, push forward, by gradual persistent motion like that of a boring tool; *fig.* to persevere by slow and laborious means to the attainment of a distant object.

1697 DRYDEN *Virg. Georg.* III. 438 They take their Flight ..boring to the West. **1867** F. FRANCIS *Angling* iii. (1880) 77 The bream has a disagreeable knack of boring head down. **1874** HELPS *Soc. Press.* ii. 23 The 'great measure' man has one or two objects respecting which he bores on throughout the greater part of his life.

d. *trans.* and *intr.* Of a horse: To thrust the head straight forward.

1731 BAILEY II, [With Horsemen] a horse is said to boar or bore, when he shoots out his nose as high as he can. **1802** C. JAMES *Mil. Dict.* (1816) 54/2. **1824** SCOTT *Redgauntlet* let. vii, The bit secured between his teeth, and his head bored down betwixt his fore-legs.

4. *trans.* To produce or make (a hole, passage, tunnel) by boring (mod. use as 1, 3). ***to bore one's way***: to advance by a boring motion.

1523 FITZHERB. *Husb.* §24 Than maye he..bore the holes with his wymble. **1535** COVERDALE *2 Kings* xii. 9 Then Ioiada the prest toke a chest, and bored an hole aboue therin. **1635** J. BABINGTON *Pyrotechn.* xxiii. 27 Then boare your holes thorow your inch board. *a* **1705** RAY (J.) These

diminutive caterpillars are able..to pierce or bore their way into a tree. **1833** HT. MARTINEAU *Manch. Strike* x. 110 Boring a hole between two flints in a yard with a rusty pair of scissors. **1853** PHILLIPS *Rivers Yorksh.* ii. 33 The passage is like a tunnel; it is in fact bored out by the water.

5. To push or thrust as by boring; now esp. in Racing language, to push out of the course.

1677 *Lover's Quarr.* 317 in Hazl. *E.P.P.* II. 266 He bor'd him out of the Saddle fair. **1884** *L'pool Mercury* 5 Mar. 5/1 In the world of racing 'to bore' is to push an opponent out of his course.

†**6.** To mock, trick, cheat, gull; ? = BOURD *v.*[1] 2.

1602 *Life T. Cromwell* II. ii. 103 One that hath gulled you, that hath bored you Sir. **1613** SHAKS. *Hen. VIII*, I. i. 128 At this instant He bores me with some tricke. **1622** FLETCHER *Span. Curate* IV. v. 43, I am laughed at, scorn'd, Baffel'd and boared, it seems.

bore (bɔə(r)), *v.*[2] [App. f. BORE *sb.*[2]]

trans. To weary by tedious conversation or simply by the failure to be interesting.

1768 EARL CARLISLE *Let.* 16 Apr. in Jesse *G. Selwyn* I. 291, I pity my Newmarket friends, who are to be *bored* by these Frenchmen. *Ibid.* 293, I have seen as yet nothing of Florence, therefore shall not *bore* you. **1774** *Private Lett. 1st Ld. Malmesbury* I. 278, I have bored you sadly with this catastrophe. **1821** BYRON in Moore's *Life* xli. 476 Hobhouse and others bored me with their learned localities. **1853** DE QUINCEY *Sp. Mil. Nun* Wks. III. 15 A man..has no unlimited privilege of boring one. **1883** *Fortn. Rev.* Feb. 186 Whereas he had expected to be dreadfully bored, he had on the contrary been greatly instructed.

bore, pa. t. and obs. pa. pple. of BEAR *v.*[1]; obs. f. BOAR, BOOR; var. BOR *dial.*, neighbour.

Boread, Boreiad ('bɔəri:æd, bɒ'ri:æd), *sb.* and *a.* [as sb. ad. Gr. Βορεάδης, Βορηιάδης, patronymic f. βορέας BOREAS; as adj. perh. suggested by Gr. βορεάς, -άδος, fem. adj., of the north wind.]

A. *sb.* A son of Boreas. **B.** *adj.* Relating to northern regions.

1854 KEIGHTLEY *Mythol. Anc. Greece & It.* (ed. 3) 418 The Boreiads there turned back. **1882** C. ELTON *Orig. Eng. Hist.* 5 Later poets..incorporated the Boread legends with travellers' descriptions..of a solar worship.

boreal ('bɔərɪəl), *a.* Also 5 boriall, 6 boryall, 7 boreall. [ad. L. *Boreālis*; see BOREAS, and -AL[1].]

1. Of or pertaining to the north; situated on the northern side; of a northern character. ***boreal signs***: the six signs of the Zodiac from *Aries* to *Virgo*. ***boreal dawn*** (rare): the *aurora borealis*. Now chiefly in *Zool.* and *Bot.*

1470 HARDING *Chron.* ccxl. *note*, Foure flodes..Ebbynge & flowynge in the see boriall. **1536** *Exhort. Northe* in Furnivall's *Ballads fr. MSS.* I. 305 The boryalle Region. **1695** WESTMACOTT *Script. Herb.* 42 Fitz Stephens describing London, tells us of a large Forrest of [Chestnut] Trees on the Boreal part of it. **1805** W. TAYLOR in *Ann. Rev.* III. 211 His pretended reforms, like the boreal dawn, glittered at a distance. **1845** POE *Ulalume*, The boreal pole. **1846** MCCULLOCH *Acc. Brit. Empire* (1854) I. 99 [Plants] all eminently alpine or boreal. **1874** COUES *Birds of N.-W.* 316 The Acadian Owl is not so boreal a bird as its congener.

2. Of or pertaining to the north wind.

1656 BLOUNT *Glossogr.*, *Boreal*, pertaining to the North-Wind. **1672** R. WILD *Declar. Lib. Consc.* 7 Such a boreal month as this March. **1720** POPE *Iliad* XXIII. 241 To gentle Zephyr and the Boreal blast. **1830** in *Blackw. Mag.* XXVIII. 941 The boreal storms are o'er.

3. Belonging to the 'boreal province' of the Mollusca.

1854 WOODWARD *Mollusca* III. (1856) 358 The boreal shells of America are described by Dr. Gould. **1873** GEIKIE *Gt. Ice Age* xv. 196 Perfect specimens of boreal and arctic shells.

4. Applied by Blytt to the next period of vegetation in Scandinavia after the arctic period, and later by others to the climate of other areas.

1876 [see ARCTIC *a.* 3]. **1939** V. G. CHILDE *Dawn Europ. Civ.* (ed. 3) i. 2 A continental Boreal phase, characterized by summers longer and warmer than to-day, but severe snowy winters. **1946** L. D. STAMP *Britain's Struct. & Scenery* xiv. 157 The abrupt change from a cold or 'Boreal' climate to the milder, damper 'Atlantic' climate. **1963** *Field Archaeol.* (Ordnance Survey) (ed. 4) 23 The application of the techniques of pollen analysis and Carbon 14 investigations have shown conclusively that the site belongs to the Boreal climatic phase which succeeded the last Ice Age, and that it may be dated with some confidence to 8,000–7,500 B.C.

boreal, obs. form of BERYL.

bore'alis. Short for AURORA BOREALIS.

1790 BURNS *Tam O'Shanter*, Or like the borealis race, That flit ere you can point their place.

'borealize, *v.* *nonce-wd.* [f. BOREAL + -IZE.] *intr.* To adopt northern manners or pronunciation.

1864 LOWELL *Biglow P.* in Poet. Wks. (1879) 235/2 Spenser..borealized in his pastorals.

borean ('bɔərɪən), *a.* [f. BORE-AS + -AN.] Pertaining to the north wind; northern.

1645 QUARLES *Sol. Recant.* i. 6 It blusters at the Borean Gates. **1866** J. ROSE *Virg. Georg.* 58 The borean blast.

Boreas ('bɔərɪæs). Also 4 Borias. [a. L. *Boreas*, a. Gr. βορέας north wind.] The north-wind; the god of the north-wind. Now only in *Mythol.* and in poet. or humorous personification.

1398 TREVISA *Barth. De P.R.* XI. iii. (1495) 388 Borias the Northern wynde arysyth. *c* **1450** HENRYSON *Dog, Wolf & Sh.*, Boreas, with blastis bitterly. **1579** SPENSER *Sheph. Cal.* Feb. 226 The blustring Boreas did encroche. **1635** QUARLES *Embl.* I. ii. (1718) 10 Blust'ring Boreas blows the boiling Tide. **1718** POPE *Iliad* II. 1025 Boreas beats the hoarse-resounding shores. **1863** MARY HOWITT *F. Bremer's Greece* II. xvii. 193 Boreas had decided otherwise, and blew up against us a terrible north wind.

boreau, var. of BOURREAU, *Obs. Sc.*, hangman.

borecole ('bɔəkəʊl). Also 8 boorcole. [prob. ad. the Du. name *boerenkool* lit. 'peasant's cabbage'.] A loose or open-headed variety of the cabbage, cultivated under the name of Kale.

1712 ARBUTHNOT *Hist. John Bull* (1755) 24 His children.. live upon salt herring, sowre crud, and borecole. **1813** C. MARSHALL *Garden.* xv. (ed. 5) 222 Borecole or cale is a hardy green. **1850** *Gard. Chron.* 276 Borecole also called Kail.

bored (bɔəd), *ppl. a.*[1] Also 7 boared. [f. BORE *v.*[1] + -ED.] Pierced, perforated; cylindrically hollow. Said of a gun, with modifying words prefixed, as ***chamber-, taper-bored.***

1513 DOUGLAS *Æneis* IV. Prol. 154 Halding opinioun der of a borit bane. **1578** *Chr. Prayers* in *Priv. Prayers* (1851) 506 Thou stretchest out thy bored hands. **1607** TOPSELL *Four-f. Beasts* 473 They also had a care to cover all the floor with..dry boared boards. **1692** in *Smith's Seaman's Gram.* II. ii. 91 He ought..to know whether truly bored, or taper bored. **1720** POPE *Iliad* VII. 305 From their bored shields the chiefs their javelins drew. **1808** J. BARLOW *Columb.* III. 415 From his bored ears contorted serpents hung.

bored (bɔəd), *ppl. a.*[2] [f. BORE *v.*[2] + -ED.] Wearied, suffering from ennui.

1823 BYRON *Juan* XIII. xcv, Society is now one polished horde, Formed of two mighty tribes, the Bores and Bored. **1861** SALA *Tw. round Clock* 99 He seems the most bored, the most indifferent spectator there.

boredom ('bɔədəm). [f. BORE *sb.*[2] + -DOM.]

1. = BOREISM.

1864 *Realm* 10 Feb. 1 The complete art of boredom. **1879** GEO. ELIOT *Theo. Such* xv. 273 The male could assert his superiority and show a more vigorous boredom.

2. The state of being bored; tedium, ennui.

1852 DICKENS *Bleak Ho.* II. xxviii. 253 [His] chronic malady of boredom. **1876** GEO. ELIOT *Dan. Der.* II. xxx. 264 A man whose grace of bearing has long been moulded on an experience of boredom.

3. The class of bores as a whole.

1883 *Gd. Wds.* 115 Boredom rejoiced—gossip clapped her hands.

†**'boree**[1]. *Obs.* Also bory. [ad. F. *bourrée* 'a rustic dance belonging originally to Auvergne' (Littré).] A kind of dance, a bourrée.

1676 ETHERIDGE *Man of Mode* IV. i. (1684) 55, I am fit for Nothing but low dancing now, a Corant, a Boreè, Or a Minnuét. *c* **1730** SWIFT *Tom & Dick* Wks. 1755 IV. I. 261 Dick could neatly dance a jig, But Tom was best at borees.

boree[2] (bɔə'ri:). [f. BORE *v.*[2] + -EE[1] 2.] A person who is bored.

1841 J. S. MILL *Let.* 1 Mar. in *Wks.* (1963) XIII. 466 Instead of being the *boree* on the subject of an unfinished article I have a strong vocation for being the *borer* in respect of it. **1872** BUTLER *Erewhon* ix. 79 They would be consigned to the Hospital for Incurable Bores, and made to work at being bored..; in fact..they would be kept as professional borees.

boree[3] ('bɔəri:). [Aboriginal *booreah* fire.] A variety of myall, *Acacia pendula*, found in Eastern Australia.

1878 'R. BOLDREWOOD' *Ups & Downs* iii. 29 Myall and boree belts of timber. **1889** J. H. MAIDEN *Usef. Native Plants* 363 'Weeping', or 'True myall'... Called 'Boree' by aboriginals, and often 'Boree', or 'Silver-leaf Boree', by the colonists of Western New South Wales. **1934** *Bulletin* (Sydney) 7 Nov. 24/1 Gidya and boree are good in most places [as fence posts].

boreen (bɔ:'ri:n). *Anglo-Irish.* Also bohreen, bohereen, bohir-. [f. Irish *bóthar* (pronounced bo:hər), a road + *-een*, diminutive suffix, a. Ir. *-ín*.] A lane, a narrow road; also *transf.* an opening in a crowd. (Used only when Irish subjects are referred to.)

1841 S. C. HALL *Ireland* I. 77 At my brother's, a piece down that boreen. *Ibid.* 287 Wheresomever he went, the people made a bohreen for him. **1882** R. DOWNEY *Congreve's Doom* in *Tinsley's Mag.*, At length we reached a narrow boreen, down which we drove. **1899** SOMERVILLE & 'Ross' *Irish R.M.* 138, I thought you were a dead man when you faced him at the bohereen. **1920** *Cornh. Mag.* Oct. 494 A campaign among bogs and bohireens. **1921** *Blackw. Mag.* Jan. 11/1 The grass-grown bohereen leading over the crest of the hill. **1953** N. FITZGERALD *Midsummer Malice* xv. 189 The quarter of a mile of bohereen that connected the stables to the main road.

boreism ('bɔərɪz(ə)m). Also borism. [f. BORE *sb.*[2] + -ISM.] The characteristic behaviour of bores; the practice of being a bore.

1833 M. SCOTT *Tom Cringle* xvi. (1859) 401 Borism is fast attaining a head it never reached before. **1839** H. ANDERSON *Haileybury Observ.* i. 20 An intolerable mixture of impertinence and boreism.

†**'borel.** *Sc. Obs.* Also 5- boral(e, 6–7 borrel. [f. BORE *v.*[1] + -EL, as in *shovel.*] A boring tool, a wimble, an auger. Also *attrib.*

1488 *Acta Dom. Concilii* 106 (JAM.) A womyll, a borale price xid. **1549** *Compl. Scot.* 11 Ane knyf, ande ane borrel. **1611** *Rates* (JAM.) Borrels for wrights, the groce iiil. *a* **1801** HOGG *Hunt of Eildon* 321 (JAM.) Ane round and boral hole.

borel, var. of BORREL, BUREL, *Obs.*

borelaps, obs. form of BURLAPS.

borelich, borely, obs. ff. BURLY.

†**bo'remes.** Corrupted form of BOUTS-RIMÉS.

1687 MRS. BEHN *Emperor of M.* I. iii. Wks. 289 I'll make some Boremes on Love. *Ibid.* 290 Who writ these Boremes?

borer ('bɔərə(r)). Also (only in sense 2) 6 boryer, 7 borier, borrier. [f. BORE *v.*[1] + -ER[1]; the forms in *-ier*, *-yer*, may be influenced by Fr. words in *-ière*, as *tarière* borer.]

1. One who bores or pierces.

1483 *Cath. Angl.* 37 A Borer; *forator.* **1839** CARLYLE *Chartism* iv. 138 The millions are, and must be skilless, ploughers, delvers, borers. **1879** in *Cassell's Techn. Educ.* II. 10 To enable the borer to make a complete section of the strata.

b. A horse that 'bores'.

1872 LEVER *Ld. Kilgobbin* vi. 41 The best bit for a 'borer'.

c. A name given to the Myxine or Hag-fish; also to the *Teredo* or shipworm; and to various insects which bore through wood, etc.

1789 *Phil. Trans.* LXXIX. 68, I should conceive it a preservative against the Borer, so destructive to ships in this part of the world. **1841** ORDERSON *Creol.* ii. 9 The borer, a grub peculiar to the sugar cane, made such..ravage. **1879** ATCHERLY *Boërland* 238 The depredations caused by an insect called the borer. **1884** *Longm. Mag.* Mar. 525 The Hagfish or Borer..penetrating the captured cod or ling.. devours the soft parts.

2. An instrument for boring: **a.** the tool employed for boring through rocks; **b.** the apparatus attached to the tail of boring-insects.

1572 J. JONES *Bathes Buckstone* 2 a, Boryers, such as mynerall men use in searching ore. **1623** WHITBOURNE *Newfoundland* 75 Taps, Boriers, and Funnels. **1633** T. STAFFORD *Pac. Hib.* vii. (1821) 556 With all the yron borriers, seven peeces in all. **1797** *Phil. Trans.* LXXXVII. 326 At the time the borer burst through. **1802** PALEY *Nat. Theol.* (1817) 155 The awl or borer fixed at the tails of various species of flies. **1883** *Pall Mall G.* 6 Sept. 8/2 The borer having come in contact with a dynamite cartridge previously unexploded.

boresome ('bɔəsəm), *a.* [f. BORE *sb.*[2] + -SOME.] Tending to be a bore, boring. So **'boresomeness.**

1868 LD. R. GOWER *Rec. & Remin.* (1903) 150 So little real enjoyment to make up for so much loss of time and boresomeness. **1895** *Nineteenth Cent.* Sept. 474, I spent a boresome fortnight at Aden. **1905** E. GLYN *Viciss. Evangeline* 152 They were all casual and indifferent to their poor wives! and boresome, and bored!! **1925** P. A. SCHOLES *Second Bk. Gramophone Rec.* p. xii, There is..a degree of boresomeness in some of Beethoven's compositions.

boreson, obs. form of BAUSON, badger.

boresprit, obs. form of BOWSPRIT.

borestaff, obs. f. *boarstaff*: see BOAR 2.

borethyl: see BOR-.

boretree, variant form of BOURTREE.

borewe, obs. form of BORROW.

‖**borg** (bɔrg, bɔ:g). [ON. and Da. *borg*, the equivalent form to OE. *burȝ*, BOROUGH, q.v.] Used by Kingsley in the specific sense of: One of the 'Danish boroughs' in England.

1866 KINGSLEY *Herew.* (1875) Prel. 11 Round by Leicester and the five borgs of the Danes.

borg, borghe, borh, var. BORROW *sb. Obs.*

borgeis, -es, -eys, obs. forms of BURGESS.

borgeon, -goune, obs. forms of BURGEON.

borȝen, pa. pple. of BERGH *v. Obs.* to shelter.

borhs-ealdor, variant of BORSHOLDER.

boric ('bɔərɪk), *a. Chem.* [f. BOR-ON + -IC.] Of or pertaining to boron; containing boron in chemical combination, as ***boric chloride*** (BCl_3), ***boric oxide*** (B_2O_3); ***boric acid***, formerly called, because prepared from borax, ***boracic acid*** (H_3BO_3).

1869 ROSCOE *Elem. Chem.* 152 Boracic or Boric Acid. **1873** WATTS *Fownes' Chem.* 216 The vapour of boric chloride.

boride ('bɔəraɪd). [f. BOR-ON + -IDE.] A primary compound of boron with a metallic element.

1863 WATTS *Dict. Chem.* I. 169 Heated on platinum-foil before the blowpipe, it forms a fusible boride of platinum.

borier, obs. form of BORER.

borillia, obs. variant of BARILLA.

1685 BOYLE *Motion* ii. 11 Borillia or some other fixed salt.

boring ('bɔərɪŋ), *vbl. sb.*[1] [f. BORE *v.*[1] + -ING[1].] **1.** The action of piercing, perforating, making a bore-hole, etc.; also *concr.* = BORE-HOLE.

c **1440** *Promp. Parv.* 44 Borynge, or percynge, *perforacio, cavatura.* **1544** *MS. Acc. St. John's Hosp., Canterb.*, Payd for boryng of a ladder ij*d.* **1626** BACON *Sylva* §352 The Boring of holes in that kinde of wood. **1708** J. C. *Compl. Collier* (1845) 13 Do you not use Boreing sometimes in Sinking? **1860** TYNDALL *Glac.* II. §19. 328 Count Rumford boiled water by the heat developed in the boring of a cannon. **1861** W. FAIRBAIRN *Addr. Brit. Assoc.*, In various mines, borings, and Artesian wells.

2. *attrib.* and *Comb.*, as ***boring-apparatus, -bench, -block, -machinery, -mill, -room, -tool***; also **boring-bar**, the suspended bar which carries the bit for boring cannon; **boring-bit** = *bore-bit* (see BORE *sb.*[1]); **boring-gauge**, an appliance for limiting the action of the boring tool to the required depth; **boring-rod** = *bore-rod* (see BORE *sb.*[1])

1667 PRIMATT *City & C. Build.* 26 You find by your Boring-rods that you have a good seam of Coles. **1833** J. HOLLAND *Manuf. Metals* II. 102 The boring-bench is composed of two stout beams of timber. *Ibid.* The [gun-] barrel is in the next place transferred to the boring-mill. **1845** STOCQUELER *Handbk. Brit. India* (1854) 174 The instrument-room, in which are arranged the various boring-bars, bits, and knives. **1860** TYNDALL *Glac.* II. §9. 271 M. Agassiz had iron boring-rods carried up the glacier, with which he pierced the ice. **1884** MARVIN *Region Etern. Fire* xii. 196 The pump draws the oil as freely . . as when the basin was first tapped by the boring bit.

boring ('bɔərɪŋ), *vbl. sb.*[2] [f. BORE *v.*[2] + -ING[1].] The practice of annoying and wearying others; behaving as a bore.

1868 HELPS *Realmah* iii. (1876) 40 Boring has become a fine art. **1880** GRANT WHITE *Every-Day Eng.* 304 It [interviewing] . . makes boring a paid profession.

† **'boring**, *vbl. sb.*[3] *Obs. rare*$^{-1}$. [f. BOREE[1], F. *bourrée*, as 'chasing' from *chassée*.] A certain step in dancing.

1775 SHERIDAN *Rivals* III. iv. (1883) 113, I must rub up my balancing, and chasing, and boring.

boring ('bɔərɪŋ), *ppl. a.*[1] [f. BORE *v.*[1] + -ING[2].] **1.** That bores or perforates; *esp.* applied to certain insects and molluscs. **boring sponge**, a saltwater sponge of the genus *Cliona*, which bores shells.

1853 DE LA BECHE *Geol. Observ.* xxvi. 485 There were bare patches of carboniferous limestone in the sea, and into these the boring animals of the time burrowed. **1878** HUXLEY *Physiogr.* 208 The perforations in the column of the temple are the work of boring shell-fish. **1881** R. HUNTER et al. *Encycl. Dict.* **1885** *Encycl. Brit.* XVIII. 107/2 *Cliona*, the boring sponge, destroys the shells and so injures the oyster.

2. Of a horse: That thrusts his head forward.

1875 'STONEHENGE' *Brit. Sports* II. III. i. §3. 523 In every way, therefore, it acts well with a boring horse.

boring ('bɔərɪŋ), *ppl. a.*[2] [f. BORE *v.*[2] + -ING[2].] That annoys, wearies, or causes ennui. Hence **'boringly** *adv.*

1840 T. HOOK *Fitzherbert* III. iv. 66 Emily was patiently enduring . . Miss Matthews's boring vanities. *a* **1845** HOOD *Incend. Song* xiii, Burn all bores and boring topics. **1840** T. HOOK in *New Month. Mag.* LX. 429 Frank's attempts to moralize, not tediously, boringly or cantingly.

'boringness. [f. BORING *ppl. a.*[2] + -NESS.] The quality of being boring or annoying.

1893 *Sketch* 316/2 His boringness is a quality inherent in him... Boringness springs, surely, in some measure from want of tact. **1971** *Daily Tel.* 29 Apr. 6/6 The brutishness and boringness of . . Eskimo village life.

borioun, obs. form of BURGEON, bud.

borish ('bɔərɪʃ), *a.* [f. BORE *sb.*[2] + -ISH.] Tedious, wearisome.

1766 H. ST. JOHN *Let.* 9 Dec. in Jesse *G. Selwyn* II. 101 It would be vastly too *borish* in a letter. **1767** J. CRAWFORD *Let.* March, *Ibid.* 153 He suffered so little during the operation of trepanning that . . he felt it quite *borish.* **1864** *Soc. Sc. Rev.* 100 When Music and other gentle arts which once cheered him become borish.

borish, obs. form of BOARISH, and BOORISH.

borism, variant of BOREISM.

‖ **'borith.** [a. late L. *borith*, a. Heb. *bōrīth*, rendered in A.V. 'sope'; earlier versions followed the Vulgate in retaining the Heb. word.] A plant yielding an alkali used for cleansing (? *Saponaria officinalis*).

1382 WYCLIF *Jerem.* ii. 22 If thou wasshez thee with clensing cley, and multeplie to thee the clensende erbe boreth [**1388** borith, **1535** COVERDALE herbe of Borith]. **1468** *Medulla Gramm.*, Boryth, Ffullere gres. **1552** ABP. HAMILTON *Catech.* (1884) 23 The herbe callit Borith quhilk hais greit vertue of clenging. **1678** BP. GLOUCESTER *Expos. Catech.* 171 It is no water-work, no, not if you put to it Nitre, much sope, Fullers-earth, or Borith. **1730** in BAILEY.

borize ('bɔəraɪz), *v.* [f. BOR-AX + -IZE.] To infuse a preparation of borax into the veins of an animal intended for food. Hence **'borized** *ppl. a.*

1884 W. M. WILLIAMS *Borized Meats* in *Gentl. Mag.*, The borized haunch remained perfectly untainted . . The circulation of the borized blood might be continued.

borler, var. of BURELLER, *Obs.*, clothworker.

borley ('bɔːlɪ). *dial.* A boat used by trawlers about the estuary of the Thames.

1864 *Daily Tel.* 18 May, The trawlers, sailing in boats known as 'Borleys'.

borlich, obs. form of BURLY.

bormethyl: see BOR-.

born (bɔːn), *pple.* and *a.* Forms under BEAR *v.* [In modern use the connexion with *bear* is no longer felt; the phrase *to be born* has become virtually an intr. verb. See BEAR *v.* 43, 44.]

A. Senses of *to be born.*

1. To be brought forth as offspring, to come into the world. (See BEAR *v.* 44.)

2. *fig.* **a.** Of things: To come into existence (chiefly *poet.* and rhetorical). **b.** in *Theol.* of persons, *to be born of God*: to become a child of God; *to be born again*: to undergo the new birth, become or be regenerate.

1382 WYCLIF *John* iii. 3 But a man schal be born aȝen [**1388** borun aȝen, TINDALE boren a newe, **1611** borne againe]. —— *1 John* iv. 7 Each man that loueth his brother, is born [**1388** borun, TINDALE and **1611** borne] of God. **1593** HOOKER *Eccl. Pol.* Pref. i. §1 All that would but seem to be born of Him. **1857** HEAVYSEGE *Saul* (1869) 127 Lo, the breaking light is born! **1859** TENNYSON *Vivien* 381 Some sudden turn of anger born Of your misfaith.

3. With sbs. or adjs., or complementary phrases, as *to be born a poet, an Englishman*; *to be born blind, lucky, rich*, etc., i.e. to be so by the conditions of one's birth, by capacities implanted at birth, or the like; ***to be born under a lucky star, with a silver spoon in one's mouth***, proverbial phrases denoting a fortunate destiny, or inherited wealth. *to be born to* (an inheritance, certain relationships, etc.): to inherit by right of birth; to be destined to from birth. Similarly with infin., as *to be born to suffer, to be hanged*, etc. Also *born and bred*: see BREED *v.* 11; *born in the purple*: see PURPLE *sb.* 2 d; *born yesterday*: see YESTERDAY *adv.* 2.

a **1000** *Boeth. Metres* xxvi. 46 Gif he to þæm rice wæs on rihte boren. **1382** WYCLIF *Matt.* ii. 1 Wher is he, that is borun kyng of Jewis. **1610** SHAKS. *Temp.* I. i. 35 If he be not born to be hanged our case is miserable. **1697** DRYDEN *Virg. Georg.* IV. 463 Born to bitter Fate. **1750** JOHNSON *Rambl.* No. 148 ¶9 Those who were born to his protection.

4. Of qualities, tastes, aptitudes, *to be born in, with* (a person): to be implanted at birth.

1710 NICHOLLS *Comm. Common Prayer* Rrr b, There is a sort of Original Corruption in our Nature . . born with us into the World.

B. Attrib. uses of the pa. pple.

1. Said of persons:

a. generally = that (ever) was born, as 'Can any born man deny it?' *born man* (*obs.*), a native.

c **1550** *Virgilius* in Thoms *E.E. Rom.* 22 She was the greatest borne woman that was than there aboute. **1582-8** *Hist. James VI* (1804) 147 This Bell was a borne man in Stirline. **1667** MILTON *P.L.* IV. 324 Goodliest man of men since born.

b. That has been born of such a quality or condition, as *a born orator, a born Englishman*; very common in *born fool*, and the like. Often following the sb., as *a poet born.*

c **1330** *Arth. & Merl.* 7790 Ywain bastard y-bore. *c* **1386** CHAUCER *Merch. T.* 1790 Thyn owene squier and thy born man. **1551-6** ROBINSON tr. *More's Utop.* 131 Borne aduersaries and enemies one to an other. **1582** N. T. (Rhem.) *Mark* vii. 26 The woman was a Gentile, a Syrophœnician borne. **1742** RICHARDSON *Pamela* III. 89, I, a poor helpless Girl . . shall put on Lady-airs to a Gentlewoman born. **1861** *Sat. Rev.* XII. 38/1 Lord John and Mr. Walpole both have their weaknesses; but neither of them is a born fool. **1863** KINGSLEY *Water Bab.* vi, She was a lady born. **1878** MORLEY *Diderot* I. 286 The resource of the born journalist.

c. Qualifying another adj., as in *born free* (obs. in attrib. use, cf. FREEBORN), *born-blind.*

1393 GOWER *Conf.* I. 68 Of thilke bore free kinde. **1517** TORKINGTON *Pilgr.* (1884) 52 Our savyor gaff sight to the born blynde man. **1878** MORLEY *Diderot* I. 85 The born-blind are at first without physical delicacy.

d. Preceded by adv., adj., or sb., forming combs., indicating (*a*) time or order of birth, as *eldest-, youngest-born*, poet. or rhetorical synonyms for 'eldest', 'youngest' (often used as quasi-sbs.), *last-, latest-, newly-born*; (*b*) place of birth or origin, as *cloud-, country-, Danish-, sea-born*; (*c*) the quality or rank of a person's parentage, as *gently-, lowly-, nobly-born* = of gentle, lowly, noble birth; (*d*) condition at or by birth, as *blind-, free-, poor-born.* Cf. BASE-, FIRST-, HIGH-, LOW-, NEW-, TRUE-, WELL-BORN, etc.

1382 WYCLIF *Luke* ii. 7 And sche childide her firste born sone. **1642** FULLER *Holy & Prof. St.* II. xxiv. 149 Gentilely born on both sides. **1684** DRYDEN in Roscom. *Ess. Transl. Verse* Pref. (1709) 4 Authors nobly born will bear their part. **1697** DRYDEN *Virg. Georg.* IV. 142 Better born, and of a nobler Kind. **1783** AINSWORTH *Lat. Dict.* (Morell) I, Blind born, *cæcigenus.* **1837** CARLYLE *Fr. Rev.* II. v. i. 247 Pet son (her last-born?) of the Scarlet Woman. *a* **1861** MRS. BROWNING *Lady Gerald. Courtsh.*, Men call him lowly born. **1867** FREEMAN *Norm. Conq.* I. iv. 189 The Danish-born Bernard.

2. Of qualities, aptitudes, etc.: That was born in or with a person; innate, inherited.

1742 RICHARDSON *Pamela* III. 243 This . . must be born Dignity—born Discretion. **1833** GEN. P. THOMPSON *Exerc.* (1842) III. 465 It is part of our born-thralldom.

3. Phr. (*one's*) ***born days***: one's lifetime. *colloq.*

1742 RICHARDSON *Pamela* III. 383 He never was so delighted in his born Days. **1826** DISRAELI *Viv. Grey* VI. i. 286 You shall rue it all your born days.

born (bɔːn), *v. U.S.* [Irreg. f. BORN *pple.*] **1.** *trans.* To cause to be born, to deliver (a child), to bring into existence. *rare.*

1932 W. FAULKNER *Light in August* xvii. 371 Byron Bunch borning a baby. *Ibid.* xviii. 403, I took care of his woman for him and I borned his child for him. **1982** *Washington Post* 19 Jan. D1 Stress has a way of borning art and gifted people.

2. *intr.* To come to birth, to be born. Chiefly as *pres. pple.*, *ppl. a.*, and *vbl. sb.* Also *fig.* Cf. ABORNING *adv.* and *pred. a.*

1932 W. FAULKNER *Light in August* xv. 330 The talk. It went here and there about the town, dying and borning again like a wind or a fire. **1960** S. PLATH *Colossus* (1967) 9 The small birds converge, converge With their gifts to a difficult borning. **1966** W. STYRON *Confessions of Nat Turner* III. 340 While yanking a borning calf from its mother's womb Moore suffered a bizarre and fatal accident. **1980** *Christian Science Monitor* 11 Feb. B11 'Astronomy of the Ancients' is a collection of eight articles from the borning interdisciplinary field known as archaeoastronomy. **1983** *Ibid.* 29 Mar. 20 We soon discovered that rehabilitating wildlife . . was a highly expensive hobby. As the 'borning season' influx rose . . , we suffered a shortage of shelter space.

born-, see BURN-.

born-again, *a.* orig. *U.S.* Also **born again.** [f. BORN *pple.* + AGAIN *adv.*, after John iii. 3: see BORN *pple.* A. 2 b.]

a. Of, pertaining to, or characterized by (an experience of) new birth in Christ or spiritual renewal; of a Christian: placing special emphasis on this experience as a basis for all one's actions, evangelical.

1961 *Church & People* Nov.-Dec. 185 (Lancaster-Oslo/Bergen corpus) Each was a born-again Christian. **1962** *Ibid.* Mar.-Apr. 64 A visiting preacher asked one of our congregation the other day, 'Are you born again?' — and got the answer, 'Not yet, — but I'm coming that way!' **1970** *Redemption Tidings* 15 Jan. 12/7 Testifying to a born again experience, each declared that 'now they must seek the Lord to lead them'. **1976** *National Observer* (U.S.) 10 July 5/1 Strauss is insulting everybody in sight, with the possible exception of born-again Jimmy Carter of Georgia, who may be our next President. **1976** *Time* 27 Sept. 94/2 As a born-again Christian, Alabama State Auditor Bettye Frink prayed hard as she tried to decide whether it was fair to her family for her to pursue politics. **1977** *National Observer* (U.S.) 15 Jan. 12/2 Thirteen years ago, the Gallup Poll found only 20 per cent of Americans had undergone the 'born again' experience. **1977** *Time* 26 Dec. 41/1 Encouraged by the presence of a born-again Southern Baptist in the White House, . . the far-flung residents of the new Bible Belt are loosely lumped together under the name Evangelicals. **1981** *Times* 14 Sept. 16/6 The 'born again' fundamentalist 'moral majority' movement in the United States . . is closely tied in with the charismatic movement in that country. **1984** E. FAIRWEATHER *Only Rivers Run Free* vi. 319 It's different for Protestant women, we're not so hooked on the church, except for those born-again Christians.

b. *fig.* Regenerate, revitalized; characterized by the extreme enthusiasm of the newly converted or re-converted.

1977 *Time* 19 Dec. 56/2 On their way to *gourmandise*, a curious thing has happened to born-again American cooks: they have rediscovered the glorious raw ingredients and inimitable provincial dishes of their own country. **1980** *Psychology Today* Aug. 45 (*heading*) China's born-again psychology. **1981** *Times* 27 Jan. 12/7 One of the Bill's most outspoken critics, the born-again Labour Party which has decided . . to end the consensus that once existed on this issue, also says the Bill is sexist. **1982** *Observer* 2 May 7/4 Nott has never been a true, born-again monetarist. **1985** J. RABAN *Foreign Land* iv. 57 They're a bit born-again about smoking now. **1985** *Listener* 18 Apr. 25/1 The former sinner . . had become a born-again Muslim.

borne (bɔən), *ppl. a.* Forms: see BEAR *v.*

1. a. Carried, sustained, endured, etc. Used attrib. chiefly in such constructions as 'patiently borne injuries', 'the breeze-borne note'.

1605 SHAKS. *Macb.* III. ii. 42 The shard-borne Beetle.

b. ***light borne***, easily guided, not hard-mouthed; said of horses. ***water borne***, see quot.

1611 COTGR., *Alegerir vn cheval à la main*, to . . cause a horse to be light borne. **1627** CAPT. SMITH *Seaman's Gram.* ix. 45 Water borne is when there is no more water than will iust beare her from the ground.

2. a. *Comb.*, with adverbs, as ***borne-down, borne-in***, etc. See *bear down, bear in*, etc. under BEAR *v.*

1600 CHAPMAN *Iliad* XV. 354 In such a borne-up kind The Trojans overgat the Wall. **1637** RUTHERFORD *Lett.* clxx. (1862) I. 399 Intimated and borne-in assurance of His love. **1679** KING in *Spirit of Popery* 23 The born-down and Ruined Interest of our Lord and Master. **1878** BROWNING

La Saisiaz 10 Blushing 'Good Night', rosy as a borne-off bride's.

b. With prefixed sb., as ***air-***, ***carrier-***, ***chair-***, ***glider-borne***: see the sbs. (See 1944 *Amer. Speech* XIX. 222 f.)

borne, obs. f. BOURN; var. BERNE, *Obs.*, man.

‖**borné** (bɔrne), *a.* [Fr., pa. pple. of *borner* to limit.] Limited in scope, outlook, mental equipment, etc.

1795 J. MOORE *Diary* 27 May (1904) I. v. 153 His mind is *borné* and illiberal to a degree. **1850** *Househ. Words* 3 Aug. 434/1 The Rockvilles remained high, proud, bigotted, and *borné*. **1873** J. S. MILL *Autobiogr.* vi. 193 A jobbing and *borné* local oligarchy. **1936** T. WATTS-DUNTON in G. K. Chesterton *Autobiogr.* xiii. 282 Anyone so *borné* as poor Browning was. **1961** *Partisan Rev. Anthol.* (1962) 259 Certain crimes, certain characters, in their impudence or awfulness, have the power of making us feel *bornés*.

Bornean (ˈbɔːnɪən), *a.* and *sb.* Also 9 **Borneon.** [f. *Borneo* (see below) + -AN.] **A.** *adj.* Of or pertaining to Borneo, the largest island in the Indonesian Archipelago. **B.** *sb.* A native of Borneo.

1812 J. HUNT in H. Keppel *Exped. Borneo* (1846) II. p. xxxi, The fruit-bearing trees which enrich and adorn the Indian continent offer, on the Borneon shore, all their kindred varieties. **1839** J. BROOKE *Jrnl.* 19 Sept. in *Ibid.* I. iv. 78 Let me speak it to the honour of the Borneons, that they neither cock-fight nor smoke opium. **1850** KINGSLEY *Alton Locke* II. xv. 222 A baby-ape in Bornean forests. **1863** *Boys' Own Mag.* II. 396 Such a course is quite impracticable with a Bornean. *Ibid.* 511 And here I may say was an end of my Bornean adventures. **1920** *Q. Rev.* July 175 Their ancient Italian forefathers..were clearly once at much the same grade of social development as the Bornean tribes. **1926** A. HUXLEY *Jesting Pilate* II. 228 Genuine and aboriginal Borneans. **1965** P. WAYRE *Wind in Reeds* xv. 215 A trio of Bornean Great Argus and several Greater Bornean Crested Fireback Pheasants as well as a number of the rare Chestnut Flanked Bornean Tree Partridges.

borned, variant of BURNED *a. Obs.*, burnished.

Borneo (ˈbɔːniːəʊ). The name of a large island in the Indian Archipelago. *Attrib.* in ***Borneo camphor***, the camphor extracted from the *Dryobalanops camphora*, also the tree itself; ***Borneo caoutchouc***, a kind of india-rubber obtained from Borneo. Hence **borneene** (ˈbɔːniːiːn), **borneol** (ˈbɔːniːɒl), organic compounds chiefly obtained from the Borneo camphor tree; **bornesite** (ˈbɔːnɪsaɪt) 'a sweet volatile substance occurring in the caoutchouc of Borneo' (Watts *Dict. Chem.* I. 626.)

1876 HARLEY *Mat. Med.* 703 The Borneo Camphor is one of the giants of the vegetable world. *Ibid.* Fluid hydrocarbon called camphor oil or borneene. *Ibid.* 680 A hydrocarbon isomeric with..borneol. **1884** ROSCOE & SCHORLEMMER *Chem.* III. 553 By subjecting Borneo caoutchouc to pressure, a liquid is obtained from which bornesite is left on evaporation.

Bornholm (ˈbɔənhəʊm). [The name of a Danish island in the Baltic Sea.] Used *attrib.* in **Bornholm disease**, an epidemic virus disease characterized by acute pain in the intercostal muscles; epidemic pleurodynia.

[**1932** E. SYLVEST in *Bull. de l'Office intern. d'hygiène publique* XXIV. 1431 La Maladie de Bornholm.] **1933** *Brit. Med. Jrnl.* 4 Nov. 817/2 'Bornholm' disease. **1962** *Lancet* 12 May 1016/1 Quite sharp pains, similar to those in Bornholm disease.

bornite (ˈbɔənaɪt). *Min.* [ad. G. *bornit* (1845), f. the name of Ignatius von *Born*, an Austrian mineralogist (1742–91): see -ITE[1].] A brittle reddish-brown sulphide of copper and iron; also called *purple copper ore* or *erubescite*.

1854 DANA *Syst. Min.* (ed. 4) 38 Erubescite. Bornite, *Haid.* Variegated Copper. **1896** *Times* 21 Aug. 10/3 The great bornite mine at Nelson [British Columbia]. **1946** J. R. PARTINGTON *Gen. & Inorg. Chem.* xiii. 325 The commonest ores of copper are sulphides of copper and iron: chalcopyrite ..and bornite or erubescite or variegated copper ore. **1965** G. J. WILLIAMS *Econ. Geol. N.Z.* viii. 98/2 The Bonanza section of Maria mine—where covellite was reported with a little bornite.

boro(o, var. of BORROW, *Obs.*, a pledge, etc.

boro- (ˈbɔərəʊ). *Chem.* Combining form of BORON, as in **boroˈfluoride**, a compound of fluoride of boron with a metallic fluoride; **boroˈtungstate**, a salt formed by the combination of boric and tungstic acids with the same base; **boroˈglyceride**, a compound of boric acid with glycerine, used as an antiseptic; also in *Min.*, **boroˈcalcite**, native borate of calcium.

1869 ROSCOE *Elem. Chem.* 153 Boron forms a borofluoride. **1882** *Athenæum* 8 April 448/2 Prof. Barff described his new antiseptic compound boro-glycerid ($C_3H_5Bo_3$). **1881** *Nature* XXIII. 236 Borotungstate of sodium.

borohydride (ˌbɔərəʊˈhaɪdraɪd). *Chem.* [f. BORO- + HYDRIDE.] A compound containing the radical $-BH_4$, or a substituted form of this radical. Hence **borohydride reduction**, selective reduction of a compound by a borohydride.

1940 *Jrnl. Amer. Chem. Soc.* LXII. 3422 Its probable structure has led us to adopt the name aluminium borohydride. *Ibid.* 3430 The basic structures of the aluminium, beryllium and lithium borohydrides are closely related. **1961** W. GERRARD *Org. Chem. Boron* x. 136 Selectivity of reduction can be achieved by employing sodium borohydride in conjunction with a particular solvent. **1965** H. O. HOUSE *Mod. Synthetic Reactions* ii. 40 Sodium borohydride reductions of α, β-unsaturated compounds are only rarely complicated by reduction of the carbon-carbon double bond.

boron (ˈbɔərɒn). *Chem.* [f. BOR-AX, with the ending of CARB-ON, the element being extracted from borax, and resembling carbon in some of its properties.] **a.** One of the elementary bodies; a non-metallic solid, not fusible at any known temperature. It is obtained as a dark brown or greenish brown powder (***amorphous boron***); and in a less pure form as crystals (***adamantine boron***). In some of its properties it resembles carbon and silicon. Symbol B. **boron hydride**, any of a series of compounds of boron and hydrogen; at one time considered as potential rocket fuel, and among the earliest examples of electron-deficient compounds; = BORANE.

1812 SIR H. DAVY *Chem. Philos.* 315, I first procured boron in October, 1807, by the electrical decomposition of boracic acid. **1869** ROSCOE *Elem. Chem.* 151 Boron combined with oxygen and sodium is found as borax in nature. **1879** F. JONES in *Jrnl. Chem. Soc.* XXXV. 41, I am not aware that any attempt has been made since 1809 to obtain boron hydride. **1933** A. STOCK *Hydrides of Boron & Silicon* iii. 40 The yield of boron hydride..was better if they used phosphoric instead of hydrochloric acid for decomposing the boride. **1955** *Q. Rev.* (*Chem. Soc.*) IX. 176 The boron hydrides and some of their derivatives are examples of electron-deficient compounds. **1961** *New Scientist* IX. 484 These boron hydrides appeared to be of academic interest only until..the need for rocket fuels became apparent.

b. Examples in *Nucl. Physics.*

1938 *Proc. Camb. Phil. Soc.* XXXIV. 290 (*title*) The Disintegration of Boron by Slow Neutrons. *Ibid.* 291 By such measurements on the image of the cloud track resulting from the boron disintegration we have been able to determine the..origin of the He and Li particles. **1949** ROSSI & STAUB *Ionization Chambers & Counters* viii. 189 The construction of a highly sensitive boron chamber that can be used for detecting neutrons of all energies. *Ibid.* 194 These detectors have been named long boron counters. **1957** *Gloss. Terms Nucl. Sci.* (*A.S.A.*) 21/1 Because of its high absorption of neutrons, boron may be used (e.g., in the form of boron steel) as a control absorber in thermal nuclear reactors. **1963** B. FOZARD *Instrumentation Nucl. Reactors* iii. 30 Typical sensitivities for a boron-coated reactor control ionisation chamber.

boronia (bɒˈrəʊnɪə). [f. name of Francesco *Borone*, an Italian botanist (1769–94).] A plant of the rutaceous genus so named, a sweet-scented Australian shrub.

1852 G. C. MUNDY *Antipodes* I. 76 The Boronias shoot up their slender stems..towards the sun. **1896** *Melburnian* 28 Aug. 53 (Morris), The scent of boronia and the odour of wattle-blossom greet us from baskets of the flower-girl. **1926** K. S. PRICHARD *Working Bullocks* v. 55 Ti-tree, boronia-bushes, and prickly acacia. **1966** *Times* 11 Nov. (W. Aust. Suppl.) p. iv/2 The scent of the boronia's monk-brown-and-golden bells.

borosilicate (ˌbɔərəʊˈsɪlɪkət). [f. BORO- + SILICATE.] A silicate incorporating some boric oxide. ***borosilicate glass***, silicate glass containing boric oxide, used esp. in heat-resistant glassware.

1817 T. THOMSON *Syst. Chem.* (ed. 5) III. 409 Family of Borosilicates. **1933** RUTHERFORD *Coll. Papers* (1965) III. 343 The fact that our accelerating tube was a large cylinder of pyrex, a borosilicate glass, strengthened the supposition that the whole effect might be due to boron. **1947** *Endeavour* July 117/1 Potash glasses give a purer blue than the corresponding sodium glasses, and..borosilicates yield a reddish hue. **1965** PHILLIPS & WILLIAMS *Inorg. Chem.* I. xiv. 553 Soda glass is conveniently worked at a lower temperature than borosilicate glass, and the latter at a lower temperature than quartz glass.

borou, obs. form of BORROW *v.*

borough (ˈbʌrəʊ, ˈbʌrə). Forms: 1 burȝ, buruȝ, 1–3 burh, 2 burch, bure(g)h, (burehg), beriȝ, 2–3 buruh, 3 burrh (*Orm.*), burwe, buri, 3–4 burȝ, buruȝ, borh, borȝ, boruȝ, boru, 4 burw, burȝe, borȝ(e, bourȝ, borou, borwȝ, borwgh, borw(e, borgh(e, 4–5 burghe, 4–6 (also *Sc.* 7–9) burgh, borogh, 4–7 borowe, 5 burwgh, borowgh, burwhe, borugh(e, burwe, bourg, 5–6 bourgh, 5–7 burrow(e, 6 borrowe, (bourg), burow, 6–7 boroughe, 6–8 burrough, (7 burrowghe, 8 borrough), 6– borough. *Dat. sing.* 1 byriȝ, burȝe, 2 birie, berie, 3 biri, burie, buri. [Common Teut.: OE. *burȝ, burh* = OFris. *burch*, OS. *burg* (MDu. *burch, borch*, Du. *burg*), OHG. *burug* (MHG. *burc(g-)*, mod.G. *burg*), ON. (Sw., Da.) *borg*, Goth. *baurgs*:—OTeut. **burg-s* str. fem. App. f. same root as OTeut. **berg-an* str. vb. 'to shelter': see BERGH *v.*; but the phonology is not quite clear. In German and ON. the word is recorded chiefly in the primary sense of 'fortress, castle', but there are traces of the sense of 'town, civic community', which is found in Goth. and OE., and may therefore be assumed to have been developed in OTeut. Of the immense variety of spellings current in ME., *burrough* became the prevalent one in early mod. Eng., but was subsequently displaced by *borough* in England and Ireland, while the form established in Scotland was BURGH, q.v. The Danish BORG and Fr. BOURG have also been used by historical writers in special senses. See also BURROW, BERRY *sb.*[3]

Like other fem. consonantal stems, the OE. *burȝ* had vowel change (*byriȝ*) in gen. and dat. sing., and nom. acc. plural, which survived in dat. sing. to the 13th c. This dative, *biri, berie, buri*, was also at times used for the nominative; whence the modern *Bury, -bury*, in place-names.]

†**1. a.** A fortress, castle, or citadel. *Obs.* (Unequivocal instances of this sense are rare, even in OE. In quot. 1394 the word denotes simply a large building; and 1425 is quite doubtful.)

c **820** *Kentish Gloss.* in Wr.-Wülcker *Voc.* 63 *Ad arcem et ad mœnia*, to burȝe and to wealle. *a* **1000** *O.E. Chron.* an. 920 Eadweard cyning..ȝetimbrede þa burȝ. [**1394** *P. Pl. Crede* 118 We buldeþ a burwȝ a brod and a large. *c* **1425** WYNTOUN *Cron.* VIII. xiii. 125 Castellis, Bowrrowys and Fortalys.]

†**b.** A court, a manor-house. Hence prob. in place-names, *e.g.* Edgeware Bury, Hertingford Bury.

c **1175** *Cott. Hom.* 231 And þider ȝeclepien alle his underþeod þat hi bi éne féce to his curt (berie) come sceolde. *c* **1250** *Gen. & Ex.* 2257 He ledde hem alle to Iosepes biri. [**1576** LAMBARDE *Peramb. Kent* (1826) 377 Bury, or Biry.. was used for a court, or place of assembly.]

†**2. a.** A fortified town; a town possessing municipal organization (cf. OE. *burhwaru* body of citizens); more generally, any inhabited place larger than a village. (The three notions were originally co-extensive. When the word became restricted to the mod. sense (3) its wider sense passed to *town.*) *Obs.*

c **893** K. ÆLFRED *Oros.* II. viii. §1 Hie binnan þære byriȝ up eodon..ond þa burȝ [*10th c. MS.* burh] mid ealle awestan. *c* **1000** *Ags. Gosp.* Matt. xxi. 17 Of þære byriȝ. *c* **1160** *Hatton G.* ibid., Of þare beriȝ. *c* **1175** *Cott. Hom.* 225 Hi woldan wercen ane burch · and enne stepel binnan þara birie. *c* **1205** LAY. 218 He makede ane heȝe burh. *c* **1250** *Gen. & Ex.* 1053 Ȝet sat Loth at ðe burȝes gate. *c* **1325** *E.E. Allit. P.* B. 1666, I haf bigged Babiloyne, burȝ alþerrychest. **1480** CAXTON *Chron. Eng.* v. (1520) 43 b/2 Cytees, and boroughs, and townes that the Saxons hadde destroyed. **1483** *Cath. Angl.* 48, A Burghe *burgus*.

†**b.** *fig.* Cf. BURROW shelter, which Feltham may have confounded with *borough*.

1627 FELTHAM *Resolves* I. lii. Wks. (1677) 82 The mind is then shut up in the Burrough of the body.

3. a. A town possessing a municipal corporation and special privileges conferred by royal charter (hence the sovereign is said *to create a borough*). Also a town which sends representatives to parliament. (A ***municipal borough*** often differs in territorial extent from the ***parliamentary borough*** of the same name.) The word is commonly restricted to towns which do not possess the more dignified title of CITY. For the Scottish uses, see BURGH.

(Early examples are necessarily not distinct in sense from the preceding.)

[*c* **1380** *Sir Ferumb.* 283 Be it castel, burgh, outher Cite. **1398** TREVISA *Barth. De P.R.* XIV. ii. (1495) 466 Aournyd wyth many grete cytees and boroughes.] **1512** *Act. 4 Hen. VIII*, xi, The Bourgh of Lymyngton with thappurtenaunces. **1574** tr. *Littleton's Tenures* 35 a, The aunciente townes called Boroughes bee the moste auncient and eldest Townes that bee within England. **1587** FLEMING *Contn. Holinsh.* III. 1276/1 To this man King Henrie the third..did grant that his towne of Wigan should be a burrow. **1652** *Proc. Parliament* No. 34. 2083 A list of the Burroughs that have since assented to the Union. **1718** *Free-thinker* No. 66. 84 Your Counties, and your Burroughs.. send you into Parliament. **1738** *Hist. Crt. Excheq.* ii. 20 Several of the Demesne Lands were given to Burroughs. **1827** HALLAM *Const. Hist.* (1876) III. xiii. 38 Edward VI created fourteen boroughs. **1845** STEPHEN *Laws Eng.* II. 357 A 'borough' is properly a town or city represented in parliament, although the term has occasionally (as in the Municipal Corporation Act) a wider signification.

b. *the Borough*: esp. that of Southwark. Cf. 5.

[**1559** *Mirr. Mag., Jack Cade* xxi, To Southwarke borow where it lay a night.] **1797** *Ann. Reg.* 28 A dreadful fire broke out yesterday morning in the High-Street in the Borough. **1886** *Daily News* 18 Dec. 6/2 Fire in the Borough.

c. ***to own a borough, to buy a borough***: to possess or to buy the power of controlling the election of a member of parliament for a borough. ***close borough, pocket borough***, a borough 'owned' by some person. ***rotten borough***: one of the boroughs which, before the passing of the English Reform Bill in 1832, were found to have so decayed as no longer to have a real constituency.

1771 SMOLLETT *Humphr. Cl.* (1815) 246 The practice of buying boroughs, and canvassing for votes. **1812** SIR F. BURDETT in *Examiner* 12 Oct. 656/1 They will no more part with their rotten boroughs. **1817** G. ROSE *Diaries* (1860) I.

33 To suppress what were called the rotten boroughs. **1867** MORLEY *Burke* 104 Wilkes proposed to disfranchise the rotten boroughs.

d. An incorporated town or village; a town having a warden or chief burgess as its official head. *U.S.*

1718 in *Pennsylvania Col. Rec.* III. 58 The said town might be erected into a Borough by a Charter of Incorporacon. **1854** *Stat. State Connecticut* 329 The wardens and a majority of the burgesses of any such borough, may, in like manner, authorize such an alley to be kept at any place in any such city or borough. **1925** G. P. KRAPP *Eng. Lang. in Amer.* I. iii. 178 Now that the word Manhattan has been legalized as the name of the Borough of Manhattan, it is possible it may become colorlessly official and lose some of its romantic glamour.

e. (*a*) In New Zealand, a village, township, or town having a special governing body called a borough council. (*b*) In New South Wales, a municipal corporation of not less than 1,000 inhabitants and not more than 9 square miles in area. In Victoria, such a municipality of not less than 300 inhabitants.

1865 R. P. WHITWORTH *Baillière's Vict. Gazetteer* 59 Brunswick is a borough township,..in the..electoral district of E. Bourke boroughs. **1867** *Acts N.Z. 31 Vict.* No. 24 §29 There shall be in and for each single borough a council consisting of nine councillors. **1874** *Silver's Handbk. Australia & N.Z.* (ed. 2) 131 At the end of 1871 there were sixty-four corporate towns and boroughs, containing within their municipal limits about one-half the population. A borough must not have an area of more than nine square miles.

f. Any of the five administrative divisions of New York City (see quot. 1948).

1897 *Independent* 11 Mar. 306/1 The Charter provides.. that the Borough of Brooklyn may have a professionally conducted school system. **1948** *Chicago Tribune* 18 Mar. III. 4/5 The jubilee commemorates the 50th anniversary of the consolidation of the boroughs of Manhattan, Brooklyn, Bronx, Queens and Staten Island into New York City. **1970** *N.Y. Times Encycl. Almanac* 222/2 Thus the city today consists of five boroughs, each a county in its own right: Manhattan is New York County; Brooklyn is Kings County; Staten Island is Richmond County; and Queens and the Bronx bear the same county as borough names. **1986** *New Yorker* 3 Feb. 90/3 On January 8th,..the borough president of Queens, who is also the Democratic boss of that borough ..had spent much of the day at City Hall.

g. An administrative district of Greater London in which services, etc., are provided by a local authority. Cf. METROPOLITAN *a.* 2a.

1899 *Act* 62 & 63 *Vict.* c. 14 § 1 The whole of the administrative county of London, exclusive of the City of London, shall be divided into metropolitan boroughs (in this Act referred to as boroughs). **1963** *Act* 11 & 12 *Eliz. II* c. 33 §1 II. 1 The boundary between the London boroughs numbered 6 and 17 respectively..in the existing metropolitan borough of Woolwich shall be the..centre of the navigable channel of the River Thames at low water. **1976** *Times* 21 May 2/5 Dr. Douglas Chambers, the coroner, asked whether it might not be desirable for checks to be made in other London boroughs.

h. In Alaska, a territorial and administrative division corresponding to a county elsewhere in the United States.

1956 *Fairbanks* (Alaska) *Daily News-Miner* 6 Feb. 7 All local government powers shall be vested in boroughs and cities. The State may delegate taxing powers to boroughs and cities only. **1966** R. A. COOLEY *Alaska* viii. 103 The creation of new units of government, the boroughs, has brought in its wake yet another series of problems... The boroughs are only now coming into existence. At the present time there are nine of them. **1974** *Encycl. Brit. Macropædia* I. 413/1 State and borough governments have difficulty in providing the usual range of services because of the limited extent of the economy.

†**4.** At Richmond, Yorkshire, and perhaps other northern old corporate towns: A property held by BURGAGE, and formerly qualifying for a vote for members of parliament. Cf. BOROUGH-HOLDER.

1715 *Lond. Gaz.* No. 5296/4 A Very large Burrough, standing in..the Market-place of Richmond in Yorkshire, consisting of three Dwelling Houses, and two large shops.

†**5.** In 14th to 16th c. sometimes used for the suburbs of a city, the portion lying outside the wall. Cf. contemporary use of F. *bourg*.

c **1380** *Sir Ferumb.* 1767 Til þay wer passed þe borwgh. *c* **1450** *Merlin* xviii. (1877) 291 Kynge Arans hadde all day assailed the Castell of Arondell, but..nothinge thei wonne, saf only thei hadde brente the bourgh withoute. **1523** LD. BERNERS *Froiss.* I. cxc. 225 The gate..bytwene the.. borowe and the cytie. [At Oxford, the suburb of St. Clement's, east of the Cherwell, is traditionally called 'the Borough'.]

6. Archæological and historical uses.

a. Adopted to translate Gr. δῆμος and L. *pagus* in the sense of township or district.

a **1747** ABP. POTTER in T. Mitchell *Aristoph.* (1822) II. 160 The Athenians..delivered in their names, together with the names of their father and borough. **1770** LANGHORNE *Plutarch* (1879) I. 81/2 Numa..divided the country into.. portions, which he called pagi, or boroughs. **1850** MAURICE *Mor. & Met. Philos.* III, Socrates was born in a little burgh of Attica.

b. *Eng. Hist.* in various *arch.* forms: used by some writers on the Old English period. See also BORG, BOURG, BURG, BURGH.

1872 E. ROBERTSON *Hist. Ess.* Introd. 11 The Burh, of burgh of early days. **1875** STUBBS *Const. Hist.* I. v. 92 The 'burh' of the Anglo-Saxon period was simply a more strictly organised form of the township. *Ibid.* 93 *note*, The five Danish burhs..had not only special privileges of their own, but a common organization.

7. *Comb.* and *attrib.*

†**a.** Obs. law terms used *Hist.* by writers of 16th c. onwards; most recent writers retain the OE. spelling: **burgh-bote** [OE. *burh-bót*; cf. BOOT *sb.*[1]], a tax for the repair of fortresses; **burgh-breche** [OE. *burh-bryce*; cf. BREACH], close-breaking, burglary; **burgh-mote, borough-moot** [OE. *burh-ȝemót*; cf. MOOT], the judicial assembly of a borough.

1647 N. BACON *Hist. Disc.* xxxiii. 82 Power to charge one another with the maintenance of the Fortifications by an imposition called Burghbote. **1844** LINGARD *Anglo-Sax. Ch.* (1858) I. vi. 221 Burgh-bot, or contribution towards the maintenance of the burghs or places of defence. **1387** TREVISA *Higden* Rolls Ser. II. 95 Burghbreche a Frensche *blesmure de court ou de cloys.* **1598** TATE in Gutch *Coll. Cur.* I. 4 *Borrowbreach* is interpreted *Civitas rupta.* **1641** *Termes de la Ley* 44 Burbreach..trespasses done in Citie or Borough against the peace. *a* **1400** *Vsages of Wynchestre* in *Eng. Gilds* 350 At þe borghmot of seynt mychel. **1747** CARTE *Hist. Eng.* I. 311 A court or burghmote was held thrice a year for determining all causes between the inhabitants. **1872** E. ROBERTSON *Hist. Ess.* 130 The later county court of the Vicecomes or Sheriff..held three times a year as a Burh-gemote in the leading burgh of the district. **1880** *Antiquary* June 255 The ancient Burghmote horn of Ipswich.

†**b.** Other obs. compounds: **borough-folk** (OE. *burh-folc*), the people of a town; **burgh-kenning**, coined by Stow as an etymological rendering of BARBICAN (!); **burh-were**, *pl.* **-weren** [OE. *burhwaru, -ware, -waran*], the people or community of a town, the townsmen.

c **1200** *Trin. Coll. Hom.* 89 þat burh folc hihten þe heȝe strete. *c* **1250** *Gen. & Ex.* 1853 Emor..And his burgefolc fellin in wi. **1598** STOW *Surv.* xxxiii. (1603) 304 A Burgh-Kening or Watch Tower of the Cittie. *c* **1205** LAY. 28368 Iherden þa burh-weren [**1275** borh-men] hu hit was al ifaren. *Ibid.* 28392 Hi bi-hehte þere burȝe-were auer mare freo laȝe.

c. *attrib.* and *Comb.* in sense 3, as *borough-accountant, -architect, -bailiff, -surveyor*; **borough council** [COUNCIL 10], a local council which conducts the affairs of a borough; **borough court**, a court of limited jurisdiction held in a borough by special privilege; **borough-rate**, a rate levied by the municipality of a borough; **borough sessions**, a court held by the recorder of a borough, usually quarterly, established under the Municipal Corporations Act of 1835. Also with reference to parliamentary representation, as *borough-constituency, -election, faction, -influence, -patron, -politics, -slave, -traitor, -tyrant, -voter*, etc.; **borough-jobber, borough-jobbing** = BOROUGH-MONGER, -MONGERING;

1812 CRABBE *Tales, Patron* 1 A *borough-bailiff, who to law was trained. **1866** BRIGHT *Sp. Irel.* 2 Nov. (1876) 193 Wherever the *borough constituencies are so small. **1879** *Contemp. Rev.* XXXIV. 695 One change is imperatively called for—the getting rid of the incubus of aldermen in the city and *borough councils. **1900** G. B. SHAW *Let.* 31 Oct. (1972) 189 Candidates for appointments should be examined by some public educational body entirely independent of the Borough Council. **1918** *Existing Law Boroughs Penn.* xxvi. 220 The borough council may fill any vacancy in their body until the municipal election next following. *a* **1974** R. H. CROSSMAN *Diaries* III. 484 As a result of the [Maud] proposals, 124 county and borough councils and over 1,000 district councils would disappear. **1985** *Whitaker's Almanack 1986* 620/1 The Greater London Council and the six metropolitan county councils are to be abolished and most of their functions made the responsibility of the existing borough and district councils. **1769** BLACKSTONE *Comm.* Index, *Borough courts. **1959** JOWITT *Dict. Eng. Law* I. 266/2 Borough courts..are now of little importance, most business having been transferred.. to the county court. *a* **1797** H. WALPOLE *Mem. Geo. II.* (1847) II. xi. 373 He would be no *borough-jobber. **1803** BRISTED *Pedest. Tour* II. 345 Exaltation by the usual gradations of *borough-jobbing, of courtierizing, and a peerage. **1811** *Edin. Rev.* XVII. 258 Having..prohibited the sale of seats by *borough-patrons. **1863** H. COX *Instit.* III. ix. 730 Householders..paying poor-rates and *borough-rates. **1835** *Act 5 & 6 Will. IV* c. 76 §110 *marg.*, Offenders committed to *Borough Sessions whose Jurisdiction is taken away to be tried in the adjoining County. **1813** COBBETT *Pol. Reg.* XXXIII. 81 Like a set of *borough-slaves, submitting to choose a second member at the dictation of Sir Francis Burdett.

borough, obs. form of BURROW, rabbit-hole, mound, and shelter; and of BROUGH.

Borough-English (ˈbʌrəˈɪŋglɪʃ). [A partial translation of the Anglo-French *tenure en Burgh Engloys*, tenure in (an) English borough: according to Blackstone so called because prevailing in certain boroughs, and because it was English as distinguished from French.]

A custom or tenure in some parts of England, by which the youngest son inherits all the lands and tenements.

1327 *Year Bk. 1 Edw. III*, 12, pl. 38 (ed. 1679) Il ad en Notingham deux tenures, s. Burgh Engloys and Burgh Fraunceyes..toutes les tenements dont launcestre morust seisi en Burgh Engloyes devient descender a le puisne fitz. **1531** *Dial. Laws of Eng.* I. xx. (1638) 35 In Burghenglish the younger sonne shall enjoy the inheritance, and that in conscience. **1656** in BLOUNT. **1667** E. CHAMBERLAYNE *St. Gt. Brit.* I. III. v. (1743) 181 In other [places] the youngest son inherits all the Land by a Custom called Borough-English. **1862** *Sat. Rev.* 5 July 13 The extraordinary scene that would ensue if Parliament should, in one of its idle moments, suddenly enact that the custom of Borough-English should prevail through the realm. **1882** F. POLLOCK in *Macm. Mag.* XLVI. 360 *note*, The custom of borough-English abounds in Kent, Sussex, Surrey, the neighbourhood of London, and Somerset. In the midlands it is rare, and north of the Humber..it does not seem to occur.

borough-head, incorrect f. BORROW-HEAD.

borough-holder (ˈbʌrəˌhəʊldə(r)). [f. BOROUGH + HOLDER.] In certain Yorkshire boroughs: A person who holds property by burgage tenure: see BOROUGH 4. Modern dictionaries explain the word as = BORSHOLDER; possibly this is the meaning in quot. 1738.

1712 *Lond. Gaz.* No. 5036/3 The humble Address of the Mayor..Aldermen and Assistants of the..Borough of Rippon..and of several Gentlemen and Borough-holders. **1738** *Hist. Crt. Excheq.* ii. 27 The King's Borrough-Holders in every County.

†**ˈborough-kind.** *Obs. rare*$^{-1}$. [? f. BOROUGH-ENGLISH, after GAVELKIND.] = BOROUGH-ENGLISH.

1577 HARRISON *England* II. ix. (1877) 203 Burrow kind is where the youngest is preferred before the eldest.

boroughlet (ˈbʌrəlɪt). *rare.* [f. BOROUGH + -LET, dim. suffix.] A diminutive borough or town.

1864 H. MAYHEW *German Life & Mann.* I. 5 The moors ..from which the..boroughlet..is said to derive its name.

†**borough-man.** *Obs.* [OE. *burhman*; see BOROUGH and MAN.] A townsman, citizen, burgess. **b.** In some Yorkshire boroughs: A burgage tenant, BOROUGH-HOLDER.

c **1000** ÆLFRIC *Voc.* in Wr.-Wülcker *Voc.* 140 *Urbanus*, burhsita, uel burhman. *c* **1205** LAY. 12441 Moni riche burh-mon þer wende beon bliðe anan. *a* **1225** *Ancr. R.* 350 Pilegrimes..bikumen nout buruhmen iðe worldes buruh. *c* **1400** *Destr. Troy* XXI. 8570 þai bere the burgh-men abacke to the bare walles. **1708** *Lond. Gaz.* No. 4424/10 The Burgesses, Borough-men, Gentlemen and other substantial Inhabitants within the Borough of Thirsk.

borough-master (ˈbʌrəˌmɑːstə(r)). Also burough-, burgh-, bourg-: and see BURGOMASTER. [f. BOROUGH + MASTER; in sense 1 imitated from Du. *burgemeester*.]

†**1.** A Dutch or Flemish burgomaster; sometimes used incorrectly, and also extended to similar functionaries in other foreign countries (e.g., quot. 1625 relates to Poland). **b.** The head of the municipality of certain Irish boroughs. *Obs.*

1494 FABYAN *Chron.* VII. 436 And some of the borough maisters of the sayde towne [Bruges]. **1590** GREENE *Neuer too late* (1600) 14 The richest Merchant or grauest Burghmaster. **1625** PURCHAS *Pilgrim* II. 1421 The Borrow-masters sell Wine. **1696** *Lond. Gaz.* No. 3178/4 The Borough Master, Burgesses, and Commonalty of the Borough of Bayle in Ireland.

2. The patron or 'owner' of a BOROUGH (3c).

a **1832** BENTHAM *Mem.* Wks. 1843 X. 237 Members..are supposed to speak the sentiments of the borough-master who puts them in.

boroughmonger (ˈbʌrəˌmʌŋgə(r)). [f. BOROUGH + MONGER.] One who trades in parliamentary seats for boroughs. (A sarcastic designation coined about the end of the 18th c., and very frequently used in the discussions on electoral reform up to 1832.) Hence **ˈboroughmonger** *v. rare*; **ˈboroughmongering** *vbl. sb.* and *ppl. a.*; **ˈboroughmongery**, the arts and practices of a boroughmonger.

1794 MATHIAS *Purs. Lit.* (1798) 309 An impudent, unqualified intrusion of Borough mongering Mercers. **1809** *Sir Fr. the Reformer* 9 He swears eternal detestation To borough-mongers of the nation. **1820** *Blackw. Mag.* VII. 677 Worse even than base boroughmongry. **1831** SYD. SMITH *Wks.* (1867) II. 215 The awful danger of extinguishing Borough-mongers. **1836** HOR. SMITH *Tin Trump.* (1876) 68 Boroughmongers—an extinct race of beasts of prey. **1844** DISRAELI *Coningsby* IV. iv. 126 The boroughmongering of our own times. **1846** HT. MARTINEAU *Hist. Peace* II. IV. iii. 417 By this [Reform] bill, the practice of boroughmongery was cut up by the roots. **1847** L. HUNT *Men, Wom. & Bks.* I. xiii. 215 'Never borough-mongered with it,' says the peer. **1865** BRIGHT *Sp. Reform* 18 Jan. (1876) 335 The Reform Bill..disturbed the boroughmongers to a remarkable degree. **1879** *Edin. Rev.* April 497 They represented either Downing Street or a score of boroughmongering peers.

borough-reeve (ˈbʌrəriːv). Forms: 1 **burhȝeréfa** (also *Hist.* in 9), 2 **burhreve**, 9 **borough-reeve.** [f. BOROUGH + REEVE.]

†**a.** A governor of a town or city; *esp.* the official who before the Norman Conquest represented the king's authority for fiscal and other purposes in boroughs, as the *scír-ȝeréfa* (SHERIFF) did in shires. The office seems to have been substantially identical with that of PORTREEVE.

c **1000** ÆLFRIC *Gloss.* in Wr.-Wülcker *Voc.* 110 *Prætor* uel *præfectus*, uel *quæstor*, burhȝerefa. *c* **1225** *Leg. Kath.* 1927 Com a burhreve [orig. *urbis prefectus*] as þe þat wes þes deoueles budel. [**1861** PEARSON *Early & Mid. Ages Eng.* I. 84 The præfectus, or burh-gerefa, was rather a royal than a civic officer.]

b. The chief municipal officer in certain unincorporated English towns, before the Municipal Corporations Act, 1835.

1808 *Chron.* in Ann. Reg. 325/1 The weavers assembled.. near Manchester..Mr. Starkie, the Boroughreeve strove to persuade them to disperse, but in vain. **1846** MCCULLOCH *Acc. Brit. Empire* (1854) II. 191 The officer of the king, called port-reeve or borough-reeve. **1881** MORLEY *Cobden* I. 121 He was intolerant of the small politics of the Borough-reeve and the Constables. **1885** *Manch. Exam.* 20 Mar. 8/4 He filled the office of boroughreeve, or chief magistrate, of Salford in 1839.

boroughship (ˈbʌrəʃɪp). *rare.* [Two words: (1) f. BOROUGH + -SHIP, answering in formation (though without historical connexion) to OE. *burhscipe*; (2) f. OE. *borh* pledge, security (see BORROW) + -SHIP.]

1. A township; the fact of constituting a borough or township.

c **1000** ÆLFRIC *Gloss.* in Wr.-Wülcker *Voc.* 144 *Municipium*, burhscipe. **1862** *Macm. Mag.* Mar. 415 They could not have kept up tribeship, and they took instead of it, their boroughship,—which..consisted in a making up of social tribes on neighbourhood, instead of kindred on blood.

2. The condition of being security for the good behaviour of neighbours; FRANK-PLEDGE.

1864 *Reader* 23 July 98/3 The..institution of boroughship, or lawbinding of the landholders as pledges, each for the other's lawful behaviour.

†**ˈborough-ˌtenure.** *Obs. rare.* = BOROUGH-ENGLISH.

a **1670** HACKET *Abp. Williams* II. (1692) 197 Their young brothers, by burrough-tenure, have got the estate from them.

ˈborough-town. *arch.* Forms: see BOROUGH. [f. BOROUGH + TOWN. Cf. OE. *burhtún* enclosure surrounding a castle (as in the place-name *Burton*).]

A town which is a borough. Still sometimes applied to Irish municipal boroughs. Cf. BURROWS-TOWN (*Sc.*).

[*c* **1000** *Woman's Lament* 31 (Gr.) Sindon burȝtunas breruin beweaxne.]

1382 WYCLIF *Joshua* vii. 2 Of the burȝtown [**1388** the citee] Bethel. **1393** LANG. *P. Pl.* C. IV. 112 Hit ys noȝt semly ..in cyte ne in borwton þat vsurers oþer regratours..Be fraunchised for a free man. **1480** CAXTON *Chron. Eng.* ccxliii. 288 Thurgh every Cyte and good Burgh tounes in Englond. **1601** HOLLAND *Pliny* (1634) I. 88 One Borough Towne of Romane Citizens. *a* **1674** CLARENDON *Hist. Reb.* I. I. 67 Edenborough..was but a Burrough Town within the Diocess of Saint Andrews. **1839** CAPPER *Topogr. Dict.* 1052 Wexford, a seaport..shire, assize, and borough town.

borow(e, obs. form of BORROW *v.*

†**ˈborowe, ˈborou**, *a. Obs.* [? corruption of BORREL (though this form does not appear there).] ? Homely, unlearned. Also as quasi-*sb.*

1579 TOMSON *Calvin's Serm. Tim.* 953/1 He vseth that borowe kinde of speache. **1611** BROUGHTON *Require Agreem.* 21 Our Lordes Prayer..in vulgar Greeke for the borous.

borrachio, var. of BORACHIO, *Obs.*, wine-skin.

borral-tree. *Sc. rare*⁻¹. Meaning uncertain; perhaps 'hollowtree': Jamieson suggests that Hogg may have meant BOUR TREE; on which conjecture the word has since been given in dictionaries and books on botany as an actual name of the Elder.

1818 HOGG *Brownie* I. 216 Round the hillock, on the lea, Round the auld borral tree, Or bourock by the burn-side.

borratose: see BORATO.

borrel, borel (ˈbɒrəl), *a. arch.* Forms: 4 borel(l, burel(l, 5 borelle, 6 borrell, *Sc.* burell, burrell, 7–9 borrel, borel. [Conjectured to be an attrib. use of *borel*, BUREL *sb.* 'coarse clothing'; the adj. and the sb. appear in the same forms in 14th c., but in Eng. writers from Caxton onwards the adj. is *borrel*, *borel*, while the sb. is regularly *burrel*, *burel*. Sense 2 seems to be a development of 1, which appears much earlier. See BOROWE.]

†**1.** Belonging to the laity. *Obs.* (or *arch.*)

1377 LANGL. *P. Pl.* B. x. 286 And þanne shal borel clerkes ben abasched, to blame ȝow or to greue. *c* **1386** CHAUCER *Sompn. T.* 164 And moore we seen of cristes secree thynges Than burel [*so in 4 MSS.*, *Heng.* burell, *Corpus* borell, *Harl.* borel] folk al though they weren kynges. *a* **1420** OCCLEVE *De Reg. Princ.* 52 Some of hem [priests] ben as borelle folkes be. *c* **1575** GASCOIGNE *Fruites Warre* xxviii, Bycause they covet more than borrell men. **1860** WARTER *Sea-Board & D.* II. 473 As with the lay and borrel man, so too with Bishop, Priest, or Deacon.

2. Unlearned, rude; rough. *arch.* (In quot. 1513 said of spears; cf. BOISTOUS, BOISTEROUS.)

1513 DOUGLAS *Æneis* Prol. 48 Weill ma I schaw my burell busteous thocht. *Ibid.* VII. xii. 56 Bayr in thair handis lance stavis and burrell speris. **1572** GASCOIGNE *Flowers* Wks. (1587) 111 My borrell braine is all too blount To give a gesse. **1625** GILL *Sacr. Philos.* I. 63 His words seeme borrel and rude. **1727** *Cowell's Law Dict.* s.v. *Bordel*, Borel-folkes, drunkards, and epicures, which the Scotch now call burielfolk. **1828** SCOTT *F.M. Perth* v, A coarse, ignorant, borrel man like me. **1870** MORRIS *Earthly Par.* I. I. 318 Lo, such are borel folk.

borrel, var. of BOREL, *Sc.*, an auger.

‖**borrico** (boˈriko). Also borico. [Sp., dim. of *burro.*] A little donkey. (Only an alien word.)

1648 GAGE *West Ind.* iv. (1655) 13 We travailed like Spanish Dons upon our little Boricoes, or Asses. **1838** SPARKS *Biogr.* IX. vi. 228 Our boys..make a Pope and a Devil of old cast clothes, mount them on a borrico.

Borrovian (bɒˈrəʊvɪən), *sb.* and *a.* [f. the name of George *Borrow* (1803–81) English writer + -IAN, after *Harrovian*, etc.] **A.** *sb.* **1.** A student or admirer of George Borrow. **2.** The diction characteristic of Borrow's works. **B.** *adj.* Of, relating to, or characteristic of Borrow or his writings.

1888 *Reflector* 8 Jan. 26/1 The born Borrovian—for men are born Borrovians, not made. **1900** W. I. KNAPP in *Borrow's Lavengro* 568/2 *Engro* (mere *ending*), Borrovian for 'master', 'fellow', 'chap'. **1904** *Daily Chron.* 21 July 3/6 Bampfylde Moore Carew, who, born with a genius for roving truly Borrovian, ran away from school to become King of the Gypsies. **1956** F. SWINNERTON *Background with Chorus* vi. 49 Edmund Gosse, no Borrovian, anonymously and poohpoohingly reviewed..*George Borrow and his Circle.*

ˈborrow, *sb. Obs.* exc. *Hist.* with the exception of sense 5. Forms: 1 borȝ, 1–3 borh, 2–4 borȝ, (3 barh), 3–4 boru, borewe, 4 borou, *Sc.* borwch, (bourgh), 4–5 borwe, 4–7 borow(e, borgh(e, 5 *Sc.* borch(e, (brugh, borough), 6 boro, borge, (*Sc.* broche), 6–7 borrowe, 6–7, 9 borrow, (9 *Hist.* borh, borch). [OE. *borȝ*, *borh* str. masc., = MHG. *borc*, *borg*, Du. *borg* pledge, loan, f. root of OTeut. **berg-an* str. vb. to protect: see BERGH *v.* Senses 4 and 5 are f. BORROW *v.*¹]

†**1.** A thing deposited as security, a pledge; a guarantee, bail; suretyship; ransom, deliverance. ***to borrow***: as a pledge. ***to lay to borrow***: to put in pledge, to pawn. In senses 1 and 2 already obsolete or archaic in England in Spenser's time; but retained in *Sc. Law.*

a **975** Thorpe's *Laws* I. 274 (Bosw.) Ic wille, ðæt ælc mann sy under borȝe. *c* **1175** *Lamb. Hom.* 73 Heore godfaderes and heore godmoderes scullen..ben to borȝes et þe fonstan. *a* **1300** *Cursor M.* 23792 þat soru, þat nakins borgh us fra mai boru. **1375** BARBOUR *Bruce* I. 625 Thartill in-to borwch draw I Myn herytage. *c* **1385** CHAUCER *L.G.W.* 2105 Hauyth here of myn herte blod to borwe If that ye wele. *c* **1386** CHAUCER *Knts. T.* 764 Ech of hem hadde leyd his feith to borwe. *c* **1460** *Sir Penny* vii. 5 Withouten brugh & wed. **1542–3** *Act 34–35 Hen. VIII*, xxvii. §58 Pledges or borows to pay the kinges fine. **1579** SPENSER *Sheph. Cal.* May 150 Nay..by my deare borrow [*gloss.* that is our Saviour, the commen pledge of all men's debts to death]. **1631** RUTHERFORD *Lett.* 19 (1862) I. 80 It cannot stand with His honour to die in the borrows (as we use to say) and lose thee. **1814** SCOTT *Wav.* I. xv. 228 [They] concussed them into giving borrows (pledges), to enter into captivity again. **1860** C. INNES *Scotl. Mid. Ages* 184 If a thief could find no borch he was hanged.

†**b.** Hence in OE. and early ME. ***on, to borrow***: on security, by way of loan. *Obs.*

a **900** Thorpe's *Laws* I. 52 (Bosw.) Gif ðu feoh to borȝe selle. *c* **975** *Rushw. Gosp.* Matt. v. 42 þæm þe wille on borȝ nioma æt þe ne beo unȝeþwære. *a* **1300** *Cursor M.* 6144 Fra þis folk..þe folk of israel to boru Asked silueren vessel.. And clathes. **1418** in Jeffrey *Hist. Roxburghsh.* IV. i. 89 The Earl not having occupied the land, let the same 'to borch' to the abbot on May 1418.

†**2.** Of persons: A surety, hostage; bail, deliverer from prison. *Obs.*

a **1000** *Laws of Æthelred* i. 1. in Thorpe's *Laws* 119 Sette ȝetreowe borȝas. *a* **1200** *Trin. Coll. Hom.* 17 Here godfaderes sullen..ben here boreȝes toȝenes Gode. *c* **1205** LAY. 31077 Ich wulle his on barh beon [*c* **1275** borh]. *a* **1340** HAMPOLE *Psalter* 497 Answere for me, that is, be borgh of myn amendynge. **1377** LANGL. *P. Pl.* VII. 81 For beggeres borwen euermo and her borghe is god almyȝti. **1470** HARDING *Chron.* ccxix. iv. 4, I shalbe youre borowe. *a* **1541** WYATT *De profundis*, *Ps.* cxxx, From depth of death..Thee have I called, O Lord, to be my borrow. **1552** ABP. HAMILTON *Catech.* 190 The godfather and godmother..ar maid borrowis or souerteis for the barne. **1609** SKENE *Reg. Maj.* 8 He may recover the possession of the lands, he findand ane borghe. **1819** SCOTT *Ivanhoe* II. x. 176 Retain as borrows my two priests.

†**b.** ***I dare be borrow***, etc.: 'I'll warrant', 'I'll be bound'. *Obs.*

c **1430** LYDG. *Min. Poems* (1840) 41 The womman was woo, I dare be borwe. *c* **1460** *Towneley Myst.* 231, I shalle be his borghe to-yere He felys no more payn.

†**c.** ***to find*** (***take***) God, Mahoun, St. Blase, St. George, etc. ***to borrow***, i.e. as security for one's truth, good faith, or honour; later as an asseveration = In God's name, By St. George, St. George to speed! ***St. John to borrow!*** a Scotch formula at parting (= ***au revoir***), as to the origin of which see quot. 1470. *Obs.*

a **1330** *Otuel* 305 Ich wole finde mahoun to borwe, Ich wile be redi erliche to morwe. *c* **1386** CHAUCER *Sqrs. T.* 596, I hidde fro hym my sorwe And took hym by the hond, seint John to borwe. **1393** GOWER *Conf.* II. 34 But I dare take God to borwe. **1423** JAS. I. *King's Q.* xxiii, With mony 'fare wele' and 'sanct Iohne to borowe'. *c* **1470** HENRY *Wallace* III. 336 Thar leyff thai tuk, with conforde..Sanct Ihone to borch, thai suld meyt haille agayne. **1529** SKELTON *Albany* 506 Sainct George to borrowe, Ye shall have schame and sorrowe. **1530** LYNDESAY *Papyngo* 701 We sall..mak ȝow saif: we fynd sanct Blase to borgh. **1535** STEWART *Cron. Scot.* II. 519 All salbe weill, I find ȝow God to borrow. **1548** HALL *Chron.* (1809) 416 Now sent George to borowe, let us set forward. **1566** UDALL *Royster D.* IV. viii. 77 What then? Saincet George to borow, our Ladies Knight.

3. *Hist.* (usually with obs. spelling.) A *friðborh* (lit. 'pledge of peace') or tithing, which in early England was an association of ten neighbouring householders who were jointly answerable before the law, 'so that if one of the ten men offend, the other nine may bring him to right'; afterwards called ***liberum plegium*** and FRANKPLEDGE, the word *frið* 'peace' having been corrupted into 'free'. There is no direct evidence that in OE. *borh* was used as = *friðborh*, but in 16th c. *borowe* appears as a synonym of 'tithing' or 'frankpledge', and from that period to the present time many writers have confused it with BOROUGH. Cf. BORROWHEAD, BORSHOLDER.

1581 LAMBARDE *Eiren.* I. iii. (1588) 15 The chiefe men of the free pledges within that Borow or Tithing. **1872** E. ROBERTSON *Hist. Ess.* 119 Every Borowe or Tything.

4. A borrowing. *rare*⁻¹.

1611 SHAKS. *Wint. T.* I. ii. 39 Of your Royall presence, Ile adventure The borrow of a Weeke.

5. *Golf.* The amount which one 'borrows' (see BORROW *v.*¹ 2d) to allow for the slope of the green.

1862 R. CHAMBERS *Rambling Remarks* 24 The boy puts the 'putter' into your hand, but before applying it to the ball, it will be well for you to examine the ground between it and the hole. You observe possibly that it slants a little; in that case, a 'borrow' is required *up* the slant, and that borrow you must make. **1913** *Country Life* 29 Nov. 759 The player who does not put his approach shots very near the hole will be constantly calculating the 'borrow' of entertaining undulations. **1958** *Times* 13 Oct. 14/2 Wolstenholme..had a long downhill putt..but he did not give it quite enough borrow. **1973** *Times* 24 May 10/1 Miss Parker hooked her tee shot at the short 15th and, with a poor chip, lay 20ft from the hole. But down went the putt, the borrow exactly measured.

6. *Comb.* and *attrib.*, as (in sense 1) **borrow-breach** (only *Hist.*, OE. *borh-bryce*), breach of covenant; **borrow-roll** (Sc. *borgh-row*), a mortgage-roll. Also BORROWGAGE, BORROW-GANG, BORROW-HEAD, BORROWHOOD, BORSHOLDER.

a **900** K. ÆLFRED *Laws* iii. in Thorpe's *Laws* 28 (*title*) Be Borȝ-bryce. *Ibid.* Ærcebiscepes borȝes-bryce..ȝebete mid þrim pundum. *c* **1550** SIR J. BALFOUR *Practicks* (1754) 38 The Serjand aucht to present attachiamentis and borghrowis that ar fundin in his handis. **1844** LINGARD *Anglo-Sax. Ch.* (1858) II. i. 7 'The bot of borhbryce', or penalty for breach of covenant.

†**ˈborrow**, *a. Obs. rare*⁻¹. Meaning and origin uncertain: said of the pitch of a wall.

1679 PLOT *Staffordsh.* (1686) 162 These [walls of blast furnace] according as they may be pitched less transhaw, or more borrow; will mend..or alter the nature of the Iron.. The Iron made in a borrow work is much more tough.

borrow (ˈbɒrəʊ), *v.*¹ Forms: 1 borȝian, 3 boru, 3–5 borwe, 4–5 borou, borewe, 4–6 borowe, (5 boro(o, bourowe, bor(o)wyn, borwon, borwne), 5–6 borow, (6 burow), 7 borrowe, 4– borrow. [OE. *borȝian*, f. *borȝ*, *borh* pledge, surety (BORROW *sb.*); cf. OHG. *borgên* to take heed, f. **borg* (?object of care), MHG., mod.G. *borgen* to borrow, f. MHG. *borg* pledge.]

I. To give security for, take on pledge.

1. *trans.* **a.** To take (a thing) on pledge or security given for its safe return; **b.** To take (a thing) on credit, on the understanding of returning it, or giving an equivalent; *hence*, to obtain or take the temporary use of (a thing recognized as being the property of another, to whom it is returnable). Const. *of*, rarely *from*, formerly *at*.

The essential notion of borrowing originally was the *security* given for the safety of the thing so taken: the essential notion now is that the thing is the property of another and liable to be *returned*, the only security given being often the undertaking, formal or implied, that it shall be so returned when we have used it.

a **1000** *Lamb. Psalm* xxxvi[i]. 21 (Bosw.) Borȝaþ se synfulla and na ȝefillþ. *c* **1000** *Ags. Gosp.* Matt. v. 42 þam þe wylle æt þe borȝian ne wyrn þu him. **1297** R. GLOUC. 393 He ..leyde..hys broþer to wedde Normandye, And borwede of hym þervppe an hondred þousend marc. *a* **1340** HAMPOLE *Pr. Consc.* 3219 Thai may nathyng begg ne borowe. *c* **1430** *Syr Gener.* 8775 Whi he bourowed it of him soo. **1535** COVERDALE *2 Esdr.* v. 3 Let vs borowe money of the kinge vpon vsury. **1552** HULOET, Borowe of Peter to paye Paule.. wher as a man doth Borow of one to paye an other. **1651** HOBBES *Leviath.* II. xxii. 116 If the person of the Body Politique..borrow mony of a stranger. **1769** *Junius Lett.* I. 4 This nation will not bear..to see new millions borrowed. **1860** TYNDALL *Glac.* I. §22. 156, I borrowed a handkerchief from Lauener.

c. *Arith.* In *Subtraction*, when the number to be subtracted in one denomination is greater than that of the minuend, To transfer to the

latter mentally the equivalent of a unit of the next higher denomination, compensating or 'paying back' for this at the next step in the process.

1594 BLUNDEVIL *Exerc.* I. (ed. 7) 91 Take 6 out of nothing, which will not bee, wherefore you must borrow 60. **1881** FITCH *Lect. Teaching* xi. 326, '9 from 3 I cannot; Borrow 10'.

2. *fig.* **a.** To render oneself indebted for; to make temporary use of (something not one's own); used, e.g. of temporal possessions, with notion of their being only *lent* to us, not given. More usually of immaterial things: as, to adopt (thoughts, expressions, modes of conduct) from another person, or (words, idioms, customs, etc.) from a foreign language or people; to obtain (a temporary favour) by request; to derive (one's authority, etc.) from another, as opposed to holding it by inherent right; to draw (a comparison, inference, suggestion) from some source alien to the subject in hand; to adopt (something) for other than its normal purpose. Const. *from*, *of*, formerly *at*.

As applied to the adoption of foreign words or customs, it properly implies that the adoption is merely temporary; but this restriction is now often disregarded, esp. by writers on philology; cf. LOAN-WORD.

a **1225** *Ancr. R.* 204 Þet is riht religiun, þet euerich.. boruwe et tisse urakele worlde so lutel so he euer mei, of mete, of cloðe, of eihte. *c* **1380** WYCLIF *De Dot. Eccles.* Sel. Wks. III. 434 Wiþout autorite borewid of oþer. **1398** TREVISA *Barth. De P.R.* VIII. xvii. (1495) 325 The mone hath no lyght of herself, but borowyth and takyth of the plente of the sonne. **1423** JAS. I. *King's Q.* I. v, I in purpose, at my boke, To borowe a slepe, at thilke tyme began. **1549** LATIMER *Serm. bef. Edw. VI.* (Arb.) 80 Let hym borowe example at Salomon. **1595** SHAKS. *John* v. i. 51 Inferior eyes That borrow their behauiours from the great. **1600** HOLLAND *Livy* XXIV. xxii. 524 You were best therefore to borrow [*sumeret*] some respite of time of the Embassadours. **1697** DRYDEN *Virg. Georg.* I. 96 Borrow part of Winter for thy Corn. **1706** A. BEDFORD *Temple Mus.* vi. 113 The Rabbies would.. borrow Words from other Languages. **1763** J. BROWN *Poetry & Mus.* xi. 184 Their [the Romans'] Music and Poetry was always borrowed and adopted. *a* **1847** R. HAMILTON *Rew. & Punishm.* iv. (1853) 185 The illustrations are borrowed from the fowls of heaven and from the flowers of the field. **1875** JOWETT *Plato* (ed. 2) IV. 15 No man can be happy who, to borrow Plato's illustration, is leading the life of an oyster.

b. *to borrow trouble*: to go out of one's way to meet trouble. *U.S. colloq.*

1854 H. H. RILEY *Puddleford & its People* ix. 119 Bird, you're allers bor'ring trouble. **1934** J. H. WALLIS *House of Murder* xiii. 128 Don't borrow trouble, Mr. Gundlach... If the hand doesn't pain any more, it will probably be all right. **1963** D. B. HUGHES *Expendable Man* (1964) vi. 182 Let's not borrow trouble.

c. In organ-building: see BORROWED *ppl. a.* 2 b.

1894 T. ELLISTON *Organs & Tuning* 63 Borrowing from one stop to form part of another is undesirable; the wind coming sometimes from one source, and at other times from another, or from both sources, make it impossible for the note to be always in tune... The Pedal Organ is somewhat exempt from the faults of borrowing, inasmuch as usually only one note is used at a time. **1902** J. W. HINTON *Organ Constr.* (ed. 2) 64 *Borrowing*, arranging a certain number of pipes so as to be common to two or more stops. **1905** T. CASSON *Pedal Organ* 24, I once tried the experiment of borrowing the Quint from a manual Bourdon. *Ibid.* 27 The borrowing must be economical; that is, it must cost less in room or money, or both, than actual independent pipes. **1927** *Organ* VII. 75 While he was about it, the builder might have borrowed this 'creamy' bourdon into the pedal.

d. *trans.* and *intr.* *Golf.* (See quots.)

1897 *Encycl. Sport* I. 472/1 *Borrow*, to play a ball up a hill or slope, instead of straight across it, so that the slope will cause the ball to return towards the hole. **1909** VAILE *Mod. Golf* 55 You allow for the slope.. and the curve.. will be the result if you have correctly estimated length and the amount you ought to 'borrow'... In golfing language, 'always borrow enough'. *Ibid.* 64 Both these cuts may be used when putting across a slope to hold the ball up against the natural tendency to run down a hill. If they are used it will obviously be unnecessary to 'borrow' so much in allowing for the slope.

†**II.** To be surety for, be good for, ransom, save.

†**3.** *trans.* To be surety for, go bail for; to ransom, redeem, release by paying a ransom. *Obs.*

a **1300** *Cursor M.* 23792 Þat soru þat nakins borgh us fra mai boru. **1377** LANGL. *P. Pl.* B. IV. 109 He shal rest in my stokkes, And þat as longe as he lyueth · but lowenesse hym borwe. *c* **1530** PALSGR. 461 If thou be taken prisoner.. I wyl nat borowe the. **1609** SKENE *Reg. Maj.* 107 Gif the Lord of the Court, to quhom the defender is borrowed, hes diverse Courts; he quha borrowes him, sall assigne to the persewer ane certaine day and place. *c* **1783** *Ballad 'Young Bekie'* iv. in Child *Ballads* II. 466/1 O gin a lady woud borrow me, At her stirrup-foot I woud rin.

†**4.** *transf.* **a.** To give security or safety to; to lease, rescue, save; to defend, protect. (With this cf. BERGH *v.* to protect. See also BURȜEN *v.*) *Obs.*

a **1300** *Cursor M.* 5286 Me borud noght bot godd allan. *c* **1350** *Med. MS.* in *Archæol.* XXX. 368 Yat day fro feueres it schall yᵉ borwe. *a* **1400** *Cov. Myst.* (1841) 421, I pray to God.. That he us borwe fro synfulle shame. **1522** *World & Child* in Hazl. *Dodsl.* I. 269 Some good word that I may say To borrow mans soul from blame.

†**b.** *absol.* To warrant, 'be bound', assert confidently. Cf. BORROW *sb.* 2 b. *Obs.*

c **1475** *Sqr. lowe Degre* 451, I shall borowe for seven yere He shall not wedde my doghter dere. **1590** GREENE *Neuer too late* (1600) 24 Wonder twas in her eyne Fire and water should combine: If th' old saw did not borrow, Fire is loue, and water sorrow.

borrow ('bɒrəʊ), *v.*² *Naut.* [Derivation uncertain; connexion with BORROW *v.*¹ 2 (as if it were 'to borrow, encroach upon, what belongs to the land or the wind') seems far-fetched; possibly the original sense was 'to shelter': see BURROW.]

intr. 'To approach closely either to land or wind.' Smyth *Sailor's Word-bk.* 1867.

1622 R. HAWKINS *Voy. S. Sea* (1847) 108 It is not good to borrow neere the shore, but to give it a fayre birth. **1702** *Lond. Gaz.* No. 3781/4 No Ship to borrow nearer the Harbour than that Perch. **1860** *Merc. Mar. Mag.* VII. 70 To borrow on the breakers of the spit to within 8 or 10 fathoms.

borrowable ('bɒrəʊəb(ə)l), *a. rare.* [f. BORROW *v.*¹ + -ABLE.] That can be borrowed.

1821 L. HUNT *Indicator* No. 73 (1822) II. 168 That description of property which may emphatically be called borrowable. **1885** *Pall Mall Budget* 19 June 31/1 'Buyable' as well as borrowable from the circulating libraries.

†'**borrowage.** [f. BORROW *sb.* and *v.* + -AGE.]

1. Suretyship.

c **1440** *Promp. Parv.* 44 Borwage, *fidejussio.*

2. The act of borrowing from another.

1577 HARRISON *England* II. viii. (1877) 176 Requiting him with the like borowage as he hath vsed toward me in his discourse.

borrowe, obs. form of BOROUGH, BORROW.

borrowed ('bɒrəʊd), *ppl. a.* [f. BORROW *v.*¹ -ED.]

1. Taken on loan. *borrowed days*: in Cheshire, the first eleven days of May, so called because in Old Style they belonged to April; see BORROWING *vbl. sb.*¹ c. *borrowed time*: an unexpected extension of time, esp. of a person's life.

c **1440** *York Myst.* xxxi. 105 A borowed bene sette I noght be hym. **1646** SIR T. BROWNE *Pseud. Ep.*, So it is usual among us.. to ascribe unto March certain borrowed days from April. **1688** *Answ. Talon's Plea* 27 The Palace.. where he resides, being but a borrowed house. **1855** MACAULAY *Hist. Eng.* IV. 245 He rode away.. on a borrowed horse, which he never returned. *Scotch Pop. Rime*, But when the borrowed days were gane, The three silly hoggs cam hirplan' hame. **1898** *E.D.D.* s.v., A man who lives on borrowed time lives on trespass-ground. Ay, all mine is borrowed time, noo. **1939** R. CHANDLER *Big Sleep* xviii. 148 Brody was living on borrowed time. **1961** R. JEFFRIES *Evidence of Accused* iii. 26 After the age of forty-five one's living on borrowed time.

2. *transf.* and *fig.* **a.** Taken or used at second-hand, not one's own; assumed, counterfeit, 'put on'; adopted or adapted for the nonce. *borrowed light*, (*a*) reflected light (see quot. 1834); also *fig.*; (*b*) see quot. 1963.

1571 GOLDING *Calvin on Ps.* i. 1 A borowed maner of speech. **1596** SPENSER *F.Q.* III. xii. 14 Her bright browes were deckt with borrowed haire. **1621–31** LAUD 7 *Serm.* (1847) 8 Most of the later divines are for the borrowed sense. **1657** BP. H. KING *Poems* 139 Even such is man, whose borrow'd light Is streight call'd in, and paid to night. **1762** HUME *Hist. Eng.* (1806) V. lxvii. 81 [Bedlow] had travelled over many parts of Europe under borrowed names. **1834** MRS. SOMERVILLE *Connex. Phys. Sc.* xxxvi. (1849) 408 If comets shine by borrowed light. **1880** F. HALL in *19th Cent.* Sept. 426 Has borrowed English been a peculiarity of the last two or three centuries? **1934** H. G. WELLS *Exper. Autobiogr.* I. ii. 39 Behind the shop was an extremely small room, the 'parlour', with a fireplace, a borrowed light and glass-door upon the shop and a larger window upon the yard behind. **1963** *Gloss. Build. Terms (B.S.I.)* 13 *Borrowed light*, a glazed.. opening in an internal wall or partition designed to admit light.

b. In organ-building, said of a pipe, a stop, or a set of them which is sounded at the expense of another or is incomplete of itself and is eked out by the use of pipes of another stop or set.

1840 in GROVE *Dict. Mus.* (1880) II. 600/2 'Borrowed' Solo Organ. **1880** *Ibid.* 595/1 Choir Organ. 2 real stops; 4 borrowed... Borrowed by communication from the Great Organ. *Ibid.* 595/2 The extra department consisted of a complete borrowed organ of 13 stops derived from the Great Organ. *Ibid.*, Second Great Organ. 13 borrowed stops.

borrowee (ˌbɒrəʊ'iː). *rare.* [f. as prec. + -EE.] One from whom something is borrowed.

1885 *Spectator* 13 June 779/2 Nobody ever met a borrower who was not savage at a refusal, unless the borrowee were a bank.

borrower ('bɒrəʊə(r)). [f. as prec. + -ER.]

1. One who takes a thing on security or on credit.

c **1440** *Promp. Parv.* 44 Borware [**1499** borower], *mutuator, sponsor.* **1602** SHAKS. *Ham.* I. iii. 75 Neither a borrower, nor a lender be. **1677** YARRANTON *Eng. Improv.* 15 Here are both to the Lender and Borrower great Advantages. **1776** ADAM SMITH *W.N.* I. II. iv. 360 Sober people are universally preferred as borrowers. **1875** JOWETT *Plato* (ed. 2) V. 314 The borrower should be under no obligation to repay either capital or interest.

2. *transf.* and *fig.* One who adopts a thing, uses it temporarily, or takes it at second-hand.

1605 SHAKS. *Macb.* III. i. 27, I must become a borrower of the Night, For a darke houre, or twaine. **1750** HARRIS *Hermes* Wks. (1841) 236 We have been remarkable borrowers, as our multiform language may sufficiently shew. **1876** M. ARNOLD *Lit. & Dogma* 215 He.. would not have become thus a borrower from Jesus.

†'**borrow-gage.** *Obs.* [f. BORROW *sb.* + GAGE; the two words being equivalents from different langs.] Pledge.

1303 R. BRUNNE *Handl. Synne* 9576 Þou settest þy selfe yn borghe gage.

†'**borrowgang.** *Obs.* Forms: 4 borghegang, 4 *Sc.* borowgange, (erron. borrowgane), 7 *Sc.* borrowgang(e. [f. BORROW *sb.* + GANG (act of going); app. implying the existence of a phrase 'to go borrow'; cf. *to go bail.*] Suretyship; the responsibility incurred by a surety.

1303 R. BRUNNE *Handl. Synne* 9582 Quyte þe weyl oute of borghegang. *a* **1375** ? BARBOUR *St. Egipciane* 967, I kepyt nocht þe borowgane I drew hyr ine. **1609** SKENE *Reg. Maj.* 48 The pledges.. either.. confes their borrowgange.. or they deny the samine.

†**borrow-head**¹ ('bɒrəʊhɛd). *Obs.* exc. *Hist.* [f. BORROW *sb.* 3 + HEAD; cf. BORSHOLDER. The fuller form *friðborhheved* occurs in the (Latin) Laws of Edward the Confessor xx. Writers from the 16th c. onwards have often confounded BORROW *sb.* 3 with BOROUGH; hence the incorrect form *borough-head*, commonly adopted in dictionaries.] Originally the head of a *friðborh* or tithing (see BORROW *sb.* 3); the word, with its synonyms BORSHOLDER, HEADBOROUGH, afterwards came to denote a parochial officer, now called a Petty Constable.

1581 LAMBARDE *Eiren.* I. iii. (1602) 13 Borowhead, Borsholder and Tythingman, bee three severall names of one selfe same office and do signifie The chiefe man of the free pledges within that Borowe or Tything. **1613** SIR H. FINCH *Law* (1636) 336 The conseruator of peace.. In a Tything [is called] a petie Constable, Borsholder, Head-Borough, Third-borough, Boroughhead, Tything-man, or Chiefe pledge. **1857** TOULM. SMITH *Parish* 121 Tything-man, borsholder, borrowhead, headborough, chief-pledge, or provost.

†'**borrowhead**², **-hood.** *Obs.* [f. BORROW *sb.* 2 + -HEAD, -HOOD.] Suretyship.

c **1380** WYCLIF *Sel. Wks.* III. 10 Þe boruheed of Crist þat witnessiþ ech trewe mannis truþe. ? *a* **1500** *Robin Hood* (Ritson) I. i. 955 Of the borowe hode thou spekest to me Herde I never ere.

borrowing ('bɒrəʊɪŋ), *vbl. sb.*¹ [f. BORROW *v.*¹] The action of the verb BORROW (senses 1, 2); taking on loan, taking at second-hand, etc.; also *concr.*, that which is borrowed.

1539 TAVERNER *Erasm. Prov.* 46 The Englysh prouerbe.. testyfyeth that he that goeth a borowynge, goeth a sorowynge. **1562** J. HEYWOOD *Prov. & Epigr.* (1867) 15 Sauying by borowyng, tyll we be in det. *a* **1630** S. PAGE in Spurgeon *Treas. Dav.* Ps. li. 3 Our food and raiment, the necessaries of life, are borrowings. **1642** FULLER *Holy & Prof. St.* II. xxiii. 147 Confession puts the difference betwixt stealing and borrowing. **1830** COLERIDGE *Table T.* 111 So borrow as to repay by the very act of borrowing. **1882** J. W. LEGG *Liturgical Colours* II. 14 These colours.. seem to be a modern borrowing from Rome.

†**b.** In certain obsolete phrases: *to do, give, lend borrowing*: to lend. *to take borrowing*: to borrow. *to ask in borrowing*: to ask as a loan.

c **1380** WYCLIF *Wks.* (1880) 277 Þat.. borwyng and lynynge be frely don to pore men. **1382** —— *Prov.* xxii. 7 He that taketh borewing, seruant is of the usurer. *Ibid. Luke* vi. 34 If ȝe ȝyuen borwynge to hem, of whiche ȝe hopen to take aȝen, what grace is to you? *c* **1570** *Leg. Bp. St. Andrews* in *Scot. Poems 16th C.* (1801) II. 328 Sowmes of silver fra him [he] ast In borrowing. **1573** *Sege Edinb.* ibid. II. 287 Lend vs ane borrouing of ȝour auld blak bellis.

c. *borrowing days*: the last three days of March (Old Style), said in Scottish folk-lore to have been borrowed by March from April, and supposed to be specially stormy.

1549 *Compl. Scot.* 38 The borial blastis of the thre borouing dais of marche. **1791** *Statist. Acc. Scotl.* I. 57 Born in the borrowing days. **1818** SCOTT *Hrt. Midl.* xxviii, The bairns' rime says, the warst blast of the borrowing days couldna kill the three silly poor hog-lams.

borrowing ('bɒrəʊɪŋ), *vbl. sb.*² *Naut.* [f. BORROW *v.*²] Sailing close to land or to the wind.

1622 R. HAWKINS *Voy. S. Sea* (1847) 117 The norther part of the bay hath foule ground, and rockes under water; and therefore it is not wholesome borrowing of the mayne.

'**borrowing**, *ppl. a.* [f. BORROW *v.*¹ + -ING².] That borrows. Hence '**borrowingly** *adv.*

1640 BROME *Sparagus Gard.* I. iii, I hope you will not.. urge me beyond patience with your borroughing attempts. *Ibid.* Your countenance.. lookes so borrowingly. **1855** DICKENS *Dorrit* ix, They eyed him with borrowing eyes. **1866** CRUMP *Banking* vii. 148 As an import to the lending country, and as an export to the borrowing country.

'**borrow-pit.** [app. f. BORROW *v.*¹] In civil engineering, an excavation formed by the removal of material to be used in filling or embanking. Also '**borrow-hole**.

1893 KIPLING *Day's Work* (1898) 2 Tiny asses climbing out of the yawning borrow-pit below with sackfuls of stuff. **1901** *Practitioner* Mar. 258 'Borrow-holes' in railway embankments. **1907** *Notes on Books* June 267/2 An easily applied check on borrow-pit measurements.

† '**borrowship.** *Obs. rare.* = BORROWAGE.
c **1440** *Promp. Parv.* 44 Borwage [K. borweshepe], *fidejussio.*

borsch (bɔːʃ, bɔrʃtʃ). Also **borscht, borshch, bortsch.** [Russ. *borshch.*] A Russian soup of several ingredients, esp. beetroot and cabbage.
1884 J. PAGET *Let.* 2 Sept. in *Mem. & Lett.* (1901) II. vi. 346 A real Russian dinner—first there was a strange thing called Borsch. **1927** *Blackw. Mag.* Sept. 294/1 Caviare, crimson bowls of bortsch, with thick seasoned cream. **1929** *Daily Tel.* 22 Jan. 7/6 The borscht is a delicious consommé of beef and duck, ham, beetroot. **1939** *Collier's* 21 Jan. 40/1 The other new words came in a steady flood: Big time..the borscht circuit (Catskill Mt. summer resorts booking life-of-the-party m.c.'s). **1963** V. NABOKOV *Gift* iii. 153 She was slowly mixing a white exclamation mark of sour cream into her borshch.

borsella (bɔːˈsɛlə). [Perversion of It. PROCELLO.] In glass-making, an instrument for modifying the form of vessels.
[**1699** tr. *H. Blancourt's Art of Glass* 31 The Instruments mark'd E. serve to finish the Work, which the Italians call *Ponteglo, Passago, Procello, Spiei*, and also *Borsello*, whereof we want the Figure.] **1823** G. CRABB *Technol. Dict., Borsella* (Mech.), an instrument with which glass makers contract or extend their glasses at pleasure.

borsholder (ˈbɔːshəʊldə(r)). *Obs.* exc. *Hist.* Also 6 **borsolder**, 6–8 **bosholder**, 7 **bursholder**, 9 in historical writers **bors-, borhs-ealdor.** [The spelling *borghesaldre* in the AF. Statutes of the Realm (I. 223) points to OE. **borȝes aldor*, f. *borȝes*, gen. case of *borh* (BORROW *sb.* 3) + ALDER *sb.*² Not connected with BOROUGH.]
The chief of a tithing (BORROW *sb.* 3) or frank-pledge; afterwards a parish officer identical in functions with the Petty Constable (= BORROWHEAD, HEADBOROUGH, TITHINGMAN). (Also *fig.*)
1536 *Act 28 Hen. VIII*, x, Euery..hedborowe, thyrdborowe, borsholder, and euery other lay officer. **1609** SIR E. HOBY *Letter to T.H.* 3, I dispatched this paper, as my Borsholder. **1618** DALTON *Country Just.* in Halliwell *Shaks.* VI. 324 There be other officers of much like authority to our constables, as the borsholders in Kent, the third-borow in Warwickshire, and the tythingman and burrow-head, or headborow, or chiefe-pledge in other places. **1678** *Lond. Gaz.* No. 1357/1 His Majesty doth hereby strictly Charge all Constables, Churchwardens, Headboroughs, Tythingmen, Borsholders, and other Parish Officers. **1768** BLACKSTONE *Comm.* I. 356 The antient headboroughs, tithing-men, and borsholders, were made use of to serve as petty constables. **1857** TOULM. SMITH *Parish* 15 Elsewhere, the name headborough, and elsewhere that of borsholder, was and is in use. **1872** E. ROBERTSON *Hist. Ess.* 114 The..Parish Constable and beadle, representatives of the Borh's Ealdor and the Bode or messenger of the Court.

Borstal, borstal (ˈbɔəstəl). [Name of a village near Rochester in Kent.] In full ***Borstal institution***: a reformatory for 'juvenile adults', conducted according to the method first put into practice at the reformatory at Borstal and adopted afterwards elsewhere. Also *attrib.* So *Borstal system*: a system established in 1908 whereby young persons convicted of criminal offences between the ages of 16 and 23 may be sent to a Borstal institution for a period of reformative training, usu. 3 years, after which they are released subject to further supervision by the ***Borstal Association***. Hence **Borˈstalian**, an inmate of a Borstal.
[**1902** *Encycl. Brit.* XXXII. 8/1 In 1901..a 'juvenile-adult reformatory' was opened at Borstal, near Rochester, by the conversion of a part of the existing convict prison.] **1907** *Daily Chron.* 6 June 5/4 The 'Borstal prisoner'. **1907** *Borstal System* 2 Every lad who is imprisoned in Dartmoor or Borstal passes into the care of the Borstal Association on his discharge. **1917** *Times* 7 Feb. 5/6 Four youths have escaped from the Borstal Institution, Rochester. **1921** *Glasgow Herald* 15 Nov. 6 The Borstal boys have five meals a day at Portland. **1923** (*title*) The Borstalian. **1951** *Lancet* 3 Mar. 519/1 The only open borstal for girls is at East Sutton. *Ibid.* 519/2 A survey of 300 borstal girls. **1957** *Encycl. Brit.* III. 924/1 There are now in England four Borstal institutions—at Chatham, Feltham and Portland for youths, and that for girls at Aylesbury. **1958** *Observer* 19 Oct. 21/6 There are sharp sketches of fellow Borstalians.
Also *transf.* as *adj.*
1936 'J. TEY' *Shilling for Candles* x. 112 Grant thought how Borstal she was in spite of her soignée exterior. That air of resentment against the world in general and her own fate in particular was very familiar to him.

'**borstall.** *local.* Also 7 **bostal.** [? f. OE. *beorh* a hill (BARROW *sb.*¹) + OE. *stīȝel(e*, STILE. But the explanation 'seat on the side or pitch of a hill' given by Bp. Kennett (see Halliwell), suggests OE. **beorh-steall.*] (See quot.)
1674 RAY *S. & E. Country Wds.* 59 *Bostal*, a way up a hill. Suffolk. **1880** L. J. JENNINGS *Rambles among Hills* 199 One of the steep paths up the hillside known in the South Down district as bostalls or borstalls. **1884** *Contemp. Rev.* Aug. 330 The steep paths which wind up to the summit [of the Downs] retain their Saxon name of borstalls.

† **borstax.** *Obs. rare*⁻¹. ? Some kind of axe.
c **1300** *Song Husbandm.* in *Pol. Songs* 151 Mi bil ant my borstax.

borsten, obs. form of BURST.

borstyan, variant of BUSTIAN, *Obs.*, cloth.

bort (bɔːt). Also 7 **bourt**, 9 **boart.** [Possibly a. OF. *bord, bort*, bastard; the word is used in mod.F. (Littré, supplement) as *bord* and *bort*, but is not in Cotgr. 1611.] The fragments removed from diamonds in cutting, when too small for jewellery; also diamonds of too coarse a quality for jewellery: used to make diamond powder.
1622 MALYNES *Anc. Law-Merch.* 74 The Flat Diamonds, which are in the superficies of the Bourt of Diamonds, and are impure, commonly beaten therefore into powder for the vse of the other Diamonds, that are cut and polished by the Millne. **1698** FRYER *Acc. E. India & P.* III. iii. 113 A flat Press, where under Steel-wheels the Diamonds are fastned; and with its own Bort are worn into what Cut the Artist pleases. **1817** JAS. MILL *Brit. India* I. II. viii. 353 In a flat press, where under steel wheels, the diamonds are fastened, and with its own bort are worn into what cut the artist pleases. **1884** F. BRITTEN *Watch & Clockm.* 129 Drills are selected from needle-shaped pieces of bort. **1959** *Times* 18 Nov. 21/1 The diamonds produced in the laboratory..are similar to so called boart or abrasive grit.

boru(gh, boruwen, obs. forms of BORROW.

boru(ȝ, obs. form of BOROUGH.

'**boruret.** *Chem.* [f. BOR-ON + -URET.] Earlier name for a boride, now generally disused.
1847 in CRAIG.

Borussian (bəʊˈrʌʃən), *sb.* and *a.* [f. med.L. *Borussi* pl. or *Borussia* (app. etymologizing perversion of stem *Prūs-*, as if f. Slavonic *po* by, alongside + *Russia*): see -IAN.] = PRUSSIAN.
1607 TOPSELL *Four-F. Beasts* 211 They [elks] are..found ..in the wood Hercynia, and among the Borussian-Scythians. **1608** —— *Serpents* 23 The auncient Borussians, worshipped a naturall Serpent of the earth. **1718** T. PURNEY *Chevalier de St. George* 49 As regal Beast From Dwolm Borussian bursts. **1882** *Encycl. Brit.* XIV. 702/1 The Lithuanian stem was divided into three main branches:—the Borussians or Prussians; the Letts..and the Lithuanians. **1921** *Trans. Scott. Eccles. Soc.* 126 So far as they are free from Wendish or Borussian admixture. **1925** *Contemp. Rev.* Jan. 72 The country was occupied by aboriginal tribes of Finns, Letts, Lithuanians, Borussians, and Poles or kindred Slavs.

borw(ȝ, obs. form of BOROUGH, BURROW.

borwch, borwe-n, obs. forms of BORROW.

† '**borwen.** *Obs. rare.* [? Parallel form of BURIEN:—OE. *byrȝen*] A mound, heap.
1570 LEVINS *Manip.* 60 A Borwen, *cumulus.*

borzoi (ˈbɔːzɔɪ). Also 9 **barzoi.** [a. Russ. *borzóĭ*, a male dog of the breed called *borzáya*, f. *bórzyĭ* swift.] A breed of dog, also called the Russian or Siberian wolf-hound.
1887 *Field* 14 May 679/1 The Russian barzoi, or Siberian wolfhound, is one of the noblest of all dogs. **1892** *Pall Mall Gaz.* 11 Feb. 7/2 The Grand Duke owns seventy of these barzois or Russian wolfhounds. **1892** *Field* 5 Mar. 325/1 There seems to be a general feeling among owners of Borzois that the time has now arrived for the successful starting of a special club. **1895** *Westm. Gaz.* 9 Oct. 7/2 The Borzois Club is going to be remodelled, but I am glad to hear..that there is no immediate intention of altering the existing scale of Borzoi points. **1945** C. L. B. HUBBARD *Observer's Bk. Dogs* 30 The Borzoi arrived in England about 1875. **1969** *Times Lit. Suppl.* 6 Mar. 236/4 One inevitably comes up with Gollancz's yellow jackets,..Alfred A. Knopf's borzoi colophon, and so on.

bos = *behoves*: see BUS *v. Obs.*; also obs. f. BOSS.

bosa, var. of BOZA, an oriental drink.

bosard(e, obs. form of BUZZARD.

boscage, boskage (ˈbɒskɪdʒ). Also 5 **buscage**, (7 **boxage**). [ME. *boskage*, a. OF. *boscage* (mod.F. *bocage*) wooded country, a thicket:—late L. *boscāticum*, f. late L. *boscu-m* wood: see -AGE; cf. the It. equivalent *boscaggio.*]
1. A mass of growing trees or shrubs; a thicket, grove; woody undergrowth; sylvan scenery.
c **1400** *Ywaine & Gaw.* 1671 Als he went in that boskage, He fond a letil ermytage. **1483** CAXTON *G. de la Tour* I ij b, She..suffred so moche euylle and meschyef in the buscage. **1522** SKELTON *Why nat to Court* II. 50 And with such corage Hunte the boskage. **1626** BACON *New Atl.* (1650) 1 A Land Flat to our sight, and full of Boscage. **1719** J. AUBREY *Surrey* IV. 173 Thick Boscages of Box-Trees. **1830** TENNYSON *Dream Fair Women* 243 The sombre boskage of the wood. **1858** CARLYLE *Fredk. Gt.* II. VII. vii. 260 The cool boscages and orangeries of the place.
†**2.** The pictorial representation of wooded landscape; also, a decorative design imitating branches and foliage. *Obs.*
1610 FOLKINGHAM *Art Survey* II. vi. 58 Compartiments are Blankes or Figures bordered with Anticke Boscage or Crotesko-woorke. **1624** WOTTON *Archit.* (1672) 59 Chearful Paintings in Feasting and Banquetting Rooms..Landskips and Boscage, and such wild works in open Tarraces. **1679** *The Confinement* 57 Boscage within each Chamber must be shown, Or the mean pile no Architect will own.
†**3.** *Law.* (Meaning disputed; see quots.) *Obs.*
1483 CAXTON *Gold. Leg.* 145/2 He gaf to them of that hows the fee ryall of that buscage. **1598** MANWOOD *Lawes Forest* xii. §1 (1615) 88 To be quit of Boscage..is to be discharged of paying any duetie for windfall woods. **1672** *Cowell's Interpr., Boscage*, is such sustenance as Wood and Trees yield to Cattel, viz. Mast. **1753** CHAMBERS *Cycl. Supp., Boscage* sometimes denoted a tax or duty laid on wood brought into the city.

† **boscaresque,** *a. Obs. rare*⁻¹. [f. It. *bosco* wood, or perh. *boscareccio* (Florio) woody; after *picturesque.* (Cf. F. *boscaresque*, used by Rousseau.)] Picturesque with sylvan scenery.
a **1734** NORTH *Lives* II. 181 His garden was exquisite, being most boscaresque.

bosce, obs. form of BOSS.

‖ **bosch**¹ (properly bɔs, usually bɔʃ). Also **bosh.** [Du. *bosch* a wood, BUSH.] Used by the Dutch settlers in South Africa, and thence in *comb.*, as: **bosch-bok**, an antelope of South Africa, the Bush-buck; **bosch-man** = BUSHMAN (the word used in Holland, however, is *boschjesman*); **bosch-vark**, a species of wild pig in South Africa.
1786 tr. *Sparrman's Voy. Cape G.H.* 271, I saw and gave chase to the bosch-bok. **1834** PRINGLE *Afr. Sk.* 76 The boschbok oft would bound away. *Ibid.* iii. 161 The boschvark, or wood-swine. **1854** H. MILLER *Footpr. Creat.* ix. (1874) 156 The degraded boschmen of creation.

bosch², **bosh** (bɒʃ). [In full, *bosch butter*, i.e. artificial butter manufactured at 'sHertogenbosch or 'Bosch' (Bois-le-duc) in Holland.] An imitation of butter, otherwise called BUTTERINE, usually consisting of oleomargarine with a small proportion of genuine butter. Also **bosch butter.**
1879 *Echo* 7 Apr. 3/4 It was known in the trade by the name of 'bosh'. **1880** *Daily News* 26 Feb. 5/2 Oleomargarine ..is generally sold in this country under the name of 'butterine', but it is also known commercially by the more expressive term 'bosch'.

Bosch(e: see BOCHE.

boschayle, var. of BUSHAILE, *Obs.*, copse.

bosche, boscher, obs. ff. BUSH, BUTCHER.

† **bosco.** *Obs.* ? Distortion of BOSS.
1654 GAYTON *Fest. Notes* II. iii. 42 The boscos, and suboscos (I mean) the dulapes and the jawy part of the face.

bose (bəʊs), *sb.*¹ Colloq. abbrev. of BOSUN.
1912 J. MASEFIELD in *English Rev.* XII. 376 The bose half blind, Spat. **1927** J. SAMPSON *Seven Seas Shanty Book* 47 A handy Bose and a handy Sails.

Bose (bəʊz), *sb.*² The name of S. N. *Bose* (see BOSON) used *attrib.* in place of BOSE-EINSTEIN, as ***Bose condensation, statistics.***
1931 *Sci. Abstr.* A. XXXIV. 187 The Bose statistics. **1932** *Physical Rev.* XL. 1029 One can as yet not decide from isotherm measurements alone whether or not real gases obey the Bose statistics. **1967** J. WILKS *Liquid & Solid Helium* xi. 309 A perfect gas of even atomic mass should obey Bose statistics, and exhibit a Bose condensation below a certain temperature. **1968** C. G. KUPER *Introd. Theory Superconductivity* ix. 156 This formalism is a generalization of the quantum mechanics of a single particle to a system of many non-interacting particles obeying Bose statistics.

bose (bəʊs), *v.* [cf. E.D.D. *Boss* v.³ to bang, *Boss* adj. hollow, empty (= BOSS *a.*).] To test (ground) for the presence of buried structures by noting the sound of percussion from a weighted rammer. So '**boser**, an instrument used for this purpose; '**bosing** *vbl. sb.*, the action or process of testing ground in this way.
1929 *Antiquity* III. 231 The plan made by Dr. Curwen, based upon 'bosing' and excavation, is full of interest. **1930** *Ibid.* IV. 30 The 'boser' can easily be made out of a narrow cylindrical tin filled with about 8 lbs. of lead. **1953** R. J. C. ATKINSON *Field Archæol.* (ed. 2) i. 31 The first of these [methods], known as '*bosing*', consists in percussing the surface of the ground with a weighted rammer and listening to the sound thus produced. Over undisturbed ground the sound is dull;..over a filled-up ditch or pit it changes to a more resonant note... A heavy pick-axe may be used as a boser.

bose, obs. form of BOOSE, BOSS, BUSH.

Bose-Einstein (ˌbəʊzˈaɪnstaɪn). *Physics.* [The names of S. N. *Bose* (see BOSON) and Albert *Einstein* (1879–1955), German-born American physicist.] ***Bose-Einstein condensation***, in a system of bosons, the existence of a proportion of the particles in a zero-energy state when the temperature is below a certain value; ***Bose-Einstein particle*** = BOSON; ***Bose-Einstein statistics***, a type of quantum statistics used with systems of indistinguishable particles which have the property that any number can occupy the same quantum state; cf. *Fermi-Dirac statistics.*
1928 *Proc. Physical Soc.* XL. 329 In the Bose-Einstein statistics λ is essentially positive. **1938** *Physical Rev.* LIV. 947 (*heading*) On the Bose-Einstein condensation. **1948** MOTT & SNEDDON *Wave Mech. & its Applications* xi. 354 Field theory for Bose-Einstein particles. **1955** H. B. G. CASIMIR in W. Pauli *Niels Bohr* 131 The remarkable feature

of Bose-Einstein condensation is that a sizable fraction of the particles is forced by the statistics into.. a state which should have curious and essentially non-classical properties. **1968** C. G. KUPER *Introd. Theory Superconductivity* ix. 156 A collection of particles obeying Bose-Einstein statistics has a wave function which is symmetrical under the interchange of any two particles.

bosey: see BOSIE.

bosh (bɒʃ), *sb.*[1] [Origin unknown; senses 1 and 2 may be of distinct derivation. Sense 1 has been compared with Ger. *böschen* to slope. The plur. form is due to the fact that blast-furnaces were formerly of square section, and the 'boshes' were the *four* sloping walls of the lower portion.]

1. *pl.* In a blast-furnace, the lower part of the shaft, sloping downwards from the belly, or widest part, to the hearth.

1679 PLOT *Staffordsh.* (1686) 162 Where these oblique walls terminat, which they term the boshes. **1864** *Q. Jrnl. Science* I. 492 The body and boshes being made of distinct truncated cones.

2. 'A trough in which bloomary tools (or, in copper-smelting, hot ingots) are cooled.' Raymond *Mining Gloss.* 1881.

†**bosh** (bɒʃ), *sb.*[2] *Obs.* [Origin unknown: perhaps a corruption of F. *ébauche* outline, rough-hewn figure.] An outline, rough sketch. Hence (?) ***to cut a bosh***: to make a figure, to make an imposing, swaggering appearance.

1726 AMHERST *Terræ Fil.* xlvi. 245 Who has handsomer tie-wigs, or more fashionable cloaths, or cuts a bolder bosh than Tom Paroquet? *Ibid.* 247 Laughing at everybody.. that does not cut as bold a bosh as they do. **1751** *Student* II. 287 A man who has learned but the bosh of an argument, that has only seen the shadow of a syllogism.

bosh (bɒʃ), *sb.*[3] *slang* or *colloq.* [a. Turk. *bosh* empty, worthless; the word became current in Eng. from its frequent occurrence in Morier's novel *Ayesha* (1834), which was extremely popular, especially in the 'Standard Novels' edition 1846.]

1. Contemptible nonsense, 'stuff'; trash; foolish talk or opinions.

[**1834** MORIER *Ayesha* I. 219 This firman is *bosh*—nothing. *Ibid.* I. 283 The parts [of the Koran] which are taken from the Christian Bible are divine; [the other parts] are spurious. They are *bosh*—nothing.] **1850** P. CROOK *War of Hats* 19 Some nameless bosh—seduction—or crim. con. **1863** KINGSLEY *Water Bab.* (1878) 174 And were pure bosh and wind. **1864** MISS YONGE *C'tess Kate* xii. 212 Don't talk bosh out of your books. **1885** *Illustr. Lond. News* 23 May 539/2, I can write something that is not bosh.

2. *int.* Stuff and nonsense! Humbug!

1850 C. KINGSLEY *Let.* 31 May in *Life & Works* (1902) VII. 28 Theirs is now discovered not to be a necessary trade. Bosh! The question is this—[etc.]. **1852** DICKENS *Bleak Ho.* xxi, Bosh! It's all correct. *Ibid.* xxiv, Bosh, what's my head running against!

bosh, *sb.*[4] *slang.* [ad. Romany *bosh-* to crow, fiddle, etc., a. Skr. *vāś*-to low, bellow.] A fiddle. *Comb.*: **bosh-faker, -killer, -man**, one who plays a fiddle.

1846 *Swell's Night Guide* 47 A boshman every Tuesday night for hopping and chaunting. **1859** HOTTEN *Dict. Slang, Bosh*, a fiddle. *Bosh-Faker*, a violin player. **1865** F. H. NIXON *Peter Perfume* 102 'Boshman' in the old-hand vernacular signifies a fiddler. **1876** W. GREEN *Cheap Jack* 231 Can you rocker Romanie, Can you fake a bosh? **1935** X. PETULENGRO *Romany Life* xxxiii. 119 Rudy and Adolphus were the *bosh*-killers (we spoke English Romany now); I played the melodeon.

†**bosh**, *v.*[1] *Obs.* [f. BOSH *sb.*[2]] *intr.* To cut a dash; to make a show; to flaunt.

1709 STEELE & SWIFT *Tatler* No. 71 ¶8 When to the plain Garb of Gown and Band a Spark adds an inconsistent long Wig, we do not say now he Boshes, but there goes a Smart Fellow. **1726** AMHERST *Terræ Fil.* xxxiii. 180 Bosh it about town in lace ruffles.

bosh (bɒʃ), *v.*[2] *slang.* [f. BOSH *sb.*[3]] *trans.* To make of no effect; to spoil; to humbug.

1870 *Macm. Mag.* XXI. 71 You 'bosh' his [a man's] joke by refusing to laugh at it; you 'bosh' his chance of sleep by playing upon the cornet all night in the room next to him. **1883** MISS BRADDON *Gold. Calf* xiv, Boys would get on capitally with Jardine. They'd never try to bosh him.

bosh: see BOSCH[2].

bosher ('bɒʃə(r)). *slang.* [f. BOSH *sb.*[3] + -ER.[1]] One who talks 'bosh' or nonsense.

1913 D. H. LAWRENCE *Let.* 17 Jan. (1932) 94 Don't ever mind what I say. I am a great bosher, and full of fancies that interest me. **1939** H. G. WELLS *Holy Terror* I. iii. 89 'The man's a blatant bosher.' 'He's not. He knows exactly what he is up to.'

bosholder, obs. form of BORSHOLDER.

bosh-shot: see BOSS-SHOT.

boshy ('bɒʃɪ), *a.* [f. BOSH *sb.*[3] + -Y[1].] Of the nature of bosh; contemptible, worthless.

1860 J. M. ATKINSON *Let.* 6 May in *Richmond-Atkinson Papers* (1960) I. x. 577 The concentration of 'boshy' gossip in town is wearisome. **1864** 'MARK TWAIN' *Sk. Sixties* (1927) II. 132, I read your boshy criticisms on the opera with the most exquisite anguish. **1882** 'F. ANSTEY' *Vice Versâ* iv, There was no dancing, only boshy games and a conjuror.

bosie ('bəʊzɪ). *Austral.* Also **bosey**. [Hypocoristic f. the name of B. J. T. *Bosanquet*, an English cricketer: see -IE.] = GOOGLY *sb.* Also *attrib.*, as ***bosie ball, bowler, bowling***.

1912 *Australasian* 2 Mar. 481/2 Then he lifted the 'Bosie' bowler high to the on. **1920** E. R. WILSON in P. F. Warner *Cricket* ii. 74 The 'googly' or 'Bosie ball' as it was afterwards christened in Australia. **1927** *Observer* 13 Feb. 23/6 The finest exponent of 'Bosie' bowling in the world. **1930** C. V. GRIMMETT *Getting Wickets* i. 22 It was at this time that I learned to bowl the 'bosie' or 'googly'—an off-break with a leg-break action. **1954** A. G. MOYES *Austral. Batsmen* xiv. 186 The changes in bowling style and tactics.. from off-spin to speed, to 'boseys'.

bosjesman: see BUSHMAN.

bosk (bɒsk). Also 3-4 **boske**, (9 **bosque**, *rare*). [The early ME. *bosk(e* was a variant of *busk*, BUSH; *bosk* and *busk* are still used dialectally for BUSH; but the modern literary word may have been evolved from BOSKY.]

†**1.** A bush. *Obs.* exc. *dial.*

1297 R. GLOUC. 547 Hii houede vnder boskes. *c* **1300** *Prov. Hendyng* xx, Vnder boske shal men weder abide, quoþ Hendyng. *c* **1325** *E.E. Allit. P.* B. 322 Boþe boskez & bourez & wel bounden penez.

2. A thicket of bushes and underwood; a small wood.

1814 SCOTT *Ld. Isles* v. xv, Meantime, through well-known bosk and dell, I'll lead where we may shelter well. **1847** TENNYSON *Princ.* i. 110 Blowing bosks of wilderness. **1862** LYTTON *Str. Story* II. 82 Every bosk and dingle. **1878** H. PHILLIPS *Poems fr. Span. & Germ.* 69 In a flowery bosque there flies a bird. **1885** *Century Mag.* 544 It is planted with pleasant little bosks and trim hedges.

Hence †**boske addre**, lit. 'bush-adder': a viper, a serpent (L. *coluber*).

1382 WYCLIF *Ex.* vii. 9 Tak thin ȝerde, and throw it bifore Pharao, and be it turned into a bosk eddre.. The ȝerde.. was turnyd into a boske addre.

boskage, variant of BOSCAGE.

boske(n, obs. form of BUSK *v.* to prepare.

bosker ('bɒskə(r)), *a. Austral.* and *N.Z. slang.* Now *obsolescent*. Also formerly **'boscar, 'boshter**. [Origin unknown.] Good, excellent, delightful. Cf. BONZER *a.* Hence as *sb.*

1906 E. DYSON *Fact'ry 'Ands* i. 1 'She's er little boshter!' he said vehemently. 'Y' orter seen 'er.' *Ibid.* xii. 151 He promised to show Feathers a 'boshter knack for passing out gazobs'! **1909** A. H. ADAMS *Galahad Jones* i. 8 It's a 'bosker' castle. **1911** C. E. W. BEAN *'Dreadnought' of Darling* xxxv. 314 'That's it—my word, it's a bosker, that is' the driver whispered to the Sydney passenger. **1911** 'KIWI' *On Swag* vii. 14 We gave him a boscar funeral. **1916** *Anzac Book* 36 'A boshter night for a walk,' I remarked, buttoning my coat about me. **1922** A. E. MULGAN *Three Plays N.Z.* 36 That's a boscar song. **1926** I. M. PEACOCKE *His Kid Brother* iv. 54 What bosker fun. **1943** F. SARGESON in *Penguin New Writing* XVIII. 63 It turned out a bosker day. **1952** A. GRIMBLE *Pattern of Islands* 68 'Cripes!' he said. 'She's a fair bosker, ain't she, son!'

bosket, bosquet ('bɒskɪt). [18th c. a. F. *bosquet*, ad. It. *boschetto*, dim. of *bosco* wood. See also the earlier forms BUSHET, BUSKET; and cf. BOUQUET.] A plantation in a garden, park, etc., of underwood and small trees; a thicket.

1737 MILLER *Gard. Dict.*, *Bosquets*.. are small Compartments of Gardens.. form'd of Trees, Shrubs, or tall large growing plants. **1828** SCOTT *F.M. Perth* I. 316 There are bushes and boskets enough by the river side. **1833** T. HOOK *Parson's Dau.* II. viii. 238 A gravel circle encompassing a bosquet of laurel, laurestinus and holly. *a* **1847** MRS. SHERWOOD *Lady of Manor* IV. xviii. 27 Nothing was to be seen but stiff parterres, trim avenues, close bosquets, grottoes, and Chinese bridges. **1859** L. OLIPHANT *China & Japan* I. xii. 237 Charming little boskets with mossy seats.

Hence **bo'squettish** *a.*

1881 *Academy* No. 491. 252 To him plants become bosquettish.

boskiness ('bɒskɪnɪs). [f. BOSKY *a.*[1] + -NESS.] The quality of being bosky.

a **1844** in W. H. Maxwell *Sports & Adv. Scotl.* (1855) iv. 57 Tangled.. boskiness. *c* **1860** *Imperial Gaz. Scotl.* I. 222. **1863** HAWTHORNE *Old Home* (1879) 56 A shadowy secluded grove, with winding paths among its boskiness.

Boskop ('bɒskɒp). [The name of a place in the Transvaal, South Africa.] In *attrib.* use with *man, race*, etc.: of or belonging to the early type of man indicated by the skull of the late Pleistocene period found at Boskop. Hence **'Boskopoid** *a.* [-OID], characterized by the type of skull found at Boskop; also as *sb.*

1915 *Nature* 5 Aug. 615/2 The Boskop man was of the Neanderthal race, but more advanced in intelligence. **1926** *Bantu Studies* II. 219 Comparison has been made mainly with the Boskopoid remains from Zitzikama reported upon .. during the last two years, and with the descriptions of the original Boskop remains. **1948** A. L. KROEBER *Anthropol.* (ed. 2) iii. 108 Undoubtedly Neanthropic is the Boskop type. .. The Boskop type skulls are massive and large. **1959** J. D. CLARK *Prehist. S. Afr.* iv. 97 The physical types belonging with the earlier occupation levels at this site were in fact 'Bush-Boskopoids'. **1966** E. PALMER *Plains of Camdeboo* vii. 118 The Middle Stone Age people—the Boskop race—of South Africa were not one race but several.

bosky ('bɒskɪ), *a.*[1] [f. BOSK (not recorded between 14th and 19th c., but preserved in dial.) + -Y; or alteration of BUSKY, after It. *boscoso.*] Consisting of or covered with bushes or underwood; full of thickets, bushy. (Also *transf.*)

1593 PEELE *Chron. Edw. I.* (1874) 407 In this bosky wood Bury his corpse. **1610** SHAKS. *Temp.* IV. i. 81 My boskie acres, and my vnshrubd downe. **1634** MILTON *Comus* 312 And every bosky bourn. **1757** DYER *Fleece* (1807) 79 The bosky bourns of Alfred's shires. **1810** SCOTT *Lady of L.* III. xiv, The bosky thickets. **1851** H. MELVILLE v. 33 A brown and brawny company with bosky beards.

bosky ('bɒskɪ), *a.*[2] *dial.* or *slang.* [perh. a humorous use of prec., with the notion of 'overshadowed' or 'obscured'.] Somewhat the worse for drink, tipsy.

1730-6 BAILEY, *Bosky*, half or quite fuddled. **1824** *Blackw. Mag.* XVI. 573 He may be tipsy, bosky, cut, or anything but drunk. **1843** T. HOOK in *New Month. Mag.* LX. 11 Became, to use a colloquial expression, uncommonly bosky.

†**bosman.** *U.S. Obs.* Also **bosseman**. [ad. Fr. *bosseman* (cf. G. *bootsmann* boatswain).] = BOWSMAN. *Obs.*

[**1807** C. C. ROBIN *Voyages* II. 212 Les rameurs sont distribués également de chaque côté; à l'arrière est le patron qui gouverne, et en avant un homme, nommé bosman, une perche à la main, sonde les lieux où l'on craint de toucher.] **1876** *Scribner's Monthly* Jan. 404/2 A man in the bow called the *bosman*, who generally wielded a sort of a boathook, watched the course. **1906** *Trans. Kansas State Hist. Soc.* 1905-6 IX. 272 The captain of the boat, called the 'patron', did the steering, and his assistant, called the 'bosseman', stood on the bow, pole in hand, and gave directions to the men at the cordelle.

Bosniac ('bɒznɪæk). Also **-ak**. [ad. F. *Bosniaque*, or G. *Bosniake*, ad. Russ. *Bosnyak.*] = BOSNIAN *sb.*

1836 *Penny Cycl.* V. 231/1 The inhabitants of Bosnia are composed of Bosniaks, a race of Sclavonian origin. **1848** E. LEAR *Jrnl. of Landscape Painter in Albania* (1851) 17 The packed Wallachians, and Bosniacs, and Jews started crampfully from the deck. **1920** *Edin. Rev.* Oct. 218 The ruling race absorbed large numbers of Christians, Greeks, Slavs, and later on Albanians and Bosniacs.

Bosnian ('bɒznɪən), *a.* and *sb.* [f. *Bosnia*: see -IAN. Cf. F. *bosnien.*] **A.** *adj.* Of or pertaining to Bosnia, a province of Yugoslavia. **B.** *sb.* A native of Bosnia.

1788 [see SERVIAN *sb.*]. **1830** C. FRASER *Hist. War in Bosnia* 17 A number of females who, like the ancient Bosnian women, acquired the courage of heroes. *Ibid.* 63 Mohammed set off with five or six thousand horsemen, Bosnians. **1836** *Penny Cycl.* V. 230/1 The Verbas, another Bosnian river, rises in the heart of the country. **1847** [see TURK[1] 2]. **1847** MRS. A. KERR tr. *Ranke's Hist. Servia* 167 He opposed to the great Bosnian army about 1500 men. **1924** *Contemp. Rev.* Nov. 620 'The Bosnians are never satisfied', we were told. **1949** L. DURRELL *Spirit of Place* (1969) 103 The Bosnian peasants in their dramatic costume.

bosom ('bʊzəm), *sb.* Forms: 1 **bósm, bósum**, 2-3 **bosm, bosem**, *Orm.* **bosemm**, 3-6 **bosum** (in 6 only *Sc.*), 4-7 **bosome**, (6 **bosym, bowsum, boosome**), 4- **bosom**. [OE. *bósm* = OFris. *bósm*, OS. *bósom* (MDu. *boesem*, Du. *boezem*), OHG. *buosam* (MHG. *buosem*, mod.G. *busen*):—WGer. **bôsm-* (not in EGer.). Remoter etymology unknown: it has been conjectured that **bôsmo-* stands for **bôh-smo*, f. **bôhu-*:—OAryan **bhâghu-s* arm (BOUGH); the word would then, like the partially synonymous FATHOM, primarily mean the space embraced by the two arms.]

I. 1. a. The breast of a human being; also *poet.* of a bird, etc.

c **1000** ÆLFRIC *Numb.* xi. 12 Ðæt ic hiȝ bære on minum bosume, swa fostormodor deþ cyld. **1382** WYCLIF *John* xiii. 23 Oon of his disciplis was restinge in the bosum of Jhesu. *c* **1440** *York Myst.* xv. 104 A baren broche by a belle of tynne At youre bosom to be. **1592** SHAKS. *Ven. & Ad.* 646 Within my bosom.. My boding heart pants. **1697** DRYDEN *Virg. Georg.* IV. 19 Progne, with her Bosom stained in Blood. **1847** TENNYSON *Princ.* II. 88 Doves That sun their milky bosoms on the thatch. **1864** —— *Aylmer's F.* 687 The babe Too ragged to be fondled on her lap, Warm'd at her bosom?

b. The enclosure formed by the breast and the arms. ***in one's bosom***: clasped to one's breast. Now only *arch.*, and chiefly in fig. Scriptural phrases, e.g. ***in Abraham's bosom*** (cf. *Luke* xvi. 22): in the abode of the blessed dead.

c **1175** *Lamb. Hom.* 53 Alse heo heom [heore euencristene] walde in to heore bosme puten. *c* **1200** ORMIN 19391 Iesu Crist.. þatt inn hiss Faderr bosemm iss. **1382** WYCLIF *Mic.* vii. 5 Hir that restith in thi bosum. **1420** *E.E. Wills* (1882) 47 That he resseyue me yn-to þe brode bosum off his mercy. **1578** *Gude & Godlie Ballates* (1868) 36 Quhen Lazarus he saw.. In his bosome. **1816** W. HOLLAR *Dance Death* xix. 53 Death.. attacks this warrior, in the bosom of victory. **1866** NEALE *Seq. & Hymns* 162 The child was in Abraham's bosom.

c. ***wife of one's bosom***: orig. a Hebraism adopted in the Bible of 1611; but its Eng. use is influenced by senses 6 a and b. (The similar

phrase ***husband of one's bosom***, *Deut*. xxviii. 56, never became current.) Hence, ***to take to one's bosom***: to marry.

1611 BIBLE *Deut.* xiii. 6 The wife of thy bosome. *Ibid.* xxviii. 56 The husband of her bosome. **1747** HERVEY *Medit.* (1753) II. 53 The Wife of his Bosom may expire by his Side. **1814** T. JEFFERSON *Corr.* (1830) 233 Not even the wife of his bosom. **1881** W. PITT LENNOX *Plays, &c.* I. 37 The woman he had taken to his bosom.

†**d.** *transf.* The womb. *Obs.*

971 *Blickl. Hom.* 5 Heo onfeng on hire medmycclan bosm God Fæder Sunu. *c* **1200** *Trin. Coll. Hom.* 131 Of alle þe bernes, þe ben boren of wifes bosem. **1535** STEWART *Cron. Scot.* II. 411 Sonnis als of thair bosumis tha bair.

e. *pl.* In recent use, a woman's breasts. *colloq.*

1959 C. MACINNES *Absolute Beginners* 68 Snaps of the Dean sell like hot ice-cream among vintage women with too many bosoms and time on their hands. **1961** L. HUGHES *Ask your Mama* 72 Sojourner..Bared her bosoms, bared in public To prove she was a woman. **1965** I. FLEMING *Man with Golden Gun* v. 70 She gave him a quick glimpse of fine bosoms as she bent to the door of the icebox. **1978** C. BEATON *Parting Years* 2 Can you really imagine that is the way the arm comes out of the socket? Look at their bosoms—they're nowhere near where they should be. Have you ever seen a naked woman? **1986** *Observer* 2 Mar. 60/1 She was larger than lifesize: enormous buttocks and stomach, with two medium-sized watermelons for bosoms.

2. *fig.* Applied to the surface of the sea, a lake, a river, or the ground: with various associations from the literal sense.

a **1000** *Andreas* 444 (Gr.) Of brimes bosme. **1595** SHAKS. *John* IV. i. 3 When I strike my foot Vpon the bosome of the ground. **1697** DRYDEN *Virg. Georg.* III. 557 [A river] which before Tall Ships of Burthen on its Bosom bore. **1750** G. HUGHES *Barbados* 220 From the bosoms of some of the upper leaves rise small pedicles. **1816** G. S. FABER *Orig. Pagan Idol.* III. 11 A small island was consecrated in the bosom of a deep lake. **1837** WORDSWORTH *Tour Italy* Sonn. xxvi, Tossed on the bosom of a stormy sea. **1873** BLACK *Pr. Thule* x. 160 The broad bosom of the stream.

3. *transf.* **a.** The part of the dress which covers the breast; also the space included between the breast and its covering.

b. *spec.* Considered as the receptacle for money or letters, formerly answering to modern use of 'pocket'. **c.** ***to give*** (***requite***, etc.) ***into one's bosom*** (a Hebraism derived from the Bible).

a **1121** *O.E. Chron.* an. 1086 (Laud MS.) Mid his bosum full goldes. *c* **1250** *Gen. & Ex.* 2811 In hise bosum he dede his hond. *c* **1386** CHAUCER *Chan. Yem. Prol. & T.* 565 This Chanon took out a Crosselet Of his bosom. **1388** WYCLIF *Luke* vi. 38 Thei schulen ȝyue in to ȝoure bosum a good mesure. **1526** *Pilgr. Perf.* (W. de W. 1531) 1 b, A synguler iewell to bere in my bosom. **1580** BARET *Alv.* B 958 To put money in ones bosom. **1684** BUNYAN *Pilgr.* II. 10 That thou put this Letter in thy Bosome. **1834** MARRYAT *P. Simple* xii, A large frill to his bosom.

d. The front of a shirt. *U.S.*

1863 *Horticulturist* (Albany, N.Y.) Dec. 4 Shirt and bosom makers. **1872** *N.Y. Times* 24 Apr. 8 Advt. (Hoppe), Shirts made to order, with beautifully embroidered Bosoms. **1945** B. A. BOTKIN *Lay My Burden Down* 51 Please don't let my gal see under my coat, 'cause I got on a bosom and no shirt.

4. A curved recess; a cavity, hollow interior; a sinus. [Cf. Lat. *sinus*]

†**a.** The hull or the hold of a ship. *Obs.*

a **1000** *Cædmon's Gen.* 1306 (Gr.) Gescype scylfan on scipes bosme. *c* **1205** LAY. 7849 Scipen gunnen helden. Bosmes þer rendden: Water in wende.

†**b.** *Phys.* The cavity of the stomach; one of the chambers of the heart; a recess or angle in which two bones meet. *Obs.*

1578 BANISTER *Hist. Man* I. 29 The vj bone is fastened to the angular bosome of the Postbrachiall bones. **1610** BARROUGH *Meth. Physick* III. i. 101 The bosome of the stomack. **1662** J. CHANDLER *Van Helmont's Oriat.* 178 There is Hedge or Partition between both bosomes of the Heart.

†**c.** A concave bend in a coast-line, or the part of the sea embraced by it; a bay. *Obs.*

c **1325** *E.E. Allit. P.* C. 107 Þe blyþe breþe at her bak þe bosum he fyndes. **1533** BELLENDEN *Livy* I. (1822) 449 The bosum of the seyis, quhare the Venicianis dwellis. **1600** FAIRFAX *Tasso* xix. viii, Where into creeks and bosoms blind A winding hill his corners turn'd and cast. **1685** R. BURTON *Eng. Emp. Amer.* iv. 70 They were..cast upon a bosom of the South Cape of Massachusets Bay.

d. *poet.* The 'belly' or curvature of a sail before the wind. (Cf. BOSOM *v.* 1.)

1872 BLACKIE *Lays Highl.* 7 A strong south-wester blowing Strained the bosom of their sail.

e. *Mech.* The recess or depression round the eye of a millstone; the 'breast' or curvature of a plough-share; also in *Shipbuilding*, the concave curvature of a frame.

1813 A. YOUNG *Agric. Essex* I. 134 This degree of roundness and fulness in the bosom [of a plough] is necessary on heavy ground. **1869** SIR E. REED *Ship Build.* viii. 149 The beam-plate is run into the bosom of the frame and rivetted to it.

5. a. Expressing a local relation: The interior, the midst: sometimes a development of sense 4, but often with a reference to one of the senses 'embrace' (1 b), 'bosom of garment' (3 b), and 'womb' (1 d).

1489 CAXTON *Faytes of A.* I. xxv. 79 Enuyrone thyn aduersaryes..wythin the bosom of thyn ooste. **1595** SPENSER *Col. Clout* 243 Fishes..Which in the bosome of the billowes breed. **1663** BOYLE *Usefulness Nat. Philos.* I. iv. 66 Quick-silver..will swallow up Gold, and hide it in its Bosom. **1849** ROBERTSON *Serm.* Ser. I. ii. (1866) 37 The seed lying in the genial bosom of the earth. **1861** GEO. ELIOT *Silas M.* I Deep in the bosom of the hills.

b. fig. ***in the bosom of one's family***: in the privacy of the domestic circle (usually also implying family affection and confidence). ***in the bosom of a church*** (or other association): within the inner circle of its membership. And the like.

a **1600** HOOKER (J.) They which live within the bosom of that church. **1803** JANE PORTER *Thaddeus* i. (1831) 2 Within the bosom of his family. **1833** I. TAYLOR *Fanat.* i. 13 In the bosom of the Church rests the hope of the conversion of the world. **1839** THIRLWALL *Hist. Greece* VII. 173 The traitors whom Athens had..cast out from her bosom. **1873** MORLEY *Rousseau* I. 37 He was publicly received into the kindly bosom of the true church.

6. *fig.* The breast considered as the seat of thoughts and feelings. Cf. HEART.

a. The repository of secret thoughts and counsels: hence used for 'inward thoughts' (quot. 1604). †***to be of*** (a person's) ***bosom***: to be entrusted with his secrets. ***friend of one's bosom***: cf. BOSOM FRIEND.

a **1225** *Ancr. R.* 148, I mine boseme..is al mi hope iholden. **1382** WYCLIF *Job* xxxi. 33 If I..hilede in my bosum my wickenesse. **1590** SHAKS. *Mids. N.* I. i. 216 Emptying our bosomes, of their counsell sweld. **1604** —— *Oth.* III. i. 58 You shall haue time To speake your bosome freely. **1605** —— *Lear* IV. v. 26, I know you are of her bosome. *a* **1643** W. CARTWRIGHT *Lady Errant* III. i. (1651) 29 We enterchange Bosoms, and counsels, thoughts and souls. **1712** STEELE *Spect.* No. 428 ⁋2 The man..is shunn'd to-day by the Friend of his Bosom. **1813** T. JEFFERSON *Corr.* (1830) 194 A confidential communication..deposited in his bosom, and never meant to trouble the public mind.

b. The seat of emotions, desires, etc.: hence used for 'desire' (quot. 1603).

c **1175** *Lamb. Hom.* 105 Wreðe hafð wununge on þes dusian bosme. **1595** SHAKS. *John* iv. i. 32 His words do take possession of my bosome. **1603** —— *Meas. for M.* IV. iii. 139 You shal haue your bosome on this wretch. **1625** BACON *Ess.* Ep. Ded. (Arb.) 498 They come home to Mens Businesse and Bosomes. **1764** GOLDSM. *Trav.* 364 Far from my bosom drive the low desire. **1818** *Gentl. Mag.* LXXXVIII. II. 153 The cause comes home to the bosom of every man under the British Government. **1842** TENNYSON *Amphion* 102, I will not vex my bosom.

†**7. a.** Transferred to a person. (Cf. the similar use of ***hand, heart, head***, etc. for their possessor.)

1599 SHAKS. *Hen. V*, II. Cho. 21 A nest of hollow bosomes. **1608** MIDDLETON *Mad World* II. i, I'll pawn my credit for him, an honest, trusty bosom. **1651** JER. TAYLOR *Holy Living* (1727) 249 He is the proper object and bosom to whom the restitution is to be made. **1756** C. LUCAS *Ess. Waters* II. 198 Inscribed to a Bosom fraught with every Social Virtue.

b. *ellipt.* for BOSOM FRIEND.

1913 A. N. LYONS *Simple Simon* I. vi. 90 He's a darling. He and me are bosoms. **1959** B. RUCK *Romantic Afterthought* xxvii. 138, I don't go in for buddies and 'bosoms'.

II. *Comb.* and *attrib.*

8. General relations, chiefly attributive: **a.** Worn upon or carried in the bosom: as in ***bosom-book, -brooch, -pin, -vesture***.

1617 *Janua Ling* Advt. ad fin., If not as a manuall or pocket-booke, yet a pectorall or *bosome-booke, to be carried twixt jerkin and doublet. **1835** HAWTHORNE *Amer. Note-bks.* (1871) I. 7 The bar-keeper had one of Benton's mint-drops for a *bosom-brooch. **1831** CARLYLE *Sart. Res.* II. v, The *bosom-vesture of Summer.

b. Pertaining to the bosom as the seat of thoughts and feelings: as in ***bosom-balm, -broil, -comfort, -devil, -hell, -peace, -prophecy, -throe***, etc.

1742 YOUNG *Nt. Th.* II. 171 Our thoughts at enmity; our *bosom-broil. *a* **1656** BP. HALL *Soliloquies* 61 Guiltiness..like a *bosom-devil would ever torment itself. **1674** FLATMAN *Agst. Thoughts* 7/4 These anguishes, this *bosome-Hell. **1659** FLATMAN *Dooms-day Th.* 66 When..Conscience..all our *bosom-secrets breaks. **1858** HOOD *Hero & L.* xvii, The agony and *bosom-throe.

c. Cherished in the bosom: hence usually = dear, beloved, 'darling': as in ***bosom-child, -sin, -son, -vanity, -vice, -wickedness***.

1862 GOULBURN *Pers. Relig.* 179 The *bosom-adder of vanity. **1838** WORDSW. *To Sleep*, Dear *Bosom-child we call thee. **1620** SANDERSON *Serm.* I. 142 Far off from medling with his *bosom sin. **1740** WESLEY *Wks.* (1872) XIV. 327 Their bosom sins, or the sins which did most easily beset them. **1678** *Yng. Man's Call.* 143 Turn away your eyes from *bosome vanities. **1705** STANHOPE *Paraphr.* III. 61 If..some One darling *Bosom-vice be left unmortified.

d. Intimate, confidential: as in ***bosom-communion, -counsel, -friendship, -interest, -lover***.

1650 T. GOODWIN *Wks.* (1865) X. 557 How canst thou think God should..take thee into immediate *bosom-communion with himself? **1619** KING *Serm.* 19 Did he then thinke..of a *bosome enemie? **1860** C. PATMORE *Faithf. for Ever* 89 Take no wife Who to your stooping feels she owes Her name; such debts make *bosom-foes. **1742** YOUNG *Nt. Th.* I. 340 Like *bosom friendships to resentment sour'd. **1596** SHAKS. *Merch. V.* III. iv. 17 Anthonio..the *bosome louer of my Lord.

e. locative with pple. or ppl. adj., as in ***bosom-reigning, -stricken*** (other examples in 9).

1645 QUARLES *Sol. Recant.* Eccles. iv. 5 With yauning lips, and *bosome-folded hands. **1637** PRESTON *Mt. Ebal* (1638) 32 We must confesse our beloved *bosome-raigning sinnes. **1855** SINGLETON *Virgil* II. 474 The *bosom-stricken dames their woman's shout Raise to the stars of heaven.

9. Special comb.: †**bosom-bird**, *fig.* a bosom friend; **bosom-deep** *a.* (*adv.*), up to the bosom (cf. *ankle-deep*); **bosom-felt** *ppl. a.*, = HEARTFELT; **bosom-hung** *ppl. a.*, hanging down upon the bosom; †**bosom-mischief**, ? the root of the mischief; †**bosom-partner**, a wife; †**bosom-piece**, ? a piece of attire covering the bosom; *fig.* a bosom friend; †**bosom-sermon**, one learnt by heart and recited; †**bosom-slave**, a concubine; **bosom-staff**, an instrument used in testing the straightness of the faces of millstones (see 4 e).

1655 TRAPP *Marrow Gd. Auth.* (1868) 836/2 One of his *bosom-birds, Porphyry. **1882** ROSSETTI *Rose Mary* III. vi, She had waded *bosom-deep Along death's bank in the sedge of sleep. **1771** SMOLLETT in Anderson *Brit. Poets* (1795) X. 959/2 His *bosom-felt wo. *a* **1662** HEYLIN *Laud* I. 161 Eunomius, the *bosom-mischief of those times. **1633** FORD *Love's Sacr.* I. i. (1839) 76 The *bosom-partner of my lord. **1619** BEAUM. & FL. *Valentin.* II. iii, Was I your *bosom-piece for this? **1594** CAREW *Huarte's Exam. Wits* (1616) 149 Which these cannot bring about, who haue conned *bosome-sermons. **1728** THOMSON *Spring* 1131 Let eastern tyrants, from the light of heaven Seclude their *bosom-slaves.

B. as *adj.* Private, confidential, intimate.

1640 HABINGTON *Hist. Edw. IV*, 224 Lewys freeing himselfe from so bosome an enemie by poysoning Charles. **1648** SYMMONS *Vind. Chas. I*, 307 He tells her in his most bosom expressions, that, etc.

bosom ('bʊzəm), *v.* [f. prec. sb.]

†**1.** *intr.* To form a bosom; to belly. ? *Obs.*

c **1375** BARBOUR *Troy-bk.* II. 1699 Thai..halit wp þare salis hie That bowsummit with þe wyndis blast.

2. *trans.* To put into the bosom.

1598 SYLVESTER *Du Bartas* I. vii. (1641) 60/2 Bosoming his hand. **1819** B. W. PROCTOR (B. Cornwall) *Dram. Sc.*, *A. Wentworth* i, I like to see you bosom them [violets].

3. *trans.* To take to the bosom, embrace; *fig.* to receive into intimate companionship.

1605 SHAKS. *Lear* V. i. 13, I am doubtful that you have been conjunct, And bosom'd with her. **1633** FORD *Broken H.* IV. i. (1811) 296 Ixion, aiming To embrace Juno, bosomed but a cloud. **1634** HEYWOOD *Maidenh. Lost* I. Wks. 1874 IV. 106 A Prince hath bin repulst, and meanest persons Bosom'd. **1840** E. ELLIOTT *Vill. Patriarch* Poet. Wks. 55 He has long been bosomed with me.

†**b.** *intr.* To have familiar intercourse. *Obs. rare.*

1633 FORD *Love's Sacr.* IV. i, You were wont To bosom in his counsels. **1637** HEYWOOD *Dialogues* II. 121 She..Doth with this Monster bosome, drinke, and eat.

4. *transf.* and *fig.* To carry or enclose in the bosom; to embosom.

1632 MILTON *Allegro* 78 Towers and battlements..Bosom'd high in tufted trees. **1634** —— *Comus* 368 The sweet peace that goodness bosoms ever. **1792** WORDSW. *Descript. Sk.* Poet. Wks. I. 72 Como, bosomed deep in chestnut groves. **1817** BYRON *Manfred* I. i. 115 Space bosom'd not a lovelier star.

5. *fig.* To hide (a secret) in the bosom; to take to heart, keep in mind. Also with *up*.

1606 DAY *Ile of Gulls* B iv b, Ile bosome what I thinke. **1613** SHAKS. *Hen. VIII*, I. i. 112 Bosome vp my counsell. **1839** BAILEY *Festus* xiv, Be mine, dear maid, the loves, and thou Shalt ever bosom them as now.

†**6.** To wound or hit in the bosom. *nonce use.*

1631 HEYWOOD *Maid of West* III. Wks. 1874 II. 295, I bosom'd him at every second thrust.

bosomed ('bʊzəmd), *ppl. a.* [f. BOSOM *sb.* and *v.* + -ED.] **a.** Having a bosom, shaped like the bosom; swollen with wind (as a sail). **b.** Enclosed, hidden; confined in the bosom, bated (breath).

a **1650** CRASHAW *Sosp. d'Her.* xviii, Like two bosom'd sails. **1667** MILTON *P.L.* v. 127 The Groves, the Fountains, and the Flours That open now thir choicest bosom'd smells. **1730** THOMSON *Autumn*, From the bottoms of the bosomed hills. **1867** J. MARTINEAU *Chr. Life* (ed. 4) 344 Say, with bosomed breath, 'Lo, God is here!'

'bosomer. *rare.* [f. BOSOM *v.* + -ER[1].] One who or that which bosoms, in various senses.

a **1821** KEATS *Sonn.* Wks. (1884) 363 Blue! 'Tis the life of heaven..The bosomer of clouds. **1884** LD. HOUGHTON *In Gondola* in *Mem. Many Sc.* 98 Bosomer of the poet's wearied mind, Dear boat!

,bosom 'friend, bosom-friend.

1. A specially intimate or beloved friend.

1590 GREENE *Never too Late* (1600) 56 There is nothing better than a bosom friend with whom to conferre. **1650** HUBBERT *Pill Formality* 221 His..inward bosome friends. **1699** SHAFTESB. *Inq. conc. Virtue* ii. (1708) 2 The secrets of the breast unfolded to a bosom-friend. **1878** BOSW. SMITH *Carthage* 13 Polybius..was the bosom friend of her destroyer.

†**2.** *transf.* An article of wearing apparel to protect the bosom from cold. *Obs.* (Cf. *comforter*.)

1802 *Hull Packet* 28 Sept. 2/2 Handkerchiefs, tippets, bosom friends and other articles peculiarly adapted to the ensuing season. **1838** *Workwoman's Guide* xi. 275 Some persons do not hollow out bosom friends, but knit them square or oblong.

'bosomful, *a. rare.* Bosomy, full-bosomed.

1870 JOAQUIM MILLER *Memory & Rime* (1884) 17 A moon of spring, High wheeling, vast and bosomful.

'bosoming, *vbl. sb.* [f. BOSOM *v.* + -ING[1].] A taking into one's bosom; embracing.

1624 HEYWOOD *Gunaik.* IV. 169 Their bedding and boosooming.

bosoming ('bʊzəmɪŋ), *ppl. a.* [f. as prec. + -ING[2].] Embracing, embosoming.

1852 D. MOIR *Even. Sketch.* Poet. Wks. II. 232 With bosoming boughs round Musselburgh hang Its clumps of ancient elm-trees. **1871** R. ELLIS *Catullus* lxi. 177 In Thee love lighteth a bosoming Flame.

bosomy ('bʊzəmɪ), *sb.* [f. BOSOM *sb.* + -Y[1].]

1. Full of sheltered recesses or hollows.

1611 COTGR., *Sinueux*..bosomie..full of hollow turnings. **1860** L. HUNT *Poems* 234, I beheld in momentary sun, One of thy hills gleam bright and bosomy.

2. Of a woman: having a prominent bosom.

1928 BLUNDEN *Undertones of War* xiv. 156 A most formidable woman of bosomy immenseness. **1952** *Landfall* VI. 114 A rare young creature, straight and slender yet bosomy. **1967** *Coast to Coast 1965–6* 250 Glossy photos of bosomy girls.

boson ('bəʊzɒn). *Nuclear Physics.* [f. the name of the Indian physicist S. N. *Bose* (1894–1974) + -ON.] Any particle which has a symmetric wave-function and which therefore obeys Bose-Einstein statistics; also *attrib.* Cf. FERMION. Also **intermediate boson,** a boson postulated to exist as a quantum or intermediary of weak interactions.

1947 P. A. M. DIRAC *Princ. Quantum Mech.* (ed. 3) ix. 210 The new statistics was first studied by Bose, so we shall call particles for which only symmetrical states occur in nature *bosons.* **1953** M. SCHÖNBURG in *Nuovo Cimento* X. 429 When the coordinates and momenta are given at the time t = 0, we must take for bosons (28a)..and for fermions (28b). **1955** W. PAULI *N. Bohr* 33 The coupling between one Boson field and one Dirac field. **1955** D. TER HAAR in *Rev. Mod. Physics* XXVII. 312/2 Fermi-Dirac particles. Such particles are sometimes called *fermions* and the Bose-Einstein particles, *bosons.* **1958** *Physical Rev.* CX. 1482/2 The existence of such a heavy boson..will itself lead to the occurrence of decays which are not found in nature, and which would not occur in any detectable amount if there are no intermediate bosons. **1961** POWELL & CRASEMANN *Quantum Mech.* xii. 453 Particles whose spin is an integral multiple of *ħ* are bosons. **1965** *New Statesman* 17 Sept. 393/3 One of these tracks may well be the first sign of the existence of the long-sought particle of matter called intermediate boson.

boson, obs. form of BOATSWAIN.

boss (bɒs), *sb.*[1] Forms: 3–5 boce, 4–5 boos, 4–6 bos, 5 bose, 5–6 *Sc.* boys(s, 6–8 bosse, (7 bosce), 6– boss. [ME. *boce, bos,* a. OF. *boce* (mod.F. *bosse*) = ONF. *boche* BOTCH, It. *bozza*; perh. connected with OHG. *bôz-an* = BEAT *v.* In ME. *boss* and *botch* are partly synonymous, but the former is not recorded in the sense 'pimple, boil', nor the latter in the sense 'boss of shield', 'ornamental stud'.]

1. a. A protuberance or swelling on the body of an animal or plant; a convex or knob-like process or excrescent portion of an organ or structure; in 16th c. applied to the lobe of the liver, spleen, etc.; as now used it seems partly transf. from 3.

1386 CHAUCER *Parson's T.* ¶ 349 Somme of hem shewen the boce of hir shape. **1541** COPLAND *Guydon's Quest. Chirurg.*, It yssueth out of the bosse of the lyuer. **1658** ROWLAND *Mouffet's Theat. Ins.* 990 It [the grashopper] is of a blackish green colour, having on each side two bunches or bosses of the same colour. **1677** GREW *Anat. Fruits* v. §13 In the Centre of the Case, stands a great Parenchymous Boss. **1775** *Phil. Trans.* LXV. 414 The large branches..covered with great bosses and knobs of gum. **1878** BARTLEY tr. *Topinard's Anthrop.* II. xii. 488 The Frontal bosses are often confluent. **1882** VINES *Sachs' Bot.* 421 The cuticularised exospore, generally provided with ridges, bosses, spines, or granulations.

†**b.** *spec.* A hump or hunch on the back. *Obs.*

a **1300** *Cursor M.* 8087 Crumpled knes and boce [*Gött.* bouch] on bak. *c* **1440** *Gesta Rom.* (1879) 396 Entred a dwerfe..hauyng..a bose in his back, and Crokid fete. **1835** KIRBY *Hab. & Inst. Anim.* I. ii. 62 The ox of Surat is stated to have two of these bosses or humps.

†**c.** A protuberance made by padding the dress. *Obs.*

c **1380** WYCLIF *Sel. Wks.* III. 124 In þis pryde synnen wymmen in makyng of hor bosis.

†**d.** The big bulk of an animal; a bulky animal.

1399 LANGL. *Rich. Redeless* III. 98 But tho all the berlingis brast out at ones..That bosse [the bear] was unbounde and brouute to his owene. **1657** REEVE *God's Plea* Ep. Ded. 3 An Elephant thus praised for his great Bosce, or a fat Bull of Basan for his wellfleshed flanks.

†**e.** A fat woman. *Obs.*

1579 LYLY *Euphues* 115 If she be well sette, then call hir a Bosse. **1586** MARLOWE *1st Pt. Tamburl.* III. iii, Disdainful Turkess, and unreverend boss. **1632** SHERWOOD s.v. *Bosse,* A fatt Bosse, *femme bien grasse et grosse.*

2. A knoll or mass of rock; in *Geol.* applied chiefly to masses of rock protruding through strata of another kind.

1598 SYLVESTER *Du Bartas* I. vii. (1641) 59/1 Here from a craggy Rocks steep-hanging boss..A silver Brook in broken streams doth gush. **1839** MURCHISON *Silur. Syst.* I. xxxvi. 483 This little boss of Ludlow rocks has been thrust up through the environing coal measures. **1863** A. RAMSAY *Phys. Geog.* 31 In the midst of a tract of mica-schist..a boss of granite rises. **1879** RUTLEY *Stud. Rocks* iii. 15 Eruptive rocks which have formed intrusive bosses, or dykes.

3. a. A round prominence in hammered or carved work, etc.; *e.g.* a raised ornament in bookbinding (in earlier use, *esp.* the 'umbo' or round knob, often of precious metal, which occupied the centre of the cover); one of the metal knobs on each side of the bit of a bridle (F. *bossette*); a metal stud used for ornament. †*in boss*: in high relief; cf. F. *en bosse.*

1382 WYCLIF *Isa.* iii. 18 The Lord shal don awei the ournement of shon, and boces, and beȝes. **1395** *E.E. Wills* (1882) 5 A basyn of siluer with boses apon the brerdes. *c* **1440** *Promp. Parv.* 41 Boce or boos of a booke or oþer lyke [*H.* booce], *turgiolum.* **1563–87** FOXE *A. & M.* I. 232/2 The bosses of his Bridle were worth a great treasure. **1651** DAVENANT *Gondibert* II. VI. xlvi, Where all harmonious Instruments they spie Drawn out in Bosse. **1660** PEPYS *Diary* 2 Nov., In the afternoon I..saw some silver bosses put upon my new Bible. **1662** EVELYN *Chalcogr.* (1769) 18 Those who..work in bosse with the puntion. **1719** DE FOE *Crusoe* I. 349 The Bosses of the Bridle had stuck in his Teeth. **1879** *Print. Trades Jrnl.* XXVI. 8 Enriched with elaborate metal bosses.

b. *spec.* The convex projection in the centre of a shield or buckler.

c **1386** CHAUCER *Miller's T.* 80 A brooch sche baar..As brood as is the boos of a bokeler. **1483** *Cath. Angl.* 37 A Bose [*A.* Boste] of a buclere, *vmbo.* *a* **1547** SURREY *Æneid* II. 287 Hidden behind her targetes bosse they crept. **1611** BIBLE *Job* xv. 26 He runneth vpon him..vpon the thicke bosses of his bucklers. **1729** T. COOKE *Tales, Prop. &c.* 117 See on his Shield's thin Boss the Greecian stand. **1815** ELPHINSTONE *Acc. Caubul* (1842) I. 17 A shield of steel, the bosses and rim of which were set with diamonds and rubies.

c. *transf.* and *fig.*

1791 COWPER *Odyss.* I. 65 In yonder woodland isle, the central boss Of Ocean. **1860** TYNDALL *Glac.* I. §5. 39 The sunbeams struck his crown, and converted it into a boss of gold. **1881** GRANT ALLEN in *Knowledge* No. 4. 66 A bee..flies straight towards the blossom and settles on the little boss of carpels in the centre.

†**d.** = BOSSELL. *Obs. rare.*

1497 *Accts. Founder's Guild* in *Archæol. Jrnl.* XLIII. 165 A maser wt a boos and an hert of siluer ouer gilted. **1499** *Ibid.* 167 A masar wt a hollow boyss prynted with a hewar.

e. *Arch.* An ornamental projection in a vault at the intersection of the ribs.

1823 RUTTER *Fonthill* 9 Bosses of foliage and fruit..cover the intersections. **1849** FREEMAN *Archit.* 393 The spandrils, cornices, and bosses allow of any amount of enrichment. **1884** *Church Bells* 6 Sept. 940 In the roof are bosses, on one of which is carved a bear and ragged staff, for Beauchamp.

f. *Mech.* 'The enlarged part of a shaft, on which a wheel is keyed, or at the end, where it is coupled to another' (Webster). *Ship-building.* The projecting part of the stern-post of a screw steamer, which is pierced for the shaft of the propeller to pass through. (Cf. F. *bosse* nave of a wheel.)

1869 SIR E. REED *Ship Build.* iv. 70 The boss on the post was forged in the usual manner. *Ibid.* xx. 436 Where a plate has a large amount of twist, such as boss plates, etc., special means are employed to ensure accuracy. **1878** MARKHAM *Gt. Frozen Sea* xi. 157 The ice formed so quickly in the 'boss' that it..prevented the shaft from entering.

g. A soft pad used in ceramics and glass-manufacture for smoothing and making uniform the colours applied with oil to a glass or porcelain surface, and for cleaning gilded surfaces.

1860 URE *Dict. Arts* (ed. 5) III. 506 The 'boss' is made of soft leather. *a* **1877** KNIGHT *Dict. Mech.* s.v. *Bossing,* The bossing is laid on with a hair-pencil, and leveled with a boss of soft leather. **1879** E. C. HANCOCK *Amat. Pott. & Glass Painter* 49 The boss consists of a lump of cotton wool, screwed up, as it were, in two or three thicknesses of fine soft linen. **1961** M. JONES *Potbank* xii. 44 Bert..polished it [*sc.* a plate] with a boss—a piece of cloth stuffed with wool.

h. The central portion of the propeller of an aeroplane.

1916 H. BARBER *Aeroplane Speaks* iv. 121 If a weight..placed in a bolt-hole on one side of the boss fails to disturb the balance, then the propeller is usually regarded as unfit for use.

4. A sort of die used by cutlers.

1831 J. HOLLAND *Manuf. Metals* I. 213 From this foundation plate rises the bed or boss. *Ibid.* II. 23 It [the fork] in this red hot state is next placed in a cut steel boss or die, upon which another boss exactly adapted is made to fall.

5. *attrib.* and *Comb.*, as **boss-*maker*;** †**boss-backed** *a.*, hump-backed; **boss-nail** (see quot.); **boss-stone,** the stone fixed at the intersection of the ribs in groined vaulting; **boss-tip,** the point of the boss of a shield; **boss-work.**

1639 HORN & ROBOTHAM *Gate Lang. Unl.* xvi. (1643) §175 For the bosbacked (bunch-backt) camell serves in stead of a waggon. **1580** HOLLYBAND *Treas. Fr. Tong, Bosseteur,* a *bossemaker. **1697** EVELYN *Numism.* i. 11 Leather Money, through which a small *boss-nail of Silver was struck in the middle. **1879** SIR G. SCOTT *Lect. Archit.* II. 212 They made the upper surface of the *boss-stone horizontal. **1855** SINGLETON *Virgil* I. 294 And on his buckler's *boss-tip idly hung. **1697** *Lond. Gaz.* No. 3347/8 A Cane Couch embroidered with *Boss-work upon green Velvet.

†**boss,** *sb.*[2] *Obs.* Also bosse. [Of uncertain etymology: perh. only a sense of the prec. Compare, however, F. *buse, buise* conduit, though this alone could not give *boss,* unless through assimilation to the preceding.]

'A water conduit, running out of a gor-bellied figure', Bailey 1731: chiefly in 'the Boss of Billingsgate'.

c **1520** W. DE WORDE (*title*) Treatyse of a Galaunt, with the Maryage of the Fayre Pusell the Bosse of Byllyngesgate unto London Stone. **1539** *Godly Sayng* in Furnivall *Ballads fr. MSS.* I. 315 When the bosse of byllyngate wa[x]ythe so merye To daunce with a bagpype at scala celi, & the crose of chepeside dothe kepe a scole of fence. **1603** STOW *Surv.* (1842) 160/1 Then have ye a boss of sweet water in the wall of the churchyard. **1657** HOWELL *Londinop.* 85 Bosse Alley, so called of a Bosse of Spring-water. **1731** in BAILEY.

†**boss,** *sb.*[3] *Obs. Sc.* Also 4 bose, 5–7 boce. [Origin obscure: cf. OF. *busse* cask; also Du. *bus* 'box', *bos* (orig. the same) 'package, bundle, truss'.]

1. A cask; *esp.* a small cask; a leathern butt or bottle for wine, etc.

c **1375** ? BARBOUR *St. Cecile* 532, I cane wele find þi poweste lik a bose, of wynd þat fillit ware. **1489** *Act. Dom. Conc.* 129 (JAM.) Twa chalder of mele out of a boce..thre malvysy bocis price of the pece viiis. vid. *c* **1505** DUNBAR *Friars of Berwik* 157 Haif thair ane pair of bossis, gud and fyne Thay hald ane gallone full of Gascone wyne. **1552** LYNDESAY *Monarche* 2579 Thocht sum of ȝow be gude of conditione, Reddy for to ressaue new recent wyne, I speik to ȝow auld bosis [*v.r.* boisis bossis] of perditione. *c* **1565** R. LINDSAY *Chron. Scotl.* (1728) 82 To send for two bosses of wine..The bosses were of the quantity of two gallons the piece. *c* **1570** *Leg. Bp. St. Andrews* in *Scot. Poems 16th C.* II. 338 Tua leathering bosses he hes bought. *c* **1600** BUREL in Watson *Coll. Poems* II. 26 (JAM.) Cryis..As wind within a boce.

2. *old boss*: a term of contempt applied to persons (*Sc.*). Cf. sense 1, quot. 1552. [But it may be a distinct word: cf. ON. *bossi,* Sw. *buss* fellow. See discussion in Jamieson.]

1566 KNOX *Hist. Ref.* (1732) 34 (JAM.) Hay Dean of Restalrig, and certane auld bosses with him. *Ibid.* Wks. 1846 I. 127 The Bischope preached to his jackmen, and to some old bosses of the toune.

boss, *sb.*[4] Also 6 boos, 7–8 bosse. [? a. MDu. *bosse, busse,* mod.Du. *bos, bus* = BOX.] A plasterer's tray, a hod.

1542 *MS. Acc. St. John's Hosp., Canterb.*, Bowht a trowell a boos and a syffe. **1611** COTGR., *Clifoire,* a Plaisterers tray, or bosse. **1677** MOXON *Mech. Exerc.* (1703) 248 A Bosse, made of Wood, with an Iron Hook, to hang on the Laths, or on a Ladder, in which the Labourer puts the Morter which the Tyler uses. **1875** GWILT *Archit.* Gloss.

†**boss** (bɒs), *sb.*[5] *Obs.* exc. *dial.* [? corruption of BASS *sb.*[2]; but cf. Du. *bos* bottle of straw.] A seat consisting of or resembling a bundle of straw; a hassock.

1695 WESTMACOTT *Script. Herb.* 179 Bull-Rushes make Bosses and Bed-mats best. **1727** SWIFT *Gulliver* IV. ii. Round which they sat on their haunches upon bosses of straw. **1841** S. C. HALL *Ireland* I. 83 The family sit on stools and bosses (the boss is a low seat made of straw).

boss (bɒs), *sb.*[6] [ad. Du. *baas* master (older sense 'uncle'), supposed to be related to Ger. *base* female cousin, OHG. *basa* 'aunt'.]

a. An orig. American equivalent of 'master' in the sense of employer of labour; applied also to a business manager, or any one who has a right to give orders. In England at first only in workmen's slang, or humorously, = 'leading man, swell, top-sawyer'; now in general use in Britain.

[*a* **1649** J. WINTHROP *Hist. New England* (1908) I. 166 Here arrived a small Norsey bark..with one Gardiner, an expert engineer or work base [= Du. *werk-baas*], and provisions. **1653** F. NEWMAN et al. *Let.* May in E. Hazard *Hist. Collections* (1794) II. 236 From our Place of Residence at the Basses house in the Monhatoes.] **1806** W. IRVING *Let.* 26 May in P. M. Irving *Life & Lett.* (1862) I. xi. 138, I had to return, make an awkward apology to boss, and look like a nincompoop. **1813** LD. YARMOUTH *Let.* 12 Dec. in E. Taylor *Taylor Papers* (1913) vii. 98 There are some peasants watching, one of whom has frightened the boss with an alarm of a sortie. **1822** J. FLINT *Lett. Amer.* 9 *Master* is not a word in the vocabulary of hired people. *Bos,* a Dutch one of similar import, is substituted. **1830** GALT *Lawrie T.* III. ii. (1849) 86 The overseer of the roads..could give me employment as a boss, or foreman. **1868** W. WHITMAN *To Working Men* (Rossetti) 102 Were I to you as the boss employing and paying you, would that satisfy you? **1870** MISS BRIDGMAN *R. Lynne* II. ix. 187 We shall have one of the head bosses of the medical profession down here. **1936** G. B. SHAW *Millionairess* Pref. 106 A born boss is one who rides roughshod over us by some mysterious power that separates him from our species and makes us fear him. *Ibid.* 128 Clearly we shall be boss-ridden in one form or another. **1937** 'G. ORWELL' *Road to Wigan Pier* viii. 157 The accent and manners which stamp you as one of the boss class. **1962** *Listener* 16 Aug. 238/1 Most people make mistakes when they start a new job, and it is irritating for the boss.

b. In American politics, a manager or dictator of a party organization.

1882 H. SPENCER in *Standard* 31 Oct. 5/7 Those who framed your Constitution never dreamed that twenty thousand citizens would go to the poll led by a 'boss'.

c. *attrib.* Of persons: master, chief. Of things: most esteemed, 'champion'. Now esp. in U.S. slang: excellent, wonderful; good, 'great'; masterly.

1836 in J. R. COMMONS *Doc. Hist. Amer. Industr. Soc.* (1910) IV. 287, I am a boss shoemaker. **1840** J. P. KENNEDY *Quodlibet* 221 Charley Moggs, long known as the boss loafer of Bickerbray. **1848** W. E. BURTON *Waggeries* 63 (Th.), 'How d'ye do, folks?'..'is the boss devil to hum?' **1860** BARTLETT *Dict. Amer.* s.v., We hear of a boss-carpenter, a boss-bricklayer, boss-shoemaker, etc. instead of master-carpenter, etc. **1877** BESANT & RICE *Son of Vulc.* I. xiv. 150 'Good God A'mighty in heaven!' said the boss boatman, who was a religious man. **1881** *N. York Nation* 3 Feb., No country in the world could make such a boss-show as the United States. **1884** *Lisbon* (*Dakota*) *Star* 29 Aug., The boss thresher of Ransom county. *Ibid.* 10 Oct., They are of the 'Welcome' variety, and are the boss oats. **1961** *Metronome* Apr. 32 The arrangements by Clayton are effortless and elegant—he has always been a boss arranger. **1964** L. HAIRSTON in J. H. Clarke *Harlem* 288 That's boss, Baby—the best I ever seen. **1967** P. WELLES *Babyhip* xxxv. 256 'I'm going with you to New York.'.. 'Yeah?' she said, 'you're going with me. Oh, I think that's boss... It's just boss. It's truly, truly, boss. Maybe, I'll keep the *Kama Sutra* for us.' **1970** T. SOUTHERN *Blue Movie* 17 And her mouth was boss beauty; her lips were like young Rita Hayworth's..; and her teeth were..perfect. **1984** M. AMIS *Money* 41, I have to tell you right off that Martina Twain is a real boss chick by anyone's standards.

d. *Comb.* **boss-boy** *S. Afr.* (see BOY *sb.*[1] 3 e); **boss-cocky, -cockie** *Austral. slang* [COCKY *sb.*[2] 2], a farmer who employs labour and works himself; hence in extended use, a person in authority; **boss-man** (orig. *U.S.*) = BOSS *sb.*[6] a; **boss of** (or **over**) **the board** [BOARD *sb.* 2 d] *Austral.* and *N.Z.*, the overseer of a shearing-shed.

1898 MORRIS *Austral. English* 46/1 Boss-cockie. **1916** J. B. COOPER *Coo-oo-ee* i. 16 Mrs. Muller, before she married the German, was Kate Hardley, the daughter of a boss cockie farmer fifty miles away. **1928** 'BRENT OF BIN BIN' *Up Country* xiii. 218 Rab was the boss cocky of it [*sc.* an orchestra]. **1969** *Coast to Coast 1967–8* 5 But what was her place now? She was a kind of boss cocky. **1934** C. CARMER *Stars fell on Alabama* (1935) IV. iv. 212 When old man Huckaby died a year ago Wade came up to the house and stayed night and day, waiting on the old boss-man. **1965** H. GOLD *Man who was not with It* xii. 103 Bossman on the biggest power-generator Sunday school show in the South-land. **1969** J. WAINWRIGHT *Big Tickle* 25 Divisional Chief Superintendent Sullivan..was boss-man of North End Division. **1896** H. LAWSON *While Billy Boils* xiv. 89 There are tally lies..and lies about getting the best of squatters and bosses-over-the-board. *Ibid.* xlii. 253 The third shearer was telling a yarn... 'So I said to the boss-over-the-board, "you're a nice sort of a thing," I sez.' **1901** M. FRANKLIN *My Brilliant Career* xxii. 186 A big strike among the shearers when the narrator had been boss-of-the-board out beyond Bourke. **1948** V. PALMER *Golconda* vii. 51 Macy the Battler, they had called him at his last shearing-shed after he had tackled a nagging boss-of-the-board.

boss (bɒs), *sb.*[7] *U.S.* [app. the same word as Eng. dial. (south-western) *borse, boss, buss* six-months-old or half-grown calf (1790 Grose *Prov. Dict.*, etc.).] A word used in addressing a cow. (Cf. BOSSY *sb.*) Also, the American bison.

1800 in *Wash. Hist. Quart.* (1928) XIX. 268 The Indians traded..Tongues and Bosses. **1848** BARTLETT *Dict. Amer.*, *Boss*, among the hunters of the prairies, a name for the buffalo. **1874** *Rep. Vermont Board Agric.* II. 706 So-o-o boss! There, you've kicked it over—All that milk, now, I declare! **1901** *Nation* 18 Apr. 314/2 The call 'Co' boss is familiar to most of the inhabitants of our Northern States and Canada.

boss, *sb.*[8] = BOSS-SHOT.

1898 *Eng. Dial. Dict.* s.v., He then tried to jump the ditch to the big stone, but in his hurry he made a boss and fell into the water.

BOSS (bɒs), *sb.*[9] *S. Afr.* Also B.O.S.S., Boss. [Acronym, f. the initial letters of *B*ureau *o*f (properly: for) *S*tate *S*ecurity.] The state security service of the Republic of South Africa, established in 1969 and renamed National Intelligence Service in 1978.

1969 *Post* (S. Afr., Golden City ed.) 15 June 14 Now, from baasskap and boozeskap to BOSSskap. You've probably read about B.O.S.S. The letters stand for Bureau of State Security. **1970** *Cape Argus* 30 Jan. 1 The public outcry over the implications of certain aspects of the so-called B.O.S.S. legislation. **1971** *Guardian Weekly* 27 Nov. 9/1 The group is convinced that there have been between eight and 20 BOSS agents working in Britain. **1973** T. SHARPE *Indecent Exposure* ii. 18 'I have here', he said, brandishing the directive from BOSS, 'orders from Pretoria.' **1974** *Eastern Province Herald* (S. Afr.) 15 May 2 Allegations that Boss has been secretly funding Shaka's Spear, the Zulu opposition party. **1983** *National Law Jrnl.* (U.S.) 8 Aug. 6/2 Gordon Winter..was a spy with South Africa's secret police—the Bureau of State Security (BOSS).

boss (bɒs), *a. Sc.* Also 6 bois, bos, 7 bosse. [perh. connected with BOSS *sb.*[3], where some quotations refer to hollowness. But the notion may be 'turgid, swollen'; cf. BOSS *sb.*[1], *v.*[1]]

Hollow. *lit.* and *fig.* **boss window**: bay window.

1513 DOUGLAS *Æneis* II. ii.[i.] 73 With the straik, The bois cavys sowndit and maid a dyn. *c* **1565** R. LINDSAY *Chron. Scotl.* 235 (JAM.) The lordis..who war entred in the bos window. **1597** LOWE *Chirurg.* (1634) 231, I use a little Instrument of silver, that is bosse or hollow within. **1719** RAMSAY *Wks.* (1848) I. 156 If these be solid ware or boss. **1834** H. MILLER *Scenes & Leg.* xii. (1857) 180 Making boss professions of goodwill.

b. Empty.

a **1758** RAMSAY *Poems* I. 285 (JAM.) He said, he gloom'd, and shook his thick boss head. **1832–53** *Whistle-Binkie* (Sc. Songs) Ser. II. 89 I'm sure ye're neither boss nor dry.

c. Without resources, powerless.

a **1600** A. HUME *Ep. G. Moncrief*, They are bot stocks and stanes; bos, deif and dumb. **1768** ROSS *Helenore* 21 (JAM.) He's nae boss, six score o' lambs this year.

boss (bɒs), *v.*[1] Also 4 boosen, 5 bos, boce, 5–6 booce. [f. BOSS *sb.*[1]]

†**1. a.** *trans.* To make to project, to stuff out. *Obs.*

c **1380** WYCLIF *Sel. Wks.* III. 124 Soche men þat boosen hor brestis.

†**b.** *intr.* To swell out, project. *Obs.*

c **1400** *Destr. Troy* 3022 The here of hir hede, huyt as the gold, Bost out vppon brede bright on to loke. *c* **1449** PECOCK *Repr.* II. ii. 138 Ymagis boocing and seemyng as thouȝ thei were going and passing out of the wal. **1540** RAYNALD *Birth Man* I. vii. (1634) 29 The middle part of the wombe port.. where it bosseth downeward..hangeth pendant wise. **1542** UDALL *Erasm. Apophth.* 235 a, With a great bunche, which, bossyng out, made him crookebacked.

2. a. *trans.* To fashion in relief; to beat or press out into a raised ornament, to emboss.

c **1400** *Destr. Troy* 1564 Ymagry ouer all amyt þere was.. Bost out of þe best þe byg toures vmbe. **1530** PALSGR. 459/1, I booce or to boce out, as workemen do a holowe thynge. **1881** *Porcelain Wks. Worcester* 21 The workman..bosses it [the clay] with a wet sponge, and presses it into every line of the pattern.

b. In ceramics, to smooth a surface of boiled oil on pottery by means of a boss (BOSS *sb.*[1] 3 g).

1860 URE *Dict. Arts* (ed. 5) III. 506 A coat of boiled oil adapted to the purpose being laid upon the ware with a pencil, and afterwards levelled, or as it is technically termed 'bossed', until the surface is perfectly uniform. **1879** [see BOSSING *vbl. sb.*[1] d]. **1881** [see BOSS *v.*[1] 2, where this quot. is wrongly placed].

3. To furnish or ornament with bosses.

c **1626** *Dick of Devon.* III. ii. in Bullen *O. Pl.* (1883) II. 46 But was ever English horse thus Spanish bitted and bossd! **1650** FULLER *Pisgah* IV. vi. 112 Either only studded or bossed therewith. **1664** PEPYS *Diary* (1879) III. 5 Thence to the clasp-makers to have it [my Chaucer] clasped and bossed. **1849** RUSKIN *Sev. Lamps* i. x. 20 Do not let us boss our roofs with wretched half-worked blunt-edged rosettes. *fig.* **1583** STUBBES *Anat. Abus.* II. 50 Then shall your mouth be bossed with the lather.

boss (bɒs), *v.*[2] *colloq.* (orig. *U.S.*) [f. BOSS *sb.*[6]] *trans.* To be the master or manager of; to manage, control, direct. ***to boss it***: to act as master.

1856 *Nat. Intelligencer* 3 Nov. (Bartlett) The little fellow that bosses it over the crowd. *a* **1860** *Pluribustah* (Bartlett) Let his Woman's Rights companion Boss the house. **1866** *Reader* 3 Nov. 913 Bossed by Uncle Andreas Darling, day by day the dwelling grew. **1882** SALA in *Illust. Lond. News* 25 Feb., The gentleman..bossing the band of pioneers. **1882** W. D. HAY *Brighter Britain* I. vi. 166 The way that Old Colonial 'bossed' them round was an edifying sight to see. **1933** C. A. MACDONALD *Pages from Past* v. 62 He 'bossed' a timber-cutting camp. **1944** R. LEHMANN *Ballad & Source* I. iv. 35 'Well, I won't be bossed by her,' she said gruffly.

boss (bɒs), *v.*[3] *dial.* and *slang.* [Cf. BOSS-EYED, BOSS-SHOT.] *trans.* To miss or bungle (a shot); *gen.* to bungle, make a mess of. Also *absol.*

1887 *N. & Q.* III. 236/2 To boss is schoolboy slang for 'to miss'. **1889** BARRÈRE & LELAND *Dict. Slang* s.v., To *boss* anything, to make a mess of it, to spoil it. **1898** *Eng. Dial. Dict.* s.v., He had six shies at the cocoa-nuts, and he bossed every time. **1903** 'MARJORIBANKS' *Fluff-Hunters* 74 You're simply bossing up the whole show by philandering with a widow.

boss, dial. f. BUSS *v.*, to kiss.

1691 RAY *N.C. Wds.* s.v. *Osse*, Ossing comes to bossing. Prov. Chesh.

bossage ('bɒsɪdʒ). *Arch.* [a. F. *bossage*, f. *bosse* a projection, BOSS *sb.*[1]]

1. (See quot.)

1730–6 BAILEY, *Bossage* [with Architects] is a Term used of any Stone that has a Projecture, and is laid in its Place uncut, to be afterwards carved into mouldings, capitals, etc.

2. 'Rustic work, which seems to advance before the naked of a building, by reason of indentures or channels left at the joints.' (Gwilt.) Also *attrib.*, as in ***bossage work***.

1704 HEARNE *Duct. Hist.* (1723) II. III. 395 Built of two Stories high, in Bossage Rustick. **1819** *Banquet* 71 The fretted bossage, from the ceiling ript, Crumbles to powder in the yawning crypt. **1845** FORD *Handbk. Spain* VI. 472 The bossage work resembles that of Merida and Alcantara.

Hence **'bossaged** *ppl. a.*

1855 *Fraser's Mag.* LI. 268 A large massive palazzo, whose rough bossaged front descended into the water.

bossa nova (ˌbɒsə 'nəʊvə). [Pg. *bossa* tendency + *nova* fem. sing. of *novo* new.] A style of Brazilian music related to the samba; a dance performed to this music.

1962 *Daily Mail* 2 Nov. 14/4 In a hesitant way the bossa nova is already starting. At Edmundo's club..his band plays bossa nova while the customers perform their own version, a kind of lazy samba. **1962** *New Statesman* 21 Dec. 911/1 In Brazil *bossa nova* is in no sense a dance. It is a way of playing and singing. **1963** *New Yorker* 8 June 99 (Advt.), And shop for Brazilian antiques and bossa nova records. **1967** *Guardian* 22 Apr. 5/6 The same band handles bossa nova, rock-and-roll, and rhythm-and-blues with equal panache.

bossdom ('bɒsdəm). orig. *U.S.* [f. BOSS *sb.*[6] + -DOM.] The condition of being a boss; that which constitutes the sphere of influence of a political boss; the control of politics by bosses.

1888 J. B. BRYCE *Amer. Commonw.* II. lxiii. 462 The extinction of the Boss himself and of bossdom. **1893** *Black & White* 1 Apr. 383/1 He was going to make John Bull realise that his days of bossdom were over. **1894** *Citizen* (Albion, Mich.) 293 It is not healthy for a party, if the few are allowed to do all and say all. That way Rings and Bossdom lie.

bosse, obs. form of BOSS.

bossed (bɒst), *ppl. a.* Also 6–7 bost(e. [f. BOSS *sb.*[1] and *v.*[1]]

1. Made to swell out or project, rounded out.

1541 R. COPLAND *Guydon's Quest. Chirurg.*, [The thigh bone] is receyued in the pyt of the hukcle bone and is somwhat bossed outwarde. **1578** BANISTER *Hist. Man* I. 35 Where the Patel is thickest, and bossed forth like the middest of a buckler. **1615** CROOKE *Body of Man* 81 The arteries..are straight and euen without any bossed knottes at all. **1644** J. CARTER *Nail & Wheel* (1647) 21 They [nails] have great and glorious bossed and gilded heads.

2. Raised or beaten in relief, embossed; also, portrayed in relief.

1536 in *Antiq. Sarisb.* (1771) 195 Two pair of Censers, silver and gilt, of bossed work. **1675** *Lond. Gaz.* No. 1002/4 Stoln out of Westminster Abbey..Two large Silver Candlesticks, Boss'd and Gilt. **1833** TENNYSON *Poems* 83 With chalices of curious wine..And bossèd salvers. **1850** BLACKIE *Æschylus* II. 189 Upon his shield he bears..a woman Leading with sober pace an armed man All bossed in gold.

3. Furnished with bosses or projecting ornaments.

1611 BP. HALL *Serm.* v. 55 Lucian compares his Grecians, to a fair, gilt, bossed book. **1655** FULLER *Ch. Hist.* VII. 424 One of His Play-Fellows proffered Him a bossed-plated Bible to stand upon. **1705** HEARNE *Diary* (1885) I. 120 [A book] covered with velvet and boss'd with Silver. **1868** MORRIS *Earthly Par.* II. 131 Leaping up, he took The reins in hand and the bossed leather shook.

b. Studded, ornamented.

1586 WEBBE *Eng. Poetrie* (Arb.) 82 Weedes meete for a princely mayden, Boste with Ermines white. **1596** SHAKS. *Tam. Shr.* II. i. 355 Fine Linnen, Turky cushions bost with pearle. *a* **1627** MIDDLETON *Black Bk.* Wks. V. 567 Hangers, all bost with pillars of gold.

bosselated ('bɒsəleɪtɪd), *ppl. a. Phys.* [f. F. *bosselé*, pple. of *bosseler* to mould into small protuberances.] Formed into small protuberances.

1873 G. FLEMING tr. *Chauveau's Anat. Domest. Anim.* 412 The large colon..is bosselated, plicated, and traversed by longitudinal bands. **1876** GROSS *Dis. Bladder, &c.* 135 Tuberous fibroma..occurs, especially in young subjects, as a bosselated..tumor in the vicinity of the trigone.

†**'bossell.** *Obs.* [dim. of BOSS *sb.*[1]; perhaps already in OF.] The 'print' or ornamental medallion fixed in the bottom of a 'mazer' or drinking bowl: = BOSS *sb.*[1] 3 d.

1495 *Will of Rogers* (Somerset Ho.) Grete masser wt the Image of S. James in the bossell thereof. **1497** *Will of Butside* (ibid.) A masser wt a turnyng bossell wt a brode bonde. **1498** *Will of T. Johnson* (ibid.) A grete bossell of siluer.

bosset ('bɒsɪt). [a. F. *bossette*, dim. of *bosse* BOSS *sb.*[1]] A small protuberance or knob.

1859 TODD *Cycl. Anat. & Phys.* V. 517/2 The male calf of the Red Deer at the sixth month differs from the female.. in having two small elevations or 'bossets'.

boss-eyed, *a. dial.* and *slang.* [Cf. BOSS *v.*[3], BOSS-SHOT.] Having only one good eye; squint-eyed, cross-eyed. Also *fig.* oblique, crooked, one-sided.

1860 HOTTEN *Dict. Slang* (ed. 2). **1882** CHAMBERLAIN *W. Worc. Gloss.*, *Boss-eyed*, squinting. **1890** [see BOSS-SHOT]. **1898** *Eng. Dial. Dict.* s.v., The horse shied and we ran up against the gate-post, and knocked the step of the cart all boss-eyed. **1959** I. & P. OPIE *Lore & Lang. Schoolchildren* xi. 214 It is unlucky for a cross-eyed woman to look at you. .. When somebody who is boss-eyed goes by you spit on the ground.

boss-fern. A book-name for species of 'buckler-fern' or *Nephrodium.* (Britten and Holland.)

bossiness[1] ('bɒsɪnɪs). [f. BOSSY *a.*[1] + -NESS.] The quality of being bossy.

1870 RUSKIN *Aratra P.* i. §21 A pleasant bossiness or roundness of surface.

bossiness[2] ('bɒsɪnɪs). [f. BOSSY *a.*[2] + -NESS.] The quality of being bossy or overbearing.

1928 J. DEVANNY *Dawn Beloved* I. ii. 19 She savagely resented any 'bossiness'. **1958** *Listener* 30 Oct. 699/1 The bossiness and love of power so often characteristic of dwarfish persons of insecure social status.

bossing ('bɒsɪŋ), *vbl. sb.*[1] Also 5 bocynge. [f. BOSS *v.*[1]] The action of the verb BOSS[1]: **a.** swelling; **b.** ornamenting with bosses; **c.** (meaning obscure: see quot. 1480).

c **1440** *Promp. Parv.* 41 Bocynge or strowtynge, *turgor.* **1480** CAXTON *Chron. Eng.* II. (1520) 17/1 Two other wayes he made in bossynge through out the lande, the one is called Fosse, and that other Fosse dyke. **1583** GRINDAL *Will* Wks.

(1843) 459, I give..ten pounds towards the clasping, bossing, and chaining of the same [books].

d. In ceramics, the process of smoothing the surface of colour applied to pottery over a coating of boiled oil; also, the coating of oil used for this purpose.

a **1877** KNIGHT *Dict. Mech.*, *Bossing*, ground-laying the surface of porcelain in an unfinished state, to form a basis of adherence for the color... The bossing is a coat of boiled oil, to hold the color. **1879** E. C. HANCOCK *Amat. Pott. & Glass Painter* 49 When the oil has become somewhat set, so as to be 'tacky' to the finger, it is ready for the second process, called 'bossing'.

bossing ('bɒsɪŋ), *vbl. sb.*[2] *U.S.* [f. BOSS *v.*[2]] The practice of acting as a 'boss'.

1864 SALA in *Daily Tel.* 23 Dec., They won't do a stroke of work if they can help it..They like 'bossing'. **1884** *Manch. Exam.* 13 Aug. 5/4 The 'bossing' of railways is a practice not exclusively confined to the United States.

bossism ('bɒsɪz(ə)m). *U.S.* [f. BOSS *sb.*[6] + -ISM.] The system in which political parties are controlled by 'bosses' or 'wire-pullers'.

1881 *Scribner's Mag.* Aug. 616 The event shows also that the days of 'bossism' are closing. **1883** *American* VI. 88 If Bossism and Hubbellism were found..to be still the potential forces.

† **'bossive**, *a. Obs. rare.* [f. BOSS *sb.*[1] + -IVE (suggested perhaps by F. *bossu* hump-backed).] Crooked, deformed.

1658 OSBORN *Adv. Son* (1673) 47 Wives do worse than miscarry, that go their full time of a Fool with a Bossive birth. —— *Jas. I.* Wks. 513 Here lies..Little Bossive Robin.

† **'bossment.** *Obs. rare.* [f. BOSS *sb.*[1] + -MENT. Cf. *embossment*.] The formation of a hump.

1541 R. COPLAND *Guydon's Formul.* Y iij, For the gibbosite & bocement Auycen aloweth emplastrum de acoro.

boss-ship, bossship ('bɒsʃɪp). orig. *U.S.* [f. BOSS *sb.*[6] + -SHIP.] The rule or position of a boss or bosses, esp. in politics.

1882 *Nation* 2 Nov. 371/3 To enable Mahone to build up a new..boss-ship in Virginia. **1889** 'MARK TWAIN' *Conn. Yankee* xiii. 160 The thing that would have best suited..my nature would have been to resign the Boss-ship and get up an insurrection. **1894** *Voice* (N.Y.) 6 Sept., It was thought to be an auspicious time to shake off the 'bossship' exercised by Mr. Platt for many years. **1928** D. H. LAWRENCE *Lady Chatt.* xiii. 217 'But who is boss of the show?' she asked. 'The men who own and run the industries'... 'They don't take their boss-ship seriously enough,' she said.

boss-shot. *dial.* and *slang.* [See BOSS *v.*[3]] A bad shot or aim; *fig.* an unsuccessful attempt.

1890 FARMER *Slang*, *Boss*, to miss one's aim; to make such a shot as a boss-eyed person would be expected to make. Boss-shot is a common phrase. **1898** *Eng. Dial. Dict.* s.v., A bad shot with a stone is called a boss-shot. **1912** W. DEEPING *Sincerity* xviii. 141 Harkness made a clutch at the bow, but Master Brandon was too quick for him. He retreated three paces, grinning. 'Boss shot, that!' **1919** E. H. JONES *Road to En-dor* (1920) xxviii. 300 The student..made two boss shots before he hit the bull.

Also in corrupt form **bosh-shot**.

1939 'G. ORWELL' *Coming up for Air* III. i. 181 The Nazis chop people's heads off..and sometimes the executioner makes a bosh shot. **1959** 'O. MILLS' *Stairway to Murder* vii. 80 You haven't been having another bosh shot at the Crown Jewels, have you?

bossy ('bɒsɪ), *a.*[1] [f. BOSS *sb.*[1] + -Y[1].]

1. Swelling in, or like, a boss; projecting in rounded form.

1543 TRAHERON *Vigo's Chirurg.* I. iii. 3 The fourme of the heed..is also bossie, and bouncheth out in the fore and in the hynder partes. **1667** MILTON *P.L.* I. 716 Nor did there want Cornice or Freeze, with bossy Sculptures grav'n. **1668** CULPEPPER & COLE *Barthol. Anat.* I. xiv. 33 The tuberant or bossie part of the Liver. **1879** T. HARDY *Return Native* i. 20 This bossy projection..occupied the loftiest ground of the heath.

2. Having bosses or prominences.

1812 H. & J. SMITH *Rej. Addr.* ix. (1873) 75 Survey this shield, all bossy bright. **1851** RUSKIN *Stones Ven.* II. vi, Bossy beaten work of mountain chains. **1876** GEO. ELIOT *Dan. Der.* II. xviii. 146 Mab had..a bossy irregular brow and other quaintnesses.

bossy ('bɒsɪ), *a.*[2] [f. BOSS *sb.*[6]] Given to acting as 'boss' or leader. *colloq.* (orig. *U.S.*).

1882 *Harper's Mag.* Dec. 108/1 There was a lady manager who was dreadfully bossy. **1902** *Westm. Gaz.* 16 June 3/1 They cannot forget his often irritating ways and his decided tendency to be 'bossy'. **1933** N. COWARD *Design for Living* I. i. 7 Personally, I never cared for her very much. A bossy woman.

bossy ('bɒsɪ), *sb. U.S.* [Eng. dial. (south-western), dim. of *boss*, BOSS *sb.*[7]] = BOSS *sb.*[7]; a calf or cow. Also *bossy-calf*, *-cow*.

1844 'J. SLICK' *High Life N.Y.* II. 181 She only bust out in a new spot; and, like a great bossy calf, I had to jine in again. **1848** BARTLETT *Dict. Amer.*, *Bossy*, a familiar name applied to a calf. **1863** 'G. HAMILTON' *Gala-Days* 95 Bossy starts from the post, tail up in a hand gallop. **1907** *N.Y. Even. Post* 25 Feb. 3 He..will go out to interview a bossy [cow] who has eaten her last wisp of hay. **1911** H. QUICK *Yellowstone N.* xii. 314 A notion o' what it means to incorporate the fruit of the nest [*sc.* eggs] with the bossy. **1927** H. CRANE *Let.* 19 Mar. (1965) 291, I had just landed in town after three months with the bossy cows.

bost(e, obs. form of BOAST.

bost, var. BOAST *v.*[2]

‖ **bostangi** (bɒ'stændʒɪ). Also bostangee, -dgy. [a Turk. *bostānjī* 'a soldier of one of the corps of guards of the Sultan's palace' (Redhouse); lit. 'keeper of the garden', f. *bostān* (Pers.) a garden.] A Turkish guard of the palace.

1694 *Lond. Gaz.* No. 2989/1 A Capigi, with several Bostangies was dispatched after him to bring him back. **1717** LADY M. W. MONTAGUE *Lett.* 31 I. 106 He was preceded..by the spahis and bostangees (these are foot and horse-guards). **1753** HANWAY *Trav.* (1762) II. XIII. ii. 286 One of the principal officers of the bostangis. **1813** J. C. HOBHOUSE *Journey* 812 The Bostandgys and other attendants immediately formed a line.

bostar, obs. form of BOASTER.

bosthoon (bɒ'stuːn). *Irish.* Also bostoon. [ad. Ir. *bastún* whip made of green rods, soft or spiritless fellow.] An awkward fellow; a tactless, senseless person.

1833 W. CARLETON *Traits* I. 65 Sure only for this, I say, you bosthoon..where 'ud the purty colleen be? **1841** S. C. & A. M. HALL *Ireland* I. 75 Ye grate Bosthoon. **1914** JOYCE *Dubliners* 197 Is this what we pay rates for?.. To feed and clothe these ignorant bostooms [*sic*]. **1932** D. JOHNSTON *Moon in Yellow River* I. 20 Are you the ignorant bosthoon that's banging and hammering away at my knocker? **1933** DAVIES & THOMSON tr. *O'Sullivan's 20 Yrs. A-Growing* xvii. 227 Remember your ancestors! Strike the bostoon! **1970** M. KENYON *100,000 Welcomes* xii. 105 If it hadn't been for that seethin' bosthoon Dempsey we'd have had it wrapped up.

† **'boston**[1]. *Obs.* (see quot.)

1534 *Eng. Ch. Furniture* (1866) 203 An altar cloth of red silke powtheryd with flowres called boston.

'Boston[2]. [The name of the city of Boston in Massachusetts.]

1. A game at cards, allied to whist, named after the siege of Boston in the American War of Independence, to which the technical terms of the game refer. [a. F. *Boston*: see Littré, and the *Académie des Jeux*.]

1800 *Sporting Mag.* XVI. 185/2 (*heading*) Rules for the Game of Cards called Boston. *Ibid.* 186/1 The eldest hand ..if he thinks..that he can get five tricks or more, played as at Whist, says Boston. [**1805** *Académie Univ. des Jeux* s.v. *Whist*, Tarif du jeu de Boston Whist.] **1820** in HOYLE. **1850** Bohn's *Handbk. Games* 295 Boston..very much resembles Whist, and is somewhat like Quadrille. **1866** *Daily Tel.* 10 June 5/1 The French national game of Boston, which was invented in honour of a certain Transatlantic infusion. **1880** *Libr. Univ. Knowl.* II. 791 Boston, a game at cards, played by 4 persons, with 2 packs [one dealt, the other cut for trumps].

2. A variation of the waltz. Also *Boston dip* (*waltz*) (see quot. 1885); *Boston two-step*, a variation of the two-step.

1879 *Amer. Punch* Oct. 116/1 The Hardshell Baptists will not dance even the Boston Dip Waltzes. **1885** A. DODWORTH *Dancing* 73 *Boston*... When stepping with the right foot, the left knee is slightly bent, producing the dip, from which the name Boston Dip was derived. **1887** *Courier-Journal* (Louisville) 8 May 12/8 The young English baron..[was] dancing the Boston with Miss Bazaine. **1913** E. SCOTT *All about the Boston* 21 Mr. Henry Zay wrote: 'I have danced the "Boston" for twenty years (I am an American) and say emphatically that there is no set figure that can be called the "Boston". It is a series of steps or figures—such as the ordinary waltz-step, the "dip", the "run", the "reverse"', etc. *Ibid.* 24 At the present time the term 'Boston' is applied to the kind of movement that in its best and most graceful form would be far more consistently described as Rectilineal or Diagonal waltzing. **1918** A. BENNETT *Pretty Lady* iii. 11 Do play for me. Play a boston —a two-step.

3. Boston baked beans chiefly *U.S.*, a dish consisting of haricot beans baked with salt pork and molasses; occas. in *sing.*; **Boston (bull) terrier**, a small smooth-coated terrier originating in Massachusetts from a crossing of the bulldog and terrier; also *ellipt.* and *attrib.*; **Boston crab**, a wrestling hold (see quot. 1961).

1853 MRS. A. L. WEBSTER *Improved Housewife* 147 *Boston baked beans. **1904** *Omaha Bee* 16 Aug. 4 The maker of Boston baked bean pots is dead, but the fame of the Boston baked bean is perpetual. *c* **1938** *Fortnum & Mason Price List* 60/2 Boston baked beans..per tin 1/3. **1982** S. B. FLEXNER *Listening to Amer.* 62 The dish of beans cooked with saltpork and molasses wasn't widely called *Boston baked beans* until the 1850s. **1894** *Outing* (U.S.) Mar. 465/1 After much discussion the name of *Boston Terrier was finally selected because all other names indicating the origin of the dog were more or less in conflict with those of older breeds. **1907** F. T. BARTON *Terriers* ix. 90 The so-called *Boston terriers* appear to be but indifferent specimens of the bull-terrier cropped. **1945** C. L. B. HUBBARD *Observer's Bk. Dogs* 31 Boston Bull-Terrier... The breed was recognized by the American Kennel Club in 1893. **1948** *Chicago Tribune* 4 Apr. (Grafic Mag.) 20/4 The Boston originated from a cross between the English bulldog and the white English terrier. **1955** W. W. DENLINGER *Complete Boston* I. iv. 112 The correct Boston neck fits neatly into and between long shoulders. **1961** WEBSTER, **Boston crab*, a professional wrestling hold in which the aggressor sits on the buttocks of a prone opponent and pulls upward on the opponent's legs. **1962** *Spectator* 13 Apr. 480 The Boston Crab looks pretty agonising. **1985** *Time* 15 Apr. 105/1 It can be no small feat of strength and precision to execute an atomic knee drop, a figure-4 leg lock, or the dreaded Boston crab.

Hence **'Boston** *v. intr.*, to dance the Boston. *colloq.*

1913 A. N. LYONS *Simple Simon* III. vi. 328 He was saying to her 'Do you Boston?' **1920** S. LEWIS *Main St.* i. 2 Scores recited more accurately and dozens Bostoned more smoothly.

Bostonese (bɒstə'niːz). *U.S.* [f. *Boston*, Mass. + -ESE.] **a.** *collect.* Natives or inhabitants of Boston (see also quot. 1785). **b.** (See quot. 1888[2].)

1785 J. HADFIELD *Englishman in Amer.* 29 June (1933) 61 He asserted he had tomahawked and scalped 50 Bostonese, a name they [*sc.* Indians in Canada] give generally to the Americans of the States. **1876** *Cincinnati Enquirer* 17 June 3/2 His reply was not negro at all, it was purest Bostonese. **1888** *N.Y. Herald* 29 July (Farmer), There were a number of people present, principally Bostonese. **1888** FARMER *Americanisms*, *Bostonese*..is a method of speech or manners supposed to be specially affected by the residents of that city. **1925** *N.Y. Times* 8 Sept. 24/3 Squire Sam Jones..in the second innings surrendered four runs to the Bostonese. **1948** MENCKEN *Amer. Lang.* Suppl. II. 179 The educated speech of the State..is 'untainted by Bostonese'.

Bostonian (bɒ'stəʊnɪən), *sb.* and *a.* [f. as prec.]

A. *sb.* A native or inhabitant of Boston.

1682 J. W. *Let. from N.-Eng.* 7 These *Bostonians* enrich themselves by the ruine of Strangers. **1698** C. MATHER *Bostonian Ebenezer* Title-p., The Bostonians. **1774** H. WALPOLE *Let.* 2 Feb. (1904) VIII. 418 The Bostonians have canted three hundred chests of tea into the ocean. **1847** W. I. PAULDING *Noble Exile* in *Amer. Comedies* 107 Nay..we Bostonians have the reputation of being Bostonians wherever we go. **1897** C. M. FLANDRAU *Harvard Episodes* 18 When I say 'a Bostonian'..I mean of course a Bostonian that one knows. **1965** *Listener* 3 June 835/3 To be a poet in the age of Eliot, to grow up in the shadow of a frosty Bostonian.

B. *adj.* Belonging or native to Boston.

1698 C. MATHER (*title*) The Bostonian Ebenezer. **1794** HUMPHREYS *Industry* 15 Where Bostonian maids, with songs, prepare The canvass wings. **1920** *Chambers's Jrnl.* 15 May 374/1 His carefully nuanced Bostonian accent.

† **'bostrell.** *Obs. rare.* [? f. med.L. *bostar* a cow-house.] ? A bull or cow not full-grown.

1559 *Will of A. Lloyd, N. Wales* (Somerset Ho.), Two calves & a bostrell.

bostrychoid, -al (bɒstrɪ'kɔɪd, -əl), *a. Bot.* [f. Gr. βόστρυχ-ος curl or lock of hair + -OID + -AL[1].] 'Having the form or character of a ringlet or bostryx.' Gray *Bot. Text-bk.* 1880.

1875 A. W. BENNETT tr. *Sachs's Botany* 157 A Helicoid (bostrychoid) Dichotomy.

‖ **bostryx** ('bɒstrɪks). *Bot.* [a. Gr. βόστρυξ, var. of βόστρυχος, curl.] 'An uniparous helicoid cyme.' Gray *Bot. Text-bk.* 1880.

bosun, bo'sun, var. BOATSWAIN, representing the common pronunciation ('bəʊs(ə)n).

1868 W. S. GILBERT *Bab Ballads* 85 And a bo'sun tight, and a midshipmite, And the crew of the captain's gig. **1894** STEVENSON & OSBOURNE *Ebb-Tide* I. v. 77 He had a bo'sun's chair rigged over the rail..and went overboard with a pot of paint. **1930** 'GREENHORN' *Tinker, Tailor* vi. 134 We were swung alongside in a bosun's chair to scrape the dirt off the masts and spars. **1963** *Times* 26 Feb. 12/6 The bo'sun's call is the object one sees..hanging on a chain round the neck of the sailor on duty at the gangway of a British warship. Some people..call it a pipe.

Boswell ('bɒzwɛl). The name of James *Boswell* (see BOSWELLIAN *a.*), used allusively for: a constant companion or attendant who witnesses and records what a person does.

1858 O. W. HOLMES *Autocrat Breakf.-Table* (*sub-title*), Every man his own Boswell. **1891** A. CONAN DOYLE *Adv. Sherlock Holmes* (1892) 6, 'I think that I had better go, Holmes.' 'Not a bit, Doctor. Stay where you are. I am lost without my Boswell.' **1932** N. MITFORD *Christmas Pudding* iii. 41, I never thought of biography, but of course that's the very thing for me... May I be your Boswell, darling?

Boswellian (bɒz'wɛlɪən), *a.* and *sb.* Also Boswellean. [f. *Boswell*, the name of Dr. Johnson's friend and biographer, + -IAN.]

A. *adj.* Resembling Boswell as a biographer.

1843 CARLYLE *Past & Present* II. i. 54 The 'Chronicle', or private Boswellean Notebook, of Jocelin. **1855** *Rambler* III. 485 The average Englishman..has been bored by the Boswellian adoration of the Corsican Paoli. **1884** *Graphic* 21 June 607/2 Mr. Hatton..puts down everything with more than Boswellian minuteness.

B. *sb.* A student or admirer of Boswell.

1908 *Daily Chron.* 11 Nov. 3/4 Their appearance in print was hailed with pleasure by Johnsonians and Boswellians. **1921** *Glasgow Herald* 29 Jan. 13 Johnsonians and Boswellians alike will therefore receive with joyful gratitude Dr. J. T. T. Brown's paper.

So **'Boswellism**, the characteristic manner or style of Boswell as a biographer.

1825 MACAULAY *Ess.* (1860) I. 58 That propensity which, for want of a better name, we will venture to christen Boswellism. **1875** F. HALL in *Lippincott's Mag.* XV. 345 A rooted aversion to anything like Boswellism.

'Boswellize, *v.* **1.** *intr.* To write in Boswell's style; **'Boswellizing** *vbl. sb.*

1838 *Fraser's Mag.* XVII. 488 Boswellizing became in fashion. **1856** R. VAUGHAN *Mystics* (1860) I. 7 But I have been Boswellizing to you about the past history of these friends of mine.

2. *trans.* To treat in the Boswellian manner; to observe and record the actions, etc. of (someone).

1837 J. G. Lockhart *Mem. Sir W. Scott* IV. v. 151 Private lucubrations..designed to *Boswellize* Scott. **1855** *Tait's Mag.* XXII. 444/2 We had rather the many-sided man should remain to us the mystery he is, than be Boswellised after the fashion which is now current. **1912** A. Lang *Shakespeare, Bacon & Gt. Unkn.* ii. 29 There was no enthusiastic curiosity about him; nobody Boswellised any playwright of his time.

bosyne, var. of buysine *Obs.*, trumpet.

bot, bott (bɒt), *sb.*[1] Usually in *pl.* **bots, botts** *Sc.* **bats, batts.** [Etymology unknown: connexion with bite is phonologically inadmissible.]

1. a. A parasitical worm or maggot; now restricted to the larvæ of flies of the genus *Œstrus.* The name is considered to belong properly to the larva of *Œ. equi*, inhabiting the digestive organs of the horse, but is applied also to that of *Œ. bovis* (the gadfly), found under the skin of cattle, and to that of *Œ. ovis*, found in the frontal sinus of sheep. ***the botts*** is sometimes used as sing., as the name of the disease caused by these parasites. Also *fig.*

1523 Fitzherb. *Husb.* §102 The bottes is an yll dysease, and they lye in a horse mawe, and they be an inche long white coloured, and a reed heed, and as moche as a fyngers ende. *a* **1529** Skelton *Agst. Scottes* 171 The roughefoted Scottes We have well eased them of the bottes. **1568** *Jacob & Esau* I. i, in Hazl. *Dodsl.* II. 189 He hath either some worms or botts in his brain. **1617** Markham *Caval.* I. 64 All foales naturally..are euer subiect to great aboundance, both of Mawwormes, Grubbes, and Bots. *a* **1722** Lisle *Husb.* (1757) 465 Groundsel and savine are good against the worms, commonly called the bots in horses. **1836** *Penny Cycl.* V. 261/2 The hole made by the bot [in the beast's hide] in his escape will apparently close. **1918** E. Pound *Pavannes* 36 Mosher's propagandas That are the nation's botts, collicks and glanders. **1922** Wodehouse *Clicking of Cuthbert* v. 109 Like a sheep with the botts. **1951** Colyer & Hammond *Flies Brit. Isles* xxiii. 294 Bots do not appear to be the cause of permanent damage to their hosts.

fig. **1602** *Return Parnass.* I. ii. (Arb.) 13 Some of them are at this instant the bots and glanders of the printing house. **1647** Ward *Simp. Cobler* 72 [The Irish] are the very offall of men..the Bots that crawle on the Beasts taile.

b. 'Ludicrously applied to a bowel complaint in men, *Selkirks.*; also used to denote a colic, *West Scotl.*' (Jamieson).

1721 Ramsay *Poems* 30 She never ran sour Jute [liquor], because It gee's the Batts. **1816** Scott *Old Mort.* vii, 'The last thing ye sent Cuddie, when he had the batts.' **1844** H. Stephens *Bk. Farm* II. 178 Going out to work..with a full stomach, may bring on an attack of batts or colic.

c. *Austral.* and *N.Z. slang.* (See quots. 1919 and 1941.)

1919 Downing *Digger Dial.* 13 Bott, (1) a cadger; (2) a useless person; (3) a hanger-on. **1941** Baker *N.Z. Slang* vi. 51 In early uses *bot* is rendered as a germ, doubtless from *bot-fly*. From this comes the phrase of greeting, *How are the bots biting?* By the 1920's a *bot* is being used extensively for a troublesome person, for a persistent borrower, a financial parasite... Of fairly recent development in New Zealand is the phrase *to have the bot*, to be sick or out of sorts, moody or disagreeable. **1960** J. Fingleton *Four Chukkas to Austr.* 63 One of..the officials was berating Pressmen..as a 'lot of bots who wanted everything for nothing'.

2. Used as an expression of execration. (Cf. pox.)

1584 *3 Ladies Lond.* I. in Hazl. *Dodsl.* VI. 257 A bots on thy motley beard! **1606** *Sir G. Goosecappe* IV. ii. in Bullen *O. Pl.* (1884) III. 65 A botts a that stincking word odorous, I can never hitt on't. **1719** D'Urfey *Pills* (1872) IV. 124 Bots on them all, Both great and small.

3. *Comb.*: **bot-worm**; **bot-bee, bot-fly**, an insect of the genus Œstrus, whose eggs produce the bots; **bot-hole**, a hole in a hide made by a bot in escaping.

1852 T. Harris *Insects New Eng.* 499 The various insects, improperly called bot-bees, are two-winged flies. **1819** Rees *Cycl.* s.v., *Œ. ovis*, the sheep bot-fly..*Œ. tarandi*, the reindeer bot-fly. **1816** Kirby & Sp. *Entomol.* (1843) I. 121 The Tanners also prefer those hides that have the greatest number of bot-holes in them, which are always the best and strongest. **1847** Carpenter *Zool.* §733. **1877** *Rep. Vermont Dairym. Assoc.* VIII. 105 Grub-in-the-head is a bot-worm, ..cousin to the bots in horses.

bot, bott (bɒt), *sb.*[2] Colloq. abbrev. of bottom *sb.* 1 b.

1922 Joyce *Ulysses* 527 Spank your bare bot right well, miss, with the hair-brush. **1951** Auden *Nones* (1952) 54 The cute little botts of the sailors. **1959** I. & P. Opie *Lore & Lang. Schoolchildren* xiii. 301 A kick up the bot for being a clot.

bot, bót, OE. form of boot *sb.*[1], occas. used by modern historical writers in reference to OE. law and custom in senses 5, 5 b, 9, 10 of that word.

bot, obs. form of boat *sb.*, boot, bout = about, but; obs. pa. t. of bite.

bot (bɒt), *v. Austral.* and *N.Z. slang.* [f. bot, bott 1 c.] *intr.* (See quot. 1941.) So **'botting** *vbl. sb.*

1934 *Bulletin* (Sydney) 7 Nov. 46/2 Settle up when I sell me next picture... Never did like botting on a bloke. **1941** Baker *N.Z. Slang* vi. 52 *To bot*, to borrow money, to impose on others, and *botting*, the practice. *To bot on* a person is widely used..*cold botting* is a straight-out request for food at house-doors.

‖**bota** ('bota). [Sp.] **1.** A small leather bottle for holding wine.

1832 W. Irving *Alhambra* 20 His bota, or leathern bottle, which was of portly dimensions, filled to the neck with choice Valdepeñas wine. **1923** *Blackw. Mag.* Aug. 180/2 The *bota* was unslung, and we all toasted one another in tarry wine. **1940** E. Hemingway *For whom Bell Tolls* xxi. 267 Give me the *bota* with wine.

2. A boot, esp. for riding. *U.S.*

1834 A. Pike *Prose Sk. & Poems* 138 The men with their pantalones of cloth,..the botas of striped and embroidered leather. **1901** *Out West* June 481 She..looked up..at the pretty red-stained *botas* studded with silver buttons. **1967** 'La Meri' *Sp. Dancing* (ed. 2) 149 *Botas*, Spanish dancing boots, male.

botallackite (bəʊ'tæləkaɪt). *Min.* [f. the *Botallack* mine, Cornwall: see -ite[1].] A name given by A. H. Church in 1865 to a variety of atacamite containing a large proportion of water.

1865 A. H. Church in *Jrnl. Chem. Soc.* III. 213. **1868** Dana *Syst. Min.* (ed. 5) 121 Botallackite occurs at the Botallack mine, Cornwall, in thin crusts of minute interlacing crystals, closely investing killas.

botanic (bəʊ'tænɪk), *a.* and *sb.* [ad. med.L. *botanicus*, a. Gr. βοτανικός, f. βοτάν-η plant: see -ic; perh. the immediate source is F. *botanique*, which occurs in Cotgrave, 1611.]

A. *adj.* Pertaining to the science or study of plants, to botany. (Now mostly superseded by botanical, exc. in names of institutions founded many years ago, as 'The Royal Botanic Society', 'The Botanic Gardens'.)

1656 Parkinson in *Phil. Trans.* LXIII. 84 *note*, Discovered in a botanic excursion by J. Tradescant. **1677** Plot *Oxfordsh.* 149 Our very Learned Botanic Professor. **1678** Cudworth *Intell. Syst.* 326 That Ancient Botanick Book mentioned by Galen. **1678** Phillips, *Botanical* or *Botanic*, belonging to Herbs or Plants. **1736** Thomson *Liberty* II. 140 Where..Hymettus spread..to botanick hand the stores of health. **1762–71** H. Walpole *Vertue's Anecd. Paint.* (1786) V. 21 He probably engraved the botanic figures for Lobel's Observations. **1842** Tennyson *Amphion* x, They read Botanic Treatises, And Works on Gardening thro' there.

B. *sb.* †**1.** One skilled in plants, a botanist. *Obs.*

1657 W. Coles *Adam in Eden* To Rdr., The Botanick is as commonly puzzled as satisfied. **1676** Worlidge *Bees* (1691) 38 A tree esteemed..by our modern Botanicks.

†**2.** Chiefly in pl. *botanics.* [cf. *physics*, *mathematics*.] The science of plants; = botany. *Obs.*

1698 *Phil. Trans.* XX. 463 Such as are advanced in the Knowledge of Botanicks. **1725** De Foe *Voy. round World* (1840) 182 He had no skill in botanicks. **1758** *Monthly Rev.* 592 Supereminent skill in botanics.

botanical (bəʊ'tænɪkəl), *a.* [f. prec. + -al[1].] Concerned with the study or cultivation of plants, pertaining to botany.

1658 Sir T. Browne *Gard. Cyrus* II. 499 The Persian Gallants who destroyed this Monarchy, maintained their Botanicall bravery. **1767** Barrington in *Phil. Trans.* LVII. 214 When a stranger, from botanical or other curiosity, goes to the top of a Welsh mountain. **1797** Holcroft *Stolberg's Trav.* III. lxxxvii. (ed. 2) 442 A large botanical garden. **1830** Lyell *Princ. Geol.* xxxviii. (1850) 591 Botanical Geography. A comparison of the plants of different regions. **1873** Morley *Rousseau* II. 75 In his botanical expeditions.

botanically (bəʊ'tænɪkəlɪ), *adv.* [f. prec. + -ly[2].] In a botanical manner; in relation to botany; according to the principles or technical language of botany.

1757 Da Costa in *Phil. Trans.* L. 229 *note*, Scheuchzer has arranged the fossile plants botanically. **1793** W. Curtis *Bot. Mag.* VI. 215 In its improved, or to speak more botanically, in its monstrous state. **1848** C. A. Johns *Week at Lizard* 291 It is botanically distinguished from the other ..Heaths, by its anthers. **1870** Yeats *Nat. Hist. Comm.* 102 Botanically, this is the region of palms.

†**'botanism.** *Obs.* [ad. L. *botanism-us*, a. Gr. βοτανισμός; cf. botanize and -ism.] = botany.

1668 D. Lloyd *Mem.* 316 Competent skill in..Physick, and the two parts belonging to it, Chirurgery and Botanism. **1727** Bradley *Fam. Dict.*, *Film*, a Term in Botanism.

botanist ('bɒtənɪst). [a. F. *botaniste*; cf. prec. and -ist.] One who studies botany.

a **1682** Sir T. Browne *Tracts* 61 That diligent botanist Bellonius. **1683** Robinson in Ray *Corr.* (1848) 135, I intend to write to the best botanist..of this, or perhaps any, age. **1770** Gray in *Corr. w. Nicholls* (1843) 107, I rejoice to see you are so great a gardener and botanist. **1874** Helps *Soc. Press.* iv. 63 The..botanists who come to..be instructed by the plants at Kew.

botanize ('bɒtənaɪz), *v.* [ad. mod.L. *botanizāre*, ad. Gr. βοτανίζειν to gather plants; cf. botanic and -ize.]

1. *intr.* To seek for plants for botanical purposes; to study plants botanically.

1767 Mrs. Delany *Lett.* Ser. II. I. 168 They will botanize charmingly (and I shall come in for some scraps of knowledge). **1775** Masson in *Phil. Trans.* LXVI. 296 In the day-time they retire to the woods, which renders it very dangerous to botanize there. *a* **1841** Wordsw. *Poet's Epitaph*, Philosopher! a fingering slave, One that would peep and botanize Upon his mother's grave?

2. *trans.* To explore or examine botanically. Hence **'botanized** *ppl. a.*

1861 Geikie *E. Forbes* x. 285 To botanize the islands thoroughly. **1866** Kingsley *Herew.* i. 49 The world was not to him as to us, round, circumscribed, mapped, botanized.

botanizer ('bɒtənaɪzə(r)). One who botanizes.

1849 Curzon *Visits Monast.* 238 The botanizer, however, was dead enough.

botanizing ('bɒtənaɪzɪŋ), *vbl. sb.* [f. as prec. + -ing[1].] The action of seeking for plants, or of studying plants botanically. Often *attrib.*

1794 Mathias *Purs. Lit.* (1798) 399 In this botanizing age, it should not pass without observation. [? *ppl. a.*] **1835** Beckford *Recoll.* 183 By getting out of his vehicle and botanizing by the roadside. **1859** G. Wilson *E. Forbes* iv. 103 The..professor led his students, each summer's Saturday, on a botanizing march. **1883** *Harper's Mag.* Oct. 706/2, I..had my botanizing tin on my back.

botanizing ('bɒtənaɪzɪŋ), *ppl. a.* [f. as prec. + -ing[2].] That searches for or examines plants.

†**bo'tano.** *Obs.* [ad. It. *bottana.*] (See quot.)

1611 *Rates* (Jam.), Botanos or peeces of linnin litted blew, the peece iiil. **1670** *Ibid.* Botanoes or blew lining. **1660** *Act 12 Chas. II*, iv. Sched., Botanoes per piece *xs.*

botano-, repr. Gr. βοτανο-, combining form of βοτάνη plant; cf. botanic, botany. Hence in 17th c. were formed many short-lived compounds in imitation of those of astro-. †**bota'nographer**, †**bota'nographist**, one who describes plants. †**bota'nography**, the (or a) description of plants. †**bota'nologer**, a botanist. †**botano'logical** *a.*, relating to botany. †**bota'nology**, botany. **'botano,mancy** (incorrectly †**'botomancy**), divination by plants. †**bota'nomical** *a.* [wrongly formed, cf. *astronomical*], botanical. †**bo'tanomy**, botany.

1682 *Weekly Mem.* 271 Collected out of all writers, as well ..*Botanographers and physicians as Lexicographers. **1662** Fuller *Worthies* (1840) II. 496 Doctor Bowle, my worthy friend, and most skilful *botonographist. **1731** Zollman in *Phil. Trans.* XXXVII. 219 We still want a *Botanography, or Description of the Plants. **1658** Sir T. Browne *Gard. Cyrus* i. 102 The wisedom of that eminent *Botanologer [Solomon]. *Ibid.* iv. 175 The Tree..which stricter *Botanology will hardly allow to be Camphire. **1755** Johnson *Dict.*, *Botanology.* **1610** Healey *St. Aug. Citie of God* 294 Divination..by Hearbes, *Botonomancy. **1640** E. Chilmead tr. *Ferrand's Love Melanch.* 176 Botanomancy.. is done by the noise or crackling that knee holme, box, or bay leaues make when they are crushed betwixt one's hands or cast into the fire. **1653** Urquhart *Rabelais* III. xxv, To have the truth of the matter..disclosed unto you by *botomancy. **1861** W. Smith *Dict. Bible* I. 442 Botanomancy. **1656** Blount *Glossogr.*, *Botomical* or rather **Botanomical*, pertaining to hearbs. **1716** M. Davies *Ath. Brit.* III. 37 Chiron..cultivated Botanomy.

botany ('bɒtənɪ). [f. botanic after analogy of sbs. in *-y* related to adjs. in *-ic*, as *astronomy* and *astronomic*.]

1. The science which treats of plants.

1696 Ray *Philos. Lett.* (1718) 290 The great difficulties the lovers of Botanie are forced to encounter. **1706** Hearne *Rem. & Coll.* (1885) I. 233 A man much inclined to Botanny. **1710** M. Henry *Exp. Song of Sol.* iv, Solomon was a great master in botany. **1880** Gray *Struct. Bot.* Introd. 1 The two Biological Sciences..Zoology and Botany.

2. Short for 'Botany Bay'. Usually *attrib.* as in ***Botany wool***: orig. wool from Botany Bay, but now applied to all Australian wool. ***Botany yarn***: yarn made from this wool.

1882 *Daily News* 4 Mar., A fair business is doing in botany yarns. **1883** *Times* 27 Aug. 9/5 English & Botany wools are in fair request. **1883** *Daily News* 17 Sept. 2/3 Fine Botany wools are still the most in favour.

b. Short for *Botany wool.*

1884 W. S. B. McLaren *Spinning* vi. 116 When the material is very short Botany, the advantage is not so great. .. It is confined to commission combers and Botany spinners. **1900** *Daily News* 16 Oct. 2/6 In the botany trade it is difficult for spinners to obtain orders.

Botany Bay. [So called by Captain Cook on account of the great variety of plants collected there by the botanist who accompanied him.] Proper name of a place in New South Wales, formerly a convict settlement; hence proverbially used in sense of 'transportation'; also *fig.*

1812 *Examiner* 19 Oct. 666/1 The famished wretch..is sent to the whipping-post or to Botany Bay. **1821** Byron *Juan* III. xciv, Such names at present cut a convict figure, The very Botany Bay in moral geography. **1841** Marryat *Poacher* vi, They are..sent off to Botany Bay.

†**botar.** [Prob. a fictitious word evolved from botargo.] (See quot.)

1769 Pennant *Zool.* III. 279 Of the roes of the female [Mullets] which are called Botar, is made Botargo.

botargo (bəʊ'tɑːgəʊ). Also 6 **botarge**, 7 **buttargo, butargo, puttargo**, 8 **boutargue**, (9 **boutaraga**), *Pl.* **-oes, -os.** [a. It. *botargo*, *botarga* (now *buttarga*), ad. Arab. *buṭarkhah* 'preserved mullet-roe', in

Makrizi A.D. 1400 (in pl. *buṭārikh*, whence It. var. *bottarica*), ad. Coptic *outarakhon*, which the Arab. word renders in a glossary published by Kircher; f. Coptic *ou-* indef. article + Gr. ταρίχιον pickle. See Quatremère in *Journal des Savants*, Jan. 1848. (Fr. form *boutargue*, occas. found in Eng.)]

A relish made of the roe of the mullet or tunny.

1598 *Epulario* H ij b, To make Botarge, a kind of Italian meat, fish spawn salted. **1615** G. SANDYS *Trav.* 93 Salt, Buttargo, and Cassia being now the principall [commodities]. **1616** CAPT. SMITH *Descr. New Engl.* 16 (Arb.) 197 Mullet and Puttargo. **1620** —— *New-Engl. Trials* Wks. (Arb.) 240 Mullit, Caviare, and Buttargo. **1653** URQUHART *Rabelais* I. xxi, Hard rowes of mullet called Botargos. **1661** PEPYS *Diary* 5 June, Drinking great draughts of claret, and eating botargo, and bread and butter. **1702** W. J. *Bruyn's Voy. Levant* xlii. 170 They..take out the Spawn, of which..they make Boutargue. **1730** SWIFT *Panegyr. Dean* Misc. (1735) V. 141 And, for our home-bred British Cheer, Botargo, Catsup, and Caveer. **1813** HOBHOUSE *Journ.* 693 Boutaraga, or the roes of fish, salted and pressed into rolls like sausages. **1840** HOOD *Kilmansegg* xxviii, That huge repast, With its loads & cargoes Of drink & botargoes, At the birth of the Babe in Rabelais. **1852** SCHMITZ *Niebuhr's Anc. Hist.* I. 140.

botcard, ? for *bottard* = BATTARD a cannon.

c **1565** R. LINDSAY *Chron. Scotl.* 143 Two great Botcards.

botch (bɒtʃ), *sb.*[1] Forms: 4 (**bouch(e), boch, 4–5 bocche, 5–7 boche, 5 bohche, booche,** (6 *Sc.* **boiche**), **4–6 botche, 6– botch.** [ME. *boche*, *bocche*, a. ONFr. *boche* (mod.Picard *boche*, Norm. *bosche*) = OF. *boce* (now *bosse*) ulcer, botch, a common Romanic word (Pr. *bossa*, It. *bozza*, of same meaning; It. *boccia*, Sp. *bocha* ball):—med.L. *bocia*, *-um*: see BOSS *sb.*[1], and cf. BOUCH(E *sb.*[2]]

†**1.** A hump; a swelling; a tumour, wen, or goître; = BOSS *sb.*[1] 1. *Obs.*

1382 WYCLIF *Isa.* xxx. 6 Berende..vp on the bocche [**1388** botche] of camailes ther tresores. **1398** TREVISA *Barth. De P.R.* XV. xxxi, Many men wonen ny3e þe mounteynes, and þey haue gret bocches..under þe chyn, of ofte use of snowe and water. *c* **1450** *Nominale* in Wr.-Wülcker *Voc.* 707 *Hic gibbus*, a boche in bake. **1481** CAXTON *Myrr.* II. xiv. 99 Plente of wymmen that haue botches vnder the chyn. **1519** HORMAN *Vulg.* 30 The bounche or botche [*gibbus*] is so boystous that it can unneth be bounde vp with a trussar.

†**2.** A boil, ulcer, or pimple. Also *fig.* as 'spiritual botch'. *Obs.* exc. *dial.*

1377 LANGL. *P. Pl.* B. xx. 83 Byles, and bocches and brennyng agues. **1486** *Bk. St. Albans* C vij, Booches that growe in a hawkes jowe. **1547** BOORDE *Brev. Health* vii. 9 In Englishe it [*Ulcera*] is named byles or botches. **1634** CANNE *Necess. Separ.* (1849) 96 This great wickedness, which causeth spiritual botches and sores. **1667** MILTON *P.L.* XII. 180 Botches and blaines must all his flesh emboss. **1785** BURNS *Address Deil* xviii, While scabs and botches did him gall, Wi' bitter claw. **1875** ROBINSON *Whitby Gloss.* (E.D.S.) *Botches*, sore places.

†**b.** *spec.* A tumour from which horses suffer, *esp.* in the groin. *Obs.*

1579 GOSSON *Sch. Abuse* (Arb.) 19 It is the custome of the flye to leaue the sound places of the Horse and suck at the Botch. **1607** TOPSELL *Four-f. Beasts* 308 A botch..in the hinder parts betwixt the thighs. **1706** PHILLIPS, *Botch*..a Sore in the Groin of a Horse.

3. Boils or sores as a malady; an eruptive disease or plague, as 'the botch of Egypt'. *arch.* or *Obs.*

1388 WYCLIF *Deut.* xxviii. 27 The Lorde smyte thee with the botche [**1382** byil] of Egipt. **1526** TINDALE *Rev.* xvi. 2 There fell a noysom and a sore botche apon the men. **1534** *Aberdeen Reg.* V. 16 (JAM.) Ane seyknes & smyttand plaig callit the boiche. **1570** LEVINS *Manip.* 177 Botch, *pestilentia*. **1842** SIR H. TAYLOR *Edwin* III. viii, The Lord shall smite him with the botch of Egypt.

botch (bɒtʃ), *sb.*[2] [f. BOTCH *v.*[1] (Sometimes indistinguishable from fig. use of the prec.)]

1. A botched place or part, a flaw or blemish resulting from unskilful workmanship.

1605 SHAKS. *Macb.* III. i. 133 To leaue no Rubs nor Botches in the Worke. **1645** MILTON *Tetrarch.* Wks. 1738 I. 244 Let it stick as a notorious botch of deformity.

2. *fig.* **a.** A clumsy patch; a meaningless or unsuitable word added for the sake of rime or metre.

1693 DENNIS *Impart. Critick* iii. 25 Every Epithet is to be look'd upon as a Botch, which does not add to the thought. **1707** SWIFT *On Union* Wks. 1755 IV. I. 283 By way of botch She piec'd it up again with scotch. **1780** WESLEY *Wks.* (1872) XIV. 341 In these Hymns there is no doggerel, no botches. **1861** A. B. HOPE *Eng. Cathedr. 19th C.* 220 The difficulties of accommodation are honestly recognized and boldly grappled with, not by botches and makeshifts.

†**b.** A mark like a clumsy patch, a blotch. *Obs.*

1715 *Lond. Gaz.* No. 5365/4 The other 4 [Sheep] cropt on the Right Ear, and a black Botch on the Left Hipp.

3. a. A bungled piece of work. So *botch-work*.

1648 HERRICK *Hesper.* I. 104 Learne of me what woman is, Something made of thred and thrumme; A mere botch of all and some. **1845** LD. CAMPBELL *Chancellors* (1857) III. lvi. 130 When the writer tries to be light and airy, we have such a botch as might have been expected. **1870** HAWTHORNE *Eng. Note-bks.* (1879) I. 187, I have made a miserable botch of this description. **1876** HAMERTON *Intell. Life* II. ii. 406 Vastness of the interval, that separates botch-work from handicraft.

b. *fig.*

1864 ELIZ. MURRAY *E. Norman* I. 159 The men were not to be trusted, most of them being convicts, or 'botches' of one kind or other.

4. a. = BOTCHER *sb.*[1] *dial.*

1855 *Whitby Gloss.*, *A Botch*, a cobbler.

b. = BOTCHER[1] 3. *dial.* and *colloq.*

1829 J. KENNEY *Illust. Stranger* II. i. 24 Some botch of an embalmer, who had not done justice to Your princely remains. **1868** J. C. ATKINSON *Gloss. Cleveland Dial.* 59 He's nobbut an aud *botch*. He's mair lahk t'mar an t'mend.

botch (bɒtʃ), *v.*[1] Also 4 **bocchyn**, 5–6 **botche.** [ME. *bocche-n*, of uncertain etymology: having apparently no original relation to BOTCH *sb.*[1], though the words may have subsequently influenced each other. Prof. Skeat suggests for the vb. a LG. origin, comparing MDu. *butsen*, (1) to strike, beat, (2) to repair (Oudemans), app. related to Du. *botsen* to knock, dash, Ger. dial. *butschen*, *butzen* to strike, knock; according to Franck an onomatopœic word of echoic origin. But the sense 'repair' in Du. *butsen* seems to be recent, while in English it appears in Wyclif: also there is no sense 'knock' in English, so that connexion with the continental words is very doubtful. Perhaps the Eng. word is an onomatopœia related in its genesis to 'patch'; cf. Ger. *batzen* to patch. See BODGE.]

1. *trans.* To make good or repair (a defect, damage, damaged article); to patch, mend. Now only: to repair clumsily or imperfectly. Often with *up*.

1382 WYCLIF *2 Chron.* xxxiv. 10 That thei enstoren the temple, and eche feble thingus thei bocchyn [**1388** reparele alle feble thingis]. **1530** PALSGR. 461/1, I botche or patche an olde garment..I haue botched my hosen at the heles. **1551** ROBINSON tr. *More's Utop.* (Arb.) 69 Sicke bodies..to be kept and botched up. *a* **1680** BUTLER *Rem.* (1759) II. 200 He does not mend his Manners, but botch them with Patches of another Stuff and Colour. **1863** FAWCETT *Pol. Econ.* IV. ii. 535 Botching and patching each single tax.

b. *absol.* To do repairs; to patch clumsily.

1580 TUSSER *Husb.* (1878) 166 Cobble and botch, ye that cannot buie new. **1730** SWIFT *Dan Jackson's Pict.* Wks. 1755 IV. I. 249 At last I'm fairly forc'd to botch for't. **1815** SCOTT *Guy M.* xxi, I labour and botch..and produce at last a base caricature. **1865** [see BOTCHING *vbl. sb.*[2]]

2. To spoil by unskilful work; to bungle.

1530 PALSGR. 461/1 To botche or bungyll a garment as he dothe that is nat a perfyte workeman. **1663** PEPYS *Diary* 26 Apr., Tom coming, with whom I was angry for his botching my camlott coat. **1850** BLACKIE *Æschylus* I. 293 This chorus seems hopelessly botched..and all attempts to mend it are more or less unsatisfactory. **1858** HAWTHORNE *Fr. & It. Jrnls.* I. 292 The greatest bungler that ever botched a block of marble.

3. *fig. trans.* To put or stitch together clumsily or unskilfully; to construct or compose in a bungling manner. Often with *up*, *together*.

1561 T. NORTON *Calvin's Inst.* III. v. (1634) 319 Augustines booke of repentance..botched of good and bad by some scraper together. **1678** CUDWORTH *Intell. Syst.* I. iv. 411 An ill-agreeing Drama, botch'd up of many impertinent Intersertions. **1768** TUCKER *Lt. Nat.* II. 124 One or two of Horace's purple rags botched together with coarse seams of abuse.

b. To add as a patch.

1589 *Pappe w. Hatchet* (1844) 39 Botching in such frize iestes vppon fustion earnest. **1656** [see BOTCHING *vbl. sb.*]

†**botch**, *v.*[2] ? *nonce-wd.* [f. BOTCH *sb.*[1]] To mark with botches.

1699 GARTH *Dispens.* II. (1700) 22 Young Hylas, botch'd with Stains to foul to name.

botched (bɒtʃt), *ppl. a.* [f. BOTCH *v.*[1] + -ED.] Mended or patched in a bungling manner; clumsily put together; cobbled. Hence **'botchedly** *adv.*

1568 DK. NORFOLK in Campbell *Love-lett. Mary Q. Scots* App. 27 You schall make but boched work yf you doe not sowndlie and perfectlye conclude thowes dyfferencys. **1733** G. CHEYNE *Eng. Malady* I. x. §4 This Cement never makes them the same continued Organ, scarce any thing but a botch'd or clouted one. **1752** HUME *Idea Perf. Commw.* Ess. (1777) I. 524 The common botched and inaccurate governments seem to serve the purposes of society. **1831** CARLYLE *Sart. Res.* I. viii, A botched mass of tailors' and cobblers' shreds. **1879** *Spectator* 31 May 681 The Peace is a botched-up affair, bringing Great Britain nothing, etc. **1642** H. MORE *Song of Soul* II. III. III. lxvii, Thus patch they Heaven more botch'dly then old cloths.

botcher[1] ('bɒtʃə(r)). Also 4 **bochour**, 5 **botchare.** [f. BOTCH *v.* + -ER[1].]

1. A mender, repairer, or patcher. Also *fig.*

1499 *Promp. Parv.* 42 Botchare of olde thinges, *resartor*. **1629** FORD *Lover's Mel.* I. ii. (1811) 134 Physicians are the bodys coblers, rather the botchers of mens bodies. **1863** MRS. C. CLARKE *Shaks. Char.* ix. 225 Lepidus was a peace-botcher from timidity.

2. *spec.* †**a.** A cobbler. *Obs.*

c **1375** ? BARBOUR *St. Marcus* 78, He saw a bochour mend al[d] schone, & gef hyme his scho for to mend. **1610** COOKE *Pope Joan* in *Harl. Misc.* (Malh.) IV. 70 That John the Twenty-second was 'filius veteramentarii resarcitoris videlicet solearum'; that is, the son of a botcher.

b. A tailor who does repairs.

1530 PALSGR. 200/1 Botcher of old garments, *rauavdevr*. **1552** HULOET, Bodger, botcher, mender, or patcher of olde garmentes. **1589** R. HARVEY *Pl. Perc.* 14 There is a Shomaker, there is a Cobler: a Tailor, and a Botcher. **1663** BAXTER *Div. Life* 31 A sorry Taylor may make a Botcher, or a bad Shoomaker may make a Cobler. *a* **1734** NORTH *Lives* (1826) II. 409 Like a botcher in a paltry hut, sat cross-legged. **1783** COWPER *Lett.* 23 Sept., Though but a botcher, which is somewhat less than a tailor. **1841** MARRYAT *Poacher* xxviii, I had to examine..their trousers, and hold weekly conversation with the botcher, as to..repairs.

†**c.** ? A jobber. (Sense doubtful; cf. *botcheries* and *brokerages* in quot. 1624 under BOTCHERY.)

c **1510** BARCLAY *Mirr. Good Mann.* (1570) G iv, Be no towler, catchpoll nor customer, No broker nor botcher, no somner nor sergeaunt..The moste of this number liueth..by fraudes and by polling.

3. One who does a thing bunglingly; a clumsy maker up *of*; an unskilful workman, a bungler.

c **1440** *Promp. Parv.* 42 Bochchare or vncrafty [**1499** botchar], *iners*. **1581** J. BELL *Haddon's Answ. Osor.* 288 This Pope Boniface yͤ botcher of yͤ Decretalls. **1654** TRAPP *Comm. Job* xiii. 4 Ye are not onely..forgers, but..botchers. **1700** CONGREVE *Way of World* V. i, To become a botcher of second-hand marriages. **1885** R. BRIDGES *Nero* II. i, Thou miserable, painful, hackney-themed Botcher of tragedies.

botcher[2] ('bɒtʃə(r)). A young salmon; a grilse.

1801 T. SELWYN *MS. Let. to A. Selwyn*, We have Salmon and we have botcher If the fisher man chance to cotch her. **1875** *Times* 26 Aug., Formerly grilse, or botchers, were far more plentiful than they have been. **1886** *Athenæum* 3 Apr. 459/3 The two-year-old salmon, the grilse or 'botcher'.

'botcheress, *nonce-wd.* A female botcher.

1813 *Sismondi's Lit. Eur.* (1846) II. xxv. 173 A botcheress of lost reputations.

†**'botcherly**, *adj.*, *adv.* *Obs.* [f. BOTCHER[1].]

A. *adj.* [-LY[1].] Bungling, unworkmanlike.

1603 FLORIO *Montaigne* III. xii. (1632) 595 A number of such botcherly-patchcotes..wherewith to enamell this treaty, etc. **1653** W. LAWSON *Angling* in Arb. *Garner* I. 193 It is botcherly, hinders the biting, and sometimes cuts the line.

B. *adv.* [-LY[2].] After the manner of a botcher; unskilfully.

1607 *Schol. Disc. agst. Antichr.* I. i. 47 Painted or grauen, cunningly drawne or botcherly made.

botchery ('bɒtʃərɪ). [f. BOTCHER[1]: see -ERY.] A botcher's work; clumsy or awkward workmanship or its result; patchwork.

1608 *World of Wonders* 235 (L.) If we speak of base botchery. **1674** R. GODFREY *Inj. & Ab. Physic* Pref., I, who always hated Botchery, might have real Art. **1732** DE FOE, etc. *Tour Gt. Brit.* (1769) I. 277 Disgrace this fine Piece, and make it mere Botchery. **1880** WEBB tr. *Goethe's Faust* Prel. 10 Your pretty masters, with their botchery.

b. ? Jobbery: cf. BOTCHER[1] 2 c.

1624 BP. MOUNTAGU *Gagg* 35 Those manifold botcheries, and brokerages of your Romish church.

botchily ('bɒtʃɪlɪ), *adv.* [f. BOTCHY *a.*[2] + -LY[2].] In a botchy manner.

1882 *Good Literature* 29 Apr., The inelegant and botchily printed catalogues.

†**'botching**, *vbl. sb.*[1] *Obs. rare*[−1]. [f. BOTCH *sb.*[1] + -ING[1].] The forming of botches or boils.

1398 TREVISA *Barth. De P.R.* VII. xxxi. (1495) 245 By botchynge of the lounges all the body is wasted.

botching ('bɒtʃɪŋ), *vbl. sb.*[2] [f. BOTCH *v.*[1] + -ING[1].] The action of repairing or mending; clumsy patching; unskilful or bungling work.

c **1440** *Promp. Parv.* 5 A bocchement, or a bocchynge, *augmentum*. *a* **1535** FISHER *Wks.* 358 O corruptible body which..dayly needeth reprations and botching vp with meate and drinke. **1656** SANDERSON *Serm.* (1689) 392 The botching in of a course shred into a fine garment. **1691** T. H[ALE] *Acc. New Invent. &c.* 98 That patching and botching with Solder. **1719** DE FOE *Crusoe* (1840) I. ix. 159, I set to work a-tailoring, or rather indeed a-botching. **1865** RUSKIN *Eth. Dust* v. (1883) 87 All doubt, and repenting, and botching, and retouching, and wondering what it will be best to do next, are vice, as well as misery.

botching ('bɒtʃɪŋ), *ppl. a.* [f. BOTCH *v.* + -ING[2].] That botches; repairing, jobbing; bungling.

1598 FLORIO, *Taccola*..a patching, or botching piece of worke, a bungling. **1661** S. PARTRIDGE *Double Scale Proportion* To Rdr., The fault is in the botching Taylor, not in the stuffe. **1834** H. MILLER *Scenes & Leg.* xxviii. (1857) 424 An old botching carpenter.

†**'botchment.** *Obs. rare.* [f. BOTCH *v.* + -MENT.] An addition, a 'make-up'.

c **1440** *Promp. Parv.* 5 A bocchement, *augmentum*. *Ibid.* 42 Bochment [**1499** botchement], *additamentum*. **1526** SKELTON *Magnyf.* 1126 Gyve me thy dogge, and I am content, And thou shalt have my hawke to a botchment.

botchour, obs. form of BUTCHER.

†**'botchy**, *a.*[1] *Obs.* [f. BOTCH *sb.*[1] + -Y[1].] Pertaining to, or of the nature of, a botch; covered with botches or excrescences.

1398 TREVISA *Barth. De P.R.* V. xxiv. (1495) 132 The grystels the fyrst of whyche is knotty and botchy. *c* **1450** *Nominale* in Wr.-Wülcker 710 *Gibbosus*, bochy. **1606** SHAKS. *Tr. & Cr.* II. i. 6 Were not that a botchy core. **1768** TUCKER *Lt. Nat.* II. 331 We may claim Mahometism as a botchy excrescence or spurious offspring of the Gospel.

botchy ('bɒtʃɪ), *a.*^{2} [f. BOTCH *sb.*^{2} + -Y^1.] Full of botching or bungling work.

1879 G. M. HOPKINS *Let.* 10 Mar. (1935) 24 Each verse a work of art, no botchy places.

†**bote.** *Obs. rare*$^{-1}$. Some kind of tool.

c **1325** *Coer de L.* 4357 Some caught a bote, and some a hach, And broughton to tymbyr and rach.

bote, ME. form of BOOT *sb.*^{1}, occas. used since the 16th c. by legal and historical writers in legal senses of OE. *bót*: **a.** Repair; **b.** estover; **c.** compensation; **d.** expiation. For quots. see BOOT *sb.*^{1} 5, 5 b, 9, 10.

bote, obs. f. BOAT *sb.*, BOOT, BUT; obs. pa. t. BITE.

botefeu, var. of BOUTEFEU, *Obs.*, an incendiary.

botel (bəʊ'tɛl). orig. *U.S.* Also **boatel.** [Blend of BOAT *sb.* and HOTEL *sb.*] A hotel catering for boat-owners (see quot. 1960).

1956 *N.Y. Times* 3 June 25 A 'boatel' in the park for the overnight accommodation of yachtsmen and outboard-boat operators. **1959** *Woman's Day* July 28/2 The area is accessible only by boat or sea-plane, and there are no automobiles on the island. Hence the Inn at Windigo Harbor and the Lodge at Rock Harbor are referred to as botels rather than motels. **1960** *Daily Tel.* 20 Aug. 7/1 Boatel. It means what you would expect: a waterfront hotel where you can bring your own boat, or hire one, and have the best of both worlds by spending your holiday sailing yet being able to live ashore in warm, dry comfort. **1962** *Ocean Times* (R.M.S. 'Queen Mary') 20 Oct. 8/1 (Advt.), Boulters Inn Botel..situated on the River Thames. **1969** *Daily Tel.* 11 Jan. 19/3 It will include two hotels, flats, 'boatels', yacht clubs.

2. A ship with the facilities of a hotel. Also *attrib.*

1959 *Listener* 31 Dec. 1162/1 (Advt.), A new concept of river cruising by the botels 'Amsterdam' and 'Arnhem'. **1962** *Times* 3 Jan. 2/3 'Botel cruises' through the heart of Europe.

botel, boteler, obs. form of BOTTLE, BUTLER *sb.*

†**'botemay.** *Obs. rare.* [Some kind of corrupted form of *bitumen*: cf. It. *bitume.*] Bitumen.

c **1300** *K. Alis.* 4763 Pilers of brass and botemeys. *Ibid.* 6189 Above, and byneothe, is heore heolyng, With botemay, that wol clyng, That no water, salt no cler, Heom to derye hath no power.

†**boten, botne,** *v. Obs.* Also 5 booten, -ne. [ME. *botn-en*: inceptive vb. f. *bót*, BOOT *sb.*^{1}: of earlier rise than the verb BOOT^1. In form intr. but also taken as trans. = BEET *v.*^{1}, BOOT *v.*^{1}]

1. *intr.* To become better; to amend or recover health, be healed.

a **1225** *St. Marher.* 22 Ant comen dumbe ant deaue to hire bodi as hit lei, ant botneden alle. *c* **1325** *Chron. Eng.* 768 Ase me him in towmbe dude, A wodmon botnede y the stude.

2. *trans.* To make better in health; to heal, cure.

a **1225** *Leg. Kath.* 2523 þat healeð alle uueles & botneð men of euch bale. *c* **1350** *Will. Palerne* 1055 þei were botned of here bales strong. **1362** LANGL. *P. Pl.* A. VII. 179 Blynde and Bedraden weore Botned [*v.r.* botind; B. VI. 194 bootned, C. IX. 188 botnede] a þousent.

†**botener, botner.** *Obs. rare*$^{-1}$. [f. BOTEN *v.* + -ER^1.] A healer; a restorer.

a **1400** *Hymn Virg.* v. in T. Warton *Eng. Poetry* (1840) II. 109 Heil botenere of everie bodi blynde.

†**botening, botning,** *vbl. sb. Obs.* [f. BOTEN *v.* + -ING^1.] Healing, cure; help.

1303 R. BRUNNE *Handl. Synne* 11029 A wode man touchede on hys [Paschasius'] bere..And anone he hadde botenyng. *c* **1315** SHOREHAM 96. *c* **1430** *Chev. Assigne* 370 And þus þe botenynge of god browʒte hem to honde.

boterace, -ras, -rasse, obs. ff. BUTTRESS.

botere, obs. form of BUTTER.

†**'boterel.** *Obs. rare*$^{-1}$. [a. OF. *boterel*, dim. of *bot* toad.] A toad.

c **1340** *Ayenb.* 187 Vor he ne may naȝt þolye þane guode smel of þe ilke smerieles namore þanne þe boterel þane smel of þe vine.

‖**'boterol.** *Her.* [ad. F. *bouterolle* the tip of a scabbard; but the word has many other meanings, and it is not clear which is intended.] Some kind of charge borne on a shield.

1864 BOUTELL *Heraldry Hist. & Pop.* xix. §5 (ed. 3) 315 Three boterols gules.

†**'botew.** *Obs.* Also 5 butwe, buttwe, butewe, 6 botowe, boatew(e. [f. *bote*, BOOT *sb.*^{3}: cf. F. diminutives in *-eau.*] ? A short boot.

c **1440** *Promp. Parv.* 45 Botew, *coturnus, botula, crepita.* **1463** *Ripon Ch. Acts* 159, j par de buttwe shon. **1481** *Gild Cordwainers Exeter* in *E.E. Gilds* 332 All wete lethere and drye botez, botwez, schoez, pyncouz, galegez. **1483** *Cath. Angl.* 49 A Butewe, *ocreola.* *a* **1529** SKELTON *Magnyf.* 765 A betell, or a botowe [*printed* batowe] or a buskyn lacyd. **1555** *Fardle Facions* II. xii. 269 The Bisshoppes..xv. holy garmentes..His boatewes, his Amice, an Albe.

†**bot-fork.** *Obs.* [Perh. f. *bot*, var. of BAT *sb.*^{2} + FORK. Mätzner suggests OF. *botte* 'bottle' of hay, Stratmann Du. *bot*, blunt.] ? A forked stick.

c **1350** Wright's *Lyric P.* xxxix. 110 Mon in the mone stond ant strit, on is bot forke is burthen he bereth.

both (bəʊθ), *a.* and *adv.* Forms: 2–3 **baðe, baþe,** bathe, 2–6 **boðe, boþe,** bothe, (3 **beþe, beoðe**), 4–6 **booþ, -th,** (6 boeth), 7 boath, 4– **both;** also 3–5 **boðen, -þen, -then,** 5 **bothyn;** *north.* 3–5 **bathe, bath,** 4–6 **baithe,** 5–6 **bayth,** 6–8 **beath,** 4– **baith.** *Genit.* 3 **bathre, baiþer,** 3–4 **baþer(n,** 4 **bothers, -es,** 5 **bothes, -is,** (4–6 **bothe**), 7–8 **both's.** [early ME. *bāðe* (genitive *bāðre*) was app. a. ON. *báðar* m., *báðir* fem., *bæði, báði* neut. (genitive *báðra*) = OS. *bêðia* m. f., *bêðiu* neut., OHG. *bêde* and *beide* m., *bêdâ, beido* fem., *bēdiu, beidiu* neut.; an extended form of the simple word found in Goth. as *bai* masc., *ba* neut., and in OE. as *béȝen, bá* (see BO). No trace of this extended form appears in OE.; the simpler form *bei*, BO existed side by side with *both* until 14–15th c., when the former died out.

The suffix in ON. *báðar* and the equivalent forms is believed to be unconnected with that in Goth. *bajôþs* both (declined as sb. plur.), and to represent the definite article (in Goth. *þai, þô*) which seems to have coalesced with the simple *bai, ba* owing to the tendency to say 'both the' instead of merely 'both'; cf. Goth. *ba þô skipa* 'both the ships' *Luke* v. 8. The constructions of *both* in Eng. follow those of the earlier BO and to some extent those of ALL; examples of its use as attribute to a sb. plur. without intervening possessive, demonstrative, or article, do not appear until after BO had become obsolete.]

A. *adj.* **I.** Proper sense and normal uses.

The one and the other; referring to two specially designated persons or things, implying that two and no more are so designated, and emphasizing the fact that neither of them is excepted from the statement made; equivalent to 'the two, and not merely one of them'.

The following Constructions occur:

1. *absolutely.* From 14th c. sometimes *the both* (obs.). In early mod.Eng. sometimes inflected as a sb., with genitive *both's.*

c **1200** ORMIN 250 Baþe wærenn alde. *a* **1300** *Cursor M.* 666 Bath he sette in þare fre will. **1330** R. BRUNNE *Chron.* 269 It turnes bot tille þe boþe, if Godes grace may stond. **1616** B. PARSONS *Mag. Charter* 26 Judge no cause in hand, Before boths talke thou understand. *a* **1620** A. HUME *Brit. Tong.* (1865) 34 For exemple of beath, and to conclud this treatesse. **1697** DRYDEN *Virg. Georg.* III. 352 He..resents his Wounds, His ignominious Flight, the Victor's Boast, And more than boath, the Loves, which unreveng'd he lost. **1715** *Let.* in *Wodrow Corr.* (1843) II. 38 That the business be tried, and both sides allowed to counter-question both's witnesses. **1752** JOHNSON *Rambl.* No. 197 ¶13 The old gentlewoman considered herself wiser than both. **1848** MACAULAY *Hist. Eng.* II. 113 Both were Tories: both were men of hot temper and strong prejudices.

2. In *apposition* with a plural sb. or pronoun.

When referring to the subject of a sentence, *both* was in early ME. usually separated from it, and placed after the vb. or whole predication. This is still common dialectally. In the literary language, *both* is still placed after the verb *be* (occasionally also after *become, seem, appear*, etc.), and after the auxiliary in a compound tense.

c **1175** *Cott. Hom.* 223 þa weran boðe deadlice. *a* **1225** *Ancr. R.* 10 Noþeleas heo weren wel beoðe. *a* **1300** *Havelok* 1680 Loke þat ye comen beþe. *a* **1300** *Cursor M.* 793 Al for noght þai ette it bath. *c* **1400** *Gamelyn* 625 As they stoode talkyng bothen in-feere. *c* **1580** LYLY *Euphues* (1636) K 12, I wish you were both married. **1622** MABBE tr. *Aleman's Guzman D'Alf.* I. 255 They were both equall in state and condition. **1836** DICKENS *Pickw.* x, We are both men of the world. *Mod.* They seem both very obstinate. They have both gone. The brothers might both have come.

3. In *attributive* relation to a plural sb.:

a. with a defining word (demonst. or poss. adj., 'def. article', genitive case, etc.): *Both* precedes the defining word, as 'both my friends saw it'. It may also (with greater emphasis) follow the sb., esp. when the subject of the sentence, as 'my friends both saw it'. (In this case it further follows the verb *be* or an auxiliary, as' my friends had both seen it': cf. 2).

The constructions are the same when there is ellipsis of the sb. after demonst. or poss. pron., as 'I need both these', 'these are both mine'. For the colloq. *both of* before sb. see 6.

1297 R. GLOUC. 376 Wo so by Kyng Wyllames day slou hert oþer hynde, Me ssolde putte oute boþe hys eye. **1394** *P. Pl. Crede* 224 A greet cherl and a grym..Wiþ a face..as a bagge honged On boþen his chekes. **1548** LATIMER *Ploughers* (Arb.) 25 To lette or hinder boeth these kyndes. **1588** A. KING *Canisius' Catech.* 84 Thay..in auld tymes had baith ye kynds in publick vse. **1632** MILTON *Allegro* 32 Laughter holding both his sides. **1785** BURNS *Twa Herds* xii, Baith the Shaws, That aft hae made us black and blae. **1870** TENNYSON *Gareth & L.* 80 Both thy brethren are in Arthur's hall.

†**b.** Formerly *both* was sometimes placed between the defining word and the substantive.

c **1430** *Bk. Hawkyng* in *Rel. Ant.* I. 297 Knyt the bothe endes with a threde. *c* **1449** PECOCK *Repr.* II. xi. 216 Whether he entendid these bothe effectes, or the oon of hem oonli. **1551** RECORDE *Pathw. Knowl.* I. Def., The middle partes nother bulke vp, nother shrink down more then the bothe endes. *c* **1615** CHAPMAN *Odyss.* III. 572 To plate the both horns round about with gold. **1649** RAINBOWE *Sermon* 2 A King whose both hands God had filled with blessings of every kind. **1830** tr. *Aristophanes' Knights* 85 He..with his both hands, scoops up from the public funds.

c. without defining word. *Both* regularly precedes the sb., but in lively or humorous address may sometimes follow it, as in quot. 1597. *both ways*: in both respects.

1526 *Pilgr. Perf.* (W. de W. 1531) 34 Bothe wayes suche desyres be vnlawfull. **1593** HOOKER *Eccl. Pol.* Pref. v. §3 A solemn declaration made on both parts. **1597** SHAKS. *2 Hen. IV*, III. ii. 308 Fare you well, Gentlemen both. **1628** HOBBES *Thucyd.* (1822) 105 Shew not yourselves both ways inferior to your ancestors. **1712** ADDISON *Spect.* No. 499 ¶2 Very agreeable young people of both sexes. **1798** CANNING in *Anti-Jacobin* 9 July (1832) 208 Much may be said on both sides. **1849** RUSKIN *Sev. Lamps* iv. §26 So they have..a pair of horns: but not at both ends. **1879** LOCKYER *Elem. Astron.* v. §35. 206 In Russia..it is customary to give both dates.

4. In *attrib.* relation to a plural pronoun:

a. in nom. or obj. *Both* follows the pronoun, as 'they both went'. (With *be* and auxiliaries it further follows the verb: cf. 2). In ME. *both* might precede the pronoun, 'both they went'; of this usage *both which* still occurs; but the regular modern construction with *both* preceding the pronoun is 'both of us', 'both of whom', 'both of which' (see 6).

c **1320** *Metr. Hom.* 55 Baithe thai gan his wai to lette. *c* **1386** CHAUCER *Reeves T.* 271 He myghte doon vs bathe [*Camb.* bothe; *Corp.* boþ(e] a vileynye. **1472** MARG. PASTON *Lett.* 689 III. 37 The Holy Ghost kepe you bothyn. **1475** CAXTON *Jason* 37 b, Bothe they toke a good palfraye. **1549** *Marriage Serv.*, So long as you both shall live. **1597** J. PAYNE *Royal Exch.* 43 Then would yt..make bothe theme the better to love one another. **1610** SHAKS. *Temp.* I. ii. 241 The time 'twixt six and now Must by vs both be spent most preciously. **1611** BIBLE *2 Peter* iii. 1 In both which [epistles] I stir vp your pure minds. **1816** J. WILSON *City Plague* II. i. 14 They both speak of death. **1848** MACAULAY *Hist. Eng.* II. 114 The papers found in the strong box..had converted them both to the true faith.

†**b.** in genit. pl. with a sb., as *our, your, her* (= their), *their bather, bother, bothens, botheres*, etc. (afterwards *both*, which sometimes preceded the pron.) = of us, you, them both. *Obs.*

Latterly the sb. often improperly took the plural form by attraction of the pronoun; this idiom is still in vulgar use, as 'It is both your faults,' 'she is both their mothers'.

a **1300** *Cursor M.* 1254 In þat way sal þou find forsoth þi moders and mine our bather slogh. *Ibid.* 23958 þair baiþer paines aght to be mine. **1377** LANGL. *P. Pl.* B. XVI. 165 Cryst toke þe bataille, Aȝeines deth and þe deuel · destruyed her botheres myȝtes. *c* **1430** LYDG. *Bochas* I. ix. (1544) 19 b, This was concluded by their both assente. **1479** *Bury Wills* (1850) 54 As moste beste can be advysed by ther botheris counsell. **1513** MORE *Rich. III.* Wks. (1557) 54/1 [To be] here as a saintuary man to their both dishonour and obloquy. **1536** *St. Papers Hen. VIII*, I. 509 Ye take uppon you to set order bothe to them and Us, your bothe Sovereigne. **1592** SHAKS. *Rom. & Jul.* II. iii. 51 Both our remedies Within thy helpe and holy physicke lies. **1601** —— *All's Well* I. iii. 169 Were you both our mothers. **1627** HAKEWILL *Apol.* (1630) 167 Both their haire was as white as was possible. **1699** BENTLEY *Phal.* Pref. 9 It was both our misfortunes that he committed the whole affair to the care of his Bookseller. **1752** MRS. LENNOX *Female Quix.* (1820) II. 29 These sentiments which now cause both our unhappiness.

5. In *attrib.* relation to two substantives or pronouns (or a sb. and pron.) coupled by *and*, the same constructions obtain as in 3: as 'both John and I came', 'John and George both came', 'the brother and sister are both dead', but this is practically indistinguishable from the adverbial use in B 1.

6. With *of*: *both of* is now used before pronouns and pronominal words, instead of the simple *both* (see 4). The use with a sb., as 'both of these arguments', is colloquial, but scarcely ever occurs in literature.

1590 SHAKS. *Err.* V. i. 291, I am sure you both of you remember me. **1602** —— *Lear* III. i. 27 The hard Reine which both of them hath borne. **1611** BIBLE *Gen.* xxii. 8 They went both of them together. **1875** JOWETT *Plato* (ed. 2) I. 80 Both of us often talk to the lads. **1878** MORLEY *Crit. Misc.* I. 211 With both of them, more than with other poets.

II. Transferred senses and abnormal uses.

7. In certain pleonastic combinations, †*both two, twain* (cf. OE. *bá twá*); *both the two*; †*all both* (cf. G. *alle beide*): all synonymous with *both* (so also in adverbial use; see B 2 b).

c **1275** LAY. 2399 Mid childe hii weren boþe two. *c* **1325** *E.E. Allit. P.* B. 155 Byndez byhynde, at his bak, boþe two his handez. *c* **1300** *Cursor M.* 635 (Gött.) Naked war þai bath tway. **1485** CAXTON *Paris & V.* (1868) 18 Bothe two were throwen to the erthe. **1523** LD. BERNERS *Froiss.* (1812) I. 621 They were bothe two armed. **1571** T. FORTESCUE *Forest Hist.* 129 Yet would he retain with hym still Silan and Sasilas, all both Lacedemonians. **1587** GOLDING *De Mornay* Pref. 4 From both twaine of them, wee drawe..the trueth of our Scriptures. *c* **1600** SHAKS. *Sonn.* xlii, Both find each other, and I lose both twain. **1846** GROTE *Greece* II. xviii. (1854) III. 365 Both the two cities reached a high pitch of prosperity.

8. Synonymous with 'the two' in phrases *either* (*neither, whether*) *of both, of the both* (*obs.* or *dial.*); *between both.* (*arch.*)

1443 *Pol. Poems* (1859) II. 214 Attween bothen..Crist Jhesu send us pees. **1489** CAXTON *Faytes of A.* I. xxiv. 75 There abode not one man alyve of neythre of bothe partyes. **1489** *Will of Harryngton* (Somerset Ho.) Whether of the both it shall fortune. **1544** ASCHAM *Toxoph.* (Arb.) 27 We be borne for neither of bothe. **1584** WHETSTONE *Mirour* 27 b, The coveitous man is the worst of both. **1067** TOPSELL

Serpents 607 Either of both abhorreth one the other. **1766** GOLDSM. *Vic. W.* xxxii, The argument was supported, for some time, between both, with equal obstinacy. **1856** J. R. BALLANTYNE *Aphor. Sánkhya Philos.* 38 'Between both', i.e. between Soul and not-Soul, both together.

†**9.** Used as a sing. (cf. G. *beides*). *Obs. rare*⁻¹.

1721 R. KEITH *T. à Kempis' Vall. Lillies* ii. 22 Both is a very great Evil.

B. *adv.* (*conj.*)

1. Preceding two homogeneous words (sbs., adjs., vbs., advbs., or preps.) or phrases, coupled by *and*, *both* adds emphasis to the sentence by suggesting a contrast with the statement as it would have been had one of the terms been omitted. ***both..and*** is thus nearly = *not only..but*. (*Both* in this construction is not now preceded by a genitive case or an adj. of any kind, as in quots. 1641, 1690, 1834).

As *both..and* corresponds to the Latin *et..et*, it is usual to class *both* as a conjunction; but it more properly belongs to the same grammatical category with EVEN. This use of *both* arises out of the construction in A 5, and in 'both the king and the queen spoke', 'the king and the queen both honour him', 'Mercury and Venus are both inferior planets', *both* may still be viewed as an adjective in attributive relation to the two substantives. But in the extended use 'both juster and kinder' or 'both by day and by night', 'he both walks and runs', it can no longer be so treated.

1154 *O.E. Chron.* (Laud MS.) an. 1137 Bathe be nihtes . & be dæies. *c* **1175** *Lamb. Hom.* 143 For to deme baþe þe gode and þe uuele. *c* **1250** *Gen. & Ex.* 899 He was boðen king and prest. *a* **1300** *Havelok* 958 Boþen heye men and lowe. *c* **1320** *Cast. Love* 497 Boþe Ich and Merci We beclepeþ þe dom for-þi. *a* **1400** *Cov. Myst.* (1841) 94, I shal send for hem, bothyn fere and nere. **1528** LYNDESAY *Dreme* Prol. 20 Because vnblomit was baith bank and braye. **1641** HINDE *J. Bruen* vi. 24 A faire image of this young Gentle-mans both wants and weaknesses. **1690** LOCKE *Hum. Und.* II. xxi. §9 All its both Motion and Rest, come under our Idea of Necessary. **1766** GOLDSM. *Vic. W.* ii. (1806) 7, I looked upon this as a masterpiece both for argument and style. *a* **1834** COLERIDGE *Remains* (1836) III. 375 This idle argument is the favourite both shield and sword of the Romanist. **1837** J. H. NEWMAN *Par. Serm.* (ed. 3) I. viii. 114 It is both severe and indulgent. **1662** *Bk. Com. Prayer, Visit. Sick*, Both now and evermore.

b. Extended to more than two objects.

c **1386** CHAUCER *Knts. T.* 1440 To whom bothe heuene and erthe and see is sene. *c* **1430** LYDG. *Bochas* I. vii. 18 She was also bothe ioly, fayre, and good. **1523** LD. BERNERS *Froiss.* (1812) I. 351 Bothe prelates, bysshoppes, abbottes, barownes, and knyghtes. **1591** SHAKS. *1 Hen. VI*, v. v. 107 Margaret shall now be Queene and rule the King; But I will rule both her, the King, & Realme. **1592** — *Ven. & Ad.* 747 Both favour, savour, hue and qualities. **1612** BRINSLEY *Lud. Lit.* 283 Rewards..giue all kinde of hartning..both to Masters, Vshers, and Schollars. **1678** BUNYAN *Pilgr.* I. (1862) 37 To help them, both by awakening of them, counselling of them, and profferring to help them. **1782** JOHNSON *Lett.* 2 Mar., Both Williams, and Desmoulins, and myself are very sickly. **1798** COLERIDGE *Anc. Mar.* VII. xxii, He prayeth well, who loveth well Both man and bird and beast. *c* **1839** DE QUINCEY *Wks.* XV. (1863) 140 For both Chaucer and Shakespeare and Milton.

2. *Both* may follow, instead of preceding (as in 1), the two words or phrases connected by *and*; now only in the case of two sbs. (two pronouns, or sb. and pronoun) subjects of the same plural verb, but formerly (and still dialectally) in all other cases. In this use *both* may often be replaced by *too* or *also*.

a **1225** *Ancren R.* 14 Of fleschliche vondunges, & of gostliche boðe. *c* **1230** *Hali Meid.* 5 Widewen..& weddede baðe. *c* **1240** *Lofsong.* 205 Ich habbe i-suneged ine mete . and in drunche boðe. **1394** *P. Pl. Crede* 31 þe cofres of cristendam · & þe keye boþen. **1467** JOHN PASTON *Lett.* 573 II 303 He had shrevyn Master Brakley, and how-syllyd hym bothe. **1470–85** MALORY *Arthur* IV. xiii, I am sore hurte and he bothe. *Ibid.* (1816) II. 405 My broder Gareth loved hym ..and alle his bretheren, and the kynge, bothe. **1561** T. HOBY tr. *Castiglione's Covrtyer* (1577) P vij, It shalbe good for him and me both. **1600** W. BARLOW *Serm.* (1601) A v a, Malice marres logike and charitie both. **1683** BURNET tr. *More's Utopia* Pref., His setting out so barbarous a practice ..is so wild and so immoral both. *Mod.* I have seen your brother and your sister both. *Mod. dial.* He can sing and dance both.

†**b.** ***both two*** (in same sense). *Obs.*

1413 LYDG. *Pylgr.* v. xi. (1483) 102 The scorpyon..byteth and styngeth bothe two at ones. **1513** BRADSHAW *St. Werburge* (1848) 57 And founder was also Of dyuers holy places and monasteryes both two.

†**3.** After a negative or word implying exclusion, *both* was formerly sometimes used instead of *either*. (Cf. ALL A 4.)

1470–85 MALORY *Arthur* XVIII. v, Of that I will not fayle you, nor her bothe. **1608** TOPSELL *Serpents* 608 This snake ..sunk down from altar clean, without both harm or noise.

C. *Comb.*, as †**both-hands**, a factotum (cf. *one's right-hand*); **both-handed** *a.*, using both hands with equal ease; whence ***both-handedness***; †**both-like** *a.*, resembling both; †**both-side** *a.*, derived from a like source on both sides; **both-sided** *a.*, viewing both sides, taking both sides into account; whence ***both-sidedness***.

a **1637** B. JONSON (Ogilvie) He is masters *both-hands, I assure you. *a* **1637** B. JONSON, etc. *Widow* IV. ii. in *Dodsley* (1780) XII. 295 [He] half cozens his belly..if he dine among ..*both-handed feeders. **1653** HOLCROFT *Procopius* II. 40 Bent his bow (being both-handed) and killed Jabdas horse. **1883** *Student* III. 284 The tendency to what might be called *Both-handedness in the use of the brush. **1883** *St. James's G.* 27 Feb. 5 In old age however there is a marked tendency to both-handedness. **1628** GAULE *Pract. The.* 145 Twixt God and Man; Is now brought forth to both, of *both-like Nature. **1623** LISLE *Ælfric on O. & N.T.* Ded., By Vertue met in *both-side Royall blood. **1879** H. SPENCER *Data of Ethics* vi. 99 *Both-sided conceptions. **1874** — *Stud. Sociol.* xvi. 397 Dangers from the want of a due *both-sidedness.

both(e, obs. form of BOOT, BOOTH, BOTH.

botham, -em, obs. form of BOTTOM *sb.*

bother (ˈbɒðə(r)), *v. colloq.* Also 8 bodder, *Sc.* **bauther**, **bather**. [Etymology unknown; the earliest instances occur in the writings of Irishmen (T. Sheridan, Swift, Sterne), and the word has long formed part of the vocabulary of the comic Irishman of fiction and the stage. This suggests an Anglo-Irish origin; but no suitable etymon has been found in Irish.

The Irish *bódhar* deaf, *bódhairim* I deafen (suggested by Crofton Croker), and *buaidhirt* trouble, affliction, *buaidhrim* I vex (proposed by Garnett) alike labour under the difficulty that the spoken words do not suggest *bodder* or *bother*. Wedgwood would identify the word with *pother*: could *bother* be an Anglo-Irish corruption of the latter?]

†**1.** *trans.* To bewilder with noise; to confuse, muddle; to put into a fluster or flutter. *Obs.*

1718 T. SHERIDAN *To Swift* in *Swift's Wks.* (1824) XV. 107 With the din of which tube my head you so bother. **1832–53** *Whistle-Binkie* (Sc. Songs) Ser. I. 22 The hearts of the maids, and the gentlemen's heads, were bother'd, I'm sure, by this Irishman.

2. a. *trans.* To give trouble to; to pester, annoy, worry. Also *refl.*, and in phrase ***to bother one's head, one's brains***: to trouble oneself with thinking.

a **1745** SWIFT *Dial. Hibern. Style* Wks. VII. 156 Lord I was bodderd t'other day with that prating fool Tom. **1753** *Dial. betw. Swift & Prior* 123 You boddered me enough with many of these Articles, already. **1762** STERNE *Let.* in Traill *Sterne* vi. 81 Civility thus uniform wearies and bodders me to death. **1768** FOOTE *Devil on Sticks* III, Don't let him bother us, with his yea and nay nonsense. **1852** E. FORBES *Let.* in Wilson & Geikie *Life* xiv. 506 A point that has bothered Prestwich, D'Archiac, and Dumont. **1878** JOAQUIN MILLER *Songs Italy* 127 Whether you bother your brain or no.

b. In the imperative (logically 3rd pers. sing. with implied subject after analogy of verbs of cursing) as a mild imprecation; also ***bother it!*** and absol. ***bother!*** as an exclamation indicating annoyance (confused with the *sb.*; cf. BOTHERATION).

1840 DICKENS *Old C. Shop* xxxiii. 281 To this amorous address Miss Brass briefly responded 'Bother!' **1844** — *Mart. Chuz.* xlix. 564 'Bother Mrs. Harris!' said Betsey Prig... 'I don't believe there's no sich a person!' **1850** MRS. STOWE *Uncle Tom's C.* xxi. 215 Oh, bother! don't plague me, Emily! **1855** THACKERAY *Rose & Ring* xvi. (1866) 106 'Bother your album!' says Bulbo. **1877** *Fraser's Mag.* Oct. *Clericality*, Bother the parson!

3. *intr.* and *absol.* To give trouble to others or to oneself; to make a fuss; to be troublesome.

a **1774** FERGUSSON *Election* Poems (1845) 42 Lang's their debatin' thereanent, About protests they're bauthrin'. **1787** WOLCOTT (P. Pindar) *Ode upon Ode* Wks. 1794 I. 411 If musicians miss but half a bar, Just like an Irishman she starts to bother. **1850** CARLYLE *Latt.-d. Pamph.* vii, Make money; and don't bother about the Universe. **1863** HAWTHORNE *Pilgr. Boston* in *Old Home* (1879) 178 We bothered a good while about getting through a..lock. **1863** KINGSLEY *Water-Bab.* iii. 119 To prevent the Cythrawl Sassenach from coming bothering into Wales.

†**4.** *intr.* and *trans.* (?) To blarney, to 'humbug'.

1803 BRISTED *Pedest. Tour* I. 101 Sufficient documents to enable me to *bother* about it, so that I could not easily be detected. *Ibid.* 152 As..Cowan..would be less likely to be convicted of some unfortunate blunder..than myself, I desired him to go down and *bother* them well.

bother (ˈbɒðə(r)), *sb.* [f. prec. vb.]

†**1.** (?) Blarney, humbug, palaver. *Obs.* Cf. BOTHER *v.* 4, BOTHERING.

1803 BRISTED *Pedest. Tour* I. 267 Among an ignorant.. peasantry the *bother* must consist of coarse and broad flattery laid on with a trowel. **1822** HONE *Slap at Slop Facetiæ* 24 In wishing that the Press should be securely chained, the Members of this Society have no desire to limit their own bother.

2. Petty trouble, worry; disturbance, 'fuss'.

1834 M. SCOTT *Cruise Midge* (1859) 283 We had a little bother with him at first. **1846** B. BARTON *Selections* (1849) 43 Without more putter and bother than the thing is worth. **1852** THACKERAY *Esmond* III. i. (1876) 277 The right divine, about which Dr. Sacheverel and the High Church party in England were just now making a bother. *a* **1884** P'CESS ALICE *Mem.* 147 Mountain air Weber wants me to have, and quiet, away from all bothers.

botheration (bɒðəˈreɪʃən). *colloq.* Formerly also **bodderation**. [f. prec. + -ATION.] The act of bothering; petty vexation or annoyance; often used as an exclamation.

1797 *Sporting Mag.* Mar. 342/1 After a long *botheration*.. Mr. Lucius Concannon was convicted. **1801** SOUTHEY in *Life* (1850) II. 138, I would fairly see it out, and witness the whole boderation. **1814** J. CHALMERS *Let.* in *Life Chalmers* I. 452 Formal visits and complimentary calls, and invitations and botherations of all sorts. **1819** *Abeillard & Hel.* 18 As Pat says, Sure 'tis bodderation. **1841** C. J. LEVER *C. O'Malley* xv. 81 'It's for Counsellor Kinshella, below-stairs'... 'Bethershin.' **1847** C. M. YONGE *Scenes & Char.* vii. 67 'Rachel is going away.'.. 'Rachel! Rachel! botheration!' roared Reginald. **1850** CARLYLE *Latter-d. Pamph.* ii. 7, I for my own part, so left with paper and ink, and all taxes and botherations shut out from me. **1861** *Crt. Life at Naples* 80 'Botheration!' was the muttered reply. **1867** G. MEREDITH *R. Feverel* xxiv. (1885) 183 The pipe that allayeth botheration.

bother-headed (ˈbɒðəˌhɛdɪd), *ppl. a.* [f. BOTHER *sb.* + -HEADED.] Muddle-headed, stupid. Hence ˌ**bother'headedness**.

1872 LYTTON *Parisians* IV. vi, I..am awfully bother-headed. **1836** *Fraser's Mag.* XIII. 546 Most Bœotian botherheadedness.

bothering (ˈbɒðərɪŋ), *vbl. sb.* [f. BOTHER *v.*]

†**a.** (?) Palavering, 'humbugging'. *Obs. rare.*

b. Giving or taking trouble, worrying, perplexing.

1803 BRISTED *Pedest. Tour* I. 76 The art and mystery of bothering, whose chief efficacy resides in a facility of talking an infinite deal of nothing with readiness and volubility. **1806** W. TAYLOR *Month. Mag.* XXII. 536 It [ambiguity] is a learned word for what the English call bothering, which is derived from *both*. **1884** E. GURNEY in *Mind* Jan. 120 Any sort of argument or bothering.

ˈbothering, *ppl. a.* [f. as prec. + -ING².] Troubling, annoying, worrying.

1821 CLARE *Vill. Minstr.* I. 122 The bothering bustle of the wind. **1875** M. PATTISON *Casaubon* 103 Trifling talk, but very bothering.

botherment (ˈbɒðəmənt). *colloq.* [f. as prec. + -MENT.] = BOTHER *sb.* 2.

a **1851** J. COOPER (Stratm.) 'Twould be a botherment to a living soul to lose so much money. **1854** *Blackw. Mag.* LXXV. 11 They had abundant botherments upon the road. **1855** *Whitby Gloss.*, *Botherments*, troubles, difficulties.

bothersome (ˈbɒðəsəm), *a.* [f. as prec. + -SOME.] Troublesome, annoying.

1834 M. SCOTT *Cruise Midge* (1863) 61 It was rather a bothersome matter to navigate between the rows of them. **1850** DE MORGAN *Let.* in *Mem.* (1862) 209 And so Logical Systems are bothersome.

botheum, -om, -on, obs. forms of BUTTON.

bothome, obs. form of BOTTOM *sb.*

bothrenchyma (bɒˈθrɛŋkɪmə). *Bot.* Also bothrenchym. [f. Gr. βόθρ-ος pit + ἔγχυμα infusion: cf. PARENCHYMA.] Pitted tissue; tissue consisting of pitted vessels. Hence **bothrenchymatous** (-ˈkɪmətəs), *a.*

1835 LINDLEY *Introd. Bot.* (1848) I. 56 Pitted Tissue, or Bothrenchym. *Ibid.* 184 Bothrenchymatous and vascular tissue. **1870** BENTLEY *Bot.* 40 Pitted or Dotted Vessels constitute by their combination Pitted Tissue.. Bothrenchyma.

Bothrodendron (bɒθrəʊˈdɛndrɒn). *Bot.* [mod.L., f. Gr. βόθρος pit + δένδρον tree.] A genus of fossil plants, found in coal measures (cf. LEPIDODENDRON); also (with lower-case initial), a plant of this genus.

a **1835** LINDLEY & HUTTON *Fossil Flora Gt. Brit.* II. 97 Bothrodendron. Stem not furrowed, covered with dots. Scars of cones, obliquely oval. **1862** BURTON *Bk. Hunter* I. 2 Your other hard names—your ichthyodorulite, trogontherium, lepidodendron, and bothrodendron. **1902** *Encycl. Brit.* XXXI. 413/2 The cuticles of a Bothrodendron.

bothul, obs. form of BUDDLE, corn-marigold.

bothum, bothun, obs. forms of BUTTON.

bothy, bothie (ˈbɒθɪ). *Sc.* Also 8 bothay. [Of uncertain history: Irish and Gaelic have *both* 'hut' (dim. *bothan*), and Gael. has dim. *bothag*; but as the *th* in Gael. has been mute for many centuries, it is not easy to see how these could have given *bothy*. Cf. BOOTH.]

1. A hut or cottage; *spec.* a building consisting of one room in which the unmarried men servants on a farm are lodged together, or in which masons, quarrymen, etc. lodge together. (Bothies of women have also been recently tried, as a substitute for the 'Bondage' system.)

[**1570–87** HOLINSHED *Scot. Chron.* (1806) I. 19 Arran otherwise called Botha after St. Brandons time who dwelled there in a little cottage which (as all other the like were in those daies) was called Botha.] **1771** PENNANT *Tours Scotl.* (1790) 124 A Sheelin or Bothay, a cottage made of turf. **1854** H. MILLER *Sch. & Schm.* ix. (1857) 174 The sort of life that is spent in bothies and barracks. **1876** GRANT *Burgh Sch. Scot.* II. xv. 511 *note*, The children came..to attend school in a small bothy.

2. *attrib.*, as in ***bothy-life***, ***-man***, ***-system*** (in reference to farm bothies).

1854 H. MILLER *Sch. & Schm.* ix. 192 The influences of ..the barrack, or rather bothy life. *Ibid.* (1858) 239 Ninety-nine out of every hundred of our bothy-men. *Ibid.* xi, What has since been extensively known as the bothy system.

Hence **ˈbothyism**, the farm-bothy system.

1864 *Cornh. Mag.* Nov. 618 Looking only at what may be called well-regulated bothyism, it is difficult to conceive how such a system can be defended.

† **'botillage.** *Obs. rare*⁻¹. [a. F. *bottelage*, f. *bottel-er* to put up in bundles. Cf. BOTTLE *sb.*³] The act of tying up in 'bottles' or bundles.
1576 in Nichols *Progr. Q. Eliz.* II. 48 Measuring, carriage, and botillage of wheat.

botken, -kin, obs. forms of BODKIN.

botlere, botles(se, obs. ff. BUTLER *sb.*, BOOTLESS.

botling ('bɒtlɪŋ). Also bottlin(g. [cf. Du. *bot* stumpy.] The fish called chub or chevin (*Cyprinus cephalus*).
a **1613** J. D[ENNYS] *Secr. Angling* in Arb. *Garner* (1877) I. 175 The peel, the tweat, the botling, and the rest. **1653** T. BARKER *Art Angling*, It [salmon-roe] is a special bait for dace or dare, good for chubb, or bottlin, or grayling. **1833** J. RENNIE *Alph. Angling* 105 The chub, chevin, or bottling neither affords good sport to the angler nor a good dish.

botme, botom, obs. forms of BOTTOM *sb.*

† **'botment.** *Obs. rare.* [f. *bot*, BOOT *sb.*¹ + -MENT. (The later form would have been *bootment*.)] Amendment, remedy.
c **1440** *York Myst.* xix. 90 þer may no botment be.

botoné, -ée, -y ('bɒtəʊneɪ, -ɪ). *Her.* Also 7 bottony, 8 botonny. [a. OF. *botoné*, mod.F. *boutonné* covered with buds.] Having an ornament of three knobs or bud-like projections resembling a trefoil leaf; hence sometimes called *trefoiled* or *treffled*.
1572 BOSSEWELL *Armorie* II. 64 b, S. beareth Sable, two Delphines d'Argent . . betwene sixe Crosses Botony. **1760** PORNY *Heraldry* (1777) Gloss., *Botonny*. **1827** *Gentl. Mag.* XCVII. II. 533 A cross botoné. **1864** BOUTELL *Heraldry Hist. & Pop.* xv. (ed. 3) 182 The crosslets are *botonée*.

† **botorescle.** *Obs. rare*⁻¹. [? Cf. F. *bouterolle* scabbard tag.]
1463 *Bury Wills* (1850) 41, I beqwethe to William Lawshull my botorescle set in gold with nedil werk.

botoume, obs. form of BOTTOM *sb.*

† **bo'tozio.** *Obs. rare*⁻¹. ? = It. *bottaccio* cask.
1622 R. HAWKINS *Voy. S. Sea* (1847) 150 Five hundred botozios of wine.

† **botraille.** *Obs. rare*⁻¹. Meaning uncertain: can it be an early form of BUTTRESS? cf. next.
c **1430** LYDG. *Min. Poems* (1840) 170 Paterfamulias, wise and expert . . Shulde sette botraille atweyne derk and lighte.

botreaux, botreulx, obs. forms of BUTTRESS.
1569 NEWTON *Cicero's Old Age* 46 a, The strong botreaux of the Romaine people. **1552** HULOET, Botreulx or butrese of a brycke wall.

bo-tree ('bəʊtriː). [f. Singhalese *bo*, corruption of Pāli *bodhi* (Skr. *bodhi*) the bo-tree, more fully called *bodhi-taru*, f. *bodhi* 'perfect knowledge', *taru* 'tree'; it having been under such a tree that Gautama attained the enlightenment which constituted him 'the Buddha'. In Singhalese *Bogaha* (*gaha* a tree).] The *ficus religiosa* or pīpal tree, specifically allied to the Banyan.
[**1681** R. KNOX *Hist. Ceylon* 18 This tree they call Bogahah; we the God-Tree.] **1862** MRS. SPEID *Last Years Ind.* 276 The Banyan, par excellence, sometimes called the Bo-tree, is the specially sacred tree of the Bhuddhists. **1871** ALABASTER *Wheel of Law* 20 *note*, This Bo or Bodhi tree is the tree under . . which Buddha attained to omniscience.

† **'botriform,** *a. Obs. rare.* [f. Gr. βότρ-υς bunch of grapes + -FORM.] = BOTRYOIDAL.
1805 T. WEAVER tr. *Werner's Fossils* 84 Rounded particular forms, as botriform, globular, kidney-form. **1806** *Ann. Rev.* IV. 889 Fistuliform and botriform, are less proper than the received . . fistulous, and botryoidal.

botrycymose (,bɒtrɪsaɪ'məʊs), *a. Bot.* [f. Gr. βότρυ-ς cluster of grapes + CYMOSE.] See quot.
1880 GRAY *Bot. Text-bk.* 399 *Botry-cymose*, Racemes or any botryose clusters cymosely aggregated.

botrylle (bɒ'trɪl). *Zool. rare.* [ad. mod.L. *botryllus*, as if ad. Gr. *βότρυλλος, dim. of βότρυς cluster of grapes.] A genus of tunicate molluscs, giving its name to the family *Botryllidæ*. The Lat. name is usually adopted unchanged. Hence **bo'tryllian** *a.*, belonging to the family Botryllidæ.
1835 KIRBY *Hab. & Inst. Anim.* I. vii. 219 Sometimes they are parasitic: thus a species of botrylle envelopes, like a cloak, certain ascidians. **1849–52** TODD *Cycl. Anat. & Phys.* IV. 1208/2 The botryllian group of Tunicates.

botryoid ('bɒtrɪɔɪd), *a.* [ad. Gr. βοτρυοειδής, f. βότρυ-ς cluster of grapes: see -OID.] Resembling a cluster of grapes.
1747 MORTIMER in *Phil. Trans.* XLIV. 432 Smooth polished Knobs, in Form like to the botryoïd Iron Ore.

botryoidal (bɒtrɪ'ɔɪdəl), *a.* = prec.
1816 CLEAVELAND *Min.* 544 Earthy arseniate of cobalt . . occurs in crusts, which are sometimes reniform or botryoidal. **1841** TRIMMER *Pract. Geol.* 74 Minerals presenting an aggregation of large sections of small globes are called botryoidal.

botryolite ('bɒtrɪəʊlaɪt). *Min.* [f. as prec. + λίθος stone: see -LITE.] See quots.
1850 DANA *Geol.* xv. 605 Datholite . . presenting the radiated spheroidal forms of the variety botryolite. **1852** W. PHILLIPS *Min.* (Brooks and Miller) 411 Botryolite . . is merely an amorphous variety of datholite.

botryose (,bɒtrɪ'əʊs), *a. Bot.* [f. as prec. + -OSE.] Bearing flowers in clusters or racemes, which develop successively from the base upward.
1880 GRAY *Struct. Bot.* v. 144 *note*, The kinds of Inflorescence are all reducible to two types . . the Indeterminate and Determinate . . Also named by Eichler the Cymose and Botryose types.

bott (bɒt). [cf. BAT *sb.*²]
1. The name given by lace-makers to the cushion on which lace is woven.
1849 in CRAIG.
2. 'In founding, a clay plug used to close a hole against molten iron' (Cent. Dict. Suppl. 1909). Also *attrib.* So **'botting** *vbl. sb.* (see quot. *a* 1877).
a **1877** KNIGHT *Dict. Mech.*, *Botting*, restopping the tapping-hole of a furnace after a part of its charge has been allowed to flow therefrom. **1888** *Lockwood's Dict. Mech. Engin.*, Bott Stick. **1900** J. SHARP *Mod. Foundry Pract.* 144 A round ball of this [loam] is placed on a disc of iron at the end of an iron rod, and is forced into the tap-hole . . when it is wished to stop a tapping out with the bott or bod stick.

bott(e, obs. form of BOAT *sb.*, BOOT.

bott, see BOT.

† **botte.** *Obs.* or *dial.* ? A brand or marking on sheep.
1641 BEST *Farm. Bks.* (1856) 12 The manner is to give lambes a tarre marke before they goe to the field, and our usuall way is to give them only the botte on the farre buttocke, and sometimes to run the edge of the botte downe the neare liske.

† **bottebolt,** var. of *butt-bolt*: see BUTT *sb.*

‖ **bottega** (bot'tega). [It. *bottega* small shop, studio, f. L. *apothēca*: see APOTHEC.] An artist's workshop or studio, esp. in Italy.
1900 F. LITCHFIELD *Pott. & Porc.* vii. 198 The group of ateliers or *bottegas* in . . Italy . . where work of this kind was carried on by individual artist potters, and their assistants or pupils. **1934** *Burlington Mag.* July 30/1 A frieze of blue terra-cotta from the bottega of Andrea della Robbia.

‖ **bottekin** ('bɒtkɪn). [cf. OF. *bottekin* (*botekin*) 'dimin. de botte' (Godef.).] A kind of small fancy boot. Cf. BOOTIKIN.
1882 *Standard* 19 Sept. 5/1 We live in a time of tight-lacing, high heels, and bottekins.

bottelle, obs. form of BOTTLE.

Böttger ('bœtgər). The name of J. G. *Böttger* (1682–1719), a German maker of porcelain, used *attrib.* to designate a type of red stoneware.
[**1850** J. MARRYAT *Hist. Pott. & Porc.* 233 *Böttcher Ware*, a fine red stoneware which was made by a chemist of that name, at Dresden, and which led to the discovery of porcelain in Europe.] **1869** LADY C. SCHREIBER *Jrnl.* (1911) I. 32 Böttger tankard. *Ibid.* 43 Two white Dresden teapots . . and a red Böttger one. **1925** W. W. WORSTER tr. *Hannover's Pott. & Porc.* III. iii. 43 The Plaue ware is . . thicker in the body and coarser in its shape than Böttger ware.

bott-hammer ('bɒt,hæmə(r)). [ad. G. *bott-hammer*, f. *botten* to break flax + *hammer* HAMMER *sb.*] A wooden hammer used to break the stalks of flax.
1858 SIMMONDS *Dict. Trade*, *Bott-hammer*, a wooden block with a long bent helve or handle, and having channels or flutings under its face used to beat flax. *a* **1877** KNIGHT *Dict. Mech.*, *Bott-hammer*, a wooden mallet with a fluted face, used in breaking flax upon the floor to remove the boon.

Botticellian (bɒtɪ'tʃɛlɪən), *a.* [f. the name of Sandro *Botticelli* (1444–1510), Florentine painter: see -AN.] Having the characteristics of Botticelli's work. Also **Botticell(i)'esque** *a.* and **Botti'celli** *attrib.*
1890 G. B. SHAW in *Star* 28 Apr. 2/3 Her slim figure, Tuscan school profile, and Botticellian grace. **1927** *Observer* 8 May 7 Mr. Berenson traces the original Botticellian type of the head. **1929** P. ASHBURNER in *Oxf. Poetry* 3 Quivering Botticelli leaves Tantalize the water-plants. **1934** S. BECKETT *More Pricks than Kicks* 256 Enormous breasts . . Botticelli thighs. **1939** *Burlington Mag.* Feb. 100/1 All the Botticelliesque material. *Ibid.* June 298/1 Pollaiuolesque-Botticellesque forms. **1966** COX *Illustr. Dict. Hairdressing & Wigmaking* 23/2 *Botticelli style*, from the hair style depicted on women in his painting 'Spring'. **1967** *Coast to Coast 1965–6* 173 The . . lacquer-red of their lipsticks had caused . . even Botticellian schoolgirls to feel barbaric.

bottine ('bɒtiːn). Also 6 *Sc.* botyn(e. [a. F. *bottine*, dim. of *botte* boot. Adopted in Sc. in 16th c., and independently in Eng. in 19th.]
1. A buskin, a large boot partly covering the leg.
1513 DOUGLAS *Æneis* I. vi. 57 With rede botynis on thair schankis hie. **1884** J. G. BOURKE *Snake Dance* i. 4 The women in the Pueblos north of Santa Fé . . wear a bottine, or legging, shaped somewhat like a Wellington boot.
2. A light kind of boot worn by ladies and children, a half-boot.
c **1845** C. BRONTË *Professor* (1857) I. xii. 194 Large feet tortured into small bottines. **1866** *Illust. Lond. News* 2 June 546 The fashionable bottines have merely the toes of leather, the remainder of the boot being of some thin textile fabric. **1876** GEO. ELIOT *Dan. Der.* 367 Some white gloves and some new bottines.

† **'bottle,** *sb.*¹ *Obs.* Forms: 1 botl, 2–3 buttle, (*Orm.*) bottl, 4– bottle. [OE. *botl*, corresp. to OS. *bodl*, OFris. *bodel*, ON. *ból* (:—*boðl*):—OTeut. *þoþlo-, from *bu-*, *bo-* 'dwell', with instrumental suffix *-þlo* = *-pro* (Gr. -τλο-, -τρο-). Cf. BOLD *sb.*¹] A dwelling, habitation, building.
[In place-names, as *Harbottle*, *Newbottle*, *Morbattle*.]
c **1000** *Ags. Gosp.* St. Matt. xxvi. 3 Ða wæron ȝesamnode þa ealdras þæra sacerda . . to þæra sacerda botle. *c* **1105** *Gloss.* in Wr.-Wülcker 552 *Palatium*, kinelic botl. *a* **1200** *Trin. Coll. Hom.* 185 Elch bilefful man þe is þider iboden shal finden þare his buttle. *c* **1200** ORMIN 2788 þe laffdiȝ Marȝe comm Till Zacariȝess bottle.

bottle ('bɒt(ə)l), *sb.*² Forms: 4 botel, 5 bottelle, botill, botyll, 5–6 botell(e, bottell, 6–7 botle, bottel, 6– bottle. [a. OF. *bouteille*, also *botel*, common Romanic = It. *bottiglia*, Sp. *botella*, Pg. *botelha*:—late L. *buticula*, dim. of late L. *butis*, *buttis* vessel, BUTT.]
1. a. A vessel with a narrow neck for holding liquids, now usually made of glass; originally of leather.
c **1375** WYCLIF *Serm.* Sel. Wks. II. 147 þes newe hoolis, þat ben maad in oold botelis. *c* **1380** *Sir Ferumb.* 510 Ȝunder at my sadel boȝe hongeþ o botel, Ful of baume. **1436** *E.E. Wills* (1882) 108 A pere of botell of siluer. *a* **1529** SKELTON *C. Clout* 652 Ye were wonte to drynke Of a lether bottell. **1611** BIBLE *Jer.* xix. 1 Goe and get a potters earthen bottell. **1716** ADDISON *Freeholder* No. 34. Boisterous Clubs, that . . throw Bottles at one another's Heads. **1836** DICKENS *Pickw.* vii, Bottles, glasses, and dessert were placed on the table.
b. The quantity (of liquor) which a bottle can hold, a bottleful. Cf. CUP, GLASS. Often *attrib.* (preceded by a numeral), as *a three-bottle man*: i.e. who drinks three bottles of wine at a sitting.
1687 [MONTAGUE & PRIOR] *Hind & P. Transv.* 2 [We] never trouble our heads with National concerns, till the third bottle has taught us as much of Politicks, as the next does of Religion? **1751** CARLYLE in Ramsay *Remin.* iii. (ed. 1864) Being a five-bottle man, he could lay them all under the table. **1791** BOSWELL *Johnson* 99 Port wine, of which he then sometimes drank a bottle. **1812** L. HUNT in *Examiner* 11 May 289/1 Six-bottle Ministers and plenitudinous Aldermen. **1821** BYRON in Moore *Life* xli. 472.
c. *fig.* in phrases of Biblical origin (after *Job* xxxviii. 37, *Matt.* ix. 17).
1560 BIBLE (*Geneva*) *Job* xxxviii. 37 Who can cause to cease the bottels of heauen? **1599** *Broughton's Lett.* iii. 13 The bottles of the clowdes, as Iob calleth them. **1635** SWAN *Spec. M.* iv. §2 (1643) 58 The aire is often clear, and those bottles of rain are not always there. **1651** HOBBES *Leviath.* IV. xlv. 366 These old empty Bottles of Gentilism. *a* **1677** BARROW *Serm.* Wks. 1716 II. 72 The wide seas . . supplying the bottles of heaven with water.
d. *to pass the bottle of smoke*: to give countenance to a conventional falsehood, to cant.
1855 DICKENS *Dorrit* I. xxxiv, To help myself in my turn, and pass the bottle of smoke. *Ibid.* To keep up the pretence as a labour and study, and patience . . and all the rest of it —in short, to pass the bottle of smoke, according to rule.
e. A baby's feeding-bottle. *to bring up on the bottle*: said of an infant reared by means of a feeding-bottle instead of at its mother's breast.
1848 THACKERAY *Pendennis* I. iii. 25 His first socks . . his bottle, and other interesting relics of his infancy. **1858** —— *Virginians* I. xviii. 141 Baby . . is bawling out on the stairs for his bottle. **1966** *Child Care* (*Brit. Med. Assoc.*) 21 An expectant mother who . . has decided . . to put the baby on the bottle is probably influenced by one or more of the following objections.
f. A hot-water bottle.
1857 MRS. GASKELL *Let.* 9 Oct. (1966) 889 We got *two* great bottles& slept together & heaped shawls on us to get warm. **1967** R. MACKAY *House & Day* 142 The bottle's in your bed. I put a wee flask on the table. Ovaltine. **1968** R. V. BESTE *Repeat Instructions* xiv. 147 I've just put a kettle on for my bottle.
g. In various *slang* uses. (*a*) Phr. *no bottle* no good; bad(ly), useless(ly).
1846 *Swell's Night Guide* 76 She thought it would be no bottle, cos her rival could go in a buster. **1931** W. F. BROWN in *Police Jrnl.* Oct. 501 When he got up the steps, he had a mouthpiece who was no bottle.
(*b*) A collection or share of money.
1893 P. H. EMERSON *Signor Lippo* v. 12 We never count the denarley on the pitch, but put each man's bottle into the sack just as it is till sharing time. **1928** *Radio Times* 2 Nov. 302/1 His [*sc.* a busker's] show ended, he passes along the line with his hat and proceeds to investigate the contents, or 'bottle'. **1939** J. B. PRIESTLEY *Let People Sing* x. 256 Knocker brought out some money. . . 'Not much bottle. A nicker, half a bar.'
(*c*) A reprimand. *Naval.*
1938 'GIRALDUS' *Merry Matloe Again* 177 A 'bottle' from the captain of the quarter-deck who is usually the ugliest P.O. in the ship. **1950** G. H. JONES *Worst Enemy* 220 Others came in to see me over-anxious to please, full of 'yes, sirs' expecting always to be given what is called a 'bottle'.
(*d*) Courage, spirit, 'guts'; *esp.* in phr. *to lose one's bottle*, to lose one's nerve.

This use prob. derives from the phrase _no bottle_ 'no good, useless' (sense 1 g(a) above). It is however often popularly associated with the rhyming slang term _bottle and glass_ = 'arse' and other similar expressions.

1958 F. Norman _Bang to Rights_ 62 We all began to ask each other..why he hadn't made a dash for it. 'What's the matter Frank, your bottle fallen out?' **1965** _Sunday Times_ 30 May 24/3 It's the worst that could be said about you, that you'd lost your bottle. **1969** _It_ 4–17 July 11/2 You've gotta have a helluva lot of bottle to do something like that, and I believe that Morrison did it out of sheer contempt. **1978** P. Marsh et al. _Rules of Disorder_ iii. 73 Clowns in the social world of soccer fans..aspire to being hooligans but lack the 'bottle' to succeed in such a role. **1982** A. Price _Old 'Vengeful'_ vii. 114 Danny's real hard, and got a certain amount of bottle. **1985** _T.V. Times_ 31 Aug.–6 Sept. 17/1, I don't think I handled the intrusion so well. I tend to lose my 'bottle'.

2. _transf._ The practice of drinking. _over a (the) bottle_: while drinking; at the wine: see over.

1709 Steele _Tatler_ No. 2 ¶1 My Spark flies to the Bottle for Relief. **1762–71** H. Walpole _Vertue's Anecd. Paint._ (1786) III. 240 Most of his performances were produced over a bottle. **1848** Macaulay _Hist. Eng._ II. 258 A dull man whose chief pleasures were derived from his dinner and his bottle.

attrib. **1712** Addison _Spect._ No. 507 ¶2 Our bottle conversation is so infected with them, that, etc.

†**3. a.** Something resembling a bottle; as: the seed-vessel of a plant, the honey-bag of a bee. _Obs._

1609 C. Butler _Fem. Mon._ vi. (1623) O iij, The Nectar or liquid hony the Bees gather with their tongues, whence they let it downe into their bottles which are within them like unto bladders. **1616** Surfl. & Markh. _Countr. Farm_ 499 The cocke heads, bells, or bottells which beare the seeds.

b. _colloq._ A thermionic valve.

1940 in _Chambers's Techn. Dict._ **1945** _Electronic Engin._ XVII. 424 Vacuum bottles..had to be produced on an ever-increasing scale.

4. _Comb._ and _Attrib._, as (sense 1) †_bottle-ale_ (also _attrib._), †_-beer_, _-belly_, _-case_, †_-cider_, _-conjuror_, _-cork_, †_-drink_, _-faucet_, _-filter_, _-maker_, _-rinsing_, _-room_, _-stand_, _-stopper_, _-works_; (sense 2) _bottle-bravery_, _-companion_, _-friend_, _-swagger_, _talk_; also _bottle-bellied_, _-like_, _-shaped_ adjs.

1586 Webbe _Eng. Poetrie_ (Arb.) 37 A Booke in Ryme..in commendations of Copper noses or *Bottle Ale. **1597** Shaks. _2 Hen. IV_, ii. iv. 140 Away you Bottle-Ale Rascall. **1641** French _Distill._ v. (1651) 122 It will tast as quick as *bottle beer. **1820** W. Irving _Sketch-bk._, _J. Bull_ (D.) Some choleric, *bottle-bellied old spider. **1807** Southey _Espriella's Lett._ (1814) II. 203 A..thick-headed fellow, with a *bottle belly and a bulbous nose. **1830** Galt _Lawrie T._ vi. viii. (1849) 290 His fits of *bottle-bravery. **1711** Addison _Spect._ No. 89 ¶1 Sam..is a very good *Bottle-Companion. **1755** _Gentl. Mag._ XXV. 65 *Bottle-conjurors, and persons who will jump down their own throats. **1746** W. Dunkin in P. Francis tr. _Horace's Ep._ ii. ii. 134 The Felon's Fork Defac'd the Signet of a *Bottle-Cork. **1791** _Chron._ in _Ann. Reg._ 6/2 He carried home all the bottle-corks he could come at. **1940** Dylan Thomas in _Life & Lett._ 274 A bursting sea with bottlecork boats. **1683** Tryon _Way to Health_ 164 All such *Bottle-Drinks are infected with a yeasty furious foaming matter. **1849–52** Todd _Cycl. Anat. & Phys._ IV. 1193/1 The *bottle-like form of the Ascidia. **1483** _Act 1 Rich. III_, xii. §1 Weavers, Horners, *Bottlemakers, and Coppersmiths. **1711** _Customs' Notice_ in _Lond. Gaz._ No. 4862/5 Bottle-makers, and other Dealers in..Skins. **1695** _Lond. Gaz._ No. 3114/4 Glass Works, Stone and Earthen *Bottle Works. **1733** P. Miller _Gard. Dict._ (ed. 2) s.v. _Cucurbita_, The Fruit of some Species is long, of others round or *Bottle-shap'd. **1952** A. G. L. Hellyer _Sanders' Encycl. Gardening_ (ed. 22) 426 Bottle-shaped fruits.

5. Special comb.: **bottle-age**, the length of time that a wine, etc., has remained in the bottle; **bottle-arsed** _a._ (_Printers' slang_), of type: wider at one end than at the other; **bottle-baby**, a baby reared by means of a feeding-bottle; **bottle bank**, a collection point (usu. one or more covered skips) to which members of the public can take empty bottles for recycling; also _attrib._; †**bottle-bearer**, one who carries a bottle, a butler (cf. _cup-bearer_); **bottle-boot**, 'a leather case to hold a bottle while corking' (Ogilvie); **bottle-boy**, an apothecary's assistant; **bottle-charger**, an apparatus for charging bottles with a liquid under pressure; **bottle-chart**, a chart of ocean surface currents compiled from data obtained by means of bottles thrown from ships and subsequently picked up at a distance; †**bottle-clay**, clay of which earthenware bottles were made; †**bottle-coaster**, a stand on which decanters were passed round the table; **bottle-drainer**, a frame in which inverted bottles are placed to drain; †**bottle-dropsy**, dropsy affecting the abdomen only; **bottle-end**, a round of glass resembling the bottom of a bottle, used in windows; **bottle-fed** _a._, (of an infant or young animal) brought up on the bottle (see sense 1 e); cf. _breast-fed_; hence (as back-formation) **bottle-feed** _v. trans._; **bottle-feeding** _vbl. sb._, feeding (_e.g._ of infants) by means of a bottle; **bottle-fish**, the _Saccopharynx ampullaceus_, a fish which can inflate its body so as to resemble a leathern bottle; **bottle-glass**, a bottle-shaped glass (_obs._); the coarse kind of glass of which common bottles are made; also _attrib._; **bottle-gourd**, a kind of flask-shaped gourd (_Lagenaria vulgaris_); **bottle-grass** _U.S._, a variety of foxtail grass, esp. _Setaria viridis_; **bottle-green** _a._, of a dark green colour, like bottle-glass; as _sb._ this colour; **bottle-heath**, bell-heather (_Erica tetralix_); **bottle-house**, a building in which bottle-glass is made; **bottle-imp**, an imaginary imp inhabiting a bottle; also, a Cartesian devil, a hollow figure suspended in a bottle of water; **bottle-jack**, (_a_) a jack for roasting meat, shaped like a bottle; (_b_) applied to an escapement in a clock or watch resembling that of a bottle-jack; (_c_) a kind of lifting-jack (Knight _Dict. Mech._, _a_ 1877); †**bottle-man**, a servant or official who has charge of bottles; **bottle-nest** (= _bottle-tit_); **bottle-opener**, an implement for opening bottles; **bottle-ore**, a kind of sea-weed (bladder-wrack, _Fucus vesiculosus_); **bottle-party**, a party to which each guest contributes a bottle (of wine, etc.); also an establishment, usu. a night-club, where drinks ordered in advance are served after licensed hours; †**bottle-pear**, a kind of pear so called from its shape; **bottle-rack** (= _bottle-drainer_); **bottle-screw**, a corkscrew; **bottle-shaker**, an apparatus used in centrifugation; **bottle-shop**, a shop licensed to sell wines and spirits only in the bottle; †**bottle-slider, -slide**, a tray for a decanter (= _bottle-coaster_); **bottle-stone**, a variety of obsidian; **bottle-stoop** (_Med._), a block of wood with a groove on the upper surface, so sloped that the contents of a bottle placed upon it may be easily removed with a knife in dispensing; **bottle store** (_a_) _S. Afr._ = _bottle-shop_; (_b_) a place where bottles are stored; **bottle-swallow**, an Australian bird, a species of martin; **bottle-tit**, **bottle-tom**, the Long-tailed Tit (_Parus caudatus_), from the shape of its nest; **bottle-track**, the track taken in the ocean by a bottle thrown overboard at a given point; cf. **bottle-chart**; **bottle-washer**, one who or a machine which washes bottles; also (_humorous_) one who looks after affairs, a factotum; **bottle-windowed** _a._, having windows made up with bottle-ends (see above). Also bottle-brush, etc.

1959 _Spectator_ 28 Aug. 255/3 It..will be better still with a little more *bottle-age. **1770** Luckombe _Hist. Printing_ 233 It [_sc._ the type] drives out, or gets in, either at the head, or the foot, and is, as Printers call it, *_Bottle-arsed_. **1838** Timperley _Printers' Man._ 64. **1890** Farmer _Slang_, _Bottle-arsed_, type thicker at one end than the other—a result of wear and tear. **1893** _Daily News_ 9 Mar. 2/7 Was it what you call a *bottle-baby? **1905** _Westm. Gaz._ 23 Oct. 4/1 Wanted, nurse for night duty only; one thoroughly accustomed to bottle babies. **1963** M. McCarthy _Group_ x. 221 Most of our babies are bottle babies. **1977** _Grocer_ 27 Aug. 7/1 (_heading_) *Bottle banks start. **1979** _Observer_ 30 Dec. 3/8 The Glass Manufacturers' Federation has sponsored the Bottle Bank scheme (with 125 skips in 45 towns), to recycle the glass from bottles. **1984** _Which?_ Aug. 355/3 Why not take your old non-returnable glass bottles to your local bottle bank instead of throwing them away? **1580** Hollyband _Treas. Fr. Tong_, _Vn sommelier_, a *bottle bearer. **1656** Trapp _Comm. Matt._ ix. 17 Certain heretics called..bottle-bearers, because they bare a bottle on their backs. **1857** Kingsley _Two Y. Ago_ i. (D.) He..fulfilled the ideal of a *bottle-boy. **1679** Plot _Staffordsh._ (1686) 122 *Bottle clay, of a bright whitish streaked yellow colour. **1801** Mar. Edgeworth _Belinda_ v, Their father pushing them on together, like two decanters in a *bottle-coaster. —— _Angelina_ iii, Angelina's letter was..found in a *bottle-drainer. **1562** Turner _Baths_ 3 The *bottel dropsey whych is about the stomack. **1907** W. De Morgan _Alice-for-Short_ ix. 92 A..window..filled with what some called *bottle-ends, and others German rounds. **1907** _Westm. Gaz._ 10 Apr. 10/1 This might be one of the causes of..infantile mortality, especially amongst *bottle-fed children. **1960** _Farmer & Stockbreeder_ 29 Mar. 65/2 She has built up an enterprise which last year bottle-fed 80 lambs. _Ibid._ 84/3 The other three [lambs] are being bottle-fed. **1962** _Guardian_ 12 Jan. 8/7, I breast-fed one and bottle-fed the other at alternate feeds. **1966** _Ibid._ 28 Oct. 10/5, I watched two of them bathing and bottle-feeding the tiny babies. _c_ **1865** _Circ. Sc._ I. 362/1 *Bottle-feeding will be preferable to the employment of a wet-nurse. **1626** Bacon _Sylva_ §213 Take therefore a Hawks-Bell..and hang it by a thred within a *Bottle-Glass. **1702** _Lond. Gaz._ No. 3821/8 A Round Bottle-Glass-House 94 Foot High, and 60 Foot broad. **1765** Delaval in _Phil. Trans._ LV. 24 Several pieces of green bottle glass. **1875** Ure _Dict. Arts_ II. 651 The coarsest and simplest form of this manufacture is bottle-glass. **1861** Miss Pratt _Flower. Pl._ II. 309 The *bottle-gourds (_Lagenaria_)..being shaped like flasks. **1814** J. Green in _Trans. Soc. Promotion Useful Arts_ III. 121 Panicum viride. *Bottle grass. **1840** Dewey in _Mass. Zool. & Bot. Surv.: Plants_ 244 _Setaria_. Bottle Grass. **1816** Coleridge _Statesm. Man._ (1817) 360 Black, blue, or *bottle-green. **1862** _Enquire Within_ 112 From the darkest bottle-green..to the lightest pea-green. **1863** Kingsley _Water-Bab._ i. 13 Red fly-catchers, and pink *bottle-heath, and sweet white orchis. **1875** Ure _Dict. Arts_ II. 652 A *bottle-house has generally eight other furnaces. **1822** De Quincey _Confess._ Wks. I. 106 The letter would poison my very existence, like the *bottle-imp. **1862** _Catal. Internat. Exhib._ II. xxix. 5598 *Bottle imps. **1947** _Antiquity_ XXI. 105 A toy known sometimes as a Bottle-imp, sometimes more grandly as a Cartesian Devil or Diver. **1845** E. Acton _Mod. Cookery_ (ed. 2) vii. 155 The *bottle-jack..is wound up like a watch, by means of a key. **1850** Denison _Clock & Watchm._ 50 The bottle-jack or 'vertical' pallets. **1860** _Ibid._ (ed. 4) 35 The bottle-jack escapement is precisely the same as in De Vick's clock. **1869** Curzon _Visit Monast._ 283 Twisting round and round like a leg of mutton hanging to a bottle jack. **1630** J. Taylor (Water P.) _Farew. Tower bottles_, Each *Bottleman (but I) Had alwayes a crack'd crowne or a black eye. **1634** _Althorp MS._ in Simpkinson _Washingtons_ Introd. 19 To the porters musicians and bottlemen for their rewardes. **1931** _Kansas City Times_ 17 Dec. 20 There were a few keys and a corkscrew and *bottle-opener in the bunch. _a_ **1953** Dylan Thomas _Quite Early One Morning_ (1954) 31 Why should the bottle-opener be under the hall-stand? **1756** W. Borlase _Observ. State Scilly Isl._ 120 The gross *Bottle-ore, which has hollow nobs or pustules in it, is reckoned to make the best kelp. **1926** C. Beaton _Diary_ 9 Dec. in _Wand. Years_ (1961) 151, I was invited to Madge Garland's *bottle-party. **1931** A. Powell _Afternoon Men_ I. i. 23 'Is it a bottle party?' 'You'd better bring a bottle of something,' said Barlow, 'in case there isn't anything to drink at all.' **1937** _Daily Herald_ 26 Jan. 4/5 There may also be provisions to deal with bottle parties. **1601** Holland _Pliny_ I. 439 Peares take their name..of the forme of their neck, as the *Bottle-peares. **1846** _French Dom. Cookery_ 323 Rinse them [bottles] as they become empty, and invert them on the *bottle-rack. **1702** _Phil. Trans._ XXIII. 1367 A close spiral revolution like the Worm of a *Bottle Screw. **1775** J. Granger _Biogr. Hist. Eng._ (ed. 2) III. 148 Her hair is dressed in many formal curls, which nearly resemble bottle-screws. **1938** Masefield _Dead Ned_ 133 A clasp-knife having at its back a bottle-screw. **1969** E. H. Pinto _Treen_ 60 Corkscrews, also known as bottle screws, screws, and steel worms, were being made in Tudor times. **1913** _Oxford Univ. Gaz._ 4 June 943/2 Motor driven centrifuge and *bottle-shaker. **1929** _Times_ 30 Jan. 9/7 These were what were known as '*bottle shops', and could not sell less than a bottle of spirits and a half-bottle of wine at any one time. **1785** _Lounger_ No. 86 As harmless as e'er a *bottle-slider at the table. **1815** Scott _Guy M._ xxxvi, His head crowned with a bottle-slider, his eye leering with an expression betwixt fun and the effects of wine. **1862** G. H. Mason _Zululand_ ii. 17 Another..formerly kept a small *bottle store. **1944** J. A. Lee in D. M. Davin _N.Z. Short Stories_ (1953) 104 There are rats in the bottle store, dozens of them! **1950** _Cape Times_ 17 June (W.-e. Mag.) 5 As soon as the bottlestore opens, the _mailer_ is there. He gets his regulation two bottles and takes this to the shebeen. **1898** Morris _Austral Engl._ 47/2 *_Bottle-Swallow_, a popular name for the bird _Lagenoplastis ariel_, otherwise called the Fairy Martin... The name refers to the bird's peculiar retort-shaped nest. **1851** Mayhew _Lond. Labour_ II. 72 The *Bottle-tit..has a long hanging nest like a bottle. **1837** _Southern Lit. Messenger_ III. 656 They have yet founded no city to themselves..but are willing to remain the boot-cleaners and the *bottle-washers of the whites. **1865** _Derby Mercury_ 1 Mar., Thoroughly cleaned by the steam bottle-washer. _a_ **1887** _Mod. colloq._ Head cook and bottle-washer of the establishment. **1894** _Daily News_ 8 Mar. 8/6 (Advt.), Handy man as Bottlewasher or Kitchen Porter. **1928** _East End Star_ May 3/3 She is Superintendent, Treasurer, cook and bottlewasher. **1899** Kipling _Stalky_ 224 A little *bottle-windowed, half-dairy, half-restaurant, a dark-browed, two hundred-year-old house.

bottle ('bɒt(ə)l), _sb._³ Forms: 4–6 botel, 5 bottelle, 5–6 botell(e, 6 bottel, 6–7 bottell, 7 botle, 6– bottle. [a. OF. _botel_, dim. of *_bot_, masc. form = _botte_ bundle.]

1. A bundle of hay or straw: now somewhat local in use. _**to look for a needle in a bottle of hay**_: to engage in a hopeless search. Cf. _Needle in a haystack_.

_c_ **1386** Chaucer _Maunc. Prol._ 14 Al-though it be nat worth a Botel hey. _c_ **1485** _Digby Myst._ (1882) ii. 85 A peck of otys and a botell of haye. **1530** Palsgr. 620 He is aboue in the haye lofte makynge botelles. **1578** _Scotter Manor Roll_ in Peacock _N. Linc. Gloss._ (E.D.S.) s.v., No man shall gett anie bottells of furres [i.e. furze]. **1592** Greene _Upst. Courtier_ (1871) 4 b, He..gropeth in the dark to find a needle in a bottle of hay. **1617** in Hearne _Coll._ (1885) I. 53 Hay being 20_s._ a load, the Penny Bottle ought to wey 3½. **1798** D. Graham _Wks._ II. 120 Shaking down two bottles of straw. _a_ **1845** Hood _Lost Heir_ ii, A child as is lost about London streets..is a needle in a bottle of hay.

2. bottle-horse, a horse for carrying bundles or packages, a pack-horse.

1461–83 _Ord. R. Househ._ 75 This office [of Sellar] hath a sumpter-man and horse, and also a bottle-horse. **1469** _Ibid._ (1790) 97 Item, A maile horse and a botell horse.

bottle ('bɒt(ə)l), _sb._⁴ _Bot._ [Partly corruption of _boþel_, buddle; partly a special use of bottle _sb._¹, from the shape of the ovary or calyx in some of the plants so named.] The popular name of several plants, chiefly with adj. denoting colour, as blue-bottle, q.v.; **white bottle**, _Silene inflata_; **yellow bottle**, _Chrysanthemum segetum_ (= buddle); **bottle of all sorts**, the _Pulmonaria officinalis_ 'no doubt in allusion to the flowers of two different colours'. See Britten and Holland.

1573 Tusser _Husb._ (1878) 95 Herbes, branches, and flowers, for windowes and pots. Botles, blew, red and tawnie. **1633** _Gerard's Herbal_ ii. ccli. 734 The Violet-coloured Bottle or Corne-floure.

'**bottle**, _sb._⁵ _Obs._ Corruption of boltel.

1660 Bloome _Archit._ A a, _Astragulus_, a bottle and fillet .._Echinus_ a bottle cut with edges... _Torus_, any bottle.

bottle ('bɒt(ə)l), _v._¹ [f. bottle _sb._²]

1. _trans._ To put into a bottle for the purpose of storing or keeping. Often with _up_. _**to bottle off**_: to transfer (liquors) from the cask into bottles.

1641 French _Distill._ v. (1651) 122 Let it stand a week, and then bottle it up. **1650** H. More in _Enthus. Triumph._ (1656) 111 How so subtil a thing as this Anima is can be either barrel'd up, or bottled up, or tied up in a bag, etc. **1769** Mrs. Raffald _Eng. Housekpr._ (1778) 321 Let it stand seven weeks, then bottle it. **1807** Southey _Espriella's Lett._ (1814)

III. 272 You might as reasonably attempt to dissect a bubble, or to bottle moonshine. **1882** *Garden* 18 Mar. 183/3 Keeping Grapes after they are bottled. **1885** H. CONWAY *Fam. Affair* ix. 70 They were very busy bottling off a quarter cask of sherry.

2. *fig.* To store up as in bottles; to keep under restraint (anger or other feelings); to shut *up*, *in*, *down*, *out*.

1622 T. SCOTT *Belg. Pismire* 53 Vapours..boteled vp in cloudes. *a* **1711** KEN *Anodynes* Poet. Wks. 1721 III. 429 He ..Bottles my Tears, accepts my Prayers. **1853** H. DRUMMOND in *Croker Papers* (1884) III. xxviii. 268 Twenty years of wrath bottled up. **1854** H. MILLER *Sch. & Schm.* xxii. 486 To anticipate the process of being ourselves bottled in, by bottling the country out. **1865** *Sat. Rev.* 7 Jan. 23/1 To catch and bottle up his now evaporated 'Spirit of the East'.

3. *Printing.* To make bottle-arsed.

1877 *Design & Work* 15 Sept. 341 The letters stand fair and square on the shank—that is, not 'bottled', as we say in the trade. 'Bottling' arises from the following cause—imperfect locking up, or lines badly spaced out... The risk of getting 'bottled' letter is, however, not very great... Amateurs are in..danger of 'bottling' their own letter.

4. *intr.* To collect money. So **'bottling** *vbl. sb. slang.* Cf. BOTTLE *sb.*² 1 g (*b*).

1934 P. ALLINGHAM in *Evening News* 9 July 11/3 He is an expert at that delicate part of the business [street entertaining] known as 'bottling', which means the art of persuading people to put money into your hat. **1936** W. A. GAPE *Half Million Tramps* vi. 159, 'I only sing the old favourite songs. You can "bottle" until you learn some.'.. To 'bottle' is the slang term for collecting. **1939** ADELER & WEST *Remember Fred Karno?* iii. 47 They commenced operations, performing as often as they could draw a crowd, and collecting, or 'bottling', before the crowd dispersed.

5. *trans.* To admonish. *Naval slang.*

1946 J. IRVING *Royal Navalese* 37 To bottle someone is to dress them down very thoroughly.

6. *intr.* With *out*: to lose one's nerve (see BOTTLE *sb.*² 1 g(d)); to back out of an action at the last minute, 'chicken out'. *slang.*

1979 *Listener* 8 Mar. 343/3 This is the big crime, for them: if they are informers or if they don't have the courage to do a crime. They, as they say, 'bottle out'. **1979** *Daily Tel.* 12 Sept. 19/7 Asked if she went on the robbery, she said: 'I was supposed to, but I bottled out.' **1980** S. MCCONVILLE in Michaels & Ricks *State of Lang.* 527 He was challenged and he *bottled out.* **1985** *Times* 17 July 12/1 Why did Ken Livingstone 'bottle out' and vote to set a legal GLC rate?

'bottle, *v.*² ? *dial.* [f. BOTTLE *sb.*³: cf. F. *botteler.*] To make *up* (hay) into bottles.

1611 COTGR., *Boteler*, to botle or bundle vp. **1653** URQUHART *Rabelais* I. xxiv, They..did recreate themselves in botteling up of hay.

bottle-brush. [f. BOTTLE *sb.*² + BRUSH.]

1. A brush for cleaning bottles, with bristles diverging on all sides from a central stem.

1713 DERHAM *Phys.-Theol.* 190 *note*, Antennæ; plain in the Female [Gnat], in the Male feathered, somewhat like a Bottle-brush. **1883** *Leisure Ho.* 473/1 Suggestive of gigantic feather-brushes, or rather bottle-brushes.

2. *Bot.* **a.** The popular name of the Horse-tail (*Equisetum*) and Mare's-tail (*Hippuris vulgaris*), from their shape. Also applied to various other plants or flowers (see quots.); *bottle-brush grass*: *Asperella hystrix.* **b.** Also applied to an Australian shrub, the *Banksia marginata* (Rhind's *Veg. Kingd.* 1874, 711), and to the *Metrosideros floribunda* (*The Garden* 10 June (1882) 417/3).

1843 J. TORREY *N.Y. Nat. Hist. Surv.*: *Flora* II. 478 Bottle-brush Grass... Moist, rocky woods, and along shady ravines: not rare. **1852** G. C. MUNDY *Our Antipodes* I. ii. 76 The Bottle-brush, one of the most characteristic plants of the bush..has rough, twisted branches, and a leaf something like the holly. Sir Joseph Banks gave it the botanical name of Banksia. **1883** A. EASTHER *Gloss. Dial. Almondbury* 15 *Bottlebrush*, a plant otherwise called Common Spurry, or Farmer's Ruin: *Spergula arvensis*... Another plant bears the same name—the Mare's Tail, or *Hippuris vulgaris.* **1883** *Encycl. Brit.* XX. 174/1 Bottlebrush [in Queensland], the *Callistemon lanceolatus.* **1923** D. H. LAWRENCE *Kangaroo* xviii. 397 Gold red bushes of the bottle-brush tree. **1957** P. WHITE *Voss* iii. 70 Belle had a spray of the crimson bottlebrush that she had torn off recklessly. **1961** *Amat. Gardening* 30 Sept. Suppl. 8/3 *Callistemon*..the unusual flowers..have a mass of prominent stamens giving the appearance of a bottle brush. This has given rise to the popular name of bottle brush plant. **1967** *Southerly* XXVII. 199 The flame of bottle-brush.

3. *attrib.* and in *comb.*

1851 *Q. Rev.* Dec. 40 Bottle-brush-flowered, zigzag-leaved, grey-tinted, odd-looking things. **1885** LADY BRASSEY *The Trades* 265 The..*Entada scandens*..bears an insignificant yellow, bottle-brush, acacia-like flower.

bottlebump, dial. var. BUTTERBUMP, bittern.

'So called on our east coast.' SMYTH *Sailor's Word-bk.*

bottled ('bɒt(ə)ld), *ppl. a.* [f. BOTTLE *sb.*² and *v.*¹]

†**1.** Resembling a bottle, protuberant, swollen.

1594 SHAKS. *Rich. III*, I. iii. 242 Why strew'st thou Sugar on the Bottel'd Spider, Whose deadly Web ensnareth thee about? **1768** TUCKER *Lt. Nat.* I. 448, I..saw a black bottled spider as big as myself. **1768** WALES in *Phil. Trans.* LX. 109 Their noses small, and..what is generally termed bottled. **1769** FALCONER *Dict. Marine* (1789) C c iij b, The chambers of mortars..are spherical..conical, bottled or concave.

2. Kept or corked up in a bottle. *bottled gas*, gas stored in liquid form in portable containers.

1660 BOYLE *New Exp. Phys.-Mech.* xxviii. 217 A Vessel full of bottl'd drink. **1662** FULLER *Worthies* II. 115 This is believed..the Original of bottled-Ale in England. **1769** MRS. RAFFALD *Eng. Housekpr.* (1778) 359 Any kind of bottled fruit. **1829** SOUTHEY *Sir T. More* II. 345 Brisk reputations, indeed, are like bottled twopenny, or pop. **1837** MARRYAT *Dog-Fiend* xlviii, Give them some bottled beer. **1930** *Engineering* 4 July 28/2 In the United States, 'bottled' gas, in the form of liquified propane and butane..is employed. **1960** *News Chron.* 20 July 6/6 The little bottled gas cookers are just like ordinary ones.

3. *fig.* **a.** Kept under restraint, pent up.

1840 HOOD *Up Rhine* 45 One with whom he could pour out his bottled-up grievances. **1853** C. BRONTË *Villette* xvi, He fumed like a bottled storm.

b. Stored up, concentrated.

1872 W. W. READE *Martyrdom of Man* 399 Life is bottled sunshine.

c. *bottled lightning*: (*a*) = LIGHTNING *sb.* 2; (*b*) concentrated vigour or energy; also *attrib.*

1839 DICKENS *Nickleby* xlix. 489 Bring in the bottled lightning, a clean tumbler, and a corkscrew. **1899** W. JAMES *Talks* 209 To all who looked upon her an impression as of 'bottled lightning' was irresistibly conveyed. *Ibid.* 210 There are plenty of bottled-lightning temperaments in other countries, and plenty of phlegmatic temperaments here.

4. *slang.* Drunk; intoxicated.

1927 *N.Y. Times* 9 Jan. (*heading*) British pilot tells police, 'If you say I am bottled, I will agree.' **1932** A. HUXLEY *Brave New World* v. 91 Bottled as she was..Lenina did not forget to take all the contraceptive precautions prescribed by the regulations. **1939** J. B. PRIESTLEY *Let People Sing* iii. 64 The gov'nor must be good an' bottled.

bottleful ('bɒt(ə)lfʊl). [f. BOTTLE *sb.*² + -FUL.] As much as a bottle will contain.

c **1865** in *Circ. Sc.* I. 119/1 Collecting a bottleful of the gas.

bottle-head. [f. as prec. + HEAD.]

†**1.** A var. of BEETLE-HEAD (see BEETLE *sb.*¹ 3); a stupid fellow. *Obs.* or *arch.*

1654 GAYTON *Fest. Notes*, Is it the custom of your country, you bottle-head, to use knight-errants after this manner? **1815** SCOTT *Guy M.* xliv, But why, for a blind bottlehead, did ye not ask the guineas?

†**2.** Some plant. *Obs.*

1713 PETIVER in *Phil. Trans.* XXVIII. 188 Purple Salamanca Bottle-head. Ray 324. 8.

3. The Bottle-nosed Whale (so-called); see BOTTLE-NOSE 2.

1819 REES *Cycl.* s.v., *Bottle-head*, a species of whale.

Hence †**'bottle-headed** = *beetle-headed*; 'void of wit'. Grose 1796.

bottle-holder ('bɒt(ə)lˌhəʊldə(r)). [f. as prec. + HOLDER.] One who holds a bottle; *spec.* one who waits on a pugilist at a prize-fight: *fig.* a second, a backer, a supporter.

1753 SMOLLETT *Ct. Fathom* (L.) An old bruiser makes a good bottle-holder. **1816** SCOTT *Antiq.* xxxix, Tutors, dependents, and bottle-holders of every description. **1858** CARLYLE *Fredk. Gt.* I. IV. v. 442 His Majesty's bottle-holder in that battle with the Finance Nightmares and Imbroglios.

So **'bottle-holding** *vbl. sb.*, backing, supporting.

1884 *Pall Mall G.* 5 Apr. 3/1 The Spectator..does a good deal of injudicious bottle-holding for Mr. Chamberlain.

bottle-neck, bottleneck ('bɒt(ə)lnɛk). [f. BOTTLE *sb.*² + NECK *sb.*¹] **1.** The neck of a bottle (see NECK *sb.*¹ 11 a).

1922 JOYCE *Ulysses* 423 A room lit by a candle stuck in a bottleneck.

2. A narrow entrance to or stretch in a road, comparable to the neck of a bottle in shape; *gen.* a narrow or confined space where traffic may become congested.

1896 [see sense 4 below]. **1907** *Westm. Gaz.* 21 Aug. 5/2 The bottle-neck, known as London-road, at the Elephant and Castle. **1915** W. J. LOCKE *Jaffery* x. 123 Through the bottle-neck of Brentford,..we crawled as fast as we were able. **1928** *Britain's Industr. Future* (*Liberal Ind. Inquiry*) IV. xxiii. 314 Any failure to maintain dock and harbour facilities ..results in delays... Ports then become the 'bottle-necks' of ocean traffic and congestion results.

3. *fig.* Anything obstructing an even flow of production, etc., or impeding activity, etc.

1928 *Observer* 15 July 10/3 It is hoped to make one side of the higher science forms of the school a bottle-neck through which boys of special intelligence..may pass. **1936** *Economist* 14 Mar. 581/1 Frequent complaints of deliveries falling into arrears..reveal the existence of numerous 'bottlenecks'. **1947** *Ann. Reg. 1946* 13 Import programmes, the bottleneck of which was no longer shipping, but finance. **1968** *Brit. Med. Bull.* XXIV. 192/2 The technology, therefore, exists; the bottle-neck..is in the education and training of those whose activities can benefit from its effective use.

4. *attrib.* and *Comb.* Also quasi-*adj.*, = BOTTLE-NECKED *ppl. a.*

1896 *Daily News* 26 Dec. 3/1 The widened portions at Holloway and elsewhere are rendered useless by narrow, bottle-neck approaches to Finsbury-park. **1898** *Ibid.* 19 Oct. 3/1 [He] called Old Jewry 'a bottle-neck-shaped street'. **1908** *Daily Graphic* 21 Mar. 13/3 Our desire at present is to look so feminine that bottle-neck shoulders are praised. **1938** L. MACNEICE *Earth Compels* 7 The bottle-neck harbour collects the mud.

bottle-neck, bottleneck ('bɒt(ə)lnɛk), *v.* [f. prec.] *trans.* To confine or impede in a bottleneck; to pass (something) through a bottleneck.

1928 *Daily Express* 12 June 3/4 He is 'bottle-necked' between Hungerford Bridge and the Hotel Cecil. **1933** *Planning* I. VIII. 8 It is easier to organise an export trade, which is necessarily bottlenecked through one channel. **1954** *Information Please Almanac 1955* 35 *Bottleneck*, to delay progress; to hold up a process, especially at a critical point.

So **'bottle-necked** *ppl. a.*, shaped like the neck of a bottle.

1932 H. SIMPSON *Boomerang* vii. 140 No bottle-necked alleys to delay them.

bottle-nose ('bɒt(ə)lˌnəʊz). Also 6 **bytyl-**. [f. as BOTTLE *sb.*² + NOSE. In sense 1 pronounced and usually written as two words.]

1. A nose resembling a bottle, a swollen nose. (With the form *bytyl-nose* = *beetle-nose*, cf. the confusion of *bottle-head* and *beetle-head.*)

[**1547** BOORDE *Brev. Health* cclxxxvi. 94 b, There be two kyndes [of polypus], the one is a bytyl nose.] **1635** BRERETON *Trav.* (1844) 94 Captain Ragg..famous..for his great bottle nose. **1748** SMOLLETT *Rod. Rand.* i. **1811** BYRON *Hints fr. Hor.* 58 Black eyes, black ringlets, but—a bottle nose!

2. The Bottle-nosed Whale: a name given to several of the Dolphin family, *esp.* the genus *Hyperoödon.*

1668 T. SMITH *Voy. to Constant.* in *Misc. Curiosa* (1708) III. 15 We saw..several Bottle-noses, fish of about three yards long. **1775** DALRYMPLE in *Phil. Trans.* LXVIII. 397 Some bottle noses, and vast flocks of flying fish. **1807** HOME *ibid.* XCVII. 97 The bottle-nose porpoise and large bottle-nose whale. **1854** R. OWEN in *Circ. Sc. Org. Nat.* I. 278 The great bottle-nose or hyperoodon. **1863** KINGSLEY *Water-Bab.* vii. 279 Razor-backs, and bottle-noses.

†**3.** A dial. name of the puffin. *Obs.*

1678 RAY *Willughby's Ornith.* 325 The Bird called in South-Wales Gulden head, Bottle-nose and Helegug.

'bottle-nosed, *a.* [f. prec. + -ED.] Having a bottle nose.

1568 *Like will to Like* in Hazl. *Dodsl.* III. 311 My dame called thee bottle-nosed knave. **1591** HARINGTON *Orl. Fur.* XLIII. cxxviii, A Gipsen..blab-lipt, beetle-browd, and bottle-nozed. **1863** BUCKLAND *Cur. Nat. Hist.* Ser. II. 325 A bottle-nosed whale..cast ashore from the Thames in 1783. **1865** DICKENS *Mut. Fr.* iii, The bottle-nosed regular customer.

bottle-o(h ('bɒt(ə)ləʊ). *Austral.* and *N.Z. colloq.* Also **bottle-o-er.** [f. BOTTLE *sb.*² + O *int.*] A collector of empty bottles.

1906 E. DYSON *Fact'ry 'Ands* xvi. 217 Half-a-dozen of them would have died for the bibulous comp. despite the bottle-o's stock garnered in the trouser fringe. **1914** *Bulletin* (Sydney) 14 May 36/2 Bottle-o Bill and his tart Could join in the catchy refrain. **1915** E. N. G. POULTON in *Countess of Liverpool's Gift Bk.* 95 He was the great panjandrum of his 'profession', the King of Bottle-O-ers. **1943** *Coast to Coast 1942* 105 A bottle-o followed him crying cheerily, 'Bottles, bottles, any empty bottles.' **1954** *Ibid. 1953–4* 161 They must pay for what they took; no thieving like other bottle-ohs. **1967** D. WHITTINGTON *In Search of Australian* 90 'What do you do for a living?'..'I'm the local bottle-O'.

bottler ('bɒtlə(r)), *sb.*¹ [f. BOTTLE *sb.*² and *v.*¹ + -ER.]

†**1.** A bottle-maker. *Obs.*

1415 *York Myst.* Introd. 22 Pouchemakers, Botellers, Capmakers.

2. One who bottles liquor.

1878 F. WILLIAMS *Midl. Railw.* 349 The bottling room, where the bottler is at work.

bottler ('bɒtlə(r)), *sb.*² and *a.* *Austral.* and *N.Z. slang.* [Cf. BONZER *a.*] (Something or somebody) excellent.

1890 'R. BOLDREWOOD' *Col. Reformer* x. 154 He's a bottler, that's what he [*sc.* a horse] is. **1941** BAKER *N.Z. Slang* vi. 51 Of children's terms..we may note..*bottler* and *snozzler*, descriptive of something superlative or excellent, both as nouns and adjectives. **1959** G. SLATTER *Gun in Hand* 239 Congratulations boy, a glorious try, a real bottler, you won the game.

bottle-tree ('bɒt(ə)ltriː). [f. BOTTLE *sb.*² + TREE *sb.*] An Australian tree of the sterculia family, either the Queensland tree *Sterculia rupestris* or the similar *Sterculia diversifolia* of Victoria, so called from the bottle-like shape of its trunk.

1846 C. P. HODGSON *Remin. Australia* 264 The sterculia or bottle-tree is a very singular curiosity. It generally varies in shape between a soda water and port wine bottle. **1885** MRS. C. PRAED *Head Stat.* 179 In dense scrub, where the bottle-trees rose weird and white. **1889** J. H. MAIDEN *Useful Native Plants* 60 A 'Kurrajong'. The 'Bottle-tree' of N.E. Australia, and also called 'Gouty-stem'. **1891** *'Coo-ee'* 284 A great white bottle tree, its trunk perfectly bare. **1931** F. D. DAVISON *Man-Shy* (1934) vii. 107 Through open bottle-tree country. **1958** R. STOW *To Islands* 52 Not far from the aerodrome strip there, under the bottle tree.

bottlin(g, variant of BOTLING.

bottling ('bɒtlɪŋ), *vbl. sb.* [f. BOTTLE *v.*¹ + -ING¹.] The act of putting into, or keeping in, bottles; *fig.* keeping under restraint. Often with *up.*

1594 PLAT *Divers Chem. Concl.* 14 The bottleing uppe of your best Ale. **1626** BACON *Sylva* §46 You may drink it well after 3 daies Botteling. **1691** SWIFT *Athen. Soc.* Wks. 1755

IV. I. 235 An art as vain as bottling up of winds. **1830** M. DONOVAN *Dom. Econ.* I. 309 The bottling of the cider.

bottom ('bɒtəm), *sb.* Forms: 1 botm, 3-4 **boþem, -om, -um, botham, -em, -um,** 5 **botym, botme,** 5-7 **botome, bottom(e, botoume,** 6-7 **bothom(e,** 9 *dial.* **botton,** 6- **bottom;** *north.* **bodome, -dom, -dum,** *mod.Sc.* **boddem.** [OE. *botm* str. masc., representing WGer. **boþm-*, whence OS. *bodom*, OHG. *bodam*, MHG., Du. *bodem*, mod.G. *boden*; the ON. *botn* appears to point to **boþno-* as the OTeut. form; but both may have been OTeut.: cf. Gr. *πυθμήν*, also Skr. *budhná*, L. *fundus* (for **fud-nus*):—Aryan **bhudhno-*.

The phonology of the Teut. forms is not yet clearly explained; the ME. variants *boþom boddom* also present difficulties.]

I. The lowest surface or part of anything.

1. a. The lowest part of anything, considered as a material thing; the lower or under surface, that surface of a thing on which it stands or rests; the base. Applied *spec.* to the keel of a ship (cf. 7), the circular end of a cask, etc. Proverb, 'Every tub (vat) must stand on its own bottom'.

a **1000** *Cædmon's Satan* 721 (Gr.) þa he on botme [þære helle] stod. *c* **1050** *Ags. Gloss.* in Wr.-Wülcker *Voc.* 181 *Cimba uel carina*, scipesbotm. **1382** WYCLIF *Wisd.* v. 10 A step is not to finde, ne a path of his [a ship's] botme in the flodis. *c* **1425** *Seven Sag.* (P.) 809 The credyl bothume turnyd on hyghe. *c* **1460-70** *Bk. Quintessence* 5 þat þe necke of þe glas be turned dounward, and þe botum be turned vpward. **1651** HOBBES *Leviath.* III. xxxviii. 242 A pit without a bottome. **1727** SWIFT *Gulliver* III. i. 180 It appeared to be a firm substance, the bottom flat, smooth and shining. **1768** ROSS *To the Begging* (JAM.), I'll then unto the cobler And cause him sole my shoon An inch thick i' the boddom. **1769** MRS. RAFFALD *Eng. Housekpr.* (1778) 289 Boil your artichoke bottoms in hard water. **1848** MACAULAY *Hist. Eng.* xiii. (1872) III. 38/2 Barrels with the bottoms knocked out served the purpose of chimneys. *Mod.* A drawer with a false bottom.

b. The sitting part of a man, the posteriors, the seat. (Colloq.) Also, the 'seat' of a chair.

1794-6 E. DARWIN *Zoon.* (1801) III. 253 So as to have his head and shoulders much lower than his bottom. **1835** J. WILSON *Noctes Ambr.* xxxix. (1864) IV. 79 The Dunghill cock..hides his head in a hole..unashamed of the exposure of his enormous bottom. **1837** CARLYLE *Fr. Rev.* II. IV. i. 185 Patriot women take their hazel wands, and fustigate..broad bottom of priests. **1885** *Leisure Ho.* Jan. 47/1 Women and children will be found caning or rushing the 'bottoms'.

c. ***bottoms up!***: a call or toast to finish one's drink to the last drop. Cf. BOTTOMER c. Hence as *adv. phr.*

1917 G. J. NATHAN (*title*) Bottoms up. **1928** *Vanity Fair* Dec. 79 Bottoms up to Vanity Fair! **1934** S. KINGSLEY *Men in White* I. iii. 48 Come on! Bottoms up! *She smiles back at him, and drains the glass.* **1934** J. O'HARA *Appt. in Samarra* (1935) iv. 119 The old priest..drank his highball almost bottoms up. **1964** L. NKOSI *Rhythm of Violence* 51, I say bottoms up both to women and to glasses! [He raises his glass.]

2. a. The ground or bed under the water of a lake, sea, or river. Hence ***to go to the bottom***: to sink, founder; to be wrecked.

a **1000** *Beowulf* 3016 þa heo to botme com. *c* **1325** *E.E. Allit. P.* C. 144 þe wawes..Durst nowhere for roȝ arest at þe bothem. *c* **1400** MAUNDEV. xxx. 300 Men may see the botme of the See. *c* **1460** *Towneley Myst.* 90 Now..to the botham is it sonken. **1583** STANYHURST *Æneis* I. (Arb.) 21 Soom synck too bottoms, sulcking thee surges asunder. **1635** N. CARPENTER *Geog. Del.* III. ix. 149 So great an abundance of water, that they can neither find the bottome or bounds thereof. **1697** DRYDEN *Virg. Georg.* IV. 618 The Sun..darting to the bottom, bak'd the Mud. **1730** A. GORDON *Maffei's Amphit.* 376 The Bottom is very good anchoring Ground. **1812** J. WILSON *Isle of Palms* II. 22 Down to the bottom must she go With all who wake or sleep. **1821** SHELLEY *Prometh. Unb.* II. ii. 73 The oozy bottom of clear lakes and pools.

b. ***to touch bottom***: to reach the lowest point. ***to have no bottom***: to be unfathomable, inexhaustible, etc. Often *fig.*

1682 SIR T. BROWNE *Chr. Mor.* 63 Forgetting..the vicissitude of good and evil, they apprehend no bottom in felicity. **1886** *Pall Mall G.* 22 Apr. 11/2, I do not believe we have touched bottom; I believe the reduction will go on.

†3. A deep place, a depth, either in the sea or land; an abyss. *Obs.*

a **1000** *Cædmon's Gen.* 361 (Gr.) He hæfð us befylled fyres to botme. *c* **1325** *E.E. Allit. P.* B. 1030 He bode in þat boþem [the Dead Sea] broþely a monyth. **1611** BIBLE *Wisd.* xvii. 14 The same sleepe..came vpon them out of the bottomes of ineuitable hell. **1667** MILTON *P.L.* VII. 289 So low Down sunk a hollow bottom..Capacious bed of Waters. **1697** DRYDEN *Virg. Georg.* IV. 557 In the Carpathian Bottom makes abode The Shepherd of the Seas. **1703** MAUNDRELL *Journ. Jerus.* (1721) Add. 4 A great..Rock, separated by a great gulph or natural bottom, from the land. **1759** BORLASE in *Phil. Trans.* L. 504 They called to their companions above to be drawn up from the bottoms.

4. a. The bed or basin of a river. **b.** Low-lying land, a valley, a dell; an alluvial hollow. Now esp. *U.S.*

c **1325** *E.E. Allit. P.* B. 383 Vch boþom watz brurd-ful to þe bonkez eggez. **1481** *Ripon Ch. Acts.* 347 Head-rack Bothome. **1513** DOUGLAS *Æneis* VII. Prol. 57 Bank, bra, and boddum blanschit wolx and bair. **1576** LAMBARDE *Peramb. Kent* (1826) 239 They [streams] all passe in one bottome to Wie and to Canterbury. **1613** W. BROWNE *Brit. Past.* II. i. (1772) II. 2 Past gloomy bottomes and high-waving woods. **1687** A. LOVELL tr. *Bergerac's Comic. Hist.* I. 177 Do you perceive, said he to me, what bottom we are going down into? **1732** LEDIARD *Sethos* II. IX. 294 This bottom, or inclosure..was about two hundred paces broad. **1803** T. JEFFERSON *Writ.* (1830) III. 504 There are on the borders of the rivers some rich bottoms, formed by the mud brought from the upper country. **1837** PECK *Gaz. Illinois* I. 3 The term 'bottom' is used throughout the west to denote the alluvial soil on the margin of rivers, usually called 'intervals' in New England. **1851** C. CIST *Cincinnati* 18 Cincinnati itself is built on an ancient alluvial plain, lying in two levels called the 'upper and lower bottoms'. **1907** MULFORD *Bar-20* xx. 200 They crawled to the last line of brush and looked out over an extensive bottom. **1942** W. FAULKNER *Go down, Moses* i. 33 Messing around up yonder in the bottom all last night!

c. In gold-mining, the channel of an old river (also called the gutter) containing rich deposits of gold; also, the layer below it. *Austral.*

1855 W. HOWITT *Land, Labour & Gold* I. xiii. 223 We have a hole within a few feet of the bottom, which I am confident will turn out well. **1887** HAYTER *Christmas Adv.* 5 (Morris), We reached the bottom, but did not find gold.

5. a. The lowest part of anything, considered as a place or position in space; the lowest point or locality, the 'foot'. Said both of vertical direction, and of the lowest point, on a slope.

a **1300** *Cursor M.* 1699 In þe boþem [of the ark] sal be na stall For al þeir filth sal þedir fall. *c* **1340** *Gaw. & Gr. Knt.* 2143 Til þou be broȝt to þe boþem of þe brem valay. **1526** TINDALE *Matt.* xxvii. 51 The vayle of the temple dyd rent in twayne from the toppe to the bottome [**1382** WYCLIF, fro the heiȝest til doun; **1388** to the lowest]. **1598** SHAKS. *Merry W.* III. v. 13 If the bottome were as deepe as hell, I shold down. **1664** EVELYN *Kal. Hort.* (1729) 204 Cutting the..Roots a little, especially at bottom. **1853** LYTTON *My Novel* III. xxiv, Two cherry trees, standing at the bottom of the Park. **1863** KINGSLEY *Water-bab.* 14 At the bottom of a hill they came to a spring. **1873** MORLEY *Rousseau* I. 296 Rousseau was alone at the bottom of his garden.

b. *fig.* in phr. ***from*** (***to***) ***the bottom of the heart***, etc.

1549 *Bk. Com. Prayer, Commun. Serv.* Rubr., If one of the parties..be content to forgive from the bottom of his heart all that the other hath trespassed against him. **1557** NORTH *Gueuara's Diall Pr.* (1619) 146/2, I loue thee from the bottome of my stomacke. **1585** ABP. SANDYS *Serm.* (1841) 334 From the bottom of my heart I confess with St. Paul, *Minimus sum.* **1802** MAR. EDGEWORTH *Moral T.* (1816) I. x. 83 He wished, from the bottom of his heart, that he had a thousand. **1848** MACAULAY *Hist. Eng.* I. 169 Worthless men ..to the very bottom of whose hearts he saw.

c. The foot of a page; the last place in a list or class; the lower end of a table, in point of dignity or precedence.

1658 ROWLAND *Mouffet's Theat. Ins.* 916 The rest he placed in the bottom of the wax, that is, in the last part of his will. **1863** A. J. HORWOOD *Yearbks. 30 & 31 Edw. I.* Pref. 32 The case at the bottom of p. 141 acknowledges the rule. **1866** C. D. YONGE *Naval Hist. Eng.* I. xi (L.), Justice was satisfied by his being placed at the bottom of the list of post-captains. **1884** MRS. CRAIK *G. Helstone* 246 Mr. Beresford's genial face at the bottom of his table, did more to give zest to the viands than an appetizing sauce.

d. *Mining.* Usually *pl.* The lowest workings in a mine. Also *attrib.*, as ***bottom captain, coal, worker.***

1778 PRYCE *Min. Cornub.* 174 The Bottom-Captains, whose business is to see that the common men perform due labour down in the mine. **1860** *Eng. & For. Mining Gloss.* (ed. 2) 5 *Bottoms*, the lowest workings either in a stope, level, or elsewhere. **1883** GRESLEY *Gloss. Coal-mining*, *Bottom*, the bottom of the shafts and roadways, &c., near the shafts. **1892** *Daily News* 26 Feb. 5/6 It comprises about 280,000 miners, of whom 200,000 are 'bottom workers'. **1900** *Daily Express* 28 June 7/3 There is an immense quantity of coal known locally as 'bottom coal' practically intact. **1967** *Gloss. Mining Terms (B.S.I.)* VIII. 7 *Bottom coal* (bottoms, floor coal), the lowest part of a seam, which may or may not be extracted.

e. The part of a boot or shoe below the uppers; the sole, heel, and shank.

1841 *Penny Cycl.* XXI. 410/2 The employing master.. prepares and sorts the sole or bottom-stuff for the maker. **1881** *Instr. Census Clerks* (1885) 76 Bottom Finisher. **1886** *Encycl. Brit.* XXI. 831/1 He then pares off inequalities and 'levels the bottoms'. **1911, 1921** [see *bottom-scourer* in 19].

6. a. *transf.* The deepest or most remote part of a recess, bay, or the like; the farthest point, or inmost part.

1603 R. JOHNSON *Kingd. & Commw.* 117 Venice..is a city seated at the bottome of the Adriatique sea. **1634** W. WOOD *New Eng. Prosp.* I. i, At the bottome [of Massachusetts Bay] ..are situated most of the English plantations. *a* **1674** MILTON *Hist. Mosc.* i. Wks. (1851) 476 The way thither is through the western bottom of Saint Nicholas Bay. **1791** BURKE *App. Whigs* Wks. VI. 20 Mahomet hid in the Bottom of the sands of Arabia. **1856** KANE *Arct. Exp.* I. viii. 82 Almost at the bottom of this indentation.

b. *fig.*

1587 GOLDING *De Mornay* viii. 100 Trogus Pompeius beginneth his Historie at the bottome of all antiquitie.

7. a. ***bottom*** (***of a ship***): generally, as in 1 (where see quots.); *spec.* 'the part of the hull of a ship which is below the wales' (Adm. Smyth); also, the hull as a whole; *hence*, A ship, boat, or other vessel.

1522 WOLSEY in Fiddes *Life* (1726) 64 To bring their wines upon strangers bottoms. **1540** *Act 32 Hen. VIII*, xiv, Laden..in any shyppe botome or vessell of this realme of England. **1600** HOLLAND *Livy* XXXIII. xxxvii. 845 They.. passed over the Po in small bothomes and punts. **1665** *Lond. Gaz.* No. 11/4 They were bound for Bordeaux with several others, all Dutch Bottoms. **1697** DAMPIER *Voy.* (1729) I. 143 When they come to Panama, [they] dispose of the Goods and Bottom together. **1770** LANGHORNE *Plutarch* (1879) I. 138/2 Amintas..and Sosicles..who sailed in one bottom, bore down upon him. **1817** BYRON *Beppo* xcvii, He transferr'd his lading..to another bottom. **1883** *American* VII. 162 Goods imported in foreign bottoms.

b. *fig.*

1636 FEATLY *Clavis Myst.* vii. 85 All private mens estates are ventered in the bottome of the Common-wealth. **1697** *Establ. Test.* 2, I do not pretend..to meddle with the Needle and Compass of the Publique Bottom. **1799** J. ROBERTSON *Agric. Perth* 442 In no bottom can it be more safe than in land. **1824** SCOTT *St. Ronan's* x, I wish Clara's venture had not been in such a bottom.

8. † a. The dregs, sediment of liquors; the last portion of the wine in a cask (*obs.*). **b.** In *Copper-smelting* (see quot.).

1660 HOWELL *Dict.*, *Bottom*, or the settling of liquor at the bottom. **1703** *Lond. Gaz.* No. 3963/3 The White Wines..at 40*l.* per Tun, the White Bottoms at 10*l.* **1870** *Eng. Mech.* 18 Feb. 547/3 Known as black copper or 'bottoms'. **1881** RAYMOND *Mining Gloss.*, *Bottoms*, in copper-smelting, the impure metallic copper..which separates from the matt, and is found below it.

9. ***bottom of a wig***: the portion hanging down over the shoulder. ***full bottom***: short for 'full-bottomed wig'.

1851 THACKERAY *Eng. Hum.* II. 89 The fathers of theology did not think it decent to appear except in a full bottom.

II. That which underlies or supports a thing.

†10. a. That upon which anything is built or rests; the foundation. *Obs.*

c **1440** *Promp. Parv.* 45 Botme, or fundament, *basis.* **1647** H. MORE *Song of Soul* II. App. civ, All the stately works and monuments Built on this bottome. **1660** SHARROCK *Vegetables* 39 That canon will certainly hold longer which is best built in the bottome. **1674** ALLEN *Danger Enthus.* 5 Several Orders among the Papists have been built upon the same Bottom.

†b. The ground under a plant; the soil in which it grows. *Obs.*

a **1620** J. DYKE *Worthy Commun.* (1640) To Rdr., A plant that growes upon its own bottom. **1649** BLITH *Eng. Improv. Impr.* To Husb., No less than may..yield good bottome and rooting to the corn.

11. *fig.* **a.** A foundation, basis, footing.

a **1620** J. DYKE *Worthy Commun.* (1640) 194 Hee comes off from all bottom he hath in himselfe and in nature. **1675** BROOKS *Gold. Key* Wks. 1867 V. 155 This glorious name Shaddai, was a noble bottom for Abraham to act his faith upon. **1697** *Snake in Grass* (ed. 2) p. xv, This was the Bottom upon which the Quakers first set up. **1718** PENN *Life* in Wks. 1726 I. 136 If we could not all meet upon a Religious Bottom, at least we might upon a Civil One. **1788** PRIESTLEY *Lect. Hist.* v. xxxvi. 262 Authority established on the same bottom with the privileges of the people.

b. Phrase. ***to stand on one's own bottom***: to act for oneself, be independent.

1606 HOLLAND *Sueton.* 97 Hee had used also before, to stand upon his owne bothom. *a* **1656** BP. HALL *Content.* 45 Man, though he..stand upon his own bottome, yet [is] he not a little vvrought upon by examples. **1680** MORDEN *Geog. Rect.* (1685) 106 Everyone endeavours to stand on their own bottom. **1788** REID *Aristotle's Log.* vi. §1. 129 When reason acquires such strength as to stand on its own bottom.

c. In fig. phrases: ***the bottom falls*** (or ***drops***) ***out of***: there is a collapse of; ***to knock the bottom out of***: see KNOCK *v.* 6 b.

1637 RUTHERFORD *Let.* 9 Sept. (1664) 144 The bottom hath fallen out of both their wit and conscience at once. **1868** *Iowa Agric. Soc. Rep. 1867* 64 The bottom has at length dropped out of this humbug. **1872** 'MARK TWAIN' *Roughing It* (1873) lviii. 420 Gould and Curry soared to six thousand three hundred dollars a foot! And then—all of a sudden, out went the bottom and everything..went to ruin and destruction! **1923** WODEHOUSE *Inimit. Jeeves* iv. 45, I felt as if the bottom had dropped out of things with a jerk. **1926** E. M. DELL *Black Knight* I. x, 'I try to take things as they come.'..'And when the bottom falls out of everything—what do you do then?' **1957** M. BANTON *W. Afr. City* vi. 103 In the 1930s the bottom fell out of the market in ginger and coffee.

12. The fundamental character, essence, reality. Phrases. ***to search, etc., to the bottom***: to examine thoroughly, to find out the real character of. ***at*** (***the***) ***bottom***: in reality, as distinguished from superficial appearances. ***to be at the bottom of***: to underlie, to be the real author or source of.

1577 HARRISON *England* II. i. (1877) 12 When the pope understood the botome of the matter. **1594** T. B. *La Primaud. Fr. Acad.* II. 391 There is nothing in man which.. God..searcheth not vnto the bottome. **1600** TOURNEUR *Transf. Metamorph.* lviii, Doth demonstrate presently The bottome of his mind effectually. **1651** *Proc. Parliament* No. 94. 1446 The examination of that business to the bottom. **1683** *Apol. for Prot. France* vi. 88 The Clergy in the bottom judges that the Pope has Right to lay an Ecclesiastical Censure upon the Kingdom of France. **1711** STEELE *Spect.* No. 43 ¶5 We are by no means yet sure, that some People are not at the Bottom on't. **1720** OZELL tr. *Vertot's Rom. Rep.* III. XIV. 325 Antony, at the Bottom, very indifferent about this Revenge, pretended to be in earnest. **1748** ANSON *Voy.* III. x. (ed. 4) 544 If this matter was examined to the bottom. **1773** MONBODDO *Language* (1774) I. I. iv. 42 In order to get at the bottom of this question. **1780** SHERIDAN *Sch. Scand.* I. i. 8 Every body was sure there was some reason for it at bottom. **1809-10** COLERIDGE *Friend* (1865) 75 With whomsoever we play the deceiver and flatterer, at the bottom we despise. **1838** DICKENS *Nickleby* xxiii. 215 He's a good pony at bottom. **1848** MACAULAY *Hist. Eng.* I. 387 The Jesuits were at the bottom of the scheme. **1866** ARGYLL *Reign Law* vi. (1871) 320 That which is really at the bottom of all this ambiguity of language. **1873** MORLEY *Rousseau* II. 171 It is bad, because it is at bottom, a superstition.

†**13.** A pecuniary 'foundation' or 'basis' for commercial enterprise; capital, resources; *hence*, financial stability, commercial standing. *Obs.*

1662 FULLER *Worthies* (1840) II. 451 Beginning on a good bottom left him by his father. **1787** T. JEFFERSON *Writ.* (1859) II. 206, I know of no mercantile house in France of surer bottom.

14. Physical resources, 'staying power', power of endurance; said esp. of pugilists, wrestlers, race-horses, etc.

1774 GOLDSM. *Anim. Nat.* II. 106 Though the Savages held out and, as the phrase is, had better bottoms, yet for a spurt the Englishmen were more nimble and speedy. **1790** BEWICK *Quadr.*, *Race Horse* (1800) 7 What is called in the language of the turf, bottom. **1822** BYRON *Juan* VIII. cx, [He] died all game and bottom. **1835** *Penny Cycl.* III. 421/2 They ..have their manes and tails cropped..under the supposition that it adds to their strength and bottom. **1862** R. PATTERSON *Ess. Hist. & Art* 180 For solidity, bottom, and a courage that never wavers, they [British troops] are incomparable.

†**15. a.** A clew or nucleus on which to wind thread; also a skein or ball of thread. Also *fig.* *Obs.*

c **1440** *Promp. Parv.* 45 Botme of threde. **1490** CAXTON *Eneydos* xxxi. 120 He must take wyth hym a botom of threde. **1555** EDEN *Decades W. Ind.* I. v. (Arb.) 85 Of gossampine cotton ready spunne foure great bottomes. **1611** COTGR., *Fondrillon*, a bottom to wind silke, thread or yarne on. **1614** RALEIGH *Hist. World* II. 367 He received from her [Ariadne] a bottome of thred. *c* **1645** HOWELL *Lett.* (1650) I. 267, I will twist up what I know upon as narrow a bottom as may be shut up within the compass of this letter. **1698** S. CLARK *Script. Just.* 112 It's high Time now to wind up my Bottoms. **1731** SIR E. PEYTON *Div. Catastr. Ho. Stuarts* 64, I have ravelled out the Pieces to wind up this Bottom. **1754** BP. WARBURTON *Lett. fr. Late Prelate* (1809) 168 So you see I am winding up my bottoms.

†**b.** The cocoon of a silkworm. *Obs.*

1609 *Mulb. Trees* in *Harl. Misc.* (Malh.) III. 86 Upon the branches..the wormes will fasten themselues, and make their bottomes. **1655** GURNALL *Chr. in Arm.* xiii. §3 (1669) 42/2 The Silk-worm..works her self out of her bottom. **1665** *Phil. Trans.* I. 88 The manner of winding their Silk from their Bottoms.

†**16.** ? The lap. *Obs.*

1725 BRADLEY *Fam. Dict.* II. s.v. *Lithotomy*, The Operator lays the sick Person upon a soft pillow, in the Bottom or Lap of some Strong Man.

17. *Particle Physics.* [An arbitrary choice of name.] The name of (a quark carrying) a flavour with a charge of $-\frac{1}{3}$; symbol *b*.

1977 *Sci. News* 13 Aug. 100/1 Once the charmed quark was in the picture, symmetry principles and other considerations led to openings for a fifth and a sixth. The last two have been designated rather whimsically 'truth' and 'beauty' although in a recent statement Lederman names them more prosaically 'top' and 'bottom'. **1977**, **1978** [see TOP *sb.*¹ 18]. **1979** *N.Y. Times* 13 Feb. C2 The upsilon, formed of a bottom quark and a bottom antiquark, is 10 times more massive than the proton. **1980** *Sci. Amer.* Jan. 28/2 A first order of business for the new accelerators will be filling in the blanks in the catalogue of hadrons, particularly those that incorporate top and bottom quarks in their structure. **1983** *McGraw-Hill Yearbk. Sci. & Technol.* *1984* 282/2 The recently discovered *B* meson..is stable, providing the first direct evidence for the existence of a very heavy quark, carrying a new flavor, called beauty or bottom.

III. *Attrib.* and *Comb.*

18. *simple attrib.* or *adj.* Of or pertaining to the bottom; lowest, basal, fundamental; last. (Hence superlative BOTTOM-MOST.)

1561 T. NORTON *Calvin's Inst.* I. 8 b, The presumptuous boldnesse..is throwen downe euen to the bottome point of the earth. **1677** MOXON *Mech. Exerc.* (1703) 221 The bottom width of the Hollow. **1685** W. ADAMS *Dedham Pulpit* (1840) 97 This is the bottom cause. **1885** *Pall Mall G.* 2 Dec. 3/1 The bottom political fact just now. **1885** *Boston (Mass.) Jrnl.* 20 Dec. Advt., All kinds of Horse Furnishings at Bottom Prices.

19. General comb., chiefly attrib., in senses **a.** At the bottom, forming the bottom, as ***bottom-discharge***, ***-rock*** (also *fig.*), ***-water***; ***bottom-heavy*** adj.; **b.** That remains on the bottom (of sea, river, etc.); done at or near the bottom, as ***bottom-fish***, ***-fishing***, ***-liver***, ***-living***, ***-trailing***; **c.** That belongs to or forms the bottom of anything, as ***bottom-board***, ***-timber***; **d.** *fig.* Fundamental, as †***bottom-ground***; **e.** Of or pertaining to low-lying ground, as ***bottom-glade***, ***-grass***, ***-land***; **f.** (sense 1 b) ***bottom-pincher***, ***-pinching***.

1881 C. A. EDWARDS *Organs* 42 The *bottom board is made of thick pine. *a* **1877** KNIGHT *Dict. Mech.*, **Bottom-discharge Water-wheel*, a turbine from which the water is discharged at the bottom instead of at the sides. **1900** *Daily News* 24 Oct. 7/7 Orders for 160 bottom-discharge trucks have been placed in America. **1847** ANSTED *Anc. World* vi. 106 *Bottom-fish, living on offal and on the invertebrated groups. **1830** HOWITT *Seasons, Mar.* 59 His sport is.. confined to *bottom-fishing. **1634** MILTON *Comus* 532 Hard by i' the hilly crofts That brow this *bottom-glade. **1592** SHAKS. *Ven. & Ad.* 236 Within this limit is relief enough; Sweet *bottom-grass, and high delightful plain. *a* **1679** T. GOODWIN Wks. 1865 X. 431 The reason or *bottom-ground of all that wickedness. **1927** *Sunday Times* 6 Mar. 7/3 The double basses are generally too plentiful at these concerts, and..they too often made the music sound *bottom-heavy. **1882** H. LANSDELL *Through Siberia* I. 220 We had a splendid view of the noble Yenesei at sunset, of its verdant *bottom-lands on either side. **1927** HALDANE & HUXLEY *Animal Biol.* xii. 302 They are all marine and essentially *bottom-livers. **1881** *Jrnl. Microsc. Soc.* Jan 68 The porcellanous Foraminifera..are known to be exclusively *bottom-living species. **1959** J. BLISH *Case of Conscience* xii. 119 He was fundamentally nothing more complicated than a *bottom-pincher. **1939** AUDEN & ISHERWOOD *Journey to War* 53 Their horse-play, *bottom-pinching..and endless jokes about *les poules*. **1955** AUDEN *Shield of Achilles* ii. 41 The honking bottom-pinching clown. **1864** DANA *Text-Bk. Geol.* (1874) 45 In Great Britain, the whole thickness above the unfossiliferous *bottom-rocks is about 100,000 feet. **1887** C. B. GEORGE *40 Yrs. on Rail* v. 93 About the time I had reached bottom rock in my financial troubles,..I met A. B. Pullman. **1856** KANE *Arct. Exp.* II. xxvi. 266 The ice had strained her *bottom-timbers. **1822** *Edin. Rev.* 300 They gave us our elementary lesson of *bottom-trailing. **1878** HUXLEY *Physiogr.* 152 The surface freezes while the *bottom-water remains several degrees warmer.

20. Special comb., as **bottom-bed**, the lowest stratum of a formation of rocks; **bottom-boarding**, the bottom-planks of a boat; **bottom-boards**, boards at the bottom of a boat serving to protect the outer planking; **bottom-cargo**, the cargo carried in the hold; **bottom-dish**, that placed at the lower end of the table; **bottom dog** = UNDERDOG (cf. *top dog* s.v. TOP *sb.*¹ 34); also *attrib.*; so **bottom-doggy** *a.*, pertaining to or characteristic of a bottom dog; **bottom dollar** *U.S.*, (one's) last dollar, usu. in collocations with *bet*; **bottom drawer**, lit. the lowest drawer of a chest of drawers, etc., in which a woman stores clothes, linen, etc., in preparation for her marriage; **bottom facts** *U.S.*, the fundamental facts; **bottom fermentation**, that during which the yeast cells collect at the bottom of the liquid; also *attrib.*; **bottom gear**, the lowest-speed gear (see GEAR *sb.* 7) in a motor; **bottom-heat**, heat supplied to plants through the soil; **bottom-ice**, ice which forms on the bottom of a river or sea; **bottom-land**, **bottomland** *U.S.*, low-lying land, esp. a stretch of level land near a river; = BOTTOM *sb.* 4 b; also *attrib.*; **bottom-lift** (see quot.); **bottom-line**, (*a*) the lower part of a fishing-line; (*b*) orig. *U.S.*, the last line of a profit-and-loss account, showing the final profit (or loss); also *loosely*, the net profit; *fig.*, the final analysis or determining factor; the point, the crux of the argument; **bottom-moraine**, débris dropped from icebergs on the bottom of the sea; **bottom-planks** the outer planking of the bottom of a boat; **bottom-plate**, (*a*) an iron plate in a printing-press; (*b*) the set of knives forming the bed of a pulping machine in paper-making; **bottom prairie** *U.S.*, a prairie lying along the bank of a river; **bottom-sampler**, a grab for dredging samples from the sea-bottom; hence ***bottom-sampling*** ppl. a. and vbl. sb.; **bottom-scourer**, an operative who smooths the 'bottoms' of boots and shoes; **bottom-set bed** *Geol.* (see quots.); **bottom-side** = sense 1 a; **bottom timber** *U.S.*, timber growing in bottom-lands; **bottom-tool**, a tool used in wood-turning; **bottom-up**, **-upwards** *adv.*, in an inverted position, upside-down; †**bottomward**, the part near the bottom; **bottom-wigged** *a.*, wearing a wig with full bottom; **bottom-wind** (see quot.); **bottom wool** (see quot.); **bottom yeast** = *bottom fermentation* yeast.

1845 P. B. BRODIE *Hist. Fossil Insects* 58 Hard blue limestone, ('*bottom bed') with Ostrea, Modiola minima, and other shells. **1900** G. SWIFT *Somerley* 110 At the risk of tearing out what was left of the *bottom-boarding, we hauled her on to the beach. **1861** T. HUGHES *Tom Brown at Oxford* I. xi. 192 I've larded the *bottom boards under my seat so that not a drop of water will..come through. **1883** *Man. Seamanship for Boys' Training Ships* 84 Q. What are bottom boards? A. Long pieces of wood nailed together, which lay from the stern sheets to the bow. **1840** MARRYAT *Poor Jack* xxiii, Our *bottom cargo consisted of..crockery. **1747** H. GLASSE *Art of Cookery* ix. 94 A collar of Fish in Ragoo... This is a fine *Bottom-dish. **1796** MRS. GLASSE *Cookery* v. 79 A porcupine of a breast of veal..is a grand bottom-dish. **1884** *Boston (Mass.) Jrnl.* 12 July, I can't help sympathizing with the *bottom dog [in a fight]. **1926** D. H. LAWRENCE *Plumed Serpent* vi. 119 There was a touch of bottom-dog insolence about her. **1927** *Daily Express* 12 Aug. 9/5 The award will be received with disappointment by..the 'bottom dogs' of the service. **1925** D. H. LAWRENCE *Let.* 2 Apr. (1962) II. 832 *Canaille* of the most *bottom-doggy order. **1857** *San Francisco Call* 24 Jan. 4/1 Sometimes, however, luck will run against him, and..he 'slips up for his *bottom dollar'. **1866** *Congress. Globe* Mar. 1474/1 His opinion is that a State can go out of the Union and he is willing to bet his bottom dollar on his judgment. **1904** HARBEN *Georgians* v. 43 You bet yore bottom dollar I'm open to criticism myself. **1958** *Dissent* V. I. 80 And I'd bet my bottom dollar that Negro hipsters, among themselves, often put down the whites. **1886** R. HOLLAND *Gloss. Cty. Cheshire* 407 If a young woman were to buy a set of teathings, or a tablecloth, or what not, and were asked what use she had for such things, she would answer, 'Oh! they're to put in my **bottom drawer*.' **1902** A. BENNETT *Anna of Five Towns* xiii. 343 The bride took all the house-linen to her husband... As soon as a girl had passed her fifteenth birthday, she began to sew for the 'bottom drawer'. **1959** *Woman's Own* 14 Feb. 58/3 She had been saving furiously for her 'bottom drawer' ever since she became engaged. **1877** *N.Y. Tribune* 17 Mar. (Bartlett), Curiosity has been on the tiptoe these many weeks to know the *bottom facts. **1883** 'MARK TWAIN' *Life Mississippi* xlii. 393 Though there ain't only one or two ways when you come down to the bottom facts of it. **1902** *Encycl. Brit.* XXVI. 367/1 In the Continental **bottom-fermentation* system, the pitching and fermentation take place at a very low temperature. **1905** J. L. BAKER *Brewing Industry* 100 Brewer's yeast (*Saccharomyces cerevisiæ*) is divided into two classes, top fermentation and bottom fermentation yeast. **1923** *Westm. Gaz.* 2 Feb., A stiff climb on *bottom gear brings Mosul.. in sight. **1968** *Listener* 1 Aug. 140/3 Still our red-hot old bus engines ploughed on uphill in bottom gear. **1882** *Garden* 14 Jan. 26/3 The cuttings..are planted out in frames in a gentle *bottom-heat. **1882** GEIKIE *Geol.* II. II. §6. 111 Water-ice is formed..by the freezing of the layer of water lying on the bottom of rivers, or the sea (*bottom-ice, ground-ice, anchor-ice). **1728** *Boston News-Letter* 23–30 May 2/2 Fifty Acres of..Meadows and Meadow *Bottom Land. **1841** C. CIST *Cincinnati* 66 The larger streams are now found meandering through alluvial plains called 'bottom lands'. **1903** *N.Y. Even. Post* 12 Sept., The tract consists of a bottom land along the Ohio River, and a plateau elevated 300 feet above the bottom land. *Ibid.* 19 Sept., To complete the maturity of the bottomland crops. **1926** *Chambers's Jrnl.* 1 May 345/1 The lakes and sloughs ran in a vast network over the bottom lands. **1961** L. MUMFORD *City in History* xiii. 405 A discouraging site: bottomland, bordered by a swamp on the Potomac side. **1881** RAYMOND *Mining Gloss.*, **Bottom-lift*, the deepest lift of a mining-pump, or the lowest pump. **1837** KIRKBRIDE *Northern Angler* 91 The *bottom or casting-line must consist of three lengths of twisted gut. **1967** *San Francisco Examiner* 8 Sept. 35/7 George Murphy and Ronald Reagan certainly qualified because they have gotten elected. I think that's the *bottom line. **1970** R. TOWNSEND *Up the Organization* 76 All overheads should be brought down to the bottom line for bonus purposes. **1982** *Sci. Amer.* Oct. 14/2 The bottom line is that invention is much more like falling off a log than like sawing one in two. **1984** *Observer* 26 Feb. 37/2 So much goddam effort has gone into improving profitability right down to the bottom line. **1882** *Nature* XXV. 470 The Devonian rocks..are covered with a thick sheet of typical *bottom-moraine. **1891** KIPLING *Light that Failed* ii. 27 The whale-boat..chose to hit a hidden rock and rip out half her *bottom-planks. *a* **1877** KNIGHT *Dict. Mech.*, **Bottom-plate* (printing), a plate of iron belonging to the mold of a printing-press, on which the carriage is fixed. *a* **1884** *Ibid.* Suppl., *Bottom-plate* (paper-making), the gang of knives forming the concave or bed beneath the cylinder of a rag-grinding machine or pulping engine. **1804** J. ORDWAY in *Wis. Hist. Coll.* (1916) XXII. 95 A beautiful *Bottom Prarie ..about 2000 acres of Land covered with wild rye and wild potatoes. **1882** WORTHEN *Econ. Geol. Illinois* II. 73 The latter are the so-called 'ridge prairies', while the former are sometimes designated as 'bottom prairies'. **1911** PETERSEN & JENSEN *Danish Biol. Station Rep.* XX. 73 By means of *bottom-samplers..it is shown that the uppermost brown layer of the sea-bottom must be regarded as dust-fine detritus. **1959** A. HARDY *Fish & Fisheries* v. 104 Petersen's quantitative bottom-sampling grab. **1911** F. SELLERS in *Rep. Labour & Social Conditions in Germany* III. 95 *Bottom-scourers 24*s.* (Frankfurt per week). 12*s.* to 16*s.* (Leeds per week). **1921** *Dict. Occup. Terms* (1927) §429 *Scourer*,.. designated according to parts upon which he works, *e.g.* bottom or naumkeag scourer, heel scourer. **1905** CHAMBERLIN & SALISBURY *Geol.* iii. 191 The sediment rolled at the bottom of the current is dumped on reaching the steep slope, and constitutes the inclined *fore-set* beds... The material in suspension is carried farther, settles more gradually, and constitutes the **bottom-set* beds. **1942** C. A. COTTON *Geomorphology* (ed. 3) xv. 206 In a delta some of the silt layers are covered over by advancing fore-set beds, and then become the *bottom-set beds* of the delta. **1856** COZZENS *Sparrowgr. Papers* vii. 88 It was vexatious enough to see our lawn *bottom-side up on a festive occasion. **1869** *Rep. U.S. Commissioner Agric.* *1868* 327 Put the box in a pan of water and turn it nearly bottom-side up. **1964** *New Scientist* 12 Mar. 686/1 The regions above and below the height of maximum density are generally referred to as the 'topside' and 'bottomside'. **1834** PECK *Gaz. Illinois* II. 150 The *bottom timber consists of oaks [etc.]. **1874** J. W. LONG *Amer. Wild-fowl Shooting* ix. 150 How much better walking it is in this bottom-timber than in the woods of New England. *a* **1877** KNIGHT *Dict. Mech.*, **Bottom-tool*.., a turning-tool having a bent-over end, for cutting out the bottoms of cylindrical hollow work. **1858** *Merc. Mar. Mag.* V. 67 A ship *bottom-up..might easily be taken for a 'danger'. **1694** *Lond. Gaz.* No. 3006/4 More towards the middle to the *bottomward. **1884** *Harper's Mag.* Oct. 801/2 Our heavy *bottom-wigged monarchy outlived that.. invader. **1849** G. SOAME *New Curios. Lit.* I. 151 The *Bottom-Wind has its name from being supposed..to arise from the bottom of those lakes which are situated amongst mountains. **1848** H. W. HAYGARTH *Bush Life Australia* v. 47 The wool nearest the skin, or, as it is called, the '*bottom wool', which is the hardest to cut, but the most weighty and valuable. **1910** *Encycl. Brit.* X. 278/1 It has not..been possible to transform a typical top yeast into a permanent typical *bottom yeast.

bottom (ˈbɒtəm), *v.* [f. prec.]

1. *trans.* To put a bottom to. Cf. BOTTOMED 1.

1544 *Coventry Acc.* in T. Sharp *Dissert.* (1825) 185 Item payd for bottomyng a cressyt vjd. *Mod.* Send this saucepan to be new bottomed.

†**2.** *fig.* **a.** To find a bottom or foundation for; to serve as a bottom for; to establish firmly. *Obs.*

1656 J. BENTHAM *Two..Treat.* (1657) To Rdr., Such grounds..as may sufficiently bottome the Negative in the controversie. **1677** HALE *Prim. Orig. Man.* I. i. 8 We stand in need of the discoveries of sense..to bottom any sound conjecture concerning the Nature, Causes, and effects of the things in Nature. **1685** F. SPENCE *House Medici* 248 He affected to bottom his own repute by disclosing the ignorance of others.

b. ***to bottom upon***: to set upon a foundation; to base, found, ground upon; also *refl.*

1637 SANDERSON *Serm.* II. 88 Upon this base the apostle had bottomed contentation. **1678** NORRIS *Coll. Misc.* (1699) 241, I may not..bottom myself upon such a centre, as will moulder away. *a* **1703** BURKITT *On N.T.* Matt. xi. 6 Such as ..bottom their expectations of heaven and salvation upon him. **1824** COLERIDGE *Aids Refl.* App. xvi, To bottom all our

convictions on grounds of right reason. **1860** FORSTER *Gr. Remonstr.* 67 He bottomed it strongly on the precedents and language of law.

†**c.** *intr.* (for *refl.*) To rest as upon a foundation; to be based, grounded. *lit.* and *fig. Obs.*

c **1630** RISDON *Surv. Devon* §5 (1810) 19 Smallridge takes its name from..a very slender ridge, and bottoms on three parts thereof. **1660–3** J. SPENCER *Prodigies* (1665) 212 In all Knowledg which bottoms upon Experience Men should attend indifferently to any kind of Instances. *a* **1704** LOCKE *Posth. Wks.* (1706) 61 Readily take a view of the Argument, and..see where it bottoms. **1732** BERKELEY *Alciphr.* I. 12. **1790** BURKE *Fr. Rev.* 20 All the oblique insinuations concerning election bottom in this proposition.

†**3.** To wind (as a skein). *fig. Obs.* Cf. BOTTOM *sb.* 15.

1591 SHAKS. *Two Gent.* III. ii. 53 As you vnwinde her loue from him..You must prouide to bottome it on me. **1612** DRAYTON *Poly-olb.* vii. 104 As neatlie bottom'd up as nature forth it drew.

4. a. *trans.* to reach the bottom of; to drain to the bottom, to empty. Also *intr.* To reach the bottom.

1808 *Cumbrian Ballads* liii. 119 They push'd round a glass like a noggin, And bottom'd the greybeard complete. **1845** *Whitehall* xii. 79 The provost..in return bottomed the goblet. **1875** 'STONEHENGE' *Brit. Sports* I. I. xi. §7 A cap..is placed upon the point and pushed into the case till it bottoms. **1882** JEFFERIES *Bevis* I. ix. 140 He bottomed with his feet and stood upright [in the pond].

b. *fig.* To get to the bottom of, examine exhaustively, understand thoroughly.

1785 R. CUMBERLAND in *Observer* No. 102 That mystery is thoroughly bottomed and laid open. **1817** COLERIDGE *Biog. Lit.* I. x. 176 Openly declaiming on subjects..which they had never bottomed. **1860** SMILES *Self-Help* vii. 195 He had bottomed the whole inquiry.

c. *intr.* Of prices, trade, etc.: to reach the lowest level. Also with *out.*

1892 *Daily News* 17 Nov. 7/1 Discount rates appear to have bottomed for the time. **1920** *Glasgow Herald* 6 Sept. 9 Others with shallower purses are content to wait until prices have bottomed. **1958** *Times* 14 July 13/3 With the recession apparently having bottomed out there is now much less insistence..that the Government take some vigorous action. **1969** *Daily Tel.* 21 Apr. 2/1 This is not the time to go liquid. If the index bottoms at 420 unless your timing is absolutely spot on it will pay to sit tight and ride out the squalls. **1970** *Ibid.* 10 Feb. 19/4 Analysts saw the advance as part of the market's 'bottoming out' pattern.

5. a. *trans.* In mining, to reach the bottom of (a mine); to reach a point (in a mine) beyond which further mining is useless; also *absol.*, to get down to the bed-rock or clay; to reach earth which contains gold. So ***to bottom on***: to strike or reach (gold); also *fig.* **b.** *intr.* Said of a claim, etc.: to be worked to the bottom. *Austral.* and *N.Z.*

1853 E. CLACY *Lady's Visit to Gold Diggings of Austral.* v. 73 Their hole had been fairly 'bottomed', a nice little nest of nuggets discovered. **1858** MCCOMBIE *Hist. Victoria* xv. 219 In their anxiety to bottom their claims, they not seldom threw away the richest stuff. **1890** 'R. BOLDREWOOD' *Miner's Right* I. viii. 214 As soon as the main body of block claims began to bottom, gold flowed in with almost fabulous profusion. *Ibid.* II. xiii. 25 Though they had a week's start of us, we bottomed on the same day, and by nightfall the field was aware that Olivera's half-share men had bottomed another duffer. **1892** R. WARDON *McPherson's Gully* 14 They shifted their pegs to fresh ground and again 'set in'—and again bottomed on gold! **1900** H. LAWSON *On Track* 143 One day Peter..told us that his party expected to 'bottom' during the following week. *Ibid.*, Later came the news that 'McKenzie and party' had bottomed on payable gold. **1926** J. DOONE *Timely Tips for New Australians* Gloss., To 'bottom on to gold', to strike gold. To succeed. **1963** A. LUBBOCK *Austral. Roundabout* 79 Shafts have been sunk 'blind',..on the chance of bottoming on 'opal-dirt'.

6. *intr.* In mechanics, to strike or touch the bottom or far end (see quot. *a* 1877).

a **1877** KNIGHT *Dict. Mech.* s.v., Cogs are said to bottom when their tops impinge upon the periphery of the co-acting wheel. A piston which strikes or touches the end of its cylinder is said to bottom. **1959** *Motor Manual* (ed. 36) v. 123 The spring deflections with a full load will become excessive and the vehicle will 'bottom' if a bad bump is encountered.

7. *Electr.* (See quot. 1960.).

1946 *Electronic Engin.* XVIII. 143 A master oscillator produces a sine wave... This is amplified and squared by 'bottoming' a valve anode. **1948** *Ibid.* XX. 63 To operate the screen grid on its negative resistance portion the anode must 'bottom'. **1954** K. W. GATLAND *Devel. Guided Missile* (ed. 2) 237 When a valve 'bottoms' its anode can draw no more current. **1960** H. CARTER *Dict. Electronics* 32 *Bottoming*, a thermionic valve is said to 'bottom' when, by reason of the potential applied to one or other of its grids, the anode current falls to zero.

† **'bottomage.** *Obs.* = BOTTOMRY.

1678 in PHILLIPS; hence in BAILEY, etc.

bottomarie, -ery, obs. forms of BOTTOMRY.

bottomed ('bɒtəmd), *ppl. a.* [f. BOTTOM *sb.* and *v.* + -ED.]

1. Having a bottom; furnished with a bottom of some special material or form; usually in composition, as ***foul-, full-, gravel-, sharp-bottomed.***

1559 *Richmond. Wills* (1853) 135 One trussin bedde bothomed with girth webbe. **1590** GREENE *Fr. Bacon* (1630) 29 In Frigats bottom'd with rich Sethin planks. **1702** W. J. *Bruyn's Voy. Levant* xxxvi. 139 We came into a chamber 18 foot long..the Roof being sharp bottom'd. **1710** *Lond. Gaz.* No. 4691/4 Wearing a light brown Wig, sometimes full bottomed. **1742** R. BLAIR *Grave* 326 Nor margin of the gravel-bottom'd brook. **1841** ORDERSON *Creol.* xvi. 192 Leather-bottomed chairs. *c* **1850** *Rudim. Navig.* (Weale) 100 Vessels..full-bottomed for large cargoes. **1859** F. GRIFFITHS *Artil. Man.* (1862) 114 Unless the shot are bottomed.

b. Covered at the bottom, having as a bottom or foundation.

1799 J. ROBERTSON *Agric. Perth* 485 Most of our extensive mosses are bottomed by clay. **1872** *Daily News* 28 Feb., A narrow creek flanked with warehouses, and bottomed with its fœtid deposit.

2. Founded, based, grounded; mostly *fig.*

c **1645** HOWELL *Lett.* (1650) I. 395 It was far from being any opinion..bottomed upon weak grounds. **1823** LAMB *Elia* Ser. II. x. (1865) 298 Our literary talk..was bottomed well; had good grounds to go upon. **1874** MORLEY *Compromise* 134 A strong and well-bottomed character.

Hence † **'bottomedness**, the quality of resting upon a sure foundation, stability.

1642 ROGERS *Naaman* 19 The freedome, bottomednesse, and unchangeablenesse of the promise.

bottomer ('bɒtəmə(r)). [f. BOTTOM *v.* + -ER[1].] **a.** One who puts a bottom to anything. **b.** One who works at the lowest station. **c.** A draught in which the cup is drained to the bottom.

1723 *Lond. Gaz.* No. 6194/7 Elizabeth Squibb..Cane-Chair Bottomer. **1876** BLACKMORE *Cripps* III. xvi. 259 He firmly restricted good feeling..to three good bumpers, and a bottomer. **1881** RAYMOND *Mining Gloss.*, *Bottomer*, the man stationed at the bottom of a shaft in charge of the proper loading of cages, etc. *a* **1887** *Shop Notice-board.* A. B. Chair-caner, Rush-bottomer.

bottoming ('bɒtəmɪŋ), *vbl. sb.* [f. BOTTOM *v.* + -ING[1].] **1. a.** The action of putting a bottom to anything. **b.** The action of setting on a sure basis. **c.** *concr.* An under layer, a foundation.

1526 *MS. Acc. St. John's Hosp., Canterb.*, Payd for botomyng of a basket. **1642** ROGERS *Naaman* 179 So farre as may further him in the bottoming of the soule in mercy. **1646** H. LAWRENCE *Comm. Angells* Table, Our hopes differ from others..in the bottoming of them by expectation. **1823** MCADAM *Road-making* 49 These previous beds of stone are called the bottoming. **1846** MCCULLOCH *Acc. Brit. Empire* (1854) II. 51 A road..with a foundation or bottoming of large stones.

d. *attrib.*, as **bottoming-hole**, the open mouth of a glass-making furnace; **bottoming-tap**, a square-edged tap for cutting an internal thread uniformly to the bottom of a hole.

1839 URE *Dict. Arts* 582 This spheroid having become cool and somewhat stiff, is next carried to the bottoming hole. *a* **1877** KNIGHT *Dict. Mech.*, *Bottoming-hole*, the open mouth of a furnace at which a globe of crown glass is exposed during the progress of its manufacture, in order to soften it and allow it to assume an oblate form. *a* **1884** *Ibid.*, Suppl., *Bottoming tap*, one for carrying the thread of full size to the bottom of the hole.

2. *Austral.* In mining, the process of reaching bed-rock. Cf. BOTTOM *v.* 5.

1890 'R. BOLDREWOOD' *Miner's Right* I. vii. 189 The bottoming of three or more shafts on the supposed line of lead shall be a sufficient test.

3. *Electr.* See BOTTOM *v.* 7.

bottomless ('bɒtəmlɪs), *a.* [see -LESS.]

1. That has no bottom.

c **1325** *E.E. Allit. P.* B. 1022 For hit [the Dead Sea] is brod & boþemlez, & bitter as þe galle. **1535** COVERDALE *Job* xxxvi. 16 So shall he kepe the..from the bottomlesse pytte that is beneth. **1607** TOPSELL *Four-f. Beasts* 325 Let his neck be yoked in an old bottomless pail. **1641** MILTON *Ch. Govt.* II. Wks. (1851) 180 Unlesse her bottomlesse gorge may be satisf'd with the blood of the Kings daughter the Church. **1710** PALMER *Proverbs* 172 Jupiter puts the discourses and promises of lovers into a bottomless bag. **1860** DICKENS *Uncomm. Trav.* xi, How knowingly (with a sheaf and a bottomless chair at our back) we should lounge on bridges.

b. *fig.* Without foundation, baseless.

1563 DAVIDSON *Confut. Kennedy* in *Misc. Wodrow Soc.* (1844) 241 The rest of his lessone..is on ane boddomles ground. **1642** PRINCE RUPERT *Declar.* 6 Strange, false and bottomlesse untruths. **1866** CRUMP *Banking* viii. 175 Speculators..are often encouraged in their bottomless enterprises by obtaining credits with certain companies.

2. *fig.* Inexhaustible, unfathomable.

1526 TINDALE *Doctr. Treat.* (1848) 400 The judgments of God are bottomless. **1545** BRINKLOW *Lament.* (1874) 86 Oh ye dispisers of the bottomlesse mercy of God. **1640–4** SIR J. CULPEPPER in Rushw. *Hist. Coll.* III. (1692) I. 31 Besides the bottomless Perjury of an *Et cætera*. **1743** TINDAL tr. *Rapin's Hist. Eng.* II. XVII. 129 Bottomless graces and immeasurable benefits. **1826** SCOTT *Woodst.* (1832) 190 He must be bottomless if I cannot sound him before the night's out.

Hence **'bottomlessly** *adv.*, unfathomably; **'bottomlessness**, bottomless state or quality.

1627–8 FELTHAM *Resolves* xix. (1636) 65 Who..is so bottomlessly ill, as to love vice, because it is vice? **1642** ROGERS *Naaman* 180 That wearisomenesse of Selfe, never settled, that bottomelessenesse, never grounded. **1854** THOREAU *Walden* xvi. 306 Men will believe in the bottomlessness of a pond without taking the trouble to sound it.

'bottommost, *a. superl.* [f. BOTTOM *sb.* 18 + -MOST; cf. *topmost.*] That is at the very bottom, lowest.

1861 SALA *Tw. round Clock* 206 The bottommost round of the sporting ladder. **1880** MRS. PARR *Adam & E.* xxi. 292 To set..all the folks..bottommost side upwards. **1884** *Public Opinion* 3 Oct. 427/1 We might arrive at the 'bottommost' lock before nightfall.

† **'bottomrer.** *Obs.* In 7 bodomerer. [f. BOTTOMRY *v.* + -ER[1].] One who lends money on a bottomry bond.

1682 SCARLETT *Exchanges* 253 The sum of the damage..must be deducted from the Sums that *D. E.* and *G.* are to receive, they being as Bodomerers or Assurers.

bottomry ('bɒtəmrɪ). Also 7 **bottommarie, -y, bodomery,** 8 **bottomree, bottomery.** [f. BOTTOM *sb.* 7 + -RY, after Du. *bodmerij.*] A species of contract of the nature of a mortgage, whereby the owner of a ship, or the master as his agent, borrows money to enable him to carry on or complete a voyage, and pledges the ship as security for repayment of the money. If the ship is lost, the lender loses his money; but if it arrives safe, he receives the principal together with the interest or premium stipulated, 'however it may exceed the usual or legal rate of interest'. Also *attrib.*, as in ***bottomry-bond, -money.***

1622 MALYNES *Anc. Law-Merch.* 171 The name Bottommarie is deriued by the Hollanders from the Keele or Bottome of a ship..The money so taken vp by the master of the ship, is commonly done vpon great necessitie..the vse payed for the same is verie great, at 30, 40, and 50 *pro cent.* without consideration of time. **1663** PEPYS *Diary* 30 Nov., A master of a ship who had borrowed twice his money upon the bottomary. **1682** SCARLETT *Exchanges* 253 Amongst conditional bills, Bills of Bodomery may be reckoned, that is, Bills that are made upon the Keele of the Ship, which are accidentially conditional. **1708** *Termes de la Ley* 86 Bottomry. **1741** JOHNSON *Debates Parl.* (1787) I. 218 It is a common practice to take money upon bottomree. **1748** ANSON *Voy.* I. i. 9 The remaining [£] 5000 they raised on bottomry bonds. **1755** MAGENS *Insurances* I. 26 We have no fixed Laws..in England, for settling partial losses on Bottomry-Monies. **1842** PARK *Mar. Insur.* II. xxii. 869 In this consists the difference between bottomry and respondentia, that the one is a loan upon the ship, the other upon the goods. **1848** ARNOULD *Mar. Insur.* I. iii. 76.

bottomry ('bɒtəmrɪ), *v.* [f. prec.] *trans.* To pledge (a ship) as security for money lent: see prec.

1755 MAGENS *Insurances* I. 26 A Master cannot bottomry his whole Ship at a place where her Owners reside. **1848** ARNOULD *Mar. Insur.* III. viii. (1866) II. 931 The repairs abroad for which the ship was bottomried had been done by strangers.

† **'bottomy,** *a. Obs.* [f. BOTTOM *sb.* + -Y[1].] Lying in a 'bottom', low-lying.

1635 SWAN *Spec. M.* (1670) 156 Caused by the Waters..settling themselves in those declive and bottomy places.

bottony, variant of BOTONÉ.

botty ('bɒtɪ). *slang.* [f. BOTTOM *sb.* 1 b + -Y[6].] (See quot. 1874.)

1874 HOTTEN *Slang Dict.* 94 *Botty*,..an infant's posteriors.—*Nursery.* **1922** JOYCE *Ulysses* 759 Like a wellwhipped childs botty. **1924** R. FIRBANK *Prancing Nigger* v. 36 De time de scorpion bit her botty.

botuliform ('bɒtjʊlɪ͵fɔːm), *a.* [ad. mod.L. *botuliformis*, f. L. *botulus* sausage: see -FORM.] Sausage-shaped.

1861 HENSLOW, *Dict. Bot. Terms.*

botulin ('bɒtjuːlɪn). *Med. rare.* [f. L. *botul-us* sausage + -IN[1].] Botulinus toxin (see below). So **botu'linic** *a.*, derived from, pertaining to botulin; **botulinum** (bɒtjuː'laɪnəm) [mod.L.], specific name of the bacillus of botulism, used *attrib.*; **botu'linus** [mod.L. (E. van Ermengem 1896, in *Centralbl. f. Bakteriol.* XIX. 443)], former specific name of the bacillus of botulism, used *attrib.*, as **botulinus toxin**, an exceptionally powerful neurotoxin produced by the bacillus *Clostridium botulinum*, usu. in preserved foods that have been imperfectly sterilized.

1890 BILLINGS *Med. Dict.* 178/2 *Botulinic acid*, Buchner's name for a substance found in poisonous sausages. **1899** *Clinical Jrnl.* 7 June 112/2 An efficient antitoxin for the botulinic poison. **1900** DORLAND *Med. Dict.* 117/1 *Botulin*, a poisonous ptomain sometimes found in preserved meats: it is produced by *Bacillus botulinus.* **1902** MUIR & RITCHIE *Man. Bacteriol.* (ed. 3) xvi. 382 The properties of the botulinus toxin..have been found to correspond closely,..with the toxins of diphtheria and tetanus. **1910** F. W. MOTT in *Allbutt's Syst. Med.* (ed. 2) VII. 185, I have observed also in experimental poisoning by botulin, absinthe, phosphorus, and other poisons,..that the neurons are not equally affected. **1928** W. GILTNER *Elem. Text Bk. Gen. Microbiol.* xviii. 243 The bacteria either split the protein of the food into a toxic molecule..or they secrete a true toxin, —botulinum toxin, while growing in the food. **1929** W. BULLOCH in *Syst. Bacteriology* III. 380 In preserved vegetables..antigenic substances are formed capable of absorbing complement in the presence of ordinary botulinus antitoxin. *Ibid.* 386 Botulinus toxin is unaffected by peptic digestion. *Ibid.* 394 Botulism can hardly arise from the ingestion of botulinus spores. *Ibid.* 397 The botulinus serum should be a polyvalent one. **1962** *Jrnl. Neuropath. & Exper. Neurol.* XXI. 610 Botulinus toxin in its purified form is the most toxic biological substance known. **1970** *Daily Tel.* (Colour Suppl.) 20 Feb. 21 Six ounces of botulinus toxin is enough to kill everybody in

Britain (or North America) if it is distributed in the right way.

botulism ('bɒtjuːlɪz(ə)m). *Med.* [ad. G. *botulismus* (also in Engl. use), f. L. *botul-us* sausage: see -ISM.] Poisoning caused by eating food, usu. imperfectly preserved, that contains botulinus toxin.

1878 W. B. WOODMAN tr. *von Ziemssen's Cycl. Med.* XVII. 539 In the larger towns, botulismus occurs extremely seldom. **1887** A. M. BROWN *Anim. Alkaloids* 156 In Germany it is known by the term *botulism*, a form of poisoning of the organism observed to result from the ingestion of putrefying meats. **1899** *Clinical Jrnl.* 7 June 112/1 This disease or botulism is quite different in its nature. **1922** H. ZINSSER *Textbk. Bacteriol.* (ed. 5) xxxvi. 742 Botulismus toxin is produced under conditions of strict anaërobiosis. **1922** *Times* 6 Sept. 7/3 He had no doubt the deaths in this case were due to botulism, for which disease antitoxins..had proved disappointing. **1959** *Science* 25 Sept. 769/2 In botulism the immediate cause of death is usually a paralysis of the skeletal musculature.

botume, -ym, obs. forms of BOTTOM *sb.*

boture, obs. form of BITTERN, BUTTER.

boty(e, botyng(e, obs. f. BOOTY, BOOTING.

bou, boua, obs. forms of BOUGH, BOW, BOA.

bouat, var. of BOWET, *Sc.*, a lantern.

boucan, boucasin, var. BUCCAN, BOCASIN.

†**bouce Jane.** *Obs. rare*$^{-1}$. A dish in olden cookery, consisting of minced fowl boiled in milk with pot-herbs, currants, etc.

c **1420** *Anc. Cookery* in *Ord. R. Househ.* A. (1790) 431.

†**bouche,** *sb.*^{1} *Obs.* Also 5–7 bouch. See also BOUGE *sb.*^{2} [a. F. *bouche* lit. 'mouth'.]

1. An allowance of victual granted by a king or noble to his household, his attendants on a military expedition, etc. Only in (or with reference to) the phrase ***to have bouche of (in) court*** = F. *avoir bouche à (en) cour* lit. 'to have mouth at court'.

a **1440** *Sir Degrev.* 998 The eorl..ffayre hym gan praye To dwel at hys costage, At bouche and court and wage. **1441** *Plumpton Corr.* Introd. 55 The said people..kept the said towne of Ripon like a towne of warr, takeing some *vid.* a day, & xiid. a day, & bouch of court. **1526** *Househ. Ord.* in *Thynne's Animadv.* (1865) Introd. 38 For their Bouch in the morning, one chet loafe, one manchet, one gallon of ale. **1589** PUTTENHAM *Eng. Poesie* 45 [The emperor] called for Virgil and gave him not onely a present reward, with a good allowance of dyet; a bouche in court, as we use to call it. **1601** in F. TATE *Househ. Ord. Edw. II*, §49 (1876) 31 He shal have for his bouch, iiijd ob. a dai. **1662** FULLER *Worthies* I. 173 All having Bouch of Court, (bread and beer) and six pence a day.

2. Mouth; esp. in phrase ***ball, bullet in (en) bouche***; cf. also *ball* or *bullet in mouth*.

1583 STANYHURST *Æneis* III. (Arb.) 92 Heere loa behold Boreas from bouch of north blo Pelorus Oure ships ful chargeth. **1591** GARRARD *Art Warre* 76 The valiant repulse of a sodaine invading enimie by Bawll en bouche. **1650** SIR W. BUTLER in Carlyle *Cromwell's Lett. & Sp.* Let. cxxiii, With their drums beating, colours flying, matches burning, and bullet in bouch. [**1708** *Lond. Gaz.* No. 4479/5 The Garrison is to march out..with loaded Arms, flying Colours, Drums beating, Match lighted, Ball in Mouth.]

3. *à bouche*: (see quot.)

1864 BOUTELL *Heraldry Hist. & Pop.* iii. (ed. 3) 14 In these shields a curved notch is cut out, for the lance to pass through, in the dexter chief; when thus pierced the shield was said to be *à bouche*.

†**bouche,** *sb.*^{2} *Obs.* Also 6 bowche. [App. variant of BOTCH *sb.*^{1}, confused with BOUGE *sb.*^{1}] A hump, swelling.

a **1300** *Cursor M.* 8087 (Gött.) Crumplid knes, and bouch [*v.r.* bouche, boce] on bac. **1538** *Bury Wills* (1850) 135, iij candylstyke of lattyn, on sylver pece wyth the bowche of the letter in the botom.

bouche (buːʃ), *sb.*^{3} Often written bush; see BUSH *sb.*^{2} [prob. f. BOUCHE *v.* to plug.] A metal plug which is drilled to form the vent or touchhole of a cannon.

1862 F. GRIFFITHS *Artil. Man.* (ed. 9) 186 Bouches, vents. **1867** SMYTH *Sailor's Word-bk.*, *Bush*, or *Bouche*..the plug ..screwed into the metal of the gun at the place of the vent, which is then drilled in it.

†**bouche,** *sb.*^{4} ? misprint for *benche* or *boncke*.

1481 CAXTON *Reynard* (Arb.) 39 Thise traytours..ben now most preuy of counseyl aboute the kynge, and sytte by hym on the hye bouche.

bouche, *v.* [prob. a. F. *boucher* to plug.]

1. *trans.* To insert into (a cannon) the metal plug in which the vent is drilled: see BOUCHE *sb.*^{3}, BUSH *sb.*^{2} Hence **bouching** *vbl. sb.*

1781 *Phil. Trans.* LXXI. 264 If these pieces were bouched with iron..they would stand fire. **1862** F. GRIFFITHS *Artil. Man.* 52 *Bouching a gun* is fixing a pure copper vent into it.

†**2.** (See quot.) *Obs. rare.*

1721 BAILEY, *Bouched him*, stopped his mouth. *O. Phrase.*

‖**bouchées** (buʃe), *sb. pl.* *Cookery.* [a. F. *bouchée* 'mouthful', f. *bouche* mouth.] Small baked confections, patties. Also *sing.* and *attrib.*

1846 SOYER *Cookery* 153 The bouchées must be cut with a fluted cutter not larger than half-a-crown piece. **1928** BLUNDEN *Undertones of War* iii. 27 Their front windows.. exhibited..chocolate bouchées in silver paper. **1960** *Good Housek. Cookery Bk.* 48/2 *Bouchées*, very small pastry cases filled with a savoury mixture, and served as after-dinner savouries, or with cocktails. Special tins, like miniature patty pans (called bouchée moulds), are used to bake the pastry cases.

†**boucher.** *Obs.* Also bowchyer, bowger. [*Boucher* appears to be a corruption of *bowger*, and this a deriv. of *bowge*, BOUGE 'bag, wallet,' perh. in sense of 'purse'; but cf. BOWSER^{1}.] A treasurer, cashier, bursar.

c **1450** *Gregory's Chron.* 139 At the same tabylle the bowgerys of the chauncery. **1494** FABYAN VII. 586 At ye same table sat the bowchyers of the Chauncery. **1583** STANYHURST *Æneis* I. 29 Pigmalions riches..that pinchepeny boucher.

boucher, obs. form of BUTCHER.

boucherize ('buːʃəraɪz), *v.* [f. *Boucherie* the name of a French chemist + -IZE.] *trans.* To impregnate timber with sulphate of copper as a preservative. Hence **'boucherizing** *vbl. sb.*

1871 CULLEY *Handbk. Prac. Telegraphy* 363 The method of boucherising may be described as follows.

†**bouchet.** *Obs.* [? Application of F. *bouchet* a drink composed of sugar, cinnamon, and water.]

1706 PHILLIPS, *Bouchet* (Fr.), a round white Pear, about the bigness of a midling Bergamot, with a fine tender Pulp, and sugar'd Juice; being ripe about the middle of August. **1755** in JOHNSON. **1847** in CRAIG: and in other mod. Dicts.

bouchon (buʃɔ̃). [a. F. *bouchon* plug.] A cylindrical brass plug, tubular at the ends, to be inserted in the plate of a watch when the bearings are considerably worn. (The bouchon is a patent article of French manufacture: the English means of effecting the same purpose is called BUSHING.)

1884 F. BRITTEN *Watch & Clockm.* 35 A bouchon is selected as small as the pivot will admit.

boucht, var. form of BOUGHT.

bouchue, var. or misspelling of BUCHU.

†**'bouchy,** *a.* *Obs. rare.* [? f. BOUCH(E *sb.*^{2} + -Y^{1}.] Bulging, convex.

1398 TREVISA *Barth. De P.R.* v. li. (1495) 168 The thies ben..bouchy afore and haue two sharpnesses.

bouck, boucle, obs. forms of BUCK, BUCKLE.

‖**bouclé** (bukle), *a.* [Fr., = buckled, curled.] (See quot. 1909.) Hence as *sb.*, a yarn of looped or curled ply; fabric made from this.

1895 *Montgomery Ward Catal.* 30/3 Boucle Cloth..plain, smooth weave, over the surface of which is the boucle effects, produced by curly mohair noils of same colors, woven irregularly through the cloth, and having the appearance of silk tufts. **1909** WEBSTER *Bouclé*, woven so as to have a knotted and curled appearance, by using a two-ply yarn one thread of which is partly drawn out into a loop. **1930** *News Chron.* 6 Oct. 13/2 Another good fabric..is bouclé coating, an all-wool material with a bouclé surface. **1960** *Which?* Feb. 39/2 *Bouclé.* Fabric named from its fancy looped yarn, which gives characteristic, uneven surface. Often in wool, silk and viscose rayon. Used for dresses and coats. **1960** *Times* 14 Mar. 15/1 Dior's two-piece of navy bouclé wool. **1964** *Which?* Sept. 284/2 *Loop* or *bouclé*, a compound yarn with loops at regular intervals.

‖**boucon.** *Obs.*$^{-0}$ [F. *boucon* 'a bit, morsell, mouthfull; especially such a one as is empoisoned' (Cotgr.), 'mets ou breuvage empoisonné' (Littré), = Pr. *bocon*, It. *boccone* 'morsel'.]

1706 PHILLIPS, *Boucons* (Fr. in *Cookery*), Veal-stakes rolled up with thin fat slices of Bacon and Gammon. **1730–6** BAILEY.

†**boud.** *Obs.* or *dial.* Also 5 boude, 5–7 bowde, 6 bowd, 8 bood, 9 bude. [Of unknown origin; identity with OE. *budda*, ME. *bod(de* in *scharnboddes* dung-beetles, has been conjectured.] A weevil; an insect or worm which breeds in malt, etc. Also in *comb.*, as ***boud-eaten.***

c **1440** *Promp. Parv.* 46 Bowde, malte-worme, *gurgulio.* **1580** TUSSER *Husb.* (1878) 52 Bowd eaten malt, for health or for profit, find noysome thou shalt. **1691** RAY *S. & E. Country Wds.*, *Bouds*, weevils, an insect breeding in malt. **1713** *Lond. & Countr. Brew.* III. (ed. 2) 222 In some Counties they call it Bood, others Pope, and Whool. **1867** SMYTH *Sailor's Word-bk.*, *Bude*, an old name for the biscuit-weevil.

boud, = behoved: see BUS *v.*

‖**'bouderie.** *rare.* [F. *bouderie.*] Pouting.

1854 THACKERAY *Newcomes* II. 239 Practise artless smiles upon him, gentle little bouderies, tears.

boudget, obs. form of BUDGET *sb.*

‖**boudin** (budɛ̃). [Fr.] A blood-sausage, a black pudding; also, force-meat shaped like a sausage. Also ***white boudin*** [Fr. *boudin blanc*], a white pudding.

1845 E. ACTON *Mod. Cookery* xiii. 279 Small mushrooms ..stewed quite tender in butter may be mixed with the boudin after it is taken from the mortar. **1861** MRS. BEETON *Bk. Househ. Managem.* 472 *Boudins* of a long shape, the size of the dish they are intended to be served on. **1947** M. LOWRY *Under Volcano* i. 25 Puddings known as black or blood puddings..*boudin*, don't you know, Jacques. **1967** C. DURRELL tr. *R. Oliver's French at Table* viii. 316 The hors d'œuvre..were..solid stuff: sausage, white *boudin*, truffled pasties.

boudin, var. BOLDEN *ppl. a.* *Sc. Obs.* swollen.

‖**boudoir** (budwar). [a. F. *boudoir* lit. 'a place to sulk in', f. *bouder* to pout, sulk.] **a.** A small elegantly-furnished room, where a lady may retire to be alone, or to receive her intimate friends. Formerly sometimes applied to a man's private apartment.

1781 HAYLEY *Tri. Temper* II. 130 As the French boudoir to the Gothic tower, Such is the peer, whom fashion much admires, Compar'd in person to his ancient sires. **1785** COWPER *Let. to J. Hill* 25 June, I write in a nook that I call my boudoir. **1786** J. ADAMS *Diary* Wks. 1851 III. 405 In what he calls his boudoir—a little room between his library and drawing-room. **1851** KINGSLEY *Yeast* ii. 24 Argemone was busy in her boudoir (too often a true boudoir to her). **1886** MORLEY *Crit. Misc.* I. 31 The paltry affairs of the boudoir and the ante-chamber.

b. *transf.* The occupants of a boudoir.

a **1830** HAZLITT *Vulgarity*, The callous insensibility of the drawing room and boudoir.

c. *attrib.*

1803 *Lett. Miss Riversdale* III. 92 The duke had fitted up these pretty little *boudoir* recesses. **1858** BAGEHOT *Coll. Works* (1965) II. 50 The *Lady of the Lake* is a sort of *boudoir* ballad. **1903** *Daily Chron.* 17 Jan. 8/4 A dressing gown..is sometimes glorified..into a compromise between a dressing gown and a teagown, and then is known as a boudoir gown. **1912** in A. ADBURGHAM *Shops & Shopping* (1964) xxii. 258, 2 boudoir caps, at 18/9. **1914** WYNDHAM LEWIS *Let.* 2 Apr. (1963) 59 The boudoir suggestiveness and Yellow Book Gallicisms. **1937** M. SHARP *Nutmeg Tree* vii. 78 Mrs. Packett was sitting up in bed wearing a very smart boudoir-cap. **1966** COX *Illustr. Dict. Hairdressing & Wigmaking* 23/2 *Boudoir helmet*, a decorated hair net of silk or other suitable material for wear by a woman in her boudoir to keep her hair in position during her toilet activity.

Hence **boudoi'resque** *a.* [see -ESQUE], of the kind appropriate to a boudoir. **'boudoirize** *v.* [see -IZE], to sit in or frequent a boudoir.

1880 MRS. C. READE *Brown Hand & White* II. iii. 59 How fond modern French painters seem to be of boudoiresque humanity. **1883** *Harper's Mag.* July 321/1 'It is a sweet hour', said Glorvina..'It is a *boudoirising* hour', said I.

boue, bouwe, obs. forms of BOW *v.*

boueer, bouel, obs. ff. BOOR, BOWER, BOWEL.

bouerd, var. of BOURD *sb.* and *v.* *Obs.*, jest.

†**'bouerie.** *Obs. rare*$^{-1}$. [ad. Du. *bouwerij*, f. *bouwer* peasant: cf. BOWERY, BOOR.] Boorishness.

1577 HOLINSHED *Descr. Brit.* II. ix. 178 King John..did extinguish it [the ordeal]..as flat lewdnesse and bouerie.

bouet, var. of BOWET, *Sc.*, a lantern.

bouf, boufaleau, obs. ff. BEEF, BUFFALO *sb.*

†**'bouffage.** *Obs. rare*$^{-1}$. [a. OF. *bouffage* 'any meat that (eaten greedily) fils the mouth, and makes the cheeks to swell; cheeke-puffing meat' Cotgr.] A satisfying meal.

1672 SIR T. BROWNE *Let. to Friend* ix. (1881) 134 His inwards and flesh remaining could make no bouffage, but a light bit for the grave.

‖**bouffant(e** (bufɑ̃, -ɑ̃t), *a.* [F. *bouffant*, *-ante*, pr. pple. of *bouffer* to swell.]

a. *Dressmaking.* Puffed out, bulging.

1880 *Cassell's Mag.* June 441 Dress improvers are coming in..and all the Parisian short dresses are more or less bouffante. **1883** *Ibid.* Nov. 756/2 Mantles..are..quite short at the back, and bouffant.

b. Of a hair-style: puffed out; arranged in a swelling or fluffy style. Hence as *sb.*, such a hair-style.

1955 *Vanity Fair's Guide for Bride* 52 René..designed a simple hairstyle... Watch that smooth but bouffant silhouette. **1959** S. GIBBONS *Pink Front Door* xx. 232 Her eyes glistened dreamily within their little burrow of white wool and *bouffant* fair hair. **1959** *Sunday Times* 27 Sept. 21/1 The bouffant, hair-styler's joy and milliner's grief. **1966** *Economist* 9 Apr. 130/1 Since lofty bouffant hairdos have long been favoured here, Spain had a head start in the manufacture of..switches, chignons, postiches, wiglets and wigs.

†**bouffe**^{1}. *Obs.* [cf. F. *bouffée* puff of wind or steam, f. *bouffer* to swell the cheeks.] A puff.

1475 CAXTON *Jason* 74 He apperceyuid many bouffes of flambe..springe into the ayer.

‖**bouffe**^{2} (buf). [a. F. *bouffe*, ad. It. *buffa* jest.] Short for *Opéra bouffe* comic opera: see OPERA.

bouffon, boufoon, obs. ff. BUFFOON.

‖**Bougainvillæa** (buːgeɪnvɪ'liːə, commonly buːgən'vɪlɪə). Also **-ea, -ia.** [Named after the Fr. navigator Bougainville 1729–1811.] A genus of tropical plants of the order *Nyctaginaceæ*, having flowers almost concealed by large leafy bracts.

1866 *Treas. Bot.* I. 160/2 *Bougainvillæa spectabilis* is a climbing shrub or small tree, with alternate leaves and small spines. **1881** MRS. PRAED *Policy & Pass.* I. 145 A wide verandah..festooned by bougainvillea. **1883** *Sunday Mag.* Sept. 547/2 Cascades of bougonvillias, passion-flowers, banksias and roses.

'bougar ('buːgə(r)). *Sc.* Etymology unknown.
1. *pl.* 'Cross spars, forming part of the roof of a cottage, used instead of laths.' Jamieson.

a **1550** *Christis Kirke Gr.* xiv, With bougars of barnis thay beft blew kappis. **1858** M. PORTEOUS *Souter Johnny* 28 This braw lid Made frae the bougars o' the Kirk.

2. *Comb.*, as **bougar-stakes**, 'the lower part of rafters, that were set on the ground in old houses'; **bougar-sticks**, 'strong pieces of wood fixed to the..rafters of a house by wooden pins'.

†**bouge**, *sb.*[1] *Obs.* or *dial.* Also 4–6 **bowge.** [a. OF. *bouge* (also *boulge, buge, buche*, Godef.) a small leather bag or wallet:—L. *bulga* a leathern bag, also the womb; of Gaulish origin (Festus): OIr. *bolg, bolc*, a sack. The variant BULGE is found still earlier, and runs parallel to *bouge* in senses 1 and 2; 2 has also the variant form BULCH; 3 has the parallel and later form BILGE.]

†**1.** A wallet or bag, *esp.* one made of hide; a skin-bottle; = BULGE *sb.* 1. *Obs.*

1387 TREVISA *Higden* (Rolls Ser.) VII. 385 His malys were i-serched his bouges and his trussynge cofres. **1388** WYCLIF *Ps.* xxxii. 7 He gaderith togidere the watris of the see as in a bowge [**1382** botel]. *c* **1440** *Promp. Parv.* 46/1 Bowge, *bulga*. *c* **1470** *Hors, Shepe, & G.* (1822) 7 By draught of horse fro ryuers & wellis Bouges be brought to brewars for good ale. **1557** PAYNELL *Barclay's Jugurth* 96 He charged bottels and bowges to the hydes of the same beaste. **1600** HOLLAND *Livy* XXI. xxvii. 408 Fastning their apparrell to bouges of lether like bladders [*in utres*].

b. *Her.* Cf. BOUGET.

1572 BOSSEWELL *Armorie* II. 30b, D. beareth Or, three water bowges Sable in chefe.

†**2.** A swelling, a hump; = BULGE *sb.* 2. *Obs.*

1398 TREVISA *Barth. De P.R.* v. xl. (1495) 155 The caas of the galle is a certayne skynne sette vppon the bowges of the lyuer. *c* **1430** in Wyclif *Lev.* xxi. 20 (MS. S.) If he hath a botche *or a bouge on his bak.* **1483** *Cath. Angl.* 38 A Bowge, *gibbus, struma.*

3. The protuberant part of a cask; = BILGE 2.

1741 *Compl. Fam. Piece* I. v. 266 Then give it Vent at the Bouge, with a Hole made with a Gimblet. **1750** W. ELLIS *Mod. Husbandman* IV. ii. 109 Turning the cask sideways, on its bouge, immediately cork up the lower holes. **1867** SMYTH *Sailor's Word-bk.* 122 *Bouge* or *Bowge and Chine*, or *Bilge and Chimb*, the end of one cask stowed against the bilge of another. **1875** PARISH *Sussex Dial.*, *Bouge*, a water cask. The round swelling part of a cask.

4. A cowrie. *rare.* [a. F. *bouge* 'coquillage servant de monnaie aux Indes' (Boiste).]

1875 JEVONS *Money* iv. 24 The cowry shells, which, under one name or another—chamgos, zimbis, bouges, etc.

5. *Comb.*, as (sense 1) *bouge-maker, -man*; **bowge-work**, bulged or raised work.

1530 PALSGR. 187 *Faysevr de bahus*, a lether coofer maker or a bouge maker. *c* **1500** *Cocke Lorelles B.* 10 Tankarde berers, bouge men, and spere planers. **1596–7** BOND in *Hist. Croydon* App. (1783) 154 The windoes with bowge worke.

†**bouge**, *sb.*[2] *Obs.* Also 5 **bowge**, 7 **budge.** Corrupt form of BOUCHE *sb.*[1], court-rations; also used by Ben Jonson in the sense of 'provisions'.

1461–83 *Ord. R. Househ., Liber Niger Edw. IV*, 19 The Lyvery for horses at bouge of Court, of gentlemen & many other, &c. now is lefte. **1540** *St Papers Hen. VIII*, I. 623 Every of them to have lyke bouge of courte. **1611** COTGR., *Avoir bouche à Court*, to eat and drinke scotfree, to haue budge-a-Court, to be in ordinarie at Court. *a* **1616** B. JONSON *Love Restor.* 87 A bombard man, that brought bouge for a Countrey Lady or two that fainted..with fasting. —— *Mercurie Vind.* Wks. (1692) 377, I am to deliver the buttry in, so many firkins of aurum potabile, as it delivers out bombards of budge to them.

†**bouge**, *sb.*[3] *Obs. rare.* A species of trout.

1705 *Act 4 Anne* viii, *Bouges*, otherwise called Sea Trouts.

†**bouge**, *sb.*[4] *Obs. rare*[−1]. (possibly misprint.) A horsehair noose.

1725 BRADLEY *Fam. Dict.* I. s.v. *Ducks*, Fasten your Collars or slipping Bouges to the End of your Stick.

bouge, *sb.*[5] In silver manufacture, a hollow running round any article.

†**bouge**, *v.* *Obs.* Also 5–7 **bowge**, 6 **boulge, budge.** [f. BOUGE *sb.*[1]: there are also partially differentiated variants BILGE, BULGE, and BULCH.]

1. *trans.* To stave in a ship's bottom or sides, cause her to spring a leak; = BILGE *v.* 1.

1485 CAXTON *Trevisa's Higden* VII. xxvi (1527) 284 He..toke..one of the Soudans grete shyppes..and bowged and thyrled it in yᵉ nether syde. **1577** HOLINSHED *Chron.* III. 15/2 Sir Anthonie Oughtred folowing the Regent at the sterne, bowged hir in diverse places, and set hir powder on fire. *Ibid.* II. xvii. (1877) 288 Our ships will either bowge those of other countries or put them to flight. **1580** NORTH *Plutarch* (1676) 460 He had fewer galleys than they, yet he budged divers of theirs and sunk them. **1600** HOLLAND *Livy* XXI. l. 421 One vessell..was bouged and pierced [*perforata*].

2. *intr.* To suffer fracture in the bilge; = BILGE *v.* 2.

a **1577** GASCOIGNE *Voy. Holland*, Lest therupon Our shippe should bowge.

3. To swell out, to bulge; = BULGE *v.* 3.

1398 [see BOUGING.] **1647** H. MORE *Song of Soul* I. I. xlvi, From this first film all bulk in quantity Doth bougen out. **1851** S. JUDD *Margaret* ii. 6 When it reaches the stone that bouges out there.

bouge, obs. form of BUDGE.

†**bouged**, *ppl. a.* *Obs.* [f. BOUGE *v.* + -ED.] Having the bottom staved in; = BULGED 2.

1580 H. GIFFORD *Gilloflowers* (1875) 146 Not halfe so fast the bowdged shippe, The water in doth drinke.

†**bougeron.** *Obs. rare.* [OF.] A sodomite.

c **1400** *Rom. Rose* 7024 If ther be castel or citee Wherynne that ony bougerons be. **1675** COTTON *Poet. Wks.* (1765) 192 Thou now speak'st perfect, Bougeroon.

bouget ('buːdʒɪt). *Her.* Also 6 **boget**, 7 **bowget.** [Earlier spelling of BUDGET *sb.*] A representation of an ancient water vessel, consisting of a yoke with two leathern pouches, or buckets, attached.

[**1486** *Bk. St. Albans, Her.* B iv b, Gorgys be called in armys water bulgees.] **1592** WYRLEY *Armorie* 136 Who did in gules three siluer Bogets bear. **1688** R. HOLME *Armory* III. vi. 75 He beareth Or, a Water Bowget, Sable. **1859** TURNER *Dom. Archit.* III. II. vii. 250 Two shields of arms, on one of which are three water bougets.

†**bouget.** Misprint or bad spelling for BOUGHT, the bend of the elbow.

1548 VICARY *Englishm. Treas.* (1626) 30 Till it appeare in the bouget of the arme.

bough (baʊ), *sb.* Forms: 1–2 **bóh, bóᵹ**, 2–4 **boȝ**, 2–3 **boȝh, bou**, 3 **bohu, bohw, bouh, buȝ**, 3–4 **bugh**, 3–5 **bogh**, 3–7 **bow**, 4 **boghe, (boght), boow, bouȝ(e, bouw, bowȝe, buh**, 4–6 **bowe**, 5 **boe**, *Sc.* **bwy**, 5–6 *Sc.* **bew**, 5–7 **boughe**, 6 **bewch, boowe, bouwe**, 5–9 *Sc.* **beugh**, 5– **bough.** [Common Teut.: OE. *bóᵹ, bóh* = OHG. *buog* (MHG. *buoc*, mod.G. *bug*) shoulder, foreleg; MDu. *boech*, Du. *boeg*, ON. *bôg-r* shoulder, bow of a ship:—OTeut. **bôgu-z*:—Aryan **bhāghu-s*, Skr. *bāhu-s* arm. foreleg, Gr. *πᾶχυς* fore-arm.

The sense 'bough of a tree' appears to be of exclusively Eng. development; the Bow of a ship is ultimately the same word, but of recent adoption from Scandinavian or Low German. Notwithstanding a certain fitness of sense, this word is in no way related to the vb. stem **beug-*, OE. *búg-an* to BOW.]

†**1.** The shoulder of an animal. *Obs.*

c **1000** ÆLFRIC *Ex.* xxix. 22 þu nymst þone rysle of þam ramme..& þone swyþran boh. ? *a* **1400** *Morte Arth.* 188 Seyne bowes of wylde bores with þe braune lechyde.

2. A limb, leg. *Sc.*

c **1550** A. SCOTT in *Evergreen* II. 183. xvi, Ryde down this brae, Thocht ye suld brek a beugh. **1706** in Watson's *Coll. Poems* I. 46 (JAM.) Came and tuik her by the beugh.

3. a. One of the larger limbs or offshoots of a tree, a main branch; but also applied to a smaller branch.

c **1000** *Ags. Gosp.* Matt. xxi. 8 Sume heowun þæra treowa boᵹas [*c* **1160** *Hatton* boᵹes]. *c* **1200** *Trin. Coll. Hom.* 219 þe huuemeste bou of þe treuwe. *c* **1200** ORMIN 10002 All cwike & grene boȝhess. *c* **1250** *Gen. & Ex.* 608 A grene oliues boȝ. *a* **1300** *Cursor M.* 8291 Apon a bogh þan can he seit. *c* **1420** *Anturs of Arth.* iv. (1842) 2 Vndur boes thay byde. **1423** JAS. I. *King's Q.* xxxv, From beugh to beugh thay hippit and thai plaid. *c* **1450** HENRYSON *Mor. Fab.* 45 The Bewes braid blomed about mine head. *c* **1500** *God speed Plough* 30 Our payment shalbe a styk of A bough. **1555** EDEN *Decades W. Ind.* III. x. 183, To couer the same with bouwes. **1653** WALTON *Angler* 154 Fasten that line to any bow. **1716–8** LADY M. W. MONTAGUE *Lett.* I. xxxviii. 150 Followed by a man dressed in green boughs. **1875** B. TAYLOR *Faust* I. xxi. 182 Boughs are groaning and breaking.

†**b.** *transf.* and *fig.* A main branch, as of a vein or artery; a branch of a family, or of anything metaphorically referred to as a tree. *Obs.*

a **1225** *Ancr. R.* 336 Bigin uormest et prude, & sech alle þe bowes þerof. *a* **1300** *Cursor M.* 24274 All sal be sauued thoru a man þat born es on þis bogh. **1330** R. BRUNNE *Chron.* 40 He wedded þe dukes douhter..þre bouwes of þam spronge. **1526** *Pilgr. Perf.* (W. de W. 1531) 54b, The religyous persone shold not..haue..deed bowes ne corrupte braunches. **1668** CULPEPPER & COLE *Barthol. Anat.* I. vi. 12 The Boughs of the Vein..are sent unto the transverse Muscle.

4. *transf.* A gallows: cf. similar use of *tree*. *Legal Proverb.* 'The father to the bough, the son to the plough': supposed to mean that, according to Kentish custom, attainder for felony does not deprive a man's children of the succession to his property. *arch.*

1590 SWINBURN *Testaments* 53 Or in Kent in Gauelkind..for there it is said, the father to the boughe, and the son to the ploughe. **1596** SPENSER *State Irel.* Wks. (1862) 553/2 Some..have beene for their goods sake caught up, and carryed straight to the bough. **1870** MORRIS *Earthly Par.* III. IV. 77 If she doom thee to the bough.

5. *Comb.*, as **bough-flecked** *a.*, flecked by the partial shadow of boughs (*poet.*); **bough-house**, (*a*) *U.S.*, a temporary structure made of boughs; (*b*) *dial.*, see quot. 1852; **bough-runes**, Stephens's name for the runic characters modified so as to resemble branching trees; also **boughless** adj.

1870 MORRIS *Earthly Par.* III. IV. 404 The *bough-flecked dazzling light of mid-day shone. **1811** WILSON *Amer. Ornith.* III. 111 Their destroyers construct for themselves lurking holes made of pine branches, called **bough-houses.* **1852** *N. & Q.* 17 Apr. 371/2 Witnesses spoke of a 'bough-house', and the explanation given was, that certain houses where beer, &c. was sold at fair-time only had boughs outside to indicate their character. **1882** MRS. CHAMBERLAIN *Gloss. West Worcs. Words* 4 *Bough-house*, house opened at fair-time only, for the sale of liquor. (Pershore.) Suppressed 1863. **1894** *Outing* (U.S.) July 281/1 Down in the bough house the campers reclined. **1946** BLUNDEN *Shelley* i. 20 To the July Fair..folk came in from the country by hundreds and thousands, and 'bough houses' for their refreshment crowded the roadways. **1839** *Fraser's Mag.* XX. 345 A birch-tree, entirely *boughless, branchless, and twigless. **1868** G. STEPHENS *Runic Mon.* I. 240 The Ice-runes are read in the same way as the *Bough-runes on the Maeshoue stones. **1669** J. WORLIDGE *Syst. Agric.* (1681) 249 Field-fares and *Bow-thrushes.

†**bough**, *v.*[1] *Obs.* [f. prec. sb.] **a.** *trans.* To strip of boughs. **b.** *intr.* To send out boughs.

1523 FITZHERB. *Husb.* §132 Dresse the wode and bowe it clene, and cut it at euery byght. **1852** [see BOUGHED].

†**bough**, *v.*[2] *Obs.* exc. *Sc.* (pron. baʊx) [f. the sound; cf. BOW-WOW.] *intr.* To bark as a dog. Hence **'boughing** *ppl. a.*

1566 STUDLEY *Seneca's Agamem.* (1581) 155b, Nor barke with any boughinge throate.

bough, obs. form of BO[2], BOW.

†**'boughage.** *Obs.* [f. BOUGH *sb.*[1] + -AGE: cf. *branchage*.] Boughs collectively.

1594 CAREW *Tasso* (1881) 71 High Firres, Beeches, and Holmes of thicke bowage.

boughed (baʊd), *ppl. a.* [f. BOUGH *sb.* and *v.*[1] + -ED.] **a.** Having boughs (chiefly with descriptive adj., as ***dark-boughed, low-boughed***); also, covered or shaded with boughs. **b.** Stripped of (its) boughs.

c **1400** *Lay le Freine* 169 An asche..fair and heighe, Wele y-bowed. **1725** SLOANE *Jamaica* II. 304 They build their nests in low bough'd trees. **1805–6** COLERIDGE *3 Graves* III. iii, A mossy track all over boughed. **1852** TUPPER *Proverb. Philos.* 391 The tree is felled, and boughed, and bare. **1877** M. ARNOLD *Grande Chartreuse*, Many a dark-bough'd pine.

boughery ('baʊərɪ). *nonce-wd.* [f. BOUGH + -ERY; cf. *rookery*.] A structure of boughs.

1855 *Household Wds.* XII. 435 Each family was squatted down under a few gum-tree boughs..all except the unmarried young men, who were located in groups at bougheries of their own.

boughie, obs. form of BOUGHY.

bough-pot ('baʊpɒt). *arch.* or *dial.* Also 7 **bow-pott**, 7– **bow-pot.** [f. BOUGH *sb.* + POT: cf. BEAU-POT.] A pot or other vessel for holding boughs, etc., for ornament; a flower-pot; in 19th c. also a bunch of flowers, bouquet.

1583 J. HIGINS *Junius' Nomenclator* 388 Bough-pots, or flower pots set in the windows of private houses. **1665** PEPYS *Diary* 13 Sept., The wind..flung down a great bow-pott that stood upon the side-table. **1777** SHERIDAN *Sch. Scand.* III. iii, Not..a twig but what's in the bough-pots out of the window. **1841** *Blackw. Mag.* L. 206 Bough-pots decorate their windows. **1848** THACKERAY *Van. Fair* i, 'We have made her a bow-pot.' 'Say a bouquet..'tis more genteel.' **1884** *Leisure Hour* Apr. 233/1 Removed to make place [in grates] for the 'bough-pots', or posies.

†**bought**, *sb.*[1] *Obs.* Forms: α. 5 **bouȝt, bowght**, 6 **boughte, bught(e**, 4–7 **bought**; β. 6 **bowt(e**, 6–7 **bout.** [A comparatively late word (certain only from 15th c.); parallel in its senses to BIGHT, ME. *byȝt*, OE. *byht*; and corresp. in form and sense to MLG. *bucht* (whence modG. *bucht*, Du. *bocht*, Da. and Sw. *bugt*). The Eng. word may also have been from LG.; but more probably it arose out of an assimilation of *byght* to BOW *v.*, or was itself formed from BOW on the pattern of *byght*, etc. (cf. *Bucht* in Grimm). When the guttural became weak or mute, *bought* began apparently to be associated with the adv. *'bout, about* (see 2 b, quot. 1435), and in 16–17th c. was commonly spelt *bout*, whence, with special development of sense, the current BOUT, *sb.*[2] q.v.]

†**1. a.** A bend or curve; *esp.* a hollow angle or bend in the animal body. Cf. BIGHT 1. *Obs.*

α. **1519** HORMAN *Vulg.* 25b, There is a scabbe in the bought of myne arme [*in ancone*]. **1530** PALSGR. 200/2 Bought of the arme, *le ply du bras.* **1551** RECORDE *Pathw. Knowl.* I. vii, To make a plumbe lyne..on the vtter or inner bughte [of a circle]. **1610** MARKHAM *Masterp.* II. lxv. 327 Ouerthwart the very bought or inward bent of the knee. **1658** FRANCK *North. Mem.* (1821) 159 On the bought of her near buttock was branded a remarkable patch.

β. **1609** C. BUTLER *Fem. Mon.* (1634) 40 If there be any crook or bout in the Belt. **1634** T. JOHNSON *Parey's Chirurg.* XVI. xxxiii. (1678) 364 If the elbow be dislocated..some put some round thing into the bout of the elbow.

†**b.** A bending in a coast-line, mountain-chain, etc. Cf. BIGHT 3. *Obs.*

α. **1480** CAXTON *Chron. Eng.* ccxxiii. 222 They..met the baillol and his companye at an hongyng bought of the more.
β. **1587** FLEMING *Contn. Holinshed* III. 1331/2 To enter in at the great chanell of Middleborough by the bout of the foreland. **1610** HOLLAND *Camden's Brit.* I. 643 In the very boute well neere of the shore. **1675** *Pennsylv. Archives* I. 34 Over agt the Boute aboue Verdrick-teige-hooke.

†**2. a.** The bend or loop of a rope, string, or chain; the part between the ends or points of attachment (cf. BIGHT 2); the fold of a cloth, etc.; a turn or involution; also *fig.*, and in *comb.* as ***bought-wise***.
α. *c* **1460** J. RUSSELL *Bk. Nurture* in *Babees Bk.* (1868) 129 Draw streight þy clothe, & ley þe bouȝt on þe vttur egge of þe table. **1570** LEVINS *Manip.* 217 A Bought, *plica.* **1611** BIBLE *1 Sam.* xxv. 29 *marg.*, In the midst of the bought of a sling. **1616** SURFL. & MARKH. *Country Farm* 712 Net.. fastened bought-wise unto the end of a long pole.
β. **1562** *Inv. Q. Mary's Dresses* in *Sat. Rev.* (1863) 12 Dec. 764/2 [Fardingales..expanded by whalebones] bowtis of quhaill horne. **1575** BANISTER *Chyrurg.* II. (1585) 279 Let it be tyed first with ij inuolutions or bowtes. **1632** MILTON *L'Allegro* (1863) 140 In notes, with many a winding bout Of linkèd sweetness long drawn out. *a* **1648** LD. HERBERT *Life*, One curl rising by degrees above another, and every bout tied with a small ribband.

b. A coil, fold, or 'knot' formed by the body of a serpent, the tail of a horse, etc. Now *poet.* (revived by Tennyson).
α. [*c* **1300** *K. Alis.* 4712 Of theose bought was heore croune.] *c* **1435** *Torr. Portugal* 558 Abowght the schyld he lappyd yt ther, Torrent the bowght asondyr schere. **1591** SPENSER *Virg. Gnat* 255 He..wrapt his scalie boughts with fell despight. **1633** H. COGAN *Pinto's Trav.* xxxv. (1663) 140 An Adder of Brass, infolded into I know not how many boughts.
β. **1596** SPENSER *F.Q.* I. xi. 11 His huge long tayle..Whose wreathed bouts when euer he vnfoldes.
1872 TENNYSON *Gareth & Lynette* p. 16 The dragon-boughts and elvish emblemings Began to move, seethe, twine and curl. **1906** C. M. DOUGHTY *Dawn in Britain* IV. xv. 148 Like as some serpent, which..in the sun, displays her glittering boughts.

†**3.** (cf. BOUGHT *v.*[1] quot. 1521.) *Obs.*
1480 CAXTON *Chron. Eng.* lxviii, The beme of that sterre was bryghter than the sonne and at the bouȝt of the beme appered a dragons hede. *Ibid.* lxix, The hede of the dragon that is seyn at the bought of the beem.

bought, bught (bauxt, bʌxt), *sb.*[2] *Sc.* Also bowght, boucht, bucht. [Etymology obscure: it answers in form to the prec.; but the connexion of sense is uncertain. The Gael. *buchd* appears to be from Lowl. Sc.]
1. A sheep-fold; *spec.* a pen for confining ewes at milking-time.
1513 DOUGLAS *Æneis* IX. ii. 64 As we se..The wyld wolf ..Abowt the bowght [*v.r.* boucht] plet al of wandis tyght. **1813** HOGG *Kilmeny* xxiv, Broke from their boughts and faulds.
2. 'A square seat in a church, a table-seat.' Jam.
3. *Comb.*, as *bought-door, -seat.*
1807 HOGG *Mt. Bard* 27 (JAM.) The bught door is always carefully shut at even.

†**bought,** *v.*[1] *Obs.* Also 6 bowght, bowt, 8 *Sc.* bught. [f. BOUGHT *sb.*[1]] *trans.* and *intr.* To bend, wind, fold; to link.
1521 FISHER *Wks.* 324 Nor a syngle beme of the sonne is nothynge so myghty as whan it is doubled and bowghted in itselfe by reboundynge and reflexyon. **1555** *Fardle Facions* I. vi. 100 Nature hath made..hollow Guttres, and Criekes into the maigne lande, bowtyng and compassyng in and out. **1832** *Whistle-Binkie* (Sc. Songs) I. (1853) 121 When the canvassin' cam' round, the member walk'd about, And bughted i' the Provost's arm.

bought, bught, *v.*[2] *Sc.* [f. BOUGHT *sb.*[2]]
1. *trans.* To pen or fold (sheep). Hence **'boughting** *vbl. sb.*
1724 RAMSAY *Tea-T. Misc.* (1733) I. 72 At boughting-time to leave the plain In milking to abide thee. **1792** BURNS *My ain kind Dearie*, The eastern star Tells bughtin-time is near, my jo.
2. *gen.* To inclose, fence in; hence **'boughted** *ppl. a.* **bouchting-blanket,** 'a small blanket, spread across a feather-bed, the ends being pushed in under the bed at both sides' (Jamieson).
1807–10 TANNAHILL *Bonnie Wood Craigie Lee*, The mavis, down thy bughted glade, Gars echo ring frae every tree.

bought (bɔːt), *ppl. a.* [pa. pple. of BUY, which see for forms.]
a. Purchased; freq. in comb. ***dear-bought*** (cf. *dere abought* under ABYE). ***bought-book***: (*Comm.*) a book for keeping an account of bought goods. ***bought-in***, ***bought-out***: purchased from an outside source (*i.e.* not raised or produced on one's own premises). (See also BUY *v.* 6, 8.) **b.** *fig.* (see senses of BUY) Ransomed, gained by a sacrifice; also bribed, etc. †***bought plea***: a groundless accusation.
1599 PORTER *Angry Wom. Abingd.* (1841) 104 Tis an olde prouerbe..bought wit is the best. **1636** RUTHERFORD *Lett.* lxxv. (1862) I. 193 This was but a bought plea and I was a fool. **1646** CRASHAW *Delights of Muses* (1652) 134 More than ..a bought blush, or a set smile. **1700** DRYDEN *Palamon & Arc.* 1687 Bought senates and deserting troops are mine. **1796** BURKE *Regic. Peace* ii. Wks. VIII. 230 Dear-bought advantages. **1849** FREESE *Comm. Class-bk.* 101 The Bought, or, Bills of Parcels Book, into which are entered the particulars of all goods bought. **1894** *Daily News* 8 June 9/6 Several parcels have been cleared since the late auctions, at the bought-in prices. **1947** N. BALCHIN *Aircraft Builders* 26 Joint committees on..materials, sub-contracting, and bought-out parts, and spares. **1960** *Farmer & Stockbreeder* 16 Feb. 109 Bought-in store cattle.

boughten ('bɔːt(ə)n), *ppl. a.* [irreg. f. BOUGHT *ppl. a.* by assimilation to *foughten.*] = BOUGHT *ppl. a.* Used *poet.* for the sake of metre; otherwise only *dial.* and in U.S. in application to purchased as opposed to home-made articles.
1793 COLERIDGE *Robespierre* III. Wks. III. 36 The Commune's villain friendship, And Henriot's boughten succours. **1805** SOUTHEY *Madoc in W.* xiv, Whose faith Reck'd not of boughten prayers, nor passing bell. **1825** *Bro. Jonathan* I. 131 Leather shoes, and white, 'boughten' stockings.

†**'boughtling.** *Obs. rare.* In 3 boghtling. [? f. BOUGHT *pa. pple.* of BUY + -LING.] One bought or ransomed.
a **1300** *Cursor M.* 17262 [I] euer..haf thoght..O þi boghtlinges hu þou boght.

†**boughty** ('baʊtɪ), *a. Obs.* [f. BOUGHT *sb.*[1] + -Y[1].] Bent, curved; having one or several bends.
1570 LEVINS *Manip.* 111 Boughty, *intricatus.* **1611** COTGR., *Cornu*, crooked, or boughtie, like a horne. —— s.v. *Asne*, Bowed, boughtie, or bowing.

bough-wough, var. form of BOW-WOW.

boughy ('baʊɪ), *a.* Also 6–7 boughie. [f. BOUGH *sb.* + -Y[1].] Abounding in boughs.
1570 LEVINS *Manip.* 111 Boughy, *ramosus.* **1610** G. FLETCHER *Christ's Vict.* in Farr's *S.P.* (1847) 62 Her watchman, arm'd with boughie crest. **1832** J. WILSON in *Blackw. Mag.* XXXI. 988 Surprising Sir Ralph..on briary, broomy, and boughy ground. **1848** THOREAU *Maine W.* i. (1867) 37 The drear and boughy wilderness.

‖**bougie** (buʒi). [a. F. *bougie* wax candle, from *Bougie* (Arab. *Bijiyah*), a town in Algeria which carried on a trade in wax.]
1. A wax-candle, a wax-light.
1755 *Mem. Capt. P. Drake* II. ii. 40 Supplied with.. Bougies, otherwise Wax-lights, for their own Apartments. **1817** MAR. EDGEWORTH *Tales & Novels* (Rtldg.) IX. xii. 109 Snatching up a bougie, the wick of which scattered fire behind him, he left the room. *c* **1865** LETHEBY in *Circ. Sc.* I. 97/1 Stearic candles will supersede every other description of *bougie.*
2. *Med.* A thin flexible surgical instrument made of waxed linen, india-rubber, metal, etc., for introduction into the passages of the body, for the purpose of exploration, dilatation, or medication.
An *armed* or *caustic* bougie has a piece of caustic fixed within its extremity.
1754–64 SMELLIE *Midwif.* III. 513 He introduced a large bougie which went up a great way. **1758** J. S. tr. *Le Dran's Observ. Surg.* (1771) 222 Bougies, contrived of waxed Linen rolled up. **1804** ABERNETHY *Surg. Observ.* 201, I introduced a small hollow bougie..into the œsophagus, and injected half a pint of milk and water.

bougil, obs. form of BUGLE.

†**'bouging,** *vbl. sb. Obs.* [f. BOUGE *v.* (sense 3) + -ING[1].] A swelling, protuberance.
1398 TREVISA *Barth. De P.R.* v. xl. (1495) 155 The galle is a membre hote and drye sette on the bowgyng of the lyuer. *Ibid.* v. xlii. (1495) 159 Roundnes of guttes and bowgynge and foldynge is nedefull. *Ibid.* v. li. (1495) 168 The inner bowchynge and roundenes of the thies.

†**'bougoun.** *Obs. rare*[−1]. ? Some kind of musical instrument.
c **1325** *Allit. P.* B. 1416 Bougounz busch batered so þikke.

†**bougre.** *Obs. rare.* [a. F. *bougre*, OF. *boulgre* a 'Bulgarian', a heretic:—late L. *Bulgarus* an inhabitant of Bulgaria.] A heretic.
1340 *Ayenb.* 19 He..ne belefþ þet he ssolde, ase deþ þe bougre and þe heretike. *Ibid.* 134 Vor þet byeþ þe bougres and þe heretiks proude uorlore.

bouh, obs. form of BOUGH, BOW.

bouillabaisse (buːjə'beɪs, -'bɛs). [Fr., ad. mod. Prov. *bouiabaisso.*] A dish of Provençal origin, composed of fish stewed in water or spiced white wine. Also *fig.*
1855 THACKERAY *Miscell.* I. 44 This Bouillabaisse a noble dish is—A sort of soup or broth, or brew, Or hotch-potch of all sorts of fishes. **1902** *Westm. Gaz.* 9 July 2/1 Let it be noted that the greater variety of fish employed to fashion a *bouillabaisse*, the greater the grace and excellence of the same. **1911** R. W. CHAMBERS *Common Law* x. 305 Only art is one delicious bouillabaisse to him. **1932** H. SIMPSON *Boomerang* viii. 175 His wife had skill in the preparation of bouillabaisse. **1966** [see BOUTIQUE b].

bouilli ('buːjiː). Also 7 buollie, 8 bouillé, -ie. [a. F. *bouilli*, pa. pple. of *bouillir* to boil.] Boiled or stewed meat, *esp.* beef. Also *attrib.*
1664 BUTLER *Hud.* II. i. 598 French Cooks use Their Haut-gusts, Buollies, or Ragusts. **1753** SMOLLET *Ct. Fathom* (1784) 116/1 The knight indulged upon his soup and bouillé. **1821** KITCHENER *Cook's Oracle* (ed. 4) 145 Beef Bouilli..is fresh beef gently simmered by a slow fire.

bouillie: see BOOLY.

‖**bouillon** (bujɔ̃). Also 8 bouillion. [F. *bouillon*, f. *bouillir* to boil.]
1. a. Broth, soup. Also in *comb.* **bouillon cube,** a cube of beef (or other meat) extract with seasonings.
1656 in BLOUNT *Glossogr.* (as Fr.) **1725** BRADLEY *Fam. Dict.* s.v. *Sorrel*, Bouillons or thin Broth. *c* **1865** *Circ. Sc.* I. 343/2 What in France is sold under the name of bouillon-cakes, is nothing but gelatine. **1934** in WEBSTER. **1954** E. DAVID *Ital. Food* 39 Chicken bouillon cubes..are quite excellent. *Ibid.*, The same firm also make good beef bouillon cubes. **1960** *Sunday Express* 10 Apr. 15/4 A little light stock made from a bouillon cube.
b. A broth used as a medium for the culture of bacteria. Also *attrib.*
1887 T. M'C. ANDERSON *Treat. Dis. Skin* 289 Injections made under the skin with Bouillon of recent cultivation..set up gangrene of the skin. **1897** *Jrnl. Path. & Bacteriol.* IV. 183 Peptone Bouillon at 37° C.—A cloudiness appears in the broth in 12–18 hours. **1903** *Daily Chron.* 21 Oct. 10/1 Five cubic centimetres of a highly poisonous bouillon culture of certain bacteria (streptococci) was injected under the skin of the ears of rabbits. **1909** *Practitioner* Nov. 591 Five decigrams of a bouillon culture of streptococcus of erysipelas.
2. A saline 'bath', or solution of an alkali, in which wool is steeped previous to dyeing.
1791 HAMILTON *Berthollet's Dyeing* I. I. II. i, Wool Boiled in a bath with saline substances—this is called the bouillon.
3. An excrescence of flesh in the foot of a horse.
4. In *Dressmaking.* A puffed fold.
1869 *Daily News* 4 Mar., Her Serene Highness..wore a blue satin train, trimmed with bouillonnes of white tulle.

bouk. Now only *Sc.* and *dial.* Forms: 1–3 búc, 2–4 buke, 3–4 bouk, 3–6 bouke, 5 bowke, 6 buike, 7 buick, 8–9 buik, 4– bouk. [OE. *búc* belly = OS. *bûc*, Du. *buik*, OHG. *bûh, bûch*, MHG. *bûch*, mod.G. *bauch* belly, ON. *bûk-r* trunk of the body:—OTeut. **bûko-z.* The prevailing sense in ME. is the same as in ON., from which it may have been taken. As early as 15th c. this word was confounded with BULK *sb.*, which afterwards usurped most of its senses, and has superseded it in literary use. The modern dial. and Sc. *bouk* seems to be partly a survival of ME. *bouk*, partly the regular descendant of ME. *bolk*, BULK.]
†**1.** The belly, paunch, or abdomen. *Obs.*
c **1000** ÆLFRIC *Hom.* (1846) II. 270 Þat husel is..betwux toðum tocowen, and into þam buce asend. *c* **1175** *Lamb. Hom.* 25 Þe heo wulle underfon..cristes licome in his sunfulle buke. **1486** *Bk. St. Albans* B vij b, Whan yowre hawke hath wormys in hir bowke.
2. The trunk of the body; hence the body of a man or animal. After 14th c. only *Sc.* and *dial.*
a **1225** *Ancr. R.* 134 Þe hwule þet mi soule is in mine buke. *a* **1225** *Juliana* 70 Er þe bodi wið þe buc beo isundret from hire heauet. **1330** R. BRUNNE *Chron.* 174 A bouke of a motoun. *c* **1330** *Arth. & Merl.* 7189 That the heued fleighe fram the bouk. **1513** DOUGLAS *Æneis* I. ix. 100 Ane hundreth busteous bowkis of swyne. **1591** R. BRUCE 11 *Serm.* X ij b, They cary their heartes out of their buikes as it were. **1794** BURNS *Batt. Sheriff-muir* ii, They rush'd and push'd..And monie a bouk did fa', man. **1832–53** *Whistle-Binkie* (Sc. Songs) Ser. I. 85 Mony a bonny buik lay cauld.
†**b.** *transf.* Applied to the body or interior of a church. *Obs.* (Cf. BULK.)
c **1420** *Chron. Vilod.* 340 A lowe in to þe bouke of þe chirche was send. **1499** *Will of Bannfeld* (Somerset Ho.), To be buried in the bouke of the Church.
3. = BULK in its modern senses: Magnitude in three dimensions, volume; largeness of volume, bulkiness; the greater portion of anything. Only mod. *Sc.* and *dial.*
1697 CLELAND *Poems* 78 (JAM) Though old Colquhoun should bear the buick o't. **1805** J. NICOL *Poems* II. 3 (JAM.) The blades, accordin to their bouk He partit into bands. **1826** J. WILSON *Noct. Ambr.* Wks. 1855 I. 148 I'll weigh't against its ain bouk, lead only excepted, o' ony ither material noo extant. **1855** *Whitby Gloss.*, *Bouk* (pron. *Book*), bulk, size, substance.

bouk, dial. f. BOLK *v. Obs.* to belch; and BOWK, a pail.

bouk(e, obs. and Sc. form of BUCK.

†**bouked,** *ppl. a. Obs.* [f. BOUK + -ED.] Having a protuberance.
c **1300** *K. Alis.* 6265 Schorte y-swerred..And bouked byfore and byhynde. **1513** DOUGLAS *Æneis* III. vi. 127 Quhar, in hir bowkit bysme, that hellis belth, The large fludis suppis thrise in ane swelth.

†**'bouksome,** *a. Sc. Obs. rare.* Also buksome, -sum, bulksome. [App. f. BOUK + -SOME; but influenced in sense and partly in form by BULK; see BUXOM *a.*[2]] Corpulent, portly; occupying large space, bulky; *fig.* great, powerful, influential.
1600 *Act. Jas. VI*, (1814) 209 (JAM.) Andro had ane vther dowblet..and wes mair buksum. **1708** M. BRUCE *Lect. & Serm.* 33 (JAM.) Where Christ grows ay bulksomer in the bosom. *Ibid.* Christ is buksome in heaven. **1785** *Poems Buchan Dial.* 12 (JAM.) Laggert wi' this bouksome graith You will tyne haaf your speed.

bouky, Sc. form of BULKY.

boul, bool. *Obs.* exc. *Sc.* and *north. dial.* (bul). Also 6 boule, *Sc.* bowle, bulis (*pl.*), 8–9 bool. [perh. a. MDu. *boghel* or MLG. *bogel* (mod.Du. *beugel*, Ger. *bügel*) bow, hoop, ring, f. stem of OTeut. **beugan* to bend, BOW.]

1. Anything bent into a curve; a curvature. *Sc.*

1513 DOUGLAS *Æneis* III. viii. 55 A port thair is.. In maner of a bow maid bowle [*v.r.* boule] or bay. **1808** JAMIESON s.v., 'The bool of the arm', when it is bent, i.e. the curvature.

2. *esp.* The curved or semicircular handle of a pail, tea-kettle, pint-stoup, etc.; the annular part of a key; the holes in scissors for the thumb and finger. **bouls, bools,** a movable handle of two parts for a pot, called also *clips*. *Sc.* and *north. Eng.*

1560 *Aberdeen Reg.* V. 24 (JAM.) Ane pair of pot bulis. **1570** LEVINS *Manip.* 218 Y^e Boule of a potte, *ansa, capulum.* **1816** SCOTT *Antiq.* III. 359 Gloss., 'To come to the hand like the boul o' a pint-stoup'.. as easily and agreeably as the handle of a drinking vessel comes to the hand of a tippler.

3. A child's hoop for bowling. *dial.* (N.E. England.)

boul, obs. form of BOWL *sb.*

boulangerite (buːˈlɑːndʒəraɪt, -æ-). *Min.* [f. *Boulanger* name of a French mineralogist + -ITE.] A native sulphide of antimony and lead.

1868 DANA *Min.* §122 Embrithite is from the locality of boulangerite at Nertschinsk.

Boulangism (buːˈlænʒɪz(ə)m). [ad. F. *Boulangisme*, f. the name of Georges Ernest Jean Marie *Boulanger* (1837–91), French general and politician.] The principles and methods of Boulanger and his party who, from about 1886 to 1889, advocated a policy of militarism and revenge against Germany. So **Bouˈlangist** *a.* and *sb.*

1888 *Times* 16 Mar. 5/4 Nothing proved that Boulangism had anything in common with Bonapartism. **1888** *Appletons' Ann. Cycl. 1887* 292/1 Boulangist Demonstrations... Crowds gathered around the Opera cheering Boulanger. **1889** F. TURNER *General Boulanger* 197 Another method invented by the Government to crush out Boulangism was the employment of numbers of police spies to watch the General, Count Dillon, and all the principal members of the National party. **1889** *St. James's Gaz.* 16 Jan. 10/2 The source of the Boulangist election expenditure is a burning question in France. *Ibid.* 3 Aug. 9/2 Fifteen telegraph clerks, reported to the Postmaster-General as Boulangists. **1954** A. J. P. TAYLOR *Struggle for Mastery* 315 If there had ever been a Boulangist crisis, it was now over.

bould-, obs. form of BOLD-.

boulder, bowlder (ˈbəʊldə(r)), *sb.*[1] Also *dial.* boother, bowder. [Shortened f. BOULDER-STONE.]

1. A water-worn rounded stone, varying in size, but properly larger than a pebble, used frequently for paving and building purposes; a cobble.

1617 MARKHAM *Caval.* I. 57 Paued with pibble boulder, or some other kind of small stone. **1811** PINKERTON *Petral.* I. 265 Brown clay slate, in bowlders, found in the bed of the Alecnundra. **1837** CARLYLE *Fr. Rev.* I. v. ix. 256 The Bastille..sinks day by day..its ashlars and boulders tumbling down continually. **1871** TYNDALL *Fragm. Science* (ed. 6) I. vi. 209 Fastened the sail at the top, and loaded it with boulders at the bottom.

2. *spec. Geol.* A large weather-worn mass or block of stone, frequently carried by natural forces to a greater or less distance from the parent rock, and generally lying on the surface of the ground, or in superficial deposits; an erratic block.

1813 BAKEWELL *Introd. Geol.* (1815) 73 Some of the vertical beds of rock covering the granite contain.. boulders. **1830** LYELL *Princ. Geol.* I. 369 Enormous rounded boulders..of trachyte and basalt. **1859** DARWIN *Orig. Spec.* xii. 335 Erratic boulders have..been noticed on the Rocky Mountains.

fig. **1858** HAWTHORNE *Fr. & It. Jrnls.* (1872) I. 14 The first Napoleon..a great boulder in history.

3. *transf.* A lump or mass of some material; *spec.* in *Mining*, a large detached piece of ore found away from the regular lode. Also *attrib.* in the sense of 'big, lumpy'.

1861 SALA *Tw. round Clock* 173 Its boulders of whitening, and its turpentine-infected bundles of firewood. **1862** DANA *Man. Geol.* 537 Boulders of Native Copper have been found. **1882** *Pall Mall G.* 31 May 4/1 The birds will have..all of the seed; the boulder clods will never cover it.

4. *Comb.*: ***boulder-strewed, -strewn*** adjs.; **boulder-belt,** a belt of boulders deposited by a glacier on melting; **boulder-clay,** a clayey deposit belonging to the ice-age, and containing boulders, etc.; **boulder-drift** = *boulder-formation*; **boulder-flat,** a tract of country strewed with boulders; **boulder-formation,** a formation or deposit consisting of mud, clay, etc., in which boulders are embedded; **boulder-head,** a kind of sea-wall; **boulder-pavement,** a bed of boulders naturally arranged; **boulder-paving,** paving made of boulders; **boulder-period,** the geological epoch in which boulder-formations were being produced, the Ice Age or Glacial Period; **boulder-train,** boulders deposited by the melting of a glacier; **boulder-walls** (see quot.).

1894 J. GEIKIE *Gt. Ice Age* (ed. 3) 742 In some instances these *boulder-belts are all the marginal morainic representatives that can be detected over considerable tracts. **1859** H. MILLER *Sketch-Bk. Pop. Geol.* i. 30 The *boulder-clay exhibits certain unique appearences. **1878** HUXLEY *Physiogr.* xvii. 282 An icy sea, from which the boulder clay and glacial gravels were deposited. **1884** DAWSON IN *Handbk. Canada* 324 Stratified sands and gravels overlying the boulder-clay. **1876** PAGE *Adv. Text-bk. Geol.* xix. 355 The *boulder-drift is a bold and clearly-defined formation. **1884** J. COLBORNE *With H. Pasha* 44 The road across this *boulder-flat consisted of numerous pathways running side by side. **1845** DARWIN *Voy. Nat.* ix. (1873) 180 Fragments of primitive rocks derived from the surrounding *boulder-formation were very numerous. **1894** J. GEIKIE *Gt. Ice Age* (ed. 3) 523 Here and there '*boulder-pavements' occur. **1845** DARWIN *Voy. Nat.* viii. 174 The ice-transporting *boulder-period. **1897** *Outing* (U.S.) XXIX. 339/2 A wearisome tramp over the *boulder-strewed mountain side. **1897** *Daily News* 5 May 3/1 Arta Hill, bleak and boulder strewn. **1899** *Westm. Gaz.* 11 Dec. 8/1 The precipitous *boulder-strewn heights. **1967** *Oceanogr. & Marine Biol.* V. 135 *Boulder trains between drumlins along the New England coast are effective means of such protection. **1738** CHAMBERS *Cycl.*, **Boulder-walls*, a kind of walls built of round flints or pebbles, laid in a strong mortar.

ˈboulder, bolder, *sb.*[2] The bulrush (*Scirpus lacustris*); 'the rush used for bottoming chairs'.

1847–78 HALLIWELL, *Bolder.* **1884** G. C. DAVIES *Norfolk Broads* iii. 24 The weeds and boulders (or clumps of flags).

boulder (ˈbəʊldə(r)), *v.* [f. BOULDER *sb.*[1]] To make into boulders. (Perh. only in pa. pple.)

1839 MURCHISON *Silur. Syst.* I. xxxix. 540 They may have been carried down by streams to the shores, and have been long bowldered there.

bouldering (ˈbəʊldərɪŋ), *vbl. sb.* [f. prec. + -ING[1].] **1.** The action of prec. verb; paving with boulders; *concr.* boulder-stones laid as a pavement.

1880 L. WALLACE *Ben-Hur* 409 The bouldering of the pavement was rough.

2. *Mountaineering.* Practice climbing on large boulders.

1920 G. W. YOUNG *Mountain Craft* iv. 152 The introduction to climbing customarily..is practice upon single rocks, low cliffs, quarries and erratic boulders, with or without the aid of a rope held from above. This 'bouldering', or problem climbing,..is of little use as commencing practice. **1954** W. NOYCE *South Col* iv. 63 John spotted a pointed boulder some thirty feet high by the wayside. Daring routes were made up it; and henceforward bouldering..became a popular pastime.

boulder-stone (ˈbəʊldəstəʊn). Forms: 3–6 bulder-ston(e, 7 boother-, bowther-stone, 8–9 bowlder-stone, 7– boulder-stone. [Etymology obscure. With ME. *bulderston*, cf. Sw. dial. (E. Gothl.) *bullersten* a large stone in a stream, one which makes a rumbling noise in the water, as opposed to *klappersten* a smaller pebble; f. Sw. *buller* noise, roar, *bullr-a* to roar, rumble + *sten* = STONE. This gives a passable sense; but no corresponding word is known elsewhere in Swedish, Old or New, Icelandic, Norwegian, or Danish; so that actual relation between the North. Eng. and Swedish dialect word cannot be asserted.

No words answering to Sw. *buller, bullra*, exist in Old or New Icelandic; but Da. has *bulder* 'tumbling noise', *buldre* 'to racket, rattle, make a noise'. If either these words were in use in North. Eng., or a compound **buldersteen* in Da., it would be natural to find here the origin of the Eng. word; but no such connecting links are found. The verb and sb. seem indeed to exist in the Sc. *buller* 'to bellow, roar', *buller* 'bellowing, roar, loud gurgling sound', but this is not quite the shade of sense required, while the form it would yield is not *bulder-, bowlder-, bowther-*, or *boother-*, as actually found in North. Eng. dial., but **bullerstane*, which is not found.]

A rounded water-worn stone larger than a pebble, a cobble-stone (= BOULDER *sb.* 1). Also, in later use, = BOULDER 2.

a **1300** *Havelok* 1790 He gripen sone a bulder ston, And let it fleye. **1523** FITZHERB. *Husb.* §15 Bulder stones..wold weare the yren to soone. **1635** BRERETON *Trav.* (1844) 101 The best paved street with bowther stones..that I have seen. **1792** *Gentl. Mag.* Apr. 350 Large bowlder stones. **1861** MRS. NORTON *Lady La G.* I. 224 The ground is rough with boulder stones. **1879** JENKINSON *Guide to Lake Dist.* 148 *Borrowdale*..The Bowder Stone is an immense detached block..computed to weigh 1971 tons. **1884** S. E. DAWSON *Handbk. Canada* 295 A very singular plateau, covered to a great depth with rounded boulder-stones.

bouldery (ˈbəʊldərɪ), *a.* [f. BOULDER[1] + -Y[1].] Characterized by the presence of boulders.

1859 *All Y. Round* No. 36. 219 Constantinople..with.. its loose bouldery trottoir. **1876** PAGE *Adv. Text-bk. Geol.* xiii. 217 The bouldery conglomerates that flank the Grampians. **1878** H. M. STANLEY *Dark Cont.* II. xii. 347, 400 yards from the bouldery wall, rose a lengthy and stupendous cliff line. **1882** BLACKMORE *Christowell* II. x. 219 The ground was uneven though not bouldery.

†**boule**[1]. ? *Obs.* [app. a variant spelling of BOLL, BOWL, a hemispherical dish.] A measure of lead ore: see quot.

1449 *Excheq. Records* in Risdon *Surv. Devon* Introd. 18, 144 Bouls of Glance Oar. **1670** PETTUS *Fodinæ Regales* s.v. *Boule*, cited in TAPPING *Gloss. Lead-mining Terms* 1851 (E.D.S.) 24 *Boule* or *Dish*, a certain measure wherewith the miners are accustomed to measure out the duties to the church and king..it formerly contained about half a peck.

boule[2] (buːl). An altered form of the word commonly spelt BUHL. See BOULLE.

boule[3] (ˈbaʊliː, ˈbuːleɪ). [a. Gr. βουλή senate.] A legislative council of ancient Greece, originally aristocratic and consisting of the heads of families, later consisting of representatives chosen by lot.

1846 GROTE *Hist. Greece* II. I. xx. 89 The Boulê, or council of chiefs, and the Agora, or general assembly of freemen. **1905** *Spectator* 4 Mar. 318/2 The Boulé, which answers practically to the House of Commons.

‖**boule**[4] (bul). [Fr., = BOWL *sb.*[2]]

1. A game resembling roulette (see quot. 1911). Also *attrib.*

1911 *Encycl. Brit.* XXI. 308/2 In recent years there has been a tendency to supplant the *petits chevaux* at French resorts by the *boule* or ball game..; in this a ball is rolled on a basin-shaped table so that it may eventually settle in one of a number of shallow cups, each marked with a figure. **1928** *Daily Tel.* 10 July 15/5 Rooms for boule and baccarat. **1937** M. ALLINGHAM *Dancers in Mourning* i. 3 A shower of counters on a *boule* table.

2. A French form of bowls, played on rough ground, usu. with metal balls. Also in pl. form.

1924 W. J. LOCKE *Coming of Amos* xvii. 220, I..aided her to play a childish game of boule. **1942** W. SIMPSON *One of our Pilots* iv. 107 Groups of soldiers were playing 'boules', a crude form of bowls played on rough ground, which was very popular in France. **1953** F. STARK *Coast of Incense* ii. 96 The game of boule—bowls without the bowling-green.

boule, obs. form of BOWL.

boulene, boulin, obs. forms of BOWLINE.

boulespret, obs. form of BOWSPRIT.

boulet (buːleɪ). [a. F. *boulet* BULLET, dim. of *boule* ball: cf. BOWL *sb.*[2]]

†**1.** A small globe, sphere, or ball. *Obs.*

1605 TIMME *Quersit.* III. 86 Thou shalt put them into a small boulet of oake. **1677** GALE *Crt. Gentiles* II. III. 204 The Agnus Dei..is made like to those bulles or boulets of waxe, which they hang about the neckes of children.

2. *techn.* 'A horse whose fetlock or pastern-joint bends forward, and out of its natural position' (Webster). [A misuse of the F. word, which means 'fetlock'; a horse which has its fetlock out of place is said to be *bouleté*.]

boulevard (ˈbuːl(ə)vɑːd, ‖bulvar); *rarely* **-vart.** [a. F. *boulevard*, older *-vart, -ver*; app. corrupted from a Teut. word = Ger. *bollwerk* BULWARK; cf. Sp. *baluarte*, It. *baluardo* bulwark.]

a. A broad street, promenade, or walk, planted with rows of trees. Chiefly applied to streets of this kind in Paris, or to others which it is intended to compare to them. Now freq. (esp. in *U.S.*), a wide or well laid-out street or avenue.

(The French word originally meant the horizontal portion of a rampart; hence the promenade laid out on a demolished fortification.)

1769 H. WALPOLE *Let.* 30 Aug. (1857) V. 183 She and I went to the Boulevard last night after supper. **1772** *Weekly Mag.* 21 May 233/2 We made the circuit of the city on the boulevards. **1816** J. SCOTT *Vis. Paris* (ed. 5) 65 The Boulevarde, goes round the capital, and was originally its boundary. **1871** M. COLLINS *Mrq. & Merch.* III. xii. 288 I'm fond of its Boulevarts busy. **1875** *Scribner's Monthly* Sept. 541/2 The boulevard which started from Lincoln Park, connects the Central and Douglas Parks, and then continuing [etc.]. **1881** MORLEY *Cobden* II. 128 The massacre of unarmed citizens on the boulevards. **1903** A. B. HART *Actual Govt.* 328 Hence have grown up systems of boulevards, broad, winding, and well-surfaced, reaching from park to park and often from city to city. **1938** J. CARY *Castle Corner* 65 A head and face that might have belonged to any senior military club or Cheltenham boulevard. **1958** A. SILLITOE *Sat. Night & Sun. Morning* xi. 153 They took a long walk back to her house, by the boulevard that bordered the estate.

b. *attrib.* and *Comb.* **boulevard theatre**: see quot. 1961; so ***boulevard farce***, etc.

1838 *Times* 24 Feb. 5/2 The scribblers of the French Boulevard-theatres are its real masters. **1918** W. HUTCHINSON *Doctor in War* (1919) xviii. 260 The superb, boulevard-wide..military roads of the Italian engineers. **1928** T. E. LAWRENCE *Lett.* (1938) 613 I'm always reading the Frenchmen I like: none of them boulevard idols. **1929** *Observer* 17 Nov. 11/3 The piece is not only amusing. It deserves to be judged by a higher standard than the mere boulevard farce. **1941** KOESTLER *Scum of Earth* 48 The boulevard press..tried to prove that France was fighting a war for democracy. **1961** *Times* 17 Jan. 4/1 The expression 'boulevard theatre', which up to a few years ago was in current use to describe that part of French theatrical production whose principal aim was to amuse..becomes nowadays less and less useful.

c. *N. Amer.* A dual carriageway; an arterial road, main highway, or freeway.

1929 [see *three-lane* s.v. THREE B. III 1]. **1933** M. McKERNAN in *Life in U.S.* 210 The tourist booming along the Kansas-Colorado boulevard sees only a stretch of monotony that burns his eyeballs. **1936** MENCKEN *Amer. Lang.* (ed. 4) 546 Boulevard, in some American cities, has of late taken on the meaning of a highway for through traffic, on entering which all vehicles must first halt. In England such a highway is commonly called an arterial road. **1976** L. DILLS *CB Slanguage Dict.* (rev. ed.) 19 *Boulevard*, expressway (SE). **1979** *Washington Post* 22 Feb. C1/6 Alex Haley swings out of a parking lot onto a busy Los Angeles boulevard, his bronze and green 250 SL Mercedes nosing along.

Hence (in newspapers) **boule'vardian** *a.*, **boule'vardish**, **'boulevardy** *a.*, **'boulevardize** *v.*
1864 *Sat. Rev.* XVIII. 27/2 The boulevardizing of Paris has..caused great misery to the poor.

boulevarded ('buːlvɑːdɪd), *a.* [f. BOULEVARD + -ED².] Provided with boulevards.
1891 *Pall Mall Gaz.* 21 Dec. 1/3 An ideal of a boulevarded London. **1897** *19th Cent.* June 931 It has no boulevarded, Parisianised streets. **1951** DYLAN THOMAS *Let.* Jan. (1966) 352 O evergreen..boulevarded..cradle of Persian culture.

‖**boulevardier** (bulvardje). Also boulevardeer (buːləvɑː'dɪə(r)). [Fr.: f. *boulevard*, see BOULEVARD.] One who frequents a boulevard.
1879 F. HARRISON *Choice Bks.* (1886) 24 As hard..as it seems to a Parisian boulevardier to live in a quiet country. **1882** *Society* 28 Oct. 11/2 The abandoned boulevardier only looks with pity on the young enthusiasts. **1916** H. L. WILSON *Somewhere in Red Gap* ix. 374 Roystering blades from Pittsburgh or boulevardeers from Bucyrus—not a New Yorker in sight.

†**boulever'sation.** *Obs. rare*⁻¹. [f. next + -ATION.] An overturning or upsetting.
1667 E. CHAMBERLAYNE *St. Gt. Brit.* I. (1684) 64 The late Bouleversations or overturnings.

†**bouleverse,** *v. Obs. rare.* Also 7 boulverse. [a. F. *bouleverse-r* to turn as a ball, f. *boule* ball, *verser* to turn.] *trans.* To upset, overturn.
1673 MARVELL *Reh. Transp.* II. 369 It would raise a very great disorder..to bouleverse [ed. **1674** boul-verse] so, and overturn the signification of all words.

‖**bouleversement** (bulvɛrsmɑ̃, bʊl'vɜːsmənt). [F.; f. *bouleverse-r* to overturn: see prec.] A turning upside down, a violent inversion.
1814 SCOTT *Let.* in *Life* xi. (Chandos) 251 There is need for a previous bouleversement of every thing. **1832** *Blackw. Mag.* XXXI. 553 The bouleversement of ideas..which a revolution produces. **1877** W. THOMSON *Voy. Challenger* I. iii. 185 The bouleversement of the dredge had plainly been caused by the twist in the new line.

boulge, boulke, obs. forms of BULGE, BULK.

boulimy, var. form of BULIMY.

Boulle (buːl). [f. the name of André-Charles *Boulle* (1642–1732), French cabinet-maker.] The correct form of the word commonly spelt BUHL. Cf. BOULE².
1875 POLLEN *Anc. & Mod. Furnit.* (1875) 95 Boul marquetry, which owes its name to the maker..André Charles Boule. **1876** *Encycl. Brit.* IV. 446/1 Boulle-work is a kind of inlaying and ornamentation of cabinet-work. **1883** *Scotsman* 9 May 11/8 Old Bronze Groups..on magnificent coloured Boule Pedestals. **1910** *Ibid.* 322/2 The most splendid and sumptuous specimens of Boulle are diminishing in number. **1955** R. FASTNEDGE *Eng. Furn. Styles* xi. 257 Boulle furniture was favoured in some quarters.

boulspret, -sprit, obs. forms of BOWSPRIT.

boulster, obs. form of BOLSTER.

boult, -er, var. of BOLT *v.*¹ to sift, -ER.

†**boultel.** *Obs.* Also 5–6 bultell(e. [a. OF. **buletel*, earlier *buretel* (now *bluteau*) meal-sieve; f. *buleter*, *bureter* (now *bluter*) to BOLT *v.*¹] A kind of cloth specially prepared for sifting; a sieve (= BOLTER¹ 2); hence degree of fineness as determined by the fineness of the sieve.
1266 *Act 51 Hen. III.* (*Assisa Panis*), Panis de coquet de eodem blado et eodem bultello, ponderabit, etc. [*transl.* **1618**, Bread Cocket of a farthing of the same Corne and bultell, shall weigh, etc.] *c* **1460** J. RUSSELL *Bk. Nurture* 164 in *Babees Bk.* (1868) 128 Let hit renne in iiij. or vj. bagges; gete þem, if þow may, of bultelle clothe. **1477** *Lanc. Wills* (1884) 3 Half a pece bultell price iijs., j Dosen bultell price xvjd. *a* **1502** ARNOLD *Chron.* (1811) 206 A balle bultell conteyneth xxxvi. half pecis. *a* **1610** in Gutch *Coll. Cur.* II. 12 They bake two loaves for one penny..good paste, and boutell, and lawfull size. **1638** PENKETHMAN *Artach.* G iv b, For his Boult ell *od.* 2*q.* **1660** *Act 12 Chas. II*, iv. Sched., Boultel Rains the piece viii.*s.*

boultell, boultle, boultine: see BOLTEL.

boulter ('bəʊltə(r)). Also bolter. [Deriv. unknown: see also BULTER, BULTEY.] A long fishing-line armed with a large number of hooks.
1602 CAREW *Cornwall* 34 a, These Hakes..are taken..with the boulter [*ed.* **1811** bolter] which is a Spiller of a bigger size. **1848** C. A. JOHNS *Week at Lizard* 243 Spillers and boulters are long stout lines, to which are attached several hundred baited hooks, with an anchor and waste-line furnished with corks at the end. **1883** *Fisheries Exhib. Catal.* 126 Bolter, Card containing thirteen sizes of hooks.

Boulton ('bəʊltən), *a.* [The name of a firm of glove-manufacturers.] Of the thumb of a glove: cut with a shaped piece extending upwards into the palm.
1922 *Daily Mail* 12 Dec. 1 Real Kid Nappa Gauntlet Gloves,..boulton cut thumb. *Ibid.*, Mocha Gloves:..Pique sewn, boulton thumb. **1929** *Penberthy's Sale Catal.* Mar. 24 An ideal Glove for hard service. Boulton cut. *Ibid.* 26 Men's English Tan Cape,..Boulton cut.

bouman ('baʊmən, 'buːmən). *Sc.* [app. f. BOW *sb.*⁴] The tenant of a BOWING.
1752 *Stewart's Trial* (*Scots Mag.* Sept. 458), John MacCol, bouman, having the charge of milk-cows upon a farm or shealing belonging to Stewart of Appin. **1886** STEVENSON *Kidnapped* xii. 108 The farmers and the crofters and the boumen..wringing their very plaids to get a second rent. *Ibid.* 204 *note*, A bouman is a tenant who takes stock from the landlord and shares with him the increase.

bouman, obs. form of BOWMAN.

boumbard, obs. f. BOMBARD.

boumet = *baumet*, obs. pa. pple. of BALM *v.*

†**boun** (baʊn), *v. Obs.* or *arch.* Forms: 3 bune(n, 4–9 boun(e, bown(e, bowen, 5 *Sc.* bowyn, 9 boon. [f. *boun*, older form of BOUND *ppl. a.*¹ The word appears to have become obsolete in literary use *c* 1600; revived by Sir W. Scott.]
†**1.** *trans.* To prepare, make ready. *Obs.*
a **1375** *Joseph Arim.* 414 þe kyng boskes lettres anon, to bounen his bernes. *Ibid.* 472 To boune mo bernes. **1515** *Scottish Field* 213 in *Chetham Misc.* (1856) II, Then the bishop full boldlie bowneth furth his standart.
b. *refl.* To prepare oneself, get ready (often in connexion with *busk*); to betake oneself, have recourse *to* (anything).
a **1300** *Cursor M.* 11920 Ioseph..buned him to wend againe. *c* **1400** *Destr. Troy* 827, I would boune me to batell, and take my bare aunter. **1515** *Scottish Field* 83 in *Chetham Misc.* (1856) II, He did buske and bowne him, to go on his message. *a* **1575** PILKINGTON *Exp. Nehemiah* (1841) 353 They buskle and bowne themselves to this work. **1600** FAIRFAX *Tasso* III. xxx. 45 The villaine, who to flight him bound. **1808** SCOTT *Marm.* IV. xxii, Each ordering that his band Should bowne them with the rising day. **1847** BARHAM *Ingol. Leg.* (1877) 243 St. Medard hath boon'd himself for the task. **1866** J. ROSE *Virgil* 99 Soon must we boun' us for a loftier song.
2. *intr.* (for *refl.*) To get ready, prepare; to dress.
c **1375** BARBOUR *Troy-bk.* II. 2852 Than thocht hime at þat ymage gay Bouned to pass frome hime away. **1513** DOUGLAS *Æneis* VII. Prol. 97, I crocit me, syne bownit for to sleip. *Ibid.* XIII. Prol. 46 Euery thing..Bownis to tak the hail-sum nychtis rest Eftir the days laubour. **1674** RAY *N.C. Wds.* 7 *To Boun* and *unboun*, to dress and undress. **1815** HOGG *Pilgr. Sun* I. xvi, For then the fairies boun' to ride And elves of Ettrick's greenwood shaw.
3. *intr.* To betake oneself *to* (a place), set out, go.
c **1325** *E.E Allit. P.* B. 1398 Barounes at þe sidebordes bounet ay where. *c* **1375** BARBOUR *Troy-bk.* II. 2712 Pirrus bowned to Delphos yle. *a* **1455** HOLLAND *Houlat* xviii, But bownis out of Babilon with all obedience. *a* **1540** *Peebles to Play* i. 5 At Beltan, when ilk bodie bounes To Peebles to the play. **1552** LYNDESAY *Monarche* 6312 The blysfull byrdis bownis to the treis. **1805** SCOTT *Last Minstr.* V. xxx, Till Lord Dacre's band Were bowning back to Cumberland.

boun, obs. form of BON, BOON, BOUND *ppl. a.*

bounce (baʊns), *sb.*¹ [see BOUNCE *v.* (The first three senses appear nearly simultaneously, and their order here is purely provisional.)]
1. A heavy and usually noisy blow caused by something big; a sounding knock, thump.
a **1529** SKELTON *Ware the Hauke* 86 He gave her a bounce Full upon the gorge. **1583** STANYHURST *Æneis* III. (Arb.) 88 With ramping bounce clapping neer to the seacoast Fierce the waters ruffle. **1629** FORD *Lover's Mel.* I. i. (1839) 2 Blustering Boreas..thumps a thunder bounce. **1761** *Brit. Mag.* II. 506 A noise from the next room, conveyed in distinct bounces against the wainscot. **1824** MISS MITFORD *Village* Ser. II. (1863) 247 His knock at the door was a bounce that threatened to bring the house about our ears.
†**2.** The loud burst of noise produced by an explosion; the explosion itself. *Obs.* (See BOUNCE *interj.* in the same sense, occurring 1523.)
[**1552** HULOET, Bounce, noyse, or thump.] **1595** SHAKS. *John* II. 462 He speakes plaine Cannon fire, and smoake, and bounce. **1702** DE FOE *Reform. Manners* Concl. 44 These are the Squibs and Crackers of the Law, Which hiss and make a Bounce, and then withdraw. **1719** HALLEY in *Phil. Trans.* XXX. 990 The rattling Noise like small-Arms, heard after the great Bounce on the Explosion over Tiverton. **1766** CAVENDISH *ibid.* LVI. 149 With 7 parts of inflammable to 3 of common air, there was a very gentle bounce or rather puff.
3. a. A leap, a bound. ***on the bounce***: in continual spasmodic movement.
1523 SKELTON *Garl. Laurel* 1318 He brought out a rabyll Of coursers and rounsis With lepes and bounsis. **1570** LEVINS *Manip.* 220 A Bounce, leape, *saltus.* **1729** ATTERBURY *Misc. Wks.* V. 131 It will not be so much upon the bounce as formerly. **1809** W. IRVING *Knickerb.* IV. x. (1849) 242 The testy little governor..appears with one annoyance and the other to have been kept continually on the bounce. **1884** *Chr. World* 10 July 513/1 In each bounce or throw of the ball.
b. An act of bouncing or ejecting. Also *fig. colloq.* (orig. *U.S.*).
1876 *N.Y. Times* 23 June 1/5 Tilden is no stronger than he was, although his friends are already playing the 'bounce' game that was so successful at Cincinnati. **1877** BARTLETT *Dict. Amer.* (ed. 4) Add., *Bounce.* To get the ***grand bounce*** is to be dismissed from service; particularly from an office under government. **1906** E. DYSON *Fact'ry 'Ands* ix. 119 Pee give him er bounce off ther land. *a* **1910** 'O. HENRY' *Rolling Stones* (1916) 125 'Had you ever thought' I asks, ..'of giving her the bounce yourself?' **1966** 'E. LATHEN' *Murder makes Wheels go Round* i. 8 At the other companies ..the big boys who went to jail got the bounce.
4. a. (from 2.) A loud or audacious boast; a boastful falsehood; *abstr.* impudent self-assertion, swagger.
1714 STEELE *Lover* (1723) 93 This is supposed to be only a Bounce. **1733** CHEYNE *Eng. Malady* III. iv. (1734) 301 It was a wild Bounce of a Pythagorean, who defy'd any one to, etc. **1824** GALT *Rothelan* II. v. ix. 261 It is, I own, a brave bounce to aspire to the daughter of so proud an earl. **1829** DE QUINCEY *Murder* Wks. IV. 21 The whole story is a bounce of his own. **1866** W. G. WARD *Ess.* (1882) II. 107 Here is bounce and swagger with a vengeance.
b. *colloq.* A boastful, swaggering fellow.
1812 J. H. VAUX *Flash Dict.*, *Bounce*, a person well or fashionably drest is said to be a *rank bounce.*
5. A buoyant rhythm. Also *attrib. colloq.* (orig. *U.S.*).
1937 *Amer. Speech* XII. 45/1 *Bounce*, a light medium-fast tempo with a light accent on the first and third beats. **1956** G. CHISHOLM in S. Traill *Play that Music* iii. 41 Medium Bounce Tempo. **1958** B. ULANOV *Hist. Jazz in Amer.* xxv. 350 *Bounce*, used by some musicians, especially Duke Ellington, to describe a particularly buoyant beat.
6. *Comb.* **bounce-flash** *Photogr.*, reflected flash-light.
1952 J. F. W. FRERK *All about Flash Photogr.* 25 Splash or Bounce Flash. This is a way of using diffused flash light only, by directing the flash against the ceiling. **1953** A. MATHESON *Leica Way* 176 For very soft and even illumination..fire the flash at a light wall or ceiling, utilizing the reflected light... This 'bounce-flash' illumination needs either a stronger flash bulb or a larger aperture than direct light.

bounce (baʊns), *sb.*² A name of the Dogfish (*Scyllium Canicula*).
a **1709** RAY *Syn. Pisc.* 22. **1861** COUCH *Brit. Fishes* I. 11 Bounce = Nurse Hound.

bounce (baʊns), *v.* Forms: 3 **bunsen**, 4–7 **bounse**, 6–7 **bownce**, 6– **bounce**. [The origin of BOUNCE *v.*, *sb.*¹, *int.* (*adv.*) is obscure, and their mutual relations complicated. ME. *bunsen* agrees in form and meaning with mod.Du. *bons* a thump, *bonzen* (LG. *bunsen*, HG. dial. *bumbsen*) to beat, thump, thwack; but there is no early record of these words, and perh. they may be related to the Eng. word merely as parallel onomatopœic formations. Early in 16th c. we find the interjectional use of *bounce* (= LG. and HG. dial. *bums!*) to imitate the report of a gun or other loud sudden noise, and (a little later) to express sudden or violent movement. About the same time the vb. (previously seldom occurring) became common in its original sense 'to beat', but with the notion of noise or vehemence more conspicuous—'to knock, bang'; it also acquired the senses 'to make a banging or explosive noise', and 'to make a sudden or violent movement of a bounding nature'. The sb. is also found in all these senses early in the 16th c. Whether these were natural developments of the original sense, as expressing phenomena which often accompany a knock or thump, or at least are present in the bang of cannon (which had come into use just before these extensions of *bounce*), or whether there has been influence of any other words is not clear. The development of sense however is to a great extent parallel to that of BANG, which has dialectally even the sense of '*bounce* into a room', etc.]
I. To beat, thump, trounce, knock.
†**1.** *trans. Obs.*
a **1225** *Ancr. R.* 188 Þer ʒe schulen iseon bunsen ham mit tes deofles bettles. **1387** TREVISA *Higden* Rolls Ser. I. 281 Þis Pypinus gat Charles þat heet Tutidis of *tundere*, þat is 'bete and bounse'. **1560** *Nice Wanton* in Hazl. *Dodsl.* II. 167 Yet Salomon sober correction doth mean, Not to beat and bounce them to make them lame. **1596** SPENSER *F.Q.* III. xi. 27 And wilfully him throwing on the gras Did beat and bounse his head and brest full sore. **1652** BENLOWES *Theoph.* x. xxxix. 184 We seem'd to knock at hell, and bounce the firmament. **1682** N. O. *Boileau's Lutrin* III. 186 I'le trounce and bounce thee for 't i' th' Spiritual Court. **1727** SWIFT *Gulliver* III. ii. 184 Bouncing his head against every post. **1801** MAR. EDGEWORTH *Good Fr. Gov.* (1831) 122 She has taught me to read without bouncing me about and shaking me.
†**2.** *intr.* To knock loudly, *esp.* at a door. *Obs.*
1570 B. GOOGE *Popish Kingd.* IV. 38 On the Thursday Boyes and Girles do runne in euery place, and bounce and beate at euery doore. **1591** LYLY *Endym.* IV. ii. 56 Come my browne bils wee'l roare Bownce loud at taverne dore. **1656** TRAPP *Comm. Matt.* V. 20 They shall come knocking and bouncing, with 'Lord, Lord, open unto us'. **1708** SWIFT *Wks.* (1841) II. 256 Another bounces as hard as he can knock.

II. To make a loud explosive noise, to talk loudly or bigly.

†**3. a.** *intr.* To make a noise of explosion, to go 'bang'. *Obs.*

1552 HULOET, Bouncen or cracke, *crepo.* *c***1700** in Hearne *Coll.* II. 456 Fir'd the Train, And made it bounce louder and louder. **1719** RAMSAY *Wks.* (1848) I. 149 Where cannon bounced and rearing horses pranced.

b. *trans.* To slam, to bang (a door).

1786 WOLCOTT (P. Pindar) *Ep. Boswell* Wks 1794 I. 321 What though against thee porters bounce the door.

4. a. *intr.* To talk big, bluster, hector; to swagger. ***to bounce out (with)***: to blurt out 'roundly'.

*c***1626** *Dick of Devon* II. iv. in Bullen *O. Pl.* II. 38 Are you bouncing? Ile no further. *a***1659** CLEVELAND *Gen. Poems* (1677) 137 There he bounceth out with his εὕρηκα. **1758** JOHNSON *Idler* No. 28 ¶5 Let him bounce at his customers if he dares. **1765** BP. LOWTH *Let. to Warburton* 14 He.. bounces, blusters, and swaggers, as if he were really sovereign Lord. **1848** THACKERAY *Van. Fair* lxv, 'She's the finest lady I ever met in my life', bounced out the Major. **1872** F. W. ROBINSON *Wrayford's W., Tito's Troubles*, You must not let the big boys bounce.. over him too much.

b. *trans.* To proclaim with bounce.

*a***1652** BROME *Queen* I. iii. 6, I may not hear these wonders bounc'd.

5. *trans.* To talk big at; to bully. In modern colloq. use, To 'blow up', scold roundly.

*a***1626** FLETCHER *Nt. Walker* IV. i, I doe so whirle her to the Counsellors chambers.. and bounce her for more money. **1812** J. H. VAUX *Flash Dict.*, *To bounce a person out of any thing*, is to use threatening or high words, in order to intimidate him, and attain the object you are intent upon. **1883** *Manch. Exam.* 30 Nov. 5/2 French statesmen persuaded themselves.. that they could 'bounce' their opponents out of a slice of territory in Tonquin. *Mod. colloq.* The clerk was well bounced for his carelessness.

III. *intr.* To move with a sudden bound.

6. a. To bound like a ball; to throw oneself about: *esp.* said of an elastic or bounding movement by a heavy or bulky body. In early use *to bounce it* (said of a woman dancing): cf. L. *humum pulsare* 'to thump or pounce the ground'.

1519 *Interl. Four Elem.* in Hazl. *Dodsl.* I. 35 She will bounce it, she will whip, Yea, clean above the ground! **1589** *Gold. Mirr.* (1851) 54 See where one bounseth in a players gowne. **1601** SHAKS. *Per.* II. i. 26, I saw the porpus, how he bounced and tumbled. **1743-4** MRS. DELANY *Autobiog.* (1861) II. 254 My heart bounced for joy at the news of your good house. **1787** BEST *Angling* (ed. 2) 35 When you have struck him, he will plunge and bounce in the water very much. **1802** I. MILNER *Life* xiv. (1842) 261 All in one instant, it bounced into my mind, that there must be an opening in the said brass rods. **1812** H. & J. SMITH *Rej. Addr.* 40 Nine centuries bounced he from cavern to rock. **1839** BAILEY *Festus* v, God puts his finger in the other scale, And up we bounce, a bubble. **1851** O. W. HOLMES *A Song of '29*, A cannon bullet rolling Comes 'bouncing' down the stairs. *a***1859** DE QUINCEY *Bentley* Wks. VI. 84 The judges bounced like quicksilver. **1883** BROWNING *J. Hakkadosh* in *Jocoseria* 127 Yet is the Ruach (.. The imparted Spirit) in no haste to bounce From its entrusted Body. *Mod.* This ball is split, and will not bounce at all.

b. *trans.* To cause to rebound. Also *transf.*, to cause to be reflected.

1876 'MARK TWAIN' *Tom Sawyer* i. 9 I'll take and bounce a rock off'n your head. **1929** WODEHOUSE *Summer Lightning* iii. 76 He poised the tennis-ball and.. bounced it on the silver medallist's back. **1950** *Sci. News* XV. 67 A beam of electrons is 'bounced off' the surface (in a vacuum) and collected on a photographic plate. **1959** *Daily Tel.* 16 May 1/1 An experiment was now in hand for bouncing radio waves from the planet Venus. **1959** I. & P. OPIE *Lore & Lang. Schoolch.* vii. 114 Repeated while bouncing two balls against a wall.

c. *intr.* Of a cheque: to be returned to the drawer because there are insufficient funds to meet it. Occas. *trans.*, to present (such a cheque).

1927 *New Republic* 26 Jan. 277/2 'Bouncer'.. may be either (1) a rubber check returned by the bank as no good, or (2) the person who passes (bounces) the rubber check. **1928** *Sunday Express* 2 Dec. 2/6 'Rubber checks', i.e., the type that comes bouncing back from the bank. **1943** HUNT & PRINGLE *Service Slang* 16 *Bounce*, to be returned by the Bank [of a dud cheque]. **1951** *News Chron.* 12 Dec. 4/4 If a customer draws a cheque for £25 when there is only £20 in his balance, the cheque will 'bounce'—it will be returned to the customer who paid it in with the uncomplimentary remark, 'Insufficient funds'. **1955** *Times* 25 Aug. 9/4 If.. you.. then bounce a cheque, you will be in trouble.

d. *trans.* To bowl a bouncer or bouncers at (a batsman). See BOUNCER 6. *Cricket colloq.*

1960 I. PEEBLES *Bowler's Turn* viii. 63 He was a magnificent hooker, and few fast bowlers bounced him a second time. **1985** *Times* 9 Apr. 22/4 Fast bowlers of every country now bounce non-batsmen.

7. To come or go as unceremoniously as a tossed ball, to throw oneself with excess of physical momentum; to burst unceremoniously *into*, *out of*.

1679 *Hist. Jetzer* 4 The Receiver, Cook, and Mr. Novice, came bouncing in. **1827** SCOTT *Diary* in *Lockhart* xxiv, The French.. bounce in at all hours and drive one half mad with compliments. **1851** HELPS *Comp. Solit.* iv. (1874) 45 The market-gardener's wife, little attended to, bounces out of the room. **1883** LD. SALTOUN *Scraps* I. iii. 264 The innkeeper's wife bounced into the room.

8. a. *trans.* To discharge suddenly from employment. *U.S.* [Of uncertain origin.]

1884 *Boston (Mass.) Jrnl.* 3 Oct. 2/3 Speaker Carlisle has bounced his clerk, Mr. Nelson, for telling tales out of school. **1885** *Milnor (Dakota) Teller* 5 June 5/2 Tuller, Judge Hudson's imported clerk of the court at Lisbon, is likely to be bounced, and Hugh Doherty appointed.

b. *trans.* To eject summarily. Chiefly *U.S. colloq.* Cf. BOUNCER 5.

1877 BARTLETT *Dict. Amer.* (ed. 4) 62, I daresn't go in there; the bar-tender's drunk, and I might get bounced. **1883** [see BOUNCER 5]. **1891** C. ROBERTS *Adrift Amer.* 128 Here I jumped another train and got 'bounced' at Bernalillo.

c. To throw over (as a suitor). *U.S. colloq.*

1893 'O. THANET' *Stories Western Town* 213 You don't suppose it would be any use to offer Esther a cool hundred thousand to promise to bounce this young fellow?

bounce (baʊns), *int.* and *adv.* Also 6 bowns, bounse, 6-7 bownce. [The stem of the vb. or sb. interjectionally: cf. the corresponding use of Ger. *bums*, *bumps*, as in *bums geht die Thür* (Grimm).]

A. *int.* **a.** Imitating the sound of a gun. **b.** Expressing sudden, violent movement.

1523 SKELTON *Garl. Laurel* 624 With that I herd gunnis russhe out at ones, Bowns, Bowns, Bowns! that all they out cryde. **1590** *Pasquil's Apol.* I. D ij b, Bounse, thers a gunne gone off, doe not the Bishops quake at thys? **1597** SHAKS. *2 Hen. IV*, III. ii. 303 Bownce would hee say, and away againe would hee goe. **1608** ARMIN *Nest Ninn.* (1880) 59 Bownce is the worlds motto there, till they discharge the braine of all good abearing. **1852** HOOD *Lamia* iii. 44 At every step—Bounce! when I only thought to stride a pace, I bounded thirty.

B. *adv.* With a BOUNCE (senses 1, 2, 3).

1604 DEKKER *Honest Wh.* Wks. 1873 II. 82 The Turkes gallies are fighting with my ships, Bownce goes the guns. **1750** GRAY *Let.* in *Poems* (1775) 216 The Heroines.. bounce into the parlour enter'd. **1789** WOLCOTT (P. Pindar) *Expost. Ode* xii. Wks. 1812 II. 242 Bounce on my dear *os frontis* falls the lead. **1847** BARHAM *Ingol. Leg.* (1877) 95 Bounce went the door, In came half a score Of the passengers, sailors, and one or two more. **1864** MISS YONGE *New Ground* xv, Something came bounce against the door.

bounceable (ˈbaʊnsəb(ə)l), *a.* *colloq.* Also bouncible. [f. BOUNCE *v.* + -ABLE.] Inclined or given to bounce. Hence **ˈbounceably** *adv.*

1830 S. WARREN *Diary Phys.*, *Grave Doings*, He became quite 'bouncible', and ranted about the feat. **1876** BLACKMORE *Cripps* xii. 69 Beckley.. as good as told the latter lady not to be 'so bounceable'. **1838** DICKENS *O. Twist* xxviii, There's no call to tell a man he is, so bounceably.

†**bounced**, *ppl. a.* *Obs.* [f. BOUNCE *v.* + -ED.[1]] Beaten, knocked about.

1519 HORMAN *Vulg.* in *Promp. Parv.* 55 He came home with a face all to bounced, *contusâ*.

bouncer (ˈbaʊnsə(r)). [f. BOUNCE *v.* + -ER.[1]]

1. One who bounces (sense 4 of the vb.).

1762 FOOTE *Lyar* III. (1776) 56 Nor is the character of my son to be blasted with the breath of a bouncer. **1776** in *Priv. Lett. 1st Ld. Malmesbury* I. 351 The Nabob, the greatest Bouncer of all those Bouncers, comes out of gaol. **1876** *World* No. 115. 20 The old maid.. does not stand the slightest chance unless she be of the gushing bouncer class.

2. a. A boaster, bully, swaggering liar. **b.** in *Thieves' slang* (see quot. 1862).

1833 MARRYAT *P. Simple* xxxi, He's a.. kind fellow enough, but.. Such a *bouncer!* **1862** MAYHEW *Crim. Prisons* 46 Bouncers and besters who cheat by laying wagers.

3. A 'bouncing' or 'thumping' lie.

1805 G. COLMAN *J. Bull* II. iii. (L.) You know.. what a bouncer you told me.

4. A large specimen of its kind; a 'thumper'.

1842 DE QUINCEY in *Blackw. Mag.* July 127/2 The stone must be a bouncer. **1872** TAUNT *Map Thames* 15 See, I've got a roach, and a bouncer. *Colloq.* She was a bouncer.

5. One engaged to eject undesirable or unruly persons from a saloon, ballroom, etc.; a 'chucker-out'. *colloq.* (orig. *U.S.*).

1865 *Nat. Police Gaz.* (U.S.) 29 Apr. 4/2 Old Moyamensing is almost as famous for its lawless gangs of boys and young men, as it was in the days of the 'killers' and 'bouncers'. **1883** *Daily News* 26 July 4/8 The Bouncer.. is merely the English 'chucker out'. When liberty verges on licence and gaiety on wanton delirium, the Bouncer selects the gayest of the gay, and—bounces him. **1888** A. C. GUNTER *Mr. Potter* xx, Several of the fighting brigade of the establishment, that in American slang would be termed 'bouncers'. **1903** A. ADAMS *Log Cowboy* xiii. 204 The bouncer of the dance hall of course had his eye on our crowd. **1938** WODEHOUSE *Summer Moonshine* i. 19 He held down a job for a time as bouncer at some bar. **1961** *Evening Standard* 21 Aug. 12/6 Bouncers required for dance Sat. evenings.

6. A ball that bounces high; *spec.* in *Cricket*, one that rises sharply off the pitch.

1913 *Cricket* 305/2 Every bowler pitches short sometimes, and when.. he does so the resultant.. 'bouncer'.. is no more than an ordinary risk. **1955** *Times* 24 June 14/1 Heine's first ball, a bouncer, was as the drawing of a sword.

bounch(e, var. of BUNCH.

bouncing (ˈbaʊnsɪŋ), *vbl. sb.* [f. BOUNCE *v.*]

1. Striking, knocking, banging, thumping.

1583 STANYHURST *Æneis* II. (Arb.) 59 With rip rap bouncing thee ram to the chapter is hurled. **1589** NASHE *Almond for P.* 13 a, Hauing worn out three or four pulpits with the vnreasonable bounsing of his fists. **1870** L'ESTRANGE *Miss Mitford* I. vi. 176 A noise of shouting, knocking, and bouncing.

†**2.** The making of loud, explosive noise; banging.

1598 BARRET *Theor. Warres* V. v. 167 To heare the bouncing of the Cannon. **1652** J. WORDSWORTH tr. *Sandeval* 327 Great clamors of men and bouncing of guns.

3. Bragging, blustering; boastful exaggeration, lying; *colloq.* a good scolding.

1634 HEYWOOD *Witches Lanc.* IV. Wks. 1874 IV. 29, I doe not like the bouncing of good Offices. **1687** T. BROWN *Saints in Up.* Wks. 1730 I. 72 Calling of names and giving the lie.. swaggering and bouncing. **1773** JOHNSON in *Boswell* II. 68 Nothing can be poorer than his mode of writing: it is the mere bouncing of a schoolboy. **1885** YOUNG *Two Sides of Sh.* iv, A great protection against bouncing and rudeness.

4. A sudden bounding movement.

1611 COTGR., *Balotade*, a bounding, or bousing, as, of a football, or high going horse. **1774** GOLDSM. *Nat. Hist.* (1862) I. x. 52 A rocking of the earth to and fro, and sometimes a perpendicular bouncing.. of the same.

5. *Firework-manuf.* (See quot.)

1888 W. H. BROWNE *Firework Making* 15 Furnishing the squib with its report is called bouncing. *Ibid.* 43 Bouncing, or giving to the saucisson its report.

6. *Comb.* **bouncing-pin**, an apparatus for measuring 'knocking' in an internal combustion engine; also *attrib.*

1930 *Engineering* 10 Jan. 44/1 This sleeve.. carries a bouncing-pin mechanism. **1934** *Jrnl. R. Aeronaut. Soc.* XXXVIII. 354 Instructions for setting of the bouncing-pin contacts. *Ibid.*, Then remove the diaphragm and bouncing pin.

ˈbouncing, *ppl. a.* [f. BOUNCE *v.* + -ING[2].] That bounces: in various senses of the verb relating alike to loudness, brag, and vigorous or ungainly movement. Often also (like 'thumping, whacking, whopping, strapping', and other words meaning vigorous striking) used with the sense of 'big', esp. 'big rather than elegant or graceful'. ***bouncing putty***: a soft elastic silicone polymer (see quot. 1950).

(In many of the quotations the exact shade of meaning is doubtful.)

1579 SPENSER *Sheph. Cal.* Aug. 61, I saw the bouncing Bellibone. **1588** *Marprel. Epist.* (Arb.) 34 Can they not be satisfied with the blessing of this braue bounsing priest? **1602** *Return from Parnass.* IV. i. (Arb.) 50, I am well prouided of three bounsing wenches. **1606** J. RAYNOLDS *Dolarny's Prim.* (1880) 97 The bounsing Doa, vnto the brakes did come. **1611** *Coryat's Crudities* Pref. Verses, Oh for a bonny blith and bounsing ballet To praise this Odcomb'd Chanticleere. **1662** FULLER *Worthies* (1840) 363 His mother.. lay down her burthen at Elmeby.. where this bouncing babe Bonner was born. **1736** H. WALPOLE *Corr.* (1820) I. 8 A bouncing head of, I believe, Cleopatra. **1743** MRS. DELANY *Autobiog. & Corr.* (1861) II. 237 [She] is as bouncing as ever, and as loud. **1773** GOLDSM. *Stoops to Conq.* 111, I never saw such a bouncing swaggering puppy since I was born. **1807** T. JEFFERSON *Writ.* (1830) IV. 101 The bouncing letter he published, and the insolent one he wrote to me. **1813** WAUGH *Let.* in *Mem.* v. (1839) 310 An inexperienced, bouncing but well-disposed young woman. **1837** J. LANG *New S. Wales* II. 378 It has even given birth to a school of oratory in the colony—the bouncing school, it may be styled. **1841** MRS. MOZLEY *Fairy Bower* iv, She was ..bold Belle, and bouncing Belle, and every thing but bonny Belle. **1847** BARHAM *Ingol. Leg.*, *St. Cuthb.*, Stephen de Hoaques.. had told all the party a great bouncing lie. **1944** J. G. E. WRIGHT *U.S. Patent 2,541,851* (1951), Novel compositions which because of their unusual properties may best be described as 'bouncing putties'. **1950** *Jrnl. Brit. Interplan. Soc.* IX. 56 Another contribution by General Electric is 'bouncing putty', a viscous and highly resilient silicon material previously used as a core for golf balls. The idea is that certain delicate equipment is buried in the material and shocks thereby distributed evenly over the entire surface of the instruments.

Hence **ˈbouncingly** *adv.*, boastfully, blusteringly.

*a***1677** BARROW *Pope's Suprem.* (L.) Pighius said, bouncingly, the judgement of the apostolical see.. is far more certain.

bouncing-Bet (ˌbaʊnsɪŋ ˈbɛt). [f. prec. + *Bet* for Elizabeth.] A popular name for the Soapwort (*Saponaria officinalis*).

1884 *Harper's Mag.* Oct. 740/2 The bouncing-bets and sweet-williams. **1884** MILLER *Plant-n.*, Bouncing Bet, *Saponaria officinalis*.

bouncy (ˈbaʊnsɪ), *a.* [f. BOUNCE *v.* + -Y[1].]

1. That bounces; having a buoyant manner.

1921 *Chambers's Jrnl.* Jan. 1/2 The little, bouncy man waved his umbrella in excitement. **1928** *Sunday Dispatch* 2 Sept. 15 Once more George.. forestalled the bouncy Irishman. **1962** C. WATSON *Hopjoy was Here* ix. 105 He sounded jolly bouncy over the phone.

2. Resilient, springy.

1926 *Sunday at Home* Jan. 220/2 This big, old house with the bouncy sofa and springy chairs.

bound (baʊnd), *sb.*[1] Forms: 3 bunne, (4-5 ? boune), 6-7 bowne, 4-6 bond(e, bounde, 5-7 bownd(e, 4- bound. [a. OF. *bodne, bone, bune, bonne, bunne*, also *bunde, bonde*, 13th c. AF. *bounde*; in med.L. *bodena, bodina* (*bonna, bunda*):—earlier *butina* (Leg. Ripuar.) = meta, limes. The phonetic history of the Fr. word is difficult; see Littré *bonde* and *borne*, and cf. BOURNE.]

†**1.** A landmark indicating the limit of an estate or territory. *Obs.* exc. in *comb.*

*c***1205** LAY. 1313 þa comen heo to þan bunnen þa Hercules makede. *c***1300** *K. Alis.* 5593 Ymages of moundes, That men clepeth Ercules boundes.

2. a. The boundary line of a territory or estate; *gen.* a limit or boundary, that to which anything extends in space.

1387 TREVISA *Higden* Rolls Ser. V. 299 Osca passed nowher his fader bondes. **1483** *Act 1 Rich. III*, vi. §1 The contract..was made..within the Bounds and Jurisdiction of the same Fair. **1523** LD. BERNERS *Froiss.* I. xlvi. 62 The frenche kynge..commaunded them to kepe the bondes of Flanders, on payne of their lyues. **1551** RECORDE *Pathw. Knowl.* II. Introd., A platte forme..is inclosed with lines as with his boundes. **1615** SIR R. BOYLE in *Lismore Papers* (1886) I. 77 This day..I made the bownds perfect between my Lands of Kilrobistown. **1635** N. CARPENTER *Geog. Del.* II. ii. 19 A right line is the shortest betwixt his owne bounds. **1752** HUME *Ess. & Treat.* (1777) 290 The bounds of all the European kingdoms are..nearly the same they were 200 years ago. **1809** BAWDEN tr. *Domesday Bk.* 239 Thormer is situate within the bounds of the Castle of Ilbert. **1839** YEOWELL *Anc. Brit. Ch.* (1847) 19 The apostle travelled to the utmost bounds of the West.

b. Phrases. *to beat the bounds*: see BEAT *v.* 41. †*to gain bounds of*: to outstrip.

1653 URQUHART *Rabelais* II. Prol., Perceiving the prey by force of flight to have gained bounds of her.

c. *pl.* The limit or boundary beyond which soldiers, sailors, students, schoolchildren, etc., resident in a particular building, quarters, or area, may not pass. Now chiefly in ***out of bounds***, outside or beyond this boundary.

1681 R. KNOX *Hist. Ceylon* IV. ix. 156 Plain reason would tell him, that we being prisoners were without our bounds. *c* **1805** *Regul. Sherborne School*, Every other part of the town is out of School bounds, except the Church-Yard. **1857** HUGHES *Tom Brown* I. ix, The chief offenders..were flogged and kept in bounds. **1865** *Blackw. Mag.* Apr. 472/1 The reason of putting the river out of bounds was the danger incurred by boys who could not swim. **1890** A. CONAN DOYLE *Firm of Girdlestone* v. 32 A lad coming up to an English University..must be within bounds at a fixed time. **1895** [see OUT OF *prep. phr.* III]. **1909** D. SLADEN *Trag. Pyramids* xiii. 201 The decree of the General, which made the Considines out of bounds for the Army, like a Mohammedan festival. **1965** M. SPARK *Mandelbaum Gate* ii. 43 She got into the car and made him drive out of school bounds, miles away.

3. a. *pl.* The territory situated on or near a boundary; a border-land; also land within certain limits, a district, neighbourhood, tract.

1340 *Ayenb.* 206 He [Lot] ssolde guo out of þe cite of sodomme, and alle þe boundes. **1536** BELLENDEN *Cron. Scot.* (1821) I. Introd. 41 In all boundis of Scotland..is gret plente of haris. *a* **1649** DRUMM. OF HAWTH. *Hist. Scot.* (1655) 12 The Chiefs and Principals of the Families in these bounds. **1651** HOBBES *Leviath.* I. x. 46 Marquises..were Counts that governed the Marches, or bounds of the Empire. **1823** SCOTT *Peveril* I. vii. 126 These rascals, who come hither to annoy a noble lady on my bounds.

b. *sing.*

1596 SHAKS. *1 Hen. IV*, v. iv. 90 When that this bodie did containe a spirit, A Kingdome for it was too small a bound.

c. In *Tin-mining.* The area or extent of ground taken in by a miner.

1696 *Lond. Gaz.* No. 3184/3 Owners of the Tyn Bounds, and Adventurers in Tyn Mines. **1881** RAYMOND *Mining Gloss.*, *Bounds* (Cornw.), a tract of tin-ore ground.

4. *fig.* A limit with reference to immaterial things, as duration, lawful or possible action, feeling, etc.

1393 GOWER *Conf.* III. 22 Of abstinence he wot no bounde. **1535** COVERDALE *Job* xiv. 5 Thou hast apoynted him [man] his boundes, he can not go beyond them. **1634** T. JOHNSON *Parey's Chirurg.* VII. xvi. (1678) 181 Let this be the bound of Sweating, when the patient begins to wax cold. **1690** LOCKE *Hum. Und.* I. i. §3 It is..worth while, to search out the Bounds between Opinion and Knowledge. **1737** H. WALPOLE *Corr.* (1820) I. 17, I should be out of all bounds, if I was to tell you half I feel. **1799** MACKINTOSH *Bacon & Locke* Wks. 1846 I. 332 He sometimes carried beyond the bounds of calm and neutral reason his repugnance to doctrines. **1856** FROUDE *Hist. Eng.* (1858) I. iii. 188 It..prevented anarchy from breaking bounds.

5. *Comb.* and *Attrib.*, as ***bound-line***, ***-mark***, ***-oak***, ***-road***, ***-stone***, where *bound* = BOUNDARY. **bound(s)-beater**, one who takes part in the ceremony of beating the bounds; **bound(s)-beating**, the ceremony of beating the bounds.

1850 MRS. BROWNING *Poems* II. 223 All Europe's *bound-lines,—drawn afresh in blood. **1623** LISLE *Ælfric on O. & N.T.* Pref. ¶17 We can neither know well..the names of places and *bound-markes of our own country. **1826** SCOTT *Malachi Mal.* ii. 31 Such a bound-mark as I have described. **1706** HEARNE *Coll.* (1885) I. 242 Yᵉ first was a *Bound-Oak. **1584** *Wodrow Soc. Misc.* 424 His side of the *Bound Rode. **1909** *Essex Rev.* XVIII. 188 After the perambulation there was a dinner, jointly with the Little Leighs *bounds-beaters, at the inn. **1927** *Sunday at Home* June 553/2 The religious part of the *bounds-beating was prohibited. **1602** CAREW *Cornwall* 129a, The one..somewhat curiously hewed..It should seeme to be a *bound-stone. **1855** MERIVALE *Rom. Emp.* (1865) IV. xxxiii. 78 The divisions of land..continued to be known by these bound-stones down to a late period of the empire.

bound (baʊnd), *sb.*² [f. BOUND *v.*²; but cf. F. *bond* of same meaning.] An elastic spring upward or onward; a leap made in an onward career: said both of inanimate bodies and animals, while *leap* is used only of the latter. Phrases. †*to take at the (first) bound*: to take up at the first opportunity, at the outset; to do at once. *to take before the bound*: to be beforehand with. ***at a bound***: by an instantaneous movement. ***to advance by leaps and bounds***: to make startlingly rapid progress.

a **1553** UDALL *Royster D.* (Arb.) 70 If you coulde haue take it vp at the first bounde, We should..pastime haue founde. **1596** SHAKS. *Merch. V.* v. 73 Youthful and vnhandled colts Fetching mad bounds. **1642** FULLER *Holy & Prof. St.* v. xvi. 422 They resolved to take the matter at the first bound. *c* **1645** HOWELL *Lett.* (1650) II. 29 'Tis good then to put wings unto them, and to take the ball before the bound. **1667** MILTON *P.L.* IV. 181 Th' arch-fellon..At one slight bound high overleap'd all bound Of Hill or highest Wall. *a* **1719** ADDISON (J.), The horses started with a sudden bound. **1839** BAILEY *Festus* vii, At every bound I see, I feel The earth rush round. **1848** W. BARTLETT *Egypt to Pal.* ii. (1879) 26 He plunges at a bound into the east.

bound (baʊnd), *ppl. a.*¹ Forms: 3–4 bun, bune, 4–5 bon(e, 4–9 boun(e, bown(e, -nn(e, 6 bond, 7–9 *dial.* boon(e, 9 *dial.* bawn, 6– bound. [a. ON. *búinn*, Norweg. *büen*, pa. pple. of *búa* to get ready, appearing first in the north as *būn*, afterwards in ME. *boun*; the added *d* in the mod. form may be due in part to its being regarded as the pa. pple. of the derived verb BOUN, and in part to confusion with BOUND *ppl. a.*² = obliged; but cf. other instances as in *Mahound*, *sound*, *compound*, *astound*, for *Mahoun*, *soun*, *compoun*, *astoun*, also the vulgar *gownd*, *drownd*, etc.]

†**1.** Ready, prepared: said both of persons and things. Of persons: Dressed, attired. Also (in 14th c.) At hand, present. Often pleonastically ***ready boun***, ***ready and boun***. *Obs.*

c **1200** ORMIN 2329 Loe her icc amm ammbohht all bun To follȝhenn Godess wille. *a* **1300** *Cursor M.* 11595 Son was ioseph redi bun. *Ibid.* 14376 Namli þas þat has ben bune [*Trin.* nere] Quen he vpraisid lazarune. *c* **1386** CHAUCER *Franklin's T.* 775 She was bown to goon the wey forth right. **1393** LANGL. *P. Pl.* C. III. 173 And bed hem alle ben boun beggeres and opere. *c* **1400** *Destr. Troy* 2756 Bowne on hor best wise in hor bright wedis. **1470** HARDING *Chron.* viii. i, He to paye was so readye and bowne For his vitayle. **1513** BRADSHAW *St. Werburge* 162 At the north-gate they were redy bowne. *c* **1550** *Scot. Poems 16th C.* II. 133 Pluck vp ȝour herts, and make ȝow bowne. **1602** SHAKS. *Ham.* III. iii. 41 Like a man to double businesse bound, I stand in pause where I shall first begin. **1768** ROSS *Helenore* 93 (JAM.) The squire..to find her shortly makes him bown. **1810** SCOTT *Lady of L.* IV. iii, A band of war Has for two days been ready boune. **1813** HOGG *Queen's Wake* 147 Earl Walter..For battle made him boun'. **1853** G. JOHNSTON *Nat. Hist. E. Bord.* I. 228 These..are boon to ride the Borders as in the good olden time.

2. Prepared or purposing to go, starting, directing one's course, destined. With *for* (*to*, *into* obs.), or adv. of motion. Phrases, ***homeward bound***, ***outward bound***.

c **1400** *Ywaine & Gaw.* 3788 When thai saw him theder bown. *c* **1440** *Gesta Rom.* I. xii. 33 Deere frend..whodir art thou bone? **1513** DOUGLAS *Æneis* IX. vii. 21 Quhidder ar ȝe boun, ȝe schaw ws plane. **1590** GREENE *Arcad.* (1616) 51 A Barke bound for Arcadie. **1602** SHAKS. *Ham.* IV. vi. 10 Th' Ambassadours that was bound for England. **1709** ADDISON *Tatler* No. 156 ¶1 We may see the Son of Ulysses bound on the same Expedition. **1748** ANSON *Voy.* III. viii. (ed. 4) 490 He gave out at Macao, that he was bound to Batavia. **1801** SOUTHEY *Thalaba* x. xi, You see a Traveller, Bound upon hard adventures. **1848** MACAULAY *Hist. Eng.* I. 635 The ships which were bound for New England were crowded. **1866** SIR J. HERSCHEL *Fam. Lect. Sc.* 206 Bound on we know not what errand.

fig. **1548** E. GESTE *Pr. Masse* 118 Where oure confessyon is bounde, lette oure hartes be represented. *c* **1593** SPENSER *Sonn.* viii, Angels come to lead fraile mindes to rest In chast desires, on heavenly beauty bound.

3. With infinitive, = about (to), going (to), in a fair way (to). Only *dial.*; to be distinguished from the similar use of BOUND *ppl. a.*², though the latter construction was perhaps suggested by this.

The phrase *He is bound to win* would, in northern dial., mean merely 'He is going to win'; in literary Eng. it means 'He must necessarily win', the word here being BOUND *ppl. a.*² (Cf. also sense 1, quots. 1470, 1602.)

1864 ATKINSON *Whitby Gloss.* s.v., 'I believe it is boun to be wet', going to be rain. **1862** *Life among Colliers* 31 He was so violently sicke he declared he was bound to die.

bound (baʊnd), *ppl. a.*² Also 4–6 bounde, 5 boun, bonde. *North.* bund, bun. [pa. pple. of BIND *v.*: shortened from BOUNDEN.]

1. a. Made fast by a tie, confined; fastened down; bandaged: also *fig.*

1552 ABP. HAMILTON *Catech.* 263 A synnar bund with the band of syn..is oblissit to thole paine for his syn. **1570** LEVINS *Manip.* 221 Bound, *ligatus, deuinctus.* **1665** J. SPENCER *Prophecies* 74 These Orators have confest themselves greatly straitned and bound up. **1694** W. SALMON *Iatrica* I. iii. 94/2 The Spasm..not being able to get over the bound place, is hindered from coming to the Head. **1818** BYRON *Mazeppa* xi, My bound and slender frame Was nothing to his angry might.

†**b.** *transf.* of a woman: Pregnant. Cf. BAND *sb.*¹ 1 c, BEND *sb.*¹ 1 d, BOND *sb.*¹ *Obs.*

a **1400** *Relig. Pieces fr. Thornton MS.* (1867) 89 Þe byrde so bryghte with birdyne ȝode bun. *c* **1450** *Lay Folks Mass Bk.* 71 We sal pray also for all women þat er bun with childer in þis parichin. **1513** DOUGLAS *Æneis* VII. vi. 103 Quhilk, bund with child, dremit scho did furth bryng.

†**2.** Kept fast in bonds or in prison. *Obs.*

1382 WYCLIF *Isa.* xlii. 7 That thou shuldyst bringe out fro closing the bounde. **1555** EDEN *Decades W. Ind.* (Arb.) 50 To delyuer the bounde owt of pryson. **1611** BIBLE *Heb.* xiii. 3 Remember them that are in bonds, as bound with them.

3. Confined in the bowels, costive. †Also of a cough: Tight, dry (*obs.*).

1530 PALSGR. 306/2 Bounde in the belye, *serre au ventre.* **1579** J. JONES *Preserv. Body & Soul* I. xv. 28 The Nurse..shall take such medicines when she is bounde. **1607** TOPSELL *Four-f. Beasts* 165 They suffer inflamation and are bound in the belly. **1664** PEPYS *Diary* (1879) III. 1 If you are bound or have a fit of yᵉ Stone. **1757** WHYTT in *Phil. Trans.* L. 574 Her cough is still bound. **1777** FYNNEY *ibid.* LXVII. 459 She was always in the extremes of being too loose or too bound.

4. a. Tied in the same bundle; intimately connected. ***bound up in*** or ***with***: (*fig.*) having common interests *with*, 'wrapped *up*' *in*, dependent upon.

1611 BIBLE *Gen.* xliv. 30 His life is bound vp in the lads life. **1712** STEELE *Spect.* No. 449 ¶2 The only Child of a decrepid Father, whose Life is bound up in hers. **1788** T. JEFFERSON *Corr.* (1830) 316, I consider their happiness as bound up together. **1841** DISRAELI *Amen. Lit.* (1867) 160 Chaucer, in his political life, was bound up with the party of John of Gaunt. **1857** DICKENS *Little Dorrit* (Hoppe) Seeing us so bound up in Pet. **1873** MORLEY *Rousseau* I. 50 A rapid and volatile constitution..is insensibly bound up with sensibility.

b. *Philol.* Designating a grammatical element, such as the present participial ending *-ing*, the adverbial ending *-ly*, etc., which occurs only in combination with another ('bound' or 'free') form.

1926 L. BLOOMFIELD in *Language* II. 155 A form which may be an utterance is *free.* A form which is not free is *bound.* Thus, *book, the man* are free forms; *—ing.., —er..* are bound forms. **1957** S. POTTER *Mod. Ling.* iv. 78 *Book-s*..consists of two morphemes, the free form *book* and the bound form *-s* (bound because it cannot be used independently).

†**5.** Cohering; of glutinous consistency. *Obs.*

1635 J. BABINGTON *Pyrotechn.* xix. 23 These oyles must be ..wrought up, till you finde your mixture bound like dough.

6. Of books: Provided with a binding or cover (see BIND *v.* 10). Const. *in* (leather, vellum, cloth, etc.).

1708 HEARNE *Coll.* (1885) II. 159 It was..a bound book. **1711** ADDISON *Spect.* No. 37 ¶2 Tales in Verse by Mr. Durfey: Bound in Red Leather, gilt on the Back. **1848** MACAULAY *Hist. Eng.* I. 474 Presenting the sovereign with a richly bound copy of the English Bible.

7. a. Under obligations (of duty, gratitude, etc.); Const. a person, or the duty owed. **b.** Having entered into a contract binding to service, as 'a bound apprentice'.

c **1470** HENRY *Wallace* IV. 57 War noucht I was bonde in my legiance. **1579** LYLY *Euphues* (Arb.) 33 It was doubted whether he were more bound to Nature..or to Fortune. **1591** SHAKS. *1 Hen. VI*, II. i. 37 Shall this night appeare How much in duty, I am bound to both. **1645** G. DANIEL *Poems* Wks. 1878 II. 73 For everie Man Is bound to his owne heart. *a* **1656** BP. HALL *Occas. Medit.* (1851) 61 How much am I bound to God, that hath given me eyes. **1752** JOHNSON *Rambl.* No. 201 ¶7 He that is not yet hardened by custom..thinks himself bound by his word. **1856** FROUDE *Hist. Eng.* (1858) I. i. 11 Whoever owned land, was bound to military service.

c. With *infinitive*: Compelled, obliged; under necessity (esp. logical or moral); fated, certain; also in *U.S.* determined, resolved (sc. to go, etc.).

(In dialects *tied* is used in the same sense, as 'That horse is tied to win'.)

c **1360** *Song Deo Gratias* in *E.E.P.* (1862) 129 A noþer is boun to begge his bred. *c* **1400** *Destr. Troy* 9474 Þai were boun to gyffe bake, & the bent leue. **1558** KNOX *First Blast* (Arb.) 5 We in this our miserable age are bounde to admonishe the world. **1607** FLETCHER in *Shaks. C. Praise* 72 Speake, I am bound to heare. **1711** STEELE *Spect.* No. 52 ¶3 We hold our selves in Gratitude bound to receive..all such Persons. **1844** MRS. HOUSTON *Yacht Voy. Texas* I. 2, I was bound to be pleased with the arrangements. **1868** FREEMAN *Norm. Conq.* II. App. 587 The lioness was bound to bring forth only a single cub. **1883** MISS BRADDON *Ishmael* v, Life is a waiting race, in which the best horse is bound to win.

8. In *comb.*: Preceded by a sb. in instrumental relation, or by an adj. used adverbially, as ***hard-***, ***love-***, ***wind-***, ***wood-bound***; often with reference to books, as ***cloth-***, ***morocco-***, ***parchment-bound***; **full-bound**, **whole-bound**, bound entirely in leather; **half-bound**, having the back only, or back and corners, of leather, the rest of the binding being cloth or paper. Also HIDE-BOUND, IRON-BOUND, WEATHER-BOUND, q.v.

1704 *Lond. Gaz.* No. 4021/3 Iron and Wood-bound Cask, old Yards, Boats. **1735** POPE *Prol. Sat.* 181 Who..strains from hard-bound brains eight lines a year. **1847** LD. G. BENTINCK in *Croker Papers* (1884) III. xxv. 143, 800 grain-laden ships..lying wind-bound..in the gat of Gibraltar. **1873** KINGSBURY in *Speaker's Comm.*, *Song. Sol.* vi. 12 The soul..is here the love-bound heart. **1881** MORLEY *Cobden* I. 6 His little parchment-bound diary of expenses. *a* **1887** *Bookseller's Catal.*, The plates whole bound in russia, extra, gilt edges, the text half bound russia neat.

9. For *I'll be bound*, and other uses, see BIND *v.*

¶ = BOND *a.* Subject to servitude, in bondage. *Obs.* [Due to the later association of BOND with *bonds* and *bound*: cf. however sense 7 b, and BOUNDEN 2 b.]

1532 HERVET *Xenophon's Househ.* (1768) 22 Bounde men haue as great nede to be comforted..as other fre men. **1754** ERSKINE *Princ. Sc. Law* (1809) 113 All the colliers in Scotland, who were bound colliers at the time..shall be free from their servitude.

bound (baʊnd), *v.*[1] [f. BOUND *sb.*[1]; not found before the end of 14th c. Cf. OF. *bonner*, now *borner*:—med.L. *bodināre, bonāre, bundāre*.]

†**1.** *trans.* To set bounds to, limit; to confine within bounds; to mark (*out*) the bounds of. *Obs.*

1393 GOWER *Conf.* III. 103 Was [Asia] that time bounded so, Wher..Nile..falleth Into the see Alexandrine. **1523** FITZHERB. *Surv.* Prol., All these maners..shulde be..bounded and valued in euery parte. **1602** WARNER *Alb. Eng.* Epit. (1612) 358 Caritick with his Britons..were lastly chased and bounded by them from out all parts. **1603** KNOLLES *Hist. Turks* (1638) To Rdr., And with his word boundeth in the raging of the sea. **1623** BINGHAM *Xenophon* 135 Before they had parcelled, and bounded out the ground. **1667** MILTON *P.L.* XII. 370 He shall..bound his Reign With earth's wide bounds. **1762** FALCONER *Shipwr.* II. 228 In vain he..bounds the distance by the rules of art.

b. *fig.*

1393 GOWER *Conf.* I. 218 God..hath al thinge bounded. **1554** *Act 1 & 2 Phil. & Mary* viii. §38 Such whose Right, Title or Interest is bounded or taken away. **1647** *Answ. Lett. to Dr. Turner* 19 The Apostles..did in their latter dayes..bound out that power which still we do call Episcopacy. **1690** LOCKE *Hum. Und.* I. iv. §12 Exercise of his Faculties was bounded within the Ways, Modes, and Notions of his own Country. **1799** MACKINTOSH *Bacon & Locke* Wks. 1846 I. 329 Such facts bound our researches in every part of knowledge. **1842** H. E. MANNING *Serm.* (1848) I. xi. 151 It makes a man..bound himself about by his own horizon. **1850** MRS. JAMESON *Leg. Monast. Ord.* 3 His views were not bounded by any narrow ideas of expediency.

†**c.** *intr.* To limit itself; be limited. *Obs. rare.*

1705 *Luctus Brit.* 141 Nor bounds thy Praise to Albions narrow coast.

2. *trans.* To form the boundary of.

1601 HOLLAND *Pliny* I. 73 Lecheum of the one hand, and Cenchræa of the other, do bound out and limit the said streights. **1622–62** HEYLIN *Cosmogr.* III. (1673) 1/1 Asia is bounded on the West, with the Mediterranean. **1824** W. IRVING *T. Trav.* I. 257 A line of blue hills that bounded the landscape. **1879** FROUDE *Cæsar* xxi. 351 He crossed the little river Rubicon, which bounded his province. **1884** BOWER & SCOTT *De Bary's Phaner. & Ferns* 37 The cavity..is..bounded by the lateral walls of the neighbouring..cells.

†**b.** To enclose, confine, contain; also with *in*.

1595 SHAKS. *John* II. i. 431 Whose veines bound richer blood then Lady Blanch? **1606** —— *Tr. & Cr.* IV. v. 129 My Mothers bloud Runs in the dexter cheeke, and this sinister Bounds in my fathers.

3. intr. *to bound on*: to abut upon, adjoin. *to bound with*: to have the same boundaries as. *arch.*

c **1570** THYNNE *Pride & Lowl.* (1841) 10 These breeches I did bound on on either side. **1601** HOLLAND *Pliny* I. 109 Troas..bounds on the coast of Hellespontus. **1622** CALLIS *Stat. Sewers* (1647) 87 The Banks..belong to the subject, whose lands do but and bound thereon. **1637** EARL MONMOUTH *Romulus & Tarquin* 241 Bounding upon madness, it [melancholy] brings men to sublimity. **1792** T. JEFFERSON *Corr.* 164 They bound on us between two and three thousand miles. **1858** BEVERIDGE *Hist. India* III. 269 Territories..bounding with those of British India on the west.

bound (baʊnd), *v.*[2] [ad. Fr. *bondir*, which signified only to 'resound' till the 15th c., when the meaning of to 'rebound, spring' first appears, perh. f. L *bombitāre* to hum, f. *bombus* a humming noise. (With the earlier Fr. sense cf. quot. 1601 in 1.)]

†**1.** To recoil, rebound. *Obs.*

1593 SHAKS. *Rich. II*, I. ii. 58. **1601** —— *All's Well* II. iii. 314 Why these bals bound, ther's noise in it. **1633** G. HERBERT *Temple, Assurance* vii, Thou hast cast a bone Which bounds on thee, and will not down thy throat.

2. *intr.* To spring upwards, leap; to advance with leaps or springs: said both of inanimate and animate objects. Also *fig.*

1592 SHAKS. *Ven. & Adon.* 265 He leaps, he neighs, he bounds. **1599** —— *Hen. V*, III. vii. 13 He bounds from the Earth, as if his entrayles were hayres. **1663** BUTLER *Hud.* I. I. 431 And yet so fiery he would bound, As if he grieved to touch the Ground. **1711** POPE *Temple F.* 333 Thro' the big dome the doubling thunder bounds. **1751** JOHNSON *Rambl.* No. 167 ¶6 Our hearts bound at the presence of each other. **1798** WORDSW. *Tintern Abbey* 69 Like a roe I bounded o'er the mountains. **1816** BYRON *Ch. Har.* III. ii, The waves bound beneath me as a steed That knows his rider. **1853** LYTTON *My Novel* VI. vii. 290 She would..bound forward.

†**3.** *trans.* To make (a horse) leap. *Obs.*

1586 WARNER *Alb. Eng.* VIII. xxxviii. 190 Whether that he trots, or turnes, or bounds his barded Steede. **1599** SHAKS. *Hen. V*, v. ii. 146.

bound (baʊnd), *v.*[3] Aphetic form of ABOUND.

1568 T. HOWELL *Arb. Amitie* 72 If we bound in store: Commodities then offreth made a Salue for euery sore.

bound (baʊnd), *v.*[4] *rare.* [variant of BOUN *v.*] *refl.* To direct one's course. *intr.* To go, lead.

1596 SPENSER *F.Q.* I. x. 67 The way that does to heaven bownd. **1821** JOANNA BAILLIE *Lady G.B.* xiv, She ere stroke of midnight bell, Did bound her for that dismal cell.

bound, obs. form of BOND, BOON.

'boundable, *a.* [f. BOUND *v.*[1] + -ABLE.] Capable of being bounded or limited.

1667 H. MORE *Div. Dial.* iii. §33 (1713) 268 The Extremes themselves are boundable.

†**'boundage.** *Obs.* [f. BOUND *sb.*[1] and *v.*[1] + -AGE.]

a. The action of marking out the bounds or limits. **b.** The bounds taken as a whole; the compass, extent.

1598 MANWOOD *Lawes Forest* xx. §2 (1615) 147 The boundage of the Forest was then so great..that it was almost impossible for any man..to liue within the daunger thereof. **1610** FOLKINGHAM *Art of Surv.* II. ii. 49 Boundage is the compassing and describing of Plots with their buttalls, metes, bounds and Coastage.

†**'boundal.** *Obs.* [f. BOUND *sb.*[1] + -AL[1].] *pl.* Bounds, limits.

a **1670** HACKET *Abp. Williams* I. (1692) 22 Dr. Davenant..kept him within the even boundals of the cause.

boundance, aphetic f. ABUNDANCE, q.v.

†**'boundant,** *a. Obs.* [Erroneous form of BOUNDEN, q.v.] **a.** Obligatory. **b.** Obliged.

1649 FULLER *Just Man's Fun.* 23 It is..the boundant dutie of..pious people. **1654** —— *Two Serm.* Ep. Ded., Your Ladyships boundant Orator, Thomas Fuller.

boundary ('baʊndərɪ). Also 7 **bundary.** [f. BOUND *sb.*[1] + -ARY[1] B 2.] **1. a.** That which serves to indicate the bounds or limits of anything whether material or immaterial; also the limit itself.

1626 BACON *Sylva* §328 Corruption is a Reciprocall to Generation: And they Two, are as Natures two Termes or Bundaries. **1690** LOCKE *Hum. Und.* II. xxiii. (1693) 168 The simple Ideas we receive from Sensation and Reflection, are the Boundaries of our Thoughts. **1751** JOHNSON *Rambl.* No. 178 ¶3 Providence has fixed the limits of human enjoyment by immoveable boundaries. **1860** TYNDALL *Glac.* I. §6. 43 The dots representing the boundaries of the ridges.

b. *attrib.*, as in ***boundary-dispute, -ditch, fence, -keeper, -line, -mark, -treaty, -wall***; also **boundary dog** *Austral.* and *N.Z.* (see quot. 1945); **boundary layer**, the layer of fluid adjacent to a moving body; esp. in *Aeronaut.*, the layer of air adjacent to an aircraft in motion; **boundary light** (see quot. 1951); **boundary-rider** *Austral.* and *N.Z.*, one who rides round the fences of a station, and repairs them when broken; hence ***boundary-riding***.

1850 A. LAWRENCE *Official Desp. to J. M. Clayton*, I have said nothing about the *boundary-disputes of Nicaragua and her neighbours. **1941** *Oxoniensia* VI. 87 One of the field-systems attached to the..settlement may probably be identified in the *boundary-ditches on the lower half of the air-photograph. **1876** D. KENNEDY *Colonial Trav.* xv. 196 The first [dog] seen was a *boundary dog, chained to a break in a fence, to prevent sheep straying from one run to another. **1945** BAKER *Austral. Lang.* iii. 72 A sheep dog chained to a kennel at a gateway..to prevent sheep passing through is called a *boundary-dog.* **1857** R. B. PAUL *Lett. fr. Canterbury* ii. 27 The *boundary fence which separates the poor man from the rich. **1926** M. L. SKINNER in *Adelphi* May 794 Somebody's boundary fence beyond the railways. **1933** L. ACLAND in *Press* (N.Z.) 16 Sept. 15/7 **Boundary keeper*, a shepherd who keeps sheep from passing an unfenced boundary. **1922** J. M. BURGERS in *Proc. K. Akad. Wetensch. (Amsterdam)* XXIII. 1097 We can calculate the distribution of the vorticity and the current in the *boundary layer, when we suppose the velocity outside the boundary layer to be known. **1924** *Flight* 20 Nov. 737/1 The deductions from the boundary layer theory gave a rather poor approximation to the truth. **1949** O. G. SUTTON *Science of Flight* ii. 48 The air, because of its viscosity, sticks to the surface of a moving body, and forms a boundary layer. **1937** *Reports & Mem., Aeronaut. Res. Committee* No. 1793 p. 1, Light signals used in aviation..at the aerodrome ..*boundary lights. **1951** *Gloss. Aeronaut. Terms (B.S.I.)* III. 23 *Boundary lights*, lights defining the boundary of a landing area. **1705** in *Rec. Col. Rhode Island* (1858) III. 528 The *boundary lines between this her Majesty's Collony..and her Majesty's Province of the Massachusetts Bay. **1842** H. E. MANNING *Serm.* (1848) I. xii. 167 He that lives on a dubious boundary-line. **1875** JOWETT *Plato* (ed. 2) V. 180 The boundary line which parts the domain of law from that of morality. **1878** MORLEY *Diderot* 198 The reign of truth was hindered by the artificial *boundary-marks. **1865** *Australasian* 15 July 13/4 The shepherds and *boundary-riders of the past and present. **1890** E. W. HORNUNG *Bride from Bush* xviii. 279 A boundary-rider..sees that the sheep in his paddock 'draw' to the water, that there is water for them to draw to, and that the fences and gates are in order. **1944** *Living off Land* iv. 94 There are no boundary riders on these cattle holdings. **1890** 'R. BOLDREWOOD' *Col. Reformer* I. x. 149 You'll have messages to carry, *boundary riding to do. **1830** CARLYLE in *For. Rev. & Cont. Misc.* V. 23 These were fair conditions of a *boundary-treaty. **1864** *Theol. Rev.* Mar. 11 Between science and theology..it is impossible to build a *boundary-wall.

2. *Cricket.* **a.** The bounds or limit-line of a cricket field.

1867 *J. Lillywhite's Cricketers' Compan.* 7 Always agree at starting..what are the boundaries. **1899** W. G. GRACE *Cricket. Remin.* ii. 23 There were no fixed boundaries at Lord's when I first played there. **1905** H. A. VACHELL *Hill* xii. 248 [He] cut the sixth ball to the boundary. **1920** E. R. WILSON in P. F. Warner *Cricket* 64 Boundaries..were adopted at Lord's for the Eton *v.* Harrow match of 1866.

b. A hit to the boundary; also, the number of runs allowed for the hit.

1896 *Westm. Gaz.* 24 July 5/2 His placing on the leg side, especially off Giffen, was extremely fine, and gave him several boundaries. **1910** *Ibid.* 26 Feb. 16/2 A four boundary is often the result. **1955** *Times* 13 July 8/6 He then hit Goddard almost for 6 to long-on and hooked him for another vivid boundary.

c. *attrib.*, as ***boundary-bye, -hit, -play, -stroke***.

1887 F. GALE *Game Cricket* IX. xvi. 270 'Boundary byes' ought to be abolished..the batsmen being entitled to run as many as they could. *Ibid.* 268 There were no boundary hits. **1896** *Westm. Gaz.* 7 Feb. 3/1 A splendid display of true cricket relieved by free 'boundary' play. **1905** *Ibid.* 15 June 7/1 It was not until the third over of the match that he opened the scoring with a boundary-stroke.

bound-bailiff. A name given by Blackstone to the sheriff's officer in explanation of the vulgar term BUM-BAILIFF, q.v.

1768 BLACKSTONE *Comm.* I. 346 The sheriff being answerable for the misdemesnors of these bailiffs, they are therefore usually bound in a bond for the due execution of their office, and thence are called bound-bailiffs.

†**bounde.** *Obs.* [var. of BOND *sb.*[2]] A husbandman, peasant, serf.

c **1320** *Seuyn Sag.* 582 Kanst thou me telle gode bounde Whi hit is so short wering? *c* **1330** *Arth. & Merl.* 27 Tho that the bounde y-seighe this, Anon he start for diol y-wis.

bounded ('baʊndɪd), *ppl. a.* [f. BOUND *v.*[1] + -ED.] That has bounds or limits; that has its limits marked. Also with instrumental sb., as in ***horizon-bounded***. †**b.** (quot. 1685, American.) ? Marked so as to serve for a boundary. *Obs.*

c **1600** JAS. I. *Sonn.* in Farr's *S.P.* (1848) 1 The bounded waves, and fishes of the seas. **1685** *Col. Rec. Penn.* I. 128 Such as Cutt or fall Marked or bounded trees. **1756** BURKE *Subl. & B.* Wks. 1842 I. 43 Progression..alone can stamp on bounded objects the character of infinity. **1812** BYRON *Ch. Har.* I. xxxi, Immense horizon-bounded plains succeed. **1850** TENNYSON *In Mem.* xlvi, O Love, thy province were not large, A bounded field. **1881** MAXWELL *Electr.* I. 16 Bounded surfaces are limited by one or more closed lines.

c. *fig.* Limited, circumscribed.

1709 POPE *Ess. Crit.* 221 The bounded level of our mind. **1827** HALLAM *Const. Hist.* (1876) II. x. 255 A king of England could succeed only to a bounded prerogative. **1865** M. ARNOLD *Ess. Crit.* i. (1865) 14 In some directions Burke's view was bounded.

†**bounded,** improperly for BOUND, BOUNDEN.

1586 FERNE *Blaz. Gentrie* Ep. Ded., The author therof (as he is specially bounded) shall stand. **1636** HEYWOOD *Challenge* I. i. Wks. 1874 V. 13 What bounded service have you ever done my beauty? *a* **1711** KEN *Hymnar.* Wks. 1721 II. 85 Thou..dost..keep the Tempter bounded in his chain. **1819** CRABBE *T. of Hall* VII. 344 To this fair vision I, a bounded slave, Time, duty, credit, honour, comfort gave.

†**'boundedly,** *adv. Obs. rare*[−1]. [f. BOUNDED *ppl. a.* + -LY.] Within certain limits only, finitely.

1674 N. FAIRFAX *Bulk & Selv.* 156 Gods making a boundedly perfect world, from his unboundedly perfect power.

'boundedness ('baʊndɪdnɪs). [f. as prec. + -NESS.] The quality of being bounded; limited extent or range.

1674 N. FAIRFAX *Bulk & Selv.* 65 Its [the world's] boundedness..arising unavoidably from its very kind. **1795** SOUTHEY *Lett. Spain* (1799) 57 A mountainous track is well adapted for moonlight by the boundedness of its scenery. **1886** M. ARNOLD in *19th Cent.* 647 The boundedness and backwardness of their spirit.

bounden ('baʊndən), *ppl. a.* [The fuller form of BOUND *ppl. a.*[2] f. BIND *v.*, q.v. for Forms.]

†**1.** = BOUND, in literal senses: Made fast by tie, band, or bar; tied, fastened, clamped. *Obs.*

c **1325** *Coer de L.* 5123 Bounden coffres, and gret males. *c* **1325** *E.E. Allit. P.* B. 322 Both boskez & bourez & wel bounden penez. **1375** BARBOUR *Bruce* VII. 115 Ane of thame apon his hals A mekill bundyn weddir bare. **1382** WYCLIF *Gen.* xlii. 35 Thei founden in the mouth of the sackis boundun moneys. **1856** LONGF. *Beowulf's Exp. Heort* 56 The men shoved off..the bounden wood [*Beow.* 438 wudu bundenne].

†**b.** Pregnant. *Obs.* Cf. BOUND *ppl. a.*[2] 1 b.

c **1400** *Destr. Troy* 13718 Ho boundyn with barne with þe bold Pirrus.

†**c.** Of notes in music: Connected by a bind.

1609 DOULAND *Ornithop. Microl.* 40 The Accidents of simple Notes..are also the Accidents of the bounden Notes.

2. Made fast in bonds or in prison. Also as quasi-*sb. arch.*

a **1300** *Cursor M.* 13103 He..þat sale Boru þe bunden folk o bale. **1388** WYCLIF *Isa.* xlii. 7 That thou schuldest lede out of closing togidere a boundun man. *a* **1533** FRITH *Disput. Purgatory* (1829) 153 Thou hast..brought out thy bounden prisoners out of the pit. **1778** BP. LOWTH *On Isa.* (ed. 12) 384 *notes*, The proclaiming of perfect liberty to the bounden. **1870** TENNYSON *Pelleas & Ett.* 306 Her knights..thrust him bounden out of door.

b. *fig.* In bondage, subject. *arch.* (Cf. BOND.)

c **1480** *Ragman Roll* in Hazl. *E.P.P.* 75 Ye so bowendyn han mayd hym and so thrall. **1596** SPENSER *Hymn Beauty* 281 That I her bounden thrall by her may liue. **1820** SCOTT *Abbot* xxxvii, Make me your bounden slave for ever.

†**c.** Tied with the bonds of matrimony. *Obs.*

1426 AUDELAY *Poems* (1844) 6 For thou art boundon, go were thou goo. *c* **1450** *How wise man, etc.* 133 in Hazl. *E.P.P.* I. 175 Laddys that ar bundyn..That can not rewle ther wyves aryȝt.

3. Under obligation, legal or moral; obliged, compelled, enforced. *arch.*

a **1300** *Cursor M.* 12117 Þou es vnder and þar-in bunden. **1547** in *Newminster Cartul.* (1878) 316 Thabouebounden Rychard Tyrrell. **1809** R. LANGFORD *Introd. Trade* 106 The above bounden Thomas Abbot. **1872** LIDDON *Elem. Relig.* i. 19 Here God is represented as the bounden Companion of a man's life.

4. Under obligation on account of favours received; obliged, beholden, indebted (*to*). Also as quasi-*sb.* (*obs.*). The usual modern sense.

1530 PALSGR. *Ep. Ded.* 4 To whom for their benefytes I was so highly bounden. *c* **1585** *Faire Em* i. 222, I thank your highness, whose bounden I remain. **1595** SHAKS. *John* III. iii. 29, I am much bounden to your Maiesty. **1621** BOLTON *Stat. Irel.* (an. 28 Eliz.) All us your most bounden and obedient subjects. **1642** T. TAYLOR *God's Judgem.* I. I. vi. 9 He is the more bounden and beholden to him. **1765** H. WALPOLE *Otranto* iv. 64, I am bounden to your charity. **1854** THACKERAY *Newcomes* xvi, Why need we be bounden to others?

5. *esp.* in phr. ***bounden duty***. So occas. also *discipline*, *obedience*.

(A curious corruption *bound and duty* is occasionally found.)

1530 PALSGR. *Ep. Ded.* 5 My most bounden duetie to obey. **1559** *Bk. Com. Prayer, Commun. Serv.*, We beseche the to accept this our bounden duty and seruice. **1563** SHUTE *Archit.* A ij b, I according to my bound and duety shall pray to God for your long life and prosperous Raygne. **1701** *Lond. Gaz.* No. 3751/5 Our bounden Duty..to Your Majesty. **1833** HT. MARTINEAU *Manch. Strike* iv. 45 It was his bounden duty to accept the office. **1844** S. MAITLAND *Dark Ages* Introd. 10 Many more had..departed from their bounden discipline.

† **bounden**, *a.*, corruptly for BOUND *ppl. a.*^{1} 2.

1821 JOANNA BAILLIE *Met. Leg. Colum.* xxix, Were bounden for their course.

† **'boundenly**, *adv. Obs. rare*$^{-1}$. [f. prec. + -LY^2.] According to bounden duty.

1583 tr. *Ochin's Serm.* Ep. Ded. (L.) Your ladishippes daughter, most boundenly obedient.

bounder ('baʊndə(r)), *sb.*^{1} Also 6 **bowndor**, 7 **boundier**. [f. BOUND *v.*^{1} + -ER^1: but see sense 4.]

I. 1. One who sets or marks out bounds or limits. *lit.* and *fig.*

1570 LEVINS *Manip.* 73 A Bounder, *terminator*. **1610** HOLLAND *Camden's Brit.* I. 745 Umpiers and Bounders between diuerse Shires. *a* **1619** FOTHERBY *Atheom.* II. vii. §6 (1622) 274 The Bounder of all these, is onely God himselfe: who..is the Bounder of all things.

†**2.** One who occupies a district bounding another, a borderer. *Obs.*

1542 UDALL *Erasm. Apophth.* 105 b, The bordreers or bounders inhabityng round about any place are called in greke Ἀμφικτυονες.

†**3.** One who occupies a 'bound' or tract of tin-ore ground. See BOUND *sb.*^{1} 3 c. ? *Obs.*

1702 *Lond. Gaz.* No. 3773/1 The humble Address of the Landlords, Bounders, Adventurers, and Miners, within the County of Cornwal. **1708** *Ibid.* No. 4458/1 The Owners, Bounders, Adventurers..concerned in Tin..at Truroe.

II. 4. A limit, a boundary; a landmark: prob. a corruption of BOUNDURE [cf. *border*], taken as *bounder* 'that which bounds'. *arch.* or *dial.*

1505 *Will* in *Ripon Ch. Acts* 304 The howse..and the bowndor therof. **1564** GRINDAL *Fun. Serm.* Wks. (1843) 27 They..only builded it for a bounder and for a testimony. **1598** STOW *Surv.* xxxiii. (1603) 293 The Postes there placed as a Bounder. **1619** J. KING *Serm.* 14 Mine old age,—for that is the bounder of nature. **1622-62** HEYLIN *Cosmogr.* II. (1682) 135 The River Ob, the East Bounder of Russia. **1635** BRATHWAIT *Arcad. Pr.* 139 From the flowry boundiers of his Empire. **1839** STONEHOUSE *Axholme* 64 The inquisition of 'the bounder' of Hatfield Chase, taken in 1607. **1855** *Whitby Gloss.*, *Bounders*, landmarks or boundaries, fences.

5. *Attrib.* and *Comb.*, as ***bounder-mark***, ***-stone***.

1666 *Peramb. Danby* in Atkinson *Provinc. Danby* (1863) The exact distance between each bounder mark and other. **1634** WITHER *Emblemes* 161 The bounder-stones held sacred heretofore. **1672-5** COMBER *Comp. Temple* (1702) 567 To seize on his Neighbour's Field, or remove his Bounder-stone. **1863** ATKINSON *Provinc. Danby*, *Bounder-stoups*, upright stones..serving to mark limits or boundaries.

bounder ('baʊndə(r)), *sb.*^{2} [f. BOUND *v.*^{2} + -ER.^{1}]

†**1.** *slang.* A four-wheeled cab or trap, so called from the bounding motion of the vehicle in passing over rough roads. *Obs.*

1842 *Hints to Freshmen* (Hotten, 1865), The man who drives has a well-appointed 'bounder' of his own. **1859** HOTTEN *Dict. Slang*, *Bounder*, a four wheel cab. **1865** *Ibid.*, *Bounder*,..a University term for a trap.

2. A person of objectionable manners or antisocial behaviour; a cad. Also in milder use as a term of playful abuse. (Occas. applied to a woman.) *colloq.*

a **1889** in Barrère & Leland *Dict. Slang* (1889) s.v., If I ordered the particular hat I desired I should be taken for a bounder. **1889** *Ibid.*, *Bounder* (university), a student whose manners are despised by the *soi-disant élite*, or who is beyond the boundary of good fellowship...(society), a swell, a stylish fellow, but of a very vulgar type. **1890** *Times* 2 May 13/5 To speak of a man as a bounder is to allude to him as an outsider or cad. **1899** W. ARCHER *Study & Stage* 48 That is an anti-social proceeding, the conduct of a 'bounder'. **1912** A. BRAZIL *New Girl at St. Chad's* viii. 126 Flossie is a bounder! **1917** J. ADAMS *Student's Guide* 27 A prig is one who has too much self-respect, a bounder one who has too little. **1919** WODEHOUSE *Damsel in Distress* vi. 70 He had been marched up the Haymarket in the full sight of all London by a bounder of a policeman. **1930** W. S. MAUGHAM *Cakes & Ale* xvii. 195 Women..adore a bounder.

† **'bounder**, *v. Obs.* [f. BOUNDER *sb.*^{1}] To bound.

1636 *N. Riding Rec.* IV. 51 A place boundering on Holtby. **1797** BEWICK *Brit. Birds* I. 292 The chin and upper part of the neck are yellow, boundered by a black line.

† **'boundered.** *Obs. rare.* [f. prec. + -ER^1.] = BOUNDER *sb.*^{1} I.

1610 HOLLAND *Camden's Brit.* I. 156 If any man would.. accuse me as a false bounderer and surveior.

bounderish ('baʊndərɪʃ), *a.* [f. BOUNDER *sb.*^{2} 2 + -ISH^1.] Having the character or characteristics of a bounder. So **'bounderishly** *adv.*, **'bounderishness.**

1899 E. PHILLPOTTS *Human Boy* 35 With all his bounderishness, he was awfully clever. **1921** D. H. LAWRENCE *Sea & Sardinia* 265 He smoked his cigarette bounderishly. **1928** *Sunday Dispatch* 23 Dec. 12 An awfully bounderish and unbearable sort of young man. **1959** *Guardian* 30 Sept. 7/1 The hero's Nietzschean vitality and young bounderishness.

† **'boundify**, *v. Obs. rare*$^{-1}$. [f. BOUND *sb.*^{1} + -FY.] *trans.* To set bounds to; to confine.

1598 SYLVESTER *Du Bartas* II. iii. I. (1641) 145/1 Untill this Day..Within straight lists thou hast been boundifi'd.

† **'bounding**, *vbl. sb.*^{1} *Obs.* [f. BOUND *v.*^{1}]

1. The action of forming or marking a limit of, or setting up a boundary to. Also with *out*.

1543 *Act 35 Hen. VIII*, xvii. §7 The..meting and bounding of the said fourth Part of the said Woods. **1602** CAREW *Cornwall* 136 When a Myne is found..the first discouerer..at the foure corners of his limited proportion, diggeth vp three Turfes, and the like (if he list) on the sides, which they terme Bounding. **1614** RALEIGH *Hist. World* II. 272 In bounding out their proper lands.

2. Abuttal, marching; boundary.

1552 HULOET, Bowndynge or buttynge of thre fieldes ioynynge together. **1703** DE FOE *Orig. Power People* in *Misc.* 159 Buttings and Boundings of Land. **1750** G. HUGHES *Barbados* 6 The buttings and boundings of several tenements near this bay.

3. *fig.* A limiting, confining, or restricting.

1608 HIERON *Wks.* I. Q 99 Neither is it..any straightning or bounding of Gods Spirit. **1658** in Burton *Diary* (1828) III. 316 This is a bounding of our power.

bounding ('baʊndɪŋ), *vbl. sb.*^{2} [f. BOUND *v.*^{2}] A leaping or springing, esp. in an elastic way.

1617 MARKHAM *Caval.* II. 199 It fortifies a horse exceedingly in his boundings and hie salts. **1712** ADDISON *Spect.* No. 321 ¶6 His [Satan's] bounding over the Walls of Paradise. **1769** FALCONER *Dict. Marine* (1789) G g iv, The bounding of a flat stone thrown horizontally into the water. **1841** MACAULAY *Comic Dram. Restor.*, *Ess.* (1854) II. 569/2 Amidst the bounding of champagne corks.

bounding ('baʊndɪŋ), *ppl. a.*^{1} [f. BOUND *v.*^{1} + -ING^2.] That bounds, or forms a boundary to.

1593 SHAKS. *Lucr.* 1119 A gentle flood..the bounding banks o'erflows. **1789** BURNS *Banks of Frith* ii, Where bounding hawthorns gaily bloom. **1850** TENNYSON *In Mem.* xvii, Thro' circles of the bounding sky. **1881** MAXWELL *Electr. & Magn.* I. 17 The region has one bounding surface.

†**b.** With *on*: Bordering on. *Obs.*

1597 WARNER *Alb. Eng.*, *Æneidos* 317 A part of Thrace called Cressa, bounding on Mygdonia. **1600** HOLLAND *Livy* XXVII. xxx. 691 e, A citie..bounding upon the Ocean.

bounding ('baʊndɪŋ), *ppl. a.*^{2} [f. BOUND *v.*^{2} + -ING^2.] **1. a.** That bounds, leaps, or springs. Also *fig.*

a **1667** COWLEY *Greatness* Wks. 1710 II. 746 Playing at Nuts and Bounding Stones, with little Syrian and Moorish Boys. *a* **1700** DRYDEN *Ceyx & Alcyone*, *Fables* 363 Then o'er the bounding Billows shall we fly. **1783** COWPER *Task* VI. 327 The bounding fawn, that darts across the glade. **1837** MARRYAT *Dog-Fiend* xxiv, With what a bounding heart did [he] step into the boat! **1884** *Daily News* 1 Apr. 5/1 The days of a bounding revenue have not come back.

b. Of the pulse.

1879 *St. George's Hosp. Rep.* IX. 783 A very bad illness, marked by headache, bounding, hardly compressible pulse.

c. *fig.* Increasing by leaps and bounds.

1887 *Charity Organis. Rev.* III. 230 And yet, those.. bounding vagrancy returns!

2. = BOUNDERISH *a. colloq.*

1904 *Spectator* 31 Dec. 1089/1 A certain repulsion excited by his 'bounding' behaviour. **1924** H. A. VACHELL *Quinney's Adv.* 169, I caught him looking at that bounding Tommy Loring.

Hence **'boundingly** *adv.*

1838 *Monthly Mag.* 524 Away the bark boundingly goes.

boundless ('baʊndlɪs), *a.* and *sb.* [f. BOUND *sb.*^{1} + -LESS.] **A.** *adj.* Without bounds or limits; illimitable; unbounded, unlimited.

1592 *No-body & Some-b.* (1878) 288 He..Fills all the boundless country with applause. **1592** SHAKS. *Rom. & Jul.* II. ii. 133 My bounty is as boundlesse as the Sea. *a* **1625** FLETCHER *Mad Lover* IV. i. 16 She is a Princes and by that rule boundles. **1750** JOHNSON *Rambl.* No. 55 ¶6 With a boundless profusion of compliments. *a* **1796** BURNS *Farew. Eliza*, Boundless oceans roaring wide. **1848** MACAULAY *Hist. Eng.* I. 450 A boundless command of the rhetoric in which the vulgar express hatred and contempt. *a* **1859** — *ibid.* V. 562 The Revolution opened to the Churchills a.. boundless prospect of gain.

Hence **'boundlessly** *adv.*, and **'boundlessness**.

1674 N. FAIRFAX *Bulk & Selv.* 22 God..is boundlesly far and wide of me. **1823** BYRON *Age of Bronze* xiv, Blood and treasure boundlessly were spilt.

a **1619** DANIEL *Coll. Hist. Eng.* (1626) 107 Their boundlessnes came to be brought within some limits. **1682** NORRIS *Hierocles* 99 The boundlessness of desire. **1854** J. ABBOTT *Napoleon* (1855) I. xxiv. 374 She also knew the boundlessness of his ambition.

B. *sb.* That which has no bounds, the illimitable.

1909 *Westm. Gaz.* 10 July 3/2 We, a handful of men, concerning ourselves deeply in small matters, are brought face to face with the boundless.

'boundly, *a. rare*$^{-1}$. ? Subject to bounds, finite: the opposite of *boundless*. Or ? Bounden.

1817 KEATS *Sleep & Poetry* 209 O ye..Whose congregated majesty so fills My boundly reverence, that I cannot trace Your hallow'd names in this unholy place.

'boundness. [f. BOUND *pa. pple.* of BIND.] The condition of being bound or under obligation.

a **1866** J. GROTE *Exam. Util. Philos.* viii. 144 This boundness of us to duty.

† **'boundsome**, *a. Obs. rare.* [f. BOUND *sb.*^{1} + -SOME.] Held within bounds, finite.

1674 N. FAIRFAX *Bulk & Selv.* 15 The analogy that is between us, and other timesome and boundsome beings.

† **'boundure.** *Obs.* [f. BOUND *sb.*^{1} + -URE. Cf. *closure*, *seizure*.] A bounding or limiting, limitation; limit or bound. Cf. BOUNDER *sb.*^{1} 4.

1654 EARL MONM. tr. *Bentivoglio* 458 Large boundeurs were restored to the Towns of Breda etc. **1655-60** STANLEY *Hist. Philos.* (1701) 378/1 The boundure of that which is limited. **1634** SIR T. HERBERT *Trav.* 254 The boundure of Alexander's march into India being in the tract obscure.

boune, obs. f. BOON, and BOUND *a.* prepared.

boung, boungle, obs. ff. BUNG, BUNGLE.

[**bouning** (Mätz.) error for *bouuing* = BOWING.

c **1400** *Apol. Lollards* 62 Al bouuing doune.]

bounny, var. of BUNNY, *Obs.*, a swelling.

bounteous ('baʊntɪəs), *a.* Forms; 4-5 **bontyvous, bountyveus, bountevous(e, -euous(e, 5 bontyvese, bonteuous, bountyuous,** *superl.* **bounteest, 6 bountuous, 5- bounteous.** [ME. *bontyvous*, *bountevous*, f. OF. *bontif*, *bontive* benevolent, full of goodness (f. *bonté* goodness; see BOUNTY) + -OUS. Afterwards altered so as to appear f. *bounté*, BOUNTY + -OUS.]

1. Of persons or agents: Full of goodness; in modern use, always: Full of goodness to others, beneficent; generously liberal, munificent.

c **1374** CHAUCER *Troylus* I. 883 Ne y neuere saw a more bountevouse Of her astate. **1413** LYDG. *Pylgr. Sowle* V. xiv. 79 We thanken the..Of thy full bounteous benyuolence. **1477** EARL RIVERS (Caxton) *Dictes* 22 Be bonteuous to alle thoos that seke sciences. **1526** *Pilgr. Perf.* (W. de W. 1531) 19 b, His bountuous liberalite and mercy. **1605** SHAKS. *Macb.* III. i. 98 Euery one According to the gift which bounteous Nature Hath in him clos'd. **1606** — *Ant. & Cl.* IV. ii. 10 Lets to night Be bounteous at our Meale. **1681** DRYDEN *Abs. & Achit.* 872 Colleges on bounteous Kings depend. **1732** POPE *Hor. Sat.* II. ii. 60 Oyl, tho' it stink, they drop by drop impart, But sowse the cabbage with a bounteous heart. **1738** WESLEY *Hymn 'Come Holy Spirit,'* Thou bounteous Source of all our Store. **1871** R. ELLIS *Catullus* lxiv. 22 Born in bounteous ages.

†**b.** Of prowess; Valiant: see BOUNTY 1 b. *Obs.*

a **1440** *Sir Degrev.* 311 The knyghtus..in batelle so bountyveus. *c* **1485** *Digby Myst.* (1882) III. 952 The bounteest, and the boldest onder baner bryth.

2. Of things: Proceeding from bounty; generously or freely bestowed, 'liberal', plentiful, ample in size or amount, abundant.

1542 UDALL *Erasm. Apophth.* 341 a, To bee honoured with moste high & bounteous rewardes. **1697** DRYDEN *Virg. Georg.* I. 248 The promis'd Blessing of a Bounteous Crop. **1751** JOHNSON *Rambl.* No. 181 ¶4 The consequences which such a bounteous allotment [in a lottery] would have produced. **1790** COWPER *Iliad* I. 29 To accept the bounteous price. **1842** TENNYSON *Gardener's D.* 138 The bounteous wave of such a breast As never pencil drew. **1878** MORLEY *Diderot* II. 68 The land where production has been so noble, so bounteous, so superb.

'bounteously, *adv.* [f. prec. + -LY^2.] In a bounteous manner; with generous liberality; munificently; freely, plentifully, largely, amply.

1531 ELYOT *Gov.* I. xx, Ye may..bounteousely rewarde me. **1590** SPENSER *Muiopot.* 151 Feeding vpon their pleasures bounteouslie. **1601** SHAKS. *Twel. N.* I. ii. 52, I prethee (and Ile pay thee bounteously) Conceale me what I am. *a* **1649** DRUMM. OF HAWTH. *Biblioth. Edinb. Lectori* Wks. (1711) 222 Great spirits..learn to forget what they bounteously bestow. *a* **1843** SOUTHEY *Inscript.* xxxv. Wks. III. 153 Never had benignant nature shower'd More bounteously..Her choicest gifts. **1860** TYNDALL *Glac.* 184 The glorious light..was poured bounteously over crags, and snows.

'bounteousness. [f. as prec. + -NESS.] The quality of being bounteous or liberal; liberality, munificence.

c **1440** *Promp. Parv.* 46 Bontyvasnesse [**1499** bountyuousnesse] *munificentia, liberalitas*. *c* **1485** *Digby Myst.* (1882) III. 209 Heyll, prynse of bovntyows-nesse! **1571** GOLDING *Calvin on Ps.* lxviii. 11 A signe of hys bounteousnesse in watering the land with seasonable rayne. **1655** H. VAUGHAN *Silex Scint.* 151 Poor herbs drink and praise thy bounteousness. **1852** MISS YONGE *Cameos* (1877) III. xv. 126 Warwick occupied the chief place in the eyes of the nation, from his exceeding bounteousness to the poor.

bounteth, -ith ('bu:ntɪθ). *north. dial.* [app. a. OF. *bontet, buntet* (bun'teθ), the earlier (11–12th c.) form of *bonté*, whence BOUNTY (cf. *poortith, dainteth, faith*). But the word is known only since the 15th c. (in later times only in Scotch), so that its historical connexion with the OF. word is not illustrated.]

A gift of bounty; gratuity, reward; a gift stipulated for in addition to money wages. Cf. BOUNTY 4b.

c **1440** *York Myst.* xv. 118 For I haue herde declared.. That bountith aftir rewarde. **1553** DOUGLAS *Æneis* XII. vi. 127 This is the bounteth [*v.r.* bontay] thay sal bere away. **1724** RAMSAY *Tea-t. Misc.* (1733) II. 194 Saw ye Jenny Nettles.. Her fee and bountith in her lap. **1818** SCOTT *Rob Roy* xxiv, Upon my wage, board-wage, fee, and bountith. **1834** H. MILLER *Scenes & Leg.* xi. (1857) 168 He will not away from us without his bountith.

bountied ('baʊntɪd), *ppl. a.* [f. BOUNTY + -ED.] Supported or assisted by bounties.

1788 T. JEFFERSON *Writ.* (1859) II. 524 The eighty-five ships.. bountied as the English are, will require a sacrifice of twelve hundred and eighty-five thousand livres a year.

bountiful ('baʊntɪfʊl), *a.* [f. BOUNTY + -FUL.]
1. Of persons: Full of, or abounding in, bounty; graciously liberal, generous. ***Lady Bountiful***, a character in Farquhar's *Beaux' Stratagem* (1707): since used for the great (or beneficent) lady in a neighbourhood.

1508 FISHER *Wks.* (1876) 172 Thy mercy is.. so grete and bounteful to wretched synners. *a* **1577** SIR T. SMITH *Commw. Eng.* (1609) 27 Higher stomacke, and bountifuller liberality than others. **1596** SHAKS. *1 Hen. IV*, III. i. 168 A worthy gentleman.. as bountifull as Mynes of India. **1771** *Junius Lett.* lvi. 294 How much easier it is to be generous than just, and.. men are sometimes bountiful who are not honest. **1815** SCOTT *Paul's Lett.* (1839) 11 Those facts.. affect you as a Lady Bountiful. **1830** MACAULAY *Southey's Colloq., Ess.* (1854) I. 109/1 He [the magistrate] ought to be .. a Lady Bountiful in every parish, a Paul Pry in every house. **1857** BUCKLE *Civilis.* iii. 142 The richest countries were those in which nature was most bountiful.

2. Of things: Characterized by bounty, abundantly yielding; also, ample, abundant, plenteous.

1538 STARKEY *England* 77 Our mother the ground ys so plentuous and bountyful. **1601** SHAKS. *All's Well* II. ii. 15 That's a bountifull answere that fits all questions. **1860** TYNDALL I. §27. 207 A bountiful fire of pine logs was made. **1885** *Manch. Exam.* 26 Jan. 5/3 Soil so bountiful that one day's labour is sufficient to procure three days' living.

bountifully ('baʊntɪfʊlɪ), *adv.* [f. prec. + -LY[2].] In a bountiful manner; with generous liberality, munificently, plentifully, amply.

1580 HOLLYBAND *Treas. Fr. Tong, Largement*, largely, bountifullie, liberally, abundantly. **1593** PEELE *K. Edw. I*, And in my hall shall bountifully feed. **1611** BIBLE *2 Cor.* ix. 6 He which soweth bountifully, shall reape bountifully. **1725** *Lond. Gaz.* No. 6373/2 To provide so bountifully for instructing them. **1835** MARRYAT *Olla Podr.* iii, The fruits of the earth, so bountifully bestowed.

bountifulness ('baʊntɪfʊlnɪs). [f. prec. + -NESS.] The quality of being bountiful; generous liberality, bounteousness.

1489 CAXTON *Faytes of A.* I. xxi. 66 The whiche for example of hys bountefulnes we soo often remembre. **1558** *Act 1 Eliz.* iv. §29 The Queene.. of her abundant Grace and Bountifulness, is pleased, etc. **1862** F. HALL *Hindu Philos. Syst.* 117 To give praise for the love and bountifulness of our merciful Father.

† **'bountihead.** *Obs.* (exc. as an archaism). [f. BOUNTY + -HEAD.] Bounteousness.

1596 SPENSER *F.Q.* II. x. 2 How shall fraile pen.. Conceive such soveraine glory and great bountyhed! **1621** AINSWORTH *Annot. Ps.* cxxxvi. 1 The mercy or bountihed which hee receiveth. [**1864** *Temple Bar* Dec. 43 The glorious dead Who have left us their grace and their bountihead.]

† **bountines, bountenes.** *Obs. rare.* Bounteousness. [But the standing of the word is insecure: the first instance may be *bounteues*; the second may be an error of the press.]

1512 *Act 4 Hen. VIII*, xix. Pream., The goodnes bountenes liberalitie favour.. by his Highnes shewed. **1650** HANMER *Eccl. Hist.* 176 Bountiness [1st ed. 177 bountifulnes].

bounting, obs. form of BUNTING.

bountree (*Sc.* 'buntri). [? A variant of BOURTREE; or a distinct word = *bound-tree*, f. BOUND *sb.* from being planted to mark boundaries.]

Common name in Scotland of the Elder-tree. Also *attrib*, as in ***bountree gun***.

1821 *Blackw. Mag.* Aug. (JAM.) Bountry-guns are formed of the elder tree, the soft pith being taken out. **1848** *Proc. Berw. Nat. Club* II. vi. 265 The Ash and the Bountree were also observed.

bounty ('baʊntɪ). Forms: 4 bunte, bwnte, 4–6 bonte, bounte, bountee, 5 bount, bownte, 5–6 bontie, 6 *Sc.* bontay, 6–7 bountie, -ye, 6– bounty. [a. OF. *bontet*:—L. *bonitāt-em* goodness.]

† **1. a.** Of persons: Goodness in general, worth, virtue; in *pl.* virtues, excellences; also excellent condition, high estate. *Obs.*

a **1300** *Cursor M.* 10086 þis leuedi lele, þat buntes in hir bar sa fele. **1375** BARBOUR *Bruce* II. 48 Neuir.. man sa hard sted as wes he, That eftirwart com to sic bounte. *c* **1386** CHAUCER *Clerkes T.* 359 Publissched was the bounte of hir name.. in many a regioun. *c* **1440** *Partonope* 4525 Bount, mercy, and eke mekenesse. **1485** CAXTON *Chas. Gt.* 238 Thou knowest what I haue doon for the bounte that is in the. **1513** DOUGLAS *Æneis* XIII. ii. 152 The gret Enee Quhilk in excelland vertu and bonte Excedyt all the remanent a far way. **1623** DRUMM. OF HAWTH. *Cypress Grove* Wks. (1711) 127 He is only the true and essential Bounty, so is He the only essential and true Beauty.

† **b.** Warlike prowess, valour; *rarely*, a deed of valour. *Obs.*

c **1330** *Amis & Amil.* 5 Twoo barons of grete bounte. **1375** BARBOUR *Bruce* III. 132 He thocht.. To do ane owtrageouss bounte. *a* **1400** *Morte Arth.* (Roxb.) 5 Off alle þe world the beste knight Off biaute and of bounte. *c* **1430** *Syr Gener.* 9828 His bountie fel fast to ground. **1485** CAXTON *Paris & V.* 22 What honour is comen to me by hys prowesse and by his bounte. *c* **1530** LD. BERNERS *Arthur* 243 For he is the chefe floure of bounte in all maner of chyvalry.

† **2.** Of things: Good quality or property, worth, excellence, virtue. *Obs.*

c **1300** *Beket* 1031 Gold ne passeth noȝt in Bounte so moche Leode. *c* **1314** *Guy Warw.* (A.) 825 He schal bring to þe turment þat day.. a stede of gret bounte. *c* **1450** LONELICH *Grail* xlvii. 21 Kamalot.. was of sweche bownte that alle kinges weren crowned þere sekerle. **1525** LD. BERNERS *Froiss.* II. Pref., The bountie of the same cronycles, in whom are conteygned the warres of these parties.. encorageth me. **1531** ELYOT *Gov.* II. vii. (1557) 104 Noryshyng meates and drynkes in a sycke body doe lose their bountee. **1592** WYRLEY *Armorie* 152 By his coursers bountie sir Hue Chatelon Was savd.

† **3.** Kindness, beneficence; an act of kindness, a good turn (sometimes *ironical*). *Obs.*

a **1300** *Cursor M.* 12501/2 Quar-for.. To þis dedman þat hight als þou, Ne dos þou grace o bunte nan? **1330** R. BRUNNE *Chron.* 266 For Edward gode dede þe Baliol did him mede a wikked bounte. *c* **1386** CHAUCER *Pers. T.* ¶451 Agayn wikked dede of his enemy, he shal doon hym bountee. *c* **1450** *Merlin* xii. 181 And she hym asked what bounte it was that she hadde hym don. **1483** CAXTON *Gold. Leg.* 160/2 He remembryd euyl the bountee that he did to hym. **1651** *Proc. Parliament* No. 92. 1407 Christ came the neerest to him [Peter] in a miraculous bounty.

4. a. Goodness shown in giving, gracious liberality, munificence: usually attributed to God, or to the great and wealthy, who have it in their power to give largely and liberally.

a **1300** *Cursor M.* 9531 To quam ilkan he gaf sum-thing Of his might and of his bounte. *a* **1450** *Knt. de la Tour* (1868) 137 For her bounte and goodnesse, God hath shewed mani miracles for her. **1542** UDALL *Erasm. Apophth.* 215a, Bountie and largesse is befallyng for kynges. **1579** GOSSON *Sch. Abuse* (Arb.) 40 The honourable bountye of a noble minde. **1611** DEKKER *Roar. Girle* Wks. 1873 III. 141 When bounty spreades the table, faith t'were sinne (at going of) if thankes should not step in. **1750** JOHNSON *Rambl.* No. 17 ¶4 Every other satisfaction which the bounty of Providence has scattered over life. **1839** THIRLWALL *Greece* VII. 207 The royal liberality of his nature, which delighted in acts of bounty. **1856** FROUDE *Hist. Eng.* (1858) I. iv. 302 Many of these people.. were dependent on his bounty.

b. An act of generosity, a thing generously bestowed; a boon, gift, gratuity.

c **1250** *O.E. Misc.* 36 For þise griate bunte þet ure lord yefþ. **1377** LANGL. *P. Pl.* B. XIV. 150 Men doth hym other bounte, ȝyueth hym a cote aboue his couenaunte. **1513** DOUGLAS *Æneis* VIII. Prol. 140 Sum [langis] for thar bonty or bone. **1602** *Return fr. Parnass.* II. i. (Arb.) 21 Here is.. foure pence your due, and eight pence my bounty. **1679–88** *Secr. Serv. M. Chas. II & Jas. II.* (1851) 68 To Coll^d Morrice Kingwell, bounty £1000 0. **1725** DE FOE *Voy. Round World* (1840) 103, I gave a largess or bounty of five dollars a man. **1878** MORLEY *Diderot* I. 289 The Empress added a handsome bounty to the bargain.

5. *esp.* **a.** A gift bestowed by the sovereign personally, or by the state. ***Queen Anne's Bounty***: see quots.

1708 *Royal Procl.* in *Lond. Gaz.* No. 4504/1 All such Seamen.. shall Receive as our free Gift and Royal Bounty, the respective Rewards and Allowances following.
1704 *Off. Notice* in *Lond. Gaz.* No. 4077/4 The Governors of the Bounty of Queen Anne, for the Augmentation of the Maintenance of the Poor Clergy. **1707** *Ibid.* No. 4323/3 A General Court of.. the Bounty of Queen Anne. **1768** BLACKSTONE *Comm.* I. 286 To this end she granted her royal charter.. whereby all the revenue of first-fruits and tenths is vested in trustees for ever, to form a perpetual fund for the augmentation of poor livings. This is usually called queen Anne's bounty.

b. A gratuity given to recruits on joining the army or navy; also as a reward to soldiers.

1702 *Royal Procl.* in *Lond. Gaz.* No. 3821/2 Such who shall Desert any of Our Ships of War, in Order to obtain Our intended Bounty. **1801** BLOOMFIELD *Rural T.* (1802) 52 Employment fail'd, and poverty was come; The Bounty tempted me. **1833** MARRYAT *P. Simple* (1863) 119 On his arrival at Gibraltar, he had been offered and had received the bounty. **1873** *Act 36 & 37 Vict.* lxxvii. §8 Out of any bounty or pay receivable by him.

c. A sum of money paid to merchants or manufacturers for the encouragement of some particular branch of industry.

1719 W. WOOD *Surv. Trade* 150 Whatever shall be paid the Northern Colonies as a Bounty at first, to enter heartily and chearfully upon the doing of this. **1776** ADAM SMITH *W.N.* I. I. xi. 207 In 1688 was granted the Parliamentary bounty upon the exportation of corn. *Ibid.* II. IV. v. 99 Bounties are sometimes called premiums. **1817** BABINGTON in *Parl. Deb.* 762 The evils.. arising from creating manufactures by means of a bounty from Government. **1852** McCULLOCH *Dict. Comm.* 1255 The existing bounties (draw-backs) on refined British colonial sugar are specified in the 11 & 12 Vict. c. 97.

d. A reward offered for the scalp of an American Indian, or for the body of a wanted criminal taken dead or alive. Now *Hist. N. Amer.*

1764 J. PENN in *Pennsylvania Archives* 4th Ser. (1900) III. *Papers of Governors* 292, I do.. promise, that there shall be paid.. the following several and respective premiums and Bounties for the prisoners and Scalps of the Enemy Indians that shall be taken or killed. **1886** MORLEY *Crit. Misc.* I 110 The grandson of William Penn proclaimed a bounty of fifty dollars for the scalp of a female Indian, and three times as much for a male. **1929** H. G. EVARTS *Tomahawk Rights* xii. 224 Twas the very settlers from hereabouts that.. forced Pennsylvania to put a bounty on all Injun scalps. **1947** R. SANTEE *Apache Land* iii. 34 The Mexican States offered a bounty for Apache scalps. **1970** D. BROWN *Bury my Heart at Wounded Knee* ii. 25 The Spanish, French, Dutch, and English colonists made the custom [*sc.* scalping] popular by offering bounties for scalps of their respective enemies.

e. A sum of money paid for the scalp (pelt, etc.) of each animal of a particular (usu. dangerous) species killed. Chiefly *N. Amer.*

1847, etc. [see SCALP *sb.*[1] 2 c]. **1912** *Oregonian* (Portland) 20 Oct. 5/7 Indians and others make good wages killing young coyotes and selling the pelts for bounty. **1919** C. G. ABBOTT *Friends & Foes of Wild Life* 5 Under present conditions in New York State.. the institution of a bounty system would be of little.. benefit. **1954** W. R. EADIE *Animal Control* 80 Many states pay bounties on bobcats. **1979** W. ASHWORTH *Carson Factor* vi. 61 The bounty system spread across the nation.. reaching Oregon in 1840... The first modern bounty law was passed in 1909, and during.. four years nearly ninety-two thousand coyotes were slaughtered.

f. *transf.* and *fig.* A premium or reward.

1868 M. PATTISON *Academ. Org.* 62 Scholarships.. are become a bounty upon a privileged species of education.

g. ***King's*** (or ***Queen's***) ***bounty***: a sum of money given from the royal purse to a mother who has given birth to three or more children at once.

1872 *Porcupine* 8 June 156/1 Frenchwomen are seldom recipients of the Queen's bounty. **1910** *Encycl. Brit.* IV. 324/2 King's Bounty. **1939** *Times Lit. Suppl.* 18 Mar. 162/3 Here, too, are.. 'quins' and the King's Bounty.

6. *Attrib.* and *Comb.*, as ***bounty-money***; **bounty-broker** (see quot.); **bounty-fed**, supported and encouraged by bounties; **bounty-hunter** *N. Amer.* (now *Hist.*), a person who pursues wanted criminals, etc., for the sake of rewards offered; **bounty-jumper**, *U.S.* (see quot.); **bountyless**, without bounty.

1864 SALA in *Daily Tel.* 9 Aug., A *bounty-broker is simply a crimp, or what the recruiting sergeants in Charles-street, Westminster, call a 'bringer'. **1884** *Sat. Rev.* 14 June 781/1 A countervailing duty upon *bounty-fed sugar. **1930** *U.S. Dept. Agric. Official Rec.* 27 Mar. 7/2 The arrest of these dishonest *bounty hunters has broken up the activities of thieves in the State [of Washington]. **1954** E. LEONARD *Bounty Hunters* vi. 45 Duro studied the bounty hunter silently. Within him he could feel the hatred for this man. **1964** L. COCHRAN *Wilderness* vi. 53 All but the leader [*sc.* a wolf] had met their death by eating poisoned baits set by bounty hunters. **1984** *Listener* 14 June 37/4 Fonda is an ageing bounty-hunter who brings a corpse in for the inexperienced sheriff. **1875** HIGGINSON *Hist. U.S.* 306 Bringing into the service many '*bounty-jumpers'.. who enlisted merely for money, and soon deserted to enlist again. **1864** *Daily Tel.* 9 Sept., His conscripts, *bountyless as they may be, will have to be paid. **1692** LUTTRELL *Brief Rel.* (1857) II. 524 Letters from Torbay say that they were distributing the *bounty money. **1863** *Cornh. Mag.* Mar. 443 The kit is no longer to be paid for out of the bounty-money.

bountyng, obs. form of BUNTING.

† **boup**, *v.* *Obs. rare.* To bump.

1715 BAGFORD *Let.* in *Leland's Coll.* I. Pref. 76 If he refused to do this [to salute the post] they [the Billingsgate porters] forthwith lay'd hold of him, and by main force boup'd his a—— against the post.

bouquet (bu:'keɪ, 'bu:keɪ). Also boquet. [a. Fr. *bouquet* orig. 'little wood' cognate with Pr. *bosquet*, It *boschetto* dim. of *bosco* wood. cf. BUSKET.]

1. a. A bunch of flowers, a nosegay; also *fig.*

1716–8 LADY M. W. MONTAGUE *Lett.* I. xxxii. 111 A large *bouquet* of jewels, made like natural flowers. **1768** STERNE *Sent. Journ.* (1778) II. 144 He had wrapt [paper] round the stalks of a *bouquet* to keep it together. **1785** T. WARTON *Notes on Milton* (L.) May-buskets; if busket be not there the French *bouquet*, now become English. **1791** BURKE *Corr.* (1844) III. 278 The flowers.. I.. had seen.. tied up in one *bouquet*. *a* **1845** HOOD *Sniffing a Birthd.* x, No flowery garlands—no bouquet. **1880** O. W. HOLMES in *Scribner's Mag.* XXI. 157 I'm a florist in verse and what *would* people say If I came to a banquet without my bouquet? [Cf. Fr. sense, 'petite pièce de vers pour une fête'.]

b. *fig.* A compliment, praise; phr. ***to throw bouquets***, to pay compliments.

1904 *Journalist* 28 May 89 We do not wish to say 'I told you so', or to 'throw any bouquets' in our own direction. **1907** N. MUNRO *Daft Days* xxiii. 203 I've never done throwing bouquets at myself about it ever since. **1955** *Times* 4 May 9/6 The union would inevitably receive their share of the brickbats and bouquets.

2. The perfume exhaled from wine.

1846 *French Dom. Cookery* 320 Negligence in the filling of the casks..will destroy the bouquet. *c* **1865** in *Circ. Sc.* I. 353/1 The perfume, or 'bouquet,' is something different from the odour of wine. **1873** LYTTON *K. Chillingly* IV. vii, Lifting his glass to his lips, [he] voluptuously inhaled its bouquet. **1876** BARTHOLOW *Mat. Med.* (1879) 350 Bouquet is that quality of wine which salutes the nose.

3. *transf.* **a.** A bunch of flavouring herbs. Also **bouquet garni** [F., 'garnished bouquet'] (see quots.). **b.** A large flight of rockets, as the close of a firework display. **c.** The flight of a multitude of pheasants breaking covert from the central point at which the beaters meet; this central spot itself.

1846 *French Dom. Cookery* 41 A garnished bouquet is when thyme, fennel, and bay are added to the parsley and onions. **1852** F. BISHOP *Illustr. London Cookery Bk.* 408 *Bouquet*, a bunch of parsley and scallions tied up to put in soups, &c. *Bouquet garni*, or *Assaisonné*, the same, with the addition of cloves or aromatic herbs. **1875** 'STONEHENGE' *Brit. Sports* I. I. vii. §4. 104 The shooters are now collected to the spot to which all the beaters congregate, termed the bouquet. **1879** *Times* 2 June, The great bouquet of rockets being particularly fine. **1960** *Woman* 3 Dec. 42 Classic ingredients of a bouquet garni are half a bay leaf, three or four long-stemmed sprigs of parsley, and a sprig of thyme.

bouqueted (buːˈkeɪd), *a. rare.* [f. BOUQUET + -ED².] Furnished with a bouquet or bouquets.

1860 *All Y. Round* No. 52. 34 The..lorgnetted..bouqueted..perfumed..throng.

‖**bouquetier** (buːkəˈtɪə(r), Fr. buktje). Also erron. -ière. [Fr., f. BOUQUET.] A small holder for a bunch of flowers, esp. one carried in the hand.

1786 J. WEDGWOOD *Let.* 22 July (1965) 300 It consisted of upwards of £100 worth, of vases, bouquetiers, [etc.]. **1871** A. NESBITT in W. Chaffers *Catal. Slade Coll. Glass* 80 Large Blue Bouquetière. **1875** METEYARD *Wedgwood Handbk.* 392 Bouquetier. A flower-pot,..often with a pierced cover for the insertion of the stems of flowers.

‖**bouquetin** (bukətæ̃, ˈbuːkətɪn). [F. *bouquetin*, app. for *bouc-estain*, ad. Pr. 15th c. *bocstagn*, Ger. *stein-bock*.] An animal of the Goat tribe, inhabiting Switzerland; the ibex, or steinbock.

1783 W. F. MARTYN *Geog. Mag.* II. 312 The..animals..peculiar to this country [Switzerland] are the bouquetin and the chamois. **1824** CAMPBELL *Theodric* 9 Heights browsed by the bounding bouquetin. **1882** *Cornh. Mag.* Jan. 56 I'm off to the Pyrenees to shoot bears and bouquetins.

bouquinist (ˈbuːkɪnɪst). [a. Fr. *bouquiniste*, f. *bouquin* an old book.] A dealer in second hand books of little value.

1840 *New Month. Mag.* LX. 493 The students, besides, are the property of the *bouquinists* (we want the term in our language).

bour, obs. f. BOOR and BOWER.

†**ˈbourage.** *Obs. rare.* Also bowrage. [app. an erroneous form for Fr. *bourg*.] *bourage of Saint Peter*: The suburb of Rome called the Borgo, containing St. Peter's, the Vatican, etc.

1523 LD. BERNERS *Froiss.* I. cccxxvi. 510 The romayns..came into the bowrage of saynt Peter. *Ibid.* cccxlvi. 549 They..conquered the bourage of saynt Peter.

bourage, bourrage, obs. ff. BORAGE.

Bourbon (burbɔ̃, ˈbʊəbɒn, -ən), *sb.* [f. *Bourbon l'Archambault*, a town in the department of l'Allier, France.]

1. A member of the family which long held the thrones of France and Naples, and until 1931 that of Spain; also *fig.* as in quot. 1873, and *attrib.*

1768 STERNE *Sent. Journ.* (1775) I. 5 No—said I—the Bourbon is by no means a cruel race. **1873** TRISTRAM *Moab* xiv. 254 Muleteers are certainly typical Bourbons, They learn nothing and they forget nothing.

2. *transf.* In U.S. politics: A nickname for 'a Democrat behind the age and unteachable'.

1884 *Boston (Mass.) Jrnl.* 29 Nov. 2/4 The Herald wants the Bourbons, 'the men who still swear by Andrew Jackson', sent to the rear. *Ibid.* 20 Sept., That chief of Bourbon organs, the Charleston (S.C.) News.

3. a. The former name of the island now called Réunion, in the Indian Ocean, so named in 1642 in honour of the French royal family; whence **Bourbon Palm**, a common name of the genus *Latania*, found in Réunion and Mauritius.

b. A rose belonging to a group of hybrids (*Rosa × borboniensis*) produced by *R. chinensis* and *R. damascena*, believed to have originated in Réunion (Isle de Bourbon) *c* 1825, and used as a parent of many modern varieties.

1829 LOUDON *Encycl. Plants* 446 *Rosa centifolia*... Garden Varieties... Bourbon. **1841** *Penny Cycl.* XX. 158/1 Bourbon rose..is a natural hybrid between *R. Indica* and a variety called red four-seasons. This hybrid was found among a number of the latter plants in a hedge in the Isle of Bourbon. **1852** S. WARNER *Queechy* liv, The air was full of the sweetness of damask and Bourbon varieties. **1869** S. R. HOLE *Book about Roses* 173 Of the Bourbons..there are several which are valuable additions to a general collection of Roses. *Ibid.* 174 Catherine Guillot, with Louise Odier,..are..two winsome maids of honour in waiting upon the Bourbon Queen. **1962** *Amat. Gardening* 24 Mar. 4/3 The species and older shrub roses such as the albas, Bourbons, damasks and gallicas.

c. ***Bourbon tea***: see TEA *sb.* 6.

1861 BENTLEY *Man. Bot.* 667 *Angræcum fragrans.*—The dried leaves of this fragrant species are used as a kind of tea in the Mauritius. This is commonly known as *Faham* or *Bourbon tea*.

4. (ˈbɜːbən) Whisky of a kind originally made in Bourbon County, Kentucky; a glass of this whisky. Also *attrib.* orig. *U.S.*

1846 in *Amer. Speech* (1963) XXXVIII. 158 Old Bourbon. **1850** 'M. TENSAS' *Odd Leaves from Louisiana 'Swamp Doctor'* 37, I would have sworn it was good old Bourbon whiskey. **1862** *Congress. Globe* May 2288/3 One barrel of genuine Bourbon liquor. **1957** J. BRAINE *Room at Top* vii. 75 George poured me another Bourbon. **1958** G. GREENE *Our Man in Havana* v. v. 238 Bourbon is stronger than Scotch.

5. ***Bourbon biscuit***: a chocolate-flavoured biscuit with a chocolate cream filling.

1932 L. GOLDING *Magnolia Street* v. 103 Mrs. Poyser sent in some smoked salmon and a bag of Bourbon biscuits. **1960** R. COLLIER *House called Memory* iii. 44 The chocolate biscuits, the bourbon biscuits, and the bridge rolls.

Hence [from sense 1] **Bourˈbonian**, **Bourˈbonic** *adjs.*, of or pertaining to the Bourbons; **Bourboniˈzation**, reduction under Bourbon predominance; **ˈBourbonism**, adhesion to the Bourbon dynasty, or to the Bourbon party in U.S. politics; **ˈBourbonist**, a supporter of the Bourbon dynasty.

1651 HOWELL *Venice* 177* This present Pope Innocent the tenth is as much an Austrian as the other was a Bourbonian. **1728** MORGAN *Hist. Algiers* II. iv. 271 The Burbonian and Austrian Factions. **1883** L. FIGUEROLA *Pol. Cond. Spain* in *Fortn. Rev.*, The first Bourbonic branch. **1886** SEELEY in *Academy* 6 Feb., The bourbonisation of the Continent. **1884** *Boston* (Mass.) *Jrnl.* 18 Sept., The spirit of pro-slavery Bourbonism. **1820** *Edin. Rev.* XXXIV. 3 Our travellers..occasionally take part with..Bourbonists. **1862** *Standard* 13 Dec., The Bourbonists..carried a white banner with a fleur de lys.

†**bourd**, *sb. Obs.* Forms: 4-5 burde, 4-7 bord(e, bourd(e, 5 bouerd, 5-6 bowrd(e, 5-7 boord(e, 7 boward. [ME. *bourde*, a. OF. *bourde*, Pr. *borda* 'lie, cheating, deception', of unknown origin.

Diez's proposed identification of OF. *bourde* with *behort* 'tournament, tilting', is discarded; for '*bourde* goes back to a date before the contraction of *behourt* to *bourt* could have taken place, and originally there was no connexion of sense' (P. Meyer). At a later time *behourder* was contracted to *behourder, bourder*, and thus brought into confusion with this word and its verb *bourder*: see BOURD *v.*]

An idle tale, a jest, a joke; jesting, raillery, joking, merriment, fun; a merry tale.

c **1340** *Gaw. & Gr. Knt.* 1212 Al laȝande þe lady lanced þo bourdez. **1387** TREVISA *Higden* Rolls Ser. IV. 143 He wolde torne hit to bourde and lawȝhynge. **1430** LYDG. *Chron. Troy* II. xvi, All his speche ful of bouerdes was. *c* **1430** —— *Min. Poems* 57 To be forsworn they hold it but a bord. *a* **1450** *Knt. de la Tour* (1868) 111 The kingges doughter..called hym in bourde her sone. *c* **1520** *King & Barker* 110 in Hazl. *E.P.P.* 9 Owr kyng lowhe, and had god bord. **1548** CRANMER *Catech.* 25 b, I spake not these wourdes in ernest but in borde. **1593** DRAYTON *Eclog.* VII. 208 For all thy Jests, and all thy merrie Bourds. **1606** HOLLAND *Sueton.* 63 Either in earnest or boord [*vel serio vel joco*].

b. In a bad sense: Mockery, bantering. (Probably the earlier sense, as in French.)

1320-30 *Lai le Freine* 9 Bourdes and ribaudy. **1340** *Ayenb.* 56 Þanne beyþ þe burdes and þe trufles uor entremes. **1483** CAXTON *G. de la Tour* B vj b, Al was taken for a bourd and a mocquerye. *a* **1541** WYATT in *Tottel's Misc.* (Arb.) 51 Nought moueth you my dedly mone, But stil you turne it into bordes. **1602** FULBECKE *1st Pt. Parall.* 71 If a man..should strike an other or vse broad boward against him.

c. Play, game.

1362 LANGL. *P. Pl.* A. x. 197. **1530** PALSGR. 199/2 Bourde or game, *jeu*.

†**bourd**, *v.*¹ *Obs.* [a. OF. *bourder*, f. *bourde*: see prec.]

1. *intr.* To say things in jest or mockery; to jest, joke; to make fun, make game.

1303 R. BRUNNE *Handl. Synne* 8667 How a bonde man bourdede wyþ a knyȝt. **1375** BARBOUR *Bruce* VIII. 383 A lord so sweet and debonar, So blith als and so veill bowrdand. *a* **1450** *Knt. de la Tour* (1868) 40 He herde hem clatre, laughe, iangle, and borde of highe. **1481** CAXTON *Reynard* (Arb.) 27 Ye borde and iape with me, for what I seche I fynde not. *a* **1555** BRADFORD *Wks.* 38 We shall feel it is no bourding with him. *a* **1600** in Kelly *Sc. Prov.* (1721) 56 (JAM.) Bourd not wi' bawtie (lest he bite you). *c* **1674** RAY *N.C. Wds.* s.v., Bourd neither with me nor with my honour, *Prov. Scot.* **1703** D. WILLIAMSON *Serm. bef. Gen. Assembly* 59 It is not safe to bourd with God, Conscience and Death. *a* **1758** RAMSAY *Poems* (1800) II. 175 (JAM.) Never gi'e Encouragement or bourd with sic as he.

b. To play.

c **1440** *Promp. Parv.* 44 Boordon, or pleyyn, *ludo, jocor.* *c* **1450** *Merlin* 31 Whiche..passeden thourgh the feild where childern were bourdinge. **1548** UDALL, etc. *Erasm. Par., Mark* vi. 42 Euen when he bourdeth to, or maketh any game or pastyme. **1559** *Mirr. Mag., Clifford* vi, To part his necke, and with his head to bourd.

2. *trans.* To make game of, mock, jest with.

1592 G. HARVEY *Pierce's Super.* 194 No man could..bourd a wilfull friend more dryly. **1636** JAMES *Iter Lanc.* 102 In a wan fainte palenesse bourding death.

†**bourd**, *v.*² *Obs.* Also 4-5 borde, 5 bordyn, boordon, -de, bouerd, 4-6 bourde. [f. F. *border, bourder*, contr. from *behorder* to fence, tilt, f. *behord, behort* tilting lance, tilting, tourney; see Diez. Probably confounded with prec.]

intr. To joust, tilt; to engage in a sham fight.

c **1450** *Merlin* vi. 100 And after mete..yede the barouns and the knyghtes to boorde in a feire pleyn. *Ibid.* ix. 133 After mete was the quyntayne reysed, and ther at bourded the yonge bachelers.

bourd, bourde, obs. f. BOARD *sb.* and *v.*

bourdain, -den, obs. ff. BURDEN *v.*

bourdel, obs. variant of BORDEL.

†**ˈbourder.** *Obs.* Forms: 4 burdoure, bourdeoure, bordiour, 4-9 bourdour, 5 bordere, -youre, bowrder, 6 bourder, *Sc.* burdour, 6-7 boorder, 7 boarder. [ME. *bourd(e)our*, a. AFr. *bourd(e)our*, = OF. *bordeor*, f. *border, bourder* to BOURD *v.*¹] A jester, a joker, a buffoon; a mocker.

1330 R. BRUNNE *Chron.* 204 A knyght a bourdour kyng R. hade. *c* **1375** ? BARBOUR *St. Ninian* 890 His menstrale..þat ves gud mane & gud burdoure. *c* **1440** *Promp. Parv.* 44 Bordyoure, or pleyare [**1499** bordere], *joculator.* **1483** CAXTON *G. de la Tour* C i, He is but a bourdour and a deceyuer of ladyes. **1552** HULOET, Bourder or rayler, whiche doth counterfayte those whome he mocketh. Bourder, or scoffer. **1606** J. DAVIES *2nd Husb. for Overburie's Wife* (1877) 12 Yet boord no Buffons that are boorders broad. [**1801** STRUTT *Sports & Past.* III. ii. 141 Strolling companies, composed of minstrels..bourdours or jesters, and other performers.]

bourdes, variant of BOURDIS, *Obs.*

†**ˈbourdful**, *a. Obs.* [f. BOURD *sb.* + -FUL.] Full of jesting or sport; jocose, sportive. Hence **ˈbourdfully** *adv.*, in jest, in mockery.

1388 WYCLIF *Wisd.* i. 11 *marg.*, Vndurstondun of a dedly leesing, not of a bourdeful leesing. *a* **1400** *Miracle-pl.* in *Rel. Ant.* II. 45 Bourdfully takyng Goddis biddynge or wordis or werkis is scornyng of him. *c* **1400** *Destr. Troy* 3952 [Antenor] delited hym in myrthe, Bourdfull among buernes. **1496** *Dives & Paup.* (W. de Worde) VIII. ii. 322/2 Called in latyn iocosum, that is bourdfull in Englysshe.

†**ˈbourding**, *vbl. sb. Obs.* [f. BOURD *v.*¹ + -ING¹.] Jesting, joking; buffoonery; trifling.

c **1340** *Gaw. & Gr. Knt.* 1404 In her bourdyng þay bayþen in þe morn, To fylle þe same forwardez. *c* **1449** PECOCK *Repr.* I. xx. 120 That men..schulden pleie in word bi bourding. **1566** KNOX *Hist. Ref.* Wks. 1846 I. 147 It was bitter bowrding to the Cardinall and his courte. *a* **1658** J. DURHAM in Spurgeon *Treas. Dav.* Ps. lxxxv. 8 Let them beware of bourding and dallying with God's mercy.

†**ˈbourding**, *ppl. a. Obs.* [f. BOURD *v.*¹ + -ING².] That jests, jokes, mocks, or trifles. So **bourdingly** *adv.*

1552 HULOET, Bourder or rayler..beynge of that mocking and bourdyng sort. —— Bourdingly, or in bourde, *iocose.*

†**bourdis.** *Obs.* Also burdis, bordis, bourdys, -es, -ise. [ME. *burdis, bordis, bourdis*, a. OF. *bordis, burdiz*, earlier *behordeis, bohordis*, mod.F. *béhourdis* shock of lances, tourney, f. OF. *behurt, behourt* lance, of uncertain origin; see Littré.] Tilting, fencing with lances.

1303 R. BRUNNE *Handl. Synne* 4662 Myracles and bourdys Or tournamentys of grete prys. *c* **1320** *Seuyn Sag.* (W.) 744 The leuedi stod..For to bihelde the burdis. *c* **1314** *Guy Warw.* (A.) 167 Al him preysed þer y-fere Of bordis and turnament. *c* **1350** *Will. Palerne* 1477 He was atte a bourdes þer bachilers pleide. *c* **1450** *Merlin* vi. 100 The x men..yede also to se this bourdise.

†**bourdise**, *v. Obs. rare*⁻¹. [f. prec.] *intr.* To joust, tilt.

c **1320** *Seuyn Sag.* (W.) 740 The knight was lopen on his stede, And burdised with the knightes of the lond.

†**ˈbourdly**, *adv. Obs. rare.* [f. BOURD *sb.* + -LY².] Jestingly, in jest, frivolously.

1500 *Ort. Voc.* in *Promp. Parv.* 44 *Nugaciter*, bourdly.

†**ˈbourdon**¹, **burdoun.** *Obs.* exc. *Hist.* Forms: 3-6 burdon, 4-5, 9 bordon, -un, 4-6 burdoun(e, 7 bourdon. [a. Fr. *bourdon* 'pilgrim's staff', Pr. and Sp. *bordon*, It. *bordone*, med.L. *burdōn-em*, identified by Du Cange and Diez with *burdo* mule (the name being transferred from the pilgrim's mule to his staff). Littré suggests connexion with *bourde* 'pole used to support a grounded ship', which he further refers to *behourt* lance; but here there seems some error.]

1. A pilgrim's staff.

a **1300** *K. Horn* 1092 Horn took burdon and scrippe. *c* **1320** *Syr Beves* 2063 Beues..gaf him is hors..For is bordon and is sklauin. **1362** LANGL. *P. Pl.* A. VI. 8 He bar a bordun [**1377** burdoun, **1393** bordon], I-bounde wiþ a brod lyste. **1413** LYDG. *Pylgr. Sowle* I. i. (1859) 2 Caste doune thy scrippe and thy burdon. **1652** URQUHART *Jewel* Wks. (1834) 230 With a palmer's coat upon him, a bourdon in his hand, and some few cockle shels stuck to his hat. **1849** ROCK *Ch. Fathers* II. vi. 199 [The Cathedral prior was suffered to use the silver bordon, which may..be called the prior's staff].

2. A stout staff; a club, a cudgel; sometimes app. a spear or spear-shaft.

c **1325** *Pol. Songs* 150 Beggares go with bordon and bagges. *c* **1425** WYNTOUN *Cron.* VIII. xxxviii. 56 Ilkane a gud Burdowne in hand. **1483** CAXTON *Gold. Leg.* 31/4 Helysee put hys bourdon in the water and anon the yron began to swymme. **1513** DOUGLAS *Æneis* VII. ix. 69 Ane bowrdoune

of ane lang styf tre, The poynt scharpyt and brynt ane lytill we. **1535** STEWART *Cron. Scot.* III. 311 Mony burdoun vpoun basnot brak. **1550** LYNDESAY *Sqr. Meldrum* 445 Twa nobilmen of weir..And in their handis strang burdounis.

bourdon², **burdoun** (ˈbʊədɒn). Also 4 bor-, burdoun, -don, 5 burdown. [a. F. *bourdon* the continuous bass or 'drone' of the bagpipe, the bass string of a violin, etc., also a drone bee, = Sp. *bordon*, Pg. *bordão*, It. *bordone*, med.L. *burdo* drone: possibly an imitative word: cf. the Celtic stem *durd-*, *dord-*, noise, sound.

(A conjecture that the bass-pipe of an organ, or drone of a bag-pipe may have been so called from its resemblance to a staff, BOURDON¹, is not supported by the history.)]

†**1.** The low undersong or accompaniment, which was sung while the leading voice sang a melody.

For the continuation of this sense see BURDEN, in which word it has been completely merged.

c **1386** CHAUCER *Prol.* 673 This Somonour bar to hym a stif burdoun [*v.r.* bordoun], Was neuere trompe of half so greet a soun. —— *Reeves T.* 245 His wyf bar him a burdon [*v.r.* burdoun], a ful strong. *c* **1400** *Epiph.* 1918 (Turnb. 1843) They yeve a full delectabull sond Bothe trebull and meyne and burdown. **1596** SPENSER *Astroph., Aegl.* 77 Wolues do howle and barke, And seem to beare a bourdon to their plaint.

2. a. A bass stop in an organ, usually of 16ft. tone; a similar stop in a harmonium; also the drone of a bagpipe. Also *attrib.*, as in ***bourdon stop***.

1861 MUSGRAVE *By-Roads* 55 A tone equal to the finest bourdon stop of a large church-organ. **1876** M. DAVIES *Unorth. Lond.* 195 Others murmured them [prayers] in a low bourdon kind of voice. **1882** *Musical Times* 1 Feb. 106 Organ for sale..Separate bourdon, pedals, couplers, composition pedals, etc.

b. *Bell-ringing.* (See quot. 1938.)

1927 R. CHURCH *Dream*, etc. 10 Loud peal and pæan, bourdon and burden Swinging, one voice, ringing 'Rejoice'. **1938** *Oxf. Compan. Mus.* 111/2 The lowest string of the lute and violin used to be called the bourdon, as is still the lowest bell in a ring of bells.

Bourdon³ (ˈbʊədɒn). The name of Eugène *Bourdon* (1808–84), French hydraulic engineer, used *attrib.* and in the possessive to designate his inventions: **Bourdon('s) barometer, gauge, manometer**, a pressure gauge employing a Bourdon tube; **Bourdon coil, spiral, tube**, a coiled metallic tube which tends to straighten out when pressure is exerted within it.

1859 *Negretti & Zambra's Catal. Opt. & Meteorol. Instruments* 23 Bourdon's Barometers, card dial..metal dial and plate glass front. **1864** *Negretti & Zambra's Treat. Meteorol. Instruments* 7 Bourdon's Pressure Gauge, with metal taps, adapted for all pressure below nine atmospheres. *a* **1877** KNIGHT *Dict. Mech.* s.v. *Bourdon Barometer*, The Bourdon is commonly known as the metallic barometer. **1886** *Q. Jrnl. R. Meteorol. Soc.* XII. 124 Each thermometer consists of a very thin curved metal case (a Bourdon tube). **1901** W. W. F. PULLEN *Steam Engin.* iv. 143 The Bourdon Gauge consists of an oval tube bent nearly into a complete circle, one end being fixed and the other free to move. **1923** GLAZEBROOK *Dict. Appl. Physics* III. 494/2 The Bourdon tube thermograph. *Ibid.*, The Bourdon tube thermometer is much less sensitive to change of temperature than the bimetallic thermometer. **1930** *Engineering* 14 Feb. 214/2 Any fall in pressure in the Bourdon tube will tend to open the pilot valve. **1959** H. BARNES *Oceanogr. & Marine Biol.* 121 [In the bathythermograph] the temperature-responsive unit is not a wire but a liquid in metal thermometer with a Bourdon spiral.

bourdon, obs. form of BURDEN *sb.*

†**bourdonasse.** *Obs.* [a. OF. *bourdonasse.*] A light lance or javelin with a hollow shaft.

1596 DANETT *Comines* (1614) 301 Their men of armes were all..furnished with braue plumes and goodly bourdonasses.

‖**bourdonnée** (burdɔne), *a. Her.* [Fr.] Terminating in knobs or balls.

1612 PEACHAM *Gentl. Exerc.* 153 *Cosm.* Be there no more crosses then one borne in Armes? *Eud.* Yes... The most ordenary are these... Croiseè... Composeè... Bourdonneè. **1722** NISBET *Her.* I. 119 A Cross Bourdonee, as if it were made of Pilgrims Staves, which use to have a round Ball at the Top. **1780** EDMONDSON *Heraldry* II. Gloss. **1880** *Encycl. Brit.* XI. 696/1 Originally..the arms of the cross ended in knobs like the handles of a pilgrim's staff, thence called 'bourdonnée'.

boure, obs. form of BOOR, BOWER.

boureau, var. of BOURREAU, executioner.

bouree, var. BOURRÉE.

‖**bourg** (bur, bʊəg). [F. *bourg*:—late L. *burg-us*, ad. WGer. *burg*: see BOROUGH.] Used by historical writers in the earlier sense of town or village under the shadow of a castle; or of 'continental' as distinguished from English town; occasionally also in the modern French sense of 'market town'.

c **1450** *Merlin* xv. 236 Thei brent bourgs, and townes and castelles. **1536** *Remed. Sedition* 15 b, Many bourges in Germany, haue a great nombre of Jewes in them. **1690** *Lond. Gaz.* No. 2603/1 A great Bourg called Canina. *c* **1700** *Gentl. Instr.* (1732) 266 He can only lose an abandon'd Bourg. **1840** THACKERAY *Paris Sk. Bk.* (1872) 197 They reached the bourg of Rossillon. **1859** TENNYSON *Enid* 276 Ye think the rustic cackle of your bourg The murmur of the world! **1864** SIR F. PALGRAVE *Norm. & Eng.* III. 47 The Flemings..had settled in and about the bourg and its spreading suburbs.

‖**bourgade** (burgad). Also 7 burgade, -ard. [Fr. *bourgade*, f. *bourg* a town (cf. prec.) + -ADE.] A village, or unwalled town consisting of scattered dwellings. (Now only an alien word referring to France; but in 17th c. used as English.)

1601 HOLLAND *Pliny* I. 135 Dispersed into pettie villages and burgades. **1610** —— *Camden's Brit.* 196 A proper little towne..which of two burgards..is growne, as it were, into one burgh. **1658** USSHER *Ann.* 148 He set upon the Town; being but an open burgade. **1796** MORSE *Amer. Geog.* II. 308 The canton [Uri] consists only of villages, and little towns or bourgades. **1851** SIR F. PALGRAVE *Norm. & Eng.* I. 325 A large populous bourgade..which had grown up under the protection of the Abbey.

bourgamot, obs. form of BERGAMOT.

bourgeis, bourgen, ff. BURGESS, BURGEON.

‖**bourgeois** (burʒwa, ˈbʊəʒwɑː), *sb.*¹ and *a.* Also 8 burgeois. [F. *bourgeois* (OF. *burgeis*, whence BURGESS):—late L. *burgensis*, f. *burg-us* town, ad. WGer. *burg*: see BOROUGH and BOURG.]

A. *sb.* **1.** *orig.* A (French) citizen or freeman of a city or burgh, as distinguished from a peasant on the one hand, and a gentleman on the other; *now* often taken as the type of the mercantile or shopkeeping middle class of any country. Also fem. **bourgeoise**, a Frenchwoman of the middle class.

a **1674** CLARENDON *Hist. Reb.* III. XII. 241 He liv'd in a jolly familiarity with the Bourgeois and their Wives. **1704** ADDISON *Italy* (1733) 281 Body of the Burgeois. **1794** J. COURTENAY *Pres. State Manners of France & Italy* ii. 25 Here the pretty *Bourgeoise*, drest in smiles and in charms. **1807** J. BERESFORD *Miseries Hum. Life* II. 49 A *Bourgeoise*, who is privileged by wealth..to issue cards, and lose her money, to her superiors. **1842** L. S. COSTELLO *Pilg. Auvergne* I. 149 We met several peasants and some bourgeoises from neighbouring villages. **1864** KIRK *Chas. Bold* I. viii. 385 The merchants and persons of independent means, to whom the name of bourgeois was exclusively given. **1883** *Harper's Mag.* July 265/2 The German bourgeois and his family. **1959** *Listener* 10 Dec. 1051/2 A garrulous *bourgeoise.*

2. Used disparagingly. **a.** In communist or socialist writings: a capitalist; anyone judged to be an exploiter of the proletariat.

1883 [see COMMUNIST 1]. **1886** MARX & ENGELS *Manifesto of Communists* ii. 17 The Bourgeois, not content with having the women and daughters of their wage-slaves at command, ..find it a capital amusement to seduce each other's wives. **1886** F. K. WISCHNEWETZKY tr. *Engels's Condition of Working-Class* (1892) 277 It is utterly indifferent to the English bourgeois whether his working-men starve or not, if only he makes money.

b. A socially or æsthetically conventional person; = PHILISTINE *sb.* 4. Hence ***to shock the bourgeois*** [F. *épater le(s) bourgeois*], to behave unconventionally, to utter novel opinions; so ***bourgeois-shocker***. Cf. ÉPATER.

1930 A. HUXLEY *Brief Candles* 100 It's better to be a good ordinary bourgeois than a bad ordinary bohemian..or a second-rate intellectual. **1934** R. CAMPBELL *Broken Record* ii. 48 This tame and cowardly gang of bourgeois-shockers. **1960** C. P. SNOW *Affair* v. 49 It was mildly ironic, when one thought how, as a young woman, she had shocked the bourgeois, to find her set on seeing him a cosy, bourgeois success.

B. *adj.* or *attrib.*

1. Of or pertaining to the French middle classes; also in *comb.*, as ***bourgeois-looking***.

1564–5 RANDOLPH in G. Chalmers *Mary Q. Scots* (1818) I. 123 She [Mary] saith..I sent for you..to see how like a bourgeois-wife I live. **1867** PARKMAN *Jesuits in N. Amer.* xiv. (1875) 175 She was born..of a good bourgeois family. **1871** MORLEY *Voltaire* (1886) 331 Born to be the insipid gossip of a bourgeois circle.

2. Resembling the middle classes in appearance, way of thinking, etc. Also used disparagingly: selfishly materialistic or conventionally respectable and unimaginative; = PHILISTINE *a.* 2. (See also quot. 1960.)

1764 S. FOOTE *Lyar* II. 11 Decency is..a mere bourgois plebeian quality. **1775** H. WALPOLE *Let.* 10 Aug. (1904) IX. 231 Consider how *bourgeois* it would be in me to talk of her Highness my niece. **1840** THACKERAY *Paris Sk. Bk.* (1872) 79 A regular burgeois physiognomy. **1871** LOWELL *Study Wind., Word for Winter*, A poet whose inspiration always has an undertone of *bourgeois*. **1873** SYMONDS *Grk. Poets* iii. 80 He is thoroughly *bourgeois*, to use a modern phrase. **1894** 'A. HOPE' *Dolly Dialogues* xvi. 84 '*Bourgeois*,' I observed, 'is an epithet which the riff-raff apply to what is respectable, and the aristocracy to what is decent.' **1921** SHAW *Back to Methuselah* II. 43 You and I were brought up in the old bourgeois morality... Savvy..is a Bolshevist. **1930** A. HUXLEY *Brief Candles* 189 How can you be so disgustingly *bourgeoise*, Pamela? So crass, so crawling? **1949** F. MACLEAN *Eastern Approaches* I. iii. 32 Up to a year or two before [1937] jazz, or 'dzhaz', as it was called, had been frowned on [in Russia] as bourgeois stuff. **1960** C. S. LEWIS *Studies in Words* i. 21 When I was a boy..*bourgeois* meant 'not aristocratic, therefore vulgar'. When I was in my twenties this changed... *Bourgeois* began to mean 'not proletarian, therefore parasitic, reactionary'.

3. (Cf. sense A. 2 a above.) Capitalistic, non-communist; esp. used disparagingly.

1850 H. MACFARLANE tr. *Marx & Engels's Manifesto of German Communist Party* in *Red Republican* 23 Nov. 183/2 The old Bourgeois Society with its classes, and class antagonisms, will be replaced by an association, wherein the free development of each is the condition of the free development of all. **1886** J. L. JOYNES tr. *Marx's Wage-Labour & Capital* 11 Increase of capital..cannot abolish the opposition between his [*sc.* the labourer's] interests and those of the bourgeois or capitalist class. **1928** G. B. SHAW *Intelligent Woman's Guide to Socialism* lxxiv. 369 When the Russian Communist and his western imitators speak of the proprietors and their political supporters as 'bourgeois'. **1946** KOESTLER *Thieves in Night* 90 Powder and cosmetics are banned from our stores as attributes of 'bourgeois decay'.

4. Of French wine: next in quality to wines classified as the best (see quot. 1908).

[**1846** C. COCKS *Bordeaux* II. 197 After the Second-Fourth growths, comes a list of wines known by the name of *Bons Bourgeois*.] **1908** E. & A. VIZETELLY *Wines of France* iii. 93 Below the classified growths, throughout the Bordelais, come..those which are known locally as (1) 'bourgeois', (2) 'artisan', and (3) 'peasant' wines. *Ibid.*, A superior bourgeois Médoc of 1904. **1920** G. SAINTSBURY *Notes on Cellar-bk.* iv. 49 A sound *bourgeois* wine, much above *ordinaire*. **1967** C. RAY *Compleat Imbiber* IX. 66 Some lesser classed growths, both great and *bourgeois*.

5. *Comb.*, as ***bourgeois-capitalistic, -democratic, -liberal*** adjs.; ***bourgeois-mindedness***.

1936 WIRTH & SHILS tr. *Mannheim's Ideology & Utopia* i. 28 The liberal beginnings of the bourgeois-capitalistic era. **1937** E. SNOW *Red Star over China* III. ii. 90 The Communists, of course, regarded the successful fulfilment of the 'bourgeois-democratic' revolution as a necessary preliminary for any Socialist society. **1948** J. TOWSTER *Political Power in U.S.S.R.* I. i. 10 The Soviet state arose on the ruins of the bourgeois-democratic state form. **1936** WIRTH & SHILS tr. *Mannheim's Ideology & Utopia* v. 249 The bourgeois-liberal mode of thought. **1955** H. HODGKINSON *Doubletalk* 18 The rise of 'bourgeois-mindedness'.

Hence **bour'geoisdom** [-DOM], the political ascendancy of the bourgeoisie; bourgeois people collectively.

1887 MOORE & AVELING tr. *Marx's Capital* I. p. xxx, In its rational form it [*sc.* Hegelian dialectic] is a scandal and abomination to bourgeoisdom. **1937** 'C. CAUDWELL' *Illusion & Reality* iv. 87 In its early stages bourgeoisdom requires the shattering of all feudal forms.

bourgeois (bɜːˈdʒɔɪs), *sb.*² [Conjectured to be from the name of a French printer or type-founder.] A size of printing type between Long Primer and Brevier.

1824 J. JOHNSON *Typogr.* II. ii. 16 Two lines of some Diamond will answer to one of Bourgeois. **1852** W. WILKS *Half Century* Pref., Twenty-three sheets of bourgeois leaded.

‖**bourgeoisie** (burʒwazi, ˌbʊəʒwɑːˈziː). [Fr., f. *bourgeois*: see above.] **a.** The body of freemen of a French town; the French middle class; also extended to that of other countries.

1707 *Lond. Gaz.* No. 4354/1 To the Council of the City, the Clergy, and Bourgeoisie of Vallangin. **1848** MILL *Pol. Econ.* Prelim. Rem. (1876) 12 The Commons of England, the Tiers-Etat of France, the *bourgeoisie* of the continent generally, are the descendants of this class. **1856** GEO. ELIOT *Ess.* (1884) 284 The elaborate study of the German bourgeoisie. **1883** *Spectator* 13 Oct. 1309/2 The 'political surveys' he was in the habit of addressing to the bourgeoisie of the Elgin Burghs.

b. In Communist writings: the capitalist class. Cf. BOURGEOIS A. 2 a and B. 3.

1886 F. K. WISCHNEWETZKY tr. *Engels's Condition of Working-Class* (1892) 281 We have seen..how the bourgeoisie exploits the proletariat in every conceivable way for its own benefit. **1888** S. MOORE tr. *Marx & Engels's Manifesto* 7 By bourgeoisie is meant the class of modern Capitalists, owners of the means of social production and employers of wage-labour. **1957** R. N. CAREW-HUNT *Guide to Communist Jargon* iii. 6 In present communist usage the term bourgeoisie is given, however, such an extension as to include all those who, whether they possess capital or not, have an interest in preserving the capitalist system.

bourgeoisify (buːʒˈwɑːzɪfaɪ), *v.* [f. BOURGEOIS *a.* + -IFY.] To convert to a bourgeois outlook or mode of life. (Used esp. in Communist writings.) So **bour'geoisified** *ppl. a.*

1930 tr. *Lenin's Coll. Wks.* XVIII. 44 Marx shows how..the British proletariat is becoming 'bourgeoisified'. **1937** 'C. CAUDWELL' *Illusion & Reality* iv. 75 The bourgeoisie and the bourgeoisified nobility. **1938** 'G. ORWELL' *Homage to Catalonia* v. 78 The workers' militias..must be preserved..and every effort to 'bourgeoisify' them must be resisted. **1960** *New Left Rev.* Sept.–Oct. 13/2 Temporary industrial monopoly enabled the capitalists to 'bribe' and 'bourgeoisify' the working class.

So **bourgeoisifi'cation**, conversion to a bourgeois outlook or mode of life.

1937 J. M. MURRY *Necessity of Pacifism* ii. 32 'The bourgeoisification of the English proletariat', which he [*sc.* Marx] deplored. **1938** 'G. ORWELL' *Homage to Catalonia* v. 71 A general 'bourgeoisification', a deliberate destruction of the equalitarian spirit of the first few months of the revolution, was taking place.

bourgeoi'sitic, *a.* = BOURGEOIS *a.*

1848 CLOUGH *Remains* (1869) I. 122 The boys..of the garde mobile are infected with bourgeoisitic loyalty..The Socialists..regard the whole thing as at present a failure —a bourgeoisitic triumph.

bourgeon, var. form of BURGEON.

bourger, obs. form of BURGHER (after BOURG).
1652 *Let. fr. Paris* in *Proc. Parliament* No. 157 Had they ..not been appeased by some of the Bourgers [of Paris].

bourgeys, -essy, obs. ff. BURGESS, BURGESSY.

bourgh, obs. f. BOROUGH, BURGH.

bourg(h)ol, varr. BURGOO.

bourginot, bourgoinette, var. of BURGONET.

bourgmaister. [OF. *bourgmaistre*], obs. form of BURGOMASTER.
1594 T. B. *La Primaud. Fr. Acad.* 588 In some places they have advoyers, or bourg-maisters, as in the Cantons of Switzerland, and in the free townes of Germanie.

†**bour'goigne.** [F. *Bourgogne* Burgundy.] 'The first part of the Dress for the Head next the Hair.' (*Fop Dict.* 1690.)

Bourignian (bʊ'rɪnɪən). *Ch. Hist.* [f. the name *Bourign-on* + -IAN.] Of or derived from Antoinette Bourignon, an enthusiast of Flanders in the 17th c., who held that the Christian religion consists in a certain inward feeling and divine impulse, rather than in knowledge and practice. Hence **Bou'rignianism, -'ignonism, -ist.**
1697 *State Philadelph. Soc.* 30 Since these Sheets were gone to the Press there came to my Hand a Piece, call'd Bourignianism Detected. **1836** *Penny Cycl.* V. 290 Under the name of the Bourignian Doctrine, it is..renounced by candidates for holy orders in the Church of Scotland. **1884** *Brit. & For. Evang. Rev.* Apr. 255 Dr. George Gordon of Aberdeen was deposed..for holding the principles of Bourignonism. *Ibid.* The Aberdeen Bourignonist was deposed.

bourish, obs. form of BOORISH.

bourlaw ('bʊəlɔː). A form of BYRLAW, used in the comb. **bourlawmen** in south of Scotland.
1866 *Proc. Berw. Nat. Club* 261 There is a court consisting of two bourlawmen appointed by the bailie. **1879** *S. Counties (Scotl.) Register* in *Athenæum* 16 Aug. 208 Berwickshire: Earlston: Court of Bourlawmen..The men holding this somewhat rare office are sworn when appointed to give judgment, to the best of their knowledge and ability, in cases that come before them, and their decision is understood to be absolute in point of law. Their work as Bourlawmen consists in fixing the amount of damages done by straying or pounded cattle and the like.

†**bourlet.** *Obs.* [F. *bourlet* in same sense, earlier *bourrelet*, dim. of OF. *bourrel* 'mass of flocks or wadding': a doublet of BURLET.] (See quot.)
1725 BRADLEY *Fam. Dict.* I, *Bourlet*..in Gardening..is said of the Place, where, after some Years, the Graft becomes thicker than the Stock on which it was grafted.

bourly, -ie, obs. forms of BURLY.

bourn (bɔən), *v. rare.* [f. BOURN *sb.*^{2}] *trans.* To set a limit or bounds to; to bound; to check.
1808 J. BARLOW *Columb.* IV. 338 A second world..By oceans bourn'd. **1866** J. ROSE *Virg. Ecl. & Georg.* 106 Nor rocks, nor precipice, nor torrent's force Shall bourn his headlong and resistless force.

bourn, bourne (bɔən), *sb.*^{1} Forms: (1 burn, burna, 1–3 burne), 4, 7 borne, 4– bourne, 5–7 bowrne, 6–7 boorn(e, 7– bourn. [A variant of BURN, being the form commonly used in the south of England since the 14th c. Originally pronounced like *burn, adjourn*: but the influence of the *r* disturbed the pronunciation, as in *mourn*; whence the mod. spelling and pronunciation.]

A small stream, a brook; often applied (in this spelling) to the winter bournes or winter torrents of the chalk downs. Applied to northern streams it is usually spelt BURN.
c **1325** *E.E. Allit. P.* A. 973 Bow vp to-warde þys bornez heued. **1362** LANGL. *P. Pl.* A. Prol. 8 Vndur a brod banke bi a Bourne syde. *c* **1440** *Bone Flor.* 609 Ranne bowrnes all on blode. **1576** LAMBARDE *Peramb. Kent* (1826) 260 Sundry smal brookes, or boornes. **1612** DRAYTON *Polyolb.* 3 The Bournes, the Brooks, the Becks, the Rills, the Rivilets. *c* **1630** RISDON *Surv. Devon* §281 (1810) 292 Whereout..a spring breaketh, by some called a borne. **1634** MILTON *Comus* 313 And every bosky bourn from side to side. **1657** HOWELL *Londinop.* 10 Those ancient and present Rivers, Brooks, Boorns, Pools, Wells, Conduits, and Aqueducts, which serve to refresh the City of London. **1757** DYER *Fleece* II. 383 He [Drayton] whose rustic muse..sung the bosky bourns of Alfred's shires. *a* **1856** LONGF. *Happiest Land* viii, Over mountain gorge and bourn [*rime-wd.* horn]. **1879** JEFFERIES *Wild Life S. County* 22 The villages on the downs are generally on a bourne, or winter water-course..In summer it is a broad winding trench..along whose bed you may stroll dryshod..In winter, the bourne often has the appearance of a broad brook.
fig. *c* **1430** *Hymns Virg.* (1867) 71 In þin herte blood, þat holi bourne [*rime-wd.* spurn].

bourn(e, var. of BURN *v.*^{2}, to burnish.

bourn(e, obs. f. BERNE, man, wight.
c **1325** *E.E. Allit. P.* A. 616 Where wystez þou euer any bourne abate..in his prayere?

bourne, bourn (bɔən), *sb.*^{2} Also 6–7 borne. [Early mod.Eng. *borne*, a. F. *borne* (formerly occas. *bourne*), app. = OF. *bodne, bone, boune* (see BOUND *sb.*^{1}). In Eng. in Lord Berners, and in Shakspere (seven times), then app. not till 18th c.; the modern use being due to Shakspere, and in a large number of cases directly alluding to the passage in *Hamlet*. Confused in spelling with BOURN *sb.*^{1}
(The history of *borne* in Fr. is uncertain; Littré suggests that it arose from the later *bone, boune* by the intercalation of *r*; Diez supposed a substitution of *r* for *d* in the earlier *bodne*; M. Paul Meyer says '*bodne, bosne, borne* is an admissible phonetic series, the more so that Pr. has a dim. *bózola*, and a sb. *bozolar* (borner, limiter)'.)]

†**1.** A boundary (between fields, etc.). *Obs.*
1523 LD. BERNERS *Froiss.* I. ccxii. 257 All..places, lyenge bitwene the boundes and bournes folowynge. *Ibid.* The foresayd boundes and bornes in the article of Calais. **1610** SHAKS. *Temp.* II. i. 152 Borne, bound of Land, Tilth, Vineyard none. **1611** —— *Wint. T.* I. ii. 134 One that fixes No borne 'twixt his and mine. **1731** BAILEY, *Borns*, Limits, bounds, etc. *Shakes.* **1790** COWPER *Iliad* XVIII. 679 Oft as in their course They came to the field's bourn.

2. A bound, a limit. (Approaching 3.) *arch.*
1606 SHAKS. *Ant. & Cl.* I. i. 16 Ile set a bourne how farre to be belou'd. **1727** THOMSON *Summer* 99 From the far bourne Of utmost Saturn. **1847** TENNYSON *Princ.* Concl. 100 A shout..rang Beyond the bourn of sunset. **1858** SEARS *Athan.* III. vii. 312 A sphere above the natural, and within the bourn of immortality.

3. The limit or terminus of a race, journey, or course; the ultimate point aimed at, or to which anything tends; destination, goal. (Somewhat *poetic*: often *fig.*)
[Shakspere's famous passage probably meant the 'frontier or pale' of a country; but has been associated contextually with the goal of a traveller's course.]
[**1602** SHAKS. *Ham.* III. i. 79 The dread of something after death, The vndiscouered Countrey, from whose Borne No Traueller returnes. *a* **1761** FAWKES *Sparrow* (R.) Dismal regions! from whose bourn No pale travellers return.] *c* **1800** K. WHITE *On Prayer* in *Rem.* (1839) 433 The means employed to arrive at the bourn of our desires. **1805** WORDSW. *Prel.* II. (1850) 35 The selected bourne Was now an Island. **1865** M. ARNOLD *Ess. Crit.* vi. (1865) 212 Perhaps, even of the life of Pindar's time, Pompeii was the inevitable bourne.

¶ *incorrectly* for: Realm, domain. [A misunderstanding of the passage in *Hamlet*.] *Obs.*
1818 KEATS *Endym.* III. 31 A thousand Powers keep religious state, In water, fiery realm, and airy bourne. **1827** PRAED *Poems* (1865) II. 218 No dame should come To be the queen of his bourn.

4. In comb. *bourne-stone* (formed by Carlyle from F. *borne*), a boundary stone.
1837 CARLYLE *Fr. Rev.* II. I. iii. 23 Chaumette..one already descries..on *bourne*-stone of the thoroughfares. **1858** KINGSLEY *St. Maura* 56 As you preached and prayed From rock and bourne-stone.

bourneless, bournless ('bɔənlɪs), *a. rare.* [f. BOURNE *sb.*^{2} + -LESS.] Boundless.
1755 J. GRAINGER *Ode Solitude* 117 Great God..The bournless macrocosm's Thine. **1849** *Fraser's Mag.* XL. 308 Athwart the bourneless blue no fleeting rack is driven.

bournonite ('bʊənənaɪt). *Min.* [f. the name of its discoverer, Count Bournon] Antimonial sulphide of lead and copper; a brittle opaque mineral with metallic lustre.
1805 R. JAMESON *Syst. Min.* II. 579 (Dana) Bournonite, Antimonial lead ore. **1863–79** WATTS *Dict. Chem.*, *Bournonite*..is found in the copper mines of Cornwall.

bournous, obs. form of BURNOUS.

bourock ('buːrək). *Sc.* [perh. dim. of *bour*, BOWER: see -OCK.] A little cot or hut; a small heap of stones, a mound.
1807–10 TANNAHILL *Five Friends* Poems (1846) 156 Weel wha's in the bouroch, and what is your cheer? **1816** SCOTT *Antiq.* iv, 'About this bit bourock, your honour..I mind the bigging o't'.

bourowe, obs. form of BORROW.

bourrachoe, var. BORACHIO, *Obs.*, leathern bottle.

†**bou'rreau.** *Obs.* Also 6 *Sc.* boreau, burreau, 7 boureau: see also BURRIO. [In 16th c. *boreau*, a. OF. *boreau* (earlier *borel*), now *bourreau*, of uncertain origin: see Diez and Littré. Common, in many spellings in Scotch literature.] An executioner, hangman, or torturer. Chiefly *fig.*
1549 *Compl. Scot.* 27 That samyn boreau is stikkit or hangit eftiruart for his cruel demeritis. *Ibid.* The cruel inglis men..ar boreaus ande hang men permittit be god to puneis vs. **1567** FENTON *Trag. Disc.* 208 b, Covetousnes..is thordynarie torment and contynual bourreau that trobles the mynd of thold man. **1584** J. MELVILL *Diary* (1842) 203 Bludie burreaus and crewall buchars of Sathan. **1599** JAS. I. *Βασιλ. Δωρον* (1682) 20 A Tyrannes..infamous life armeth..his owne subjects to become his burreaux. *c* **1720** PRIOR *Viceroy* (D.) The Bourreau did his worst.

‖**bourrée** (bure). Also 8 bouree. [Fr.; see BOREE.]

1. a. A lively dance, of French origin, in common time (two beats in a bar). **b.** A musical composition, written usually in duple rhythm and in two-measure phrases, in which the character of the lively dance so named is represented.
1706 J. WEAVER tr. *Feuillet's Orchesography* 57 Suppose, for example, the *Step* to be a *Bouree.* **1776** HAWKINS *Hist. Music* IV. 390 The Bouree is supposed to come from Auvergne in France; it seldom occurs but in compositions of French masters. **1879** GROVE *Dict. Mus.* I. 264/1 The bourrée is often to be found in the older suites, especially in those of Bach. **1891** *Queen* 3 Jan. 18/3 Minuet in D (No. 1) is fairly interesting, Bourrée in G (No. 2) is rather wild. **1963** *Times* 12 Jan. 4/1 An excellent set of French dancers became available. Their *bourrée* was a great delight.

2. ***bourrée step*** or ***pas de bourrée***, a sideways step in dancing in which one foot crosses behind or in front of the other.
1706 P. SIRIS *Art of Dancing* 41 (*heading*) A Table of Bourrée-Steps or Fleurets. **1710** J. ESSEX tr. *Feuillet's Treatis of Chorography* 15 One may make little hopps or Bouree steps but little hopps are more in fashion. **1786** S. J. GARDINER *Definition Minuet-Dancing* 25 The lady must then make a pá tombéz with her left Foot, and the Gentleman a pá de bouréz with his left Foot. **1830** R. BARTON tr. *Blasis's Code of Terpsichore* II. 102 Afterwards come..the *pas de bourrée* and the various movements of different kinds of pirouettes. **1957** G. B. L. WILSON *Dict. Ballet* 206 *Pas de bourrée*, lit. a bourrée step; a step probably deriving its name from the Bourrée..with which, however, it has now no apparent connexion.

‖**bourrelet** (burəle). [Fr.: also adopted in forms BOURLET, BURLET.] A ridge-like excrescence.
1859 TODD *Cycl. Anat. & Phys.* V. 477/2 The ridge or 'bourrelet' at the upper margin of the wall answers to the posterior nail-wall.

Boursault ('bʊəsɒlt). [The name of a Parisian rose-grower, Henri *Boursault* fl. *c* 1810.] A species of climbing rose originating from the Alpine rose (*Rosa alpina*), introduced in 1683; also, a rose of this species.
1826 R. SWEET *Hortus Brit.* I. 138 Rosae..Boursoulti. Boursoult's. Hybrid. 1821. **1837** T. RIVERS *Rose Amateur's Guide* 50 The Boursault Rose. (Rose Alpina.) This is a most distinct group of roses, with long, reddish flexible shoots. *Ibid.* 51 The Red Boursault is our oldest variety. **1864** S. HIBBERD *Rose Bk.* 29 The Boursault roses... The Old Red Boursault..was the first double variety of *Rosa alpina*. **1956** *Dict. Gardening* (*R.H.S.*) (ed. 2) IV. 1824/2 The Boursault Roses (hybrids of *R. alpina*, pillar roses with reddish smooth stems, sometimes without prickles).

‖**bourse** (burs, bʊəs). [a. F. *bourse* in same sense, *literally* 'purse'. The form BURSE was in regular use from *c* 1550 to *c* 1775, when it became obsolete; *bourse* is a re-adoption of the word from modern French, as an *alien* term.]

An exchange, or place of meeting for merchants; the money-market (of a foreign town). Used esp. of the French institution corresponding to the Stock Exchange in London.
[**1597** BP. HALL *Sat.* VI. i, Trampling the bourses [ed. **1599** burses] marble twice a day.] **1845** DISRAELI *Sybil* (1863) 45 With the exception of..some sombre mansions, a dingy inn, and a petty bourse, Marney mainly consisted of a variety of narrow..lanes. **1861** MOTLEY *Dutch Rep.* II. 289 It was a common subject of discussion on the Bourse at Antwerp. **1885** *Standard* 10 Apr., An arbitragist..is a person who speculates between two Bourses by the help of a partner or confrère in Paris or Berlin.

†**'bourser.** *Obs. rare*$^{-1}$. [var. of BURSAR, q.v.; cf. F. *boursier*, f. *bourse*.] A purser.
1685 *Royal Proclam.* in *Lond. Gaz.* No. 2068/1 Masters of Ships, Boursers and Mariners.

boursocrat ('bʊəsəkræt). *rare.* [f. BOURSE after *aristocrat*.] A Stock-Exchange 'magnate'.
1882 *Truth* 19 Jan. 118/1 On Twelfth-Night a Boursocrat entertained a party of relatives and friends.

bourtree ('bʊətriː). Now only *Sc.* and *north. dial.* Forms: 5 burtre, 7 burt-tree, 9 burtree, 6– bourtre(e, 7–9 *dial.* boretree, bortery, 8–9 *Sc.* bourtree. [Of uncertain phonetic form, and unknown origin. The plausible derivation from BORE *v.*^{1} (see quot. 1691) is inconsistent with the earliest and with the dialect forms; derivation from BOWER, Sc. *bour, boor* (in sense of 'arbour') answers phonetically, but is unlikely with regard to meaning. Cf. BOUNTREE.]

The Elder-tree (*Sambucus nigra*). *attrib.*, as in ***bourtree-berry, -bush***; **bourtree-gun**, a popgun made of the wood of the Elder, after the pith has been removed.
c **1450** *Nominale* in Wr.-Wülcker 228, *Hec sambucus*, a burtre. **1561** HOLLYBUSH *Hom. Apoth.* 25 b, The floures of Eldren or Bouretre. **1562** TURNER *Herbal* II. 59 b, The wod ..is very holow..lyke vnto elder or bourtre. **1579** LANGHAM *Gard. Health* (1633) 214 Eldren, or Bourtree. **1691** RAY *N.C. Wds.* 131 *Bore-tree*, elder-tree; from the great pith in the younger branches which Children commonly bore out to make potguns of them. **1786** BURNS *Addr. Deil* vi, Rustlin, thro' the boortrees comin. **1815** SCOTT *Guy M.* liii, I was behind that bourtree bush at the very moment. **1821** MRS. WHEELER *Westmorld. Dial.* 73 Bortery-berry wine. **1878** SMILES *Rt. Dick* iv. 29 The only tree that thrives..is the common bourtree or elder.

bousarde, obs. form of BUZZARD.

bousche, obs. form of BUSH (of a wheel).

bouse, bowse (buːz, baʊz), *v.*[1] Forms: 3, 6- bouse, bowse, 6-7 bowze, 7 bouz(e: see also BOOZE. [ME. *bousen*, app. a. MDu. *bûsen*, early mod.Du. *buizen* to drink to excess, corresp. to Ger. *bausen* in same sense. The origin is not quite clear: Kluge takes the Ger. vb. to be derived from *baus*, MHG. *bûs* blown-up condition, tumidity; but the Du. seems directly related to *buise* a large drinking-vessel. Both vb. and sb. occur (once) in ME.; but they seem to have become generally known in 16th c. as words of thieves' and beggars' cant, whence they passed into slang and colloquial use. Perh. the use in Falconry came down independently from ME. Most commonly pronounced (buːz), and since 18th c. often phonetically written BOOZE, q.v.]

1. *intr.* To drink; to drink to excess or for enjoyment or goodfellowship; to swill, guzzle, tipple.

c **1300** *E.E.P.* (1862) 154 Hail ye holi monkes .. depe cun ye bouse · þat is al ȝure care. **1567** HARMAN *Caveat* 32 They bowle and bowse one to another. **1592** NASHE *P. Penilesse* (ed. 2) 27 a, They lye bowzing and beere-bathing in their houses euery after-noone. **1648** HERRICK *Hesper.* (1869) 211 But before that day comes, Still I be bousing. **1790** BURNS *Tam O'Shanter* 5 While we sit bousing at the nappy. **1839** DE QUINCEY *Murder* Wks. IV. 22 He .. had the honour of bowsing with him in the evening. **1876** BROWNING *Pacchiar. etc., Epilogue* x, I were found in belief that you quaffed and bowsed (*rime-wds.* caroused, drowsed).

b. *to bouse it*: in same sense.

1623 BINGHAM *Comp. Rom. & Mod. Warres*, They play the Ruffians, and bouse it out in drinke. **1634** SIR T. HERBERT *Trav.* 156 So soone as the Sun sets, and the kettles beat, then they bowze it lustily.

2. *trans.*

a **1612** HARINGTON *Epigr.* I. 68 Thou, professed Epicure, That .. bowzest Claret wine. **1652** BROME *Jov. Crew* II. 388 For all this bene Cribbing and Peck let us then, Bowse a health to the Gentry Cofe of the Ken. **1848** B. WALSH *Aristoph. Clouds* 312 And the rascally jorum of soup that I've boused.

†**3.** *Falconry.* Of a hawk: To drink much (*trans.* and *intr.*). Cf. BOUSING *vbl. sb.* 2.

1575 TURBERV. *Falconrie* 84 With water before hir to the end she may bathe when she will and bouze as naturally they are enclined to do .. for bowzing may oftentimes preserve them from sicknesse. *a* **1682** SIR T. BROWNE *Misc. Tracts* 115 [They gave to hawks] a decoction of Cumfory to bouze.

bouse, bowse (baʊs), *v.*[2] Chiefly naut. Also 8 bowss. [Of unknown origin: confounded in the dictionaries generally with BOUSE *v.*[1] = *booze*: but this rimes with *house*.] *trans.* To haul with tackle. Also *absol.*

1593 *Sir. F. Drake Rev.* in Arb. *Garner* V. 497 Felling of great trees; bowsing and hauling them together, with great pulleys and hawsers. **1627** CAPT. SMITH *Seaman's Gram.* iii. 36 The Younkers are the young men .. for slinging the yards, bousing or trising. **1769** FALCONER *Dict. Marine* (1789) *To Bowse*, to draw on any body with a tackle .. This is pronounced *bowce*. **1816** SCOTT *Antiq.* viii, As we used to bouse up the kegs o' gin. **1840** MARRYAT *Poor Jack* xiii, We boused out our gun. **1868** WOOD *Homes without H.* xiv. 297 The nautical method of 'bowsing' up a rope.

b. *transf.*

1751 SMOLLETT *Per. Pic* xiv. (D.) Pshaw! brother, there's no occasion to bowss out so much unnecessary gum [i.e. palaver].

c. *to bowse up the jib* (fig.): to drink heavily, to make oneself 'tight'.

1837 MARRYAT *Dog Fiend* ix. **1840** —— *Poor Jack* xxii, The captain used to *bowse his jib* up pretty taut every night.

bouse, bowse (buːz, baʊz), *sb.*[1] Forms: 4 bous, 6- bouse, bowse, 8 bowze: see also BOOZE. [Related to BOUSE *v.*: also BOOZE, q.v.]

1. *colloq.* Drink; liquor. (The first quot. may mean a drinking-vessel.) About 1600 a word of vagabonds' cant.

c **1300** in Wright's *Lyric P.* xxxix, Drynke to hym deorly of fol god bous .. When that he is dronke ase a dreynt mous. **1567** HARMAN *Caveat* 34 Then doth this vpright man call for a gage of bowse, whiche is a quarte pot of drinke. **1632** MASSINGER *New Way, &c.* II. i, *Wellborn.* No bouse, nor no tobacco? *Tapwell.* Not a suck, sir. **1730-6** BAILEY, *Bowze* (with the Vulgar) any Sort of strong Liquor.

2. A drinking-bout, a carouse.

1786 BURNS *To J. Kennedy* ii, An' if we dinna hae a bouze, I'se ne'er drink mair. **1812** W. TENNANT *Anster F.* v. liii, With riot and with bouse. **1857** S. OSBORN *Quedah* iv. 53 All hands had had what they graphically termed 'a bowse-out'. **1858** CARLYLE *Fredk. Gt.* (1865) I. III. ix. 192 A good bouse of liquor now and then.

bouse (baʊs, buːs), *sb.*[2] Also 7 bous. (See quots.)

1653 MANLOVE *Lead-mines* 266 Fell, Bous, and Knockbarke, Forstid-oar and Tees. **1851** TAPPING *Gloss. Derby Leadmining* (E.D.S.), *Boose, bouse, fell, bouse ore*, lead ore in its rough state, or in other words the contents of a metalliferous vein, before the baser minerals are separated. **1866** *North Country, Durham &c., Bouse*, lead ore when picked out from the refuse rock.

bouse, bousie, var. BOOSE, BOOSY, cattle-stall.

bousen, var. of BOWSSEN *v. Obs.* to duck.

bouser ('buːzə(r), 'baʊzər). [f. BOUSE *v.*[1] + -ER[1].] One who bouses; a toper, guzzler, drunkard.

1611 COTGR. *Piailleur*, a tipler, bowser, pot-gossip. **1657** REEVE *God's Plea* 131 These common Bowsers and daily Drunkards. **1809** W. IRVING *Knickerb.* (1861) 184 This redoubtable Swede .. a huge feeder, and bouser in proportion.

'bousing, *vbl. sb.* [f. BOUSE *v.*[1] + -ING[1].]

1. Deep drinking, guzzling, tippling.

a **1529** SKELTON *Image Hypocr.* IV. 583 How they iest and iell, With bowsing and bollinge. **1567** HARMAN *Caveat* 23 The buriall was turned to bousing and belly chere. **1641** HINDE *J. Bruen* iv. 15 They .. have [not] any skill in any arts but of .. bowzing and drinking.

2. *Falconry.* (See quots.)

1575 TURBERV. *Falconrie* 243 By bouzing .. you shall have evident proofe and undoubted shewe of his disease. **1615** LATHAM *Falconry* Gloss., Bousing is when a Hawke drinketh often, and seemes to be continually thirstie.

3. *attrib.*, as ***bousing-bout, -can, -den, -house, -inn***; †**bousing ken** (*thieves' slang*), a low ale-house.

1596 SPENSER *F.Q.* I. iv. 22 In his hand did bear a bouzing can. **1594** NASHE *Unfort. Trav.* Wks. (Grosart) V. 68 Their houghs & bousing houses, which commonly are built fayrer than their Churches. **1561** AWDELEY *Frat. Vacab.* 3 The Alehouse, whych they call the Bowzyng In. **1567** HARMAN *Caveat* 83 A bousing ken, a ale house. **1652** BROME *Jov. Crew* II. Wks. 1873 III. 390 As Tom or Tib .. When they at Bowsing Ken do swill.

'bousing, *ppl. a.* [f. as prec. + -ING[2].] That bouses; given to immoderate drinking; tippling.

1569 TURBERV. *Epit. & Sonn.* (1837) 331 As Circes cup no sooner might the bowsing Greekes beguile. **1589** *Hay any Work* 33 Dumbe Johns bousing mates. *a* **1659** CLEVELAND *Inund. of Trent* 49 With a file of bowzing Comrades.

boussen, var. of BOWSSEN *v. Obs.*, to duck.

boussin'gaultite. *Min.* [f. *Boussingault*, name of a French geologist + -ITE.] A volcanic mineral product.

1865 *Athenæum* No. 1944. 130/3, *Boussingaultite*, a natural product of Tuscany, consisting chiefly of sulphate of ammonia. **1868** DANA *Min.* §651 *Boussingaultite*, a sulphate of ammonia with part of this alkali replaced by magnesia.

‖**boussyng.** *Obs. rare*[−1]. [a. MDu. *bûzinc, bunzinc*, Du. *bunsing* 'fitchew, polecat'.] A polecat.

1481 CAXTON *Reynard* (Arb.) 79 Tho cam forth many a beest anon as .. the ostrole, the boussyng and the fyret.

bouste, var. of BUSTE, *Obs.*, box.

boust(i)ous, var. BOISTOUS *a. Obs.*, boisterous.

‖**boustrophedon** (baʊstrəʊ'fiːdən, buː-), *adv.* and *a.* (*sb.*) [Gr. *βουστροφηδόν*, adv. f. *βου-στρόφος* ox-turning.] (Written) alternately from right to left and from left to right, like the course of the plough in successive furrows; as in various ancient inscriptions in Greek and other languages. Hence **boustrophe'donic** *a.*

1783 BLAIR *Rhet.* (1812) I. vii. 155 Afterwards, the Greekes adopted a new method, writing their lines alternately from the right to the left, and from the left to the right, which was called Boustrophedon. **1846** ELLIS *Elgin Marb.* II. 174 A very antient Greek inscription, written in the boustrophedon manner. **1847** GROTE *Greece* II. xi. III. 176. **1880** *Times* 6 Nov. 4/5 The usual boustrophedon manner which the Hittites affected. **1801** J. HAGER *Babylon. Inscr.* 11 The laws of Solon in boustrophedonic writing.

boustrous, obs. form of BOISTEROUS.

bousum, obs. form of BUXOM.

bousy ('buːzɪ, 'baʊzɪ), *a.*[1] [f. BOUSE *v.*[1] + -Y[1].]

1. Affected with much drinking; intoxicated, sotted; showing the effects of intoxication.

a **1529** SKELTON *El. Rumming* 17 Droupy and drowsy, Scuruy and lousy; Her face all bowsy. **1625** *Modell of Wi.* 31 With quaffing and carowsing .. she could make him bowsie beyonde all measure. **1635** *Long Meg of Westm.* ii, Neither beastly nor bowsie Sleepy nor drowsie. **1742** POPE *Dunciad* IV. 493 Rous'd at his name up rose the bousy Sire. **1842** DE QUINCEY *Herodotus* Wks. IX. 195 And every day got bousy as a piper.

2. Addicted to bousing, drunken.

1592 GREENE *Upst. Courtier* in *Harl. Misc.* (Malh.) II. 232 A seale to marke the bowsie drunkard to die of the dropsie. **1616** B. JONSON *Devil an Ass* v. vi. (1631) 164 To be greazy, and bouzy .. ragged and louzy. **1708** HEARNE *Coll.* (1885) II. 109 There's .. Royce yᵉ Bouzy.

Hence **'bousyish, bowsyish**, *a.*, rather bousy.

1832 J. WILSON in *Blackw. Mag.* XXXII. 721 The oracular lip of your Lordships .. Bowsyish Depute.

†**bout**, *sb.*[1] *Obs.* Some part of a woman's head-dress.

a **1300** *Songs Costume* (1849) 42 The bout and the barbet wyth frountel shule feȝe.

bout (baʊt), *sb.*[2] Also 6 bowt, 9 *dial.* boot. [App. a specialized sense of BOUGHT *sb.*[1] 'bending' (which in 16th c. was also spelt *bout*), perhaps influenced by association with BOUT *adv.*[2] 'about'.]

†**1. a.** A circuit, an orbit; a roundabout way. *Obs.*

a **1541** WYATT *Poet. Wks.* (1861) 152 The seuenth heauen .. In nine and twenty yeres complete and daies almost sixtene Doth carry in his bowt, the star of Saturn old. **1598** SYLVESTER *Du Bartas* I. ii. (1641) 18/1 Which in thy wide bout, boundlesse all dost bound. *a* **1655** T. ADAMS *Wks.* 1861-2 II. 14 (D.), I love not to fetch any bouts where there is a nearer way.

b. The going and returning of the plough along two adjacent furrows: also *attrib.*

1601 HOLLAND *Pliny* XVIII. xviii, They make not past two or three bouts in a land, and as many ridges. **1812** STRICKLAND *Agric. E. Yorksh.* 159 Ridging up the land into two-bout ridges. **1840** *Jrnl. Eng. Agric. Soc.* I. III. 261 Ridges .. each consisting of 2 furrows up and 2 down, or 2 bouts, as they are called.

2. a. A 'round' at any kind of exercise, a turn or spell of work; as much of an action as is performed at one time.

1575 TURBERV. *Bk. Venerie* 135 If he doe it not at three boutes it is also a forfeyture. **1617** HIERON *Wks.* (1620) II. 236 To set vpon some course of godlinesse for a bout or two. **1650** FULLER *Pisgah* III. v. 328 They had .. another bout in the same service. **1725** BRADLEY *Fam. Dict.* s.v. *Wheat*, With a broad Cast, which some do with a single Cast, and some with a double Bout, that is, to sow it twice in a place. **1819** WORDSW. *Waggoner* II. 96 When every dance is done, When every whirling bout is o'er. **1879** F. POLLOK *Sport Brit. Burmah* II. 121 [We] had long contemplated a shooting bout together.

b. *this, that bout*: i.e. occasion, turn, time.

1660 H. MORE *Myst. Godl.* v. xv. 177 He .. may well sustain the person of the Seventh for this bout. **1692** R. LESTRANGE *Josephus' Wars* VII. v. (1733) 766 The Romans did not find the Enemy asleep this Bout. **1712** STEELE *Spect.* No. 326 ¶5 The Upholsterer was called, and her Longing sav'd that bout. **1845** DISRAELI *Sybil* 295 The Lancashire lads will not come to harm this bout.

3. a. A round at fighting; a contest, match, trial of strength, physical or intellectual.

1591 SHAKS. *1 Hen. VI*, III. ii. 56 Damsell, Ile haue a bowt with you againe. **1609** ROWLANDS *Whole Crew, &c.* 8 Sometimes at the fist we haue a bout. **1726** AMHERST *Terræ Fil.* xliv. 233 A bout at cudgels. **1749** FIELDING *Tom Jones* VII. viii, The two maids .. began a second bout at altercation. **1826** SCOTT *Woodst.* (1832) 186 If there was a bout at single-stick. **1879** FARRAR *St. Paul* I. 634 At Corinth he had doubtless witnessed those wrestling bouts.

b. Used of a continued fit of drinking.

1670 MAYNWARING *Vita Sana* vi. 78 Those drunken bouts being repeated .. lay the foundation of many chronick diseases. **1715** BURNET *Own Time* (1766) I. 164 Only fit to be concluded after a drunken bout. **1842** PARK *Mar. Insur.* II. 943 To indulge in fits or bouts of drinking.

c. A fit or turn of illness, as 'a severe bout of influenza'. *dial.*

†**4.** A term used to express a certain quantity of lead ore. (See quot.) ? *Obs.*

1747 HOOSON *Miner's Dict.* v, When they have done measuring they account the whole to be so many Bouts, as suppose 24 Bouts and one half, that's sixty-four Loads; the short Bout is used where lesser quantities are raised, and the whole groove not divided into such small Parts.

5. The inward curve of a rib in a violin or similar instrument, by which the waist is formed.

1889 *Cent. Dict.* **1893** *Fiddler's Handbk.* 4 Bouts, .. the sides of the fiddle, divided into the lower, middle, and upper bouts. **1898** H. R. HAWEIS *Old Violins* iii. 35 The curve of the bouts tilted, contracted, or elongated. *Ibid.* 38 Observe the improved purfling, the bouts and mitres cut with clear intention.

†**bout**, *adv.*[1] and *prep.*[1] *Obs.* or *dial.* Forms: 1 be-útan, bútan, -on, búta, búte, 2-3 bute(n, 3 bouten, 3-6 boute, (5 bowte), 5-6 (7) bout. [ME. *boute, bouten*, early ME. *bŭte(n*:—OE. *bútan* (*búta, búte*) adv., prep., conj.: orig. *be-útan* adv. and prep. 'without', L. *extra*; a WGer. compound (= OS. *bi-ûtan, bûtan*, OHG. *bi-ûzan*, MG. *bûzen*) f. *bi* prep. 'BY, with' + *ûtan*, earlier *ûtana* (OHG. *ûzana, ûzan*, OS., OE *ûtan*), Gothic *ûtana*, orig. 'from without', *ἔξωθεν*, later simply 'without', *ἔξω*; f. *ût* OUT + *-ana* suffix with force of 'from'. Originally an adverb, but already in Gothic construed with a genitive = 'outside *of*', and in WGer. also with dative; in OE. with dat. and acc. The OE. *bútan* split up into two forms in ME.: first, as prep. and adv., this strong form *bútan, bŭte(n, boute(n, bout* (cf. OUT), which became obs. before 1600, its sense being continued by WITHOUT; secondly, as adv. and conj., a weakened form, *bŭta(n, bŭte(n*, BUT, which still continues. As *bout* became obs., *but* acquired some quasi-prepositional uses; in northern dialect, and esp. in Scotch, *but* (*bot*) had even in 14th c. the senses of ME. *bout*, and still partly retains them. See BUT.]

A. *adv.* Outside, without; out.

a **890** *O.E. Chron.* an. 867 Wæl ȝeslæȝen, sume binnan sume butan. *c* **950** *Lindisf. Gosp.* Mark xiv. 68 [Petrus] eode buta. —— John xviii. 16 Petrus uutudlice ȝestod .. to duru .. ute *vel* bute *vel* fore. *c* **1205** LAY. 3748 Scholde a quene beon king in þisse londe, & heora sunen beon bute [*c* **1275** boute]. *c* **1315** SHOREHAM 40 The signe hiis that hys boute y-do, That thynge hys grace bynne. [hys = is.]

B. *prep.*

1. Outside of, without. **a.** *of position* (with dat.).

a **1000** *Cædmon's Gen.* 1354 (Gr.) Be-utan earce bordum. *c* **1000** ÆLFRIC *Lev.* iv. 21 Butan ðære wic-stowe. *a* **1120**

O.E. Chron. (Laud. MS.) an. 1116 Ægðer ȝe binnan burȝan and butan.

b. *of motion* (with acc.).

c **950** *Lindisf. Gosp.* Mark v. 10 þætte hine ne fordrife buta ðæt lond. *c* **1000** *Ags. G.* Mark viii. 23 He..lædde hine butan þa wic. *c* **1160** *Hatton G.* ibid., Buton þa wic.

2. Without, apart from, not having, void of: esp. in phrase *bouten ende*. (Obs. in Eng. before 1500, but retained in Sc. in form *bot*, BUT, q.v.)

894 *O.E. Chron.*, Hie fluȝon ofer Temese buton ælcum forda. **971** *Blickl. Hom.* 33 Eal his lif he lifde buton synnum. *c* **1175** *Lamb. Hom.* 43 Deor, summe feðer foted, summe al bute fet. *c* **1200** ORMIN Introd. 21 To ben a butenn ende þær. *c* **1205** LAY. 23676 Arthur fehten wolde..butene cnihte [*c* **1275** boute eni cniht]. *c* **1300** *Land Cokaygne* 21 in *E.E.P.* (1862) 157, I sigge for soþ, boute were. Þer n'is lond on erthe is pere. *c* **1305** *St. Dunstan* 184 *ibid.* 39 Hi schulle wone And kynges beo bouten ende. *c* **1350** *Will Palerne* 567 As schip boute mast. **1430** LYDG. *Chron. Troy* I. vi, Bout makyng of delay. *a* **1500** *Chester Pl.* (1847) II. 55 This cote boute seame To breake it were shame. [**1631** CRAIGE *Pilgrim & H.* 6 Tumbling teares bout cease.]

b. *absol.* with obj. not expressed: Without.

a **1225** *Ancr. R.* 418 Stamin habbe hwose wule; and hwose wule mei beon buten. *c* **1400** *Trentalle* in *Epiph.* (Turnb. 1843) 80 The ton have ende that other is bowte. **1674** RAY *N.C. Wds.* 7 To be bout as Barrow was, i.e. to be without.

3. Except, beyond, more than: see BUT.

c **890** K. ÆLFRED *Bæda* III. xxiii. §4 Butan anum cnihte. *c* **1320** *Sir Beues* 53 He nas boute seue winter olde.

bout (baʊt), *adv.*[2] and *prep.*[2] In 3 bute(n, bot, 6 bout, 7- 'bout. [ME. *bute(n*, aphet. form of *abute(n*, as, in later times, *'bout* of ABOUT.]

A. *prep.* In various senses of ABOUT. (Not in literary prose.)

c **1250** *Gen. & Ex.* 566 Ðor buten Noe long swing [*MS.* swinc] he dreȝ. *a* **1300** *Cursor M.* 14106 Bise ert þou bot [*v.r.* a-bute] mani dede. *Ibid.* 21695 Quen strijf was bute þe preisthede. **1602** WARNER *Alb. Eng.* x. lvii. 250 An Agnus Dei bout her neeke, a crost-Christ in her hand. **1622** MASSINGER *Old Law* v. i, The nimble fencer..made me tear..'bout the chamber. **1821** CLARE *Vill. Minstr.* I. 17 Discourses..'Bout work being slack, and rise and fall of bread. *a* **1845** HOOD *Agric. Distress* vi, While we bargain 'bout the hay.

B. *adv.* In Nautical phr. *'bout ship* = 'put about the ship', that is, turn her head, alter her course.

1830 MARRYAT *King's Own* xvi, 'Bout ship, Mr. Pearce.

bout (baʊt), *v.* [f. BOUT *sb.*[2] 1 b.] *trans.* To plough in such a manner as to make bouts. Hence **'bouted** *ppl. a.*, ploughed in this manner.

1733 W. ELLIS *Chiltern & Vale Farm.* ii. 36 Bout it up at Allhollantide. *Ibid.* 37 In June harrow it down and bout it the same way; in July hack it overthwart, or bout it up across. **1844** *Jrnl. R. Agric. Soc.* V. I. 16 Two of these harrows cover a single ridge of four furrows; four cover an eight-furrow stretch, consisting of two ridges bouted into one. **1864** *Ibid.* XXV. II. 291 The fallows are broken up in the autumn.., ploughed back in spring, then twice across, and bouted in 27-inch ridges.

bout, obs. f. BOLT, and of BOUGHT *sb.* & *pa. pple.*

bou'tade, bou'tado. Also butado [mod.F. *boutade*, taking place of OF. *boutée* (see -ADE), f. *bouter* to thrust: for *boutado*, see -ADO.] A sally, a sudden outburst or outbreak.

1614 BACON *K. James* (L.) It was but a boutade of desire and good spirit. **1654** EARL MONM. tr. *Bentivoglio* 321 This (said he) may be termed a French Butado. **1661** *Mercurius Caledonius* 1 Mar. in Chambers *Cycl. Eng. Lit.*, All our boutadoes and capriccios. **1704** SWIFT *T. Tub* IV. 67 His first boutade was to kick both their wives..out of doors. **1865** 'OUIDA' *Strathmore* I. x. 164 One of those tantalising *boutades* that were her most cruel and certain witcheries. **1905** *Spectator* 28 Jan. 141/2 Miss Burney had the good fortune to see only the better side of the Doctor... She was seldom witness of his boutades. **1924** *Blackw. Mag.* June 783/2 A certain notoriety for boutades among my associates.

boutant: see ARC-BOUTANT.

boutaraga, -argue, variants of BOTARGO.

boutcloth, obs. f. *bolt-cloth*: see BOLT *sb.*[3]

boute, obs. form of BOOT.

† **boutefeu.** *Obs.* Also 7 beautifew, beutifew, -efeau, -w, boutfeu, boutefeau, -ieu, boutifieu, -ure, bowtifeu, 7-8 boutefew, 8 botefeu. [a. F. *boutefeu* a linstock, an incendiary, f. *bouter* to put + *feu* fire. Very common in the 17th c.] An incendiary, a firebrand; one who kindles discontent and strife; also *attrib.*

a **1598** LD. BURLEIGH *Advice Q. Eliz* in *Harl. Misc.* (1809) II. 281 The Guisards happen to serve for boutefeus in Scotland. **1622** BACON *Hen. VII*, 68 A very Boutefeu. **1641** J. JACKSON *True Evang. T.* I. 35 Close enemies of the Empire, and secret beutefeaus of rebellion. **1642** *Observ. his Majesty's Answ. Declar. Parl.* 12 Theeves and boutifures. **1656** BRAMHALL *Replic.* iii. 138 Such Bigots and Bowtifeus. **1667** *Decay Chr. Piety* xix. 364 Lusts..are confestly the boutefeaus among us. **1691** WOOD *Ath. Oxon.* II. /529 He became..a great Boutifieu & firebrand in the Church. *a* **1734** NORTH *Exam.* I. iii. ¶106. 196 Factious Boutefews, Bawlers for Property & against Popery, etc. **1754** RICHARDSON *Let.* in Mrs. Barbauld *Life* (1804) III. 106 The sanguine expectations of their boutefeu editor.

boutell, variant of BOLTEL, and BOULTEL.

bouter ('baʊtə(r)). *dial.* [f. BOUT *adv.*] (See quot.)

1834 CRABBE in *Life & Wks.* I. vi. 144 The female servants at a side table called a bouter.

† **'boute-selle.** *Obs. rare.* [a. F. *boute-selle*, f. *bouter* to put + *selle* saddle.] A trumpet-call, warning knights or cavalry to put on the saddle; = *Boot and saddle*: see BOOT *sb.*[3] 1 b.

1628 tr. *Mathieu's Powerf. Favorite* 136 At Executions, the Trumpets sounded the battaile, as the alarme, or the bouteselle [*misprinted* bonteselle], to go to death. **1649** G. DANIEL *Trinarch. Hen. V*, cli, The Towne-pent Rutters..attend to Bot et Selle. *a* **1658** CLEVELAND *Gen. Poems* (1677) 8 The sprightly Chanticlere..Sounds Boutesel [*v.r.* Bootesel] to Cupid's Knight.

† **boutgate.** *Obs. Sc.* [f. *bout*, aphet. f. ABOUT + GATE, going.] *lit.* A going about; *hence*, ambage, circumvention; equivocation, quibble.

1591 R. BRUCE *11 Serm.* T ij a (JAM.) The boutgates and deceites of the hearte of man are infinite. **1657** COLVIL *Whigs Supplic.* (1751) 138 They bring but bout-gates, and golinzies. *a* **1734** WODROW *Corr.* (1843) III. 463 Witnesses to his shifting and boutgates. **1768** ROSS *Helenore* 79 (JAM.) Nory..Made shift by boutgates to put off the day.

bouthe, obs. form of BOOTH.

bouting ('baʊtɪŋ), *vbl. sb.* [f. BOUT *sb.*[2] 1 b + -ING[1].] (See quot.) Also *attrib.*

1733 W. ELLIS *Chiltern & Vale Farm.* xxxviii. 311 Bouting, or Bouting-up, is a Half-ploughing of the Ground. *Ibid.* 312 Bouting-down, is done by making a shallow Thorough on each Side of the Ridge of the Bout. **1786** WASHINGTON *Diaries* (1925) III. 43 The field..is divided into 3 parts, by bouting Rows running crossways. **1834** *Penny Cycl.* II. 224 Sometimes (in ploughing land) two ridges are set up against each other, which is called ridging or bouting.

boutique (buː'tiːk). [F. (14th c. in Littré), f. OPr. *botica* (It. *bottega*), ad. L. *apothēca*, a. Gr. ἀποθήκη (see APOTHEC).] A small shop.

1767 J. LONG *Sel. Unpubl. Rec. Govt.* (*Fort William*) (1869) 501 The street..has been greatly encroached upon by a number of golahs, little straw huts, and boutiques. **1780** *India Gaz.* 9 Dec. (Y.), Mrs. Henpeck..is a great buyer of Bargains, so that she will often go out to the Europe Shops and the Boutiques, and lay out 5 or 600 Rupees in articles that we have not the least occasion for. **1854** *Househ. Words* IX. 43/1 A collection..presided over by a very solemn man..calling aloud at intervals to the passers-by to patronise the *boutique* at six sous. The attractions of his booth include soaps of all colours and patterns. **1859** SALA *Twice round Clock* 185 The merchants who have here [Burlington Arcade] their tiny *boutiques*. **1926** *Glasgow Herald* 18 Sept. 4 A small Sinhalese child..disappears into one of the 'boutiques' (small native shops) on the other side.

b. *spec.* A small fashion-shop or department that sells ready-to-wear clothes designed by a couturier; a small shop selling 'trend-setting' clothes or other articles, esp. for young or fashionable people. Also *attrib.*

1953 *N.Y. Times* 26 Jan. 12/5 The usual boutique sports clothes were not so evident as swirls of summer cocktail and evening dresses went by. **1954** *New Yorker* 27 Nov. 143/1 On the first floor is still another boutique, this one awave with ostrich-feather fans on new or antique mountings. **1957** *Times* 21 Oct. 13/1 Boutique departments in the big stores, designed to fill the gap between custom-made couture clothes and those made by wholesale houses are now well established. **1957** *Observer* 17 Nov. 11/3 The idea of 'Boutiques', those small shops set inside couture establishments to sell ready-to-wear. **1964** *Queen* 1 Jan. 57/2 [In] the third of the..boutiques..is a pot-pourri of pretty rococo and sometimes gilded objects, handsome ranges of household glass and china, and a special men's section. **1966** *Vanity Fair* May 116/2, I..love the look of boutique clothes. **1966** M. QUANT *Quant by Quant* 35 It was agreed that if we could find the right premises for a boutique..we would open a shop. It was to be a *bouillabaisse* of clothes and accessories..sweaters, scarves, shifts, hats, jewellery, and peculiar odds and ends.

† **boutisale.** *Obs. rare*[−1]. [f. BOOTY + SALE.] A sale of booty, in order to divide the proceeds.

1630 HAYWARD *Edw. VI*, 88 To speake nothing of the great Boutisale of Colledges and Chantries, to speake nothing of all his other particular pillages.

bouton (butɔ̃). [Fr., = button.]

1. In *pearl bouton, bouton pearl*, anglicization of *perle bouton*, a round pearl with a flat back marking the place where it was attached to the shell.

1851 *Illustr. Catal. Gt. Exhib.* III. 689 Brilliant tiara, ornamented with fine oriental pearl drops and boutons. **1907** *Daily Chron.* 5 Apr. 4/5 An exquisite pearl and brilliant necklace, formed as fifteen graduated drops, each composed of one bouton pearl, one brilliant, and one pear-shaped pearl drop. **1927** *Daily Express* 9 May 5/3 If it is a round pearl, with a flat back showing where it was attached to the shell, it will be called a 'bouton' pearl.

2. The button-like end of a honey-bee's tongue.

1886 F. R. CHESHIRE *Bees & Bee-Keeping* 95 The central and side ducts run down to that part of the tongue where the spoon, or bouton is placed.

‖ **boutonnière** (butɔnjɛr). [Fr.]

1. A spray of flowers worn in the buttonhole.

1877 B. HARTE *Story of a Mine* xi, She had distributed it to make *boutonnières* for other gentlemen. **1883** *Standard* 10 Nov. 3/2 Sir John Bennett came into court..carrying a huge bouquet, as well as a scarlet *boutonnière*. **1919** *Hist. Amer. Lit.* II. 268 He had worn a high hat, cane, and boutonnière. **1970** *Daily Tel.* 26 Feb. 17 Mr Bronson cooks and receives diners alternately..wearing a *boutonnière* in the lapel of his dark lounge suit.

2. *Surg.* An incision made in the urethra in order to extract a calculus or remove a tumour.

1884 H. THOMPSON *Tumours of Bladder* 76 The high operation is a much more formidable and hazardous proceeding than the simple boutonnière. **1908** *Practitioner* Feb. 180 A projecting intravesical lobe was wrenched out through a boutonnière incision.

boutrisse, obs. form of BUTTRESS.

‖ **bouts-rimés** (burime), *sb. pl.* [F. *bouts* ends + *rimés* rimed.] Rimed endings: see first quot.

1711 ADDISON *Spect.* No. 60. ¶8 The bouts-rimez were the favourites of the French nation for a whole age together... They were a List of Words that rhyme to one another, drawn up by another Hand, and given to a Poet, who was to make a Poem to the Rhymes in the same Order that they were placed upon the List. **1824** BYRON *Juan* XVI. l, Sonnets to herself, or bouts rimés. **1840** HOOD *Up Rhine* Introd. 4 Weary of repeating such bouts rimés as the Rhine and the land of the vine.

bouty, bouw(e, obs. ff. BOOTY, BOUGH, BOW.

bouvardia (buː'vɑːdɪə). *Bot.* [mod.L., f. the name of Dr. Charles *Bouvard* (died 1658), superintendent of the Jardin du Roi, Paris: see -IA.] Any plant of the rubiaceous genus of this name, which was introduced from Mexico and Central America, bearing handsome red, yellow, or white flowers.

1846 LINDLEY *Veg. Kingd.* 764 The fragrance or beauty..of the Gardenias,..Bouvardias, Catesbæas, &c. is unsurpassed in the vegetable kingdom. **1873** A. D. WHITNEY *Other Girls* vi. 64 Scarlet bouvardias and snowy deutzias. **1907** *Westm. Gaz.* 9 Oct. 2/1 The garden, with odorous bouvardias all awake.

bouvier ('buːvɪeɪ). [F., lit. 'cowherd'.] A breed of dog (see quots. 1934 and 1947).

1934 WEBSTER, *Bouvier des Flandres*, a powerfully built, rough-coated dog of a breed originating in Belgium. It has a slightly tousled appearance, with definite eyebrows, a mustache, and a beard. In color it ranges from fawn to black, through pepper-and-salt, and gray and brindle. **1947** G. L. HUBBARD *Working Dogs* ii. 58 The Bouvier des Ardennes is the Cattle Dog of the Belgian Ardennes... It has many rivals among other local Bouviers or Bouvier types... It appears to be a descendant of the Bouvier de Flandres. **1963** *Guardian* 5 Jan. 5/3 Among the dogs successfully trained for police work are the Rottweiller, the Reisenschnauzer, and the Bouvier.

† **bouvrage.** *Obs.* [ad. OF. *buvrage, buverage*, now *breuvage*, BEVERAGE.] Beverage, drink.

a **1815** *Culloden Papers* 184 (JAM.) Picking the pockets of the people of any ready money they have, to pay for foreign bouvrage.

bouwel, bouxome, obs. f. BOWEL, BUXOM.

bouye, obs. form of BUOY.

bouza, variant form of BOZA.

bouze, variant of BOUSE, BOOSE.

bouzouki (buː'zuːkɪ). [ad. mod.Gr. μπουζούκι; cf. Turkish *bozuk*.] In Greece, a sort of mandoline. Also *attrib.*

1952 L. MACNEICE *Ten Burnt Offerings* ii. 22 Not all The gadarene jeeps nor all the taverna bouzoukis Can utterly drown the pack that yelps on the scent. **1959** 'N. BLAKE' *Widow's Cruise* 90 The three Greek musicians were warming up with *bouzouki* songs. **1964** *Punch* 4 Nov. 700/3 A bouzouki, the most haunting sounding of all Greek musical instruments.

bouzy, boozy ('buːzɪ), *a.*[1] *Sc.* [? variant of BUSHY.] BOSKY, BUSHY.

1807 HOGG *Mount. Bard* 154 (JAM.) In a cottage, poor and nameless, By a little bouzy linn. *a* **1810** *Rem. Nithsdale Song* 67 A paukie cat..Wi' a bonnie bowsie tailie. **1808** JAMIESON s.v., A tree rich in foliage is said to have a boozy top.

'bouzy, *a.*[2] *north. dial.* Also boozy, bowsy. [Cf. Ger. *baus*, 'swollenness, inflation': see BOUSE *v.*[1]] Big, bulky, corpulent.

1807 J. STAGG *Poems* 62 Down his boozy burden fell. **1808** JAMIESON *Dict.*, *Bouzy-like*, having the appearance of distension, or largeness of size. **1875** F. K. ROBINSON *Whitby Gloss.* (E.D.S.), *Bowzy*, big-bellied.

bouzy, -ie, *a.*[3] obs. forms of BOUSY, sotted.

bovarism ('bəʊvərɪz(ə)m). Also bovarysm(e. [ad. F. *bovarysme*, f. the name of the principal character in Flaubert's novel *Madame Bovary* (1857) + -ISM.] (Domination by) a romantic or unreal conception of oneself. Hence **bovaric, bovaristic** *adjs.*; **bovarize, bovaryze** *v. trans.* and *intr.*

[**1902** J. DE GAULTIER (*title*) Le Bovarysme.] **1929** A. HUXLEY *Do what you Will* 273 By a process of what Jules de Gaultier has called 'Bovarysm'..we impose upon ourselves a more or less fictitious personality. *Ibid.* Our earnest efforts to bovaryze ourselves into imaginary unity. *Ibid.* The bovaric personage..is firmly established. **1934** T. S. ELIOT *Eliz. Essays* iii. 40, I do not believe that any writer has ever exposed this *bovarysme*, the human will to see things as they are not, more clearly than Shakespeare. **1936** A. HUXLEY *Olive Tree* 30 The French philosopher, Jules de Gaultier,

has said that one of the essential faculties of the human being is 'the power granted to man to conceive himself as other than he is'. He calls this power 'bovarism' after the heroine of Flaubert's novel Madame Bovary. *Ibid.* 31 People have bovarized themselves into the likeness of every kind of real or imaginary being. *Ibid.* 32 Realizing, if only in words, his bovaristic dreams. **1952** H. LEVIN in *Ess. in Crit.* II. 3 If to Bovarize is simply to daydream. *Ibid.* 16 An all-pervasive state of mind: Bovarism.

bovate ('bəʊveɪt). Also 7 bovatt, 8 boviat. [ad. med.L. *bovāta*, f. *bōs, bov-is* an ox; cf. -ATE[1].] An oxgang, or as much land as one ox could plough in a year; one-eighth of the carucate or ploughland; varying in amount from 10 to 18 acres according to the system of tillage, etc.

1688 R. HOLME *Armory* III. iii. 59 Bovatt of Land is as much as 15 Acres, in some places 20 Acres. **1723** H. ROWLANDS *Mona Antiqua* (1766) 122 Gavels, measured out by Boviats and Carucats. **1839** STONEHOUSE *Axholme* 345 William, the son of Roger de Beltoft, is returned as having two parts of one bovate of land. **1883** SEEBOHM *Eng. Vill. Community* 61 The full husband-land or virgate was composed of two bovates or oxgangs. [**1886** I. TAYLOR, The normal oxgangs in the Boldon Buke are 15 and 12 acres.]

bove, *adv.* and *prep.* Forms: 1 be-ufan, 1-2 bufan, bufon, 2-3 bufen, buuen, buven, buve, 3-4 boven, bove. [ME. *bove(n*, earlier *buven, bufen*:—OE. *bufan*, earlier *be-ufan*, a West Ger. compound (OS. *bi-oban*, Du. *boven*), f. *bi-*, BY, beside + *ufan* (OS. *oban*, OHG. *oban, obana*), OTeut. **ufana, ubana* from above, above, f. *uf* up + *-ana* suffix orig. expressing motion from.]

†**1.** (In OE. and early ME.) The earlier and simpler form of ABOVE. *Obs.*

The compound *a-bufan* appeared in the 12th c. in the north and n.e. as an adverbial form; by the end of 13th c. *abuven* was also prepositional, and generally used instead of *buven, buve*; and in 14th c. *bove* became obsolete. The following examples show the forms; the development of meaning will be found under ABOVE.

a **940** *Laws of Æthelstan* iv. 4 (Bosw.) Swa we her beufan cwædon. *c* **1000** ÆLFRIC *Manual of Astron.* 1 Eall swa deop under þyssre eorðan, swa heo is bufan. **1205** LAY. 26564 And smat hine buuen þan scelde. *c* **1315** SHOREHAM 117 Al that hys bove and under molde. ?*c* **1390** *Forme of Cury* (ed. Pegge) 75 Plant it boue with prunes and damysyns.

2. In modern English *'bove, bove*, is an occasional shortening of ABOVE, in verse.

1591 SPENSER *Ruines of Time* 110 Lifting up her brave heroick thought Bove womens weaknes. **1610** SHAKS. *Temp.* II. i. 118 'Boue the contentious waues. *c* **1630** DRUMMOND *Poems* Wks. (1711) 37 'Bove other far esteem'd. **1886** PLUMPTRE *Dante, Hell* I. 13 But when I reached a point 'bove which did tower A mount.

bove: see BUS *v.* = behoves.

†**bovert.** *Obs. rare*[−1]. [Cf. OF. *bouvert* a young ox or steer, f. *bœuf* ox.] ? A young ox.

?*a* **1400** *Chester Pl.* I. 129 Then hope I to have..The better in the bore as I hade before, Of this boverte.

Bovey ('bʌvɪ). [Proper name of a parish near Exeter in Devonshire.] *Bovey coal*: a lignite or brown-coal of Miocene age, occurring in beds at Bovey, and elsewhere.

1760 MILLES *Bovey Coal* in *Phil. Trans.* LI. 535 The Devonshire fossil..commonly known by the name of the Bovey Coal. **1860** FORDYCE *Hist. Coal, &c.* 31 Bovey Coal is found embedded in the pipe clays of Dorsetshire. **1861** MRS. BEETON *Bk. Househ. Managem.* iii. 32 Of coal there are various species; as, pit..cannel..bovey, jet, &c.

boviate, obs. form of BOVATE.

bovicide ('bəʊvɪsaɪd, 'bɒvɪ-). [f. L. *bōs, bov-is* ox + -CIDE; cf. L. *bovicīdium* slaughtering of cattle.] A slayer of oxen; *humorously* a butcher.

1678 PHILLIPS (*App. affected Wds.*) *Bovicide*, a killer of Oxen, a Butcher. **1832** *Blackw. Mag.* XXXI. 321 He had been a Bovicide.

'**boviculture.** [f. as prec. + CULTURE.] Cattle-rearing. (*Affected.*)

1876 *Daily Tel.* 4 Dec., The old epoch of boviculture.

'**bovid**, *a.* [f. as prec. + -ID.] Of or pertaining to the ox family, or *Bovidæ* of Zoologists, a family of Ruminating animals, having simply rounded horns, and no lachrymal sinuses.

boviform ('bəʊvɪfɔːm), *a.* [f. as prec. + -FORM.] Having the form of an ox, ox-like.

1678 CUDWORTH *Intell. Syst.* I. v. 673 There were once produced..Chimæras..mixtly Boviform and Hominiform.

bovine ('bəʊvaɪn), *a.* [ad. L. *bovīnus*, f. *bōs, bov-* ox; cf. F. *bovine*.] Belonging to, or characteristic of, the ox tribe. Also *ellipt.* = bovine animal.

1817 G. S. FABER *Eight Dissert.* (1845) I. 405 The worship of the bovine Apis. **1865** *Athenæum* No. 1969. 103/3 No wild bovine is now known in Syria. **1877** J. ALLEN *Amer. Bison* 468 Particularly bovine, also, is the satisfaction they take in rubbing themselves against trees.

2. *fig.* Inert, sluggish; dull, stupid; cf. *bucolic*.

1855 O. W. HOLMES *Poems* 235 Where bovine rustics used to doze and dream. **1879** *Contemp. Rev.* 291 Neither in the ranks of bovine Toryism nor of rabid Radicalism.

bovinely ('bəʊvaɪnlɪ), *adv.* [f. BOVINE + -LY[2].] In a bovine, dull, or inert manner.

1900 CROCKETT *Joan of Sword Hand* xxxiv. 227 Seydelmann..simpered bovinely down upon the girls. **1902** *Daily Chron.* 7 Nov. 5/2 The slow-witted politician, bovinely chewing the cud of his correspondent's schemes.

Bovril ('bɒvrɪl). Also bovril. [f. L. *bōs, bovis*, ox, cow.] **1.** The proprietary name of a concentrated essence of beef, invented in 1889 by J. Lawson Johnston. Also *fig.*

1889 *Athenæum* 18 Aug. 187/1 He ought to have drunk nothing but water, or at most a comforting cup of bovril. **1924** T. E. LAWRENCE *Lett.* (1938) 452 Your work..is the essence of thought, a variety of mental Bovril. **1935** AUDEN & ISHERWOOD *Dog beneath Skin* 12 Tourists, to whom the Tudor cafés Offer Bovril and buns upon Breton ware.

2. Facetious alteration of BROTHEL *sb.* 3.

1936 R. ACKLAND *After October* I. 49, I had to take a job as a sort of dancing partner, and the place was practically a bovril. **1948** S. P. B. MAIS *Caper Sauce* xii. 124 I'm not having my house turned into a Bovril.

bovrilize ('bɒvrɪlaɪz), *v.* [f. prec. + -IZE.] *trans.* To concentrate the essence of; to epitomize, condense.

1901 *Daily News* 11 Jan. 5/1 Here..is one of these 'bovrilised' announcements..: Wanted, Sit. as Comp. by Eng. lady, 35; good Fr.; good refs.; would trav. R.R., 100. **1902** *Daily Chron.* 22 Aug. 8/7 He must give us not life, but the essence of it—a bovrilised version, as it were. **1902** *Academy* 13 Dec. 655/2 His fondness for bovrilising thought ..into so small a compass of words that the sentences are really too 'meaty'. **1928** *Musical Times* Nov. 1003 The exercises..are short enough not to fatigue the attention, and they bovrilise the difficulties or virtues admirably.

bovver ('bɒvə(r)). *slang.* Also (*rarely*) bovva. [Repr. Cockney pronunc. of BOTHER *sb.*] Trouble, disturbance, or fighting, esp. caused by skinhead gangs. Freq. in Comb., as **bovver bird**, the female counterpart of a *bovver boy*; **bovver boot**, a heavy boot with toe-cap and laces, of a kind characteristically worn by skinheads; **bovver boy**, a hooligan; *spec.* one of a gang of skinhead youths.

1969 *New Society* 13 Nov. 762/1 'We show 'em because they're useful if there's a bit of bovver.' Bother is the crophead word for fight; indeed, a lot of them call their footwear 'bovver boots'. **1970** *Observer* 11 Jan. 28/4 It was called *The Aggro Boy* and centred around a football match in general and two bovva boys in particular. **1970** *Pix* (Austral.) 29 Aug. 7/1 In Britain,..skinheads and their 'bovver birds' came into fashion around last April. **1972** DANIEL & MCGUIRE *Paint House* ii. 24 Around the Collinwood there was about twenty on average but with bovver there was sometimes more than that. **1977** *Daily Express* 29 Jan. 7/4 Tybalt... This most menacing of Verona's bovver-boys. **1980** *Daily Tel.* 6 May 19 Yesterday at Brighton..police..confiscated hundreds of pairs of laces from 'bovver boots' so that the youngsters wearing them could not kick anyone. **1983** *Listener* 20 Oct. 27/2 Mr Hanna is the nearest thing *Newsnight* has to a bovver boy, but that is not to say that he is a vulgar or crude person.

†**bovy.** *Obs. rare*[−1]. (See quot.)

1547 BOORDE *Introd. Knowl.* 167 There is[in Bohemia] a beast called a Bouy lyke a Bugle..a vengeable beast.

bow (bəʊ), *sb.*[1] Forms: 1 boȝa, 3-4 boȝe, (3 bou), 3-7 bowe, 4 bouwe, boghe (boȝ), 4-5 boowe, 6 boe, (boll), 4- bow. [Com. Teut.: OE. *boȝa*, corresp. to OFris. *boga*, OS. *bogo* (MDu. *booghe*, Du. *boog*), OHG. *bogo* (MHG. *boge*, mod.G. *bogen*), ON. *bogi* (Sw. *båge*, Da. *bue*):—OTeut. **bugon-*, f. stem *bug-* of *beugan*, to bend.]

I. 1. a. *gen.* A thing bent or fashioned so as to form part of the circumference of a circle or other curve; a bend, a bent line.

Not actually exemplified in OE., but entering into numerous compounds, as *elnboȝa* elbow, *hring-boȝa* 'ring-bow,' a coiled snake, *rén-boȝa* rain-bow, *stán-boȝa* 'stone-bow,' an arch, *boȝa-net* bow-net. In ME. the general sense was often supplied from French by *arch*, but *bow* is occasional. (In quot. 1387, it is quite possible that *bowe* is the Norse *bug-r* bend, bowing, the bend of a river.)

1387 TREVISA *Higden* (1865) II. 87 From þe bowe of the ryuer of Humber. **1541** ELYOT *Image Gov.* 100 The Theatre was a place made in the fourme of a bowe, that hath a great bente. **1846** ELLIS *Elgin Marb.* II. 13 The floating drapery describes a bow above her head.

b. *Calligraphy.* A curved stroke forming part of a letter.

1914 E. A. LOEW *Beneventan Script* vii. 127 The important elements of which the letters are composed are.. the bow, the tall upright stem, [etc.]. **1957** N. R. KER *Catal. MSS. Anglo-Saxon* p. xxx, The bow of p is regularly open in the early manuscripts.

II. Specific uses.

2. A rainbow. (Mostly contextual or poetical for the compound.)

a **1000** ÆLFRIC *Gen.* ix. 14 Æteowþ min boȝa on ðam wolcnum. *c* **1000** *Sax. Leechd.* I. 284 Heo þone heofonlican boȝan mid hyre bleoȝe efenlæce. *c* **1340** *Cursor M.* 1977 (Fairf.) Quen þou þat boghe may se þer-oute of suche flode haue þou na doute. **1382** WYCLIF *Ecclus.* xliii. 12 See the bowe, and blisse hym that made it. **1597** DRAYTON *Mortimer.* 53 The bowe appeares to tell the flood is donne. *c* **1630** DRUMM. OF HAWTH. *Poems* Wks. (1711) 56/2 Ropes make of the rainy bow. **1667** MILTON *P.L.* XI. 865 A dewie Cloud, and in the Cloud a Bow. **1728** THOMSON *Spring* 203 Bestriding earth, the grand ethereal bow. **1850** TENNYSON *In Mem.* cxxii. 190 Every dew-drop paints a bow.

†**3.** An arch (of masonry), as in a gateway, or bridge. *Obs.* exc. *dial.*

a **1000** *Beowulf* (Z.) 2719 Ða stan boȝan stapulum fæste. *c* **1325** *E.E. Allit. P.* A. 323 Þurȝ drwry deth boȝ vch ma dreue. **1382** WYCLIF *Prov.* xx. 26 He bowith in vpon hem a stonene bowe. *c* **1386** CHAUCER *Prol.* 125 After the scole of Stratford atte Bowe [*Cambr. MS.* stratforthe at the bowe]. **1483** *Cath. Angl.* 31/1 A Bowe of a bryge. **1513** DOUGLAS *Æneis* VI. x. 10 Thai portis with thair stalwart bow and brace. **1513-75** *Diurnal Occurrents* (1833) 211 At Bessie Beaties hous, in the passage to the over boll. **1570-87** HOLINSHED *Scot. Chron.* (1806) II. 327 Their heads were set ..on the neither-bow. **1862** BARNES *Rhymes Dorset. Dial.* II. 75 By the mossy brudge's bow.

4. a. A weapon for shooting arrows or similar missiles, consisting of a strip of elastic wood or other material, bent by means of a string stretched between its two ends; the arrow is impelled by the recoil which follows the retraction of the string. Phrases. ***to bend*** or ***draw a bow, to shoot with*** (formerly *in*) ***a bow. bows and bills!*** the cry of alarm raised in the English camp in old times. See also CROSS-BOW, STONE-BOW.

a **1000** *Gnomic Vers.* 154 (Gr.) Boȝa sceal stræle. *c* **1205** LAY. 6471 Enne boȝe swiðe strong. *a* **1225** *Ancr. R.* 250 He tobrekeð his bowe. **1340** *Ayenb.* 45 An archer..nom his boȝe. **1382** WYCLIF *1 Kings* xxii. 34 A maner man bente a boowe. *a* **1400** *Cov. Myst.* 45 My bowe xal I drawe. **1557** *Tottel's Misc.* 265 He claymed Cupides boe. **1562** HEYWOOD *Prov. & Epigr.* (1867) 61 Many a man speaketh of Robyn hood, That neuer shot in his bowe. *a* **1572** KNOX *Hist. Ref.* 28 (JAM.) The schout ryises, Bowes and Billis!..whiche is a significatioun of extreim defence. **1597** SHAKS. *2 Hen. IV*, III. ii. 48 Hee drew a good Bow..hee shot a fine shoote. **1607** DEKKER *Northw. Hoe* v. Wks. 1873 III. 80 Its better to shoot in a bowe that has been shot in before. **1671** MILTON *P.R.* III. 305 They issue forth, steel bows and shafts their arms. **1830** SIR J. HERSCHEL *Stud. Nat. Phil.* III. iii. (1851) 273 The bow of Ulysses, which none but its master could bend. **1877** BRYANT *Among Trees* 96 While yet the Indian hunter drew the bow.

b. *transf.* A bowman (in plural).

c **1511** *1st Eng. Bk. Amer.* (Arb.) Introd. 34/2, x. M. knyghtes..vi. M. crosse bowes, xv. M. longe bowes, and xl. M. othere men. **1577** HOLINSHED *Chron.* III. 1259/1 There was among these a thirtie bowes with a bagpipe. **1825** SCOTT *Talism.* x, A strong guard of bills and bows.

c. *fig.* with many phrases: e.g. ***to have two*** (***many***, etc.) ***strings to one's bow***: to have two (or many) resources or alternatives. ***to draw the longbow***: to make exaggerated statements (*colloq.*). † ***the bent of one's bow***: one's intention, inclination, disposition, 'calibre' (cf. BENT *sb.*[2] 8, 9). † ***to shoot in*** (***another's***) ***bow***: to practise an art other than one's own. † ***by the string rather than the bow***: by the most direct way. Proverb, ***a bow too long bent waxes dull***: relaxation is desirable; hence in other allusive phrases.

c **1532** SIR ADRIAN FORTESCUE in *Oxf. Dict. Proverbs* (1948) 59/1 A bowe that is longe bent, will waxe dulle. **1562** J. HEYWOOD *Prov. & Epigr.* (1867) 30 Ye haue many stryngis to the bowe. *Ibid.* 165, I haue the bent of his bowe, that I know. **1579** LYLY *Euphues* (Arb.) 116 My counsaile is that thou have more strings to thy bow than one. **1678** BUTLER *Hud.* III. i. 3 As he that has two strings t' his bow, And burns for love and money too. **1690** W. WALKER *Idiomat. Anglo-Lat.* Pref. 4 To save..the labour of turning from place to place with references, which to some is tedious and to all unpleasing who love to go by the string rather than by the bow. **1721** J. KELLY *Scot. Proverbs* 33 A Bow o'er bent will weaken. *Eng.* All Work and no Play makes *Jack* a dull Boy. **1783** AINSWORTH *Lat. Dict.* (Morell) I. s.v. *Bent*, I have got the bend of his bow, *ego illius sensum pulchrè calleo.* **1812** JANE AUSTEN *Mansf. P.* viii. (D.) Miss Bertram.. might be said to have two strings to her bow. **1817** KEATS *Let.* 5 Sept. (1931) I. 38 But let us refresh ourself from this depth of thinking, and turn to some innocent jocularity—the Bow cannot always be bent. **1824** BYRON *Juan* XVI. i, They ..draw the long bow better now than ever. **1876** C. M. YONGE *Womankind* xi. 80 A strain which makes it very desirable..to unbend the bow, by a journey abroad, a sea-side sojourn.

†**d.** ***to bend*** or ***bring*** (***a person***) ***to one's bow***: i.e. to one's will, inclination, or control. ***to come to*** (***a person's***) ***bow***: to become compliant or subject. (Here there may have been later association with BOW *sb.*[2])

1631 *Foxe's A. & M.* III. xii. 880/2 Perceiuing they could not bend him vnto their bowe. **1633** H. COGAN *Pinto's Trav.* lxxii. (1663) 294 All this he did cunningly, hoping by this means to bring him to his bowe with less peril. **1650** HUBBERT *Pill Formality* 22 To bear such sway and rule over others that they must have all men come to their bow. **1675** BROOKS *Gold. Key* Wks. (1867) V. 497 Neither Darius, his presidents, nor princes, could ever bring Daniel to their bow. **1682** BUNYAN *Holy War* 30 Mansoul being wholly at his beck, and brought wholly to his bow. **1697** DAMPIER *Voy.* (1729) II. II. 5 The Dutch..have lately endeavoured to bring the King..to their Bow.

e. ***Cupid's bow***: see CUPID 1 b.

†**5. a.** A yoke for oxen. *Obs.* or *dial.*

c **1400** *Destr. Troy* 901 [Oxin] als..bowande to þe bowes as any bestes might. **1523** FITZHERB. *Husb.* §5 His oxen or horses, and the geare that belongeth to them, that is to say, bowes, yokes, landes, stylkynges, wrethynge temes. **1600** SHAKS. *A.Y.L.* III. iii. 80 As the Oxe hath his bow sir, the horse his curb, etc. **1669** WORLIDGE *Syst. Agric.* (1681) 322 Bow, an Ox-bow or Yoak. **1721** BAILEY, *Bow*, or Ox-Bow, a Yoke of Oxen. *C*[*ountry Word*].

b. *pl.* Two pieces of wood laid archwise to fit a horse's back, give the saddle its due form, and keep it tight: see SADDLE-BOW.

6. *Music.* **a.** [from 4.] The appliance with which instruments of the violin class are played, being a rod of elastic wood with a number of horse-hairs stretched from end to end, which is drawn across the strings, and causes them to sound. (It was formerly curved, with a cord instead of the hairs, thus resembling an archer's bow.)

1580 HOLLYBAND *Treas. Fr. Tong, L'Archet d'vn rebec*.. the bowe of a viole. **1776** BURNEY *Hist. Mus.* (1789) I. 271 The bow now in use was.. unknown to the ancients. **1807** ROBINSON *Archæol. Græca* v. xxiii. 537 They struck the strings sometimes with a bow, and sometimes only with the fingers. **1880** GROVE *Dict. Mus.* II. 632 [Paganini] made his staccato by throwing the bow violently on the string.

b. [f. BOW *v.*] A single passage of the bow across the string.

1838 W. GARDINER *Music of Nat.* 120 In Beethoven.. we find many bars included in one bow.

c. *transf.* Part of an insect's wing resembling a violin-bow in function.

1836–9 TODD *Cycl. Anat. & Phys.* II. 928/2 When the wings are rubbed briskly together these rasps or bows produce a loud grating against some projecting nervures.

7. Applied to parts of the body resembling a bow.

†**a.** The iris of the eye. **b.** The eye-brow. *Obs.*

1611 COTGR., *Arc*.. the bow, or Iris of the eye. **1729** T. COOKE *Tales* 64 The Bows her Eyes above. *Ibid.* 103 How have I prais'd thy Cheeks where Roses blow! How dwell'd with Wonder on thy sable Bow!

†8. An arc of a circle. *Obs.*

1594 BLUNDEVIL *Exerc.* III. I. (ed. 7) 274 The circular line .. is called *arcus*, in English the bow. **1660** BLOOME *Archit.* B iij, Where that Circle cutteth the 12 part.. divide above the bowe thereof.. in foure. **1674** N. FAIRFAX *Bulk & Selv.* 68 The motion would be.. a bow or arch of a circle. *Ibid.* 117 A wheel of manifold rims.. would make out uneven bows of circles, in even shares of time.

†9. 'An astronomical instrument formerly used at sea, consisting of only one large graduated arc of 90°, three vanes, and a shank or staff.' Smyth *Sailor's Word-bk.*

1696 PHILLIPS, *Bow*, a Mathematical Instrument to take heights. [**1706** *Ibid.* A Mathematical Instrument, formerly us'd by Seamen to take the height of the sun.]

10. An instrument for drawing curves, especially of large radius, consisting of a rigid beam, and a strip of wood, steel, or the like, which is bent into the required shape by means of screws.

1706 PHILLIPS, *Bow*, a Beam of Wood or Brass, with three long Screws that direct a Lath of Wood or Steel to any Arch; being commonly us'd to make Draughts of Ships, Projections of the Sphere, etc. [So BAILEY 1731, JOHNSON, etc.]

11. **a.** A ring or hoop of metal, etc. forming a handle. Cf. BAIL *sb.*², BOUL.

1611 COTGR. s.v. *Anneau*, The bow (or vpmost part) of a key. **1685** *Lond. Gaz.* No. 3054/4 A pair of Scissars with silver Bowes. **1730** SAVERY in *Phil. Trans.* XXXVI. 328 It.. lifted a Key by the Bow. **1833** J. HOLLAND *Manuf. Metals* II. 39 Fancy scissors with shanks and bows of gold. **1863** ATKINSON *Danby Provinc.*, *Bow*, a semicircular hoop or handle to anything, as a basket, a backstone or a pail. **1884** F. BRITTEN *Watch & Clockm.* 36 The ring of a watch case by which it is attached to the watch guard is.. called a bow.

b. The guard of a sword-hilt, or of a trigger.

1701 *Lond. Gaz.* No. 3723/4 A silver-hilted Sword without a Bow. **1881** GREENER *Gun* 328 The lever being so shaped and adjusted as to form the bow.

c. A bent strip of wood or metal to support the hood, cover, etc. of a vehicle; a bail or slat.

d. A curved piece of metal used to make contact with an overhead wire in electric traction; = *bow trolley* (see 19 below). Also *attrib.*

1909 *Cent. Dict.* Suppl., *Bow-spring*, in electr. traction, the spring which keeps the bow spread out, when a bow is used to take current from a trolley-wire.

e. A leg of a pair of spectacles; also, the frame of either of the lenses. *U.S.*

1711 in *Essex Inst. Hist. Coll.* (Salem, Mass.) IV. 187/1 To Madam Rebekah Brown, I give my spectacles with gold bows. **1847** LONGF. *Evang.* I. iii. 4 Glasses with horn bows Sat astride on his nose. **1890** *Harper's Mag.* Oct. 720/1 A pair of ancient silver-rimmed spectacles from which the bows were lost.

12. *Arch.* **a.** (See quots.)

a **1723** WREN in Gwilt *Archit.* 1006 The vaults of the nave .. are supported.. by the bowes or flying buttresses. *Ibid.* Gloss. *Bow*, the part of any building which projects from a straight wall. It is sometimes circular and sometimes polygonal on the plan, or rather formed by two exterior obtuse angles. Bows on polygonal plans are called canted bows. [Hence *Bow-window*.]

b. Short for BOW-WINDOW.

1885 *Harper's Mag.* Mar. 547/1 Two little windows.. replaced by an ample bow.

13. A name of various instruments or tools consisting of a curved piece of wood, with a string extending from one extremity to the other; used, e.g. by smiths, etc. for turning a drill; by turners for turning wood; by hatters for separating the fibres of fur or wool.

1875 URE *Dict. Arts* II. 784 *Hat Manuf.*, After the fur is thus driven by the bow from one end of the hurdle to the other, it forms a mass called a bat.

14. An Indian musical instrument.

1872 MATEER *Travancore* 217 The favorite instrument is the bow. A series of bells of various sizes is fastened to the frame of a gigantic bow, and the strings are tightened so as to produce a musical note when struck.

†15. A bow's length, used as a measure of length in archery: chiefly in *fig.* phrases. *Obs.*

1592 GREENE *Upst. Courtier* in *Harl. Misc.* (Malh.) II. 224 Alas! proud princox, you pearch a bow to hie. —— *Disput.* 2 No, no, Nan, you are two bowes downe the wind. **1607** MIDDLETON *Michaelm. Term* IV. i, I am not a bow wide of your mind, sir. **1649** G. DANIEL *Trinarch., Rich. II*, xi, Some men will haue an ayme Sixe Bowes beyond the Levell wch they made.

16. **a.** 'The doubling of a string in a slip-knot' (J.); a single-looped knot. **b.** A double-looped ornamental knot into which ribbons, etc., are tied (the usual sense). **c.** A necktie, ribbon, etc., tied up in such a knot. So ***bow-knot.***

1547 SALESBURY *Welsh Dict.*, *Kwlwm dalen*, a bowe knot. **1671** CROWNE *Juliana* III. 33 What knot? a bow-knot? A bow-knot saucy-chops? ha! can you tye your nose of a bow-knot? **1676** WISEMAN (J.), Make a knot and let the second knot be with a bow. **1768** STERNE *Sent. Journey* (1778) I. 5 Tying up the ribband in a bow-knot, [I] returned it to her. **1861** MRS. STOWE *Pearl Orr's Isl.* I. v. 30 When he had once seated himself in a double bow-knot at a neighbor's evening fireside. **1874** *Queen* 8 Aug., The sleeves were.. ornamented with bows of brown faille. *a* **1887** *Mod.* Her sash was tied in a bow. **1896** *Godey's Mag.* Apr. 446/2 A woman with her back doubled into a bow-knot.

III. *Attrib.* and *Comb.*

17. *attrib.* or as *adj.* Bent like a bow, bowed.

1592 SHAKS. *Ven. & Ad.* 619 On his bow-backe, he hath a battell set, Of brisly pikes. **1678** *Lond. Gaz.* No. 1272/4 He is aged about 25 years.. a bowe nose a little sharp and reddish. **1703** *Ibid.* No. 3951/4 Lewis Branson.. with fair Hair and bow Legs. **1832** MARRYAT *N. Forster* vi, A little fat man with bow legs.

18. Obvious comb., as ***bow-chest, -maker; bow-bending, bow-like, -played, bow-shaped*** adjs.

a **1688** VILLIERS (Dk. Buckhm.) *Poems* (1775) 142 *Bow-bending Cupid. **1515–24** in E. Lodge *Illustr. Brit. Hist.* (1838) I. 2 To my Lord D'Arcy, by 3 warrants; bows of yew, 4074.. *bow chests and arrow chests, 240. **1611** SPEED *Theat. Gt. Brit.* xxxii. (1614) 63/1 Whose East coasts lye *bowe-like into the German ocean. **1859** R. BURTON *Centr. Afr.* in *Jrnl. Geog. Soc.* XXIX. 310 [Lips] pointed in the centre with that bowlike form which Europeans hold beautiful. **1864** *Hist. Violin* in *Eng. Mech.* (1870) 11 Feb. 536/2 John Dodd was.. England's best *bow-maker. **1836** DUBOURG *Violin* ix. (1878) 274 The construction of *bow-played instruments. *a* **1887** *Mod.* A *bow-shaped curvature.

19. Special comb. **bow-and-arrow** *attrib.*, belonging to or characteristic of the period when the bow and arrow was the chief weapon of war; **bow-arm**, the arm that holds the bow (in archery or in violin-playing); **bow-beaked** *a.*, having a curved beak; **bow-bender**, ? a bow-bearer; **bow-bent** *a.*, bent like a bow, bowed; **bow-boy**, a boy with a bow (applied to Cupid); **bow-brace**, a guard to protect the left arm from the friction of the bowstring; †**bow closet**, a closet in a recess in the wall of a room; **bow-drill**, a drill turned by means of a bow, the string of which is twisted round the drill (see sense 13); **bow-fin**, a kind of fish (*Amia calva*); **bow-houghed** *a.*, having crooked hips; **bow-instrument**, an instrument played with a bow, as a violin; **bow-iron** (see quot.); **bow-key** *U.S.* = *bow-pin*; **bow-knot** (see sense 16); †**bow-lap**, a term describing a particular posture of the leaves of a plant (see quot.); †**bow-marks**, butts for archery; **bow-meeting**, a meeting for the practice of archery; **bow-necked** *a.*, having a curved neck; **bow-(neck)tie**, a necktie in the shape of a bow (sense 16 b); **bow-pen**, **bow-pencil**, a bow-compass with a pen or pencil; **bow-pin**, a key or cotter to fasten the bow of an ox-yoke; **bow-saw**, a saw with a narrow blade stretched in a strong frame as the bowstring in the bow; **bow-spring**, a bow-shaped spring; **bow-stock**, the stock or longitudinal beam of a cross-bow; †**bow-tree**, the wooden part of an archer's bow; **bow trolley**, a device for collecting the current from an overhead wire in electric traction; †**bow-ward**, a nick in the end of the stem of a key where it joins the bow (see sense 11); **bow-whip** *U.S.* (see quot.); **bow-woman** (*nonce-wd.*), a female archer; **bow-wood**, the wood of the Osage Orange (*Maclura aurantiaca*).

1899 *Westm. Gaz.* 27 July 2/2 We may yet work back to the *bow-and-arrow period if modern inventions make war with their aid too grotesquely horrible and difficult. **1907** *Macm. Mag.* Oct. 935 Bow-and-arrow men. **1860** *Archer's Guide* 44 The Brace buckles round the *bow-arm, to prevent the string hurting it. **1881** BROADHOUSE *Mus. Acoust.* 167 A steady and practised use of the bow-arm. **1791** COWPER *Iliad* XVI. 521 Two vultures.. *Bow-beak'd, crook-talon'd. **1719** J. AUBREY *Surrey* III. 74 Sir Thomas Carwarden, Kt. .. was *Bow-Bender to King Henry VIII. **1592** GREENE *Groat's-w. Wit* (1874) 13 Hee would stroake his *bowbent leg, as though he went to shoote loue arrows from his shins. **1628** MILTON *Vac. Exerc.* 69 A sibyl old, bow-bent with crooked age. **1592** SHAKS. *Rom. & Jul.* II. iv. 16 His heart cleft with the blind *Bowe-boyes but-shaft. **1758** MRS. DELANY *To Mrs. Dewes* 542 A little shell ornament for my *bow closet. **1865** TYLOR *Early Hist. Man.* ix. 243 The *bow-drill is a most ancient and well known boring instrument. **1880** GUNTHER *Fishes* 372 The *'Bow-fin' or 'Mud-fish' is not uncommon in.. fresh waters of the United States. **1672** *Phil. Trans.* VII. 5064 One of the G. Dukes Musicians, & plays on all *Bow-Instruments. *a* **1877** KNIGHT *Dict. Mech.*, **Bow-iron*, the staple on the side of a wagon-bed which receives the bows of the tilt or cover. **1859** J. YOUNG in B. Young et al. *Jrnl. Discourses* VI. 230/2 You that have on such a yoke had better pull out the *bow-keys. **1913** M. STACPOOLE *Monte Carlo* vi. 63 He was wearing a rather exaggerated *bow necktie. **1672** GREW *Anat. Plants* I. iv. § 16 There is the *Bow-Lap, where the leaves are all laid somewhat convexly one over another, but not plaited. **1877** *All Y. Round* 29 Sept. 186 The character of these *bow-meetings varies. **1858** LYTTON *What will he do* II. iv, Showy, *bow-necked, long-tailed.. hybrids. **1869** *Eng. Mech.* 19 Mar. 574/2 In tracing a circle with a *bow-pen. **1856** *Mich. State Agric. Soc. Trans. 1855* VII. 55 Sample *bow pins. **1677** MOXON *Mech. Exerc.* (1703) 102 The Frame or *Bow-Saw. **1840** *Civil Engin. & Arch. Jrnl.* III. 56/2 A vertebrated carriage.. with *bow-spring bearers and buffers. **1897** *Sears, Roebuck Catal.* 223/2 Gentlemen's silk *bow ties. For turn-down collar. **1910** *Westm. Gaz.* 24 Jan. 3/1 He wore a check suit.. and a pink cotton bow-tie. ? *c* **1500** *Robin Hood* (Ritson) I. i. 288 Lytell Johan toke none other mesure But his *bowe tre. **1901** *Trans. Amer. Inst. Elect. Engin.* 111 (Cent. Dict. *Suppl.* s.v. *Trolley*), *Bow trolley. **1902** *Encycl. Brit.* XXVIII. 98 On the continent of Europe considerable use has been made of bow trolleys, which consist of light metallic bow-shaped structures.. running along on the under side of the wire against which they rub. **1677** MOXON *Mech. Exerc.* (1703) 23 H the Shank .. K the *Bow-ward, L the bow. **1890** *Harper's Mag.* Oct. 718/1 His whip was the fashionable '*bow whip' of the period, common enough now, to be sure, with a long lash, tapering down to a fine silk 'snapper' on the end. **1877** *All Y. Round* 29 Sept. 188 The performances of the bowmen are decidedly distanced by those of the *bowwomen. **1866** *Treas. Bot.*, s.v. *Maclura*, Its elastic yellow wood is called *Bow-wood, from its being used by the Indians for making bows.

bow (baʊ), *sb.*² [f. BOW *v.*¹ 9.]

An inclination of the body or head in salutation and in token of respect, reverence, submission, etc.; an obeisance. ***to make one's bow***: to retire, leave the stage.

a **1656** COWLEY *Liberty* Wks. 1710 II. 686 That I do you with humble Bows.. adore. **1710** STEELE *Tatler* No. 16 ¶ 2 Making Bows till his Buttons touch'd the Ground. **1766** [C. ANSTEY] *Bath Guide* xi. 156 Shewing them how.. to make a good Bow. **1769** *Junius Lett.* xxxv. 164 She received him.. with bows, and smiles. **1863** GEO. ELIOT *Romola* I. vi, She returned Tito's bow.

1791 DK. LEEDS *Polit. Mem.* (1884) 156 In which case I should think myself obliged to make my bow. **1875** J. THOMSON *Life W. Thomson* ix. 133 The old farmer.. is making his bow—passing off the stage never again to return.

¶ Cf. also phrases under BOW *sb.*¹ 4 d.

bow (baʊ), *sb.*³ *Naut.* Also 7 **bowe**, 8 **bough**. [Recorded only since 1600. Corresp. in form and sense to LG. *bûg*, Du. *boeg*, Da. *boug*, *bov*, Sw. *bog*, all with senses 'shoulder of man or beast', and 'bow of a ship'. The older Teut. forms were ON. *bóg-r*, OHG. *buog* (MHG. *buoc*), MDu. *boech* 'shoulder of man or beast', OE. *bōȝ*, *bóh* 'shoulder, upper arm', and 'bough of a tree':—OTeut. **bôgu-z*. corresp. to Gr. *πᾶχυς*, *πῆχυς*, and Skr. *bāhu-s* 'arm'. *Bow* is thus in origin the same word as BOUGH, but while the latter has come down direct from OE. in one of the OE. senses, *bow* has been adopted at a later time from LG., Du., or Da., in the special sense of the 'shoulders' of a boat or ship, developed in the maritime speech of one or other of these, but not known to OE. or ME. *Bough* and *bow* have thus widely diverged, the earlier meaning of 'shoulder, arm', not being retained by either. (Not related to BOW *sb.*¹, nor to BOW *v.*¹, though probably now associated with the latter in the popular etymological consciousness, as appears from most attempts to explain it.)]

1. **a.** 'The fore-end of a ship or boat; being the rounding part of a vessel forward, beginning on both sides where the planks arch inwards, and terminating where they close, at the rabbet of the stem or prow, being larboard or starboard from that division'. Smyth *Sailor's Word-bk.* Also in *pl.* 'bows', i.e. the 'shoulders' of a boat.

1626 CAPT. SMITH *Accid. Yng. Seamen* 11 The bend, the bowe, the hawse. **1627** —— *Seaman's Gram.* ii. 10 The Bow is the broadest part of the Ship before, compassing the Stem to the Loufe. **1703** *Lond. Gaz.* No. 3923/3 She had cut her Anchors from the Bow. **1727** A. HAMILTON *New Acc. E. Ind.* II. l. 220 The Sea.. broke over the Ship, carrying away .. two Anchors from the lee Bough. **1772–84** COOK *Voy.* (1790) I. 166 At day-break [we] observed the others [rocks] under our bows. **1828** SCOTT *F.M. Perth* III. 81 A number of boats.. having their several pipers in the bow. **1840** R. DANA *Bef. Mast* x. 24 Baggage, which we put into the bows of the boat. **1833** M. SCOTT *Tom Cringle* ii. 44 We saw a large West Indiaman suddenly.. stand across our Bows. **1882** *Daily Tel.* 12 Sept. 2/2 The sea washes noisily against the weather bow.

b. An object is said to be ***on the bow*** when within 45° of the point right ahead.

1626 CAPT. SMITH *Accid. Yng. Seamen* 18 He stands right a-head; or on the weather bow, or ley bow. **1762–9** FALCONER *Shipwr.* III. 124 Cliffs they view Faintly along the larboard bow descried. **1883** *Law Times Rep.* XLIX. 332/1

A steamer..bearing about three or four points on the starboard bow of the Clan Sinclair.

c. *attrib.*

1875 Bedford *Sailor's Pocket Bk.* i. (ed. 2) 22 A Column is said to be in *Two Bow Lines* when the ships are ranged on each bow of a single ship.

d. *bow(s on*, with the bow of the vessel turned towards the object considered or in view.

[**1856** T. Williams *Fiji & Fijians* I. vi. 205 The commander ordered it to be run with its bows on the shore.] **1877** *Design & Work* 218/2 To hit a craft coming bows on. **1893** Kipling *Many Invent.* 104 A galley coming up bow-on. **1903** *Westm. Gaz.* 15 June 3/1 The 'standard type' has equal offensive strength in all directions—whether bows-on or broadside. **1967** *Jane's Surface Skimmer Systems 1967–68* 49 The flat bottom hull..permits the craft to run bow-on to any flat, sloping bank to embark passengers.

2. *transf.* The rower nearest to the bow. (*colloq.*)

1830 Marryat *King's Own* xxxii, In bow forward!—way enough. **1860** Hughes *Tom Brown Oxford* xxxiii, The last man whom Tom would have chosen as bow in a pair oar.

3. *Comb.*, as *bow-anchor, -port, -sheet, -side, -timber*; †**bow-chase, bow-chaser** (see quots); **bow-fast**, a hawser at the bow to secure a vessel to a wharf (see fast); **bow-grace, bow-grease**, 'a kind of frame or fender of old junk placed round the bows and sides of a ship to prevent her receiving injury from floating ice or timbers' (Smyth *Sailor's Word-bk.*); (also called bongrace, and in some way connected with that word); **bow-oar**, the oar nearest the bow; *transf.* the man who pulls this oar; also, in a whale-boat, the foremost oar but one; **bow-pieces**, 'the ordnance in the bows' (Smyth *Sailor's Word-bk.*); **bow-wave**, (*a*) *Naut.* the wave set up at the bows of a ship under way; (*b*) *transf.* a shock wave produced in front of a body passing through the air. See also bowline, bowman[2], bowsprit.

1627 Capt. Smith *Seaman's Gram.* vii. 29 The first, second, and third Anchor..are called *Bow Anchors. **1871** Tyndall *Fragm. Sc.* vi. (ed. 6) I. 205 Both port and bow anchors were cast in deep waters. **1769** Falconer *Dict. Marine* (1789) **Bow Chace*, a cannon..in the fore-part of a ship to fire upon any object a-head of her. **1836** Marryat *Midsh. Easy* xvii, Firing only her *bow-chasers. *c* **1850** *Rudim. Navig.* (Weale) 106 The former [ports] are made for the purpose of firing upon an enemy ahead, and are called bow-chasers. **1867** Smyth *Sailor's Word-bk.*, *Bow-chasers*, two long chase-guns placed forward in the bow-ports to fire directly ahead. **1822** *Western M. Rev.* III. 354 His *bow-fast (a grape vine) parted, and his frail bark put to sea without a pilot. **1913** Masefield *Daffodil Fields* 30 The bowfast was cast off, the screw revolved. **1851** Melville *Moby Dick* II. xxx. 205 Being the savage's bowsman—that is, the person who pulled the *bow-oar in his boat (the second one from forward). **1867** *Harper's Mag.* Oct. 655/1 That man, the smallest of the lot, is the 'Bow Oar'. **1627** Capt. Smith *Seaman's Gram.* xiii. 60 Begin with your *bow peeces. **1829** Marryat *F. Mildmay* iii, I was looking out of the *bow-port. **1837** —— *Dog-Fiend* xxii, The men had thrown their pea jackets under the *bow-sheets. **1885** *Where Chineses Drive* 5 The oarsman on the *bow-side strokes. **1877** W. H. White *Man. Naval Archit.* 450 The position of the crest of the last wave in the train of waves that follow the *bow wave ..exercises a very sensible effect on the resistance. **1949** S. P. Llewellyn *Troopships* 32 Porpoises..leaping and plunging in the bow-wave. **1959** J. L. Nayler *Dict. Aeronaut. Engin.* 238 For a sharp nosed wedge of semi-angle θ at zero incidence with the bow wave attached. **1962** *Listener* 1 Mar. 370/1 It was most probably the supersonic bow wave from a large meteorite falling through the atmosphere.

†**bow** (buː), *sb.*[4] *north. dial. Obs.* Also 4– bu. [a. ON. *bú* farming, a farm, farm stock, stock of cattle on a farm, corresp. to OE., OS. *bû* dwelling, habitation, OHG. *bû* dwelling, culture, tillage, building (MHG. *bû, bou*, mod.G. *bau*, Du. *bouw* tillage, building):—OTeut. **bôwo-m*, f. *bŭ-* L. 'colĕre'. Only ON. had the sense 'live-stock, cattle', whence the north. Eng. and Sc. word.]

1. The stock of cattle on a farm, a herd.

a **1300** *Cursor M.* 6744 Qua stelis scep, or ox, or cu, To sla or sell of oþer bu, Oxen fiue for an he pai. **1513** Douglas *Æneis* vi. i. 86 Sevin ȝoung stottis that ȝok buir nevir nane, Brocht from the bow [*grege*]. *Ibid.* vii. ix. 139 Fyve bowis of ky [*armenta*]. **1535** Stewart *Cron. Scot.* (1858) I. 58 For his reward that tyme to haif ane kow, Quhair he thocht best out of the kingis bow. **1568** *Bannatyne Poems* 145 (Jam.) A flok or two, A bow of ky. [**1866** Edmondston *Shetl. & Orkney Gloss.* 14 *Bû*, a term used in old deeds to denote cattle.]

2. *Comb.* **bow-house**, cattle-house.

1861 C. Innes *Sk. Early Sc. Hist.* iii. 375 The bow-house (cattle-house) was rated at so much 'kain' or produce, in butter and cheese.

†**bow, bowe**, *sb.*[5] *Sc. Obs.* [prob. (buː) from an earlier *bulle* or *boule* (papal) bull (cf. *fow, fou'* = *full*; *pow, pou'* = *pull, pool*, etc.): for sense cf. F. '*bulles* provisions d'un bénéfice; les bulles d'un évêché, d'une abbaye' (Littré). See bull *sb.*[2]] The provisions of a benefice granted by the Pope.

1513–75 *Diurn. Occurr.* (1833) 28 To waill all the bowis of the benefices. **1529** Lyndesay *Complaynt* 223 Be his Bowis war weill cumit hame, To mak seruyce he wald thynk schame. **1535** —— *Satyre* 3401 My Lords, how haue ȝe keipit ȝour thrie vows? Indeid, richt weill, till I gat hame my bows. **1566** Knox *Hist. Ref.* Wks. 1846 I. 274 Maister Johne Gray..past to Rome for expeditioun of the bowes of Ross to Maister Henry Sinclare.

Bow (bəʊ), *sb.*[6] The name of a make of china originally manufactured at the Bow China Manufactory at Stratford-le-Bow in Essex.

1753 *Derby Mercury* 9 Mar. in Jewitt *Ceramic Art* (1878) I. vii. 200 Bow China Warehouse was opened on Wednesday, the 7th of February, near the Royal Exchange, in Cornhill, London,..where it will continue to be sold in the same manner as formerly, at Bow. **1863** W. Chaffers *Marks & Monograms* 138 A punch bowl of Bow china. **1869** Lady C. Schreiber *Jrnl.* (1911) I. 2 Small broken Bow figure. *Ibid.* 31 An imperfect..'Dovecote' of Chelsea or Bow. **1961** *Connoisseur* Dec. 310 Three dated specimens of Bow porcelain..have been purchased by the British Museum.

bow (baʊ), *v.*[1] Pa. t. and pple. bowed (baʊd). Forms: *Inf.* 1 búȝan, 2–3 buȝe(n, 3 bouȝe(n, buwe(n, buen, bouwe, buch, 4 boowe(n, boȝ(e, boghe, bu(e, bou(e, bugh, bouh, buu, 4–5 bogh, 4–7 bowe, 5 bow-in, -yn, 6 bough, 6–8 boow, 4– bow. *Strong pa. t.* 1 béaȝ, béah (*pl.* buȝon), 2–3 beh (*pl.* buȝen), 3 bæh, bah, beoh, beih, bieh, (*pl.* bæhȝen, buȝeȝen, buhȝen, biȝen, bowen), 4 beiȝ, beȝgh, bey(ȝ, bugh, (*pl.* boȝen). *Strong pa. pple.* 1 boȝen, 3–4 (i)boȝen, (i)buwen, 4 bowe(n. *Weak pa. t.* 3 boȝede, bouwed, 4 boȝed, boghed, -id, -ud, bued, buud, boued, boud, bowede, -ide, -id, -et, 4– bowed. *Weak pa. pple.* 4 (i)bowed, 4–6 bowid, -yd, boude (*Sc.* bewchit, bowit), 4– bowed. [Orig. a strong vb.: OE. *búȝan* (pa. t. *béah, buȝon*, pple. *boȝen*), corresp. to OS. **bûgan*, (MDu. *bûghen*, MLG. *bûgen*, Du. *buigen*); also with different vowel in the present stem, OHG. *biogan* (MHG. and mod.G. *biegen*), ON. **bjúga* (pa. t. pl. *bugum*, pple. *boginn*), Goth. *biugan* (pa. t. *baug*, *bugum*, pple. *bugans*):—OTeut. stem **beug-* f. root *bug-*, apparently identical with Skr. *bhuj-* to bow, bend, L. *fugere*, Gr. *φεύγ-ειν* to flee; although the expected Teut. form corresponding to these would be *buk-*. The causal of this was OTeut. *baugjan*, OE. *bíeȝan*, *býȝan*, weak verb: see bey *v.* In early ME. there was some confusion of forms in writing, due to the ambiguous use of *u* for both OE. *ú*, and Fr. *u* = *ü*, OE. *y*. As early as the 13th c. *bow* began to usurp the sense of *bey*, which became obs. in the 14th c.; and coincidently with this extension of sense, *bow* began to take a weak pa. t. and pa. pple.

(This is one of several vbs. in which the LG. langs. (OE., OFris., OS., Nether-Frankish) have *û* against the *iu* of Gothic, ON. *jú*, OHG. *io*.)]

I. Intransitive uses. (Rarely trans. by ellipsis.) In the literal senses 1–4 superseded by bend.

†**1.** To assume a bent or crooked shape, position, or attitude; to bend. *Obs.* exc. *dial.*

a **1000** *Holy Rood* 36 (Gr.) þær ic þa ne dorste..buȝan oððe berstan. *a* **1300** *Cursor M.* 11683 Bogh þou til vs..þou tre. *c* **1374** Chaucer *Anel. & Arc.* 186 Hir daunger made him..bowe and beende. *c* **1430** *Hymns Virg.* (1867) 73 My backe bowiþ, myn iȝen ben soore. **1526** Tindale *Phil.* ii. 10 That in the name of Jesus shuld every knee bowe. **1562** J. Heywood *Prov. & Epigr.* (1867) 152 Better boowe then breake. **1603** Shaks. *Meas. for M.* iii. i. 26 Like an Asse, whose backe with Ingots bowes. **1618** Bp. Hall *Serm.* v. 110 Let the smith strike a bar..though it be iron, it bows. **1677** Moxon *Mech. Exerc.* (1703) 14 When you chuse Iron, chuse such as bows oftenest before it break. *Mod. Sc.* A pin bows more easily than a needle.

†**2.** To turn; to turn aside, off, or away; to turn back, retreat; to swerve, decline. Also *fig. Obs.*

a **1000** Ælfric *Man. Astron.* in *Pop. Treat. Sc.* 10 Heo næfre ne byhð ne ufor ne nyðor. —— *Ex.* xxxii. 8 Hiȝ buȝon raðe of þam wæȝe. *c* **1175** *Lamb. Hom.* 117 Buh from euele and do god. *a* **1300** *Cursor M.* 19379 þai..neuer..ne buud fra cristen trouth. **1382** Wyclif *Baruch* iv. 12 Thei bowiden awei fro the lawe of God. **1548** Udall, etc. *Erasm. Par.* Pref. 9 Boughed neyther to the ryghte hande ne to the lefte. **1580** Hollyband *Treas. Fr. Tong, Decliner*, to decline, to bowe from.

†**b.** (in wider sense) To bend one's course, turn or direct one's steps, wend one's way, make one's way, go, betake oneself. (Sometimes, with appropriate context, = flee.) *Obs.*

a **1000** Ælfric *Ex.* xxi. 13 Ic ȝesette him hwæder he buȝan sceal. *c* **1205** Lay. 5559 Heo iseiȝen Brennes buȝe [*c* **1275** comen] heom to-ȝennes. *Ibid.* 14273 Forð he gon buȝen [*c* **1275** wende]. *c* **1275** *Ibid.* 9351 Hamund to þane wode fleh and touward þe see he bieh. *c* **1325** *E.E. Allit. P.* A. 973 Bow vp to-warde þys bornez heued. **1330** R. Brunne *Chron.* 141 Henry in Inglond wonnes..& wille not bouh. **1382** Wyclif *John* v. 13 Ihesu bowide him fro the cumpany. *c* **1400** *Destr. Troy* 9490 þen fled all in fere, and the fild leuit, Bowet to þere bastels with bale at þere herttes.

†**c.** *to bow in*: to turn in, enter. *Obs.*

c **1380** Wyclif *Sel. Wks.* III. 5 þis cumfort bowiþ into myn herte. *Ibid.* 7 If clensid it[þe soule] kepiþ clene, bowynge þerenne abundantly grace of parfiȝt knowynge of virtues.

†**3.** To have a curved direction, to lie or proceed in a curve; to curve, to be deflected. *Obs.*

c **893** K. Ælfred *Oros.* i. i. §9 Nilus seo ea..west irnende ..and þonan norþ buȝende ut on þone Wendelsæ. **1388** Wyclif *Isa.* lix. 8 The pathis of hem ben bowid to hem. **1530** Palsgr. 461 The toppe of Charyng crosse hath bowed downwardes [*se est decliné*] many a daye. **1535** Coverdale *Numb.* xxiii. 28 The toppe of mount Peor yt Boweth towarde the wyldernesse. **1601** Holland *Pliny* I. 118 The very coasts of this streight Bosphorus..boweth and windeth like a curb to Mæotis. **1607** Topsell *Four-f. Beasts* 316 Another hot sharp Iron like a Bodkin, somewhat bowing at the point. **1756** Mrs. Calderwood *Jrnl.* in *Athenæum* No. 2984. 10/2 The ridge of the boat, which bows like an arch.

†**b.** *fig.* To have an inclination; to tend. *Obs.*

1562 Turner *Herbal* ii. 108 b, Peares are temperat, in a mean betwene heat and cold, or they bow a litle to coldnes.

†**4.** To stoop or lower the head and upper part of the body, esp. in condescension. *Obs.* (or *arch.*)

c **1200** *Trin. Coll. Hom.* 121 Ure drihten..beih of heuene to mannen. *a* **1240** *Lofsong* in *Cott. Hom.* 211 Heie helinde, beih þe to me, and buh to mine bonen. *c* **1300** in Wright *Lyric P.* xxv. 70 Thin heved doun boweth to suete cussinge. **1534** Ld. Berners *Gold. Bk. M. Aurel.* (1546) C vij b, It is necessarie..to remount to very high thinges, leste it bowe vnto lowe and yl thinges. **1842** Tennyson *Dora* 101 She bow'd upon her hands..She bow'd down And wept in secret.

5. To bend the neck under a yoke; *hence*, to become a thrall or subject; to submit, yield, render obedience *to*.

Beowulf 2918 Se byrn-wiȝa buȝan sceolde. *a* **1000** *O.E. Chron.* an. 913 Him beaȝ god dæl þæs folces to. *c* **1175** *Lamb. Hom.* 91 þa underfengen heo his lare and buȝen to fulehte. *a* **1240** *Lofsong* in *Cott. Hom.* 205 Ich habbe ofte ibuwen to alle mine þreo i-fon. *a* **1300** *Cursor M.* 14496 All þis werld til him sal buu. *a* **1340** Hampole *Psalter* lxxx[i]. 11 My folke boghed noght til my worde. *c* **1386** Chaucer *Wyf's Prol.* 440 On of us tuo mot bowe douteles. **1531** Elyot *Gov.* (1580) 174 A man should not bowe for any Fortune or trouble of minde. **1682** Dryden *Satyr to Muse* 149 Under Iron Yokes make Indians Bow. **1808** J. Barlow *Columb.* iii. 436 They bow in silence to the victor's chains. **1862** Stanley *Jew. Ch.* (1877) I. xviii. 344 He at last bows to the inevitable course of events. **1871** Freeman *Norm. Conq.* (1876) IV. xvii. 57 Winchester..bowed to William some while before his coronation.

†**b.** (Also construed with a dative appearing afterwards as a simple obj.): To obey. *Obs.*

c **1205** Lay. 7295 ȝif heo me wulleð buȝen [*c* **1275** bouwe]. *a* **1225** *Ancr. R.* 198 þet child þet ne buhð nout his eldre. **1375** Barbour *Bruce* ix. 753 Till at thou knaw The richt, and bow it as thou aw. *c* **1400** *Destr. Troy* 507 Tho obeit the bolde, and bowet hir fader.

6. To bend the body, knee, or head, in token of reverence, respect, or submission; to make obeisance. (Emphasized by *down*: const. *to*, *before*.)

a **1000** Ælfric *Numb.* xxv. 2 [Israhela bearn] to þam hæþenȝilde buȝon. *c* **1200** *Trin. Coll. Hom.* 199 Buȝe we to þe stone. *c* **1205** Lay. 22482 Swa he on his cneowen bæh. *a* **1240** *Orison* in *Cott. Hom.* 191 To þe ich buwe and mine kneon ich beie. *a* **1300** *Cursor M.* 11629 (Gött.) *title*, Hou þe tre boued to saint mari. **1593** Hooker *Eccl. Pol.* i. viii. § 11 Shall I bow to the stock of a tree? **1611** Bible *Esther* iii. 5 Haman saw that Mordecai bowed not, nor did him reuerence [Wyclif, bowid not kne; Coverdale, bowed not the knee]. **1611** —— *Ps.* xcv. 6 O come, let vs worship and bowe downe[Coverd. ourselues]: let vs kneele before the Lord our maker. **1667** Milton *P.L.* i. 111 To bow and sue for grace With suppliant knee. **1781** Gibbon *Decl. & F.* III. xlix. 114 An hundred princes bowed before his throne. **1871** Morley *Rousseau* (1873) II. 267 That which asks us to bow down and worship God as a 'stream of tendency'.

7. To incline the body or head (*to* a person) in salutation, acknowledgement of courtesy, polite assent, etc.; to make or give a bow.

1651 *Proc. Parliament* No. 93. 1428 Then he bowed to the Court and Councel. **1698** Dryden *Virg. Æneid* ii. 186 With graceful action bowing thus began. **1709** Steele & Add. *Tatler* No. 81 ¶4 He bowed to Homer, and sat down by him. **1837** Dickens *Pickw.* ii, 'My friend, sir, Mr. Snodgrass', said Mr. Winkle..Doctor Slammer's friend bowed. **1848** Macaulay *Hist. Eng.* I. 150 He smiled, bowed, and extended his hand graciously to the lips of the colonels and majors. *Mod.* Her Majesty acknowledged the cheers by bowing graciously as she drove along. He bowed to her as usual, but she looked straight before her, and passed on.

b. *trans.* To express by bowing.

1606 Shaks. *Ant. & Cl.* ii. iii. 3 All which time, before the Gods my knee shall bow my prayers to them for you. **1821** Keats *Isabel* xxiv, Lorenzo..Bow'd a fair greeting. **1884** *Punch* 20 Dec. 294/2 Mr. Punch bows his acknowledgments to 'Good Words'. *Mod.* Mr. B—— bowed his assent.

c. To usher *in* or *out* with a bow, or bows; so *to bow* (any one) *up* or *down* (*stairs, etc.*).

1819 Crabbe *T. of Hall* iii. 60 Argue he could not, but in case of doubt, Or disputation, fairly bow'd it out. **1833** Ht. Martineau *Briery Creek* ii. 31 Returning from bowing out Dr. Sneyd with much civility. **1851** Thackeray *Eng. Hum.* iii. (1858) 114 He and his chamberlains bow her up the great stair to the state apartments.

d. *intr. to bow out*: in fig. use, to retire (gracefully); to retreat or withdraw; to resign. *colloq.* (orig. *U.S.*).

1942 Berrey & Van den Bark *Amer. Thes. Slang* §213/4 *Retract; withdraw; 'back out'*,..bow out. **1943** L. Browne *See what I Mean* xvi. 109. It was a case of bow down or bow out. **1959** *Times* 19 Mar. 18/3 Yesterday Norwich fully deserved to win, yet had to bow out and are left behind in the shadows. *a* **1975** Wodehouse *Sunset at Blandings* (1977) ii. 22 When I found that his club was the Athenaeum, crawling ..with bishops and no hope of anyone throwing bread at anyone, I bowed out. **1985** *Times* 2 July 1/5 (*caption*) Virginia Wade bowing out of the singles in her last Wimbledon.

II. 8. Reflexive uses. The pronoun was perhaps originally dative, but was at length treated as a simple object, as in III. *Obs.* or *arch.*

a. in sense 1.

a **1225** *Ancr. R.* 266 Buh þe, he seið, aduneward..þeo buhð hire, þet to his fondunde beieð hire heorte. *a* **1300** *Cursor M.* 11683 (Gött.) Boue þe till vs..þu tre. *c* **1300** in Wright *Lyric P.* xvi. 54 Hire loue..beh him to me over bord. *c* **1430** *Chev. Assigne* 335 He bowethe hym down & ȝeldethe vp þe lyfe. **1611** BIBLE *Eccles.* xii. 3 When..the strong men shall bowe themselues.

b. in sense 2.

c **1205** LAY. 7499 Beiene þa eorles buȝen heom [*c* **1275** wende] togaderes. **1382** WYCLIF *John* v. 13 Ihesu bowide him fro the cumpany. *c* **1430** *Chev. Assigne* 265 An holy abbot was þer-by & he hym þeder bowethe.

c. in sense 5.

a **1300** *Cursor M.* 19132 Bot mani turnd þar and..To baptim tak þam-seluen buud. *Ibid.* 19529 þe folk was in þat tun to þe baptiszing þam buud.

d. in sense 6.

a **1300** *Cursor M.* 8961 Dun sco bugh hir to þe grund [*v.r.* bowid hir]. *Ibid.* 10902 To goddes sande scho gan hir bow [*Cott.* bu]. **1535** COVERDALE *Dan.* ii. 46 [He] fell downe vpon his face, and bowed him self vnto Daniel. **1611** BIBLE *Ex.* xx. 5 Thou shalt not bow downe thy selfe to them.

e. in sense 7.

a **1626** BACON *New Atl.* 11 He bowed himself a little to us. *Ibid.* 15 At which speech we all rose up and bowed our selves.

III. Causative uses, in which *bow* has taken the place of the obs. causal BEY.

9. *trans.* To cause (a thing) to bend; to force or bring into a curved or angular shape; to inflect, curve, crook. *arch.* and *dial.* (as in *Sc.*).

a **1300** *K. Horn* 427 Armes heo gan buȝe, Adun he feol iswoȝe. **1502** ARNOLDE *Chron.* (1811) 164 Take a graff and bowe it in bothe endes. **1598** J. DICKENSON *Greene in Conc.* (1878) 133 Tender twigges may with ease be bowed. **1600** HOLLAND *Livy* XXI. lviii. 427 They could hardly bend and bow their joints. **1613** SHAKS. *Hen. VIII*, II. iii. 36 A threepence bow'd would hire me. **1626** BACON *Sylva* §426 Take a low Tree, and bow it. **1680** BAXTER *Answ. Stillingfl.* Pref. A iij b, Iron is too stiff for me to bow. **1875** DARWIN *Insectiv. Pl.* viii. 194 The tentacles after a time being bowed backwards.

†**b.** *fig. Obs.*

1599 SHAKS. *Hen. V*, I. ii. 14 God forbid..That you should fashion, wrest, or bow your reading..With opening Titles miscreate. **1662** FULLER *Worthies* (1840) III. 289 Latin words are bowed in their modern senses. **1678** BUTLER *Hud., Lady's Answ.* 156 Marriage, at best, is but a Vow: Which all Men either break, or bow.

c. esp. ***to bow the knee***: i.e. to bend it in adoration or reverence.

1382 WYCLIF *Phil.* ii. 10 That in the name of Ihesu ech kne be bowid. —— *1 Kings* xix. 18 Seuen thousand of men of whom the knees ben not bowid before Baal. **1580** BARET *Alv.* B 1067 To make courtesie or to bowe the knee. **1875** B. TAYLOR *Faust* II. II. iii. 142 To Ops and Rhea have I bowed the knee.

†**10.** To cause to turn in a given direction; to incline, turn, direct; *fig.* to incline or influence (the mind). *Obs.*

a **1300** *Cursor M.* 17588 His blissing to þaa men he buus. *c* **1380** WYCLIF *Sel. Wks.* III. 422 As þof þei wolde bowe him [God] as maysters of his conseile. *c* **1449** PECOCK *Repr.* I. i. 7 He or sche ouȝte bowe awey her heering, her reeding and her vndirstonding. **1513** DOUGLAS *Æneis* XIII. vi. 106 All our prayeris and requestis kynd Mycht nowder bow that dowr mannis mynd. **1651** HEWSON *Let.* in *Proc. Parliament* No. 92. 1413 The Lord God hath abundantly bowed their hearts and affections..to the Parliament. **1705** PENN in *Pa. Hist. Soc. Mem.* X. 17 You may..bow him to better manners and gain him.

¶ In ***to bow the ear, the eye***, there appears to be a mixture of the notion of 'direct or turn with attention', and of 'bend the head downwards'. See senses 10 and 11.

c **1230** *Hali Meid.* 3 Bihald & buh þin eare. **1535** COVERDALE *Ps.* xxx[i]. 2 Bowe downe thine eare to me, make haist to delyuer me. **1578** *Gude & Godlie Ballates, Lament. Sinner* i, Bowing doun Thy heavenly eye. **1579** SPENSER *Sheph. Cal.* Jan. 16 Bowe your eares vnto my dolefull dittie. **1611** BIBLE *Ps.* lxxxvi. 1 Bow downe thine eare, O Lord, heare me.

11. To bend (anything) downwards; to incline, to lower (often in *fig.* expressions).

c **1205** LAY. 15740 þe nunne beh hire hæfde adun. [*a* **1225** *Ancr. R.* 130 Ase brid vleoinde buhð þet heaued lowe (perh. this = *byhð*, from BEY *v.*).] *a* **1300** *Cursor M.* 11690 Yeit it [þe tre] boghud dun ilk bogh. **1382** WYCLIF *Isa.* xxxi. 3 The Lord shal boowen [**1388** bowe doun] his hond. **1601** SHAKS. *All's Well* I. ii. 43 And bow'd his eminent top to their low rankes. **1747** HERVEY *Medit. & Contempl.* (1818) 192 Wave, ye stately Cedars..wave your branching heads to Him who meekly bowed his own on the accursed tree. **1842** TENNYSON *Dora* 103 She bowed down her head, Remembering the day when first she came. **1871** FREEMAN *Norm. Conq.* (1876) IV. xvii. 95 Lanfranc refused to bow his shoulders to such a burden.

b. *fig.* To bend (a thing) in submission.

a **1300** *Cursor M.* 15291 þis suete iesu..þat bued sua his lauerd-hede to buxumnes of therll. *c* **1440** HYLTON *Scala Perf.* (1494) II. xvi, Yf he woll bowe his wyll to God.

12. To cause to stoop, to crush (as a load does).

1671 MILTON *Samson* 698 With sickness and disease thou bow'st them down. **1725** POPE *Odyss.* XI. 239 And bow his age with sorrow to the tomb. **1738** WESLEY *Psalms* (1765) lvii, To Thee let all my Foes submit, Who hunt and bow my Spirit down. **1855** MACAULAY *Hist. Eng.* IV. 97 The load which had bowed down his body and mind.

bow (bəʊ), *v.*[2] [f. BOW *sb.*[1] 6.] *trans.* and *intr.* To play with or use the bow (on a violin, etc.).

1838 W. GARDINER *Music Nat.* 202 A single bar of music ..may be bowed fifty-four different ways. **1861** *Times* 16 Oct., His artists and amateurs bow and finger in thoroughly good style. **1864** G. MEREDITH *Emilia* xxv. 194 How differently he bows from the other men, though it is only dance music.

bow (baʊ), *v.*[3] *Naut.* [f. BOW *sb.*[3]] *trans.* Of a ship: To cut (the water) with the bow.

1858 *Merc. Mar. Mag.* V. 199 Sea very turbulent..ship bowing it admirably. **1867** SMYTH *Sailor's Word-bk.*, *Bowing the sea*, meeting a turbulent swell in coming to the wind.

bow, bowe, obs. forms of BOLL[2], BOUGH.

†**'bowable,** *a. Obs.* [f. BOW *v.*[1] + -ABLE.]

1. That may be bowed or bent; flexible, pliable.

1483 *Cath. Angl.* 38 Bowabylle, *vbi* pliabylle. **1583** STUBBES *Anat. Abus.* (1877) I. 76 It is flexible and bowable to any thing a man can desire. **1611** COTGR., *Ployable*, pliable, bowable, bendable.

2. *fig.* Complaisant.

c **1449** PECOCK *Repr.* 200 Make the patroun (that is to seie Crist) to be to us inclineable or boweable or redi to heere us. **1623** WODROEPHE *Marrow Fr. Tongue* 323 (L.) If she be a virgin, she is pliable or bowable.

Hence **'bowableness.**

c **1475** *Found. St. Barthol. Ch.* I. xxvii. (1886) 63 The synowys were dryed up & alweys lackid bowablenesse.

bowall(e, -aly, -ayl, obs. forms of BOWEL.

bowall, obs. form of BOLE[3], *Sc.*, recess.

a **1600** *Aberdeen Reg.* (JAM.) All fyir that cumis in [is carried into] the kirk to be keepit in the bowall in the wall.

bowand, obs. Sc. form of BOWING.

boward, variant of BOURD, *Obs.*, a jest.

bowat, variant of BOWET, a lantern.

bow-backed ('bəʊ,bækt), *a.* [prob. f. BOW *sb.*[1] (but perh. in sense a. from BOWE *ppl. a.*, bowed, crooked) + BACK.] **a.** Having the back permanently bent, crook-backed. **b.** Having the back arched, as an angry cat.

Hence **bow'backedness.**

1470 HARDING *Chron.* clvii. iii, This Edmond..Brokebacked and bowbacked bore, Was vnabled to haue the monarché. **1587** FLEMING *Contn. Holinshed* III. 1311/2 When they wax crooked & bow backt. **1847** TENNYSON *Princ.* VI. 339 The two great cats..Bow-back'd with fear. **1864** *N. Brit. Rev.* Dec. 405 By a sudden effort.. overcoming his bowbackedness.

bow-bearer ('bəʊ,bɛərə(r)). [f. BOW *sb.*[1]]

1. One who carries a bow.

a **1600** *Rob. Hood* (Ritson) II. xii. 70 Bow-bearer after mee.

2. An under-officer in a forest, who looked after trespasses affecting vert and venison.

1538 LELAND *Itin.* VI. 95 §4 Ther be 9. Kepers, to Raungers, a Bowberer, and the Lord Wardein. **1610** HOLLAND *Camden's Brit.* I. 723 Bowbearer to King William Rufus. **1820** SCOTT *Monast.* xviii, We will name this youth bow-bearer in the forest granted to us by good King David. **1837** HOWITT *Rur. Life* V. ii. (1862) 377 This forest..has also two rangers, a bowbearer, and landwarden.

Bow-bell, -bells. The bells of Bow Church, i.e. St. Mary-le-Bow, formerly 'Seyn Marye Chyrche of þe Arches', in Cheapside, London (so called from the 'bows' or arches that supported its steeple. Cf. ARCH.) This church having long had a celebrated peal of bells, and being nearly in the centre of the City, the phrase 'within the sound of Bow-bells' has come to be synonymous with 'within the City bounds'. Also *attrib.*, as in ***Bow-bell cockney.*** *transf.* A loud tongue (*obs.*).

1600 ROWLANDS *Lett. Humours Blood* iv. 65, I scorne..To let a Bowe-bell Cockney put me downe. **1611** *Coryat's Crudities* Pref. Verses, Peale thy praise with Roupe & Bowbell clapper. **1616** T. ADAMS *Soul's Sickn.* Wks. 1861 I. 499 The tenor or bow-bell is the abused creatures. *a* **1659** CLEVELAND *Talkative Wom.* 38 Thy Tong..That Tom a Lincoln and Bow-bell. **1884** *Punch* 30 Dec. 294/2 Having been born within the sound of Bow Bells, he cannot help being a son of Cockaigne.

†**'bowbert, -art, -ard.** *Obs. Sc.* [app. a. OF. *bobert* 'stupid fellow, lout' (Godef. quotes 'li fous bouviers li fous bobers', and 'c'est un bobers, un soz noez'): cf. Swiss Romance *bobet* 'sot, bête'.] A sluggish fellow, a dull lout. Also *attrib.* or as *adj.* (Only in Gawin Douglas.)

1513 DOUGLAS *Æneis* I. vii. 33 Fra their hife Expellis the bowbart [*v.r.* buobert] beist, the faynt drone be. *Ibid.* XI. xiv. 18 Quhou happynnis this..That ȝe sal evir sa doillit and bowbartis [*v.r.* bowbardis] be Onwrokyn sik iniuris to suffyr heir.

bow-case ('bəʊkeɪs). [f. BOW *sb.*[1] 4.] A case in which a bow is kept. In 16–17th c. applied humorously to a lean starveling, a 'bag of bones'.

1464 *Mann. & Househ. Exp.* 267 Item, for a bowcas, viijd. **1544** ASCHAM *Toxoph.* (Arb.) 119 A bowecase of ledder is not the best. **1599** MARSTON *Sco. Villanie* III. x. 222 Poore budge face, bowcase sleeue, but let him passe. **1605** *Tryall Chev.* II. i. in Bullen *Old Pl.* (1884) III. 289 Bowyer a Captayne? a Capon..a Yellow-hammer, a bow-case. **1874** BOUTELL *Arms & Arm.* ii. 34 The bow of the Greek hero, when in the field, was carried in a bow-case.

bowcer, var. of BOWSER[1], *Obs.*, treasurer.

bowch, obs. form of BOUCH(E, BULGE.

bowcher, -yer, obs. ff. BUTCHER, BOUCHER.

bow-compass ('bəʊ,kʌmpəs), **-compasses** (-ɪz). [f. BOW *sb.*[1] + COMPASS.]

1. A pair of compasses with the legs jointed so that the points can be bent inwards; also applied to any compasses made for drawing small circles. (Commonly called *bows*; when the legs are kept apart by a spring, *spring bows.*)

1796 HUTTON *Math. Dict.* I. 315/1 *Bow Compasses* or *Bows*, are a small sort of compasses, that shut up in a hoop, which serves for a handle.

2. = BOW *sb.*[1] 10.

bowd(e, dial. f. BOLD *a.*; var. of BOUD, *Obs.*

bowden, -in, var. BOLDEN *v.* and *ppl. a. Sc. Obs.* to swell, swollen.

bowder, dial. form of BOULDER.

†**'bowdled,** *ppl. a. Obs.* [Origin obscure.] Having the feathers ruffled; swelled out.

1587 HARRISON *England* II. vii. (1877) 169 Much heare left on the cheekes will make the owner looke big like a bowdled hen.

bowdlerize ('baʊdləraɪz), *v.* [f. the name of *Dr. T. Bowdler*, who in 1818 published an edition of Shakspere, 'in which those words and expressions are omitted which cannot with propriety be read aloud in a family': see -IZE.] *trans.* To expurgate (a book or writing), by omitting or modifying words or passages considered indelicate or offensive; to castrate.

1836 GEN. P. THOMPSON *Let.* in *Exerc.* (1842) IV. 124 Among the names..are many, like Hermes, Nereus..which modern ultra-christians would have thought formidably heathenish; while Epaphroditus and Narcissus they would probably have *Bowdlerized*. **1869** *Westm. Rev.* Jan., It is gratifying to add that Mr. Dallas has resisted the temptation to Bowdlerize. **1881** SAINTSBURY *Dryden* 9 Evil counsellors who wished him to bowdlerise glorious John. **1883** *Ch. Times* 703/4 It [Henry IV] is Bowdlerized, to be sure, but that is no evil for school purposes.

Hence **'bowdlerism, ,bowdleri'zation, 'bowdlerized** *ppl. a.*, **'bowdlerizer, 'bowdlerizing,** *vbl. sb.* and *ppl. a.*

1869 *Pall Mall G.* 4 Aug. 12 We doubt whether Juvenal.. can be read with advantage at the age when Bowdlerism, as a moral precaution, would be desirable. **1878** *Athenæum* 6 Apr., False squeamishness or inclination to Bowdlerism. **1882** *Westm. Rev.* Apr. 583 The bowdlerization..is done in an exceedingly awkward and clumsy fashion. **1879** F. HARRISON *Choice Bks.* (1886) 63 A Bowdlerised version of it would be hardly intelligible as a tale. **1886** HUXLEY in *19th Cent.* Apr. 489 We may fairly inquire whether editorial Bowdlerising has not prevailed over historic truth.

†**'bow-draught.** *Obs.* [f. BOW *sb.*[1] + DRAUGHT, from the phrase *to draw a bow.*] A bowshot; the distance a bow will carry.

1375 BARBOUR *Bruce* VI. 58 A place..that weill twa bowdraucht was, Fra thai the vattir passit had. *c* **1400** MAUNDEV. viii. 96 Fro thens a Bowe draughte, toward the Southe. **1470–85** MALORY *Arthur* I. xv, They come as nyghe kynge Bors as a bowe draughte. **1716** *Let.* in Wodrow *Corr.* (1843) II. 133 The kirk being about two bow draughts at most out of the road.

bowdshett, obs. form of BUDGET *sb.*

'bow-dye. [Named from *Bow* near Stratford in Essex, where dyers particularly carried on their works in the 17th c. (Bow took its name from the single-arched bridge built there across the Lea in the reign of Henry I, to replace the ford of the old Roman Road which gave name to Stratford, and Old Ford; cf. BOW *sb.*[1] 3.)]

A scarlet dye; also *attrib.* or as *adj.* Hence **bow-dye** *v.*, to dye scarlet; **bow-dyed** *ppl. a.*; **bow-dyer.**

a **1659** CLEVELAND *Obsequies* 9 Or can his Bloud *Bow-die* th' Egyptian Sand. **1676** TEONGE *Diary* (1825) 151 Flemingoes flye all about..they are blew and bow-dye. **1688** *Lond. Gaz.* No. 2346/4, 3 pieces of Bow-dy'd Serges. **1691** T. H[ALE] *Acc. New Invent.* 51 The Invention of the Scarlet or Bow-dye. **1703** *Art's Improv.* 13 As to the fading of the Bow-Die, and the Water-colours. **1745** DE FOE *Eng. Tradesm.* iv. (1841) I. 25 He goes in partner with C. D., a scarlet-dyer, called a bow-dyer, at Wandsworth.

†**bowe,** *ppl. a. Obs.* [ME. *bowe*:—earlier *bowen*:—OE. *boȝen*, pa. pple. of *buȝan*, to BOW.] Bowed, bent, crooked.

a **1000** *Beowulf* 5646 Wyrm woh-boȝen wealden ne moste. *a* **1500** *E.E. Misc.* (Warton Club) 11 Now age is croppyn one me ful stylle, He makyt me hore, blake, and bowe.

bowed (baʊd), *ppl. a.*[1] [f. BOW *v.*[1] + -ED[1].]

1. Bent, curved, crooked; (see the verb).

The ordinary northern word for 'bent', as *a bowed pin, a bowed street.*

1483 *Cath. Angl.* 38 Bowed, *clinatus, deuexus.* **1562** J. HEYWOOD *Prov. & Epigr.* (1867) 152 Boude wands serue for sumwhat. **1674** N. FAIRFAX *Bulk & Selv.* Contents, The springiness of..boughed bodies. **1674** GREW *Anat. Plants* I. iv. §8 And if the Leaf have but one main Fiber, that also is postur'd in a bowed or Lunar Figure; as in Mint and others. **1785** BURNS *Halloween* iv, A runt was like a sowtail Sae bow't that night. **1874** BOUTELL *Arms & Arm.* vii. 114 These shields were generally 'bowed' on their front face, that is, they generally presented a convex external contour. **1885** *Times* 4 June 10/2 He [a horse] had been under suspicion on account of a 'bowed tendon' from his earliest appearance on the turf.

2. Bent down under a load, weight of years, etc.

1848 KINGSLEY *Saint's Trag.* II. xi. 134 How you'll welcome us, Returned in triumph, bowed with paynim spoils. **1864** TENNYSON *En. Ard.* 704 Enoch was so brown, so bow'd, So broken. **1864** MISS YONGE *Trial* II. 18 A mute smoothing of his bowed shoulders.

b. *fig.*

1382 WYCLIF *Baruch* ii. 18 The soule that..goth bowid, and meekid. **1873** SYMONDS *Grk. Poets* vii. 228 Nay, do not pine thus, bowed beneath my burden.

bowed (bəʊd), *ppl. a.*[2] [f. BOW *sb.*[1] and *v.*[2] + -ED[1].] Furnished with a bow (in various senses); played with a (violin) bow. In *Her.* = EMBOWED.

1425 *Acts Jas. I.* (1597) §60 ȝeamen..sufficientlie bowed and schafted, with sword and buckler and knife. **1823** RUTTER *Fonthill*, The window is to the west, large and bowed. **1837** HT. MARTINEAU *Soc. in Amer.* III. 88 The young women, in cotton gowns and braided and bowed hair. **1838** G. HOGARTH *Musical Hist.* II. 153 Quartets, and trios, for bowed instruments. **1885** *Pall Mall G.* 4 May 4/1 The 'bowed' passages were much too rapid.

bowed (baʊd), *ppl. a.*[3] [f. BOW *sb.*[3] + -ED[2].] Furnished with a bow; prob. only in *comb.*

1747 W. HORSLEY *The Fool* (1748) II. 300 Full-bowed Ships..will make better Way through the Water.

bowedness ('baʊdnɪs). [f. BOWED *ppl. a.*[1] + -NESS.] Bowed or bent condition.

1801 W. TAYLOR in *Month. Mag.* XI. 503 Humility..fear ..and disgrace..superinduce on the bodily frame a sloping or bowedness of attitude.

bowel ('baʊɪl) *sb.*[1] Forms: 3 buel, 4 bewelle, bouel, 4–6 **bowele, bowelle,** 5 **bawelly, boel, bowalle, bowaly, bowyle, boyell,** 5–8 **bowell,** 3– **bowel.** [ME. *buel, bouel,* a. OF. *boel, buel, bouel,* masc. (also *boele, buele, bouele* fem.) = Pr. *budel,* It. *budello*:—late L. *botellus* pudding, sausage (Martial), in late pop.L. 'a small intestine', dim. of *botulus* a sausage (cf. also PUDDING).]

I. *sing.*

1. One of the divisions of the alimentary canal below the stomach; an intestine, a gut. Now rare in the singular exc. in medical use.

c **1325** *E.E. Allit. P.* C. 293 In a bouel of þat best he [Jonah] bidez on lyue. **1393** GOWER *Conf.* II. 265 She toke her after the bowele Of the seewolf. **1481** CAXTON *Myrr.* II. vi. 75 They [the Olyphaunts] haue to fore them in maner of boyell grete and large. **1552** HULOET, Brasten bowell, *bubonocele.* **1884** *Nature* 27 Mar. 497/1 The seat of the disease, namely, the bowel.

†**b.** Gut (as a material). *Obs.*

c **1420** *Liber Cocorum* 5 Harpe strynges made of bowel.

†**c.** Any internal organ of the body. *Obs.*

c **1440** *Promp. Parv.* 46 Bowalle or bowelle, *viscus.* **1620** VENNER *Via Recta* viii. 169 These two bowels, especially the liuer, doe vehemently desire sweete things. **1674** R. GODFREY *Inj. & Ab. Physic* 118 The Stomach..so useful and necessary a Bowel that no Animal lives without it. **1782** T. ARNOLD *Insanity* II. 65 No bowel is more frequently mutilated..than the brain.

II. *plural* collectively.

2. The intestines or entrails; the portions of the intestinal canal contained within the abdomen.

a **1300** *Cursor M.* 16505 His buels [*later MS.* boweles] all, vte at his wambe þai wrang. *c* **1300** *K. Alis.* 4668 Theo bowelis weoren y-nomen out, And for-brent. **1398** TREVISA *Barth. De P.R.* v. xlii. (1495) 158 The bowelles ben cominly called the guttes. **1562** TURNER *Herbal* II. 111 a, Good for the brekinge and bursting of the bowelles. **1611** BIBLE *Ezek.* vii. 19 They shall not satisfie their soules, neither fill their bowels. **1667** MILTON *P.L.* II. 800 They return, and howle and gnaw My Bowels, their repast. **1758** JOHNSON *Idler* No. 17 ¶7 The anatomical novice tears out the living bowels of an animal. **1804** ABERNETHY *Surg. Observ.* 154 [It] brought on so violent an affection of his bowels. **1813** J. THOMSON *Inflammation* 189 Bathing the feet and legs gives relief in inflammation of the bowels.

†**b.** The (external) belly. *Obs. rare.*

1703 *Lond. Gaz.* No. 3932/4 Several Warts on him [a horse], one on his Ear, one on his Breast and Bowels.

c. The interior or inside of the body; also *fig.* Cf. *womb, heart, bosom, breast sb.* (rarely *sing.*)

1532 MORE *Confut. Tindale* Wks. 497/2, I shall gyue my law in their bowele. *c* **1561** G. CAVENDISH *Life Wolsey* (1825) I. 136, I do both lack wit in my poor old head, and cunning in my bowels. **1583** GOLDING *Calvin on Deut.* vi. 33 God will not haue vs to fall..to pulling out of his bowels as they doe which will needes bee searching out of measure. **1611** BIBLE *Gen.* xv. 4 But he that shall come foorth out of thy owne bowels.

3. *transf.* (Considered as the seat of the tender and sympathetic emotions, hence): Pity, compassion, feeling, 'heart'. Chiefly *pl.*, and now somewhat *arch.* Cf. HEART, BREAST *sb.*

1382 WYCLIF *Phil.* i. 8 Hou I coueite ȝou alle in the bowelis of Jhesu Crist. *c* **1440** *Gesta Rom.* 24 Whenne she sawe his blody serke, all her bowelis weere troubelyd more than tunge may telle. **1611** BIBLE *Phil.* ii. 1 If any bowels and mercies. **1651** *Proc. Parliament* No. 110. 1695 Want of bowels in preaching towards them who are in hazard to perish. **1655** FULLER *Waltham Abb.* (1840) 274 Bloody Bonner..full (as one said) of guts, and empty of bowels. **1685** CROWNE *Sir C. Nice* I. 5 The family is a sad family, and I tarry out of pure bowels. **1708** *Lond. Gaz.* No. 4427/2 To shew their Bowels for their Country. **1798** CANNING in *Anti-Jacobin* 14 May (1852) 104 'Twould have moved a Christian's bowels To hear the doubts he stated. **1832** LYTTON *Eugene A.* ii, I am a man that can feel for my neighbours. I have bowels—yes I have bowels. **1865** CARLYLE *Fredk. Gt.* V. XIII. i. 2 Had idle readers any bowels for him; which they have not.

b. In various archaic phrases as: ***bowels of compassion, mercies, pity,*** etc.

1526 *Pilgr. Perf.* (W. de W. 1531) 110 b, Close not your bowells of charite from them. **1611** BIBLE *Coloss.* iii. 12 Put on therefore..bowels of mercies. **1642** SIR T. BROWNE *Relig. Med.* II. §2 Upon the bare suggestion and bowels of pity. **1794** GODWIN *Cal. Williams* 279 The law has neither eyes, nor ears, nor bowels of humanity. **1873** MORLEY *Rousseau* II. 218 *note*, It has none of the yearnings of the bowels of tenderness.

4. The interior of anything; heart, centre. Cf. BELLY *sb.* 9.

1548 LD. SOMERSET *Epist. Scots* 243 Be we not in yͤ bowels now of the realme? **1584** WHETSTONE *Mirour Mag.*, Dicinghouses..within the bowelles of the Citie of London. **1589** *Hay any Work* A iij, Thou wilt enter into the bowels of the cause in hand. *a* **1593** H. SMITH *Wks.* (1867) II. 265 Three days and three nights in the bowels of the earth. **1696** WHISTON *Th. Earth* II. 78 All Volcano's or subterraneous Fires, are in the Bowels of some Mountain. **1769** BLACKSTONE *Comm.* IV. 364 That monster in true policy.. a body of men, residing in the bowels of a state, and yet independent of it's laws. *c* **1860** FARADAY *Forces Nat.* vi. 164 Brought together in the bowels of the earth.

†**5.** Offspring, children. *Obs.* [Cf. L. *viscera.*]

[**1526** TINDALE *Philem.* 12 Receave him, that is to saye myne awne bowels. **1559** MORWYNG *Evonym.* 343 Sum put to it wormes or bowels of the earth.] *a* **1593** H. SMITH *Serm.* (1871) I. 289 We should not spare our own bowels. **1603** SHAKS. *Meas. for M.* III. i. 29 Thine owne bowels which do call thee, sire. **1682** SIR T. BROWNE *Chr. Mor.* I. vii, Men.. bowelless unto others, and merciless unto their own bowels.

III. 6. *Comb.* (of *bowel-*), as ***bowel-complaint; -like, -racking*** adjs.; also, **bowel-deep**, up to or as high as the middle; **bowel-galled** *a.*, ? applied to a horse whose belly is fretted with the girth; †**bowel-gazer, -prier**, one who inspects the entrails of sacrificed animals for religious purposes, a haruspex; hence **bowel-gazing, -prying; bowel-hive, -hives** *Sc.*, a popular name for infantile enteritis and similar affections; **bowel-hive grass**, a herbalists' name for *Alchemilla arvensis* or Parsley-piert (Britten and Holland).

1828 SCOTT *Rev. Davy's Salmonia* (1849) 260 *Bowel-deep in the stream. **1587** GOLDING *De Mornay* xxii. 335 Seneca saith..that the *Bowelgasers were inuented for nothing els but to holde the people in awe. *Ibid.* xxxii. 521 Where be..your Oracles, your *Bowelgazings and your Sacrifices? **1715** PENNECUIK *Tweeddale* 7 (JAM.) The rickets in children, which they call the *Bowel-hyve. **1863** *Rept. Registrar Gen. Scot.*, 'Bowel-hives' (or 'bull-hives'), the vernacular name under which is included enteritis, convulsions, diarrhœa, dysentery, and teething. **1839–47** TODD *Cycl. Anat. & Phys.* III. 549/1 The stomach [of *Iulus*] is long and *bowel-like. **1600** HOLLAND *Livy* XLII. xxx. 1132 The *Bowell-priers [*aruspices*]..declared, That..they should make speed. *Ibid.* 287 (R.) The *bowell-prying soothsaier.

bowel *sb.*[2], rare variant of BOLE *sb.*[3], recess.

1834 H. MILLER *Scenes & Leg.* vi. (1857) 76 Little square recesses, termed bowels or boles.

bowel ('baʊɪl), *v.* Also 4 **bouwel(en,** 5 **bowaylyn, bowellyn,** 7 **bowell.** [f. BOWEL *sb.*[1] Cf. OF. *boeler.*]

1. *trans.* To take out the bowels of, disembowel.

1330 R. BRUNNE *Chron.* 329 Fro þe galweis quik þei lete him doun, & bouweld him alle hote. **1440** J. SHIRLEY *Dethe K. James* (1818) 27 Many of the other traitours were boweld all qwik. *c* **1440** *Promp. Parv.* 46 Bowaylyn, *eviscero.* **1566** GASCOIGNE *Jocasta* Wks. (1587) 95 In thy sacred name I bowel here This sacrifice. **1655** FULLER *Ch. Hist.* IX. 169 Five Seminaries..were hanged, bowelled, and quartered for treason. **1725** BRADLEY *Fam. Dict.* II. s.v. *Sprain*, Take a.. Whelp, flea and bowel him. **1861** DIXON *Bacon* x. §6 Coke, bent on hanging and bowelling all these miserable wretches.

†**2.** *fig.* To stir the bowels of, move or arouse the compassion of. *Obs. rare.*

1645 RUTHERFORD *Tryal & Tri. Faith* (1845) 270 He was bowelled in heart, his bowels were moved with compassion.

bowel, obs. var. of BOWL *sb.*[2]

bowelled ('baʊɪld), *ppl. a.* [f. BOWEL *sb.*[1] and *v.* + -ED.] **a.** Having the bowels removed, disembowelled. **b.** Having bowels or recesses.

1589 FLEMING *Virg. Georg.* I. 17 The strings or little veines (Of boweld beasts). **1606** G. W[OODCOCKE] *Ivstine* 2 b, A Hare was brought..readye bowelled. **1622** HEYLIN *Cosmogr.* I. (1682) 252 Bowelled with mines, or clothed with sheep. **1727** THOMSON *Summer* 133 To the bowelled cavern darting deep.

bowelless ('baʊɪllɪs), *a.* [f. BOWEL *sb.*[1] + -LESS.] Without bowels; without compassion or pity; merciless, unfeeling.

1649 JER. TAYLOR *Gt. Exemp.* I. ii. 64 The most cruell and bowellesse hangmen. **1752** YOUNG *Brothers* IV. i, Bowelless severity! **1863** W. B. JERROLD *Sign. Distress* 35 Bowelless imitators of their cries of agony.

'**bowelling,** *vbl. sb.* [f. BOWEL *v.* + -ING[1].] The extracting of the bowels, disembowelling.

c **1440** *Promp. Parv.* 46 Bowalynge, *evisceracio.* **1681** *Lond. Gaz.* No. 1621/4 Without Embalming, Bowelling, or Wraping in Sear-cloth.

†'**bowelly,** *a. Obs. rare.* [f. BOWEL *sb.*[1] + -LY[1].] Having 'bowels', compassionate, sympathetic.

a **1637** N. FERRAR 110 *Consid.* (1638) 184 From this bowelly affection..it proceeds that a man loues God aboue all things. **1655** GURNALL *Chr. in Arm.* xxii. (1669) 482/1 So we may pray with a more bowelly sense of their wants for them.

bowen, obs. form of BOUN *v.*

bowenite ('bəʊɪnaɪt). *Min.* [f. the name of George T. *Bowen*, 19th-cent. American mineralogist: see -ITE[1].] A hard, compact, translucent form of serpentine, resembling nephrite.

1850 DANA *Syst. Min.* (ed. 3) 265 Bowenite..as Bowen states, differs from nephrite in containing a large percentage of water. **1911** *Encycl. Brit.* XV. 123/1 The green jade-like stone known in New Zealand as *tangiwai* is bowenite, a translucent serpentine with enclosures of magnesite.

bower (baʊə(r), 'baʊə(r)), *sb.*[1] Forms: 1 **búr,** 2–3 **bur,** 3 **bure,** 3–6 **bour,** 3–7 **boure, bowr,** 4 **bor,** 4–7 **bowre,** 5 **bowur,** 6 **boire,** 9 (**bowre**), *dial.* **boor,** 5– **bower.** [OE. *búr* dwelling, etc., corresp. to OS. *bûr* neut., OHG. *búr* masc. (MHG. *búr*, mod.G. *bauer* bird-cage), LG. *buur, bur* m., ON. *búr* (Sw. *bur*, Da. *buur*):—OTeut. **bûro(m*:—Aryan *bhūrom*, f. *bhu*, in Teut. *bŭ-* to dwell. Hence NEIGHBOUR (OE. *néah-ȝebúr*) and BOOR.]

1. A dwelling, habitation, abode. In early use *lit.* A cottage; in later use a poetical word for 'abode'.

Beowulf (Z.) 2455 On his suna bure. *a* **1000** *Chart. Eadrea* in *Cod. Dipl.* V. 336 To ðen haȝan; andlang haȝan bur. *c* **1325** *E.E. Allit. P.* A. 963 Bryng me to þat bygly bylde, & let me se þy blysful bor. **1567** STUDLEY *Seneca's Hippol.* (1581) 75 The whilst the fire shall burne These bones, set ope his buriall bower. **1568** *Like will to L.* in Hazl. *Dodsl.* III. 353 Of all iniquity thou art the bow'r. **1579** SPENSER *Sheph. Cal.* Sept. 97 The blacke bowre of sorrowe [*gloss.* hell]. **1712** ADDISON *Spect.* No. 281 ¶11 Our Historians describe the Apartments of Rosamond's Bower. **1810** SCOTT *Lady of L.* I. xii, The primrose pale, and violet flower, Found in each cliff a narrow bower.

b. *esp.* a vague poetic word for an idealized abode, not realized in any actual dwelling.

c **1600** SHAKS. *Sonn.* cxxvii. 7 Sweet beauty hath no name, no holy bower. **1644** MILTON *Areop.* (Arb.) 46 The bowr of earthly blisse. **1770** GOLDSM. *Des. Vill.* 5 Dear lovely bowers of innocence and ease. **1781** COWPER *Hope* 164 Plucks amaranthine joys from bowers of bliss. **1858** NEALE *Bernard de M.* 34 O! princely bow'rs, O land of flow'rs.

c. A fancy rustic cottage or country residence.

1810 SCOTT *Lady of L.* I. xv, In that soft vale, a lady's bower. **1862** *Athenæum* 30 Aug. 270 Miss Helen Campbell ..gave an entertainment in his honour, at her bower in the Clachan Glen.

†**d.** A covered stall or booth at a fair. *rare.*

1506 in Glasscock *Records St. Michael's* 31 Rec. on michelmas day for standing of bowers wᵗn th chirchyerde ixd.

2. An inner apartment, *esp.* as distinguished from the 'hall', or large public room, in ancient mansions; *hence*, a chamber, a bed-room. Still in *north. dial.*; in literature only *archaic* and *poetic.*

c **1000** ÆLFRIC *Voc.* in Wr.-Wülcker 124 *Cubiculum*, bedcofa *vel* bur. *c* **1200** *Trin. Coll. Hom.* 139 He..ches þere crundel to halle · and eorðhole to bure. *c* **1205** LAY. 29218 þer inne he bulde ænne bur. *a* **1300** *Cursor M.* 3921 A godd had laban in his bure. *c* **1386** CHAUCER *Nonne Prestes T.* 12 Fful sooty was hir bour and eek hire halle. *c* **1440** *Promp. Parv.* 46 Bowre, chambyr, *thalamus, conclave.* *c* **1460** in *Babees Bk.* (1868) 13 In halle, yn bowre, or at þe borde. **1535** STEWART *Cron. Scot.* II. 616 Euerilk office, baith in hall and bour. **1596** SPENSER *Astroph.* 28 Merily masking both in bowre and hall. **1674** RAY *N.C. Wds.* 7 Boor, the Parlour, Bedchamber or inner room. *Cumb.* **1814** SCOTT *Ld. of Isles* III. vii, Now torch and menial tendance led Chieftain and knight to bower and bed. **1851** *Cumbld. Gloss.*, *Boor*, the inner room. **1868** FREEMAN *Norm. Conq.* II. ix. 357 His sons ..carried him to the king's own bower.

b. Especially applied to a lady's private apartment; a boudoir. Now only *poetic.*

a **1000** *Cædmon's Gen.* 109 (Bosw.) On bure, ahof bryd Abrahames hleahtor. *a* **1300** *Cursor M.* 4411 Was neuer don to leuedi mar Scam..þan..Ioseph soght on me in her bour. *c* **1325** *Coer de L.* 879 The kynges doughter lay in her boure. *c* **1380** *Sir Ferumb.* 2165 Sayde þᵉ heþen kyng 'In my doȝtere bour þar þay ben'. **1810** SCOTT *Lady of L.* v. viii, Love-lorn swain in lady's bower. **1850** MRS. BROWNING *Rom. of Page* x, Her bower may suit thee ill! **1866** KINGSLEY *Herew.* viii. 135 She enticed him into her bower.

3. A place closed in or overarched with branches of trees, shrubs, or other plants; a shady recess, leafy covert, arbour.

The first two quots. rather anticipate than illustrate this use of the word.

[*c* **1325** *E.E. Allit. P.* C. 437 He busked hym a bour..Of hay & of euer-ferne & erbez a fewe. **1509** FISHER *Wks.* 232 Caused an yue tree to sprynge vp sodeynly rounde aboute his boure.] **1523–5** LD. BERNERS *Froiss.* I. LXXX. (R.) To lodge in bowers of trees, more nerer to the towne. **1596** SHAKS. *1 Hen. IV*, III. i. 210 Ditties..Sung by a faire Queene in a Summers Bowre. **1667** MILTON *P.L.* IV. 246 Where the unpierc't shade Imbround the noontide Bowrs. **1706** ADDISON *Rosamond* I. i, The bower, that wanders In meanders, Ever bending..Glades on Glades. **1727** BRADLEY *Fam. Dict.* I. s.v., Care must be had that you do not confound the Word Bower with Arbour; because the first is always built long and arch'd, whereas the second is either round or square at Bottom, and has a sort of Dome or Ceiling at the Top. **1827** KEBLE *Chr. Y.* 5th Sund. aft. Easter, A gracious rain, freshening the weary bower.

4. A structure reared by the bower-bird.

1869 NICHOLSON *Zool.* lxvi. (1880) 625 These curious birds have the habit of building very elaborate bowers.. These bowers are wholly independent of their nests. **1884** GRANT ALLEN in *Pall Mall G.* 20 Sept. 3/2 He had brought a bower of the Australian bower-birds over to England.

5. *Attrib.* and *Comb.*, as ***bower eaves***, ***-enshaded***, ***-head***, etc.; **bower-may** (*arch.*) = BOWER-MAIDEN; **bower-page**, a lady's attendant (*arch.*); †**bower-thane** (see quot.); †**bowre-window** (see quot.). Also BOWER-BIRD, -MAIDEN, -WOMAN.

1842 TENNYSON *Margaret* v, Look out below your *bower-eaves. **1816** L. HUNT *Rimini* III. 442 *Bower-enshaded kisses. *a* **1825** *Ballad 'Fair Annie'* xi. in Child *Ballads* III. (1885) 76/1 She is up to her *bower-head, To behold both sea and land. **1870** MORRIS *Earthly Par.* III. IV. 48 No life of bliss Like sewing gold mid *bower-mays. **1830** C. CLARKE *3 Courses* 17 The striplings..more adapted to be *bower-pages to those high-born dames. **1845** THORPE tr. *Lappenburg's Hist. Eng.* (L.) The chamberlain, or *bower-thane, was also the royal treasurer. **1805** REPTON *Landscape Gard.* 178 Large recesses or bays, sometimes called *bowre windows, and now bow windows.

bower ('bəʊə(r)), *sb.*[2] [f. BOW *sb.*[1] and *v.*[2] + -ER.]

†**1.** A maker of bows; a bowyer. *Obs.*

c **1440** *York Myst.* xxix. 254 The Bowers and Fleccheres. **1466** *Mann. & Househ. Exp.* 367, I payd to the bower fore dyverse gere, vjs. **1483** *Cath. Angl.* 38 A Bower, *arcuarius.* **1733** P. LINDSAY *Interest Scot.* 56 The Bowers, Fletchers, and several others.

2. One who plays with a bow on a violin or other stringed instrument.

1668 SHADWELL *Sullen Lov.* II. Wks. 1720 I. 43 He is a most incomparable Bower, he has..the most luxurious Bow-hand of any man in Europe.

bower ('baʊə(r)), *sb.*[3] [f. BOW *v.*[1] + -ER[1].]

1. One who bows, stoops, etc.; (see BOW *v.*[1])

1630 PRYNNE *Lame Giles* 44 The Anti-puritan bowers at the name of Iesus. **1641** R. BROOKE *Eng. Episc.* II. vii. 113 Bowers and Cringers. **1849** *Life J. Skinner* iv. (1884) 60 When the bow is made, the bower walks out of the room.

2. One who bends anything.

1580 NORTH *Plutarch* 4 A wreather or bower of Pine-apple trees. **1921** *Dict. Occup. Terms* (1927) §278 *Bower, fish hook bower*,..sets, feeds and operates small fly press which bends fish hooks and forms ring at end.

†**3.** That which causes to bend; *esp.* a muscle.

1596 SPENSER *F.Q.* I. viii. 42 His rawbone armes, whose mighty brawned bowrs Were wont to rive steele plates. **1611** COTGR., *Flecheurs*, benders, pliers, bowers..the muscles that serue to bow the joynts of the fingers.

bower ('baʊə(r)), *sb.*[4] [f. BOW *sb.*[3] + -ER[1]: cf. *three-decker*, etc.]

1. The name of two anchors, the ***best-bower***, and ***small-bower***, carried at the bows of a vessel; also the cable attached to such anchor.

1709 *Lond. Gaz.* No. 4521/2 Our small Bower..was drove through our Ship's Bow. **1748** ANSON *Voy.* I. vii. (ed. 4) 101 To cut their cable, and leave their best bower behind them. **1769** FALCONER *Dict. Marine* (1789) I b, Three good cables; the *sheet* cable, and the two *bowers*; best and small. **1842** MARRYAT *P. Keene* xxxix. 278, I shall back the best bower with the sheet, and let go the small bower at the same time. **1867** SMYTH *Sailor's Word-bk.* 124 Starboard being the best bower, and port the small bower.

2. More fully called ***bower-anchor***, ***-cable***.

1652 *Proc. Parliament* No. 142. 2223 My..best bower Ancher hooked in one of his Ports. **1748** ANSON *Voy.* II. ii. (ed. 4) 186 A violent gust of wind..instantly parted our small bower cable. **1772–84** COOK *Voy.* (1790) VI. 2107 A great piece of ice..brought home the small bower anchor. **1837** CARLYLE *Fr. Rev.* I. IV. iv. 179 By sure bower-anchor hangs and swings the tight war-ship.

fig. **1823** BYRON *Juan* XII. iii, Theirs is the best bower-anchor, the chain cable Which holds fast other pleasures. **1874** SPURGEON *Treas. Dav.* Ps. lxxxix. 1 The divine faithfulness..is the bower anchor of the soul.

†'**bower**, *sb.*[5] *Obs.* [a. Du. *bouwer* or Ger. *bauer*: see BOOR.] A peasant, husbandman.

c **1430** LYDG. *Min. Poems* (1840) 192 Of tilthe of lande treteth the boueer. *a* **1563** BALE *Sel. Wks.* (1849) 191 Done to death in Frisland by the bowers of the country for teaching a strange religion.

†'**bower**, *sb.*[6], '**bowess.** *Obs. rare.* [f. BOUGH *sb.* + -ER (prob. after BRANCHER), for which the fem. -ESS was afterwards substituted.] (See quots.)

c **1460** *Bk. Hawkyng* in *Rel. Ant.* I. 293 When they [young hawks] begynne to feder..they woll drawe them oute of here neste, and clambre over bowes, and come agayn to here neste, and then beth clepid bowers. **1486** *Bk. St. Alban's* A ij b, They will..draw to bowis..then thay be clepit Bowessis. **1706** PHILLIPS, *Bower* or *Bowess* (in *Falconry*), a young Hawk so nam'd, when she draws any thing out of her Nest, and covets to clamber on the Boughs.

bower, *sb.*[7] *Sc.* [f. BOW *sb.*[4] herd of cattle + -ER[1]. Pronounced in Sc. ('buːər, 'baʊər).] A tenant who rents a herd of cows along with their pasture and fodder from a proprietor or farmer, and makes what profit he can out of their produce, after paying the rent; or who gives his labour as his share, and divides profits with the proprietor of the stock. Cf. BOUMAN.

bower ('baʊə(r)), *sb.*[8] [a. Ger. *bauer* peasant, one sense of which is 'knave at cards'.] In the game of Euchre the name of the two highest cards—the knave of trumps, and the knave of the same colour, called *right* and *left bower* respectively.

a **1871** BRET HARTE *Heathen Chinee*, At last he put down a right bower, Which the same Nye had dealt unto me. **1884** *Detroit Free Press* Oct. (Negro Orator) De black man has de bowers in his hand.

bower (baʊə(r), 'baʊə(r)), *v.* [f. BOWER *sb.*[1]]

1. *trans.* To embower; to enclose. *lit.* and *fig.*

1592 SHAKS. *Rom. & Jul.* III. ii. 81 When thou did'st bower the spirit of a fiend In mortall paradise of such sweet flesh? **1798** SOUTHEY *Eng. Eclog.* i, Jessamine..canopied And bower'd and lined the porch. *a* **1860** M. ARNOLD *Sch. Gipsy* iii.

†**2.** *intr.* To lodge, shelter, make one's dwelling.

1596 SPENSER *F.Q.* VI. x. vi, Trees of honour..Spredding pavilions for the birds to bowre.

bower, var. of BOUGHER.

bower-anchor: see BOWER *sb.*[4]

Bower-Barff ('baʊə bɑːf). *Metallurgy.* [The names of G. and A. S. *Bower* and F. S. *Barff*, 19th-cent. American engineers.] **Bower-Barff process**: a development of the Barff process (see quots. and BARFF). Hence **Bower-Barffed** *ppl. a.*, treated by this process; **Bower-Barffing** *vbl. sb.*, treatment by this process. (Also with lower-case initials.)

1884 G. BOWER in *Trans. Soc. Engin. 1883* 59 The coating consists of a film of magnetic oxide, and is produced directly by the Barff process, and indirectly by the joint process of the author and his son. So long as these were worked independently, the one was called the Barff, the other the Bower process; but now that the various English patents are in the hands of one company, they are worked together and the process is called the Bower-Barff process. **1940** *Chambers's Techn. Dict.* 106/2 *Bower-Barffing*, an anti-corrosion process applied to sanitary ironwork. **1944** *Jrnl. Iron & Steel Inst.* CL. 83 The Bower-Barff process in which the steel is heated to about 800° C. for 20 min. first in air, then in superheated steam and finally in a producer-gas atmosphere. **1952** *Archit. Rev.* CXI. 138/2 A pan of twenty gallons working capacity in bower-barffed cast-iron.

bower-bird ('baʊəbɜːd). **1.** The name given to several Australian birds belonging to the Starling family, remarkable for their habit of building bowers or 'runs', and adorning them with feathers, bones, shells, etc. These are not used as nests, but as places of resort.

1847 CARPENTER *Zool.* §395. **1884** [see BOWER *sb.*[1] 4].

2. *fig.* A person who collects ornaments, odds and ends, etc. (see also quot. 1943). Also *attrib.* Hence as *v. intr.*, to pick up odds and ends.

1926 FOWLER *Mod. Eng. Usage* 193/2 Such bower-birds' treasures as *au pied de la lettre*, *à merveille*. *Ibid.* 194/1 Every writer..who suspects himself of the bower-bird instinct should make and use some such classification system. **1941** K. TENNANT *Battlers* xxvii. 301 George the Bower-bird.. was..prowling around deserted camps, swooping on rubbish. *Ibid.*, I don't want him bower-birding round this camp. **1943** BAKER *Austral. Slang* (ed. 3) 13 *Bower bird*, a petty thief.

bowered (baʊəd, 'baʊəd), *ppl. a.* [f. BOWER *v.* + -ED.] Shaded, embowered; furnished with bowers.

1746 J. WARTON *Approach of Summer* (R.) Plac'd thy green and grassy shrine, With myrtle bower'd and jessamine. **1829** SOUTHEY *Sir T. More* I. 42 A high hill top, nor bowered with trees, nor broken by the plough. **1878** H. PHILLIPS *Poems fr. Span. & Germ.* 33 The bowered hut of mossy thatch.

'**bowering**, *ppl. a.* [f. as prec. + -ING[2].] Embowering, shading, covering.

a **1717** PARNELL *Gift of Poetry* (R.) Its bowering borders kiss the vale beneath. **1850** JEAN INGELOW *Two Margarets* i, She mus'd..In winding walks, and bowering canopies.

†**bowering**, *sb. Obs.* (?)

? *a* **1400** *Chester Pl.* II. (1847) 58 Shorte armed is he, To the bowering of this tree He will not well laste.

'**bowerless** ('baʊəlɪs), *a.* [f. BOWER *sb.* + -LESS.] Without a bower or bowers.

1837 *New Month. Mag.* LI. 115 How flowerless, bowerless, budless, and blossomless!

'**bowerlet.** [see -LET.] A small bower.

1830 *Fraser's Mag.* I. 411 The rich Herder..she accommodates in a pretty bowerlet of four sides, or pages.

†'**bowerly**, *a. Obs.* exc. *dial.* [Cf. BURLY; also BOWER *sb.*[3] 3.] Large; stout, burly.

1542 UDALL *Erasm. Apophth.* 184 b, He had seen..right greate and bowerly images. **1794** WOLCOTT (P. Pindar) *Ep. to Bruce* Wks. II. 478 The bowerly hostess, for a cart-horse fit. **1864** CAPERN *Devon Provinc.*, *Bowerly*, stout, rotund. **1880** MRS. PARR *Adam & E.* xxi. 298 Eve's a fine bowerly maid. **1880** MISS COURTNEY *W. Cornw. Gloss.*, *Bowerly*, burly; corpulent. **1880** T. COUCH *E. Cornw. Gloss.*, *Bowerly*, stately and comely.

'**bower-maid, -,maiden.** *arch.* Also 4–5 bur-, bour-, boure-. [f. BOWER *sb.*[1] 1.] A chamber-maid; a lady in waiting.

c **1308** *Sat. People Kildare* ix. in *E.E.P.* (1862) 175 Goddes bourmaidnes and his owen spouse. *c* **1330** *Arth. & Merl.* 6486 A burmaiden he hadde fair and schene. *c* **1440** *Promp. Parv.* 56 Burmayden, *pedissequa, ancilla.* *c* **1450** *Gloss.* in Wr.-Wülcker 623 *Abra*, bowre-mayde. **1884** TENNYSON *Becket* 121 Only my best bower-maiden died of late.

bowers, bowiers mustard: see BOOR.

'**bower-,woman.** *arch.* Also 4–5 bour-, 5 bur-. [f. BOWER *sb.*[1] 1.] A chamber-woman, a waiting-woman.

c **1380** WYCLIF *Sel. Wks.* II. 9 þis gospel telliþ not how Marie tok a bourwoman, but went mekeli in hast to salute her cosyn. *c* **1400** *Ywaine & Gaw.* 1711 A lady, twa bourwemen alswa. *c* **1450** *Gloss.* in Wr.-Wülcker 691 *Hec abra, ancilla*, burwoman. **1820** SCOTT *Monast.*, The shepherd's wife..who in better days had been her own bowerwoman.

bowery ('baʊərɪ), *sb. U.S.* [ad. Du. *bouwerij* 'husbandry', 'farm'.] **a.** A farm; a 'plantation'. *obs.* exc. in **the Bowery**: in New York City, an area of a squalid and wretched character noted for its cheap places of amusement and frequented by homeless vagrants.

1787 M. CUTLER in W. P. & J. P. Cutler *Life & Corr.* (1888) I. 305, I..left the city by way of the Bowery. **1809** W. IRVING *Knickerb.* (1861) 116 His abode which he had fixed at a bowery, or country-seat, at a short distance from the city, just at what is now called Dutch Street. **1842** —— *Braceb. Hall* II. 225 He had purchased a farm, or, as the Dutch settlers called it, a bowerie. *c* **1844** R. H. COLLYER *Lights & Shadows Amer. Life* 7 The crowd and bustle of business in Chatham Street, and the Bowery. **1876** BANCROFT *Hist. U.S.*, The [Dutch] emigrants were scattered on boweries or plantations. **1930** E. POUND *XXX Cantos* xxviii. 130 Stiff as a cigar-store Indian from the Bowery.

b. *attrib.*, in sense 'of, pertaining to, or characteristic of the Bowery'; **Bowery boy**, a rough or rowdy of a type at one time characteristic of the Bowery.

1840 *Daily Picayune* (New Orleans) 28 Aug. 2/1 The Bowery boys of New York have..eclipsed the nice young men of Baltimore. **1852** C. A. BRISTED *Upper Ten Thousand* 29 Its occupants are of not-to-be-mistaken Bowery cut—veritable b'hoys. **1856** *Spirit of Times* 1 Nov. 149/1 Starflower of the blooming Bower-y girls. **1882** J. D. McCABE *New York* 642 The original 'Bowery Girl' must have been made of a rib of the original 'Bowery Boy', so exactly was she his counterpart. **1884** *Thompson St. Poker Club* 14 Mr. Tooter Williams and the odor of a Bowery cigar entered together. **1924** J. BUCHAN *Three Hostages* xviii. 263 'Hell!' he cried, with a torrent of Bowery oaths. *a* **1952** E. J. BRADY in R. Ward *Penguin Bk. Austral. Ballads* (1964) 185 The Bowery gal she knows 'er know; The Frisco gal is silly.

Hence '**boweryish** *a.*, smacking of the Bowery in New York.

1846 POE *Wks.* (1864) III. 109 Elevating the tone of this 'Editor's Table' (which its best friends are forced to admit is a little Boweryish).

bowery ('baʊərɪ), *a.* [f. BOWER *sb.*[1] + -Y[1].] Of the nature of a bower; embowering, leafy.

1704 POPE *Windsor For.* 262 Bow'ry mazes and surrounding greens. **1824** MISS MITFORD *Village* Ser. I. (1863) 21 Shaded..by wild overgrown shrubs, bowery acacias. **1876** M. B. EDWARDS *John & I*, xxi. 170 The boweriest part of the garden.

bowess: see BOWER *sb.*[6]

bowet ('baʊɪt, Sc. 'buət). *Sc.* Forms: 5 bowyt, 5–6 bowett, 6–9 bowat, 9 booit, bouat, bouet, buat, 6– bowet. [perh. (as suggested by Way) a. F. *boite* (in Berry, according to Littré, *bouete*) box, case; or rather from its med.L. equivalent *boeta*: cf. 'abscondet ignem in boeta in secreto' Du Cange, where see also *Lucerna Boeta.*]

A small lantern.

1440 *Promp. Parv.* 46/1 Bowett, or lanterne, *lucerna, lanterna.* **1552** ABP. HAMILTON *Catech.* 121 Sa aucht ye to use the law or command of God, as a Torche, Bowat or Lanterin. **1686** G. STUART *Joco-Ser. Disc.* 61 A twinkling light set..In little Bowet. **1814** SCOTT *Wav.* II. xv. 229 McFarlane's buat [i.e. the moon]. **1864** R. REID *Old Glasgow* 395 Ladies frequently made use of hand bowets, having plates of thin horn in lieu of glass.

bowgard, obs. form of BUGGER.

bowge, variant of BOUGE, bag, wallet.

bowge, obs. form of BOUGE, BULGE, *v.*

†**bowger**[1]. *Obs.* [prob. a. OF. **bougier*, f. *bouge*, bag, wallet: see BOUGE. Cf. BOUCHER, BOWSER[1].] A purser, treasurer.

c **1450** *Gregory's Chron.* 139 At the same tabylle the bowgerys of the chancery.

†bowger^2. The name in St. Kilda of the Puffin.
1698 MARTIN *St. Kilda* (1753) 34 (JAM.) The Bowger, so called by those in St. Kilda..is of the size of a pigeon. 1766 PENNANT *Zool.* (1768) II. 485.

bowget, obs. form of BUDGET *sb.*.

bowght, etc., obs. form of BOUGHT, etc.

bowgle, obs. form of BUGLE, ox.

bow-hand ('bəʊhænd). [f. BOW *sb.*^{1} + HAND.]
1. The hand which holds the bow in archery, i.e. the left hand. Hence, †(*wide*) *on the bow-hand*: wide of the mark, 'out'.
1588 SHAKS. *L.L.L.* IV. i. 135 Wide a' th bow hand, yfaith your hand is out. 1596 SPENSER *State Irel.* Wks. (1862) 520/2 He shootes wyde on the bow hand, and very far from the marke. 1611 CHAPMAN *Iliads* XIII. 534 Atrides' dart of Helenus the thrust out bow-hand struck. 1613 BEAUM. & FL. *Coxcomb.* I. iii, I am much o' the bow-hand else. 1828 SCOTT *F.M. Perth*, I. 24 You are on the bow-hand still, Smith. 1871 BROWNING *Balaust.* (1881) 26 Thou must arm The bow-hand.
2. The hand which holds the bow of a violin, etc., i.e. the right hand; *transf.* style of playing.
1668 SHADWELL *Sullen Lov.* II. Wks. 1720 I. 43 He has.. the most luxurious Bow-hand of any man in Europe.

bow-head ('bəʊhɛd). [f. BOW *sb.*^{1} + HEAD *sb.*] In full *bow-head whale*. The Arctic right whale, *Balæna mysticetus*.
1887 *Pall Mall Gaz.* 8 Sept. 2/2 A bow-head whale preparing to 'sound'. 1888 *Encycl. Brit.* XXIV. 523/2 The 'bowhead' of the Okhotsk Sea and Behring Strait. 1896 KIPLING *Seven Seas* 129 Hath he..Spoke on the ice with the Bow-head—followed the Sabre-tooth home? 1938 *Geogr. Jrnl.* XCII. 371 The mammoth bowhead whale.

bowiare, bowier, obs. forms of BOWYER.

bowie^1 ('baʊɪ, 'bɔːwɪ). *Sc.* [Of uncertain origin: it has been referred to F. *buie* water-vessel; it is possibly a dim. of *bowe* = BOLL or BOWL.] A low shallow tub or pail; a wooden milk-bowl.
1538 *Aberdeen Regist.* V. 16 (JAM.) Ane stand, a bowy. *a*1774 FERGUSSON *Poems* (1789) II. 56 (JAM.) I' the far nook the bowie briskly reams. 1816 SCOTT *Old Mort.* Introd. 10 [He] makes them into spoons, trenchers, bickers, bowies, and so forth. 1853 G. JOHNSTON *Nat. Hist. E. Border* I. 136 Scrubbers for cleaning milk bowies.
Hence **bowieful**.
1805 J. NICOL *Poems* I. 143 (JAM.) Thar bowiefu's o' kail fu' strang. 1818 HOGG *Brownie Bodsb.* II. 45 (JAM.) Davie.. brought me a hale bowiefu' o' milk.

'bowie^2. Short for BOWIE-KNIFE.
1850 KINGSLEY *Alt. Locke* xxvii (D.), I took the precaution of bringing my bowie and revolver with me.
Hence **'bowieism**, the use of the bowie-knife.
1844 *For. Q. Rev.* XXXIV. 118 Arkansas is the head-quarters of Bowieism.

bowie, obs. form of BUOY.

bowie-knife ('bəʊɪnaɪf). [f. the name of one Colonel Bowie (see last quot.); originally, according to Bartlett, 'pronounced *boo-ee*' ('buːɪ)] A large knife, with a blade from ten to fifteen inches long and above an inch broad, curved and double-edged near the point, carried as a weapon in the wilder parts of the United States.
1842 DICKENS *Amer. Notes* (1850) 32/2 A sewing society.. which..never comes to fisty cuffs or bowie-knives as sane assemblies have been known to do elsewhere. 1850 MRS. STOWE *Uncle Tom* xxviii. 268 St. Clare received a fatal stab in the side with a bowie-knife. 1858 O. W. HOLMES *Aut. Breakf.-t* 21 The American bowie-knife is the same tool [*gladius*] modified to meet the daily wants of civilized society. 1885 *Daily News* 11 Feb. 5/3 The hunting-dagger which belonged to the redoubtable Colonel James Bowie, and which has served as the pattern of all subsequent bowie-knives..is a formidable double-edged weapon, with a horn handle and a curved blade fifteen inches long and an inch and a quarter wide at the hilt.
Hence **'bowie-kniving** *vbl. sb.*
1861 SALA *Tw. round Clock* 350 Not impossible to imputations of gouging, bowie-kniving and knuckle-dusting.

'bowing, *sb. Sc.* [app. f. BOW *sb.*^{4}] A stock farm with the stock on it.
1808-79 JAMIESON *Dict.* s.v., *To tak a farm in a bowin*, to take a lease of a farm in grass, with the life stock on it; this still remaining the property of the landholder, or person who lets it. *Ayrs.* 1863 *Glasgow Her.* 11 Sept., To let near Balloch, a Bowing of 20 Cows.

bowing ('bəʊɪŋ), *vbl. sb.*^{1} [f. BOW *v.*^{1} + -ING^1.]
1. a. Bending, curving, twisting; flexure, inclination.
1398 TREVISA *Barth. De P.R.* XVIII. xvi. (1495) 776 The cokatryce pressith not his bodi wyth moche bowynge. 1481 CAXTON *Reynard* (Arb.) 28 Without bowyng of your legges. 1570 BILLINGSLEY *Euclid* I. def. viii. 3 A plaine angle is an inclination or bowing of two lines, the one to the other. 1610 GUILLIM *Heraldry* II. iv. 44 A Bunched Line is carried with round reflections or bowings vp and downe.
†b. Inflexion (of the voice). *Obs.*
1561 NORTON *Calvin's Inst.* III. xx. 435 The Reader should sound his words with so small a bowing of his voice, that it should be liker to one that readeth than to one that singeth.

†2. *concr.* A curved or bent part; a bending, bend, or flexure; a joint. *Obs.* exc. *dial.*
1519 HORMAN *Vulg.* 26 Amoste at euery bonys ende is a grystell: that lyeth betwene the bowynge lyke a mattresse. 1587 FLEMING *Contn. Holinshed* III. 1339/2 On the outside of the bowing of the arch were painted three goddesses. 1681 *Willis' Rem. Med. Wks.*, It descends to the bowing of the Elbow. 1864 CAPERN *Devon Prov.*, *Bewings*, joints.
3. The action of inclining the body or head in salutation, etc.; the making of an obeisance; also *attrib.*, as in *bowing acquaintance*.
1616 PURCHAS *Pilgr.* (1864) 22 After often bowings, and touching the ground with his head. 1660 MILTON *Free Commw.* 429 The perpetual bowings and cringings of an abject People. 1807 J. BERESFORD *Miseries Hum. Life* II. xviii. 164 A horse with an unceasing trick of nodding..his head up and down, as if he had a bowing acquaintance with every thing he meets. 1862 *Cornh. Mag.* VI. 852 One makes a sort of pleasant bowing acquaintance with the several women. 1876 GREEN *Sh. Hist.* 497 The bowings at the sacred name.

bowing ('bəʊɪŋ), *vbl. sb.*^{2} [f. BOW *v.*^{2} + -ING^1.]
1. a. The playing of (a violin, etc.) with a bow; the method or style of handling the bow. **b.** 'The particular manner in which a phrase or passage is to be executed, and the signs by which such a manner is usually marked.' Grove. (Cf. *fingering*.)
1838 W. GARDINER *Music Nat.* 121 Modern writers accurately mark the bowing of every passage. 1865 tr. *Spohr's Autobiog.* I. 14 My bowing particularly displeased him. 1881 BROADHOUSE *Mus. Acoust.* 160 Stringed instruments are made to sound either by striking, plucking, or bowing.
2. *Hat-making.* The process of distributing the fibres for felting by means of the 'bow'.
1842 WHITTOCK *Bk. Trades* 293 (Hatter), Each article undergoes a process..termed 'bowing'.

bowing ('baʊɪŋ), *ppl. a.* [f. BOW *v.*^{1} + -ING^2.]
1. That bends or inclines; inclined, bent (*obs.*).
*c*1440 *Gesta Rom.* xlviii. 216 With bowinge knees þey worshipid him. *c*1470 HENRY *Wallace* III. 215 On bowand treis [thai] hangit thaim rycht thar. 1674 N. FAIRFAX *Bulk & Selv.* 68 The nearer the eye comes to a great thing that is bowing, the less bowing it seems. 1728 YOUNG *Love Fame* IV. (R.), And then he can out-bow the bowing dean.
b. *fig.* Yielding, submissive, obedient.
*a*1340 HAMPOLE *Pr. Consc.* 7987 Alle thing tylle þam salle be boghand. *c*1400 *Destr. Troy* 901 [þe orible oxin]..as bowande to þe bowes as any bestes might. 1844 KINGLAKE *Eothen* xxv. 325 The readily-bowing mind of the oriental.
†2. That may be bent; flexible, pliant. *Obs.*
1483 CAXTON *Gold. Leg.* 331/2 His fyngers and his toes.. were bowyng and hoole as they hadde be newely buryed. 1551 TURNER *Herbal* F v b, To make hoopis of, and twygges for baskets it is so bowing. 1570 LEVINS *Manip.* 136 Bowing, *lentus, flexilis.*

†'bowingly, *adv. Obs.* [f. prec. + -LY.] In a curving or bending manner or direction.
1552 HULOET, Bowynglye, lyke a bowe, *arcuatim. Ibid.* Bowynglye, *procliue, recurue.* 1594 BLUNDEVIL *Exerc.* III. I. (ed. 7) 271 A right line is that which goeth right from one point to another, and not bowingly.

†'bowingness. *Obs.*$^{-0}$ [f. as prec. + -NESS.] Bending quality.
1580 HOLLYBAND *Treas. Fr. Tong.*, *Flechissure*, bought, or bowingnesse.

bowk, bouk (baʊk). *local.* [perh.:—OE. *búc* bulging vessel, pitcher, also 'belly', see BOUK, and cf. BUCKET.]
†1. A milk pail; a pail. *Obs.* or *dial.*
*c*1000 ÆLFRIC *Judges* vii. 20 Hi tobræcon þa bucas. 1663 P. HENRY *Diary* 15 June (1882) 139 A mayd..who coming from milking fell down with the Bowk on her head and dyed. 1879 MISS JACKSON *Shropsh. Gloss.*, *Bouk* (obsolescent), a pail with an upright handle, used for various purposes of brewing, dairy-work, etc.
2. A large tub or bucket used in coal-mines.
1865 *Engineer* 1 Dec. 16/3 Three men..were lowered down the shaft in a bowk or tub. 1869 *Echo* 28 June, They then..got into the water bowk, which they were using as a skip. 1882 *Law Reports* 357 A workman..killed through falling from a 'bowk', in which he was being drawn up the pit shaft.

bowk, north. form of BUCK, BULK.

bowk, variant of BOLK *v. Obs.* to belch.

'bow-kail. *Sc.* ['So called from the circular form of this plant.' (Jamieson—a very doubtful conjecture.) The Sc. pronunc. is ('bukel, 'bʌu-).] Cabbage.
1785 BURNS *Halloween* iv, Will..wander'd thro' the bow-kail. *Ibid.* ix, Poor Willie, wi' his bow-kail runt.

bow-knot: see BOW *sb.*^{1} 16.

†bow-krickel. *Obs.* [corrupt. ad. Ger. *baumgrille* 'tree-cricket'; see BALM-CRICKET.] A cicada.
1658 ROWLANDS *Mouffet's Theat. Ins.* 989 In Germany and England I do not hear that there are any Grashoppers to be found, but if they be, they are in both Countreys called Bow-krickels, or Baulm Krickets.

bowl (bəʊl), *sb.*^{1} Forms: 1 bolla, 2-7 bolle, (5 boole), 6-7 boll, 6 boule, 7 boul, bowle, boal, 7-9 bole, 7- bowl. *Pl.* bowls, (in 1 bollan, 2-3 -en). [Com. Teut.: OE. *bolla* = MDu. *bolle*, Du. *bol*, ON. *bolli* wk. masc.; cogn. with OHG. *bolla* (MHG. *bolle*), wk. fem., 'bud, round pod, globular vessel'; hence OE. *heafodbolla* 'brainpan, skull'; f. root **bŭl-* 'to swell, be swollen'; cf. also OHG. *bolôn*, MHG. *boln* to roll. The normal modern spelling would be BOLL which came down to 17th c. in sense of 'round vessel', and is still used in sense of 'round seed-vessel'; but the early ME. pronunciation of *-ōll* as *-ōwl* (cf. *roll, poll, toll*, etc.), has left its effects in the modern spelling *bowl* in the sense of 'vessel', which is thus at once separated in form from other senses of its own (see BOLL *sb.*^{1}), and confounded with BOWL *sb.*^{2} a ball, from Fr. *boule*.]
1. a. 'A [round] vessel to hold liquids, rather wide than deep; distinguished from a cup, which is rather deep than wide.' J. Usually hemispherical or nearly so.
Historically, a *bowl* is distinguished from a *basin* by its more hemispherical shape; a 'basin' being proportionally shallower and wider, or with the margin curved outward, as in the ordinary wash-hand basin; but the actual use of the words is capricious, and varies from place to place; in particular, the ordinary small earthenware vessels, used for porridge, soup, milk, sugar, etc., which are historically *bowls*, and are so called in Scotland and in U.S., are always called in the south-east of England, and hence, usually in literary English, *basins*. The earlier usage remains in *salad-bowl, finger-bowl* (now also *basin*), *punch-bowl*, and the *convivial* or *social bowl* (see b).
*c*1000 *Sax. Leechd.* I. 300 Genim..twegen bollan fulle wæteres. *c*1205 LAY. 19783 Heo comen to þare welle and heore bollen feolde. *c*1386 CHAUCER *Chan. Yem. Prol. & T.* 657 Bryngeth eek with yow a bolle or a panne ful of water. *c*1440 *Promp. Parv.* 43 Bolle, dysche, *cantare.* Bolle, vesselle, *concha, luter.* 1474 CAXTON *Chesse* 12 A boole of coppre. 1481 —— *Reynard* (Arb.) 113 A grete bolle full of scaldyng water. 1563 HYLL *Art Garden.* (1593) 150 Set either a boule or pan of water. 1625 PURCHAS *Pilgrimes* II. 1735 They dig deepe pits in the earth, and wash the earth in great bolls, and therein they find the gold. 1646 SIR T. BROWNE *Pseud. Ep.* VII. xiii. (1686) 300 Water in a boal. 1833 HT. MARTINEAU, *Briery Crk.* iii. 49 Cups and basins which the younger girl had washed in the wooden bowl. 1850 MRS. STOWE *Uncle Tom* xvii. 163 John will..give the baby all the sugar in the bowl.
b. *esp.* as a drinking vessel; whence *the bowl*, drinking, conviviality.
*c*950 *Lindisf. Gosp.* John xix. 29 Bolla *vel* copp full of æcced. *c*1205 LAY. 14994 þene bolle heo sette to hire chin. *c*1325 *E.E. Allit. P.* B. 1511 In bryȝt bollez, ful bayn birlen þise oþer. 1414 *Test. Ebor.* (1836) I. 362 Lego..unum ciphum de argento, qui vocatur le Bolle. 1548 LATIMER *Ploughers* (1868) 35 As manie as drancke of the pardon boll should haue pardon. 1576 LAMBARDE *Peramb. Kent* (1826) 319 One onely wassailing cup or Bolle walked round about the boorde. 1594 SHAKS. *Rich. III*, V. iii, 72 Giue me a Bowle of Wine. 1651 *Miller of Mansfield* 9 Nappie Ale..in a browne Bole. 1663 COWLEY *Verses & Ess.* (1669) 107 The Beechen Bowl fomes with a floud of Wine. 1706 ADDISON *Rosamond* II. vi, Quickly drain the fatal Bowl. 1805 SOUTHEY *Madoc in W.* xv, O'er the bowl they commun'd. 1811 *Let. fr. Son to Mother* 11, I fly to the bowl; thence quaff short oblivion.
fig. and *transf.*
*c*1025 ÆLFRIC *Saints' Lives St. George* I. 312 Ænne mycelne bollan mid bealuwe afylled. 1393 LANGL. *P. Pl.* C. XXI. 410 þi drynke worth deþ and deop helle þy bolle. *c*1575 GASCOIGNE *Fruites Warre* (1831) 212 Hope brings the boll whereon they all must quaffe. 1649 JER. TAYLOR *Great Exemp.* II. Add. x. 9 The World presents us with faire language..these are the outsides of the bole. 1871 MORLEY *Voltaire* (1886) 15 The tiny bowl of a man's happiness was spilt upon the ground.
c. With prefixed substantive, as *ale-, sugar-, etc.*
1562 J. HEYWOOD *Prov. & Epigr.* (1867) 153 Drownd theyr soules in ale boules. 1615 G. SANDYS *Trav.* 39 Accustomed..of their sculs to make drinking-bolles. 1709 *Tatler* No. 42 ¶13 A Mustard-Bowl to make Thunder with.
†d. A tub or round vessel for other purposes.
*a*1000 *Cursor M.* 5524 (Gött.) Apon þair neckes sal þai bere Bollis [*Cott.* hott = hod] wid stan and wid mortere.
2. *transf.* The contents of a bowl, a bowlful.
1530 PALSGR. 459 This felowe blussheth lyke a butchers bolle. 1605 CAMDEN *Rem.* 130 New named with a bole of wine powred vpon their heads. 1617 *Janua Ling.* 814 The butler hath drunke up a whole bolle. *a*1764 LLOYD *Satyr & Pedlar* Poet. Wks. 1774 I. 59 A bowl prepar'd of sav'ry broth. 1847 TENNYSON *Princ.* v. 214 Nor robb'd the farmer of his bowl of cream.
3. a. The more or less bowl-shaped part of any vessel or utensil; e.g. of a cup or flagon, tobacco-pipe, spoon, candlestick; the scale-pan of a balance.
1386 RYMER *Fœdera* XVIII. 143 One cupp, the boll thereof agett ovall fashion called the Constables Cupp, with an aggett in the foote. 1398 TREVISA *Barth. De P.R.* XIX. cxxxi. (1495) 940 The weyght is rightfull whan both the bolles hangyth euen. 1611 BIBLE *Zech.* iv. 2 A candle-sticke all of gold, with a bowle vpon the top of it. 1679 PLOT *Staffordsh.* (1686) 197 Which so well resembled..[a tobacco pipe] both in the boll and heel. 1692 in Capt. Smith *Seaman's Gram.* II. xxxi. 144 The Bole or Bore of the Morter, next to the Wad. 1814 SCOTT *Wav.* I. ix. 123 The grotesque face on the bole of a German tobacco-pipe. 1840 R. DANA *Bef. Mast.* xix. 55 They smoke a great deal..using pipes with large bowls. 1885 *Mag. of Art* Sept. 458/2 The bowl of the spoon.
b. The basin of a fountain, etc.

1575 LANEHAM *Let.* (1871) 52 A fayr formed boll, of a three foot ouer: from wheans sundrye fine pipez did distill continuall streamz intoo the receyt of the Fountayn. **1870** F. WILSON *Ch. Lindisf.* 90 The bowl [of the font] is dated 1664.

c. A bowl-shaped natural basin.

1860 TYNDALL *Glac.* I. §23. 165 The rim of a flattened bowl quite clasped by the mountains.

d. A football stadium (no longer necessarily bowl-shaped). Freq. in the names of particular stadia. Cf. ROSE BOWL 2, *Super-Bowl* s.v. SUPER- 6c. *U.S.*

1913 *Yale Alumni Weekly* 4 July 1073/1 I voice the thanks of all Yale graduates for the 'Bowl'... I am glad that Yale.. prefers the good old word 'bowl' with its savor of manly English sport, to the 'coliseum' of the Romans or the 'stadium' of the Greeks. **1923** *Pasadena* (Calif.) *Star-News* 1 Jan. 1 Cheered to the echo,..a crowd of about 50,000 people in the great Rose Bowl, Pasadena's new Stadium in the Arroyo Seco. **1931** E. LINKLATER *Juan in Amer.* II. xii. 135 To see a good game people would drive for many miles and the bowl was generally well filled. **1975** *New Yorker* 8 Dec. 35/3 It was pleasant indeed to be sitting in the Yale Bowl among sixty-six thousand people, all of them intelligent-looking. **1987** *Washington Post* 23 Mar. A 7/2, Three banks backed Robbie's plan to build a stadium..30 miles north of Miami's downtown crumbling Orange Bowl.

†**4.** *Naut.* (See quot.) *Obs.*

1627 CAPT. SMITH *Seaman's Gram.* v. 20 The Top, Cap, or Bowle, which is a round thing at the head of either Mast for men to stand in. **1668** WILKINS *Real Char.* II. xi. §iv. 281 Parts of Vessels..fixed and upright; or the upper parts of these, round and prominent: Mast-Top, Boul. **1721–1800** BAILEY, *Bowl* [in a ship], a round space at the Head of the Mast for the Men to stand in.

5. The blade of an oar. (Cf. bowl of spoon in 3.)

1805 SOUTHEY *Madoc in Azt.* xxv. Wks. V. 367 Oars From whose broad bowls the waters fall and flash.

6. (See quot.)

1884 *British Almanack & Comp.* 32 The nets..are further buoyed up by small kegs, called 'bowls'.

7. *Comb.*, as **bowl-basin, -cup, -shaped** adj.: also **bowl-barrow**, a prehistoric mound of the shape of an inverted bowl; **bowl-fellow**, a drinking companion; **bowlful**, the content of a bowl; † **bowl-piece**, a piece (of plate) of the form of a bowl; **bowl-weft** (see quot.)

1812 R. COLT-HOARE *Anc. Hist. S. Wilts.* 21 *Bowl *Barrow.* This is, I think, the most ordinary shaped barrow, and more frequently met with than any of the others. **1846** KNIGHT *Old England* 7 On every side of Stonehenge we are surrounded with barrows. Some are of the shape of bowls, and some of bells..Long-barrow, bowl-barrow, bell-barrow. **1607** *Althorp MS.* in Simpkinson *Washingtons* Introd. 6 *Boll basons (whereof one hath brinkes) iiij. **1420** *E.E. Wills* (1882) 45–6 A *bolle cuppe i-keueryd of syluer. Also a bolle pece. **1509** BARCLAY *Shyp of Folys* (1570) 16 She and her *boul felowes sitting by the fire. **1611** BIBLE *Judg.* vi. 38 A *bowle full of water. **1725** BRADLEY *Fam. Dict.* II. s.v. *Juice*, A Bowlful of the Juice. **1459** *Test. Ebor.* (1855) II. 235, Duas pecias argenti et coopertas vocatas *boll-peces. **1479** *Inv. Plate* in *Paston Lett.* III. 273, J grete boll pees, with a cover. **1864** *N. & Q.* Ser. III. VI. 459/1 *Bowl-weft ..applied to materials abstracted by weavers in Lanarkshire ..to exchange it with travelling hawkers for bowls and other earthenware dishes.

¶ See also BOLL, BOULE.

bowl (bəʊl, baʊl), *sb.*[2] Forms: 5–7 boul(e, bowle, (7 bowel), 7– bowl; *Sc.* and *north. dial.* boul, bool. [ME. *boule*, a. F. *boule* ball:—L. *bulla* 'bubble', hence, 'round thing, ball'. The French pronunciation (bul), is retained in Sc. and parts of Northumbria, now often written *bool*; the normal English would be (baʊl) as in *foul, fowl*, which still prevails in nearly all the dialects from Yorkshire to Devon, and thence to Kent; the pronunciation (bəʊl), a corruption due to graphic confusion with BOWL *sb.*[1], appears to have originated in London and its neighbourhood, but has extended elsewhere with the use of the vb. in cricket.]

†**1. a.** A sphere, globe, ball. *Obs.* in lit. Eng.

1413 LYDG. *Pylgr. Sowle* v. xiv. (1483) 107 God made this grete world..round as a boule. **1449** *Excheq. Records* in Risdon *Surv. Devon.* Introd. 18, 144 Bouls of Glance Oar. **1549** *Compl. Scot.* vi. 54 The mune is ane thik masse, round lyik ane boule or bal. **1556** *Chron. Gr. Friars* (1852) 25 The wedercoke, crosse, & the bowle of Powlles stepulle. **1594** BLUNDEVIL *Exerc.* III. I. (ed. 7) 273 But if such body bee round as a boule, Spheare or Globe. **1609** HOLLAND *Amm. Marcell.* XVII. iv. 84 A bowle or globe of brasse [*sphæra ahenea*]. **1623** LISLE *Ælfric on O. & N.T.* Ded. xii, No roaring brazen throat Shall belch out iron boules. **1644** NYE *Gunnery* (1670) 20 The bowl rowling up and down in the sieve. **1670** *Lassels Voy. Italy* I. (1698) 117 The six Boules of his [the Medici] Arms.

b. Retained dialectally either in the general sense, or in special uses.

In S. Shields, a water-worn or other rounded stone, such as were formerly used for paving the streets, is called a 'bool'.

1839 MURCHISON *Silur. Syst.* I. xxxii. 440 Small concretionary nodules of impure limestone, here called bowls by the workmen. *Mod. Sc.* A butter bool, rock bool, sugar bool. As round as a bool.

2. *spec.* A globular or round solid body used to play with: **a.** *esp.* in the game of Bowls (see 3) played on a bowling-green: A body of hard wood, originally spherical, but now made slightly oblate on one side and prolate on the other, so as to run with a BIAS (q.v.). ***carpet-bowls***, used in a drawing-room form of the game, are globular, and of china or earthenware. **b.** Also, those of wood, used in skittles, nine-pins, and the like, which in some parts of the country (e.g. Somersetshire) are spherical, in others much flattened or cheese-shaped. (It is not possible to separate **a** and **b** in the quotations.)

c **1420** OCCLEVE *De Reg. Princ.* 24 To..pleye at the balle or boule. *c* **1440** *Promp. Parv.* 46 Bowlyn or pley wythe bowlys, *bolo.* ?*c* **1475** *Sqr. lowe Degre* 804 An hundreth Knightes.. Shall play with bowles in alayes colde. **1556** RECORDE *Cast. Knowl.* 111 A litle altering of the one side, maketh the boul to run biasse waies. **1588** *Marprel. Epist.* (1843) 54 O well bowlde, when John of London throwes his bowle, he will runne after it, and crie rub, rub, rub. **1611** MARKHAM *Countr. Content.* in Strutt *Sports & Past.* (1876) 363 Flat bowles being best for allies, your round byazed bowles for open grounds of advantage. **1691** NORRIS *Pract. Disc.* 126 The fortune of the Boul does [depend] upon its delivery out of the Hand. **1692** BENTLEY *Boyle Lect.* ii. 71 A Bowl thrown upon a smooth Bowling-green. **1768** TUCKER *Lt. Nat.* I. 509, I have a bowl in my hand and want it to touch the jack at the other end of the green. **1836** HOR. SMITH *Tin Trump.* (1876) 112 It is not every rogue that, like a bowl, can gain his object the better by deviating from the straight line. **1863** *Tyneside Songs* 87 War the bowl there, Harry Wardle's myed a throw.

fig. **1618** MYNSHUL *Ess. Prison* (1638) 17 To bee a bowle for every alley, and run into every company, proves thy mind to have no bias. **1625** BACON *Ess.* (Arb.) 185 Which set a Bias vpon the Bowle, of their owne Petty Ends.

†**c.** A billiard ball. *Obs.*

1530 PALSGR. 200/2 Bowle to playe at the byles, *bille.* **1695** ALINGHAM *Geom. Epit.* 29 Suppose one bowl at the point *a* ..and *c d* the Billiard Table.

d. *Sc.* A marble, used by boys in play; or, in some parts, only the larger kind used at 'bonce'. (In Sc. *bool.*)

1826 J. WILSON *Noct. Ambr.* Wks. 1855 I. 110 Frae the size o' a peppercorn to that o' a boy's bools.

e. A delivery of the ball in cricket: now usually *ball.*

1862 *Chambers's Encycl.* III. 320/1 At the end of every four bowls, the bowler, wicket-keeper, long-stop, and fielders, change places.

f. A turn in the game of bowls; also, the delivery of the ball.

1889 in *Cent. Dict.* **1894** E. T. AYERS *Bowls* (ed. 2) 80 'Driver' on such occasions often comes in for reproach after an unsuccessful bowl.

3. *pl.* A game played with bowls:

a. on a bowling-green, or in a drawing-room (*carpet-bowls*); **b.** in a bowling-alley (*obs.* exc. in dialects where the name 'bowls' is still applied to 'skittles', as in Somerset); †**c.** formerly (apparently) also applied to Billiards (*obs.*). (It is not easy to identify the sense in individual quotations: the game played in *alleys* was apparently skittles or something analogous.)

1495 *Act 11 Hen. VII*, ii. §5 Noon apprentice..[shall] pley..at the Tenys, Closshe, Dise, Cardes, Bowles nor any other unlawfull game. **1549** CHALONER *Erasm. on Folly* O iij a, To the dyse, to tables, to cardes, or to boules. **1577** HOLINSHED *Chron.* III. 893/2 Tables, dice, cards, and bouls were taken and burnt. **1588** *Marprel. Epist.* (Arb.) 19 Who goeth to bowles vpon the Sabboth? **1593** SHAKS. *Rich. II*, III. iv. 3 What sport shall we deuise here in this Garden?.. Madame, wee'le play at Bowles. **1606** DAY *Ile of Guls* III. ii. Clear the green. The Duke is coming to bowls. **1612** T. TAYLOR *Comm. Titus* ii. 14 Cards, dice, bowles, bouls, vnprofitable Companie. **1661** PEPYS *Diary* 5 June, Sir W. Pen and I went home with Sir R. Slingsby to bowles in his ally. *a* **1687** PETTY *Pol. Arith.* Pref., To play well at Tennis, Billiards, or Bowels. **1755** OLDYS *Life Raleigh* Wks. 1829 I. 104 The captains and commanders were..at bowls upon the Hoe at Plymouth. **1844** DICKENS *Lett.* (1880) I. 117, I caught him..playing bowls in the garden. **1873** B'NESS BUNSEN in Hare *Life* I. ii. 55 The gentlemen played at bowls in the spacious bowling-green.

d. *Sc.* The game of marbles.

Mod. Co' way an' play a game at the bools.

4. The roller or anti-friction wheel in a knitting-machine on which the carriage traverses.

5. *Comb.*, as †**bowl-alley**, a long narrow space where a game of bowls was played, a skittle-alley: **bowl-room** (see quot.).

1628 EARLE *Microsm.*, *Bowl-Alley* 101 A *Bowl-Alley is the place where there are three things thrown away beside Bowls, to wit, time, money, and curses, and the last ten for one. **1634** RAINBOW *Labour* (1635) 30 The most goodly.. ground in..your Citie, the Bowle-allies and Dice-houses. **1753** CHAMBERS *Cycl. Supp.* s.v. *Bowling, Bowl-room*..is when a bowl has free passage, without striking on any other.

bowl (bəʊl), *v.*[1] [f. BOWL *sb.*[2]: so med.L. *bolāre*, f. *bolus*: cf. mod.F. *bouler*, f. *boule*.]

I. Senses derived from the game of bowls.

1. a. *intr.* To play at bowls; to trundle or roll a bowl, etc. along the ground.

1440 *Promp. Parv*, 46/1 Bowlyn or pley wythe bowlys, *bolo.* **1570** LEVINS *Manip.* 218 To Boule, *mittere globum.* **1589** *Hay any Work* 33 To bowle but seuen dayes in a weeke, is a very tollerable recreation. **1588** SHAKS. *L.L.L.* IV. i. 140 Sir, challenge her to boule [rimes with *foule, oule*]. **1589** COOPER *Admon.* 57 Your iesting at the bishop for bowling vpon the Sabboth. **1603** KNOLLES *Hist. Turkes* (1621) 1119 Some they put in the ground up to the chin, and..with yron bullets bowled at their heads. **1705** HICKERINGILL *Priest-cr.* I. (1721) 46 They may well win, that bowl alone. **1863** *Tyneside Songs* 87 Ye'll fynd them boolin' there.

b. *trans.* ***to bowl*** (*one*) ***to death*** (cf. 1603 in prec.), ***out of his money***, etc.

1598 SHAKS. *Merry W.* III. iv. 91, I had rather be set quick i'th earth And bowl'd to death with Turnips. **1818** SCOTT *Rob Roy* iii, Bowled you out of it at Marybone.

2. a. *trans.* To cause to roll, to send with a rolling or revolving motion (a bowl, a hoop, etc.).

1580 HOLLYBAND *Treas. Fr. Tong.*, *Iallet*, a little boule to cast & boule farre. **1602** SHAKS. *Ham.* II. ii. 518 Boule the round Naue down the hill of Heauen. **1686** GOAD *Celest. Bodies* II. i. 124 We must Fix the Sun, and Bowl the Earth about. **1742** YOUNG *Nt. Th.* IX. 1277 Who bowl'd them flaming thro' the dark profound. **1819** JANE TAYLOR *Philosopher's Scales*, Last of all the whole world was bowled in at the grate. **1863** KINGSLEY *Water Bab.* (1878) 4 Bowling stones at the horses' legs as they trotted by. *Mod.* Children bowling their hoops.

b. *trans.* To carry or convey on wheels, i.e. in a carriage or other vehicle.

1819 SHELLEY *Peter Bell* II. xiv, The wretched fellow Was bowled to Hell in the Devil's chaise.

3. *intr.* To move like a bowl or hoop along the ground, to move by revolution; to move on wheels (esp. ***to bowl along***), said of a carriage, or those who ride in it: also *transf.* of a ship.

[**1611** SHAKS. *Wint. T.* IV. iv. 338 They haue a Dance..if it be not too rough for some, that know little but bowling.] **1759** JOHNSON *Idler* No. 54 ¶4 A fashionable lady..bowling about in her own coach. **1780** COWPER *Progr. Err.* 438 The carriage bowls along. **1859** MASSON *Brit. Novelists* iii. 186 The moon bowling fearfully through clouds. **1863** *Cornh. Mag.* Feb., When the good ship is bowling along in the quiet moonlight. **1872** BLACK *Adv. Phaeton* xvi. 221 We bowled through the little village of Overton.

II. Senses connected with cricket.

4. a. *intr.* To launch or 'deliver' the ball at cricket.

Originally, the ball was actually *bowled* 'or trundled' along the ground: by the successive stages of *underhand* 'bowling' above the ground (used before 1800), *round-arm* or *round-hand* (introduced *c* 1825, and at first disallowed, as being 'throwing'), and the more recent *over-hand* or *over-arm*, 'bowling' has reached a stage, at which its practical difference from 'throwing' is a matter on which authorities are at variance.

1755 *Game at Cricket* 7 (penes M.C.C.), *Laws for the Bowlers*, The Bowler..when he has bowl'd one Ball, or more, shall bowl to the Number of Four before he changes Wickets, and he shall change but once in the same Innings. **1770** J. LOVE *Cricket* 2 Expert to Bowl, to Run, to Stop, to Throw. **1847** TENNYSON *Princess* Prol. 81 A herd of boys with clamour bowl'd And stump'd the wicket. **1879** *Sat. Rev.* 5 July 21 It is easy work bowling to men who have lost heart. **1880** W. G. GRACE in *Boy's Own Paper* II. 716 A man is now not only allowed to bowl as high as he likes, but a great many of our so-called bowlers deliberately throw.

b. ***to bowl with one's head***: to bowl intelligently; ***to bowl short***: to pitch the ball short of a good length; ***to bowl over the wicket***: to bowl with the bowling-arm nearest to the bowler's wicket; opp. ***to bowl round*** (or formerly ***outside***) ***the wicket***: to bowl with the bowling-arm away from the bowler's wicket.

1851 J. PYCROFT *Cricket Field* ii. 20 How is it that Clarke's slow bowling is so successful?.. 'You see, sir, they bowl with their heads.' *Ibid.* viii. 161 Playing him back all day if he bowls short, and hitting him hard along the ground whenever he overpitches. **1854** *Ibid.* (ed. 2) xi. 265 Any round-armed bowler (who does not bowl 'over the wicket'). **1887** F. GALE *Game Cricket* 154 Learning to play a round-arm bowler, bowling round the wicket. **1893** R. DAFT *Kings of Cricket* xiii. 230 Harrison..seems to me to bowl better 'with his head' than he used to formerly. **1955** *Times* 9 May 15/1 On Saturday he bowled over the wicket.

5. *trans.* in various constructions. **a.** To bowl *the ball.* Also, **b.** To bowl *the bails off*, to bowl *the wicket* (*down*). **c.** To bowl *a batsman* or *player* (*out*): to get him 'out' by bowling the bails off. **d.** To bowl *an over.* **e.** To put on (a player) to bowl in a cricket match.

1719 in H. T. Waghorn *Dawn of Cricket* (1906) 5 The Kentish men were bowled out. **1736** in —— *Cricket Scores* (1899) 14 When there were but two, and one wicket to bowl down. **1744** *Laws of Cricket* in *Dict. Arts & Sci.* (1755) IV. 3459/1 The bowler..when he has bowled one ball, or more, shall bowl to the number four before he changes wickets. *Ibid.*, If..the player is bowled out. *Ibid.*, If the wicket is bowled down, it is out. **1746** in 'Bat' *Cricket Man.* (1850) 80 Harris...o. b[owled] by Hadswell. **1755** *Game at Cricket* 8 Though..the Player be bowl'd out. *Ibid.* 9 If the wicket is bowl'd down, it's out. **1774** in *Q. Rev.* No. 316. 463 It was necessary to 'bowl the bail off'. **1833** *New Sporting Mag.* Sept. 325 Floyer bowls the over. **1862** F. *Lillywhite's Cricket Scores* I. 415 His underhand bowling..was so fast that it was not always safe to bowl him. **1879** *Sat. Rev.* 5 July 21 When he was not bowling wickets, he was..making catches. **1880** W. G. GRACE in *Boy's Own Paper* II. 716 Let him bowl a few balls every day. **1880** *Boy's Own Bk.* 105 His object being to bowl down the wicket. *Ibid.* All the players on one side are bowled, caught, or run out. **1881** *Daily News* 9 July 2 Richards was bowled for a good and useful 23. **1882** PARDON *Austral. in Eng.* 111, I think he might have bowled Boyle more. **1885** *Lillywhite's Cricketer's Ann.* 175 (M.C.C. Laws) The ball must be bowled. If thrown or jerked, the Umpire shall call 'No Ball'. (A distinct action of the elbow distinguishes a *throw.*) **1888** R. H. LYTTELTON *Cricket* xi. 343 Mr. Ward bowled thirty-two overs for 29 runs. **1955** A. ROSS *Australia 55* 96 Hutton bowled Tyson and Statham for an hour.

6. Hence *fig.* (*colloq.* or *slang*). To bowl (a person) *out, over, down.*

1793 *Sporting Mag.* 29 Sept. 371 Field-tennis threatens ere long to bowl out cricket. **1805** CAPT. CRUMBY *Let.* in *19th Cent.* No. 273. 721 He wished me to be made acquainted with it [*sc.* Ld. Nelson's memorandum], that in the event of his being 'bowl'd out' I might know how to conduct the ship. **1812** J. H. VAUX *Flash Dict.* s.v. *Bowled out*, [A thief] when he is ultimately taken, tried, and convicted, is said to be bowled out at last. **1829** MARRYAT *F. Mildmay* iii, I hope plenty of the lieutenants are bowled out. **1865** DICKENS *Mut. Fr.* i. 274 I'll bowl you down. **1867** TROLLOPE *Claverings* II. xii. 147 You certainly did bowl her over uncommon well. **1870** MISS BRIDGMAN *R. Lynne* I. ix. 127 He had been bowled over by one of them. **1885** *Illustr. Lond. News* 6 June 572 The horse that is favourite at starting ..is more frequently 'bowled over'.

†**bowl,** *v.*[2] *Obs.* To pass the convivial bowl, to booze. See BOLL *v.*[2], BOLLING, BOLLER.

bowl, bowle (bəʊl). *v.*[3] *north. dial.* [perh. identical with MDu. *bōghelen* to curve, crook, f. *bōghel*, now *beugel*, a bow, hoop, ring: cf. BOUL *sb.*] To curve, to crook (Jamieson).

1513 [see BOWLAND].

Hence **bowld, bowled** *ppl. a.*

1818 HOGG *Brownie* II. 226 (JAM.) Get away wi' ye! ye bowled-like shurf. **1863** *Tyneside Songs* 6 Bowld Sandy Bowes—young Cuckoo Jack.

†'**bowland,** *ppl. a. Obs. Sc.* [app. pr. pple. of BOWL *v.*[3]] Curving, crooked, hooked.

1513 DOUGLAS *Æneis* III. iv. 15 With handis like to bowland birdis clewis. *Ibid.* VI. ix. 135 Ane hiddeous grip with busteous bowland beik His maw immortale doith pik.

bowlder, var. of BOULDER *sb.*[1]

†**bowl-dish.** *Obs.* Forms: see BOWL *sb.*[1] A bowl-shaped dish, a bowl.

1530 PALSGR. 199/2 Boledysshe or a bole, *jatte.* **1577** B. GOOGE *Heresbach's Husb.* (1586) 137 Take a great bowle-dish. **1712** *Grt. Brit. Honeycombe, MS.* (N.) The boy was throwing of a bole-dish of water over his fish. **1725** BRADLEY *Fam. Dict.* s.v. *Sallet*, A large wooden Bowl-dish.

bowle, var. of BOUL, *Obs.*, a bend, a handle.

bow-legged ('bəʊlɛgd), *a.* [f. *bow-legs* + -ED.] Having crooked or outwardly bent legs; bandy-legged. (Huloet identified it with *knock-kneed.*)

1552 HULOET, Bowe legged, as he that hath his legges bowed inwarde, narrow at the knees. **1601** HOLLAND *Pliny* I. 350 Wry legged, *Vatiæ*, and *Vatinii* (bow-legged). **1686** *Lond. Gaz.* No. 2137/4 A black and white gelt Dog.. bowe-leg'd. **1697** *Ibid.* No. 3287/4 Talks very lowd, bow Legg'd, walks briskly. **1863** HUXLEY *Man's Place Nat.* 28 When he walks in the erect posture, he turns the leg and foot outward, which occasions him..to seem bow-legged.

bowler[1] ('bəʊlə(r)). [f. BOWL *v.* + -ER[1].]

1. One who bowls; one who plays at bowls.

c **1500** *Cocke Lorelles B.* (1843) 11 Bowlers, mas shoters, and quayters. **1609** B. JONSON *Sil. Wom.* I. i. (1616) 531 Every bowler, or better o' the greene. **1707** FARQUHAR *Beaux' Strat.* I. i. 4 A profess'd Pick-pocket, and a good Bowler. **1801** STRUTT *Sports & Past.* III. vii. 236 Modern bowlers have usually three or four [bowls].

2. *Cricket.* The player who bowls or 'delivers' the ball at the wicket. Also *bowler's* (or *bowlers'*) *match*: a cricket match in which the bowling is superior to the batting; *bowler's wicket*: one more favourable to the bowler than to the batsman.

1722 *Weekly Jrnl.* 21 July 2296/1 The Taylor was a good bowler. **1755** [see BOWL *v.* 4]. **1770** J. LOVE *Cricket* 15 Hodswell, of Dartford..celebrated Bowler. **1848** THACKERAY *Van. Fair* xiii, He..was the best batter and bowler, out and out, cf the regimental club. **1863** *Baily's Mag.* Aug. 360 It was a bowlers' match all through. **1876** *Ibid.* June 415 Much..will depend on..whether it is a batsman's or a bowler's wicket on the day of the match. **1888** *Sat. Rev.* 2 Sept. 312/2 It was clearly to be a bowler's match. **1895** *Badminton Mag.* Aug. 132 Any one can bowl on a bowler's wicket.

bowler[2] ('bəʊlə(r)). [f. BOWL *sb.*[1] or *v.*[2] + -ER[1].]

†**1.** A deep drinker; a drunkard: see BOLLER I.

2. A workman who shapes the bowl of a spoon.

1879 *Cassell's Techn. Educ.* IV. 413/2 The 'bowler' who domes up the broad end into the semblance of a bowl.

bowler[3] ('bəʊlə(r)). *colloq.* [f. BOWL *sb.*[2], quasi *bowl-hat.*] **a.** A low-crowned stiff felt hat, a 'billy-cock'. Also *bowler-hat.*

1861 *Sat. Rev.* 21 Sept. 297 We are informed that he.. wore, or rather carried in his hand, a white bowler hat. **1882** PEBODY *Eng. Journalism* xxi. 158 The Ministers, in bowlers and pea-jackets, are to be found upon the shore of highland lochs.

b. *fig.* As a symbol of civilian life (as opposed to service in the armed forces), or of the process of demobilization. Hence *bowler-hatting* vbl. sb. Occas. in extended use, with reference to dismissal.

1925 FRASER & GIBBONS *Soldier & Sailor Words* 34 *To be given one's bowler*, to be demobilised and returned to civil life. **1928** 'IAN HAY' *Poor Gent.* iv. 74 Nelson and Trafalgar put the bowler hat on that scheme. **1931** BROPHY & PARTRIDGE *Songs and Slang, 1914–18* (ed. 3) 287 *To be given one's bowler*, to be demobilized. *To get a bowler hat*, to be sent home, to be 'sacked'. Officers' slang; applied only to major and higher officers. **1953** *Economist* 8 Aug. 372/1 Little has been said..to suggest that the settlers have any agreed programme to offer—beyond the 'bowler-hatting' of colonial civil servants of whom they have made scapegoats. **1959** *Observer* 4 Jan. 11/3 He [*sc.* Lord Mountbatten] did not ask for his bowler hat when Mr. Sandys reorganised defence a short time ago.

Hence **bowler-hatted** *adj.*, (*a*) wearing a bowler-hat; (*b*) civilian, demobilized.

1909 M. BEERBOHM *Yet Again* 47, I picture him frock-coated, bowler-hatted, and evidently nervous. **1950** E. HYAMS *From Waste Land* 16 The bowler-hatted City gent. **1959** *Economist* 30 May 841/2 Those warriors who want to spend vastly more on defence are mostly either bowler-hatted or arm-chairborne.

bowlespret, obs. form of BOWSPRIT.

'**bowless,** *a.* Without a bow (in various senses).

1845 ELIZA COOK *Poems* Ser. II. 235 The bowless blind boy [*viz.* Cupid]. **1861** *Temple Bar* I. 282 His bow-less white neckcloth. **1905** *Daily Chron.* 25 Mar. 3/2 Her slippers were even bowless.

bowline[1] ('bəʊlaɪn). *Naut.* Forms: 4 **bouline, bawelyne,** 5 **bowelyne,** 5–6 **bowlyne,** 6 **boulene, bolyn, bollene, bollinge,** 6–9 **bowling,** 7 **bolin(e, bow-lin, boulin, bow line** 7–8 **boling,** 8–9 **bow-line,** 6– **bowline.** [In sense 1, in most modern Teutonic langs.: Sw. *boglina*, Da. *bovline*, Du. *boeglijn*, Ger. *bulien*; whence also F. *bouline*, It., Sp., Pg. *bolina*. In all the Teut. langs. it is connected in form with the ship's BOW, which seems to be the derivation; though, as it is found in Eng. several centuries before *bow*, it does not appear whence we received it, nor why the pronunciation does not agree with that of BOW.

The alleged ON. *bóglína* occurs only in the *þulur*, a rimed glossary composed prob. in Orkney, and full of foreign terms.]

I. 1. A rope passing from about the middle of the perpendicular edge on the weather side of the square sails (to which it is fastened by three or four subdivisions, called 'bridles') to the larboard or starboard bow, for the purpose of keeping the edge of the sail steady when sailing on a wind.

c **1325** *E.E. Allit. P.* C. 104 Sprude spak to þe sprete þe spare bawe-lyne. *c* **1330** R. BRUNNE *Chron.* (K.O.) Bouline. *c* **1450** *Pilgrim's Sea-Voy.* 25 in *Stacions Rome* (1867) 38 Hale the bowelyne! now, vere the shete. **1549** *Compl. Scot.* vi. 40 Hail out the mane sail boulene. **1594** GREENE *Look. Glasse* (1861) 134 We sail'd amain and let the bowling fly. **1622** HEYLIN *Cosmogr.* IV. (1682) 87 That piece of Tackle which our Mariners now called the Bolin. **1636** B. JONSON *Discov.*, Tell them of the main-sheet, and the boulin. **1666** *Lond. Gaz.* No. 31/1 Without cutting his Bowlings, or discharging one Gun. **1773** *Gentl. Mag.* 143, I haul'd up my bowlines, and to the wind laid. **1832** MARRYAT *N. Forster* xlvii, Let go the main-top bowling.

2. Short for *bowline-knot* (see 4).

1823 F. COOPER *Pioneer* xxiv. (1869) 107/2 It would have been more ship-shape to lower the bight of a rope, or running bow-line below me.

3. *on a bowline*: said of a ship when close-hauled, (i.e. with the bow-line) so as to sail close to the wind.

1625 PURCHAS *Pilgrimes* IV. 1174 The wind was so narrow that we stood upon a bowling. **1840** R. DANA *Bef. Mast* x. 24 We were..obliged to..come upon a taut bowline. **1834** M. SCOTT *Cruise Midge* (1859) 480 Running in for San Andreas on a bowline. **1867** SMYTH *Sailor's Word-bk.* s.v., The ship sails on a bowline, or stands on a taut bowline.

4. *Comb.*: **bowline-bend,** a mode of fastening ropes together with two bow-line knots; **bowline-bridle** (see 1); **bowline-cringle,** an eye through which a bowline-bridle is fastened; **bowline-knot,** a simple but very secure knot, used in fastening the bowline-bridles to the cringles.

c **1860** H. STUART *Seaman's Catech.* 44 A fore course has one *bowline bridle and two cringles. **1627** CAPT. SMITH *Seaman's Gram.* v. 27 The *Boling knot is..fastened by the bridles into the creengles of the sailes. **1850** *Petrel* I. 83 Oh, that we had a bowline knot, to let down to him!

II. In *Ship-building.* '*Bowlines* are longitudinal curves representing the ship's fore-body cut in a vertical section.' Smyth *Sailor's Word-bk.*

†**bow-line**[2]. *Obs.* [f. BOW *sb.*[1] + LINE.] An arc of a circle.

1551 RECORDE *Pathw. Knowl.* I. xxii, Draw a cord or stryngline crosse the circle, then deuide into .ij. equall partes, both that corde, and also the bowe line, or arche line, that serueth to that corde. *Ibid.* I. xi, A bowline.

bowling ('bəʊlɪŋ), *vbl. sb.* [f. BOWL *v.*[2]]

1. Playing at bowls; the action of rolling a bowl or other round body.

1535 *Act 27 Hen. VIII*, xxv, Any open plaieng house or place for common bowling. **1612** BACON *Studies, Ess.* (Arb.) 13 Bowling is good for the Stone and Reines. **1705** HICKERINGILL *Priest-Cr.* II. vi. 66 They go to Shooting or Bowling as soon as Afternoon Service is done. **1801** STRUTT *Sports & Past.* III. vii. 235. **1879** *Daily News* 2 Sept. 3/1 Bowling was at all times a mild species of recreation.

2. *Cricket.* **a.** The action of 'delivering' the ball.

1755 *Game at Cricket* 6, *Laws.* **1859** *All Y. Round* No. 13. 306 Jim..go in: cut over the slow bowling. **1879** *Sat. Rev.* 5 July 21 Oxford was once more aided by the bowling of Mr. Jellicoe.

b. The strength or resources of the bowlers in a cricket team.

1845 W. DENISON *Cricketer's Compan.* (ed. 2) p. viii, Their great deficiency..is in bowling. **1893** R. DAFT *Kings of Cricket* xiii. 234 Surrey..possesses plenty of bowling and of quite the best quality.

c. *fig.*

1959 *Listener* 6 Aug. 222/2 A Minister at question time trying to stand up to accurate opposition bowling.

3. *Comb.*, as *bowling-day, -ground, -night*; **bowling-crease,** the line from behind which the bowler 'delivers' the ball in cricket; **bowling saloon** *U.S.*, a building equipped with bowling-alleys.

1755 *Game at Cricket* 6, *Laws*..The Bowling-Creases must be cut in a direct line from each Stump. *Ibid.* 8 If he delivers the Ball, with his hinder Foot over the Bowling-Crease, the Umpire shall call no Ball. **1842** DICKENS *Amer. Notes* I. vi. 208 A painted lamp directs you to the Bowling Saloon, or Ten-Pin alley. **1880** *Boy's Own Bk.* 105 Within the return-crease..and behind the bowling-crease, the bowler must stand when he delivers the ball.

bowling, variant of BOLLING *sb.*

'**bowling-'alley.** An alley or long enclosure for playing at bowls or skittles: cf. ALLEY 4.

1555 *Act 2 & 3 Phil. & M.* ix, Licence..for the having.. of any Bowling-Allies. **1612** ROWLANDS *Knave of Clubs*, At Bedlam bowling-alley, late Where citizens did bet. **1703** *Art's Improv.* I. 9 The Use of them, in Paving the Streets, and laying of bowling-Allies. **1884** *Harper's Mag.* Jan. 298/2 The establishment of a good bowling-alley.

'**bowling-green.** A smooth level lawn or green for playing bowls upon. (Hence a common simile 'as level (or smooth) as a bowling-green'.)

1646 EVELYN *Mem.* (1857) I. 227 The whole country flat and even as a bowling-green. *a* **1695** WOOD *Life* (1848) 267 Trained privately in New Coll. bouling-green. **1800** MAR. EDGEWORTH *Lottery* ii, Going to a bowling-green tea-party this evening. **1825** WATERTON *Wand. S. Amer.* I. i. 120 An immense plain..as level as a bowling-green.

bowlke, obs. form of BULK.

bowln(e, obs. f. BOLLEN, swollen.

bowlster, bowlt, obs. ff. BOLSTER, BOLT *v.*[1], [2].

'**bowly,** *a. Sc.* Also **bowlie, boolie.** [perh. f. BOW *sb.*[1] or [2] + -LY[1]; but cf. BOWL *v.*[3] and BOUL.] Bent, rounded.

1821 GALT *Ann. Par.* 131 It was of the goose species, only with short bowly legs. **1864** J. BROWN *Plain Wds. Health* 87 Your bowly back, your huge arms.

bowman[1] ('bəʊmən). Also 4–5 **boumon.** [f. BOW *sb.*[1] + MAN.]

1. A man who shoots with a bow; *esp.* a fighting man armed with a bow.

1297 R. GLOUC. 378 Spermen auote & bowmen, & al so arblastes. *c* **1400** *Destr. Troy* 5536 He was boumon of the best. **1581** J. BELL *Haddon's Answ. Osor.* 492 You are a prety bow man but your luck is very ill. **1598** BARRET *Theor. Warres* I. i. 3 Were there such bowmen as were in the old time. **1611** W. BARKSTED *Hiren* (1876) 105 Saturn wounded by loues little bowman. **1839** THIRLWALL *Greece* III. 375 Heavy infantry, with bowmen and slingers.

†**2.** Some kind of fish. *Obs.*

1610 W. FOLKINGHAM *Art of Survey* IV. iii. 63 Conger, Lampson, Bowman, Soles.

3. bowman's root: a name given to certain plants: *Gillenia trifoliata*, *Euphorbia corollata*, and *Isnardia alternifolia.*

bowman[2] ('baʊmən). *Naut.* [f. BOW *sb.*[2] + MAN.] The oarsman who sits nearest to the bow of a boat.

1829 MARRYAT *F. Mildmay* xix, The bowman holding on with the boat-hook. **1840** R. DANA *Bef. Mast* xxiii. 71 The bow-man had charge of the boat-hook and painter.

Bowman[3] ('bəʊmən). *Anat.* [The name of Sir William *Bowman* (1816–1892), English surgeon.] Used in the possessive in *Bowman's capsule*: a Malpighian capsule; *Bowman's glands*: tubular glands in the olfactory mucous membrane; *Bowman's membrane*: the anterior elastic lamina (see quot. 1900).

1882 D. B. DELAVAN in T. E. Satterthwaite *Man. Histol.* (ed. 2) xxii. 372 Bowman's glands, peculiar to the olfactory mucous membrane, are found in it in large numbers. A. MAYER in *Ibid.* xiv. 206 Bowman's capsule is composed of a structureless basement-membrane surrounding each glomerulus. **1898** W. H. H. JESSOP *Man. Ophthalmic Surgery* v. 69 The anterior homogeneous membrane (Bowman's). **1900** E. H. STARLING *Elem. Hum. Physiol.* (ed. 4) x. 445 The glomerular epithelium acts simply as a filter allowing the water and salts of the blood-plasma to pass into Bowman's capsule. **1900** C. H. MAY *Man. Diseases of Eye* viii. 112 Bowman's membrane is a thin, homogeneous membrane which separates the corneal epithelium from the proper substance of the cornea. **1927** HALDANE & HUXLEY *Animal Biol.* iv. 115 The end of the kidney tubule..is dilated to form a capsule (Bowman's Capsule).

bown(e, -nn(e, obs. ff. BOON, BOUN, BOUND.

bownce, bowns, obs. forms of BOUNCE.

bownd, -en, obs. form of BOUND, -EN.

bow-net ('bəʊnɛt). [f. BOW *sb.*[1] + NET: possibly the original form of the thing explained the name.]

1. A kind of trap used for lobsters, crayfish, etc., consisting now of a cylinder of wicker-work closed at one end and having a narrow, funnel-shaped entrance at the other; also called, a bow-weel.

a **1000** ÆLFRIC *Voc.* in Wr.-Wülcker 167 *Nassa* bogenet, *uel* leap. *Ibid.* 181 *Nassa*, æwul, *uel* boganet. **1552** HULOET, Bowe nette or weele, *nassa.* **1607** TOPSELL *Four-f. Beasts* 37 They take them in bow-nets..whereinto they enter for the food, but being entrapped cannot go forth again. **1639** HORN & ROB. *Gate Lang. Unl.* xxxviii. §427 A Fisherman fisheth with a bownet or weel, in a river. **1883** G. C. DAVIES *Norfolk Broads* xix. 145 Bow-nets set in the runs..for tench and eels.

2. A kind of net attached to a bow or arch of wood or metal, used by fowlers.

1875 'STONEHENGE' *Brit. Sports* I. IV. i. §4. 293 [Hawks] must be captured either by the bow-net or the hand-net.

bownogh, var. of BONAGH, *Obs.*, an Irish soldier.

bownte, obs. form of BOUNTY.

bow-pot, variant of BOUGH-POT.

bowpres, var. of BEAUPERS *Obs.*, a fabric.

bowr, bowre, obs. ff. BOWER *sb.*[1], [3].

bowrd(e, bowrder, var. of BOURD, BOURDER.

†**bowrugie.** *Obs. Sc.* [A corrupt derivative of BURGESS or ad. Fr. *burgeoisie*.] The 'Burgesses' or third estate of the Scottish Parliament.

c **1470** HENRY *Wallace* VIII. 4 In Sanct Jhonstoun.. assemblit clerk, barown, and bowrugie.

†**bowse**, *sb. Obs. rare.* [a. MDu. *buis* gun: cf. BUS and HARQUEBUS.] A harquebus.

1556 *Chron. Gr. Friars* (1852) 42 All London musterd in harnes, morys pykes, bowses, hand gons, and whytt cottes.

bowse, bowsie, var. of BOUSE, BOUSY.

†'**bowser**[1]. *Obs.* Also bowcer, bowsier. [Derivation uncertain: perhaps a corruption of AF. *bourser*, OF. *boursier*, BURSAR, f. *bourse*, purse.

Notwithstanding the form *bowcer*, and the agreement in sense with BOWCHER, the two words can hardly be identical, since there was no OF. *boucier, bouchier*, with suitable sense. But the two *bowser* and *bowger*, (*bowcher*) may have been confused in English.]

A treasurer, bursar. Hence '**bowsery**, a bursar's office, a bursary.

1534 HEN. VIII. *Liber Regis* (1786) p. xi, To serche and knowe the..names of the..almoner, bowser, hospyteler. **1552** R. HUTCHINSON *Serm. Lord's Supper* (1842) 225 Masters of colleges do call their stewards and bowsers to an account and audit. **1626** *Scogin's Jests* (N.) Had every night the keys of the bowcery and buttery delivered. **1631** T. POWELL *Tom of All Tr.* 149 To be head Bowsier of the Colledge. **1721–1800** BAILEY, *Bowser*, the Purser, or Treasurer of a College.

bowser[2] ('baʊzə(r)). [Trade name.] A petrol pump (chiefly *Austral.* and *N.Z.*); also, a petrol tanker used for fuelling aircraft, tanks, etc. Also *transf.*

1921 *Trade Marks Jrnl.* 26 Oct. 2060 Bowser... Oil and petrol pumps. S. F. Bowser & Company Incorporated... Fort Wayne..State of Indiana. **1934** *Bulletin* (Sydney) 18 July 11/4 In those days there was but one [petrol] pump storage system—the Yankee line, manufactured by one Bowser... 'Bowser' had gained general acceptance, at least in Australia. **1935** 'H. ADAIR' *Wanted a Son* II. viii. 228 They came to a petrol pump—a 'bowser' Alec called it. **1942** W. SIMPSON *One of our Pilots* 18 The hundred odd vehicles of our M.T. columns—petrol bowsers, tractors,..etc. **1943** *Amer. Speech* XVIII. 87 [In New Zealand] a pump at a filling-station is a *bowser*. **1963** D. IRVING *Destruction of Dresden* III. iii. 139 The bowsers were waiting to top up the tanks once again. **1968** P. SHARP *Railway Stations* 16 A water bowser (or tank on wheels) refills the cisterns in the roof of the coaches for the kitchens and toilets.

bowshot ('bəʊʃɒt). Forms: 3–5 bow(e)-schote, 6 -shote, bow-shotte, 7–8 bowshoot(e, 7– bowshot. [f. BOW *sb.*[1] + SHOT *sb.*] The distance to which an arrow can be shot from a bow.

c **1300** *K. Alis.* 3491 A bowe-schote fro the brynke. *c* **1450** LONELICH *Grail* xiii. 316 More than fowre bowschote. *c* **1532** LD. BERNERS *Huon* xcv. 308 Themperour..auaunsyd hym selfe a bowe shote before his companye. **1652** COTTERELL *Cassandra* I. v. 474 Within a Bow-shoot of their gates. **1734** tr. *Rollin's Anc. Hist.* (1827) II. II. 101 Within bowshot of it. **1814** SCOTT *Wav.* viii, About a bow-shot from the end of the village.

bowsie, var. of BOOZY, BOUSY.

bowsman ('baʊzmən). [ad. Fr. *bosseman* BOSMAN, misunderstood as 'bow's-man'.] = BOWMAN[2]: used of a man positioned at the bow without an oar, having certain specified duties.

1776 M. COCKING *Jrnl.* 10 Mar. in *Pubn. Hudson's Bay Rec. Soc.* (1951) XIV. 37 He..will make a proposal to them for employing Canadians to be engaged by him for a term of years at Montreal to serve as Bowsmen. **1804** LEWIS in *Jrnls. Lewis & Clark Exped.* (1904) I. 34 The one not engaged at the oar [of the batteau] will attend as the Bowsman. **1840** *Knickerbocker* XVI. 270 The delicious white-fish are so numerous, that the bow's-man takes his scoop-net and literally dips them into the boat. **1851** MELVILLE *Moby Dick* II. xii. 107 The mutineer was the bowsman of the mate. **1935** *Geogr. Jrnl.* LXXXV. 271 Not only the steersman but the bowsman. **1968** R. M. PATTERSON *Finlay's River* 63 The six members of Black's crew..consisted of bowsman and steersman, and four middlemen.

bowsom(e, -sum, obs. forms of BUXOM.

†**bowson** obs. dial. f. BAUSON, badger.

1617 ASSHETON *Jrnl.* (1848) 18 We had a bowson: wee wrought him out and killed him.

bowsprit ('bəʊsprɪt). Forms: α. 4 bouspret, 6 boespritte, 7– bowsprit; β. 6–7 boresprit, 7 boresprit, boar-spright; γ. 6 boltspreet, 7 boultspret, 7–9 boltsprit; δ. 7 boldspreet; ε. 7 bolesprit, bowle-, boulspret, boule spret, -sprit. [Found in all the mod. Teut. langs.: Du. *boegspriet*, LG. *bogspret*, Ger. *bug-*, *bogspriet* (from LG. or Du.), Sw. *bogspröt*, Da. *bogspryd*; in all connected with the ship's BOW, and with a word, in OE. *spréot* pole (ME. *spret, spreet*), Du. *spriet* spear, javelin, Sw. *spröt* insect's feeler. Cf. also OHG. *spriuzan*, MHG. *spriuzen* to prop. The origin seems to lie between LG., Du., and English: in the latter *spréot* was itself used in a nautical sense in OE. and ME. (see SPRIT). But against the compound *bow-sprit* being of English rise, are the late appearance of *bow* in the language, and the numerous perverted forms with *bore, boar, bolt, bold, bole, bowle*, which seem to show that the connexion with *bow* was not evident to English sailors, either in sense or pronunciation. (Quotations for the word are very rare before 1590.)]

1. A large spar or boom running out from the stem of a vessel, to which (and the jib-boom and flying jib-boom, which extend beyond it) the foremast stays are fastened.

α. *c* **1330** R. BRUNNE *Chron.* (K.O.) Bouspret. *a* **1500** *Chester Pl.* (MS. 1592) I. (1843) 48 With toppe-castill and boe-spritte. **1634** BRERETON *Trav.* I. 169 The bow-sprit or sprit-sail [mast] which stands sloping even over the beak-head. **1700** TYRRELL *Hist. Eng.* II. 833 Their Bowsprits armed with Iron. **1805** in Nicolas *Disp. Nelson* VII. 189 *note*, Found the bowsprit badly wounded, and bowsprit-shrouds shot away. **1842** DICKENS *Amer. Notes* (1850) 56/2 By the water side, where the bowsprits of ships stretch across the footway. **1875** 'STONEHENGE' *Brit. Sports* II. VIII. i. §3 The forward rig also changed, from the bumpkin bowsprit and one head sail, to a long running bowsprit and full-sized flat jib.

β. **1594** W. PHILLIPS *Linschoten's Trav.* in Arb. *Garner* III. 428 Our boresprit touched the shore. **1610** SHAKS. *Temp.* I. ii. 200 On the Top-mast, The Yards and Boresprit, would I flame distinctly. *a* **1623** tr. *Camden's Hist. Eliz.* III. (1688) 413 Brake her Fore mast or Boresprit. **1655** HEYWOOD *Fortune by Land.* IV. Wks. 1874 VI. 416 Our Mainsail, Boar-spright, and our Mizen.

γ. **1591** PERCIVALL *Sp. Dict., Cevadera*, the saile of the boltspreet. **1600** HAKLUYT *Voy.* (1810) III. 125 The yce.. touched their boltsprit. **1627** CAPT. SMITH *Seaman's Gram.*, Boultspret Ladder..made fast ouer the Boulspret to get vpon it. **1719** DE FOE *Crusoe* (1869) 294 She had lost her Maintop-mast, Fore-mast and Boltsprit. **1815** SCOTT *Ld. of Isles* I. xiv. 12 Her boltsprit kissed the broken waves.

δ. **1652** *Proc. Parliament* No. 170 Putting out the Parliaments Jack on the Boldspreet end, and the English Ensign on the Poop.

ε. **1617** MINSHEU *Sp. Dict., Bauprez*..the bole-sprit of a ship. **1626** CAPT. SMITH *Accid. Yng. Seamen* 15 The fore mast, misen and bowlespret..the boulespret hath no bow lines. **1634** SIR. T. HERBERT *Trav.* 182 Her bole-sprit broke our mizen shroudes. **1691** T. H[ALE] *Acc. New Invent.* 120 From the extremity of the Boulsprit to the Lanthorn.

†2. *fig.* The human nose. *humorous. Obs.*

1690 SHADWELL *Am. Bigot* V. Wks. 1720 IV. 295 Thy.. nose, that bolt-sprit of thy face. **1691** —— *Scowrers* V, They do not consider the tenderness of my bolt-sprit.

†'**bowssen**, *v. Obs.* Also boossen, bous(s)en, bowsen. [ad. Cornish *beuzi* 'to immerge, drown', according to Williams 'a later form of *bedhy, bidhy*, or *budhy*, Breton *beuzi*, Welsh *boddi* to drown: (*Bidhyzi*, mentioned by Borlase, is a different word, being 'a late form of *bedidhia* to dip, baptize', Breton *badeza*, Welsh *bedydhio*, ad. L. *baptizā-re*.)]

trans. To immerse or duck (in a holy well). Hence '**bowssening** *vbl. sb.*

1602 CAREW *Cornwall* 123 a, There were many bowssening places, for curing of mad men..if there appeared small amendment he was bowssened againe and againe. **1758** BORLASE *Cornwall* 302 The Cornish call this immersion Boossenning, from Beuzi or Bidhyzi, in the Cornu-British, and Armoric, signifying to dip or drown. **1856** J. ALLEN *Hist. Liskeard* iv. 46 The spring..is said to have been used for bowsening or plunging an insane person suddenly, in order to restore him. **1865** L'ESTRANGE *Yachting W. Eng.* 300 Holy wells..used as bowssening, or ducking pools for the cure of madness.

†**bowstaff.** *Obs.* Pl. **bowstaves.** [f. BOW *sb.*[1] 4.] A stick to be made into a bow.

[**1394** in Hakluyt *Voy.* I. 167 In the yeere of our Lord 1394 ..werke, wax, osmunds, and bowstaues, to the value of 1060 nobles.] **1436** *Pol. Poems* (1859) II. 171 Osmonde, coppre, bow-staffes, stile, and wex. **1540** *Act 32 Hen. VIII*, xiv, For euery xxiiii. bundelles of bowstaues xxvis. viiid. **1641** *Termes de la Ley* 172 Garble is to sort and chuse the good from the bad as the Garbling of Bowstaves. **1720** *Stow's Surv.* (ed. Strype 1754) II. v. xiii. 304/2 Bow Staves and arrows at low prices.

bowstar, -ster, -stowre, Sc. ff. BOLSTER.

†**bow-sting.** *Obs. Sc.* = BOWSTAFF.

1551 *Aberdeen Reg.* V. 21 (JAM.) Valit bowstingis, price of the scoir vi ll. Scottis money.

†'**bowstowre.** *Obs. rare.* [perh. a. OF. *bosteor, var. of *bouteor*, f. *bouter* (also *boster*) to strike, knock, as in 'bosterent a la porte' (Godef.).]

perh. = Striker, knocker (a battering-ram).

c **1425** WYNTOUN *Cron.* VIII. xxxiv. 23 Browcht a Gyne, men callyd Bowstowre For til assayle that stalwart towre.

Bow-street ('bəʊstriːt). A street in London near Covent-Garden, in which the principal metropolitan police-court is situated: hence **Bow-street officer, -runner**, etc., a police officer.

1812 *Examiner* 19 Oct. 663/1 Supported by a Bow-street Officer. **1838** DICKENS *O. Twist* xxx, 'It's the runners!' ..'The what!'..'The Bow-street officers.'

bow-string, bowstring ('bəʊstrɪŋ). [f. BOW *sb.*[1] + STRING *sb.*]

1. The string of a bow; also *fig.*

1486 *Bk. St. Albans* B vi, Tho saame lewnes þou shalt fastyn slackely as a bowstryng vnocupyede. **1564** *Act 8 Eliz.* x. §4 An Armouror, Fletcher or maker of Bowstrings. **1626** BACON *Sylva* §993 Sound will be conveyed to the Eare, by striking upon a Bow-string, if the Horne of the Bow be held to the Eare. **1809** CAMPBELL *Gertrude* III. xiv, The bow-string of my spirit was not slack. **1814** SCOTT *Ld. of Isles* VI. xxii, At once ten thousand bow-strings ring, Ten thousand arrows fly!

2. As used in Turkey for strangling offenders.

1603 KNOLLES *Hist. Turks* (1638) 258 [He] commanded the executioner presently to strangle him with a bow string. **1768** TUCKER *Lt. Nat.* II. 79 The Turks can now.. discharge their ministers by other methods than the bow-string. *a* **1839** PRAED *Poems* (1865) II. 45 As if apprenticed to the work, He ties the bowstring round the Turk.

3. *Attrib.* and *Comb.*, as ***bowstring-maker***; **bow-string bridge**, a bridge consisting of an arch and horizontal tie, to resist the horizontal thrust; hence **bowstring-girder**; **bowstring hemp**, plants of the genus *Sanseviera*, N.O. *Liliaceæ*, found both in Africa and India, of the fibres of which bow-strings are made.

1530 PALSGR. 200/2 Bowstryng maker *faisevr de cordes a larc.* **1724** *Lond. Gaz.* No. 6249/6 William Boyworth..Bow-string-maker. **1866** *Treas. Bot.* s.v. *Sanseviera*, The Bowstring Hemps are stemless perennial plants.

bowstring ('bəʊstrɪŋ), *v.* [f. prec. sb. The pa. t. and pple. ought to be *bowstringed*, but *bowstrung* is also found, from the vb. *to* STRING.] *trans.* To strangle with a bow-string.

1803 *Edin. Rev.* I. 359 The vizier who commands a vanquished army..is generally bowstringed. **1840** POE *Wks.* 1864 I. 132 It was high time for her to get up and be bow-strung. **1884** *Graphic* 23 Aug. 204/2 He took his bow and bowstrung him.

Hence '**bowstringer** and '**bowstrung** *ppl. a.*

1820 BYRON *Juan* V. cxlvii, His lately bowstrung brother caused his rise. **1839** STONEHOUSE *Axholme* 426 The first settler was chief of the bow stringers who attended his [the Conqueror's] army.

bowsum, obs. form of BOSOM, BUXOM.

bowsy, variant of BOUSY, BOOZY.

bowt(e, obs. form of BOLT, BOUT, BOUGHT.

bowtel(l, variant of BOLTEL, a plain circular moulding.

bowthe, bowther, obs. ff. BOOTH, BOULDER.

bowtifew, var. of BOUTEFEU, *Obs.*, an incendiary.

bow-weed, corruptly **bow-wood**. A popular name of *Centaurea nigra*: cf. BULLWEED.

BRITTEN & HOLLAND cite *Appendix* to GERARD.

bow-window ('bəʊ-'wɪndəʊ). [f. BOW *sb.*[1]]

1. A Bay-window segmentally curved on plan; called in *A.P.S. Dict. Arch.*, a *Bow Bay-window*.

Often used as co-extensive with *bay-window*, whence 'such absurdities of diction as "square bow windows"'. *Bay-window* is generic, *bow-window* specific, and of much later rise, this form of bay being rare in earlier times.

1753 RICHARDSON *Grandison* (1781) VI. xxiv. 136 The other seats of the bow-window. **1794** REPTON *Landscape Gard.* (1805) 178 Large recesses or bays, sometimes called bowre windows, and now bow windows. **1816** JANE AUSTEN *Emma* II. ix. 198 A string of dawdling children round the baker's bow-window. **1850** THACKERAY *Pendennis* xxxv. (1884) 339 His common lounge was the bow-window of White's.

2. *slang.* A big belly.

1840 MARRYAT *Poor Jack* i, A very large man..with what is termed a considerable *bow-window* in front.

Hence '**bow-,windowed**, having bow-windows; also (*slang*) big-bellied.

1868 HOLME LEE *B. Godfrey* ix. 44 The upstairs bow-windowed room. **1850** THACKERAY *Pendennis* xxxiv. (1884) 334 Look at that very bow-windowed man.

bow-wise ('bəʊwaɪz), *adv.* [f. BOW *sb.*[1] + -WISE.] In the form or figure of a bow.

1398 TREVISA *Barth. de P.R.* VIII. xvii. (1495) 320 Now she [the mone] shewyth herself shape a bowe wyse and now as a cercle. **1583** STANYHURST *Æneis* III. (Arb.) 87 The hauen from the eastcoast, in bowewise, crooked apereth. **1842** MRS. BROWNING *Grk. Chr. Poets.* (1863) 61 Streaked bow-wise, with a livid white and red.

bow-wow, *int.* and *sb.* Also 7 bowgh-wawgh, bough-wough, 8 bough waugh. [Imitative. Other forms are BAUGH, BOUGH, BAW-WAW, q.v.]

1. ('baʊ'waʊ) An imitation of the barking of a dog.

1576 LAMBARDE *Peramb. Kent* (1826) 233. [See BAW-WAW.] **1610** SHAKS. *Temp.* I. ii. 382 Harke, harke, bowgh wawgh: the watch-Dogges barke. **1651** OGILBY *Æsop* (1665) 53 Bough wough, Whose that dare break Into my master's House? **1682** OTWAY *Venice Pres.* III. i. 35 Now, bough waugh, waugh, bough waugh (Barks like a dog). **1855** BROWNING *Holy-Cross Day* in *Men & Wom.* II. 160 Bow, wow, wow,—a bone for the dog!

2. a. as *sb.* The bark of a dog; also *fig.*

1785 [see BARKING *ppl. a.*[1] 2 b]. **1826** GALT *Last of Lairds* xviii. 165 It's a sore thing for a man to be frightened into his first marriage by the bow wow o' a kirk session. **1849** W. IRVING *Crayon Misc.* 211 With a deep-mouthed bow-wow. **1854** GILFILLAN *Beattie's Poems* Introd. 16 The deep bow-wows of Johnson's talk.

b. *attrib.* ('baʊwaʊ), as in ***bow-wow theory***, applied in ridicule to the theory that human speech originated in the imitation of animal sounds.

1826 SCOTT *Jrnl.* 14 Mar. (1939) I. 135 The Big Bow-wow strain I can do myself like any now going. **1864** MAX MÜLLER *Sc. Lang.* Ser. II. 87 The strong objection..to what I called the Bow-wow and the Pooh-pooh theories. **1883** *Century Mag.* XXVI. 33 Advocates of the 'Bow-wow' theory of the origin of language may find convincing facts among the Zuñis.

c. quasi-*adj.* Dog-like, snarling, barking.

1785 LD. PEMBROKE in Boswell *Jrnl. Tour Hebrides* 8 Dr. Johnson's sayings would not appear so extraordinary, were it not for his *bow-wow way.* **1854** H. MILLER *Sch. & Schm.* (1858) 344 He could recite in the 'big bow-wow style'.

3. *transf.* A dog. *humorous* or as *nursery term.* Also *to go to the bow-wows*: to go 'to the dogs'. *jocular colloq.*

1785 GROSE *Dict. Vulgar T., Bow-wow,* the childish name for a dog. *a* **1800** COWPER *Beau's Reply* (D.) Nor some reproof yourself refuse From your aggrieved bow-wow. **1839** DICKENS *Nickleby* lxiv. 617 It is all up with its handsome friend, he has gone to the demnition bow-wows. **1893** W. K. POST *Harvard Stories* 114 Everything was going to the bow-wows. **1917** H. A. VACHELL *Fishpingle* xiii. 263 He was going fast to the bowwows before I went to India. **1931** R. CAMPBELL *Georgiad* i. 20 All the bow-wows, poodles, tykes and curs.

bow-wow (baʊ'waʊ), *v.* [f. prec.] *intr.* To bark; also *fig.* to snarl, growl. Hence **bow-'wower, bow-'wowing.**

1832 MARRYAT *N. Forster* i, To be snarled at, and bow-wowed at, in this manner, by those who find fault. *a* **1845** HOOD *To Hahnemann* vi, Stop his *bow-wow-ing.* **1850** CARLYLE *Latt.-day Pamph.* viii, To be bullied and bowowed out of your loyalty to the God of Light.

bowy, obs. form of BOUGHY *a*, and BOWIE.

bowyang ('bəʊjæŋ). *Austral.* and *N.Z.* Also boyang. [f. dial. *bowy-yanks* (see *E.D.D.*), *bow-yankees* (see Halliwell), leather leggings. Cf. also *Sc. Nat. Dict.* s.v. *Booyangs, Bonanks.*] A band or strap worn about the trousers below the knee, esp. by labourers.

1893 *Warracknabeal Herald* 22 Sept., To those not in the cult of 'boyang worship', it may be necessary to explain that the two straps used to hitch the lower part of labourers' trousers are 'boyangs'. **1927** J. DEVANNY *Old Savage* 121 He missed his bowyangs dreadfully. **1948** A. P. GASKELL in *Coast to Coast 1947* 259 Progressive all right... I was the first in my district to appear at a dance without bowyangs. **1956** G. BOWEN *Wool Away!* (ed. 2) ii. 15 Without bowyangs, and with sheep working on the legs all the time, trousers would soon work down. **1965** *N.Z. Listener* 26 Feb. 15/1 *Bow-yangs,* laces tied around the trouser legs below the knee to prevent drag when shearers bend over.

bowyer ('bəʊɪə(r)). Forms: 3 bowiare, 5 bowȝere, 6 bowere, bowyere, 6 boier, bowier, 7 boweyer, 6- bowyer. [f. BOW *sb.* + -YER: cf. *lawyer.*]

1. One who makes, or trades in, bows.

1297 R. GLOUC. 541 The bowiares ssoppe hii breke & the bowes nome ech on. *c* **1440** *Promp. Parv.* 46 Bowȝere [**1499** bowyere], *arcuarius.* **1514** FITZHERB. *Justyce Peas* (1538) 92 Every boier make..two bowes of elme. **1544** ASCHAM *Toxoph.* (Arb.) 20 No man will be offended—excepte it be summe fletchers and bowiers. **1697** *View Penal Laws* 8 Concerning Bowyers and the making and keeping of Bows. **1862** MARSH *Eng. Lang.* xii. 182 The arrow-makers, or fletchers..had as full a vocabulary as the bowyers.

2. A bowman, an archer. Also *attrib.*

c **1440** *Promp. Parv.* 46/1 Bowȝere..*architenens.* **1725** POPE *Odyss.* VIII. 260 Who boldly durst defy the Bowyer God. **1808** SCOTT *Marm.* II. xv, His Norman bowyer band. **1870** BRYANT *Iliad* I. v. 156 The bowyer-god, Apollo.

Bowyers mustard: see BOOR.

bowza, variant of BOZA, a drink.

bowze, bowzy, var. of BOUSE, BOUSY.

bowzey, obs. form of BOOSY *dial.*, cow-stall.

box (bɒks), *sb.*[1] *Bot.* Also 4-7 boxe. [OE. *box,* ad. L. *bux-us* box-tree, Gr. *πύξος.*]

1. A genus (*Buxus*) of small evergreen trees or shrubs of the N.O. *Euphorbiaceæ*; specially *B. sempervirens*, the Common or Evergreen Box-tree, a native of Europe and Asia; a shrub with deep-green leaves of a thick leathery texture. It is much used in ornamental gardening, *esp.* in a dwarfed variety (***dwarf*** or ***ground box***) for the edgings of flower-beds.

931 *Chart. Æðelstan* in *Cod. Dipl.* V. 195 Of ðere ȝemear-codan æfsan to ðon readan slo..of ðam treowe to ðere wican æt ðam boxe. *a* **1000** ÆLFRIC *Voc.* in Wr.-Wülcker 139 *Buxus,* box. **1382** WYCLIF *Isa.* lx. 13 The fyrr tree, and box, and pyne tree togidere. *c* **1420** *Anturs of Arth.* vi, Vndur a lefe tale Of box and of barbere byggyt. **1551** TURNER *Herbal* G vj a, The wood of boxe is yelowe and pale. **1578** LYTE *Dodoens* VI. xxxii. 699 The smal Boxe is called of some in Latine, *Humi Buxus*: that is to say, Ground Boxe, or Dwarffe Boxe. **1713** *Guardian* No. 173 (1756) II. 360 There ships of myrtle sail in seas of box. **1830** TENNYSON *A Spirit haunts,* Fading edges of box beneath. **1836** *Penny Cycl.* VI. 75/2 The Majorca box..is a handsomer plant..with broader leaves, and a more rapid growth.

2. The wood of the box-tree, BOX-WOOD; much used by turners and wood-engravers. Also *fig.*

c **1385** CHAUCER *L.G.W.* 867 Pale as box sche was. **1398** TREVISA *Barth. De P.R.* XVII. xix, Also of boxe beþ boxes made to kepe in muske and oþer spicerye. **1553** EDEN *Treat. New Ind.* (Arb.) 16 *Rhinoceros*..of the colour of boxe. **1635** J. BABINGTON *Pyrotechn.* 1 You must get of the best drie Box you can finde. **1677** MOXON *Mech. Exerc.* (1703) 347 Made on Box or Brass of most Mathematical Instrument Makers. **1852** MCCULLOCH *Dict. Comm.* 189 Box is a very valuable wood. It is of a yellowish colour, close-grained, very hard, and heavy.

3. *Comb.* and *Attrib.*

a. *attrib.* Of box or box-wood; pale as box.

1382 WYCLIF *Isa* xxx. 8 Wryt to it vp on a box table. **1598** E. GILPIN *Skial.* (1878) 43 Their box complexions..Their iaundice looks. **1677** *Lond. Gaz.* No. 1245/4 One Box Comb. One Pocket Handkerchief. **1693** W. ROBERTSON *Phraseol. Gen.* 276 Boxteeth, teeth as yellow as box. **1714** *Fr. Bk. of Rates* 359 The Trade of Ivory-Combs, and also Horn-Combs, and Box-Combs. **1884** *Cassell's Fam. Mag.* Feb. 141/2 Anything..in the way of box edging.

b. *Comb.*, as ***box-bordered, box-like*** adj.; **box-berry,** the fruit (and plant) of the winter-green of America (*Gaultheria procumbens*); **box-edged** *a.*, having a border of box plants; so ***box-edge*** (cf. quot. 1884 under 3 a); **box-elder, -alder,** a North American tree, the Ash-leaved Maple (*Acer negundo*); **box-gum** *Austral.*, one of various species of *Eucalyptus* (cf. c below). **box-holly,** a name of Butcher's broom (*Ruscus aculeatus*); **box-slip,** a slip of box inlaid in the beechwood of some carpenters' planes in order to give durability to the edge; **box-thorn,** common name for shrubs of the genus *Lycium*, esp. *L. barbarum.* Also BOX-TREE, BOX-WOOD.

1851 S. JUDD *Margaret* II. i. 162 The path was strewn with old claret *boxberries. **1884** *Harper's Mag.* Oct. 661/2 A *box-bordered plat. **1932** AUDEN *Orators* II. 63 Between *box-edges, past the weathering urns. **1909** *Cent. Dict.* Suppl., *Box-edged. **1945** E. WAUGH *Brideshead Revisited* 71 The box-edged walks of the kitchen gardens. **1866** *Treas. Bot.* 781/1 The *Box Elder..is sometimes introduced into English shrubberies. **1887** D. MACDONALD *Gum Boughs* 7 The clumps of *box-gums clinging together for sympathy. **1661** LOVELL *Hist. Anim. & Min.* 79 They [Rhinoceroses] have..a *Boxe-like colour. **1678** W. SALMON *Pharm. Lond.* I. iv. 74 *Lycium, Pyxacantha, Buxea spina*..*Boxthorn. **1846** MRS. LOUDON *Ladies' Comp. Flower-Gard.* 130 *Lycium, Solanaceæ,* Boxthorn.

c. Applied with distinguishing epithet to several other plants, as **bastard box,** *Polygala chamæbuxus*; **flowering box,** *Vaccinium Vitis-Idæa*, having leaves like those of the box; **grey box,** *Eucalyptus dealbata* of S. Australia; † **prickly box,** the box-thorn (*Lycium*), also the butcher's broom, *Ruscus aculeatus* (Lyte); **Queensland box,** *Lophostemon macrophyllus*; **red box** (of New South Wales), *L. australis*; **spurious box,** *Eucalyptus leucoxylon*, of S. Australia; **Tasmanian box,** *Bursaria spinosa.* Applied to many Australasian species of *Eucalyptus* (see quots.), *Tristania conferta* (bastard, brisbane, brush, red, or white box), and some other trees: see Morris *Austral English.*

1578 LYTE *Dodoens* VI. xiii. 674 Butchers broome..is called..in base Almaigne, Stekende palme, that is to say, Prickley Boxe. *Ibid.* xxxiii. 699 Prickley Boxe is a tree not much vnlyke to the other Boxe. **1820** J. OXLEY *Jrnl. Two Exped. into N.S. Wales* 15 The timber, dwarf box, and gum trees (all eucalypti), with a few cypresses and camarinas. *Ibid.* 227 The country..thickly timbered, chiefly with the species of eucalyptus called box. **1866** LINDLEY & MOORE *Treas. Bot., Box*..White, of Australia, *Eucalyptus albens.* Yellow, of Australia, *Eucalyptus melliodora.* **1889** J. H. MAIDEN *Usef. Native Pl. Australia* 121 Native box..is greedily eaten by sheep,..usually a small scrub, in congenial localities it develops into a small tree. *Ibid.* 468 *Eucalyptus hemiphloia*... This is a common 'Box' of New South Wales and Queensland. **1964** R. HOLT in R. Ward *Penguin Bk. Austral. Ballads* 198 Gidgee, myall, box and jarrah.

box (bɒks), *sb.*[2] Also *Sc.* boxse, boxe. [OE. *box* neut. or masc.: it is not clear whether this was (1) another sense of *box*, the name of the tree, (2) an independent adoption of L. *buxum* boxwood, in the sense of a thing made of box, or (3) an altered form of L. *pyx-is* (*puxis,* med.L. *buxis*) box: see PYX. In favour of the latter cf. OHG. *buhsa* fem. (MHG. *buhse, bühse,* Ger. *büchse,* MDu. *busse, bosse,* Du. *bus, bos*) on OTeut. type **buksja-*, ad. L. *pyxis* or Gr. *πύξις* box. As the latter was f. *πύξος* box-wood, the L. form of which was *buxus,* late and med.L. had many forms with initial *b,* as *buxis, buxida, buxta, boxta, bosta, bossida* (cf. BOIST), from some of which the Teutonic forms might well be derived.]

I. 1. A case or receptacle usually having a lid; **a.** orig. applied to a small receptacle of any material for drugs, ointments, or valuables; **b.** gradually extended (since 1700) to include cases of larger size, made to hold merchandise and personal property; but (unless otherwise specified) understood to be four-sided and of wood.

a **1000** ÆLFRIC *Voc.* in Wr.-Wülcker 124 *Pixis,* bixen box. *c* **1000** *Ags. Gosp.* Matt. xxvi. 7 Ða ȝenealæte him to sum wif, seo hæfde box [Vulg. *alabastrum*] mit deorwyrðe sealfe. *c* **1200** *Trin. Coll. Hom.* 145 Hie nam ane box ȝemaked of marbelstone and hine fulde mid derewurðe smerieles. **1393** LANGL. *P. Pl.* C. XIV. 54 As þe messager..bereþ bote a boxe a breuet þer-ynne. *c* **1440** *Promp. Parv.* 46 Box or boyste, *pixis.* **1480** *Cath. Angl.* 39 A Box, *pixis.* **1526** *Pilgr. Perf.* (W. de W. 1531) 286 b, The swete oyntement..was closed and shutte in the boxe. **1580** BARET *Alv.* B 1083 Boxes or chestes where grocers put there spices and wares. **1592** SHAKS. *Rom. & Jul.* V. i. 45 And about his [the apothecary's] shelues A beggerly account of emptie boxes..thinly scattered, to make vp a shew. **1611** BIBLE *2 Kings* ix. 1 Take this boxe of oile in thine hand. —— *Transl. Pref.* 1 Certaine bare themselves as auerse from them as from..boxes of poison. **1677** *Lond. Gaz.* No. 1263/4 Three Silver Boxes, one for Sugar, one for Pepper, and one for Mustard. **1751** JOHNSON *Rambl.* No. 171 ⁋7 My landlady..took the opportunity of my absence to search my boxes. **1862** BURTON *Bk.-hunter* I. 15 His spoil, packed in innumerable great boxes. **1875** URE *Dict. Arts* II. 471 Sand and loam (packed tightly into metal boxes, called flasks).

c. *fig.*

1606 SHAKS. *Tr. & Cr.* V. i. 29 Why thou damnable box of enuy thou. *a* **1618** RALEIGH *Rem.* (1664) 89 It is an essentiall property of a man truly wise, not to open all the boxes of his bosome. **1653** WALTON *Angler* 220, I have several boxes in my memory in which I will keep them all very safe.

d. *Austral.* and *N.Z.* A mixing up of different flocks of sheep; also *transf.*; also with *up.* Cf. sense 21 and BOX *v.*[1] 5 b.

1872 C. H. EDEN *My Wife & I in Queensland* iii. 67 Great care must of course be taken that no two flocks come into collision, for a 'box', as it is technically called, causes an infinity of trouble. **1941** BAKER *N.Z. Slang* v. 39 A *box-up,* a state of confusion, and *to be in a box,* to be in a confused state of mind, in a quandary.

2. With various substantives indicating its purpose, position, etc., as ***bonnet-, cartridge-, coal-, collecting-, dirt-, hat-, letter-, light-, match-, missionary-, money-, pepper-, pill-, pillar-, poor-, sand-, savings-, snuff-, tar-, touch-box***; also DICE-BOX, and with a more specific signification, ***fire-, smoke-, steam-box,*** etc.

1638 SHIRLEY *Mart. Soldier* IV. iii. in Bullen *Old. Pl.* (1882) I. 236 The Sand of a Scriveners Sand-boxe. **1709** STEELE *Tatler* No. 79 ⁋1, I made her resign her Snuff-Box for ever. **1722** *Lond. Gaz.* No. 6068/8 One Pepper-box, two Salts. *c* **1730** SWIFT *Directions Housemaid,* Leave a pail of dirty water, a coal-box, a bottle, a broom. **1808** R. PORTER *Trav. Sk. Russ. & Swed.* (1813) I. i. 11 A broad belt, to which hangs an unwieldly cartridge-box. **1875** URE *Dict. Arts* III. 1079 *Water-Meter,* A dirt box is attached to each end of the meters. **1883** *Fisheries Exhib. Catal.* 217 Cigar boxes, jewel boxes, handkerchief boxes, glove boxes, match boxes.

3. In various contextual applications: † **a.** The pyx or receptacle for the consecrated host; † **b.** A surgeon's box, used as a cupping-glass (cf. BOIST); **c.** A ballot-box; **d.** A dice-box; **e.** A letter-box; **f.** The receptacle for infants at the gate of a foundling hospital.

1297 R. GLOUC. 456 þe box ek, þat hong ouer the weued, myd Godes fless & blod. **1533** ELYOT *Cast. Helth* (1541) 61 Application of boxes about the stomake, in hot feuers, are to be eschewed. **1549** THOMAS *Hist. Italic* (1561) 79 Boxes, into whiche, if he wyll, he may let fall his ballot. **1556** *Chron. Gr. Friars* (1852) 55 Spekyng agayne the sacrament of the auter..callyd it Jacke of the boxe. **1562** BULLEYN *Sicke Men, &c.* 52 b, Aplie boxis with skariffaction. **1604** BRETON *Pass. Sheph.* III. in *Spenser's Wks.* (Grosart) III. Introd. 29 Or to see the subtle fox, How the villain plies the box. **1680** COTTON in Singer *Hist. Cards* 332, I have seen a losing gamester greedily gnawing the innocent box. **1753** CHAMBERS *Cycl. Supp.* s.v. *Box,* Our sharpers have opportunities of playing divers tricks with the box, as palming, topping, slabbing. *a* **1853** A. OPIE *Bank Note,* It is ..necessary that a person whom I can trust should put the letter in the box. **1873** MORLEY *Rousseau* I. 118 The new-born child was dropped into oblivion in the box of the asylum for foundlings.

g. A receptacle or pigeon-hole at a post office in which letters to a subscriber are placed; hence, a similar receptacle or the like at a newspaper office in which replies to an

BOX 462 BOX

advertiser are placed. orig. *U.S.* Cf. *box-letter, box number, box-rent* (sense 24).

1832 [see *box-letter*]. **1833** B. F. Hallett *Trial E. K. Avery* 43 E. K. Avery had a private box at my office. **1897** E. W. Brodhead *Bound in Shallows* 242 The following evening Dillon found in his post-office box a letter of one line. **1919** Wodehouse *My Man Jeeves* 119 My address will be Box 341, *London Morning News*. **1971** *Times Lit. Suppl.* 23 Apr. 487/2 The Times Canadian Service Division, Box 490, King City, Ontario.

h. (See quot.)

1889 *Atalanta* June 597/1 For flower-painting never use what is technically termed 'box', viz.: the muddy colour.. that is left on the sides of the colour-box from former usage.

i. = safe *sb.* 1 b. *slang* (orig. *U.S.*).

1904 'No. 1500' *Life in Sing Sing* xiii. 261 We got a country jug on our first touch, but the box wasn't heavy enough for five. **1904** H. Hapgood *Autobiogr. of Thief* vi. 120 He was one of the most successful box-men (safe-blowers) in the city. **1926** J. Black *You can't Win* viii. 89 We've got the combination of that box, kid. *Ibid.* ix. 104 Shorty was one of the patricians of the prison, a 'box man' doing time for bank burglary.

j. *colloq.* A gramophone, wireless set, or television set; spec. ***the box***: television; a television set. Cf. *magic box*.

1924 T. E. Lawrence *Lett.* (1938) 436, I..play Beethoven & Mozart to myself on the box. **1930** Kipling *Limits & Renewals* (1932) 208 It was one of his prerogatives to announce what the Man in the Box [*i.e.* wireless announcer] said about the sick Padishah. **1950** G. Marx *Let.* 6 Dec. (1967) 168, I have solved the television problem by having a remote control installed on the ugly box. **1958** *Observer* 18 May 14/2 'Contradiction is the very moving principle of the world!' The Box, with its abrupt switches from the trivial to the profound, is always providing illustrations to Hegel's pet dictum. **1963** E. Humphreys *Task* I. xi. 120, I saw one of your plays, Dicky. On the old box.

k. A coffin. *slang.*

Cf. quot. 1674 s.v. black *a.* 1 a.

1925 Fraser & Gibbons *Soldier & Sailor Words* 34 *The box*, a coffin. **1957** 'W. Henry' *Jesse James* 66 Personally, I'll believe he's dead when the box is shut and covered up.

4. a. *esp.* A money-box, containing either private or public funds, often with a defining word added.

c **1386** Chaucer *Cook's T.* 26 Ffor often tyme he foond his box [*v.r.* boxe] ful bare. **1393** Langl. *P. Pl.* C. I. 97 And boxes ben [broght] forþ [I-] bounden with yre. **1552-3** *Inv. Ch. Goods Stafford* 87 The poore mans box. *a* **1555** Lyndesay *Tragedy* 70, I purcheist—for my proffect singulare, My Boxsis and my Threasure tyll auance,—The Byschopreik of Merapose, in France. **1580** Baret *Alv.* B 1079 A boxe for almes or the poore mens boxe. **1607** Shaks. *Timon* III. i. 16 Nothing but an empty box, Sir, which..I come to intreat your Honor to supply. **1766** Goldsm. *Vic. W.* iv, He..was to have a halfpenny on Sunday to put into the poor's box.

b. *transf.* The money contained in such a box; a fund for a particular purpose. Cf. *box-club*.

1389 in *Eng. Gilds* (1870) 5 He schal haue of þe comune box xiiijd. *Ibid.* 7 Alle þe costages that be mad aboute hym be mad good of the box. **1439** *E.E. Wills* (1882) 113, I bequeth to the..Comune Box..vjs. viijd. **1621** Burton *Anat. Mel.* II. iii. VII. (1651) 356 With ordinary gamesters, the gains go to the box. **1775** Johnson *Lett.* cxii. (1788) I. 234 The ladies..pay each twopence a week to the box. **1830** Galt *Lawrie T.* I. ii. (1849) 5 She applied in her auld days for a recommendation to get her put upon the box.

5. Short for Christmas-box, q.v.

a **1593** H. Smith *Serm.* (1866) II. 240 The law is like a butlers-box, play still on till all come to the candestick. **1611** Cotgr., Such a box as our prentices beg before Christmas. **1621** W. Mason *Handf. Ess.* C ij, As an apprentices box of earth, apt he is to take all, but to restore none till hee be broken. **1629** Taylor *Wit & Mirth* in Brand *Pop. Ant.* (1870) I. 270 Westminster Hall..is like a Butler's Box at Christmas amongst gamesters: for whosoeuer loseth, the Box will bee sure to bee a winner. **1668** Pepys *Diary* 28 Dec., Called up by drums & trumpets; these things & boxes having cost me much money this Christmas. **1712** Steele *Spect.* No. 509 ¶3 The beadles & officers have the impudence at Christmas to ask for their box.

6. A box under the driver's seat on a coach; hence in general the seat on which the driver sits.

1625 *Knappe's Patent* No. 31 A devise whereby the coachman without comyng from his boxe shall..keepe the hinder wheeles from turninge. **1669** Evelyn *Mem.* (1857) II. 42 Our coachmen so drunk, that they both fell off their boxes on the heath. **1753** Chambers *Cycl. Supp.* s.v. *Box*, *Coach-box*, a place under the coachman's seat, wherein he puts what may be wanted for the service of the coach or horses. **1812** Jane Austen *Mansf. Pk.* (1870) I. viii. 67 The barouche would hold four perfectly well..independent of the box. **1884** Q. Victoria *More Leaves* 116 Brown as always, unless I mention to the contrary, on the box.

7. A box and its contents; hence a variable measure of quantity.

c **1305** *Judas* 131 in *E.E.P.* (1862) 110 If þe boxes hadde ibeon isolde..þe teoþing þerof was þrettie pans. **1377** Langl. *P. Pl.* B. XIII. 194 Haued nouȝt Magdeleigne more for a boxe of salue þan zacheus. **1706** Phillips, *Box* is also taken for an uncertain quantity of some Commodities; as of Prunelloes, 14 Pounds; of Quick-silver, from one to two Hundred Weight; of Rings for Keys, two Gross, etc. **1716** *Lond. Gaz.* No. 5438/4 Two Quarter Boxes of Lace and Edgings. **1852** McCulloch *Dict. Comm.* 667 Exportation of Sugar from Havannah in 1849: 614,366 boxes at 400 lbs. **1875** Jowett *Plato* (ed. 2) V. 36 He who is to be a workman should have his box of tools when he is a child. **1886** *Illust. Lond. News* 3 July 2/3 A 'box of whistles', otherwise an organ.

II. A compartment or place partitioned off for the separate accommodation of people or animals.

8. a. A seated compartment in a theatre, at first specially for ladies; often qualified, as ***front-, private-, side-, stage-, upper-***, etc. In *pl.* collectively for a distinct part of the auditorium.

(As *box*, when this sense arose, had not acquired the sense of a *large* wooden chest, but was chiefly an apothecary's pill box or ointment pot, or perhaps a 'jewel-box', its transference to the theatrical use was more remarkable than it seems to us with our notions of large 'boxes' for goods. Could it be at first humorous or jocular, with some reference to 'casket', 'jewel box', or 'box of ointment very precious'?)

1609 Dekker *Gull's Horn-bk.*, I mean not into the lords roome, which is now but the stages suburbs. No, these boxes..are contemptibly thrust into the reare. **1632** Massinger *City Mad.* II. ii, (*Anne*) The private box ta'en up at a new play For me and my retinue. **1667** Pepys *Diary* (1877) V. 60 We were forced to go into one of the upper boxes at 4*s.* a piece. **1755** Johnson *Dict.*, *Box*, the seats in the playhouse where the ladies are placed. **1779** Sheridan *Critic* I. i. 443 Applications from all quarters for my interest ..from ladies to get boxes. *a* **1845** Hood *United Fam.* xvi, Nine crowded in a private box. **1881** *Daily News* 12 Sept. 2/3 The auditorium, the boxes, upper circle, and gallery.

b. *transf.* The occupants of the boxes; *esp.* the ladies.

a **1700** Dryden (J.) The boxes and the pit Are sovereign judges of this sort of wit. *a* **1704** T. Brown *Persius* i. Prol. Wks. 1730 I. 51 Nor [I] from the tender boxes e'er Yet have drawn one pitying tear. **1711** Addison *Spect.* No. 40 Let him behave himself..abjectly towards the fair one, and it is ten to one but he proves a favourite of the boxes.

9. A compartment partitioned off in the public room of a coffee-house or tavern.

1712 Steele *Spect.* No. 266 ¶4, I went to an Inn in the City..I waited in one of the boxes. **1782** Cowper *Let. to Hill* 7 Dec., I see you in your box at the coffee-house. **1871** M. Collins *Mrq. & Merch.* I. ix. 290 An ancient coffee-room, divided into boxes in the snug old fashion.

10. a. Short for jury-box, witness-box.

1822 Lamb *Elia, Roast Pig*, Without leaving the box.. they brought in a simultaneous Verdict of Not Guilty. **1837** Dickens *Pickw.* xxxiv, Mr. Winkle entered the witness-box. Mr. Phunky ought to have got him out of the box with all possible dispatch. **1848** Macaulay *Hist. Eng.* II. 385 The jury appeared in their box. **1880** *Daily Tel.* 4 Nov., By his country, represented by twelve men in a box, he will be tried.

b. = confessional *sb.* 2 a.

1922 Joyce *Ulysses* 726, I wonder did he know me in the box.

11. a. Applied to an old square pew in a church, to a prison-cell, and the hinder compartment in a boat.

1709 *Let. to Ld. M[ayor]* 4 Some who sat in the Stalls and Boxes at St. Paul's titter'd. **1834** Ainsworth *Rookwood* III. v. (1878) 200 In a box of the stone jug I was born. **1867** Smyth *Sailor's Word-bk.*, *Box*, the space between the backboard and stern-post of a boat, where the coxswain sits.

b. *U.S.* The station occupied by various players in baseball; esp. either of the spaces in which the pitcher or the batter stands.

1881 *Detroit Free Press* 26 Sept. 1/5 Weidman..will have to go into the box for the remaining four games. **1909** *Collier's* 15 May 14/1 The pitcher was now contained in a box six feet square. **1944** Runyon *R. à la Carte* (1946) vi. 95 Putting the zing on Bill Terry for not taking Walker out of the box when Walker is getting a pasting from the other club.

c. *Cricket.* = gully *sb.*[1] 2 d.

1913 *Daily Mail* 7 July 9/2 Splendid catch anywhere near the wicket, especially in 'the box'. **1926** *Ibid.* 29 June 10/2 Hobbs was caught in that nondescript position which is variously known as 'the box' and 'the gully'.

12. A separate compartment or stall for a horse, etc., in a stable, or a railway truck. Also ***horse-box. loose box***: one in which the animal is free to move about.

1846 W. Andrew *Ind. Railw.* (ed. 2) 14 The horses came out of the horse boxes..as fresh as when they went into them. **1886** *Sat. Rev.* 6 Mar. 327/2 To get cast in a loose box half as big as a barn. *Ibid.* 328/1 [A racehorse]..found huddled up in the corner of his box, shaking from head to foot.

III. A box-like shelter; a hut, or small house.

13. a. A place of shelter for one or more men; as a sentry's, signalman's, or watchman's box; a sportsman's hiding-place while shooting.

b. *spec.* on the *Railway*. A small structure, generally on raised supports, from which the signals, switches, etc., of a section of a railway are worked.

1714 Gay *Trivia* II. 176 The Centry's Box. **1835** Hood *Dead Robbery* iii, The Watchman in his box was dosing. **1884** Speedy *Sport* x. 176 Grouse are not slow to discover any movement in the 'box'.

c. Short for *telephone box*.

1935 G. Greene *England Made Me* I. 16, I rang up..from a box in the Circus. **1961** 'T. Hinde' *For Good of Company* i. 16 Tony seized the phone and held it out of the box towards him.

14. A small country-house; a residence for temporary use while following a particular sport, as a ***hunting-, shooting-, fishing-box***.

1714 Ellwood *Autobiog.* 233, I took a pretty Box for him ..a mile from me. **1756** *Gentl. Mag.* XXVI. 445 And purchases his country box. **1756** J. Warton *Ess. Pope* (1782) III. I. 108 His father retired from business..to a little convenient box, at Binfield. **1825** Cobbett *Rur. Rides* 200 Rawlinson, who..has a box and some land here. **1873** Tristram *Moab* xi. 213 Some of these he may have employed to erect here a hunting-box.

IV. Technical usages.

15. A case for the protection of a piece of mechanism from injury, dust, etc. **a.** The case in which the needle of a compass is placed. ***Box and Needle*** (see quot.).

[When the cardboard with the points was not attached to the needle, but was fixed to the box, the box would have to be turned each time the ship changed its direction (see quot. 1613); hence may have arisen the expressions in Box *v.*[1] 12.]

1613 M. Ridley *Magn. Bodies* 105 If the ship turne anything about, the boxe of the compasse must also be turned. **1696** Phillips, *Box and Needle*, an Instrument used in surveying of Land, and finding out the situation of any side, by pointing one end of its needle towards the North. **1753** Chambers *Cycl. Supp.*, *Box and Needle*, in Navigation, is the same with the compass. **1755** Johnson, *Box*..the case of the mariner's compass.

†**b.** The case (i.e. inner case) of a watch. Also the barrel. *Obs.*

1675 *Lond. Gaz.* No. 1008/4 Lost..a plain round Watch ..the Box and Out-case of Gold. **1678** *Ibid.* No. 1305/4 A round Watch.. in a silver Box engraven, a plain silver out Case. **1740** Cheyne *Regimen* 320 Like a Spring in the Box of a Watch. **1751** in Chambers *Cycl.*

c. The case of a lock; also, the socket on a door-jamb which receives the bolt.

1679 Plot *Staffordsh.* (1686) 376 These Locks they make either with brass or iron boxes so curiously polish't. **1875** Ure *Dict. Arts* III. 139 A bolt shoots from the box or lock ..and catches in some kind of staple or box fixed to receive it.

d. A group of aircraft flying in close formation. Also *attrib.*

1941 *Battle of Britain Aug.-Oct. 1940* 13 Enemy bomber formations were also protected by a box of fighters. **1946** G. Gibson *Enemy Coast Ahead* ix. 121 They looped and rolled in perfect box formation. **1951** O. Berthoud tr. *Clostermann's Big Show* I. 45 The Luftwaffe would not in fact have time to concentrate on the first box.

e. *Mil.* An enclosed area heavily defended in all directions.

1942 *Hutchinson's Pict. Hist. War* 10 June–1 Sept. 125 The best defended 'box' will not hold out very long against greatly superior armoured strength. **1944** *Return to Attack* (Army Board, N.Z.) 9/1 'Baggush by the sea' was the fortress 'box' on the Mediterranean shore originally constructed in 1940 by the first contingent to leave New Zealand.

f. A light shield worn by cricketers to protect the genitals.

1950 N. Cardus *Second Innings* iv. 90 Not every player in those days used a 'box'. **1964** I. Fleming *You only live Twice* xi. 139 'What is a box?' 'It is what our cricketers wear to protect those parts when they go out to bat. It is a light padded shield of aluminium.'

16. a. A metal cylinder in the nave of a cart or carriage wheel, which surrounds the axle. **b.** The case in which the journal of a shaft, axle, etc., revolves; a journal-box, a bearing. (Cf. bush *sb.*[2])

1711 *Lond. Gaz.* No. 4935/4 Cast Iron Boxes, for the Wheels of all manner of Carriages. **1753** Chambers *Cycl. Supp.* s.v., Box of a wheel, the aperture wherein the axis turns. **1811** Wellington in Gurw. *Disp.* VIII. 351 You will let him have..brass boxes from wheels. **1885** Unwin *Elem. Machine Design* 229 Axle-boxes are peculiarly formed journal-bearings.

17. The piston of a pump; the case containing the valve; also the upper part of a pump-stock.

1626 Capt. Smith *Accid. Yng. Seamen* 12 The Pumpe.. the pumpes chaine, the spindle, the boxe, the clap. **1769** Falconer *Dict. Marine* (1789) G iv, The pump-spear.. draws up the *box*, or piston, charged with the water. **1867** Smyth *Sailor's Word-bk.* s.v., Each ordinary pump has an upper and lower box; in the centre of each box is a valve opening upwards.

18. A cavity made in the trunk of a tree to collect its sap; cf. box *v.*[1] 7.

1720 Dudley *Maple Sugar* in *Phil. Trans.* XXXI. 27 The Box you make may hold about a Pint. **1856** Olmsted *Slave States* 339 If we enter, in the winter..a 'turpentine orchard', we come upon negroes engaged in making boxes, in which the sap is to be collected the following spring.. These 'boxes'..are cavities dug in the trunk of the tree.

19. *Printing.* **a.** One of the cells into which a typecase is divided.

1696 Phillips s.v. *Case*, The Printers call a Case a division of little Boxes where they put the Letters of the Alphabet. **1875** Ure *Dict. Arts* III. 643 The upper case, having ninety-eight boxes, contains the capital and small capital letters (etc.)..in the lower case, having fifty-four boxes, are disposed the small letters (etc.).

b. A space enclosed within borders or rules, esp. one to draw attention to a heading, an announcement, etc. Cf. box *v.*[1] 3 d.

1929 F. A. Pottle *Stretchers* 317 Its scare heads and leaded sub-heads, its boxes and rules. **1933** P. Macdonald *Myst. Dead Police* v. 36 In the centre of the page, inset in a black-edged 'box' and different type, was a condensed biography of the arrested man. **1957** Steinbeck *Pippin IV* 58 Louella Parsons had a front-page box headed: *Will Clotilde come to Hollywood?*

20. *Founding.* In sand-moulding, the case containing the sand in which the mould is made; a 'flask'.

1875 Ure *Dict. Arts* II. 476 Boxes constitute an essential and very expensive part of the furniture of a foundry.

V. 21. a. Phrases. *to be in the* (formerly *a*) ***wrong box***: to be in a wrong position, out of the right place. ***to be in a box*** (colloq.): to be in a fix,

in a 'corner'. So *to be in the same box*: to be in a similar (unhappy) predicament.

[The original allusion appears to be lost; was it to the boxes of an apothecary? Cf. [Cæsar Borgia] appoincted poysoned coumfettes for a Cardinall that dined with his father, but the father hym selfe was serued of the wronge boxe and died. W. THOMAS *Hist. Italie* 1549.]

a **1555** RIDLEY *Wks.* 163 (D.) If you will hear how St. Augustine expoundeth that place, you shall perceive that you are in a wrong box. **1607** WALKINGTON *Opt. Glass* 17 Socrates said, laugh not, Zophyrus is not in a wrong box. *a* **1659** CLEVELAND *Coachman* 12 Sir, faith you were in the wrong Box. **1679** *Hist. Jetzer* 13 The Father Confessor saw himself in a wrong box. **1685** H. MORE *Para. Proph.* 252 You should find your self in a wrong Box. **1836** MARRYAT *Midsh. Easy* x. 31 Take care your rights of man don't get you in the wrong box. **1865** H. SEDLEY *M. Rooke* 143 If I weren't in something like the same box as his'n. **1884** RIDER HAGGARD *Dawn* xlvii, Well, we are in the same box. **1911** H. WALPOLE *Mr. Perrin* v. 92 He always told himself that all the members of the staff were in the same box.

b. *Austral.* and *N.Z.* colloq. phrases: *(one) out of the box*: an excellent person or thing; *(to be) a box of birds*: (to be) fine, excellent.

1931 F. D. DAVISON *Man-Shy* (1934) v. 74 She's one out of the box, all right. **1943** F. SARGESON in *Penguin New Writing* XVII. 73 'Hello Terry,' he said, 'how's things?' 'A box of birds,' Terry said. **1947** D. M. DAVIN *For Rest of Lives* xxx. 146 Everyone is a box of birds, still celebrating being alive. **1949** H. WADMAN *Life Sentence* 11 Well, anything very good of its kind is 'one out of the box'.

VI. *Comb.* and *Attrib.*

22. *simple attrib.* Belonging to a box or boxes; coming from boxes.

1883 *Harper's Mag.* Nov. 880/1 The coigne of vantage in the box tier. **1885** *Daily News* 14 July 2/2 New laid eggs.. cannot be competed against by the foreign or 'box' eggs.

23. General comb.: **a.** objective, as *box-maker*, *-making*, *-opener*, *-scraper*, *-setter*; *box-turning* adj. **b.** attributive, (*a*) of a box, as *box-lid*; (*b*) of the nature of, or resembling a box, as *box-keelson*, *-lock*, *-stall*, *-stove*, *-stringer*; (*c*) pertaining to a box in a theatre, etc., as *box-book* (hence *box-book-keeper*), *-circle*, *-lobby*, *-opener*, *-seat*, *-ticket*; also *box-like* adj.

1783 *London Chron.* 22 Nov. 501/2 A box lobby Puppy comes in at half price, and immediately goes to the *box-book to see *who's there.* **1812** *Dramatic Censor 1811* 294 For the benefit of Mr. Spring, Box book-keeper. **1849** *Theatrical Programme* 4 June No. 1, p. 12 Mr. Massingham the obliging and gentlemanly box-book keeper of the Princess's Theatre, takes his benefit on Friday next. **1812** *Examiner* 9 Nov. 713/2 The *box-circle at the Theatres. **1827** *Gentl. Mag.* XCVII. II. 501 Whatever has been on the *box-lid.. is unfortunately wholly defaced. **1836** DUBOURG *Violin* ix. (1878) 277 An ugly, bluff, *box-like pattern [of violin]. **1858** W. ELLIS *Vis. Madagasc.* iii. 54 The little box-like room. **1783** *Box lobby [see *box-book* above]. **1842** Box-lobby [see LOBBY *sb.* 2 a]. **1730** SAVERY in *Phil. Trans.* XXXVI. 326 A common Door Key of an Iron *Box-Lock. **1645** PAGITT *Heresiogr.* (ed. 4) 133 The Author of this Sect was one Iohn Hetherington, a *Boxe-maker. **1878** MRS. STOWE *Poganuc P.* vii. 55 Carried the *boxstove into the broad aisle of the meeting-house. **1869** SIR E. REED *Ship-build.* ix. 168 *Box-stringers are formed on the beam ends. **1768** *Pennsylvania Gaz.* in G. O. Seilhamer *Hist. Amer. Theatre* (1888) I. xxii. 247/1 After the tea equipage was removed, one of the gentlemen produced some *box tickets for the play. **1866** M. MACKINTOSH *Stage Reminisc.* 175 For the evening performance there were so many 'box' tickets taken that we had to remove the barrier and enlarge our reserved seat accommodation.

24. Special comb.: **box-annealing** *vbl. sb.*, a process of annealing in which the metal is enclosed in a metal box or pot to prevent oxidation; also *attrib.*; hence **box-anneal** *v.*; **box-back** *a.*, designating a coat or jacket of which the back has a squared, box-like appearance; **box-barrage**, an artillery barrage concentrated on a particular 'box' or area; **box-barrow**, a barrow with upright sides and front; **box-beam**, an iron beam with a double web; **box-bill** (see quot.); **box-board** (orig. *U.S.*), board suitable for making boxes; also *attrib.*; **box-camera**, (*a*) (see quot. 1842); (*b*) a hand camera of the form of a box; **box-cañon**, **-canyon** *U.S.*, a narrow canyon having a comparatively flat bottom and vertical walls; **box-car** *U.S.*, a large closed-in railway goods wagon; **box-cart** *U.S.*, a cart having a box-shaped body; **box-chronometer**, a marine chronometer with gimbal arrangements like a ship's compass; **box-churn**, a churn resembling a box in shape; **box-cloth**, a thick coarse cloth material, usually of a buff colour, from which riding garments are made; also applied to the colour; **box-club**, a society for mutual aid in distress, a friendly or provident society; **box-coat**, a heavy over-coat worn by coachmen on the box, or by those riding outside a coach; **box-coil**, a heating apparatus consisting of a coil of straight tubes joined at the ends, and occupying a cubical space; **box-coloured** *a.*, coloured by immersion in a box or tray of dye; **box-coupling**, an iron collar used to connect the ends of two shafts or other pieces of machinery; **box-crab**, a crab of the genus *Calappa*, which when at rest resembles a box; **box-cutter**, a person employed in cutting out the material for boxes; **box-day** = BOXING-DAY; also one of the days in the vacation appointed in the Court of Session (Scotl.) for the lodgment of papers ordered to be deposited in the Court (cf. BOX *v.*[1] 4, BOXING *vbl. sb.*); **box-desk**, a desk of a box-like shape; **box-drain**, a drain of quadrangular section; **box-feeding**, rearing cattle with each animal in a box or separate stall of the stable; **box-fish**, a name of the trunk-fish, *Ostracion*; **box-fitter**, a worker in an iron and steel foundry who attaches fittings and adjusts the parts of the moulding boxes; **box-food**, food which is given to animals in a box; **box-frame**, (*a*) the enclosed space in a window-frame for sash windows, in which the balance-weights are hung; (*b*) a frame or framework shaped like a box; also *attrib.*; see also quot. 1931; **box-girder**, an iron girder resembling a box, the four sides being fastened to one another by angle-irons; (see quot. 1865); **box-grain**, a grain given to leather in which lines are crossed in rectangular fashion; **box-groove** (see quot.); **box gutter**, a gutter of rectangular cross-section; **box-hand**, (*a*) (see quot.); (*b*) a person engaged in the manufacture or packing of boxes; (*c*) the compositor who sets up the type for stop-press news; **box-hat** *colloq.*, a tall (silk) hat; = BOXER[4] 1; **box-head**, (*a*) an indented heading in a printed article; (*b*) the freshwater squaw-fish, *Ptychocheilus oregonensis*; **box-hook**, a hook used to handle, close, or raise boxes; **box-house** *U.S.*, a square-built house suggestive of a box; **box-iron**, a smoothing iron with a cavity to contain a heater; also *attrib.*; **box junction**, a road junction with a grid of yellow lines painted on the road forbidding the road-user to enter the junction area until his exit is clear; also *ellipt.*; **box-keeper**, (*a*) the keeper of the dice and box at a gaming table; (*b*) an attendant at the boxes in a theatre; so **box-keeperess**; **box-key** = *box-spanner*; **box-kite**, (*a*) a toy kite having the form of a box; (*b*) a kite invented by Lawrence Hargrave, of Sydney, Australia, consisting of two light rectangular boxes secured together horizontally, formerly used in meteorological experiments; cf. HARGRAVE; (*c*) = **box-kite aeroplane**, an early form of biplane in which the arrangement of the planes resembled a box-kite; **box-letter** *U.S.*, a letter placed in a private box at a post office instead of being sent out and delivered to the addressee; **box-level**, a surveyor's level consisting of a glass-covered box instead of a level and tube; **box-loom**, a loom with more than one shuttle-box at either end of the lathe; **box lunch** *U.S.*, a packed lunch; **box-man**, a man who carries a box; **box-master** *Sc.*, a treasurer; **box-mattress** = *box-spring*; **box-meat**, meat packed in boxes for transport; **box-metal**, a metallic alloy of copper and tin, or of zinc, tin, lead, and antimony for bearings; **box-money**, (*a*) money collected in boxes; (*b*) a payment to the keeper of the dice-box at each throw; in *pl.* simply *boxes*; **box-motion**, the machinery for operating the shuttle-boxes of a loom; **box number**, the number of a 'box' (sense 3 g) at a post office or newspaper office; **box-nut**, a screw nut with a closed end; **box-ottoman**, an ottoman (OTTOMAN *sb.*[2] 1) with a hinged upholstered lid forming the seat, with a receptacle below; **box-oyster** *local U.S.*, a fine large oyster, formerly packed in boxes instead of barrels; **box-plan**, a plan of the boxes or seats in a theatre; **box-pleat**, a double pleat or fold in cloth; so **box-pleated** *ppl. a.*, **box-pleating** *vbl. sb.*; **box-rent** *U.S.*, the charge for a private post office box; **box-room**, a room for storing boxes, trunks, etc.; **box-seat**, the driver's seat on the box of a coach (see sense 6); (in quot. 1838, a seat on the roof of an early type of railway-carriage); **box-set**, a theatrical scene closed in with walls and ceiling; **box-shutter**, a shutter that folds back into a box, also called *boxing-shutter*; **box-slater** (*Zool.*), a name of the genus *Idothea* of Isopods; **box-sleigh**, a sleigh with a box-like body; **box-spanner**, a spanner with a socket-head at one or both ends which fits over the nut, etc., to be turned; **box-spring**, one of a set of spiral springs contained in a box-like mattress frame; **box-square**, a metal-working tool used for marking parallel lines on round shafts; **box-stair** (see quot.); **box-staircase** *U.S.*, a closed staircase; **box-staple**, the staple on a door-post into which the bolt of a lock is shot, when the staple is so shaped that it covers the end of the bolt; **box-stone** *Geol.*, a rounded piece of brown sandstone containing a fossil; **box-strap**, a flat bar bent at right angles to confine a square bolt or projection; **box-string**, a string-board of a staircase in which the ends of the steps are entirely boxed in, also called *close string*; **box-swivel**, a swivel designed to prevent a fishing-line from tangling; **box-tail**, a box-shaped stabilizer of a biplane; **box-tappet**, a cam for working the shuttle-boxes of a loom; **box-tenon**, a tenon at an angle; **box-timbering**, the lining of a shaft with rectangular plank frames (Raymond *Mining Gloss.*); **box-toe**, in boots and shoes, a toe with a stiff, strong lining; **box-tool(s**, an attachment to a lathe consisting of tools secured in a box-shaped holder (Lockwood); **box-top**, the top of a box; *spec.* a voucher attached to the packaging of groceries, etc., which offers a free gift or comprises part of a special offer; **box-tortoise**, **-turtle** (see quot.); **box-trap**, a trap, shaped like a box, used for capturing animals; **box-tricycle**, a tricycle with a box in which articles can be carried; **box-valve**, a short rectangular section of a pipe, containing a valve; **box-van**, a van with a flat roof; **box-wagon**, *U.S.* = *box-car*; (*b*) an open wagon with a box-shaped body; **box-wallah** (*Anglo-Ind.* see WALLAH) (*a*) a native itinerant pedlar in India; (*b*) a shopkeeper, retailer, or business-man; **box-wrench** = *box-spanner*. Also BOX-BED.

1929 *Jrnl. Iron & Steel Inst.* CXX. 483 Normalised sheets command a much higher price in the United States than material which has been *box-annealed. **1928** *Ibid.* CXVIII. 356 The American Rolling Mill Co... has built a series of twelve *box-annealing furnaces. **1930** *Engineering* 2 May 583/1 (*heading*) Normalising and box-annealing of sheets. **1946** R. BLESH *Shining Trumpets* (1949) viii. 196 In their tight '*box-back' coats, the players blasted away. **1918** in F. A. POTTLE *Stretchers* (1929) 116 Germans put over a *box barrage entirely around the wood, hemming our boys in. **1941** *Hutchinson's Pict. Hist. War* 19 Mar.–13 May 16 Our airmen.. had to make their way through an intense box barrage. **1941** *Illustr. London News* CXCVIII. 207 (*caption*) British artillery, responsible for the most severe 'box barrage' of the campaign, pounding away at Tobruk just before our troops entered. **1837** CARLYLE *Fr. Rev.* II. I. xi. 69 Yoked in long strings to *box barrow or over-loaded tumbril. **1881** RAYMOND *Mining Gloss.*, **Box-bill*, a tool used in deep boring for slipping over and recovering broken rods. **1841** *Amer. Almanac for 1842* 116/2 Paper Sheathing, binders, wrapping, and *box boards. **1910** R. W. SINDALL *Paper Technology* (ed. 2) 240 *Box boards*, used for box-making of all kinds, and manufactured from mechanical wood pulp, old waste papers, hemp, &c. **1932** F. LLOYD WRIGHT *Autobiogr.* (1945) IV. 273 The box-board cabins.. are to be connected by a low staggered box-board wall. **1842** FRANCIS *Dict. Arts* s.v. *Camera Obscura*, The *box camera is constructed as follows: procure a box, about 14 inches long E, having another box sliding in it F; the inner box having but one end, and in the centre of that end a double convex lens. **1902** *Encycl. Brit.* XXXI. 690/1 Single-magazine Box Camera. **1873** J. G. BOURKE *Jrnl.* 21 Mar. (D.A.E.), We descended into a *box cañon and made camp. **1947** *Canadian Alpine Jrnl.* June 91 We were unable to follow this route (with a pack-horse) beyond a box canyon. **1856** *Mich. State Agric. Soc. Trans. 1855* VII. 334 There are on the road.. 11 four-wheeled *box cars. **1898** *Engineering Mag.* XVI. 69 The Illinois Central equipment was of the standard box-car type. **1890** *Harper's Mag.* Mar. 569/2 Jim.. returned with the *box-cart and horse. **1875** BEDFORD *Sailor's Pock. Bk.* v. (ed. 2) 190 In winding up *box-chronometers, the chronometer should be inverted carefully in its gimbals. **1844** H. STEPHENS *Bk. Farm* II. 341 For a *box-churn, whether horizontal or vertical, the plunger should make about 60 revolutions per minute. **1853** *Jrnl. R. Agric. Soc.* XIV. I. 70 In the box-churn the whey often escapes through the spindle-hole. [**1748** LADY SHERARD *Let.* 17 Oct. in M. M. Verney *Verney Lett.* (1930) II. xxxiii. 244 He had two *box clothes and no harness.] **1890** *Peel City Guardian* 29 Mar. 3/5 We saw it in emerald green velvet to stone box cloth. **1898** H. GRAVES et al. *Cycling* 20 We are not aware of the existence of all-wool box-cloth. **1766** ENTICK *London* IV. 239 Scots-hall, a corporation for the relief of the poor.. people of Scotland.. founded by James Kinnier.. who obtained.. letters patent to incorporate a *box-club of his countrymen for this purpose. **1807** VANCOUVER *Agric. Devon* (1813) 464 Box clubs.. have much extended since the law passed for making them corporate. **1822** W. IRVING *Braceb. Hall* (1845) 60 The travellers' room is garnished.. with *box-coats, whips of all kinds. **1861** EMERSON *Cond. Life* 90 Dress makes a little restraint.. But the box-coat is like wine: it unlocks the tongue. *a* **1884** KNIGHT *Dict. Mech.* Suppl., **Box Coil*, a steam or hot-water coil of many members, occupying a cubical space comparable in its proportions to a box. **1903** L. A. FLEMMING *Pract. Tanning* 80 Sumac-tanned skins.. are usually *box-colored, that is, dyed in trays or dye boxes. **1901** *Daily Chron.* 10 Sept. 10/7 *Box cutter.. wanted, for box factory at Watford. **1864** BURTON *Scot Abr.* I. v. 302 The handsel.. has fallen into disuse, having been superseded by that great institution the *Box-day. **1905** *Daily Chron.* 21 Nov. 5/6 Two 'paltry pieces' of silk and a *box-desk were among the gifts. **1848** *Gard. Chron.* 769 Three methods of feeding cattle are.. Hemel-feeding, Stall-feeding, and *Box-feeding. **1839–47** TODD *Cycl. Anat. & Phys.* III. 969/1 The.. *box-fishes.. have their entire body.. enclosed in a dense case of armour. **1920** *Glasgow Herald* 18 Sept. 8 An agreement under which fitters, pattern-filers, and *box-fitters in the Glasgow area are to receive an advance of 5*s.* 6*d.* per week. **1886** C. SCOTT *Sheep-farming* 129 If it be intended to use *box food, the sheep require to

be trained to eat from the boxes when hoggs. *a* **1877** Knight *Dict. Mech.*, **Box-frame*, a casing behind the window-jamb for counterbalance-weights. **1931** Roget *Dict. Electr. Terms* (ed. 2) 34/2 *Box-frame motor*, an ironclad motor without a split frame, as in some traction motors. **1948** *Archit. Rev.* CIV. 187 Concrete box-frame construction. **1865** Brande & Cox *Dict. Sci.*, etc., **Box Girder*, a form of girder resembling a box, made out of boiler plate, fastened together by means of angle irons, which are riveted respectively to the top and bottom plates. **1874** Thearle *Naval Archit.* 73 The complex and varied systems of box-girder keels and keelsons. **1914** H. R. Procter *Making of Leather* 133 If the drawing down is repeated across the skin, a square or '*box' grain is formed. **1881** Raymond *Mining Gloss.*, **Box-groove*, a closed groove between two rolls, formed by a collar on one roll, fitting between collars on another roll. **1876** *Encycl. Brit.* IV. 503/1 Parallel or *box-gutters are necessary next parapets where a curb roof is formed. **1954** *Highway Engin. Terms* (*B.S.I.*) 23 *Box gutter*, a drainage channel or gutter of rectangular cross section. **1796** *Sporting Mag.* IX. 126/2 The profits of this trade were immense. There was what they called the *box-hands, that is, if a person threw three times together successfully, he gave one silver piece to the use of the house. **1833** *Fraser's Mag.* VIII. 194 The avowed profits of keeping a table of this kind is the receipt of a piece for each box-hand,—that is, when a player wins three times successively, he pays a certain sum to the table; and there is an aperture in the table made to receive these contributions. **1921** *Dict. Occup. Terms* (1927) §449 *Box hand, box man*, .. fills monorail bogies with *masse cuite*. *Ibid.* §522 *Box hand, fudge box hand*, a compositor who sets up type, for 'latest news' or 'stop press', which is put into a box and inserted in stereo cylinder. *Ibid.* §554 *Box hand, box maker*, .. turns up, to form box side, pieces of cardboard already cut to shape and creased. **1886** F. T. Elworthy *Dial. W. Somerset* 86 He had on a *box-hat too! **1919** J. C. Snaith *Love Lane* xvi. 73 Broadcloth trousers allied to a prehistoric box-hat. **1909** Jacobus et al. *Standard Bible Dict.* p. xxii, The larger articles [in the Standard Bible Dictionary] will be found to be divided into sections by *box-heads... This is done to facilitate easy cross-reference. *a* **1884** Knight *Dict. Mech.* Suppl., **Box Hook*. 1. A hook used in handling boxes; somewhat like a cotton-hook, which see. 2. A hook made on the plan of a cant-hook; used in closing boxes packed full of fish. 3. Hooks used in pairs in swinging boxes from a lifting-tackle. **1881** *Rep. Indian Affairs* (U.S.) 83 Some *box-houses constructed for the purpose. **1746** Miles in *Phil. Trans.* XLIV. 56 *Box-Irons for smoothing Linen-Clothes. **1723** *Lond. Gaz.* No. 6195/6 John Brown .. Box-Iron-maker. **1966** *Guardian* 30 Dec. 14/5 So successful have London's yellow *box junctions been in easing the traffic flow, that the Greater London Council is proposing 33 more... The Ministry of Transport first introduced the boxes with their warning 'Do not enter the box until your exit is clear' three years ago. **1680** Cotton in Singer *Hist. Cards* 335 If you be not careful and vigilant, the *box-keeper shall score you up double or treble boxes. **1693** W. de Britaine *Hum. Prudence* 141 Playing at Dice .. the Box-keeper is commonly the greatest Winner. **1728** Vanbrugh & Cib. *Prov. Husb.* v. iii. 112 She hears the Boxkeepers, at an Opera, call out—The Countess of Basset's Servants! **1855–7** Thackeray *Misc.* II. 346 (D.) The *box-keeperess popped in her head, and asked if we would take any refreshment. *a* **1877** Knight *Dict. Mech.*, **Box-key*, an upright key, used for turning the nuts of large bolts, or where the common spanner cannot be applied. **1898** *Science Siftings* 17 Dec. 137/1 A few of the principal shops are now offering *box kites. **1908** *Westm. Gaz.* 11 May 4/1 The double box-kite aeroplane with which Mr. Farman won the Archdeacon Prize in Paris recently. **1918** H. Barber *Aeroplane Speaks* Pl. vi, In 1909 came the semi-Wright biplane... Then the first box-kite flown by Mr. Grace at Wolverhampton. *Ibid.* Pl. xii, The Curtiss bi-planes .. the box-kite type, 1909, on which Mr. Curtiss won the Gordon-Bennett Race at Reims. **1928** C. F. S. Gamble *North Sea Air Station* xx. 351 By means of a 5-foot linen box-kite and spare aerial with which I had been experimenting at Yarmouth we were able to get into and keep into [*sic*] constant wireless communication with Yarmouth. **1832** *U.S. Postal Regul.* 43 *Box-letters. **1909** *Century Dict.* Suppl., *Box-loom. **1954** J. L. Morse *Unicorn Bk. 1953* 179 It went into such details as allowing troops twenty minutes for their *box lunches. **1960** G. Sanders *Mem. Professional Cad* ii. vii. 157 The crowd outside the Chapel of the Psalms had brought box lunches, bawling babies, and hula hoops. **1873** *Contemp. Rev.* XXI. 741 The treasurer of an ordinary Friendly Society, in Scotland, is sometimes its '*box-master'. **1885** D. Beveridge *Culross* II. 155 The privilege of having a deacon and box master of their own. **1928** *Daily Mail* 7 Aug. 1/2 (Advt.), You can enjoy *all* the luxury and comfort of the most expensive *Box Mattress. **1906** *Daily Chron.* 7 June 5/4 The import of '*box' meat. **1866** Geo. Eliot *F. Holt* II. 193 Accommodation for narrative bagmen or *boxmen. **1557** *Order of Hospitalls* F v b, An Yerelybooke for Collections, Legacies and Benevolences, *Boxe Mony. **1753** Chambers *Cycl. Supp.* s.v. *Box*, Betters have the advantage over casters as they have no box-money to pay. **1894** T. W. Fox *Mech. Weaving* 393 The ever-increasing number of different *box motions. **1923** D. L. Sayers *Whose Body?* iv. 67 Here's our advertisement... Perhaps it would have been safer to put a *box number. **1888** *Lockwood's Dict. Mech. Engin.*, Box Nut. **1912** 'K. Mansfield' *Scrapbk.* (1939) 7 *Box-ottomans and beds. **1811** C. Mathews *Let.* 1 July in Mrs. Mathews *Mem. C. M.* (1838) II. vi. 126, I have an immense *box-plan already; and I expect a good house. **1912** A. Bennett *Matador of 5 Towns* 246 The box-plan could be consulted at the principal stationers. The Alexandra Hall contained no boxes whatever, but 'box-plan' was the phrase sacred to the occasion. **1883** *Daily News* 22 Sept. 3/3 The .. material, arranged in *box-pleats from the waist. **1883** *Myras's Jrnl.* Aug., Narrow box-pleated blouse paniers finish the corsage. **1882** *Society* 14 Oct. 24/2 The width of a skirt necessary for kilting or box-pleating is always three times as much as for a plain one. **1841** *Congress. Globe* 20 Feb., App. 343/2 [I proposed] to cure the abuse growing out of *box-rents. **1881** *Congress. Rec.* Mar. 2283/1 Postal funds are such funds as arise from box rents and from the sale of postage-stamps. **1927** Conan Doyle *Case-Bk. S. Holmes* ix. 248 My mind is like a crowded *box-room with packets of all sorts stowed away therein. **1838** *Osborne's Guide to Grand Junction Railway* 107, I will suppose you mounted on the *box seat. **1849** De Quincey in *Blackw. Mag.* Oct. 488/2 The public took to bribing, giving fees to horse-keepers, &c., who hired out their persons as warming-pans on the box-seat. **1853** 'C. Bede' *Verdant Green* xii. 116 Mr. Verdant Green tipped for the box-seat. **1889** *Cent. Dict.*, *Box-set. **1933** P. Godfrey *Back-Stage* xi. 143 Ceiling-pieces were introduced and box-sets for domestic interiors with real doors and windows. **1869** Nicholson *Zool.* xxxii. (1880) 305 Other well-known Isopods are .. the *box-slaters (*Idothea*). **1888** *Lockwood's Dict. Mech. Engin.*, *Box Spanner. **1962** *Which?* (Suppl.) Apr. 67/1 The Austin A60 had a grease gun, nave plate remover and box spanner. **1895** *Montgomery Ward Catal.* 621/1 Wire Mattresses... *Box Spring: has 72 spiral steel japanned springs covered with .. tow. **1927** *Daily Tel.* 11 May 17/7 (Advt.), All the beds are fitted with boxsprings and hair overlays of the finest quality. **1902** P. Marshall *Metal Tools* 18 A *box-square is an elongated form of square, the chief use of which is for marking parallel lines on round shafts or spindles. **1901** R. Sturgis *Dict. Arch.*, **Box Stair*, one made with two closed strings, so that it has a boxlike form of construction. **1907** M. H. Norris *Veil* i. 5 Returning to the hall he opened the door of a box stair-case, ascending unconsciously on tiptoe a broad flight of shallow stairs to an immense attic. *a* **1877** Knight *Dict. Mech.*, **Box-staple* (Carpentry), the box or keeper on a door-post, into which is shot the bolt of a lock. **1870** E. R. Lankester in *Q. Jrnl. Geol. Soc.* XXVI. 499, I have .. spent a good deal of time in working at the nodules, which I propose to call '*Box-stones', since the name of 'boxes' has been applied to those which exhibit the remains of a shell on being broken open by the phosphate-diggers of Suffolk. **1893** Geikie *Geol.* (ed. 3) 1009 Rounded pieces of brown sandstone, known as 'box-stones', evidently derived from the denudation of a single horizon, and enclosing casts of marine shells. *a* **1877** Knight *Dict. Mech.*, **Box-strap*, a flat bar, bent at the middle, to confine a square bolt or similar object. **1847** Stoddart *Angler's Comp.* 138 The *box-swivel is a very necessary part of the minnow-tackle. **1909** *Westm. Gaz.* 23 Oct. 9/1 His Voisin biplane, .. with its *box-tail wagging high in the air. **1894** T. W. Fox *Mech. Weaving* 287 A lateral motion .. is given to the short shafts by *box tappets and lever connections. **1909** Webster, *Box toe. **1913** W. H. Dooley *Man. Shoemaking* 181 Box Toe, used to hold up the toe of the shoe so as to retain the shape. It is generally of sole leather, but often made of canvas or other material and stiffened with shellac or gum. **1937** *Amer. Speech* XII. 101 *Hook* is that part of the commercial which urges you to send in the *box tops. **1967** I. Hamilton *Man with Brown Paper Face* ii. 27 He used to send in all the box-tops for the do-it-yourself handcuff kit. **1843** *Penny Cycl.* XXV. 72 Genus Pyxis. This genus is the only Land *Box Tortoise. By means of this sort of moveable door or lid, the Pyxis .. can shut itself up in a sort of box. **1770** G. Cartwright *Diary* 26 Sept. (1792) I. 39, I made a *box-trap for martens, and set it on the opposite side of the river. **1785** T. B. Hazard *Jrnl.* 2 Apr. (1930) 78/2 Made door for Box Trap for Biger Babcock Junr. **1936** *Discovery* July 227/2 Shrews .. escaped between the wires of box-traps. **1896** *Daily News* 8 Oct. 9/2 The father of the deceased said his son was in the habit of riding a *box tricycle. **1856** Emerson *Eng. Traits* 125 The same men .. shut down their valve, as soon as the conversation approaches the English church. After that, you talk with a *box-turtle. *a* **1884** Knight *Dict. Mech.* Suppl., **Box Valve*, a box section in a pipe containing a valve, and having a cover for access. **1908** *Westm. Gaz.* 30 Mar. 5/2 A light *box-van. **1847** H. Bushnell *Address Hartford Co. Agric. Soc.* 14 To .. live on the coarsest fare, to ride in a *box waggon or cart. **1874** *Congress. Rec.* Apr. 3377/2 A small .. covered carriage, sufficient to enable a Bureau officer to come to the Capitol .. upon a rainy day like this, and not be soaked in a 'box-wagon'. **1886** *Encycl. Brit.* XX. 247/1 Open or box waggon. *a* **1847** Mrs. Sherwood *Lady of Manor* III. xxi. 263 The *box-wallas or sundook-wallas, are native pedlars. **1865** *Pall Mall G.* 3 Aug. 11/1 As to the poor boxwallah, the memsahib is a good deal to blame. **1889** Kipling *From Sea to Sea* (1899) I. i. 7 This Young Man must have been a delight to the Delhi boxwallahs. **1956** W. Slim *Defeat into Victory* 133 It was the 'Box Wallahs', the commercial community, who in those hot, anxious months .. turned Eastern India into a base and workshop .. for Burma.

box (bɒks), *sb.*³ Also 4–5 boxe. [ME. *box*: of unknown origin; perh. related to an OTeut. **boki-*, whence MDu. *bōke*, *bōke*, early mod.Du. *beuk*, MHG. *buc* blow, stroke, MDu. *bōken*, MHG. *bochen* to strike, slap; but in this case the formation remains unexplained. It has also been compared with Da. *bask* blow, stripe, but no intermed. links have been found. More probably, it is of native English origin; it may be an onomatopœia, or have arisen from some fig. or playful use of box *sb.*² (Mahn compares Gr. *πύξ* 'with clenched fist', which might have been to the purpose if 'box' had begun as school slang.)]

†**1.** A blow; a buffet. *Obs.* exc. as in 2.

c **1385** Chaucer *L.G.W.* 1388 Hadde in armys manye a blode box [*v.r.* boxe]. ? *a* **1400** *Morte Arth.* (Roxb.) 93 With his burlyche brande a box he hyme reches. **1580** Baret *Alv.* B 1076 To giue one a boxe or blowe with the fist. **1647** H. More *Song of Soul* iii. App. lxv, The Shrow him beat with buffes and boxes. **1727** Swift *Gulliver* ii. v. 136 The bird .. gave me so many boxes with his wings on both sides of my head and body .. that, etc.

2. *spec.* A blow on the ear or side of the head with the hand; a slap, a cuff.

c **1440** *Promp. Parv.* 46 Box or buffett, *alapa*. **1589** (*title*) Pappe with an Hatchet .. Or a Countrie cuffe, that is a sound boxe of the eare for the idiot Martin to hold his peace. **1594** Nashe *Unfort. Trav.* 64 My owne mother gaue I a boxe on the eare too. **1599** Shaks. *Hen. V*, iv. vii. 133 To take him a boxe a'th ere. **1601** *Sherley's Trav.* (1863) 9 Sir Anthonies brother gaue the captaine a sound boxe. **1676** D'Urfey *Mad. Fickle* ii. i. (1677) 11 A Box oth' Ear for a Prologue, you know. **1712** Addison *Spect.* No. 317 ¶35 Gave Ralph a box on the Ear. **1876** Green *Short Hist.* vii. §3. 363 She [Elizabeth] met the insolence of Essex with a box on the ear.

box (bɒks), *v.*¹ [f. box *sb.*², which yields a large number of disconnected uses.]

1. a. *trans.* To furnish or fit with a box.

1481–90 *Howard Househ. Bks.* (1841) 190 My Lord paid me .. for boxyng a peyre wheles. **1844** *Regul. & Ord. Army* 102 For a box trigger-plate, including new trigger, and boxing ditto, and fitting the same fit for service, 1*s.* 3*d.*

b. To give a Christmas-box (*colloq.*); whence *boxing-day*.

†**2.** *trans.* To bleed by cupping; to cup. *Obs.* Cf. boist *v.*

1477 Earl Rivers (Caxton) *Dictes*, The ij to boxe and lete blode. **1533** Elyot *Cast. Helth* (1541) 60 Of scarifyeng called boxyng or cuppyng. **1543** Traheron *Vigo's Chirurg.* ii. xix. 30 To boxe, or cuppe the place wyth depe scarificatyon.

3. a. To put into a box.

1586 Cogan *Haven Health* cvii. (1636) 108 If it [Marmalade] be stiffe, then take it off and box it, while it is warm. **1616** Surfl. & Markh. *Countr. Farm* 424 Straine it, and boxe it after you haue strewed sugar in the boxe. **1741** *Compl. Fam. Piece* i. iii. 239 Lay them drying .. then box them. **1860** Gosse *Rom. Nat. Hist.* 26 Here is the 'copper underwing', that seems so unsuspicious that nothing appears easier than to box it. **1884** *Pall Mall G.* 4 July 6/1 Eighty girls are employed in sorting cigars and boxing them.

b. *to box up*: to 'put up' in a box: also *fig.*

1672 Marvell *Reh. Transp.* i. 192 The Sentences shall be boxed up in several paragraphs. **1674** Flatman *To Mr. Austin* 16 Thus John Tradeskin starves our greedy eyes, By boxing up his new found Rarities. **1823** J. Badcock *Dom. Amusem.* 147 Box up the refined potass carefully.

c. *to box in* or *up*: to enclose in a box or casing.

1864 *Jrnl. R. Agric. Soc.* XXV. ii. 354 Provision should be made, when practicable, to fence in or 'box up' the moving parts... It would be very easy to box up the gearing of a fixed thrasher... It would also be impossible to completely box-in a chaff-cutter. **1919** *Autocar Handbk.* (ed. 9) 129 In other cars the motor is boxed in nearly air-tight by a shield underneath and a closed bonnet above.

d. *Printing.* To enclose within rules; to print with a border. Also with *in*.

1904 Goodchild & Tweney *Technol. & Sci. Dict.* 65/1 *Box in*, a term indicating that rules should be placed round as a border. **1924** W. M. Raine *Troubled Waters* xxii. 229 A leaded advertisement .. boxed to draw more attention.

4. To lodge a document in a Law Court.

1868 *Act 31 & 32 Vict.* c. §63 The Court may order such documents as appear necessary to be printed and boxed.

5. a. To confine as in a box, or in uncomfortably narrow limits; often with *up*, *in*.

1710 Swift *Tatler* No. 238 ¶3 Box'd in a Chair the Beau impatient sits. **1824** Mrs. Sherwood *Waste Not* ii. 5 How do you like being boxed up with the old lady? **1865** Cameron *Malayan Ind.* 83 The wall of jungle which boxes in each plantation.

b. To mix up or allow to be mixed up (different flocks of sheep). Also const. *up*, and *absol.* *Austral.* and *N.Z.*

1864 *Puketoi Diary* 19 Apr. (MS.), Lambs boxed. **1871** Lady Barker *Christmas Cake* iv. iii. 278 Tom's sheep were always coming to grief .. and never a week passed without his getting boxed. That's mixed-up, ma'am. **1881** A. C. Grant *Bush Life in Queensland* I. 253 All the mobs of different aged lambs which had been hitherto kept apart were boxed up together. **1888** 'R. Boldrewood' *Robbery under Arms* III. xii. 168 After they'd got out 20 or 30 they'd get boxed, like a new hand counting sheep, and have to begin all over again. *a* **1889** in Barrère & Leland *Dict. Slang* s.v., Now, mind yourselves, for if you box, You'll play the mischief with the flocks. **1959** H. P. Tritton *Time means Tucker* 16/2 In the event of two mobs getting 'boxed' they would have to be taken to the nearest yard and drafted out.

6. *trans.* and *intr.* To fit compactly as in a box; *techn.* to fit with a scarf joint.

1794 Martyn *Rousseau's Bot.* xxix. 459 Savin has opposite, erect, decurrent leaves, with the oppositions boxed into each other along the branches. *c* **1850** *Rudim. Navig.* (Weale) 152 Its lower end scarphs or boxes into the keel. **1867** Smyth *Sailor's Word-bk.* 126 The stem is boxed when it is joined to the fore end of the keel by a side scarph.

7. *trans.* To make an excavation in the trunk of (a tree) for the sap to collect.

1720 Dudley *Maple Sugar* in *Phil. Trans.* XXXI. 27 You box the Tree. **1755** *Gentl. Mag.* XXV. 551 Turpentine .. gathered by boxing the pitch-pine trees. **1865** *Morning Star* 5 Apr., The trees after being 'boxed' begin to produce turpentine immediately.

8. To partition *off* into boxes.

1869 *Daily News* 30 May, The fronts of the galleries have been snugly boxed off.

9. *slang.* To overturn in his box (e.g. a watchman).

1851 Thackeray *Eng. Hum.* ii. (1858) 59 Were they all .. hunting in the country, or boxing the watch? **1852** —— *Esmond* ii. v. (1876) 196 The incorrigible young sinner, was abroad boxing the watch, or scouring St. Giles's.

10. *Sc.* To wainscot, to panel walls with wood. (Jamieson.)

11. To take with, or appeal to, the box audience of a theatre, etc.

1672 Villiers (Dk. Buckhm.) *Rehearsal* (Arb.) 29 It shall read .. and act and plot and shew, ay, and pit, box and gallery, I gad, with any Play in Europe. **1831** Macaulay *Moore's Byron*, The rants of Byron's rhyming plays would have pitted it, boxed it, and galleried it, with those of any Bayes or Bilboa.

12. Naut. *to box the compass*: **a.** (see quot.)

1753 Chambers *Cycl. Supp.*, *Boxing*, among sailors, is used to denote the rehearsing the several points of the compass in their proper order. **1836** Marryat *Midsh. Easy* xviii, I can raise a perpendicular .. and box the compass. **1867** Smyth *Sailor's Word-bk.*, To Box the Compass. Not only to repeat the names of the thirty-two points in order

and backwards, but also to be able to answer any and all questions respecting its division.

b. *fig.* To go round to the direct opposite; to make a complete turn.

1815 *Scribbleomania* 213 Cobbet..Has box'd every point of the compass to Gammon. **1833** *Fraser's Mag.* VIII. 29 The *Mercury*..boxed round the political compass, following instinctively its old employer—Interest. **1869** BLACKMORE *Lorna D.* xliii. (D.) The wind would regularly box the compass..in the course of every day, following where the sun should be.

13. ***to box off***: to turn the head of a vessel by hauling the head-sheets to windward and bracing the headyards aback; to box-haul. ***to box about***: to sail up and down, often changing the direction.

1832 MARRYAT *N. Forster* xxii, You must box her off. **1836** *Fraser's Mag.* XIV. 571 He often boxed about, in his Highland yacht, for a week together. **1853** KANE *Grinnell Exp.* xxiii. (1856) 185 While thus boxing about on one of our tacks.

box (bɒks), *v.*^{2} [f. BOX *sb.*^{3} According to Mätzner, Franck, Kluge, etc., the mod.Du. *boxen*, LG. *baksen*, *baaksen*, Ger. *baxen*, *boxen*, Da. *baxe*, Sw. *baxas*, *boxas*, are all from English.]

1. *trans.* orig. To beat, thrash; *later*, to strike with the fist, to cuff, to buffet: *now* usually, to strike (the cheek, ear, etc.) with the hand.

1519 HORMAN *Vulg.* 137 §17 He was boxed out of the place: as he had been a started hare. **1589** R. HARVEY *Pl. Perc.* 12 To boxe a shadowe, and beate their knuckels against a bare wall. **1601** SIR J. OGLE in Sir F. Vere *Comm.* 150 He ..must sit with his hands bound, whilest boyes and devils come and box him about the ears. *a* **1661** HOLYDAY *Juvenal* 206 Xerxes commanded them to give the sea 300 strokes with a scourge, and to box it. **1666** PEPYS *Diary* 20 Jan., I become angry, and boxed my boy..that I do hurt my thumb. **1704** STEELE *Lying Lover* II. (1747) 31 Lettice—I'll down right box you—Hold your Tongue, Gipsy. **1783** AINSWORTH *Lat. Dict.* (Morell) I. s.v. *Ear*, Boxed on the ear, *colaphis*, vel *alapis*, *cæsus*. **1837** DISRAELI *Venetia* I. ix. (1871) 42 Attempting to box her son's ears. **1876** BLACK *Madcap V.* i. 3 I've a good mind to box your ears.

fig. **1674** R. GODFREY *Inj. & Ab. Physic* 29 To have our ears weekly boxt about with the Philosophers-stone, Horizontal Gold and Noble Mercury.

2. a. *intr.* To fight with fists; now mostly of purely athletic practice with boxing-gloves.

1567 STUDLEY *Seneca's Hippolytus* (1581) 64 b, The naked Fist found out To scratch and cuffe, to boxe and bum. **1682** DRYDEN *Epil. Banks' Unhappy Fav.* 33 'Tis just like children when they box with pillows. **1765** TUCKER *Lt. Nat.* II. 170 Two men boxing together in the next street. **1790** COWPER *Odyss.* VIII. 124 To leap, to box, to wrestle and to run. **1819** BYRON *Juan* II. xcii, For sometimes we must box without the muffle. *a* **1859** DE QUINCEY *Autobiog. Sk.* Wks. I. 36 To box..was in those days a mere necessity of schoolboy life at public schools.

b. ***to box it out***, etc.: cf. *to fight it out*.

1697 COLLIER *Ess. Mor. Subj.* I. (1709) 132 Clowns may Box if off, and be quiet. **1702** DE FOE *More Reform.* Pref. 2 The Englishmen fairly Box it out.

c. ***to box on***: to continue boxing or fighting; also *fig. colloq.*

1919 DOWNING *Digger Dial.* 13 *Box on*, (1) continue; (2) fight. **1954** F. C. AVIS *Boxing Ref. Dict.* 14 *Box*, an order of the referee to the contestants to carry on with the contest; also..Box On. **1959** 'D. BUCKINGHAM' *Wind Tunnel* vii. 61, I would face her with Paddy's story and then 'box-on' from there. **1965** *New Statesman* 7 May 725/1 However clever and facile I was, I lost friends and failed to influence people. But I boxed on.

d. ***to box clever***: to behave cleverly; to use one's wits. *slang.*

1936 J. CURTIS *Gilt Kid* vi. 62 He knew, however, that he would have to box clever. **1950** A. BARON *There's no Home* 210 If you box clever and keep your mouth shut,..you ought to be able to count on a suspended sentence.

3. a. *trans.* To fight (another) with fists.

1694 R. L'ESTRANGE *Fables* (1699) 343 The Ass..look'd on, till they had box'd themselves a weary. **1749** FIELDING *Tom Jones* XVI. ii, Box thee for a bellyfull. **1803** BRISTED *Pedest. Tour* I. 359 If they were to..box each other.

b. colloq. or dial. phr. ***to box Harry***: to go without a meal; to have a poor meal so as to save expense.

1823 'JON BEE' *Slang* 16 *Box-harry*, to go without victuals. Confined truants, at school, without fire, fought or boxed an old figure nicknamed 'Harry', which hung up in their prison —to keep heat. **1862** G. BORROW *Wild Wales* II. i. 3 Those [commercial travellers] whose employers were in a small way of business, or allowed them insufficient salaries, frequently used to 'box Harry', that is have a beef-steak, or mutton-chop, or perhaps bacon and eggs..instead of the regular dinner of a commercial gentleman. *Ibid.* Having made arrangements for 'boxing Harry' I went into the tap room. **1902** *N. & Q.* 7 June 450/1 An old woman..was telling me that she had only by her a very poor supply of seed [potatoes], and finished up by ejaculating, 'Never mind, I must box Harry...' When questioned..she said..she must needs do without. *Ibid.* 5 July 13/2 '*Box Harry*'. This is well known in the Northern Counties in the sense of doing things 'on the cheap'... In Mr. Page's instance the woman seems to have meant she must beg some potatoes to make up the deficiency.

4. *transf.* To strike with the fore-paw.

a **1711** GREW (J.) A leopard is like a cat; he boxes with his forefeet, as a cat doth her kitlins.

boxage, obs. form of BOSCAGE.

Box and Cox. The name of a farce written by J. M. Morton (1811-91) in 1847, in which two characters, John Box and James Cox, occupy the same apartment (the one by day and the other by night); hence applied allusively to an arrangement in which two persons take turns in sustaining a part, occupying a position, or the like.

1881 *Punch* 3 Sept. 100/1 This sort of Box and Cox life in a cabin. **1927** C. E. RAVEN *Creator Spirit* iii. 78 Representing mind and body as playing a perpetual game of Box and Cox. **1959** *Spectator* 14 Aug. 180/2 The French Community..shares, Box-and-Coxwise, the Luxembourg Palace with the French Senate.

box-bed. [f. BOX + BED.] A bed having the form of a large box with wooden roof, sides, and ends, opening in front with two sliding panels or shutters; often used in cottages in Scotland: sometimes also applied to a bed arranged so as to fold up into a box.

1801 R. GALL *Tint Quey* 173 She clauchtit down wi' speed The bowet aff the box-bed head. **1883** *Longm. Mag.* Apr. 648 The cottage being divided into two small apartments by the box-beds erected in a line.

box-calf. [Named about 1890 by Edward L. White, of White Bros. & Co., Boston, Mass., U.S.A., after Joseph *Box*, bootmaker, of London. (The picture of a calf in a box was adopted as an advertising device.)] A calfskin tanned with chrome salts and having a grain of rectangularly crossed lines. Cf. *box-grain*.

[**1899** *Moniteur de la Cordonnerie* 437 (Bonnaffé *Dict.*).] **1904** P. N. HASLUCK *Leather Working* 15 Box Calf.—The grain side is the face of this leather. It is somewhat like firm ooze calf, only black. **1906** A. WATT *Leather Manuf.* (ed. 5) 356 In box-calf it is usual to grain two ways only, once from the head to the tail, and then from belly to belly. **1908** TROTMAN *Leather Trades Chem.* 143 Ordinary chromed box-calf shavings containing 5·7 per cent. of chromic oxide.

boxed (bɒkst), *ppl. a.* [f. BOX *v.*^{1} + -ED.] Enclosed in, or as in, a box; confined within uncomfortably narrow limits. Frequently with *up*. Also with *in*. ***boxed shutters***: shutters folding into boxings.

1589 WARNER *Alb. Eng.* V. xxiii. 115 Their [*i.e.* Papists'] skaer-spright water, boxed Boans, their hoasts. **1865** J. D. BURN *Three Years among Working-classes in U.S.* 254 It is often dangerous for a person with boxed-up notions to try the experiment of letting them loose in company. **1885** HUGH CONWAY *Fam. Affair* xxxiv. 314 The fearful room with its boxed-up odour of death. **1900** *Times* 15 Mar. 8/1 The boxed machinery. **1905** *Westm. Gaz.* 29 Aug. 10/1 The reception and despatch of the boxed fruit. **1939** N. COWARD *Play Parade* II. p. x, *Boxed in.* Part of Stage surrounded by a three or fourfold Scene set down to the Proscenium or False Proscenium. **1960** *Times* 16 Sept. 16/7 The acoustics of the theatre..giving a boxed-in sound to the score.

box-elder: see BOX *sb.*^{1} 2 b.

boxen ('bɒksən), *a. arch.* [f. BOX *sb.*^{1} + -EN^{1}.]

1. Of or pertaining to the box-tree or box-trees.

1578 LYTE *Dodoens* VI. xxxi. 699 The lye in which Boxen leaves have been stieped, maketh the heare yellow. **1697** DRYDEN *Virg. Georg.* II. 613 Cytorus, ever green With Boxen Groves. *c* **1800** K. WHITE *Clift. Gr.* 54 Beneath the boxen hedge reclined. **1835** *Fraser's Mag.* XII. 543.

2. Made of or resembling box-wood.

[*c* **1000** ÆLFRIC *Voc.* in Wr.-Wülcker 124 *Pixis*, bixen box.] **1566** STUDLEY *Seneca's Agamem.* (1581) 147 b, The hollow boxen pype..doth geue a solemne sound. **1637** J. POCKLINGTON *Altare Chr.* 42 Powder to turne my boxen teeth into Ivory. **1710** PHILIPS *Pastorals* vi. 17 A Boxen Haut-Boy, loud, and sweet. **1790** COWPER *Iliad* xxiv. 344 The sculptured boxen yoke.

boxer^{1} ('bɒksə(r)). [f. BOX *v.*^{1} + -ER^{1}.] One who puts things up in boxes.

1871 *Echo* 8 Feb., The material passes..through the hands of..an 'examiner', and..a 'boxer'.

'boxer^{2}. [f. BOX *v.*^{2} + -ER^{1}.] **1.** One who boxes or fights with his fists; a pugilist.

1742 FIELDING *J. Andrews* III. ix, A stout fellow and an expert boxer. **1875** JOWETT *Plato* (ed. 2) I. 154 As if I had received a blow from the expert hand of a boxer.

2. (With capital initial.) A member of a Chinese secret society organized in the late 19th century, whose primary aim was to save the Chinese empire (and was consequently anti-dynastic); the movement inspired the attack on foreigners in Pekin in 1900. Also *attrib.*

The name represents Chinese *i ho chuan* or *chuen*, lit. righteous harmony boxers (fists).

1900 *Westm. Gaz.* 26 Apr. 8/4 A number of Boxers attacked a village where some Chinese Catholics live. *Ibid.* 25 May 5/2 The 'Boxer' menace in China continues to excite anxiety. *Ibid.* 7 June 5/7 A Boxer force was for several weeks drilling..within sight of the foreign concession. **1902** *Encycl. Brit.* XXIX. 228/2 The faith which he [*sc.* Sir Robert Hart] put in the Chinese made him turn a deaf ear to the warnings of the threatening Boxer movement in 1900. **1933** *Granta* 19 Apr. 358/2 No one could have believed that the brutal sadism to which for a moment it gave rein had survived the Boxer rising. **1959** *Chambers's Encycl.* II. 477/2 The Boxers indulged in a cult of magic.

3. Special Comb. **boxer shorts** orig. *U.S.*, long loose-fitting underpants for men, similar in design to the shorts worn by boxers in the ring.

1944 *Apparel Arts* Mar. 88/2 Do you have any *boxer shorts with elastic waistbands? **1968** 'D. HALLIDAY' *Dolly & Singing Bird* vii. 68 A young man..in very small boxer shorts and a peaked cap. **1983** *Listener* 3 Feb. 19/3 You can always..don your string vest and boxer shorts and bang hell out of a rowing machine.

Hence **Boxerism** ('bɒksərɪz(ə)m), the conduct and practices of the Boxers in China.

1901 *Westm. Gaz.* 11 Apr. 1/2 It is scarcely surprising.. that Boxerism is still lurking beneath the surface. **1907** *Daily Chron.* 28 Sept. 1/7 An outbreak of Boxerism has taken place in China.

boxer^{3}. [f. BOX *sb.*^{1} + -ER^{1}.] A boxwood pegtop.

1840 *Peter Parley's Ann.* 85 I'll give you my two pegs for your boxer. **1853** *N. & Q.* 1st Ser. VIII. 63/1 Schoolboys call tops made of boxwood, *boxers*. **1881** F. Y. *Ev. Man his own Mech.* II. ii. 267 'Boxers', as they [*sc.* spinning tops] are called from the material of which they are made, are considered to be the best.

'boxer^{4}. [? f. BOX *sb.*^{2} + -ER^{1}.] **1.** *dial.* A tall hat.

1877 *Legends in Dial. of Gloucestershire* 51 Twur genelmen wi' boxers on. **1884** H. D. RAWNSLEY in *Trans. Wordsworth Soc.* VI. 163 Wearing a big wideawake, or a bit of an old boxer.

2. A bowler or billycock hat. *Austral.*

1897 *Argus* 9 Jan. 14/2 (Morris), And will you wear a boxer that is in a battered state? **1904** *Westm. Gaz.* 9 June 12/1 In Melbourne..a..man in the ordinary Sunday suit of a worker, a boxer hat, and a blue shirt with a white collar.

boxer^{5}. [G., a. Eng. BOXER^{2}.] A smooth-coated, square-built, fawn or brindle breed of dog of the bulldog type, originating in Germany.

1934 *Hutchinson's Dog Encycl.* I. 184 Boxer. This dog, which appears to derive from the 'Dogues' that had been made use of, during past centuries, for animal-baiting, is very little known in Britain. **1952** KOESTLER *Arrow in Blue* 200 My dog Jessy—the first of a long series of Alsatians, Welsh sheep dogs, Boxers and St. Bernards. **1958** F. KING *Man on Rock* vi. 170 They cost you a fortune, big dogs. A pal of mine has a boxer, a German boxer, that's what they call it.

box-ful ('bɒksfʊl). [f. BOX *sb.*^{2} + -FUL.] As much as a box will contain.

1848 THACKERAY *Bk. Snobs* 106 Whole boxfuls of Parr's Life Pills. **1884** STEVENSON *New Arab. Nts.* 62 He watched beside the fatal boxful of dead flesh.

box-haul ('bɒkshɔːl), *v.* [f. BOX *v.*^{1} 13 + HAUL.] To veer a ship round on her heel, when it is impracticable to tack or make a great sweep. 'The helm is put a-lee, the head-yards braced flat aback, the after-yards squared, the drivers taken in, and the head-sheets hauled to windward; when she begins to gather stern-way the helm is shifted and sails trimmed.' Smyth *Sailor's Word-bk.* Hence **'box-hauling** *vbl. sb.*

1769 FALCONER *Dict. Marine* (1789) *Box-hauling* is generally performed when the ship is too near the shore to have room for veering in the usual way.

box-holly: see BOX *sb.*^{1} 2 b.

boxi'ana. *nonce-wd.* [See -ANA.] Notes about boxing and boxers.

1819 MOORE *Epist. fr. Tom Cribb* 22 Boxiana, disgrace to thy page!

boxing ('bɒksɪŋ), *vbl. sb.*^{1} [f. BOX *v.*^{1} and *sb.*^{2}]

I. From the vb.

1. a. The putting into, or providing with, a box. Various technical uses: see quots.

1607 HIERON *Wks.* I. 359 What boxing them vp to preuent embezeling! *a* **1877** KNIGHT *Dict. Mech.*, *Boxing*,..the fitting of the shoulder of a tenon in the surface of the timber, which is mortised for the reception of the tenon. **1884** F. BRITTEN *Watch & Clockm.* 36 Boxing-in..implies, in addition to the actual fixing of the movement, the fitting and connecting the winding stem. *a* **1884** KNIGHT *Dict. Mech.* Suppl., *Boxing Machine*, a machine for boring out the boxes of hubs. **1900** *Coal & Metal Miners' Pocketbk.* (ed. 6) 574 Boxing, a method of securing shafts solely by slabs and wooden pegs. **1903** *Daily Chron.* 10 Mar. 10/5 Wheeler.. one used to rivetting and boxing. **1913** W. H. DOOLEY *Man. Shoemaking* 180 *Boxing*, a term used to designate the stiffening material placed in the toe of a shoe to support it and retain the shape; such as leather, composition of leather and paper, wire net..etc.

b. *Law.* The lodgement of pleadings and other documents in court.

1863 *Act 31 & 32 Vict.* c. §71 The Court may dispense with the printing and boxing of any portions of the same.

†**2.** The applying of 'boxes' or cupping-glasses in surgical treatment; cupping. Hence ***boxing-glass***: a cupping-glass. *Obs.*

1519 HORMAN *Vulg.* 40 Launsynge, serchynge, cuttynge, rasynge, boxynge, and cuppynge. **1562** TURNER *Baths* 17 Let hym set cuppes or boxynge glasses upon his shulders. **1610** BARROUGH *Meth. Physick* I. v. (1639) 7 If age or weaknesse do prohibite bloud-letting, you must use boxing.

3. *Naut.* = BOX-HAULING.

1769 FALCONER *Dict. Marine* (1789) *Boxing*, an operation ..similar to box-hauling. It is performed by laying the head-sails..aback..in order to throw the ship's head back into the line of her course.

II. From the sb.

4. a. A structure or work of boxes.

a **1845** HOOD *Incend. Song* vi, Burn the boxing! Burn the Beadle!

b. A wooden casing, conduit, etc., constructed after the manner of a box; the lining of a well.

1867 *Trans. Ill. Agric. Soc. 1865–6* VI. 319 A water pipe or boxing eighteen inches in the clear is laid under ground to the centre of the yard. **1907** M. H. NORRIS *Veil* v. 44 Its [*sc.* a well's] slimy, moss-covered stone boxing. **1950** *N.Z. Jrnl. Agric.* May 483/2 Material should be rammed well as the walls are being built... The boxing may be removed the day following placing.

5. *Ship-building.* A square piece of dry hard wood used in connecting the frame timbers of a ship (Smyth *Sailor's Word-bk.*); also a scarf joint.

c **1850** *Rudim. Navig.* (Weale) 100 The term Boxing is also applied to the scarph of the lower piece of the stem, let flatwise into the fore-foot. **1860** H. STUART *Seaman's Catech.* 65 A scarph, called the flat scarph, or boxing scarph.

6. (See quot.)

1823 P. NICHOLSON *Pract. Build.* 220 Boxings of a Window—The two cases, one on each side of a window, into which the shutters are folded.

7. *Austral.* and *N.Z.* (See quots. and BOX *v.*^{1} 5 b.)

1871 LADY BARKER *Christmas Cake* IV. iii. 278 We calls it boxing when your sheep go and join another mob feeding close by, and you can't tell one from another except by the brand or the ear-mark. **1959** H. P. TRITTON *Time means Tucker* 16/2 Getting his sheep mixed-up with the travelling mob .. was known as 'boxing-up'.

boxing (ˈbɒksɪŋ), *vbl. sb.*^{2} [f. BOX *v.*^{2} + -ING^1.]

1. The action of fighting with fists; now usually applied to a pugilistic encounter in which the hands are covered with well-padded leather gloves. Also *transf.* of the action of animals.

1711 ADDISON *Spect.* No. 115 ¶8 This .. gives a Man all the pleasure of Boxing, without the Blows. **1753** CHAMBERS *Cycl. Supp.* s.v., We may distinguish three species of boxing; the first, where both the hands and head were absolutely naked, as is practised among us. **1824** W. IRVING *T. Trav.* I. 343 The noble science of boxing keeps up the bull-dog courage of the nation. **1856** KANE *Arct. Exp.* II. xv. 164 The hugging, pawing, and boxing, which characterize the black and grisly bears.

2. *attrib.* and in *comb.*, as ***boxing-glove, -match***, etc.

1714 *Spect.* No. 629 ¶17 He .. hath had six Duels and four and twenty Boxing-Matches in Defense of his Majesty's Title. **1813** *Examiner* 11 Jan. 26/2 The Professor .. put himself in a boxing attitude. **1875** JOWETT *Plato* (ed. 2) V. 398 We should put on boxing-gloves, that the blows and the wards might be practised.

Boxing-day. The first week-day after Christmas-day, observed as a holiday on which post-men, errand-boys, and servants of various kinds expect to receive a Christmas-box. So also ***Boxing-night, Boxing-time***.

1833 in A. MATHEWS *Mem. C. Mathews* (1839) IV. viii. 173 To the completion of his dismay, he arrives in London on *boxing*-day. **1837** DICKENS *Pickw.* xxxii. 343 No man ever talked in poetry 'cept a beadle on boxin' day. **1837** —— in *Bentley's Misc.* Mar. 296 The most turbulent sixpenny gallery that ever yelled through a boxing-night. **1849** G. SOANE *New Curios. Lit.* 317 The feast of Saint Stephen is more generally known amongst us as Boxing-Day. **1871** *Hood's 'Comic Ann.'* 59 It was the Saturday before the Monday Boxing Night. **1877** PEACOCK *N. Linc. Gloss.* (E.D.S.) *Boxing-time*, any time between Christmas-day, and the end of the first week in January. **1884** *Harper's Mag.* Dec. 9/1 In consequence of the multiplicity of business on Christmas-day, the giving of Christmas-boxes was postponed to the 26th, St. Stephen's Day, which became the established Boxing-day.

box office, box-office. [BOX *sb.*^{2} 8 a.]

1. The office at which seats may be booked for a theatrical performance or other entertainment (orig. for the hiring of a box). Also *attrib.*

1786 BETSY SHERIDAN *Jrnl.* (1960) 77 After we had nearly reach'd the Box Office a cry of Pick-pocket raised a general confusion. **1812** *Examiner* 5 Oct. 631/2 Those who apply first for places at the Box-Office. **1812** J. & H. SMITH *Rej. Addresses* 74 Close to Mr. Spring's Box office door, I've stood and eye'd the builders. **1929** J. B. PRIESTLEY *Good Compan.* II. iv. 327 The box office was at the entrance to the Pier.

2. The financial element of such a performance; *ellipt.* or *attrib.* (and *transf.*), success(ful) in attracting or appealing to an audience; = DRAW *sb.* 3; by extension, the paying audience.

1904 G. B. SHAW *Let.* 6 Dec. (1956) 44, I dont want to sacrifice my aim to the box office. **1907** *Daily Chron.* 16 May 3/5 The box-office value of every artist of prominence. **1923** G. B. SHAW in *Shaw on Theatre* (1958) 163 All that Mr Bridges Adams can do is to pretend that the front of the existing stage is a forestage, and make the box office pretend. **1926** GALSWORTHY *Silver Spoon* II. viii. 183 'Don't know why he keeps on an amateur like that.' 'Box office, dear boy; she brings the smart people.' **1932** A. HUXLEY *T. H. Huxley* in *Huxley Mem. Lectures 1925–32* 17 This kind of popular science is thoroughly popular in the other, the box-office sense of the word. **1935** WODEHOUSE *Luck of Bodkins* xxiv. 304 Exactly the touch the treatment needed to make it box-office. **1936** *Amer. Speech* XI. 221 Our play may have turned out to be good ticket or good b[ox] o[ffice]. **1960** *Observer* 11 Dec. 40/7 Mr. Khrushchev's box office performance at the United Nations. **1962** *Listener* 8 Mar. 446/2 His canny equation of box-office and genuine artistic ambition.

boxom(e, -um, obs. forms of BUXOM.

box-thorn: see BOX *sb.*^{1} 2 b.

ˈ**box-tree.** [OE. *boxtreow*, f. BOX *sb.*^{1} + *treow* TREE.] **a.** The Box, *Buxus sempervirens* and other species; = BOX *sb.*^{1} 1.

c **1000** ÆLFRIC *Gram.* vii. 20 *Hæc buxus*, þis boxtreow. *c* **1386** CHAUCER *Knts. T.* 444 Lik was he to byholde The box-tree, or the asschen deed and colde. *c* **1440** *Promp. Parv.* 46 Box tre, *buxus.* **1601** SHAKS. *Twel. N.* II. v. 18 Get ye all three into the box tree. **1852** MCCULLOCH *Dict. Comm.* s.v. *Boxwood*, In 1815, the box trees cut down on Box-hill .. produced upwards of 10,000*l.*

b. Applied to many Australasian species of *Eucalyptus*. Cf. BOX *sb.*^{1} 3 c.

1827 HELLYER in Bischoff *Van Diemen's Land* (1832) 168, I found the stump of a withered box tree. **1849** STURT *Narr. Exped. Central Australia* I. 116 The flats of the Darling .. are .. lightly wooded, having low and useless box-trees (the *Gobero* of Sir Thomas Mitchell), growing on them. *a* **1882** KENDALL *Poems* (1886) 19 Keen, fitful gusts, .. Fleet down by whistling box-tree butt. **1940** A. W. UPFIELD *Bushranger of Skies* xx. 193 I've put in half a handful of box-tree seeds. They'll act like a double dose of painkiller.

boxty (ˈbɒkstɪ). *Irish.* (See quot. 1880.)

1880 W. H. PATTERSON *Gloss. Antrim & Down* 11 Boxty, or *Boxty-bread*, a kind of bread made of grated raw potatoes and flour; it differs from 'potato bread', or 'potato cake', of which cold boiled potatoes form the principal part. **1949** 'M. INNES' *Journeying Boy* xiii. 162 Gracie's boxty is very eatable, very eatable indeed. **1969** *Observer* 12 Jan. 33 Boxty Bread—otherwise Boxty-in-the-Pan, Boxty Pancakes and Boxty-on-the-griddle .. are all made with potatoes. *Boxty* is eaten on Hallow-e'en, mostly in the north.

ˈ**boxwood.** [f. BOX *sb.*^{1} + WOOD *sb.*]

1. The wood of the box-tree; much used by turners, wood-engravers, and in the manufacture of mathematical and musical instruments.

1652 *Proc. Parliament* No. 131. 2025, 834 Logs of Box wood. **1767** RICHARDSON in *Phil. Trans.* LVIII. 20 Two .. of brass, and two of box-wood. **1855** SINGLETON *Virgil* II. 351 Inlaid in boxwood, or in ebony.

2. The tree or shrub itself.

1768 BOSWELL *Corsica* i. (ed. 2) 49 Its honey hath always been accounted better, by reason of the boxwood and yew. **1871** M. COLLINS *Mrq. & Merch.* II. vii. 197 Fringes of boxwood grew here and there.

3. American boxwood, *Cornus florida*; a deciduous tree of North America, having very heavy close-grained wood, the bark of which is used as a substitute for Peruvian bark; **Jamaica boxwood**, *Tecoma pentaphylla*.

4. *attrib.*

c **1865** J. WYLDE in *Circ. Sc.* I. 314/1 Boxwood charcoal answers best. **1880** *Printing Times* 15 May 116/1 One or two remaining Abkhasian boxwood forests.

†ˈ**boxy**, *a.*^{1} *Obs. rare.* [f. BOX *sb.*^{1} + -Y^1.] Of or like boxwood.

1552 HULOET, Boxie or of Boxe. **1608** TOPSELL *Serpents* 677 This egge is .. sometimes of a boxy .. colour. **1658** ROWLAND *Mouffet's Theat. Ins.* 959 Two cornicles like feathers, of a yellow or boxie colour.

boxy (ˈbɒksɪ), *a.*^{2} [f. BOX *sb.*^{2} + -Y^1.]

1. Resembling a box in shape; comparable to a box.

a **1861** T. WINTHROP *John Brent* (1883) xxvi. 222 A frowzy county town, with a dusty public square, a boxy church, and a spittley court-house. **1883** W. HARCOURT in A. G. Gardiner *Life* (1923) I. 492 A tall boxy house will not look well there. **1928** *Observer* 26 Feb. 20/2 A very covered and boxy effect. **1959** *Landfall* XIII. 122 Her nose was flat, with square boxy nostrils.

b. *spec.* Of clothes: having a squared appearance.

1936 *Times* 10 June 19/6 It may be of pique or linen in a short boxy swagger style. **1960** *Woman* 23 Apr. 15/1 A good, firm binding that gives a tailored look to a boxy jacket.

2. Of the feet of a horse or mule: high and narrow.

1908 *Animal Managem.* 224 'Mule', 'boxy', 'narrow', or 'club' feet are the opposite of 'flat'. *Ibid.* 271 The feet [of the mule] are narrow and boxy, as compared with the horse.

3. Of recorded or reproduced sound: lacking a full range of tone; sounding as if enclosed in a box.

1941 *Time* 14 Apr. 55/1 The recording—taken from a radio performance—sounds boxy. **1952** *Times Lit. Suppl.* 12 Dec. 812/2 The recording is unthinkably boxy. **1962** A. NISBETT *Technique Sound Studio* ii. 50 The results seem to sound more boxy than they should.

boy (bɔɪ), *sb.*^{1} Forms: 4 boi, boiȝe, bay, 4–7 boye, 5 bey, 6 boie, 4– boy. [ME. *boi, boy*, of obscure origin: app. identical with E. Frisian *boi, boy* 'young gentleman'; considered by many to be identical with Du. *boef* (buːf) 'knave', MDu. *boeve*, prob. (according to Franck) adopted from MHG. *buobe* (in mod.G. *bube* 'knave', dial. 'boy, lad').

It has been proposed to explain *bo-y* as dim. of *bo*, and this short for **bobo* the W.Ger. type of *buobe, bube.* The latter is actually found in MHG. only from about the 14th c. Its Teutonic standing is doubtful: see Grimm, Schade, Kluge. (The original sense being uncertain, the order of senses here observed is only provisional.)]

1. A male child below the age of puberty. But commonly applied to all lads still at school, as such; and parents or sisters often continue to speak of their grown-up sons or brothers as 'the boys'.

c **1300** *Beket* 88 ȝunge childerne and wylde boyes also .. scornede hire. ?*a* **1400** *Morte Arth.* 3123 Boyes in þe subarbis bourdene ffulle heghe. *c* **1440** *York Myst.* xix. 270 So may þat boy be fledde. **1535** COVERDALE *Zech.* viii. 5 The stretes of the citie shalbe full of yonge boyes and damselles [**1382** WYCLIF infauntes and maydens; **1388** yonge children and maidens; **1611** boyes and girles]. **1538** BALE *Thre Lawes* 966 Come, axe me blessynge, lyke praty boyes apace. **1588** SHAKS. *L.L.L.* IV. i. 122 When King Pippin of France was a little boy. **1653** WALTON *Angler* 46 The very boyes will learn to talk and swear. **1752** JOHNSON *Rambl.* No. 198 ¶3 The sailor hated to see tall boys shut up in a school. **1812** BYRON *Ch. Har.* II. xxiii, Ah! happy years! once more who would not be a boy? **1844** A. WELBY *Poems* (1867) 97 A noble sturdy boy is he, and yet he's only five. *Prov.* All work and no play makes Jack a dull boy.

2. a. Applied playfully, affectionately, or slightingly, to a young man, or one treated as such.

c **1320** *Seuyn Sages* (W.) 1351 Was nowt the boi of wit bereued. *c* **1440** *York Myst.* xxix. 89 Sir Knyghtis, do kepe þis boy [Peter] in bande. *Ibid.* xi. 247 þis boyes [Moses and Aaron] sall byde here in oure bayle. **1580** NORTH *Plutarch* 42 (R.) This boy who was made overseer of them was commonly twenty years of age. **1592** SHAKS. *Rom. & Jul.* III. i. 135 Thou wretched Boy that didst consort him here, Shalt with him hence. **1599** —— *Much Ado* V. i. 79 If thou kilst me, boy, thou shalt kill a man. **1722** *Daily Post* 19 Mar., He is a fat, chubby boy, aged about 20 or thereabouts. *a* **1791** WESLEY *Serm.* lxxxiii. Wks. 1811 IX. 434 Every one has his hobby-horse! Something that pleases the great boy for a few hours.

b. Used instead of 'man' in certain localities; e.g. in Cornwall, in Ireland, in the far West of the United States. Cf. B'HOY.

1730 SWIFT *Dick's Var.* Wks. 1755 IV. I. 264 Let the boys pelt him if they dare. **18..** *Song, 'St. Patrick was a gentleman'*, No wonder that our Irish boys should be so free and frisky! **1847** *Paddiana* I. 263 Judge Moore having decided in my hearing, that in Ireland the word 'Boy' has no reference to age. **1867** HEPWORTH DIXON *New America* i, These Western boys (every man living beyond the Missouri is a Boy, just as every woman is a Lady). **1880** *W. Cornwall Gloss.* (E.D.S.) s.v., There are no men in Cornwall; they are all Cornish boys. **1908** *Westm. Gaz.* 16 Oct. 11/2 In Ireland anyone who is not married is called a boy... John Gillan, the 'boy', a sturdy young man, then gave evidence.

c. In expressions of encouragement or admiration, etc., esp. ***that's the boy!*** (see ATTABOY).

[**1843** T. C. HALIBURTON *Attaché* xxv. 61/2 It's a great advantage havin' the minister with you. He'll fell the big stiff trees for you; and I'm the boy for the saplin's.] **1902** J. J. BELL *Wee Macgreegor* ii. 13 'If a beast wis gaun fur to pu' ma heid aff,' remarked Macgregor, who had grown suddenly bold, 'I-I-I wud—I wud gi'e't a kick!' 'Ye're the boy!' said his father. **1932** E. WALLACE *When Gangs came to London* ii. 26 'Ain't you the boy!' he said. **1936** J. CURTIS *Gilt Kid* xvi. 166 'Got it?' echoed Scaley. 'That's the boy.' **1962** H. HOOD in R. Weaver *Canad. Short Stories* (1968) 2nd Ser. 205 John's the boy. Oh, he's a sharp lad is John.

†**3. a.** A servant, slave. *Obs.* Now only when a boy in sense 1 or 2.

c **1350** *Will. Palerne* 1705 Sche .. borwed boiȝes cloþes .. & bogeysliche as a boye · busked to þe kychene. *c* **1430** LYDG. *Bochas* II. v. 46 b, With his sweorde, but she [Lucretia] would assent Her and a boye he would prent I-fere. **1535** COVERDALE *1 Sam.* ii. 13 The prestes boye came, whyle the flesh was seething. **1588** T. L. *To Ch. of Rome* (1651) 9 By David his Boy, whom his heart approved. **1601** F. TATE *Househ. Ord. Edw. II*, §94 (1876) 56 That none of the kings meignee .. charetter or sompter boy .. keepe his wife at the court. **1764** T. JEFFERSON *Corr.* Wks. 1859 I. 190 You mention one [letter] you wrote last Friday, and sent by the Secretary's boy. *Mod.* The doctor's boy, sir!

†**b.** A camp-follower. *Obs.*

1599 SHAKS. *Hen. V*, IV. iv. 82 The French might haue a good pray of vs, if he knew of it, for there is none to guard it [the luggage] but boyes. *Ibid.* IV. vii. 1 Kill the poyes and the luggage, 'Tis expressly against the Law of Armes.

c. 'In Southern India and in China a native personal servant is so termed, and is habitually summoned with the vocative '*Boy!*' (Yule). Also applied to male negro slaves of any age; in the South Seas to Polynesians kidnapped in 'the labour trade'.

1609 HAWKINS in Purchas *Pilgr.* 211 My boy Stephen Grovenor. **1681** R. KNOX *Hist. Ceylon* 124 We had a black boy my Father brought from Porta Nova to attend upon him. **1850** MRS. STOWE *Uncle Tom* xxx, 'Now up with you, boy! d'ye hear?' said the auctioneer to Tom. **1875** THOMSON *Malacca* 228 A faithful servant or boy, as they are here called, about forty years of age. **1884** *Pall Mall G.* 16 Aug. 1/2 The vessel is granted a licence to carry so many 'boys', as the native men are called.

d. In combination with other words, as LINK-BOY, POST-BOY, POT-BOY.

e. In S. Africa, a Coloured or Native labourer or servant of any age. So ***boss boy***, a Coloured or Native overseer; ***Cape boy***, a Cape Coloured man or boy.

1812 A. PLUMPTRE tr. *Lichtenstein's Trav. S. Afr.* I. I. viii. 119 A Hottentot .. expects to be called by his name if addressed by any one who knows it; and by those to whom it is not known he expects to be called Hottentot .. or boy. **1833** J. PHILIP in *Lett. Amer. Missionaries* (1950) 40 An example of a native boy at Pacaltsdorp conducting a small school. *Ibid.* 42 A school on the British system taught by a Hottentot boy. **1896** *Spectator* 2 May 629 A Cape 'boy' fighting at Bulawayo is .. a coloured native enlisted and drilled within the Colony. **1906** *Daily Chron.* 11 Apr. 3/6 One white man in the mine is expected to 'boss' forty blacks or Chinese, which he cannot do with safety, in fact the black

'boss-boy' is left to do much of the blasting. **1963** *Times* 2 May 12/7 The Johannesburg city council, which employs thousands of Africans in jobs ranging from welfare officers to dustmen, has banned the use of the word 'boy' to describe any of them.

f. (*the*) *boy*: champagne. *slang.*

The derivation is uncertain: see Barrère & Leland *Dict. Slang*, Farmer *Slang*.

1882 *Punch* 11 Feb. 69/1 He'll nothing drink but 'B. & S.' and big magnums of 'the Boy'. **1882** O. Wilde *Let.* 12 May (1962) 117 You and I will sit and drink 'Boy' in our room. **1929** *Melody Maker* Jan. 20/2 Lord Delamere came up to them with a foaming magnum of champagne and said, 'Well, boys! you've given us a glorious time! What do you say to a beaker of "the boy"?'

g. From 1918 to 1924, the lowest rank in the Royal Air Force.

1918 *Army Orders* Nov. 35 The following additional column will be *inserted* in the table of corresponding ranks.. Royal Air Force..Air Mechanic, 3rd Class. Private, 2nd Class. Clerk, 3rd Class. Boy. **1924** *R.A.F. King's Regulations* I. p. vii, Airman, or Airmen. These words, wherever they occur, will be held to include a warrant officer, a N.C.O., an aircraftman, and a boy.

†**4.** As a term of contempt: Knave, varlet, rogue, wretch, caitiff. *Obs.* [In early quotations, not always to be distinguished from BOIE, executioner.]

c **1300** *K. Alis.* 4376 He..threow him over arsun; And saide, 'ly ther vyle bay!' *c* **1325** *E.E. Allit. P.* A. 805 In Iherusalem watz my lemman slayn & rent on rode with boyez bolde. *c* **1440** *Promp. Parv.* 29/1 Bey or boy, *scurrus*. **1562** Bulleyn *Bk. Simples* 76 a, Through a very vile coward or boie, often the valiaunt man is slaine. **1588** *Marprel. Epist.* (Arb.) 28 Calling him boy, knaue, varlet, slanderer. **1607** Shaks. *Cor.* v. vi. 101, 104, 117.

5. Used in familiar address, often with the epithets 'my', 'old'. *old boy* (see also OLD *a.* 8 a). Hence *to old-boy* vb.

1601 Shaks. *Twel. N.* II. iv. 122 But di'de thy sister of her loue my Boy? **1620** —— *Temp.* II. ii. 56 To sea, boys, and let her goe hang. **1712** Arbuthnot *John Bull* (1727) 79 Fear not, old boy; we'll do it, I'll warrant thee. **1742** Richardson *Pamela* III. 380 Never fear, old Boy, said Sir Charles, we'll bear our Parts in Conversation. **1878** Miss Broughton *Cometh up as Fl.* xv. 163 Old boy'ing each other.

6. a. In various connexions, indicating a member of fraternity or band, as in ***Peep of Day Boys***, a secret organization in Ireland; ***Roaring Boys***, riotous fellows of the time of Elizabeth and James I.; also ***the old boy*** *U.S.*, the devil; ***yellow boys***, guineas.

c **1590** Greene *Tu Quoque* in *Dodsley* VII. 25 (N.) This is no angry, nor no roaring boy, but a blustering boy. **1609** B. Jonson *Epicœne* I. iv. (N.) The doubtfulness of your phrase ..would breed you a quarrel once an hour with the terrible boys. **1659** *Leg. Capt. Jones* (Halliw.), In hope to get such roaring boys as he. **1712** *Whig & Tory* iii. 34 He [Sacheverell] had Meat, and Drink, and yellow Boys. **1802** *Balance* (Hudson, N.Y.) 14 Oct. 317 (Th.), The devil has been nick-named the old boy. **1837–40** Haliburton *Clockm.* (1862) 140 As we invigorate the form of government (as we must do, or go to the old boy). **1831** Carlyle *Sart. Res.* III. x. 331 In Ireland..Ribbonmen, Cottiers, Peep-of-Day Boys. **1854** M. J. Holmes *Tempest & Sunshine* xv. 203 Where the old boy is your mistress? **1953** A. Miller *Crucible* (1956) I. 32 The Church's enemies relied no less upon the Old Boy to keep the human mind enthralled.

b. A rough or rowdy (e.g. of the streets); freq. *pl.* in ***the boys*** = criminals; *spec.* the thieves and swindlers who frequent race-courses.

1834 *Knickerbocker* III. 34 The landlord after telling me not to mind the *boys*, went about his business. **1840** *Daily Picayune* (New Orleans) 28 Aug. 2/1 The Bowery boys of New York have..eclipsed the nice young men of Baltimore. **1843** *Punch* 29 Apr. 179/2 The comments and cheers of those very important members of street society, the boys. *a* **1889** in Barrère & Leland *Dict. Slang*, Cleansing the rings from..those criminal scoundrels known as the boys. **1938** F. D. Sharpe *S. of Flying Squad* i. 13 Down goes the Squad the night before to greet 'the boys' at the turnstiles. *Ibid.* v. 64 Word went round among the 'boys' that the takings had been hefty.

c. *pl.* Men of the armed forces; soldiers. So ***boys in blue***: see BLUE *sb.* 3 b.

1861 O. W. Norton *Army Lett.* (1903) 19 It was then announced that the whole thing was a canard, started just to keep the boys quiet. **1881** F. E. Weatherly *Old Brigade* 2 Where are the boys of the Old Brigade? *c* **1915** L. G. Ford (*song*) *Keep the Home Fires Burning*, Turn the dark cloud inside out, Till the boys come home. **1959** M. Shadbolt *New Zealanders* 36 The time when we would watch the boys swing, bayonets flashing,..towards the grey waiting ships.

d. *pl.* Members of a group sharing common interests; one's fellows or habitual companions; esp. in colloq. phr. ***one of the boys***: one who belongs to such a group; *spec.* one who conforms to its interests or practices, 'a good sport'. *colloq.* So ***jobs for the boys***, appointments for one's supporters or favourites.

1886 *Lantern* (New Orleans) 8 Sept. 3/1 When he happens in with the boys, he can enjoy himself. **1889** W. Skey *Pirate Chief* 195 He goes on Sundays to the 'pub.' And sits among 'the boys'. **1893** *Ladies' Home Jrnl.* Nov. 20/3 She doesn't want to be treated like a lady because she wants to be 'one of the boys'. **1905** M. Beerbohm in *Sat. Rev.* 11 Nov. 620/1 On him, somehow, the blight of the theatre has not fallen... He is not, and may never become, 'one o' the boys'. **1930** Wodehouse *Very Good, Jeeves!* vii. 192 A chummy lion-tamer—a tamer who, after tucking the lions in for the night, relaxes in the society of the boys. **1939** I. Baird *Waste Heritage* v. 63 He..stopped to watch a half-dozen of the boys playing blackjack. **1950** D. & C. Christie *His Excellency* I. i, It's just a political racket—Jobs for the Boys. **1955** M. Gilbert *Sky High* i. 19 'It wasn't exactly a popular appointment, was it?' 'It certainly wasn't,' said the General. .. 'Jobs for the Boys.' **1969** *New Yorker* 3 May 64/3 He doesn't do it by being one of the boys. That's not his nature. He's a lone wolf.

e. With defining word or phrase prefixed = men (of the kind indicated by the defining element). (Cf. *backroom boy*.) *colloq.*

1941 F. & R. Lockridge *Murder out of Turn* iv. 39 The B.C.I. boys will be along. **1945** A. Huxley *Time must have Stop* xxx. 288 Just a little bit of Wordsworth, say the blue-dome-of-nature boys. *Ibid.* 291 Adler and Freud, the Dialectical Materialism boys and the Behaviourists. **1958** *Spectator* 7 Feb. 167/2 The public relations boys could really go to town. **1963** R. Parker tr. *Solzhenitsyn's One Day in Life of Denisovich* 36 Oh no, he wasn't ill, the security boys were keeping him back.

7. *Comb.* (in which 'boy' often approaches the force of an adjective); **a.** appositive, indicating sex, as ***boy-angel***, ***-baby***, ***-brood***, ***-child***, ***-cousin***, ***elephant***; or immaturity, as ***boy-actor***, ***-bridegroom***, ***-crusader***, ***-ensign***, ***-God***, ***-husband***, ***-king***, ***-lover***, ***-man***, ***-officer***, ***-poet***, ***-spouse***; or with words added which indicate the assumption of another personality, as in ***boy-girl***, ***-harlot***, ***-wench***; also **boy-bishop**, the boy elected by his fellows to play the part of bishop from St. Nicholas' Day to Innocents' Day; **b.** attributive (of or pertaining to boys), as ***boy-kind***, ***-nature***; **c.** obj. gen. with vbl. sb., as ***boy-queller***. Also **boy-blind** *a.*, blind as a boy; **boy-crazy** *a.*, (of a girl) eager to associate with boys; **boy-farm** *slang*, a school (cf. FARM *sb.*[2] 7); so ***boy-farmer***; **boy friend**, **boy-friend** *colloq.*, a male friend; *spec.* a woman's favourite male escort or companion; also with implication of an illicit relationship, a paramour; occas., the associate of a homosexual; **boy-rid** *a.*, overdone with boys (after the analogy of BED-RID); **boy-storied** *a.* that of which stories are told by boys; ***boy-like*** adv. and adj.

1861 A. K. H. B. *Recreat. Country Parson* Ser. II. 69 The popularity of the *boy-actor Betty. **1762–71** H. Walpole *Vertue's Anecd. Painting* V. 35 Six *boy-angels playing on musical instruments. **1881** *Atlantic Monthly* Jan. 89/1 They are baby socks. They are always blue. And so they all have to be given to the *boy babies. **1820** Scott *Abbott* xiv, To give place to..the *Boy-Bishop, and the Abbot of Unreason. *a* **1625** Fletcher *Love's Pilgr.* (L.), Put case he could be so *boy-blind and foolish. **1863** M. L. Whately *Ragged Life Egypt* viii. 63 The parents gave way..aided by the indifference of the *boy-bridegroom. **1879** Browning *Ivan Ivanov.* 138 Poor Stiopka..first Of my *boy-brood. **1601** Holland *Pliny* II. 301 The haire of yong *boy-children..is held to be a singular remedy for..the gout. **1878** Black *Green Past.* ii. 10 As her *boy cousin had said she was a trifle serious. **1923** *Cosmopolitan* Sept. 72/2 Going *boy-crazy at fifty. **1955** 'C. H. Rolph' *Women of Streets* 151 Ena became boy-crazy early. **1886** *Q. Rev.* April 529 A fault..which the *boy-ensigns and pages..shared with their parents. **1890** W. Morris *News from Nowhere* v. 43, I had best say nothing about the *boy-farms which I had been used to call schools. **1901** *Daily Chron.* 16 Sept. 2/6 The professional *boy-farmers..are naturally trying to supply what is desired. **1896** E. Turner *Little Larrikin* iv. 41 He went on ahead with his *boy-friend. **1909** G. W. E. Russell *Coll. & Recoll.* 330 The young ladies..meet their boy-friends at all hours and places. **1929** Wodehouse *Summer Lightning* ii. 53 'Who is this Pilbeam?' he demanded. 'Pretty much the Boy Friend, I take it, what?' **1953** E. Taylor *Sleeping Beauty* ix. 156 Boy-friend of my mother's just come in. **1957** J. Braine *Room at Top* xxx. 242 Pansies only use pubs for picking up boy friends. **1816** Byron *Seige Cor.* xxx, We kneeling see Her and the *boy-God on her knee. **1570** Drant *Serm.* in Dibdin *Libr. Comp.* 76 This Romish Church defendeth..concubines, and *boy-harlots. **1876** M. Collins *Blacksmith & Schol.* I. vi. 157 She held herself haughtily aloof from the mankind and *boykind of New Bratton. **1864** Pusey *Lect. Daniel* iii. 152 A *boy-king..is restored at once..by his own people. **1850** Mrs. Stowe *Uncle Tom* ix. 73 Two boys, who, *boy-like, had followed close on her heels. **1865** Tylor *Early Hist. Man.* xii. 337 The *boy-man laughed to himself, but said nothing. **1876** Hamerton *Intell. Life* x. x. 391 The necessities of the *boy-nature. **1762** Wesley *Jrnl.* 13 June (1827) III. 93 Two or three *boy-officers. **1883** S. Waddington *Clough* 46 These indicate..the feelings and tendencies of the *boy-poet at this early age. **1606** Shaks. *Tr. & Cr.* v. v. 45 Come, come, thou *boy-queller, shew thy face. **1823** Lamb *Elia* (1860) 82 He is *boy-rid, sick of perpetual boy. **1848** Kingsley *Saints' Trag.* Notes 245 The princess was laid in the cradle of her *boy-spouse. **1816** L. Hunt *Rimini.* II. 235 *Boy-storied trees, and love remember'd spots. **1586** Warner *Alb. Eng.* II. xi. 51 Not so much as by the tongue the *Boy wench was bewraid.

8. Phrases. ***boy and girl*** (also with hyphens), *attrib. phr.*, pertaining to or involving a boy and a girl; applied esp. to a juvenile attachment; ***boy-meets-girl*** (*colloq.* esp. *attrib.*), referring to a copybook romance; ***boy next door*** (*colloq.*), the young man in a conventional romance; a simple, unsophisticated young man; ***boys will be boys***: an expression of resignation towards childish ways.

1841 Dickens *Barn. Rudge* xxvi. 84, I have found it necessary to take some active steps towards setting this boy and girl attachment quite at rest. **1870** L. M. Alcott *Old-Fashioned Girl* viii. 132 It's only a boy-and-girl fancy, that will soon die a natural death. **1934** P. Bottome *Private Worlds* v. 54 It was what people called 'a boy and girl affair', but they can go quite deep. **1945** 'A. Gilbert' *Don't Open Door!* ix. 80 The murder..had more of those features that make a crime fascinating to the general public. There was no boy-meets-girl element. **1947** *Landfall* I. 45 This immediately..reduces the story to the familiar Hollywood formula of boy-meets-girl. **1955** T. Sterling *Evil of Day* viii. 80 The boy-next-door parody was meant to amuse her. **1958** *Photoplay* Oct. 54/1 His whole build-up is based on The Boy Next Door—the boy who's within reach of every girl fan. **1848** Thackeray *Van. Fair* xiii. 112 And as for the pink bonnets..why boys will be boys. **1858** C. M. Yonge *Christmas Mummy* ix. 131 All he had ever known against Asaph Harper was keeping company with the like of them: but boys would be boys. **1964** Wodehouse *Frozen Assets* iii. 50, I tried to tell him that boys will be boys and you're only young once.

9. (*oh*) ***boy!*** *a* colloq. (orig. *U.S.*) exclamation of shock, surprise, excitement, etc.; freq. used to give emphasis to a statement that follows it. Cf. ATTABOY.

1917 *Amer. Mag.* Mar. 13/1 'I told that dame I was Kid Hanlon.'..'Oh, boy!' I yells. **1927** *Punch* 7 Sept. 263 Oh, boy, I feel good! **1930** D. H. Lawrence *Nettles* 17 And they blushed, they giggled, they sniggered, they leered..and said: Oh boy!..that's pretty hot! **1934** M. Hodge *Wind & Rain* I. i. 18 Boy! They don't wear a damned thing! **1942** L. D. Rich *We took to Woods* (1944) ii. 34 Maine guides have a legend of quaintness to uphold, and boy! do they uphold it. **1958** 'N. Shute' *Rainbow & Rose* i. 2, I slithered in over the fence and put her [*sc.* the aeroplane] down and boy! was I glad to be on the ground!

† **boy**, *sb.*[2] *Obs. rare.* [a. OF. *boie*, *buie*:—L. *boia*, pl. *boiæ* 'a collar for the neck'.] A gyve, fetter.

1375 Barbour *Bruce* x. 763 Schir peris lumbard that ves tane..thai fand in presoune, fettirit with boyis, sittand.

boy (bɔɪ), *v.* [f. BOY *sb.*[1]] In various nonce-usages. **a.** *intr.* To play the boy, act as a boy; **b.** *trans.* To call (one) 'boy'; **c.** To represent (a woman's part) on the stage, as boys did before the Restoration; **d.** To furnish or supply with boys.

1568 *Jacob & Esau* II. ii. in Hazl. *Dodsl.* II. 211 So prattling, so trattling, so chiding, so boying. **1573** G. Harvey *Letter-Bk.* (1884) 48 If he boied me now..I hard him not. **1606** Shaks. *Ant. & Cl.* v. ii. 220, I shall see Some squeaking Cleopatra Boy my greatnesse. **1616** Beaum. & Fl. *Knt. Malta* II. iii. (R.), *Boy* did he call me..I am tainted.. Baff'd and boy'd. *a* **1635** Corbet *Poems* (1807) 126 But wert girl'd and boy'd. **1650** H. More in *Enthus. Tri.* (1656) 126 How ready the world will be to boy him out of countenance. **1655** Fuller *Hist. Camb.* (1840) 142 The gates were shut, and partly *man-ned*, partly *boy-ed*, against him.

boy, boye, obs. ff. BUOY.

boyage ('bɔɪɪdʒ). *rare.* [f. BOY *sb.*[1], app. with a confusion of -AGE suffix and AGE *sb.*] Boyhood.

1622–62 Heylin *Cosmogr.* III. (1673) 104/1 When Alexander in his Adolescency or Boyage was sacrificing to the gods. **1798** Bloomfield *Farmer's Boy* (1817) Pref. 23 Putting the little events of my boyage into metre.

boyang, var. BOWYANG.

‖**boyar, boyard** (bəʊ'jɑː(r), 'bɔɪəd). Forms: 6 boiaren, 7 bojar, boyaren, 7– boyar, 8– boyard. [a. Russ. *boyárin*, pl. *boyáre* 'grandee, lord':—earlier *bolyárin*, prob. f. OSlav. root *bol-* great; but Miklosich would connect it with Turkish *boj* stature, *boïjlu* high; Dahl, and others, with Russ. *boi* 'war', which may have influenced the later form. The word occurs in Byzantine Greek as *βοϊλάδαι*, *βολιάδαι*; Bulg. *bolerin*, Serv. *bolyar*, Rouman. *boiér*.]

A member of a peculiar order of the old Russian aristocracy, next in rank to a *knyaz* or 'prince', who enjoyed many exclusive privileges, and held all the highest military and civil offices: the order was abolished by Peter the Great, and the word is in Russia only a historical term, though still often erroneously applied by English newspaper writers to Russian landed proprietors. In Roumania the *boiér* still existed (*c* 1887) as a privileged class. (The Eng. *boyar* appears to have been taken from the plural; *boyard* is an erroneous French spelling.)

1591 G. Fletcher *Russe Commw.* (1856) 46 The emperours of Russia giue the name of counsellour to diuers of their chiefe nobilitie..These are called Boiarens. *a* **1618** Raleigh *St. Maxims* in *Rem.* (1661) 43 As the Turk, his Ianizaries; the Russe, his Boyarens. **1676** *Lond. Gaz.* No. 1077/1 Then the Bojars, which are the most eminent persons in this Countrey. **1698** Luttrell *Brief Rel.* (1857) IV. 432 The czar..has caused 200 of the boyars in his country to be put to death. **1796** Morse *Amer. Geog.* II. 77 Not only the common people but many of the boyards or nobles. **1858** *Times* 28 Aug. 10/1 The Boyards [of Roumania] are not an aristocracy of birth or wealth; they are simply a privileged class. **1865** *Spectator* 11 Feb. 151 The older families of Russia retain the traditions of the boyars and of their power to a dangerous degree. **1879** R. S. Edwards *Russ. at Home* I. 202 The rich 'boyars' (as foreigners persist in styling the Russian proprietors of the present day).

Hence '**boyardism**.

1848 *Tait's Mag.* XV. 482 Boyardism stands a good chance of being vanquished by democracy [in Roumania].

‖**boyau** ('bɔɪəʊ). Also boyeau. [F. *boyau* 'the alimentary canal', and as below:—OF. *boel*: see BOWEL.] *Fortif.* 'A branch of a trench; a zig-zag; a trench in rear of a battery, forming a

communication with the magazine; a small gallery of a mine.' Stocqueler *Milit. Encycl.* 1853.

1847 in CRAIG. **1862** F. GRIFFITHS *Artil. Man.* (ed. 9) 263 *Zig-zags*, or *Boyeaux of communication*, are trenches made for the approaches from the parallels to the besieged place.

boycott ('bɔɪkɒt), *v.* Formerly also **Boycott.** [f. the name of Capt. Boycott, an Irish landlord, who was the original victim of the treatment described.] *trans.* To combine in refusing to hold relations of any kind, social or commercial, public or private, with (a neighbour), on account of political or other differences, so as to punish him for the position he has taken up, or coerce him into abandoning it. The word arose in the autumn of 1880, to describe the action instituted by the Irish Land League towards those who incurred its hostility. It was speedily adopted by the newspapers in nearly every European language (e.g. F. *boycotter*, Du. *boycotten*, Ger. *boycottiren*, Russ. *boĭkottīrovat*, etc.).

1880 *Times* 20 Nov. 10/1 The people of New Pallas have resolved to 'Boycott' them and refused to supply them with food or drink. **1880** *Daily News* 13 Dec. 3/1 Already the stoutest-hearted are yielding on every side to the dread of being 'Boycotted'. **1880** *Illust. Lond. News* LXXVII. 587/1 To 'Boycott' has already become a verb active, signifying to 'ratten', to intimidate, to 'send to Coventry', and to 'taboo'. **1881** *Q. Rev.* 117 The lineal ancestors of the Land League 'boycotted' the poet. **1886** *Times* 2 Feb. 10/1 On September 19, 1880, Mr. Parnell formulated the law of boycotting in the town of Ennis, county Clare.

b. *transf.* and *fig.*

1881 *Spectator* 22 Jan. 119 Dame Nature arose..She 'Boycotted' London from Kew to Mile End. **1881** *Daily News* 19 May 5/3 You cannot Boycott human nature. That entity..always gets the better of the Boycotter in the long run. **1882** L. STEPHEN *Swift* vii. 157 Briefly, the half-pence were to be 'Boycotted'.

Hence **'boy,cotted** *ppl. a.*, **,boyco'ttee, 'boy,cotter, 'boy,cotting** *vbl. sb.*, **'boyco,ttism;** also **'boycott** *sb.* = *boycotting*; (U.S.) an application of boycotting.

1880 J. DILLON *Speech at Cashel* 17 Nov. (*Times* 19 Nov. 6/1) They had yet to study a branch of new Land law known as Boycotting. **1880** *Times* Dec. 9 They also do not feel warranted in regarding the threat of Boycott as one which comes within the Act. **1880** *Daily News* 25 Dec. 6/3 So long as a railway station is near him, the 'Boycottee', if he have only two or three servants to stand firm, can practically bring the Boycotters to their wits' end. **1881** GLADSTONE in *Standard* 28 Oct. 3/3 The neighbours of the Boycotted man refuse to hold any intercourse with him and his family; they will not eat with him, drink with him, buy from him, or sell to him. **1881** LD. DERBY in *19th Cent.* Oct. 481 Capital [in Ireland] is timid; boycotting, intimidation, and outrage do not attract it. **1881** *Declaration* in *Standard* 19 Feb. 3/6 We loathe and detest the very idea of a man seeking his ends by murder, by outrage, by Boycottism. **1883** MONIER WILLIAMS *Rel. Thought Ind.* I. xviii. 472 India has furnished examples of Boycotters and Boycottees, for many centuries. **1885** *Pall Mall G.* 19 Nov. 3/2 Those who have continued to hire Chinese labour and patronize the same since the Boycott.

boydekyn(ne, obs. form of BODKIN.

boydom ('bɔɪdəm). *rare.* [f. BOY *sb.*[1] + -DOM.] The estate or characteristics of boys.

1880 *Scribn. Mag.* June 312 An abnormal development of boydom.

boyell, obs. form of BOWEL.

boyer ('bɔɪə(r)). Also 9 boier. [a. Du. *boeijer* a smack.] A sloop of Flemish construction, with a raised work at each end. Smyth *Sailor's Word-bk.*

a **1618** RALEIGH in *Remains* (1661) 167 By their fashioned Ships called *Boyers, Hoybarks, Hoyes*..made to hold great bulke of Merchandize. **1642** MRQ. HERTFORD *Let. to Queen* 6 Master Knolles a servant of the king went in the boyer. **1882** *Standard* 25 Dec. 3/3 It has beauties of its own quite equal to those of xebec, felucca, or boier all put together.

†**'boyery.** *Obs.* [f. BOY *sb.*[1] + -ERY.] Boyhood.

1580 NORTH *Plutarch* (1676) 42 They called..the greatest boyes Melirenes: as who should say, ready to go out of boyery. **1656** DUGARD *Gate Lat. Unl.* §199. 55 Infancy is ignorant of itself, boyerie is passed over in sports.

boyey ('bɔɪɪ), *a.* [f. BOY *sb.*[1] + -Y[1].] Having the characteristic qualities of a boy.

1885 MRS. MOLESWORTH *Carrots* i, He was a very boy-ey boy, very much inclined to look down upon girls in general. **1902** *Harmsworth Lond. Mag.* June 494/2 A delightfully boyey boy.

boyhood ('bɔɪhʊd). [f. BOY *sb.*[1] + -HOOD.]

(Johnson has only the quotation from Swift, and says 'This is perhaps an arbitrary word'. It occurs in no edition of Bailey.) Cf. BOYISM 3.

a. The state of being a boy; the time of life during which one is a boy; also *fig.* the early period of anything. **b.** Boys taken collectively. **c.** Boyish feeling; light-heartedness.

a **1745** SWIFT (J.), Look at him, in his boyhood, through the magnifying end of a perspective, and in his manhood, through the other. **1802–25** SYD. SMITH *Ess.* 117 (Beeton's ed.) All the bloody boyhood of the Bog of Allen. **1828** D'ISRAELI *Chas. I*, I. ii. 8 Princes are unfortunate enough to be flattered even in their boyhood. **1829** HOOD *Eug. Aram* iii, Turning to mirth all things of earth As only boyhood can. **1842** TENNYSON *Sir Launc.* 19 In the boyhood of the year. **1886** MRS. A. HUNT *That other Pers.* I. 206 The turbulent mass of..gesticulating boyhood.

boyis, *pl.* fetters: see BOY *sb.*[2]

boyish ('bɔɪɪʃ), *a.* [f. BOY *sb.*[1] + -ISH[1].]

1. Of or pertaining to boys or boyhood.

1548 UDALL *Erasm. Par. Luke* iii. (R.) Big laddes..grou quite awaye from the pureness of babehood to boyish wantonnesse. **1604** SHAKS. *Oth.* I. iii. 132 Euen from my boyish daies. **1761** STERNE *Tr. Shandy* III. lxxv, From the first hours of our boyish pastimes. **1873** SYMONDS *Grk. Poets* vi. 164 In the bloom of manly or of boyish strength.

2. Boy-like; puerile.

1579 FULKE *Heskins' Parl.* 60 This is such a boyish sophisme as I am ashamed to aunswere it. **1663** COWLEY *Verses & Ess.* (1669) 143 The beginning of it is Boyish, but of this part..I should hardly now be much ashamed. **1848** MACAULAY *Hist. Eng.* II. 195 Boyish vanities, and no part of the real business of life.

boyishly ('bɔɪɪʃlɪ), *adv.* [f. prec. + -LY[2].] In a boyish manner, like a boy.

1581 J. BELL *Haddon's Answ. Osor.* 64 And the same question repeateth agayne and agayne very boyeshly. **1807** A. M. PORTER *Hungar. Bro.* I. i. 29 To hide the sensibility, which boyishly he blushed at. **1849** STOVEL *Introd. Canne's Necess.* 107, Boyishly exclaiming, 'No bishop, no king'.

boyishness ('bɔɪɪʃnɪs). [f. as prec. + -NESS.] Boyish or boylike quality or state.

1552 HULOET, Boyeshnes, *puerilitas.* **1611** COTGR., *Puerilité*..boyishnesse, childishnesse..simplicitie. *a* **1791** WESLEY *Husb. & Wives* v. Wks. 1811 IX. 75 Behaviour, that ..savours of a kind of boyishness. **1881** J. HAWTHORNE *Fort. Fool* I. i, To the end of his life there was a deep fund of boyishness in him.

boyism ('bɔɪɪz(ə)m). [f. BOY *sb.*[1] + -ISM.]

1. The characteristic nature of a boy.

a **1790** T. WARTON in Sir E. Brydges' *Milton* (1853) 566 Perhaps the real boyism of the brother..is to be taken into the account. **1826** DISRAELI *Viv. Grey* I. i. (1878) 1 The spirit of boyism began to develop itself.

2. A boyish characteristic or trait; a puerility.

1700 DRYDEN *Fables* Pref. (Globe) 498 A thousand such boyisms which Chaucer rejected. **1717** GARTH *Ovid's Met.* Pref., These are some of our poet's boyisms.

†**3.** Boyhood. *Obs.*

1810 REV. R. POLWHELE *Poet. Register* 48 The progress of Genius in boyism and in youth.

boykin ('bɔɪkɪn). [f. BOY *sb.*[1] + -KIN.] A little boy: used as a term of affection.

1547 SALESBURY *Welsh Dict., Herlotyn,* boykyn. **1658** BROME *New Acad.* I. i. 3 Where's my Boykin? my Friskoe? my Delight? *a* **1687** COTTON *Æneid Burl.* II. (1692) 80 I'm fixt to go along With thee, my boykin, right or wrong. **1822** T. MITCHELL *Aristoph.* II. 316 This species, boykin? cruet or sea-spider?

boyl, boylster, obs. forms of BOIL, BOLSTER.

boyla ('bɔɪlə). [Native name.] An aboriginal Australian sorcerer.

1865 W. HOWITT *Discov. Australia* I. 386 A superstitious notion that by eating them [*sc.* mussels] he should subject himself to the absolute power of boylas, or evil sorcerers. **1966** W. S. RAMSON *Austral. Eng.* vi. 129 Several of these words, notably..*boyla* and *koradji*, 'an aboriginal medicine-man or witchdoctor', are used only in their original and specific senses.

†**'boyly,** *a. Obs.* [f. BOY *sb.*[1] + -LY[1].] Boyish.

1552 HULOET, Boylye or boyesh, or pertaynynge to a boye. **1563–87** FOXE *A. & M.* III. 595 What a stout boyly Heretick is this? How malapertly he answereth?

boyn(e, boynard, obs. ff. BOON *sb.*, BOINARD.

boyne (bɔɪn). *Sc.* Also boy(e)n, boin. A flat shallow tub or bowl (cf. BOWIE).

1821 GALT *Ann. Par.* 46 (JAM.) Her seam..had fallen into a boyne of milk. —— *Ayrsh. Leg.* 265 (JAM.) The lasses were ..standing upright before the boyns on chairs, rubbin the clothes. **1826** J. WILSON *Noct. Ambr.* Wks. 1855 I. 97 Take a peck of purtatoes and put them into a boyne.

boyo ('bɔɪəʊ). *colloq.* and *dial.* (chiefly *Anglo-Irish*). Also boyoh. [f. BOY *sb.*[1]] Boy, lad; esp. as a jovial form of address.

1870 G. M. HOPKINS *Jrnl.* (1937) 133 Irish expressions.. *Boyo, Lado* = Boy and a half, [etc.]. **1898** J. MACMANUS *Bend of Road* 258 While there's a whack in the belt, boyo, I'll lay-on ye. **1907** G. B. SHAW *John Bull's Other Island* 80 There was..me bould English boyoh in front at the machinery. **1914** JOYCE *Dubliners* 201 If you want a thing well done..go to a Jesuit. They're the boyos have influence. **1938** J. CARY *Castle Corner* 46 The wee boyo grows like the Corners. **1943** P. CHEYNEY *You can always Duck* i. 11 There was nothin' too bad to say about that boyo. **1953** DYLAN THOMAS *Under Milk Wood* (1954) 30 *Nogood Boyo.* Me, Nogood Boyo, up to no good in the wash-house. **1955** K. AMIS *That Uncertain Feeling* xvii. 235 Get along home, there's good boyos. **1960** G. AVERY *Elephant War* iii. 49 Well, my boyo, you're in a hurry this fine morning.

boy scout: see SCOUT *sb.*[4] 2 c.

boysenberry ('bɔɪzən-, 'bɔɪsənbɛrɪ). [f. the name of Rudolph *Boysen*, 20th-cent. American horticulturist who developed it + BERRY *sb.*[1]] The fruit of a bramble, a hybrid of several plants of the genus *Rubus*; also, the bramble that bears this fruit.

1935 *Market Growers Jrnl.* 1 Dec., The Boysenberry is a cross between Cuthbert raspberry, Loganberry and blackberry. **1941** *Reader's Digest* Oct. 89/1 Boysenberry pies baked by Mrs. Knott. **1945** *Greelay* (Colorado) *Daily Tribune* 15 Mar. 10/7 Eldorado [blackberry] is plenty hardy, but Boysenberries both thorny and thornless must be covered thru the winter. **1956** *Dict. Gardening* (R.H.S.) Suppl. 98/1 *Boysenberry*, July–Aug. Large, purplish-black when ripe. Juicy but acid.

boyship ('bɔɪʃɪp). [f. BOY *sb.*[1] + -SHIP.] The personality of a boy. (A mocking form of address.)

1608 DAY *Hum. out of Breath* I. iii. (1860) 12 Your boy-ship hath so sought us, that we have found you. *a* **1634** RANDOLPH *Poems* (1638) 21 Must we then allow Your Boy-ship leave to shoot at whom you please?

boy's-love. A popular name for Southernwood, *Artemisia Abrotonum*, also called, in some districts, *lad's love*.

1863 KINGLAKE *Crimea* II. 267 The nosegay of 'boy's love' that used to be set by the Prayer-Book of the Sunday maiden. **1876** BESANT & RICE *Gold. Butterfly* xiv. 115 Stocks, pansies, boy's-love, sweet-william—used to be cultivated for their perfume.

boys'-play. Amusement for boys; trifling, child's-play.

1596 SHAKS. *1 Hen. IV*, v. iv. 76 You shall finde no Boyes play heere, I can tell you. **1672** MARVELL *Reh. Transp.* I. 249 Princes..are past such boyes-play. **1812** L. HUNT IN *Examiner* 21 Dec. 814/1 Most of his tragedies..are little better than so much gigantic boy's-play.

boyst(e, boystous, var. of BOIST, BOISTOUS.

boyte, obs. form of BOOT *sb.*[1]

†**boyter.** *Obs.* A bird of prey; ? a Buzzard.

1648 GAGE *West Ind.* xii. (1655) 45 Hawkes, Kites, Boyters (which are very many in those parts).

boytle, obs. f. BEETLE, a mallet.

†**'boytrye.** *Obs. rare*[—1].

1542 BRINKLOW *Complaynt* (1874) 26 If the kyng knewe what boytrye were there [in the Marshalsea] vsed, I think he wold neuer suffer them more to kepe court.

‖**boyuna** (bəʊ'juːnə). [Tupi *boi-una*, 'serpens obscurus' (Martins). Carried by the Portuguese from Brazil to Ceylon.]

a. A large water-snake of Brazil of dark colour (?*Boa aquatica*). **b.** A harmless snake of Ceylon.

1774 GOLDSM. *Nat. Hist.* (1862) II. III. iii. 429 The Boyuna of Ceylon is equally a favourite among the natives.

‖**boza, bosa** ('bəʊzə). Also booza, bouza, boosa. [Turkish *bōza* 'a kind of thick white drink made of millet fermented' (Redhouse).]

A popular acidulated drink in Egypt, etc., made by fermenting an infusion of millet-seed, with the addition of certain astringent substances; also an inebriating preparation of darnel-meal, hemp-seed and water.

1656 BLOUNT *Glossogr., Boza*, a drink in Turky made of seed, much like new mustard, and is very heady. **1706** tr. *L. Lemery's Treat. Aliments* III. ii. 292 The Bosa, so much esteemed by the Arabs and Egyptians, is a Composition made of the Leaves and Seed of Bangue. **1847** CRAIG, *Bosa.* **1849** SOUTHEY *Comm.-pl. Bk.* Ser. II. 45 The Booza makers are a very necessary corporation in a camp. **1879** C. R. LOW *Jrnl. Gen. Abbott* i. 97 We get plenty of supplies; grain, boosa, sheep, cows..are brought into camp.

bozo ('bəʊzəʊ). Orig. and chiefly *U.S. slang.* [Origin unknown.] A person, fellow.

1920 *Collier's* 11 Dec. 5/3 The weaknesses of the other bozo. **1921** *Ibid.* 11 June 5/1 Joe is the bozo which I write all them letters to from France. **1924** WODEHOUSE *Bill the Conqueror* vi. 134 If there's one bozo in this world I got no use for it's a little squirt that double-crosses his pals. **1935** S. LEWIS *It can't happen Here* xi. 104 Come on, you bozos! **1961** *Encounter* Apr. 26 Frank, the grey bozo behind the counter.

bozoar, obs. form of BEZOAR.

‖**bozzetto** (bɒt'setəʊ, -z-). Pl. bozzetti. [It., dim. of *bozzo* rough stone, sketch, alt. of *bozza*: see BOSS *sb.*[1]] A small rough model for a larger sculpture; also, a sketch for a larger painting.

1935 *Burlington Mag.* Oct. 144/2 A bozzetto..which was shown at the Exhibition of Venetian pictures. **1936** *Ibid.* Apr. 169/1 A plastic figure, a bozzetto, a workshop model. **1944** *Ibid.* Nov. 280 The terracotta is a bozzetto for the statue. **1959** *Times* 23 Mar. 3/3 Drawings and prints, marble busts and terracotta *bozzetti*.

bozzom, bozzum, dial. name of the Ox-eye (*Chrysanthemum Leucanthemum*), or the Yellow Ox-eye (*Chrysanthemum segetum*).

1847 in HALLIWELL.

bra[1] (brɑː). Formerly also (as *sing.*) **bras.** Colloq. abbrev. of BRASSIÈRE. Also *attrib.*

1936 W. B. M. FERGUSON *Somewhere off Borneo* i. 26 She wore nothing but a'bras', the briefest of French knickers, and the sheerest of white silk hose. **1936** *New Yorker* 28 Mar. 7 (Advt.), Bras..50 c. **1937** *Night & Day* 30 Sept. 27 (Advt.), The Bra is one of the famous 'Alphabet' Bra's. **1948** *Punch* 2 June iii/1 (Advt.), The two-piece is Rayon-Lastex

with a bra adjustable in three..ways. **1959** *Manch. Guardian* 3 July 5/6 Elasticated sides and reinforced bra top. **1968** J. IRONSIDE *Fashion Alphabet* 66 *Bra-slip*, petticoat or slip with top part shaped like a brassière and giving the support of a brassière.

bra^2 (brɑː). *Quantum Mech.* [f. BRA(CKET: cf. KET.] A vector in Hilbert space that is the complex conjugate of a ket and is symbolized by <|. Freq. as ***bra vector***.

1947 P. A. M. DIRAC *Princ. Quantum Mech.* (ed. 3) i. 19 We shall call the new vectors bra vectors, or simply bras, and denote a general one of them by the symbol <|, the mirror image of the symbol for a ket vector. **1957** F. MANDL *Quantum Mech.* (ed. 2) v. 102 The ket and bra vectors correspond to the column and row vectors of matrix algebra. **1972** J. M. JAUCH in Salam & Wigner *Aspects Quantum Theory* ix. 164 These examples..show how Dirac's bra and ket notation, so effective as an operational device, may be based on a mathematically rigorous foundation. **1973** S. WIEDER *Foundations Quantum Theory* iii. 47 The inner product **b**. **a** is a complex scalar obtained by multiplying the bra form of **b** by the ket form of a. **1974** [see KET].

bra, obs. form of BRAE.

‖**braaivleis** (ˈbrɑːɪfleɪs). *S. Afr.* [Afrikaans, lit. 'grilled meat', f. *braai* to grill + *vleis* meat, FLESH.] An out-door meal, esp. a picnic, at which meat is grilled; a barbecue.

1939 A. W. WELLS *S. Afr.* 410 Some Afrikaans words are used in English conversation, e.g...*braaivleis*. **1942** *Cape Times* 6 Nov. 3 A braaivleis in aid of war funds will be held at Alto, Helderberg. **1947** *Ibid.* 22 Dec. 9/7 Braaivleis Grillers. **1955** J. PACKER *Valley of Vines* ii. 30 A braaivleis is a sort of barbecue, Hal. We cook our steaks and chops out of doors on the embers.

Hence **braai** *sb.* and *v. trans.* and *intr.*

1959 *Cape Argus* 10 Mar. 9/9 Buy and braai your own meat. **1959** *Cape Times* 11 Apr. 4/2 Chicken Braai at Somerset West. **1961** *Cape Argus* 11 Mar. 8/8 We picnic and we braai.

braas, obs. and dial. form of BRACE.

†**braasny**, *a.* *Obs.* *rare*$^{-1}$. [A modification of *brasen* BRAZEN, with -Y; cf. *yrony*, *yron* in quot.] Like brass.

1382 WYCLIF *Deut.* xxviii. 23 Be heuene that is aboue thee braasny [**1388** brasun]; and the lond that thou tredist yrony [**1388** yrun].

brab (bræb). Also brabb. [? corruption of Pg. *brava* wild, *palmeira brava* being the Portuguese name. Written also *brab(b-tree.*]

The Palmyra palm (*Borassus flabelliformis*).

1698 FRYER *Acc. E. India* 76 (Y.) Another Tree called Brabb, bodied like a Cocoe. **1766** GROSE *Voy. E. India* I. 48 (Y) A few brab-trees, or rather wild palm-trees (the word *brab* being derived from *brabo*, which in the Portuguese signifies wild). **1859** R. BURTON *Centr. Afr.* in *Jrnl. R.G.S.* XXIX. 81 A screen of brab-trees.

brabant (brəˈbænt). [f. the name of the Duchy of Brabant. As applied to a coin, the word is a mistranslation of a passage in Hemingburgh (see first quot.), where *Brabantium* is not a sb., but an adj. agreeing with *scaldingorum.*] A term recently applied (in error) to a base coin of Flemish manufacture circulated in England in the 13th c.

[*c* **1350** W. HEMINGBURGH *Chron.* (ed. Hamilton) II. 187 Mercatores enim alienigenæ introduxerant in Angliam monetas..pessimi metalli, pollardorum, crocardorum, scaldingorum Brabantium, aquilarum..et aliorum diversorum nominum.] **1840** RUDING *Ann. Coinage* I. 201 These coins were..distinguished by the names of pollards, crocards, scaldings, brabants, eagles. **1866** ROGERS *Agric. & Prices* I. 178 Scaldings, Brabants, Eagles.

†**braˈbantie.** *Obs.* *rare*$^{-1}$. [perh. f. *Brabant* (see prec.). Cf. Sp. *brabante* a sort of linen.] A garment worn by soldiers in the 16th c.

1591 GARRARD *Art Warre* I. 18 A straite brabantie and gascaine is to be worne.

brabble (ˈbræb(ə)l), *v.* *Obs.* or *arch.* exc. *dial.* Also 6 **brabbel, brabil, -el,** 6–8 **brable.** [Derivation obscure: usually identified with Du. *brabbelen* to confuse, stammer, jabber (cf. BRABBLING *vbl. sb.* 2), but it is doubtful whether the history of the senses in Eng. supports this. Cf. BRAWL, BABBLE.

Skinner conjectured a corruption of med.L. *parabolare*, to harangue, discourse (? a forensic or university term), cf. Welsh *parablu* to speak. Du Cange has 'tota die *parabolare* per scripturas,' which agrees with sense 1. With 'womanish brabble' cf. the proverb 'ubi mulieres ibi parabolæ.']

1. *intr.* To dispute captiously or obstinately; to cavil or quibble. Const. *with*, *against* a person; *about*, *on*, *at*, *for* a thing.

c **1500** *Pore helpe* 96 in Hazl. *E.P.P.* III. 256 They wolde not haue you playe To dryue the tyme away; But brabble on the Byble. **1548** UDALL, etc. *Erasm. Par. Mark* x. 24 They did not crie, and brable agaynst him. **1579** J. FIELD *Calvin's Serm.* Ded., And then they brable with us about the translation. **1614** RALEIGH *Hist. World* II. v. v. §9. 609 He thought it no fit season to brabble at the Law. **1621** BP. MOUNTAGU *Diatribæ* 538 What have we brabbled, and contended for all this while?

2. To quarrel about trifles; *esp.* to quarrel noisily, brawl, squabble. Cf. BRABBLE *sb.* 3.

c **1530** H. RHODES *Bk. Nurture* in *Babees Bk.* (1868) 92 Brable not thou with thy neyghbour. **1590** GREENE *Never too late* (Wks. 1882) VIII. 136 Though Mars and Venus brabled, they were friends after brawls. **1653** HOLCROFT *Procopius* III. 78 While they were thus brabling for the spoiles. **1675** COTTON *Poet. Wks.* (1765) 220 If I reach one of you a Douse, You'll learn more Manners than to brabble.

3. = BABBLE *v.*

1570 LEVINS *Manip.* 126 To Brabil, *multum loqui*. **1875** *Lanc. Gloss.* (E.D.S.) *Brabble*, to chatter noisily.

ˈ**brabble,** *sb.* [f. prec.]

†**1.** A quibble, a captious objection or dispute.

1581 J. BELL *Haddon's Answ. Osor.* 227/2 To confounde.. the Sophisticall brables of all other adversaries. *a* **1626** BP. ANDREWS *Serm.* ix. (1641) 105 True righteousnesse leadeth to peace, not to questions and brabble. **1674** MARVELL *Reh. Transp.* II. 312 It is not worth the Readers trouble to interesse him in such a foolish brabble.

†**2.** A frivolous or paltry action at law. *Obs.*

1598 R. BERNARD *Terence's Andria* IV. v, To go follow sutes and brabbles in law. **1668** WILKINS *Real Char.* 271 In Judicial Affairs..those less general words of Suit, Controversie..Case, Cause, Action..Brabble. **1677** HOBBES *Odyss.* 150 The judge ariseth from his seat, Ending the brabbles of contentious men.

3. A paltry altercation, noisy quarrel.

1566 GRINDAL *Lett.* Wks. (1843) 289 To declare a womanish brabble that happened yesternight in a church in London. **1599** SHAKS. *Hen. V*, IV. viii. 69 *Fluellen*..Keepe you out of prawles and prabbles and quarrels. **1641** MILTON *Ch. Discip.* II. Wks. (1851) 54 To make a Nationall Warre of a Surplice Brabble, a Tippet-scuffle. **1860** MOTLEY *Netherl.* (1868) II. xv. 229 To spend the time in private brabbles and piques..is not a good course.

†**b.** A brawl, skirmish, or petty war. *Obs.*

1577 HOLINSHED *Chron.* III. 1145/1 In the which brabble it happened the capteins horsse to be slaine vnder him. **1601** SHAKS. *Twel. N.* V. i. 68 Heere in the streets..In priuate brabble did we apprehend him. **1622** HEYLIN *Cosmogr.* III. (1682) 168 A matter of more consequence than these Scythian brabbles.

4. Discordant babble.

1861 *Temple Bar* Oct., *Sev. Sons Mam.* xxvi, The myriad-tongued brabble had ceased. **1868** BROWNING *Ring & Bk.* IV. 34 To hear the rabble and brabble, you'd call the case Fused and confused past human finding out.

ˈ**brabblement.** *arch.* Also brable-. [f. as prec. + -MENT.] Cavilling, quibbling (*obs.*); noisy quarrelling, contentious uproar (now chiefly *dial.*).

1556 ABP. PARKER *Psalter* cvi. 16 They provokt with wrath ..Aaron..wyth foolish brablementes. *a* **1563** BALE *Sel. Wks.* (1849) 176 Are not Christ and his disciples teachers sufficient enough..but we must have unsavoury brabblements? **1593** NASHE *Christ's T.* 68 b, Contention..is euer in Armes, neuer out of brabblements. **1824** *Craven Dial.* 23 Hees ollas agait o' some brabblement. **1876** *Daily News* 28 Sept. 5/3 The Commune was a time of extraordinary 'brabblement'—to use a word of Carlyle's.

brabbler (ˈbræblə(r)). *arch.* Also 6 brabeler, 6–8 brabler. [f. as prec. + -ER^1.] One who brabbles: †**a.** a caviller, quibbler (*obs.*); **b.** a quarrelsome person, brawler.

1548 THOMAS *Ital. Gram.* (1567) *Cinciglione*, is a dronken brabeler. **1553–87** FOXE *A. & M.* (1596) 1877/2, I am no brabler in the scripture. **1577** HOLINSHED *Chron.* II. 84 Brablers and ale-house quarrellers. **1647** *Depos. Cast. York* (Surtees) 10 He is..a brabler and a quarreller. **1713** BP. GIBSON *Articles Visit.* in Toulm. Smith *Parish* (1857) 94 Is he a brabler, brawler..seditious party?

†ˈ**brabblery.** *Obs.* In 6 brablarie. [f. BRABBLE + -RY.] Wrangling.

1567 DRANT *Horace Epist.* I. xviii. F iij, An other vseth brablarie [*rixatur*] For very gotish wol.

brabbling (ˈbræblɪŋ), *vbl. sb.* [f. BRABBLE *v.*]

1. †**a.** Cavilling, 'hair-splitting' (*obs.*). **b.** Wrangling, noisy quarrelling.

1532 MORE *Confut. Tindale* Wks. 410/2 To beare and abide the brablyng of Tindals tonge. **1561** T. NORTON *Calvin's Inst.* (1634) Pref., With..sophisticall brabblings. **1614** RALEIGH *Hist. World* I. 172 The brabblings of the Aristotelians. **1645** in Somers *Tracts* I. 35 The Trade of Brabbling and Pettifogging. **1865** CARLYLE *Fredk. Gt.* I. III. iii. 148 Brabblings, scufflings, objurgations.

†**2.** A confusion, a jumble. *Obs.*$^{-0}$

1530 PALSGR. 617/2, I make a brablyng, *je barbouille.*

ˈ**brabbling,** *ppl. a.* *arch.* [f. as prec. + -ING^2.]

†**a.** Disposed to cavil or quibble, (*obs.*); **b.** litigious, quarrelsome; **c.** tumultuous, riotous.

1549 COVERDALE *Par. Erasm. Gal.* v. 14 The brablyng law with so many rules. **1577** HARRISON *England* II. ii. (1877) 53 In a brabling fraie, one of hir men was slaine. **1603** H. CROSSE *Vertues Commw.* (1878) 63 Violent extortion, brabling suites, and vniust vexations. **1633** P. FLETCHER *Elisa* xxii, Brabbling lawyers' brawls. [**1855** MOTLEY *Dutch Rep.* II. viii. (1866) 294 Commerce would have no security at Antwerp 'in those brabbling times'.]

ˈ**brabblingly,** *adv.* *arch.* [f. prec. + -LY^2.] In a captious or contentious manner.

1565 JEWEL *Def. Apol.* (1611) 43 We will deale herein neither bitterly, nor brablingly.

‖**brabeum** (brəˈbiːəm). *Obs.* *rare.* [late L. *brabēum*, a. Gr. βραβεῖον.] A prize, premium, reward.

1675 *Phil. Trans.* X. 549 Young architects to be encouraged by certain brabeums or prices.

brab-tree: see BRAB.

bracc, var. of BRACK^1, *Obs.*, noise.

braccate (ˈbrækeɪt), *a.* [ad. L. *brac(c)āt-us*, f. *brāc(c)æ* trousers, breeches: see -ATE^2.]

Ornith. Having the legs fully covered with feathers.

1847 in CRAIG.

‖**braccio** (ˈbrattʃo). Pl. **braccia.** [It. *braccio*, lit. 'an arm', hence a measure of length.] An Italian measure of length: nearly two English feet.

1760 RAPER in *Phil. Trans.* LI. 782 The braccio of Florence. **1855** BROWNING *Old Pict. at Flor.*, The Campanile..Shall soar up in gold full fifty braccia.

†**brace,** *sb.*^{1} *Obs.* Forms: 5 **braas, brace,** 6 **brache, brase.** [a. F. *bras*:—L. *brāc(c)hium*, lit. an arm.] An arm; esp. an 'arm' of the sea or other large body of water. ***Brace of St. George*** = med.L. *brachium Sancti Georgii* (Du Cange): the Bosporus or the Hellespont.

c **1400** MAUNDEV. xi. 126 He schal..passe the wature, that ys cleped the Brace of seynt George. **1477** CAXTON *Jason* 103 b, Guided his boot ouer the braas. **1481** —— *Myrr.* II. iii. 67 That renneth a longe thurgh the Royame of ynde, And departeth in to many armes or braces. **1506** GUYLFORDE *Pilgr.* (1851) 67 Y^e sayd streyghtes, otherwyse called the brache of seynt George. *c* **1530** LD. BERNERS *Arth. Lyt. Bryt.* (1814) 142 The stroke..cut asonder a great brase of a benche, that stode before the bedde.

brace (breɪs), *sb.*^{2} Also 5–7 **brase** 6–7 **brache,** 6 **bresse,** 7 **brasse,** 9 (*dial.*) **braas.** [Orig. a. OF. *brace*, *brache*, *brase* (fem. sing.) the two arms, esp. the width of the two arms:—L. *brāc(c)hia*, pl. of *brac(c)hium* the arm. But senses 7 onwards appear to be chiefly taken from or influenced by certain senses of BRACE *v.*^{1}, and might perhaps be better treated as a separate word.]

I. Uses of the general sense 'pair of arms'.

†**1. a.** The portion of a suit of armour covering the arms. (At first 'a pair of brace', but afterwards applied to the covering of one arm.) *Obs.*

c **1340** *Gaw. & Gr. Knt.* 582 Wel bornyst brace vpon his boþe armes. **1430** LYDG. *Chron. Troy* III. xxii, Some..ne wolde fayle To haue of mayle a payre brase. **1483** *Cath. Angl.* 39 A brace, *defensorium*, *brachiale*. *a* **1605** MONTGOMERIE *Poems* (1821) 7 On his left arm, ane brace. **1611** COTGR., *Bracats*, Brasses, or Vambrasses; armor for the armes.

†**b.** ? A coat of armour. *Obs.*

1601 SHAKS. *Per.* II. i. 133 'It hath been a shield 'Twixt me and death';—and [he] pointed to this brace.

†**c.** A state of defence or of preparation for war.

1604 SHAKS. *Oth.* I. iii. 24 Cyprus..stands not in such Warrelike brace.

†**2.** A measure of length, orig. representing the length of the extended arms; cf. FATHOM. (The French *brasse* was 1·62 metres (Littré) = about 64 inches.) *Obs.*

1599 HAKLUYT *Voy.* II. i. 211 They haue built a tombe.. a brace and an halfe high. **1613** PURCHAS *Pilgr.* VIII. xiv. (1614) 815 This fiery concauity..goes down two hundred and fifty braces or yards. **1710** W. MATHER *Yng. Man's Comp.* (1727) 399 Giving diversity of Names to their Measures; as the Yard, Ell, Goad, Aulne, Brace.

†**3.** An embrace; *fig.* in quot. *Obs.*

1589 *Pasquil's Ret.* 4 Hee fell into the brace of Rome again.

†**4.** An arch of a bridge. Cf. SPAN of arch. *Obs.*

1483 *Cath. Angl.* 39 A Brace of a bryge, or of a vawte; *sinus*, *arcus*.

5. *Sc.* A mantel-shelf. Cf. **brace-piece** in VI; also ***window-brace*** 'the part of a window on which the sash rests' (Jamieson).

1806 TRAIN *Poet. Rev.* 101 A dreadfu' knell came on the brace.

6. A carpenter's tool, having a crank handle, and a socket or pad to hold a 'bit' for boring.

1567 *Wills & Inv. N.C.* (1835) 268, V wombles, iij percers bittes and a brace xx^d. **1832** BABBAGE *Econ. Manuf.* xvii. (ed. 3) 153 Braces for carpenters, with 12 bits. **1833** J. HOLLAND *Manuf. Metal* II. 128 The joiner when boring with a brace and bit.

II. That which clasps, tightens, secures, connects. Cf. BRACE *v.*^{1} 3.

7. a. A clasp, buckle, clamp, or other connecting piece or fastener.

c **1440** *Promp. Parv.* 46 Brace of a balke, *uncus*, *loramentum*. **1571** *Wills & Inv. N.C.* (1835) 362 On^m iij^c claspes for collers..iij boxes of bresses ij^s vj. **1580** HOLLYBAND *Treas. Fr. Tong*, *Agraphe*, a buckle of a gyrdle, a claspe, a brace. **1607** TOPSELL *Four-f. Beasts* 177 Some thick collar or brace, so as he [the Fox] can never bite it asunder. **1639** HORN & ROB. *Gate Lang. Unl.* xlix. §545 *marg.*, The braches bind down and hold fast the dormans to the studs. **1790** COWPER *Odyss.* I. 561 Fasten'd it with bolt and brace secure. **1868** G. STEPHENS *Runic Mons.* I. 295 This Bronze Brace..has belonged to a Sword-sheath of wood.

b. *Dentistry.* A wire device for straightening the teeth.

1952 *News Chron.* 8 July, If she wears corrective glasses or braces on her teeth, pretty hair makes her less conscious of her handicaps. **1952** M. MCCARTHY *Groves of Academe* (1953) iv. 56 They had been routed to the dentist for braces.

†**8.** The fibula of the leg. A transl. of L. *fibula* lit. 'brooch' or 'buckle'. Cf. *brace-bone* in VI.

1656 DUGARD *Gate Lat. Unl.* §223. 61 The Fibula, or Brace, or lesser focile.

9. A strap bearing a buckle, or otherwise adapted to be drawn tight and fastened: **a.** for tightening the joints of armour. (Perh. only a mod. inference from BRACE *v.*^{1})

1852 MISS YONGE *Cameos* (1877) II. iii. 29 His own thrifty hands mended the brace.

b. One of a pair of straps of leather or webbing used to support the trousers; a suspender. (In quot. 1816 with pun on BRACE *sb.*^{3}; cf. BRACER^1 1, quot. 1799.)

1798 JANE AUSTEN *Let.* 27 Oct. (1952) 23 There were no narrow braces for children and scarcely any notting silk. 1806 J. BERESFORD *Miseries Hum. Life* I. x. 261 When dressing in violent haste—your braces becoming suddenly ..entangled. 1816 'QUIZ' *Grand Master* I. 20 It broke, and .. Carried away both stays and braces. 1824 *Craven Dial.* 17 They gee 'em two names, a braas an a gallows. 1848 THACKERAY *Van. Fair* iii. (1853) 15, I have embroidered for you a very beautiful pair of braces.

c. A strap serving as a handle (*fig.* in quot.).

1592 BP. ANDREWES *Serm.* (1843) V. 504 Our faith is the braces or handle whereby we take hold.

10. a. A leathern thong which slides up and down the cord of a drum, and is used to regulate the tension of the skins, and thus the pitch of the note. (cf. BRACE *v.*^{1} 4.) †**b.** Also the cord itself (*obs.*).

1596 *Edw. III*, II. ii. 26 Go.. hang him in the braces of his drum. *a* 1735 DERHAM (J.) The little bones of the ear-drum do in straining and relaxing it, as the braces of the war-drum do in that. 1880 GROVE *Dict. Mus.* I. 466/1 This cord is tightened by means of leather braces. *Ibid.* 466/2 The heads are tightened by cords and braces.

c. *transf.* Tension.

a 1697 HOLDER (J.) The laxness of the tympanum when it has lost its brace or tension.

11. ***brace of a coach***: one of the stout leathern straps by which the body of a carriage is suspended from the springs.

1720 GAY *Poems* (1745) I. 174 See yon bright chariot on its braces swing. 1794 W. FELTON *Carriages* (1801) I. 226 The bodies of Carriages are suspended from the springs by braces.

12. *Naut.* (See quot. 1850.)

c 1850 *Rudim. Navig.* (Weale) 100 *Braces*, straps of iron, copper, or mixed metal, secured with bolts and screws to the stern-post and bottom planks. In their after ends are holes to receive the pintles by which the rudder is hung. 1869 SIR E. REED *Ship-build.* xiii. 247 The rudder was hung to three braces, riveted to the hollow-plate stern-post.

13. A slender bandage or cord fastened round a decoy-bird's body. Cf. *brace-bird* in VI.

1768 PENNANT *Zool.* II. 332 These birds [the decoys] are secured.. by what is called a brace.

14. A sign } used in writing or printing, chiefly for the purpose of uniting together two or more lines, words, staves of music, etc. Sometimes, but less correctly, used in plural to denote square brackets [ ].

1656 BLOUNT *Glossogr.* s.v., With Printers a Brace is that which couples two or more words together. 1806 CALLCOTT *Mus. Gram.* i. 3 When a Staff is wanted for each hand they are joined together by a Brace. 1824 L. MURRAY *Eng. Gram.* I. 413 A Brace } is used in poetry at the end of a triplet. 1841 J. R. YOUNG *Math. Dissert.* iii. 129 The first term within the braces. 1880 MUIRHEAD *Gaius* Introd. 12, I have had recourse to.. braces [ ] and marks of parenthesis.

III. 15. Two things taken together; a pair, a couple. Often a mere synonym for *two*, as in cricketing language 'A hit B for a brace'; see c.

In this sense the plural is also *brace*, as in *two or three brace*, *several brace*.

a. *orig.* of dogs. (Perhaps the band or cord with which dogs were coupled in coursing was called a *brace*; cf. sense 13 and LEASH.)

1430 LYDG. *Chron. Troy* I. vi, This ylke lease of thre.. All sodeynly was tourned to a brase. *c* 1440 *Promp. Parv.* 46 Brace of howndys. 1593 SHAKS. *3 Hen. VI*, II. v. 129 Edward and Richard like a brace of Grey-hounds.. Are at our backes. 1602 DEKKER *Satirom.* Wks. 1873 I. 226 *Sir Vaugh.* I indited a brace or two more. *Asi.* He makes hounds of us ..a brace quoth a? 1816 SCOTT *Bl. Dwarf* ii. 15 He summoned to his side the brace of large greyhounds.

b. of other animals, *esp.* certain kinds of game.

1570 LEVINS *Manip.* 6 A Brace of Deere, *duo damae.* 1651 FULLER *Abel Rediv. Erasmus* (1867) I. 83 Hammond and Urswick sent him a brace of geldings. 1715 *Lond. Gaz.* No. 5371/4 A brace of Trouts. 1741 *Compl. Fam.-Piece* II. i. 317 A Brace or Leash of Live Partridges. 1851 KINGSLEY *Bad Squire* 28 A few more brace of game. 1867 F. FRANCIS *Angling* v. (1880) 178, I rose and hooked six brace of capital fish.

c. of things. (More correctly when united or paired, as in *a* ***brace of pistols.***) ***a brace of shakes***: see SHAKE *sb.*^{1} 2 h. Hence in *Cricket*: ***a brace*** (***of ducks***), a score of nought in both innings of a match; ***to bag a brace***, to score nought in both innings.

1583 STUBBES *Anat. Abus.* (1877) 75 Their Parents owe a brase of hunndred pounds more than they are worth. 1630 M. GODWYN *Annales England* 232 Robert Ket.. had gathered a fortune of a brace of thousands. 1642 FULLER *Holy & Prof. St.* III. vii. 167 Borrowing of thy neighbour a brace of chambers for a night. 1719 DEFOE *Crusoe* 200 The two Muskets I loaded with a Brace of Slugs each. 1725 *Lond. Gaz.* No. 6372/3 Shot through the Left Arm with a Brace of Bullets. 1755 MRS. C. CHARKE *Life* 45 A heavy Blunderbuss, a Muscatoon, and two Brace of Pistols. 1832 HT. MARTINEAU *Ireland* v. 85 Three brace of pistols. 1867 *J. Lillywhite's Cricketers' Compan.* 57 Tom Humphrey achieved the feat of 'bagging a brace'. 1891 W. G. GRACE *Cricket* xi. 329 In 1868, he got me out for a brace of 'ducks' at Neath. 1903 P. F. WARNER in H. G. Hutchinson *Cricket* xiv. 398 More than one well-known cricketer has 'bagged a brace' there. 1912 A. A. LILLEY *Twenty-four Years Cricket* v. 65 Noble and Gregory.. were thus dismissed for a 'brace'. 1929 *Chicago Sunday Trib.* 25 Aug. I. 3/7 They found Edward Barnett.. and his brother.. sleeping with a brace of automatics under their pillows.

d. of persons. (Chiefly with a touch of humour or contempt.)

1606 WARNER *Alb. Eng.* XIV. xci. (1612) 370 Clargie-men .. Pluralitie that huddle, haue also their brace of wiues. 1655 FULLER *Ch. Hist.* II. ii. §84 I. 213 A brace of Brethren, both Bishops. 1768 GOLDSM. *Good-n. Man* III. i, I'll undertake to set down a brace of dukes. 1847 TENNYSON *Princ.* v. 453 A lusty brace of twins may weed her of her folly. 1863 MRS. C. CLARKE *Shaks. Char.* xix. 483 Thorough specimens of a brace of vulgar demagogues.

IV. That which imparts rigidity or steadiness; cf. BRACE *v.*^{1} 6.

16. A strip or band of metal used for support, e.g. in mounting bells.

1730 *Churchw. Accts. Holy Cross, Canterb.*, Casting All ye braces for ye bells. 1880 GROVE *Dict. Mus.* I. 219/2 Bells.. are first carefully secured by iron bolts and braces. 1885 *Manch. Exam.* 21 July 6/5 The pieces of copper were furnished.. with iron braces, intended to give them rigidity.

17. a. *Building* and *Mech.* A timber or scantling used in a roof or other trussed framework to stiffen the assemblage of pieces composing it; a piece of timber or iron used to strengthen the framework of a vessel, bridge, pier, etc.; a stay used to steady a printing press.

1530 PALSGR. 200/2 Brace of an house, *brace.* 1616 BULLOKAR, *Braces*, In building it signifieth the peeces of timber which bend forward on both sides and beare up the rafters. 1677 MOXON *Mech. Exerc.* (1703) 141 The Quarters and Braces between the principal Posts.. are fitted in. 1823 P. NICHOLSON *Pract. Build.* 155 To keep the timbers from descending, two braces are introduced. 1838 F. SIMMS *Public Wks. Gt. Brit.* II. 25 Diagonal braces of cast iron. 1841 *Penny Cycl.* XXI. 395/2 A method of counteracting the arching of a ship by braces of iron. 1867 SMYTH *Sailor's Word-Bk.* 127 Braces are plates of iron.. used to bind efficiently a weakness in a vessel.

b. In the theatre, a rod or length of timber used to brace a flat.

1866 W. DAVIDGE *Footlight Flashes* xv. 151 They are called braces, and are used for sustaining the weight of cottages, trees, and set pieces of all kinds. 1941 N. COWARD *Australia Visited* vii. 46 The actors stumble around.. making believe that a few chairs, braces, and empty sugar-boxes are the palace of a King.

V. Technical uses of obscure origin.

18. in *Mining.*

1881 RAYMOND *Mining Gloss.*, *Brace*, the mouth of a shaft.

19. in *Agriculture.*

1807 VANCOUVER *Agric. Devon* (1813) 119 Near the point of the share, a comb or brace rises, and.. is inserted about midway in the perpendicular bar.

VI. 20. *Comb.* and *Attrib.*, as ***brace-button***, ***braces-maker***; also **brace-bird**, a decoy-bird secured by a brace (see 13); †**brace-bone**, the fibula; **brace-drill**, a boring tool shaped like a brace; **brace-head, -key**, an attachment at the top of a column of boring-rods, by means of which these are turned; **brace-piece**, *Sc.*, a mantel-piece; **brace-rod**, a connecting rod used to support or give rigidity to any part of a structure; **brace-shot** *U.S.* = BRACKET *sb.* 5 b.

1885 *Pall Mall G.* 10 Oct. 4/2 The *brace bird is generally a goldfinch. 1634 T. JOHNSON *Parey's Chirurg.* XV. ii. (1678) 327 The *brace-bone serves for the sustaining of the muscles, and not of the body as the leg-bone doth. 1875 URE *Dict. Arts* I. 439 The *brace-head, or cross-head, with the four handles held by the borers. 1836 DICKENS *Sk. Boz* (1850) 149/2 A retired glove and *braces maker. 1844 H. STEPHENS *Bk. Farm* I. 428 In this plough.. there is usually applied a *brace-rod V. 1907 *Westm. Gaz.* 27 Dec. 4/2 On a special collar of the enclosed propeller-shaft are two brace-rods, extending triangular fashion to the sleeves of the live axle. 1914 R. H. DAVIS *With the Allies* (1915) 134 To find the range the artillery sends what in the American army are called *brace shots.

brace (breɪs), *sb.*^{3} *Naut.* Also 7 **brase**. [a. F. *bras* (*de vergue*) of same meaning (lit. 'arm'); assimilated to BRACE *sb.*^{2} It is less probable that Fr. *bras* in this sense is an adaptation of the Eng. word, which would then be a special application of BRACE *sb.*^{2} II.] A rope attached to the yard of a vessel for the purpose of 'trimming' the sail.

1626 CAPT. SMITH *Accid. Yng. Seamen* 28 Ease your mayne brases. 1762 FALCONER *Shipwr.* II. *note*, The lee-brace confines the yard so that the tack will not come down to its place. 1840 R. DANA *Bef. Mast* v. 10 We were obliged to steady the booms and yards by guys and braces.

b. *attrib.*, as in ***brace-block***, ***-man***, ***-pendant.***

c 1860 H. STUART *Seaman's Catech.* 49 Brace men attend their braces. 1867 SMYTH *Sailor's Word-Bk.* 127 Brace pendants are lengths of rope, or.. chain, into which the yard-arm brace-blocks are spliced.

brace (breɪs), *v.*^{1} Also 4–7 bras(e, 6 brais(s, 7 **breace**. [ad. OF. *bracie-r* to embrace, f. *brace* the two arms; but some of the senses are taken directly from those of BRACE *sb.*^{2} q.v.]

†**1.** *trans.* To put the arms round, embrace. *Obs.*

c 1375 ? BARBOUR *St. Thomas* 135 In armys cane brase þame bath. *c* 1430 *Syr Gener.* 3324 In his armes he can hir brace. 1526 SKELTON *Magnyf.* 1578 A baby to brace and to basse. 1570 LEVINS *Manip.* 6 To Brace, *amplecti.*

2. To encompass, surround, gird, encircle; also, *causally*, to put round, make to surround. (Now usually with some notion of 3 combined.)

1513 DOUGLAS *Æneis* IX. vi. 140 Euryll.. hes this jowell [a girdle] hynt, About his sydis it brasing. 1579 SPENSER *Sheph. Cal.* Sept. 124 Bigge Bulles of Basan brace hem about. 1782 COWPER *Gilpin* 122 He seem'd to carry weight, With leathern girdle braced. 1835 AIRD *Chr. Bride* I. v, A flowing wood the middle mountain braced.

3. To clasp, fasten up tightly, gird: sometimes with a reference to one or other of the senses of BRACE *sb.*^{2}

c 1325 *Coer de L.* 5649 Anon did hote Faste that men scholde it brace. ? *a* 1400 *Morte Arth.* 1182 Stryke of his hevede.. brace it in yryne, And sett it on the barbycane. 1530 LYNDESAY *Papyngo* 938 They haue ane Boumbard, braissit vp in bandis. 1562 LEIGH *Armorie* (1597) 10 b, A Souldior.. caused his man to brace him in a male. 1695 BLACKMORE *Pr. Arth.* IV. 566 He ne'er before had brac'd the Helmet on. 1725 POPE *Odyss.* x. 19 The adverse winds in leathern bags he brac'd. 1810 CRABBE *Borough* v. Wks. 1834 III. 105 His short stout person he is wont to brace In good brown broad-cloth. 1870 BRYANT *Iliad* VIII. I. 255, I brace my armor on for war.

4. To make tight or tense; to stretch, strain (*esp.* the skin of a drum). Cf. BRACE *sb.*^{2} 10.

c 1440 *Promp. Parv.* 46 Bracyn, or sette streyte, *tendo.* 1595 SHAKS. *John* v. ii. 169 A drumme is readie brac'd, That shall reuerberate all, as lowd as thine. 1730 SWIFT *Panegyr. Dean* Wks. 1755 IV. I. 142 Then gluttony.. Brac'd like a drum her oily skin. 1777 ROBERTSON *Hist. Amer.* III. 443 Bracing the back of the bow with a kind of thread. 1802 PALEY *Nat. Theol.* iii. (1827) 445 In a drum the pelt is carried over a hoop, and braced as occasion requires.

5. a. To 'string up' (nerves, sinews, etc.), give firmness or tone to. So also ***to brace up.***

1736 GRAY *Let.* in *Poems* (1775) 9 His vigorous arm he try'd.. Brac'd all his nerves, and every sinew strung. 1740 CHEYNE *Regimen* 66 Medicines, to brace and wind up the Stomach. *c* 1750 SHENSTONE *Elegies* ix. 14 They gave you toils, but toils your sinews brace. 1847 L. HUNT *Men, Women, & Bks.* I. iii. 40 Would to Heaven his nerves had been as braced up as his face. 1879 CHR. ROSSETTI *Seek & F.* 56 Winter which nips can also brace.

b. *fig.* Also refl. ***to brace oneself*** (cf. *to gird oneself*); also ***to brace one's heart, energies***, etc., in sense of summoning up resolution for a task. Also freq. with *up.*

a 1500 *Chaucer Poem* in Todd *Illustr.* 299 Arysyng full lyghtely my sylfe did brase. 1805 WORDSW. *Prel.* I. (1850) 8 An earnest longing rose To brace myself to some determined aim. 1816 JANE AUSTEN *Emma* I. vii. 113 It was ..necessary to brace her up with a few decisive expressions. 1836 THIRLWALL *Greece* II. xv. 306 Nothing now remained but to brace every nerve for the battle. 1876 GREEN *Short Hist.* i. §4. 39 Under Offa Mercia first really braced herself to the completion of her British conquests. 1887 M. CORELLI *Thelma* I. xvii, He paused—then suddenly bracing himself up, added [etc.]. 1891 HARDY *Group of Noble Dames* ix. 230 It gave him an opportunity to brace himself up. 1903 'No. 7' *25 Years in 17 Prisons* xii. 125 When I heard the words 'sad news'.. I braced myself up, clenched my teeth.. and prepared to hear the worst.

c. *intr.* ***to brace up***: to brace oneself; to pull oneself together for an effort; also, to take a drink for this purpose. *orig. U.S.*

1809 *Deb. Congress* 20 Jan. 1148 We have been.. bracing up; we have had plenty of good wine. 1817 S. R. BROWN *Western Gaz.* 354 If the stomach be foul.. take an emetic, and then brace up with bark. 1845 C. M. KIRKLAND *Western Clearings* 62 He braces up for the occasion. *a* 1910 'MARK TWAIN' *Myst. Stranger* (1916) 130 All that was needed.. was that Wilhelm should brace up and do something that should cause favorable talk. 1958 M. DICKENS *Man Overboard* ix. 145 Don't make a scene, Mum... Brace up.

6. a. To render firm or steady by binding tightly.

1785 COWPER *Task* I. 41 A lattice-work, that braced The new machine, and it became a chair. 1803 WELLINGTON in Gurw. *Disp.* I. 488 The spring lines are then lashed diagonally from one boat to the other to brace them tight. 1870 ROLLESTON *Anim. Life* 144 They are braced by ligaments.

b. More generally: To fix, render firm, set rigidly or firmly down. Also *fig.*

1849 THOREAU *Week Concord Riv.* Thursd. 315 With their fore feet braced, they sustained the rushing torrent in their rear. 1873 HOLLAND *A. Bonnic.* xiii. 222 Braced by them as I was, Mr. Mullens made no headway against me. 1876 WHYTE-MELVILLE *Katerfelto* ix. 98 He braced his foot in the stirrup to afford a purchase for her ascent.

7. To join firmly, couple together.

1826 E. IRVING *Babylon* I. III. 210 Which event is again braced to the former parts of the book.

†**brace**, *v.*^{2} *Obs.* Also 6 brase. [prob. a use of BRACE *v.*^{1} (see esp. sense 5): but cf. also OF. *braçoier* to swing the arms about (as a sign of pride; cf. quot. in Godef. 'Orgueus va des bras brachoiant, Des espaules espauloiant').] To bluster, domineer; to assume a defiant attitude; chiefly in phrase *to face and brace.*

1447–8 SHILLINGFORD *Lett.* (1871) 23 He can.. braule, bragge and brace, lye and swere well to. *a* 1529 SKELTON *Agst. Scottes* 33 Such boste make To face and brace All voyd of Grace. 1549 LATIMER *Serm. bef. Edw. VI* (Arb.) 152 Men .. woulde face it and brace it and make a shewe of vpryght dealynge. *a* 1563 BECON *Fortr. Faithf.* (1844) 599 They gripe, they nip, they face, they brase, they semble.. to maintain and set forth their unnoble nobility.

brace (breɪs), *v.*^{3} *Naut.* Also 7 breace. [ad. F. *brasser* (also *brasseyer*), of same meaning; or f. BRACE *sb.*^{3}] *trans.* To move or turn (a sail) by means of braces. Hence, with various adverbs and prepositions, as ***brace aback***, to draw (the yards) in, so as to lay the sails aback; ***brace about, abox*** (see quots.); ***brace by***, to brace (the yards) in contrary directions on the different masts; ***brace in***, to lay (the yards) less obliquely athwartships; ***brace round*** = *brace about*; ***brace sharp*** (see quot.); ***brace to***, to ease the lee- and draw in (the weather-braces) so as to assist in tacking; ***brace up***, to put (the yards) into a more oblique position. Also *absol.* in prec. uses.

1669 STURMY *Mariner's Mag.* I. ii. 16 Breace the Foresail ..to the Mast. **1675** *Lond. Gaz.* No. 3073/3 He Braced to and fell a-stern. **1762** FALCONER *Shipwr.* II. 908 Brace the foremost yards aback. **1769** —— *Dict. Marine* (1789) *Brasser sous le vent*, to brace to leeward, or brace-up the yards. **1832** MARRYAT *N. Forster* xi, The yards [were] braced by. **1840** R. DANA *Bef. Mast* xxii. 66 Her yards were braced sharp up. **1867** SMYTH *Sailor's Word-bk.* 127 *To brace about*, to turn the yards round for the contrary tack. *To brace abox*, a manœuvre to insure casting the right way, by bracing the head-yards flat aback (not square). *To brace sharp*, to cause the yards to have the smallest possible angle with the keel, for the ship to have head-way.

b. *transf.* (humorous.)

1834 M. SCOTT *Cruise Midge* (1863) 34 We braced up sharp round a right-angled corner of our pestiferous path.

brace, *a. U.S. slang.* [? attrib. use of BRACE *sb.*^{2}] ***brace game***, a game in which there is concerted cheating; ***brace box***, in faro, a dealing box designed to facilitate cheating.

1875 *Chicago Tribune* 25 Aug. 8/1 The brace game flourishes..to cheat the gambling fraternity. **1908** S. E. WHITE *Riverman* vi. 58 'I tell you, you can't win!' cried Newmark disgustedly. 'It's a brace game pure and simple.' **1908** G. H. LORIMER *J. Spurlock* vi. 116 Life's not even a gamble in this age of commercialism, fo' Fo'tune deals from a brace box.

brace, variant of BRAZE *v. Obs.*

braced (breɪst), *ppl. a.*^{1} [f. BRACE *v.*^{1} + -ED.]

1. Strained, strengthened, girt, etc.; cf. the verb.

1633 P. FLETCHER *Purple Isl.* v. xl, Where stands a braced drumme, whose sounding head..Gives instant warning. **1847** BARHAM *Ingol. Leg.* (1877) 265 In Mariner's dress, with cutlass braced. **1862** RUSSELL in *Times* 27 Mar., The deck..is supported by heavy braced oak beams.

†**b.** *fig.* = Contracted. *Obs. rare.*

1534 WHITTINTON *Tullyes Offices* I. (1540) 31 Nothynge of so strayte and brased stomake and so poore.

2. *Her.* Interlaced or linked together. Also written *brased.*

1562 LEIGH *Armorie* (1597) 105 b, He beareth..iij Cheuronnels, brased on the baste Or. **1766** PORNY *Heraldry* (1787) 150 A Man's Heart Gules, within two equilateral triangles braced Sable.

braced, *ppl. a.*^{2} *Naut.* [f. BRACE *v.*^{3} + -ED.] Turned or moved by means of braces.

1762 FALCONER *Shipwr.* I. 228 Yards alternate square and sharply braced. **1881** *Times* 21 Dec., The vessel was hove to ..with yards braced up.

†**'bracel.** *Obs. rare.* [a. OF. *bracel*:—L. *bra(c)chiāle* bracelet, f. *bra(c)chium* arm.] A bracelet.

c **1535** DEWES *Introd. Fr.* in Palsgr. 907 The bracel, *le bracelet.*

braceless ('breɪslɪs), *a.* [f. BRACE *sb.*^{2} + -LESS.] Without a brace or braces.

1859 F. MAHONEY *Rel. Father Prout* 233 Braceless breeches.

bracelet ('breɪslɪt). Forms: 5- **bracelet**, 5 **brasselat**, 6 **bracelette**, **bracellette**, **brasche-**, **brase-**, 7 **bras-**, **brasselet**. [a. OF. *bracelet*, dim. of OF. *bracel*: see BRACEL.]

1. a. An ornamental ring or band worn on the arm or wrist.

1438 *E. E. Wills* (1882) 110 A Bracelet of Gold. **1488** *Invent. Jas. III* in Tytler *Hist. Scot.* (1864) II. 391 A brasselat of gold, with hede & pendes of gold. **1549** *Compl. Scot.* 120 I tuke his croune fra his hede, and his brascheletis fra his armis. **1611** SHAKS. *Cymb.* v. v. 416 The Bracelet of the truest Princesse That euer swore her Faith. *a* **1634** RANDOLPH *Poems* (1638) 13 Upon her arme a braslet hung. **1717** LADY M. W. MONTAGUE *Lett.* II. xliv. 19 She wore large diamond bracelets. **1839** THIRLWALL *Greece* II. 348 The collars and bracelets, with which the Persians.. adorned their persons.

b. *Palmistry.* A wrinkle crossing the wrist at its junction with the hand.

1883 FRITH & ALLEN *Chiromancy* 125 The Rascette or 'bracelets'..will be found in two or three distinctly marked lines underneath the hand. **1891** *Chambers's Encycl.* VII. 727 These last (the bracelets), if well marked, strengthen the effect of the line of life, each bracelet indicating thirty years of life.

c. A narrow band of hair left on the legs of an animal after it has been clipped.

1904 *Windsor Mag.* Jan. 290/1 The only sign of hair being on the ears and the 'bracelets' around the legs.

†**2.** Applied to ornaments of similar shape worn on other parts of the person. *Obs.*

1624 CAPT. SMITH *Virginia* I. 3 In her eares were bracelets of pearle. **1684** BUNYAN *Pilgr.* II. (1862) 339 About Christiana's neck the Shepherds put a Bracelet. **1684** BURNET tr. *More's Utopia* 106 Their Caps were covered with Bracelets set full of Pearls and other Gems.

3. A fetter for the wrist, a gyve, hand-cuff.

1816 SCOTT *Harold Dauntl.* IV. viii, His bracelets of iron —his bed in our towers. **1883** *Pall Mall G.* 21 Sept. 12/1 Punishment used for refractory prisoners in Sing Sing:—Tight steel bracelets are fastened about the wrists.

4. A piece of armour covering the arm.

1580 HOLLYBAND *Treas. Fr. Tong, Vn gardebras*, the bracelets of an armour. **1864** BURTON *Scot Abr.* III. ii. 135 Armed with..headpiece and bracelets.

5. *Her.* = BARRULET.

6. *Comb.* Also **braceletless** *a.*, without bracelets.

1655 MRQ. WORCESTER *Cent. Inv.* Index 4 A Bracelet-alphabet [to write..by stringing of Bracelets.] **1801** SOUTHEY *Thalaba* VI. xxvi, Their ancles bound with bracelet-bells. **1873** MISS BROUGHTON *Nancy* I. 84 Barbara is locketless, braceletless, chainless.

braceleted ('breɪslɪtɪd), *ppl. a.* [f. prec. + -ED^2.] Furnished with a bracelet or bracelets.

1630 J. TAYLOR (Water-P.) *Wks.* III. 98 She's ring'd, she's braceletted, she's richly tuff'd. **1843** *Blackw. Mag.* LIV. 338 Her many-braceleted arms. **1885** C. E. CRADDOCK *Proph. Smoky Mount* i. 25 His prisoner braceleted with the..hand-cuffs.

†**'bracement.** *Obs. rare*$^{-1}$. [f. BRACE *v.*^{1} + -MENT.] (See quot.)

1677 GREW *Anat. Fruits* iii. §7 The Bracement or Reticulation of the Vessels.

bracer^1 ('breɪsə(r)). [f. as prec. + -ER^1.]

1. That which clamps, binds, etc.; a cincture, bandage, brace; †also a pair of braces (*obs.*).

1579 J. JONES *Preserv. Body and Soul* I. xix. 34 Vsing instruments..as Brasers, Wastes, or bodies, made eyther of paper bordes, plate, or Cardes, etc. to make them slender. **1626** CAPT. SMITH *Accid. Yng. Seamen* 11 Bindings, knees, boults, trunions, brasers. **1730** A. GORDON *Maffei's Amphit.* 213 By reason of the Concatenation of the Stones and Iron Bracers. **1799** *Specif. J. Foster's Patent* No. 2361 Making a bracer or sling for..keeping up breeches. **1876** GEO. ELIOT *Dan. Der.* VIII. lx. 543 The chest..was made heavy by ornamental bracers and handles.

†**2.** ? The 'enarme' or strap for holding the buckler on the arm. *Obs. rare*$^{-1}$. (But cf. next word.)

1612 BEAUM. & FL. *Cupid's Rev.* IV. 419 Take down my Buckler..and fetch a nail or two: and tack on bracers.

3. That which braces (the nerves); *hence* a tonic medicine (a common sense in 18th c., now *obs.*). *spec.* A drink taken to brace one up (*colloq.*, orig. *U.S.*).

1740 CHEYNE *Regimen* p. ix, Bark, Bitters and Steel, and such Astringents and Bracers. **1826** SCOTT in *Lockhart* (1839) VIII. 204 Adversity is to me a tonic and a bracer. **1829** *Savannah* (Ga.) *Mercury* 1 July (Th.), If I take..a cooler at nine, a bracer at ten, a whetter at eleven,..who has a right to complain? **1830** *Fraser's Mag.* I. 182 As a bracer to the nerves, [I] slipped into the provision-basket a handful of..bottles. **1877** J. HABBERTON *Jericho Road* 12 Treat him to whisky; he needs a bracer. **1924** WODEHOUSE *Bill the Conq.* xx. 288 He took some worms and slipped them a stiff bracer. **1951** M. KENNEDY *Lucy Carmichael* II. iii. 113 We're all going into the Swan for a bracer... Do come..and have a drink before your drive back.

'bracer^2. Forms: 4-6 **braser**, 5 **bracere** (in Cath. Angl.), **brassure**, 6 **bracher**, 6-7 **brasar**, 7 **bracert**, **brasser**, 4- **bracer**. [a. OF. *brasseüre* (L. type **bracchiātūra*, f. *bracchium* arm); influenced by the synon. Fr. *brassard*, and by analogy of -ER: cf. *bordure, border.*]

The portion of a suit of armour covering the arm. Also a sort of guard for the wrist used in archery, in fencing, and in playing games at ball.

c **1386** CHAUCER *Prol.* 111 Vp on his arm he baar a gay bracer. ? *a* **1400** *Morte Arth.* 1859 Brasers burnyste bristez in sondyre. **1545** ASCHAM *Toxoph.* (Arb.) 108 A bracer serueth..to saue his arme from the strype of the strynge. *Ibid.* (1654) 146, I sawe a man whyche vsed a brasar on his cheke. **1570** LEVINS *Manip.* 72 A Bracher, *brachiale.* **1611** MARKHAM *Countr. Content.* I. viii. (1668) 47 A mans Arm arm'd in a bracer of wood. **1624** CAPT. SMITH *Virginia* II. 31 His arrow head he quickly maketh with a little bone, which he ever weareth at his bracert. **1734** tr. *Rollin's Anc. Hist.* (1827) II. IV. 259 Presented him with a helmet, bracers & bracelets all of gold. **1801** STRUTT *Sports & Past.* II. iii. 89 A round hollow bracer of wood to cover the hand and lower part of the arm, with which he struck the ball. **1886** WOOD *Man & Handiwk.* 241 Modern archers possess..a sort of gauntlet called a bracer.

†**'bracery.** *Obs. rare*$^{-1}$. [? Short for EMBRACERY.] Embracery, corruption.

1540 *Act 32 Hen. VIII*, ix, *title*, The bill of bracery and buying of titles. **1886** in *Law Q. Rev.* Oct. 484 Our laws did manifest a great..jealousy of..bracery and the buying of pretenced titles.

braces, suspenders: see BRACE *sb.*^{2} 9 b.

brach (brætʃ). *arch.* Forms: 4-5 *pl.* **braches**, **-ez**, 5 **bracke**, **brasche**, 6 **braach**, **bratche**, 7 **bratch**, 6-7 **brache**, 6- **brach**. [ME. *braches* pl., prob. a. OF. *brachès*, *brachez*, pl. of *brachet* (med.L. *brachētus*), dim. of *brac* (accus. *bracon*), a common Romanic word (Pr. *brac*, *bracon*, It. *bracco*, Sp. *braco*, med.L. *bracco*, *-ōnem*), a. OHG. *bracco* (MHG. *bracke*) a hound hunting by scent. From this pl. *braches* was app. educed an English sing. *brache*, *brach*. (F. *braque* masc. is a modern form, prob. from It. or MHG.)]

A kind of hound which hunts by scent; in later Eng. use, always feminine, and extended to any kind of hound; a bitch-hound.

c **1340** *Gaw. & Gr. Knt.* 1142 Braches bayed þerfore & breme noyse maked. *Ibid.* 1563 The best of his brachez. **1467** *Househ. Exp.* 558 A ȝonge brasche of halfe ȝere holde. **1490** CAXTON *Eneydos* xv. 54 Theyr brackes retches and bloode houndes. **1594** CAREW *Huarte's Exam. Wits* x. (1596) 131 A braach, to hunt and bring the game to his hand. **1596** NASHE *Saffron Walden* T, And so it is with his bratche or bitche-foxe. **1611** MARKHAM *Countr. Content.* (1649) 27 When your Bratch is neere whelping..you shall separate her from other hounds. **1686** *Gentl. Recreat.* II. 27 in *Cath. Angl.* 39 A brach is a mannerly name for all hound-bitches. **1811** W. SPENCER *Poems* 78 Many a brach, and many a hound Attend Llewellyn's horn. **1848** KINGSLEY *Saint's Trag.* II. i. 63 We'll..pamper the brach till we make her a wolf. **1864** H. KINGSLEY *Hillyars* xxiii, Let them take their braches and lie down.

b. *fig.* A term of abuse. Cf. BITCH.

1610 B. JONSON *Alch.* I. i, Away this brach. *a* **1652** BROME *Cov. Gard. weeded* IV. i, Thou greedy Brach.

†**'brachal.** *Obs. rare*$^{-1}$. [app. ad. It. *bracciale*, of same meaning; cf. L. *bracchiāle*, f. *bracchium* arm.] Protective armour for the arm.

1658 J. BURBERY *Christina Q. Swedland* 466 The Cavaliers ..were armed on the breast and the back, with brachals and gauntlets.

brache, -er, obs. forms of BRACE, BRACER.

†**'brachell.** *Obs. rare*$^{-1}$. = BRACHET; (prob. an error: a female bloodhound is meant).

c **1470** HENRY *Wallace* v. 25 In Gyllisland thar was that brachell brede.

brachelytrous (bræ'kɛlɪtrəs), *a.* [f. mod.L. *brachelytr-a* (f. Gr. βραχ-ύς short + ἔλυτρον case, sheath) + -OUS: cf. F. *brachélytre.* (A more correct form would be *brachyelytrous.*)] Pertaining to the *Brachelytra*, a division of the beetles distinguished by the shortness of their wing-sheaths.

1847 *Proc. Berw. Nat. Club* II. 233 Brachelytrous insects forming the family Staphylinidæ.

brachen, obs. Sc. form of BRACKEN.

brachet ('brætʃɪt). *arch.* Also 4 **brachete**, 5 **brachett**, 9 **bratchet**. [a. F. *brachet*, dim. of *brac*: see BRACH, and BRATCHET.]

1. = BRACH.

[**1262** in *Athenæum* 20 Aug. (1881) 241 Cum octo brachettis et quatuor Leporariis.] *c* **1340** *Gaw. & Gr. Knt.* 1603 Brachetes bayed þat best. **1483** *Cath. Angl.* 39 A Brachett, *oderensicus.* **1557** *K. Arthur* (Copland) III. v, There came rennynge in a whyte hart..and a whyte brachet next hym. **1808** SCOTT *Marm.* II. Introd. 40 The Bratchet's bay From the dark covert drove the prey.

2. A little brat, a child: see BRATCHET.

†**'brachetour.** *Obs. rare.* [ad. med.L. *braciātor* brewer (prob. through an AFr. **brachetour*; cf. ONF. *brachier* = OF. *bracier*, mod. *brasser* to brew).] A brewer.

1598 KITCHIN *Courts Leet* (1675) 28 If any Butcher, Brachetour, Baker..&c. conspire..not to sell victual but at certain prices.

brachial ('brækɪəl, 'breɪkɪəl), *a.* Also 6 **brachiall**. [ad. L. *brāchiālis*, f. *brāchium*, *bracchium* an arm (see -AL^1); cf. F. *brachial.*]

1. Belonging to the arm; chiefly in *Phys.*, as ***brachial vein, artery, nerve, muscle, ganglion***, etc.; also ***brachial tooth***, an obs. name for the styloid process of the ulna. Rare in non-technical use.

1578 BANISTER *Hist. Man* III. 42 Two distinct orders of Brachiall bones. **1726** MONRO *Anat. Nerves* (1741) 66 It contributes to form the brachial Nerves. **1841** CATLIN *N. Amer. Ind.* (1844) II. lviii. 225 Inferior in brachial strength.

2. Of the nature of, or resembling, an arm. (*Zool.*)

1835 KIRBY *Hab. & Inst. Anim.* II. xvii. 106 Twelve tentacles rather smaller than the brachial ones. **1836** TODD *Cycl. Anat. & Phys.* I. 36/2 The mouth, surrounded by four brachial appendages.

brachial, *sb.* [f. the adj.]

1. = *brachial artery, vein*, etc.: see BRACHIAL *a.* I.

1859 TODD *Cycl. Anat. & Phys.* V. 542/1 The brachials and femorals are split up..into hair-like capillaries.

2. *Zool.* **a.** One of a series of bones in fishes to which the pectoral fins are attached.

1873 MIVART *Elem. Anat.* 162 The fourth or lowest of the four *brachials* which together may represent the humerus, and to which the fin-rays are attached.

b. One of the calcareous plates in the branches of a crinoid.

1888 ROLLESTON & JACKSON *Anim. Life* 572 The joints of the arms [in Crinoids] are termed *brachials.* **1962** D. NICHOLS *Echinoderms* ii. 24 The skeletal pieces supporting the arms are called *brachials.*

brachiate ('brækɪeɪt, 'breɪkɪət), *a.* [ad. L. *brāchiāt-us* armed, f. *brāchi-um* an arm: see -ATE².] *lit.* Having arms; in *Bot.* having branches in pairs running out nearly at right angles with the stem and crossing each other alternately.

1835 LINDLEY *Introd. Bot.* (1848) I. 169 When the branches diverge nearly at right angles from the stem, they are said to be brachiate. **1880** GRAY *Bot. Text-bk* 399.

brachiate ('brækɪeɪt), *v.* [As from BRACHIATE *a.*; see -ATE³.] *intr.* (See quot. 1948.) So **'brachiating** *ppl. a.* and *vbl. sb.*; **brachi'ation**, the act of brachiating; **'brachiator**, an animal that brachiates.

1899 *Proc. Zool. Soc.* 7 Mar. 306 The hand of the Chimpanzee is adapted for brachiation. *Ibid.* 305 The arm of the Chimpanzee is that of the brachiators, anthropoids like the Orang and Gibbon, which use the arms as one of the main organs of locomotion. **1932** J. S. HUXLEY *Probl. Rel. Growth* vii. 238 Man..is undoubtedly descended from brachiating ancestors with relatively long arms. **1934** WEBSTER *Brachiate* v.i. **1948** WEINER in *New Biol.* V. 70 Their [*sc.* apes'] ability to brachiate, that is to swing their way from branch to branch by their arms. **1957** *Antiquity* XXXI. 191 They lacked the brachiating specializations of modern apes. **1962** D. MORRIS *Biology of Art* v. 143 A hanging and swinging form of locomotion termed brachiation.

brachie, var. of BRACKY *a. Obs.* saltish.

brachiferous (bræ'kɪfərəs), *a. Zool.* [mod., f. L. *brāchi-um* arm + -FEROUS.] Arm-bearing.

1877 HUXLEY *Anat. Inv. An.* iii. 138 The brachiferous disk suspended by four pillars. **1880** *Syd. Soc. Lex.*, *Brachiferous disc*, the floor of the subumbrellar cavity in the Rhizostomidæ.

brachigerous (bræ'kɪdʒərəs), *a. Zool.* [f. as prec. + -GEROUS.] = prec.

1836 TODD *Cycl. Anat. & Phys.* I. 36/2 Groups into which the acalephæ have been divided..5. Brachigerous.

brachio-cephalic (,brækɪəʊsɪ'fælɪk), *a. Anat.* [ad. mod.L. *brachiocephalicus*, f. Gr. βραχίων arm + κεφαλή head; cf. κεφαλικός of or pertaining to the head.] Pertaining to both arm and head: applied chiefly to the blood-vessels common to the arms and head.

1836–39 TODD *Cycl. Anat. & Phys.* II. 850/1 The.. brachio-cephalic artery. **1849–52** *Ibid.* IV. 1408/2 This great vein..is formed by the union of the two brachio-cephalic veins.

brachiopod ('brækɪəʊpɒd). *Zool.* Pl. 'brachiopods, also in mod.L. form **brachiopoda** (brækɪ'ɒpədə). [ad. mod.L. *brachiopoda*, sb. pl. f. Gr. βραχίω-ν arm + πούς, ποδ- foot.]

A bivalve mollusc distinguished by having, on each side of the mouth, a long spiral arm, used in procuring food. Also *attrib.*

1836 *Penny Cycl.* V. 310/2 The generative system of the Brachiopoda. *Ibid.* 311/1 The Brachiopods..are stationary. **1859** DARWIN *Orig. Spec.* xi. (1878) 307 Certain Brachiopods have been but slightly modified from an extremely remote geological epoch. *Ibid.* ii. (1872) 35 Brachiopod shells.

Hence **brachi'opodist**, one versed in the study of brachiopods; **brachi'opodous** *a.*, of or resembling the brachiopoda.

1836 *Penny Cycl.* V. 310/2 The spiral disposition of the arms is common to the whole of the brachiopodous genera.. hitherto..examined. **1881** *Q. Jrnl. Geol. Soc.* 215 Nothing is left undone by that distinguished brachiopodist.

Brachiosaurus (,brækɪəʊ'sɔːrəs). *Palæont.* [mod.L., f. Gr. βραχίω-ν arm + σαῦρος lizard.] A genus of huge dinosaurs, with the forelegs longer than the hind legs; also, an animal of this genus.

1903 E. S. RIGGS in *Amer. Jrnl. Sci.* XV. 299 The term *Brachiosaurus altithorax* is therefore proposed in recognition of the great size and unusually long humerus of this specimen. *Ibid.* 306 The thoracic centra.. of *Brachiosaurus* ..range from 39 to 43 centimeters in length. **1931** *Discovery* May 142/2 A large dinosaur, which is perhaps allied to the brachiosaurus. **1934** W. E. SWINTON *Dinosaurs* vii. 90 There is little doubt that *Brachiosaurus* was an immense creature.

brachish, obs. form of BRACKISH.

brachisto-, comb. form of Gr. βράχιστος, superl. of βραχύς short, as in ‖**brachistocephali** (bræ,kɪstəʊ'sɛfəlaɪ), men or races with the shortest skull; **brachistocephaly** (-'sɛfəlɪ), the quality of having the shortest type of skull. Cf. BRACHYCEPHALIC. Also **brachistochrone** (bræ'kɪstəkrəʊn) [Gr. χρόν-ος time], the curve in which a body descending to a given point under the action of gravity will perform its journey in the shortest possible time; the curve of quickest descent.

1866 HUXLEY *Preh. Rem. Caithn.* 85 Sub-divide the Brachycephali into Eurycephali..and Brachistocephali. *Ibid.* 111 Of these, but one reaches the limits of brachistocephaly. *a* **1774** GOLDSM. *Surv. Exp. Philos.* (1776) I. 153 The curve of a cycloid, which was afterwards called by the hard name of a Brachystochrone, or the line of quickest descent. **1877** E. THOMAS tr. *Lange's Materialism* I. 122 The falling body reaches the goal more quickly upon the brachystochrone than upon an inclined plane.

‖**brachium** ('breɪkɪəm, 'brækɪəm). *Biol.* [L. *bra(c)chium*, the arm, spec. the fore-arm.] In Mammalia, the upper arm from the shoulder to the elbow.

1731 in BAILEY Vol. II. **1847** CRAIG [in the modern use]. **1877** HUXLEY & MARTIN *Practical Biol.* 160 Each fore limb is divided into *brachium*, *antebrachium*, and *manus*, which correspond with the arm, fore-arm, and hand in man.

brachman, obs. form of BRAHMIN.

brachy-, comb. form of Gr. βραχύ-ς short, as in **'brachyblast** [Gr. βλαστός sprout, shoot] = SPUR *sb.*¹ 7 a. **brachycatalectic** (,brækɪkætə'lɛktɪk), *a. Prosody* [cf. CATALECTIC, Gr. βραχυκατάληκτος], wanting one foot or two syllables. **brachyceral** (bræ'kɪsərəl), **brachycerous** (bræ'kɪsərəs), *a. Ent.* [Gr. κέρας horn], having short 'horns' or antennæ. **brachy'cranial** *a.*, having a short cranium or head. **,brachydi'agonal** *a. Cryst.*, pertaining to the shorter lateral axis of a rectangular prism; also as *sb.* **brachydome** (-dəʊm), *Cryst.* [see DOME], a 'dome' or prism whose face is parallel to the brachydiagonal axis. **brachyelytrous**: see BRACHELYTROUS. **brachymetropy** (-'mɛtrəpɪ) [Gr. μέτρ-ον measure + ὤψ, ὠπ-ός eye], near- or short-sightedness. **brachypinacoid, -koid** (-'pɪnəkɔɪd), *a. Cryst.* [Gr. πίναξ, πίνακ-ος board, tablet], pertaining to either of the two planes which in the Orthorhombic system are parallel to the vertical and brachydiagonal axes respectively. **brachypleural** (-'pl(j)ʊərəl), *a.* [Gr. πλευρ-ά rib], having short ribs. **brachypterous** (bræ'kɪptərəs), *a.* [Gr. πτερ-όν wing], short-winged: applied to certain species of diving-birds; also applied to insects; hence **bra'chypterism**, the state or condition of being brachypterous. **brachytypous** (bræ'kɪtɪpəs), *a. Min.* [Gr. τύπ-ος form, type], of a short form.

1895 W. R. FISHER *Schlich's Man. Forestry* IV. III. ii. 402 The fungus [*sc.* larch-blister] can gain admission only through wounds, frequently of brachyblasts eaten by *Coleophora laricella.* **1821** *Blackw. Mag.* X. 386 The ancients had no such verse as the Iambic trimeter brachycatalectic. **1875** W. HOUGHTON *Sk. Brit. Ins.* 107 Another brachyceral fly. **1875** BLAKE *Zool.* 283 The brachycerous Dipterans comprise..the Gad-flies. **1902** *Biometrika* I. 462 In both races platycephaly is associated with brachycranial characters. **1868** DANA *Min.* Introd. 25 The short lateral or brachydiagonal [axis]. *Ibid.* 26 The planes form what is called a *brachydome*, they being parallel to the shorter lateral axis. **1879** RUTLEY *Stud. Rocks* x. 119 In the direction of the..brachydiagonal it is hyacinth-red. *Ibid.* 97 The cleavages, which are parallel to the base and brachypinakoid. **1881** *Academy* 22 Oct. 315 Macropleural and brachypleural types. **1937** *Discovery* Mar. 91/2 This brachypterism, as it is termed, occurs also in the Orthoptera and Rhynchota. **1939** *Nature* 15 Apr. 645/2 Ruwenzori provides numerous examples of species of insects which are either short winged (brachypterous) in the female or in both sexes... Apart from this phenomenon of 'brachypterism' no obvious cases of adaptation to mountain conditions among insects were noted. **1842** BRANDE *Dict. Sci.* 163/1 *Brachypterous*, in ornithology, when the folded wings of a bird do not reach to the base of the tail.

brachycephal ('brækɪsɪfæl). [Back-formation from BRACHYCEPHALIC *a.*] A brachycephalic person.

1901 G. SERGI *Mediterranean Race* i. 12 The present populations of southern Germany are in great part brachycephals, among whom mesocephals are rare and dolichocephals quite isolated. **1928** V. G. CHILDE *Most Anc. East* x. 234 The European beakers were made and used by brachycephals. **1930** C. G. SELIGMAN *Races of Africa* vi. 132 Short to medium brachycephals, with a stature rather under 65 inches.

brachycephalic (,brækɪsɪ'fælɪk), *a.* Also **-kephalic.** [f. BRACHY- + Gr. κεφαλή head: cf. κεφαλικός of or pertaining to the head.] *lit.* Short-headed: used in *Ethnology* to denote skulls of which the breadth is at least four-fifths of the length: opposed to DOLICHOCEPHALIC.

1849–52 TODD *Cycl. Anat. & Phys.* IV. 1355/2 The Cranium is Mongoliform and brachycephalic. **1851** D. WILSON *Preh. Ann.* (1863) I. ix. 281, I have met with Brachycephalic Scots. **1866** HUXLEY *Preh. Rem. Caithn.* 83 Skulls with a cephalic index of 0·8, or more, are Brachycephalic. **1877** DAWSON *Orig. World* 427 The brachy-kephalic head.

So **brachycephales**, more freq. **-cephali** [mod.Latin], men with brachycephalic skulls. **brachy'cephalism**, the condition of being brachycephalic. **brachy'cephalous**, *a.* = *brachycephalic.* **brachy'cephaly** = *brachycephalism.*

1865 *Reader* No. 113. 227/1 A race of brachycephales. **1863** A. RAMSAY *Phys. Geog.* (1878) 581 They belong mainly to the Brachycephali or broad-skulls. **1880** *Nature* 8 Jan. 224 The skull ranges from brachycephalism in the Siberians and Peruvians to extreme dolichocephalism in the Eskimo. **1883** K. BLIND in *Academy* Mar. 17 190/1 Brachykephalism in Asia Minor. **1872** tr. *Figuier's Hum. Race* Introd. 25 A short cranium is styled brachycephalous. **1871** DARWIN *Desc. Man* I. I. iv. 148 Short men incline more to brachycephaly.

brachydactyly (,brækɪ'dæktɪlɪ). *Path.* [f. BRACHY- + Gr. δάκτυλ-ος finger + -Y³.] Abnormal shortness of the digits. So **,brachy'dactylism**; **,brachy'dactylous** *a.*

1881 *Syd. Soc. Lex.* I, *Brachydactylous*, short-fingered. **1886** STEDMAN in *Buck's Handbk. Med. Sci.* III. 498/2 A loss of one or two phalanges only (brachydactylism). **1906** *Green's Encycl. & Dict. Med. & Surg.* I. 460/1 *Brachydactyly* (shortness of the digits). **1908** *Lancet* 25 Apr. 1212/1 Dr. H. Drinkwater read a paper on Brachydactyly —a Study in Heredity, giving an account of a brachydactylous family. **1944** K. MATHER in Darlington & Mather *Genes, Plants & People* (1958) xii. 131 Traits, like brachydactyly, inherited in this way, could virtually be wiped out in one generation.

brachygraphy (bræ'kɪgrəfɪ). Also 7 **-graphie**, and (erron.) 7 **brachyo-**, 7–8 **brachi-**. [a. F. *brachygraphie*, f. Gr. βραχύ-ς short + -γραφία writing.] The art or practice of writing with abbreviations or with abbreviated characters; shorthand, stenography. Also *attrib. Obs.* except as a designation of certain old systems of shorthand, esp. that of Gurney (see quot. 1778).

1590 P. BALE (*title*) The art of brachygraphie, that is, to write as fast as a man speaketh treatably. **1600** NASHE *Summer's Last W.* in Hazl. *Dodsl.* VIII. 41 If I wist there were any such knavery, or Peter Balis brachygraphy. **1667** E. CHAMBERLAYNE *St. Gt. Brit.* I. III. x. (1743) 226 Therein are taught..Calligraphy, Brachigraphy or Shorthand, etc. **1778** J. GURNEY *Brachygr.* Pref. 1 Brachygraphy..is extremely antient, (for we read of its being practised in the Roman Senate). **1884** *Leeds Merc. Wkly. Suppl.* 15 Nov. 8/3 The system of brachygraphy in which the contents of the volume were shrouded.

b. *fig.*

1656 tr. *Hobbes' Elem. Philos.* (1839) 316 The brachygraphy of the analytics, and an art..of registering with brevity..the inventions of geometricians. **1715** tr. *Pancirollus' Rerum Mem.* II. x. 334 These Curiosities are the Brachigraphy or Short-hand of Art.

bra'chygrapher, a shorthand-writer; **brachy'graphic, -al**, of or pertaining to brachygraphy.

1633 T. ADAMS *Comm. 2 Pet.* i. 9 By brachygraphical characters they will take a sermon verbatim. **1654** GAYTON *Fest. Notes* I. 8 (R.) He asked the brachygrapher, whether he wrote the notes of that sermon. **1782** *Gentl. Mag.* LII. 219 Memoirs of the most eminent brachygraphers.

brachylogy (bræ'kɪlədʒɪ). Also 7 **brachil-**, 8 **brachyology.** [ad. Gr. βραχυλογία, in med.L. *brachiologia*, f. βραχύ-ς short + -λογία speech: see -LOGY. Cf. F. *brachylogie.*] Conciseness of speech, laconism; *concr.* a condensed expression.

[**1589** PUTTENHAM *Eng. Poesie* (Arb.) 222 Brachiologa, or the Cutted comma.] **1623** COCKERAM, *Brachilogies*, short speeches. **1716** M. DAVIES in *Athen. Britan.* II. To Reader xlv, In the Poet's Brachyology, Aliquisque malo fuit usus in illo. **1866** ELLICOTT *On 2 Thess.* iii. 7 A simple and intelligible brachylogy. **1882–3** SCHAFF in *Herzog's Encycl. Rel. Knowl.* III. 2293 Delitzsch specifies brachylogy as characteristic of its [the Talmud's] style.

brachyodont ('brækɪədɒnt), *a.* Also **brachydont.** [f. BRACHY- + ὀδούς (ὀδοντ-) tooth.] Designating teeth with short or low crowns and well-developed roots.

1883 W. H. FLOWER in *Encycl. Brit.* XV. 430/1 Modification of [the selenodont form] from a brachyodont to a hypsodont type. **1884** *Geol. Mag.* 548 Detached upper molars of a smaller form, with a brachydont..structure. *Ibid.*, Several lower molars and a fragment of a mandible from Hempstead indicate a brachydont anthracotheroid. **1891** [see BILOPHODONT *a.*]. **1968** R. ZANGERL tr. *Peyer's Compar. Odontology* 191 The teeth of the earliest monodelphous mammals..are at the same time brachyodont—low-crowned and provided with well-developed roots.

brachyurous, -ourous (brækɪ'ʊərəs), *a. Zool.* [f. mod.L. *brachyura*, (f. Gr. βραχύ-ς short + οὐρά tail) + -OUS.] Pertaining to the *Brachyura*, one of the three tribes of Decapod Crustacea, distinguished by the non-development of the abdomen or 'tail', including the crab and its congeners.

1828 KIRBY & SP. *Entomol.* xlviii. IV. 462 Brachyurous Decapod Crustacea. **1849–52** TODD *Cycl. Anat. & Phys.* IV. 1302/2 In all other..Brachyourous Decapods yet observed, a real metamorphosis takes place. **1877** HUXLEY *Anat. Inv. An.* vii. 379 The Spiders stand in somewhat the same relation to the Scorpions, as the brachyurous to the macrurous Crustacea.

So **brachy'ural, -'oural** *a.*, **brachy'uran, -'ouran** *adj.* and *sb.* [cf. -AL¹, -AN.]

1852 DANA *Crust.* I. 33 Not consistent with Brachyural type. **1877** HUXLEY *Anat. Inv. An.* vi. 350 The Anomuran condition passes into that of the young Brachyuran.

bracing ('breɪsɪŋ), *vbl. sb.*¹ [f. BRACE *v.*¹]

1. The action of embracing (*obs.*), girding, binding tightly, lacing up, strengthening: see the verb.

1536 BELLENDEN *Cron. Scot.* (1821) II. 53 Ane devill in forme of woman..quhilk..tistit him, be voluptuous brasing, to hir plesoure. *a* **1631** DONNE *Serm.* lxxvii. 779 a, The Brasing & beating of our Drums in the Pulpit. **1826** MISS MITFORD *Village* Ser. II. (1863) 277 Oh the lacing, the

bracing, the bonneting, the veiling. **1856** FROUDE *Hist. Eng.* I. 78 The moral sinew of the English must have been strong indeed when it admitted of such stringent bracing.

2. An appliance or arrangement for tying, fastening, supporting, or strengthening. *lit.* and *fig.*

1849 W. FITZGERALD *Whitaker's Disput.* 5 The Roman synagogue..hath need continually of new supports and bracings. **1861** *Times* 7 Oct., There were bracings on the top of the girders, which would have the effect of steadying them. **1883** *Law Times Rep.* XLIX. 139/1 The standards were not secured by any ties or bracings of any kind.

3. *attrib.* (or ? the *ppl. a.*), as in ***bracing-girdle, -rope***; **bracing-chain**, a chain used to bind together the sides of a wagon bearing a heavy load.

1552 HULOET, Bracynge gyrdle, *subcingulum.* **1827** STEUART *Planter's G.* (1828) 295 Fixing or loosening the bracing-ropes.

†**bracing**, *vbl. sb.*² *Obs.* Also 6 brasing. [f. BRACE *v.*² + -ING¹.] The action of assuming a bold or defiant attitude. In phrase ***facing and bracing***.

1481 CAXTON *Reynard* 115 Whiche wyth grete facing and bracyng oppresse the poure peple. **1541** R. BARNES *Wks.* (1573) 290/1 My Lordes, leue of your fasing and your brasing: for our Lord..will at length not bee out faced. **1571** GOLDING *Calvin on Ps.* xii. 5. 39 Their importunate facing and bracing in woordes [orig. *improba verborum jactantia*].

'bracing, *ppl. a.* [f. as prec. + -ING².] That braces, girds, etc. Now used chiefly of the air or climate; formerly of tonic medicines.

1750 RUTTY in *Phil. Trans.* LI. 476 A powerful..bracing ..medicine. **1821** KEATS *Isabel* xxiv, With belt and spur and bracing huntsman's dress. **1850** MRS. STOWE *Uncle Tom* xv. 129 The cold of a more bracing climate. **1871** NAPHEYS *Prev. & Cure Dis.* I. v. 154 Dry heat is bracing.

Hence **'bracingly** *adv.*, in a bracing manner, so as to brace. **'bracingness**, bracing quality.

1874 ELLACOMBE in *Church Bells* 15 Sept. (1883) 808/1 The bolts had better be put in bracingly, that is, not perpendicularly. **1876** *Fortn. Rev.* Mar. 341 [The Engadine] has what may be termed a graduated scale of bracingness.

brack (bræk), *sb.*¹ Also 2–3 bracc (*Orm.*), 6 *Sc.* brek, 6–7 bracke, 6–8 brak. See BRECK. [Two formations: (1) in Ormin a. ON. *brak* (= OE. *ȝebræc*, OS. *gibrak*) creaking noise, f. OTeut. *brekan* to break: cf. L. *fragor*, f. stem of *frangĕre*. (2) In later use, a parallel form to BREAK *sb.*, f. BREAK *vb.*]

I. ME., from ON. *brak*.

†**1.** Noise, outcry. *Obs.*

c **1200** ORMIN 1178 Shep iss all unnskaþefull..& makeþþ itt nan mikell bracc. *Ibid.* 1186 Jesu Crist..toc þildiliȝ wiþþutenn bracc, þatt mann himm band. **1513** DOUGLAS *Æneis* XIII. vi. 85 For all the brek and sterage that hes bene.

II. mod., f. BREAK *v.* Cf. BREAK *sb.*, BRECK.

†**2.** A breaking, breach, rupture. Still *Sc.*

1540 RAYNALD *Byrth Man.* II. vi. (1634) 130 Heale this brack and wound by sowing both sides of it together again. *a* **1599** in Hakluyt *Voy.* III. I. 81 They beat the sayd bulwarke and wall in such wise, that they made great bracks. *a* **1619** FOTHERBY *Atheom.* Pref. 6 To repaire all the ruines and seuerall bracks of it. **1669** WORLIDGE *Syst. Agric.* (1681) 322 A Breck, or Brack, a gap in a Hedge.

†**b.** *fig.* A rupture, quarrel. *Obs.*

1600 HOLLAND *Livy* XXV. xxix. 570 Hippocrates and Epicides..made the brack, & were the troublers and disturbers of this peace. **1608** CHAPMAN *Byron's Conspir.* Plays 1873 II. 236 That can mend The brack betwixt us.

3. A flaw in cloth. Also *fig.* (Now chiefly *dial.*)

[**1530** PALSGR. 200/2 Brake in clothe, *rentreture*.] **1552** *Act 6 Edw. VI*, vi. §1 Over-stretching them upon the Tenter, and then stopping with Flocks such Bracks as shall be made. **1597** LYLY *Euphues* (Arb.) 33 The finest veluet [hath] his bracke. **1636** FEATLY *Clavis Myst.* lxix. 888 The needle fils not up the bracke or rent. **1840** BROWNING *Sordello* v. 400 The knack Of keeping fresh-chalked gowns from speck and brack. **1873** MISS BRADDON *Str. & Pilgr.* I. vi. 62 'She sent me a gownd last week..a regular good one, not a brack in it'.

†**4.** A broken piece, fragment, atom. *Obs.*

c **1615** CHAPMAN *Odyss.* XVII. 249 A cord, that would not slip For knots and bracks about the mouth of it. **1644** DIGBY *Nat. Bodies* Ded. (1658) 14 Many bracks and short ends which cannot be spun into an even piece. **1647** N. FAIRFAX *Bulk & Selv.* 79 The least brack of body cannot be broken a pieces, because 'tis already the least.

†**5.** Breach, breaking, violation. *Sc.*

1658 *Presbyt. Strathbogie Rec.* in Hessey *Sunday* (1880) 217 The said day A.C...was delaitit for brak of Sabbath.

†**6.** Break of continuity, 'fault' in mining. *dial.*

1747 HOOSON *Miner's Dict.* S ii, After crossing of Pees, Tees, Braks, Jumbles, or what other disorder may happen that the vein cannot be easily made out.

†**7.** 'A stripe of uncultivated ground, between two *shots* or plots of land.' (Jamieson.) Cf. BREAK *sb.* 12. *Sc.*

†**8.** A sudden breaking out of water; a sudden heavy fall of rain; a flood when the ice breaks; a quantity of snow, earth, or debris shooting from a hill. *Sc.*

†**brack**, *sb.*² *Obs. rare.* [prob. identical with prec.: cf. connexion of L. *rūpes* with *rumpĕre* to break, and BREAK *sb.*] A cliff, crag, or rock.

c **1530** *Hickscorner* in Hazl. *Dodsl.* I. 185 Thrown in a raft, and so about borne On rocks or bracks for to run. **1598** FLORIO, *Bricche*, crags, cliffs, or brackes in hills.

brack, *sb.*³ [f. Ger. *bracken* to examine or sort goods. Cf. BRACK *v.*, BRACKER.] The system of official sorting of goods or produce in vogue at the principal Baltic ports.

1734 *Treaty Eng. & Russ.* in Magens *Insurances* II. 592 The Brack shall be equitably established.

†**brack**, *sb.*⁴ *Obs.* [App. a shortened form of BRACKEN.] = BRACKEN¹.

1482 *Monk of Evesham* (Arb.) 40 A full depe valeye..set with bocis and brackys on euery syde hangyng owte. **1627** DRAYTON *Agincourt* 182 They fed on Fearne & brack. **1675** EVELYN *Terra* (1776) 36 Vegetables abounding in fixed Salts ..as Pease-haulm, Bracks.

†**brack**, *sb.*⁵ *Obs. rare*⁻¹. [? ad. F. *braque*, *brague*, breeching for cannon.] ? Breeching for cannon; or perh. = BRACKET *sb.* 3.

1622 R. HAWKINS *Voy. S. Sea* 213 Our hatches upon our bolts, our brackes in our deckes and gunner roome.

brack, *a.* and *sb.*⁶ Also 6 brak, bracke. [prob. (as a nautical word) a. Du. *brak* brackish (whence Ger. *brackwasser* brackish water); identified by Franck with MDu. *brak* worthless.]

A. *adj.* Salt, briny, brackish. ? *Obs.*

1513 DOUGLAS *Æneis* v. xiii. 28 ȝet [= pour] the cleir wyne furth in fludis brak [L. *salsos fluctus*]. **1786** tr. *Sparrman's Voy.* I. 255 The Brak rivers have got this appellation from the quality of their waters, which are brackish or saltish. **1827** SOUTHEY in *Q. Rev.* XXXV. 117 Living upon beef and brack water.

†**B.** *sb.* Salt water, brine; the sea. *Obs.* (Only in Drayton, and apparently not in general use then, as the gloss 'salt water' is given in the margin.)

1591 DRAYTON in Farr's *S.P.* (1845) I. 133 Drags their fat carkasse through the foamie bracke. **1627** —— *Agincourt* 185 The Sunne..Shall with the Fishes shortly diue the Brack.

brack, *sb.*⁷ [Abbrev. of BARNBRACK; cf. Ir. *breac* speckled.] An Irish cake or loaf containing seeds or fruit; = BARNBRACK.

Quots. 1855 prob. represent attempts to render Irish *bairghean breac* BARNBRACK.

1855 E. ACTON *Mod. Cookery* (rev. ed.) xxvi. 546 Rich Brawn Brack, or Borrow Brack. *Ibid.*, To convert the above into the popular Irish 'speckled bread', or *Brawn Brack*.. add to it three ounces of carraway-seeds. *Ibid.* xxvi. 555 Common *brown brack*, or Irish seed-cake. **1959** J. O'DONOVAN *Visited* xxix. 182 She..made tea and sliced a home-made brack. **1960** *Guardian* 10 Dec. 12/6 Breads, bracks, baps, scones.

brack (bræk), *v.* [ad. Ger. *bracken* to sort or inspect goods, f. *brack* 'inferior goods, refuse'.] *trans.* To sort or select (goods, produce, etc.) (at the Baltic ports). Cf. BRACK *sb.*³, BRACKER. Hence **bracked** *ppl. a.*

1858 HOMANS *Cycl. Comm.* 1343 All flax and hemp shipped from Memel must be bracked or assorted by sworn selectors. **1883** *Scotsman* 30 July 7/6 Tallow, bracked, about 51*s.*

brack(e, obs. form of BRAKE, BRACH; and Sc. pa. t. of BREAK *v.*

†**bracked**, *ppl. a. Obs.* In 7 brackt. [f. BRACK *sb.*¹] Having a brack or flaw (in texture).

1612 J. DAVIES *Muses Sacr.* (1877) 77 A feate Embroderer that hath a piece of Velvet brackt t'embroder on.

bracken¹ ('bræk(ə)n). Also 4–9 **braken**, 5 **brakan, bracon**, (7 **braking**), 8 **brachen** (*Sc.*), 8–9 **breckan** (*Sc.*), **breckon** (*north. dial.*). [ME. (northern) *braken*, app. representing an ON. **brakni*, whence Sw. *bräken*, Da. *bregne* 'fern' (? and, by corruption, Icel. *burkni* 'common fern'.)

The alleged OE. *bracce* wk. fem. is merely a guess of Cockayne's (*Leechd.* III. 315) from the place-name *Braccanheal* Bracknell (which may possibly be from a personal name Bracca). It could not, in any case, be the predecessor of ME. *braken*. Cf. BRAKE *sb.*¹, BRACK *sb.*⁴]

1. a. A fern; *spec.* (in modern writers) *Pteris aquilina*, the 'Brake'. (In the north all large ferns are *brackens*; *Pteris aquilina* is merely the most conspicuous and best known, from the masses in which it grows.) Southern writers often make *bracken* collective. Also *attrib.*

c **1325** *E.E. Allit. P.* B. 1675 þou..most..byte on þe bent of braken & erbes. **1483** *Cath. Angl.* 40 A Braken, *filix.* **1523** FITZHERB. *Surv.* 6 b, Yet may he lawfully..selle all the wode, brome, gorse, fyrs, braken, ferne, busshes. **1548** TURNER *Names of Herbes* (1881) 38 The commune Ferne or brake, which the northerne men cal a bracon. **1563** *Richmond. Wills & Inv.* (1853) 169 Burning brakens. **1649** BLITHE *Eng. Improv. Impr.* (1653) 124 Goss, Broom, Braking, &c. **1775** LIGHTFOOT *Flora Scot.* (1789) 653 Flowering Fern or Osmund Royal: Royal Brachens *Scotis.* **1787** BURNS *Halloween* xxvi, Amang the brachens, on the brae. **1810** TANNAHILL *Gloomy Winter's now awa'*, Feathery breckans fringe the rocks. **1813** HOGG *Queen's Wake* 2 I found thee in the braken glen. **1878** BLACK *Green Past.* ii. 13 Withered brackens coming up in solitary stalks of green.

b. A shade of brown resembling the colour of turning bracken; a warm orangey-brown.

1923 *Weekly Dispatch* 8 Apr. 14 (Advt.), Shades include Nigger, Bracken, Brown, Tan, Grey. **1978** *Morecambe Guardian* 14 Mar. 33 (Advt.), Mini 1000 in bracken, one owner.

2. *Comb.*, as †**bracken-bush**, a large plant or clump of fern or bracken; **bracken-clock**, the Rose-beetle (*Phyllopertha horticola*).

1483 *Cath. Angl.* 40 Brakanbuske, *filicarium, felicetum.* **1884** G. BRAITHWAITE *Salmon. Westmrld.* vi. 27 The bracken-clock, or rose-beetle.

Hence **brackened** ('bræk(ə)nd), *a.*, overgrown with bracken.

1884 W. C. SMITH *Kildrostan* I. i. 32 Brackened braes and craggy hills.

†**'bracken**². *Obs.* [ad. Gael. and Ir. *breacan*, f. *breac* spotted or chequered.] A tartan plaid worn by Highlanders and northern Irishmen. (See M. Hickson *Irel. 17th C.* I. 257.)

1652 *News fr. Low Countr.* 2 The Scottish Brackin. **1653** *Exam. D. Mac Gillmartin* in M. Hickson *Irel. 17th C.* (1884) I. 277 Had seen his mother's bracken in the hands of the soldiers. **1828** SCOTT *F.M. Perth* III. 57 I am as familiar with brogues and bracken as if I had worn them myself.

†**'brackener**. *Obs. rare.* Also brakk- [a. OF. *braconier* (= mod.F. *braconnier*, now used in sense of poacher) a keeper of hounds, f. *bracon* hound: see BRACH.] A servant who attended to the hounds.

1490 CAXTON *Eneydos* xv. 54 Rennynge houndes went wyth the brakkenere for to be atte the reysynge of the beest. *Ibid.* The brackener hadde dystourned the herte in to his busshe.

brackeny ('bræk(ə)nɪ), *a.* [f. BRACKEN¹ + -Y¹.] Abounding in bracken.

1834 A. CUNNINGHAM *Burns* 136/2 The brackeny glens.. of the North are more welcome..than the sunny vales of Italy.

bracker ('brækə(r)). [a. Ger. *bracker*, f. *bracken* to sort goods.] A government inspector or sorter of goods at the Baltic ports. See BRACK *sb.*³ and *v.*

1734 *Treaty Eng. & Russ.* in Magens *Insurances* II. 592 The Brackers shall be answerable for the Quality of the Goods. **1858** HOMANS *Cycl. Comm.* 1635 Linseed..The year of its growth is stamped on the barrel by sworn inspectors (*brackers*). *Ibid.* 1792 When a shipment of tallow is made, the agent is furnished by the selector (*bracker*) with a sample from each cask.

bracket ('brækɪt), *sb.* Also 6–7 **bragget**, 7 **braget(t**, 8 **brecate, brockett**. [The earliest form *bragget* appears to be (either directly or through F. *braguette*) ad. Sp. *bragueta*, dim. of *braga*:—L. *brāca*, sing. of *brācæ* breeches; the form *bracket* is a corruption, perh. influenced by It. *bracheta*, dim. of *braca*:—L. *brāca*.

The Eng. senses are difficult to account for, but may in part be based on unrecorded senses of the Sp., It., or Fr. words. Prof. Skeat suggests that the 'bracket' of architecture may have been so called from its resemblance to the 'codpiece' of a pair of breeches (Sp. *bragueta* meant both 'codpiece' and 'bracket'). Further, a name suggested by 'breeches' may naturally have been applied to an apparatus consisting of two limbs set at an angle, like the 'bracket' of shipbuilding, or to appliances used in pairs, like the 'brackets' of a gun-carriage. Then, as a bracket of any kind was generally used for support, the erroneous etymology from L. *brachium* 'arm' or its Romance derivatives presented itself, and seems to have affected the development of senses. Cf. also OF. *bracon* and *braquant* 'supporting beam'.]

1. a. In *Building*, a piece of stone, wood, or metal projecting from a wall, and having a flat upper surface which serves as a ledge to support a statue, the spring of an arch, a beam, shelf, etc.; usually carved or sculptured, and sometimes employed merely as a decoration; under the name of bracket are included the CORBEL and the CONSOLE.

1580 BARET *Alv.* B 1099 A Bragget or staie..in building to beare vp the sommer or other part. **1664** EVELYN tr. *Freart's Archit.* 136 Modilions..are a kind of Bragets to the Corona. **1707** J. MORTIMER *Art. Husb.* 564 Let your Shelves be laid upon Brackets. **1845** PARKER *Gloss. Archit.* I. 60. **1859** TURNER *Dom. Archit.* III. 213 The angel bracket of an oriel window.

b. A small (usually ornamental) shelf, or set of two or three shelves, for the wall of a room.

1635 *Althorp MS.* in Simpkinson *Washingtons* Introd. 70 Bragetts for the drawinge room. **1714** *Lond. Gaz.* No. 5214/3 Gilt Brocketts, Desks, and Book Cases. **1756** MRS. CALDERWOOD *Jrnl.* (1884) 75 Above the lintel..[are] brecates set out for china. **1810** JEBB *Corr.* II. 5 You shall have..a bracket for your books. **1881** *Mechanic* §735 Brackets which are short small shelves may also be fixed to the wall.

c. *transf.* (? with allusion to BRACT.)

1860 RUSKIN *Mod. Paint.* V. VI. iii. 14 The little brackets, which project beneath each bud and sustain it.

2. In *Carpentry, Shipbuilding*, etc.: A support consisting of two pieces of wood or metal joined at an angle, or of a single piece bent at an angle. Also *attrib.*, as ***bracket plate***.

1627 CAPT. SMITH *Seaman's Gram.* ii. 11 The brackets are little carued knees to support the Galleries. *c* **1850** *Rudim.*

Navig. (Weale) 100, *Brackets*, short crooked timbers, resembling knees, for support or ornament. The Hair Bracket is the boundary of the aft-part of the figure head. **1879** *Cassell's Techn. Educ.* IV. 363/2 The principal transverse frames are made up of.. bracket plates.

3. One of the two 'cheeks' or side-pieces of a gun-carriage, which support the trunnions of a piece of ordnance; also used of the entire carriage of a gun mounted on board ship or in a casement.

1753 CHAMBERS *Cycl. Supp.*, *Cheeks* of a mortar, or Brackets.. are made of strong planks of wood.. they rise on each side of the mortar, and serve to keep her at what elevation is given her. *c* **1860** H. STUART *Seaman's Catech.* 5 Brackets—transom—fore axletree. **1880** *Encycl. Brit.* (ed. 9) XI. 311 The trail [of gun-carriage] consists of two side brackets.

4. A metal pipe, usually of ornamental shape, projecting from the wall of an apartment, at once to support and supply the gas lamps or burners.

1876 GWILT *Archit.* §2264 e, The outer arm of the bracket ..should be protected on the top by a hanging shade.

5. a. One of two marks of the form [ ] or ( ), and in mathematical use also {}, used for enclosing a word or number of words, a portion of a mathematical formula, or the like, so as to separate it from the context; in typography, esp. applied to 'square brackets' (formerly called crotchets), the 'round brackets' being designated 'parentheses'. Sometimes improperly applied to the 'vinculum' or horizontal line over the writing, serving in algebra the same purpose as brackets; also to the 'brace' { used for coupling together two lines of writing or printing (cf. BRACKET *v.*); hence *brackets* is used *fig.* for 'the position of being bracketed equal, equality'.

1750 G. FISHER *Instructor* (ed. 10) 23 [ ] Brackets or Crochets, generally include a Word or Sentence, explanatory of what went before. **1824** L. MURRAY *Eng. Gram.* I. 413 Crotchets or Brackets [ ] serve to enclose a word or sentence, which is to be explained in a note, or the explanation itself, or a word or sentence which is intended to supply some deficiency, or to rectify some mistake. **1859** BARN. SMITH *Arith. & Algebra* (ed. 6) 194 A Bracket ( ) or {}, or [ ]. **1883** *Standard* 12 Feb. 2/6 On a shorter course Regnard is not unlikely to earn brackets.

b. *transf.* The (specified) distance between a pair of shots fired, one beyond the target and one short of it, in order to find the range for artillery; chiefly in the phrase ***to establish a bracket***.

1899 *Daily News* 6 Dec. 5/7 At first I fire at 3100 yards, and if I find that my shot is short I fire a second round, say at 3300, in order to go beyond the object. If I see that my shot does go over I am satisfied that I have established what is called 'a long bracket', that is to say, I have found two ranges, 200 yards apart, between which the object must lie. .. I.. fire another shot to shorten the distance within which I can then know that the target must be. This we call, on the same principle as the other, 'a short bracket'. **1916** 'BOYD CABLE' *Action Front* 42 The German gun had got its bracket. **1927** *Blackw. Mag.* Apr. 476/2 The shell passed over the ship, to be followed by a second one which fell short, establishing a 'bracket', which.. is all that a gunner desires.

c. A group bracketed together as of equal standing in some graded system, as ***income bracket***: a class of persons grouped according to income.

1880 BP. GOODWIN in *Macm Mag.* No. 246. 477 Sedgwick was in the first bracket. **1932** *N.Y. Times* 1 May III. 1/3 The most striking fact in vital statistics is the increase in the upper-age brackets. **1940** *Jrnl. R. Aeronaut. Soc.* XLIV. 506 The general bracket of utilisation within which the aeroplanes will fall. **1940** F. SCOTT FITZGERALD *Let.* 18 Mar. (1964) 66 Competent people with a little pull have no trouble finding places in the same income brackets. **1943** *Gen* 2 Jan. 29/1 Once he got in the upper brackets, fistically speaking. **1952** *News Chron.* 15 July 6/8 'At my age,' he [*sc.* an athlete] added, 'I have only two years left in the top bracket.' **1956** 'M. INNES' *Appleby plays Chicken* v. 43 They were both from the same social bracket.

d. *Skating.* A series of turns resembling a bracket or 'brace' (see sense 5). Also *attrib.*

1892 [see COUNTER *sb.*[4] 6]. **1901** *Encycl. Sport* IV. 366/1 Three turns and bracket turns are accomplished upon two edges. *Ibid.* 370/1 *Turn loops* are turns worked into the form of a loop, and *Bracket loops* are brackets skated in a similar way. **1935** *Times* 14 Nov. 6/7 The great stumbling block in this test for the average skater is the bracket figure. **1967** *Daily Tel.* 3 Mar. 14/7 She coolly executed a smooth change-edge loop figure and an equally accurate bracket-change-bracket.

6. *Comb.* and *Attrib.*, as **bracket-bolt**, an iron bolt securing a mortar to its brackets; **bracket-burner, -light**, a gas-bracket; = sense 4; **bracket clock**, a clock designed to stand on a shelf or wall-bracket; **bracket-crab**, a crab or windlass designed for attachment to a wall or post; **bracket fungus, mushroom**, any fungus which grows on trunks of trees forming a bracket-like projection; **bracket-shelf**, a form of bracket used as a shelf; **bracket-stair, -staircase** (see quot.); **bracket system** (see quot.); **bracket-trail**, in *Gunnery*, a trail composed of two or more timbers or irons, opposed to *block trail*; **bracket-wise** *adv.*, after the manner of, or so as to resemble, a bracket.

1753 CHAMBERS *Cycl. Suppl.* s.v. *Cheeks*, Bolts of iron which go through both cheeks, both under and behind the mortar.. are called the *bracket-bolts. **1876** GWILT *Archit.* §2293 j, Fix.. *bracket burners in passages. **1894** F. J. BRITTEN *Former Clock & Watchmakers* 185 *Bracket or pedestal clocks.. were in favour before.. the long-case variety. The earliest English wooden bracket clock cases were of the square pattern. **1958** 'W. HAGGARD' *Slow Burner* i. 13 The handsome bracket clock on the table. **1909** *Cent. Dict.* Suppl., *Bracket fungus. **1910** *Encycl. Brit.* IV. 366/2 *Bracket-fungi.* The term 'bracket' has been given to those hard, woody fungi that grow on trees or timber in the form of semicircular brackets. **1927** *Observer* 28 Aug. 18/1 The so-called *bracket mushrooms that chiefly flourish in rotting trunks have been platforms rather than brackets. **1876** GWILT *Archit.* §2183 A *Bracket Staircase is one which has an opening or well.. and is supported by landings and carriages. *Ibid.* In *bracket stairs the internal angle of the steps is open to the end. **1874** THEARLE *Naval Archit.* 86 The *Bracket System is the development.. of the transverse and longitudinal systems combined, by which iron-clad ships have been built since their introduction. **1865** C. H. OWEN *Elem. Lect. Artillery* (ed. 4) 62 The travelling carriages for siege guns had *bracket trails, but those now made.. are similar in construction to the 40-pr. block trail carriage. **1884** *Pall Mall G.* 5 Dec. 11/2 Timbers.. are pushed out *bracketwise.. layer above layer.

'bracket, *v.* [f. prec.]

1. *trans.* To provide with brackets; to enclose (words, expressions, formulæ, etc.) within brackets.

1870 JEBB *Sophocles' Elect.* (ed. 2) 14/2 Dindorf.. brackets the line as spurious.

2. To couple or connect (two or more lines of writing, etc.) by means of a brace; *esp.* so to connect two or more names of equal merit in a class-list; hence *fig.* to mention two persons or things together so as to imply that they are equal or have something in common.

1861 *Sat. Rev.* 23 Nov. 557 We entirely approve of his.. reluctance to be bracketed with a person of this sort. **1868** FREEMAN *Norm. Conq.* (1876) II. ix. 348 It is bracketted with the massacre of Saint Brice. **1869** *Daily News* 30 Jan. Only four times beaten for both prizes, as often bracketed.

3. *intr.* To project like a bracket.

1855 FERGUSSON *Handbk. Archit.* IX. iv. 428 A number of small imitations of arches, bracketing one beyond the other.

4. To find the range for artillery by means of a bracket or series of brackets (BRACKET *sb.* 5 b). Also *trans.* Hence **'bracketing** *vbl. sb.*

1909 in WEBSTER. **1914** *Times* 12 Oct. 7/4 They [*sc.* the Germans] dispense to a great extent with the method of ranging known by us as 'bracketing', especially when acting on the defensive, and direct fire by means of squared maps and telephone. **1916** J. BUCHAN *Greenmantle* xxi. 293 The shell dropped ten yards to our right. A second later another fell behind us... 'They know their business. They're bracketing.' **1926** 'J. J. CONNINGTON' *Death at Swaythling Court* xvi, I took the liberty of bracketing the Lethal Ray machine.. on Swaythling Court. **1957** M. K. JOSEPH *I'll soldier no More* (1958) 187 In the distance, a puff of smoke suddenly appeared... Almost looks as if we're being bracketed.

bracket, variant of BRAGGET.

'bracketed, *ppl. a.* [f. BRACKET *v.* + -ED.] Furnished with, or enclosed in, brackets; coupled by a bracket with another name.

c **1865** *Circ. Sc.* I. 455/2 A bracketed quantity. **1885** *Athenæum* 6 June 729/3 Bracketed sentences or paragraphs.

'bracketing, *vbl. sb.* [f. as prec. + -ING[1].]

1. The action of furnishing, coupling, uniting, with brackets.

1869 SWINBURNE *Ess. & Stud.* (1875) 214 Byron and Shelley.. I protest against the bracketing of the two names. **1876** GLADSTONE in *Contemp. Rev.* June 20 The bracketing, in which no less than eight systems will.. be presented to view.

2. *Arch.* A wooden framework or skeleton, consisting of wooden ribs nailed to the ceiling, joists, and battening, for the purpose of supporting a cornice, cove, or other moulding.

1823 P. NICHOLSON *Pract. Build.* 138 Cove-bracketing is the finish of the top of the faces of a room, adjacent to the cornice. **1876** GWILT *Archit.* §2088 Thus the general form of the bracketing will be obtained.

Brackett ('brækɪt). *Physics.* The name of Frederick Sumner *Brackett* (b. 1896), U.S. physicist, used *attrib.* to designate a series of lines discovered by him in 1922 (*Astrophysical Jrnl.* LVI. 154) in the infra-red part of the spectrum of atomic hydrogen, with wave numbers represented by the formula $R(1/4^2 - 1/m^2)$ (where R is the Rydberg constant and m = 5, 6,...), of which the first line is at 4·04 micrometres and the series limit is at 1·46 micrometres.

1930 PAULING & GOUDSMIT *Structure of Line Spectra* i. 3 There have since been discovered other hydrogen series.. the Lyman series.. the Paschen series.. the Brackett series. **1967** [see LYMAN]. **1970** [see PFUND].

brackish ('brækɪʃ), *a.* Also 6 **brakkische**, **brachish**, 7 **brakish**. [f. BRACK *a.* + -ISH[1].]

1. Of a somewhat salt or saline taste; partly fresh, partly salt.

1538 LELAND *Itin.* VII. 139 The Water is a litle brakkische. **1594** MARLOWE *Dido* I. ii, The southern wind with brackish breath. **1703** MAUNDRELL *Journ. Jerus.* (1721) 83 Fresh Water he call'd it, but we found it brackish. **1878** HUXLEY *Physiogr.* 128 This saltness increases until the water becomes decidedly brackish.

2. *fig.* and *transf.* **a.** Spoilt by mixture, as of sea-water with fresh. **b.** Nauseous, distasteful. **c.** Nautical (quots. 1867 and 1881).

1611 SPEED *Hist. Gt. Brit.* IX. vi. (1632) 514 Retaining at this day the [English] language.. though brackish with the mixture of vulgar Irish. **1867** SMYTH *Sailor's Word-bk.* Introd. 7 The pithy conciseness of the brackish tongue renders it eminently useful on duty. **1871** ROSSETTI *Dante at Ver.* lv, The bread.. Seemed brackish, less like corn than tares. **1881** SMYTH *Cycle Celest. Obj.* (ed. 2) 2 Certain brackish rhymes.

† **'brackish**, *v. Obs. rare*[−1]. [f. BRACKISH *a.*] *trans.* To render brackish.

1637 HEYWOOD *Dial. Jup. & Io* Wks. 1874 VI. 267 O, brackish not your waters with your teares.

'brackishness. [f. as prec. + -NESS.] The quality of being salty or brackish; also *fig.*

1571 GOLDING *Calvin on Ps.* Ep. Ded. 5 The bitter fountaine Exampeus.. with its brackishnes marreth the sweete river Hipanis. *a* **1631** DONNE *Biathan.* 175 Some of those acts of ours.. may at the first Tast have some of the Brackishnes of Sin. **1682** WHELER *Journ. Greece* I. 13 Their Cisterns preserve water (without the least brackishness) always sweet. **1796** MORSE *Amer. Geog.* I. 694 Spirituous liquors.. used to correct the brackishness of the water.

† **'brackle.** *Obs.*[−0] [var. of BROCKLE, f. stem of OE. *brecan* to BREAK.] (See quot.)

1710 A. J. *Eng. Portug. Dict.*, To carry away rubble or brackle of an old decayed house.

brackman, obs. form of BRAHMIN.

† **'brackmard.** *Obs.* exc. *Hist.* Also 9 **braquemard.** [a. F. *braquemart* a short broad sword: see Littré.] See quots.; also *attrib.*

1653 URQUHART *Rabelais* I. xliv, He drew his brackmard or horseman's sword. *Ibid.* With his great brackmard sword, laid such load upon those runaways, that, etc. **1874** BOUTELL *Arms & Arm.* ix. 177 The *braquemard*, or *cutlass*.. has a straight flat wide blade, that is pointed and very sharp at either edge.

bracks: see BRAXY, *Sc.*, disease of sheep.

† **'brackwoort.** *Obs. rare.* [prob. corruption of *bracket* BRAGGET, with assimilation of the last syllable to WORT[2].] Used by Harrison to denote a portion of wort reserved from a former brewing, which, spiced and sweetened, was added to beer to promote fermentation and improve the flavour.

1577 HARRISON *England* 169 This she reserveth by itself unto further use.. calling it Brackwoort on Charwoort.. She addeth to hir brackwoort or charwoort half an ounce of arras.

† **'bracky**, *a.*[1] *Obs.* Also 7 **brachie**. [f. BRACK *sb*[6] + -Y[1].] = BRACKISH *a.*

1593 DRAYTON *Eclog.* iv. 90 Men, Sea-Monsters, swam the bracky Flood. **1603** KNOLLES *Hist. Turks* (1621) 795 The water becometh brachie.

fig. **1583** STANYHURST *Æneis* IV. (Arb.) 101 Netled with theese brackye nouels [L. *rumore amaro*].

bracky, *a.*[2] [f. *brack*, var. of BRAKE *sb.*[1] and BRAKE *sb.*[2]; the two being confused.] **a.** = BRACKENY. **b.** Of the nature of a brake or thicket.

a **1618** SYLVESTER *Job Triumph.* (1620) 945 The brackie barren wildernesse. **1628** COKE *On Litt.* 4 b, A brackie ground is called *filicetum, ubi filices crescunt.*

Braconid ('brækənɪd), *a.* and *sb.* [f. mod.L. *Bracon* + -ID[3].] **A.** *adj.* Of or belonging to the Braconidæ, a family of small ichneumon flies. **B.** *sb.* A fly of this family.

1893 in *Funk's Stand. Dict.* **1913** *Oxf. Univ. Gaz.* 4 June 961/1 The Braconids *Caelinus niger* and *Pezomachus fasciatus.* **1916** *Canadian Entomologist* XLVIII. 89 *Dinocampus americanus*.. a common Braconid parasite of many of the larger species of Coccinellids. **1957** E. B. FORD *Butterflies* (ed. 3) vi. 109 [The Ichneumons are] again divided between the true Ichneumons (family Ichneumonidae) and the closely related Braconids (family Braconidae).

bract (brækt). Also bracte; and in L. form **bractea**, *pl.* **bracteæ**, also occas. **bracteas**. [ad. L. *bractea* (formerly used unchanged) a thin plate or leaf of metal, gold-leaf; cf. Fr. *bractée.*]

1. *Bot.* **a.** A small modified leaf, or scale, growing immediately below the calyx of a plant, or upon the peduncle of a flower.

1770 ELLIS in *Phil. Trans.* LX. 520 Under this flower-cup are four floral leaves, or bracteæ. **1794** MARTYN *Rousseau's Bot.* xiii. 149 A lateral leaf to each calyx, which Linnæus calls the.. bracte. **1807** J. E. SMITH *Phys. Bot.* 22 The Lavenders.. have coloured bracteas. **1835** LINDLEY *Introd. Bot.* (1848) I. 309 There are.. no exact limits between bracts and common leaves. **1884** J. E. TAYLOR *Sagac. & Mor. Plants* 103 In the Yew.. some bracts become aborted.

b. *attrib.*, as in ***bract-sheath***; also deriv. **'bractless** *a.* ***bract-like*** adjs.

1847 CRAIG, *Bractless*, without bracts. **1847** W. E. STEELE *Field Bot.* 167 S[piranthes] *autumnalis*, root-leaves oblong, those of stem bract-like. **1870** HOOKER *Stud. Flora* 415

Carex præcox..bract-sheaths short. **1911** F. O. BOWER *Plant-Life on Land* iv. 64 The calyx sprang from bract-like leaves.

2. *Zool.* A similar appendage found in some of the Hydrozoa.

1878 BELL *Gegenbauer's Comp. Anat.* 97 Nutritive, generative, and tentacular individuals are generally placed together in groups, in such a way that there is one bract to a group.

bracteal (ˈbræktiːəl), *a.* [f. L. *bracte-a* BRACT + -AL[1].] Pertaining to, or of the nature of, bracts.

1770 *Phil. Trans.* LX. 523 The flower of the *Gordonia Lasianthus*..with its calyx and bracteal leaves.

bracteate (ˈbræktiːət), *a.* and *sb.* [ad. L. *bracteātus*, f. *bractea*: see BRACT.] **A.** *adj.*

1. *Bot.* Having bracts, bearing bracts.

1845 LINDLEY *Sch. Bot.* (1858) v. 57 Flowers in heads or dense spikes, bracteate. **1870** HOOKER *Stud. Flora* 291 Whorls many-flowered, axillary, or in leafy bracteate heads.

2. Formed of metal beaten thin; applied chiefly to coins, medals, or ornaments made of thin plates of gold or silver, the design being hollow on the under side and convex on the upper.

1866 *Athenæum* No. 1996. 139/1 Two Danish bracteate ornaments.

B. *sb.* A bracteate coin or metal; also *attrib.*

1845 PETRIE *Eccl. Archit. Irel.* 213 Bracteates..coined by the first two propagators of Christianity in Denmark and Sweden. **1868** G. STEPHENS *Runic Mon.* II. 505 Few of the earlier Bracteate-stamps can be directly connected with 'classical' prototypes.

ˈbracteated (-eɪtɪd), *a.* = BRACTEATE I.

1852 E. HAMILTON *Flora Homœop.* II. 24 Flowers..in dense..bracteated corymbs.

bracted (ˈbræktɪd), *ppl. a.* [f. BRACT + -ED[2].] Furnished with bracts.

1854 in OGILVIE.

bracteiform (ˈbræktiːɪfɔːm), *a.* [mod. f. L. *bractea* (see above) + -FORM; cf. Fr. *bractéiforme*.] Bract-shaped, bract-like.

1870 HOOKER *Stud. Flora* 280 *Mentha aquatica*..leaves ovate-oblong or cordate, upper bracteiform.

bracteolate (bræk'tiːəleɪt, ˈbræktiːəleɪt), *a.* [f. next. + -ATE[2].] Furnished with bracteoles.

1830 LINDLEY *Nat. Syst. Bot.* 86 Calyx 5-lobed, sometimes bracteolate at the base. **1872** OLIVER *Elem. Bot.* II. 142 Sweet Violet. Bracteolate irregular flowers.

bracteole (ˈbræktiːəʊl). [ad. L. *bracteola* (also used unchanged) a thin leaf of gold, also (mod.), a small bract.] A small bract, a bractlet.

1830 LINDLEY *Nat. Syst. Bot.* 165 Calyx..occasionally with 2 bracteolæ at the base. **1876** HARLEY *Mat. Med.* 709 Calyx usually surrounded by three narrow bracteoles.

bracteose (brækti:ˈəʊs), *a.* [f. L. *bracte-a* BRACT + -OSE.] (See quot.)

1880 GRAY *Bot. Text-bk.* 400 Bracteose—Full of, or with conspicuous bracts.

bractlet (ˈbræktlɪt). [f. BRACT + -LET.] A minute or secondary bract.

1835 LINDLEY *Introd. Bot.* (1848) I. 310 When the bracts are very small they are called bractlets. **1842** GRAY *Struct. Bot.* v. (1880) 142 Bractlets are bracts of a secondary or ultimate order.

brad (bræd). Also 3–6 **brod**, 5 **brode**. [A variant of BROD, which in its more general sense has retained the older form; the change of vowel is perhaps due to dialect pronunciation.]

1. A thin flattish nail of the same thickness throughout, but tapering in width, having a small 'lip' on one edge, instead of a head.

1295 in Rogers *Agric. & Prices* II. 490 [Elham, 300 brods]. *c* **1440** *Promp. Parv.* 53 Brode, hedlese nayle, *clavus acephalus*. *c* **1450** *Nominale* in Wr.-Wülcker *Voc.* 727 *Hic aculius*, a brad. **1526** *Pilgr. Perf.* (W. de W. 1531) 254 With moost buystous broddes of yren nayled them fast to yᵉ sayd tree. **1582** *Wills & Inv. N.C.* (1860) II. 67, xv hondert latt brods 6/. **1677** MOXON *Mech. Exerc.* (1703) 158 Brad, is a Nail to Floor Rooms with. **1823** P. NICHOLSON *Pract. Build.* 220 Brad, a small nail, having no head except on one edge. **1831** J. HOLLAND *Manuf. Metals* I. 194 Brads or spikes.. sometimes made nearly a foot in length for the shipwright's or builder's use. **1881** *Mechanic* §218 A light hammer with a small face..for driving brads.

2. *slang.* (See quots.)

1812 J. H. VAUX *Flash Dict.*, *Brads*, halfpence; also money in general. **1841** MARRYAT *Poacher* vi, 'Have you any brads?'..'What are those?'..'Any money, to be sure.'

brad, *v.* [f. prec.] *trans.* To fasten with brads.

1794 W. FELTON *Carriages* (1801) I. 5 The pannels are.. bradded on the surfaces of the framing. **1881** *Mechanic* §626 Each flange can then be bradded in its place.

†**brad**, *ppl. a. Obs.* [var. of BRED, pa. pple. of BREDE *v.*[1]] Roasted, broiled.

c **1340** *Gaw. & Gr. Knt.* 891 Summe baken in bred, summe brad on þe gledez.

brad, obs. form of BREAD, BROAD.

bradawl (ˈbrædɔːl). [app. f. BRAD *sb.* + AWL, denoting an awl for making holes to insert brads; though the ON. *bragð-alr* lit. 'twirling awl', a fire-drill, suggests a different derivation.]

A kind of small boring tool, a sprig-bit.

1823 P. NICHOLSON *Pract. Build.* 238 Brad-awl..is the smallest tool used for boring. **1881** *Mechanic* §262 The bradawl varies in..diameter of the steel shaft from $\frac{1}{16}$ in. to $\frac{1}{8}$ in. or $\frac{3}{16}$ in.

Bradbury (ˈbrædbərɪ). [The name of John Swanwick *Bradbury*, Secretary to the Treasury 1913–19.] Former colloquial name for a currency note of £1. (Cf. FISHER[2].)

[**1914** *Punch* 21 Oct. 342/3 Not a burglar on our books for the last six weeks..not a coiner, not a note expert. And they had the opportunity of their lives with the John Bradbury notes!] **1917** *Punch* 22 Aug. 128 Parting with three Bradburys and three shillings. **1920** *Oxf. Tracts Econ. Subj.* No. 27. 4 The 'Bradbury', nominally a pound, and by statute legal tender for a pound of debt, has lost, from its abundance, a part of its purchasing power. **1926** G. FRANKAU *Masterson* xvi, Cynthia had decided to 'risk a couple of Bradbury's each way'.

†**ˈbradden**, *v. Obs. rare*$^{-1}$. [app. f. BREED *v.*, or BROOD *v.*, in same sense.

(The Shropsh. Gloss. has '*bradling*, brooding, as a hen over her chickens', '*broodle*, to breed' (= BROOD *v.*[2]); Halliw. has '*broodle*, to cuddle, *north.*'; also '*bradow*, to spread, to cover'. With the latter cf. BROAD, BREDE *v.*[2])]

trans. To breed or 'brood', to hatch.

1653 E. CHISENHALE *Cath. Hist.* 12 An upstart youngling, that wind-egge of a tumult, which being braddened under a Toad of France, is become a staring Cockatrice.

braddishing, obs. form of BRATTICING.

brade, obs. f. BRAID, BREAD, BREDE *sb.*, BROAD.

Bradenham (ˈbræd(ə)nəm). [Trade-name.] Applied *attrib.* to a dark, sweet-cured ham. Also *ellipt.*

1906 *Daily Chron.* 24 Sept. 7/2 Next door the Wiltshire Bacon Curing Company shows a decided novelty in 'Bradenham' hams and chaps. They are perfectly black, a result achieved, it is said, by curing with treacle. **1927** D. L. SAYERS *Unnatural Death* I. vi. 68 Tell me how it comes that your little waitress and her railway clerk come down to Epping Forest to regale themselves on sandwiches made from coal-black, treacle-cured Bradenham ham? **1959** *Hist. Wiltshire (V.C.H.)* IV. 223/1 In 1897 the company [*sc.* the Wiltshire Bacon Curing Co. Ltd.] took over the Bradenham Ham Co. and since it was wound up in 1921 'Bradenham' hams, cured by a secret recipe, have been manufactured by the Wiltshire Bacon Co. **1960** *House & Garden* Apr. 111/2 There are counters of hams including Bradenhams (the coal-black ham).

Bradford (ˈbrædfəd). Shortened form of *Bradford-on-Avon*, the name of a town in Wiltshire, used *attrib.* in ***Bradford clay*** (see quots.). Hence **Bradˈfordian** *a.*

1858 [see BATHONIAN *a.* 2]. **1903** GEIKIE *Textbk. Geol.* (ed. 4) II. VI. 1142 Its [*sc.* Forest Marble's] lower portion near Bradford-on-Avon is a grey marly clay with thin layers of tough limestone and calcareous sandstone about 10 feet thick, and this argillaceous band has been separately designated the Bradford clay. **1910** *Encycl. Brit.* IV. 372/1 *Bradford clay*, a thin, rather inconstant bed of clay or marl situated in England at the base of the Forest Marble, the two together constituting the Bradfordian group in the Bathonian series of Jurassic rocks.

Bradleian (ˈbrædlɪən, -ˈliːən), *a.* Also **Bradleyan.** [f. *Bradley* (see below) + -AN.] Of, pertaining to, or characteristic of: (*a*) the English idealist philosopher Francis Herbert Bradley (1846–1924) or his writings; or (*b*) his brother, the Shakespearean critic Andrew Cecil Bradley (1851–1925).

1905 W. JAMES in *Jrnl. Philos.* 2 Mar. 115 It gets rid of any need for an Absolute of the Bradleyan type. **1909** —— *Pluralistic Universe* ii. 71 The functions of the bradleian absolute are in this particular identical with those of the theistic God. **1943** E. L. MASCALL *He who Is* vi. 77 Idealistic philosophies of the Bradleian type are so unsatisfactory. **1961** *Listener* 21 Dec. 1083/2 He does not try to put Othello back on the Bradleian pedestal.

bradoon, var. form of BRIDOON.

Bradshaw (ˈbrædʃɔː). Colloquial designation of 'Bradshaw's Railway Guide', a time-table of all railway trains running in Great Britain, the earliest form of which was first issued at Manchester in 1839 by George *Bradshaw* (1801–53), printer and engraver. (Ceased publication in 1961.) Also *transf.* and *fig.*

1847 F. A. KEMBLE *Let.* in *Records of Later Life* (1882) III. 289 You ask me what book I read now to put me to sleep —why, Murray's 'Handbook for France'..and the foreign 'Bradshaw'. **1851** *Fraser's Mag.* Jan. 126/1 It is always dangerous to travel upon the faith of an old Bradshaw. **1914** 'BARTIMEUS' *Naval Occasions* xi. 77 The young Doctor looked up from the year-old 'Bradshaw' with which he was wont to enliven moments of depression by arranging mythical week-ends at friends' houses in various parts of England. **1923** J. M. MURRY *Pencillings* 201 Reading reviews is a minor and fascinating science like the study of the continental Bradshaw. **1954** J. MASTERS *Bhowani Junction* xxx. 257 The girl's a walking Bradshaw. **1959** *Times* 20 May 11/7 It would be the easiest thing in the world for a new D.N.B. to become the Tom Tiddler's ground of historical specialists and so to cease to count as more than a 'Bradshaw' for students. **1961** *Economist* 18 Mar. 1047/1 Poor *Bradshaw* is, no doubt, irreplaceable. His approaching demise, in May, is one that countless thousands precipitately and inconsolably mourn.

Hence **ˈBradshaw** *v.*, (*a*) *trans.* to make a 'Bradshaw' for; (*b*) *intr.* (*R.A.F. slang*) to follow a railway in flying. Hence **ˈBradshawing** *vbl. sb.*

1887 MRS. D. DALY *Digging & Squatting S. Australia* 253 Mr. Westgarth says: 'If the through route of Central Australia is some day to be Bradshawed.' **1946** E. C. CHEESMAN *Brief Glory* ii. 21, I knew the only thing to do was to 'Bradshaw': in other words to follow the railways. **1946** A. PHELPS *I couldn't care Less* iii. 25 Bradshawing can sometimes lead into trouble... I dislike following a railway except in extreme emergency when forced to fly low.

brady-, comb. form of Gr. βραδύ-ς slow, as in **bradyˈcardia** [Gr. καρδία heart], slowness of the pulse; **bradykinin** (-ˈkaɪnɪn) [Gr. κίν-ησις motion + -IN[1]], a polypeptide stimulating the action of the visceral muscles; **bradyˈphrasia** [Gr. φράσις speech], slowness of speech due to mental defect or disease; **ˈbradyseism** [SEISM], a slow rise and fall of the earth's crust.

1890 BILLINGS *Med. Dict.* I. 182/1 Bradycardia. **1908** J. MACKENZIE *Dis. Heart* 133 True bradycardia..only occurs when all the chambers of the heart participate in the slow action. **1965** J. POLLITT *Depression & its Treatment* ii. 13 Bradycardia. **1949** M. ROCHA E SILVA et al. in *Amer. Jrnl. Physiol.* CLVI. 261 (*title*) Bradykinin, a hypotensive and smooth muscle stimulating factor released from plasma globulin by snake venom and by trypsin. **1878** J. A. MCCREERY tr. *von Ziemssen's Cycl. Med.* XIV. 816 We find bradyphrasia and paraphrasia developed in a similar manner in conditions of morbid hebetude and intellectual weakness. **1896** *Daily News* 11 Feb. 6/2 The slow movements, or bradyseisms..were those which had resulted in the formation of continents. **1959** A. A. G. SCHIEFERDECKER *Geol. Nomencl.* 196/2 *Bradyseism*, slow movement of the ground especially recognizable by an upheaval, subsidence or a shifting of shore line *Ibid.* 268/1 *Bradyseism*, slow vertical movements of the earth's crust, caused by volcanic action.

†**bradypepsy** (ˈbrædɪˌpɛpsɪ), **-ˈpepsia.** *Obs.* Also 6–7 **bradypepsie**, 7 **bradio-**, **bradupepsia**, **bradyspepsy.** [ad. Gr. βραδυπεψία, f. βραδύ-ς slow + πέψ-ις cooking, digestion: cf. Fr. *bradypepsie*.] Slowness of digestion. (Freq. in 17th c.)

1598 SYLVESTER *Du Bartas* (1621) 210 The dog-hunger or the bradypepsie. **1688** R. HOLME *Armoury* II. xvii. 429 Bradupepsia, is when meat is long in digesting. **1710** T. FULLER *Pharm. Extemp.* 397 A bitter colluvies brings Queasiness..Bradypepsy.

bradypeptic (-ˈpɛptɪk), *a.* (*sb.*) [cf. PEPTIC.] Slow of digestion: also *fig.*

1879 G. MEREDITH *Egoist* III. xi. 240 For facts, we are bradypeptics to a man, sir.

bradypod, -pus (ˈbrædɪpɒd, -pəs). [ad. Gr. βραδύπους, -ποδ- slow-footed, f. βραδύ-ς slow + πούς foot.] A member of the family of edentate mammal quadrupeds represented by the Sloth. Hence **braˈdypodal** *a.*, pertaining to the bradypods.

1833 *Penny Cycl.* I. 230/2 Both these genera were formerly included..under the common name of Bradypus or Sloth. **1843** *Ibid.* XXV. 502/1 The bradypodal modifications of the jaws.

brae (breɪ, *dial.* breː, brɪə, briː). Now only *Sc.* and *northern dial.* Forms: 4 **bro**, 4–8 **bra**, 5–6 (*Sc.*) **brai**, 5–7 **bray(e**, (6 **braue**), 6–7 **bray**, **braie**, 6– **brae**, 8–9 (*dial.*) **brea**, **breea.** [Evidently a. ON. *brá* = OE. *brǽw*, *bréaw* eyelid, OS. *brâwa*, *brâha*, OHG. *brâwa* (MHG. *brâ*, Ger. *braue*) eyebrow:—OTeut. **brǣwâ-*: cf. BROW and BREE.

The phonetic history is clear: *bro*, *bra*, *brae* answer to ON. *brá*, as *blo*, *bla*, *blae* do to *blá*. The word must have passed through the sense of 'eye-brow' to 'brow of a hill', *supercilium* (cf. OE. *éaȝhill* 'eye hill' = eyebrow); but no quotations illustrating the change appear. The Eng. form *bro* has long been obs., and in spoken use *brae* is now exclusively northern and mainly Scotch, though occurring in recent literary English.]

1. The steep bank bounding a river valley. Frequent in the collocation 'banks and braes'.

1330 R. BRUNNE *Chron.* 310 þer to þe rayne bigan, and flowand bank and bro. **1375** BARBOUR *Bruce* IV. 372 Vnder ane bra [thai] thair galay dreuch. **1483** *Cath. Angl.* 39 Bra, *ripa*. **1536** BELLENDEN *Cron. Scot.* (1821) I. 235 Gret slauchter was maid on the brayis of this river. **1615** G. SANDYS *Trav.* 99 Slow Nile with low-sunke streames shall keepe his braies. **1791** BURNS *Banks of Doon* (vers. 3) i, Ye banks and braes o' bonie Doon. **1803** WORDSW. *Ellen Irwin*, Upon the braes of Kirtle. **1855** *Whitby Gloss.*, *Breea*, the brink or bank of a river.

2. A steep, a slope, a hill-side. (Called in south of England a *hill*, as in Ludgate or Holborn Hill; in the north a 'hill' is always a mount or eminence with a summit, and with slopes or 'braes' on all sides of it, as in 'the Calton Hill'.)

1425 WYNTOUN *Cron.* VIII. xxvi. 7 The Scottis men come til a bra. **1535** STEWART *Chron. Scotl.* II. 524 Vnder ane bra quhair tha thocht it to hyde. **1548** PATTEN *Sped. Scotl.* (Arber *Garner* III. 62) The hill (for so they call a *Bray*). **1600** FAIRFAX *Tasso* IX. xcvi. 178 On that steepe bray Lord Guelpho would not than Hazard his folke. **1634** S. RUTHERFORD *Lett.* (1862) xli, At the very overgoing of the brae and mountain. **1716** *Lond. Gaz.* No. 5415/2 The Braes of Mar. **1799** J. ROBERTSON *Agric. Perth* 146 The farmers.. in the breas. **1820** SCOTT *Monast.* ii, The steep braes rose

abruptly over the little glen. **1822** Bewick *Mem.* 10 A steep but low 'brae'. **1830** Praed *Poems* (1865) I. 179, I have seen thee gaze Upon these birks and braes.

3. *Comb.*, as *brae-face*, *-head*, *-side*; also, **brae(s)-laird**, 'a proprietor of land on the southern declivity of the Grampians' (Jamieson); **brae-man**, one who lives among the hills; *spec.* one who lives on the southern slopes of the Grampians.

1799 J. Robertson *Agric. Perth* 422 The brea-faces..are better fitted for sheep than cattle. **1818** Scott *Rob Roy* xxvi, He..took to the brae-side, and became a broken-man. **1823** —— *Quentin D.* ii, 'I am, master' answered the young Scot, 'a braeman'. **1854** H. Miller *Sch. & Schm.* (1858) 535 A splendid bonfire blazing from the brae-head.

brag (bræg), *sb.*[1] Also 5–8 **bragg(e**, 6 **braggue**. [The etymology of brag *sb.*[1], *vb.*, *adj.*, and their mutual relations are uncertain. There are several related words in 16th c. French, *braguer* 'to flaunt, brave, brag', *bragueur*, *braguerie*; *bragard* 'gay, gallant, braggard, braggadochio-like', *bragarder* 'to brave it, to brag, vaunt', *bragardise*, etc. (all in Cotgr.); but as these appear so late, while some of the Eng. words go back to 1300, the latter cannot be referred to a French origin (though the later *braggart* and *braggery* may). The words are not in other Romanic langs., and their origin has been variously sought in Celtic and in Norse: see Diez. It is doubtful whether the *adj.* or *sb.* is the earlier in Eng.; both appear before the vb. The order of senses is also uncertain.

Diez conjectured that the Fr. might be from ON. *brak* 'creaking noise' (Sw. *brak* bounce, Da. *brag*), *braka* (Da. *brage*) 'to creak, crack, *insolenter se gerere*' Haldorss.; others have suggested ON. *bragr* 'the best, the foremost, the boast or toast (of anything)'; also 'poetry'. See Diez, Wedgwood, Skeat.]

†**1.** A loud noise, the bray of a trumpet. (Cf. brag *v.* 1.) *Obs.*

1513 Douglas *Æneis* ix. viii. 105 Bot than the trumpettis weirly blastis aboundis, Wyth terribill brag of brasin bludy soundis.

2. Arrogant or boastful language (in earlier examples usually in phrase *brag and boast*); boasting, boastful assertion. (Phrase ***French brag***, common in 16th c.; also used in sense 3.)

c **1360** *Know Thyself* in *E.E.P.* (1862) 132 Vr bost vr brag is sone ouerbide. **1387** Trevisa *Higden* Rolls Ser. III. 427 [These words] haveþ more of brag and of boost. *c* **1440** *York Myst.* xlvi. 225 His bragge and his boste is he besie to bid vs. **1513** Douglas *Æneis* xi. vii. 127 With brag and bost [*v.r.* braik and boist] or wapynnis, he Me doith awayt. **1548** Udall, etc. *Erasm. Par. Luke* xxiv. 53 Not makyng vauntes and braggues of their weorkes. **1548** Hall *Chron.* (1809) 192 Melune..and diuerse other tounes, yelded and turned at a proude crake, or a Frenche bragge, without stroke striken. **1600** Shaks. *A.Y.L.* v. ii. 34 Cesars Thrasonicall bragge of I came, saw, and ouercome. **1753** Richardson *Grandison* (1781) IV. 242 My Uncle..sometimes reminds me of what he calls my former brags. **1877** Mrs. Oliphant *Makers Flor.* xv. 354 He has thus held his place..not without a certain brag of his strength.

b. in *proverb.*

1618 *Barnevelt's Apol.* E iv b, Bragge is a good Dog still. **1752** Johnson *Rambl.* No. 197. ¶3 When I envied the finery of any of my neighbours, [my mother] told me that 'Brag was a good dog, but Holdfast was a better.'

†**3.** Show, pomp, display; pompous demeanour or carriage. *Obs.*

1494 Fabyan vi. ccxii. 227 The bragge or pompe of the worlde. *a* **1553** Udall *Royster D.* (Arb.) 48 Ye must haue a portely bragge after your estate..Vp man with your head and chin. **1577** Holinshed *Chron.* III. 850/1 They were all French in apparell, yea, and in French vices and brags. **1632** G. Herbert *Temple*, *Content*, The brags of life are but a nine days wonder.

4. *concr.* That which is boasted of; the 'boast'.

1538 Leland *Itin.* II. 52 This [the Fair is] one of the Bragges of the Toun. **1634** Milton *Comus* 745 Beauty is nature's brag.

5. A person who brags, a braggart, a boaster.

1671 J. Webster *Metallogr.* xv. 233 They [Chymists] are nothing but vain and ignorant brags. **1881** Evans *Leicester. Gloss.* (E.D.S.), *Brag*, a boaster.

6. A game at cards, essentially identical with the modern game of 'poker'. The name is taken from the 'brag' or challenge given by one of the players to the rest to turn up cards equal in value to his. See also quotations. Also *attrib.*, as in ***brag-party***.

1734 Seymour *Compl. Gamester* 20 The main Thing by which the second Stake is to be won, is called the Brag, which..gives the Game its Denomination. **1749** H. Walpole *Lett. H. Mann* (1834) II. cxcix. 265 Methodism is more fashionable than any thing but brag; the women play very deep at both. **1822** *Encycl. Brit.* s.v., A pair of aces is the best brag, a pair of kings the next, and so on. **1855** Geo. Eliot in Cross *Life* (1885) I. 356 One night we attempted 'Brag' or 'Pocher.' **1859** J. Lang *Wand. India* 16 Two young gentlemen were victimized last night at the brag party.

b. *fig.* with a reference to sense 2. ***to play a game of brag***: to try which can impose on or get the better of the other by boasting.

1883 *Fortn. Rev.* Dec. 895 The two countries may be still only engaged in a game of brag.

†**brag**, *sb.*[2] *Obs.* exc. *dial.* [Derivation unknown.] A large nail.

[**1371** Rogers *Agric. & Prices* (1866) I. xx. 500 York gives two unique names 'brags' and 'scot-nails' under the year 1371.] *c* **1440** *York Myst.* xxxiv. 95 Here are bragges þat will noght faile. **1702** Thoresby in *Phil. Trans.* XXV. 1864 Brags, or great Iron Nails.

†**brag**, *sb.*[3] *Obs. rare.* (See quot.)

c **1682** J. Collins *Mak. Salt* 25 In..Surrey, their Wheatfields were formerly much annoyed with Smut or Brag.

brag (bræg), *a.* and quasi-*adv.* Also **bragge**. [See brag *sb.*[1]]

†**1.** Spirited, brisk, lively, mettlesome, valiant. *Obs.*

a **1300** Wright's *Lyric P.* (1842) 24 That maketh us so brag and bolde, and biddeth us ben blythe. *c* **1350** *Will. Palerne* 3048 Best of his bodi boldest & braggest in armes. **1600** Holland *Livy* xxv. xxxix. 579 e, The Romanes..lustie and brag for their new victorie, began to make a fray. **1610** G. Fletcher *Christ's Vict.* i, The bragge lambes ranne wantoning about.

†**2.** Boastful (*of*). *Obs.*

c **1315** Shoreham 110 Prede..That ketheth wordes bragge. **1560** Daus tr. *Sleidane's Comm.* 119 b, They are as bragge and as proude as pecockes. **1655** Gurnall *Chr. in Arm.* i. (1669) 75/1 Not the braggest Philosopher among the Gentiles.

†**3.** quasi-*adv.* Haughtily, boastfully. *Obs.*

c **1350** *Will. Palerne* 2352 Summe þat bere hem now brag schuld blede or euen. *c* **1394** *P. Pl. Crede* 706 Hy schulde nouȝt beren hem so bragg. **1572** R. H. *Lauaterus' Ghostes* (1596) 41 They vaunted and bare themselues very brag on their priuiledges. **1579** Spenser *Sheph. Cal.* Feb., Seest how brag yond bullock beares..his pricked eares?

†**4.** *Comb.* **brag-brained**, head-strong. *Obs.*

1648 *Petit. Eastern Assoc.* 20 Whirl-crown'd, and bragg-braind Opinionists.

5. Prime, first-rate, surpassingly good. *U.S.*

1836 *Jeffersonian* 5 May 96 (Th.), The Moselle was a new brag boat, and had made several quick trips. **1857** *Knickerbocker* Sept. 292 Isaac had once been the 'brag hand' of the plantation. **1893** *Outing* (U.S.) XXII. 92/1 His [*sc.* the pup's] sire was the brag runner of the country. **1904** W. N. Harben *Georgians* xvi. 160 A boy that blowed an army bugle come, an' the brag singer, a young man that sung 'Whar is my wanderin' boy to-night?'

brag (bræg), *v.* Also 4–7 **bragge**, 6 **brage**, **braggue**, *Sc.* **braig**. [See under brag *sb.*[1]]

†**1.** *intr.* Of a trumpet: To sound loudly; also, to make a loud sound (with a trumpet); *trans.* to sound (a trumpet). Cf. brag *sb.*[1] 1.

1382 Wyclif *Josh.* vi. 5 Whanne the voyce of the trompe ..in ȝoure eeris braggith [**1388** sowne]. ? *a* **1400** *Morte Arth.* 1484 Thane þe Bretones boldely braggene þeire tromppez. *Ibid.* 4108 Bremly the brethemen bragges in troumppes.

2. *intr.* and *refl.* To vaunt, talk boastfully, boast oneself. (In earlier examples chiefly in conjunction with *boast*.) Const. (*on*, *in*, obs.) *of*, *about*.

1377 Langl. *P. Pl.* B. xiii. 281 For-why he bosteth and braggeth with many bolde othes. **1543** Hen. VIII *Parl. Speech* 24 Dec., If I see a Man boast and brag himself, I cannot but deem him a Proud Man. *c* **1645** Howell *Lett.* (1688) II. 389 The fashion of his Face which..he hath no cause to brag of. **1647** W. Browne *Polex.* i. 225, I will no more brag in being one of his slaves. **1728** Morgan *Algiers* II. ii. 234 Nor has our [Nation] abundance of Reason to brag of its superabundant Regularity. **1786** Wolcott (P. Pindar) *Ode R. A's* x. Wks. 1812 I. 154 Garrick, on whom our Nation justly brags. **1858** Gladstone *Homer* III. 562 The disposition of the Trojan chief to brag.

†**b.** To swagger, strut, 'show off'. *Obs.*

a **1553** Udall *Royster D.* (Arb.) 64 Idle loytrers, braggyng vp and downe. **1578** T. N. *Conq. W. India* 40 They should ..not thus bragge in other mens land. **1589** R. Harvey *Pl. Perc.* (1860) 28 You shal haue a lame Iade, bridle and brag it vp and downe Smithfield.

fig. **1588** Shaks. *L.L.L.* v. ii. 683 She's quick, the child brags in her belly alreadie: 'tis yours [i.e. Braggart's].

3. *trans.* **a.** To defy proudly, challenge; also, to bully, threaten. *Obs.* exc. *dial.* **b.** To impose upon or overawe by boasting (*mod.*, perhaps with allusion to game of brag).

1551 Ascham *Let.* Wks. 1865 I. ii. 257 Two fair castles of either side of Rhene..one bragging the other. *a* **1555** Ridley *Wks.* 115 They will outface, brace, and brag all men. **1584** J. Carmichael *Let.* in *Misc. Wodrow Soc.* (1844) 438 The King..boasting the poor, and bragging the rich. **1823** Scott *Quentin D.* I. 60 (D.) An artist who might brag all Paris. **1843** *Proc. Berw. Nat. Club* II. 58 Amateurs from one part of the county..by challenging or *bragging* those of the vicinity..provoked a vigorous competition. **1876** Whyte-Melville *Katerfelto* xviii. 202 Our old Duke wasn't to be bragged at such a game as that.

4. To boast of, vaunt, lay boastful claim to.

1588 A. King *Canisius' Catech.* 224 Na man quha braigs confidence and certantie of ye remission of his sinnes. **1600** S. Nicholson *Acolastus* (1876) 54 Euery stalke Brags the sweete blossomes he is blest withall. **1611** Shaks. *Cymb.* v. iii. 93 He brags his seruice. **1625** K. Long *Barclay's Argenis* (1636) 389 These which bragge their skill in controversies. **1790** Morison *Poems* 82 (Jam.) Ye'll brag high rank, Or heaps o' siller.

5. To declare or assert boastfully, to boast. Const. with *obj. inf.* (obs.) or *subord. cl.*

1563–87 Foxe *A. & M.* III. 878 The very meanest.. bragged that they had bathed their hands in the blood of a Lutheran. **1627** P. Fletcher *Locusts* iii. xxviii, That eye, and eare, Which being blind, and deafe, bragges best to see, and heare. *a* **1659** Cleveland *Rebel Scot* i, No more let Ireland brag her harmless nation Harbours no venom. **1725** Ramsay *Gentle Sheph.* v. iii, I'll..brag for aye that I was ca'd the aunt O' our young lady. **1870** Bryant *Iliad* viii. I. 248 Bragged that each of you would be a match For fivescore Trojans.

6. In the game of brag (see brag *sb.* 6).

1734 Seymour *Compl. Gamester* 21 The best Cards you can have really to brag of are a Pair Royal of Aces.

braga-beaker ('brɑːga,biːkə(r)). Also **brage-goblet**, etc. [f. ON. *braga-* in *braga(r)full* the cup drunk at funeral feasts.] A cup from which a toast is drunk.

Quots. 1847 and 1851 show that some writers, mistaking the etymology, thought the word was connected with Bragi, the god of poetry in Norse mythology.

1839 G. Stephens tr. *Tegnér's Frithiof's Saga* 270 Thus should he stand opposite the Brage-goblet, first make a vow, and then drink out the Bumper. **1847** I. A. Blackwell in T. Percy tr. *Mallet's Northern Antiq.* 549 Bragi's bumper—the Bragafull. **1851** B. Thorpe *Northern Mythol.* I. 190 At guilds the Bragarfull, or Bragi-cup was drunk. **1854** W. B. Jerrold (*title*) A brage beaker with the Swedes: or, notes from the North in 1852. **1921** *Public Opin.* 15 July 61/3 Wielding Thor's hammer and drinking from the braga-beaker in the hall.

†**bra'gance.** *Obs. rare*$^{-1}$. [prob. a. OF. **bragance*, f. *braguer* to brag; or ? directly f. brag *v.*[1]] Bragging, boasting.

c **1460** *Towneley Myst.* 99 He can make purveance, With boste and bragance.

bragard, -rie, obs. var. of braggart, -ry.

braget(t, obs. form of bracket *sb.*

Bragg (bræg). The name of Sir William Henry *Bragg* (1862–1942) and of his son Sir William Lawrence *Bragg* (born 1890), English physicists, used *attrib.* or in the possessive to designate certain laws, effects, etc., in *Physics* (see quots.).

1913 *Phil. Mag.* XXV. 618 The air equivalent of the carbon was calculated from Bragg's law to be about 78 per cent. of the whole stopping power. **1920** Rutherford in *Proc. R. Soc.* A. XCVII. 387 It can readily be calculated from Bragg's rule. **1923** *Phil. Mag.* XLV. 121 The fact that Bragg's law cannot be strictly true seems to have been pointed out first by Darwin. **1930** Rutherford in *Proc. R. Soc.* CXXIX. 214 When this average size was plotted against the distance from source to chamber, the familiar Bragg ionisation curve was obtained. **1931** *Physical Rev.* XXXVIII. 1420 In this investigation, regular Bragg reflections from the face of crystals oscillating and non-oscillating have been observed in order to notice any variation in intensity or line width. **1934** C. Meyer *Diffraction of Light* viii. 294 Bragg's law, taken literally, states that a given wave-length will be reflected in a given spectral order only when the glancing angle takes a *unique* value θ. **1940** *Chambers's Techn. Dict.* 108/2 *Bragg method*, a method of investigating crystal structure by means of X-rays. **1950** F. Gaynor *Concise Encycl. Atomic Energy* 32 *Bragg angle*, the glancing angle for x-rays reflected by planes of a crystal. **1957** *Gloss. Terms Nucl. Sci.* (*A.S.A.*) (1958) 21/2 *Bragg curve*, a curve showing the average number of ions per unit distance along a beam of initially monoenergetic ionizing particles.

†**bra'ggade.** *Obs. rare*$^{-1}$. [f. brag *v.* + -ade.] Brag; boasting.

1762 in *Ann. Reg.* 40/1 His conversation..was..strongly tinctured with vanity, braggade and impertinence.

braggadism: see braggartism.

†**bragga'docian**, *a.* and *sb.* *Obs.* Also **bragadocian, -chian, braggadoccion, -kean, -tian.** [f. braggadoci-o + -an.]

A. *adj.* Of the nature of a braggadocio, given to vaunting. **B.** *sb.* = braggadocio. Hence **bragga'docianism.**

1599 *Broughton's Lett.* ii. 10 Thrasonicall Braggadoccion self-boasting. **1631** R. H. *Arraignm. Whole Creature* xi. §1. 99 [They] magnifie their skill with braggodokean and bumbasted words. **1654** Trapp *Comm. Job* xxxii. 5 To censure Elihu, for a palpable Bragadochian. **1716** M. Davies *Athen. Brit.* III. *Dissert. Pall. Angl.* 20 While the Romanists were venting their bragadocian Lyes. **1624** Bp. Mountagu *Gagg* Pref. 18 Take not this for an enlargement or braggadocianisme.

†**bragga'docie**, *v.* *Obs. rare*$^{-1}$. [f. next.] To pride or vaunt (oneself); = brag *v.* 2.

a **1688** G. Villiers (Dk. Buckhm.) *Restoration* Epil., One Who bragadocied still himself upon Being infallible.

braggadocio (brægə'dəʊʃɪəʊ), *sb.* (and *a.*) Also 6–8 **braggadoche**, 7–8 **bragodocia**, **brahgadochio**, **bragado-**, **braggadoccio**, **-chio**, **-sier.** [A name formed from brag after the analogy of Italian augmentatives in *-occhio*, *-occio*, given by Spenser to his personification of Brag, Vainglory.

(Formerly also pronounced (-kɪəʊ), which was perhaps Spenser's usage.)

1590 Spenser *F.Q.* ii. iii. Argt., Vaine Braggadocchio, getting Guyons horse, is made the scorne of knighthood trew.]

1. An empty, idle boaster; a swaggerer.

1594 Nashe *Unfort. Trav.* 15 These..goose-quill Braggadoches were mere cowards and crauens. **1618** Raleigh *Rem.* (1644) 233 Whatsoever the Bragadochio, the Spanish Ambassadour saith. **1714** *Wentworth Papers* (ed. Cartwright) 430 They did Web wrong that said he was a braggadosier. **1759** H. Walpole *Corr.* 343 (ed. 3) III. 321

You are spies, if you are not bragadochios. **1832** CARLYLE in *Fraser's Mag.* V. 382 He..had much of the sycophant, alternating with the braggadocio.

2. The talk of such a person, empty vaunting.
a **1734** NORTH *Exam.* Pref. 14 Without a Braggadocio this may be styled a New Work. **1822** SOUTHEY *Lett.* (1856) III. 358, I found..that this was half blunder, half braggadocio. **1878** H. SMART *Play or Pay* i. 8 Though his assertions might appear all braggadocio, it was not so.

B. *attrib.* or *adj.*; and in *comb.* as **braggadocio-like** *adv.*
1600 J. LANE *Tom Tel-troth* 126 And makes them brave it braggadochio-like. *a* **1613** OVERBURY *A Wife, etc.* (1638) 92 A Braggadochio Welshman. **1829** CARLYLE in *For. Rev. & Cont. Misc.* III. 123 [He] evidently writes with great gusto, in a lively braggadocio manner. **1862** AINSWORTH *Tower Lond.* (1864) 279 Xit kept up his braggadocio air and gait.

braggar, obs. variant of BRAGGER.

braggart ('brægət), *sb.* and *a.* Also 6 bragart, 7 bragard, (braggate), 7-9 braggard. [a. 16th c. F. *bragard*, f. *bragué-r* to brag; see -ARD.]
A. *sb.* A vain bragger, one who brags much.
a **1577** GASCOIGNE *Wks.* (1587) 74 In braggarts bote which set it selfe on sands. **1592** SHAKS. *Rom. & Jul.* III. i. 105 A Braggart, a Rogue..that fights by the booke of Arithmeticke. **1612** T. JAMES *Jesuits' Downef.* 4 As if they were..bragging braggates of Toledo. **1641** J. JACKSON *True Evang. T.* ii. 128 Marshall Biron will dye like a mad man, and Parry like a braggard. **1812** COLERIDGE, *Braggard.* **1856** THACKERAY *Christmas Bks.* (1872) 86 The real master of the school is Prince.. pitiless with fools and braggarts.
B. *adj.* and *attrib.* Bragging, vainly boastful.
1613 R. C. *Table Alph.* (ed. 3), *Bragard*, fine, trime, proude. **1735** POPE *Donne Sat.* IV. 201 Truth! shall I quit thee For puffing, braggart, puft nobility? **1846** ARNOLD *Hist. Rome* III. xlvi. 347 If in his lifetime he indulged in.. braggart language. **1882** FARRAR *Early Chr.* II. 66 Braggart self-confidence.
Hence, **braggart-like** *adv.* and **braggartly** *a.*
a **1845** HOOD *Last Man* xxiv, To see him lording so braggart-like. **1611** CHAPMAN *Iliad* III. Comm. (1857) 79 Whoever saw true learning..vouchsafe mansion in any.. braggartly spirit.

braggartism ('brægətɪz(ə)m). Also 6 bragadisme, 6-7 bragardisme, 7 braggadesme, bragarisme. [f. BRAGGART (but cf. BRAGGER) + -ISM.] The characteristic practice of a braggart; bragging. So also † **braggarist** = BRAGGART.
1591 SHAKS. *Two Gent.* II. iv. 164 What Bragadisme is this? **1601** CORNWALLYES *Ess.* II. xxix. (1631) 30 Ostentation, and bragarisme. **1618** *Barnevelt's Apol.* C iij, Now this..vaine-glorious fellow..enters afresh into his bragarisme. *c* **1626** *True Relat.* in Arb. *Garner* I. 609 Which they in their braggadesme enforced so far. **1848** THACKERAY *Bk. Snobs* 76 The British Snob, for..braggartism in his way, is without a parallel.

'braggartry. [f. BRAGGART + -RY.] = prec.
1598 FLORIO *Dict.* To Rdr. A viij b, Whose thrift is usurie ..whose valour bragardrie. **1877** tr. *Lange's Materialism* II. 67 To turn their fearlessness into..braggartry.

bragged (brægd), *ppl. a.*[1] [f. BRAG *v.*]
a. Boasted of, vaunted. †**b.** Boastful, vaunting.
1580 SIDNEY *Arcadia* III. 319 Lycurgus more bragged and neere his brothers humour. **1599** *Broughton's Lett.* viii. 28 Your much bragd-of Concent. **1607** SHAKS. *Cor.* I. viii. 12 That was the whip of your bragg'd Progeny.

† **bragged**, *ppl. a.*[2] *Obs.* [In first quot. prob. misprint for *bagged*; thence copied into the later.] With young, in pup.
1575 TURBERV. *Venery* 188 You shall hardly take a bytch-foxe when she is bragged and with cubbe. **1677** *Gentleman's Recreat.* I. 106. **1741** *Compl. Fam.-Piece* II. i. 294 When a Bitch Fox is bragged, and with Cub, she is hardly to be taken.

bragger ('brægə(r)). Also 4-7 **-ar.** [f. BRAG *v.* + -ER[1].] **1.** One who brags; a boaster or blusterer.
1362 LANGL. *P. Pl.* A. VII. 142 To Pers þe plouh Mon [one] profrede his gloue, A Brutiner, A Braggere. *c* **1530** H. RHODES *Bk. Nurture* in *Babees Bk.* (1868) 103 Be..no busy bragger of the vertues with the which thou art indued. **1663** KILLIGREW *Parson's Wed.* I. i. in *Dodsley* (1780) XI. 377 Nothing shall privilege your bragger's tongue to abuse me. **1830** GALT *Lawrie T.* I. vi. (1849) 19 The figure of the bragger set all present into a roar of laughter.
2. *Card-playing.* In the game of brag, a nine or knave (see also BULLET *sb.*[1] 6). *U.S.*
1807 [see BULLET *sb.*[1] 6]. **1938** H. ASBURY *Sucker's Prog.* 21 In American Brag there were eight 'braggers'—the jacks and nines of each suit.

braggery ('brægərɪ). Also 6 bragerie, 7 braggry. [f. prec. + -Y; or a. F. *braguerie.*]
1. Bragging; vaunting speech.
c **1571** tr. *Buchanan's Detect. Mary* in Campbell's *Love-lett. Mary* (1824) 142, I could rehearse his glorious vain braggeries in France. **1576** NEWTON *Lemnie's Complex.* (1633) 197 It is a meere vanity and foolish braggry. **1830** MRS. BRAY *Fitz of F.* xxi. (1884) 172 Falsehood, braggery.. a cruel heart, are fiends that walk in flesh and bones.
†**2.** Rabble. *Obs. rare.*
1548 HALL *Chron.* (1809) 610 All the nobles of the Frenche courte were in garments of many colours, so that thei were not knowen from the braggery. **1577** HOLINSHED *Chron.* III. 861/1 Vagabonds, plowmen, labourers, and of the bragerie, wagoners and beggers.

bragget ('brægɛt). Forms: 4-7 bragg-, bragat, -et(t, 4-9 bragg-, bragot(te, 4-7 braket, 6 brogat, 8-9 bracket, 6- bragget; 9 (*Sc.*) bragwort, bregwort. [a. Welsh *bragawd*, earlier *bracaut* = Ir. *bracát*:—OCeltic **brăcāta*, f. the OCeltic word given by Pliny and Columella, in the acc. *bracem*, as the Gaulish name of a kind of grain, whence Welsh *brag*, OIr. *brac*, mod.Ir. *braich* malt. The forms *brackwoort*, *bragwort*, *bregwort* indicate an association with WORT[2]; a late Sc. form is *bragwud*; see also BRAGOES.]
A drink made of honey and ale fermented together; latterly the honey has been replaced by sugar and spice. Also *attrib.* in *Braggot Sunday*. See also BRACKWOORT.
c **1386** CHAUCER *Milleres T.* 75 Hir mouth was sweete as bragot [*v.r.* braket] or the Meeth. *c* **1420** *Pallad. on Husb.* III. 812 In bragot then or wyne or meeth hem kepe. **1586** COGAN *Haven Health* ccxxxviii. (1636) 267 To make Bragget. Take three or foure galons of good Ale or more. *c* **1618** FLETCHER *Woman's Prize* III. ii, Out upon her, How she turned down the Bragget! **1727** BRADLEY *Fam. Dict.*, *Bragget*, a Drink made with Honey and Spice. **1802** SIBBALD *Chron. Scot. Poetry* Gloss. (JAM.) *Bragwort*, mead, a beverage made from the dregs of honey. **1821** *Blackw. Mag.* Jan. 405 (JAM.) The Scottish bregwort, or mead, so plentiful at a harvest supper. **1841** GRESLEY *For. Arden* 107 Bracket, a preparation of ale with honey. **1872** HARDWICK *Trad. Lanc.* 78 Mid Lent Sunday is likewise called Braggat or Braggot Sunday, from the custom of drinking 'mulled' or spiced ale on that day.

bragget, obs. form of BRACKET *sb.*

bragging ('brægɪŋ), *vbl. sb.* [f. BRAG *v.* + -ING[1].] The action of BRAG *v.*
1399 *Pol. Poems* (1859) I. 401 Ffor braggynge and ffor bostynge. **1549** OLDE *Erasm. Par., 1 Thess.* ii. 1 We came not unto you, with bragging and staring. **1604** *Meet. Gallants at Ordin.* 24 Such a bragging and a cracking. **1866** LIVINGSTONE *Jrnl.* (1873) I. v. 128 An ebullition of beer bragging.

bragging ('brægɪŋ), *ppl. a.* [f. BRAG *v.* + -ING[2].] That brags; boastful, swaggering, etc.
1530 PALSGR. 306/2 Braggyng, *brague.* **1649** ROBERTS *Clavis Bibl.* 140 That proud bragging Gyant Goliath. **1700** DRYDEN *Cock & F.* 134 No bragging coxcomb, yet no baffled knight. *c* **1815** JANE AUSTEN *Northang. Abb.* (1833) II. xv. 207 They were..a forward, bragging, scheming race.

braggingly ('brægɪŋlɪ), *adv.* [f. prec. + -LY[2].] In a bragging manner; boastfully, ostentatiously.
1540 COVERDALE *Fruitf. Less.* v. Wks. I. 398 Not lordly and braggingly. **1656** TRAPP *Comm. Luke* xviii. 12 He braggingly made a gift of that which he was bound to pay.

braggite ('brægaɪt). *Min.* [f. BRAGG + -ITE[1].] (See quots.)
1932 BANNISTER in *Min. Mag.* XXIII. 188 This being the first new mineral to be isolated and determined by X-ray methods, it may very appropriately be named braggite in honour of Sir William H. Bragg and his son Prof. W. L. Bragg, the pioneers of the new method for the investigation of crystals. **1940** C. M. RICE *Dict. Geol. Terms* 52/1 *Braggite*, sulphide of platinum, palladium, and nickel, (Pt, Pd, Ni) S, tetragonal, as minute grains in the concentrates of the Bushveld norite, Transvaal.

braggle, -ing, rare var. of BROGGLE, -ING.

bragite ('brægaɪt). *Min.* [ad. Norw. *bragit* (D. Forbes and T. Dahll 1854, in *Nyt Mag. Naturvidenskab.* VIII. 227), f. *Bragi*, a Scandinavian deity: see -ITE[1].] A variety of fergusonite found in Norway and Sweden.
1868 DANA *Syst. Min.* (ed. 5) 276, 525. **1896** CHESTER *Dict. Min.* 38 *Bragite*, a mineral occurring in brown, tetragonal crystals, not fully examined, but referred both to zircon and fergusonite.

bragless ('bræglɪs), *a.* [f. BRAG *sb.*[1] + -LESS.] Without brag or vain boast.
1606 SHAKS. *Tr. & Cr.* v. ix. 5 Yet braglesse let it be.

† **bragly** ('bræglɪ), *adv. Obs.* [f. BRAG *a.* + -LY[2].] Ostentatiously, briskly, nimbly.
1579 SPENSER *Sheph. Cal.* Mar. Seest not thilke same hawthorne studde, How bragly it begins to budde? *a* **1717** PARNELL *Poet. Wks.* (1833) 20 The faeries bragly foot the floor.

bragman, obs. var. of BRAHMIN.

bragodocia, obs. form of BRAGGADOCIO.

† **'bragoes.** *Obs. rare.* Corruption of BRAGGET.
1605 MARSTON *Dutch Court.* v. i, Good ale, perrys, bragoes, syder..was the true auncient British and Troyan drinks.

bra-goose, ? erroneous f. BRANT-GOOSE.
1749 T. SHORT in Thompson *Ann. Influenza* 26.

bragout, ? = *brag-out*: see BRAG *v.*
1592 GREENE *Def. Conny-catch.* Wks. (Gros.) XI. 80 He pronounst his wordes like a bragout, and helde up his head like a Malt-horse. *Ibid.* 74 All these Nouelties doth this pipned Bragout boast on.

braguette (brə'gɛt). Also brayette. [OFr.] A piece of armour of the fifteenth century corresponding to the cod-piece.
1867 W. MCDOWALL *Hist. Dumfries* xxvii. 349 His bulky dagger-proof coat of green velvet and scarlet braguette. **1895** *Oracle Encycl.* I. 180/1 Brayette and loin-guard.

bragwort, -wud, Sc. var. of BRAGGET.

Brahm, Brahma (brɑːm, 'brɑːmə). Also Brahme. [ad. Skr. *Brahmā*, masc., *Brahma*, neut., nom. of *Brahman.*] **a.** The supreme God of post-Vedic Hindu mythology. **b.** In the later pantheistic systems, the Divine reality, of which the entire universe of matter and mind is only a manifestation. Hence **'Brahmahood**, the state of Brahma; absorption into the divine essence.
1785 WILKINS tr. *Bhagvat* viii. 55 Brahm is that which is supreme and without corruption. **1827** COLEBROOKE *Misc. Ess.* (1837) I. 339 While a man sleeps without dreaming, his soul is with Brahme. **1840** H. H. WILSON *Vishnu Purána* 284 Sages who are the sons of Brahmá, or Brahmans. **1862** F. HALL *Refut. Hindu Philos. Syst.* 194 When the soul.. becomes convinced, that..itself is Brahma..it escapes from further vicissitude, and realizes Brahmahood.

Brahma, shortened f. BRAHMAPOOTRA.

‖ **brahmacharya** (ˌbrɑːmə'tʃɑːrɪə). [ad. Skr. *brahmacárya*, f. *brahman* prayer, worship + *carya* conduct.] Purity of life, esp. regarding sexual matters; celibacy; sexual self-restraint; freq. used with reference to the life and teachings of M. K. Gandhi. Hence ˌ**brahma'chari**, one who practises brahmacharya.
1920 M. K. GANDHI *Self-Restraint v. Self-Indulgence* (1947) I. ix. 70 The word in Sanskrit corresponding to celibacy is *Brahmacharya*, and the latter means much more than celibacy. *Brahmacharya* means perfect control over all the senses and organs. For the perfect *Brahmachari* nothing is impossible. **1925** *Ibid.* ii. 39 There can be no two opinions about the necessity of birth control. But the only method handed down from ages past is self-control or *brahmacharya.* **1958** J. V. BONDURANT *Conquest of Violence* i. 12 The opinion that a satyagrahi must be a vegetarian, must observe *brahmacharya* (continence), must develop *aparigraha* (non-possession) and must manifest other ideal Gandhian attributes. **1962** A. HUXLEY *Island* v. 56 He had been brought up to reverence the Ideal of Purity. '*Brahmacharya*, if you know what that means.' **1969** R. SHANKAR *My Music* ii. 58 He strongly insists that the students follow *brahmacharya*—for the disciple, a traditional Hindu way of life that includes only the absolute essentials of material needs.

Brahman, etc.; see BRAHMIN, etc.

Brahmapootra (brɑːmə'puːtrə). [Attrib. use of the name of the river.] A variety of domestic fowl, said to have been first brought from Lakhimpur, on the River Brahmaputra, in 1846; now usually abbreviated as *Brahma.*
1851 in Wright *Bk. Poultry* (1885) 245 The only question is whether they are Grey Shanghaes or Brahmapootras. **1885** WRIGHT *Bk. Poultry* 268 The most common error..is that of confounding the Brahma type with the Cochin.

Brahmi ('brɑːmiː). [Skr.] The name of one of the oldest alphabets of India, probably of Semitic origin.
1895 G. BUHLER *Orig. Indian Brāhma Alphabet* 33 The Brāhmī lipi is the real old Indian alphabet, which was popularly used in the third century B.C. all over India. **1902** *Encycl. Brit.* XXXIII. 901/2 The alphabets of India all spring from two sources: (*a*) the Kharoṣṭhī, (*b*) the Brāhmī alphabet. **1920** *Blackw. Mag.* May 621/2 A long inscription in Brahmi characters of about 150 B.C. **1963** A. H. DANI *Indian Palaeogr.* iii. 28 This similarity hardly leaves any doubt that Indian Brāhmī was created on the basis of the North Semitic letters.

Brahmic ('brɑːmɪk), *a.* [f. Skr. *brahma*, combining form of *brahman* (see BRAHM) + -IC.] Pertaining to the Indian society known as the Brahmo Somāj, or to the older one called Brahma Sabhā.
1852 *Calcutta Rev.* XVII. xvii, The foundation of the Brahmic creed is identical with that of the Deistic. **1869** *Echo* 9 Oct., Accepting what is now called the Brahmic covenant.

Brahmin, Brahman ('brɑːmɪn, -mən). Forms: 5-7 **bragman**, 6 **bramane**, 7-9 **brachman(e, -min**, 7 **brackman, braman, -men, -mine, -miny**, 8-9 **bramin**, 8- **brahmin**, 9 **brahman.** [ad. Skr. *brāhmana*, f. *brahman* praise, worship; some of the older Eng. forms were derived from or influenced by the Greek spelling βραχμᾶνες (pl.), L. *brachmāni*, *-es*, and med.L. corruptions; the form *Brahmin*, a corruption of the Indian vernacular pronunciation, is still all but universal in popular use; during the present century Orientalists have adopted the more correct *Brahman*, which (often written *Brâhman* or *Bráhman*) is employed by most writers on India.]
a. A member of the highest or priestly caste among the Hindus.
1481 CAXTON *Myrr.* II. v. 70 Other peple whiche ben callyd..bragman whiche ben fayrer than they to fore named. **1553** EDEN *Treat. New Ind.* (Arb.) 17 Their Priestes (called *Bramini*). **1599** HAKLUYT *Voy.* II. I. 252 The Bramanes which are their priests. **1634** SIR T. HERBERT *Trav.* 50 An ancient Braminy, a devout Wretch. **1650** BULWER *Anthropomet.* iii. 66 The Bramines of Agra mark themselves in the Forehead. **1656** BLOUNT *Glossogr.*, *Brackmans*, a sect of Philosophers in India. **1676** DRYDEN

Aurengz. III. i, Take the preaching Brachman hence. **1684** BURNET *Th. Earth* III. iii. 17 The modern Indian philosophers, the reliques of the old bragmans. **1711** POPE *Temple F.* 100 And Brachmans, deep in desert woods rever'd. **1753** HANWAY *Trav.* (1762) II. xv. i. 406 *note*, He was fond of the brachmins or indian priests. **1835–41** THIRLWALL *Greece* liv. (L.) A whole community of Brahmins may have preserved the purity of their blood. **1842** PRICHARD *Nat. Hist. Man* 163 Aryavarta was the Holy Land of the Brahmans.

b. *fig.* spec. A member of the upper class of Boston, Mass., U.S.A.

1823 BYRON *Juan* XIII. lxxxiii, Thirty-three Of highest caste—the Brahmins of the ton. **1859** O. W. HOLMES *Elsie V.* i. Title, The Brahmin caste of New England. **1881** *Homes & Haunts of our Elder Poets* 155 To be a missionary of Boston culture.. must have pleased the anxious thought of this medical Brahmin. **1931** J. T. ADAMS *Epic of Amer.* viii. 219 The West.. was dominating the American outlook, in spite of the smug Boston Brahmins. **1963** M. MCCARTHY *Group* ii. 45 Their exact social position in Boston, which Kay greatly over estimated—they were not 'Brahmins', horrid word, at all.

c. *attrib.*, as in ***Brahman-slayer***; also **Brahmin beads**, the corrugated seeds of *Elæocarpus*, used by the Brahmins and others as necklaces; **Brahmin ox** (cf. BRAHMINEE *a.*), a humped variety of the ox; †**Brahmin-pope**, a chief Brahmin (*obs.*).

1613 PURCHAS *Pilgr., Descr. India*, All men, and the King himselfe, adore the Bramen-Pope. **1847** CARPENTER *Zool.* §269 The Zebu or Brahmin Ox. **1856** *Farmer's Mag.* Jan. 10 There were also some other crosses.. between the Brahmin and our own native races. **1858** MUIR *Sanskr. Texts* I. 161 The city had been robbed of its glory by those Brahman-slayers.

Hence **Brahmanhood** (ˈbrɑːmənhʊd), the rank or position of a Brahmin.

1840 H. H. WILSON *Vishnu Purána* 405 Who.. obtained Brahmanhood through devotion. **1866** *Reader* 17 Mar. 269 The issue of such marriage being admissible to the Bráhmanhood in the seventh generation.

Brahminee (brɑːmɪˈniː), *sb.* Also **Brahmini**. [a. Skr. *brāhmaṇī*, fem. of *brāhmana* BRAHMIN.] A female Brahmin.

1794 SIR W. JONES *Inst. of Menu* x. 66 Begotten by a S'údra on a Bráhmeni. **1858** BEVERIDGE *Hist. India* II. IV. i. 13 A Brahmini or female Brahmin. **18..** SIR A. C. LYALL *Song*, in *N. & Q.* 26 Feb. (1887) 87 My mother was a Brahmanee.

Brahminee (ˈbrɑːmɪniː), *a.* Also **Brachmany, Brahmany, Brahminy, Braminy**. [f. BRAHMIN, prob. after anal. of native Indian derivatives like *Bengalee* (*Bengālī*), etc.] Pertaining to the Brahmin caste; appropriated to the Brahmins. ***Brahminee bull*** = Brahmin ox; ***Brahminee duck***, the *Casarca rutila*; ***Brahminee fig-tree***, the 'Banyan' (*Ficus Indica*); ***Brahminee kite***, the *Haliastur Indicus* (Balfour *Cycl. India* I. 437, where the spelling is *Brahmany*).

1811 MRS. SHERWOOD *Henry & Bearer* 30 Under the shade of a Braminee fig-tree. *c* **1813** —— *Stories Ch. Catech.* xx. 73 No answer.. was made.. excepting by the pigeons and brahminee kites. **1830** MARRYAT *King's Own* xlii, He.. took away a Brachmany.. girl. **1884** *Macm. Mag.* No. 292. 303 Everywhere we see the inevitable Brahminy kite. **1885** LADY BRASSEY *The Trades* 99 The cattle.. feeding peacefully beside Brahminee bulls.

Brahminic, -manic (braˈmɪnɪk, -ˈmænɪk), *a.* [f. BRAHMIN + -IC.] Pertaining to the Brahmins.

1862 MAX MÜLLER *Chips* (1867) I. 225 The earlier systems of Brahmanic philosophy. **1865** MURDOCH *Mosheim's Eccl. Hist.* 716 *note*, The corruption of the Brahminic religion.

Brahˈminical, -ˈmanical, *a.* Also 9 Brahmenical, Braminical. [f. as prec. + -ICAL.] = prec.

1809 WILFORD *Sacr. Isles* in *Asiat. Res.* IX. 71 Many Bráhmenical families. **1870** MAX MÜLLER in *Fraser's Mag.* Apr. 448 The Brahmanical body of religious doctrines. **1883** SEELEY *Expans. Eng.* 268 The brahminical period comes to an end.

Brahˈminicide, -ˈmanicide. [f. BRAHMIN + -CIDE.] **a.** One who has killed a Brahmin. **b.** The act of killing a Brahmin.

1811 W. WARD *Hist. Hindoos* (1817) 96 If the husband be a bramhŭnicide. **1836** B. HODGSON in *Asiat. Res.* XX. 127 That enumeration is as follows: 1.. brahmanicide. **1872** MONIER WILLIAMS *Skr. Dict.* 692 *Brahmahatyā*.. Brahmanicide.

Brahminism, -manism (ˈbrɑːmɪnɪz(ə)m, -mənɪz(ə)m). [f. BRAHMIN + -ISM.] The principles and practice of the Brahmins.

1816 G. S. FABER *Orig. Pagan Idol.* I. 86, I shall in future use the terms Buddhism and Brahmenism. **1846** MAURICE *Relig. World* I. ii. (1861) 54 Hindoo patriots.. have dreamed of bringing back the first state of Brahminism. **1877** tr. *Tiele's Hist. Relig.* 118 The Vedic religion gives birth to Brâhmanism.

Hence **Brahminist, -manist; Brahministic** *a.*; **Brahminize** *v.*

1816 G. S. FABER *Orig. Pagan Idol.* I. 124 The doctrine of a succession of worlds is held no less decidedly by the Buddhists than by the Brahmenists. **1862** R. PATTERSON *Ess. Hist. & Art* 427 The Brahminised Tamul race in the south. **1883** MONIER WILLIAMS *Relig. Thought in Ind.* ii. 42 They proceeded to Brahmanize the popular songs of the people. **1886** *N.Y. Forum* Mar. 42 Sometimes this Brahministic baptism was performed by the bank of a sacred river.

Brahmism (ˈbrɑːmɪz(ə)m). Also **Bramism**. [f. BRAHM + -ISM.]

†**a.** The religion of Brahma. *Obs.* **b.** The tenets of the Indian society called Brahma Sabhā, or of the more recently founded Brahmo Somaj. Cf. BRAHMOISM.

1813 *Month. Rev.* LXXI. 478 The Bramism of the Hindoos. **1852** J. MULLENS (*title*) Vedantism, Bráhmism, and Christianity examined and compared.

Brahmoism (ˈbrɑːməʊɪz(ə)m). [f. Bengali *Brāhmo* in *Brāhmo* (or *Brāhma*) *Samāj* society worshipping the supreme spirit (BRAHMA) + -ISM.] A reformed Hinduism of a theistic character founded by Ram Mohun Roy in 1830. So **ˈBrahmo, ˈBrahmoist**, a follower of Brahmoism; also *attrib.*

1857 DASS *Supreme Being of Brahmo Theol.* 7 There is an impassable gulf which separates unitarian Christianity from Brahmoism. **1862** C. H. MANUEL *Destiny of Human Life* 17 Brahmoism—pure Theism—is essentially anti-idolatrous. **1870** *Contemp. Rev.* XIII. 232 Which has raised Brahmoism from a small Hindoo sect into a comprehensive religion. *Ibid.* 239 A congregation of Brahmos. *Ibid.* XV. 131 The Brahmoists of both sections may already be numbered by thousands. **1885** BALFOUR *Cycl. India* I. 438 Brahmoism has carried on a crusade against the institution and usages of caste. **1927** P. C. RAY *Life of C. R. Das* iii. 25 He married according to Brahmo rites (Act 3 of 1873) Basanti Devi.

Brahmsian (ˈbrɑːmzɪən), *a.* and *sb.* [f. *Brahms* (see def.) + -IAN.] **A.** *adj.* Of, relating to, or characteristic of the German composer Johannes Brahms (1833–97) or his music. **B.** *sb.* A follower or admirer of Brahms. So **ˈBrahmsite** *a.* and *sb.*

1894 G. B. SHAW *Music in London 1890–94* (1956) III. 145 A German Brahmsite critic proclaims them the latest products of the great school in chamber music. *Ibid.* 146 It was at one of these recent Brahmsian Populars that Mr Oswald sang some vocal pieces. **1929** C. A. PHILLIPS tr. *Niemann's Brahms* xxviii. 355 A few typically Brahmsian technical formulas. **1947** C. GRAY *Contingencies* ii. 59 An exclusive and esoteric cult such as that of the Brahmsians. **1949** *Penguin Mus. Mag.* July 85 The early 'renaissancers' were Brahmsites. **1963** *Listener* 7 Feb. 264/3 It used dated features like Brahmsian minor-key themes.

Brahui (brəˈhuːɪ), *sb.* and *a.* Also 9 **Braho(o)e**. **A.** *sb.* A pastoral people of Baluchistan; a member of this people; their language. **B.** *adj.* Of or pertaining to the Brahui or their language.

1816 H. POTTINGER *Trav. Beloochistan* iv. 54 The Belooches.. are divided into two great classes, severally known by the appellations of Belooche and Brahoöe. *Ibid.*, The Brahoöekee is.. so dissimilar [from Persian] in its sound and formation, that I never recollect to have remarked in it a single expression in any way approaching the idiom of Persian. **1826** J. C. PRICHARD *Physical Hist. Mankind* (ed. 2) II. v. iii. 11 These nations are the Belooches.. and the Brahoöes. *Ibid.* 12 The Brahoöes are divided into a great number of petty tribes. **1844** *Ibid.* (ed. 3) IV. x. 63 We must mention the Brahúi, who are divided into a number of different tribes. **1848, 1875** [see BALUCH]. **1873** H. W. BELLEW (*title*) From the Indus to the Tigris... Together with a synoptical grammar and vocabulary of the Brahoe language. **1924** *Blackw. Mag.* Jan. 113/2 Luckily we were dealing with Brahuis not Mahsuds. **1932** W. L. GRAFF *Language* 414 The Brahui dialect, isolated in Baluchistan. **1943** S. K. CHATTERJI *Lang. & Linguistic Problem* 8 Brahui (207,000) in Baluchistan, a remnant of the great Dravidian bloc of western India. **1953** W. J. ENTWISTLE *Aspects of Lang.* xi. 347 The Dravidian languages of the Deccan have left behind them a solitary outpost in the Brahui of Baluchistan.

brai, variant of BRAE, BRAYE.

braid (breɪd), *sb.* Forms: 1 **brægd-, bræ̆d-, bréd-**, (1–2 **ȝebreȝd, ȝebræȝd**), 3–6 **breid(e**, 4–5 **breyd(e**, 4–6 **brayd(e, braide**, 5–6 **brade**, 6 (**bray**), 6–7 **breade**, 7 (**bredd**), 4– **braid**. [Partly:—OE. *bræȝd-* = ON. *bragð* neut.:—OTeut. *bragdo-m*, f. str. vb. **bregdan, bragd* (see BRAID *v.*[1]), and partly aphet. form of OE. *ȝebreȝd*, f. *breȝdan* to BRAID. All the senses are closely paralleled by those of ON. *bragð*, which may possibly to some extent have influenced the Eng. word. The archaic BREDE *sb.*[3] used in modern poetry (in sense 4) began as a mere orthographical variant of *braid* (*breade*).]

I. Sudden movement.

†**1.** A sudden or brisk movement; a start, jerk; a twist, wrench, strain. *Obs.* [cf. BRAID *v.*[1] I.]

[*a* **1000** *Phœnix* 57 (Gr.) Nis þær.. ne winterȝeweorp ne wedra ȝebreȝd.] **1297** R. GLOUC. 22 Þer was mony a strong breid, so þat ribbes þre þe geant brek of Corineus. *a* **1300** *Cursor M.* 7169 Sampson.. gaue a braid [*v.r.* breid] sa fers and fast, þat all þe bandes of him brast. *c* **1385** CHAUCER *L.G.W.* 1166 Sche waylith and sche makith manye a breyde. *c* **1430** *How Good wife taught Dau.* in *Babees Bk.* (1868) 41 Go þi silf þerto & worche an houswijfes brayde. *c* **1485** *Digby Myst.* III. (1882) 1148 Loke, boy, þou do it with a brayd! **1626** in *Hum., Wit & Sat. 17th C.* (1883) 384 The woman.. gave a braid with her head.

†**b.** A sudden assault or onset, an attack. *Obs.*

1340 HAMPOLE *Pr. Consc.* 1925 Ilk man.. Aght to drede þe bitter dedes brayde. *c* **1430** *Syr Gener.* 3805 Of that braide Abel was war, That the baner of Perse bare. **1565** GOLDING *Ovid's Met.* XIII. (1593) 301 To have Ulisses ever as companion at the braid. **1609** HOLLAND *Amm. Marcel.* XVIII. ii. 106 Whither in that doubtfull braid they were driven.

c. An aim to strike, the launching of a blow; sometimes a blow.

Still in this sense in mod.Scotch.

? *c* **1450** *Kyng & Hermit* 364 in Hazl. *E.P.P.* (1864) 26 The frere.. gafe the coppe sych a breyd, That well nyh of iȝede. **1513** DOUGLAS *Æneis* XIII. Prol. 147 Syne to me wyth his club he maid ane braid.

†**d.** *fig.* An outburst of passion, envy, or anger; a freak, a whim. *Obs.*

a **1450** *Knt. de la Tour* (1868) 54 Thei.. fytithe ayenst.. the braydes of the fyre of lecherye. *c* **1500** *New Notbroune Mayd* 435 in Hazl. *E.P.P.* III. 18 His irous brayde Wyll not be layed. **1532** MORE *Confut. Tindale* Wks. 442/2 He bringeth.. onely a rashe malicioue frantike braide. **1540** HYRDE *Vives' Instr. Chr. Wom.* (1592) U iv, You women.. weene to gouverne.. nations with the braids of your stomackes.

†**2.** *transf.* [Cf. ON. *auga-bragð* 'twinkling of an eye', moment.] A moment, short space of time. In the phrases ***at, in a braid*** the meaning varies between 1 and 2. *Obs.*

a **1300** *Cursor M.* 16722 Þe toþer theif him gaf ansuer, and blamed him a-braid. *c* **1325** *E.E. Allit. P.* B. 539 Vche best at a brayde [hyȝez] þer hym best lykez. *a* **1400** *Cov. Myst.* (1841) 231 He wylle byn here within a brayde. *c* **1430** *Syr Tryam.* 78 'Owt upon the, thefe!' sche seyde in that brayde. **1592** *Chester Pl.* (1847) II. 155 Now goe we forthe all in a breade. **1657** TRAPP *Comm. Job* xlii. 16 For a short braid of adversity.

II. A trick, deception.

†**3.** An adroit turn; a trick or subtilty. (Cf. BRAID *v.*[1] II.; ON. *bregðask* to change unexpectedly, disappoint, deceive; OE. *bræȝd-boȝa* a deceitful bow; also F. *tour* a 'turn,' a trick). *Obs.*

[*c* **950** *Lindisf. Gosp.* Matt. xiii. 22 ȝebræȝdas ðæra wlenca underdelfes þæt word.] *a* **1000** Thorpe's *Laws* I. 160 (Bosw.) He hit dyde butan brede [*v.r.* bræde] and biȝswice. *c* **1250** *Bestiary* 672 in *O.E. Misc.* 21 Ðis elp he reisen on stalle; and tus atbrested ðis huntes breid. **1330** R. BRUNNE *Chron.* 164 Full stille away he went, þat was a theues braid. **1570** REDFORDE *Songs* (1848) 60 Beware, good maides, Of all such braydes.

III. Plait.

4. Anything plaited, interwoven, or entwined; *esp.* A plait of human hair. In 19th c. sometimes applied to the flat bands of hair, worn at one time by ladies over the side of the face, as in early portraits of Queen Victoria.

1530 PALSGR. 200/2 Braydes of a womans heer, *tresses*. **1564** GOLDING *Justine* 54 (R.) [Alexander] cutte the wrethes [of the Gordian knot] a sonder with a sworde, and.. found the ends of the knottes wythin the braides. **1740** SOMERVILLE *Hobbinol* iii. (1749) 163 Her plaited Hair behind her in a Brede Hung careless. **1834** M. SCOTT *Cruise Midge* (1859) 272 Her hair plaited in three distinct braids that hung down her back. **1864** *Soc. Sc. Rev.* The hair is done up in a braid at the back. **1865** TROLLOPE *Belton Est.* i. 11 Wearing on her brow thin braids of false hair.

b. Since the 17th c. the variant BREDE has been used poetically in the sense of 'plait', and modern writers also use *braid* in the transferred and vague senses, mentioned under BREDE *sb.*[3] 3.

[**1643** MILTON *Divorce* vi. Wks. (1851) 33 His silk'n breades untwine, and slip their knots. **1697** DRYDEN *Ess. Georg., Virg.* (1721) I. 201 A curious Brede of Needle-work.] **1708** I. PHILIPS *Cyder* (1807) 88 And puzzles the beholder's eye That views the wat'ry braid. *c* **1800** K. WHITE *Contempl.* 71 We'll watch, in eve's ethereal braid. *c* **1818** HEBER *To Hairbell*, Most I love thine [the hairbell's] azure braid. **1856** BRYANT *Ages* xxvi, All blended, like the rainbow's radiant braid.

5. A string or band with which the hair is confined or entwined.

1576 GASCOIGNE *Steele Gl.* Epil. 12 But curle their lockes with bodkins and with braids. **1634** MILTON *Comus* 863 In twisted braids of lilies knitting The loose train of thy amber-dropping hair. **1717** POPE *Sappho & P.* 85 Nor braids of gold the varied tresses bind. **1799** COLERIDGE *Dark Ladie*, My jet black hair in pearly braids. **1816** SCOTT *Jock o' Hazeld.* iii, A chain of gold ye sall not lack Nor braid to bind your hair. **1830** TENNYSON *Day-dream* 82 Jet-black hair.. streaming from a braid of pearl.

6. *mod.* A woven fabric of silken, woollen, cotton, gold or silver thread in the form of a band, used for trimming or binding articles of dress.

1706 PHILLIPS, *Braid*, a small Lace, a Chain, or Edging. **1868** *Ladies' Treasury* 9 Morning dress.. trimmed in pattern with black mohair braid. **1882** BECK *Draper's Dict.*, *Braid*.. not properly solely applicable to the fillet or binding which the name now represents.

b. A narrow flat band woven of linen thread, with an open-work border on each side, used to form the outline of the pattern in point-lace work. ***Honiton braids***: braids intended for use in making Honiton lace.

1874 *Cassell's Househ. Guide* I. 225 The materials required will be.. several yards of point lace braid. **1886** *Daily News* 17 May 3/6 Honiton braids are dull of sale.

7. *Comb.* as **braid-comb**, 'a back comb for a lady's hair.'

†**braid** (breɪd), *a.* (or *ppl. a.*) *Obs. rare*[−1]. [Of doubtful meaning and origin; perh. short for

braided in some sense; cf. OE. *bregden*, deceitful, also BRAIDIE *a.*] ? Deceitful.

1601 SHAKS. *All's Well* IV. ii. 73 Since Frenchmen are so braide, Marry that will, I liue and die a Maid.

braid (breɪd), *v.*[1] Pa. t. and pple. braided. Forms: 1 breȝdan, (bræȝdan), brédan, 3 breden, 3-4 breide(n, 4-5 breyde, 4-6 brayd(e, (5 brede, 5-7 brade, 8 *dial.* breead), 5- braid. *Pa. t.* 1 bræȝd, bræ̃d, *pl.* bruȝdon, brúdon, 3 bræid, breod, *pl.* brudden, 3-4 breid(e, 4 brede, 4-5 breyde, 4-6 braid(e, brayd(e, 5-6 brayed, brayded, 7 bred, bradde, 4- braided. *Pa. pple.* 1 broȝden, bróden, 3-5 broiden, 4 brayden, brawden, browden, 4-6 broyden, 5 brait, -ed, brayded, 7 breaded, 8- braided, *dial.* breed. [Com. Teut.: OE. *breȝdan* (pa. t. *bræȝd, bruȝdon*, pple. *broȝden*) = OS. *bregdan* (MDu. *breiden*, Du. *breien*), OHG. *brettan* (MHG. *bretten*), ON. *bregða*:—OTeut. **bregd-an* (extended from **breg-*), with root-meaning 'to pull quickly hither and thither, to move suddenly to and fro'. In OE. the *ȝ* of the root was often omitted, with lengthening of the vowel (*brédan, bræ̃d, brúdon, bróden*), but the diphthongal form (*breyde*, etc.) prevailed in ME. The pa. pple. had in 13-15th c. the form *broyden*, in 14-16th *browden*, sometimes in 14-15th c. *brawden*; the phonetic history of which presents some difficulties. By 1400 the original strong pa. t. was displaced by the weak *brayded*, which in the 15th c. had also extended to the pa. pple., though *browden* continued in Sc. at least till 1600. From the strong forms of the pa. pple. appear to have arisen the newer synonymous weak verbs BROID, BROWD, BRAWDE q.v.; see also BROIDER, *browder*, *brawder*.]

I. To make a sudden jerky movement (originally off or away to one side).

†**1.** *trans.* To make a sudden movement with (the hand, foot, etc.); to brandish (a spear); to deal (a blow). In OE. const. with instrumental case, afterwards treated as simple object. *Obs.*

a 1000 *Beowulf* 1033 þær ȝit . . mundum bruȝdon. *c* 1300 *K. Alis.* 7373 On a stede wel y-dyght: He ryt his spere braydyng. *c* 1325 *Coer de L.* 411 Another stroke he hym brayde. *c* 1450 HENRYSON *Mor. Fab.* 75 The Wolfe braid foorth his fute, the Man his hand. *c* 1505 DUNBAR in *Maitland Poems* 5 (JAM.) I wald na langer beir on brydil, bot braid up my heid.

†**2.** To draw (a sword, knife, etc.). (Const. orig. with instrumental case as in 1; cf. ON. *bregða sverði*; but in later OE. app. regarded as an application of sense 3.) *Obs.*

[*Beowulf* 3333 Ic þy wæpne ȝebræd.] *a* 1000 *Battle of Maldon* 163 Byrhtnoð bræd bill of scæðe. *c* 1205 LAY. 15260 Heo breoden ut þe sæxes. 1330 R. BRUNNE *Chron.* 229 þe envenomed knyfe out braid, & gaf Edward a wounde. *c* 1450 HENRYSON *Mor. Fab.* 30 Out of his breste ane bill can hee braid. *c* 1500 *Felon Sewe Rokeby* in Bell *Anc. Ballads* (1857) Hee brayded out hys brande.

†**3.** To jerk, snatch, wrench, fling, etc., with a sudden effort; freq. with *up, down, out*. *Obs.*

a 1000 *Battle of Maldon* 154 Se . . bræd of ðæm beorne blodiȝne gar. *c* 1200 *Trin. Col. Hom.* 217 Ich triste þat he . . wille of þis werȝes grune mine fet breiden. 1297 R. GLOUC. 22 A gret ok he wolde breide a doun, as it a smal ȝerde were. *c* 1384 CHAUCER *H. Fame* 1678 Oute hys trumpe of golde he brayde . . and set it to his mouth. 1388 WYCLIF *Ps.* xxiv. [xxv.] 15 He schal breide awey my feet fro the snare [1382 he shal pullen up]. *a* 1400 *Octouian* 461 And breyde away with hard roun The grypes wynge.

†**b.** *Naut. to braid up (the sails)*. *Obs.*

c 1400 *Destr. Troy* 1945 [He] braid vp a brode saile, hade brethe at his wille. 1627 CAPT. SMITH *Seaman's Gram.* ix. 40 Brade vp close all them sailes.

†**4.** To deliver with a brisk action. *Obs.*

c 1325 *E.E. Allit. P.* A. 711 Burnez her barnez vnto hym brayde. *c* 1340 *Gaw. & Gr. Knt.* 2377 He . . brayde broþely þe belt to þe burne seluen.

†**5.** *intr.* To start, usually out of sleep or a swoon; to awake; also to start or burst into motion; to rush, spring, or dart; *fig* to start ('out of one's wit'); also used *refl.* in same sense. *Obs.*

c 1205 LAY. 26454 Walwain bræid to sweorden. *a* 1300 *Havelok* 1282 Of his slep a-non he brayd. *c* 1380 *Sir Ferumb.* 299 For angre sche braid hure wel neȝ wod. *c* 1386 CHAUCER *Franklin's T.* 299 ffor verray wo out of his wit he breyde. *c* 1440 *Generydes* 165 Right sodenly he braydid and he wooke. *c* 1450 HENRYSON *Mor. Fab.* 20 They braded ouer the bent, As fire off flint. 1513 DOUGLAS *Æneis* I. ii. 51 Furth at the ilk port wyndis braid in a rowt. 1603 *Philotus* cxxix, Quhat is the mater . . Quhat garris yow braid?

†**b.** *trans.* To rouse, startle. *Obs. rare.*

c 1325 *E.E. Allit. P.* A. 1169 þat brathe out of my drem me brayde.

†**6.** *intr.* To break forth abruptly into speech; to burst into a cry. *Obs.*

c 1000 *Guthlac* 878 (Gr.) Wop ahofon, hleoðrum bruȝdon. *c* 1400 *Ywaine & Gaw.* 2072 The lyon . . brayded als he had bene wode. *a* 1547 EARL SURREY *Æneid* iv. 476 And foorth in rage at last thus gan she brayde.

†**b.** *trans.* To ejaculate, burst out with. *Obs.*

1562 LEIGH *Armorie* 166 His irefull hart straight braided out wrothful wordes.

II. To change suddenly or abruptly.

†**7.** *intr.* To make a change. Const. with instrumental case (cf. ON. *bregða búi, tiöldum*, to change one's abode, strike tents). Only in OE.

a 1000 *Cædmon's Exodus* 222 (Gr.) Brudon feldhusum [= they struck their tents].

†**8.** *intr.* To change in colour or appearance. In OE. with instrumental case (or *on* = into). *Obs.* Cf. BRAIDED b.

a 1000 *Salomon & Sat.* 150 (Gr.) Næfre hie ðæs syllice bleoum bregdað. *a* 1000 *Guthlac* 882 (Gr.) Bruȝdon eft awyrȝdo wærloȝan on wyrmes bleo. *c* 1430 LYDG. *Bochas* III. i. (1554) 69 b, With thy giftes who that hath to done Of chaunges braideth ofter than the Mone. —— *Min. Poems* 24 All worldly thing braidith upon tyme.

†**9.** *refl.* To assume an appearance, act a part.

c 1205 LAY. 6667 þe king hine bræid [*c* 1275 breid] sæc alse þeah hit seoð weore.

†**10.** intr. *to braid of*, formerly *after*, *on*: to take after, resemble, be like. Still *dial.* [Cf. ON. *bregðr einum til eins.*]

c 1205 LAY. 6895 Wel he braid [*c* 1275 dude] on deade efter his alderen. *c* 1430 LYDG. *Bochas* III. xxi. 93 b, Which froward monster . . Braydeth on Hidra. *c* 1505 DUNBAR *Discr. in Asking* 13 Sum schamis to ask, as braidis of me. 1691 RAY *N.C. Wds.*, *Breid of, Brade of*, to be like in conditions: 'Ye breid of the miller's dog; ye lick your mouth or the poke be ope'. 1864 ATKINSON *Whitby Gloss.* s.v., 'You breead o' me, you don't like noise'.

III. To pull a thread to and fro, intertwine. [A Common Teutonic sense.]

11. *trans.* To twist in and out, intertwine, interweave, plait; to embroider; to make (a garland, cord, fabric) by intertwining, twisting, or plaiting. (Now in ordinary Eng. only *poet.* or *dial.* except as applied to the hair, in which use it appears to be now interpreted as 'to arrange in braids'.)

c 1000 ÆLFRIC *Gram.* xxviii. §5. 176 *Plecto*, ic brede net. *a* 1225 *Ancr. R.* 236 For pine . . he breideð þe crune of blisse. *a* 1250 *Owl & Night.* 645 Mi nest . . is broiden al abute. *a* 1300 *Cursor M.* 1008 Wit blis and beild broiden best. 1393 GOWER *Conf.* III. 237 They taughten him a lace to braide. 1530 PALSGR. 471/1, I broyde heare, or a lace, or suche lyke. *Je tortille*, Brayde your heare up. 1686 GOAD *Celest. Bodies* III. iii. 475 They are Plaited and Breaded in the same Twine. 1753 HOGARTH *Anal. Beauty* v. 28 Part of the hair of their heads, braided together from behind. 1848 MRS. JAMESON *Sacr. & Leg. Art* (1850) 211 The rich golden hair partly braided. 1883 G. C. DAVIES *Norfolk Broads* xxxii. 249 They [the nets for eel-sets] are braided or made in the winter. 1884 *Harper's Mag.* July 303/1 She . . wove rag carpets . . braided rugs, etc.

b. *transf.* To 'thread the mazes' of the dance; to cross and recross.

1813 SCOTT *Trierm.* III. xxi, When the whirlwind's gusts are wheeling, Ours it is the dance to braid. 1875 B. TAYLOR *Faust* xxi. I. 181 Here winds away, and in a hundred divided veins the valley braids.

IV. [Mod. f. BRAID *sb.* 5 and 6.]

12. *trans.* To bind or confine (the hair) with a braid or ribbon, or something equivalent. (Retained by modern poets from *braid the hair* in sense 11, but applied in another sense.)

1793 SOUTHEY *Triumph. Wom.* 31 With roseate wreaths they braid the glossy hair. 1810 SCOTT *Lady of L.* III. v, Yet ne'er again to braid her hair The virgin snood did Alice wear. 1813 —— *Rokeby* III. xxviii, A weary lot is thine, fair maid . . To pull the thorn thy brow to braid.

13. *trans.* **a.** To ornament or trim with braid. **b.** To outline (a design for point-lace work) by means of braid (see BRAID *sb.* 6 b). **c.** To manufacture braid; to weave (material) into braid (see also BRAIDER, BRAIDING-MACHINE).

1848 MISS YONGE *Abbey Ch.* xi. 232 You have been six months braiding that frock. 1874 *Cassell's Househ. Guide* I. 225 When the whole design has been braided. *Mod.* 'They braid slippers for curates.'

†**braid**, *v.*[2] *Obs.* [Prob. aphetic f. ABRAID *v.*[2], UPBRAID; but as ON. *bregða* was used in this meaning, it may perhaps be a sense of BRAID *v.*[1]] *trans.* To upbraid, reproach.

c 1325 *Body & Soul* 257 in *Map's Poems* (1841) 343 Thou . . me thus breidest of myn un-hap. *c* 1440 *Promp. Parv.* 49 Breydyn or vpbreydyn, *impropero*. 1553 BRENDE *Q. Curtius* VIII. 8 Thou wilt braid me with the saving of his life. 1562 J. HEYWOOD *Prov. & Epigr.* (1867) 56 Better dissemble it . . Than to broide him with it. 1608 SHAKS. *Per.* I. i. 93 'Twould 'braid yourself too near for me to tell it.

braid, *v.*[3] [App. a dial. corruption of BRAY *v.*[2], by confusing *brayed, braid, braided*. Given by Forby and Halliwell as East Anglian. Not in Bailey, nor Johnson; taken app. from Halliwell into Webster and other recent Dicts.] *trans.* To intermix; 'to mingle by rubbing in some fluid or soft substance'.

1853 *Hints Yng. Housewives* 31 The plain old-fashioned starch . . is braided up with cold water. *Ibid.* 118 Braid a teaspoonful of flour with a little of the cream.

braid, obs. and Sc. f. BROAD.

braid, obs. f. BREAD and BREDE breadth.

braided ('breɪdɪd), *ppl. a.* [wk. pa. pple. of BRAID *v.*[1]] In some senses of the vb.: **a.** Plaited, woven, entwined; *fig.* tangled, intricate, as a dance. †**b.** *braided wares*: goods that have changed colour, tarnished, faded. *Obs.* **c.** Embroidered; *fig.* rippled, as water by the wind. **d.** Trimmed with braid, as 'a braided coat' (*mod.*).

1494 FABYAN VII. ccxxiv. 251 For that tyme clerkes vsed busshed and brayded hedys. 1599 MARSTON *Sco. Villanie* I. iii. 185 To yeeld his braided ware a quicker sale. 1653 GATAKER *Vind. Annot. Jer.* 183 They may the better help to vend such braided wares. 1710 STEELE *Tatler* 245 ¶2 Bracelets of braided Hair. 1721 BAILEY, *Braided*, faded, that hath lost its colour. 1742 COLLINS *Ode Poet. Char.* 48 In braided dance their murmurs join'd. 1758 JOHNSON *Idler* No. 13 ¶8 She has boxes filled with . . braided shoes. 1812 BYRON *Ch. Har.* I. lxxxi, With braided tresses bounding o'er the green. 1821 SHELLEY *Prometh. Unb.* I. 860 That planet-crested shape swept by on lightning-braided pinions. 1848 THACKERAY *Vanity Fair* xxviii, A braided frock-coat and duck trowsers. 1865 TENNYSON *Mourner* 10 The swamp . . With moss and braided marish-pipe. 1885 *Century Mag.* XXIX. 501, I sought . . the place Of the wind-braided waters.

e. Applied to a stream that divides, esp. at low water, into several channels.

1901 *Science* 15 Nov. 778/1 This extensive deposit . . is the product of aggradation by braided or laced streams. 1940 *Geogr. Jrnl.* XCVI. 352 Three major types of rivers, actively downcutting, balanced meandering, and aggrading or braided.

braider[1] ('breɪdə(r)). [f. BRAID *v.*[1] + -ER.[1]] **a.** One who makes or applies braids. **b.** A part of a sewing machine, used for stitching braid on cloth. **c.** A braiding-machine.

1866 TOMLINSON *Cycl. Useful Arts* III. 622 Subsidiary pieces of apparatus . . the hemmer, the binder, the braider. 1874 KNIGHT *Amer. Mech. Dict.* I. 355 The sizes of flat braiders most in use are those braiding 53 and 65 strands.

†'**braider.**[2] *Obs.* [f. BRAID *v.*[2]] An upbraider.

1552 HULOET, Brayder or caster in teeth with a good turne past.

†'**braidie**, *a. Sc. Obs. rare.* [f. BRAID *sb.* 3 + -IE, -Y[1].] Deceitful. Hence '**braidieness**.

a 1600 MONTGOMERIE *Poems* (1821) 54 Sir, I have sein them baith, In braidieness & lye aback Escape.

braiding (breɪdɪŋ), *vbl. sb.*[1] [f. BRAID *v.*[1]]

1. a. The action of plaiting, embroidering, etc.; also the action of making or applying braid. **b.** Braids collectively. **c.** Braided work; *transf.* embroidery; also *fig.*

c 1440 *Promp. Parv.* 49 Bredynge of lacys or oþer lyke, *laqueacio, nectio, connectio.* 1540 HYRDE *Vives' Instr. Chr. Wom.* I. ix. (R.) Let not the outward apparell of women bee decked with the brayding of hir haire. 1831 J. WILSON in *Blackw. Mag.* XXIX. 288 Some delicate braidings . . along the calm of the Great Blue Sea of Heaven. 1849 THACKERAY *Pendennis* xxiii, A gentleman enveloped in mustachios, whiskers, fur collars, and braiding.

2. braiding-machine, one for weaving braid.

1874 KNIGHT *Amer. Mech. Dict.* I. 355 Braiding-machines are made of all sizes.

†'**braiding**, *vbl. sb.*[2] *Obs.* [f. BRAID *v.*[2]] Upbraiding.

1552 HULOET, Braiding or casting in teath.

braidism ('breɪdɪz(ə)m). *Med.* [f. the surname *Braid.*] The process of producing sleep or trance by causing the patient's attention to be intensely concentrated on some visual object; this process, which had long been practised under the name of MESMERISM, was first scientifically applied, and its effects accounted for, by Dr. James Braid in 1842.

(Braid's own name for the process was HYPNOTISM, which is still the one most frequent in scientific use; the popular term MESMERISM is not employed by medical writers, as it is understood to imply an explanation of the phenomena differing from that of Braid.)

1882 BASTIAN in Quain's *Dict. Med.* 132 Braidism certainly deserves more attention than it has received. *Ibid.* 973 The too ready adoption of hypnosis or Braidism may do harm rather than good.

braie. [a. F. *brai* resin, also a compound used for calking ships. Cf. BRAY *v.*[3]] (See quot.)

1871 *Daily News* 12 May, A material for insulating telegraphic wires named 'braie' . . which was a preparation of coal tar.

braie, braik: see BRAE, BRAYE, BRAKE, BREAK.

brail (breɪl), *sb.*[1] Also 5-6 brayl(e, -ll(e, 7 brale, braile. [a. OF. *brail*, earlier *braiel*:—L. *brācāle* 'breech-girdle, waist-belt for keeping up the breeches', form *brācæ* breeches; hence girdle, cincture, in other senses; in sense 1 *braiel* occurs in Wace.]

1. *pl.* Small ropes fastened to the edges of sails to truss them up before furling.

a 1450 *Pilgrims Sea-Voy.* 33 in *Stacions Rome* (1867) 38 Y howe! trussa! hale in the brayles! 1627 CAPT. SMITH *Seaman's Gram.* v. 22 The Brales are small ropes reeued thorow Blockes . . with them we furle or farthell our sailes acrosse. 1762-9 FALCONER *Shipwr.* II. 287 The sailors . . man the enfolding brails. 1885 NORRIS *A. Vidal* III. 224 Catch hold of those brails, and haul on them when I tell you.

b. ? A rope attached to a fishing net for a similar purpose.

1883 *Fisheries Exhib. Catal.* 195 Minnow gangs, brails, gangings, used in various sea fisheries. 1883 ABBOTT in

Glasgow Weekly Her. 14 July 8/1 Some [of the fish]..made their way between the brail and the net.

2. A girdle used to confine a hawk's wings.

1828 SEBRIGHT *Hawking* 12 The brail..is a thong of soft leather with a slit..along the middle. **1875** 'STONEHENGE' *Brit. Sports* I. IV. i. §6. 295 When first hooding her, the brail should be used.

3. *pl.* The feathers about a hawk's rump; also *attrib.*, as in ***brail-feathers***.

1486 *Bk. St. Albans* A viij b, The same federis ye shall call the brayles or the brayle federis. **1575** TURBERV. *Bk. Falconrie* 278 All the brayles and smal fethers of the trayne. **1611** COTGR., *Brayeul*, feathers about a hawkes fundament, called by our Faulconers the brayle.

brail, *sb.*[2] [ad. F. *brelle* in same sense: see Littré.] In the American timber trade: A number of logs held together by ropes and booms, forming part of a raft.

1879 *Lumberman's Gaz.* 1 Oct. This part of the Slough is wide and deep, and is used for coupling up the strings into brails and rafts.

brail (breɪl), *v.* Also 7 braile, brale. [f. BRAIL *sb.*[1]] *trans.*

1. To haul *up* (the sails) by means of the brails.

1625 SIR R. GRANVILLE in *G. Granville's Wks.* (1732) 293 My Lord Essex did Brail up his Foresail. **1762** FALCONER *Shipwr.* II. 26 'Brail up the mizen quick!' the Master cries. **1834** M. SCOTT *Cruise Midge* (1863) 95 The frigate hauled down the jib and brailed up the spanker.

2. To confine (a hawk's wings) with a brail.

1643 *Parables on Times* 9 Not content to braile and clip their wings onely. **1828** SEBRIGHT *Hawking* 13 He should be carried on the fist..with his wing brailed.

brailed, *ppl. a.* [f. prec. + -ED.]

a. Confined by a brail (said of a hawk's wings). **b.** ***brailed worm***: perh. a ringed worm [? from extended sense of OF. *braiel* girdle; see BRAIL *sb.*[1]]

1496 *Bk. St. Albans, Fysshynge* 26 In May the grene worme: a lytyll breyled worme. *a* **1653** G. DANIEL *Idyll on G. Herbert* 5 My long-brail'd Pineons..I cannot spread.

c. Hauled (*up*, etc.) by means of brails. So **'brailing** *vbl. sb.* (also of a tent and *fig.*).

1856 G. CUPPLES *Green Hand* xiv. 138 The brailed foresail. **1902** C. J. CORNISH *Naturalist Thames* 8 A furling and brailing-up of the rain-clouds. **1910** F. H. LAWRENCE *Let.* 19 Aug. in *Home Lett. T. E. Lawrence* (1954) 600 They had left a piece of the tarpaulin outside the brailing of the tent. **1921** *Spectator* 7 May 589/1 The brailing up of the loose-footed sail. **1924** *Weekly Westm. Gaz.* 13 Sept. 568/3 The brailed brown mainsail of a barge. **1939** *War Illustr.* 16 Dec. 440/2 A bell-tent with sandbagged brailing. **1964** C. WILLOCK *Enormous Zoo* v. 96, I looked out under the brailing of the tent.

Braille (breɪl). Also **braille**. The name of the French teacher of the blind Louis *Braille* (1809–52) used *attrib.* to designate a system of embossed printing for the blind, perfected by him in 1834. Also *ellipt.*

In this system the symbols for the letters, etc., are composed of raised dots arranged in different ways. It was adopted as the standard system in England by the British and Foreign Blind Association, 1869–70.

1853 E. C. JOHNSON *Tangible Typogr.* 22 System Braille..a system of raised dots..this new arbitrary system of dots [has been] adopted throughout the French schools. **1871** T. R. ARMITAGE *Educ. Blind* i. 8 A modification of the Braille system has been suggested by Dr. Russ, of New York. *Ibid.* iii. 21 The reasons which have induced the Council to adhere to the original Braille, are briefly these:—1st. The Braille type is very generally diffused [etc.]. **1887** A. M. SULLIVAN *Let.* 2 June in H. Keller *Story of my Life* (1903) III. ii. 324, I gave her my braille slate to play with, thinking that the mechanical pricking of holes in the paper would amuse her. **1891** *Daily News* 21 Feb. 5/4 The assistant transcribed her answers, written in Braille, into the ordinary characters. **1930** J. M. RITCHIE *Concerning the Blind* vii. 126 Braille has reached the proud position of being the one and only system now in use. *Ibid.* 127 There was a dearth of music in Braille.

Hence as *v. trans.*, to transcribe or print in Braille; to mark in Braille. So **'Brailler** (see quot. 1951); **'Braillist**, a person who transcribes Braille.

1909 *Daily Chron.* 15 July 4/4 A worker who is both a skilled musician and a skilled Braillist. **1944** A. ROHRBACK *Volunteer Braille Transcribing* 5 Qualified braillists began the transcription of books for libraries and schools for the blind. **1951** *Sci. News Let.* 1 Dec. 352/1 Brailler, a typewriter for the blind... The only moving part is the Brailling unit which carries a small embossing head across the page. **1956** *Bookseller* 20 Oct., A select list of new titles Brailled and added to stock. **1964** *Listener* 5 Mar. 394/1 Their [*sc.* blind people's] cookers can be brailled for temperature markings.

brain (breɪn), *sb.* Forms: 1 **brægen** (**breȝn**), **brægn**, **braȝn**, **braȝen**, 3 **braȝen**, **breine**, 3–6 **brayn(e**, 4–7 **braine**, 5–6 **brane**, 3– **brain**. [OE. *bræȝ(e)n* = LG. *brägen*, Du. and Fris. *brein* (not found in HG., Scand., or Goth.):—OTeut. type **bragno(m)*, perh. related to Gr. *βρεχμός* forehead.]

1. a. The convoluted mass of nervous substance contained in the skull of man and other vertebrates. By some earlier scientific writers restricted to the anterior portion (in Latin *cerebrum*) as opposed to the posterior portion (BRAINLET, *cerebellum*); but this distinction is now expressed by the Lat. words, which have been adopted in scientific use, and *brain* in technical as well as in popular language includes the entire organ; it is also applied by extension to the analogous but less developed organs of invertebrate animals.

In 16th c. it became usual to employ the pl. instead of the sing. when mere cerebral substance, and not a definite organic structure, was meant; this usage still continues: we say 'a dish of brains', 'a disease of the brain'.

c **1000** *Ags. Ps.* vii. 16 On his bræȝn astiȝe his unriht. *c* **1000** *Sax. Leechd.* I. 358 Bares bræȝen ȝesoden..ealle sar hyt ȝeliðeȝaþ. *a* **1100** *Voc. in Wr.-Wülcker Voc.* 305 *Cerebrum*, braȝen. *c* **1205** LAY. 1468 His blod and his brain [*c* **1275** braȝen] ba weoren to-dascte. **1297** R. GLOUC. 446 Kyng Henry brayn, and gottes, and eyen ybured were At Reynys in Normandye. **1393** GOWER *Conf.* II. 176 The wit and reson..Is in the celles of the brain. *c* **1460** *Towneley Myst.* 209 (Mätz.) Lo here a crowne of thorne, to perche his brane within. **1486** *Bk. St. Albans* B iiij, Rewarde youre hawke with the Brayne and the necke. **1578** BANISTER *Hist. Man* v. 78 The quadruplication of Dura mater..lyeth betwene the brayne and Cerebellum. **1598** SHAKS. *Merry W.* III. v. 7 Ile haue my braines tane out and butter'd. **1653** WALTON *Angler* 179 Pearch..have in their brain a stone. **1772** PRIESTLEY *Inst. Relig.* (1782) II. 389 The power of thinking..depends..upon the brain. **1824–8** LANDOR *Imag. Conv.* (1846) 460 The power of thinking is no more in the brain than in the hair. **1880** HUXLEY *Cray-Fish* iii. 105 A transversely elongated mass of ganglionic substance termed the Brain or cerebral ganglion.

b. Phrases. ***to dash, knock out a person's brains***: i.e. by a blow. ***to blow out*** (***any***) ***one's brains***: to shoot oneself or another in the head.

1607 SHAKS. *Timon* I. i. 193 To knocke out an honest Athenians braines. **1831** CARLYLE *Sart. Res.* II. vi, Establish himself in Bedlam; begin writing Satanic Poetry; or blow out his brains. **1859** *Autobiog. Beggar-boy* 95 [He] demanded his money, or he would blow out his brains. **1864** TENNYSON *Boädicea* 68 Dash the brains of the little one out.

†**2.** *transf.* Marrow; the pith or heart of the growth at the top of a date-palm. *Obs.*

1552 HULOET, Brayne, or marrow of the legge, *musculus*. **1601** HOLLAND *Pliny* I. 386 These [date-trees] haue in the very head and top, a certain pleasant..marow, which they terme, The braine.

3. a. Considered as the centre of sensation, the organ of thought, memory, or imagination. (From 16th c. onwards the pl. has been preferred in familiar use and idiomatic phrases, but not in dignified language, exc. when more than one brain is referred to.)

c **1230** *Hali Meid.* 35 Of breines turnunge þin heaued [schule] ake. *c* **1384** CHAUCER *H. Fame* 24 To grete feblenesse of her brayne. **1536** *Remed. Sedition* p. ii b, Full of bones, but voyde of brayne. **1604** JAMES I *Counterbl.* 103 The Nose being the proper Organ and conuoy of the sense of smelling to the braines. **1697** DRYDEN *Virg. Georg.* II. 674 Ye sacred muses, with whose Beauty fir'd My Soul is ravish'd, and my Brain inspir'd. **1845** DISRAELI *Sybil* (1863) 275 'You have a clear brain and a bold spirit; you have no scruples..You ought to succeed.' **1875** STUBBS *Const. Hist.* II. 512 Was that plan the conception of any one brain?

fig. **1844** KINGLAKE *Eothen* ii. (1878) 17 The accomplished Mysseri..was in fact the brain of our corps. **1861** M. ARNOLD *Pop. Educ. France* Pref. 23 Frenchmen proclaim..Paris to be the brain of Europe.

b. Phrases. ***to break*** (obs.), ***beat, busy, cudgel, drag, puzzle one's brains***: to exert oneself in thought or contrivance. ***to crack one's brain(s)***: to render oneself insane. ***to have*** anything (***e.g.*** music, bicycling, any object of admiration or antipathy) ***on the brain***: to be crazy on the subject of; also, ***to have got*** (something) ***on the brain***. ***to turn one's brain***: to render giddy, hence *fig.* to bewilder, to render vain or imprudent. † ***a dry brain*** (Shaks.): a dull or barren brain void of thinking power. † ***a hot brain***: an inventive fancy. † ***boiled brains***: hot-headed fellows.

1530 PALSGR. 350 We breake our braynes for nought. **1577** STANYHURST *Descr. Irel.* in *Holinshed* VI. 32 To beat his braines in the curious insearching of deep mysteries. **1600** SHAKS. *A.Y.L.* II. vii. 38. **1602** —— *Ham.* v. i. 63 Cudgell thy braines no more about it. **1611** —— *Wint. T.* III. iii. 64; IV. iv. 701. **1742** YOUNG *Nt. Th.* VIII. 513 An eminence, tho' fansy'd, turns the brain. **1847** TENNYSON *Princ.* IV. 136 While I dragg'd my brains for such a song. **1848** KINGSLEY *Saint's Trag.* II. iii, I puzzled my brains about choosing my line. **1862** MRS. GASKELL *Lett.* (1966) 698 Our poor people would get work, and..we should not be killed with 'Poor on the Brain', as I expect we shall before the winter is over. **1869** *Congress. Globe* Jan. 182/2 The Gazette seems to have the franking privilege 'on the brain'. **1884** CROMER *Let.* 11 Mar. in Marq. of Zetland *Lord Cromer* (1932) ix. 100, I have got it on the brain that much writing is not a good thing for the moment. **1900** C. M. YONGE *Modern Broods* i. 12 Child, I believe you have bicycles on the brain. **1911** A. BENNETT *Hilda Lessways* II. iv. 173 Tom..had for the moment got Beethoven on the brain. **1957** M. SPARK *Comforters* v. 108 Caroline had it very much on the brain that her phantom should be outwitted in this one particular.

c. An electronic device that performs complicated operations comparable to those of the human brain; *spec.* an electronic computer. Cf. *electronic brain*.

1934 *Scoops* 10 Feb. 15/2 An attempt to construct a mechanical man who can think..is to be made by the Massachusetts Institute of Technology. The 'Brain' of the new robot is an accomplished fact. **1945** *War Illustr.* 7 Dec. 492/1 The 'brain' of the shell is a fuse, a tiny radio set—transmitter, receiver and aerial all combined—in the nose of the shell. **1951** R. KNOX *Stimuli* III. xxi. 129 Recently the Press recorded the invention of a calculating machine... They called it a 'brain'. **1952** *Economist* 1 Nov. 305 Univac, the 'Giant Brain', an electronic automatic computer. **1954** K. W. GATLAND *Devel. Guided Missile* (ed. 2) iv. 109 In the self-homing device we have a 'brain unit' capable of making high-g turns and of operating..control entirely beyond human capabilities.

4. *fig.* Intellectual power, intellect, sense, thought, imagination. (From 16th c. often plural.)

1393 GOWER *Conf.* III. 4 That is nought for lake of braine. **1526** TINDALE *1 Tim.* vi. 4 He wasteth his braynes aboute questions. **1571** GOLDING *Calvin on Ps.* ix. 12 David did not vpon his oun brayn appoint God a dwelling place there. **1618** *Barnevelt's Apol.* G iij, Hee that hath any brayne, sees hee is not well in his wittes. **1732** POPE *Ess. Man* II. 47 Tricks to shew the stretch of human brain. **1763** CHURCHILL *Candidate* (R.) Let those who boast the uncommon gift of brains, The laurel pluck. **1861** T. BROWN *Horæ Subs.* Ser. I. 171 'Pray, Mr. Opie, may I ask you what you mix your colours with?'..'With brains, sir!' was the gruff reply.

b. Phrases. † ***to bear a brain***: to be cautious, thoughtful, have brains. ***to suck*** (or ***pick***) ***a person's brains***: to elicit and appropriate the results of his thought. † ***of the same brain***: in the same strain of thought, similarly conceived. (But cf. ***of the same bran***.)

1526 SKELTON *Magnyf.* 1422, I counsel you, bere a brayne. **1592** G. HARVEY *Pierces Super.* 120 Some potestats ..will by fittes beare a braine. **1652** BP. HALL *Invis. World* I. viii, These [tales] and a thousand more of the same brain. **1808** SCOTT *Marmion* VI. xvi, Eustace, thou bear'st a brain.

c. *colloq.* A clever person; so ***the brains***: the cleverest person (in a group, etc.); a 'master-mind'. (Cf. 1844 *fig.* quot. for sense 3 a.)

1914 W. OWEN *Let.* 21 Dec. (1967) 309 This gentleman is, all round, an 'interesting' pupil, and what the French call 'a Brain'. **1923** E. WALLACE *Capt. Souls* xxxv. 197, I felt like a fourth form boy listening to a 'brain', and found myself being respectful! **1925** H. LEVERAGE in *Flynn's* 3 Jan. 693/1 *Brains*, the one who works out plans for a robbery. **1954** 'N. BLAKE' *Whisper in Gloom* I. vi. 75 The Brain's got what it takes. **1958** *Times* 20 Jan. 5/5 Admiral Sir William Wynter, 'the brains' of the victory.

5. *Comb.*; general relations.

a. attributive: Of the physical brain, as ***brain-ache, -atoms, -capacity, -chamber, -condition, -cortex, -giddiness, -matter, -softening, -symptom***; of the brain as the seat of intelligence, as ***brain-chart, -fancy, -labour, -power, -war, -work***.

1862 LYTTON *Str. Story* II. 280 His crown, with its *brain-ache of care. **1936** *Discovery* Nov. 351/2 The largest [skull on record] is that of Turgenev, the Russian novelist, which had a *brain capacity of 2,030 c. cm. **1870** GLADSTONE *Prim. Homer* (1878) 61 The poetical unity of Homer's *brain-chart. **1890** W. JAMES *Princ. Psychol.* I. vi. 162 Certain *brain-conditions occur together which, if they occurred separately, would produce a lot of lower states. *Ibid.* x. 399 We speculate on the brain-condition during all these different perversions of personality. *Ibid.* xiv. 567 The amount of activity at any given point in the *brain-cortex is the sum of the tendencies of all other points to discharge into it. **1657** BROME *Queene's Exch.* IV. i, The *brain-giddiness of these wilful Lords. **1864** TENNYSON *Aylmer's F.* 447 Prodigal of all *brain-labour he. **1878** HOOKER & BALL *Marocco* 150 By their superior *brain-power. **1883** *Harper's Mag.* June 125/1 *Brain-softening or degeneration of the spinal cord. **1845** GEO. ELIOT *Let.* 13 June (1954) I. 195 It always gives one satisfaction to see the evidence of *brain work. **1871** M. COLLINS *Mrq. & Merch.* III. xi. 252 Men who are wise do no brainwork save in summer. **1931** J. S. HUXLEY *What dare I Think?* ii. 69 Pure brain-work like that of a mathematician.

b. objective and objective-genitive; as ***brain-wright*** sb.; ***brain-breaking, -fretting, -purging, -smoking, -spattering*** adjs.

1616 HOLYDAY *Persius* 317 *Brain-purging, hellebore. *a* **1654** SELDEN *Engl. Epin.* iii. §19 *Brain-smoaking liquors. **1823** BYRON *Juan* IX. iv, War's a *brain-spattering..art. **1602** DAVIES *Mirum in Mod.* 7 (D.) The *Brayn-wrights skill And wisdome infinite.

c. instrumental and locative: as ***brain-begot, -born, -bred, -cracked, -crazed, -fevered, -spun, -strong*** adjs., also ***brain-worker*** sb.; ***brainlike*** adj.

1596 FITZ-GEFFRAY *Sir F. Drake* (1881) 22 Joves *braine-borne Pallades. **1812** BYRON *Ch. Har.* II. vii, With *brain-born dreams of evil. **1630** J. TAYLOR (Water P.) *Wks.* III. 122/2 His *braine-bred Daughter. **1657** BROME *Queene's Exch.* III. Wks. 1873 III. 497, I fear he's *brain-crack'd, lunatick. **1652** —— *North. Lasse* I. v Wks. III. 11 The Master and the man both *brain-cras'd. **1849** TODD *Cycl. Anat. & Phys.* IV. 141/2 Cerebral substance..replaced by a *brain-like matter. **1832** J. C. HARE in *Philol. Mus.* I. 643 *Brain-spun systems of metaphysics. **1863** DASENT *Jest & Earnest* (1873) II. 273 True it is, as the saw goes, 'Bairns are brain-strong'. **1878** HOLBROOK *Hygiene of Brain* 91 A farmer may be a *brain-worker.

6. Special combinations: **brain-axis** = *brain-stem*; **brain-ball**, the brain of an enemy slain in combat made into a ball by mixing it with lime and preserved as a trophy; † **brain-being, -brat**, a creature of the fancy; **brain-box**, the skull; † **brain-break**, a conception that overtasks the brain; **brain-cap**, the upper part of the skull; **brain-case** (= *brain-box*); **brain-cell**, one of the cells forming the tissue of the brain; **brain-centre**, any nerve-centre in the brain, esp. one of those supposed to be the controlling centres of

particular functions; also *fig.*; **brain-child** *colloq.*, the product of a person's mind; an invention; **brain-coral**, coral resembling in form the convolutions of the brain; **brain-crack**, a craze or crotchet; **brain damage**, physical injury to or deterioration of the brain that leaves its function permanently and substantially impaired; hence **brain-damaged** *a.*; **brain death**, irreversible loss of function in the cerebrum and brain-stem of such a degree that respiration and circulation continue only if artificially maintained; so **brain-dead** *a.*; **brain drain**, phrase used *colloq.* of the 'loss' of highly trained or qualified people by emigration, particularly to the U.S.; **brain-dressed** *a.*, of skins, dressed with a liquor prepared by boiling deer brains; **brain-fag**, exhaustion of the brain by prolonged mental strain; **brain-fagged** *a.*, suffering from brain-fag; **brain-fever**, a term for inflammation of the brain, 'and also for other fevers, as typhus, with brain complications' (*Syd. Soc. Lex.*); **brain-fever bird**, an Indian hawk-cuckoo (*Cuculus varius*) having a persistent cry; **brain-lit** *a.*, enlightened by thought; **brain-mantle**, the upper part of the brain; **brain-mass**, (*a*) material quantity of brain; (*b*) the brain, regarded as a material object; **brain-path**, one of a number of supposed lines of conduction in the brain, along which nervous impulses come to travel more readily than by other routes; also *attrib.*; **brain-picker**, one who 'picks' the brains of another (cf. PICK $v.^1$ 9); **brain-racking** *vbl. sb.*, racking of the brain; mental torture or anguish; also *ppl. a.*; **brain-sand**, minute particles of gritty substance found chiefly in the pineal gland; **brain scan**, a scan of the brain to ascertain the distribution of radioactivity in it following the intravenous administration of a radio-isotope (used as a diagnostic aid for tumours); **brain scanner**, an apparatus for performing a brain scan; so **brain scanning** *vbl. sb.*; **brain-shed**, the scattering of brains; †**brain-squirt**, a childish attempt at reasoning; **brain-stage**, the imagination; **brain-stem**, the central trunk of the brain upon which the cerebrum and cerebellum are set, and which continues downwards to form the spinal cord; **brain-stone** (= *brain-coral*); **brain-storm**, (*a*) 'a succession of sudden and severe phenomena, due to some cerebral disturbance' (Gould 1894); (*b*) *U.S. colloq.* = *brain-wave* (c); (*c*) *U.S.*, a concerted 'attack' on a problem, usu. by amassing a number of spontaneous ideas which are then discussed; also *attrib.*; so as *v.*, to make such an attack; hence **brain-storming** *vbl. sb.* and *ppl. a.*; **brain-stuff**, (*a*) medicine for the brain; (*b*) the product of thinking; ideas; **brain-sugar** (see quot.); **brain-teaser** or **-twister** (orig. *U.S.*), a difficult problem; a puzzle; **brain-trick**, a cunning device; **brain-tunic**, a membrane enveloping the brain; **brain-vibration**, an excitation or nervous discharge in the brain; **brain-wave**, (*a*) a hypothetical telepathic vibration; (*b*) (usu. in *pl.*) a measurable electrical impulse in the brain; (*c*) *colloq.*, a sudden inspiration or bright idea; **brain-worm**, a worm infesting the brain; *fig.* a wriggling disputant. Also BRAIN-PAN, BRAINSICK, BRAIN-WOOD.

1894 GOULD *Dict. Med.* 233 **B[rain] axis*, that portion of the brain-substance including the island of Reil, the basal ganglia, the crura, pons, medulla, and cerebellum. [**1809** D. O'CONNOR tr. *Keating's Gen. Hist. Ireland* I. 279 Ceat.. placed his ball of brains in a sling.] **1904** *Westm. Gaz.* 9 July 5/1 The old king, who sat with the *brain-ball on his head. **1907** *Folk-Lore* June 228 Mesgegra's brain-ball, an object that could be slung from a sling. **1659** FULLER *App. Inj. Innoc.* (1840) 450 A mere wit-work, or *brain-being, without any other real existence. **1630** R. H. in J. Taylor (Water P.) *Wks.* Pref. Verses, One Bacchus, and some other Venus urges, To blesse their *brain-brats. **1895** A. H. KEANE *Ethnology* iii. 46 The *brain-cap of many savages has been found to be larger and heavier than that of some higher races. **1741** MONRO *Anat.* (ed. 3) 78 The several Bones of which the *Brain-case consists. **1887** W. JAMES *Coll. Ess. & Rev.* (1920) 290 Even in the case of congenital defect of the extremities, the *brain-centres might feel in the usual ancestral way. **1902** —— *Var. Relig. Exper.* ix. 212 Our emotional brain-centres strike work, and we lapse into a temporary apathy. **1904** *Westm. Gaz.* 3 Mar. 1/3 From its brain-centre in the middle of the floor of the New York Stock Exchange the recording instruments of the Exchange Company print out continuously the news of the transactions. **1881** *Household Words* 1 Oct. 450/2 The *brain-children [*i.e.* novels] of the illustrious dead. **1882** SWINBURNE *Lett.* (1960) IV. 284 The most unlucky and despised of all my brain-children. **1921** WODEHOUSE *Jill the Reckless* xvii. 254 The almost maternal yearning to see his brain-child once more, which can never be wholly crushed out of a young dramatist. **1958** J. CANNAN *And be a Villain* iv. 81 How well I know that filing system. It was my own brain-child. **1709-11** PETIVER *Gazophyl.* Decas Sept. 6/2 Tab. 68 Common American *Brain Corall... So call'd for its likeness to humane Brains. **1936** RUSSELL & YONGE *Seas* (ed. 2) vii. 162 The well-known Meandrina or Brain-coral. **1851** THACKERAY *Eng. Hum.* (1866) 107 What would Sir Roger de Coverley be without..his charming *brain-cracks? **1951** *Pediatrics* VII. 212 Several clinical reports have described the association of insulin hypoglycemia in juvenile diabetes with psychiatric disturbances or *brain damage. **1959** *Jrnl. Chronic Dis.* IX. 223 Brain damage in the aged..is presumed present when there is evidence of defects of orientation, memory, and comprehension. **1974** PASSMORE & ROBSON *Compan. Med. Stud.* III. II. xxxv. 71/2 A confusional or delirious state may be the first indication of the presence of structural brain damage. **1954** *Pediatrics* XIV. 479/1 '*Brain damaged' children. **1959** *Jrnl. Chronic Dis.* IX. 221 Aged mentally ill persons fall into several groups. The largest group of seriously disordered persons are the aged who are chronically ill, many of whom are brain damaged. **1983** *Listener* 1 Sept. 14/3 Our third child was born brain-damaged. **1976** *Time* 12 Apr. 50 Because Karen was not '*brain dead', few lawyers were surprised when Judge Robert Muir ruled against any 'pulling of the plug'. **1986** *Telegraph* (Brisbane) 12 June 5/5 A 17-day-old boy who last night was given the heart of a brain-dead infant.. gave no sign of rejecting the new organ. **1964** *Jrnl. Amer. Med. Assoc.* 12 Oct. 113/2 Medicolegal texts do not mention the consideration of *brain death by EEG. **1974** *Times* 5 Apr. 18 He insists that the donor heart should still be beating when the operation to remove it starts. That is possible only when the concept of 'brain death' is accepted and at present would probably not be ethically permissible in Britain. **1979** *Removal of Cadaveric Organs for Transplantation* (Health Depts U.K.) 11/1 This Working Party accepts the view held by the Conference of Royal Colleges that death can..be diagnosed by the irreversible cessation of brain-stem function—'brain death'. In diagnosing brain death the criteria laid down by the Colleges should be followed. **1984** *Listener* 29 Mar. 8/2 The *Panorama* on brain-death apparently challenged medical orthodoxy. **1963** P. FAIRLEY in *Evening Standard* 7 Jan. 1/2 Nearly one quarter of Britain's best young scientists and technologists are being magnetised to jobs in North America. About 10 per cent are settling there. This is the shock finding of experts who have spent months investigating the '*brain drain' across the Atlantic. **1964** *News Front* Apr. 15 The United Kingdom is deeply concerned about its 'brain drain'. **1887** *Harper's Mag.* June 61/2 These [deerskin leggings] were prepared of *brain-dressed skins that perfectly turned the rain and dew. **1851** DUNGLISON *Dict. Med. Sci.* (ed. 8) 596 A hypochondriacal condition,..termed by some *cerebropathy*; by others, **brain-fag*. **1884** W. JAMES in *Mind* IX. 17 In states of extreme brain-fag the horizon is narrowed almost to the passing word. **1903** MCFAUL *Ike Glidden* ii. 13 He continued in this brain-fagged and mentally-deranged condition for several weeks. **1833** MARRYAT *P. Simple* (1863) 367, I had a *brain-fever, which lasted six or seven days. **1885** MARCHIONESS OF DUFFERIN in *Vice-regal Life in India* (1890) ii. 30 The 'brainfever' bird repeats his name over and over again until he nearly gives you the malady itself. **1901** *Badminton Mag.* Mar. 243 The ceaseless, irritating cry of the brain-fever bird. **1879** G. H. LEWES *Problems* III. III. 416 The *corona* (what the Germans call the **Brain-mantle* because it *covers* the other parts). **1894** H. ELLIS *Man & Woman* v. 105 The cerebrum, or brain-mantle. **1879** G. H. LEWES *Problems* III. II. 67 The popular argument.., showing more *brain-mass to be accompanied by greater..intelligence, breaks down. **1915** E. R. LANKESTER *Diversions of Naturalist* 270 The mere shape of the brain-mass. **1890** W. JAMES *Princ. Psychol.* II. xvii. 8 As the currents vary, and the *brain-paths are moulded by them, other thoughts with other 'objects' come. **1892** —— *Coll. Ess. & Rev.* (1920) 319 The brain-path theory based on reflex action..helps them to analyze their cases. **1925** C. FOX *Educ. Psychol.* 143 Fall back on brain-paths to account for the phenomena of memory. **1810** LADY LYTTELTON *Let.* 11 Feb. (1912) 94 He will meet a formidable body of *brain-pickers. **1963** *Times* 25 Mar. 15/1 Very successful farmers are apt to be inveterate brain-pickers. **1892** 'MARK TWAIN' *Amer. Claimant* i. 4 My very footfalls time themselves to the *brain-racking rhythm. **1897** *Daily News* 30 Mar. 8/1 It is this that causes the English in South Africa so much brain-racking. **1905** *Westm. Gaz.* 22 Mar. 1/3 It was a noisy..monster..and began its torturing, brain-racking persecution at eight in the morning. **1905** *Daily Chron.* 29 Sept. 3/3 Some less brain-racking railway guide. **1857** DUNGLISON *Med. Lex.* 718/1 *Pineal Gland...* It almost always contains sabulous particles, Sabulum conarii, *Brain Sand, Pineal Sand. **1873** T. H. GREEN *Introd. Pathol.* (ed. 2) 75 The corpora amylacea..are very liable to become calcified, and they then constitute one form of'brain sand'. [**1960** *Southern Med. Jrnl.* (Nashville, Tennessee) LIII. 418/2 Many modifications in the equipment had to be made ..before cerebral scans of good quality could be obtained.] **1961** *Acta Radiologica Suppl.* CCI. 29 A *brain scan may be abnormal in two different ways:..areas of increased uptake and..areas of decreased uptake may be shown. **1973** *Daily Colonist* (Victoria, B.C.) 21 June 2/1 A brain scan is a painless procedure. **1985** O. SACKS *Man who mistook Wife for Hat* xv. 127, I obtained a brainscan, and this showed that she had indeed had a small thrombosis or infarction in part of her right temporal lobe. **1964** *Symp. Med. Radioisotope Scanning* (Internat. Atomic Energy Agency) II. 81 (*heading*) Design & function of a *brain scanner for clinical use. **1974** *Radiology* CX. 109 This new technique involves the use of an EMI brain scanner. **1986** *Economist* 26 Apr. 16/2 The magnets used in brain scanners owe much to those developed for past accelerators. **1961** in *Biol. Abstr.* (1962) XXXVIII. 1320/1 (*heading*) A theoretical evaluation of *brain scanning systems. **1974** R. M. KIRK et al. *Surgery* xiv. 270 Brain scanning after introducing a radioactive substance intravenously..is an extremely useful and painless technique. **1857** GEN. P. THOMPSON *Audi Alt.* I. xxiii. 83 The subordinates have resisted in a way that ended in blood and *brain-shed. **1654** G. GODDARD in Burton *Diary* Introd. (1828) I. 68 They were but bugbears and *brain-squirts. **1879** G. H. LEWES *Probl. Life & Mind* 3rd Ser. III. xiv. 416 That large portion of the neural axis which Germans call the **Brain-stem*. **1927** HALDANE & HUXLEY *Anim. Biol.* vi. 142 When we are 'doing nothing' the cortex is all the time inhibiting the postural centres in the brain-stem from producing rigidity. **1681** GREW *Musæum* II. v. i. 244 A flat Horney Shrub..Rooted in a kind of *Brain-Stone. **1758** BORLASE *Nat. Hist. Cornw.* 240 The fossil corals ..such as brain-stone. **1855** KINGSLEY *Glaucus* 34 A beautiful madrepore or brainstone on your mantelpiece, brought home from some Pacific coral-reef. **1871** T. R. JONES *Anim. Kingd.* (ed. 4) 112 The beautiful structures known as *Meandrinæ*, or 'brain-stones'. **1907** *Daily Chron.* 13 Feb. 7/5 Ordeals of mind which formed a *brain-storm or mental explosion. **1908** *Westm. Gaz.* 8 Aug. 4/3 In the closing years of his active life, Ruskin had suffered from recurrent brain-storms. **1922** *Daily Mail* 2 May 5/4 If he were crossed he had brain storms which took the form of violent temper and depression. **1925** *College Humor* Feb. 43/2 He had a brainstorm. **1932** *Amer. Speech* VII. 329 *Brain storm*, a sudden and usually fortunate thought. **1947** I. ASIMOV in E. Crispin *Best SF II* (1962) 103 When our missing robot failed of location anywhere..we brain-stormed ourselves into counting the robots left. **1953** *Manch. Guardian Weekly* 12 Feb. 3 They carry behind their every brain-storm the authority of the White House. **1953** *San Francisco Exam.* 15 Mar. (Pict. Rev. Sect.) 4/2 Alex Osborn..has contributed to American business a new technique and terminology—the 'brain storm session'. **1955** *N.Y. Times* 6 Nov. F3/5 They are being taught..how to brainstorm their way to conclusions concerning subjects ranging from world affairs to specific engineering puzzles. **1957** *Britannica Bk. of Yr.* 512/1 *Brainstorming*, the pooling of ideas towards the solution of a special problem. **1959** C. WILLIAMS *Man in Motion* vi. 66 A sort of preliminary brain-storming session. **1911** W. OWEN *Let.* 21 Nov. (1967) 97 The borrowed-*brainstuff which I imbibed to help me through the Exam.—Sanatogen. **1933** H. G. WELLS *Shape of Things to Come* v. § 8. 426 The abundant release of brain-stuff, the mental plenty which has resulted from the organization of material plenty. **1948** E. H. W. MEYERSTEIN *Let.* 9 Nov. (1959) 352 Ethel Smyth..used his brainstuff as a libretto for her cantata. **1901** DORLAND *Med. Dict.* (ed. 2), *Cerebrose*, *brain-sugar, $C_6H_{12}O_6$; a principle derivable from the brain-substance, and sometimes found in diabetic sugar. **1923** H. C. WITWER *Fighting Blood* iv. 105 While you're puzzling over that *brain teaser, I'll get back to Judy. **1966** OGILVY & ANDERSON *Excurs. Number Theory* vi. 82 Here are some of the super brain-teasers that Sierpinski asks us to ponder. **1922** *John Martin's Big Bk. for Little Folk* 256 Fascinating *brain twisters never so hard as to discourage nor so easy as to fail of sustained interest. **1942** R. G. COLLINGWOOD *New Leviathan* xvi. 116 This is a famous brain-twister planted upon the world by Kant and Fichte. **1890** W. JAMES *Princ. Psychol.* I. v. 129 Then the last *brain-vibration would discharge downward into the motor tracts. **1905** A. R. WALLACE *My Life* II. 309 Thought or brain-vibrations, may be carried by the ether to other brains. **1869** C. READE *Put Yourself in his Place* (1870) II. ii. 67 Now that very afternoon, as if by the influence of what they call a *brain-wave, Grace Carden..was moved to ask [etc.]. **1871** A. T. RITCHIE *Lett.* (1924) 147 You must have sent a brain wave, for oddly enough we had all just read the book..when your letter came saying you too had been reading it. **1886** *Proc. Soc. Psych. Research* Oct. 178 Such expressions as 'brain-waves' (Knowles), 'mentiferous ether' (Maudsley).. testify to this natural, though premature, desire to ticket or identify a force which..cannot at present be correlated with nerve-force [etc.]. **1890** *Harper's Mag.* Apr. 744/1 Lucilla, with what she was fond of terming a brain wave, comprehended the situation. **1916** *Blackw. Mag.* Aug. 264/1 Then the wirers got brain waves, saw the folly of their first orders,..and began to panic terribly. **1917** W. PETT RIDGE *Amazing Years* xi. 160 It's a brain wave... Aunt Weston, how bright you are! **1926** GALSWORTHY *Escape* II. vi. 72 Look here! I've got a brain-wave. Let's all go into Widecombe in the car? **1935** *Discovery* Jan. 1/1 By means of electrical records made through the skull various states of the brain can be recognised; but the 'brain waves' thus recorded do not appear to be the result of thought-action. **1959** *Listener* 1 Oct. 534/3 Study of the activity of the brain of puppies with the electro-encephalograph for 'brain waves'..reveals a juvenile type of wave form. **1645** MILTON *Colast.* Wks. (1851) 364 This *Brain-worm against all the Laws of Dispute, will needs deal with them heer.

†**brain**, *a. Obs.* [Cf. BRAINISH.] Furious, mad.

c **1340** *Gaw. & Gr. Knt.* 286 If any..Be so bolde in his blod, brayn in hys hede. **1513** DOUGLAS *Æneis* XI. xvii. 73 He walxis brayne in furour bellicall. **1809** J. SKINNER *Collect. Poetry* 126 (JAM.), I wat right weel he was fu' brain.

brain (breɪn), *v.* Also 4–6 **brayne**, 5–6 **brane**, 7 **braine**. [f. the sb.]

1. *trans.* To dash (any one's) brains out; to kill by dashing out the brains.

1382 WYCLIF *Isa.* lxvi. 3 That sleth a beste, as that brayne a dogge. **1489** CAXTON *Faytes of A.* II. xxxvii. 156 Thenne shall they of the towne brayne hem with stones. **1596** SHAKS. *1 Hen. IV*, II. iii. 24 If I were now by this Rascall, I could braine him with his Ladies Fan. **1615** G. SANDYS *Trav.* 45 Hee desperately brained himselfe. **1691** WOOD *Ath. Oxon* I. 31 He was most cruelly murder'd, by being brain'd like an Ox. **1884** TENNYSON *Becket* 201 Methought they would have brain'd me with it, John.

fig. **1603** SHAKS. *Meas. for M.* v. i. 401 It was the swift celeritie of his death..That brain'd my purpose.

†**2.** To conceive in the brain. *Obs. rare.*

1611 SHAKS. *Cymb.* v. iv. 147 Such stuffe as Madmen Tongue and braine not.

3. To furnish with a brain.

1882 W. WEEDEN *Soc. Law Labor* 94 Both the labor and capital must be headed, brained, as it were, with thought.

Hence, ˈ**brainer**, ˈ**braining** *vbl. sb.*

c **1440** *Promp. Parv.* 47 Braynynge, or kyllynge, *excerebracio*. **1842** DE QUINCEY *Wks.* (1863) XIII. 306 Not only the stone must be a bouncer..but it ought to be..a good brainer, viz., splinting-jagged.

brained (breɪnd), *a.* [f. BRAIN *sb.* + -ED^2.] Furnished with a brain or brains. Usually with adj. prefix, as *addle-*, *dry-*, *dull-*, *feeble-*, *hot-*, *nimble-*.

c **1440** *Promp. Parv.* 47 Branyd or full of brayne. **1528** PAYNELL *Salerne Regim.* F iv b, Feble brayned folkes. **1610** SHAKS. *Temp.* III. ii. 7 If th' other two be brain'd like vs, the State totters. *a* **1704** T. BROWN *Sat. on Quack* Wks. 1730 I. 63 That hot brain'd sot Thy father. **1819** SHELLEY *Peter Bell*

VI. xx, A mad-brained goblin for a guide. **1866** MOTLEY *Dutch Rep.* IV. v. 633 The addle-brained Oberstein.

brainge (breɪndʒ), *v. Sc.* Also **braindge, breinge, breenge** (briːndʒ). *intr.* To force or move oneself with clumsy violence.

1786 BURNS *To Auld Mare* xii, Thou never braing't, an' fetch't an' fliskit.

brainge (breɪndʒ), *sb. Sc.* Also **braindge.** [f. prec.] A violent and clumsy rush or bounce.

1789 DAVIDSON *Seasons* 35 (JAM.) Baith wi' a brainge, Sprang, hap and sten, out o'er a nettle. **1858** M. PORTEOUS *Souter Johnny* 30 Ye'll wi a braindge Jerk aff the Mune.

brainily ('breɪnɪlɪ), *adv.* [f. BRAINY *a.* + -LY².] In a brainy fashion; with clever use of the wits. So **'braininess.**

1922 *Daily Mail* 21 Nov. 10 Lewis's tactics..were extremely bad. There was no suggestion of braininess. **1923** *Ibid.* 29 May 12 Against Lewis,..he certainly fought brainily.

brainish ('breɪnɪʃ), *a. Obs.* or *arch.* [f. BRAIN *sb.* + -ISH¹.] Headstrong, passionate.

1530 PALSGR. 307/1 Braynisshe, hedy, folisshe, selfe wylled. **1602** SHAKS. *Ham.* IV. i. 11 And, in his brainish apprehension, killes The vnseene good old man. **1603** DRAYTON *Heroic Ep.* Pref., The Worke might in truth be judged Braynish. **1850** BLACKIE *Æschylus* I. 104 Thy son.. whom unwittingly of life I reft, In a brainish moment.

brainless ('breɪnlɪs), *a.* Also 6 **brainsless.** [f. BRAIN *sb.* + -LESS.]

1. Devoid of brain; that has had the brain removed, 'pithed'.

c **1440** *Promp. Parv.* 47 Braynles, *incerebrosus.* **1547** *Life 70 Abps. Canterbury* To Rdr., A very charnell howse off brainslesse unlearned skulles. **1611** SPEED *Hist. Gt. Brit.* VII. xxxvi. (1632) 389 A brainlesse body. **1875** H. WOOD *Therap.* (1879) 176 The experiments on brainless frogs.

2. †**a.** Insane, mentally diseased, imbecile. *Obs.*

1496 *Dives & Paup.* (W. de W.) v. xxiv. 230 Yf the prynce be..frentyke or braynles. *c* **1500** *Blowbol's Test.* in Halliw. *Nugæ P.* 9 Braynles as a Marshe hare. **1625** tr. *Gonsalvio's Sp. Inquis.* 164 Some caught vncurable diseases and paines in the head, and became almost brainlesse.

b. Foolish, irrational; wanting intelligence, thought, or self-control.

c **1470** *Hors, Shepe, & G.* (1822) 21 As souldyours that braynles be & wood. **1575** CHURCHYARD *Chippes* (1817) 127 George Carey, I haue receyved your braynlesse letter. **1797** COLERIDGE *Poems* (1862) 36 The apostate by the brainless rout adored. **1863** *Cornh. Mag.* Feb., To what shifts a brainless man is put about.

Hence **'brainlessly** *adv.*, **'brainlessness.**

1610 HEALEY *St. Aug. Citie of God* VI. vi. (1620) 232, I think no man so brainelessly sottish. **1884** *Century Mag.* Nov. 59 A good deal of hard swearing at his brainlessness.

†**'brainlet.** *Obs.* [f. BRAIN *sb.* + -LET, transl. L. *cerebellum* 'little brain'.] The cerebellum.

1668 CULPEPPER & COLE *Barthol. Anat.* III. ii. 130 The Cerebellum, Brainlet, or petty-brain. *a* **1720** GIBSON *Farrier's Guide* I. iv. (1738) 35 Cerebellum, or Brainlet.

brain-pan ('breɪnpæn). *arch.* [f. BRAIN *sb.* + PAN.] That which contains the brain; the skull.

c **1400** MAUNDEV. xxxii. 234 The Brayn Panne of a ded Man. **1535** COVERDALE *Judg.* ix. 53 A woman cast a pece of a mylstone..and brake his brane panne. **1711** STEELE *Spect.* No. 167 ⁋3 To settle my Head and cool my Brain-pan. **1872** HARDWICK *Trad. Lanc.* 205 The skull of a fossil elephant.. commonly believed to be the brain-pan of an enormous giant.

b. *transf.* (Cf. *head, noddle, skull.*)

a **1641** BP. MOUNTAGU *Acts & Mon.* (1642) It is a starveling conceit of Innovating brain-pans.

brainsick ('breɪnsɪk), *a.* [f. BRAIN *sb.* + SICK.]

1. Diseased in the brain or mind; addle-headed, mad, foolish, frantic.

1483 CAXTON *G. de la Tour* xiv. 20 Nor foles that are brayne sik. **1549** LATIMER *Serm. bef. Edw. VI.* (Arb.) 84 What ye brain-sycke fooles..do ye beleue hym? **1648** *Hunting of Fox* 25 Some head-strong brain-sick Sectaries. **1733** SWIFT *Legion Club* Wks. 1755 IV. I. 206 A queer Brain-sick brute, they call a peer. **1848** MACAULAY *Hist. Eng.* I. 591 This man, at once unprincipled and brainsick.

†**b.** as *sb. Obs.*

1606 SYLVESTER *Du Bartas* I. iv. Wks. (Grosart) 150 (D.) Some brainsicks liue there now-a-daies.

2. Of things: Proceeding from a diseased mind.

1571 GOLDING *Calvin on Ps.* viii. 3 With braynsik madnesse. **1790** COWPER *Odyss.* IV. 616 The brainsick fury seiz'd him. **1856** R. VAUGHAN *Mystics* (1860) I. 278 The spasmodic movements of a brainsick disinterestedness.

Hence **brainsickly** *a.* and *adv.*, **brainsickness.**

1605 SHAKS. *Macb.* II. ii. 46 To thinke So braine-sickly of things. **1823** *Blackw. Mag.* XIII. 415, I am not so brain-sickly as to dwell on gloomy reverie. **1541** PAYNELL *Catiline* xxxv. 54 Wherto shuld we reherse the furious brain-sykenes of Cethegus?

brain trust, brains trust. [transf. sense of TRUST *sb.* 7.] **a.** The name (usu. in form *Brain Trust*) given to a group of experts appointed in 1933 to advise the American President F. D. Roosevelt on political and economic matters. **b.** (usu. *brains trust*) A group of persons assembled (orig. in *Broadcasting*) to give their impromptu views on topics of current or general interest. Both forms (in Britain usu. *brains trust*) also used *transf.* of any group of experts.

Quot. 1910 is a chance occurrence of the expression *brain trust*; the main use began in 1933.

1910 in *Amer. Speech* (1957) XXXII. 57 Brain trust. **1929** *Papers Michigan Acad. Sci., Arts & Lett.* X. 281/2 *Brain Trust* (Am.), the General Staff. **1933** *Sun* (Baltimore) 17 Aug. 8/6 The 'brain trust' of the gang chooses a city for the 'operation' located within a hundred miles of a State boundary line. **1933** *Newsweek* 2 Sept. 4/1 The President's Brain Trust, a little band of intellectuals. **1934** H. G. WELLS *Exper. Autobiogr.* II. ix. 791 The new President..was calling these new brains into consultation. Some journalist ..invented the phrase the 'Brains Trust'. *Ibid.* 792 This Brains Trust movement. **1937** *N.Y. Times* 28 Mar. Mag. 4/2 The 'brain trust' of the C.I.O. are men who have read widely, thought deeply on industrial questions, and might be characterized..as 'intellectuals'. **1937** C. ODETS *Golden Boy* I. iii. 45 The people who'll pay to watch a 'brain trust' you could fit in a telephone booth! **1939** *Amer. Speech* XIV. 246 The term *brains trust*..was originally used by James Kieran during the campaign of 1932. He used the plural, *brains.* **1940** *War Illustr.* 5 Jan. 546 'Brains Trust' of the R.A.F. in France. **1941** *New Statesman* 27 Sept. 304/3 A question sent in to the B.B.C. by a schoolboy of eleven was discussed by the Brains Trust on Sunday. **1941** *Manch. Guardian Weekly* 5 Dec. 365/4 In one unit the commanding officer, a captain, and a private form the Brains Trust. **1945** 'R. CROMPTON' *William & Brains Trust* i. 13 It was the time when the Brains Trust movement, so rashly started by the B.B.C., was sweeping England. Every town, every village, every parish, every street had its Brains Trust, at whose meetings earnest seekers after knowledge discussed the scientific, political or economic problems of the day. **1962** *Lancet* 1 Dec. 1180/1 A brains trust discussed practical health education of village parents. **1968** A. HAILEY *Airport* I. viii. 83 There were other sessions, some of them 'brain trust' affairs involving Kennedy aides.

Hence **brain(s) truster**, a member of a brain(s) trust.

1934 *Sun* (Baltimore) 28 Mar. 3/3 The Roosevelt 'brain trusters'. **1953** *Manchester Guardian Weekly* 23 Apr. 2 Foreign Ministers, advisers, and anonymous brain trusters. **1958** *New Statesman* 1 Feb. 127/2 He believes the Brains-trusters really are equipped to pronounce themselves upon, virtually, anything.

'brainwashing. orig. *U.S.* [f. BRAIN *sb.* + WASHING *vbl. sb.* I. *fig.*] The systematic and often forcible elimination from a person's mind of all established ideas, esp. political ones, so that another set of ideas may take their place; this process regarded as the kind of coercive conversion practised by certain totalitarian states on political dissidents. Also *attrib.* and *transf.* Hence, by back-formation, **brainwash** *v. trans.*, to practise brainwashing on; **brainwashed** *ppl. a.*; **brainwasher**, one who practises it.

1950 E. HUNTER in *New Leader* 7 Oct. 7/2 'Brain-reform' is the objective, popularly referred to as 'brain-washing'. **1952** *Times* 26 May 41/1 Ai Tze-chi was Red China's chief indoctrinator or, as he was generally called, Brainwasher No 1. **1953** *Manch. Guardian Weekly* 21 May 15 You refer to brainwashing. You feel..that you have been brow-beaten? **1953** *Sat. Even. Post* 31 Oct. 10/1 The anticommunist soldiers..may be blackmailed or brain-washed or third-degreed. **1955** *Times* 10 June 7/4 Snake-charmers..have so far failed in their attempts to brain-wash the serpents. **1955** *Harper's Mag.* July 16 On this subject—and others—the Texans have brain-washed themselves so thoroughly [etc.]. **1955** *Times* 31 Aug. 8/5 Realistic 'brain-washing' procedures for those who are 'captured'. **1957** D. J. ENRIGHT *Apothecary's Shop* 225 (*title*) The Brain-Washed Muse. Some Second Thoughts on Tradition. **1968** M. WOODHOUSE *Rock Baby* viii. 83 There was something attractive, in an off-beat, screwy sort of way, about the idea of psycho-analysing a brain-washed robot.

brain-'wood. (after 14th c. only *Sc.*) [f. BRAIN *sb.* + WOOD *a.*, OE. and ME. *wód* mad.] Frenzied in brain or mind; mad.

a **1340** HAMPOLE *Pr. Consc.* 6707 For hungre þai sal be als brayne-wode. *c* **1375** ? BARBOUR *St. Alexis* 214 ȝouland as half brawne wod. *c* **1425** WYNTOUN *Cron.* VIII. xiii. 51 He swa mankyd, as brayne-wode Kest fast wyth þe Stwmpe þe Blode In-til Willame Walays face. *a* **1550** *Christis Kirke Gr.* xxii, Quhyn thay had beirit lyk baitit bullis, And branewod brynt in bails.

brainy ('breɪnɪ), *a.* [f. BRAIN *sb.* + -Y¹.] That has plenty of brains; acute, clever.

1845 LEIGH HUNT *Let.* 19 July (1862) II. 104 That was a good, hearty, brainy, valuable bit of existence you gave us the other night. **1874** *Sex & Educat.* 25 Men here are for the most part wiry, sinewy, nervous, and brainy. **1883** D. WHEELER *By-Ways of Lit.* iii. 42 The culture [in monasteries] was of a more brainy sort. **1951** J. CANNAN *And All I Learned* x. 174 All of them had passed except poor old Timothy and she had to confess that he wasn't at all brainy. **1956** M. DICKENS *Angel in Corner* xi. 228 Betty's fiancé was an undersized but brainy boy.

braird (brɛəd), *sb.* Properly *Sc.* (brerd, brird), but now sometimes used by Eng. writers. Also 5-6 **brerd**, 6-8 **breird, brierd**, 8 **breard, brere.** [The same word with BRERD; the OE. *brerd* probably, like the Teut. cognates, had the senses of 'point, spike, blade of grass', as well as that of 'edge', though the former are recorded only for the form *brord.*] The first shoots of grass, corn, or other crops.

c **1450** HENRYSON *Mor. Fab.* 3 The corne abreird. —— 59 Now it is Lent, now it is hie on brierd. **1513** DOUGLAS *Æneis* XII. Prol. 77 The cornis croppis and the beris new brerd. **1721** KELLY *Scottish Prov.* 328 There is no breard like midding breard. *c* **1817** HOGG *Tales & Sk.* V. 11 Hares surprised..among the early braird. **1859** TENNENT *Ceylon* 25 The delicate braird that springs after the surface has been annually burnt.

braird (brɛəd), *v.* [f. prec.] *intr.* Of corn, etc.: To sprout, to appear above the ground.

c **1450** HENRYSON *Fables* 1904 (*Anglia* IX. 337) The wickit thocht begynnis for to breird. **1513** DOUGLAS *Æneis* II. ix [viii]. 60 With schyning skyn new brerd. **1865** *Carter's Gard. & Farmer's Vade-M.* 11. After the seed has brairded, it may be well to cover it by hand-hoeing. **1883** *Trans. Highl. Soc. Agric.* Ser. IV. XV. 38 The potatoes..came up..not quite as straight as a line when brairding. **1884** *Times* 20 June 4 Present sowings [in swedes and turnips] may braird well.

Hence **brairded, brairding, breirding.**

1765 RUTHERFORD *Lett.* I. lxxiii. (JAM.) I find a little breirding of God's seed in this town. **1854** *Phemie Millar* 35 The freshly brairded fields.

brairds, var. of BREARDS, *Sc.*

brais, braiss, obs. form of BRACE.

†**braise**, *v.*¹ *Obs. rare.* [? corruption of BRAY, influenced by BRUISE. Possibly in both quots. the correct reading is *bruysing.*] *trans.* To bruise, to bray. Hence **'braising** *vbl. sb.*

a **1500** *Gold. Litany* in Maskell *Mon. Rit.* (ed. 2) III. 270 The lyftyng vp of thi most holy body on the crosse, and the sore braysyng thereof. **1557** *Richmond. Wills* (1853) 100 Ij braysenge morters with ij pestles xxˢ.

braise (breɪz), *v.*² Also **braize, braze.** [a. Fr. *braiser*, f. *braise*, hot charcoal.] To cook *à la braise*; i.e. to stew in a tightly-closed pan (properly with a charcoal fire above and below), the meat being surrounded with slices of bacon, herbs, etc.

1797 *Lond. Art Cookery* 149 Serve this ragoo under two ducks, cut into quarters, and brazed in a well seasoned braze. **1846** *French Domest. Cookery* 41 *Braise*: to stew meat tender with fat bacon.

Hence **braise** *sb.*, braised meat, or the preparation for braising with. Also **braised** *ppl. a.*, **'braiser** *sb.* [partly ad. F. *braisière*], **'braising** *vbl. sb.* used *attrib.* in ***braising-kettle, -pan.***

1769 MRS. RAFFALD *Eng. Housekpr.* (1778) 93 Add some of the braize liquor (if any left). **1797** *Lond. Art Cookery* 148 Stew them [chickens' feet] in a braze. *Ibid.* 149 [see vb.] **1825** *French Domest. Cookery* 376 To dress a dish à la braise you must have a braising-pan. *a* **1880** MRS. HENDERSON in Webster *Supp.* s.v., A braising kettle has a deep cover which holds coals; consequently the cooking is done from above, as well as below.

†**brait.** [? mistake for BORT.] 'A name given by jewellers to the rough diamond.'

1706 in PHILLIPS. **1721-1790** in BAILEY; and in mod. Dicts.

braith, -ful, -ly, Sc. forms of BRATH, etc.

braize, variant of BREEZE *sb.*³

brak (brak, bræk), *a.* and *sb. S. Afr.* Also (rarely) **brack.** [Afrikaans, = brackish.] **A.** *adj.* Brackish; alkaline. **B.** *sb.* Brackishness; alkalinity; alkaline soil. Cf. BRACK *a.* and *sb.*⁶

1793 tr. *Thunberg's Trav.* II. xii, *Brak-water* is water stagnating in valleys and low places; it contains a kind of brine, and tastes more or less saltish. **1827** G. THOMPSON *Trav. & Adv. S. Afr.* I. II. iii. 447 We procured each of us a draught of very brack water. **1890** A. MARTIN *Home Life Ostrich Farm* v. 82 The ground must be 'brack', a peculiar kind of soil which, though loose and friable, is not porous. This brack is often used to cover the flat roofs of the houses. *Ibid.* 94 It..gave me the first experience of a big rain—and of a *brack* roof. **1947** *Cape Times* 13 Mar. 6/5 The reckless over-watering of some irrigated lands, leading to the development of brak. **1955** L. G. GREEN *Karoo* xi. 133 The *gannabos*..flourishes in the *brak* soil. **1959** *Cape Argus* 21 Nov. 1/3 Some cattle have died from drinking the brak water which always follows after protracted droughts.

C. *Comb.* **brakbush**, name of various salt-loving plants, esp. species of *Atriplex, Salicornia* and *Salsola.*

[**1824** BURCHELL *Trav.* II. i. 21 A shrubby species of *Atriplex*, probably the *A. candicans.* Yet the name of *Brak-boschjes* does not exclusively belong to this plant.] **1844** J. BACKHOUSE *Narr. Visit S. Afr.* 502 The best places for cattle in these deserts are those which are saline, and afford the scrubby *Atriplex*... These are termed 'brak-places' and such shrubs are called 'Brak-bushes'. **1863** J. S. DOBIE *S. Afr. Jrnl.* 1 Sept. (1945) 122 He picked up some seed of brackbush (considered good for sheep).

brak, obs. pa. t. of BREAK; obs. f. BRACK, BRAKE.

brakan, -en, obs. ff. BRACKEN.

brake (breɪk), *sb.*¹ [ME. *brake*, not found in northern writers, said by Turner (1562) to be the equivalent of the northern *braken*: see BRACKEN. It was possibly a shortened form: perh. due to *braken* being assumed by southern speakers to be a plural: cf. *chick, chicken*, also BRACK *sb.*⁴ But it may also possibly be a parallel form from the same root. BRAKE *sb.*² appears too late for us to assume that this word could in any way be derived from it; though in recent use

they are probably often assumed to be the same word, as if the 'brake' were a plant that grows in 'brakes' or vice versa.]

1. Fern, bracken.

*c*1325 W. DE BIBLESW. in Wright *Voc.* 156 *Feugere*, a brake. *c*1440 *Promp. Parv.* 47 Brake, herbe or ferme. 1562 TURNER *Herbal* II. A ij b, *Filix femina*..is the commen ferne or brake whiche the Norther men call a braken. 1669 W. SIMPSON *Hydrol. Chym.* 189 Those who burn brakes for their ashes. 1768 TUCKER *Lt. Nat.* II. 685 Self-conceit grows..out of ignorance, as heath and brakes do from barren sands. 1842 TENNYSON *Day Dr., Sleep Pal.* vi, A wall of green Close-matted, bur and brake and briar. 1862 ANSTED *Channel Isl.* II. viii. (ed. 2) 181 The common brake (*pteris aquilina*).

2. *Comb.* and *Attrib.*, as **brake-bush**, **-fern**, **-root**; **brake of the wall**, the common polypody.

*c*1440 *Promp. Parv.* 47 Brakebushe or fernebrake, *filicetum.* 1561 HOLLYBUSH *Hom. Apoth.* 39a, Take..sixe unces of the rotes of Brak of the wal or Polipody. 1626 BACON *Sylva* §83 The making of Glass, of a certain Sand and Brake-Roots.

brake (breɪk), *sb.*[2] Also 7 bracke, 8–9 break(e. [cf. MLG. *brake*, connected with *breken* to BREAK, and originally meaning tree-stumps or broken branches, but also used (esp. in the phrase *busk unde brake*, bush and brake) in the exact sense of the Eng. word. See Schiller-Lübben. The historical relation of the Eng. to the LG. word is unknown.]

A clump of bushes, brushwood, or briers; a thicket. Also *attrib.*, as in *brake-axe*.

*c*1440 [see BRAKE[1] 2]. Fernebrake, *filicetum.* 1563 *Mirr. Mag., Jane Shore* xviii, What scratting bryers do growe upon such brakes. 1590 R. PAYNE *Descr. Irel.* (1841) 6 A simple workeman with a Brake axe will cleaue a greate Oke. 1635 N. CARPENTER *Geog. Del.* II. xvi. 282 Their Houses were caues, their pallaces brackes or thickots. 1667 MILTON *P.L.* IV. 175 So thick entwin'd, As one continu'd brake, the undergrowth Of shrubs. 1772–84 COOK *Voy.* (1790) IV. 1290 Rendered almost impassable..by breaks of fern, shrubs, and fallen trees. 1821 SHELLEY *Adonais* xviii, The amorous birds now pair in every brake. 1850 MRS. STOWE *Uncle Tom* xiv. 121 He saw again the cane brakes and cypresses of gliding plantations.

brake (breɪk), *sb.*[3] Also 5 braoke, brakene (sense 3), 6 braake, 8 *Sc.* braik (sense 2), 9 break. [Identical with MLG. *brake*, or ODu. *braeke*, mod.Du. *braak* a flax-brake (whence F. *braquer* to brake flax), f. Du. *breken* to BREAK. The resemblance of the sb. to the cognate Eng. verb apparently gave rise to the extension of sense by which *brake* became a generic name of implements used for breaking or crushing. The form *brakene* in Promp. Parv. may possibly represent the pl. of the MLG. or Du. word.]

1. A toothed instrument for braking flax or hemp.

*c*1450 in Wr.-Wülcker *Voc.* 608 *Rupa*, a braoke. *Ibid.* 696 *Hec rupa*, a brake. 1451 *Test. Ebor.* III. 119, j brake ijd. 1552 HULOET, Brake for flaxe or hempe. 1611 COTGR., *Brioche*, a brake for hempe. 1615 MARKHAM *Eng. Housw.* (1660) 132 You may then at your pleasure break it [flax]..in a brake of wood. 1704 *Dict. Rust. et Urb.*, *Brake* or Flax-Blake; is two pieces of timber, with teeth. 1858 CARPENTER *Veg. Phys.* §516 A very simple machine is used for this purpose, termed a break. 1869 SPON *Dict. Engineering* I. 629 Fig. 1285 shows [a] Hemp and Flax Brake.

2. A baker's kneading-machine. Hence **brakesman, break(s)man**, a man who operates a baker's kneading-machine; **brake-** (or **break-**) **staff** (see quots.).

*c*1440 *Promp. Parv.* 46 Bray or brakene, baxteris instrument, *pinsa.* 1567 THOMAS *Ital. Gram.*, *Macinella*, a braake to knede dowe withall, or to brake liue hempe. 1580 BARET *Alv.* B 1108 A Brake, *frangibulum*, Plin. *mactra.* 1617 MARKHAM *Caval.* VI. 15 You shall kneade..first with handes ..lastly with the brake. 1836 P. BARLOW in *Encycl. Metrop.* (1845) VIII. 801/2 [The dough] is deposited on a strong wooden platform or table, called a *break*, to be operated upon by the breaksman, who seizes a strong lever called a *break-staff*, with which he presses down the dough. 1845 DODD *Brit. Manuf.* V. 23 Ships' biscuits..made by hand... The dough was..taken from the trough and put on a wooden platform called the break. On this platform worked a roller, called the break-staff... One end..was loosely attached by a kind of staple to the wall, and the breakman, riding or sitting on the other end, worked the roller to and fro over the dough, by an uncouth jumping or shuffling movement. 1921 *Dict. Occup. Terms* (1927) §433 *Brake operator, brakesman, breaksman*,..is one of two men who operate brake machine for compressing, with rollers, kneaded paste into sheets, preparatory to biscuit stamping.

3. In *Brewing* and similar processes: A wooden mill to crush green fruits, hops, etc.

1534 *Eng. Ch. Furniture* (1866) 187 A brake to make verjoyce with. 1571 *Wills & Inv. N.C.* I. (1835) 360, j brake wth the tonge & pynn viij[d]. 1616 SURFL. & MARKH. *Countr. Farm* 425 You shall put them [hops] into a..wooden Brake, and there crush, grind, or bruise them.

4. A heavy harrow for crushing clods. Also called *brake-harrow*.

1785 BURNS *2nd Ep. Lapraik* 2 An' pownies reek in pleugh or braik. 1844 STEPHENS *Bk. of Farm* II. 532 The brake-harrow is only an enlargement of the common implement.. Brakes are made of various forms.

5. An instrument resembling a pair of scissors set wide open, for peeling the bark from willows for basket-making.

1824 *Mech. Mag.* II. 223 My new invented brake for taking the bark off willows. 1880 JEFFERIES *Hodge & M.* II. 89 The willows are carried to the brakes.

brake (breɪk), *sb.*[4] [Perhaps a. OF. *brac*, oblique case of *bras* an arm; cf. F. *braquer le timon* to turn the rudder, *braquer un canon* to point a cannon.]

1. A lever or handle for working a machine.

†**a.** The winch of a crossbow (only in phrase *bows of brake*); hence a crossbow, ballista, or similar engine. *Obs.* exc. *Hist.*

*c*1380 *Sir Ferumb.* 3276 And wyþ boȝes eke of brake for to schute þykke. 1393 LANGL. *P. Pl.* C. XXI. 293 Setteþ bowes of brake and brasene gonnes. *c*1440 *Partonope* 1149 The bowes of brake are bent in hast. 1552 HULOET, Brake, or crosbowe, *ballista.* 1600 HOLLAND *Livy* XXI. xi. 400g, With ordinance of quarell shot, brakes, and other artillerie. 1600 FAIRFAX *Tasso* XVIII. xliii. 324 Not rammes, not mightie brakes, not slings alone. 1840 BROWNING *Sordello* IV. 372 Arbalist, catapult, brake, mangonel.

b. The handle of a pump.

1626 CAPT. SMITH *Accid. Yng. Seamen* 12 The pumpes brake. 1627 —— *Seaman's Gram.* ii. 8 The handle we call the brake. 1762–9 FALCONER *Shipwr.* II. 466 At either pump they ply the clanking brake. 1831 LARDNER *Pneumat.* vi. 314 The piston is worked..in common pumps by a lever, called the brake.

c. A lever forming part of the apparatus for boring coal.

1851 *Coal-tr. Terms Northumbld. & Durh.* 10 A Brake.. consists of a lever..12 feet long; the fulcrum..2 feet from the end above the bore-hole. 1855 G. GREENWELL *Mining Eng.* 109 A brake is a simple lever..having an iron crook attached from which the [boring] rods are suspended by a piece of rope.

2. *Comb.*, as **brake-pump**, a pump worked by a brake; **brake-sieve** (*Mining*), a rectangular sieve worked by a lever or brake.

1881 *Daily Tel.* 28 Jan., A couple of men..laid hold of the brake pump. 1881 RAYMOND *Mining Gloss.*, *Brake-sieve*, a jigger, operated by a hand-lever.

†**brake**, *sb.*[5] *Obs.* Also 5 breake. [Of uncertain origin: possibly identical with the prec. sb. (cf. F. *braquer un chariot* 'to turn, set, or bend a chariot on the right or left hand' Cotgr.); more probably a. ODu. *braeke* (see BRAKE *sb.*[3]), occurring in the sense of a nose-ring for a draught ox; or extended use of BRAKE *sb.*[3], due to influence of the verb BREAK (a horse).]

A bridle or curb. (Said in Chambers *Cycl. Supp.* 1753 to be a synonym of BARNACLE[1].) *Obs.*

1430 LYDG. *Chron. Troy* I. v, Both bridell, breake & reyne. 1552 HULOET, Brake, or sharpe snaffle for a horse. 1557 Tottell's *Misc.* (Arb.) 187 The brake within the riders hande, Doth strayne the horse. 1563–87 FOXE *A. & M.* III. 819 Many..lost their lives to shake off this most rough brake. 1587 TURBERV. *Trag. T.* (1837) 94 Hardir brakes doe breake the mouth too much. 1753 CHAMBERS *Cycl. Supp.*

brake, *sb.*[6] [Origin, possible connexion with prec., and sequence of senses uncertain.]

†**1.** A cage of iron or wooden bars; a trap; *fig.* a snare, difficulty, dilemma. *Obs.*

*a*1529 SKELTON *Elynour Rum.* 325 It was a stale to take The devyl in a brake. 1548 UDALL, etc. *Erasm. Par. Luke* Pref. 6b, So should I in this matier stand in a streight brake. 1553 BRENDE *Q. Curtius* I. 10 Because of hys fercenes, kept him [Bucephalus] within a brake of iron barres. 1572 FORREST *Theoph.* 1022 No more hy myndede to come in his [the Devil's] brake. 1625 BURGES *Pers. Tithes* 79 He.. sought to wind himselfe out of the brakes of Tithes due by Diuine Right. 1640 SHIRLEY *Opportunity* (N.) He is fallen into some brake, some wench has tied him by the legs.

2. A framework intended to hold anything steady; a frame in which a horse's foot is placed when being shod; also in *Ship-building* (see quot.).

1609 C. BUTLER *Fem. Mon.* v. (1623) Kij, Then make a Brake behind the stoole of foure stakes, 2 two foot, and 2 foure feet long. 1869 SIR E. REED *Shipbuild.* xx. 436 The plate is heated and bent to the form of the bed or brake.

†**b.** fig. *to set one's face in a brake*: to assume an immovable expression of countenance. *Obs.*

1607 CHAPMAN *Bussy D'Amb.* Plays 1873 II. 8 Or (like a Strumpet) learne to set my lookes In an eternal Brake. 1608 —— *Byrons Trag.* ibid. II. 280 See in how graue a Brake he sets his vizard. 1609 B. JONSON *Sil. Wom.* IV. vi. (1616) 583 Some..that haue their faces set in a brake!

†**3.** An instrument of torture; a rack. *Obs.* exc. *Hist.* [Perh. this belongs rather to BRAKE *sb.*[3]]

1530 PALSGR. 463/1, I brake on a brake, or payne banke. 1539 T. CROMWELL in *St. Papers Hen. VIII.* I. 602, I am advised..to go the Toure, and see hym sett in the brakes. 1642 FULLER *Holy & Prof. St.* IV. xiii. 301 A daughter of the Duke of Exeter invented a brake or cruel rack. 1720 *Stow's Surv.* (ed. Strype 1754) I. I. xiv. 66/2 The Brake or rack, commonly called the Duke of Exeter's daughter because he was the deviser of that torture. 1855 BROWNING *Ch. Roland* xxiv, That wheel, Or brake..that harrow fit to reel Men's bodies out like silk?

†**4.** A turner's lathe. [Perh. a different word.]

*c*1570 THYNNE *Pride & Lowl.* (1841) 50 In..doublet leveled by lyne, Poynted and bottoned as in a brake. 1609 HOLLAND *Amm. Marcel.* XXXIII. vi. 228 As if the whole space were wrought round by a Turners brake.

brake (breɪk), *sb.*[7] Also break. [Etymology uncertain; prob. an application of the sense of 'lever' (BRAKE *sb.*[4]), or perh. of that of 'curb' (BRAKE *sb.*[5]); since F. *frein*, It. *freno*, literally 'bridle', are used in this sense. This being so, the spelling *break* would be due to 'popular etymology', because it 'breaks' the motion.]

1. An apparatus for retarding the motion of a wheel by means of pressure applied to the circumference; usually consisting of a wooden block or an iron or steel band, and of a lever for pressing it against the tire. Also *fig.* of any retarding agency.

α. 1772–82 W. BAILEY *Machines Soc. Arts* I. 149 Z, Which occasionally draws down the brake on the periphery of the walking wheel. 1792 *Trans. Soc. Arts* X. 233 The means will appear to be the gripe or brake at the top. 1825 N. WOOD *Railroads* 78 The brake or lever, which is called a 'convoy'. 1851 *Coal-tr. Terms Northumbld. & Durh.* 10 *Brake*..a band of iron caused by a lever to press upon a..wheel. 1863 TYNDALL *Heat* i. 9 The brake is applied, and smoke and sparks issue from the wheel. 1875 WHITNEY *Life Lang.* viii. 149 A powerful brake to check his arbitrary action.

β. 1838 *Public Wks. Gt. Brit.* 52 That every carriage should be provided with a break. 1839 S. C. BREES *Railw. Pract.* Gloss. 287 *Break* or *Convoy* to Railway Carriages. a hand lever worked by the breaksman. 1862 *Macm. Mag.* Oct. 455 This loom is fitted with Sellers' 'break' for stopping the loom. 1870 HUXLEY *Lay Serm.* xi. (1874) 246 To act as a sort of break.

2. Short for 'brake-van'.

1885 *Daily News* 5 Feb. 6/3 One of the suspected men.. travelled in the guard's brake.

3. *Comb.* and *Attrib.*, as **brake-apparatus**, **-band**, **-bar**, **-beam**, **-block**, **-lever**, **-pedal**, **-power**, **-rod**, **-shoe** (see quots.); also **brake-compartment**, **brake-van**, or simply *brake*, the compartment or the carriage in a train which contains the brake apparatus; **brake-cylinder** (see *brake-pipe*); **brake-drum**, a cylinder attached to a wheel or hub, upon which the brake shoe presses; **brake fluid**, specially formulated liquid for use in hydraulic brakes; **brake-gear**, the whole braking apparatus of a motor-car or train; **brake-handle**, a hand lever controlling a brake, taking the place of the usual brake-wheel; **brake-horse-power** (see HORSEPOWER); **brake lining**, a strip of fabric attached to the face of a brake-shoe to increase friction and provide a renewable surface; **brake mean effective pressure** (see quot.); **brake parachute** *Aeronaut.*, a parachute attached to the tail of an aeroplane and opened to serve as a brake; **brake-pipe**, the pipe of an automatic air-brake, which conveys compressed air to the cylinders operating the brakes of a railway train; **brake-strap**, a strap which surrounds the pulley of a brake worked by friction; **brake-wheel**, the wheel by which the brakes are worked.

1885 *Daily News* 5 Feb. 6/3 The spare *brake apparatus.. in..the last carriage but one..He saw the man get out of the *break-compartment. *a*1877 KNIGHT *Dict. Mech.* I. 356/2 The air-pipe under each car makes connection by a branch with..a..*brake-cylinder. 1896 *Cosmopolitan* XX. 420/1 A *brake-drum of peculiar construction placed under the seat. 1908 *Westm. Gaz.* 4 June 4/2 Inside the brake-drum..are four stout spiral springs. 1931 R. F. KUNS *Automotive Service* iii. 200 This cylinder is filled with fluid, usually termed the *brake fluid, composed of alcohol and glycerin or similar nonfreeze liquids. 1959 *Motor Man.* (ed. 36) viii. 216 Any topping-up must be done only with genuine hydraulic brake fluid. 1984 B. FRANCIS *AA Car Duffer's Guide* 104 The piston seal is leaking and brake fluid has got on the linings. 1908 *Daily Chron.* 2 Jan. 6/4 It was far more important for a man to look to his *brake gear than to his speed gear. 1902 *Ibid.* 16 July 8/4 The woman climbed out at the back, using the *brake-handle as a step. 1927 *Brake horsepower [see *break mean effective pressure* below]. 1903 *Daily Chron.* 27 Jan. 7/5 *Brake-levers shall be fitted..on both sides of wagons. 1921 *Daily Colonist* (Victoria, B.C.) 6 Apr. 6/1 (Advt.), We do more than tell you that Raybestos is good *Brake Lining. 1927 *Daily Tel.* 11 May 18/6 (Advt.), The well-known Top Dog brake-lining. 1962 *Which?* (Car Suppl.) Oct. 134/1 The figures for brake lining life..are calculated. 1927 V. W. PAGÉ *Mod. Aircraft* (1928) vii. 302 *Brake mean effective pressure—The net unit pressure which, if applied during the power strokes to the pistons of an engine having no mechanical losses, would produce the given brake horsepower at the stated speed. 1942 H. S. ZIM *Parachutes* 251/1 (*index*) *Brake parachute. 1903 R. J. MECREDY *Dict. Motoring* 33 The motion of the *brake pedal causes mechanism..to close the two halves inward and grip the brake drum. 1906 D. LEECHMAN *Autocar Handbk.* xv. 117 In many cars the brake pedal is coupled up to the clutch, so that applying the brake automatically disengages the motor from the driving gear. 1886 *Encycl. Brit.* XX. 249/1 The brake can be at once released by restoring the pressure in the *brake-pipe. 1878 F. WILLIAMS *Midl. Railw.* 557 Lest ..there should be any deficiency in the *brake power. 1874 KNIGHT *Amer. Mech. Dict.* I. 357 *Brake-shoe, that part of a brake which is brought in contact with the object whose motion is to be restrained. 1835 URE *Philos. Manuf.* 53 The frame..acts, of course, upon the slide-pieces..which hold the *brake-strap. 1897 *Outing* (U.S.) June 262/1 Right thumb on spool of reel, left thumb in leather brake-strap. 1885 *Manch. Exam.* 15 May 5/7 An invention for coupling and uncoupling railway rolling stock direct from the engine or *brake-van. 1864 *Times* 30 Dec. He was always in the break-van where the line was on an incline. 1873 B. STEWART *Conserv. Force* ii. §48 On a dark night sparks are seen to issue from the *break-wheel.

brake, variant of BRACK, small particle.

1586 J. HOOKER *Girald. Irel.* in *Holinshed* II. 87/2 To the last brake of sinister surmises.

brake, var. of BREAK, a kind of carriage.

† **brake**, a. Obs. rare. [? f. BREAK v.] ? Fragile.
1616 SURFL. & MARKH. Countr. Farm 447 Those of Glasse must not be of brake mettall, but of Crystall earth well armed.

brake (breɪk), v.[1] Also 7 break, 9 Sc. brack (sense 3). [f. BRAKE sb.[3]]
1. trans. To beat and crush flax, hemp, etc.
1398 [see below]. **1523** FITZHERB. Husb. §42 But howe it [flax] shulde be sowen..dryed, beaten, braked. **1611** COTGR., Brayer du lin, to brake, or dresse flax. **1727** BRADLEY Fam. Dict. s.v. Drying, Hemp or Flax..may be spread upon a Kiln..in order to dry it upon the same, and then to brake it.
2. To break (clods) with a harrow.
1800 J. HEADRICK Com. Board Agric. II. 260 The land [should be] again cross-ploughed..and afterwards braked.
3. To knead (dough).
1832-53 Whistle-binkie in Sc. Songs Ser. III. 71 My bannock to brack, an' my errand to rin.
Hence **braked** ppl. a., **'braking** vbl. sb.
1398 TREVISA Barth. De P.R. xvii. clx. (1495) 708 Wyth moche brakyng, heckelynge and robbyng. **1649** BLITHE Eng. Improv. Impr. (1652) 252 Instead of braking..there they altogether pill it. **1653** WALTON Angler 107 The body is.. bound with black braked-hemp.

brake, v.[2] Obs. [f. BRAKE sb.[6] 3] To torture on the 'brake' or rack; to rack.
1530 PALSGR. 463 The false murdrer was braked thrise or ever he would confesse the trouthe.

† **brake**, v.[3] Obs. rare. [Cf. BRACK sb.[5]: perhaps ad. early It. bracare, or braccare: Florio (1611) has 'Braccare, to bracke or mount ordinance'; and 'Bracare, to breech; also to bind about with iron plates; also to stocke a piece'.]
trans. To mount (cannon); cf. BRACK sb.[5]
1579 FENTON Guicciard. I. 35 Cannons..were braked and planted with an incredible diligence. Ibid. IV. 151 After he had braked his artillerie. Ibid. (1618) 363 Against the which place, they within the towne..braked a great peece.

brake, v.[4] [f. BRAKE sb.[4]] intr. To attend to a winding engine. Hence **'braking** vbl. sb.
1857 SMILES Stephenson iii. 17 Paying some attention to the art of brakeing. **1862** —— Engineers III. 32 Young Stephenson couldn't brake, and..never would learn to brake, he was so clumsy.

brake (breɪk), v.[5] [f. BRAKE sb.[7]] **1.** trans. To apply a brake to (a wheel); also transf.
1868 Daily News 3 Sept., The kicked-off waggons were braked. **1881** PALGRAVE Visions of Eng. 23 Earth her pace.. delays, Braked by the tides.
2. intr. To be checked by a brake. Also with up.
1891 E. S. ELLIS Check 2134 ii. 13 He felt the train braking up for the Station. **1937** J. SQUIRE Honeysuckle & Bee 149 A car suddenly braked to a standstill outside the door.

† **brake**, v.[6] Obs. Also Sc. braik. [perh. repr. an unrecorded OE. *bracian, f. bræc, which occurs in the sense of 'phlegm, mucus, saliva'; cf. ODu. braeken, MLG. and mod.Du. braken to vomit; allied to BREAK (cf. Ger. sich brechen).]
trans. and intr. To spue, vomit.
c**1325** E.E. Allit. P. C. 340 And þer he brakez up þe buyrne [Jonah], as bede hym oure lorde. **1388** WYCLIF Prov. xxiii. 8 Thou schalt brake out [1382 spewen out] the metis, whiche thou hast ete. **1393** LANGL. P. Pl. C. VII. 431 And as an hounde þat et gras, so gan ich to brake. c**1440** Promp. Parv. 47 Brakyn, or castyn or spewe, vomo. **1535** LYNDESAY Satyre 624, I lay braikand lyk a brok. Ibid. 4357.
¶ Cf. to break wind: see BREAK v. 47.
Hence **'braking**, vbl. sb.
1398 TREVISA Barth. De P.R. xvii. cvi. (1495) 669 Mynte of gardens abateth wyth vynegre brakynge and castyng that comyth of feblynes of the vertue retentyf. c**1440** Promp. Parv. 47 Brakynge or parbrakynge, vomitus. **1768** Ross Helenore 56 (JAM.) That gut and ga' she keest with braking strange.

brake (breɪk), arch. pa. t. of BREAK.

brakeage, breakage ('breɪkɪdʒ). [f. BRAKE sb.[7] + -AGE.] The action of a brake in stopping a train, etc. Also attrib.
1864 Daily Tel. 6 Aug., If they thought Inspector Darby had been the cause of want of breakage by not seeing that the train had its proper number of guards. **1869** Eng. Mech. 24 Dec. 363/3 The breakage power of the tender is not sufficient.

brakeless ('breɪklɪs), a. [f. BRAKE sb.[7] + -LESS.] Not provided with a brake.
1880 Daily Tel. 8 Oct., Disasters have befallen brakeless trains. **1886** Century Mag. Apr. 855/1 Here we were..in a lonely mountain road..with a brakeless machine.

braken, variant form of BRACKEN, fern.

brakesman ('breɪksmən). Also **brakeman, breaksman**. [In sense 1, f. BRAKE sb.[4] + MAN; in sense 2, referred to BRAKE sb.[7]; for the form cf. craftsman, marksman, sportsman.]
1. In Coal-mining: see quot.
1851 Coal-tr. Terms Northumbld. & Durh. 10 Brakesman, the engineman who attends to the winding machine. **1866** JEVONS Coal Quest. (ed. 2) 258 George Stephenson was brakesman to the fixed engine.

2. The man in charge of the brake-apparatus of a railway train.
1833 Amer. Railroad Jrnl. II. 738/1 Two brakemen $450.00. **1838** Civil Engineer & Architect's Jrnl. I. 388/1 The engine was thrown off the line..and the 'breakman' so dreadfully injured that his life is despaired of. **1861** OLMSTED Cotton Kingd. I. 161 A brakeman told me this delay was not very unusual. **1865** Morn. Star 1 Feb., At the time of the accident he had been employed as a breaksman about three weeks. **1883** Harper's Mag. Jan. 212/2 The brakeman bawled out, 'Tannery Town!' **1921** Daily Colonist (Victoria, B.C.) 22 Mar. 1/5 Mr. Murdock asserted that $5.12 was not too much for a railway brakeman for an eight-hour day or a run of 100 miles. **1967** Boston Herald 1 Apr. 1/3 Railroad conductors and brakemen were barred Friday from proceeding with a nationwide railroad strike.

braket, variant of BRAGGET.

braking ('breɪkɪŋ), vbl. sb. [f. BRAKE v.[5] + -ING[1].] The action of applying a brake (to a wheel); also attrib., as **braking distance** (see quot. 1950).
1904 Daily Chron. 15 June 6/7 A clever braking arrangement secures a representation of the difficulites encountered in running on the metals. **1905** Ibid. 13 Feb. 3/7 Frictional braking is jarring, uncertain, difficult of gradual application, and most destructive to the parts concerned. **1909** Westm. Gaz. 16 Sept. 5/1 Fixed to these chains is a braking band. **1950** U.S. Bur. Publ. Roads Highway Capacity Manual 18/1 Braking distance, the total distance traversed by a vehicle while it is being brought to rest, measured from the position of the vehicle at the instant the brake shoe touches the brake drum. **1964** Times 11 Feb. 11/7 Drivers moving at speeds above their vision-and-braking distances.

brakkener, variant of BRACKENER. Obs.

braky ('breɪkɪ), a. [f. BRAKE sb.[1] or [2] + -Y. The sense is not very distinctly brought out by writers.] Overgrown with brushwood or fern.
1636 B. JONSON Discov., Redeem arts from their rough and brakey seats, where they lay hid. **1775** ADAIR Amer. Ind. 7 To secure them from the brambles and braky thickets. **1790** A. WILSON Sheph. Dream Poet. Wks. 11 High on the summit's brow, or braky glen..they fed. **1855** SINGLETON Virgil I. 8 Far hanging from the braky cliff.

braky, var. of BRACKY a.

† **brald**, pa. pple. Sc. Obs. rare-[1]. [cf. Du. brallen to adorn.] Dressed, decked, arrayed.
c**1571** SIR R. MAITLAND Solace in Age, The fairast wenche in all this toun..in hir best goun, Rycht braivlie brald.

brall(e, -ar, -er, -ing: see BRAWL, etc.

Brama, an(e, obs. f. BRAHMA, BRAHMIN.

Bramah (properly 'brɑːmə, often 'brɑːmɑː). Attrib. or syntactical use of the name of Joseph Bramah (1749-1814), designating machines, etc. invented by him, as **Bramah-key** (also short **Bramah**) **-lock, -pen; Bramah's press**, a hydraulic machine constructed to produce enormous pressure.
1836 DICKENS Sk. Boz ii. (1850) 166 Testing the influence of their patent Bramahs on the street-door locks to which they belonged. **1875** URE Dict. Arts III. 140 The Bramah lock has been long celebrated. **1846** G. WRIGHT Cream Sci. Knowl. 55 Bramah's press..is on the principle of the hydrostatic bellows.

Bramantesque (brɑːmənˈtɛsk), a. [ad. It. Bramantesco, f. the name of Bramante d'Urbino (1444-1514), a celebrated Italian architect.] Designating the style of architecture now known as Renaissance.
1883 C. C. PERKINS Handbk. Ital. Sculp. 182 note, The artist who introduced Renaissance architecture, then called Bramantesque, into Lombardy. **1908** E. WHARTON Hermit 162 The Library cupola assumed a Bramantesque grace.

'bramantip. Logic. A mnemonic word, representing the first mood of the fourth figure of syllogisms, in which the two premisses are universal affirmatives, and the conclusion a particular affirmative.
1870 BOWEN Logic vii. 200.

Bramathere (ˈbrɑːməθɪə(r)). [f. Brama = BRAHMA + Gr. θηρίον wild animal.] A genus of fossil animals, remains of which are found in India.
1879 LE CONTE Elem. Geol. 499 The Sivathere..seems to have combined the characters of a Ruminant and a Pachyderm. The Bramathere was a similar animal.

brambel, obs. form of BRAMBLE.

† **'bramberry**. Obs. or dial. [f. BRAME[2] + BERRY sb.[1]; cf. OHG. brâmberi, MHG. brâmber, mod.G. brombeere blackberry: see next.] The brambleberry or blackberry.
1599 A. M. Gabelhouer's Bk. Physic 166/2 Take the rootes of Bramberryes..& wash them in water. **1864** Yorksh. Provinc. (Kirkby), I have sold a good few Bramberries.

bramble[1] ('bræmb(ə)l). Forms: 1 brémel, brǽmel, brǽmbel, 1-4 brembel, 2 brimbel, 3 brimbyl, 4 brembil, -bul, brimbil, 5 bremmyll, brymbyl(l, brymmeylle, 5-6 brymble, 5-9 bremble

(in 9 dial.), 6 brambel, brombille, brymmil, 6-bramble. [OE. brembel, brǽmbel, later form (with euphonic b, and consequent shortening of vowel) of brémel, brǽmel, masc.:—OTeut. type brǽmilo-z, dim. of the word, of which the simplest forms are OE. bróm BROOM:—WGer. *brǽm:—OTeut. *brǽmo-z, and WGer. *brâma 'thorny shrub' (OHG. brâma, MDu. brame, Du. braam, MLG. braam):—OTeut. brǽmâ- str. fem. Cf. mod.G. brombeere brambleberry, blackberry. See also BROOM.]
1. A rough prickly shrub; spec. the blackberry-bush (Rubus fruticosus).
c**1000** ÆLFRIC Gen. iii. 18 Ðornas and bremelas heo asprit ðe. c**1000** Sax. Leechd. I. 192 Genim þas wyrte þe man erusti, & oðrum naman bremel [v.r. brǽmbel] nemneð. Ibid. II. 290 Wiþ utwærce brembel þe sien beзen endas on eorþan. c**1175** Cott. Hom. 223 Se eorðe..sylðe þornes and brembles. a**1300** Cursor M. 924 Brembel [v.r. brimbyl] and thorn it sal te yeild. **1382** WYCLIF Job xxxi. 40 For whete be sprunge to me a brimbil. **1481** CAXTON Reynard (Arb.) 95 Tho cam we in a felde ful of brome and brembles. **1513** DOUGLAS Æneis III. ix. 110 My wrechit fuid wes berreis of the brymmill. **1562** TURNER Herbal II. U iv b, The bramble bindeth, drieth and dieth heyre. **1697** DRYDEN Virg. Georg. III. 678 Their defenceless Limbs the Brambles tear. **1751** JOHNSON Rambl. No. 161 ⁋1 Tully sought amidst bushes and brambles the tomb of Archimedes. **1861** DELAMER Fl. Gard. 111 There is a double white-flowered variety of the common Bramble.
fig. **1644** MILTON Educ. (1738) 136 That asinine feast of sow-thistles & brambles which is commonly set before them. **1779** JOHNSON L.P., Dryden (1816) 351 The roses had not yet been plucked from the bramble.
2. Comb. and Attrib., as **bramble-brake, -brier, -bud, -bush, -leaf, -thread, -wood**; also **bramble-bond**, a bramble-shoot used to bind straw in thatching, etc.; **bramble-brand**, a parasitic fungus (Aregma rubi) which appears on the bramble; **bramble-cure**, a superstitious practice formerly employed in country districts for the cure of disease (cf. bramble-loop); **bramble-flower**, the flower or blossom of a bramble; also the Dog-rose (Rosa canina); **bramble-loop**, the loop formed by a bramble-shoot bent round so as to root itself into the ground again; **bramble-rose**, the white trailing dog-rose. Also BRAMBLE-BERRY.
1854 J. HOGG Microsc. II. i. (1867) 294 *Bramble Brand, hypogenous with a dull red stain on the upper surface. c**1000** Ags. Voc. in Wr.-Wülcker Voc. 269 Tribulus, *brǽmbelbrǽr. **1579** LANGHAM Gard. Health (1633) 87 Bramble breer, or Blackberry. **1579** SPENSER Sheph. Cal. June 7 The *Bramble bush, where Byrds..their tunes attemper. **1846** SOWERBY Brit. Bot. (1864) III. 163 An incautious approach to a *Bramble-bush. **1866** Treas. Bot. II. 996/1 In Cornwall the *bramble-cure is only employed for boils. **1591** SPENSER Virgil's Gnat xi, This with sharpe teeth the *bramble leaves doth lop. **1866** Treas. Bot. II. 996/1 We have heard of cows that were..dragged through the *bramble-loop. **1713** C'TESS WINCHELSEA Misc. Poems 291 The Woodbind and the *Bramble-Rose.

'bramble[2]. Shortened form of BRAMBLING.
1674 RAY Eng. Birds 83 The Bramble or Brambling.
Hence (or from BRAMBLE[1]) **bramble-finch** = BRAMBLING; also **bramble-net**, 'a net for catching birds, a hallier' Phillips 1706.
1865 Derby Merc. 25 Jan., Mr. Scrimshaw also sent three grey parrots, a macaw..and bramblefinches. **1881** Standard 2 Mar. 5 The Act..omits the bramblefinch.

brambleberry ('bræmb(ə)l,bɛrɪ). The 'berry' or fruit of the bramble: a blackberry.
c**1000** Sax. Leechd. III. 8 Drince seoca of brǽmel berian зewrungene oft. **1552** HULOET Brymble berry, morum. **1655** MOUFFET & BENN. Health's Improv. (1746) 314 Bramble-berries or Black-berries..are..nourishing to a weak Stomach. **1727** BRADLEY Fam. Dict. s.v. Flux, The Powder of Snails burnt with the Powder of Bramble-berries. **1852** Gard. Chron. 54 In Scotland [and north of England] black currants are called 'Blackberries', and the fruit of Rubus fruticosus is called 'Bramble-berries'.

brambled ('bræmb(ə)ld), ppl. a. [f. BRAMBLE[1] + -ED[2].] Covered with or full of brambles.
a**1790** T. WARTON Ode iii. (R.) Forlorn she sits upon the brambled floor. **1880** BLACKMORE M. Anerley I. xviii. 322. Their crane had been left in a brambled hole.

brambling ('bræmblɪŋ). Also 6 bramlin(e, 7 brambline, bramlin. [= Ger. brämling, prob. f. WGer. *brâma BRAMBLE + -LING.]
A bird (Fringilla montifringilla) belonging to the finch-tribe; the Mountain Finch.
1570 LEVINS Manip. 133 A Bramlin, bird, montifringella. **1655** MOUFFET & BENN. Health's Improv. (1746) 188 Bramblings are a kind of small Birds, feeding chiefly upon Seeds. **1882** Proc. Berw. Nat. Club IX. 504 The Brambling, or Cock of the North, was rather a rare winter visitor.

brambly ('bræmblɪ), a. [f. BRAMBLE[1] + -Y[1].] Full of brambles; of the nature of brambles; thorny.
1581 MULCASTER Positions 86 Rough, brambly, and bushy groundes stuffe the head. **1611** COTGR., Ronceux..bramblie, brierie. **1710** PHILIPS Past. iv. (R.) Hark, how they warble in that brambly bush. **1860** TENNYSON Brook, I murmur under moon and stars In brambly wildernesses.

†**brame**[1]. *Obs. rare*−1. [Prob. ad. It. *brama* 'earnest desire or wishing'.] Longing.

1596 Spenser *F.Q.* iii. ii. 52 Through..hart-burning brame, She shortly like a pyned ghost became.

†**brame**[2]. *Obs.* [Identical in form with MDu. and MHG. *brâme* of same meaning: see bramble. But the OE. form corresponding to these is *bróm* giving ME. *brome* (broom). See bramberry.] A brier or bramble.

c **1425** *Voc.* in Wr.-Wülcker 646 *Hec tribulus*, brame.

'**brame**, *v.* [a. F. *brame-r* to cry as an animal (elephant, ox, deer, etc.).] ? To roar, bluster, rage. Hence '**braming**.

1865 Neale *Hymns Parad.* 6 Winter braming, summer flaming.

Bramene, etc.: see Brahmin, etc.

bramkersine, obs. form of brankursine.

Bramley ('bræmlɪ). [f. the name of Matthew *Bramley*, an English butcher, in whose garden at Southwell, Notts., this apple is said to have been first grown *c.* 1850 (see 1931 *N. & Q.* 14 Nov. 351/2).] A type of cooking apple; in full *Bramley('s) seedling*.

1900 *Gardening* 3 Mar. 1 Vigorous-growing varieties, especially Bramley's..will make strong wood. **1902** *Encycl. Brit.* XXVIII. 530/1 For storing, the cooking sorts favoured now are..Bramley's Seedling, Golden Noble, and Lane's Prince Albert. **1957** E. Hyams *Speaking Garden* 34 No matter how sour and sharp the apples used—for example, Bramleys. **1959** *Listener* 19 Nov. 907/1, 4 medium-sized Bramley cooking apples.

bramlin(e, obs. form of brambling.

Bramling ('bræmlɪŋ). *local.* Also **Brambling**. [The name of *Bramling* Farm, Ickham, Kent, where the first sets were raised.] A species of hop.

1899 *Westm. Gaz.* 15 Sept. 9/3 In many of the important parishes the Bramlings are all picked. **1902** *Times* 22 Sept. 11/6 Both the Bramlings and the Goldings have grown out fairly satisfactorily.

Bramoism, variant of Brahmism.

bran (bræn), *sb.*[1] Forms: 3-4 **bren**, 5 **brenne**, **bryn(e**, 6 **brene**, 5-7 **branne**, 3- **bran**. [a. OF. *bren*, *bran*; cf. Pr. and Sp. dial. *bren*, It. dial. *brenno*, *brinnu*, *bren*, *bran*. A Celtic etymology is usually alleged, but the words quoted, Bret. *brenn*, Welsh *bràn*, Gael. *bran*, appear to be adopted from Fr. and Eng. The sense of 'filth, excrement', which belongs to *bren* or *bran* in mod.Fr., is not recorded in OFr.; if this were the primary sense, we might compare Welsh *braen*, Ir. *brean*, Gael. *breun*, which have in composition the sense of 'manure'.]

1. a. The husk of wheat, barley, oats, or other grain, separated from the flour after grinding; in technical use, the coarsest portion of the ground husk (see quot. 1883).

a **1300** *Cursor M.* 15524 He wil þe sift nu if he mai, as man dos corn or bran. *c* **1325** *Gloss. W. de Biblesw.* in Wright *Voc.* 155 *Le furfre*, bren. *c* **1386** Chaucer *Reeve's T.* 133 In stide of flour yet wol I yeue hem bren. **1464** *Mann. & Househ. Exp.* 254 My mastyr payd..for bred and brenne, vj.*s.* **1547** Boorde *Brev. Health* §377 Made with..the bran of benes. **1620** Venner *Via Recta* i. 18 There is a kinde of abstersiue faculty in the bran. **1756** Nugent *Gr. Tour Italy* III. 344 They have an academy called *La Crusca* (a word which signifies *bran*, alluding to the sifting of the flour). **1883** *Knowledge* 24 Aug. 120/1 The husk is separated in different degrees of coarseness; 'bran', 'pollard', & 'sharps'..bran being the coarsest.

b. *fig.* and *transf.* (Proverbial phrases, ***to sift to the bran, to take the flour and leave the bran.***)

1577 Hellowes *Gueuara's Fam. Ep.* 237 You bestowed so much branne in the worlde. **1607** Shaks. *Cor.* i. i. 150 All From me do backe receiue the Flowre of all, And leaue me but the Bran. **1639** J. Clarke *Parœmiol.* 326 The Devils meale is halfe branne. **1654** Jer. Taylor *Real Pres.* Aj, Nothing which had not been already considered, and sifted to the bran. **1659** Gauden *Tears Ch.* 182 The ignorant vulgar (who are the bran and coarser sort of people).

†**2.** Scurf in the hair. *Obs.* (Cf. Gr. *πίτυρον*, L. *furfur*.)

1578 Lyte *Dodoens* i. lxxiii. 110 The lye..doth clense the heare from all bran or white scurffe. **1580** Baret *Alv.* B 1133 Full of branne or skurfe.

3. *Comb.*, chiefly attrib. (containing bran as an ingredient), as ***bran-biscuit, -bread, -cake, -loaf, -mash, -poultice, -tea, -water***; also **bran-bath**, a bath taken in water in which bran has been steeped; **bran-boil** (*Calico Printing*), a boiling of the fabrics in bran-water in order to remove colouring matters from them; †**bran-dance** *U.S.* (see quot. 1833); **bran-drench**, a bath of bran and water in which leather is placed to remove the lime used in liming; **bran-duster**, a machine for 'dusting' or clearing away flour from bran; **bran-pie** (see pie *sb.*[2] 2); **bran-stuffed** *ppl. a.*, stuffed with bran; **bran-tub** = *bran-pie*; also *fig.*

1875 Ure *Dict. Arts* I. 463 There is no advantage in adding soap to the *bran boil. *c* **1425** *Gloss.* in Wr.-Wülcker *Voc.* 657 *Panis furfurius*, *branbred. **1870** *Daily News* 28 Oct., An order that..no bread should be made in..Metz except bran bread. **1833** *Sk. D. Crockett* 148 This is the famous *bran-dance of the west, and derives its name from the fact that the ground is generally sprinkled with the husk of Indian meal. **1887** *Harper's Mag.* Dec. 61/2 It all kem about from that thar bran dance. **1883** Haldane *Workshop Rec.* Ser. ii. 373 *Bran-drench..is prepared by soaking wheaten-bran in cold water..and straining the extract. **1849** *Rep. Comm. Patents* (U.S.) 374 No. 6952.—Improvement in *Bran Dusters. **1838** *Penny Cycl.* XII. 309/1 A *bran-mash is given after a day of more than usual fatigue. **1862** F. Griffiths *Artill. Man.* (ed. 9) 221 Let ample bran mashes be given. **1838** I. Taylor *Home Educ.* 265 Wooden, waxen, and *bran-stuffed personages that crowd..the drawing-room. **1849** C. Brontë *Let.* in Mrs. Gaskell *Life* (1857) II. 91 The pains..return..but I combat them steadily with pitch plasters and *bran tea. **1858** C. Parry in E. Parry *Mem.* vii. (1870) 173 It quite reminded me of the *bran-tub itself as I unpacked each separate article. **1909** *Westm. Gaz.* 22 Apr. 8/2 Sideshows will contain the ever-popular phrenologist's tent and bran-tub. **1963** *Times Lit. Suppl.* 26 Apr. 313/3 This is a mathematical bran-tub. **1875** Ure *Dict. Arts* I. 463 The clearing process..by boiling in *bran-water.

†**bran**, *sb.*[2] *Obs.* Also 7 **brann(e**. [Prob. special use of bran *sb.*[1], suggested by the L. phrase *ejusdem farinæ*; influence from brand would seem probable, but that word does not appear to have had the required sense so early.] Sort, class, quality.

1610 Bp. Hall *Apol. Brownists* 59 Their Popes supremacy, infallibility..and a thousand other of this branne. **1647** Jer. Taylor *Dissuas. Popery* iii. (1686) 225 They add more particulars of the same Bran. **1672** Marvell *Reh. Transp.* i. 237 A particular bran of persons who will..be accounted the Church of England. *Ibid.* ii. 327 Magnifyed and esteemed..by those of your Bran and Leaven.

†**bran**, *sb.*[3] *Obs.* Also **brane**. [a. F. *bran(e* 'a kind of unreclaimable wild Oxe in Provence and Languedoc' (Cotgr.), ad. pseudo-Latin *branus*, *brana*, a misreading of *brauus*, *braua*; cf. mod. Pr. *brau* bull.] A name applied to some imperfectly known animal, described as a wild ox.

1688 Holme *Armoury* ii. ix. 170 Markham..calls it a Buffle, or Wild Oxe; others call them Brans, or Branes, or Wild Oxen.

†**bran**, *sb.*[4] *Obs. rare*−1. [The original Latin document (printed in Riley's *Mon. Gildhallæ* II. 118) has *brannum*; Riley also cites *brenna* from Gervase of Canterbury, apparently the freshwater bream; cf. *branling*, brandling; also barne.] Some kind of fish.

1720 *Stow's Survey* (ed. Strype 1754) II. v. xxvi. 464/2 A better Bran, Sard, and Betule for 3*d*.

bran (bræn), *v.* [f. bran *sb.*[1]] *trans.* To 'clear' maddered goods by boiling in bran-water. Hence **branning** *vbl. sb.*

brancard ('bræŋkəd). Also 6 **brancorde**, 7 **brankard**. [a. F. *brancard* a litter, f. *branche* branch.] A horse-litter.

1592 Unton *Corr.* (1847) 301 His hurt will not suffer him to ryde but in a brancorde. **1613** Purchas *Pilgr.* viii. xi. 795 An image of wood, like to a man, set vpon an azure-coloured stoole, in a brankard or litter. **1752** Lady M. W. Montague *Corr.* lxiv. III. 125 My bed was placed on a brancard. **1879** R. S. Edwards *Russ. at Home* I. 310 Had I seen the brancard in which Charles XII. was carried at the battle of Pultawa?

brances, var. of *brasses*: see brass (*Min.*).

branch (brɑːnʃ, -æ-), *sb.* Forms: 3 **bransch**, 3-6 **brance**, 4 **bronch**, 4-6 **braunche**, 4-7 **branche**, **braunch**, 5 **brawnche**, 3- **branch**. [a. F. *branche* branch:—late L. *branca* paw of an animal.]

I. A material offshoot.

1. A portion or limb of a tree or other plant growing out of the stem or trunk, or out of one of the boughs; in a more specific sense, a *branch* is understood to be smaller than a bough and larger than a shoot or spray.

a **1300** *Cursor M.* 1321 He.. sau..a mekil tre, Wid branchis fele of barc al bare. *c* **1325** *E.E. Allit. P.* B. 487 A bronch of olyue. *c* **1385** Chaucer *L.G.W.* 2681 Sche quakyth As doth the braunche that sepherus shakyth. *c* **1449** Pecock *Repr.* i. vi. 29 As the sprai cometh out of the braunche, the braunche out of the bouȝ. **1552** Abp. Hamilton *Catech.* 82 A stark brance of ane Aik tree. **1667** Milton *P.L.* vii. 433 From Branch to Branch the smaller Birds with song Solac'd the Woods. **1704** Pope *Autumn* 75 Now golden fruits on loaded branches shine. **1873** Morley *Rousseau* I. 169 To construct hovels of branches and clay.

2. *transf.* **a.** Anything analogous to a limb of a tree, in being a lateral extension or subdivision of a main trunk; e.g. of a mountain range, a river, a road or railway, an artery or vein, etc.

1297 R. Glouc. 152 þe oþer hadde sene branches..And toward þe Yrische see..þei drowe. **1603** R. Johnson *Kingd. & Commw.* 221 Therein are saide to be three and twenty braunches of the mount Atlas. **1696** Whiston *Th. Earth* ii. 104 Tho' the particular place..be now under Water, and a Branch or Bay of the Great Ocean. **1787** Winter *Syst. Husb.* 99 The branches, or smaller drains are from twenty to forty, or fifty feet a-part. **1791** *Act 31 Geo. III* c. 65 (Preamble), To make and maintain One other Rail or Waggon Way, or Stone Road, with Branches therefrom. **1831** R. Knox *Cloquet's Anat.* 644 From the aorta therefore arise secondary trunks, branches, twigs and ramuscules in great number. **1831** in *N. & Q.* (1868) II. 102/1 The railroad is not supposed to answer vastly well, but they are making a branch to Warrington. **1840**, **1846** [see *branch-railway*, *-line* in sense 12]. **1862** Stanley *Jew. Ch.* (1877) I. xiv. 276 The vast army fled far through the eastern branch of the plain. **1874** Boutell *Arms & Arm.* ix. 173 From these guards curved branches proceed..to the pommel. **1878** F. Williams *Midl. Railw.* 359 It is a branch of the Great Northern.

b. *U.S. spec.* A small stream or brook.

[**1624** John Smith *Hist. Virginia* ii. 23 Here doth the river divide it selfe into 3 or 4 convenient branches.] **1663** in *North Carolina Col. Rec.* (1886) I. 20 That Parcell of land.. Beginning at a small creek or Branch. **1796** B. Hawkins *Lett.* 25, I came to a branch covered with reeds. **1832** J. Hall *Leg. West* (1833) 27 He proceeded cautiously towards a rivulet, or in the vernacular of the country, a branch, that meandered along the foot of the hill. **1835** W. Irving *Tour Prairies* 188 Most of the 'branches', or streams, were dried up. *Ibid.* 307 In 'branch' or brook water. **1917** Mathewson *Sec. Base Sloan* v. 67 An' there's a branch close by it too, mighty nice tastin water, Mas Wayne.

c. One of the subdivisions of a deer's horn; a 'start,' antler, or shoot; *transf.* a horn anciently worn as part of a woman's head-dress.

1485 *Bk. St. Albans* E. iiij, Too braunchis first pawmyd he most haue. **1598** Manwood *Lawes Forest* iv. §6 (1615) 46 In a Bucke they say [of the antlers], Bur, Beame, Braunch, Aduancers, Palme, and Spellers. **1661** Lovell *Hist. Anim.* The horns are only on the Males, and have 6 or 7 branches. **1847** Tennyson *Princ.* Concl. 98 A shout rose again, and.. shook the branches of the deer.

1483 Caxton *G. de la Tour* D viij, Many of them caste away their braunches and hornes.

d. One of the arms of a candelabrum or chandelier. Hence †A chandelier, esp. of the kind used in churches. *Obs.*

[**1476** *Will* (Somerset Ho.), Ad sustentacionem luminis beate marie virginis vocati le Branche.] **1525** *Churchw. Accts. St. Dunstan's, Canterb.*, Taperys that where sparyd of the braunche before the Rode. **1552** Huloet, Candlestycke called a braunche. Candlestycke with thre braunches or lightes. **1709** E. W. *Life Donna Rosina* 135 A Chrystal Branch fill'd with Wax Candles. **1794** G. Adams *Nat. & Exp. Philos.* III. xxix. 180 You may find how long a branch is which hangs down from the roof of a church.

e. *poet.* The human arm (or hand). *rare.*

1588 Shaks. *Tit. A.* ii. iv. 18 What sterne vngentle hands Hath..made thy body bare Of her two branches.

†**3.** A branch-like figured pattern in embroidery or ornamental work: cf. branch *v.* 6, branched 2 b.

1606 Peacham *Art Drawing* 35 In diapering.. maintaining one branche or the same work throughout.

†**4.** A definite complex structure or form, as the characteristic form of man or any animal.

1668 Culpepper & Cole *Barthol. Anat.* i. xxviii. 68 The Particles of the Seed..agitated only by the Heat of the womb..fall into the Branch of a Livewight. *Ibid.* The Divine Shape of..Man is alwaies one and the same..How could that Branch be formed without the Mind?

II. Figurative applications suggested by the *relation* of a branch to the tree.

5. Connected with the notion of a 'genealogical tree'.

a. One of the portions into which a family or race is divided according to the differing lines of descent from the common ancestor; hence a division of a nation, or of a 'family' in any *fig.* sense, such as that of a group in scientific classification.

a **1300** *Cursor M.* 5657 (Gött.) þat branch [*Cott. MS.* brance] of kin cald iuus was, þat cam of iacob sonis iudas. *a* **1581** Campion *Hist. Irel.* viii. (1633) 24 Cast out by the collaterall braunches of Cham. **1793** Burke *Corr.* (1844) IV. 135, I do not flatter myself, that the English branch of the Jacobin family is a jot better than the French. **1839** Thirlwall *Greece* I. 147 They are Minyans; a branch of the Greek nation. **1848** Macaulay *Hist. Eng.* I. 219 Both the branches of the great House of Austria sprang to arms.

†**b.** A child, descendant; cf. *scion*. *Obs.* exc. in humorous use; (quot. 1807 contains an allusion to *Psalm* cxxviii. 3). Cf. *olive-branch*.

1535 Coverdale *Jer.* xxiii. 5, I wil rayse vp the rightuous braunch of Dauid. **1577** Holinshed *Chron.* II. 12/1 Bastolenus a branch of Japhet..brought thither the same kind of speech. **1605** Camden *Rem.* 93 Robert the sonne of Maldred, a braunch of an olde English familie. **1753** Watts *Coronat. Day* xiii. 49 Poet. Wks. 1782 VII. 150 Mark that young branch [*footnote*, Prince William] of rising fame. **1791** Boswell *Johnson* (1816) I. 22 Of which [family] the poet was a branch. **1807** Crabbe *Par. Reg.* i. 478 Now of that vine he'd have no more increase, Those playful branches now disturb his peace.

c. In devotional literature applied to Christ, with allusion to *Isa.* xi. 1, *Zech.* iii. 8, vi. 12, etc.

1535 Coverdale *Zech.* vi. 12 Beholde, the man whose name is the braunche. **1719** Watts *Hymns* i. l. ii, He [God] makes the Branch of promise grow. **1831** *Wesley's Hymns* Supp. No. 650 Branch of Jesse's stem, arise.

6. a. With express or implied reference to a metaphorical tree, root, or stock: One of the consequences deducible from a general principle; one of the effects resulting from a cause.

1526 *Pilgr. Perf.* (W. de W. 1531) 131 b, Which is..the thyrde braunche in the tree of grace. **1719** Watts *Hymns* i. lvii. v, Wild and unwholesome as the root Will all the branches be. **1756** Burke *Subl. & B.* Wks. 1842 I. 40 This

branch rises..from terrour, the common stock of every thing that is sublime.

b. *to destroy (anything) root and branch*: to destroy it utterly, to destroy both the thing itself and all its effects; originally suggested by the wording (derived from *Mal.* iv. 1) of the London Petition of Dec. 11, 1640 for the total abolition of episcopal government (see quot.). Hence, ***root-and-branch petition, root-and-branch bill***, this petition, and the bill embodying its proposals, laid before parliament in 1641; ***root-and-branch party***, the party by which the bill was supported; also (with more general meaning) ***root and branch policy, reform***, a 'radical' policy or reform involving the total abolition of some existing institution.

[**1611** BIBLE *Mal.* iv. 1 The day that cometh shall burn them up..that it shall leave them neither root nor branch. **1640** *Petition* in Rushw. *Hist. Coll.* (1721) IV. 93 That the said government, with all its dependencies, roots, and branches, be abolished. **1655** FULLER *Ch. Hist.* VIII. ii. §6 It was vain to strike at the branches, whilest the roote of all Hereticks doth remain.] **1641** LORD SAY & SELE in *Ho. Lords* in Cobbett *Parl. Hist.* (1807) II. 806 The question..is not, Whether episcopacy..shall be taken away root and branch. *a***1674** CLARENDON *Hist. Reb.* III. (1843) 94/1 Sir Harry Vane, and shortly after Mr. Hambden..were believed to be for root and branch; which grew shortly after a common expression. **1655** LESTRANGE *Chas. I*, 184, The Scotish fires had..burnt up to nothing Episcopacy both root and branch. **1867** MORLEY *Burke* 180 The root and branch policy of the Tudors. *Ibid.* 237 Privilege and immunity were then cut up root and branch. **1884** GARDINER *Hist. Eng.* IX. xcvi. 299 The Root-and-Branch party knew well that they could not ..count on a majority.

c. In medieval theology, one of the subordinate classes coming under the category of any one of the seven deadly sins, or of any venial sin.

*a***1300** *Cursor M.* 26363 Gastly sin [es]..lust and pride, And þair bransches þat springes wide. **1340** *Ayenb.* 9þer by zome bronches þet ne byeþ naȝt dyadlich zenne. *c***1386** CHAUCER *Pers. T.* ¶15 Of this roote [pride] springen general braunches; as ire, envye, accidie. **1393** LANGL. *P. Pl.* C. XVII. 264 Ypocrisie is a braunche of pruyde. **1615** HIERON *Wks.* I. 603 The raging sins of the first Table, as well as the more notorious branches of the second.

7. a. A division of a subject; a subdivision of a general concept or notion; a department of any study, pursuit, or employment; freq. in phraseological combinations, (where *department* may be substituted), as ***branch of activity, industry, study***, etc. Also ***branch of the revenue, of the prerogative***, etc.

1509 HAWES *Past. Pleas.* XI. xl, As to the fourth part, Pronouncyacyon, I shal it shewe anone..Wyth many braunches of it. **1596** SHAKS. *Merch. V.* II. ii. 66 The sisters three, and such branches of learning. **1651** HOBBES *Leviath.* II. xxvi. 141 Fidelity..a branch of naturall Justice. *a***1674** CLARENDON *Hist. Reb.* III. (1843) 114/1 Thus fell that high court [the star-chamber], a great branch of the prerogative. **1712** STEELE *Spect.* No. 288 ¶3 Indian Silks were formerly a great Branch of our Trade. **1727** SWIFT *Gulliver* I. vi. 66 Their learning..flourished in all its branches. **1756** C. LUCAS *Ess. Waters* Pref., One branch of quackery. **1762** HUME *Hist. Eng.* (1806) V. lxvii. 109 The king's revenue lay under great debts and anticipations; those branches granted in the year 1669 and 1670 were ready to expire. **1813** JANE AUSTEN *Pride & Prej.* iii. 10 She was obliged to seek another branch of the subject. **1839** THIRLWALL *Greece* I. 239 The Phœnicians..introduced letters, along with other branches of knowledge.

b. One of the divergent directions along which a line of thought may be followed out; a division of a complex proposition, question, argument, discussion, demand, legislative enactment, etc.

1542–3 *Act 34–35 Hen. VIII*, v. §3 It is conteined in the ..statute, within diuers articles and branches of the same. **1632** *Star Chamb. Cases* (1886) 102, I thinke these as branches of the first charge are charged in the bill. **1696** WHISTON *Th. Earth* IV. v. 377 The first Branch of this Proposition. *a***1700** in Rushworth *Hist. Coll.* III. II. ii. 980 [*heading*] The Branch of a letter from the Arch-bishop of Canterbury to Dr. Hall..dated..the 11th of November 1639. *Ibid.* 1347 (*heading*, an. 1640) A Branch of the Lord Digby's Speech about Episcopacy. **1783** AINSWORTH *Lat. Dict.* (Morell) 1, A branch [of discourse], *caput.* **1818** CRUISE *Digest* VI. 307 The express declaration of the testator in almost every branch of his will.

8. A component portion of an organization or system, a part of a larger unity. ***branch of the legislature***, one of the houses or chambers into which the legislative body is divided.

1696 WHISTON *Th. Earth* Introd. 11 The bare Earth..is but one of the Members or Branch. **1712** ADDISON *Spect.* No. 287 ¶5 A mixt Government consisting of three Branches. **1768** BLACKSTONE *Comm.* IV. 258 This branch of the legislature, which represents the people. **1839** YEOWELL *Anc. Brit. Ch.* xiii. (1847) 150 The Roman Church was a sound and uncorrupt branch of the Catholic Church.

9. A local office of business, subordinate to the main or head office, as the 'branch' of a bank or other establishment.

1817 *Petition* in *Parl. Deb.* 215 This London Union Society..establishing branches and affiliations. **1875** JEVONS *Money* (1878) 257 Important banks, each possessing numerous branches.

III. 10. The certificate held by a brother of the Trinity House; also that given by the Trinity House to pilots who have passed an examination as to their competence. Cf. *branch-pilot* in 13.

1865 ESQUIROS *Cornwall* 237 He received a branch, the name given to a certificate bearing the signature of the Society.

IV. 11. In various techn. senses [chiefly after Fr. *branche*]: in *Arch.* the rib of a Gothic vault; in *Zool.* (see quot. 1881); in *Mech.* the beam or axle of a pump or similar machine; also, a bolt or strap with arms; in *Harness-making*, a pair of parallel levers passing through the ends of a curb-bit, and provided with rings or loops for the curb-chain, etc.; in *Fortification*, the wing of a horn- or crown-work; also, one of the boyaux of a zigzag approach. The word is also used of the metal piece on the end of a hose, to which the nozzle is screwed (also, the hose itself); and of each of the sides of a horse-shoe.

1659 LEAK *Water-wks.* 17 The said Levers shalbe also fitted to two arms or branches. **1793** SMEATON *Edystone L.* §38 There were two large branches fixed near the center, for taking hold of the two sides of a large upright piece of timber. **1838** *Penny Cycl.* XII. 296/1 The defenders of their branches could not have avoided firing upon one another. **1881** *Nature* XXIV. 463 Branches—The cell-bearing portions of the zoarium of Glauconome..or Synocladia. **1884** E. L. ANDERSON *Mod. Horsemanship* I. v. 18 The branches should be long or short, as the rider wishes a mild or a severe bit. **1897** *Daily News* 22 Nov. 7/3 Engineer Heather..ordered his men to drop their 'branches' and run. **1945** S. SPENDER *Citizens in War* 46 Two firemen may then have to stand for hours holding the 'branch'..from which the water proceeds. **1959** R. COLLIER *City that wouldn't Die* viii. 132 Swing your branch to the left, son—give the Shoe Lane corner a drink.

V. *Comb.* and *Attrib.*

12. General relations: **a.** (in sense 1), objective with ppl. adj., vbl. sb., or agent-noun, as ***branch-bearing, -gatherer***; locative and instrum. (*poet.*), as ***branch-charmed, -embellished, -rent***; attrib. (pertaining to a branch), as ***branch-bud***; also ***branch-like*** adj.; **b.** (in sense 2) attrib. (having the character of a branch), as ***branch-line*** (of railway), ***-road, -root, -vein***; **c.** (in sense 9) as ***branch bank, -establishment, -office.***

1796 *Boston Directory* 302 *Branch Bank, State street. **1832** *Chambers's Edin. Jrnl.* I. 162/3 The conductors of the branch banks give no loans..without consulting with their masters. **1567** MAPLET *Gr. Forest* 56 Pearserthnut..is in leafe and *braunch bearing like to Cicer. **1882** VINES *Sachs' Bot.* 370 The deciduous *branch-buds of *Bryum annotinum* may also be considered as organs of reproduction. *a***1821** KEATS *Hyperion*, Tall oaks, *branch-charmed by the earnest stars. **1597** DRAYTON *Mortimer.* 110 Notingham..Crowne of the beautious *branch-embellish'd soyle. **1483** *Cath. Angl.* 41 A *Brawnche gederer, *frondator.* **1852** TUPPER *Proverb. Philos.* 167 With dull malignant stare watcheth the *branch-like boa. **1846** *Penny Cycl.* Supp. II. 667/2 When ..in working *branch lines, a carriage must be sent through for the accommodation of only two or three passengers. **1885** *Law Rep.* XXIX. *Chancery Div.* 219 The company had no *branch office of its own in England. **1840** *Act 3–4 Vic.* xcvii. §18 Effecting communication between such railway and any..*branch railway. **1820** KEATS *Lamia* 13 Vales deflower'd, or forest-trees *branch-rent. **1831** *Deb. Congress* 1 Mar. 830 The opening of *branch roads. **1842** DICKENS *Amer. Notes* I. iv. 149 Except when a branch-road joins the main one, there is seldom more than one track of rails. **1884** BOWER & SCOTT *De Bary's Phaner. & Ferns* 362 *Branch-roots of Dracæna reflexa..have a thoroughly typical structure. **1858** W. ELLIS *Visits Madagasc.* ix. 242 At the adjacent *branch station..we remained a week. *c***1400** in *Rel. Ant.* I. 190 Fro '*basylica*'..A *branche veyn spryngeth up ful bolde.

13. Special combinations: **branch-bottom** (in *U.S.*), see quot.; **branch-building** *a.*, building in branches; **branch-chuck** (*Mech.*), a chuck having four branches turned up at the ends, and furnished with screws; **branch-coal**, a provincial name for anthracite; **branch house**, an offshoot of a religious community, business firm, etc.; **branch-island**, an island beside a river formed by an ANABRANCH; **branch library**, a library other than the main one in an area; hence ***branch librarian***; **branch-pilot**, a pilot who holds a Trinity House certificate; **branch-point** *Math.*, a point in the complex plane at which two or more branches of a function of a complex variable coincide; †**branch-stand** *v.*, 'to make a Hawk take the Branch, or leap from Tree to Tree, till the Dog springs the Partridge' (Phillips, 1706); **branch wines**, a translation of Pg. *vinos de ramo*, wines made for home consumption; **branch-work**, ornamental figured patterns (cf. 3).

1880 *New Virginians* I. 82 The land being what is called *branch-bottom, i.e. alluvial in character. **1868** WOOD *Homes without H.* xxvii. 514 We shall take first the *branch-building mammalia. **1840** K. H. DIGBY *Mores Cath.* x. i. 9 Cisteaux, the mother house of the order, [was] founded..in 1098... La Ferté was the first *branch house. **1872** GEO. ELIOT *Middlem.* VI. lxi. 346 There was a branch house at the west end. **1834** J. R. JACKSON in *Jrnl. R. Geogr. Soc.* IV. 79 Thus, such branches of a river as after separation re-unite, I would term anastomosing-branches; or, if a word might be coined, anabranches, and the islands they form, *branch-islands. **1938** H. A. SHARP *Branch Libraries* iii. 62 A superintendent of branches..is necessarily a mediary between the chief and the *branch librarian. **1862** MRS. GASKELL *Let.* 16 June (1966) 689 Would it be much trouble for you to enquire from him [*sc.* Mr. Mudie] whether he has any *Branch-Library in Paris..? **1927** *Cmd. 2868* (*Publ. Libr. Rep.*) 66 The branch library is the most important form of library extension. **1864** *Times* 10 Dec., The first *branch pilot who offered his services..was bound to be accepted. **1878** CAYLEY in *Proc. Lond. Math. Soc.* IX. 32 There are certain points V called *branch-points (Verzweigungspuncte), such that to each point V there correspond two united points..and n-2 other distinct points. **1966** E. G. PHILLIPS *Topics Complex Analysis* ii. 20 On traversing loop A in the positive sense, the straight pieces have no effect on $f(z)$ since they do not contain a branch point. **1833** C. REDDING *Hist. Mod. Wines* viii. (1836) 226 The wine country of the Douro is again subdivided..into, first, Factory wines..and secondly, *Branch wines. **1702** W. J. *Bruyn's Voy. Levant* ix. 32 Intermixed with *Branch-works that make a glorious shew. **1842** TENNYSON *Pal. Art* 95 Branch-work of costly sardonyx.

branch, *v.* [f. prec. sb.: cf. F. *brancher.*]

I. *intr.* **1.** To bear or put forth branches; sometimes with *forth, out.* Also *fig.*

1382 WYCLIF *Ecclus.* xxxix. 19 Floureth floures, as lilie; ȝyueth smel, and braunceth in to grace. **1552** HULOET, Braunchen, or haue braunches, *frondeo.* **1611** SHAKS. *Wint. T.* I. i. 27 There rooted betwixt them then such an affection, which cannot chuse but braunch now. **1759** tr. *Duhamel's Husb.* II. i. (1762) 127 Gave the earth round these plants a good stirring before they branched. **1882** VINES *Sachs' Bot.* 478 They branch even before they reach the ground.

2. *transf.* and *fig.* To throw out branches or offshoots; to separate into branches, ramify. Freq. const. *from, into.* Now almost always with *out.*

1398 TREVISA *Barth. De P.R.* III. ix. (1495) 54 The fyfthe synewe braunchyth and comyth in bowes to the Instrumentes of towchynge. **1756** BURKE *Subl. & B.* Introd. Wks. I. 129 What subject does not branch out to infinity? **1853** ROBERTSON *Serm.* Ser. III. iii. (1872) 31 It branches, therefore, into a twofold division. **1862** H. SPENCER *First Princ.* I. v. §32 (1875) 117 Consequences..that go on branching out more widely as years progress.

b. To spring out, as a branch or branches from the stem or root; to deviate from an original direction, strike off in a new path; to diverge from a central point; in mod. use chiefly with adv. *out, off*, less freq. *away.*

*c***1400** *Destr. Troy* 8750 Beamys of bright sun, þat braunchis olofte. **1711** ADDISON *Spect.* No. 247 ¶2, I have known a woman branch out into a long dissertation upon the edging of a petticoat. **1799** *Scotl. described* (ed. 2) 13 Many inferior ranges, here and there, branch out from them on all sides. *c***1811** FUSELI *Lect. Art* v. (1848) 463 If it branch not out of the subject. **1839** YEOWELL *Anc. Brit. Ch.* xi. (1847) 112 From this point..branched most of the great roads into the interior. **1870** MAX MÜLLER *Sc. Relig.* (1873) 163 A very early concentration of speech from which these dialects branched off. **1871** FREEMAN *Norm. Conq.* (1876) IV. xviii. 212 The Foss Way..branched off from the Eastern gate. **1884** *Macm. Mag.* Oct. 431/2 An excellent street..branches away from the quay, and leads into a vast square.

†**3.** To spring, arise, or descend from a common stock or parentage; also, *to be branched* (in the same sense). *Obs.*

1583 STANYHURST *Æneis* I. (Arb.) 18 That from thee Troians should branch a lineal ofspring. **1609** HIERON *Wks.* I. Ded. A ij, All those young plants, which..haue branched from you both. **1631** WEEVER *Anc. Fun. Mon.* 544 These Butlers are branched from Sir Raph Butler. **1639** FULLER *Holy War* III. xviii. (1840) 146 They were a younger house of the Waldenses, and branched from them.

II. *trans.*

4. To divide (anything) into branches; to spread out (anything) in the manner of branches.

1700 W. KING *Transactioneer* 10 The ends of the Twigs are branched into bunches of Flowers. **1795** SOUTHEY *Joan of Arc* I. 48 The dark yew..branch'd there its naked roots. **1864** TENNYSON *Aylmer's F.* 221 Jewels..Sprinkled about in gold that branch'd itself Fine as ice-ferns.

5. *fig.* To arrange or set *out* in branches. *arch.*

1628 PRYNNE *Cens. Cozens* 10 We branch the matter of this Booke into points of Doctrine and substance. **1673** *Lady's Call.* I. v. §32, I shall not need to branch out devotion into the several parts. **1789** BENTHAM *Princ. Legisl.* xviii. §56 The whole system of offences..is branched out into five classes. **1810** *Month. Rev.* LXII. 496 If a Gothic story be branched out in the forms of the Shakspearean drama.

6. To adorn or embroider with gold or needlework representing flowers or foliage. Cf. BRANCH *sb.* 3. Also *fig.*

1596 SPENSER *F.Q.* II. ix. 19 The traine whereof loose far behind her strayd, Braunched with gold and perle. **1611** FLETCHER *Philast.* v. iv. 37 May the Moths branch their Velvets. *Ibid.* Branch me his skin in flowers like a sattin. **1859** TENNYSON *Enid* 631 Enid fell in longing for a dress All branch'd and flower'd with gold.

7. To furnish with branches or branching horns. Also *fig.*

1633 FORD *Broken Hrt.* II. i. 250 The city housewives.. Cull, kiss, and cry sweetheart, and stroke the head Which they have branch'd.

branchage ('brɑːnʃɪdʒ, -æ-). [f. BRANCH *sb.* + -AGE: cf. F. *branchage.*] Branches in the mass.

1868 BROWNING *Ring & Bk.* x. 274 Leafage and branchage vulgar eyes admire. **1873** —— *Red Cott. Night-C.* 652 In the main ash-avenue Under the blessing of its branchage-roof.

branchar, -er: see BLANCHER[1].

branched (brɑːnʃt, -æ-), *ppl. a.* [f. BRANCH *sb.* and *v.* + -ED.]

1. Provided with branches. *lit.* and *fig.* (Cf. senses of the sb.; often combined with numeral or other adjs., as ***double-***, ***five-***, ***many-branched.***)

c **1350** *Will. Palerne* 753 Vnder a tri appeltre..þat was braunched ful brode. **1567** STUDLEY *Seneca's Hippolytus* (1581) 56 The Elme displayes his braunched armes. **1668** WILKINS *Real Char.* 157 A double branched brow-antler. **1841** MRS. BROWNING *House Clouds* 29 A spacious hall.. Branched with corridors sublime. **1877** R. J. MORE *Under Balkans*, A lighted triple-branched wax taper.

†**2. a.** Divided, distributed; descended (from a family or an ancestor). (Cf. BRANCH *v.* 3-5.) *Obs.*

1429 *Pol. Poems* (1859) II. 141 Royal braunched, descended from two lynes.

b. Adorned with a figured pattern in embroidery, gilding, chasing, etc. Cf. BRANCH *v.* 6.

1509 HAWES *Past. Pleas.* XXVII. xxxii, The rofe was braunched curiously Of the beten golde both gaye and glorious. **1552** H. W. KING *Invent. Ch. Goods* (1885) 15 A cope of blew and Braunched Damaske..xxs. **1601** SHAKS. *Twel. N.* II. v. 54 Calling my Officers about me, in my branch'd Veluet gowne. **1703** *Lond. Gaz.* No. 3895/4 Seven Silver Spoons..branched on the tops.

3. Hence in Arch. ***branched work***, the carved foliage on friezes and monuments.

4. Chem. ***branched chain***: an open chain (CHAIN *sb.* 5 g) of atoms having one or more side chains. Freq. *attrib.*

1889 G. M'GOWAN tr. *Bernthsen's Text-bk. Org. Chem.* i. 43 The boiling point becomes lowered continuously the more the carbon atom chain is branched. **1903** A. J. WALKER tr. *Holleman's Text-bk. Org. Chem.* I. 46 In branched chains there are carbon atoms which are directly linked to three or four others. *Ibid.*, Branched-chain compounds are often distinguished by the prefix *iso.* **1939** *Jrnl. R. Aeronaut. Soc.* XLIII. 42 Straight-run petrols..and branched-chain paraffins are the outstandingly useful aviation fuels. **1946** *Nature* 14 Dec. 863/1 One fundamental approach to this problem was based on fatty acids with branched-chains.

branchellion (bræŋˈkɛlɪɒn). [a. Fr. *branchellion*, shortened by Savigny from the earlier *branchiobdellion* lit. 'a leech having gills'; cf. BRANCHIO- and Gr. βδέλλα leech.] A species of Annelid, a leech which attacks fishes and tortoises.

1847 in CRAIG. **1876** BENEDEN *Anim. Parasites* 113.

brancher[1] (ˈbrɑːnʃə(r), -æ-). [f. BRANCH *v.* + -ER[1].] That which bears or puts forth branches.

1610 FOLKINGHAM *Art of Survey* I. ii. 43 The thin brauncher [vine] needs a battle soyle to enlarge the Dilation. **1651** *Reliq. Wotton.* (1685) 77 If their Child be not such a speedy spreader and brancher, like the Vine.

ˈbrancher[2]. Also 5 brauncher, brawncher. [a. AF. *brancher = F. *branchier*, f. *branche* BRANCH.] A young hawk (or other bird) when it first leaves the nest and hops about the branches.

?*a* **1400** *Morte Arth.* 190 Þareby braunchers in brede bettyr was never. **1486** *Bk. St. Albans* ij b, After saynt Margaretis day..they bene calde Brawncheris. **1575** TURBERV. *Bk. Falconrie* 69 The brancher is she that followeth the old hawke from braunch to braunch. **1727** BRADLEY *Fam. Dict.* s.v. *Canary Bird*, Those of the first year ..are term'd Branchers. **1808** JAMIESON, *Branchers*, young crows, after leaving the nest, and betaking themselves to the boughs or branches. *Teviotd.* **1873** *Daily News* 19 July 5/7 We have a cage with a 'brancher' (a young linnet).

b. *fig.* A young child.

1833 M. SCOTT *Tom Cringle* xvi. 389 My home..with all my pretty little tender branchers hopping about me.

branchery (ˈbrɑːnʃərɪ, -æ-). [f. BRANCH *sb.* + -ERY.] Branches collectively. *lit.* and *fig.*

1830 COLERIDGE *Ch. & St.* (1839) 131. **1847** SARA COLERIDGE in *Biog. Lit.* Introd. 125 All the branchery of mystic beliefs and superstitious practices. **1855** BAILEY *Mystic* 85 That tree..From whose umbrageous branchery human fruit..In sacred ripeness dropped.

†**b.** Applied by Grew to: The ramifications of the endocarp in an apple or other fruit.

1674 GREW *Anat. Plants* I. vi. §2 The Branchery is nothing else but the Ramifications of the Lignous Body throughout all the parts of the Parenchyma. **1753** CHAMBERS *Cycl. Supp.* s.v. *Apple*, The branchery, or vessels are only ramifications of the woody part of the branch.

branch-hircin, obs. form of BRANKURSINE.

‖**branchiæ, branchia** (ˈbræŋkɪiː, ˈbræŋkɪə), *sb. pl.* Also obs. ME. pl. braunches. [L. *branchia*, pl. *branchiæ*, ad. Gr. βράγχια gills, pl. of βράγχιον (in sing. meaning a fin).]

The organs of respiration in fishes, etc.; gills.

1398 TREVISA *Barth. De P.R.* v. xxxv. (1495) 147 Some beestes haue no lounges but they haue braunches in stede of lounges. **1674** GREW *Anat. Trunks* I. iii. §26 Fishes having their Branchiæ; Land-Animals their Lungs. **1854** BUSHNAN in *Circ. Sc.* (1865) II. 23/2 The Pulmonary Arachnidians.. breathe by..pulmonary branchia. **1866** WOOD *Nat. Hist.* (1874) 627 The double gills or branchiæ.

branchial (ˈbræŋkɪəl), *a.* [f. L. *branchi-æ* (see prec.) + -AL[1]: cf. Fr. *branchial.*] Pertaining to, of the nature of, or resembling gills. **branchial arch**, one of a series of bony or cartilaginous structures supporting the gills of fishes and amphibians, and found embryonically in mammals.

1801 *Phil. Trans.* XCI. 246 The branchial appendages.. are of a deep blood colour. **1836** TODD *Cycl. Anat. & Phys.* I. 115/2 The bilocular heart of fishes is entirely branchial. **1875** *Encycl. Brit.* I. 757/2 There is no trace of any fourth branchial arch, such as exists in tadpoles and in young salamanders. **1936** J. T. JENKINS *Fishes Brit. Is.* (ed. 2) 7 The variation in the structure of the gills and their supporting branchial arches.

branchiate, -ated (ˈbræŋkɪeɪt, -eɪtɪd), *a.* [f. as prec. + -ATE[2] + -ED.] Having, or characterized by, branchiæ or gills.

1836 TODD *Cycl. Anat. & Phys.* I. 107/2 Ciliated, branchiated, and pulmonated classes. **1870** ROLLESTON *Anim. Life* Introd. 62 In Branchiate Vertebrata there is no epidermal skeleton.

branchiferous (bræŋˈkɪfərəs), *a.* [f. mod.L. *branchifer* (f. *branchiæ* gills + *-fer* bearing) + -OUS.] Bearing or furnished with gills.

1854 WOODWARD *Mollusca* (1856) 98 The development of the branchiferous gasteropods may be observed..in the common river-snails.

branchiform (ˈbræŋkɪfɔːm), *a.* Also branchiiform. [f. L. *branchi-æ* gills + -FORM.] Like or resembling gills.

1845 *Proc. Berw. Nat. Club* II. 146 Articulations.. branchiform, being chiefly adapted for respiration. **1852** DANA *Crust.* I. 612 There are..branchiiform appendages.

branchiness (ˈbrɑːnʃɪnɛs, -æ-). [f. BRANCHY + -NESS.] Branchy quality or condition. Also *fig.*

1611 COTGR., *Branchage*, branchinesse; thicknes, or store of branches. **1804** W. TAYLOR in *Ann. Rev.* II. 323 The metaphysical generalizations display..a fibrous branchiness of argument. **1806** *Month. Mag.* XXI. 416 A bush differs from a tree in that its branchiness begins at the very root.

branching (ˈbrɑːnʃɪŋ, -æ-), *vbl. sb.* [f. BRANCH *v.*]

1. The action of throwing out branches, or of diverging in the manner of branches; ramification; *concr.* a collection of branches. Also *fig.*

1578 BANISTER *Hist. Man* v. 71 With diuers orders of braunchynges they embrace it. **1684** T. BURNET *Th. Earth* I. 232 We have before compar'd the branchings of these rivers..to the ramifications of the arteries in the body. **1724** WATTS *Logic* 348 Finish your whole argument with as few inferior branchings as reason will admit. **1882** VINES *Sachs' Bot.* 207 Dichotomous branching is frequently repeated in one and the same plane.

2. The action of decorating with flowers or foliage, in embroidery, gilding, engraving, etc.

1622 HEYLIN *Cosmogr.* III. (1673) 53/2 The branching of Satins..being amongst many others, one of their Inventions.

ˈbranching, *ppl. a.* [f. as prec. + -ING[2].]

1. That branches; that puts forth branches.

1382 WYCLIF *Jer.* xvii. 2 Ther braunching trees in heeȝe mounteynes. **1645** MILTON *Arcades* 86 Under the shady roof Of branching elm. **1725** POPE *Odyss.* XIII. 122 High at the head a branching Olive grows. **1842** TENNYSON *Vere de Vere* 27 Not thrice your branching limes have blown.

2. Spreading, ramifying, diverging; also, rambling, diffuse.

1720 POPE *Iliad* XXI. 446 The branching streams. **1810** SOUTHEY *Kehama* XVIII. vii, In branching veins. **1864** BURTON *Scot Abr.* II. i. 128 The Burnets..were a branching family.

3. Bearing antlers, antlered.

1667 MILTON *P.L.* VII. 470 The swift Stag..Bore up his branching head. **1718** POPE *Iliad* III. 37 So joys a lion, if the branching deer..his bulky prize, appear.

branchio- (ˌbræŋkɪəʊ), also incorrectly **brancho-**, combining form of Gr. βράγχια gills, as in **ˌbranchio-ˈanal** *a.*, pertaining to the branchiæ and anus. **ˌbranchio-ˈcardiac** *a.*, belonging to the gills and heart. **ˌbranchio-ˈgasteropod**, *pl.* **-poda, -pods**, a gasteropod which breathes air through water; also, any gasteropod. **ˌbranchio-ˈpallial** *a.*, pertaining to the gills and mantle of molluscs. **ˌbranchio-paˈrietal** *a.*, pertaining to the gills and wall of the atrium (of molluscs).

1856 HUXLEY in Woodward *Mollusca* 446 The part.. behind [the mantle] becomes the branchio-anal surface. **1836** TODD *Cycl. Anat. & Phys.* I. 206/2 The blood.. returns to the heart by means of the branchio-cardiac vessels. **1877** HUXLEY *Anat. Inv. An.* viii. 505 In all.. Branchiogasteropods, the mantle secretes a cuticular shell. **1880** BASTIAN *Brain* 84 The 'auditory saccules'..are connected with this great branchio-pallial ganglion. **1856** WOODWARD *Mollusca* III. 334 The branchial sac is connected with the wall of the atrium by (branchio-parietal) vessels.

branchiopod (ˈbræŋkɪəˌpɒd). Pl. **-opods, -opoda** (-ˈɒpədə). [f. BRANCHIO- + Gr. πούς, ποδ-ός foot: cf. Fr. *branchiopode.*] *lit.* 'Gill-footed,'—a member of the Crustacean order distinguished by having the gills upon the feet. Also *attrib.*

1826 KIRBY & SP. *Entomol.* IV. 81 In the..Branchiopod Crustacea the long dorsal vessel is also found. **1836** TODD *Cycl. Anat. & Phys.* I. 755/2 In the Branchiopods..the body consists of a long series of rings. **1862** WOOD *Nat. Hist.* 732 The gills are attached to the feet, and they are therefore termed Branchiopoda.

Hence **ˌbranchiˈopodous** *a.*

1836 TODD *Cycl. Anat.* I. 692/1 The young of Balanids.. closely resemble some of the branchiopodous crustacea.

branchiostegal (bræŋkɪˈɒstɪgəl), *a.* [f. BRANCHIOSTEGE (or its elements) + -AL[1].]

1. Pertaining to the membrane which protects a gill chamber; covering or protecting the gills.

1749 *Phil. Trans.* XLVI. 128 Slender cartilaginous Bones ..analagous to the brancheostegal Bones of other Fishes. **1872** MIVART *Elem. Anat.* 478 The branchiostegal membrane..is supported by the branchiostegal rays.

2. quasi-*sb.* for *branchiostegal ray.*

1849-52 TODD *Cycl. Anat. & Phys.* IV. 1144/2 Slightly curved rays..called branchio-stegals.

branchiostegan (bræŋkɪˈɒstɪgən). [f. mod.L. *branchiosteg-i* (cf. next) + -AN.] A member of the *Branchiostegi*, an old order of cartilaginous fishes having free gills covered by a membrane.

1847 in CRAIG.

branchiostege (ˈbræŋkɪəʊˌstiːdʒ), *a.* [a. Fr. *branchiostège*, f. BRANCHIO- + Gr. στέγ-ειν to cover] Covering the gills (= BRANCHIOSTEGAL).

Hence **branchiostegite** (-ˈɒstɪˌdʒaɪt). [app. after Gr. στεγίτης, erroneously taken as an agential sb. from στέγειν], the membrane covering the gills. Also **branchiostegous** (-ˈɒstɪgəs), *a.* (*a*) having gill-covers; (*b*) = BRANCHIOSTEGAL.

1748-52 SIR J. HILL *Hist. Anim.* 220 (JOD.) The branchiostege membrane contains ten, eleven, or twelve bones. **1769** PENNANT *Zool.* III. 164 The number of its branchiostegous rays are seven. **1774** GOLDSM. *Nat. Hist.* (1862) II. III. i. 294 The cartilaginous, or..branchiostegous tribe of fishes. **1880** HUXLEY *Cray-Fish* 25 This flap..is called the Branchiostegite because it covers the gills or branchiae.

branchiostomous (bræŋkɪˈɒstəməs), *a.* [f. BRANCHIO- + Gr. -στομος -mouthed + -OUS.] Having the gills in connexion with the mouth.

1881 OWEN in *Nature* XXIV. 499 In fishes the double function of the mouth is retained—all are 'branchiostomous'.

branchireme (ˈbræŋkɪˌriːm). [f. L. *branchi-æ* gills + *rēm-us* an oar.] An organ in the branchiopod entomostraca which serves the double purpose of respiration and of locomotion. Cf. quot.

1835 KIRBY *Habits & Inst. Anim.* II. xvii. 133 Jointed legs, that terminate in a fasciculus of setiform branches.. also connected with the respiration of the animal..might be denominated Branchiremes.

branchite (ˈbræŋkaɪt). *Min.* [ad. G. *branchit* (P. Savi 1842, in *Neues Jahrb. f. Mineralogie* 459), f. the name of J. *Branchi* of Pisa: see -ITE[1].] A mineral resin found in fossil pine wood.

1851 DANA *Man. Min.* 97 *Branchite*, found with coal, especially brown coal, and resembling wax or tallow. **1883** *Encycl. Brit.* XVI. 429/1 Branchite,..is similar [to Scheererite].

branchless (ˈbrɑːnʃlɪs, -æ-), *a.* [f. BRANCH *sb.* + -LESS.] Without, or destitute of, branches.

1611 COTGR., *Tronçonner*..to make headlesse, branchlesse. **1834** AIRD *Nebuchadn.* I. ii. 53 Beneath her branchless palm must Judah sit.

b. *fig.* and *transf.*

1606 SHAKS. *Ant. & Cl.* III. iv. 24 Better I were not yours Then your so branchlesse. **1848** W. BARTLETT *Egypt to Pal.* iii. (1879) 39 About midway of this branchless course it enters Egypt.

branchlet (ˈbrɑːnʃlɪt, -æ-). Also 8 **branchilet.** [f. as prec. + -LET.] A little branch, a shoot; in *Bot.* a smaller branch growing from a larger one (rendering L. *ramulus*); *fig.* a small division or offshoot.

1731 BAILEY, *Branchilet*, a little Branch. **1820** LINDLEY *Monogr. Roses* Introd. 21, I have found it necessary to make a distinction between branches and branchlets. **1881** MIVART *Cat* 279 The dorsal branch divides at the carpus into two branchlets. **1883** E. ARNOLD *Nt. Slaughter* in *Ind. Idylls* 241 There perched A thousand crows..some on branchlets.

brancho-, incorrect form of BRANCHIO-.

branch-ursine, obs. form of BRANKURSINE.

branchy (ˈbrɑːnʃɪ, -æ-), *a.* [f. BRANCH *sb.* + -Y[1].]

1. Bearing branches; full of, covered with, or consisting of branches.

1382 WYCLIF *2 Kings* xvii. 10 And vndir al braunchy tree. **1480** CAXTON *Ovid's Met.* XIV. xv, Com to me, into this braunchy wood. **1661** K. W. *Conf. Charac.* (1860) 89 Called arms, for their hard branchey resemblance. **1725** POPE *Odyss.* v. 313 [Trees]..lopp'd and lighten'd of their branchy load. **1820** COMBE (Dr. Syntax) *Consol.* I. 134 The cedar, The branchy monarch of the wood. **1850** BLACKIE *Æschylus* I. 35 The outspread olive's branchy shade.

2. *transf.* Putting forth offshoots, or divisions; wide-spreading, ramifying; also (of deer) bearing horns, antlered.

1606 N. Baxter *Man Created* in Farr's *S.P.* (1848) 238 Within a branchie filme there lyeth the braine. 1676 J. Beaumont in *Phil. Trans.* XI. 731, I have a piece of branchy spar. 1830 T. Hamilton *C. Thornton* (1845) 99 The deer.. stood..tossing high their branchy foreheads. 1830 Tennyson *Talking Oak* 273 The fat earth feed thy branchy root.

branck, -vrsin, obs. ff. BRANK, -URSINE.

brancorde, obs. form of BRANCARD.

brancorne; see BRANTCORN.

brand (brænd), *sb.* Also 1-7 **brond(e**, 4 **bront, broond**, 5 **bronnd**, 6 *Sc.* **broynd**, 7 **bran**, 9 *dial.* **bron**. [Com. Teut.: OE. *brand, brǫnd* = OFris. *brand* (MDu. *bran(d)*, Du. *brand*) OHG., MHG. *brant* (mod.G. *brand*), ON. *brand-r*:—OTeut. **brando-z*, f. *bran-* pret. stem of **brinn-an* to BURN + suffix *-do*, as in WORD.]

I. Act, means, or result of burning.

†1. Burning, conflagration, destruction by fire.

a 1000 *Beowulf* 4258 Hy hine ne moston..bronde forbærnan. *c* 1300 *K. Alis.* 1856 They..stete fuyre, and wilde bronnd, Anon in kyng Daries lond.

2. A piece of wood that is or has been burning on the hearth; also *poet.* a torch, a match or linstock (see quot. 1810).

c 950 *Lindisf. Gosp.* John xviii. 3 Judas..cuom ðidir mið lehtfatum & brondum & woepnum. *a* 1000 *Dan.* 246 (Gr.) Bæron brandas on bryne fyres. *c* 1175 *Lamb. Hom.* 81 He wule aquikien and al þe brond tenden. *a* 1300 *Cursor M.* 7154 Vn-to þair tails fir he band, Foluand ilk fox a brand. 1477 Earl Rivers *Dictes* (Caxton) 16 Scornyng..wastith loue as the fiere doth the bronde. *a* 1547 Surrey *Æneid* IV. 505 With burial brandes I absent shall thee chase. *a* 1674 Milton *Hist. Mosc.* Wks. 1738 II. 129 So cold..that the very Sap of their Wood-fewel burning on the fire, freezes at the Brand's-end. 1735 Somerville *Chase* II. 409 Like Flocks of Sheep they fly Before the flaming Brand. 1810 Campbell *Batt. Baltic* i, By each gun the lighted brand, In a bold determined hand. 1835 W. Irving *Tour Prairies* 41 The brands of one of their fires were still smoking.

3. *transf.* and *fig.*

†a. *collect.* or in *pl.* The fire on the hearth. *Obs.* or *dial.*

a 1300 *Prov. Hendyng* 109 Este bueþ oune brondes, quoþ Hendyng. 1862 Barnes *Rhymes Dorset Dial.* I. 129 She warm'd em some cider avore the bron.

b. ***a brand from the burning*** or ***from the fire*** (in allusion to *Zech.* iii. 2 and *Amos* iv. 11): a person delivered from imminent danger.

1382 Wyclif *Zech.* iii. 2 Wher this is not a dead brond rauyshid of the fijr. 1535 Coverdale *ibid.* Is not this a brande taken out of the fyre? 1779 Wesley *Hymns* (1831) 170 O Jesus, of thee I inquire, If still thou art able..The brand to pluck out of the fire. 1822 R. Cox *Life Fletcher* ii. 17 His prayer hence was, 'Save me, Lord, as a brand snatched out of the fire'.

c. The torches of Cupid and the Furies.

c 1385 Chaucer *L.G.W.* 2252 The furyes thre with all hir mortall bronde. 1579 Lyly *Euphues* (Arb.) 112 So shalt thou easely..quench the brandes of Cupide. 1611 Shaks. *Cymb.* II. iv. 91 Two winking Cupids..nicely Depending on their Brands. 1795 Burke *Let.* Wks. 1842 II. 245 The meditations of the closet have..inflamed armies with the brands of the furies.

d. ***Jove's*** or ***God's brand***: the lightning. ***Phoebus' brand***: the burning rays of the sun. With a blending of the sense 'weapon': (cf. Milton's 'flaming brand' of the archangel in *P.L.* XII. 643).

1513 Douglas *Æneis* VIII. vi. 20 Into this land Saturnus com, fleand gret Jovis brand. 1596 Spenser *F.Q.* I. viii. 21 Where th' Almighties lightning brond does light. 1620 T. Peyton *Parad.* in Farr's *S.P.* 177 A smoky hill, which sends forth fiery brands Of burning oyle, much like the sword the tree of life doth keepe. 1885 H. H. Gibbs tr. *Integer Vitae* in *Nat. Rev.*, And o'er me Phœbus' fiery brand, Fierce beating from above.

e. Applied to persons. Cf. *firebrand.*

1608 Armin *Nest Ninn.* 4 And you of our Innes of Court, nimble braind brands that burne without smoking.

4. a. The mark made by burning with a hot iron.

1552 Huloet, Bronde, or marke made with a whote yron. 1601 Holland *Pliny* I. 220 The marke or brand of a buls head which was imprinted vpon his [Bucephalus'] shoulder. 1722 De Foe *Moll Fl.* (1840) 219 My comrade, having the brand of an old offender, was executed. 1851 Longf. *Gold. Leg.* iv. v, I see the scar, The brand upon your forehead.

b. *fig.* A sign or mark, sometimes in a general sense, but usually (with reference to the practice of branding criminals) conveying the idea of disgrace; a stigma, a mark of infamy.

1597 Hooker *Eccl. Pol.* v. lxv. §11 To mark that age with the brand of error and superstition. 1628 Prynne *Cens. Cozens* 98 Are they not a public brand and blemish to our Church? 1651 Cleveland *Poems* 24 No Fellon is more letter'd, though the brand Both superscribes his shoulder and his hand. 1726 De Foe *Hist. Devil* II. vi. (1840) 244 The devil could go nowhere without this particular brand of infamy. 1853 Marsden *Early Purit.* 324 The brand of that day's infamy will never disappear from the annals of Massachusetts.

c. A trade-mark, whether made by burning or otherwise. (Applied to trade-marks on casks of wines or liquors, timber, metals, and any description of goods except textile fabrics.)

1827 *Motley v. Downman* 3 Mylne & Craig *Law Rep.* 4 The proprietors have added the brand mark 'Margam' on each box. 1881 *Mechanic* §155. 53 Timbers from Swedish ports are marked on the ends with red letters or brands.

d. *spec.* A mark of ownership impressed on cattle, horses, etc., by branding. Also *attrib.* and *Comb.*, as **brand blotter**, one who steals cattle and obliterates the ownership-marks. Chiefly *U.S.*

1665 in *Conn. Public Rec.* (1852) II. 28 They shal enter such saile..in the said brand booke. 1667 *Ibid.* 58 For yr brand of horses they shal have ye letter V on ye near buttock. 1707 *Boston News-Let.* 10 Feb. 2/2 A prety large bright bay Gelding, having a Brand on his near Buttock of this form d. 1869 C. L. Brace *New West* xxii. 288 The brands, both of cattle and horses,..are controlled by law in California. 1888 *Century Mag.* Apr. 860 A man must have natural gifts, as well as great experience, before he becomes a good brand-reader. 1910 W. M. Raine *B. O'Connor* 107 You red-haided [= headed] son of a brand blotter. 1930 L. G. D. Acland *Early Canterbury Runs* iv. 77 He was probably D. A. or J. D. Brittan, who registered a brand between them in 1854. 1963 A. Lubbock *Austral. Roundabout* 147 A brand-forger with a dozen aliases.

e. A steer or other animal bearing a particular brand-mark. *U.S.*

1881 G. W. Romspert *Western Echo* 186 It is seldom they kill their own brands. 1903 A. Adams *Log Cowboy* vii. 90, I must have inspection papers before I can move a brand out of the county in which it is bred.

5. An iron instrument for making marks by burning, or (quot. 1828) for cauterizing a wound.

1828 Scott *F.M. Perth* II. 159 The more I felt the pain his knife and brand inflicted, the better was my chance of recovery. 1860 W. Collins *Wom. White* II. v. 321 Pain and fear and grief written on her as with a brand.

6. (*transf.* from 4 c.) A particular sort or class of goods, as indicated by the trade-marks on them.

1854 Miss Warner *Old Helmet* I. 266 The ale was of a superior brand. 1864 *Reader* 25 June 803 The most renowned dealers whose brand passes muster. 1880 *Print. Trades Jrnl.* XXXI. 14 The perfume of this brand of wax is delightful. 1883 *Harper's Mag.* Aug. 451/1 There are special brands of steel wire for the shrouds and stays.

7. A species of blight in plants, causing the leaves and young shoots to look as though they were burnt; called also BURN (cf. Ger. *brand*).

1639 Horn & Robotham *Gate Lang. Unl.* vi. §52 If it be over heated, it turns to brand or mildew. 1861 Miss Pratt *Flower. Plants* III. 386 Of truly parasitic plants some..are known by the common names of Mildew, Rust, Brand, etc. 1881 Whitehead *Hops* 58 There are special forms of these fungi, known as rust or brand.

II. 8. The blade of a sword or similar weapon, and hence (like 'blade') the sword itself. [So also in Icel. and in later times in OF. and MHG. *brant*: possibly from its flashing in the light.]

†a. Blade, weapon. *Obs.* (exc. as in b).

c 1050 *Will of Æthelstan Æth.* in Thorpe *Dipl.* 559 Ic ȝean Eadmunde minon breðer þæs swurdes þe Offa cyng ahte.. and anes brandes. *c* 1380 Wyclif *Serm.* Sel. Wks. I. 26 A swerd or a knyf..Thei myȝten..wiþdrawe þes brondis þat þus done harme.

b. A sword. (Cf. the poetical use of 'blade'.) A poetical use, though in the present century writers of romance have used it in prose as an archaism.

a 1000 *Beowulf* 2912 Hine syððan no brond ne beadomecas bitan ne meahton. *c* 1205 Lay. 15239 He scal leosen þa hond þurh his aȝene brand. *c* 1340 *Gaw. & Gr. Knt.* 1584 Braydez out a bryȝt bront, & bigly forth strydez. *c* 1400 *Destr. Troy* 7926 And I thi bane for to be with my brond egge. *c* 1440 *York Myst.* xxix. 142 Yone boy with a brande Brayede me full nere. *a* 1541 Wyatt *Psalm* xxxvii. 14 They have unsheathed eke their bloody bronds. 1667 Milton *P.L.* XII. 643 Th' Eastern side..Of Paradise..Wav'd over by that flaming Brand. 1718 Pope *Iliad* v. 105 On his broad shoulder fell the forceful brand. 1820 Scott *Abbot* iii, There ne'er was gentleman but who belted him with the brand. 1873 Symonds *Grk. Poets* v. 124 My wealth's a burly spear and brand.

9. *attrib.* (sense 6) and *Comb.*, as **brand-image**, the impression of a product in the minds of potential users or consumers; also *transf.* and *fig.*, the general or popular conception of some person or thing; **brand-name**, a trade or proprietary name; also *transf.*

1958 M. Mayer *Madison Avenue U.S.A.* iii. 59 David Ogilvy, of Ogilvy, Benson & Mather, apostle of the 'brand image'. *Ibid.* iii. 63 Ogilvy's brand-image advertising.. works essentially on the consumer's conscious mind in an effort to convince him that brand A, technically identical with brand B, is somehow a better product. 1959 *News Chron.* 14 July 4/6 In the jargon of the P.R. trade, there is as yet no 'brand image' for the Prime Minister of Japan. 1960 K. Amis *New Maps of Hell* ii. 45 Space-opera with a full complement of BEMs and a small staff of mad scientists attended by scantily clad daughters constitutes..the main brand-image of science fiction. 1961 *Guardian* 27 May 6/2 Methods..used to determine brand loyalty among smokers. 1922 *Hotel World* 25 Mar. 9 (*heading*) Brand names on menus? 1950 A. H. Sayer et al. *Economics in our Democracy* IV. xiii. 99 Each package has a brand name, which identifies the product as having been made by a certain manufacturer. 1952 E. Partridge *From Sanskrit* 49 The association existed long before any Scotch whisky received the brand-name *the real Mackay*. 1958 *Spectator* 27 June 836/2 The brand-name wrapped loaf. 1960 *20th Cent.* Sept. 234 Mr. Wesker's enemies dismiss him as a mere brand-name oversold by the theatrical Left.

brand (brænd), *v.* Also 4-6 **brond(e**, 5 **bronne**. [f. prec.]

1. *trans.* To burn with a hot iron, whether for the purpose of marking the flesh (as in the case of criminals or slaves), or of cauterizing as a surgical operation; also *fig.*

c 1400 *Apol. Loll.* 103 Hauing þer consciens iren brondit. *c* 1440 *Promp. Parv.* 53 Bronnyn wythe an yren [1499 brondyn], *cauterizo.* 1615 G. Sandys *Trav.* 109 Both men and women do brand their armes for the loue of each other. 1753 *Scots Mag.* Feb. 97/1 The former is to be branded and imprisoned. 1850 Mrs. Stowe *Uncle Tom* xi. 91 Has been branded in his right hand with the letter H.

2. a. To mark indelibly, as a proof of ownership, as a sign of quality, or for any other purpose; to impress (a word, letter, or device) by way of brand. *spec.* to mark (cattle or horses) with a brand.

1587 Golding *De Mornay* xii. 177 Thou wouldest that God should at leastwise brond him with the broade arrow. 1644 in *Conn. Public Rec.* (1850) I. 118 Owners..shall earemarke or brand all their Cattle and swyne that are aboue halfe a yeare old. 1652 [see BRANDED *ppl. a.*[2] 1 a]. 1669 in *Springfield* (Mass.) *Rec.* (1899) II. 101 There are many horses to be branded. 1681 Cotton *Wond. Peak* (ed. 4) 43 Every step did brand Assured footing in the yielding sand. 1765 Washington *Diaries* (1925) I. 216 Calves and Yearl[in]gs branded on the Right Shoulder GW. 1805 Luccock *Nat. Wool* 113 When sheep are not branded with pitch, or any other substance injurious to the staple. 1869 C. L. Brace *New West* xxii. 288 Each owner..lassoed the cattle which were his, branding the calves and those whose marks were somewhat obliterated. 1879 *Cassell's Techn. Educ.* IV. 253/2 The mark was the letters 'M. C.' branded on tin-plates.

b. *fig.* To set a mental mark of ownership upon; also, to impress (a fact, an event) indelibly on one's memory.

1602 Warner *Alb. Eng.* XI. lxiii. (1612) 273 The greene knight, be whoso he shall, her heart had branded hers. 1848 Kingsley *Saint's Trag.* v. i. 226 To brand upon your thoughts How she was once a woman. 1875 Jowett *Plato* (ed. 2) III. 531, I was able to recall every word of this, which is branded into my mind. 1879 Farrar *St. Paul* (1883) 114 Words and utterances..branded indelibly upon the memory.

3. *fig.* To mark or stamp with infamy, stigmatize.

1625 Bacon *Atheism, Ess.* (Arb.) 337 All..are branded with the Name of Atheists. *a* 1674 Clarendon *Hist. Reb.* (1702) I. III. 215 They..intended by some Vote to Brand him, and make him odious. 1771 Cumberland *West Ind.* IV. iv, Brand me for a coward if I baulk you. *a* 1853 Robertson *Lect.* ii. 61 Dare we brand infidelity with hard names?

brand, obs. form of BRAWNED.

‖**brandade** (brɑ̃dad). [Fr., ad. Pr. *brandado*, lit. 'thing which has been moved, shaken'.] In full *brandade de morue.* A Provençal dish made from salt cod.

1825 *Fr. Domestic Cookery* 195 (*heading*) Brandade of salt cod. 1866 H. Toogood *Treas. Fr. Cookery* 46 (*heading*) Cod.—brandade de morue. 1877 E. S. Dallas *Kettner's Bk. Table* 84 The first recipe for a brandade..was written by Grimod de la Reynière. 1951 R. Campbell *Light on Dark Horse* xxi. 294 Nothing is better, says a Provençal proverb, for reviving and remaking a man than living in the clear sunlight, speaking Provençal, eating 'brandade', and drinking the good red wine of Provence. 1966 'K. Nicholson' *Hook, Line & Sinker* v. 64 Brandade de Morue ..cod fillets cooked with garlic, cream, olive oil, lemon juice and a teeny suggestion of fennel.

[**branded**, misreading for *brauded* embroidered; so also *brandur* for *braudur* embroidery.

c 1440 *Gaw. & Gol.* II. iii, Here belt was of blunket.. Branded with brende golde. *Ibid.* II. iv, His brene and his basnet..With a brandur abought, al of brende golde.]

'branded, *ppl. a.*[1] *Obs.* exc. *dial.* [A northern var. of *brended*, later BRINDED.] Brindled.

1561 *Richmond. Wills* (1853) 148, I geve to Henry Todd an oxe calfe in Peknell, color branded. 1607 Topsell *Four-f. Beasts* 126 A spotted, branded, party coloured dog is not approved. 1611 Chapman *Iliad* XXI. 217 They saw a branded serpent sprawl..amongst them from above. *a* 1800 *Ballad, 'Lads of Wamphray'* iii. in Scott *Minstr.*, The brokit cow and the branded bull. 1880 Patterson *Antrim & Down Gloss.*, *Branded, brannet*, of a red colour with streaks or bands, applied to cattle.

branded ('brændɪd), *ppl. a.*[2] [f. BRAND *v.*]

1. a. Marked with a hot iron. b. Bearing a trade-mark, or mark of quality.

1652 *Proc. Parliament* No. 159. 2502 Advt., A light grey Mare..branded with E. *a* 1704 T. Brown *Sat. Quack* Wks. 1730 I. 64 A branded villain. 1880 *Daily Tel.* 30 Apr., There is no alteration in branded iron.

c. Labelled with a trade or proprietary name; having a brand-name.

1897 *Daily News* 16 Dec. 7/2 A customer asked for a certain branded ham. 1946 D. L. Sayers *Unpopular Opinions* 128 Any proposal to control the marketing of branded goods..will be violently opposed, on the loftiest hygienic grounds, by the papers that carry the branded advertising.

2. *fig.* Marked with infamy, stigmatized.

1601 R. Yarington *Two Lament. Traj.* v. ii. in Bullen *O. Pl.* IV, Bronded with a marke of Shame. 1654 *Curia Politiæ* 100 Why should that branded Politician make feare and love impossible and inseparable? 1878 Bosw. Smith *Carthage* 265 Branded with the defeat of Cannæ.

† **'branded**, *ppl. a.*[3] *Sc. Obs. rare*[−1]. [Cf. F. *brandir* to fasten two pieces of wood together with a peg.] ? Firmly secured; perh. error for *bandit*.

1535 STEWART *Cron. Scot.* I. 350 Ane brig.. Rycht stark of tymmer.. Brandit and bond, and festnit richt fest.

bran-deer. A loose adaptation of Ger. *brandhirsch*, 'a stag with dark-brown breast.' Grimm.

1774 GOLDSM. *Nat. Hist.* II. v. (1862) I. 327 A kind of stag, named by the ancients the Tragelaphus, and which the natives call the bran deer.

brandeis, obs. Sc. form of BRANDISH.

brandelede, obs. var. of BRANDRETH.

† **brandellet.** *Obs. rare*[−1].

c **1325** *Coer de L.* 322 His pusen therwith gan gon, And also his brandellet bon, Hys vyser and his gorgere.

† **'brandenburgh.** *Obs.* [f. the name of a city in Prussia, famous for woollen manufactures. So Fr. *brandebourg*.] A morning gown.

1676 ETHEREDGE *Man of Mode* IV. ii. (1684) 61 Y' have a very fine Brandenburgh on, Sir Fopling. **1691** *Fop Dict. Supp.*, *Brandenburgh*, a Morning Gown.

† **'brandenburgs.** *Obs.* [Prob. so called because worn in the army of the Elector of Brandenburg, afterwards king of Prussia; cf. Fr. *brandebourg*, 'boutonnière avec ornement' (Boiste).] *pl.* **a.** The ornamental facings to the breast of an officer's coat.

1753 HANWAY *Trav.* (1762) I. VII. xcii. 422 [The Prussian King] in his regimentals, which are a blue cloth frock with silver brandenburgs. *a* **1771** SMOLLETT *Humph. Cl.* (1815) 225 He wore a coat.. trimmed with Brandenburgs, now totally deprived of their metal.

b. (Also **brande(n)bourgs.**) Ornamental trimmings (see quot. 1882) on a woman's dress, in fashion from about 1870 to 1910.

1873 *Young Englishwoman* Mar. 130/2 One [mantle].. is fastened in front with brandenbourgs, finished off with macarons and round balls of the same style. **1882** CAULFEILD & SAWARD *Dict. Needlew.* 44/2 *Brandenbourgs.* Synonymous with 'Frogs'. A button formed somewhat in the shape of a long and narrow barrel, smaller at the ends than the middle, and made of silk on a wooden foundation. **1891** *Queen* 17 Jan. 103/1 Costumes of Hussar-blue cloth with black braid brandebourgs. **1902** *Daily Chron.* 8 Nov. 8/3 The fulness of the fronts is finished with brandebourgs of silk cords. **1909** *Westm. Gaz.* 17 July 15/1 It hangs rather full from the waist, is open in front, or caught with Brandenburgs of braid or tinsel.

brander ('brændə(r)), *sb.*[1] [f. BRAND *v.* + -ER.] One who brands.

1860 RAWLINSON *Herodotus* VII. xxxv. IV. 36 He [Xerxes] bade the branders take their irons and therewith brand the Hellespont.

'brander, *sb.*[2] *Obs.* exc. *Sc.* and *north. dial.* Also 5 **brandyr**, 6 **brandire.** [Variant of BRANDIRON.] A gridiron. See also BRANDISE, BRANDIRON, BRANDRETH.

c **1450** *Gloss.* in Wr.-Wülcker 626 *Tripos*, brondyre. **1587** in Wadley *Bristol Wills* (1886) 251 My great pan and brandire and Pykes thervnto belonginge. **1708** *Inv.* in E. W. Dunbar *Soc. Life Moray* 212 (D.) A frying-pan, two branders. **1815** SCOTT *Guy M.* xxiv, A couple of fowls.. reeking from the gridiron or brander.

brander ('brændə(r)), *v.*[1] Chiefly *Sc.* and *north. dial.* [f. prec.] *trans.* and *intr.* To cook on the gridiron, broil, grill. Hence **'brandered** *ppl. a.*, **brandering** *vbl. sb.*, as in ***brandering steak.***

c **1782** SIR T. SINCLAIR *Scott. Dial.* 172 (JAM.) The Scots also say *to brander* for to broil meat. **1814** SCOTT *Wav.* lxiv, 'I'll brander the moor-fowl that John Heatherblutter brought in this morning.' *c* **1817** HOGG *Tales & Sk.* III. 37 Brandered kidneys. **1848** FORSTER *Life Goldsm.* I. iv, A brandered chop served up.

'brander, *v.*[2] [prob. f. BRANDER *sb.*[2], as if 'to arrange cross-bars in the form of a gridiron'; but cf. F. *brandir* under BRANDED *ppl. a.*[2]]

Hence **'brandering** *vbl. sb.*, 'the covering of the under-side of joists with battens... to nail the laths to, in order to secure a better key for the plaster of a ceiling' (Spon *Dict. Engineer.* 1869.)

branderer, ? erron. form of *brauderer*, BROIDERER: but the passages are obscure.

1387 TREVISA *Higden* Rolls Ser. III. 77 [Tullus Hostilius].. vsede purpur, a maner reed cloþinge of kynges and branderers and rueeres [orig. *purpura et fascibus usus est*]. *c* **1530** in Gutch *Coll. Cur.* II. 287 Deliveryd to my said Lordis Branderars of his Copis in small Perle.. poiss. iiij oz. *Ibid.* II. 289 Deliveryd in gilte spangillis for my Lordis Footmen Coolis to Stevyn Humble Branderer poiss. clvj oz.

brandewine, early form of BRANDY.

brande(y)rne, -hirne, var. of BRAND-IRON.

brand-goose: see BRANT *sb.*

brandied ('brændɪd), *ppl. a.* [f. BRANDY *v.*] Mixed, treated, or 'fortified' with brandy.

1833 C. REDDING *Mod. Wines* iv. (ed. 2) 66 The brandied wines of Portugal. **1871** MORLEY *Crit. Misc.* (1886) I. 287 The wine of truth is in his cup a brandied draught.

brandified ('brændɪfaɪd), *ppl. a.* [As if f. a vb. *brandify*: see -FY.] **1.** Affected by brandy.

1863 *Spring & Summ. Lapl.* 31 He had already got some such notion into his muddled, brandified old head.

2. Mixed or treated with brandy.

1841 THACKERAY *Mem. Gormandising* in *Wks.* (1900) XIII. 576 A brandyfied liquor called sherry. **1877** G. EASTON *Wine of Cana*, Brandified and whiskeyfied wines.

branding ('brændɪŋ), *vbl. sb.* [f. BRAND *v.*]

1. The action of marking with a hot iron, as a surgical operation; or of burning a mark upon a criminal, or an article for sale.

c **1440** *Promp. Parv.* 53 Brondynge, *cauterizacio.* **1660** R. COKE *Justice Vind.* 14 Anything.. received into the senses, be it whipping, branding or hanging. **1764** HARMER *Observ.* vi. xvi. 261 Whipping and branding with the flower-de-lis among the French. **1846** McCULLOCH *Acc. Brit. Empire* (1854) I. 631 The gutting.. of the herrings, and the branding of the barrels. **1849** GROTE *Greece* II. xl. V. 128. *fig. a* **1649** DRUMM. OF HAWTH. *Hist. Jas. V*, Wks. (1711) 90 It would be an everlasting branding their honour, if timorously.. they show their backs to their enemies.

2. *attrib.*, as in ***branding-corrall, -iron, -yard***; **branding-chute** *U.S.*, a gradually narrowing enclosure into which cattle are driven to be branded.

c **1440** *Promp. Parv.* 53 Brondynge yren, *cauterium.* **1583** GOLDING *Calvin on Deut.* xiv. 80 Despisers of God.. haue the said bronding yron searing within them. **1863** W. PHILLIPS *Speeches* xi. 259 His broad bosom scarred all over with the branding-iron. **1881** *Gentl. Mag.* Jan. 64 The branding-yard [for cattle]. **1882** *Lippincott's Mag.* May 429/2 Several small fenced enclosures.. and a branding-chute are soon completed. **1885** *Pall Mall G.* 20 Mar. 3/2 The cows and calves.. are driven into the branding corrall. **1911** MULFORD *Bar-20 Days* xx. 197 Johnny Nelson waited.. on the platform of the branding chute.

'branding, *ppl. a.* [f. BRAND *v.* + -ING[2].]

1. That scorches or marks by burning.

1811 BYRON *Curse of Min.* xi, In many a branding page and burning line. **1850** TENNYSON *In Mem.* ii, Nor branding summer suns avail To touch thy thousand years of gloom. **1868** LD. LYTTON *Chron. & Char.* II. 127 The branding bolt, that rent The skies asunder.

2. That brands or stigmatizes.

1853 C. BRONTË *Villette* xxiii. (1876) 250 It was a branding judgment. **1877** FARRAR *My Youth* i. 4 He felt the branding finger upon his brow.

† **'bran,diron.** *Obs.* exc. *dial.* Also 4 **brandhirne**, 5–6 **-eyrne, -erne, -yren**, 6 **brond-**; other forms under BRANDER *sb.*[2] [f. BRAND + IRON.]

1. A kitchen utensil, commonly a gridiron, but the name is transferred to other articles, as andirons (still *dial.* in Kent), a stand for a kettle, a trivet. See the synonymous BRANDER *sb.*[2], BRANDISE; also BRANDRETH.

1381 *Eng. Gilds* 233 Seven dozens of 'vesselles du peutre'; a 'brandhirne'. **1411** *Inv.* in Turner *Dom. Archit.* III. iv. 153, j brandeyrne. **1424** *E.E. Wills* (1882) 56 A peyre rakkes of yryne, and to branderes. **1552** HULOET, Brond-yron, or Andyron. **1580** BARET *Alv.* B 1126 A Brandiron or posnet, *chytra.* **1596** *Wills & Inv. N.C.* II. 271, j brande-iron, that the kettle standes on. **1730** DAVIES in *Phil. Trans.* XXXVI. 445 The Brand-Irons and Legs thereof were strained. **1886** R. JEFFERIES in *Pall Mall Budget* 2 Dec. 9/1 What are usually called dog-irons on the hearth are called brand-irons, having to support the brand or burning log.

¶ **2.** Taken by Spenser, and by Quarles after him, in the sense of: A sword [= BRAND *sb.* 8].

1596 SPENSER *F.Q.* IV. iv. 32 And with his brondiron round about him layd. **1621** QUARLES *Argalus & P.* (1678) 100 [He] Vnsheath'd his furious Brand-iron. *Ibid.* (1708) 122 The stout Amphialus.. Up heav'd his thirsty brandiron.

† **3. brand-iron-wise**, in the shape of a gridiron.

1555 EDEN *Decades W. Ind.* (Arb.) 381 Southeast.. is thre trees lyke a brandierwyse.

† **brandise** ('brændɪs). *Obs.* exc. *dial.* Also 1 **brand-isen**, 9 **brandice.** [OE. *brand-isen*, f. *brand* burning + *isen* iron: but the history of the word between OE. and modern times is uncertain.] A trivet; perhaps used also in the other senses of BRANDER *sb.*[2], BRANDIRON.

c **1000** ÆLFRIC *Voc.* in Wr.-Wülcker 127 *Andena vel tripes*, brandisen. **1872** HARDWICK *Trad. Lancashire* 133 The brandice. **1874** HARDY *Madding Crowd* xxii. (1882) 152 There was a great black crock upon the brandise.

brandish ('brændɪʃ), *v.* Forms: 4–5 **braundis-, ise(n, -ish, -issh, -ysch, -ische**, 5 **brawndesche, branych** (*Cath. Angl.*), 4–6 **brandiss, -issh, -isch**, 6 *Sc.* **brandeis**, 5– **brandish.** [a. Fr. *brandiss-* lengthened stem of Fr. *brandir*, a common Romanic word (L. type **brandire*), f. Teut. BRAND, a sword.]

1. *trans.* To flourish, wave about (a sword, spear, dart, club, or other manual weapon) by way of threat or display, or in preparation for action.

a **1340** HAMPOLE *Psalter* vii. 13 He sal braundis his swerd. **1382** WYCLIF *Ps.* vii. 13 But ȝee shal ben convertid, his swerd he shal braundishen. **1475** CAXTON *Jason* 15 b, [They] brandished their speris and escried their enemyes. **1583** STANYHURST *Æneis* II. (Arb.) 54 They brandish weapons sharp edgde. **1611** BIBLE *Ezek.* xxxii. 10, I shall brandish my sword before them. **1727** SWIFT *Gulliver* II. vii. 161 Draw their swords at once, and brandish them in the air. **1824** DIBDIN *Libr. Comp.* 726 You may brandish your mother of pearl paper-cutter. **1848** MACAULAY *Hist. Eng.* II. 488 A great crowd.. of young peasants, brandishing their cudgels. **1874** BOUTELL *Arms & Arm.* ii. 40.

b. *fig.*

c **1325** *E.E. Allit. P.* A. 346 Þoȝ þou daunce as any do, Braundysch & bray þy braþez breme. **1648** MILTON *Tenure Kings* (1650) 3 Lawes which they so impotently brandish against others. **1697** COLLIER *Ess. Mor. Subj.* II. (1709) 152 They love to be always brandishing their Advantage. *a* **1764** LLOYD *Fam. Let. Rhimes* Wks. 1774 II. 78 Your eyes that brandish burning darts. **1867** J. MARTINEAU *Chr. Life* (ed. 4) 370 Brandishing the threat of infliction.

c. To flourish about, move vigorously (the limbs, the head, etc.); also used of a snake darting out its tongue, of a lion flourishing its tail, etc. Somewhat *arch.*, if not *obs.*

? *a* **1400** *Morte Arth.* (Roxb.) 117 The knight þan braundisshid yche a bone. **1610** G. FLETCHER *Christ's Vict.* (1632) 22 And every one brandisht his fiery tongue. **1834** PRINGLE *Afr. Sk.* viii. 260 He was now beginning to.. brandish his tail.

2. *absol.* To flourish one's weapons or limbs; to make a flourish or display; to swagger.

c **1340** *Alisaunder* 1122 That hee nas loose in no lime.. To byte, ne to braundise. *c* **1350** *Will. Palerne* 2321 Breme burnes.. Brandissende wiþ gret bost. *c* **1430** *How Gd. Wyf taugt Dau.* in *Babees Bk.* (1868) 39 Braundische not with þin heed. *c* **1505** DUNBAR *Dance* 33 He brandeist lyk a beir. **1533** BELLENDEN *Livy* IV. (1822) 338 Brandisand throw the army.

3. *intr.* (for *refl.*) Of a sword, = To be brandished.

a **1649** DRUMM. OF HAWTH. *Hist. Scot.* (1655) 2 Your Swords.. should brandish to set him on his Royall throne. **1800** SCOTT *Lady of L.* VI. xviii.

† **4.** *trans.* Of the sun or other luminary: To dart forth, scatter (rays of light); also (rarely) to irradiate, render luminous. *Obs.*

1598 SYLVESTER *Du Bartas* II. i. IV. (1641) 108/1 His brows seem brandisht with a Sun-like fire. **1653** H. MORE *Conject. Cabbal.* (1713) 215 This light of Righteousness.. may not brandish its rays in the empty field. **1656** BLOUNT *Glossogr.*, *Brandish*, to make to.. glister with gentle shaking or moving.

† **b.** *intr.* To glitter, gleam, flash, coruscate.

1552 HULOET, Brandysh, or glytter, lyke a sworde, *corusco.* **1598** SYLVESTER *Du Bartas* II. i. IV. (1641) 109/1 Thine eyes already (now no longer eyes; But new bright stars) do brandish in the skyes. *Ibid.* (1608) 78 Orion, Eridanus, the Whale.. Through Heavens bright arches brandish up and down. [**1884** STEVENSON *New Arab. Nts.* 237 A branch of flame shot brandishing through the aperture.]

'brandish, *sb.* [f. prec.] An act of brandishing; a flourish or wave (of a weapon).

1599 B. JONSON *Cynthia's Rev.* v. x, I can wound with a Brandish. **1709** ADDISON *Tatler* No. 157 ¶ 11 Tosses of the Head, and Brandishes of the Fan. **1816** BYRON *Siege of Cor.* xxii, The reply was the brandish of sabre and spear.

† **'brandish**, *a. Obs. rare.* [f. BRANDY + -ISH[1].] Of the quality of, or resembling brandy.

1683 TRYON *Way to Health* 560 A strong sulpherous brandish Spirit, that has no other operation than common Brandy or Spirit of Wine.

brandished ('brændɪʃt), *ppl. a.* [f. BRANDISH *v.* + -ED[1].] Made to vibrate; flourished, waved.

1583 STANYHURST *Æneis* II. (Arb.) 67, I doe se theyre brandisht tergats. **1667** MILTON *P.L.* XII. 633 The brandisht Sword of God before them blaz'd. **1709** STEELE *Tatler* No. 34 ¶ 4 Some Body.. has called a fine Woman dancing, a Brandished Torch of Beauty. **1813** SCOTT *Rokeby* v. xxxii, His brandished faulchion's sheer descent!

brandisher ('brændɪʃə(r)). [f. BRANDISH *v.* + -ER[1].] One who brandishes or flourishes a weapon.

c **1600** CHAPMAN *Iliad* xx. 146 O Phœbus, brandisher of darts. **1860** W. G. CLARK *Vac. Tour* 46 The brandishers of daggers were persons from the well-fed, well-dressed orders.

brandishing ('brændɪʃɪŋ), *vbl. sb.* [f. BRANDISH *v.* + -ING[1].]

1. The action of flourishing (weapons).

c **1440** *Promp. Parv.* 48 Brawndyschynge, *vibracio.* **1655** *Theophania* 92 By the brandishing of their weapons in the air we knew the fight was not yet ended. **1821** JOANNA BAILLIE *Wallace* xiv, With hopeful, wanton brandishing.

b. *fig.*

1690 LOCKE *Hum. Und.* IV. xvii, He who shall employ all the force of his Reason only in brandishing of Syllogisms. **1766** FORDYCE *Serm. Yng. Wom.* (ed. 4) I. v. 193 The brandishings of wit in the hand of ill-nature.

† **2.** Flashing, coruscating. *Obs.*

1552 HULOET, Brandishinge, or glytteryng, *coruscatio.*

3. A corrupt form of BRATTISHING.

1846 PARKER *Concise Gloss. Arch.*; and in mod. Dicts.

brandishing ('brændɪʃɪŋ), *ppl. a.* [f. BRANDISH *v.* + -ING[2].] **a.** Vibrating, quivering. † **b.** Gleaming, flashing, sparkling.

1581 W. WARREN (*title*) The brandishing brightnes off an English Gentlewoman. **1658** ROWLAND *Mouffet's Theat. Ins.* 1130 They move in a brandishing manner. **1660** BOYLE

New Exp. Phys.-Mech. i. 25 The vehement agitation, and brandishing motion.

† **'brandishment.** *Obs. rare*$^{-1}$. [f. BRANDISH *v.* + -MENT.] The action of brandishing.
1640-1 LD. J. DIGBY *Sp. in Ho. Com.* 9 Feb. 14 Their Brandishment of the spirituall sword. **1655** *Theophania* 180 The brandishment of his Sword was no less terrible.

brandisite ('brændɪsaɪt). *Min.* [ad. G. *brandisit* (1846), f. the title of Clement, Count of *Brandis*, after whom the mineral was named: see -ITE[1].] A variety of seybertite.
1868 DANA *Syst. Min.* (ed. 5) 508. **1883** *Encycl. Brit.* XVI. 413/2 Brandisite is similar [to Clintonite].

brandiss, obs. f. BRANDISH *v.*

† **'brandle,** *v. Obs.* [ad. F. *branler*, found in both senses; the *d* may be due to an acquaintance with the earlier Fr. form *brandeler*, but more probably is merely phonetic, as in *spindle*; cf. also BRANGLE, BRANLE, BRANSLE, BRANTLE.]
a. *trans.* To shake, shock, cause to waver. **b.** *intr.* To become unsteady, to totter, waver.
1606 LD. NORTHAMPTON *Proceed. agst. Garnet* G g b. Subiects cannot be too curious, when the State brandles. **1621** BACON *Hen. VII*, 96 It had like to have brandled the fortune of the day. **1655** LESTRANGE *Chas. I.* 112 Gave him so terrible a shock, as made his Vantguard to brandle.

brandless ('brændlɪs), *a.* [f. BRAND *sb.* + -LESS.] That has no brands, or wood for fuel.
1849 ROCK *Ch. of Fathers* IV. xi. 96 The hearth that had all day long been cold and brandless.

† **'brandlet.** *Obs. rare*$^{-1}$. [f. BRAND *sb.* + -LET.] A bird: perh. the *Brandtail* or Redstart.
1576 GASCOIGNE *Compl. Philomene* Prol. 31 The Brandlet saith, for singing sweete and softe (In hir conceit) there is none such as she.

brandlet, variant of BRANDRETH, *Obs.*

brandling ('brændlɪŋ). [f. BRAND *sb.* + -LING; from the colour or markings.]
1. A worm of a red colour variegated with rings or bands of brighter colouring, used as bait by anglers.
1651 T. BARKER *Art of Angling* (1820) 3 Brandlin. **1653** WALTON *Angler* 94 For a Brandling, hee is usually found in an old dunghil. **1741** *Compl. Fam.-Piece* II. ii. 336 The Brandlings are generally found in Cow or Hog's Dung. **1854** BADHAM *Halieut.* 274 A gudgeon being incapable of refusing a lively young brandling. **1880** *Boys Own Bk.* 264 The brandling and gilt tail are excellent bait for Perch.
2. *dial.* A local name of the salmon parr; formerly regarded as a species of trout.
c **1730** BURT *Lett. N. Scotl.* (1818) I. 121 A little trout.. called in the North of England a branlin. **1802** J. WILSON (Congleton) *MS. Let. 17 Apr. to J. Boucher, Brandling*, a small Trout. *Cumb.* **1880-84** J. DAY *Fishes Gt. Britain* II. 68 The Salmon.. From one to two years old, before it has gone to the sea, it is known as a parr, pink, smolt, smelt, salmon-fry, sprag, or salmon-spring, samlet, brandling, fingerling, etc., etc.

† **'brandling,** *ppl. a. Obs.* [f. BRANDLE *v.*, cf. BRANLING.] Tottering, unsteady, wavering.
1605 RALEIGH *Introd. Hist. Eng.* (1693) 36 Before the settling of the Government whilest it was new and brandling. **1611** COTGR., *Branslant*, brandling.. reeling, staggering, wauering.

brand-mark ('brænd-ˌmɑːk). [f. BRAND + MARK.] The mark left by a branding-iron: also *fig.*
1655-60 STANLEY *Hist. Philos.* (1701) 143/1 A Brand-mark, which declared the ill disposition of the owner. **1684** *Lond. Gaz.* No. 1990/4 An old Brandmark on the farther Leg behind. **1879** FARRAR *St. Paul* II. 580 Or borne in his mortal body such evident brand-marks of the Lord.
Hence **brand-marked** *ppl. a.*
1678 *Lond. Gaz.* No. 818/4 Brand marked with two P's counter-placed. **1847** *Nat. Encycl.* I. 331 The *Acheus Ai*, or brand-marked sloth.

brand-new, ('brænd 'njuː), *a.* Also **bran-new,** *Sc.* **brank-, brent-new.** [f. BRAND *sb.* + NEW, as if fresh and glowing from the furnace; cf. Shakspere's *fire-new.*] Quite new, perfectly new.
c **1570** FOXE *Serm. 2 Cor.* v. 63 New bodies, new minds.. and all thinges new, brande-newe. **1714** GAY *What d'ye call it?* II. v. 28 'Wear these Breeches Tom; they're quite bran-new.' **1790** BURNS *Tam o' Shanter*, Nae cotillon brent new frae France. **1821** CLARE *Vill. Minstr.* I. 38 When villagers put on their bran-new clothes. **1824** SCOTT *St. Ronan's* I. 56 (JAM.) Yeomen with the brank new blues and buckskins. **1858** CARLYLE *Fredk. Gt.* II. VII. iii. 183 The whole Saxon Army.. all in beautiful brand-new uniforms. **1871** MORLEY *Voltaire* (1886) 131 A bran-new vaudeville.
Hence in same sense (chiefly *dial.*) the double forms **brand-fire-new, brand-span-new, brand-spander-new.** Also **brand-newness.**
1825 *Bro. Jonathan* I. 151 Bran-fire, noo, as I'm alive. **1830** H. ANGELO *Remin.* I. 57 His feet were thrust into a bran-span new pair of fashionable pumps. **1855** *Whitby Gloss., Brandnew, Brandspandernew*, fresh from the maker's hands, or 'spic and span new'. **1870** HAWTHORNE *Eng. Note-bks.* (1879) I. 108 This brand-newness makes it seem much less effective.

† **'brandon.** *Obs. rare.* Also **brandom.** [a. F. *brandon* burning wisp of straw, etc.: com. Romanic:—L. type **brandōn-em*, f. Teut. *brand* burning.]
1. A torch. *lit.* and *fig.* (Frequent in Drummond.)
a **1649** DRUMM. OF HAWTH. *Shadow of Judgm.*, Her right hand swings a brandon in the air. —— *Poems* 14 His [Cupid's] Darts.. all for nought him serve as doth his Brandom.
‖**2.** A kind of French rustic dance (see Littré).
1755 *Gentl. Mag.* XXV. 175 The Brandons were celebrated in many cities in France the first Sunday of Lent, round bonfires of straw, whence they had their name.

brandreth ('brændrɪθ). Also 5 **branderith, brandryt(h(e,** 5-6 **-rethe,** 6 **brandrate, -ereth, brendreth,** 6-8 **brandrith;** also with substitution of *l* for *r* 5 **brandelede, branlet,** 5-6 **brenlede** (Wr.-Wülcker 769), **-delette.** [a. ON. *brand-reið* a grate, f. *brand-r* brand, burning + *reið* carriage, vehicle: cf. OE. *brandrod* for *brandrád*, (*Corpus Gl.*, Wr.-Wülcker 5, 38), and *brandred*, *-rida* ('andena', *ibid.* 349, 266); OHG. *brantreita.*]
†**1.** A gridiron; a tripod or trivet of iron. (Originally a grate supported on three legs on the hearth: hence the apparent variety of definitions.) *Obs.* exc. *dial.*
1400 *Test. Ebor.* (1836) I. 268 Unum par tongis, unum flechok, unum branderith. *a* **1450** *MS. Lincoln. Med.* f. 283 (Halliw.) Take grene ȝerdis of esche, and laye thame over a brandrethe. **1533** BELLENDEN *Livy* I. (1822) 90 Thay band ane brandreth of irne, with mony grete stanis, to his crag. **1590** *Inv.* in *Eng. Ch. Furniture* (1866) 248 Item ij brandrethes and an apple iron. **1663** *Inv. Ld. J. Gordon's Furniture*, A droping pan; a brandereth of iorn; ane ladle and fork. **1727** BRADLEY *Fam. Dict.*, *Brandrith*, a Trevet or other Iron Utensil to set a Vessel on over the Fire. **1875** *Lanc. Gloss.* (E.D.S.) *Brandreth*, a gridiron.
2. A framework of wood for various purposes, as a stand for a cask, or for a hay-rick; a substructure of piles to support a house; also a fence or rail round the opening of a well.
1483 *Cath. Angl.* 40 A Brandryth to set begynnyge [*v.r.* byggyng] on, *loramentum.* **1573** *Lanc. Wills* (1857) III. 62 A brandereth where upon the barrell laye. **1659** HOOLE *Comenius' Vis. World* (ed. 12) 93 Wells.. are compassed about with a brandrith, lest any should fall in. **1837** HOWITT *Rur. Life* III. vi. (1862) 279 There was.. the brandreth, or frame on which a rick once stood.
†**3.** (See quotation.) *Obs.*
1688 R. HOLME *Armory* III. viii. 53 The Brandret or Mill-rinde, a cross like Iron laid in the Upper Stone to turn it.

'brandtail. Name of a bird, the Redstart or Firetail.
1802 MONTAGU *Ornith. Dict.*, *Brantail.*

brandtite ('bræn(d)taɪt). *Min.* [ad. Sw. *brandtit* (1888), f. the name of Georg *Brandt*, Master of the Swedish Mint: see -ITE[1].] Hydrated arsenate of calcium and manganese occurring in crystal form near Pajsberg in Sweden.
1896 CHESTER *Dict. Min.*

brandur, misreading for *braudur*: see BRANDED.

brandy ('brændɪ), *sb.* Also 7 **brandwine, brandewine, brandy-wine, brandee.** [The orig. form *brandwine, brandewine* is a. Du. *brandewijn* 'burnt' (i.e. distilled) wine. In familiar use abbreviated as *brandy* as early as 1657; but the fuller form was retained in official use (customs tariffs, acts of parliament, etc.) down to the end of 17th c., being latterly, as the spelling shows, regarded as a compound of *brandy + wine.*]
1. a. Properly an ardent spirit distilled from wine or grapes; but the name is also applied to spirits of similar flavour and appearance, obtained from other materials.
α. **1622** FLETCHER *Beggar's Bush* III. i, Buy any brand-wine, buy any brand-wine? *c* **1650** *Roxb. Ballads* (1886) VI. 320 It is more fine than Brandewine, The Butterboxes' Poison. **1652** *Proc. Parliament* No. 153. 2391 Laden with Woolls, Brandy Wine and Salt. **1697** *View Penal Laws* 173 No Aqua-Vitæ or Brandy-Wine shall be imported into England. **1719** D'URFEY *Pills* (1872) V. 23, I was entertained, With Kisses fine, and Brandy Wine.
β. **1657** COLVIL *Whigs Supplic.* (1751) Introd. 5 The late Dutch war.. occasioned the bringing in of such superfluity of brandy. **1663** HICKERINGILL *Jamaica* 78 Of your Wine and Brandee, you'le be free. **1790** BURNS *Scots Prol.* 4 Does nonsense mend, like brandy, when imported? **1848** KINGSLEY *Saint's Trag.* III. ii. 158 And take his snack of brandy for digestion.
b. A drink of brandy. Similarly ***brandy-and soda*** (cf. *B. and S.* s.v. B. III.)
1884 G. MOORE *Mummer's Wife* (1887) 193 The brandies and sodas supped in the dressing room. **1900** E. GLYN *Visits Elizabeth* 253 Charlie had two brandies-and-sodas instead of his usual glass of milk. **1903** *Daily Chron.* 11 Nov. 5/2 Took a brandy before going to kirk, lest I should smell of whisky in the house of the Lord! **1932** E. BOWEN *To North* xvii. 174 They would want two brandies.
c. *fig.* Something that stimulates or excites.
1903 G. B. SHAW *Man & Superman* III. 99 Hell is full of musical amateurs: music is the brandy of the damned. **1930** M. ENTHOVEN tr. *Janni's Machiavelli* 80 Machiavelli is the most glorious distiller of political brandy who has ever existed.
2. *Comb.* and *attrib.*, as ***brandy-cag, -devil, -dough, -flask, -keg, -man, -merchant, -shop,*** and in the names of drinks as ***brandy and soda, brandy and water, brandy-flip, -posset, -punch,*** etc.; † ***brandy-face; brandy-faced, -burnt, -sodden*** adjs.; also **brandy-ball,** a kind of sweet; **brandy-butter,** a hard sauce made of brandy and butter; **brandy-cherry** = cherry-brandy; also cherries preserved in brandy; so **brandy-peach,** etc.; **brandy paper,** paper steeped in brandy; **brandy-smash** *U.S.* (see quot. 1909 and SMASH *sb.*[1] 5); **brandy-snap,** wafer-like gingerbread. Also BRANDY-BOTTLE, BRANDY-PAWNEE.
1825, 1849 *Brandy-ball [see HARD-BAKE]. **1862** MAYHEW *Crim. Prisons* 51 Buttons, that have much the appearance of small brandy-balls. **1838** HAWTHORNE *Amer. Note-bks.* (1871) I. 161 A large.. *brandy-burnt, heavy-faced man. **1939** 'VIVETTE' in A. L. Simon *Concise Encycl. Gastronomy* I. 29/2 In U.S.A., a *Hard Sauce* is made with one measure of fresh butter to two of castor sugar... In England, a similar sauce is called **Brandy Butter* or *Rum Butter.* **1795** WOLCOTT (P. Pindar) *Lousiad* II. Wks. 1812 I. 227 And for a cruet stands a *brandy-cag. *a* **1687** COTTON *Aeneid II. Burl.* (1692) 83 Whether 't was that she.. Fainted for want of *brandy-cherry. **1853** *Harper's Mag.* VII. 275/2 A swine drunk on brandy-cherry stones is disgusting. **1885** C. M. YONGE *Two Sides of Shield* II. v. 101 And there was Miss Hacket getting brandy cherries and strong coffee. **1820** SHELLEY *Œdipus Tyr.* I. i, Fat martyrs to the persecution Of stifling turtle-soup and *brandy-devils. **1799** G. SMITH *Laboratory* I. 21 Supplied with *brandy dough. *a* **1687** COTTON *Aeneid II. Burl.* (1692) 85 You goodman *Brandy-face, unfist her. **1861** SALA *Tw. round Clock* 284 Hulking labourers and *brandy-faced viragos, squabbling at tavern doors. **1833** MARRYAT *P. Simple* (1863) 168 I've emptied the *brandy-flask; and that's a bad job. **1865** E. BURRITT *Walk to Land's E.* 62 Articles of food and drink.. such as egg-nog and *brandy-flip. **1865** *N. Brit. Rev.* Sept. 227 Ula informed me that he had lost the *brandy-keg. **1723** *Lond. Gaz.* No. 6172/9 Henry Gillum.. *Brandyman. *a* **1771** SMOLLETT *Humph. Cl.* (1815) 139 After some unsuccessful essays in the way of poetry, he commenced *brandy-merchant. **1769** MRS RAFFALD *Eng. Housekpr.* (1778) 227 Tie them down with *brandy papers over them. **1781** HAYLEY *Tri. Temper* III. 467 Eager she plies them with a *brandy peach. **1769** MRS. RAFFALD *Eng. Housekpr.* (1778) 309 To make a *Brandy Posset. **1689** SEWALL *Diary* (1878) I. 306 In the Lord's Hall Guy's Pot was filled with *Brandy Punch. **1818** SCOTT *Rob Roy* xxvi, Mr. Jarvie compounded .. a very small bowl of brandy-punch. *a* **1719** ADDISON *Play-house* (R.) Forgets his pomp.. And to some peaceful *brandy-shop retires. **1850** A. W. THAXTER *Poem before Iadma* 7 Or didst thou at the Pemberton absorb a *brandy-smash? **1909** *Cent. Dict.* Suppl., *Brandy-smash*, a drink made by mixing brandy with crushed ice and putting a few sprigs of mint in the glass. **1871** M. COLLINS *Mrq. & Merch.* I. ix. 300 Send me.. a.. supply of *brandy and soda. **1854** WHYTE MELVILLE *Gen. Bounce* (1855) I. ix. 203 Sufficient to destroy the ideal in the most *brandy-sodden brain. **1829** MARRYAT *F. Mildmay* xi, A hot.. glass of *brandy-and-water.

† **'brandy,** *a. Obs. rare*$^{-1}$. [see BRANDED *ppl. a.*[1]] = BRANDED *ppl. a.*[1]
1608 TOPSELL *Serpents* 734 'Squalidus albenti color est.' In English, brandy colour.

'brandy, *v.* [f. BRANDY *sb.*]
1. *trans.* To mix or treat with brandy.
a **1848** MARRYAT *R. Reefer* xliv, [He] scolded Quasha for not brandying his sangaree. **1855** *Fraser's Mag.* LI. 647 The French do not brandy up their wines for home consumption.
2. To refresh or fortify with brandy.
1837 DICKENS *Pickw.* v, When his guests had been washed, mended, brushed, and brandied. **1862** B. TAYLOR *Home & Abr.* Ser. II. ii. 120 At the Six-Mile House, our horses were watered, and the passengers brandied.
b. *to brandy it*: to drink brandy in excess.
a **1819** WOLCOTT (P. Pindar) *Wks.* (1830) 138 He surely had been brandying it, or beering.

brandy-bottle ('brændɪ-ˌbɒt(ə)l), *sb.*
1. A bottle (for) containing brandy; also *fig.*
1676 ETHEREDGE *Man of Mode* I. i. (1684) 3 Go, you are an insignificant Brandy Bottle. **1765** TUCKER *Lt. of Nat.* II. 179 Putting his mouth to the brandy bottle.
2. *Bot.* A local name of the Yellow Water-lily (*Nuphar luteum*).
1846 MRS. LOUDON *Ladies' Comp. Flower-Gard.* 201 The popular name is Brandy Bottle, from the flowers smelling like brandy. **1863** PRIOR *Plant-n.* 28 Brandy-bottle, from the shape of the seed-vessel, the yellow water-lily.

brandy-cowe (? 'brændɪkaʊ). Washings of brandy-casks, used in making spurious wines.
1829 in C. Redding *Hist. Mod. Wines* xv. (1836) 339 In addition to these may be introduced brandy-cowe (the washings of brandy-casks).

brandy-pawnee (ˌbrændɪ'pɔːnɪ). [f. BRANDY + Hind. *pānī* water; an East Indian camp-word.] Brandy-and-water.
1816 'QUIZ' *Grand Master* Pref., And died at last with brandy pauny. **1848** THACKERAY *Van. Fair* lvii, The refreshment of brandy-pawnee which he was forced to take.

brandyren, var. of BRANDIRON.

brandy-wine, early form of BRANDY.

brane, obs. form of BRAIN, BRAN.

branewod, *Sc.* var. of BRAIN-WOOD *a. Obs.*

bran-fire-new: see under BRAND-NEW.

branfulness ('brænfʊlnɪs). *rare*$^{-1}$. [f. as if from **branful* full of bran + -NESS.] The state of being full of bran (like unsifted flour): hence *fig.*
1879 G. MEREDITH *Egoist* I. Prel. 3 The realistic method ..is mainly accountable for our present branfulness.

brang, Sc. pa. t. of BRING *v.*

brangill, brangland: see BRANGLE *v.*

† **'brangle**, *sb.*^{1} *Obs.* [Phonetic variant of BRANLE *v.*; cf. BRANGLE *v.*^{1}, also BRANDLE, BRANSLE, BRANTLE.]
1. A shake, an impulse, a setting in motion; = F. *branle*, BRANLE, BRANSLE.
1652 URQUHART *Jewel* Wks. (1834) 266 Forced, for want of a convenient agent to give them the due brangle, to lye immobile. **1653** —— *Rabelais* II. xv. (1737) II. 123 Gave it the brangle, hurling it with all their force down the hill.
2. A kind of dance; = F. *branle*, BRANLE, BRANSLE, BRANTLE. (Only *Sc.*)
1513 DOUGLAS *Æneis* XIII. ix. 107 Vpstart Troianis, and syne Italianis, And gan do dowbill brangillis. **1549** *Compl. Scot.* vi. 66 It vas ane celest recreation to behald thei.. braulis and branglis..vitht mony vthir lycht dancis.

† **'brangle**, *sb.*^{2} *Obs.* exc. *dial.* [f. BRANGLE *v.*^{2}: cf. F. *branle.*]
1. A brawl, wrangle, squabble.
1600 HOLLAND *Livy* IV. xxxv. 162 i, Run desperatly and blindly into a world of brangles and troubles. **1686** GOAD *Celest. Bodies* I. xvi. 105, I will not press this too much, because it may occasion a Brangle. **1722** DE FOE *Mem. Cavaliers* (1840) 154 The feuds and brangles of this parliament. **1875** *Lanc. Gloss.*, *Brangle*, a quarrel or squabble.
2. ? A state of confusion, a muddle.
1865 *Morning Star* 26 May, The bill had got into that unfortunate state which the right hon. gentleman..was in the habit of calling a 'brangle'.

† **brangle** ('bræŋg(ə)l), *v.*^{1} *Obs.* [A phonetic variant of BRANLE *v.*, a. Fr. *branler*: cf. BRANDLE *v.*]
1. *trans.* To shake; to brandish, flourish (a sword, etc.); to wag (the head); to sway to and fro, cause to totter.
1513 DOUGLAS *Æneis* XII. ii. 111 The schaft he schuike, and branglis lustely. **1653** URQUHART *Rabelais* III. xlv, Charmides shook and brangled his head. *a* **1684** LEIGHTON *Serm.* xxviii. 414 Will the pillars be brangled.
b. *fig.* To shake (in mind), cause to waver.
a **1600** THROGMORTON in Sir. J. Melvil *Mem.* (1683) 61 Retaining the hearts of those you have gained already, recovering of those who are brangled. **1634-46** ROW *Hist. Kirk* (1842) 426 The people were brangled and shaken with contrarie doctrines. **1730** T. BOSTON *Mem.* vii. 208 In case it should misgive it would brangle me terribly.
c. To render uncertain.
1608 *Merry Devil Edm.* in Hazl. *Dodsley* X. 228 The title [to some land] is so brangled with thy debts.
2. *intr.* To shake, totter.
1513 DOUGLAS *Æneis* XI. xi. [x.] 119 The tree branglis bosting to the fall. **1549** *Compl. Scot.* vii. 68 Ane croune of gold, hingand, & brangland, that it vas lyik to fal doune.

† **'brangle**, *v.*^{2} *Obs.* or *arch.* Also 6 *Sc.* **brangill.** [perh. a particular use of prec., influenced in meaning by WRANGLE (14th c.), and possibly by BRABBLE, BRAWL, with which it is nearly synon.] *intr.* To wrangle, squabble, dispute contentiously.
1553 DOUGLAS *Æneis* VIII. Prol. 125 That brangillis [*ed. Small* braulis] thus with thi boast. **1598** SYLVESTER *Du Bartas* II. i. II. (1641) 93/1 Flesh & bloud will brangle, And murmuring Reason with th' Almighty wrangle. **1684** tr. *Agrippa's Van. Arts* lxxxiii. 292 With what Heat..they brangle about the sick-mans bed. **1868** BROWNING *Ring & Bk.* I. 241 Thus wrangled, brangled, jangled they a month.

branglement ('bræŋg(ə)lmənt). [f. BRANGLE *v.*^{2} + -MENT; but cf. F. *branlement.*] A wrangle, a disorderly dispute.
1617 COLLINS *Def. Bp. Ely* II. x. 446 The Bishop would not rush into this new branglement. **1830** *Blackw. Mag.* XXVIII. 179 A specimen of conjugal branglement. **1879** *Cornh. Mag.* Dec. 688 He declined to hold a branglement with a blockhead.

† **brangler** ('bræŋglə(r)). *Obs.* or *arch.* [f. as prec. + -ER^1.] A wrangler, brawler.
1611 COTGR., *Altercateur*, a brabler, brawler, brangler. **1684** tr. *Agrippa's Van. Arts* 333 Such as are egregious Branglers..make a noise with uncouth words. **1820** SCOTT *Monast.* xxviii, Drawn into a quarrel by a rude brangler.

† **'brangling** ('bræŋglɪŋ), *vbl. sb.*^{1} *Obs.* [f. BRANGLE *v.*^{1} + -ING^1.] Shaking, agitation; also, mental perturbation.
1585 JAMES I. *Ess. Poesie* (Arb.) 70 Who set the earth on her fundations sure, So as her brangling none shall euer see. **1597** MONTGOMERIE *Cherrie & Slae* xx, My veines with brangling lyk to brek.

'brangling, *vbl. sb.*^{2} [f. BRANGLE *v.*^{2} + -ING^1.] Noisy and turbulent disputing; squabbling.
1611 COTGR., *Altercation*, altercation..wrangling, brangling. **1622** T. STOUGHTON *Chr. Sacrif.* x. 136. **1726** SWIFT *To a Lady* Wks. 1755 IV. I. 295 Drives out brangling and contention. **1830** D'ISRAELI *Chas. I*, III. xiii. 288 The branglings and heart-burnings of their unsettled heads.

† **'brangling**, *ppl. a.*^{1} *Obs.* Also 6 *Sc.* **brangland.** [f. BRANGLE *v.*^{1} + -ING^2.] Shaking, tottering; vibrating, quivering. Also *fig.*
1513 DOUGLAS *Æneis* X. viii. 107 The brangland speyr. **1613** DANIEL *Coll. Hist. Eng.* 108 Before the settling of the government whilest it was new and brangling. **1653** URQUHART *Rabelais* III. xlv, Such a brangling agitation and moving.

'brangling, *ppl. a.*^{2} [f. BRANGLE *v.*^{2} + -ING^2.] Wrangling, quarrelsome, contentious.
1621 BURTON *Anat. Mel.* II. iii. VII, A brangling knaue. **1728** SWIFT *Mullinix & Tim.* Wks. 1755 III. II. 208 These brangling jars of Whig and Tory.

brank (bræŋk), *sb.*^{1} *Obs.* or *dial.* Also 6 **branke,** 7 **branck.** [Derivation unknown.
The plant was introduced from Asia in 14th or 15th c. perh. by the Turks; cf. its various names, L. *frumentum Turcicum*, Ger. *heide(n)kraut*, F. *blé sarrasin*, Pol. *poganka*, Boh. *pohanka* lit. 'heathen, Turkish'. There is a certain similarity of sound between the last and *brank*, but nothing is known of any connexion.]
Buckwheat (*Fagopyrum esculentum*).
1577 B. GOOGE *Heresbach's Husb.* (1586) 40 b, You may sowe Bucke, or Branke, as they call it. **1677** *Lond. Gaz.* No. 1227/4 A Dutch built Hoy, laden with 14 Tuns of Buck, or Branck. **1730** T. COX *Magna Brit.* V. 275 The Eastern parts ..produce Plenty of Branke and Hemp. **1815** W. JOHNSON tr. *Beckmann's Hist. Invent.* (1846) I. 430 It is grown [in] Norfolk and Suffolk, where it is called brank.

brank, *sb.*^{2}: see BRANKS^1.

† **brank** (bræŋk), *v.*^{1} *Sc. Obs.* [app. f. *brank*, sing. of BRANKS^1.] *trans.* To bridle, restrain; to put in the branks. Also *fig.*
1574 *Glasgow Burgh. Rec.* in Wilson *Sc. Archæol.* 692 Gif thai flyte to be brankit. *a* **1600** *Scot. Poems 16th C.* (1801) II. 194 We sall gar brank you Before that time trewly. **1664** *Mem. Dr. Spottiswode* (1811) 74 (JAM.) They feared also that their estaittes might be branked.

† **brank**, *v.*^{2} *Obs.* exc. *Sc.* and *dial.* [Of uncertain origin. Cf. Ger. *prangen* 'to adorn oneself, vaunt, brag', for which MHG. had *brangen* (also *brankieren*); perh. the Eng. word was adapted from an equivalent LG. form. Cf. PRANK. Jamieson connects it with the prec., through the notion of 'bridle up oneself'.] Hence **'branking, -and** *ppl. a.*
1. *intr.* Of horses: To prance, to toss the head.
? **1400** *Morte Arth.* 1861 They hewene, With brandez of browne stele brankkand stedez! **1513** DOUGLAS *Æneis* XI. xii. 7 Stedis apon thar strait born bridillis brankand fast.
2. Of persons: To march in a confident or demonstrative fashion; to strut; to prance, prank.
c **1550** LYNDESAY *Pedder Coffeis* 37 He cumis brankand throw the toun. **1725** RAMSAY *Gentle Sheph.* IV. ii, Her brankan wooer taks his horse, To strut a gentle spark at E'nburgh cross. **1811** MRS. GRANT *Highland Superst.* II. 260 When Donald came branking down the brae Wi' twenty thousand men. **1862** H. KINGSLEY *Ravenshoe* xlvii, They came branking into some pot-house.

† **brank(e.** *Obs. rare.* Also **braunk.** [a. OF. *branc* (*branc de l'espée* sword-blade), taken by Diez as a variant of *brant* = BRAND, though, as the Pr. form is *brenc*, this appears doubtful.]
A brand, a sword. App. only in Caxton.
1480 CAXTON *Ovid's Met.* XII. xii, He..bete hym with his branke of steel. *c* **1489** —— *Sonnes of Aymon* i. 28 Soo heued uppe the duke his branke of stele, and smote Lohier. *Ibid.* 81 His braunk of stele.

brankard, obs. form of BRANCARD.

brank-new, corruption of BRAND-NEW.

branks^1 (bræŋks). Rare sing. **brank**; also as sing. *a branks* (cf. *a bellows*). [A Scotch word found in use since the 16th c.: etymology unknown. It has been compared with ME. *bernak* (BARNACLE) and BRAKE; also with Ger. *pranger* the pillory, *pranger* a barnacle for a horse; and with Du. *prang* a fetter.]
(Jamieson was prob. right in taking sense 2 'bridle' as the earlier (cf. BRANK *v.*): but as the history is so uncertain, the senses are here placed simply in the chronological order of the available quotations.)
1. A scold's bridle; an instrument of punishment used in the case of scolds, etc., consisting of a kind of iron framework to enclose the head, having a sharp metal gag or bit which entered the mouth and restrained the tongue.
1595 in *Munic. Acc. Newcastle* (1848) 41 Paide for caring a woman throughe the towne for skoulding, with branks, 4*d.* **1652** in E. Henderson *Kirk-Session Rec. Dumfermline* 18 Nov., She shall stand at the tron, with the branks on hir mouth. **1772** PENNANT *Tours Scotl.* (1774) 80 The Brank.. is a sort of head piece, which opens and encloses the head of the impatient. **1858** T. N. BRUSHFIELD *Obsol. Punishmts.* 6 It has been called..a Brank, the Branks, a pair of Branks, the Scold's Bridle, Gossip's Bridle, and..[in 1623] 'a Brydle for a curste queane'. Branks were in active use in Scotland many years before their introduction into England. **1869** SPURGEON *J. Ploughm. Talk* vi. 45 In Walton Church.. there is a brank or scold's bridle.
2. 'A sort of bridle... Instead of leather, it has on each side a piece of wood joined to a halter, to which a bit is sometimes added; but more frequently a kind of wooden...muzzle.' Jamieson.
1657 COLVIL *Whigs Supplic.* (1751) 114 Some ask'd.. Why sodds for saddle, and branks for bridle. **1787** BURNS *Death & Dr. Hornb.*, Its shanks They were as thin, as sharp an' sma' As cheeks o' branks. **1849** *Tait's Mag.* XVI. 568 His cheeks clapped together like a pair of dismantled branks.

branks^2. [Perh. an application of BRANKS^1 in the sense of a gag; but cf. BRANCHUS and BRANCOS.] The mumps.
1794-6 E. DARWIN *Zoon.* (1802) III. 365 Mumps, or branks, is a contagious inflammation of the parotis. **1860** RAMSAY *Remin.* v. (ed. 18) 115 I've had..the branks.

brank-ursine (bræŋk'ɜːsɪn). Forms: 6 **bramkersine, branke ursyne,** 6-7 **-ursine,** 7 **branckvrsin,** 7-9 **brank-ursin,** 8 **branch-ursine, -hircin,** 7- **brank-ursine.** [ad. med.L. *branca ursīna* lit. 'bear's claw', cf. F. *branc-*, *branche-ursine*, which may be the immediate source.]
Bear's breech, Acanthus. (Erroneously applied to the Cow-parsnip (*Heracleum Sphondylium.*)
1551 TURNER *Herbal* (1568) I. Bj, Acanthus is called of ye barbarus wryters *branca ursina*, in English branke Ursyne. **1563** HYLL *Art Garden.* (1593) 98 Take..of the roots of Bramkersine..a quarter of a pound. **1610** MARKHAM *Masterp.* II. clxxiii, Branckvrsin is a wonderfull great mollifier. **1783** AINSWORTH *Lat. Dict.* (Morell) II, *Acanthus*, the herb branch-hircin, as having leaves like a goat's horn; or brank-ursin, or bear's-foot, from its shagginess. **1833** *Penny Cycl.* I. 68/2 The brank-ursine is identical with the common architectural and sculptural acanthus.

branky ('bræŋkɪ), *a. Sc.* [f. BRANK *v.*^{2} + -Y.] Showy, gaudy.
1789 BURNS *Batt. Killiecrankie* i. Whare hae ye been sae brankie, O?

† **'branle**, *sb. Obs.* [a. F. *branle.*]
1. Wavering, agitation, (?) confusion.
1581 SAVILE *Tacitus' Hist.* ii. (1591) 78 The Legion incensed with griefe..put them of the first [legion] in branle [*impulit primanos*].
2. A kind of dance, and the kind of music suitable to it; = BRANGLE *sb.*^{1} 2, BRANSLE 2, BRANTLE.
1674 BOYLE *Mech. Hypoth.* 34 Branles, Sarabands, Jigs, and other..Tunes. **1820** SCOTT *Abbot* xxxi, She led the last branle.

† **'branle**, *v. Obs. rare*$^{-1}$. [a. F. *branle-r* 'to shake'; ulterior origin uncertain. Diez and Littré connect it with *brandir* to BRANDISH, the former taking it for a deriv. form **brandoler*, the latter from *brandeler*, found in OF. with the senses of both *brandir* and *branler*. Cf. BRANDLE, BRANGLE.] To agitate, toss about, bandy.
1654 JER. TAYLOR *Real Pres.* xii. 28 This new question began to branle the words of Type and Antitype.

† **'branlie**, *a. Obs. rare*$^{-1}$. [? f. BRAN *sb.*^{1} + -LY^1.] Pale yellow.
1589 FLEMING *Virg. Georg.* III. 39 Woorst colour is in [horsses] white, or branlie [horsse like box].

branlin(g, dial. form of BRANDLING.

† **'branling**, *vbl. sb. Obs. rare*$^{-1}$. [f. BRANLE *v.* + -ING^1.] A wavering or agitation.
1646 HOWELL *Lustra Ludov.* *3 There are branlings and trepidations amongst them.

† **'branling**, *ppl. a. Obs.* [f. BRANLE *v.* + -ING^2.] Wavering, vacillating, insecure.
c **1645** HOWELL *Lett.* v. 47 Whosoever was found pendulous, or brangling [ed. **1713** branling] in his Religion. **1646** —— *Lustra Ludov.* 169 Notwithstanding the branling hazardous stand he was at.

branne, obs. form of BRAN.

branner ('brænə(r)). [f. BRAN *sb.*^{1} + -ER^1.]
1. An operative who cleans tinned plates with bran.
1881 *Instr. Census Clerks* (1885) 94 White Branner. **1921** *Dict. Occup. Terms* (1927) §279 *Branner*, a tinman's helper attending branning machine,..sometimes specifically designated according to whether black or white plates are being cleaned, e.g., black branner, white branner.
2. A machine for removing the oil from tinned plates by means of bran and slaked lime.
1902 *Sci. Amer.* 1 Nov. 290/2 As the plates leave the tin pot, they have upon them a thin coating of oil which has to be removed... They are put into a branner which is located conveniently at the side of the tinning machine.

bran-new: see BRAND-NEW.

branning: see BRAN *v.*

branny ('brænɪ), *a.* [f. BRAN *sb.*^{1} + -Y^1.] Consisting of, abounding in, or resembling bran.
1533 ELYOT *Cast. Helth* (1541) 88 Called branny residence, in Latin *furfurea*. **1783** S. CHAPMAN in *Med. Commun.* I. 273 A branny sediment. **1877** ROBERTS *Handbk.*

Med. (ed. 3) I. 138 The epidermis comes off in small, branny scales.

† **'branskate,** *v.* *Obs. rare.* [ad. Du. *brandschatten* = Ger. *brandschatzen*, f. *brand* burning + *schatz* treasure, orig. tribute. (The German word has also been used for the nonce.)]

To put (a place) to ransom, or subject to a payment, in order to avoid pillage or destruction. Hence **'branskating** *vbl. sb.*

1721 STRYPE *Eccl. Mem.* II. I. 328 The French King should ask reckoning of Albright of that he had branskated. *Ibid.* The soldiers.. finding themselves wealthy and rich of the branskating and spoil.

† **'bransle.** *Obs.* Also 8 **bransel.** [a. F. *bransle* (16th c.), a graphical variant of *branle*: see BRANLE, also BRANGLE, BRANTLE.]

1. Movement, perturbation. *rare.* (= BRANGLE *sb.*[1] 1, BRANLE *sb.* 1.)

1603 FLORIO *Montaigne* III. ix. (1632) 565 Observe.. the motions and bransles of the Heavens.

2. A kind of dance; also, a song for dance music. (= BRANGLE *sb.*[1] 2, BRANLE *sb.* 2, BRANTLE.)

1596 SPENSER *F.Q.* III. x. 8 Now making layes of love.. Bransles, ballads, virelayes. **1597** MORLEY *Introd. Mus.* 181 The *bransle de poictou* or bransle double is more quick in time.. but the straine is longer, containing most vsually twelue whole strokes. **1829** SCOTT *Anne of G.* 344 The youthful couple went off to take their place in the bransle.

brant (brænt), *sb.* (Also BRENT q.v.) [Derivation and original application uncertain: in Sw. *brandgås* (Icel. *brandgás* only in the *þulur*) is the sheldrake or bergander; in Ger., *brandgans* is according to some the sheldrake, but with Grimm = *Anser fuscus*, the Black or Velvet Duck; in English, *brant*, *brant-goose* was long confounded with the barnacle goose. Early naturalists (Gesner, Aldrovandus, etc.) were content to derive the name from *βρένθος* an unidentified water-bird mentioned by Aristotle; later etymologists have suggested *brended* or BRANDED, brindled, and BRAND fire, burning, perh. in sense of dusky black, or sooty colour; but in the absence of knowledge where the name arose, and to what bird it was originally applied, nothing can be determined.]

The smallest species of wild goose (*Bernicla brenta*) breeding in high northern latitudes, and visiting the British coasts in winter. Formerly confounded with the allied Barnacle-goose. Also **brant-goose** (in 8 casually **bran-, brand-goose**; in Eng. authors since Pennant more commonly BRENT-GOOSE q.v.).

1544 TURNER *Avium praecipuarum* 23 Prior anser a nostris hodie *branta* et *bernicla* vocatur. **1601** HOLLAND *Pliny* I. 301 Such egs not only Doues doe bring, but.. geese and Brants, or the female Barganders. **1624** CAPT. SMITH *Virginia* II. 27 In winter there are.. Geese, Brants, Ducke. **1668** CHARLETON *Onomast.* 98 The *Barnacle* or *Scots-goose* or *Clak-guse*, quae eadem forte est cum Branta seu *Brentho*. **1676** T. GLOVER in *Phil. Trans.* XI. 626 Cormorants, Brants, Shield-fowl. **1836** W. IRVING *Astoria* (1849) 332 The country abounded with.. swans, wild geese, brant. **1855** LONGF. *Hiaw.* I. 103, I have given you brant and beaver.

b. 1597 GERARDE *Herbal* 391 Foules, whom we call Barnakles; in the north of England Brant geese. **1668** WILKINS *Real Char.* II. v. 156 One is black from the breast to the middle of the belly, called Brant Goose, Bernicla or Brenta. **1678** RAY *Willughby's Ornith.* 360, I am of opinion that the Brant-Goose differs specifically from the Bernacle, however writers of the History of Birds confound them. **1750** E. SMITH *Compl. Housewife* 7 To chuse a goose, wild goose, and Bran-goose. **1766** *Phil. Trans.* LVI. 212 He mentions the brand geese first. **1863** KINGSLEY *Water-B.* vi. 269 Swans and brant geese, harlequins and eiders.

† **brant** (brænt), *a.* and *adv.* *Obs.* exc. in *north. dial.* [OE. *brant*, *brǫnt* 'high, steep', corresp. to ON. **brant-r*, whence Icel. *bratt-r*, Sw. *brant*, Da. *brat*; not known in other Teut. langs. Found in literature in 16th c., and still used in north. Eng. dial.: the Sc. form is BRENT, q.v.]

A. *adj.* **1.** Lofty, steep, sheer, precipitous.

a **1000** *Elene* 238 (Gr.) Leton þa ofer fifelwæȝ famiȝe scriðan bronte brimþisan. *a* **1000** *Andreas* 273 (Gr.) þæt þu us ȝebrohte brante ceole.. on þære mæȝðe! **1544** ASCHAM *Toxoph.* (Arb.) 58 A man maye.. syt on a brante hyll syde. **1821** MRS. WHEELER *Cumbld. Dial.* App. 7 Our brant fells. **1822** J. BRIGGS *Rem.* 106 in *Lanc. Gloss.* (E.D.S.) Ye'll find it a lang way an' varra brant.

2. Of the forehead: Unwrinkled; see BRENT.

1483 *Cath. Angl.* 41 Branit [*v.r.* brante], *abrugatus*.

B. *adv.* Straight, straight up; erectly, steeply.

a **1400** *Alexander* (Stevenson) 124 Apon the bald Bucipelon brant up he sittes. **1544** ASCHAM *Toxoph.* (Arb.) 87 Hawarde.. slew kyng Jamie.. euen brant agenst Flodon hil.

Hence † **'brantness,** steepness.

1641 BEST *Farm. Bks.* (1856) 1 If hee bee a dodded tuppe, yow may knowe him best by the brantnesse of his foreheade, which appearith high and sharpe.

brant, var. of BRAND, blight. See also BRUNT.

† **brant-barley.** *Obs. rare.* Quaking-grass.

1597 GERARD *Herbal* I. lv. 74 *Briza*, is called.. in English Brant Barley.

† **'brantcorn.** *Obs.* Also 7 (in Cotgr.) brancorne. [a. MDu. *brantkoren* (Ger. *brandkorn*): cf. BRAND *sb.* 7 + CORN.] Blight, smut (*Uredo segetum*).

1578 LYTE *Dodoens* IV. xvii. 471 Blight or Brantcorne.. insteede of a good eare, there cometh up a black burnt eare, ful of blacke dust or powder. **1646** SIR T. BROWNE *Pseud. Ep.* 335 Brant corne and trees blacke by blasting.

brant-fox ('bræntfɒks). [ad. Ger. *brand-fuchs*, Du. *brand-vos*; in Sw. *brandräf*, Da. *brandræv*; f. *brand* burning, ? burnt colour.] An English adaptation of the German name of a variety of the fox, chiefly distinguished by a greater admixture of black in its fur; according to Grimm, it has black feet, ears, and tail.

1864 in WEBSTER, and in later Dicts.

brant-goose: see BRANT *sb.*

† **'brantle.** *Obs.* [Phonetic var. of BRANDLE.] A kind of dance; = BRANGLE *sb.*[1] 2, BRANLE *sb.* 2, BRANSLE *sb.* 2.

1662 PEPYS *Diary* 31 Dec., They danced the Brantle. **1846** *Sir R. de Coverley* 229 Asking a thousand questions.. respecting certain brantles and corantos.

'branular, *a. rare.* [A spurious formation from BRAIN, ? after *grain*, *granular*.] Pertaining to or affecting the brain.

1857 I. TAYLOR *World of Mind* 634 Either a trick, practised upon me, or it might be a branular illusion.

braquemard: see BRACKMARD.

† **braquet.** *Obs.* See quot.

1753 *Public Advertiser* 3 Oct. 3/3 Exceeding fine Braquet Red Wine of Nice.

bras, brasaill, -sel, -sell, brasand, brasar: see BRASS, BRAZIL, BRACING, BRACER.

brasche, -let, obs. ff. BRACH, BRASH[1], BRACELET.

brase, obs. form of BRACE *v.* and BRAZE *v.*

braselet, obs. form of BRACELET.

brasen, braser, obs. forms of BRAZEN, BRACER.

† **'braser.** *Obs. rare.* = BRAZIER[1].

1465 *Paston Lett.* 533 II. 249 Roberd Lovegold, braser.

‖ **'brasero.** Also 7 **brasera, braziero.** [Sp.: = Fr. *brasier*.] = BRAZIER[2].

1652 URQUHART *Jewel* Wks. (1834) 234 A char-coale fire burning in a silver brasero. **1683** EVELYN *Diary* 4 Oct., Chimney furniture, sconces, branches, braseras. *a* **1683** SIDNEY *Disc. Govt.* (1714) 383 A Braziero of Coals brought into his Chamber. **1841** BORROW *Zincali* (1843) I. 241 A huge brasero of flaming charcoal.

† **brasey, brasill.** *Obs.* [Cf. F. *brasiller*, 'faire griller promptement sur la braise'; also BRAISE.] A mode of cooking: see BRAISE.

c **1440** *Anc. Cookery* in *Househ. Ord.* (1790) 435 Boor in Brasey. *Ibid.* 446 Eles in Brasill.

brash (bræʃ), *sb.*[1] Chiefly *dial.* Also 6 **brasche.** [perh. onomatopœic, with associations of *break*, *brast*, etc. and of *crash*, *dash*, etc. In senses 2, 3, perhaps distinct, with other associations, e.g. *rash*, and *splash*.]

† **1.** An attack, assault; a bout. *Sc.* and *n. dial.*

1573 *Scot. Poems 16th C.* II. 292 At the bak wall wes the brasche they gaue. *a* **1600** MONTGOMERIE *Poems* (1821) 195 Curage bydis the brash. **1638** H. ADAMSON *Muses Thren.* Introd. 8 (JAM.) The last brashe was made by a letter of the prime poet of our Kingdome. **1724** RAMSAY *Evergreen* II. (*title*) A Brash of Wouing.

2. A slight attack of sickness or indisposition; *esp.* one arising from a disorder of the alimentary canal. Hence ***teething-brash, weaning-brash.***

1785 BURNS *Sc. Drink* xv, Wae worth that brandy, burning trash, Fell source o' monie a pain an brash. *a* **1800** *Gay Goss-Hawk* 79 in Scott *Minstr.*, As gin she had ta'en a sudden brash, And were about to die.

3. An eruption of fluid. **a.** ***water-brash:*** an eructation or belching of water (acid, bitter, etc.) from the stomach, pyrosis. **b.** A sudden dash or burst of rain. Cf. BLASH.

1811 WILLAN *Gloss. W. Riding*, *Brash*, a sudden sickness, with acid rising into the mouth. **1825** JAMIESON, *Water-brash*. **1849** *Blackw. Mag.* LXVI. 684 The wind returned.. with an occasional brash of rain. **1856** EMERSON *Eng. Traits* Wks. 1874 II. 60 He is a churl with a soft place in his heart, whose speech is a brash of bitter waters. **1875** *Lanc. Gloss.* (E.D.S.) 52 *Brash*, an eruption. [*Water-brash* in most of the E.D.S. northern and north. midl. Glossaries.]

brash (bræʃ), *sb.*[2] [perh. a corrupt form of F. *brèche*; cf. It. *breccia* of same meaning: but see BRASH *a.*[1]] A mass or heap of fragments; applied to (*a*) loose broken rock forming the highest stratum beneath the soil of certain districts: rubble; (cf. *corn-brash*); (*b*) fragments of crushed ice, hence ***brash-ice;*** (*c*) refuse boughs or branches, hedge clippings, twigs. Also *attrib.*

a **1722** [implied in BRASHY *a.*[1]]. **1787** WINTER *Syst. Husb.* 283 The soil a loam, on a stone brash clay. **1837** MACDOUGALL tr. *Graah's Greenland* 62 A stream of loose brash-ice proceeding from the ice-blinks. **1853** KANE *Grinnell Exp.* xiv. (1856) 102 Icy fragments or 'brash'. **1882** in *Standard* 2 Sept. 2/4 On the light stone brash estates birds are very small and scarce.

brash (bræʃ), *a.*[1] Now chiefly in *U.S.* [perh. onomatopœic; ? influenced by *break* and *rash.*] Fragile, brittle: used chiefly of timber.

1566 DRANT *Wail. Hierim.* K viij, Their cracklinge hydes, britle and brashe as dryed barke of tree. *c* **1850** *Nat. Encycl.* I. 618 *Brash*, [Americanism] for brittle. **1860** *Merc. Mar. Mag.* VII. 168 A species of oak, very brash when newly cut. **1860** BARTLETT *Dict. Amer.*, *Brash*, Brittle. In New England .. used.. of wood or timber that is brittle.

brash, *a.*[2] [? Connected with prec. or with BRASH *sb.*[1]] **1. a.** Hasty, rash, impetuous; (orig. *U.S.*), impulsive, assertive, impudent; crude, insensitive; flashy. Also as *adv.*

(Quots. 1837 and 1889 are U.S.)

1824 *Craven Dial.* 24 What a brash raggald! **1837** R. M. BIRD *Nick of Woods* I. viii. 120 Strannger thar's as brash as a new hound in a b'ar fight. **1875** *Lanc. Gloss.* (E.D.S.), *Brash*, hasty. **1889** 'C. E. CRADDOCK' *Despot of Broomsedge Cove* ii. 27 Ye notice how turrible brash Josiah Preen be,—can't wait fur pa'son ter summons him. **1928** *Punch* 4 Apr. 374/2 He was going out in his brash street-suit with the flash tie. **1946** J. B. PRIESTLEY *Bright Day* viii. 248 That feeling of inevitable national superiority.. which makes decent people seem brash and insensitive. **1948** W. SANSOM *South* 114 The dogs of Italy do not chase cats like their brash northern brothers. **1950** R. MACDOUGALL *To Dorothy, A Son* in *Plays of Yr.* 418 The room has the lurid, brash appearance of an American cocktail bar. **1956** A. WILSON *Anglo-Saxon Att.* I. i. 7 This brash young American little knew what sore places he was invading with his clumsy fingers. **1958** *Oxf. Mag.* 1 May 390/2 One of those amiable institutions which survive in an alien age until they stand directly challenged by some brash newcomer.

b. Hard, harsh, rough. Also as *adv.* *U.S.*

1868 *Putnam's Mag.* Dec. 675/1 See here,.. you are playing this a little too brash. **1872** SCHELE DE VERE *Americanisms* 446. **1880** A. W. TOURGÉE *Bricks without Straw* 116 He was pretty brash wid me, an 'llowed ter hit me wid a stick. **1896** G. ADE *Artie* iii. 23, I swore I'd get next, no matter what kind of a brash play I had to make. **1904** W. H. SMITH *Promoters* 51 We won't rob 'em entirely; there isn't any use in being altogether too brash.

2. Active, quick. Also as *adv.* *U.S.*

1884 'MARK TWAIN' *Huck. Finn* 62 When I got to camp I warn't feeling very brash, there warn't much sand in my craw. **1888** 'C. E. CRADDOCK' *Keedon Bluffs* 63 Whar's that buckeye tree ye war a-goin ter cut down fur me so brash? **1891** M. E. RYAN *Pagan of Alleghanies* 118, I ain't so brash in the timber as I'd like to be.

† **brash,** *v.*[1] *Obs.* Also 9 **brasch.** [Cf. BRASH *sb.*[1], also BRUSH *v.*[2] and ME. *brissen.*] *trans.* (and *absol.*) To assault, attack; to breach (a wall or other defence). Also *fig.*

c **1565** R. LINDSAY *Cron. Scot.* (1814) 309 (JAM.) His captanes.. war all hanged when he had brasched and wone the hous. **1570–3** R. BANNATYNE *Jrnl.* (1806) 274 (JAM.) They suld have brashit the wall whair thair batter was made. **1629** SIR W. MORE *True Crucif.* 195 (JAM.) Whose breast did beare, brash't with displeasure's dart, A bruised spirit and a broken heart. **1638** FARLEY *Emblems*, Death lies in ambush .. And brasheth where our sconces weakest be.

brash (bræʃ), *v.*[2] [See BRASH *sb.*[2] and cf. BRUSH *v.*[2] 7.] *trans.* To remove the lower branches of (a tree). Also with *up*. Hence **'brashing** *vbl. sb.*

1950 *Q. Jrnl. Forestry* XLIV. 72 As a fire precaution.. a belt 30 ft. wide should be completely brashed up as soon as possible. *Ibid.* 75 'Brushing up or brashing' means the removal of the lower boughs up to 5 to 7 ft. **1959** W. K. RICHMOND *Brit. Birds of Prey* xiii. 150 Forestry Commission plantations before they have been 'brashed'.

brashly ('bræʃlɪ), *adv.* orig. *U.S.* [f. BRASH *a.*[2]] In a brash manner.

1865 'MARK TWAIN' *Sk. Sixties* (1926) 179, I mixed into this business a little too brashly—so to speak—and without due reflection. **1884** *Mexican Let.* in *Boston (Mass.) Jrnl.*, Aug., This department of business that started off so brashly has played out. **1949** *Here & Now* Oct. 11/3 A brashly self-confident member of an Opposition which had had the confidence largely knocked out of it. **1952** C. DAY LEWIS tr. *Virgil's Aeneid* v. 104 What that exhibitionist yonder So brashly relies on. **1957** 'E. FERRARS' *Furnished for Murder* iii. 25 An energetic, rather brashly handsome woman.

'brashness[1]. orig. *U.S.* [f. BRASH *a.*[1]] Brittleness.

1864 *Ret. Agric. Soc. Maine* 54 They [*sc.* sheep] become very fat in the summer, which increases the brashness of the wool. **1929** *Ann. Appl. Biol.* XVI. 41 The term 'brashness' arose in America, and is now in common use in the timber trade of both this country and the U.S.A. In this paper its use will be restricted to that condition of timber.. which produces a peculiar 'carroty', short, fracture.

'brashness[2]. orig. *U.S.* [f. BRASH *a.*[2]] The state or quality of being brash, impetuous, crude, etc.

1883 *N. York Paper* in *Pall Mall G.* 9 July 11/1 Vanderbilt, with all his brashness on the road, is timid in the street. **1894** P. L. FORD *Honorable P. Stirling* (1898) xliii. 258 'That is a bargain,' he said, with a brashness simply disgraceful in a good business man. **1957** *Guardian* 9 Sept. 4/4 One needs.. a maximum of brashness in out-staring curious sightseers. **1958** J. CAREW *Wild Coast* v. 62 His front of brashness was his way of finding out how far he could go.

brashy ('bræʃɪ), *a.*[1] [f. BRASH *sb.*[2] + -Y[1].] Of the nature of brash; broken, crumbly, fragmentary.

a **1722** LISLE *Husb.* (1757) 106, I have eight or nine acres of brashy ground. **1857** PAGE *Adv. Text-bk. Geol.* xvii. (1876) 311 Calcareous grits, and shelly 'brashy' sandstones. **1878** MARKHAM *Gt. Frozen Sea* iv. 51 The ice was of a soft 'brashy' nature..from one to three feet in thickness.

'brashy, *a.*[2] *Sc.* Also **braushie.** [f. BRASH *sb.*[1] 3.] Characterized by brashes of rain; showery.

1805 NICOL *Poems* I. 114 (JAM.) Thro' monie a speat O' braushie weather. **1865** *Gd. Words* June 466 The spring had been very brashy and cauld.

brasier(e, -yer, obs. forms of BRAZIER.

brasik, var. of BRASSIK, *Obs.*, cabbage.

Brasil, -sile, -sill, obs. ff. of BRAZIL.

brasill: see BRASEY.

†**brask,** *v. Obs. rare. trans.* ? To brush, graze.

1674 COTTON *Voy. Ireland* III. 156 The ferry-boat brasking her sides 'gainst the weeds.

braslet, obs. form of BRACELET.

brasque (brɑːsk, -æ-), *sb.* [a. F. *brasque* in same sense; accord. to Littré, connected with *braser* to solder.] 'A lining for crucibles or furnaces; generally, a compound of clay, etc. with charcoal dust.' Raymond *Mining Gloss.*

1871 *Trans. Amer. Inst. Mining Eng.* I. 108 A thin coating of clay or brasque (a composition of powdered charcoal and clay in varying proportions). **1875** URE *Dict. Arts* II. 1023 Partially filling it with..charcoal or brasque.

brasque (brɑːsk, -æ-), *v.* [f. BRASQUE *sb.*] *trans.* To line with brasque. Hence **brasqued** *ppl. a.*

1880 *Encycl. Brit.* XIII. 319/2 The bed of this latter [finery] is 'brasqued' or lined with charcoal powder moistened and rammed in. **1885** *Spons' Mechanics' Own Bk.* 17 If brass be heated in a brasqued crucible.

brass (brɑːs, -æ-), *sb.* Forms: 1–2 bræs, 2 bres, 3 breas, 3–5 bras(e, 4–7 brasse, 3- brass. [OE. *bræs*, of unknown origin: not found elsewhere. (It has been compared with OSw. *brasa* fire, *brasa* to flame, Da. *brase* to roast; but no connexion has been traced. The alleged ON. *bras* 'solder' is a figment.)]

I. 1. a. *Historically*: The general name for all alloys of copper with tin or zinc (and occasionally other base metals). To distinguish alloys of copper and tin, the name BRONZE has subsequently been adopted (Johnson 1755–73 explains the new word *bronze* as 'brass'). Hence

b. In strict modern use, as distinguished from 'bronze': A yellow-coloured alloy of copper and zinc, usually containing about a third of its weight of zinc.

The OE. *bræs* was, usually at least, an alloy of copper and tin (= BRONZE); in much later times the alloy of copper and zinc came gradually into general use, and became the ordinary 'brass' of England; though in reference to ancient times, and esp. to the nations of antiquity, 'brass' still meant the older alloy. When works of Greek and Roman antiquity in 'brass' began to be critically examined, and their material discriminated, the Italian word for 'brass' (*bronzo, bronze*) came into use to distinguish this 'ancient brass' from the current alloy. ***Corinthian brass***: a reputed alloy of gold, silver, and copper.

c **1000** ÆLFRIC *Gram.* vi. 15 *Aes*, bræs oððe ar. *c* **1150** *Voc.* in Wr.-Wülcker 550 *Æs*, bres. *c* **1200** ORMIN 17417 He shollde melltenn brass. *a* **1225** *Juliana* 30 Brune of wallinde breas. *c* **1250** *Gen. & Ex.* 3898 Moyses ðor made a wirme of bras. *a* **1300** *Cursor M.* 5903 Þe king hert wex herd as bras. **1477** EARL RIVERS (Caxton) *Dictes* 67 Men take glasses, bras and other suche thinges for as moche gold. **1552–3** *Inv. Ch. Goods Stafford* 12 On chales of silver..ij of brasse, a sensor of brasse, ij candelstikes of brase. **1623** B. JONSON in *Shaks. C. Praise* 141 O, could he but have drawne his Wit..in Brasse. **1718** LADY M. W. MONTAGUE *Lett.* II. liii. 74 Inscriptions on..tables of brass. **1781** THOMPSON in *Phil. Trans.* LXXI. 327 Brass in a very fine powder, commonly called brass dust. **1865** BARING-GOULD *Werewolves* iv. 34 A compound like Corinthian brass into which many pure ores have been fused.

c. Taken as a type of hardness, imperishableness, insensibility, etc.

1388 WYCLIF *Job* vi. 12 Nethir my strengthe is the strengthe of stoounus, nether my fleisch is of bras. *c* **1600** SHAKS. *Sonn.* cxx, Unless my nerves were brass or hammer'd steel. **1613** —— *Hen. VIII*, IV. ii. 45 Mens euill manners liue in Brasse, their Vertues We write in Water.

†**d.** *transf.* Copper. *Obs.*

1382 WYCLIF *Deut.* viii. 9 Of the hillis of it ben doluen metallys of brasse [**1535** COVERDALE and **1611** thou mayest dig brass(e)]. **1617** MORYSON *Itin.* I. II. iv. 177 Mines of Iron and Brass.

e. A wide-spread miner's name for iron pyrites in coal. Cf. BRAZIL[2].

1829 S. GLOVER *Hist. Derby* I. v. 234 Many of the coal-seams..have considerable quantities of brasses or drosses in them, which are lumps of iron pyrites. **1879** *Cassell's Techn. Educ.* IV. 271/1 Detached masses of pyrites..are called 'brasses' by the colliers.

f. in *Organ-building*. (See quot.)

1852 SEIDEL *Organ* 167 A great portion of the pipes are often composed of brass. This is nothing but a mixture or composition of lead and tin. *Ibid.* Good brass consists either of fifteen parts pewter and one part lead, or of fourteen parts pewter and two parts lead.

2. Used elliptically for various things made of brass: esp.

a. A sepulchral tablet of brass (or latten), bearing a figure or inscription, laid down on the floor or set up against the wall of a church.

1613 *MS. Acc. St. John's Hosp., Canterb.*, Payd for fasting of the brass of the graves in the chaunsells *vd.* **1654** EVELYN *Mem.* (1857) I. 317 The soldiers had lately knocked off most of the brasses from the grave-stones. **1732** DE FOE *Tour Gt. Brit.* (1769) II. 279 Merchants, as they are called on the Brasses over their Monuments. **1851** D. WILSON *Preh. Ann.* (1863) II. IV. ix. 456 A small mural brass. **1861** *Sat. Rev.* 22 June, Once a zealous 'rubber', on asking whether there were any 'brasses' in a church, was guided, in answer, to the brass handles of the pew doors. **1874** BOUTELL *Arms & Arm.* x.

b. A bearing or block for a shaft.

1731 BEIGHTON in *Phil. Trans.* XXXVII. 5 The Wheel lies with its two Gudgeons..upon two Brasses. **1790** *Specif. J. Wood's Patent* No. 1744 The brasses or friction rollers for the necks and bearing of the crank to work in. **1823** R. BUCHANAN *Millwork* 264 Produce unequal wear on the gudgeons and brasses.

c. A brazen vessel: cf. *copper*. (*rare.*)

1810 SOUTHEY *Kehama* XVII. i, Huge as a Ship that travels the main sea Is that capacious brass.

d. Musical instruments of brass.

[**1382** WYCLIF *1 Cor.* xiii. 1 As bras sownnynge or a symbal tynkynge.] **1832** L. HUNT *Poems* 208 Ev'n the bees lag at the summoning brass. **1876** G. B. SHAW *How to become Mus. Critic* (1960) 10 A good deal of piccolo, drum, and cymbal, relieved by an effective melody for the brass. **1885** *Truth* 11 June 928/1 There are not enough of them [fiddles]; the brass blows them all to pieces. **1926** WHITEMAN & MCBRIDE *Jazz* ix. 195 Musicians recognize four general classes of instruments in speaking of the orchestra—strings, wood winds, brasses, and the battery of traps.

e. *slang* (orig. *U.S.*). Senior officers in the armed forces (in allusion to their brass or gold insignia); 'brass-hats' collectively; esp. ***the big*** (or ***top***) ***brass***. Also *transf.* and *attrib.*

1899 *Boston Herald* 26 July 4/8 It was not a big brass general that came; But a man in khaki kit. **1945** *Life* 2 July 13/3, I don't suppose that Congress and the Big Brass would ever agree to that. **1949** *Bulletin* (Philad.) 14 Sept. 4/1 The top police brass spreads out a hot carpet for the local cops. **1951** E. AMBLER *Judgment on Deltchev* xvii. 204 Some of his revelations..were deeply shocking to the Anglo-American brass. **1951** *Economist* 15 Dec. 1463/1 The 'high brass' of American business was also well represented at the meeting. **1952** *Newsweek* 19 May 21 Top Pentagon brass are taking the aviation-gasoline restriction seriously. **1959** A. C. CLARKE *Across Sea of Stars* 123 The general was unaware of his *faux pas*. The assembled brass thought for a while.

f. *Typogr.* A brass block or die, esp. one used for a design or lettering on the cover of a book. Often with defining word.

1930 M. SADLEIR *Evol. Publishers' Binding Styles 1770–1900* 90 Such lettering was printed from a specially cut binding-brass... This brass was sometimes discarded and plain type lettering employed. **1951** S. JENNETT *Making of Books* 175 The brass from which the lettering and decoration is blocked on a modern book.

g. *slang.* = *brass nail.*

1934 [see sense 7]. **1952** N. STREATFEILD *Aunt Clara* 161 If Mr. Willis thought she was a brass, he had got another think coming... If you looked at those brown eyes you could see she was innocent as a baby. **1958** F. NORMAN *Bang to Rights* 10 His old woman who was a brass on the game.

3. Money.

†**a.** Copper or bronze coin; also *fig. Obs.*

1362 LANGL. *P. Pl.* A. III. 189 Beere heor bras on þi Bac to Caleys to sulle. [Perhaps belongs here.]

1526 TINDALE *Matt.* x. 9 Posses not golde, nor silver, nor brasse yn youre gerdels. **1599** SHAKS. *Hen. V*, IV. iv. 19 Luxurious Mountaine Goat, offer'st me Brasse? **1775** CRABBE *Inebriety*, Where canvass purse displays the brass enroll'd.

b. Money in general, cash. *slang* or *dial.*

1597–8 BP. HALL *Satires* I. iii. 58 (D.) Shame that the muses should be bought and sold For every peasant's brass. **1601** HOLLAND *Pliny* II. 486 *Obæerati*..pressed with the heauy burden of brasse, *i.* debt. **1794** BURNS '*What can a young lassie*', His auld brass will buy me a new pan. **1811** BYRON *Hints fr. Hor.* 548 Who ne'er despises books that bring him brass. **1848** C. BRONTË *J. Eyre* (1857) 349 'You've like no house, nor no brass, I guess?' **1871** E. PEACOCK *Ralf Skirl.* III. 27 You wouldn't have gone near him..if it hadn't been for his brass.

4. a. *fig.* Taken as a type of insensibility to shame: hence, Effrontery, impudence, unblushingness.

[**1588** SHAKS. *L.L.L.* v. ii. 395 Can any face of brasse hold longer out?] **1642** FULLER *Holy & Prof. St.* v. x. 395 His face is of brasse, which may be said either ever or never to blush. **1682** DRYDEN *Satyr to Muse* 236 And like the Sweed is very Rich in Brass. *a* **1734** NORTH *Exam.* III. viii. ¶17 The Author hath the Brass to add, etc. **1780** MAD. D'ARBLAY *Diary & Lett.* I. 318, I entered the room without astonishing the company by my brass. **1853** LYNCH *Self-Impr.* 45 An empty, vaunting person, who has brass enough to face the world.

b. Colloq. phr. ***as bold as brass***: very bold(ly) or impudent(ly); brazen-faced(ly).

1789 G. PARKER *Life's Painter* 162 He died damn'd hard and as bold as brass. An expression commonly used among the vulgar after returning from an execution. **1849** LYTTON *Caxtons* I. I. iv. 27 Master Sisty (coming out of the house as bold as brass) continued rapidly [etc.]. **1922** S. J. WEYMAN *Ovington's Bank* xvii. 188 Seeing as he hung back I up to him bold as brass.

II. *Attrib.* and *Comb.*

5. a. *simple attrib.*: (Made) of brass, brazen. (In former times sometimes united with hyphen.)

1408 *E.E. Wills* (1882) 15 A bras pot. **1420** *Ibid.* 46, I petit brase morter. **1475** *Bk. Noblesse* 84 Alle othir golde, silver, and brasse money. **1650** R. STAPYLTON *Strada's Low-C. Warres* x. 3, 15 great Brasse-Cannon. **1652** *Proc. Parliament* No. 34. 2081, 5 small brasse guns. **1710** HEARNE *Coll.* II. 363 The Antients us'd Brass Arms before Iron ones. **1720** *Stow's Surv.* (ed. Strype 1754) II. v. xvii. 363/2 We recieve ..also Whalebone Train Oil, Brass Battery. **1724** SWIFT *Drapier's Lett.* Wks. 1755 V. II. 147 Whoever received or uttered brass coin. **1776** *Hist. Europe* in *Ann. Reg.* 36/1 Brass field pieces. **1876** HUMPHREY *Coin Coll. Man.* xvi. 196 Not worth a brass button.

b. Colloq. phr. ***to come*** (or ***get***) ***down to brass tacks*** (or ***nails***): to concern oneself with basic facts or realities. orig. *U.S.*

1897 H. A. JONES *Liars* I. 23 Come down to brass tacks. What's going to be the end of this? **1903** *N.Y. Sun* 28 Nov. 3 This bold sister was the first..to get down to brass tacks in a discussion of the scandal. **1911** H. QUICK *Yellowstone N.* xi. 288 When you come down to brass nails. **1927** *Daily Express* 20 June 2 (Advt.), Let's get down to Brass Tacks. **1932** T. S. ELIOT *Sweeney Agonistes* 25 That's all the facts when you come to brass tacks: Birth, and copulation, and death. **1953** L. A. G. STRONG *Personal Remarks* 10 When we put theories aside, and come down to brass tacks.

6. General comb.: **a.** objective or obj. genitive, as ***brass-caster***, ***-finisher***, ***-founder***, ***-foundry***; ***-finishing*** adj.; **b.** instrumental, as ***brass-armed***, ***-bound*** (also *fig.*), ***-mounted***, ***-shapen***; **c.** similative, as ***brass-bold***, ***-bright***, ***-coloured***, ***brass-like***; **d.** parasynthetic, as ***brass-browed***, ***-footed***, ***-fronted***, ***-handled***, ***-headed*** (†***-head***), ***-hilted***, ***-plated***, ***-scaly***, ***-studded***, ***-tipped***, etc.

1583 STANYHURST *Æneis* II. (Arb.) 45 A *brasse bold merchaunt in causes dangerus hardye. **1880** G. M. HOPKINS *Poems* (1918) 50 Now the other was brass-bold. **1867** W. MORRIS *Jason* VI. 110 The *brass-bound tiller. **1901** *Daily Chron.* 29 Aug. 3/1 The soldierly old brass-bound General. **1913** W. DE LA MARE *Peacock Pie* 88 His brass-bound cart. **1908** HARDY *Dynasts* III. v. vi. 451 The flames making the faces of the crowd *brass-bright. **1630** PRYNNE *Anti-Armin.* 238 Dare any *brasse-browed Arminian be so shamelessly absurd. **1725** POPE *Odyss.* XXIV. 607 The *brass-cheek'd helmet. **1851** RUSKIN *King Gold. River* i, A very large nose, slightly *brass-coloured. **1621** BURTON *Anat. Mel.* III. ii. v. i. (1651) 544 She taught him how to tame the fire-breathing *brass-feeted Bulls. **1879** *Melbourne Argus* 24 Dec. 2/1 The same rates are paid in the fine *brassfinishing shops. **1601** HOLLAND *Pliny* II. 486 A third society..of *brasse-founders. **1716** *Lond. Gaz.* No. 5450/3 A *Brass Foundery is..building at Woolwich. **1613** HEYWOOD *Braz. Age* II. ii. Wks. 1874 III. 212 And these our *brasse-head buls. **1692** *Lond. Gaz.* No. 2804/4 A *Brass-hilted Sword. **1598** CHAPMAN *Iliad* VIII. 36 His *brass-hooved winged horse. **1877** A. B. EDWARDS *Up Nile* xix. 536 An antique *brass-mounted firelock. **1591** GREENE *Maiden's Dr.* Wks. 1881–3 XIV. 306 *Brass-renting Goddesse, she cannot lament. **1590** SPENSER *F.Q.* I. xi. 11 His long *bras-scaly back. **1583** STANYHURST *Æneis* ii. (Arb.) 67 Brandisht tergats, and *brasshapen harneise. **1858** LONGFELLOW *M. Standish* IV. 53 A Bible, Ponderous, bound in leather, *brass-studded, printed in Holland. **1862** MAYHEW *Crim. Prisons* 32 Gaugers with their *brass-tipped rules.

7. Special comb. and phrases: **brass band**, a band of musicians with wind instruments of brass; **brass bason**, a basin of brass, also *fig.* a barber or surgeon barber; **brass-blacking**, a dead black surface given to brass ornaments by treatment with chemicals; **brass-bounder**, (*a*) see quot. 1890; (*b*) an apprentice on board ships of English companies, so called from the brass on his uniform; **brass-colour**, (*a*) a preparation used to colour objects to resemble brass; (*b*) a preparation of oxidized brass used to stain glass to various tints of blue and green; †'**brasscut**, a copperplate engraving (cf. *woodcut*); **brass edge** (see quot.); †**brass-face**, an impudent person; **brass farthing**, an emphatic equivalent of *farthing* in depreciatory expressions; **brass-foil**, **brass-latten**, Dutch leaf or Dutch gold made by beating out plates of brass very thin; **brass-hat** *slang*, an officer of high rank in the British army (or other Service), so called from the gilt insignia on his cap; hence ***brass-hatted*** adj.; **brass-helmeted** *a.*, wearing a brass helmet; †**brass-leaf** = *brasscut*; **brass lump**, a miners' term for massive iron pyrites or marcasite; **brass-man**, one who plays a brass musical instrument; **brass nail** [rhyming slang for TAIL *sb.*[1]], a prostitute; †**brass-plate**, copper-plate for engraving; **brass plate**, a plate of brass, bearing an inscription, e.g. on or at a door or gate, bearing the resident's name; also a monumental 'brass' (2 a); **brass-plater** *slang*, a man of the professional class; **brass-powder**, a powder consisting of copper or one of its alloys used in varnish; **brass-rag**, in slang (orig. *Naut.*) phr. ***to part brass-rags***, to quarrel; **brass-rubbing**, the process of rubbing a brass (see RUB *v.*[1] 1 e); also, the impression thus obtained; so ***brass-rubber***; **brass rule**, a strip of brass, type-high, used to separate lines or columns of type; '**brass-smith**, an artificer in brass; '**brass-work**, artificers' work in brass; *pl.* an establishment for making or working in brass; '**brass-worker**, an artificer in brass.

1834 C. BRONTË in W. Gérin *C. Brontë* (1967) vi. 84 There are to be five *brass bands each consisting of two trumpets, three bombardones, [etc.]. **1837** HAWTHORNE in *Democratic*

Rev. Oct. 35 A company of summer soldiers, .. attended by the 'brass band'. **1849** *Theatrical Programme* 9 July 44 The Brass Band on the Lawn will perform an admired Selection of Popular Overtures. **1861** *N. Brit. Rev.* Nov. 392 The gentlemen of the Brass Band. **1871** M. COLLINS *Mrq. & Merch.* II. vi. 170 The brass band plays horribly. **1599** BP. HALL *Sat.* IV. i. 162 Esculape! how rife is phisicke made When ech *brasse-basen can profess the trade. *a* **1884** KNIGHT *Dict. Mech.* Suppl., **Brass-blacking*, a dead black color; used freely with French optical instruments. **1890** FARMER *Slang*, **Brass-Bounder* (nautical), a midshipman. **1927** *Blackw. Mag.* Sept. 374/2 There were none but sailors, brass-bounders, stewards. **1797** *Encycl. Brit.* III. 519/2 The finest *brass-colour is made with powder brass.., diluted into a varnish. **1839** URE *Dict. Arts* 169 Brass Colour.. is prepared by exposing for several days thin plates of brass upon tiles in the *leer* or annealing arch of the glass-house, till it be oxidized into a black powder. **1662** J. BARGRAVE *Pope Alex. VII.* (1867) 70 With all the scenes in excellent *brasscutts. **1884** F. BRITTEN *Watch & Clockm.* 36 *Brass Edge in common watch movements, [is] a brass rim fitted round the pillar plate. **1647** LILLY *Chr. Astrol.* cvii. 538 An impudent fellow, a *Brasse-face, yet of good understanding. **1642** ROGERS *Naaman* 33 As bare and beggarly as if he had not one *brasse farthing. **1880** BESANT & RICE *Seamy Side* x. 78, 'I care not one brass farthing.' **1893** KIPLING *Many Invent.* 210, I tell you der big *brass-hat pizness does not make der trees grow. **1940** *War Illustr.* 5 Jan. 546/1 No one today hears sarcastic reference to 'brass hats', the traditional term for the staff officers of the High Command. **1903** KIPLING *Traffics & Discov.* (1904) 73 There's a crowd of *brass-'atted blighters there which will say I've been absent without leaf. **1917** 'TAFFRAIL' *Off Shore* 82 The brass-hatted potentate who regards our quarterly list of breakages with a horny and unsympathetic eye. **1897** *Westm. Gaz.* 22 Nov. 9/1 The *brass-helmeted firemen. **1677** MOXON *Mech. Exerc.* (1703) 53 A thin piece of *Brass-latin. **1654** GAYTON *Fest. Notes* III. i. 66 In the book..a great Cut or *Brasse leafe. **1674** *Phil. Trans.* IX. 222 Pieces of the ordinary Fire-stones or Marcasite of the Coal-pits which here we call **Brass-lumps*. **1757** WALKER in *Phil. Trans.* L. 146 It is.. exceeding ponderous, and of a shining yellow colour, and is called by the miners brass lumps. **1872** T. HARDY *Under Greenwood Tree* I. I. iv. 50 They should ha' stuck to strings. Your *brass-man, is brass—well and good; your reed-man, is reed—well and good. **1958** B. RUST in P. GAMMOND *Decca Bk. of Jazz* iv. 60 These two fine brassmen made good jazz. **1934** P. ALLINGHAM *Cheapjack* 317 *Brass* (**Brassnail*), prostitute. **1938** F. D. SHARPE *S. of Flying Squad* i. 15 Ladies whom the Underworld calls 'brass nails'. **1655** MRQ. WORCESTER *Cent. Inv.* §100 All..of these Inventions..shall be Printed by *Brass-plates. **1771** *Encycl. Brit.* III. 511/1 The compositor..puts..this slip of brass-plate..in the composing-stick. **1836** DICKENS *Sk. Boz* I. 96 A brass-plate on the private door with 'Ladies School' legibly engraved thereon. **1860** MRS. GASKELL *Right at Last*, I saw a brass-plate with Doctor James Brown upon it. **1894** Brass plate [see PLATE *sb.* 5 b]. **1921** *Glasgow Herald* 9 Apr. 6 Steelworkers and bankers, ship-platers and '*brass-platers', 'workers' and 'parasites', we shall all have to take off our coats. **1839** URE *Dict. Arts* 169 Only so much of the *brass powder and varnish should be mixed at a time as is wanted for immediate use. **1898** W. P. DRURY *Tadpole of Archangel* 141 The graceful figures stiffened, passing each other with ..eyes fixed on futurity... 'Don't you *know* that we've parted *brassrags?' *Ibid.* 142 When 'Pincher' Martin, Ordinary, and 'Nobby' Clarke, A.B., desire to prove the brotherly love..with which each inspires the other, it is their..custom to keep their brasswork cleaning rags in a joint ragbag. But, should relations..become strained between them, the bag owner casts forth upon the deck..his sometime brother's rags; and with the parting of the brassrags hostilities begin. **1903** KIPLING *Traffics & Discov.* (1904) 49 You'll shut your mouth..or you an' me'll part brass rags. **1922** MRS. A. SIDGWICK *Victorian* vii, If you dare to use that word flapper in my hearing..we part brass rags. **1959** *Economist* 14 Mar. 979/2 He seems to have finally parted brass rags with the Arab nationalists and President Nasser. **1856** *Athenæum* 17 May 626 The quiet haunts of the *brass-rubber. **1886** C. M. YONGE *Chantry House* II. xiv. 135 Her greatest achievement in *brass-rubbing, a severe and sable knight. **1890** H. W. MACKLIN *Monumental Brasses* ii. 27 Brass-rubbings are greatly improved by being mounted. **1897** (*title*) The Oxford Journal of Monumental Brasses, being the Journal of the Oxford University Brass-Rubbing Society. **1952** E. COXHEAD *Play Toward* ii. 68 He'd cycled over with one of your girls, and they were taking brass rubbings in the church. **1831** CARLYLE *Sart. Res.* II. iv. Has he not seen the Scottish *Brasssmith's Idea? **1664** *Phil. Trans.* I. 25 In the *Brass-works of Tivoli. **1689** *Lond. Gaz.* No. 2509/4 Black Japan Gilt Brass-work. **1761** WESLEY *Jrnl.* 13 Sept., Employed in the neighbouring brass-works. **1805** *Chron.* in *Ann. Reg.* 378/1 The brass work being over-heated. **1723** *Lond. Gaz.* No. 6171/10 Benjamin Gibbons ..*Brassworker.

brass (brɑːs, -æ-), *v.*[1] [f. prec.: cf. *to tin.*]

1. a. *trans.* To coat with brass by electro-plating or otherwise.

c **1865** G. GORE in *Circ. Sc.* I. 213/1 Solutions used for coppering or brassing iron. *Ibid.* 222/1 Copper articles may be superficially brassed.

b. *fig.* To cover with effrontery. *to brass it* (colloq.): to put on a face of brass, to behave with effrontery.

1859 *Times* 18 Mar. 8/6 To wipe his mouth and brass his brow, and charge us with underrating our fellow countrymen.

2. *intr.* To pay *up*. Also *trans. slang.*

1898 J. D. BRAYSHAW *Slum Silhouettes* 147 Now..p'raps you'll pay the man. Go on—brass up! *Ibid.* 150 Along comes Mister Internashonal, an' brasses up every stiver o' that twenty-eight quid. **1939** F. THOMPSON *Lark Rise* vi. 119 Husbands and sons at work 'brassed up' on Friday nights. **1949** WODEHOUSE *Mating Season* viii. 79 What did he soak him? Five quid?.. And Gussie brassed up and was free?

3. *slang* (orig. *Services*'). **a.** (See quot. 1925.) **b.** (See quot. 1943.)

1925 FRASER & GIBBONS *Soldier & Sailor Words* 35 *To brass off*: to grumble. **1943** HUNT & PRINGLE *Service Slang* 16 The verb *brass off* means to tell off severely. **1964** V. CANNING *Scorpio Lett.* iv. 75 After I'd brassed you off for pinching my parking space.

† **brass**, *v.*[2] *Obs. rare*[−1]. [a. OF. *brasse-r* to burn.] ? To burn, to scorch.

1481 CAXTON *Myrr.* III. xv. 167 They rested them not by the grete fyres ne brassed not as som doo now.

brassage ('bræsɪdʒ). [a. F. *brassage*, f. *brasser* to stir together melted metals.] A mint-charge levied to cover the expense of coining money.

1806 *Edin. Rev.* VII. 275 Not content with levying..a brassage. **1884** *Times* 20 Mar. 11 They might take *brassage* or 'mint charge' to mean the equivalent of the cost of coining.

brassard (brəˈsɑːd). Also **brassart**. [a. F. *brassard*, f. *bras* arm; see -ARD.]

1. Armour for the upper part of the arm. (Only *Hist.*)

1830 JAMES *Darnley* x. 47/1 This brassard is a little too close. **1834** PLANCHÉ *Brit. Costume* 122 Brassarts connect the shoulder with the elbow-pieces. **1866** *Fortn. Rev.* I Sept. 152 Talbot is wearing brassards and a tabard.

2. A badge worn on the arm; an armlet.

1870 *Daily News* 21 Sept., Brassards seem to be obtainable for the asking. **1879** FIFE-COOKSON *Armies of Balkans* vii. 100 An English doctor who..had the white brassard with the red crescent on his arm.

brassate ('bræseɪt). *Chem.* [f. BRASS-IC + -ATE[4].] A salt of brassic acid.

1863 WATTS *Dict. Chem.* I. 655 Brassate of sodium gives by analysis 8.5 per cent. soda.

brasse (bræs). [Cf. LG. *brasse* (Schiller and Lübben), Ger. *brassen* a bream (cf. BRASSEM).] A name of a fish of the perch family.

1847 CRAIG, *Brasse*, the pale-spotted perch.

brasse, -lat, -let, obs. ff. BRACE, -LET.

brassed (brɑːst, -æ-), *ppl. a.* Also 4 **brased**, 7 **brast**. [f. BRASS + -ED.] **1.** Made of, or overlaid with brass: also *fig.*

a **1300** *E.E. Psalter* cvi[i]. 16 Yhates [that] brased ware, And slottes irened. **1611** CHAPMAN *Iliad* XVII. 425 Both cast Dry solid hides upon their necks, exceeding soundly brast. *a* **1734** NORTH *Lives* I. 363 None so brassed in this kind as demure pretenders who complain of popery and arbitrary power.

2. With *off*: disgruntled, 'fed up', 'browned off'. *slang* (orig. *Services*').

1941 J. SOMMERFIELD in *Penguin New Writing* VIII. 46 I'm brassed off waiting. **1943** P. BRENNAN et al. *Spitfires over Malta* 12 Very tired and brassed off, we bundled our kit on our shoulders. **1959** I. JEFFERIES *13 Days* x. 158, I thought you was brassed off!

Brassell, obs. form of BRAZIL.

‖ **'brassem.** *Obs.* [a. Du. (and MDu.) *brasem* bream; = OS. *bressemo*, OHG. *brahsema* (MHG. *brahsem*, *brasme*, *brahsen*, Ger. *brassen*): BREAM.] A kind of fish; ? a sea-bream.

1731 MEDLEY *Kolben's Cape G.H.* II. 196 There are two sorts of Brassems in the Cape Sea. **1772–84** COOK *Voy.* (1790) I. 322 The brassem is found only about the cape. Of this fish there are two sorts.

brassen, obs. form of BRAZEN.

brasser, obs. f. BRACER; see BALLOON 1, 10.

1650 WELDON *Crt. Jas. I.* (1817) 47 Lifting up his hand over his head with a Ballan brasser.

‖ **brasserie** (brasəri). [Fr., orig. = brewery, f. *brasser* to brew.] A beer saloon, usually one in which food is served.

1864 *Realm* 15 June 8/3 May his monument outlive all other *brasseries*! **1887** *Athenæum* 1 Jan. 10/3 [They] are delighted to earn a cheap reputation at the *café* or the *brasserie*. **1888** *Pall Mall Gaz.* 6 Mar. 4 The employment of girls in brasseries, which have so evil a name. **1926** *Sunday at Home* June 536/1 You are impressed at once by the contrast of the innumerable *brasseries* and restaurants with our wretched public-houses.

brasset ('bræsɪt). [? A bad form of BRASSARD.] ? = BRASSARD.

1751 CHAMBERS *Cycl.*, s.v. *Armor*, A compleat Armor antiently consisted of a casque or helm, a gorget, cuirasse, gantlets, tasses, brassets, cuisses, and covers for the legs, to which the spurs were fastened. **1831** BREWSTER *Nat. Magic.* xii. (1833) 306 A cuirass with its brassets.

brassey, brassie: see BRASSY *sb.*[2]

brassic ('bræsɪk), *a.* [f. next.] Pertaining to or derived from the genus *Brassica*.

1879 WATTS *Dict. Chem.* I. 655 Colza oil is a mixture of two glycerides, which yield by saponification brassic acid.

‖ **brassica** ('bræsɪkə). *Bot.* [L.; = cabbage.] A genus of cruciferous plants, containing the cabbage in its many varieties, the turnip, rape, etc.

1832 *Veg. Subst. Food* 258 Some species of brassica..was introduced into this country by the Romans. **1854** BUSHNAN in *Circ. Sc.* (*c.* 1865) II. 27/2 The leaves of the various species of brassica.

brassière ('bræsɪɛə(r), -ɪə, -z-). Also **brassiere**. [Fr., orig. (17c.) bodice, now chiefly in pl. 'leading strings (of infant)'.] A woman's undergarment worn to support the breasts.

1911 *Daily Colonist* (Victoria, B.C.) 5 July 3/7 (Advt.), Brassieres of fine cambric, lace and embroidery trimmed. **1912** *Queen* 27 July 10 (Advt.), The Stylish Figure of To-Day requires a Brassiere. **1936** W. HOLTBY *South Riding* IV. vi. 262 Her young body, partially covered by pink brassière, trunks, [etc.]. **1961** J. HELLER *Catch-22* (1962) iv. 39 An unhooked brassiere was as close as you ever hoped to get to Paradise.

† **'brassik.** *Obs. rare.* Also **brasik**. [ad. L. *brassica*: see BRASSICA] Cabbage.

c **1420** *Pallad on Husb.* IX. 53 Rave as brassik for vyne as ille is fonde. *Ibid.* x. 137 Nowe brasik to growe For November plauntyng.

'brassil. Iron pyrites; coal containing pyrites: see BRAZIL[2].

brassily ('brɑːsɪlɪ, -æ-), *adv.* [f. BRASSY *a.* + -LY[2].]

1. With impudence or brazen confidence.

1889 in *Cent. Dict.* **1952** S. KAUFFMANN *Philanderer* iv. 61 He doesn't mind sticking his bespectacled face into things and grinning broadly and brassily.

2. With a brassy noise.

1898 KIPLING *Day's Work* 94 Its band playing clashily and brassily a popular but impolite air.

brassin, obs. f. BRAZEN.

brassiness ('brɑːsɪnɪs, -æ-). [f. BRASSY *sb.*[1] + -NESS.] Brassy quality or appearance. Also *fig.*

1731 in BAILEY II. **1847** *Proc. Berw. Nat. Club* II. No. 5. 238 The brassiness of the elytra. **1921** H. CRANE *Let.* 17 Oct. (1965) 67, I have the apparent brassiness to call myself a person of rather catholic admirations. **1952** S. KAUFFMANN *Philanderer* iv. 61 But there was more to Perry than.. brassiness or quick brain. **1958** *Listener* 4 Dec. 964/3 He [*sc.* a horn player] seems to have acquired..the characteristic mellow tone free from any disagreeable brassiness.

brassing ('brɑːsɪŋ, -æ-), *vbl. sb.* [f. BRASS *v.*[1] + -ING[1].] The process or art of coating with brass.

c **1865** G. GORE in *Circ. Sc.* I. 222/2 Another liquid which he uses for brassing.

attrib. *Ibid.* 223/1 All the brassing solutions..are imperfect.

brassish ('brɑːsɪʃ, -æ-), *a.* Somewhat brassy.

1774 MRS. DELANY *Lett.* Ser. II. II. 473 A little brassish coperish, goldish thread-like stuff.

Brasso ('brɑːsəʊ, -æ-). [f. BRASS *sb.*] The proprietary name of a preparation for polishing brass and other metals.

1905 *Trade Marks Jrnl.* 24 May 670 *Brasso*... Preparations for polishing Metals and other articles, included in Class 50. Reckitt and Sons, Limited,.. Yorkshire; Manufacturers. **1925** *Glasgow Herald* 24 Mar. 8 A tin of Brasso, oily rag. **1936** C. DAY LEWIS *Friendly Tree* iii, Anna had once seen a duck dive its head and emerge with the top of a Brasso tin in its beak and swallow it. **1942** A. L. ROWSE *Cornish Childhood* 83 Friday..was the day on which the scales and weights in the shop were cleaned: whether it was..the smell of the brasso, I don't know, but I disliked Friday.

brassure, obs. form of BRACER.

brassy ('brɑːsɪ, -æ-), *a.* Also 6 **brassie, -ye.** [f. BRASS *sb.* + -Y[1].]

1. Consisting of or covered with brass.

1583 STANYHURST *Æneis* I. (Arb.) 32 Thee stayrs brassye grises stately presented. **1599** MARSTON *Sco. Villanie* II. vi. 200 That dreamed of Imagery, Whose head was gold, brest siluer, brassie thigh. **1880** L. WALLACE *Ben-Hur* 328 On the left the brassy legions of Caesar.

2. Of the nature or appearance of brass, in colour, sound, taste, etc.

1789 MRS. PIOZZI *Journ. France* I. 426 [It] left a brassy taste in my mouth for a whole day. **1803** *Phil. Trans.* XCIII. 68 Of a pale brassy colour. **1847** MOTHERWELL *Spirits of Light* Hark, to their trumpets' brassy blare. **1857** KINGSLEY *Two Y. Ago* I. 65 The sky..is brassy green.

3. *fig.* with many varieties of sense.

a. Hard as brass, pitiless, unfeeling.

1596 SHAKS. *Merch. V.* IV. i. 31 And plucke commiseration of his state From brassie bosomes.

b. Having a 'face of brass', unblushing, impudently confident, or forward.

1576 LAMBARDE *Peramb. Kent* (1826) 156 To make them blush..were they never so brassie and impudent. **1690** *Def. Dr. Walker* 2 A brassy Impudence. **1792** J. WOLCOTT (P. Pindar) *Churchw.*, Betty was too brassy, We never keep a servant that is saucy. **1846** DOUGLAS JERROLD *Chron. Clovernook* Wks. IV. 415 A brassy confidence in his face.

c. Of brass, as opposed to 'golden'; debased yet pretentious.

1586 FERNE *Lacies Nobilitie* 2 This present age, which is growne so harde and brassye, for the golden dayes are long sithence ouer-passed. **1842** TENNYSON *Amphion* ix, In such a brassy age I could not move a thistle.

d. Harsh and feelingless in tone, like a brass instrument; having a strident artificial tone.

1865 M. ARNOLD *Ess. Crit.* 74 That hard, brassy, over-stretched style. **1870** *Daily News* 26 July 5 Its brassy clangour of quickly-recurring rhymes. **1884** J. A. SYMONDS *Shakspere's Predecessors* 508 Aretino..proved his originality by creating a new manner, brassy and meretricious.

e. In medical use, describing a cough.

1880 BARWELL *Aneurism* 91 Severe brassy cough. **1895** *Oracle Encycl.* II. 221/2 The patient..awakens..with a peculiar cough, called by physicians 'brassy'.

ˈbrassy, *sb.*[1] *Sc.* Also bressie. [Cf. BRASSE.] A fish, 'the ancient Wrasse' (Jamieson).

1710 SIBBALD *Fife* (1803) 128 *Turdus vulgatissimus Willoughboei*: I take it to be the same our fishers call a *Bressie*.

brassy (ˈbræsɪ), *sb.*[2] *Golf.* Also **brassey, brassie.** [f. BRASS *sb.* + -Y[6].] A wooden club shod with brass.

1888 *Daily News* 2 July 5/1 The golfer will hunt for his 'brassey' in vain. **1889** LINSKILL *Golf* iii. 20 A brassey is very similar to a wooden niblick, but..the sole of the head is shod with a plate of brass as a protection to the wood and bone. **1890** [see CLEEK *sb.* 1 b]. **1929** WODEHOUSE *Mr. Mulliner Speaking* vi. 203 John Gooch, smiting vigorously with his brassie.

b. *ellipt.* for *brassy shot.*

1906 *Daily Chron.* 22 May 9/5 He sliced his drive badly, but played a perfect brassey to within four yards of the pin. **1909** *Ibid.* 22 Apr. 8/4 His tee shots and brassies being of fine length and direction.

c. *attrib.*, as ***brassy player, shot, stroke.***

1894 *Westm. Gaz.* 21 Dec. 7/2 To the third hole in, he got away a fine tee shot, which he followed by a good brassy stroke to the green. **1897** *Ibid.* 30 Dec. 7/3 Mr. Ramsay Islay ..killed a seagull on the wing with a brassey shot. **1904** *Ibid.* 1 Jan. 3/1 He is a good brassy player.

brast, *v.*, northern form of BURST.

a **1300** *Cursor M.* 7170 Þat all þe bandes of him brast. *c* **1450** *Songs & Carols* 51 (Mätz.) Tyll both hys eyen in watyr gan brast. **1513** DOUGLAS *Æneis* XII. Prol. 39 The fyry sparkis brastyng fra his ene. **1818** BYRON *Ch. Har.* I. lxxviii, Mid wounds, and clinging darts, and lances brast. **1865** MISS LAHEE *Betty o' Yep's T.* 10 in *Lanc. Gloss.* (E.D.S.) s.v., Laughin' fit to brast their soides.

brast, obs. form of BRASSED.

brastle (ˈbræs(ə)l), *v.* [OE. *brastlian*, ME. *brastlien*; cf. MHG. *barsteln*, Sw. *prassla.* But the modern (Scotch) use may be a recent onomatopœia. Cf. BRATTLE, BRUSTLE.]

†**1.** *intr.* To crackle, clatter; to roar (as flames).

c **1000** ÆLFRIC in Thorpe *Hom.* II. 508 (Bosw.) Ðæt treow brastliende sah to ðam halʒan were. *c* **1205** LAY. 27463 Sceldes brastleden.

2. To rush with clattering noise, or with excited haste. *Sc.*

1826 J. WILSON *Noct. Ambr.* Wks. 1855 I. 234 Plouterin in the dubs, or brastlin up the braes. **1835** *Blackw. Mag.* XXXVIII. 156 A small trout or two brastled away to the other side of the shallow.

Brasyle, -lle, obs. forms of BRAZIL.

brasyn, brasynge, obs. ff. BRAZEN, BRAZING.

brat (bræt), *sb.*[1] *Obs.* exc. *dial.* Also 1 **bratt**, 6 **bratte.** [Of Celtic origin. OE. (Northumbrian) *bratt* was prob. adopted from OIrish *brat(t* masc., 'cloth', esp. as a covering for the body, 'plaid, mantle, cloak' (cf. Gael. *brat* 'haircloth for a kiln, apron; covering, mantle, veil', OWelsh **breth* (or **brath*), pl. *brith, bryth,* applied to the swaddling-clothes of an infant: the mod. Welsh *brat* 'pinafore, rag', is merely the Eng. word.]

1. A cloth used as an over-garment, *esp.* of a coarse or makeshift character.

†**a.** (in OE.) A cloak. **b.** in *midl.*, *west.*, and *north. dial.*, A child's pinafore; a woman's or girl's pinafore or apron. (See also quot. 1962.) **c.** *contemptuously.* A rag, or article which is 'a mere rag'. Hence **ˈbratful**, apronful.

c **950** *Lindisf. Gosp.* Matt. v. 40 Ðæm seðe wil..cyrtel ðin to niomanne forlet eac hrægl *vel* hæcla *vel* bratt [*L.* pallium, *Ags.* wæfels, *Rushw.* hryft]. *c* **1386** CHAUCER *Chan. Yem. Prol. & T.* 329 A brat [v.r. bak] to walken in by day-light. **1529** MORE *Supplic. Souls* Wks. 337/2 There is none so poore as we, yt haue not a bratte to put on our backes. **1570** LEVINS *Manip.* 37 A Bratte, *panniculus.* **1691** RAY *N.C. Wds.* 8 *Bratt*, a course Apron, a Rag. **1775** J. COLLIER (Tim Bobbin) *Tummus & M.* 60 Th' treacle butter cake stickt to Seroh's brat. **1786** BURNS *The Author's Earnest Cry* xxiv, Sowp's o' kail an' brats o' claise. **1867** E. WAUGH *Owd Blanket* i. 19 in *Lanc. Gloss.*, A brat-full o' guinea gowd. **1885** MRS. LYNN LINTON *Chr. Kirkland* I. i. 15 The women held their aprons ('brats' we called them). **1959** *Times* 15 Oct. 14/6 The picking basket or pail was rejected in favour of the 'brat', a long apron made from a meal sack into which the potatoes were first picked. **1962** J. B. PRIESTLEY *Margin Released* I. iii. 24, I..had put on the chequered overall known locally as a 'brat'.

2. A jacket for a sheep's back.

1862 J. WILSON *Farming* 487 This 'Brat'..prevents the wool from parting over the spine.

†**3.** Rubbish, beggarly stuff. Cf. BEGGARY 5. *Obs.*

1656 DUGARD *Gate Lat. Unl.* §336. 93 The Threshers—with a whisk of feathers purge it from the refuse—& with a siev from the brat or beggery.

4. (*Sc.*) The tough film or skin which forms on porridge, rice pudding, and the like.

1795 *Statist. Acc.* XV. 8 *note* (JAM.) *Brat*, a cover or scurf. **1864** J. BROWN *Jeems* 11 Saying his grace over our bickers [of porridge] with their brats on.

brat (bræt), *sb.*[2] Also 6–7 **bratt(e.** [Of uncertain origin: Wedgwood, E. Müller, and Skeat think it the same word as the prec., but evidence of the transition of sense has not been found.]

'A child, so called in contempt' J. In 16th and 17th c. sometimes used without contempt, though nearly always implying insignificance; the phrase ***beggar's brat*** has been common from the first.

c **1505** DUNBAR *Flyting* 49 Irsche brybour baird, wyle beggar with thy brattis. **1557** *Tottel's Misc.* (Arb.) 109 Yong brats, a trouble: none at all, a maym it seems to bee. *a* **1577** GASCOIGNE in Farr's *S.P.* (1845) I. 35 O Abrahams brats, O broode of blessed seede. **1583** STANYHURST *Æneis* I. (Arb.) 25 What syn hath Æneas, my brat, committed agaynst the? *a* **1593** H. SMITH *Wks.* (1866–7) I. 197 Where any sectary hath one son, Machiavel hath a score, and those not the brats, but the fatlings of the land. **1650** CROMWELL in Carlyle *Lett. & Sp.* (1871) III. 9, I should be glad to hear how the little brat doth. **1712** STEELE *Spect.* No. 479 ¶1 The noise of those damned nurses and squalling brats. **1750** JOHNSON *Rambl.* No. 15 As cheap as any two little brats can be kept. **1808** SCOTT *Mem.* in *Lockhart* i. (1842) 8/1, I felt the change from being a single indulged brat, to becoming a member of a large family, very severely. **1879** DIXON *Windsor* II. vi. 65 Repulsed in her appeal for mercy like a beggar's brat.

b. *fig.* Offspring, product.

1678 CUDWORTH *Intell. Syst.* I. v. 891 An ignoble and bastardly brat of fear. **1720** ORMOND in *Swift's Lett.* (1766) II. 9 The South-sea was said to be my lord Oxford's brat. **1790** WOLCOTT (P. Pindar) *Ep. S. Urban* Wks. 1812 II. 257 Ambitious that the Brats my Rhymes Should see the Gentlefolks of future times.

brat (bræt), *sb.*[3] Also **bratt.** [A variant of BRET.] A fish: the turbot, birt, or bret. Also *attrib.*, as in ***brat-net.***

1759 *Chron.* in *Ann. Reg.* 68/2 It..had a head like a turbot or Bratt. **1883** *Fisheries Exhib. Catal.* 12 Brat or Turbot Net complete.

brat (bræt), *sb.*[4] *Mining.* [perhaps akin to BRAT[1], 2.] 'A thin bed of coal mixed with pyrites or carbonate of lime.' Bainbridge *Law of Mines* 1856.

brat (bræt), *v. rare.* [f. BRAT *sb.*[1]] *trans.* To wrap up in a brat or clout.

1570 LEVINS *Manip.* 37 To Bratte, *panniculis circumdare.* **1862** [see BRATTING *vbl. sb.*].

bratch, -et, obs. forms of BRACH, BRACHET.

†**ˈbratchel.** *Obs.* [perh. from BRAKE *v.*[1] or *sb.*[3]: cf. *sack, satchel.*] 'The husks of flax set on fire' (Jamieson).

1815 *Clan-Albin* I. 77 (JAM.) The blaze of a bratchel, and above all the superlative joys of a waulking.

bratchet (ˈbrætʃɪt). Also in 6 **bratchart, bratshard.** [Apparently the same word as BRACHET: cf. the application of *whelp, cub,* etc. to a child; but perhaps associated with BRAT *sb.*[2] as if a diminutive of that.]

1. = BRACHET.

2. A little brat, a child. (*contemptuous* or *playful.*)

a **1600** MONTGOMERIE *Flyting* 284 That bratchart in ane busse vvas borne. **1832–53** *Whistle-binkie* (Sc. Songs) Ser. III. 74, I..took the bratchet [Cupid] on my knee.

attrib. **1821** SCOTT *Kenilw.*, To play child-keeper..to be plagued with a bratchet whelp.

bratful, var. BRETFUL, *Obs.*; see also BRAT *sb.*[1] 1.

†**brath**, *sb. Obs.* Also 3 **braþþe** (*Orm.*), 4 (? braith), **brath(e.** [Ormin's *braþþe* appears to imply a formation from *braþ*, BRATH *a.* + -TH[1] (:—OE. *-þo*) as in *length, wrath* (:—OE. *wrǽþ-þo*).] Impetuosity, violence, wrath, ire.

c **1200** ORMIN 1233, & dafftelike leden þe, wiþþutenn bracc and braþþe. *Ibid.* 4707 Clene of braþþe. *c* **1325** *E.E. Allit. P.* B. 916 In þe brath of his breth þat brennez alle þinkez. *c* **1375** ? BARBOUR *St. Christina* 275 Al þai bestis socht hyme to Ine mykil brath. *c* **1400** *Destr. Troy* 5075 Priam..Bade hom blynn of hor brathe.

†**brath, braith,** *a. Obs.* Also 3–4 **braþ.** [ME. *braþ*, a. ON. *bráðr*; which became in midland Eng. BROTH(E. The northern dial. retained *brath*, spelt in 15–16th c. Sc. *braith, brayth.*] Impetuous, violent, wrathful.

c **1200** ORMIN 7164 Forr ȝiff þe riche mann iss braþ, & grimme. *a* **1300** *Cursor M.* 16164 For to do his breth to bu of him þat was ful brath. *c* **1340** *Gaw. & Gr. Knt.* 1909 Þer bayen hym mony braþ houndez. *c* **1440** *Syr Gowghter* 108 And afterwarde wax breme and brathe. *c* **1470** HENRY *Wallace* XI. 171 Nese, mouth and eyn Throuch the braith blaw, all byrstit out of blud.

brathe, variant of BRAYTHE *v. Obs.*

†**ˈbrathel.** *Obs. rare*—[1]. Variant of BRETHEL, BROTHEL, wretch, worthless person.

1542 UDALL *Erasm. Apoph.* 24 a, The scoldyng of brathels is no more to bee passed on then the squekyng of welle wheles.

†**ˈbrathful, braithful,** *a. Obs.* Also 6 **breth-, breithfull.** [cf. BROTHFUL.] Violent, wrathful.

1513 DOUGLAS *Æneis* X. vi. 155 With brethfull [*v.r.* braythful] blastis. *Ibid.* XII. viii. 133 All kynd of wreth and breithfull ire now he Leyt slip at large.

†**ˈbrathly, braithly,** *a.* and *adv. Obs. north. dial.* and *Sc.* Also 4 **brathely.** [f. BRATH, BRAITH *a.* or BRATH *sb.* + -LY. Cf. BROTHELY.]

A. *adj.* Impetuous, violent, angry.

a **1455** *Houlate* II. 14 (JAM.) The battellis so brym brathly and blicht. **1513** DOUGLAS *Æneis* I. ii. 11 [Eolus] braithlie tempestis by his power refrenis.

B. *adv.* Impetuously; furiously, violently.

a **1300** *Cursor M.* 2240 Brathli þai þis werk bigan. *Ibid.* 21400 Brathli on his fas he brast. ? *a* **1400** *Morte Arth.* 3220 This comlyche kynge..Bownnys brathely to bede. *c* **1400** *Melayne* 255 Barouns ondir blonkes fate Braythely ware borne doun. *c* **1470** HENRY *Wallace* VI. 212 The bailful teris bryst braithly fra hys eyne.

bratishing, obs. form of BRATTICING.

bratling (ˈbrætlɪŋ). [f. BRAT *sb.*[2] + -LING.] A little brat, an infant.

1652 BROME *Jov. Crew* II. Wks. 1873 III. 387 The Bratling's born, the Doxey's in the Strummel. **1796** COLERIDGE in Cottle *Remin.* (1847) 100 We are all—wife, bratling, and self, remarkably well.

‖**brattach** (ˈbratəx). [Gaelic (and Irish) *bratach* fem. (Manx *brattagh*) a standard, banner, flag, f. *brat* cloth.] An ensign, banner, or flag.

1828 SCOTT *F.M. Perth* vi, No five of each clan have a rusty shirt of mail as old as their brattach.

bratte, obs. form of BRAT.

brattery (ˈbrætərɪ). [f. BRAT *sb.*[2] + -ERY.] A collection of brats, a nursery. (*contemptuous.*)

1788 LD. SHEFFIELD in *Ld. Auckland's Corr.* (1861) II. 220 We hope the Brattery will continue well. **1834** BECKFORD *Italy, &c.* I. 4 The apartment above my head proves a squalling brattery.

brattice (ˈbrætɪs), *sb.* Forms: α. 3 **brutaske**, 4 **brytasqe**, 5 **betrax** (= *bretask*). β. 4 **brutage**, 4–5 **bretage**, 5 **bretayge, britage, brytege,** (9 *Hist.* **bretache, brattish**). γ. 4–5 **bretais, -ays,** 5 **bretise, -asce, -ys, -is, brettys, bertes, bartes.** δ. 9 (sense 2) **brettis, brattice, -ish.** [Found in many types: α. ME. *brutaske, brytasqe*, a. ONF. *breteske, -aske, -esque*: β. ME. *brutage, bretage*, etc., a. AFr. *bruteshe* (Matt. Paris), OF. *bretesche*, mod.F. *bretèche*: γ. ME. *bretasce, -ais, -is*, etc., a. OF. *bretesce, bretasce.* The OF. *breteske, -esche, -esce* (rarely *bertesque, -esche, -ece*), correspond to Pr. *bertresca*, It. *bertesca* (*baltresca*), med.L. *bretachia, bertescha, breteschia*, etc. Of uncertain origin; according to Mahn (to whom Diez adheres) prob. a derivative of Ger. *brett* board, with Romanic suffix *-esca*, with sense of 'boarding', 'boardwork'. The early forms in *bru-, bry-*, app. of English or Anglo-French origin, are due perhaps to the obscurity of the first vowel. The 15–16th c. forms in *ber-, bar-* were northern: see BRATTICING. The original sense became obs. before 1500. To modern times the word has come down in local use, chiefly in connexion with coal-mining, in the forms *brettis* (Derbyshire), *brattice* (Newcastle, etc.), *brattish.* Although *brettis* is the best form etymologically, *brattice* has become more generally known, and accepted in literary use; *brattish* has given the architectural *brattishing.*]

The general sense is 'boarding, planking, a structure of boards'. Hence *spec.*

†**1.** A temporary breastwork, parapet, or gallery of wood erected on the battlement of a fortress, for use during a siege. *Obs.*

α. type *breteske.*

1297 R. GLOUC. 536 Atte laste hii s[s]ende Al the brutaske withoute, & the brugge brende. *c* **1380** *Sir Ferumb.* 3315 Þe kernels..wer broke & schente, & þe brytasqes on þe tour an heȝe dulfuly a-doun wer caste. *c* **1440** *Promp. Parv.* 50/1 Betrax of a walle, *propugnaculum.*

β. type *bretesche, bretage.*

c **1325** *E.E. Allit. P.* B. 1190 Bigge brutage of borde bulde on þe walles. *c* **1350** *Will. of Palerne* 3001 Here walles were broke · wiþ engynes strong, here bretages al a-boute · forbrent & destroyed. *c* **1430** WYCLIF *Song Sol* viii. 9 (Lamb. MS.) If it is a wal, bilde we theronne siluerne touris, *ethir britagis.* *c* **1450** *Gloss. Garlande's Dict.* in Wright's *Voc.* 130 *Propugnacula*, brytegys. *c* **1475** *Voc.* in Wr.-Wülcker 784 *Hoc propinaculum*, a bretayge. [**1851** TURNER *Dom. Archit.* II. v. 193 A drawbridge with a bretache above it. **1861** *Sat. Rev.* 6 Apr. 345/2 A very graphic report..describing the siege of that place in 1240, makes frequent mention of.. brattishes, breastworks or turrets of timber.]

γ. type *bretesce*, ? *bretis.*

c **1380** WYCLIF *Serm.* (Sel. Wks.) I. 191 Bi þis weye mai no man eende þe laste bretais of þis tour. *c* **1400** *Ywaine & Gaw.* 163 A bretise brade. *c* **1425** WYNTOUN *Cron.* VIII. xxvi. 233 (JAM.) To mak defens and brettys. *c* **1440** *Promp. Parv.* 50 Bretasce [**1499** bretays], *propugnaculum.* *c* **1450** *Voc.* in Wr.-Wülcker 731 *Hoc signaculum*, a bretys. *c* **1500** *Lancelot* 873 Towart ther bretis. *Ibid.* 1005 A bertes. *Ibid.* 2897 To the bartes to behold and see. [**1885** C. OMAN *Art of War* 59 The brattice was a wooden gallery fitted with apertures in its floor, and running along the top of the wall.]

b. The 'battlement' of a cup.

1465 *Test. Ebor.* (1855) II. 272, j. peciam argenti stantem cum uno bretis.

2. In form *brattice* (dial. also *brattish*): A partition, generally of deal. **a.** (esp.) A partition for the purpose of ventilation in the shaft of a coal-pit (***shaft brattice***), or in a drift, or other working of a colliery (***drift, headways,*** or ***board brattice***).

1851 *Coal-tr. Terms Northumbld. & Durh.* 11 Shaft or main brattice is usually made of 3-inch Memel plank.. Common brattice is made of ½-inch American deal.. It is nailed to props set for the purpose (called brattice props). **1860** *Times* 10 Dec. 10/2 Where only one shaft is sunk..a downcast and an upcast are created by running an airtight partition, or 'brattice' to the bottom. **1883** *Standard* 23 Nov. 3/7 Gas still showed..on both sides of the brattice.

b. A partition of boards in a room. *dial.*

1851 TURNER *Dom. Archit.* I. vi. 201 A rude partition, called a brattish, rises to the eaves **1863** ATKINSON *Danby Provinc., Brattice,* a wooden partition, serving to divide a closet or store room into two parts.

c. A lining of timber to a shaft or a headway in a pit.

1881 RAYMOND *Mining Gloss., Brettis* (Derb.), a crib of timber filled up with slack or waste. —— *Brettis-way,* a road in a coal-mine, supported by brettises built on each side after the coal has been worked out.

3. In form *brattish*: 'A shelf: also a seat with a high back. *north. dial.*' (Halliwell.)

4. *attrib.* in sense 2, as **brattice-cloth**, stout tarred cloth used in mines instead of wooden bratticing; *brattice-nail, -work*; *brettis-way*: see 2 c.

1885 *Engineer* 15 May (*Advt.*) John Marsden, manufacturer of Tarred, Oiled, and Fire-Proof Brattice Cloth. **1880** *Daily Tel.* 5 Oct., The miner..scratched with the point of a rusty brattice nail the farewell letter to his wife.

brattice (ˈbrætɪs), *v.* In 5 **bretexe.** [f. prec.]

†**1.** (in obs. form *bretexe*): *trans.* To fortify with a wooden breastwork. *Obs.*

1430 LYDG. *Chron. Troy* II. xi, Euery towre bretexed was so clene.

2. *to brattice up*: to line the sides of a shaft, or the like, with planking or boarding.

1862 *Times* 21 Jan., The stone was all carefully bratticed up. **1869** BLACKMORE *Lorna D.* lviii (D.), A great round hole or shaft bratticed up with timber.

bratticing (ˈbrætɪsɪŋ). Also in 4 **briteysing,** 5 **bretaysynge,** 6 *Sc.* **bertising, -ene,** 6–9 BRATTISHING, dial. **braddishing.** [f. BRATTICE *v.* (or *sb.*) + -ING¹.]

†**1.** (In the obs. forms): The furnishing of the ramparts of a castle, etc., with temporary (wooden) parapets or breastworks; the parapet and its works collectively. *Obs.*

c **1380** WYCLIF *Sel. Wks.* I. 191 þe hiȝest part of his tour is briteysing of charite. **1483** *Cath. Angl.* 43/1 A bretasynge, *propugnaculum.* **1651** *Rec. Pittenweem* in *Statist. Acc.* IV. 376 That the town's colours be put upon the bertisene [= bertising] of the steeple.

(From the preceding illiterate Sc. spelling *bertisene*, Sir Walter Scott appears to have evolved the grandiose BARTIZAN, vaguely used by him for *bretising* or *bratticing*, and accepted by later writers as a genuine historical term.)

2. Brattice-work in a coal-pit.

1866 *Morning Star* 18 Dec. 6/2 The 'braddishing' or tarred sheet at an opening near him being suddenly carried away. **1868** *Even. Standard* 25 Aug., That might easily have been remedied by bratticing or air-pipes. **1883** *Standard* 23 Nov. 3/7 By means of bratticing he was able to explore the place.

3. *Arch.* See BRATTISHING.

bratting (ˈbrætɪŋ), *vbl. sb.* [f. BRAT *v.* + -ING¹.] The covering with a brat; *spec.* covering the backs of sheep with a cloth or apron.

1862 J. WILSON *Farming* 487 Where the bratting plan has been adopted, the usual rate of mortality has been reduced.

brattish (ˈbrætɪʃ), *a.* [f. BRAT *sb.*² + -ISH.] Of or befitting a brat; childish.

1879 BEERBOHM *Patagonia* vi. 99 By the time they [children] abandon their brattish ways.

brattish, dial. var. of BRATTICE.

brattishing (ˈbrætɪʃɪŋ). A variant of BRATTICING, used in *Architecture*, in sense: A cresting of open carved work on the top of a shrine.

1593 *Rites & Mon. Ch. Durh.* (1842) 35 Ther was a brattishing on the fore parte of the wainscott or rowffe, very fynely and curiously wrought. **1845** *Gloss. Gothic Archit.* I. 69 *Brattishing.* **1851** PUGIN *Rood Screens* 32 A very elaborate screen of carved oak, surmounted by open bratishing. **1862** G. SCOTT *Westm. Abbey* (ed. 2) 68 A piece of cresting or brattishing. **1867** H. T. ELLACOMBE in *Trans. Exeter Dioc. Archit. Soc.* I. 106 Surmounted by a brattishing of Tudor flower in burnished brass.

¶ Also a *dial.* var. of BRATTICING in other senses.

brattle (ˈbræt(ə)l), *sb.* Chiefly *Sc.* Also 6 **brattill, brattyll.** [This and its verb are onomatopœic, prob. with association of *break, brast* and *rattle*; cf. also *brabble, brastle.*]

1. A smart rattling sound, *esp.* of something breaking or bursting.

c **1505** DUNBAR *Turnament* 73 His harnass brak and maid ane brattill. **1513** DOUGLAS *Æneis* IX. xi. 96 The hydduus scheild abufe him mayd a brattyll. **1839** W. CARLETON *Fardorougha* (ed. 2) 81 There comes an accidental brattle of thunder. **1865** LIVINGSTONE *Zambesi* xxi. 426 [Each] striving which can produce the loudest brattle while turning. **1870** *Daily News* 3 Sept. 5 The brattle of a drum under my window.

2. The sound or onset of sharp rattling blows.

a **1600** MONTGOMERIE *Poems* (1821) 75 Ȝe dou not byde a brattill. **1786** BURNS *Winter Nt.* iii, Or silly sheep, wha bide this brattle O' winter war.

3. The sound of scampering feet; a resounding scamper, rush, or spurt.

a **1758** RAMSAY *Poems* (1844) 79 Bauld Bess flew till him wi a brattle. **1785** BURNS *To a Mouse* i, Thou need na start awa ..Wi' bickerin brattle. **1828** J. WILSON in *Blackw. Mag.* XXIV. 294 A breast-brushing brattle down the brae.

brattle (ˈbræt(ə)l), *v.* Chiefly *Sc.* [See prec.]

1. *intr.* To produce a forcible rattling noise.

1513 DOUGLAS *Æneis* VII. Prol. 133 Branchis brattlyng, and blayknit schew the brays. *a* **1849** MANGAN *Poems* (1859) 51 Harsh engines brattled night and day.

b. with cognate object.

1852 D. MOIR *Winter Wild* vii, His iron heels..Brattling afar their under-song.

2. To rush with rattling noise, as a mountain brook over a stony bed; to bicker. Orig. *Sc.*

1834 H. MILLER *Scenes & Leg.* xxxi. (1857) 457 A mossy streamlet comes brattling from the hill. **1853** G. JOHNSTON *Nat. Hist. E. Bord.* I. 18 Many little livelier runlets that brattle down the green hills on each side. **1882** *Macm. Mag.* Oct. 472 The becks that brattle through the brake.

3. To run with brattling feet; to scamper. *Sc.*

1725 RAMSAY *Gent. Sheph.* I. ii, Our twa herds come brattling down the brae. **1826** *Blackw. Mag.* XIX. 382 Brattle not away so, ye foolish lambs.

brattling (ˈbrætlɪŋ), *vbl. sb.* [f. BRATTLE *v.* + -ING¹.] The action of the verb to BRATTLE; the production of harsh rattling sounds.

a **1771** SMOLLETT *Humph. Cl.* (1793) I. 34 The bursting, belching, and brattling of the French horns. **1809** W. IRVING *Knickerb.* (1861) 35 His voice sounded not unlike the brattling of a tin trumpet. **1821** BYRON *Sardan.* III. i. 394 As a lute's [voice] pierceth through the cymbal's clash, Jarr'd but not drown'd by the loud brattling.

brattling (ˈbrætlɪŋ), *ppl. a.* [f. BRATTLE *v.* + -ING².] That brattles: see the verb.

1820 W. IRVING *Sketch-bk.* (1849) 420 The hoarse brattling tone of a veteran boatswain. **1826** J. WILSON *Noct. Ambr.* Wks. 1855 I. 136 To gie them [dogs]..a brattlin run o thretty miles after a fox. **1860** J. KENNEDY *Horseshoe R.* i. 11 A rough and brattling mountain torrent. **1863** JEAN INGELOW *Poems* 178 She wondered by the brattling brook, And trembled with the trembling lea.

'brattock, *local.* [dim. of BRAT *sb.*²] A tiny brat, a young one.

1858 *Chamb. Journ.* X. 108 A solitary pair of eider-ducks may sometimes venture to rear their progeny of 'brattocks' on the rock.

bratty (ˈbrætɪ), *a. colloq.* (orig. *U.S.*). [f. BRAT *sb.*²: see -Y¹.] Of a child or adolescent: spoiled, badly-behaved; of an adult: immature, given to behaving like a spoiled child.

1961 in WEBSTER. **1973** M. AMIS *Rachel Papers* 15 Chinless elitist and bratty whey-faced lordling that I most unquestionably was, my move to London had nothing to do with any antipathy towards themselves, nor towards the village. **1977** M. FRENCH *Women's Room* (1978) ii. 115, I.. took care of *your* bratty kids all day. **1980** J. WENNER in S. Terkel *Amer. Dreams* 397, I was always considered bright or spoiled or precocious or bratty. **1985** *Maledicta* VIII. 235 John McEnroe, the bratty tennis champ pictured as cute on his BIC razor commercials, 'is as cute as a razor nick'.

‖**bratwurst** (ˈbrɑːtvʊrst). Pl. **bratwürste.** [G.] A type of German sausage.

1911 *Cosmopolitan* Feb. 314/1 See that I have blutwurst, brattwurst, and mettwurst every day for breakfast. **1932** L. GOLDING *Magnolia Street* I. viii. 128 The gentile guests drank beer and ate *Bratwurst*. It was a real German party. **1962** *Punch* 11 July 51/2 We ate two delicious *Bratwürste* apiece.

braugham, dial. var. BARGHAM, a horse-collar.

1807 J. STAGG *Poems* 14 Kit gat a braugham in his han', Wi' veng'ance whurl'd it at him, The collar leeghted roun' his neck, An' to the fluir it pat him.

braul(e, obs. form of BRAWL.

braun(e, braunfalne, obs. ff. BRAWN, -FALLEN.

braunce, braundise, obs. ff. BRANCH, BRANDISH.

braunite (ˈbraʊnaɪt). *Min.* [Named after Mr. *Braun* of Gotha (Dana).] An anhydrous oxide of manganese, a brittle dark brownish-black mineral occurring both crystallized and massive.

1839 *Penny Cycl.* XIV. 380/2 Braunite..before the blow-pipe melts and effervesces slightly with borax. **1869** ROSCOE *Elem. Chem.* 233 Manganese sesquioxide..occurs in nature as the mineral braunite.

‖**brava** (ˈbrɑːva), *int.* and *sb.* [It., fem. of BRAVO *int.* and *sb.*²] A term of approbation addressed to a woman: excellent! well done! Hence as *sb.*, an exclamation of *brava!*

1803 *Lett. Miss Riversdale* I. 92 Lord Grantin.. encouraged me with *bravas*! **1943** C. KNIGHT *Affair of Fainting Butler* iv. 43 The secretary looked dourly at the black object for a moment, then..clapped it into her mouth and swallowed without so much as a sip of water. 'Brava!' exclaimed Hinckley, applauding with hands held high. **1951** P. BRANCH *Wooden Overcoat* xi. 117 'Brava!' said Hugo calmly. 'I couldn't have done better myself.' **1977** *Washington Post* 9 May B7/4 To have enforced this would have been to deprive an opera audience of its favourite indoor sport, cheering arias and crying 'brava'. **1984** *N.Y. Times* 22 July I. 44/1 Alicia de Larrocha..played a Mozart concerto, won protracted bravas, and..eclipsed everything else on the Mostly Mozart program.

†**bra'vade.** *Obs.* [a. F. *bravade,* (according to Littré) ad. It. *bravata* bragging, boasting, f. *bravare* to brag, boast, f. *bravo*: see BRAVE. Cf. also Sp. *bravada,* and see -ADE.] = BRAVADO.

1579 J. STUBBES *Gaping Gulf* C vj, Euen so will it be harder then yron for Englishmen to digest..the french insolencies and disdaynefull brauades. **1676** *Packet Adv. to Men of Shaftesb.* 40 What occasion or need his Lordship had of this high Bravade. **1778** ROBERTSON *Hist. Amer.* II. v. 80 He..disregarded this vain bravade. **1833** *Fraser's Mag.* VIII. 304 He ventured, by way of bravade, upon a single glass of claret.

†**bra'vade,** *v. arch.* or *Obs.* [f. prec. sb.]

1. *intr.* To look brave, assume a bold or defiant front. *to bravade the street*: to swagger along it.

1634-46 ROW *Hist. Kirk* (1842) 464 Ilk shaimles lowne, With his silk goune, Bravades the street. **1637** GILLESPIE *Eng. Pop. Cerem.* Ord. C iij, The Archbishop of Spalato commeth forth..stoutly brandishing and bravading. **1667** R. LAW *Mem.* (1818) 18 The Dutch fleet bravading there attacks the river.

2. *trans.* To dare, brave, defy.

1676 ROW *Contn. Blair's Autobiog.* xii. (1848) 479 The Dutch navy bravades the English upon their coast.

Hence **bra'vading** *vbl. sb.* and *ppl. a.*

1812 J. HENRY *Camp. agst. Quebec* 88 Many..wrote and spoke of this bravading..with much applause. **1820** SCOTT *Monast.* ix, Listening to the bravading tales of gay Christie. **1823** *Blackw. Mag.* XIII. 278 Sir Joshua..with his arm a-kimbo, bravading cap, and chosen air of importance.

bravado (brəˈveɪdəʊ, -ˈvɑːdəʊ), *sb.* Also 6–7 **brauado, braueado,** 7 **brauardo, bravadoe, brevada;** *pl.* **bravadoes** (also **-os**). [ad. Sp. *bravada* and F. *bravade*: see BRAVADE and -ADO².]

1. Boastful or threatening behaviour; ostentatious display of courage or boldness; bold or daring action intended to intimidate or to express defiance; often, an assumption of courage or hardihood to conceal felt timidity, or to carry one out of a doubtful or difficult position.

Now usually in the singular, without *a*: less commonly *a bravado* or in *pl.*

1599 HAKLUYT *Voy.* II. I. 287 It was not that Spanish brauado. **1626** *Caussin's Holy Crt.* 62 To sound vain-glorious Brauado's. **1630** BRATHWAIT *Eng. Gentl.* (1641) 110 These Gamesters, who in a bravado will set their patrimonies at a throw. **1645** MILTON *Colast.* Wks. (1851) 362 Hee retreats with a bravado, that it deservs no answer. **1678** BUNYAN *Pilgr.* I. 128 Notwithstanding all his Bravadoes, he [Shame] promoteth the Fool, and none else. *a* **1707** BP. PATRICK *Serm. 1 Sam.* xvii. 8 To have been done out of a bravado. **1800** WEEMS *Washington* x. (1877) 119 To hear their bravadoes, one would suppose, etc. **1816** JANE AUSTEN *Emma* II. viii. 181 A sort of bravado—an air of affected unconcern. **1824** SCOTT *Redgauntlet* Introd., A series of idle bravadoes. **1853** ROBERTSON *Serm.* Ser. III. xvii. 214 We may do it in bravado or in wantonness.

†**b.** *to make* or *give a bravado*: to make a display in the face of the enemy, to offer battle. *Obs.*

1600 HOLLAND *Livy* III. lx. 128 When they made bravadoes, and challenged them to come forth and fight, not one Romane would answer them again. **1617** MORYSON *Itin.* II. II. ii. 164 That some foote should bee drawne out of the Campe, to give the Spaniards a brauado. **1688** *Lond. Gaz.* No. 2361/3 A Party of the Moors making a Bravado.

c. *attrib.*

1583 STUBBES *Anat. Abus.* II. 50 The barbers..haue one maner of cut called the French cut..one of the brauado fashion. **1844** DISRAELI *Coningsby* v. iv. 204 It is a day..of hopes and fears..bravado bets and secret hedging.

†**2.** A swaggering fellow, a hector, a bravo. *Obs.* [app. after Sp. masculines in *-ado* already used in Eng., as *desperado, renegado,* etc. Cf. *bravo.*]

1653 A. WILSON *Jas. I* 28 Roaring Boys, Bravadoes, Roysters, &c. commit many insolencies. **1668** PEPYS *Diary* 28 Feb., The Hectors & bravadoes of the House. **1817** COLERIDGE *Biog. Lit.* II. xxi. 121 But idlers and bravadoes.. must beware. **1825** KNAPP & BALDW. *Newgate Cal.* III. 397/2 Webb..was the greatest bravado.

Hence **bra'vadoism.** *rare.*

1833 *Fraser's Mag.* VIII. 527 Was..his apparent strength and defiance, real weakness and bravadoism?

bravado (brəˈveɪdəʊ, -ˈvɑːdəʊ), *v.* [f. prec. sb.] *intr.* To show bravado, talk defiantly, put on a bold face. Hence **bra'vadoing** *vbl. sb.* and *ppl. a.*

1800 MAR. EDGEWORTH *Belinda* I. iv. 72, I bravadoed to Harriet most magnanimously. **1809-12** —— *Almeria* Wks. 1832 VII. 283 Notwithstanding her bravadoing air, [she] was frequently perplexed and anxious. **1826** *Blackw. Mag.* XIX. Pref. 9 There was..much bravadoing and even apparent offers of battle. **1840** T. HOOK *Fitzherbert* III. xvii. 333 They tried to bravado it out.

†**bravashing,** *ppl. a. Obs. rare*⁻¹. [f. F. *bravache* 'a Swaggerer, Swash-buckler' (Cotgr.), ad. It. *bravaccio* bully (f. *brav-o* +

-*accio*, pejorative suffix) + -ING².] Boasting, swaggering.

1652 URQUHART *Jewel* Wks. (1834) 255 Which he did do ..in a lofty and bravashing humour, that, etc.

brave (breɪv), *a.*, *sb.*, *int.* [a. F. *brave*, not an original Fr. word, but adapted from It. *bravo* brave, gallant, fine: cf. Sp. and Pg. *bravo*, Pr. and Cat. *brau*. Ulterior derivation uncertain. Nearly all the Eng. senses may have been adopted from French. Cf. BRAW.

(Prof. Storm would associate *bravo* (in Sp. also *bravio*) with OIt. *braido*, *brado* wild, savage, which is also a sense of Sp. and Pg. *bravo*; cf. Pr. *braidiu* fiery, spirited (horse). These he would refer to a Latin type **brabidus*, formed from *rabidus* mad, fierce, of the existence of which there appears to be other evidence. See *Romania* 1876, p. 170. A more recent conjecture (*Romania* XIII. 110) tries to derive it from *barbarus*, but this does not suit Pr. *brau*.)]

A. *adj.*

1. a. Of persons and their attributes: Courageous, daring, intrepid, stout-hearted (as a good quality).

1485 CAXTON *Paris & V.* Prol., It is very good to relate the brave deeds. **1591** SHAKS. *1 Hen. VI*, III. ii. 134 A brauer Souldier neuer couched Launce. **1642** FULLER *Holy & Prof. St.* II. xviii. 118 Innocence and Independance make a brave spirit. **1644** MILTON *Educ.* (1738) 137 High hopes of living to be brave men, and worthy Patriots. **1732** POPE *Mor. Ess.* I. 115 Who combats bravely is not therefore brave. He dreads a Death-bed like the meanest slave. **1769** *Junius Lett.* iii. 16 A brave man has no rules to follow but the dictates of his courage. **1839** THIRLWALL *Greece* II. 233 For six days they made a brave defence. **1848** MACAULAY *Hist. Eng.* II. 157 Extolled by the great body of Churchmen as if he had been the bravest and purest of martyrs.

b. absol. *the brave* (now only pl.).

1697 DRYDEN *Alexander's F.* 15 None but the brave deserves the fair. **1726** GAY *Fables* I. i. 33 The brave Love mercy, and delight to save. **1782** COWPER *Loss Roy. George* 1, Toll for the brave! The brave that are no more. **1852** TENNYSON *Wellington* viii, To glorious burial slowly borne Follow'd by the brave of other lands.

2. Finely-dressed; = Sc. BRAW; splendid, showy, grand, fine, handsome. (Rare in 18th c.; in 19th c. apparently a literary revival, or adopted from dialect speech.)

1568 *Like will to L.* in Hazl. *Dodsl.* III. 312 To go more gayer and more brave, Than doth a lord. **1570** LEVINS *Manip.* 42 Braue, *splendidus*. *a***1593** H. SMITH *Wks.* (1866–7) I. 150 The lilies which are braver than Solomon. **1612** HEYWOOD *Apol. Actors* Author to Bk., One man is ragged, and another brave. **1624** CAPT. SMITH *Virginia* I. 11 At length he came to most braue and fayre houses. **1677** MOXON *Mech. Exerc.* (1703) 257 Lord Montague's brave House in Bloomsbury. **1810** SCOTT *Lady of L.* II. xvi, Now might you see the tartans brave. **1855** BROWNING *Bp. Blougram's Apol.*, His coat..Brave with the needlework of noodledom.

3. *loosely*, as a general epithet of admiration or praise: Worthy, excellent, good, 'capital', 'fine', 'famous', etc.; 'an indeterminate word, used to express the superabundance of any valuable quality in men or things' (J.). *arch.* (Cf. BRAW *a.*)

a. of persons.

1600 SHAKS. *A.Y.L.* III. iv. 43 O that's a braue man, hee writes braue verses, speakes braue words. **1603** *Mournef. Dittie* in *Shaks. C. Praise* 56 You Poets all, brave Shakspeare, Johnson, Greene. **1673** *Ess. Educ. Gentlewom.* 29 Zeuxes and Timanthes were brave Painters. **1679** PENN *Addr. Prot.* I. §5 (1692) 20 Many brave Families have been ruin'd by a Gamester. **1740** J. CLARKE *Educ. Youth* (ed. 3) 57 His Son is a brave Scholar.

b. of things.

1577 NORTHBROOKE *Dicing* (1843) 102 Nowe are the braue and golden dayes. **1599** SHAKS. *Much Ado* v. iv. 130 Ile deuise thee braue punishments for him. **1605** —— *Lear* III. ii. 79 This is a braue night to coole a Curtizan. **1653** WALTON *Angler* 104 We wil make a brave Breakfast with a piece of powdered Bief. **1798** SOUTHEY *Eng. Eclog.* ii, Here she found..a brave fire to thaw her. **1834** —— *Doctor* xxii. 51 Knowledge is a brave thing. **1850** MRS. BROWNING *Poems* I. 5 Here's a brave earth to sin and suffer on!

c. ***brave new world*** (also with capital initials): the title of a satirical novel (1932) by Aldous Huxley (after Shakespeare's *Tempest* v. i. 183) portraying a society in which 'progress' has produced a nightmarish 'utopia'; freq. used allusively.

1933 *Ann. Reg. 1932* 35 The driving force that sweeps Mr. Huxley on to presenting every nook and cranny of his Brave New World to the fiercest light of inquiry is the heart-corroding disgust he feels for human society as it will become according to his vision. **1935** H. G. WELLS *Things to Come* x. 93, I will *go* for this Brave New World of theirs—tooth and claw. **1947** J. HAYWARD *Prose Lit. since 1939* 16 The practice and particularly the theory of agriculture were the subject of many of these treatises on post-war planning—'blueprints'..of a brave new world.

d. ***brave west winds***, the strong prevailing westerly winds in 'the Roaring Forties'.

1883 [see FORTY *sb.* 4].

4. *Comb.*, chiefly parasynthetic, as ***brave-hearted***, ***-horsed***, ***-minded***, ***-sensed***, ***-spirited***, ***-spiritedness***.

1617 HIERON *Wks.* II. 313 Termes of Worth, of Gallantrie, of Braue-spiritednesse, and the like. **1631** WEEVER *Anc. Fun. Mon.* 636 That braue-spirited politicke-wise Lord. **1663** in Spalding *Troub. Chas. I.* (1829) 12 The earl of Angus..and thirty other brave-horsed gentlemen, came to the Bog. **1873** SYMONDS *Grk. Poets* iii. 70 The whole people mourns..for the death of a brave-hearted man.

5. quasi-*adv.* = BRAVELY. (Now only *poet.*)

1596 SPENSER *F.Q.* I. iv. 8 There sat most braue embellished..A mayden queene. **1721** STRYPE *Eccl. Mem.* I. I. xlvi. 345 Noble and brave-built structures. **1808** SCOTT *Marm.* I. x, The trumpets flourish'd brave. **1870** MORRIS *Earthly Par.* III. IV. 184 Better housed, or braver clad.

B. *sb.* [in sense 1, directly from F. *brave*.]

1. a. A brave man, a warrior, soldier: since 1800 applied chiefly to warriors among the North American Indians [after the French in N. America].

1601 CHESTER *Love's Mart.* (1878) 55 We haue no cause to feare their forreine braues. *a***1611** CHAPMAN *Iliad* III. 463 Advance Thy braues against his single power. **1763** CHURCHILL *Proph. Fam.* Poems I. 118 The race of Roman braves Thought it not worth their while to make us slaves. **1823** BYRON *Island* III. ii, The wave Is hurl'd down headlong, like the foremost brave. **1837** W. IRVING *Capt. Bonneville* (1849) 96 The chiefs leading the van, the braves following in a long line, painted and decorated. **1841** CATLIN *N. Amer. Ind.* (1844) I. vi. 35 A Blackfoot brave whose portrait I have painted.

b. A bravo, bully; a hired assassin. *Obs.* or *arch.*

1598 SYLVESTER *Du Bartas* II. iii. IV. (1641) 187/1 Ador'd of Flatterers, Of Softlings, Wantons, Braves and Loyterers. **1611** CORYAT *Crudities* 275 There are certaine desperate and resolute villaines in Venice called Braves. **1649** MILTON *Eikon.* 25 Happy times, when Braves and Hacksters were thought the fittest to defend the King. **1675** DRYDEN *Aurengz.* I. i. 96 Morat's too insolent, too much a Brave. **1693** W. ROBERTSON *Phraseol. Gen.* 277 A brave (or fellow hired to revenge a quarrel of another, *sicarius*. **1865** SIR K. JAMES *Tasso* II. XI. xxxvi, Ye sneaking, skulking braves.

2. A bravado. *arch.*

1590 GREENE *Never too late* (1600) 52 Suppose..that beautie hath given him the braue. **1598** SYLVESTER *Du Bartas* II. iii. IV. (1641) 182/1 Marcheth amain to give the Town a brave. **1600** HEYWOOD *1 Edw. IV.* Wks. 1874 I. 54 Leaue off these idle braues of thine. **1662** FULLER *Worthies* I. 33 Bitter was the Brave which railing Rabsheca sent to holy Hezekiah. **1840** BROWNING *Sordello* v. 432 A whole life's braves Should somehow be made good. **1878** SIMPSON *Sch. Shaks.* I. 75 Stucley waited about the court and amused the Councillors with his braves and brags.

†**3.** Finery, splendour = BRAVERY 3. *Obs.*

1602 WARNER *Alb. Eng.* XI. lxvii. 285 Sixe score Concubines, that seem'd so many Queenes for braue.

†**C.** *interj.* [Cf. BRAVO.] Capital! Excellent! Bravo! *Obs.* or *dial.*

*a***1593** MARLOWE *Jew of M.* II. ii, Oh, brave, master! I worship your nose for this. **1749** FIELDING *Tom Jones* XV. ii, O brave!..my cousin has you, I find. **1862** BARNES *Rhymes Dorset Dial.* I. 148 O brave! What wages do 'e mëan to gi'e?

brave (breɪv), *v.* [a. F. *brave-r* to act the brave toward, etc., f. *brave* BRAVE.]

I. *transitive.*

1. To treat with bravado; to challenge, defy.

1546 *St. Papers Hen. VIII*, XI. 107 Leest the Frenchmen might take occasion..to have braved Your Majestie. **1590** GREENE *Orl. Fur.* (1599) 9 Ile beard and braue thee in thy proper towne. **1603** KNOLLES *Turks* (1621) 94 Braving them (if they were men) to come out. **1636** HEYWOOD in *Ann. Dubrensia* (1877) 69 Ossa and Pelion, that so brave the sky. *a***1764** LLOYD *Actor* Poet. Wks. 1774 I. 12 Braving monarchs in his Saviour's cause. **1884** TENNYSON *Becket* 100, I must hence to brave The Pope, King Louis, and this turbulent priest.

†**2.** To threaten, menace. *Obs.*

*a***1619** BP. COWPER in Spurgeon *Treas. Dav.* Ps. cxix. 19 He braved him with banishments.

3. To meet or face (danger) with bravery; to encounter, defy. (The ordinary current sense.)

1776 GIBBON *Decl. & F.* I. xvii. 436 The adventurous Leander braved the passage of the flood. **1797** MRS. RADCLIFFE *Italian* i, Do not brave the utter darkness of these ruins. **1832** HT. MARTINEAU *Life in Wilds* i. 4 Poverty induces them to brave danger. *a***1876** J. H. NEWMAN *Hist. Sk.* I. IV. iv. 409 They braved the severe weather of that climate. **1884** *Pall Mall G.* 4 Jan. 2/1 The school braves successfully the ordeal of annual inspection.

†**4.** To make brave, embolden, encourage. *Obs.*

*a***1593** H. SMITH *Wks.* (1866–7) I. 172 We may see..how a gay coat..or a gold ring, can brave a man's mind.

†**5.** To make splendid; to deck out, adorn. *Obs.*

1590 *Exhort. Her Maj. Subj.* in *Harl. Misc.* I. 172 Brave not yourselves in gold, silk, and silver. **1594** SHAKS. *Rich. III*, v. iii. 279 He [the sun] should haue brau'd the East an houre ago. **1596** —— *Tam. Shr.* IV. iii. 125 Thou [the tailor] hast brau'd manie men. **1625** BACON *Love*, *Ess.* (Arb.) 445 How it [love] braves, the Nature, and value of things.

†**6.** To boast; 'to carry a boasting appearance of' J. ***to brave out***: to display boastfully, show off. ***to brave oneself***: to boast or pride oneself *in*.

1581 J. BELL *Haddon's Answ. Osor.* 44b, Points, which you seeme specially to have called out, that in them you might brave out yᵉ nimblenes of your witte, and eloquence of toung. *a***1626** BACON (J.) Both particular persons and factions are apt enough to flatter themselves or, at least, to brave that which they believe not. **1644–52** J. SMITH *Sel. Disc.* VII. i. (1821) 309 They rather proudly braved themselves in their knowledge of the Deity, etc.

II. *intransitive* (and const. *to brave it*).

7. To boast, glory, vaunt. ***to brave it***: to swagger, act the bravo. Now in ***to brave it out***. (Perh. rather sense 3?)

1549 DK. SOMERSET in Strype *Eccl. Mem.* II. I. xxii. 180 The Frenchmen..will brave much of this. **1597** J. PAYNE *Royal Exch.* 14 These fellows wyll brave yt out, how slender so ever they be within. **1613** W. BROWNE *Brit. Past.* II. v. (1772) II. 188 Nevermore let holy Dee O're other rivers braue. **1627** BP. HALL *Psalmes Met.* x. 3 The wicked braues and boasts In his vile and outragious thought. **1702** C. MATHER *Magn. Chr.* III. III. (1852) 542 That peace might brave it among you. **1817** WILBERFORCE in *Parl. Deb.* 1693 Braving about the liberties of his country. **1855** TENNYSON *Maud* IV. v. 17 However we brave it out, we men are a little breed.

†**8.** *intr.* To dress splendidly, to make a gay show; freq. also *to brave it*. *Obs.*

1583 T. WATSON *Poems* (Arb.) 60 Thou glasse, wherein my Dame hath such delight, As when she braues, then most on thee to gaze. **1592** DANIEL *Compl. Rosamond* (1717) 52 And live in Pomp to brave among the Best. *a***1632** BP. M. SMYTH *Serm.* 130 To strowt it, and to stout it, and to braue it in costly apparell.

9. To act bravely, to be brave. *rare.*

1884 W. C. SMITH *Kildrostan* I. ii. 265 Haunted With the young craving For doing and braving In the world's battle.

brave: see BRAVY.

†**bra'veer**, *v.* *Obs. rare*⁻¹. [f. BRAVE: cf. *domineer*, and -EER¹.] To act the bravo towards.

1652 URQUHART *Jewel* Wks. (1834) 240 He dandleth the sword in his hand, as if he were about to braveer us.

bravely ('breɪvlɪ), *adv.* [f. BRAVE *a.* + -LY².]

1. In a brave manner; valiantly, fearlessly.

1590 SHAKS. *Mids. N.* v. i. 148 He brauely broacht his boiling bloudy breast. **1695** LD. PRESTON *Boeth.* IV. 177 Against whose Power vertue can bravely stand. **1795** SOUTHEY *Joan of Arc* II. 211 Still we struggled bravely! *c***1860** M. ARNOLD *Emped. on Etna* II. i, The..quiet man May bravelier front his life.

2. In a showy manner; gaily, splendidly, finely, handsomely; = *Sc.* BRAWLY.

*c***1505** DUNBAR *Blyth Aberdeen* vi, With quhyt hattis all browderit rycht brav[elie] (*rime wds.* bewtie, sweitlie). **1570** B. GOOGE *Pop. Kingd.* III. (1880) 36b, Hir Image doe they bravely decke with sumptuous show to sight. **1603** KNOLLES *Hist. Turks* (1621) 373 He saw Zacharias come forth bravely mounted. **1636** DAVENANT *Wits* (1673) 184 The Chamber's bravely hung.

3. Worthily, excellently, capitally, well: cf. BRAVE *a.* 3; also BRAWLY. Chiefly *dial.*

*c***1600** *Rob. Hood* (Ritson) II. xxvi. 72 None of them could pass these men, So bravely they do shoot. **1606** SHAKS. *Tr. & Cr.* I. ii. 198 Here's an excellent place, heere we may see most brauely. **1684** BUNYAN *Pilgr.* II. (1862) 199 He lives bravely where he is. **1864** ATKINSON *Whitby Gloss.* s.v., 'How do you?'—'I am quite bravely, thank you'..To get on bravely, is to prosper or 'speed bravely'. **1874** BLACKIE *Self-Cult.* 15 A man may live, and live bravely, without much imagination. **1884** BLACK *Jud. Shaks.* xii, The wench looks bravely well.

†**'braveman.** *Obs.* A 'fine gentleman'.

1608 DEKKER *Belman Lond.* Wks. 1884–5 III. 88 To be a Begger is to be a Braueman, because 'tis now in fashion for very braue men to Beg.

'braven, *v.* *rare*⁻¹. [f. BRAVE *a.*: cf. *brighten*, etc.] *trans.* To make brave, embolden.

1865 J. TAYLOR *Words & Pl.* 26 The failures which seemed only to braven the resolution and to nerve the courage.

'braveness. [f. BRAVE *a.* + -NESS.] The quality of being brave; BRAVERY.

1589 PUTTENHAM *Eng. Poesie* (Arb.) 182 More obseruable to the Greekes and Latines for the brauenesse of their language, ouer that our is. **1592** WARNER *Alb. Eng.* VIII. xli. 201 The beautie and the brauenes of the Person. **1603** HOLLAND *Plutarch's Mor.* 306 (R.) The brauenesse of the exploit. **1650** WELDON *Crt. Jas. I*, 42 Astonied at the bravenesse of our Embassie, and the handsome Gentlemen. **1679** OATES *Narr. Popish Plot* 32 To encourage the Friends to braveness of mind. [Not in JOHNSON 1755.] **1927** *Daily News* 14 May 4/3, I was much moved by the braveness and sincerity of the works I read.

braver ('breɪvə(r)). [f. BRAVE *v.* + -ER¹.] One who braves, or faces, danger or an enemy; also *formerly*, a braggart, boaster.

1589 NASHE in *Greene's Menaphon* (Arb.) 16 Who..would carrie the bucklers full easilie from all forreine brauers. **1591** PERCIVALL *Sp. Dict.*, *Fanfarron*, a bragger, a brauer. **1827** *Gentl. Mag.* XCVII. II. 42 Buonaparte..the undaunted braver of every difficulty. **1846** DICKENS *Lett.* (ed. 2) I. 156 Such a braver of conventionalities never wore petticoats.

bravery ('breɪvərɪ). [prob. a. F. *braverie* the action of braving, f. *braver* to BRAVE, or ad. It. *braveria*, f. *bravare* to BRAVE.]

†**1.** The action of braving or acting the bravo; daring, defiance; boasting, swaggering; bravado. ***a bravery***: an act of bravado. ***in***, ***upon***, or ***for a bravery***: in bravado, in defiance, in display of courage or daring, as a brag. *Obs.*

1548 PATTEN *Exped. into Scotl.* in Arb. *Garner* III. 98 The Scots continued their bravery on the hill. **1614** RALEIGH *Hist. World* III. 93 The whole Campe (not perceiving that this was but a bravery) fled amaine. *a***1631** DONNE *Ess. Div.* (1651) 63 No Man is an Atheist, however he pretend it and serve the Company with his Braveries. **1671** MILTON *Samson* 1243 Ere long thou shalt lament These braveries, in irons loaden on thee. **1814** SOUTHEY *Roderick* XXIV, No time, said he, is this for bravery.

1577 HARRISON *England* II. xii. (1877) 241 In a braverie to show what store he had. **1594** NASHE *Unfort. Trav.* 14. **1603** KNOLLES *Hist. Turks* (1621) 92 Certaine of the souldiers upon a bravarie adventured to mount the wall. **1614** RALEIGH *Hist. World* III. 95 Hee made a stand, rather in a bravery, than with purpose to attempt..any further. **1666** TEMPLE *Let.* Wks. 1731 II. 23 We sate for four Hours, and in Bravery I drank fair like all the rest.

2. Daring, courage, valour, fortitude (as a good quality). In earlier quotations not clearly separable from sense 1. (The ordinary current sense.)

1581 SIDNEY *Apol. Poetrie* (Arb.) 56 He receiued more brauerie of minde, bye the patterne of Achilles, then by hearing the definition of Fortitude. **1613** J. H. *Lives Norman Kings Eng.* 150 Full of inward braverie and fiercenesse. **1732** LAW *Serious C.* xxiv. (1761) 465 The noblest bravery that an human mind is capable of. **1769** *Junius Lett.* i. 8 The bravery..of the Commander-in-chief. **1837** HT. MARTINEAU *Soc. Amer.* III. 116 What can a woman be, or do, without bravery? **1859** TENNYSON *Elaine* 113 Lancelot, the flower of bravery.

3. Display, show, ostentation; splendour.

1570 HOLINSHED *Scot. Chron.* (1806) I. 29 Their apparel was not made for braverie & pompe. **1573** TUSSER *Husb.* (1878) 204 The brauerie of this world..likened is, to flowre of grasse. **1600** HOLLAND *Livy* XXXIV. iv. 855 a, Wastfull and sumpteous bravery of women. **1673** CAVE *Prim. Chr.* I. vi. 144 The churches began to excel in costliness and bravery. *a* **1716** SOUTH *12 Serm.* (1717) III. 390 A Festival, designed chiefly for..joyfull Piety, but generally made only an occasion of Bravery. **1843** PRESCOTT *Mexico* VI. i. (1864) 338 All their wonted bravery of apparel. **1874** C. GEIKIE *Life Woods* v. 78 The leaves are in all their bravery.

b. *concr.* Finery, fine clothes; = *Sc.* BRAWS.

1563 *Homilies* II. vi (1859) 309 Preparing ourselves in fine bravery, to wanton, lewd, and unchaste behaviour. **1591** SPENSER *M. Hubberd* 608 All the braverie that eye may see. *a* **1618** RALEIGH *Rem.* (1644) 100 Exceed not in the humour of rags and bravery. **1636** SYMPSON *Law-breakers*, Have I borrowed the forehorse bells, his plumes, his braveries. **1862** *Times* 26 June 11/1 Tens of thousands..in their decent Sunday bravery. **1870** MORRIS *Earthly Par.* I. I. 86 There stood our guide, decked out with braveries.

†**c.** An adornment, an embellishment. *Obs.*

1577 HOLINSHED *Chron.* I. 55/1 Such painting of their bodies..they esteemed a great brauerie. **1599** HAKLUYT *Voy.* I. I. 224 They vse for a brauerie to make great holes in their eares. *Ibid.* (1810) III. 598 Their teeth are all filed, which they doe for a braverie.

†**d.** A thing of beauty or interest, a thing to exhibit. *Obs.*

1583 GOLDING *Calvin on Deut.* cvi. 650 A relike to be showed for a brauerie. **1650** FULLER *Pisgah* 426 Two eminent braveries, First, the Golden Vine..The other was that Golden Eagle. **1657** W. COLES *Adam in Eden* To Rdr., What fairer objects..than these painted Braveries?

†**e.** A fine thing, a matter to boast or be proud of. *Obs.*

a **1626** BP. ANDREWES *Pattern Catech. Doct.* (1846) 150 In a vain glory we think it a bravery and a magnificent thing to swear. **1638** FORD *Fancies* II. i. 145 'Twere a bravery, Could you forget the place.

†**4.** Mere show, ostentatious pretence. *Obs.*

1628 HOBBES *Thucyd.* (1822) 95 This is not now rather a bravery of words..than real truth. *a* **1640** MASSINGER *Old Law* II. i, Worth itself is lost, And bravery stands for 't. **1681** BURNET *Hist. Ref.* II. 241 [They] measured counsels more by the bravery than the solidity of them.

†**5.** A gallant, a beau; also *collect.* gallants, grandees, chivalry. *Obs.*

1609 B. JONSON *Sil. Wom.* I. iii. (1616) 536 Hee is one of the Braueries, though he be none o' the Wits. **1633** MASSINGER *City Mad.* II. i, Sitting at the table with The braveries of the kingdom. *a* **1652** BROME *Queene's Exch.* I. ii, Whole Sholes of upstart Braveries. *a* **1670** HACKET *Abp. Williams* (1692) I. 162 (D.) The Grandees also, and others of the Castilian Bravery.

bravie, var. of BRAVY, *Obs.*, a prize.

braving ('breɪvɪŋ), *vbl. sb.* [f. BRAVE *v.* + -ING[1].] The action of the verb to BRAVE.

1615 CHAPMAN *Odyss.* XXI. (R.), With so proud a straine Of threats and brauings. **1627** SANDERSON *Serm.* (1681) 92 If after all this Braving he should be Out-dared with big looks. **1763** C. JOHNSON *Reverie* II. 127 All their braving shall not make me quit the advantages of my situation. **1817** J. H. FRERE *K. Arthur* I. x, True point of honour, without pride or braving.

† **'braving**, *ppl. a. Obs.* [f. as prec. + -ING[2].]

1. That braves; daring, defiant, boasting.

1579 J. STUBBES *Gaping Gulf* D iij b, These braving English gentlemen are as farre from the wisedom of theyr noble auncesters..as from theyr courage. **1605** *Play Stucley* 1073 in *Sch. Shaks.* (1878) I. 201 Braving braggart..Look to thyself. **1679** PRANCE *True Narr. Pop. Plot* 6 He spoke openly, and in a braving manner. **1748** RICHARDSON *Clarissa* (1811) II. xxxii. 198 No blustering, braving lover.

2. Showy, resplendent; high-sounding, stately.

1600 FAIRFAX *Tasso* IX. lxxxii. 175 Fine And brauing in his Turkish pompe he shone. **1633** P. FLETCHER *Elisa* II. xxxiv, The flowers..Spreading their braving colours to the skie. **1649** J. H. *Motion to Parl.* 41 A many large and braving Titles.

† **'bravingly**, *adv. Obs.* [f. prec. + -LY[2].] In a braving manner; boastfully, defiantly.

1616 SHELDON *Miracles of Antichr.* 4 (L.) Bravingly, in your epistle to Sir Edward Hobby, you end thus. **1631** BRATHWAIT *Whimzies* 47 Hee domineeres bravely; beares himselfe toward his ragged regiment bravingly.

'bravish ('breɪvɪʃ), *a.* [f. BRAVE *a.* + -ISH[1].]

a. Somewhat brave or defiant. **b.** *dial.* Considerable, pretty fair; cf. BRAVE.

1538 *St. Papers Henry VIII*, III. 83 He is so hawte and chafing that men be aferde to speke to him, doubting his bravishe lightnes. **1880** MRS. PARR *Adam & E.* xxvii. 382 ''Tis a bravish spell since you and me were together.'

bravissimo: see BRAVO.

† **'bravity.** *Obs.* Also 6 bravite. [a. F. *braveté* (16th c. in Littré): see BRAVE and -ITY.] = BRAVERY (in various senses).

1546 *St. Papers Hen. VIII*, XI. 100 They see wherunto all the French kinges..gret offres and bravites be cum unto. **1547** *Life 70th Abp. Canterb.* B vj *marg.*, Sumtuous feastinge ..great coste in brauitie and Lordly pompe. **1596** BUREL *Queen's Entry Edinb.*, Quhois bravities can scarce be tauld. **1689** J. WELWOOD *Let.* in Walker *Remark. Pass.* 23 (JAM.) Brave opportunities for shewing forth the bravity of spirit in suffering.

bravo ('brɑːvəʊ), *sb.*[1] Pl. bravoes (-os). [a. It. *bravo*: cf. BRAVE. Long naturalized in Eng., whence a pronunciation ('breɪvəʊ) in some Dicts.]

1. A daring villain, a hired soldier or assassin; 'a man who murders for hire' (J.); a reckless desperado.

1597 DANIEL *Civ. Wars* III. lxxii, This bravo cheers these dastards all he can. **1632** MASSINGER *Maid of Hon.* IV. v, Setting-on your desperate bravo To murder him. **1668** R. LESTRANGE *Vis. Quev.* (1708) 217 Cassius and my self were but your Bravos. **1711** STEELE *Spect.* No. 136 ⁋3, I have been three Nights together dogged by Bravoes. **1761** HUME *Hist. Eng.* I. vii. 155 Those bravoes, or disorderly soldiers, with whom every country in Europe..abounded. **1813** SHELLEY *Q. Mab* IV. 178 The hired bravos who defend The tyrant's throne. **1876** GREEN *Short Hist.* viii. §6. 528 While the bravoes of Whitehall laid hands on their leaders.

†**2.** = BRAVADO. *Obs. rare.*

1609 B. JONSON *Sil. Wom.* III. vi. (1616) 563 Is this your Brauo, ladies? **1713** *Lond. & Countr. Brew.* IV. (1743) 289 For keeping them to a great Age out of a Bravo.

bravo ('brɑːvəʊ), *int.* and *sb.*[2] Also in superl. form bra'vissimo. [a. It. *bravo*, superl. *bravissimo* most excellent.] Capital! excellent! well done!

1761 COLMAN *Jealous W.* i. (L.) That's right—I'm steel—Bravo!—Adamant—Bravissimo! **1817** BYRON *Beppo* xxxii, His 'bravo' was decisive. **1875** JOWETT *Plato* (ed. 2) I. 232 Bravo, Heracles, brave words, said he.

Hence, as *sb.* An exclamation of *bravo!* a cheer.

1844 LD. BROUGHAM *A. Lunel* III. v. 149 He escaped to bed before any bravo could be heard. **1855** O. W. HOLMES *Poems* 29 Whose thousand bravos roll untired along.

bravo ('brɑːvəʊ), *v.* [f. BRAVO *sb.*[1] and *int.*] *trans.* †**1.** = BRAVE *v.* 1, 2. *Obs.* **2.** To greet with 'bravo!'

1732 *Col. Rec. Penn.* III. 496 Treated with great contempt insulted and bravoed by those of Maryland. **1831** MISS FERRIER *Destiny*, [He] was bravoed and applauded.

† **bra'vour, braveur.** *Obs.* [a. F. *bravoure*, ad. It. *bravura* bravery, f. *bravo* BRAVE. (North's *braveur* was a mistaken form, app. after *grandeur*, *hauteur*, etc.).] Valour, bravery, spirit; bravado.

1695 *Whether Parl. be not dissolved, &c.* 57 The People want bravour to push the Defence of their Liberties. *a* **1734** NORTH *Lives* III. 226 He carried himself with a sort of braveur against cold. —— *Exam.* (1740) 555. *Ibid.* 572.

‖**bravura** (brə'v(j)ʊərə). [It.: = bravery, spirit.]

1. Display of daring or defiance; brilliancy of execution, dash; attempt at brilliant performance.

1813 *Examiner* 3 May 282/1 *A Thunder Storm* [picture] has a bravura both of conception and execution. **1845** *Blackw. Mag.* LVIII. 260 The great vice of the present day is bravura—an attempt to do something beyond the truth. **1865** CARLYLE *Fredk. Gt.* X. XXI. vi. 123 Most shameful this burning of Habelschwert by way of mere bravura. **1879** *Athenæum* No. 2709 The idea, spontaneous and thrillingly simple, has none of their bravura.

2. A passage or piece of music requiring great skill and spirit in its execution, written to task the artist's powers. Also *transf.*

1788 'PASQUIN' *Childr. Thespis* (1792) 136 In the lofty bravuras she copies the spheres. **1822** W. IRVING *Braceb. Hall* (1849) 44 Listening to a lady amateur skylark it up and down through the finest bravura of Rossini or Mozart. **1846** DE QUINCEY *Syst. Heavens* Wks. 1854 III. 196 A short bravura of John Paul Richter..I call it a bravura, as being intentionally a passage of display and elaborate execution.

3. *attrib.* in the musical sense.

1802 *Edin. Rev.* I. 217 What a Scotch or Irish melody is to a bravura singer. **1845** E. HOLMES *Mozart* 121 The bravura style of violin playing. *Ibid.* 253 The bravura passages should subserve good musical ideas. **1850** L. HUNT *Autobiog.* I. vi. 232 His popular, and not very refined style of bravura-singing. **1880** GROVE *Dict. Mus.* I. 272/1 Bravura songs, requiring a compass and a power of execution out of the common.

Hence **bra'vuraish** *a.*

1879 *Art Jrnl.* June 113 This accomplished artist's bravuraish handling and colouring.

† **'bravy.** *Obs.* Also 7 brave, bravie, brayvy. [f. med.L. *bravium*, *brabīum*, ad. Gr. βραβεῖον prize.] A prize, reward.

1676 BULLOKAR, *Brave*, the prize given to him that wins in Games of exercise. **1678** PHILLIPS (*App.*), *Bravie* (old word), a reward. [**1829** S. TURNER *Hist. Eng.* III. II. xi. 48 Any vulgar sport where bravium was contended for.]

braw (brɔː), *a.*, *sb.*, *adv. Sc.* Also bra'. [Sc. form of BRAVE, in old pronunciation (brɑːv): cf. *ca'* = *calve*, *ha'*, *hae* = *have*, etc.]

A. *adj.*

1. = BRAVE *a.* 2; finely-dressed; splendid, showy.

1724 RAMSAY *Tea-t. Misc.* (ed. 9) I. 8 She was the brawest in a' the town *c* **1774** C. KEITH *Farmer's Ha'*, Put on your best array, And let's be braw. **1785** BURNS *Cotter's Sat. Nt.* iv, To show a braw new gown. **1816** SCOTT *Old Mort.* v, 'Ye think yoursell a braw fellow enow; and troth..there's na fault to find wi' the outside.' *Ibid.* vi.

2. = BRAVE 3; worthy, excellent, capital, fine.

c **1565** R. LINDSAY *Cron. Scotl.* (1728) 584 (JAM.) The recorder of Barvick..maid ane braw speech to his majestie. **1739** A. NICOL *Poems* 27 (JAM.) 'Tis unka bra', When ilka thing yields pleasure. **1814** SCOTT *Wav.* xxxix, 'Ow ay, sir! a braw night', replied the lieutenant. **1827** J. WILSON *Noct. Ambr.* Wks. 1855 I. 357 Peter my braw man..bring but a bottle o' primrose wine.

3. Hence phrases ***braw and able***, ***braw and canty***, ***braw and soon***, etc.: cf. the similar use of *fine*, *nice*.

1768 ROSS *Helenore* 52 (JAM.) Look'd braw and canty whan she came in by.

B. *sb. pl.* = BRAVERY 3; fine clothes, finery.

1724 RAMSAY *Tea-t. Misc.* (1733) I. 100 When she glaicks paughty in her braws. **1795** MACNEILL *Will & Jean*, Thousands had mair braws and siller, But were ony half sae fair? **1818** SCOTT *Hrt. Midl.* xvi, 'But, Madge, the lads only like ye when ye hae on your braws.'

† **brawde**, *v. Obs.* Also braud. [See BROWD and BRAID *v.*]

1. *trans.* To embroider. Hence **brawded** *ppl. a.*

1483 *Cath. Angl.* 41 To Brawde, *epigramare*. **1509** HAWES *Past. Pleas.* 200 A goodly garment, Brauded with perle. **1572** *Scot. Poems 16th C.* II. 252 Buft brawdit hois, coit, dowblet, sark and scho.

2. To braid, plait, intertwine.

1555 *Fardle Facions* II. viii. 175 Rushes..they braude together muche like oure figgefraile.

brawden: see BROWDEN *pa. pple.*

brawderer, -y, obs. ff. BROIDERER, -Y.

† **'brawdster.** *Obs.* [f. BRAWDE *v.* + -STER.] A woman (or man) who embroiders.

c **1450** *Voc.* in Wr.-Wülcker 692 *Hec palmaria*, a brawdster. **1483** *Cath. Angl.* 41 A Brawdestere, *epigramator*, *epigramatrix*.

brawl (brɔːl), *sb.*[1] Also 5–7 brall(e, braul(e, brawle. [f. BRAWL *v.*[1]]

1. A noisy turbulent quarrel, a 'row', a squabble.

c **1460** *Towneley Myst.* 190 (Mätz.) Thou has long had thi wille, and made many bralle. *c* **1550** *Scot. Poems 16th C.* II. 181 Mony leisings make mony braul. **1561** T. NORTON *Calvin's Inst.* II. 151 They folishly moue a brawle about the name of First begotten. **1655** FULLER *Ch. Hist.* III. 86 Wheresoever any braule began, in London, it ended alwayes in the Old-Jury, with pillaging of the people therein. **1720** WATTS *Hymn*, Whatever brawls disturb the street, There should be peace at home. **1824** W. IRVING *T. Trav.* II. 242 Astounding the neighbourhood with midnight brawl and ruffian revelry. **1876** GREEN *Short Hist.* vii. §7. 421 He perished at thirty in a shameful brawl.

†**2.** Noisy exclamation, clamour. *Obs.*

1581 J. BELL *Haddon's Answ. Osor.* 1 b, I shall have.. confuted the most foolish and spitefull braules of Osorius. *Ibid.* 68 Of opinion that your bare braules, shalbe receaved as infallible truthes. **1611** BIBLE *Ecclus.* xxvii. 14 Their braules make one stop his eares.

† **brawl**, *sb.*[2] *Obs.* Also 5 browle. [prob. f. BRAWL *v.*[1], with which at least it was associated in use: but it may have been at first identical with ME. *broll*: see BROLL *sb.*] A brawler, a bravo, a bully.

(Some of the following quotations are quite uncertain.)

c **1440** *York Myst.* xxx. 6 What brawle þat with brawlyng me brewis. *Ibid.* xvi. 38 What browle þat is brawlyng his brayne loke ȝe brest. **1652** NEEDHAM tr. *Selden's Mare Cl.* 5 Why not this Bag to mee then too, thou brawl. **1725** BAILEY *Erasm. Colloq.* 34 I'm his Swabber..his Book-keeper, his Brawl, his Errand boy. [Cf. BROLL *sb.*]

† **brawl**, *sb.*[3] *Obs.* Also 6–7 brall(e, 6–8 braul(e. [f. BRAWL *v.*[2], or a. F. *branle*, f. *branler*, *brandeler*: cf. BRANGLE.]

1. A particular pace or movement in dancing.

1521 COPLAND *Introd. Frenche* 16 For to daunce ony bace daunce there behoueth .iiii. paces, that is to wite syngle, double: repryse, & braule. **1531** ELYOT *Gov.* (1580) 71 They [the motions] may be well resembled to the braule in daunsing.

2. A kind of French dance resembling a cotillon.

a **1541** WYATT *Poet. Wks.* (1861) 182 And in this brawl as he stood entranced. **1549** *Compl. Scot.* vi. 66 Dansand base dansis, pauans, galȝardis, turdions, braulis and branglis. **1580** SIDNEY *Arcad.* 72 Holding hand in hand daunce as it were in a braule. **1588** SHAKS. *L.L.L.* III. i. 9 Will you win your loue with a French braule? **1611** COTGR., *Bransle*, a brawle or dance, wherein many (men and women) holding by the hands sometimes in a ring, and otherwhiles at length moue altogether. **1711** BUDGELL *Spect.* No. 67 ⁋2 The Lacedæmonians..made their Hormus (a Dance much resembling the French Brawl) famous. **1750** GRAY *Let.* in *Poems* (1775) 214 My grave Lord-Keeper led the brawls. **1840-2** BARHAM *Ingol. Leg.*, *Aunt Fanny*, At some court

Fancy-Ball..you may Fancy King Charles, I say, stopping the brawl.

b. The air or music of this dance.

c **1600** *Distracted Emp.* IV. i. in Bullen *O. Pl.* (1884) III. 225, I had thought to have whysteld hym a braule for makinge me daunce attendance.

†**c.** *fig.* [Cf. F. *mener, ouvrir le branle*; Eng. 'Lead, open the ball.']

a **1649** DRUMMOND *Hist. Jas. III.* Wks. (1711) 43 The Kennedies..take the occasion..[to] change the brawl of state.

†**brawl,** *sb.*[4] *Obs.* Also braul. 'A blue and white striped cloth manufactured in India.' Craig.

1725 *Lond. Gaz.* No. 6388/2 The following Goods, viz... Allejaes, Brawls, Bombay Stuffs. **1788** CLARKSON *Impol. Slave Tr.* 104 Blue cloths, Brawles, Bejutapants, Callicoes.

brawl, *sb.*[5] dial. var. of BROLL, *Obs.* brat.

brawl (brɔːl), *v.*[1] Also 5–6 brall(e, braul(e, braull. [Late ME.; origin and primary sense uncertain: mod.Du. has *brallen* to brag, boast, mod.Ger. dial. *brallen* to shout, roar, both apparently recent, and of unknown origin. (Franck thinks the Du. prob. echoic, with influence of various other words.) ON. *bralla* 'to trick, job', does not suit the sense. F. *brailler* to shout, make a din, bawl, found in 14th c. (which Littré thinks a deriv. of *braire* to bray) approaches the sense, but could not phonetically be the source of the Eng. word. Mätzner separates *brall* to make a noise, and *brawl* to quarrel, but such a division does not appear tenable.]

1. *intr.* 'To quarrel noisily and indecently' (J.); to wrangle; to squabble. (In very early use and in Shaks. 1597 it was perhaps simply 'to contend, strive, quarrel'.)

1375 BARBOUR *Bruce* I. 573 That brwyss, that presumyt swa Aganys him to brawle or ryss. *c* **1440** *Promp. Parv.* 48/1 Brawlyn or strywen, *litigo, jurgo.* **1474** CAXTON *Chesse* 125 Gyue thou place to hym that brawleth or chideth. **1530** ELYOT *Gov.* I. xxii, Men do braule, whan betwene them is altercation in wordes. **1548** COVERDALE *Erasm. Par. 1 Cor.* i. 10 To fyght and braule with woordes, is agaynste honestie. **1597** SHAKS. *2 Hen. IV*, I. iii. 70 His diuisions (as the Times do braul) Are in three Heads. **1609** BIBLE (Douay) *Gen.* xxvi. 21 They brawled likewise, and he called the name of it, Enmitie. **1741–3** WESLEY *Jrnl.* (1749) 92 Expell'd the society ..Three, for quarrelling and brawling. **1853** LYNCH *Self-Improv.* iv. 100 A gentleman will not brawl with everybody, nor indeed brawl with anybody.

†**b.** *trans.* To chide, scold, revile. *Obs.*

1474 CAXTON *Chesse* 36 Brawlyng and betyng hym as his seruaunt. **1483** —— *G. de la Tour* G v b, She that brawled and reproched her of her husbondes. *a* **1529** SKELTON *Why nat to Court* 593 His servauntes menyal He doth revyle and brall. *a* **1649** DRUMM. OF HAWTH. *Idea* Wks. (1711) 220 They will essay to brawl the present form of state and church-government.

2. *intr.* To raise a clamour, make a disturbance; in early use sometimes to brag or boast loudly. (*to brawl in church* technically includes any speaking other than as prescribed in the Prayer Book.)

1447–8 SHILLINGFORD *Lett.* (1871) 23 He can.. braule, braygе, and brace, lye and swere well to. *c* **1460** *Towneley Myst.* 141 Begyn he to bralle, many men cache skorne. **1513** DOUGLAS *Æneis* XII. viii. 84 Now brawland in this place, now voustand thar. **1523** LD. BERNERS *Froiss.* I. clxiv. 203 And belles began to braule, wherby it myght well be knowen that ther was besynesse in hande. **1552** *Act 5 & 6 Edw. VI*, iv. § 1 If any Person..by Words only, quarrel, chide or brawl in any Church or Churchyard. **1579** TOMSON *Calvin's Serm. Tim.* 16/2 They brall as cattes & doggs in an vnknown language. **1594** SHAKS. *Rich. III*, I. iii. 324, I do the wrong, and first begin to brawle. **1837** CARLYLE *Fr. Rev.* II. V. v. 66 Patriotism..may brawl and babble yet a little while.

†**b.** *refl.* To boast oneself loudly. *Obs.*

?*a* **1400** *Morte Arth.* 1349 Loo! how he brawles hyme for hys bryghte wedes.

c. *trans.* To utter clamorously.

1563 *Mirr. Mag., Rivers* x, No matter what they brall. **1597** SHAKS. *2 Hen. IV*, II. i. 71 What are you brauling here? **1832** TENNYSON *Pal. Art* 210, I care not what the sects may brawl.

3. *intr.* Of a stream: To make a noise of conflict in its rapid course over stones, etc.

1600 SHAKS. *A.Y.L.* II. i. 32 The brooke that brawles along this wood. **1809** W. IRVING *Knickerb.* II. iv. (1849) 109 The late dimpling current began to brawl around them. **1814** SCOTT *Ld. of Isles* III. xii, A wild stream..Came brawling down its bed of rock. **1869** SPURGEON *J. Ploughm. Talk* 43 Shallowest brooks brawl the most.

4. with *compl.* (*trans.*) To drive or force *down*, *out*, etc., by brawling.

1595 SHAKS. *John* II. i. 383 Till their soule-fearing clamours haue braul'd downe The flintie ribbes of this contemptuous Citie. **1726** DE FOE *Hist. Devil* I. iv. (1840) 57 Juno was within an ace of brawling him out of heaven. **1837** CARLYLE *Fr. Rev.* I. I. v. vii. 155 So must Paris..brawl itself finally into a kind of sleep.

†**brawl,** *v.*[2] *Obs.* Also braul. [Possibly ad. F. *branle-r* to move from side to side: cf. *vamure, vaward* for *avantmur, van-ward.*] *intr.* To move to and fro, vibrate, waver, quiver.

1375 BARBOUR *Bruce* XII. 131 Quhen he hys fayis saw braw-land sua, In hy upon thaim gan he ga. *c* **1450** *Merlin* xiv. 206 The dragon hadde a wide throte that the tounge seemed braulinge euer.

brawler ('brɔːlə(r)). Also 6 braller, brauler, *Sc.* brallar. [f. BRAWL *v.*[1] + -ER[1].]

1. One engaged in or given to brawls; a quarrelsome, wrangling fellow; a breaker of the peace.

1377 LANGL. *P. Pl.* B. XVI. 43 Bakbiteres breke-cheste brawleres and chideres. **1387** TREVISA *Higden* Rolls Ser. IV. 209, I-slawe with swerdes of comoun contakkours [or brawlers, *gladiatorum*]. *c* **1440** *Promp. Parv.* 48 Brawlere, *litigator.* *a* **1593** H. SMITH *Wks.* II. (1867) 253 If they be dicers, swearers, drunkards, brawlers. **1735** OLDYS *Raleigh* Wks. 1829 I. Thou shalt be in as much danger in contending with a brawler in a private quarrel as in a battle. **1855** MACAULAY *Hist. Eng.* IV. 654 A tavern brawler.. swaggering drunk about the streets.

2. A noisy contentious talker.

c **1510** J. INGLIS *Gen. Satyre* ix, Sic brallaris and bosteris, degenerait fra their natures. **1581** J. BELL *Haddon's Answ. Osor.* 2 This prattling brawler hath framed a long discourse. **1692** WASHINGTON tr. *Milton's Def. Pop.* xii. (1851) 246 That Clause in the Coronation Oath, which such a brazen-fac'd Brawler as you call fictitious. **1713** BP. GIBSON *Art. Visitation* in Toulm. Smith *Parish* (1857) 94 Is he a brabler, brauler, contentious, seditious party? **1837** CARLYLE *Fr. Rev.* II. II. v. v. 65 A blustering Effervescence, of brawlers and spouters.

brawling ('brɔːlɪŋ), *vbl. sb.*[1] [f. BRAWL *v.*[1]]

1. Noisy quarrelling; wrangling; contention, 'row'.

1393 LANGL. *P. Pl.* C. XVII. 360 For brawelynge and bac-bytynge and beryng of false wittnesse. *c* **1440** *Promp. Parv.* 48/1 Brawlynge, *jurgium.* **1661** BRAMHALL *Just Vind.* vi. 154 That *insana laurus*, which causeth brawling and contention. **1657** COLVIL *Whigs Supplic.* (1751) 40 Soldiers forging ale-house brawlings.

2. Clamour; indecent or offensive noise; scolding.

c **1440** *York Myst.* xxx. 142 Þat boy for his brawlyng Were bettir be vn-borne. **1562** J. HEYWOOD *Prov. & Epigr.* (1867) 64 My braulyng at home, makith him banket abrode. **1581** J. BELL *Haddon's Answ. Osor.* 43 Your unmeasurable braulyng hath altogether weryed me. **1596** SHAKS. *1 Hen. IV*, II. ii. 6 Peace ye fat-kidney'd Rascall, what a brawling dost thou keepe. **1794** BURKE *Imp. W. Hastings* Wks. XVI. 78 Noise and brawlings of criminals..raving at the magistrate. **1883** *Congregationalist* May 387 A procedure which was brawling in church, and a brawling of a very bad type.

3. The confused din of a stream or torrent.

1837 HAWTHORNE *Amer. Note Bks.* (1871) I. 59 No noise but the brawling..of the stream. **1859** JEPHSON *Brittany* ix. 139, I could hear the brawling of the little river beneath. **1884** GILMOUR *Mongols* 153 The brawling of the torrent rose mingled with the sound of the flail.

†'**brawling,** *vbl. sb.*[2] *Obs.* [f. BRAWL *v.*[2] + -ING[1].] Motion from side to side, quivering.

?*a* **1400** *Morte Arth.* 2176 Þat braste at þe brawlyng, and brake in þe myddys!

brawling ('brɔːlɪŋ), *ppl. a.* [f. BRAWL *v.*[1] + -ING[2].] That brawls: **a.** Noisily quarrelsome, wrangling; **b.** Clamorous, noisy, bawling; **c.** Flowing with noise and commotion, as a brook.

1535 COVERDALE *Prov.* xix. 13 A braulynge wife is like the topp of an house, where thorow it is euer droppynge. **1591** ASCHAM *Scholem.* (1863) 130 For all.. those brauling Bulles of Basan. **1633** T. ADAMS *Exp. 2 Peter* ii. 20 The beating mallet upon the brawling metal disquiets him. **1726** THOMSON *Winter* 69 The brawling brook And cave, presageful, send a hollow moan. **1820** SCOTT *Abbot* ii, A brawling ruffian, and a common stabber. **1879** SEGUIN *Black For.* xi. 183 A chasm..through which a narrow brawling trout-stream makes its way.

†'**brawlingly,** *adv. Obs. rare.* [f. prec. + -LY[2].] In brawling manner.

1552 HULOET, Brawlynglye..*rixose.* **1579** J. JONES *Preserv. Body & Soul* I. xi. 22 Let the doggish Philosopher ..neuer so brawlingly prate to the contrarie.

brawlsome ('brɔːlsəm), *a.* [f. BRAWL + -SOME, after *quarrelsome.*] Given to brawls, quarrelsome.

1845 *Whitehall* xvi. 112 'Tis not in good liquor to be brawlsome.

brawly ('brɔːlɪ), *adv. Sc.* Also brawlies. [f. BRAW *a.* + -LY[2].] Finely; excellently, well.

1794 BURNS *Charley my Darling* iv. Brawly well he ken'd the way To please a bonie lass. **1816** SCOTT *Old Mort.* x, He can hit a mark brawly. **1818** —— *Hrt. Midl.* xxix, You Cameronian bodies ken that brawlies.

brawn (brɔːn), *sb.* Forms: 4 brahun, 4–6 braun(e, 4 brawen, 4–7 brawne, (5 browne), 6 brawyne, 5– brawn. [a. OF. *braon, braoun* (*braion*) fleshy part, muscle, particularly the most fleshy part of the hind leg, originally a part suitable for roasting, corresp. to Pr. *bradon*; ad. WGer. *brâdo*, f. *brâdan* to roast (see BREDE *v.*[1]). The specific sense 'boar's flesh' is exclusively of English development, and characteristic of English habits.]

1. Fleshy part, muscle; *esp.* the rounded muscles of the arm, leg and thumb.

c **1325** *Gloss W. de Biblesworth* in Wright *Voc.* 148 En la jambe [the caalf] est la sure [brahun]. *c* **1386** CHAUCER *Knts. T.* 1280 Hise lymes grete, hise brawnes harde and stronge. **1398** TREVISA *Barth. De P.R.* v. xxvii. (1495) 136 The armes ben..coueryd wyth skinne brawne and strenges with fleshe amonge. *c* **1420** *Pallad. on Husb.* IV. 675 Take oxen yonge.. in brawnes rising greet. **1568** *Jacob & Esau* II. ii. in Hazl. *Dodsley* II. 209 My teeth I can scarcely charm From gnawing away the brawn of my very arm. **1608** MIDDLETON *Mad World* II. vii, Is not your honour sore about the brawn of the arm? **1617** MARKHAM *Caval.* II. 49 Your thombe close vpon the reynes, with the brawne thereof turned toward the pomell of your saddle. **1718** POPE *Iliad* XVI. 374 His blow.. transpierced his thigh, Tore all the brawn. **1769** BLACKSTONE *Comm.* IV. 360 All laymen who are allowed this privilege shall be burnt with a hot iron in the brawn of the left thumb. **1865** HOLLAND *Plain T.* viii. 27 God makes a man of bone, brawn and blood.

b. *spec.* The arm, the calf of the leg, the buttock.

1382 WYCLIF *Job* xxii. 9 The brawnes [**1388** schuldres; Vulg. *lacertos*; **1611** arms] of moderles childer thou tobrosedist. **1581** NUCE *Seneca's Octavia* 175 Sir Brutus sterne, his brawnes and armes did dight, His soueraigne liege to slayne by force and might. **1607** SHAKS. *Cor.* IV. v. 126 Once more to hew thy Target from thy Brawne. **1864** *Glasgow Her.* 24 Sept., Stiffish a little, with a peculiar sensation about the brawns.

c. *transf.* and *fig.*

1601 HOLLAND *Pliny* I. 470 The outside..of the leaf hath in it certain strings, sinues or veins, brawns and ioynts. **1883** H. GEORGE *Progr. & Pov.* 388 Liberty is..the brawn of national strength, the spirit of national independence.

†**2.** The muscle or flesh of animals as food.

c **1340** *Gaw. & Gr. Knt.* 1631 Suche a brawne of a best.. Ne such sydes of a swyn, segh he never are. **1393** LANGL. *P. Pl.* C. XVI. 67 Braun and blod of þe goos, bacon and colhoppes. *c* **1440** *Anc. Cookery* in *Househ. Ord.* (1790) 430 Then take the braune of hennes, or of capons, and bray hom. **1513** *Bk. Keruynge* in *Babees Bk.* (1868) 279 Bytwene the foure membres laye the brawne of the capon. **1519** HORMAN *Vulg.* 164 b, He hath eate all the braune of the lopster. **1601** HOLLAND *Pliny* I. 297 While one loues nothing but the leg [of a fowl], another likes and praises the white brawne alone. **1655** MOUFFET & BENN. *Health's Improv.* (1746) 150 Mingling the Brawns of Peacocks with Porks Flesh. **1656** *Shepherd's Kal.* xxvii, In the winter shepheards do eat beef ..Brawn of Harts, Hinds and all kind of venison.

b. In Coverdale and the 'Great Bible', used to render Heb. *ḥēleb* 'fat', where Geneva, 1611, and Rev. V. have 'grease'. (The orig. meaning is uncertain. The Septuagint, Vulgate, Wyclif, Douay, following a different pointing of the Heb. *ḥālāb*, render 'is curdled like milk'.)

1535 COVERDALE *Ps.* cxviii. [cxix.] 70 Their herte is as fat as brawne.

3. *spec.* The flesh of the boar. (Often defined as 'brawn of a boar', even in 16th c.) In recent use, the flesh of a boar (or swine), collared, boiled, and pickled or potted. [With the restriction of application we may compare the restriction of *bacon*, a deriv. of *back*, to the cured back and sides of the pig.]

1377 LANGL. *P. Pl.* B. XIII. 62 Wombe-cloutes and wylde braune & egges yfryed with grece. *c* **1386** CHAUCER *Franklin's T.* 526 Brawen of the tusked swyn. *c* **1440** *Promp. Parv.* 48 Brawne of a bore, *aprina.* *c* **1460** *Towneley Myst.* 89 Lay furthe of oure store, Lo here browne of a bore. **1570** LEVINS *Manip.* 44 Brawne, *caro callata, aprina, callum.* **1614** MARKHAM *Cheap Husb.* (1623) 129 The best feeding of a Swine for Larde, or a Boare for Brawne. **1641** MILTON *Animadv.* (1851) 200 Is a man therefore bound..at noon to Brawn, or Beefe? *a* **1704** T. BROWN *Pleas. Ep.* Wks. 1730 I. 110 Private deliberations over brawn and guest-ale. **1781** *Westm. Mag.* II. 47 This turban for my head is collar'd brawn! **1828** SOUTHEY *Ep. A. Cunningham*, Whether ham, bacon, sausage, souse or brawn.

4. *transf.* A boar (or swine) as fattened for the table. *dial.* Cf. BACON *sb.*

?*a* **1400** *Morte Arth.* 1095 Brokbrestede as a brawne, with brustils fulle large. **1601** *Ord. R. Househ.* (1790) 288 The Serjeant of the Larder hath for his fee..the feete cut off at the first joynt of every braune spent in the Queenes house. **1630** J. TAYLOR (Water P.) *Gt. Eater Kent* Wks. I. 144/2 What say you to the Leafe or Flecke of a Brawne new kild? **1705** SUSANNA WESLEY in Eliza Clarke *Life* (1886) 55 To spread a report that my own brawn (boar) did this mischief. **1791** COWPER *Iliad* IX. 258 With the flesh of sheep And of a fatted brawn. **1807** STAGG *Poems* 18 Loud as brawns war snowran.

5. Hardened or thickened skin, the result of continued friction; also *fig.* L. *callum.*

1578 LYTE *Dodoens* IX. lxvii. 744 The hard skinne or brawne that is in the handes or feete, which is gotten by labour. **1617** HIERON *Wks.* 1619–20 II. 374 Corsiues for the eating out that dead flesh which is in their hearts, & for the paring off that brawne which is growne vpon them. **1639** FULLER *Holy War* II. xiv. (1840) 69 Witness the brawn on his hands and knees made with continual praying. **1639** HORN & ROB. *Gate Lang. Unl.* xxv. § 320 A brawn [thick skin] from hardning.

6. *Attrib.* and *Comb.*, as *brawn-bands*, *-buttock*; *brawn-fed*, *-like* adjs.; †**brawn-fallen** *a.*, shrunken in flesh, thin, skinny.

1653 PLAT *Gard. Eden* 67 Binding the bark..with a packthred, or rather with *brawn-bands, will keep roses long from blowing. **1601** SHAKS. *All's Well* II. ii. 19 The barbers chair..fits..the *brawn-buttock, or any buttock. **1579** LYLY *Euphues* (Arb.) 127 Were not Milo his armes *brawne-fallen for want of wrastlyng. **1606** CHAPMAN *Gentl. Usher* Plays 1873 I. 288 Leane and brawn-falne; I and scarsly sound. **1703** FARQUHAR *Inconstant* I. (D.) For our women here in France, they are such lean brawn-fall'n jades. **1567** DRANT *Hor. Epist.* xv. E vj, That I may cum *brawne fed. **1849–52** TODD *Cycl. Anat. & Phys.* IV. 1393/2 The surrounding cellular texture..puts on a *brawn-like character.

brawn (brɔːn), *v.* [f. prec.]

1. *trans.* To harden; to render callous; also *fig. Obs.* (at least in *fig.* sense).

1571 GOLDING *Calvin on Ps.* xlii. 5 Those which have bin enured to miserie from theyr chyldhood, wer brauned. **1593** NASHE *Christ's T.* 13 b, If thou hadst not embrued or brawned thine owne hands..in blood. **1641** BAKER *Chron.* 29/2 With continual kneeling her knees were brawned. **1653** A. WILSON *Jas. I.* 91 Industry brawns and hardens the Armes.

2. *intr.* To become hard or callous.

1839–47 TODD *Cycl. Anat. & Phys.* III. 254/2 This cutaneous cancer..consists of a brawning induration.

3. *trans.* To fatten (a boar).

1655 MOUFFET & BENN. *Health's Improv.* (1746) 147 The best Way of brawning a Boar is this..Before Christmas he will be sufficiently brawned with continual lying, and prove exceedingly fat, wholesome and sweet. *a* **1843** SOUTHEY *Nondescr.* iv, Pigs were made for man..born to be brawn'd And baconized.

†4. *intr.* To grow fat. (Of a boar.) *Obs.*

1580 TUSSER *Husb.* xv. (1878) 40 At Mihelmas safely go stie vp thy Bore..better he brawneth if hard he doo lie.

brawnche, brawndesche, obs. forms of BRANCH, BRANDISH.

brawned (brɔːnd), *ppl. a.* Also 6 **brand**. [f. BRAWN + -ED.]

1. Well-furnished with muscle; having well-developed arms, thighs, and legs; muscular, brawny.

c **1505** DUNBAR *Tua Mariit Wemen* 429 To see quhat berne is best brand, or bredest in schulderis. **1523** FITZHERB. *Husb.* §75. **1565** GOLDING *Ovid's Met.* VIII. (1593) 190 Right dreadfull was to see His brawned necke. **1577** B. GOOGE *Heresbach's Husb.* (1586) 115 Thies large and well brawned. **1609** HOLLAND *Amm. Marcell.* XXX. IX. 397 His bodie was well brawned [*lacertosus*], musculous and strong.

2. Covered with thickened skin; hardened, callous: chiefly *fig. Obs.* (at least in *fig.* sense.)

1583 STANYHURST *Æneis* I. (Arb.) 24 O deere companions ..Brawnd with woorse venturs. **1612** T. TAYLOR *Comm. Titus* ii. 14. 514 A brawned conscience begets defence of sinne. *a* **1656** BP. HALL *Sel. Thoughts* §63 Not so brawned under the rod that we should not feel it.

†3. Fattened as a boar. *Obs.*

1552 HULOET, Brawned, or hard of flesh, lyke a boore. **1583** GOLDING *Calvin on Deut.* clxxxi. 1125 They became fatte..and as it were so brawned that they were readie to burst with greace. **1601** DENT *Pathw. Heaven* 172 Fatting themselues like Boares..till they be well brawned.

†'**brawnedness.** *Obs. rare*⁻¹. [f. prec. + -NESS.] Callousness.

1635 R. BOLTON *Comf. Affl. Consc.* iii. 103 An insensible brawnednesse..impressed upon their conscience.

brawner ('brɔːnə(r)). [f. BRAWN *v.* + -ER: cf. *porker*.] A boar fattened for the table.

1708 W. KING *Cookery* (R.) Send up the brawner's head. **1809** *Edin. Rev.* XIII. 341 The misery of the brawner.

brawniness ('brɔːnɪnɪs). [f. BRAWNY + -NESS.]

1. Muscular quality; muscularity.

1684 CHARNOCK *Wks.* II. 150 The brawniness of his arm. **1828** SCOTT *F.M. Perth* ii, The length and brawniness of his arms.

†2. Callousness, insensibility. *Obs.*

a **1645** J. DOD in Spurgeon *Treas. Dav.* Ps. xiv. 5 A brawniness hath overgrown their consciences. **1656** TRAPP *Comm. Eph.* iv. 18 Hardness, brawniness, a hoof upon their hearts. **1692** LOCKE *Educ.* §113 This Brawniness and Insensibility of the Mind, is the best Armour we can have.

†'**brawnness,** obs. var. of BRAWNINESS.

1398 TREVISA *Barth. De P.R.* VII. lix. (1495) 273 The membres of the heed dispose their superfluytees..to the brawnesse of the throte and soo comyth Squynancye. **1598** FLORIO, *Callosita*, hardnes, brawnnes.

brawny ('brɔːnɪ), *a.* Also 6–7 **brawney, -ie**. [f. BRAWN *sb.* + -Y¹.]

1. Characterized by muscle or muscular strength.

1599 MARSTON *Sco. Villanie* II. v. 195 O, brawny strength is an all-canning charme. *a* **1644** QUARLES *Argument* in Farr's *S.P.* (1848) 134 Would any strive with Samson for renowne, Whose brawney arme can strike most pillars down? **1741** WATTS *Improv. Mind* (1801) 346 Samson and Goliath would have lost..their brawny limbs, in the course of half a century. **1842** LONGF. *Vill. Blacksmith* i, The muscles of his brawny arms Are strong as iron bands.

†b. Of a fruit: ? Fleshy. *Obs.*

c **1420** *Pallad. on Husb.* III. 742 Oxe dounge about her rootes..The pomes sadde and brawny wol it gete.

2. Characterized by hardened skin.

1613 *Life Will. I.* in *Select. Harl. Misc.* (1793) 26 After her death, her knees appeared brawny and hard, with much kneeling at her devotions. *a* **1638** MEDE *Wks.* III. 678 That which is seared, becomes more hard and brawny. **1702** ECHARD *Eccl. Hist.* (1710) 335 His knees became hard and brawny as a Camels. **1879** T. BRYANT *Prac. Surg.* II. 252 The disease appears as a brawny infiltration of the breast.

†3. *fig.* Callous, hardened, unfeeling. *Obs.*

1596 BP. BARLOW *3 Serm.* i. 43 If his heart yarne not, it is brawnie. *a* **1638** MEDE *Apost. Later Times* 118 A hard and a brawny Conscience, which hath no feeling in it. *a* **1694** TILLOTSON *Serm.* clxxv. (1743) IX. 4105 Some men..by sin ..bring themselves into a brawny and insensible condition.

4. *Comb.*, chiefly parasynthetic, as ***brawny-chined, -fisted, -hearted, -limbed,*** etc.

a **1639** W. WHATELEY *Prototypes* II. xxxiv. (1640) 165 So brawney-hearted, that they would but laugh at Christ himselfe if he should bid them weepe. **1725** POPE *Odyss.* xx. 204 Three porkers for the feast, all brawny-chined, He brought. **1870** *Daily News* 14 Nov., Of all the ladies of Belleville they are..the brawniest-fisted.

Braxton Hicks ('brækstən hɪks). *Obstetrics.* Also with hyphen. The name of John *Braxton Hicks* (1823–97), English obstetrician, used *attrib.* and in the possessive to designate spontaneous, irregular, usually painless contractions of the uterus that occur during pregnancy (described by Hicks in *Trans. Obstetr. Soc.* (1872) XIII. 216).

1905 H. JELLETT *Man. Midwifery* III. ii. 229 The occurrence of painless and intermittent contractions of the uterus which are perceptible from the third month of pregnancy onwards was first determined by Braxton Hicks. .. It is consequently known as Braxton Hicks' sign. **1928** W. G. LEE *Childbirth* vi. 62 Inasmuch as these intermittent or Braxton-Hicks contractions of the uterus are..a constant feature of the latter part of pregnancy, the occurrence of pain has prognostic value at this time as an indication that the intensity of uterine contractions has increased. **1985** E. SLOANE *Biol. of Women* (ed. 2) x. 340/2 During the last few weeks of pregnancy, the spontaneous painless Braxton Hicks' contractions that have been occurring all along, become stronger.

braxy ('bræksɪ), *sb.* and *a. Sc.* Forms: see below. [Etymology and even form uncertain: Jamieson has the forms *braik* (sing.), *bracks* (pl.), *braxes* (pl.), and *braxit*, as well as *braxy*. Either the latter is orig. an adj. *brax-y*, formed from a collective pl. *bracks, brax* (cf. *peasy, poxy*), or it is an erroneous sing. deduced from *braxes*, as if this were *braxie-s*. Prob. 'the *bracks*' is the original, being a special use of the pl. of BRACK in some sense derived from BREAK. Cf. OE. *bræc* rheum, catarrh, also *bræc-cōðu* and *bræc-sēocnes* falling sickness, *bræc-sēoc* ill with falling sickness. As examples of the ways in which names of diseases are treated, we may compare *pox* for *pocks, axis, axes, axys* (often as pl.) for *access, jaundys* pl. for *jaundice*.]

1. The popular name in Scotland of splenic apoplexy in sheep; an inflammatory disease of the internal parts, rapid and fatal in its effect.

1791 *Statist. Acc. Scotl.* IV. 8 (*Lethnot, Forf.*) A disease which is here called the *Braxes*. —— *Ibid.* 242 (*Barry, Forf.*) Among the shepherds it is called the *Bracks*. —— *Ibid.* II. 440 (*Selkirk*) The braxy as some call it. **1793** *Ibid.* IX. 326 The sheep that died of the braxy in the latter end of autumn. **1822** W. NAPIER *Store-farming* 58 The sickness or braxy has been very fatal in many parts of this country.

2. as *adj.* Characterized by this disease, as ***braxy-sheep, mutton***; also *absol.* the flesh of a braxy sheep, or, generally, of one that has died by disease or accident.

1785 BURNS *Ep. W. Simson* xix, While moorlan herds like guid, fat braxies. **1854** H. MILLER *Sch. & Schm.* ix. (1857) 165 Two tall pyramids of braxy mutton heaped up each on a corn-riddle. **1863** N. MACLEOD in *Gd. Words* 503 The occasional dinner luxury of Braxy,—a species of mutton which need not be too minutely inquired into. **1880** *Cornh. Mag.* June 691 Braxy is the flesh of sheep which have died a natural death, by flood, drift, or disease.

Hence **braxied** *ppl. a.*

1870 STEWART *Lochaber* xix. (1883) 112 A tender lamb or braxied sheep.

bray (breɪ), *sb.*¹ [f. BRAY *v.*¹, or a. OF. *brai, brait* 'cry', f. *braire*.]

†1. Outcry; a loud cry, a shriek. *Obs.*

a **1300** *K. Alis.* 2175 So gret bray, so gret crieyng Ffor the folk there was dyeyng. *c* **1450** *Merlin* xviii. 300 The lady vndirstode the brayes and the cries that the bretheren made a-boute hir. **1552** EDW. VI. *Lett.* lxii. (Roxb.) 87 You cannot yet ask leave to return..till this bray do cease. **1558** PHAËR *Æneid* IV. Liij b, Thrise she sounding fell, and there upon she gaue a braye. **1596** SPENSER *F.Q.* IV. viii. 62 The Tyrant selfe came forth with yelling bray.

2. The cry peculiar to some animals, esp. the ass; *humorously* of the human voice.

1650 T. BAYLY *Herba Parietis* 37 No brayes of asses, nor of bulls. **1728** POPE *Dunciad* II. 251 Sore sighs Sir Gilbert, starting, at the bray..So swells each wind-pipe; Ass intones to Ass. **1798** WORDSW. *Peter Bell* I. 55 The Ass sent forth A long and clamorous bray! **1834** H. AINSWORTH *Rookwood* I. iii, A snorting bray [of a buck] was heard. **1870** LOWELL *Among my Bks.* I. (1873) 338 The solemn bray of one pedagogue was taken up and prolonged in a thousand echoes.

3. *transf.* A loud harsh sound produced by natural agencies, brass musical instruments, etc.

1593 SHAKS. *Rich. II*, I. iii. 135 With harsh resounding Trumpets dreadfull bray. **1813** SCOTT *Trierm.* III. xvii, And with rude crash and jarring bray The rusty bolts withdraw. **1821** JOANNA BAILLIE *Met. Leg.*, *Wallace* lxxxi. 9 The white churned foam with angry bray. **1884** J. COLBORNE *With Hicks Pasha* 121 Unearthly shrieks and brays from brass instruments and horns.

4. *fig.*

1929 E. SITWELL *Gold Coast Customs* 17 The bray Of the eyeless mud. **1953** C. DAY LEWIS *Ital. Visit* i. 21 A great Elgarian clash and bray of sunshine.

†**bray,** *sb.*² *Obs.* [f. BRAY *v.*²] A baker's pestle.

c **1440** *Promp. Parv.* 46 Bray or brakene, baxteris instrument, *pinsa*.

bray (breɪ), *sb.*³ *Her.* Also **brey**. [a. OF. *braie, braye*, *breie, now *broie*.]

1. A semicircular figure representing a barnacle or bit to restrain a restive horse.

1863 C. BOUTELL *Man. Her.* 45 *Breys*, barnacles for a horse's nose, used in breaking the animal. **1864** —— *Her. Hist. & Pop.* (ed. 3) xv. 175 Three breys or barnacles in pale or.

2. (Corresponding to Fr.) A tool used for breaking hemp, used as a bearing.

1882 CUSSANS *Handbk. Her.* 109 A Hemp-brey is really the same instrument as a Horse-brey, except that they were used for different purposes, and that the former is in Armory always represented as being upon a wooden stand.

bray (breɪ), *v.*¹ Also 4–7 **brai(e, braye**. [ME. *braie, braye*, a. F. *brai-re* (11th c. in Littré) 'to cry' (now only of the ass), = Pr. *braire* to cry, Rumansch *bragir*, med.L. *bragire* (Diez): perh. of Celtic origin, f. a stem *brag-* cogn. with L. *fragor*; cf. OIr. *braigim* 'pedo' (Thurneysen). The original sense would thus be 'to make a crackling, grating, or jarring noise'.]

†1. *intr.* To cry out, to utter a loud harsh cry; *esp.* of grief or pain. *Obs.*

a **1300** *Cursor M.* 22607 He sal here it [heaven] cri to wonder, bath cri and brai for dute and drede. **1413** LYDGATE *Pylgr. Sowle* II. xliv. (1859) 50 Now, wepeth, yellyth, cryeth, brayeth, as besyly as ye can. **1502** *Ord. Crysten Men* v. ii. (1506) 358 For to cry & to braye in wepynge & in playnynge. **1513** DOUGLAS *Æneis* I. v. 120 The horrible tirrant wth bludy mouth sall bray. **1552** HULOET, Bray or cry lamentably. **1596** SPENSER *F.Q.* I. viii. 11 The Gyant.. loudly brayd with beastly yelling sound. **1613** R. C. *Table Alph.* (ed. 3) *Exclaime*, bray, or cry out.

b. predicated of the cry.

1596 SPENSER *F.Q.* I. vi. 7 Her shrill outcryes and shrieks so loud did bray.

2. Of animals: formerly the cry of horses, oxen, deer, etc.; now chiefly used of the ass.

1380 *Sir Ferumb.* 3669 Þat hors..faste gan neye and loud braye. **1393** GOWER *Conf.* I. 144 And though him lacke vois of speche..He [Nebuchadnezzar] kneleth in his wise and braieth To seche mercy. **1481** CAXTON *Myrr.* II. vi. 77 Thenne he [an elephant] begynneth for to braye, crye and waylle. **1534** LD. BERNERS *Gold. Bk. M. Aurel.* (1546) Q, There is not so croked a hors, but yf he see a mare, he wille braie ones or twise. **1560** BIBLE (*Geneva*) *Ps.* xlii. 1 As the Hart brayeth for the riuers of water [cf. **1611** *marg.*]. **1614** RALEIGH *Hist. World* III. iv. §4 The first Horse that brayed. **1633** P. FLETCHER *Purple Isl.* I. xvii, What cares an asse for arts: he brayes at sacred Muses. **1697** DRYDEN *Virg. Georg.* III. 575 Stags..pitifully bray. **1715** GAY *Trivia* II. (R.) Before proud gates attending asses bray. **1726** THOMSON *Winter* 824 As..they [deer]..piteous bray. **1877** A. B. EDWARDS *Up Nile* iv. 91 The donkey kicks up his heels and brays.

b. *contemptuously* of the human voice.

1635 A. STAFFORD *Fem. Glory* (1869) 90 Hee vehemently braies out against my Rhetoricall flowers. **1642** H. MORE *Song of Soul* I. II. cxxxii. **1692** WASHINGTON tr. *Milton's Def. Pop.* v. (1851) 159 None ever brayed so learnedly. **1876** BLACKIE *Songs Relig. & Life* 229 With fervid wheels pursue, Though thousands bray around thee.

3. *transf.* Of wind, thunder, musical instruments, etc. (now esp. of the trumpet): To make a loud harsh jarring sound.

1340 *Ayenb.* 73 Þer þou sselt yzy..ver bernynde, brenston stinkinde, tempeste brayinde. **1485** CAXTON *Chas. Gt.* (1880) 165 A ryuer..whyche..renneth so fast and brayeth. **1570** B. GOOGE *Pop. Kingd.* III. 928 Till in the loftie heauens darke, the thunder bray no more. **1695** BLACKMORE *Pr. Arthur* VIII. 375 Swords clash with Swords, Bucklers on Bucklers bray. **1757** GRAY *Bard* II. iii, Heard ye the din of battle bray? **1805** SCOTT *Last. Minstr.* I. vi, They watch to hear the war-horn braying. **1812** J. & H. SMITH *Rej. Addr.* xvii. (1873) 162 Brays the loud trumpet, squeaks the fiddle sharp. **1852** SEIDEL *Organ* 180 The reed-registers must not rattle or bray. **1872** BLACKIE *Lays Highl.* 79 Little reck they, how the storm may bray.

b. Of a place: To resound in like manner.

1607 SHAKS. *Timon* II. ii. 169 Euery roome Hath blaz'd with Lights, and braid with Minstrelsie. **1728** POPE *Dunciad* II. 260 Walls, steeples, skies bray back to him again.

4. *trans.* To utter harshly (cries, sounds, etc.). Often with *out*.

c **1325** *E.E. Allit. P.* A. 346 Braundysch & bray þy braþez breme. **1531** ELYOT *Gov.* II. vi, Roryng and braiying out wordes despyteful. **1579** FULKE *Heskins' Parl.* 4 What asse of Acarnania wold braye out suche a reason? **1588** GREENE *Pandosto* (1843) 23 Pandosto..in a fury brayed out these bitter speeches. **1602** SHAKS. *Ham.* I. iv. 11 The kettle Drum and Trumpet thus bray out The triumph of his Pledge. **1667** MILTON *P.L.* VI. 209 Arms on Armour clashing bray'd Horrible discord. **1854** THACKERAY *Newcomes* II. 286 His men of brass..who were accustomed to bray 'See the Conquering Hero comes'. **1860** *Sat. Rev.* X. 421 A Brass band brayed welcome at the terminus.

b. To give forth with a cry or bray.

1567 STUDLEY *Seneca's Hippol.* (1581) 56 Where Zephyrus most milde Out brayes his baumy breath. **1596** SPENSER *F.Q.* II. i. 38 As gentle hynd..Braies out her latest breath.

bray (breɪ), *v.*² Also 5–7 **braie, braye**. [ME. *brayen*, a. OF. *breie-r* (mod.F. *broyer*), corresp., according to Diez, with Pr. and Sp. *bregar*, It. *brigare*. Storm would derive the Romanic words from Teut. *brek-an* to break.]

1. *trans.* To beat small; to bruise, pound, crush to powder; usually in a mortar.

1382 [see BRAYED *ppl. a.*] *c* **1420** *Liber Cocorum* (1862) 26 Take, bray tho brawne of aȝt capon. *c* **1440** *Promp. Parv.* 47 Brayyn, or stampyn in a morter, *tero*. *c* **1470** *Bk. Quintessence* 11 Take þat blood..and braie it wiþ þe .10. part of comen salt. **1525** LD. BERNERS *Froiss.* II. lxii. [lxv.] 212 The Englysshmen were fayne to gather the thystelles in the feldes, and braye them in a morter. **1610** MARKHAM *Masterp.* II. c. 383 Stoppe the foot with nettles and salt braid together. *c* **1615** CHAPMAN *Odyss.* x. 268 That foul Cyclop

that their fellows bray'd Betwixt his jaws. **1703** Maundrell *Journ. Jerus.* (1732) 86 The Kernels of this Fruit the Arabs bray in a Mortar. **1850** Thackeray *Pendennis* lv. (1884) 541 So she was to be turned out of doors—or brayed alive in the double gilt pestle and mortar.

b. *fig.*; freq. with ref. to *Prov.* xxvii. 22.

1535 Coverdale *Prov.* xxvii. 22 Though thou shuldest bray a foole with a pestell in a morter like otemeell, yet wil not his foolishnesse go from him. **1583** Stubbes *Anat. Abus.* ii. 78 The word of God is not preached vnto them, and as it were braied, punned, interpreted and expounded. **1610** B. Jonson *Alch.* ii. iii, Sir, with an Argument, He'll bray you in a mortar. **1626** T. H. *Caussin's Holy Crt.* 302 We must bray togeather, the matters of prayer, as Aromatique spices, with the discussion of our understanding. **1664** Butler *Hud.* ii. *Heroic Epist.* 35 Nor being..bray'd so often in a Mortar, Can teach you wholesom Sense, and Nurture. **1855** Browning *Men & Wom., Pretty Woman*, But for loving, why, you would not, sweet, Though we prayed you, Paid you, brayed you In a Mortar.

2. Technical uses: †**a.** To crush flax or hemp with a brake. [F. *broyer le chanvre.*] *Obs.*

1398 Trevisa *Barth. De P.R.* xvii. xcvii. (1495) 663 Flexe is..beten and brayd and carflyd. **1530** Palsgr. 462/2, I bray in a brake, as men do hempe.

b. To temper and spread printing-ink.

1688 [see brayer²]. **1706** in Phillips. Hence in Bailey, etc.

c. To pound and scour (woollen cloth).

1879 *Cassell's Techn. Educ.* IV. 342/1 The newly-woven cloth requires to be scoured or brayed in order to remove the oil..and the size.

3. To beat, thrash. *dial.*

1808 *Cumbr. Ballads* xxxiv. 77 She brays the lasses, starves the lads. **1864** Atkinson *Whitby Gloss.* s.v., I'll bray thy back for thee.

†**bray**, *v.*³ *Obs. rare.* [a. F. *bray-er* to pitch (a ship), f. *brai* pitch, resin.] To pitch (a ship).

1600 Hakluyt *Voy.* (1810) III. 383 Our men sought all meanes to recouer rosen in the woodes..to bray the vessel.

bray (breɪ), *v.*⁴ *S. Afr.* Also ‖brei, brey. [ad. Afrikaans *brei*, f. Du. *breien* braid *v.*¹] *trans.* To prepare, dress (the skin of an animal).

[**1822** W. J. Burchell *Trav.* I. xv. 351 The trunk of a tree is fixed up near the hut, for the purpose of preparing (or, as they call it, *breyen*) leathern *reims*.] *a* **1835** J. Goldswain *Chron.* (1946) 20 Six or eight sheep skins wich they bray or rub them in thear hands. **1840** W. C. Harris *Game & Wild Animals S. Afr.* i. 4 The hide, when brayed, is employed by the Colonists for *riems*, or thongs. **1897** 'F. Macnab' *On Veldt & Farm Bechuanaland* iv. 53 They..were always busy braying a skin, sewing a karross [etc.]. **1925** S. C. Cronwright-Schreiner in *Centenary Bk. S. Afr. Verse* 61 The hardy Boer..cut the strip And brei'd and rolled and hammered it round to make the Wagon-whip. **1934** R. Campbell *Broken Record* vii. 170, I shot two seals,..brayed their skins and sold them to tourists for motoring coats. **1934** 'N. Giles' *Ridge of White Waters* i. ix. 109 Their clothes, patched from skins they breyed themselves. **1952** S. Cloete *Curve & Tusk* (1953) ix. 85 A kilt of breyed skin. **1955** E. A. Ritter *Shaka Zulu* xvii. 203 Everyone lay down to sleep—the maidens on their mats with well brayed skins as blankets.

†**bray.** In phr. *at a bray*, app. for *at a braid* = on a sudden, unawares; see braid.

1549–62 Sternhold & H. *Ps.* cxix. 110 Although the wicked layd their nets, To catch me at a bray.

bray(e, obs. form of brae.

†**'brayable**, *a. Obs. rare*⁻⁰. [f. bray *v.*² + -able.] Capable of being crushed or pounded.

1611 Cotgr., *Brisable*, burstable, breakeable, brayable.

brayd(e, brayed, var. of braid.

†**'brayded**, *ppl. a. Obs. rare*⁻¹. Erroneous form for brayed, as if from a present-stem *brayd*.

1561 Hollybush *Hom. Apoth.* 18 a, Take a dishfull of brayded or beaten barlye.

†**braye.** *Obs.* Also 6 brey, 6–7 braie. [a. F. *braie* = med.L. *braca* dike, embankment: of unknown origin.] A military outwork; a mound or bank defended by palisades and watchtowers. ***false braye*** (ad. Fr. *fausse braie*): an advanced parapet surrounding the main rampart.

1512 *Act 4 Hen. VIII*, i §1 To make Bulwerkes, Brayes, Walles, Diches, and al other fortificacions. **1546** *St. Papers Hen. VIII*, XI. 205 He knowith of no newe fortification.. saving only a newe braye about their fort. **1575** Laneham *Let.* (1871) 2 A fayre Park on the one side, which by the Braiz is linked too the castl on the South. **1577** Holinshed *Chron.* II. 857 The king that was walking aloft on the braies of the wals. **1599** Hakluyt *Voy.* II. 122 A Brey and Cortaine without was battered by the forts. **1645** Symonds in *United Serv. Mag.* (1842) ii. 467 There is..a pallizado above the false bray. **1653** Urquhart *Rabelais* iii. Prol., Contrived platforms, barricadoed the false brayes.

brayed (breɪd), *ppl. a.* [f. bray *v.*² + -ed.]

1. Beaten small, bruised, pounded.

1382 Wyclif *1 Sam.* xxv. 18 Fyue busshellis of brayid corn. **1575** Turberv. *Bk. Falconrie* 333 With a little salte brayed verie small. **1811** Pinkerton *Petral.* II. 265, I only found a dust composed of brayed marble.

†**2.** *brayed ware*: app. a confusion for *braided ware* = damaged or faded goods; see braided.

1603 Harsnet *Pop. Impost.* 25 The silly Conie was caught; she was seazed upon for brayed wares.

brayen, early form of brain.

brayer¹ ('breɪə(r)). [f. bray *v.*¹ + -er¹.] One who brays; *esp.* an ass.

1598 Florio, *Russo*..a snorter, a brayer, one that is hoarse. **1728** Pope *Dunciad* ii. 246 Sound forth, my Brayers, and the welkin rend. **1876** G. Roslyn *Geo. Eliot in Derbysh.* 54 She had a pony and he had a donkey. He could not make the brayer go.

brayer² ('breɪə(r)). *Printing.* [f. bray *v.*² + -er¹.] A wooden muller or pestle used to rub down and temper the ink.

1688 R. Holme *Armory* ii. iii. 56 Brayer, is a round wooden Rubber, flat at the bottom, it is used in the Inke-block to Bray and Rub Inke. **1824** J. Johnson *Typogr.* II. 524 He brings forward a small quantity of ink..which he rubs well with the brayer.

Hence **'brayer** *v. trans.* To spread or rub fine.

1824 J. Johnson *Typogr.* II. 524 Care should be observed not to brayer out much [ink] at a time.

brayer³ ('breɪə(r)). [Deriv. uncertain: cf. F. *brayer* in various technical senses; or ? bray *v.*²] Part of a compound lever for raising or depressing the 'runner' or upper grindstone in a corn-mill, being the transverse piece which supports the end of the 'bridge-tree'.

1770 J. Ferguson *Lect.* (1805) I. 83 The end S is let into a beam Q R, called the brayer. **1822** Imison *Sc. & Art* I. 69 The end M of the brayer is raised or depressed at pleasure.

‖**brayera** (brɑːˈjɛərə). [Named after Brayer, a foreign physician.] A genus of Rosaceous trees, the only known species of which (*B. anthelmintica*) is a native of Abyssinia. **b.** A medicinal preparation of the flowers and tops of this tree, called also Cusso, valued as an anthelmintic. Hence also **'brayerin**, a bitter acrid resin found in Cusso.

1875 H. Wood *Therap.* (1879) 601 Brayera is a most efficient remedy against the tapeworm.

brayette: see braguette.

braygirdle, -gurdylle, var. of breechgirdle.

braying ('breɪɪŋ), *vbl. sb.*¹ [f. bray *v.*¹]

†**1.** Loud or harsh crying, hoarse shouting. *Obs.*

1547 Boorde *Brev. Health* ccclxxiv. 119 b, A mans voyce the which may have dyvers impedimentes as horsnes, brayenge. **1576** Newton tr. *Lemnie's Complex.* (1633) 121 With too much and too violent braying out.

2. The crying of various animals, now *esp.* of the ass. Hence *contemptuously* of the human voice.

c **1440** *Promp. Parv.* 47 Brayynge yn sownde, *barritus.* **1590** Greene *Never too late* (1600) 28 The young Tigers follow the braying of their olde sire. **1684** tr. *Agrippa's Van. Arts* cii. 363 The untuneable braying of Asses. **1826** Scott *Woodst.* (1832) 177 At the braying of the first wild ass.

3. Of musical instruments.

1704 Rowe *Ulyss.* i. i. 63 The Braying of the Minstrel's Noise. **1884** *Leisure Hour* June 374/1 The braying and droning of trumpets and bagpipes.

braying ('breɪɪŋ), *vbl. sb.*² [f. bray *v.*² + -ing¹.] The action or process of pounding, as in a mortar; also *attrib.*, as in *braying-stone.*

c **1440** *Promp. Parv.* 47 Brayynge, or stampynge, *tritura.* *a* **1680** Butler *Rem.* (1759) II. 222 His discourse is like the braying of a Mortar, the more impertinent the more voluble and loud.

braying ('breɪɪŋ), *ppl. a.* [f. bray *v.*¹ + -ing².]

1. That brays; that makes a loud harsh sound.

1572 Gascoigne *Flowers* Wks. (1587) 47 Thus with a braying sigh his noble tongue he stayde. **1652** Benlowes *Theoph.*, Wits..By braying Beasts condemned are. **1782** Cowper *Gilpin* 203 While he spake, a braying ass Did sing most loud and clear. **1807** Byron *Newstead Abb.* xiv, The braying trumpet and the hoarser drum.

2. *fig.*

1922 E. Sitwell *Façade* 15 The hard and braying light.

brayl(e, brayn, obs. f. brail, brain.

brays, var. of breeze *sb.*³

1865 Jevons *Coal Quest.* (ed. 2) 313 It became customary to mix coke and brays or small coal with the charge of fuel.

brayste, *v. Obs.* [? var. of *breste*, burst.]

c **1400** *Rowland & Ot.* 986 Schall none of my men the brayste.

Braysyle, obs. form of Brazil.

brayt. *Obs. rare*⁻¹. [perh. a. OF. *brait* cry; see bray *sb.*¹: but cf. braid *v.*¹] A cry, yell.

c **1450** *Merlin* xiv. 216 Sonygrenx..turned to flight, and caste a grete brayt and an orible.

†**braythe, breythe**, *v. Obs. rare.* Also 6 brathe, breat. [perh. a. ON. *bregða* to move swiftly, start: etymologically identical with OE. *brægdan* braid *v.*¹] *intr.* To rush or 'fly' *up.*

c **1325** *E.E. Allit. P.* B. 1421 Wyne..warmed his hert & breyþed vppe in to his brayn. **1561** Hollybush *Hom. Apoth.* 5 a, When the same is inflamed and breateth up into the heade. *Ibid.* 5 b, Hote bloode, that lyeth in the harte, and bratheth vp into the braynes. *Ibid.* 7 Undigested vapor, braythynge vp, and troubling the braynes.

braze (breɪz), *v.*¹ Also 1 brasian, 6 brasen. [OE. *brasian*, f. *bræs*, brass; but as no examples are found in ME., the 16th c. verb may have been formed anew on the analogy of *glaze, graze.*]

1. *trans.* To make of brass; to cover or ornament with brass.

[*c* **1000** Ælfric *Gram.* xxxvi. 215 *Aero*, ic brasiȝe.] **1552** Huloet, Brasen, or make with brasse, *æro.* **1611** Cotgr., *Bronzer*, to Braze; to make of, or couer with, brasse. *c* **1615** Chapman *Odyss.* xv. (R.) A caldron or a tripod, richly braz'd. **1693** W. Robertson *Phraseol. Gen.* 278 To braze or cover with brass.

2. *fig.* **a.** To make hard like brass, harden, inure; **b.** 'to harden to impudence' (J.) (Cf. *brazen-faced.* But some view this as a sense of braze *v.*², taken as = harden in the fire.)

1602 Shaks. *Ham.* iii. iv. 37 And let me wring your heart ..If damned Custome haue not braz'd it so, That it is proofe and bulwarke against Sense. **1608** Armin *Nest Ninn.* (1842) 1, I am brazed by your fauours, made bould in your ostended curtesies. **1616** Breton *Good & Bad* (1616) 31 His face is brazed that he cannot blush. **1648** Jenkyn *Blind Guide* iii. 62 You reply nothing, but new braze your face. **1833** *Fraser's Mag.* VIII. 707 Custom has so brazed the whole fraternity to these nefarious practices.

3. *transf.* To colour like brass.

1864 W. Story *Roba di R.* xix. 402 The sunset brazes with splendour the throbbing sky. **1866** Lowell *Poet. Wks.* (1879) 372 Clouds That braze the horizon's western rim.

braze (breɪz), *v.*² Also 6 brase. [? a. F. *brase-r* to solder, in OF. *braser* to burn; prob. a. ON. **brasa* to fire, expose to fire (cf. Sw. *brasa* to flame, Du. *brase* to roast). But the modern Eng. and French sense 'solder' does not come obviously from 'fire': one might suppose that in Eng. it was taken from or influenced by braze *v.*¹: but whence then the F. *braser*?]

†**1.** To fire, expose to the action of fire. *Obs.*

1581 Lambarde *Eiren.* iv. iv. 458 If any arrowhead Smith haue not well boiled, brased and hardened at the point with steele..such heads of arrowes..as he hath made.

2. To solder (with an alloy of brass and zinc).

1677 Moxon *Mech. Exerc.* (1703) 12 You may have occasion sometimes to Braze..a piece of work; but it is used by Smiths only, when their work is so thin, or small, that it will not endure Welding. **1835** Sir J. Ross *N.-W. Pass.* ii. 12 So much worn, as to require a piece to be brazed to it, to restore its thickness. **1875** 'Stonehenge' *Brit. Sports* i. v. xi. §1. **1881** Greener *Gun* 235 It is a common practice with foreign makers to braze their barrels together from end to end.

braze (breɪz), *sb.* [f. braze *v.*²] The process of brazing; a brazed joint. So **'brazeless** *a.*

1897 *Westm. Gaz.* 6 Dec. 9/1 Among the other novelties are the brazeless but fixed joints shrunk together. **1898** *Ibid.* 16 Apr. 6/1 The other process, which is described as brazeless. **1934** Webster, Braze. **1955** *Brazing Man.* (Amer. Welding Soc.) iii. 21 The American Welding Society defines a brazing filler metal as a metal to be added in making a braze.

braze, obs. form of braise.

brazed (breɪzd), *ppl. a.* [f. braze *v.*¹ + -ed¹.] Made or covered with brass; also *fig.* brazened, rendered shameless.

The first quotation is uncertain: can it be from braze *v.*²?

1583 Stanyhurst *Æneis* i. (Arb.) 32 Thee beams with brazed copper were costlye bepounced. **1773** Johnson in *Boswell* (1831) III. 83 Tytler advanced with his front ready brazed. **1884** *Nonconf.* 13 Mar. 258/2 Questions..talked about with staggering audacity in the brazed communities of the States.

brazeletta, -e, -o, obs. forms of braziletto.

brazen ('breɪz(ə)n), *a.* Forms: 1 bræsen, 2–7 brasen, 4 brassen, 4–5 brasun, 4–6 brasin, -yn, 5–6 brason, 6 brassin, 7 brassen, brazon, 6– brazen. [OE. *bræsen*, f. *bræs*, brass; see -en¹.]

1. Made of brass.

a **1000** *Lamb. Psalter* xvii[i]. 35 (Bosw.) Þu ȝesettest swa swa boȝan bræsenne earmas mine. *c* **1200** Ormin 17424 þatt brasene neddre. *a* **1300** *Cursor M.* 12193 Als a chim or brasin [*v.r.* brassen, brasen] bell. *c* **1400** *Apol. Loll.* 90 Heþun men had sex kyndis of similacris, cleyen, treen, brasun, stonun, silueren & golden. **1444** *Test. Ebor.* (1855) II. 112 My best brasyn pottis. **1552** Abp. Hamilton *Catech.* 52 A brassin ymage. **1593** Shaks. *Rich. II*, iii. iii. 33 Brazen Trumpet. **1602** —— *Ham.* i. i. 73 Brazon Cannon. **1662** J. Chandler *Van Helmont's Oriat.* 85 Let there be a brassen Bottle. **1740** Swift *Let. Mrs. Whiteway* 29 Apr., In Phalaris's brazen bull. **1875** Jowett *Plato* (ed. 2) I. 142 Like brazen pots, which when they are struck continue to sound.

b. Referring to the strength rather than the actual material of brass; hence, strong as brass.

1382 Wyclif *Jer.* xv. 20 And I shal ȝyue thee to this puple in to a strong brasene wal. **1561** T. Norton *Calvin's Inst.* Pref., He may breake it [the earth] with all the iron and brasen strength, with all the golden and syluer glistering therof. **1574** tr. *Marlorat's Apocalips* 24 As a brazen wall agaynst all the land of Juda. **1593** Shaks. *3 Hen. VI*, ii. iv. 4 Wer't thou inuiron'd with a Brazen wall. **1873** Morley *Rousseau* II. 26 A region..which the spirit of their time had shut off from them with brazen barriers.

2. *transf.* and *fig.* Resembling brass in colour, sound, etc. (Often to be referred back to Homer's οὐρανὸς χάλκεος, πολύχαλκος, ὄπα χάλκεον.)

1596 Spenser *Hymn Heav. Beautie* 263 Wks. 1842 V. 428 Heavenly notes and carolings..that filles the brasen sky. **1606** Shaks. *Ant. & Cl.* iv. viii. 36 Trumpeters, with brazen

dinne blast you the citties eare. **1611** CHAPMAN *Iliad* XVIII. 191 His brazen voice once heard. **1667** MILTON *P.L.* VII. 496 The Serpent..with brazen Eyes And hairie Main terrific. *Ibid.* XI. 713 The brazen Throat of Warr had ceast to roar. **1784** COWPER *Task* IV. 104, I..Hear the faint echo of those brazen throats. *a* **1827** LONGF. *Burial of Minn.* i, The glory that the wood receives At sunset in its brazen leaves. **1856** BRYANT *Summer Wind* 16 Bright clouds, Motionless pillars of the brazen heavens.

3. *fig.* Hardened in effrontery; shameless.

1573 [see BRAZEN-FACE 1]. **1588** T. L. *To Ch. Rome* (1651) 11 Seeking (after their hard and brazen progenitors) t'establish a righteousnesse..of their owne. *a* **1639** W. WHATELEY *Prototypes* I. xix. (1640) 220 A brazen forehead, that is never a whit abashed. **1731** SWIFT *To Gay*, I knew a brazen minister of state, Who bore for twice ten years the public hate. **1853** ROBERTSON *Serm.* Ser. III. v. 70 The outcast woman whom human scorn would have hardened into brazen effrontery. **1869** PARKMAN *Disc. Gt. West.* x. (1875) 124 A rare monument of brazen mendacity.

4. Phrases. ***brazen age***: the third of the four mythological ages of mankind, said to come between the silver and the iron age. † ***brazen dish***: 'the standard dish or measure by which the wooden dishes for measuring the lead duties in Derbyshire are gauged' (Tapping's *Gloss. Lead Mining Terms* 1851).

1631 *Star. Chamb. Cases* (1886) 90 The deputy Barre Masters, measured the oare with a brasen dish. **1841** ELPHINSTONE *Hist. India* I. 257 These last bear some resemblance to the golden, silver, brazen, and iron ages of the Greeks.

5. *Comb.*, chiefly parasynthetic: **a.** *lit.* (often transl. Gr. χαλκο-, χαλκεο-), as ***brazen-floored, -footed, -gated, -headed, -hilted, -hoofed, -mailed, -pointed***; **b.** (*fig.*), as ***brazen-barking, -browed, -fisted, -fronted, -lunged***. Also BRAZEN-FACE, -ED.

1651 MORE in *Enthus. Tri.* (1656) 276 As Dionysius calls him, that *brazen-barking Cerberus. **1682** SIR T. BROWNE *Chr. Mor.* 42 Noon day vices & *brazen-brow'd iniquities. **1791** COWPER *Odyss.* VIII. 397 The *brazen-floor'd abode Of Jove. **1855** KINGSLEY *Heroes* IV. (1868) 132 The two *brazen-footed bulls. **1842** J. B. FRASER *Allee Neem.* I. 255 Thou *brazen-fronted knave. **1832** TENNYSON *Œnone* 137 The *brazen-headed spear. **1726** AMHERST *Terræ Fil.* xxxi. 165 A new bob-wig, and a *brazen-hilted sword. **1567** GOLDING *Ovid's Met.* VII. (1593) 155 The *brazen-hooffed bulles. **1596** FITZ-GEFFRAY *Sir F. Drake* (1881) 22 Encarving characters of memorie, In *brasen-leav'd books of eternitie. **1870** BRYANT *Iliad* I. I. 20 The Achaian warriors, *brazen-mailed.

brazen ('breɪz(ə)n), *v.* [f. the adj.]

1. *trans.* ***to brazen (out)***: to face impudently or as with a face of brass. Also with indefinite obj. ***to brazen it out.***

a **1555** LATIMER *Serm. & Rem.*, To brazen it. [K. Oliphant.] **1679** *Hist. Jetzer* Pref. A ij, Father Ireland.. brazen'd out the Court, and Hector'd the King's Evidence with one Witness upon another. **1712** ARBUTHNOT *John Bull* 86 He would talk saucily, lye, and brazen it out. **1763** BICKERSTAFF *Love in Village* III. ix, Would you brazen me, too? Take that (*boxes him*). **1777** SHERIDAN *Trip Scarb.* v. ii, I am resolved to brazen the brunt of the business out. **1873** DIXON *Two Queens* II. x. x. 212 The deed was done, and must be brazened out.

2. *trans.* To harden, make bold or reckless.

1884 TENNYSON *Becket* 193, I fear [they] Are braced and brazen'd up with Christmas wines For any murderous brawl.

brazen-face. [f. BRAZEN *a.* 3.]

1. As two words: An unabashed or hardened countenance. † ***to set a brazen face upon***: to meet with a bold front, to brazen out.

1573 G. HARVEY *Lett.-Bk.* (1884) 26 He purposid..to set a good brasin face on the matter. **1588** *Marprel. Epist.* (Arb.) 34 Hath not your brother London a notable brazen face to vse these men so for their owne?

2. As one word: A brazen-faced person.

1598 SHAKS. *Merry W.* IV. ii. 141 Well said Brazon-face, hold it out. **1682** N. O. *Boileau's Lutrin* II. 14 Not warn'd, the Brazen-face would out be flying Against the State.

brazen-faced ('breɪz(ə)nfeɪst), *a.* In 6 also **brazenfast.** [f. prec. + -ED².] With bold unblushing front, impudent, unabashed.

1571 GOLDING *Calvin on Ps.* xii. 5 With such brazenfaste boldnesse. **1605** SHAKS. *Lear* II. ii. 30 What a brazen-fac'd Varlet art thou to deny thou knowest me. **1619** *Pasquil's Palin.* (1877) 142 Blush (if you can) and are not brazen-faced. **1677** GILPIN *Dæmonol.* (1867) 82 Such open and brazen-faced assertions. **1846** *Sir R. de Coverley* II. 182 The brazen-faced termagant.

b. *humorously*, of things.

1864 MISS BRADDON *Doctor's Wife* i. 5 A big, new, brazen-faced house in the middle of the queer old High Street.

Hence **'brazen-facedly** (-feɪstlɪ), *adv.*

1624 GATAKER *Transubst.* 174 Onely boldly and brasin-facedly avouching that, etc. **1829** WILSON in *Blackw. Mag.* XXV. 384 She looked at you brazen-facedly.

brazenly ('breɪz(ə)nlɪ). *adv.* [f. BRAZEN *a.* + -LY².] In a brazen, impudent manner.

1714 MANDEVILLE *Fab. Bees* (1728) 12 All the Rogues cry'd brazenly Good Gods, had we but Honesty! **1840** CARLYLE *Heroes* vi. 313 That the..Christian Church.. brazenly went about pretending to pardon men's sins for metallic coined money. **1880** E. KIRKE *Garfield* 56.

'brazenness. [f. BRAZEN *a.* + -NESS.]

1. Brazen quality or appearance.

1731 in BAILEY II. **1755** in JOHNSON; and in mod. Dicts.

2. Effrontery, impudence.

1861 ELSIE GARRETT in *Gd. Words* 409 Stately, powerful comeliness, a thought defiant, but not to brazenness.

brazenry ('breɪz(ə)nrɪ). [f. as prec. + -RY.] Brazen assertion; a matter of brazenness.

1868 KINGLAKE *Crimea* IV. iv. 57 Coming from Lord Lucan, this language was no vulgar brazenry.

† **braze'raine.** *Obs. rare*⁻¹. = BRAZIER².

1623 FAVINE *Theat. Hon.* II. xii. 167 Throwe strong Gummes and Perfumes into the Cassolet and Brazeraine burning continually.

brazier¹ ('breɪzɪə(r), -ʒ(ɪ)ə(r)). Forms: 5-6 brasyer, 6 braseer, 5-8 brasier, 6- brazier. [f. BRAZE *v.* (or ? BRASS *sb.*) + -IER; cf. *glazier, grazier.*] One who works in brass.

c **1400** *Destr. Troy* 1589 Belmakers, bokebynders, brasiers fyn. *c* **1440** *Promp. Parv.* 47 Brasyere, *erarius.* **1503** *Act 19 Hen. VII*, vi. §1 The seid Craftez of Peweterer and Braseer. **1530** PALSGR. 200/2 Brasyer, *fondevr.* **1613** SHAKS. *Hen. VIII*, v. iv. 42 He should be a Brasier by his face. **1724** SWIFT *Drapier's Lett.* Wks. 1755 V. II. 15 Mr. Wood made his half-pence of such base metal..that the brazier would hardly give you above a penny of good money for a shilling of his. **1852** MISS YONGE *Cameos* (1877) II. xxviii. 301 A brazier named Lambert..began to harangue the people.

brazier² ('breɪzɪə(r), -ʒ(ɪ)ə(r)). Forms: 7-8 brasiere, 8 brazire, 8- brazier (9 brasier). [a. F. *brasier*, f. *braise* hot coals. The spellings *brasiere, brazire*, indicate an earlier pronunc. (-'ɪə(r)), as in *grenadier*, etc.; cf. BRASERO.] A large flat pan or tray for holding burning charcoal, etc.

1690 *Fop Dict.*, *Brasiere*, a large Vessel, or moving-Hearth of Silver for Coaks, transportable into any Room, much used in Spain. **1766** SMOLLETT *Trav.* 122 They warm their apartments with a brasiere of charcoal. **1792** *Gentl. Mag.* LXII. I. 238 Two brazires were constantly kept burning in it. **1865** DICKENS *Mut. Fr.* iii. 13 The fire was in a rusty brazier, not fitted to the hearth.

braziery ('breɪzɪərɪ, -ʒ(ɪ)ərɪ). [f. BRAZIER¹ + -Y³.] Brazier's work; also *concr.*

1795 J. AIKIN *Manchester* 294 Wigan has long been noted for..braziery work..The braziery is now on the decline. **1805** W. TAYLOR in *Ann. Rev.* III. 244 Hence an increased consumption of braziery and pottery. **1872** YEATS *Techn. Hist. Comm.* 355 The making of brass tubing is another branch of braziery.

Brazil¹ (brə'zɪl). Forms: 4-7 brasile, brasill, 4-8 brasil, 5 brasyl(l)e, braysyle, 6 brasell, brasyll, brasaill, brassell, bresyle, 6-7 brazel(l, bresil(l, 7 brasel, brazile, -ill, 7- brazil. [? a. Sp. (also Pg.) *brasil* or It. *brasile*; corresp. to F. *brésil*, Pr. *bresil, brezilh*, in OF. *berzi, bresis*, OIt. *verzino*, in med.L. ? *brezellum, brasilium, bresillum, braxile*: of unknown origin; perh. a corruption of an oriental name of the dye-wood originally so called. On the discovery of an allied species, also yielding a dye, in South America, the territory where it grew was called *terra de brasil*, 'red-dye-wood land', afterwards abbreviated to *Brasil* 'Brazil'. *Brazil-wood* was thus not named from the country, but the converse was the case. Formerly pronounced in Eng. '*brazil*, as shown by rimes and spellings.

Conjectural etymologies are F. *briser* to break, *brésiller* to crumble (as if the wood arrived in a broken state); also F. *braise*, Sp. *brasa* 'glowing coal' (from its colour); also Arab. *wars* saffron, in some parts perhaps pronounced *vars, vers* (cf. It. *verzino*). See Diez, Littré.]

I. The substance.

1. Originally, the name of the hard brownish-red wood of an East Indian tree, known as Sappan (*Cæsalpinia Sappan*), from which dyers obtain a red colour. After the discovery of the New World, the name was extended and gradually transferred to the similar wood of a South American species (*C. echinata*), which has given its name to the land of Brazil, and to other species, natives of the West Indies and Central America, 'all valuable to the dyer, producing various tints of red, orange, and peach colour'.

1386 [see 2]. *c* **1440** *Promp. Parv.* 47 Brasyle, *gaudo uel lignum Alexandrinum.* **1544** ASCHAM *Toxoph.* (Arb.) 113 As for brasell, Elme, Wych and Asshe, experience doth proue them to be but meane for bowes. **1553** EDEN *Treat. New Ind.* (Arb.) 20 *Presilium* or brasyll, cometh from Darnasseri.. almost cc. leages from Calicut. **1553** —— *Decades W. Ind.* I. IV. (Arb.) 80 None other trees then brasile, whiche the Italians caule *Verzino.* *Ibid.* 199 Of the bresyle. **1594** BLUNDEVIL *Exerc.* v. (ed. 7) 570 The Province Brasilia tooke his name of the wood called Brasill. **1623** S. HARWOOD *Propag. Plants* III. ii. (1668) 85 A little hand-bill..helved of Ivory, box, or brasil. **1801** STRUTT *Sports & Past.* II. i. 53 Bows were sometimes made of brazil.

b. Now usually called **Brazil-wood.**

1530 PALSGR. 200/2 Brasell tre to dye with, *bresil.* **1559** MORWYNG *Evonym.* 209 Of the coloure of the bresill wode. **1604** E. G. tr. *Acosta's Hist. Indies* IV. xxix. 289, 130 quintalles of Bresill wood. **1678** SALMON *Pharmacop. Lond.* iv. 38 Brasil shrub, cold and dry and astringent. **1732** *Acc. Workhouses* 86 Grinding Brazil Wood, and other things for dying. **1853** TH. ROSS tr. *Humboldt's Trav.* III. xxvii. 141 To mark the finest trunks of Brazil-wood. **1868** *Treas. Bot.* 188.

c. *attrib.* Of Brazil-wood; also *fig.*

1577 *Will of W. Olyuer* (Somerset Ho.), Unto John Maclee my brasyll staffe. **1598** MARSTON *Met. Pigmalion's Image* Sat. 2. 145 Blesse his sweet honour's running brasell boule. **1613** W. BROWNE *Brit. Past.* II. iii. (1772) II. 118 Her left hand held a knotty Brasill bow. **1624** T. SCOT *2d Pt. Vox Pop.* 7 Resting himselfe vpon a little Brasill staffe. **1710** *Lond. Gaz.* No. 4654/3, 1 Coffee-Pot with a Brasil Handle.

d. Taken as the type of hardness (whence formerly turned into bowls for bowling): thence the simile ***as hard as brazil*** still common dialectally, and sometimes explained as referring to the next word. Pronounced ('bræzɪl, 'bræz(ə)l).

1635 QUARLES *Embl.* III. v. (1718) 146 Are my bones brazil, or my flesh of oak? *Ibid.* I. x. (1718) 42 Turn thou my Brazil thoughts anew. **1877** PEACOCK *N.W. Linc. Gloss.* (E.D.S.) s.v. 'It's as hard as brazil'. **1879** MISS JACKSON *Shropsh. Gloss.* **1879** *Athenæum* 19 July 73 'As hard as Brazil', is a common saying over a great part, perhaps the whole, of England.

†**2.** The dye-stuff and dye yielded by this wood.

c **1386** CHAUCER *Nun's Pr.* '*End-Link*' 13 His colour for to dyghen With brasile [-il, -ill] ne with greyn of Portyngale. *c* **1475** *E.E. Misc.* (1855) 77 To make brasyle to flouryche letterys or to reule with bokys. **1532-3** *Act. 24 Hen. VIII*, ii, Diers..haue vsed deceyuable waies in dyeng with brasell and such other lyke subtilties. **1546** *Inv. Ch. Goods Surrey* 107 Item for brassell xij*d.* **1578** LYTE *Dodoens* v. ii. 547 One may write as faire a red as with roset made of Brasill. **1627** BACON *Sylva* §857 A small Quantity of Saffron will Tinct more then a very great Quantity of Brasil. **1669** W. SIMPSON *Hydrol. Chym.* 41 The Alkalizate Salts are used..in water for the extraction of Brasil.

b. *transf.* Stuff dyed with brazil, 'scarlet' cloth.

1389 R. WIMBELDON *Serm.* (Helmingham MS. 34. See also Foxe *A. & M.* I. 626/1) Allas, allas, þat greete cite þat was cloþid wiþ bys and purpur and brasile [Rev. xviii. 16 κόκκινον, *cocco*, 'scarlet'].

c. *attrib.*

a **1600** in Nichols' *Progr. Q. Eliz.* III. 510 A saufegarde of brasell-colour. **1703** *Art's Improv.* I. 28 Wash it over several times with Brasil Water, till you like the Colour.

II. The country, and its products.

3. A large country of South America, also called 'the Brazils'. Also *attrib.* and in *comb.*

1555 EDEN *Decades W. Ind.* (Arb.) 385 The Portugales.. sayle to America or the lande of Brasile. **1709** *Lond. Gaz.* No. 4532/3 Loaden..with Brazil-Sugar. **1712** W. ROGERS *Voy.* (1718) 53 The Portuguese nam'd it Brazile, from the red wood of that name. **1864** *Times* 26 Oct., A first-class railway for the Brazils. **1875** BEDFORD *Sailor's Pocket-bk.* iv. (ed. 2) 108 The Brazil Current is a branch of the Equatorial. **1883** BURTON & CAMERON *To Gold Coast* I. i. 18 The voyager bound Brazilwards.

4. Brazil-nut: the seed of *Bertholletia excelsa* (N.O. *Lecythidaceæ*), a lofty tree which forms large forests in Brazil; the fruit consists of a round wooden capsule, packed with about two dozen of these triquetrous 'nuts'.

1830 LINDLEY *Nat. Syst. Bot.* 116 The Souari..Nuts, or Brazil Nuts of the shops, the kernel of which is one of the most delicious fruits of the nut kind. **1852** TH. ROSS tr. *Humboldt's Trav.* II. xxiii. 390 Juvia-trees, which furnish the triangular nuts called in Europe the almonds of the Amazon, or Brazil-nuts. **1864** BATES *Nat. Amazon* viii. 230 Colossal examples of the Brazil nut tree.

Hence **Bra'zilian** *a.* and *sb.*

1607 TOPSELL *Four-f. Beasts* 19 By Brasilians..they are.. called Sagoines. *Ibid.* 705, I take it to be a Brasilian Hedghog. **1628** DRAKE *World Encompassed* 14 It is not likely that many doe use it to that end, which the Brasilians doe. *c* **1650** in *Phenix* (1708) II. 364 Those barbarous Brasilians. **1769** WATSON in *Phil. Trans.* LIX. 380 The Brasilean plants. **1825** C. WATERTON *Wanderings in S. Amer.* ii. 95 The Brazilians were told, that..education would go on. **1836** MARRYAT *Pirate* vii, There were..Brazilians. **1851** K. H. DIGBY *Compitum* V. viii. 313 Accompanying him to the Brazilian frontier. **1860** [see ARGENTINE *sb.*² 1]. *a* **1910** W. JAMES *Memories & Stud.* (1911) i. 9 Certain officials of the Brazilian empire smiled. **1961** G. DURRELL *Whispering Land* vi. 153 Two pigmy Brazilian rabbits, with ginger paws and white spectacles of fur round their eyes.

brazil ('bræzɪl), *sb.*² *dial.* Also **brassil, brazill, brazzil, brazzle.** [? f. BRASS. Perh. better spelt *brassil*; but *brazzle* is the common dialect pronunciation.]

1. A miners' name in the midland counties for iron pyrites.

1747 HOOSON *Miner's Dict.* O ij, Brassil, a ponderous shining Substance, we do not know that it is of any Value to hold any Metal at all. **1879** MISS JACKSON *Shropsh. Gloss.* s.v., Brazil is found chiefly in the 'yard coal'. **1884** PROF. C. LAPWORTH (in letter), I have heard the remark 'the coal is a poor one and full of brazzle'.

2. Coal containing much pyrites; *spec.* applied to ' the middle seam of the Great Thick Coal of South Staffordshire, which is characterized by the unfailing presence of a seam of iron pyrites, and has been locally known as the *Brazzles* from time immemorial; hence transferred to other hard coals of similar character.' (Prof. C. Lapworth).

1853 JUKES *Geol. S. Staff. Coalf.* 35 *note*, Brassil is a term generally used to denote a rough impure coal; sometimes to denote the presence of much iron pyrites. **1859** —— *Geol. Survey Mem. S. Staff. Coalf.* 173.

¶ *as hard as brazil*: see prec.

braziletto (bræzɪˈlɛtəʊ). Forms: 7 **brasiletta, brazilette,** 7–8 **brazel(l)etto,** 8 **brazil(l)etta,** 9 **brazilletto,** 7– **brasiletto,** 8– **braziletto.** [? ad. Sp., Pg. *brasilete* 'Jamaica-wood', dim. of *brasil*, BRAZIL-(wood).] One or more species of dyewood, inferior to Brazil-wood, imported from Jamaica and adjacent islands (*Cæsalpinia brasiliensis* and *crista*; now generally referred to a distinct genus *Peltophorum*).

1656 *Cromwell's Bk. Rates, Woods*, Brazeletto or Jamaica wood. **1661** HICKERINGILL *Jamaica* 22 Abundant plenty of choice Timber trees and Wood for the Dyer's use, as Fustick, Brasiletta. **1686** *Lond. Gaz.* No. 2186/1, 12 thousand pounds of Brazilette wood. **1725** SLOANE *Jamaica* II 184 Brasiletto-wood is very like Log-wood.. It grows in Jamaica. **1782** P. H. BRUCE *Mem.* XII. 418 Two negroes..at work for their master in the woods, cutting brazilletta. **1789** *Act 27 Geo. III*, xiii. Sched. s.v. *Wood*, Brazilletto or Jamaica Wood for dyers. **1868** *Treas. Bot.* 858 *Peltophorum Linnæi*, otherwise called *Cæsalpinia brasiliensis* yields the orange-coloured dyewood..Braziletto-wood. The wood of *P. Vogelianum*, which is a native of Brazil, is also called Braziletto or Sobrazil. **1884** MILLER *Plant-n.*, *Cæsalpinia crista*, Bahama Braziletto.

brazilianite (brəˈzɪlɪənaɪt). *Min.* [f. BRAZIL[1] 3 (where it was first discovered) + -IAN + -ITE[1] 2 b.] †**1.** = WAVELLITE. *Obs.*

1818 J. MAWE *Descr. Catal. Min.* (ed. 3) 54 Wavellite ..*Brazilianite*. Occurs massive; botroidal; and crystallized in flat rhombic prisms.

2. A mineral consisting of a basic phosphate of sodium and aluminium.

1945 POUGH & HENDERSON in *Amer. Mineralogist* XXX. 574 The authors decided that such an important mineral should bear the name of its country of origin... Our.. choice was *brazilianite*. **1947** *Times* 9 Jan. 7/4 A new mineral of gem quality named Brazilianite.

brazilin (ˈbræzɪlɪn). [f. BRAZIL + -IN.] The red colouring-matter of Brazil-wood.

1863 WATTS *Dict. Chem.* I. 656 Brazilin crystallises by spontaneous evaporation in reddish yellow needles.

brazilite (brəˈzɪlaɪt). *Min.* [ad. G. *Brazilit* (Hussak 1892, in *Neues Jahrb. für Min.* II. 141), f. BRAZIL[1] 3 (where it was first discovered) + -ITE[1] 2 b.] = BADDELEYITE.

1893 L. FLETCHER in *Min. Mag.* X. 158 Since the results of the above investigation [on Baddeleyite]..a description of a new mineral, *Brazilite*, has appeared in the *Neues Jahrbuch für Mineralogie*..as part of a letter sent by Dr. Hussak from Brazil. *Ibid.* 160 Dr. Hussak, with characteristic courtesy, offers to simplify mineralogical nomenclature by withdrawing the name Brazilite. **1955** [see BADDELEYITE].

brazing (ˈbreɪzɪŋ), *vbl. sb.* [f. BRAZE *v.*[1], [2] + -ING[1].] The action of the verbs BRAZE; **a.** passing over hot coals; **b.** soldering; **c.** coating with brass.

1551 TURNER *Herbal* 81 It maketh black scarres to be whyte, and taketh awaye the blacke colour of brasynge. **1869** *Student* II. 73 All the joints..are made tight by soldering or brazing. **1886** *Cyclist* 25 Aug. 1194/1 Wanted, a good bicycle fitter, able to do his own brazing.

brazire, obs. form of BRAZIER[2].

brazzle: see BRAZIL *sb.*[2]

bre, obs. variant of BREE, *Sc.*

breach (briːtʃ), *sb.* Also 3–6 **breche,** 5 **bryg,** 6 *Sc.* **brache,** 7 **bretch,** ? 8 **breech.** [ME. *breche*, partly perh. repr. OE. *bryce*, *brice* (:—OTeut. **bruki-z* from **brek-*: see BREAK), which however gave in early ME. BRUCHE; partly a. F. *brèche*, in same sense but chiefly concrete. The obvious relation of *break*, *breach*, as in *speak*, *speech*, would tend to make *breche*, *breach* the prevailing form.]

I. The action of breaking.

†**1. a.** The physical action of breaking; the fact of being broken; breakage, fracture. *Obs.*

a **1000** *Guthlac* 670 (Gr.) Ne sy him banes bryce. *a* **1300** *Cursor M.* 8220 (Gött.) Sua depe the rotis samen kest miht ne man þeden winne widuten breche [*v.r.* brekyng]. **1610** HOLLAND *Camden's Brit.* I. 346 By violence of bretch and ruins great. **1629** GAULE *Holy Madn.* 295 The casuall breach of a Crystall Glasse. **1676** HALE *Contempl.* I. 52 The breach of a vein..may put a period to all those pleasures.

†**b.** *breach of the day*: 'break' of day. *Obs.*

1579 FENTON *Guicciard.* XIV. (1599) 667 The assault began about the breach of the day.

2. The breaking of waves on a coast or over a vessel; hence, the nautical phr. ***clean, clear breach.***

1601 SHAKS. *Twel. N.* II. i. 23 Before you tooke me from breach of the sea. **1719** DE FOE *Crusoe* iii, She [the boat] would be dashed in..pieces by the breach of the sea. **1867** SMYTH *Sailor's Word-bk.* 129 *Clear breach*, the waves rolling clean over without breaking..*Clean-breach*, when masts and every object on deck is swept away.

3. *fig.* The breaking of a command, rule, engagement, duty, or of any legal or moral bond or obligation; violation, infraction: common in such phrases as ***breach of contract, covenant, faith, promise, trust.***

[*c* **1025** *Eccl. Laws of Cnut* 24 Wið æþhwylcne æwbryce.] **1382** WYCLIF *Jer.* iii. 13 To the Lord thi God thou hast do lawe breche. *c* **1440** *York Myst.* v. 143 Lorde, Eue garte me do wronge and to þat bryg me brought. **1533–4** *Act 25 Hen. VIII*, xvii, Attempted the breche or violacion of the same statutes. **1573** G. HARVEY *Lett.-bk.* (1884) 13 Better then the breach of ani custum. **1588** SHAKS. *L.L.L.* II. i. 170 Receiue such welcome..As Honour, without breach of Honour may Make tender of. **1605** —— *Lear* I. ii. 162 Nuptial breaches. **1612** T. TAYLOR *Comm. Titus* iii. 1 Who..liue in the breach of Gods commaundement. **1636** MASSINGER *Bashful Lover* IV. ii, A virtue, and not to be blended With vicious breach of faith. **1659** HAMMOND *On Ps.* xxv. 7 The breaches innumerable, wherewith I have..offended against thee. **1711** STEELE *Spect.* No. 262 ¶7 Nor shall I look upon it as any Breach of Charity. **1764** REID *Inquiry* ii. §6. 109 They can..break them and be punished for the breach. **1803** WELLINGTON in Gurw. *Disp.* II. 174 In breach of your promises to me. **1833** HT. MARTINEAU *Manch. Strike* iv. 53 Convicted of a breach of contract. **1834** ARNOLD *Life & Cor.* (1844) I. vii. 379 What it would be a breach of duty in me to omit. **1879** STUBBS *Const. Hist.* II. xvi. 370 The breach of the truce by the Scots.

b. *spec.* and *techn.*, as **breach of arrestment,** illegal disposal of property which has been 'attached', or placed under the control of a law-court; **breach of close,** unlawful entry upon private ground, trespass; **breach of (the) peace,** an infringement or violation of the public peace by an affray, riot, or other disturbance; **breach of pound,** the action of breaking into a pound or similar enclosure without right or warrant; **breach of prison,** escape of a prisoner from confinement; **breach of privilege,** a violation of the rights of a privileged body; **breach of promise,** *gen.* as in prec. sense; *spec.* = breach of promise to marry.

1590 SHAKES. *Com. Err.* IV. i. 49 You vse this dalliance to excuse Your breach of promise to the Porpentine. **1613** [see PROMISE *sb.* 1]. **1650** R. STAPYLTON *Strada's Low-C. Warres* ii. 30 They..might fairly declaim against [it] by the name of Breach of Priviledge. **1671** F. PHILIPPS *Reg. Necess.* 50 For the breach of the peace 120 shillings. **1786** PALEY *Mor. Philos.* (ed. 2) III. I. xvi. 164 God will punish false swearing with more severity than a simple lie, or breach of promise. **1817** *Parl. Deb.* 796 The Speaker said..the House should pronounce, whether the passage in the work..was or was not a breach of privilege. **1865** *Derby Mercury* 1 Mar., Alleged contempt of that House, and a breach of its privileges. *Mod.* The damages in a breach-of-promise case. **1895** G. B. SHAW *Shaw on Theatre* (1958) 61 Trial by Jury is..unintelligible except as a satire on..the breach-of-promise suit. **1949** M. MEAD *Male & Female* xv. 299 Breach-of-promise cases are a silly excrescence in a world in which women do half the proposing.

c. In colloq. use, short for *breach of promise*.

1840 DICKENS *Old Cur. Shop* viii, There's the chance of an action for breach. **1905** *Daily Chron.* 16 Aug. 6/7 'The breach action was not brought by her,' said Mr. Burnett, opening the present proceedings on behalf of the major. *Ibid.*, At the breach trial.

†**4.** An irruption *into*; an infringement *upon*; an inroad, injurious assault. *Obs.*

1579 LYLY *Euphues* (Arb.) 100 The Axiomaes of Aristotle ..have sodeinley made..a breach into my mind. **1611** BIBLE *1 Chron.* xiii. 11 The Lord had made a breach vpon Vzza. **1647** WARD *Simp. Cobler* 58 Your connivence with the Irish butcheries, your forgetfull breaches upon the Parliament. *a* **1674** CLARENDON (J.) This breach upon kingly power. **1751** ADDISON *Freeholder* No. 13. 77 Innocent of the great Breach which is made upon Government.

5. a. A breaking of relations (*of* union or continuity).

1625 BACON *Unity in Relig., Ess.* (Arb.) 423 Nothing, doth so much..drive Men out of the Church, as Breach of Unity. **1768** BLACKSTONE *Comm.* III. 162 By the breach and dissolution of..the relation itself. **1775** DE LOLME *Eng. Const.* I. i. (1784) 14 They completed the breach of those feeble ties. *Mod.* It could not be done without a breach of continuity.

b. *absol.* A break-up of friendly relations; rupture, separation, difference, disagreement, quarrel.

1573 G. HARVEY *Lett.-bk.* (1884) 17 A little breach betwixt thes twoo and me was the tru and onli caus of al thes sturs. **1580** BARET *Alv.* B 1201 Breach of friendes. **1604** SHAKS. *Oth.* IV. i. 238 There's falne betweene him, & my Lord, An vnkind breach. **1713** BURNET *Own Time* (1766) II. 87 A great breach was like to follow. **1862** STANLEY *Jew. Ch.* (1877) I. ix. 186 The nearest approach to a breach was.. when their monument of stones was mistaken..for an altar.

6. The leaping of a whale clear out of the water.

a **1843** *Penny Cycl.* XXVII. 294/2 The breach may be seen in a clear day from the mast-head at a distance of six miles.

II. The product of breaking.

7. A physically broken or ruptured condition of anything; a broken, fractured, damaged, or injured spot, place, or part; an injury.

†**a.** of the body. *Obs.*

1398 TREVISA *Barth. De P.R.* VII. lv. (1495) 270 Yf that breche [hernia] is grete and olde and wyth brekyng of the synewe it is sondred vneth or neuer. **1559** MORWYNG *Evonym.* 118 It cureth also fistulas, old breaches, and temporall byles. **1665** G. HAVERS *P. della Valle's Trav. E. India* 395 Shewing him his hand and his other breaches.

b. A disrupted place, gap, or fissure, caused by the separation of continuous parts; a break.

1530 PALSGR. 201/1 Breche where water breke in, *breche*. **1555** EDEN *Decades W. Ind.* (Arb.) 320 The yearth hath many great chynkes or breaches. **1624** CAPT. SMITH *Virginia* v. 174 The salt water..entred at the large breaches of their poore wooden castle. **1653** MANTON *Exp. James* iii. 5 Small breaches in a sea-bank let in great inundations. **1750** JOHNSON *Rambl.* No. 79 §11 The crew implore the liberty of repairing their breaches.

c. *esp.* 'A gap in a fortification made by a battery' (J.). Hence ***to stand in the breach*** (often *fig.*).

1597 SHAKS. *2 Hen. IV*, II. iv. 55 To come off the Breach, with his Pike bent brauely. **1598** BARRET *Theor. Warres* V. iv. 138 To ruinate their Curtine, and make good breaches. **1611** BIBLE *Ps.* cvi. 23 Had not Moses his chosen stood before him in the breach [COVERDALE, gap]. **1665** MANLEY *Grotius' Low-C. Warrs* 363 The Town was easily gained by Scaling Ladders, and Breaches. **1712** STEELE *Spect.* No. 428 ¶2 No Soldier entering a Breach adventures more for Honour. **1799** WELLINGTON *Let.* in Gurw. *Disp.* I. 30 On the 3rd of May the breach appeared to be practicable. **1814** SCOTT *Wav.* xiii, Being the first to mount the breach.

d. *fig.*

1605 SHAKS. *Lear* IV. vii. 15 Cure this great breach in his abused Nature. **1649** JER. TAYLOR *Gt. Exemp.* III. Ded. Let., To bind up the great breaches of my little fortune. **1657** —— in *Four C. Eng. Lett.* 106 By your wise counsel and comfort stand in the breaches of your own family. **1710** SHAFTESB. *Charac.* (1737) III. 397 An unhappy Breach in my Health.. forc'd me to seek these foreign Climates. **1722** DE FOE *Moll Fl.* (1840) 132 Vice breaks in at the breaches of decency. **1836** MARRYAT *Midsh. Easy* xviii. 63 To heal the breach in his wounded honour.

†**8.** Surf made by the sea breaking over rocks; broken water, breakers. *Obs.*

1624 CAPT. SMITH *Virginia* (1629) 19 We found many shoules and breaches. **1626** —— *Accid. Yng. Seamen* 18 A shoule, a ledge of rockes, a breach, a shallow water. **1707** *Lond. Gaz.* No. 4380/3 The Royal Anne..saw several Breaches, and soon after, the Rocks above Water.

†**9.** A break in a coast, a bay, harbour. *Obs.* Cf. BREAK *sb.*[1] 7 b.

1611 BIBLE *Judges* v. 17 Asher continued on the sea shore and abode in his breaches [*Vulg.* portubus, WYCLIF hauens].

†**10.** A break in continuity, an interruption, interval; a division marked by breaks or intervals.

1589 PUTTENHAM *Eng. Poesie* I. xix. (Arb.) 57 By breaches or diuisions to be more commodiously song to the harpe. *Ibid.* xxvi. 65 This Epithalamie was deuided by breaches into three partes..The first breach was song at the first parte of the night. **1590** SPENSER *F.Q.* III. iv. 35 And all her sister Nymphes..Supplide her sobbing breaches with sad complement.

11. A condition of broken relations; a gap in sentiment or sympathy.

1745 WESLEY *Answ. Ch.* 1, I do not want..to widen the Breach between us. **1816** SCOTT *Antiq.* v, The breach was speedily made up between them. **1863** BRIGHT *Sp. Amer.* (1876) 138 Create an everlasting breach between the people of England and the people of the United States of America.

12. A piece of land broken up by the plough. *dial.*

1594 PLAT *Jewel-ho.* I. 43 *marg.*, Erith breaches [that surrounded leuell at Erith]. —— *New Sorte of Soyle* 44 That exceeding fertilitie which I have herd commended in those two breaches, even by the severall farmers thereof.

1864 CAPERN *Devon Provinc.*, *Breach*, a plot of land prepared for another crop.

breach (briːtʃ), *v.* [f. the sb.]

1. *trans.* To make a breach in (a wall, defence, natural boundary, etc.); to break through.

1803 WELLINGTON *Let.* in Gurw. *Disp.* II. 479 If the wall ..should be breached when the place shall be stormed. **1817** JAS. MILL *Brit. India* II. IV. iv. 149 The English had breached the fort. **1845** DARWIN *Voy. Nat.* xx. (1852) 477 Every reef of the fringing class is breached by a narrow gateway in front of the smallest rivulet. **1878** HUXLEY *Physiogr.* 193 It often happens that the lava..breaches one side of the conical hill.

b. *fig.*; *spec.* in Financial and Stock Exchange jargon, to go beyond (above or below) (a figure). Cf. BREAK *v.* 9 c.

1547 BOORDE *Brev. Health* ccliii. 85 b, [Obliviousness] may come to yonge men and women whan theyr mynde is bryched.

1979 *Economist* 23 June 81/1 When the ecu limits are breached, the offending currency is supposed to take action. **1982** *Observer* 17 Oct. 18/3 London's 'FT' 30-share index breached the 600 mark. **1984** *Economist* 10 Mar. 52/2 So far, Mr Nakasone has not dared to breach the 1% mark.

†**2.** *intr.* To make or cause a breach; to quarrel, separate. *Obs.*

1573 TUSSER *Husb.* 2nd Ep. Ded. xi, At first for want of teaching, At first for trifles breaching. **1641** R. BROOKE *Eng. Episc.* I. ix. 52 If the Church will breach (with the Anabaptists).

3. *Naut.* Of whales: To leap out of the water.

a **1843** See BREACHING. **1854** *Chamb. Journ.* I. 53 'There she blows again!.. There she breaches.' **1866** KINGSLEY *Herew.* v. 115 They saw a whale spouting and breaching.

breach(e, obs. form of BREECH.

breached (ˈbriːtʃt, ˈbriːtʃɪd), *ppl. a.* [f. prec. + -ED.] Pierced or cleft with a breach; rent, torn. Also *fig.*

1547 BOORDE *Brev. Health* ccliii. 85 b, A medecine for Bryched persones, I do nat knowe. *a* **1649** DRUMM. OF HAWTH. *Poems* Wks. (1711) 35/2 Conquering squadrons.. Entring a breached city. **1762–9** FALCONER *Shipwr.* II. 719 Our sea-breach'd vessel. **1854** H. MILLER *Sch. & Schm.* (1858) 255 Attired in a sadly-breached suit of Aberdeen grey.

ˈ**breacher.** [f. as prec. + -ER[1].] One who makes or commits a breach.

1697 *Disc. Swearing* 16 There is a very terrible Threatning annext against the Breachers of it [a commandment].

ˈbreachful, *a.* [f. BREACH *sb.* + -FUL.] Full of breaches.

1864 in WEBSTER.

†**ˈbreachily**, *adv. Obs. rare.* [f. BREACHY *a.*[1] + -LY[2].] In a 'breachy' manner.

1662 J. CHANDLER *Van Helmont's Oriat.* 115 New [cheese] waxeth breachily sharp, which doth easily stir up torments or wringings in a soure stomach.

ˈbreaching, *vbl. sb.* [f. BREACH *v.* + -ING[1].]

1. The action of making a breach in, or of breaking through (a wall, etc.): also *attrib.*

1803 WELLINGTON *Let.* in Gurw. *Disp.* II. 479 If the wall should be so bad as not to require breaching. **1833** *Fraser's Mag.* VIII. 317 The subsequent breaching of the Spanish fortresses. **1855** PRESCOTT *Philip II*, I. IV. iii. 417 The breaching artillery consisted of forty-three guns. **1878** *Macm. Mag.* Jan. 252/1 The breaching of tanks from excessive rain.

2. See quot., and cf. BREACH *sb.* 6 and *v.* 3.

a **1843** *Penny Cycl.* XXVII. 294/2 Other habits of this whale, such as 'breaching', or leaping clear out of the water and falling back again on its side. **1885** *Longm. Mag.* 407.

†**ˈbreachy**, *a.*[1] *Obs.* or *dial.* [Cf. BRACKY.] Brackish. (In Chandler, perh. 'of alkaline taste'.)

1662 J. CHANDLER *Van Helmont's Oriat.* 158 Writers have distinguished..Odours, and Savours, as sweet, bitter, salt, sharp, breachy, soure. **1875** PARISH *Sussex Gloss.* (E.D.S.), *Breachy*, brackish, applied to water.

breachy (ˈbriːtʃɪ), *a.*[2] Chiefly *U. S.* [f. BREACH + -Y[1].]

1. Of horses and cattle: Apt to break fences, and get out of inclosures.

1780 E. PARKMAN *Diary* (1899) 275 To my sorrow, my Oxen have been breachy at Mr. Isaac Parker's and let in Cattle with them into his Cornfield. **1800** Addison *Amer. Law Rep.* 258 McKinney's horses were breachy. **1810** *Nat. Hist.* in *Ann. Reg.* 628/2, I never saw a breachy Tunis sheep. **1838** HALIBURTON *Clockm.* I. 141 They are the most breachy of the two and ought to go to pound themselves. **1899** A. BROWN *Tiverton Tales* 133 That cussed breachy cow.. hooked it [*sc.* a fence] down.

2. Characterized by breaches.

bread (brɛd), *sb.*[1] Forms: 1 bréad, 2–3 bread, (2 brad), 2–3 bræd, 2–7 bred, (3–5 bredd), 3–6 brede, (4 bryad, bryead), 4–6 breed(e, 5–7 breade, 6– bread, 5– *Sc.* breid, (6–7 bredde, 7 braid, 9 *dial.* brade). [OE. *bréad*, pl. *bréadru*: repr. WGer. **braud*, and corresp. to OFris. *brâd*, OS. *brôd* (MDu. *broot-de*, Du. *brood*, LG. *brôd*, *brood*), OHG., MHG. *brôt* (Ger. *brod*, *brot*); ON. *brauð* (Sw., Da. *bröd*):—OTeut. **braudoz-*, a neuter *-os* stem, not preserved in Gothic. The original Teutonic name for bread survives in the modern LOAF (OE. *hláf*, OHG. *hleib*, ON. *hleifr*, Goth. *hlaifs*, *hlaibs*, OTeut. **hlaibo-z*) formerly in all the langs. in the sense of 'bread' and 'loaf'. *Braudoz-*, *brôd*, *bréad*, appears to have originally meant 'piece, bit, fragment, L. *frustum*': but already in OS. and OHG. it had the acquired sense of 'bread'; 'OHG. shows no clear distinction of meaning between *brôt* and *hleib*' (Sievers). In OE. *bréad* is rare: the later Blickling Glosses have the pl. *bréadru*, 'frusta' (i.e. 'pieces, bits'). The other examples are all Northumbrian, in the Lindisfarne (& Rushw.) gloss; viz. *John* xiii. 27, 30 translating *buccella*, the 'mouthful' given to Judas, for which the Ags. Gospels have *bitan*, Wyclif *morsel*, Rhemish *morsel*. In verse 26 where the Vulgate twice renders the same Gr. word (ψωμίον bit, piece) by 'panem', later versions 'bread', the Ags. has *hláf*, Lindisf. *laf*, which seems to show that *bréad* was not yet identified with *panis*. But in *John* vi. 23, *bréad* actually represents *panem* of the Vulgate (= ἄρτον), and *hláf* of the Ags. version: where however *broken bread* is in question. Before 1200 *bread* had quite displaced *hláf* as the name of the substance, leaving to the latter the sense 'loaf' which it has since retained. It thus appears that a word originally meaning 'piece, bit, *frustum*', has passed through the senses of 'piece of bread', 'broken bread', into that of 'bread' as a substance; while at the same time the original word for 'bread, loaf, *panis*' has been restricted to the undivided article as shaped and baked, the 'loaf'. The Lowland Scotch and north. dial. use of *piece* illustrates anew the first step in this transition, for it is the regular word for a piece of bread, as in 'give the bairn a piece', 'a beggar asking a piece', a 'piece-poke', a 'gie's-a-piece' i.e. a beggar.

So also in Slovenish, '*kruh*, "bread" is literally "a piece, something broken off"' (Miklosich, *Etym. Wbch. Slav. Spr.* 143).

With *brôd*, *bréad*, Prof. Sievers connects the Ger. *brosame* crumb, in OHG. *brôsma*, OS. *brôsmo*:—OTeut. *braudsmon-*, the sense of which confirms the original meaning of **braudoz-*, and points to some root having the sense of 'break'. OE. *bréotan* does not answer phonetically. (The preceding facts are, of course, quite inconsistent with the conjecture that *bread* is a deriv. of the verb-root *bru* to BREW.)]

I. †**1.** (Only in OE.) Bit, piece, morsel (of food). See above in Etymology.

2. a. A well-known article of food prepared by moistening, kneading, and baking meal or flour, generally with the addition of yeast or leaven.

c **950** *Lindisf. Gosp.* John vi. 23 Neh ðær stoue ðær ȝeeton þæt bread [*Ags. Gosp.* þone hlaf]. *c* **1175** *Cott. Hom.* 233 Hi hadden brad and win and vii sandon. *c* **1200** *Moral Ode* 191 in *Trin. Coll. Hom.* 225 We ȝieueð..a steche of ure breade. *c* **1200** ORMIN 1590 þerrflinng bræd iss clene bræd. *a* **1300** *Cursor M.* 15233 Takes and etes o þis bred, For fless þan es it min. **1340** *Ayenb.* 107 A zop of hot bryead. *c* **1383** WYCLIF *Sel. Wks.* III. 443 þis sacrid ooste is verrey Goddis body and verrey breede. **1413** LYDG. *Pylgr. Sowle* v. xiii. (1483) 104 This breed and this wyn the hyhe kyng blessith with his hand. *c* **1440** *Bone Flor.* 1004 Be hym y sawe in forme of bredd, When the preest can synge. **1562** J. HEYWOOD *Prov. & Epigr.* (1867) 30 Better is halfe a lofe than no bread. **1600** HOLLAND *Livy* XLVIII. 1237 To chew his bare bread. **1609** SKENE *Reg. Maj.* 151 They make not breid agreand to the money. **1655** MOUFFET & BENN. *Health's Improv.* 236 Bread and Cheese be the two targets against death. **1713** *Lond. & Country Brew.* II. (1743) 94, I do not care how white my Bread is. **1799** tr. *H. Meister's Lett.* 228 You write *bread*, and you pronounce it *bred*. **1843** HOOD *The Shirt* v, O God! that bread should be so dear, And flesh and blood so cheap!

b. The plural has been used as a literalism of translation (*obs.*); also in sense of 'kinds of bread'; and *colloq.* of individual portions or helpings of bread.

1547 BOORDE *Brev. Health* Pref. 4 They must knowe the operacyon of all maner of breades, of drinkes, and of meates. **1579** FULKE *Heskins' Parl.* 140 Three sundry breades are mentioned by Christe. **1609** BIBLE (Douay) *Ps.* xl. 10 The man also..who did eate my breades. —— *Prov.* xii. 11 He that tilleth his land, shall be filled with breads. **1865** *Pall Mall G.* 11 Oct. 3 By two o'clock we were all seated, nibbling at our breads in a famished way.

c. *to break bread*: (*a*) to break it for one's own mouthfuls; hence to eat or partake of bread or food; (*b*) (from N.T.) to break it for distribution to others, to dispense bread, or *fig.* the bread of life; also to break the sacramental bread in the Communion of the Lord's Supper, to administer or join in the Communion.

a **1300** *Cursor M.* 12559 Noþer durst þai..ne brek þair brede, ne tast þair mes, Till he war cummen til þair des. **1382** WYCLIF *Lam.* iv. 4 The litil childer askeden bred, and ther was not that shulde breke to them. —— *Acts* xx. 7 Whanne we comen for to breke breed, Poul disputide with hem. —— *Mark* xiv. 22 Jhesus took bred, and blessinge brak, and ȝaf to hem. *c* **1430** *Syr Gener.* 3067 Elles brede mot I neuer breke. **1583** STUBBES *Anat. Abus* II. 74 To breeke the bread of life to their charges. **1598** SHAKS. *Merry W.* I. iv. 161 An honest maid as euer broke bread. **1607** —— *Timon.* I. ii. 48 The fellow that sits next him, now parts bread with him. **1813** BYRON *Br. Abydos* II. xvi, Not all who break his bread are true. **1878** H. SMART *Play or Pay* i, The sole stranger that has broken bread with the ——th Hussars this evening.

d. Often phraseologically combined with the name of some other article eaten or drunk with it, as ***bread and milk, meat, salt, water***: **bread and cheese**, *fig.* for plain fare, needful food, victuals, living; also, a child's name for the young leaves of the Hawthorn, the Wood-Sorrel or 'Cuckoo-bread', and one or two other plants; **bread and milk**, bread saturated with boiling milk; also, the Cuckoo-flower (*Cardamine pratensis*); † **bread and salt**, an old form of oath, whence *to take bread and salt*, to swear; **bread and wine**, the 'elements' in the Communion. Also BREAD AND BUTTER. See also WATER *sb.* 2 a.

1589 in H. Hall *Soc. in Eliz. Age* (1886) 219 *Bread and cheese, *vid.* **1598** SHAKS. *Merry W.* II. i. 140, I loue not the humour of bread and cheese. **1795** WOLCOTT (P. Pindar) *Lousiad* III. Wks. 1812 I. 247 Morpheus..gave To brainless Authors, bread and cheese, and fame. **1857** HUGHES *Tom Brown* iii, Cut with their bread-and-cheese knives. **1875**, etc. [see E.D.D.]. **1952** F. WHITE *Good Eng. Food* I. vi. 69 Hawthorn..the budding leaves of which..are called by the children 'bread and cheese'. **1691** WOOD *Ath. Oxon* II./332 He taught School..to gain *bread and drink. **1785** R. BROMFIELD in *Med. Commun.* II. 24 A *bread and milk poultice. *a* **1869** CONINGTON *Misc. Writ.* (1872) I. 247 To our taste it savours too much of the bread and milk of the nursery. **1575** J. STILL *Gamm. Gurton* v. ii, No other wight, save she, by *bred and salt. **1599** SHAKS. *Hen. V*, v. i. 9. **1604** DEKKER *Honest Wh.* v. ii, He took bread and salt..that he would never open his lips. **1552** ABP. HAMILTON *Catech.* 18 The propir mater..of this haly sacrament, quhilk is *breid and wyne. **1886** MORLEY *Crit. Misc.* I. 298 He was willing to continue the [Communion] service..on condition that he should not himself partake of the bread and wine.

e. With qualifying words, as **black bread**, a coarser dark kind made of some inferior grain; **native bread**, an underground fungus (*Mylitta australis*) eaten by Australian aborigines; also BROWN-BREAD, q.v. For *ammunition bread*, *barley-bread*, etc., see first element of comb.

1863 WATTS *Dict. Chem.* I. 657 The coarser kinds of bread, such as the..*black bread of Germany. **1549–62** STERNHOLD & H. *Ps.* cxxvii. 2 Feeding full hardly with *browne bread. **1616** MARKHAM *Countrey Farm* v. xx. 578 Of the meale wholly together..is made *houshold bread. And when the greatest of the branne is taken away, then there is usually made thereof citizens bread. **1866** *Treas. Bot.* II. 769/1 The *Native Bread of Australia..when dry becomes extremely hard and horny. **1884** *Times* 14 Aug. 3 A fungoid plant, the Tasmanian native bread, weighed, when fresh, 37 lbs.

f. In proverbial and other expressions, as † ***bread of wheat***, † ***God's bread, 'od's bread***: i.e. the sacramental bread: an obs. form of adjuration or oath. † ***to bake any one's bread***: see BAKE *v.* 6. ***to know on which side one's bread is buttered***: to have the sense to know where one's interest lies. ***to take the bread out of one's mouth***: to take away his livelihood, to take from a person what he is on the very point of enjoying. ***bread buttered on both sides***: great good fortune, lucky circumstances.

c **1380** *Sir Ferumb.* 2986 Wel sone hur bred was y-bake: hure lif-dawes wern ago. *a* **1500** *Songs & Carols 15th C.* (1856) 4 The eldest dowter swor, be bred of qwete. **1562** J. HEYWOOD *Prov. & Epigr.* (1867) 71, I know on which syde my bread is buttred. **1592** SHAKS. *Rom. & Jul.* III. v. 177 Gods bread, it makes me mad. **1681** *Roxb. Ballads* (1886) VI. 173 'Ods Bread, she's jealous I trow! **1708** MOTTEUX *Rabelais* IV. xvi, You little Prigs, will you offer to take the Bread out of my Mouth? **1837** LOCKHART *Scott* (1839) I. 206 *note*, Wherever Walter goes he is pretty sure to find his bread buttered on both sides. **1845** J. W. CROKER in *Papers* (1884) III. xxiv. 47 Lord Johnny dashed forward to take the bread out of his [Peel's] mouth.

g. ***bread and circuses*** [tr. L. (Juv. *Sat.* x. 80 Duas tantum res anxius optat, Panem et circenses.)], used allusively for food and entertainment, esp. when provided by a government to assuage the populace.

1914 H. P. EDEN (*title*) Bread and circuses. **1924** KIPLING *Debits & Credits* (1926) 217 Rome has always debauched her beloved Provincia with bread and circuses. **1937** 'N. BLAKE' *There's Trouble Brewing* i. 23 Bread and circuses, with me figuring as the circus. **1967** *Listener* 16 Mar. 373/1 The almost Roman outpouring of stale bread and dull circuses in what is supposed to be the more 'entertaining' side of television.

3. † **a.** (With *pl.*) A loaf, a roll; also, a broken piece, or fragment, of bread. *Obs.*

c **1325** *E.E. Allit. P.* B 1405 Burnes berande þe bredes vpon brode skeles. *c* **1450** HENRYSON *Tale of Dog* 38 Ane certane breid, worth five schillings or mair. **1526** *Pilgr. Perf.* (W. de W. 1531) 192 The xii baskettes of breedes yt remayned..in ye great myracle of our lorde. **1535** COVERDALE *1 Kings* xix. 6 At his heade there was a bred [WYCLIF loaf] baken on the coles. **1609** SKENE *Reg. Maj.* 134 Gif ane man is taken..with ane bread, the price of ane halfe pennie. **1643** PRYNNE *Sov. Power Parl.* II. 32 Scarce a penny bread a day to support their lives.

b. In full ***altar-bread***. A sacramental wafer. Usu. *pl.*

1849 Altar-breads [see ALTAR B. II]. **1877** J. D. CHAMBERS *Div. Worship* 352 The Breads being now on the Corporal. **1899** W. J. S. SIMPSON *Mem. W. S. Simpson* 154 An iron instrument for stamping the altar breads.

4. a. Taken as a type of ordinary food or victual. (Perhaps from the Lord's Prayer.) ***bread of idleness***: food not worked for; so similar phrases, as ***bread of affliction***, etc. †***full of bread***: full-fed.

c **1175** *Lamb. Hom.* 63 Gif us to dei ure deies bred. **1340** *Ayenb.* 110 Vayre uader oure bryad of eche daye yef ous to day. **1382** WYCLIF *Isa.* xxxiii. 16 Bred to hym is ȝoue, his watris ben feithful. **1388** —— *Deut.* xvi. 3 Thou schalt ete breed of affliccioun. *c* **1400** *Destr. Troy* 13549 Me bus, as a beggar, my bred for to thigge. **1535** COVERDALE *Ex.* xxiii. 25 So shal he blesse thy bred & thy water [WYCLIF, looues, and watris]. **1593** SHAKS. *Rich. II*, III. i. 21 Eating the bitter bread of banishment. **1602** SHAKS. *Ham.* III. iii. 80 He tooke my Father grossely, full of bread. **1611** BIBLE *Prov.* xxxi. 27 She..eateth not the bread of idleness [WYCLIF, idil bred; COVERDALE bred with ydilnes]. —— *Ezek.* xvi. 49 Pride, fulnesse of bread, and aboundance of idlenesse was in her. *a* **1700** DRYDEN *Ovid's Met.*, *Pythag. Philos.* 132 If men.. chaw with bloody teeth the breathing bread. **1832** MARRYAT *N. Forster* xi, You cannot eat the bread of idleness on board of a man-of-war. **1842** TENNYSON *Lady Clare* 26, I speak the truth, as I live by bread!

b. *fig.*

c **1380** WYCLIF *John* vi. 35, I am breed of lyf. **1542–60** BECON *Potat. for Lent.* Wks. (1843) 105 Touch not the thievish breads of perverse doctrine. **1660** JER. TAYLOR *Worthy Commun.* i. § 1. 21 The holy Sacrament..the bread of elect souls. **1875** HAMERTON *Intell. Life* x. iv. 358 The daily bread of literature and art.

5. a. Livelihood, means of subsistence.

1719 DE FOE *Crusoe* i, I was under no necessity of seeking my bread. **1727** A. HAMILTON *New Acc. E. Indies* II. xxxv. 31 Poor miserable Fishers, who get their Bread out of the Water, to keep them from starving. **1777** BURKE *Corr.* (1844) II. 170 The bread of a family depends on that man's paralytic hand. **1802** MAR. EDGEWORTH *Moral T.* (1816) I. 205 You..make your bread by your..pen. **1822** BYRON *Vis. Judg.* xcvi, He meant no harm in scribbling..'twas..his bread. **1848** MACAULAY *Hist. Eng.* II. 142 Many officers.. arbitrarily deprived of their commissions and of their bread.

b. ***in good bread***: in a good living or position (?*obs.*); ***in bad bread***: in a bad state, in difficulties; in disfavour *with* a person. *dial.* and *U.S.*

1763 in *Essex Inst. Hist. Coll.* (1913) XLIX. 139 Mr. Barnard..is now in good bread, and seems loth to affront his people by telling them plainly of these public sins. **1778** *Ibid.* (1907) XLIII. 11 Old England I beleve is got into Bad Bread. *Ibid.* 16 Hope it is the French Fleet, if not we shall be in Bad Bread, but we must see it out with them. **1785** GROSE *Dict. Vulgar T.* s.v. *Bread*, In bad bread; in a disagreeable scrape, or situation. **1825** JAMIESON *Suppl.* s.v. *Bread*, *To be in bad bread*, to be in a dilemma, or in an evil

taking. **1894** P. H. HUNTER *J. Inwick* xviii. 223, I saw fine I was gaun to be in bad breid wi' baith sides.

c. Money. *slang* (orig. *U.S.*).

[**1939** RAMSEY & SMITH *Jazzmen* (1940) iii. 63 Inside the low, smoky room, the musicians sweated for their bread.] **1952** *Down Beat* 18 June 15 If I had bread (Dizzy's basic synonym for loot) I'd certainly start a big band again. **1965** L. W. HOLT in J. H. Clarke *Harlem* 207 There won't be much 'cake' unless the brothers should happen to get some *bread* to buy it with. **1967** C. DRUMMOND *Death at Furlong Post* iii. 28 So me with all that bread.. maybe a week, and then I get the plane.

6. Extended to various preparations of the composition or nature of bread. †**a.** Pie-crust; pastry. *Obs.*

a **1300** *Cursor M.* 4487 A lepe.. Wit bred þat i bar on mi heued. *c* **1420** *Anturs of Arth.* xxvii, Briddes bacun in bred. ?*c* **1475** *Sqr. lowe Degre* 319 Wyth byrdes in brede y bake.

†**b.** Sea-biscuit. *Obs.*

1651 *Proc. Parliament* No. 84. 1289 We have taken..2 casks of Bread, and one barrel of Pease in one Vessel. **1746** in W. Thompson *R.N. Advoc.* (1757) 18 The Bread..is all good, but..it has been..long aboard. **1793** PITT in G. Rose *Diaries* (1860) I. 128, I rather imagine he uses the term bread, as synonymous with biscuit.

c. Other preparations of corn or flour. *U.S.*

1863 *Life in South* II. 237 An abundant supply of cold chicken, ham, and 'breads', as all the variety of corn cakes, waffles, hot rolls, and hominy are called.

7. Short for BEE-BREAD. (In 17th c. pollen.)

1676 GREW *Anat. Flowers* v. §1 That Body which Bees gather and carry upon their Thighs, and is commonly called their Bread.. The Bread is a Kind of Powder; yet somewhat moist.

II. *attrib.* and *Comb.*

8. *simple attrib.* Of bread, *esp.* as a material (***bread pudding***, etc.); about or for bread, as ***bread riots***.

1723 J. NOTT *Cook's & Confectioner's Dict.* P. §235 To make a Bread-pudding. **1783** S. CHAPMAN in *Med. Commun.* I. 287 A bit of..light bread pudding. **1860** MAYNE *Expos. Lex.* 170/1 The bread poultice, used as emollient in ordinary cases. **1883** *Harper's Mag.* Mar. 578/2 The crusts saved for a bread pudding. **1968** *Listener* 26 Sept. 423/2 The secret of a good bread pudding is adding enough spices and fruit, especially currants.

9. General comb.: **a.** attributive, as ***bread-bag***, ***-bin***, ***-binge***, ***-cart***, ***-chest***, ***-crust***, ***-food***, ***-hutch*** (*c* 1440), ***-knife***, ***-pan***, ***-paste***, ***-pill***, ***-rack***, ***-rasp***, ***-roll***, ***-sauce***, ***-tax***, ***-tray***, ***-wagon***, ***-weevil***; **b.** objective or obj. gen., as ***bread-baker***, ***-baking***, ***-chipper***, ***-chopper***, ***-cutter***, ***-earner***, ***-earning***, ***-grate*** (1587), ***-grater***, ***-maker***, ***-making***, ***-seller***, ***-taking***, ***-taxing***, ***-wanting***; **c.** parasynthetic, as ***bread-faced***.

1729 BYRD *Field Jrnl.* in *Colonial Rec. N. Carolina* (1886) II. 795 The woods..tore the very deer skins that guarded the *Bread bags. **1864** *Daily Tel.* 4 Oct., A 'bread-bag knot'..is the old boatswain's trap to catch a thief at his biscuit-store. **1723** *Lond. Gaz.* No. 6195/5 Henry Browning..*Bread-Baker. **1757** W. THOMPSON *R.N. Advoc.* 21 Being on a Subject of *Bread baking. **1593** *Wills & Inv. N.C.* II. (1860) 227 Two jackes, one *bread-binge. **1638** PENKETHMAN *Artach.* Kb, The *Bread-Carts..comming from Stratford towards London, were met at the Miles end. **1616** R. C. *Times' Whis.* II. 775 Some *bread-chipper or greasy cooke. **1597** SHAKS. *2 Hen. IV*, II. iv. 342 Call me Pantler, and Bread-chopper. **1882** A. BAIN *J. S. Mill* v. 193 Mill has done more than any single person for the *bread-earners of the sex. **1587** *Wills & Inv. N.C.* II. (1860) 149 Item, ij minsinge knives, and a *breadgrate of tynn. **1624** *Althorp MS.* in Simpkinson *Washingtons* Introd. 55, 2 frying pannes, 4 peales, and a *bread grater. *c* **1440** *Promp. Parv.* 48 *Brede-huche, *turrundula*. **1833** *Chambers's Jrnl.* II. 285/3 With a *bread-knife arrested in his surprised hand. **1861** MRS. BEETON *Bk. Househ. Managem.* 991 Taking care..that butter-knife and bread-knife are in their places. **1857** ELIZA ACTON *Eng. Bread-bk.* II. iv. 178 A skilful *bread-maker. *Ibid.* I. iii. 29 Old methods of 'panification', or *bread-making. *Ibid.* II. iv. 154 It is well to warm the *bread-pan or tub, and the flour also. *Ibid.* II. 98 A substance similar to *bread-paste or dough. **1892** G. & W. GROSSMITH *Diary of Nobody* xiii. 172 Daisy and Lupin..began throwing *bread-pills at each other. **1747** H. GLASSE *Art of Cookery* i. 4 Some love *Bread-Sauce in a Bason. **1884** *Manch. Exam.* 4 Dec. 5/3 A decision of great importance to bakers and *breadsellers. **1640** R. CAREW in *Doidge's West. Count. Ann.* (1882) 211 None departed..till after the *breade taking. **1863** DE MORGAN in *Athenæum* 10 Oct. 467 The abolition of the *bread-tax. **1841** GEN. P. THOMPSON *Exerc.* (1842) VI. 52 Old saws impressed on him by a *bread-taxing clergy. **1695** *Lond. Gaz.* No. 3091/3, 200 of the Enemies Horse..were come..to intercept our *Bread-Wagons. **1710** *Ibid.* No. 4714/2 To halt..for..our Baggage and the Bread-Waggons.

10. Special comb.: **bread-artist**, a casual term applied to one who prosecutes an art or profession simply to gain a living; **bread-barge** (*Naut.*), an oval tub in which bread is placed for mess; †**bread-bearer**, an officer of the royal household; **bread-berry**, bread steeped in hot water and seasoned or sweetened, pap (cf. ALEBERRY); **bread-board, breadboard**, (*a*) a board on which bread is cut, dough kneaded, etc.; (*b*) *slang*, a name given to a board on which an experimental electric circuit, etc., is set out; hence as *v. trans.*, to make a flat model of (such a circuit, etc.); so '**breadboarding** *vbl. sb.*; †**bread-brake**, a kneading trough or machine; **bread-controller** = *bread-steward*; **bread-crust bomb** *Geol.* (see quot. 1909); **bread-dust**, powdered bread or biscuit; **bread-flake** (*dial.* **brade-fleigh**), a wooden frame or rack upon which oat-cakes are placed to dry and harden; †**bread-god**, contemptuous term for the consecrated host; **bread-jelly** (see quot. 1868); †**bread-lepe**, a bread-basket; **bread-line** (orig. *U.S.*), (*a*) a queue of poor people waiting to receive bread or other food given as charity; also *fig.*; (*b*) = *subsistence level*; **bread-meal**, (*a*) meal for household or brown bread (*dial.*); (*b*) sometimes used for rock-meal (Ger. *berg-mehl*); **bread-nut**, the seed of the *Brosimum alicastrum*; **bread-powder**, baking-powder; **bread-purveyor** = *bread-steward*; **bread-room**, a room for keeping bread, esp. *Naut.* 'a place parted off below the lower deck, close abaft, for keeping the bread'; also *slang*. = BREADBASKET 2; **bread-root**, the name of one or two plants producing edible tubers or bulbs, *spec.* a species of Psoralea (*P. esculenta*), and *Camassia esculenta* or Quamash; also the root itself; **bread-science, -study**, a science or study pursued as a means of gaining a livelihood; †**bread-skep** = *bread-lepe*; **bread-steward** (see quot.); **bread-stick**, a long slender roll of crisp bread; **bread-ticket** (orig. *U.S.*), (*a*) a ticket entitling the possessor to bread; (*b*) *fig.* = *meal ticket* b; **bread-trade**, the buying and selling of bread; also, a branch of trade pursued as a means of gaining a livelihood; **bread-unit**, a unit of value in rationing bread; †**bread-worship**, the worship of the host, ARTOLATRY; whence **bread-worshipper**; †**bread-wright**, a baker.

1831 CARLYLE *Sart. Res.* II. iv, The *Bread-artist can travel contentedly round and round..and realize much: for himself victual. **1840** R. DANA *Bef. Mast* xxxii. 123 The *bread-barge and beef-kid were overhauled. **1647** HAWARD *Crown Rev.* 28 *Breadbearer: Fee, £1 10s.4d. **1741** *Compl. Fam.-Piece* I. i. 43 Let the Child's Diet be..a thin *Bread-berry. **1864** J. BROWN *Plain Wds. Health* 44 Giving the baby..thin bread-berry once a day..so as gradually to wean it. **1857** *Mrs. Putnam's Receipt Book* 3 Mix..the dough; roll it on a *bread-board about an inch thick. **1940** *Amateur Radio Handbk.* (ed. 2) vi. 106/2 The simplest and cheapest style is the baseboard or 'breadboard' layout, where the various stages are assembled in a row along a wooden base. **1948** *Gloss. Computer Terms* (U.S. Office of Naval Res. Special Devices Center: M.I.T. Servomechanisms Lab. Rep. R—138) 4 *Breadboard*, a roughly constructed experimental model of a circuit. **1952** R. F. JONES in W. Sloane *Stories for Tomorrow* (1955) ii. 75 Breadboard lay-outs were assembled with maximum care. **1953** *Electronic Engin.* XXV. 143 Drift was encountered in the initial 'breadboard' model. *Ibid.* 417 During the late 1920's the supporting panel or 'breadboard' for the components tended to become horizontal in the box. **1956** R. A. HEINLEIN *Door into Summer* (1960) iii. 44, I could bread-board a rig for that. **1959** *New Scientist* 26 Mar. 695/1 Years would be lost by breadboarding, since it required..the redesign of an operating breadboard model into a submarine hull. **1967** H. HARRISON *Technicolor Time Machine* (1968) ix. 86 I'm afraid a good deal of the circuitry was breadboarded. **1564** *Wills & Inv. N.C.* (1835) 223 Two cawels and a *breadbrayk iiijs. **1909** *Cent. Dict.* Suppl., **Bread-crust bomb*, a somewhat rounded mass of igneous rock, ejected in a volcanic eruption, whose surface presents an appearance similar to that of baked bread, as if the interior had expanded beyond the stretching capacity of the surface crust. **1938** *Nature* 18 June 1106/1 Origin of breadcrust bombs of the peléan type. **1856** KANE *Arct. Expl.* II. xx. 199 Two bags of *bread-dust. **1840** S. BAMFORD *Life of Radical* I. 234 (*Lanc. Gloss.*) The large *bread-flake in the kitchen was speedily unthatched. **1866** E. WAUGH *Ben an' th' Bantam* i. 11 (*Lanc. Gloss.*) A brade-fleigh or bread-rack, which was suspended from the ceiling, like a great square harp. *a* **1555** LATIMER *Serm. & Rem.* (1845) 260 Requiring to know if their *bread-god had flesh..as our dear Redeemer had. *a* **1631** DONNE *Serm.* lviii. 585 When they had made their Bread-God, they poysoned the Emperour with that Bread. **1853** MRS. GASKELL *Cranford* xi. 208 Mrs. Forrester made some of the *bread-jelly, for which she was so famous, to have ready as a refreshment. **1868** M. JEWRY *Warne's Model Cookery* 661/1 *Bread Jelly*... Take the crumb of a penny roll; cut it into thin slices, and toast them... Put them into a quart of spring water. Let it simmer over the fire till it has become a jelly. Strain..and flavour..with a little lemon juice and sugar. *c* **1250** *Gen. & Ex.* 2078 Me drempte ic bar *bread-lepes ðre. **1900** *Lippincott's Mag.* LXV. 3 [Story by A. B. Paine entitled] The *Bread Line. *Ibid.* 12 That's the bread line. They get a cup of coffee and a loaf of bread every night at twelve o'clock. **1909** H. N. CASSON *Life C. H. McCormick* 12 This..republic could not develop beyond the struggle for food. It was chained to the bread-line. **1929** *Dundee Courier* 7 Nov., My life has been spent among people..close to the bread line. **1959** *New Statesman* 28 Feb. 294/3 The average African family in the urban areas lived calamitously below the bread-line. **1863** ATKINSON *Provinc. Danby*, **Bread-meal*, flour with the coarsest bran taken out..such as..produces 'brown-bread'. **1756** P. BROWNE *Jamaica* 372 *Bread-Nut. The fruit boiled with salt fish..has been frequently the support of the negroes. **1866** *Treas. Bot.* I. 171/2 Bread-nut. **1627** CAPT. SMITH *Seaman's Gram.* ii. 12 The *Bread-roome is commonly vnder the Gun-roome. **1794** LD. HOOD in Nicolas *Disp. Nelson* (1845) I. 483 *note*, Put all you can get into your bread-room. **1841** *Penny Cycl.* XIX. 94/2 *P. esculenta*, the *bread-root of North America, is cultivated along the banks of the Missouri. **1860** F. ROWAN *Schleiermacher's Life & Lett.* I. 159 He has not studied any so-called *bread-science. **1496** *Dives & Paup.* VIII. xvii. 344/2 The ryche man shal gyue answere..of euery cromme of brede in his *bredeskep. **1857** ELIZA ACTON *Eng. Bread-bk.* 13 *note*, *Panetier du Roi*, *bread-steward, bread-purveyor, or bread-controller, whose office was to regulate the distribution of bread in the royal household, and who had supreme authority over all the bakers of the kingdom. **1909** *Cent. Dict.* Suppl., **Bread-sticks*, bread-dough rolled into sticks and baked: served with bouillon, soup, or tea. **1936** J. DOS PASSOS *Big Money* 470 Picking up a breadstick and snapping it into his mouth. **1831** CARLYLE *Sart. Res.* II. iv, Is it not well that there should be what we call Professions or *Bread-studies (*Brodzwecke*) preappointed us? **1876** GEO. ELIOT *Dan. Der.* III. xxiii. 194 If you resolve to take art as a bread-study. **1855** *Chicago Times* 21 Mar. 3/1 Entering a bake-shop and stealing therefrom *bread tickets to the value of $16. **1956** I. BROMIGE *Enchanted Garden* III. iv. 164, I wanted so much more... Not just a bread ticket. I wouldn't care how poor we were. **1858** J. MARTINEAU *Stud. Chr.* 326 These pursuits..sink into mere *bread-trades. **1946** *Lancet* 6 July 29/2 The ration will be measured in *bread units. A 1 lb. 12 oz. loaf will cost 4 bread units, 1 lb. of flour 3 bread units, and 1 lb. of flour confectionery 2 bread units. **1641** SANDERSON *Serm.* II. 8 A shrewd appearance of their idolatrous *bread-worship. **1574** *Life 70th Abp. Canterb.* To Rdr., Superstitious Archsacrificers, and principall *breadworshippers. *c* **1250** *Gen. & Ex.* 2077 Quað ðis *bred-wriȝte, liðeð nu me.

bread (brɛd), *v.* [f. BREAD *sb.*[1]] *trans.* **a.** *Cookery.* To dress with bread-crumbs. **b.** To clean by rubbing with bread. **c.** To provide with daily bread.

1629 PARKINSON *Parad.* II. iii. 476 Some doe use the pouder of the herbe dryed..to mixe with grated bread, to breade their meate. **1727** BRADLEY *Fam. Dict.* I. s.v. *Fish pottage*, Flowering and breading them after they have been dip'd in beaten Eggs. **1797** E. CHAMBERS *Let.* 29 Nov. in *Papers of J. Steele* (1924) I. 152 What [corn] I have..will Scarcely Bread the Negroes. **1825** *Fr. Dom. Cookery* Gloss. 376 Cutlets, fish, etc. are usually breaded thus. **1879** TOURGEE *Fool's Err.* xviii. 91 They had enough to bread themselves. **1884** F. BRITTEN *Watch & Clockm.* 108 Instead of rubbing with pith the work may be carefully breaded.

bread(e, var. of BREDE.

bread and 'butter. (Often written with hyphens, esp. when used *attrib.*)

1. a. Bread spread with butter; also *attrib.* Also *attrib.* and *comb.*, as ***bread-and-butter pudding***; ***bread-and-butterless*** adj.

1630 WADSWORTH *Sp. Pilgr.* iii. 15 Euery one hath..a peece of bread and butter. **1711** ADDISON *Spect.* No. 323 ⁋6 Eat a slice of Bread and butter, drank a dish of Bohea. **1729** E. SMITH *Compl. Housewife* (ed. 3) 81 A Bread and Butter Pudding... Take a two-penny Loaf..spread it in very thin slices [etc.]. **1817** BYRON *Beppo* xxxix, The Nursery still lisps out in all they utter—Besides, they always smell of bread and butter. **1822** KITCHINER *Cook's Orac.* 449 Bread and Butter Pudding. **1849** [see TEALESS *a.*]. **1853** MRS. GASKELL *Cranford* i. 14 He..lessened the pretty maid-servant's labour by waiting on empty cups, and bread-and-butterless ladies. **1883** ROE in *Harper's Mag.* Dec. 50/2 She likes bread and butter and..realities.

b. *dial.* A slice of bread and butter.

1853 W. D. COOPER *Gloss. of Provincialisms in Sussex*, *Bread and butters*, slices of bread buttered. **1927** W. E. COLLINSON *Contemp. Eng.* 54, I well remember the disgust we children felt at a lady..who always said a bread and butter, where we used *a piece of bread and butter*.

2. Taken as a type of every day food; the means of living; hence *attrib.* in many elliptical and allusive expressions. See also QUARREL *v.* 1 a.

1732 SWIFT *Let.* 12 Aug. (1965) IV. 60 Your quarrelling with each other upon the subject of bread and butter is the most usual thing in the world. **1738** —— *Polite Conv.* I. 17, I won't quarrel with my Bread and Butter for all that: I know when I'm well. **1836–7** SIR W. HAMILTON *Metaph.* (1859) I. i. 6 By the Germans, the latter [i.e. the professional or lucrative sciences] are usually distinguished as the *Brodwissenschaften*, which we may translate, 'The Bread and Butter Sciences'. **1844** H. TWISS *Life Ld. Eldon* I. vi. 119 Young man, your bread and butter is cut for life. **1870** LOWELL *Among my Bks.* Ser. I. (1873) 222 Life lifted above the plane of bread-and-butter associations. **1884** *Harper's Mag.* Dec. 92/2 Industries were not so plenty..that men could afford..to quarrel with their bread and butter. **1886** *Contemp. Rev.* May 663 Journalists who frankly avow what is called the bread-and-butter theory of their craft. **1929** *Publishers' Weekly* 30 Nov. 2588/1 The old stand-bys, the bread-and-butter books in every department. **1939** A. CHRISTIE *Murder is Easy* xii. 128 One mustn't quarrel with one's bread and butter. **1955** *Times* 11 May 6/1 Providing furniture for new houses was the bread and butter of the industry.

3. ***no bread and butter of mine***: no matter affecting my material interests, no business of mine.

1764 FOOTE *Mayor of G.* I. i, However, it is no bread and butter of mine.

4. a. *attrib.*; *spec.* Of or pertaining to the age when bread-and-butter is extensively consumed; boyish, girlish; *esp.* (cf. quot. 1817 in 1) school-girlish.

a **1625** BEAUM. & FL. *Hum. Lieut.* III. vi, Ye bread-and-butter rogues, do ye run from me? **1807** W. IRVING *Salmag.* (1824) 180 These little, beardless, bread and butter politicians. **1861** TROLLOPE *Barchester T.* xli. (D.) A lady at any rate past the wishy-washy bread-and-butter period of life. **1865** *Pall Mall G.* 13 May 4 Would feel that they were tittered at as bread-and-butter Misses.

b. bread-and-butter letter orig. *U.S.*, a letter of thanks for hospitality; cf. COLLINS. Also *ellipt.*

1901 HOWELLS *Pair of Patient Lovers* 82 His prompt bread-and-butter letter. **1933** N. STREATFEILD *Tops & Bottoms* xxiv. 308 Please *never* write me bread-and-butter letters. **1964** E. BOWEN *Little Girls* III. i. 164 Rude? Should have written a bread-and-butter?

Hence (with reference to sense 4) **bread-and-butterhood, -butterishness, bread-and-buttery** *a.*

1884 LADY MAJENDIE *Out of Element* III. xxiv. 321, I think the ties of bread-and-butterhood are stronger than any later ones after all. **1843** *Blackw. Mag.* LIII. 80 They.. emerge..into the full and perfect imago of little.. gentlemen, and little ladies, without any of those intermediate conditions of laddism, hobble-de-hoyism, or bread-and-butterishness. **1859** G. MEREDITH *R. Feverel* xiii. (1885) 90 His future bride is now pinafored and bread-and-buttery. **1882** MRS. RIDDELL *Struggle for Fame* xxvi, You [an authoress] are rather bread-and-buttery still.

ˈbread-basket.

1. *lit.* A basket for holding bread, or in which bread is handed round.

1552 HULOET, Bread basket, hamper, or hutch. **1780** WILSON in *Phil. Trans.* LXX. 457 A bread-basket was filled with snow. **1849** COBDEN *Speeches* 66 To indemnify themselves by putting their hands into your bread-baskets.

2. *slang.* The stomach.

1753 FOOTE *Englishm. Paris* I. (1763) 15 Made the Soupe-maigre rumble in his Bread-basket. **1763** C. JOHNSTON *Reverie* I. 135 Hitting him a plump in the bread-basket. **1803** BRISTED *Pedest. Tour* I. 46 Our landlady, who was standing..with her mouth wide open, and her hands locked together..resting on her prominent breadbasket. **1850** KINGSLEY *Alt. Locke* xxxiii. (D.) 'What do you think o' that now in a policeman's bread-basket?'

3. *slang.* A large bomb containing smaller bombs; esp. in MOLOTOV *bread-basket.*

1940 [see MOLOTOV]. **1941** *Word Study* Nov. 1/1 A few radio commentators and newspapermen have applied the phrase *Goering*, or *Goering's, breadbasket* to a similar type of bomb dropped sometimes by the Germans in raids over London. **1944** J. H. FULLARTON *Troop Target* xxiv. 179 Lone bombers dropping 'bread-baskets' which spew scores of tiny bombs over a wide area.

bread-corn (ˈbrɛdkɔːn).

1. Corn or grain for making bread. An expression that comes down from a time when 'corn' had a much wider sense than it now bears in England or America; cf. *peppercorn*, and in OE. *senepes corn* mustard seed.

1362 LANGL. *P. Pl.* A. VII. 58 A Busschel of Bred corn he bringeþ þer-Inne. **1398** TREVISA *Barth. De P.R.* XVII. lxiv, Many medle benes with bred corne, to make þe bred þe more heuy. **1610** P. HOLLAND *Camden's Brit.* II. 219 The inhabitants..use in steed of bread-corne, dried fish. **1770** LANGHORNE *Plutarch* (1879) I. 251/2 A great quantity of bread-corn was brought into Rome. **1846** MCCULLOCH *Acc. Brit. Empire* (1854) I. 477 Rye..the bread-corn of Germany and Russia. **1857** ELIZA ACTON *Eng. Bread-bk.* iv. 53.

2. *spec.* 'Corn to be ground into *bread-meal*, not to be used for finer purposes' (*N. Linc. Gloss.*).

attrib. **1669** BOYLE *Contn. New Exp.* II. (1682) 28, I made Paste of Bread-corn-meal, without Leaven.

ˈbread-crumb, *sb.* **a.** (Properly two words) A crumb of bread; *esp.* (in *pl.*) bread crumbled down for dressing fried fish, boiled ham, etc. **b.** The crumb or soft part of bread, as distinct from the crust. Hence **ˈbread-crumby** *a.*

1769 MRS. RAFFALD *Eng. Housekpr.* (1778) 35 Strew over them bread crumbs. **1831** CARLYLE *Sart. Res.* II. ii, To carry forth my supper (bread-crumb boiled in milk), and eat it out of doors. **1879** GEO. ELIOT *Theo. Such* iv. 85 He was.. acceptable in society as a part of what we may call its bread-crumb. **1881** MISS BRADDON *Asph.* 19 Thin slices of carmine ham, with a bread-crumby edge.

bread-crumb, *v.* [f. the sb.] *trans.* To dip in bread-crumbs in preparation for cooking. Hence **bread-crumbed** *ppl. a.*; **bread-crumbing** *vbl. sb.*

1846 SOYER *Cookery* 103 Egg and bread-crumb each piece. **1854** —— *Shilling Cookery* 35 The heads when cooked may be egged and bread-crumbed over. **1877** E. S. DALLAS *Kettner's Bk. Table* 179 The plain cutlets and the breadcrumbed ones. *Ibid.* 228 For breadcrumbing, the French plan is to dip the cutlet into oil or butter and then to roll it in crumbs. **1927** *Daily Express* 17 Nov. 5/2 The chicken was 'egged and breadcrumbed' in readiness for the dish.

breade, var. of BRAID, BREDE.

breaded (ˈbrɛdɪd), *ppl. a.* [f. BREAD *v.* + -ED.] Treated or dressed with bread, bread-crumbs, etc.

1616 MARKHAM *Countrey Farm* v. xxi. 581 Such..may drinke of breaded water, that is to say, water wherein rie bread hath beene well beaten and laboured. **1727** BRADLEY *Fam. Dict.* I. s.v. *Galantine*, A Pig may also be garnished with its Skin well breaded. **1879** E. S. BRIDGES *Round the World* 27 Veal cutlets plain and breaded.

breaded, var. of BREDED, plaited.

breaden (brɛd(ə)n), *a.* [f. BREAD *sb.* + -EN[1].] Made or consisting of bread. †*breaden god*: a polemical term for the consecrated host.

1579 FULKE *Confut. Sanders* 696 They might as well see him burne his breaden Gods. **1609** SIR E. HOBY *Let. Mr. T. H.* 84 Your breaden doll in a shauelings hand. **1624** T. TAYLOR *2 Serm.* i. 23 So must every man worship the breaden, brazen, woodden, and golden gods. **1626** HAKEWILL *Comparison* 11 Their bredden Idoll in the consecrated host. **1633** T. ADAMS *Exp. 2 Peter* ii. 1 Delighted to behold the breaden god carried in a box. **1680** H. MORE *Apocal. Apoc.* 354. **1702** C. MATHER *Magn. Chr.* IV. ii. (1852) 47. **1827** J. IVIMEY *Pilgr. of 19th C.* iii. 101 No objection to their manufacturing and eating their breaden God. **1839** J. ROGERS *Antipapopr.* VIII. ii. 242 The worship ..of a breaden and winemade God.

bread-fruit (ˈbrɛd-fruːt). [f. BREAD *sb.* + FRUIT.] The farinaceous fruit of a tree; *esp.* that furnished by *Artocarpus incisa* of the South Sea Islands, etc., of the size of a melon, and having a whitish pulp of the consistency of new bread. Also short for 'Bread-fruit tree'.

1697 DAMPIER *Voy.* (1729) I. 296 The Bread-fruit (as we call it) grows on a large Tree as big and high as our largest apple trees..it is as big as a Penny-loaf, when Wheat is at five shillings the Bushel. **1748** ANSON *Voy.* III. ii. (ed. 4) 417 A kind of fruit..called by the Indians Rima, but by us the Bread-Fruit. **1772–84** COOK *Voy.* (1790) V. 1623 Covered with cocoa-palms and bread-fruit trees. **1845** DARWIN *Voy. Nat.* xviii. (1852) 403 The bread-fruit conspicuous from its large, glossy and deeply digitated leaves. **1866** *Treas. Bot.* I. 96/2 The bread-fruit..is prepared by baking it in an oven heated by hot stones.

†**ˈbreadiness.** *Obs. rare.* [f. BREADY + -NESS.] The quality or fact of being bread.

1624 GATAKER *Transubst.* 182 Calvin, Beza and many more..who..maske with great wordes the naked breadinesse of their Protestanticall Sacrament.

†**ˈbreadish,** *a. Obs. rare*[−0]. [f. BREAD *sb.* + -ISH[1].] Of the nature of bread. Hence **ˈbreadishness.**

1688 BP. OXFORD *Reasons for Abrog. Test.* 22 They could not onely separate the Matter and Form, and Accidents of the Bread from one another, but the Paneity or Breadishness it self from them all.

bread-kind (ˈbrɛdkaɪnd). [f. BREAD *sb.* + KIND *sb.*] Food like bread; esp. a West Indian name for yams, sweet potatoes, and similar food-stuffs.

1697 DAMPIER *Voy.* 311 The Mindanao People live 3 or 4 months of the year on this food for their Bread kind. **1712** W. ROGERS *Voy. round World* 376 At which Allowance we have not above 12 Days at most, being all the Bread Kind we have in the Ship. **1891** *Wesleyan Meth. Mag.* May 362 A brown woman..with a load of 'bread-kind' on her head. **1899** W. P. LIVINGSTONE *Black Jamaica* v, The principal food consisted of what is locally called 'bread-kind'; yams, sweet potatoes, cocos, plantains.

breadless (ˈbrɛdlɪs), *a.* [f. BREAD *sb.*[1] + -LESS.] Without bread; without food.

1377 LANGL. *P. Pl.* B. XIV. 160 Beggeres aboute Midsomer bredlees þei soupe. **1733** P. WHITEHEAD *State Dunces* (R) Plump peers, and breadless bards alike are dull. **1847** *Tait's Mag.* XIV. 793 The terrible sufferings of a thousand breadless families. **1864** *Athenæum* 777/1 They who, half-fed, feed the breadless.. These are Charity's disciples.

Hence **ˈbreadlessness.**

1860 MRS. P. BYRNE *Undercurr. Overl.* II. 93 The crime of poverty then is thus classified; first mendicancy, or the state of 'breadlessness'; secondly vagrancy, or the state of 'homelessness'.

breadliness. *nonce-wd. daily breadliness*: fellowship in earning or partaking of 'daily bread'.

1863 MRS. GASKELL *Sylvia's L.* xxxix. (D.) Because of any fellowship or daily breadliness between us two.

breadness (ˈbrɛdnɪs). [f. BREAD + -NESS.] In discussions on Transubstantiation: The quality of being bread, bread-quality, 'breadiness'.

1866 *Church Times* 28 Apr., The idea that there is no substance, that is to say, no breadness of the Bread remaining. **1867** PEARSON *Early & Mid. Ages Eng.* I. 613 He asserted that the individuality of the bread (its breadness) was exchanged for the individuality of Christ (his humano-divinity).

bread-stich, var. of *brede-stitch*; see BREDE *sb.*[3] 4.

bread-stuff (ˈbrɛdstʌf). [f. BREAD + STUFF.] Material for bread; grain, flour: now usually in *pl.*

1793 T. JEFFERSON *Writ.* (1859) III. 509 France receives favorably our bread stuff, rice, wood, etc. **1845** DISRAELI *Sybil* (1863) 282 'Take my breadstuffs and I'll give you a cheque at sight on the Pennsylvanian Bank.' **1847** LD. G. BENTINCK in *Croker Papers* (1884) III. xxv. 142 Loaded with 1800 tons of breadstuffs.

breadth (brɛdθ). Also 6 bredeth(e, bredthe, breth, 6–7 bredth, 7 breadthe. [A late formation on the earlier *breade*, BREDE, by analogy with *leng-th, streng-th*, etc.: see -TH[1].]

1. a. Measure or distance from side to side of a surface; width, extent across. Also *fig.*

1523 *Act 14 & 15 Hen. VIII*, vi, One other way..of as greate largeness in bredeth or larger than the said olde way. **1570** BILLINGSLEY *Euclid* I. def. 2 A line is length without breadth. **1599** SHAKS. *Much Ado* v. i. 11 Measure his woe the length and bredth of mine. **1653** HOLCROFT *Procopius* II. 41 A rock stretching far in bredth. **1742** RICHARDSON *Pamela* III. 118 Let the World go as it will, we shall have our Length and our Breadth at last. **1870** F. WILSON *Ch. Lindisf.* 79 The breadth, across the transepts, is 54 feet.

b. *to a hair's breadth*: with minute exactness of measure, to a nicety. Cf. HAIR-BREADTH.

1598 SHAKS. *Merry W.* IV. ii. 4, I professe requitall to a haires bredth. **1709** STEELE *Tatler* No. 36 ¶2 Lady Autumn knows to an Hair's Breadth where her Place is in all Assemblies and Conversations.

2. a. A piece (of cloth, etc.) of the full breadth, without reference to its length; a width.

1584 *Inv.* in Scott *Kenilw.* Notes, A fayre quilte of crymson sattin vj breadths. **1673** GREW *Anat. Roots* iv. §19. 73 The several Plates or Bredths of a Floor-Mat. **1743** R. MAXWELL *Sel. Trans.* 398 (JAM.) The number of biers or scores of threads in the breadth of the said cloth. **1874** CHR. ROSSETTI *Sp. Likenesses* 50 These breadths must be run together, three and three.

b. An extent or area as measured by its breadth: the length not being expressly considered.

1601 HOLLAND *Pliny* I. 119 Cause it to inlarge it selfe into a bredth on the left hand as far as to the riuer Cyrus. **1813** *Examiner* 4 Jan. 6/1 Large breadths of lands..are left unsown. **1864** *Realm* 29 June 4 Only a given breadth can yearly be sown with grain crops. **1876** GEO. ELIOT *Dan. Der.* I. iii. 13 Green breadths of undulating park.

3. Extent, distance in general, length.

1595 SHAKS. *John* IV. ii. 99 That blood which ow'd the bredth of all this Ile, Three foot of it doth hold. **1601** —— *All's Well* III. ii. 26 If there bee bredth enough in the world, I will hold a long distance. **1608** —— *Per.* IV. i. 37 He will repent the breadth of his great voyage.

4. *fig.* **a.** Largeness (of mind, sentiment, or view), liberality, catholicity; also, wide or broad display of a quality.

1847 GROTE *Greece* (1862) III. xxviii. 45 Breadth of common sentiment and sympathy between Greek and Greek. **1852** TREVELYAN *Life Macaulay* (1876) I. vi. 391 The press found occasion to attack Macaulay with a breadth and ferocity of calumny. **1878** MORLEY *Condorcet* 75 Turgot shows a breadth and accuracy of vision.

b. Undue freedom or lack of decorum in dealing with indelicate matters; grossness or licence of expression. (Cf. BROAD *a.* 6c, BROADNESS 2.)

1873 W. C. HAZLITT *Feudal Period* Pref. p. ix, A few of them exhibit a breadth which is scarcely consonant with modern ideas of decorum.

5. *Art.* A broad effect: see quots.

1788 SIR J. REYNOLDS *Disc.* (1876) 84 A greater breadth and uniformity of colour. *c* **1811** FUSELI *Lect. Art* v. (1848) 465 Breadth, or that quality of execution which makes a whole so predominate over the parts as to excite the idea of uninterrupted unity amid the greatest variety..is a judicious display of fulness, not a substitute of vacuity. **1857** RUSKIN *Elem. Drawing* 311 Good composers are always associating their colours in great groups..and securing.. what they call 'breadth', that is to say a large gathering of each kind of thing into one place; light being gathered to light, darkness to darkness, and colour to colour. **1885** *Athenæum* 30 May 700/3 Simplicity, harmony, and breadth combine in these pictures with a restfulness which is truly admirable.

6. *Comb.* (*Naut.*), as **breadth-line,** 'a curved line of the ship lengthwise, intersecting the timbers at their respective broadest parts' (Weale); **breadth-riders** *sb. pl.*, 'timbers placed nearly in the broadest part of the ship...so as to strengthen two or more timbers' (Adm. Smyth).

breadthen (ˈbrɛdθən), *v.* [f. prec.: after *lengthen.*] *intr.* To increase in breadth; to broaden, widen.

1809 W. TAYLOR in Robberds *Mem.* II. 278 The inroads of mediocrity are ever breadthening. **1884** A. FORBES in *Eng. Illustr. Mag.* Apr. 455/2 As I painted, the picture breadthened on the canvas.

breadthless (ˈbrɛdθlɪs), *a.* [f. as prec. + -LESS.] Without breadth.

1642 H. MORE *Song of Soul* II. II. vi, The term of latitude is breadthlesse line. **1854** SIR W. HAMILTON in *Stewart's Wks.* Advt. 9 *note*, The realizing, not only to imagination but to sight, of breadthless lines.

breadthways, -wise (ˈbrɛdθweɪz, -waɪz), *adv.* [see -WAYS, -WISE.] In direction of the breadth.

1677 MOXON *Mech. Exerc.* (1703) 240 Roof Tiles..made Circular breadthways like a half Cylinder. **1758** *Elaboratory* 23 A course of bricks laid breadthways. **1864** H. SPENCER *Illust. Progr.* 161 Each finger-breadth was..equal to four grains of barley placed breadthwise. **1866** *Reader* 797 Some crossing it lengthways and some breadthways.

bread-tree (ˈbrɛdtriː). [f. BREAD + TREE.] A name sometimes given to the bread-fruit tree; also to several other trees of which the produce is used as food, as *Gardenia edulis, Encephalartos caffer.*

1786 tr. *Sparrman's Voy.* I. 346 On a height..grew the bread-tree (*brood-boom*) of the Hottentots. **1823** BYRON *Island* II. xi, The bread-tree..yields The unreap'd harvest of unfurrow'd fields. **1834** PRINGLE *Afr. Sk.* vi. 204 The Hottentot bread-tree, a species of palm.

bread-winner (ˈbrɛdwɪnə(r)).

1. One who supports himself and those dependent upon him by his earnings.

1821 GALT *Ann. Parish* 162 (JAM.) What war is when it comes into our hearths, and among the bread-winners. **1863** MISS MULOCH *Mistr. & Maid* xi. 122 Many a young fellow of his age was the stay and bread-winner of some widowed mother or sister. **1880** A. HUTH *Buckle* I. iii. 198 The age at which the bread-winners marry.

2. The tool, art, or craft with which any one earns his living.

1818 SCOTT *Br. Lamm.* II. 255 (JAM.) 'I'se gang hame, —and then get my bread-winner' [a fiddle]. **1821** GALT *Ann. Par.* 174 (JAM.) An aged woman, who has but the distaff for her bread-winner. **1870** LOWELL *Among my Bks.* Ser. I.

(1873) 190 That art which was..the bread-winner alike for soul and body.

So **ˈbread-winning** *vbl. sb.* and *ppl. a.*

1875 HELPS *Anim. & Mast.* vi. 142 Of course, it has nothing to do with bread-winning pursuits. **1879** M. PATTISON *Milton* 13 His aim is far above breadwinning. **1879** GEO. ELIOT *Theo. Such* xvi. 290 The sort of public spirit that scamps its bread-winning work.

† **ˈbreadwort.** *Obs. rare.* [f. *bread*, BREDE, plait, intertwining + WORT.] The Knot-grass.

1783 AINSWORTH *Lat. Dict.* (Morell) 11, *Polygonon*..the herb knotgrass, or breadwort.

† **ˈbready,** *a. Obs.* [f. as prec. + -Y¹.] Characterized by, or of the nature of, bread; breaden.

1550 BP. HOOPER *Serm. on Jonas* v. Wks. 527 Honorius the third, Bishop of Rome, commanded this new bready god to be honoured, anno 1226. **1624** GATAKER *Transubst.* 89 They endeavour with Epithets and wordes to cover the bready nakednesse thereof. **1633** W. AMES *Agst. Cerem.* II. 520 The..Masse-god is made..of a bready substance.

break (breɪk), *v.* Pa. t. broke (brəʊk). Pa. pple. broken (ˈbrəʊk(ə)n), broke. Forms: 1 brecan (*Northumb.* brican), 2–5 breken, 3–6 breke, 6–7 breake, 6– break; (also 2–3 breoken, 3–4 brec, 4 brek, 4–5 breek, 5 brakyn, byrkyn, 6 *Sc.* brek, breik, 7 breack). *Pa. t. sing.* 1–3 bræc, 2–4 brac, (*Orm.* bracc), 3–5 (& 6 *Sc.*) brak, 4– (*Sc.*) brack; also 2–3 brec, 3 breac, 4 brek, breck, 4–5 breek, breke, 6 breake, 4–8 brake; *pl.* 1 brǽcon, (2 breaken, breoken), 2–4 breken, 3–4 breke, 4 breeken; also 3–5 braken, (2–5 *north.* brak, 4 brac, 4– brack); *sing.* and *pl.* 4–6 (7–9 *arch.*) brake, 6– broke, (6 brooke, 7 broak). *Pa. pple.* 1 brocen, 2–3 ibroken, 3– broken, (3–5 brokun, -yn, 4–5 y-broke), 4– broke, (7 broak, brake, 8 *Sc.* breaken). [OE. *brecan* (*bricþ*, pa. t. *bræc*, *brǽcon*, pa. pple. *brocen*), corresp. to OFris. *breka*, OS. *brekan*, (MDu., Du. *breken*), OHG. *brehhan* (MHG., mod.G. *brechen*), Goth. *brikan* (pa. t. *brak*, *brêkum*, pple. *brukans*):—OTeut. stem *brek-*, corresp. to L. *frag-* (*frang-o*, *frēgi*, *fractum*), Aryan **bhreg-*. The original short vowels of the present stem and pa. pple were lengthened in ME., though *breck*, *brick*, and *brocken* are still retained dialectally. The normal pa. t. *brak*, *brack* (= OE. *bræc*, Ormin's *bracc*), remains in the north; the normal plural in ME. was *brēken*, *breeke(n*, which would have become *breake* in 16th c.; but by the operation of levelling, we find also a ME. sing. *brēk*, *breek*, and a (north.) pl. *brak*, *brack*; a pl. *braken* occurs in Layamon, and in late ME. *brāke* became the regular form both in sing. and pl., which, being retained in the Bible of 1611, is still familiar as an archaic form. But early in the 16th c., if not before, *brake* began to be displaced by the modern *broke*, formed after the pa. pple. Of the pa. pple., *broken* is still the regular form, but from the end of the 14th c. this was often shortened to *broke*, which was exceedingly common in prose and speech during the 17–18th c., and is still recognized in verse.]

(Many of the uses of this verb are so contextual, that it is difficult, if not impossible, to find places for them in a general scheme of its signification: when not found here, they may be sought under other words of the phrase.)

I. To sever into distinct parts by sudden application of force, to part by violence. Often with an adjunct indicating result, as in *to break asunder*, *in pieces*, *small*. See also *break up*.

1. a. *trans.* generally.

a **1000** *Psalm* ii. 9 (Spelm.) Swa swa fæt tiȝelen ðu bricst hi. *c* **1175** *Lamb. Hom.* 79 Me brekeð þe nute for to habbene þene curnel. *a* **1300** *Cursor M.* 6542 Þe tables þat in hand he bare, To pees he þam brak right þar. **1398** TREVISA *Barth. De P.R.* v. xx. (1495) 125 The thynge that is kytte and broke bi the foreteeth. *c* **1440** *Promp. Parv.* 49 Brakyn a-sunder cordys and ropis. **1589** WARNER *Alb. Eng.* v. xxvii. 137 Spurres hewen off the heeles, and Swords broke ouer head. **1601** BP. BARLOW *Serm. Paules Crosse* 17 A threefold rope is not easily broken. **1652** *Proc. Parl.* No. 136. 2130 His Coach was broke to peeces. **1653** WALTON *Angler* 123 He should not have broke my line by running to the Rods end. **1700** BLACKMORE *Job* 70 All my members were in pieces broke. **1710** STEELE *Tatler* No. 222 ¶3 A natural Inclination to break Windows. **1799** G. SMITH *Laboratory* II. 261 He [the fish] will certainly break you, as we term it (that is, snap your line) and make his escape. **1814** SCOTT *Ld. Isles* VI. xiv, I've broke my trusty battle-axe.

b. *intr.* for *refl.*

c **1175** *Lamb. Hom.* 83 Þet gles ne brekeð. *c* **1230** *Hali Meid.* 15 Þat hit ne breke ne beie. *a* **1300** *Cursor M.* 4389 He drou, sco held, þe tassel brak. *c* **1400** MAUNDEV. ii. 13 Thei breken for dryenesse, whan Men meven hem. **1526** *Pilgr. Perf.* (W. de W. 1531) 47 Anone it breketh, and so shedeth the wyne. **1601** SHAKS. *Twel. N.* I. v. 24 If both [points] breake, your gaskins fall. **1860** TYNDALL *Glac.* II. §17. 317 The glacier was evidently breaking beneath our feet.

2. In various spec. uses, as

† **a.** To rend or tear (cloth, paper). Still in s.w. dial. (See also BROKEN.)

a **1000** *Beowulf* 1511 Sae deor moniȝ hilde tuxum here syrcan bræc. **1382** WYCLIF *John* xxi. 11 The nett..ful of grete fischis..the nett is not brokun. *c* **1489** CAXTON *Sonnes of Aymon* i. 37 There had you seen many a gowne torne and broken. **1516** T. ALLEN in Lodge *Illust. Brit. Hist.* (1838) I. 23 After the sight thereof, your Lordship should break or burn it [the letter]. **1557** *Order of Hospitalls* G ij, Mending of such [sheets, etc.] as shalbe broken from time to time.

b. To cut up (a deer); to tear in pieces (a fox), also with *up*; to carve (a fowl), also with *out*, *up* (obs.).

c **1320** *Sir Tristr.* 452 Bestes þai brac and bare. **1513** *Bk. Keruynge* in *Babees Bk.* (1868) 267 Breke that egryt. *Ibid.* 277 Take the capon by the legges..& breke hym out. **1588** SHAKS. *L.L.L.* IV. i. 58 Boyet, you can carue, Breake vp this Capon. **1810** SCOTT *Lady of L.* IV. v, Raven..watching while the deer is broke. **1875** BUCKLAND *Log-bk.* 155 Like hounds breaking up a fox.

† **c.** To comb (wool) roughly, being the first process in carding. *Obs.* or *arch.*

1511–12 *Act 3 Hen. VIII*, vi. §1 Every Clothier..which shall..delyver to eny persone eny Wolle to breke, kembe, carde, or spynne. **1514** *Act 6 Hen. VIII*, ix. §1 The Breaker or Kember to deliver again..the same Wooll so broken and kembed.

† **d.** To wreck (a ship). *Obs.*

1382 WYCLIF *1 Kings* xxii. 48 Thei ben broken in Aziongober [**1611** BIBLE The shippes were broken at Ezion Geber]. **1535** STEWART *Cron. Scot.* II. 529 Ane schip..wes brokin on ane sand. **1547–64** BAULDWIN *Mor. Philos.* (Palfr.) xi. 167 When the ship is broken, [they] may swim and escape. **1611** BIBLE *Jonah* i. 4 The ship was like to be broken.

e. To destroy the completeness of; to take away a part from; to divide, part (a set of things). *Spec.* to change (a banknote or the like). *to break with*: to divide and share with. Cf. *to break bulk*, 43.

1741 RICHARDSON *Pamela* xvii. (L.) You should have given them [4 guineas] back again to your master: and yet I have broken them. **1808** JAMIESON *Scot. Dict.*, To Break a Bottle: to open a full bottle; especially when it is meant only to take out part of its contents. **1821** CLARE *Vill. Minstr.* I. 67 My last-earn'd sixpence will I break with thee. **1844** DICKENS *Mart. Chuz.* xliii. 494 It was the same note; he hadn't broken it. **1880** W. H. PATTERSON *Gloss. Antrim & Down* 12 Can you break that pound note for me? *a* **1888** *Mod.* The shopkeeper would not break the set. **1959** N. MAILER *Advts. for Myself* (1961) 81 He stretched himself out,..thinking..of the thrill of breaking a five-dollar bill.

† **f.** To dissolve (parliament), disband (a regiment). *Obs.*; cf. *break up*, 57 d.

1685 *Lond. Gaz.* No. 1997/2 The Regiments he brought into the Emperors Service are broken. **1715** BURNET *Own Time* II. 209 The Earl of Danby's prosecution was the point on which the parliament was broken. **1763** *Brit. Mag.* IV. 106 Lord Robert Sutton's regiment..having refused to be broke. **1788** PRIESTLEY *Lect. Hist.* v. xl. 291 The Grand Seignior can neither touch the public treasure, [nor] break the Janizaries.

† **g.** *intr.* (or *refl.*) *Obs.*

1601 SHAKS. *All's Well* IV. ii. 11 The Army breaking, My husband hies him home.

h. In *Music*: To break a CHORD, a NOTE, q.v.

i. In leather manufacture, to scrape a skin smooth and clean on the flesh side.

1842 *Penny Mag.* XI. 215/2 The lamb-skins having been steeped in water, 'broken' on the flesh side, and drained. **1845** DODD *Brit. Manuf.* V. 187 The goat-skins are..soaked in water..to soften them, and then undergo the process of 'breaking'.

j. *Phonology.* To cause breaking (BREAKING *vbl. sb.* 1 e) of (a vowel). Also *intr.*

1845 J. M. KEMBLE in *Proc. Philol. Soc.* II. 135 Not satisfied with transforming *i* into *ë*, before *h*, *l*, *m*, it [*sc.* Anglo-Saxon] broke the vowel into *ëo*. **1871** F. A. MARCH *Compar. Gram. Anglo-Saxon* I. 11 Before a consonant combination beginning with *l*, *r*, *h*, it [sc. *a*] breaks to *ea*. *Ibid.* 20 *l*, *r*, *h*, oftenest before a consonant, break foregoing *a* to *ea*. **1959** A. CAMPBELL *Old Eng. Gram.* v. 56 *æ* was broken, and appears as *ea*..before *r* followed by a consonant.

k. *to break the wicket* (Cricket): to dislodge a bail or the bails in stumping or running out a batsman.

1875 F. GALE in *Baily's Mag.* Sept. 274 He took her [*sc.* the ball] close to the bails and just broke the wicket. **1901** *Strand Mag.* June 616/1 The ball was thrown in from the field, the bowler took it, and broke the wicket, so as to run the batsman out.

l. (See quot. 1889.) orig. *U.S.*

1889 *Cent. Dict.* s.v., *To break a gun*, to open it by the action. **1956** M. PROCTER *Pub Crawler* 125 With the casual ease of long practise he 'broke' the gun and ejected the six rounds.

3. In phrases: ***to break bread***: see BREAD, 2 c. ***to break a lance with***: to enter the lists against, enter into competition with. ***to break blows, words with***: to exchange blows, words with. † ***to break a straw with***: to fall out with (*humorous*).

971 *Blickl. Hom.* 37 Brec þinne hlaf þearfendum mannum. **1589** GREENE *Menaph.* (Arb.) 85 Breaking a few quarter blowes with such countrey glances as they coulde. **1590** SHAKS. *Com. Err.* III. i. 75 A man may breake a word with you sir, and words are but winde. **1591** —— *1 Hen. VI*, III. ii. 51 Breake a Launce, and runne a-Tilt at Death. **1603** FLORIO *Montaigne* III. viii. (1632) 520, I shall breake a straw or fall at ods with him that keepes himselfe so aloft. **1862** THORNBURY *Turner* I. 263 In 1800 Turner entered classical ground to break a lance with Claude.

4. *trans.* and *intr.* To burst. Of an abscess or boil: To burst the surface, so that the contents escape. Sometimes also of a vein, blood-vessel, etc.

1398 TREVISA *Barth. De P.R.* VII. xxi. (1495) 239 Yf the postume of the eere be broke it is knowe by rennynge of quytter. **1533** ELYOT *Cast. Helth* (1541) 38 A boyle or impostume comen forthe and broken. **1557** NORTH *Gueuara's Diall. Pr.* (1582) 452 b, They brake the vaines of their hands and feete, and offered the bloud thereof. **1576** LAMBARDE *Peramb. Kent* (1826) 408 As the evill humor ..(gathered to a boyle, or head) will easily breake. **1592** SHAKS. *Ven. & Ad.* 460 The berry breaks before it staineth. **1602** —— *Ham.* IV. iv. 28 This is the imposthume of much wealth and peace, That inward breaks. **1652** CULPEPPER *Eng. Physic.* 17 Laid warm on a Boil [it] will ripen and break it. **1711** *Lond. Gaz.* No. 4894/2 Most of their Bombs break before they fall. **1802** R. REECE *Med. Guide* (1850) 306 Boils ..after they break..require only to be kept clean.

5. Said in reference to the rupture of a surface: **a.** To part or lay open the surface of (anything), as of land (by ploughing, etc.). Also *to break up*, 57 f: and see *to break ground*, 44.

1499 *Promp. Parv.* 49 Breken claddis, *occo*. **1526** *Pilgr. Perf.* (W. de W. 1531) 23 Our soyle or lande is our hertes, whiche we..breke with the plough of abstynence. **1552** HULOET, Break land with a plough, *obfringo*. **1697** DRYDEN *Virg. Eclog.* VIII. 97 Verse breaks the Ground, and penetrates the Brake. **1813** BYRON *Giaour* i, No breath of air to break the wave. **1847** LONGF. *Ev.* I. ii. 114 The merry lads ..breaking the glebe round about.

b. To crack or rupture (the skin); to graze, bruise, wound, as in phrase ***to break one's head***. ***to break Priscian's head***: to violate the rules of grammar.

c **1305** *Jud. Iscariot* 50 in *E.E.P.* (1862) 108 Children..he wolde smyte, And breke here armes and here heued. *c* **1489** CAXTON *Sonnes of Aymon* x. 256 Atte the fallyng that he made, he brake alle his browes. **1590** SHAKS. *Com. Err.* II. i. 78 Backe slaue, or I will breake thy pate a-crosse. **1592** —— *Rom. & Jul.* I. iii. 38 Euen the day before she broke her brow. **1711** BUDGELL *Spect.* No. 161 ¶3 A Ring of Cudgel-Players..breaking one another's Heads. **1785** R. CUMBERLAND *Observer* No. 22 §6 Observe how this..orator breaks poor Priscian's head for the good of his country. **1883** *Daily Tel.* 10 July 5/4 Does Shakespeare never break Priscian's head?

c. *intr.* Of the surface of water: to present a broken appearance, caused by water-bloom (see quots. and BREAKING *vbl. sb.* 2 c). *dial.*

1873 G. C. DAVIES *Mountain, Meadow, and Mere* 16 The Ellesmere water..*breaks*. Every summer..the water becomes full of some matter held in suspension... The other meres do not *break* to such an extent. **1887** T. DARLINGTON *Folk-Speech of S. Cheshire* 128 Bar-mere's bin *breekin'* this afternoon.

6. *intr.* To crack without complete separation. Formerly said of a bell; hence possibly, from the similarity of the sound emitted, of a boy's voice on reaching the age of puberty.

1486 *Bk. St. Albans* D iij, That thay [the bells on a hawk's neck] be hoole and not brokyn and speciall in the sowndyng place. **1667** PEPYS *Diary* 21 Aug., This morning come two of Captain Cooke's boys, whose voices are broke; and are gone from the Chapel. **1706** A. BEDFORD *Temple Mus.* ix. 172 Lads, when their Voices did Break, or Alter. **1880** in Grove *Dict. Mus.* I. 703/2 His voice began to break.

II. With regard chiefly to the state or condition produced: to break so as to disable, destroy cohesion, solidity, or firmness, crush, shatter.

7. a. *trans.* To crush, shatter (*e.g.* a bone). ***to break the leg*** or ***arm***: i.e. the bones of the limb.

a **1000** *Ags. Gosp.* John xix. 32 [Hi] bræcon ærest ðæs sceancan þe mid him ahangen wæs. *a* **1300** *Cursor M.* 21145 A wicked iuu..him brac his harn panne. **1382** WYCLIF *Ex.* ix. 25 Eche treo of the cuntree it [the hail] breke togidere. *c* **1460** *Towneley Myst.* 142, I shuld with this steylle brand Byrkyn alle his bonys. **1599** HAKLUYT *Voy.* II. II. 331 [19] The elephant..with the poise of his body breaketh him. **1759** tr. *Duhamel's Husb.* I. xv. (1762) 100 When the distemper'd grain is broke. **1836** MARRYAT *Midsh. Easy* xxxiii, Break my leg!—break my leave, you mean?

b. ***to break on the wheel***: to bind a criminal to a wheel, or similar frame, and break his limbs, or beat him to death; so † ***to break on the torture***: to put to the torture, dislocate on the rack, etc. ***to break one's back*** or ***neck***: to dislocate the bones of the back or neck; also *fig.* to overpower, render nugatory, crush. ***to break the neck of a journey, a piece of business***, etc.: to get through the most serious part of it. ***to break the back of a ship***: to break the keel and keelson, dislocate the framework of the centre, so that the two ends tend to fall apart.

a **1300** *Cursor M.* 22202 Ouer hogh to lepe his hals to brek. *c* **1400** *Gamelyn* 712, I ne hadde broke his nekke, tho I his rigge brak. **1579** FENTON *Guicciard.* VII. (1599) 289 To break the necke of the wicked purposes and plots of the French. **1586** WARNER *Alb. Eng.* II. x. 47 Her good-man..kindly bad her breake her necke, olde Jade. **1598** GRENEWEY *Tacitus' Ann.* XI. vii. (1622) 148 Being broken on the torture, he confessed nothing. **1610** SHAKS. *Temp.* III. ii. 26, I had rather cracke my sinewes, breake my backe, Then you should such dishonor vndergoe. **1634** MASSINGER *Very Wom.* v. iv, Rack him first, and after break him Upon the wheel. **1690** LUTTRELL *Brief Rel.* (1857) II. 147 A Dutch man of war..run upon the sands and broke her back. **1735** POPE *Prol. Sat.* 308 Who breaks a butterfly upon a wheel? **1864** *Times* 24 Dec., The..delusion that a single campaign would 'break the neck of the rebellion'. **1878** MORLEY *Diderot* I. 201 A country where youths were broken on the wheel for levity in face of an ecclesiastical procession.

c. ***to break the heart***: to kill, crush, or overwhelm with sorrow. Also *intr.* (for *refl.*)

c **1386** CHAUCER *Knts. T.* 96 Hym thoughte þat his herte wolde breke. **1593** DRAYTON *Eclog.* x. 93 Thou with thine Age, my Heart with sorrow broke. **1605** SHAKS. *Macb.* IV. iii. 210 The griefe that do's not speake, Whispers the o'refraught heart, and bids it breake. **1713** ADDISON *Cato* III.

iii. 31 Thy disdain Has broke my heart. **1832** Tennyson *Œnone* 31 My heart is breaking and my eyes are dim. **1848** Macaulay *Hist. Eng.* II. 253 The great calamity which.. had almost broken his heart.

d. *Cricket.* ***to break one's duck('s egg)***: to score one's first run in an innings, thus avoiding a 'duck' (duck *sb.*[1] 7).

1867 G. H. Selkirk *Guide to Cr. Ground* ii. 26 If he makes one run he has 'broken his duck's egg'. **1900** W. A. Bettesworth *Walkers of Southgate* 19 Parr broke his duck, but could get no further, being bowled by Atkinson for one run. **1912** A. Brazil *New Girl at St. Chad's* vii. 112 Her first ball, being a wide, served to increase the confidence Honor had felt in breaking her duck.

8. † **a.** To dissolve (anything hard or coherent).

1579 Langham *Gard. Health* (1633) 81 The herbe boyled or drunke raw with Wine breaketh the stone. *a* **1648** Digby *Closet Open.* (1677) 87 Set them [honey and water] over so gentle a fire as you might endure to break it in the water with your hand.

b. *intr.* To dissolve, relax. As said of a frost there may be some admixture of the notion of a break of continuity (*branch* V). Also of weather: to change suddenly, esp. after a long settled period. Cf. sense 57 h.

1530 Palsgr. 754/2 It thaweth, as the weather dothe, whan the frost breaketh. **1570–87** Holinshed *Scot. Chron.* (1806) I. 273 The frost breake and the snowe melted. **1607** Topsell *Four-f. Beasts* 291 His Cough breaketh more and more. **1681** Dryden *Abs. & Achit.* 287 Or if they shou'd, their Interest soon would break. **1767** Watson in *Phil. Trans.* LVII. 444 On the next day..the frost broke. **1887** Yeats *Lett.* (1954) I. 51 The weather breaking might send me off any time, as my uncle stops here only so long as it is fine. **1930** W. S. Maugham *Cakes & Ale* viii. 91 The weather broke suddenly.

c. Of prices of commodities, stocks, etc.: to fall suddenly or sharply. orig. *U.S.*

1870 W. W. Fowler *Ten Yrs. in Wall St.* 435 Gold had broken to 87, and then..ran up to 194. **1899** *Daily News* 15 May 2/6 Under the influence of Mr. Flower's death, what are known as Flower stocks broke in overwhelming volume. **1929** *Times* 30 Oct. 14/1 Prices broke far below the previous low levels of the year.

9. a. *trans.* To demolish, smash, destroy, ruin; to defeat, foil, frustrate (things material or immaterial); *esp.* to defeat the object of (a strike) by engaging other workers.

a **1300** *Cursor M.* 12018 Thoru envie and wreth and tene [He] brack þe lackes al bi-dene. **1513** More *Edw. V* (1641) 13 Each laboureth to breake that the other maketh. **1535** Coverdale *Ps.* lxxxviii [ix]. 10 Thou breakest the proude, like one that is wounded. **1678** N. Wanley *Wonders* v. i. §103. 468/2 Ferdinand the third..broke the Great power of the Swedes. **1719** De Foe *Crusoe* xiv, The number of them broke all my measures. **1871** Freeman *Norm. Conq.* (1876) IV. xvii. 47 Their moral force was utterly broken. **1905** [implied in *strike-breaker*, strike *sb.* 20]. **1914** *Round Table* Mar. 367 The farmers contributed the bulk of the power that..broke the strike.

b. To nullify or set aside (a will) by legal methods.

1891 *Melbourne Argus* 12 Dec. 11/8 [New York.] Under the law [she] would be entitled to one-half of the estate, should the will be broken.

c. To better (a record, a score, etc.). Also in Financial and Stock Exchange jargon, = breach *v.* 1 b. (See record *sb.* 5 d.)

1886 [see record *sb.* 13 a]. **1909** Webster s.v., He broke the record for the high jump. **1955** F. Brown *Angels & Spaceships* 171 Up to that hole he [*sc.* a golfer] had an excellent chance to break a hundred. [**1959** *Economist* 21 Feb. 705/2 There is now a firm conviction that the [Dow-Jones industrial] average will break through 650 this year.] **1964** G. W. Cooke *Stock Markets* xxv. 339 Both averages continued the rise in October 1962, and the industrial broke its previous high in September 1963. The rail average broke above its 1959 and 1961 highs. **1981** *Times* 25 Apr. 19/5 The index failed to break the 600 level. **1984** *Financial Times* 28 Feb. iv. p. vi/2 The Tokyo Stock Exchanges got off to a good start this year with the Dow Jones index breaking the historical yen 10,000 mark for the first time in early January.

d. To win against (an opponent's service) in lawn tennis or a similar game. Also *intr.* or with *through*.

1959 *Times* 2 July 3/1 Mackay saved his next game, broke to 8–7 in an uproar, and served out heroically for the set. *Ibid.* 4 July 3/7 He broke service in the first game. **1961** *Ibid.* 4 July 4/1 True, Wilson..did break for 2–4 and then move to 3–4. **1964** *Observer* 1 Nov. 19/1 Sangster broke service in the ninth game and went on to win 6–4. *Ibid.*, Sangster broke through Bungert's service in the fifth game.

e. To disprove (an alibi).

1932 D. L. Sayers *Have his Carcase* xxv. 338 I'll break that alibi if I die for it. **1961** 'N. Blake' *Worm of Death* ix. 128 He had just seen an apparently broken alibi rendered intact again by a few words. **1984** *Daily Tel.* 22 June 12/3 Parry, however, had had an alibi which Mr Wilkes is confident that he has broken.

10. *trans.* To shiver or dash in pieces a wave, billow, or moving mass of water, as a rock or other obstacle does; also *intr.* said of waves, etc. when they dash against an obstacle, or topple over and become surf or 'broken water' in the shallows. (But in the 'breaking' of waves, the sea, etc., various other senses are often combined: see the quots.)

c **1375** Barbour *Bruce* iii. 699 Wawys wyd [that] brekand war. **1593** Shaks. *Lucr.* 1440 Their [the waves] ranks began To break upon the galled shore. **1697** Dryden *Virg. Georg.* iii. 406 About him, and above, the Billows broke. *a* **1744** Pope (J.) That tumult in the Icarian sea, dashing and breaking among its crowd of islands. **1795** Southey *Joan of Arc* viii. 306 Some huge promontory whose broad base Breaks the rough wave; the shiver'd surge rolls back. **1842** Tennyson, Break, break, break On thy cold gray stones O Sea! **1860** *Merc. Mar. Mag.* VII. 259 In heavy..weather Point Pinos breaks the swell.

11. a. To ruin financially, make bankrupt (a person or bank). ***to break the bank***: formerly also in the sense 'to become bankrupt'.

(*To break the bank*, in Gambling means to clear out the amount of money which the proprietor of the gaming table has before him: see bank *sb.*[3] 4.)

1612–15 Bp. Hall *Contempl. O.T.* xix. vii, The holiest man may be deep in arrearages, and break the bank. **1644–7** R. Stapylton *Juvenal* 123 Meer expence in paper breaks you all. *a* **1674** Clarendon *Hist. Reb.* (1703) II. vii. 330 The necessities of the Army still pressed us..to break the Merchants here. **1705** Tate *Warriour's Welc.* x. 7 Britain's Gen'ral came..and broke the Bank of Fame. **1850** Thackeray *Pendennis* lvi. (1884) 548 He had seen his friend ..break the bank three nights running at Paris.

b. *intr.* (for *refl.*) To become bankrupt, to 'fail' (commercially). Now less usual.

1596 Shaks. *Merch. V.* iii. i. 120 Hee cannot choose but breake. **1661–2** Pepys *Diary* 19 Jan., Our merchants here in London do daily break. **1678** Butler *Hud.* iii. iii. 248 By which some Glorious Feats atchieve, As Citizens, by breaking, thrive. **1793** Ld. Spencer in *Ld. Auckland's Corr.* (1862) III. 82 Hutchinson is going to break, and to show the world that honesty is the best policy. **1856** Emerson *Eng. Traits* v. 89 In trade, the Englishman believes that nobody breaks who ought not to break. **1879** H. George *Progr. & Pov.* v. i. (1881) 250 A bank breaks..and on every side workmen are discharged.

12. a. *trans.* To crush the strength of, wear out, exhaust; to weary, impair, in health or strength.

1483 Caxton *Gold Leg.* 224/1 He was broken with the hete of the sonne and wyth labour. **1583** Babington *Commandm.* Ep. Ded., Your servants, that breake both bodie and braines in your affaires. **1666** Pepys *Diary* (1879) VI. 78 Whom I have not seen since he was sicke..he is mightily broke. **1715** Burnet *Own Time* II. 340 Lord Essex told me he was much broken in his thoughts. **1725** Pope *Odyss.* xii. 143 O worn by toils, oh broke in fight. **1857** Ruskin *Pol. Econ. Art* 16 None had been broken by toil.

† **b.** So ***to break one's brain, mind, wind*** (cf. broken-winded). *Obs.*

c **1340** Hampole *Prose Treat.* 37 He sall mowe breke his heuede and his body and he sall neuer be þe nerre. **1530** Palsgr. 464/1, I breake my brayne to do hym good. **1547** Boorde *Brev. Health* §321 Breaking a mans mynde about many matters the whiche he can nat comprehende. **1596** Shaks. *1 Hen. IV*, ii. ii. 13 If I trauel but foure foot..further a foote I shall breake my winde. **1597** Morley *Introd. Mus.* 77, I shall neuer leaue breaking my braines til I finde it. **1647** Ward *Simp. Cobler* 22 It would breake his [the Devil's] wind and wits to attend such a Province. **1690** W. Walker *Idiom. Anglo-Lat.* 70 He breakes his brains with studying.

c. *intr.* To fail in health, decay, give way. See also *to break up*, 57 i.

1713 Swift *Cadenus & V.* Wks. 1755 III. ii. 15 I'm sorry Mopsa breaks so fast. **1804** G. Rose *Diaries* (1860) II. 194 The Archbishop..is breaking fast. **1876** Trevelyan *Life & Lett. Macaulay* II. vii. 2 His health was breaking fast.

13. To crush in spirit or temper; to discourage; to overcome, prevail upon (*obs.*).

[**1513** Douglas *Æneis* viii. vii. 33 Aurora wyth hyr teris so the brak, For tyl enarme hir child.] **1618** Bolton *Florus* ii. xvii. 144 Cato..brake the hearts of the Celtiberians..by certaine encounters. **1667** Milton *P.L.* v. 887 That Golden Scepter Is now an Iron Rod to bruise and breake Thy disobedience. *a* **1674** Clarendon *Hist. Reb.* (1704) III. xv. 458 By breaking their Fortunes and Estates, he had not at all broken their Spirits. **1752** Hume *Ess. & Treat.* (1777) I. 192 A person..easily broken by affliction. **1855** Macaulay *Hist. Eng.* IV. 96 The slaughter of Aghrim had broken the spirit of the army.

14. a. To reduce to obedience or discipline, tame, train (horses or other animals, also human beings); to subject or habituate *to*. Now also *to break in* 53 a.

1474 Caxton *Chesse* 32 His hors wel broken. **1519** Horman *Vulg.* 254 It is better to breke a mannys owne people in warr than to hyre straungers. **1542** Udall *Erasm. Apoph.* 80 a, The same children he broke and taught how to awayte on their parentes. **1596** Shaks. *Tam. Shr.* ii. i. 148 Why then thou canst not break her to the Lute? **1605** Bacon *Adv. Learn.* ii. xiii. §7 (1873) 156 Cicero himself being broken unto it by great experience. **1668** Pepys *Diary* 14 Dec., About breaking of my horses to the coach. **1688** R. Holme *Armoury* ii. 149/2 To Break or Back a Colt is the first riding of him. **1766** Goldsm. *Vic. W.* x, They had never been broken to the rein. **1824** Miss Mitford *Village* Ser. i. (1863) 113 Whose dog hath he broken?

b. ***to break from.*** Cf. also *break of*, 33 b.

1530 Palsgr. 464/2, I breake a yonge beest from his wylde condyscions.

III. To violate.

15. To violate, do violence to; to fail to observe or keep; to transgress. (The opposite of *to keep sacred* or *intact*.) Said esp. in reference to

a. a law, commandment, rule, requirement; a thing sanctified by law or ordinance, as the Sabbath, the king's peace, a sanctuary. † ***to break time*** (in Music): to fail to keep time.

a **1000** *Cædmon's Daniel* 299 (Gr.) Yldra usse..ðin bibodu bræcon. **1023** *Chart. Canute* in *Cod. Dipl.* IV. 24 Gif ænig is ðæt ȝewilnað to brekenne..ðas ure ȝefæstnunge. *c* **1175** *Lamb. Hom.* 79 He..brec cristes heste. *c* **1200** *Trin. Coll. Hom.* 179 þat..brecð grið þar he hit healde sholde. *a* **1300** *Cursor M.* 11992 Hu iesus brickes vr halidai. *Ibid.* 13808 þou carl, qui brekes þou vr lau? *c* **1375** Wyclif *Serm.* Sel. Wks. II. 95 He brac þe Sabot. **1377** Langl. *P. Pl.* B. ii. 82 Unboxome and bolde to breke þe ten hestes. **1591** Spenser *Virgil's Gnat* lix, Cruell Orpheus..Seeking to kisse her, brok'st the gods decree. **1593** Shaks. *Rich. II*, v. v. 43 Keepe time: How sowre sweet Musicke is, When Time is broke, and no Proportion kept? **1668** Marvell *Corr.* ci. Wks. 1872–5 II. 255 We had broke no privelege of the Lords. **1678** Butler *Hud.* iii. iii. 592 He Ingag'd the Constable to seize All those that would not break the Peace. **1771** *Junius Lett.* liv. 284 The laws have..been shamefully broken. **1850** Thackeray *Pendennis* lxi. (1884) 603 As refined as Mrs. Bull, who breaks the King's English.

b. a contract or covenant of any kind; a treaty, indenture, league, truce, peace, or the like.

911 *O.E. Chron.* (Parker MS.) Her bræc se here on Norð hymbrum þone frið. **1340** *Ayenb.* 16 Prede brek uerst uelaȝrede and ordre. *c* **1440** *Promp. Parv.* 50 Breke conuenant, *fidifrago*. **1513** Douglas *Æneis* xii. v. Advt., Quhou Iuturna..Breikis the peax, and hasty batale sent. **1552** Huloet, Breake truce, *fœdus frangere*. **1763** *Brit. Mag.* IV. 372 Which made me break my indentures, and run away. **1791** Burke *App. Whigs* Wks. VI. 150 The contract is thereby broke. **1873** Burton *Hist. Scot.* V. lvii. 153 The English were the first to break the peace.

c. an oath, promise, pledge, vow, one's word, (one's) faith.

a **1000** *Beowulf* 4132 þonne bioð brocene, að-sweord eorla. *c* **1205** Lay. 705 Brutus him swar an æð, breken þat he hit nælde. *c* **1340** *Cursor M.* 10674 Hir vou to breke. **1496–7** *Act 12 Hen. VII*, xii. Pream., In breking his seid promys. **1552** Huloet, Breake fayth, othe, or promyse. **1593** Shaks. *2 Hen. VI*, v. i. 91 False King, why hast thou broken faith with me? —— *Rich. II*, iv. i. 214 God pardon all Oathes that are broke to mee. **1664** Butler *Hud.* ii. ii. 138 Some, to the Glory of the Lord, Perjur'd themselves and broke their word. **1752** Johnson *Rambl.* No. 201 ¶9 A promise is never to be broken. **1848** Macaulay *Hist. Eng.* II. 79 The king would gladly have broken his word. *Ibid.* (1857) II. 471 That men who are in the habit of breaking faith should be distrusted when they mean to keep it is part of their just and natural punishment.

d. † ***to break spousehood*** (ME.), ***wedlock, matrimony*** (16th c.): to break the marriage vow, commit adultery. ***to break a marriage***: to dissolve or annul it, obtain a divorce.

c **1175** *Lamb. Hom.* 143 þe sunfulle Men þet spushad brekeð. **1530** Tindale *Gen.* Prol., David, though he brake wedlock. **1535** Coverdale *Matt.* xix. 18 Thou shalt not breake wedlocke. —— *Luke* xvi. 18 Who so euer putteth awaye his wife and marieth another breaketh matrimony. **1844** Ld. Brougham *Brit. Const.* xiv. (1862) 212 His desire to break his first marriage from his wish to espouse Anne Boleyn.

† **e.** ***to break day***: to fail to keep an appointed time (for payment, etc.). *Obs.*

c **1300** *Beket* 769 Com to morwe..that thu thane dai ne breke. *c* **1386** Chaucer *Chan. Yem. Prol. & T.* 487 That in no wise he breke wol his day. *c* **1590** Marlowe *Jew of M.* i. ii. 340 If we break our day, we break the league. *c* **1610** Rowlands *Terrible Batt.* 8 Sirrha, your day is broke, ile keepe your pawne. **1642** Rogers *Naaman* To Rdr., Breaking daies, promises, yea oathes and vowes.

f. ***to break ship***: to fail to rejoin a ship on the expiration of leave.

1905 'Q' *Shining Ferry* iii. xviii, I brought across a sailor-looking chap... Thinks I, 'You've broken ship, my friend.' **1907** *Daily Chron.* 3 Apr. 1/7 The serious offence of 'breaking ship'. **1909** *Ibid.* 28 June 8/7 In the afternoon he broke ship, but was undiscovered.

IV. To make a way through, or lay open by breaking; to penetrate; to open up.

16. a. To burst (a barrier) so as to force a way through it. Also *to break open*: see 17 b.

a **1000** *Byrhtnoth* 277 Eadweard bræc ðone bordweall. *a* **1200** *Moral Ode* 92 in *E.E.P.* (1862) 27 Ne brecð neuer-euft crist helle dure. *c* **1325** *E.E. Allit. P.* B. 1239 He brek þe bareres as bylyue. **1384** Chaucer *Mother of G.* 86 And broken been the yates eek of helle. **1607** Shaks. *Cor.* i. i. 210 They..sigh'd forth Prouerbes That Hunger broke stone wals. **1766** Gibbon *Decl. & F.* I. xvi. 419 The doors were instantly broke open. **1860** Smiles *Self-help* i. 10 Admiral Hobson..broke the boom at Vigo, in 1702.

b. To solve (a code or cipher); to decipher.

1928 P. Buranelli et al. *Cryptogram Bk.* p. ii, We were amazed at the ease with which anyone could break a coded message. **1931** *N. & Q.* 30 May 379/2 Their centre in New York receives messages by the thousand in a code that has not yet been broken. **1956** C. Simak *Time & Again* xxxv. 168 No one else could break the language in which his notes were written.

17. a. To enter (a house, an enclosed place, etc.) by breaking part of its circuit; to enter by force or violence. Cf. *to break open*, or *into*, 42; and *to break up*, 57 j. (See housebreaker.) In modern use, only in phr. ***to break and enter***: see breaking *vbl. sb.* 1 c.

851 *O.E. Chron.* [The Danes] bræcon Contwara burȝ and Lundenburȝ. *a* **1123** *Ibid.* an. 1102 þeofas..breokan þa minstre of Burh. *c* **1305** *Jud. Iscariot* 73 in *E.E.P.* (1862) 109 Iudas brac þe ȝard anon. **1393** Langl. *P. Pl.* C. xxi. 383 [þou] by-glosedest hem and bygyledest hem and my gardyn breke. **1483** *Cath. Angl.* 42 To Breke garth, *desepire*. **1495** *Act 11 Hen. VII*, lix. Pream., Evyll disposed persones.. intendyng..to have broken the hous of your seid Subget. **1533–4** *Durham Depositions* (Surtees) 49 The said Dicson did break the churche of West Awkelande. *c* **1677** Marvell *Growth Popery* 29 Clauses most severe..one for breaking all Houses whatsoever on suspicion of any such Pamphlet. **1745** Wesley *Wks.* (1872) XII. 69 Shall George Whitfield be charged with felony, because John Wesley broke a house? **1768** Blackstone *Comm.* III. 209 Every unwarrantable entry on another's soil the law entitles a trespass by breaking his close. **1797** Tomlins *Jacob's Law-Dict.* I. Bb3/3 To break and enter a *shop*..is not burglary, but only larceny. **1817** [see enter *v.* 10 d]. **1959** A. Sillitoe *Loneliness Long-Dist. Runner* 11 There's a shop to break and enter. **1961** J. Maclaren-Ross *Doomsday Bk.* i. iv. 56 He broke-and-entered through a back window.

b. ***to break open***: to open or enter by breaking. Cf. also *to break up*, 57 j.

1590 SHAKS. *Com. Err.* III. i. 73 Go fetch me something, Ile break ope the gate. **1593** —— *Lucr.* 446 She, much amazed, breaks ope her lock'd-up eyes. **1621** QUARLES *Esther* (1638) 89 Break ope the leaves, those leaves so full of dread. **1623** MEADE in Ellis *Orig. Lett.* I. 289 III. 150 The king siezes upon all the Merchants Letters from Spain, breaks them open. **1652** *Proc. Parliament* No. 109 Advt., His stable being broke open, was stoln one Brown bay gelding. **1753** W. DOUGLASS *Brit. Settlem. N. Amer.* 287 They broke open his house and carried him from his naked Bed. **1853** *Arab. Nts.* (Rtldg.) 266 The very robbers who had broken open and pillaged his house.

18. To make or produce (a hole, opening, passage, way, etc.) by breaking.

c **1320** *Seuyn Sag.* (W.) 1261 An hole thai bregen. **1633** P. FLETCHER *Purple Isl.* XI. xii, A renting sigh way for her sorrow brake. **1698** in *Select. Harl. Misc.* (1793) 387 Morgan set his soldiers to break avenues for their marching out. **1705** HEARNE *Coll.* 5 Oct. (1885) I. 52 Dalton being forc'd to break way. **1835** I. TAYLOR *Spir. Despot.* ii. 70 Their predecessors who have broke a path upon this field of noble and expansive good will. **1865** TYLOR *Early Hist. Man.* ii. 20 A way for thought is already broken.

19. To escape from (an enclosed place) by breaking part of the enclosure, as in ***to break prison*** or ***jail***; also ***to break bounds***.

c **1300** *Beket* 48 Gilbert and his felawes siththe..Prisoun breke. **1482** CAXTON *Chron. Eng.* cclvii. 336 The prysoners of Newgate brake theyr prison. *c* **1593** SPENSER *Sonn.* lxxiii, My hart..Breaking his prison, forth to you doth fly. **1674** J. B[RIAN] *Harv.-Home* viii. 52 Who is himself; and breaks the jayl, must die. **1790** BURKE *Fr. Rev.* 8 Am I to congratulate an highwayman..who has broke prison, upon the recovery of his natural rights? **1813** BYRON *Giaour* 534 The faithless slave that broke her bower. **1816** JANE AUSTEN *Emma* III. vii. 116 You had..broken bounds yesterday, and run away from your own management. **1856** [see BOUND *sb.*[1] 4]. **1857** BUCKLE *Civilis.* I. xii. 670 A hatred and jealousy which broke all bounds. *Mod.* Scholars gated for a week for breaking bounds.

20. a. ***to break covert*** or ***cover***: to start forth from a hiding-place; also absol. *to break*; cf. 37, 39.

1602 *Return fr. Parnass.* II. v. (Arb.) 31, [I] stood to intercept from the thicket: the buck broke gallantly. **1859** JEPHSON *Brittany* ix. 149 The wolf, a cub, broke cover in fine style. **1859** TENNYSON *Enid* 183 They break covert at our feet.

b. ***to break water*** or ***soil***: said of a stag.

1486 *Bk. St. Albans* E vij b, Then brekyth he water ther to take yow tent. **1575** TURBERV. *Venerie* 241 When he goeth quite through a ryver or water, we say he breaketh soyle. **1607** TOPSELL *Four-f. Beasts* 91 They love the lakes and strong streams, breaking the floods to come by fresh pasture.

21. a. To penetrate (as light breaks the darkness, sound the air). Cf. 41.

1599 SHAKS. *Hen. V*, III. iii. 40 Whiles the mad Mothers, with their howles confus'd, Doe breake the Cloudes. **1676** DRYDEN *Virg. Georg.* IV. 666 All her fellow Nymphs the Mountains tear With loud Laments, and break the yielding Air. **1795** SOUTHEY *Joan of Arc* IV. 44 To-morrow's sun, Breaking the darkness of the sepulchre. **1813** BYRON *Giaour* 1145 What beam shall break my night? **1839** THIRLWALL *Greece* III. 265 Only one ray of hope broke the gloom of her prospects. **1871** SWINBURNE *Songs bef. Sunrise, Eve of Rev.* 49 The night is broken eastward; is it day?

b. *intr.* Said of the darkness (*rare*).

1594 SHAKS. *Rich. III*, V. iii. 86 Flakie darkenesse breakes within the East.

22. a. † ***to break one's mind*** (***heart***): to deliver or reveal what is in one's mind (*obs.*). ***to break news, a matter, a secret***: to make it known, disclose, divulge it; now implying caution and delicacy.

c **1450** LONELICH *Grail* xxxvi. 274 Al ȝowre herte thanne to me breke. **1474** SIR J. PASTON *Lett.* 747 III. 118 To whom she brake hyr harte and tolde hyr y[t] she sholde have hadde Mast[r] Paston. **1525** LD. BERNERS *Froiss.* II. lxii. [lxv.] 212 A squyer of Bretayne, to whome he had broken his mynde. **1528** GARDINER in Pocock *Rec. Ref.* I. 101 His holiness demanded whether the king's highness had at any time broken this matter to the queen. **1683** *Penn. Archives* I. 83, I broke y[e] bussiness to Pr. Aldrix. **1712** STEELE *Spect.* No. 455 ¶3 She began to break her Mind very freely..to me. **1712** ARBUTHNOT *John Bull* 102 With a design to break the matter gently to his partners. **1759** DILWORTH *Pope* 64 After a short acquaintance..he broke his mind to him upon that subject. *a* **1779** G. COLMAN in G. Colman (Jun.) *Posth. Lett.* (1820) 339 Here it may be resolved..that she shall break the secret of their marriage to the old Earl. **1840** HOOD *Up Rhine* 1 Now, however, I have some news to break.

†**b.** Hence, *intr.* to break *with* (rarely *to* a person), *of* or *concerning* (a thing). *Obs.*

1463 *Paston Lett.* 473 II. 134 He kept not his owyn councell but brak to every man of it. **1529** MORE *Comf. agst. Trib.* II. Wks. 1188/1 Wyth hym she secretely brake, and offered hym ten ducates for hys labour. **1591** SHAKS. *Two Gent.* III. i. 59, I am to breake with thee of some affaires. **1599** —— *Much Ado* I. i. 328 Then after to her father will I breake. **1612** DRAYTON *Poly-olb.* Song xii. 200 With him to breake Of some intended act. **1614** RALEIGH *Hist. World* v. vi. §8 To this effect Scipio brake with the Consul.

c. To publish or reveal (an item of news); to make available for publication. (Cf. sense 39 b.) *Journalists' colloq.*

1906 G. W. PECK *Bad Boy with Circus* 21 (Weingarten). **1935** M. M. ATWATER *Murder in Midsummer* xxviii. 262 Are you breaking the story in the morning papers? **1961** 'B. WELLS' *Day Earth caught Fire* vii. 108 But she didn't break the story.

23. *trans.* ***to break a jest***: to utter, crack a joke. So ***to break a sigh, a smile***, etc.

1589 *Pappe w. Hatchet* B, Your Knaueship brake your fast on the Bishops, by breaking your iests on them. **1599** SHAKS. *Much Ado* II. i 152 Hee'l but breake a comparison or two on me. **1655** FULLER *Ch. Hist.* v. III. 119 On the Scaffold (a place not to break jests, but to break off all jesting) he could not hold. **1709** SWIFT *Adv. Relig.* Wks. 1755 II. I. 107 He is ..in continual apprehension that some pert man of pleasure should break an unmannerly jest. *a* **1774** GOLDSM. *Double Transf.* 57 Jack..often broke A sigh in suffocating smoke. **1795** SOUTHEY *Joan of Arc.* x. 151 Welcoming his gallant son, He brake a sullen smile. **1833** *Fraser's Mag.* VIII. 54 The landlord and waiter..were not suffered to do any thing, save to break their jokes on the members.

24. To open, commence, begin. In certain obs. phrases, as to ***break parle, break trade***. Also at Billiards: ***to break the balls***: to make a stroke from the formal position in which the balls are placed at the beginning of a game, or after a foul stroke. In Billiards (Snooker, Pool, etc.): now also *intr.* and with *off*. (But cf. 31.)

1588 SHAKS. *Tit. A.* v. iii. 19 Romes Emperour and Nephewe breake the parle. **1788** FALCONBRIDGE *Afr. Slave Tr.* 12 After permission has been obtained for breaking trade..the captains go ashore. **1850** BOHN *Handbk. Games* 565 *Breaking the balls* is to take them all off the table, place the red on its spot, and..begin again from the baulk. **1893** *Funk's Stand. Dict.* I. 234/2 *Break*..*i*[*ntr*]...*Games.* To make the first play, as in pool. **1949** J. DAVIS *How I play Snooker* 170 (*heading*) Breaking off. **1957** R. HOLT *Teach yourself Billiards & Snooker* 8 The winner of the toss or 'stringing' thus has choice of balls, and of 'breaking' (commencing the game) or asking his opponent to 'break'. **1965** J. PULMAN *Tackle Snooker this Way* xi. 56 After winning the toss in the professional game we never think of allowing our opponent to 'break off'.

V. To make a rupture of union or continuity by breaking.

* *of union.*

25. a. *trans.* To break a bond, or anything that confines or fastens; to disrupt; hence to dissolve, loosen. Also *fig.* often with *asunder*.

a **1225** *St. Marher.* 18 Alre kingene king brec nu mine bondes. **1382** WYCLIF *Judges* xvi. 9 She criede to him, Philistien upon thee, Sampson, The which brak the boondis. **1535** COVERDALE *Ps.* ii. 3 Let us breake their bondes a sunder. **1578** TIMME *Calvin on Gen.* 241 The ambition of Nimrod, brake the bonds of this modesty. **1717** POPE *Eloisa* 173 Death, only death, can break the lasting chain. **1837** NEWMAN *Par. Serm.* (ed. 3) I. xv. 226 Distrust ..breaks the very bonds of human society. **1855** MACAULAY *Hist. Eng.* IV. 95 The spell which bound his followers to him was not altogether broken.

b. *intr.* (for *refl.*) See also 1 b for literal use.

c. *Naut. trans.* To free and shake out (a flag or sail which has been furled); also with *out*.

1889 *Times* 6 Aug. 8/3 The Royal Standard was broken on board the Victoria and Albert, and immediately H.M.S. Valorous..began to fire a salute. **1899** *Daily News* 9 Oct. 6/2 The Columbia broke out her spinnaker. **1901** *N. & Q.* 9th Ser. VII. 176/2 When a standard is 'broken' it is unfurled after being hoisted. **1928** *Daily Tel.* 20 Mar. 13/7 The Afghan standard was broken from the Majestic's mainmast. **1945** C. S. FORESTER *Commodore* 36 A black ball was soaring up the mast, and as it reached the block a twist of the seaman's wrist broke it out.

26. a. *trans.* To make a rupture in (the ranks of the enemy). (Also in one's own ranks, by quitting them, or fleeing.)

c **1205** LAY. 27506 Þene sceld-trume breken: þe Bruttes þer heolden. **1375** BARBOUR *Bruce* XII. 217 And luk ȝhe na vay brek aray. *c* **1400** *Destr. Troy* 6679 Mony batels he broke, buernes he slough. *c* **1460** FORTESCUE *Abs. & Lim. Mon.* (1714) 46 Nor yet to may breke a mighty Flote gatheryd of Purpose. *c* **1532** LD. BERNERS *Huon* (1883) 344 He drew his swerde..& brake the thyckest presse. **1636** MASSINGER *Bashf. Lover* II. iii, He dies that breaks his ranks Till all be our's. **1769** FALCONER *Dict. Marine* (1789) A a iij, It cannot easily break the enemy's line. **1803** MUNRO in Owen *Wellesley's Disp.* 790 After breaking their infantry, your cavalry..was not sufficiently strong to pursue any distance. **1842** TENNYSON *Two Voices* 155 The foeman's line is broke.

b. *absol.* Said of a band of fighting men: to break their ranks, fall into disorder; also of the ranks.

1598 BARRET *Theor. Warres* I. i. 4 To perform execution if the enemie break or flie. **1781** T. JEFFERSON in Sparks *Corr. Amer. Rev.* (1853) III. 308 They broke twice, and ran like sheep. **1824** MACAULAY *Ivry* 43 Their ranks are breaking like thin clouds before a Biscay gale. **1878** BOSW. SMITH *Carthage* 221 The 4,000 Roman cavalry..broke and fled.

c. *intr.* (for *refl.*) Said of clouds, mists, etc.: to divide, disperse.

1826 DISRAELI *Viv. Grey* VIII. iv. 485 The storm cannot last long thus..I am sure the clouds are breaking. **1875** GREEN *Short Hist.* viii. §1. 448 Cromwell saw the mists break over the hills of Dunbar.

d. *intr.* Bridge. Of the outstanding cards in a suit: to be distributed (evenly: i.e. favourably from the declarer's point of view; etc.) between opponents.

1952 *Bridge Mag.* Apr. 36/2 If the spades break no worse than four-two and the trumps three-one, establishment of the spade suit should be easy. **1959** *Listener* 8 Jan. 84/1 The trumps broke badly and the contract was down. *Ibid.* 19 Nov. 904/2 The diamonds failed to break. **1981** H. W. KELSEY *Bridge* ii. 29 The 4-1 trump split was a bit of a blow, but the slam would still be safe enough if either the spades or the diamonds broke evenly. **1983** V. MOLLO *Winning Bridge* i. 5 As the trumps didn't break kindly either, he had to concede defeat.

** *of continuance or continuity.*

†**27.** *trans.* To cut short, stop, bring to a sudden end. ***to break the siege***: to raise the siege. *Obs.*; but see *to break off*, 54 a.

1330 R. BRUNNE *Chron.* 111 (Mätz.) Our tale wille we no breke, bot telle forth the certeyn. *c* **1386** CHAUCER *Melibeus* ¶77 Wel ny alle atones bigonne they to rise for to breken his tale. **1387** TREVISA *Higden* Rolls Ser. II. 415 Penthesilea.. brak þe sege of þe Grees. **1534** MORE *Answ. Poysoned Bk.* 1058/2 A better then we both shall breake the strife betwene vs. *a* **1553** UDALL *Royster D.* IV. iv, Will ye my tale break? **1709** STRYPE *Ann. Ref.* I. xlvii. 510 To use means to break the match.

28. a. To interrupt the continuance of (an action); to stop for the time, suspend.

c **1400** *Rom. Rose* 6224 Love..brake his tale in the spekyng As though he had hym tolde lesyng. **1580** BARET *Alv.* B 1200 The workes be broken and remaine vnperfite for a time. **1712** ADDISON *Spect.* No. 321 ¶11, I would not break the Thread of these Speculations. **1848** MACAULAY *Hist. Eng.* I. 513 He was the first country gentleman..to break that long prescription.

b. ***to break one's fall, one's journey, the force of a blow.***

1848 MACAULAY *Hist. Eng.* II. 117 His fall, though thus broken, was still a fall. **1858** SEARS *Athan.* III. ii. 265 An awful plunge downward with nothing to break the fall. **1880** *Standard* 14 Dec., Count Hatzfeldt..breaks his journey at this capital to-day.

29. To interrupt the continuance of (a state); to disturb: esp. **a.** ***to break one's sleep*** or ***rest***; **b.** ***to break silence, stillness***. (See SILENCE.)

1597 SHAKS. *2 Hen. IV*, IV. v. 69 For this, the foolish ouer-carefull Fathers Haue broke their sleepes with thoughts. **1623** BINGHAM *Xenophon* 139 You shall put to death a man, that hath broken many a sleepe for you. **1706** ESTCOURT *Fair Examp.* I. i. 9, I hope your ill Luck did not break your Rest last Night. **1710** STEELE *Tatler* No. 222 ¶3 Keeping them awake, or breaking their Sleep when they are fallen into it. **1768** STERNE *Sent. Journ.* (1778) I. 176, I was not disposed to break silence. **1853** ROBERTSON *Serm.* Ser. III. xi. 138 There are but three things which can break that peace. **1853** KINGSLEY *Hypatia* xi. 126 Not a sound..broke the utter stillness of the glen.

c. ***to break one's fast***: to put an end to fasting by eating; *esp.* to eat after the night's fast, take the first meal of the day; to breakfast.

c **1400** *Beryn* Prol. 71 Ete & be merry, why breke yee nowt yeur fast? **1523** FITZHERB. *Husb.* §149 Be vppe betyme & breake thy faste before day. **1586** COGAN *Haven Health* ccxiii, These old men brake their fast commonly with honey. **1620** VENNER *Via Recta* viii. 171, I aduise them, not to be altogether fasting till dinner, but to breake their fast. **1653** WALTON *Angler* i. 2 My purpose is to be at Hodsden.. before I break my fast. **1665** EVELYN *Mem.* (1857) I. 375, I brake fast this morning with the King. **1808** SCOTT *Marm.* I. xxxi, And knight and squire had broke their fast.

30. a. To interrupt the uniformity of any quality; to qualify, allay.

1839 THIRLWALL *Greece* I. 183 An uniform tenor of life, broken only by the exertions necessary to satisfy the simplest animal wants. **1877** A. B. EDWARDS *Up Nile* vii. 177 Not a tree, not a hut..broke the green monotony of the plain. **1885** *Spectator* 18 July 950/2 He..breaks for a few hours the terrible sameness of a dull..sordid life.

b. Of colours: To modify a colour by mixing it with some other colour. Also *break down* 51 e, and *broken colours* (see BROKEN).

1753 CHAMBERS *Cycl. Supp.* s.v. *Broken*, A colour is said to be broken, when it is taken down or degraded by the mixture of some colour.

31. To alter abruptly the direction of (a line). ***to break a ball*** (at Cricket): to make it change its direction on touching the ground. ***to break joint***: said of stones or bricks in a building, when the lines of junction are not continuous. ***to break sheer***: see SHEER.

1616 SURFL. & MARKH. *Country Farm* 101 He [the ox] breaketh not vp his taile, but suffereth it to draw all along after him. **1660** BLOOME *Archit.* B, This Pillar is broken perfectly. **1753** CHAMBERS *Cycl. Supp.* s.v., The ray of incidence..is, as it were, broken and bent into another direction. **1793** SMEATON *Edystone L.* §42 Breaking joint one course upon the other. **1884** *Lillywhite's Cricket Comp.* 29 Cooper..has the faculty of breaking a ball two or three feet. **1884** W. G. GRACE in *Pall Mall G.* 3 Oct. 2/1 He says that a fast bowler can 'break' both ways, but admits that this cannot be done with precision.

32. a. *intr.* To deviate or start off abruptly from a line or previous course; to project; to fall off. Also with *away*, *off*; see 54 c.

1677 MOXON *Mech. Exerc.* (1703) 36 Examine..whether the Worm..do not break into Angles. *Ibid.* 279 Let the Keystone break without the Arch. **1687** *Lond. Gaz.* No. 2297/8 Stray'd or stolen..a black Mare..breaks high in the forehead. **1873** TRISTRAM *Moab* vii. 125 The plain.. breaking away abruptly in limestone precipices to a great depth. **1879** B. TAYLOR *Stud. Germ. Lit.* 240 The narrative continually breaks into dialogue.

b. In *Cricket*. A ball bowled is said to break when it changes its course after it has pitched: the bowler causes this by his delivery. It is said ***to break back*** when it breaks in from the off, ***to break in***, when it breaks from the leg side.

1847 W. DENISON *Cricketer's Companion* p. xix, The tendency of his bowling is to make the ball break back from the 'off', to the 'leg'. **1866** 'CAPT. CRAWLEY' *Cricket* 36 A.. ball breaking in from the leg-side. **1882** *Daily Tel.* 17 May, Clean bowled by a trimmer from Barnes, the ball apparently breaking back.

c. Of flowers: To burst into a diversity of colours under cultivation.

1835 LINDLEY *Introd. Bot.* (1848) II. 249 We have known the dahlias from a poor single dull-coloured flower break

into superior forms and brilliant colours. **1846** Mrs. Loudon *Ladies Comp. Flower Gard.* 303 All seedling Tulips, when they first flower, are..of a dull uniform colour; and to make them break, that is, to produce the brilliant and distinct colours which constitute the beauty of a florist's flower, a variety of expedients are resorted to.

VI. To sever or remove by breaking.

33. a. *trans.* To separate by breaking a connexion. (See *break away*, *off*, *out*.)

a **1200** *Trin. Coll. Hom.* 93 Brokene boȝes. *a* **1300** *Cursor M.* 15024 Bifor þair king þe childer kest Branches þai brak o bogh. *a* **1340** Hampole *Pr. Consc.* 2078 For þe dede his mynde away þan brekes. **1382** Wyclif *Deut.* xxiii. 25 Thou shalt breek eeris, and with the hoond brisse. **1611** Bible *Gen.* xxvii. 40 Thou shalt breake his yoke from off thy necke. *Mod.* Great boughs broken from the trees.

b. *to break* (*any one*) *of a practice* or *habit*: to cause him to discontinue it. Perh. orig. belonging to 14 b.

1612 Bacon *Greatness of Kingd., Ess.* (Arb.) 482 Neither must they be too much broken of it [danger], if they shall be preserued in vigor. **1701** W. Wotton *Hist. Rome* v. 74 He ..Broke them of their warm Baths. **1748** J. Mason *Elocut.* 11 A thick mumbling Way of speaking; which he broke himself of by declaiming with pebbles in his mouth. **1816** *Life W. Havergal* (1882) 15 His only fault is in preaching too fast, but he is trying to break himself of this. **1865** M. Arnold *Eug. de Guérin, Ess. Crit.* (1875) 165 When she wants to break a village girl of disobedience to her mother.

34. a. *intr.* To sever a connexion abruptly; to cease from relation *with*, quarrel *with*. See also *to break off*, 54 f.

1591 Shaks. *Two Gent.* ii. v. 19 *Speed.* Shall he marry her? *Launce.* No, neither. *Sp.* What, are they broken? **1607** —— *Cor.* iv. vi. 48 It cannot be The Volces dare breake with vs. **1687** R. Lestrange *Answ. Diss.* 39 They Brake, upon This Point. **1734** tr. *Rollin's Anc. Hist.* xx. §1 (1827) IX. 2 The Romans break with Perseus. **1859** Masson *Milton* I. 616 Charles broke with his Third Parliament in March 1628–9. **1872** Freeman *Gen. Sketch* xv. §14. 324 Ready to break with the past altogether.

b. In boxing or wrestling, to separate from one's opponent after a clinch; esp. as an order from the referee. Also with *away* (see sense 50 d).

1932 Wodehouse *Hot Water* vi. 114 Next thing you know they're rolling on the floor, and me acting as referee and telling them to break. **1966** 'J. Hackston' *Father clears Out* 199 Tom, who was also referee, told them to break, and both girls still kept hanging on.

35. ***to break an officer***; to cashier, deprive him of his commission, degrade him from his rank.

1695 *Lond. Gaz.* No. 3135/3 Three other Colonels are broke. **1717** De Foe *Hist. Ch. Scot.* iii. 73 Whether he was not broke for Cowardise I am not certain. **1787** Nelson in Nicolas *Disp.* (1845) I. 243 That no Officer could serve under him, and that sooner or later he must be broke. **1840** R. Dana *Bef. Mast* xvii. 46 From the time that he was 'broken', he had had a dog's berth on board the vessel. **1867** Smyth *Sailor's Word-bk.*, *Break*, to deprive of commission, warrant, or rating, by court-martial.

VII. Intransitive senses implying movement accompanied by the breaking of ties or barriers; to burst.

36. *intr.* To escape or depart by breaking ties or barriers (physical or immaterial); to depart by a forcible or sudden effort, to escape from restraint. Often with *loose*, *free*: see also *to break away*, 50 c.

a **1000** *Phœnix* 67 Wæter wynsumu..of ðære moldan tyrf brimcealdu brecað. *a* **1000** *Andreas* 513 (Gr.) We brecað ofer bæþweᵹ. **1423** Jas. I. *Kingis Q.* cxv, [Thay] breken louse, and walken at thaire large? **1535** Coverdale *Dan.* ii. 1 Had Nabuchodonosor a dreame..and his slepe brake from him. **1628** Digby *Voy. Medit.* (1868) 65 My boate broke from my sterne with a man in her. **1711** Steele *Spect.* No. 262 ¶4 When I broke loose from that great Body of Writers. **1810** Scott *Lady of L.* ii. xxxiv, Then Roderick from the Douglas broke. **1846** Ruskin *Mod. Paint.* I. ii. i. vii. §3. 74 The great historical painters..who had broken so boldly.. from the trammels of this notion. **1877** R. H. Hutton *Ess.* VII. Pref., Illusions from which..men have had the courage to break free. **1878** Morley *Crit. Misc.* Ser. i. 220 A world that had broken loose from its moorings.

37. To come out or emerge by breaking barriers; to burst forth, rush out with sudden violence. Const. *upon*. See also *to break forth*, 52; *out*, 55.

a. of words, laughter, sounds, etc.

1330 R. Brunne *Chron.* 55 (Mätz.) Bituex þam and þe messengers broþefulle wordes brak. **1596** Spenser *F.Q.* ii. iii. 24 Twixt the perles and rubins [i.e. teeth and lips] softly brake A siluer sound. **1709** Pope *Ess. Crit.* 628 But rattling nonsense in full vollies breaks. **1833** Ht. Martineau *Fr. Wines and Pol.* i. 12 Cries of grief and despair broke from them at every step. **1837** Lytton *Athens* I. 477 Loud broke the trumpets The standards..were raised on high. **1876** Green *Short Hist.* i. §4. 38 Verses of his own English tongue broke from time to time from the master's lips.

b. of an attacking party.

c **1400** *Destr. Troy* 13014 A busshement of bold men breke hym vpon. **1598** Grenewey *Tacitus' Ann.* i. xiv. (1622) 27 Vntill the enemy, with hope to breake vpon them, should draw neere. **1614** Raleigh *Hist. World* v. i. §10. 573 They brake back furiously upon their own footmen.

c. of natural phenomena, as a storm, light, etc.

1693 Dryden *Ovid's Met.* i. l. 483 in *Examen Poeticum* 31 A second Deluge, o're our heads may break. **1875** Dawson *Dawn of Life* i. 3 First bright streaks of light that break on.. night and death. **1961** L. van der Post *Heart of Hunter* i. i. 37 The country where the rains had broken. **1965** *Listener* 3 June 828/1 The monsoon, heaviest in the world in that area, had broken.

d. Of fish: To rise to the bait.

1885 *Harper's Mag.* Jan. 216/1, I tried to fool them with sham colored feathers; but no, sir, they [the fish] never broke.

e. *Athletics.* To get off the mark prematurely at the start of a race. Also with *away*.

1897 *Encycl. Sport* I. 55/2 While the runner has his hands on the ground he cannot 'break away' from the mark, and if a runner 'breaks away' he is, under the A.A.A. rules, put back a yard. **1959** *Observer* 26 July 24/6 H. Smit..broke twice in the 100 yards and should by international rules have been disqualified.

38. a. A person is also said ***to break into arms, rebellion, weeping, a laugh***, etc.

1588 Shaks. *Tit. A.* iii. i. 216 Do not breake into these deepe extreames. **1670** Cotton *Espernon* i. ii. 46 To which ..he was further necessitated by the King of Navarre's breaking into Arms. **1866** Kingsley *Herew.* xii. 170 She broke into wild weeping. **1871** A. R. Hope *My Schoolb. Fr.* (1875) 110 We broke into a titter. **1872** Black *Adv. Phaeton* iv. 42 The pony broke into a brisk trot. **1876** Green *Short Hist.* vi. §2 (1882) 275 In Kent..the discontent broke into open revolt.

b. To make a dash; to set off at a run. So ***to break back***: to set off running in a reverse direction. *U.S.*, *Austral.*, and *N.Z.*

1834 Crockett *Narr. Life* ii. 11 He gathered about a two year old hickory, and broke after me. *Ibid.* xiv. 96 When my lead dog..raised his yell, all the rest broke to him. **1835** A. B. Longstreet *Georgia Scenes* 125 The way she [*sc.* a horse] now broke for Springfield 'is nothing to nobody'. **1889** A. Reischek *Story of Wonderful Dog* vi. 34 If the sheep broke he ordered a second dog to assist. **1907** S. E. White *Arizona Nights* v. 98 The cattle would attempt to 'break' past the end and up the valley. **1933** E. Jones *Autobiogr. Early Settler* xii. 59 If a mob [of sheep]..broke back,..the rest of us would have to wait while the shepherd on whose beat the sheep had broken back, went for them. **1946** F. Davison *Dusty* ix. 96 With the dogs so far forward, the rearmost sheep..had a chance to break back.

c. Of a horse, esp. in trotting or pacing: to change gait; to lose a level stride. orig. *U.S.*

1839 *Spirit of Times* 13 July 222/3 While Awful was ahead, and his backers were counting the spoils in advance, he broke! **1852** C. A. Bristed *Upper Ten Th.* 26 Suddenly the pacer stops short and capers. He is used up and has 'broken'. **1908** *Springfield Weekly Republican* 8 Oct. 2 A trotter in a race breaks, that is, loses his level stride and reverts to an impossible kind of gallop which is not permitted by the rules. **1969** *Sydney Morning Herald* 24 May 27/3 Yogi Hall, who started 10–9 on favourite in the Trotters' Handicap, was barred because he broke badly during the running.

39. a. To issue forth, come forth suddenly into notice, come as a surprise. Const. *from*, *upon*, *into*.

1711 Steele *Spect.* No. 41 ¶5 He thought fit to break from his Concealment. **1712** Pope *Messiah*, See heav'n..break upon thee in a flood of day. **1750** Johnson *Rambl.* No. 79 ¶7 The anxieties that break into his face. **1830** H. Rogers *Ess.* I. i. 9 There is no author who so often breaks upon his readers with turns of thought, for which they are totally unprepared. **1853** Kane *Grinnell Exp.* xv. (1856) 107 Here ..the Greenland shore broke upon us. **1884** W. C. Smith *Kildrostan* 43 Only the lap of the rippling wave Broke on the hush of their solitude.

b. Of an item of news: to become public or available for publication. *Journalists' colloq.*

1934 F. Baldwin *Innoc. Bystander* (1935) ix. 188 The papers have left me alone for a long time... I was sick with worry when..Merry acted the fool. But nothing broke. **1936** E. Ambler *Dark Frontier* x. 163 You'll give us an exclusive when the story does break, I hope. **1938** E. Waugh *Scoop* ii. i. 111 A big story is going to break.

c. To happen, occur. *slang* (orig. *U.S.*).

1914 *Sat. Even. Post* 15 Aug. 8/1 They say my homer was lucky..but, believe me, it was time things broke for me. They been breakin' for him all his life. **1934** Webster s.v., Things are breaking right for me. **1936** J. Curtis *Gilt Kid* xi. 118 Everything'll break good.

40. Of buds, flowers, roots, etc.: To sprout out, come forth, burst into flower or leaf, expand.

c **1325** *Rel. Ant.* I. 124 When blosmes breketh on brere. **1868** Darwin *Anim. & Pl.* II. xiii. 31 In..carrot-beds a few plants often 'break'—that is, flower too soon. **1882** *Garden* 18 Mar. 187/1 Vigorous young [vine] rods..will require dexterous handling to get them to break evenly.

41. a. To burst out of darkness, begin to shine; as the *day*, *morning*, *daylight*. Const. *on*, *upon*. Many varieties of this expression appear, often mixed with other uses of *break*, as 'the darkness is breaking'; cf. 'the clouds are breaking' in 26 c.

1535 Coverdale *Isa.* xxi. 12 The watchman answered: The daye breaketh on. **1599** Shaks. *Hen. V*, iv. i. 88 Brother Iohn Bates, is not that the Morning which breakes yonder? **1611** Bible *Gen.* xxxii. 26 Let me goe, for the day breaketh [Coverd. breaketh on]. **1647** J. Hall *Poems* 92 The day Breakes clearer on them. **1772–84** Cook *Voy.* (1790) V. 1688 Till day began to break upon them. **1829** I. Taylor *Enthus.* x. 259 When..the first beams of sound philosophy broke over the nations. **1836** Kingsley *Lett.* (1878) I. 33 Ere the sun had broken on the earth. **1871** Morley *Voltaire* (1886) 23 The darkness seems breaking.

†**b.** *trans.* To cause to break. *Obs.*

1509 Hawes *Past. Pleas.* i. xiv, Golden Phebus..With cloudes redde began to break the daye.

42. a. *intr.* (and with *indirect pass.*) To enter by breaking barriers; to make a forcible or violent entrance *into* a place; to make an irruption. (Formerly expressed by *break* trans.: see 17.)

1398 Trevisa *Barth. De P.R.* v. xxxv. (1495) 147 That colde ayre breke not sodaynly in to the herte. *c* **1400** *Destr. Troy* 11937 Þai..Brekyn into bildynges, britnet the pepull. **1628** Hobbes *Thucyd.* (1822) 55 The Lacedemonians afterwards brake into Attica. **1677** Moxon *Mech. Exerc.* (1703) 158 Carpenters with their Ripping Chissel do often Break in to Brick-walls; that is, they cut holes. **1883** *Law Rep. Queen's B.* XI. 590 The prosecutor's house was feloniously broken into and entered.

b. To get *into*, or make a sudden appearance in, some occupation, activity, etc. *colloq.* (orig. *U.S.*).

1899 *Chicago Daily News* 10 May 6/1 Nichols will be anxious to break into the game pretty soon. **1907** *Collier's* 5 Oct. 11/2 Mr. F. C. Wheeler..decided recently for the first time in his life to break into print. **1939** J. Dell *Nobody ordered Wolves* i. 7 Phillip was one of the countless thousands whose consuming ambition was to 'break' into the motion picture industry.

VIII. Phrases and combinations.

* *Phrases.*

43. ***to break bulk*** (cf. 2 e): 'to open the hold and take out goods thence' (*Capt. Smith's Seaman's Gram.* 1692); to destroy the completeness of a cargo by taking out a portion, to begin to unload.

1575 in *Hist. Glasgow* (1881) 117 Breking bowk [of a cargo]. **1587** *St. Paper Office* Domest. Corr., To bring them [ships] into this realme without breaking bulke. **1622** Malynes *Anc. Law-Merch.* 195 All Merchants ships being laden, haue alwaies..beene permitted to breake bulke below, or at Tilburie-Hope. **1668** Marvell *Corr.* xcviii. Wks. 1872–5 II. 257 An impeachment..against Sir W. Penn, for breaking bulke in the East India prizes. **1709** Steele *Tatler* No. 106 ¶2 Whether he would break Bulk, and sell his Goods by Retail. **1792** Burke *Negro Code* Wks. 1842 II. 424 The faithful execution of his part of the trust at the island where he shall break bulk. **1833** Marryat *P. Simple* v, He was breaking Casks out of the hold. **1883** *Times* 24 Mar. 6 The whole [cargo of tea] can be sampled and sold the moment the steamer breaks bulk.

44. ***to break*** (***the***) ***ground*** (cf. 5 a):

a. To dig through the surface of ground, especially when covered with turf; to plough up ground for the first time, or after it has lain long in pasture. See also *to break up*, 57 f.

1712 Prideaux *Direct. Ch. Wardens* (ed. 4) 76 The Fee for breaking the soil [for a grave] belongs to them. *Mod.* (U.S.) It takes three farm-horses of good weight to break prairie-land.

b. Of an army: To begin digging trenches.

1678 *Lond. Gaz.* No. 1320/3 We hear the French are breaking ground, as if they intended a formal Siege. **1810** Wellington in Gurw. *Disp.* VI. 200 The enemy broke ground before Ciudad Rodrigo on the night before last.

c. *fig.* To commence operations, take the first steps, do pioneer work.

1709 *Lond. Gaz.* No. 4555/3 Last Night we broke Ground. **1830** De Quincey *Bentley* Wks. VI. 56 One of those who first broke ground as a pioneer in the great field of Natural Philosophy. **1834** *Blackw. Mag.* XXXV. 792 They have broken no ground from which they have not been driven. **1840** Carlyle *Heroes* i, Could I thus, as it were, not exhaust my subject, but so much as break ground upon it.

d. *Naut.* 'Break-ground. Beginning to weigh, or to lift the anchor from the bottom.' Smyth *Sailor's Word-bk.*

1752 Beawes *Lex Mercat.* 116 If..the ship *breaks ground*, and arrives at her port.

e. *Boxing.* (See quot. 1897.)

1889 E. B. Michell *Boxing* iii, in W. H. Pollock et al. *Fencing*, etc. 154 The proper style of breaking ground or shifting, or slipping, is by movements to the right. **1897** *Encycl. Sport* I. 139/1 *Break ground*, to take up a fresh position to the right or left.

45. ***to break the ice*** [cf. quot. 1710]: to prepare the way, take the preliminary steps, make a beginning; sometimes, in modern use, with a reference to the coldness or stiffness of first intercourse with strangers. See also Ice *sb.* 2 b.

1602 Warner *Alb. Eng.* xi. lxii. 273 Caboto whose Cosmographie and selfe-proofe brake the Ice To most our late Discouerers. **1610** Guillim *Heraldry* To Rdr., I have broken the Ice, and made way to some after-commers. **1611** Cotgr., *Acheminer*, to commence, breake the ice. **1683** D. A. *Art Converse* 15 The Ice being thus broken, another will utter her mind on the same matter. **1710** Steele *Tatler* No. 7 ¶6 The Ice being broke, the Sound is again open for the Ships. **1775** Sheridan *Duenna* ii. ii, So! the ice is broke, and a..civil beginning too! **1853** H. Rogers *Ecl. Faith* 28, I availed myself of a pause in the conversation to break the ice in relation to the topic which lay nearest my heart.

46. ***to break square***, or ***squares*** [of uncertain origin: cf. 2 e]: to interrupt or violate the regular order; commonly in the proverbial phrase, ***it breaks no square***, i.e. does no harm, makes no mischief, does not matter.

1576 Foxe *A. & M.* 986 The missyng of a few yeares in this matter, breaketh no great square in our story. **1594** T. B. *La Primaud. Fr. Acad.* II. 116 There are but fewe that breake not square oftener in eating & drinking too much then to litle. **1633** Herbert *Temple, Discharge* vii, Man and the present fit! if he provide [i.e. look into the future], He breaks the square. **1640** Fuller *Joseph's Coat* vii. (1867) 179 Would so small a matter have broken any squares? **1671** Dryden *Even. Love* iii. i, 'Tis no matter; this shall break no Squares betwixt us. **1760** Sterne *Tr. Shandy* (1802) II. v. 152 This fault in Trim broke no squares with them.

47. ***to break wind***: to void wind from the stomach or bowels. [But cf. brake *v.*⁵ to void from the stomach.]

[**1540** Lyndesay *Satire* 7624, I lay braikand like ane brok. —— 4367 Sche blubbirt, bokkit, and braikit still.] **1552** Huloet Belke, or bolke, or breake wynde vpwarde. **1606** Holland *Sueton.* 171 He would give folke leave to breake winde downward and let it goe even with a crack at the very

bourd. **1636** HEALEY tr. *Theophrast. Char.* 45 He lying along, belcheth or breaketh wind. **1795** J. WOLCOTT (P. Pindar) *Lousiad* Wks. 1812 I. 269 Had the Thunderer but broke wind.

48. ***to break even*:** **a.** *intr.* In *Faro* (see quot.). *U.S.*

1909 *Cent. Dict.* Suppl. s.v., *To break even*, in *faro*, to bet that each card will win or lose an even number of times on the deal.

b. To emerge from a transaction, enterprise, etc., with balancing gains and losses. orig. *U.S.*

1914 S. LEWIS *Our Mr. Wrenn* 33 To go bumming around like you do and never have to worry about how the firm's going to break even. **1920** *Flight* XII. 508/2 What must we earn to 'break even'? **1950** J. DEMPSEY *Champ. Fighting* ii. 12 He and I broke even in our three four-rounds bouts. **1958** *Listener* 2 Oct. 498/1 Today a novel needs to sell 5,000 copies for a publisher to break even.

** *Combined with adverbs*:

49. break across. 'In tilting, when the tilter by unsteadiness or awkwardness suffered his spear to be..broken across the body of his adversary, instead of by the push of the point' (Nares). Cf. Shaks. *A.Y.L.* III. iv. 44.

1580 SIDNEY (N.) One said he brake across, full well might it so be.

To break asunder: see 25.

50. break away.

a. *trans.* [from 33.] To sever or remove by breaking.

1420 *E.E. Wills* (1882) 45 A branche of þe couercle [is] y-broke away. **1781** COWPER *Expost.* 501 The lamp that with awaking beams, Dispell'd thy gloom and broke away thy dreams. **1855** COSTELLO *Stor. Screen* 77 Those who..broke away the bars which kept him prisoner.

b. *intr.* (for *refl.* of a.)

1860 TYNDALL *Glac.* I. §11. 70 The snow..broke away from the foot and fell into the chasm.

c. *intr.* [from 36.] To start away with abruptness and force; to go off abruptly; to escape by breaking from restraint. Also *fig.*

1535 COVERDALE *Jer.* lii. 6 The souldyers brake awaye, and fled out of the cite by night. **1590** SHAKS. *Com. Err.* IV. iv. 1 Feare me not man, I will not breake away. *c* **1610** MIDDLETON etc. *Widow* I. i. in *Dodsley* (1780) XII. 234 When thieves are taken, and break away twice or thrice one after another. **1852** TUPPER *Proverb. Philos.* 317 A dappled hart hath flung aside the boughs and broke away. **1872** BLACK *Adv. Phaeton* xii. 164 If people break away from the ordinary methods..they must take their chance.

d. *Boxing.* (See quot.)

1897 *Encycl. Sport* I. 139/1 *Break away*, to get away from an opponent. **1904** A. J. NEWTON *Boxing* viii. 67 So clinched, they remain..on the lookout for an opportunity to break away in the most favourable manner. **1923** [see CLINCH *v.*[1] 2 e].

To break back (Cricket): see 32 b.

51. break down.

a. *trans.* [from II.] To break (anything) so that its parts fall to the ground; to demolish, destroy, level with the ground. Also of things *fig.*

1382 WYCLIF *Isa.* v. 5, I shal breke down his wal. **1611** BIBLE *ibid.*, Breake downe the wall thereof. **1742** WESLEY *Wks.* (1872) I. 353 They..brake down part of the house. **1876** J. H. NEWMAN *Hist. Sk.* I. I. i. 9 They would be powerful to break down; helpless to build up. **1878** MORLEY *Diderot* II. 29 He will not, however, on that account break down the permanent safeguards.

b. [from 7.] To break into small pieces; to crush; to decompose.

1859 JEPHSON *Brittany* iv. 42 With delicious light French roll broken down into it. **1883** *Athenæum* 29 Dec. 871/1 The molecule of arabic acid, $C_{89}H_{142}O_{74}$, is broken down.

c. [from 12–13.] To crush or prostrate in strength, health, courage, etc.

1853 *Arab. Nts.* (Rtldg.) 274 So much was he already broken down by affliction, sorrow and terror. **1873** MORLEY *Rousseau* I. 28 The character of Jean Jacques was absolutely broken down. **1885** *Manch. Exam.* 6 Sept. 5/4 He has been consistently anxious to break down the power in Egypt of the Turkish pashas.

d. *intr.* (for *refl.*) To fall broken or in ruins; to collapse, give way, fail utterly, prove of no avail; to give way, as the back sinews of a horse's leg (whence the technical use in 1831, 1864). Also of an engine, a machine, vehicle, or the like: to cease to function, esp. through the fracture or dislocation of a part.

1831 YOUATT *Horse* xvi. (1872) 373 A slight injury..is called a sprain of the back sinews or tendons; and when it is more serious, the horse is said to have broken down. **1837** *United Service Jrnl.* May 112 One of her engines 'broke-down', as it is technically called. **1856** SIR B. BRODIE *Psychol. Inq.* I. iii. 93 The mind may break down all at once under some sudden affliction. **1864** LD. PALMERSTON in *Daily Tel.* 26 Aug., It often happens that a very good-looking horse breaks down. **1865** TROLLOPE *Belton Est.* xxix. 345 The task before her was..so difficult that she almost broke down in performing it. **1875** JOWETT *Plato* (ed. 2) III. 204 If this definition of justice breaks down. **1880** MCCARTHY *Own Times* III. xl. 223 His health almost suddenly broke down. **1904** KIPLING *Traffics & Discoveries* 314 They knew my car had broken down. **1958** *Times* 9 Sept. 4/6 Congestion that might be caused when a vehicle breaks down.

e. [from 30.] To tone down, qualify.

1867 TIMBS & GULLICK *Painting* 303 Breaking down the warm lights with colours of the opposite quality. **1882** *Standard* 9 Oct. 2/7 He had used 'white' sugar for 'breaking down' some gin. **1882** *Printing Times & Lithogr.* 15 Feb. 35 Another class of tones is formed by breaking down orange with its complementary colour blue.

f. *trans.* To divide (logs) into timber (see quot. 1922).

1878 *Technol. Dict.* (ed. 3) II. 84/1 *To break down timber*, ..débiter le bois..en planches, etc. **1883** M. P. BALE *Saw-Mills* iii. 35 The band-sawing machine can..be used for breaking down heavy logs. **1922** R. C. BRYANT *Lumber* 451 *Break down*, v. 1. To reduce large logs to a size which can be sawed on the main log saws in a sawmill. 2. To cut a log into cants. (Pacific Coast Forests.) **1927** J. F. STEWART *Man. Forest Engineering & Extraction* xiii. 171 The logs..are broken down to suitable sizes by this saw.

g. To analyse or classify (figures, statistics, etc.). orig. *U.S.*

1934 WEBSTER, *Break down*,..to separate (an account or a budget) into its component parts or subdivisions. **1941** *Amer. Speech* XVI. 45 A vast amount of raw material has been broken down for classification. **1948** *Hansard Commons* CDXLVIII. 1663 The programme account..is not broken down as between the Home, Light, and Third Programmes.

h. To stop (something objectionable); to 'give over'; esp. in ***break it down***: stop it, 'come off it'. *Austral.* and *N.Z. colloq.*

1941 *Coast to Coast 1941* 127 Ah, break it down, feller. Everybody knew you had her on the town. **1943** *N.Z.E.F. Times* 15 Mar. 6/5 Break down the swearing. **1944** L. GLASSOP *We were Rats* I. v. 35 'Break it down,' I said, 'nothing would interest me less.' **1949** J. R. COLE *It was so Late* 13 'Break it down!' Wood shouted from the telephone. 'I can't hear a thing.'

52. break forth.

a. *intr.* [from 37.] To make a rush forward.

1552 HULOET, Breake forth or out, *prorumpo.* **1611** BIBLE *Exod.* xix. 22 Lest the Lord breake forth vpon them. **1646** BUCK *Rich. III*, II. 61 Forth breakes King Richard towards the Earle.

b. Of flame, light, passion, war, disease, etc.: To burst out, break out.

1535 COVERDALE *Isa.* lix. 8 Then shal thy light break forth as yᵉ mornynge. **1561** NORTON & SACKV. *Gorboduc* III. i, The fire..breakes forth with double flame. **1596** SHAKS. *1 Hen. IV*, III. i. 27 Diseased Nature oftentimes breakes forth In strange eruptions. **1597** DRAYTON *Mortimer.* 11 A little sparke..Breakes forth in flame. **1611** BIBLE *Ex.* ix. 10 A boyle breaking forth with blaines. **1626** BACON *Sylva* §384 Many Diseases..break forth at particular times. **1660** STANLEY *Hist. Philos.* (1701) 85/2 In the second year..broke forth a War. **1712** STEELE *Spect.* No. 302 ¶5 In Emilia..it [religion] does not break forth into irregular Fits and Sallies of Devotion. **1848** MACAULAY *Hist. Eng.* I. 645 It was not only against the prisoners that his fury broke forth. **1871** FREEMAN *Norm. Conq.* IV. xviii. 224 He breaks forth into full light in the course of the next year. **1875** BRYCE *Holy Rom. Emp.* vi. (ed. 5) 85 These were the feelings that..broke forth in the shout of Henry.

c. [from 36.] To break loose from restraint.

1605 SHAKS. *Lear* I. iv. 222 Breaking forth In ranke and not to be endur'd riots. *a* **1639** W. WHATELEY *Prototypes* II. xxix. (1640) 135 You young men that have too much broken forth.

†**d.** [from 40.] To spring or sprout out vigorously. *Obs.*

1674 GREW *Anat. Trunks* vi. §4 The Trunk-Roots break forth all along it.

e. [from 38] To burst into utterance; to exclaim with sudden outburst.

1526 TINDALE *Gal.* iv. 27 Breake forth and crye thou that travelest not. **1611** BIBLE *Isaiah* xiv. 7 They breake foorth into singing. **1725** POPE *Odyss.* XVI. 482 The Prince breaks forth; proclaim What tydings, friends? **1882** *Sun* 14 May 6/5 The anti-lacrossers cheered and broke forth with [a ditty].

53. break in. **a.** *trans.* = 14.

1785 BURKE *Sp. Nab. Arcot's Debts* Wks. 1842 I. 326 Suppose his highness not to be well broken in to things of this kind. **1840** MACAULAY *Clive* 3 Savages..who had not broken in a single animal to labour. **1850** MRS. STOWE *Uncle Tom* xix. 198, I broke a fellow in, once. **1856** F. PAGET *Owlet of Owlst* 97 She must be well broke in to the smell of tobacco.

b. *intr.* [from 42.] To force one's way in, enter forcibly or abruptly; to make an irruption.

1552 HULOET, Breake in, *irrumpo.* **1614** RALEIGH *Hist. World* IV. v. §6. 514 Ptolemy's army brake in without resistance. **1615** G. SANDYS *Trav.* Ded., The wild beasts..hauing broken in vpon them. **1711** ADDISON *Spect.* No. 131 ¶8 When an unexpected Guest breaks in upon him. **1749** FIELDING *Tom Jones* XV. v, I am afraid..I break in upon you abruptly. **1884** *Mehalah* iv. 50 Lest he should be broken in on from the cellar.

c. To infringe ***upon*** or interfere with; to interrupt or disturb suddenly or unexpectedly.

1657 Burton's *Diary* (1828) II. 79 Bring in a Bill, which is as effectual. Otherwise business will break in upon you. **1748** CHESTERF. *Letters* II. 81 Some little passion or humour always breaks in upon their best resolutions. **1765** BLACKSTONE *Comm.* I. 70 Whenever a standing rule of law..hath been wantonly broke in upon by statutes or new resolutions. **1806** G. ROSE *Diaries* (1860) I. 251, I would..break in upon these [arrangements] to call in Clarges Street. **1820** W. IRVING *Sketch-bk.* (1859) 5 Those sudden storms which will sometimes break in upon the serenity of a summer voyage. **1882** SHORTHOUSE *J. Inglesant* II. 378 The booming of cannon broke in upon the singing of the psalms.

d. To interpose abruptly in a conversation.

a **1719** ADDISON (J.) The doctor..with a deep voice and a magisterial air breaks in upon conversation, and drives down all before him. **1807** ANNA M. PORTER *Hungar. Bro.* 78 'You remember the circumstances', added the marshal, seeing Charles about to interrupt him, 'but I'll not be broken in on'. **1828** SCOTT *F.M. Perth* I. 18 Feeling the certainty of being right..the father broke in. **1875** JOWETT *Plato* (ed. 2) III. 9 In the discussion..Glaucon breaks in with a slight jest.

e. [from 39.] To burst or flash *upon.*

1713 BERKELEY *Hylas and P.* iii. ad fin., A new light breaks in upon my understanding. **1742–3** *Observ. Methodists* 14 Fresh Emanations of Divine Light break in upon..my Soul. **1836** J. GILBERT *Chr. Atonem.* ii. (1852) 42 Had these lights but broken in upon an earlier period. **1865** DICKENS *Mut. Fr.* xii, Not the faintest flash of the real state of the case broke in upon her mind.

f. (See quot.).

1823 P. NICHOLSON *Pract. Builder* 220 To Break in—To cut or break a hole in brick-work, with the ripping-chisel for inserting timber, etc.

g. In paper-manufacture, to subject (rags) to a process of washing and pulping.

1865 *Chambers's Encycl.* VII. 243 They are thoroughly washed and partly pulped; or, as it is technically called, *broken in.*

h. To bring (virgin land) into cultivation. Also **breaking-in** vbl. sb. *Austral.* and *N.Z.* (orig. *dial.*: see *E.D.D.* and *Sc. Nat. Dict.*)

1891 R. WALLACE *Rural Econ. Austral. & N.Z.* i. 24 The single-furrow plough is employed to break in the land. *Ibid.* vi. 109 Such results are only expected for a few years after breaking in until the wood ashes left after burning the bush are exhausted. **1939** E. E. VAILE *Pioneering Pumice* v. 99, I was breaking in some country about two and a half miles from the homestead. **1950** *N.Z. Jrnl. Agric.* Feb. 141/1 In many parts of the North Island, farm country still offers a stubborn resistance to breaking-in.

54. break off.

a. *trans.* [from 27.] To discontinue (anything) abruptly; to put a forcible, abrupt, or definite end to.

c **1340** HAMPOLE *Prose Treat.* 29 þou sall..breke of þat. **1526** *Pilgr. Perf.* (W. de W. 1531) 151 Vouchsafe..to interrupte and breke of the swete quietnes of contemplacyon. **1597** MORLEY *Introd. Mus.* 117 Now wil I breake off my intended walke. **1611** BIBLE *Dan.* iv. 27 Breake off thy sinnes by righteousnesse. **1649** MILTON *Eikon.* 2 The first parlament he broke off at his coming to the Crown. **1712** HUGHES *Spect.* No. 554 ¶7, I might break off the account of him here. **1712** ADDISON *Spect.* No. 295 ¶4 We find several Matches broken off upon this very Head. **1855** MACAULAY *Hist. Eng.* III. 255 The conferences were soon broken off.

b. *intr.* To leave off or stop abruptly.

c **1340** HAMPOLE *Prose Treat.* 29 When þou hase bene besye vwtwarde..þou sall breke offe and come agayne to þi prayers. **1588** SHAKS. *L.L.L.* v. ii. 262 Not one word more my maides, breake off, breake off. **1589** PUTTENHAM *Eng. Poesie* III. xii. (Arb.) 178 When we begin to speake a thing, and breake of in the middle way. **1641** J. JACKSON *True Evang. T.* II. 122 We must not here breake off; let us continue on the story. **1727** DE FOE *Syst. Magic* I. ii. (1840) 42 Upon this their consultation broke off. **1841** MACAULAY in Trevelyan *Life* (1876) II. ix. 111 He may break off in the middle of a story.

c. = 32.

1725 DE FOE *Voy. round World* (1840) 129 She found the shore break off a little, and soon after a little more. **1833** *Regul. Instr. Cavalry* I. 30 The front rank break off to the left.

d. *trans.* [from 33.] To sever or detach completely by breaking.

1530 PALSGR. 465/1, I breake of a pece or porcyon of a thyng from the hole. **1611** BIBLE *Ex.* xxxii. 2 Breake off the golden earerings which are in the eares of your wiues. **1710** STEELE *Tatler* No. 15 ¶1 To the End of that Stamen of Being in themselves which was broke off by Sickness. **1759** B. MARTIN *Nat. Hist. Eng.* I. Cornw. 4 Part of one of them has been broke off.

e. *intr.* To detach oneself abruptly *from.*

1606 SHAKS. *Ant. & Cl.* I. ii. 132, I must from this enchanting Queene breake off. **1862** STANLEY *Jew. Ch.* (1877) I. x. 198 A Jewish sect..which professes to have broken off from Israel at this time.

f. [from 34.] To sever connexion or relation (*with*), to separate.

1647 W. BROWNE *Polex.* II. 73 To breake off instantly with the enemies of his greatnesse and religion. **1667** PEPYS *Diary* 27 July, The King and my Lady Castlemaine are quite broke off, and she is gone away. **1709** STEELE *Tatler* No. 36 ¶1 False Lovers, and their shallow Pretences for breaking off. **1827** SCOTT *Surg. Dau.* II. 158 Her ungrateful lover was now occupied with the means, not indeed of breaking off with her entirely, but, etc.

g. *trans.* To draw off sharply, withdraw completely *from.*

1607 TOPSELL *Four-f. Beasts* 107 Then must the retreat be sounded, and..the Dogs be broken off. **1700** J. LAW *Counc. Trade* (1751) 155 At whose pains..ought the people of this kingdom be broken off from this habit of idleness.

h. [from 28 b.] To intercept and repel.

1791 SMEATON *Edystone L.* §338 A sloping Bank..to break off the fury of the sea.

†**i.** *intr.* [from 24.] To start, begin. *Obs.*

1591 LYLY *Sappho* II. iii. 177 Then shall wee have sweet musique. But come, I will not breake off.

j. *Naut.* (See quot.)

1867 SMYTH *Sailor's Word-bk.* s.v. *She breaks off from her course*: applied only when the wind will not allow of keeping the course; applies only to 'close-hauled' or 'on the wind'. *Broken off*, fallen off, in azimuth, from the course.

to break on: see 41.

55. break out.

a. *trans.* [from 33.] To force out by breaking.

1611 BIBLE *Ps.* lviii. 6 Breake out the great teeth of the young lyons. *Mod.* To break the glass out of a window, the teeth out of a rake, etc.

b. *intr.* [from 37.] To burst or spring out from restraint, confinement, or concealment. Said of persons and things material, also of fire, light, etc.

a **1000** *Beowulf* 5085 Geseah þa..stream ut þonan brecan of beorȝe. *c* **1205** LAY. 30854 þat he [the pick] brac ut

biforen under his breaste. *c* **1340** HAMPOLE *Pr. Consc.* 4465 Bot at þe last þai sal breke out And destroy many landes obout. **1382** WYCLIF *Isa.* lviii. 8 Thanne shal breken out as morutid thi liȝt. *Ibid.* xxxv. 6. **1576** LAMBARDE *Peramb. Kent* (1826) 261 Those very welles or springs..whereof the one breaketh out of the ground about Stallesfield. **1647** *Sectary Dissected* 17 What an ambush of Banditi is here broken out against the poor Statutes? **1679** W. LONGUEVILLE in *Hatton Corr.* (1878) 183 Sunday last a fire or two broke out in ye citty. **1763** WESLEY *Jrnl.* 21 Aug., The sun broke out several times, and shone hot in my face. **1885** *Manch. Exam.* 6 July 5/1 A fire broke out and spread with great rapidity.

c. Said of a morbid eruption on the skin; also of an epidemic disease.

1535 COVERDALE *Levit.* xiii. 12 Whan the leprosy breaketh out in the szkynne. **1640** FULLER *Abel Rediv.* (1867) II. 143 There brake out a grievous pestilence in that city. **1661** LOVELL *Hist. Anim. & Min.* 327 The measells, which are little swellings, red, breaking out in the skinn. **1711** ADDISON *Spect.* No. 16 ¶2 Those Blotches and Tumours which break out in the Body. **1842** TENNYSON *Walk. to Mail* 71 The same old sore breaks out from age to age. **1851** DIXON *W. Penn* xxxi. (1872) 298 The yellow fever broke out in Philadelphia.

d. A person, or his body, is also said to ***break out*** (***in*** or ***into*** boils, etc.).

c **1300** *Beket* 2421 His flesch bigan to breken out: and rotede and foule stonk. **1552** HULOET, Breake oute, or braste oute, as a mannes face doth with heate. **1651** HOBBES *Leviath.* (1839) 309 The bodies of children..breaking out into biles and scabs. **1690** *Lond. Gaz.* No. 2596/4 He is a short..Man, his Lips broke out. **1769** GOLDSM. *Rom. Hist.* (1786) II. 144 His face was all broke out into ulcers. **1819** L. HUNT *Indicator* No. 7 (1822) I. 56 He used to break out in enormous biles and blisters.

e. Said of exclamations, feelings, passions, traits; of discord, riot, war, rebellion, etc.

1580 BARET *Alv.* B 1201 Laughter breaketh out soudainlie. **1598** DRAYTON *Heroic. Ep.* II. 35 My Heart must breake within, or Woes breake out. **1649** MILTON *Eikon.* iv. (1851) 360 Besides this, the Rebellion in Ireland was now broke out. **1715** BURNET *Own Time* II. 406 His speech was suppressed for some days, but it broke out at last. **1845** S. AUSTIN *Ranke's Hist. Ref.* I. 429 The natural antagonism between them soon broke out. **1847** L. HUNT *Men, Women, & Bks.* II. xi. 274 Traits of him still break out. **1848** MACAULAY *Hist. Eng.* I. 163 Formidable riots broke out in many places. **1850** W. IRVING *Goldsm.* xxix. 284 His goodness of heart, which broke out on every occasion.

f. Persons or other agents are also said to ***break out into*** or ***in*** some manifestation of feeling or some action. (N.Z. examples refer to a drinking bout.) See also *E.D.D.*

1480 CAXTON *Descr. Brit.* 19 A metrer breketh out in this maner in praysing of this cite. **1599** SHAKS. *Much Ado* I. i. 24 Did he breake out into teares? **1655** FULLER *Ch. Hist.* IX. 83 Thomas Piercy..brake out into open Rebellion against the Queen. **1711** ADDISON *Spect.* No. 45 ¶6 She broke out into a loud Soliloquy. **1795** SOUTHEY *Joan of Arc* VIII. 316 The exultant French Break out in loud rejoicing. **1875** JOWETT *Plato* (ed. 2) I. 185 Ctesippus again breaks out, and again has to be pacified by Socrates. *a* **1888** *Mod.* He's not a confirmed dipsomaniac, but only breaks out now and again. **1898** J. BELL *In Shadow of Bush* xvii. 101 Davie..had thought it best on the one occasion in which Dan had broken out, to give him a wide berth. **1904** *N.Z. Illustr. Mag.* IX. 429 Bill did 'break out'.

g. *trans.* To open up (a receptacle or the like) and remove its contents; to get (articles) out of a place of storage; hence, to prepare (food or drink) for consumption. *colloq.* (chiefly *U.S.*).

[**1832** MARRYAT *P. Simple* (1834) v, He was breaking Casks out of the hold.] **1840** R. H. DANA *Bef. Mast* xiv, There is always a good deal to be done in the hold: goods to be broken out. **1849** N. KINGSLEY *Diary* (1914) 22 Broke out our chests to-day, found all our things in good order. *Ibid.* 73 They broke out the baggage room to-day to get iron for various purposes. **1877** *Fraser's Mag.* XV. 221 Afterwards the fish are *broken out* and washed, and then packed in wooden hogshead casks. **1962** K. ORVIS *Damned & Destroyed* vi. 47, I went home and broke out a fresh bottle of Scotch. **1968** C. BURKE *Elephant across Border* vi. 236 'Break out some more coffee.' Lori made more coffee.

h. *intr.* Of a goldfield: to come into operation. Also *transf. Austral.* and *N.Z.*

1862 E. HODDER *Memories of N.Z. Life* 180 The Mammoth Caverns, which have been discovered since the diggings broke out. **1873** TROLLOPE *Australia & N.Z.* II. xxiii. 380 When Gold 'broke out', as the phrase goes, on the western side of the Middle Island. **1894** C. J. O'REGAN *Voices of Wave & Tree* 14 When the Coast broke out, we roughed it thro' the bush. **1901** 'M. FRANKLIN' *My Brilliant Career* ii. 11 Ere the diggings had broken out on Bruggabrong, our nearest neighbour..was seventeen miles distant.

56. break through. [f. branch VII. *Through* is here originally a preposition, and the analysis is *to break through-a-fence*, not *to break-through* a fence, but the prep. tends to attach itself to the vb. as in L. *perfringĕre*, and is sometimes used absol. as an adverb.]

a. *trans.* To penetrate (a barrier of any kind) by breaking it; to force one's way through.

c **1400** *Destr. Troy* 5827 He hit hym so hetturly..þat he breke þurgh the burd to the bare throte. **1697** DRYDEN *Virg. Georg.* IV. 528 Hypanis, profound, Breaks through th' opposing Rocks. **1711** STEELE *Spect.* No. 53 ¶8 A Satyr peeping over the silken Fence, and threatening to break through it.

fig. **1597** HOOKER *Eccl. Pol.* v. xlix. §6 Neither are they able to break through those errors wherein they are settled. **1798** FERRIAR *Illustr. Sterne* ii. 24 Wit, like beauty, can break through the most unpromising disguise. **1847** L. HUNT *Men, Women, & Bks.* II. xi. 262 Those conventional hypocrisies of which most people are ashamed, even when they would be far more ashamed to break through them.

b. To burst through restraints of, transgress.

1712 BUDGELL *Spect.* No. 401 ¶7, I purpose to break through all Rules. **1749** FIELDING *Tom Jones* I. iii, A custom he never broke through on any account. **1808** T. JEFFERSON *Writ.* (1830) IV. 129, I was unwilling it should be broke through by others.

c. To project abruptly through.

1860 TYNDALL *Glac.* I. §11. 80 Two rocks break through the snow.

d. *absol.*

1526 TINDALE *Matt.* vi. 19 Where theves breake through and steale. **1659** Burton's *Diary* (1828) IV. 273 The Chair broke through and rose without a question. **1690** LOCKE *Educ.* §70 After Corruption had once broke thro'.

57. break up.

a. *trans.* [from 1.] To break into many parts; to disintegrate.

1752 BEAWES *Lex Mercat.* 52 If a ship be broken up or taken to pieces..and afterwards..be rebuilt..she is now another, and not the same ship. **1864** *Derby Mercury* 7 Dec., The steel pieces were broken up, and the iron ones were beaten up into bars. **1875** JOWETT *Plato* (ed. 2) IV. 7 He cannot understand how an absolute unity..can be broken up into a number of individuals. **1876** J. H. NEWMAN *Hist. Sk.* I. I. ii. 54 Heraclius succeeded in..breaking up the Persian power.

b. To rend or tear: see 2 a.

c. To cut up, carve: see 2 b.

d. [from 2 f.] To dissolve, disband, put an end to, give up; as in to break a regiment, gang, parliament (*obs.*); to break up a house, household, housekeeping, school, an assembly. Colloq. phr. ***break it up***: (*a*) *imp.* disperse; stop (a fight); (*b*) *U.S.* (see quot. 1946).

1483 *Act 1 Rich. III*, ii, Many worshipful Men..were compelled by Necessity to break up their Housholds. *c* **1500** *Song* in *Rel. Ant.* I. 117 To brek upe the scole. **1647** WARD *Simp. Cobler* 12 Glad to heare the Devill is breaking up house in England, and removing somewhether else. **1721** *Lond. Gaz.* No. 5977/2 They..broke up their Assembly. **1833** MARRYAT *P. Simple* xxix, My uncle..had..broken up his housekeeping. **1875** JOWETT *Plato* (ed. 2) I. 70 We fairly gave way and broke up the company. **1936** S. KINGSLEY *Dead End* II. 113 Break it up!.. Come on, break it up!..go on home! Go on, break it up! **1946** MEZZROW & WOLFE *Really the Blues* 371 *Break it up*, bring the house down. **1947** 'N. BLAKE' *Minute for Murder* vii. 149 A policeman..forced his way..through the crowd, shouting '..Stand aside! Break it up!' **1959** *Encounter* Aug. 28/2 If someone had stepped in and said, 'break it up',..all would have gone well.

e. *absol.* and *intr.* from preceding. *spec.* of a school.

1535 COVERDALE *Isa.* xxxvii. 36 So Sennacherib the kinge of the Assirians brake vp, and dwelt at Niniue. **1536** WRIOTHESLEY *Chron.* (1875) I. 52 The twentith daie of Julie, the Convocation brooke upp at Poules. **1606** G. W[OODCOCKE] *Ivstine* 14 b Euery one bethinking how he might priuly breake vp, and steale home to resist the Enemy. **1612** DRAYTON *Poly-olb.* v. 77 Then vp the Session brake. **1707** C. MORDAUNT *Let.* 5 May in E. Hamilton *Mordaunts* (1965) iv. 74 Wee break up the Saturday after next and I desiare if you be in town to send for me. **1740** RICHARDSON *Pamela* II. 364 When you break up next, my Dear, said he, if you're a good Girl, you shall make your new Aunt a Visit. *a* **1855** C. BRONTË in *Cornh. Mag.* (1860) Apr. 495, I wrote ..to the friends of my pupils, notifying the day when we break up. **1882** *Boy's Own P.* IV. 283 A few days later the school broke up for the summer holidays.

f. *trans.* [from 5.] To open up (ground) with the spade or plough.

1557 TUSSER *100 Points Husb.* lxi, In January, husbandes will breake vp their lay. **1611** BIBLE *Jer.* iv. 3 Breake vp your fallow ground. *a* **1771** SMOLLETT *Humph. Cl.* (1815) 192 The roads having been broke up by the heavy rains in the spring, were..rough. **1787** WINTER *Syst. Husb.* 129 The beginning of October is the best season for breaking-up old pasture-lands.

†**g.** *intr.* [from 5 b.] = *break out*, 55 d. *Obs.*

1561 HOLLYBUSH *Hom. Apoth.* 1 a, [It] maketh the skin stronge, harde, and also cleane, that it break vp no more.

h. [from 8 b.] Of frost, (formerly) of an epidemic: To give way, cease. Of any kind of weather: to change.

1544 *Late Exped. Scot.* (1798) 10 And for asmoch as the myst yet contynued, and dyd not breake..we concluded, if the wether did not breake vp, to haue encamped our selues vpon the same ground. *a* **1586** SIDNEY *Arcadia* (1912) II. ix. 202 The weather breaking up, they were brought to the maine lande of Pontus. **1626** BACON *Sylva* §383 In Barbary, the Plagues break up in the Summer Moneths. **1801** NELSON in Nicolas *Disp.* (1845) IV. 355 Before the frost broke up at Cronstadt.

i. [from 12 c.] To fail in physical organization.

†**j.** *trans.* [from 16, 17.] To burst open (a barrier), make forcibly way into (a house), open forcibly (a letter, box, etc.).

1523 LD. BERNERS *Froiss.* I. cccxxii. 501 With great axes they brake vp the dore. **1552** HULOET, Breake vp a wryt or letter, *resigno*. **1578** TIMME *Calvin on Gen.* 199 The Lord brake up the floodgates of the waters. **1646** *Burd. Issach.* in *Phenix* (1708) II. 309 If any should offer violence to break up the Doors. **1682** BUNYAN *Holy War* 278 When we had broken it [the letter] up and had read the contents thereof. **1700** BLACKMORE *Job* 108 He in the dark Breaks houses up, on which he set his mark. **1712** PRIDEAUX *Direct. Ch.-Wardens* (ed. 4) 87 If any Person doth in the Night-time break up the Church. **1827** CARLYLE *Germ. Rom.* III. 223 Fixlein..broke up the presentation as his own.

†**k.** *absol.* [from prec.] *Obs.*

1528 TINDALE *Doctr. Treat.* (1848) 203 Let the judges.. not break up into the consciences of men. **1535** COVERDALE *Matt.* vi. 20 Where theues nether breake vp nor yet steale.

l. To begin or commence operations upon.

1688 *Lond. Gaz.* No. 2344/4 There was 500 Acres of Fresh Grass..broak up on May Day. **1711** ADDISON *Spect.* No. 60 ¶4 As a Mine not broken up.

†**m.** *intr.* [from 39.] To transpire. *Obs.*

1584 J. CARMICHAEL *Let.* in *Wodrow Soc. Misc.* 418 The murder of the Prince of Orange first brack up and came by speciall post.

†**n.** [from 40.] To burst (into flower). *Obs.*

c **1450** HENRYSON *Mor. Fab.* 45 The blossomes blyth brack vp on banke and bra.

o. *trans.* To disconcert, upset, disturb; to excite; *spec.* (orig. *U.S.*) to convulse with laughter. Also *intr. colloq.*

1825 J. CONSTABLE *Let.* 23 Oct. (1964) II. 404 She says, her sister is going to be married—& that she fears it will break her up. **1860** O. W. HOLMES *Prof. Breakf.-t.* i. 11 This episode broke me up, as the jockeys say, out of my square conversational trot; but I settled down to it again. **1895** 'MARK TWAIN' in *N. Amer. Rev.* Jan. 61 Well, humour is the great thing, the saving thing,..so, when M. Bourget said that bright thing about our grandfathers, I broke all up. **1895** *Harper's Mag.* Sept. 545/2 A most pathetic stream of arguments and blasphemy, which broke Joan all up, and made her laugh as she had not laughed since she played in the Domremy pastures. **1902** L. BELL *Hope Loring* 240 What language you use!.. If you knew how it breaks me up when you use slang! **1959** H. GARDNER *So What Else is New?* 2 The remark broke up the other people in the elevator, but the diminutive culprit continued to stare defiance. **1967** *New Yorker* 21 Jan. 52 The number broke the place up, and Marsala invited me back to play that night. **1968** *Listener* 4 Jan. 27/3 The camera had only to turn to Tommy Cooper for the audience to break up with laughter.

☞*Phrase-key* of BREAK *v.* (in addition to the adverbial combinations):—*b* one's back, 7 b; *b* ball, 31; *b* balls, 24; *b* bank, 11; *b* in billiards, 24; *b* blows with, 3; boils *b*, 4; *b* bonds, 25; *b* bounds, 19; *b* brain, 12 b; *b* bread, 3; buds *b*, 40; *b* bulk, 43; *b* cloth, 2 a; *b* cover, covert, 20; *b* in cricket, 31; day *b*, 41; *b* day, 15 c; *b* deer, 2 b; *b* fall, 28 b; *b* fast, 29 c; fish *b*, 37 d; flowers *b*, 32 c, 40; *b* fowl, fox, 2 b; *b* free, 36; frost *b*, 8 b; *b* ground, 44; *b* of habit, 33; *b* one's head, 5 b; *b* one's heart, 7 c, 22; *b* horse, 14; *b* house, 17; *b* ice, 45; *b* into, 38, 42; *b* jail, 19; *b* jest, 23; *b* joint, 31; *b* journey, 28 b; *b* a lance with, 3; *b* law, 15; *b* loose, 36; *b* marriage, matrimony, 15 d; *b* matter, 22; *b* one's mind, 12 b, 22; morning *b*, 41; *b* one's neck, 7 b; *b* news, 22; *b* oath, 15 c; *b* officer, 35; *b* on, 39, 41; *b* open, 17 b; *b* parle, 24; *b* parliament, 2 f; *b* peace, 15; *b* in pieces, 1; *b* of practice, 33; *b* Priscian's head, 5 b; *b* prison, 19; *b* promise, 15 c; *b* ranks, 26; *b* regiment, 2 f; *b* rest, 29; *b* sheer, 31; *b* ship, 2 d; *b* siege, 27; *b* sigh, 23; *b* silence, sleep, 29; *b* small, 1; *b* smile, 23; *b* soil, 20 b; *b* spirit, 13; *b* spousehood, 15 d; *b* square(s, 46; *b* stillness, 29; *b* a straw with, 3; *b* on torture, 7 b; *b* trade, 24; *b* upon, 39, 41; *b* vein, 4; voice *b*, 6; *b* water, 20 b; waves *b*. 10; *b* on wheel, 7 b; *b* wind, 12 b, 47; *b* with, 2 e, 22 b, 34; *b* wool, 2 c; *b* one's word, 15 c; *b* words with, 3.

break-. The verb-stem in composition forming sbs. or adjs.

I. With verb + object.

1. Forming *sbs.*, as **break-bones**, the Ossifrage or Osprey; **break-bulk**, one who breaks bulk, a captain that abstracts part of his cargo; **break-circuit**, a device for opening and closing an electric circuit; **break-club** (*Golf*), any obstacle on which the player might break his club; †**break-forward**, an alleged old name of the hare; †**break-gap**, that which opens a passage; †**break-hedge**, a trespasser; †**break-league**, a breaker of a league or treaty; †**break-love**, a disturber or destroyer of love; †**break-net**, the Dog-fish or Thresher; †**break-peace**, a peace-breaker; †**break-promise**, a promise-breaker; †**break-pulpit**, a boisterous preacher; †**break-vow**, a breaker of vows; **breakwind**, (*a*) *dial.* a disease of sheep; (*b*) a screen or protection against the wind.

1881 A. C. GRANT *Bush Live Queensl.* xxix. II. 133 One of the men..has managed to stop the *break-aways. **1838** POE *A. G. Pym* Wks. 1864 IV. 123 It is frequently called the *break-bones, or osprey peterel. **1622** R. HAWKINS *Voy. S. Sea* (1847) 166 To smother their owne disloyalties, in suffering these *breake-bulks to escape. *a* **1884** KNIGHT *Dict. Mech.* Suppl., **Break-circuit*, an arrangement on an electro-magnetic or magneto-electric instrument, by which an operator can open or close the circuit at pleasure. **1857** Chambers *Inform.* II. 67, *Lifting of *Break-clubs.*—All loose impediments within twelve inches of the ball may be removed on or off the course when the ball lies on grass. *c* **1300** *Names of Hare* in *Rel. Ant.* I. 13 The make-fare, the *breke-forwart. **1645** PAGITT *Heresiogr.* (1662) Ep. Ded., The *break-gap to all those mischiefs that flowed in upon the King. **1573** TUSSER *Husb.* (1878) 33 Keepe safe thy fence, scare *breakhedge thence. **1583** STANYHURST *Æneis* IV. (Arb.) 113 Al faythlesse *break leages. *Ibid.* 143 Like a *breaklooue mak'bat adultrer. **1583** J. HIGINS *Junius' Nomenclator*, *Breakenet, a sea-dog or dogfishe. **1623** MINSHEU *Sp. Dict.*, *Lamia*, a certaine dog-fish called a Breaknet. **1593** *Pass. Morrice* 73 Our only *breakepeace. **1600** SHAKS. *A.Y.L.* IV. i. 196, I will thinke you the most patheticall *breake-promise. **1589** *Marprel. Epit.* F, Som of our bishops are very great *breakepulpits. **1583** STANYHURST *Æneis* IV. (Arb.) 444 This *breakuow naughtye. **1596** SHAKS. *John* II. ii. 569 That Broker, that still breakes the pate of faith. That dayly breake-vow. **1823** HOGG *Sheph. Cal.* I. 110 It never saw either braxy or *breakwind. **1833** in W. S. Ramson *Austral. Eng.* (1966) 95 Breakwind. **1862** J. S. DOBIE *S. Afr. Jrnl.* 26 Sept. (1945) 32 A tarpaulin hung on weather side for a break-wind. **1863** *Fraser's Mag.* Mar. 282/2 What the Australians call a 'breakwind', *i.e.*, a pent roof, looking like the falling flap of a large bird-trap. **1875** *Encycl. Brit.* II. 317/2 The Norway maple..is a hardy tree, used as a breakwind in exposed situations on the east coast. **1890** *Athenæum* 18 Oct. 516/1 [Tasmanians] were frequently content with a mere break-wind in lieu of any covered structure. **1934** A. RUSSELL

Tramp-Royal vii. 54 The only form of shelter I needed was a small breakwind.

2. Forming *adjs.*, as **break-axe**, that breaks axes, as in **break-axe tree**, *Sloanea Jamaicensis*; **break-bone**, bone-breaking, as in **break-bone fever**, the *dengue*, an infectious eruptive fever of warm climates; also *ellipt.*; **break-covert**, that breaks covert; †**break-dance**, disturbing, turbulent; **break-teeth** or **-tooth**, difficult to pronounce. See also BREAK-BACK, BREAK-NECK.

1756 P. BROWNE *Jamaica* 250 The *Brake-axe Tree. It is so very hard that it is found a difficult matter even to cut it down. **1862** *N.Y. Tribune* 16 May, Another fever, to which the natives [of the south-western United States] give the name..of *Breakbone. **1866** A. FLINT *Princ. Med.* (1880) 1073 Excruciating pains in the head, eyes, muscles of the neck, loins, and extremities are prominent traits of the affection; hence the name breakbone fever. **1885** LADY BRASSEY *The Trades* 395 A ship with several cases of 'Dengue', or 'Breakbone fever' on board. **1820** KEATS *Isabella* xxviii, The *break-covert blood-hounds. **1586** J. HOOKER *Girald. Irel.* Ep. Ded., This brainesicke and *breakedanse Girald of Desmond..did breake into treasons. **1788** GROSE *Dict. Vulgar T.* (ed. 2), **Break-teeth Words*, hard words, difficult to pronounce. **1825** H. WILSON *Mem.* I. 48 Not to put in any break-teeth long words. **1827** SCOTT *Jrnl.* 11 Feb. (1939) II. 21 The Admiral with the break-tooth name.

II. With the vb. used attrib. = *breaking*; as ***break-iron***, etc.; **break crop**, in arable farming: a different kind of crop sown to break the continuity in repeated sowing of cereals; **break-dancing** orig. *U.S.*, a style of dancing popularized by U.S. Blacks, often individual or competitive, and characterized by a loud insistent beat to which dancers perform energetic and acrobatic movements, sometimes spinning around on their backs on the pavement or floor (pioneered during the late 1970s by teams of Black teenaged dancers in the south Bronx, N.Y.); also **break-dancer**; **break-piece** = BREAK *sb.*[1] 17 a; **break-roll**, one of a pair of rollers between which wheat-grains are split; **break-signal**, a signal used to separate distinct parts of a telegraphic message.

1967 *Punch* 10 May 687/2 Other..*break crops include roots, oats, and oil seed rape. **1971** *Country Life* 23 Sept. 771/1 The break crop was needed firstly to restore the drain on fertility as a result of successive cereal crops. **1984** 'D. ARCHER' *Ambridge Years* 114 Rape provides a very useful 'break crop' by preventing some of the diseases you can get if you plant corn over and over again on the same land. **1982** *Village Voice* (N.Y.) 21 Sept. 61/1 The Smurf is a fusion dance..a dance incorporating smoothed out elements of *break dancing. *Ibid.* 31 Aug. 55/2 Men in battery-powered visors lit up and dimmed,..break dancers broke. **1983** *Daily News* 23 Sept. 18 They are young street dudes, nearly all of them black, anywhere from 10 to 23 years old, and what they are doing is a new style of dancing known as 'breaking' or 'break dancing'. It is the first new dance phenomenon in the cities in more than a decade. **1984** *New Yorker* 5 Mar. 43/2 The Bronx is very bebop—street music with a heavy, funky brass beat—which is good for electric boogie and break-dancing. **1985** *Sunday Tel.* (Colour Suppl.) 3 Feb. 32/4 The streets of New York and Los Angeles might twitch with coke-sniffers, break-dancers and the denizens of the eighties, but the old America was not dead yet. **1881** *Mechanic* §383. 166 The *break-iron by which the shaving is turned in its upward course. **1842** FRANCIS *Dict. Arts* Q 2 b/1 The fore part of the spindle is terminated by a wire, and a *break piece at the end of it. **1879** G. PRESCOTT *Sp. Telephone* 253 An electromagnet with a self-interrupting breakpiece attached to its armature. **1910** *Encycl. Brit.* X. 551/2 The first pair of *break-rolls used to be called the splitting rolls, because their function was supposed to be to split the [wheat] berry longitudinally down its crease. **1876** PREECE *Telegraphy* 287 These parts are separated from each other by a distinct signal, called the *break signal.

break (breɪk), *sb.*[1] Also 4 **brek**, 5–6 **breke**, 5–7 **breake**. [f. BREAK *v.*]

1. a. An act of breaking; breakage, fracture.

a **1300** *Cursor M.* 6344 Wit-vten ani brek or brist. *Ibid.* 8044 Wit-vten brek of ani bogh. *c* **1440** *Promp. Parv.* 49 Breke, or brekynge, *ruptura, fractura.* **1870** *Standard* 12 Dec., The great operation had been stopped by the break of a bridge of boats.

b. With adverbs, expressing the action of the corresponding verbal combinations (BREAK *v.* 48–57); as **break-away**, **break-in**, **break-out**, (also *Austral.* and *N.Z. slang*, a drinking bout), BREAK-DOWN, BREAK-UP, etc; **break-back**, a sudden backward movement (see also sense 5, and BREAK-BACK *a.* 2).

1885 *Times* 4 June 10/3 After several *breaks away the 12 competitors were despatched to an excellent start. **1920** *Blackw. Mag.* Feb. 196/2 This '*break-back' of his had certainly been a brilliant achievement. **1960** E. S. & W. J. HIGHAM *High Speed Rugby* xvii. 239 If the scrum-half tries a blindside run, the flank will follow him round just far enough to make a break-back impossible. **1856** KANE *Arc. Expl.* II. vii. 83 My joy at this first *break-in upon its drudgery. **1903** *Daily Chron.* 10 Feb. 6/4 There was a further break-in of the river bank. **1944** *Times* 22 July 4/4 A successful break-in by the British..is never exploited by pursuit. **1820** SCOTT *Abbot* xxvi, They would be sure to make a *break-out if the officers meddled with the auld Popish witch-wife. **1870** *Standard* 12 Dec., On the break-out of the war. **1888** 'R. BOLDREWOOD' *Robbery under Arms* I. xi. 128 He saw him once in one of his break-outs, and heard him boast of something he'd done. **1908** W. H. KOEBEL *Anchorage* 49 A break-out doesn't seem to oil your tongue to run any more'n usual. **1947** *Ann. Reg. 1946* 24 The Russian break-out from the Baranovo bridgehead. **1958** *Economist* 29 Nov. 764/1 Nothing is more important than a British breakout from the rigid positions of the cold war.

2. ***break of day*** or ***morn***: the first appearance of light, the dawn. So ***break of June***: the beginning or opening days of June.

1584 LODGE *Alarum, Forb. & Prisc.* 21 b, The careful Marriner..sought for his Loade starre, and at breake of morning..found it out. **1597** DRAYTON *Mortimer.* 107 The misty breake yet proues a goodly day. **1647** W. BROWNE *Polex* II. 205 At the fifth dayes break, those that were in the top of the maine Mast began to cry, Land **1708** *Lond. Gaz.* No. 4471/3 Lieutenant-General Dedem was..order'd to march Yesterday at break a-Day. **1755** YOUNG *Centaur* vi. (1757) IV. 252, I see the break of their moral day. **1812** J. WILSON *Isle of Palms* III. 749 Now dim, now dazzling like the break of morn. **1820** KEATS *Isabella* IV. 26 A whole long month of May in this sad plight Made their cheeks paler by the break of June.

3. †An irruption, a breaking in. *Obs.*

c **1565** R. LINDSAY *Chron. Scot.* (1728) 57 The Englishmen had wasted so much on the borders, without any occasion or break of him to England.

†**4. a.** A breaking forth, a burst (of sound). *Obs.*

1750 [R. PULTOCK] *Life P. Wilkins* xxxiii. (1883) 90/1 The order of their flight was admirable, and the break of the trumpets so great..that I wondered how they could bear it.

b. An act of breaking out or away (see BREAK *v.* 49 c and 55 b); a rush or dash; an escape; freq. with *to make.* orig. *U.S.*

1833 *Sk. & Eccentr. D. Crockett* 82 Just before I got there, the old bear made a break and got loose. **1846** J. J. HOOPER *Adv. Simon Suggs* (1851) xii. 143, I maid a brake on a bee line for Urwinton. **1888** T. ROOSEVELT in *Cent. Mag.* May 49 Our three men..understood perfectly that the slightest attempt at a break would result in their being shot down. **1910** [see JAIL *sb.* 2]. **1929** 'G. DAVIOT' *Man in Queue* vi. 65 The man had gone to ground instead of making a break for it.

c. *Hort.* A bud or shoot that sprouts from a plant-stem. Also *attrib.*, as ***break bud*** (see quot. 1954).

1933 *Jrnl. R. Hort. Soc.* LVIII. 99 There are varieties too that on natural break buds are not good. *Ibid.*, Secure the plants well at the top break. **1954** A. G. L. HELLYER *Encycl. Garden Work* 30/2 A break is a branch or fork. *Ibid.* 31/1. If a rooted chrysanthemum cutting is left to its own devices, it will after a time, produce an abortive flower bud at the top of the stem, which will prevent further lengthening of this particular stem and force it to produce side shoots or breaks. In consequence, this abortive flower bud is often known as the 'break bud'. **1959** *Listener* 22 Oct. 706/1 From these [shoots], new breaks will appear which will produce the blooms for next season.

5. *Cricket.* A 'twist' or deviation of the ball from its previous direction on touching the ground. ***break-back***: the breaking in of a ball from the off side (i.e. with a right-handed bowler).

1851 PYCROFT *Cricket Field* vii. 137 Look hard for the twist, or a 'break' will be fatal. **1855** *F. Lillywhite's Guide to Cricketers* 21 Without a 'break-back', the thing is impossible with any but an over-pitched ball. **1866** *Jerks in from Short Leg* 74 The break-back removing a bail destroys in a moment the vision of triumph. **1881** *Standard* 18 June 3/1 Steel beat him with the break, and Hone stumped him well. **1881** *Macm. Mag.* XLIII. 288/2 By virtue of a good pitch and a break back. **1884** I. BLIGH in *Lillywhite's Cricket Ann.* 7 Considerable command over the ball in respect of pitch and break. **1886** *Daily News* 22 July 5/1 Mr. Tylecote..was bowled by an unplayable break-back of Mr. Spofforth's.

6. a. *Billiards.* A consecutive series of successful strokes; the number of points thus scored. **b.** Similarly in *Croquet.*

1865 *Times* 10 Apr., Mr. Russell vastly improved in his play, making some very excellent breaks. **1874** J. HEATH *Croquet Player* 55 Do not let the balls you are playing on in your break get too close together. **1883** *Land & Water* 10 Feb. 99 It is evidently possible, given the necessary nerve and skill, for breaks of 500 and upwards to be made on the billiard tables of the present make.

7. a. A broken place, gap, or opening: of more general application than BREACH.

a **1300** *Cursor M.* 14012 Þar sco fand ani breck or sare, Wit hir smerl sco smerd þare. **1539** *Act 31 Hen. VIII*, v, It shalbe lawfull..to make dere leapes and breakes in the said hedges. **1688** J. CLAYTON in *Phil. Trans.* XVII. 987 At the breakes of some banks, I have found veins of Clay. **1691** T. H[ALE] *Acc. New Invent.* 97 Where these Holes or Breaks are met with. **1836** MACGILLIVRAY tr. *Humboldt's Trav.* ii. 39 The Peak of Teyde..appeared in a break above the clouds. **1879** SEGUIN *Black For.* xiv. 236 He might wander..without finding a break in the mountain wall.

†**b.** An opening, a bay. *Obs.*

1557 PAYNEL *Barclay's Jugurth* 80 For about the extreme partes of Affrike be ij brekes of the sea [L. *sinus*] nere together.

8. An interruption of continuity: **a.** in anything material; *spec.* in geological strata, a fault; also in the deck of a ship (see quot. 1850).

1725 DE FOE *Voy. round World* (1840) 264 The hollow channel in the middle where there was a kind of fall or break in it. **1747** HOOSON *Miner's Dict.* Y viij b, Signs of some Break, Chun, or Vein. **1791** SMEATON *Edystone L.* §209 Probably with several breaks, as is usual in the arrangement of the Strata of the earth. **1832** MARRYAT *N. Forster* xxxii, Captain Drawlock walked to the break of the gangways. **1840** R. DANA *Bef. Mast* xiii. 32 Foster went as far as the break of the deck, and there waited for him. *c* **1850** *Rudim. Navig.* (Weale) 101 *Break*, the sudden termination or rise in the decks of some merchant ships, where the aft and sometimes the forepart of the deck is kept up to give more height between decks.

b. in a course of action or time. *spec.* of a trotter or pacer, the act of breaking away from a level stride (cf. BREAK *v.* 38 c) (orig. *U.S.*).

1689 SHERLOCK *Death* iii. §4 (1731) 114 It makes a Break in our Lives. **1830** LYELL *Princ. Geol.* I. 134 This remarkable break in the regular sequence of physical events. **1839** *Spirit of Times* 13 July 222/3 It was as bad a break as we ever saw. *a* **1867** H. WOODRUFF *Trotting Horse of Amer.* (1868) i. 41 The penalty of a break was such that the rider.. would be afraid to push his horse up to the top of his speed. **1878** LADY HERBERT *Hübner's Ramble* I. xii. 184 The run is 5,000 miles without a break. **1878** MORLEY *Diderot* I. 252 He would pass a whole month without a day's break, working ten hours a day at the revision of proof-sheets. **1903** A. D. MCFAUL *Ike Glidden* xxii. 200 When rounding into the home stretch his horse broke, and suddenly went to a wild swerving break that carried him to the complete outside of the track. **1968** *Wanganui Chron.* 15 Nov. 6/3 Stylish Major, the beaten favourite on Tuesday after going into a break trying to match the early pace.

c. in a discourse or composition; in the rhythm of a verse; also in printed matter. Occas. *attrib.*, as in *break-line*.

1627 CAPT. SMITH *Seaman's Gram.* A iiij b, You finde the word in the Margent in that breake [paragraph] against it. **1710** SWIFT *Tatler* No. 230 ¶6 The Breaks at the End of almost every Sentence. **1779** JOHNSON *Dryden, L.P.* (1816) IX. 393 The Alexandrine..invariably requires a break at the sixth syllable. **1885** *Law Rep. Queen's B.* XIV. 727 There is no break in the section, and the words 'in any highway', govern all that follows.

d. Marks [– – –] employed in print or writing to indicate abrupt pauses.

1733 SWIFT *On Poetry* Wks. 1755 IV. I. 186 In modern wit all printed trash is Set off with num'rous breaks – – – and dashes —. **1862** T. TROLLOPE *Marietta* I. x. 183 An unlimited supply of question stops, marks of admiration, italics and breaks.

e. A short interval between lessons, usu. in the middle of morning or afternoon school. Also *transf.* Cf. *coffee-break*, *tea-break*.

1861 H. SPENCER *Educ.* ii. 65 Short breaks during school-hours, excursions into the country,..in these and many like traits, the change may be discerned. **1913** C. MACKENZIE *Sinister Street* I. I. vi. 94 Well, see you to-morrow in the break, young Fane. **1921** S. THOMPSON *Rough Crossing* ii. §1, At 'break' Elizabeth met Lilian again. **1933** MRS. C. S. PEEL *Life's Enchanted Cup* xi. 133 In many workrooms no morning break was permitted... We finally decided that.. the girls should be allowed a ten minutes' break at 11 o'clock.

f. On the Stock Exchange, a sudden decline in prices. *U.S.* (Cf. BREAK *v.* 8 c.)

1870 J. K. MEDBERY *Men & Myst. Wall St.* 203 To endure an occasional 'break' in stocks. **1931** *Economist* 23 May 1110/2 The trend continued downwards, with particularly sharp breaks among high-priced stocks.

g. *slang.* A collection taken in aid of a prisoner awaiting trial or recently discharged.

1879 *Macmillan's Mag.* Oct. 502/1 The mob got me up a break (collection). **1896** A. MORRISON *Child of Jago* xxv. 252 Get up a 'break' or subscription to pay for his defence.

h. The angle between the brim and crown of a hat.

1881 in OGILVIE.

i. A mistake, blunder; esp. in phr. ***a bad break***: a serious mistake. *colloq.* (orig. *U.S.*).

1884 E. W. NYE *Baled Hay* 200 Possibly science may be wrong. We have known science to make bad little breaks. **1887** F. FRANCIS *Saddle & Mocassin* 146 You've made one or two bad breaks since you've been in town. **1902** G. H. LORIMER *Lett. Merchant* 311 When a clerk makes a fool break, I don't want to beg his pardon for calling his attention to it. **1905** KIPLING *Actions & Reactions* (1909) 26 We're.. moving in worlds not realised, and we shall make some bad breaks. **1931** WODEHOUSE *If I were You* vii. 82 He'd always be worrying..for fear he was going to make a break of some kind.

j. A freak or abnormal development from the parent stock.

1921 *Conquest* Sept. 491/3 These 'mutations', 'sports' or 'breaks', as they are variously called. **1933** *Jrnl. R. Hort. Soc.* LVIII. 388 We are always looking out for natural breaks or variations.

k. *Broadcasting.* (See quot. 1941); *spec.* in phr. ***natural break*** (see quot. 1962).

1941 *B.B.C. Gloss. Broadc. Terms* 5 *Break*, interruption, either momentary or prolonged, in the transmission of a programme. **1959** *Manch. Guardian* 11 Aug. 4/5 The only reason grandpappy hasn't been on television is that he never could learn to wait for the natural breaks. **1962** *Rep. Comm. Broadc. 1960* 72 Fourth among the main specific duties laid upon the [Independent Television] Authority is the obligation to ensure that advertisements do not occur except at the beginning or end of programmes, or in natural breaks in them... What was meant by the term was a break which would have occurred even had there been no advertisement: for example, in the interval between the acts of a play, or at half-time in football matches.

9. *Music.* **a.** The point of separation between the different registers of a voice. **b.** 'In an organ stop: The sudden alteration of the proper scale-series of pipes by returning to those of an octave lower in pitch' (Stainer and Barrett).

1881 C. A. EDWARDS *Organs* 153 As a rule on modern organs the breaks are made on the C sharp keys. **1883** CURWEN *Standard Course* 105/2 Passages running across the 'break' can be sung with an even quality of voice. *Ibid.* 107/1 The break between the upper and lower thick registers is easily noticed in male voices.

c. In jazz, a short solo or improvised phrase; a passage of a few bars during which an

instrumentalist plays unaccompanied. orig. *U.S.*

1926 A. NILES in W. C. Handy *Blues* 8 The notes.. which follow this rest, fill in the following break, and themselves are called 'the break', or 'the jazz'. **1927** *Melody Maker* Apr. 377/1 Now try a two-bar break composed of Type A and Type B. **1958** P. OLIVER in P. Gammond *Decca Bk. of Jazz* i. 21 Of each line of four bars, he may sing only two or three, allowing room for an instrumental or vocal 'break'.

10. a. Something abruptly breaking the line, or level; an irregularity, roughness, knot, etc. *spec.* rough, irregular country; broken country (*local U.S.*).

1756 BURKE *Subl. & B.* Wks. I. 241 The fine variation is lost in wrinkles, sudden breaks, and right lines. **1771** SIR J. REYNOLDS *Disc.* iv. (1876) 362 A portrait-painter.. leaves out all the minute breaks.. in the face. **1787** BEST *Angling* (ed. 2) 168 *Break*, a knot in the joint of a rod. **1820** J. C. GILLELAND *Ohio & Miss. Pilot* 171 Some of the breaks rise in deep circular glens called coves. **1902** WEBSTER *Suppl.*, *Break*.., a line of cliffs, and associated spurs and small valleys, at the edge of a mesa. (*Western U.S.*) **1903** CLAPIN *Dict. Amer.* 74 *Break*, a rough, irregular piece of ground. (Neb.) **1918** S. S. VISHER *Geogr. S. Dakota* 117 Badlands or 'breaks' afforded protection from winter storms.

b. *Archit.* (see quots.)

1685 EVELYN *Diary* (1827) III. 178 Windows and Columns at the break and entrance of free-stone. **1807** HUTTON *Course Math.* II. 88 The breaks of the windows themselves are 8 feet 6 inches high, and 1 foot 3 inches deep. **1823** P. NICHOLSON *Pract. Build.* 441 Any portion of the exterior side of a building which protrudes itself towards the spectator, is denominated a projection or break.

c. A broken or disturbed portion on the surface of water. *U.S.*

1852 *Trans. Mich. Agric. Soc.* III. 231 They will make a break in the water near the shore with their tail. **1897** 'MARK TWAIN' *Following Equator* ix. 109 With.. the 'break' spreading away from its head, and the wake following behind its tail.

11. A number of chests of tea, a lot or consignment.

1864 *Times* 4 Nov. Breaks of Canton scented orange pekoe. **1883** *Ibid.* 24 Mar. 6 In a break of 600 chests you will find an absolute uniformity of weight, both of package and contents and of quality.

12. A portion of ground broken up for cultivation; a tract distinct in surface or appearance.

1674 RAY *S. & E. Count. Wds.* 60 *Break*, land plowed the first year after it hath lain fallow in the sheep walks. *Norf.* **1767** A. YOUNG *Farmer's Lett. People* 11, I have.. seen Breaks of wheat of five quarters per acre. **1794** *Statist. Acc. Scot.* XI. 152 Such farms as are divided into 3 inclosures, or, as they are commonly called, breaks. **1878** BLACK *Green Past.* II. 14 Young rabbits.. scurried through the dry heather to the sandy breaks. **1883** *Nature* XXVII. 446 The 'break' or oasis, believed.. to exist in the interior of Greenland.

13. *dial.* A large number or quantity.

1808 JAMIESON *Break*, a considerable number of people, a crowd; as a break of folk, *Fife*. **1880** *W. Cornwall Gloss.* (E. D. S.), *Brake*, a large quantity: particularly applied to flowers, as a 'brake of honeysuckle'. **1884** G. C. DAVIES *Norfolk Broads* xxxii. 247 The sky was cloudless, & the stars remarkably brilliant.. Alluding to the 'break' of stars above us, the man said that it foretold rough stormy weather.

14. In type-founding, a surplus piece of metal remaining on the shank of a newly cast type.

1683 MOXON *Mech. Exerc., Printing* 370 *Break*,.. the Mettle that is contiguous to the Shank of a New Cast Letter: This Break is formed in the Mouth-piece of the Letter-mould, and is called a Break, because it is always broke from the Shank of a Letter. **1843** HOLTZAPFFEL *Turning* I. 324 The breaks, or the runners, of the types are first broken off. *a* **1877** KNIGHT *Dict. Mech.*

15. The quantity of hemp which is prepared or sold in one year. *U.S.*

1796 *Mass. Mercury* 29 Apr. (Cent. Dict.), Best St. Petersburg clean Hemp of the break of the year 1796. **1907** *Daily Chron.* 7 Mar. 6/6 A 'break' of hemp, which in America means the quantity sold in a year.

16. A portion of a crop of turnips, etc., set aside for sheep to feed on.

1805 R. W. DICKSON *Pract. Agric.* II. 672 Removing them [*sc.* sheep] to fresh portions or breaks every eight or ten days. **1886** C. SCOTT *Sheep-farming* 48 A certain breadth or portion of the turnips, called a 'break', the extent of which is regulated by the number of sheep to be put on. **1933** L. ACLAND in *Press* (N.Z.) 23 Sept. 13/7 *Break*, a temporary division made in a paddock so that stock shall feed off the turnips, etc., in sections. **1950** *N.Z. Jrnl. Agric.* May 461/1 Breaks of winter forage crops such as turnips or chou moellier.

17. a. *Electr.* and *Telegraphy.* An apparatus for interrupting or changing the direction of an electric current; a commutator.

1854 *Tomlinson's Cycl. Useful Arts* I. 580/1 The other pole.. communicates.. with the little wheel, called the break, the circumference of which is partly of metal and partly of wood or ivory, so as to interrupt and renew.. the metallic connexion. *a* **1877** KNIGHT *Dict. Mech.*

b. *Electr.* The action of breaking contact in an electric circuit; the position in which contact is broken (in phr. *at break*). See also MAKE *sb.*² 9.

1875 F. GUTHRIE *Magn. & Electr.* 206 The automatic make and break. Fig. 181 shows the 'hammer break'. **1876** *Nature* XIV. 62/2 The increase of excitability was manifested towards make, and scarcely at all towards break.

18. *colloq.* A chance, an opportunity; a piece of good luck; freq. with defining word, as ***an even break***: an equal or fair chance. orig. *U.S.*

1911 H. QUICK *Yellowstone N.* v. 126 It's allus an even break whether they'll stan' and freeze in their tracks, or chase after some bunch of.. natives. **1911** MULFORD *Bar-20 Days* xxiii. 231 Now he wanted an 'even break', where once he would have called all his wits into play to avoid it. **1918** —— *Man fr. Bar-20* xiii. 128 If th' stakes are high an' the breaks anywhere near equal, I'll risk my last dollar or my last breath. **1926** J. BLACK *You can't Win* xxi. 331, I could 'take' the spot if I got a fair break on the luck. **1928** *Daily Express* 11 July 12 The chances in the 'quarter-mile' seem to give the Americans only an even break for a first place. **1930** *Publishers' Weekly* 8 Feb. 705/2 These buyers and their stores get what are known as 'the breaks'. **1938** G. GREENE *Brighton Rock* II. i. 62 A break like that's *too* good. *Ibid.* 72 We had a lucky break. **1948** L. A. G. STRONG *Trevannion* 196 Give the boy a break, they thought indulgently.

19. *Boxing.* The act of separating after the contestants have been in a clinch.

1928 *Daily Express* 2 Aug. 13/5 Lewis was disqualified for hitting on the break.

20. *attrib.* **break-lathe**, a lathe having a portion of its bed open or removable so as to admit work of larger diameter; **break-line** *Typogr.*, the last line of a paragraph.

1883 *Encycl. Brit.* XV. 154/1 Break lathes.. were made by Mr. (now Sir Joseph) Whitworth as long ago as 1840. **1683** MOXON *Mech. Exerc., Printing* 226 Nor do good Compositers account it good Workmanship to begin a Page with a Break-line. **1808** STOWER *Printer's Gram.* 163 Part of a word, or a complete word in a break line, if it contain no more than three or four letters, is improper. **1824** J. JOHNSON *Typogr.* II. 90 To take a comprehensive view of the copy,.. to notice.. the number of break lines. **1967** *Hart's Rules for Compositors* (ed. 37) 56 Break-lines should consist of more than five letters, except in narrow measures.

break, *sb.*² Also **brake**. [Derivation not quite certain: app. f. BREAK *v.*, in the sense 'to break a horse'; but it is said in Knight's *Amer. Mech. Dict.* to be a general name for the fore-part or frame of a carriage, so that it may possibly be an application of BRAKE *sb.*⁵]

1. A large carriage-frame (having two or four wheels) with no body, used for breaking in young horses.

1831 LOUDON *Cycl. Agric.* (ed. 2) 1002 The training of coach-horses commences with.. driving in a break or four-wheeled frame. **1865** *Derby Mercury* 1 Mar., A horse-breaker's drag, or break, with two horses harnessed to it.

2. A large wagonette.

1856 C. M. YONGE *Daisy Chain* I. xxvi. 285 Norman's fate conveyed him to the exalted seat beside the driver of the break. **1874** LADY BARKER *N. Zealand* iv. 23 In their comfortable and large break with four horses. **1882** *Proc. Berw. Nat. Club* IX. III. 451 A brake and four conveying a large party. **1884** P'CESS ALICE *Mem.* 72 Louis drove me and his two brothers in a break. **1885** *Manch. Exam.* 23 Apr. 5/2 The large brakes which convey pleasure-seekers.

break, var. spelling of BRAKE *sb.*², ³, ⁵, ⁷, *v.*¹

breakable ('breɪkəb(ə)l), *a.* and *sb. pl.* [f. BREAK *v.* + -ABLE.] **A.** *adj.* Capable of being broken, frangible.

1570 LEVINS *Manip.* 2 Breakable, *fragilis*. **1611** COTGR., *Brisable*, burstable, breakeable. **1646** FULLER *Wounded Consc.* (1841) 278 Christ's bones were in themselves breakable. **1844** *Proc. Berw. Nat. Club* II. XII. 100 Breaking the eggs and every other thing breakable.

B. *sb. pl.* Things which are capable of being broken.

1820 BYRON *Let.* 12 June in R. E. Prothero *Lett. & Jrnl. Byron* (1901) V. 44 Mother Mocenigo will probably try a bill for breakables. **1904** H. G. WELLS *Food of Gods* I. iv. 117 The child was born with good intentions. 'Padda be good, be good,' he used to say as the breakables flew before him. **1909** —— *Tono-Bungay* I. ii. §4 There was a plaster of Paris horse to indicate veterinary medicines among these breakables.

Hence **'breakableness**.

1856 RUSKIN *Mod. Paint.* III. IV. xv. §13 The character on which he fixes first is frangibility—breakableness to bits.

breakage¹ ('breɪkɪdʒ). [f. BREAK *v.* + -AGE.]

1. The action or fact of breaking.

1813 WELLINGTON in Gurw. *Disp.* X. 373 There has already been much breakage. **1827** *Q. Rev.* XXXV. 151 The breakage of the crockery was the grand coup-de-théâtre. **1831** CARLYLE *Sart. Res* II. ii, In their [children's] wanton breakages and defacements, you shall discern a creative instinct.

b. *Music.* The change in the quality of the voice in passing from one 'register' to another.

1883 CURWEN *Standard Course* 105/2 It is remarkable that the change of breakage into this register should be just an octave higher than that into the thin register.

2. The results of breaking; loss or damage caused by breaking.

1848 ARNOULD *Mar. Insur.* (1866) II. III. i. 667 A certain per centage is fixed.. as the ordinary amount of leakage and breakage for which the Underwriter is in no case liable. **1849** FLEESE *Comm. Class-Bk.* 77 When gold dust, or the precious metals in ore, are bought, the loss of weight or off-fall in refining, called in some places breakage.

3. An interruption caused by breaking; a break.

1871 FARRAR *Witn. Hist.* i. 36 Here then are miracles.. breakages in the unbroken continuity. **1881** STOKES in *Nature* No. 626. 614 If there was a breakage in the cable something like 300 miles off.

4. *Naut.* (see quot.)

1867 SMYTH *Sailor's Word-bk.* 130 *Breakage*, the leaving of empty spaces in stowing the hold.

breakage², var. form of BRAKEAGE.

break-away, breakaway ('breɪkəweɪ). Pl. **break-aways, breaks-away.** [f. phr. *to break away*: see BREAK *v.* 50.]

1. The action of breaking away; severance.

1897 *Badminton Mag.* IV. 421 A big break-away occurs in the ranks [of flying rooks]. **1909** *Daily Chron.* 13 July 1/4 The owners report that there is no 'breakaway' from the agreement. **1923** *Glasgow Herald* 1 Feb. 6 A challenging breakaway from rhythm. **1923** *Daily Mail* 31 May 13 There is a natural breakaway of the water on one side into a bog. **1950** H. READ *Educ. for Peace* iv. 55 A complete break-away from a pedagogic tradition which had its origins in the Revival of Learning.

2. *Austral.* **a.** A panic rush of animals, usually at the sight or smell of water; a stampede.

1891 'The Breakaway', title of picture by Tom Roberts at Victorian Artists' Exhibition (Morris *Austral Eng.*).

b. An animal that leaves the herd.

1893 *Argus* 29 Apr. 4/4 (Morris), The smartest stock horse that ever brought his rider up within whip distance of a breakaway.

3. In various sports, the act of breaking away or getting free. **a.** *Athletics, Racing.* A false start to a race. **b.** *Boxing.* The getting away from one's opponent or the separating of the contestants after a spell of in-fighting. **c.** *Association Football.* A sudden rush of a player or players with the ball towards the opponents' goal (esp. after a period of pressure); in *Rugby Football* used esp. of the action of a player moving quickly away from the scrummage. **d.** *Cycling.* (See quots. 1961); also, a cyclist who is leading in a race.

1885 *Times* 4 June 10/3 After several breaks away the 12 competitors were despatched to an excellent start. **1906** *Daily Chron.* 7 Sept. 9/4 They scored from a breakaway. **1909** *Westm. Gaz.* 29 Nov. 12/2 The visitors fully deserved their win, for, save for a few spasmodic breaks-away by the home team, they were pressing continually. **1928** *Daily Mail* 9 Aug. 14/1 A bad preliminary breakaway, which delayed the start. **1930** I. M. B. STUART *Theory Mod. Rugby Practice* vi. 111 The wing forwards would be well advised.. to.. hold themselves in readiness for a quick break-away. **1961** F. C. AVIS *Sportsman's Gloss.* 149/1 *Breakaway*, a sudden and significant opening up of a gap in advance of the main group of riders in a cycle race. **1961** PARTRIDGE *Dict. Slang* Suppl. 1013/2 *The breakaway*, those competitors who have established a substantial lead: racing cyclists' coll.: since ca. 1925. **1961** *Times* 7 June 5/6 The exception to the general massing of the riders were the early breakaways of Jacobs.. and Tarr.

4. *attrib.* or as *adj.* That breaks away or has broken away; seceding.

1934 in WEBSTER. **1949** KOESTLER *Promise & Fulf.* III. i. 310 The so-called 'General Zionists' and the 'Progressive Party', a break-away group of the former. **1951** *Engineering* 13 July 56/2 Breakaway unions were condemned by.. the Minister of Labour. **1961** *Listener* 28 Dec. 1116/2 The 'breakaway' province of Katanga.

b. *spec.* in *Rugby Football.* Applied to a forward in the side row of the scrummage. Also *ellipt.*

1954 J. B. G. THOMAS *On Tour* 114 A twenty-eight-year-old salesman and tall breakaway forward. **1955** *Times* 22 Aug. 3/1 The breakaway men, Fry, Retief, and Ackermann, covered a vast amount of ground and showed great speed in the open. **1969** *Australian* 24 May 36/7 Other NSW Country forwards who could force their way into the State side tomorrow are breakaway Dick Cocks, and prop Ross Turnbull.

break-back, *sb.*: see BREAK *sb.*¹ 1 b, (*Cricket*) 5.

'break-back, *a.* [f. BREAK *v.* + BACK *sb.*¹; cf. BREAK-NECK.] **1.** That breaks the back; crushing, over heavy.

1556 J. HEYWOOD *Spider & F.* lxxii. 16 Our breakbacke burdens. **1607** J. DAVIES *Summa Tot.* 21 (D.) All breake-backe Crosses which we vndergo. **1822** W. COBBETT *Rur. Rides* (1885) I. 104 All the break-back and sweat-extracting work.

2. Of a roof: having the lower portion at a different angle from the upper. Also *ellipt.* as *sb. U.S.* ? *Obs.*

1856 S. G. GOODRICH *Recoll. of Lifetime* (1857) I. 78 The house.. was a low edifice.. two stories in front; the rear being called a *breakback*, that is, sloping down to a height of ten feet. **1859** BARTLETT *Dict. Amer.* (ed. 2), *Break-back*, a term applied to a peculiar roof, common in the country, where the rear portion is extended beyond the line of the opposite side, and at a different angle. The addition thus acquired is used as a wash-room, a storehouse, or for farming implements.

break-down (breɪkdaʊn; see below). [f. the verbal phrase *break down* (see BREAK *v.* 51).

In this and similar verbal formations, the stress seems primarily to be even ('*break* '*down*), or with stronger force on the adv. (,*break* '*down*); but in familiar and well-established expressions (as sense 2), there is a tendency to take the combination without analysis as a single word, and to say '*break,down*, or even '*breakdown*: this is also regularly done in attributive use, (as in ' 'breakdown 'gang').]

1. a. The act of breaking and falling down; a ruinous downfall, a collapse. *lit.* and *fig.*

1832 MARRYAT *N. Forster* xxii, These unfortunate *break downs*. **1835** BROWNING *Paracelsus* III. 70 The break-down of my general aims. **1883** CHALMERS *Local Govt.* 152 Any break-down or hitch in the working of the sanitary laws.

b. *esp.* A fracture or dislocation of machinery resulting in a stoppage. Hence *attrib.*, as in ***break-down gang, train.***

1838 *Civil Engineer* I. No. 11. 296/1 *Railway Casualties*—obstructions from cattle wagons and breaks down. **1852** J. LUDLOW *Master Engineers, &c.* 105 Double pay for overtime caused by break-down or accident. **1863** *Times* 6 Apr., Break-down gangs from Peterborough and Grantham. **1866** *Standard* 15 Sept. 4/5 A mine where there had been a breakdown. **1893** *Funk's Standard Dict.*, *Breakdown van* (Gt. Brit.), a wrecking-car. **1933** in *Amer. Speech* (1942) XVII. 4/2 Morton, my car's outside Savarin's... Get your breakdown lorry round for it. **1953** A. SMITH *Blind White Fish in Persia* i. 22 One of its hands..prepared the breakdown lorry.

c. Of the animal functions, or health (esp. of the mental powers); spec. ***nervous breakdown***: (a case of) neurasthenia; a vague term for any severe or incapacitating emotional disorder.

1858 J. H. BENNET *Nutrition* iv. 91 A complete breakdown of the general health. **1875** M. PATTISON *Casaubon* 465 Walter Scott had the first warning of his own break-down in similar symptoms. [**1904** J. LONDON *Sea-Wolf* xxxvi. 290 There had been his terrific headaches, and we were agreed that it was some sort of brain break-down.] **1905** A. BENNETT *Sacred & Profane Love* III. i. 212, I read in the papers..that you were suffering from neurasthenia and nervous breakdown. **1907** J. LONDON *Iron Heel* x. 141 Hints were made of mental breakdown on his part. **1927** J. S. HUXLEY *Relig. without Rev.* iv. 125 The phase of conflict ended with that crash known generally as a 'nervous breakdown'. **1930** B. RUSSELL *Conquest of Happiness* 75 One of the symptoms of approaching nervous break-down is the belief that one's work is terribly important. **1959** J. BRAINE *Vodi* v. 82 He was never seen at the school again. The official explanation was a complete nervous breakdown.

d. *Electr.* The sudden passage of electric current through an insulating medium. Also *attrib.*, as **breakdown voltage**, the voltage required to cause a break-down.

1915 F. W. PEEK *Dielectric Phenomena* vi. 154 The moisture may even be removed from the space between the electrodes by the action of the field, in which case its presence would not be detected by low-voltage breakdowns. *Ibid.* 155 The relative breakdown voltages of gaps in oil, at 60 cycles, and for impulse voltages..are given. **1962** SIMPSON & RICHARDS *Junction Transistors* iv. 67 The voltage V_B at which this sudden decrease in resistance occurs is called the breakdown voltage.

e. Chemical or physical decomposition. Also *attrib.*, as **breakdown product**, a product resulting from the disintegration of a substance.

1928 A. B. CALLOW *Food & Health* 24 Certain chemical compounds when eaten cause a flow of gastric juice. The chief of these substances are the break-down products of proteins (peptones, etc.). **1959** *Listener* 2 July 38/2 Organic materials of a fibrous nature..encourage green water and algae during the inevitable breakdown processes. **1961** *Lancet* 19 Aug. 395/2 Hæmoglobin breakdown was completely inhibited.

f. An analysis or classification (of figures, statistics, etc.). Cf. BREAK *v.* 51 g.

1936 HARRISON & MITCHELL *Home Market* 140 Such families were extremely few and their breakdown according to density was impossible. **1948** *Observer* 18 Apr. 4/5 The latest threat to clarity is the use of 'breakdown' to mean 'analysis' or 'classification'. **1957** *Times* (Canada Suppl.) 12 Nov. p. viii/1 Figures rose..to 73,578 for the corresponding period this year. The breakdown of this..figure was English 47,240, Scots 15,124, Irish 9,646, Welsh 1,568.

2. 'A riotous dance, with which balls are often terminated in the country. A dance in the peculiar style of the negroes.' Bartlett *Dict. Amer.* (U.S.; but frequently humorously in Eng.)

a **1864** *New Eng. Tales* (Bartlett), Don't clear out when the quadrilles are over, for we are going to have a break-down to wind up with. **1877** BURNAND *'Ride to Khiva'* 11 Clog-dancers, or nigger duettists, at a Music Hall with a breakdown. **1881** *Gd. Words* XXII. 41/2 The men followed with a fiendish 'breakdown'.

3. *Sawmilling.* (See quot. 1957.) Also (*N.Z.*) applied to the building in which the initial cutting of timber from logs is done. Also *attrib.* Cf. *breaking-down.*

1923 C. M. MALFROY *Small Sawmills* 17 The laying of the foundations of the breakdown should first be proceeded with. *Ibid.*, The logging delivery-tram, mill log-skids, engine, breakdown bench. **1943** *Amer. Speech* XVIII. 85 The cleared tracks..carry logs to the mill, where it is handled by a *break-down man.* **1957** *Brit. Commonw. Forest Terminol.* II. 33 *Breakdown*, the initial operation in converting from the round, by sawing a log longitudinally into cants, and, by extension, cants into large timber, preparatory to further manufacture.

breaker[1] ('breɪkə(r)). Also 2–6 breker, (5–6 *Sc.* -ar). [f. BREAK *v.* + -ER[1].] He who or that which breaks (in various senses of verb.).

1. a. One who breaks, crushes, or destroys; so ***breaker off***, etc.; and with defining sb. as HOUSE-BREAKER, SHIP-BREAKER, etc., q.v.

c **1175** *Lamb. Hom.* 83 Ne mihte nawiht brekere bon icloped. *c* **1535** DEWES *Introd. Fr.* in *Palsgr.* 1040 The peas ..is..breker of strife. **1563** *Homilies* II. *Fasting* II. (1859) 288 A breaker of his fast. **1597** T. PAYNE *Royal Exch.* 14 They become eyther breakers or banckerers. *a* **1649** DRUMM. OF HAWTH. *Cypress Grove* Wks. 118 Death..is the reasonless breaker off of all actions. **1840** CARLYLE *Heroes* iv. 193 A Breaker of Idols. **1847** TENNYSON *Princ.* II. 143 Horn-handed breakers of the glebe.

b. *spec.* One who cards wool. (cf. BREAK *v.* 2 c.)

1514 *Act 6 Hen. VIII*, ix. §1 The Breaker or Kember to deliver again..the same Wooll so broken and kembed. **1764** BURN *Poor Laws* 156 Three weavers and spoolers, two breakers, etc.

c. One who makes known (tidings, etc.).

1864 TENNYSON *Aylmer's F.* 594 A breaker of the bitter news from home.

2. a. One who transgresses or violates a law, oath, convention, etc.

1382 WYCLIF *2 Macc.* xiii. 7 It bifelle the breker of lawe for to die. **1483** *Cath. Angl.* 42 A Breker or tryspaser; *preuaricator, transgressor.* **1535** COVERDALE *Ezek.* xvi. 38 A breaker of wedlocke and a murthurer. **1596** SHAKS. *1 Hen. IV*, I. ii. 132 He [Falstaff] was neuer yet a Breaker of Prouerbs: He will giue the diuell his due. **1765** BLACKSTONE *Comm.* I. 350 Constables..may apprehend all breakers of the peace. **1864** H. SPENCER *Illustr. Univ. Progr.* 61 Some courageous breaker of conventions.

b. In comb. with defining sb., as COVENANT-, LAW-, SABBATH-BREAKER, etc., q.v.

3. One who subdues, tames, or trains. Also *breaker in*, and in *comb.*, as HORSE-BREAKER.

1552 HULOET, Breaker of horse, or other beast brutysh. **1828** SCOTT *F.M. Perth* I. 23 The breaker of mad horses —the tamer of wild Highlandmen. **1834** *Fraser's Mag.* IX. 93 A breaker-in of dogs. **1860** *Encycl. Brit.* XX. 220 Whenever the dog in advance points, it is the breaker's duty to make all the rest that acknowledge the scent to point.

4. a. That which breaks; as a break-water (*obs.*), a harrow (see quot. 1799). In many comb., as COAL-, ICE-, ROCK-BREAKER, q.v.

1661 HICKERINGILL *Jamaica* 47 There is no landing..by reason of the fury of the waves (not pacified by any Breakers). **1799** J. ROBERTSON *Agric. Perth* 96 Some [harrows] are made large enough to be a draught for two horses, which are distinguished by the name of Breakers.

b. *spec.* The name of various machines for crushing the dried stems of flax or hemp, and for performing the first operation in carding cotton, etc.

1817 *Parl. Deb.* 1059 The stems of flax and hemp..are passed through two machines, the first called a breaker, the second a rubber. **1875** URE *Dict. Arts* I. 972 After passing through the first or 'breaker card', the cotton is put through the 'finisher'. **1879** Cassell's *Techn. Educ.* IV. 274/2 The slivers produced by the breakers, as the first set of engines is called.

c. In paper-manufacture, a machine in which rags, etc., are washed and partly pulped. Also *attrib.*, as ***breaker-plate.***

1880 J. DUNBAR *Pract. Papermaker* 71 It may be mentioned that the breaker-plate ought to be sharp when starting to blottings. **1902** *Encycl. Brit.* XXXI. 456/1 The next step is that of washing and 'breaking in', which takes place in an engine called the 'breaker'. **1963** R. R. A. HIGHAM *Handbk. Papermaking* ii. 23 Different types of breakers are available for use with rag, wood pulp sheets, waste paper and broke.

d. In anthracite mining, an apparatus for breaking, sizing, and cleaning coal for the market.

1885 *Encycl. Brit.* XVIII. 501/2 The 'breaker', an anthracite invention and a monster of destruction, is an edifice of wood and iron 100 feet high,..with rollers set with teeth to crush the larger lumps, with bolting screens to separate the sizes. **1900** *Coal & Metal Miners' Pocket-bk.* (ed. 6) 574 *Breaker Boy*, a boy who works in a coal breaker.

e. In cheese-making, an implement for breaking the curd into small pieces.

1844 *Jrnl. R. Agric. Soc.* V. I. 88 The first process of breaking down the curd in the cheese-tub is..performed by a breaker or curd-cutter.

5. A heavy ocean-wave which breaks violently into foam against a rocky coast or in passing over reefs or shallows. ***Breakers ahead!*** 'the common pass-word to warn the officer of broken water in the direction of the course'.

1684 I. MATHER *Remark. Provid.* (1856) 43 If the Providence of God had not by the breakers given them timely warning they had been dashed to pieces. **1740** WOODROOFE in Hanway *Trav.* (1762) I. IV. lix. 275 When there is any sea, the breakers are visible. **1845** DARWIN *Voy. Nat.* xiv. (1852) 305 The great wave broke in a fearful line of white breakers. **1864** TENNYSON *En. Ard.* 51 Along that breaker-beaten coast. *Ibid.* 549 Till hard upon the cry of 'breakers' came The crash of ruin. **1879** BEERBOHM *Patagonia* 3 Suddenly we heard a shout of 'Breakers ahead!' and every one turned pale.

†**6.** A kind of firework. *Obs.*

1630 J. TAYLOR (Water P.) *Wks.* III. 118/1 Rackets, Crackers, Breakers and such like, giues blowes and reports without number. **1635** J. BABINGTON *Pyrotechn.* xxxvi. 43 Your reports or breakers for this work shall be made as follows.

7. A horse that breaks (BREAK *v.* 38 c). orig. *U.S.*

a **1867** H. WOODRUFF *Trotting Horse in Amer.* (1868) xxiii. 201 Although a trotter of remarkably fine speed and power, he was such a bad breaker. **1965** *Weekly News* (N.Z.) 8 Dec. 59/2 Breaking horses have always been a problem... There is an alarmingly high percentage of breakers.

breaker[2] ('breɪkə(r)). *Naut.* [Commonly believed to be a corruption of Sp. *bareca* or *barrica*; cf. BARECA, BARRICO.] A small keg or cask.

1833 MARRYAT *P. Simple* xxxiii, A breaker or two (that is, small casks holding about seven gallons each) of water was put into each boat. **1835** —— *Jac. Faithf.* xx, The purser sent a breaker of spirits on shore. **1875** BEDFORD *Sailor's Pocket Bk.* vi. (ed. 2) 227 They will be found very useful for carrying both provisions and water, and stow better than breakers.

† '**breakeress.** *Obs. rare.* In 4 brekeresse. [f. prec. + -ESS.] A woman who breaks.

1382 WYCLIF *Jer.* iii. 7 The brekeresse of lawe, Juda, hir sister. —— 8 The lawe brekeresse.

break-even ('breɪk'iːv(ə)n). orig. *U.S.* [f. *to break even* (see BREAK *v.* 48 b).] Usu. *attrib.*: designating or pertaining to the point at which one 'breaks even' (see BREAK *v.* 48 b); of or pertaining to a balance of expenditure and revenue, profit and loss, etc.

1938 *Barron's National Financial Weekly* 14 Nov. 27/3 Tire companies in the first half of the year were around the break-even point on the average. **1948** *Jrnl. R. Aeronaut. Soc.* LII. 688/2 By matching the right size of aeroplane to the stage length, 'break-even' fares of between fourpence and sixpence per passenger mile could be achieved. **1949** *Ibid.* LIII. 199/2 Sales of 400 aircraft would be required before the constructor reached 'break-even' point and recovered his outlay. **1952** A. E. BENN *Management Dict.* 66 *Break-even point*, that point at which the level of balance is equal, as the level of production at which there will be no profit or loss. **1958** *Times* 12 Dec. 12/1 (*heading*) Earliest possible 'break-even'. *Ibid.*, Steps necessary to achieve the earliest possible break-even date. **1965** *Listener* 1 July 9/2 Half the tenants..can afford a break-even rent.

breakfall ('breɪkfɔːl). [f. BREAK *v.* 28 b + FALL *sb.*[1]] In judo, a movement whereby the impact of a fall is diminished. Hence as *v. intr.*, to execute a breakfall.

1906 MIYAKE & TANI *Game of Ju-Jitsu* v. 35 The sideways break-fall..may nearly always be used when you are pitching forward on to your head. **1954** E. DOMINY *Teach yourself Judo* ii. 20 Spend 5 minutes on breakfalls. *Ibid.* iii. 36 As he begins to fall you must let go of his jacket with your right hand so that he can breakfall.

breakfast ('brɛkfəst), *sb.* Also 5 brekfast, 6 breke-, breck-, 6–7 breakefast. [f. BREAK *v.* 29 c + FAST.]

1. That with which a person breaks his fast in the morning; the first meal of the day.

1463 *Mann. & Househ. Exp.* 224 Exspensys in brekfast, xj. *d.* **1491** *Act 7 Hen. VII*, xxii. Pream., Ye were at your brekefast. **1528** MORE *Heresyes* IV. Wks. 251/1 That men shoulde go to masse as well after sowper as before brekefast. **1594** LADY RUSSELL in Ellis *Orig. Lett.* I. 233 III. 40 Becawse I here your Lordship meaneth to be gon early in the morning, I am bowld to send your pale thin cheecks a comfortable little breckfast. **1762** GOLDSM. *Nash* 46 People of fashion make public breakfasts at the assembly-houses. **1793** COWPER *Lett.* 25 Apr., My only time for study is now before breakfast. **1819** SHELLEY *Peter Bell Third* III. xii, Dinners convivial and political..Breakfasts professional and critical. **1860** TYNDALL *Glac.* I. §27. 207 My assistants were preparing breakfast.

2. a. Occas. in wider sense: That which puts an end to a fast, a meal.

1526 TINDALE *Heb.* xii. 16 Esau which for one breakfast solde his right. **1591** SHAKS. *Two Gent.* v. iv. 34, I would haue beene a break-fast to the Beast. *a* **1700** DRYDEN (J.) The wolves will get a breakfast by my death.

b. = WEDDING-*breakfast.*

1848 THACKERAY *Van. Fair* xv. 132 We'll have a wedding, Briggs, and you shall make the breakfast, and be a brides' maid. **1903** G. B. SHAW *Man & Superman* IV. 167 I'm off for my honeymoon... Oh don't say that, Violet. And no wedding, no breakfast.

3. *Comb.* and *attrib.*, as ***breakfast-bell***, †***-board***, ***-china***, ***-cloth***, ***-cup***, ***-food***, ***-hour***, ***-nook***, ***-parlour***, ***-party***, ***-room***, ***-service***, ***-stall***, ***-table***, ***things***, ***-time***, ***-tray***; **breakfast-set**, the crockery in use at breakfast; **breakfast television, TV** orig. *U.S.*, television broadcasting in the morning, esp. at or around breakfast time; **breakfast-time television, TV** orig. *U.S.* = *breakfast television* above.

1842 T. MARTIN in *Fraser's Mag.* Dec., The *breakfast-bell had sounded. **1544** *Privy Purse Exp. P'cess Mary* (Madden) 149 Item paid..for mending the *Brekefaste-borde and fyre-Shovell. **1811** JANE AUSTEN *Sense & Sens.* I. ii. 26 The set of *breakfast china is twice as handsome as what belongs to this house. **1929** E. BOWEN *Joining Charles* 124 Breakfast-china..with a red rim. **1778** G. L. WAY *Learning at Loss* I. 107 Dipping the Corner of the *Breakfast Cloth into his Tea-cup. **1850** DICKENS *Dav. Copp.* xxv. 270 A clean breakfast-cloth. **1834** CARLYLE *Fr. Rev.* II. VI. vii. 365 In remote streets, men are drinking *breakfast-coffee. **1762** BOSWELL *London Jrnl.* 12 Dec. (1950) 81, I ordered some large *breakfast cups. **1911** A. BENNETT *Hilda Lessways* I. v. 47 Her big breakfast-cup full of steaming tea. **1898** *Ladies' Home Jrnl.* Feb. 28/1 (Advt.), Ralston Health Club *Breakfast Food. **1941** M. ALLINGHAM *Traitor's Purse* vii. 75 The familiar cartons of breakfast food. **1811** L. M. HAWKINS *Countess & Gertrude* I. v. 80 An unforeseen indisposition..kept her ladyship in almost hopeless doubt during her *breakfast-hour. **1876** C. M. YONGE *Womankind* xiii. 92 It is very unfortunate that most people's breakfast hour coincides with this only period permitted for religious teaching. **1931** *Kansas City Times* 9 Oct., A cute little room called the *breakfast nook. **1958** J. CANNAN *And be a Villain* iii. 50 You can come into my kitchen..there's a breakfast nook, as they calls it in the books. **1802** C. WILMOT *Let.* 14 Feb. in *Irish Peer* (1920) 43 If 'Italy is the Garden of Europe',..Scotland the *breakfast Parlour, and so on, I really think one may say France is the 'Drawing-room'. *c* **1815** JANE AUSTEN *Northang. Ab.* (1833) II. vii. 142 She found her way to the breakfast-parlour. **1814** JANE AUSTEN *Mansf. Park* II. x. 232 Sir Thomas asked Crawford to join the early *breakfast party. **1871** MORLEY *Crit. Misc.* (1886) I. 298 The hard geniality of some clever college-tutor of stiff manners, entertaining undergraduates at an official breakfast party. **1732** SARAH, DUCHESS OF MARLBOROUGH *Let.* 4 July (1943) 36 The rooms I mean, is that where the

red velvet bed stands and the room next to it, which they call the *breakfast room. **1837** LOCKHART *Scott* VII. 404 A charming breakfast-room which looks to the Tweed. **1838** J. ROMILLY *Camb. Diary* 16 Oct. (1967) 156 She ordered a beautiful *breakf. service for him. **1855** TROLLOPE *Warden* viii. 122 The breakfast-service on the table was equally costly and equally plain. **1939** A. THIRKELL *Before Lunch* ix. 249, I shall give you a breakfast service and a very large Persian cat. *c* **1815** JANE AUSTEN *Northang. Ab.* (1833) II. vii. 143 The elegance of the *breakfast set. **1853** DICKENS *Bleak Ho.* xlvii. 449 A *breakfast-stall at a street corner. **1762** T. CHIPPENDALE *Gentleman & Cabinet-Maker's Director* (ed. 3) 8 Two Designs of *Breakfast-Tables. One hath a Stretching-Rail...The other hath a Shelf. *a* **1817** JANE AUSTEN *Northanger Abbey* (1818) II. v. 67 Never in her life before had she beheld half such variety on a breakfast-table. **1838** DICKENS *O. Twist* 144/1 A well-spread breakfast-table. **1971** *Life* 10 Dec. 68/2, I felt I had performed reasonably well on midnight radio and *breakfast television from Boston to San Francisco. **1984** S. TOWNSEND *Growing Pains A. Mole* 144 At 6.25 I woke my parents up by shouting loudly up the stairs that Breakfast Television was starting. **1980** *Economist* 12 July 93/3 Channel Four..is meant to start then [*sc.* in 1982] (so too is *Breakfast TV, but its revenue is likely to be less than 1% of total TV advertising). **1987** *Financial Times* (Weekend Suppl.) 21 Feb. p. xviii/8 There was nothing to divert me except Breakfast TV. **1980** *Economist* 26 Jan. 18 What the IBA wants from contenders is profitability. The only major innovation it is encouraging is national *breakfast-time television. **1952** *N.Y. Times* 20 Jan. II. 11/1 *Breakfast-time TV has been a commercial success in some cities outside of New York. **1987** *Maclean's Mag.* 13 Apr. 46 She describes the England around her with Dickensian sweep: the New Right, the Falklands War, new technology, breakfast-time TV. **1841** 'M. A. TITMARSH' in *Britannia* 15 May 315/2 All the *breakfast things begin to clatter. **1960** 'J. BELL' *Wellknown Face* iv. 37 She had moved both cups off the little tray to make room for her breakfast things. **1599** LADY M. HOBY *Diary* 25 Sept. (1930) 74 After I had praied I walked in the garden tell *break fast time. **1725** DE FOE *Voy. round World* (1840) 276 Even before breakfast-time. **1815** SCOTT *Guy M.* xlv, He had ridden the whole day since breakfast-time. **1865** MRS. GASKELL *Wives & Daughters* (1866) II. xxi. 210 Mrs. Gibson breakfasted in bed... Her own private letters always went up on her *breakfast-tray. **1893** E. F. BENSON *Dodo* (ed. 3) I. iv. 82 He met a footman carrying a breakfast-tray.

breakfast ('brɛkfəst), *v.* [f. prec.]

1. *intr.* To break one's fast (see BREAK *v.* 29 c); to take the first meal of the day.

1679 EVERARD *Popish Plot* 11 After break-fasting peaceably. **1752** JOHNSON *Rambl.* No. 200 ¶6 A back room, where he always breakfasted when he had not great company. **1883** FROUDE *Short Stud.* IV. II. ii. 181 If an undergraduate now and then breakfasted with his tutor, the undergraduate was shy.

2. *trans.* To provide with breakfast, entertain at breakfast.

1793 T. JEFFERSON *Writ.* IV. 83 They will breakfast you. **1885** M. PATTISON *Mem.* 50, I was breakfasted by Copleston.

'breakfaster. One who breakfasts.

1845 SYD. SMITH *Irish Rom. Cath. Ch.* Wks. 1859 II. 334/1 'Oh, don't you know what has happened?' said the sacred breakfaster. **1864** *Realm* 13 Apr. 6 There are plenty of bad breakfasters.

'breakfasting, *vbl. sb.* [f. as prec. + -ING[1].] The taking of breakfast. Also *attrib.*, as in ***breakfasting-house, -place, -time.***

1732 DE FOE, etc. *Tour Gt. Brit.* (1769) II. 172 Now turned into a Breakfasting-House. **1741** RICHARDSON *Pamela* II. 177 We have made but sorry Breakfastings. *a* **1771** SMOLLETT *Humph. Cl.* (1815) 68 Yesterday..she went by herself to a breakfasting in one of the rooms.

'breakfastless, *a.* [see -LESS.] That is without a breakfast.

1795 SOUTHEY *Lett. fr. Spain* (1799) 41 After having travelled twenty miles..almost breakfastless. **1868** BROWNING *Ring & Bk.* VII. 835 He may go breakfastless and dinnerless.

break-front ('breɪk'frʌnt). [f. BREAK- + FRONT *sb.*] Used esp. *attrib.*: a piece of furniture having a front of which the line is broken by a curve or angle.

1928 *Daily Tel.* 24 July 12/2 A large break-front sideboard. **1955** R. FASTNEDGE *Eng. Furn. Styles* vii. 168 Some prominence was given to the library breakfront bookcase. **1962** *Times* 19 Apr. 15/3 The very stately Chippendale break-front had glazed locked doors.

break-in: see BREAK *sb.*[1] 1 b

breaking ('breɪkɪŋ), *vbl. sb.* [f. BREAK *v.* + -ING[1].] The action of the vb. BREAK.

1. a. in transitive senses.

c **975** *Rushw. Gosp.* Luke xxiv. 35 On brecunge breodes. *a* **1300** *Cursor M.* 8044 (Gött.) Widuten breking of any bow. **1382** —— *Sel. Wks.* III. 521 Cristis disciplis knewen him in brekynge of þe breed. **1514** in Glasscock *Rec. St. Michael's Bp. Stortford* (1882) 33 For brekyng of Ground in the cherche at the buryyng of her husband. **1533–4** *Act 25 Hen. VIII*, xviii. §1 Spinninge, cardinge, breakinge, and sorting of wolles. **1589** PUTTENHAM *Eng. Poesie* (Arb.) 258 Euery poore scholler..cals it the breaking of Priscians head. **1590** SHAKS. *Com. Err.* III. i. 74 Breake any breaking here, and Ile breake your knaues pate. **1722** WOLLASTON *Relig. Nat.* ix. 202 Burnings, crucifixions, breakings upon the wheel. **1813** *Examiner* 18 Jan. 42/2 A breaking of windows on the ground-floor. **1823** LOCKHART *Reg. Dalton* I. iv. (1842) 19.

b. with an adverb: see the vb.

1607 HIERON *Wks.* I. 270 No breaking off of olde sinnes. **1610** *MS. Acc. St. John's Hosp., Canterb.*, For breacking owt of a tre. **1842** DICKENS *Amer. Notes* I. viii. 307 Blowings-up in steam-boats and breakings down in coaches. **1850** MRS. STOWE *Uncle Tom* xxiii. 226 Dodo..was now getting his breaking in, at the hands of his young master. **1864** BURTON *Scot Abr.* II. i. 77 A general breaking-open of the prisons. **1868** W. COLLINS *Moonst.* (1871) 234 The breaking-off of the engagement. **1957** J. S. HUXLEY *Relig. without Rev.* viii. 198 The breaking-down of other substance.

c. The act of forcing a passage into another person's house or other building; freq. in phr. ***breaking and entering***, = HOUSEBREAKING.

1617 [see HOUSEBREAKING]. **1729** G. JACOB *Law-Dict.* O1/2 If a Thief unlocks a Door, or draws the Latch of a Room, to rob..these are a Breaking. **1797** TOMLINS *Jacob's Law-Dict.* I. Bb3/1 A Felony at common law, in (1) *breaking and entering* (2) the *mansion house* of another..to the intent to commit some *felony*. **1855** [see BURGLARY[1] a]. **1939** N. MARSH *Overture to Death* viii. 93 A breaking and entering job at Moorton Park with..her ladyship's jewellery gone.

d. In woollen manufacture, the operation by which short combed slivers are combined and made into continuous lengths. Also ***breaking-in.***

1843 *Penny Cycl.* XXVII. 554/1 The breaking being thus effected, the sliver of wool proceeds to a large bobbin or cylinder. **1915** R. BEAUMONT *Woollen & Worsted* 631 The piece, having been scoured, milled, dried, and tentered, is evenly damped, raised, or raised across before being passed onto the teazle machine. This is called 'breaking-in'.

e. *Phonology.* [After G. *brechung.*] = FRACTURE *sb.* 5. Also applied to different sound changes in Old Norse and other Germanic languages.

1871 F. A. MARCH *Compar. Gram. Anglo-Saxon.* I. 20 *Breaking* is the change of one vowel to two by a consonant. **1874** A. J. ELLIS *E. E. Pronunc.* IV. xi. 1270 Grimm considers breaking mainly due to the action of a following *r, h.* **1937** *Language* XIII. 123 (*title*) Breaking in Old Norse and Old English. *Ibid.*, Under breaking I include here the change of a front vowel in a stressed syllable to a diphthong by the influence of following velar elements whether these be consonants in the same syllable [in O.E.] or vowels in the next [in O.N.].

2. a. in intransitive senses.

1647 FULLER *Good Th. in Worse T.* (1841) 74 Pref., The difference betwixt downright breaking and craving time of their creditors. **1662** GERBIER *Princ.* 39 A noise of breaking of their Waves on the Shoar. **1719** DE FOE *Crusoe* (1840) xiii, The breaking of the sea upon their ship. **1727** —— *Eng. Tradesm.* vii. (1841) I. 47 Breaking is the death of a tradesman. **1874** BLACK *Pr. Thule* 8 The breaking of the waves along the hard coast.

b. with an adverb.

1535 COVERDALE *Job* xxx. 14 Yᵉ breakynge in of waters. **1563** *Homilies* II. *Disobedience* I. (1859) 551 The breach of obedience and breaking in of rebellion. **1711** ADDISON *Spect.* No. 39 ¶5 Abrupt Pauses and Breakings-off in the middle of a Verse. **1719** DE FOE *Crusoe* (1840) iii, My breaking away from my parents.

c. ***breaking (of the meres)*** = WATERBLOOM. Cf. BREAK *v.* 5 c.

1884 W. PHILLIPS in *Trans. Shrops. Archæol. Soc.* VII. 285 The breaking is called in German 'Wasserblüthe' (water-blossom). **1927** WEST & FRITSCH *Treat. Brit. Freshwater Algae* 451 The phenomena of 'water-bloom' and the 'breaking of the meres' are due to the sudden and often periodical appearance of large quantities of a few species of Myxophyceae. **1948** *New Biol.* V. 21 This 'water bloom' or 'breaking of the meres' may be quite sudden.

3. ***breaking of the day***: daybreak, dawn.

1523 LD. BERNERS *Froiss.* I. xviii. 25 In the brekyng of the daye ii. trompettis of Scotland mette with the Englisshe scout-watche. **1611** BIBLE *Gen.* xxxii. 24 There wrestled a man with him, vntill the breaking of the day. **1658** A. FOX tr. *Wurtz' Surg.* II. xviii. 128 At mornings near the breaking of the day they are most pained.

†**4.** A breach or gap. *Obs.*

a **1300** *E.E. Psalter* cv[i]. 23 He suld am have for-lorn; If noght Moises..Had standen in brekinge in his sight. **1676** MOXON *Print Letters* 24 The Breakings and Wants in the Arches you must work in by hand.

5. A piece of land newly broken up. (*U.S.*)

1883 *Pamphlet Jamestown* (*Dakota*) *Board of Tr.*, He earned enough besides, with what he raised on his breaking, to keep himself.

6. ***breaking-out***: an eruption; an outburst.

1552 HULOET, Breakyng out of chyldrens mouths called exulceration. *a* **1649** DRUMM. OF HAWTH. *Hist. Jas. III.* Wks. 44 The authors of every breaking-out and sedition. **1652** FRENCH *Yorksh. Spa* xv. 115 The Scab, the Itch, the Scurff..and all such breakings out. **1783** F. MICHAELIS in *Med. Commun.* I. 356 There appeared a breaking-out on the forehead. **1854** H. MILLER *Sch. & Schoolm.* xxv. (1857) 544 On the breaking out of the controversy.

7. ***breaking up***, = BREAK-UP.

1463 *Bury Wills* (1850) 34, I wil that my household be kept hool to gedyr..vj hool wykkes aftir my dissees and at the brekyng vp I wil myn executours and they haue a good dyner to gedyr. **1612** BRINSLEY *Lud. Lit.* 195 To giue them Theams before their breaking vp at noone. **1726** AMHERST *Terræ Fil.* xlii. 222 Many a school-boy has done more than this for his breaking-up task. **1768** TUCKER *Lt. Nat.* II. 625 It is presumed the boy will come home at breakings-up. **1832** *Nat. Philos.* (U. K. S.) II. *Pneum.* Introd. 70 The breaking-up of the monsoons is the name given by sailors to the shifting of the periodical winds.

8. *attrib.* as in ***breaking(-up) plough; -weight; breaking-crop***, the first crop on newly broken ground; ***breaking-down***, the action of converting a log into sawn timber; also *attrib.*; cf. BREAK *v.* 51 f and BREAK-DOWN 3; ***breaking-down rollers*** (see quot.); ***breaking-engine***, (*a*) in paper-manufacture, a machine for washing and pulping rags, a breaker; (*b*) in woollen-manufacture, a carding-machine; ***breaking-frame***, a machine for drawing out the slivers in spinning wool; ***breaking-off***, the removal of the piece of surplus metal from newly-cast type; also *attrib.*; ***breaking-point***, (*a*) the point, or degree of stress, at which a particular material breaks; (*b*) *fig.* the point at which a person's strength or endurance fails, or at which a situation becomes critical; ***breaking-rollers***, an apparatus for the mechanical kneading of dough; ***breaking-strain, -strength, -stress***, the strain or stress required to break a particular material or object.

1813 VANCOUVER *Agric. Devon* 181 It has occurred..for lay oats to have been made the breaking-crop. **1883** M. P. BALE *Saw-Mills* xxxviii. 331 *Breaking down*, in sawing, is dividing the baulk into boards or planks. **1913** A. I. CARR *Country Work & Life in N.Z.* xxiv. 40 'Breast' benches (where the flitches from the breaking-down saw are cut into commercial sizes) are still used in many mills. **1922** R. C. BRYANT *Lumber* iv. 81 The breaking down of the log continued until it was reduced to a size which could be worked by the saws C and D. **1949** E. DE MAUNY *Huntsman in Career* 162 The scream of the bandsaws on the breaking-down bench. **1839** URE *Dict. Arts* 860 Two pairs of rollers, which, from being used to consolidate the metal by rolling whilst hot, are termed breaking-down rollers. *a* **1877** KNIGHT *Dict. Mech.*, *Breaking-engine*, the first of a series of carding-machines, to receive and act on the lap from the lapper; it has usually coarser clothing than the finishing-cards. **1880** J. DUNBAR *Pract. Papermaker* 71 When furnished in the breaking-engine, wash thoroughly before letting down the roll. **1875** URE *Dict. Arts* III. 1163 The slivers..are drawn out and extended by the rollers of the breaking-frame. **1683** MOXON *Mech. Exerc.*, *Printing* 176 Breaking off is commonly Boys-work: It is only to Break the Break from the Shanck of the Letter. **1839** URE *Dict. Arts* 1261 From the breaking-off boy the types are taken to the rubber. **1921** *Dict. Occup. Terms* (1927) §279 *Breaker.., breaker-off, breaker-off boy* [also *breaking-off boy*], breaks off superfluous wedge-shaped piece of metal, which adheres to lower surface of type when type leaves casting machine, by pressing lower surface of type against table. **1853** *Knickerbocker* XLII. 593 The great 'breaking-plough'..goes tearing..through the roots and grubs. **1899** PITMAN *Key to Business Corresp.* 23 The breaking point of the yarn is guaranteed to be not less than 36 pounds weight for 120 yards. **1908** H. G. WELLS *War in Air* iv. 102 Elaborating the apparatus of war, until the accumulating tensions should reach the breaking-point. *Ibid.* xi. 353 Under the stresses of the war their endurance reached the breaking point. **1922** JOYCE *Ulysses* 365 Transparent stockings, stretched to breaking point. **1845** DODD *Brit. Manuf.* V. 24 The dough is..placed under the breaking-rollers..which perform the office of kneading. **1886** S. W. MITCHELL *R. Blake* xix. 181 The engineer speaks of the breaking-strain in material; the breaking-strain in morals was near for Octopia. **1888** [see STRAIN *sb.*[2] 9]. **1902** *Encycl. Brit.* XXXIII. 11/2 A medium steel..showed a breaking strength of 39 tons per square inch. **1960** *B.S.I. News* Jan. 2 The belt has a breaking strength of 2 tons and weighs only a little over 2 lb. **1940** *Chambers's Techn. Dict.* 111/1 Breaking stress. **1959** *Chambers's Encycl.* XIII. 224/2 Once the breaking stress has been measured it is easy to calculate the permitted working stress by dividing by the appropriate factor of safety. **1781** M. PATTEN *Diary* (1903) 438 Our 4 oxen and breaking up plow helped james Walker break up. **1851** *Illust. Lond. News* 4 Jan. 10 The breaking weight being 30 tons.

breaking ('breɪkɪŋ), *ppl. a.* [f. BREAK *v.*]

1. That breaks, in various senses (chiefly *intr.*) of the verb.

1590 SHAKS. *Com. Err.* II. ii. 128 A drop of water in the breaking gulfe. **1593** —— *Rich. II*, III. ii. 3 Your late tossing on the breaking Seas. **1655** S. ASHE *Fun. Serm. 18 June* 11 He was ready to fall upon idolatrous Israel with breaking blowes. **1674** FAIRFAX *Bulk & Selv.* 51 Beams differently breaking or refrangible. **1678** MANTON *Wks.* (1871) II. 190 His ruinous and breaking condition. **1713** YOUNG *Last Day* II. 187 Breaking dawn Rouz'd the broad front. **1769** FALCONER *Dict. Marine* (1789) *Ecume*, the froth or foam of a breaking sea. **1814** SOUTHEY *Roderick* xxiv, Within her breaking heart. **1820** BYRON *Juan* v. cliv, To save the credit of their breaking bank. **1881** *Daily News* 9 July 2 Lucas was bowled for a breaking ball.

b. with *down, in, up*, etc.

1853 KANE *Grinnell Exp.* xxxviii. (1856) 347 The first breaking-in day of Spring. **1858** GREENER *Gunnery* 237 An apparently crazy and breaking-up constitution displays itself most clearly. **1879** MACCARTHY *Own Times* II. 306 The confusion was that of a breaking-down system.

2. In comb. with sbs., as *heart-breaking*, etc.

1874 ALDRICH *Prud. Palfrey* vii. (1885) 116 It was heart-breaking work sometimes and back-breaking work always.

3. ***breaking-joint***: see BREAK *v.* 31 and JOINT *sb.*

break-neck ('breɪk,nɛk), *a.* and *sb.* [f. BREAK *v.* 7 b + NECK.]

A. *adj.* Likely to break the neck; endangering the neck or life; headlong (of speed, etc.); precipitous (of roads, rocks).

1562 J. HEYWOOD *Prov. & Epigr.* (1867) 16 My..breakneck fall. **1618** BOLTON *Florus* III. i. 164 Break-neck clifs, and high over-hanging places. **1809** *Edin. Rev.* XV. 62 A break-neck road from Madrid to San Ildefonso. **1882** B. RAMSAY *Recoll. Mil. Serv.* I. v. 131 To ride a breakneck pace round Jacko Hill.

†**B.** *sb. Obs.* 'A fall in which the neck is broken; a steep place endangering the neck' (J.); *fig.* destruction, ruin.

1563 *Homilies* II. *Idolatry* (1859) 251 Such a stumbling-block for his own feet and others that may perhaps bring at last to breakneck. **1579** TOMSON *Calvin's Serm. Tim.* 289/2 The question is not of any light fall, but it is a deadly breaknecke. **1624** F. WHITE *Reply Fisher* 527 They may..

fall with a breake-necke, downe to Hell. **1649** W. Dell *Way of Peace* 115 The very break-neck of the Churches peace and unity. **1653** Gataker *Vind. Annot. Jer.* 137 To work the downfall and break-neck of mens souls.

†**b.** One who risks breaking his neck. *Obs.*

1598 Florio, *Scauezzacóllo*, a breakeneck, a halter-sack, a wag.

'break-off, *sb.*

1. The action of breaking-off: see break *v.* 54, *esp.* discontinuance, severing of relations.

1860 Forster *Gr. Remonstr.* 169 The sudden and impetuous break-off from the party with whom he had acted so zealously.

2. In a musket or rifle: The metal work of the stock of a gun into which the breech of the barrel fits.

1804 *Hull Adv.* 21 Jan. 4/1 The left hand then seizes the shaft of the stock and the right hand dislodges the barrel from the 'Break-off'. **1844** *Regul. & Ord. Army* 106 For a new break off filed up, fitted, and hardened. **1858** Greener *Gunnery* 250 With the breeches in the percussioned state, break-offs fitted and locks jointed.

break-out: see break *sb.*[1] 1 b

'break point. [break-.] Also with hyphen and as one word. **1. a.** The place or time at which an interruption or change is made.

1878 G. Prescott *Speaking Telephone* 192 The break-point, where the current is interrupted. **1960** R. M. Currie *Work Study* x. 116 When breaking the job down into elements..use audible points in the work, such as the snap of a switch,..as element break-points. **1977** *R.A.F. News* 30 Mar.–12 Apr. 1/3 This choice will be open to those officers who decide to leave at either of the two 'breakpoints' rather than complete the full sixteen years. **1983** *N.Y. Times* 11 Dec. vi. 142/1 There is a statistically significant association between fragile sites and breakpoints leading to chromosome rearrangements in cancer cells.

b. *Computing.* A place in a computer program where the normal execution of instructions would be interrupted, esp. by another program.

1948 J. P. Eckert in *Moore School Lectures 1946* 30 June (1985) 441 In a test run, if the final answers did *not* agree with the correct answers for the test run, the operator would have recourse to a set of what were termed 'break points'. **1960** Cooke & Markus *Electronics & Nucleonics Dict.* 56/1 *Break point*, a place in a computer routine at which a special instruction is inserted to stop a digital computer for a visual check of progress, if desired. **1983** *Your Computer* (Austral.) Aug. 63/1 Now, the return address is the address *after* the breakpoint, so we must decrement the program counter before storing it away.

2. a. = *breaking-point* s.v. breaking *vbl. sb.* 8.; also, the point at which the situation in question changes, a turning point.

1959 *Times* 22 May 9/2 Imports of woollen goods into the United States reached the 'breakpoint' of 13,500,000 lb. **1966** *Jrnl. Canad. Operational Res. Soc.* 114 *Break point*, the critical level of combat capability, measured by some explicit function of game variables, below which the unit is considered unable to persist in its assigned mission. **1968** *Economist* 17 Aug. 70/2 Chiefly at issue is the 'break point' for reducing commissions on such 'volume' transactions. **1983** *Christian Science Monitor* 26 Aug. 17 It [*sc.* drought] has ruined crops, dried wells, and sent millions of peasants streaming into the region's already overtaxed cities. Last week, the situation reached breakpoint.

b. *spec.* in *U.S. Law*, a figure above which a fee for a non-profit-making lawyer would be excessive in relation to his overheads.

1983 *Federal Reporter* (U.S.) (1984) DCCXI. 1136/2 The windfall aspect of the award would be eliminated by selecting $75 per hour as a 'breakpoint', and fees for plaintiffs' [counsel] would not be calculated at rates higher than the $75 per hour figure. **1984** *Legal Times* 16 Jan. 9 When hours were correlated to income, Gary R. Lietz.. commented, 'The breakpoint of diminished returns on income appears after 54 hours per week'.

3. *Lawn Tennis.* A point which would win the game for the player(s) receiving service; the situation at which the receiver(s) may break service by winning such a point.

1975 *Tennis USA* Apr. 20/3 When the match began, he had four break points against Jimmy in the second game but was unable to convert the opportunity. **1980** *Times* 2 July 10/3 In the fourth game, Fibak had two break points. **1983** M. Navratilova *Tennis my Way* 160 She used to throw examples of match situations at me and then explain what I should do..such as play aggressively at break point up, defensively at break point down.

'breakshuach. *Sc.* Also **breakshugh, breckshaw.** [Derivation and correct form of second element unknown: it cannot be connected with OE. *bræc-séoc* epileptic.] The dysentery in sheep.

1799 *Ess. Highl. Soc.* III. 411 (Jam.) Dysentery or Braxy, *Breckshaw.* *c* **1817** Hogg *Tales & Sk.* IV. 199 There is a disease among sheep, called by shepherds the Breakshugh, a deadly sort of dysentery. **1822** W. Napier *Pract. Store-farming* 139 It [draining] prevents a great many of the diseases to which sheep are liable, and particularly breakshuach, rot, foot-rot, and braxy.

breakstone ('breɪkstəʊn). [f. break *v.* + stone; a transl. of L. *saxifraga.*] A name given by herbalists to the Saxifrages; and vaguely to plants supposed to be related to them.

1688 R. Holme *Armoury* ii. 111/1 Of the Saxifrage, or Breakstone, the husks are brownish green. **1712** tr. *Pomet's Hist. Drugs* I. 5 It has obtain'd the Name of Saxifrage, and by a great many that of Break-Stone. **1846** Sowerby *Brit. Bot.* (ed. 3) *Breakstone*, Parsley Piert, *Alchemilla arvensis.* **1863** Prior *Plant-n.* 28.

break-through, breakthrough ('breɪkθruː). [f. phr. *to break through*: see break *v.* 56; cf. G. *durchbruch.*] **1.** An act of breaking through (a barrier of any kind); spec. *Mil.*, an advance penetrating a defensive line or the like; also *fig.*, esp. (*a*) *U.S.* a sudden increase in prices or values; (*b*) a significant advance in knowledge, achievement, etc.; a development or discovery that removes an obstacle to progress. Also *attrib.*

1918 *Daily Express* 5 Nov. 1/2 The attempted break-through for which the English and French have again been striving on a front of over thirty-seven miles was frustrated. **1921** A. Lunn *Alpine Ski-ing* vii. 98 A break-through into a crevasse can be instantly checked. **1936** *Mind* XLV. 248 Barriers have to be erected having negative valence if a break-through be attempted. **1937** A. L. Rowse *Sir R. Grenville* vii. 154 Drake had captured 200,000 ducats of the King's property..in his break-through into the South Sea. **1944** *Times* 8 Feb. 4/4 British tanks..have been forced to renounce their break-through attempt. **1949** *Amer. Speech* XXIV. 174 A strong and sudden increase [in the market] is a *breakthrough.* **1957** *Economist* 23 Nov. 736/1 The break-through to industrial prosperity began with the First Industrial Revolution. **1958** *Listener* 11 Sept. 376/2 The technological break-through which allowed both the United States and the U.S.S.R. to produce H-bombs within a year of each other.

2. Special Comb.: **breakthrough bleeding,** bleeding from the uterus occurring between a woman's menstrual periods, esp. as a side-effect of some contraceptive pills.

1958 G. Pincus et al. in *Amer. Jrnl. Obstetr. & Gynecol.* LXXV. 1336 In about 8 per cent of women..a breakthrough bleeding occurred before the nineteenth day of medication. **1962** [see spotting *vbl. sb.* 5]. **1963** J. H. Burn *Drugs, Med. & Man* (ed. 2) XV. 156 When oestrogens (such as stilboestrol) are used alone.., the lining membrane of the uterus..is not maintained intact during the intervals between the periods, and 'break-through' bleeding occurs. **1968** J. H. Burn *Lect. Notes Pharmacol.* (ed. 9) 93 The function of the progestogen is to prevent 'break-through' bleeding in the mid-cycle. **1974** M. C. Gerald *Pharmacol.* xxiv. 427 Breakthrough bleeding or failure to menstruate may also occur. **1983** *Oxf. Textbk. Med.* I. x. 85/1 Breakthrough bleeding as well as contraceptive failure can occur in women on rifampicin or enzyme-inducing anticonvulsants.

break-up, *sb.* [f. verbal phr. *to break up*: see break *v.* 57. For the stress see break-down.] The action or fact of breaking up; disruption, separation into parts, disintegration (*lit.* and *fig.*); e.g. decay of animal functions; change from fine or settled weather, or from frost; dispersal or dissolution of a meeting, company, society, or system. **break-up price** or **value,** the price or value of assets at the break-up of a concern.

1795 Ld. Auckland *Corr.* (1862) III. 292 The sudden break-up of Lord Fitzwilliam's Government in Ireland. **1836** S. Laing *Trav. Norway* (L.) The break-up of the cold weather soon followed. **1836–9** Todd *Cycl. Anat. & Phys.* II. 630/1 The break-up which..follows..morbid alterations of the heart. **1864** *Times* 23 Dec., The sounds of mirth and song that usually mark the break-up of a large English school. **1878** Browning *Poets Croisic* xxxvii, An epitaph On earth's break-up. **1899** *Westm. Gaz.* 4 Dec. 10/2 A trade valuer was examined to show that he had advised the Grices to sell their business..at a break-up price. **1902** *Ibid.* 15 Nov. 7/1 At break-up values the assets of the company would pay 10s. in the pound to preference shareholders. **1930** *Economist* 1 Feb. 233/1 Shares of most of them are now selling below or close to their 'break-up' asset value. **1968** *Globe & Mail* (Toronto) 17 Feb. B8 The breakup value is no more than 10 cents a share.

attrib. **1843** J. T. Coleridge in *Arnold's Life & Corr.* (1844) I. i. 11 One break-up party was held in the junior common room at the end of each term.

breakwater ('breɪkwɔːtə(r)). [f. break *v.* + water.]

1. Anything that breaks the force of the waves at a particular place, *esp.* a solid structure of rubble and masonry erected to form or protect a harbour, etc.

1769 Falconer *Dict. Marine* (1789) *Break-water*, the.. hull of some old..vessel, sunk at the entrance of a small harbour, to..diminish the force of the waves. **1791** Smeaton *Edystone L.* §100 The house-reef may..be considered as a pier, break-water, or bulwark to vessels lying there. **1846** G. N. Wright *Cream Sci. Knowledge* 58 The most remarkable Break-waters are those of Cherbourg in France, and Plymouth in England. **1856** Kane *Arct. Expl.* I. iii. 36 This berg is a moving break-water. **1857** Page *Adv. Textbk. Geol.* iii. 60 And present breakwater-like their natural slopes to the action of the waves.

fig. **1854** H. Miller *Sch. & Schm.* 332 A breakwater..to protect from that grinding oppression of the poor by the poor. **1875** *Fortn. Rev.* Mar. 333 A religious breakwater.

2. In other uses: **a.** A groyne or barrier on the beach to retain shingle; **b.** (See quot. 1769).

1721 Perry *Daggenh. Breach* 116 Several low narrow Jetties, (or Break-Waters) extending from the top of the Beach down to the Low Water Mark. **1769** Falconer *Dict. Marine* (1789) *Break-water* is also a sort of small buoy, fastened to a large one in the water, when the buoy-rope of the latter is not long enough to reach from the anchor..to the surface of the water. The use of this break-water is therefore to shew where the buoy swims.

bream (briːm), *sb.* Forms: 4 breem, brem, 4–7 breme, 5 breeme, 6–7 breame, 7– bream. [ME. *breme*, a. F. *brême*, in OF. *bresme* (med.L. *bresmia*), ad. Teutonic: cf. OS. *bressemo*(:—*brehsmo*), also with *a*, OHG. *brahsema* (whence med.L. *braximus*), MHG. *brahsem*, *brasme*, Ger. *brassen*, MDu. and Du. *brasem*:— WGer. *brahsm-* and *brehsm-*; perh. f. stem of *brehwan* to glitter, sparkle. (The word has no connexion with barse.)]

1. The common name of a fresh-water fish (*Abramis brama*) called also Carp-bream, which inhabits lakes and deep water, and is distinguished by its yellowish colour and the high arched form of its back. Also the genus (*Abramis*, family *Cyprinidæ*) to which this belongs, including also the White Bream (*A. blicca*) and other species.

c **1386** Chaucer *Prol.* 350 Many a Breem [*v.r.* brem, breme] and many a luce in Stuwe. **1462** *Mann. & Househ. Exp.* 561 My master putt into the said ponde, in grete bremes, xij. **1539** *Act 31 Hen. VIII*, ii. §1 Pykes, breames, carpes, tenches, and other fysshes. **1616** Surfl. & Markh. *Country Farm* 506 If you intend the pond for Carpe or Breame. **1653** Walton *Angler* 174 The Bream..is a large and stately fish..long in growing. **1769** Pennant *Zool.* III. 309 The bream is an inhabitant of lakes—or the deep parts of still rivers. **1870** Morris *Earthly Par.* I. i. 167 Look up and down..And note the bubbles of the bream.

2. a. Applied also to some acanthopterygious sea-fishes, of the genus Pagellus (family *Sparidae*), and genus *Labrus* (family *Labridæ*), as the Sea Bream (*P. centrodontus*), Spanish Bream (*P. erythrinus*).

c **1460** J. Russell *Bk. Nurture* 578 in *Babees Bk.* (1868) 156 Carpe, Breme de mere, & trowt. **1655** Mouffet & Benn. *Health's Improv.* (1746) 238 Breams of the Sea be of a white and solid Substance. **1840** R. Dana *Bef. Mast* vii. 16 There were cod, breams, silver-fish, and other kinds.

b. Any of various fishes of the family Centrarchidæ, or sun-fishes, resembling the common European bream. *U.S.*

1634 W. Wood *New Eng. Prospect* ii. xvi. 90 Catching of Pikes, Pearches, Breames, and other sorts of fresh water fish. **1791** W. Bartram *Trav. Caroline* 176 The golden bream or sun-fish, the red bellied bream..also abound here. **1884** Goode *Nat. Hist. Aquatic Anim.* 406 The Blue Sun-fish—*Lepomis pallidus*..is known as the 'Blue Bream'. **1965** A. J. McClane *Standard Fishing Encycl.* 143/2 Bream. A regional colloquialism (Southern United States) for various sunfishes, usually pronounced as 'brim'.

3. *Comb.* **bream-backed:** (of a horse) having a high ridged back.

1723 *Lond. Gaz.* No. 6190/7 Stolen..a sorrel Nag.. bream back'd. **1834–43** Southey *Doctor* cxciii. (D.) He was not..hollow-backed, bream-backed, or broken backed.

bream (briːm), *v.*[1] Also 7 breem. [Of uncertain origin: known only since 1600. It has been conjecturally referred to Du. *brem* 'broom, furze', and to Eng. *broom*, as a deriv. vb., or a dialect variant: but evidence is lacking. Conjectures identifying the word with *bren*, burn, are unsupported exc. by the analogy of Ger. *ein Schiff brennen*, F. *chauffer le vaisseau*, *donner le feu.*]

trans. To clear (a ship's bottom) of shells, seaweed, ooze, etc., by singeing it with burning reeds, furze, or fagots, thus softening the pitch so that the rubbish adhering may be swept off. Cf. broom *v.*

1626 Capt. Smith *Accid. Yng. Seaman* 3 For calking, breaming, stopping leakes. **1627** —— *Seaman's Gram.* ii. 13 Breaming her, is but washing or burning of all the filth with reeds or broome. **1628** Digby *Voy. Medit.* (1868) 60 There I careend and breemed my shippes with verie great diligence. **1779** Forrest *Voy. N. Guinea* 260 On the 8th we breamed the vessel's bottom. **1875** *Fortn. Rev.* Aug. 206 Bonfires of brushwood, lighted to bream the sharp-bowed craft.

bream, *v.*[2] Also 6 breme (*dial.*), breme. Variant of brim *v.*[1] said of a boar or sow.

1577 B. Googe *Heresbach's Husb.* (1586) 127 The female camel of Bactria, feeding upon the mountaines amongest the wilde Boares, is oftentimes breamed of the boare, and conceaveth. **1863** Atkinson *Provinc. Danby*, *Brim, breme*, to desire the boar; to serve the sow.

†**breame.** *Obs. rare*[−1]. [Known only in the passage cited: if correct, cf. Ger. *breme*, MHG. *breme*, *brem*, OHG. *bremo* masc., answering to an OTeut. *bremon- masc., parallel to *brimisi- fem., whence OHG. *brimissa*, Ger. *bremse*: see brimse.] Breese, gadfly; = brimse.

1589 Fleming *Virg. Georg.* iii. 41 *note*, A kind of flieng vermin that stingeth cattell, a horseflie, breame, a breese.

breame, var. of breem *a. Obs.*

†**'breamet.** *Obs.* Also 5 bremate, bremette. [? dim. of bream: but cf. OF. '*bremat* = *brême*' Godef.] A young, or small, bream.

1462 *Mann. & Househ. Exp.* 561 My master putt in the said ponde, in male bremetes, xij. **1496** *Bk. St. Alban's, Fishing* 29 Ye shall angle for hym [a bream]..wyth a redde worme..And for bremettis take maggotes.

breamflat ('bri:mflæt). [f. BREAM *sb.* + FLAT.] A fish, the White Bream.

1836 *Penny Cycl.* V. 374/1 *Brama blicca* (the white bream, or bream flat)..is of a silvery or bluish-white hue.

breaming ('bri:mɪŋ), *vbl. sb.* [f. BREAM *v.*[1] + -ING[1].] The clearing of a ship's bottom by burning. Hence *breaming-fuel, -hook.*

1627 CAPT. SMITH *Seaman's Gram.* ii. 13. 1628 DIGBY *Voy. Medit.* (1868) 61 The inconueniencie of breeming aloft to pay the shippe ouer with pitch. 1759 COLEBROOKE in *Phil. Trans.* LI. 51 Corruptly called breaming, for brenning or burning. 1769 FALCONER *Dict. Marine* (1789), *Chauffage*, breaming-fuel. *Fourches de Carene*, breaming-hooks.

breard, breare, obs. forms of BRAIRD, BRIER.

breards (brɪədz), *sb. pl. Sc.* [The same as BRAIRD, in sense of 'short ends or points'.] 'The short flax recovered from the first tow by a second hackling' (Jamieson). Cf. *backings.*

1733 P. LINDSAY *Interest Scot.* 161 Dressing and stapling the Lint..into fine drest Flax, fine drest Tow, common Tow, Backings, and Breards. 1804 *Edin. Even. Courant* 1 Sept. (JAM.) White and blue breards, fit for spinning yarn.

breast (brɛst), *sb.* Forms: 1-4 **breost**, 3-8 **brest**; (also 4 *Kent* **bryest**, 4-5 **breest, breste**, 4-6 *north.* **breist**, 5-6 **brist, birst**), 6- **breast**. [OE. *bréost* = OFris. *briast*, OS. *briost*, *breost*, ON. *brjóst*, (Sw. *bröst*, Da. *bryst*) neuter, answering to an OTeut. type **breusto(m)*: represented in Goth. by *brusts* fem. pl. (no sing.):—OTeut. **brust-s* consonantal fem., 'prob. originally inflected as a dual' (Kluge), whence OHG. (MHG., mod.Ger.) *brust* fem., MLG. (MDu., Du.) *borst* fem. (with metathesis of *r*). The term is confined to Teutonic, there being no common Indo-Europ. name for the breast. As to the form and derivation, see below. OE. *éo* became normally ME. *ē*, *ee*, mod. *ee* (i:), and in Sc. and north dial. *breast* rimes with *priest*; but in Standard Eng., the *e* has been shortened before the two consonants; the spellings *breast* and *brest* run side by side from 16th to 18th c.; in current usage we spell *breast* and pronounce *brest*.

The difference of vowel in OTeut. **breust-*, **brust-* is explained by the fact that all monosyllabic consonantal stems had originally shifting stress, with corresponding ablaut (**breust-s*, **brust-óz*); the neuter gender in OE., OS., and ON. by the supposition that **breust-s* was orig. inflected as a dual (the two breasts) of which the nom. and acc. **breustô-* would later become **breust*, *bréost*, which after the loss of the dual would naturally be treated as neuter pl., as in other known instances. Even in senses 2, 5, the plural was usual in OE., as exclusive in Gothic. **Breust-* cannot be connected with *berstan*, *brestan* to burst: but it may be related to the OS. verb. *brustian* to bud, and be a root-noun from a vb. **breust-an* (see Lexer under *brust*), a specialized derivative of **breut-an* (i.e. **breut-stan*, **breustan*; cf. **brek-stan*, *brestan*, f. *brek-an*). The 'breasts' would thus be orig. the *mammæ* or paps, likened to 'buds' or 'sprouts'. See further Kluge *Beiträge* VIII. 510.]

I. 1. a. Each of the two soft protuberances situated on the thorax in females, in which the milk is secreted for the nourishment of their young; the mamma; also the analogous rudimentary organ of males, the mammilla. Hence, in phrases ***to give, have, put to, the breast***; an infant ***at the breast, past the breast.***

(Properly said of women, but sometimes of the lower animals.)

c 1000 *Ags. Gosp.* Luke xi. 27 þa breost [*Lindisf.* titto, *vel* breosto] þe ðu suce. *c* 1000 *Sax. Leechd.* I. 182 Wiþ innoþes sare, & þæra breosta. *a* 1300 *Sarmun* lviii. in *E.E.P.* (1862) 7 þat soke þe milk of maidis brest. *c* 1305 *St. Kath.* 249 in *E.E.P.* (1862) 96 Here breostes hi to-drowe Fram hire bodi mossel mele. 1387 TREVISA *Higden* Rolls Ser. VII. 39 [The virgin Mary] took here brest [*mamillam*] out of here bosom. 1542-3 *Act 34 & 35 Hen. VIII*, viii. §1 As womens brestes being sore. 1605 SHAKS. *Macb.* I. v. 48 Come to my Womans Brests And take my Milke for Gall. 1647 W. BROWNE *Polex.* I. 237 When she was past the breast, he chose many young gentlemen of his Court to be of her guard. 1649 BP. REYNOLDS *Hosea* i. 1 The fruitfulness of the womb, and of the brests. 1688 *Lond. Gaz.* No. 2371/4 His Majesty was pleased to order that the Breast should be given him. 1709 STEELE *Tatler* No. 15 ¶2 One Country Milch-Wench, to whom I was..put to the Breast. 1843 MACAULAY *Prophecy of Capys* xiv, Thou, that..hast tugged at the she-wolf's breast. 1863 GEO. ELIOT *Romola* (1878) I. 122 An amulet worn close under the right breast.

b. Hence *fig.* Source of nourishment.

1611 BIBLE *Pref.* 1 Upon whose breasts againe themselues doe hang to receiue the Spirituall and sincere milke of the word. 1611 SPEED *Theat. Gt. Brit.* xix. (1614) 37/1 Cambridge, the other brest and nurse-mother of all pious literature. 1788 WESLEY *Wks.* (1872) VII. 185 The sacraments are not dry breasts. 1872 YEATS *Growth Comm.* 249 'Husbandry and cattle rearing', he says, 'are the two breasts whence France is nourished'.

2. a. The front of the thorax or chest, the fore-part of the body, lying between the neck and the belly. (In OE. usually in the plural, for original dual.)

Beowulf (Z.) 552 Beado hrægl broden on breostum læg golde gegyr[wed]. *c* 1000 *Ags. Gosp.* John xiii. 25 þa he hlinode ofer ðæs hælendes breostum [*Lindisf. G.* onufa breost ðæs hælendes]. *a* 1225 *Ancr. R.* 34 Beateð ower breoste. *c* 1380 WYCLIF *Serm.* Sel. Wks. I. 27 He smote upon his breest. 1398 TREVISA *Barth. De P.R.* v. xxxiii. (1495) 144 The breste is the ouer bony parte betwene the pappes and teetes. 1440 J. SHIRLEY *Dethe K. James* (1818) 23 The sayde hongman toke a rope, and knyt hit fast aboute thare birstes, undre thaire harmeholes. 1584 POWEL *Lloyd's Cambria* 97 On his backe or brest. 1596 SHAKS. *Merch. V.* IV. i. 252 You must cut this flesh from off his breast. 1634 T. JOHNSON tr. *Parey's Chirurg.* XI. (1678) 270 Muskets..may be called Breast-guns, for that they are not laid to the cheek, but against the breast. 1678 BUNYAN *Pilgr.* I. 71 He threw a flaming Dart at his brest. 1843 MACAULAY *Lake Regillus* xxviii, Herminius smote Mamilius Through breast-plate and through breast.

b. The part of a garment or a piece of armour covering the breast.

1651 *Proc. Parliament* No. 119. 1846, 310 backs with their brests, and 10 Head pots. *a* 1678 CLARENDON *Hist. Reb.* (1703) II. VI. 31 To procure old Backs, and Breasts, and Pots, with Pistols. 1830 *Fraser's Mag.* II. 436 Beruffled breasts and wrists were the order of the day.

c. The bosom.

1650 HUBBERT *Pill Formality* 15 It is a dangerous thing to harbor a Traytor within your brest.

†3. Occasionally extended to the whole upper portion of the body, the thorax or chest. *Obs.*

a 1340 HAMPOLE *Pr. Consc.* 679 þe body of þat tre þar-by Es þe brest with þe bely. 1661 LOVELL *Hist. Anim. & Min.* 302 The breast as to its anterior part hath two clavicles and the os pectoris..the posterior part hath two shoulders and twelve vertebra's. 1754-64 SMELLIE *Midwif.* I. Introd. 33 A perforation must be made..into the cavity of the breast. 1766 CHESTERF. *Lett.* 404 IV. 241, I am glad to hear that your breast is so much better.

4. a. The corresponding part in the body of the lower animals.

a 1400 *Chester Pl.* I. (1843) 31 Upon thy breste thou shalte goe and eate the earth. *c* 1440 *Promp. Parv.* 49 Breeste of a beste, *pectus.* 1513 DOUGLAS *Æneis* VIII. iv. 181 The rouch byrsis on the brest and crest Of that..wilde beist. 1592 SHAKS. *Ven. & Ad.* 296 Broad breast, full eye, small head, and nostril wide. 1710 PRIDEAUX *Orig. Tithes* ii. 78 The wave brest and heave shoulder of the peace Offerings. 1826 KIRBY & SP. *Entomol. Lett.* (1828) IV. 542 Nipping the breast will kill many small Lepidoptera.

b. As a joint or other piece of meat.

1530 PALSGR. 910 The gygot, a brest, *le gigot.* 1710 ADDISON *Tatler* No. 255 ¶3 Antipathy..to a Cheshire Cheese, or a Breast of Mutton. 1832 *Fraser's Mag.* V. 529 They were charged with stealing a breast of mutton.

5. a. *fig.* and *transf.* The seat of the affections and emotions; the repository of consciousness, designs, and secrets; the heart; *hence*, the affections, private thoughts and feelings. (Commonly pl. in OE.)

a 1000 *Cædmon's Gen.* (Gr.) 656 Mæg ðin mod wesan bliðe on breostum. *c* 1175 *Lamb. Hom.* 183 Ihesu..Min bliþe breostes blisse. *c* 1230 *Hali Meid.* 7 þe þat herest him þat al welt in wið in þi breoste. *c* 1430 *Hymns Virg.* (1867) 2 How y hadde ledde my lijf so zore, I putt it freischli in-to my brist. 1513 DOUGLAS *Æneis* V. iv. 134 The fauorable fortoun ..gan the breistis of the vther avance. 1600 CHAPMAN *Iliad* XV. 581 Their herdsmen wanting breasts To fight with lions. 1607 SHAKS. *Cor.* III. i. 258 What his Brest forges, that his Tongue must vent. *a* 1643 W. CARTWRIGHT in *Dodsley* (1780) X. 221 That man of peace there, Hath been trusted with Kings breasts. 1667 MILTON *P.L.* IX. 730 Can envie dwell In heav'nly brests? 1711 STEELE *Spect.* No. 30 ¶3 Our Statutes are..recorded in our own Breasts only. 1750 GRAY *Elegy* xv, Some village Hampden, that with dauntless breast The little tyrant of his fields withstood. 1839 THIRLWALL *Greece* II. 368 What motives were predominant in the breast of Pausanias.

†b. *on breast*: in or by heart. *Obs.*

a 1560 ROLLAND *Crt. Venus* I. 45 Maist part was my prayers to con Knowit on breist.

c. ***to make a clean breast***: to make a full disclosure or confession.

1752 CAMERON in *Scots Mag.* (1753) Oct. 508/1 He pressed him..to make a clean breast, and tell him all. 1861 *Sat. Rev.* 23 Nov. 524 A clean breast must be made of everything. 1878 BLACK *Green Past.* xxiii. 184, I may as well make a clean breast of it.

†6. *transf.* The place where the lungs are situated; *hence*, breath, voice in singing. *Obs.*

1547 J. HEYWOOD *Four P's* in *Dodsley* (1780) I. 67, I have some syght in syngynge, But is your brest any thynge sweet? *a* 1553 UDALL *Royster D.* (Arb.) 14 So loe, that is a breast to blowe out a candle. 1601 SHAKS. *Twel. N.* II. iii. 19 By my troth the foole has an excellent breast. I had rather then forty shillings I had..so sweet a breath to sing, as the foole has. 1621 FLETCHER *Pilgr.* III. vi. (N.) Let's hear him sing, he has a fine breast. 1711 STRYPE *Parker* 9 (N.) Queristers, after their breasts are changed.

†7. A broad even front of a moving company; hence ***in, of, on (a) breast*** = ABREAST. *Obs.*

1647 MAY *Hist. Parl.* III. i. 10 A narrow Lane, where onely foure of a breast could march. 1653 URQUHART *Rabelais* I. liii, Six men at armes..might together in a breast ride all up to the very top. 1686 R. P. in *Phil. Trans.* XX. 382 The Current of Water came down..with a Breast as if it would have drowned the whole Towns. 1725 *Lond. Gaz.* No. 6382/3 The Register, in Breast, with the Secretary. 1788 *Lond. Mag.* 200 To admit the passage of three carriages and two horses on a breast. 1807 ROBINSON *Archæol. Gr.* IV. xix. 405 The ships went three or more in a breast.

8. Applied to various surfaces or parts of things analogous in shape, position, etc. to the human breast; the forefront, face, swelling or supporting surface. †In *military* use, a breastwork; see BREAST *v.* 4.

c 1400 *Destr. Troy* 5930 In the brest of the batell þere buernes were thicke. 1601 SHAKS. *Jul. C.* I. iii. 51 The crosse blew Lightning seem'd to open The Brest of Heauen. 1793 SMEATON *Edystone L.* §96 The seas broke against the overhanging Breast of the rock. 1806 *Act 46 Geo. III*, cliii, No pier, quay, wharf, jetty, breast, or embankment, shall be erected. 1812 J. WILSON *Isle of Palms* I. 27 The waves that lend their gentle breast In gladness for her couch of rest. 1814 WORDSW. *Excurs.* IV. 627 Upon the breast of new-created earth Man walk'd. 1872 JENKINSON *Guide Eng. Lakes* (1879) 200 Along the tolerably smooth breast of the hill.

9. In various technical uses: **†a.** *Anatomy.* A portion of the hand (see quot.). **b.** *Agriculture.* The forward part of the mould-board of a plough. **c.** *Arch.* (see quot. 1823); also, the part of a wall between a window and the floor; an obs. name of the *torus* of a column (spelt *Brest* by Bailey and Johnson). **d.** *Mining.* (see quot. 1881); also, the wooden partition which divides the shaft of a coal-mine into two compartments. **e.** The curve in a fork just above the prongs. **f.** *Mech.* 'A bush connected with a small shaft or spindle'; also, the swelling or bulging part of a nave or hub. **g.** *Carpentry.* The under surface of a handrail, rafter, or rib of a dome. **h.** A large roller or cylinder in a carding-machine. Also *attrib.*, as ***breast cylinder.***

1541 R. COPLAND *Guydon's Quest. Chirurg.*, In the thyrde coniunction be foure bones longer than the other. And that coniunction is called the brest of the hande or pecten. 1727-51 CHAMBERS *Cycl.*, *Brest* or *Breast*, in architecture, a term used by some for that member of a column otherwise called the *tore.* 1770 *Monthly Rev.* 307 Placed just under the breast of the chimney. 1807 VANCOUVER *Agric. Devon* (1813) 115 There is little apparent curve in its breast or mould-board. 1823 P. NICHOLSON *Pract. Build.* 434 The solid parts of the walls, between the funnel or flues, and the rooms, are called the breasts of the chimnies. 1881 RAYMOND *Mining Gloss.*, *Breast.* 1. The face of a working. 2. In coal mines, the chamber driven upwards from the gangway, on the seam, between pillars of coal left standing, for the extraction of coal. 3. That side of the hearth of a shaft-furnace which contains the metal-notch. *a* 1884 T. LISTER in W. S. B. McLaren *Spinning* (1884) x. 229 A breast large enough to entitle it to the name of a cylinder. 1884 *Implement & Mach. Rev.* 1 Dec. 6701/2 The..plough..has, together with the ordinary mould board, a digging breast. 1888 *Encycl. Brit.* XXIV. 659/1 Against the lickerin revolves the 'angle-stripper', the function of which is to remove the wool..and deliver it over to the great breast cylinder.

II. Combinations.

10. Comb. (*attrib.*) of obvious meaning; as ***breast-bow, -button, -cord, -girdle, -guard, -key, -milk, -piece, -pin, -pocket; breast-deep, breast-rending*** adjs.

1847 *Life Mrs. Sherwood* vi. 87 She always wore a *breast bow to answer the bow on her cap. 1862 THACKERAY *Philip* II. 256 A certain *breast-button of his old coat. 1879 E. ARNOLD *Lt. Asia* IV. (1881) 105 Took down the silver bit and bridle chains, *Breast-cord, and curb. 1588 SHAKS. *Tit. A.* V. iii. 179 Set him *brest deepe in earth, and famish him. 1388 WYCLIF *Jer.* ii. 32 Whethir..a spousesse schal forȝete hir *brest girdil? 1578 *Richmond. Wills* (1853) 281 A budged, j male pinyen, and a *brestgard, ijs. 1840 *Penny Cycl.* XVII. 241/1 Parapet..is termed in German *Brustwehr*, or breast-guard. 1803 BRISTED *Pedest. Tour* II. 122 Spilling an abundance of water upon her *breastkerchief, and wetting her bosom. 1813 SIR. R. WILSON *Diary* II. 202 A person conversant in all matters.. and who possesses the *breast-key of the magnates. 1650 JER. TAYLOR *Holy Living* (1727) 124 Fed with a little *breast-milk. 1785 M. GARTHSHORE in *Med. Commun.* II. 37 It was supported by breast milk. 1611 COTGR., *Brichet*, the brisket or *breast-peece. 1825 SCOTT in *Lockhart* (1839) VIII. 120, I hate fine waistcoats and *breast pins upon dirty shirts. 1772 NUGENT *Hist. Friar Gerund* I. 172 In the *breast-pocket of his large cloak. 1625 K. LONG *Barclay's Argenis* IV. x, *Brest-rending care.

11. Special combs.: **breast-backstays** *Naut.*, long ropes serving to aid in supporting the masts against an oblique headwind (cf. BACKSTAY); **breast-band**, a girdle or band passing round the breast; also *spec.* = *breast-rope*; **breast-beating**, an exaggerated and ostentatious demonstration of woe, remorse, etc.; **†breast-brooch** = BREASTPLATE 2; **†breast-bundel**, a breast-girdle; **breast-casket** = *breast-gasket*; **breast-chain**, a chain used for the same purpose as a *breast-strap*; **†breast-clout**, a bib; **breast-collar**, a broad pulling strap passing round the breast of a horse, used instead of a neck-collar; **breast-cut**, the cut of meat from the breast, brisket; **breast-drill**, a drill against which the workman bears his breast while drilling; **breast-fast**, 'a large rope or chain, used to confine a ship's broad-side to a wharf or quay, or to some other ship' (Smyth *Sailor's Word-bk.*); **breast-fed** *a.*, (of infants) fed at the mother's breast; so ***breast-feeding*** (opposed to *bottle-feeding*); ***breast-feed*** vb.; **†breast-flap** (see quot.); **breast-gasket** *Naut.*, a rope, cord, or other piece of plaited stuff used to tie up the bunt of a sail, and secure it to the yard; **breast-girth**, (*a*) measurement around the breast; (*b*) (see quot. 1958); **breast-glass** (see quot.); **breast-harness**, harness in which a breast-band is used in place of a collar; **breast-height**, (*a*) the interior slope of a parapet in fortifications; (*b*) the height of a man's chest above ground-level, usually taken as 4 ft. 3 in. (in some countries 4 ft. 6 in.), the standard height used for measuring

the 'girth, diameter and basal area of standing trees'; **breast-hoe**, a hoe pushed by the breast; **breast-hooks**, 'large pieces of compass-timber fixed within and athwart the bows of the ship, of which they are the principal security, and through which they are well bolted' (Weale); **breast-knees** *sb. pl.*, timbers placed in the forward part of a vessel across the stem to unite the bows on each side; **breast-knot**, a knot or bow of ribbon, etc. worn on the breast; † **breast-lap** = *breast-flap*, BREASTPLATE 2; † **breast-lin** (*Ormin*), lit. breast-linen, linen breastplate; **breast-line**, the rope along which are ranged the pontoons of a military bridge, and to which they are fastened; **breast-mill**, a mill driven by a breast waterwheel; **breast-moulding**, moulding done upon the panel beneath a window; **breast-pain**, a disease in horses; **breast-pang**, the *Angina pectoris*; **breast-peat** (see quot.); † **breast-pit**, the hollow of the breast; † **breast-probe**, a probe for examining the cavity of the breast; **breast-pump**, an instrument for drawing milk from the breast by suction; **breast-rail** *Naut.*, the upper rail of the balcony, or of the breastwork at the forepart of the quarter-deck; **breast-roll**, the cloth beam of a loom; **breast-rope** *Naut.*, a rope for securing the yard-parrels; a rope for supporting the leadsman while sounding; **breast-shore**, each of a line of props transversely supporting a vessel in dry dock; **breast-strap** *Harness*, a strap fixed at one end to the collar and supporting the pole of the vehicle; **breast-stroke** *Swimming*, a stroke in which the breast is squarely opposed to the water, the arms are pushed forward and outwards in a wide arc, and the legs perform a frog-like action; also as *v. intr.*; so ***breast-swimming***; **breast-wall**, a wall supporting a bank of earth, etc., a retaining wall; **breast-weed**, a herbaceous plant (*Saururus cernuus*) having broad heart-shaped leaves and small white flowers, the Lizard's tail; **breast-wimble**, a kind of gimlet or auger upon which the breast presses in working; **breast-wood**, collective name for young shoots of fruit trees trained on espaliers or against walls. Cf. also BREAST-HIGH, -PLATE, -WORK, etc.

1769 FALCONER *Dict. Marine* (1789) E ij, *Breast-back-stays and after-back-stays; the intent of the former being to sustain the top-mast when the force of the wind acts upon the ship sidewise. **1840** R. DANA *Bef. Mast* xxv. 82 Setting up the weather breast-backstays. **1837** W. IRVING *Capt. Bonneville* (1849) 135 *Breast-bands, saddle and crupper, are lavishly embroidered. **1952** *Granta* 15 Nov. 10/1 There are times when the noise of *breast-beating and intellectual self-analysis sounds like a drum and fife band. **1969** *Nature* 9 Aug. 550/2 A proper and urgent concern for the environment is overtaken by self-indulgent breast-beating. **1382** WYCLIF *Ex.* xxviii. 15 The *breest broche [**1611** breastplate] forsothe of dom thou shalt make with werk of dyuerse colours. —— *Jer.* ii. 32 Whether forȝete shal . . the womman spouse of hir *brest-bundle [**1388** -girdil]. *c* **1325** *Gloss W. de Biblesw.* in Wright's *Voc.* 143 *Une bavere*, a *brestclut. **1801** W. FELTON *Carriages* II. 156 Neck Collars, and Saddles instead of *breast Collars and housings. **1825** S. & S. ADAMS *Compl. Serv.* 76 The Joints of Beef, according to the London method of cutting. Brisket or *Breast-cut. **1865** TYLOR *Early Hist. Man.* ix. 243 Known among the Oriental nations as the *breast-drill. **1627** CAPT. SMITH *Seaman's Gram.* vii. 30 A *Breast-fast is a rope . . fastened to some part of the Ship forward on, to hold her head to a wharfe. **1903** *Daily Chron.* 15 Jan. 5/2 The death rate was thirty times as high in children fed on cow's milk as in those *breast-fed. **1909** *Daily Chron.* 3 June 6/4 This figure including those breast-fed by the mothers. **1928** *Daily Express* 29 Feb. 3 Taken regularly—both before and after the birth—[it] enables nearly every mother to *breast-feed her baby. **1904** *Fabian News* XIV. 25/1 The decline of *breast-feeding. *a* **1536** TINDALE *Table Words Ex.* I. 419 *Breastlap*, or **breastflap*, is such a flap as thou seest in the breast of a cope. **1909** *Daily Chron.* 3 June 3/3 'Weak heart', or 'insufficient *breast-girth', or other physical defect. **1958** J. HISLOP *From Start to Finish* 167 *Breast-girth*, strap made of webbing which goes from one side of the saddle to the other (being attached to the girths) and stops the saddle from slipping back. **1880** *Syd. Soc. Lex.*, **Breast glass*, a flattened glass vessel, with an opening large enough to receive the nipple, placed on the breast to catch . . milk. **1932** *Forestry* VI. 53 The common *breast-height form-factor, which represents the ratio between the volume of the tree and that of a cylinder with the same height and the same girth or diameter as that of the tree at breast height. **1787** WINTER *Syst. Husb.* 174 The intervals should be hoed with a running or *breast hoe of twelve inches broad. **1748** ANSON *Voy.* II. iv. (ed. 4) 221 One *breast-hook was broken. **1840** R. DANA *Bef. Mast* ii. 4 Her stern and breast-hooks dripping. **1860** H. STUART *Seaman's Catech.* 68 What are the breast hooks for? To unite the sides of the ship together forward; they are generally made of iron. **1716** ADDISON *Freeholder* No. 11 (1725) 69 The influence of this Beautiful *Breast-Knot. **1824** MISS MITFORD *Village* Ser. I. (1863) 119 A black lace tippet . . parting at the middle, to display a gay breast-knot. **1535** COVERDALE *Ecclus.* xlv. 10 In the *brestlappe there was a goodly worke, wherin was fastened light and perfectnesse. **1581** MARBECK *Bk. of Notes* 75 Those Vrim and Thumim, which the Priest bare in his breast lappe. **1577** tr. *Bullinger's Decades* (1592) 334 The brest-lap of iudgement. *c* **1200** ORMIN 955 Off þatt preostess shulldrelin, & offhiss *breostlin baþe. Summwhatt icc habbe showedd ȝuw. **1674** PETTY *Disc. R. Soc.* 99 Seen in all *Breast- and Undershot-Mills. **1821** R. TURNER *Abridgm. Arts & Sc.* 266 Water-mills are of three kinds: undershot mills, breast mills, and overshot mills. **1844** T. GRAHAM *Dom. Med.* 324 Excepting in the case of *breast-pang, very active exercises daily. **1802** *Agric. Surv. Peebles* 208 (JAM.) [He] digs the peat, by driving in the spade horizontally with his arms; this peat is designed *breast-peat. **1398** TREVISA *Barth. De P.R.* XVII. xxi, Sode in vinegre and leyde with a sponge to þe *breste pit. **1758** J. S. *Le Dran's Observ. Surg.* (1771) 200 The Admission of the *Breast-Probe. **1861** MRS. BEETON *Bk. Househ. Managem.* 1036 Every mother . . should be provided with a *breast-pump, or glass tube, to draw off the superabundance. **1924** J. S. FAIRBAIRN *Gynæcol. with Obstetrics* v. xxi. 406 The use of a breast-pump. **1831** G. PORTER *Silk Manuf.* 215 The cloth-beam or *breast-roll to which the ends of the warp are attached. **1627** CAPT. SMITH *Seaman's Gram.* v. 20 Parrels . . with the helpe of the *Brest-rope doth keepe the Yard close to the Mast. **1825** H. GASCOIGNE *Nav. Fame* 52 Forward he leans, and far the balance leaves, The Breastrope trusting while the lead he heaves. **1860** H. STUART *Seaman's Catech.* 42 See the breast ropes properly secured. **1894** W. H. WHITE *Man. Naval Archit.* (ed. 3) 322 The shores under the bilges and bottom take part of the weight, and the '*breast shores' assist in maintaining form. **1867** C. STEEDMAN *Man. Swimming* 93 There are four distinct kinds of motions for the arms, and the same number and kind for the legs, used in the common plain or *breast-stroke. **1922** E. RAYMOND *Tell England* II. vii. 237 Other flies fell into my tea, and did the breast-stroke for the side of the mug. **1928** *Daily Express* 18 Feb. 5/1 He . . breast-stroked away toward the setting moon. **1867** C. STEEDMAN *Man. Swimming* 106 Its [*sc.* side swimming's] superiority over *breast swimming. **1601** HOLLAND *Pliny* XVII. xv, The French Vibrequin or *brest-wimble, which gently and quickely boreth a hole, and hurteth not the wood. **1882** *Garden* 354/2 To allow a free and unrestricted growth of *breastwood unto the middle of July.

breast (brɛst), *v.* [f. prec. sb.]

1. *trans.* To apply or oppose the breast to (waves, wind, a steep ascent); to stem, face, meet in full opposition. ***to breast a fence, horse***, etc.: to mount by springing so as to bring the breast over.

1599 SHAKS. *Hen. V*, III. Prol. 13 Bresting the loftie Surge. **1646** SIR T. BROWNE *Pseud. Ep.* 128 It observes not a constant respect unto the mouth of the wind, but variously converting doth seldome breast it right. ? *a* **1700** *Ballad 'Fause Foodrage'* xxii. in Scott *Minstr. Sc. Bord.*, You shall learn . . Right well to breast a steed. **1870** MORRIS *Earthly Par.* I. 171 The horse began to breast the hill. **1874** BLACKIE *Self-Cult.* 79 A swimmer . . breasting the big waves.

b. *fig.*

1850 PRESCOTT *Peru* II. 29 Prepared to breast the difficulties of the sierra. **1862** GOULBURN *Pers. Relig.* IV. (1873) 318 Breasting its perils . . gallantly.

c. ***to breast oneself***: to oppose one's breast *to*; so ***to breast it out*** (cf. *face it out*).

1815 *Hist. J. Decastro, &c.* III. 114 To breast it out against difficulties, dangers, sin, and the devil. **1863** W. PHILLIPS *Speeches* i. 6 Civil government breasting itself to the shock of lawless men.

d. ***to breast aside***: to breast so as to push aside.

1853 KANE *Grinnell Exp.* xliv. (1856) 406 We gradually force ahead, breasting aside the floes.

2. *intr.* To press forward with the breast.

? *a* **1700** *Red Squair* in *Ever Green* (1824) II. 225 Breisting owre the Brae. **1786** BURNS *Salut. to Mare* xiv, Thou never lap, an' sten't and breastit, Then stood to blaw.

† **3.** *trans.* To give the breast to; *fig.* to nourish. *Obs. rare.*

1573 TUSSER *Husb.* (1878) 27 In good corne soile to nest thee, Where pasture and meade may brest thee.

† **4.** To defend in front or with a breastwork.

1591 LAMBARDE *Arch.* (1635) 172 The Offenders, which were . . so brested, sided, and backed with a many friends. **1624** CAPT. J. SMITH *Virginia* III. vi. 60 Their pallizadoed towne . . brested about with brests very formally.

5. *trans.* To apply the breast to.

1820 KEATS *Isabella* lix. 470 She hurried back, as swift As bird on wing to breast its eggs again.

6. ***to breast up a hedge***: to cut away the branches on one side so that the main upright stems are laid bare.

breast-beam ('brɛstbiːm).

1. *Naut.* One of the beams at the fore-part of the quarter-deck and round-house, and after-part of the forecastle.

1850 *Rudim. Navig.* (Weale) 95.

2. *Weaving.* The horizontal wooden beam in the front of a loom.

1790 A. WILSON *Groans fr. Loom*, While a bad web was his theme, The breast-beam supported his head. **1875** URE *Dict. Arts* III. 1114 The breast beam . . is supported at its end upon brackets.

3. The front cross-beam of the frame of a locomotive.

breast-board ('brɛstbɔəd).

1. The earth-board or mould-board of a plough.

1649 BLITHE *Eng. Improv. Impr.* (1653) 190 The Shield-board, some call Breast-board, or Earth-board, or Furrow-board. **1725** BRADLEY *Fam. Dict.* s.v. *Plough*, The Earth board, Mould board, Breast board, Throw board.

2. *Mining.* 'Planking placed between the last set of timbers and the *face* of a *gangway* or *heading*, in quicksand or loose ground' (Raymond).

3. *Rope-making.* A loaded carriage to which the yarn-ends are attached at the foot of the rope-walk.

breastbone ('brɛstbəʊn). The thin flat bone running down the front of the thorax, and articulated by cartilages with the ribs; the sternum.

a **1000** *Ags. Gloss.* in Wr.-Wülcker 158 *Pectusculum*, breostban. *c* **1380** *Sir Ferumb.* 1623 On was clouen in-to þe chynne: another to þe brust-bon. *a* **1400** *Isumbras* 455 The beryns he hitt appone the hode, Thorowe the breste-bane it wode. **1646** SIR T. BROWNE *Pseud. Ep.* 183 Inclining to the spine or brestbone. **1863** KINGSLEY *Water-bab.* iv. 147 The leap-frogs you make out of a goose's breastbone.

breasted ('brɛstɛd), *ppl. a.* [f. BREAST *sb.*]

1. Having a breast; *esp.* in comb., as ***big-, narrow-, open-, wide-, flat-breasted***.

c **1314** *Guy Warw.* (1841) 261 As a somer it is brested bifore in the brede. *c* **1420** in *Rel. Ant.* I. 232 A Woman . . fayre brested. **1522–4** CAPON in Fiddes *Wolsey* (1726) coll. 103 Syngyng men byn . . very well brested. **1544** ASCHAM *Toxoph.* (Arb.) 126 The bygge brested shafte is fytte for hym. **1626** COCKERAM III, *Chymæra*, a Monster . . brested like a Lyon. **1711** J. DISTAFF *Char. Don Sacheverellio* 9 Times are altered since you went open Breasted. **1741** MONRO *Anat.* (ed. 3) 311 [They] become . . flat breasted.

2. Ornamented or decorated on the breast.

1829 *Blackw. Mag.* XXV. 80 Breasted with the cross, they roam on to the Holy Land.

breastful ('brɛstfʊl). *rare.* [f. as prec. + -FUL.] As much as fills the breast; also *fig.*

1856 MRS. BROWNING *Aur. Leigh* VI. 191 The hungry beggar-boy . . Bears yet a breastful of a fellow-world To this.

breast-high ('brɛsthaɪ), *a.*, *adv.*, *sb.*

A. *adj.* As high as the breast. *spec.* in *Forestry*: cf. *breast-height* s.v. BREAST *sb.* 11.

1677 MOXON *Mech. Exerc.* (1703) 157 Part of the Battlement being Breast high. **1716** *Lond. Gaz.* No. 5472/2 The Water was Breast high. **1823** J. BADCOCK *Dom. Amus.* 207 The rider has a breast-high support ascending from his seat. **1905** *Terms used in Forestry & Logging* 7 *Breasthigh*, at or having a height of $4\frac{1}{2}$ feet above the ground.

B. *adv.*

1. To the height or depth of the breast.

1580 SIDNEY *Arcad.* (J.) The river itself gave way unto her, so that she was straight breast-high. **1678** *Massacre in Irel.* 8 They saw one like a Woman rise out of the River breast-high. **1854** J. ABBOTT *Napoleon* (1855) I. xxxv. 556 Some . . wading breast high, reached the opposite bank.

2. Said in *Hunting* of the scent when it is so strong that the hounds go at a racing pace with their heads erect.

1858 KINGSLEY *Ode to N.-E. Wind* 30 Hark! the brave North-Easter! Breast-high lies the scent. **1868** R. EG.-WARBURTON *Hunt. Songs* lvi, When we fly with a scent breast high, and a galloping fox before us.

C. *sb.* A tunnel or horizontal entrance into a coal-mine, so low that the miner has to stoop: in Lancash. dial. ***breast-hee***.

1850 BAMFORD *Tim Bobbin* Introd. 3 in *Lanc. Gloss.* (E.D.S.) The collier brought his coal to daylight at the mouth of a . . breast-hee, generally opening out not unlike a large black sough, on some hill-side. **1857** E. WAUGH *Lanc. Sk.* 44 *ibid.*, At the mouth of a lonely breast-hee on his native moor-side.

'**breastie.** *Sc.* Diminutive of BREAST *sb.*

1785 BURNS *To Mouse* 1, Wee sleekit, cow'rin tim'rous beastie, O, what a panic's in thy breastie!

breasting ('brɛstɪŋ), *vbl. sb.* [f. BREAST *sb.* and *v.* + -ING[1].]

1. a. The action of confronting or opposing with the breast, of ascending the breast of a slope, etc. **b.** *concr.* A covering for the breast, breastwork.

1817 SOUTHEY *Morte Arth.* I. Introd. 60 'The French', says the chronicler of Pero Nino . . 'arm the horses with head pieces and breastings of leather'. **1836** LANDOR *Lett. Conserv.* 76 The current of evil is only to be stemmed by the united weight and breasting of the people. **1870** *Daily News* 7 Dec., Its flanking fire would have prohibited the breasting of the slope toward Villiers.

2. *techn.* The curved channel in which a breast water-wheel works.

breastless ('brɛstlɪs), *a.* Without breasts.

1854 BLACKIE in *Blackw. Mag.* 265 Before his spear the Amazon yields . . The breastless host. **1861** *Three Barriers* 88 These breastless tribes are Birds, Reptiles, and fishes.

† '**breastlet.** *Obs. rare.* [See -LET.] A small piece of meat from the breast.

a **1571** JEWEL *On Matt.* ix. 37 Whensoever the ox, or calf, or sheep . . was offered unto God . . the priest for his share had the breastlet which covered the heart.

breast-plate ('brɛstpleɪt). [f. BREAST *sb.* + PLATE, q.v. for Forms.]

1. A piece of armour for protecting the breast; also, any plate worn on the breast.

c **1386** CHAUCER *Knts. T.* 2120 Som wol ben armed in an haubergeon And in bristplate. **1535** COVERDALE *Ephes.* vi. 14 Hauing on the breast-plate of righteousnesse. **1678** BUNYAN *Pilgr.* I. 62 Sword, Shield, Helmet, Breastplate. **1814** SCOTT *Ld. Isles* VI. xxxii, A lance's point Has found his breastplate's loosen'd joint. **1833** J. HOLLAND *Manuf. Metals* II. 11 The

breast-plate.. with a little steel boss in the centre and straps attached to fasten it over the workman's belly. **1844** *Regul. & Ord. Army* 158 The Bayonet Belt is to be then fitted in front, and wherever it crosses the Pouch Belt, there the Breast-Plate is to be placed.

2. A folded piece of embroidered linen worn on the breast of the Jewish high-priest, and adorned with twelve precious stones, representing the twelve tribes. Cf. *Exod.* xxviii. xxxix.

1581 MARBECK *Bk. of Notes* 75 In the Ephod or in the brest plate were .12. precious stones. **1611** BIBLE *Ex.* xxviii. 4 A breastplate [WYCLIF breest broche, racional; COVERDALE brestlappe], and an Ephod, and a robe. **1667** MILTON *P.L.* III. 598 The Twelve that shon In Aarons Brest-plate. **1868** MARRIOTT *Vest. Chr.* 79.

3. In various technical uses: as **a.** *Building.* A breast-summer. **b.** *Mech.* A plate in which the butt end of a drill is inserted when the pressure is applied by the breast in boring. **c.** = BREAST-PLOUGH. **d.** A strap or arrangement of straps passing across the breast of a riding-horse and attached to the saddle and saddle-girths. **e.** *Zool.* The under part of the horny case of a tortoise or turtle; the plate covering the lower side of the thorax of some insects. **f.** The inscription-plate on a coffin.

1667 PRIMATT *City & C. Build.* 59 Summers, Brest-plates, with Joysts, Rafters, and Window-frames. **1677** MOXON *Mech. Exerc.* (1703) 7 The Drill-Plate, or Breast-Plate.. hath an hole punched a little way into it, to set the blunt end of the Shank of the Drill in. **1704** *Dict. Rust. et Urb.* s.v. *Burning*, A Breastplayt to pare off the Turff. *a* **1720** W. GIBSON *Diet of Horses* viii. (ed. 3) 127, I have seen horses sometimes galled and fretted by buckling their Breast-plates too tight. **1845** DARWIN *Voy. Nat.* xvii, We lived entirely upon tortoise-meat; the breast-plate roasted.. with the flesh on it is very good. **1849** in Southey *Comm.-pl. Bk.* Ser. II. 586 A butterfly.. through a very remarkable opening in the breast-plate, emitted a great quantity of a sort of froth. **1864** *Derby Mercury* 7 Dec., The outer shell of the coffin was of oak.. upon the breast-plate was an inscription recording the name and age of the deceased.

ˈbreast-plough. 'A sort of Plough driven by main force with one's breast, commonly used in paring the Turf in Burn-beating' (Worlidge *Syst. Agric.* (1681) 322).

1725 BRADLEY *Fam. Dict.* s.v. *Trenching Spade*, Some of these Spades.. are made with one side turned up like the Breast-Plow. **1869** BLACKMORE *Lorna D.* xv, We must.. labour as at a breast-plough.

Hence **ˈbreast-plough** *v.*, and **ˈbreast-ploughing** *vbl. sb.*

1846 J. BAXTER *Libr. Pract. Agric.* II. 183 The breast-ploughing on these soils is easy.

breastsummer, bressummer (ˈbrɛsəmə(r)). Also **breastsommer, bressomer, bressumer, brestsummer.** [f. BREAST *sb.* + SUMMER *sb.*² (a. F. *sommier* beam).] A 'summer' or beam extending horizontally over a large opening, and sustaining the whole superstructure of wall, etc.; e.g. the beam over a shop-front, the lower beam of the front of a gallery, and the like.

1611 COTGR., *Contrefrontail*, the brow-peece.. of a dore; a haunse, or breast summer. **1727** BRADLEY *Fam. Dict.* s.v. *Building*, Brest-Sommers, Girders, Trimmers, and Wall-plates. **1845** *Gloss. Goth. Archit.* I. 69 Breastsummer, Bressummer.. a beam supporting the front of a building, etc., after the manner of a lintel. **1880** *Daily News* 27 Apr. 3/7 The bressummer was then burning. **1885** J. F. MOLLOY *Royalty Rest.* II. 193 Breastsummers of stout oak.

breast-wheel (ˈbrɛsthwiːl). A water-wheel, in which the water is admitted to the float-board nearly on a level with the axle.

1759 SMEATON in *Phil. Trans.* LI. 137 To examine the effects when the impulse and weight are combined, as in the several kinds of breast-wheels, etc. **1831** LARDNER *Hydrostatics* x. 203 A breast wheel partakes of the nature of the overshot and undershot wheels.

breastwise (ˈbrɛstwaɪz), *adv.* [f. BREAST *sb.* + -WISE.] Side by side, abreast.

1620 DEKKER *Dream* (1860) 24 So wide That ten caroches (breastwise) in may ride. **1673** RAY *Notes of Husb.* 130 He uses to plow with his Oxen endwayes or all in one file.. whereas breastwise it is very hard evenly to match them. **1849** GROTE *Greece* II. xxxviii. V. 24 Two lines of ships.. were moored across the strait breastwise.

breastwork (ˈbrɛstwɜːk).

1. a. *Fortif.* A fieldwork (usually rough and temporary) thrown up a few feet in height for defence against an enemy; a parapet.

1642 *Relat. Action bef. Cyrencester* 3 Gardens.. divided by many low dry stone walls, as good as Breast workes. **1645** R. SYMONDS *Diary Civ. War* (1859) 232 At Worcester Prince Maurice has made without the ditch.. a low breast-work, and a stockado without. **1693** LUTTRELL *Brief Rel.* (1857) III. 152 The English made a breastwork of the dead, to cover them in the time of action. **1809** W. IRVING *Knickerb.* (1861) 98 The mud breastworks had long been levelled with the earth. **1839** THIRLWALL *Greece* II. 346 Closing their wicker shields, and fixing them in the ground, so as to form a kind of breastwork before them. **1861** SMILES *Engineers* II. 236 The Hythe Military Canal.. protected by a breastwork on the land side.

b. *transf.* and *fig.*

1828 CARLYLE *Misc.* (1857) I. 230 Behind the outmost breastwork of gentility. **1821** DE QUINCEY *Confess.* Wks. I. 103 This watery breastwork, a perpendicular wall of water carrying itself as true as if controlled by a mason's plumb-line.

2. In various technical uses: **a.** *Naut.* 'A sort of balustrade of rails, mouldings, or stanchions which terminates the quarter-deck and poop at the fore ends' (Smyth *Sailor's Word-bk.*); see also quot. 1870. **b.** *Arch.* The parapet of a building. **c.** = BREASTING 2.

1769 FALCONER *Dict. Marine* (1789), *Breastwork*.. frequently decorated with sculpture. *c* **1850** *Rudim. Navig.* (Weale) 101 The breast-work.. serves to make a separation from the main-deck. **1870** *Daily News* 27 Sept., Having the space occupied by the turrets, funnel, hatch-ways, &c., raised seven or eight feet above the low deck. The armoured sides of this superstructure Mr. Reed calls the 'breastwork'. **1875** URE *Dict. Arts* II. 849 A good example of the form of iron buckets employed in the breast wheel.. is shown in fig. 1178: *a.* shrouding.. *e.* breastwork.

3. The brickwork or masonry forming the breast of a fire-place.

1806 *Massachusetts Spy* 23 July (Th.), On the breastwork over the fireplace was the distinct impression of a bloody hand. **1833** LOUDON *Encycl. Archit.* §79 The fire-places to have each a strong iron chimney-bar (bar for supporting the breast-work, or front side of the flues).

breasty (ˈbrɛstɪ), *a. colloq.* [f. BREAST *sb.* 1 a + -Y¹.] = BOSOMY *a.* 2.

1944 H. HUNT *Limit of Darkness* 23 The others kidded him about being breasty because of the twin bulges made by the pipe and his tobacco pouch. **1959** *Numbers* (N.Z.) IX. 38 A pretty breasty, curly haired girl in blue. **1960** *20th Cent.* Dec. 582 An Amis hero pouncing on a breasty girl.

breath (brɛθ). Forms: 1 **brǽþ**, *Anglian* **bréþ**, 2–3 **breð**, 3–6 **breth**, 4 **breeth, breeþ, breþ**(e, 4–6 **brethe**, 6 **breathe**, 6– **breath.** [OE. *brǽþ*, *bréþ* odour, smell, exhalation as of anything cooking or burning:—WGer. type **brâþ-*, OTeut. **brǣþo-z*:—Aryan **bhrêto-*, with original sense 'exhalation from heat, steam, reek', f. root **bhrē-*, Teut. **brǣ-* to burn, heat: see BREDE *v.*¹, and BROOD. Thus related to OHG. *brâdam*, MHG. *bradem*, Ger. *brodem* 'exhalation, vapour, steam':—OTeut. type **brǣþmo-z* :—Aryan ˈ*bhrē-tmo-* (cf. Skr. ˈ*ā-tman*, etc.), f. same root. The sense passed in Eng. through that of 'heated air expired from the lungs' (often manifest to the sense of smell, as in 'strong breath') to 'the air in the lungs or mouth', thus taking the place of OE. *ǽðm*, early ME. *ēþem* (see ETHEM), and ME. ANDE, ONDE, Sc. *aind*, *aynd*, from Old Norse. The original long vowel of OE. *brǽþ* has only recently been shortened; the 16th c. (breːθ) having become (brɛθ), instead of (briːθ) as in the verb BREATHE.]

†1. Odour, smell, scent. *Obs.*

c **893** K. ÆLFRED *Oros.* VI. xxxii. §2 Þa ongon se cealc mid ungemete stincan; þa wearþ Iuninianus mid þæm bræþe ofsmorod. *a* **1100** *Ags. Voc.* in Wr.-Wülcker 3 *Odor*, bræþ. *c* **1175** *Lamb. Hom.* 153 Hwenne þe nose bið open to smelle unlofne breð. *a* **1340** HAMPOLE *Pr. Consc.* 613 He may se fra his body com.. Alkyn filthe with stynkand brethe. *c* **1400** *Destr. Troy* 8804 Bawme, þat was bright, & of brethe noble.

2. †a. An exhalation or vapour given forth by heated objects, etc.; steam, smoke, reek. *Obs.*

a **1300** *Pop. Treat. Sc.* 203 (Wright) 136 Both of the see and of fersch water he draweth up the breth. *a* **1340** HAMPOLE *Pr. Consc.* 4727 Blode and fire and brethe of smoke. **1398** TREVISA *Barth. De P.R.* XVII. xxvi. (1495) 619 Whan canell is broke therof comyth a breth as it were a myste. **1561** HOLLYBUSH *Hom. Apoth.* 3 Hold thy nose over it that the vapor or hot breth ascende into thy head. **1667** MILTON *P.L.* IV. 806 Like gentle breaths from Rivers pure.

b. (with influence of sense 3): The air exhaled from anything, or impregnated with its exhalations, and retaining its characteristic odour. Also *fig.* Cf. AIR *sb.*¹.

1625 BACON *Gardens, Ess.* (Arb.) 557 Because the Breath of Flowers is farre Sweeter in the Aire.. then in the hand. **1830** TENNYSON *A Spirit haunts* 18 The moist rich smell of the rotting leaves, And the breath Of the fading edges of box beneath. **1837** NEWMAN *Par. Serm.* (ed. 2) III. x. 147 Full of the.. breath of the grave. **1874** BLACKIE *Self-Cult.* 43 What a student should specially see to.. is not to carry the breath of books with him wherever he goes.

c. with a mixture of the sense of 'puff': A little of the air, a whiff.

1873 BLACK *Pr. Thule* xxv. 424 The remote islands, where a stranger brought.. a breath of the outer world with him.

3. a. The air exhaled from the lungs, originally as made manifest by smell, or as a visible exhalation; hence *to keep* (*save, spare*) *one's breath to cool one's* (*own*) *porridge*: see PORRIDGE *sb.* 4. **b.** generally, The air received into and expelled from the lungs in the act of respiration. *to draw breath*: to inhale air, breathe; *hence*, to live: also *to spend, waste* (*one's*) *breath* (as in unprofitable speech). This is now the main sense, which colours all others.

a. *c* **1340** *Cursor M.* 3573 (Trin.) Teeþ to rote, breeþ [*earlier MSS.* ande] to stynke. *c* **1386** CHAUCER *Pardoneres T.* 224 Sour is thi breeth. **1398** TREVISA *Barth. De P.R.* V. xxxvii. (1495) 152 Changynge of breth comyth of vnyuersall corrupcion of the inner membres. **1601** SHAKS. *Jul. C.* I. ii. 249 The rabblement.. vttered such a deale of stinking breath. **1642** FULLER *Holy & Prof. St.* IV. xviii. 333 A Swede fights best when he can see his own breath. **1842** T. MARTIN in *Fraser's Mag.* Dec., You will oblige me by keeping your own breath to cool your own porridge. *Mod.* His breath smelling strong of alcohol.

b. *c* **1440** *Promp. Parv.* 50 Brethe, *anelitus.* **1535** COVERDALE *Ps.* cxxxiv[v]. 16 They heare not, nether is there eny breth in their mouthes. *c* **1534** *Pilgrim's T.* 476 in Thynne *Animadv.* App. i. 90 That ever it dreu brethe. **1697** DRYDEN *Virg. Georg.* IV. 699 Draw the vital breath of upper Air. **1712** STEELE *Spect.* No. 426 ¶2 Within ten Hours after the Breath is out of the Body. **1713** BERKELEY *Hylas & P.* iii. Wks. 1871 I. 323, I will no longer spend my breath in defence of it. **1809** W. IRVING *Knickerb.* (1861) 157 Even the inhabitants of New-Amsterdam began to draw short breath. **1842** TENNYSON *Morte d'Arth.* 148 Then spoke King Arthur, drawing thicker breath. **1850** —— *In Mem.* cxx, I trust I have not wasted breath.

c. *transf.* The wind blown into a musical instrument. *poet.*

1605 SHAKS. *Macb.* V. vi. 19 Make all our Trumpets speak, giue them all breath. **1697** DRYDEN *Virg. Georg.* II. 789 Before the Breath Of brazen Trumpets rung the Peals of Death. **1878** BROWNING *La Saisiaz* 36 But the soul is not the body: and the breath is not the flute.

d. *fig.* Taken as the type of things unsubstantial, volatile, or fleeting.

1593 SHAKS. *Lucr.* 212 A dream, a breath, a froth of fleeting joy. **1603** —— *Meas. for M.* III. i. 8 A breath thou art, Seruile to all the skyie-influences.

4. a. A gentle blowing, a puff; now usually *breath of air* or *breath of wind*; but in early times used absolutely in sense of 'wind, breeze, air in motion'.

c **1325** *E.E. Allit. P.* C. 107 Þe blyþe breþe at her bak þe bosum he fyndes. *Ibid.* 138 When boþe breþes con blowe vpon blo watteres. *c* **1400** *Destr. Troy* 3697 Þe bre and the brethe burbelit to gedur. **1627** CAPT. SMITH *Seaman's Gram.* x. 46 There is not a breath of wind stirring. **1711** STEELE *Spect.* No. 167 ¶3 The least Breath of Wind has often demolished my magnificent Edifices. **1822** SHELLEY *Hellas* 4 Sweet as a summer night without a breath. **1833** HT. MARTINEAU *Manch. Strike* vi. 67 A breath of fresh air came in. **1860** TYNDALL *Glac.* I. §18. 133 There was not a breath of air stirring.

b. In the 'breath of summer', 'of morn', etc. there is almost always an admixture, great or small, of a *fig.* use of senses 2 b, 3 a.

c **1386** CHAUCER *Prol.* 5 Whan Zephirus eek with his swete breeth Inspired hath.. the tendre croppes. *c* **1600** SHAKS. *Sonn.* liv, When summers breath their masked buds discloses. **1775** SHERIDAN *Duenna* I. i. 185 The breath of morn bids hence the night. **1821** BYRON *Sardan.* I. ii. 575 Can I not even breathe The breath of heaven?

c. *fig.* In such phrases as 'the breath of popular favour' (cf. Lat. *popularis aura*), the original notion of the breath of favouring wind which fills the sails, is much mixed with that of spoken or whispered breath, and sometimes with other of the later senses.

a **1639** WOTTON *Char. Happy Life* in *Reliq. Wotton.*, Untide unto the world by care Of Publike fame or private breath. **1692** SOUTH *12 Serm.* (1697) I. 32 The Mind can.. quickly feel the thinness of a popular Breath. *a* **1703** BURKITT *On N.T.* Mark i. 45 Christ retires from the breath of popular applause. **1790** GOUVR. MORRIS in Sparks *Life & Writ.* (1832) II. 96 They must patiently wait the breath of the Assemblée, and follow as it blows. **1874** H. REYNOLDS *John Bapt.* i. §4. 35 Forced into new attitudes by the changing breath of human appreciation.

5. a. The faculty or action of breathing, respiration. Hence, breathing existence, spirit, life; so *breath of life, breath of the nostrils.*

a **1300** *Seven Sins* 41 in *E.E.P.* (1862) 19 Þe deuil benimiþ him is breþ. **1382** WYCLIF *Gen.* ii. 7 And spiride in to the face of hym an entre of breth of lijf. *c* **1386** CHAUCER *Knts. T.* 2194 Whan with honour vp yolden is his breeth. **1587** *Mirr. Mag., Alban* lxx, Now faint I feele, my breath begins to fayle. **1611** SHAKS. *Wint. T.* V. i. 83 When your first Queene's againe in breath. **1611** BIBLE *Gen.* vii. 22 All in whose nosethrils was the breath of life. **1738** WESLEY *Psalms* No. 121. v, He guards our Souls, he keeps our Breath. **1821** CLARE *Vill. Minstr.* I. 169 Now, poor puss! thou'st lost thy breath, And decent laid the molds beneath. **1850** TENNYSON *In Mem.* xxxvi, And so the Word had breath.

b. *to catch* or *hold one's breath*: to check suddenly or suspend the act of respiration. Also *fig.*

1719 DE FOE *Crusoe* iii, I held my breath.. I was ready to burst with holding my breath. **1816** BYRON *Ch. Har.* III. lxxxiv, In his lair Fix'd Passion holds his breath, until the hour Which shall atone for years. **1833** MARRYAT *P. Simple* xlvii, 'I see her', replied I, catching my breath with joy. **1864** *Glasgow Her.* 11 June, It also catches my breath and makes me cough.

c. *to take a person's breath* (*away*): to cause him to hold his breath owing to sudden emotion; hence, to dumbfound, flabbergast.

1864 BROWNING *Likeness* in *Dram. Personæ*, He never saw .. What was able to take his breath away. **1905** T. DIXON *Clansman* 351 The daring campaign these men were waging took his breath. *a* **1910** 'MARK TWAIN' *Myst. Stranger* (1916) 14 He said it placidly, but it took our breath for a moment and made our hearts beat. **1965** *Listener* 3 June 826/1 It is the really bold planting that takes one's breath away.

6. An act of breathing; a single respiration. Hence phrases: *in* (*with*) *one* or *the same breath, at a breath*, etc.

1483 *Cath. Angl.* 43 A Breth; *vbi* ande. **1489** CAXTON *Faytes of A.* II. xxxix. 164 Taughte to.. plonge in to the watre and wyth a long breth to kepe them self therynne. **1571** *Buchanan's Detect. Mary* in H. Campbell *Love-lett. Mary Q. Scots* (1824) 148 When she cannot stay him in life, cometh she to receive his last breath? **1588** *Marprel. Epist.*

(Arb.) 3, I cannot very often at one breath come to a full point. **1634** QUARLES *Embl.* I. (1818) 58 Thou swallowest at one breath Both food and poison down. **1717** POPE *Eloisa* 333 Till ev'ry motion, pulse, and breath, be o'er. **1850** MRS. STOWE *Uncle Tom* xvii. 160 I'll fight to the last breath, before they shall take my wife and son. **1858** HAWTHORNE *Fr. & It. Jrnls.* I. 83 In the space of half a dozen breaths. **1867** FREEMAN *Norm. Conq.* (1876) I. vi. 506 The Chroniclers speak of it in the same breath with the election of Harold.

7. a. Power of breathing, free or easy breathing. Chiefly in phrases: e.g. ***out of breath***: breathing with difficulty, breathless; so ***in breath*** (obs.), ***to get, keep, lose one's breath, to put out of breath***.

1590 SHAKS. *Com. Err.* IV. i. 57 You run this humor out of breath. **1602** —— *Ham.* V. ii. 282 The King shal drinke to Hamlets better breath. **1603** KNOLLES *Hist. Turkes* (1621) 1254 The Turkes yet in breath..gave an attempt unto the high Towne. **1782** COWPER *J. Gilpin* xl, Away went Gilpin out of breath. **1810** SCOTT *Lady of L.* I. vii, Two dogs.. Unmatched for courage, breath, and speed. **1859** TENNYSON *Elaine* 421 At last he got his breath and answer'd.

b. ***to take breath***, to breathe freely, to recover free breathing, as by pausing after exertion. Also *fig.*

1581 NOWELL & DAY in *Confer.* I. (1584) G iij, Some of vs were fayne to go out of the chauncel to take breath. **1581** J. BELL *Haddon's Answ. Osor.* 401 To pause awhiles, and to take breath upon good advise, what were best to be done. **1828–41** TYTLER *Hist. Scot.* (1864) I. 112 They sat down to take breath.

8. a. Opportunity or time for breathing; exercise of the respiratory organs. Also *fig.*

1594 SHAKS. *Rich. III*, IV. ii. 24 Giue me some litle breath, some pawse, deare Lord. **1606** SHAKS. *Tr. & Cr.* II. iii. 121 He hopes it is no other, But for your health, and your digestion sake, An after Dinners breath. —— IV. v. 92 Their fight..either to the vttermost Or else a breath. **1673** TEMPLE *Observ. U. Prov.* Wks. 1731 I. 24 The great Breath that was given the States in the Heat of their Affairs.

†**b.** Of mines, etc.: ***to have breath***: to have free passage for foul air or gas. *Obs. rare.*

1599 HAKLUYT *Voy.* II. I. 83 The mine had vent or breath in two places.

9. a. *transf.* Whisper, utterance, articulate sound, speech; judgement or will expressed in words.

1377 LANGL. *P. Pl.* B. XIV. 61 þorw his breth mowen men & bestes lyuen. *Ibid.* XVIII. 319 With þat breth helle brake. **1589** J. HART *Orthogr.* 6 To use as many letters in our writing as we do voyces or breathes in speaking. **1599** SHAKS. *Much Ado* V. i. 273 Art thou the slaue that with thy breath hast kild mine innocent childe? **1612** T. TAYLOR *Comm. Titus* i. 9 Noting in one breath of Bellarmine three errors. **1720** WATTS *Div. Songs* xvii. iii, Hard names..and threatening words, That are but noisy breath. **1770** GOLDSM. *Des. Vill.* 54 A breath can make them, as a breath has made. **1785** BURNS *Cotter's Sat. Nt.* xix, Princes and lords are but the breath of kings. **1830** TENNYSON *Dream F.W.* ii, Dan Chaucer, the first warbler, whose sweet breath Preluded those melodious bursts. **1875** JOWETT *Plato* (ed. 2) V. 114 There is an undoubted power in public opinion when no breath is heard adverse to the law.

b. ***below*** or ***under one's breath***: in a low voice or whisper. ***bated breath***: see BATED *ppl. a.*

1832 LYTTON *Eug. Aram* I. iii, Hush, said Ellinor under her breath. **1865** J. USSHER *Lond. to Persep.*, The Armenian woman can only talk in her own house below her breath.

10. *Phonology.* Voiceless expiration of air, forming a hiss, whish, puff, or similar sound. *attrib.*, as in ***breath consonant***, a consonant formed by the breath in the mouth without the action of the vocal chords: such are the sounds (k, t, p, x, ʃ, s, θ, f).

1842 *Penny Cycl.* XXII. 429/2 It will be observed..that these consonants have no voice throughout their duration; that they each have breath-sound. **1867** MELVILLE BELL *Visible Speech* 49 When the breath, or the voice, is moulded by precise dispositions of the parts of the mouth. *Ibid.* 70 The Breath-glide. **1874** SWEET *Hist. Eng. Sounds* 76 To determine the laws which govern the distribution of the breath þ and f, and the voice ð and v. **1879** —— in *Philol. Soc. Trans.* 471 Swedish..final voiced stops..seem to be shorter than in English, and to have a stronger breath off-glide.

11. *Comb.*, as ***breath-bereaving***, ***-blown***, ***-catching***, ***-control***, ***-force***, ***-giver***, ***-giving***, ***-holding*** sb. and adj., ***-stopping***, ***-stream***; **breath-bubble**, a bubble blown by the breath; *fig.* an empty thing, a trifle; **breath-catching** *a.* = *breath-taking*; **breath-group** *Phonetics*, the succession of words, whether a sentence or part of a sentence, uttered without pause, in a single breath; †**breath-room**, room for breathing, breathing-space; †**breath-seller**, one who sells perfumes or scents; also, one who speaks for pay; **breath-sounds**, respiratory sounds heard in auscultation; **breath-tainted** *a.*, having tainted or foul breath; also *fig.*; **breath-taking** *a.*, surprising, thrilling, dumbfounding (cf. sense 5c, above); hence *breath-takingly* adv.; **breath-test**, measurement of the amount of alcohol in the blood by means of a breathalyser; also **breath-testing** *vbl. sb.* and *ppl. a.*

1618 BRATHWAIT *Descr. Death* in Farr's *S.P.* (1848) 270 A *breath-bereaving breath..He comes..to rid us of our feares. **1827** HOOD *Hero & L.* xxxviii, A *breath-blown dart Shot sudden from an Indian's hollow cane. **1835** BROWNING *Paracelsus* I. 30 Painted toys, *Breath-bubbles, gilded dust. **1868** MRS. H. WOOD *Flowers* in *Argosy* June, 'What's killing him?' cried Sale, with..a sort of *breath-catching. **1928** *Daily Tel.* 6 Nov. 14/5 Green, Wood and Violet..do some breath-catching tumbles. **1958** L. W. TANCOCK in *Aspects of Translation* 50 His personal endowments of voice and *breath-control. **1935** M. SCHUBIGER *Role of Intonation* 1 The amount of *breathforce (stress). **1963** *English Studies* XLIV. 60 Amplitude is not only a function of breath-force but also of vowel quality. **1609** *Metamorph. Tobacco* (Collier) 9 *Breath-giuing herbe. **1877** H. SWEET *Handbk. Phonetics* 86–7 The only division actually made in language is that into '*breath-groups'... Within each breath-group there is no pause whatever. **1909** D. JONES *Pronunc. of Eng.* 58 The following are examples of breath-groups: *Yes; Good morning; Shall we go out for a walk?* **1964** E. A. NIDA *Toward Sci. Transl.* viii. 178 In this type of translating there are several important factors (1) timing, both of syllables and breath groups. **1890** W. JAMES *Princ. Psychol.* II. xx. 174 The *breath-holding stillness of the boy playing 'I spy', to whom the seeker is near. **1937** J. R. FIRTH *Tongues of Men* iii. 40 The larynx or Adam's apple—the breath-holding, whisper-, and voice-making instrument. **1968** *Brit. Med. Bull.* XXIV. 250/1 CO_2 excretion is abolished..by breath-holding or by rebreathing. **1669** WORLIDGE *Syst. Agric.* viii. §3. 161 Leaving the Plant a little *Breath-room in the middle. **1601** CORNWALLYES *Ess.* II. xlix. (1631) 310 Call in those *breath-sellers, and perfumers. **1603** FLORIO *Montaigne* I. xxii. (1632) 52 A fourth estate of Lawyers, breathsellers, and pettifoggers. **1934** PRIEBSCH & COLLINSON *German Lang.* p. xv, A total stoppage of the outgoing *breath-stream. **1645** QUARLES *Sol. Recant.* I. 42 An old *Breath-tainted Churl. **1880** 'MARK TWAIN' *Tramp Abroad* xxxiii. 324 It was a sort of *breath-taking surprise. **1908** *Westm. Gaz.* 1 Apr. 7/3 This breath-taking assertion was made to a 'Westminster' representative. **1966** *Illustr. London News* 30 July 35 (Advt.), It tastes like a view from the top of the Eiffel Tower. Breathtaking. **1928** *Manch. Guardian Weekly* 31 Aug. 175/3 *Breathtakingly beautiful. **1966** *Economist* 12 Nov. 650/3 She has dropped her proposal for random road-side *breath-tests for drivers. **1968** *Listener* 21 Mar. 391/3 It has been forecast from recent casualty figures that the breath-test should cut deaths by 1,600 a year. **1960** *Daily Tel.* 27 Jan. 11/4 He subjected a colleague and myself to analyses of alcohol in the blood on his *breath-testing machine. **1967** *Spectator* 17 Nov. 605/2 The main object of breath testing is, of course, deterrence.

breathable (ˈbriːðəb(ə)l). [f. BREATHE *v.* + -ABLE.] Fit or agreeable to breathe, or to be inhaled; respirable.

1731 in BAILEY II. **1849** J. WILSON in *Blackw. Mag.* LXVI. 9 How breathable the atmosphere!

Hence ˈ**breathableness** (in mod. Dicts.).

breathalyser (ˈbrɛθəlaɪzə(r)). Also **-zer.** [f. BREATH + AN)ALYSER, -ZER.] (See quot. 1960[1].) Also *attrib.*

1960 *Times* 19 Jan. 7/4 The Breathalyser, an American instrument for measuring the percentage of alcohol in the blood from a breath sample, was put on view..yesterday. **1960** *Daily Mail* 19 Jan. 5/1 The Breathalyzer, the snap-test machine..for picking out drunken drivers. **1960** *News Chron.* 16 June 6/1 The breathalyser test is favoured by many. **1967** *Spectator* 20 Oct. 450/2 It may well be that the breathalyser test works and one cause of death on the roads has been banished from the scene.

Hence [as back-formation] ˈ**breathalyse** *v. trans.*, to subject (someone) to a test with a breathalyser; ˈ**breathalysed** *ppl. a.*

1967 *Times* 1 Dec. 8/3 Would it not be sensible to amend the Bill so that the police power to stop and 'breathalyse' people should be limited? **1967** *New Statesman* 29 Dec. 901/1 The matey breathalysed population drives obediently round in business-like pursuit of teenage love and entertaining kitchen furniture. **1978** *Cornish Guardian* 27 Apr. 12/3 A man..refused to be breathalysed as he lay in a hospital bed with a broken neck after a motor-cycle accident. **1983** *Financial Times* 22 Jan. 9 Hundreds of thousands of motorists..put themselves at risk of being breathalysed and prosecuted for being drunk in charge of a car.

breathe (briːð), *v.* Forms: 4 **brethi**, 4–5 **brethen**, 4–6 **brethe**, **breeth**, 5 **brethyn**, 6–8 **breath**, 5– **breathe**. [ME. *brethe(n*, f. *breth*, BREATH: not formed in OE. The verb retains the original long vowel with (ð) for (θ) between two vowels (*brethen*, etc.): cf. *mouth*, *mouths*, to *mouth*.]

I. *intr.* †**1.** To exhale, steam, evaporate. *Obs.*

a **1300** *Fragm. Pop. Sc.* (Wr.) 202 The sonne..maketh wateres brethi up as hi schulde swete. **1559** MORWYNG *Evonym.* 198 Heet them in a vessell diligently covered, that nothing breeth out. *Ibid.* 212 Close it, that the spirits brethe not out. **1560** P. WHITEHORNE *Ordering of Souldiours* (1573) 28 b, Putting them into a greate yearthen potte..lute it, or daube it very well aboute, so that it cannot breathe. **1594** PLAT *Jewell-ho.* III. 26 By this meanes a small quantity of.. water will be a long time in breathing out. **1608** SHAKS. *Per.* III. ii. 94 A warmth breathes out of her. **1670** LASSELS *Voy. Italy* (1698) II. 189 The infectious vapour which breatheth out of this sulphurous ground.

†**2.** To emit odour, to smell. Now only *fig.* with reference to sense 3.

c **1400** *Destr. Troy* 9119 Bame &..balsaum, þat brethid full swete. *c* **1468** in *Ord. R. Househ.* (1790) 40 To make amongst them other swete fumes, things to make them breathe most holesomly and delectable. **1712** POPE *Rape Lock* I. 134 All Arabia breathes from yonder box.

b. *fig.* To be redolent *of.*

1697 DRYDEN *Virg. Georg.* IV. 602 Down from his Head the liquid Odours ran, He breath'd of Heav'n, and look'd above a Man. **1832** TENNYSON *Mariana in South* vi, Old letters, breathing of her worth. **1842** —— *Audley Crt.* 7 Francis just alighted from the boat, And breathing of the sea.

3. Of animals: **a.** To exhale air from the lungs.

1398 TREVISA *Barth. De P.R.* III. v. (1495) 52 He makyth the body *spirare* (that is to brethe). **1526** TINDALE *John* xx. 22 He brethed upon them [WYCLIF, he blewe on hem], and sayde vnto them: Receaue the holy goost. **1587** GOLDING *De Mornay* ix. 122 If a man do but breath vpon them they vanish into smoke.

b. To exhale and inhale, to respire. The ordinary current sense, which colours all the others.

1377 [see BREATHING *vbl. sb.* 1]. *c* **1440** *Promp. Parv.* 50 Brethyn or ondyn, *spiro, anelo, aspiro.* *c* **1450** LONELICH *Grail* xxxviii. 389 Onnethis there brethen they myhte. **1483** *Cath. Angl.* 43 To Brethe..*spiritum trahere*..*vbi* to Ande. **1593** HOOKER *Eccl. Pol.* I. xvi. §5 When we breathe, sleep, move. **1610** SHAKS. *Temp.* IV. i. 45 Before you can say come, and goe, And breathe twice. **1726** BUTLER *Serm.* xi. 212 The Air in which we breath. **1842** TENNYSON *Morte d' Arth.* 162 And answer made King Arthur, breathing hard.

†**c.** *transf.* of plants. *Obs. rare.*

1574 HYLL *Conject. Weather* i, The seedes in the earth.. cannot then breath forth. **1664** EVELYN *Kal. Hort.* (1729) 228 Their [plants'] being kept from Breathing (as I presume to call it).

d. *trans.* To bring (*to*, *into* a state) by breathing.

1816 BYRON *Ch. Har.* III. lxxix, This breathed itself to life in Julie.

e. Of wine (uncorked and left for a while to stand): to absorb air, to oxidize, by which process the flavour of the wine is held to improve.

1951 R. POSTGATE *Plain Man's Guide to Wine* i. 27 Pretty well every wine is improved by being given an hour in which to breathe. **1959** L. DURRELL in *Holiday* Jan. 48/1 And don't drive too fast... It is bad for the wine... And tell Martine to let it rest and breathe after its journey. **1969** A. E. LINDOP *Sight Unseen* xii. 103, I opened a bottle of wine and left it to 'breathe'. **1987** B. FREEMANTLE *Charlie Muffin San* xxx. 273 There was a bottle of Margaux on the table..and another opened and breathing on a sideboard.

f. Of materials (as leather, etc.) which allow the passage of air and inhibit condensation, esp. those worn close to the body. Also *transf.*, of (a part of) the body, esp. the foot.

1969 *Sears Catal.* Spring/Summer 461/2 Upper [of shoe] breathes yet repels water, resists stains. **1970** *Motoring Which?* July 117/2 We wanted to make the material 'breathe', to check on the watertightness of the casing. **1980** *Sci. Amer.* Apr. 37/1 Because the material can 'breathe' and pass perspiration, it interferes little more than ordinary clothing with the ability of its wearer to shed heat. **1982** N. GOULD in *M. H. Jahss' Disorders of Foot* II. lxiv. 1761/1 Rubber soles are heavy and do not 'breathe'. **1984** *Daily Tel.* 16 Apr. 12/1 We go jogging in trainers which don't allow the feet to breathe.

4. To draw the breath of life; to live, exist.

1382 WYCLIF *Joshua* x. 40 Alle that myȝten breeth he slowȝ. **1594** SHAKS. *Rich. III*, I. i. 161 Clarence still breathes, Edward still liues and raignes. **1674** FLATMAN *Job* i, Few be the days, that feeble man must breath. **1713** POPE *Windsor F.* 300 What Kings first breath'd upon her winding shore. **1873** BLACK *Pr. Thule* xvii. 274 A better-intentioned fellow does not breathe.

b. with predicative sb. or adj.

1593 SHAKS. *3 Hen. VI*, III. i. 82 Why? Am I dead? Do I not breath a Man? **1608** ARMIN *Nest Ninn.* (1842) 7 The World..askt if it were possible such breathde hers to commaunde. *c* **1620** Z. BOYD *Zion's Flowers* (1855) 67 Hee'le say our house yet never breathed scant. **1826** DISRAELI *Viv. Grey* IV. iv. 153 Within five minutes you will breathe a beggar and an outcast.

c. *fig.* To live. ***to breathe through***: to animate, inform.

1732 POPE *Ess. Man* I. 275 One stupendous whole..That ..Breathes in our soul, informs our mortal part. **1862** STANLEY *Jew. Ch.* (1877) I. v. 102 Its effect on Israel..still moves and breathes amongst us. **1865** M. ARNOLD *Ess. Crit.* ix. (1875) 386 Certain governing ideas of Spinoza..which breathe through all his works.

d. *fig.* To be alive *with.*

a **1881** DISRAELI (O.) The staircase in fresco..breathed with the loves and wars of gods and heroes.

5. To take breath (see BREATH 7b); *fig.* to pause, take rest. ***to breathe again*** (fig.): to recover from anxiety, excitement, etc.; to be relieved in mind. ***to breathe freely***: to be at ease; to be in one's element.

1577 HOLINSHED *Chron.* III. 1137/1 Without giuing anie long time to the residue of the guides..to breath vpon their businesse. **1595** SHAKS. *John* IV. ii. 137 Now I breath againe Aloft the flood. **1597** HOOKER *Eccl. Pol.* V. lxv. §8 If..only to breathe between troubles may be termed quietness. **1627** CAPT. SMITH *Seaman's Gram.* xiii. 60 Let vs breathe and refresh a little. **1720** OZELL *Vertot's Rom. Rep.* II. XIV. 331 With Orders to give Antony no Time to Breathe, but to pursue him forthwith. **1839** THIRLWALL *Greece* I. 333 War was the element in which the Spartan seems to have breathed most freely. **1859** TENNYSON *Enid* 567 Twice they fought, and twice they breathed.

†**6.** fig. ***to breathe to***, ***after***: to aspire to, pant after, long to attain to. *Obs.*

1524 *St. Papers Hen. VIII*, IV. 245 The saide Archebusshop bretheth myche to honour. *a* **1593** H. SMITH *Serm.* (1866) II. 330 Let us breathe after the fountain of the living water. *a* **1602** W. WATSON *Decacord.* 154 Whilest the Spaniard was a breathing to have gotten the Kingdom, if he could. **1603** KNOLLES *Hist. Turks* (1621) 428 We see the Turkes..breathing after our destruction. **1734** WATTS *Reliq. Juv.* (1789) 257 Set it a breathing after eternal things.

7. *transf.* To give forth audible breath or sound; to speak, sing, etc.

1598 SHAKS. *Merry W.* IV. v. 2 Speake, breathe, discusse. **1607** —— *Timon* III. v. 59 You breath in vaine. **1632**

MILTON *Penser.* 151 As I wake, sweet music breathe. **1842** TENNYSON *Two Voices* 434 A hint, a whisper breathing low.

8. Of wind, air, etc.: To blow softly. (Cf. 3 a.)

1610 SHAKS. *Temp.* II. i. 46 The ayre breathes vpon vs here most sweetly. **1704** POPE *Windsor F.* 136 Where cooling vapours breathe along the mead. **1830** TENNYSON *Godiva* 55 The low wind hardly breathed for fear. **1884** W. C. SMITH *Kildrostan* 48 The wind that breathes upon the woods.

9. ***to breathe upon*** (fig.): to infect or contaminate; to tarnish (as if with breath); to taint, corrupt. Cf. *blow upon*, BLOW *v.*[1] 30.

[**1591** SHAKS. *Two Gent.* v. iv. 131 Take but possession of her, with a Touch: I dare thee, but to breath vpon my Loue.] **1820** BYRON *Mar. Fal.* v. i. 429 When the proud name on which they pinnacled Their hopes is breathed on. **1859** TENNYSON *Enid* 1799 Before the Queen's fair name was breathed upon.

II. *trans.*

10. To exhale, to emit by expiration (*out*); *fig.* to send or infuse *into*, communicate by breathing.

1382 WYCLIF *Lament.* ii. 12 Whan thei shuld brethen out ther soulis in the bosom of ther modris. **1388** —— *Gen.* ii. 7 The Lord God..brethide in to his face the brething of lijf. *c* **1590** MARLOWE *Massacre Paris* III. ii, Breathe out that life wherein my death was hid. **1593** SHAKS. *2 Hen. VI*, IV. i. 7 Who..from their misty Iawes Breath foule contagious darknesse in the ayre. **1871** R. ELLIS *Catullus* lxiv. 104 Her unvoic'd lips breathed incense faintly to heaven. **1873** MORLEY *Rousseau* I. 313 He breathed new life into them.

b. *transf.* of things.

1647 W. BROWNE *Polex.* II. 339 The resolution that hatred can breath into haughty courages. **1667** MILTON *P.L.* II. 244 His Altar breathes Ambrosial Odours. *Ibid.* III. 607 What wonder then if fields and regions here Breathe forth Elixir pure. **1782** COWPER *Table T.* 294 Place me where Winter breathes his keenest air. **1839** ARNOLD in Stanley *Life* II. ix. (1858) 140 The rocks actually breathing fragrance from the number of their aromatic plants.

c. ***to breathe one's last*** or ***one's last breath*** or ***gasp***: to die, expire.

1593 SHAKS. *3 Hen. VI*, v. ii. 40 Mountague hath breath'd his last. *Ibid.* II. i. 108 Where your braue Father breath'd his latest gaspe. **1651** *Proc. Parliament* No. 82. 1247 The kingdome, languishing and ready to breath out her last. **1714** POPE *Rape Lock* III. 158. **1850** TENNYSON *In Mem.* xcviii. 5 Where he breathed his latest breath.

11. To inhale and exhale (air, etc.), to respire; *esp.* to inhale, as in 'to breathe foul air'. Also *fig.*

1588 SHAKS. *L.L.L.* v. ii. 732, I breath free breath. **1632** SANDERSON *12 Serm.* 472 The ayre we continually breath. *a* **1704** T. BROWN *Dk. Ormond's Recov.*, Divine Alcides breathes celestial air. **1810** HENRY *Elem. Chem.* (1826) II. 605 A sensation..produced by breathing the fumes of burning sulphur. **1878** BROWNING *La Saisiaz* 17 Wreaths.. that intercept the air one breathes. *Mod.* Free as the air we breathe.

12. To give utterance to: **a.** To utter in the most quiet way; to whisper, make known, communicate.

1595 SHAKS. *John* IV. ii. 36 To this effect..We breath'd our Councell. *a* **1674** CLARENDON *Hist. Reb.* (1702) I. III. 203 Few men to whom he could breath his Conscience. **1819** SCOTT *Ivanhoe* II. i. 20 But the petition was already breathed. *a* **1847** R. HAMILTON *Rew. & Punishm.* viii. (1853) 378 No intimation of hope is breathed. *Mod.* I would not breathe it to another.

b. To utter with vehemence or passion. Also with *out*.

1535 COVERDALE *Acts* ix. 1 Saul was yet breathinge out threatnynges and slaughter agaynst the disciples of the Lorde. **1596** SPENSER *F.Q.* I. vi. 38 Two knights..Both breathing vengeaunce. **1611** COTGR. s.v. *Duc*, Both..now and then breath out horrible shrikes. **1648** JENKYN *Blind Guide* i. 3 He breathes out reproaches. **1720** OZELL *Vertot's Rom. Rep.* II. x. 153 Marius..breathed nothing but Blood and Slaughter. **1809** J. BARLOW *Columb.* III. 22 The nations ..Breathe deadly strife, and sigh for battle's blare.

c. To express, manifest, evince, display.

1667 MILTON *P.L.* I. 554 Such as..in stead of rage Deliberate valour breath'd. **1780** HARRIS *Philol. Enq.* (1841) 482 A custom breathing their liberal and noble disposition. **1792** S. ROGERS *Pleas. Mem.* II. 12 Whose language breathed the eloquence of Truth. **1846** WRIGHT *Ess. Mid. Ages* I. ii. 61 Passages which breathe the true spirit of poetry. **1862** STANLEY *Jew. Ch.* (1877) I. xiii. 251 The whole period breathes a primitive simplicity.

13. *trans.* and *refl.* To let breathe; to give breathing, or a breathing space to; to recreate.

1563-87 FOXE *A. & M.* (1596) 252/1 The Kings permission to him granted, to breath himselfe a little and to walke abrode. **1596** DANETT *Comines* (1614) 304 When we had breathed our horses, wee ridde foorth a fast trot towards the King. **1642** FULLER *Holy & Prof. St.* IV. xvi. 324 Stopping..to breath himself and the Reader. **1824** SOUTHEY *Life & Corr.* (1850) v. 177 Taking up a book for five or ten minutes, by way of breathing myself. **1835** WILLIS *Pencillings* II. liv. 122 We dismounted here to breathe our horses.

14. To excite the respiratory organs of: *hence* †**a.** to exercise briskly; to accustom *to* by exercise (*obs.*). **b.** to put out of breath, exhaust, tire.

[**1430-1525** See BREATHED 1.]

1567 TURBERV. in *Thynne's Animadv.* Introd. 143 You breath your foming steede Athwart the fields. **1598** B. JONSON *Ev. Man in Hum.* I. v. 127 Ile send for one of these Fencers, and hee shall breath you. **1601** SHAKS. *All's Well* II. iii. 271, I thinke thou wast created for men to breath themselues vpon thee. **1611** HEYWOOD *Gold. Age* II. i. Wks. 1874 III. 32 Nor haue I yet bene to these pastimes breath'd. **1658** *Whole Duty Man* i. §2. 11 He that expects to run a race will beforehand be often breathing himself. **1676** F. VERNON in *Phil. Trans.* II. 580 The Plains of Elis are..fit to breath Horses in. **1826** F. COOPER *Mohicans* (1829) II. xv. 232 The warriors who had breathed themselves so freely in the preceding struggle. **1847** TENNYSON *Princess* Prol. 113 He had breath'd the Proctor's dogs. **1884** MISS BRADDON *Ishmael* II. 183 He was a little breathed when he stood before the door.

15. To give breath to (a wind instrument); to blow.

a **1721** PRIOR *Solomon* III. Wks. (1835) II. 178 They breathe the flute, or strike the vocal wire. **1762** *Judas Macc.* III. 18 See the Godlike Youth advance, Breathe the Flutes, and lead the Dance. **1822** [see BREATHED 4].

16. ***to breathe a vein***: to give vent to it; to lance it so as to let blood. *arch.* or ? *Obs.*

1652 FRENCH *Yorksh. Spa* x. 95 Have a vein breathed. **1655** CULPEPPER *Riverius* I. xv. 53 If the Liver be hot..we must breath a Vein. **1748** RICHARDSON *Clarissa* (1811) VIII. 120 They were forced to breath a vein to bring her to herself. **1756** P. BROWNE *Jamaica* 25. **1836** MARRYAT *Japhet* iv. 10 Permitting me to breathe a vein in his own arm.

breathed, *ppl. a.* [f. BREATHE *v.* and BREATH *sb.* + -ED. In early instances it is not easy to separate the verbal from the noun-derivative, nor to fix the pronunciation.]

I. From the vb. (*now* briːðd, 'briːðɪd).

1. Exercised, put into breath, in (good) wind; esp. in ***well-breathed***, and the like.

1430 LYDG. *Chron. Troy* I. vi, Though he be best brethed to endure. **1525** LD. BERNERS *Froiss.* II. cxxxvi. [cxxxii.] 380 Rode forthe an easy passe to kepe their horses well brethed. **1596** SHAKS. *Tam. Shr.* Induct. ii, Thy gray-hounds are as swift As breathed Stags. **1637** HEYWOOD *Roy. King* v. ix. Wks. 1874 VI. 79 The Falcon better breath'd, seiz'd on the Eagle. **1678** R. LESTRANGE *Seneca's Mor.* (1702) 343 A Footman that is not breath'd, cannot keep pace with his Master's Horse. **1704** POPE *Windsor F.* 121 To plains with well-breath'd beagles we repair.

b. *fig.* † ***lust-breathed*** (in Shaks.): animated or inspired by lust, or breathing lust (cf. *well-read*, *fair-spoken*).

1594 SHAKS. *Lucr.* 3 Lust-breathed Tarquin. **1607** —— *Timon* I. i. 10 A most incomparable man, breath'd as it were, To an vntyreable and continuate goodness. **1647** WARD *Simp. Cobler* 14 It is a most toylsome taske to runne the wild-goose chase after a well breath'd Opinionist. **1681** DRYDEN *Abs. & Achit.* 631 To speak the rest, who better are forgot, Would tire a well breath'd Witness of the Plot.

2. Put out of breath, exhausted, winded.

1599 PORTER *Angry Wom. Abingd.* in Hazl. *Dodsley* VII. 358 As good as a cry of hounds, to make a breath'd hare of me!

3. Exhaled, respired, inhaled and exhaled; uttered in a breath, whispered.

1579 SPENSER *Sheph. Cal.* Jan. 40 The blossome..With breathed sighes is blowne away, and blasted. **1596** —— *F.Q.* II. iii. 7 Vile Caytiue..Vnworthie of the commune breathed aire. **1629** MILTON *Ode Nativ.* 179 No nightly trance, or breathed spell, Inspires the pale-eyed priest. **1861** SMILES *Engineers* II. 220 The exhausted or breathed air.

4. Of wind-instruments: Played upon; cf. BREATHE *v.* 15. *poet.*

1822 PROCTOR (B. Cornwall) *Lud. Sforza* i. 16 Like numbers floating from the breathed flute.

†**5.** ***breathed ware***: ? tarnished goods; 'BRAIDED ware'.

1661 DAVENPORT *City Nt.-Cap* IV. in *Dodsley* (1780) XI. 326 We vent no breath'd ware here.

II. From the sb. (brɛθt).

6. Having breath; as in ***long-breathed***: long-winded, or long-lived. (The 2 early quots. are doubtful.)

1555 *Fardle Facions* II. xi. 260 Damoselles..softe as the Silke, and breathed like the Rose. **1628** EARLE *Microcosm.* xviii. 38 The rooms are ill breath'd. **1649** SELDEN *Laws Eng.* I. lxiv. (1739) 132 Had the King been a little longer breathed with patience, he might have had his will upon easier terms. **1816** SCOTT *Antiq.* xxi, 'They werena a lang breathed generation, I reckon'. **1884** *Mind* Jan. 125 It requires a long-breathed reader to accompany him through his devious course.

7. *Phonology.* Uttered with breath as opposed to voice; surd; cf. SONANT.

1877 SWEET *Handbk. Phonetics* 31 Consonants can therefore be breathed as well as voiced.

breather ('briːðə(r)). [f. BREATHE *v.* + -ER[1].]

1. He who, or that which, breathes; one who lives, a living being, creature, animal.

c **1600** SHAKSPERE *Sonn.* lxxxi, When all the breathers of this world are dead. **1606** —— *Ant. & Cl.* III. iii. 24 She shewes a body, rather then a life, A Statue, then a Breather. **1674** N. FAIRFAX *Bulk & Selv.* 135 Those reasonless breathers that live under us. **1850** TENNYSON *In Mem.* cxviii. 6 Breathers of an ampler day.

†**2.** He who, or that which, supplies breath; *fig.* inspirer, animater.

1615 CROOKE *Body of Man* 354 Calleth it [the midriff] the breather or bellowes of the lower belly. *a* **1711** NORRIS (J.) The breather of all life does now expire.

3. a. A spell of exercise taken to stimulate the breathing, or to try the wind; cf. BREATH 8. Also, that which puts out of breath, or exhausts.

a **1836** COLMAN *Poor Gent.* iv. ii (L.) Here we are at last —that hill's a breather. **1861** WHYTE MELVILLE *Mkt. Harb.* 229 They gave the hapless 'Marathon' a spin with 'Chance', as a mere breather. **1884** *Cyclist* 13 Feb. 249/1 Cyclists are looking forward to being able to take a 'breather' during the present week.

b. A short rest in which to recover breath; a breathing-space. (Cf. BREATHE *v.* 13.)

1901 *Daily Chron.* 15 Oct. 5/4 But the horses have had their breather, and we must on. **1902** *Ibid.* 21 May 3/3 A field battery on the left had a hot time of it just at this moment, and drew out of action for a breather quite close to our guns. **1940** L. A. G. STRONG *Sun on Water* 178 He worked fast for an hour and a half, then sat back for a breather. **1959** *Daily Tel.* 9 Nov. 1/1 They stopped for a 'breather' on the hard shoulder, which is out of bounds, except for vehicles in distress.

4. One who breathes forth, speaks, proclaims.

1382 WYCLIF *Acts* ix. 1 Saul, ȝit brethere, *or blowere*, of manassis and betyng. **1603** SHAKS. *Meas. for M.* IV. iv. 31 For my Authority beares of a credent bulke, That no particular scandall once can touch But it confounds the breather. **1612** T. JAMES *Jesuits Downef.* 8 These are the very first brokers, breathers and brochers of contention abroad. **1812** L. HUNT in *Examiner* 14 Dec. 787/2 This Breather of Eloquence could not say a few decent..words.

5. In full, ***breather pipe***: a vent in the crankcase, etc., of an internal-combustion engine, for the release of excessive pressure or gases.

1929 W. FAULKNER *Sartoris* II. vi. 145 He lifted the hood and removed the cap from the breather-pipe. **1935** *Times* 22 Oct. 9/1 Here also is the oil filler with a breather. **1962** *Which?* (Car Suppl.) Oct. 136/1 Cleaning the crankcase breather.

breathful ('brɛθfʊl), *a.* [f. BREATH + -FUL.] Full of breath or air; having breath or life, alive; breathing perfume, redolent, odorous.

1583 STANYHURST *Æneid* III. (Arb.) 81 How fares Ascanius? doth he liue, and breathful abideth? **1590** SPENSER *Muiopot.* 195 Fresh Costmarie, and breathfull Camomill. **1596** —— *F.Q.* IV. v. 38 The breathfull bellows blew amaine. **1593** BARNES *Parthen.* in Arb. *Garner* V. 350 Waste breathless words! and breathful sighs increase!

breathiness, see BREATHY *a.* 2.

breathing ('briːðɪŋ), *vbl. sb.* [f. BREATHE *v.*]

1. a. Exhalation and inhalation of breath; respiration; a single act of respiration.

1377 LANGL. *P. Pl.* B. XI. 349 Some bryddes at þe bille þorwgh brethynge conceyued. **1608** HIERON *Wks.* I. 736 Forsake mee not, I pray thee, in my last breathing. **1611** SHAKS. *Cymb.* II. ii. 18 'Tis her breathing that Perfumes the Chamber thus. **1691** WOOD *Ath. Oxon.* I. 260 Our author.. surrendred up his last breathings in his house in Magd. Parish. **1815** SCOTT *Ld. of Isles* II. xxx, His breathing came more thick and fast. **1842** TENNYSON *Day Dream* 93.

b. The time in which a breath is drawn; a very short time.

1625 F. MARKHAM *Bk. Hon.* v. iv. §1 Though it be but for a breathing, or short time. **1826** DISRAELI *Viv. Grey* III. vi. 116 It was there only for the breathing of a second.

c. Power of retaining the breath, 'wind'.

1667 OLDENBURG in *Phil. Trans.* II. 431 Pearl-fishers are fed with dry and rosted meat, to give them better breathing.

d. *fig.* Influence, inspiration.

1587 GOLDING *De Mornay* v. 56 The very benefitte which we receiue by his loue, is secret and insensible through breathing which worketh in us. **1878** B. TAYLOR *Deukalion* I. ii. 23 Over all things huge and coarse There came the breathing of a regal sway.

†**2.** Time to breathe, respite, pause, rest. *Obs.*

1598 BARRET *Theor. Warres* III. ii. 88 One troupe..ready to second another, and to giue breathing one to another. **1641** J. JACKSON *True Evang. T.* I. 32 The Church had no breathing for whole twenty yeares together. **1687** *Lond. Gaz.* No. 2262/1 Having received some breathing by a Proclamation.

3. Exercise taken to stimulate the respiratory organs; a breather.

1755 *Mem. Capt. P. Drake* iv. 30, I used to go often..to take a Breathing with his Scholars. **1865** *Morning Star* 2 Feb., The Oxonians..took their first 'breathing' over the course from Oxford to Iffley and back this afternoon.

4. Utterance, divulgence.

1606 SHAKS. *Ant. & Cl.* I. iii. 14, I am sorry to giue breathing to my purpose. **1611** BIBLE *Lament.* iii. 55 Hide not thine eare at my breathing, at my crie.

5. Aspiration (*after*), longing (*for*).

a **1652** J. SMITH *Sel. Disc.* iv. 109 Those breathings and gaspings after an eternal participation of him. **1805** D. JOHNSTON *Serm. for Blind* 39 A pious mind can meditate upon God and send up holy breathings towards him. **1852** TUPPER *Proverb. Philos.* 205 Ye commune of hopes and aspirations, the fervent breathings of the heart.

6. Of the wind: Gentle blowing.

1635 SWAN *Spec. M.* v. §2 (1643) 170 Redness of the skie ..declare[s] that some spirits or windie breathings are above. **1781** COWPER *Retirement* 530 The breathings of the lightest air that blows. **1802** WORDSW. *Sonn.* '*To T. l'Ouv.*' There's not a breathing of the common wind That will forget thee.

†**7.** Ventilation; a place for air or vapour to escape, a vent, air-hole. *Obs.*

1387 TREVISA *Higden* Rolls Ser. II. 75 Stues..wiþ streite side weies of breþynge [*lateralibus angustiis spiraculi viis*]. **1480** CAXTON *Descr. Brit.* 17 Weyes of brething that wonderly cast vp hete. **1483** *Cath. Angl.* 43 A Brethynge, *spiraculum, spiramen.* **1697** DRYDEN *Virg. Georg.* I. 131 The Warmth..makes New Breathings, whence new Nourishment she takes.

8. The opening of a vein in order to let blood.

1612 WOODALL *Surg. Mate* Wks. (1653) 328 By breathing of a Veine..the partie hath bin recovered. **1641** R. LESTRANGE *Relapsed Apost.* Introd. 4 Breathing of a Vein with a Dog-whip. **1719** D'URFEY *Pills* (1872) I. 87 Till the breathing a Vein Corrects the mad Pulse into Quiet.

9. *Gram.* An aspiration, an aspirate: *spec.* (Gr. πνεῦμα, L. *spiritus*) in Greek grammar, the two signs, (ʽ) or 'rough breathing', and (ʼ) or 'smooth breathing', which indicate respectively the

presence and absence of the aspirate. See also
ASPER sb.¹, ASPIRATE sb. 2, ASPIRATION 6.

1746 T. NUGENT tr. *Port Royal Gr. Gram.*, The
Grammarians call breathing (πνεῦμα) the manner of
breathing a Syllable in pronouncing it. These breathings
are twofold; one soft and smooth .. thus ἐγώ . . The other rough
and hard .. thus ἅμα. **1864** *Athenæum* No. 1934. 672/2 The
text is furnished with breathings and accents. **1875**
SCRIVENER *Lect. Grk. Test.* 20 Breathings and accents were
added, at first very irregularly.

10. *Comb.* and *attrib.*, as **breathing-fit**, a
breathing-space, pause, rest; **breathing-hole**, a
hole or vent for air; **breathing-part, -place**, a
place or opening for breathing; a pause;
breathing-pore, a minute opening for the
passage of air, a spiracle or stoma; **breathing-
room** = *breathing-space*; **breathing-space**,
room or time to breathe; also, a rest; a period of
inactivity; so *breathing-spell*, **breathing-time**,
breathing-tube, a tube through which to
breath; **breathing-while** = *breathing-space*.

1589 *Tri. Love & Fort.* III. in Hazl. *Dodsl.* VI. 195 Here
is a *breathing-fit after hard mischance. **1805** WORDSW.
Waggoner I. 37 Many a breathing-fit he takes. **1580**
HOLLYBAND *Treas. Fr. Tong., Naseaux* . . the *breathing
holes of the nose, the nosethrill. **1856** KANE *Arct. Expl.* I.
xiii. 141 They had worked numerous breathing-holes . . in
the solid ice. **1644** BULWER *Chiron.* 44 To distinguish the
Comma's and *breathing parts of a sentence. **1382** WYCLIF
Prov. xx. 27 The lanterne of the Lord the *brething place
[Vulg. *spiraculum*] of a man. **1581** SIDNEY *Apol. Poetrie*
(Arb.) 71 That Cæsura or breathing place in the middest of
the verse. **1768** G. WHITE *Selborne* 40 The head of a fallow-
deer . . furnished with two spiracula, or breathing-places
besides the nostrils. **1836** *Penny Cycl.* V. 374/1 *Breathing-
pores . . are formed by the juxtaposition of two cells. **1678** R.
L'ESTRANGE tr. *Seneca's Morals* II. xv. 188 But they had
open Ayr, and *Breathing-Room. **1891** W. JAMES *Will to
Believe* (1897) 203 That howling mob of desires, each
struggling to get breathing-room for the ideal to which it
clings. **1650** R. STAPYLTON *Strada's Low-C. Warres* v. 130
They gave her jealousies a short *breathing-space. **1842**
TENNYSON *Locksley H.* 167 There the passions cramp'd no
longer shall have scope and breathing-space. **1878** BOSW.
SMITH *Carthage* 247 He had at least given her a brief
breathing space. **1922** D. H. LAWRENCE et al. tr. *Bunin's
Gentleman from San Francisco* 2 He had almost reached the
level of those whom he had taken as his ideals, so he made up
his mind to pause for a breathing space. **1599** SANDYS
Europæ Spec. (1632) 192 Some *breathing time to revive
himselfe, after his wearinesse. **1873** SYMONDS *Grk. Poets* iii.
68 Here was a breathing-time of indecision and suspense.
1889 *Cent. Dict.*, *Breathing-tube, in *entom.*, the respiratory
tube of certain aquatic larvæ and dipterous puparia. **1946**
Jane's Fighting Ships 1944–5 229/2 The 'Schnorkel', or
breathing tube, . . enabled submarines to remain submerged
for much longer periods. **1593** SHAKS. *Ven. & Ad.* 1142 It
shall . . Bud and be blasted in a *breathing-while. **1873**
BROWNING *Red Cott. Night-C.* 416 Turn round and look
about, a breathing-while!

ˈbreathing, *ppl. a.* [f. as prec. + -ING².]
Respiring, living; blowing; emitting
fragrance; taxing the breath, etc.; in the various
senses of the verb.

1398 TREVISA *Barth. De P.R.* v. xxxv. (1495) 147 Euery
brethynge beest hath lounges. **1591** SPENSER *Virgil's Gnat*
xxiv, Gentle murmure of the breathing ayre. **1595** SHAKS.
John II. i. 419 Rescue those breathing liues to dye in beds.
1684 BUNYAN *Pilgr.* II. 66 Christiana began to Pant, and
said, I dare say this is a breathing Hill. **1747** COLLINS *Eclog.*
III. 6 Or scent the breathing maize at setting day. **1777** SIR
W. JONES *Pal. Fortune* 26 Incense-breathing gales perfum'd
the grove. **1816** SOUTHEY *Lay of Laureate, Dream* 62 Infant
man . . Most weak and helpless of all breathing things. **1845**
HOOD *Decl. Chivalry* ix, A battle was a battle then, A
breathing piece of work.

b. *fig.* Of pictures and statues: Life-like (cf.
Vergil's *spirantia signa, æra*).

1697 DRYDEN *Virg. Georg.* II. 646 Breathing Figures of
Corinthian Brass. *c* **1750** SHENSTONE *Elegy* xi. 22 The
breathing picture and the living stone. **1813** SHELLEY *Q.
Mab* 17 That lovely outline . . fair As breathing marble.

† c. *breathing with* or *from*: fresh from. *Obs.*

c **1534** *Pol. Verg. Eng. Hist.* (1846) I. 274 Hee sawe his
enemies stand . . freshe and breathinge from the late
spoylinge of his contrie. **1603** KNOLLES *Hist. Turkes* (1621)
881 Canalis and Quirinus yet breathing with the late
slaughter of the Turkes. *Ibid.* 1227 Yet breathing with
victorie.

d. *breathing-sweat*: a profuse perspiration.

1744 WALL in *Phil. Trans.* XLIII. 216 After the second
Dose of the Powders, each of them . . broke out into an
universal breathing Sweat. **1776** ANDERSON *ibid.* LXVI. 545
It brought on a breathing Sweat.

breathingly (ˈbriːðɪŋlɪ), *adv.* [f. prec. + -LY².]
In a breathing manner; with or as with life or
animation; gently as a breath.

1830 J. WILSON in *Blackw. Mag.* XXVIII. 527 Perfect
spiritual health, breathingly embodied in perfect corporeal
flesh and blood. *a* **1859** L. HUNT *Poems* (1860) 236 A rill that
slips Over the sunny pebbles breathingly.

breathless (ˈbrɛθlɪs), *a.* [f. BREATH + -LESS.]
1. Without breath: **a.** Without respiration.

1398 TREVISA *Barth. De P.R.* v. xxiv. (1495) 134 A beest
maye not wythout peryll be bretheles by longe space. **1675**
HOBBES *Odyss.* (1677) 66 Speechless and breathless as he,
like one dead. **1766** CHALKLEY *Wks.* 250, I had a Fit of the
Phthysick, and was at Times almost breathless.

b. Lifeless, dead. (L. *exanimatus*).

1595 SHAKS. *John* IV. iii. 66 Kneeling before this ruin of
sweete life, And breathing to his breathlesse Excellence The
Incense of a Vow. **1697** DRYDEN *Virg. Eclog.* v. 27 The
Nymphs about the breathless Body wait. **1708** J. PHILLIPS

Cyder I. 25 Guard each row With the false terrors of a
breathless kite. *a* **1819** J. HOGG *Flodden F.* xiii, The fated
arrow Breathless left the royal hero.

† c. *Gram.* Unaspirated. *Obs.*

1668 WILKINS *Real Char.* 379 [Dentals] Such as are
Breathless: Sonorous D, mute T.; *Breathing* . . Dh, Th.

2. Breathing with difficulty, panting (as a
result of swift running or violent exercise); out
of breath, exhausted, spent. Also *transf.* and *fig.*

c **1450** *Merlin* xviii. 299 She was so hoorse and so brethles
that on hire feet myght she not stonde. **1591** SPENSER *M.
Hubberd* 1374 He fled All breathles. **1597** BP. HALL *Sat.* I.
vi. (R.) The lingring Spondees, labouring to delay The
breathlesse Dactiles, with a sudden stay. **1709** *Tatler* No. 43
¶7 Breathless almost, and spent in the eager Chace. **1851**
LONGF. *Gold. Leg.* IV. (Nunnery) How I remember that
breathless flight.

b. Holding one's breath, as with awe,
expectation, excitement.

1802 WORDSW. *Sonn.* 'It is a beauteous Evening' 3 The holy
time is quiet as a nun Breathless with adoration. **1823** LAMB
Elia Ser. I. xv. (1865) 121 With a breathless impatience of
recognition. **1850** ALISON *Hist. Europe* VIII. liii. 397
Europe, in breathless suspense, awaited the issue.

3. Unstirred by a breath of wind.

1815 WORDSW. *Evening Volunt.* vi, The Mere Seems firm
as solid crystal, breathless, clear, And motionless. **1881**
MISS BRADDON *Asph.* I. 238 Blue skies and sunny noontides
. . without the baking heat and the breathless atmosphere.

breathlessly (ˈbrɛθlɪslɪ), *adv.* [f. prec. + -LY².]
In a breathless manner; with caught or
suspended breath; in breathless suspense.

1837 LYTTON *Athens* II. 565 Sophocles . . carries on the
passion of the spectators to wait breathlessly the moment
when Orestes shall be discovered. **1841** ORDERSON *Creol.*
xiii. 131 'Ah'! he exclaimed breathlessly. **1861** W. COLLINS
Dead Secr. 238 Looking stedfastly, speechlessly,
breathlessly, at her blind husband.

breathlessness (ˈbrɛθlɪsnɪs). [f. as prec. +
-NESS.] Breathless condition, want of breath.

1615 BP. HALL *Contempl. N.T.* IV. xxxiii, With much toil
and sweat and breathlessness. **1626** DONNE *Serm.* 39 The
Breathlessnesse of Death. **1870** MORRIS *Earthly Par.* III. IV.
191 They must stay A little while the eager play . . for very
breathlessness.

breathy (ˈbrɛθɪ), *a.* [f. BREATH + -Y¹.]
1. Of, pertaining to, or of the nature of breath.

1528 PAYNELL *Salerne Regim.* X. ij b, That hit comforteth
breathy membres. *a* **1598** PEELE *David & B.* 485 (D.) Help
thy Bethsabe, Whose heart is pierced with thy breathly
swords. **1603** FLORIO *Montaigne* II. xvi. (1632) 353 In this
breathie confusion of bruites, and frothy chaos of reports.
1605 TIMME *Quersit.* III. 163 The more thinne and breathie
part passe by insensible transpirations. **1635** SWAN *Spec. M.*
186 (L.) Lightning is less flamy and less breathy.

2. Of the voice in singing: Having an
admixture of the sound of breathing. Hence
ˈbreathiness.

1883 CURWEN *Stand. Course* 105/2 Some deep contralto
voices, though weak and breathy in the thin register. *Ibid.*
95/2 In the 'gradual' attack, the vocal membranes are
brought together *while* the breath is being emitted . . It
causes what we call 'breathiness'.

breawe, -is, obs. forms of BREW, BREWIS.

breaze, obs. form of BREEZE *sb.²*, light wind.

breborion, earlier form of BRIMBORION.

brec, obs. pres. and pa. t. of BREAK *v.*

breccan, obs. form of BRACKEN fern.

1669 SIMPSON *Hydrol. Chym.* 332 The ashes of breccans.

breccia (ˈbrɛttʃə, ˈbrɛtʃɪə). Also 8 brechia, 9
brecchia, bricia. [a. It. *breccia* 'gravel or rubbish
of broken walls' (Florio), cogn. with F. *brèche*
breaking, breach, breccia, Sp. *brecha*, adapted
from Teutonic: cf. OHG. *brecha* breaking, f.
brechan, OTeut *brekan* to BREAK. (Used in the
name *Breccia Marble*, before its separate use in
Geology.)]

a. *Geol.* A composite rock consisting of
angular fragments of stone, etc., cemented
together by some matrix, such as lime:
sometimes opposed to *conglomerate*, in which
the fragments are rounded and waterworn.
osseous or *bone breccia*: one in which fossil
bones are found.

1774 STRANGE in *Phil. Trans.* LXV. 38 Which the Italians
call *lava brecciata*, from its resemblance to the Breccia
marbles. **1781** J. T. DILLON *Trav. Spain* 362 A kind of
brechia or pudding-stone. **1784** WEDGWOOD *Phil. Trans.*
LXXIV. 378 It had the appearance of *breccia* marble or
plum-pudding stone. **1802** PLAYFAIR *Illustr. Hutton. Theory*
7 Those pudding-stones or breccias where the gravel
consists of quartz. **1818** SCOTT *Rob Roy* (1855) 244 Deep
gullies where masses of the composite rock or breccia
tumbling . . from the cliffs have rushed to the valley. **1836**
Penny Cycl. V. 374 The name of Breccia is derived from the
well-known Breccia marble, which has the appearance of
being composed of fragments joined together by carbonate
of lime. **1851** D. WILSON *Preh. Ann.* (1863) I. i. 29
Embedded in the same breccia with flint knives.

b. *transf.* A conglomerate of gravel and ice.

1856 KANE *Arct. Expl.* I. xi. 116 Stands of the same Arctic
breccia.

c. *fig.*

1873 L. STEPHEN *Freethinking* vi. 203 His prose, at excited
moments, becomes a kind of breccia of blank verse. **1944** H.

G. WELLS *'42 to '44* 149 With this sort of breccia in their
heads, these gentlemen seem able to sleep of nights without
ordinary narcotics.

Hence **ˈbreccial** *a.*, of or pertaining to breccia.

1853 KANE *Grinnell Exp.* xxx. (1856) 259 One solid
breccial mass of impacted angularities.

brecciated (ˈbrɛtʃɪeɪtɪd). Also 8 breciated, 9
brechiated. [f. BRECCIA; cf. It. *brecciato*, pa. pple.
of *brecciare* to reduce to breccia.] Formed into a
breccia, of the structure of a breccia.

1772 PENNANT *Tour Scotl.* (1774) 218 Some are breciated
or filled with crystalline kernels. **1789** MILLS in *Phil. Trans.*
LXXX. 86 The including chert, amongst which we found
some that is brecciated. **1830** LYELL *Elem. Geol.* (1865) 458
The well known brecciated limestone of the Pyrenees. **1875**
CROLL *Climate & T.* xviii. 294 The brecciated subangular
conglomerates and boulder beds of the Old Red Sandstone.

brecciation (brɛtʃɪˈeɪʃən). *Geol.* [f. BRECCIA +
-ATION.] The fragmentation of a rock; also, a
brecciated condition.

1873 *Q. Jrnl. Geol. Soc.* XXIX. 188 We . . arrive at the
conclusion that the contortion and the 'brecciation' of the
rocks are two totally distinct phenomena. **1917** *Jrnl. Geol.*
XXV. 161 A crackle breccia, representing incipient
brecciation, is one whose fragments are parted by planes of
fission and have suffered little or no relative displacement.
1932 A. HARKER *Metamorphism* xi. 165 The cataclastic
process may be modified . . in many ways. . . In what is
properly termed brecciation, the first stage in the
breaking-down process is a fragmentation . . the individual
elements of the breccia being not separate crystals but pieces
of rock. **1969** BENNISON & WRIGHT *Geol. Hist. Brit. Isles* viii.
164 The Mannacan Beds are regarded as probable
equivalents of the Meadfoot Beds but their brecciation and
the absence of fossils frustrate definite correlation. **1971** *Sci.
Amer.* Oct. 56/3 The brecciation is the result of a
catastrophic event, probably the impact of an asteroid-sized
object, that blasted out the Imbrium basin.

brech, -e, obs. form of BREACH, BREECH.

brecham (ˈbrɛxəm, ˈbrɛçəm). *Sc.* Also 6
brechome, 8 brechan, brechem, brechom. [By
metathesis f. *bercham, bergham*, ME. *berhom*: see
BARGHAM.] The collar of a draught-horse.

1501 DOUGLAS *Pal. Hon.* 426 Raw silk brechamis ouir
thair halsis hingis. **1566** *Inventories* 171 (JAM.) Auld
brechomes and hernes. **1756** MRS. CALDERWOOD *Jrnl.*
(1884) 67 A sort of brecham about their necks. **1792** *Statist.
Acc. Scotl.* IV. 395 The straw brecham is supplanted by the
leather collar. **1818** SCOTT *Hrt. Midl.* v, Ye have set yourself
down on the very brecham that wants stitching. **1883**
Glasgow Her. 8 Sept. 3/2 A collar which rises high and stiff
at the back of his neck resembling somewhat a horse's
'brecham'.

Brechtian (ˈbrɛçtɪən), *a.* and *sb.* [f. the name
Brecht (see def.) + -IAN.] **A.** *adj.* Of, pertaining
to, or characteristic of, the German playwright
and poet Bertolt Brecht (1898–1956) or his plays
or dramatic technique. **B.** *sb.* An admirer or
follower of Brecht.

1935 *Life & Letters Today* Sept. 66 The film . . lies
halfway between the Brechtian ideal and commercial
materialism. **1948** E. R. BENTLEY *Brecht's Private Life of
Master Race* 92 The Brechtian theatre has few technical
demands to make. *Ibid.* 93 The Brechtian characters are
without hate, without love. **1958** *Times* 10 Nov. 14/2 His
delight in Brechtian visual effects. **1959** *Observer* 15 Mar.
11/3 Her stagecraft is boldly Brechtian. **1959** *Times Lit.
Suppl.* 6 Nov. 637/1 'Relaxed' is a word which Brechtians
are especially fond of applying to the Master's style of
acting.

breck. Forms: 3–5 brek, 4–5 brekke, 5 breke,
5–6 brecke, 3–7 breck. [A parallel form of BREAK
sb.¹, or a direct derivation of *brec-* stem of BREAK
v.] **† 1.** A breach, blemish, failing. *Obs.*

a **1300** *Cursor M.* 6344 He drou þam vp at first, Wit-vten
ani brek or brist. *c* **1369** CHAUCER *Dethe of Blaunche* 940
Swiche a fairenesse of a nekke . . that boon nor brekke Nas
ther non seen that mys satte. **1413** LYDG. *Pylgr. Sowle* I. xv.
(1859) 13, I that am in this brecke perylous. **1573** TUSSER
Husb. (1878) 40 Saint Michel doth bid thee amend the
marsh wal, the brecke and the crab hole. **1642** FULLER *Holy
& Prof. St.* I. xiii. 41 No breck was ever found in her veil,
so spotlesse was her conversation. **1662** —— *Worthies* III. 38
Monuments . . remaining without breck or blemish to this
day.

2. = BREAK *sb.¹* 12. Also *attrib.*; **Breckland**, a
name given to the region of brecks in Norfolk.

1787 MARSHALL *Rur. Econ. E. Norfolk, Breck* . . a large
new-made inclosure. **1837** *Penny Cycl.* VIII. 282/1 The
naked brecks (or undulating downs) of Norfolk. **1840** *Jrnl.
R. Agric. Soc.* I. IV. 360 The first damside breck meadow on
the plan. **1863** MORTON *Cycl. Agric.* II, *Breck* (Norf., Suff.),
a large field. In Northumb., etc., a portion of a field
cultivated by itself. **1879** LUBBOCK *Fauna of Norfolk* Introd.
p. viii, On the 'Breck' district the lordly Bustard roamed.
1894 *Naturalists' Jrnl.* Oct. 90 The 'brecks' . . are the upland
heaths and huge fields of this district [*sc.* south-west
Norfolk]. *Ibid.*, We at length reach a typical breckland wild
—Roudham Heath. **1897** W. RYE *Songs of Norfolk* 124 Such
cramped wild country, half rough breck land and half
marsh. **1956** O. COOK *Breckland* 59 Many of the Breckland
cottages . . have no gardens. . . This is typical of Breckland.

breck, obs. pres. and pa. t. of BREAK.

† bred. *Obs.* exc. *dial.* Forms: 2 breod, 3 brid,
3–5 brede, 6 *Sc.* breid. [Common Teut.: OE.
bred, corresp. to MDu. *bert(d-)*, Du. *berd*, OHG.
bret, Ger. *brett*:—OTeut. *bredo(m, a doublet of
*bordo(m BOARD, the two forms corresponding to

Skr. **bradha-*, **brdha-*, Aryan *'*bhredho-*, **bhr'dho-*: see BOARD.] A board; a tablet; in mod. Sc. applied to a bakeboard, and to the wooden lid of a pot, pan, water-butt, etc. (e.g. *a pan-bred*).

a **1000** ÆLFRIC *Deut.* ix. 9 Ða astah ic on þone munt, & bær þa stænenan bredu. *c* **1175** *Lamb. Hom.* 11 Þas þreo laȝe ȝewriten inne þa oðre table breode. *a* **1300** *Cursor M.* 16578 Apon þe hefd o þis rode, ouer-thwart was don a brede. *c* **1325** *E.E. Allit. P.* C. 184 He [Jonah] watz flowen..In-to þe boþem of þe bot, & on a brede lyggede. *c* **1440** *Promp. Parv.* 48 Brede, or lytylle borde, *mensula*, *tabella*, *asserulus*. **1538** *Aberd. Reg.* V. 16 (JAM.) Twa baikbreddis. **1688** HOLME *Armory* III. iii. 104 A Braide or Braed which is a broad long Board, with a hole in one end of it..upon this Cooks..carry Bread unbaked, to and from the Bake-House. **1808** JAMIESON *Sc. Dict.*, *Pot-bred*, the wooden lid of a pot. *Ass-bred* [ash-board].

b. *Comb.* † **bred-cheese**, some kind of cheese.

c **1440** *Promp. Parv.* 48/2 Bredechese [*v.r.* bredchese], *jumtata* [*junctata*].

bred (brɛd), *ppl. a.*[1] [Pa. pple. of BREED *v.*]

† **1.** Developed in the womb; hatched from the egg; brought forth. *Obs.*

c **1440** *Promp. Parv.* 48 Bredde or hecchyd, of byrdys [**1499** hetched], *pullificatus*. **1570** LEVINS *Manip.* 48 Bredde, *genitus*, *ortus*.

2. Reared, brought up, (properly) trained.

1655 GURNALL *Chr. in Arm.* vii. §1 (1669) 500/1 Paul was a bred scholar. **1711** ADDISON *Spect.* No. 108 ¶3 Being bred to no Business and born to no estate. **1719** LOUDON & WISE *Compl. Gard.* p. xxvii, The Trees or Plants to be there planted, ought to be handsome bred Plants. **1846** McCULLOCH *Acc. Brit. Empire* (1854) I. 165 The sheep bred in the county. **1863** FR. KEMBLE *Resid. Georgia* 124 Born and bred in America. **1873** MORLEY *Rousseau* I. 193 Bred in puritan and republican tradition.

b. Chiefly in *comb.*: (*a*) with sb., as ***country-***, ***court-***, ***farm-***, ***town-bred***; (*b*) with advs., as ***ill-***, ***well-bred***, of bad or good breeding.

1670 EACHARD *Cont. Clergy* 52 A town bred or country-bred similitude, it is worth nothing. **1760** GOLDSM. *Cit. W.* xciii, Court-bred poets. **1766** —— *Vic. W.* xi, A small stipend for a well-bred girl. **1845** FORD *Handbk. Spain* i. 29 No nation..is better bred or mannered than the lower classes of Spaniards. **1871** BLACKIE *Four Phases* i. 65 [This] would..be considered extremely ill-bred. **1884** BLACK *Jud. Shaks.* xxviii, The..awkwardness of a farm-bred wench.

3. Of animals: Of good breed. So with reference to the comparative purity of the breed: ***thorough-bred***, ***half-bred***, ***three-parts-bred***, etc.

1710 *Lond. Gaz.* No. 4677/4 Their Horses seem to have been bred Horses. **1787** 'G. GAMBADO' *Acad. Horsem.* (1809) 20 Nothing now is to be seen but bred horses. **1859** JEPHSON *Brittany* iii. 29 Thorough-bred horses in stalls.

¶ ***bred and born***: see BREED *v.* 10.

† **bred**, *ppl. a.*[2] [pa. pple. of BREDE *v.*[2]] Outspread; extended.

? *a* **1500** *Battle of Otterbourne* 91 (Percy *Reliques*) He durste not loke on my bred banner.

bred(d, var. of BRAID, BREDE; pa. t. of BREDE *v.*

bred(e, **bredd(e**, obs. ff. BIRD *sb.*, BREAD, BREED.

bredale, **bredeale**, obs. ff. BRIDAL.

bredbergite ('brɛdbəgaɪt). *Min.* [f. the name of B. G. *Bredberg*, who first described it: see -ITE[1].] A name given by J. D. Dana in 1868 to a variety of andradite found at Sala, Sweden, which contains a large amount of magnesium.

1868 DANA *Syst. Min.* (ed. 5) 270 Lime-Magnesia Iron-garnet; Bredbergite.

bredden, obs. form of BREADEN *adj.*

† **brede**, *sb.*[1] *Obs.* Forms: 1 **brǽde**, **bréde**, 2–5 **brede**; also 3 **brade**, **bread(e**, 6 *Sc.* **breid**. [OE. *brǽde*, Angl. *bréde*, f. OTeut. **brǣd-an*, BREDE *v.*[1], to roast. A synonymous derivative of the same root was WGer. *brâdon-*, OHG. *brâto* (Ger. *braten*) roast flesh, whence Romanic *bradon*, OF. *braon*, Eng. BRAWN.]

Roast meat. *Obs.* (but cf. SWEETBREAD.)

a **1000** *Gloss.* in Wr.-Wülcker 127 *Assura*, uel *assatura*, bræde. *c* **1205** LAY. 30583 He nom his aȝe þeh..þer of he makede brede [**1250** breade]. *a* **1250** *Moral Ode* in *Trin. Coll. Hom.* 224 Swines brade is wel swete. *a* **1250** *Owl & Night.* 1630 Me mai mid me biȝete Wel gode brede to his mete. *c* **1300** *K. Alis.* 5249 Beef and motoun, Bredes, breddes, and venysoun. ? *a* **1400** *Morte Arth.* 1049 Þare ware rostez fulle ruyde, and rewfulle bredez. *c* **1420** *Avow. Arth.* xxxi, Bothe the birds and the brede, To Carlele thay bringe. [**1535** STEWART *Cron. Scotl.* (1858) I. 87 Gif ony beist..war slane, Ilk craftisman thairof to haif ane breid.]

† **brede**, *sb.*[2] *Obs.* exc. *north. dial.* Forms: 1 **brædu**, **-o** (acc. **brǽde**), 2–3 **bræde**, **breade**, 3–7 **brede**, (4 **brade**, 5 **brēd**), 4–6 **breede**, 6–7 **breed**, **breade**, (7 **braid**), 5– *Sc.* **breid**, (6 **breyde**). [OE. *brǽdu*, *-o*; corresp. to OFris. *brêde*, LG. *brêde*, OHG. *breitî*, MHG. and mod.G *breite*, ON. *breidd* (Sw. *bred*, Da. *brede*), Goth. *braidei*: —OTeut. **braidjôn-*, abstr. sb. f. **braido-z*, in OE. *brâd* BROAD. In the 16th c. it began to be spelt *breade*, but this form was not established before the word was itself superseded in Eng. use by the new formation *bredeth*, BREADTH. *Brede* still survives in north Eng. dialects, and in Sc., where it is usually written *breid* (brid): cf. ABREID.]

1. Breadth, width.

a **1000** *Ags. Psalms* cxvii[iix]. 45 Ic on bealde brædu [Vulg. *in latitudine*] gange. **1297** R. GLOUC. 385þat folc of Ssropssyre..robbede Wurcestre ssyre in lengþe & in brede. *c* **1320** *Syr Bevis* 536 Neither alingthe ne on brade. *c* **1380** WYCLIF *Sel. Wks.* III. 89 Twenti cubitis longe and ten of breede. *c* **1400** MAUNDEV. ix. 100 In brede 150 Furlonges. **1562** J. HEYWOOD *Prov. & Epigr.* (1867) 142 Not the breade of one heare. **1551** TURNER *Herbal* (1568) B j a, The stalke is a hand brede hygher. **1875** ROBINSON *Whitby Gloss.* s.v., 'Quite full abrede', sufficient in breadth.

b. ***acre brede***: the breadth of an acre, i.e. 4 poles or perches, also called a ***fur-brede*** (cf. *furlong*). A *brede* of underwood, etc.: a slice of an acre-brede, or 4 poles broad, by 1 pole long.

c **1470** HENRY *Wallace* I. 400 Þe suerd flaw fra hym a fur breid on ye land. **1523** LD. BERNERS *Froiss.* I. ccccxx. 736 One coulde nat se an acre of brede. **1525** *Ibid.* II. clxxxvii. [clxxxiv.] 573 An acre brede of lande of fro the kynge. **1677** PLOT *Oxfordsh.* 262 Dividing them..into Acres and Braids (or bredths), every Acre containing forty braids, a braid being one pole long and four broad.

2. A piece of stuff of the full breadth.

1554 *Bury Wills* (1850) 144 Oon paire of fyne shetis of ij bredes and a halfe, and oon paier of two bredes. **1578** *Inventories* (1815) 211 (JAM.) Of claith of silver..contening threttie lang breiddis, sevin schort breidis. **1855** *Whitby Gloss*, *Breeds*, breadths of cloth. *Mod. Sc.* How monie breids will ye put in the skirt?

3. ***in, on, a brede***, mod. Sc. A-BREID: abroad.

[*c* **1205** LAY. 21995 He is imeten a bræde fif & twenti foten.] *a* **1300** *E.E. Psalter* cxviii [ix]. 45, I yhode in brede. *c* **1400** *Destr. Troy* 3022 The here of hir hede..bost out vppon brede bright on to loke. *c* **1460** *Towneley Myst.* (1836) 1 Make we hevene and erth, on brede. **1526** *Pilgr. Perf.* W. de W. 1531) 208 b, In brede it extended the armes. **1535** STEWART *Cron. Scot.* II. 610 Tha landis all on breid. **1787** BURNS *Salut. Auld Mare* xii, Spread abreed thy weelfill'd brisket. **1816** SCOTT *Antiq.* II. 245 (JAM.) The prophecy got abread in the country.

brede (briːd), *sb.*[3] *arch.* Also 7 **breade**, **bred**, 8 **breed**, **bread**. [A variant of BRAID *sb.*, in 16–17th c. *bread*(*e*; used archaically by modern poets. Cf. BREDE *v.*[3]]

1. Anything plaited, entwined, or interwoven; a plait; interweaving, braiding, embroidery; = BRAID *sb.* 4.

1643 MILTON *Divorce* I. vi. (1851) 33 His silk'n breades untwine, and slip their knots. **1689** *Lond. Gaz.* No. 2444/4 He had on..a blew Rateen Wastcoat with Silver Brede. **1697** DRYDEN *Ess. Georg.*, *Virg.* (1721) I. 201 A curious Brede of Needle-work. **1820** KEATS *Lamia* 1, Spoilt all her silver mail and golden brede. **1847** TENNYSON *Princ.* VI. 118 In glowing gauze and golden brede. **1861** LOWELL *Washers of Shroud* iv, The ancient Three..Still crooning, as they weave their endless brede.

2. A twist or plait of hair: see BRAID, *sb.* 4 b.

1696 KENNETT *Rom. Antiq.* II. IV. (1713) 253 They made use of a twist or brede of hair. *a* **1721** PRIOR *Henry & E.* 426 Thy comely tresses..In graceful breeds, with various ribbon bound. **1740** SOMERVILLE *Hobbinol* iii. (1749) 163 Her plaited Hair behind her in a Brede Hung careless.

3. Applied by the poets to things that show or suggest interweaving of colours, or embroidery, *esp.* to the prismatic colouring of the rainbow. But used by some modern writers in sense of 'colouring, dye', apparently from misunderstanding their predecessors.

1708 J. PHILIPS *Cyder* II. 67 The show'ry Arch, With lifted Colours gay..Delights, and puzles the Beholders Eye, That views the watry Brede. **1744** AKENSIDE *Pleas. Imag.* II. 118 Thro' the brede Of colours changing from the splendid rose To the pale violet's dejected hue. **1867** JEAN INGELOW *Story of Doom* I. 21 The almug, and the gophir shot their heads Into the crimson brede that dyed the world. **1869** LOWELL *Seaweed* iv, The same wave that rims the Carib shore With momentary brede of pearl and gold.

4. *Comb.* **brede-stitch** (improp. *bred-*, *bread-*).

1640 J. TAYLOR (Water P.) *Praise Needle* (ed. 12) Pref., Chain-Stitch, Brane Bred-stitch, Fishes-stitch, Irish-stitch, Queen-stitch. **1766** GOLDSM. *Vic. W.* xi, They understand their needle, breadstitch..and all manner of plainwork.

brede, *v.*[1] *Obs.* Forms: 1 **brǽdan**, **brédan**, 2–5 **brede(n**. *Pa. t.* 1 **brǽdde**, **brédde**, 2–4 **bradde**, 2–5 **bredde**. *Pa. pple.* 1 **brǽded**, **brǽdd**, 2–3 **brad**, 3–4 **bred(d**. [Common Teut.: OE. *brǽdan* (Angl. *brédan*) = OFris. *brêda*, MDu. *brâden* (Du. *braden*) str. vb., OHG. *brâtan* (MHG. *brâten*, mod.G. *braten*), str. vb. 'to roast'. OTeut. **brǣd-an* was apparently a derivative (Aryan type *bhrē-dh-*) of the verb root **brǣ-*, **brê-* (Aryan **bhrē-*) to burn, heat, warm: see BREATH, BROOD. No traces of the strong inflexions are found in OE., and the vb. passed entirely out of use *c* 1500. See also BREDE *sb.*[1]] *trans.* To roast, broil, toast.

a **1000** *Colloq. Monast.* 29 (Bosw.) We maȝon brædan ða þing ðe to brædenne synd. *c* **1175** *Lamb. Hom.* 53 He bindeð vppon þa [mousetrap] swike chese and bret hine for þon þet he scolde swote smelle. *c* **1205** LAY. 25986 His flæsce he gon breden. *a* **1225** *Juliana* 170 In led we scholle hire brede. *a* **1300** *Cursor M.* 6081 It sal noght siþen be bot bred, þis lamb. *c* **1325** *Coer de L.* 1492 Makes our mete Whether ȝe wole sethe or brede. *c* **1330** *Arth. & Merl.* 9305 Man and hous thai brent and bredden. *c* **1340** *Gaw. & Gr. Knt.* 891 Summe [fishes] brad on þe gledez. **1509** *Parl. Devylles* xii, I wyll..in hell his soule brede.

† **brede**, *v.*[2] *Obs.* or *dial.* Forms: 1 **brǽdan**, 2–5 **brede(n**, 3–7 **brede**, 6–7 **breade**, *mod. dial.* **bread**, **brede**, etc. *Pa. t.* 1 **brǽdde**, 3 **bræd**, 4 **brad**, **-de**, 4–6 **bred**, 5 **bret**, 9 **brad**. [Common Teut.: OE. *brǽdan*, corresp. to OS. *brêdian*, OHG. *breiten* (MHG. and mod.G *breiten*), ON. *breiða* (Sw. *breda*, Da. *brede*), Goth. *braidjan*, to make broad, f. *braid-s*, in OE. *brád*, BROAD.]

1. *trans.* To make broad; to broaden, dilate.

c **890** K. ÆLFRED *Bæda* I. viii. (Bosw.) Hi heora stowe bræddon. *c* **1440** *Promp. Parv.* 49 Bredyn or make more brode, *dilato*. **1674** RAY *N.C. Wds.* 8 *Breade*, to make broad, to spread.

2. *trans.* To spread out, spread about, extend.

c **1325** *E.E. Allit. P.* A. 813 For vus he lette hym..brede vpon a bostwys bem. *c* **1340** *Cursor M.* 534 As onde wiþ host in brest is bred [*Cott.* spred]. *c* **1420** *Pallad. on Husb.* XI. 101 Let brede hem, lest thai hete and be the wers. ? *a* **1600** *Scot. Field* 24 in Furniv. *Percy Folio* I. 213 On this side Bosworthe in a bancke thei bred forth their standards. **1802** J. WILSON (Congleton) *MS. Let. to J. Boucher*, Bread or brede Manure, i.e. to fling it about and spread it on the Land, is a very common Expression here; and also the Participle, as, They have brad it.

3. *intr.* To spread, extend.

c **1320** *K. Alis.* 3252 Thorugh the heorte brede the steil. *c* **1340** *Gaw. & Gr. Knt.* 1928 He were a bleaunt of blwe, þat bradde to þe erþe. *c* **1400** *Destr. Troy* 8794 The bavme . bret thurgh the bones..euer folowand the fell. **1600** DYMMOK *Ireland* (1843) 16 Thence yt [East Meath] breadeth to the Kinges county and the countie of Kildare.

4. *trans.* To overspread, cover; spread (a table).

c **1205** LAY. 18523 Bordes heo brædden. al þat folc æt & dronc. *c* **1325** *E.E. Allit. P.* B 1693 His berde I-brad alle his breste to þe bare vrþe. *c* **1400** *Destr. Troy* 383 Burdes were bred in the brade halle. *Ibid.* 1172 Þan rises þe sun, bredis with his beames all þe brode vales.

† **brede**, *v.*[3] *Obs.* In 6–7 **bread**. [A var. of BRAID *v.*: cf. the sb. BREDE[3].] *trans.* To intertwine, plait, wreathe, twist; = BRAID *v.* 11.

c **1440** *Promp. Parv.* 49 Bredynge of lacys or oþer lyke, *laqueacio*, *nectio*, *connectio*. **1501** DOUGLAS *Pal. Hon.* III. lxviii, The durris and the windois all war breddit With massie gold. **1596** SPENSER *F.Q.* III. ii. 50 Taking thrise three heares from off her head, Them trebly breaded in a threefold lace. **1686** GOAD *Celest. Bodies* III. iii. 475 They are Plaited and Breaded in the same Twine. **1695** BLACKMORE *Pr. Arth.* IX. 305 He slashed his breaded Whip.

breded, **breden**, obs. pa. t. and pple. of BREED.

breder, **-ir**, **-ur**, **-yr**, obs. pl. of BROTHER.

bredeth(e, **bredth(e**, obs. ff. BREADTH.

bredie ('briːdɪ). *S. Afr.* Also **breedi**. [Afrikaans, from Malagasy.] A stew of meat and vegetables.

1815 A. PLUMPTRE tr. *Lichtenstein's Trav. S. Afr.* II. xxxiii. 82 *Breedi* signifies in the Madagascar tongue *Spinage*; the word is brought hither by the slaves, and at present, throughout the whole colony, every sort of vegetable which, like cabbage, spinage, or sorrel, is cut to pieces and dressed with Cayenne pepper, is included under the general term *Breedi*. **1870** *Cape Monthly Mag.* Oct. 224 All sorts of vegetable '*breedies*', are importations from India. **1947** L. G. GREEN *Tavern of Seas* (1952) viii. 59 She made every variety of bredie, the stews that the Malays brought to the Cape; especially the tamatie bredie.

bredigite ('briːdɪgaɪt). *Min.* [f. the name of M. A. *Bredig* (b. 1902), German-born American chemist: see -ITE[1].] A mineral consisting of the metastable orthorhombic phase of dicalcium silicate.

1948 TILLEY & VINCENT in *Min. Mag.* XXVIII. 257 It is in recognition of Bredig's important contribution to the solution of the problem of calcium orthosilicate polymorphism that it is proposed to designate the new mineral phase bredigite. **1966** *Amer. Min.* LI. 1766 The α' (bredigite), β (larnite) and γ (unnamed) forms of dicalcium silicate (Ca_2SiO_4) occur together in the contact zone around a syenite-monozonite intrusion in Marble Canyon.

† '**breding**, *vbl. sb. Obs.* [f. BREDE *v.*[2] + -ING[1].] Broadening, spreading out.

c **1440** *Promp. Parv.* 49 Bredynge or makynge brode, *dilatacio*.

bredling: see BROADLING.

† **bree** (briː), *sb.*[1] *Obs.* exc. *north. dial.* Forms: 1 **brǽw**, **bréaw**, 3 *pl.* **breow-en**, 4–5 *pl.* **brew-is**, 5 *pl.* **bren**; also 1 **bréaȝ**, **bréȝ** (**-éȝh**, **-éhȝ**), 3 **breyh**, 3–4 **breȝe**, **breye**, *pl.* **briȝ-es**, 5 *pl.* **bregh-is**, **briys**, 6 **bryes**, *Sc.* **breis**, 5–6 **bre**, 6–7 **brie**, 5– **bree**. [OE. *brǽw*, *bréaw*, Anglian **bréw*, *bréȝ*, *bréaȝ*, masc. 'eye-lid'; according to Sievers, an *i-* stem, OTeut. type **brǣ'wi-*, *brǣ'hwi-*; cf. OFris. (*âg-*)*brê*, neut.: the corresponding word elsewhere is a fem. *â-* stem, OS. *brâwa*, *brâha* (LG. *braue*, MDu. *brauwe*, Du. *wenkbraauw* eye-brow), OHG. *brâwa*, *brâa*, *brâ*, eye-lash (MHG. *brâwe*, *brâ*, Ger. (*augen-*)*braue* eye-brow, also *-braune*, a modern corruption from the pl. *brâwen*, *brauen*, *braun*), ON. *brá*, *brǫ́* eye-lid:—OTeut. **brǣwâ*, from **brǣhwâ*. The Gothic **brêwa*, **brêhwa* is not preserved; but cf. *brahw* 'blink, twinkle', *in brahwa augins* 'in the twinkling of an eye'. This points to a radical

sense 'blinker, twinkler' as a name of the eye-lid (or eye-lash), in which case this word cannot well be referred to the same root as BROW, OTeut. *brû-* 'eye-brow', as generally assumed. Yet the two words curiously interchanged in use in different langs., and at different periods; and in continental WGer. the *brû-* forms were lost, and their place supplied by forms from *brǣwâ-*. The original sense of *brû-* was 'eye-brow'; in OE. extended and transferred to 'eye-lash', so that 'eye-brow' was distinguished as *ofer-brú*. The original sense of *brǣwâ-* was app. 'eye-lid', as in ON. and OE., but in OHG. restricted to 'eye-lash', and thence subsequently extended and transferred to 'eye-brow' (orig. *obara brâwa*), the sense 'eye-lash' being brought down to modern times by the compound *wint-brâwa*, MHG. *wint-brâ, winbrâ*, mod.Ger. *wimper*. OE. had *brú* = eye-lash (*cilium*), *brǣw, bréȝ* = eye-lid (*palpebra*); by the 13th c. *bru, brouw* passed to the sense 'eye-lid', and *brew* (*breow, breȝ, bree*) to that of 'eye-brow'; the latter sense was retained by *bree* in the north, after it had in turn been taken up by *brow* in the south. From 15th to 17th c. *bree* was used by some southern writers as = 'eye-lash', a curious reversion to what had been the original OE. sense of *brú*, BROW, q.v. (The ON. cognate *brǭ* gave BRAE.)

(The parallelism of **brû-* and **brǣwâ-* is further seen in the fact that 'eye-brows' was expressed in OHG. by *obarun brâwa, ubarbrâwo* (Graff III. 315), in OE. by *oferbrúa*, and in ME. *uvere breyhes, briȝes aboue þe eiȝes, aboue breghis*. For the phonetic explanation of the late WS. form *bréaw* from *brǣw*, see Sievers *Ags. Gram.* (ed. 2) §112, 118.)]

†**1.** The lid of the eye, the eye-lid. (In Layamon the *breow* of the first text is displaced by *brouw*, BROW in the second text.) *Obs.*

c **890** K. ÆLFRED *Bæda* IV. xxxii. § 1 (Bosw.) Unwlitiȝ swile .. his eaȝan breȝh [*palpebram oculi*] wyrde. *a* **1000** *Ags. Psalter* cxxxi[i]. 4 Gif ic .. minum breawum beode hnappunga. *c* **1000** *Sax. Leechd.* II. 38 Wiþ piccum bræwum ȝenim þreo hand fulla mucwyrte. *c* **1000** ÆLFRIC *Gloss.* in Wr.-Wülcker 156/38 *Palpebræ*, breawas. *c* **1205** LAY. 18374 þa hing his breowen adun [*c* **1275** þo heng he his brouwes adun].

2. The eye-brow: sometimes the hair, sometimes including the superciliary ridge. (Distinguished at first as *uvere breyh, briȝes above the eiȝes, aboue breghis*: since Wyclif, only *north.*: still *Sc.*)

c **1275** *XI Pains of Hell* 98 in *O.E. Misc.* 150 Sume to heore myd-þeyh, And sume to heore vuere breyh. *c* **1375** —— (*Vernon MS.*) 111 *ibid.* 226 þo þat weren vp to þe briȝes In þat flod aboue þe eiȝes. **1388** WYCLIF *Lev.* xiv. 9 That .. he shaue the heeris of the heed, and the beerd, and brewis [*supercilia*]. *c* **1400** *Destr. Troy* 3780 Blake horit aboue breghis and other Serklyt of hom seluyn. *c* **1420** *Anturs of Arth.* xxx, Bore-hedis of blakke, and brees full bold. *c* **1420** *Avow. Arth.* xxvii, Gauan bare him fro his stede, That both his brees con blede. *c* **1485** *Digby Myst.* (Mor. Wisd.) 196 For sorowe my bren I knette. **1513** DOUGLAS *Æneis* VI. vii. 96 Hir ene fixit apon the ground held sche, Moving na mair hir curage, face nor bre. **1517** HAWES *Past. Pleas.* xxix. ii, His head was greate, beteled was his browes .. His bryes brystled truely lyke a sowes. **1550** LYNDESAY *Sqr. Meldr.* 1293 He hat the Knicht abone the breis. **1768** ROSS *Helenore* (1789) 74 (JAM.) They .. lay stane still, not moving ee nor bree. *Mod. Sc.* He is dirt up to the very ee-brees.

†**3.** An eye-lash. *Obs.*

c **1450** *Voc.* in Wr.-Wülcker 631 *Cilium*, [gloss] brye. **1482** *Monk of Evesham* (Arb.) 23 The briys of hys ye lyddys beganne firste a lytil to moue. **1530** PALSGR. 201/1 Bree of the eye, *poil de loiel*. **1656** DUGARD *Gate Lat. Unl.* §205. 57 The brees (growing out of the edg of the ey-lids) .. hinder, that nothing may fall thereinto.

bree (briː), *sb.*[2] *Obs.* exc. *Sc.* Forms: 1 briw, 2 bri, 4–5 bre, 8– bree. [Derivation obscure: the ME. *bre* mod.Sc. *bree*, may be the same as the earlier ME. *bri*, OE. *briȝ, briw*, but the phonology is not clear, and the sense is not quite identical. (*Bre* might however represent **bréow*, a possible variant of *bríw*; cf. *níw, néow*, etc.) OE. *bríw, briȝ* masc. = OHG. *brîo* (*brîw-*), *brî* (MHG. *brîe, brî*, mod.Ger. *brei*), MLG. *brîg, brî*, MDu. *brî*, all masc. (Du. *brij* fem.):—OTeut. **brîwo-z*: the Goth. **breiws* is not exemplified, and the word is not in Scand. It cannot well be referred to *brŭ̆*, root of BREW, nor to *brǣ-, brê-*, to warm; Kluge suggests a root *bri* to cook.]

†**1.** A thick pottage made of meal, pulse, etc. *Obs.*

c **1000** *Sax. Leechd.* II. 88 Swa þicce swa briw. *Ibid.* 264 Wyrc him briw of wealwyrte moran. *c* **1000** ÆLFRIC *Gram.* ix. §46 *Hæc puls*, ðes briw. *a* **1200** *Voc.* in Wr.-Wülcker 547/12 *Puls*, bri.

2. Broth, juice, liquor in which anything has been steeped or boiled, or which flows from it. ***barley-bree***: malt liquor. ***herring-bree***: herring-brine. Also *fig.*

c **1420** *Liber Cocorum* 17 Perboyle thyn oysturs .. Kepe welle thy bre. *Ibid.* 49 In fat bre fresshe of befe I wene, þay schalle be soþun. **1786** BURNS *Sc. Drink* xiii, How easy can the barley-bree Cement the quarrel! **1861** RAMSAY *Remin.* Ser. II. 90 We wring't [the Lord's Prayer], an' we wring 't, an' the bree o't washes a' the lave o' our prayers. **1865** *Times* 22 Apr., 'Snow bree' is unfavourable to angling.

†**3.** *fig.* Water; the sea. *Obs.*

c **1400** *Destr. Troy* 3697 So þe bre and the brethe burbelit to gedur. *Ibid.* 12516 All the company .. With þere shippes .. were brent in the bre with the breme lowe of the leymonde laite, þat launchit fro heuyn.

bree, *sb.*[3] *north. dial.* [perh. an erroneous form from BREEZE *sb.*[2], sense 4: cf. next word.]

Disturbance, commotion, disagreement.

1790 SHIRREF *Poems* 67 (JAM.) Ye'll .. see It thro' the parish raise an unco bree. **1807** STAGG *Poems* 8 They're off wi' seck a bree. **1821** MRS. WHEELER *Westmrld. Dial.* 88 We hed a sort of a bree ont afore ea went.

bree, *sb.*[4] obs. or dial. form of BREEZE *sb.*[1] gadfly. A singular inferred from *brees*, taken as pl.

1678 A. LITTLETON *Lat. Dict.*, A bree, *asilus, tabanus*.

†**bree**, *v. Obs.* exc. *dial.* Also 4 bre, 5 *Sc.* brey. [OE. *bréȝan* to terrify, frighten (:—*bróegan*) f. *bróga* fear, terror; cf. OHG. *bruogen*.]

1. *trans.* To terrify, affright, scare.

c **1000** *Ags. Gosp.* Luke xii. 4 Ne beo ȝe breȝyde fram þam þe þone lichaman of-sleað. —— xxiv. 22 Sume wif .. us breȝdon þa wæron ær leohte æt þære byrȝene. *c* **1425** WYNTOUN *Cron.* VI. iv. 36 A Serpent .. breyd þame all standand þare-by. *c* **1505** DOUGLAS *K. Hart* I. xxiv, It culd thame bre, and biggit thame to byde. **1674** RAY *N.-C. Wds.* 8 *Bree*, to frighten. **1750** J. COLLIER (Tim Bobbin) *Wks.* 51 I'r so feerfully breed at meh hure stood on eend. **1875** in *Lanc. Gloss.* (E.D.S.) 55 He was fair breed.

2. ? *intr.* To be terrified.

c **1375** ? BARBOUR *St. Theodera* 15 Befor þe croice he [the devil] sa breis þat, quhene he It seis, þane he fleis.

breead, dial. form of BRAID *v.*

breech (briːtʃ), *sb.* Forms: 1 bréc, (bræc), 3 brych, 3–5 brech, 4–6 breche, 4–7 breeche, 6 breache, briech, bryche, 6–7 breetch, 7 brich, 7– britch, 9 breach, 5– breech. [Com. Teut.: OE. *bréc* (:—*bróec*), pl. of **bróc* fem. = OFris. *brók*, pl. *brék*, (MDu. *broec*, Du. *broek*), OHG. *bruoh* (MHG. *bruoch*, mod.Ger. *bruch*, obs. in 18th c., but still in Switz. pl. *brüch*), ON. *brók*, pl. *brœkr* (Sw. *brōk*, Da. *brōg*):—OTeut. type **brôk-s* fem. monosyl. 'article of clothing for the loins and thighs'.

Often stated to be an adoption of L. *brāca* (also *brăca, bracca*), or its Gaulish original, which was app. **brăcca*, (see BROGUE) clothing for the legs ('barbara tegmina crurum' Vergil *Æn.* XI. 777); but **brôk-s* has all the marks of an original Teutonic word = Aryan **bhrâg-s*. The Celtic *brăcca* is considered by Dr. Whitley Stokes to be phonetically descended from an earlier **brăg-na*, a derivative of the same root *bhrăg-*, and so cognate with the Teutonic.]

†**1.** A garment covering the loins and thighs: at first perh. only a 'breech-cloth'; later reaching to the knees.

a. in OE. *bréc*, plural of *bróc*.

a **1000** *Reg. St. Benot* 55 (Bosw.) Brec, *femoralia*. *a* **1100** *Voc.* in Wr.-Wülcker 328 *Femoralia*, bræc.

b. in ME. usually *brēch, breech* as a sing.

a **1100** *Cott. Cleop. Gloss.* in Wr.-Wülcker 433 *Lumbare*, gyrdel oððe brec. *a* **1225** *Ancr. R.* 420 Sum wummon .. wereð þe brech of heare ful wel i-knotted. *c* **1380** WYCLIF *Serm.* Sel. Wks. II. 3 Joon hadde neiþer coote ne breche. *c* **1400** MAUNDEV. xxiii. (1839) 250 Alle the women weren Breech, as wel as men. **1480** CAXTON *Chron. Eng.* cci. 183 The good man .. come thyder al naked sauf his breche. **1535** COVERDALE *Jer.* xiii. 1 Get the a lynnen breche, and gyrde it aboute thy loynes. **1562** J. HEYWOOD *Prov. & Epigr.* (1867) 16 To beg a breeche of a bare arst man. **1642** *Jack Puffe* 39 in Hazl. *E.P.P.* IV. 316 With out-stucke bomm, streight breech, and spit at side.

c. Now always in pl. **breeches** (ˈbrɪtʃɪz), or *a pair of breeches* (perh. not so used before 15th c.). *Breeches* are distinguished from *trousers* by coming only just below the knee, but dialectally (and humorously) *breeches* includes *trousers*.

[*c* **1205** LAY. 18028 Heo .. gripen heore cniues & of mid here breches. **1382** WYCLIF *Gen.* iii. 7 They soweden to gidre leeves of a fige tree, & maden hem brechis.] *a* **1500** *Voc.* in Wr.-Wülcker 629 *Bracce*, brechys. **1555** *Fardle Facions* I. iv. 41 Some make them brieches of the heares of their heades. **1560** BIBLE (Genev.) *Gen.* iii. 7 They sewed figge tree leaues together, and made themselues breeches. **1591** SPENSER *M. Hubberd* 211 His breeches were made after the new cut. **1661** PEPYS *Diary* 6 Apr., To put both his legs through one of his knees of his breeches. **1784** COWPER *Task* I. 10 As yet black breeches were not. **17..** *Chestnut Horse*, Dreamed of his boots, his spurs, his leather breeches, Of leaping five-barred gates, and crossing ditches. **1858** HAWTHORNE *Fr. & It. Jrnls.* II. 179 Their trousers being tucked up till they were strictly breeches.

2. a. Hence the phrase, said of a wife, ***to wear the breeches*** (***breech*** obs.): to assume the authority of the husband; to rule, be 'master'.

[**1553** T. WILSON *Rhet.* 89 As though the good man of the house weare no breeches or that the Graye Mare were the better horse.] **1568** T. HOWELL *Newe Sonn.* (1879) 151 He is a cokes: and worthy strokes, whose wife the Breeches beare. **1593** SHAKS. *3 Hen. VI*, v. v. 24 That you might still haue worne the Petticoat, And ne'er haue stolne the Breech from Lancaster. **1600** *Maides Metam.* IV. in Bullen *O. Pl.* (1882) I. 147 This is leape yeare: Women weare breeches, petticoats are deare. **1606** *Choice, Chance & C.* (1881) 22 She that is master of her husband must weare the breeches. **1665** GLANVILL *Sceps. Sci.* xvi. 100 The Female rules, and our Affections wear the breeches. **1807** W. IRVING *Salmag.* (1824) 102 The violent inclination she felt to wear the breeches.

b. Phr. ***too big for one's breeches*** or ***britches***: see BIG *a.* 3 e.

3. A term of ridicule applied to the Commonwealth coinage, suggested by the arrangement of two shields on the reverse side of the coin.

1673 LD. LUCAS *Sp. in Ho. Peers* 3 All the Parliament money called Breeches, (a fit Stamp for the Coyn of the Rump) is wholly vanished.

4. a. The part of the body covered by this garment; the buttocks, posteriors, rump, seat. (Instances of this sense before 16th c. are very doubtful: the OE. passage, so often cited, as well as the ME. ones, prob. belong to 1.)

[*c* **1000** *Sax. Leechd.* II. 146/3 Nim gate hær smec under þa brec wiþ þær ræȝe reosan. *c* **1305** *Edmund Conf.* 164 in *E.E.P.* (1862) 75 He was byneþe his brech igurd faste ynouȝ Wiþ a strong corde. **1480** CAXTON *Descr. Brit.* 40 At her brech out and home They hong their money.]

a **1533** FRITH *Disp. Purg.* (1829) 110 Then hath he made a rod for his own breech. **1599** GREENE *Alphonsus* (1861) 231 Unless I send some one to scourge thy breech. **1630** HAYWARD *Edw. VI*, 74 A lewd boy turned towards him his naked britch. **1682** N. O. *Boileau's Lutrin* II. 147 She dropt backwards upon her breech. **1751** SMOLLETT *Per. Pic.* xlvi. (1779) II. 88 Our hero .. dismissed him with a kick on the breech. **1821** BYRON *Juan* v. lxviii, Trowsers .. such as fit an Asiatic breech.

b. *spec.* in *Obstetr.*; also *ellipt.* for *breech delivery, position, presentation.*

1673 H. CHAMBERLEN tr. *F. Mauriceau's Accomplisht Midwife* II. xxiv. 201 The Chirurgeon perceiving the Child to come with the Breech foremost, ought to put it back, if he can. **1752** W. SMELLIE *Treat. Theory & Pract. Midwifery* III. iv. 323 When the legs are delivered, let him wrap a cloath round the breech of the child. **1781** A. HAMILTON *Treat. Midwifery* 244 The varieties of the *breech* are, 1st, The fore parts of the child placed to the *pubes* of the mother; 2dly, To the *sacrum*; 3dly, To either side. **1840** T. CASTLE *Blundell's Princ. & Pract. Obstetricy* IV. vi. 292 Let then, the natural efforts bring the breech to the outlet of the pelvis, then lay hold of the hips. **1903** J. W. WILLIAMS *Obstetr.* xiii. 262 If interference becomes necessary, the complete breech offers more satisfactory conditions for immediate delivery. **1958** H. SPEERT *Essays on Eponymy* lxv. 567 The 'assisted breech' has long been taught as the properly conservative method of managing most breech births. **1962** D. E. REID *Textbk. Obstetr.* xx. 532/2 During labor, as the breech descends, the shoulders must also descend. **1963** D. G. W. CLYNE *Textbk. Gynaecol. & Obstetr.* xxviii. 666 Maternal death from an uncomplicated breech is almost unknown nowadays.

c. *transf.* The hinder parts of a beast; also of its skin or fleece: cf. BREECHING 4.

1710 *Lond. Gaz.* No. 4780/4 The Hair galled off his Buttocks with a Breech Tye. **1805** LUCCOCK *Nat. Wool* 193 The breech of the fleece is large and hairy. **1868** *Daily News* 8 Dec., A steer .. like the rejected one .. about the 'breeches'. **1885** F. BOWMAN *Struct. Wool* 219 The coarsest part of the fleece .. where the wool grows in large locks with long coarse hairs .. is called the 'breach' or 'britch'. **1940** *Chambers's Techn. Dict.* 114/1 *Britch* or *breech*, a wool-sorter's term for wool obtained from the thighs and root of the tail, estimated as the lowest quality in a fleece. **1963** *Times* 6 Feb. (N.Z. Suppl.) p. v/3 Britch wool.

5. *techn.* **a.** *Gunnery.* 'The hindermost part of a piece of ordnance' (Bailey); the part of a cannon behind the bore; the corresponding part in a musket or rifle (cf. BREECH-LOADER). Also *attrib.*

1575 GASCOIGNE *Weedes* Wks. (1587) 183 The bravest peece for breech and bore that ever yet was bought. **1626** CAPT. SMITH *Accid. Yng. Seamen* 32 Her carnooze or base ring at her britch. **1664** BUTLER *Hud.* II. I. 264 Cannons shoot the higher pitches The lower we let down their Breeches. *c* **1728** SWIFT *Problem* Wks. 1755 IV. I. 301 At the breech it flashes first. **1835** MARRYAT *Olla Podr.* xvii, Muskets which load at the breech. **1879** *Cassell's Techn. Educ.* III. 308 The gun always travels with its back part, or breech, towards the horse's heads. **1874** BOUTELL *Arms & Arm.* xi. 218 The breech end of the gun.

b. Occas. used of the lower or thicker end of various instruments, tools, etc.; e.g. the thick end or 'tail' of the bolt of a lock.

1677 MOXON *Mech. Exerc.* (1703) 30 It hath an Hook returning at the Lower End of it, to fall into the Breech of the Bolt. **1793** SIR G. SHUCKBURGH in *Phil. Trans.* LXXXIII. 80 A semicircle divided with its nonius, to every 5', on the breech plate of the telescope.

c. *Ship-building.* 'The outside angle formed by the knee-timber, the inside of which is the throat' (Smyth *Sailor's Word-bk.*).

†**6.** *pl.* The roe of a cod-fish. *Obs.*

1688 R. HOLME *Armoury* II. xiv. 324 The Spawn, or Frye, is the seed of the fish: of some called Eggs; in a Cod-Fish termed the Breeches.

7. *Comb.* chiefly attrib., as ***breech-belt, case, -cloth, -clout, delivery, labour, -maker, -part, -piece*** (of a gun), ***-pocket, -rope, -sight*** (of a gun), ***-tie***. Also ***breeches-maker, -pocket***.

c **1450** *Gloss.* in Wr.-Wülcker 734 *Hoc lumbare*, a *brek-belt. ? *c* **1475** *Hunt. Hare* 206 His breche-belt all to-brast. **1774** W. SMELLIE *Treat. Theory & Pract. Midwifery* (ed. 5) III. 52 A *Breech case, from Dr. Tathwell. **1924** J. S. FAIRBAIRN *Gynæcol. with Obstetr.* III. xv. 283 In a doubtful breech case the finger should be passed along the cleft backwards and forwards. **1841** CATLIN *N. Amer. Ind.* (1844) I. xxix. 232 We found him naked, except his *breech-cloth. **1757** R. PUTNAM *Memoirs* 9 July (1903) 12 Having nothing to cover us from the Natts & Musketoes .. but a Shirt and *Breech Clout. **1897** *Outing* (U.S.) XXX. 246/1 A breech-clout for the men, and a short skirt for the women.

1947 J. Bertram *Shadow of War* vii. iv. 235 We stripped down to our *fundoshi*—a kind of Japanese breech-clout. **1882** W. T. Lusk *Sci. & Art Midwifery* x. 200 (*heading*) The configuration of the fœtus in *breech deliveries. **1964** J. M. Brudenell *Obstetr.* xi. 94 Because of the risks to the foetus breech deliveries should only be performed by an experienced obstetrician in hospital. **1885** W. S. Playfair *Treat. Sci. & Pract. Midwifery* (ed. 3) I. iii. v. 365 After a difficult *breech labour is completed the child should be carefully examined. *c* **1500** *Cocke Lorelles B.* (1843) 6 By her crafte a *breche maker. **1858** Greener *Gunnery*, They all appear to have been loaded by removing a *breech part, or chamber. **1862** F. Griffiths *Artil. Man.* (ed. 9) 190 The *breech piece is a cylinder..bored, turned, and shrunk upon the end of the barrel. **1831** Carlyle *Sart. Res.* iii. xi, A Signpost, whereon stood written that such and such a one was *Breeches-Maker to his Majesty. **1783** Cowper *Let.* 26 Jan., Some held their hands behind them..and others had thrust them into their *breeches pockets.

8. Special comb., as (sense 5 a) **breech action**, the mechanism at the breech of a gun; **breech-block**, a moveable steel block by which the breech end of the barrel in certain fire-arms is closed; **breech-lever**, a lever by which the breech-block of some cannons is screwed in place; **breech-pin**, **breech-plug**, a pin or plug closing the breech end of a gun; **breech-screw** (see quot.); (sense 4 b) **breech baby** *colloq.*, a fœtus in the womb in a breech presentation; **breech position**, in a breech presentation, any of the four possible orientations of the fœtus relative to the mother's pelvis; **breech presentation**, a presentation (presentation 8 b) in which the buttocks are the nearest part of the fœtus to the *os uteri*; (sense 1 c) **breeches-ball**, a ball of composition for cleaning breeches; **Breeches Bible**, a book-collector's name for the Geneva Bible of 1560 on account of the rendering of *Gen.* iii. 7, though this was already in Wyclif (cf. 1 c); **breeches-buoy**, a life-saving apparatus consisting of a life-buoy with suspended canvass support resembling breeches through which the legs are put; **breeches-figure**, a person who makes a good figure in breeches; so **breeches-part**, a part in which men's clothes are worn by an actress. Also breech-girdle, -loader.

The examples are arranged in alphabetical order of the second element.

1885 *Daily News* 13 Apr. 6/3 The *breech-action [of the gun] is so simple and well-balanced that it can be worked by a child. **1969** *Woman* 11 Oct. 15/1 There were two of us booked for Caesarian operations. They had decided on that for me because they thought she was a *breech baby. **1798** Jane Austen *Northang. Ab.* (1833) II. vii. 141 An expenditure in shoe-strings, hair-powder, and *breeches-ball. **1835** *Penny Cycl.* IV. 374/2 This [the Geneva] edition is often called the '*Breeches Bible', on account of a rendering given in Genesis iii. 7. **1881** Greener *Gun* 115 The *breech-blocks blew up, in consequence of..imperfect cartridges. **1880** *Boy's Own Paper* III. 52/1 A life-line, furnished with a '*breeches-buoy' (resembling a pair of canvas breeches with the legs cut off) was secured to the wreck. **1808** Hurstone *Piccad. Ambulator* II. 45 The fascinating Mrs. A—k—ns, formerly the much admired *breeches-figure on the stage. **1862** F. Griffiths *Artil. Man.* (ed. 9) 205 **Breech Lever*, a weighted arm on the end of the breech screw. **1779** T. Holcroft *Let.* 30 Oct. in Hazlitt *Mem. T. Holcroft* (1816) III. 250 Who on the stage has considerable merit in *breeches' parts, coquets, &c. **1865** *Dublin Univ. Mag.* I. 70 We do not profess special admiration of ladies in what are technically..termed breeches parts. **1727** Bradley *Fam. Dict.* s.v. *Fowling piece*, The *Breech-pin..must be somewhat above the Touch-hole. **1885** *Harper's Mag.* Mar. 632/2 A breech-pin of a gun ..was forced into the brain. **1881** Greener *Gun* 17 The *breech-plug was placed in a groove in the wooden frame. **1876** W. S. Playfair *Treat. Sci. & Pract. Midwifery* I. iii. v. 352 The phenomena of delivery in the first and third *breech positions. **1811** *Lond. Pract. Midwifery* (ed. 3) x. 190 In *breech presentations the parts are gradually and well dilated. **1962** D. E. Reid *Textbk. Obstetr.* xx. 527/1 In rare instances the diagnosis of breech presentation may be established only by use of the x-ray. **1862** F. Griffiths *Artil. Man.* (ed. 9) 205 **Breech-Screw*, a cylinder of iron with a screw turned on the outside, working in a female screw in the breech, presses the vent piece into its place when the gun is loaded.

breech (brɪtʃ, briːtʃ), *v.* Forms: 5 brek-yn, 6 breche, britch, 6- breech. [f. prec. sb.]

1. To cover or clothe with, or as with, breeches; to put (a boy) into breeches. † *to breech it* (obs.): to serve as breeches.

1468 *Medulla Gram.* in *Cath. Angl.* 42 *Bracco*, to brekyn. **1509** Barclay *Shyp of Folys* (1874) I. 167 Breche hir with plate and mayle And for all that..She shall desceyve the. **1612** Rowlands *Knaue of Harts* 13 Let vs haue..French Doublet, and the Spanish Hose to breech it. **1850** Thackeray *Pendennis* liii, Incidents which occurred about the period when the hero was breeched.

fig. **1605** Shaks. *Macb.* ii. iii. 122 Their Daggers Vnmannerly breech'd with gore.

†**2.** To whip on the buttocks; to flog. *Obs.*

1573 G. Harvey *Lett.-bk.* (1884) 33 The bois must be britch[t]. **1580** Hollyband *Treas. Fr. Tong.*, *Fesser*, to breech boyes, to scourge them. **1639** Massinger *Unnat. Comb.* i. i, Tales out of school! Take heed, you will be breeched. **1821** Scott *Kenilw.* xxiv, Thou art a prating boy, and should be breeched for thine assurance.

3. *Naut.* To secure (a cannon) by a breeching.

1757 *Lett. fr. Capt. Gilchrist* 26 July (Record Office MS.), By breaching my aftermost guns aft. **1833** Marryat *P. Simple* (1863) 28 'Now..we'll breech these guns'.

breeched, *ppl. a.* [f. prec. + -ed¹.]

1. Wearing or furnished with breeches.

c **1550** *Songs Costume* (1849) 85 Proude and paynted parragones And monstrus breched beares. **1866** Motley *Dutch Rep.* Introd. 4 The Romans divided his race respectively into long-haired, breeched, and gowned Gaul (*Gallia comata, braccata, togata*).

2. Of a gun: Provided with a breech.

1575 Gascoigne *Weedes* Wks. (1587) 185 They [a kind of gun] be..Renforced wel, and breeched like a brock. **1802** *Hull Advertiser* 18 Dec. 3/1 Old Barrels bored and breeched to shoot close and strong.

3. Of a cannon: Secured by a breeching.

1830 Marryat *King's Own* xxii, The guns [are] double-breeched.

4. *Thieves' slang.* 'Flush of money' (J. H. Vaux *Flash Dict.* 1812).

†**'breecher.** *Obs. rare*⁻⁰. [f. as prec. + -er¹.] One who flogs.

1611 Cotgr., *Fesseur*, a whipper, scourger, breecher.

'breechesless *a.*, without breeches, breechless.

1822 *Blackw. Mag.* XII. 636 Those breechesless heroes, the Sons of the Mist. **1837** *Fraser's Mag.* XVI. 670 The killing of the breechesless barbarians at Glencoe.

†**breechgirdle.** *Obs.* Forms: 3 (?), 4 **brei gurdel**, 4–5 **braygirdle, brechgerdel, -gerdle, breek girdille, breggurdel, -dle, bre-, brei-, brigirdel, -dil, brygurdel**, 5 **braygurdylle, brekgyrdylle, brygyrdyll, breke-girdul, brigirdele, brekegyrdyl, bregyrdyle**, 5–6 **brekegyrdle**, 6 **breache gyrdle.** [Corresp. to an OE. type **brécgyrdil*, whence ME. Kentish *brechgerdel*, north. *brekgyrdyl*: the latter became by assimilation (cf. *blackguard*) *breggirdel*, *bregirdel.*]

A girdle or belt worn round the loins; a belt to keep up the breeches.

a **1300** *O.E. Misc.* 193 ȝif him ne schal..his brei gurdel quakie. **1340** *Ayenb.* 205 Þe writinge zayþ þet Ieremies brechgerdel rotede bezide þe wetere. **1388** Wyclif *Jer.* xiii. 4 Take the brigirdil..which is aboute thi leendis. *c* **1400** Maundev. v. 49 Trees, that ben non hyere than a Mannes breek Girdille. **1440** *Promp. Parv.* 51/1 Brygyrdyll, *lumbare, renale.* *a* **1500** *Gloss* in Wr.-Wülcker 629 *Perysoma*, braygurdylle. **1552** Huloet, Breache gyrdle, *lumbare.*

breeching ('briːtʃɪŋ), *vbl. sb.* [f. breech *v.* and *sb.* + -ing¹.]

1. The action of clothing with breeches; *concr.* clothing for the breech or haunches (*obs.*).

1604 S. Rowlands *Look to it, etc.* D ij b, You with..The Moncky wast, the breeching like a Beare.

†**2.** A flogging. *Obs.*

1520 Whittinton *Vulg.* (1527) 26, I studye to-daye bycause I fere a brechyng. **1590** Marlowe *Edw. II*, v. iv, Aristarchus' eyes, Whose looks were as a breeching to a boy. **1594** Nashe *Unfort. Trav.* 73 Worse than an vpbraiding lesson after a britching. *a* **1613** Overbury *Char.*, *Puny-Clarke* (1638) L iij, His dreames of breeching.

b. *attrib.* as in *breeching boy*, *-scholar*, a young scholar still subject to the birch, hence *fig.* a novice. (Cf. also *whipping-boy.*)

1596 Shaks. *Tam. Shr.* iii. i. 18, I am no breeching scholler in the schooles. **1611** Cotgr., s.v. *Donat*, The duells were, as then, but breeching boyes, like Grammar Schoole boyes, but young in experience, but Nouices. **1611** Speed *Hist. Gt. Brit.* ix. xx. 23 How such a breeching-boy as hee was, durst attempt so great a wickednesse.

3. A strong leather strap passing round the breech of a shaft-horse, and enabling him to push backwards; a breech-band. Also *attrib.*

1515–24 in Lodge *Illustr. Brit. Hist.* (1838) I. 3 To William Pawn..cart-saddles, collars, harnes, and breeching. **1801** W. Felton *Carriages* II. 131 Breechings are of no use to them [horses] but in hilly places. *Ibid.* 134 It is buckled to the collar along with the breeching-strap. **1861** Musgrave *By-Roads* 174 An old female hostler, who gave us neither cruppers, blinkers, or breeching.

4. Coarse clotted wool on the buttocks of sheep.

1799 Pitt in *Commun. Board of Agric.* II. 464 The Morf fleece is almost wholly fine, with a very small proportion of breechings or daglocks.

5. *Naut.* A stout rope attached by a thimble to the cascabel of a gun, and securing the gun to the ship's side. Hence *breeching-bolt*, *-loop.*

1627 Capt. Smith *Seaman's Gram.* xiv. 65 Britchings are the ropes by which you lash your Ordnance fast to the Ships side. **1769** Falconer *Dict. Marine* (1789) *Breeching*, a rope used to secure the cannon..and prevent them from recoiling too much. **1833** Marryat *P. Simple* (1863) 100 Double breechings were rove on the guns.

6. The parts forming the breech of a gun, the breech-action.

1802 *Hull Advertiser* 18 Dec. 3/1 An improved construction of breeching. **1816** P. Hawker *Instr. Yng. Sportsmen* (1826) 35 This breeching was also patronized by the late Mr. Smith.

7. 'A bifurcated smoke-pipe in a furnace'.

breechless ('briːtʃlɪs), *a.* Also *Sc.* and *north. dial.* breekless; other Forms, see breech. [f. breech *sb.* + -less.] Without breeches; bare or naked about the buttocks.

? *a* **1400** *Morte Arth.* 1048 His brode lendez, He bekez by þe bale fyre, and breklesse hyme semede. **1470** Harding *Chron.* l. iii, This stone..On whiche yᵉ Scottish Kynges wer brechelesse set At their coronomente. **1638** *Songs Costume* (1849) 141 Some like breechless women go, The Russ, Turk, Jew, and Grecian. **1822** Scott *Pirate* v. 45 A breekless loon frae Lochaber. **1864** *Sat. Rev.* XVIII. 711/1 Even a breechless islander, of the man Friday cast, would revolt at the idea. **1864** Atkinson *Whitby Gloss.* s.v. *Breeks*, They were sarkless and breekless.

breech-loader ('briːtʃləʊdə(r)). A fire-arm in which the charge is introduced at the breech.

1858 Greener *Gunnery* 143 Under no circumstances..can a breech-loader be as safe as a solid gun. **1864** *Times* 4 Nov., One ordinary service Armstrong breechloader..and one Whitworth rifled muzzleloader. **1877** *Daily News* 5 Oct. 5/2 Steel breechloaders from Herr Krupp's factory. **1879** *Daily News* 12 Aug. 5/1 The Highland moors have been echoing to the breechloader.

breech-loading ('briːtʃləʊdɪŋ). *vbl. sb.*

A. The method of loading (fire-arms) at the breech.

1866 *Daily Tel.* 26 May, The practice made with the imperfect 'needle-gun'..proves that breech-loading.. perfectly admits of introduction into warfare. **1874** Boutell *Arms & Arm.* 219 The idea of breech-loading formed a part of the original conception of the cannon itself.

B. *attrib.* That is loaded at the breech.

1858 Greener *Gunnery* 17 Breech-loading guns cannot be made sufficiently durable to yield any reasonable return for the extra expense and trouble. **1861** *Sat. Rev.* 30 Nov. 559 This complaint..indicated an opinion that the breech-loading Armstrong 100-pounders..are not powerful guns. **1880** *Standard* 14 Dec., The 43-ton breech-loading gun.

breed (briːd), *sb.* [f. breed *v.*: the act of breeding; hence, the progeny or race in which this results.]

†**1.** breeding, generation, birth; parentage, extraction; natal or racial origin. *of breed*: of breeding age. *Obs.*

? *a* **1600** *Merch. & Son* 34 in Hazl. *E.P.P.* I. 134 Ther was not oon man in all thys londe, that bare a bettyr brede. **1607** Topsell *Four-f. Beasts* 466 Let them be young also, and of breed, Nam melior est ea ætas, quam sequitur spes, quam ea quam sequitur mors. **1610** W. Folkingham *Art Surv.* i. iv. 8 Fish, and other liuing Creatures doe differ and varie in.. peculiar attributes according to their places of Breede. **1632** G. Herbert *Temple, Providence* xxviii, Nothing useth fire, But man alone, to show his heavenly breed.

2. Race, lineage, stock, family; strain; a line of descendants from a particular parentage, and distinguished by particular hereditary qualities. (Abstract and concrete.)

a. of animals.

1553 Eden *Treat. New Ind.* (Arb.) 22 Elephantes, of greater stature, and a better broede. **1611** Bible *Deut.* xxxii. 14 Rammes of the breed of Bashan. **1653** Walton *Angler* i. 4 To destroy the very breed of those base Otters. **1722** *Lond. Gaz.* No. 6046/4 A dark brown Mare..betwixt Cart and Saddle Breed. **1810** Scott *Lady of L.* i. vii, Two dogs of black Saint Hubert's breed. **1814** Sir H. Davy *Agric. Chem.* 258 It is necessary from time to time to change, and as it were to cross the breed. **1848** Macaulay *Hist. Eng.* I. 312 Many breeds, now extinct or rare, both of quadrupeds and birds. **1859** Darwin *Orig. Spec.* i. (1873) 15 The diversity of the breeds is something astonishing.

b. of men, etc.: now often contemptuous.

1596 Spenser *Prothal.* 66 They did not seeme To be begot of any earthly seede, But rather angels, or of angels breede. *c* **1610** Rowlands *Terrible Batt.* 41 His wife is of a proud and dainty breed. **1711** Steele *Spect.* No. 52 ¶3 To mend the Breed and rectify the Physiognomy of the Family on both Sides. **1770** Gray *Corr.* (1843) 102, I never saw such a boy; our breed is not made on this model. **1843** Macaulay *Lake Regillus* xiii, Titus, the youngest Tarquin, Too good for such a breed. **1855** —— *Hist. Eng.* III. 368 Warriors of a different breed.

c. *gen.* A kind, a species, a set. Now *colloq.*

1588 Shaks. *L.L.L.* v. ii. 266 Are these the breed of wits so wondered at? **1674** N. Fairfax *Bulk & Selv.* 73 That measure of rest, and new breed of quickners that have befallen the body in the night. **1881** *Folk-Lore Record* IV. 106 The word breed is peculiarly used [in Irish folk-lore], as they speak of 'breeds of cabbages', 'breeds of potatoes', &c. **1889** 'Mark Twain' *Connecticut Yankee* xxiii. 228 All the different breeds of rockets. **1964** *Ann. N.Y. Acad. Sci.* CXV. 569 The purpose of this paper is not to propose the design and construction of new breeds of computers. **1967** *Boston Sunday Herald* 26 Mar. i. 9/3 Development Administrator Edward J. Logue—a new breed of planner.

†**d.** Of plants: A race. *Obs.*

1687 Lovell *Bergerac's Com. Hist.* I. 153 Now the Breed of that Fruit..is lost in your World.

e. A person of mixed descent; a half-breed. Also *attrib.* orig. *N. Amer.*

1870 *Canadian Illustr. News* 26 Feb. 271/3 The 'breeds' in their ire said on him they'd fire For him 'twas a regular sell, sell, sell. **1892** *Outing* (U.S.) Jan. 287/1 A tall, wiry 'Breed' hunter, called Dave, or 'Injun Dave', according to taste. **1892** *Harper's Mag.* Feb. 387/2 One-quarter of the number of 'breeds' could read and write. **1905** D. Wallace *Labrador Wild* iii. 47 Eskimos and 'breeds', the latter being a comprehensive name for persons whose origin is a mixture in various combinations and proportions of Eskimo, Indian, and European. **1926** J. Black *You can't Win* xvi. 229, I soon mastered Chinook, practicing on the two 'breed' boys.

†**3. a.** Offspring; *esp.* The young brought forth at the same time viewed collectively; a family, litter. *Obs.* (or *dial.*); now replaced by brood. Also *fig.*

1580 BARET *Alv.* B 1164 The young brede of bees. **1596** SHAKS. *Merch. V.* I. iii. 135 Lend it not As to thy friends, for when did friendship take A breede of barraine mettall of his friend? *c* **1600** —— *Sonn.* xii, And nothing 'gainst Time's scythe can make defence Save breed, to brave him when he takes thee hence. **1697** DRYDEN *Virg. Georg.* III. 225 Thy Care must now proceed To teeming Females; and the promis'd Breed. **1802** PALEY *Nat. Theol.* (1817) 147 The hen..is frightened when her supposititious breed of ducklings take the water. **1863** ATKINSON *Danby Provinc.*, *Breed*, a brood, a litter of young ones.

†**b.** ***at a breed***: at a birth. *Obs.*

a **1711** GREW (J.) She lays them in the sand..sometimes above an hundred at a breed.

†**c.** Applied to single progeny or offspring; young one, child, bairn. *Obs.*

1586 WARNER *Alb. Eng.* I. ii. 4 Cybell [had] brought to light Her second breede, a smiling boy. *Ibid.* X. lv. 253 When Junos Breed on farther bankes his passenger had set.

†**d.** *transf.* Those bred in (a place): brood.

1691 RAY *Creation* I. (1704) 75 The Sea—so render'd more salutary for the maintenance of its Breed.

4. *Comb.* **breed-cup**, **breed-prize**, a prize at a show, etc., given to the best animal of a particular breed; †**breed-goose**, **-mother**, **-ram**, a goose, etc. for breeding; †**breed-reserved** *a.*, reserved for breeding; **breed-society**, a society which is concerned with the production of a particular breed of animal. See also HALF-BREED.

1465 *Mann. & Househ. Exp.* 296 A gander, iiij. bredegese, and v. goslynges. **1611** SPEED *Hist. Gt. Brit.* V. iii. 11 The breed-reserued creatures saued in the floting Arke. **1662** FULLER *Worthies* I. 127 To give ten pound or more for a Breed-ram. **1668** MARKHAM *Way to Wealth* vi. 49 No good House-wife will breed of a young, but of an old breed-mother. **1888** *Pall Mall Gaz.* 10 Dec. 8/2 There are seven silver breed cups for the cattle classes. **1892** *Daily News* 14 Sept. 5/5 The future of stock fairs will be in some degree affected by the breed-societies. **1896** *Ibid.* 8 Dec. 5/1 The Breed Cup for shorthorns was taken by the Earl of Rosebery's 'Proud Madam'. *Ibid.* 4 Mar. 8/6 Mr. G. Jackson, of Birmingham, has the breed prize.

breed (briːd), *v.* Pa. t. and pa. pple. **bred**. Forms: *Inf.* 3–6 brede, 6–7 breede, 6– breed; *Pa. t.* and *pa. pple.* 4 breed, 4–5 bredde, 7 bread, 4– bred. (Also 6 *pa. t.* breded, *pa. pple.* breden.) [OE. *brédan* (:—*bróedan*) = OHG. *bruotan* (MHG. *brüeten*, mod.G. *brüten*):—OTeut. type **brôdjan*, f. *brôdâ-* 'warmth, fostering heat, hatching, BROOD'. *Brood*, *breed*, are analogous to *food*, *feed*, *blood*, *bleed*.]

I. *trans.* (and *absol.*)

1. a. *trans.* Said of a female parent: To cherish (brood) in the womb or egg; to bring (offspring) forward from the germ to the birth; to hatch (young birds) from the egg; to produce (offspring, children).

c **1000** ÆLFRIC *Hom.* II. 10 þæt sind beon..of ðam huniȝe hi bredað heora brod. *a* **1250** *Owl & Night.* 1633 Ich not to hwan þu bredst..þi brod. *a* **1300** *Cursor M.* 3895 Lya bred child, and hadd a sun. *Ibid.* 12223 Quat wamb him bare or brede. **1530** PALSGR. 463/2, I..brede yonge, as a woman or any other suche beest dothe. **1587** GOLDING *De Mornay* i. 7 Neither thou in begetting him, nor his mother in breeding him, did once thinke vpon the fashioning of him in hir wombe. **1588** SHAKS. *Tit. A.* II. iii. 146. **1850** MRS. STOWE *Uncle Tom* xviii. 184 A man kept me to breed chil'en for market.

†**b.** To generate. *Obs.*

1513 DOUGLAS *Æneis* x. Prol. 52 The Fader..ever bredis His Son, his word and wysdom eternall.

†**c.** *fig. Obs.*

1526 *Pilgr. Perf.* (W. de W. 1531) 75 We conceyue our owne sorowe, and breed therof..vnryghteousnes. **1595** SPENSER *Sonn.* ii, Unquiet thought! whom at the first I bred ..And sithens have with sighes and sorrowes fed.

2. *absol.* To be pregnant, to be with young or with child. (Now chiefly *dial.*)

1629 GAULE *Pract. The.* 85 So breeds the Virgin by her owne, and vnusual Seed. **1669** W. SIMPSON *Hydrol. Chym.* 352 Women breeding or with child. **1712** STEELE *Spect.* No. 430 ¶3 Lucina..was breeding, and she did nothing but entertain the Company with a Discourse upon the Difficulty of Reckoning to a Day. **1723** SWIFT *Stella at Woodp.* Wks. 1755 IV. I. 38 Like a lady breeding. **1885** STEVENSON *Dynamiter* Ded., Yours is the side of the child, of the breeding woman, of individual pity and public trust.

3. *absol.* Of animal species: To produce brood or young; to have offspring; to propagate their species.

a **1250** *Owl & Night.* 101 That other ȝer a faukun bredde. **1297** R. GLOUC. 177 In eche roche þer ys..an ernes nest, þat hii bredeþ in ywys. *c* **1440** *Promp. Parv.* 49 Bredyn or hetchyn, as byrdys, *pullifico.* **1532–3** *Act 24 Hen. VIII*, x, Rookes..do daily brede and increase throughout this realm. **1653** WALTON *Angler* 167 Most fish breed after this manner. **1802** PALEY *Nat. Theol.* (1817) 240 Mankind will in every country breed up to a certain point of distress. **1836–9** TODD *Cycl. Anat. & Phys.* II. 468/2 A mare has bred with an ass and has had a mule foal. **1859** DARWIN *Orig. Spec.* i. (1873) 7 Carnivorous animals..breed in this country pretty freely under confinement.

b. *fig.*

1599 SHAKS. *Much Ado* I. iii. 4 There is no measure in the occasion that breeds, therefore the sadnesse is without limit. **1603** —— *Meas. for M.* II. ii. 142 Shee speakes, and 'tis such sence That my Sence breeds with it. **1612–5** BP. HALL *Contempl. O.T.* (1837) II. XIX. i. 5 Kindnesses breed on themselves. **1866** ARGYLL *Reign Law* i. (ed. 4) 2 Half the perplexities of men are traceable to obscurity of thought hiding and breeding under obscurity of language.

4. *trans.* Said of countries, situations, or conditions, engendering living things; also, in the *passive*, of animals being engendered or brought into existence (without reference to parental action).

a **1250** *Owl & Night.* 1722 Theȝ heo nere i-bred a wolde, Ho was i-toȝen among mankunne. *c* **1325** *E.E. Allit. P.* C. 143 Efte busched to þe abyme þat breed fyssches. **1413** LYDG. *Pylgr. Sowle* IV. ii. (1483) 58 In these pepyns was bredde a worme. **1580** BARET *Alv.* B 1164 Rotten timber breedeth wormes. **1590** GREENE *Never too late* (1600) 9 Women are vniuersally *mala necessaria*, wheresoeuer they be eyther bred or brought vp. **1653** WALTON *Angler* 85 There be certaine waters that breed Trouts. **1675** HOBBES *Odyss.* ix. 30 Rocky is Ithaca..But breedeth able men. **1802** BINGLEY *Anim. Biog.* (1813) III. 122 This insect..is bred and nourished in bacon. **1853** *Eng. Illust. Mag.* Nov. 72 A hard place..to live in, and fit to breed a hardy race.

5. a. Of the natural production of things inanimate: now esp. in 'to breed fever' and the like; also *fig.* 'to breed bad blood' (see BLOOD), etc.

c **1325** *E.E. Allit. P.* B. 257 Hit was þe forme-foster þat þe folde bred. **1398** TREVISA *Barth. De P.R.* VIII. xxviii. (1495) 339 Oores of metall ben gendred and bred depe wythin the erthe. *Ibid.* XV. xlii. 503 Creta bredyth precyous stones. **1598** W. PHILLIPS *Linschoten's Trav.* in Arb. *Garner* III. 30 The great number of the men in the ship was the cause of breeding the same [plague]. **1607** TOPSELL *Four-f. Beasts* 496 To suck all [the milk] that their dams can breed. **1657** AUSTEN *Fruit Trees* I. 84 Figs are said to..breed store of blood. **1665** BOYLE *Occas. Refl.* (1675) 68 Green Fruit breeds Sickness in the Body. **1719** DE FOE *Crusoe* (1840) II. i. 1 What is bred in the bone will not go out of the flesh. **1863** KINGSLEY *Water-bab.* v. (1875) 225 Dirt breeds fever.

†**b.** To develop (teeth, wings, or the like). *Obs.*

1544 PHAËR *Regim. Lyfe* (1560) S v b, About the seventh moneth..after yᵉ byrthe, it is natural for a childe for to breede teeth. **1667** MILTON *P.L.* IX. 1010 Divinitie within them breeding wings. **1738** SHAW *Barbary* in Pinkerton *Coll. Trav.* XIV. 622 When the little ones [lion cubs] breed their teeth.

†**c.** To produce (products of human art). *Obs.*

1577 HOLINSHED *Chron.* II. 40/1 His pen..is dailie breeding of such learned bookes. **1699** POMFRET *Reason* 52 Those books that modern times have bred.

6. a. To give rise to, engender, develop, produce, create, cause, be the source of.

c **1200** *Trin. Coll. Hom.* 55 Estmetes þe bredeð sinnes. **1398** TREVISA *Barth. De P.R.* XVII. civ. (1495) 669 The smell of the apples of mandragora..bredyth slepe. **1542** UDALL *Erasm. Apoph.* 278 It breded & areised greate enuie and grutchyng against Caesar. **1583** STANYHURST *Æneis* I. (Arb.) 20 Noght breeds theym coomfort. **1598** BARRET *Theor. Warres* IV. i. 120 Warres may breed pouertie, and pouertie breedeth peace. **1601** SHAKS. *All's Well* II. iii. 140 Shee is young, wise, faire..And these breed honour. **1651** HOBBES *Leviath.* I. ii. 6 Lying cold breedeth Dreams of Feare. **1878** MORLEY *Diderot* II. 184 An iniquitous government breeds despair in men's souls.

b. Rarely with *forth* (obs.), *up*.

1570 ASCHAM *Scholem.* (Arb.) 42 Our reasons serue onelie to breede forth talke. **1605** *Verstegan's Dec. Intell.* (1628) Pref. Verses, The beautious light Bred foorth of Phebus bright arising rays. **1863** KINGLAKE *Crimea* (1876) I. i. 10 Acts which tended to breed up causes of quarrel.

c. *Nuclear Engin.* To produce (fissile material) in a breeder reactor.

1948 *Nature* 28 Aug. 318/1 Uranium 235..must be made to breed 'secondary' fuel from more abundant materials. **1955** *Times* 5 Aug. 9/7 The more spectacular third-stage reactor, in which nuclear fuel is 'bred'.

†**7.** with *compl.* To cause to become; to make, cause, bring (into a state, or to do something). *Obs.*

c **1460** *Launfal* 704 Sche ley doun yn hyr bedde, For wrethe syk sche hyr bredde. *c* **1465** *Plumpton Corr.* 14 God bred her to be delivered of her son Nicholas on Tewsday. **1625** BACON *Greatness of Kingd.*, *Ess.* (Arb.) 477 Such a Proportion of Land..as may breed a Subiect, to liue in Conuenient Plenty.

†**8.** To cherish, foster. *Obs.*

a **1225** *Ancr. R.* 200 þe þet bret þesne kundel, in hire breoste al is attri to Gode. *Ibid.* 222 Moni..bredeð in hire breoste sum liunes hweolp.

9. a. To take charge of or promote the engendering of (animals); to 'raise' (cattle).

c **1400** *Gamelyn* 359 þe bestis þou hast forþ bredde. **1523** FITZHERB. *Husb.* §8 For to rere and brede catell or shepe. **1676** RAY *Corr.* (1848) 121 The manner of breeding Canary-birds. **1796** MORSE *Amer. Geog.* II. 21 A great number of small cattle are bred in this province. **1859** JEPHSON *Brittany* iii. 28 A Frenchman cannot breed a foal without the assistance of the paternal government.

b. *absol.*

1859 DARWIN *Orig. Spec.* i. (1873) 24 Hardly any one is so careless as to breed from his worst animals.

c. To put (an animal) *to* (another) for breeding.

1886 C. SCOTT *Sheep-farming* 161 The ewes to which he is bred. **1955** W. W. DENLINGER *Complete Boston* 57 Half of the top bitches in the entire country may have been bred to him upon the strength of his winning record.

10. To train up to a state of physical or mental development. [This sense is evidently transferred from 1; the young creature being viewed as a rude germ to be developed by nurture.]

a. To rear (animals) so as to develop their physical qualities or intelligence.

1523 FITZHERB. *Husb.* §120 A horse mayster is he, that bieth wylde horses, or coltes, and bredeth theym. **1697** DRYDEN *Virg. Georg.* III. 85 The Generous Youth, who..to the Plough the sturdy Bullock breeds. *Ibid.* III. 186 To chuse a Youthful Steed..To breed him, break him, back him. **1774** GOLDSM. *Nat. Hist.* (1862) I. II. ii. 259 The wild ass is even more asinine..than that bred in a state of.. servitude.

b. To train up (young persons) in the arts of life; to educate, tutor, bring up. Also with complemental object, as 'to breed him a scholar, a papist', and with *to*, 'to breed him *to* a profession, *to* the law', etc. (*Bring up* is the ordinary modern equivalent in all shades of meaning.)

†(*a*) To train by education, educate, teach. *Obs.*

1570 ASCHAM *Scholem.* (Arb.) 73 One of the best Scholers that euer S. Johns Colledge bred. **1615** SIR R. BOYLE in *Lismore P.* (1886) II. 101, I sent my eldest son..into England to be bred there. **1627** DONNE *Serm.* 47 Breed them not in an opinion that such a Faith is enough. **1662** FULLER *Worthies* (1840) I. 130 Sir John Mason..was..bred in All Souls in Oxford. **1676** WYCHERLEY *Pl. Dealer* I. i. (1678) 9 She lodges in one of the Inns of Chancery, where she breeds her Son, and is her self his Tutoress in Law-French. **1706** *Lond. Gaz.* No. 4220/3 Restraining them from taking and breeding Apprentices. **1751** JOHNSON *Rambl.* No. 180 ¶1 A wealthy trader..having the ambition to breed his son a scholar, carried him to an university. **1774** T. WARTON *Hist. Eng. Poetry* Diss. II. 125 The universal ardour..of breeding almost all persons to letters. **1796** SOUTHEY *Hymn to Penates* Wks. II. 279 We grew up Together, and in the same school were bred. **1834–43** —— *Doctor* xxvi, He did not determine upon breeding him either to the Church or the Law.

(*b*) To bring up from childhood, including all the circumstances which go to form the religious persuasion, manners, position in life, and trade.

1650 BAXTER *Saint's R.* II. (ed. 5) 247 David, who was bred a Shepherd. **1697** DRYDEN *Virg. Eclog.* VIII. 60 In Desarts thou wert bred. **1715** DE FOE *Fam. Instruct.* II. i. (1841) I. 176 Thou talkest as if thou hadst been bred a heathen. **1771** FRANKLIN *Autobiog.* Wks. 1840 I. 5 Thomas was bred a smith under his father. **1813** SCOTT *Rokeby* IV. viii, He bids thee breed him as thy son. **1848** MACAULAY *Hist. Eng.* II. 239 Most of these functionaries had been bred Churchmen. **1857** BUCKLE *Civiliz.* I. vii. 341 The old traditions in which they had been bred. **1866** G. MACDONALD *Ann. Q. Neighb.* vii, I bred him to the joiner's trade, sir.

†(*c*) Also ***to breed up***. *arch.* or *Obs.*

1611 BIBLE *Pref.* 3 Boyes that are bred up in the Scriptures. **1641** HINDE *J. Bruen* iv. 14 Very few Gentlemen ..will bee at the cost to breed up two [sons] in the University. **1732** BERKELEY *Alciphr.* i. §6 Suppose that I am bred up..in the Church of England. **1741** WATTS *Improv. Mind* (1801) 4 Arithmo had been bred up to accounts all his life. **1736** PENDARVES in *Swift's Lett.* (1766) II. 229 The poor duchess is often reproached with her being bred up in Burr-street, Wapping. **1801** MAR. EDGEWORTH *Contrast* (1832) 108 Care to breed up their children well. **1836** J. H. NEWMAN *Par. Serm.* II. ix. (ed 2) 115 He was bred up in a human school.

11. ***to be born and bred***, or ***bred and born***: an alliterative phrase in which *bred* has usually sense 9, though formerly sense 1.

a **1340** HAMPOLE *Pr. Consc.* 4209 In þe first he sal be born and bredde, And in þe secunde be nuryst. **1542** UDALL *Erasm. Apoph.* 113 a, Where he was born and breden. *Ibid.* 133 b, In the same Isle born, breden, and brought vp. **1580** BARET *Alv.* B 1165 We are so borne and bredde of nature. **1601** SHAKS. *Twel. N.* I. ii. 22, I was bred and borne Not three houres trauaile from this very place. **1732** LAW *Serious C.* xviii. (ed. 2) 326 Born and bred in families that have no Religion. **1875** JOWETT *Plato* (ed. 2) I. 288 He was born and bred in your house.

II. *intr.* (for *refl.*)

12. a. To come into being or existence, as a continued process; hence, to be engendered or produced.

c **1200** *Trin. Coll. Hom.* 165 Wuremes breden in wilderne. *a* **1300** *Cursor M.* 16410 His blod on vs be, and on þaim þat of vs sal brede. *c* **1320** *Anticrist* 32 Nu sal yee her..Hu þat anticrist sal brede. *c* **1430** *Hymns Virg.* (1867) 4 Heil crowned queene..Heil þat alle oure blis in bradde! *c* **1440** *York Myst.* xxxii. 130 Woo worthe þe wombe þat I bredde ynne. **1579** GOSSON *Sch. Abuse* (Arb.) 46 The worme that breeds within it. *c* **1600** *Lyrics for Lutenists* (Collier) 14 It is a sweete delicious morne, Where day is breeding, never borne. **1626** BACON *Sylva* §696 Fleas breed principally of Straw or Mats, where there hath been a little moisture.

†**b.** Of eggs: To be hatched.

1661 LOVELL *Hist. Anim. & Min.* 108 They lay egges, which breed.

†**c.** Of vegetables, animal structures, growth, etc.: To come forth, spring, grow. *Obs.*

a **1300** in Wright's *Lyric P.* xiv. 45 Blosmes bredeth on the bowes. **1375** BARBOUR *Bruce* XVI. 68 Lewis on the branchis spredis, And blomys bricht besyd thame bredis. **1541** R. COPLAND *Guydon's Quest. Chirurg.*, Fro whens bredeth the synewes? **1668** CULPEPPER & COLE *Barthol. Anat.* III. xi. 153 Certain strong band, breeding from without, and creeping to the Cheek-bone.

†**d.** Of mineral products: To be formed naturally, be produced. *Obs.*

1398 TREVISA *Barth. De P.R.* (Tollemache MS.) XVI. iii, That stone [alabaster] þat bredeþ [*nascitur*] aboute Thebe. *Ibid.* XIX. xxiii. (1495) 877 Some colour bredeth in veynes of the erthe, as Sinopis Rubrica.

13. *fig.* To arise, originate, spring forth, make their appearance.

c **1385** CHAUCER *L.G.W.* 1156 Of which ther gan to bredyn swich a fyer. **1586** WARNER *Alb. Eng.* I. iii. 10 His high exploits, whereof such wonder bread. **1817** JAS. MILL *Brit. India* I. III. iv. 585 [He] allowed..discontents & jealousies to breed in the army.

†**14.** with *compl.* To grow or become (something). *Obs.*

c **1325** *Poem temp. Edw. II*, lxiii, Thei . . bredeth wode for wele. *c* **1325** *E.E. Allit. P.* B. 1558 þenne þe bolde Baltazar bred ner wode.

†**15.** ? To nestle, to hive; to dwell. *Obs.*

c **1325** *E.E. Allit. P.* A. 415 He Corounde me quene in blysse to brede. *c* **1340** *Gaw. & Gr. Knt.* 21 Quen þis Bretayn watz bigged . . Bolde bredden þerinne. *c* **1350** *Will. Palerne* 1782 To sum wildernesse where as þei bredde.

III. Phrases. ***to breed out***: to exhaust the breed, degenerate (*obs.*); also, to eliminate (a characteristic) by (controlled) breeding; ***to breed in and in***: to breed always with near relatives; the opposite being ***to breed out and out***.

1599 SHAKS. *Hen. V*, III. v. 29 Our madames mock at vs, and plainely say Our Mettell is bred out. **1607** —— *Timon* I. i. 259 The straine of mans bred out into Baboon and Monkey. **1819** BYRON *Juan* I. lvii, In that point so precise in each degree That they bred in and in . . Marrying their cousins—nay, their aunts and nieces. **1922** R. LEIGHTON *Complete Bk. of Dog* xii. 178 Most Irish water spaniels have bad, straight shoulders, a defect which should be bred out. **1941** J. S. HUXLEY *Uniqueness of Man* xv. 299 We could theoretically breed out much of human variety.

IV. *Comb.* formed on the verb-stem: †**breed-sleep** *a.*, sleep-breeding, soporific; †**breed-young** *a.*, having young, suckling.

1583 STANYHURST *Æneid* IV. (Arb.) 112 Hoonnie liquid sprinckling and breede sleepe wild popye strawing. **1603** FLORIO *Montaigne* (1632) Swifter then breed-yong Tiger.

breed(e, obs. form of BREAD, BREDE *sb.*² and ³.

†**'breed-bate.** *Obs.* [f. BREED *v.* + BATE *sb.*¹] One who breeds 'bate', or excites strife; a mischief-maker.

1593 *Tell-trothe's N.Y. Gift* 39 He delights not in breed-bates. **1598** SHAKS. *Merry W.* I. iv. 12 No tel-tale, nor no breede-bate. **1852** KNIGHT-BRUCE in De Gex, etc. *Law Rep.* I. 680 Referring to decent people . . and not to breedbates, barretors, or counsel whom no Inn would own.

breeder ('bri:də(r)). [f. BREED *v.* + -ER¹.]

1. a. That which breeds or produces offspring.

1588 SHAKS. *Tit. A.* IV. ii. 68 Among'st the fairest breeders of our clime. **1593** —— *3 Hen. VI*, II. i. 42 You loue the Breeder better then the Male. **1614** MARKHAM *Cheap Husb.* (1623) 136 Not good to chuse a crowing hen, for they are neither good breeders nor good layers. **1641** BEST *Farm. Bks.* (1856) 1 Hunge tuppes are . . to bee kept for breeders. **1725** BRADLEY *Fam. Dict.* II. s.v. *Pigeon*, The Pigeon called the Leghorn is . . an excellent Breeder. **1727** SWIFT *Modest Prop.* Wks. 1755 II. II. 60 There may be about two hundred thousand couple, whose wives are breeders. **1859** DARWIN *Orig. Spec.* iii. (1878) 51 The elephant is reckoned the slowest breeder of all known animals.

b. That which produces or originates; the author, source, or cause.

1572 BOSSEWELL *Armorie* III. 5 Breders, norishers, & comforters of all lyuyng thynges. **1589** R. HARVEY *Pl. Perc.* (1860) 20 Neither the breeders nor fauorites of discord. **1674** N. FAIRFAX *Bulk & Selv.* 9 That evil should alwayes flow from evil in a chain of breeders.

†**c.** A plant used for propagation. **d.** A gardeners' name for an immature, self-coloured, seedling tulip.

1601 HOLLAND *Pliny* I. 531 As for another [shoot], springing from a yeare-old branch, it is left alwaies for a breeder. **1660** SHARROCK *Vegetables* 27 Tulips without blackish bottome are noe good breeders of various coloured flowers. **1846** MRS. LOUDON *Ladies' Comp. Flower-Gard.* 303 Breeders . . are seedling Tulips before they have shown any variety of colour.

2. a. One who breeds cattle or other animals.

1531 ELYOT *Gov.* I. x, Virgile leaueth farre behynde hym all breders, hakneymen, and skosers. **1533-4** *Act 25 Hen. VIII*, i, Euery owner, grasier, fermour, breder, drouer, and brogger of this realme. **1707** *Lond. Gaz.* No. 4342/3 [To] bring a Certificate from the Breeder, of his Mare's Age. **1824** W. IRVING *T. Trav.* II. 18 He was a breeder of cattle. **1846** J. BAXTER *Libr. Pract. Agric.* II. 265.

fig. **1573** TUSSER *Husb.* (1878) 28 Let Lent well kept offend not thee, for March and Aprill breeders bee.

†**b.** A grower or producer. *Obs.*

1547 *Act 1 Ed. VI*, i. Pream., The said Breeders of the said Wools.

†**3.** One who brings up; a trainer, instructor. *Obs.*

1571 ASCHAM *Scholem.* (Arb.) 72 Tyme was whan Italie and Rome haue bene . . the best breeders and bringers vp of the worthiest men. **1602** WARNER *Alb. Eng.* XII. lxxi. 296 Of world-admired Drake . . And his braue breeder Hawkins.

4. *Nuclear Engin.* In full ***breeder reactor, pile***: an apparatus that can create more fissile material than it consumes in the chain reaction.

1948 LAPP & ANDREWS *Nucl. Radiation Physics* xvi. 401 The development of a breeder-type reactor. *Ibid.* 481 Breeder pile. **1948** *U.S. Atomic Energy Comm. 3rd Semi-Ann. Rep.* 12 The 'breeder' type of reactor, a 'nuclear chain reactor which over a period of time will actually create more fissionable material than is put into the reactor as fuel to sustain the reaction'. **1949** *Sci. Amer.* July 36 A 'breeder' reactor that would produce new fissionable atoms as fast as it used the old ones up. **1950** *Ann. Reg. 1949* 423 An engineering design for an experimental 'breeder' atomic pile had been completed. **1950** *Chemical Industries* Jan. 28/2 Of the four reactors, two are breeders and two are non-breeders. **1963** *Ann. Reg. 1962* 380 The successful operation of so-called breeder reactors, which made new fuel as they burnt their own. **1969** *Sci. Jrnl.* July 41/3 Eight or nine countries . . are hurrying to develop practical reactors that will produce more fissile material than they consume; that is, breeder reactors. *Ibid.*, Breeders are seen as opening the door to virtually unlimited energy.

breeding ('bri:dɪŋ), *vbl. sb.* [f. BREED *v.* + -ING¹.]

1. a. Bringing to the birth; hatching; production of young. ***breeding of teeth***: dentition (*obs.*).

a **1300** *Cursor M.* 3479 Hir breding was ful selcut sare, Bot hir chiltting was mikel mare. **1387** TREVISA *Barth. De P.R.* XVII. ii. (1495) 600 Grete bredynge of beestis is in suche places. *c* **1440** *Promp. Parv.* 49 Bredynge, or brodynge . . of birdys. *c* **1420** *Pallad. on Husb.* I. 635 For bredynge To set an hen on eyron ix is goode. **1544** PHAËR *Regim. Lyfe* (1560) S v b, Breedyng of teeth. **1712** *Lond. Gaz.* No. 4976/2 Illness . . occasioned by the breeding of his Teeth. **1836** *Penny Cycl.* VI. 378/2 The breeding and fattening of cattle.

†**b.** Hence (vulgarly), extraction, parentage. *Obs.*

1597 SHAKS. *2 Hen. IV*, V. iii. 111, I know not your breeding. **1606** DAY *Isle of Guls* iv. 1 *Lis.* What breeding hast had? *Man.* Very good breeding, sir; my great grandfather was a ratcatcher, my grandsire a hangman.

c. *Nuclear Engin.* The production of fissile material. Cf. BREED *v.* 6 c.

1947 G. GAMOW *One Two Three* vii. 184 The favorable and unfavorable conditions for neutron breeding. **1956** A. H. COMPTON *Atomic Quest* 324 A breeding reactor. *Ibid.*, The process by which all the uranium and thorium is made available as fission fuel is known as 'breeding'.

2. *fig.* Origination, production, development.

1549 Q. ELIZ. in Ellis *Orig. Lett.* I. 166 II. 157 That shulde be but a bridinge of a ivel wil of the people. **1587** GOLDING *De Mornay* xxvii. 426 The breeding of Kingdomes and Principalities. **1625** USSHER *Answ. Jesuit* 400 The breedings of this disease. **1664** POWER *Exp. Philos.* I. 62 The heat which was in fermentation whilst they [Minerals] were yet in breeding.

3. The rearing and training of the young; bringing up: formerly in sense of 'education'.

1577 HELLOWES tr. *Gueuara's Chron.* 91 For yᵉ breeding of children . . and the marriage of Orphans. **1653** MILTON *Hirelings* Wks. (1851) 381 [They] have had the most of thir breeding, both at School and University, by Scholarships. *a* **1704** T. BROWN *Declam. Adv.* Wks. 1730 I. 42 You had never very good breeding thus to laugh at my ingenuity. **1777** SHERIDAN *Trip Scarb.* I. i, She has her breeding within doors: the parson teaches her to play upon the dulcimer. **1859** MILL *Liberty* ii. 48 His Stoical breeding. **1864** BURTON *Scot Abr.* I. ii. 61 Royal birth and breeding.

4. The results of training as shown in personal manners and behaviour; generally used for 'good breeding', good or proper manners.

1596 SHAKS. *Merch. V.* II. vii. 33 In graces, and in qualities of breeding. **1665** BOYLE *Occas. Refl.* (1675) Pref. 14 As I fancy'd persons, of their Breeding and tempers, would talk to one another. **1689** SHADWELL *Bury F.* I. i. 122 It out does St. James Square in dressing and breeding. **1710** STEELE *Tatler* No. 21 ¶2 The Height of good Breeding. **1732** BERKELEY *Alciphr.* I. §12 Mind what men of parts and breeding say. **1771** GOLDSM. *Hist. England* III. 142 This romantic message, which was quite in the breeding of the times. **1826** DISRAELI *Viv. Grey* VII. vi. 421 Her ignorance of all breeding is amusing. **1870** GRANT WHITE *Words & Uses* (1881) 62 That tone of voice which indicates breeding rather than education, etc.

5. *attrib.*, as in ***breeding-cage, breeding-dress, -ground*** (also *fig.*), ***-habit, -hole, -place, plumage, -pond, range, -season, station, -stock, storm, territory, -time***, etc.

1936 *British Birds* XXIX. 234 In May numbers appear to be in full *breeding dress. **1856** KANE *Arct. Expl.* I. xxi. 268 Ducks . . seeking their *breeding-grounds. **1931** V. A. DEMANT *This Unemployment* i. 15 The atmosphere of acquiescence . . is the most fruitful breeding-ground of practical atheism. **1937** *British Birds* XXXI. 84 Observations concerning *breeding-habits. **1841** in *Proc. Berw. Nat. Club* I. ix. 252 The favourite . . *breeding-places of these birds. **1842** DICKENS *Amer. Notes* (1850) 118/1 A breeding-place of fever, ague, and death. **1938** *British Birds* XXXII. 19 Mr. Blake caught it and noticed the *breeding plumage and oiled underparts. **1789** WHITE *Selborne* (1851) 70 The migration of frogs from their *breeding-ponds. **1890** *Stock Grower* 1 Feb. 11/2 *Breeding range, on the Pecos River, New Mexico. **1920** E. HOWARD *Territory in Bird Life* ii. 44 The district . . lies well within the limits of the breeding range of most of our common species. *a* **1714** M. HENRY *Wks.* I. 552 It may minister some comfort and relief to a pious mother, in *breeding-sickness. **1920** E. HOWARD *Territory in Bird Life* 59 Guillemots and Razorbills return at intervals to the *breeding stations early in the season. **1840** J. MORTON in *Rep. Sel. Farms* (*Libr. Usef. Knowl.*, *Husb.* III) 17 The healthiness . . of the stock, upon this farm . . is a great inducement to keep a large *breeding-stock. **1961** *Guardian* 21 Nov. 8/5 Man . . has started a *breeding storm in his own species. **1920** E. HOWARD *Territory in Bird Life* 26 The evolution of the *breeding territory may have been influenced by relationships in the inorganic world. **1711** ADDISON *Spect.* No. 128 ¶3 Their Songs begin a little before *Breeding-time.

breeding ('bri:dɪŋ), *ppl. a.* [f. BREED *v.* + -ING².] That breeds: see the verb.

1552 HULOET, Breding, or full of breadyng, *fœtuosus.* **1593** SHAKS. *Ven. & Ad.* 260 A breeding jennet, lusty, young, and proud. **1641** MILTON *Animadv.* Wks. (1851) 195 The malignity of that breeding corruption. **1661** LOVELL *Hist. Anim. & Min.* 80 A breeding Mare. **1856** OLMSTED *Slave States* 55 A breeding woman is worth from one-sixth to one-fourth more than one that does not breed.

Hence **'breedingness.**

1674 N. FAIRFAX *Bulk & Selv.* 132 The life . . is but a frame or draught of springs, leavened into a breedingness.

†**'breedling.** *Obs.* [f. BREED *v.* + -LING.] One born and bred in a place; a native.

1663 PEPYS *Diary* 18 Sept., Over most sad fenns, all the way observing the sad life which the people of the place (which, if they be born there, they do call the breedlings of the place) do live. [Taken by Macaulay for a proper name. See *Hist. Eng.* (1855) III. xi. 41.]

breedy ('bri:dɪ), *a.* [f. BREED + -Y¹.] Breeding readily; prolific. Hence **'breediness.**

1753 *Dial. betw. Swift & Prior* 24 Our early Marriages, the Breedyness of our People. **1824** J. WILSON in *Blackw. Mag.* XII. 55 Blockheads . . are breedy, and double themselves every ten years. **1865** *Cornh. Mag.* II. 53 The life and habits of the breedy creature [the oyster]. **1883** *St. James's Gaz.* 14 Apr. 6 Hares are not such breedy creatures as rabbits.

breefe, obs. form of BRIEF.

breek (bri:k). Forms: 3–6 **breke**, 6 **breik**, 7 **breeke**, 5– **breek**. [North. Eng. and Sc. variant of BREECH *sb.*]

1. A garment covering the loins and thighs; = BREECH *sb.* 1.

†**a.** Formerly in singular. *Obs.*

a **1300** *Cursor M.* 2048 Was funden þan na breke in land. *c* **1440** *Promp. Parv.* 48 Breche or breke, *braccæ.* *a* **1528** SKELTON *Elynour Rumm.* 452 The vertue . . Of her husbands breke.

b. Now only in pl. **breeks** = BREECHES.

1552 LYNDESAY *Monarche* 985 And maid thame Breikis of leuis grene. **1632** B. JONSON *Magn. Lady* v. v, I ha' linnen Breeks on. **1651** *Proc. Parliament* No. 84. 1282 To slip off their breeks, that so they may wade up to their middle. **1814** SCOTT *Wav.* xlviii, It's ill taking the breeks off a Highlandman. **1853** KANE *Grinnell Exp.* xxx. (1856) 263 A pair of coarse woollen drawers, and a pair of seal-skin breeks over them. **1855** *Whitby Gloss.*, *Breeks*, breeches.

†**2.** The buttocks, rump, posterior. *Obs.*

1641 BEST *Farm. Bks.* (1856) 69 They beginne usually on the belly . . greasinge tayle and breeke last.

breekless, north. form of BREECHLESS.

breekums. *Sc.*, Short breeks, knee-breeches.

1832–53 *Whistle-Binkie* (Sc. Songs) Ser. II. 4 My auld uncle Watty, Wi' 's buckled knee breekums an' three cockit hattie.

†**breel.** *Obs. rare*⁻¹. [Perh. contr. form of BRETHEL.] A worthless, good-for-nothing fellow.

[*c* **1440** *Promp. Parv.* 50/1 Breyel, *brollus, brolla, miserculus.*] *c* **1485** *Digby Myst.* (1882 III. 927 Why lowtt ȝe nat low to my lawdabyll presens, ye brawlyng breelles.

breem, obs. f. BREAM; var. of BREME *a.* *Obs.*

breended, obs. form of BRINDED.

†**breer.** *Obs.* exc. in *Sc.* or north *dial.* [cf. next.] A sprout, shoot; in mod.Sc. 'the first appearance of grain above ground, after it is sown' (Jamieson).

c **1320** *Cast. Love* 123 Blosme on bouȝ and breer on rys. **1808** JAMIESON s.v. *A fine breer*, an abundant germination.

†**breer, brere,** *v.* *Sc.* or north *dial.* A variant of BRAIRD, to sprout, germinate.

c **1700** KENNET *MS. Gloss.*, To *brere* . . as corn just coming up. **1816** SCOTT *Old Mort.* viii, 'A braw night this for the rye . . the west park will be breering bravely this e'en.' **1846** BROCKETT *Gloss. N.C. Wds.*, *Brere, Brear.*

breer(e, dial. form of BRIER.

breese, obs. form of BREEZE *sb.*², BRUISE; var. of BREEZE *sb.*¹, ³.

breetch, breeth, obs. ff. of BREECH, BREATH(E.

breethreed, obs. form of BROTHERHOOD.

breeze (bri:z), *sb.*¹ Forms: 1 **briosa, breosa**, 4–6 **brese**, 5 **breze, breas**, 6 **bryze**, 6–7 **brize, brizze**, 7 **brieze, briese, breise, brise, breez**, (**bree, brye**), 4– **breese**, 7– **breeze**, (9 *arch.* **brize**). [OE. *briosa, breosa* masc.: conjecturally referred by some to BRIMSE; but there appears to be no ground for supposing any connexion.]

1. A gadfly: a name given to various dipterous insects, esp. of the genera *Œstrus* (BOT-FLY) and *Tabanus*, which annoy horses and cattle. *arch.* or *dial.* † **b.** ***sea-breeze***: a parasite infesting some fish (cf. Gr. οἶστρος). *Obs.* Also *fig.*

a **800** *Gloss.* in Wr.-Wülcker 7/20 *Asilo*, briosa. *Ibid.* 49/42 *Tabunus*, briosa. *c* **1380** CHAUCER *Balade*, I wol me venge on loue as doþe a breese On wylde horsse. **1596** SPENSER *F.Q.* VI. i. 24 As doth a steare . . With his long taile the bryzes brush away. **1601** HOLLAND *Pliny* I. 329 Certain Brees and horse-flies come of it [timber]. **1611** COTGR., *Tahon*, a Brizze, Brimsee, Gadbee, Dunflie, Oxeflie. *Tahon Marin*, the sea Brizze; a kind of worm found about some Fishes. **1641** MILTON *Ch. Discip.* II. (1851) 34 They deliver up the poor transformed heifer of the Commonwealth to be stung and vext with the breese and goad of oppression. **1661** K. W. *Conf. Charac.* (1860) 62 By the biting of this brye they run headlong after superiority. *a* **1725** POPE *Odyss.* XXII. 335 Like oxen maddened by the breeze's sting. **1850** BLACKIE *Æschylus* II. 44 O pain! pain! pain! . . The fateful brize!

†**2.** Applied vaguely to other insects. *Obs.*

a **1300** *E.E. Psalter* civ. 34 Brese, of whilk na tale ne ware. **1401** *Pol. Poems* (1859) II. 54 Whan the first angel blew . . ther rose smotheryng smoke, and brese therinne [**1611** locusts (*Rev.* ix. 3, etc.)]. *c* **1440** *Promp. Parv.* 49 Brese, *locusta.* **1483** CAXTON *Gold. Leg.* 412/3 That same tyme cam in to fraunce brezes or locustes Innumerable.

3. *Comb.*, as **breeze-fly** = BREEZE 1.

1572 MASCALL *Govt. Cattle* (1627) 34 To make that the breese-flie shall not annoy & bite cattell. 1868 WOOD *Homes without H.* xxvi. 511 Breeze Fly (*Œstrus bovis*).

breeze (briːz), *sb.*² Forms: 6–7 **brize, brieze,** 7 **brise, brese, breeze, breaze,** 7–8 **breez, breese,** 7– **breeze.** [In 16th c. *brize, brieze,* app. ad. OSp. (and Pg.) *briza* (mod.Sp. *brisa*) 'north-east wind' (though, according to Cotgrave, *brize* also occurs in Fr. (in Rabelais *a* 1550) = *bize, bise* 'north wind'). Cf. also It. *brezza* 'cold wind bringing mist or frost' (Florio), Milanese *brisa* 'cool wind from the north' (Diez). Cotgrave's *brize* = *bize,* supports the suggestion of Diez, that the word was orig. a variant of *bisa, bise* 'north east wind'. On the Atlantic sea-board of the West Indies and Spanish Main, *briza* acquired the transferred senses of 'north-east trade-wind', and 'fresh wind from the sea', in which it was adopted by the English navigators of the 16th c. The further extension to 'gentle fresh wind' generally, is English; cf. the actual F. *brise* (in the Dict. of the Academy only since 1762).]

†**1.** *orig.* A north or north-east wind; *spec.* applied within the tropics to the NE. trade-wind.

1565–89 *Hawkins' 2nd Voy.* in Arb. *Garner* V. 121 The ordinary brise taking us, which is the north-east wind. 1595 RALEIGH *Disc. Guiana* in Hakluyt *Voy.* (1600) III. 661 Against the brize and eastern wind. 1604 E. G[RIMSTON] *D'Acosta's Hist. Indies* III. iv. 128 In that Zone..the Easterly windes (which they call Brises) do raine. *a* 1618 RALEIGH *Apol.* 19 When the Easterly wind or Breeses are kept off by some High Mountaines. 1626 BACON *Sylva* §398 The great Brizes which the motion of the Air in great Circles ..produceth. 1685 *Phil. Trans.* XV. 1148 There are continual Eastern winds under the line which they call Brises. 1706 PHILLIPS, *Brizes,* or rather *Breezes,* certain Winds, which the motion of the Air in great circles doth produce, refrigerating those that live under the line.

†**2. a.** The cool wind that blows from the sea by day on tropical coasts. (This was on the Atlantic sea-board of tropical America an east or north-east wind, i.e. a *breeze* in sense 1; thence the name was extended to the 'sea-breeze' from any point of the compass.) *Obs.* exc. as in b.

1614 RALEIGH *Hist. World* I. iii. §8 These hottest regions of the World..are..refreshed with a daily Gale of Easternly Wind (which the Spaniards call the Brize). *a* 1618 —— *Inv. Shipping* 39 Southerly winds (the Brises of our Clymate) thrust them..into the Kings ports. 1627 CAPT. SMITH *Seaman's Gram.* x. 46 A Breze is a wind blowes out of the Sea, and commonly in faire weather beginneth about nine in the morning. 1628 DIGBY *Voy. Medit.* 38 Intending to goe in in the morning with the brize. 1665 G. HAVERS *P. della Valle's Trav. E. Ind.* 373 Sending a breeze, or breath, or small gale of wind daily. 1696 PHILLIPS, *Breez,* a fresh gale of wind blowing off the Sea by day. 1839 THIRLWALL *Greece* II. 307 A strong breeze which regularly blew up the channel at a certain time of the day.

b. Extended to include the counter-current of air that blows from the land by night; hence ***sea-breeze*** and ***land-breeze***.

a 1700 DRYDEN (J.) From land a gentle breeze arose by night. 1706 in PHILLIPS. 1731 BAILEY II, *Breez,* a fresh gale of wind blowing from the sea or land alternately for some certain hours of the day or night only sensible near the coast. 1782 COWPER *Loss Royal George* 9 A land-breeze shook the shrouds. 1832 MACAULAY *Armada* 31 The freshening breeze of eve unfurled that banner's massy fold.

3. a. A gentle or light wind: a *breeze* is generally understood to be a lighter current of air than a *wind,* as a *wind* is lighter than a *gale.* 'Among seamen usually synonymous with wind in general' (Smyth *Sailor's Word-bk.*).

1626 CAPT. SMITH *Accid. Yng. Seamen* 17 A calme, a brese, a fresh gaile. 1762 FALCONER *Shipwr.* I. 350 The lesser sails that court a gentle breeze. 1798 COLERIDGE *Anc. Mar.* II. v, The breezes blew, the white foam flew. 1863 C. ST. JOHN *Nat. Hist. Moray* vii. 167 The breeze was gentle, but sufficient to take us merrily over.

b. Slang phrases: ***to hit, split*** or ***take the breeze***: to depart; ***to get (have)*** or ***put the breeze up***: to get or put the wind up (see WIND *sb.*¹ 10 b).

1910 'O. HENRY' *Whirligigs* xiv. 168 We got to be hittin' the breeze. 1925 FRASER & GIBBONS *Soldier & Sailor Words* 35 *Breeze up, to have the*: to be nervous, to have the 'wind up'. 1931 RUNYON *Guys & Dolls* (1932) 29 And with this she takes the breeze and I return to the other room. 1934 D. L. SAYERS *Nine Tailors* III. 279 He got a vertical breeze up. 1948 D. BALLANTYNE *Cunninghams* 89 She was only making out she hadn't seen you so's you wouldn't get the breeze up. 1951 J. B. PRIESTLEY *Fest. Farbridge* 296 Put the breeze up me. 1959 I. & P. OPIE *Lore & Lang. Schoolch.* x. 193 Expressions inviting a person's departure, for instance:.. sling your hook, split the breeze, [etc.].

4. *fig.* **a.** A disturbance, quarrel, 'row'. *colloq.*

1785 GROSE *Dict. Vulgar Tongue, To kick up a breeze,* to breed a disturbance. 1803 WELLINGTON *Let.* in Gurw. *Disp.* II. 367 The cession would create a breeze in the Konkan. 1811 —— *ibid.* VII. 320 There was an old breeze between General —— and ——. 1837 MARRYAT *Dog-Fiend* I. xv. (L.), Jemmy, who expected a breeze, told his wife to behave herself quietly. 1865 *Sat. Rev.* 28 Jan. 119 'Don't be angry, we've had our breeze. Shake hands.'

b. A breath of news, whisper, rumour. *colloq.*

1879 STEVENSON *Trav. Cevennes* 215 There came a breeze that Spirit Séguier was near at hand. 1884 *Denver* (Colorado) *Tribune* Aug., Give us a breeze on the subject.

c. *slang.* Something easy to achieve, handle, etc. orig. *U.S.*

1928 G. H. RUTH *Babe Ruth's Own Bk. Baseball* 299 *Breeze,* an easy chance. 1958 M. DICKENS *Man Overboard* ix. 136 This will be a breeze for you. 1962 S. CARPENTER in *Into Orbit* 75 All in all, the test was a breeze.

5. *Comb.,* as ***breeze-borne, -like, -shaken, -swept, -wooing,*** adjs.

1805 J. GRAHAME *Sabbath,* On the distant cairn the watch-man's ear Caught doubtfully at times the *breeze-borne note. 1798–9 COLERIDGE *Day-Dream* ii. 5 A soft and *breeze-like feeling. 1802 WORDSW. *To H.C.,* The breeze-like motion. 1742 YOUNG *Nt. Th.* II. 300 Fate..hair-hung, *breeze-shaken, o'er the gulph A moment trembles. 1872 CALVERLEY *Fly Leaves* 4 Lingers on, till stars unnumber'd Tremble in the *breeze-swept tarn. 1894 G. BELL *Safar Nameh* 48 On the threshold of his breeze-swept dwelling. *c* 1830 J. H. GREEN *Morn. Invit. Child* 22 The bee hums of heather and *breeze-wooing hill.

breeze (briːz), *sb.*³ Also 9 **breese, braize.** [Origin somewhat uncertain: prob. a. F. *braise,* OF. *brese* burning charcoal, hot embers, also 'extinguished half-burned coal' (Littré), as *braise de boulanger* baker's breeze.]

a. Small cinders and cinder-dust, used in burning bricks, etc.; small coke and coke-dust.

1726 *Act 12 Geo. I,* xxxv, Nor any Breeze be used in the burning of any Bricks for Sale. 1751 CHAMBERS *Cycl., Breeze,* in brick-making, are small ashes and cinders, sometimes made use of instead of coals, for the burning of bricks. 1862 *Act 25 & 26 Vic.* c. 102 §89 If any person.. carry away..cinders, rubbish, ashes, or breeze from any houses. 1864 *Athenæum* No. 1928 466/3 Braize (or cinder taken from the scavenger's yard). 1875 URE *Dict. Arts* I. 505 *Breezes* (*Braise* Fr.), the dust of coke or charcoal. The coke burner applies this term to the small residual coke obtained in coke burning. The sifted ashes removed from houses is called breeze, and sold under that name to brickmakers and others. 1884 R. R. BOWKER in *Harper's Mag.* Apr. 777/1 Coke breeze (the refuse of gas-works).

b. *attrib.,* as **breeze-block,** a building-block made of 'breeze' (or some similar material) (see quot. 1923); so ***breeze-concrete***.

a 1877 KNIGHT *Dict. Mech.* I. 367/1 *Breeze-oven,* a furnace adapted for burning coal-dust or *breeze.* 1923 *Harmsworth's Househ. Encycl.* I. 521/2 *Breeze block.* Fine cinders, crushed coke, furnace clinker and burnt brick are used under the name of breeze in the construction of blocks for housebuilding...Breeze-blocks are fire-resisting, light and porous, suited for partitions and other internal walling. 1930 E. J. P. BENN *Account Rendered* ii. 10 We put up breeze-block boxes to look like houses. 1930 *Engineering* 11 July 41/3 Breeze and clinker concrete.

†**breeze,** *v.*¹ *Obs. rare.* [f. BREEZE *sb.*¹] *intr.* To buzz as a breeze or gadfly.

1688 R. HOLME *Armory* II. ix. 191 The Brize, Breezeth, or Brilleth.

breeze (briːz), *v.*². [f. BREEZE *sb.*²]

1. a. *intr.* To blow gently, as a breeze. *rare*

1682 [see BREEZING]. 1809 J. BARLOW *Columb.* IV. 624 The breathing airs..Breeze up the bay.

b. *colloq.* To move or proceed briskly; to depart. So ***to breeze in***: to arrive or enter briskly. orig. *U.S.*

1907 *Chicago Even. Post* 4 May 9 He breezed through the Louvre at such a pace that he broke all the rapid sight-seeing records. 1922 J. A. DUNN *Man Trap* ix. 129 If they show, breeze right along and forget me. 1923 WODEHOUSE *Inimit. Jeeves* iv. 51 'Ten o'clock, a clear night, and all's well, Jeeves,' I said, breezing back into the good old suite. *Ibid.* xv. 204 To..warn young Bingo to turn his coat-collar up and breeze off snakily by some side exit. 1930 W. S. MAUGHAM *Bread-Winner* I. 45 When did you breeze in, old bean? 1951 R. CAMPBELL *Light on Dark Horse* 246 My favourite brother George..breezed in to look for me.

2. ***to breeze up*** (Naut.): (of a wind) to freshen, to become stronger: also *impers.* Of a noise: to rise on the breeze.

1859 H. KINGSLEY *G. Hamlyn* xliv. (D.), The noise of the distant fight breezed up louder than ever. 1867 SMYTH *Sailor's Word-bk.,* Breezing up, the gale freshening. 1881 CLARK RUSSELL *Sailor's Sweeth.* III. vi. 292 Standing by the topsail halliards should it breeze up.

breezeless ('briːzlɪs), *a.* [f. BREEZE *sb.*² + -LESS.] Without a breeze; still, calm.

a 1763 SHENSTONE *Wks.* (1764) I. 41 A stagnant breezeless air. 1848 LYTTON *Milton,* Silent and sultry glowed the breezeless noon. 1849 C. BRONTË *Shirley* ix. 116 A still, dark day, equally beamless and breezeless.

breeze-way, breezeway ('briːzweɪ). orig. *U.S.* [f. BREEZE *sb.*¹ + WAY *sb.*¹] A roofed passage, usu. open at the sides, connecting two buildings or parts of a house.

1931 K. N. BURT *Man's Own Country* 39 A small log building attached to the end of his own ranch-house by means of what is known to the Far West as a breeze-way. This construction is a floored and roofed-over passage, open at the sides. 1952 M. MCCARTHY *Groves of Academe* (1953) ix. 170 From the other end of the breeze-way, through the open door of the dark garage, they heard Cathy's voice thinly calling. 1957 *New Yorker* 21 Sept. 39/1 Now if you don't have a floodlit crèche in the breezeway and your roof outlined with colored lights you're nobody. 1963 J. N. HARRIS *Weird World Wes Beattie* (1964) ii. 18 A modern split-level house complete with car port, breezeway and Chinese elm hedge. 1968 *Globe & Mail* (Toronto) 17 Feb. 46/9 (Advt.), Two acres of trees and lawn,..breezeway and double garage. 1969 *Sydney Morning Herald* 24 May 37/3 (Advt.), Large breezeway..connects Triple Garage to Rumpus Room.

breezily ('briːzɪlɪ), *adv.* [f. BREEZY + -LY².] In a breezy manner. Also *fig.* (see BREEZY *a.* 2b).

1865 *Morning Star* 1 June, Yesterday morning broke clearly, brightly, breezily. 1935 F. W. CROFTS *Crime at Guildford* xi. 146 'Good morning, gentlemen,' he said breezily. 1963 *New Statesman* 20 Dec. 902/3 She..refers quite breezily to her lack of relatives.

'breeziness. [f. BREEZY + -NESS.] The condition of being breezy; also *fig.*

1837 *Fraser's Mag.* XVI. 581 A sea-breeziness that we really dreaded to lose in a work written under the anti-Atlantic inspiration of Germany. 1885 *Illust. Lond. News* 8 Aug. 147/1 The breeziness of Fielding's novels.

'breezing, *ppl. a.* [f. BREEZE *v.* + -ING².] Blowing gently or freshly as a breeze.

1682 *New News fr. Bedlam* 21 We launcht our Ship..As having then some breezing prosperous Gales. *a* 1704 T. BROWN *On Beauties* Wks. 1730 I. 44 Soft breezing Zephyrs.

breezy ('briːzɪ), *a.* [f. BREEZE *sb.*² + -Y¹.]

1. Exposed to breezes, swept by the breeze.

1718 POPE *Iliad* II. 758 The warriors standing on the breezy shore. 1814 WORDSW. *Excurs.* I. 471 The shadows of the breezy elms above. 1859 CAPERN *Ball. & Songs* 137 Health laughs on every breezy hill. *Mod.* High on the breezy downs.

2. a. Attended with breezes, full of breezes, windy.

1753 GRAY *Elegy* vi, The breezy call of incense-breathing morn. 1798 WORDSW. *Lines wr. in Early Spring,* To catch the breezy air. 1840 HOOD *Up Rhine* 237 The night was breezy and cloudy.

b. *fig.* Fresh, airy; characterized by brisk vigour or activity; lively, jovial.

1870 LOWELL *Among my Bks.* Ser. II. (1873) 163 Whose breezy verse seems to float between a blue sky and golden earth. 1873 'MARK TWAIN' & WARNER *Gilded Age* li. 470 Said in almost his breezy old-time way. 1884 *American* VIII. 87 The chapter on 'Value' is particularly fresh and breezy. 1896 MRS. CAFFYN *Quaker Grandmother* 112 A strong, vigorous, breezy, old woman. 1930 W. S. MAUGHAM *Cakes & Ale* ii. 21 Roy smiled at the steward with breezy cordiality. 1942 *New Statesman* 11 July 25/1 American Jews are just like any other Americans, complete with breezy manners and deep voice. 1955 *Times* 27 Aug. 7/5 Some breezy remarks on Dutch or Flemish pictures.

bref, brefly, obs. ff. BRIEF, BRIEFLY.

breg-, in obs. forms: see BRIG-.

†**breganse,** *sb. Obs.* Cf. BRIGANDER.

1503 *Prer. of H. White* (Somerset Ho.), My best payr of breganse.

breger, var. of BRIGUER, *Obs.*

bregg(e, obs. form of BRIDGE.

bregger, -ynge, var. BRIDGER, etc. abridger.

breggurdel, bregirdil, -gyrdyle, var. of BREECHGIRDLE.

‖**bregma** ('brɛgmə). *Phys.* Pl. **'bregmata.** [a. Gr. βρέγμα front of the head.] The region of the skull where the frontal and the two parietal bones join; the sinciput; in infancy, before the sutures are closed, constituting the anterior fontanel. (Also formerly spoken of as two regions, the right and left bregmata.) Hence **breg'matic** *a.,* pertaining to the bregma.

1578 BANISTER *Hist. Man* I. 8 This Bregma is to be understode the vpper part of the head foreward, nigh to the Coronall Suture. 1754–64 SMELLIE *Midwif.* III. 41 Through one of the Bregmata. 1787 C. B. TRYE in *Med. Commun.* II. 145 Over the whole right bregma. 1857 BULLOCK *Cazeaux' Midwif.* 219 The great or anterior fontanelle is also called..the bregmatic fontanelle. 1878 BARTLEY tr. *Topinard's Anthrop.* iv. 133 The bregmatic fontanelle..is always closed before two years and a half of age.

Breguet (brəgeɪ). Also erron. **Bréguet.** The name of Abraham Louis *Breguet,* French watchmaker of Swiss origin (1747–1823), used attrib. in ***Breguet (hair)spring,*** the overcoil balance spring of a watch.

1881 F. J. BRITTEN *Watch & Clockmakers' Handbk.* (ed. 4) 63 Breguet springs are now often used for pocket chronometers instead of the helical form. 1908 *Sears Roebuck Catal.* 259/1 This movement..has 21 fine ruby jewels in gold settings, cut expansion balance, Breguet hairspring, [etc.]. 1929 G. H. BAILLIE *Watches* vii. 168 Properly, a Breguet spring should have no regulating curb pins, because the curve of the overcoil is correct only when it is of one definite length, and any movement of the curb pins alters its length and partially destroys its effect. 1952 FLOOD & WEST *Dict. Sci. & Techn. Words* (1953) 42/1 *Bréguet spring,* special form of hair-spring..in a watch.

bregynge, var. BRIDGING *vbl. sb. Obs.* abridging.

†**brehon** ('briːhən). *Obs.* exc. *Hist.* Also 6 **breighoon,** 7 **brehan.** [ad. Irish *breathamh* or *breitheamh,* pl. *breitheamhuin* (pronounced 'brɛəvɪn), in OIr. *brithem,* gen. *brithemon* 'judge', f. *breth* judgement.] An ancient Irish judge.

a 1581 CAMPION *Hist. Irel.* vi. (1633) 19 The Breighoon (so they call this kind of Lawyer) sitteth him downe on a

banke. **1596** SPENSER *State Irel.* 4 In the case of murder, the Brehon, that is their judge, will compound between the murderer and the friends of the party murdered. **1827** HALLAM *Const. Hist.* (1876) III. xviii. 345 In the territories of each Sept, judges called Brehons .. sat .. to determine controversies. **1875** MAINE *Hist. Inst.* ii. 24 They are .. the creation of a class of professional lawyers, the Brehons.

b. ***Brehon law***, the code of law which prevailed in Ireland before its occupation by the English, finally abolished in the reign of James I.

1596 SPENSER *State Irel.* 4 What is that you call Brehon Law? .. It is a rule of right unwritten, but delivered by tradition from one to another. **1614** RALEIGH *Hist. World* II. v. ii. 327 One that hath quite abolished a slauish Brehon Law. **1672** PETTY *Pol. Anat.* 375 Governed by different laws; the Irish by the Brehan law, and the English there by the laws of England. **1757** BURKE *Abridgm. Eng. Hist.* Wks. X. 334 The narrow notions of our lawyers, who abolished the authority of the Brehon law, and at the same time kept no monuments of it. **1856** FROUDE *Hist. Eng.* II. 248 The Brehon traditions—a convenient system, which was called law, but which in practice was a happy contrivance for the composition of felonies.

brei (braɪ). *Biochem.* [a. Ger., lit. 'pulp, jelly'.] Living tissue which has been ground or finely cut into a pulp for experimental purposes, sometimes with fluid added to form a suspension.

1935 *Biochem. Jrnl.* XXIX. 57 Evidently determinations of Qo_2 in tissue 'brei' must be influenced by these findings. **1946** *Nature* 19 Oct. 555/2 The brei resulting from grinding the larvae in a mortar was homogenized. **1962** A. PIRIE *Lens Metabolism Rel. Cataract* 431 (*heading*) Formation of α-glycerophosphate from glucose by intact rabbit lens or undiluted lens brei. **1976** *Nature* 22 Jan. 223/2 The tissues from six pregnant mice .. were homogenised in phosphate-buffered saline .. and the resultant tissue brei was absorbed in equal proportions (w/v) with the antisera for 30 min at 37°C.

brei, var. BRAY *v.*[4]

breid, Sc. f. BREAD, BREED, BREDE; obs. f. BRAID.

breigge, var. of BRIDGE *v. Obs.* to shorten.

breigirdil, -gurdel, var. of BREECHGIRDLE.

breik, obs. f. BREAK, BREECH.

brein(e, breird, obs. ff. BRAIN, BRAIRD.

breirdit: see BRERDED.

breise, obs. f. BREEZE *sb.*[1], gadfly.

breislakite ('braɪsləkaɪt). *Min.* Also **-ackite**. [after *Breislak*, an Italian geologist of German descent.] A woolly-looking variety of pyroxene.

1869 PHILLIPS *Vesuv.* x. 296 Hornblende, or Amphibole, including Breislakite—in ejected blocks and scoriæ on Somma and Vesuvius.

breist, obs. form of BREAST *sb.*.

breithauptite ('braɪthaʊptaɪt). *Min.* [after *Breithaupt*, a Saxon mineralogist.] Antimonial nickel, a native alloy of these two metals (Ni Sb) found in the Harz Mountains.

breither, obs. pl. of BROTHER.

breithful, var. of BRATHFUL *a. Obs.*

breitschwanz ('braɪtʃvants). Also **breitschwantz, breitswanz**. [G., = broad tail.] = BROADTAIL.

1923 *Daily Mail* 16 Apr. 15 The frilled coat had a sailor collar of dark blue breitschwanz. **1927** *Daily News* 26 Sept. 2/4 Especially good is the imitation or broadtail known as breitswanz. **1928** *Daily Express* 24 Jan. 5/4 Shaved lamb, breitschwantz, caracul, and astrakhan are seen in beige and light shades of golden brown. **1960** B. MARSHALL *Divided Lady* 119 Bice looked lovely in a Breitschwanz coat and a black hat.

brek, obs. Sc. f. BRACK *sb.*[1], outcry.

brek(e, obs. f. BREAK, BRECK, BRICK.

breke, -girdul, obs. ff. BREECH, -GIRDLE.

‖**ˌbrekeke'kex.** a. Gr. βρεκεκεκέξ, used by Aristophanes to imitate the croaking of frogs.

1607 WALKINGTON *Opt. Glass* 78 Frogs with their brekekekex brekekekex coax. **1656** TRAPP *Comm. Matt.* xxii. 33 Those Romish frogs, the Jesuits, will never have done, though never so much set down, but be still up with their hateful Brekekekex-coax-coax.

brekil, brekyl(le, obs. ff. BRICKLE, brittle.

brekke, var. of BRECK, *Obs.*

brekker ('brɛkə(r)). (*University*) *slang.* [f. BREAK(FAST *sb.* + -ER[6].] Breakfast.

1889 in BARRÈRE & LELAND *Dict. Slang.* **1900** G. SWIFT *Somerley* 66 Have you had any brekker? **1908** *Daily Chron.* 20 Apr. 4/7 A young man who looked like an undergraduate wondered when his 'brekker' would be ready. **1928** D. L. SAYERS *Unpleasantness at Bellona Club* xi. 129 He'd only that moment swallowed his brekker. **1965** J. P. CARSTAIRS *Concrete Kimono* i. 9, I complained of an undesirable brekker kipper.

brekkie, brekky ('brɛkɪ). *slang* (orig. children's). [f. BREAK(FAST *sb.* + -Y[6].] Breakfast.

1904 E. NESBIT *Phoenix & Carpet* xii. 218, I've brought your brekkie, and I've put the little cloth with clover-leaves on it. **1926** E. BOWEN *Ann Lee's* 66 Do call poor Bingo in .. and give him his brekky. **1969** *Private Eye* 25 Apr. 12, I don't reckon I feel like brekkie!

brell, obs. form of BRILL.

‖**breloque** (brə'lɔk). [F.: see Littré.] A small ornament fastened to a watch-chain.

1856 THACKERAY *Christm. Bks.* (1872) 137 His chains and breloques .. and ambrosial moustaches. **1882** A. B. HOPE *Brandreths* I. xvi. 250 His chain and his breloques wag.

brem, -e, obs. forms of BREAM.

brembel, -bil, -bul, -ble, obs. ff. BRAMBLE.

†**'brember.** *Obs.* [OE. *brember*, var. of *brembel*, BRAMBLE.] A by-form of BRAMBLE.

a **1000** *Cædmon's Gen.* 2928 (Gr.) He rom ȝeseah brembrum fæstne. *c* **1386** CHAUCER *Sir Thopas* 35 Sweet as is the brembre flour [*v.r.* brembul].

†**breme** (briːm), *a. Obs.* exc. *poet.* and *dial.* (brim) in sense 6. Forms: 1- **bréme**, 2- **breme**; also 3-6 **brem**, 3- **brim**, 3 **brime**, 4-6 **brym**, 5-6 **brymme**, **bryme**, 4-7 **breeme**, 6 **brimme**, 6-7 **breem**, (7 **breame**). [In Branch I, OE. *bróeme*, *bréme*, (*brýme*), celebrated, famous. The origin of Branch II, which did not exist in OE., and was more decidedly northern in ME. use, is at present unexplained.

The Lindisf. Gosp. has (*Matt.*, Pref. l. 10) *broemende* as a gloss of L. *fervēre*, which gives a sense related to branch II; but it is difficult to see the connexion between this and OE. *bróeme*, *bréman*. Nor can branch II be derived from OE. *bremman* to bray, roar, 'rudere, fremere', ME. BRIM *v.*, though there may have been later confusion between a 'breme' or 'brim' boar, and a 'brimming' boar.]

I. Celebrated, brilliant, clear, loud, distinct.

†**1.** Celebrated, famous, glorious (only in OE.); hence as a general epithet of admiration: Excellent, good, 'fine', 'famous'; sometimes app. = very big or strong. *Obs.*

a **1000** *Ags. Ps.* cxxxv[i]. 21 Og .. wæs swyþe breme cyning on Basane. *a* **1300** *Floriz & Bl.* 792 þilke feste was wel breme. *c* **1325** *E.E. Allit. P.* A. 862 Vchonez blysse is breme & beste. *c* **1350** *Will. Palerne* 18 A big barn and breme of his age. **1377** LANGL. *P. Pl.* B. XII. 224 How euere beste or brydde hath so breme wittes.

†**2.** Brilliant, shining, bright; *hence*, clearly seen, evident, apparent, obvious. *Obs.*

c **1340** *Alisaunder* 533 Of Barbre þe bryght God brem to beholde. *c* **1400** *Destr. Troy* 1563 Ymagry .. Of bestes and babery breme to beholde. **1526** *Pilgr. Perf.* (W. de W. 1531) 291 b, The lyght of grace .. is so breme in these holy soules. **1548** W. PATTEN *Exp. Scotl.* in Arb. *Garner* III. 106 They mustered somewhat brim in our eyes. **1581** STUDLEY *Seneca's Medea* 121 Lyfe seems the bayte to sight that lyeth brim, Death is the hooke that underlies the same. **1594** PLAT *Jewel-ho.* III. 32 So brim and glittering light. **1605** [see B.].

†**3.** Strong, distinct, or clear in sound. *Obs.*

a **1300** [see B.]. *c* **1340** *Gaw. & Gr. Knt.* 1601 There watz blawyng of prys in mony breme horne. *Ibid.* 2200 A wonder breme noyse. **1340** *Alex. & Dind.* 503 Brem briddene song [in] þe braunchus a-lofte. **1581** T. HOWELL *Deuises* (1879) 199 As a Bell sends forth the brimmest sownde, When deepest downe the Ringer plucks the frame. **1596** *Life Scanderbeg* 368 Brimme noise of the drummes, trumpets and tamborins. **1606** SYLVESTER *Du Bartas* II. II. iv. (1621) 301 But, brimmer far than in the Heav'ns, heer All these sweet-charming Counter-Tunes we hear.

†**4.** Of reports, rumours: Loudly or strongly current or prevalent, much spoken of. *Obs.*

1560 THROGMORTON in Froude *Hist. Eng.* (1881) VI. 439 The bruits were so brim of the marriage of the Lord Robert. **1529** MORE *Comf. agst. Trib.* I. Wks. 1140/2 Sith these tydinges haue comen hether so brymme of the greate Turkes enterpryse. **1565** GOLDING *Ovid's Met.* XII. (1593) 280 In their talke most breeme Was then Achilles victorie. **1617** *Argentile & C.* in Percy *Reliques* (1767) II. 243 That thou Doest hold me in disdaine Is brimme abroad.

II. Fierce, raging, rough, rugged.

†**5.** Of persons and their attributes or actions: Fierce, raging, furious; stern, wroth. *Obs.*

c **1200** ORMIN 7197 Herode king was grill & gramm, & breme, & bollȝhenn. *a* **1300** *Cursor M.* 4003 Esau coms brem and brath. *c* **1400** *Destr. Troy* 9632 Brem was þe battell vpon both haluys. *c* **1440** *Promp. Parv.* 51 Brym or fers, *ferus, ferox.* **1496** *Dives and Paup.* (W. de W.) x. Introd. 31 Whan all other synnes forsake men for elde and feblenesse, than couetyse is moost breme. **1513** DOUGLAS *Æneis* VI. v. 41 This sorofull boitman with brym [*v.r.* breme] luik. **1556** ABP. PARKER *Psalter* H iv, Amyds my foes so brymme. **1580** SIDNEY *Arcadia* II. 224 Let not pride make the brim.

†**b.** similarly of beasts; *esp.* as an epithet of the *boar* (perh. with ref. to sense of BRIM *v.*). *Obs.*

a **1300** *Cursor M.* 4899 þe sargantz þat ware brem [*v.r.* breme, brim] als bare. *c* **1420** *Sir Amadace* xvi, He come to me as breme as bare. *c* **1530** LD. BERNERS *Arth. Lyt. Bryt.* (1814) 56 Who hath the loke of a brym bore. **1535** STEWART *Cron. Scotl.* II. 461 Lyke ony lyoun he wes als brym and bald. **1550** LYNDESAY *Sq. Meldrum* 518 As brym as he had bene ane beir. *a* **1553** UDALL *Royster D.* IV. vi, Never bore so brymme, nor tost so hot. *a* **1650** *Turke & G.* 36 in Furniv. *Percy Folio* I. 92 Though ye be breme as bore.

†**c.** of a fierce flame or blaze. *Obs.* or *arch.*

c **1374** CHAUCER *Troylus* IV. 156 As breme as blase of straw yset a fyre. *c* **1400** *Destr. Troy* 860 þe fyre .. was blasound of brunston with a brem lowe. **1818** *Ballad* in *Edin. Mag.* Oct. 327 (JAM.) The sun sae breem frae hint a clud, Pour't out the lowan day.

6. Of the sea, wind, etc.: Raging, rough, fierce, stormy: an attribute of winter, taken from Lydgate by Spenser, and echoed from Spenser by later poets. It survives in living use in north. dial. as *brim*.

a **1300** *Havelok* 2233 That he sholde drenchen him In the se, that was ful brim. **1330** R. BRUNNE *Chron.* 28 Kast him in tille Temse, whan it was most brym. *c* **1400** *Destr. Troy* 3714 A brode in the breme se. **1430** LYDG. *Chron. Troy* II. xvi, The breme wynter with his frost hore. **1513** DOUGLAS *Æneis* VII. Prol. 15 Brym blastis of the northyne art. **1579** SPENSER *Sheph. Cal.* Feb. 42, Breme [*Gloss.* chill, bitter] winter with chamfred browes. **1598** DRAYTON *Heroic. Epist.* XVI. 8 On whose breeme Seas the Icie Mountaines flote. **1603** —— *Odes* x. 30 T'asswage breeme Winters scathes. **1611** COTGR., *Froid*, cold .. breame, chill. *a* **1618** J. DAVIES *Eglog.* (1772) 114 Looke how breeme winter chamfers earths bleeke face. **1748** THOMSON *Cast. Indol.* II. vii, Glad summer or the winter breme. **1808** JAMIESON s.v. *Brim*, 'A brim frost' is still a common phrase for a severe frost. *S.B.* **1824** WIFFEN *Tasso* I. vi.

†**7.** Also in ***brem valay***: rough, rugged valley; ***breres brimme***: sharp briers. *Obs.*

c **1340** *Gaw. & Gr. Knt.* 2145 To þe boþem of þe brem valay. *c* **1400** *Rom. Rose* 1836 Thisteles thikke, And breres brymme for to prikke.

B. quasi-*adv.* in the various senses: Splendidly, brilliantly, clearly; loudly; fiercely.

a **1000** *Andreas* (Gr.) 1721 Breme ȝebledsod. *a* **1300** in Wright's *Lyric P.* 44 When briddes singeth breme. *c* **1340** *Gaw. & Gr. Knt.* 781 þe bryge watz breme vp-brayde. *c* **1386** CHAUCER *Knts. T.* 841 Arcite and Palamon, That foughten breeme, as it were boores tuo. *a* **1500** *E.E. Misc.* (Warton) 65 Gabrelle schalle bloo both brymme and scrylle. **1577** tr. *Bullinger's Decades* (1592) 619 [It doth] shine out very brightly, but far more brim if we, etc. **1605** SYLVESTER *Du Bartas* I. iv. (1633) 79 The rest .. we do more brim behold. **1607** W. BARKSTED *Mirrha* (1876) 12 Eccho was pleas'd with voice resounding brim.

breme, obs. form of BREAM, a fish.

breme, obs. or dial. f. BRIM *v.*, said of swine.

†**'bremely**, *a. Obs.* [f. BREME *a.* + -LY[1].] Fierce, furious.

c **1300** *Cursor M.* 24847 (Edinb.) þaim blew on mani bremli blast. *a* **1500** *Songs & Carols 15th C.* (1847) 26 (Mätz.) That brymly best so cruell and unryd, Ther tamyd I hym.

†**'bremely**, *adv. Obs.* Also 3-5 **bremly**, 6 **brimly**: see BREME *a.* [f. BREME *a.* + -LY[2].]

1. Fiercely, angrily; *hence*, in more general senses, as hotly, vehemently, strenuously, strongly.

a **1300** *Cursor M.* 7606 For þis word was saul wrath, For oft sith was he bremli brath. *c* **1350** *Will. Palerne* 948 Wel y vnderstande whider þe belaunce bremliest bouwes. *c* **1400** *Ywaine & Gaw.* 3163 The lioun bremely on tham blist. **1513** DOUGLAS *Æneis* XII. xii. 215 As he brymly thus inforcis fast To draw the speyr. *c* **1525** SKELTON *Replyc.* 221 Bremely with your bristels Ye cobble and ye clout Holy Scripture so about. **1592** WARNER *Alb. Eng.* VIII. xliii. (1612) 207 On these doo vulgar Eares and Eyes so brimly waite and gaze.

2. Loudly, distinctly, shrilly.

c **1340** *Gaw. & Gr. Knt.* 569 Bryddez busken to bylde, & bremlych syngen. *c* **1350** *Will. Palerne* 23 And briddes ful bremely on þe bowes singe. ? *a* **1400** *Morte Arth.* 4108 Bremly the brethemen bragges in troumppes.

3. Brightly; clearly; evidently, distinctly.

1577 tr. *Bullinger's Decades* (1592) 618 The Lord will not .. reueale himself and his glorie any whit more fully and brimly. **1583** STANYHURST *Æneis* II. (Arb.) 62 My mother, the Godesse .. most brimlye dyd offer Her self to visadge. *Ibid.* III. 75 At thee wyndoors .. moonshyne brimlye dyd enter. **1589** PUTTENHAM *Eng. Poesie* III. xxv. (Arb.) 311 A man sees better and discernes more brimly his collours.

†**'bremeness.** *Obs.* In 4-5 **bremnes**, 6 **breem-**. [f. as prec. + -NESS.] Fierceness, fury.

c **1400** *Destr. Troy* 4665 Then the se wex sober, sesit the wyndis .. The bremnes abatid; blusshit the sun. *Ibid.* 10104 Pollexena, with hir pure loue, .. Abated the bremnes in his bale yre. **1540** HYRDE *Vives' Instr. Chr. Wom.* (1592) X. iv, Quietnes is of more authoritie than hastie breemnes.

bremete, bremette, obs. ff. BREAMET.

breming, var. of BRIMMING, said of swine.

1577 B. GOOGE *Heresbach's Husb.* (1586) 149 b, Shee is with pigge at the first breming.

bremit. [app. a ppl. adj. formed on BREME *a.*, unless the OE. vb. *bremman* came down.] Infuriated.

1535 STEWART *Cron. Scot.* II. 401 The Scottis than so bremit war and bald.

bremmyll, obs. form of BRAMBLE.

bremsstrahlung ('brɛmsʃtraːlʊŋ). *Nuclear Physics.* [G., lit. 'braking radiation', f. *bremsen* to brake + *strahlung* radiation.] The electromagnetic radiation produced by the retardation of a charged particle, usu. an electron passing through the field of a nucleus.

1944 W. HEITLER *Quantum Theory Radiation* (ed. 2) iii. 160 This is .. the case for the *Bremsstrahlung* (continuous X-ray emission). The Bremsstrahlung is one of the most important processes affecting the penetrating power of high-energy electrons by passing through matter. **1948** MOTT & SNEDDON *Wave Mech.* x. 275 Among [radiation] processes of the third order the most important is

'Bremsstrahlung'—the emission of radiation by an electron passing through the field of a nucleus. **1958** *New Scientist* 16 Jan. 14/1 A radiative heat loss due to this process (technically known as *bremsstrahlung* radiation). **1962** *Newnes Conc. Encycl. Nucl. Energy* 90/2 *Bremsstrahlung*.. The name (braking radiation) originates in the radiation produced when electrons are stopped in an absorber. **1965** *New Scientist* 30 Dec. 905/1 The third possibility is that the X-rays from the Crab are produced by bremsstrahlung or the braking of electrons in a hot gas cloud at a temperature of 10-100 million °K.

Bren (brɛn). [f. *Brno*, a town in Czechoslovakia, where the gun was originally made + first syllable of *Enfield*, Middlesex, England, seat of a small-arms factory.] In full, *Bren gun*. A type of light, quick-firing machine-gun. Also *attrib.*, as **Bren (gun) carrier**, a small bullet-proof tracked vehicle, designed to carry the Bren gun and its crew.

1937 *Times* 29 Sept. 6/3 Use of the Bren Gun. **1939** *War Illustr.* 28 Oct. 200 A long train of Bren gun carriers is passing towards the front. **1940** *Times Weekly* 7 Aug. 8/4 A motor-cyclist detachment of the Lancashire Fusiliers followed by their Bren carriers. **1946** KOESTLER *Thieves in Night* 67 The steady rattle of an automatic, a Lewis or a Bren.

bren, early ME. plural of BREE.

bren(e, obs. form of BRAN, BURN.

brend(e, -ing, brended, obs. ff. BURNT, BURNING, BRINDED variegated.

†**'brendice**. *Obs. rare*$^{-1}$. [a. It. *brindesi*, *brindisi*, 'a drinking or health to one' (Florio); according to Diez perverted (by popular etymology) from Ger. *bring dir's*, i.e. *ich bringe dir's zu*; whence also Fr. *brinde*: see Littré. Cf. BRINCE, BRINCH *v.*] A cup in which a person's health is drunk, a bumper.

1673 DRYDEN *Amboyna* I. i, I go to fill a Brendice to my Noble Captain's Health.

brene, -ie, -y, obs. ff. BRYN, BRINIE, corselet.

breneage. *Obs. rare*$^{-1}$. (? Burning.)

1535 *Leverton Churchw. Acc.* in *Archæol. Jrnl.* XLI. 345 (D.) To Wyllm Cortys for breneage in the fen.

breng, brenk, obs. ff. BRING, BRINK.

'brennage. *Old Law*. [A modern rendering of OF. *brennage*, *brenage*, f. *bren* BRAN; or of its med.L. form *brennagium*. Many examples of the latter are in Du Cange; it is also given in Blount, Tomlins, etc.; the Eng. form appears in mod. Dicts.] A payment in, or instead of, bran, made by tenants to feed their lord's hounds.

1753 CHAMBERS *Cycl. Supp.*, Brennage. **1847** in CRAIG.

brenne, obs. form of BRAN.

brenne, brennand(e, -ing(e, -ar, -er, obs. ff. BURN, -ING, BURNER.

brennish, bad form of BRINISH *a.*

brenstone, obs. form of BRIMSTONE.

brent (brɛnt), *a.* *Sc.* [A phonetic variant of BRANT, found in northern ME., and in Sc.]

†**1.** Steep, lofty: see BRANT. *Obs.*

c **1325** *E.E. Allit. P.* B. 379 þay..bowed to þe hyȝ bonk þer brentest hit wern. *c* **1340** *Gaw. & Gr. Knt.* 2165 Hyȝe bonkkez and brent. **1691** RAY *N.C. Wds.* 132 *Brent-brow*, a steep Hill, *Metaph.*

2. Of the forehead: **a.** Lofty, straight up, prominent. **b.** Unwrinkled, smooth.

c **1400** *Destr. Troy* 3030 With browes full brent, brightist of hewe. **1513** DOUGLAS *Æneis* VIII. xii. 14 From his blyth browis [L. *tempora læta*] brent and athyr ene The fyre twinkling. **1629** Z. BOYD *Last Battle* 678 (JAM.) At the first sight of that angrie Majestie, with brent browes and sterne countenance. *a* **1758** RAMSAY *Poems* (1800) II. 17 (JAM.) Her fair brent brow, smooth as th' unrunkled deep. **1789** BURNS *J. Anderson* i, Your bonie brow was brent.

brent (brɛnt), *sb.* [So commonly spelt by Eng. authors since Pennant; Dr. Kay also (1570) had *brend-gose*. The form usual in 16th and 17th c., and still prevalent in U.S., is BRANT, which see.]

The smallest species of wild goose (*Bernicla brenta*), a winter visitant of the British coasts. Also, more fully **brent-goose** (in 6 brend-gose).

1570 CAIUS *De var. animal.* 18 Anser Brendinus..Vulgus ..a coloris varietate a *Brendgose* nominat..*Bernded* seu *brended* id animal dicitur, quod in colore murino variegatum est albo, ut est hic anser. **1768** PENNANT *Zool.* II. 453 Mr. Willoughby, Mr. Ray, and M. Brisson very properly describe the Bernacle and Brent as different species. **1839** *Proc. Berw. Nat. Club* I. vii. 190 Brent-geese..and golden-eyes, were very plentiful. **1848** C. A. JOHNS *Week at Lizard* 333 Brent (*Anser torquatus*). **1876** DAVIS *Polaris Exp.* v. 113 Large flocks of brent-geese were seen. **1884** *Mehalah* i. 3 The barking of the brent geese as they return from their northern breeding places is heard in November.

brentid ('brɛntɪd), *a.* (*sb.*) *Entom.* Of or pertaining to the Brentides, a family of rhynchophorous beetles containing the genus *Brentus*, having a remarkable projecting proboscis.

[**1836** *Penny Cycl.* V. 390/2 Brentides..are almost entirely confined to tropical climates.] **1864** *Reader* No. 94. 488/3 A curious little Brentid insect.

brent-new, obs. form of BRAND-NEW.

breo-, earlier spelling of BRE-, BREA-.

brepho-, combining form of Gr. βρέφος babe; only in nonce-wds., as **bre'pholatry** (brɛ'fɒlətrɪ), baby-worship; **bre'phophagist**, baby-eater; **bre'photrophy** (see quot.).

1731 BAILEY II, *Brephotrophy*..an hospital for orphans. **1857** *Blackw. Mag.* LXXXII. 594 Brepholatry..means exaggerated worship of a small household Llama. **1875** E. RAE *Land of N. Wind* 265 (D.) A gentleman who affirmed that babies were excellent eating..This Brephophagist was a well-dressed and nicely-mannered man.

brer (brɛə(r)). *colloq.* (orig. *U.S.*). [Representing an American Negro or southern U.S. pronunc. of BROTHER *sb.*] Brother.

1881 J. C. HARRIS *Uncle Remus* i. 17 Arter Brer Fox bin doin' all dat he could fer ter ketch Brer Rabbit. **1889** G. B. SHAW *London Music 1888–89* (1937) 145 Last night we had Brer Jean [de Reszke] as Raoul and Brer Edouard as Marcel. **1895** KIPLING *Lett. of Travel* (1920) 107 No one seems to know particularly where Brer Coon lives.

brer, obs. form of BRIER.

†**brerd**. *Obs.* exc. *dial.* Also 1 breard, briord, 3 breord, 4 brurde, 4–5 brerde, 6 *Sc.* breird. [OE. *brerd* brim, margin; cf. OHG. *brort*, *brord* prow, margin, lip, also OE. *brord* point, prick, ON. *broddr* shaft, pike: see BRAIRD, and BROD.]

The topmost surface or edge: rim, brim, brink.

c **1000** *Ags. Gosp.* John ii. 7 Hiȝ ȝefyldon þa oþ þone brerd [*Lindisf. & Rushw.* briorde]. *c* **1050** *Ags. Gloss.* in Wr.-Wülcker 178 *Crepido*, brerd uel ofer. *c* **1200** ORMIN 14040 And filledenn upp till þe brerd Wiþþ waterr þeȝȝre fetless. *c* **1205** LAY. 23322 From breorde to grunde. *a* **1225** *Ancr. R.* 324 þe þet nappeð upon helle brerde, he torpleð ofte al in. **1382** WYCLIF *Ex.* xxxvii. 11 He made to it a goldun brerde. **1424** *E.E. Wills* (1882) 56 Six saucers of siluere merkid with a sink foil vnder þe brerdez. *c* **1475** *Cath. Angl.* 42 (MS. A) Brerde [*v.r.* Brede] of a wessille, *labrum, abses.* **1596** *Declar. etc. Melville's MS.* 279 (JAM.) Has gotten the breird to drink. *a* **1758** RAMSAY *Sc. Proverbs* (1776) 19 (JAM.) Better hain at the brierd than at the bottom. **1808** JAMIESON s.v. *Breird*, 'The brerd of the water' is..still used in Dumbartonshire for the surface of it.

¶ See also BRAIRD *sb.*

†**'brerded**, *ppl. a.* *Obs.* In 6 *Sc.* breirdit. [f. prec. + -ED.] = BRIMMED.

1535 STEWART *Cron. Scot.* (1858) I. 69 All the brym wes breirdit ouir with blude.

†**'brerd-full**, *a.* *Obs.* Also 4 brurdful. [f. as prec. + FULL; cf. BRETFULL.] Brim-full.

c **1000** ÆLFRIC *Lives of Saints* VI. 282 Brerd-ful wines. *c* **1200** ORMIN 14529 Swa summ þatt oþerr fetless wass Brerdfull off waterr filledd. *c* **1325** *E.E. Allit. P.* B. 383 Vch boþom watz brurdful to þe bonkez eggez.

brere (brɪə(r)). The original form of BRIER, BRIAR, retained in the dialects, and by mod. poets.

brerewood, a corruption of BREWARD brim.

brese, obs. form of BREEZE *sb.*^{1}, ^{2} and BRUISE.

†**'bresed**, *a.* *Obs.* Perhaps: Bristly, shaggy, rough.

c **1325** *E.E. Allit. P.* B. 1694 His browes bresed as breres aboute his brode chekes. *c* **1340** *Gaw. & Gr. Knt.* 305 Bende his bresed broȝez, blycande grene.

bresewort, obs. form of BRUISEWORT.

bresil, var. of BRISEL *Obs.*, brittle.

Bresill, -yle, obs. forms of BRAZIL^1.

breslet, variant of BERCELET, *Obs.*

bresse, obs. form of BRACE *sb.*^{2}.

bressie: see BRASSY *sb. Sc.*, a fish.

bressomer, bressumer, var. of BREAST-SUMMER.

†**brest**, *sb.* [ME., a. ON. *brestr* burst, crack, want, loss, f. *bresta* = OE. *berstan* to BURST.]

1. Damage, injury, harm, wrong.

a **1300** *Cursor M.* 17630 For wel suld all þe brest be bett. *Ibid.* 11230 þe sun beme gais thoru þe glas and cums again wit-vten brest. *Ibid.* 4283 (Trin.) What is more herte brest þen want of þing þat men loue best. *c* **1325** *E.E. Allit. P.* B. 229 Hit watz a brem brest & a byge wrache. **1564** *Brief Exam.* B iij, Without touche of brest sure and vnuiolable.

2. Failure, want.

a **1300** *Cursor M.* 6308 O water had þai ful mikel brest. *c* **1440** *Promp. Parv.* 49 Brest, or wantynge, *indigencia.*

brest, brestel, obs. ff. BREAST *sb.*, BURST, BRISTLE.

bret (brɛt), *sb.* Also 6 brytte, brite, brette, 6–7 brit, 7–8 brut, 5– brett. [Derivation and etymological form uncertain: written also *bert*, *burt*, *byrte*, BIRT q.v.]

†**1.** The name of a fish, identified in some places with the Brill, in others with the Turbot; = BIRT.

c **1460** J. RUSSELL *Bk. Nurture* 852 in *Babees Bk.* (1868) 175 Lynge, brett & fresche turbut. **1555** EDEN *Dec. W. Ind.* (Arb.) 297 Hearynges, coddes, haddockes and brettes. **1570** LEVINS *Manip.* 148 A Brit, fish, *rhombus*. **1601** J. THEYER *Dutch Fishing* in *Phenix* I. 228 All along the Coast of England..are innumerable shoals..of..Scate, Brett, Gurnet, Turbutt. **1610** FOLKINGHAM *Art of Survey* IV. iii. 63 Sturgion, Turbot, Porpuis, Seale, Bret, Tunie. **1611** COTGR., *Bertonneau*, a bret, or Turbot. **1671** RAY *Corr.* (1848) 94 What they call Bret in Lincolnshire and Yorkshire, and..in all the east part of England, is the turbut of the west country, where the name Bret is not known. **1836** YARRELL *Brit. Fishes* (1859) I. 642 Another name quoted among those in use for the Brill, namely the Brett.

2. The spawn or fry of the herring; = BRIT.

1725 DUDLEY in *Phil. Trans.* XXXIII. 262 He has seen this Whale..to take in a Sort of reddish Spawn or Brett, as some call it, that..will lie upon the Top of the Water, for a Mile together. **1867** F. FRANCIS *Bk. Angling* ix. (1880) 308 Bret, or herring sail, on which they have been feeding.

†**bret, brit**, *v.* *Obs.* or *dial.* [Cf. OE. *bréotan* to break, bruise.] *trans.* ? To bite, crop.

1578 H. WOTTON *Courtly Controv.*, The young lambes.. nibling and brettyng the toppes of the preatye pagles. **1864** CAPERN *Devon Provinc.*, *Brit*, to indent.

bretage, -ais, -asce, -ayge, -ays, obs. ff. of BRATTICE.

†**'bretcock**. *Obs.* A fish: cf. BRET.

1522 *Acc.* in *Archæol.* XXV. 449 P^d to John Syff for a brettcocke viijd. **1524** *Ibid.* 454 Bretcocke. **1526** *Househ. Exp. Sir T. Le Strange* (Addit. MS. 27448. f. 27) Item, a playce, vjd. Item, a bretcocke, iiijd.

bretelle (brə'tɛl). [Fr., strap, sling; in *pl.* braces.] Each of the ornamental shoulder-straps extending from the waist-belt in front to the belt behind of a woman's dress. Chiefly *pl.* Also *attrib.* and *Comb.*

1857 *Godey's Lady's Book* July 68/2 This bretelle makes a sufficient trimming for any simple evening-dress. **1890** *Daily News* 21 Oct. 2/1 Bretelle-shaped lines of fine passementerie in green and gold. **1896** *Ibid.* 4 July 6/3 The bodice..has frills of black chiffon passing over the shoulders in bretelle fashion. **1909** *Daily Chron.* 22 Feb. 7/5 These are arranged back and front bretelle-wise to fall over the deep, folded taffetas belt. **1932** *Daily Express* 20 Sept. 19/1 Two bretelles in front that are knotted at the centre front of the corsage.

'bretessé, bretessee, bretessy. *Her.* [a. F. *bretessé* bratticed.] Having embattlements on each side.

1572 BOSSEWELL *Armorie* II. 123 b, The field is Or, on a pale bretessee Sable. **1586** FERNE *Blaz. Gentrie* 179 Rather Crenelle then Bretessy. **1753** CHAMBERS *Cycl. Supp.*, *Bretesse*, a term used to express a line..of the same nature with what is usually called the *crenelle* or *embattled line.*

†**'bret-full**, *a.* *Obs.* Also 4 bredful, bratful, bretful. Also written *divisim*, bret full. [app. a phonetic corruption of BRERDFULL.] Full to the brim, brim-full.

c **1200** *Trin. Coll. Hom.* 167 Te lichame of iob warð bret-ful of wunden. *c* **1325** *E.E. Allit. P.* A. 126 Bred ful my braynez. **1362** LANGL. *P. Pl.* A. Prol. 41 Heor Bagges and heore Balies weren bratful I-crommet. *c* **1386** CHAUCER *Prol.* 687 His walet..Bret ful of pardon comen from Rome al hoot. *a* **1500** *Med. Receipts* in *Rel. Ant.* I. 55 Fill a mykell potte bretfull. **1616** BULLOKAR, *Bretfull*, top full.

†**breth.** *Obs.* Also berth. [a. ON. *bræði* anger, ire, haste, f. *bráðr* hasty, sudden: see BRATHE.] Ire, fury, rage.

a **1300** *Cursor M.* 7624 In breth he wald him thoru ber. *Ibid.* 18222 Als þof he brath had bene in breth. *c* **1380** WYCLIF *Sel. Wks.* III. 5 Shrift is levynge of sinne, þat turneþ þi breeþ fro me. *c* **1425** WYNTOUN *Cron.* VII. ix. 378 Thai slew, and heryid in thare berth. *c* **1460** *Towneley Myst.* 197 Whils I am in this brethe, Let me put hym to dethe.

†**brethe**, *v.* *Obs.* Also 3 breoðen; pa. pple. brothin. [OE. **bréoðan* in *abréoðan* to go to ruin, decay, degenerate. Hence BRETHEL, BROTHEL.] *intr.* To go to ruin. Pa. pple. *abroðen*, *broþin*: degenerate, dissipated, self-ruined.

[*a* **1000** *Byrht.* 242 (Gr.) Abreoðe his angin. *c* **1000** ÆLFRIC *Gram.* viii. (Z.) 32 Eala þu abroðene folc!] *c* **1205** LAY. 5807 ȝe sculleð breoðen. *Ibid.* 30415 Bruttes gunnen breoðen: balu wes on uolken. *c* **1275** *Ibid.* 5196 Ne seh[s]te leofue broþer, hou breþiþ [*c* **1205** breoðeð] þis France. *c* **1300** *Sarmun* in *E.E.P.* (1862) 6 Al þat þou wan here wiþ pine a broþin eir sal wast it al.

†**'brethel.** *Obs.* [repr. OE. **briéþel*:—OTeut. **braujilo-z*, f. **braujiu-* (OE. *bréaþ* brittle, *Leechd.* I. 260); f. stem of prec. vb.: cf. BROTHEL.] A worthless fellow, good-for-nothing, wretch.

c **1440** *York Myst.* xxvi. 179 Say, brethell, I bidde þe abide. *c* **1440** *Promp. Parv.* 50 Breþel [*printed* breyel], *brollus*. **1469** MARG. PASTON in *Lett.* 617 II. 365 We haue

lost of her but a brethele and set yt the les to hart. c1547 BALE *Sel. Wks.* (1849) 244 Old superstitious bawds and brethels.

bretheles, brethles, obs. ff. BREATHLESS.

†**'bretheling.** *Obs.* Also **briþeling, brotheling.** [f. BRETHEL + *-ing*: cf. ATHEL-ING.] = BRETHEL.

c1275 *O.E. Misc.* 184 þral vnbuxsum, Aþeling briþeling, Lond wiðute laȝe. c1320 *Syr Bevis* 2067 Beues wente alse a bretheling. c1330 *Arth. & Merl.* 164 Our princes..seyd, that her king Nas bot a bretheling. ?15.. in Furniv. *Percy Folio* I. 426 Their young king was but a brotherlinge.

†**'bretheman.** *Obs. rare*⁻¹. [f. *brethe*, BREATH + MAN.] ? A blower of a wind-instrument, a trumpeter, etc.

?a1400 *Morte Arth.* 4108 Bremly the brethemen bragges in troumppes, In cornettes comlyly, whene knyghttes assembles.

brether, -ern(e, -ir, obs. plurals of BROTHER.

brethered, -hed(e, obs. f. BROTHERHOOD, -RED.

brethil, bretil, -nesse, obs. ff. BRITTLE, -NESS.

brethren ('brɛðrɪn), special pl. of BROTHER.

†**'brethrendom.** *Obs.* [f. prec. + -DOM.] = next.

1481 in *Eng. Gilds* (1870) 317 Ye schall geve yn part of your godes to þe mantaeynyn of þis brotheryndon.

†**'brethrenhood.** *Obs.* [f. as prec. + -HOOD.] = BROTHERHOOD; fraternity.

1481 in *Eng. Gilds* (1870) 317 Ye shal not dyscouer þe counsell of þe bretherynhod.

'Brethrenism. The principles and system of the Protestant sect calling themselves *Brethren* or *Christian Brethren*, commonly called *Plymouth Brethren*, whence also ***Plymouth Brethrenism.***

1865 *Pall Mall G.* 5 The religious system known as Plymouth Brethrenism. 1883 *Bookseller's Catal.*, 55 Brethrenism.—Kelley's (W.) Lectures on the Book of Isaiah.

Breton ('brɛtən), *sb.* and *a.* [ad. OF. *Breton* (see BRITON).] **A.** *sb.* A native of Brittany; the Celtic language of Brittany. **B.** *adj.* Belonging to or characteristic of Brittany, its inhabitants, or their language. *Spec.*, designating a type of hat with a round crown and an upward-curved brim; also *ellipt.*

†*Breton tackle* (Naut.), app. the earlier form of BURTON *tackle.*

c1386 CHAUCER *Prol. Franklin's T.* (1894) 709 Thise olde gentil Britons...Of diuerse auentures maden layes. a1400 *Kyng Alisaunder* (1952) 5881 þe kynges oost..maugre Picard and Bretoun, Breken þere þe wal adoun. 1495 *Naval Acc. Hen. VII* (1896) 188 Brytton takles. *Ibid.* 198 Bretton takles. *Ibid.* 210 Breton takles. a1500 *Sir Orfeo* (Harley MS.) 16 In Brytayn þis layes arne ywryte..Of aventures þat fillen by dayes, Wherof Brytouns made her layes. 1525 [see SEE *v.* 15b]. [1592 *Surv. or Topogr. Descr. France* 42 The other three dioceses do speake a mixed language, sometimes French sometimes Britton. *Ibid.* 44 The Brittains are generally tractable, but those that are neerer the sea coast are not so courteous as the rest. 1652 HEYLIN *Cosmogr.* I. 168/1 The Britains..were questionlesse one of the first Nations that possessed any part of Gaul. See also BRITAIN *sb.*² 2, *a.* 3.] 1653 URQUHART tr. *Rabelais' Gargantua* xxxi. 139 The very barbarous Nations of the Poictevins, Bretons, Manceaux. 1818 MRS. STOTHARD *Lett. Tour Normandy* (1820) xxiv. 253 The Breton language appears to me..far more corrupted than the Welsh. *Ibid.* 254 The Bretons do not resemble in countenance either the Normans or French, nor have they much of the Welsh character. 1830 *Cambrian Q. Mag.* II. 192 The Breton-speaking Brittany. 1855 TENNYSON *Maud* xxiii. 78 Here on the Breton strand! Breton, not Briton. 1861 *Chambers's Encycl.* II. 332/1 The Breton has generally a tinge of melancholy in his disposition. 1903 [see SAILOR 4]. 1913 J. MORRIS JONES *Welsh Gram.* Introd. 1 Keltic..The P division, consisting of Gaulish, and the British group, comprising Welsh, Cornish and Breton. 1941 *Amer. Speech* XVI. 67/2 Later *Bretons* and *Sailors* were pushed, and the standard *Snap-Brim.* 1952 *Vogue* June 61 Simone Mirman's huge Breton hat in black straw. 1968 K. O'HARA *Bird-Cage* xvi. 129 A string of Breton onions. 1968 J. FLEMING *Hell's Belle* i. 49 They..ate Breton pancakes filled with cheese and mushrooms. 1969 *Listener* 6 Feb. 165/3 Local schools used to display a notice which read: 'No spitting, and no talking Breton.' And even today there is a celebrated Breton couple six of whose 13 children have never been officially registered because they insisted on giving them Breton names.

brett. A short term for BRITZKA, a kind of four-wheeled carriage.

1865 MRS. WHITNEY *Gayworthys* II. 159 Mrs. Topliff drove an open English brett.

brettice, brettis, common var. of BRATTICE.

Bretwalda (brɛt'wɔːldə). *Hist.* [OE.: occurring once in the Chronicle, where the Parker MS. (in its oldest part written *a* 900) has it thus, while the later MSS. read variously, B *brytenwalda*, C *bretenanwealda*, D and E *brytenwealda*, F *brytenweald*; and twice in a charter of King Æthelstán as *brytænwalda, brytenwalda.* See below.]

A title given in the Old English Chronicle to King Egbert, and (retrospectively) to seven earlier kings of various Old English states, said to have held superiority, real or titular, over their contemporaries; also occasionally assumed by later Old English kings: its sense can only be 'lord (or ruler) of the Britons', or 'of Britain'; cf. the Roman title *dux Britanniarum*, and the *Brettonum dux* of Beda, *rector Britanniæ* of Æthelstan. (See Rhŷs *Celtic Britain*, Freeman *N.C.I.*)

[*Note.* It is uncertain whether the later forms are genuine fuller forms, traditional equivalents, or merely etymologizing alterations of *Bretwalda* 'ruler of the Bretts' (cf. *Ælwalda, Alwealda, Ealwealda* 'All-ruler, Almighty'). The element *bryten-* occurs also in several compounds, all poetic, in the sense 'far-stretching, spacious', as in *bryten-cyning, bryten-grund, bryten-rice, bryten-wang*; whence Kemble wished to explain *brytenwalda* as 'wide ruler'. But in the charter of Æthelstán, the equivalence of 'Brytenwalda ealles ðyses iȝlandes' to 'rector totius huius Britanniae insulae' shows its identity with *Britannia.* Kemble's conjectured derivation of *bryten-* from *bréotan* 'to break' is etymologically impossible; and there can be little doubt that, even in the poetic compounds, the word is simply a poetic use of *Bryten, Breoten* Britannia, or of *Breotone* (:—*britum*) Brittōnes, Britons. These compounds may actually have been formed on the model of *bryten-walda*, or, if earlier, may have had reference to the *far-reaching extent* of Britain, as compared with any single state in it; or finally, the word *breotone* Britons, may have been taken poetically for 'men', 'people', or 'nations', as apparently in *Satan* 1. 687 *burg and breotone* cities and peoples or nations. It is not impossible that *Bretwalda* was suggested by a British title, such as **Brithon-wletic*, **Brython-wledig* = Brittonum dux.]

c855 *O.E. Chron.* an. 827 (Parker MS.) Ecgbryht..wæs se eahteða cyning, se ðe Bretwalda wæs. 934 *Charter* in *Cod. Dipl.* V. 218–9 Ic Æðelstan, Ongol-Saxna cyning and Brytænwalda eallæs [(2) Brytenwalda ealles] ðyses iȝlandæs [*Latin version* (1) Ego Æðelstanus rex et rector totius huius Britanniae insulae; (2) Ego Æðelstanus Angul-Saxonum necnon et totius Britanniae rex]. 1839 KEIGHTLEY *Hist. Eng.* I. 22 Some of the Anglo-Saxon Kings assumed a still higher title, that of Bretwalda or Ruler of Britains. 1855 MILMAN *Lat. Chr.* (1864), II. IV. iii. 239 Any Bretwalda or Supreme Sovereign. 1875 STUBBS *Const. Hist.* I. VI. 122 The existence of this hegemony, whether or no its possessor bore the title of Bretwalda, was not accompanied by unity of organisation.

bretylle, obs. form of BRITTLE.

breu-, see BREV-, BREW-.

breunnerite ('brɔɪnəraɪt). *Min.* [f. the name of Count *Breunner*, a 19th-cent. Austrian nobleman: see -ITE¹.] The name given by Haidinger to a variety of magnesite in which some of the magnesium is replaced by iron.

1825 HAIDINGER tr. *Mohs' Treat. Min.* I. 411 Brachytypous. Rhombohedral... Breunnerite. 1857 J. D. DANA *Man. Min.* (new ed.) vi. 248 *Mesitine spar*, (Breunnerite.) A carbonate of iron and manganese occurring in yellowish rhombohedrons. 1929 H. A. MIERS *Mineralogy* (ed. 2) I. III. 255 The anhydrous rhombohedral carbonate known by the name of breunnerite. 1960 W. H. DENNEN *Princ. Min.* vii. 288 *Magnesite*... Chemical varieties: Ferroan (breunnerite), manganoan, calcian.

breve (briːv), *sb.* Also 6 **breeuve,** 7 **brieve.** [A variant of *bref, brefe,* BRIEF *sb.* in same senses.]

1. A letter of authority; a royal mandate: see BRIEF *sb.* 1.

a1300 *Cursor M.* 19606 O prince o preistes..purchest he þar breue For to seke..cristen men. 1600 *Gowrie's Conspir. Select. Harl. Misc.* (1793) 197 In those parts where my lord was, they would give sundrie folks breeuves. 1626 DONNE *Serm.* 687 The Jews had license to beg, they had a Breve. a1656 HALES *Gold. Rem.* (1688) 182 Our legal business in the world must be done in certain forms of breves and writs. 1873 DIXON *Two Queens* I. II. ii. 15 He was tempted to revoke his breves.

b. *spec.* A pope's letter; = BRIEF *sb.* 2.

1536 STARKEY *England* Introd. (1871) 37 Yf you folow the breves of the pope to you directid. 1679 PULLER *Moder. Ch. Eng.* (1843) 38 Performed by..Pope Paul V, in a very smart breve, dated 1612. 1700 TYRRELL *Hist. Eng.* II. 790 The Pope..committed the Execution of his Breve to the Abbot. 1823 LINGARD *Hist. Eng.* VI. 202 The breve of dispensation produced by the queen..was an evident forgery. 1863 GARDINER *Hist. Eng.* I. ii. 79 The pope..had sent two breves to Garnet.

c. A summary, a short code of instructions, etc.

1523 *Let.* in Burnet *Hist. Ref.* II. 105 The more the said Breve cometh to light. 1651 CLEVELAND *Poems* 43 The Painters Brieve for Venus face; Item an Eye from Jane, a lip from Grace.

2. *Music.* A note of the value of two semibreves, now written white and either oblong or (more usually) oval, with one or two strokes on each side; rarely used in modern music.

1460 [see BRIEF *sb.* 8]. 1480 *Will of Bristowe* (Somerset Ho.) An Imnar [Hymner] closed wᵗ brevys and longes. 1674 PLAYFORD *Skill Mus.* I. vii. 24 The Names of Notes in the Proportion of Time are Eight, as a Large, Long, Breve, Semibreve, etc. 1706 A. BEDFORD *Temple Mus.* xi. 227 When Musick was first invented, there were but Two Notes, viz. a Long, and a Breve. 1782 BURNEY *Hist. Mus.* II. 196 The black square note, called a Breve, the first and almost only note used in Canto Fermo. 1806 CALLCOTT *Mus. Gram.* iii. 26 The Breve is a square white Note. 1863 LD. LYTTON *Ring Amasis* I. 27.

†**3.** *Gram.* A short syllable. *Obs.*

1548 HALL *Chron.* Rich. III. an. 3 (R.) This poetical schoolemayster, corector of breues and longes. 1751 CHAMBERS *Cycl.* s.v., A breve is one time, and a long two.

4. *Print.* The mark ˘ placed over a vowel to signify that it is short.

5. [Fr. *brève.*] A name sometimes given (from their short tails) to the ant-thrushes.

†**breve,** *v. Obs.* Forms: 3–4 **breven,** 4–6 **breve,** 5 **briefe,** 6 **bryve,** 6 *Sc.* **breif, brew.** [ME. *breven*, app. a. ON. *bréfa* to write (corresp. to OHG. *briofan*, OHG., MHG. *briefen*), ad. med.L. *breviāre* to draw up or send dispatches, f. *breve* a note, dispatch: see BRIEF. App. the Latin word was never adopted in OE., but early ME. *breven* may possibly have been directly from it, rather than from the ON.]

1. *trans.* (and *absol.*). To set down in writing; to indite, compose, write (a matter).

a1225 *St. Marher.* 16 In iannes ant in iembres bokes ibreuet. c1340 *Gaw. & Gr. Knt.* 2521 As hit is breued in þe best boke of romaunce. c1400 *Destr. Troy* 3736 þus he breuyt in his boke of þe breme kynges. 1470 HARDING *Chron.* xxxi. iii, As chronycles doth briefe. c1505 DUNBAR *Poems* (1884) 105 Allace! I can bot ballattis breif. a1560 ROLLAND *Crt. Venus* Prol. 319 Now pas thy wayis, thou barrant buik new breuit.

b. To enter in books of account; to 'post', make up (accounts).

a1377 in *Househ. Ord.* (1790) 10 Leveryes of men servantes, intituled Calciatura besides all wages breved. c1440 *Bk. Curtasye* in *Babees Book* (1868) 553 The clerke of þe cochyn shalle alle þyng breue. 1484 MARG. PASTON *Lett.* 881 III. 314 The mane..woll not take upon hym to breve dayly.

c. *to breve for*: to render an account for.

1478 *Liber Niger* in Pegge *Cur. Misc.* (1782) 74 That the Marshall..send such one with his rod as he will answer for on the morrow and also that he will breve for.

2. To recount, relate, state, tell.

c1325 *E.E. Allit. P.* A. 754 Breue me bryȝt, quat-kyn of priys Berez þe perle. c1340 *Gaw. & Gr. Knt.* 1488 If hit be sothe þat ȝe breue, þe blame is myn awen. a1400 *Alexander* (Stevenson) 78 Breve us thi name. 1447–8 SHILLINGFORD *Lett.* (1871) 55 Y wolde have comyned wᵗ ham to have breved the mater.

3. To note, point out.

c1340 *Gaw. & Gr. Knt.* 1436 þe best þat þer breued watz wyth þe blod houndez.

brevely, compar. **breveloker,** obs. f. BRIEFLY.

†**'brevement, brievement.** *Obs.* Also **brief-, breavement.** [f. BREVE *v.* + -MENT, or perh. directly ad. med.L. **breviāmentum*, f. *breviāre.*] The action of inditing or entering in books; *concr.* an entry.

c1475 in *Househ. Ord. Edwd. IV.* (1790) 39 All other offycers that must be at the brevement, have their breakfaste together in the Compting-house, after the breavementes be made. 1539 *Ibid.* 228–231 The Clerke of the Greencloth shall..cast up all the particular Breifments of the House after they shall be comptrolled. 1667 E. CHAMBERLAYNE *St. Gt. Britain* I. II. xii. (1743) 101 All bills of Comptrolment, parcels, and brievements are allotted and allowed by the Clerks-comptrollers.

†**'brever.** *Obs.* [f. BREVE *v.* + -ER¹.] One who makes entries in books; a book-keeper.

c1475 in *Ord. R. Househ.* 71 Noe yoman..to bere or make oute of this office any breade but by knowledge of the brevour.

brevet ('brɛvɪt), *sb.* Also 4–5 **breuette,** 8 **brevitt.** [a. F. *brevet* a note, dim. of *bref* letter, etc.: see BRIEF.]

†**1.** An official or authoritative message in writing; *esp.* a Papal Indulgence. *Obs.*

1362 LANGL. *P. Pl.* A. Prol. 71 He bonchede hem with his Breuet and blered heore eiȝen. 1377 *Ibid.* B. v. 649, I wil go fecche my box with my breuettes. 1430 LYDG. *Chron. Troy* II. xii, This worthy Kyng..Hath his breuettes and his letters sent For his lordes to holde a parlement. 1603 HOLLAND *Plutarch's Mor.* 462 He gave unto them..two brevets or letters to carrie unto the Ephori. 1652 *Proc. Parliament* No. 109. 2659 Ingaged to signifie that Bul with the Brevet and Excommunication before the King here. 1721 BAILEY, *Brevet*, a Brief, a Pope's Bull. *Old word.* a1754 CARTE in Gutch *Coll. Cur.* II. 107 Council Brevitts, though of no authority in point of Evidence, yet for Information are often useful. [Not in JOHNSON 1755.]

2. An official document granting certain privileges from a sovereign or government; *spec.* in the Army, a document conferring nominal rank on an officer, but giving no right to extra pay.

1689 BURNET *Tracts* I. 25 Had a brevet to be a Marischal of France. 1721 *Lond. Gaz.* No. 5952/2 The Duke of Chartres..holds this Employment by a Brevet only. 1811 WELLINGTON *Let.* in Gurw. *Disp.* VII. 557 Six Majors..to be promoted by brevet to the rank of Lieutenant Colonel. 1844 *Regul. & Ord. Army* 3 When Regiments or Detachments are united..in Camp..the Eldest Officer, whether by brevet or otherwise, is to command the whole.

b. *transf.* and *fig.*

1819 *Edin. Rev.* XXXI. 279 Any blockhead who could produce a sonnet..obtained a brevet of poet. 1861 *Sat. Rev.* 23 Nov. 533 The Church..offers an easy entrance to the stupid..a brevet of gentility to those who feel their need of it.

3. *attrib.* or quasi-*adj.*, as in ***brevet officer, rank.***

1781 A. Hamilton in Sparks *Corr. Amer. Rev.* (1853) III. 302, I have used the term Brevet..as signifying, in general, all officers not attached to any established corps. **1796** Morse *Amer. Geog.* I. 243 All the commissioned and brevet officers of the army and navy. **1836** *Penny Cycl.* V. 402/1 Brevet rank does not exist in the royal navy. **1868** *Regul. & Ord. Army* ¶27 Captains having the brevet rank of Field Officers..do duty as field Officers in Camp and Garrison.

b. *transf.* and *fig.*

1829 Scott *Demonol.* x. 357 One of those accredited ghost tales which attain a sort of brevet rank as true. **1856** Thackeray *Christm. Bks.* (1872) 21 The two old ladies have taken the brevet rank, and are addressed as Mrs. Jane and Mrs. Betsy.

brevet (ˈbrɛvɪt), *v.* Pa. t. and pple. breveted. [f. prec.: cf. F. *breveter.*] *trans.* To raise to a certain rank by brevet; also *fig.*

1839 *Fraser's Mag.* XX. 519 Women, in the court of France, were but just brevetted to the rank of ladies. **1879** Tourgee *Fool's Err.* iv. 18 He is colonel now; has been breveted a brigadier-general.

brevetcy (ˈbrɛvɪtsɪ). [see -cy.] Brevet rank.

1846 in Worcester; and subsequent Dicts.

†**ˈbreveter.** *Obs. rare*$^{-0}$. [f. brevet *sb.* 1 + -er.[1]] One who carries brevets.

c **1440** *Promp. Parv.* 50 Breuetowre, *brevigerulus.*

brevi- (ˈbrɛvɪ-), comb. form of L. *brevis* 'short', used as the first element of many modern scientific words: as **breviped** (ˈbrɛvɪpɛd), *a.* [L. *pes, ped-* foot], having short feet (or legs); *sb. Ornith.* a short-legged bird. **ˈbrevipen**, *sb. Ornith.* [L. *penna* feather], a short-winged bird. **brevipennate** (-ˈpɛnət), *a.* short-winged. **brevirostrate** (-ˈrɒstrət), *a.* [L. *rostrum* beak], having a short bill or beak.

1880 *Libr. Univ. Knowl.* III. 40 Brevipennes, or Brevipennates, a term for such birds as the ostrich, cassowary..and others having very short wings. **1852** Dana *Crust.* I. 134 Carapax broad..brevirostrate.

†**ˈbrevial.** *Obs.* [ad. med.L. *breviāle* in same sense, f. *brevis* short.] = breviary 2.

[**1314** *Test. Garini* (Du Cange) Legavit Hoduyno capellano melius Breviale quod habebat.] **1847** Halliw., *Breviall*, a breviary.

breviarist (ˈbriːvɪərɪst). ? *Obs.* [f. breviary + -ist.] One who writes a breviary or abstract.

1621 Bp. Mountagu *Diatribæ* 205 Wee poore simple Breuiarists know so much. **1679** Prance *Addit. Narr. Pop. Plot* 25 All Compendiums are subject to mistakes, and surely our Breviarist is not free from One.

breviary (ˈbriːvɪərɪ). Also 6–7 breuiarie, 7 breauarye, breaviary, breviari. [ad. L. *breviārium* 'summary, abridgement', from neuter of *breviārius* adj. 'abridged', f. *brevi-s* short.]

1. a. A brief statement, summary, epitome. ? *Obs.*

1547 Boorde *Brev. Health* Pref. 5 b, Namynge this booke accordyng to the matter, which is, the Breuiary of health. **1580** North *Plutarch* 421 Lucullus..layed a great wager.. that he would write the Breviary of the Marsean Wars in Verse or Prose. **1635** N. R. tr. *Camden's Hist. Eliz.* II. 139 *marg. note*, A breaviary of the Queene of Scots discourse. **1667** E. Chamberlayne *St. Gt. Brit.* I. III. x. (1743) 224 The Navy Office, Excise Office, etc. etc., are of lesser Note than can be particularized in this Breviary. **1728** Newton *Chronol. Amended* Introd. 2 Hippias, the Elean..published a breviary or list of the Olympic Victors. **1801** W. Playfair (*title*) Statistical Breviary, showing the Resources of every State in Europe.

†**b.** *transf.* and *fig.*; cf. *epitome.*

1609 Bp. Andrewes *Serm.* II. 243 This little word is a breviary of all that good is. **1628** Feltham *Resolves* I. xli. Wks. (1677) 67 In all which he is but the great worlds Breviary. **1649** Jer. Taylor *Gt. Exemp.* xv. §27 Christs discipline was the breviary of all the wisdom of the best men.

2. a. In the Roman Catholic Church, the book containing the 'Divine Office' for each day, which those who are in orders are bound to recite.

The Office consists of psalms, collects and 'lections' or readings from the Scripture and the lives of the Saints. Those who are only in 'Minor Orders', i.e. below the grade of sub-deacon, are not required to say Office.

1611 Bible *Pref.* 9 What alterations haue they made..of their Seruice bookes, Portesses, and Breuiaries. **1794** D'Israeli *Cur. Lit.* (1848) I. 17 The psalms of a breviary or the prayers of a missal. **1832** tr. *Sismondi's Ital. Rep.* viii. 178 He recited his breviary. [**1836** J. H. Newman *Tracts for Times* No. 75 The word Breviarium first occurs in..the eleventh century, and is used to denote a compendium or systematic arrangement of the devotional offices of the Church.] **1848** Macaulay *Hist. Eng.* II. 204 While breviaries and mass books were printed at Oxford under a royal licence..Baxter was in gaol; Howe was in exile.

b. *fig.*

1826 C. Butler *Grotius* xi, It was the breviary of all French aspirants to political distinction. **1877** Shields *Final Philos.* 46 Montaigne of Bordeaux..whose sprightly 'Essays', more Pagan than Christian, have been styled the breviary of free-thinkers. **1878** Morley *Diderot* II. 115 She habitually called the Spirit of Laws the breviary of Kings.

c. fig. phr. ***matter of breviary*** (= *matiere de breviaire*, Rabelais, Pantagruel IV. viii): a thing that admits of no question or doubt.

1694 Motteux tr. *Rabelais* IV. viii. 35 It is written *Mihi vindictam*, &c. matter of breviary, Mark ye me; that's holy stuffe. **1889** *Sat. Rev.* 12 Jan. 29/1 It is a matter of breviary with Gladstonians that Unionist journals are not to be trusted. **1894** *Ibid.* 27 Oct. 463 Is it not..rather matter of controversy than matter of breviary whether the distinction applies?

†**ˈbreviate,** *a. Obs.* [ad. L. *breviāt-us*, pa. pple. of *breviāre* to shorten, f. *brevis* short. Cf. abbreviate.] Abbreviated, shortened; short.

1509 Hawes *Conv. Swearers* 38 For a breuyat pleasure of worldly vanyte. **1515** Barclay *Egloges* IV. (1570) C. vj/2 By beastly surfeit the life is breviate. **1552** J. Mychell (*title*) A breuiat Cronicle contaynynge all the Kinges from Brute to this daye. **1656** *Shepherd's Kal.* viii, By sloth in the time of this breviate life we gather not goods for the life eternal.

breviate (ˈbriːvɪət), *sb.* [f. prec. adj. used subst., like the L. neuter *breviātum.*]

1. A short account, brief statement; a summary, abridgement, compendium.

1581 J. Bell *Haddon's Answ. Osor.* 226 A Breviate of all Luthers doctrine. **1650** Fuller *Pisgah* 431 What we read in Saint Luke was onely the breviate, sum, and abridgement of his Sermon. **1709** Hearne *Coll.* 10 Dec. (1886) II. 324 Begs H. to send mere breviates of his materials. **1862** P. B. Power (*title*) Breviates: or Short Texts and their Teachings. **1865** *Reader* No. 143. 341/1 A breviate of the chronicles.

b. *fig.*

1695 Tryon *Dreams & Vis.* xi. 209 God made him [man] ..a breviate of the nature of all things divine and humane.

c. *Comb.*, as ***breviate-maker.***

1611 Cotgr., *Extrayeur de proces*, a reporter, or Abridger, of Cases; a breuiate-maker.

†**2.** A brief missive or dispatch; a note. *Obs.*

1602 Warner *Alb. Eng.* XII. lxxv. (1612) 312 His Tablet sent she, and there with this breuiat by a Page. **1676** Bullokar, *Breviate*, a brief note, little or short writing. **1748** Richardson *Clarissa* (1811) VIII. xxii. 98, I send..for particulars of the fatal breviate thou sentest him this night.

†**3.** A lawyer's brief. *Obs.*

1594 *Zepheria* xx. in Arb. *Garner* V. 75 How often hath my pen (mine hearts Solicitor!) Instructed thee in Breviat of my case! **1664** Butler *Hud.* II. II. 612 As well-fee'd Lawyer on his Breviate. *a* **1734** North *Lives* (1826) I. 192 He could over night..admit his clients..and..was then prepared, next day, to peruse his breviate.

4. ? The daily portion to be read in the breviary.

1813 Hogg *Queen's Wake* 164 Wearied with the eternal strain Of formal breviats, cold and vain.

†**ˈbreviate,** *v. Obs.* [f. as prec. (or aphetic form of abbreviate).]

1. *trans.* To abbreviate, shorten.

1526 Skelton *Magnyf.* 2366 By myschefe to brevyate and shorten his dayes. **1570** Levins *Manip.* 40 Breuiate, *abbreuiare.* **1637** Heywood *Dialog.* 885 Wee'l breviat your long motions Within a few short termes.

2. To abridge; *spec.* to abstract for counsel's instruction, to brief.

1663 Manley *Sollicitor* 102 To breviate his Clyents cause fit to instruct counsel. **1679** Hobbes *Dial. Com. Laws* (1840) 57 The office of this Chancellor was..to breviate the matter of the petitions, for the easing of the Emperor.

Hence **ˈbreviated** *ppl. a.*, **ˈbreviating** *vbl. sb.*

c **1590** Marlowe *Faust.* III. 10 The breviated names of holy saints. **1633** Ford *Love's Sacr.* II. ii. (1839) 82 For the breviating the prolixity of some superfluous transmigration.

†**ˈbreviately,** *adv. Obs.* [f. breviate *a.* + -ly[2].] Shortly, briefly; compendiously.

1509 Hawes *Conv. Swearers* 6, I..Purpose to compyle here full breuyatly A lytell treatyse. *a* **1560** Rolland *Crt. Venus* I. 771 Thay can not gif senten[ce] Sa breuiatlie.

breviatic, var. of briviatic.

†**breviˈation.** *Obs.* [ad. L. *breviātiōn-em*, f. *breviāre* to shorten; or aphetic f. abbreviation.]

1. The process of shortening; summarizing.

1509 Hawes *Past. Pleas.* 30 He must nombre al the hole cyrcumstaunce Of thys mater wyth brevyacion.

2. An abbreviation or abridgement.

1580 Hollyband *Treas. Fr. Tong, Symbole*..the shorte summe or breuiation of the creede. **1657** Colvil *Whigs Supplic.* (1751) 24 Breviations stenographic.

†**ˈbreviator.** *Obs.* [a. L. *breviātor*, agent-noun f. *breviāre* to shorten.] One who makes summaries or abstracts; also = abbreviator 2.

1546 Langley *Pol. Verg. De Invent.* VIII. ii. 145 a, Pius the II did create Breuiators and set them in an Order. **1679** Prance *Addit. Narr. Pop. Plot* 20 But our Breviator, when he pleaseth, can over-look, etc. **1751** Chambers *Cycl.* s.v., At Rome, those are still called breviators, or abbreviators, who dictate and draw up the pope's briefs.

†**ˈbreviature.** *Obs.* [ad. med.L. *breviātūra* abridgement, f. *breviāre* to shorten: see -ure.] An abbreviation.

1583 J. Higins tr. *Junius' Nomenclator, Notæ*.. Abbreviatures. Notes: abbreviations, breuiatures. **1731** Bailey II, *Breviature*, an abbreviation, etc. **1857** Wright, *Breviature*, a note of abbreviation.

brevicite (ˈbrɛvɪsaɪt). *Min.* [ad. Sw. *brevicit* (Berzelius 1834, in *Arsberättelse om Framstegen i Fysik och Kemi* (1834) 179), f. *Brevig* (now *Brevik*), a town in Norway: see -ite[1].] Natrolite, as found in certain parts of Norway.

1836 T. Thomson *Outl. Min., Geol.*, etc. (ed. 7) I. 680 Brevicite. This name has been given by Berzelius to a mineral sent him by M. Strom, from Brevig, in Norway, which appears to have filled up an amygdaloidal cavity in a trachyte-looking rock. **1892** *Dana's Syst. Min.* (ed. 6) 602 Brevicite is the same as spreustein, though the name has also been used as synonymous with radiolite. *Ibid.*, Radiolite, bergmannite, spreustein, brevicite, palæo-natrolite, are names which have been given to the natrolite from the augite-syenite of southern Norway,..where it occurs fibrous, massive, and in long prismatic crystallizations.

brevier (brɪˈvɪə(r)). *Typogr.* [a. OF. or AF. **brevier*:—L. *breviārium* breviary; app. because this type was used in printing breviaries. Cf. *canon, pica, primer*, of similar origin.

Mr. T. B. Reed (*Hist. Lett. Foundries* 39) says this conjecture is not borne out by an examination of the Breviaries, most of which are printed in a considerably larger size; but that the German Brevier, corresponding to our Small Pica, is of more frequent occurrence in these works. He suggests that the name *Brevier*, like the French and German equivalent 'Petit', may mean that this, being the smallest body, was used for getting the most matter into a brief space. But this hardly explains the word *brevier.*]

The name of the type in size between Bourgeois and Minion.

1598 *Ord. Stationers' Co.* in *Hist. Lett. Foundries* (1887) 129 Those in brevier and long primer letters at a penny for one sheet and a half. **1706** Phillips, *Brevier* or *Breveer*, a small sort of Printing-Letter. **1709** *Lond. Gaz.* No. 4617/4 Printed upon Extraordinary Paper, and with a New Brevier Letter. **1721** Bailey, *Brevier*, a small sort of Printing-Letter, one degree smaller than Long Primer. **1802** Mar. Edgeworth *Mor. Tales* (1816) I. xiv. 113 A printer's devil ..may be a capital judge of pica and brevier.

‖**ˈbreviger.** *Obs.* exc. *Hist.* [med.L.: f. *brevis, breve*, brief + *-ger* -carrying.] One who carries briefs; a begging friar.

1859 *York Fabric Rolls* (Surtees) 167 *note*, Another letter of instructions for a breviger. **1859** *Sat. Rev.* VIII. 428/1 Chaucer must have had a Yorkshire breviger in his mind, when he described, in his Sompnoure's Tale, the alms-gatherer in Holderness.

breviloquence (brɪˈvɪləkwəns). *rare.* [ad. L. *breviloquentia*, f. *brevi-s* short + *loquentia* speaking.] Brevity of speech; laconism.

1656 Blount *Glossogr.*, *Breviloquence*..a brief or short form of speaking. **1678** Phillips, *Breviloquence* (Lat., a short discourse, a speaking in brief. **1721** in Bailey. [Not in Johnson.] **1863** J. Murphy *Comm. Gen.* xli. 13 A specimen of pithy breviloquence.

breviloquent (brɪˈvɪləkwənt), *a.* [ad. L. *breviloquent-em*, f. *brevi-s* short + *loquens* speaking.] Given to concise speaking, laconic.

1865 H. Merivale in *Fortn. Rev.* II. 138 They seem to anticipate the breviloquent era of Sir Rowland Hill.

‖**brevi manu.** *Law.* [L.; = with short hand.] Summarily; without legal process.

1808 in Jamieson. **1833** *Act 3 & 4 Will. IV*, xlvi. §90 Such magistrate..may..issue his warrant for removing the same brevi manu.

breviped, -pen, -rostrate, etc.: see brevi-.

†**ˈbrevit,** *v. Obs.* or *dial.* [perh. f. brevet *sb.*, with the sense of 'take by brevet' or 'warrant'.] *intr.* To forage; to 'beat about' for game; see also dial. quots. Hence **ˈbreviting** *vbl. sb.*

1600 Holland *Livy* XXII. xl. 457 Victuals, which from day to day he brevited for [*ex rapto*], to serve his present neede. *Ibid.* XXIX. xxxii. 734 Masanissa..lived for some days by the breviting and robberie of the other two horsemen. **1604** Drayton *Owl*, Breviting by night, Under pretence that she was ill of sight. **1842** Akerman *Wiltsh. Gloss.* (E.D.S. 1879) *Brevet about*, to beat about, as a dog for game. **1879** Miss Jackson *Shropsh. Gl.*, *Brevit*, to search, pry, examine inquisitively 'Who's bin brevitin' i' my drawer?' **1881** Evans *Leicester. Gl.* (E.D.S.) *Brevet*, to rummage, ransack, search..Cats are said to *brevet* after mice, dogs after rats or rabbits, etc.

brevitt, obs. form of brevet.

brevity (ˈbrɛvɪtɪ). Also 6 breuite, brevyte, 6–7 breuitie, 7 breuity, brevitie. [prob. a. AF. *brevete* (F. *brièveté*):—*brevitāt-em* 'shortness', f. *brevi-s* short: assimilated to the Latin spelling.]

1. Shortness, esp. as applied to time.

1542–3 *Act 34 & 35 Hen. VIII*, xxvii. §99 Many sutes.. cannot be tried..for breuitie of time. **1628** Feltham *Resolves* I. xxxii. Wks. (1677) 55 Miserable brevity! more miserable uncertainty of life! **1853** Robertson *Serm.* xiv. 177 The deep thought of the brevity of time.

2. The being short in speech or writing; contraction into few words, conciseness, terseness.

1509 Barclay *Ship of Fooles* (1570) 18 If that it were not for cause of breuitie, I could shewe, etc. **1574** Whitgift *Def. Aunsw.* II. Wks. 1851 I. 237, I omit them for brevity' sake. **1602** Shaks. *Ham.* II. ii. 90 Since Breuitie is the Soule of Wit..I will be breefe. **1606** Holland *Sueton.* To Rdr., Brevitie is many times the mother of Obscuritie. **1663** Butler *Hud.* I. I. 669 Brevity is very good, When w' are, or are not understood. **1732** De Foe, etc. *Tour Gt. Brit.* (1769) II. 287 On the Churn..stands Cirencester (or Cicester, for Brevity). **1811** Syd. Smith *Wks.* (1867) I. 208 Brevity is in writing what charity is to all other virtues.

3. Shortness in other relations. *rare* and *forced.*

1597 Shaks. *2 Hen. IV*, II. ii. 135, I will imitate the honourable Romaines in breuitie. *Poin.* Sure he meanes breuity in breath: short-winded. **1863** *Riddles* (Routledge) Why is wit like a Chinese lady's foot? Because brevity is the sole of it.

† 'brevy, *v. Obs. rare.* In 6 breuy. [f. L. *brevi-āre* to abridge: see BREVE.]

trans. To write down concisely. Cf. BREVE *v.*

1502 ARNOLD *Chron.* (1811) 140 Titoleuoo..hath breuied all yᵉ annuell storys of Rome.

brevyte, obs. form of BREVITY.

brew (bruː), *v.* Pa. t. and pple. brewed (bruːd). Forms: 1 bréowan, 2–3 breowe(n, 3–5 brewen, 4–7 brewe, 4– brew, (also 4–5 breu, 4–6 bru, 4–7 brue, 5 brow-yn, -ne, br(u)w-yn, 6 breawe). *Pa. t.* 1 bréaw, 3 breuȝ, 4 breuh, breu, brew; *pl.* 1 bruwon, 3 browe(n; also 3–7 brued, 4 breud, 4– brewed, 6– brew'd. *Pa. pple.* 1 (ʒe)browen, 3–4 (i-)browen, 4–5 browe, 5 bruen, brew(e, 5–6 browne, *Sc.* browin, brouin, broune; also 4– brewed, (4 ibrowt, 4–7 brued, 4–5 breud(e, 5 brewid, 7 bru'd). [Common Teut.: OE. *bréow-an* (*bréaw, bruwon*; (*ʒe*)*browen*) str. vb. = OS. **briuwan* (MLG. *bruwen*, MDu. *bruwen, brouwen*, Du. *brouwen*, wk.), OHG. *briuwan* (MHG. *briuwen, brûwen*, mod.Ger. *brauen*) str., ON. *brugga* (Sw. *brygga*, Da. *brygge*) wk.; pointing to an OTeut. verb-root **brū* (pre-Ger. *bhreu-*): cf. OHG. *brû-hûs* 'brewhouse'. Outside Teutonic, the same root is perh. to be recognized in L. *dēfrutum* new wine boiled down, and Thracian *βρῦτον* (= *φρῦτον*) beer. Cf. BROTH, and other derivatives, which show that the root *brŭ* had originally also in Teutonic a wider sense than 'brew', apparently that of 'make a decoction, infuse'. The strong pa. t. is found in ME. till the 14th c., and the str. pa. pple. to the 16th (the latter still in Sc.); but weak forms occur in the 13th.]

1. a. *trans.* Properly: To make (ale, beer, and the like) by infusion, boiling, and fermentation.

c **893** K. ÆLFRED *Oros.* I. i. §20 And ne bið ðær nænig ealo ʒebrowen mid Estum. *c* **1325** *Poem temp. Edw. II*, xxix, Gude ale & strong Wel ibrowen of the beste. *c* **1440** *Promp. Parv.* 54/1 Browne ale, or other drynke..*pandoxor.* **1535** STEWART *Cron. Scot.* II. Argt., How King Duncane send the Wyne and Aill browin with mukil Wort to King Sueno. **1570** LEVINS *Manip.* 213 To Breawe, *coquere potum.* **1591** SHAKS. *Two Gent.* III. i. 304 She brewes good Ale. **1768** BLACKSTONE *Comm.* I. 320 Malt liquors brewed for sale, which are excised at the brewery. **1813** HOGG *Queen's Wake* 69 We drank fra the hornis that never grew, The beer that was never browin. **1872** YEATS *Techn. Hist. Comm.* 124 Ale the monks themselves brewed.

b. *fig.* with conscious reference to the literal sense.

1297 R. GLOUC. 26 A luþer beuerage to here bihofþe þei browe. *c* **1325** *Coer de L.* 4365 A sorye beverage ther was browen! **1606** SHAKS. *Tr. & Cr.* IV. iv. 7 If I could temporise with my affection, Or brew it to a weake and colder pallat. **1651** CLEVELAND *Elegy Abp. Canterb.* 2 He brews his Tears that studies to lament. **1871** MORLEY *Crit. Misc.* (1886) III. 288 Why are we to describe the draught which Rousseau and the others had brewed..as maddening poison to the French?

c. To convert (barley, malt, or other substance) into a fermented liquor.

1362 LANGL. *P. Pl.* A. v. 133, I Bouhte hire Barly heo breuh hit to sulle. **1522** *Bury Wills* (1850) 118 To fynde yearelie a busshell and halffe of malte to be browne. **1713** *Lond. & Countr. Brew.* I. (1742) 70 The Charge and Profit of brewing Six Bushels of Malt for a Private Family. **1789** BURNS, O Willie brew'd a peck o' maut.

d. *absol.* (often in proverbial expressions: cf. BAKE *v.* 6.)

a **1300** *Cursor M.* 2848 Suilk als þai brued now ha þai dronken. **1451** *Pol. Poems* (1859) II. 230 Let hem drynk as they hanne brewe. **1543–4** *Act 35 Hen. VIII*, viii, Such persons as brew for theyr owne prouision, and not to sale. **1598** SHAKS. *Merry W.* I. iv. 101, I wash, ring, brew, bake, scowre, dresse meat and drinke. **1612** *Pasquil's Night-Cap* (1877) 82 You must drinke As you have bru'd; bee it small or strong. **1652** *Proc. Parliament* No. 138. 2162 The Admirall..said, that as they brewed so they should bake. **1878** SPURGEON *Treas. Dav.* Ps. cix. 17 As he brewed, so let him drink.

†**2. a.** To mix (liquors), mix with water, dilute. *Obs.*

1520 WHITTINTON *Vulg.* (1527) 15 b, This wyne is brued [*dilutum*]. **1587** HARRISON *England* II. vi. (1877) 149 That they would neither drinke nor be serued of..such [wine] as was anie waies mingled or brued by the vintener. **1579** TOMSON *Calvin Serm. Tim.* 310/2 They brue, they mingle, and confound the doctrine of the gospel with their owne dreames. **1620** VENNER *Via Recta* vi. 101 Water and fine Sugar onely brewed together. **1641** FRENCH *Distill.* v. (1651) 125 You may drop..Oil..into the Wine, and brew them well together.

†**b.** To pour (= L. *infundere*). *Obs.*

1581 MARBECK *Bk. of Notes* 1164 They..brew their new wine into new vessells. **1594** PLAT *Jewell-ho.* III. 29 Brew them a pretie while out of one pot into another.

3. a. *transf.* 'To make by mixing several ingredients' (J.), as whisky punch; or by infusion, as tea.

a **1626** BACON (J.) We have drinks also brewed with several herbs and roots, and spices. **1825** *Bro. Jonathan* I. 417 Have a care! You are brewing that for us, now. **1861** RAMSAY *Remin.* ii. (ed. 18) 37 A famous hand at brewing a good glass of whisky. **1865** *Athenæum* No. 1979. 429/1 Brewing a cup of coffee. **1868** HOLME LEE *B. Godfrey* xxiii. 124 The kettle was boiled, the tea brewed. **1875** B. TAYLOR *Faust* I. vi. 101 Canst thou..alone not brew the potion?

b. Colloq. phr. *to brew up*: to make tea.

1916 *Daily Mail* 1 Nov. 4/4 'Brew up' or 'drung up' (to make tea, over-seas expressions). **1943** A. CLIFFORD *Three against Rommel* xxxiii. 389, I thought we might brew up.

4. To concoct, contrive, prepare, bring about, cause: *spec.* **a.** evil, mischief, trouble, woe; in early use esp. with *bale, boot, bitterness, bargain*, etc.

c **1250** *Hymn Virg.* 30 in *Trin. Hom.* 256 Care of drede þat Eue bitterliche us breuȝ. *Ibid.* 257 Bale to breowe. *a* **1300** *Cursor M.* 4137 Baret rede i noght yee bru. **1377** LANGL. *P. Pl.* B. XVIII. 361 Þe bitternesse þat þow hast browe brouke it þi-seluen. *c* **1440** *York Myst.* xxix. 239 Þis brethell has brewed moche bale. *a* **1560** ROLLAND *Crt. Venus* IV. 448 Vnder the conditioun..that he brew na mair baill. **1578** T. PROCTER *Gallery Invent.* in *Heliconia* I. 105 Ulisses wife, whose chastnesse brued her fame. **1810** SOUTHEY *Kehama* XI. vi, All deadly plagues and pestilence to brew.

b. designs, projects, productions of the intellect.

c **1386** CHAUCER *Monk's T.* 3575 He brew this cursednesse and al this synne. *c* **1425** *Seven Sag.* (P.) 1284 Hys wyf.. Brewed the childys deth. **1571** GOLDING *Calvin on Ps.* xlv. 2 His heart was brewing of some notable and excellent matter. **1579** FENTON *Guicciard.* II. (1599) 66 It was beleeued his death was brued in a cup of poyson. **1649** FULLER *Just Man's Fun.* 2 They do not ponder things in their heart, but onely brew them in their heads. **1803** 'C. CAUSTIC' *Terr. Tractor.* I. 34 *note*, I could not rest quietly till I had brewed a sublime treatise.

c. natural phenomena, as rain, wind, a storm.

1530 PALSGR. 594 Foule weather as whan it rayneth snoweth or broweth, or any otherwyse stormeth. **1593** SHAKS. *3 Hen. VI*, II. ii. 156 That Sun-shine brew'd a showre for him. **1697** DRYDEN *Virg. Georg.* I. 578 The Moon ..bodes a Tempest on the Main, And brews for Fields impetuous Floods of Rain. **1765** FALCONER *Demag.* 185 Foundering in the storm himself had brew'd.

5. *intr.* To be in preparation; to be in process of mixing, concocting, production, etc.: cf. prec. senses. (The modern *to be brewing*, partly derived from an earlier *to be a-brewing*, is not altogether intrans. in origin: cf. *the house is* (*a*) *building*.)

a **1300** *Cursor M.* 118 Bituix þe ald law and þe new How crist birth bigan to brew. *c* **1460** *Towneley Myst.* 314 Your baille now brewys. **1599** *Mirr. Mag., Worcester* iii, Doubtes that dayly brue. **1610** SHAKS. *Temp.* II. ii. 19 Another Storme brewing. **1677** *Lond. Gaz.* No. 1210/2 Some hundred Barrels of Beer brewing for the use of the Troops. **1682** N. O. *Boileau's Lutrin* III. 202 Thou little thinkest What work's a brewing. **1741** RICHARDSON *Pamela* (1824) I. 82 Satisfied there is mischief brewing. **1860** HOLLAND *Miss Gilbert* ii. 20 A storm was brewing in the domestic sky.

6. *trans.* Of oysters: To produce (spawn).

1865 *Cornhill Mag.* XI. 54 The parent oyster goes on 'brewing' its spawn for some time; and it is supposed that the spawn swims about with the current for a short period before it falls.

7. *Comb.*, in which *brew* has the sense of *brewer, brewing*, as †**brew-bate**, one who stirs up quarrelling or dissension; **brew-kettle**, the vessel in which the wort and hops are boiled; †**brew-lead**, a leaden vessel used in brewing; **brew-wife**, a woman that brews, a brewster or brewster-wife. Also BREWHOUSE.

1602 FITZHERBERT *Apol.* 33 What resteth then to make these *brewbates so confident? **1369** *Test. Ebor.* (Surtees) I. 87 Plumbum meum, anglice *breuled in fournes. **1430** *Ibid.* II. 12 Unum brewlede, unum maskfatt. **1522** *Wills & Inv. N.C.* (Surtees) 106, I bequeth to my son..the brew-house as it standeth, that is to say a brewelede, with a mashefatt and a tapstone, etc. **1393** LANGL. *P. Pl.* C. VII. 354 Whederwarde he wolde þe *brew-wif hym asked. **1479** *Paston Lett.* 828 III. 244 He hath maried a bruewyf and kepeth the brue hous.

brew, *sb.*¹ [f. BREW *v.*] **a.** The action, process, or result, of brewing; the beverage, etc. brewed; sometimes used locally for 'yeast'.

c **1510** *Ch.-Wardens' Acc. St. Dunstan's Canterb.*, For a quarton of Brew jd. *ob.* **1627** BACON *Sylva* (J.) Trial..made of the like brew with potatoe roots..which are nourishing meats. **1742** YOUNG *Nt. Th.* ix. 621 The brew of thunders. **1856** KANE *Arct. Expl.* II. viii. 90 Our brew of beer..turns out excellent. **1859** J. LANG *Wand. India* 338 Give us a little drop more of that last brew.

b. *brew-up*: (a pause for) the making of tea; cf. BREW *v.* 3 b. *colloq.*

1944 A. JACOB *Traveller's War* vi. 123 The crews halted for a 'brew up' near us: some drank tea,..others took a nap. **1963** *Times* 26 Jan. 9/7 The..petrol tins which the Desert Rats found equally handy for washing in or for a 'brew-up'.

brew (bruː), *sb.*² Local var. BROW *sb.*¹ 6 b.

1887 HALL CAINE *Deemster* xxvii. 176 Nearer the cliff I found this, and this; and then down the brew itself..I saw this other one. **1891** 'L. KEITH' *Halletts* II. v. 107 He'll stand quiet enough;..it's the grass on the brew he's after. **1927** *Chambers's Jrnl.* Feb. 126/1 The brews of the ditches or hedge-bottoms.

brewage ('bruːɪdʒ). In 6–7 bruage. [f. BREW *v.* + -AGE: but prob. in its origin associated with F. *breuvage* (early forms *breuage, bruvage*) drink, BEVERAGE, whence the original wide sense.]

1. A concocted beverage; a decoction; something that has been *brewed*, a brewing.

1542 UDALL *Erasm. Apoph.* 301 a, The bruage of wyne and the iuice of hemlocke tempreed together was brought vnto hym. **1555** *Fardle Facions* II. viii. 166 Their drincke is a bruage..sometyme of Ryze, sometyme of Barlie. **1598** SHAKS. *Merry W.* III. v. 33 Ile no Pullet-Spersme in my brewage. **1644** MILTON *Areop.* (Arb.) 63 Malmsey, or some well spic't bruage. **1827** *Blackw. Mag.* XXI. 833 She.. hated rum as the devil's own brewage. **1829** PEACOCK *Misfort. Elphin* 173 The Druids..made..a mystical brewage of carefully-selected ingredients. **1848** MACAULAY *Hist. Eng.* iii. I. 335 A rich brewage made of the best Spanish wine.

b. *fig.*

1599 NASHE *Lenten Stuffe* (1871) 35 Neuer since I spouted ink, was I of worse aptitude to go through with such a mighty March brewage. **1821** *Blackw. Mag.* X. 269 Such a brewage of tempest. **1873** BROWNING *Red Cott. Nt.-Cap* 110 When her brewage—love—Was well a-fume about the novice-brain.

2. The process of brewing.

1776 PRINGLE *Health Mariners* 16 In the space of twenty-four hours their brewage is compleated. **1832** M. SCOTT in *Blackw. Mag.* XXXI. 902 A new brewage of punch took place. **1856** KANE *Arct. Expl.* I. xxix. 387 To complete my latest root-beer brewage.

3. A boiling (e.g. of salt).

c **1550** J. BALFOUR *Practicks* 87 The hundreth salt browage contenand nine score bollis.

† '**breward**, *sb. Obs.* exc. *dial.* Also 7 brerewood, 9 *dial.* brewit, bruart. [A variant of BRAIRD, BRERD; cf. OE. *breord, briord, brord.*]

1. Brim (of a hat); = BRERD.

1611 COTGR., *Aile*..the brimme, or brerewood of a hat. **1674** RAY *N.C. Wds.* 8 *Hat Bruarts*, Hat brims. *Cheshire.* **1868** E. WAUGH *Sneck-Bant* ii. 38 (*Lanc. Gloss.*) Wi' th' rain drippin' off his hat brewits.

2. Sprouting of corn, etc.; = BRAIRD.

1875 *Lanc. Gloss.* (E.D.S.) 59 A fine bruart o' strawberry.

† '**breward, brewerd**, *v. Obs.* exc. *dial.* [f. prec.: cf. BRAIRD *v.*] To sprout.

1609 BIBLE (Douay) II. 1084 The sede newly sowne to one, beginning to brewerd to an other. **1875** *Lancash. Gloss.* (E.D.S.) s.v., Yo'r taties are bruartin' finely.

† **brewe.** *Obs.* Also 6 brew, 7 brue. [Etymology unknown.] A fowl; ? a kind of snipe.

c **1460** J. RUSSELL *Bk. Nurture* in *Babees Bk.* (1868) 143 Wodcok..resteratiff þey ar, & so is the brewe. *c* **1475** *Noble Bk. Cookery* (Napier 1882) 63 A Brewe sley him in the mouthe, as a curlewe. **1513** *Bk. Keruynge* in *Babees Bk.* (1868) 276 Vntache that brewe. **1605** in *Archæol.* XIII. 341 These Foules bee nowe in seasone..Brue.

brewed (bruːd), *ppl. a.* [f. BREW *v.* + -ED.] See BREW *v.* 4.

1634 MILTON *Comus* 696 Hence with thy brewed enchantments, foul deceiver!

brewer ('bruːə(r)). Also 3–7 bruer, 4 brywer, 4–5 brewere. [f. BREW *v.* + -ER¹.]

1. One who brews; *spec.* one whose trade is to make malt liquors. *brewers' grains* (see GRAIN *sb.*¹ 4 b).

a **1300** Wright's *Relig. Songs* vii. 82 Theos false chepmen ..Backares and brueres. **1393** LANGL. *P. Pl.* C. I. 221 Bakers and brywers, bouchers and oþere. *c* **1440** *Promp. Parv.* 54 Browstar, or brewere, *pandoxator, -trix.* **1577** HARRISON *England* II. vi. (1877) 150 Ale and beere..as it pleaseth the bruer to make them. **1592** NASHE *P. Penilesse* 10 b, Brewers ..by retayling filthy Thames water, come in few yeres to be worth fortie or fifty thousand pound. **1671** in *Stow's Surv.* (ed. Strype 1754) II. 713/1 No street car, or Brewer's dray. **1732** BERKELEY *Alciphr.* ii. §4 You think a drunkard most beneficial to the brewer and the vintner. **1836** *Penny Cycl.* V. 404/2 The fining or clearing, which is sometimes done by the brewer, sometimes by the publican.

2. A concocter, contriver *of*.

1563 *Homilies* II. xiv. (1640) 191 The author and brewer of sinne, and the ruler of Hell. **1586** J. HOOKER *Girald. Irel.* in *Holinshed* II. 96/2 James de la Hide was the onlie bruer of this rebellion.

breweress ('bruːərɪs). [f. prec. + -ESS.] A female brewer. (Only occasionally used.)

1841 B. BOTFIELD *Mann. & Househ. Exp.* (Roxb.) Introd. 39 The Countess had employed a breweress at Banbury.

† **brewern, browern.** *Obs.* In 5 brewarne, browhern. [f. vb. stem *brew-* or *bru-* (see BREWHOUSE) + OE. *ærn, ern* place, closet, etc.: cf. BARN.] A brewhouse.

c **1450** *Metr. Voc.* in Wr.-Wülcker 626 *Pandoxatorium*, brewarne; *pistrinum*, bakehouse. **1453** MARG. PASTON *Lett.* 185 I. 250 The drawte chamer, and the malthouse, and the browere [*app. an error for* browerne]. **1465** *Paston Lett.* 978 III. 435 The Botere..the Browhern..the Kychyn.

brewership ('bruːəʃɪp). [f. BREWER + -SHIP.] The office or employment of a brewer.

1824 *Blackw. Mag.* XV. 197 Buxton, whose brewership unfortunately unfits him for the..lead.

brewery ('bruːərɪ). [f. BREWER; see -ERY. (Not in Johnson 1755–1773: nor Bailey 1721–1800).]

1. A place for brewing; the establishment of a public brewer; formerly called a BREWHOUSE.

1658 HEXHAM *Dutch Dict.*, Een Brouwerye, a Brewerie, or a brewing-house. **1736** J. MᶜURE *View Glasgow* 285 There is a stately Brewarie belonging to Robert Luke..adjacent to the above great Tannarie. **1772** PRIESTLEY in *Phil. Trans.* LXII. 148 Living..in the neighbourhood of a public brewery. **1791** BOSWELL *Johnson* (1831) I. 506 The brewery was to be sold. **1862** *Jrnl. Roy. Dublin Soc.* Apr. 311 The director of the college..showed me also their brewery.

b. *fig.*

1880 EARL DUNRAVEN in *19th Cent.* Sept. 446 The whole region [Colorado] is one vast brewery of storms.

†**2.** The process or trade of brewing; also, the 'trade' or body of brewers. *Obs.*

*a*1714 C. Davenant *Ess. Trade* I. 79 (L.) If they should bring any distress and trouble upon the London brewery, it would occasion the making ill drink. 1796 Morse *Amer. Geog.* II. 121 The porter brewery .. is also chiefly carried on in London.

brewes(s, -esse, brewester, obs. forms of BREWIS, BREWSTER.

† **'brewet,** another f. BROWET, *Obs.* = BREWIS.

*c*1420 *Gloss.* in Wright *Voc.* 200 *Hic garrus*, brewett. ?*a*1450 *Forme of Cury* 11 Brewet of almony.

brewhouse ('bru:haʊs). Also 4 brewhous, 5 brywhouse, brewhows(e, bruhows, 6 brewehouse. [f. vb.-stem *bru-* BREW- + HOUSE. Cf. OHG. *brû-hûs*.] A house or building in which beer is brewed; a brewery.

1373 *Test. Ebor.* I. 89 Item legavit Roberto de brewhous v marcas. *c*1386 Chaucer *Milleres T.* 3334 In al the toun nas Brewhous ne Tauerne That he ne visited. 1458 *Test. Ebor.* II. 226 The pantre, botre, kechyn, bakhows, and brewhouse. 1483 *Cath. Angl.* 45 A Bruhows, *pandoxatorium*. 1529 *Act 21 Hen. VIII*, xiii. §32 No Spiritual Person .. shall have, use, or keep any Manner of Brew-house. 1671 F. Philipps *Reg. Necess.* 362 A better house than the Brew-house which he could not thrive in at Huntington. 1677 Yarranton *Eng. Improv.* 163 You must have a Bake-house and Brew-house of your own. 1797 *Chron.* in *Ann. Reg.* 47/1 Mr. Meux's brewhouse in Liquorpond Street. 1837 Hawthorne *Twice-told T.* (1851) I. x. 176 That shall tear down the distilleries and brewhouses.

brewice, obs. form of BREWIS.

brewing ('bru:ɪŋ), *vbl. sb.* [f. BREW *v.* + -ING[1].]

1. a. The action, process, or occupation described under BREW (various senses).

1467 *Bury Wills* (1850) 46, I will that the seid Denys haue here esement in the bakhows in lawfull tyme for bruynge. 1562 J. Heywood *Prov. & Epigr.* (1867) 179 Great brewyng, small drinke. 1663 Gerbier *Counsel* 5 Nor is a Laboratorium .. fit either for Baking or Brewing. 1777 Macbride in *Phil. Trans.* LXVIII. 122 You will have a second brewing of lime-water. 1855 Macaulay *Hist. Eng.* IV. 585 Sir John Friend .. had made a very large fortune by brewing.

b. *fig.* Concoction, preparation.

1545 Joye *Exp. Dan.* xi. (R.) The miserable mutacions of kingdoms nowe .. in brewing. 1601 Holland *Pliny* xiv. vi. (R.) Such a brewing and sophistication of them they make. 1673 [R. Leigh] *Transpr. Reh.* 39 This is a Plot .. this has been a brewing any time this Thirty years. 1854 Alford in *Life* (1873) 237, I have an *Edinburgh* article in brewing.

2. The quantity of liquor brewed at once.

1626 Bacon *Sylva* (J.) A brewing of new beer, set by old beer, maketh it work again. 1753 *Scots Mag.* Aug. 393/2 Distilling the second draught of a brewing of aqua-vitæ.

3. *Naut.* A collection of black clouds betokening a storm.

4. *attrib.* and *Comb.*, †**brewing-lead,** a vessel for brewing in; **brewing-up,** (*a*) gradual formation or production; (*b*) (see quot. 1961).

1885 *Civilian* 3 Jan. 130/1 An Act .. to make it compulsory that every collection of worts be entered in the *brewing-book within one hour. 1551–60 *Inv.* in H. Hall *Soc. Elizab. Age* (1886) 152 In the Brewhouse A *Brewing Copper. 1702 *Lond. Gaz.* No. 3855/4 Utensils proper .. for a *Brewing house. 1444 *Test. Ebor.* II. 100 Lego .. i. *brewinglede. 1504 *Bury Wills* (1850) 101, I wull that they shall haue all brewyng ledys. 1694 *Lond. Gaz.* No. 2991/4 The Greyhound in Ipswich .. with a convenient *Brewing Office. 1838 Dickens *O. Twist* (1850) 110/1 A scullery, or small *brewing-place, at the end of the passage. 1766 Goldsm. *Vic. W.* xvii, We shall then have the loan of his cider-press and *brewing-tubs for nothing. 1953 R. Lehmann *Echoing Grove* 103 She began to speak .. of the first signs .. of the *brewing-up of Corrigan's psychological collapse. 1961 *Times* 7 Nov. 19/1 In Britain a thriving business has grown up in tuning and modifying the engines of existing models [of cars] to give more performance... Referred to by enthusiasts as 'brewing up', .. or merely 'hotting up'. 1863 *Times* 6 Mar., Another rickety booth holds the *brewing utensils. 1462 *Test. Ebor.* II. 256 A cesterne, the ledes, with other *brewing-vessell.

brewis ('bru:ɪs, bru:z). Forms: 3–4 broys, brouwys: see BROWIS; 5 **brewes, brus,** 6 **brewish, -ys, brues, -isse, -yse,** 6–7 **brewes, -ess, -esse, brewz,** 7 **brewice, -isse, bruesse,** 8 **brews,** 9 *dial.* **breawis,** 6– **brewis.** [ME. *browes, brouwys, brewes*, etc., a. OF. *brouetz*, in 13th c. *broez*, nominative of *brouet, broet* 'soup made with broth of meat', dim. of OF. *bro, breu*: see BROWET, of which this word is thus a doublet. It is possible that the change of *browes* to *brewes, brewis* was influenced by some popular association with OE. *briw*, pl. *briwas* soup, pottage (see BREE), or even with the vb. BREW. Cf. BROWIS, BROSE.]

1. Broth, liquor in which beef and vegetables have been boiled; sometimes also thickened with bread or meal. Now chiefly *dial.*, and applied very variously in different localities.

[1300–1525 see BROWIS.] 1526 in *Househ. Ord.* (1790) 174 Venison in brewz or mult, 1 mess, 4*d.* 1530 Palsgr. 201/2 Brewes, *brovet*. 1599 A. M. tr. *Gabelhouer's Bk. Physic* 250/2 Cut a chese to shivers, and make therof cheese brues. 1610 Holland *Camden's Brit.* I. 126 Fatned with Scottish pottage and brewesse. *c*1622 Fletcher *Prophetess* I. iii. 27 What an inundation of brewisse shall I swim in? *a*1650 *MS. Bodl.* 30. 13 b, The verie bruise of divinitie, fatt and glorious. 1719 De Foe *Crusoe* (Hotten) 297 The Liquor of the Meat, which they call Brews. 1822 Scott *Nigel* x, Mountains of beef, and oceans of brewis, as large as Highland hills and lochs. *c*1850 in E. Fowke et al. *Canada's Story in Song* (1960) 164 Tho' Newfoundland is changing fast, some things we must not lose: May we always have our flipper pie, and codfish for our brewis. 1869 Blackmore *Lorna D.* vi. (ed. 12) 35 She can't stir a pot of brewis. 1874 Mrs. Whitney *We Girls* vi. 130 One [fryingpan] was set on with the milk for the brewis. 1906 J. Lumsden *Skipper Parson* vi. 87 A popular dish in Newfoundland is 'brewis', pronounced *broose*. 1964 *Canad. Geogr. Jrnl.* Apr. 135 Only in Newfoundland were we served .. fish-and-brewis.

2. 'Bread soaked in boiling fat pottage, made of salted meat' (J.).

*c*1440 *Promp. Parv.* 53 Browesse [1499 browes], *adipatum*. 1554 Becon *Comfort. Epist.* (1844) 208 Eating beef and brewis knuckle-deep. 1580 Baret *Alv.* B 1225 Brewis, *offulæ adipatæ*. 1588 *Marprel. Epist.* 41 The B. of Glocester .. affirmed that beefe and brewesse had made him a papist. 1594 Lyly *M. Bombie* III. iv. 113 A stately peece of beefe .. in great pompe sitting upon a cushion of white brewish. *a*1625 Fletcher *Mad Lover* II. i. 8 Beefe we can beare before us linde with Brewes. 1680 Shadwell *Woman-Capt.* I. Wks. 1720 III. 347 A greasy serving-man .. whose beard stunk of beef and brewis. 1854 W. Gaskell *Lect. Lanc. Dial.* 13 in *Lanc. Gloss.* (E.D.S.) Bread soaked in broth, or in the fat that drips from meat .. is known as brewis. 1857 J. Scholes *Jaunt* 13 (*ibid.*) Drops o fat on Owdham breawis.

brewit, dial. var. of BREWARD.

brewlyng, obs. form of BROILING *vbl. sb.*[2]

brewst. [An alteration of BROWST, apparently under the impression that the latter is a Sc. dialect form, and that the English ought to follow *brew*.] A 'browst' or brewing.

1854 *Blackw. Mag.* LXXV. 529 The brewsts of the different years. 1864 Miss Yonge *Trial* I. 243 His resolution of .. drinking the brewst he had brewed for himself.

brewster[1] ('bru:stə(r)). Forms: 4 **breuster, brewester(e,** 5– **brewster,** 5 *north.* **browstar, -stere,** 6 *Sc.* **broustar, -ster, browster.** [f. BREW *v.* + fem. suffix -STER: cf. *baxter*. See also BROWSTER.]

1. *orig.* A woman that brews, a female brewer.

*c*1308 *Rel. Ant.* II. 176 Hail be ȝe, brewesters, with ȝur galuns, Potels and quarters. 1377 Langl. *P. Pl.* B. v. 306 Beton þe brewestere bad hym good morwe. *c*1425 *Voc.* in Wr-Wülcker 662 *Hec brasiatrix*, brewster. *c*1450 *Ibid.* 692 *Hec pandoxatrix*, a brewster. 1820 Scott *Abbot* xv, We will play .. in Dame Martin the Brewster's barn-yard.

2. Extended to both sexes: A brewer. (Only north Eng. and Sc. since 15th c., exc. as in 3.)

1377 Langl. *P. Pl.* B. Prol. 218 Baxsteres and brewesteres, and bocheres manye. *c*1430 Lydg. *Min. Poems* (1840) 211 Bakerys, browsterys, vyntenerys, with fressh lycour. *c*1440 *Promp. Parv.* 54 Browstar or brewere, *pandoxator, pandoxatrix*. *c*1550 Sir J. Balfour *Practicks* (1754) 15 Brouster, for his fie, five pundis. 1607 *North Riding Rec.* (1883) I. 71 Fr. Steele brewster presented for selling ale contrary to the Statute.

3. *Comb.* and *Attrib.* **brewster-wife** (*Sc.*), a woman that brews or sells malt liquors; **brewster sessions,** sessions for the issue of licenses to trade in alcoholic liquors.

*a*1774 Fergusson *Leith Races*, The *Browster wives thegither harl A' trash that they can fa on. 1818 *Burt's Lett. N. Scotl.* I. 323 *Notes*, A bad specimen of a Scotish brewster-wife. 1864 A. McKay *Hist. Kilmarnock* 128 The brewster-wives had formed a scheme for raising the price of ale. 1883 *Standard* 7 Sept., At the Canterbury *Brewster-Sessions .. all the licenses were granted except two.

Brewster[2] ('bru:stə(r)). *Physics.* [The name of the Scottish physicist Sir David *Brewster* (1781–1868).] **1.** Used *attrib.* in connection with his discoveries in optics, as **Brewster('s) angle,** the angle of incidence at the surface of a dielectric for which a wave polarized in the plane of incidence is not reflected at all, and an unpolarized wave is reflected as a plane-polarized one; **Brewster('s) fringes** (or **bands**), interference fringes produced when a beam of (white or monochromatic) light passes through two sheets of glass, etc., and undergoes different internal reflections in them; **Brewster's law** [published by Brewster in 1815], the law that the tangent of the Brewster angle is equal to the refractive index of the dielectric (in a vacuum), or to the ratio of the refractive indices of the media either side of the interface; **Brewster window,** a window in a laser, etc., so arranged as to polarize light by reflection at the Brewster angle.

[1932 Hardy & Perrin *Princ. Optics* xxix. 600 The angle of incidence for which the polarization of the transmitted light is a maximum is somewhat less than the Brewsterian angle.] 1950 Jenkins & White *Fund. Optics* (ed. 2) xxiv. 489 The physical reason why light vibrating in the plane of incidence is not reflected at *Brewster's angle lies in the transverse character of light vibrations. 1962 Corson & Lorrain *Introd. Electromagn. Fields* xi. 369 For light incident on glass with an index of refraction of 1·6, the Brewster angle is about 58°. 1980 *Sci. Amer.* Oct. 178/1 Because of the Brewster angle, however, one type of polarization is enhanced, and it quickly comes to dominate the laser process. 1984 D. C. Giancoli *Gen. Physics* xxxviii. 736 At Brewster's angle, the reflected and transmitted rays make a 90° angle to each other. 1890 T. Preston *Theory of Light* viii. 156 (*heading*) *Brewster's bands. 1934 *Discovery* July 185/2 A group of straight and parallel interference fringes (known as *Brewster's fringes) is seen through the telescope, the group consisting of a central white fringe accompanied by a few coloured fringes on either side. 1963 R. W. Ditchburn *Light* (ed. 2) ix. 359 The Brewster fringes .. are observed by means of M_1. 1976 Jenkins & White *Fund. Optics* (ed. 4) xiv. 303 The usefulness of Brewster's fringes lies chiefly in the fact that when they appear, the ratio of the two interferometer spacings is very exactly a whole number. 1882 *Encycl. Brit.* XIV. 611 (*heading*) *Brewster's law. 1937 Jenkins & White *Fund. Optics* xiv. 316 This is Brewster's law, which shows that the angle of maximum polarization depends on the refractive index and therefore varies with wave-length. 1973 R. S. Longhurst *Geom. & Physical Optics* (ed. 3) xxi. 519 If the angle of incidence for light in one direction is the polarizing angle and the directions of the incident and refracted rays are reversed, the new angle of incidence is the polarizing angle for light in the reverse direction. This follows at once from the original statement of Brewster's law. [1962 *Rev. Sci. Instruments* XXXIII. 921 (*heading*) Construction of a gaseous optical maser using Brewster angle windows.] 1965 *Appl. Phys. Lett.* VII. 244/1 In the present work a *Brewster window tube with external mirrors was used. 1984 *Nat. Geographic* Mar. 341 (caption) In some gas lasers transparent disks called Brewster windows .., slanted at a precise angle, polarize the laser's light.

2. (With lower-case initial.) A unit of measurement for the stress-optical coefficient of a material, equal to 10^{-12} m^2N^{-1} (orig. 10^{-10} cm^2 per gramme force, equal to $(10^{-12}/0.981)$ m^2N^{-1}).

1910 L. N. G. Filon in *Proc. R. Soc.* A. LXXXIII. 576 The stress-optical coefficients .. are expressed in a unit of 10^{-10} cm.[2] per gramme weight. It would be very desirable to have a short name for this unit... I propose to call it a brewster. 1938 *Jrnl. R. Aeronaut. Soc.* XLII. 570 The stress-optical coefficient of a certain soft vulcanised rubber compound is found to be 2,030 brewsters. 1980 L. Levi *Appl. Optics* II. x. 11 The difference in refractive index parallel and normal to the stress direction is readily calculated by the formula $\Delta n = SB = 10^{-12}\ S^*B^*$ where S is the stress (S^* when in units of N/m^2) and B is the stress-optic coefficient (sometimes called Brewster's constant) of the material (B^* when in units of brewsters, i.e., reciprocal pN/m^2).

Hence **Brew'sterian** *a.*

1942 *Ann. Reg. 1941* 355 An explanation of the elliptical polarisation of light reflected at the Brewsterian angle which is independent of the existence of surface films or strains in the refracting medium. 1963 R. W. Ditchburn *Light* (ed. 2) xii. 545 With most surfaces, the light reflected at the Brewsterian angle is elliptically polarized.

brewsterite ('bru:stəraɪt). [f. name of Sir David *Brewster* + -ITE.] A zeolitic mineral, belonging to the hydrous silicates, white in colour, and of uneven fracture.

1843 Portlock *Geol.* 223 Brewsterite has been stated to occur .. at the Causeway.

brewsterlinite ('bru:stəlɪnaɪt). *Min.* [f. *brewsterlin(e* + -ITE[1]; Dana orig. used *brewsterline*, f. the name of the Scottish physicist Sir David *Brewster* (1781–1868), who first described the liquid in 1823 + *-line*, prob. repr. L. *oleum* oil + -IN[1] (as in CRYPTOLIN); this he changed to *brewstoline* and then to *brewsterlinite*.] A transparent liquid of uncertain composition found in inclusions in certain minerals.

[1850 J. D. Dana *Syst. Min.* (ed. 3) v. vii. 559 Brewsterline. Fluid. Colorless... We have thought proper to recognize this fluid among minerals and name it, although yet imperfectly described. 1854 *Ibid.* (ed. 4) I. v. 471 Brewstoline.] 1864 *Ibid.* (ed. 5) 761 Brewsterlinite. A new fluid in the cavities of minerals. 1902 H. A. Miers *Mineralogy* II. xviii. 443 'Brewsterlinite' .. was investigated by Brewster, who found it to have the low refractive index 1·2. 1966 W. A. Deer et al. *Introd. Rock-Forming Min.* I. 47 Microscopic cavities are sometimes found in topaz, usually filled with a liquid: one such liquid, brewsterlinite, has a refractive index of 1·13 and has been supposed to be liquid CO_2.

brewys, brewz, obs. forms of BREWIS.

brey, variant of BRAYE, *Obs.*

brey, var. BRAY *sb.*[3]

brey, var. BRAY *v.*[4]

breyd(e, variant of BRAID.

breyer, breyr, obs. forms of BRIER.

breyfe, breyff, obs. forms of BRIEF.

breythe, variant of BRAYTHE *v. Obs.*

breze, obs. form of BREEZE.

breziline, variant of BRAZILIN.

briar, etc.: see BRIER, etc.

Briard (brɪ'ɑ:(d)). [Fr., adj. of *Brie* (region of France).] A sheep-dog of a breed of French origin.

1934 in Webster. 1938 A. Woollcott *Let.* (1946) vii. 168 The livestock there has been augmented by a Briard. He .. is known as Mugwump and is roughly the size of the National Gallery. 1948 C. L. B. Hubbard *Dogs in Britain*

191 The Briard (Chien de Brie), a French Sheepdog taken from Corsica to Egypt during the Napoleonic expedition. **1967** H. KEMELMAN *Nine Mile Walk* (1968) 156 Duke was no ordinary dog. He was a briard, a Belgian sheepdog, a huge creature with a long rough iron-grey coat, the shaggy fur covering even his face.

briareus (braɪˈɛərɪəs, ˈbraɪər(j)uːs). Proper name of a hundred-handed giant of Greek mythology; sometimes used connotatively.

1606 SHAKS. *Tr. & Cr.* I. ii. 30 A gowtie Briareus, many hands and no vse. **1852** TUPPER *Proverb. Philos.* 310 She with the might of a Briareus, is dragging down the clouds upon the mountain.

Hence **Briarean** (-ˈiːən, -ˈɛərɪən), of or relating to Briareus; hundred-handed. Also quasi-*sb.*

1599 MARSTON *Satires*, Shape-changing Proteans, damn'd Briareans. **1820** BYRON *Mar. Fal.* I. ii. 268 Could I not shatter the Briarean sceptre Which in this hundred-handed senate rules? **1883** PROCTOR *Myst. Time & Sp.* 57.

bribability, bribe- (braɪbəˈbɪlɪtɪ). [f. next: see -ITY.] The quality of being bribable; corruptibility, venality.

1832 J. TAYLOR *Records my Life* II. 232 The Doctor seems to show symptoms of Bribability. **1867** CARLYLE *Shooting Niagara* iii, Calling in of new supplies of blockheadism, gullibility, bribeability, amenability to beer and balderdash.

bribable, bribeable (ˈbraɪbəb(ə)l), *a.* (*sb.*) [f. BRIBE *v.* + -ABLE; see also -BLE.]

A. *adj.* Capable of being bribed; open to bribery; corrupt; venal.

1829 *Blackw. Mag.* XXVI. 641 The close and the bribable boroughs will not be violated. **1858** CARLYLE *Fredk. Gt.* I. v. v. 590 Grumkow, a bribeable gentleman. **1866** *Ch. Times* 31 Mar. 101/2 Give increased voting power to the bribeable classes. **1879** BAGEHOT *Lit. Studies* I. Introd. 63 A most amusing picture of the bribable electors.

B. *sb.* A corrupt or venal person.

1867 *Fortn. Rev.* July 112 The bribables..in the new constituencies.

†**ˈbribage.** *Obs. rare*⁻¹. [f. BRIBE *v.* + -AGE.] Exaction of illegal fees by officials.

1587 HARRISON *England* II. iii. (1877) 77 Yer the Scholar can be preferred, such bribage is made, that poore mens children are commonlie shut out.

†**bribble-brabble.** *Obs.* [Reduplicated form on BRABBLE.] Vain chatter or wrangling; *attrib.*

1665 HOWARD *Committee* III. (D.) You are a foolish bribble-brabble woman, that you are.

bribe (braɪb), *sb.* Also 5–6 **brybe**. [*Bribe* sb. and vb., and *brybour*, appear together in Chaucer and his contemporaries: their previous history is obscure. OF. had *bribe* in sense of 'piece of bread, frustum panis', *esp.* 'a peece, lumpe, or cantill of bread giuen vnto a beggar' (Cotgr.); the same senses occur with med.L. *briba*: see Du Cange. Cf. Walloon *brib* alms, Sp. *briba* mendicancy, It. *birba* vagabond's trade; also OF. *briber*, *brimber* to beg (*intr.*), be a mendicant, Walloon *briber*, Sp. *bribar* to lead a vagabond life, be a strolling beggar, It. *birbare* 'to play the sly knave' (Florio); also OF. *bribeur*, *brimbeur* mendicant, strolling beggar, with Sp. *bribon*, It. *birbone*, *birbante* vagrant, vagabond, and the ME. *bribour*, BRIBER sense 1; also OF. *briberie*, *brimberie*, Rouchi *briberie*, Walloon *bribreie* mendicancy. The ulterior history is quite unknown; if the sense of OF. *bribe* is the original, the order of development would appear to have been 'piece of bread', 'alms', 'living upon alms', 'professional begging'. Hence, app. from practical association, the English sense 'to steal, plunder'. The further history in English is also involved, but appears to be somewhat thus: in *bribe* sb. the early sense of 'theft, plunder, spoil', appears to have been transferred to the 'black mail' or 'baksheesh' exacted by governors and judges who abused their positions, and thus to gifts received or given for corrupt purposes, whence the later sense of the vb. The transition is best seen in the agent-noun *briber*, where we have the series, 'beggar', 'vagabond', 'thief', 'robber', 'extortioner', 'exactor of black mail', and 'receiver of baksheesh' (the Baconian sense). The sudden and startling change from the Baconian 'briber', who received douceurs, to the modern 'briber' who gives them, can be explained only by taking the latter as a separate derivative of the verb in its latest sense.]

†**1.** A thing stolen or robbed; theft, robbery; spoil, plunder. *Obs.* (The Chaucer quotation is doubtful: if the sb. is right, it might perh. have the sense of 'an alms', as in OF.)

c **1386** CHAUCER *Freres T.* 78 (*Harl. MS.*) Feyning a cause for he wolde han a bribe [*Petw. MS.* wold haue a brybe; 5 *texts read* he wolde brybe]. *c* **1440** *Pomp. Parv.* 50 Brybery or brybe, *manticulum.* **1509** BARCLAY *Shyp of Folys* (1874) II. 85 Theyr howsys stuffed with brybes abhomyn[a]bly.

2. 'A reward given to pervert the judgment or corrupt the conduct' (J.).

a. The earlier sense probably regarded it as a consideration extorted, exacted, or taken by an official, a judge, etc.; i.e. as the act of the receiver: cf. BRIBER.

1535 COVERDALE *Ecclus.* xl. 12 All brybes [**1611** briberie] and vnrighteousnes shalbe put awaye, but faithfulnes and trueth shal endure for euer. **1580** BARET *Alv.* B 1227 Buying and selling of iustice for bribes. **1601** SHAKS. *Jul. C.* IV. iii. 3 You haue condemn'd, and noted Lucius Pella For taking Bribes heere of the Sardians. **1611** BIBLE *1 Sam.* viii. 3 His sonnes..tooke bribes, and peruerted iudgement.

b. But it is now applied to a consideration voluntarily offered to corrupt a person and induce him to act in the interest of the giver, e.g. a consideration given to a voter to procure his vote.

1555 BRADFORTH in Strype *Eccl. Mem.* III. App. xlv. 130 Who they myght make their frend with brybes. **1570** LEVINS *Manip.* 113 A Bribe, *largitio.* **1607** SHAKS. *Cor.* I. ix. 38, I..cannot make my heart consent to take A Bribe. **1667** PEPYS *Diary* (1879) IV. 340 His rise hath been his giving of large bribes. **1718** POPE *Iliad* I. 40 Prayers, and tears, and bribes shall plead in vain. **1776** GIBBON *Decl. & F.* I. 115 The infamous bribe with which Julian had purchased the empire. **1839** THIRLWALL *Greece* xi. 45 Duties..which belong to the judicial character, of rejecting bribes, hearing impartially, and deciding faithfully. **1880** MᶜCARTHY *Own Times* IV. lvi. 218 Before long surely it will be accounted as base to give as to take a bribe.

†**3.** (*perh.*) Rascally or execrable behaviour; clamour. Cf. BRIBER 1 b, quot. *a* 1400. *Obs.*

a **1560** ROLLAND *Crt. Venus* IV. 306 Quhen all this brybe & boist is quite ouir blawin.

4. *Comb.*, as ***bribe-broker***, ***-brokerage***, ***-monger***; ***bribe-free***, ***-worthy*** adjs.; **bribe-service**, a service done for a bribe. Also BRIBE-TAKER, -TAKING.

1789 BURKE *Imp. W. Hastings* Wks. XIV. 236 Is it in the hands of Mr. Hastings's wicked *bribe-brokers. **1632** BROME *Novella* I. ii. Wks. 1873 I. 116 Dos he appeare *bribe-free? Is he the only officer uncorrupted? *a* **1593** H. SMITH *Wks.* (1866–7) I. 87 He would never speak to usurers and *bribe-mongers. **1788** BURKE *Imp. W. Hastings* Wks. XIII. 396, I charge him with not having done that *bribe-service, which fidelity even in iniquity requires. **1731** ARBUTHNOT *Epit. Francis Chartres*, Without *bribe-worthy service, he acquired, or more properly created, a ministerial estate. **1788** BURKE *Imp. W. Hastings* Wks. XIII. 360 To secure them against bribes by taking from the power of bribe-worthy service.

bribe (braɪb), *v.* Also 4–6 **brybe**, 5 **brybyn**, 6 **brybbe**. [See under the sb.]

†**1.** *trans.* To take dishonestly; to purloin; to steal, rob; to obtain by abuse of trust, or by extortion; to extort. *Obs.*

c **1386** CHAUCER *Cokes T.* 53 For ther is no thef withowten a lowke, That helpeth him to wasten and to sowke Of that he brybe [*v.r.* bribe] kan, or borwe may. **1401** *Pol. Poems* (1859) II. 40 He chiterith and he bribith All that he may gete. *c* **1440** *Promp. Parv.* 50/2 Brybyn, *manticulo, latrocinor.* **1494** FABYAN VII. 353 A parte was brought vnto yᵉ lordes, but yᵉ more part was stolen and brybed. **1538** BALE *Johan Baptiste* in *Harl. Misc.* I. 106 [Publican says] By me, from hens fourth, nought from the poore shall be brybed. **1552** HULOET, Polle, brybe, or extort. **1561** AWDELAY *Frat. Vacab.* 13 A licoryce knave that will swill his maisters drink and brybe his meate. **1643** PRYNNE *Power Parl.* App. 30 Great taxes and summes of money..spent vainly and riotously, and bribed out of the Kings Coffers.

†**b.** *absol.* To steal, extort, or purloin. *Obs.*

c **1386** CHAUCER *Freres T.* 78 This Somnour euere waityng on his pray ffor to somne an old wydwe a Ribibe ffeynynge a cause for he wolde brybe. *c* **1550** *Hye way Spyttel Ho.* 283 in Hazl. *E.P.P.* IV. 37 They must beg, or els go brybe, and steale.

2. To influence corruptly, by a reward or consideration, the action of (a person); to pervert the judgement or corrupt the conduct by a gift. Const. *with* a consideration, *to* an action, *to do* a thing.

1528 ROY *Rede me* (Arb.) 54 They brybe hym..for to be favoured. **1603** SHAKS. *Meas. for M.* II. ii. 145 Hark, how Ile bribe you..*Ang.* How? bribe me? *Isa.* I, with such gifts that heauen shall share with you. **1678** N. WANLEY *Wonders* V. ii. §80. 472/2 He bribed the Bishop of Rome to the empoysoning of his brother Zemes. **1681** *Trial S. Colledge* 132 Seek an occasion to tell him they were bribed off, and were forsworn. **1789** BENTHAM *Princ. Legisl.* xviii. §27 *note*, To bribe a trustee..is..to suborn him to be guilty of a breach or an abuse of trust. **1855** MILMAN *Lat. Chr.* (1864) III. VI. ii. 403 They endeavoured to bribe them with enormous pay to enter into their service. **1878** MORLEY *Diderot* II. 23 The judges were bribed.

b. *absol.* To use or apply bribes; to practise bribery.

1768 JOHNSON in Goldsm. *Good-nat. Man* Prol. 26 The bard may supplicate, but cannot bribe. **1848** MACAULAY *Hist. Eng.* II. 158 He fawned, bullied, and bribed indefatigably.

3. *trans.* To purchase or obtain by bribery. *arch.*

1718 POPE *Iliad* I. 284 And bribe thy friendship with a boundless store. **1733** SWIFT *On Poetry* Wks. IV. I. 190 To bribe the judge's vote. **1749** SMOLLETT *Regicide* I. vii. (1777) 22 Not thrones and diadems shall bribe My approbation! **1873** [see BRIBED].

4. *fig.* To gain over by some influence.

1595 SHAKS. *John* II. i. 171 With these Christall beads heauen shall be brib'd To doe him Iustice, and reuenge on you. *c* **1620** Z. BOYD *Zion's Flowers* (1855) 33 A flattering sleepe Bribes them to rest. **1665** HOWARD *Ind. Queen* IV. i, Your greater Merits bribe her to your side. **1869** BUCKLE *Civilis.* III. v. 371 The memory of which is almost enough so to bribe the judgment.

bribed (braɪbd), *ppl. a.* [f. BRIBE *v.* + -ED.]

†**a.** Obtained by bribery; stolen (*obs.*). **b.** Won over by a bribe, bought by a gift.

1576 NEWTON tr. *Lemnie's Complex.* (1633) 123 A bribed Judge, that gapes for gaine. **1598** SHAKS. *Merry W.* V. v. 27 Diuide me like a brib'd-Bucke, each a Haunch. **1813** BYRON *Br. Abydos* II. xiv, The bowl a bribed attendant bore. *c* **1873** J. ADDIS *Elizab. Echoes* (1879) 92 The bribed Judgments that he falsely meted.

bribee (braɪˈbiː). [f. BRIBE *v.* + -EE; cf. *examinee.*] The recipient of a bribe.

1858 GEN. P. THOMPSON *Audi Alt.* I. lix. 230 The bond between the briber and the bribee. **1881** *Times* 25 Jan. 8 A large number of bribees were examined.

†**ˈbribeless,** *a. Obs.* [f. BRIBE + -LESS.] Free from bribes; not to be corrupted by a bribe.

1608 TOURNEUR *Rev. Trag.* I. iv. 37 Nay, then, step forth thou Bribelesse officer! *a* **1618** RALEIGH *Pilgr.* in *Rem.* (1661) 257 From thence to Heavens bribeless Hall, Where no corrupted voices brawl. **1640** BP. REYNOLDS *Passions* (1658) 1102 Conscience is a most bribeless worker.

briber (ˈbraɪbə(r)). Forms: 4–6 **bri-**, **brybour**, 5 **briboure**, **-bowre**, **-bur**, 5–6 **bryber**, 6 **bri-**, **brie-**, **brybor**, **brybar**, 5– **briber**. [a. AF. *bribour* = OF. *bribeor*, later *bribeur*: see BRIBE *sb.*]

†**1.** A vagabond, strolling vagrant; = F. *bribeur*, It. and Sp. *bribon*. *Obs.* (The last quot. belongs doubtfully here.)

1483 *Cath. Angl.* 43 A Bribur, *circumforaneus, sicofanta.* *c* **1500** DUNBAR *Flyting* 49 Irsch brybour baird, vyle beggar with thy brattis! *a* **1600** *Hist. Pieces* in Peck *Cromwell* 30 He made his porter shut his gates To sycophants and briebors.

†**b.** Hence: Scoundrel, wretch, rascal. (Cf. a similar use of *beggar*, *vagabond*, *thief.*) *Obs.*

1387 TREVISA *Higden* Rolls Ser. II. 313 Gentilmen, for to haue dyuersite and distinccioun from suche bribours made hem rynges of gold. *a* **1400** *Cov. Myst.* 183 If any brybour do bragge or blowe aȝens my bost. *c* **1440** *York Myst.* xxvi. 169 Say, bittilbrowed bribour. **1509** BARCLAY *Ship of Fooles* (1570) 39 Ye babbling bribers, endeuour you to amende. *c* **1550** LYNDESAY *Depl. Q. Magdalene* 66 The potent Prince ..Contrair that bailfull bribour [death] had no micht.

†**2.** A thief, purloiner, or robber; a taker of blackmail; an extortioner. *Obs.*

1377 LANGL. *P. Pl.* B. xx. 260 Alle other in bataille ben yholde bribours [C. XXIII. 262 brybours] Pilours and pykehernois in eche a place ycursed. **1387** TREVISA *Higden* Rolls Ser. II. 147 So þese bribours were i-made men of þe lond [*sicque de prædonibus accolæ effecti*]. **1413** LYDG. *Pylgr. Sowle* IV. xxxiv. (1483) 83 To oppressen brybours and extorcioners. *c* **1440** *Promp. Parv.* 50 Brybowre, *manticulus.* **1461** J. PASTON in *Lett.* 384 II. 4 To lette brybers that wold a robbed a ship undyr color of my Lord of Warwyk. **1525** LD. BERNERS *Froiss.* II. x. 21 The bribours of the Countrey watched for them at the passages. **1548** CRANMER *Catech.* 100 b, Extorcioners, brybers, pollers, and piellers, deuourers of widowes houses. **1552** HULOET, Brybor. *Vide* in poller and thefe. **1563–87** FOXE *A. & M.* (1596) 145/1 By inward theeues and bribers.

†**3.** A judge or other official who levies 'blackmail' upon those to whom he should administer justice; one who exacts or accepts bribes; a bribee. Cf. BRIBE-TAKER. *Obs.*

1520 WHITTINTON *Vulg.* (1527) 13 He is a bryber, or a taker of brybes [*is est largitionis capax*]. **1549** LATIMER *Serm. bef. Edw. VI*, iii. (Arb.) 97 A bryber, a gyft taker, a gratifier of rytche men. **1586** T. B. *La Primaud. Fr. Acad.* 372 Iustice ought not to be either a briber, or respecter of persons, that is, she must neither take any thing, nor judge for anie favour. **1599** *Life Sir T. More* in Wordsworth *Eccl. Biog.* (1853) II. 80 His chancellour was a great briber and extortioner. **1605** BACON *Adv. Learn.* II. xxiii. §6 (1873) 222 A judge were better be a briber than a respecter of persons; for a corrupt judge offendeth not so lightly as a facile. **1611** RICH *Honest. Age* (1844) 13 When euery vsurer, euery briber, euery extortioner..is an honest man.

4. One who offers or gives a bribe.

1583 BABINGTON *Commandm.* (1637) Have wee never suffered these hands to feele the weight of a bribers gift to drawe us to oppression? **1692** SOUTH *12 Serm.* (1697) I. 271 Affection is still a Briber of the Judgment. [**1721** Not in BAILEY in this sense.] **1755** in JOHNSON. **1837** LYTTON *Athens* II. 246 Themistocles the most expert briber of his time. **1863** H. COX *Inst.* I. viii. 116 Bribery is a misdemeanor, punishable..in the briber and person bribed.

†**5.** A thing that bribes, a price paid. *Obs.*

1607 SHAKS. *Timon* III. v. 61 His seruice done at Lacedemon, and Bizantium, Were a sufficient briber for his life.

ˈbriberess. *rare.* [f. prec. + -ESS. Cf. OF. *briberesse* beggar-woman.] A woman who bribes.

1748 RICHARDSON *Clarissa* (1811) VI. xiii. 64 As we cluttered by the door of the fair bribress.

†**ˈbribering,** *vbl. sb. Obs.* [This and the next imply a vb. *briber*, formed on the sb. *bribour*, *briber*, in its earlier sense of 'thief'.] Thieving.

1567 HARMAN *Caveat* (1869) 60 Brought before me..as Malefactors, for bryberinge and stealinge.

†**ˈbribering,** *a. Obs.* [cf. prec.] Thieving.

c **1530** *Dyal. betw. Gentl. & Husbandm.* (Arb.) 137 (D.) It is the moost briberynge thefe That euer was.

†**ˈbriberous,** *a. Obs.* [f. BRIBER + -OUS.]

a. Rascally, thievish, given to taking bribes. **b.** Of the nature of a bribe, corrupt.

1534 WHITTINTON *Tullyes Offyces* II. (1540) 84 Such bryberous rewardes promessed. *c* **1550** *Hye way Spyttel Ho.* 387 in Hazl. *E.P.P.* IV. 44, I meane these bawdy brybrous knaves, That lodgeth them that so powles and shaves. *a* **1614** S. GRAHAME, The brib'rous minde who makes a god of gould.

bribery ('braɪbərɪ). Forms: 5 **brybre, brybory,** 5–6 **brybery,** 6 **bri-, brybry(e, bryboury, -burrye,** 6–7 **bri-, bryberie,** 6– **bribery.** [f. BRIBER + -Y[3]: see -ERY; or a. OF. *briberie*, found in earlier sense of 'mendicancy'.]

†**1.** Purloining, larceny, theft, robbery. *Obs.*

c **1386** CHAUCER *Freres T.* 67 He knew of bribryes [*v.r.* bryberyes, bryberyis, briberies, 2 *MSS.* briber] mo Than possible is to telle in yeres two. **1387** TREVISA *Higden* VII. xxiv. (Rolls Ser.) VIII. 81 Al þat were aboute hym ȝaf hem so to robberye and to bryberie [*v.r.* briborye, brybury]. *c* **1440** *Promp. Parv.* 50/2 Brybery or brybe, *manticulum.* *c* **1460** *Towneley Myst.* 194 Fy on the, fundlyng, Thou lyfes bot by brybre. **1526** SKELTON *Magnyf.* 1242 To theft and bryboury I make some fall And pyke a locke and clyme a wall. **1567** HARMAN *Caveat* (1869) 34 Charged with fellony or petye brybrye.

†**2.** Robbery with violence or force; extortion.

1523 FITZHERB. *Surv.* Prol., A gretter bribery nor extorcyon a man can nat do, than vpon his owne tenauntes, for they dare nat say nay nor yet complayne. **1557** N. T. (Genev.) *Matt.* xxiii. 25 Within they are ful of brybery and excesse. **1589** BP. COOPER *Admon.* 178 To oppresse them by couetousnesse, extortion, and briberie.

3. The exaction or taking of a bribe; 'the offence of a judge, magistrate, or any person concerned judicially in the administration of public justice, of receiving a reward or consideration from parties interested, for the purpose of procuring a partial or favourable decision' (*Penny Cycl.*). *arch.*

1549 LATIMER *Serm. bef. Edw. VI* (Arb.) 88 Brybery is a pryncely kynde of theuing. Thei wil be waged by the rich, eyther to geue sentence agaynste the poore, or to put of the poore mannes causes. *Ibid.* 113 [The deuyll] goeth about as much as he can to corrupt the men of lawe, to make them fal to bribery. **1621** ELSING *Debates Ho. Lords* (1870) 23 His estate raysed by theis briberyes. **1769** BLACKSTONE *Comm.* IV. 139 Bribery is..when a judge, or other person concerned in the administration of justice, takes any undue reward to influence his behaviour in his office. **1836** *Penny Cycl.* V. 407/1 Since the Revolution, in 1688, judicial bribery has been altogether unknown in England.

4. The act or practice of giving or accepting money or some other payment with the object of corruptly influencing the judgement or action; the offer or acceptance of bribes; *spec.* the application of such influences to gain votes at a parliamentary or other election.

1570 LEVINS *Manip.* 104 Bribery, *ambitus.* **1588** GREENE *Pandosto* (1607) 20 The simplicitie of his conscience feared him from such deceitfull briberie. *a* **1639** W. WHATELEY *Prototypes* II. xxvi. (1640) 57 Bribery is naught, that is to seeke to turne a Governour from justice by gifts, and hire him to do wrong. **1767** COWPER *Let.* 16 June, We expect, or rather experience a warm contest between the candidates for the county, the preliminary movements of bribery, threatening, and drunkenness being already taken. **1827** HALLAM *Const. Hist.* (1876) I. v. 268 This [1571] is the earliest precedent on record for the punishment of bribery in elections. **1863** H. COX *Inst.* I. viii. 116.

5. *Comb.*, **bribery-oath**, an oath administrable to a voter at a parliamentary election, declaring that he has not received a bribe for his vote.

1809 TOMLINS *Law Dict.* s.v. *Parliament* vi. (B) 3 The Bribery Oath, which must be taken as required by 2 Geo. II. c. 24.

'**bribe-,taker.** One who takes bribes.

1549 LATIMER *Serm. bef. Edw. VI* (Arb.) 88 This is the noble thefte of princes, and of magistrates. Thei are bribetakers. **1585** ABP. SANDYS *Serm.* (1841) 35 He neither was a bribe-taker, nor an extortioner. **1626** *Raleigh's Ghost* in *Harl. Misc.* (Malh.) III. 539 Gondomar..one of the four bribe-takers for the profane privileges.

So **bribe-taking** *vbl. sb.* and *ppl. a.*

1549 LATIMER *Serm. bef. Edw. VI* (Arb.) 130, I wold the Iudges woulde take forth theyr lesson, that there myghte be no more iniquitye vsed, nor brybe-takynge. **1880** *Fortn. Rev.* Feb. 221 The only people who throve were rowdies and bribe-taking judges.

bribing ('braɪbɪŋ), *vbl. sb.* [f. BRIBE *v.* + -ING[1].] The action of the verb BRIBE; †**a.** thieving; †**b.** extortion; **c.** corruption by bribes. Also *attrib.*

1549 LATIMER *Serm. bef. Edw. VI* (Arb.) 130 If there shall be brybynge, they [Judges] knowe the peryl of it. **1573** TUSSER *Husb.* x. (1878) 21 Bribing and shifting haue seldom good end. **1618** BOLTON *Florus* III. i. 161 The bribing of Scaurus came to light. **1634** SANDERSON *Serm.* II. 288 Then what crouching, and fawning, and bribing, and dawbing, to have the matter taken up in a private chamber? **1839** MARRYAT *Phant. Ship* xxxi, We may get away by bribing.

'**bribing,** *ppl. a.* [f. BRIBE *v.* + -ING[2].]

†**1.** Dishonest, thievish. *Obs.*

1542 UDALL *Erasm. Apoph.* 323 a, Verres..left nothyng behynde hym, as beeyng a taker and a brybyng feloe. **1567** HARMAN *Caveat* (1869) 74 These beastlye brybinge breeches.

†**2.** That exacts or accepts bribes; venal. *Obs.*

1592 GREENE *Art Conny catch.* Pref. 4 Some bribing officer, who threatneth to carrie him to prison, takes awaie all the monie, and lets him slip. **1621** ELSING *Debates Ho. Lords* (1870) 19 Shewing howe grievous to the comon welth a bribing Judge is. **1649** CROMWELL *Lett.* 31 Dec., They are accounted the bribingst people that are.

3. That gives bribes; that corrupts or seduces with or like a bribe.

c **1670** *Expost. Men Buckhm.* 1/2 Did he not once make you a bribeing Present of Timber? **1818** COBBETT *Resid. U.S.* (1822) 231 Bribing and corrupt boroughmongers.

‖**bric-à-brac** ('brɪkə,bræk). Written also without the accent, and as one word. [Fr.; said by Littré to be formed after the phr. *de bric et de broc* 'by hook or by crook'.] Old curiosities of artistic character, knick-knacks, antiquarian odds-and-ends, such as old furniture, plate, china, fans, statuettes, and the like.

1862 THACKERAY *Philip* I. 299 All the valuables of the house, including, perhaps, J. J.'s bricabrac, cabinets, china, and so forth. **1873** MISS BRADDON *Str. World* I. iv. 67 That bric-a-brac upon which the Bellingham race had squandered a small fortune. **1885** *Athenæum* 7 Mar. 308 Some syndicate, growing tired of bric-à-brac.

b. *attrib.*, as in ***bric-à-brac man, shop.***

1840 THACKERAY *Paris Sk. Bk.* (1872) 243 The palace of Versailles has been turned into a bricabrac shop. **1876** GEO. ELIOT *Dan. Der.* lxvii. (D.) Haven't an affair in the world.. except a quarrel with a bric-a-brac man.

c. quasi-*adj.* (*humorous.*)

1872 GEO. ELIOT *Middlem.* xliii. 13, I think he is a good fellow; rather miscellaneous and bric-à-brac,—but likable.

Hence **bric-a-bracker, bric-a-brackery.** (*colloq.* or *humorous.*)

1880 MARK TWAIN *Tramp Abr.* I. 180, I am content to be a bric-a-bracker. *Ibid.* I. 179 It is the failing of the true.. devotee in any department of bric-a-brackery.

briccol(l, obs. form of BRICOLE.

brich, obs. form of BREECH.

†**briche,** *a. Obs.* [OE. *brýce*, corresp. to OHG. *brûchi*:—OTeut. *brûki-z*, f. *brûkan* to use.] Useful, serviceable.

c **1000** *Ags. Psalter* cxviii [xix]. 35 Gelæd me on stiȝe þær ic stæpe mine on þinum bebodum bryce hæbbe. *c* **1250** *Bestiary* 379 in *O.E. Misc.* 12 We sulen hauen heuenriche, Gef we bitwixen us ben briche. —— 728 And ðeðen he sal cumen eft, And ben us alle briche.

briche, bryche, obs. variants of BIRCH.

bricht, Sc. form of BRIGHT *a.*

bricia, obs. form of BRECCIA.

brick (brɪk), *sb.*[1] Forms: 5 **breke,** (*pl.*) **brikkes,** 5–6 **bryke,** 6 **brike, brikke, bryk, bryck(e,** 6–7 **bricke,** 6– **brick.** [Found only since the middle of the 15th c.; not in the *Promptorium* 1440, or *Catholicon* 1483: prob. a. F. *brique*, in OF. also *briche*; quoted by Godefroy 1264 (*briche*) and 1457 (*brique*) in sense of 'a form of loaf', and also in OF. in sense of 'broken piece, fragment, bit', and reinforcing a negative in sense 'not a bit'. Still in Burgundian and Hainault dial., in sense 'piece', *brique de pain* 'piece of bread', in Swiss Romance 'piece, bit, débris', mod.Pr. *briga* 'débris'. It would appear therefore that the OF. word was derived in some way from the Teutonic verb *brek-an* to break (cf. F. *brèche*, ONF. *breke, breque* breaking, BREACH), and that its original sense was 'broken piece', which passed through the general sense 'piece, bit', or the specific sense 'piece of bread as baked, loaf', to that of 'piece of baked clay'. In French *une brique*, the shaped object, would thus be earlier than *la brique*, the substance; but in English the earliest examples yet found are of the substance.]

I. 1. A substance formed of clay, kneaded, moulded, and hardened by baking with fire, or in warm countries and ancient times by drying in the sun; used instead of stone as a building material.

c **1440** [See BRICK WALL *sb.*[1] I.] **1465** *Mann. & Househ. Exp.* 301, I did rekene wethe heme that makethe my breke. **1467** *Ord. Worcester* in *Eng. Gilds* (1870) 372 That no chimneys of tre..be suffred..but that the owners make hem of bryke or stone. **1535** COVERDALE *Gen.* xi. 3 Come on, let vs make bryck & burne it. And they toke bryck for stone. *c* **1543** W. CLEVE in *Dom. Archit.* III. 79 With closer of brike toured aboute your gardein. **1603** SHAKS. *Meas. for M.* IV. i. 28 Garden circummur'd with Bricke. **1776** GIBBON *Decl. & F.* I. 44 Augustus was accustomed to boast that he had found his capital of brick, and that he had left it of marble. **1788** H. WALPOLE in *Walpoliana* xiv. 8 The ruin in Kew Gardens is built with act-of-parliament brick. **1846** McCULLOCH *Acc. Brit. Empire* (1854) I. 623 By far the greater number of houses in London..are built of brick.

2. A block of this substance, or of sand and lime, concrete, and other materials, made of a definite size and shape, as an individual object; ordinarily rectangular, but also of other shapes for special purposes. (In 16th c. the pl. was often *brick.*)

c **1525** *Surv. Yorksh. Monast.* in *Yorkshire Archæol. Jrnl.* (1886) IX. 329 A litle house..coueryd wt tyle, wt a chymney of brikkes. **1535** COVERDALE *Ex.* v. 8 The nombre of the brycke which they made. **1611** BIBLE *Gen.* xi. 3 Goe to, let vs make bricke, and burne them thorowly. —— *Ex.* vi. 18 Yet shall ye deliuer the tale of brickes. **1651** *Proc. Parl.* No. 123. 1902 Our Landlords..have exacted the full taile of the Bricks, when the ground produced no straw. **1677** YARRANTON *Engl. Improv.* 136 Six hundred thousand of Bricks builds a Granary, Two Brick and half thick. **1724** *Ord. Tilers' & Brickl. Comp.* in *Lond. Gaz.* No. 6251/3 Every Brick is to be 9 Inches in Length, 4 Inches and a Quarter of an Inch in Breadth, and 2 Inches and a Quarter of an Inch in Thickness. **1823** P. NICHOLSON *Pract. Build.* 345 Called Fire-Bricks, because of their enduring the fire. **1840** MARRYAT *Olla Podr.* (Rtldg.) 256 We cannot put on a heavy roof with a brick-and-a-half wall. **1850** LAYARD *Nineveh* xiii. 342 Squares which when dried by the heat of the sun served them for bricks. **1875, 1879** Slag-brick [see SLAG *sb.*[1] 6 a]. **1922** D. M. LIDDELL *Handbk. Chem. Engin.* II. 948 At present bricks made from sand and lime are extensively used, while they have been used in Europe for 50 years.

3. A loaf shaped like a brick. Often applied to a 'tin-loaf', but the local uses vary. [Cf. the OFr. and Fr. dial. uses referred to above.]

1735 BYROM *Rem.* (1855) I. II. 615 Breakfasted upon a penny brick and tea with sugar, and ate all the brick very near. **1822** KITCHINER *Cook's Orac.* App. 508 Put a quartern of Flour into a large Basin..knead it again, and it is ready either for Loaves or Bricks. **1857** ELIZA ACTON *Eng. Bread-Bk.* II. iv. 184 The loaves technically called 'bricks', which are baked in tins. **1847–78** HALLIWELL, *Brick*, a kind of loaf. *var. dial.* **1875** URE *Dict. Arts* I. 477 The loaves known under the names of *bricks, Coburg, cottage*, and *French rolls*, being all made of the same dough.

4. *transf.* **a.** A brick-shaped block of any substance, e.g. of tea (see *brick-tea* in 10); of wood, for a child to play with; of ice-cream; also in other more consciously figurative uses. ***box of bricks***: a box of wooden blocks for a child to build with.

1827 H. E. LLOYD *Timkowski's Trav.* II. 315 A good horse was in our presence sold for about sixty bricks of tea. **1832** F. TROLLOPE *Dom. Manners* I. xix. 301 A numerous collection of large wooden bricks. **1861** C. M. YONGE *Young Step-Mother* xxix. 434 He..built up a tower with her wooden bricks. **1871** TYNDALL *Fragm. Sc.* (ed. 6) I. xii. 358 In building up crystals these little atomic bricks often arrange themselves into layers. **1875** URE *Dict. Arts* II. 507 Patent fuel..small coal and pitch, moulded together into bricks by pressure. **1884** GILMOUR *Mongols* 143 Buyers.. conspicuous from the clumsy bricks of tea which they carried. **1885** STEVENSON *Dynamiter* 191 'You see this brick?'..lifting a cake of the infernal compound [dynamite] from the laboratory-table. **1922** S. LEWIS *Babbitt* ix. 123 He gulped down a chill and glutinous slice of the ice-cream brick. **1938** R. W. LAWSON tr. *Hevesy & Paneth's Man. Radioactivity* (ed. 2) ix. 94 The α-particles..are not the ultimate bricks of which the nucleus is composed. **1939** L. MACNEICE *Autumn Jrnl.* xix. 76 Baby Croesus crawls in a pen With alphabetical bricks. **1959** I. & P. OPIE *Lore & Lang. Schoolch.* ix. 165 Cornet, Brick, and Lollipop Taste very nice when bought from the shop. **1964** F. L. WESTWATER *Electronic Computers* iii. 49 Only a limited number of electronic 'bricks', as they are called, are used. These bricks, which are circuit elements, have been thoroughly tested beforehand.

b. ***brick couching***, in embroidery, couching in which the laid threads or cords are secured by cross stitches resembling, in their arrangement, the vertical joints of brickwork. Hence ***in bricks***, in divisions resembling bricks. Cf. *brick-stitch* (sense 10 below).

1882 CAULFEILD & SAWARD *Dict. Needlew.* 180/1 The chief varieties of Flat Couching are Brick, Broad, Burden, Diagonal, and Diamond. **1911** A. DRYDEN *Church Embroid.* 112 The commonest form of stitching the gold is in bricks, each couching-stitch being in between the two stitches of the preceding line.

c. The colour of brick; brick-red.

[**1856** M. N. THOMSON *Elephant Club* 163 A [red] head of hair which the youth of America are accustomed to designate as a 'brick-top'.] **1897** *Sears, Roebuck Catal.* 21/3 Send for illustrated color card..Pink—Milwaukee Brick—Quaker Drab. [**1912** *Dialect Notes* III. 572 *Brick-topped*, red-headed.] **1922** JOYCE *Ulysses* 48 A dull brick muffler strangling his unshaven neck. **1923** *Daily Mail* 16 Jan. 1 Blanket Cloth Magyar Wrap Coats... Cream, Beaver, Mole, Nigger, Brick.

5. a. Phrase ***like bricks, like a brick***: with a vengeance, vigorously, with good will: occasionally with a clear reference to the crash with which a quantity of bricks fall, but usually only as an expression of eulogy, as in sense 6. Also (orig. *U.S.*), ***like a thousand*** (occas. ***hundred***) ***of brick(s)***; ***like a ton of bricks***: see COME *v.* 56 g.

1836 DICKENS *Sk. by Boz, Lost Cab-driver*, Out flies the fare like bricks. **1836** HILL *Yankee Stories* 32 (Weingarten *Suppl. Notes to D.A.E.*), If I don't be into him with a thousand of brick. **1840** 'SAMUEL SLICK' *Clockmaker* Ser. III. 50 If I don't pitch into Ben Parsons' ribs like a tousand of bricks. **1841** *Picayune* (New Orleans) 16 Mar. 2/2 They.. rounded the first turn pretty much in a heap like a thousand of brick. **1853** E. FORBES *Let.* in Geikie *Life* xiv. 509 Gibbs has worked like a brick. **1856** KINGSLEY *Let.* May, You fellows worked like bricks. **1856** F. PAGET *Owlet Owlst.* 139 She sits her horse as if she was part of him..hunts like..a brick. **1860** *Picayune* 27 Apr. (De Vere), He fell upon us like a thousand of bricks. **1886** R. BROWN *Spunyarn & Spindrift* vii. 123 The people at the Admiralty will be down on you like a hundred of bricks. **1896** C. JAMES *Yoke of Freedom* 161 Once let a man play me false, I'm down on him like a hundred of bricks. **1911** A. BENNETT *Hilda Lessways* III. ii. 226, I had the whole gang down on me instantly like a thousand of bricks. **1929** W. S. MAUGHAM *Writer's Notebk.* (1949) 228 I'd have had the whole community down on me like a ton o' bricks. **1967** E. GRIERSON *Crime of one's Own* xii. 98 The..gentleman..made his living by selling books, and not *those* sort of books either, or the Super would have been down on the place long since like a ton of bricks.

b. Slang phr. (orig. *U.S.*), *to have* (or *wear*) *a brick in one's hat*: to be under the influence of liquor.

1847 *Knickerbocker* XXIX. 569 A youth who came home one night..having 'a brick in his hat'. **1848** DURIVAGE & BURNHAM *Stray Subjects* 61 He wore a 'brick' within that hat. **1849** [see HAT *sb.* 5 c]. **1889** BARRÈRE & LELAND *Dict. Slang* I. 180/1 *Brick in the hat* (common), intoxicated, top-heavy.

c. *to drop a brick*: to commit a verbal indiscretion, make a 'bloomer'. *colloq.*

1923 *Punch* 3 Oct. 334 It was hinted to me pretty plainly that I had dropped a brick, as you say. **1924** GALSWORTHY *White Monkey* III. xii, I've got to keep my head shut, or I shall be dropping a brick. **1928** 'SAPPER' *Female of Species* xvii. 307 The stones of Stonehenge are little pebbles compared to the bricks you dropped, but I forgive you.

6. *fig.* (*slang* or *colloq.*) A good fellow, one whom one approves for his genuine good qualities.

1840 BARHAM *Ingol. Leg.*, *Bros. Birchington* xiii, I don't stick to declare Father Dick..was a Regular Brick. **1857** HUGHES *Tom Brown* vii. (1871) 151 What a brick not to give us even twenty lines to learn. **1864** MISS YONGE *C'tess Kate* xii. (ed. 2) 213 'She's run away, like a jolly brick!' **1870** MISS BRIDGMAN *R. Lynne* I. xviii. 318 She believed Robert was no end of a brick.

7. 'Bricks, or Briques, in *Heraldry*, are figures or bearings in arms, resembling a building of bricks' (Chambers *Cycl. Supp.* 1753).

II. *attrib.* and *Comb.*

8. *simple attrib.* or *adj.* **a.** Of brick. Similarly *brick-and-mortar*, etc.: see also MORTAR *sb.*[2] a (quots. 1863 and 1895). **b.** In the shape of a brick.

c **1440** [See BRICK WALL *sb.*[1] 1.] **1591** SPENSER *Bellay's Vis.* ii, Nor brick nor marble was the wall. **1677** MOXON *Mech. Exerc.* (1703) 129 Stone, or Brick Houses. **1753** CHAMBERS *Cycl. Supp.* s.v. *Brick*, Some also mention brick-tin, a sort of tin in that shape brought from Germany; and brick-soap, made in oblong pieces. **1851** HELPS *Friends in C.* I. 4 Red brick houses, with poplars coming up amongst them. **1865** M. ARNOLD *Ess. Crit.* iv. 138 Margate, that brick-and-mortar image of English Protestantism. **1884** *Littell's Living Age* CLXI. 88 A..brick-and-stone erection.

9. General comb.: **a.** attrib., as *brick-cart*, *-clamp*, *-colour*, *-furnace*, *-machine*, *-mason*, *-mould*, *-pit*, *-stack*, *-trowel*, *-truck*. **b.** objective, as *brick-moulder*. **c.** instrumental or parasynthetic, forming adjs., as *brick-bound*, *-built*, *-coloured*, *-floored*, *-fronted*, *-hemmed*, *-paved*, *-walled*; also *brick-building* vbl. sb.

1881 J. HAWTHORNE *Fort. Fool* I. xviii, The trim and *brick-bound conventionality of the London mansion. **1631** WEEVER *Anc. Fun. Mon.* 230 All the *bricke-building was done at his charges. *a* **1845** HOOD *Turtles* iv, Before a lofty *brick-built pile Sir Peter stopp'd. **1663** GERBIER *Counsel* 46 He must not suffer *Brick-carts to overturne the load of Bricks. **1598** FLORIO *Worlde of Wordes* 149/2 *Gioggiolino*, a kinde of colour which we call flesh-colour, or *brickcolour. **1818** W. TUCKER *Fam. Dyer & Scourer* (ed. 2) 53 To make a Brown inclining to a Brick Colour. **1708** *Lond. Gaz.* No. 4416/4 [He] had on a *Brick-colour'd Coat. **1898** COUNTESS OF ARNIM *Eliz. & German Garden* 10, I used to..go.. slowly across the *brick-floored hall. **1605** *Leverton (Lincoln) Ch.-Wardens Acc.* (MS.) 84 b, Pd. to Thoms. Jenkinson *brickmayson for vj daies whitteninge of the Churche..vijs. **1858** GLENNY *Gard. Every-day Bk.* 251 Whatever there is no room for in the Greenhouse must be consigned to the *brick-pits. **1899** *Westm. Gaz.* 7 Jan. 5/1 A *brick-stack, 60 ft. in height, fell, crashing on to the sheds. **1915** *Times* 15 Apr. 4/1 A severe bombardment of the 'brickstacks' and the enemy's trenches. **1677** MOXON *Mech. Exerc.* (1703) 245 A *Brick Trowel. **1823** P. NICHOLSON *Pract. Build.* 384 The Brick-trowel is used for spreading mortar, and likewise for cutting bricks. **1647** R. STAPYLTON *Juvenal* 184 *Brick-wall'd Babilon.

10. Special comb.: **brick-ax(e**, a double-headed axe with chisel-shaped blades, used by bricklayers; **brick-barred** *a.*, inlaid (as a floor) with rows of bricks; **brick-box**, a 'box of bricks' (see 4); **brick-bread** (cf. *brick-loaf*); **brick-burner**, one who attends to a brick-kiln, a brick-maker; **brick-clay**, clay for making bricks; in *Geol.* a fine species of clay found lying upon boulder-clay; **brick-dryer**, an oven for drying bricks before burning; **brick-end**, a broken piece or fragment of brick; **brick-loaf**, a loaf shaped like a rectangular brick (see 3); **brick-nog**, **-nogging**, a method of building in which a timber framework is filled in with brickwork; **brick-oil**, an old drug compounded of powdered brick and linseed oil; **brick-on-edge** *a.*, designating a construction built of bricks laid on their sides; **brick-pond** *U.S.*, a pond in a brickfield; **brick-press**, a machine for pressing and consolidating the moulded clay; **brick-stitch** = *brick couching* (see 4 b above); †**brickstone**, a brick; **brick-tea**, tea leaves pressed into the shape of a small brick, in which form it is imported into Russia, and also used as a medium of exchange in Mongolia; **brick-trimmer**, an arch or 'trimmer' of brickwork for receiving the hearth of a fire-place; **brickyard**, a place where bricks are made, a brickfield. Also BRICKFIELD, -KILN, -LAYER, etc.

1548–62 *Norfolk Antiq. Misc.* (1880) II. 10 A *brykaxe, a hamerax, a trowell, and a pykax. **1823** P. NICHOLSON *Pract. Build.* 389 The Brick-axe is used for..cutting off the soffits of bricks. **1885** (*title*) First lessons in arithmetic, by means of *brick-box. **1762** *Boston Selectmen's Minutes* (1887) 29 Nov., A 4*d.* loaf of *brick bread is 3 oz. less than a 4*d.* white loaf. *c* **1500** *Cocke Lorelles B.* (1843) 10 Bewardes, *brycke borners, and canel rakers. **1703** *Art's Improv.* p. xiv, Statute Laws yet in force, for the regulating of the Trades of Brick-Burners, etc. **1837** *Penny Cycl.* VII. 245/2 *Brick clay..lies in abundance upon the London clay. **1868** LOSSING *Hudson* 206 Its banks yield some of the finest brick-clay in the country. **1527** *MS. Acc. S. John's Hosp., Canterb.*, A lode of *brykendis xiiijd. **1858** *Chamb. Jrnl.* IX. 147 Enthroned on brick ends and pieces of stone. **1723** J. NOTT *Cook's & Confectioner's Dict.* No. 7 E, 'Till you have made it in the form of a *Brick-loaf. **1873** MRS. WHITNEY *Other Girls* iii. (1876) 30 A brick loaf..always seemed to me a man's perversion of the idea of bread. **1825** COBBETT *Rur. Rides* 86 The labourers' dwellings..are made of what they call *brick-nog. **1857** TURNER *Dom. Archit.* III. II. vii. 278 An old house of timber and brick-nogging. **1875** URE *Dict. Arts* I. 533 *Brick oil..is a relic of old pharmacy. **1851** *B'ham & Midl. Gardeners' Mag.* Dec. 220, I should recommend a *brick-on-edge wall being run up. **1811** *Massachusetts Spy* 9 Jan. 3/3 Two boys..were..drowned in a *brick pond in the vicinity of the city [*sc.* Philadelphia]. **1894** *Naturalist* Feb. 56 Myriophyllum alterniflorum. Blythe Nook brickponds. **1872** MRS. A. MERCIER *Our Mother Church* xvi. 348 The edge is done in '*brick' stitch, which can be easily worked by looking at the pattern. **1882** CAULFEILD & SAWARD *Dict. Needlework* s.v., Brick stitch was largely used as backgrounds in ancient embroideries. **1960** B. L. SNOOK *English Hist. Embroidery* 32 Split stitch was still used.. accompanied by laid-work, couching, brick stitch, satin stitch and long and short stitch. **1560** WHITEHORNE *Certayne Wayes* (1573) 44 a, Taking it out, you shal see it made like unto a *bricke-stone. **1827** H. E. LLOYD *Timkowski's Trav.* I. 36 The dry, dirty, and damaged leaves and stalks of the tea are..mixed with a glutinous substance, pressed into moulds, and dried in ovens. These blocks are called..on account of their shape, *brick tea. **1852** SINNETT tr. *Huc's Journ. Tartary* 18 To boil some Mongol tea—the well-known brick tea, boiled with salt. **1872** OLIVER *Elem. Bot.* II. 147 'Brick Tea', used in Central Asia, is made from common kinds and refuse, mixed with bullock's blood, pressed and dried in moulds. **1864** *Leeds Mercury* 20 Sept., He went to work at a *brick yard. **1884** *Pall Mall G.* 8 Apr. 11/2 He has succeeded in emancipating..little brickyard children from a regular Egyptian bondage.

† **brick**, *sb.*[2] *Obs.* 'The name of a sort of lamprey ...distinguished...by having a number of black transverse spots, very narrow and long' (Chambers *Cycl. Supp.* 1753).

brick (brɪk). *v.* [f. BRICK *sb.*[1]] Mostly in comb. with advbs.

1. *to brick up*: to build or close up with brickwork.

1648 *Bury Wills* (1850) 211, I desire that the passage into the vault be bricked and filled up. **1691** LUTTRELL *Brief Rel.* (1857) II. 259 Orders for bricking up their little gate leading into Whitefryers. **1794** BURKE *Imp. W. Hastings* Wks. XV. 414 Very great sums of money are bricked up and kept in vaults. **1868** E. EDWARDS *Ralegh* I. i. 9 They have bricked up the lower part of the..window.

2. *to brick over*: to cover with brick.

a **1845** HOOD *Town & Count.* xiv, See Hatton's Gardens bricked all o'er. **1863** BROWNING *Bp. orders Tomb*, Bricked o'er with beggar's mouldy travertine.

3. To line, face, or pave with brick; to imitate brickwork on a plaster surface by lining and colouring.

1825 MRS. SHERWOOD *Old Times* II. in *Houlston Tracts* I. xxiv. 7 They are now bricked in the front. **1830** D'ISRAELI *Chas. I*, III. vi. 107 The decent appearance of bricking their [house] fronts.

4. *intr.* To work with (load, make, etc.) bricks.

1884 *Pall Mall G.* 10 Sept. 7/2 Another man..was bricking at a vessel close by.

5. *U.S. slang.* (See quot.)

1863 *Daily Tel.* Aug. (Amer. Corresp.) Another favourite punishment..was that of 'bricking', which was done by bringing the knees close up to the chin and lashing the arms tightly to the knees.

brickbat ('brɪkbæt). Also 6–7 **brickbatt**. [See BRICK *sb.*[1] and BAT *sb.*[2]]

1. a. A piece or fragment of a brick; properly, according to Gwilt, less than one half of its length. It is the typical ready missile, where stones are scarce. Also *attrib.*

1563–87 FOXE *A. & M.* III. 329 She sent a brickbat after him, and hit him on the back. **1597** S. FINCHE in *Hist. Croydon* App. (1783) 153 They have filled up that trenche with..brickbatts, and rubbushe. **1726** AMHERST *Terræ Fil.* l. 269 A very numerous mob..assaulted the room..with brickbats and stones. **1823** P. NICHOLSON *Pract. Build.* 355 The three-quarter brick, or brick-bat, is called a closer. **1871** DIXON *Tower* IV. xxvii. 288 Mud and brick-bats greeted the returning guards. **1890** W. JAMES *Princ. Psychol.* I. vii. 196 The continuous flow of the mental stream is sacrificed, and in its place an atomism, a brickbat plan of construction, is preached.

b. *comb.* **brickbat-cheese**.

1784 J. TWAMLEY *Dairying* 59 To make brick bat Cheese ..put it into a wooden mould in the shape of a brick, press it a little, then dry it. **1861** MRS. BEETON *Bk. Househ. Management* 809 Brickbat cheese has nothing remarkable except its form.

c. *fig.* An uncomplimentary remark; adverse criticism.

1642 MILTON *Apol. Smect.* (1851) 275, I beseech ye friends, ere the brick-bats flye, resolve me and yourselves, is it blasphemy..for me to answer a slovenly wincer. **1929** *Daily Express* 7 Nov. 17/5 And now for the brickbats. **1955** [see BOUQUET 1 b]. **1966** *Listener* 30 June 960/3 There were some much-needed brickbats thrown at our hero's wife.

2. *Astr.* (See quots.) *colloq.*

1892 RANYARD *Proctor's Old & New Astr.* 640 Clerk Maxwell used to describe the matter of the rings [of Saturn] as a shower of brickbats, amongst which there would inevitably be continual collisions taking place. **1898** A. CLERKE et al. *Astr.* 340 It may be that collisions are infrequent in this conglomeration of 'brickbats'. **1926** H. C. MACPHERSON *Mod. Astr.* 78.

'brick,bat, *v.* [f. prec. sb.: cf. *to stone.*] *trans.* To pelt with brickbats.

1884 *Boston* (*Mass.*) *Jrnl.* 27 Oct. 7 The Republican procession was brickbatted.

brick-dust ('brɪkdʌst). [f. as prec. + DUST.]

1. Powdered brick.

1664 EVELYN *Kal. Hort.* (1729) 195 Where the Soil is Clay ..mingle it with Brick-dust. **1862** *Enquire Within* 279 The cayenne of commerce is adulterated with brick-dust.

2. A tint or colour resembling that of brickdust.

1807 OPIE *Lect. Art.* I. (1848) 247 The barren coldness of David, the brick-dust of the learned Poussin.

b. *attrib.*

1709 STEELE *Tatler* No. 9 ¶ 1 Brickdust Moll had scream'd through half a Street. **1775** CLAYTON in *Phil. Trans.* LXVI. 108 A brick-dust red. **1853** KANE *Grinnell Exp.* xviii. (1856) 135 Tinged with a brick-dust or brown stain. **1873** TRISTRAM *Moab* xiii. 249 Its leaves and fruit-pods [are] a brick-dust orange.

3. Hence **brickdust-like, brickdusty** *a.*

1856 KANE *Arct. Expl.* II. ii. 35 The brickdusty poverty of the blood. **1863** BUCKLAND *Curios. Nat. Hist.* Ser. II. (ed. 4) 205 There was a red brick-dust-like substance. **1883** *Harper's Mag.* Dec. 131/1 A light brick-dusty color.

brick-earth ('brɪk'ɜːθ). [f. BRICK *sb.* + EARTH.] Earth or clay suitable for making bricks; in *Geol.* a clayey brownish earth lying below the surface soil in the London basin.

1667 EVELYN *Mem.* (1857) II. 24 We went to search for brick-earth. **1768** TUCKER *Lt. Nat.* II. 75 Timber, stone, lime, and brick-earth for our habitation. **1878** HUXLEY *Physiogr.* xvii. 280 In many places round London the sheet of gravel is overlaid by a thin deposit of brownish loam represented on the map as brick-earth since it is largely worked by brickmakers.

bricked (brɪkt), *ppl. a.* [f. BRICK *v.*] Constructed of brick; laid or lined with brick.

1673 RAY *Journ. Low C.* 50 Fair new brickt Houses. **1708** SWIFT *Bickerstaff Detected*, Whether his grave is to be plain or bricked. **1851** *Illustr. Lond. News* 83 The bricked-up window. **1861** WHYTE MELVILLE *Mkt. Harb.* 20 Stamping up a bricked passage.

brickel, obs. form of BRICKLE *a.*

'bricken, *a.* [See -EN.] Of brick.

1851 *Ill. Lond. News* 19 Apr. 311 Commonplace bricken cottages. **1859** BARNES *Rhymes Dorset. Dial.* II. 82 Up the bricken wall did rise. **1862** MAYHEW *Crimin. Prisons* 24 London..in its every-day bricken and hard-featured reality.

† **'bricken**, *v. Obs.* (See quots.)

1691 RAY *S. & E. Co. Wds.*, *Bricken*, to bridle up the head. **1706** PHILLIPS, *Bricken*, to hold in one's Chin proudly, to bridle it.

brickette (brɪ'kɛt). Also **bricket**. [f. BRICK *sb.*[1] + -ET, -ETTE.] A small brick, esp. of ice-cream. Cf. BRICK *sb.*[1] 4 and BRIQUETTE 3.

1934 *Archit. Rev.* LXXVI. p. xlii, The paths, constructed of herringbone brickets, are both colourful and durable. **1959** *Manch. Guardian* 4 Aug. 3/6, 180 brickettes [of ice-cream] a minute. **1962** *Engineering* 4 May 597/1 Brickettes destined to become choc-bars.

brick-field ('brɪkfiːld). A field or piece of ground in which bricks are made.

1801 MAR. EDGEWORTH *Early Less.* II. *Harry & Lucy*, To go to the brick field to see how bricks were burned. **1813** *Examiner* 1 Feb. 78/2 Labourer in a brick field. **1858** W. ELLIS *Vis. Madagascar* xiii. 361 Spadefuls of soil piled up like newly made bricks in a brick-field.

'brickfielder. [f. prec. + -ER[1].] Local name in Sydney, New South Wales, for a thick cloud of dust brought over the city by a south wind from neighbouring sandhills (called the 'Brickfields'); now applied to a hot northerly wind in various regions of Australia.

1843 J. BACKHOUSE *Narr. Visit Austral. Col.* 3 Jan. 236 This kind of wind..is frequent in the summer, and coming upon the town from the direction of some brick-fields, has obtained the name of a Brick-fielder. **1853** *Fraser's Mag.* XLVIII. 515 What the Sydney people call a 'brickfielder'. **1862** CLARA ASPINALL *3 Yrs. in Melbourne* 188 A dust storm, a real 'Brickfielder' was blowing. **1886** COWAN *Charcoal Sk.*, The buster and brickfielder: Austral red-dust blizzard and red-hot simoom.

brickhil, brickill, obs. ff. BRICK-KILN.

'brickhood. The state of being of brick.

1752 H. WALPOLE *Lett.* (1837) I. 175 Almost all the walls ..are in their native *brickhood*.

bricking ('brɪkɪŋ). [f. BRICK *sb.*[1] + -ING[1].]

1. Building with brick; brickwork. Also *attrib.*

1770 in *Maryland Hist. Mag.* (1917) XII. 368 Pray defer yr Stable, Bricking in yr Garden or any other Jobs untill you have compleated the stone Wall. **1924** *Glasgow Herald* 20

Mar. 12 But between him and his coal, before ever he had sunk his bricking ring, intervened the war.

2. An imitation of brickwork, as on a plastered or stuccoed surface; in embroidery, brick-stitches collectively.

a **1877** KNIGHT *Dict. Mech.*, *Bricking*, the imitation of brickwork on a plastered or stuccoed surface. **1911** A. DRYDEN *Church Embroid.* 112 For ordinary bricking use about ten stitches to the inch.

brickish ('brɪkɪʃ), *a. slang.* [f. BRICK *sb.* 5, 6 + -ISH[1].] **1.** 'Jolly', 'fine', 'capital'.

1856 A. SMITH *Mr. Ledbury* I. xix. 149 'How's the times?' 'Brickish.'

2. = BRICKY *a.* 1

1879 G. M. HOPKINS *Poems* (1918) 41 Thou [*sc.* Oxford] hast a base and brickish skirt there. **1900** E. GLYN *Visits Eliz.* 257 She has quite a different coloured chest to the top bit that shows above her pearl collar, which is brickish-red from hunting. **1960** BETJEMAN *Summoned by Bells* i. 1 Brickish Kentish Town seen through the leaves of Highgate.

Hence **'brickishness** *slang*, the quality of being good-hearted or 'brickish'.

1906 *Daily Chron.* 26 July 3/2 Janet's sheer 'brickishness' held her faithful to her organist. **1924** F. M. FORD *Some do Not* I. vi. 163 They had talked..about the brickishness of the parson in taking her in.

brick-kiln ('brɪk-kɪln). Forms: 5 **brykekyl**, 6 **bricke keele, brycke kylne**, 7 **brick(e-kill, brick(e-kilne, (brickhil)**, 7-8 **brickill**, 8- **brickkiln**. A kiln or furnace for burning bricks.

1481 [Implied in *brick-kilner*]. **1552** HULOET, Brycke kylne, *fornax lateraria*. **1580** BARET *Alv.* B 1234 A bricke keele, *fornax lateritia*. **1611** BIBLE *2 Sam.* xii. 31 Passe through the bricke-kilne. **1701** *Phil. Trans.* XXIII. 1089 The burning of Brick in a Brickill. **1875** URE *Dict. Arts* I. 524 The common brick kiln is a rectangular building.

Hence **brick-kilner**, a brick-burner or brickmaker.

1481-90 HOWARD *Househ. Bks.* (1841) 171 Item, to the brykekyler of Eppswich viij.*d.*

bricklayer ('brɪk,leɪə(r)). Also 5 **brekeleyer**, 5-6 **bryche leyer**. [f. BRICK *sb.* + LAYER.] One who lays the bricks in building.

bricklayer's itch: a cutaneous disease produced on the hands of bricklayers through contact with lime.

1485 *Catal. Harleian MSS.* (1808) I. 285/1 Licence..to reteigne Richard Chezholme brekeleyer. *c* **1500** *Cocke Lorell's B.* (1843) 9 Tylers, bryche leyers, harde hewers. **1562** *Act 5 Eliz.* iv. §30 The Art or Occupation of a..Brick-maker, Bricklayer, Tyler. *a* **1649** DRUMM. OF HAWTH. *Conv. betw. B. J. & W. D.* Wks. 224 Ben Johnson..was..put to another craft, viz. to be a bricklayer. **1824** BYRON *Juan* XVI. lviii, A modern Goth, I mean a Gothic Bricklayer of Babel, call'd an architect. **1841** MARRYAT *Poacher* iii, He took up the profession of a bricklayer's labourer.

Hence † **bricklayery** [cf. *carpentry*] = next.

1677 MOXON *Mech. Exerc.* (1703) Title, The Arts of Smithing, Joinery, Carpentry, Turning, Bricklayery. **1703** *Lond. Gaz.* No. 3922/4 The Arts of..Turning and Bricklayery.

bricklaying ('brɪkleɪɪŋ). The art or craft of building with brick.

1484 *Catal. Harleian MSS.* (1808) I. 284/2 Artificers experte in Breke-leying. **1602** *Return fr. Parnass.* I. ii. (Arb.) 13 He were better betake himselfe to his old trade of brick-laying. **1876** GWILT *Archit.* §1889 In the country the trades of bricklaying and plastering are usually united.

† **brickle** ('brɪk(ə)l), *a. Obs.* or *dial.* Forms: 5 **brekyl(le, bryckell**, 6 **bryckel, brickel(l, brykle, bryckle**, 6- **brickle**. [A parallel form to ME. *bruchel* (-y-), pointing to OE. type **brycel*, *brycl-es* (cf. the mod. forms *much*, *mickle*, earlier Sc. *mekyl*, from OE. *mycel*, *mycl-es*):—OTeut. **brukilo-*, f. pa. pple. stem of *brek-an* (OE. *brecan*) to break; cf. the parallel BRITTLE:—OE. *brytel*:—OTeut. **brutilo-* f. pa. pple. stem of *bréotan*. See also the doublets BRITCHEL, BROCKLE, BRUCKLE.]

1. Liable to break, easily broken; fragile, brittle.

1468 *Medulla Gram.*, *Fracticeus*, brekyl. *Fragilis*, freel or brekyl. **1523** FITZHERB. *Husb.* §100 The houe before wyll be thycker, and more bryckle. **1534** MORE *On the Passion* Wks. 1398/2 As a brickell earthen pot in pieces al to frush them. **1591** SPENSER *Ruins Time* 499 Th' Altare..Was built of brickle clay. **1611** BIBLE *Wisd.* xv. 13 This man that of earthly matter maketh brickle vessels. **1663** GERBIER *Counsel* 54 Many Bricks are brickle. **1747** HOOSON *Miner's Dict.* E ij b, Where it lies in a Body of considerable thickness, it is more Brickle and Joynty. **1875** *Lanc. Gloss.* (E.D.S.) *Brickle, britchel*, fragile, brittle.

2. *fig.* Frail, weak.

c **1460** *Towneley Myst.* 101 The world..is ever in drede and brekylle as glas. **1494** FABYAN VI. ccxiv. 231 This transetory and bryckell lyfe. **1562** J. HEYWOOD *Prov. & Epigr.* (1867) 157 Man is brickell. **1609** BIBLE (Douay) *Ps.* lxxxix, Mans life as brickle as spiders web. *a* **1640** JACKSON *Wks.* (1844) I. 303 This brickle earthly life.

3. *fig.* Delicate, ticklish; requiring cautious handling.

1568 DK. NORFOLK *Let.* in H. Campbell *Love-lett. Mary Q. Scots* App. 28 You may see howe farre..I wade in this most brykle cace. **1816** SCOTT *Old Mort.* vii, 'How I am to fend for ye now in thae brickle times'.

† **'brickleness.** *Obs.* [f. prec. + -NESS.] The quality of being brickle or brittle; fragility.

1561 DAUS tr. *Bullinger on Apoc.* (1573) 216 It is called glassy because of the frailtie and bricklenes. **1671** *Will of Walling, Kendal* (Somerset Ho.), Considering the bricklenes of my state. **1689** G. HARVEY *Curing Dis. by Expect.* xxii. 178 The knowledge of the brickleness..of a Stone.

brickmaker ('brɪkmeɪkə(r)). One who makes bricks as his trade.

1465 *Mann. & Househ. Exp.* 301 The breke maker. I did rekene wethe heme that makethe my breke. **1548** *Act 2 & 3 Edw. VI*, xv. §4 No Person..shall..let or disturb any..Lime-burner, Brick-maker. **1672-95** *Roxb. Ballads* II. 474 (*title*) The Brickmaker's Lamentation. **1875** URE *Dict. Arts* I. 519 The Egyptians were great brick-makers.

'brickmaking. The trade or occupation of making bricks.

1703 *Art's Improv.* p. xii, Tanning, Brick-making, Seasoning of Wood. **1875** URE *Dict. Arts* I. 519 Brickmaking is exceedingly ancient.

brick-red ('brɪk'rɛd), *a.* Of the colour of red brick.

1810 HENRY *Elem. Chem.* (1826) II. 592 The colour of the precipitate..being much darker and more inclined to brick-red. **1843** PORTLOCK *Geol.* 105 Brick-red calcareous grits. **1882** *Garden* 25 Mar. 204/2 Of a pleasing fiery brick-red uniform colour.

'bricksetter. = BRICKLAYER. (In midlands and north.)

1865 *Spectator* 18 Feb. 182 The strike of the Manchester bricksetters. **1878** F. WILLIAMS *Midl. Railw.* 357 Half a dozen bricksetters casing the 12 ft. length.

brick wall, *sb.*[1] **1.** (Formerly often written as one word *brickwall*, or with hyphen, as still *attrib.*) A wall built of brick.

c **1440** BOKENHAM tr. *Higden* in *Engl. Stud.* X. 18 Enviround abowte with bryke wallis. **1535** COVERDALE *2 Kings* iii. 25 There remayned but the stones in the brickwall. **1611** SHAKS. *Wint. T.* IV. iv. 818 Set against a Brick-wall. **1753** CHAMBERS *Cycl. Supp.* s.v. *Brick*, Brick-walls are also found warmer and wholesomer than those of free-stone and marble.

attrib. **1785** COWPER *Task* IV. 771 That never pass their brick-wall bounds.

2. *fig.* An impenetrable barrier. Phr. ***to talk to a brick wall***, to fail to elicit any response from one's interlocutor; ***to see through a brick wall***: see WALL *sb.*[1] 18.

1886 H. BAUMANN *Londinismen* 16/2 *Brickwall*: he can see thro a brickwall *er kann durch eine Mauer sehen.* **1898** *Westm. Gaz.* 19 July 1/2 We have been putting this dilemma to Liberals and Irish and the answers which we have obtained from both have brought us to what we have called the 'Irish brick-wall'. **1909** JEROME *They and I* vii, We mustn't have to tell 'em the same thing over and over again, like we was talking to brick walls. **1936** L. A. G. STRONG *Last Enemy* 309 You're a bit second-sighted, aren't you? I mean you see farther through a brick wall than most? **1963** A. SMITH *Throw out Two Hands* iii. 36 A chain reaction followed of other similarly frustrating brick walls. **1968** G. BUTLER *Coffin Following* ii. 58 You still look as if you could see through a brick wall.

† **'brickwall**, *sb.*[2] *Obs.* [A corruption of BRICOLE, associated by popular etymology with the *brick wall* of the tennis court: 'Musicke... which, tho' Anaxias might conceiue was for his honour, yet indeede hee was but the Brick-wall to conuey it to the eares of the beloued Philoclea' (Sidney *Arcadia* 283).]

= BRICOLE *sb.* 2 Also *attrib.*

1580 HOLLYBAND *Treas. Fr. Tong.*, *Il à fait vne bricole*, he hath plaied and made a Bricke-wall. **1611** COTGR., *Bricoler*, to tosse, or strike a ball sideways; to give it a bricke wall (at Tennis). **1662** SIR A. MERVYN *Sp. Irish Affairs* 4 We come not to criminate, or to force a ball into the Dedan, but if any brick-wall expressions happen..it is rather a force upon us.

† **'brickwall**, *v. Obs.* [corruption of F. *bricoler*: see prec.] *trans.* To cause to rebound.

1596 NASHE *Saffron Walden* Wks. (Grosart) III. 20 Whiles thou mak'st a Tennis-court of their faces, by brick-walling thy clay-ball crosse vp and downe their cheekes. *c* **1600** J. CHAMBERLAIN *Lett.* (1861) 13 Tossed too and fro and brick-wald like a tennis ball from the one side to the other. *a* **1628** F. GREVILLE *Mustapha* v. (1633) 127 Brickwall your errors from one to another.

'brickwork, brick work.

1. Builders' work executed in brick.

1580 HOLLYBAND *Treas. Fr. Tong.*, *Briqueterie*, bricke worke. **1594** PLAT *Jewell-ho.* III. 78 Buildinges that consist of Brickewoorke. **1703** *Art's Improv.* I. 4 By a rod of Brick-work, is meant, Sixteen Foot and half Square, at a Brick and half thick. **1779** SHERIDAN *Critic* I. ii. (1883) 159 A Detester of visible Brickwork, in favour of the new-invented Stucco. **1874** PARKER *Illust. Gothic Archit.* II. 271 The brickwork of the [Roman] Empire..is the finest brickwork in the world.

2. Building with bricks; bricklaying.

1677 MOXON *Mech. Exerc.* 245 Tools used in Brick Work.

3. *pl.* A place where bricks are made.

1703 *Proclam.*, in *Lond. Gaz.* No. 3879/4 Owner of the Brick and Pantile Works near Tilbury Fort. **1875** URE *Dict. Arts* I. 525 In many brick-works near Paris, screw presses are now used for consolidating the bricks..in their moulds.

bricky ('brɪkɪ), *sb. colloq.* Also **brickie**. One who works with bricks, a bricklayer, a brickfield or bricklayer's labourer.

1880 D. W. BARRETT *Life & Work among Navvies* II. ii. 39 'Navvy' and 'bricky' seem to them amusing specimens of wit. **1883** J. STRATTON *Hops & Hop-p.* 133 The occupations of the people are chiefly..dustmen, brickies, sweeps. **1964** *Economist* 19 Dec. 1363/1 Something to help the brickie with corners.

'bricky, *a.* [f. BRICK *sb.* + -Y[1].] **1. a.** Made or built of brick. **b.** Full of or abounding in bricks. **c.** Of the colour of brick, brick-red.

1596 SPENSER *Prothal.* viii, Those bricky towres..Where..the studious Lawyers haue their bowers. **1610** W. FOLKINGHAM *Art of Survey* I. xi. 41 Brickie rubble. **1862** *Spectator* 29 Mar. 355 Amid the desolate bricky preparations of 'building-lease' ground. **1884** *St. James's Gaz.* 10 May 6/2 The flesh-tints are a little hot and bricky.

2. Like a 'brick' or good fellow. *slang.*

1863 J. C. ATKINSON *Stanton Grange* i, Old Milburn was the 'brickiest' master..at Elmdon.

Hence **'brickiness.**

Mod. 'The unrelieved brickiness of the place.'

bricole ('brɪkəl, brɪ'kəʊl). Also 6 **bric-, brik-, briccoll**, 7 **bricol, briccole, brickoll**, 9 **bricolle**; see also corrupt form BRICKWALL. [a. F. *bricole* (It. *briccola*, Sp. *brigola*):—late L. *briccola*. Ulterior derivation uncertain: see Littré.]

1. An ancient military engine or catapult for throwing stones or bolts.

1525 LD. BERNERS *Froiss.* II. clxxi. [clxvii.] 500 In this towre was a bricoll or an engyn whiche..dyde cast great stones. **1614** SYLVESTER *Bethulia's Rescue* III. 109 Th' Enginer..Bends here his Bricol, there his boystrous bow. **1840** L. RITCHIE *Windsor Castle* 214 The bricolle, which discharged large heavy darts with square heads.

2. In *Tennis*: The rebound of a ball from the wall of a tennis court, 'a side-stroake at Tennis wherein the ball goes not right forward, but hits one of the walls of the court, and thence bounds towards the aduerse partie' (Cotgr. 1611); also *fig.* an indirect, unexpected stroke or action. Similarly in *Billiards* (see quot.).

1598 FLORIO, *Briccola*, a brikoll or rebounding of a ball from one wall to another in a tenis court. *a* **1631** DONNE *Lett.* (1651) 65 That love, which..fell not directly, and immediately upon my self, but by way of reflection or Briccole. **1694** R. L'ESTRANGE *Fables* cccciv. 435 Couzen'd with a Bricole at Tennis. **1798** H. WALPOLE *Lett.* (1857) I. Introd. 111 Introducing two courtiers to acquaint one another, and by bricole the audience, with what had passed in the penetralia. **1863** *Hoyle's Games* (ed. Pardon) 378 The ball..will jump on reaching the cushion, especially if played bricole, across the cushion. **1880** *Boy's Own Bk.* 638, *Bricole*, a ball struck against a cushion in order to make a cannon or hazard on its recrossing the table.

3. Harness worn by men in drawing guns, where horses cannot be used or procured.

1864 in WEBSTER.

† **'bricole**, *v. Obs.* [f. prec. sb.] To cause to rebound; 'to pass a Ball, to toss it side-ways' (Phillips, 1706). See also BRICKWALL *v.*

1611 FLORIO, *Briccolare*, to brickoll from wall to wall.

† **bri'coun.** *Obs. rare.* [a. OF. *bricon*, *bricun*.] A knave.

a **1400** *Cato's Morals* 103 in *Cursor M.* App. iv, If þou be fole and bricoun and kepis noȝt in resoun.

brid, var. of BIRD *sb.*, BRED, BURD.

bridal ('braɪdəl), *sb.* (*a.*) Forms: 1 **bríd-ealo, -ealu**, 2-6 **brydale, bridale**, 3, 7- **bridal**. Also (3 **bridel**), 3-4 (*s.w.*) **brudale (y)**, 3-7 **bridall**, 4 **bruydale (bruytale, bridhale)**, 4-5 (*Kent*) **bredale**, 5 **bredeale**, 6 **brydall, brideall, brydeale, brideale**, (7 **bride hall**). [OE. *brýd-ealo* (infl. *-ealoð*), lit. 'wedding ale', 'wedding banquet or conviviality': see BRIDE *sb.* 5 (in comb.), and ALE. The analytical form, with stress (primary or secondary) on *-ale*, never died out, was very common *c* 1600, and is still used as a historical or antiquarian term: see BRIDE-ALE. On the other hand the individualized '*bridal*, with the stress and sense of *ale* quite suppressed, occurs before 1300, and remains as the living word.]

1. A wedding feast or festival; a wedding.

(The sense 'wedding feast' is distinct in early usage; by the time of Wyclif the word was often extended to include the whole proceedings of the wedding or marriage, in which use it was often made plural (cf. L. *nuptiæ*, *sponsalia*, F. *noces*, ME. *sposailes*, mod. *nuptials*); it is now chiefly poetic, except when used attributively (see 2).

1075-6 *O.E. Chron.* (Worcester MS.) þær wæs þæt bryd ealo [*Laud MS.* eala] þæt wæs manegra manna bealo. *Ibid.* (Laud MS.) Æt þam bryd ealoð [*Worcester MS.* brydlope] æt Norðwic. *c* **1200** ORMIN 14002, I þe land o Galile Wass an bridale ȝarrkedd. *a* **1300** *Cursor M.* 13363 Bridall [*v.r.* bridel, bridale] was þar broiden an. **1340** *Ayenb.* 233 Þe wyse maydines..yeden in mid þe bredgome to þe bredale. **1362** LANGL. *P. Pl.* A. II. 36 Alle þis Riche..weoren bede to þe Bruyt-ale [*v.r.* in B., C., bre-, bri-, bru-, bruy-, brydale]. **1382** WYCLIF *Song of Sol.* Argt. 73 The bridalis of Crist and of the Chirche. *c* **1440** *Gesta Rom.* (1879) 301 Þe day was sette of hire bredeale. **1552** HULOET, Brydeale, *nuptus.* **1562** J. HEYWOOD *Prov. & Epigr.* (1867) 12 It is, as telth vs this olde tale, Meete, that a man be at his owne brydale. **1575** LANEHAM *Let.* (1871) 20 A solem brydeale of a proper

coople. **1581** MARBECK *Bk. of Notes* 140 The pompe of Brideals. **1604** SHAKS. *Oth.* III. iv. 150 Such obseruancie As fits the Bridall. **1724** RAMSAY *Tea-t. Misc.* (1733) I. 89 Let us a' to the bridal, For there will be lilting there. **1808** SCOTT *Lochinvar* iii, O come ye in peace here, or come ye in war, Or to dance at our bridal, young Lord Lochinvar? **1859** TENNYSON *Enid* 231, I.. Will clothe her for her bridals like the sun.

fig. **1632** G. HERBERT *Temple, Vertue* i, Sweet day, so cool, so calm, so bright, The bridall of the earth and skie.

2. a. Since 1600, mostly used attributively, by association with adjectives (of Lat. origin) in *-al*, as *nuptial*, *natal*, *mortal*, etc. Most of the earlier attributive uses or combinations of BRIDE also reappear with *bridal*, as ***bridal bed, bowl, cake, chamber, house, knot, ring***, etc., and many of more modern character, as ***bridal cheer, day, dinner, dress, favour, morn, veil, wreath***, etc., etc., where *wedding* may always be substituted. These are sometimes unnecessarily hyphened. ***bridal suite***, in a hotel, a suite of rooms designed especially for use by a newly-married couple.

c **1440** *Promp. Parv.* 50 Brydale howse, *nuptorium.* **1596** SPENSER *F.Q.* v. ii. 3 Where and when her bridale cheare Should be solemniz'd. —— *Prothal.* 17 Adornd with dainty gemmes.. Against the brydale day. **1596** SHAKS. *Tam. Shr.* III. ii. 221 Gentlemen, forward to the bridall dinner. *Ibid.* IV. i. 181, I will bring thee to thy Bridall chamber. *c* **1600** *Lyrics for Lutenists* (Collier) 3 Shee can.. trimme with plums a bridall cake. **1611** *Ram Alley* IV. i. in Hazl. *Dodsley* X. 338 Quaffing out our bridal bowl. **1714** YOUNG *Force Relig.* I. 85 Now on the bridal-bed his eyes were cast. **1717** POPE *Eloisa* 219 For her the Spouse prepares the bridal ring. **1800** MAR. EDGEWORTH *Belinda* xix, Lady Anne Percival came.. with a bridal favour in her hand. **1810** SOUTHEY *Thalaba* VII. xxxi, Who comes from the bridal chamber? **1850** TENNYSON *In Mem.* Concl. 28 But where is she, the bridal flower.. She enters, glowing like the moon Of Eden on its bridal bower. **1874** BLACK *Pr. Thule* 9 Marching at the head of a bridal procession. **1925** N. COWARD *Fallen Angels* 11, The room decorated like a Bridal Suite. **1938** H. ASBURY *Sucker's Progr.* 265 The bridal suite was called 'Paradise'. **1970** *Woman's Own* 24 Jan. 3/2 London's Royal Garden Hotel has offered the couple a bridal suite.

b. Sometimes more distinctively adjective, in construction or in sense: = Of or pertaining to a bride, worn by a bride (e.g. *bridal bouquet, veil, wreath*); bride-like.

1748 RICHARDSON *Clarissa* (1811) II. 140 With a simpering altogether bridal. **1809** J. BARLOW *Columb.* III. 501 Nor shalt thou e'er be told, my bridal fair. **1865** MISS MULOCH *Chr. Mistake* 108 She stood, all in her fine garments, a fair, white, bridal-like vision.

c. *bridal wreath*: a Chilean shrub of the family *Saxifragaceæ* (see quot. 1962); see also quot. 1961.

1889 *Cent. Dict.*, *Bridal wreath*, the *Francoa ramosa.* **1961** F. PERRY *Shrubs & Trees for Smaller Garden* v. 139 *Spiraea* x *arguta*, Bridal Wreath. The most widely grown species, with very slender twigs festooned with dainty white flowers. **1962** *Amat. Gardening* 27 Jan. 23/1 The plant known as Bridal Wreath is Francoa ramosa and comes from Chile. It produces long sprays of white flowers in July and August.

†**3.** (*ellipt.*) *pl. rare.* = BRIDALLER.

c **1630** RISDON *Surv. Devon* §225 (1810) 239 Apparell'd in their best array, As bridals use upon their nuptial day.

'bridaller, *rare.* [f. BRIDAL + -ER[1].] One who takes part in a bridal; †**a.** a bride or bridegroom; **b.** a wedding-guest.

1640 BRATHWAIT *Ar't asleep, Husb.?* 47 There was no Activity sure a wanting in those two jovial Bridallers. **1830** HOGG in *Blackw. Mag.* XXVII. 219 The fairy bridallers descending Straight from the moon.

bridally ('braɪdəlɪ), *adv.* [f. BRIDAL 2 b + -LY[2].] In bridal attire; as for a wedding.

1836 MACREADY *Remin.* II. 25 She seemed bridally attired. **1883** SIR W. MUIR *Islam* 16 Black-eyed maidens all bridally attired.

†**'bridalry.** *Obs. rare*$^{-1}$. = BRIDESHIP.

1742 RICHARDSON *Pamela* III. 78 A poor Girl has.. but a few Weeks Courtship, and perhaps a first Months Bridalry, if that, and then she's as much a Slave to a Husband, as she was a Vassal to her Father.

'bridalty. *rare.* In 7 bridaltee. [f. BRIDAL + -TY: cf. *mayoralty, shrievalty.*] Wedding, bridal.

1633 B. JONSON *Love's Welcome* (1854) 780/2 At Quintain he, In honour of this bridaltee, Hath challeng'd either wide countee. **1845** *Whitehall* xxii. 161 There is more mirth with them than at a bridalty.

briddle, obs. form of BRIDLE.

bride (braɪd), *sb.*[1] Forms: 1 brýd, 2-4 (*Kentish*) brēd(e, 2-3 (*s.w.*) brude(ü), 3 brīd, 3-4 bryd, (4 bruyd), 4-6 bryde, 4- bride. [Common Teut.: OE. *brýd* str. fem. = OS. *brûd* (MLG. *brût*, MDu. *bruut -de*, Du. *bruid*), OHG., MHG. *brût* (mod.G. *braut*), ON. *brúðr* (Sw. Du. *brud*, Goth. *brûþs* :—OTeut. **brûði-z*; the general sense is 'bride', but in Gothic, though this sense is also evidenced by the compound *brûþfaþs* 'bridegroom' (*faþs* = Gr. πόσις for *πότις, Skr. *patis* 'lord'), the only sense actually occurring is 'daughter-in-law'; the med.L. *brūta*, OF. *bruy*, F. *bru*, Rumansch *brütt*, from OHG., have also only the sense 'daughter-in-law': cf. Gr. νυμφή 'daughter-in-law' and 'bride'. Not known outside Teutonic; though some would identify with it *Frūtis* an Italian name of 'Venus mater'. Radical sense uncertain: possibly the verb root *brū-* 'to cook, brew, make broth', a duty of a daughter-in-law in the primitive family.]

I. As separate word.

1. a. A woman at her marriage; a woman just about to be married or very recently married.

The term is particularly applied on the day of marriage and during the 'honeymoon', but is frequently used from the proclamation of the banns, or other public announcement of the coming marriage. In the parliamentary debate on Prince Leopold's allowance, Mr. Gladstone, being criticized for speaking of the Princess Helen as the 'bride', said he believed that colloquially a lady when engaged was often called a 'bride'. This was met with 'Hear! hear!' from some, and 'No! no!' from others. Probably 'bride elect' would have satisfied critics.

c **1000** ÆLFRIC *Voc.* in Wr.-Wülcker 171, *Sponsa*, bryd. *c* **1000** *Ags. Gosp.* Matt. xxv. 1 And ferdon onȝen þone brydguman and þa bryde. *c* **1160** *Hatton G.* ibid., Onȝen þanne bred-gumen and þare brede. *c* **1200** ORMIN 15337 Crisstess hird.. Iss crisstess brid onn erþe. *a* **1225** *Ancr. R.* 164 Nefde he brude ibrouht hom? *a* **1300** *Havelok* 2131 Hauelok lay on his lift side, In his armes his brihte bride. *c* **1385** CHAUCER *L.G.W.* 2622 The nyght is come the bryd shal go to bedde. *c* **1450** *Gloss.* in Wr.-Wülcker 691, *Hec domiduca*, a bryde. **1535** COVERDALE *1 Macc.* ix. 37, & brought ye bryde from Madaba with greate pompe. **1592** SHAKS. *Rom. & Jul.* I. ii. 11 Ere we may thinke her ripe to be a Bride. **1671** MILTON *Samson* 320 To seek in marriage that fallacious bride. **1858** MACKAY *Three Flowers*, Thus I won my blushing bride One happy summer-day. **1884** *Pall Mall G.* 13 Feb. 8/2 The bride.. wore a dress of white satin embroidered with pearls.

fig. **1611** BIBLE *Rev.* xxi. 9, I will shew thee the Bride, the Lambes wife. *a* **1835** MRS. HEMANS *Death-d. Korner*, The youth went down to a hero's grave, With the sword, his bride. *a* **1850** ELIZA COOK *Rover's Song*, The Ocean's my home, and my bark is my bride.

b. A girl, woman, esp. a girl-friend. *slang.*

1935 G. INGRAM *Cockney Cavalcade* ix. 146 'I must git a bride too,' announced Patsy... Patsy, like most of his class, was eager to get a girl. **1964** *Listener* 31 Dec. 1053/2 This load of squaddies.. ain't got any brides with them.

†**2.** In 15th and 16th c. denoting also a bridegroom; = spouse. *Obs.* Cf. *bride-couple* in 6.

c **1440** *Promp Parv.* 50 Bryde, infra in spowse, *sponsus, sponsa.* **1483** *Cath. Angl.* 43 A Bride; *sponsa, sponsus vir eius.* **1598** SYLVESTER *Du Bartas* II. iv. II. (1641) 211/2 Sweet Daughter dear.. Isis blesse thee and thy Bride With golden fruit. *Ibid.* II. iv. II. 213/1 Art thou not Shee, that with a chaste-sweet flame Did'st both our Brides' hearts into one heart frame?

†**3.** Occas. found = BURD 'lady, maiden', etc.; but perh. only by confusion.

Thus in the quot. from *Cursor M.* the later versions have *bride, bruyd*, for the *birde* (= BURD) of the *Cotton MS.*

a **1300** *Cursor M.* 7131 Vn-to þat birde [*Fairf.* bride, *Trin.* bruyd].. Sampson al þe soth hir tald.

4. A collector's name for the Dark Crimson Underwing moth (*Catocala sponsa*).

1860 GOSSE *Rom. Nat. Hist.* 26 Ha! the lovely 'bride'! If you can net her, you have a beauty.

II. In combination.

Bride- had originally the force of 'bridal, wedding' (the primitive marriage being essentially the acquisition of a *bride*): so in all the OE. compounds of *brýd-*. Only in modern combinations, as *bride-like, brideless*, is *bride* used in sense 1.

5. Obvious comb. **a.** = 'bridal, wedding', as ***bride-banquet, -barn, -bell, -chamber, -clothes, -day, -kiss, -people, -ring, -sheet, -sleep, -song, -wife.*** **b.** = 'bride', as ***bride-lifter, -lifting, -money; brideless, -like, -widowing*** adjs.; also in Social Anthropology, as ***bride-abduction, -capture, -purchase, -service, -wealth.***

a. **1633** FORD *'Tis Pity* IV. i, That marriage seldom's good, Where the *bride-banquet so begins in blood. **1652** BROME *Jov. Crew* IV. ii. 424 We are mist within the *Bride-Barn among the Revell rout. **1850** MRS. BROWNING *Poems* II. 29 The merry *bride-bell Rings clear through the greenwood. **1850** MRS. BROWNING *Poems* II. 46 Why glads it thee, that a *bride-day be By a word of woe defiled. *c* **1380** WYCLIF *De Dot. Eccl.* Sel. Wks. III. 440 ȝif we have þenne *brydeclopis, we shal for evere be dampned. **1830** CARLYLE *Richter* Misc. (1857) II. 150 Caroline.. bestowed on him the *bride-kiss of her own accord. **1816** JANE AUSTEN *Emma* I. i. 3 The wedding over and the *bride-people gone, her father and herself were left to dine together. **1851** KINGSLEY *Yeast* xiii. 246 Where is your *bride-ring, my fair maid? **1930** T. S. ELIOT tr. *St.-J. Perse's Anabasis* 63 Loud acclamations.. for the publication of the *bride-sheets! **1871** ROSSETTI *Eden Bower* xvii, That he may.. curse the day when the *bride-sleep took him. **1587** GOLDING *De Mornay* xxiv. 372 For *Bridesongs, they bee not wanting. **1629** FORD *Lover's Mel.* v. i, Sorrows are chang'd to bride-songs. **1567** TURBERV. *Ovid's Epist.* 51 Ne didst thou cause a marriage bed for *bridewife to be drest.

b. **1937** R. H. LOWIE *Hist. Ethnol. Theory* v. 46 There is nothing to show that it regularly accompanies *bride-abduction. **1878** E. B. TYLOR *Early Hist. Mankind* (ed. 3) x. 287 The import of the Spartan marriage, which he calls the 'form of capture', as indicating previous habit of *bride-capture. **1937** C. M. ARENSBERG *Irish Countryman* iii. 106 A last remnant of a primeval bride-capture. **1884** TENNYSON *Becket* 170 The *brideless Becket is thy King and mine. **1865** MCLENNAN *Prim. Marriage* 33 A young fellow called the *bride-lifter lifts the bride. **1871** TYLOR *Prim. Cult.* I. 65 *'Bridelifting' has been noticed as one of the regular games of the little native boys and girls. **1824** MISS MITFORD *Village* Ser. I. (1863) 117, I never saw any thing so delicate and *bride-like as she looked in her white gown. **1926** D. H. LAWRENCE *David* x. 71 Is Merab not worth the *bride-money? **1920** R. H. LOWIE *Primitive Society* vii. 178 The functionally related customs of clear-cut *bride-purchase and patrilocal residence. **1937** —— *Hist. Ethnol. Theory* xiii. 240 Kirchhoff has unearthed significant South American relations: matrilocal residence, *bride-service. **1931** E. E. EVANS-PRITCHARD in *Man* Mar. 36 There has been a considerable amount of discussion.. about an alternative expression for 'bride-price'... I may be excused for putting forward the term *'bride-wealth'. **1951** *R. Anthrop. Inst. Notes & Queries* II. iv. 116 Bride-price, bride-wealth, marriage payment, are terms used for the goods, gifts or payments transferred by the bridegroom or his family to the bride or her family on the occasion of marriage. **1832** L. HUNT *Poems* 173 The *bride-widowing sword.

6. Special comb.: †***bride-belt***, the zone or belt worn by a virgin; †***bride-bowl*** = BRIDE-CUP; ***bride-bush***, a bush hung out at the (village) alehouse in honour of a wedding; †***bride-couple***, a newly-wedded pair; ***bride-door***, the door of the BRIDEHOUSE; ***bride-knot***, a wedding favour; †***bride-leader***, the precursor of the later BRIDE-MAN, who brought the bride to the bridegroom; †***bride-mother***, one who acts the part of mother at weddings in some countries; ***bride-price***, money paid for a bride; †***bride-squire*** = BRIDEMAN; ***bride-stake***, a pole set up to dance round at a wedding; ***bride-weed***, a bride's dress or veil; ***bride-wort***, Meadow-sweet (*Spiræa Ulmaria*) ; also, American Meadow-sweet (*S. salicifolia*). Also BRIDE-ALE, BRIDE-WOMAN, q.v.

1598 SYLVESTER *Du Bartas* (1608) 376 Thou wed a wife, another 'fore thy face Shall lose her *bride-belt. **1630** B. JONSON *New Inn* Argt., Lord Beaufort.. calls for his bed and *bride-bowl to be made ready. **1654** GAYTON *Fest. Notes* II. iv. 50 His *Bride-bush, which to that purpose is very good, if a thorne or two were pluckt out of it. **1635** J. HAYWARD *Banish'd Virg.* 172 Having lodg'd the *bride-couple a-bed. **1864** ATKINSON *Whitby Gloss.* s.v. *Bride-door*, To run 'for the *bride-door'; the race for the bride's gift by young men, who wait at the church-door till the marriage ceremony is over. The prize is usually a ribbon, which is worn for the day in the hat of the winner. **1694** *Ladies Dict.* (N.), Nor was he slow in furnishing the *bride-knots and favours. **1552** HULOET, *Bryde leader, *pronubus.* **1561** DAUS tr. *Bullinger on Apoc.* (1573) 202 The Apostles as the *brideleaders.. haue brought the Church to our Sauiour, a chaste virgin. **1712** *Lond. Gaz.* No. 4987/1 The Empress Dowager with the Vice-Admiral's Lady, were the *Bride-Mothers. **1876** DIGBY *Real Prop.* iii. i. §4. 113 By early Teutonic custom.. the *bride-price, or price paid by the intending husband to the family of the bride. **1885** *Pall Mall G.* 7 Feb. 5/1 When the bride price has been paid, the girl runs away and hides.. and his friend (compare our 'best man') brings her home by force. **1633** B. JONSON *Love's Welc.*, The two *bride-squires.. were in two yellow leather doublets. **1854** SYD. DOBELL *Balder* xxiii. 123 The mist is as a *brideweed on the moon. **1863** PRIOR *Plant-n.*, **Bridewort*, from its resemblance to the white feathers worn by brides.

bride (braɪd), *sb.*[2] [a. F. *bride* bridle, bonnet-string = Pr. and Sp. *brida*, from Teutonic: cf. OHG. *brîdel*: see BRIDLE.]

†**1.** A bridle, rein. Also *fig. Obs.*

c **1300** *K. Alis.* 7627 How love heom ladde by strong bride. *a* **1300** *K. Horn* 772 Berild.. tok him bi þe bride.

2. The delicate net-work which connects the patterns in lace; also, a bonnet-string.

1869 *Latest News* 3 Oct. 5 One [bonnet].. is very pretty made of velvet and black lace; black or white tulle brides. **1883** *Mag. of Art* Dec 67/2 The delicate beauty of its white knots lightly held together by cobwebby 'brides'.

3. *Surg.* Membranaceous filaments found in the centre of abscesses or in deep wounds which prevent the escape of pus, or cause morbid adherence.

1845 *Encycl. Metrop.*, VII. 739 When the maturation [of the pustule in small-pox] is complete the 'bride'.. ruptures.

†**bride** (braɪd), *v.*[1] ? *Obs.* [f. BRIDE *sb.*[1]]

1. *intr.* To play or act the bride. (Also with *it.*)

1530 PALSGR. 465/2 This mayde brideth very well, *ceste pucelle fait lespousée tresbien.* **1596** SHAKS. *Tam. Shr.* III. ii. 253 Shall sweet Bianca practise how to bride it? *a* **1652** BROME *Eng. Moor* I. iii, Would you have brided it so lumpishly With your spruce younker?

2. *trans.* To wed, marry. Also *absol.*

1601 *Death Earl Huntington* I. ii. in Hazl. *Dodsley* VIII. 231 [He] will not bed, forsooth, before he bride. *c* **1612** FLETCHER *Two Noble Kinsmen* (L.), I knew a man.. who A lass of fourteen brided. *a* **1658** CLEVELAND *Cl. Vindiciæ* (1677) 92 This Wench he fain would have Brided.

†**bride**, *v.*[2] *Obs. rare.* [perh. f. BRIDE sb.[2]: cf. BRIDLE *v.*] *intr.* To mince, practise affectedly.

1530 PALSGR. 951 To bride, *nidger* [COTGR. *Niger*, to trifle, play the fop or nidget]. **1593** NASHE *Foure Lett. Confut.* 80 He brides it and simpers it out a crie. **1598** FLORIO, *Cincischiare*, to mince it or bride it in eating or speaking.

bride-ale, bridale ('braɪd,eɪl). [A conscious retention or restoration of the earlier analytical form of BRIDAL *sb.* [q.v.] in its early sense.]

1. A wedding-feast of the Old English type, an ale-drinking at a wedding.

1000-1500 [see BRIDAL 1]. **1540** CRANMER *Bible* Pref., Neither [is] weepinge convenient at a brideale. **1577** HARRISON *England* II. vi. (1877) 150 In feasting [the husbandmen] doo exceed after their maner: especiallie at bridales. **1589** PUTTENHAM *Eng. Poesie* (Arb.) 97 For recreation of the common people at Christmasse diners and brideales. **1621** AINSWORTH *Annot. Gen.* xxix. 22 A banquet

named in Hebr. of drinking.. Such we call a Bride-ale. **1762** HUME *Hist. Eng.* lii. (1806) IV. 97 Wakes, church-ales, bride-ales, and other cheerful festivals of the common people. **1857** TOULM. SMITH *Parish* 503. **1864** PALGRAVE *Norm. & Eng.* III. 126 The doleful bridale of Dôle. **1868** FREEMAN *Norm. Conq.* (1876) II. vii. 151 Tostig's bride, whose bride-ale had been so cruelly interrupted.

2. 'The warmed, sweetened, and spiced ale, presented to a wedding party on its return from Church' (Atkinson *Provinc. Danby, Yorkshire*, 1863).

ˈbride-bed. *arch.* [f. BRIDE- = wedding.] The nuptial couch, the marriage bed.

1532 MORE *Confut. Tindale* Wks. 575/2 Ere they went to theyr bryde bedde. **1602** SHAKS. *Ham.* v. i. 268, I thought thy Bride-bed to haue deckt (sweet Maid). **1848** KINGSLEY *Saint's Trag.* IV. i. 182 What right have I to arrogate Christ's bride-bed?

bridecake (ˈbraɪdkeɪk). Also 9 **bride's-cake.** [f. BRIDE- = wedding.] A rich, highly ornamented cake, eaten at a wedding; wedding cake.

1552 HULOET, Bryde cake, *sumanalia.* *a* **1600** *Rob. Hood* (Ritson) II. i. 211, I got a good piece Of bride-cake, and so came away. **1606** *Choice, Chance, etc.* (1881) 54 Breakefast, where a bride-cake and a messe of cream, with the help of a cold pie, staied our stomackes well. **1666** PEPYS *Diary* 17 Aug., Had a piece of bridecake sent me by Mrs. Barbary. **1822** W. IRVING *Braceb. Hall* (1849) 474 Loads of bride-cake were distributed. **1877** W. JONES *Finger-ring L.* 171 Slices of the bride-cake.

ˈbride-chamber. *arch.* The room in which a wedding is celebrated; the nuptial apartment.

1579 J. STUBBES *Gaping Gulf* C iv, To be a doleful bryde in theyr bloody brydchambers. **1611** BIBLE *Matt.* ix. 15 Can the children of the bride-chamber mourne, as long as the bridegrome is with them? **1871** MORLEY *Crit. Misc.* (1886) I. 268 Topics eternally old, yet of eternal freshness, the perennial truisms of the grave and of the bride-chamber.

ˈbride-cup. *arch.* or *Obs.* [f. BRIDE- = wedding.] **a.** A cup or bowl handed round at a wedding. **b.** A cup of spiced ingredients prepared at night for the 'bride-couple'. Also *fig.*

1554 PHILPOT *Exam. & Writ.* 241 God doth call me (most unworthy) to drink of the Bride-cup of his Son. **1562** J. HEYWOOD *Prov. & Epigr.* (1867) 15 The drynke of my bride cup I should haue forborne. **1630** B. JONSON *New Inn.* v. i, Get our bed ready, chamberlain, And, host, a bride-cup; you have rare conceits, And good ingredients. **1633** *Jack of Newbery* in *Laneham's Let.* (1871) 20 There was a fair bride-cup of silver gilt carried before her, wherein was a goodly branch of rosemary. **1822** W. IRVING *Braceb. Hall* II. 323 The butler bore before her the bride-cup.

bridegroom (ˈbraɪdgruːm). Forms: α. 1 **brýdguma,** 2-3 **brid-, brudgume,** 3 **bridgom(e,** 3-4 **bridegome,** 4 **brydgome,** (*Kentish*) **bredgome;** β. 6 **brydegrome,** 6-7 **bridegrome, -groome, bridgroome,** 6- **bridegroom.** [α. OE. *brýdguma,* f. *brýd,* BRIDE + *guma* 'man' (poetic):—*OTeut. *gumon-,* cognate with L. *homin-.* The compound was Common Teut.: cf. OS. *brûdigomo* (MDu. *brûdegome,* Du. *bruidegom*), OHG. *brûtigomo* (MHG. *briutegome,* Ger. *bräutigam*), ON. *brúðgumi* (Sw. *brudgumme,* Da. *brudgom*):—OTeut. **brúdigumon-*; not preserved in Gothic, which has *brûþfaþs* = 'bride's lord'. β. After GOME became obs. in ME., the place of *bridegome* was taken in 16th c. by *bridegrome,* f. *grome,* GROOM 'lad'.

During the 14th c. the only known examples of *bridegome* are northern or Kentish: no instances at all are known in the 15th c., and in the *Promptorium* and *Catholicon, bryde* is of both sexes: see BRIDE[1] 2. The 16th c. *brydegrome* was thus perh. really the '*bride-lad*', i.e. the lad who was a 'bride': cf. *bride-couple,* and the original senses of *bride-man, bride-woman.* Was it a new independent formation only accidentally resembling *brydegome,* or had the latter survived in some dialect, whence it was drawn forth in the 16th c. in a mistaken form?]

1. A man about to be married, or very recently married.

α. Form *brydegome.*

c **1000** *Ags. Gosp.* John iii. 28 Se ðe bryde hæfð, se is brydguma [*Lindisf.* se ðe hæfes ða bryd brydguma is]. *c* **1200** ORMIN 10393 To beon bridgume nemmnedd. *c* **1230** *Hali Meid.* 9 Gentille wimmen.. þat nabbeð hwerwið buggen ham brudgume. *a* **1300** *Cursor M.* 13424 þan left þe bridgom his bride. *a* **1300** *E.E. Psalter* xviii. [xix.] 6 Als bride-gome of his boure comand. **1340** *Ayenb.* 233 þe wyse maydines.. yeden in mid þe bredgome to þe bredale.

β. Form *bridegroom.*

1526 TINDALE *John* iii. 29 He that hath the bryde is the brydegrome. But the frende of the brydegrome, which, etc. [WYCLIF He that hath a wif is the housbonde, but the frende of the spouse, etc.]. **1535** COVERDALE *2 Esdr.* xvi. 34 The daughters shal mourne, hauinge no brydegromes. **1580** BARET *Alv.* B 1241 A Bridegroome, *sponsus.* **1596** SHAKS. *Tam. Shr.* III. i. 153 And is the Bride and Bridegroom coming home? **1791** BURNS *Lament J. Earl Glencairn* x, The bridegroom may forget the bride Was made his wedded wife yestreen. **1875** JOWETT *Plato* (ed. 2) III. 71 He.. dresses himself as a bridegroom and marries his master's daughter.

b. *fig.* Said of Christ in his relation to the Church, or as heavenly spouse of a nun.

a **1225** *St. Marher.* 19 Bring me to þi brihte bur, brudgume of wunne. **1842** TENNYSON *St. Agnes' E.* 31 For me the Heavenly Bridegroom waits.

2. *comb.* or *attrib.*

1647 COWLEY *Mistr., Gazers* iv, On the earth with Bridegroom-Heat, He [the sun] does still new Flowers beget. **1711** SHAFTESB. *Charac.* II. 396 The bridegroom-doge, who in his stately Bucentaur floats on the bosom of his Thetis.

ˈbridegroom, *v. rare.* [f. prec. sb.] *trans.* To act as bridegroom to, to wed.

1868 A. MENKEN *Infelicia* 3 A Midnight swooped down to bridegroom the Day.

ˈbridegroomship. The position of bridegroom.

a **1567** HARDING in Jewel *Def. Apol.* (1611) 81 As touching the Bridegroomeship.. Christ is the only Bridegroome of the Church.

bridehall, corrupt form of BRIDAL.

1610 HEALEY *St. Aug. City of God* 250 In the Bride-hall chamber.

ˈbridehood. [f. BRIDE + -HOOD.] The state or position of a bride.

1839 BAILEY *Festus* (1854) 319 To fit her for her bridehood.

†**ˈbridehouse.** *Obs.* or *dial.* [f. BRIDE- = wedding.] The house where a wedding is held.

1550 COVERDALE *Spir. Perle* xii. Wks. 1844 I. 133 From the.. marriage or bride-house goeth many one home heavy and sad. **1594** *Taming of Shrew* in *Halliwell's Shaks.* VI. 281 We shall have good cheere anon at the bridehouse. **1675** T. BROOKS *Gold. Key* Wks. 1867 V. 554 She may.. be brought into the bride-house with all solemnity.

bridel, bridell(e, obs. ff. BRIDAL, BRIDLE.

†**ˈbride-lace.** *Obs.* exc. *Hist.* [f. BRIDE- = wedding.]

1. A piece of gold, silk, or other lace, used to bind up the sprigs of rosemary formerly worn at weddings; the earlier form of wedding favours.

1575 LANEHAM *Let.* (1871) 21 Euery wight with hiz blu buckeram bridelace vpon a braunch of green broom (cauz rozemary iz skant thear). **1599** PORTER *Angry Wom. Abingd.* (1841) 25 A nosegay bound with laces in his hat, Bridelaces, sir. **1622** BOYS *Wks.* (1630) 531 You are a kinde friend indeed to come in hither without your wedding apparell and bride-lace. **1663** KILLIGREW *Parson's Wed.* IV. ii, Do you give these favours? Are these your bride-laces?

2. *pl.* The striped ribbon-grass, or Lady's Garters (*Phalaris arundinacea* var.).

†**ˈbridelock.** *Obs.* In 1 **brýdlác,** 3 **brudlac, -lak.** [OE. *brýdlác* (pl.) nuptials, marriage, f. *bryd-* BRIDE- + *lác* play: cf. *wedlock.*] An OE. word for 'marriage', which did not survive the 13th c.

c **1000** *Canons of Ælfric* 9 (Bosw.) Æt ðam brydlacum. *a* **1225** *Juliana* 7 To brudlac and to bed ibrohte. *c* **1230** *Hali Meid.* 9 On hare brudlakes dei.

†**ˈbridelope.** *Obs.* [late OE. *brýdlóp,* either:—**brýdhléap,* or ad. ON. *brúðhlaup, brullaup* (Sw. *bröllopp,* Da. *bryllup*) wedding; cf. OHG. *brûthlauft, -louft,* MHG. *brûtlouf,* Ger. (*arch.*) *brautlauf*; f. OTeut. *brûđi-* BRIDE + *hlaup-* run, LEAP.]

The oldest known Teutonic name for 'Wedding': lit. 'the bridal run', or 'gallop', in conducting the bride to her new home. See Grimm, *Brautlauf*: and cf. BROOSE. ? Only in OE.

c **950** *Lindisf. Gosp.* Matt. xxii. 2 Gelic.. cyne-menn seðe dyde ða brydlopa [= *nuptias*] sune his. **1076** *O.E. Chron.* (MS. D) Æt ðam brydlope æt Norðwic [*Laud MS. has* brydealoð].

ˈbridely, *a. rare.* [OE. *brýdelíc* nuptial, f. *brýd,* BRIDE: the 16th c. word may have been formed anew, as 'bridely' in sense of 'bride-like', might possibly be said now.] Nuptial, bridal.

a **1100** *Cott. Cleop. Gloss.* in Wr.-Wülcker 388 (also 530) *Dramate,* þa brydelican gewrite. **1565** GOLDING *Ovid's Met.* I. (1593) 16 The bond of bridelie bed. **1567** TURBERV. *Ovid's Epist.* 71 In spousal bande and bridely knot be tyde.

bridemaid, earlier form of BRIDESMAID.

ˈbridemaiden. *arch.* or *dial.* = BRIDEMAID, BRIDESMAID. Hence **bridesmaidenship** *sb.*

1808 SCOTT *Lochinvar* vi, The bridemaidens whispered "Twere better by far'. **1824** MISS MITFORD *Village* Ser. I. (1863) 239 The bride-maidens were only less smart than the bride. **1839** BAILEY *Festus* (1854) 300 The stars Were her immortal bridemaidens. **1884** E. SIMCOX in *19th Cent.* June 1047 Based on the widest experience of bridesmaidenship.

†**ˈbrideman.** *Obs.* or *dial.* [f. BRIDE- = wedding, or in sense 2.]

†**1.** = BRIDEGROOM. *Obs.*

1613 T. GODWIN *Rom. Antiq.* (1658) 75 The brideman did lift her over the threshold. *Ibid.* 121 The bride-man, as soon as he was married, used to cast nuts among the people.

2. A young man performing various ceremonial duties at a wedding; formerly called also *bride-leader.* (In early times the bridemen led the bride to the bridegroom.) Now = BRIDESMAN.

1663 KILLIGREW *Parson's Wed.* V. iv, Parson, I'll be your bride-man. **1670** DRYDEN *Roy. Martyr* v. ii, Betwixt her Guards she seem'd by Bride-men led. **1751** SMOLLETT *Per. Pic.* (1779) I. iv. 33 To the utter disappointment of the bridemen and maids. **1813** MAR. EDGEWORTH *Patron.* III. xxxix. 109 There is no record concerning who were the bridemen. **1830** CARLYLE in *For. Rev. & Cont. Misc.* V. 43 The evening-star, the brideman of the sun.

brideship (ˈbraɪdʃɪp). [f. BRIDE *sb.*[1] 1 + -SHIP.] The status or standing of a bride; the rank or personality of a bride.

a **1652** BROME *Novella* II. i, All her wares, For her to take her choyce to deck her Brideship. **1865** CARLYLE *Fredk. Gt.* III. VIII. vi. 50 Wilhelmina's wedding-day arrived, after a brideship of eight months.

bridesmaid (ˈbraɪdzmeɪd). Also 6-9 **bridemaid.** [The earlier form was *bridemaid,* as in *brideman* and the other compounds of BRIDE- in sense of 'bridal, wedding'; the 19th c. *bridesmaid* is due to the same perverted analysis, which has changed *brideman* into *groomsman.*]

A young unmarried woman performing various ceremonial duties at a wedding; in modern times the bridesmaids merely accompany or form the train of the bride.

α. Form *bridemaid.*

1552 HULOET, Bryde mayde, *pronuba.* **1621** QUARLES *Argalus & P.* (1678) 55 The Bride shall sit; Despair and Grief shall stand Like heartless Bride-maids upon either hand. **1747** HERVEY *Medit. & Contempl.* (1818) 22 The bride-maids, girded with gladness, had prepared the marriage-bed; had decked it with the richest covers, and dressed it in pillows of down. **1798** COLERIDGE *Anc. Mar.* VII. xviii, But in the Garden bower the Bride And Bride-maids singing are. *a* **1847** MRS. SHERWOOD *Lady of Manor* IV. xxiv. 147 Letitia, who had been my bridemaid. **1851** HAWTHORNE *Twice-told T.* (1883) 33 The widow between her fair young bridemaids.

β. *bridesmaid.* (At first *colloq.* or *epistolary.*)

1794 LD. AUCKLAND *Corr.* (1862) III. 256 It is proposed to one of your sisters to be bridesmaid at the royal marriage. **1836** DICKENS *Sk. Boz, Characters* viii. 144 The bridesmaids could sit in the front parlour and receive the company. **1840** *Ann. Reg.* 24 The royal bridesmaids are each to have a brooch. **1884** *Pall Mall G.* 13 Feb. 8/2 The bridesmaids.. wore dresses of cream soie épinglé and plush.

Hence **ˈbridemaidship,** the position or office of a bridesmaid; **ˈbridesmaiding** *vbl. sb.,* acting as bridesmaid.

1858 TROLLOPE *Dr. Thorne* iv, I won't be Augusta's bridesmaid; I'll bide my time for bridesmaiding. **1864** *Chamb. Jrnl.* 8 Oct. 642 It's your first experience of bridemaidship, and you look very nice.

ˈbridesman. [Altered from the earlier BRIDEMAN, q.v.] A young man who acts as friend or attendant of the bridegroom at a wedding, and performs various ceremonial offices for him.

1808 SCOTT *Lochinvar* iii, Among bride's-men and kinsmen, and brothers and all. **1811** W. SPENCER *Poems* 21 No common bridesmen wait us there. **1859** SMILES *Stephenson* 348 To poor Robert Gray.. who acted as his bridesman on his marriage.. he left a pension.

ˈbridewain. *north. dial.* [f. BRIDE *sb.*[1] + WAIN wagon.] The wain or wagon on which a bride's 'providing' (surmounted by the spinning-wheel adorned with blue ribbons) used to be sent to her new home; also, a carved chest in which the providing was put, when of smaller compass; the contribution made to this by friends and neighbours, the wedding presents; the occasion on which these are given, a bidding wedding.

1807 STAGG *Poems* 2 A youthfu' pair, By frugal thrift exceyted, Wad hev a brydewain, an' of course The country roun' inveyted. **1855** *Whitby Gloss., Bride-wain,* a carriage loaded with household goods, travelling from the bride's father's to the bridegroom's house. **1873** *Spectator* 23 Aug. 1069/2 One bit of furniture peculiar.. to this district [Whitby]—the 'bride-wain', or chest for wedding-clothes. **1875** *Lanc. Gloss.* (E.D.S.) *Bride-wain,* a bidden wedding. **1884** *Gd. Words* 10 The toilet service was ranged ornamentally on a carved oak bridewain in the corner.

bridewell (ˈbraɪdwəl). Also 6 **brydwelle,** 7 **bridewel, (bridlewel), bridwell.** [From *Bride Well,* i.e. (*St.*) *Bride's Well,* a holy well in London, near which Henry VIII had a 'lodging', given by Edward VI for a hospital, afterwards converted into a house of correction.]

1. A house of correction for prisoners; a place of forced labour; a gaol, prison. Also *fig.*

[**1552** *Contemp. Rev.* (1878) 773 Our suit.. is for one of your Grace's houses called Bridewell. **1560** DAUS tr. *Sleidane's Comm.* 19 b, Kynge Henry the eight.. builded a goodlye lodginge purposely for him [Charles V] vpon the Riuer of Themse, called Bridewell.] *a* **1593** H. SMITH *Wks.* (1867) II. 43 To bridewell with these rogues! **1618** BOLTON *Florus* III. xix. 233 Breaking up the worke-jayles, or bridewels, by right of Warre. **1632** MASSINGER *City Mad.* IV. i, Seek them In Bridewell or the Hole. **1679-88** *Secr. Serv. Moneys Chas. & Jas.* (1851) 147 The rebells that were imprisoned in the castle and bridewell at Taunton. **1777** HOWARD *Prisons Eng.* (1780) 5 There are very few bridewells in which any work is done, or can be done. **1885** M. DAVITT *Leaves fr. Prison Diary* I. 32 Various terms of previous imprisonments.. in county bridewells.

2. *attrib.* (With *bridewell-bird* cf. *gaolbird.*)

1589 *Pasquil's Return* B iij b, The stocke-keeper of the Bridewel-house of Canterburie. **1589** R. HARVEY *Pl. Perc.* 6 Skufling in the kennel together by the eares like bride well birds. **1596** P. COLSE *Penelope's Compl.* (1880) 167 Thy

giggish tricke, thy queanish trade, A thousand Bridewel birds hath made. **1628** EARLE *Microcosm.* xxxi. 67 The Bridewell-man, and the Beadle. **1663** KILLIGREW *Parson's Wed.* IV. ii, This is better than..Bridewell hemp, brown bread, and whip-cord. *Ibid.* I. iii, Bridewell orphans.

Hence **'bridewell** *v.*, to commit to a Bridewell; **'bridewelling** *vbl. sb.*

1687 H. CARE *Draconia* (D.) Here is bridewelling, banishing, and selling of people to slavery.

†**'bridewoman.** *Obs.*

1. (Correl. of *brideman* 1, *bridegroom*) = BRIDE.

1530 PALSGR. 201/1 Bride woman, *espousee.*

2. (Correlative of *brideman* 2) = BRIDEMAID.

1701 (*title*) Ladies' Defence, or the Bridewoman's Counsellor Answered.

bridge (brɪdʒ), *sb.*[1] Forms: 1 brycg, bricg, 2-6 brugge, 3-6 brygge, 4-6 bregge, (brige), 4-7 brigge, (5-6, 9 *dial.* brudge, bryg(e, 6 bruge), 6-7 bridg, 5- bridge; also *northern* 3- brig, 4-6 brygg, 5 bregg, brigg, 5-9 brigg. [Common Teut.: OE. *brycg* fem., identical with OFris. *brigge, bregge*, (MLG. *brugge*, MDu. *brugghe*, Du. *brug*), OHG. *brucca* (MHG., mod.G. *brücke*):—OTeut. **brugjâ-*. The corresponding ON. *bryggja* has the sense 'landing-stage, gangway, movable pier'; the ON. word for 'bridge' being *brú* fem. (Da. *bro*, Sw. *bro*). As in other OE. words in *-cg*, the northern dialect has retained hard (g) against the palatalized (dʒ) of the south.]

1. a. A structure forming or carrying a road over a river, a ravine, etc., or affording passage between two points at a height above the ground.

Bridges vary in complexity from a simple plank, or a single arch, stretching from bank to bank over a stream, to an elaborate structure of architectural or engineering skill, supported by arches, piers, girders, chains, tubes, etc.

For the different kinds, as *bascule-bridge, bowstring-bridge, chain-bridge, draw-bridge, floating-bridge, pontoon-bridge, suspension-bridge, tubular-bridge*, etc., also *Asses' Bridge*: see the first element of the compounds.

c **1000** ÆLFRIC *Gram.* ix. §39 (Z.) 63 *Hic pons*, þeos brycg [*v.r.* bricg]. *a* **1131** *O.E. Chron.* an. 1125 Men weorðon adrencte and brigges to brokene. *c* **1175** *Lamb. Hom.* 31 Dele hit wrecche monne, oðer to brugge oðer to chirche weorke. *c* **1330** *Arth. & Merl.* 7803 This bachelers hadden a bregge y-passed. *c* **1380** *Sir Ferumb.* 1679 Hit ys Mantryble þat þow sye wyþ þe grete brigge. *c* **1449** PECOCK *Repr.* III. x. 338 The brigge of Londoun. **1480** CAXTON *Chron. Eng.* cxcii. 169 The scottes hobilers went bytwene the brudge and the englysshmen. **1552-3** *Inv. Ch. Goods Stafford.* 33 To make a bruge called Hugh Bruge. **1556** *Chron. Gr. Friars* (1852) 11 The erles hede with one of hys qwarters of the lordes ware sett on London bregge. *Ibid.* 17 Thys yere sanke a parte of London brygge with two arches. **1594** SHAKS. *Rich. III*, III. ii. 72 They account his Head vpon the Bridge. **1611** SPEED *Hist. Gt. Brit.* IX. xvii. (1632) 868 [He] came hastily to the Brigge. **1660** WALPOLE in Cobbett *Parl. Hist.* (1808) IV. 145 This was so severe a bill upon the Women, that, if a bridge was made from Dover to Calais, the women would all leave this kingdom. **1685** MORDEN *Geog. Rect.* 112 Cæsar's Bridg over the Rhine is one of the antientest in Europe. **1817** BYRON *Childe H.* iv. 1, I stood in Venice, on the Bridge of Sighs, A palace and a prison on each hand. **1843** MACAULAY *Lays Anc. Rome, Horatius* lxx, How well Horatius kept the bridge, In the brave days of old.

β. The form *brig* is used from Northamptonshire northward in the local dialects, in proper names, and in literature for the sake of local colouring.

a **1300** *Cursor M.* 8945 Þai..mad a brig Ouer a litel burn to lig. **1375** BARBOUR *Bruce* x. 86 At ane Brig beneth. **1418** *Bury Wills* (1850) 3 Apd Stanewelle bregg. **1572** *Lament. Lady Scotl.* in *Scot. Poems 16th C.* (1801) II. 247 Palice, kirk, and brig, Better in tyme to beit, nor efter to big. **1647** H. MORE *Insomn. Philos.* xviii. 2 Passing as water underneath a brig. **1787** BURNS *Twa Brigs*, The Sprites that owre the Brigs of Ayr preside. **1821** CLARE *Vill. Minst.* I. 46 He loved to view the mossy-arched brigs. **1852** MISS YONGE *Cameos* (1877) IV. ix. 103 Whenever he should pass the brig of Cramond. **1875** *Lanc. Gloss.* (E.D.S.) s.v., The most southerly point of the county where 'brig' is used..is..Bamber Brig, a few miles south of Preston. **1876** TENNYSON *North. Farmer* (*new style*) xiv, I'll run up to the brig.

b. *fig.* Also *attrib.*, as ***bridge church, passage*** (see 11 b).

a **1225** *Ancr. R.* 242 ȝe beoð ouer þisse worldes see, uppen þe brugge of heouene. **1742** YOUNG *Nt. Th.* VIII. 717 Faith builds a bridge from this world to the next. **1863** E. NEALE *Anal. Th. & Nat.* 63 The bridge for thought to pass from one particular to the other. **1874** SAYCE *Compar. Philol.* i. 53 Gestures..forming the bridge by which we may pass over into spoken language. **1931** *Ann. Reg. 1930* II. 238 The replacement of the Marqués de Estella's Cabinet by a 'bridge' Government. **1950** *Time* 4 Sept. 33/1 Radio dramas have always depended on music to get listeners from one mood or scene into another, fast. In the trade, such six- or eight-bar snatches of music are called cues or 'bridges'. **1962** A. NISBETT *Technique Sound Studio* ix. 158 Effects can often be peaked as a bridge between two parts of the same scene. *Ibid.* 159 As an alternative to the simple fade-out/fade-in technique..music bridges can be used.

c. ***bridge of boats***: a roadway supported by boats moored abreast across a stream or other body of water; cf. FLYING-BRIDGE, PONTOON.

1387 TREVISA *Higden* (1865) I. 55 (Mätz.) Þere Xerxes þe kyng made ouer a brigge of schippes. **1688** *Lond. Gaz.* No. 2346/2 They had begun a Bastion at the Head of the Bridge of Boats. **1811** WELLINGTON *Let.* in Gurw. *Disp.* VII. 151 There will be no difficulty in laying a bridge of boats.

d. † ***beside the bridge***: off the track, gone astray (*obs.*). ***a gold or silver bridge***: an easy and attractive way of escape. (F. *faire un pont d'or à ses ennemis*, Littré.)

1579 FENTON *Guicciard.* II. (1599) 78 Not to stoppe the way of the enemy..but rather (according to an old councell) to make him a bridge of silver. **1652** CULPEPPER *Eng. Physic. Enl.* (1809) 338 If Pontanus say otherwise, he is beside the bridge. **1670** G. H. *Hist. Cardinals* III. I. 233 Who willingly made him a Golden Bridge, to send him going. **1755** SMOLLETT *Quix.* (1803) IV. 180 Lay a bridge of silver for a flying enemy. **1824** BYRON *Def. Transf.* II. ii. 14 A golden bridge Is for a flying enemy.

e. Proverbial phr. ***to cross a*** (or ***the***) ***bridge when one comes to it***: to deal with a problem when and if it arises; ***to burn one's bridges behind one***: to burn one's boats (see BURN *v.*[1] 9 c).

1850 LONGFELLOW *Jrnl.* 29 Apr. in *Life* (1886) II. 165 Remember the proverb, 'Do not cross the bridge till you come to it.' **1892** 'MARK TWAIN' *Amer. Claim.* 94 It might be pardonable to burn his bridges behind him. **1914** E. R. BURROUGHS *Tarzan of Apes* xxviii. 399 Because she had been afraid she might succumb to the pleas of this giant, she had burned her bridges behind her. **1930** J. C. RANSOM *God without Thunder* (1931) vii. 166 If Plato had had the opportunity, he might have become a Christian, and burned his bridges behind him. **1943** E. S. GARDNER *Case of Empty Tin* i. 13 We'll cross that bridge when we come to it.

2. Short for DRAWBRIDGE.

c **1205** LAY. 19242 Heore brugge heo duden adun. *c* **1325** *Coer de L.* 3955 Her brygges wounden up in haste, And her gates barryd faste. *c* **1470** HENRY *Wallace* IV. 262 Thai..Tuk wp the bryg or that the day was lycht.

3. a. A gangway or movable landing-stage for boats. **b.** A fixed or floating landing-stage, jetty, or pier. *Obs.* or *dial.* [The Norse senses.]

c **1375** BARBOUR *Bruce* xvii. 403 A brig thai had, for till lat fall, Richt fra the bat apon the wall. **1425** *Sc. Acts Jas. I* (1597) §59 All boate men and ferrymen..sall haue for ilke boate a treene-brigge, qwhair-with they may receiue within their boates travellers Horse vnhurte. *c* **1560** *Map* in Maitland's *Hist. Lond.* has two landing jetties marked *privy bridge* at 'privy gardens', and *Queens-bridge* at Whitehall. *a* **1600** *Map* in G. G. Scott *Gleanings Westm. Ab.* Plate 35 Old pallace bridge. Kinges-bridge. **1686** *Lond. Gaz.* No. 2170/4 Lost or stolen..at Billingsgate Stairs, or Gravesend-Bridge, an old Black leather Trunk. **1850** P. CUNNINGHAM *Handbk. Lond.*, When we read in our old writers of Ivy-bridge, Strand-bridge, Whitehall-bridge, and Lambeth-bridge, landing piers alone are meant. **1879** LEWIS & SHORT *Lat. Dict.* s.v. *Pons* II. C, A plank bridge thrown from a vessel to the shore.

4. 'A narrow ridge of rock, sand, or shingle, across the bottom of a channel.'

1812 *Examiner* 14 Sept. 590/2 It is proposed to construct a Pier on the bridge between St. Nicholas and Mount Edgecombe. **1833** MARRYAT *P. Simple* xxviii, Is there water enough to cross the bridge? The sea on the bridge was very heavy. **1835** BELL *Gaz.* II. 236 Filey-bridge. **1864** BLACK *Guide Yorks.* 110 Filey Brig..is a remarkable ridge of rocks, projecting nearly half a mile into the sea and perfectly dry at low water.

5. *Naut.* The raised narrow deck or platform extending from side to side of a steamer amidships, from which the officer in command directs the motion of the vessel. Also 'a narrow gangway between two hatchways' (Smyth *Sailor's Word-bk.*).

1843 C. BAILEY *Loss of Pegasus* 44 He afterwards went on the bridge over the paddle-wheels. **1858** *Merc. Mar. Mag.* V. 53 The Boatswain was on the bridge. **1859** *All Y. Round* No. 1. 19 The Chinese..seized the arm-chest, which was on the bridge.

6. *Phys.* **a.** The upper bony part of the nose. Also the curved central part of a pair of spectacles or eye-glasses which rests on the nose.

c **1450** *Voc.* in Wr.-Wülcker 631 The brygge of þe nose. **1483** *Cath. Angl.* 44 A Bryge of a nese, *jnterfinium.* **1530** PALSGR. 201/1 Bridge of the nose, *os du nez.* **1604** DEKKER *Honest Wh.* Wks. 1873 II. 174 Hauing the bridge of my nose broken. *a* **1659** CLEVELAND *Rupertismus* 82 Let the Zeal-twanging Nose that wants a Ridge, Snuffling devoutly, drop his silver Bridge. **1839-47** TODD *Cycl. Anat. & Phys.* III. 736/2 The Caucasian nose is..elevated at the bridge.

b. A portion of the brain which stretches in a curve between the two lobes of the cerebellum in front of the medulla oblongata.

1869 HUXLEY *Phys.* 297 [The cerebellum] sends down several layers of transverse fibres..forming a kind of bridge (called *Pons Varolii*). **1879** CALDERWOOD *Mind & Br.* 36 In one solid mass, with transverse lines, is the bridge.

7. In a violin, or similar instrument: A thin, upright piece of wood, over which the strings are stretched, and which transmits their vibrations to the body of the instrument.

1607 DEKKER *Westw. Hoe* Wks. 1873 II. 341 One of the poore instruments caught a sore mischance last night: his most base bridge fell downe. **1731** HOLDER *Harmony* 11 The string of a Musical Instrument resembling a double pendulum moving upon two centers, the Nut and the Bridge. **1832** L. HUNT *Poems* Pref. 23 It has a look like the bridge of a lute. **1848** J. BISHOP tr. *Otto's Violin* App. iii. (1875) 79 The bridge..exercises an immense influence..on the quality of the tone of the violin.

8. (*north. dial.* in form *brig*:) Applied to various utensils of more or less bridge-like form, *e.g.* a tripod for holding a pot over a fire.

1600 *Churchw. Acc. St. Margarets, Westm.* (Nicholls 1797) 26 Making a pair of butts and brigs and for the carpenters work. **1847-78** HALLIWELL *Dict.*, *Brig*, an utensil used in brewing and in dairies to set the strainer upon. *north.* A kind of iron, set over a fire is so called. **1875** *Lanc. Gloss.* (E.D.S.) *Briggs*, irons to set over the fire.

9. In various specific and technical senses:

a. A 'bridging-joist', one of those joists which, in large floors, are laid upon the main or 'binding-joists', and to which the flooring boards are secured.

1663 GERBIER *Counsel* 43 For the boarding roomes..Carpenters lay Bridges overtwhart the Joyses.

b. In a furnace or boiler: A low vertical partition at the back of the grate space of a furnace; the low partition wall between the fuel-chamber and the hearth of a reverberatory furnace; 'the central part of the fire-bars in a marine boiler, on either side of which the fires are banked' (Smyth *Sailor's Word-bk.*).

1838 *Penny Cycl.* XI. 22/1 *C* is..the bridge of the furnace, which retains the fuel in its place, and serves to direct the flame towards the roof.

c. *Iron-works.* The platform or plank-way by which ore or fuel is conveyed to the mouth of a smelting furnace.

d. *Scene-painting.* A platform suspended in front of a canvass.

1859 SALA *Gaslight & D.* ii. 23 A ladder being placed against the bridge if he wishes to descend without shifting the position of his platform.

e. *Engraving.* A board, supported at each end, used to raise the engraver's hand above the plate.

1875 URE *Dict. Arts* II. 285 What is technically called a bridge..is nothing more than a thin board for the hand to rest on. *Ibid.* 286 The bridge being laid over the plate, the process of etching may now be commenced.

f. *Billiards.* The support formed by the left hand in making a stroke. Also (chiefly *U.S.*) = REST *sb.*[1] 11 c; the (usu. cross-shaped) tip of this.

1873 BENNETT & CAVENDISH *Billiards* 31 The bridge has now to be made, on which the cue is to be laid when aiming and striking. **1893** *Rules for Billiards & Pool* (Oliver L. Briggs Co.) 9 Billiard table outfit consists of..One dozen Cues..Two Bridges... Pool table outfit consists of..Twelve Cues. Two Bridges. **1909** in WEBSTER. **1964** C. COTTINGHAM *Game of Billiards* (1984) ii. 39 A *bridge* is also an elongated cue with a notched, fanlike tip which is used for making shots that are difficult to reach, or which cannot be made with a hand bridge because of the presence of interfering balls or because of excessive distance for comfortable hand bridge. *Ibid.* iv. 57 A mechanical bridge..is held firmly on the base of the table, on an angle to the cue ball. **1978** G. FELS *Pool Simplified, Somewhat* ii. 9 The way you accomplish that is to use the mechanical bridge, also called the rake, crutch, ladies' aid, and a number of barely printable epithets. Get comfortable with the bridge; it helps you reach every conceivable shot on the table.

g. *Saddlery.* A part of the harness resembling a buckle, but without the tongue, to which strapping is looped or sewed: also the bar (or bars) joining its sides.

1801 FELTON *Carriages* II. 133 In each strap a bridge is sewed. *Ibid.* The crupper..is looped through the housing bridge, and buckled about the middle.

h. *Electr.* An electrical circuit for measuring resistance or other properties by equalizing the potential at two points. Also ***bridge circuit.***

1872 [see WHEATSTONE]. **1881** MAXWELL *Electr. & Magn.* I. 447 Four conductors of great resistance may also be arranged as in Wheatstone's Bridge, and the bridge itself may consist of the electrodes of an electrometer. **1933** A. HUND *High-Frequency Measurements* iii. 97 The system shown in Fig. 57 is a bridge circuit balanced by a direct current *I.* **1942** J. G. BRAINERD *Ultra-High-Frequency Techniques* iii. 164 Either of these circuits is equivalent to a balanced bridge circuit. **1964** *Times* 31 Aug. 7/4 The Zwislocki acoustic bridge, which measures the acoustic impedance of the ear.

i. *Dentistry.* A false tooth or teeth usually connected to natural teeth on each side. Also *attrib.*; cf. *bridge-work* (s.v. 11 b).

1883 J. L. WILLIAMS in *Dental Cosmos* Dec. 629 A bridge of the six superior front teeth. **1891** *Brit. Jrnl. Dental Sci.* XXXIV. 65 Dr. Melotte..made a small bridge of one tooth. **1963** C. R. COWELL et al. *Inlays, Crowns & Bridges* ii. 4 A gold inlay is the most suitable type of bridge retainer. **1965** H. GOLD *Man who was not with It* xxx. 281 Mrs. Nancy..gave me a smile with her new bridge.

10. In *Card-playing*: see BRIDGING 1 b. *spec.* in *Euchre* (see quot. 1891).

1859 LEVER *Davenp. Dunn* I. 251 (Hoppe) I've found out the way that Yankee fellow does the king. It's not the common bridge that every body knows. **1860** MAYHEW *Lond. Lab.* I. 266 (Hoppe). **1891** 'L. HOFFMAN' *Cycl. Card & Table Games* 95 (*Euchre*) If one side has scored four, and the other side only one, such position is known as the 'bridge'... The elder hand is the only one who should order up at the bridge.

11. *Comb.* and *Attrib.* **a.** gen., as ***bridge-arch, -builder, -building, -foot, -maker, -work; bridge-like*** adj.

1772 C. HUTTON *Bridges* 6 A *Bridge-builder should be employed. **1751** (*title*) Gephyralogia..including..an abstract of the rules of *bridge-building. **1931** J. S. HUXLEY *What dare I Think?* vi. 199 There is no such instinct, any more than there is..a bridge-building instinct. **1850** ALISON *Hist. Europe* III. xviii. §39. 567 Jourdan, having..procured the necessary *bridge-equipage, prepared to cross the river. **1536** WRIOTHESLEY *Chron.* (1875) I. 59 From Temple Barr to the *bridg-foote in Southwarke. **1704** *Lond. Gaz.* No. 4019/4 Robert Adams..near the Bridge-foot, London. **1820** SHELLEY *Cloud*, From cape to cape, with a *bridge-like

shape, Over a torrent sea. **1611** BROUGHTON *Require Agreem.* 76 The *Bridge-maker [= pontiff] of Rome is blamed of Saint Paul. **1877** *Outlines Hist. Religion* 237 No special deity claimed the services of the Pontifices, the bridge- or road-makers.

b. Special comb.: **bridge-board** (see quot.); † **bridge-bote**, an ancient tax or contribution for the repair of bridges; **bridge-building**, (*a*) see sense 11 a; (*b*) *fig.*, the promotion and development of friendly relations between countries, etc.; **bridge church**, a faith in which elements of two systems of religious belief are found together; **bridge circuit** (see 9 h); **bridge-deck** (see 5); **bridge-gutter**, a gutter formed of boards covered with lead and supported on bearers, a bridged gutter; **bridge-head**, a fortification covering or protecting the end of a bridge nearest the enemy, = F. *tête de pont*; also, any military position established in the face of the enemy, e.g. by a landing force; also *fig.*; **bridge-islet** (see quot.); **bridge-man**, the keeper of a bridge; = BRIDGE-MASTER; **bridge-money**, money levied for the construction and repair of bridges; **bridge-note**, a note in Tonic Sol-fa music which marks the transition into a new key; **bridge passage**, a transitional passage in a musical or literary composition; **bridge-pin**, part of a gun; **bridge-rail** (*a*) (see quot.); (*b*) a rail around the bridge of a ship; † **bridge-silver** = *bridge-money*; **bridge spectacles** *U.S.* = PINCE-NEZ; **bridge-stone**, a flat stone, or flag, spanning a gutter or a sunken area; **bridge-tone** = *bridge-note*; **bridge-train**, a company of Military Engineers equipped for bridge-building, and carrying all the material and appliances for floating bridges; **bridge-tree**, a splinter-bar or swingle-tree; also, the adjustable beam which supports the spindle of the 'runner' or upper stone in a grain mill; **bridge-way**, the way formed by a bridge, the road or passage running over a bridge; also, the water-way which lies beneath it; **bridge-work** *Dentistry* = sense 9 i; also, the insertion of such a bridge. Also BRIDGE-HOUSE, -MASTER, -WARD.

1876 GWILT *Archit.* Gloss., *Bridge Board*, a board into which the ends of the steps of wooden stairs are fastened. *c* **1250** *Gloss. Law Terms* in *Rel. Ant.* I. 33 *Briggebote. **1844** LINGARD *Anglo-Saxon Ch.* (1858) I. vi. 221 Bryge-bot, or contribution towards the repair of bridges and highways. **1967** *N.Y. Times* in W. Safire *New Lang. Politics* (1968) 55/1 The Senate Foreign Relations Committee advanced the Administration's East-West *bridge-building program today by approving the United States-Soviet consular treaty. **1985** *Christian Science Monitor* 11 June 21/1 This process of bridge building in Indo-US relations began with the visit of the late Prime Minister Indira Gandhi to the United States in June 1982. **1927** *Church Times* 2 Sept. 266/1 Dr. Gore accepts for it [*sc.* the Anglican Church] its description by a Lutheran as a brücke Kirche—a *bridge Church between Catholicism and Protestantism. **1812** *Examiner* 28 Dec. 821/2 General Dombrowski defended the *bridge head of Borisow. **1877** CLERY *Min. Tact.* xv. 207 When the defenders hold a bridge head or other fortified post on the river. **1930** *Economist* 22 Mar. 632/2 The Channel tunnel.. would be a hopelessly vulnerable 'bridge-head'. **1938** *Star* (Kansas City) 22 Apr. 1/1 Counterattacks had reduced insurgent bridgeheads. **1940** R. W. B. CLARKE *Britain's Blockade* 6 The Nazis aim at using these territories as bridge-heads for the attack on Britain. **1944** *Ann. Reg. 1943* 25 British troops established a bridgehead of considerable width. **1959** *Listener* 2 Apr. 583/2 Once we have secured these export bridgeheads we can of course expect greater benefits. **1867** SMYTH *Sailor's Word-bk.*, *Bridge-islet, a portion of land which becomes insular at high-water. **1648** HERRICK *Hesper.* I. 52 Let it be thy pensil's strife To paint a *bridgeman to the life. **1683** *Lond. Gaz.* No. 1862/5 The Warden, Bridgemen, and Burgesses of Your Majesties Corporation of Henley upon Thames. **1783** HAMILTON in *Phil. Trans.* LXXIII. 181 The duke's bridge-man told me also, that.. this great river was perfectly dry for some seconds. **1826** *Protests Lords* III. 70 The taxes imposed on the land in the shape of road and *bridge money. **1879** CURWEN *Mus. Theory* 54 We call the tone represented by the *bridge-note the 'Transmutation-tone.' **1927** *Melody Maker* Sept. 926/2 Rhythmic construction of introductions, *bridge passages, modulations, interludes [etc.]. **1959** *Times Lit. Suppl.* 5 June 330/5 There are no bridge passages in this book. **1962** N. DEL MAR *R. Strauss* ii. 41 There is a bridge passage based on the rising octave figure. **1741** *Compl. Fam.-Piece* II. i. 320 Let your *Bridge-Pin be something above your Touch-hole. **1851** *Coal-tr. Terms Northumbld. & Durh.* 11 *Bridge-rails.. are now much used in barrow-ways, instead of tram-plates. **1875** URE *Dict. Arts* III. 692 Beside flat rails.. we have bridge rails employed, which have the form of a reversed U. **1915** 'BARTIMEUS' *Tall Ship* i. 14 The Captain, clinging to the bridge rail to maintain his balance. **1830** J. F. WATSON *Annals Philadelphia* 180 The only spectacles she ever saw were called *'bridge spectacles', without any side supporters, and held on the nose solely by nipping the bridge of the nose. **1884** *Athenæum* 16 Aug. 209/2 Simon de Montfort's charter for the remission of gable-pence and *bridge-silver to the burgesses of Leicester. **1876** GWILT *Archit.* Gloss., *Bridge Stone, a stone laid from the pavement to the entrance door of a house over a sunk area and supported by an arch. **1879** CURWEN *Mus. Theory* 54 The notation of Transition by means of *Bridge-tones we call the 'proper notation'. **1617** MARKHAM *Caval.* v. 54 The draught-breadthes.. extend from the breast of the Horse to the *bridge-tree of the Coach. **1822** IMISON *Sc. & Art* I. 69 One end of the bridge-tree which supports the spindle rests upon the wall. **1823** *Blackw. Mag.* XIII. 335 A sort of *bridgeway betwixt this world and infinity. **1884** G. C. DAVIES *Norfolk Broads* xxi. 156 As we got under the lee of the bridge the wind failed us and we remained motionless in the bridge-way. **1883** J. L. WILLIAMS in *Dental Cosmos* Dec. 624 So far as the *'bridge-work' is concerned. **1885** I. E. & R. E. CLIFFORD (*title*) Crown, Bar & Bridge-work. **1935** WODEHOUSE *Luck of Bodkins* xxi. 267 Causing George to double up like a pocket-rule and nearly swallow his bridge-work. **1963** C. R. COWELL et al. *Inlays, Crowns & Bridges* vii. 65 Very occasionally, jacket crowns may be used as retainers in anterior bridgework.

bridge (brɪdʒ), *sb.*[2] Also 9 biritch, britch, 9– Bridge. [Etym. unascertained; prob. of Levantine origin, since some form of the game appears to have been long known in the Near East; the origin of the seemingly Russian forms *biritch, britch*, is unknown; an unrecorded Turkish form **bir-üç* 'one-three' (since one hand is exposed and three concealed) was postulated as the source in *N. & Q.* (1969), 430–1.] **a.** A card-game based upon whist. In the original form of the game the dealer or his partner (dummy) named trumps, dummy's hand was exposed after the lead, and the odd tricks varied in value according to the suit named as trumps. Now = *auction* or *contract bridge*.

The game is said to have been played in Constantinople and the Near East about 1870. Formerly also called *Bridge Whist* (see sense c below). The sense in quot. 1843 is uncertain; *biritch* in quots. 1886 is applied to the call of 'no trumps'.

[**1843** J. PAGET *Let.* 18 Apr. in *Mem. & Lett.* (1901) I. vi. 144 We improved our minds in the intellectual games of Bagatelle and Bridge.] **1886** *Biritch, or Russian Whist* 2 The one declaring may, instead of declaring trumps, say 'Biritch', which means that the hands shall be played *without trumps*. *Ibid.* 3 The odd tricks count as follows:—If 'Biritch' is declared each [odd trick counts] 10 points. *Ibid.* 4 There are four honours if 'Biritch' is declared, which are the four aces. **1898** 'BOAZ' (*title*) The Pocket Guide to Bridge. **1898** *Nat. Rev.* Aug. 809 At a game of *wint* or *bridge*. **1901** 'SLAM' *Mod. Bridge* Introd., 'Bridge', known in Turkey as 'Britch'. **1963** G. F. HERVEY *Handbk. Card Games* 131 The modern game of Bridge, more correctly Contract Bridge, to distinguish it from its now-defunct predecessors, was developed by Harold S. Vanderbilt.

b. ***auction bridge***: a variety of the game which superseded the original form. The right to name trumps and to play with the dummy goes, for each deal, to the player who undertakes to make the highest score. See also *contract bridge* s.v. CONTRACT *sb.*[1] 1 g).

1903 O. CRAWFORD in *Times* 16 Jan. 5/6 'Auction bridge'.. is more lively than dummy bridge. **1908** DALTON *Auction Bridge* p. iii, Auction Bridge is really a clever combination of the two games of Poker and Bridge. **1959** T. REESE *Bridge Player's Dict.* 18 Auction bridge, the predecessor of contract, held sway from about 1911.. to 1928, when contract began to be popular. **1960** BETJEMAN *Summoned by Bells* i. 5 Happy and tense they played at Auction Bridge.

c. *attrib.* and *Comb.*, as ***bridge-coat, -drive, -four, -party, -player, -playing*** adj., ***-scorer, -table, -whist***; **bridge-marker**, a pad on which bridge scores are noted; **bridge roll** [or ? BRIDGE *sb.*[1]], a soft, oval, bread roll.

1905 *Daily Chron.* 29 May 8/4 A dainty bridge-coat in white soft glacé silk. **1928** R. MACAULAY *Keeping up Appearances* viii. 78 She had no bridge coat, a mysterious garment apparently donned by bridge-players. **1927** *Auction Bridge Mag.* May 19/2 'Bridge Drives'.. make you go 'all out' when there is a chance of a big killing. **1914** COMPTON MACKENZIE *Sinister St.* II. III. v. 576 Michael and a large party of freshmen.. had sustained themselves with dressed crab and sleepy bridge-fours. **1953** D. PARRY *Going up—Going Down* vi. 315 Afterwards there was a bridge four and Clive played billiards. **1907** *Yesterday's Shopping* (1969) 386/3 Bridge Scoring Block.. Bridge Scoring Book.. Bridge Book. Ruled for Engagements. Scoring and Total.. Bridge Marker. **1914** 'SAKI' *Beasts & Super-Beasts* 258 'What did one send them?'..'Bridge-markers.' **1910** —— *Reg. in Russia & Other Sk.* 96 Occasionally she went to bridge parties. **1949** M. LASKI *Little Boy Lost* I. i. 9 The bridge-parties and the brittle gossip. **1899** A. G. HULME-BEAMAN *Pons Asinorum* 50 No amount of rule and precept will suffice to make a first-class Bridge player. **1967** E. LEMARCHAND *Death of Old Girl* xvii. 194 His brilliance as a bridge player. **1907** E. WHARTON *Fruit of Tree* II. xvi. 244 A cluster of young bridge-playing couples. **1967** J. SYMONS *Man who killed Himself* I. i. 10 Half a dozen bridge-playing couples. **1926** D. D. C. TAYLOR *Good Housekeeping Menu* 106 Social Tea.. Bridge Rolls and Cress, White and Brown Bread and Butter. **1951** *Good Housek. Home Encycl.* 371/2 Bridge rolls are split, buttered and filled with a variety of sweet and savoury fillings. **1908** A. BENNETT *Buried Alive* vi. 139 Manilla cigars, bridge scorers, [etc.].. seemed to be the principal objects offered for sale. **1951** R. SENHOUSE tr. *Colette's Chéri* 111 Let's.. buy playing-cards, good wine, bridge-scorers. **1905** *Daily Chron.* 27 Dec. 4/5 Are we, as they say at the bridge-table, 'content'? **1899** A. G. HULME-BEAMAN *Pons Asinorum* 46 As in Bridge Whist everybody plays his own game.

d. *ellipt.* = *bridge-party*.

1907 R. BROOKE *Let.* 7 Apr. (1968) 81 The ugly friend of the Simpson's, who won a prize at our bridge last winter. **1966** H. KEMELMAN *Saturday the Rabbi went Hungry* (1967) xx. 121 My wife gave a bridge and invited his wife.

Hence **bridge** *v.*[3] *intr.*, to play bridge; **'bridger** (cf. F. *bridgeur*, 1893), a bridge-player.

1907 MRS. H. DE LA PASTURE *Lonely Lady* xvi. 279 Miss de Courset, come and play billiard-fives,.. unless you are a bridger. Are you a bridger? **1908** *Daily Chron.* 14 Nov. 6/4 We must dine and we must 'bridge'. **1928** *Sunday Express* 27 May 15 Shall she Charleston, Blues or Bridge that evening?

bridge (brɪdʒ), *v.*[1] Forms: 1 brycgian, 3 brugge-n, 3–4 brigge(n, 7– bridge. [OE. *brycgian*, f. *brycg*, BRIDGE, *sb.*[1]; cf. OHG. *bruccôn*, MHG. *brucken, brücken*.]

1. *trans.* **a.** To make a bridge over (a river, ravine, etc.); to span with a bridge or similar means of passage. Often predicated of the thing which spans. Often with *across, over*.

a **1000** *Andreas* 1263 (Gr.), Is brycgade blæce brimrade. *c* **1205** LAY. 21276 þa al wes Auene stram mid stele ibrugged. **1375** BARBOUR *Bruce* XII. 404 Thai had befor [the] day Briggit the pollis. **1665** MANLEY *Grotius' Low-C. Warrs* 155 Now that the Schelde was thus bridged. **1718** POPE *Iliad* XXI. 274 The large trunk.. Bridg'd the rough flood across. **1846** GROTE *Greece* (1862) II. i. 21 A strait narrow enough to be bridged over. **1853** KANE *Grinnell Exp.* xlii. (1856) 388 An arch of ice.. bridging a fissure. **1879** FROUDE *Cæsar* xxviii. 485 They bridged the Rhine in a week.

† **b.** To overlay, spread over. *Obs.*

c **1200** *Trin. Coll. Hom.* 91 þe children briggeden þe wei biforen ure drihten, sume mid here cloðes. *Ibid.* Sume briggeden þe asse mid here cloðes, and sume mid boȝes þe hie breken of þe trewes.

c. To span or cross as with a bridge.

1872 MARK TWAIN *Innoc. Abr.* xiii. 91 A speculator bridged a couple of barrels with a board. **1876** GWILT *Archit.* Gloss. s.v. *Bridge-over*, The upper joists.. bridge over the beams or binding-joists, and.. are called bridging-joists.

d. *fig.*

1853 CLOUGH *Songs in Abs.* vii. 8 The wide and weltering waste above—Our hearts have bridged it with their love. **1862** SIR B. BRODIE *Psychol. Inq.* II. i. 24 To bridge over the space which separates the known from the unknown. **1879** PROCTOR *Pleas. Ways Sc.* xiii. 326 The gap between the lowest savage and the highest ape is not easily bridged.

2. To form (a way) by means of a bridge.

1667 MILTON *P.L.* x. 310 Xerxes.. Over Hellespont Bridging his way, Europe with Asia joyn'd. **1705** J. PHILIPS *Blenheim* (R.) Advance; we'll bridge a way, Safe of access.

3. *slang.* (See quot.)

1812 J. H. VAUX *Flash Dict.*, *To bridge a person*, or to throw him over the bridge, is.. to deceive him by betraying the confidence he has reposed in you.

† **bridge**, *v.*[2] *Obs.* Forms: 4 bregge, breigge, 4–5 brigge, 6 brydge. [aphet. form of *abregge*, ABRIDGE, a. F. *abréger* to shorten.] *trans.* To abridge, shorten, lessen; to curtail. Also *absol.*

1330 R. BRUNNE *Chron.* 247 Noþeles he wild haf briggid, þe fals leue & erroure. *c* **1380** WYCLIF *Sel. Wks.* II. 407 It is peril to adde or to bregge fro Cristis wordis. **1382** —— *Mark* xiii. 20 No but the Lord hadde breiggid [**1388** abredgide] tho dayes. *c* **1430–40** OCCLEVE *MS. Soc. Antiq.* 134 f. 251 a, Sorow and care Byreven man his helþe, And his dayes briggen. **1526** *Pilgr. Perf.* (W. de W. 1531) 97 An aduersary.. euer brydgynge & lettyng the in euery thynge.

Hence † **'bridgement**, an abridgement, epitome; † **'bridger**, an abridger or epitomizer; † **'bridging** *vbl. sb.*, shortening.

1382 WYCLIF *Bible, Pref. Epist.* I. 72/2 Perlipomynon, that is, the book of the olde instrument, recapitulatour, word bregger. —— *2 Macc.* ii. 32 To be grauntid to the bregger [Vulg. *brevianti*]. —— *Wks.* (1880) 74 þo þat ben cursed of god for bregynge of his hestis.. ben not ponyschid þus. *c* **1534** tr. *Pol. Verg. Eng. Hist.* (1846) I. 197 Let this compendius brigement suffice. **1559** MORWYNG *Evonymus* 320 The Breviarium or Bridgment of Arnold de Villa Nova.

bridgeable ('brɪdʒəb(ə)l), *a.* [f. BRIDGE *v.*[1] + -ABLE.] That can be bridged or spanned by a bridge. Also *fig.*

1865 CARLYLE *Fredk. Gt.* (1873) VII. XVIII. iii. 135 Wadeable, bridgeable. **1890** *Advance* (Chicago) 13 Mar., Intervening islands break this distance [60 miles] into bridgeable lengths. **1898** *Daily News* 27 July 6/2 From the young officer to the preacher of non-resistance, there is a great gulf, but bridgable.

bridged (brɪdʒd), *ppl. a.* [f. BRIDGE *v.*[1] + -ED.] Furnished with a bridge or bridges; spanned or traversed with bridges.

1611 COTGR., *Ponté*, Bridged; that hath a Bridge ouer it, or belonging to it. **1862** M. HOPKINS *Hawaii* 9 Its grassy slopes; its bridged rivulets. **1864** R. BURTON *Dahome* 12 Good roads well bridged, and a channel of mountain water.

b. bridged gutter (*Building*), 'one made with boards supported by bearers and covered above with lead or zinc' (Gwilt *Archit.*).

bridge-house ('brɪdʒhaʊs). A house connected with a bridge, for its protection or control; *spec.* the house with its officers and revenues, connected in former times with the care and repair of London Bridge.

1375 BARBOUR *Bruce* XVII. 409 [Thai] pressit thame full fast to tow Hir by the brighous to the wall. **1704** *Lond. Gaz.* No. 4069/4 A Large Wharf.. near the Bridge-House. **1766** ENTICK *London* IV. 375 Estates settled on the city or bridge-house.

bridgeless ('brɪdʒlɪs), *a.* [f. BRIDGE *sb.*[1] + -LESS.] Having no bridge, unspanned by a bridge; also *fig.*

1801 SOUTHEY *Thalaba* v. x, A free and bridgeless tide, Euphrates rolls along. **1865** CARLYLE *Fredk. Gt.* IX. xx. viii. 157 A chasm or bridgeless interstice between two ramparts. **1884** H. DRUMMOND *Nat. Law in Spir. W.* (ed. 8) 72 The bridgeless gulf between the natural and the spiritual.

b. Of the nose.

1863 GEO. ELIOT *Romola* in *Cornh. Mag.* VII. 286 His bridgeless nose and low forehead.

ˈbridgemaster. An officer having control of a bridge: formerly, in some English boroughs, a regular member of the corporation; also called *bridgeman*.

1502 ARNOLD *Chron.* 135 The said brigmastirs referred all ther maters to the said Samwell. *a* **1618** RALEIGH *Observ.* in *Rem.* (1661) 179 From any Port Town.. the Bridgemaster or the Wharfmaster.. will deliver a true Note of the number of Lasts of Herrings brought to their Wharfes. **1683** *Lond. Gaz.* No. 1860/3 The Warden, Steward, Bridgemasters, Burgesses, and other Inhabitants of the Town and Corporation of Maidenhead. **1810** WELLINGTON *Let.* in Gurw. *Disp.* V. 444 In respect to the Bridges.. there is a Bridge-Master at Abrantes who has charge of them all. **1886** *Whitaker's Almanac* 260 Officers of the city of London — Elected by the Livery.. Bridge Masters.

bridges, obs. form of BRUGES (satin).

Bridgetin (ˈbrɪdʒɪtɪn), *sb.* (*a.*) In 6 **Brygittane**, 7 **Brigidian**, 8 **Brigittin(e, Birgittin.** Also **Bridgettine.** [f. the name of *St. Bridget*, in L. *Brigidia*.] A member of a religious order founded by St. Bridget in the 14th century. Also *attrib.* and as *adj.*

1533 MORE *Answ. Poysoned Bk.* Wks. 1091/2 Frere Huskyn the frere brygittane. **1656** BLOUNT *Glossogr.*, *Brigidians*, an order of religious persons instituted by Brigidia a widow. **1753** CHAMBERS *Cycl. Supp.*, *Brigittins*, or *Bridgetins*, more properly *Birgittins*.. denominated from their foundress St. Brigit or Birgit, a Swedish lady in the fourteenth century. **1756** A. BUTLER *Lives Saints* I. 514 March 22.. St. Catherine of Sweden... See her life written by Ulpho, a Brigittine friar. **1779** —— *Ibid.* (ed. 2) X. 148 The Brigittin nuns of Sion also had leave to retire abroad. **1873** J. H. BLUNT *Pref.* to *Myr. Oure Ladye* p. xii, A Brigittine community of nuns. **1884** *Mag. of Art* Apr. 221/2 The monastery of Bridgettines.. had been founded in the year 1415. **1902** F. M. STEELE *Convents Gt. Brit.* 62 The Bridgettine Rosary consists of seven *Paters* and sixty-three *Aves*. **1969** *Observer* (Colour Suppl.) 13 Apr. 54/2 *Bridgettines*.. run guesthouses at Iver Heath, Bucks, Rome and Lugano.

bridgeward (ˈbrɪdʒˌwɔːd), *sb.* In 4 **brigge-**.

1. The keeper or warden of a bridge.

a **1000** *Battle of Maldon* (in Sweet) 85 *Ags. Reader* 136 Ðæt hi ðær brycgweardas bitere fundon. *c* **1380** *Sir Ferumb.* 1700 A geant ys maked briggeward.. þe brigge ay kepeþ hee. **1820** SCOTT *Monastery* vi, The bridge-wards have been in possession of these dues.. for more than fifty years.

2. The custody or wardship of a bridge.

c **1380** *Sir Ferumb.* 3560 Þat nyȝt.. þe brigge-warde forȝete was, þorw murȝþe of ys play.

3. *Lock-smithing.* The main ward of a key.

bridgeward (ˈbrɪdʒwəd), *adv.* [see -WARD.] Towards, or in the direction of, a bridge.

1884 *Christm. Illust. Lond. N.* 10/1, I bridgeward was bent.

† **ˈbridgewater.** *Obs.* A woollen cloth named after the place of its original manufacture.

1552-3 *Acts 5 & 6 Edw. VI*, All and euery broad cloth and clothes, called Taunton clothes, Bridgewaters and other clothes. **1607** *Act 4 Jas. I*, ii, Tauntons, Bridgewaters, and Dunsters made in the Westerne parts of Somersetshire.

bridging (ˈbrɪdʒɪŋ), *vbl. sb.* [f. BRIDGE $v.^1$ or $sb.^1$ + -ING^1.]

1. a. The action of the vb. BRIDGE.

1839 THIRLWALL *Greece* II. 252 The bridging of the sacred Hellespont. **1882** VINES *Sachs' Bot.* 136 The bridging over of the medullary rays by cambium.

b. In *Card-playing*: see quot.

1879 *Sporting Exam.* 19 Aug. 262 By slightly bending a card—termed bridging—he could force, as it were, his opponent in the game to 'cut' the cards wherever he wished.

c. *Mountaineering.* (See quots.)

1941 C. KIRKUS *Let's go Climbing* iv. 56 You are now standing astride the chimney.. left hand and foot on the left wall and the right hand and foot on the right wall. You can now climb straight up in the more natural position. This is known as bridging. **1957** R. G. COLLOMB *Dict. Mountaineering* 35 *Bridging*, a method of climbing chimneys and corners; it can also be any series of upward movements on a rock face when the legs are astride and the feet are being used on pressure holds.

2. a. Bridges viewed in the mass as so much 'work'; **b.** *Carpentry.* A bridging piece (see 3).

1884 H. W. CLARKE in *Pall Mall G.* 5 May 2/2 This sum included—ballast, heavy bridging, station buildings.

3. *Comb.* and *Attrib.*: **bridging-floor**, a floor in which bridging-joists are employed; **bridging-joist**, a small beam or joist of a flooring resting upon the binding-joists below, and supporting the boarding above; **bridging-piece**, a piece placed between two opposite beams to prevent their nearer approach (Weale).

1823 P. NICHOLSON *Pract. Build.* 118 When the supporting timbers of a floor are formed by one row laid upon another, the upper row are called bridging joists. **1876** GWILT *Archit.* §2019 A double floor consists.. of.. binding joists.. bridging joists, and ceiling joists.

ˈbridging, *ppl. a.* [f. BRIDGE $v.^1$ + -ING^2.]

1. a. Constructing or appointed to construct a bridge or bridges. (Perhaps orig. attrib. use of the vbl. sb.)

1891 *Daily News* 26 May 3/7 The bridging battalion of Royal Engineers. **1901** 'LINESMAN' *Words by Eyewitness* (1902) 94 Losing eleven men of the bridging party, and having every pontoon and plank struck by the Boer marksmen.

b. *Finance.* Providing temporary cover of a debt, etc., pending receipt of cash from a forthcoming sale or negotiation of long-term finance; *esp.* as ***bridging loan***.

1967 J. L. HANSON *Dict. Econ.* (ed. 2) 50/1 *Bridging loan*, borrowing to make a purchase ahead of receiving payment for a sale as, for example, buying a new house before selling an old one. **1970** *Which?* Mar. 75/1 Many solicitors helped buyers to go ahead, by negotiating a bridging loan. They very rarely charged for this. **1975** *Economist* 12 Apr. 105 An arrangement was made to provide Mr Stern with £5½m of bridging finance to buy the whole development. **1982** *Times* 26 Aug. 15/6 Mexico's emergency bridging loan from central banks has again been increased. **1983** *Times* 12 Oct. 21/8 A big bridging operation.. looks unlikely. **1984** *Which?* Apr. 161/1 You get tax relief against the interest on a bridging loan of £30,000 or less for up to twelve months. **1986** *Courier-Mail* (Brisbane) 20 June 7/2 Wheeler used the $200,000.. as bridging finance.

2. bridging species *Bot.*, one of a series of plant-species on which a parasitic fungus may be trained or adapted to infect species otherwise immune. Also ***bridging host***.

1903 H. M. WARD in *Phil. Trans.* B. CXCVI. 34 A certain species of grass (A) may be capable of infection by means of spores from two other host-plants (B and C), neither of which is predisposed to reciprocal infection, though both may be infected from such a 'bridging' species (A) as is referred to above. **1922** *Encycl. Brit.* XXX. 478/2 'Bridging species'. *Ibid.*, 'Bridging hosts'.

bridgroome, -gume, obs. ff. BRIDEGROOM.

bridgy (ˈbrɪdʒɪ), *a. rare.* [f. BRIDGE $sb.^1$ + -Y^1.] Abounding in bridges.

1611 COTGR. *Pontueux*, bridgie, full of bridges.

bridhale, obs. form of BRIDAL.

briding (ˈbraɪdɪŋ), *vbl. sb. rare.* [f. BRIDE $v.^1$ + -ING^1.] Wedding; being a bride.

1581 T. NUCE *Seneca's Octavia* 181 Bridinge chambers banquet wise ydrest. **1861** TROLLOPE *Framley P.* III. ix. 159 The quintessence of her briding, the outer veil.. of the tabernacle—namely, her wedding-dress.

b. See quot. (Cf. BRIDE $v.^2$)

1598-1611 FLORIO, *Sposarie*, bride tricks, puling nice tricks, bridings.

bridle (ˈbraɪd(ə)l), *sb.* Forms: 1 **bridel**, 3-4 **bridel**, **-il**, 3-6 **brydel**, 4 **briddle**, **brydille**, 4-5 **bridell**, 4-6 **brydell**, **-il**, **-ill**, 5 **bridelle**, **-ill**, **-ulle**, **-yl(le**, **brydylle**, 6 **brydle**, 4- **bridle**. [OE. *brídel* for earlier **brigdel* (cf. *brigdils* Erf. Gl. 127, *O.E. Texts* 44) has various corresp. forms in WGer.: cf. OFris. *bridel*, MLG., MDu. *breidel* (*bredel*), Du. *breidel*, OHG., MHG. *brittel*; formed with instrumental suffix like *hand-le*, *saddle*, etc., from root of *bregd-an* to pull, twitch (see BRAID); cf. Ger. *zügel* from *ziehen* to draw.]

1. a. The head-gear of the harness of a horse or other beast of burden, consisting of a head-stall, bit, and rein, by which the animal is controlled and guided. ***to give a horse the bridle***: to abandon control of him; so ***to lay the bridle on his neck***. ***to keep a horse up into his bridle***: to keep him up to the full speed allowed by the degree of restraint in which he is held by the bridle. ***to go up well to his bridle***: to be a free goer, not to hang back at the pressure applied.

a **1000** *Rune Poem* xxi. (Gr.) Se brimhengest bridles neȝymeð. *a* **1225** *Ancr. R.* 74 Bridel nis nout one iðe horses muðe. **1362** LANGL. *P. Pl.* A. IV. 20 Hong on him an heui Bridel to bere his hed lowe. *c* **1385** CHAUCER *L.G.W.* 1208 The fomy brydil with the bit of gold Governyth he. *c* **1450** *Merlin* xxii. 407 He hilde the reyne of his bridill in his lefte arme. **1526** *Pilgr. Perf.* (W. de W. 1531) 160 Whether he sholde haue also the sadell and brydell with the horse. **1601** BP. BARLOW *Serm. Paules Crosse* 59 A bridle hath raines and a bit. **1674** *Ch. & Court of Rome* 8 It being proverbial, That 'tis a greater shame to bring home the Bridle than steal the Horse. **1882** *Illust. Sporting News* 4 Feb. 502/2 Come on at a good canter—not too fast, but keep them well up into their bridles. **1884** E. ANDERSON *Mod. Horsemanship* I. v. 17 In the double bridle we have the curb bit and the snaffle.

b. Occas. applied to the bit alone; also *fig.*

c **1400** *Rom. Rose* 3299 Take with thy teeth the bridel faste. **1579** FULKE *Confut. Sanders* 657 She commaunded his bridle to be made of one nayle. **1602** WARNER *Alb. Eng.* IX. xlvii. 222 More eagerly than earst I on the brydell byte.

c. *fig.* with conscious reference to a horse.

1401 *Pol. Poems* (1859) II. 85 Who wil not amenden him, ȝeue him the brydil. **1580** NORTH *Plutarch* (1676) 362 Giving the bridle to a desperate man. **1583** GOLDING *Calvin on Deut.* ii. 8 Gods deliuering of the Children out of the Bondage of Egypt was not to lay the brydle in their necke that they might go when they listed. **1796** BURKE *Let. Noble L.* 41 Calais the key of France, and the bridle in the mouth of that power. **1833** WORDSW. *Warning*, O for a bridle bitted with remorse To stop your leaders in their headstrong course.

2. *fig.* A restraint, curb, check. *Mil.* A fortress keeping an enemy in check (cf. BRIDLE *v.* 2 b).

1340 *Ayenb.* 254 Zete ane brydel to þine couaytises. *c* **1430** LYDG. *Bochas* II. xv. (1554) 55 a, Sensualitie Holdeth the bridle of lecherous insolence. **1530** RASTELL *Bk. Purgat.* III. xv. 4 Man hath nede to have both a brydel of lawe.. & also a brydell of the drede of God. **1535** COVERDALE *2 Sam.* vii. 1. **1624** BACON *New Atl.* (1677) 257 The reverence of a mans self is, next religion, the chiefest Bridle of all Vices. **1662** FULLER *Worthies* (1840) III. 488 Thy [castles].. were first intended as bridles to their country. **1791** BURKE *Th. on Fr. Affairs* Wks. VII. 37 The blind reverence they bear to the sanctity of the Pope, which is their only bridle. **1879** FROUDE *Cæsar* xv. 233 He kept his tongue under a bridle.

3. = $BRANKS^1$ 1.

1623 *Macclesfield Corp. Rec.* in Ormerod *Hist. Cheshire* III. 385 A Brydle for a curste queane. **1658** *Worcester Corp. Rec.* in Brushfield *Obs. Punishm.* (1858) I. 7 *note*, Paid for mending the bridle for bridleinge of scoulds, and two cords for the same.. js. ijd. **1753** CHAMBERS *Cycl. Supp.* s.v., In Staffordshire they have a *bridle* for correcting scolding women. **1858** BRUSHFIELD *Obsol. Punishm.* I. 16 Another Bridle.. is a very handsome specimen, being surmounted with a decorated cross.

4. The gesture described under BRIDLE *v.* 3.

1748 RICHARDSON *Clarissa* (1811) V. xxviii. 287 'Miss Howe'.. repeated she, with a scornful bridle, but a very pretty one. **1781** COWPER *Hope* 344 The flirted fan, the bridle, and the toss.

5. Applied technically or descriptively to various things resembling a horse's bridle in their form or use: *esp.*

a. *Naut.* A stout cable, or 'fast', by which a vessel is secured to moorings; also, the short piece of rope by which the bowline is attached to the leech or edge of the sail.

1626 CAPT. SMITH *Accid. Yng. Seamen* 15 The maine bowling and bridles. **1627** —— *Seaman's Gram.* v. 27 The Boling knot is.. fastened by the bridles into the creengles of the sailes. **1769** FALCONER *Dict. Marine* (1789) Cc iij b, To this swivel-link are attached the bridles, which are short pieces of cable, well served, whose upper ends are drawn into the ship, at the mooring-ports, and afterwards fastened to the masts, or cable-bits. **1793** SMEATON *Edystone L.* §259 We came to and got in the bridle and swivel.

b. *Phys.* A ligament or membrane serving to check the motion of a part, or bind one part to another; a frænum; 'a narrow slip of living structure interposed between two orifices or the opposing walls of an abscess; a band stretching across a cicatrix' (*Syd. Soc. Lex.*); †the septum of the nose (*obs.*).

1697 DAMPIER *Voyages* (1729) III. I. 351 Pinching the Bridle of the Nose with its points, it hangs dangling from thence. *c* **1720** W. GIBSON *Farrier's Guide* I. ii. (1738) 15 An appendage called the Frænum, or Bridle, which runs.. almost to the root of the yard. **1758** J. S. *Le Dran's Observ. Surg.* (1771) Dict. Bb7b, *Frænulum*, the Bridle of the Tongue. *Ibid.* 199 The *Cystis Hernialis*.. was much contracted, forming four of five strong Bridles. **1805** *Med. & Phys. Jrnl.* I Aug. 97 Two cases of children losing their lives in consequence of cutting what is called the bridle of the tongue. **1835-6** TODD *Cycl. Anat. & Phys.* I. 603/2 Those bridles which are such frequent causes of deformity after the healing of extensive burns.

c. *Mech.* A metal strip or band uniting two parts of a machine, or limiting their motion; also, the flanges which keep a slide-valve in position.

1667 *Wilmslow Churchw. Acc.* in Earwaker *E. Cheshire* I. 115 Paid for the bridle of the clocke, and several other things about the clock and quarters. **1833** J. HOLLAND *Manuf. Metals* II. 302 The massy cast-iron frames are fastened with screws and also with wrought iron bridles. **1846** *Print. Apparatus Amateurs* 10 The pressure is applied to the front of the press by a lever, which is jointed to the upper extremity by a long bridle.

d. *Agric.* A bent piece of iron on the end of a plough-beam, to which the draught-tackle is attached; a clevis.

1840 *Penny Cycl.* XVIII. 275/1 The end of this iron, which is called a bridle, has several projecting hooks.. on which an iron ring is hung at different heights.

e. The cord or other work which strengthens or tightens the sides of a net.

c **1838** C. BATHURST *Nets* 34 If it be too large, the bridle would, instead of forming a straight line along the sides of the net, hang down loosely in loops.

f. *Fire-arms.* A small plate of metal in the interior of a gunlock, which holds the sear and tumbler in position.

1844 *Regul. & Ord. Army* 100 Bridle [of musket].. 0s. 9d. **1875** URE *Dict. Arts* II. 383 The lock, inside.. showing all the parts.. *d*, the tumbler; *e*, the bridle.

g. (See quot. 1906.)

1899 C. F. MARVIN in *Yearbk. U.S. Dept. Agric. 1898* 211 The one-point attachment of bridle.. is better suited to strong than light winds. **1906** A. F. COLLINS *Man. Wireless Telegr.* 209 *Bridle*, a cord attached to a kite that holds the latter at the proper angle in the wind; the kite-cord is attached to the bridle.

6. *Comb.*, as ***bridle-maker***; also **bridle-arm** (cf. *bridle-hand*); **bridle-bridge**, a bridge fit for the passage of a horse, but not for vehicles; **bridle-cable** (see quot.); **bridle-chain** (*Mining*), one of the 'safety-chains to support a cage if the link between the cage and rope should break' (Raymond *Mining Gloss.*); † **bridle-cull** (*Thieves' cant*), a highwayman; **bridle-cutter**, a bridle-maker; **bridle-gate**, a gate leading into a bridle-path; **bridle-hand**, the hand which holds the bridle in riding, the left hand; **bridle-path**, **-road**, **-way**, a path fit for the passage of a horse, but not of vehicles; **bridle-pin**, the pin which helps to secure the bridle of a gunlock; **bridle-port**, a port or port-hole in a ship's bow through

which 'bridles' (see 5) may be run, or chase-guns fired. Also BRIDLE-BIT, -REIN.

1833 *Regul. Instr. Cavalry* I. 116 Resting the blade upon the *bridle-arm. **1882** *Proc. Berw. Nat. Club* IX. 446 The approach to the Castle..has been from a curious old *bridle-bridge. **1793** SMEATON *Edystone L.* §139 *note*, When a vessel is moored by laying down a cable upon the ground, with an anchor at each end, then another cable attached to the middle of the ground cable, is called the *Bridle Cable. **1743** FIELDING *J. Wild* I. v. (D.) A booty of £10 looks as great in the eye of a *bridle-cull..as that of as many thousands to the statesman. **1697** *Lond. Gaz.* No. 3081/3 *Bridle-Cutters..and all other Makers, Dressers, or Workers in Leather. **1720** *Ibid.* No. 5912/4 John Rest.. Bridle-Cutter. **1868** HOLME LEE *Bas. Godfrey* lxvii. 395 The horses..stopped at a *bridle-gate. **1580** SIDNEY *Arcadia* II. (R.) In the turning one might perceive the *bridle-hand something gently stir. **1833** *Regul. Instr. Cavalry* I. 39 To govern his horse by the aid of his legs and bridle-hand. **1855** SMEDLEY *Harry Coverdale* v. 27 Remember to..keep your bridle hand low. **1652** WADSWORTH *tr. Sandoval's Civ. Wars Spain* 139 One Calahorra, and with him a *Bridle-maker. **1876** GROTE *Eth. Fragm.* v. 136 The end of the bridle-maker is subservient to that of the horseman. **1811** *Nat. Hist.* in *Ann. Reg.* 470/2 The only roads..are narrow *bridle-paths winding through the recesses of the mountains. **1881** GREENER *Gun* 263 Unscrew the *bridle-pins and remove the bridle. **1832** MARRYAT *N. Forster* xlvii, Two-and-twenty guns besides her *bridle-ports. **1833** LYELL *Princ. Geol.* III. p. xxvii, Rocks, which are seen to the left of a small *bridle-road. **1868** G. DUFF *Pol. Surv.* 53 The bridle roads across the mountains..are quite enough for camels and mules. **1760** *Chron.* in *Ann. Reg.* 67/1 Was finally determined..the cause..concerning the legality of a carriage and *bridle way through the park.

bridle ('braɪd(ə)l), *v.* Forms: 1 **brídlian**, 2-3 **bridlenn** (*Orm.*), 3 **bridlen**, 4 **bridele**, **brydelen**, 5 **brydelle**, **brydelyn**, **brydyl**, 5-6 **brydel**, 6 **bridill**, **brydell**, **brydil**, **brydle**, 6-7 **bridel**, 5- **bridle**. [OE. *brídlian*, *ȝebrídlian*, f. *bridel*, BRIDLE. Cf. OHG. *brittolôn*, MHG. *britteln*.]

1. a. *trans.* To put a bridle on (a horse), to furnish with a bridle; also (*obs.*), to guide or control with a bridle.

1393 GOWER *Conf.* I. 110 Som prick her horse aside, And bridlen hem now in nowe cote. *c* **1440** *Promp. Parv.* 50 Brydelyn, *freno.* **1530** PALSGR. 939 To bridel, *brider.* **1833** *Regul. Instr. Cavalry* I. 42 The Recruits are to be taught to saddle and bridle.

b. To furnish with a bridle in other senses.

1758 J. S. *Le Dran's Observ. Surg.* (1771) 332 The Membranes which cover the Muscles, and might bridle that Part of the Wound. *c* **1838** C. BATHURST *Nets* 34 A net is bridled at its four outer margins when it is desirable to keep the meshes square. **1858** BRUSHFIELD *Obsol. Punishm.* 13 She [a scold] was ordered to be bridled and to be led through the town.

c. (See BRIDLE *sb.* 5 g.)

1899 C. F. MARVIN in *Yearbk. U.S. Dept. Agric. 1898* 210 Two methods of bridling the kite.

2. *fig.* **a.** To curb, check, restrain, hold *in*.

c **888** K. ÆLFRED *Boeth.* xxi, Bridla þe he þa ȝesceafta nu mid ȝebridlode hæfþ. *c* **1200** ORMIN 11664 Sone iss þe bodiȝ bridledd. *a* **1225** *Ancr. R.* 74 3if eni..ne bridleð nout his tunge. **1382** WYCLIF *Isa.* xlviii. 9 In my preissing I shal bridele thee, lest thou die. **1548** UDALL *Erasm. Par.* Pref. 6 Also to bridle the insolencie. **1634** MILTON *Comus* 887 Rise, rise..And bridle in thy headlong wave. **1713** YOUNG *Last Day* I. 274 He bridles in the monsters of the deep. **1725** DE FOE *Voy. round World* (1840) 41, I bridled my passion with all my power. **1756** C. LUCAS *Ess. Waters* II. 145 How is the action of iron bridled by sulphur? **1827** HALLAM *Const. Hist.* (1876) III. 64 To bridle the clergy. **1878** BOSW. SMITH *Carthage* 397 Scipio bridled his indignation.

b. In military sense: To hold in check, control.

1615 E. GRIMSTONE *Hist. World* 86 They are bridled of all sides..by a great number of strong places. **1690** LUTTRELL *Brief Rel.* (1857) II. 105 Fortifyeing Thonon, a small place on the lake of Geneva, which will bridle that citty. **1761** HUME *Hist. Eng.* III. lvi. 99 Forts were erected in order to bridle Rochelle. **1876** GREEN *Short Hist.* ii. §6 (1882) 85 Scotland..was bridled by the erection of a strong fortress at Newcastle-upon-Tyne.

3. To throw up the head and draw in the chin, (as a horse does when reined in), expressing pride, vanity, or resentment; to assume a dignified or offended air or manner:

a. *trans.* and *refl.*

c **1480** *Ragman Roll* 129 in Hazl. *E.P.P.* 75 Ful feire brydelyn ye your cowntenaunce, And propirly unto the brest adowne. **1606** DAY *Ile of Gulls* II. iv. (1881) 52 Then doe I bridle my head like a malt-horse. **1752** FIELDING *Amelia* Wks. (1775) X. 303 'Is she,' said my aunt, bridling herself, 'fit to decide between us?' **1848** A. BRONTË *Tenant Wildf. Hall* I. iv. 71 She bridled her long neck and smiled.

b. *intr.* (See BRIDLING *vbl. sb.* 3.)

c **1460** J. RUSSELL *Bk. Nurture* in *Babees Bk.* (1868) 135 Brydelynge with brest vppon your crawe. *c* **1550** *Jack Juggler* in Hazl. *Dodsley* II. 117 She minceth, she bridleth, she swimmeth to and fro. **1706** *Reflex. upon Ridicule*, 89 Whenever you tell her she is handsom, she bridles. **1748** MRS. DEWES in *Mrs. Delaney's Corr.* (1861) II. 485 Pauline ..bridles very well. **1807** OPIE *Lect. Art* IV. (1848) 330 Smirking damsels..flaunting and bridling in all the tawdry dresses and fashionable airs of the time. **1876** MISS BRADDON *J. Haggard's Dau.* II. 87 The spinsters bridled, taking this as in somewise a personal affront.

†**c.** Formerly also *to bridle it*. *Obs.*

1590 R. HARVEY *Pl. Perc.* 18 You shal haue a lame Iade, bridle, and brag it vp and downe Smithfield..as though hee could stand on no ground for lustines. **1624** BP. M. SMYTH *Serm.* 172 Shall we bridle it or bristle it against him?

d. Now commonly *to bridle up* (occas. *back*).

1748 SMOLLETT *Rod. Rand.* (1812) I. 343 She..bridled up, assumed an air of disdain. **1759** GOLDSM. *Bee* No. 5 *Reverie*, She instantly bridles up and feels the force of the well-timed flattery. **1760-2** —— *Cit. World* lxxvi, Sometimes she..would bridle back, in order to inspire us with respect as well as tenderness. **1840** DICKENS *Old C. Shop* (C.D. ed.) 19 Everybody bridled up at this remark.

†**e.** *to bridle upon* (a thing).

1748 RICHARDSON *Clarissa* (1811) II. xviii. 119, I can not indeed but say, bridling upon it, that I have heard famous scholars often and often say very silly things. **1754** —— *Grandison* IV. xv. 110 She took to herself, and bridled upon it, the praises and graces this adroit manager gave her.

4. *intr.* of a horse: to rise to or answer the bridle.

1929 *Daily Express* 5 Jan. 7/5 Mr. Wroughton's horse never bridled well at the fence... It slipped and brushed through the fence, hardly rising.

'bridle-'bit. The bit or mouth-piece of a bridle. Hence †**bridle-bitter**, a maker of bridle-bits.

[*c* **1440** *Promp. Parv.* 37 Bytt of a brydylle, *lupatum.*] *c* **1500** *Cocke Lorelles B.* (1843) 9 Brydel bytters, blacke smythes, and ferrars. **1535** COVERDALE *2 Kings* xix. 28 Therfore wyll I put a rynge in thy nose, and a brydle bytt in thy lippes. **1640** HABINGTON *Hist. Edw. IV*, 178 Able to buy the Spurres and Bridle-bits in his Campe. **1828-41** TYTLER *Hist. Scot.* (1864) I. 189 *note*, Amid a heap of chaff and dust, lay several human bones, along with a large and powerful bridle-bit.

bridled ('braɪd(ə)ld), *ppl. a.* [f. BRIDLE *v.* + -ED.] **1.** Furnished or equipped with a bridle, in various senses; curbed, restrained, controlled.

c **1385** CHAUCER *L.G.W.* 1112 Ther nas courser well ybridled none. *c* **1400** MAUNDEV. xxiii. 253 An hors sadeled and brydeled. *c* **1430** *Stans Puer ad M.* 33 in *Babees Bk.* (1868) 29 Drinke not bridelid for haste ne necligence. **1710** STEELE *Tatler* No. 196 ¶3 A bridled Rage. **1713** YOUNG *Last Day* I. 274 The bridled monsters awful distance keep. **1852** TUPPER *Proverb. Philos.* 193 His bridled steed.

2. In names of birds, having bridle-shaped markings.

1869 *Amer. Naturalist* III. 340 Dr. Gambel..bestowed upon it the title of the Bridled Tern (*S. frenata*). **1934** *Discovery* Oct. 293/1 The recent addition of six new birds to the British Isles,..and the Bridled or Lesser Sooty Tern (*Sterna anaethetus*)—by the Council of the British Ornithologists' Union. **1935** HUXLEY & HADDON *We Europeans* iii. 98 The normal and so-called bridled variety of the guillemot, which latter has a white spectacle mark round the eye.

bridleless ('braɪd(ə)llɪs), *a.* Also 5 **brydelesse**, **brydiless**, 6 **brideles.** [f. BRIDLE *sb.* + -LESS.] Without a bridle (said of the steed or rider); *fig.* unbridled, unchecked, unrestrained.

1406 OCCLEVE *Misrule* 78 Foorth ther with he renneth brydiless. **1555** PHILPOT *Apol.* in Strype *Eccl. Mem.* III. II. App. xlviii. 153 Ashamed of their brideles, blasphemous tongues. **1802** SOUTHEY *Thalaba* VI, Away went the bridleless steed. **1878** BOSW. SMITH *Carthage* 216 The bridleless Numidian cavalry.

bridler ('braɪdlə(r)). [f. BRIDLE *v.* + -ER¹.]

1. One who bridles, restrains, or controls.

1563-87 FOXE *A. & M.* (1596) 395/1 The greatest brideler of the popes usurped power. **1611** COTGR., *Bridoye*, a goose-bridler (a nickname for a Lawyer). **1641** MILTON *Ch. Govt.* vii. Wks. (1851) 135 The only bridlers of schisme. **1877** BLACKIE *Wise Men* 111 The tamer of tigers, the bridler of bears.

†**2.** A bridle-maker. *Obs. rare.*

1652 WADSWORTH tr. *Sandoval's Civ. Wars Spain* 330 Alonso de Vera, a bridler and one of the ..Citie officers.

bridle-rein ('braɪd(ə)l'reɪn). [f. BRIDLE *sb.* + REIN.] A strap or cord attached to the bit, and serving to guide or control the horse; a rein.

1382 WYCLIF *Ecclus.* xxxiii. 27 ȝoc and brydil reyne crooken the harde necke. **1552** HULOET, Brydle reine, *lorum.* **1820** SCOTT *Abbot* xxxvi, Who but Douglas ought to hold her bridle-rein? **1833** *Regul. Instr. Cavalry* I. 104 Carry the butt under the bridle-reins.

'bridle-wise, *a.* *U.S.* [BRIDLE *sb.* I.] Of a horse: readily guided by a touch of the bridle. Also *transf.*

1840 *Picayune* (New Orleans) 6 Oct. 2 The horse was not fit for a lady to ride; he was not *bridle wise.* **1898** H. S. CANFIELD *Maid of Frontier* 100 Just like a woman. You can't never make 'em bridle-wise. **1921** *Chambers's Jrnl.* Oct. 629/1 Quick-step..was the smartest and most bridle-wise pony that ever went on shoes.

Hence **'bridle-,wisdom.**

1895 *Outing* (U.S.) XXVI. 477/1 Not that in the heat of play one relies upon this bridle-wisdom.

bridling ('braɪdlɪŋ), *vbl. sb.* [f. BRIDLE *v.*]

1. The applying of a bridle; curbing, restraining, controlling. †*bridling cast*: a stirrup glass.

c **1450** *Chaucer's Dreme* 272 The bridling hire hors. **1513** MORE *Rich. III* (1641) 220 The brideling and punishing of such as there had misgoverned themselves. **1609** BEAUM. & FL. *Scornf. Lady* II. 69 Let's have a bridling cast before you go. Fill's a new stoupe. **1684** tr. *Bonet's Merc. Compit.* III. 94 The bridling the fury of the humours. **1817** G. S. FABER *Eight Dissert.* (1845) II. 283 For the purpose of bridling the apprehended refractoriness of subjects. **1833** *Regul. Instr. Cavalry* I. 42 *Bridling*, the Bridoon touching the corners of the mouth.

2. The forming of a 'bridle' to a net.

c **1838** C. BATHURST *Nets* 34 Bridling is done..on a spool a full quarter less in circumference than the one used in the body of the net.

3. The gesture mentioned in BRIDLE *v.* 3.

1709 *Tatler* No. 104 ¶1 By her bridling-up I perceived that she expected to be treated hereafter not as Jenny Distaff. **1861** *Mrs. Delaney's Corr.* II. 485 *note*, One of the first lessons in deportment..was to hold up the head on entering a room, and to keep the chin in, which is expressed by 'bridling'. **1851** HELPS *Comp. Solit.* vii. (1874) 122 Without any bridling-up or nonsense of any kind.

'bridling, *ppl. a.* [f. as prec. + -ING².] That bridles: in various senses of the verb.

1562 PHAËR *Æneid* x. Eej, Almighty mother of gods.. That..lions yolkst with brideling bittes. **1579** J. STUBBES *Gaping Gulf* Fij, The best brydle..to keepe in proude Fraunce, are the naturally brydeling bands of the sea. **1789** WORDSW. *Even. Walk* 180 He swells his lifted chest and backward flings His bridling neck. **1795** WOLCOTT (P. Pindar) *Pindariana* Wks. 1812 IV. 206 Thy bridling chin of scorn I see.

bridoon (brɪ'du:n), **bradoon** (brə'du:n). [a. F. *bridon* in same sense, deriv. of *bride* a bridle.]

1. 'The snaffle and rein of a military bridle, which acts independently of the bit, at the pleasure of the rider'. Stocqueler.

1753 CHAMBERS *Cycl. Supp.* s.v., A horse never goes so well nor sure with a bridoon, unless he have been first broke to the bit. **1801** W. FELTON *Carriages* II. 156 Harness is frequently made without breeching or bridoon. **1803** *Sporting Mag.* XXI. 220/2 A Weymouth bridle, with bit, and bradoon, is in my opinion, preferable to any other sort for the road. **1833** *Regul. Instr. Cavalry* I. 41 The use of the Bridoon, or Snaffle-Bridle. **1862** *Catal. Internat. Exhib.* II. No. 4693 Safety Springs, for riding and driving reins, to both bits, and one rein in hand, to act on the bradoon. **1968** *Encycl. Brit.* XI. 708/2 The snaffle (also bridoon or bradoon) ..may be jointed, twisted or straight.

2. *Comb.*, as *bridoon-bit*, *-bridle*, *-chain*, etc.

1801 W. FELTON *Carriages* II. 146 The *Bridoon Bit, an additional bit..with a ring at each end for the reins to be fastened to. *Ibid.* Gloss., **Bridoon Chain*, or *Links*, small ornaments, through which the bridoon reins run. *Ibid.* II. 141 The *Bridoon-Head, or Rein, is an additional bridle with a bearing-rein. **1856** J. GRANT *Black Drag.* xxxv, Every man..grasped the *bridoon rein near the ring.

bridulle, -dyl(le, obs. forms of BRIDLE.

Brie (bri:). Also **brie.** A kind of soft cheese made in *Brie*, an agricultural district in the north of France.

[**1848** THACKERAY *Van. Fair* li. 453 An assembly.. attended by the Duchess (Dowager) of Stilton, Duc de la Gruyère,..Marchese Alessandro Strachino, Comte de Brie.] **1876** *Encycl. Brit.* V. 456 The principal kinds of cheese at present known in commerce... Camembert, Parmesan, Gruyère, Brie, Roquefort [etc.]. **1951** M. KENNEDY *Lucy Carmichael* VI. i. 276 Wives..took the bus to Fenswick in search of *brie*, because Mrs. Beauclerc had discovered a shop there which stocked imported cheeses.

briech, obs. form of BREECH.

brief (bri:f), *sb.* Forms: 3-5 **bref**, 4-5 **brefe**, 4, 7 **breef**, 5 **breyfe**, 6-7 **breefe**, **briefe**, 7 **breif**, *Sc.* **brife**, 6- **brief.** [ME. *bref*, a. OF. *bref* (12th c. *brief*):—L. *breve* 'letter, dispatch, note', in late cl. L. 'short catalogue, summary', neuter of *brevis* 'short'. From official Latin the word entered at an early period into all the Teutonic langs. Cf. ON. *bréf* (found *c* 1015), Sw. *bref*, Da. *brev*, OS., OFris. *brêf* (Du. *brief*), OHG. *briof* (9th c.; MHG., mod.G. *brief*); but it is not recorded in OE., and appears to have entered early ME. from French. Here also it has remained more distinctly an official or legal word, and has not the general sense 'letter', which it has acquired in continental Teutonic.]

Of uncertain sense:

a **1225** *Ancr. R.* 122 *note* (MS. C.) To settin wordis o bref.

I. A letter of authority.

†**1.** A writing issued by official or legal authority; a royal letter or mandate; a writ, a summons. (Translating L. *breve* and AFr. *bref* in various legal meanings.) *Obs.*

[**1292** BRITTON I. i. §4 Solum ceo qe nous les maunderoms par nos brefs [as we shall authorize by our writs]. **1330** R. BRUNNE *Chron.* 237 Edward sent his brefe to Leulyn for his land. *c* **1425** *Seven Sag.* (P.) 3203 Over alle hys lond hys bref was sente To ase[m]len a comuyn parlyment. **1621** ELSING *Debates Ho. Lords* (1870) App. 133 A breefe touching gold and silver thred read. **1641** *Termes de la Ley* 43 Briefe signifies..the proces that issues out of the Chauncery or other Courts, commanding the Sherife to summon or attach *A.* to answer to the suit of *B.* etc., but more largely it is taken for any precept of the King in writing under seale, issuing out of any Court. **1882** GUNTON in *Macm. Mag.* XLV. 450 In 1533, he was made Clerk of the Briefs in the Star Chamber.

2. A letter of the pope to an individual or a religious community upon matters of discipline. It differs from a *bull* in being less ample and solemn, and in the form in which it is written. More fully called *apostolical* or *papal brief*.

c **1460** *Towneley Myst.* 127 *Nuncius*, And, lo sirs, if ye trow not me Ye rede this brefe. **1579** FENTON *Guicciard.* (1618) 30 The Pope..reenioyned him eftsoones by another Briefe, the selfe same things. **1606** *True & Perf. Relat.* Y iv a, The receiuing of two Brieues or Bulls from the Pope. **1710** *Lond. Gaz.* No. 4678/1 The Pope has at last given the Brief of the Cruciata to the King of Spain. **1850** MRS. JAMESON *Leg. Monast. Ord.* (1863) 361 Dominick, armed with the papal brief, hastened thither. **1868** W. CARTWRIGHT in *News of World* 29 Mar., A Brief..has but the Pope's name at the

beginning—'Pius Papa IX.'—is signed by the Cardinal Secretary of Briefs, bears date from the Nativity, and is written in modern letters upon soft white parchment.

†**b.** A letter of credentials given to mendicant friars and the like. *Obs.*

1377 LANGL. *P. Pl.* B. xx. 325 The Frere..cam..to þe bisshop & his brief [C. XXIII. 327 breef] hadde In contrees þere he come in confessiouns to here.

c. *dial.* A begging petition.

1764 J. COLLIER (T. Bobbin) *Let. to R.W.* in Wks. (1862) Introd. 23 Pray advise..whether, I should not have a brief [on the death of a mare]. **1879** MISS JACKSON *Shropshire Word-bk.* (E.D.S.) *Brief*, a writing setting forth the circumstances by which a poor person has incurred loss, as by fire, the death of a horse, cow, etc. Such a one takes the brief about to collect money for his indemnification.

3. A letter patent issued by the sovereign as Head of the Church, licensing a collection in the churches throughout England for a specified object of charity; called also a *Church Brief* or *King's Letter*. *Obs.* in practice.

1588 *Marprel. Epist.* 33 Spent thirteene score pounds in distributing briefes for a gathering towards the erecting of a Colledge. **1661** PEPYS *Diary* 30 June, To church, where we observe the trade of briefs is come now up to so constant a course every Sunday, that we resolve to give no more to them. **1781** COWPER *Charity* 469 The brief proclaimed, it visits every pew, But first the squire's, a compliment but due. **1820** SOUTHEY *Lett.* (1856) III. 193 A wooden thing.. such as the churchwardens carry about in the church to collect money for a brief. **1836** *Penny Cycl.* V. 420/2 A brief was issued, in 1835, to increase the funds of the 'Society for the propagation of the Gospel in foreign parts'.

II. 4. †**a.** A letter, dispatch, note. *Obs.*

c **1400** *Destr. Troy* 794 And þan ho broght hym a bref all of brode letres, þat was comly by crafte a clerke for to rede. **1572** GASCOIGNE *Fruites of Warre* (1831) 214 She sent a brief vnto me by hir mayde. **1596** SHAKS. *1 Hen. IV*, IV. iv. 1 Hie, good Sir Michell, beare this sealed Briefe With..haste, to the lord mareshal **1652** C. STAPYLTON *Herodian* XVII. 144 When this Briefe was to the Persians born They..flatly doe their message hold in scorn.

†**b.** Writing, something written. *Obs.*

c **1450** LONELICH *Grail* xxxi. 265 And the Brefis that on the schipe weren set, Signefieth holy Scripture with-owten let. **1786** BURNS *Answ. Poet. Epist.* iii, King David, o' poetic brief, Wrocht 'mang the lasses sic mischief.

c. In various slang uses (see quots.).

1860 HOTTEN *Dict. Slang* (ed. 2) 105 *Brief*, a pawnbroker's duplicate. **1874** *Ibid.* (ed. 4) 97 *Brief*,..a raffle card, or a ticket of any kind. **1879** *Macmillan's Mag.* XL. 501/2, I.. took a brief (ticket) to London Bridge. **1889** BARRÈRE & LELAND *Dict. Slang* I. 180/1 *Brief* (prison), a note or letter. .. (Thieves), a ticket, pocket-book, pawnbroker's duplicate. **1939** H. HODGE *Cab, Sir?* xv. 217 It [*sc.* a cab-driver's licence] is also called the 'brief'. **1962** *John o' London's* 25 Jan. 82/2 A policeman's warrant card is his *brief*.

III. Something abbreviated.

†**5.** A short statement or account of something that is, or might be, more fully treated; an abridgement, epitome, abstract, summary. *Obs.*

1563 MAN *Musculus' Comm-pl.* 34b, A certain brief of those commaundementes [*summa quædam eorum præceptorum*]. **1589** NASHE *Anat. Absurditie* 5 A suruey of their follie, a briefe of their barbarisme. **1645** PAGITT *Heresiogr.* (1647) B iiij b, The Creed being a brief of the Gospel. **1691** T. H[ALE] *Acc. New Invent.* 86 A Brief of the Controversie.

†**b.** *fig.*

1595 SHAKS. *John* II. i. 103 The hand of time, Shall draw this breefe into as huge a volume. *a* **1613** OVERBURY *A Wife* (1638) 44 Each woman is a briefe of Womankind.

†**c.** *abstr.* Small compass; reduced size.

1572 GASCOIGNE *Fruites of Warre* cxci, Brought into such brief.

†**d.** A device, a motto.

1594 NASHE *Unfort. Trav.* 52 With this briefe, *Qui inuident egent*.

†**6.** A list, catalogue; an invoice, memorandum.

1590 SHAKS. *Mids. N.* v. i. 42 There is a breefe how many sports are rife. **1601** F. TATE *Househ. Ord. Edw. II*, §10 (1876) 10 He shal make a breef everi day of the parcels of al manner of things delivered & spent. *Ibid.* §47. 28 Therof aunswere daily at the briefs to the clarke of the botery. **1753** CHAMBERS *Cycl. Supp.* s.v., Briefs of the dead, *Brevia mortuorum*, were letters sent by the monks of one monastery to those of another..to inform them of the deaths or obits of their monks. **1849** ROCK *Ch. of Fathers* II. vii. 380 The Death-bill, called by some the Mortuary-Roll or Brief.

7. a. *Law.* A summary of the facts of a case, with reference to the points of law supposed to be applicable to them, drawn up for the instruction of counsel conducting the case in court. *to hold a brief*: to be retained as counsel in a case, to argue a point *for*; also *fig.* in phr. *to hold a brief for* (a person): to express oneself like an advocate rather than an unbiased and critical appraiser; freq. in neg. *to hold no brief for*: to be no advocate or supporter of; *to take a brief*: to accept the conduct of a case.

1631 *Star Chamber Cases* (1886) 39 To print or write breifes of a cause before the hearing..is to be accounted scandalous. **1709** STEELE *Tatler* No. 186 ¶3 The young Fellow..seemed to hold his Brief in his Hand rather to help his Action. **1795** GIBBON *Autobiog.* 108, I spoke as a lawyer from my brief. **1826** DISRAELI *Viv. Grey* III. viii. 128 It is the first day of the Assize, so there is some chance of a brief. **1869** SEELEY *Ess. & Lect.* I. 7 Ready as Cicero showed himself to take..a brief..from accused and guilty governors. **1888** M. ARNOLD in *19th Cent.* Jan. 24 Professor Dowden holds a brief for Shelley; he pleads for Shelley as an advocate pleads for his client. **1918** R. A. KNOX *Spiritual Aeneid* 215 When I was at Balliol, we used to adapt the phrase 'I hold no brief for So-and-so'.

b. = BRIEFING *vbl. sb.* 2.

1856 W. BAGEHOT in *National Rev.* III. 164 The calling of a constitutional statesman is very much that of a political advocate; he receives a new brief with the changing circumstances of each successive day. **1940** *Sphere* 10 Aug. 164 The pilots and navigators receive their 'briefs'. **1940** *Times* 22 Aug. 5/6 (*heading*) The 'Brief' For A Long Journey and Distant Target. **1949** *Economist* 27 Aug. 465/1 The last touches have been put to the brief which Sir Stafford Cripps and Mr Ernest Bevin will be taking with them for the Washington financial talks.

c. (See quot.) Cf. *brief-paper* (sense 11).

1923 H. A. MADDOX *Dict. Stationery* 15 *Brief*, (1) A standard size of legal bags or envelopes measuring 14 in. by 5 in. (2) A legal pattern of ruled or watermarked foolscap comprising 36 or 42 feint lines and a marginal line.

IV. Something brief or short.

†**8.** *Music.* A short note; = BREVE *sb.* 2. *Obs.*

c **1460** *Towneley Myst.* 116 What was his song? hard ye not how he crakyd it? Three brefes to a long. **1594** BARNFIELD *Sheph. Cont.* iii, No Briefes nor Semi-Briefes are in my Songs. **1609** DOULAND *Ornithop. Microl.* 39 A Breefe is a Figure which hath a body foure-square, and wants a tayle. **1658** COKAINE *Fun. Elegie on T. Pilkington*, His life..Death made it be a Briefe; Crotchets he had good store.

†**9.** *Gram.* A short syllable, = BREVE *sb.* 3. *Obs.*

c **1530** H. RHODES *Bk. Nurture* in *Babees Bk.* (1868) 71 Corrupt in speeche am I, my breefes from longes to know.

†**10.** *Cards.* A means of cheating at cards. *Obs.*

1680 COTTON in Singer *Hist. Cards* 339 The breef..Take a pack of cards and open them; then take out all the honours ..then take the rest and cut a little from the edges of them all alike, by which means the honours will be broader than the rest, so that when your adversary cuts to you, you are certain of an honour; when you cut to your adversary cut at the ends.

11. *Comb.*, as ***brief-fed*** adj.; ***brief-paper***; **brief-bag**, the blue or red bag in which a barrister carries his briefs to and from court; **brief-case**, a small case made of leather, etc., for carrying papers, documents, and the like; **brief-money**, money collected under authority of a brief.

1848 *Punch* XV. 190/1 If my *brief-bag is clear, so is my conscience. **1910** *Encycl. Brit.* IV. 562/1 English brief-bags are now either blue or red. Blue bags are those with which barristers provide themselves when first called, and it is a breach of etiquette to let this bag be visible in court. The only brief-bag allowed to be placed on the desks is the red bag, which by English legal etiquette is given by a leading counsel to a junior who has been useful to him in some important case. **1926** *Amer. Speech* I. 444/1 'Why don't you rest to-night?'..'The why is in my *briefcase.' **1954** T. S. ELIOT *Confid. Clerk* I. 15 Enter Colby Simpkins with brief case. **1967** S. BECKETT *Film* 36 He drops briefcase. **1820** T. MITCHELL *Aristoph.* I. 92 The *brief-fed spark..In haste uprises to display his powers of wit and story. **1686** LADY RUSSELL *Lett.* I. xxxiv. 88 The disposers of the *brief-money met the first time yesterday. **1796** *Archæologia* XII. 116 *Brief paper, even and thin, but yellow with age.

12. *pl.* Very short knickers (see KNICKER[2]), or trunks.

1934 *Books of To-Day* Nov. 10/1 I'm bored to tears with 'scanties', I'm sick to death of 'briefs'. **1959** 'M. NEVILLE' *Sweet Night for Murder* iii. 40 Cathy, in minute briefs and bra, struggling into her dress. **1968** J. IRONSIDE *Fashion Alphabet* 66 *Briefs*, snugly fitting panties with straight leg and crutch.

brief (briːf), *a.*, quasi-*sb.* and *adv.* Forms: 4–6 bref, breff, brefe, 5–6 bryef, breve, breue, breyf(fe, 6–7 breefe, briefe, 7 breif(e, 6– brief. [ME. *bref*, a. OF. *bref*, fem. *breve* (= Pr., Cat. *breu*, It., Sp., Pg. *breve*):—L. *brevem*, nom. *brevis*, short. The vowel has been lengthened in Eng., as in *chief*, *relief*, etc.]

A. *adj.* **1.** Of short duration, quickly passing away or ending.

c **1325** *E.E. Allit. P.* A. 268, & busyez þe aboute a raysoun bref. *c* **1400** *Beryn* 871 Goith hymselff a begging aftir in breff tyme. **1603** SHAKS. *Meas. for M.* II. ii. 118 Man, proud man, Drest in a little briefe authoritie. **1605** —— *Macb.* v. v. 23 Out, out, breefe Candle, Life's but a walking Shadow. **1828** CARLYLE *Misc.* (1857) I. 231 Some brief pure moments of poetic life. **1847** TENNYSON *Princ.* iv. 43 O tell her, brief is life but love is long, And brief the sun of summer in the North, And brief the moon of beauty in the South.

†**b.** *to be brief*: to be expeditious or hasty. *Obs.*

1606 SHAKS. *Tr. & Cr.* IV. v. 237 *Achil.* Behold thy fill. *Hect.* Nay, I haue done already. *Achil.* Thou art to breefe.

2. Occupying short time in speaking or reading; consisting of few words, short, concise.

c **1380** WYCLIF *Wicket* Argument, A verye brefe diffinition of these wordes. *c* **1430** *Hymns Virg.* (1867) 55 Ihesu spak wiþ wordis breue. **1494** FABYAN II. xxxv. 26 The more partie of wryters reherce in most breuest or shortest maner. **1547** *Act 1 Edw. VI*, iii. §16 The Curate [shall]..make..a godly and briefe exhortation. **1602** SHAKS. *Ham.* II. ii. 548 The Abstracts and breefe Chronicles of the time. *a* **1680** BUTLER *Rem.* (1759) I. 263 So 'tis in Books the chief Of all Perfections to be plain and brief. **1725** DE FOE *Voy. round World* (1840) 311, I shall give a brief account of it all. **1840** CARLYLE *Heroes* vi. 322 As the briefest definition, one might say, etc.

b. *to be brief*: to speak concisely.

1588 FRAUNCE *Lawiers Log.* I. iv. 27 As if a man, meaning to be brief, should promise that he would gallop over al the rest of his text. **1644** MILTON *Educ.* (1738) 135 Brief I shall endeavour to be. **1762–71** H. WALPOLE *Vertue's Anecd. Paint.* (1786) II. 135, I shall be but brief on the circumstances of his life.

c. Curt or abrupt in manner. *rare.*

1818 SCOTT *Hrt. Midl.* xliv, The bearing of the gracious Duncan was brief, bluff, and consequential.

3. Less usually of extent in space: Short, curtailed, limited. (Cf. 1605 in sense 1.)

1668 CULPEPPER & COLE *Barthol. Anat.* II. vi. 97 Contracting the whole Heart in a brief manner. **1824** SCOTT *St. Ronan's* vi, Wearing the briefest petticoat of any nymph of St. Ronan's. **1863** HAWTHORNE *Old Home, Leamington Spa*, A small play-place..permeated by brief paths.

†**4.** *fig.* Limited, slight, restricted. *Obs.*

1432–50 tr. *Higden* (1865) I. 71 Some men of pover and breve intellecte. **1611** SHAKS. *Cymb.* v. v. 165 Postures, beyond breefe Nature.

¶**5.** Rife; common; prevalent: often used of epidemic diseases. *dial.* (The origin of this sense is not clear: the Shaksp. quot. is generally cited as an example, but is by no means certain.)

[**1595** SHAKS. *John* IV. iii. 158 A thousand businesses are briefe in hand, And heauen it selfe doth frowne vpon the Land.] **1706** PHILLIPS, *Brief*, rife, or common. **1721–1800** BAILEY, *Brief*, common, or rife. **1848–60** BARTLETT *Dict. Amer.*, *Brief*, rife, common, prevalent. This word is..much used by the uneducated in the interior of New England and in Virginia, when speaking of epidemic diseases. **1879** *Shropsh. Gloss.*, *Brief*, prevalent, general. **1881** *Leicester Gloss.* (E.D.S.) s.v. 'Colds are very brief this east wind.'

B. quasi-*sb.*

a. *in brief*: in few words, shortly, concisely. With ellipsis of 'to speak': In short, to sum up.

1423 JAS. I *King's Q.* cxxvii, Off quhich ryght thus hir ansuere was in bref. **1595** SHAKS. *John* II. i. 267 In breefe, we are the King of Englands subjects. **1609** D. ROGERS *Harl. MS.* 1944 lf. 22 A man..published..the matter of yᵉ playes in breife. **1667** MILTON *P.L.* VI. 171 To whom in brief thus Abdiel stern repli'd. **1800–24** CAMPBELL *Cherubs* 29 Ay, and a cut-throat too;—in brief, The greatest scoundrel living. **1833** HT. MARTINEAU *Fr. Wines & Pol.* ii. 21 Charles gave in brief the story of the storm.

†**b.** *the brief*, used *absol.* like *the short*. *Obs.*

1599 SHAKS. *Hen. V*, III. ii. 126 That's the breff and the long. **1601** —— *All's Well* II. iii. 34 'Tis very straunge, that is the breefe and the tedious of it. **1601** BP. BARLOW *Serm. Paules Crosse* 48 The chiefe, and the briefe is this.

C. quasi-*adv.* **a.** Shortly, quickly; in few words, concisely. **b.** In brief.

1557 NORTH *Gueuara's Diall Pr.* (1582) 79b, In this sort I should write vnto thee briefe and touching the purpose. **1592** SHAKS. *Rom. & Jul.* III. iii. 174 It were a griefe, so brief to part with thee. **1667** MILTON *P.L.* IV. 876 Those two approached And brief related whom they brought.

b. 1600 SHAKS. *A.Y.L.* IV. iii. 151 Briefe, I recouer'd him. **1855** BROWNING *Fra Lippo*, Brief, they made a monk of me.

†**brief**, *v.*[1] *Obs.* [f. BRIEF *a.*] *trans.* To shorten, abbreviate, abridge; also with *up*.

1601 R. JOHNSON *Kingd. & Commw.* Ded. ii, Compendiousnes in briefing such varietie of matter to so small a volume. *a* **1655** T. ADAMS *Wks.* (1862) II. 135 (D.) Both thy latitude and extension are briefed up.

brief (briːf), *v.*[2] [f. BRIEF *sb.*, sense 7.]

1. *trans.* To reduce to the form of a counsel's brief.

1837 RICHARDSON s.v., It is common among English lawyers as, to brief the pleadings.

2. To put (instructions) into the form of a brief *to* a barrister. Also *fig.*

1864 G. DYCE *Bella Donna* I. 304 Being 'briefed' to Maxwell, they all fell into one common mould. **1872** LEVER *Ld. Kilgobbin* lxxiii. (1875) 397 Instructions which were briefed to him in the case.

3. a. To give a brief to (a barrister), to instruct by brief; to retain as counsel in a suit.

1862 TROLLOPE *Orley F.*, I never could look a counsel in the face again if I'd neglected to brief him with such facts as these. **1882** *Pall Mall G.* 5 Apr. 2/2 Should his master be briefed in more than one court at the same time. **1883** *Times* 12 Dec. 4 The company have briefed many of the leading men at the Bar in this case.

b. To give instructions or information to. Cf. BRIEFING *vbl. sb.* 2.

1866 LEVER *Sir B. Fossbrooke* xliv, They had not been well 'briefed', as lawyers say, or they had not mastered their instructions. **1940** *Times* 22 Aug. 5/6 These calm young men are being 'briefed' for a dangerous task. **1955** *Bull. Atomic Sci.* Apr. 119/3 Dr. McNair went to the Strategic Air Command Headquarters in Omaha to brief selected top staff officers on the results of his study. **1959** A. LEJEUNE *Crowded & Dangerous* x. 113 He handed them over to the secret police and was briefed for another job.

briefing ('briːfɪŋ), *vbl. sb.* [f. BRIEF *v.*[2] + -ING[1].]

1. The action of writing briefs. Also *attrib.*, as in ***briefing-post***, a sort of paper used for briefs.

1865 LE FANU *Guy Dev.* II. xx. 211 The paper, with its bluish briefing-post pages, and broad margin. **1869** *Daily News* 14 Aug., [Medical men] who..certify excellent briefing injuries for the use of the plaintiff's advocate.

2. The action of giving information or instructions relating to a particular situation; information of this kind. Also *attrib.*

Applied esp., in the war of 1939–45 and since, to pre-flight conferences.

1910 H. BELLOC *Pongo & Bull* ix. 133 The House'll be full... You don't want Eddie to give you any briefing, do you? **1940** *Times* 22 Aug. 5/6 Everything is ready for the 'briefing' which forms an indispensable part of every bombing raid. **1942** *Penguin New Writing* XIII. 27 His name, and the names of his crew, were quietly erased from the blackboard in the briefing-room. **1942** T. RATTIGAN *Flare Path* I. 113 Take-off 22.00. Briefing 19.45. **1942** R. STORRS in E. Kennington *Drawing the R.A.F.* 31 The precise but detached tones of the Briefing Officer. **1949** 'J. TEY' *Brat Farrar* vi. 47 It had been a wonderful briefing. For a whole fortnight..they had..rehearsed..the lie of a land he had never seen.

briefless ('bri:flɪs), *a.* [f. BRIEF *sb.*, sense 7 + -LESS.] Without a brief; (a barrister) holding no briefs, unemployed.

1824 SCOTT *St. Ronan's*, The broad shoulders of a briefless barrister. **1840** MARRYAT *Olla Podr.* (1866) 267 Arthur Ansard at a briefless table. **1860** DICKENS *Uncomm. Trav.* xiv, A few briefless bipeds..called to the Bar by voices of deceiving spirits.

Hence **'brieflessly** *adv.*, **'brieflessness**.

1842 *Punch* III. 106 The dreary ghost of brieflessness Stalk'd up and down the room. **1864** *Cornh. Mag.* Dec. 682 He often has to pass long years of brieflessness.

briefly ('bri:flɪ), *adv.* [f. BRIEF *a.* + -LY².]

1. In a way or form that occupies short time; in few words, shortly, concisely, tersely.

a **1300** *Cursor M.* 120, I sal yow schew wit myn entent, Bre[fl]i [*Fairf.* shortly] of aiþere testament. **1398** TREVISA *Barth. De P.R.* III. (1495) 48 In the forsayd bokys we haue brought in breyfly somm propryttees of bodylesse substaunce. **1494** FABYAN II. xlv. 29 Guydo..reherceth moste breuely the passe tyme of the sayd kyngs. **1502** *Ord. Crysten Men* (W. de W.) II. ii. (1506) 87 Conteynynge yᵉ .x. commaundementes ryght bryefly, ryght clerely, right easely. **1559** *Mirr. Mag., Dk. Clarence* iii, I will declare as briefly as I may. **1681** BAXTER *Acc. Sherlocke* v. 193 The judgment.. I cannot better and brieflier give you, than in the words of the Preface. **1855** MAURY *Phys. Geog. Sea* xix. §794 Such, briefly stated, are the two theories.

b. Often with ellipsis of 'to speak': In short.

1514 BARCLAY *Cyt. & Uplondyshm.* (1847) Introd. 70 Briefely, all people of good behavour. **1598** SHAKS. *Merry W.* I. iii. 47 Briefely: I doe meane to make loue to Fords wife. **1611** BIBLE *Pref.* 1 Briefly..we sooner compose our differences.

†**2.** Within a short time (measured either backward or forward); soon. *Obs.*

c **1340** *Cursor M.* 18199 (Fairf.) Tho that so breuely were doune-cast. ?*c* **1475** *Sqr. lowe Degre* 873 The kyng him graunted ther to go Upon his jorney to and fro, And brefely to passe the sea. **1606** SHAKS. *Ant. & Cl.* IV. iv. 10 *Ant.* Go, put on thy defences. *Eros.* Briefely Sir. **1607** —— *Cor.* I. vi. 16 'Tis not a mile: briefely we heard their drummes. **1611** —— *Cymb.* V. v. 106 Briefely dye their ioyes, that place them on the truth of Gyrles, and Boyes.

†**3.** In an abridged form, in brief. *Obs.*

c **1460–70** *Bk. Quintessence* 1 A treatise in Englisch brevely drawe out of þe book of quintis essenciis. **1551** (*title*) The newe greate abredgement brefly conteynynge al thactes and statutes of this Realme.

†**4.** With short (prosodic) quantity. *Obs.*

c **1500** *Partenay* 6582 Als the frensh staffes silabled be More breueloker and shorter also Then is the english lines vnto see.

'briefman. [f. BRIEF *sb.* 7 + MAN.] **a.** One who makes a brief. **b.** A copier of a manuscript.

1846 in WORCESTER; and other mod. Dicts.

briefness ('bri:fnɪs). [f. BRIEF *a.* + -NESS.]

†**1.** The quality or state of being brief: shortness (of time); *hence*, quickness, celerity. ?*Obs.*

a **1400** *Cov. Myst.* 79 We passe ovyr that, breffnes of tyme consyderynge. **1539** TONSTALL *Serm. Palm Sund.* (1823) 75 For brefenes of tyme I shal omytte to reherse them. **1605** SHAKS. *Lear* II. i. 20 Briefenesse, and Fortune worke. **1608** —— *Per.* V. ii. 15 In feather'd briefness sails are filled.

2. Shortness in speech or writing; brevity; conciseness.

1530 PALSGR. 58 The brefnesse that the frenche tong useth in soundyng of theyr wordes. **1548** UDALL *Erasm. Par. Luke* Pref. 8 For loue of briefnesse. **1569** GOLDING *Heminge's Post.* 3 For breefnesse sake I omit. **1618** BOLTON *Florus* 46 To Rdr., A most exact, and studied method of briefnesse. **1811** *Edin. Rev.* XVIII. 287 A style..characterised by a studied briefness and simplicity of diction.

brier, briar (braɪə(r), 'braɪə(r)), **brere** (brɪə(r)), *sb.*¹ Forms: 1 brǽr, brér, 2–3 brer, 3–9 brere, 4–5 breyer, 4–8 breere, 5–7 breer, 5 breyr, 6 breare, breir, 6–7 bryer, 6–8 bryar, 6– brier, briar. [OE.: WS. *brǽr*, Angl. *brér*, of unknown origin. The direct representative of the OE. and ME. word is *brere*, still usual in the dialects, and retained by the poets from Chaucer and Spenser. The rise of the variant *brier* in the 16th c. is not easy to account for, especially as the spelling *bryer* shows that this never rimed with *bier*, *tier*, but with *dyer*, *crier*. But the phonetic change was exactly parallel to, and contemporaneous with that of ME. *frere*, *freyre*, to *fryer*, *frier*, FRIAR. *Briar* is a later variant (cf. *lier*, *liar*), and is now equally common. The word is historically a monosyllable, but poets have often made two syllables of it, a pronunciation supported by the spelling *briar*.]

1. A prickly, thorny bush or shrub in general; formerly including the bramble, but now usually confined to wild rose bushes.

α. Form *brere* (*breer*, *brear*).

c **1000** *Ags. Voc.* in Wr.-Wülcker 269 *Tribulus*, bræmbelbrær. *c* **1000** *Saxon Leechd.* II. 96 Brer þe hioran on weaxaþ. *a* **1225** *Ancr. R.* 276 Breres bereð rosen, & berien. **1297** R. GLOUC. 331 As þe rose spryng of þe brer. *c* **1350** *Will. Palerne* 1809 Blake-beries þat on breres growen. *c* **1386** CHAUCER *Knts. T.* 674 Doun in the breres. **1398** TREVISA *Barth. De P.R.* XVII. clii. (1495) 704 An hegge..of breers, of thornes, and trees made. *c* **1440** *Promp. Parv.* 49 Brere, or brymmeylle. **1525–30** MORE *De Quat. Noviss.* Wks. 74/2 Foregrowen with nettels, breers, and other euil weedes. **1562** TURNER *Herbal* II. 119 The fruite of the brere called an Hep. **1595** SPENSER *Sonn.* xxvi, Sweet is the Rose, but growes upon a brere. **1596** —— *F.Q.* I. x. 35 Ragged breares. **1597** BP. HALL *Sat.* VI. i, A pipe of oat or breare. **1613** W. BROWNE *Brit. Past.* II. i. (1772) II. 32 'Mong roots, and breers, and thorns. **1747** W. MASON *Musæus*, Ne bush, ne breere, but learnt thy roundelay. **1830** TENNYSON *Poems* 76 They..from the blosmy brere Call to the fleeting year. **1865** [see 2].

β. Form *brier* (*bryer*).

[?*a* **1400** *Chester Pl.* 74 A horned weither..Amonge the breyers tyed is he. *c* **1460** *Towneley Myst.* 12 Thystyls and breyr, yei grete plente.] **1545** BRINKLOW *Lament.* (1874) 92 Do briers bringe forth figges, and thorns grapes? **1579** E. K. in *Spenser's Sheph. Cal.* Feb., Argt., The Oake and the Bryer [**1597** brier]. **1611** BIBLE *Isa.* lv. 13 In stead of the brier shall come vp the Myrtle tree. **1653** HOLCROFT *Procopius* II. 54 Throwing him among Bryers. **1720** WATTS *Mor. Songs, Sluggard* 3, I passed by his garden, and saw the wild brier. **1776** ADAM SMITH *W.N.* I. II. v. 367 Over-grown with briers and brambles. **1822** BYRON *Werner* III. i. 159 The doubts that rise like briers in our path. **1847** TENNYSON *Princ.* v. 27, I was..torn with briers.

γ. Form *briar* (*bryar*).

1552 HULOET, Bryar..a lytle or yonge bryer. **1601** SHAKS. *All's Well* IV. iv. 32 Summer, When Briars shall haue leaues as well as thornes, And be as sweet as sharpe. **1711** ADDISON *Spect.* No. 56 ¶3 He walked through Briars and Brambles. **1810** SOUTHEY *Kehama* XIII. v, Nor weeds nor briars deform'd the natural floor. **1863** STANLEY *Jew. Ch.* xv. 349 The Briar, the Bramble, the Thorn that crept along the barren side of the mountain.

b. *techn.* The stock or stem of a wild rose, on which a garden rose is grafted.

1574 HELLOWES *Gueuara's Ep.* (1577) 125 Honour is ioyned to vertue as yᵉ bryer is to the rose. **1858** GLENNY *Gard. Everyday Bk.* 213/2 Roses worked on Briars are very apt to lose by the growth of the stock.

c. With qualifications: **sweet brier**, a species of wild rose (*R. rubiginosa*) with fragrant leaves and shoots; **Austrian brier** (*R. lutea*), a climbing yellow rose; also **green brier** (*Smilax rotundifolia*); **sensitive brier**, the genus *Schronkia*.

1596 SPENSER *F.Q.* III. xi. 36 A sweet breare. **1626** BACON *Sylva* §562 There is also upon Sweet, or other Bryer, a fine Tuft..of Moss. **1728** THOMSON *Spring* 105 The verdant maze Of sweet briar hedges. **1861** DELAMER *Fl. Gard.* 138 As yet, a double Austrian briar is a desideratum. **1882** *Garden* 27 May 373/1 Austrian Copper Brier is arranged in a low silver-gilt cup with small twigs of Sweet Brier.

2. Brier-bushes collectively.

c **1340** *Cursor M.* 924 (Fairf.) Brere [*Cott.* brembel] and þornes hit sal þe ʒilde. **1382** WYCLIF *Hosea* x. 8 Cloote and breere shal stye on the auters of hem. **1590** SHAKS. *Mids. N.* III. i. 110 Through bogge, through bush, through brake, through bryer. **1821** SHELLEY *Adonais* xviii, Build their mossy homes in field and brere. **1865** S. EVANS *Bro. Fabian's MS.* 59 They dolve a grave..And covered it with brere.

3. a. A branch or twig of a brier. †**b.** A thorn of a brier (*obs.*)

1393 LANGL. *P. Pl.* C. VII. 402 Hit hadde be wexed with a wips of breres. *a* **1400** *Rom. Rose* 858 Hir flesh so tendre, That with a brere smale and slendre Men myght it cleve. *a* **1674** CLARENDON *Hist. Reb.* (1702) I. Pref. 7 A Crown of Briers and Thorns. **1818** BYRON *Beppo* iv, Walk about begirt with briars.

4. *fig.* (*pl.*) Troubles, difficulties, vexations: in modern use with conscious reference to the literal sense. Hence † ***to leave in the briers*, *be in the briers*, *get out of the briers*** (all obs.).

1509 HAWES *Examp. Virt.* xiv. 298 Fatal brerys whiche be contrareyous. **1526** *Pilgr. Perf.* (W. de W. 1531) 12 b, The bryers and perylles of this worlde. **1563** FOXE *A. & M.* I. 208/1 Leaving the Bishops, and such others, in the Briers. **1575** CHURCHYARD *Chippes* (1817) 95 Now is hee free, that hapneth in the breares. **1625** SANDERSON *Serm.* (1681) I. 133 Helping a great offender out of the bryars. **1674** EARL KINCARDIN in *Lauderd. Papers* (1885) III. xlv. 75 Wee..were glade to get out of the briers at that rate. **1770** *Monthly Rev.* 35 The Netherlanders..had freed themselves from the Romish briars. **1794** BLAKE *Songs Exper., Gard. Love* 12 Priests..binding with briars my joys and desires.

5. *attrib.* and *Comb.*, as ***brier-ball*, *-berry*, *-bush*, *-flower*, *-leaf*, *-stalk***; †**brier-bell**, the bedeguar of the wild rose; **brier-coal**, ? charcoal made of twigs, etc.; †**brier-crook**, an implement for removing briers; **brier-rose**, **brier-tree**, the Dog-rose.

1694 W. WESTMACOTT *Script. Herb.* 30 *Briar-balls dried and powdered. **1728** BRADLEY *Dict. Bot.* s.v. *Cynosbatos*, This Rose is apt to bring now and then..a *Bryar-Bell, or a Spongiola, which is a Bunch of Threds, of a red Colour. **1626** BACON *Sylva* §577 The latest [Fruits] are..Grapes, Nuts, Quinces, Almonds, Sloes, *Brier-berries. **1562** TURNER *Herbal* II. 118 b, Of the *Brere bushe or Hep tre or Brere tre, *Rubus canis*. **1591** PERCIVALL *Sp. Dict.*, *Carçal*, a brier bush, *Rubetum*. **1626** BACON *Sylva* §775 Small-coal or *Briar-coal poured upon Char coal make them last longer. **1483** *Cath. Angl.* 43 A *Brerecruke, *falcastrum*. *c* **1325** *E.E. Allit. P.* B. 791 Of ble as þe *brere flour. **1766** WESLEY *Jrnl.* 17 Sept., Applying a *brier-leaf. **1810** SCOTT *Lady of L.* I. xi, The *brier-rose fell in streamers green. **1870** MORRIS *Earthly Par.* I. II. 481 The briar-rose, Rustling outside within the flowery close. **1882** *Garden* 10 June 411/3 Bouquets of pink Brier Roses. **1624** CAPT. SMITH *Virginia* I. 10 Bring forth a *bryer stalke.

brier, briar ('braɪə(r)), *sb.*² [Formerly *bruyer*, a. F. *bruyère* heath, erroneously identified with the prec. word.] The White Heath (*Erica arborea*), a native of the south of France, Corsica, etc., the root of which is extensively used for making tobacco-pipes (introduced into England about 1859); also a pipe of this wood. So **brier-root**, **brier-wood**; **brier-wooder** (*nonce-wd.*), a smoker of a brier pipe.

1868 *Tobacco Trade Rev.* Feb. 8 (*Advt.*) Health pipe: in Bruyer Wood. *Ibid.* Ap. 11 Joseph Izod, Importer of Meerschaum and Bruyer Pipes. *Ibid.* Brier Wood, Lava, Clay, and China Pipes. **1869** *Ibid.* Jan. 9 Briar Pipes. *Ibid.* Mch. 13 The substances used are meerschaum..briar-root. **1882** *Graphic* 16 Dec. 683/2 Nowadays, every third man you meet has a cigarette or a 'briar' in his mouth. **1884** MILLER *Plant-n.*, Briar Root of which Pipes are made. *Erica arborea.* **1885** M. E. BRADDON *Wyllard's Weird* i, He sat..lazily puffing at his black briarwood. **1886** *Harper's Mag.* Dec. 27 There is the ever-ready brier-root pipe loaded with Caporal. **1886** *Tinsley's Mag.* July 53 Yet I hope he is not vulgarer than the briar-wooders. *a* **1888** *Mod.* Do you really prefer a brier to a meerschaum? **1891** 'L. KEITH' *The Halletts* xxviii, Pass me the brier-root. **1909** *Daily Chron.* 23 July 3/3 A briar being his constant companion while writing.

†**brier**, *v. Obs. rare*⁻¹. In 7 bryre. [f. BRIER *sb.*¹] *trans.* To catch or annoy like briers.

1601 WEEVER *Mirr. Mart.* A v b, Some way..was knottie, othersome would bryre me.

briered, briared ('braɪəd), *ppl. a.* [f. BRIER *v.* or *sb.* + -ED.] Caught or entangled in briers; bound or covered with briers. Also *fig.*

a **1554** HOOPER in Spurgeon *Treas. Dav.* Ps. lxxvii. 20 As the shepherd is careful of his entangled and briered sheep. **1702** C. MATHER *Magn. Chr.* II. App. (1852) 183 New England was miserably briared in the perplexities of an Indian war. *a* **1823** BLOOMFIELD *Poems* (1845) 50 New-briar'd graves.

briery, briary ('braɪərɪ), *a.* [f. BRIER + -Y¹.]

1. Full of or consisting of thorns or briers; brambly, thorny.

1549 COVERDALE *Erasm. Par. James* 28 It taketh no rote in a briery place. **1581** STUDLEY *Seneca's Hippolytus* 64 Up and downe the breary Brakes. **1623** SIR J. BEAUMONT *Transfigur.* in Farr's *S.P.* (1848) 144 By steepe and briery paths ye must ascend. **1748** RICHARDSON *Clarissa* (1811) I. 223 Over briery enclosures. **1846** KEBLE *Lyra Innoc.* (1873) 154 Dews.. glist'ning clear, Thro' their brown or briery screen. **1876** BLACKMORE *Cripps* ii. 11 A briary thicket.

†**2.** Of or pertaining to briers. *Obs. rare.*

1593 NASHE *Christ's T.* (1613) 31 Her possessors neuer escape briery scratches.

3. *fig.* Of the nature of briers; vexing.

1604 T. WRIGHT *Passions* I. iii. 11 Those spinie braunches of briarie passions. **1648** EARL WESTMORELAND *Otia Sacra* (1879) 41 Choak'd with the Brierie Cares of this world. **1876** BANCROFT *Hist. U.S.* II. xxiii. 84 To go forth into the briery and brambly world.

†**briery, briary**, *sb. Obs.* [f. BRIER + -Y: see -ERY.] A place overgrown with briers.

1552 HULOET, Bryary or place where bryars growe. **1585** in *Academy* (1882) 25 Mar., Fifty acres of turbary, sixty acres of scrub and briery.

brieve (bri:v). *Scotch Law.* Also 7 breive, briefe, brife. [Another form of BRIEF *sb.*] A writ or precept issued from Chancery in the Sovereign's name, directing trial to be made of certain points specified.

Before the institution of the Court of Session (1532) a *breve* or *brieve* was the prescribed form of Summons issued for any cause; afterwards it was limited to the (Latin) Writ from Chancery addressed to the Judge Ordinary or Sheriff for trial by him and a jury of special questions in which the Court of Session had no original jurisdiction. These Brieves have all fallen into desuetude or been abolished by statute, except in one or two cases (e.g. in the appointment of a tutor-at-law to a minor), where also other forms of proceeding are now usually preferred.

1609 SKENE *Reg. Maj.* 87 Restis to speik of Brieves currant, quhilk are pleadable, that is the brieve of distres (or poynding) for debt, the Brieve of convention..The Brieve of Dissaisine. The Brieve of Protection, and breaking of the Kings peace. The Brieve of Bondage. The Brieve of Warandice. **1868** *Act 31–32 Vic.* c. §101 The brieves of furiosity and idiotry hitherto in use are hereby abolished.

brievement, var. of BREVEMENT. *Obs.*

brig (brɪg). Also 8 brigg. [Abbreviation of BRIGANTINE. Cf. *cab*, *mob*, *zoo.*, etc.] **1. a.** A vessel (*a*) originally identical with the *brigantine* (of which word *brig* was a colloquial abbreviation); but, while the full name has remained with the unchanged brigantine, the shortened name has accompanied the modifications which have subsequently been made in rig, so that a *brig* is now

(*b*) A vessel with two masts square-rigged like a ship's fore- and main-masts, but carrying also on her main-mast a lower fore-and-aft sail with a gaff and boom.

A brig differs from a *snow* in having no try-sail mast, and in lowering her gaff to furl the sail. Merchant snows are often called 'brigs'. This vessel was probably developed from the brigantine by the men-of-war brigs, so as to obtain greater sail-power.

1720 *Lond. Gaz.* No. 5848/4 The Ship Blessing, 50 Tuns Burthen, a Brigg..belonging to St. Ives in Cornwall. **1753** *Scots Mag.* Apr. 195/2 Two guarda costa brigs and a sloop of war. **1769** FALCONER *Dict. Marine* (1789) *Brig*, or *Brigantine*, a merchant ship with two masts..It is variously applied, by the mariners of different European nations, to a peculiar sort of vessel of their own marine. **1800** NELSON *Let.* 18 Feb. in Duncan *Life* (1806) 121 The El Corso brig. **1845** DARWIN *Voy. Nat.* i. 1 Her Majesty's ship Beagle, a

ten-gun brig..Sailed from Devonport. **1854** J. STEPHENS *Centr. Amer.* 2 Four ships, three brigs, sundry schooners.

(*c*) 'A hermaphrodite brig has a brig's foremast and a schooner's mainmast' (Dana *Bef. the Mast* 1840, Gloss.); = BRIGANTINE 3.

b. A place of detention, orig. on board a ship; a military or naval prison. *slang* (orig. *U.S.*).

1852 *Knickerbocker* XXXIX. 404 In less than a minute I was in the 'brig', in double irons. *Ibid.*, They call the place where prisoners are confined, 'the brig'. **1934** A. WOOLLCOTT *While Rome Burns* 13 Our dreamy old mess sergeant was even then languishing in the brig, awaiting trial. **1956** J. MASTERS *Bugles & Tiger* xxii. 293 My friends were hauled off to spend a day in the brig.

2. *Comb.* **'brig-rigged** *a.*, rigged as a brig; **brig-schooner**, a hermaphrodite brig, or brigantine (Smyth *Sailor's Word-bk.*).

1796 NELSON in Nicolas *Disp.* II. 177 Transports—La bonne Mère, two hundred and fifty tons, Brig-rigged.

brig, northern form of BRIDGE.

brigade (brɪˈgeɪd), *sb.* Forms: 7 brigada, -do, 7 briggad, 7–9 brigad, 7– brigade. [a. F. *brigade* (15th c.), ad. It. *brigata* 'company, crew, rout of good fellows' (Florio), f. *brigare* to brawl, wrangle, fight, f. late L. *briga* (It., Pr. *briga*, Fr. *brigue*) strife, contention. See -ADE. In 17th c. also in the form *brigada*, and improperly *brigado*: see -ADO. Milton accented *'brigad*, which has been followed by some later poets in the non-technical sense 2 a.]

†**1.** A company or 'crew' of people. *Obs.*

a **1649** DRUMM. OF HAWTH. *Hist. James V*, Wks. (1711) 199 Ye are such a brigade of papists, and antichristian crew. **1650** HOWELL *Revol. Naples* (1664) 117 All that huge Brigade of peeple.

2. a. *gen.* A large body or division of troops.

a **1649** DRUMM. OF HAWTH. *Hist. James V*, Wks. (1711) 91 He would..bring such war-like brigades of French and Germans. **1649** LILLY *Peculiar Prognost.* 6 Some motion of our Armies or stragling Brigadoes. **1667** MILTON *P.L.* I. 675 Thither wing'd with speed A numerous Brigad hasten'd. **1776** GIBBON *Decl. & F.* I. 16 The peace establishment of Hadrian..was composed of no less than thirty of these formidable brigades. **1855** SINGLETON *Virgil* II. 208 What kings by war Were roused, what brigads, following each, filled up The champaign.

b. *spec.* A subdivision of an army, consisting formerly of two regiments or squadrons; but the composition now varies in different countries. In the British Army, an infantry unit consisting usually of three battalions and forming part of a division, or a corresponding armoured unit (for some time the word was used only of a unit of artillery).

1637 MONRO *Exped. with Mackay's Regt.* II. 184 Twelve companies thus complete would make up three squadrons.. which..would make a complete briggad of foote. **1642** CHARLES I. in *Declar. Lords & Comm.* 19 May 31 A party.. who commanded a Brigado. **1645** CROMWELL *Lett. & Sp.* (Carl.) 14 Sept., Colonel Welden, with his brigade, marched to Pile Hill. **1702** *Lond. Gaz.* No. 3832/2 The Duke of Vendosme left..four Brigades of Foot near the place. **1855** MACAULAY *Hist. Eng.* III. 437 Marlborough, to whom William had confided an English brigade consisting of the best regiments of the old army of James. **1855** TENNYSON *Charge L. Brigade* i, 'Forward, the Light Brigade! Charge for the guns!' he said. **1886** *Whitaker's Alm.* 163 *Field Artillery*; 1st Brigade: Dépôt, Newcastle.

3. A band of persons more or less organized for purposes of fighting, hunting, etc.; also a disciplined band of workers wearing a uniform, e.g. *fire-brigade*, *shoe-black brigade*. ***boys' brigade***, an organization of the boys connected with a church or mission, for purposes of drill and instruction; begun in Glasgow in 1884.

1806 HUTTON *Course Math.* I. 219 *note*, A brigade of sappers consists generally of eight men, divided equally into two parties. **1837** W. IRVING *Capt. Bonneville* I. 166 The rest were organized into three brigades, and sent off in different directions, to subsist themselves by hunting the buffalo. *Ibid.* 30 The various brigades of trappers. **1887** *Chr. Leader* 3 Mar. 134/3 The Boys' Brigade..Ladytown Free Church, Arbroath, has started a company of this brigade.

4. *Comb.* and *Attrib.*, as ***brigade depot***, ***ribbon***; **brigade group** (see quot. 1953); **brigade-major**, a staff officer attached to a brigade, who assists the brigadier in command, and acts as the channel through which orders are issued and reports and correspondence transmitted.

1810 WELLINGTON *Let.* in Gurw. *Disp.* V. 598 A Brigade Major appears to me to be a necessary appointment in Cadiz. **1844** *Regul. & Ord. Army* 59 The Brigade-Major, or an orderly Adjutant, is to be constantly in the Lines of the Camp of the Brigade. **1873** *Ibid.* §5 Brigade depots are..to be inspected. **1945** *Diamond Track* (Army Board, N.Z.) 6/1 A brigade group with vehicles moving at 100 yards intervals. **1948** LINDSELL & BENOY *Lindsell's Mil. Organization* (ed. 27) 26 The Territorial Army is in future therefore to include ..Four independent infantry brigade groups. **1953** E. SMITH *Guide to Eng. Traditions* 9 There may even be a composite 'brigade group', in which three infantry battalions are supported by a regiment of artillery, a squadron of Royal Engineers, and signal and transport units, &c.

brigade (brɪˈgeɪd), *v.* [f. prec.]

1. *trans.* To form into a brigade or brigades; to join (a regiment or other body of troops) with others so as to form a brigade.

1805 *Ann. Rev.* III. 240 A shire is too large a division for brigading together the resident men in arms. **1837** *Blackw. Mag.* XLI. 37 The firemen..have been combined into one body—'brigaded', as the rather affected phrase is. **1878** *N. Amer. Rev.* CXXVI. 85 My regiment was brigaded with the Sixth, Seventh, and Eighth Regiments.

2. *loosely.* To form (people) as if into a brigade; to combine, associate.

a **1859** DE QUINCEY *Whiggism* Wks. VI. 100 Brigaded with so many scowling republicans are to be found..nearly one-half of our aristocracy. **1878** LADY HERBERT tr. *Hübner's Ramble* II. iii. 537 Men, who were brigaded, and always ready to trouble the public.

brigadier (brɪgəˈdɪə(r)). Also 7 brigadeere. [? a. Fr. *brigadier* (not in Cotgr. 1611), f. *brigade*: see above.]

1. More correctly **brigadier-general**: A military officer in command of a brigade; the status ranks between a major-general and a colonel, but is only local or temporary, being generally held by the senior colonel of the regiments or battalions brigaded together.

1678 SIR C. LYTTELTON in *Hatton Corr.* (1878) 162 It shall not rest upon him if I be not made a brigadeere. **1690** *Lond. Gaz.* No. 2573/4 His Majesty sent Monsieur de la Meloniere, Brigadier-General, with 5 Regiments. **1703** *Ibid.* 3916/1 He has appoint 4 Brigadiers General. **1809** WELLINGTON *Let.* in Gurw. *Disp.* IV. 484, I appointed Colonel Low to be a Brigadier General. **1844** *Regul. & Ord. Army* 3 Officers serving on the Staff in the capacity of Brigadier-Generals are to take Rank..from their Commissions as Colonels in the Army, not from the dates of their appointments as Brigadiers.

†**2.** ***brigadier-wig***: see quot. *Obs.*

c **1770** *J. Granger's Lett.* (1805) 280 A full wig tied back in one curl is a Major, in two curls is a Brigadier. **1772** GRAVES *Spirit. Quix.* III. xiii. (D.) A man..in a brigadier wig and grave habit. **1818** SCOTT *Hrt. Midl.* li, He..pushed back his brigadier wig.

briga'diership. [f. BRIGADIER + -SHIP.] The rank or office of a brigadier.

1826 MISS MITFORD *Village* Ser. II. (1863) 337 The good Colonel—fie upon me to forget his brigadiership!—the good General. **1861** W. SARGENT *André* 450 Arnold also got a brigadiership from the English.

brigading (brɪˈgeɪdɪŋ), *vbl. sb.* [f. BRIGADE *v.* + -ING[1].] The action of forming into brigades.

1815 WELLINGTON *Let.* in Gurw. *Disp.* XII. 391, I have delayed the brigading of the cavalry. **18..** LANDOR *Wks.* (1868) II. 61 Angels are not promoted by brigading with sappers and miners. **1870** *Pall Mall G.* 22 Oct. 12 Paris..is busy with the goose step, marching, counter-marching, and brigading.

brigado, obs. form of BRIGADE.

brigalow (ˈbrɪgələʊ). *Austral.* Also bricklow. [ad. native name *būriagalah*.] Any one of several species of acacia, esp. *A. harpophylla*. Also *attrib.*

1847 LEICHHARDT *Jrnl.* i. 4 The Bricklow Acacia, which seems to be identical with the Rose-wood Acacia of Moreton Bay. **1862** KENDALL *Poems* 79 Good-bye to the Barwan and brigalow scrubs. **1885** MRS. C. PRAED *Head Stat.* xvii, We are not fit for anything but store-cattle, we are all blady grass and brigalow scrub. **1901** F. CAMPBELL *Love* 263 Long shafts of silvery moonlight creep in between the waving branches of blue gum and brigalow. **1935** *Bulletin* (Sydney) 5 June 46/4 Some clumpy brigalow country. **1936** A. RUSSELL *Gone Nomad* i. 4, I am cattle-banging in western Queensland, the scent of the brigalow and mulga in my nostrils. **1957** P. WHITE *Voss* viii. 202 After the midday halt, which was spent in the shade of some brigalow scrub.

†**brigancy.** *Sc. Obs. rare*[−1]. [f. *brigan*, BRIGAND: see -ACY, -CY.] Violence; brigandage.

1513 in Pitcairn *Crim. Trials* i. 91 For common Oppression of the lieges, common Brigancie, etc. **1584** *Sc. Acts Jas. VI* (1814) 305 (JAM.) Be way of hame sukkin, brigancie and forthocht fellony.

brigand (ˈbrɪgənd). Forms: 4 bregaund, 5 brigaunt, brygaunt, 5–7 brigant, 6 brigane, brygand, 6–8 brigan, 6– brigand. [ME. a. OF. *brigand* (14th c. in Littré) = Pr. *bregan* irregular soldier; prob. ad. It. *brigante*, of which the primary meaning might be 'skirmisher', f. *brigare*: see BRIGUE *v.* and BRIGADE. It occurs in med.L. in 14th c. in the forms *brigancii*, *brigantii*, *brigantini*, *brigantes* as the name of 'une maniere de gens d'armes courant et apert, à pié'.]

†**1.** A light-armed, irregular foot-soldier. *Obs.*

? *a* **1400** *Morte Arth.* 2096 Thane bowmene of Bretayne.. Bekerde with bregaundez of ferre in tha laundez. **1460** CAPGRAVE *Chron.* 312 The brigauntis of the Frenssh side took the Kyngis cariage. **1523** LD. BERNERS *Froiss.* I. xlvii. 66 The duke..entred into Heynalt..and iiii. c. speares, besyde the brigantes, came before Quesnoy. **1557** PAYNEL *Barclay's Jugurth* 104 More lyke a skyrmishe amonge brygandes and rouers, then to any appointed or ordered bataylе. **1795** SOUTHEY *Joan of Arc* x. 250 Archers of unequalled skill, Brigans and pikemen.

2. One who lives by pillage and robbery: a freebooter, bandit; especially a member of one of the gangs of desperadoes infesting the mountainous districts of Italy, Spain, Turkey, etc.

1421 SIR H. LUTTRELL in Ellis *Orig. Lett.* II. 27 I. 85 Ther ys no steryng of none evyl doers, saf byonde the rivere of Sayne..of certains brigaunts. *c* **1489** CAXTON *Sonnes of Aymon* iv. 125 We have slayne soo many theves and brygauntes that I canne not number theym. **1570–87** HOLINSHED *Scot. Chron.* (1806) I. 392 It was taken from him by certain Brigants and robbers. **1656** BLOUNT *Glossogr.*, *Brigand*, a Footman armed..In old time when those kind of Soulders marched, they held all to be good prize, that they could purloin from the people, and thereupon this word now signifies also a Theef, purse-taker, or High-way robber. **1792** A. YOUNG *Trav. France* 154 Those troops of brigands, reported to be formidable. **1841** SPALDING *Italy & It. Isl.* III. 257 The Neapolitan brigands. **1876** FREEMAN *Norm. Conq.* V. xxii. 29 Such names as brigands and murderers are not uncommonly used by established governments to describe those who are in revolt against their authority.

3. *attrib.*

1522 *World & Child* in Hazl. *Dodsley* I. 251 Brigand harness I have beaten to back and to bones. **1816** J. SCOTT *Vis. Paris* (ed. 4) Pref. 19 The wild brigand spirit. **1859** *Autobiog. Beggar Boy* 128 He wore a sailor's dress, with a sort of brigand hat.

brigand, *v. rare.* [f. the sb.] *passive*: To be attacked by brigands.

1886 *Century Mag.* Apr. 856/1 Here we ought to have been briganed.

brigandage (ˈbrɪgəndɪdʒ). [a. 15th c. F. *brigandage*, f. *brigand*; see prec. and -AGE.]

1. The practice of brigands; highway-robbery, freebooting, pillage; †*concr.* an incursion, depredation by brigands (*obs.*).

1600 HOLLAND *Livy* XXXVIII. xlv. 1011 e, A privat brigandage and robberie. **1728** MORGAN *Algiers* II. v. 318 The Corsairs of Barbary, have extended their Brigandages even upon the Coasts of Provence. **1826** SCOTT *Quentin D.* i, The brigandage of the Free Companies. **1884** MAHAFFY in *Contemp. Rev.* XLVI. 96 Brigandage..was too often the outcome of shocking tyranny and injustice.

2. Brigands collectively.

1875 MERIVALE *Gen. Hist. Rome* i. (1877) 4 A stronghold for the unsettled brigandage of the country round.

†**'brigander**[1]. *Obs.* Forms: 5 bregaunter, -ander, breggandire, brigaunder, 5–6 brygander, -yr, brigander, 6 -inder, bregandier. [f. BRIGAND, on some obscure analogy: there is no such form in French.]

1. Body-armour for foot-soldiers; = BRIGANDINE I.

1420 *Test. Ebor.* (1836) I. 397 Unum par de bregaunters, cum tota reliqua armatura mea. **1450** JOHN PASTON *Petit.* in *Lett.* I. 106 A thowsand persones..arrayd in maner of werre, with curesse, brigaunders, jakks, salettes, gleyfes, bowes, etc. **1497** *Will of Sympson* (Somerset Ho.), Pair briganders, paire leg harneys, a paire of gussettes. **1543** GRAFTON *Contn. Harding* 497 The Duke of Buckyngham stoode harnessed in olde euell fauoured bryganders. **1611** SPEED *Hist. Gt. Brit.* IX. xviii. (1632) 915 Harnessed in olde rusty briganders.

2. A soldier wearing a brigander.

1525 LD. BERNERS *Froiss.* II. clix. [clv.] 438 The aragonoys shulde serue hym..with ii. hundred speares at their coste and charge, and a thousande crosbowes, and a thousande brigaunders.

†**brigander**[2]. App. corrupt f. BRIGADIER.

1647 HAWARD *Crown Rev.* 22 Brigander. Fee, £10.

brigander, obs. f. BERGANDER, sheldrake.

brigan'desque, *a.* [f. BRIGAND *sb.* + -ESQUE, after *arabesque*, etc.] After the style of a brigand.

1883 *Gd. Words* July 421/2 Now a shepherd would appear with his brigandesque hat.

brigandess (ˈbrɪgəndɪs). *rare.* [f. BRIGAND + -ESS.] A female brigand.

1865 MOENS *Eng. Trav. & It. Brigands*, Here I discovered that five of the band were brigandesses. **1869** *Echo* 6 Feb., Women with black brows and harsh voices—brigandesses by appearance.

brigandin(e, early form of BRIGANTINE.

brigandine, brigantine (ˈbrɪgəndiːn, -tiːn). Forms: 5 brigantyn, (bregandyrn, -ardyn), brig-, bryga(u)ndyn(e, (*Sc.* brikcane-, brekanetyne), 5–6 brigandyne, 6 bregendine, (? 7 brigintine), 6– brigandine, -tine. [Late ME., a. OF. *brigandine* (15th c. in Littré): i.e. armour for a brigand (in the original sense): see -INE.]

1. 'Body armour composed of iron rings or small thin iron plates, sewed upon canvas, linen, or leather, and covered over with similar materials' (Planché *Cycl. Cost.*); orig. worn by foot-soldiers and at first in two halves, hence in early quots. in plural or as ***pair of brigandines***; less strictly perh. = 'coat of mail, corslet'. See BRIGANDER.

c **1456** *Eng. Chron.* (Camden) 66 Armed in a peire of brigaundynez. **1465** *Paston Lett.* 99 I. 134, J peyr of Bregandyrns kevert with blew fellewet and gylt naile, with legharneyse, the vallew of the gown and the bregardyns viij *li.* **1489** *Acta Dom. Concilii* 132 (JAM.) The said Schir Mongo haid the brikcanetynes contenit in the summondis. **1548** UDALL, etc. *Erasm. Par. Mark* Pref. 4 They haue theyr brigandyne, theyr souldiers girdle. **1567** *Lanc. Wills* II. 86

A payre of bregendines. **1591** Garrard *Art Warre* 9 The Halberdier, who is armed either with Brigandine or Corslet. **1611** Bible *Jer.* xlvi, Furbish the speares, and put on the brigandines [Wyclif habiriownus; Coverd. brestplates; Vulg. *loricis*]. **1671** Milton *Samson* 1120 Put on all thy gorgeous arms, thy helmet And Brigandine of brass, thy broad habergeon. **1808** Scott *Marm.* v. ii, Their brigantines, and gorgets light. **1825** —— *Talism.* (1854) 337 He had finished adjusting his hauberk and brigandine. **1874** Boutell *Arms & Arm.* viii. 146 A brigandine..which is covered over with small iron plates of various forms, and may be called a studded tunic.

2. *attrib.*

1863 J. G. Nichols *Herald & Geneal.* June 438 Edward Lyttelton..in a white dress having a peascod-shaped body, probably of brigandine armour.

'brigandine ('brɪgəndɪn), *a. rare.* [f. brigand + -ine[1].] After the manner of a brigand.

1832 *Fraser's Mag.* V. 149 Their ominous and brigandine salutation, 'Siste Viator'.

brigandish ('brɪgəndɪʃ), *a.* [f. brigand *sb.* + -ish[1].] Pertaining to or resembling a brigand. Hence **'brigandishly** *adv.*

1877 *Daily News* 7 July 6/2 To restrain in some degree their brigandish tendencies. *Ibid.* 5/7 His attire is brigandishly picturesque.

'brigandism. [f. brigand + -ism.] The life or practices of brigandage.

1865 Maffei *Brigand Life* II. 24 Tempted to throw themselves into the wild vortex of brigandism. **1877** *Daily News* 26 July 5/7 The lovely mountain gorge celebrated in the annals of brigandism.

† **'brigandize,** *sb. Obs. rare*⁻¹. [a. rare F. *brigandise* (anno 1427 in Godef.), f. *brigand*: cf. *merchand-ise*.] Brigandage.

1609 Holland *Amm. Marcell.* xvii. xi. 94 Better fitted for brigandize than open fight in the field. *Ibid.* xxiii. iii. 221 Men meet for warlike brigandize and robberie.

brigandry ('brɪgəndrɪ). [f. brigand + -ry.] = brigandage, brigandism.

1909 *Westm. Gaz.* 17 Apr. 2/3 The Mafia, and the spirit which gave it life, is likewise passing into history, for mere brigandry can never earn the respect once paid to the aristocracy of murder. **1980** *Guardian Weekly* 28 Dec. 14/2 Today the rebels wound, mutilate, and kill civilians: where do you draw the fine line between subversion and brigandry?

brigane, brigant, obs. ff. brigand.

† **brigan'taille.** *Obs. rare*⁻¹. [f. *brigant*, brigand: cf. *bataille*, *canaille*.] Perhaps: The fighting of irregular troops or free-lances, guerilla warfare; or brigandage, pillage by free companies.

1393 Gower *Conf.* I. 11 The chirche keie in adventure Of armes and of brigantaille Stood no thing than upon bataille.

briganted, var. of *briganded*.

1872 Hardwick *Trad. Lanc.* 13 Briganted, fighting thieves.

brigantine[1] ('brɪgəntiːn). Forms: 6 **brigandyn(e -tyne, bryg-,** 6–7 **brigandine,** 7 **bregantine,** 6– **brigantine;** also 6 **bergantine,** 6–7 **vergantine.** [16th c. *brigandyn*, a. F. *brigandin* (now *brigantin*), ad. It. *brigantino* (med.L. *brigantinus* found *a* 1400), perh. in its orig. sense 'skirmishing vessel': cf. brigade and brigand. The Spanish is *bergantin*, OSp. *vergantin*: these forms also occur in Eng. writers translating, or compiling, from Spanish sources.]

† **1.** *orig.* A small vessel equipped both for sailing and rowing, swifter and more easily manœuvred than larger ships, and hence employed for purposes of piracy, espionage, reconnoitring, etc., and as an attendant upon larger ships for protection, landing purposes, etc. Used by the seafaring nations of the Mediterranean. (In English only a historical term: Littré gives *brigantin* in this sense, but perh. it is only *Hist.* in French also.)

1525 Ld. Berners *Froiss.* II. clxxi. [clxvii.] 498 To saue ourselfe, it is best we sende formost our lytell shyppes, called Brigandyns, and let vs tary in the mouthe of the hauyn. **1553** Eden *Treat. New Ind.* (Arb.) 28 Commanded a foyst and two brigantines to be furnished..which being prepared in the yere of Christ 1492, Columbus departed. **1555** —— *Decades W. Ind.* i. ii. (Arb.) 70 Owre men..settinge forewarde with their ores the brigantine. **1580** Baret *Alv.* B 1256 A brigantine or ship sent out to espie. **1611** Cotgr., *Brigantin*, a low, long, and swift Sea-vessel, bigger then the fregat, and lesse then a foist, and hauing some 12 or 13 oares on a side: we call it also a Brigantine. **1670** *Lond. Gaz.* No. 500/2 An excellent Bregantine of 28 Oars. **1715** *Ibid.* No. 5332/1 Brigantines of 44 Oars and carrying 150 Men each. **1769** Falconer *Dict. Marine* (1789), *Brigantin*, a small light vessel, navigated by oars and sails: but differing extremely from the vessel known in England by the name of brig or brigantine. **1820** S. Rogers *Italy, Brides of V.* (1839) 225 The youths were gone in a light brigantine.

β. **1555** Eden *Decades W. Ind.* (Arb.) 108 Twoo smaule shyppes commenly cauled bergantines or bryganatynes. **1648** Gage *West Ind.* x. (1655) 40 Cortez thinking that place the most convenient to launch his Vergantines.

† **2.** Applied (loosely) to various kinds of foreign sailing and rowing vessels, as the galleon, galliot, etc. *Obs.* exc. in poetic or rhetorical use.

1552 Huloet, Brigantyne, or litle Barke, or Shyppe. **1579** Fenton *Guicciard.* (1618) 246 Reuictualled Pisa continually with a Gallion and other Brigandines. **1690** *Lond. Gaz.* No. 2603/1, 24 Galeots or Brigantines, 10 Felucca's. **1748** Anson *Voy.* i. iv. (ed. 4) 53 The next day but one we spoke with a Portuguese Brigantine. **1769** Falconer *Dict. Marine* (1789), *Brigantine*, a term variously applied by the mariners of different European nations to a peculiar sort of vessel of their own marine. **1851** Longf. *Gold. Leg.* v. *At Sea*, A galley of the Grand Duca, That..Convoys those lazy brigantines Laden with wine and oil from Lucca.

3. A two-masted vessel, carrying square sails on her foremast, which is rigged like a ship's foremast; her main or after-mast is the main-mast of a schooner, and in Falconer's time, like that mast, carried a square topsail: but is now entirely fore-and-aft-rigged.

1695 *Lond. Gaz.* No. 3115/4 At His Majesty's Yard at Chatham, [was launched] a Brigantine named the *Swift*. **1725** De Foe *Voy. round World* (1840) 53 Resolving..to mast her not as a sloop but as a Brigantine. **1790** Beatson *Nav. & Mil. Mem.* I. 280 The St. Pedro brigantine, belonging to and from Ferrol..was taken by the Ambuscade privateer of London. **1870** Anderson *Missions Amer. Brd.* II. xxxv. 314 A brigantine of one hundred and fifty-six tons ..built for the especial use of the Micronesian Mission.

brigantine[2]. var. of brigandine, armour.

† **brigan'tiner.** *Obs. rare*⁻¹. [f. brigantine[1] + -er.] One of the crew of a brigantine.

1555 Eden *Decades W. Ind.* ii. i. (Arb.) 108 They which were in the bryganntyne..Ancisus..commaunded..to turne backe ageyne. The brigantiners obeyed and folowed hym.

brige, obs. form of brigue, strife.

brige, brigg, brigge, obs. ff. bridge.

bright (braɪt), *a.* and *sb.* (Compar. brighter, -est.) Forms: 1 **beorht, berht, byrht, bryht,** 1–3 **breht,** 2–4 **briht,** 3–4 **briȝt,** 4–5 **bryȝt, bryght,** 4– **bright.** Also 2–3 **brict,** 2–4 **bricht,** 3–5 **brith,** 4 **brit, brith(e, brigth,** 5 **bryth, bryȝth;** *Sc.* 4–6 **brycht,** 4– **bricht.** [Common Teut., though now lost in all the langs. exc. English: OE. *beorht* (:—*berht*) = OS. *berht*, *beraht*, OHG. *beraht*, *bereht* (MHG. *berht*), ON. *bjartr*, Goth. *bairhts*:—OTeut. **berhto-z*, from a stem **berh*:—Aryan *bhrag-*, whence also Skr. *bhrāj-* to shine, and L. *flagrā-re* to blaze, *flamma* flame. The metathesis of *breht* for *berht* occurs already in Lindisf. Gloss.]

A. *adj.* (In general, the opposite of *dull*.)

1. Shining; emitting, reflecting, or pervaded by much light.

a. said of luminaries.

a **1000** *Metr. Boeth.* xxii. 22 Berhtre þonne se leoma sie sunnan on sumera. *a* **1000** *Guthlac* 1258 (Gr.) Þa cwom leohta mæst..scinan beorht ofer burȝsalu. *c* **1175** *Lamb. Homilies* 39 Seofesiðe brihtre þene þa sunne. *c* **1391** Chaucer *Astrol.* ii. §2 The altitude of the Mone, or of brihte sterres. **1513** Douglas *Æneis* iii. Prol. 1 Hornyt Lady, paill Cynthia, nocht brycht. **1526** Tindale *Rev.* xxii. 16 The bright mornynge starre. **1601** Shaks. *All's Well* i. i. 97 That I should loue a bright particuler starre. **1747** Hervey *Medit. & Contempl.* (1818) 17 They will shine with brighter beams ..in their Lord's everlasting kingdom. **1879** Lockyer *Elem. Astron.* ii. ix. 51 One of the brightest lights that we know of —the lime-light.

b. of polished metals, precious stones, and other objects whose surfaces naturally reflect light.

a **1000** *Rood* 66 (Gr.) On beorhtan stane. *c* **1220** *Bestiary* 71 in *O.E. Misc.* 3 It makeð his eȝen briȝt. **1377** Langl. *P. Pl.* B. Prol. 168 A belle of brasse Or of briȝte syluer. *c* **1440** *Promp. Parv.* 52 Bryghte swerde, *splendona*. **1552** Lyndesay *Monarche* Prol. 152 In habyte gaye and glorious, Brychtar nor gold or stonis precious. **1597** Gerard *Herbal* i. xl. §5. 58 Bright Wheate..this kinde is fower square, somwhat bright and shining. **1652** *Proc. Parliament* No. 170 A great box of bright new cast bullets. **1723** Sheffield (Dk. Buckhm.) *Wks.* (1753) I. 40 Teeth so bright, and breath so sweet. **1802** Bingley *Anim. Biog.* (1813) I. 34 The eyes of the amphibia are in general large and bright. **1842** Macaulay *Horatius* xxi, The long array of helmets bright.

c. of illuminated surfaces, of the day in sunshine, etc.

a **1000** *Elene* 822 (Gr.) In þære beorhtan byriȝ, þær is broðor min. *c* **1340** *Cursor M.* 13541 (Fairf.) Wirk..quen þe day lastis brit. *c* **1470** Henry *Wallace* i. 288 Apon ye morn, quhen yat ye day was brycht. **1526** *Pilgr. Perf.* (W. de W. 1531) 129 Our soule irradiate or made bryght with the lyght of the aungell. **1737** Pope *Hor. Epist.* i. i. 138 The evening bright and still. **1832** Macaulay *Armada* xxxvi, That time of slumber was as bright and busy as the day. **1871** R. Ellis *Catullus* viii. 3 Bright once the days and sunny shone the light on thee.

d. of transparent substances: Clear, translucent.

1709 Steele *Tatler* No. 100 ⁋1 Which had purified the whole Body of Air into such a bright transparent Æther, as made every Constellation visible. *a* **1730** Fenton (J.) While the bright Seine t' exalt the soul With sparkling plenty crowns the bowl. *a* **1748** Thomson (J.) From the brightest wines He'd turn abhorrent.

e. *fig.* Lit up with happiness, gladness, or hope. Also, hopeful, encouraging, cheering.

1751 Johnson *Rambl.* No. 165 ⁋3 The brightest hours of prosperity have their clouds. **1815** Moore *Lalla R., Fire-worshippers*, Bright hours atone for dark ones past. **1839** J. Romilly *Cambridge Diary* 14 Jan. (1967) 162 She is..very talkative & disposed to look on the bright side of every thing. **1871** Freeman *Norm. Conq.* (1876) IV. xviii. 193 Chances of deliverance brighter than any that had offered themselves. **1917** C. Mathewson *Sec. Base Sloan* xiii. 174 Toonalta's chance to pull the game up high and dry looked bright.

† **2.** Clear or luminous to the mental perception.

a **1000** *Guthlac* 815 (Gr.) Gif hy halȝes word healdan woldun beorht in breostum. *c* **1200** *Trin. Coll. Hom.* 119 þe holi gost..alihte hem of brihtere and of festere bileue. **1741** Watts *Improv. Mind* (J.) He must not proceed too swiftly, that he may with more ease, with brighter evidence, and with surer success, draw the learner on.

3. Of persons: 'Resplendent with charms' (J.); beautiful, fair. *arch.*

c **1250** *Hymn Virg.* 14 in *Trin. Coll. Hom.* 255 Nis non maide..swo fair, so sschene, so rudi, swo bricht. *a* **1300** *Havelok* 2131 In his armes his brithe bride. *c* **1420** *Sir Amadace* lviii, That ladi gente That was so bryȝte of ble. *c* **1460** in *Babees Bk.* (1868) 15 In chambur among ladyes bryȝth. **1593** Shaks. *Lucr.* 490 By thy bright beauty was it newly bred. **1605** —— *Macb.* iv. iii. 22 Angels are bright still, though the brightest fell. *c* **1600** *Bessie of Bednal Grene* ii. ii, He had a faire daughter of bewty most bright. **1704** Pope *Windsor F.* 232 Like the bright beauties on thy banks below. **1817** Coleridge *Sibyl. Leaves* (1862) 279 A bright lady, surpassingly fair.

4. a. Of vivid or brilliant colour: used also with names of colour, as ***bright red***.

1375 Barbour *Bruce* v. 10 The treis begouth to ma Burgeonys and brycht blwmys alsua. **1655–60** Stanley *Hist. Philos.* (1701) 406/2 The kinds of colour are..Ten, Black, White, and the rest between them, Yellow, Tawney, Pale, Red, Blew, Green, Bright, Grey. **1697** Dryden *Virg. Georg.* iii. 128 His Colour Gray; For Beauty dappled, or the brightest Bay. **1704** Pope *Past., Spring* 31 Here the bright crocus and blue violet grew. *a* **1835** Mrs. Hemans *Better Land*, Strange bright birds, on their starry wings. **1836** Hawthorne *Amer. Note-bks.* (1871) I. 20 Wild rose-bushes ..with their deep, bright-red seed-vessels.

b. *spec.* Denoting tobacco of a light shade or colour. Also *bright-leaf*. orig. *U.S.*

1765 in *Amer. Hist. Rev.* (1921) XXVII. 71 Saw some of the bright coloured tobaco which sels So Dear in foreign markets. It is of a light yelow Coulour... The Inhabitants call it bright tobacco. **1933** *Discovery* Aug. 250/2 The [Cacao] moths have a preference for bright-leaf kiln-cured tobacco. *Ibid.*, Enormous stocks of Rhodesian bright tobacco.

5. Of sounds: † **a.** Clear, shrill, ringing. **b.** Said of the mental effect of a note.

a **1000** *Cod. Exon.* 79 b (Bosw.), Sum hafaþ beorhte stefne. *a* **1250** *Owl & Night.* 1681 For boþe we habbeþ stefne brihte. *c* **1250** *Gen. & Ex.* 2780 God sente a steune briȝt and heȝ. **1872** J. Curwen *Standard Course* 4/2 They are the bold ..tones of the scale..but they differ in the manner of their boldness, one being brighter, another stronger, etc.

6. Illustrious, glorious, splendid. (Lat. *clarus*.)

a **1000** *Ags. Psalter* cxxi[i]. 6 Biddað eow bealde beorhtere sibbe. *a* **1340** Hampole *Psalter* Metr. Pref. 60 To buske vs to the blysse ful brigth. **1548** Udall, etc. *Erasm. Par. Matt.* ii. 13 Bryght and notable with miracles. **1593** Shaks. *Lucr.* 1491 Troy had been bright with fame and not with fire. **1660** Barrow *Euclid* (1714) Pref. 1 Some of a brighter Genius. *a* **1687** Cotton (J.) This is the worst, if not the only stain, I' th' brightest annals of a female reign. **1734** Pope *Ess. Man* iv. 282 The wisest, brightest, meanest of mankind. **1783** Watson *Philip III.* (1793) I. ii. 232 Exhibited a bright example of the most heroic valour.

7. a. Lively, cheerful, brilliant or animated in conversation, vivacious; the opposite of *dull*.

1605 Shaks. *Macb.* iii. ii. 28 Be bright and Iouiall among your Guests. **1710** Steele *Tatler* No. 208 ⁋4, I would rather be in his Company than that of the brightest Man I know. **1885** *Manch. Exam.* 15 May 6/1 He turned up today as jaunty and bright as a young buck of twenty-five.

b. ***bright young thing*** (etc.), a member of the younger generation in fashionable society (esp. in the 1920s and 1930s), noted for exuberant and outrageous behaviour (cf. thing *sb.*[1] 10 a).

1927 *Punch's Almanack* 7 Nov. [8] Since a section of the 'Bright Young People' literally 'set the Thames on fire', things have been a little quiet. **1928** D. H. Lawrence *Phoenix II* (1968) 526 *Show* me somebody, then! And she shows me some guy, or some bright young thing. **1929** G. K. Chesterton *The Thing* iv. 38 If the bright young thing cannot be asked to tolerate her grandmother..why should the grandmother..have tolerated the bright young thing? **1931** R. Aldington *Colonel's Daughter* iii. 142 The Bright Young Idiots, who seem determined to queer the whole pitch to the puritans, by being as vicious as they can. **1936** *Morning Post* 15 July 14/5 There is a section of the community..whose life seems to consist of cocktail and sherry parties, cabarets and midnight revelries... These are decadent 'bright young things'. **1953** S. Spender *Creative Element* 159 Dreams of the Old England and the Bright Young Things.

8. Of thought, conversation, writings, etc.: Animated with wit or imagination, lively, clever, brilliant, sparkling.

1709 Steele *Tatler* No. 31 ⁋10 You'll certainly print this bright Conversation. **1779** Johnson *L.P., Pope* Wks. 1787 IV. 109 If he has brighter paragraphs, he has not better poems. **1858** O. W. Holmes *Aut. Breakf. T.* ii. 10, I really believe some people save their bright thoughts as being too precious for conversation. **1884** R. W. Church *Bacon* ix. 220 Some bright touch of his incorrigible imaginativeness.

9. a. Displaying great intelligence; quick-witted, clever. (In standard English used chiefly in speaking of children or one's inferiors.)

1741 Watts *Improv. Mind* (1801) 24 Before we proceed in finishing a bright character by conversation. **1824** W. Irving *T. Trav.* I. 203, I began life unluckily by being the wag and bright fellow at school. **1883** Gilmour *Mongols* xxxii. 367 A few soldiers not of the brightest or bravest type.

1885 *Harper's Mag.* Feb. 385/1 The child will be extra bright. *Mod.* (Ironical) He is a bright specimen!

b. Sharp, keen, watchful.

1840 R. DANA *Bef. Mast* xxxi. 117 We kept a bright lookout—one man at each bow. **1860** *Merc. Mar. Mag.* VII. 41 The look out..is not a very 'bright' one.

10. a. *Comb.*: chiefly parasynthetic, as ***bright-bloomed, -cheeked, -costumed, -eyed*** (also *transf.*), ***-faced, -featured, -haired, -harnessed, -headed, -studded, -witted***, etc.

1558 PHAËR *Æneid* IX. C c ij b, Brightheaded Phœbus.. Beheld..bothe Latines hoasts and Troyan fort. **1592** GREENE *Poems* 85 Bright-eyed his Phillis was. **1598** CHAPMAN *Iliad* I. 294 Bright-cheek'd Briseis. **1632** MILTON *Penser.* 23 Bright-haired Vesta. **1786** COWPER *Gratitude* 13 This wheel-footed studying chair..Bright-studded to dazzle the eyes. **1827** KEBLE *Chr. Y.*, 25th Sund. aft. Trin. i, The bright-hair'd morn is glowing. **1850** MRS. BROWNING *Poems* II. 46 Thy little bright-faced son. **1881** O. WILDE *Burden of Itys* in *Wks.* (1948) 724 Light-winged and bright-eyed miracle of the wood! **1920** A. HUXLEY *Leda* 13 The bright-eyed bliss Perished. **1959** *Times* 24 Nov. 3/6 Arthur Jacobs's bright-eyed, allusive libretto.

b. bright emitter (see quot. 1931); so ***bright-emitting*** adj.; **bright lights**, the city, as a place of entertainment; urban gaiety; **bright-line**, (*a*) *Physics*, applied to a discontinuous spectrum consisting of bright lines resulting from radiation from an incandescent vapour or gas; (*b*) *Photogr.*, applied to a view-finder in which the area of the picture appears framed by a white line; **bright work**, polished metal-work on ships, etc.

1923 *Pop. Wireless Weekly* 24 Nov. 463/3 A new low-consumption valve, of the *bright emitter type. **1931** *B.B.C. Year-Bk.* 437/2 *Bright Emitter*, a thermionic valve in which the filament gives its normal emission only when heated to a high temperature so that it glows brightly. **1943** *Gloss. Terms Telecomm.* (*B.S.I.*) 29 **Bright-emitting cathode*, a cathode, usually of pure metal, designed to be used at a relatively high temperature (e.g., above red heat). **1922** SINCLAIR LEWIS *Babbitt* v. 66 A nice expensive vacation in New York..with the *bright lights and the bootlegged cocktails. **1938** F. D. SHARPE *S. of Flying Squad* iv. 43 She went back to live with her mother and promised not to come up again near the bright lights. **1890** G. F. CHAMBERS *Handbk. Astron.* (ed. 4) II. 371 The spectra of *bright-line stars. *Ibid.* 372 The meteorites in nebulæ giving a bright-line spectrum. **1954** R. H. BOMBACK *Basic Leica Technique* iii. 39 The most compelling new feature of the Leica M.3 is ..the Measuring Bright Line Viewfinder. *Ibid.* 40 Superimposed on the field of view is the 'Bright Line' contour which shows clearly the extent of the image covered by any one of the three standard lenses. **1959** *Which?* Nov. 158/2 One camera had a 'brightline' viewfinder—the area of the picture was framed by a white line when seen through the viewfinder. **1841** *South. Lit. Mess.* VII. 769/2 It was a part of my duty..to superintend the cleaning of the *'bright work'. **1912** 'AURORA' *Jock Scott, Midshipman* i. 10 The bright-work on the quarter-deck..shone like silver. **1933** MASEFIELD *Conway* III. 92 The lower deck was the show deck... There was..much brasswork and bright-work upon it. **1962** *Times* 25 May 18/5 The external brightwork, including the bumpers [of a motor car].

c. In colloq. phr. ***bright-eyed and bushy-tailed***, alert and enthusiastic; lively or active. [From conventional descriptions of the squirrel (cf. def. at SQUIRREL *sb.* 1 a).] orig. *N. Amer.*

1953 B. MERRILL *Bright Eyed & Bushy Tailed* (song) 2 If the fox in the bush and the squirr'l in the tree be, Why in the world can't you and me be Bright eyed and bushy tailed and sparkelly as we can be. **1968** H. HARRISON *Technicolor Time Machine* xiv. 139 You look very bright-eyed and bushy-tailed this morning. **1975** *Latin Amer.* 5 Sept. 275/3 Arthur Schlesinger returns to his old hobby horse of defending the bright-eyed and bushy-tailed spirit in which he first proposed the Alliance for Progress. **1985** *Times* 13 June 15/1 Britain's largest quoted [investment] trust..has amply demonstrated how successful the bright-eyed and bushy-tailed approach can be.

B. *sb.*

1. Brightness, light. *arch.* (*poet.*)

c **1250** *Gen. & Ex.* 143 De sunnes briȝt, Is more ðanne ðe mones liȝt. *c* **1374** CHAUCER *Troylus* II. 815 What is the sunne wors of kynd right, Thogh that a man, for feblenes of eyen, May not endure to se on it for bright? **1598** ROWLANDS *Betray. Christ* 57 O Sunne whose shine is heav'ns eternall bright. **1636** *Ariana* 17 Acknowledging here so much brights and beauties. **1667** MILTON *P.L.* III. 380 Dark with excessive bright thy skirts appeer. **1839** BAILEY *Festus* (1848) 59/2 Others..whose forms for utter bright Are indefinable.

†**2.** A beautiful woman, a 'fair'. *Obs.*

c **1325** *E.E. Allit. P.* A. 754 Breue me, bryȝt, quat-kyn of priys Berez þe perle so maskellez. *c* **1470** HENRY *Wallace* v. 607 Throuch bewte off that brycht. *c* **1505** DUNBAR *Poem*, 'In secreit place this hyndir nycht,' I hard ane beyrne say till ane bricht.

bright (braɪt), *adv.* Forms: 1 **beorhte**, 2–4 **brihte, briȝte.** [from the adj. with adverbial *-e*, through the loss of which it was, *c* 1400, levelled with the adj.]

1. a. = BRIGHTLY.

a **1000** *Beowulf* 3039 Geseah blacne leoman beorhte scinan. *a* **1000** *Metr. Boeth.* xxxvii. §2 Ða godan scinað beorhtor þonne sunne. *c* **1200** ORMIN 2138 Hit swiþe brihhte shineþþ. *a* **1300** *Cursor M.* 8295 Þis angel þat sa bright[e] scan. **1340** *Ayenb.* 156 Grat nyed þet þe man yzy bryte ane his left half. *c* **1385** CHAUCER *L.G.W.* 163, ffor sekyrly his face schon so bryhte. **1596** SHAKS. *Merch. V.* v. i. 1 The moone shines bright. **1827** KEBLE *Chr. Year* All Saints vi, The spires that glow so bright. *Ibid.* S. Peter xiv, He dreams he sees a lamp flash bright.

†**b.** Clearly, ringingly. *Obs.*

a **1250** *Owl & Night.* 1656 Heo..song so schille and so brihte.

c. Phr. ***bright and early***: very early in the morning. orig. *U.S.*

1837 W. IRVING *Capt. Bonneville* II. ii. 17 Captain Bonneville and his three companions set out, bright and early, to rejoin the main party. **1900** *Daily News* 18 July, Persons desirous of being present at this gathering should be there bright and early. **1926** 'J. J. CONNINGTON' *Death at Swaythling Court* xvi. 286 Next morning I got up bright and early.

2. *Comb.*, as ***bright-beaming, -burning, -shining,*** †***-splendent***. It blends with the adj. in such as ***bright-dyed, -tinted***, which may be analysed as *bright(ly)* + *tinted*, or *bright tint* + *-ed*. See BRIGHT *a.* 10.

1588 SHAKS. *Tit. A.* III. i. 69 What foole hath..brought a faggot to bright burning Troy? *c* **1590** MARLOWE *Faust.* vii. 47 The..situation of bright-splendent Rome. **1593** SHAKS. *3 Hen. VI*, v. iii. 3 This bright-shining day. **1795** BURNS *Their groves o' sweet myrtle* i, Where bright-beaming summers exalt the perfume.

†**bright**, *v. Obs.* [OE. *beorhtian* to shine bright (corresp. to Goth. **bairhtôn*), f. *beorht* bright; the ME. *bright-en* (trans.) corresponds to an OE. *bierhtan* = Goth. *bairhtjan*; but it may be a transitive extension of the OE. intr. vb.]

1. *intr.* To be bright, shine.

c **890** K. ÆLFRED *Bæda* III. xix. (Bosw.) Ðær his ȝeearnunge oft miclum mæȝenum scinaþ and beorhtiȝaþ. *a* **1000** *Ags. Psalms* cxliii. 7 Þine liȝetta leohteð and beorhteð. *c* **1425** *Seven Sag.* (P.) 1997 The clerkys..made ham at ese that nyght, Til on morwen the day bryght.

b. Of sound: To be clear, to ring.

a **1000** *Beowulf* 2326 Beorhtode benc-sweȝ.

2. *trans.* To make bright, illumine.

a **800** *Vesp. Ps.* xli. 9 In deȝe onbead dryhten mildheortnisse his and on naeht ȝebirhte. *a* **1225** *Ancr. R.* 384 Luue, þet schireð & brihteð þe heorte. *c* **1400** *Destr. Troy* 815 Ryses the sun, Brightis all the burghe and the brode valis. **1686** GOAD *Celest. Bodies* I. v. 14 He [the Sun] brighteth the Air into a chearful Saphir.

bright, bad form of BRITE *v. Obs.*

brighten ('braɪt(ə)n), *v.* [ME. *brightn-en*, corresp. in form to OE. **beorhtnian*, in Northumbrian *berhtnia, ȝeberhtnia* to make bright, f. *beorht* bright. It is possible that the mod.Eng. word is a new formation on *bright*: cf. BRIGHT *v.*]

1. *trans.* To make bright.

[*c* **950** *Lindisf. Gosp.* John xiii. 32 God ȝeberhtnade hine on hine seolfne.] **1583** STANYHURST *Æneis* II. (Arb.) 53 Thee strand flames fyrye doe brighten. *a* **1700** DRYDEN (J.) As her celestial eyes Adorn the world, and brighten up the skies. **1805** SCOTT *Last Minstr.* II. xxiv, When the dawn of day Began to brighten Cheviot gray. **1831** CARLYLE *Sart. Res.* III. vi, Brightening London smoke itself into gold vapour.

b. *fig.*

1597 SHAKS. *2 Hen. IV*, II. iii. 17 There were two Honors lost..For Yours, may heauenly glory brighten it. **1667** MILTON *P.L.* IX. 634 Hope elevates, and joy Bright'ns his crest. **1872** BLACK *Adv. Phaeton* xxvi. 354 This sort of talk brightened up the spirits of our party.

2. *intr.* To become bright; to be bright, shine. Often with *up*.

a **1300** *Cursor M.* 9933 Þat castel brightnes..Ouer al þat curt on lenght and brede. **1704** POPE *Past., Spring* 72 The flowers begin to spring, the skies to brighten. **1768** BEATTIE *Minstr.* I. xxx, The rainbow brightens to the setting sun! **1819** BYRON *Juan* II. lxxxix, The boy's eyes..Brighten'd. **18..** SOUTHEY *Lodore* 58 And whitening and brightening.

b. In various fig. senses (see BRIGHT *a.*).

1709 POPE *Ess. Crit.* 421 How the style brightens, how the sense refines. **1732** BERKELEY *Alciphr.* I. 183 The Man of Raillery..shall instantly brighten up, and assume a familiar Air. **1875** JOWETT *Plato* I. 239 He brightens up and is wide awake when Homer is..recited.

'**brightened**, *ppl. a.* [f. prec.] Made bright.

1795 SOUTHEY *Joan of Arc* VII. 323 Their brighten'd tide.

'**brightener.** [f. as prec. + -ER[1].] One who or that which brightens. *spec.* in *Electro-plating* (see quots.).

1796 MISS BURNEY *Camilla* IX. viii, The brightener of my every view. **1832** *Blackw. Mag.* XXXI. 252 The richest brightener of the happiest years. **1924** BLUM & HOGABOOM *Princ. Electroplating* xviii. 293 It is possible to produce bright silver deposits from solutions containing very small amounts of carbon disulphide. (CS_2), which serves as a 'brightener'. **1930** FIELD & WEILL *Electro-Plating* vii. 94 A number of materials are not infrequently added to the cyanide copper bath to improve the quality of the deposit. These are commonly called 'brighteners'.

brightening ('braɪt(ə)nɪŋ), *vbl. sb.* [see -ING[1].]

1. The action of making or becoming bright; illumination. *lit.* and *fig.*

1552 HULOET, Bryghtnyng, or brandishynge, *vibratio.* **1674** N. FAIRFAX *Bulk & Selv.* 51 The brightning of our Island. **1712** STEELE *Spect.* No. 461 ¶4 Bestow upon it a few Brightnings from your Genius.

2. In various technical uses: see quots.

1854 SCOFFERN in *Orr's Circ. Sc.* Chem. 506 The cupelling process..may be known to have been continued sufficiently long by a peculiar appearance, termed 'brightening', assumed by the silver bead. **1879** G. GLADSTONE *Calico Printing* in *Cassell's Techn. Educ.* I. 198/2 Brightening..is for the purpose of bringing up the colours to their full brilliance.. This is attained by passing the goods through a soap bath two or more times. **1882** *Artist* 1 Feb. 63/1 A fine pearly grey for brightening or light shading.

'**brightening**, *ppl. a.* [see -ING[2].] Becoming or making bright. *lit.* and *fig.*

1725 POPE *Odyss.* IV. 346 Each bright'ning grace the genuine Greek confessed. **1810** SOUTHEY *Kehama* XXII. xi, A smile Dawn'd in his brightening countenance. **1860** TYNDALL *Glac.* I. §11. 75 Clear and sharp against the brightening sky. **1884** *Athenæum* 1 Mar. 272/3 Brightening prospects.

†'**brighthede.** *Obs.* [ME., f. BRIGHT *a.* + *-hede*, -HEAD.] = BRIGHTNESS.

a **1340** HAMPOLE *Psalter* vi. 4 Þe bryghthed & þe pees of godis light. *Ibid.* xv. 5 Þou restores til þaim þe knawynge of my brighthede.

brightish ('braɪtɪʃ), *a.* [f. BRIGHT *a.* + -ISH[1].] Somewhat bright.

1577 DEE *Relat. Spirits* I. (1659) 173 These seem somewhat brightish. **1800** HERSCHEL in *Phil. Trans.* XC. 266 Brightish-green, inclining to white.

brightly ('braɪtlɪ), *adv.* [OE. *beorhtlíce, brihtlice*, f. *beorht*, BRIGHT + *-lice*, -LY[2].] In a bright manner; brilliantly, clearly.

c **1000** *Ags. Gosp.* Mark viii. 25 Swa þæt he beorhtlice [**1160** *Hatton* brihtlice] eall ȝeseah. *a* **1225** *Ancr. R.* 154 Þenne..schule ȝe al þis brihtliche understonden. *Ibid.* 170 Te brihtluker iseon ine heouene Godes brihte nebscheft. *c* **1250** *Gen. & Ex.* 3491 Ðo so spac god so briȝt-like, ðat alle he it herden. *a* **1300** *Cursor M.* 3320 A gold ringe þat brihtly schane. **1340** *Ayenb.* 150 Hi zyeþ briȝtliche..and al aboute ham. **1587** GOLDING *De Mornay* xv. (1617) 265 Some brightlyer and some dimlier. **1596** SHAKS. *Merch. V.* v. i. 94 A substitute shines brightly as a King Vntill a King be by. **1725** POPE *Odyss.* XIV. 569 Till brightly-dawning shone The Morn. **1863** GEO. ELIOT *Romola* I. xx. (1880) I. 273 A long narrow room, painted brightly like the other. **1882** HOWELLS in *Longm. Mag.* I. 51 The grass is..brightly green.

brightness ('braɪtnɪs). [OE. *beorhtnes, brehtnis*, f. as prec. + -NESS.] The quality of being bright; brilliancy, clearness; vivacity, quickness of intellect, etc. (see BRIGHT *a.*).

c **950** *Lindisf. Gosp.* John v. 40 Brehtnise from monnum ne onfoe ic. *c* **1000** *Ags. G.* Luke ii. 9 And godes beorhtnes him ymbe-scean. *c* **1200** *Trin. Coll. Hom.* 13 Six werkes of brictnesse. **1330** R. BRUNNE *Chron.* (1810) 103 A brightnesse com fro heuen. **1413** LYDG. *Pylgr. Sowle* v. v. (1859) 76 Sterres..castyng oute bemes of huge bryghtnyes. **1592** SHAKS. *Rom. & Jul.* II. ii. 19 The brightnesse of her cheeke would shame those starres. *a* **1721** PRIOR *Solomon* III. (R.) Vex'd with the present moment's heavy gloom, Why seek we brightness from the years to come? —— (J.) The brightness of his parts..distinguished him in an age of great politeness. **1851** RUSKIN *Mod. Paint.* II. III. II. v. §15 Brightness of colour is altogether inadmissible without purity and harmony.

Bright's Disease. *Med.* [f. the name of Dr. R. Bright, whose researches, published in 1827, established the nature of the disease.] 'A generic term including several forms of acute and chronic disease of the kidney usually associated with albumen in the urine' (*Syd. Soc. Lex.*); granular degeneration of the kidneys.

1831 GRAVES in *Lond. Med. Gaz.* Dec., That obstruction of the glandular tissue to which the name of Bright's disease has been attached. **1843** —— *Syst. Clin. Med.* xxxiv. 540, I regard albuminous urine as a sign of Bright's kidney. **1866** A. FLINT *Princ. Med.* (1880) 863.

†'**brightshine.** *Obs. rare.* [f. BRIGHT *a.* + SHINE.] Lustre.

1586 FERNE *Blaz. Gentrie* 147 The brightshine of all princely virtues. **1618** BAYNE *On Eph.* i. (1643) 33 No more doth the darknesse of affliction obscure the bright-shine of this grace toward us.

'**bright-smith.** *rare.* [f. BRIGHT *a.* + SMITH.] A worker in 'white' or bright iron and tin.

1831 J. HOLLAND *Manuf. Metals* I. 156 The modern blacksmith is distinguished from the whitesmith, or brightsmith, as the latter has sometimes been called.

'**brightsome**, *a. arch.* [f. BRIGHT *a.* + -SOME: cf. *gladsome, darksome.*] Partaking of or exhibiting brightness, bright-looking. (A vaguer word than *bright*, leaving more to the imagination.)

1558 PHAËR *Æneid* IX. (1560) B b iij, His hie helme..that brightsome beames reflecting shone. **1577** HOLINSHED *Chron.* I. 99/2 Men of so brightsome countenances. *c* **1590** GREENE *Fr. Bacon* vi. 13 As brightsome as the Paramour of Mars. **1635** J. HAYWARD *Banish'd Virg.* 108 The night..is yet very brightsome and cleare. **1855** SINGLETON *Virgil* II. 154 Let me strew Their brightsome blossoms.

Hence '**brightsomeness.** *arch.*

1548 HALL *Chron.* (1809) 734 The brightsomenes of the gold. **1849** ROCK *Ch. of Fathers* II. vi. 283 The brightsomeness of the Gospel was dimmed.

Brigidian, Brigittin, var. of BRIDGETIN, *Obs.*

brigirdel, variant of BREECHGIRDLE.

†**brignole.** *Obs.* [Fr. (in same sense), named from *Brignoles* a town of Provence.] A kind of dried plum. (Littré.)

1721 C. KING *Brit. Merch.* I. 181 Capers, Olives, Brignoles, Parchment, etc.

†**bri'gose**, *a. Obs.* [ad. med.L. *brigōsus*, f. *briga*: see BRIGUE *sb.*] = next.

1679 PULLER *Moder. Ch. Eng.* (1843) 206 Which two words,—as conscious that they were very brigose and severe if too generally taken,—therefore he softens, etc.

†ˈ**brigous**, *a. Obs.* [a. AF. **brigous* = OF. *brigeus*, later *brigueux*, med.L. *brigōsus*, cf. BRIGUE.] Of or pertaining to strife or disagreement; factious, disputable.

1387 TREVISA *Higden* Rolls Ser. III. 203 þe iuges sigh þat þe cause was brigous [*dubiosum*]. *c* **1440** *Promp. Parv.* 51 Brygows, or debate-makar, *brigosus*. **1519** HORMAN *Vulg.* 128 Beware of such brygous matters.

brigs, obs. form of BRUGES (satin).

‖**brigue** (brig), *sb.* Forms: 4–5 brige, bryge, brygge, brigge, 5 (?) bryke, 7– brigue. [a. F. *brigue* (14th c. in Littré) = med.L. *briga*, It. and Pg. *briga*, Sp. and Pr. *brega*. Of uncertain origin: see Diez. The word and its derivatives are extensively developed in Italian: see BRIGAND, etc. Adopted in Eng. in the 14–15th c.; then again from modern Fr. about 1700.]

†**1.** Strife, quarrel, contention. *Obs.*

[*c* **1380** cf. BRIKE.] *c* **1386** CHAUCER *Melibeus* ¶716 Myne Aduersaries han bigonnen this debaat and brygge [*v.r.* brige, brigge]. *c* **1440** *Promp. Parv.*, Bryge or debate, *briga*, *discensio*. **1496** *Dives & Paup.* (W. de W.) IV. xxiv. 192 Yf they passe ther tyme by retchelesnesse or by bryge, the bysshop shall ordeyne. **1678** LITTLETON *Lat. Dict.*, A brigue or quarrel. *Lis, contentio* [*briga*].

‖**2.** Intrigue, faction. [from mod.F.; much used in the first half of the 18th c.] *Obs.* (exc. casually).

1701 *Jura Pop. Anglicani* 29 They must set afoot Factions and Brigues. **1720** OZELL tr. *Vertot's Rom. Rep.* I. III. 171 The Cabals and Brigues of the Patricians. **1752** HUME *Pol. Disc.* xii. 296 Sufficient to prevent brigue and faction. **1753** *Dial. betw. Swift & Prior* 134 Violent and ill-judg'd Brigues and Feuds. **1867** J. THOMSON *L'Anc. Régime* 13 He in recompense got Fierce struggle with brigue and plot.

†**brigue** (brig), *v. Obs.* [f. prec., or a. F. *brigue-r* to contend, intrigue for = It. *brigare* to brawl, brabble, strive for. But sense 1 appears to be related to BRIKE: see *Briga, brica* in Du Cange; It. *imbrigare* 'to molest, embroil'; also, to entangle, Florio.]

†**1.** *trans.* To ensnare, trap, beguile. *Obs.*

c **1380** WYCLIF *Sel. Wks.* III. 416 þo fende hafs caste þis snare for to bryge men. **1387** TREVISA *Higden* Rolls Ser. II. 367 Men were so i-briged [CAXTON begyled] þat þey couþe nouȝt come out.

2. *intr.* To intrigue; to solicit by underhand methods; to canvass. (Chiefly *Sc.* in 16–18th c.)

1588 A. KING *Canisius' Catech.* 109 Then efteruart nother brigued, or desyred, nother violentlie inuaded yᵉ Bishoprick. **1706** LD. BEILHAVEN *Sp. in Sc. Parlt.* 11, I don't think any one Post of the kingdom worth the briguing after. **1726** WODROW *Corr.* (1843) III. 270 They are already beginning to brigue and cabal. *a* **1808** BP. HURD (L.), I am too proud to brigue for admission.

†**b.** *trans.* To obtain by intrigue. *Obs.*

1758 SIR J. DALRYMPLE *Ess. Hist. Feudal Prop.* 170 Kenneth III. brigued a contrary law from his barons.

Hence **briguing** *vbl. sb.*

1704 SWIFT *T. Tub* i, By briguing and caballing. **1837** CARLYLE *Fr. Rev.* II. II. v. v. 64 Briguing, intriguing, favouritism . . goes on there.

†**brigueless.** *adv. Obs. rare.* In 5 brygeless. [f. BRIGUE + -LESS; = F. *sans brigue*.] Without cavil or dispute; with undisputed title.

1415 OCCLEVE *Oldcastle* 164 *Anglia* v. 28 Land . . þat thy fadir huld in reste and pees . . And his fadir before him brygeless.

†ˈ**briguer.** *Obs.* [ad. F. *brigueur*, f. *briguer*: see BRIGUE *v.*] A contentious person, a quarrelsome wrangler.

1496 *Dives & Paup.* (W. de W.) x. x. 385/2 There shal no shrewe, no bryger, no lechour . . entre in to this cyte. *c* **1600** BUREL *Pilgr.* in Watson's *Coll. Poems* II. 46 (JAM.) As bregers and tygers, Delyts in blud to be.

brikcanetyne, obs. Sc. form of BRIGANDINE.

†**brike.** *Obs.* Also 5 bryke. [a. ONF. *brique*, *bricque*, var. of *briche*, *brice*, trap, gin.] A trap, a snare; a 'fix', a dilemma.

c **1380** WYCLIF *Sel. Wks.* III. 128 If a man falle in bryke [*v.r.* brygge] for worldly richesses. *c* **1386** CHAUCER *Monkes T.* 400 Geniloun Oliver . . Broughte this worthy king in such a bryk [*v.r.* brike, bryke]. **1413** LYDG. *Pylgr. Sowle* IV. xxxv. (1483) 83 Ne hit belongeth nought to suche offycers for the kynges profite to meue newe brykes. *a* **1420** OCCLEVE *De Reg. Princ.* 176 They rekke not what brike her lorde be ynne.

brike, brikke, obs. forms of BRICK.

brikell, obs. form of BRICKLE.

brill (brɪl), *sb.*[1] Also 5 brell, prylle. [Origin and etymological form (*brill*, *prill*, or *perl*) unknown.

(The Cornish *brilli*, contr. of *brithelli* (pl. of *brithel*) 'mackerel' (Williams), agrees in phonetic form, but has no connexion in sense, and there is no evidence of confusion as to the two fish. The English is also probably older than the contracted form of the Cornish word.)]

A kind of flat-fish (*Rhombus vulgaris*), allied to, and resembling the Turbot, but inferior in flavour.

1481–90 *Howard Househ. Bks.* (1841) 105 For . . ij solys, a prylle, and xij. whytynges. *Ibid.* 120 For an haddok and a brell vj.d. **1740** R. BROOKES *Art of Angling* Index, Brill or Pearl. **1830** M. DONOVAN *Dom. Econ.* II. 181 The brill is longer and narrower than the turbot: the brill has scales on both sides, the turbot has thorns on the back and no scales on the other side. **1873** MISS BROUGHTON *Nancy* I. 81, I have heard . . that he does not care about brill, but worships John Dory.

†**brill**, *sb.*[2] *Obs.* (See quot.)

1688 R. HOLME *Armoury* II. 154/1 The Brills in the hair on the Eye-lids [of a horse]. **1725** BRADLEY *Fam. Dict.* II. s.v. *Horse*, To begin with the Hair . . 5. The Cronet, which is the Hair that grows over the Top of the Hoof. 6. The Brills, being the Hair on the Eye-lids.

brill (brɪl), *a.* colloq. abbrev. of BRILLIANT *a.*

1981 *New Standard* 2 June, *Brill* (as in plays, films, books), brilliant. **1982** *Pony Club Ann.* 14/1 What a brill idea. **1983** *Guardian* 10 Dec. 14/8 It may have been an awful night . . but the meat and potato pies were brill. **1984** M. AMIS *Money* 63 Maybe he's brill in the bag. **1985** *Punch* 23 Jan. 24/3 She is the only one of the three who has ever been interested in how a car works. . . She's brill, for a twelve-year-old. **1986** *Sunday Express Mag.* 10 Aug. 14 (Advt.), Here's a clue. Fab brill Hellmann's Mayonnaise.

†**brill**, *v. Obs. rare.* [Expressive of the sound.] *intr.* To make a sharp vibratory sound, as an insect by the rapid vibration of its wings.

1688 R. HOLME *Armoury* II. ix. 191 Voices of Bees, Worms, Serpents.—The Brize Breezeth or Brilleth.

‖**2.** Adaptation of Du. *brullen* to roar.

1863 W. BALDWIN *Afr. Hunting* 114 Two lionesses brilling savagely.

‖ˈ**brillant.** *Obs.* Also 7 brillain. [F. *brillant* sb., brilliance, brilliancy (subst. use of *brillant* BRILLIANT.)] Brilliancy.

1676 ETHEREDGE *Man of Mode* III. ii. (1684) 36 The brillain of so much good language, Sir, has much more power than the little beauty I can boast. **1678** T. RYMER *Trag. of Age* 6 He gives a lustre and brillant which dazzles the sight.

brillant, obs. form of BRILLIANT *a.*

‖**brillante** (brilˈlante), *a. Music.* [It. *brillante* bright, sparkling.] A term prefixed to a passage or movement, when it is to be played or sung in a gay and sparkling style.

†**brille**, *v. Obs. rare*⁻¹. [a. F. *brille-r* to shine: see BRILLIANT.] *intr.* To shine.

1727 LADY M. W. MONTAGUE *Let.* IV. clxv. 171 The town never was fuller, and some people brille in it who brilled twenty years ago.

brilliance (ˈbrɪljəns). [f. BRILLIANT: see -ANCE. No corresponding word in Fr.]

1. Intense or sparkling brightness or radiance, lustre, splendour.

[Not in JOHNSON 1755–73.] **1755** YOUNG *Centaur* i. (1757) IV. 107 How far wit can set wisdom at defiance, and, with its artful brilliances, dazzle common understandings? **1830** TENNYSON *Ode to Mem.* 20 Fruits Which in wintertide shall star The black earth with brilliance rare. **1879** HOWELLS *L. Aroostook* xxii. 243 The brilliance of a lamp that shot its red across the gloom. **1882** *Macm. Mag.* 64 Roderigues stands out well between the blue brilliances of sky and sea.

2. *fig.*

1779 JOHNSON *L.P.*, *Pope* Wks. IV. 75 A scholar with great brilliance of wit. **1808** J. BARLOW *Columb.* I. 198 New strength and brilliance flush'd his mortal sight. **1842** H. ROGERS *Introd. Burke's Wks.* (1842) I. 3 Both [the brothers Burke] possessed much of the brilliance of mind which so eminently distinguished Edmund. **1880** L. STEPHEN *Pope* 17 The story is told . . with his usual brilliance by Macaulay.

¶ *brilliance* and *brilliancy* are to a great extent synonyms: *brilliancy*, however, is more distinctly a quality having degrees; as in the comparative *brilliancy* of two colours.

brilliancy (ˈbrɪljənsɪ). [see prec. and -ANCY.]

The quality of being brilliant; shining quality, lustrousness; shining brightness. **a.** *physical.*

1747 HERVEY *Medit. & Contempl.* (1818) 89 It . . throws a brilliancy into the water of the diamond that is hardening on its rock. **1755** in JOHNSON. **1772** PENNANT *Tours Scotl.* (1774) 323 An amazing brilliancy of colors. **1856** RUSKIN *Mod. Paint.* IV. v. x. §3. 125 The apparent connection of brilliancy of colour with vigour of life, or purity of substance. **1878** HUXLEY *Physiogr.* 75 This brilliancy is rapidly lost . . on exposure to the atmosphere.

b. *non-material.*

1796 BURKE *Regic. Peace* Wks. VIII. 398 What new brilliancy then does it throw over the prospect. **1842** MISS MITFORD in L'Estrange *Life* III. ix. 157 She is full of life, and spirit, and brilliancy. **1850** MERIVALE *Rom. Emp.* (1865) I. ii. 69 The consciousness of deserved popularity added brilliancy to his wit. **1864** *Sat. Rev.* 475/1 Brilliancy and shallowness are commonly received synonyms. The best device for exciting the most solemn distrust is to accuse a man of brilliance.

c. with *plural.*

1858 HAWTHORNE *Fr. & It. Jrnls.* II. 96 Its concentrated brilliancies and magnificences. **1868** —— *Amer. Note-bks.* (1879) II. 145 The autumnal brilliancies.

brilliant (ˈbrɪljənt), *a.* (*sb.*) Also 7–8 brillant. [a. F. *brillant* shining, pr. pple. of *briller* to shine, corresp. to Pr. and Sp. *brillar*, Pg. *brilhar*, It. *brillare*, commonly taken as formed on a L. type **berillāre*, f. late L. *berill-us* (Isid.), L. *beryllus* BERYL. Littré notices that the verb is not found in Fr. before the 16th c., when it appears to have been taken from one of the cognate langs.]

1. a. Brightly shining, glittering, sparkling, lustrous.

1681 BLOUNT *Glossogr.*, *Brillant* (Fr.), glittering, sparkling, shining. **1696** PHILLIPS, *Brilliant*, glittering, casting forth a sparkling Light. **1720** KERSEY, *Brillant* [as in BLOUNT & PHILLIPS]. **1791** HAMILTON *Berthollet's Dyeing* I. Introd. 1 The beauty of brilliant colours. **1859** GEO. ELIOT *A. Bede* 60 There is always a stronger sense of life when the sun is brilliant after rain. **1878** HUXLEY *Physiogr.* 75 As brilliant as a piece of polished silver.

b. *Photogr.* Applied to a type of reflecting view-finder (see quot. 1958).

1894 *Photogram* Oct. 247/1 The 'Adams Brilliant' finder is a new departure of considerable importance. **1896** *Photography Ann.* 1895 429 Brilliant view finders are now becoming the rule. **1937** *Miniature Camera Mag.* Jan. 92/1 With the additional aid of a 'brilliant' viewfinder. **1958** M. L. HALL *Newnes Compl. Amat. Photogr.* iii. 40 Many simple cameras are fitted with so-called brilliant finders—simply a metal container with a lens in front, a mirror set at 45°, and another which receives the image and into which the user looks.

c. *brilliant cut*: in *Glass-cutting.* (See quot. 1962.)

1933 *Archit. Rev.* LXIV. 22/1 The glass panel with the brilliant-cut (that is engraved with emery wheel) figure had real beauty. **1953** *Glass for Glazing* (*B.S.I.*) 21 (*caption*) Types of brilliant cut. **1962** *Gloss. Terms Glass Ind.* (*B.S.I.*) 26 *Brilliant cut*, a decorative process in which designs are produced on flat glass with abrasive and polishing wheels.

2. *fig.* **a.** Of qualities and actions: Splendid, illustrious, distinguished, striking the imagination.

1758 LADY M. W. MONTAGUE *Lett.* IV. cx. 109 The carnival is expected to be more brilliant than common, from the great concourse of noble strangers. **1769** *Junius Lett.* xxiv. 114 Wit is oftentimes false, though it may appear brilliant. **1848** MACAULAY *Hist. Eng.* I. 242 A man of solid, though not brilliant parts. **1867** DICKENS *Lett.* (1880) II. 312 It is impossible that prospects could be more brilliant.

b. Of persons: Very distinguished or celebrated; *esp.* distinguished by talent and cleverness; having showy good qualities.

1848 MACAULAY *Hist. Eng.* I. 531 The stern and pensive William relaxed into good humour when his brilliant guest appeared. *Ibid.* II. 230 He found a brilliant circle of noblemen and gentlemen assembled. **1871** MORLEY *Voltaire* (1886) 7 Fontenelle was both brilliant and far-sighted.

c. In weakened use: amazing, 'fantastic'. *colloq.*

1971 [see BAGGY *sb. pl.*]. **1983** J. KELMAN *Not, not while Giro* 17 Man man who would've thought of me getting paid back money like that. Brilliant. **1984** S. TOWNSEND *Growing Pains A. Mole* 15, I allowed Pandora to visit me in my darkened bedroom. We had a brilliant kissing session.

†**B.** as *sb.* = BRILLANT. *Obs.*

1691 *Fop Dict.* Suppl., The Brilliant of Language. Sharpness and wittiness of Expression. **1694** CONGREVE *Double Dealer* II. i. (Jod.) Some distinguished quality, as for example the bel air, or brilliant of Mr. Brisk.

ˈ**brilliant**, *sb.* Also 7–8 brillant. [a. F. *brillant* in same sense, subst. use of *brillant* adj.]

1. A diamond of the finest cut and brilliancy.

(The *brilliant* differs from the *rose*, in having horizontal faces on its upper and under sides, called the *table* and the *collet* respectively, which are surrounded and united by facets, while the upper surface of the rose rises into a dome, and is covered with facets. The French brilliant consists of two truncated pyramids placed base to base. Watts.)

1690 *Lond. Gaz.* No. 2609/4 Lost . . a square Diamond Brilliant, weighing eight grains. **1700** DRYDEN *Gd. Parson* 139 This brillant is so spotless and so bright He needs no foyl. **1749** FIELDING *Tom Jones* v. i, The jeweller knows that the finest brilliant requires a foil. **1832** BABBAGE *Econ. Manuf.* xvi. (ed. 3) 148 A brilliant which has successively graced the necks of a hundred beauties.

b. *attrib.* and in *comb.*

1705 *Lond. Gaz.* No. 4160/4 Lost . . two single Brilliant Drops. **1709** *Ibid.* No. 4617/4 A Rose Diamond Ring, set with a large Brilliant Stone. **1713** *Ibid.* No. 5139/4 Ten Diamonds, all Brilliant cut. **1748** MRS. DELANY *Autobiog.* (1861) II. 487 He has given her a very fine pair of brilliant earrings. **1761** WILSON in *Phil. Trans.* LII. 444 Six of these gems are cut brilliant fashion.

†**2.** A kind of silken fabric. *Obs.*

1719 J. ROBERTS *Spinster* 345 Many woollen stuffs, and stuffs mixed with silk, and even silks themselves . . such as brilliants and pulerays, antherines and bombazines.

3. 'A brisk, high mettled, stately horse, that has a rais'd neck, a high motion, excellent haunches' (Bailey vol. II. 1731); also in Craig 1847.

4. A species of firework.

1875 URE *Dict. Arts* III. 682 *A fixed brilliant* . . gun powder, 16; steel-filings, 4.

5. The smallest type used in English printing, being a size less than 'diamond'. (A fancy name, suggested by *pearl*, *ruby*, *diamond*.)

1875 URE *Dict. Arts* III. 640 The smallest is called Brilliant, but is seldom used.

ˈ**brilliant**, *v. rare.* [f. BRILLIANT *a.*] *trans.* To cut as a brilliant.

1752 BEAWES *Lex Mercat.* 777 The Diamonds . . to which they have given the name of Nayffez or dwarf Points . . are naturally brillianted. **1784** H. WALPOLE *Corr.* IV. 377 (D.) The new Bristol stones . . would pass on a more skilful lapidary than I am for having been brillianted by a professed artist.

ˈ**brilliantine.** [a. F. *brillantine*, f. *brillant*.]

1. A cosmetic for imparting a gloss to the hair.

1884 *Harper's Mag.* Oct. 706/1 The same devotion to starch and brilliantine.

2. A fine, shiny, textile fabric used for dress and lining material. Chiefly *N. Amer. Obs.* exc. *Hist.*

1873 A. D. WHITNEY *Other Girls* iii. 15 The underskirt was the identical black brilliantine that had done service all the spring. **1895** *Montgomery Ward Catal.* Spring & Summer 6/2 Brocaded Mohair Brilliantines, rich and lustrous as silk. **1911** *Daily Colonist* (Victoria, B.C.) 23 Apr. 24/2 (Advt.), 2000 yards White Brilliantine, in stripe, check and floral. Very special value, 10¢. **1948** *Amer. Fabrics* V. 143/1 *Brilliantine*, cloth in which a birdseye pattern is woven into the material on the Jacquard loom. **1969** N. W. PARSONS *Upon Sagebrush Harp* xiii. 68 A dress length of new copen blue brilliantine.

brilliantined (brɪljən'tiːnd), *a.* [-ED[2].] Dressed with brilliantine (sense 1).

1906 *Daily Chron.* 6 Apr. 9/5 Their adipose cheeks and brilliantined hair. **1926** *Chambers's Jrnl.* May 315/2 A sleek and pear-shaped gentleman heavily brilliantined and scented. **1967** A. WILSON *No Laughing Matter* I. 11 Thickly brilliantined heads.

'brilliantly, *adv.* [f. BRILLIANT *a.* + -LY[2].] In a brilliant manner, with brilliant effect; brightly, glitteringly, splendidly.

[Not in JOHNSON 1755–73.] **1813** *Examiner* 22 Mar. 186/1 The last campaign..terminated not only brilliantly but gloriously. **1815** *Scribbleomania* 33 True star..With radiance poetic, most brilliantly clear. **1855** MACAULAY *Hist. Eng.* III. 615 No other large Irish town is so well cleaned, so brilliantly lighted. **1882** PEBODY *Eng. Journalism* xvi. (1882) 120 He could write and write brilliantly, in clear, terse, and vigorous English.

'brilliantness. = BRILLIANCY.

1755 in JOHNSON; whence in later Dicts.

'brilliantwise, *adv.* [f. BRILLIANT *sb.* + -WISE.] After the manner of a brilliant.

1839 BAILEY *Festus* xxix. (1848) 337 Senses fined, And pointed brilliantwise.

†**brim,** *sb.*[1] *Obs.* Forms: 1–6 brim, 1–4 brym, 4 brymme. [OE. *brim* surf, (*poet.*) the sea = ON. *brim* surf, sea; prob. f. the stem *brem-* roar, rage: see BRIM *v.*[1] It became obs. in ME.; but was perhaps used by Spenser.] An old poetical word for the sea; also, 'flood', water.

Beowulf 847 (Gr.) Wæs on blode brim weallende. *c* **937** *Battle Brunanburh* in *O.E. Chron.*, Siþþan eastan hider Engle and Sexe up becomon ofer brade brimu Brytene sohtan. *c* **1000** *Voc.* in Wr.-Wülcker 177 *Æquor*, brym, sæ. *c* **1290** *Land Cokaygne* 156 in *E.E.P.* (1862) 160 Hi..lepith dune in-to the brimme, And doth ham sleilich for to swimme. *c* **1340** *Gaw. & Gr. Knt.* 2172 A balȝ berȝ bi a bonke þe brymme [? *sea* or *shore*] bysyde. *a* **1400** *Leg. Rood* (1871) 125 In middes þe brig was ouer þe brim. **1596** SPENSER *F.Q.* v. ix. 35 The bright sunne, what time his fierie teme Towards the westerne brim [perh. = edge, horizon] begins to draw.

brim (brɪm), *sb.*[2] Forms: 3–7 brimme, brymme, 3–6 brym, 3, 7 brime, 6 bryme, 7 brimm, 4– brim. [ME. *brimme, brymme*, of uncertain etymology: cf. ON. *barmr* brim, Ger. *bräme* fem. 'margin, border, fringe', MHG. *brem* str. neut. 'edging, border'.]

I. *orig.* The border, margin, edge, or brink:

†**1. a.** of the sea, or any piece of water: Coast, shore, bank, brink. (Now only as a transferred application of 4.)

c **1205** LAY. 4472 His cniþtes..to þare sæ færden, þar laien bi þan brimme. *a* **1300** *K. Horne* 196 Ure schip bigan to swymme To þis londes brymme. **1398** TREVISA *Barth. De P.R.* XIII. xii. (1495) 447 In the brymme of the deed see groweth most fayr apples. **1534** LD. BERNERS *Gold. Bk. M. Aurel.* (1546) Llij, The flud of Nyle shulde flowe ouer his brymmes. **1597** GERARD *Herbal* II. xxxvi. §16. 249 The bayche and brimmes of the sea. **1856** BRYANT *Ages* xxviii, His willing waves yon bright blue bay Sends up, to kiss his decorated brim.

†**b.** In this sense formerly used without any defining addition. (Now only by ellipsis.)

c **1275** LAY. 17030 Þe cnihtes hine funde þar he sat bi brimme [*c* **1205** stronden]. *c* **1325** *E.E. Allit. P.* B. 365 Watz no brymme þat abod vnbrosten bylyue. **1375** BARBOUR *Bruce* XIV. 339 In a richt fair place..Lawch by a brym. *c* **1460** *Emare* 349 A boot he fond by the brym. **1596** SPENSER *F.Q.* VI. iii. 34 Whenas Calepine came to the brim..His heart with vengeance inwardly did swell. **1830** TENNYSON *Arab. Nts.* 16 The citron-shadows in the blue: By garden porches on the brim, The costly doors flung open wide.

†**2. a.** of other things. *Obs., arch.* or *dial.*

1525 LD. BERNERS *Froiss.* II. xxiii. 57 On the brimme of the dykes..he caused to stryke of the heedes of all the prisoners. **1578** LYTE *Dodoens* II. xxii. 173 Like to the common Belfloure, but..not so deepely cut about the brimmes or edges. **1596** SPENSER *F.Q.* IV. iii. 34 Upon the brim of his brode-plated shield. **1591** LYLY *Sapho* II. iv. 179 Let thy love hang at thy hearts bottome, not at the tongues brimme. **1601** HOLLAND *Pliny* II. 394 Escars that grow about the brims of vlcers. **1657** W. COLES *Adam in Eden* cxxx, The flowers..of a whitish colour washed about the brims with a little light carnation. **1716** *Lond. Gaz.* No. 5470/4 The Brims of the Ears black. **1862** BARNES *Rhymes Dorset Dial.* II. 185 E vell vrom the brim Ov a cliff.

†**b.** An edging or border (distinct from the surface).

a **1610** FLETCHER *Faithf. Sheph.* IV. i. 225 A brim Of sailing Pines that edge yon Mountain in. **1732** *Acc. Workhouses* 56 A slate with broad brims.

†**3.** *fig.* The 'brink' (of despair, the grave, etc.).

1549 COVERDALE *Erasm. Par. Rom.* Prol., Brought unto the very brymme of desperacion. **1622** A. COURT *Constancie* I. 48 The quarrels..haue brought him to the brimme of his graue. **1641** MILTON *Prel. Episc.* (1851) 80 This cited place lyes upon the very brimme of a noted corruption. **1649** JER. TAYLOR *Gt. Exemp.* II. viii. 75 He..is at the margin and brim of that state of final reprobation.

II. 4. a. Now *esp.* The edge, margin, or 'lip' of a cup, bowl, basin, or anything of similar shape artificial or natural. (Formerly often *pl.*) spec. ***brim of the pelvis*** or ***pelvic brim***: the part of the pelvis that forms the boundary of the superior pelvic aperture and separates the false or greater pelvis above from the true or lesser pelvis below; also, the aperture itself. Also *ellipt.*

1562 J. HEYWOOD *Prov. & Epigr.* (1867) 54 Better spare at brym than at bottem. **1570** LEVINS *Manip.* 131 Yᵉ Brim of a cup, *labrum.* **1586** J. HOOKER *Girald. Irel.* in *Holinshed* II. 93/2 Under the brim of his scull. **1611** BIBLE *2 Chron.* iv. 2 He made a molten Sea of ten cubites, from brim to brim. *a* **1695** WOOD *Life* (1848) 260 A vessel or a bason notched at the brimms. **1718** J. CHAMBERLAYNE *Relig. Philos.* (1730) II. xvii. §40 They will see it run over the Brims of the Glass like bottled Beer. **1754–64** [see PELVIS 1]. **1810** *Encycl. Lond.* I. 646/2 From the brim of the pelvis upwards. **1830** LYELL *Princ. Geol.* (1875) I. II. xxv. 622 On arriving at the brim of the Crater. **1885** R. & F. BARNES *Syst. Obstetr. Med.* II. xiii. 627 The filling up of the brim, and even of a part of the pelvic cavity sometimes, by the breech. **1957** D. SINCLAIR *Introd. Functional Anat.* xxi. 275 This basin is very incomplete, and ends centrally in a fairly abrupt rim of bone called the pelvic brim.

b. in *full to the brim*, and the like. Often *fig.*

1601 SHAKS. *All's Well* II. iv. 48 To make the comming houre oreflow with joy, And pleasure drowne the brim. **1606** —— *Ant. & Cl.* III. xiii. 18 He will fill thy wishes to the brimme. **1608** —— *Per.* II. iii. 50 A cup that's stored unto the brim. **1782** HAN. MORE *Belshaz.* II. 74 Fill me that massy goblet to the brim. **1814** CARY *Dante's Inf.* VI. 6 Thy city, heap'd with envy to the brim. **1875** B. TAYLOR *Faust* I. vi. 111 Quickly fill the beaker to the brim.

5. a. The upper edge or surface of water. *arch.* or *poetic.*

a **1552** LELAND in *Sat. Rev.* 13 Dec. (1885) 802 [Bremes] ons frayed approach not in the bryme of the water that yere agayne. **1571** DIGGES *Pantom.* III. xiv. S ij b, Marke..where the brimme of the water now toucheth. **1611** BIBLE *Josh.* iii. 15 The feet of the Priestes..were dipped in the brimme of the water. **1687** A. LOVELL tr. *Bergerac's Com. Hist.* I. 168 They are Fish that never rise to the brim of the Water. **1808** SCOTT *Marm.* VI. xv, Not lighter does the swallow skim Along the smooth lake's level brim.

†**b.** The surface of the ground. *Obs.*

1572 J. JONES *Bathes of Bath* II. 11 b, Neither is the place of the fyre under the brimme of the earth.

6. The projecting edge or marginal rim of a hat.

1592 SHAKS. *Ven. & Ad.* 1089 His bonnet on, Under whose brim the gaudy sun would peep. **1663** GERBIER *Counsel* 12 The broad Brim of a good Hat. **1665–9** BOYLE *Occas. Refl.* IV. xix. (1675) 279 Upon ones Drinking Water out of the Brims of his Hat. **1716–8** LADY M. W. MONTAGUE *Lett.* I. xxxviii. 154 A high-crowned hat without brims. **1831** CARLYLE *Sart. Res.* III. x. 332 They sometimes invert the hat, and wear it brim uppermost.

7. *techn.* ? The thickened marginal portion, or 'sound-bow', of a bell.

[**1697** DAMPIER *Voy.* I. (1729) 411 In the middle of the Floor stood a rusty Iron Bell on its Brims.] *a* **1849** MANGAN *Poems* (1859) 47 Brim and rim it gleams. **1872** ELLACOMBE *Bells of Ch.* i. 5 A bell should measure: in diameter at the mouth, fifteen brims; in height to the shoulder, twelve brims.

8. *Naut.* (See quot.)

1769 FALCONER *Dict. Marine* (1789) *Rim*, or *Brim*, a name given to the circular edge of any of the tops. **1867** in SMYTH *Sailor's Word-bk.*

9. *Comb.*, as **brim-charged**, filled to the brim.

1583 STANYHURST *Æneis* III. (Arb.) 87 Anchises a goold boul massye becrowning With wyne brym charged.

brim, *sb.*[3] [f. BRIM *v.*[1]] (See quot.)

1572 MASCALL *Govt. Cattle, Hogges* (1627) 274 To make them goe to brim, or take the boare, it shall be good to giue them barley. **1610** GUILLIM *Heraldry* III. xiv. (1660) 166 You shall say Boare goeth to his Brymme. **1727** BRADLEY *Fam. Dict.*, *Brim*, a Term relating to Swine; a Sow is said to go to Brim when she goes to Boar.

†**brim,** *sb.*[4] *Obs.* exc. *dial.* A bad, vicious woman. Cf. BRIMSTONE 4.

1730–6 BAILEY, *Brim* [q. a Contraction of Brimstone], a common Strumpet. **1764** T. BRYDGES *Homer Travest.* (1797) I. 173 Can mortal scoundrels thee [Hera] perplex, And the great brim of brimstones vex? **1808** JAMIESON, *Brim*, a cant term for a trull, *Loth.*

brim (brɪm), *sb.*[5] *U.S.* and *Austral.* var. of BREAM *sb.* In U.S. *spec.* the long-eared sunfish (*Lepomis auritus*); cf. BREAM *sb.* 2 b.

1795 J. SCOTT *U.S. Gazetteer* Hᵛ, A great variety of fish, as rock, mullet,..brim, and sturgeon. **1887** *Harper's Mag.* July 270/1 If they could slip away..there would be a diminished number of 'brim' and 'goggle-eye' in the ditch. **1894** *Outing* (U.S.) XXIII. 403/2 The brim, a small, red fish, which is excellent fried. **1898** MORRIS *Austral Eng.* 52/2 The popular pronunciation is *Brim*, and the fishes are all different from the various fishes called *Bream* in the northern hemisphere. **1936** *Amer. Speech* XI. 314/1 *Brim*, black perch. **1945** BAKER *Austral. Lang.* xii. 214 Popular fish-names peculiar to the Australian include: *brim* for bream. **1954** *Sydney Morning Herald* 24 May 8 Cod up to nine pound and brim up to seven.

brim (brɪm), *v.*[1] Forms: 5 bryme, brymmyn, 5–7 brymme, 6 breame, breme, 7 brime, brimme, 7– brim, (9 *dial.* breme). [In 15th c. *brymme*, in the 16th c. and mod. dial. also *breme*, corresp. to *brym*, BREME *a.*; either formed from the latter, or (though not found in ME.) actually descended from OE. *bremman* to roar, rage, corresp. to OHG. *breman*, MHG. *bremen* to rage, roar, MDu. and Du. *bremen, bremmen*, from an old Teut. root *brem-*, cogn. with L. *fremĕre.* In early mod.Du. *bremen* had also the sense 'desire violently', and LG. *brummen* (a derivative form) is said of the sow seeking the boar.]

1. *intr.* Of swine: To be 'in heat', rut, copulate.

c **1420** *Pallad. on Husb.* III. 1051 Nowe bores gladly brymmeth. *Ibid.* 1070 The sonner wol thei [sows] brymme ayeine and brynge Forth pigges moo. **1483** *Cath. Angl.* 44 To Bryme, *subare.* **1591** PERCIVALL *Span. Dict.*, *Berriondez de puerca*, when a sow is briming, *subatio.* **1616** BULLOKAR, *Brime*, a terme used among hunters when the wilde Boare goeth to the female. **1725** BRADLEY *Fam. Dict.* s.v. *Sow*, To make a Sow Brim or take Boar. **1863** ATKINSON *Danby Provinc.*, *Brim, breme*, 1. to desire the boar; 2. (as applied to the boar), to serve the sow.

2. *trans.* Said of a boar.

1552 HULOET, Brymme a sowe, as when a bore doth get pigges. **1577** B. GOOGE *Heresbach's Husb.* (1586) 127 Is oftentimes breamed of the boare, and conceaveth. **1601** HOLLAND *Pliny Nat. Hist.* I. 304. **1725** BAILEY *Erasm. Colloq.* 452 Every Boar to brim his Sow. **1863** [see 1].

†**brim, brime,** *v.*[2] *Obs. rare.*

intr. To be fertile, develop fruit, to BREED (sense 11 c).

c **1250** *Gen. & Ex.* 118 God..erðe brimen and beren dede. *Ibid.* 1128 Men seið ðe treen..Waxen in time and brimen.

brim (brɪm), *v.*[3] Also 7 brimme. [f. BRIM *sb.*[2]]

1. *trans.* To fill (a goblet, etc.) to the brim. Also *absol.*

1611 HEYWOOD *Gold. Age* I. i. Wks. 1874 III. 14 Fetch me his heart, brimme me a bowle With his warme bloud. **1805** SOUTHEY *Madoc in W.* II, The board was spread anew, Anew the horn was brimm'd. **1813** COLERIDGE, *Remorse* v. i. 108 As I brimmed the bowl, I thought on thee. **1850** TENNYSON *In Mem.* cvi. 16 Fetch the wine, Arrange the board and brim the glass.

b. *fig.* and *transf.*

1844 A. WELBY *Poems* (1867) 70 Softly brimming my young eyes with tears. **1853** BOWRING in *Fraser's Mag.* XLVIII. 351 All my heart was brimmed with bliss. **1878** GILDER *Poet & Master* 9 Not tears, but jollity..brim the strong man-child's eyes.

2. *intr.* To be or become brim-full. ***to brim over***: to overflow *with.* (The ppl. adj. BRIMMING is found from Milton onward.)

1818 KEATS *Endym.* II. 997 Where I brim Round flowery islands. **1858** HAWTHORNE *Fr. & It. Jrnls.* II. 70 The bustle of the market..went on within or brimmed over into the streets. **1873** GEIKIE *Gt. Ice Age* xxvi. 353 The Gulf of Bothnia appears to have brimmed with ice. **1874** T. HARDY *Madding Crowd* I. xxix. 322 He brimmed with deep feeling as he replied.

†**3.** *trans.* To provide with a brim. *Obs.*

1623 COCKERAM II, To brim a thing, *marginate.*

brim *a.*: see BREME.

brimbel, -bil, -byl, obs. forms of BRAMBLE.

‖**brimborion, -um.** Also 7 breborion. [Fr.; formerly *bre-, briborion*; according to Littré a perversion of *breviārium* 'breviary', whence 'foolish charmes or superstitious prayers, vsed by old and simple women against the toothache, and any such thredbare and mustie rags of blind devotion' (Cotgr.).] 'A thing without value or use' (Littré); trash, nonsense.

1653 URQUHART *Rabelais* I. xxi, He mumbled all his Kiriele and dunsical breborions. **1786** MAD. D'ARBLAY *Diary & Lett.* III. 8 Talking to your royal mistress, or handing jewels and colifichets and brimborions, baubles, knick-knacks, gewgaws. **1880** WEBB *Goethe's Faust* II. vii. 164 As when their scruples you overcome With all sorts of brimborium.

†**brim-fill,** *v. Obs. rare.* [f. BRIM *sb.*[2] + FILL *v.*] *trans.* To fill up to the brim.

1615 T. ADAMS *Blacke Dev.* 71 The cup of his iniquity [will be] brimfilled. *c* **1620** Z. BOYD *Zion's Flowers* (1855) 33 Sins our city doe brime fill. **1647** CRASHAW *Poems* 203 Thy brimfill'd bowls of fierce desire.

brimfir, variant of BRINFIR, *Obs.*

brim-full, brimful (see below), *a.* Orig. written as two words. [f. BRIM *sb.*[2] + FULL: properly pronounced ('brɪm'fʊl); cf. *half full, quite full*, and the like; erroneously ('brɪmfʊl), by association with adjs. like *mindful.*]

1. Full to the brim; on the point of overflowing.

1530 PALSGR. 307/1 Brimfull, *plain.* **1542** RECORDE *Gr. Artes* (1640) 401 [Archimedes] putting the Crowne..into the vessel of water brim full..marked, how much water did run out. **1597** SHAKS. *2 Hen. IV*, III. i. 67 His Eye brim-full of Teares. **1697** *Phil. Trans.* XIX. 516 A little Box, which I filled Brim full. **1703** MAUNDRELL *Journ. Jerus.* (1721) 51 Yet it is always brim full. **1720** GAY *Poems* (1745) I. 88 Her eyes with tears brim full. **1860** KINGSLEY *Misc.* I. 173 Rivers..brimful in the longest droughts.

b. Of the eyes: Full of tears. (This appears to be always '*brimful* in the poets: cf. *tearful.*)

1700 DRYDEN *Sigism. & Guisc.* 681 Her brimful eyes, that ready stood..Released their watery store. **1786** BURNS *Farewell St. James's Lodge*, With melting heart, and brimful eye.

2. *fig.*

1579 TOMSON *Calvin's Serm. Tim.* 116/2 Brimme full of venime against God. **1604** SHAKS. *Oth.* II. iii. 214 The peoples hearts brim-full of feare. **1706** *Reflex. upon Ridicule* 292 A woman brim-full with the notion of her beauty. **1794** *Gold. Age* in *Poet. Register* (1807) 401 And sing, brimful of thee, in tuneful strain. **1830** TENNYSON *Dream Fair Wom.* 12 My heart, Brimful of those wild tales. **1850** THACKERAY *Pendennis* xxxvii, Brimfull of health, and life, and hope. **1876** J. H. NEWMAN *Hist. Sk.* II. II. ii. 234.

brimfully. *adv. rare.* [f. prec. + -LY[2].] So as to be brim-full.

1854 *Tait's Mag.* XXI. 333 Wilson was brimfully, nay, overflowingly, imbued with the poetic element.

brimfulness. *Obs.* [f. as prec. + -NESS.]

[Johnson quotes for this the following passage from Shaks., where the reading is *brim 'fulnesse* in two words (like *brim full*) with *brim* in attributive relation to *fulness*.]

1599 SHAKS. *Hen. V*, I. ii. 150 The Scot..Came pouring like the Tyde into a breach With ample and brim fulnesse of his force. **1891** HARDY *Tess* xxvii, The brimfulness of her nature breathed from her.

'briming. (*Cornwall.*) The phosphorescence of the sea; = BURNING 3. Cf. BRINY 2.

1836 YARRELL *Fishes* II. 103 A master seaner..forms a judgment by the extent of the brining in his sean. **1880** *E. Cornwall Gloss.*, Briming. —— *W. Cornw. Gl.*, Brimming.

brimless ('brɪmlɪs), *a.* Without a brim.

1615 G. SANDYS *Trav.* 76 High-crowned brimlesse caps of beaten gold. **1824** MISS MITFORD *Village* Ser. I. (1863) 14 He with the brimless hat. **1887** *Chambers's Jrnl.* IV. 1 A round, brimless sailor's cap.

brimmed (brɪmd), *ppl. a.*[1] See BRIM *v.*[1]

1552 HULOET, Brymmed sowe, *sus subata.*

brimmed (brɪmd, 'brɪmɪd), *ppl. a.*[2] [f. BRIM *v.*[3] and *sb.*[2]]

1. Filled to the brim; brim-full.

1624 HEYWOOD *Gunaik.* III. 161 Me thinkes a cup of gold Stands brim'd before me. **1637** MILTON *Comus* 924 May thy brimmed waves for this Their full tribute never miss. **1821** KEATS *Lamia* 639 A cup he took Full brimm'd. **1877** M. ARNOLD *Poems* II. 59 This brimmed unwrinkled Rhine.

2. Having a brim, as a hat, etc. Chiefly in composition, as ***broad-***, ***narrow-***, ***wide-brimmed***.

1606 HOLLAND *Sueton.* 75 Hee never walked..without a broad brimd Hat upon his head. **1711** ADDISON *Spect.* No. 44 ¶8 In ordinary Comedies, a broad and a narrow brim'd Hat are different Characters. **1884** *Pall Mall G.* 31 Mar. 4/2 He has a brimmed hat to keep the sun from his head.

brimmer ('brɪmə(r)), *sb.* [f. BRIM *v.*[3] + -ER[1].]

1. A thing that fills to the brim; a swelling wave.

1652 BENLOWES *Theoph.* I. xviii, Swell us a lustie Brimmer ..So vast, that none may spie the coast.

2. A brimming cup or goblet.

1663 COWLEY *Cutter Coleman St.* V. vi, Boy! Fill a Brimmer, Nay fuller yet, yet a little fuller. **1697** DRYDEN *Virg.* (1806) II. 253 Nor ceas'd to draw, Till he the bottom of the brimmer saw. **1728** GAY *Begg. Op.* III. xii, Not one so sure can bring Relief As his best Friend, a Brimmer. **1826** SCOTT *Woodst.* iv. (1846) 63 Accustomed to feed the flame of their loyalty with copious brimmers.

3. A hat with a brim. Cf. *bowler*. Now chiefly *local*; spec. a straw hat.

Cf. *Local rhyme* (*Birmingham*). Straw brimmer, Ate the donkey's dinner.

a **1652** BROME *Songs* (N.) Now takes his brimmer off. **1670** EACHARD *Cont. Clergy* 136 Twisting the ends of his Girdle, and asking him the price of his Brimmer. **1888** LOWSLEY *Gloss. Berks. Words*, *Brimmer*, a hat. **1893** DARTNELL & GODDARD *Gloss. Words Wilts.*, *Brimmer*, a broad-brimmed hat. **1902** *Pall Mall Gaz.* 14 Apr. 2/3 The early brimmer marked a conspicuously daring spirit here and there against the crowd of silk hats.

brimmer ('brɪmə(r)), *v.* [f. prec.] *trans.* and *absol.* To fill and drink (brimmers of wine). Hence **'brimmered** *ppl. a.*

1838 *Fraser's Mag.* XVII. 313 Is he not seen at the Athenæum, dinnering and brimmering? **1831** HOGG in *Fraser's Mag.* IV. 380 The brimmer'd glass in every hand.

brimming ('brɪmɪŋ), *vbl. sb.*[1] [f. BRIM *v.*[1]] The action of the verb BRIM[1]: said of swine.

1530 PALSGR. 824/2 A brimmyng as a bore or sowe doth, *en rouyt.* **1601** HOLLAND *Pliny* I. 230 They stand lightly to the first brimming. **1616** SURFL. & MARKH. *Countr. Farm* I. xxiv. 106 They begin to grow hot and goe a brimming. **1671** CHARENTE *Let. Customs Tafiletta* 46 The wild Boars are most furious creatures, especially in Brimmin time.

brimming ('brɪmɪŋ), *vbl. sb.*[2] [f. BRIM *v.*[3] + -ING[1].] Being full to the brim, overflowing.

1837 HT. MARTINEAU *Soc. in Amer.* III. 73 The gushing talk of Judge Story, the brimmings of a full head and heart. **1878** G. MEREDITH in *Macm. Mag.* Oct., Something friends have told her fills her heart to brimming.

'brimming, *ppl. a.* [f. BRIM *v.*[3] + -ING[2].]

1. That rises to the brim of its vessel, basin, or bed; that fills to overflowing.

1667 MILTON *P.L.* IV. 336 They..in the rinde, Still as they thirsted, scoop the brimming stream. **1857** EMERSON *Poems* 42 The brimming brook invites a leap. **1864** TENNYSON *Brook* 64 And out again I curve and flow, To join the brimming river.

fig. **1864** *Spectator* 424 All true poetry really requires a brimming vitality of feeling and impression.

2. Of a vessel: Brim-full, full to overflowing.

1697 DRYDEN *Virg. Past.* III. 43 To store the Dairy, with a brimming Pail. **1725** POPE *Odyss.* XX. 317 Wine rosy bright the brimming goblets crowned. **1845** DISRAELI *Sybil* (1863) 48 To fill the brimming cup.

3. *advb.*

1848 W. E. AYTOUN *Danube & Eux.* 10, I am brimming full and red.

'brimmingly, *adv.* [f. prec. + -LY[2].] In a brimming manner, up to the brim. Also *fig.*

1826 T. ATKINSON *The Spate* in *Casquet Lit.* I. 196/1 The ..stream..filled it brimmingly. **1876** MRS. WHITNEY *Sights & Ins.* xv. 161 She was brimmingly happy.

brimmy ('brɪmɪ), *a.* [f. BRIM *sb.*[2] + -Y[1].] Of a hat: having a wide brim; broad-brimmed.

1896 A. MORRISON *Child of Jago* 112 The brimmy tall hat. **1908** *Westm. Gaz.* 28 Mar. 2/2 The cult flew..to big buttons on parachute-skirted coats,..to brimmy hats, brimmier hats, brimmiest hats, brimless hats. **1970** *Daily Tel.* 9 Nov. 10/2 She still had..a brimmy black hat.

†**brimse.** *Obs.* exc. *dial.* Also 7 **brimsee, brimesey,** 9 *dial.* **brimps.** [First found in 16th c.: identical with ON. *brims* (Fritzner); also Ger. *bremse*:—OHG. *primisa* (Graff), *brimissa* (Kluge), perh. f. *brem-* to roar, in sense of 'boom, buzz loudly'. In Eng. prob. from Norse, though early evidence is wanting.] A gadfly; = BREEZE *sb.*[1]

1579 GOSSON *Apol. Sch. Abuse* (Arb.) 64 They..lashe out their heeles as they had caught the brimse. **1608** TOPSELL *Serpents* 769 Those great horse-flies or ox-flies and brimsees that in summer season vex cattle. **1610** GUILLIM *Heraldry* III. xxi. 166 The Flie..of some is called the Gad-bee, and of others the Dun-fly, Brimesey, or Horse-fly. **1611** COTGR., *Tahon*, a brizze, Brimsee. *Oestre Iunonique*, a gad-bee, brimsey, brizze. *Mod. Kent Provinc.*, The brimps bite the cows so much they don't know what to do.

brimstone ('brɪmstən). Forms: *α.* 3 (?), 4–5 **brin-, brynstan(e, -ston(e, brenston, -stoon,** (4 *Kent.* **bernston,** *north.* **bronstane, brunstan(e),** 4–6 **brunston(e,** 5–6 **bronston,** 6 **byrnstone, brontstane, brint-, bryntstane, -stone,** 8– *Sc.* **brunstane.** *β.* 4–5 **brimstan(e, -ston, -stoon, brymston(e, -stoon(e, (brem-, brom-, brumstone,** 5 **brymestone,** 7 **brimestone),** 6– **brimstone;** *mod.Sc.* **brumstane.** [ME. *brin-, bren-, brun-, brimston*, late OE. (12th c.) *brynstán* (MS. Vesp. D. XIV, f. 163), app. f. *bern-, brinn-*, stems of BURN *v.* + STONE *sb.*; cf. ON. *brenni-steinn* sulphur; also, for the form, OE. *berne-lác* burnt-offering. An identical formation in other Teut. langs. (MDu. and MLG. *bernsteen*, Du. *barnsteen*, Ger. *bernstein*) is used with the sense 'amber'. The transposition in *bern-, bren-* was inherited from the vb.; the subsequent change to *brim-* may have been due to association with the adj. *brim*, BREME 'fierce': cf. quot. *c* 1400 in 1 *α*.

The uncertainty of form in ME. may be estimated by the fact that the printed ed. of Wyclif (Forshall and Madden) has in the two texts the following varieties:—*Gen.* xix. 24 brenstoon, brynston; *Deut.* xxix. 23 brimstoon, brymston; *Job* xviii. 15 brumston, brymston; *Ps.* x. 7 brunston, brymston; *Isa.* xxx. 33 brunston, brymstoon.]

1. Formerly the common vernacular name for SULPHUR. Now used chiefly when referring to its inflammable character, and to the biblical use in *Gen.* xix. 24 and *Rev.* xix. 20; or in speaking of old-fashioned prescriptions, as 'brimstone and treacle'.

α. *a* **1300** *Cursor M.* 2842 Our lauerd raind o þam o-nan, Dun o lift, fire and brinstan [*other MSS.* brimston]. **1340** HAMPOLE *Pr. Consc.* 6746 Fire and brunstan and stormes with wynde. **1340** *Ayenb.* 130 þou gest in-to helle huer þou sselt yuinde ver and bernston. **1375** BARBOUR *Bruce* XVII. 612 Lynt and hardiss with brynstane. **1393** LANGL. *P. Pl.* C. XXI. 291 Brynston [*v.r.* brymston, bremston] boilaunt brennyng out-casteþ hit Al hot on here heuedes. *a* **1400** *Cov. Myst.* (1841) 308 In bras and in bronston [*v.r.* brenston] the brethellys be brent. *c* **1400** *Destr. Troy* 860 þe ffyre..was blasound of brunston with a brem lowe. *c* **1450** *Nominale* in Wr.-Wülcker 683 *Hoc fulgur*, bornston. **1523** SKELTON *Garl. Laurel* 631 The blast of the byrnstone blew away his brayne. **1536** BELLENDEN *Cron. Scotl.* (1821) I. 136 Birnand flammis of pik, roset and brintstane. **1552** ABP. HAMILTON *Catech.* 92 With brontstaine and fyre. **1791** BURNS *Ep. J. Maxwell* iii, Rake them, like Sodom and Gomorrah In brunstane stoure. **1875** ROBINSON *Whitby Gloss. Brunstan*, or *Burnstan*, burning-stone or brimstone.

β. *a* **1300** *Cursor M.* 2888 Fir and brimstan was þe wrake. **1382** WYCLIF *Job* xviii. 15 Brumston be sprengd in his tabernacle. *c* **1386** CHAUCER *Chan. Yem. Prol. & T.* 271 Sal Armonyak and the ferthe Brymstoon [*v.r.* brymston, brunston, bremston(e, bromstone]. **1489** CAXTON *Faytes of A.* II. iv. 96 Enoyncted with oyle and brymestone. **1570** LEVINS *Manip.* 168 Brimstone, *sulphus.* **1611** BIBLE *Rev.* xix. 20 Both were cast aliue into a lake of fire burning with brimstone. **1672** R. WILD *Declar. Lib. Consc.* 14 An itch, which is too hard for butter and brimstone to cure. **1691** HARTCLIFFE *Virtues* xli. **1755** SMOLLETT *Quix.* (1803) II. 47 Every fiend may stink of brimstone. **1796** MRS. GLASSE *Cookery* xxii. 346 Fire a large match dipped in brimstone. **1840** R. DANA *Bef. Mast* xxix. 98 We..made a slow fire of charcoal, birch bark, brimstone, and other matters. **1863** KINGSLEY *Water-bab.* v. 207 She dosed them with..salts and senna, and brimstone and treacle.

b. *fire and brimstone!* an ejaculation of 'strong language'.

1601 SHAKS. *Twel. N.* II. v. 56 *To.* Fire and Brimstone! *Fa.* O peace, peace. **1604** —— *Oth.* IV. i. 245.

2. ***vegetable brimstone***: the inflammable spores of *Lycopodium clavatum* and *Selago*, sometimes employed in the manufacture of fireworks.

1866 in *Treas. Bot.*

3. *fig.*

1601 SHAKS. *Twel. N.* III. ii. 22 To put fire in your Heart, and brimstone in your Liuer. **1709** CHANDLER *Effort agst. Bigotry* 15 Such Mens new acquired Light having too much Brimstone in it. **1828** CARLYLE *Misc.* (1857) I. 120 Like a person of breeding, and without any flavour of brimstone.

4. A virago, a spit-fire. Cf. BRIM *sb.*[4]

1751 SMOLLETT *Per. Pic.* (1779) I. vi. 54 She is..not a brimstone, like Kate Coddle. **1788** *Walpoliana* xlii. 21 Oh! Madam..he had such a brimstone of a wife! **1824** W. IRVING *T. Trav.* II. 29 A tragedy queen, and a brimstone to boot.

5. ***brimstone butterfly***: an early butterfly with wings of a sulphur colour, *Gonepteryx Rhamni*.

1827 *Butterfly Collect. Vade Mec.* 87. **1860** GOSSE *Rom. Nat. Hist.* 5 The delicate 'brimstone' comes bounding over the fence.

6. *Attrib.* and *Comb.*: **a.** *simple attrib.* Of, pertaining to, or resembling brimstone; **b. brimstone match**, a match or splinter of wood having its end dipped in brimstone; **brimstone moth**, a species of moth of sulphur colour, *Rumia cratægata*; **brimstone-wort**, a plant, Sulphur-wort, *Peucedanum palustre* (and *officinale*).

a. *c* **1590** MARLOWE *Faust.* viii. 18 The most intolerable book for conjuring that e'er was invented by any brimstone devil. **1616** HOLYDAY *Juvenal* 240 Flames begun By brimstone-plot. **1786** BURNS *Sc. Drink* xx, And bake them up in brunstane pies. **1791** HAMILTON *Berthollet's Dyeing* I. I. I. iv. 67 A fine brimstone colour. **1840** DICKENS *Barn. Rudge* vi, Asserted his brimstone birth and parentage.

b. **1594** PLAT *Chem. Conclus.* 15 The rest of the fats have not received..the brimstone match. **1657** REEVE *God's Plea* 23 The furnace-brand, the brimstone-match of that cursed man. **1739** DESAGULIERS in *Phil. Trans.* XLI. 177 When Brimstone Matches are burning. **1812** SIR H. DAVY *Chem. Philos.* 299 Sulphuret of phosphorus..applied to a common brimstone match inflames when gently rubbed. **1859** W. COLEMAN *Woodlands* (1862) 112 The curious twig-like caterpillars of the Brimstone Moth. **1678** A. LITTLETON *Lat. Dict.*, Brimstone-wort, an herb, *Peucedanum.* **1863** PRIOR *Plant-n.* 29 *Brimstonewort*, from its roots yielding, as W. Coles says, 'a yellow sap which waxeth quickly hard, and dry, and smelleth not unlike to brimstone'.

†**'brimstonish,** *a. Obs. rare* [f. BRIMSTONE + -ISH[1].] Sulphurous; somewhat sulphur-coloured.

1562 TURNER *Bathes* 7 The water of this bath is knowen to be..a small part brimstonish. **1727** BRADLEY *Fam. Dict.* s.v. *Anemone*, Outer leav'd brimstonish thrum'd Green.

brimstony ('brɪmstənɪ, -nɪ), *a.* [f. BRIMSTONE + -Y[1].] **a.** Of, pertaining to, or resembling brimstone.

1382 WYCLIF *Rev.* ix. 17 Thei that saten on hem hadden fijry haberiouns, and iacynctines, and brunstony [**1535** COVERD. of a yalowe and brymstony coloure]. **1398** TREVISA *Barth. De P.R.* (Helmingham MS.) XIII. i, Yf þe grounde is brymstony, oþer of slyme. **1670** W. SIMPSON *Hydrol. Ess.* 96 The sulphurous and brimstony matter. **1830** JAMES *Darnley* xxii. 98/2 A sort of brimstony smell.

b. *transf.* and *fig.* Sulphurous, fiery.

1885 *Chambers's Jrnl.* Aug. 22 That brimstony old reprobate next door. **1924** SCHOLES *1st Bk. Gramophone Rec.* 93 The betrayer..came to a bad and brimstony end.

Hence **'brimstoniness.**

1398 TREVISA *Barth. De P.R.* VII. xxxv. (1495) 249 Glaysynesse and brenstonynesse and other suche.

brin, obs. form of BRINE, BURN.

†**'brinage.** *Obs. rare*[−1]. In 7 brynage. [f. BRINE + -AGE.] Briny quality.

1610 FOLKINGHAM *Art of Survey* I. vi. 13 Waters..of so brackish a Brynage, that they wil be conuerted to Salt by boyling.

†**brince, brinche,** *v. Obs. rare.* [Contracted from BRENDICE; or directly f. It. *brins, brinsi* 'a health or drinking to one. Also I drinke to you' (Florio 1611).] *trans.* To drink to, pledge; also *causal*, to make, or give, to drink.

1556 ABP. PARKER *Psalter* lxxv. 211 The good at brynke the cleare doth drynke, God brinche them gently so. *a* **1572** HARDING in *Jewel's Wks.* (1848) IV. 335 Luther first brinced to Germany the poisoned cup of his heresies. **1598** LYLY *Moth. Bomb.* ii. 1 (N.), I carouse to Prisius, and brinch you mas Sperantus.

brinded ('brɪndɪd), *a. arch.* Forms: 5 **brende,** 5–8 **brended,** 7 **breended,** 6– **brinded.** [Primary form app. *brended*, whence on one side BRANDED, q.v., on the other *brinded*. *Brende*, which occurs in Lydgate, is identical with one of the contemporary forms of *burnt, burned* (see BURN *v.*); nevertheless, taken with the fuller *brended*, it points to a secondary vb. *brend-en*, a possible derivative of *brand* 'burning, brand'. The sense appears to be 'marked as by burning' or 'branding'. Prof. Skeat compares Icel. *bröndóttr*

brindled, f. *brand* fire-brand.] Of a tawny or brownish colour, marked with bars or streaks of a different hue; also *gen.* streaked, spotted; brindled.

1430 LYDG. *Min. Poems* 202 On them she wyl have a bonde, As weel of bayard as of brende [*rime-wd.* rende] And yit for sorelle she wyl stonde. **1496** *Bk. St. Albans, Fysshynge* 28 A grete brended flye that bredith in pathes of medowes. **1589** GREENE *Menaph.* (Arb.) 86 Ah, Doron.. thou art as white As is my mothers Calfe, or brinded Cow. **1605** SHAKS. *Macb.* IV. i. 1 Thrice the brinded Cat hath mew'd. **1611** COTGR., *Quatroillé*, diuersified, pide, or breended, streaked with one colour vpon another. **1621** MARKHAM *Prev. Hunger* (1655) 54 Your brended Cattell haue euer the goodliest Heads. **1667** MILTON *P.L.* VII. 466 The Tawnie Lion.. Rampant shakes his Brinded main. **1717** TICKELL *Epist.* Wks. (1807) 117 Thy brinded boars may slumber undismay'd. **1774** JOHNSON *West. Isl.* Wks. X. 416 They have a race of brinded greyhounds. **1820** SHELLEY *Witch Atl.* vii, The brinded lioness led forth her young.

brindle ('brɪnd(ə)l), *a.* and *sb.* [App. deduced from *brindled*, as if this consisted of *brindle* + *-ed.*]

A. *adj.* = BRINDED, BRINDLED.

1676 *Lond. Gaz.* No. 1145/4 A.. white Mastiff Dog with half his face brindle, and large brindle spots on his sides. **1765** TUCKER *Lt. Nat.* I. 497 Two fine cows, one brindle and the other white. **1807–8** W. IRVING *Salmag.* xviii. (1860) 403 The old lady.. lost.. a brindle cow. **1862** *Sat. Rev.* 5 July 19 The longhorned [English cattle].. of which brindle or brindle and white are common colours. **1886** *Engineer* 1 Oct. 265 The quotation of brindle bricks at date is about 18s. per 1000.

B. *sb.* **a.** Brindled colour. **b.** A brindled dog.

1696 *Lond. Gaz.* No. 3242/4 An old Dutch Mastiff.. of a lightish Brindle. **1710** *Ibid.* No. 4747/4 Lost.. a Lurcher Bitch, a Brindle with a black Mussel. **1748** RICHARDSON *Clarissa* (1811) VIII. xli. 156 The artificial jet, however, yielding apace to the natural brindle. **1824** MISS MITFORD *Village* Ser. I. (1863) 65 Of the three dogs, the first a brindle, the second a yellow.

brindle, *v. dial.* 'To be irritated, to show resentment, to bridle up.'

1875 *Lanc. Gloss.* (E.D.S.) 58 He brindled up as soon as aw spoke to him.

brindled ('brɪnd(ə)ld), *a.* [A variant of the earlier BRINDED, prob. by assimilation to such words as *kindled, mingled*, perh. with some feeling of a diminutive sense.] 'Streaked, tabby, marked with streaks' (J.).

1678 *Lond. Gaz.* No. 1328/4 Lost or stolen.. a large light brindled gelt Mastiff Dog. **1718** POPE *Iliad* XI. 378 The brindled lion, or the tusky boar. **1753** SMOLLETT *Ct. Fathom* (1784) 116/2 His beard.. was of a brindled hue. **1817** J. SCOTT *Paris Revisit.* (ed. 4) 100 The mustachoes which hid the expression of the human mouth under a brindled tuft of hair. **1870** EDGAR *Runnymede* 186 A brindled bull. **1886** *Engineer* 1 Oct. 265 The brindled brick trade.. is an important Staffordshire industry.

brine (braɪn), *sb.* Forms: 1 bryne, 3–4 brin, 4 briyn, 4–7 bryne, 6 bryn, (7 broyn), 4– brine. [OE. *brýne, bríne*, corresp. to MDu. *brîne* fem., Du. *brijn* neuter, also Flem. *brijne, brēne* fem. Ulterior history unknown.]

1. Water saturated, or strongly impregnated, with salt; salt water.

a **1000** ÆLFRIC *Gloss.* in Wr.-Wülcker 128 *Salsugo, muria*, bryne. *a* **1300** *Cursor M.* 6348 Siþen þai faand.. Water bitter sum ani brin [*v.r.* brine, bryne]. **1382** WYCLIF *Jer.* xvii. 6 The lond of briyn [**1388** saltness]. *c* **1420** *Pallad. on Husb.* III. 39 Olde bryne atte tree and vyne a feest is. *c* **1440** *Promp. Parv.* 51 Bryne of salt, *salsugo.* **1544** PHAËR *Regim. Lyfe* (1560) X ij b, Take a good quantity of bryn which is made of water and salt. **1578** LYTE *Dodoens* V. xxi. 578 They keepe and preserue the leaues.. in brine or pickle. **1626** BACON *Sylva* §790 Broyn, when it is salt enough, will bear an Egg. **1657** W. FENNER *2nd Pt. Christ's Alarm* 28 God hath been laying rods in brine for thee. **1669** *Phil. Trans.* IV. 1063 Six Tuns of Brine yield one tun of Salt. **1753** CHAMBERS *Cycl. Supp.* s.v., There is sand found in all the Staffordshire brines after coction. *a* **1848** MARRYAT *R. Reefer* ix, Those were the times of large schools, rods steeped in brine (*actual fact*).

2. The water of the sea; the sea. (Chiefly *poet.*)

1598 SYLVESTER *Du Bartas* I. iii. (1641) 22/1 Such is the German Sea.. and such th' Arabian Brine. **1610** SHAKS. *Temp.* I. ii. 211 All but Mariners Plung'd in the foaming bryne. **1637** MILTON *Lycidas* 95 On the level brine Sleek Panope with all her sisters played. **1738** C. WESLEY *Psalms* (1765) cxlvii, While Monsters.. lash the foaming Brine. **1805** WORDSW. *Waggoner* III. 85 The unluckiest hulk that stems the brine. **1841** LONGF. *Ballad Fr. Fleet* vii, The great ships.. sank like lead in the brine.

3. = Briny tears. *poet.*

1592 SHAKS. *Rom. & Jul.* II. iii. 69 Iesu Maria, what a deale of brine Hath washt thy sallow cheekes for Rosaline? **1593** —— *Lucr.* 796 Seasoning the earth with showres of siluer brine. **1604** DEKKER *Honest Wh.* Wks. 1873 II. 115, I should be well seasoned, for mine eyes lye in brine.

4. *Attrib.* and *Comb.* **a.** General, as ***brine-bath, -house, -pit, -spring, -tub, -water, -well; brine-bound, -dripping, -soaked***, adjs.

1588 SHAKS. *Tit. A.* III. i. 129 And made a brine pit with our bitter teares. **1648** HERRICK *Hesper., Gt. Boast*, Look in his brine-tub, and you shall find there Two stiff blew pigs-feet. *c* **1682** J. COLLINS *Making of Salt* 20 It is called a Brine-House, to retain store for Winter Boyling. **1774** JOHNSON in *Boswell* (1831) III. 130, I tasted the brine water, which contains much more salt than the sea water. **1817** *Parl. Deb.* 740 Supposed to be not a common brine spring. **1841** *Penny Cycl.* XX. 368/2 The Cheshire brine-springs are from twenty to forty yards in depth. **1849** MACAULAY *Hist. Eng.* I. 317 The salt which was obtained by a rude process from brine pits. **1855** SINGLETON *Virgil* I. 233 Brine-dripping limbs. **1860** PIESSE *Lab. Chem. Wonders* 33 In Cheshire there are salt beds: these produce.. brine wells. **1861** COLLIER *Hist. Eng. Lit.* 419 His brine-soaked coat. **1866** HOWELLS *Venet. Life* xii. 179 Brine-bound Venice.

b. Special comb.: **brine-evaporator**, an apparatus for evaporating brine so as to deposit the salt; **brine-gauge**, a salinometer or salt-gauge; **brine-man**, one who superintends the making of brine; **brine-pan**, a shallow iron vessel in which brine is evaporated; also, a shallow pit, or basin, in which brine is evaporated by the action of the sun; **brine-pump**, a pump used for removing the brine which collects at the bottom of a steamer's boilers; **brine-seeth**, a salt boilery; **brine-shrimp** (see quot.); **brine-smeller**, one who examines a district with a view to the discovery of beds of salt; **brine-valve**, a valve in a boiler which is opened to allow the escape of water saturated with salt; **brine-worm** = *brine-shrimp.*

c **1682** J. COLLINS *Making of Salt* 30 A skilful *Brineman will govern and direct 3 or 4 Labourers. *Ibid.* 19 Before it be transmitted into the shallow *Brine-Pans. **1732** DE FOE, etc. *Tour Gt. Brit.* (1769) 395 Middlewich.. noted for making Salt, where are two excellent *Brine-seeths. **1836** *Penny Cycl.* V. 343/1 The Brine-worm or *Brine-shrimp, *Cancer Salinus* of Linnæus.. is about half an inch in length. **1860** GOSSE *Rom. Nat. Hist.* 74 At Lymington in Hampshire, the reservoirs of concentrated brine are always peopled by.. a sort of shrimp.. commonly known as the *brine shrimp. **1878** F. WILLIAMS *Midl. Railw.* 558 A *'brine smeller'.. expressed his belief that mines might be opened.

brine (braɪn), *v.* [f. BRINE *sb.*] To treat with brine: to steep, soak, pickle, wet, suffuse with brine.

Hence **brined** *ppl. a.*

1552 HULOET, Bryned or layde in powder, or salte water. **1573** TUSSER *Husb.* (1878) 167 Some corneth, some brineth. **1608** *Merry Devil Edm.* in *Dodsley* (1780) V. 261 I'll make the brined sea to rise at Ware. **1677** PLOT *Oxfordsh.* 39 'Tis yearly practiced thus to brine their Fields. *a* **1722** LISLE *Husb.* (1752) 156, I had wheat brined and limed for sowing. **1822** BEDDOES *Bride's Trag.* I. i, His cheeks with grief y-brined. *c* **1842** LANCE *Cott. Farm.* 11 Two and a half bushels of Wheat to the acre, after brining and liming. **1883** *Standard* 3 Aug. 6/6 Hides.. brined at full prices, salted at last sale's rates.

brineless ('braɪnlɪs), *a.* [f. BRINE *sb.* + -LESS.] Without brine or salt.

1791 E. DARWIN *Loves of Pl.* 111, Where vast Ontario rolls his brineless tides. **1870** LOWELL *Among my Bks.* Ser. I. (1873) 362 The brineless tears of a flabby remorse.

Brinell (brɪ'nɛl). The name of J. A. *Brinell* (1849–1925), Swedish engineer, used *attrib.* to designate his method (introduced *c.* 1900) of measuring the hardness of substances. (See quot. 1954.)

1915 *Proc. Amer. Soc. Test. Materials* XV. 47 (*title*) Relation between Brinell Hardness and Scleroscope Hardness. *Ibid.*, There was very little difference noted in the hardness at the center, or the outside, and a Brinell test was then made... The diameter of the depression was measured under a microscope and the corresponding Brinell number calculated. **1916** *Metal Industry* 25 Aug. 236 (*title*) Testing non-ferrous metals for hardness: application of the Brinell method. *Ibid.*, A series of combined microscopic and Brinell hardness tests. **1954** *Gloss. Terms Iron & Steel* (*B.S.I.*) I. 7 *Brinell hardness test*, a test to determine hardness by pressing a hard steel ball of known diameter under a standard load into the surface of the material and measuring the diameter of the indentation produced.

briner ('braɪnə(r)). [f. BRINE *v.* + -ER[1].] A salt boiler, a salter.

c **1682** J. COLLINS *Making of Salt* 4 When the Briners go to cleanse it, they cannot abide in above half an hour. **1748** *Phil. Trans.* XLV. 363 The Lees of Ale and Beer are now generally rejected by the marine Salt-Boilers; except in the West of England, where the Briners.. use them. **1759** B. MARTIN *Nat. Hist. Eng.* II. 246.

† **'brinfir.** *Obs. rare.* Also brimfir, brendfier. [Only in *Gen. & Ex.*: app. f. *brenn-en* to burn + FIRE: but see BRIMSTONE.] Fierce burning fire: applied as a name for brimstone.

c **1250** *Gen. & Ex.* 754 For mannes sinne ðus it is went, brent wið brimfir, sunken and shent. *Ibid.* 1110 Sone so loth ut of sodome cam brend-fier-rein ðe burȝe bi-nam. *Ibid.* 1164 To-ward sodome he saȝ ðe roke And ðe brinfires stinken smoke.

bring (brɪŋ), *v.* Pa. t. and Pa. pple. brought (brɔːt). Forms: *Inf.* 1 bringan, brengan, 2–5 bringen, 3–6 bringe, bryngen, 4–6 brynge, 4–7 bryng, 4– bring, (3 bringhe, brynke, 3–4 brengen, 4–5 breng, 5 bryngyn). *Pa. t.* 1–3 bróhte, 2 brochte, 3 broȝte, brouhte, 4 brouȝt(e, broȝt, broht, browȝt, browghte, (brohut), 4–6 broughte, 4–7 broght, 5 browte, 4– brought, (6 brohute, *Spenser* braught, 6– *Sc.* brocht, 9 *dial.* brong, brung). *Pa. pple.* 1–4 bróht, 3 broucht, 3–4 ybroȝt, ibrouȝt, 4 brout, browt, browht, ybrouȝt, brouht, 4–5 broȝt, (brouth), 4–6 broght, ybrought, 5 ibrowghte, (bryght), 5–6 browght, broughte, 4– brought, (6 browte, ibrout, browth, 6– *Sc.* brocht, 9 *dial.* brung). [Common Teut.: OE. *bring-an, bręngean* (pa. t. *bróhte*, pple. *bróht*), corresp. to OFris. *branga, bringa*, OS. *brengian, bringan* (MDu. *brenghen*, Du. *brengen*), OHG. *bringan* (MHG. and mod.G. *bringen*), Goth. *briggan* (= *bringan*), pa. t. *brâhta*, pple. *brâhts*. Beside the type *bring-an*, the Saxon group has also **brangjan, bręngian, bręngean, bręngan*, app. after *þankjan*; from *bringan*, OE. had also a rare strong pa. pple. *brungen* (mod. dial. *brung*), to which later dialects have added a strong pa. t., so as to conjugate, *bring, brang, brung*. The stem is not known outside of Teutonic.]

I. Simply.

1. To cause to come along with oneself; to fetch. It includes 'lead' or 'conduct' (F. *amener*) as well as 'carry' (F. *apporter*); it implies motion towards the place where the speaker or auditor is, or is supposed to be, being in sense the causal of *come*; motion in the opposite direction is expressed by *take* (Fr. *emmener, emporter*).

a. by carrying or bearing in one's hand, etc.

c **950** *Lindisf. Gosp.* John ii. 8 Dæleð nu & brengeð ðæm aldormen. *c* **1175** *Lamb. Hom.* 101 Ða ileafullen brohton heore gersum. *c* **1200** *Trin. Coll. Hom.* 47 Hie brohte þat child mid hire in to þe temple. *a* **1225** *Ancr. R.* 114 Ne brouhten heo him to presente ne win, ne ale, ne water. *a* **1300** *Cursor M.* 21588 To rome men suld a-noþer [del of cros] breng. **1340** *Ayenb.* 211 Þe messager þet none lettres ne brengþ. **1526** *Pilgr. Perf.* (W. de W. 1531) 14 They solde theyr possessyons, and brought the pryce therof. **1697** DRYDEN *Virg. Georg.* III. 16, I.. shall in Triumph come From conquer'd Greece, and bring her Trophies home. **1728** POPE *Dunciad* II. 383 The ponderous books two gentle readers bring. **1839** THIRLWALL *Greece* I. 335 He was to bring his shield home, or to be borne upon it. **1885** H. O. FORBES *Nat. Wand.* III. viii. 258 The flotsam harvest which the river was continually bringing down.

b. by leading, conducting, propelling, etc.

a **1000** *Beowulf* 1829 (Gr.) Ic ðe þusenda þeȝna bringe. *c* **1175** *Cott. Hom.* 221 God þa hine brohte into paradis. *c* **1250** *Gen. & Ex.* 737 Ðu fare.. to a lond ic ðe sall bringen him. *a* **1300** *Cursor M.* 3832 His doghtur yonder.. Bringand his beistes till þe well. *Ibid.* 5182 Ha yee broght him wit you hider? **1526** *Pilgr. Perf.* (W. de W.) 38 b, Brynge me here ye wyldest bull that is. **1565–73** COOPER *Lat. Dict.*, *Subducere naues*, to draw or bring ships to land. **1631** HEYWOOD *Fair Maid W.* I. III. i, There's a prize Brought into Falmouth Road. **1747** CARTE *Hist. Eng.* I. 192 These two princes, bringing with them a number of their vassals. **1884** BLACK *Jud. Shaks.* xxxiii, The horses were now brought round. **1885** H. O. FORBES *Nat. Wand.* III. viii. 258 At length a bend of the river brought me in sight of the European.. quarter of the city.

c. as by an attractive force.

c **1300** *Beket* 488 The Kynges coronement that so moche folc broȝte there. **1697** DRYDEN *Virg. Georg.* IV. 644 What Buis'ness brought thee to my dark Abode? **1857** BUCKLE *Civiliz.* xiv. 844 For mere purposes of social enjoyment men were brought into contact, who.. had nothing in common. *Mod.* What brings him here?

d. Colloq. phr. ***to bring home the bacon*** (fig.): to succeed in an undertaking; to achieve success.

1924 WODEHOUSE *Ukridge* viii, It may be that my bit will turn out to be just the trifle that brings home the bacon. **1928** *Daily Express* 10 Aug. 3/5 If I fail to 'bring home the bacon' I will give £10 to any charity selected by your ladyship. **1946** P. LARKIN *Jill* 33 The College takes a number of fellows like him to keep up the tone.. but they look to us to bring home t' bacon.

†**2.** To convoy, escort, accompany (a person) on his way. *Obs.* exc. *dial.*

c **1450** *Merlin* i. 20 He brought the on wey hider-warde a grete part. **1599** SHAKS. *Much Ado* III. ii. 3 Ile bring you thither my Lord, if you'l vouchsafe me. **1611** TOURNEUR *Ath. Trag.* II. ii. 48 The skie is dark; we'll bring you o'er the fields. **1611** BIBLE *Gen.* xviii. 16 Abraham went with them, to bring them on the way. **1862** BARNES *Rhymes Dorset Dial.* I. 18 *note*, To bring woone gwain: to bring one going; to bring one on his way.

3. a. ***to bring an answer, word, tidings***, etc.

a **1000** *Genesis* 651 (Bosw.) He ða bysene from Gode brungen hæfde. *a* **1300** *Cursor M.* 3965 Þe messagers him broght answar. *Ibid.* 17920 Comen am I.. Bodeworde of him for to bryng. *c* **1440** *Syr Gener.* 2195 They brought hym word ayenward thei were comyng. ? *a* **1500** *Adam Bel* 441 in Ritson *A.P.P.* 22 He shall you breng worde agayn. **1590** SHAKS. *Com. Err.* IV. iii. 37, I brought you worde an houre since that the Barke *Expedition* put forth to night. **1651** *Proc. in Parl.* No. 83. 1274 Advt., The party that brings tidings of him. **1864** TENNYSON *Sea Dreams* 258 She brought strange news.

†**b.** *ellipt.* = *bring word*, report. *Obs.*

1602 SHAKS. *Ham.* V. ii. 204 Young Osric, who brings back to him, that you attend him in the hall. **1606** —— *Ant. & Cl.* IV. xiii. 10 Hence Mardian, And bring me how he takes my death to th' Monument.

4. *fig.*, and in such expressions as ***to bring tears into the eyes, a blush to the cheek***, etc.

a **1000** *Metr. Boeth.* xi. 59 Winter bringeð weder unȝemet cald. *c* **1200** *Trin. Coll. Hom.* 258 He mai blisse bringe. **1382** WYCLIF *Jer.* xlv. 5 Y shal bringe euel vp on eche flesh, seith the Lord. **1535** COVERDALE *Ps.* xlv[i]. 8 What destruccions he hath brought vpon ye earth. **1752** JOHNSON *Rambl.* No. 207 ⁋2 Every hour brings additions. **1849** THACKERAY *Pendennis* cxxxiv, Those lines.. brought tears into the Duchess's eyes. **1850** TENNYSON *In Mem.* ii, The seasons bring the flower again, And bring the firstling to the flock. **1871** MORLEY *Voltaire* (1886) 21 To persuade us that the occasion invariably brings the leader whom its conditions require.

b. of things or actions bringing their results or consequences: To cause one to have, to procure.

c **1450** *Merlin* xiv. 229 A thynge that brought hym more mys-ese. **1577** HANMER *Anc. Eccl. Hist.* (1619) 273 A pillar resembling the forme of a crosse..bringing great admiration to the beholders. **1580** BARET *Alv.* B 1302 Liberall studies bring refuge and comfort in aduersitie. **1598** SHAKS. *Merry W.* v. v. 243 Cursed houres Which forced marriage would have brought vpon her. **1736** BUTLER *Anal.* I. iii, Rashness..and wilful folly, bringing after them many inconveniences and sufferings. **1832** TENNYSON *Miller's D.* 229 The loss that brought us pain.

†5. To deduce, derive, infer. *Obs.*

1591 SHAKS. *1 Hen. VI*, II. v. 77 Whereas hee From Iohn of Gaunt doth bring his Pedigree. **1605** CAMDEN *Rem.* (1637) 73 Hadrian, Lat... Gesner bringeth it from the Greeke Ἀδρὸς, Grosse or wealthy. **1692** RAY *Disc.* III. v. (1732) 376, I shall bring them from higher or more remote causes. **1713** SWIFT *Cadenus & V.* Wks. 1755 III. II. 12 Conclusions..From premisses erroneous brought.

6. a. To prefer or lay (a charge or accusation); to institute, set on foot (an action at law); to advance, adduce (a statement or argument).

c **1000** *Ags. G., John* xviii. 29 Hwylce wrohte bringe ȝe onȝean þysne man. **1382** WYCLIF *ibid.* What accusing brynge ȝe aȝens this man? **1574** tr. *Littleton's Ten.*, A write of right that a man bringeth. **1663** PEPYS *Diary* 14 June, Sir J. Minnes brought many fine expressions of Chaucer. **1715** BURNET *Own Time* II, The story he had sworn against the queen: which he brought only to make it probable that Wakeman..was in it. **1767** BLACKSTONE *Comm.* II. 197 If he ..puts in his claim and brings his action within a reasonable time. **1768** *Ibid.* III. III. 121 An indictment may be brought as well as an action. **1802** MAR. EDGEWORTH *Mor. Tales* (1816) I. xiii. 104 Arguments..brought by his companions in their..master's justification. **1875** JOWETT *Plato* (ed. 2) I. 316 He brings a wonderful accusation against me.

b. *to bring home*: see HOME.

1795 NELSON in Nicolas *Disp.* II. 104, I..demand..that the person..do fully, and expressly bring home his charge. **1871** R. H. HUTTON *Ess.* (1877) I. 34 The import of his action is brought home to him with the most vivid conviction.

7. a. = *bring forth*: to give birth to, bear. **b.** = *bring in*: to produce, yield, 'fetch'.

1523 FITZHERB. *Husb.* §66 The damme of the calfe shall.. brynge an other by the same time of the yere. **1535** COVERDALE *Habb.* iii. 17 The londe shall bringe no corne. **1664** BUTLER *Hud.* II. I. 466 What is Worth in any thing But so much money as 'twill bring? **1779** JOHNSON *Waller, L.P.* 224 Written when she had brought many children. **1795** SOUTHEY *Joan of Arc* II. 141 At one birth She brought the brethren. **1831** J. M. PECK *Guide for Emigrants* 47 The bottoms..will bring three or four crops of corn without manure. **1834** *Encycl. Metrop.* XXII. 365/2 They [*sc.* ferrets] breed twice a year, bringing five or six at a time. **1843** *Amer. Pioneer* II. 172 The moose is an animal similar to the deer... They usually bring two young at a time.

c. *to bring into the world*: to give birth to.

1607 SHAKS. *Cor.* v. iii. 125 Thy Mothers wombe That brought thee to this world. **1848** S. BAMFORD *Early Days* i, I was brought into the world on the 28th February.

8. *fig.* To cause to come *from, into, out of, to,* etc. a certain state or condition, or *to be* or *do* something; to cause to become.

Especially with prepositional and other phrases which are used also with *come* and *be*, and other verbs, most of which will be found under the sb. or other word in question.

a. with *on, in* (obs.), *into*:

as *to bring in good estate, debt, a plight*; *in dread, fear, in* or *on sleep* (later *a-sleep*; see e.); *in doubt, in hate, in question, in wit*; *on day* (= to light), *in* or *on life's day* (= to life); *into bands, difficulties, trouble*; *into action, harmony, contact, shape,* etc.

1297 R. GLOUC. 491 The King adde Normandie in god stat ibrouȝt al. *a* **1300** *Cursor M.* 615 In bale he broght vs and in care. **1387** TREVISA *Higden* II. 403 Pelias brouȝte Iason in witte [*suadet Jasoni*] for to fette þe goldene flees. **1398** —— *Barth. De P.R.* VI. iv. (1495) 191 Nouryces brynge the chyldren softely..on slepe. *c* **1400** *Destr. Troy* 13804 He was drecchit in a dreame, & in dred broght. **1535** COVERDALE *Judg.* Contents xvi, Dalila..bryngeth him in dotage. **1551-6** ROBINSON tr. *More's Utop.* (Arb.) 33 You shall bryng your selfe in very good case. **1593** HOOKER *Eccl. Pol.* I. x. §9 To bring themselves into hatred. **1596** SPENSER *F.Q.* VI. XII. xxxix, Yet none of them could ever bring him into band. **1602** W. WATSON *Decacordon* 260 Brought many of them into bands and other great dangers. **1736** BUTLER *Anal.* I. iv, Persons..by a course of vice, bring themselves into new difficulties. **1818** CRUISE *Digest* II. 402 It hath formerly been attempted to be brought in question. **1854** H. VICARS in *Memorials* viii. 162 Every thought brought into obedience to him. **1863** E. NEALE *Anal. Th. & Nat.* 191 All others, with which it is brought into accordance.

b. with *from, of, out of*:

as †*to bring of, out of, life* or *life's day* (formerly *o lifes dawe, o dawe, adaw,* corruptly *on daw*: cf. ADAW *v.*) = to kill; *out of order, shape, tune*; *out of patience, temper*.

a **1300** *Cursor M.* 1072 Wid murther he broght his broþer o lijf. *Ibid.* 5096 Þis hunger tide þat sal bath mani man and wijf..bring o þair lijf. *Ibid* 7808 Þat i suld him bring o dau [*Fairf.* on liues dawe]. *Ibid.* p. 990 *Resurr.* 356 We wend þat he alle Israel of woo suld haf broght. *c* **1305** *Jud. Iscariot* in *E.E.P.* (1862) 109 Ȝut were his fader betere habbe ibroȝt him of dawe. —— *St. Kenelm* 93 *ibid.* 50 If heo miȝte bringe þat child of lyfdawe. **1523** LD. BERNERS *Froiss.* I. ccxxvi. 301 They were discomfyted, and brought out of ordre by force of armes. **1530** PALSGR. 469/1 His great crammyng in of meate hath brought him out of shape. *Ibid.* 468/2, I can bring hym out of pacyence with the waggyng of a strawe. **1533** ELYOT *Cast. Helth* (1541) 62 They bringe a man from the use of reason. **1600** SHAKS. *A.Y.L.* III. ii. 262 Thou bring'st me out of tune.

c. with *to*:

as *to bring to a close, end, head, issue, pitch*; *to bearings, cure, rights*; *to death, hardness, idleness, mischief, nought, obedience, shame*; *to account, book, hand, light, trial*; *to mind, reason, recollection, remembrance*; *to bed* (see BED 6 c); *to oneself* (= to one's senses).

c **1175** *Lamb. Hom.* 103 þan men..to deþe bringeð. *c* **1230** *Hali Meid.* 15 þat ti wil were ibroht to werke. **1297** R. GLOUC. 376 þat hii nere to ssame ybroȝt. *a* **1300** *Cursor M.* 12759 His sermon þat mani man broght to resun. *Ibid.* 20122 þe seke brouȝte sche to bedde [*Cott.* broght to þair bedd]. *c* **1305** *St. Lucy* in *E.E.P.* (1862) 101 Dame Entice hire moder..þat hire to womman brouȝte. *c* **1340** *Ayenb.* 128 þe holy gost..þe seneȝere..brengþ ayen to him-zelue. *c* **1374** CHAUCER *Boeth.* III. ii. 99 Alle thinges ben referred and browht to nowht. *c* **1440** *Promp. Parv.* 51 Brynge to mynde, *reminiscor.* **1530** PALSGR. 468/2 He fell in so great a swoune that we all had ynoughe a do to bring hym to hym selfe. *Ibid.* 470/1 Tyme bringeth the truthe to lyght. **1535** COVERDALE *Mark* viii. 26 He was brought to right againe & sawe all clearly. **1611** BIBLE *Pref.* 1 Certaine worthy men haue been brought to vntimely death. **1624** MASSINGER *Renegado* I. iii, Are you amazed? I'll bring you to yourself. **1651** *Proc. Parl.* No. 88. 1343 All things now seem to bee brought to a good head. **1711** ADDISON *Spect.* No. 89 ¶1 He hoped that matters would have been long since brought to an Issue. **1715** DE FOE *Fam. Instruct.* I. vii. (1841) I. 136 You will never bring me to your beck. **1749** FIELDING *Tom Jones* II. iv, Mrs. Partridge was, at length..brought to herself. **1767** BLACKSTONE *Comm.* II. 89 Lest..the guardian should have received the value, and not brought it to account. **1806** CANNING *Fragm. Oration* 4 I'm like a young lady just bringing to bed. **1839** THIRLWALL *Greece* VII. lvi. 161 The prosecutors brought Demosthenes to trial first. **1865** DICKENS *Mut. Fr.* III. xv, I'll bring this young man to book. **1875** JOWETT *Plato* (ed. 2) I. 430 There is no greater pleasure than to have Socrates brought to my recollection. **1882** STEVENSON *Men & B.* (1886) 58 Jean was brought to bed of twins.

d. with *under, upon*:

as *to bring under the hand of, under foot*; *upon one's knees,* etc.

1535 COVERDALE *Judg.* iii. 30 Thus were the Moabites broughte vnder the hande of the children of Israel. **1552** HULOET, Bryng vnder obeysaunce or subiection. **1618** BOLTON *Florus* (1636) 121 Antiochus thus brought under-foot. **1652** *Proc. Parliament* No. 34. 2078, I hope a short time will bring them all upon their knees.

e. with *adjs.* and their equivalents:

as *to bring acquainted, low*; formerly also *at one, clean, faulty,* etc.

c **1386** CHAUCER *Knts. T.* 253 Oure lynage..That is so lowe y-brought by tyrannye. ? *a* **1400** *Morte Arth.* 1093, I.. was of blysse i-browghte alle bare. **1523** LD. BERNERS *Froiss.* I. xii. 11 To the entent that he shulde bryng hym on that case fauty. *c* **1530** —— *Arth. Lyt. Bryt* (1814) 365 He brought aslepe who so ever he touched. **1534** —— *Gold. Bk. M. Aurel.* (1546) G g vj b, I shall bryng thee at one with the Senate. **1668** SHADWELL *Sullen Lov.* I. i, I'll..bring you acquainted with this Lady. **1677** MOXON *Mech. Exerc.* (1703) 202 If you have not at first brought your Work clean. **1681** R. KNOX *Hist. Ceylon* Pref., He will bring you acquainted with the Inhabitants. **1703** SAVAGE *Lett. Antients* xlv. 110 The Distemper..which brought you so low. **1870** LOWELL *Study Wind.* 93 Bringing men acquainted with every humor of fortune.

f. with *subord. clause* (obs.) or *infinitive*:

as *to bring to be, bear, boil, to bring to pass* (= bring about, cause to happen).

c **1175** *Lamb. Hom.* 17 Bide for him..þet crist hine bringe þet he icherre from þan uuelnesse. *a* **1300** *Cursor M.* 1578 Was nan þam moght bring to reclaim. **1535** COVERDALE *Wisd.* x. 11 Wyszdome..brought to passe the thinges that he wente aboute. **1583** STUBBES *Anat. Abus.* II. 100 If it could be brought to passe. **1690** LUTTRELL *Brief Rel.* (1857) II. 70 Our men brought some of our guns to bear. **1719** DE FOE *Crusoe* (1840) I. viii. 136, I brought the plank to be about three inches thick. **1756** C. LUCAS *Ess. Waters* I. 85 It is..harder to bring the heavy acid of vitriol to boil.

9. To cause (a person or oneself) to come (to a certain course of action, etc.); to induce, persuade, prevail upon.

1611 BIBLE *Pref.* 1 Certaine..could not be brought for a long time to give way to good Letters. **1666** PEPYS *Diary* (1879) IV. 29 All children love fruit, and none brought to flesh, but against their wills at first. **1701** W. WOTTON *Hist. Rome* Commod. i. 196 She could not bring her self to give Crispina the Precedence. **1839** THIRLWALL *Greece* I. 209 They could not bring themselves to believe, that etc. **1846** D. JERROLD *Chron. Clovernook* Wks. 1864 IV. 412 A woman may be brought to forgive bigamy, but not a joke.

10. *Naut.* To cause to come or go into a certain position or direction; chiefly in phrases: *to bring by the board* (see BOARD *sb.* 12 b); *by the lee* (see LEE); *to the wind* (see WIND).

1695 LUTTRELL *Brief Rel.* (1857) III. 437 The French.. had his main mast brought by the board before he struck. **1719** DE FOE *Crusoe* (1858) 200 Her main-mast and fore-mast were brought by the board, that is to say, broken short off. **1836** MARRYAT *Midsh. Easy* xix, Gascoigne went to the helm, brought the boat up to the wind. **1858** *Merc. Mar. Mag.* V. 293, I was awoke by the ship being brought to the wind.

II. *Combined with adverbs.* (See also sense 1, and the adverbs, for the non-specialized combinations.)

11. bring about.

a. To cause to happen, bring to pass, occasion, accomplish, effect.

c **1450** *Merlin* i. 7 The deuell was right gladde that he hadde brought this a-bouten. **1480** CAXTON *Chron. Eng.* ccıv. 186 Yf that thyng myght be brought aboute. **1530** PALSGR. 466/1, I bringe aboute my purpose. **1641** J. JACKSON *True Evang. T.* I. 12 To bring his ends, and designes about. **1753** *World* No. 20. 107 Another proof of what people of fashion may bring about. **1848** MACAULAY *Hist. Eng.* I. 239 He..had borne a chief part in bringing about the marriage. **1876** J. H. NEWMAN *Hist. Sk.* I. I. iii. 139 The atrocities of the Greeks brought about a retaliation from the Latins.

†**b.** To cause to come round or make a complete revolution; to complete. *Obs.*

1588 SHAKS. *L.L.L.* v. ii. 808 There stay vntill the twelue Celestiall Signes Haue brought about their annuall reckoning. **1593** —— *3 Hen. VI*, II. v. 27 How many Houres brings about the Day.

c. To turn round; also *fig.* to reverse, convert.

1677 MOXON *Mech. Exerc.* (1703) 181 A thin String.. would not so well bring heavy Work about. **1694** ECHARD *Plautus* 152 He [Jove] knows each man that's perjur'd, or bribes his Judge to gain his cause; upon which, he brings it about i' th' upper Court. *a* **1745** SWIFT *Excell. New Song*, Now my new benefactors have brought me about. **1841** CATLIN *N. Amer. Ind.* (1844) II. liii. 152, I had brought it [a canoe] about with a master hand.

d. To restore to consciousness, or to health, = *bring round,* **a.**

1854 DICKENS *Hard Times* (Tauchn.) 66 That will bring him about or nothing will.

12. bring again.

a. See sense 1 and AGAIN.

†**b.** To restore to consciousness. *Obs.* Cf. to *bring about, round, to.*

1636 *Ariana* 177 The rest..laboured to bring mee againe, and by force of remedies I opened my eyes. *Ibid.* 320 They brought her againe with water they threw upon her.

13. bring away.

a. See sense 1 and AWAY.

†**b.** To extricate, detach, free, deliver. *Obs.*

a **1300** *Cursor M.* 16246 For þi stat þou aght to spek: to bring þi self a-wai.

14. bring back.

To cause to return (to a place or state); to restore, recover, recall.

1662 *Bk. Com. Prayer, Chas. Martyr*, Yet didst thou..at length by a wonderful providence bring him back. **1861** EARL STANHOPE *Life W. Pitt* I. i. 42, I trust the country air will bring back her strength. **1864** LONGF. *Wayside Inn, Interl. to Torquem,* This brings back to me a tale. **1886** BURTON tr. *Arab. Nts.* (abr. ed.) I. 286, I..went out after him, and brought him back secretly to the city.

15. bring down.

a. To cause to fall to the ground; to overthrow; to kill or wound (a flying bird, or other animal). Also with aircraft as *obj.*

a **1300** *Cursor M.* 63 Ar he sua brathly don be broght. **1535** COVERDALE *Baruch* v. 7 God is purposed to brynge downe all stoute mountaynes. **1768** S. BENTLEY *River Dove* 9 The Partridge, here oft as it flies, The Sportsman brings down with his Gun. **1798** MILLER in Nicolas *Disp. Nelson* (1846) VII. p. clv, *Zealous*..raked the *Guerrier*, brought down her foremast. **1917** 'CONTACT' *Airman's Outings* 23 Perhaps a German machine had been brought down. *Ibid.* 178 To 'bring down'..an enemy was extremely difficult.

b. To cause (punishment, judgements, etc.) to alight *on, upon.*

1662 *Bk. Com. Prayer, Chas. Martyr*, The crying sins of this Nation, which brought down this heavy judgement upon us. **1865** *Times* 2 Jan., To bring down on themselves the hostility of the most powerful maritime State.

c. *fig.* To lower, humble, abase.

1535 COVERDALE *Ps.* xvii[i]. 27 Thou shalt..bringe downe the hye lokes of the proud. **1768** STERNE *Sent. Journ.* (1778) II. 21, I could not bring down my mind to think of it. **1875** H. E. MANNING *Mission H. Ghost* x. 279 Every thing that could be used to bring down his great constancy.

d. To reduce, lessen, lower (price); to simplify.

1596 SHAKS. *Merch. V.* I. iii. 45 He lends out money gratis, and brings downe The rate of vsance here with vs in Venice. **1651** *Proc. Parliament* No. 94. 1450 Which I hope will bring down the price of corn there. **1719** SWIFT *To Yng. Clergyman* Wks. 1755 II. II. 5 Terms brought down to the capacity of the hearer. **1748** SMOLLETT *Rod. Rand.* xii. 27 At last however she was brought down to five, which he paid.

e. To continue (information, etc.) to a later date (cf. *Bring up* k).

1881 *Daily Tel.* 27 Dec., The annual abstract..brings down the information to June, 1881. **1885** *Bookseller* July 648/2 Information accurate and brought down to date.

f. *to bring down the house, gallery,* etc.: to evoke such demonstrative applause as threatens or suggests the downfall of the building.

1754 *World* II. No. 76. 125 His apprehension that your statues will bring the house down. **1870** LOWELL *Study Wind.* 384 Every sentence brought down the house, as I never saw one brought down before. **1884** SYMONDS *Shaks. Predecess.* x. §x. 403 The interview..must have brought down the gallery.

16. bring forth.

a. To produce, give birth to, bring into being, bear, yield (offspring; fruit, flowers, etc.; natural products; products, effects, results).

c **1200** ORMIN 1937 Þær brohhte ȝho þatt wasstme forþ Off all unnwemmedd wambe. *a* **1225** *Ancr. R.* 134 Bringen vorð briddes. **1388** WYCLIF *Ps.* ciii. 14 And thou bringist forth hei to beestis. *c* **1440** *Gesta Rom.* (1878) 233 He had weddid to wyf a yonge gentilwoman, the whiche conseyuid, and browte forthe a faire sone. *c* **1440** *Promp. Parv.* 51 Brynge forthe frute, *fructifico.* **1526** *Pilgr. Perf.* (W. de W. 1531) 47 b, Yᵉ tree neuer bryngeth forth floures ne fruytes, but fyrst it has borne & brought forth leues. **1535** COVERDALE *Wisd.* xix. 10 The grounde brought forth flyes in steade of catell. **1553** EDEN *Treat. New Ind.* (Arb.) 8 Places most apte to bring forth gold, spices, and precious stones. *c* **1600** SHAKS. *Sonn.* xxxviii, Let him bring forth Eternal numbers to outlive long date. **1605** —— *Macb.* I. vii. 72 Bring forth Men-Children onely. **1615–68** W. LAWSON *New Orchard* 49 Young Heifers bring not forth Calves so fair..as when they be come to be old kine. **1875** JOWETT *Plato* (ed. 2) V. 123 He never thought of what the future might bring forth.

†**b.** To bring up, rear, breed (animals). *Obs.*

c **1305** *St. Kenelm* 135 in *E.E.P.* (1862) 51 His norice þat him hadde ifed, & mid hire mulc forth ibroȝt. *c* **1400** MAUNDEV. 72 The Sarazines bryngen forthe no Pigges. *c* **1430** *Syr Gener.* 879 From a childe she him forth broght.

†**c.** To utter, express; to put forth, adduce, advance. *Obs.*

a **1300** *Cursor M.* 12138 To bring forth sli talking. **1382** WYCLIF *Ecclus.* xx. 29 A wys man in wrdis shal bringe forth hymself. *c* **1440** *Promp. Parv.* 51 Bryngyn forthe or shewyn forthe, *profero.* **1532** MORE *Confut. Tindale* Wks. 475/2 The places of Scripture whiche Helvidius broughte furth for the contrarye. **1606** SHAKS. *Tr. & Cr.* I. iii. 242 If that he prais'd himselfe, bring the praise forth. **1611** BIBLE *Isa.* xli. 21 Bring foorth your strong reasons.

†**d.** To bring to light, or public view. *Obs.*

a **1225** *Ancr. R.* 144 Euerich idel word bið þer ibrouht forð. **1599** SHAKS. *Hen. V.* Prol. 10 On this vnworthy Scaffold to bring forth So great an Obiect. **1601** —— *All's Well* v. iii. 151 To bring forth this discou'rie. **1605** —— *Macb.* III. iv. 125 Augures and vnderstood Relations haue.. brought forth The secret'st man of Blood. **1606** —— *Ant. & Cl.* v. ii. 219 The quicke Comedians Extemporally will stage vs.. Anthony Shall be brought drunken forth.

17. bring forward.

a. See sense 1 and FORWARD.

b. *Building.* See quot.

1823 P. NICHOLSON *Pract. Build.* 417 Bringing forward is a term applied to priming and painting new wood added to old work, or old work which has been repaired, so that the whole shall appear alike when finished.

c. *Book-keeping.* To carry on a sum from the bottom of one folio to the top of another where the account is continued.

Mod. A clerkly error in the amount brought forward.

18. bring in. a. See sense 1 and IN *adv.*

b. To introduce (customs, etc.).

c **1384** WYCLIF *De Eccl.* Sel. Wks. III. 345 To assente wiþ suche falseheed bringiþ in ofte heresies. **1611** BIBLE *2 Peter* ii. 1 False teachers.. who priuily shall bring in damnable heresies. **1690** LOCKE *Govt.* I. vi. §58 Manners, brought in and continued amongst them. **1753** *World* No. 10 Near two years ago the popish calendar was brought in.

c. To bring (money) into the purse or pocket.

1538 BALE *Thre Lawes* 1199 Thys crede wyll brynge in moneye. *a* **1716** SOUTH (J.) The sole measure of all his courtesies is.. what revenue they will bring him in. **1814** *Lett. fr. England* II. xxxviii. 83 And by the time they are seven or eight years old bring in money. **1855** COSTELLO *Stories fr. Screen* 85 'What does it bring you in?' says she.

†**d.** To introduce, place (a person) in a position or station. *Obs.*

1604 SHAKS. *Oth.* III. i. 53 He.. needs no other Suitor, but his likings to bring you in againe. **1676** *Hatton Corr.* (1878) 123 If his designe had succeeded of bringing in Sʳ Edward Deering. **1709–10** STEELE *Tatler* (J.) Since he could not have a seat among them himself, he would bring in one who had more merit.

e. To introduce (an action into a court of law or a bill into Parliament).

1602 MANNINGHAM *Diary* 16 Dec., I brought in a moot with John Bramston. **1652** *Proc. Parliament* No. 144. 2266 A day was appointed to bring in the Act. **1848** MACAULAY *Hist. Eng.* II. 121 He learned that a law, such as he wished to see passed, would not even be brought in. **1876** TREVELYAN *Macaulay* II. ix. 133 Sergeant Talfourd brought in a measure devised with the object of extending the term of Copyright in a book to sixty years.

f. To introduce (into consideration, discussion); to adduce (by way of illustration, argument, etc.).

1602 SHAKS. *Lear* III. vi. 37 I'll see their trial first. Bring in the evidence. **1631** WEEVER *Anc. Fun. Mon.* 122, I will bring in for example the Bells of the Parish Church of Winington. *a* **1745** SWIFT (J.) Quotations are best brought in, to confirm some opinion controverted. **1847** L. HUNT *Men, Women, & Bks.* I. iv. 87 Providence is.. to be brought in, humbly, when man comes to the end of his own humble endeavours.

†**g.** = *bring on*; to lead to, cause. *Obs.*

1586 COGAN *Haven Health* (1636) 98 Which.. sometime bringeth in fevers.

†**h.** To reduce to allegiance, or submission. *Obs.*

1596 SPENSER *State Irel.* (J.) Such a strong power of men, as should perforce bring in all that rebellious rout.

i. See quot.

1753 CHAMBERS *Cycl. Supp.* s.v., Bringing in a horse, in the manege, is the keeping down his nose, when he boars, and tosses it up to the wind. A horse is brought in by a strong hard branch.

j. Of a jury: To bring in a verdict, hence *colloq.* to 'find' as 'The jury brought him in guilty.' Also *ellipt.* and *transf.*

1684 [see VERDICT *sb.* 2]. **1804** *Sporting Mag.* XXV. 127/2 The jury.. brought in a verdict for the plaintiff. **1841** T. HOOD in *New Monthly Mag.* LXI. 272 The Jury debated from twelve till three What the verdict ought to be And they brought it in as Felo de Se, 'Because her own Leg had killed her!' **1865** MEREDITH *Rhoda Fleming* xviii, He's mad... There ain't a doubt as t'what the doctors 'd bring him in... Lunatic's the word! **1905** CONAN DOYLE *Return of Sherlock Holmes* 385 The coroner's jury brought in the obvious 'Wilful murder'. **1931** D. L. SAYERS *Five Red Herrings* xxix. 351 'If the jury are sensible people, they'll bring it in self-defence or justifiable homicide.'.. They brought it in manslaughter. **1938** 'N. BLAKE' *Beast must Die* I. 12 A verdict of manslaughter was brought in against some person or persons unknown. **1960** 'J. BELL' *Well-Known Face* xiv. 149 And Mrs. Prentice, too? The jury brought that in suicide.

k. = *to bring to* (see 25 f).

1860 J. CARGILL *Otago, N.Z.* 29 Open land is covered with either fern or grass,.. and is easily brought in. **1860** RUSKIN in *Cornhill Mag.* Nov. 561 Bringing in of waste lands. **1950** *N.Z. Jrnl. Agric.* Oct. 371/1 Swedes and turnips.. their usefulness as feed for dairy cows and in the bringing in of new land.

19. bring off.

a. To bring away from (a position or condition); *esp.* by boat from a ship, wreck, the shore.

1656 H. MORE *Antid. Ath.* II. ix. (1712) 68 That thence the atheist may be the more easily brought off to the acknowledgement of the existence of a God. **1676** HOBBES *Iliad* II. 183 Thus he the People brings Off from their purpose. **1701** *Lond. Gaz.* No. 3770/3 A Granadier.. swam over the River and brought off a Ferryboat. **1840** R. DANA *Bef. Mast* xxv. 79 Going ashore.. to bring off the Captain.

b. To deliver, rescue, acquit. *arch.*

[**1297** R. GLOUC. 379 ȝyf God me wole grace sende, Vorto make my chyrchegon, & bringe me of þys bende. *c* **1300** *Harrow. Hell* 61 Y shal the bringe of helle pyne.] **1606** SHAKS. *Tr. & Cr.* v. vi. 25 Ile be tane too, Or bring him off. **1699** BENTLEY *Phal.* 237 It will not bring Phalaris off; unless his Advocate can shew, etc. **1715** DE FOE *Fam. Instruct.* I. iv. (1841) I. 84, I cannot tell what you will say then to bring yourself off. **1751** CHESTERFIELD *Lett.* III. cclxx. 237. **1863** MRS. C. CLARKE *Shaks. Char.* xvi. 391 The injuring party.. is brought off triumphantly.

†**c.** To demonstrate, establish clearly. *Obs.*

1674 N. FAIRFAX *Bulk & Selv.* 37 To bring it but cleverly off, how ten thousand years between should not be time between.

d. To carry to a successful issue; to achieve.

1928 *Sat. Rev.* 27 Oct. 550/2 Theorizing about anything so personal.. seems a forlorn endeavour; but Mr. Beresford has brought it off. **1936** *Discovery* Aug. 241/1 He strains forward.. and.. brings off one of his special 'stunts' of marksmanship. **1952** M. LASKI *Village* ii. 40 They each hoped to goodness Daisy could bring it off.

20. bring on.

a. To lead forward or on, conduct (*Obs.*); to cause to advance, advance the growth of.

c **1230** *Hali Meid.* 17 þe stude & te time þat mahten bringe þe on mis for to donne. **1602** SHAKS. *Ham.* III. i. 9 When we would bring him on to some Confession of his true state. **1606** —— *Ant. & Cl.* III. ii. 44 The Aprill's in her eyes, it is Loues spring, And these the showers to bring it on. **1621** BURTON *Anat. Mel.* I. ii. II. vi. (1651) 88 Voluntary idleness.. gently brings on like a siren, a shooing horn, or some sphinx to this irrevocable gulf. **1629** PARKINSON *Paradisus* 25 According to.. the temper of the climate.. to bring them on earlier or later, as it doth with all other fruits. **1847** DICKENS *Dombey* xiv. 132 But he said.. that study would do much... 'Bring him on, Cornelia! Bring him on!' **1848** THACKERAY *Van. Fair* lii. 464 Briggs was a capital mistress for him, and had brought him on.. famously in English. **1932** A. J. WORRALL *Eng. Idioms* ix. 61 His trainer brought on the horse in fine style.

b. To produce, cause (illness, a state of things).

1671 MILTON *Samson* 373 These evils.. I myself have brought them on. **1766** GOLDSM. *Vic. W.* xviii, This.. might have brought on a relapse. **1814** WORDSW. *Excursion* I. 609 And poverty brought on a petted mood And a sore temper. **1817** JAS. MILL *Brit. India* II. v. v. 167 A battle was brought on. *Mod.* A cold which brought on influenza.

c. To bring into formal consideration or discussion, introduce.

1715 BURNET *Own Time* II. 197 Why must an attainder be brought on? **1878** SEELEY *Stein* III. 322 Metternich announced his intention of bringing on the subject.

d. *techn.* To fasten, fix, join, weld together.

1691 T. H[ALE] *Acc. New Invent.* 22 The Workmen were bringing on an ordinary Straits-sheathing with Wood upon one of his small Ships. **1852** A. RYLAND *Assay Gold & S.* 97 He found that the spoon and ladle were not made in one piece.. but that the parts bearing the marks were 'inserted', or 'brought on'.

e. To produce (a play, etc.) on the stage. (Quot. 1768 is perh. sense 20 a.)

1768 A. DOW *Let.* 16 July in *Corresp. D. Garrick* (1831) I. 306, I think it very unnecessary to submit the tragedy to any man's judgment but yours. Take it with you to the country; make your objections: if they can with facility be removed, I shall request the favour of you to bring it on. **1932** A. J. WORRALL *Eng. Idioms* ix. 61 Mr. Blank is bringing on his show at His Majesty's [Theatre].

f. To bring forward or into action; *spec.* in *Cricket*, to put (someone) on to bowl. So in *U.S. colloq.* phr. ***bring on your bears***, a defiant challenge to an adversary to do his worst.

1860 *Baily's Monthly Mag.* Sept. 429 Hayward and Parr were then brought on [as bowlers]. **1886** *Chicago Tribune* 13 Sept. 4/3 Bring On Your Bears. What with offensive Ministers and erratic Consuls,.. burden after burden of trouble has been laid upon Secretary Bayard's shoulders. *Ibid.*, He can request England or Canada.. to bring on their bears. **1904** P. F. WARNER *Recov. Ashes* xiii. 261 Arnold was brought on, and in his first over clean bowled Duff. **1954** WODEHOUSE & BOLTON *Bring on the Girls* i. 11 He says: 'Bring on the girls!' It is the panacea that never fails... The impresario has his way. The girls are brought on.

21. bring out. (See also sense 1 and OUT.)

†**a.** To separate or detach (any one) from; to deprive, do (any one) out *of*. *Obs.*

c **1400** *Destr. Troy* 8633 And the lede with a launse out of lyue broght. *a* **1450** *Knt. de la Tour* (1868) 65 To bringe hem oute of her good name. **1462** *Paston Lett.* 456 II. 108, I have bought salt and other thyngs, whiche hathe brought me out of myche sylvir. **1623** LISLE *Ælfric on O. & N.T.* Pref. 11 To bring the people out of love with the.. Bible.

†**b.** To produce, yield. *Obs.*

1545 ASCHAM *Toxoph.* (Arb.) 93 The grounde is plentifull.. whiche.. bryngeth out corne. **1607** SHAKS. *Timon* IV. iii. 188 Enseare thy Fertile and Conceptious wombe, Let it no more bring out ingratefull man.

c. To express, utter.

1665 BOYLE *Occas. Refl.* IV. xv. (1675) 257 Any thing, how contrary soever to Piety, or right Reason.. if Men can bring it out.. neatly wrapt up in Raillery.

d. To bring into clearness, distinctness, or prominence; to develop and display (talent).

1605 SHAKS. *Lear* v. iii. 163 That haue I done, And more, much more, the time will bring it out. *a* **1700** DRYDEN (J.), These.. as they boldly press, Bring out his crimes, and force him to confess. **1823** J. BADCOCK *Dom. Amusem.* 39 The exact kind of preparation which is calculated to bring out the writing. **1832** *Athenæum* 389 If the talent does exist.. such will be the only way to bring it out. **1874** HELPS *Soc. Press.* i. 3 The moon.. brought out the river and adjacent buildings resplendently. **1875** JOWETT *Plato* (ed. 2) I. 76 The antagonism of the two characters is still more clearly brought out.

e. To introduce (a young lady) formally into 'society'; to announce (a company, a foreign loan, or the like) for public subscription.

1790 *Loiterer* 23 Jan. 12 A young woman seldom did well who was *brought out* before she was eighteen. **1823** BYRON *Juan* XII. xxxi, [They] Begg'd to bring *up* the little girl, and '*out*', For that's the phrase that settles all things now, Meaning a virgin's first blush at a rout. *Mod.* That loan was brought out by Messrs. Baring in 1852.

f. To produce before the public; to place upon the stage (a play or opera); to publish (a book).

1818 BYRON in Moore's *Life* (1838) 376 They have brought out Fazio with great and deserved success at Covent Garden. **1851** *Illust. Lond. News* 354 'Robert le Diable' was originally brought out by Meyerbeer. **1878** MORLEY *Diderot* 164 It was resolved to bring out the ten volumes.. in a single issue. **1882** PEBODY *Eng. Journalism* xx. 148 Proposed that he should bring out an evening paper.

g. To exhibit, shew. (With complement.)

1705 ARBUTHNOT *Measure, Weights, &c.* (L.) But those experiments bring out the denarius heavier.

h. *to bring out one's bat* (in *Cricket*) = to carry it (out) (see CARRY *v.* 53 c).

1833 J. MITFORD in *Gentl. Mag.* Sept. 236/1 Tom [Walker] scored the amazing number of 95 runs in his first innings, and brought his bat out with him. **1870** *Times* 15 July 12/5 Mr. Green.. brought out his bat with the total at 198.

22. bring over. (See also sense 1 and OVER.)

To influence to come to one's own side or party (from an opposite one); to convert.

1724–5 SWIFT *Wks.* (1841) II. 23 By these.. means, he soon brought over both parties to him. **1771** GOLDSM. *Hist. Eng.* II. 221 The house of commons was brought over to second his request. **1848** MACAULAY *Hist. Eng.* II. 347 Able to bring over a great body of his disciples to the royal side. **1878** BOSW. SMITH *Carthage* 283 In vain, however did he attempt.. to bring over Cumæ, Naples, and Puteoli.

23. bring round. (See also sense 1 and ROUND.)

a. To restore (a person) from a fainting-fit or an attack of illness.

1834 'A VIRGINIAN' *Kentuckian in New York* I. vi. 94 You want something to make your blood circulate: a small taste or two would soon bring you round. **1864** TENNYSON *En. Ard.* 842 Dead!.. I warrant, man, that we shall bring you round.

b. To complete a set of changes in bell-ringing.

1883 *Birmingh. Daily Post* 19 Oct. 7 A peal of.. grandsire majors which was successfully rung and brought round in capital style, in four hours and fifty-five minutes.

c. To persuade; to convert *to* an opinion.

1862 TROLLOPE *Rachel Ray* I. xiii. 259 Don't you think you could say something civil to Mr. Tappitt, so as to—to bring him round again? **1889** BRIDGES *Feast of Bacchus* IV. 1055 You've got.. your father Brought nicely round: and all through my good management. **1932** A. J. WORRALL *Eng. Idioms* ix. 62 With some difficulty I brought him round to my way of thinking.

24. bring through. (See sense 1 and THROUGH.)

spec. To treat successfully through the stages of an illness.

Mod. The doctor hopes to be able to bring him through.

25. bring to.

a. *Naut.* (*trans.*) To fasten, tie, bend.

1681 *Lond. Gaz.* No. 1666/4 In the night they mended their Rigging, brought new Sails to the Yards. **1867** SMYTH *Sailor's Word-bk.*, *Bring-to*, to bend, as to bring-to a sail to the yard.

b. To cause (a ship) to come to a standstill.

1753 *Scots Mag.* Aug. 415/2 A guarda costa.. fired a gun to bring them to. **1769** FALCONER *Dict. Marine* (1789), *To Bring to*, in navigation, to check the course of a ship.. by arranging the sails in such a manner that they shall counteract each other. **1803** NELSON in Nicolas *Disp.* (1845) V. 81 At 6.30 brought to the Vrow Agneta, Dutch Brig.

c. *intr.* (for *refl.* or *absol.*) Of a ship or her crew: To come to a standstill; *transf.* to stop, 'pull up'.

1697 *Lond. Gaz.* No. 3287/3 The 5 French brought to a Stern. **1709** *Ibid.* 4521/2 They came within Random shot, and then brought to. **1748** ANSON *Voy.* (ed. 4) I. iv. 49 The Commodore made a signal for the ships to bring to. **1790** BEATSON *Nav. & Mil. Mem.* 278 Near 3 in the afternoon, when she brought to. **1845** DARWIN *Voy. Nat.* vii. (1879) 136 We brought to in a narrow arm of the river. **1861** HUGHES *Tom Brown Oxf.* II. i. 4 Here let us bring to.. and try to get acquainted with the outside of the place before the good folk are about.

†**d.** *trans.* To cause to acquiesce or be complaisant. *Obs.*

1748 RICHARDSON *Clarissa* xvi. I. 93 Proud spirits may be brought to. **1749** FIELDING *Tom Jones* XVIII. xii, I was forced to use a little fatherly authority to bring her to.

e. To restore to consciousness or to health. Cf. 8 c. *bring to oneself.*

1789 Burns *Ep. Dr. Blacklock*, I ken'd it still your wee bit jauntie Wad bring ye to. **1844** G. Gleig *Lt. Dragoon* v. (1856) 45 Our lieutenant..fainted..The French guard brought him to by shaking. **1850** Mrs. Stowe *Uncle Tom's C.* xxxiii. 299 'I'll bring her to!' said the driver with a brutal grin. 'I'll give her something better than camphire!'

f. To bring (land) into good condition. *U.S.*

1814 in *Amer. Speech* (1947) XXII. 273 To *bring to* a piece of land—to bring it into a state of cultivation, or rather perhaps into a state fit for cultivation. **1838** H. Colman *Rep. Agric. Mass.* 77 One of these gentlemen..has found this sort of land after it was thus 'brought to' extremely favorable to the growth of rye.

bring together: see sense 1 and TOGETHER.

26. bring under. To bring into subjection, subdue.

1563 *Homilies* ii. *Repentance* iii. (1859) 548 Who will bring me under for my works? **1597** Hooker *Eccl. Pol.* v. xlii. §3 Either yielding through fear, or brought under with penury. **1618** Bolton *Florus* i. xi. (1636) 31 Lucius Quinctius chiefly brought them under. **1705** Stanhope *Paraphr.* III. 40 That, which brought under the Reluctancies of Humane Nature. *a* **1834** Moore *Minstrel Boy*, The foe-man's chain Could not bring his proud soul under.

27. bring up.

a. To bring into a higher position; to elevate, raise, rear, build up; to raise to a point or amount, etc. See senses of *up*.

1297 R. Glouc. 369 þe abbey of Came..he rerde in Normandye..He broȝte vp mony oþer hous of relygyon al so. **1477** Earl Rivers (Caxton) *Dictes* 142 Yf he see that fortune raise and bring up som other of lower degre. **1611** Shaks. *Wint. T.* iv. iv. 544 Your discontenting Father, striue to qualifie And bring him vp to liking. **1677** Moxon *Mech. Exerc.* (1703) 141 The next Work the Carpenter has to do, is to bring up the Stairs. *Ibid.* 129 The Celler-Walls to be brought up by a Brick-layer with Brick. **1885** Sir E. Kay in *Law Times' Rep.* LII. 370/1 The [amount] to which the undivided profit would be brought up.

b. To rear from childhood; to educate, breed.

1483 Caxton *G. de la Tour* F vij, The child whiche hadde be secretely nourisshed and brought up cam to his enherytaunce. **1511-2** *Act 3 Hen. VIII*, iii. §1 To enduce and lern theym and bryng them uppe in shotyng. **1588** A. King *Canisius' Catech.* 50 Fosterit, teachit, and brocht vp in continuall exercise. **1611** Bible *Isa.* i. 2, I haue nourished and brought vp children. **1711** Addison *Spect.* No. 105 ¶4 A Man who has been brought up among Books. **1875** Jowett *Plato* (ed. 2) IV. 122 The doctrines in which he had been brought up. **1879** *Cassell's Techn. Educ.* IV. 70/1 The ordinary farmer brings up a lot of calves every year.

c. To introduce to general notice; to bring into vogue. ? *Obs.*

1483 Caxton *G. de la Tour* D vij b, To hasty in takynge ony newe thynges brought up. **1530** Palsgr. 470/2 He hath brought up a newe custome..To bringe up newe lawes is a perlous worke. **1693** W. Robertson *Phraseol. Gen.* 284 She brings up a fashion grown out of use. **1741** Richardson *Pamela*, The Torture is not used in England, and I hope you won't bring it up.

†**d.** To raise, originate, give utterance to (a report), etc. *Obs.*

1535 Coverdale *Numb.* xiii. 32 And of the lande that they had searched, they brought vp an euell reporte amonge the children of Israel. **1611** *Ibid.* xiv. 36 Bringing vp a slander vpon the land.

e. To bring into the presence of authority; to bring before a tribunal, or for examination.

1823 J. Badcock *Dom. Amusem.* 64 Being brought up..to answer at Bow-street office. **1865** *Reader* 8 July 30 Candidates would be expected to bring up so many books of Scott. **1885** *Law Times* LXXIX. 139/1 A writ of *certiorari* to bring up an order made by the justices.

f. *Naut.* To bring to anchor, or to a standstill.

1820 *Blackw. Mag.* VIII. 317, I was all at once..as the sailors say, brought up by an invisible fence. **1840** R. Dana *Bef. Mast* xxv. 80 They let go the other anchor..and brought the vessel up.

g. *intr.* To come to anchor; *hence*, to come to a stand, to stop, 'pull up'.

1769 Falconer *Dict. Marine* (1789) *To Bring-up*, a provincial phrase peculiar to the seamen in the coal-trade, signifying to anchor. **1790** Beatson *Nav. & Mil. Mem.* 321 The Rippon..brought up against the Morne Rouge Battery. **1856** Kane *Arct. Exp.* I. xxix. 386 At last the floe brought up against the rocks. **1858** Sears *Athan.* iv. 32 Expect when they die to..bring up at some good place. **1884** Anstey *Giant's Robe* vi, Mr. Lightowler brought up sharply opposite the end of an inclined covered staircase..where they left the dog-cart.

h. To bring under notice or consideration; to recall to notice (a by-gone matter).

1875 Jowett *Plato* I. 212 If I had said anything last year, I suppose that you would bring that up..Are you such an old fool..that you bring up now what I said at first? *Mod.* 'I am glad the matter has been brought up.'

i. To develop, produce.

1823 J. Badcock *Dom. Amusem.* 169 Chromate of potash ..brings up a yellow colour.

j. To vomit. (*colloq.*)

1719 Defoe *Further Adventures of Robinson Crusoe* 200 Then I grew sick, and reached to vomit, but could not; for I had nothing in my Stomach to bring up. *Ibid.* 201 My Stomach loathed the Sugar, and brought it all up again. **1746** T. Tomkyns tr. *Lamotte's Gen. Treat. Midwifry* ii. xxi. 213 A little cough, which kept encreasing till it brought up a little purulent spittle. **1945** M. Dickens *Thursday Afternoons* viii. 234 Hoping that Ugly [*sc.* a dog] would manage to swallow whatever it was he had taken before he brought it up.

k. *to bring up arrears, lost ground*, etc.

1788 Dibdin *Mus. Tour* xii. 43 By way of clearing my ground, or, as the Sailors call it, bringing up lee-way. **1859** Jephson *Brittany* viii. 131 The afternoon was spent in bringing up my arrears of correspondence. **1865** E. Burritt *Walk Land's E.* 445 Bringing up a long arrearage of writing. *Mod.* Has the narrative been brought up to date?

l. ***bring up the rear (arrear)***: see REAR.

m. To lead (troops, etc.) to the scene of action.

1885 U. S. Grant *Pers. Mem.* I. 415 The troops from Corinth were brought up in time to repel the threatened movement without a battle.

bringall, -gela, var. spellings of BRINJAL.

bring-and-buy, *adj. phr.* Descriptive of a charity bazaar, stall, etc., to which people bring objects for sale, and buy those brought by others. Also *ellipt.*

1932 *N.Z. Home & Country* 1 Dec. 20/1 A 'Bring and Buy' stall was held, the proceeds to be donated to the Plunket Society. **1950** S. Ertz *Prodigal Heart* xii. 210 A recent 'Bring and Buy' bazaar in aid of the Crippled Boys' Home. **1952** A. Christie *Mrs. McGinty's Dead* xiv. 115 'I got it at the B. and B. at Christmas.' 'B. and B.?'..'Bring and Buy... You bring things you don't want, and you buy something.' **1967** *Span* July 4 A bring and buy sale and lunch was held at Mrs. Miriam Stevens' house on Boars Hill on June 8th.

bringer ('brɪŋə(r)). [f. BRING *v.* + -ER[1].]

1. One who or that which brings (see various senses of the verb).

c **1340** *Cursor M.* 10161 (Trin.) Joachim bringere of bote. **1471** Earl of Oxford in *Paston Lett.* 669 III. 5 The brynger of thys letter. **1535** Tindale *Tracy's Test.* 6 A peacemaker, and bringer into grace and favour. **1597** Shaks. *2 Hen. IV*, i. i. 100 Yet the first bringer of vnwelcome newes Hath but a loosing Office. **1775** Adair *Amer. Ind.* 443 A pretended great bringer of rain. **1841** Emerson *Misc.* (1855). 158 The scholar must be a bringer of hope. **1881** H. H. Gibbs *Double Standard* 67 Their sterling amount would be at the credit of the bringer.

b. *spec.* See quot.

1864 Sala in *Daily Tel.* 9 Aug., A bounty-broker is simply a crimp, or what the recruiting sergeants in Charles-street, Westminster, call a 'bringer'.

2. With *back, in, out, up*, etc. ***bringer up***, one who rears or educates.

c **1386** Chaucer *Wife's T.* 340 Povert is..A ful gret brynger out of busynesse. **1529** Wolsey in *Four C. Eng. Lett.* 11 Your olde brynger up and lovying frende. **1581** Sidney *Apol. Poetrie* (Arb.) 71 They were first bringers in of all ciuilitie. **1604** Edmonds *Observ. Cæsar's Comm.* 130 The bringers-up or last rancke called Tergiductores. **1742** C. Wesley in Southey *Life Wesley* (1820) II. 26 Bringers-in of the Pretender. **1840** Carlyle *Heroes* iv. 210 A bringer back of men to reality. **1865** Bushnell *Vicar. Sacr.* ii. ii. (1868) 156 He is the Captain, or bringer on, of salvation.

bringing ('brɪŋɪŋ), *vbl. sb.* [f. BRING *v.* + -ING[1].]

1. A causing to come to a point of reference or to a state (see various senses of the verb).

1433 *E.E. Wills* (1882) 92 As towchyng my bryngyng on erth. **1651** Hobbes *Leviath.* iii. xxxiv. 210 The bringing of Gods people into the promised land. **1663** Gerbier *Counsel* 77 The sawing, and bringing of the Timber to a square. **1884** Black *Jud. Shaks.* xxxiv, The riding to London, and the bringing of thy father.

2. With *forth, in*, etc.: see advb. combs. of verb. ***bringing up*** (*Naut.*): see BRING *v.* 27 f.

1603 Shaks. *Meas. for M.* iii. ii. 153 Let him be but testimonied in his owne bringings forth, and hee shall appeare..a Scholler. **1691** T. H[ale] *Acc. New Invent.* 6 Materials employed in the bringing on, and stripping off the Wood-sheathing. **1769** Falconer *Dict. Marine* (1789) *Bringing-to*, is generally used to detain a ship in any particular station. **1853** R. Hunt *Man. Photogr.* 222 The bringing-out of the Picture. **1908** *Westm. Gaz.* 1 July 7/4 The 'Patrol' lost her anchor and cable in bringing up.

3. ***bringing up***, rearing, training, education, breeding.

1526 *Pilgr. Perf.* (1531) 50 His naturall father and mother, of whom he hath his body and bryngynge vp. **1602** *Return fr. Parnass.* ii. iv. (Arb.) 26 Sir you must pardon my father, he wants bringing vp. *a* **1617** Hieron *Aarons Bells* (1623) 6 By his bringing vp in Pharaohs courte. **1864** Tennyson *En. Ard.* 87 To..give his child a better bringing-up.

4. *attrib.* **bringing money**, money formerly paid by a recruiting officer to a recruit on his joining the forces.

1892 *Rep. Comm. Terms & Cond. Service in Army* 63 The Committee have found a strong consensus of opinion that the reintroduction of bringing-money would probably give a great stimulus to recruiting.

†**brinie, brynie** ('brɪnɪ). *Obs.* Forms: 2 brenie, 3 brunie, 3-4 brinie, bruny, 4 brunye, brini, brynye, breny. [ME. *brunie* (ü), *brynie, brinie, brenie*, a. ON. *brynja* (Da. *brynie*, Sw. *brynja*), corresp. to OE. *byrne* from **brynne*, OHG. *brunja, brunna* (MHG. *brunje, brünje, brünne*, also mod.G.) corslet, Goth. *brunjô* breast-plate:—OTeut. **brunjôn-*. Whether the latter was adopted from OSlav. *bronja* 'coat of mail', or the OSlav. from Teut., or both from a common source (cf. OIr. *bruinne* 'breast') is uncertain; the word is not connected with BURN *v.* The Teut. word was adopted in late L. or Romanic: cf. med.L. *brunia, -ea, bronia*, OFr. *brunie, bronie, bruigne, brugne, brogne, bruine, broine, broune*, Pr. *bronha, broingna*. The ME. *brunie* corresponds exactly to the Norman-French form, but the phonology of the parallel *brinie, brenie*, points to the Scandinavian as the original source. The regular ME. form from the OE. word would have been *byrn* (see BURNE), and from Scand. *brynie*: through contact of these and metathesis of *r*, there are also found the forms BRYN, and BYRNIE.]

Armour for the body; a coat of mail, cuirass, breastplate. Hence **brynied, brenyed** *ppl. a.* Mailed.

c **1175** *Cott. Hom.* 243 Sceold, helm, and brenie. **1205** Lay. 1553 þah he hefden brunie on. *Ibid.* 6718 And burne [**1275** brunie] he wurp on rigge. *a* **1300** *K. Horn* 591 þe fole schok þe brunie þat al þe curt gan denie [to din]. *a* **1300** *Havelok* 1775 Bernard..caste a brinie up on his rig. *c* **1320** *Sir Tristr.* 191 þurch brinies brast þe blod. *c* **1330** *King of Tars* 949 With helm on hed and brunye briht. *c* **1380** *Sir Ferumb.* 3024 Many was þe helm & brynye briȝt: þat þar was cloue. ? *a* **1400** *Morte Arth.* 316. Brenyede knyghtes. *c* **1440** *Syr Gowghter* 415 in Utterson's *E.P.* I. 179 Blode thorow brenyys brast.

brininess ('braɪnɪnɪs). Briny quality.

1883 *Sat. Rev.* 1 Dec. 709 A very briny book indeed. Its brininess is perhaps of a somewhat factitious kind.

brining ('braɪnɪŋ), *vbl. sb.* [f. BRINE *v.*]

1. The application of brine.

1787 Winter *Syst. Husb.* 268, I deem the practice of common brining to be only useful for destroying small insects.

2. The removing of brine from a steamer's boiler.

1875 Bedford *Sailor's Pocket Bk.* v. (ed. 2) 212 If obliged to use sea water for the feed, let the process of brining be as constant and continuous as possible.

brinish ('braɪnɪʃ), *a.* Also (6 brennish), 6-7 brynish. [f. BRINE *sb.* + -ISH[1].]

1. Of the nature of brine; somewhat briny, saltish; of or pertaining to the sea. †***brinish brink***: the sea-shore.

1588 Shaks. *Tit. A.* iii. i. 97 Expecting euer when some enuious surge, Will in his brinish bowels swallow him. **1609** Heywood *Brit. Troy* xi. liii, Neere to the brinish brinke. *a* **1639** S. Ward *Coal fr. Altar, Serm.* (1862) 74 Like brinish lights, they sparkle and spit at others. **1796** Morse *Amer. Geog.* I. 634 Streams of brinish water. **1822** *Blackw. Mag.* 410 One almost tastes the brinish air.

b. Applied to tears.

1580 Lyly *Euphues* (Arb.) 355 The brynish water that falleth from mine eyes. **1595** Barnfield *Cassandra* lxv, Whose body she emballms, With brennish teares. **1642** Prynne *Sov. Antid.* Concl. 31 Which he shall with brinish teares repent. **1692** E. Walker *Epictetus' Mor.* xlix, When some sad Passion tries To draw the brinish Humour from your Eyes.

2. *fig.* Bitter, nauseous.

a **1617** Hieron *Wks.* II. 475 These brinish inuectiues are vnsauory. **1649** Ambrose *Media* iii. (1652) 50 What brinish sorrows and great indignation against sin?

'brinishness. Brinish state or quality.

1755 in Johnson; and in mod. Dicts.

‖**brinjal, -jaul** ('brɪndʒɔːl). *Anglo-Indian.* Forms: 7 berenjaw, 8 bringela, brinjalle, berenjal, biringal, 8-9 bringal, brinjal, -jaal, -jall, -jaul. Also (from Arab. and Pers.) 7 *pl.* pallingenies, 8 bedin-janas, 9 badenjân, badingân. [Anglo-Indian adaptation of Pg. *bringella, bringiela*, earlier *beringela* = Sp. *berengena, al-berengena*, ad. Arabic (*al*)-*bāđinjān*. The latter is a. Pers. *bādin-gān*, ad. Skr. *vātin-gaṇa*, all applied to the same fruit. (See below.)]

The Anglo-Indian name of the fruit of the Egg-plant (*Solanum Melongena*).

[Few names even of plants exemplify so fully the changes to which a foreign and unintelligible word is liable under the influence of popular etymology and form-association. Cognate with the Sp. *alberengena* is the Fr. *aubergine*, dial. *albergine, albergaine, albergame*, also without the *al-*, *belingèle*, and, with *m* for *b*, *merangène, melongène*, botanical Lat. *melongēna*, It. *melanzana, mela insana* (= mad apple). All these go back to the Arabic *bāđinjān*, and ultimately to Skr. *vātin-gāna*, whence also Hindustāni *baingan, began*. The Malay *berinjalā*, prob. from Pg., illustrates the Anglo-Indian form (see Devic, and Yule). In the West Indies *brinjalle* has been further corrupted to *brown-jolly*. The Sanskrit name is said to mean 'the class (that removes) the wind-disorder (windy humour)', a meaning supposed to connect it with *vārttāku*, another name of the same plant, which is said to have a *māruta-nāśin* or 'wind-removing' effect. (J. T. Platts.)]

1611 N. Dounton in Purchas *Pilgr.* I. 298 (Y.) Diuers sorts of prouisions to wit..Pallingenies, cucumbers. **1673** Fryer *Acc. E. India & P.* (1698) 104 (Y.) The Garden.. planted with Potatoes, Yawms, Berenjaws, both hot plants. **1789** *Seir Mutakherin* III. 229 (Y.) He lived on raw Bringelas, on unripe mangoes, and on raw red pepper. **1789** Saunders in *Phil. Trans.* LXXIX. 86 Melons, gourds, brinjals, and cucumbers. **1810** Maria Graham *Jrnl. Resid. India* 24 (Y.), I saw..two acres covered with brinjaal. **1861** Swinhoe *N. China Camp.* 374 Sweet Potatoes, brinjalls, ground nuts, and buck wheat. **1866** *Treas. Bot.* II. 1070/1 Brinjals..are of the size and form of a goose's egg, and usually of a rich purple colour.

‖**brinjarry** (brɪn'dʒɑːrɪ). *Anglo-Ind.* Also 6 banjara, 7-9 bunjara, 8 bandjarrah, benjarry, brinjary, 8-9 binjarree, -jarry, 9 brinjaree, -jarree, bunjarrah, -jarree, vanjarrah. [corruption of Urdū *banjārā*, according to Wilson deriv. of Skr. *vanij* trade: influenced, some think, by Pers. *birinj* rice (Col. Yule).

Called in Bombay *vanjārā*.] A travelling grain and salt merchant of the Deccan.

[*c* **1632** *Life of Mohabut Khan* in J. Briggs *Acc. Bunjaras* (Y.) The very first step..was to present the Bunjaras of Hindostan with elephants, horses, and cloths.] **1793** DIROM *Camp. India* 2 (Y.) His convoy of brinjarries had been attacked. **1794** E. MOOR *Narr. Little's Detachm.* 131 The Bandjarrahs..This very useful class of Hindoos, generally, but we think, improperly called Brinjarries. **1798** WEBBE in Owen's *Disp. Wellington* 9 To open our rear for the admission of Brinjaries. **1799** KIRKPATRICK *ibid.* 173 As many Benjarries as possible. **1800** WELLINGTON in Gurw. *Disp.* I. 146 No Brinjarries in yet. **1804** —— in Owen's *Desp.* 425 His Highness shall collect as many Bunjarrahs as possible. **1813** FORBES *Oriental Mem.* I. 206 (Y.) We met there a number of Vanjarrahs, or merchants. *a* **1876** MEADOWS TAYLOR in *Life* II. 17 (Y.) Brinjarries, or carriers of grain.

brink (brɪŋk). Forms: 3-4 **brenk**, 3-6 **brynke**, 5-6 **brynke**, 5-7 **brinke**, 6 **brinck**, 3- **brink**. [ME. *brink* (*brenk*), not known in OE.; corresp. to MDu. *brinc* (Du. *brink*), MLG. *brink* 'edge of a field, grass-land, side of a hill, hill' (whence mod.G. *brink* 'green hill, grass-land'), Sw. *brink* 'descent of a hill', Da. *brink* 'steepness, precipice, declivity', all masc., cogn. with ON. *brekka* fem. (:—*brinkâ*) 'slope, hill-side, hill'. The Eng. word was prob. from Scandinavian. In sense *brink* formerly ran parallel with BRIM.]

1. The edge, margin, or border of a steep place, such as one might fall over, e.g. the 'brink' of a precipice, chasm, pit, ditch, grave. ***on the brink of the grave*** (fig.): near death. [This is the specific current sense, which now also affects the use of 2, and entirely colours the figurative use in 5; but it is doubtful whether the first two quotations do not rather belong to 2.]

a **1300** *Ancr. R.* 242 Þe horse þet is scheouh, and blencheð uor one scheadewe upo þe heie brugge, and falleð adun into þe watere of þe heie brugge [*MS. Titus D.* xviii. brinke]. *c* **1325** *E.E. Allit. P.* B. 384 Vche a dale so depe þat demmed at þe brynkez. *c* **1386** CHAUCER *Frankl. T.* 130 And caste hir eyen dounward fro the brynke [*v.r.* brinke, brenke]. —— *Merch. T.* 157, I am hoor and old, And almost at [*v.r.* on] my pittes brinke. ? *a* **1400** *Chester Pl.* 68 Your owine childe for to spill Upon this hilles brinke? **1588** SHAKS. *Tit. A.* II. iii. 241 Of this deepe pit..I haue no strength to plucke thee to the brinke. **1667** MILTON *P.L.* II. 918 The warie fiend Stood on the brink of Hell and look'd a while. **1709** BERKELEY *Ess. Vision* §148 He shall come to the brink of a precipice. **1853** KANE *Grinnell Exp.* xxxix. (1856) 355 Upon the brink of the cleanly-separated fissures. **1871** MORLEY *Voltaire* (1886) 209 Tottering on the brink of the grave. **1878** HUXLEY *Physiogr.* 170 The church..is now on the very brink of the cliff.

2. The edge of the land bordering a piece of water, as a river, lake, the sea: formerly = 'bank, shore, brim'; now *esp.* when this rises abruptly from the water: thus running into sense 1.

a **1300** *K. Horn* 141 Schup, bi þe se flode..Bi þe se brinke. *a* **1300** *Cursor M.* 1766 Þe burnes ouer þe brink [*Fairf.* brenk] it brast. **1382** WYCLIF *Gen.* xli. 3 Thei weren fedde in the brenke of the flood [**1611** vpon the brinke of the riuer]. **1387** TREVISA *Higden* Rolls Ser. I. 65 By þe see brynkes [*juxta marium margines*]. **1480** CAXTON *Descr. Brit.* 17 A ryall cite vpon the brinke of twede. **1483** —— *Gold. Leg.* 58/2 They sawe thegypcyens lyeng deed upon the brynkes of the see. **1553** EDEN *Treat. New Ind.* (Arb.) 7 Azron Gaber, by the brinke of the redde sea. **1697** DRYDEN *Virg. Georg.* III. 22 Reeds defend the winding Water's Brink. **1796** MORSE *Amer. Geog.* II. 36 Their habitations on the brink, or in the neighborhood of some lake. **1847** GROTE *Greece* II. iii, On the brink of the sea. **1855** MACAULAY *Hist. Eng.* III. 630 They marched..to the brink of the Boyne.

†**3. a.** The brim of a vessel; = BRIM 4. *Obs.* or *dial.*

1382 WYCLIF *2 Chron.* iv. 2 He maad..a ȝoten se of tenn cubitis fro brynke vnto brynk. *c* **1440** *Promp. Parv.* 52 Brynke of a wesselle. *a* **1500** *Songs & Carols* (1847) 56 Fyll the cope by the brynk. **1523** FITZHERB. *Husb.* §148 Thou muste spare at the brynke and not at the bottom. **1542** BOORDE *Dyetary* xii. (1870) 265 Fat doth swymme aboue in the brynkes of the stomache. **1598** DRAYTON *Heroic. Ep.* xxi. 151 A Bowle of Nectar, fill'd up to the Brinke. **1727** SWIFT *Baucis & Phil.* Wks. 1755 III. II. 33 Fill'd a large jug up to the brink.

b. The brim of a hat. *dial.*

1821 CLARE *Vill. Minstr.* II. 68 With weather-beaten hat of rusty brown, Stranger to brinks, and often to a crown.

†**4. a.** *gen.* A margin, border, edge. *Obs.* or *arch.*

1388 WYCLIF *Exod.* xxv. 24 Make to it a goldun brynke. *c* **1420** *Pallad. on Husb.* I. 813 In places wete or moist make evry brynke Two foote in heght. *c* **1432-50** tr. *Higden* (1865) I. 309 In the brynkes of the lesse Asia. **1508** *Balade agst. Tymes*, Prudence and policy are banyst our al brinkis. *a* **1535** MORE *Wks.* (1557) 81 The ytch of a sore leg, whan thou clawest about the brinkes. **1562** BULLEYN *Soarnes* 20 b, The brinkes of the wounde, must be oiled with Rosed omphacine. **1607** TOPSELL *Four-f. Beasts* 381 His ears erected upright, as the ears of a Cat..the farthest brinkes or edges, and also his latter may be bended on the other side. **1724** T. HEARNE *Pref. R. Glouc.* §25. 81 In one part of this MS. at the very bottom, just on the Brink of a Page. **1812** BYRON *Ch. Har.* Wks. (1846) 14/2 *note*, All these are coop'd within one Quarto's brink.

†**b.** *fig. arch.*

1629 WHITTOCK in Rushw. *Hist. Coll.* (1659) I. 688 Now we are but upon the brink and skirts of the Cause. **1821** SHELLEY *Prometh. Unb.* II. v. 1 On the brink of the night and the morning.

5. *fig.* The very verge of some state, time, event, or action: now *esp.* in the phrases ***on, to, from the brink of**, a discovery, ruin, destruction, death, eternity, anarchy, revolution, absurdity*, etc.

1330 R. BRUNNE *Chron.* 122 Scho dred þer assaute, hunger was at þe brynk. **1607** SHAKS. *Timon* v. i. 159 You..Surprize me to the very brinke of teares. **1671** MARVELL *Corr.* cxcii. Wks. (1872-5) II. 384 It is impossible we should rise before the very brinke of Easter. *a* **1677** BARROW *Serm.* (1686) III. 191 Old men..visibly stand upon the brink of eternity. **1722** DE FOE *Moll Fland.* (1840) 297, I was at the very brink of destruction. *a* **1745** SWIFT *Wks.* (1841) II. 63 To save them from the brink of ruin. **1758** JOHNSON *Idler* No. 19 ⁋3 [They] follow them to the brink of absurdity. **1818** MRS. SHELLEY *Frankenst.* (1865) 61 Sometimes on the very brink of certainty I failed. **1876** FREEMAN *Norm. Conq.* V. xxiv. 367 As conqueror, he brought us to the brink of feudal anarchy; as despot, he saved us from passing the brink. **1884** *Graphic* 158/3 The secret..on the brink of discovery.

b. with *inf.* (obs.) or *gerund*: On the very point of. (Now of something momentous or perilous.)

1702 T. SMITH in *Pepys' Diary* VI. 240 Upon the brink to complete fourscore. **1720** OZELL *Vertot's Rom. Rep.* I. IV. 228 You were upon the Brink of falling a Prey to our Enemies. **1788** LD. SHEFFIELD in *Corr. Ld. Auckland* II. 223 Trevor was on the brink of going to Petersburg. **1807-8** W. IRVING *Salmag.* xx. (1860) 468, I was on the brink of treating you with a full broadside. **1865** DICKENS *Mut. Fr.* xvi, She is on the brink of being sold into wretchedness for life.

c. *spec.* the verge of war. Hence **'brinkmanship** [-MANSHIP], the art of advancing to the very brink of war but not engaging in it; also *transf.* and *fig.*; hence (as a back-formation), **'brinkman**, one who practises brinkmanship; **'brinkmanlike** *a.*

[**1840** MILL *Let.* 30 Dec. in *Wks.* (1963) XIII. 459 They had been brought to the brink of a war.] **1956** *Life* 16 Jan. 78 Says Dulles '..Of course we were brought to the verge of war... If you try to run away from it, if you are scared to go to the brink, you are lost... We walked to the brink and we looked it in the face.' **1956** *N.Y. Times* 26 Feb. 1/5 He [*sc.* Adlai Stevenson] derided the Secretary [*sc.* J. F. Dulles] for 'boasting of his brinkmanship—the art of bringing us to the edge of the nuclear abyss'. **1958** *Ann. Reg. 1957* 183 Anglo-French 'brinkmanship' over Suez had failed to stop at the brink. **1958** S. POTTER *Supermanship* 127 Brinkmanship is a clever way of describing the Dulles attitude. *Ibid.*, Krushchev is the true Brinkman: his existence depending.. on enemy-at-the-gatemanship. **1958** *Times* 11 Nov., Jackson Pollock..was..one to whom every new painting was..almost an act of spiritual brinkmanship. **1958** *Economist* 27 Dec. 1134/1 He [*sc.* Potter] is about to plunge, brinkmanlike, into International Lifemanship. **1967** *Spectator* 18 Aug. 177/3 A policy of muddling through, of economic brinkmanship.

6. *Comb.* †**brink-full**, full to the brink, brimfull; **brinkless**, without any brink or border.

1553 BALE *Gardiner's Obed.* G vij, With an emptie and free minde and not already brynke full. **1565** GOLDING *Ovid's Met.* VIII. (1593) 207 The hunger of his brinklesse maw the gulfe that naught might fill.

'brinker. *nonce-word.* [f. BRINK + -ER¹.] One living on the brink or border.

1871 *Daily News* 13 Sept., Freeholders and copyholders of manors and 'brinkers' of commons.

brinks, *v.* [? corrupt form or spelling.] = BRINCH *v.*

1568 *Like will to L.* in Hazl. *Dodsley* III. 339 That we may toss the bowl to and fro, and brinks them all carouse-a.

brin-, brintstane, -stone, obs. ff. BRIMSTONE.

brint, obs. pa. pple. of BURN.

briny ('braɪnɪ), *a.*¹ [f. BRINE *sb.* + -Y¹.]

1. Of or pertaining to brine or to the sea; saturated with salt.

1612 DRAYTON *Poly-olb.* xi. 172 Those two renowned Wyches, The Nant-wyche and the North, whose either brynie well For store and sorts of Salts make Weever to excell. **1697** DRYDEN *Virg. Past.* II. 32, I stood Upon the Margin of the briny Flood. **1799** S. TURNER *Anglo-Sax.* (1840) I. IV. i. 263 Vast solitudes and briny marshes. **1878** HUXLEY *Physiogr.* 73 Fresh water is constantly distilled from the briny ocean.

b. Applied to tears.

1608 T. DAVISON in Farr's *S.P.* (1845) II. 330 A bryney showre Of teares. **1718** POPE *Iliad* IX. 18 Down his wan cheek a briny torrent flows. **1728** A. RAMSAY *Robt., Richy, & S.*, Ilka briny tear Ye shed for him.

briny, *a.*² (? *sb.*) [Cf. OE. *bryne*, BRUNE, and BURNING *sb.* 3.] Phosphorescent, ? phosphorescence (of the sea).

1602 CAREW *Cornwall* 26 b, If the sea-water bee flashed with a sticke or oare, the same casteth a bright shining colour, and the drops thereof resemble sparckles of fire, as if the waues were turned into flames, which the Saylers terme Briny. **1880** *W. Cornw. Gloss.*, *Briny*, phosphorescent.

briny ('braɪnɪ), *sb. colloq.* or *joc.* Also **briney**. [f. BRINY *a.*¹] The sea, the ocean.

1831 J. BANIM *Smuggler* I. xii. 276 What is he to do without a sharp 'un to chaffer with the Parleys across the briney? *Ibid.* III. 40 He was seen at t'other side of the briny. **1880** H. EVANS *Brighton Beach Loafer* (1888) 6 Tales of unutterable woe and adventures undergone on the 'briny'.

‖**brio** ('brio). [It. *brio* mettle, fire, life; in the musical phrase *con brio*.] Liveliness, vivacity, 'go'.

1734 J. CONSTABLE *Refl. Accuracy Style* iv. 140 Their hardy and venturesome expressions..does often give a kind of vigour and *Brio* (if the word is sufficiently naturaliz'd) to their lines. **1855** THACKERAY *Newcomes* xxii, Painted with all his well-known facility and brio. **1881** *Contemp. Rev.* June 879 Italian Society in spite of its ready wit, its brio and its inborn gracefulness had not..the peculiar charm of French and Spanish Society.

‖**bri'oche.** [Fr.: see Littré.] A kind of cake made of flour, butter, and eggs; sponge-cake.

1826 MISS MITFORD *Village* Ser. II. (1863) 298 To discover the merits of brioche and marrangles and eau de groseille. **1873** *St. Paul's Mag.* II. 585 She..settled down to her chocolate and brioches.

‖**briolette** (briolɛt). [mod.Fr.; also *brignolette*, *brillolette*, ? *briller* to sparkle.] A pear-shaped diamond, having facets cut in all directions.

1865 *Illustr. Lond. News* 11 Mar. 243 This diamond..is what is called a briolette—that is, a solid drop. **1884** *Birmingh. Weekly Post* 23 Aug. 3/7 It will weigh..in lozenge shape, briolette, about 300 carats.

brionine, briony, var. of BRYONIN, BRYONY.

‖**briquet** (brikɛ). [Fr.] A steel for striking light from a flint; a representation of this; esp. *Her.*, one of the ornaments used to form the collar of the order of the Golden Fleece.

1824 SCOTT *St. Ronan's* III. iv. 90 Lighting one [*sc.* a cigar] with his *briquet*. **1913** W. OWEN *Let.* 27 Dec. (1967) 223 However the *Briquet* is precisely the thing I want. They are very common in France. **1920** *Edin. Rev.* Oct. 314 The cross and briquet of Burgundy. **1952** J. B. OLDHAM *Eng. Blind-Stamped Bindings* 63 *Briquet*, a conventional representation of a steel for striking a light.

briquetage (brɪkə'tɑːʒ). *Archæol.* Also **bricquetage**, **briquettage**. [F. *briquetage*.] Objects fashioned of burnt clay (see also quot. 1960).

1902 *Amer. Anthropol.* IV. 162/2 The name 'bricquetage' is given to masses of oven-baked clay found in heaps in the region of Vic and elsewhere. **1908** *Athenæum* 28 Mar. 391/2 The clay objects mentioned above, to which the Committee have provisionally given the non-committal name of 'briquetage'. **1960** *Lincs. Archit. & Archæol. Soc.* VIII. 70 The word 'briquetage'..can be used to include debris produced by so many different activities, from potting and salting to corndrying, and it can also include material which may be purely domestic, such as the remains of hearths and chimneys, or the clay walls of buildings which have been burnt.

briquette (brɪ'kɛt, 'brɪkɪt), *sb.* Also **briquet**. [Fr. *briquette* in same sense, dim. of *brique*, BRICK. The F. word *briquet* (which is not a dim. of *brique*) has not this meaning.]

1. A block or slab of artificial stone.

1883 *Hampstead Express* 7 Apr. 1/2 Patent Victoria Stone —Tensile Strain, average of 10 briquets (see Reid, on Concrete), 794 lbs. per square inch.

2. A block of compressed coal-dust, usu. with addition of a binding substance such as pitch.

1884 *Pall Mall G.* 8 Jan. 9/2 Works for the compressing of coal briquettes. **1886** *Manchester City News* 30 Oct., The manufacture of briquettes, or machine-made coal, consists simply of the transformation of 'smudge', or very small coal ..into solid blocks, weighing about 11¼ lb. each. This result is attained by adding to the coal about eight per cent. of pitch. **1963** *Ann. Reg. 1962* 509 Exports of coal, coke, and briquettes decreased.

3. A small block of ice-cream. Cf. BRICKETTE.

1927 W. C. COLLINSON *Contemp. Eng.* 16 Cyclists selling ice-cream briquettes.

briquette (brɪ'kɛt), *v.* [f. the sb.] *trans.* To form (coal-dust, etc.) into briquettes. So **briquetted** *ppl. a.*, **briquetting** *vbl. sb.*

1898 *Eng. Mechanic* 7 Oct. 194/1 Briquetting Sawdust. **1916** LANTSBERRY tr. *Franke's Handbk. Briquetting* I. 621 Briquetting of Sawdust, and other Waste Wood. These materials can generally be briquetted fairly readily without a binding material. **1928** *Daily Tel.* 25 Sept. 11/5 The Yallourn briquetting plant of the State Electricity Commission of Victoria. **1962** *Times* 26 Mar. 5/3 They also intended to develop a briquetted fuel.

brisance ('briːzɑ̃s). [f. F. *brisant*, pres. pple. of *briser* to break.] The shattering effect of such high explosives as nitroglycerine and gun-cotton. (See also quot. 1935.) Also *attrib.*

1915 A. MARSHALL *Explosives* 390 It has been proposed by Bichel to use the expression $\frac{mv^2}{2}$ for the 'brisance' or violence of the blow given by an explosion, *m* being the mass of gas evolved and *v* the velocity of the detonation. *Ibid.* 320 For the brisance test quantities of 10 g. were used. *Ibid.* 407 *marg.*, Brisance meter. **1935** *Discovery* Feb. 43/2 Little is yet known as to the exact nature of brisance, or the property of detonating at the slightest shock, which these explosives possess.

brisant ('briːzɑ̃), *a.* [Fr.: see prec.] Of explosives: shattering, smashing, breaking.

1905 LARSEN tr. *Bichel's New Meth. Test. Explosives* 18 In this translation the word 'brisant' (explosives) has sometimes been used in preference to the rather inadequate expression 'high'. **1906** *Times* 14 Mar. Although these brisant substances belong directly to chemistry. **1918** COLVER *High Explosives* 594 The genuine brisant explosives can only be detonated by means of the energy of a primary explosive.

†**brise.** *Obs. rare.* (See quot.)
1616 SURFL. & MARKH. *Countr. Farm* 92 Afterward let him draw a Brise or two made fast in the yoke [*margin*, A Brise is a kind of ground that hath lyen long vntilled]. **1721–1800** in BAILEY.

brise, obs. form of BREEZE and BRUISE.

‖**brisé** (brize). *Dancing.* [Fr., pa. pple. of *briser* to break.] Any movement in which the feet or legs are beaten together in the air.
1786 S. J. GARDINER *Def. Minuet-Dancing* 54 The Steps generally made use of in Cotillions are..Assemblée, Brizée, [etc.]. **1830** R. BARTON tr. *Blasis's Code of Terpsichore* II. vi. 78 An attitude upon one leg, as in..the *cabriole, brisés* and the *ronde-de-jambe en l'air*. **1952** KERSLEY & SINCLAIR *Dict. Ballet Terms* 19 A single *brisé* can begin with one foot on the other ankle.

‖**brise-bise** ('bri:zbi:z). Also erron. **brise-à-bise, bris-à-bris**; colloq. **brisby.** [Fr., lit. 'wind-breaker'.] A curtain of net or lace for the lower part of a window. Also *attrib.*
1912 *Queen* 10 Aug. 266/1 Brise-bise curtains of striped net. **1923** *Daily Mail* 14 Feb. 1 (Advt.), Cream Hem-stitched Lace and Insertion Casements and Brise Bise. *Ibid.* 17 Apr. 14 Insertion Brise a bise. *Ibid.* 29 May 15 The *Brise-bise* Lace Curtain (familiarly called a 'Brisby'). *Ibid.* 14 Aug. 1/3 Cotton net..suitable for gowns, bris-à-bris.

†'**brisel, brisil, bresil.** *Obs.* [ME. *brusell(ü), brysl, brysell, bresil*, on OE. type **brýsol*, f. *brýsan* to crush, break.] Brittle, fragile.
1303 R. BRUNNE *Handl. Synne* 8568–71 þoghe þat hys flesshe be brysl and brym. *c* **1325** *Metr. Hom.* 120 Brukel [*Camb. MS.* brusell] blod and bane. —— 154 For fleys es brokel [*Camb. MS.* brysell] als wax, and neys. *a* **1340** HAMPOLE *Psalter* ii. 11 The pote of laire is bresil and soen will breke. —— ciii. 30 That thai ere dust and erth: that is, brisil and erthly. **1483** *Cath. Angl.* 44 Brysille, *fragilis.* **1802** J. SIBBALD *Chron. Sc. Poetry* Gloss. (JAM.) *Brissal*, brittle.

†**briser.** *local.* [app. a phonetic variant of BRISURE, BRUSURE, act of bruising, breaking, or crushing.] (See quot.)
1774 A. HUNTER *Georgical Ess.* (1803) IV. 321 In the month of September, a slight ploughing and preparation is given to the field, destined for beans and parsnips the ensuing year. In this country, this work is called briser.

‖**brise-soleil** (bri:zsɒ'leı). [Fr., lit. 'sun-breaker'.] A device (whether a perforated screen, louvers, or projections) for shutting out direct or excessive sunlight.
1944 *Archit. Rev.* XCV. 69 Two main types of sun-baffle have been devised..: the pierced concrete screen or 'cambogé'; and the quebra-sol or brise-soleil. **1962** *Listener* 15 Nov. 805/1 As in a modern *brise-soleil*, the two horizontal projections—balcony and roof—give shelter from the high midday sun.

brisewort, variant of BRUISEWORT.

brish, obs. form of BRUSH.

brish, *v.* Dial. var. BRUSH *v.*[2] 7. Also *intr.* Hence **brishing** *vbl. sb.*
1636 in PARISH & SHAW *Dict. Kentish Dial.* (1887) 19 For shredinge of the ashes and brishinge of the quicksettes..vj[d]. **1914** KIPLING *Diversity of Creatures* (1917) 377 The first wood down is sere and small,..The brishings off the hills. **1916** BLUNDEN *Harbingers* 59 The morning hedger with his brishing-hook. **1920** —— *Waggoner* 25 No hedger brished nor scytheman swung.

brisk (brısk), *a.* and *sb.* Also 7 **briske, brisque.** [First found in end of 16th c.; evidently familiar to Shakspere and his contemporaries. Derivation uncertain: Welsh *brysg* (used of briskness of foot) occurs in a poem of the 14th c. This appears to answer in form to OIr. *brisc*, Ir. *briosg*, Gael. *brisg*, Breton *bresk*, 'brittle', 'crumbly'; but it is not easy to connect the senses.
It is however possible that *brisk* is identical with F. *brusque* (which appears as *bruisk* in Sc. *c* 1560, and as *bruske* as early as 1600); at least Cotgr. gives *brisk* as a translation of *brusque*, and the words appear to have influenced each other in early use. See BRUSQUE.]

A. *adj.*

1. Sharp or smart in regard to movement (in a praiseworthy sense) quick and active, lively.

a. of persons. (Sometimes used of disposition = 'cheery, sprightly, lively', but this is now chiefly *dial.*)
[**1560** T. ARCHBALD *Let.* in Keith *Hist. Scotl.* (1734) 489 (JAM.) Thir ar the imbassadoris..thai depart wondrous bruisk.] **1592** SHAKS. *Rom. & Jul.* I. v. 16 Chearly Boyes, Be brisk awhile. **1611** COTGR., *Brusque*, briske, liuely, quicke, etc. *Ibid. Frisque*, friske, liuely, iolly, blithe, briske, fine, spruce, gay. **1613** R. C. *Table Alph.*, *Brisque*, quick, liuely, fierce. **1725** DE FOE *Voy. round World* (1840) 298 A company of bold, young brisk fellows. **1828** SCOTT *F.M. Perth* I. 5 The brisk, alert agent of a great house in the city. **1882** PEBODY *Eng. Journalism* xvi. 120 A bright, brisk lad, fresh from Oxford.

b. of actions and motions. (The prevalent modern use.)
1684 BUNYAN *Pilgr.* II. 101 To enter with him a brisk encounter. **1690** LOCKE *Hum. Und.* IV. xi. §5 It must needs be some exteriour Cause, and the brisk acting of some Objects without me. **1756** BURKE *Subl. & B.* Wks. I. 245 A slow and languid motion [of the eye] is more beautiful than a brisk one. **1777** WATSON *Philip II* (1839) II. 213 He made a brisk attack upon one of the gates. **1855** PRESCOTT *Philip II*, I. I. vii. 91 He..opened a brisk cannonade on the enemy. **1863** GEO. ELIOT *Romola* II. xxii, The brisk pace of men who had errands before them.

c. of trade: Active, lively.
1719 W. WOOD *Surv. Trade* 339 When Trade is brisk, Money..is more in view. **1832** HT. MARTINEAU *Hill & Vall.* iv. 49 The demand for iron was so brisk. **1833** —— *Br. Creek* iii. 64 A brisk traffic took place in the remaining articles.

d. of wind, fire, etc.
1725 POPE *Odyss.* XII. 184 Up sprung a brisker breeze. **1759** ROBERTSON *Hist. Scot.* I. III. 203 At last a brisk gale arose. **1796** MORSE *Amer. Geog.* I. 133 New and brisk fountains of water rise at spring tides. **1837** M. DONOVAN *Dom. Econ.* II. 269 The brisk fire should..be only employed when the meat is half roasted.

e. of purgatives.
1799 *Med. Jrnl.* II. 236 He had a brisk cathartic given him. **1815** *Scribbleomania* 207 *note*, They've drench'd her with cathartics brisk.

2. In allied senses, chiefly unfavourable.
†**a.** Sharp-witted, pert; curt. †**b.** 'Fast' of life. †**c.** Over hasty. †**d.** Unpleasantly sharp of tone. (With c, d, cf. Fr. *brusque.*) **e.** Quickly passing, brief.
1601 SHAKS. *Twel. N.* II. iv. 6 These most briske and giddy-paced times. **1665** GLANVILL *Sceps. Sci.* Addr. 13 Divers of the brisker Geniusses, who desire rather to be accounted Witts, then endeavour to be so. **1667** EVELYN in *Four C. Eng. Lett.* 108 The smoothest or briskest strokes of his Pindaric lyre. **1667** PEPYS *Diary* (1877) V. 422 The Surveyor began to be a little brisk at the beginning. *a* **1674** CLARENDON *Hist. Reb.* I. I. 8 When that brisk and improvident Resolution was taken. **1676** ETHEREDGE *Man of Mode* I. i. (1684) 11 He has been, as the sparkish word is, Brisk Upon the Ladies already. **1700** *Penn. Archives* I. 138, I send y[ee] y[e] Coots [= Court's] Lett[r] w[ch] is very brisk. **1739** CIBBER *Apol.* vii. 214 The briskest loose Liver or intemperate Man. [**1879** BROWNING *Ned Bratts* 23 Some trial for life and death, in a brisk five minutes' space.]

†**3.** Smartly or finely dressed; spruce. *Obs.*
1590 MARLOWE *Edw. II*, I. iv. ad fin., I have not seen a dapper jack so brisk. **1596** SHAKS. *1 Hen. IV*, I. iii. 54 To see him shine so briske, and smell so sweet. **1603** *Patient Grissil* 17 My brisk spangled baby will come into a stationer's shop.

4. Of liquors: Agreeably sharp or smarting to the taste; effervescent, as opposed to 'flat' or 'stale'. (So It. *brusco*, Fr. *vin brusque* in Cotgr.) Similarly of the air: Fresh, keen, stimulating.
1597 SHAKS. *2 Hen. IV*, v. iii. 48 A Cup of Wine, that's briske and fine. **1697** POTTER *Antiq. Greece* III. ix. (1715) 75 Brisk Wines and Viands animate Their Souls. **1741** BROWNRIGG in *Phil. Trans.* LV. 242 The brisk and pungent taste of the acidulæ. **1776** SIR W. FORBES in Boswell *Johnson* II. 404 A bottle of beer..is made brisker by being set before the fire. **1837** DISRAELI *Venetia* I. ii, The air was brisk. **1846** J. JOYCE *Sci. Dialogues* vii. 213 You see of what importance air is to give to all our liquors their pleasant and brisk flavour. **1877** L. MORRIS *Epic Hades* II. 198.

†**5.** Sharp to other senses; distinct, vivid.
†**a.** to the hearing. *Obs.*
1660 BOYLE *New Exp. Phys.-Mech.* I. 21 There is..produced a considerably brisk noise. **1667** PRIMATT *City & C. Build.* 51 Bricks well burnt..if you strike them with any thing, will make a brisk sound.

†**b.** to the sight. *Obs.*
a **1727** NEWTON (J.) Had it [my instrument] magnified thirty or twenty-five times, it had made the object appear more brisk and pleasant.

6. *Comb.* **a.** adverbial, as *brisk-going, sparkling*; **b.** parasynthetic, as *brisk-spirited.*
1711 *Lond. Gaz.* No. 4868/4 A..Cart Horse..brisk Spirited. **1831** CARLYLE *Sart. Res.* II. iii. 132 Like a strong brisk-going undershot-wheel. **1837** —— *Fr. Rev.* II. III. i. 128 Our brisk-sparkling assiduous official person.

†**B.** *sb.* **a.** A 'brisk' or smart person; a gallant, a fop. (Cf. A 3 above.) **b.** A lively, forward woman, a wanton.
1621 BURTON *Anat. Mel.* III. iii. I. ii. (1651) 604 A yong gallant..a Fastidious Brisk, that can wear his cloaths well in fashion. **1689** N. LEE *Princ. of Cleve* (N.) The forward brisk, she that promis'd me the ball assignation.

brisk (brısk), *v.* [f. the adj.]

1. *trans.* To make brisk; to freshen, enliven, animate, exhilarate, quicken. Now with *up* or (colloq.) *about.*
1628 FELTHAM *Resolves* I. lxxxiv. 261, I like a cup to briske the spirits. **1666** J. SMITH *Old Age* 112 The blood in the Arteries newly brisked in the fountain. **1710** T. FULLER *Pharm. Extemp.* 321 Bennet Pills..exalt and brisk up the..heavy Blood. **1829** E. JESSE *Jrnl. Nat.* 241 That portion of vital air which brisks up animality without consuming the sustenance of life. **1864** DICKENS *Mut. Fr.* I. ix, We want to brisk her up, and brisk her about. **1879** STEVENSON *Trav. Cevennes* 15 Modestine brisked up her pace.

2. *intr.* (for *refl.*) *to brisk about*: to move about briskly. *to brisk up*: to come up briskly; to become brisk, to behave or move in a brisk manner. (Also without *up.*)
1727 MORETON *Apparitions* 195 The lady..brisking up to him as if she would fight him. **1830** in WEBSTER, *Brisk up*,..to come up with life and speed; to take an erect, or bold attitude. **1881** MRS. HOLMAN HUNT *Childr. Jerus.* 169 He was up and brisking about. **1884** L. B. WALFORD *Nan* II. 76 After this adventure, we seemed..to brisk up afresh. **1915** H. L. WILSON *Ruggles of Red Gap* (1917) iii. 40 As I brisked out of bed the following morning at half-after six. **1916** 'BOYD CABLE' *Action Front* 170 The rattle of rifle fire dwindled away at times to separate and scattered shots, brisked up again and rose to a long roll. **1938** L. MACNEICE *Earth Compels* 40 You should see her in jodhpurs Brisking in to breakfast from a morning canter. **1966** *Listener* 24 Nov. 764/1 Claire..brisks up the even flow of strictly grammatical dialogue.

3. †**a.** *trans.* To smarten *up*; to dress finely, to trim. *Obs.* **b.** *intr.* (for *refl.*)
1592 GREENE *Disput. Conny-catcher* Wks. (Grosart) X. 204 Doest thou maruell to see me thus briskt? **1613** BEAUM. & FL. *Hon. Man's Fort.* II. i, Prune and briske myself in the bright shine Of his good Lordships fortune. **1637** G. DANIEL *Genius of Isle* 45 Whilst Neptune, to court Amphitrite doth briske. **1710** PALMER *Proverbs* 259 The young cock..stood brisking up his comb and gills. **1861** TROLLOPE *T. All Countries* 193 Susan brisked up a little for the occasion [a wedding] and looked very pretty as bridesmaid.
Hence **brisked** *ppl. a.*, '**brisking** *vbl. sb.*
1644 BULWER *Chiron.* 109 The brisked spirits. **1717** KILLINGBECK *Serm.* 223 (L.) For the relief of our natures; for the brisking up our spirits.

brisken ('brısk(ə)n), *v.* [f. BRISK *a.* + -EN[5].]

1. *trans.* To make brisk or lively. Also with *up.*
1799 A. YOUNG *Agric. Linc.* 451 Let your fuel be coke, which bears the bellows to brisken the fire, without raising a flame. **1838** *Eclectic Rev.* I. 551 Briskening the then dull tenor of periodical criticism. **1901** *Daily Chron.* 27 Dec. 3/3 The Coronation, they think, may brisken up trade generally. **1905** E. F. BENSON *Image in Sand* i. 8 Sir Henry briskened his pace a little.

2. *intr.* To become brisk, to speed up.
1876 W. MATHEWS *Getting on in the World* (1884) Ser. II. iii. 68, I heartily wish that business may brisken a little. *a* **1909** *Scribner's Mag.* (Webster), Meanwhile our artillery fire briskened. **1965** *Guardian* 27 Oct. 8/7 Leduc describes it with awe, then briskens.
Hence '**briskening** *vbl. sb.* and *ppl. a.*
1901 E. F. BENSON *Luck of Vails* I. i. 4 These agreeable influences..seemed to produce a briskening effect on the two. **1907** *Athenæum* 23 Mar. 364/1 This piece, with briskening of the action, will prove diverting. **1927** *Scots Observer* 4 June 17/2 A briskening of the air.

brisket ('brıskıt). Forms: 5 **brusket(te**, 6 *Sc.* **briscat**, (7 **bysket**, 8 *Sc.* **bisket**), 7– **brisket.** [Identical in meaning, and apparently in form, with F. *brechet* (in Cotgr. *bruchet*, in 16th c. *brichet*, 14th c. *bruschet, brischet*, which Littré derives from the Eng.; but this seems unlikely. The Breton *bruchet* and Welsh *brysced*, appear to be adopted from Fr. and Eng. respectively.]

1. The breast of an animal, the part immediately covering the breast-bone. Also, as a joint of meat.
c **1450** *Nominale* in Wr.-Wülcker 704 *Hoc pectusculum*, a bruskette. **1483** *Cath. Angl.* 46 A Brusket, *pectusculum.* **1535** STEWART *Cron. Scot.* I. 87 The wricht [had] the neiris and the briscat & maw. **1610** MARKHAM *Masterp.* II. lvi. 306 He will be very hollow vpon the bysket towards the fore-boothes. **1611** COTGR., *Ars*..the breast, or brisket of a horse. **1709** ADDISON *Tatler* No. 148 ¶1 The Black Prince was a professed Lover of the Brisket. **1769** MRS. RAFFALD *Eng. Housekpr.* (1778) 117 Bone a brisket of beef, and make holes in it with a knife. **1820** SCOTT *Monast.* xvii, It is a hart of grease too, in full season, and three inches of fat on the brisket. **1866** KINGSLEY *Herew.* xv. 204 As shaggy as a stag's brisket. **1873** E. SMITH *Foods* 48.

b. *Sc.* The human breast.
1789 FERGUSSON *Poems* II. 113 (JAM.) Their glancin een and bisket bare. **1790** MORISON *Poems* 15 (JAM.) Wi' kilted coats, White legs and brisket bare.

2. *attrib.*, as in *brisket-beef, -bone.*
1587 TURBERV. *Trag. T.* (1837) 37 The brisket bone. **1637** B. JONSON *Sad Sheph.* I. ii, The brisket bone, upon the shoon Of which a little gristle grows. **1697** DAMPIER *Voy.* (1729) I. 302 Their flesh is as hard as Brisket Beef.

briskish ('brıskıʃ), *a.* Pretty brisk.
1865 CARLYLE *Fredk. Gt.* XVI. vii. VI. 208 A briskish trade of his own in the Dresden marts.

briskly ('brısklı), *adv.* [f. BRISK *a.* + -LY[2].] With brisk motion or action; sharply, smartly, quickly, energetically, vigorously, actively.
1665 BOYLE *Occas. Refl.* IV. i. (1675) 168 My Drowsiness..made me briskly enough bid him..let me alone. **1676** LISTER in *Ray's Corr.* (1848) 124 [Lycopodium] will fire briskly in a flame. **1702** *Lond. Gaz.* No. 3809/6 The Cannon..kept firing very briskly. **1719** W. WOOD *Surv. Trade* 200 Manufactures proceeded briskly. **1812** SIR H. DAVY *Chem. Philos.* 125 A piece of dry silk..briskly rubbed against a warm plate of polished flint glass. **1839** tr. *Lamartine's Trav. East* 161/1 He sprang briskly to his feet. **1868** BROWNING *Ring & Bk.* IX. 1488 You urge him all the brisklier to repent.
†**b.** Smartly, in reference to dress. *Obs.*
1592 GREENE *Upst. Courtier* in *Harl. Misc.* (Malh.) II. 228 A..fellow..briskly apparelled, in a blacke taffata doublet, and a spruce leather jerkin with christall buttons.

briskness ('brısknıs). [f. as prec. + -NESS.] The quality of being brisk; smartness or sharpness of motion; liveliness, quickness, activity.
a **1655** R. ROBINSON in Spurgeon *Treas. Dav.* Ps. lxv. 10 [The rain] begets a kind of briskness in the sensitive creatures. **1674** N. FAIRFAX *Bulk & Selv.* 125 To leap forth into nimble freaks and brisknesses. **1839** *Sat. Mag. Suppl.* June 253/2 The animals..are not remarkable for briskness of motion. **1879** H. GEORGE *Progr. & Pov.* IX. iii, The increased briskness of trade.

b. Agreeable sharpness of taste, freshness; effervescent quality. Also *transf.* (of air) and *fig.*
1727 BRADLEY *Fam. Dict.* s.v. *Cask*, The Briskness of the Drink [cider]. **1816** L. HUNT *Rimini* I. ix, A balmy briskness comes upon the breeze. **1879** *Cassell's Techn. Educ.* I. 215 Champagne and other sparkling wines owe their briskness to the presence of carbonic acid. **1880** *Times* 26 July 9/4 Topics that have lost their briskness.

†**c.** Abrupt blunt manner; brusqueness. *Obs.*
1668 PEPYS *Diary* 13 Nov., There is no way to rule the King but by brisknesse, which the Duke of Buckingham hath above all men.

'brisky, *a.* [Cf. *blacky*, etc., and see -Y.] Of brisk nature. Also *fig.*
1590 SHAKS. *Mids. N.* III. i. 97 Most brisky Iuuenall, and eke most louely Iew. **1894** *Cornh. Mag.* Jan. 43 As we proceed, stopping regularly at every wayside public-house, many of the passengers betray symptoms of becoming 'brisky'. **1905** *Daily Chron.* 14 Mar. 6/7 The lamb.. gambols about the farm in as brisky a manner as any of its companions.

brisling ('brɪslɪŋ, 'brɪz-). Also **bristling.** [Norw., Da. *brisling* sprat.] A small, sardine-like fish of the herring family, which is widely distributed in the north-east Atlantic and the North Sea, and is cured and tinned for use as food.
1902 WEBSTER Add., Bristlings. **1913** *Times* (Weekly ed.) 14 Nov., 'Skipper Sardines' were bristling, or sprats. **1915** *Law Rep.* K. B. Div. III. 742 The brisling is the nearest approach to the sardine which the Norwegian seas provide. **1926** *Spectator* 2 Jan. 11/2 If the brisling fisheries fail the Stavanger Theatre shows a loss. **1969** A. WHEELER *Fishes Brit. Isles & N.-W. Europe* 132 In Norway.. the resultant sprats, seasoned and canned in oil, are sold as 'brislings'.

†**brisok.** *Obs. rare*$^{-1}$. [Cf. Welsh *bresych* cabbage, a. L. *brassica*; and see BRASSIC.] A wild cabbage.
a **1340** HAMPOLE *Psalter* xxxvi. 2 The kale, that he says, not ere of garthis bot of gressis, that grouys bi thaim ane in the feld, as brisokis.

brisque (brɪsk, brisk). [Fr.] In bézique and other card games, a privileged card, such as the aces and tens in bézique; also the name of a card game.
1870 'CAVENDISH' *Bézique* 8 Brisque (queen of spades and knave of diamonds, now called bézique), scored 40. Curiously enough, brisque did not exist in the game of *Brisque* itself. **1890** 'BERKELEY' *Bézique & Cribbage* 10 If the loser's score, with his brisques, is less than 1,000, he is said to be rubiconed. **1963** G. F. HERVEY *Handbk. Card Games* 20 Every Ace and 10 that a player holds in the tricks that he has won is scored for at the rate of 10 points each. They are known as brisques.

brisque, obs. form of BRISK.

brissal, var. of BRISEL, *Obs.*, brittle.

brisse(n, brissour(e, obs. ff. BRUISE, BRUSURE.

brissel, -il, -le, obs. ff. BRISTLE, BIRSLE.

†**'brissel-cock.** *Obs.* [Etymology uncertain; cf. BRISTLE *v.* 2. Jamieson conjectures *Brazil-cock.*] A kind of fowl; 'a turkey-cock' (Jam.).
c **1565** LINDESAY (Pitscottie) *Chron.* (1728) 146 (JAM.) There was.. Swan, partridge, plover, duck, drake, brissel-cock and pawnies, black-cock and muir-fowl, capercaillies.

brist, ME. variant of BREST, 'defect, want'.
a **1300** *Cursor M.* 6344 Wit-vten ani brek or brist. **1340** HAMPOLE *Pr. Consc.* 6205 Loverd when saw we þe haf hunger or thirst Or of any herber haf grete brist. *c* **1450** *Erle of Tolous* 833 Hys wyfe had seche a bryste.

brist, obs. f. BREAST *sb.*, BURST.

bristle ('brɪs(ə)l), *sb.* Forms: 3–5 **brustel**, 4 **brestel, brostle**, 4–5 **bru-, bristil, brestle**, 5 **bru-, brystyl(le, burstyll**, 6 **brisle, bristel(l**, 6–7 **brissel, brissle**, 6– **bristle**. [ME. *brustel, brostle*, corresp. to MDu. *borstel* (*burstel*), Du. *borstel* masc., LG. *börssel* fem.: a deriv. of the simpler form found in OE. *byrst*, ON. *burst* fem., OHG. *burst* masc., *borst* neut., *bursta* weak f. (MHG. *borst, bürst*, m. and n., *borste* f., Ger. *borste* f.): see BIRSE. The OTeut. form of the root-syllable is **bors-*, pointing to Aryan **bhers-*: cf. Skr. *bhṛshti-s* 'point, prong, edge'. There may have been an OE. **brystl*, and OS. **brustil*, as direct source of the ME. and LG. forms.]

1. *prop.* **a.** One of the stiff hairs that grow on the back and sides of the hog and wild boar; used extensively by brushmakers, shoemakers, etc.
[*a* **1000** *Sax. Leechd.* I. 156 Hyre twigu beoð swylce swinen byrst.] *c* **1314** *Guy Warw.* (A) 3680 Nought worth the brestel of a swin. *c* **1320** *Sir Beves* 747 His Brostles were gret and long. *c* **1380** WYCLIF *Serm.* Sel. Wks. II. 148 As bristil bryngiþ in þe þreed. **1398** TREVISA *Barth. De P.R.* XVIII. lxxxvii. (1495) 836 Sewetours call them brustyls and sewe therwyth. *c* **1440** *Promp. Parv.* 52 Brystylle or brustylle [**1499** burstyll], *seta*. **1553** EDEN *Treat. New Ind.* (Arb.) 16 Couered with bristels or bigge heares. **1601** SHAKS. *Twel. N.* I. v. 3, I will not open my lippes so wide as a brissle may enter. **1605** CAMDEN *Rem.* 35 Their brissels more than half shed. **1735** SOMERVILLE *Chase* I. 377 High on their bent Backs erect Their pointed Bristles stare. **1870** YEATS *Nat. Hist. Comm.* 300 Bristles are the stiff, glossy hairs growing on the backs of wild and domesticated swine. **1875** URE *Dict. Arts* I. 533 In 1864 our Imports of Bristles were.. 2,346,135 lbs.

b. *transf.* A filament of material other than natural bristle in the head of a brush, freq. with defining word as ***nylon*** (*wire*, etc.) ***bristle***.
a **1935** T. E. LAWRENCE *Mint* (1955) xxii. 76 Six of us and six wire brushes: but these were mangy things, with half their bristles missing. **1954** [implied at *nylon-bristled* adj. s.v. NYLON 6 b]. **1969** *Sears Catal.* Spring/Summer 869/3 Double brush... 1 side has wire bristles for removing snarls; other side natural bristles for smoothing hair.

2. *gen.* A short, stiff, pointed or prickly hair or similar appendage on other animals; the short hairs on the face of men when thickened and stiffened by shaving.
a **1300** *K. Alis.* 6621 The delfyn.. rerith up his brustelis grymme. **1481** CAXTON *Myrr.* II. vi. 71 Peple that.. haue brestles aboute their mosell lyke swyne. **1591** LYLY *Endym.* II. iii. 29 That chin.. shall be filled with brissels as hard as broome. **1611** BARREY *Ram Alley* II. i, When I was young.. And wore the brissel on my upper lip. **1753** CHAMBERS *Cycl. Supp.* s.v., Cats bristles [whiskers] have a large solid pith in the middle. **1828** STARK *Elem. Nat. Hist.* II. 129 Some of the Annelides possess a third kind of bristles, which M. Savigny terms hooked bristles.

3. In plants: 'A stiff hair or any slender outgrowth which may be likened to a hog's bristle' (Gray); a setaceous appendage or *seta*.
1731–59 P. MILLER *Gardener's Dict.* s.v. *Cnicus*, Striated seeds.. encompassed at the top with a crown of stiff bristles. **1800** E. DARWIN *Phytologia* xiv. 348. **1807** J. E. SMITH *Phys. Bot.* 228 Some species of Galium are admirably characterized by the bristles of their leaves.. being hooked backward or forward. **1875** DARWIN *Insectiv. Pl.* 322 Tipped with a stiff short bristle.

4. fig. ***to set up one's bristles***: to show temper, resistance, or pride; to bristle up, 'put up one's back'. ***to set up any one's bristles***: to arouse such feelings in him. And similar phrases.
1533 FRITH *Ep. Chr. Rdr.* Wks. (1829) 460 Cruel adversaries which set up their bristles, saying, Why, then, shall we do no good works? **1583** GOLDING *Calvin on Deut.* liii. 316 Should the Jewes.. set vp their bristles against God. **1589** COOPER *Admon.* 198 It is good to teach vs to pull downe our brissels, when we waxe proude. **1771** SMOLLETT *Humph. Cl.* (1815) 121 The more she strokes him, the more his bristles seem to rise. **1873** GOULBURN *Pers. Relig.* IV. iii. 271 The feeling that he is to be lectured.. sets a man's bristles up.

5. *attrib.* and *Comb.*: as ***bristle brush***; ***bristle-armed, -backed, -bearing, -leaved, -like, -pointed, -shaped*** adjs.
1601 HOLLAND *Pliny* II. 512 Cleanse it lightly with a wing or a bristle brush. **1614** SELDEN *Titles Hon.* Pref. D ij, Bristled on the back like Hogs.. as if you should say, Bristle-backt. *a* **1845** HOOD *Lycus Cent.*, The bristle-backed boar. **1847–9** TODD *Cycl. Anat. & Phys.* IV. 51/1 Delicate bristle-shaped processes or setæ. *Ibid.* IV. 404/1 Bristle-like organs. **1848** W. GARDINER *Flora Forfarsh.* 204 Bristle-pointed oat. **1863** J. A. BREWER *Flora Surrey* 277 Bristle-leaved Bent-grass.. plentiful on Bagshot Heath.

6. Special comb., as **bristle-bird**, a name given to certain Australian reed-warblers; **bristle-dice**, dice into which bristles were fixed to influence their position when thrown; **bristle-fern**, *Trichomanes radicans*; **bristle-grass**, the genus *Setaria*; **bristle-herring**, a genus (*Chatoessus*) of the herring family, in which the last ray of the dorsal fin is prolonged into a whip-like filament; **bristle-moss**, the genus *Orthotrichum*; **bristle-worm**, a chætopod; **bristleworts** *sb. pl.*, Lindley's name for the order *Desvauxiaceæ*, small tufted herbs with bristly leaves.
1827 VIGORS & HORSFIELD in *Trans. Linnæan Soc.* XV. 232 He [*sc.* Mr. Caley] calls it in his notes *'Bristle Bird'. **1865** GOULD *Birds Australia* I. 343 Sphenura longirostris... Long-billed Bristle-bird. **1911** LUCAS & LE SOUËF *Birds Australia* 330 The Bristle-birds have a shy disposition, and live in reed-beds and thickets. **1967** M. SHARLAND *Birds of Sun* 177 Such species as emu, bristle-bird and two or three other 'historical' kinds. **1532** *Dice Play* (1850) 28 *Bristle dice, be now too gross a practice to be put in use. **1680** COTTON in Singer *Hist. Cards* 335 This they do by false dice, as.. By bristle-dice. **1863** KINGSLEY *Water-bab.* 195 The Connemara heath, and the *bristle-fern of the Turk waterfall. **1863** PRIOR *Plant-n.*, Bristle-fern, from the bristle that projects beyond its receptacle. **1841** *Penny Cycl.* XXI. 299/1 Setaria... Two [species] are indigenous in England, *S. verticellata* and *S. viridis*, and called *bristle-grass. **1961** R. W. BUTCHER *Brit. Flora* II. 1025 The Green Bristle-grass is a loosely tufted annual with bent or erect stems 4–24 in. (10–60 cm.) high. **1844** SIR W. HOOKER *Brit. Flora* II. 57 **Bristle-moss*; from the calyptra being generally clothed with hairs. **1908** *Westm. Gaz.* 8 Aug. 16/3 There is.. a similarity in the eyes of the *bristle-worm to those of the fly. **1941** J. S. HUXLEY *Uniqueness of Man* ix. 192 Certain marine bristle-worms (Polychaetes).

bristle ('brɪs(ə)l), *v.*[1] Also 5 **brustel, brystylle**, 7 **brizle, brisle, brusle, brussel, -sle, -tle, brystle**, 9 (*dial.*) **brisle, brizzle**. [f. prec. sb. See also BRUSTLE *v.*]

I. *intr.*

1. Of hair, quills, etc.: To be, become or stand, stiff and bristly. ***to bristle up***: to rise like bristles.
1480 CAXTON *Ovid's Met.* XIII. cxlv, The heer on my body .. is longe and brustelith lyke brustelis. **1611** FLORIO, *Arricciare*.. ones haire to stare or stand on end, to brizle. **1680** OTWAY *Hist. Marius* 58 His Beard brussled. **1725** POPE *Odyss.* XI. 392 Ere the harvest of the beard began To bristle on the chin. **1748** SMOLLETT *Rod. Rand.* xxxvi, My hair bristled up. **1824** W. IRVING *T. Trav.* II. 105 Mustachios bristling from under his nose. **1861** HOLLAND *Less. Life* i. 16 The man who rises in the morning, with his feelings all bristling like the quills of a hedge-hog.

2. Of animals: To raise the bristles, as a sign of anger or excitement. **b.** Of persons: To display temper or indignation, to 'show fight.' Also with *up*.
1549 OLDE *Erasm. Par. 1 Tim.* vi. 2 It is not semely that.. they should bristle againste their maisters. **1611** DEKKER *Roar. Girle* I. Wks. 1873 III. 145 Now is my cue to bristle. **1688** J. CLAYTON in *Phil. Trans.* XVIII. 133 The howling of the Dogs he supposed.. made her [the sow] come furiously brisling. **1830** FOSTER in *Life & Corr.* (1846) II. 160 Without bristling into anger. **1837** DISRAELI *Venetia* I. xiii, 'You shall do no such thing', said Mrs. Cadurcis, bristling up. **1861** HUGHES *Tom Brown Oxf.* I. ix. 160 There now! don't bristle up like a hedgehog.

3. To be or become bristly; to be thickly set *with* (bristly points).
1606 *Sir G. Goosecappe* I. ii. in Bullen *Old. Pl.* (1884) III. 16 If your French wood brystle, let him alone. **1650** FULLER *Pisgah* IV. ii. 32 Brisling with bushes and over-grown with wood. **1837** CARLYLE *Fr. Rev.* v. ix. (1872) I. 179 All France to the utmost borders bristles with bayonets. **1850** MERIVALE *Rom. Emp.* (1865) I. i. 33 The sea-line.. bristles with projecting headlands.

b. *fig.*, as in ***to bristle with difficulties***.
1864 BURTON *Scot Abr.* II. i. 105 A Latin preface.. bristling with Greek quotations. **1875** HAMERTON *Intell. Life* II. i. 51 The fine arts bristle all over with technical difficulties.

4. To be actively or aggressively astir *with*.
1844 KINGLAKE *Eothen* xv. (1878) 181 Bristling with zeal. **1884** *Evangelical Mag.* Jan. 36 The old place once more bristled with life

II. *trans.*

5. To erect stiffly (hair, etc.) like bristles: chiefly in a temper of hostility. Also with *up*.
1595 SHAKS. *John* IV. iii. 149 Now.. Doth dogged warre bristle his angry crest. **1612** BP. HALL *Contempl. O.T.* XXI. ii, So do savage beasts bristle up themselves.. when they are in danger of loosing the prey. **1775** ADAIR *Amer. Ind.* 309 [Bears] champing their teeth, and bristling their hair, in a frightful manner. **1793** W. ROBERTS *Looker-on* No. 65 (1794) III. 8 Those aspiring asparagus, that bristle up their vegetable spears. **1863** KINGSLEY *Water-bab.* iv. 153 He would.. bristle up his feathers, just as a cock-robin would.

b. *fig.*
1596 SHAKS. *1 Hen. IV*, I. i. 98 Which makes him.. bristle vp The crest of Youth against your Dignity. **1598** CHAPMAN *Iliad* I. 192 Thetis's son at this stood vex'd, his heart Bristled his bosom. **1615** ADAMS *Politic. Hunting* Wks. 1861 I. 8 The great one bristles up himself, and conceits himself higher by the head than all the rest.

6. To furnish with a bristle or bristles; to make bristly.
1678 A. LITTLETON *Lat. Dict.*, To bristle a shooe-makers thread. *Inseto.* **1787** BEST *Angling* (ed. 2) 37 Your hook should be bristled, that is.. fasten a hog's bristle under the silk. **1850** TENNYSON *In Mem.* cvii. iii, Ice.. bristles all the brakes and thorns To yon hard crescent.

7. To cover as with bristles, to cause to bristle.
1837 CARLYLE *Fr. Rev.* (1857) I. II. III. iv. 321 Bristle yourself round with cannon. **1848** LYTTON *Harold* VI. vi, He would bristle all the land with castles.

8. To ruffle violently, exasperate.
1872 BLACKIE *Lays Highl.* 40 The black squall.. Bristles the soft lake to a Fury.

†**'bristle**, *v.*[2] *Obs.* exc. *dial.* In 5 **brystylle**, 6 **bristell, brisle, burstle**, 7 **brusle, brustle**, (9 *dial.* **brizzle, bruzzle**). [The forms *brusle, brustle*, suggest adoption from 15–16th c. Fr. *brusle-r* to burn, Pr. *bruslar*, It. *brustolare*; but the earlier *bristle, brissle*, makes this derivation doubtful, as does also the Sc. form BIRSLE.]

1. *trans.* To render the surface of (anything) crisp with heat; to toast, scorch, parch.
Hence **'bristled** *ppl. a.*
1483 *Cath. Angl.* 44 To Brystylle, *vstillare.* **1553** DOUGLAS *Æneis* VII. ix. 109 Blunt styngis of the brissillit tre [*MSS.* byrsillit]. **1562** TURNER *Bathes* 17 Let him perche or bristell at the fyre Nigella Romana. —— *Herbal* II. (1568) 93 The perched or burstled peasen.. called in Northumberland Carlines. **1691** RAY *N.C. Wds.*, 'The sun bristles the hay' i.e. dries it; 'brusled pease' i.e. parched pease. **1876** *Mid.-Yorksh. Gloss.* (E.D.S.), *Brizzle* or *Bruzzle*, to scorch, near to burning; to broil. **1877** *Holderness Gloss.* (E.D.S.) *Bruzzled-peas.*

2. *intr.* (for *refl.*) To become crisp with heat.
1788 *Gentl. Mag.* I. 189 They [peas] will then parch, crack, as we provincially [Northumberland] call it, bristle.

bristled ('brɪs(ə)ld), *ppl. a.* [f. BRISTLE + -ED.]

1. Covered, set, or tipped with bristles or stiff prickly hairs; rough and prickly, bristly.
a **1300** *K. Alis.* 5722 His rigge was bristled as with sharp sithen. *c* **1374** CHAUCER *Boeth.* 148 þe bristled[e] boor. **1509** HAWES *Past. Pleas.* xxix. ii, His bryes brystled truely lyke a sowes. **1578** LYTE *Dodoens* IV. xlvi. 505 The eares are.. more bristeled or bearded. **1607** SHAKS. *Cor.* II. ii. 96 With his Amazonian [C]hinne he droue The brizled Lippes before him. **1697** DRYDEN *Virg. Georg.* III. 397 The bristled Boar .. New grinds his arming Tusks. **1730** SOUTHALL *Bugs* 19 Has six Legs.. jointed and bristled as the Legs of a Crab.

2. Of hair or feathers: **a.** Stiff like bristles. **b.** Erect, raised, 'on end'.
1553 EDEN *Treat. New Ind.* (Arb.) 16 In the sted of a tayle, a mane, or rough and bristeled heare. **1631** *Celestina* I. 22 By thy brizzled beard. **1832** A. WILSON *Amer. Ornith.* I. 169 The hen hurries about with hanging wings and bristled feathers. **1836–9** TODD *Cycl. Anat. & Phys.* II. 84/2 With bristled mane and haggard eye.

3. Set as with bristles; bristling.
1676 HOBBES *Iliad* III. 183 The brissled Ranks Of th' armed Greeks. **1796** MORSE *Amer. Geog.* II. 309 The.. central range.. bristled with pointed rocks. **1833** I. TAYLOR *Fanat.* vi. 159 Through bristled ramparts and triple lines of shields.

4. Furnished with a bristle.
1794 *Gold. Age* in *Poet. Reg.* (1807) 407 Arm'd with a bristled end and glittering awl.

† **bristler** ('brɪslə(r)). *Obs. rare*$^{-1}$. [f. as prec. + -ER[1].] He who or that which bristles; a boar.
1607 TOPSELL *Four-f. Beasts* 181 He hath many attributes among the learned, as..bristler, wanderer.

bristletail ('brɪs(ə)lteɪl). A wingless insect (*Machilis maritima*) having the abdomen terminated by bristly appendages which assist it in leaping.
1706 PHILLIPS, *Bristle-tails*, a sort of Flies, some of which have one Bristle, others two..in their Tail. **1865** GOSSE *Land & Sea* (1874) 97, I found several colonies of that curious insect the seaside bristletail.

'**bristliness.** In 7 brizlinesse. [f. BRISTLY + -NESS.] Bristly quality.
1611 FLORIO, *Hirsutezza*, brizlinesse, hairinesse, shagginesse. [In mod. Dicts.]

bristling ('brɪslɪŋ), *vbl. sb.* In 6–7 **brustling.** [f. BRISTLE *v.*[1] + -ING[1].] The action of the verb BRISTLE; the rising on end of the hair.
1591 PERCIVALL *Sp. Dict., Enerizamiento*..bristling of the haire. **1872** DARWIN *Emotions* Introd. 12 The bristling of the hair under the influence of extreme terror.

'**bristling,** *ppl. a.*[1] [f. as prec. + -ING[2].]
1. a. Of hair, etc.: That rises or stands stiffly on end. **b.** Of persons: Bristly, rough, shaggy.
1607 TOPSELL *Four-f. Beasts* 356 They have a like bristling mane growing on the back-bone. **1762** BEATTIE *Triumph Mel.* vii, Fear's cold hand erects his bristling hair. **1850** MRS. STOWE *Uncle Tom's C.* ix. 77 He was a great, tall, bristling Orson of a fellow.
c. *fig.*
a **1639** W. WHATELEY *Prototypes* I. xix. (1640) 226 'Tis nothing but pride that sets up these bristling thoughts in you. **1864** *Linnet's Trial* I. II. iii. 220 The bristling tone natural to a man who has quite made up his mind on a subject, but who feels by no means certain that he shall be able to justify it in argument. **1877** PEACOCK *N.-W. Lincoln. Gloss.* (E.D.S.). 'There's a bristling breeze to-day, maister.'
2. Presenting a rough or prickly aspect, thickly armed (with sharp points, or with points of antagonism). Cf. L. *horridus*.
1598 DRAYTON *Heroic. Ep.* VI. 33 The brisling Reeds mov'd with soft Gales, did chide me. **1600** HEYWOOD *1 Edw. IV*, Wks. 1874 I. 25 Her bristling spires, her battled towers. **1843** PRESCOTT *Mexico* V. iv. (1864) 300 The little army..with its bristling array of long swords and javelins, stood firm. **1855** SINGLETON *Virgil* I. 99 So thick upon the roofs doth pattering leap The bristling hail.
b. *fig.*
1871 BLACKIE *Four Phases* I. 106 Religions..fenced with bristling dogmas. **1880** CLEMENSHAW *Wurtz' Atom. The.* 45 The theory..bristling with hypotheses and full of uncertainties.

'**bristling,** *ppl. a.*[2] [f. BRISTLE *v.*[2]] Scorching; burning without flame.
1561 HOLLYBUSH *Hom. Apoth.* 37 a, Diseased with the fretting or briseling stone. **1866** HOWELLS *Venet. Life* iii. 36 The pot full of bristling charcoal.

bristling, var. BRISLING.

'**bristly** ('brɪslɪ), *a.* Also 6 **brizlie, brissly,** 7 **brislie, brisly, bristlie.** [f. BRISTLE *sb.* + -Y[1].]
1. Set with bristles or short stiff hairs; setose.
1591 PERCIVALL *Sp. Dict., Erizado*, rough, bristly. **1626** BACON *Sylva* §781 The leaves..are somewhat bristly. **1697** DRYDEN *Virg. Georg.* ii. 98 The Mastful Beech the bristly Chestnut bears. **1718** POPE *Iliad* XVI. 994 The roaring lion meets a bristly boar. **1870** HOOKER *Stud. Flor.* 15 Capsule globose, sessile, bristly.
b. *fig.*
1872 *Daily News* 25 July, An intelligent and acceptable Republic—not that fierce and chafing thing made up of bristly laws. **1872** *Globe* 5 Aug., That kind of bristly temper which is always on the look-out for causes of offence.
2. Of the nature of or like bristles.
1592 SHAKS. *Ven. & Ad.* 620 On his bow-back he hath a battle set Of bristly pikes. **1645** G. DANIEL *Poems* Wks. 1878 II. 65 If I Have bristlie haire. **1735** SOMERVILLE *Chase* II. 58 Rough bristly Stubbles. **1857** W. COLLINS *Dead Secr.* (1861) 70 A ring of bristly iron-grey hair projected like a collar.
3. Thickly set with sharp or defiant points.
1865 CARLYLE *Fredk. Gt.* XVI. ii. VI. 152 The Chevalier..scans a little the frowning buttresses, bristly with guns.

Bristol ('brɪstəl). In 1 **Brycgstów,** 3–5 **Brigestou, Brycstoue,** 4–7 **Bristow.**
1. A city of England upon the Wiltshire or Lower Avon, famous since early times for its maritime trade and manufactures, and giving its name to various commercial and natural products.
2. a. Short for 'Bristol-stone': see 4.
1618 N. FIELD *Amends Ladies* I. i, To the unskilful owners eyes, alike The Bristol [*v.r.* Bristow] sparkles as the diamond. **1818** *Edin. Even. Cour.* 22 Oct. (JAM.) Studded with what was once the vogue, bristow.
b. Applied to a type of porcelain or pottery similar to Delft ware manufactured in Bristol.
1776 J. WEDGWOOD *Let.* 24 Jan. (1965) 190, I believe this to be true of nearly all our present compositions in England and France, except the Bristol. **1784** H. WALPOLE *Descr. Strawberry-Hill* 13 A cup and saucer, white with green festoons, of Bristol porcelaine. **1787** *Bristol Gaz.* Jan. in W. Chaffers *Marks & Monogr.* (1863) 138 (Advt.), Bristol Pottery, Temple Backs. **1869** LADY C. SCHREIBER *Jrnl.* (1911) I. 66 There is no Bristol, no Plymouth, scarce any characteristic Bow. **1873** H. OWEN *Two Cent. Ceramic Art Bristol* xiii. 328 Previous to the year 1859, Bristol delftware was unknown to collectors. **1900** F. LITCHFIELD *Pott. & Porc.* vii. 91 Many specimens of Bristol porcelain are unmarked. **1969** V. C. CLINTON-BADDELEY *Only Matter of Time* 28 Four milk white cups and saucers with a blue and gold band, which Mrs. Bazeley was prepared to describe as late Bristol, though..they might be early New Hall.
c. Applied to an opaque coloured (esp. blue) or white glass manufactured in Bristol.
1880 LADY C. SCHREIBER *Jrnl.* (1911) II. 292 An exquisite pair of Bristol glass candlesticks. **1882** *Ibid.* 393 Smelling bottles of fine Bristol glass. **1939** O. LANCASTER *Homes Sweet Homes* 36 Bristol glass candlesticks. **1948** M. ALLINGHAM *More Work for Undertaker* xxiv. 283 Oh, is that the glass Lawrence drank from?.. They're old Bristol. **1966** J. GLOAG *Sentence of Life* vii. 73 He glanced back at the bristol blue lamp.
3. *pl.* (with lower-case initial). *Rhyming slang* [ellipt. for *Bristol Cities* = titties (TITTY[3])]. The breasts.
1961 in PARTRIDGE *Dict. Slang* Suppl. **1962** R. COOK *Crust on its Uppers* ii. 30 These slag birds used to go trotting upstairs.., arses wagging and bristols going. **1969** J. LEASOR *They don't make them like that any More* vi. 194 She was in her early twenties, with a wonderful pair of bristols; I could see their outline, firm and round, against her dress. **1969** *Observer* 2 Feb. 28/3 The main point (or should it be points?) of this programme is Miss Barbara Windsor's bristols which are..well-developed.
4. *Attrib.*, as **Bristol-board,** a kind of pasteboard with a smooth surface; **Bristol-brick,** a siliceous material made in the form of a brick, used for cleaning cutlery; **Bristol cream,** the proprietary name of a type of sherry (see quot. 1959); cf. *Bristol milk*; **Bristol-diamond, -gem, -stone,** a kind of transparent rock-crystal found in the Clifton limestone near Bristol, resembling the diamond in brilliancy; also *attrib.*; **Bristol-fashion** (*Naut.*), in good order; **Bristol milk** (see quots.); **Bristol Non-such,** a plant, *Lychnis Chalcedonica*; † **Bristol-red,** a dye; **Bristol-water,** the water of warm springs at Clifton near Bristol, used medicinally.
1809 R. LANGFORD *Introd. Trade* 63, 2 Do. Royal *Bristol Bds. **1883** *Harper's Mag.* 861/2 Mr. Evers painted..portraits on..Bristol-board. **1886** *Trade Marks Jrnl.* 23 June 580 **Bristol Cream*. John Harvey & Sons, Denmark Street, Bristol..Sherry. **1924** J. BUCHAN *Three Hostages* iv. 57, I had a glass of the Bristol Cream for which the club was famous. **1959** W. JAMES *Word-Bk. of Wine* 32 *Bristol Cream*, an oloroso sherry blended by Harvey's of Bristol from wines imported from several sources in Spain. **1596** LODGE *Wits Miserie* 33 A counterfeit chain..*Bristow diamonds. **1624** GATAKER *Transubst.* 65 Bastard pearles, Bristow diamonds, and glasse bugles. **1662** S. P. *Acc. Latitude Men* in *Phenix* II. 517 To distinguish between a true Gem and a Bristol Diamond. **1884** F. BRITTEN *Watch & Clockm.* 215 Rock crystal..also known as 'Bristol'..diamond, is also used by watch jewellers. **1840** R. DANA *Bef. Mast* xx. 61 Everything on board 'ship-shape and *Bristol fashion'. **1867** SMYTH *Sailor's Word-bk., Bristol fashion and shipshape.* Said when Bristol was in its palmy commercial days..and its shipping was all in proper good order. **1707** E. WARD *Hud. Rediv.* II. iii. (N.) The cap..Was set with *Bristol jems. **1644** PRYNNE & WALKER *Fiennes' Trial* 78 Good store of *Bristoll milk, strong wines and waters. **1662** FULLER *Worthies, Bristol* (D.) 'Bristol Milk:' this metaphorical Milk, whereby Xeres or Sherry Sack is intended. **1848** MACAULAY *Hist. Eng.* I. iii. (D.) A rich beverage made of the best Spanish wine, and celebrated..as Bristol milk. **1668** WILKINS *Real Char.* 102 London Tuft, Sweet John, Sweet William; *Bristow Nonsuch. **1551** *Will* in Peacock *N.-W. Linc. Gloss.* (E.D.S.) s.v., One kyrtyll of *bristowe read whiche were her mothers. **1646** SIR T. BROWNE *Pseud. Ep.* 78 Diamond..Chrystall, *Bristoll stones. **1837** LOCKHART *Scott* (1839) IV. 353 A good-humoured lass..who wore as many diamonds as if they had been Bristol Stones. **1739** BYROM *Remains* (1856) II. I. 243, I wish I could drink a glass of *Bristol water in uncle Josiah's company. **1817** T. J. PETTIGREW *Mem. J. C. Lettsom* III. 314 Bristol Water is most proper for the patient's common drink.
5. *attrib.* in ordinary sense; also sometimes with reference to 'Bristol diamonds'.
1651 CLEVELAND *Poems* 32 You that dim Jewells with your Bristoll-sense.

brisure (brizyr, 'brɪʒ(j)ʊə(r)). Also **brizure.** [a. F. *brisure* fracture, breakage; also used in the heraldic and military senses. See also BRUSURE.]
1. *Her.* A variation of, or addition to, a coat of arms, marking the relation of a younger branch of the family to the main stock; a difference.
1623 FAVINE *Theat. Hon.* I. i. 11 The plaine Paternall Armes, without any Brisure. **1868** CUSSANS *Hand-bk. Her.* XXIV. 299 The Bordure Company was formerly employed as a Brisure to indicate illegitimate descent.
2. *Fortif.* A break in the general direction of a rampart or parapet; *spec.* of the parapet of the curtain adjacent to a bastion constructed with orillons.
1706 PHILLIPS, *Brisure*, a Line drawn from four to five Fathom, which is allow'd to the Courtin and Orillon, to make the hollow Tower, or to cover the conceal'd Flanks. **1836** *Penny Cycl.* V. 439/2.
† **3.** Variant of BRUSURE. *Obs.*

briswort, variant of BRUISEWORT.

brit, britt (brɪt), *sb.*[1]
1. A local name of the young of the Herring and Sprat (*Clupea harengus*, and *sprattus*); also the spawn of these.
1602 CAREW *Cornwall* 32 a, The Pilcherd..were wont to pursue the Brit, vpon which they feede, into the hauens. **1851** H. MELVILLE *Whale* II. xlviii. 131 We fell in with vast meadows of brit, the minute, yellow substance, upon which the Right Whale largely feeds. **1880–84** F. DAY *Fishes Gt. Brit.* II. 232 Britt along the Devonshire coast, consists either of young sprats or young herrings. *Ibid.* 233 The Town Council of Exeter annually make an official whitebait repast upon 'britt'. [The author discusses at length the identity of the 'britt', and shows that the name includes both species, which are at some seasons taken together, at others separately.]
2. *transf.* The fry of other fish, as the mackerel.
1886 R. C. LESLIE *Sea-painter's Log* viii. 161 The mackerel brit, or small fry.

† **Brit, Brett,** *sb.*[2] (and *a.*) *Obs.* Forms: 1 Bret(t, Bryt(t, Brit(t, 4 Brett, 6 Brit, Britt, (9 *Hist.* Brett). [OE. *Bret* (pl. *Brettas*) a Briton: cf. OCeltic (and L.) *Britto*; but the OE. form points rather to a variant OCelt. stem **Britt-os*, whence perh. the *Brittia* of Procopius. Hence *Brettisc, Bryttisc*, BRITISH.]
A. *sb.* A Briton: the ordinary name in the O.E. Chronicle; in Scotland applied to the Strathclyde Britons till *c* 1300, when the 'Laws between the Scots and the Bretts' were abolished by Edward I; in later usage only historical. **B.** *adj.* British.
O.E. Chron. an. 890 Butueoh Brettum and Francum, and Brettas him wiþ ȝefuhton [*Laud MS.* Bryttum, Brittas]. **1535** STEWART *Cron. Scot.* II. 230 Brit langage for to speik and vse, So that the Britis culd nocht weill refuse. *Ibid.* 471 All Albione wes in gude rest and peice; Bot[h] Scot and Brit, and Inglismen also. *c* **1630** RISDON *Surv. Devon* §225 (1810) 238 'Twixt Britts and Saxons. **1873** MURRAY *Dial. S.C. Scotl.* 3 The Bretts or Welsh of Strathclyde long retained their special laws as distinct from the laws of Scotland.

Brit, *sb.*[3] Colloq. shortening of BRITON *sb.* 1 c or BRITISH(ER. Also *attrib.* or as *adj.*
1901 'LINESMAN' *Words by Eyewitness* (1902) 62 The Brit is at his old game. **1948** P. WYNDHAM LEWIS *Let.* 3 June (1963) 443 Are you trying to fool the Brit Public..? **1961** S. PRICE *Just for Record* viii. 69 Your working-class Brit is a glutton for celebrities. **1969** R. PETRIE *Despatch of Dove* II. 106 Goddam Limey! You're a Brit.

† **brit, britt,** *v. Obs.* [app.:—OE. *bryttian* to divide into fragments:—**brutjôjan*, f. **brutjon-* divider, f. *brut-* pa. pple. stem of *breutan* to break, divide. Cf. ON. *brytja* to chop in pieces.] *trans.* To cut in pieces; = BRITTEN 3.
1330 R. BRUNNE *Chron.* 244 His hede þei of smyten..þe dede body þe[i] britten on four quarters corn [*i.e.* corven].

brit, variant of BRET, BRITE.

britage, obs. form of BRATTICE.

Britain ('brɪt(ə)n), *sb.*[1] Forms: 3–5 **Bretayne, Breteyn(e,** 4–5 **Brutayne,** 5 **Bretaingne,** 5–6 **Brytayne,** 6 **Britan, Brytayn, Britayn(e, Briteigne;** *Sc.* **Bretane, Bertane, Bartane;** 6–7 **Brittaine, Britaine,** 6– **Britain.** [ME. *Bretayne, -eyne*, a. OF. *Bretaigne*:—L. *Brittannia* or *Brittānia*, the island of Britain. (Lat. *Britannia* would have given F. *Bri-, Breaigne.*) The OE. name was *Breoton, Breoten, Bryten, Breten*, pointing back to a WGer. **Brituna*; also, *Breoton-lond, Breten-lond.* OCeltic had apparently no name for the island as distinct from the people. (With 16th c. Sc. *Bertane, Bartane*, cf. *Dumbarton.*)]
1. a. The proper name of the whole island containing England, Wales, and Scotland, with their dependencies; more fully called Great Britain; now also used for the British state or empire as a whole.
After the OE. period, *Britain* was used only as a historical term, until about the time of Henry VIII and Edward VI, when it came again into practical politics in connexion with the efforts made to unite England and Scotland; in 1604 James I was proclaimed 'King of Great Britain'; and this name was adopted for the United Kingdom, at the Union in 1707. After that event, *South Britain* and *North Britain* are frequent in Acts of Parl. for England and Scotland respectively: the latter is still in occasional (chiefly postal) use. (So *West Britain*, humorously or polemically for 'Ireland'.) *Greater Britain* is a modern rhetorical phrase for 'Great Britain and the colonies', 'the British Empire', brought into vogue in 1868.
a **855** *O.E. Chron.* Introd., Gaius Iulius se Casere ærest Romana Breten-lond ȝesohte. *c* **890** K. ÆLFRED *Bæda* I. i, Breoton is ealond.
1297 R. GLOUC. 22 And aftur Brut ys owne nome he clepede hit Breteyne. 82 Bretayne. *a* **1375** *Joseph Arim.* (Vernon MS.) 232 Þe Auenturus of Brutayne. *c* **1428** *Arthur* 265 Maximian kyng of Bretaingne Conquered al France and Almayne. *c* **1500** *Lyfe Jos. Armathy* (W. de W.) lf. 4 Ioseph of Aramathia..came in to grete Brytayne. *c* **1505** DUNBAR *'Schir for ȝour Grace'* 11 Fairest and best In Bartane. *c* **1515** *Prophecy of Bertlington*, The French wife shal beare the Sonne Shal weild al Bretane to the sea. **1542** HEN. VIII *Declar. Scots* B iv b, Brutus of whom the realme than callyd Brytayn toke fyrst that name. **1547** J. HARRISON *Exhort. Scottes* H vj, Yᵉ names of both subiectes & realmes ceassing, & to be changed into yᵉ name of Britain & Britons, as it was at first, & yet stil ought to be. **1548** N. BODRUGAN *Epitome* A v b, England the only supreme seat of thempire of greate Briteigne. **1604** *Procl. Jas. I*, 24 Oct., King of Great Britain, France, and Ireland. **1630** WADSWORTH *Sp. Pilgr.* vii. 69 His Majesty of great Britaine. **1665** MANLEY *Grotius' Low-C.*

Warrs 779 King James..obliterating the names of Scots and English, would have both to be united and grow up into one Kingdome..to be called Britain. **1667** DRYDEN *Ann. Mirab.* Ded., To the Metropolis of Great Britain, the most renowned and late flourishing city of London. **1707** *Act of Union* xi. §1 That the two Kingdoms of England and Scotland shall..be united into one Kingdom by the Name of Great Britain. **1710** *Act 9 Anne* vi. §4 To export and transport from Great Britain into Ireland. **1718** *Act 5 Geo. I*, xi. §16 The importation of Tar and Pitch from North-Britain into any part of South-Britain. **1729** *Act 2 Geo. II*, xxxv. §12 In several Parts of North Britain commonly called Scotland. *Ibid.* Brought..to that part of Great Britain called England. **1740** THOMSON *'Rule Britannia'*, When Britain first, at Heaven's command, Arose from out the azure main. *c* **1800** DIBDIN *'I sailed from the Downs'*, So adieu to the white cliffs of Britain. **1832** *Act 2 & 3 Will. IV*, lxxv. §1 In that part of the United Kingdom called *Great Britain*, and..that part of the United Kingdom called *Ireland*. **1868** C. W. DILKE (*title*) Greater Britain: Travels 1866–67.

b. *pl.* with reference to the several dominions and dependencies of Great Britain; cf. *Britt. (Omn.)* (= of (all) the Britains) in the legend on coins.

1897 EARL OF ROSEBERY in *Daily News* 5 July 4/5 'Regina Britanniarum'—the Queen of the Britains... She is sovereign, not of one or two, but of numberless Britains, all self-supporting. **1901** *Westm. Gaz.* 11 Dec. 2/2 Lord Rosebery has succeeded with his cry of 'All the Britains', as the three letters 'Omn' on the new coins are to testify... Our King henceforth is to be King of All the Britains.

†**2.** The duchy of Brittany or Bretagne in France; also called Little Britain, Britain the less. *Obs.*

?*a* **1400** *Morte Arth.* 36 Burgoyne and Brabane and Bretayne the lesse. *c* **1530** LD. BERNERS (*title*) Arthur of lytell Brytayne. **1605** CAMDEN *Rem.* (1637) 113 Out of places in Britaine came the families of Saint Aubin, Morley, etc. **1622** BACON *Hen. VII*, Wks. (1860) 339 Re-annexing of the duchy of Britain to the crown of France..by marriage with the daughter of Britain.

† **Britain**, *sb.*² and *a.* *Obs.* Forms: 6 **Brytane, -aine, Brittayne,** 6–7 **Britaine,** 7 **Brittan, Brittain(e,** 6–8 **Britan, Britain.** [ad. L. *Brit(t)ann-us, Brittān-us*, Briton, British. (The L. *Brit(t)anni* or *Brittāni* appears to correspond to the Gr. *Βρεττανοί*, and was perh. adopted from the Greeks of Massilia. The nearest Celtic form is the Irish pl. *Bretain*, genitive *Bretan, Brettan*, which may repr. an OCeltic *Bret(t)an-i* pl., distinct from *Britton-es*, whence BRITON, q.v.)]

A. *sb.* **1.** A Briton (i.e. an ancient Briton).

1547 J. HARRISON *Exhort. Scottes* Civb, Yet wil I not affirme that Scottes be mere Britaynes, or Englishe men mere Britaynes. **1570** LEVINS *Manip.* 19 A Brytane, *Britanus. Ibid.* 200 Brittayne. **1579** FULKE *Confut. Sanders* 561 As Ninnius a Britaine doeth testifie. **1605** CAMDEN *Rem.* (1637) 9 The Britaines..The Britains, the most ancient people of this Isle. *Ibid.* 40 The Brittans. *Ibid.* 54 The Britans. **1611** SHAKS. *Cymb.* I. iv. 28 Heere comes the Britaine. **1702** ECHARD *Eccl. Hist.* (1710) 549 The northern Britains and Caledonians.

2. A native of Bretagne in France; a Breton.

1594 BLUNDEVIL *Exerc.* v. (ed. 7) 567 Called new France, because the Brittans which are Frenchmen did first discover it. *a* **1618** RALEIGH *Invent. Shipping* 9 The French Brittains who were then esteemed the best Brittaine Sea men.

B. *adj.* **1.** Ancient British.

1563–87 FOXE *A. & M.* (1596) 48/1 Joseph of Arimathea ..among the Britaine people. **1576** LAMBARDE *Peramb. Kent* (1826) 167 There bee moreover Brytaine bricks, in the walles of the Church. **1601** HOLLAND *Pliny* I. 87 The Britan ocean. **1641** MILTON *Prel. Episc.* 18 Our Brittaine Bishops ..were remarkable for nothing more then their poverty.

2. British, in the modern political sense. **Britain Crown**, a gold coin struck by James I, orig. valued at 5*s.*, afterwards at 5*s.* 6*d.* (Cf. BRITISH CROWN.)

1609 BIBLE (Douay) Pref., To teach and feede al Britan people. *c* **1620** A. HUME (*title*) Of the Orthographie of the Britan Tongue. **1866** CRUMP *Banking* x. 224 James I—Gold [Coins]—Rose-royal..quarter-sovereign, Britain-crown.

3. Of French Bretagne; Breton.

c **1645** HOWELL *Lett.* (1650) I. 390 The Britan..is a dialect of the Welsh.

† **'Britainer, 'Britaner.** *Obs.* = prec.

1570 LEVINS *Manip.* 84 Of Britayn, Britaner, *Britannus.* **1622** PEACHAM *Compl. Gentl.* xix. (1634) 239 They are faine to have it of the Britainers, Hollanders, and from the Azores Ilands. **1709** J. JOHNSON 27 Apr. in *Ballard MSS.* XV. 46 He is the Miracle of a North-britainer.

Britannia (brɪ'tænɪə). [L. *Britannia*, anciently *Brittannia, Brittānia* (which was Bæda's spelling), corresp. to Gr. *Βρεττανία* (Diod. Sic.), f. *Brittanni* or *Brittāni* = Gr. *Βρεττανοί*: see BRITAIN *a.*]

1. The Latin name of Britain; a poetic name for Britain personified as a female; the female figure on coins, etc., emblematic of Britain.

c **893** K. ÆLFRED *Oros.* I. i. §11 þæt lond þe mon bryttania [*later MS.* bryttannia] hætt. *Ibid.* 28 Brittannia þæt igland.. On brettannia. [**1586** CAMDEN (*title*) Britannia, seu florentissimorum regnorum Angliæ, Scotiæ, Hiberniæ.. descriptio. **1637** —— Britannia, transl. newly into English by P. Holland.] **1666–7** PEPYS *Diary* 25 Feb., The King's new medall, where, in little, there is Mrs. Stewart's face.. and a pretty thing it is, that he should choose her face to represent Britannia by. **1716** *Lond. Gaz.* No. 5404/3 The Figure of a Woman, commonly called Britannia. **1740** THOMSON *Song, 'Rule Britannia'.* **1762–9** FALCONER *Shipwr.* I. 3 Of famed Britannia were the gallant crew. **1798** NELSON in Duncan *Life* (1806) 101 Britannia still rules the waves. **1818** BYRON *Juan* I. iv, Nelson was once Britannia's god of war. **1864** *N. & Q.* Ser. III. V. 37/1 The earliest coin ..with the figure of Britannia is a copper half penny of 1672.

†**2.** *Comm.* = *Britannia Linen*: see 3. *Obs.*

1676 DAMPIER *Voy.* II. II. 110 Broad-cloth, Serges.. Britannias, Hollandilloes, Iron-work, etc.

3. a. *attrib.* in commercial terms; *esp.* **Britannia-metal**, an alloy of tin and regulus of antimony, resembling silver in appearance.

1706 *Lond. Gaz.* No. 4189/4 Coarse unwatered Camblets ..Britannia Linen..broad Germany Linen. **1817** *Brownell's Sheffield Directory* 73 Britannia Metal Manufacturers. [In earlier directories called 'White Metal'.] **1849** DICKENS *Dav. Copp.* 586 Of course we have something in the shape of spoons..but they are Britannia metal. **1882** *Pall Mall G.* 30 June 1/1 Prince Bismarck's oft-quoted.. saying, that 'Speech was silvern and silence golden; but that first to speak and then to run away was Britannia metal'.

b. *ellipt.* = *Britannia metal*, or an article made of this. Also *attrib.*, made of Britannia metal.

1814 W. BENTLEY *Diary* Feb. (1914) IV. 237 He had begun the work of the Britania Ware. **1840** *Picayune* (New Orleans) 28 July 1 Britannia Table and Tea Spoons. **1852** A. CARY *Clovernook* 91 The cupboard.., where the china and britannia were wisely set for show. **1887** M. E. WILKINS *Humble Romance* 107 Pouring the tea from the shiny britannia teapot into the best pink china cups. **1970** *Globe & Mail* (Toronto) 28 Sept. 26/6 What is Britannia ware? It is a very fine type of pewter made by a spinning process instead of being cast.

Hence **Bri'tannian** *a.* = BRITISH.

1589 *Gold. Mirr.* (1851) 14 Wicked weesels, fled from Britanian grounds. **1613** PURCHAS *Pilgr.* VIII. v. 760 Our Britannian hopes, Prince Henrie and Duke Charles. *a* **1840** E. ELLIOTT *Withered W. Flowers* I. Our Britannian shore.

Britannic (brɪ'tænɪk), *a.* [ad. L. *Britannic-us* of Britain, or perh. F. *Britannique.*] Of Britain, British. Used in *His* or ***Her Britannic Majesty***.

1641 MILTON *Ch. Discip.* II. (1851) 69 [Thou] didst build up this Britannick Empire. **1695** BLACKMORE *Pr. Arth.* 237 The Britannic Hero. **1709** STEELE *Tatler* No. 6 ¶12 Envoy Extraordinary from her Britannick Majesty. **1796** MORSE *Amer. Geog.* II. 208 On a clear day the three Britannic kingdoms may be seen from this island. **1848** W. K. KELLY tr. *L. Blanc's Hist. Ten Y.* I. 473 His Britannic majesty maintained with St. Petersburg relations of amity.

Hence **Bri'tannically** *adv.*: in British fashion; in reference to Great Britain.

1716 M. DAVIES *Ath. Brit.* II. 11 Whereupon an Active Disobedience very Brittanically ensuing. **1805** *Ann. Rev.* III. 178 This extended portion..is rather locally than britannically interesting. **1869** *Student* II. 183 Several captures of the almost (Britannically) fabulous 'Bath White'.

† **bri'tannic**, *sb.* *Obs.* [a. L. *britannica* (*herba*) 'water-dock' (Lewis and Short).] A herb, app. the Water-dock (*Rumex hydrolapathum*).

1567 MAPLET *Gr. Forest* 34 *Britannick*, or English Herb hath the very looke of the greatest Sorrell. **1601** HOLLAND *Pliny* II. 269 The herbe Britannica..transported vnto vs out of Britaine.

britannicize (brɪ'tænɪsaɪz), *v.* [f. BRITANNIC *a.* + -IZE.] *trans.* To make Britannic or British in form or character.

[**1811** *Ann. Reg. 1809* Pref. p. iv, Such measures as may *Britannize*, as it were, all the other Grecian islands.] **1887** W. F. RAE *Miss Bayle's Romance* xvii, American gentlemen are 'brittannicized Indians'. **1921** *Spectator* 16 Apr. 487/2 St. Paul did not fight a lifelong battle against judaizing the Christian Church in order that we should britannicize it nowadays.

† **Bri'tannish.** *a.* *Obs. rare.* = BRITISH.

1611 SPEED *Theat. Gt. Brit.* (1614) 1/2 Other Ilands.. under the shadow of Great Albion are also accounted Britannish.

† **'Britany.** *Obs.* Also **Britanie, -annie, -anny, Brittany.** [ad. L. *Britannia.*]

1. Britain, Great Britain.

1579 E. K. in *Spenser's Sheph. Cal.* Sept. 151 Gloss., King Edgare..reigned here in Britanye. **1581** SAVILE *Tacitus Hist.* I. ii. (1591) 2 Brittany al conquered, not al retained. **1596** SPENSER *F.Q.* III. iii. 52 All Britany doth burne in armes bright. **1608** HIERON *Defence* II. 79 The Lords inheritance in this Ile of Britanie. **1611** GUILLIM *Heraldrie* III. xvii. 162 By whose glorious issue, Great Britanny now enioieth the height of Glorie and Happinesse. **1662** GUNNING *Lent Fast* 35 Lucius, first Christian King of Britanny.

2. The Roman provinces of *Britannia Prima* and *Secunda*.

1658 W. BURTON *Itin. Antonin.* 85 York..the more antient Metropolis of the Diocese of the Britainnies.

3. The French province of Bretagne: 'Little Britany'; commonly spelt Brittany.

britch, var. BREECH.

britch. Variant of BREECH *sb.*, esp. in sense 4. (See also quot. 1940.) Also in phr. *too big for one's britches*: see BIG *a.* 3 e.

1885 [see BREECH *sb.* 4 c]. **1940** *Chambers's Techn. Dict.* 114/1 *Britch* or *breech*, a wool-sorter's term for wool obtained from the thighs and root of the tail, estimated as the lowest quality in a fleece. **1963** *Times* 6 Feb. (N.Z. Suppl.) p. v/3 Britch wool.

† **'britchel**, *a.* *Obs.* exc. *dial.* Forms: 3 **bruchel**, 8–9 (*dial.*) **britchel.** [ME. *bruchel* (ü):—OE. *brycel*; cf. BRICKLE.] Liable to break; brittle.

a **1225** *Ancr. R.* 164 þis bruchele uetles is bruchelure þene beo eni gles. *c* **1230** *Hali Meid.* 13 Hwen þu hare liflade i þi bruchele flesch wiðute bruche leadest. **1674** RAY *N.C. Wds.* 8 Brichol [*printed* brichoe], brittle. *Var. Dial.* and *Chesh.* **1857** J. SCHOLES *Jaunt to see Queen* 47 in *Lanc. Gloss.*, As britchel as egg-shells.

† **brite**, *v.* *Obs.* exc. *dial.* Also 8–9 **brit.** [Cf. ON. *brjóta*, Sw. *bryte*, Da. *bryde* to break, destroy (*trans.*), corresp. to OE. *bréotan* to break, burst.] *intr.* Of grain, hops, etc.: To become over-ripe and shatter.

1669 WORLIDGE *Syst. Agric.* viii. §1 (1681) 152 It preserves the Hops from briting or shedding. *Ibid.* 323 *Brite* or *bright*: Barley, Wheat, and other Grain, and Hops are said to brite when they are over-ripe and shatter. **1674** RAY *S. & E.C. Wds.* 60. *a* **1722** LISLE *Husb. Gloss.* in *F. Wds.* (E.D.S.) *Brit*, to shed; to fall. **1883** PRIOR (*in let. to Editor*), In dry weather the grain falls from ears of wheat in the reaping and in Wiltshire is said to brit out.

briteysing, obs. form of BRATTICING.

brith, obs. form of BIRTH, BRIGHT.

brither, Sc. form of BROTHER.

Briticism ('brɪtɪsɪz(ə)m). orig. *U.S.* Also **Britticism.** [f. BRIT(ISH (or a possible *Britic*) after *Gallicism, Scotticism*, etc.] A phrase or idiom characteristic of Great Britain, but not used in the English of the United States or other countries.

1868 R. G. WHITE in *Galaxy* Mar. 335 This use of the word is a widespread Briticism. **1883** *Boston (U.S.) Jrnl.* 17 Sept., A well arranged handbook of Briticisms, Americanisms, Colloquial Phrases, etc. **1885** *Sat. Rev.* 28 Nov. 709 The American critic is within his right when he retorts at once that the use of 'directly' in place of 'as soon as' is a Britticism.

Briticization (ˌbrɪtɪsaɪ'zeɪʃən). Also **Britticization.** [f. as BRITIC(ISM + -IZE + -ATION after *Anglicization*, etc.] The process of making British (esp. with reference to the ancient Britons), or the result of this.

1953 K. JACKSON *Lang. & Hist. Early Brit.* 702 The *Bern-* and *Birn-* of Nennius are not British but are Britticisations of Latin *Bernicia*. **1955** *Antiquity* XXIX. 86 The consequent re-Britticization of Dumfriesshire.

britil, obs. form of BRITTLE.

British ('brɪtɪʃ), *a.* (*sb.*) Forms: 1 **Brettisc, Bryttisc, Brittisc (Brytisc),** 4 **Bruttische,** 5 **Brytysshe,** 6 **Brutish,** 7 **Brittish, Brytysh,** 6– **British.** [OE. *Brettisc*, etc., f. *Bret*, pl. *Brett-as, Bryttas, Brittas*, the natives of ancient Britain, the Britons: see BRIT and -ISH. The modern spelling is influenced by Latin.]

1. a. Of or pertaining to the ancient Britons. Now chiefly in ethnological and archæological use.

a **855** *O.E. Chron.* an. 508 Her Cerdic and Cynric ofsloȝon ænne Brettisc [*Laud MS.* Bryttiscne] cyning. *a* **1000** *Ibid.* (Laud) Introd., Her sind on þis iȝlande fif ȝeþeode · Englisc and Brittisc and Wilsc, and Scyttisc and Pyhtisc and Boc Leden. *a* **1100** *Ibid.* an. 1075 Se ylca Raulf wæs Bryttisc on his moder healfe, and his fæder wæs Englisc. **1605** SHAKS. *Lear* III. iv. 189 Fie, foh, and fumme, I smell the blood of a Brittish man. *c* **1645** HOWELL *Lett.* (1650) I. 377 He calls.. Helen an English woman; whereas, she was purely British, and that there was no such nation upon earth called English at that time. **1780** COWPER *Boadicea* i, The British warrior queen, Bleeding from the Roman rods. **1870** KNIGHT *Hist. Eng.* i. 3 A road, acknowledged to be British, still crosses Salisbury Plain.

b. Of or pertaining to the Celtic (Brythonic) language of the ancient Britons; later, = Welsh, occas. Cornish. Also as *sb.*

c **1205** *Layaman's Brut* (1847) (E.E.T.S.) 13393 Nu ic þe wulle teche. Bruttisce spæche. **1387** TREVISA *Higden* (Rolls) II. 79 þis citee..in Brittische speche heet Caerleon,..and Chestren in Englisshe. **1550** W. SALESBURY *Brief & Plain Introd. Welsh* sig. A. i, A briefe and a playne introduction, teachyng how to pronounce the letters in the British tong, (now commenly called Walsh). *Ibid.* sig. B. i, In Britishe or Walshe in euery worde hath the true pronunciation of A in latine. **1637** HOLLAND tr. *Camden's Britannia* 472 It coupleth it selfe with the Yare, which the Britans called *Guerne*..of Aldertrees, no doubt, so termed in British wherewith its overshadowed. **1662** *Act of Uniformity* 13–14 *Chas. II*, iv. §27 That the Book [of Common Prayer] hereunto annexed be truly and exactly translated into the British or Welsh Tongue. **1712** *Life St. Winefride* 61 *Wen* in the Old British Tongue signifies *White*. **1838** W. HOWITT *Rural Life Eng.* II. xvi. 380 The British tongue here [in Tintagel] lingered till lately. **1962** G. GRIGSON *Shell Country Bk.* I. 112 Knowing no British, they would take this word *avon* for a name. **1972** W. B. LOCKWOOD *Panorama of Indo-European Langs.* vi. 67 It is plain that the Celtic spoken in Britain was a language of the same general type as Gaulish; the two were closely related languages... We may call it British... It is often useful to be able to refer to Gaulish and British together; we may then speak of Gallo-Brittonic.

2. a. Of or belonging to Great Britain, or its inhabitants. In the earlier instances only a geographical term adopted from Latin; from the time of Henry VIII frequently used to include English and Scotch; in general use in this sense

from the accession of James I, and in 17th c., often opposed to *Irish*; legally adopted at the Union in 1707. Now chiefly used in political or imperial connexion, as *the British army*, *British colonies*, *British India*, etc., *British ambassador*, *consul*, *residents*, etc.; also in scientific and commercial use, as *British plants*, *British butterflies*, *British spirits*.

1387 TREVISA *Higden* (1865) I. 271 Gallia..is i-closed aboute..wiþ þe Bruttische occean in þe west side. 1398 —— *Barth. De P.R.* xv. lxvi. (1495) 512 Fraunce..endyth in the north at Brytysshe Occean. 1570–87 HOLINSHED *Scot. Chron.* (1806) I. 43 Amongst the Irish Scotishmen..the petition of the British Scots. 1604 J. DEE in Hearne *Coll.* (1885) I. 64 This Britysh Empire. 1643 *Script. Reas. for Defens. Armes* 76 The extirpation of the Brittish Nation, and Protestant Religion in that kingdome [Ireland]. 1699 GARTH *Dispens.* I. 7 How have I kept the Brittish Fleet at ease? 1706–7 *Act of Union 6 Anne* xi. §1 art. 8 Without any mixture of British or Irish salt. 1769 BURKE *Pres. St. Nat.* Wks. II. 187 Every British merchant in Petersburgh. 1841 W. SPALDING *Italy & It. Isl.* II. 393 His strange discussions on the British constitution. 1855 TENNYSON *Maud* I. xiii. ii, A stony British stare. 1882 *Garden* 18 Feb. 112/1 Our common British Ivy.

b. British Empire: the empire consisting of Great Britain and the other British possessions, dominions, and dependencies; now replaced by the British Commonwealth (see COMMONWEALTH 4 c). Cf. EMPIRE *sb.* 5 b.

1604 J. DEE *Pet. to King*, God..make your Maiestie to be the most blessed and Triumphant Monarch, that euer this *Brytish* Empire, enioyed. 1768 GOLDSMITH (*title*) The present state of the British Empire in Europe, America, Africa and Asia, containing a concise account of our possessions in every part of the globe, [etc.]. 1813 HECTOR CAMPBELL (*title*) The Impending Ruin of the British Empire, its Cause and Remedy considered. 1884, etc. [see COMMONWEALTH 4 c]. 1887 [see EMPIRE *sb.* 5 a]. 1902 *Encycl. Brit.* XXXIII. 393/1 The British Empire League and the Imperial Trade Defence League endeavour to promote inter-Imperial trade.

c. British Isles: a geographical term for the islands comprising Great Britain and Ireland with all their offshore islands including the Isle of Man and the Channel Islands (see ISLE *sb.* 1).

1621 HEYLIN *Microcosmus* 243 (*page-heading*) The British Isles. 1792 A. YOUNG *Trav. France* II. 343 A territory, naturally so inconsiderable as the British isles, on comparison with France. 1888 A. J. JUKES-BROWNE *Building of Brit. Isles* 1 There have been many different arrangements of land and sea over the area where the British Isles now stand. 1916 G. B. SHAW *Androcles & Lion* Pref. p. li, Practically all the white inhabitants of the British Isles and the North American continent. 1960 C. DAY LEWIS *Buried Day* ii. 32 He was for ever buying, selling or exchanging books, many of them worthless, with correspondents all over the British Isles.

d. British English: the English language as spoken or written in the British Isles; *esp.* the forms of English usual in Great Britain, as contrasted with those characteristic of the U.S.A. or other English-speaking countries.

[1869 ELLIS *E.E. Pronunc.* I. 20 Practically the speech of the American English is archaic with respect to that of the British English.] 1892 H. SWEET *New Eng. Gram.* I. 224 The influence of the vulgar London or 'Cockney' dialect is stronger in Australasian than in British English. 1926 H. W. FOWLER *Mod. Eng. Usage* 52/2 These words do not mean in American..use what they mean in British English. 1932 R. W. CHAPMAN *'Oxford' English* 540 This expression may be current in America, but it is not British English. 1967 'J. CROSS' *To Hell for Half-a-crown* x. 130 The English that Neumann was babbling was not..British English..but American.

†**3.** Of or belonging to Brittany, Breton. *Obs.*

1602 CAREW *Cornwall* 131 b, One of their auncestours..entertained a British Miller, as that people, for such idle occupations, proue more hardie then our owne.

4. *ellipt.* as *sb. pl.* British people, soldiers, etc.

1641 in Miss Hickson *Irel. 17th C.* (1884) II. App. U. 363 [In county Monaghan] there being a little plantation of British, the rebels plundered the town. 1652 *Ibid.* (1884) I. xxxix. 245 As the Irish rebels marched through the said parish they murdered all the British they could lay their hands on. 1708 *Lond. Gaz.* No. 4459/3 The British had not a Man kill'd or wounded. 1844 H. H. WILSON *Brit. India* II. vii. II. 269 Appearances began to assume an aspect most unfavourable to the British.

5. *Comb.*, as ***British-born***, ***-built***, ***-owned*** adjs., ***British-man***; **British crown**, a gold coin current in the reign of Charles I.; **British disease**, loosely applied to any fault or disorder considered typical of the British as a nation, esp. proneness to industrial unrest; cf. *English disease* (c) s.v. ENGLISH *a.* 2 e; **British gum**, a commercial name of dextrin; **British-Israelite** = ANGLO-ISRAELITE; so **British-Israel** (*attrib.*), **British-Israelism**; **British Restaurant**, a government-subsidized restaurant opened during the war of 1939–45; **British school**, a public elementary school, on the non-denominational or unsectarian basis of the 'British and Foreign School Society'; **British Standard Time**, the time system introduced in Britain on 18 Feb. 1968, which is the same as Central European Time and is equivalent to the extension of Summer Time throughout the year; **British Summer Time** = SUMMER-TIME 2; **British thermal unit** (see THERMAL *a.* 2); **British warm** (see WARM *sb.*[2] 2).

1796 MORSE *Amer. Geog.* II. 108 Numbers of *British-born subjects. 1756 *Act 29 Geo. II*, xxxiv. §18 *British built Ships or Vessels. 1866 CRUMP *Banking* x. 224 Charles I—Gold [coins]—Three-pound piece, angel, unite, double-crown, *British-crown. 1971 *Guardian* 6 Mar. 11/5 The disruption is caused, in Ford's eyes, by the '*British Disease'—constant, unpredictable strikes. 1979 *Dædalus* Winter 14 The British, after years of vivisecting their malaise (the 'British disease'), see a brighter future thanks to the combination of luck—the North Sea oil—and..rediscovering self-restraint and incomes discipline. 1984 *Financial Times* 4 Feb. 4 The British disease in this context..is high levels of overtime, much higher than on the continent. 1860 MAYNE *Exp. Lex.*, **British Gum* (*Chem.*), term for a species of gum into which starch is converted when exposed to a temperature between 600° and 700°..used as a substitute for gum Arabic in calico printing and other processes. 1907 (*title*) The *British-Israel Ecclesia. 1920 S. C. (*title*) *British-Israelism. 1934 *Times Lit. Suppl.* 1 Feb. 77/2 Are all the present millions of *British-Israelites mad? 1948 'N. SHUTE' *No Highway* v. 133 He has been in trouble with the police arising out of his activities with the British Israelites. 1711 SHAFTESB. *Charac.* (1737) III. 144 Had it happen'd to one of us *British-men to have been born at sea, cou'd we not therefore properly be call'd British-men? 1858 *Merc. Mar. Mag.* V. 308 *British-owned ..vessels. 1941 W. S. CHURCHILL *Minute* 21 Mar. in *Grand Alliance* (1950) 663, I hope the term 'Communal Feeding Centres' is not going to be adopted... I suggest you call them *'British Restaurants'. 1950 A. WILSON *Such Darling Dodos* 152 Returning from lunch at the British Restaurant. 1967 *Times* 24 Oct. 11/3 The Secretary of State for Home Affairs announced on June 23 that a bill will be introduced early next session to extend 'summer time' permanently throughout the year... We understand that the name *British Standard Time is being considered; this is ambiguous, is likely to lead to confusion and misunderstanding and should be rejected. 1970 A. P. HERBERT *In Dark* 11 By the beginning of February some real advantages will at last be seen to flow from British Standard Time. 1930 *British Summer Time [see B.S.T. *s.v.* B III]. 1958 L. R. MUIRHEAD *Blue Guide to Northern Spain* (ed. 2) p. cxxxvi, Railway time is now 1 hour later than Greenwich time, and coincides with British Summer Time when the latter is in force. 1970 A. P. HERBERT *In Dark* 90 We arrived punctually at one o'clock Local Time, two o'clock Newfoundland Government Time, 1730 British Summer Time and 1530 Greenwich Mean Time.

6. ***the best of British luck***, an expression of encouragement, often with the ironical implication that good luck will not be forthcoming. Also ellipt. ***best of British***.

1961 C. WITTING *Driven to Kill* i. 12 Here's my P.S.V. badge if you want to take the number—and the best of British luck to you. 1963 L. MEYNELL *Virgin Luck* ii. 39 As soon as they [*sc.* kittens and young birds] can fend for themselves they get shoved out into the world and the best of British luck to them. 1965 EVA-LIS WUORIO *Z for Zaborra* 190 The best of British luck to you. 1967 W. KEENAN *Lonely Beat* vii. 74 'Best of British.' With that the reporter vanished.

Hence **British-hood, Britishness.**

1883 A. FORBES in *Ninet. Cent.* Oct. 722 Their British-hood manifests itself in things big and in things little. 1872 S. MOSTYN *Perplexity* III. iii. 46 His thorough Britishness.

Britisher ('brɪtɪʃə(r)). [f. BRITISH + -ER: cf. *foreign-er*.

(Apparently of U.S. origin, and chiefly used by, or attributed to, Americans. Mr. R. Grant White has strongly disclaimed its use in U.S., but Mr. Fitzedward Hall has known it as of American currency all his life. Prof. Freeman, in his *Impressions of U.S.*, thinks it arose during the War of Independence, when the opposing forces were known as 'American' and 'British' (not 'English'), and 'Britisher' was the natural substantive from the latter. Mr. F. treats the word more dispassionately than those who denounce it as an 'odious vulgarism'. See his work.)]

A British subject; a native or inhabitant of Great Britain (as distinguished from an American citizen).

1829 MARRYAT *F. Mildmay* xx, [American mate *loquitur*] 'Are we going to be bullied by these..Britishers?' 1868 *Spectator* 14 Nov. 1325 Mr. Reverdy Johnson..was so complimentary to England..and to Britisher institutions. 1879 T. E. C. LESLIE in *Academy* 23 Even tawdry rhetoric is venial compared with the sin of using such an odious vulgarism as the word Britisher for Englishman or Briton. 1883 FREEMAN *Impressions U.S.* iv. 29, I always told my American friends that I had rather be called a Britisher than an Englishman, if by calling me an Englishman they meant to imply that they were not Englishmen themselves. *Ibid.* vi. 43 The American is really more called on to know about British matters than the Britisher is called on to know about American matters. 1884 STEVENSON *New Arab. Nts.* 38 His tweed suit..identified him as a Britisher.

Britishism ('brɪtɪʃɪz(ə)m). [f. BRITISH *a.* + -ISM.] The characteristic qualities of the British; with *a* and *pl.*, any of these qualities; a British peculiarity, form of expression, or the like (cf. BRITICISM).

1894 *Harper's Mag.* Jan. 315 Doubtless he could use 'Britishisms' if he chose. *Ibid.*, Nor should we advise an American statesman to attempt a 'Britishism'. 1906 *Daily Chron.* 20 Oct. 4/4 Americanism yet Britishism, cosmopolitanism but Imperialism. 1915 SANDAY *Meaning of War* 80 For the Englishman, *Britishism* (Britentum) and civilization..are one and the same. 1927 *Observer* 20 Nov. 11/1 These are a few of the concrete Britishisms which engage the vigilance of Chicago's mayor. 1959 *Encounter* Dec. 54 Almost all his characteristics were British..sometimes they were Britishisms exaggerated.

Britishly ('brɪtɪʃlɪ), *adv.* [f. BRITISH *a.* + -LY[2].] †**1.** In the ancient British tongue. *Obs. rare.*

1654 VILVAIN *Enchir. Epigr.* VI. xxiii, Glassenbury, Brytishly cald Inis Avalon.

2. After the manner of the British, in British fashion.

1892 STEVENSON & OSBOURNE *Wrecker* xxiii. 362 Britishly chuckle-headed. 1892 F. E. TROLLOPE *That Wild Wheel* xiv, I shall come home..to grumble, Britishly, on my half-pay. 1900 *Daily News* 3 Mar. 6/1 As he took up his position, very Britishly in front of the fire. 1904 *Windsor Mag.* Jan. 294/1 A certain sedate and Britishly respectable old codger. 1968 *Economist* 13 Apr. 64/2 Rioting very Britishly in front of the City Hall.

Britishness ('brɪtɪʃnɪs). [f. BRITISH *a.* + -NESS.] †**a.** The conditions of the ancient Britons. **b.** The quality or character of the British.

1682 W. RICHARDS *Wallogr.* 88 Primitive Brittishness was never acquainted with the habiliment of a Shirt. 1872 W. CLARK RUSSELL *Perplexity* xxvi, There were Frank's pure eyes, his clear-cut nose,..his manliness, his high-bred air, and, if I may coin a word, his thorough *Britishness*. 1904 *Daily Chron.* 9 Sept. 3/2 As Napoleon pulverised ancient kingdoms..so Hazlitt hurled himself courageously at the solid mass of complacent Britishness.

britle, obs. form of BRITTLE.

Brito- ('brɪtəʊ), comb. form f. L. *Brit(t)o* BRITON, used:

1. In sense 'belonging to the ancient Britons and..', as ***Brito-Pictish***, ***Brito-Roman*** adjs.

1654 VILVAIN (*title*) Enchiridium Epigrammatum Latino-Anglicum; an epitome of essais, Englished out of Latin... Containing six Classes or Centuries of 1. Theologicals. 2. Historicals. 3. Heterogeneals. 4. Bryto-Anglicals. 5. Miscellaneals. 6. Mutuatitials. 1860 *Chambers's Encycl.* I. 376/2 Of Roman or Brito-Roman manufacture. 1926 *Glasgow Herald* 25 Oct. 6 A long list of British or Brito-Pictish ministers.

2. In sense 'British and..', as ***Brito-arctic***, ***Brito-Canadian***, ***Brito-Japanese***. Also **Brito-centric** *a.*, having Britain as the centre.

1866 A. BELL *Hist. Canada* II. 321 In brief, what is denounced as a crime in a Gallo-Canadian shall pass for public virtue in a Brito-Canadian. 1898 *Geogr. Jrnl.* XI. 134 It is evident, therefore, that the basalts of Cape Flora and Hooker island are similar to types widely distributed in the Brito-arctic volcanic province. 1905 *Westm. Gaz.* 11 Sept. 2/3 'Anglo-Japanese' certainly is an easier form than 'Brito-Japanese'. 1924 R. MACAULAY *Orphan Island* xvi. §3 The world, as viewed from Orphan Island, wore a curious, Brito-Centric aspect.

Briton ('brɪt(ə)n, -ən), *sb.* (*a.*). Also 3 **Brytone, Brutone,** 5 **Breton(e,** 6 **Bryton, Bryttane, Bruton.** [ME. *Breton*, a. F. *breton*:—L. *Brittŏn-em*, nom. *Britto* 'a native of Britain'. The most correct L. form was *Britto*, *Brittŏn-em*, pl. *Brittŏn-es*, a. OCeltic **Britto*, pl. **Britton-es*, whence Welsh collective pl. *Brython*. The ME. *Bryton*, *Bruton* show various etymological influences; the modern *Briton* is assimilated to the erroneous L. form *Brito*, pl. *Britŏn-es*, found in MSS. (The earlier name by which the Romans spoke of this people was *Britanni*, or *Brittāni*, *-anni*, which appears to have been a Goidelic name; but after the conquest of Britain, this was gradually superseded by *Brittones* the name given to themselves by the Brythonic people of the south of the island. Only the latter survived in living use: Bæda's regular form is *Bretto*, *-ones*; and F. *Breton* represents a L. form with *-tt-*; *Britōnem*, *Britōnem*, would have given *Brion*, *Breon*. The OE. name was *Brettas*, *Bryttas*: see BRIT *sb.*[2])]

A. *sb.* **1.** A native of Britain: **a.** In History and Ethnology: One of the race who occupied the southern part of the island at the Roman invasion, the 'ancient Britons'. †**b.** A Welshman. **c.** Since the union of England and Scotland: A native of Great Britain, or of the British Empire; much used in the 18th c.; now chiefly in poetic, rhetorical, or melodramatic use, and in phrases dating to the 'Rule Britannia' period, as 'to work like a Briton', 'as tough as a Briton', etc. ***North Briton***: a Scotchman.

1297 R. GLOUC. 2 Þis was þo in Engolond Brytones [*v.r.* Brutones] were y-wys. ? *a* 1400 *Morte Arth.* 1449 Thane the Bretons brothely brochez theire stedez. *c* 1428 *Arthur* 15 Bretones ȝaf hym þat name. 1547 J. HARRISON *Exhort. Scottes* C j b, As they were called Kynges of Britayne, so was yᵉ general name of the people Brytons. *Ibid.* G v b, When these hateful termes of Scottes and Englishemen, shalbe abolisshed, and blotted oute for euer, and we shal al agre in the onely title and name of Britons. 1586 WARNER *Alb. Eng.* II. xiii. 63 He was Father vnto Brute: and thus the Brutons bring Their petigree from Jupiter. 1667 E. CHAMBERLAYNE *St. Gt. Brit.* I. III. iii. (1743) 161 So the Britons, Hugh ap Owen, etc. 1679 DRYDEN *Tr. & Cress.* Prol. 1 See, my loved Britons, see your Shakespeare rise. 1740 THOMSON *'Rule Britannia'*, Britons never will be slaves. 1760 GEO. III. in G. Rose *Diaries* (1860) II. 189, I glory in the name of Briton. 1817 WOLFE *Burial Sir J. Moore* vi, Little he'll reck if they let him sleep on In the grave where a Briton has laid him. 1839 THIRLWALL *Greece* I. 227 The ancient Britons. 1851 D. WILSON *Preh. Ann.* II. III. viii. 486 The aboriginal Briton. 1886 TENNYSON *Exhib. Ode*, Britons, hold your own!

†**2.** A Breton or native of Brittany.

†**B.** *adj.* = BRITISH. *Obs.*

1547 J. HARRISON *Exhort. Scottes* F ij, In the Englishe and Briton histories. **1571** J. MAITLAND *Admon. Earl of Mar*, Thay forcit the Briton folks to flit. **1596** SPENSER *F.Q.* II. x. 49 Yet oft the Briton Kings against them [the Romans] strongly swayd. *c* **1605** ROWLEY *Birth Merl.* IV. v. 344 To enlarge the Briton bounds. *Ibid.* v. ii. 350 To be invested with the Briton crown.

†**'Britoner.** *Obs.* Also 4–5 **Bretoner, Brytoner(e, Brutiner, Brutener, Bretener, Britonere.** 'An inhabitant of Brittany, a Frenchman, used as a term of reproach' (Skeat *Gloss. P. Pl.*).

1362 LANGL. *P. Pl.* A. VII. 142 A Brutiner, a Braggere, a-bostede him alse. *Ibid.* 163 And buffetede þe brutiner aboute boþe his chekes. [**1377** B. VI. 156, 178 Brytonere.. Britoner; **1393** C. IX. 152, 173 brytonere..brutener.]

Britoness ('brɪtənɪs). *rare.* A female Briton.

1591 SPENSER *Ruines Time* 106 Bunduca, Britonnesse.. That..with the Romanes fought. **1832** MACAULAY *Burleigh, Ess.* 1854 I. 227/1 Such outward marks of servitude as the haughty Britoness [Queen Elizabeth] exacted. **1864** TENNYSON *Boadicea* 55 The yellow-ringleted Britoness.

Britonic, var. BRITTONIC *a.* and *sb.*

britschka, britska, variants of BRITZKA.

†**'britted,** *ppl. a. Obs.* exc. *dial.* [f. *brit*, dial. form of BRITE *v.* + -ED¹.] Of grain, hops, etc.: Shattered by over-ripeness.

a **1722** LISLE *Husb.* (1752) 108 Soon, if the ground be wet, britted corn will grow. **1850** BRAVENDAR in *Jrnl. R. Agric. Soc.* XI. I. 167 The loss of the britted beans.

†**'britten,** *v. Obs.* Forms: 1 **brytnian**, 3 **briten**, 3–4 **britten**, 4 **britton, bryttyn(e, bretten, -on, bryton, brutten,** (also *pa. t.* and *pple.* **brittnet, britned, -et, brutned),** 4–5 **brittun, -yn,** 5 **brytten, (brytn-is, britn-is, britynn-it),** *Sc.* **bertyn (bertn-it), bartyn (bartn-it).** [OE. *brytnian*:—OTeut. **brutjinôn*, f. **brutjon-*, in OE. *brytta* distributor, dispenser, f. stem *brut-* of **breutan* to break, divide: cf. BRITTLE.]

1. *trans.* To distribute, dispense. (Only in OE.)

a **1000** *Beowulf* 4756 þara ðe in Swio-rice sinc brytnade.

2. To divide.

c **1200** ORMIN 14178 þiss werelld..iss dæledd and brittnedd onntill daless þre.

3. To cut or hew in pieces; to kill, slay, butcher.

a **1300** *Cursor M.* 8720 God it wit-schild þat þou britten [*v.r.* briten, brettyn] sua mi child. *c* **1350** *Will. Palerne* 1073 þe douȝti duk..bet adoun burwes, & brutned moche peple. ?*a* **1400** *Morte Arth.* 106 He salle..Bryne Bretayne þe brade, and bryttyne thy knyghtys. *Ibid.* 1487 With brandes of broune stele they brettened maylez. *c* **1400** *Destr. Troy* 1971 Drawen as a dog & to dethe broght: Brittonet þi body into bare qwarters. *c* **1470** HENRY *Wallace* III. 400 Sothroune men yat bertynit war to deide. **1513** DOUGLAS *Æneis* II. 114 Cruell Pyrrus, Quhilk brytnys the son befor the faderis face. **1535** STEWART *Cron. Scot.* I. 334 Tha bertynd hir, baith bodie, bane and blude.

b. *Hunting.* To cut up or 'break' (a boar or deer); cf. BRITTLE *v.*

c **1340** *Gaw. & Gr. Knt.* 1339 Siþen britned þay þe brest, & brayden hit in twynne. *c* **1420** *Avow. Arth.* xvii, Sethun brittuns he the best, As venesun in forest. **1535** STEWART *Cron. Scot.* II. 192 Quhen he wes bertnit to gif the houndis blude. *Ibid.* 431 Tha bar[t]nit thame lyke ony bludie deir.

Brittish, obs. form of BRITISH.

brittle ('brɪt(ə)l), *a.* Forms: 4 **britul, -il, (bretil, brethil),** 5 **brityll, brittyll, (bretylle), brytyl,** 5–6 **brytell, brytyl,** 6 **bri-, bryttell, britle, brittil, brytel, bryttle,** 6–7 **brittel,** 6– **brittle.** [ME. *britul, britil, bretil*:—OE. **brytel*:—OTeut. **brutilo-*, f. *brut-* pa. pple. stem of **breutan*, OE. *bréotan* to break. See also BROTEL, BRUTEL, and cf. BRICKLE.]

1. a. Liable to break, easily broken; fragile, breakable; friable (*obs.*).

1382 WYCLIF *Lev.* vi. 22 The bretil vessel forsothe in the which it [the flesh] is sothun. **1398** TREVISA *Barth. De P.R.* XVI. xxxvi. (1495) 564 Bras that is fusile and molte is bryttel vnder the hamour. **1532** MORE *Confut. Tindale* Wks. 398/1 With betle browes & his brittle spectacles of pride and malice. **1615** CROOKE *Body of Man* 33 Some are fragile or brittle..as Bones. **1669** WORLIDGE *Syst. Agric.* IV. §1 (1681) 35 A brittle soil..Is best for Corn. **1878** HUXLEY *Physiogr.* 159 The ice being brittle, cracks and snaps.

†**b.** Liable to destruction, perishable, mortal.

c **1380** WYCLIF *Serm.* Sel. Wks. II. 258 þei traveilen..to take britul crowne here, but men traveilen in Goddis cause to take a crown þat never may faile. **1509** FISHER *Wks.* I. 176 These brytell bodyes of ours. **1622** FLETCHER *Sea Voy.* II. ii, No goddess, friend, But made of that same brittle mould as you are. **1777** SIR W. JONES *Seven Fount.* 55 How dim the rays that gild the brittle earth.

c. *Metallurgy.* Applied to a type of fracture of material (see quot. 1946).

1930 *Engineering* 14 Feb. 231/1 A typical brittle-material fracture. **1946** *Gloss. Metallurg. Terms* (Firth Brown) 27 In a brittle fracture, metal fails by cleavage because its cohesion is exceeded. **1965** *New Scientist* 15 Apr. 173/1 The important characteristic of a brittle fracture is that a crack can propagate under a stress which is less than the design stress..and can cause complete failure of a structure.

†**2.** *fig.* That breaks faith; inconstant, fickle.

1521 *St. Papers Hen. VIII*, I. 73 Such brittle people as they [the Irish] bee, in whome is moche crafte, and litle or noo faithe. **1538** BALE *Thre Lawes* 175 Hys bryttle nature, hys slyppernesse to waye. **1622** T. SCOTT *Belg. Pismire* 15 Never did Age so abound with such brittle spirits as this.

3. *fig.* Frail, weak; insecure, unstable, transitory.

c **1555** HARPSFIELD *Divorce Hen. VIII* (1878) 202 Easy for the King to overthrow this brittle and frail clergy. **1559** *Mirr. Mag., Hen. VI*, xviii. 4 To shew by patarne of a prince, how brittle honour is. **1657** W. FENNER *2nd Pt. Christ's Alarm* 25 Consider how brittle your hearts are. **1692** DRYDEN *Eleonora* xiv. 6 A second Eve..As beauteous, not as brittle as the first. **1799** SHERIDAN *Pizarro* III. iii, The brittle tribute of his praise. **1817** JAS. MILL *Brit. India* I. III. iv. 615 The brittle materials of an Indian army.

4. *attrib.* and *Comb.*: *brittle-minded* adj.; **brittle heart** (see quot. 1938); **brittle silver ore**, the mineral Stephanite; **brittle-star**, a name applied to several species of star-fish of the genus *Ophiocoma*; **brittle-worts**, Lindley's name for the *Diatomaceæ*.

1934 DADSWELL & LANGLANDS in *Jrnl. Council Sci. & Ind. Res., Australia* VII. 190 (*heading*) *Brittle heart in Australian timbers. **1938** —— in *Empire For. Jrnl.* XVII. 58 Brittle heart has been defined as that central portion of the tree which is extremely brittle and of comparatively low strength. **1887** W. JAMES *Let.* 2 July in R. B. Perry *Thought & Char. of W. J.* (1935) I. 376 My narrow and *brittle-minded bachelor state. **1843** *Proc. Berw. Nat. Club* II. 49, *O. neglecta*, Grey *Brittle Star. **1863** G. KEARLEY *Links in Chain* vi. 119 The Brittle stars are extremely abundant around most parts of our coast. **1861** H. MACMILLAN *Footnotes Page Nat.* 170 The diatoms or *brittle-worts.. form a wonderful microcosm.

†**'brittle,** *v.*¹ *Obs.* Also 3 **brutle**, ? 6 **britle**, 7 **bryttle.** [A freq. form from BRIT, BRITTEN *v.*] *trans.* To cut to pieces; to cut up (a deer).

c **1275** *O.E. Misc.* 92 Seynt Thomas wes biscop, and barunes him quolde, Heo brutlede him. *a* **1650** *Boy & Mantle* in Child *Coll. Ballads* (1861) I. 15 He britled the bores head Wonderous weele. **1865** S. EVANS *Bro. Fabian* 58 The bravest man That ever brittled a deer.

†**'brittle,** *v.*² *Obs.* [f. BRITTLE *a.*] *trans.* To make brittle or friable.

1743 MAXWELL *Sel. Trans. Soc. Agric.* 109 (JAM.) The clay..which will be brittled by the winter frosts.

†**'brittle-brattle.** *Obs.* Reduplicated deriv. of BRATTLE.

1535 LYNDESAY *Satyre* 621 Quhill all the raipis beguith to rattil..Quhen all the sails playd brittill brattill.

'brittlely, *adv.* Also **brittly.** [f. BRITTLE *a.* + -LY².] In a brittle manner.

1580 BARET *Alv.* B 1335 Brittlely; frailely, *fragiliter.* *a* **1638** MEDE *Wks.* I. xxix. 140 The divided toes..are in a sort (though but brittlely) united together. **1678** A. LITTLETON *Lat. Dict.*, Brittly, *fragiliter.* **1852** SMITH *Eng. & Fr. Dict.*, Brittlely, Brittly, *avec fragilité.* **1923** D. H. LAWRENCE *Birds, Beasts & Flowers* 44 Almond tree..Grey, lavender sensitive steel, curving thinly and brittly up in a parabola. **1929** W. FAULKNER *Sartoris* IV. 304 Ridges skeletoned brittlely with frost. **1949** M. MEAD *Male & Female* v. 120 The Mundugumor have faced new events brittlely. **1958** *Spectator* 18 July 86/1 This facile Neapolitan, whose music and plot are brittly innocent of modulation.

brittleness ('brɪt(ə)lnɪs). [f. BRITTLE *a.* + -NESS.] The quality of being brittle; fragility.

1488 CAXTON *Chast. Goddes Chyld.* 95 Thou sholdest know..thyne owne bretilnesse and unmighte to stonde. **1548** HALL *Chron.* (1809) 547 Remembrynge the brytilnes of your promise. **1669** WORLIDGE *Syst. Agric.* viii. §1 (1681) 154 The brittleness of the inner stalk. **1862** GOULBURN *Pers. Relig.* 202 The extreme brittleness and frailty of the human will. **1869** ROSCOE *Elem. Chem.* 178 Hardness, brittleness, and tenacity, are physical properties of great importance.

†**'brittlety.** *Obs. rare*⁻¹. [f. BRITTLE *a.* after *frailty, subtlety*, etc.] Brittleness, frailty.

1652–3 *Will of Sir T. Pelham* (Somerset Ho.) Considering the brittletie and uncertayntie of this present life.

†**'brittling,** *vbl. sb. Obs.* [f. BRITTLE *v.*¹ + -ING¹.] The cutting up (of a deer or boar).

a **1500** *Chevy Chase* (MS. Ashmole 48) 17 To the quyrry then the Perse went To se the bryttlynge off the deare. *Ibid.* 26 'Leave of the brytlyng of the dear', he sayd.

'brittling, *sb.* [f. BRITTLE *a.*: cf. the scientific name *Anguis fragilis.*] 'The slow-worm' (Halliwell).

'brittlish, *a. rare.* Somewhat brittle.

1648 HEXHAM *Dutch Dict.*, Broosken, fraile, Tender, or Brittellish.

†**'brittly,** *a. Obs.* [f. BRITTLE *a.* + -Y¹.] Somewhat brittle or friable.

1698 *Phil. Trans.* XX. 221 A soft britly Matter.

brittly, *adv.* See BRITTLELY *adv.*

Brittonic (brɪ'tɒnɪk), *a.* and *sb.* Also **Britonic.** [f. Old Celtic **Britton-* BRITON + -IC.] **A.** *adj.* Of or pertaining to the ancient Britons; *spec.* = BRYTHONIC *a.* **B.** *sb.* The Brythonic language.

1923 *Glasgow Herald* 16 Feb. 11 The extensive Britonic and Bangor missions. **1926** *Ibid.* 25 Oct. 6 The Brittonic, or British, missionaries completed the Christianisation of the Northern Britons. **1953** K. JACKSON *Lang. & Hist. Early Brit.* 3 Until fairly recently, the term *Brythonic*, coined by Rhys, was regularly used to describe the language brought to Britain by the bearers of that variety of primitive Celtic speech known as *P-Celtic*... Of late there has been an increasing tendency to use *Brittonic* instead. *Ibid.* 154 A Brittonic-speaking population. **1960** REANEY *Orig. Eng. Place-Names* v. 87 Brittonic was still spoken in Somerset and Dorset at the end of the seventh century. *Ibid.* 88 Here Brittonic names are rare.

britzka, britzska ('brɪtskə, Pol. 'britʃka). Also **britschka, britzschka, britska.** [a. Polish *bryczka* (*cz* = tʃ) 'a light long travelling wagon', dim. of *bryka* goods-wagon.] An open carriage with calash top, and space for reclining when used for a journey.

1832 *Fair of May Fair* III. *Special License* ix. 372 Mrs. Parkyns..stipulated that her daughter should have a britschka built by Adams. **1839** *Sat. Mag.* Supp. Aug. 86/1 The annexed cut represents a britzschka. This form was brought from Germany about a dozen years ago. **1844** DISRAELI *Coningsby* v. vi. 213 Order the britska round as usual. **1848** THACKERAY *Van. Fair* lxii, Lord Bareacre's chariot, britzka and fourgon. **1866** MISS BRADDON *Lady's Mile* ii. 14 The fashionable world had gone homeward in barouches, landaus, britzskas and phaetons.

†**brivi'atic,** *a. Obs. rare.* [According to a note to the first quot. f. OSp. *brivion* (Sp. *bribon*) 'a loytring fellow that will not worke, but goe from Town to Town, from house to house, to begge a piece of bread and a Dish of drinke'. See BRIBE.] Of vagrants or mendicants.

1623 MABBE *Aleman's Guzman d'Alf.* I. 190 She made me study the Briviatick Art. *Ibid.* II. 95 Themselues with their breviaticke Art may lie wallowing in the durt.

Brix (brɪks). The name of A. F. W. *Brix* (1798–1890), a German scientist, used *attrib.* of a hydrometer calibrated according to the ***Brix** scale*, a scale for the measurement of the specific gravity of a sugar solution. Also used *absol.*

1897 G. L. SPENCER *Handbk. Chemists Beet-Sugar Houses* 55 The Brix and Baumé Scales. The degree Brix is the percentage by weight of sucrose in a pure sugar solution. **1910** *Chem. Abstr.* IV. 684 In basing conclusions upon results by apparent Brix the relationship of apparent to actual solids must always be borne in mind. **1912** C. A. BROWNE *Handbk. Sugar Analysis* iii. 45 The Brix hydrometer or spindle is supplied in a variety of forms. **1959** *Encycl. Brit.* XI. 996/1 The Brix saccharometer simply indicates percentage of sugar by weight when read in sugar solutions at 17·5° C.

†**'brixle, brixel,** *sb. Obs.* Also 4 **brixil, bricsl.** [a. ON. *brigzl, brigzli*, 'blame, shame'.] Shame, reproach.

a **1300** *Cursor M.* 10319 þi brixel, bale, and þin vpbraid, þat isacar þe prist þe said. *Ibid.* 24044 þat brixel [*v.r.* bricsl], beting, crone o thorn. *Ibid.* 28196 Wit flitt, wit brixil, striue and strut, myn euencristen haue i hurt.

†**'brixle,** *v. Obs.* Also 4 **bruxle.** [a. ON. *brigzla* 'to upbraid'.] *trans.* To reproach, reprove, upbraid. Hence **'brixling** *vbl. sb.*

a **1300** *Cursor M.* 10287 For þis brixling, for þis vp-braid. *c* **1325** *E.E. Allit. P.* C. 345 þenne a wynde of goddez worde efte þe wiȝe bruxlez.

briyn, obs. form of BRINE.

briz, brizz, *v.* Sc. form of BRUISE (sense 5).

brize, brizze, obs. forms of BREEZE.

brizle, brizzle, -lie, etc.; see BRISTLE, BRISTLY.

bro (brəʊ). A written or colloq. abbrev. of BROTHER *sb.* Pl. *bros.* (joc. pronounced brɒs), in the title of a firm.

a **1666** EVELYN *Diary* an. 1638 (1955) II. 20, I accompanyd my Eldest Bro (who then quitted Oxford) into the Country. **1860** E. WALFORD *County Families* 49 (Advt.), Bass's East India Pale Ale..Berry, Bros., & Co. **1905** W. M. GALLICHAN *Cheshire* 161 Notice the old timbered house now occupied by Messrs George Bros., ironmongers. **1937** PARTRIDGE *Dict. Slang* 94/2 Bro. Brother: Charterhouse: C. 20. **1940** 'N. BLAKE' *Malice in Wonderland* ix. 132, I must.. report to my bro on the sinister bloke we've just chased off.

bro, obs. form of BRAE, BROO, BROW.

broach (brəʊtʃ), *sb.*¹ Forms: 4–9 **broche**, 6 **brotche**, 6–9 **broch**, 6, 9 **brooch**, 9 *dial.* **brotch**, 6– **broach.** [ME. *broche*, a. F. *broche* (13th c. in Littré), ONF. *broke, broque*; corresp. to Pr. and Sp. *broca*, It. *brocca* 'a carver's great fork' (Florio):—Rom. or late L. **brocca* spike, pointed instrument, akin to *broccus, brocchus* adj. in *brocchi dentes* projecting teeth. The same word as BROOCH, the senses having been differentiated in spelling.]

I. A tapering pointed instrument or thing.

†**1.** A pointed rod of wood or iron; a lance, spear, bodkin, pricker, skewer, awl, stout pin. *Obs.* in general sense exc. *dial.*

c **1305** *Disp. Mary & Cross* 55 in *Leg. Rood* 135 A Broche þorw-out his brest born. **1448** *MS. R. Glouc.* Gloss. 628 A broche of brennyng fure was putte þurghe an horne, that was putt in his fondement in to K. Edward Seconds body. **1480** CAXTON *Chron. Eng.* clv. 137 He prykked the tode thurgh with a broche. **1548** THOMAS *Rules Ital. Gram.* in *Promp. Parv.* 52, *Stocco*, an armyng swoorde made like a broche. **1658** R. WHITE tr. *Digby's Powd. Symp.* (1660) 127

Make red-hot a broach or fire-shovel. **1674** RAY *N.C. Wds.* 8, *Broach*..signifies also a Butchers-prick.

2. *esp.* Such a pointed instrument used for roasting meat upon; a spit.

?*a***1400** *Morte Arth.* 1029 Thre balefulle birdez his brochez þey turne. *c***1420** *Liber Cocorum* 16 Do opon a broche, rost hom bydene A lytel. *c***1440** *Promp. Parv.* 52 Broche or spete, *veru.* **1598** BARCKLEY *Felic. Man* v. (1603) 373 Shee..put him upon the broach, and roasted him. **1622** BACON *Hen. VII*, 36 Hee turned a Broach that had worne a Crowne. **1697** DRYDEN *Virg. Georg.* II. 547 Entrails shall..drip their Fatness from the Hazle Broach. **1820** SCOTT *Ivanhoe* iv, Wild-fowl..brought in upon small wooden spits or broaches. **1872** TENNYSON *Lynette* 475 Set To turn the broach.

b. A spit for spitting herring; a similar instrument used in *Candle-making* for suspending the wicks for dipping.

*c***1440** *Promp. Parv.* 52 Broche for spyrlynge or herynge, *spiculum.* **1875** URE *Dict. Arts* I. 680 The dipping room is furnished with..a large wheel for supporting the broaches.

†**3.** ? A taper: often mentioned along with torches; but in some cases (e.g. quot. 1504) explained as a spike on which to stick a candle.

1377 LANGL. *P. Pl.* B. XVII. 244 Hew fyre at a flynte..But thow have towe to take it with, tondre or broches, Al thi laboure is loste. *c***1420** *Anturs of Arth.* xxxv, Troches and broches and stondartis bi-twene. **1504** *Eng. Gilds* (1870) 327 A broche wt a fote. ij new torches.

4. †**a.** A spindle. *Obs.* or *Sc.*

*c***1440** *Promp. Parv.* 52 Broche of threde, *vericulum.* **1483** *Cath. Angl.* 44 A Broche for garn, *fusillus.* **1513** DOUGLAS *Æneis* VII. xiv. 59 Hir womanly handis..Na spyndill vsit, nor brochis of Mynerve. **1824** MACTAGGART *Gallovid. Encycl.*, *Broaches*, Wooden spindles to put pirns on, to be wound off.

b. A shuttle used in weaving tapestry.

1783 *Encycl. Brit.* X. 8536/1 They serve to keep the warp open for the passage of broaches wound with silks, woollens, or other matters used in the piece of tapestry. **1878** MRS. SKETCHLEY tr. *A. de Champeaux's Tapestry* 2 The material for the woof is wound on a wooden shuttle, called a 'broach' or 'flute'. **1888** *Encycl. Brit.* XXIII. 212/1 The design [of tapestry and pile carpets] is formed by short stitches knotted across the warp with a wooden needle called a broach.

5. A piece of tough pliant wood, pointed at each end, used by thatchers for fixing their work.

*c***1440** *Promp. Parv.* 52 Broche for a thacstare, *firmaculum.* **1787** W. MARSHALL *Norfolk* II. 64 To prevent the wind from blowing it off..he pegs it down slightly with 'double broaches'. **1843** *Jrnl. R. Agric. Soc.* IV. II. 366 Thatcher for labour, brotches, etc., at 7*s.* 6*d.* **1863** MORTON *Cycl. Agric.* Gloss., *Broaches*..rods of hazel, etc., split and twisted for use by the thatcher.

6. A church spire; also, formerly, an obelisk. Now technically restricted as in quot. 1876.

1501 *MS. S. Lincolnsh. Churchw. Acc.*, For trassyng & makyn moldes to the brooch. **1665** in *Bp. Cosin's Corr.* (Surtees) II. 121 The lead and timber of the two great broaches at the west end of the church. **1715** tr. *Pancirollus' Rerum Mem.* I. II. xiv. 99 Augustus Cæsar brought two of these Broaches or Spires to Rome. **1854** H. MILLER *Sch. & Schm.* xiv. (1857) 348 The Masonry a-top that had supported the wooden broach. **1876** GWILT *Archit.* 959 The most frequent spire is that called a *broach*, when it does not rise from within parapets, but is carried up on four of its sides from the top of the square tower.

7. *Venery.* 'A start of the head of a young stag, growing sharp like the end of a spit' (Bailey).

1575 TURBERV. *Venerie* 52 They beare not their first head which we call Broches..until they enter the second yere of their age. **1616** BULLOKAR, *Broches*, the first head or hornes of a Hart or stagge. **1623** COCKERAM I, *Pollard*, Broach is the next [start] growing aboue the Beame antler. **1677** N. COX *Gentl. Recreation* (1706) 65 The first is called *Antlier*; the second *Surantlier*..The little Buds or Broches about the *Top*, are called *Croches.* **1774** GOLDSM. *Nat. Hist.* (1862) I. II. v. 324 The stag's horns are called his *head*; when simple, the first year they are called *broches.*

8. †**a.** A tusk or canine tooth (*obs.*). **b.** One of the teeth of a carding-comb, in a woollen mill.

1607 TOPSELL *Four-f. Beasts* 125 These [shepherds' dogs] ought to be well faced..a flat chap, with two great broches, or long, straight, sharp teeth. **1837** WHITTOCK *Bk. Trades* (1842) 483 To place the wool on one of his combs the steel brooches of which are triple.

†**9.** A surveyor's arrow used with the chain. *Obs.*

1616 SURFL. & MARKH. *Countr. Farm* 519 The Measurer must be prouided of tenne or twelue arrowes, otherwise called little broches, or prickes..to guide the chayne.

10. A general name for tapered boring-bits, or tools for enlarging or smoothing holes, generally of polygonal form with several cutting edges, sometimes round and smooth for burnishing, as in watchmaking; a similar tool used in dentistry; an instrument for broaching or tapping casks. In *Lock-making*, the pin in a lock which enters the barrel of the key.

1753 CHAMBERS *Cycl.*, Among us, *broach* is chiefly used for a steel instrument wherewith to open holes in metals. **1786** *Phil. Trans.* LXXVI. 28, I took a five-sided broach, which opened the hole in the brass. **1846** W. JOHNSTON *Beckmann's Hist. Invent.* I. 228 A piece of timber..like the handle of a broch. **1859** J. TOMES *Dent. Surg.* 415 Broaches for destroying and withdrawing the pulp should be very fine, elastic and flexible. **1884** F. BRITTEN *Watch & Clockm.* 36 A round broach..for burnishing brass holes.

11. A narrow pointed chisel used by masons.

†**12.** 'A musical instrument, the sounds of which are made by turning round a handle' (Bailey 1730–6). *Obs.*

II. from the verb.

13. A perforation or boring.

1519 HORMAN *Vulg.* 192b, That he shulde nat make a broche or do any harme. **1607** TOPSELL *Four-f. Beasts* 259 The old Horses have longer and thinner teeth..there are certain broaches or wrinckles in their teeth. **1684** *Bucaniers Amer.* iii. 32 Making an incision, or broach in the body, from thence gently distilleth a sort of Liquor.

†**14.** Phrase. ***a broach, on broach***: with a perforation or tap; esp. ***to set a (on) broach***: to tap and set running; also *fig.* (Now written ABROACH.) Also ***in broach.***

*c***1440** *Promp. Parv.* 52/2 Brochyn or settyn a vesselle abroche, *attamino.* **1513** *Bk. Keruynge* in *Babees Bk.* (1868) 266 Whan ye sette a pype on broche, do thus. **1532** MORE *Confut. Tindale* Wks. 355/2, I see..heresyes so sore sette a broche in some vnhappy heartes. **1579** TOMSON *Calvin's Serm. Tim.* 172/1 Wee haue in part set this matter on broch. **1606** EARL NORTHAMPTON in *True & Perf. Relat.* Gg2a, When it [this doctrine] was first set on broach. **1826** DISRAELI *Vivian Grey* II. xii. 169 As fine a barrel of ale in broach as you ever tasted.

III. *Attrib.* and *Comb.*, as (sense 5) ***broach-river***; ***broach-splitting***; (sense 6) ***broach-spire, -steeple***; **broach-turner**, a turn-spit; **broach-wood**, wood suitable for making broaches or spits.

1921 *Dict. Occup. Terms* (1927) §499 *Broach river; rives timber with a cleaver, and shapes the pieces of timber with a hand knife to form broaches, *i.e.* pointed implements used in thatching. **1848** RICKMAN *Goth. Archit.* 154 The *broach-spires of Northamptonshire. **1899** RIDER HAGGARD in *Longman's Mag.* Mar. 410, I found..Rough Jimmy..employed in splitting broaches to be used for thatching stacks. This is the process of *broach-splitting. **1616** SURFL. & MARKH. *Countr. Farm* 446 A head of Brasse, made after the fashion of a *broch steeple. **1532** MORE *Confut. Tindale* Wks. 549/1 The *broche turner..may let the spitte stande. **1872** TENNYSON *Lynette* 750 Dish-washer and broach-turner, loon! **1836** MARRYAT *Japhet* xiv, We were cutting hazel *broach wood in the forest.

broach (brəʊtʃ), *sb.*[2] In 7 baroche. [Place-name.] A Surat cotton grown in the *Broach* district, Gujarat State, India.

1617 R. COCKS *Diary* (Hakl. Soc. 1883) I. 330 We gave our host..a peece of backar baroche to his children to make them 2 coates. **1877** *Encycl. Brit.* VI. 482/2 The principal sorts [of Surats] are Hingunghât, Oomrawuttee, Broach, Dhollera, and Dharwar. **1959** *Chambers's Encycl.* II. 587/1 Raw 'Broach' cotton.

broach, *a. rare.* [attrib. use of sb.] Like a broach or spit; in *Arch.* broach-shaped.

1721 in BAILEY. **1849** FREEMAN *Archit.* 384 Instead of being broach, they began to spring out of the middle of the tower.

broach (brəʊtʃ), *v.*[1] Forms: 4–6 **broche**, 5–7 **broch**, 6 **broache**, (8 *dial.* **broych**), 6– **broach**. [f. BROACH *sb.*[1]: cf. F. *brocher*, Pr. *brocar*, *brochar*, It. *broccare*, f. *broche*, *broca*, *brocca* sb. Cf. BROKER.]

†**1.** *trans.* To pierce, stab, thrust through. *Obs.*

1377 LANGL. *P. Pl.* B. v. 212 To broche hem with a [pak-] nedle. *c***1400** *Destr. Troy* 9539 He was brochit þurgh the body with a big speire. **1557** *K. Arthur* (Copland) I. xvi, He broched ye hors of kynge Ban through and through. **1583** STANYHURST *Æneis* II. (Arb.) 52 His feet..with raynes of bridil ybroached. **1599** *Warn. Faire Wom.* II. 130 With the piercing steel Ready to broach his bosom. **1631** GOUGE *God's Arrows* III. §95. 364 Edward 2..was cruelly broached to death with an hot iron spit.

†**2.** *spec.* **a.** To prick with spurs; to spur. *Obs.*

1330 R. BRUNNE *Chron.* 277 Þer stedes broched þei fast, *c***1420** *Anturs of Arth.* xxxix. **1475** CAXTON *Jason* 15b, Which broched their horses with their spores. **1513** DOUGLAS *Æneis* VI. xv. 82 With spurris brocheand the fomy steidis sydis. *c***1530** LD. BERNERS *Arth. Lyt. Bryt.* (1814) 61 The capytayne of theym broched his horse agenst Arthur.

†**b.** *absol.* To spur, 'prick'. *Obs.*

*c***1380** *Sir Ferumb.* 3657 Clarioun..Comeþ by-fore faste brochyng, On ys stede of Araby. *c***1400** *Destr. Troy* 10033 Troiell..brochit in bremely his brother to venge. *c***1489** CAXTON *Sonnes of Aymon* ii. 63 The frenshemen brochyng with ye spore as fast as theyr horses might renne.

†**c.** *const.* To broach (spurs) *to* (a horse). *rare.*

1523 LD. BERNERS *Froiss.* I. 632 They broched their spurres to their horses, and so retourned to Andwarpe.

†**3. a.** To transfix (meat) with a spit which may hold it while roasting; to spit. *Obs.*

*c***1420** *Liber Cocorum* 26 Hit broch thou shalle, Then do hit to fyre and rost hit alle. **1483** *Cath. Angl.* 44 To Broche, *verudare.* **1530** PALSGR. 471/1 Whan you have broched the meate, lette the boye tourne. **1623** FAVINE *Theat. Hon.* v. i. 49 Broching it, and then turning it at the fire himselfe.

†**b.** To stick (something) *on* a spit or pointed weapon which transfixes it; to spit. *Obs.*

1557 *K. Arthur* (Copland) v. v. 5 Thre damoysels turnyng thre broches, wheron were broched xii yonge children late borne lyke yonge byrdes. **1599** SHAKS. *Hen. V*, v. Prol. 32 Bringing Rebellion broached on his Sword. **1655** *Theophania* 172 Percianus..walks as if he were broached upon a stake. **1704** WORLIDGE *Dict. Rust. et Urb.* s.v. *Basting of Hemp*, Broaching them, or spitting them upon long sticks.

4. a. To pierce (a cask, etc.) so as to draw the liquor; to tap.

*c***1440** *Promp. Parv.* 52 Brochyn or settyn a vesselle broche, *attamino.* **1530** PALSGR. 471/1, I broche a wyne vessel, *je perce.* **1579** FENTON *Guicciard.* I. 31 It is too daungerous to broach a vessell of poyson. **1659–60** PEPYS *Diary* (1879) I. 87 We broached a vessel of ale that we had sent for among us. **1707** FARQUHAR *Beaux' Strat.* I. i. 2 Here, Tapster, broach Number 1706. **1876** BANCROFT *Hist. U.S.* V. xliii. 25 A pipe of wine was broached.

b. Also with the liquor as object.

1650 BAXTER *Saints R.* I. v. §1 (1654) 49 For you, Christians, is this wine broached. **1713** *Lond. & Countr. Brew.* I. (1742) 80 Time for broaching such Beer. **1866** KINGSLEY *Herew.* iii. 77 French wine which had just been broached.

c. *fig.*, and of a vein, blood.

1573 G. HARVEY *Letter-bk.* (1884) 9 So cunning..to bru, and so reddi to broche debate. **1575** J. STILL *Gamm. Gurton* II. iii, Ye see..one end tapt of this my short devise. Now must we broche t'other to. **1663** BUTLER *Hud.* I. II. 489 Bloud was ready to be broach'd. **1817** J. GILCHRIST *Intell. Patrimony* 157 He could wrench out a tooth, broach a vein, splice a bone. **1871** BROWNING *Pr. Hohenst.* 1867 One way I bid broach the blood O' the world.

5. *transf.* and *fig.* To pierce or break into, in order to liberate or extract something; to 'tap' (a bed of coal or other mineral).

1583 STANYHURST *Æneis* I. (Arb.) 20 With poyncted flatchet thee mountan he broached. **1592** GREENE *Disput.* Addr. 1, I haue broacht vp the secretes of vice. **1650** FULLER *Pisgah* 371 A Countrey..where God broached a rich vein of gold for this particular purpose. **1839** MURCHISON *Silur. Syst.* I. xxxv. 470 The uppermost coal bed..was termed the 'broachcoal,' as being the index by which the rich field was broached or tapped. **1847** MILLER *First Impr.* x. 167 The Dudley coal field seems to have been broached just in time.

6. To give vent or publicity to; to give out; to begin conversation or discussion about, introduce, moot. (The chief current sense.)

1579 TOMSON *Calvin's Serm. Tim.* 49/1 To broch a newe and straunge doctrine. **1593** HOOKER *Eccl. Pol.* Pref. v. §3 To broach my private conceit I should be loth. **1614** T. ADAMS *Divell's Banket* 52 Euery Nouelist..must broach new opinions. **1712** ADDISON *Spect.* No. 457 ⁋2 Last Friday's Letter, in which I broached my Project of a News-Paper. **1796** MORSE *Amer. Geog.* I. 317 *note*, He [Dr. Franklin] broached the idea of the American Philosophical Society. **1860** MOTLEY *Netherl.* (1868) II. xiv. 203 Failing in that we broached the third point.

7. *techn.* To pick, indent, or furrow the surface of stone with a narrow-pointed stone-chisel called a broach, or puncheon. (The kind of work produced varies in different localities.)

1544 *Chapel Roll* in *Gloss. Goth. Archit.* (1845) I. 74 In hewinge, brochinge, and scaplyn of stone for the chapell. **1703** THORESBY *Let. Ray*, *To broych*, or *broach*, as Masons an Atchler, when with the small point of their ax, they make it full of little pits or small holes. **1808** JAMIESON, *To broach*, to rough-hew. **1876** GWILT *Archit.* 1236 The face of the stone should be previously droved, and then broached.

8. To enlarge and finish (a drilled hole) with a 'broach' or boring-bit. Also with adv. *out.*

1846 HOLTZAPFFEL *Turning* II. 572 Flutes and clarionets are first perforated with the nose-bit, and then broached with taper holes. **1859** *Ibid.* IV. 363 The work being removed from the chuck, the hole is broached out to size. **1889** HASLUCK *Model Engin. Handybk.* viii. 91 The hole in cross-head for piston-rod will have to be broached out.

broach (brəʊtʃ), *v.*[2] *Naut.* [perh. a use of BROACH *v.*[1], in sense of 'turn' (as on a spit).]

1. *intr.* in phrase, ***to broach to*** (said of the ship): to veer suddenly so as to turn the side to windward, or to meet the sea.

1705 DAMPIER *Voy.* II. iii. 6 If the Ship..should prove unruly, as..by her broaching to against all endeavours, which often happens, when a fierce gust comes. **1762–9** FALCONER *Shipwr.* II. 639 If broaching sideway to the sea, Our dropsied ship may founder by the lee. **1800** A. DUNCAN *Mariner's Chron.* (1804) II. 77 She lost her steerage way, broached-to, and upset, the sea rolling over and over. **1829** MARRYAT *F. Mildmay* v, The vessel..broached to, that is, came with her broadside to the wind and sea. **1840** R. DANA *Bef. Mast* xxxii. 126 They hove the wheel up just in time to save her from broaching to.

2. *trans.* To cause (the ship) to veer or swerve to windward, to bring with her broadside to the wind and sea.

1762–9 FALCONER *Shipwr.* II. 376 Broach the vessel to the westward round. **1875** BEDFORD *Sailor's Pocket-bk.* vi. 229 It too often happens that some of the men catch crabs with their oars, and broach the boat to.

Hence **'broaching-to** *vbl. sb.*

1762–9 FALCONER *Shipwr.* III. (1819) 98 They dread her broaching-to. **1875** BEDFORD *Sailor's Pocket-bk.* vi. 218 The one great danger, when running before a broken sea, is that of broaching-to.

broached (brəʊtʃt), *ppl. a.* Also 6 broched. [f. BROACH *v.*[1] + -ED.]

1. Pierced, tapped, set running.

1633 FORD *Broken Hrt.* v. ii, It [the blood] sparkles like a lusty wine new broach'd. **1652** BENLOWES *Theoph.* II. lxii, Each broached Vein. **1847** DISRAELI *Tancred* IV. xii, Oxen roasted whole, and broached hogsheads.

2. Set on foot, started, introduced.

1547 *Homilies* I. *Contention* I. (1859) 134 He is of the new sort..he is a new-broached brother. **1548** HALL *Chron.* (1809) 457 Thys broched and begonne enterprice. **1612** T. TAYLOR *Comm. Titus* i. 2 New broached novelties. **1789** GOUV. MORRIS in Sparks *Life & Writ.* (1832) I. 315 The business now broached.

3. Of stone: Chiselled with a 'broach'.

1625 *Minutes of Town Council* in *Hist. Glasgow* xxi. (1881) 181 The stane work thairof to be small brotchet work. **1876** GWILT *Archit.* 1236. **1880** *Archaeol. Aeliana* VIII. 157 The murus would be built..with broached stones at Ouseburn, and plain stones elsewhere.

broacher ('brəʊtʃə(r)). Also 6-7 **brocher**. [f. BROACH *v.* + -ER¹.]

1. One who broaches: chiefly in sense 6 of the vb.

1587 FLEMING *Contn. Holinshed* III. 1555/2 Ballard..who was the first brocher of this treason. **1628** EARLE *Microcosm.* xii. (Arb.) 33 A broacher of more newes then hogs-heads. **1674** N. FAIRFAX *Bulk & Selv.* 51 Our happy wonder of ingenuity, and best broacher of new light, Mr. Isa. Newton. **1710** TOLAND *Refl. Sacheverell's Serm.* 11 Pernicious Broachers of a Doctrine. **1886** G. ALLEN *Darwin* vi. 104 Among all broachers of new theories.

†2. A spit. *Obs.*

1700 DRYDEN *Fables* (1721) 157 On five sharp broachers rank'd the roast they turn'd. **1725** POPE *Odyss.* XIV. 91 Smoaking back the tasteful viands drew, Broachers and all.

3. One who broaches holes.

1921 *Dict. Occup. Terms* (1927) §200 *Broacher; broaching machinist*; a driller who enlarges or smooths out core hole, a hole previously drilled, using a broach or reamer in a drilling machine.

broaching ('brəʊtʃɪŋ), *vbl. sb.* Also 6 broching(e. [f. BROACH *v.*¹ + -ING¹.]

1. Piercing, spitting; tapping (a cask), etc.

1611 COTGR., *Afforage*..wine..paied upon the broaching of euery vessell retailed. **1615** MARKHAM *Eng. Housew.* II. ii. (1668) 69 The spitting and broaching of meat.

2. Introduction, mooting, origination of opinions.

1577 HANMER *Anc. Eccl. Hist.* (1619) 355 Continuall arguing, and broching of intricate quirks. **1600** DEKKER *Gentle Craft* i. (1862) 10 He sets more discord of a noble house By one day's broaching in his pickthank tales, Than can be salved again in twenty years. **1835** WORDSW. *Let. to B. Montagu* 1 June, The first broaching of the Reform Bill.

3. The first liquor run from a cask on tapping it.

1659 GAUDEN *Fun. Serm. Bp. Brownrig* (1660) 143 The first broachings of a vessel. **1662** FULLER *Worthies* (1840) III. 171 His mother did not carelessly cast away his youth (as the first broachings of a vessel).

4. a. The chiselling of stone with a broach.

1876 GWILT *Archit.* §1914 If broaching is performed without droving..it is never so regular. **1880** *Archaeol. Aeliana* VIII. 285 The broaching or crosshatching and other conventionalities of the Romans.

b. The action or operation of enlarging and finishing a drilled hole. (Cf. BROACH *v.*¹ 8.) Also *attrib.*, as ***broaching machine, machinist.***

1846 HOLTZAPFFEL *Turning* II. 575 For large works, broaching machines are employed. **1888** *Lockwood's Dict. Terms Mech. Engin.* s.v., Broaching is chiefly done in a drilling machine or a lathe. **1921** Broaching machinist [see BROACHER 3].

5. *Comb.* **broaching-bit** (see quot.); **broaching-thurmal, -thurmer, -turner**, a chisel for 'broaching' stone.

1881 RAYMOND *Mining Gloss.*, *Broaching-bit*, a tool used to restore the dimensions of a bore-hole which has been contracted by the swelling of the marl or clay walls.

'broaching, *ppl. a.* [f. BROACH *v.*¹ + -ING².] Piercing, stabbing.

1566 DRANT *Horace Sat.* I. F vij b, Morishe pykes, and brochyng speares.

broad (brɔːd), *a.* (*sb.*, *adv.*) Forms: 1 brád, 2-3 brad, 3-6 brod, 4-6 brode, 6 broode, 4-5 brood, 6- broad. Also *north.* 3-4 brad, (bradd), 4-5 brade, 4- *Sc.* braid. *Compared* broader, -est (1 brǽdre, brádre; brádost; 4-5 braddere, braddest; bredder). [Common Teut.: OE. *brád*, identical with OFris. *brêd*, OSax. *brêd* (MDu. *breet -d-*, Du. *breed*), OHG. (MHG. and mod.G.) *breit*, ON. *breið-r*, (Sw., Da. *bred*), Goth. *braiþ-s*:—OTeut. **braido-z*: no related words are known even in Teutonic, except its own derivatives: see BREADTH, BREDE.]

A. *adj.* 1. a. Extended in the direction measured from side to side; wide. Opposed to *narrow*.

a **1000** *Cædmon's Gen.* 994 (Gr.) Brad blado. *c* **1000** *Ags. Ps.* cxxxvi[i]. 1 Ofer Babilone bradum streame. *c* **1205** LAY. 7635 þe stelene brond swiðe brad [*c* **1275** brod] and swiðe long. *a* **1340** HAMPOLE *Psalter* viii. 7 Swa by the brad way thai ga till hell. **1375** BARBOUR *Bruce* I. 386 With banys gret & schuldrys braid. *c* **1380** WYCLIF *Wks.* (1880) 249 þe brode weie to helle. *c* **1440** *York Myst.* xxxii. 19 My forhed both brente is and brade. *c* **1449** PECOCK *Repr.* 374 Noman is without a place long and brood. **1480** CAXTON *Chron. Eng.* cxxxiv. 113 To make his foreste lenger and bredder. **1552** ABP. HAMILTON *Catech.* xxvi. 121 The braid..way of deadly syn that leidis to hel. **1580** SIDNEY *Arcadia* 239 About his neck he wore a brode and gorgeous collor. **1598** BARRET *Theor. Warres* IV. i. 95 The Broad square is the battell which conteineth more, or as much, as twise so many men in front, as in flank. **1611** BIBLE *Job* xi. 9 Broader then the sea. *a* **1762** LADY M. W. MONTAGUE *Lett.* II. xlvi. 30 Not half so broad, as the broadest part of the Thames. **1846** J. BAXTER *Libr. Pract. Agric.* I. 417 A broad chest is an excellence in a hunter.

b. = in transverse measurement.

a **1000** *O.E. Chron.* (Laud MS.) Introd., Brittene igland is ehta hund mila lang and twa hund brad. **1297** R. GLOUC. 1 Foure hondred myle brod from Est to Weste. *c* **1384** CHAUCER *H. Fame* 792 A litel rounded as a sercle Paraventure brode as a covercle. **1587** FLEMING *Contn. Holinshed* III. 1981/1 A twentie score brode from banke to banke aboue. **1601** HOLLAND *Pliny* I. 76 Almost an acre and a halfe broad. **1664** EVELYN *Kal. Hort.* (1729) 199 A Leaf no broader than a Three-pence. **1885** *Pall Mall G.* 23 Feb. 11/1 The later *Scouts* are to be 5 ft. longer and 2 ft. broader.

c. Applied technically to certain fabrics, now or originally distinguished by their width, as BROAD CLOTH, q.v., *broad glass* (D 2); also ***broad silk*** as distinguished from silk ribbons; whence ***broad-silk-loom, -weaver, broad stuffs, broad trade, broad weaver.***

1682 *Lond. Gaz.* No. 1762/4 Mr. John Guile, Broad-Weaver..in Spittle-fields. **1723** *Ibid.* No. 6189/4 John Jacobs..Broad Silk Weaver. *Ibid.* No. 6190/9 Richard Gardner..Broad-Weaver. **1727** DE FOE *Eng. Tradesm.* xxi, We now make at home all the fine broad-silks, velvets, brocades. **1826** *Annual Reg.* 59/1 The throwsters, the broad trade manufacturers, and the dyers admitted their superiority..But the ribband manufacturers, etc. **1841** *Penny Cycl.* XIX. 490/1 A recent contrivance by which the broad-silk loom had been made applicable to ribbon-weaving. **1883** *American* V. 262 The finest broad-silks.. were produced in Macclesfield.

†d. ***broad gold, money***: see BROAD-PIECE.

1688 *Lond. Gaz.* No. 2352/2 Exchanging of Broad Mony for Clipt. **1702** *Ibid.* No. 3814/4 A Piece of Broad Gold of K. Charles I. in his Armour. **1724** *Ibid.* No. 6300/2 Two Persons have been offering to change Broad Gold for Guineas..They had 68 Broad Pieces.

e. Of bran: consisting of large particles.

1908 *Animal Managem.* 98 Two varieties are distinguished as 'broad' or 'fine'; in 'broad' bran the wheat husk is more or less whole and gives the article a flaky appearance.

2. a. Less definitely as to direction (e.g. where *length* is not applicable, or not in question): Of great extent, extensive, wide, ample, spacious.

a **1000** *Elene* 917 (Gr.) Is his rice brad. *c* **1205** LAY. 5087 In ænne bradne feld [*c* **1275** in to one brode felde]. *a* **1300** *Cursor M.* 8530 Ouer al þis werld brade. *c* **1394** *P. Pl. Crede* 118 We buldeþ a burwȝ, a brod and a large. ? *a* **1400** *Morte Arth.* 106 He salle..Bryne Bretayne þe brade. *c* **1440** *Promp. Parv.* 52 Brode or large of space, *spaciosus.* **1526** *Pilgr. Perf.* (W. de W. 1531) 7 The hole brode worlde. **1671** MILTON *P.R.* II. 339 In ample space under the broadest shade. **1784** COWPER *Task* II. 22 Human nature's broadest, foulest blot. **1814** A. WILSON *Rab & Ringan*, As though braid Scotland had been a' his ain. **1843** LEVER *J. Hinton* vii. (1878) 47 The broad and swelling lands, that stretched away..far as the eye could reach.

†b. Of time. *Obs.*

c **1325** *E.E. Allit. P.* B. 659 Fro mony a brod day byfore ho barayne ay byene.

†3. a. Large in amount, ample, plentiful. *Obs.*

a **1000** *Beowulf* 6201 Beagas and brad gold. *a* **1225** *Ancr. R.* 102 Mid brod schome & sunne. *a* **1300** *Cursor M.* 3713 His brade [*v.r.* brood] blissing he him gaue. *c* **1325** *E.E. Allit. P.* B. 584 Hit is a brod wonder.

†b. Abounding, full *of*. *Obs.*

a **1300** *Cursor M.* 24744 Sua brad of hir blis es þe wai. *c* **1320** *Sir Tristr.* 177 Of folk þe feld was brade.

4. a. Wide open; fully expanded.

971 *Blickl. Hom.* 23 Hie hine..mid bradre hand sloȝan. *c* **1000** *Ags. Gosp.* Matt. xxvi. 67 Sume hine sloȝan on hys ansiene mid hera brada handen. *a* **1300** *Cursor M.* 17837 Til heuen þai lifted þair eien brade. **1607** DEKKER & WEBSTER *Hist. Sir T. Wyat* 19 Wee stand high in mans opinion, and the worldes broad eye.

b. *esp.* Of day, daylight, etc.

1393 GOWER *Conf.* II. 107 Ful oft, whan it is brode day. **1530** PALSGR. 201/2 Broode daye, *grant jour.* **1579** FULKE *Refut. Rastel* 722 We do not light wax candels in yᵉ brod day light. **1664** *Decay Chr. Piety* (J.) It no longer seeks the shelter of night and darkness, but appears in the broadest light. **1690** LOCKE (J.) If children were left alone in the dark, they would be no more afraid than in broad sunshine. **1732** BERKELEY *Alciphr.* iv. §3 A solitary walk before it was broad daylight. **1821** SHELLEY *Prometh. Unb.* II. ii. 25 Awake through all the broad noonday. **1828** SCOTT *F.M. Perth* III. 149 It cannot be concealed..it will all out to the broad day. **1879** LOCKYER *Elem. Astron.* iii. xxiv. 125 The comet of 1843 ..was visible in broad daylight.

5. a. Plainly displayed before the mental vision; plain, clear, obvious; 'pronounced', emphatic, explicit.

c **1374** CHAUCER *Boeth.* II. v. 49 How brode sheweþ þe errour and þe folie of ȝow men. *a* **1577** GASCOIGNE *Voy. Holland*, I name no man, for that were brode before. **1699** BENTLEY *Phal.* 184 Surely this is a hint broad enough. **1709** STRYPE *Ann. Ref.* Introd. §1. 8 Mary, Queen of Scotland, and the Dauphin..gave broad signs of their pretences to the Crown of England. **1825** SCOTT *Talisman* (1863) 215 He understands or guesses thy meaning—be not so broad, I pray thee. **1861** PARKER *Goth. Archit.* I. v. (1874) 161 There is no broad line of distinction. *Mod.* The hint is too broad to be mistaken.

b. Most apparent; prominent, outstanding, general, main. (Opposed to 'subordinate', 'minute'.)

1860 KINGSLEY *Misc.* I. 10, I merely take the broad facts of the story. **1869** HUXLEY in *Sci. Opinion* 28 Apr. 486/2 A knowledge of [the] broad outlines [of a subject]. **1885** *Manch. Exam.* 6 May 5/1 The broad features of the accident.

c. Denoting a type of phonetic transcription in which separate symbols are used only to denote distinctive sound units (phonemes); opp. *narrow*.

1877 H. SWEET *Handbk. Phonetics* 105 The different values of each of the vowel signs in this system, which I will call 'Broad Romic', in apposition to the scientific 'Narrow Romic', as indicating only *broad* distinctions of sound. **1908** —— *Sounds of English* 9 A broad notation is one which makes only the practically necessary distinctions of sound in each language, and makes them in the simplest manner possible, omitting all that is superfluous. **1912** *Princ. Internat. Phonetic Assoc.* 14 A *broad* transcription may be more accurately defined as a transcription obtained by using the minimum number of symbols requisite for representing without ambiguity the sounds of one language independently of other languages. **1932** D. JONES *Outl. Eng. Phonetics* (ed. 3) x. 50 A transcription of the type 'one letter per phoneme' is called a Broad Transcription. *Ibid.* 305 The transcription used in this book is not the broadest possible.

6. Of language (or the speaker): a. Plainspoken, outspoken (often in a bad sense); unreserved, not mincing matters.

1588 in *Harl. Misc.* (1809) II. 81, I..have been very often ashamed to hear so broad speeches of the King and the Pope. *a* **1611** CHAPMAN *Iliad* I. 224 His wrath, that this broad language gave. **1654** GATAKER *Disc. Apol.* 77 Without anie broad or uncivil language. **1710** STEELE *Tatler* No. 208 ¶3 A fulsom Way of commending you in broad terms. **1827** HALLAM *Const. Hist.* vii. (L.) The broadest and most repulsive declaration of all the Calvinistic tenets. **1870** JEBB *Sophocles' Electra* (ed. 2) 36/1 She now repeats the avowal in broader terms.

†b. Coarse, unrefined, vulgar. *Obs.*

1490 CAXTON *Eneydos* 2, I toke an olde boke, and..the englysshe was so rude and brood that I coude not wele vnderstande it. **1589** R. HARVEY *Pl. Perc.* (1860) 19 Speake a broad word..amongst huntsmen in chaze, you shall be leasht for your labor: as one that disgraceth a gentlemans pastime..with the termes of a heardsman.

c. Loose, gross, indecent.

1580 NORTH *Plutarch* (1676) 39 To sport one with another, without any broad speeches or uncomly jests. **1611** COTGR., *Vn gras*, a broad, or bawdie, tale. **1628** EARLE *Microcosm.* xlix. (Arb.) 70 Onely with broad and obscœne wit. *a* **1700** DRYDEN *Ovid's Art of Love* I. 882 Broad words will make her innocence afraid. **1824** W. IRVING *T. Trav.* I. 278 Laughing outrageously at a broad story. **1882** TRAILL *Sterne* 15 A collection of comic but extremely broad ballads.

7. a. Of pronunciation: Perhaps orig.: With 'wider' or 'lower' vowel-sounds (i.e. with the back or the front oral cavity more dilated); but commonly used of a strongly-marked dialectal or vulgar pronunciation of any kind, e.g. 'broad Yorkshire', 'broad Devonshire', 'broad Cockney'. ***Broad Scotch***: the Lowland Scotch vernacular.

1532 [see C 3]. **1580** A. GOLDING *Pref. Verses* in *Baret's Alv.*, The diffrence..Of brode North speech and Sowthren smoothednesse. **1697** POTTER *Antiq. Greece* I. i. (1715) 3 The Ancient Greeks pronounc'd the letter α broad like the Diphthong αυ, as in our English word All. **1724** DE FOE *Mem. Cavalier* (1840) 236 A broad north-country tone. **1787** BURNS *Brigs of Ayr* 167 In plain braid Scots hold forth a plain braid story. **1848** MACAULAY *Hist. Eng.* I. 320 His oaths..were uttered with the broadest accent of his province. **1859** *Blackw. Mag.* Sept. 255/2 Broad Yorkshire talked all over the ship. **1877** SWEET *Phonetics* 18 In the broad London pronunciation this lengthening of originally short vowels is extremely common.

†b. Of sound: Full, deep, low in pitch. *Obs.*

1607 TOPSELL *Four-f. Beasts* 258 The females have a shrill and sharper voice then the males, which is fuller and broader.

8. Unrestrained, kept within no narrow bounds; going to full lengths.

1602 SHAKS. *Ham.* III. iv. 2 His prankes haue been too broad to beare with. **1815** *Scribbleomania* 127 Kenny possesses some requisites for broad farce. **1820** W. IRVING *Sketch Bk.* I. 207 She was the picture of broad, honest, vulgar enjoyment. **1875** JOWETT *Plato* (ed. 2) I. 183 The mirth is broader, the irony more sustained.

†9. Widely diffused; spread all abroad. *Obs.*

1605 SHAKS. *Macb.* III. iv. 23 As broad, and generall, as the casing Ayre.

10. Having a wide range, extensive; widely applicable, inclusive, general.

[**1741-2** H. WALPOLE *Lett. H. Mann* I. 93 The Tories..if Tories there are, for now one hears of nothing but the Broad Bottom; it is the reigning cant word, and means, the taking all parties and people indifferently into the ministry.] **1871** MORLEY *Voltaire* (1886) 45 Intellectual education in the broadest sense that was then possible. **1875** STUBBS *Const. Hist.* III. xxi. 619 Personal feeling must be sacrificed to save ..broader principles. **1875** HAMERTON *Intell. Life* x. v. 387 A broad rule..applicable to all imaginable cases.

11. Characterized by breadth of opinion or sentiment; liberal, catholic, tolerant, allowing wide limits to 'orthodoxy'. (Cf. BREADTH 4, BROAD CHURCH.)

1832 L. HUNT *Poems* 226 With his broad heart to win his way to heaven. **1850** [See BROAD CHURCH]. **1873** LOWELL *Among my Bks.* Ser. II. 323 Keats had the broadest mind. **1886** MORLEY *Crit. Misc.* I. 78 Even good opinions are worth very little unless we hold them in a broad, intelligent and spacious way.

12. *Art.* Characterized by artistic 'breadth'; executed with a view to general effect rather than to special details. Cf. 5 b, and see BREADTH 5.

1862 GROTE *Greece* II. liv. IV. 561 A portrait of him drawn in colours broad and glaring. **1879** SALA in *Daily Tel.* 8 May, Two broad, powerful, and vividly expressed portraits. **1885** *Athenæum* 30 May 702/3 Broad and rich in tone and colour.

13. Phrases. † ***in the broad or the long***: in one way or another. ***it's as broad as it's long*** (or ***as long as it's broad***): it comes to the same thing either way, it makes no difference.

1682 SCARLETT *Exchanges* 171 If the Principal..doth force his factor one way or other, in the broad or the long, to make up his Disbursements. **1687** R. L'ESTRANGE *Answ. Diss.* 6 Whether the Church of England-Men Reject the Roman Catholiques, or the Roman Catholiques Reject the Church of England-Men, 'tis Just as Broad as it is Long. *a* **1704** —— (J.) It is as broad as long, whether they rise to others, or bring others down to them. **1775** GOUV. MORRIS in Sparks *Life & Writ.* (1832) I. 55 It is as long as it is broad —the more [troops] that are sent to Quebec the less they can send to Boston. **1848** KINGSLEY *Saint's Trag.* II. ix. 113 The

sharper the famine, the higher are prices, and the higher I sell, the more I can spend..and so it's as broad as it's long.

B. *sb.* [mostly elliptical.]

†**1.** Breadth: only in phrase ***in, on, o, a brode***; now represented by ABROAD *adv.*

a **1300** *Cursor M.* 347 þis werld.. Seit for to be on lang and brad. *c* **1420** *Anturs of Arth.* xxxv, Beddus brauderit o brode. **1456** *Paston Lett.* 281 I. 386 The straungiers ar soore a dradde, and dar not come on brode.

2. The broad part, the full breadth (of the back, the foot, etc.).

1741 MONRO *Anat.* (ed. 3) 294 The Broad of the Foot. *Mod.* To lie on the broad of one's back.

†**3.** = BROADCLOTH. *Obs.*

c **1500** ARNOLDE *Chron.* (1811) 73 Clothes called fyn brodes of the makyng of Essex.

†**4.** = BROAD-PIECE. *Obs.*

1710 *Lond. Gaz.* No. 4672/4 A..Purse, with 30 Guineas and 5 Brodes in it. **1726** AMHERST *Terræ Fil.* xlii. 224 Presenting one of the collectors with a broad (piece) or half a broad. **1763** SNELLING *Gold Coin* 28 (L.) When the twenty shilling pieces, commonly called guineas, were coined in the reign of Charles II, then the unites of the Commonwealth, Charles I, and James I, received the name of broads or broad-pieces.

5. In East Anglia, an extensive piece of fresh water formed by the broadening out of a river.

1659 SIR T. BROWNE *Let.* 16 Nov. (1946) 351 Such deluges..might..settle lakes and broades. [**1711** *Act 9 Anne* in *Lond. Gaz.* No. 4870/2 Fens, Lakes, broad Waters, or other Places of resort for Wild Fowl.] **1787** MARSHALL *Norfolk* (E.D.S.) *Broads*, fresh-water lakes (that is, broad waters; in distinction to narrow waters, or rivers). **1812** SOUTHEY *Lett.* (1856) II. 307 A broad is the spread of a river into a sheet of water. **1844** E. JESSE *Sc. & Tales Country Life* I. 82 The graceful bendings of the stream, sometimes opening into shallow broads. **1884** G. C. DAVIES (*title*) Norfolk Broads and Rivers; or, the Waterways, Lagoons, and Decoys of East Anglia.

attrib. **1883** *Academy* 8 Dec. 377/1 The artistic aspect of the Broad district.

6. *slang.* (*pl.*) Playing cards.

1789 G. PARKER *Life's Painter* xv. 129 Who are continually looking out for flats, in order to do them upon the broads, that is, cards. **1812** J. H. VAUX *Flash Dict.*, *Broads*, cards; a person expert at which is said to be a good *broad-player*. **1834** H. AINSWORTH *Rookwood* IV. ii, I nick the *broads*. **1860** HOTTEN *Dict. Slang* (ed. 2) 105 *Broads*, cards. **1938** SHARPE *S. of Flying Squad* xviii. 193 xx. 219 They..were also playing the Broads on the trains.

7. *Turning.* A tool having a disc or angular end with a sharpened edge used for turning the insides and bottoms of cylinders.

1846 HOLTZAPFFEL *Turning* II. 515 The broad..requires to be held downwards or underhand.

8. A woman; *spec.* a prostitute. *slang* (orig. and chiefly *U.S.*).

1914 JACKSON & HELLYER *Vocab. Criminal Slang* 19 *Broad*,..A female confederate; a female companion; a woman of loose morals. **1915** G. BRONSON-HOWARD *God's Man* II. ii. 131 Listen, broad,..you got your roasting clothes on to-day and you better take 'em off quick or I'll slam you one in the kisser. **1927** HEMINGWAY *Men without Women* 114 There were a couple of broads sitting at the next table. **1928** *Amer. Speech* III. 218 *Broad*, a plump, shapely girl; the words [*sic*] sometimes carries a disparaging moral significance. **1931** E. LINKLATER *Juan in Amer.* II. xvi. 177 Slummock..had got into a jam with a broad; no ordinary broad, but a Coastguard's broad. **1962** *John o' London's* 25 Jan. 82/3 Prostitutes are variously termed *tarts, toms, broads*.

C. *adv.* [in OE. a distinct word *bráde*, ME. *brode*: but on the mutescence of final *-e*, levelled with the adj.]

1. a. In a broad or extensive way; broadly, widely, fully; far, abroad.

a **1000** *Cædmon's Gen.* 223 (Gr.) Fison brade bebuᵹeþ. **1297** R. GLOUC. 417 Þur blod sprong & wende aboute brode & wyde. *c* **1350** *Will. Palerne* 753 A tri appeltre..þat was braunched ful brode. **1590** SPENSER *F.Q.* Prol., Whose praises..To blazon broad emongst her learned throng. *a* **1744** POPE (J.) Broad burst the lightnings, deep the thunders roll.

†**b.** With eyes wide open, with a stare. *Obs.*

c **1386** CHAUCER *Chan. Yem. Prol. & T.* 867 Though ye looken neuer so brode and stare. *c* **1430** *Hymns Virg. &c.* (1867) 37 Summe staren broode & moun not se.

2. a. Outspokenly, unreservedly.

c **1386** CHAUCER *Knts. T.* 741 Crist spak himself ful broode in holy writ. *c* **1440** *York Myst.* xix. 89 Thou burdis to brode! **1607** SHAKS. *Tim.* III. iv. 64 Who can speake broader, then hee that has no house to put his head in? **1850** MRS. STOWE *Uncle Tom's C.* v. 29 We don't quite fancy when women and ministers come out broad and square, and go beyond us in matters of either modesty or morals.

†**b.** *to laugh broad*: to laugh freely, without restraint, grossly.

1643 MILTON *Divorce* Introd. (1851) 6 The brood of Belial ..will laugh broad perhaps. **1658** W. BURTON *Itin. Anton.* 50 The wise men of the age will laugh broad at these.. enquiries.

3. With a broad pronunciation or 'accent'; with the vowels of dialectal or vulgar speech.

c **1532** DEWES *Introd. Fr.* in Palsgr. 899 Ye shal pronounce your *e* as ye do in latyn, almost as brode as ye pronounce your *a* in englysshe. **1596** *Edw. III*, II. i. 12 And then spoke broad, With epithets & accents of the Scots. *Mod.* 'We Devonshire men speak very broad.'

4. ***broad awake, broad waking***: fully awake, wide awake.

1583 STANYHURST *Æneis* II. (Arb.) 53 From sleepe I broad waked. **1626** T. H. *Caussin's Holy Crt.* 152 We dreame broad-waking. **1666** J. SMITH *Old Age* (ed. 2) 127 Then shall he be broad awake. **1736** WESLEY *Wks.* (1872) I. 29 Being in bed, but broad awake. **1844** G. S. FABER *Eight Dissert.* II. 352 The bard seems to have been broad awake.

5. *Naut.* (Cf. LARGE, WIDE.)

1860 *Merc. Mar. Mag.* VII. 82 A light was seen broad on the port bow [i.e. a good deal to the left of the point right ahead].

D. *Comb.* [from *adj.* and *adv.*]

1. General. **a.** parasynthetic, as ***broad-backed, -based, -beamed*** (also *transf.*; cf. BEAM *sb.*[1] 16 b), ***-bladed, -bodied, -bosomed, -bottomed, -boughed, -breasted, -buttocked, -chested, -eared, -eyed, -flapped, -fronted, -headed*** (1530), ***-hearted, -hoofed, -horned, -limbed, -listed, -margined, -minded, -nosed, -shouldered, -skirted, -souled, -sterned, -striped, -tailed, -toed, -wayed, -wheeled, -winged***, etc., etc.; **b.** adverbial, as ***broad-built, -flashing, -grinning, -spread, -spreading***, etc.

1651 *Advt.* in *Proc. Parliament* No. 81 A short Sorrell Mare..*broad backed. **1857** EMERSON *Poems* 49 We will climb the broad-backed hills. **1769** *Phil. Trans.* LIX. 310 A *broad-based pyramid. **1835** I. TAYLOR *Spir. Despot.* vi. 263 A broad-based hierarchy. **1883** *Harper's Mag.* Feb. 395/1 Brown-sailed, *broad-beamed old luggers. **1945** M. DICKENS *Thursday Afternoons* ii. 77 George in his broad-beamed blue shorts and striped fisherman's jersey. **1875** JOWETT *Plato* (ed. 2) I. 160 The fruit of the *broad-bosomed earth. **1702** *Lond. Gaz.* No. 3837/4 A Silver Tankard, *broad bottom'd. **1804** LD. ELDON in G. Rose *Diaries* (1860) II. 79 Forming an administration upon those broad-bottomed principles. **1647** H. MORE *Song of Soul* II. App. xxxiv, The *broad-breasted earth, the spacious skie. **1797** COLERIDGE *Christabel* I. vi, The huge broad-breasted, old oak tree. **1768** WALES in *Phil. Trans.* LX. 109 Their persons ..seem to be low; but pretty *broad built. **1662** FULLER *Worthies* (1840) III. 288 He had, as I may say, a *broad-chested soul, favourable to such who differed from him. **1870** BRYANT *Iliad* I. III. 92 That other chief Taller and broader-chested than the rest. **1606** SHAKS. *Ant. & Cl.* I. v. 29 *Broad-fronted Cæsar. **1530** PALSGR. 307/1 *Brode-heeded, *embrabile*. **1838** *Proc. Berw. Nat. Club* I. VI. 163 Cover the wood with broad-headed nails. **1719** DE FOE *Crusoe* (Hotten) 414 A very generous *broad-hearted Man. **1585** *Act 27 Eliz.* xvii, Any cloth..of like making called *Broad-listed Whites. **1599** MARSTON *Sco. Villanie* 167 Base blew-coates, tapsters, *broad-minded slaues. **1882** LD. BLANDFORD in *Daily News* 7 Feb. 3 No more broad-minded than..the Church they have seceded from. **1591** PERCIVALL *Sp. Dict.*, *Espaldudo* *broad shouldered, *scapulosus*. **1842** PRICHARD *Nat. Hist. Man* 178 Robust, broad-shouldered, with dark complexion. **1809** W. IRVING *Knickerb.* (1861) 115 A *broad-skirted coat with huge buttons. **1687** *Lond. Gaz.* No. 2211/4 A duskish brown bald Mare, *broad spread. **1591** SPENSER *Ruins of Time* 452 *Broad spreading like an aged tree. **1802** BINGLEY *Anim. Biog.* (1813) I. 467 The *Broad-tailed Sheep. **1816** G. COLMAN *Br. Grins, Mr. Champern.* i. (1872) 296 Like *broad-wheeled wagons without springs. **1816** KEATS *To brother George*, The *broad-wing'd sea-gull never at rest.

2. Special comb.: **broad aisle** or †**alley** *U.S.*, the main aisle or passage in a church or meeting-house; **broad band**, (*a*) (see quots.); (*b*) *Electr.* a band (see BAND *sb.*[2] 14) with a wide range of frequencies; also *transf.* and *attrib.*; **broad-banded** *a.*, having broad bands of colour as a distinctive marking, esp. defining a species of armadillo; **broad bean** (see BEAN *sb.* 1); **broad-bill**, (*a*) a name for several birds having broad bills, *esp.* the Shoveller and Spoonbill; (*b*) in full ***broadbill swordfish***: the swordfish *Xiphias gladius*; **broad-billed** *a.*, having a broad bill, esp. defining a species of sandpiper; **broad-blown** *a.*, in full bloom, full-blown; **broad-brow, broadbrow** [f. as HIGHBROW, etc.] *colloq.*, a person of broad tastes or interests, not a highbrow or a lowbrow; **broad-eyed** *a.*, having large eyes, with eyes wide open; **broad-glass**, window-glass; also *attrib.*, as ***broad-glass-house, -maker***; **broad-headedness** *Ethnol.*, brachycephaly; **broad-horn**, a kind of flat boat used on American rivers; **broad jump** = *long jump* (see JUMP *sb.*[1] 1 b); **broad-lace**, a woollen material about four inches wide, used as an ornamental border in carriage upholstery; **broad-leaf** (*Bot.*), a tree (*Terminalia latifolia*) found in Jamaica; also a local name for the Greater Plantain (*Plantago major*); (also) a settlers' name for a New Zealand tree *Griselinia littoralis*; **broadloom** *a.*, applied to a carpet woven in broad widths; also *absol.*; **broad-man** = *broadsman* (a); **broad-mindedness**, the condition of being liberal or tolerant in thought or opinion; **broad money**, a measure of the amount of money available in an economic system, according to a broad definition of money including, in addition to notes and coins, various kinds of bank deposit and sometimes also deposits held elsewhere; cf. *M2, M3* s.v. M III. 9 and contr. with *narrow money* s.v. NARROW *a.* 1 c; **broad-mouthed** *a.*, having a broad mouth; also (of words) plain-spoken, insolent (*obs.*); **broad-seed** (*Bot.*), the English name of the genus *Ulospermum*; **broad-set** *a.*, stoutly formed, thick-set; **broad-silk**, (see sense A 1 c.); **broadsman**, (*a*) (*dial.*), one who lives near the Norfolk Broads; (*b*) *slang* a card-sharper; **broad-spectrum** *a.* (orig. *U.S.*), of a drug, effective over a wide range of diseases or micro-organisms; **broad-spoken** *a.*, using plain language, plain-spoken; **broad stone** = ASHLAR 1, FREESTONE[1] 1; **broad trade** (see sense A 1 c.); **broadwalk** chiefly *U.S.*, a wide street, pavement, or foot-path; a promenade; **broad-weaver** (see sense A 1 c.).

1807 *Massachusetts Spy* 25 Mar. (Th.), Another pew at the right hand of the *broad aisle, esteemed the pleasantest in said house. **1887** *Harper's Mag.* Dec. 161/2 Miss Flint shall have pew No. 40 in the broad aisle. **1731** in H. S. Sheldon *Doc. Hist. Suffield* 250 Whether the *Broad alley in the meeting House should be fil'd up. **1806** *Intelligencer* (Lancaster, Pa.) 21 Oct. (Th.), Mr. Deming was sitting in the Pew east of the broad Alley. **1629** BOYD *Last Battell* 643 (JAM.) The verie euill thoughts of the wicked in that day shalbe spread out and laide in *broad-band before the face of God. **1847** HALLIWELL, *Broad-band*, corn laid out in the sheaf on the band, and spread out to dry after rain. North: [see also Jamieson, and Atkinson *Provinc. Danby* s.v.] **1956** HEFLIN *U.S.A.F. Dict.* 92/2 *Broadband*, a band having a wide range of frequencies. **1960** H. CARTER *Dict. Electronics* 32 Broad-band radio systems. **1962** H. C. WESTON *Sight, Light & Work* (ed. 2) vi. 186 By accepting this 'broad-band' objective it is possible to simplify the application of the method. **1904** *Westm. Gaz.* 8 Sept. 10/1 The *broad-banded species (*Xenurus unicinctus*) is a rare creature [*sc.* armadillo] from Surinam. **1783** BRYANT *Flora Diætetica* 83 The common *Broad Bean is a native of Egypt. **1819** REES *Cycl.* s.v. *Vicia*, The long-pods, broad Spanish, and white-blossomed bean. **1634** *Althorp MS.* in Simpkinson *Washingtons* Introd. 23, Teales 7—Peckards 3—*Broad-bills 5. **1802** G. MONTAGU *Ornith. Dict.* (1833) 55. **1927** Z. GREY *Tales of Swordfish* iii. 107 Few novices at the game ever held a broadbill longer than a few moments. *Ibid.* iv. 125 There were never any flukes in broadbill swordfishing. *Ibid.* vii. 157 The broadbill swordfish was the one fish in the world which could not be caught through luck. **1969** *Guardian* 8 Mar. 7/5 If you are dedicated to catching marlin swordfish and broadbills, it is an obsession. **1839** PEABODY in *Zool. & Bot. Surv. Mass.: Birds* 367 The *Broad billed Sandpiper..is very rare in the United States. [**1602** SHAKS. *Ham.* III. iii. 81 With all his Crimes *broad blowne, as fresh as May.] **1855** TENNYSON *Maud* I. xiii. 9 His face..Has a broad-blown comeliness red and white. **1877** DOWDEN *Shaks. Primer* vi. 72 Bottom in his broad-blown self-importance. **1927** A. P. HERBERT in *Punch* 12 Jan. 51/1 (*title*) Ballads for *Broad-brows. **1927** *Observer* 11 Sept. 21/1 It is no longer highbrow versus lowbrow. We are all broadbrows, and what we want to listen to depends on our mood. **1929** H. G. WELLS *King who was King* i. §2. 22 The Broadbrow is as anxious not to be 'arty' as the Low-brow and as terrified of the cheap and obvious as the High-brow. *a* **1611** CHAPMAN *Iliad* VIII. 173 *Brood-eyed Joves proud will. **1655** H. VAUGHAN *Silex Scint.* I. (1858) 23 Some fast asleepe, others broad-eyed. **1679** PLOT *Staffordsh.* (1686) 122 The glass-houses, both for Vessells and *broad-glass. **1710** *Lond. Gaz.* No. 4723/3 Any broad Glass-house within the Kingdom. **1712** *Ibid.* No. 4951/4 Broad Glass, or Window-Glass..sold by any of the Broadglass-makers. **1875** URE *Dict. Arts* II. 651 Next to it in cheapness of material may be ranked broad or spread window-glass. **1890** T. H. HUXLEY in *20th Cent.* Nov. 758 In the extreme north ..marked *broad-headedness is combined with low stature ..in the Lapps. **1839–40** W. IRVING *Wolfert's R.* (1855) 193 A flat-bottomed family boat, technically called a *broad-horn. **1846** DODD *Brit. Manuf.* VI. 132 The lace employed ..is used as a binding or edging for various parts of the interior [of a coach]; the finest is called *'broad-lace'. **1756** P. BROWNE *Jamaica* 255 *Broad-leaf Tree..grows to a very considerable size. **1875** URE *Dict. Arts* I. 534 Broad Leaf, the *Terminalia latifolia*, a tree, native of Jamaica. **1879** W. N. BLAIR *Building Materials of Otago* 155 There are few trees in the bush so conspicuous, or so well known as the broad-leaf. **1908** W. P. REEVES *N.Z.* iv. 94 The foliage which the broadleaf puts forth quite eclipses the leaves of most of the trees upon which it rides. **1956** *N.Z. Timber Jrnl.* July 54/1 *Broadleaf*, Griselinia littoralis Raoul. Cornac. Papaumu. A small tree of N.Z. with wide distribution from sea-level to beyond timber line. **1925** *Carpet & Rug World* Apr. 50/3 Belgrade *Broadloom Carpet. **1954** *Archit. Rev.* CXV. 138/1 Broadloom carpets are woven generally at widths of 10/4, 12/4, 14/4 and 16/4. **1963** *Which?* Mar. 70/2 Many carpets are sold as 'broadloom'. This is not a type, but a width. **1884** G. C. DAVIES *Norfolk Broads* xix. 145 The *Broadman's food is chiefly fish and fowl. **1893** *Athenæum* 2 Dec. 770/3 There was a rare combination in him of bigotry and *broad-mindedness. **1979** *Papers & Proc. Amer. Econ. Rev.* LXIX. II. 333/1 The *broader money stocks M_2..M_5. **1981** *Banker* July 48/2 In this case it is the velocity of broad money eg M_3, that is relevant, not narrow money). **1985** *Times* 9 Oct. 21/1 The Chancellor is still keeping a beady eye fixed on his other monetary indicator, £M_3 (broad money, in English though not in American). **1594** GREENE *Selimus* Wks. (Grosart) XIV. 286 Your squared words And *broad-mouth'd tearmes. **1864** *Mag. for Young* May 179 A broad-mouthed glass jar. **1708** *Lond. Gaz.* No. 4465/6 A plain *broad-set light gray Mare. **1858** W. ELLIS *Vis. Madagascar* ii. 47 He was..rather broad-set than corpulent. **1860** HOTTEN *Dict. Slang* (ed. 2) 105 **Broadsman*, a card sharper. **1882** *Blackw. Mag.* Jan. 100 The fixed belief among a large number of Broadsmen is that they breed upon the land. **1938** SHARPE *S. of Flying Squad* xviii. 193 Broadsmen, or three card sharpers, kept the Flying Squad busy in its early days. **1952** *Sci. Amer.* Apr. 49/3 They are known as the *broad-spectrum drugs, because each of them attacks a wide range of infections. **1954** S. DUKE-ELDER *Parsons' Dis. Eye* (ed. 12) x. 121 The 'broad spectrum' antibiotics..are clinically effective against both Gram-positive and Gram-negative organisms. **1969** *Times* 3 Mar. 5/8 The new concept of integrated pest control was discussed... It means avoiding the broad spectrum chemicals and changing lines of attack. **1703** T. N. *City & C. Purchaser* 56 *Broad-stone ..the same with Free-stone,..so called, because they are raised broad and thin out of the Quarries. **1842** GWILT *Archit.* Gloss., *Broad Stone*, the same as free-stone. **1930** H. M. TOMLINSON *All our Yesterdays* i. 3 A number of seamen, ironworkers, and dockers, idled in groups about the

*broadwalk beneath. **1939** *Florida* (Federal Writers' Project) II. 178 Oceanfront Park, with its..concrete broadwalk and privately operated amusement pier. **1985** *Financial Times* 7 June 12/7 Virginia Beach is one of the nicest east coast resort cities, with a broadwalk that runs three and one-half miles along clean sand and challenging waves.

broad, Sc. form of BOARD: cf. BROD.

1535 STEWART *Cron. Scot.* (1858) I. 3 Part tha fand in ald broades of bukis. **1801** MACNEILL *Poems* (1844) 67 Window broads just painted red.

†**broad,** *v. Obs.* Also 4 *north.* brade. [f. the adj.] *trans.* To broaden, spread abroad, expand.

a **1250** *Owl & Night.* 1312 þe (a)mansing is so ibroded. *a* **1340** HAMPOLE *Psalter* cxviii[xix]. 32 When thou bradid [*dilatasti*] my hert. Bradynge of hert is delytynge of rightwisnes. **1399** LANGL. *Rich. Redeless* II. 141 þe blessid bredd brodid his wyngis.

broad acres. In phr. (*the land of the*) *broad acres*: Yorkshire. So **broad-acred** *a.*, of or characteristic of Yorkshire. Cf. ACRE 1 b.

1898 *Windsor Mag.* VII. 696/2 Yorkshire has in recent years..played its matches in various parts of the broad-acred shire. **1907** *Minister's Gaz. Fashion* Oct. 182/1 'There's a trip in fra' Leeds, my lad,' explained the man from broad acres. **1908** A. N. COOPER (*title*) Across the Broad Acres. **1928** *Sunday Express* 17 June 12/6 A redfaced ..man of the broad-acred type. **1928** *Sunday Dispatch* 8 July 22/3 The youth of the Broad-acres.

broad-arrow, -head: see ARROW III.

ˈ**broad-axe.** An axe with a broad head, used for hewing timber, and formerly in war.

1352 MINOT *Poems* (1825) 29 To batail..With brade ax, and with bowes bent. *c* **1400** *Epiph.* 737 (Turnb. 1843) Summe had twybyll, brodax, and nawger. *c* **1450** *Gloss. Garlande* in Wright *Voc.* 137 *Dolabra*, (gloss.) brode axe. **1530** PALSGR. 201/2 Broode axe, *hache large.* **1855** W. SARGENT *Braddock's Exped.* 84 A roof of puncheons, rudely shaped with the broad-axe. **1876** BANCROFT *Hist. U.S.* III. xvi. 494 They..split open his doors with broad-axes.

ˈ**broad-brim.** *colloq.*

a. A hat with a broad brim. **b.** A nickname for one who wears such a hat; a Quaker.

1749 FIELDING *Tom Jones* III. VII. x. 78 This the Quaker had observed, and this..inspired honest *Broadbrim* with a Conceit. **1797** LAMB *Lett.* iii. (1837) I. 75 The congregation of broad-brims..were too much for his gravity. **1855** S. LOVER *Handy Andy* xxxvi, 'Now [fire] once through my broad-brim', quoth Ephraim. **1863** SALA *Capt. Danger.* I. x. 310 There are hearts of gold among those Broadbrims.

Hence **broad-brimmed** *a.*; **broad-brimmer,** a broad-brimmed hat (*colloq.*).

1688 *Lond. Gaz.* No. 2350/4 One silver broad brim'd Bason. **1716** LADY M. W. MONTAGUE *Lett.* I. iii. 12 The parson clapped on a broad brimmed hat. **1860** *Heads & Hats* 13 Flat caps and broad-brimmers were..fashionable. **1872** HARDWICK *Trad. Lanc.* 156 The wild huntsman may always be recognised by his broad-brimmed hat.

broadcast (ˈbrɔːdkɑːst, -æ-), *a.*, *adv.*, *sb.* [f. BROAD *adv.* + CAST *pa. pple.*] **A.** *adj.*

1. a. Of seed, etc.: Scattered abroad over the whole surface, instead of being sown in drills or rows. **b.** Of sowing: Performed by this method.

1767 A. YOUNG *Farmer's Lett. People* 115 The sowing is either in the broad-cast mode, or by drilling. **1831** SIR J. SINCLAIR *Corr.* II. 424 No broad-cast sowing can equal it. **1842** LANCE *Cott. Farmer* 19 On broad-cast turnips, thirty bushels of lime per acre, was the quantity used.

2. *fig.* **a.** Scattered widely abroad, widely disseminated. **b.** Wide, as if scattering seed broadcast.

1785 BURKE *Sp. Nab. Arcot's Debts* Wks. IV. 205 With a broad-cast swing of his arm, he squanders over his Indian field a sum, etc. **1875** STUBBS *Const. Hist.* III. xviii. 135 Broadcast accusations.

3. Disseminated by means of radio or television.

1922 *Times* 6 Apr. 17/7 Request to the Postmaster-General to consider the desirability of including weather forecasts in any broadcast distribution of information by wireless telephony. **1924** *Wireless World* 3 Sept. 664/1 Broadcast Announcements in Two Languages. **1936** *Discovery* Apr. 124/2 Mr Thornton's broadcast talks on exotic music are widely known.

B. *adv.* Only in phr. *to sow, scatter, throw,* etc. *broadcast.* **a.** in *Agric.*

1832 *Veg. Subst. Food* 38 Scattering the seed..over the whole surface..is..called sowing broad-cast. **1846** J. BAXTER *Libr. Pract. Agric.* I. 83 Seed sown either broadcast or in drills.

b. *fig.*

1814 SIR R. WILSON *Diary* II. 391, I have..thrown broad-cast a fruitful grain, and converted the soil of my banishment into a field that ought to be rich in future produce. **1876** GREEN *Short Hist.* vi. §6 (1882) 334 A host of spies were scattered broadcast over the land.

C. *sb.* **1.** Broadcast sowing, or mode.

1796 C. MARSHALL *Garden.* xv. (1813) 60 At broad-cast, trample the seed in with the feet. **1797** HOLCROFT *Stolberg's Trav.* (ed. 2) III. lxxx. 224 The corn has not been sown with broad-cast. **1866** ROGERS *Agric. & Prices* I. iii. 50 The rate of seed to the acre..where broadcast is adopted.

2. The action or an act of broadcasting by radio or television. Also *attrib.*

1922 *Daily Mail* 8 Aug. 7/3 (heading) World Broadcast. **1924** REITH (*title*) Broadcast over Britain. **1924** *Westm. Gaz.* 4 Dec., The Postmaster-General's power to include control over broadcast receivers. **1926** *Glasgow Herald* 16 Nov. 9 The ban on the broadcast of controversial topics. **1955** *Times* 10 May 10/3 Whether Sir Winston Churchill will make a sound or television broadcast for the Conservative Party.

ˈ**broadcast,** *v.* [f. as prec. + CAST *v.*]

1. To scatter (seed, etc.) abroad with the hand.

1813 A. YOUNG *Essex Agric.* I. 333 They sow..the barley ..spraining the first [half]; and broad-casting the second. **1836** MONTGOMERY *Poet's Portfolio* 248 Sow in the morn thy seed..Broad-cast it o'er the land. **1846** *Jrnl. R. Agric. Soc.* VII. II. 591 It is preferable to broadcast the guano.

2. *fig.* To scatter or disseminate widely.

1829 I. TAYLOR *Enthus.* iv. 270 The doctrine of missionary zeal..has been broad-cast over Christendom. **1880** RUSKIN *Lett. to Clergy* 369 Showing his detestation of the sale of indulgences by broadcasting these gratis from his pulpit.

3. To disseminate (a message, news, a musical or dramatic performance, or any audible or visible matter) from a radio or television transmitting station to the receiving sets of listeners and viewers; said also of a speaker or performer. Also *absol.*

Inflected pa. t. and pa. pple. *broadcast* (cf. BROADCAST *a.* 3); occas. *broadcasted.*

1921 *Discovery* Apr. 92/1 The [wireless] station at Poldhu is used partly for broadcasting Press and other messages to ships, that is, sending out messages without receiving replies. **1922** *Daily Mail* 8 Aug. 7/3 The largest and most powerful wireless station that can broadcast to the world. *Ibid.* 11 Nov. 7 Government arrangements for broadcasting. **1924** *Daily News* 13 Dec. 6/7 The speech broadcast to our homes to-day. **1956** M. W. STEARNS *Story of Jazz* (1957) xvi. 188 Coon-Sanders..and Henry Halstead broadcasted over the radio.

Hence ˈ**broadcasted** *ppl. a.*, = BROADCAST *a.* 3. Now *rare.*

1923 *Glasgow Herald* 3 Feb. 8 In cities the 'broadcasted' entertainment can never prove a serious rival to the theatre and concert hall. **1924** *Ibid.* 28 Aug. 7 The crowning event was the broadcasted evening service at Spurgeon's Tabernacle on Sunday.

broadcaster (ˈbrɔːdkɑːstə(r), -æ-). [f. BROADCAST *v.* + -ER[1].] **1.** A person whose speech, performance, etc., is broadcast on radio or television; also, a broadcasting company, station, or instrument.

1922 *Daily Mail* 30 Nov. 8 The Prince of Wales..made a great hit as a 'broadcaster'..when he delivered a message by wireless to the Boy Scouts. **1923** *Weekly Dispatch* 28 Jan. 2 When such music is the fare the broadcasters offer. **1926** C. R. BOYD FREEMAN *Towards Answer* i. 35 Imagine all 'wireless' installations being not only receivers but broadcasters. **1955** *Times* 27 Aug. 6/1 A frequent broadcaster and pamphleteer in favour of the all-German talks.

2. A machine for sowing seeds broadcast.

1934 in WEBSTER. **1960** *Times* 15 Feb. 19/2 The main implements are, in fact, the broadcaster, the forage harvester, [etc.].

broadcasting (ˈbrɔːdkɑːstɪŋ, -æ-), *vbl. sb.* [f. BROADCAST *v.* + -ING[1].] The action of BROADCAST *v.* 3. Also *attrib.* or as *ppl. a.*, as ***British Broadcasting Company*** or ***Corporation*** (abbrev. *B.B.C.*, q.v. as separate entry).

1922 *Glasgow Herald* 21 Apr. 10 The 'broadcasting' of pre-determined material of public interest from central stations. *Ibid.* 1 May 10 Whether the 'broadcasting' station itself shall be under or independent of official control. **1922** *Westm. Gaz.* 19 Oct., The British Broadcasting Company will broadcast news, information, concerts, lectures, educational matter, speeches, weather reports, and theatrical entertainments. **1926** *Encycl. Brit.* III. 1046/2, Feb. 23 1920 saw the opening of the first wireless telephone broadcasting service in the world, when a programme of vocal and instrumental music..was transmitted. **1962** (*title*) Report of the Committee on Broadcasting, 1960.

Broad Church. [See BROAD *a.* 11.]

A designation popularly applied to members of the Church of England who take its formularies and doctrines in a broad or liberal sense, and hold that the church should be comprehensive and tolerant, so as to admit of more or less variety of opinion in matters of dogma and ritual. Also sometimes applied to the corresponding school of opinion in other churches. (Often *attrib.*)

The phrase came into vogue about 1848, and is framed on the analogy of the far older 'High Church' and 'Low Church'; but it is not used in the same manner, the Broad Churchmen, so called, not having, like the High and the Low Church, a party organization, and seldom acting together as a party. According to the Master of Balliol (Prof. Jowett), the term was first proposed in conversation, in his hearing, by A. H. Clough, and became colloquially familiar in Oxford circles, a few years before 1850. In 1850 Dean Stanley claimed in an article on the Gorham Controversy in the *Edinburgh Review*, that the Church of England as a whole is of necessity neither 'High' nor 'Low', but *broad*, in which there was evidently a reference to the term as one superior to party. But in 1853 the Rev. W. J. Conybeare, in an article in the same Review on 'Church Parties', used 'High', 'Low', and 'Broad', as recognized party designations. Already in the 17th c. Dryden had referred (*Hind & P.* iii. 160) to the more tolerant divines of the church as 'your sons of latitude', (l. 187) 'your sons of breadth', (l. 229) 'your broadway sons'.

[**1850** STANLEY in *Edinb. Rev.* July 266 There is no need ..for minute comparison of the particular formularies of the Church to prove..that it is, by the very conditions of its being, not High or Low, but Broad.] **1853** W. J. CONYBEARE in *Edin. Rev.* XCVIII. 330 Side by side with these various shades of High and Low Church, another party of a different character has always existed in the Church of England. It is called by different names; Moderate, Catholic, or Broad Church, by its friends; Latitudinarian or Indifferent by its enemies. Its distinctive character is the desire of comprehension. Its watch-words are Charity and Toleration. *Ibid.* 273 The three great parties which divide the Church of England..commonly called the Low Church, the High Church, and the Broad Church parties. **1860** *Quart. Rev.* Oct. 497 The authoress [Geo. Eliot] is neither High-Church nor Low-Church, but a tolerant member of what is styled the Broad-Church party. **1884** *Edinb. Rev.* July 198.

Hence **Broad-Churchism, Broad-Churchman.**

1870 F. D. MAURICE *Letter* in *Life* (1884) I. xii. 184 They [the Liberals] are called Broad Churchmen now, and delight to be called so. But their breadth seems to me to be narrowness. **1874** GLADSTONE *Ritualism* in *Cont. Rev.* Oct. 673 Some of those clergy who are called Broadchurchmen.

broadcloth, broad cloth (ˈbrɔːdklɒθ, -ɔːθ). [f. BROAD + CLOTH. In *Act 1 Rich. III*, viii., an. 1482, 'broad cloths', two yards within the lists, are distinguished from 'streits', one yard wide within the lists.] Fine, plain-wove, dressed, double width, black cloth, used chiefly for men's garments. (The term is now used to imply quality rather than width, which may vary considerably; the 'double' merely represents that the piece is creased or folded double, i.e. with its two 'lists' brought together; a process not adopted with cloth of less than 54 inches wide.) Also *attrib.*

a **1420** OCCLEVE *De Reg. Princ.* 452 There gothe no lesse in a mannes typette Than of brode clothe a yerd. **1465** *Mann. & Househ. Exp.* 316, Ij. peces of blak brodeclothe, conteynenge in lengthe xlviij. yerdes. **1483** *Act 1 Rich. III*, viii. §1 Any manner woollen Clothes, called broad Clothes. **1577** HARRISON *England* II. v. (1877) 132 The wares that they carrie out of the realme are for the most part Brode clothes. **1632** MASSINGER & FIELD *Fatal Dowry* v. i, A thrifty cap, composed of broad-cloth lists. **1720** GAY *Poems* (1745) I. 72 Ye weavers all your shuttles throw, And bid broad-cloths and serges grow. **1833** HT. MARTINEAU *Cinn. & Pearls* v. 97 You dressed in broad-cloth, and I in silk.

fig. **1601** BP. BARLOW *Defence* 222 That is Christ in the broad-cloth, in the whole peece.

Hence **broad-clothier,** a dealer in broad-cloth.

1720 *Lond. Gaz.* 5878/6 Richard Rider..Broad Clothier.

broaden (ˈbrɔːd(ə)n), *v.* [f. BROAD *a.* + -EN[1]. Johnson says 'I know not whether this word occurs, but in the following passage', viz. that from Thomson in sense 1. But the same author had used *broadened* in the trans. sense.]

1. *intr.* To become broad or broader; to widen. Also with *out.*

1727 THOMSON *Summer* 1600 Low walks the sun, and broadens by degrees, Just o'er the verge of day. **1824** BYRON *Juan* XVI. lxxxviii, Smiles around Broadening to grins. **1832** TENNYSON '*You ask me why*' iii, Where Freedom broadens slowly down From precedent to precedent. **1888** MRS. H. WARD *R. Elsmere* I. iii. 79 Her round comfortable face brightened and broadened out into a beaming smile. **1894** B. HARRADEN *In Varying Moods* vii, The narrow, dull, everyday existence broadened out into many interesting possibilities.

2. *trans.* To make broad or broader; to widen, dilate. *lit.* and *fig.*

1726 [see BROADENED]. **1792** ROBERTS *Looker-on* (1794) I. 321 A constitution..so broadened, by experience, to the compass of our wants and the demands of our nature. **1861** A. B. HOPE *Eng. Cathedr. 19th C.* vi. 214 For this object the nave should be proportionably broadened. **1867** in E. B. Denison *Life Bp. Lonsdale* (1868) 240 He was a High Churchman of the old school, broadened by experience. **1871** BLACKIE *Four Phases* i. 74 To broaden his conception of morality and religion.

broadened (ˈbrɔːd(ə)nd), *ppl. a.* [f. prec. + -ED[1].] Made or become broad; dilated.

1726 THOMSON *Winter* 132 With broaden'd nostrils..The ..heifer snuffs the..gale. **1821** JOANNA BAILLIE *Met. Leg., Colum.* xlix. 16 From ocean rose her broaden'd disk.

broadening (ˈbrɔːd(ə)nɪŋ), *vbl. sb.* [f. as prec. + -ING[1].] Expansion in breadth, dilatation.

Mod. Newspaper. These Norfolk Broads are broadenings or reaches of the river.

broadening (ˈbrɔːd(ə)nɪŋ), *ppl. a.* [f. as prec. + -ING[2].] Becoming broad; expanding, dilating.

1850 MRS. BROWNING *Poems* II. 12 Within the broadening dark. **1859** R. BURTON *Centr. Afr.* in *Jrnl. R.G.S.* XXIX. 114 Up a gradually broadening valley.

broad-faced (ˈbrɔːdfeɪst), *a.*

1. Having a broad face.

1607 W. N. *Barley-Breake* (1877) The broad-fac'd Owle. **1790** BOSWELL *Johnson* (1811) III. 71 Loud obstreperous broad-faced mirth. **1882** J. HAWTHORNE *Fort. Fool* I. xv, A composed, broadfaced, straightforward old man.

†**2.** *fig.* Undisguised, open. *Obs.*

1643 *Myst. Iniq.* 43 Such broadfaced iniquity, that no mask..would fit it. **1648** JENKYN *Blind Guide* i. 12 Two broadfaced falsities. **1678** B. R. *Let. Pop. Friends* 7 The Treason appears too broad-faced.

broad gauge. The wider distance at which the rails are laid on some railways, involving a

corresponding width of carriage. See GAUGE. Often *attrib.* (also *fig.*). Hence **'broad-gauged** *a.*

(The broad gauge of the Great Western Railway, in England, is 7 feet, as against the ordinary gauge of 4 ft. 8½ in.)

1844 [see NARROW GAUGE]. **1858** BRANNAN in F. J. Meine *Tall Tales of S.W.* (1930) 255 The Univarsalists..get on the broad gage and goes the hull hog-ah! **1864** *Times* 24 Dec., A through broad-gauge train was due. **1865** *Ibid.* 25 Jan., If the broad gauge may be unnecessarily wide the narrow gauge is too narrow. **1868** M. PATTISON *Academ. Org.* iv. 102 We wish to maintain one broad-gauge line of refining education. **1881** *Chicago Times* 4 June, Everything broad-gauged and in liberal proportions.

broadish ('brɔːdɪʃ), *a.* Somewhat broad.

1793 *Phil. Trans.* LXXXIII. 179 A broadish pressure, as that of a finger. **1866** CARLYLE *Remin.* I. 207 The broadish little street.

Broadland ('brɔːdlənd). [f. BROAD *sb.* 5 + LAND *sb.*] The district of the Broads; East Anglia, or a section of it. Also *attrib.* Hence **'Broadlander.**

1889 H. M. DOUGHTY (*title*) Summer in Broadland. **1899** *Daily News* 27 Dec. 6/4 The sluggish streams and low meadows of the Norfolk Broadland. **1902** N. EVERITT (*title*) Broadland Sport. **1903** W. A. DUTT et al. *Norfolk Broads* vi. 78 Among the characteristic Broadlanders..the wherrymen are the most numerous and conspicuous. **1926** *Daily Tel.* 6 Aug. 5/2 Broadland bream at this season are particularly partial to stewed wheat.

'broad-leaved, *a.* Also -leafed. **a.** Having broad leaves: often in *Bot.* a specific distinction (= L. *latifolius*). †**b.** Broad-brimmed (*obs.*).

1552 HULOET, Brode leafed, *latifolium.* **1563** B. GOOGE *Eglogs* viii. (Arb.) 62 This pleasaunte Brodeleaued Beech. **1769** BARRINGTON in *Phil. Trans.* LIX. 34 The Wych (or broad-leaved) elm. *a* **1834** COLERIDGE *Eolian Harp* 4 With white flowered jasmin and the broad-leaved myrtle. **1861** COLLIER *Hist. Eng. Lit.* 176 A broad-leafed low-crowned hat of Flemish beaver. **1882** *Garden* 18 Feb. 112/1 The broad-leaved Butcher's-broom.

c. spec. in *Forestry* (see quot. 1957).

1905 *Terms Forestry & Logging* 39 *Hardwood*, a broad-leafed, or dicotyledonous, tree. **1927** *Forestry* I. 14 Scots Pine..in natural forests was almost always associated with a broad-leaved species, generally birch. **1953** H. L. EDLIN *Forester's Handbook* viii. 122 The current rate of planting of the broadleaved trees, or hardwoods is much lower than that of the conifers. **1957** *Brit. Commonw. Forest Terminol.* II. 33 *Broadleaved tree*, one belonging to the Dicotyledonous group of Angiosperms and producing timber known commercially as hardwood... The use of this term in certain African countries to distinguish trees having relatively large leaves as compared with *Acacias* is deprecated.

†**'broadling, 'broadlings,** *adv. Obs.* In 3 bredlinge, 6 *Sc.* braid-, breadlingis, 7 bradelings. [f. BROAD *a.* + -LING(S.] Broadwise, with the broad or flat side; extended, flat; broadly.

c **1200** *Trin. Coll. Hom.* 61 He wile smite bredlinge mid swuerde and brisen, oðer mid egge and cleuen. **1535** STEWART *Cron. Scot.* II. 119 Wes borne than braidlingis on his bak. *a* **1605** BANNATYNE *Jrnl.* 173 (JAM.) He straik ane of them breadlingis with his sword. **1606** BIRNIE *Kirk-Burial* (1833) 20 It brake not in bradelings, but as it were by degrees. *a* **1701** SEDLEY *Pindar. Ode* Wks. (1766) 16 So have I seen the warbling lark..The narrow compass of a cage forget, And broadling o'er a turf in silent pleasure sit.

broadly ('brɔːdlɪ), *adv.* [f. BROAD *a.* + -LY².]

1. In a broad manner; widely, extensively.

1599 SANDYS *Europæ Spec.* (1632) 124 When the world.. should looke about so broadly, and search so narrowly. **1697** DRYDEN *Virg. Georg.* III. 126 The Colt..Barrel belly'd, broadly back'd. **1873** MORLEY *Rousseau* I. 309 Two channels, flowing broadly apart. **1884** BOWER & SCOTT *De Bary's Phaner. & Ferns* 162 A broadly elliptical cavity.

2. *fig.* With a broad or general view; generally.

1856 SIR B. BRODIE *Psychol. Inq.* I. iii. 91 He has laid down the rule too broadly. **1860** TYNDALL *Glac.* II. §22. 346 Broadly considered, two classes of facts are presented.

3. Outspokenly, openly; manifestly, markedly, decidedly; fully.

1624 BEDELL *Lett.* iv. 81 [It] made them talke and write of it broadly. **1651** BAXTER *Inf. Bapt.* Apol. 16 Mr. T.'s greatest friends, did the broadlyest speak..of his being foiled. **1753** *Scots Mag.* Jan. 2/2 The janisaries..pretty broadly hinted their inclination. **1871** BLACKIE *Four Phases* I. 154 Looking the man broadly in the face. **1876** GREEN *Short Hist.* v. §3 (1882) 233 Wyclif broadly asserted that no man could be excommunicated by the Pope.

4. With broad pronunciation. See BROAD *a.* 7.

1580 BARET *Alv.* B 1341 To speake more brodely: to ioine wordes so..that vowels meete together gapingly.

5. *Art.* With artistic breadth. See BREADTH 5.

1875 FORTNUM *Maiolica* xii. 132 Broadly treated grotesques..in camaïeu of greenish grey on a blue ground.

'Broadmoor. The name of an institution in the village of Broadmoor, south-eastern Berkshire, for the treatment of mental patients under special conditions on account of their dangerous, violent, or criminal propensities (formerly, housing the criminally insane). ***Broadmoor patient***: a former designation of a criminal lunatic.

1868 *Jrnl. Mental Sci.* XIV. 216 Dr. Meyer gives the following account of the singularly liberal arrangements made by the Council at Broadmoor as relates both to the wages and well-being of the servants. **1914** E. G. O'DONOGHUE *Story of Bethlehem Hospital* xxxv. 345 Broadmoor was built under the provisions of the Act passed in 1860 (23 and 24 Vict. c. 75). The asylum was completed in..1863. **1948** *Act 11 & 12 Geo. VI* c. 58 §62(2) The expression 'criminal lunatic' shall cease to be used; and there shall be substituted for it wherever it occurs in any enactment the expression 'Broadmoor patient'. **1960** K. JONES *Mental Health* 223 The Royal Commission on Mental Illness and Mental Deficiency, 1954–7..suggested that consideration should be given to the question of whether Broadmoor procedures could be assimilated to those for other patients. **1976** *Milton Keynes Express* 18 June 9/4 A man who attacked a policeman with a builder's hod and used it to fend off six other officers and a police dog at Bletchley, has been sent to Broadmoor.

broadness ('brɔːdnɪs). [f. as BROADLY *adv.* + -NESS.] The state or quality of being broad; breadth.

1. *lit.* (Now mostly superseded by *breadth.*)

1388 WYCLIF *Deut.* xxxiii. 20 Gad is blessid in broodnesse. **1486** *Bk. St. Albans, Her.* C vij b, And it be dyuidid after the longnes or after the brodenes. **1526** *Pilgr. Perf.* (W. de W. 1531) 245 Infynyte..in depnes, heyght, brodnesse & length. **1643** J. STEER tr. *Exp. Chyrurg.* xvi. 66 About the broadnesse of the palme of the hand. **1730** *Magna Brit.* V. 805/1 Bretford..hath its Name from the Broadness of the Ford..over the Avon.

2. *fig.* Plainness of speech; coarseness, indelicacy.

a **1700** DRYDEN (J.), I have used the cleanest metaphor I could find, to palliate the broadness of the meaning. **1861** CRAIK *Hist. Eng. Lit.* I. 524 (L.) Broadness and indelicacy of allusion.

broad pendant, pennant. A swallow-tailed tapering flag at the mast-head of a man of war; carried by a commodore. See PENDANT.

†**broad-piece.** *Obs.* A name applied after the introduction of the guinea in 1663 to the 'Unite' or 20 shilling-piece ('Jacobus' and 'Carolus') of the preceding reigns, which were much broader and thinner than the new milled coinage.

1678 *Narr. Murd. Godfrey* 6 He..found..four broad pieces of Gold. **1690** *Lond. Gaz.* No. 2549/4, 17 false Guineas, and two false Broadpieces. **1691** LOCKE *Money* Wks. 1727 II. 47 The Broad-Pieces that were coined in King James I. time for 20*s.* nobody will now part with under 23*s.* or more. **1712** ARBUTHNOT *John Bull* (1755) 53 Others.. picked up guineas and broad-pieces. **1816** SCOTT *Old Mort.* iii, An old miser..with whom a broad piece would at any time weigh down political opinions.

broad seal, *sb.* The Great Seal of England. Also *transf.*

1536 WRIOTHESLEY *Chron.* (1875) I. 51 Letter patent under the Kinges brode seale. **1576** LAMBARDE *Peramb. Kent* (1826) 227 Advaunced to the keeping, first of the privie, and then of the broad seale. **1641** SYMONDS *Serm. bef. Ho. Comm.* D b, As if they had had the broad seale of heaven for them. **1679** *Trial Langhorn* 27 Two Pardons under the Broad Seal. **1762–71** H. WALPOLE *Vertue's Anec. Paint.* (1786) III. 172 Being allowed 200*l.* for each broad seal.

†**'broad-seal,** *v. Obs. rare*⁻¹. [f. prec.] *trans.* To seal with the broad seal; *fig.* to warrant, sanction, authorize.

1599 B. JONSON *Cynthia's Rev.* v. vi. 75 Thy presence broad-seales our delights for pure.

broadshare ('brɔːdʃɛə(r)), *a.* Of a plough: Having a broad share.

1862 J. WILSON *Farming* 110 Broadshare or paring ploughs are much used..in the autumn cleaning of stubbles.

Hence **'broadshare** *v.*

1856 *Farmer's Mag.* Jan. 23 The practice of broadsharing the stubbles immediately after harvest. **1863** MORTON *Cycl. Agric.* II. Gloss., *Broad-sharing* (Kent), ploughing shallow and wide with a broad share, without turning it over.

broadsheet ('brɔːdʃiːt). [f. BROAD *a.* + SHEET.] A large sheet of paper printed on one side only; = BROADSIDE *sb.* 3. Also *attrib.*

1705 HEARNE *Coll.* (1885–6) I. 18 A new Edition..on a Broad Sheet. **1874** MOTLEY *J. Barneveld* II. xviii. 252 Ballad-mongers and broadsheet vendors. **1878** —— *Diderot* II. 18 Pamphlets, broadsheets, sarcasms flew over Paris.

broadside ('brɔːdsaɪd), *sb.* [Formerly two words: BROAD *a.* + SIDE *sb.*]

1. a. *Naut.* 'The whole of that side of a ship above the water which is situate between the bow and the quarter' (Smyth *Sailor's Word-bk.*).

1591 GARRARD *Art Warre* 89 That they turne their broad sides as if they should encounter the enemie. *a* **1618** RALEIGH *Roy. Navy* 26 To plant great red Port-holes in their broad sides. **1742** WOODROOFE in Hanway *Trav.* (1762) I. II. xxiii. 98 They let the vessel run with her broad side ashore. **1769** FALCONER *Dict. Marine* (1789) H ij, A squall of wind laid the ship on her broadside. **1833** MARRYAT *P. Simple* (1863) 106 A heavy sea struck us on the broadside.

attrib. **1862** THORNBURY *Turner* I. 292 It is a broadside view, and represents the Redoubtable as sinking.

b. ***broadside to*** (or ***and***) ***broadside***: with the side of one ship to that of another; *transf.* side by side, close to each other.

1696 KENNETT *Rom. Antiq.* II. IV. (1713) 241 If they happen'd to swing broad-side to broad-side. **1769** FALCONER *Dict. Marine* (1789), To lie alongside of; to be broadside and broadside.

c. ***broadside on, broadside to,*** (***a broadside*** obs.): with the side of the vessel turned fully to the object considered; transversely, across the length.

1716 *Lond. Gaz.* No. 5475/3 He had ranged his Ships..a Broadside cross the River. **1800** A. DUNCAN *Mariner's Chron.* (1804) II. 82, I desired them not to come broadside-to, but stern-on. **1840** R. DANA *Bef. the Mast* xv. 41 We drifted down, broadside on, and went smash into the Lagoda.

d. Of the side of something other than a ship.

1632 RUTHERFORD *Lett.* xxiv. (1862) I. 95 He will lay the door on the broadside and come in. *c* **1661** *Argyle's Last Will* in *Harl. Misc.* (1746) VIII. 30/1 [Argyle]..stood firm on his own Interest, and could oppose a Broadside to every Emergency of Fortune. **1868** LOCKYER *Heavens* (ed. 3) 340 A line 95,000,000 miles in length, looked at broadside on at this distance, would appear but as an imperceptible point. **1884** SPEEDY *Sport* xiv. 233 They stopped and looked round, showing their broadsides the one just above the other. *Ibid.* xviii. 322 Being at close range, and broadside on, the two largest were shot dead.

2. 'The whole array, or the simultaneous discharge, of the artillery on one side of a ship of war' (Smyth *Sailor's Word-bk.*).

1597 SHAKS. *2 Hen. IV*, II. iv. 196 Feare wee broad-sides? No, let the Fiend giue fire. *a* **1599** HAKLUYT *Voy.* II. II. 63 The great shippe shot at vs all her broad side. **1630** WADSWORTH *Sp. Pilgr.* ii. 8 The man of warre..gaue vs a broade side with his Ordnance. **1748** ANSON *Voy.* II. v. (ed. 4) 237 We..had a broad-side ready to pour into her.

fig. **1833** MARRYAT *P. Simple* (1863) 82 At this last broadside of mine, my father and all my brothers raised a cry of horror.

3. A sheet of paper printed on one side only, forming one large page; = BROADSHEET.

1575 CHURCHYARD *Chippes* (1817) 43 Richard Harvey.. before 1563, had printed in a broadside, a decree..betwene Churchyarde and Camel. **1691** WOOD *Ath. Oxon.* I. 2 In one Sheet in 4to as also on a broad side of a Sheet. **1818** SCOTT *T. Landl.* Ser. II. IV. 263 The Broadside containing the last dying speech and confession of M. Murdochson. **1861** WRIGHT *Ess. Archæol.* II. xxiii. 261 Many of the fabliaux and comic poems were issued as broadside ballads.

4. *attrib.* **broadside array** *Radio*, an aerial array having its directional effect perpendicular to the elements of the array.

1932 F. E. TERMAN *Radio Engin.* xiv. 511 The Broadside Array. The simple broadside antenna array consists of a number of antennas spaced at uniform distances along a horizontal line and connected so as to be excited in phase. **1959** DAVIES & PALMER *Radio Studies* iii. 31 Aerials of large size can be constructed by connecting together large numbers of dipole or yagi elements. Such aerials are known as broadside arrays.

'broadside, *adv.* **1.** With the side turned full (*to* a given point or object).

1870 HOOKER *Stud. Flora* 455 Spikelets..inserted broadside to the rachis. **1884** SPEEDY *Sport* xiv. 231 As he was passing broadside he afforded an excellent shot.

2. *Printing.* Of letterpress, illustrations, tables, etc.: set sideways. Also as *adj.*, of a page so set (see quot. 1948); and *sb.* Chiefly *U.S.*

1925 *Univ. Chicago Press Man. Style* (ed. 8) 143 Set long box-headings broadside (i.e., vertically) so as to read up from the bottom of the text page. **1948** *Words into Type* (Appleton-Century-Crofts) 539 A broadside table or illustration is one printed with the top at the left side of the page, requiring a quarter turn of the book to the right to be in position for reading. **1957** R. A. HEWITT *Style for Print* iii. 30 All broadside illustrations, whether printed with the text or inset, should have their legends on the right-hand side of the page, i.e. in the inner margin on a left-hand page and the outer margin on a right-hand page.

'broadside, *v.* [f. the sb.] *intr.* Of a motor cycle in dirt-track racing: to skid and slide in the cinders as part of a deliberate manœuvre when the rider is 'hugging' a corner. Also in extended use of a car, pedal cycle, etc., esp. in a controlled sideways skid.

1930 *Aberdeen Press & Jrnl.* 28 Mar. 1 (*caption*) A dirt-track rider broadsiding at Crystal Palace, London. **1967** *Autocar* 28 Dec. 24/3 The car broadsided for 100 yards before turning over. **1969** *N.Z. Listener* 16 May 16/1 In the early days of 'dirt-track' the people came to see the extreme slides made by the machines as they were raced into the cinder-strewn corners. Later, specially-designed machines enabled the riders to hug the corners without 'broadsiding'.

'broadsider. *nonce-wd.* One who collects (printed) broadsides.

1862 BURTON *Bk.-hunter* I. 18 Not a black-letter man..or an Elzevirian, or a broadsider, or an old-brown-calf man.

'broadsiding, *vbl. sb.* **1.** The firing of broadsides.

1858–65 CARLYLE *Fredk. Gt.* II. IV. x. 38 Byng's Seafight, done..with due emphasis of broadsiding. *Ibid.* IV. XII. xii. 277 Vernon..attacks certain Castles so-called, with furious broadsiding.

2. The skidding of a motor cycle (see BROADSIDE *v.*).

1932 *Daily Express* 25 June 17/5 Forty-six miles an hour does not seem much to the uninitiated, but it is the broadsiding that makes dirt-track cycling what it is.

broadsword ('brɔːdsɔəd). [f. BROAD *a.* + SWORD.] 'A cutting sword with a broad blade' (J.). Also *attrib.*

[*a* **1000** *Byrhtnoth* 15 (Gr.) Ða he healdan mihte brad swurd.] *c* **1565** LINDESAY (Pitscottie) *Chron.* an. 1559 The master of Lindsay struck him on the head with a broad-sword. **1789** MRS. PIOZZI *Journ. France* I. 243 The Highland broad-sword is still called an Andrew Ferrara. **1799** ROWLANDSON (*title*) Hungarian and Highland Broadsword Exercise. **1843** PRESCOTT *Mexico* I. 359 They killed two of the horses, cutting through their necks with their stout broadswords..at a blow.

b. *transf.* (pl.) Men armed with broadswords.

1855 MACAULAY *Hist. Eng.* III. 330 Lochiel, surrounded by more than six hundred broadswords.

c. *Comb.*, as ***broadsword-shaped*** adj.

1870 ROLLESTON *Anim. Life* 22 The scapula, a broadsword-shaped bone.

broadtail ('brɔːdteɪl). The skin or pelt of a young Persian lamb, having a lustrous moiré appearance. Also *attrib.* Cf. BREITSCHWANZ.

1892 H. POLAND *Fur-Bearing Animals in Commerce* 330 Persian Lamb takes a brilliant dye... The *Broadtail*, or *Breitschwanze*, is probably..the unborn Persian Lamb; it is undoubtedly the skin about which so much..has been written, as to slaying the parent sheep for the sake of its skin. 1898 *Westm. Gaz.* 13 Jan. 3/2 A broadtail cycling suit is the latest whim in the Bois. *Ibid.* 3 Nov. 3/2, I can as strongly commend black broadtail. It is a fur very easy to manipulate. 1899 *Ibid.* 21 Sept. 3/2 The coat of black broadtail, or caracal, or Persian lamb or astrachan, all varieties of a species, is prophesied as the pet garment this winter. 1927 *Observer* 20 Nov. 21 Long waistcoats of ermine or squirrel or broad-tail. 1963 *Retail Trading-Standards Assoc. Bull.* Aug./Sept. 3/1 The following names [for furs] may be used notwithstanding the general rule:—*Animal*, Lamb (Persian). *Accepted Trade Name*, Broadtail Persian or Persian Broadtail.

'broadway. (Now usually as two words.) **a.** A wide open road or highway, as opposed to a narrow lane or byway. From the former practice of treating it as a compound, it has often come to be the proper name of a street, as the *Broadway* in New York, Hammersmith, Stratford-le-Bow, etc.

*a*1613 OVERBURY *Crumms fr. K. James' Table* Wks. (1856) 277 Where there is a broadway besides, what need I tread nere the borders of vice? 1876 BROWNING *Pacchiarotto* 92 Duty and love, one broadway, were the best.

b. (With cap. initial.) Used allusively with reference to the theatres for which Broadway in New York is famous. Also *attrib.* and in *Comb.*

1881 *Harper's Mag.* Apr. 712/2 Another suggests some Broadway idea. 1907 ZANGWILL *Ghetto Comedies* 269 He had heard vaguely of 'Hamlet'—as a great play that was acted on Broadway. *Ibid.* 271 The 'happy endings' of Broadway. 1925 O. SITWELL *Poor Young People* 35 A widow-theme That is..Ancien-Régime More than Broadway-American.

c. *attrib.* Applied by Dryden to the more tolerant divines of the English Church who were for widening its basis, called before (line 160) 'sons of latitude', and (line 187) 'sons of breadth'. Cf. the modern BROAD CHURCH.

1687 DRYDEN *Hind & P.* III. 229 Your broad-way sons wou'd never be too nice To close with Calvin, if he paid their price.

broadway, -ways, -wise ('brɔːdweɪz, -waɪz), *adv.* [f. BROAD *a.* + -WAYS, -WISE.] In a lateral direction, breadthways, laterally.

1593 R. HARVEY *Philadelphus* 44 Some [trees] are rooted broadway, as Elmes. 1693 EVELYN *De la Quint. Compl. Gard.* II. 62 Prop'd with Pearches, most broadwise, and some crosswise. 1756 FRANKLIN *Lett.* Wks. 1840 VI. 181 Sheet-lead sinking in water broadways, cannot descend near so fast as it would edgeways. 1848 DICKENS *Dombey* 213 Standing it [a letter] longwise and broadwise on his table.

Broadwood ('brɔːdwʊd). A piano made by John Broadwood (1732–1812) or by the London firm founded by him. Also *attrib.*

1832 W. GASKELL *Let.* 17 Sept. in A. B. Hopkins *Eliz. Gaskell* (1952) iii. 52 First to buy the piano (a Broadwood). 1888 G. B. SHAW *London Music 1888–89* (1937) 46 The ensemble of the three Broadwood grands was not so dreadful as might have been expected. 1895 KIPLING *Song of Banjo* in *New Rev.* June 602 You couldn't pack a Broadwood half a mile—You mustn't leave a fiddle in the damp. 1969 *Listener* 14 Aug. 225/1 A Broadwood of 1787.

broak(e, broakadge, broaker, etc., obs. ff. of BROKE, BROKAGE, BROKER, etc.

brob (brɒb). [prob. related to North dial. '*brob* to prick with a bodkin' (Grose): cf. *brad, brod, brog*, etc.] 'A peculiar spike, driven alongside the end of an abutting timber to prevent its slipping' (Raymond *Mining Gloss.* 1881).

1874 in Knight's *Amer. Mech. Dict.*

Brobdingnag ('brɒbdɪŋˌnæg). Often incorrectly **Brobdignag.** The name given by Swift in *Gulliver's Travels* to an imaginary country where everything was on a gigantic scale. Hence used *attrib.* as: Of, or pertaining to, that country; of huge dimensions; immense; gigantic.

(Swift subsequently wrote a mock letter from 'Captain Gulliver' to his cousin Sympson (purporting to be dated 27 April 1727, but first published in Dublin ed. 1735), complaining that *Brobdingnag* had been erroneously printed for *Brobdingrag*; but this was only a feint to mystify the public by a pretended solicitude for minute accuracy. The early editions have all *Brobdingnag*. See CRAIK *Life of Swift* (1882) 535–7.)

1731 POPE *Mor. Ess.* iv. 104 Such a draught As brings all Brobdignag before your thought. 1814 SOUTHEY in *Q. Rev.* XI. 65 The houses..have the appearance of Brobdingnag beehives. 1840 CARLYLE *Heroes* I. 56 Huge untutored Brobdignag genius.

Hence **Brobdingnagian** (brɒbdɪŋ'nægɪən), *a.* and *sb.* Also **-dig'nagian, -naggian. a.** *adj.* = BROBDINGNAG.

1728 MORGAN *Algiers* II. v. 319 Brobdingnaggian Leagues would scarce suffice. 1797 GODWIN *Enquirer* I. vii. 61 The final triumph of my Brobdingnagian persecutor. 1870 DISRAELI *Lothair* lxxxi. 428 A bran-new brobdingnagian hotel. 1881 GRANT ALLEN *Evolutionist at large* i, Known to our Brobdingnagian intelligence as grains of sand.

b. *sb.* An inhabitant of Brobdingnag, a giant, a person of huge size.

1729 T. COOKE *Tales, Prop. &c.* 119 In Wit we Brobdignaggians are. 1835 T. HOOK *G. Gurney* II. v. (L.) 'Sally!' screamed the Brobdingnagian..'a gentleman wants a bed!'

brobill, var. of BURBLE *v. Obs.*

broc, obs. f. BROOK; var. BROKE *Obs.*, breach.

Broca ('brəʊkə). The name of the French surgeon and anthropologist Pierre Paul *Broca* (1824–80), applied (chiefly in the possessive case) to anatomical features, etc., discovered by or named after him (see quots.). ***Broca's aphasia***, motor aphasia; ***Broca('s) area***, part of the premotor cortex in the inferior frontal convolution of the brain, concerned with the movements required for speech; ***Broca's point***, the centre of the external auditory meatus; ***Broca's table***, a graduated table of skin-colours.

1875 *Encycl. Brit.* II. 111/1 The colour of the eyes and hair is also to be defined accurately by Broca's table. 1877 *Jrnl. Mental Sci.* XXII. 406 Case of Sudden and Complete 'Aphasia' and Partial 'Right Hemiplegia', Lesion of 'Broca's Convolution'. 1884 T. G. STEWART *Dis. Nervous Syst.* ii. 22 This includes what has been named Broca's convolution, from his having made out its relation to aphasia. 1890 W. JAMES *Princ. Psychol.* I. ii. 40 Broca's region is homologous with the parts ascertained to produce movements of the lips, tongue, and larynx. 1898 BEEVOR *Dis. Nervous Syst.* xix. 283 The speech centre of Broca, situated in the posterior part of the left third frontal convolution. *Ibid.* 285 Motor aphasia.. is caused by a lesion of..Broca's centre. 1905 W. D. HALLIBURTON *Handbk. Physiol.* (ed. 7) xlviii. 689 In the higher apes..faradisation of the Broca area does not evoke vocalisation. 1911 *Ibid.* (ed. 10) xlviii. 729 That Broca's area is the chief speech centre has for long been a matter of doubt among physiologists and pathologists. 1959 *Psychol. Rev.* LXVI. 46/1 Broca's aphasia, indistinguishable from that caused by damage of Broca's area.

brocade (brəʊ'keɪd), *sb.* Forms: 6–8 **brocardo,** 7–8 **brocado, brocard,** 8 **brochad,** 7– **brocade.** [The form *brocado* was a. Sp., Pg. *brocado*, corresp. to It. *broccato* 'cloth of gold and siluer' (Percivall, Florio), lit. 'bossed' or 'embossed stuff', in form masc. pa. pple. of *broccare* 'to boss, to stud, to set with great-headed nails', f. It. *brocca* (Sp. *broca*) a boss or stud, the same word as F. *broche*, Eng. BROACH, q.v. For the change to -ADE see that ending; the form *brochad* seems influenced by F. *brocher* (cf. BROCHE *v.*). (It is not clear whether the forms *brocardo, brocard*, and F. *brocart*, are corruptions of *brocado*, or distinct formations with the suffix *-ardo, -art*, -ARD.)]

1. A textile fabric woven with a pattern of raised figures, originally in gold or silver; in later use, any kind of stuff richly wrought or 'flowered' with a raised pattern; also a cloth of gold and silver of Indian manufacture.

1563–99 HAKLUYT *Voy.* II. 215 (*Ormus*) Cloth of silke, brocardo, and divers other sortes of marchandise come out of Persia. 1656 BLOUNT *Glossogr.*, *Brocado*, cloth of gold or silver. 1691 LOCKE *Money* Wks. 1727 II, Whose Wife must spread a long Train of Brocard. 1695 MOTTEUX *St. Olon's Morocco* 149 Very rich Gold and Silver Brocades. 1702 W. J. *Bruyn's Voy. Levant* vii. 24 A sort of Bonnet of Brocardo or Cloth of Gold. 1709 *Lond. Gaz.* No. 4540/6 Bed Damasks, rich flower'd Sattins, Brochads, etc. *c*1720 PRIOR *Phyllis' Age*, Stiff in Brocard, and pinch'd in stays. 1734 POPE *Ess. Man* IV. 186 One flaunts in rags, one flutters in brocade. 1751 CHAMBERS *Cycl.* s.v., At present, any stuff of silk, satin, or even simple taffety, when wrought, and enriched with flowers, etc., obtains the denomination of brocade. 1841 ELPHINSTONE *Hist. Ind.* I. 310 Gold and silver brocade were also favourite, and perhaps original, manufactures of India. 1859 GEO. ELIOT *A. Bede* 53, I mean to bring out my best brocade, that I wore at your christening twenty years ago.

fig. 1861 CRAIK *Hist. Eng. Lit.* II. 267 (L.) The gorgeous brocade does not hide the true fire and fancy beneath.

2. (See quot.)

1869 *Eng. Mech.* 12 Nov. 215/2 Gold is not put on any paper-hangings, it is a preparation called leaf metal, or a powder called brocade or bronze.

3. *attrib.* Of or resembling brocade; **brocade-matting,** a floor matting of Japanese manufacture consisting of a texture of reeds and cotton yarn with a coloured design woven upon it; **brocade-shell,** a variegated species of cone-shell, *Conus geographicus.*

1711 ADDISON *Spect.* No. 15 ¶4 A Brocade Waistcoat or Petticoat are standing Topicks. 1745 BAKER *Don Quix.* I. I. v. 31 This curious Cap and his fine brocard Cope will make him outshine the Sun-Dial. 1812 SOUTHEY *Omniana* II. 283 Somewhat in the brocade fashion of Gongora. 1847 BARHAM *Ingol. Leg.* (1877) 281 Her rich brocade gown sat upright in its place. 1902 *Encycl. Brit.* XXIX. 696/2 The 'brocade-matting' industry of Okayama.

bro'cade, *v.* [f. prec.] To work with a raised pattern (chiefly in pa. pple.).

Mod. Newspaper, The bodice and train were brocaded with sprays of lilac on a ground of apple-blossom pink.

brocaded (brəʊ'keɪdɪd), *a.* Also 7 **brocado'd,** 8 **brokaded.** [f. prec. + -ED[2].]

1. Worked or woven in the style of brocade; ornamented with brocade.

1656 BLOUNT *Glossogr.* s.v., We call that Brocado'd Silk or Satten, which is wrought or mixed with Gold or Silver, and sometimes that is called Brocado'd Silk, which is wrought with several colours of silk. 1714 GAY *Araminta*, Brocaded Flow'rs o'er the gay Mantoe shine. 1843 LEVER *J. Hinton* iii. (1878) 10 Rich curtains of heavy brocaded silk.

2. Dressed in brocade.

1767 *St. James's Chron.* Oct., An oyster-wench *in puris naturalibus* is a more desirable object than a brocaded monster.

brocage, variant of BROKAGE.

brocale, -aly, variant of BROKALY.

brocard[1] ('brəʊkəd). [a. F. *brocard*, akin to med.L. *brocarda, brocardicorum opus*, a name given to the 'sentences' of Burchard or Brocard, bishop of Worms in the 11th c., who compiled twenty books of 'Regulæ Ecclesiasticæ'.]

1. *Law.* An elementary principle or maxim.

*a*1624 SWINBURNE *Spousals* (1686) 184 Because the Brocardes or contrary Conclusions, rather breed brabbles, than pacifie Contentions. 1759 FOUNTAINHALL *Decisions* I. 243 (JAM.) Alledged, He was minor, and so *non tenetur placitare super hæreditate paterna.* Answered, The brocard meets not. 1785 ARNOT *Trials* (1812) 298. 1825 SCOTT *Betrothed* Introd., *Societas mater discordiarum* is a brocard as ancient and as veritable. 1862 M. NAPIER *Mem. Visct. Dundee* II. 10 *Dolus latet in generalibus* is a brocard of the civilians.

2. *gen.*

1836–7 SIR W. HAMILTON *Metaph.* xiii. I. 234 *note*, The scholastic brocard pointing to the difficulties of the study of self: *Reflexiva cogitatio facile fit deflexiva.* 1856 FERRIER *Inst. Metaph.* 261 The scholastic brocard, which has been adopted as the tenth counter-proposition, is the fundamental article in the creed of..'the sensualists'.

‖**3.** Biting speech, cutting gibe. (A French sense.)

1837 CARLYLE *Fr. Rev.* II. III. iii. 143 Lameth..is met in those Assembly corridors by nothing but Royalist *brocards*; sniffs, huffs, and open insults.

†**'brocard**[2]. *Obs.* [F. *brocart.*] = BROCKET.

1607 TOPSELL *Foure-f. Beastes* 122 These Brocards are as great in quantity as other vulgar Hartes, but their bodies are leaner. [1611 COTGR., *Brocart*, a kind of swift stag, which hath but one small branch growing out of the stemme of his horne.]

brocard[3], obs. form of BROCADE *sb.*

‖**brocatelle** (brɒkə'tɛl). Also 7 **brocatall,** 8 **brocatel(l.** [F. *brocatelle*, earlier *brocatel*, 'tinsell, or thin cloth of gold, or silver' (Cotgr.), ad. It. *broccatello*, 'thin tinsel of gold'; dim. of *broccato* (see BROCADE *sb.*).]

1. An imitation of brocade, usually made of silk or wool, used for tapestry, upholstery, etc., now also for dresses. Both the nature and the use of the stuff have changed in recent years. Also *attrib.*

1669 EVELYN *Diary* 9 July (D.) Chaire and deske.. cover'd with Brocatall..and cloth of gold. 1753 CHAMBERS *Cycl. Supp.*, *Brocatell*..an ordinary kind of stuff made of cotton, or coarse silk, in imitation of brocade; chiefly used for tapestry and other furniture. 1875 URE *Dict. Arts* I. 534 *Brocatelle.* Linsey-woolsey is so called in France. A silk material which is used for lining carriages. 1884 *Pall Mall G.* 14 Feb. 11/2 The garish charms of satin brocatelle, which has a crimson ground, with a gold border.

2. = next.

1756 NUGENT *Gr. Tour, France* IV. 44 Columns of antient Greek Brocatelle.

‖**brocatello** (ˌbrɒkə'tɛləʊ). Also **-tella, -telli.** [It. *brocatello de Sienna*, so called from its brocade-like colouring: see prec.] A kind of variegated marble, clouded and veined white, grey, yellow and red, yellow usually prevailing; Sienna marble.

1752 CHAMBERS *Cycl.* s.v. *Marble*, There is also another kind of antient Brocatella dug near Adrianople. 1839 *Penny Cycl.* XIV. 409/1 The beautiful Brocatello or Brocade marble of Italy and Spain. 1875 URE *Dict. Arts* I. 534 *Brocatelli Marble*, an artificial marble made from fragments of natural marbles united by means of an artificial cement.

broccoli, brocoli ('brɒkəlɪ). [a. It. *broccoli*, pl. of *broccolo* cabbage-sprout or top, dim. of *brocco* shoot or stalk (see BROACH).]

One of the cultivated forms of the cabbage (*Brassica oleracea botrytis asparagoides*), the young inflorescence of which forms a close fleshy edible head: in its origin a more robust and hardy variety of the cauliflower. Broccoli is distinguished as *green, purple*, and *white*, the last hardly distinguishable from cauliflower, except in being in season in winter or early spring.

1699 EVELYN *Acetaria* 16 The Broccoli from Naples. 1730–6 BAILEY, *Brocoli*, an Italian Plant of the Colly-Flower Kind. 1732 POPE *Hor. Sat.* II. ii. 138 Content with little, I

can piddle here On brocoli and mutton round the year. **1737** MILLER *Gard. Dict.* s.v. *Brassica*, There are several kinds, viz. the Roman, Neapolitan, and black Broccoli. **1881** *Proc. Berw. Nat. Club* IX. iii. 568 Winter vegetables, such as Celery, Brussel Sprouts, Brocoli.

b. *Comb.*, *broccoli-like* adj.

1873 FERGUSON in *Land of Moab* 376 That sharp brocoli-like acanthus, which distinguishes the age of Justinian.

†**broch**[1]. *Obs. rare.* [ad. F. *broc*, also *broche*, large jug: see Littré.] See quot.

1679 BLOUNT *Anc. Tenures* 51 One iron Broch, which was a great Pot or Jug to carry Liquid things.

broch[2], **brogh**, **brough.** *Archæol.* Forms: 7 brogh, 7–9 brugh, 8–9 brough, burg(h, 9 broch. [n.e. Scottish, a. ON. *borg* (Da. *borg*) castle, stronghold (the ON. equivalent of OE. *burh*: see BOROUGH, BURGH). (*Broch* is the spelling adopted by the Society of Antiquaries of Scotland. Variously pronounced (brox, brʌx).)]

A structure of prehistoric times, examples of which are numerous in the Orkney and Shetland Isles, and adjacent mainland of Scotland, being a sort of round tower, having an outer and an inner wall of dry stone, the interstitial space containing little chambers for human habitation, while the open central area might be used for cattle.

1654 *Blaeu's Atlas, Map of Orkney & Shetl.*, The ancient Brugh of Mousa. The Brugh of Byrsa. **1693** J. WALLACE *Description of Orkney* 26 The many Houses and villages in this Countey which are called by the name of *Brogh*. **1701** BRAND *Descr. Orkney* 18 (JAM.) These houses are also called Burghs. **1806** NEILL *Tour Orkney* 80 (JAM.) We viewed the Pechts Brough, or little circular fort. **1851** D. WILSON *Preh. Ann.* II. III. iii. 101 A class of structures peculiar to Scotland, generally known as Brughs or Pictish towers. **1883** *Academy* 6 Oct. 235 These Brochs..are towers that somewhat remind us of lighthouses.

broch, obs. form of BROACH, BROOCH.

brochad, brochage: see BROCADE *sb.*, BROKAGE.

‖**brochan** ('brɒxən). *Sc.* Also 8 **brachan, brochin.** [Gael. *brochan* porridge, gruel.] 'Oatmeal boiled to a consistence somewhat thicker than gruel' (Jamieson); thin porridge, drammock.

1700 KING *Transactioneer* 53 The usual remedy is Giben drank upon Brochan. **1716** MARTIN *West. Isles* 12 (JAM.) They drank brochan plentifully, which is oat-meal and water boiled together. **1790** PENNANT *Tour Scotl.* 358 Their common food is Brochan, a thick meal-pudding with milk. **1860** RAMSAY *Remin.* iii. (ed. 18) 59 Breeks and brochan.

brochantite ('brɒʃəntaɪt). [After *Brochant de Villiers*, a French mineralogist: see -ITE.] A mineral belonging to the hydrous sulphates, occurring in thin, rectangular, green crystals.

1865 *Athenæum* No. 1949. 316/2 Minerals of the Brochantite group. **1868** DANA *Min.* 665 Crystals of brochantite of a fine green color.

†**broche**, *v. Obs.* [Obs. spelling of BROACH *v.* (which does not appear with this sense) = F. *brocher* to stitch, brocade.] *trans.* To stitch, work with raised figures. Hence **broched** *ppl. a.*, worked with raised figures or designs in gold, silver, etc., on a ground of silk or satin; brocaded, embroidered.

1480 *Wardrobe Acc. Edw. IV* (1830) 134 Clothe of golde as well of the grounde of velvet as of satyn ground som broched with golde. *c* **1520** *Treatise of Gallant* (W. de W.) 22 Newe broched doublettes. **1601** HOLLAND *Pliny* I. 260 The cassock broched and studded with scarlet in broad guards. **1834** PLANCHÉ *Brit. Costume* 234 Broched or guarded with goldsmith's work.

‖**broché** ('brəʊʃeɪ, Fr. brɔʃe), *a.* [Fr., pa. pple. of *brocher* to stitch: see BROCHE *v.*] **1.** Of a material, esp. silk: woven with a pattern on the surface. Also *sb.*, a material of such a texture.

a **1877** KNIGHT *Dict. Mech.*, *Broché-goods*, goods embroidered or embossed. **1880** *Drapers' Jrnl.* 27 May 5/2 Bodice of broché front breadths. *Ibid.*, A chip hat to match the dark shade of broché. **1882** CAULFEILD & SAWARD *Dict. Needlework*, *Broché*, a French term denoting a velvet or silk textile, with a satin figure thrown up on the face. **1898** *Queen* 1 Jan. 31/2 Some silk crépon gauzes, rich brochés, and fancy velveteen.

2. Of an unbound or paper-covered book: stitched.

1889 in *Cent. Dict.* **1952** J. CARTER *ABC for Bk. Collectors* 127 A continental book in its original wrappers (*broché*).

‖**bro'chette.** [F. *brochette* (14th c. in Littré), dim. of *broche*, BROACH.]

1. ? *Obs.***a.** A small broach, spit, or pointed stick. **b.** in *Cookery*: see quot. 1706.

1483 CAXTON *Gold. Leg.* 363/4 Thyrten knottes which were ful of brochettes of smale nedles and theron smale rynges. **1706** PHILLIPS *Brochette*, a Skewer to stick in Meat. In *Cookery* a particular manner of frying and stewing Chickens, etc. **1730–6** in BAILEY. **1756** *Dict. of Arts and Sci.* s.v. *Bell*, You must come again to the first face of the brochette or stick A.

2. A pin or bar used to fasten medals, orders, etc., to the coat or uniform of the wearer.

1849 THACKERAY *Pendennis* I. xxvi. 255 He wore three little gold crosses in a brochette on the portly breast of his blue coat. **1896** *Daily News* 5 Mar. 7/5 M. Faure wore his brochette of Russian Orders.

†**'brochity.** *Obs. rare*⁻⁰. [ad. L. *broc(c)hitas* projectingness of the teeth, f. *broc(c)hus*: see BROACH.] (See quots.)

1623 COCKERAM I, *Brochitie*, crookednesse. **1656** BLOUNT *Glossogr.*, *Brochity* (*brochitas*), crookedness properly of teeth or tushes. **1678** PHILLIPS, *Brochity* (old word), crookedness, especially of Teeth. So BAILEY, etc.

brochure (brɔʃyr, 'brəʊʃjʊə(r), -ʃə(r)). [Fr.; lit. 'a stitched work', f. *brocher* to stitch: see -URE.] A short printed work, of a few leaves merely stitched together; a pamphlet. Also, *spec.* a small pamphlet or booklet describing the amenities of a place, etc.

1765 CHESTERF. *Lett.* 387 (1792) IV. 214 Monsieur de Vergy published in a *brochure* a parcel of letters. **1840** *Times* 28 Apr., His present brochure is interesting from the subject of which it treats. **1865** *Q. Rev.* Apr. 345 His series of editions was accompanied by a bye-play of brochures, grammatical or critical, written in the intervals of press-labour. **1882** *Ch. Q. Rev.* Oct. 40 The famous brochure of Dr. Drake called The Memorial of the Church of England. **1925** *Brit. Hotels* (E. J. Burrow & Co.) 136/2 Torquay, Allerdale Hotel. Situated in own spacious grounds... Write for illustrated brochure (inclusive terms). **1935** *Punch* 10 July 36/2 Innumerable hotels in England offer to send me an 'Illustrated Brochure on request'. **1963** V. NABOKOV *Gift* v. 316 The sun's impact restores the deficiency..and the brazen body no longer experiences shame. All this sounds like a nudist brochure.

brock (brɒk), *sb.*[1] Chiefly *dial.* Forms: 1, 4 broc, 3–7 brocke, 4–5 brokk(e, 4–6 brok, 6 broke, 3– brock. [OE. *broc*, from Celtic: in OIr. *brocc*, Ir. and Gael. *broc*, Welsh and Cornish *broch*, Breton *broc'h*:—OCeltic **broccos*, prob. cogn. w. Gr. φορκός grey, white; cf. the Eng. name *gray*, *grey*.]

1. A badger: a name, in later times, associated especially with the epithet *stinking*.

c **1000** *Sax. Leechd.* I. 326 Sum fyþerfete nyten is, þæt nemnað taxonem, þæt ys broc on englisc. *c* **1205** LAY. 12817 Heo hudeden heom alse brockes. **1398** TREVISA *Barth. De P.R.* (Helmingham MS.) XII. x, The blak rauen is frende to þe foxe, and þerfore he fyȝteþ with þe brokke. *c* **1400** *Ywaine & Gaw.* 98 It es ful semeli, als me think, A brok omang men forto stynk. *c* **1440** *York Myst.* xxix. 117 He lokis like a brokke, Were he in a bande for to bayte. *a* **1528** SKELTON *Agst. Garnesche* 55 She seyd your brethe stank lyke a broke. **1552** HULOET, Brocke or badger, or graye beast, *taxo*. **1637** B. JONSON *Sad Sheph.* I. iv. 32 Or with pretence of chasing thence the Brock, Send in a curre to worrie the whole Flock. **1786** BURNS *Twa Dogs* 96 They gang as saucy by poor folk, As I wad by a stinking brock. **1816** SCOTT *Antiq.* xxi, 'I..rub shouthers wi' a bailie wi' as little concern as an he were a brock'. **1869** *Daily News* 30 July, Purses, made of a fox's head and skin, or that of a brock.

†**b.** *catachr.* confused with the beaver. *Obs.*

1387 TREVISA *Higden* Rolls Ser. I. 327 White beres, bausons, and brokkes [*ursi albi, fibri, et castores*]. *Ibid.* VI. 205 þat place hatte Beverlay and heet Brook his lay, for many brokkes..come þider out of þe hilles. **1483** *Cath. Angl.* 44 A Brokk, *castor, beuer*. **1591** PERCIVALL *Sp. Dict.*, *Bivaro*, a badger or brocke, *fiber*, *castor*.

2. A stinking or dirty fellow; one who is given to 'dirty tricks'; a 'skunk'.

a **1600** PEELE *Jests* II. 289 This self-conceited brock. **1601** SHAKS. *Twel. N.* II. v. 114 Marrie, hang thee, brocke. **1725** RAMSAY *Gent. Sheph.* IV. i, Ye'll gar me stand! ye shevelling-gabbit brock. **1880** *Antrim & Down Gloss.* (E.D.S.), *Brock*, a dirty person; one who has a bad smell.

3. *Attrib.* and *Comb.*, as *brock-breasted*, *-faced* adjs. (referring to the streaked face of the badger); †**brock-skin**, a badger-skin (in Wyclif app. due to confusion of L. *mēles*, *mēlis*, with *mēlōta* Gr. μηλωτή sheepskin, f. μῆλον); †**brock-wool**, hair of the beaver (see 1 b.).

? *a* **1400** *Morte Arth.* 1095 *Brok-brestede as a brawne, with brustils fulle large. **1824** *Craven Dial.* 22 Th' *brock-faced branded stirk. **1382** WYCLIF *Hebr.* xi. 37 Thei wenten aboute in *brok skynnes [Vulg. *in melotis*], and in skynnes of geet. **1526** *Pilgr. Perf.* (W. de W. 1531) 246 b, Goynge about in gotes & brockes skynnes. **1500** *Ort. Voc.* in *Promp. Parv.* 53 *Fibrina vestis*..a clothe of *brocke woll.

brock, *sb.*[2] *dial.* [OE. *broc*; cf. ON. *brokkr* 'a trotter, of a horse' Vigf.] ? A horse, a trotting horse; an inferior horse, a jade.

c **1000** *Sax. Leechd.* II. 184 Secen him broc on onrade. *c* **1386** CHAUCER *Friar's T.* 243 The Cartere smoot and cryde ..Hayt Brok, hayt Scot, what spare ye for the stones. **1586** WARNER *Alb. Eng.* II. x. 47 She stumbled headlong downe.. hoyst Brock, her good-man saide; And thirdly falling, kindly bad her breake her necke, olde Iade. **1847–78** HALLIWELL, *Brock*, a cow, or husbandry horse.

brock, *sb.*[3] *dial.* [Of uncertain origin: possibly a corruption of L. *brūcus*, *brūchus*: see BRUKE. The two senses may have no connexion.]

†**1.** ? = L. *ophiomachus* (Vulg. *Lev.* xi. 22), a kind of locust: cf. BRUKE. Only OE.

c **1050** *Ags. Voc.* in Wr.-Wülcker 460 *Ophiomachus*, broc.

2. The larva of the frog-hopper, which produces the cuckoo-spit; also the insect itself. *mod. dial.*

1788 MARSHALL *E. Yorks.* (E.D.S.), *Brock*, a young grasshopper [2nd ed. 1796 substitutes '*cicada spumaria*, the cuckowspit insect']. 'He sweats like a brock!' **1875** ROBINSON *Whitby Gloss.* (E.D.S.), *Brock*, the cuckoo-spit, 'sweating insect', or frog-hopper, the 'cicada spumata', found upon leaves in an immersion of froth. **1877** in *Holderness Gloss.* (E.D.S.).

brock, *sb.*[4] ? *Obs.* [contr. of *brocket.*] = BROCKET.

c **1515** *Berkeley Castle, MS. Forester's Acc.*, Item a brocke at ffrantonys parke. **1677** N. COX *Gentl. Recreation* I. (1706) 6, I..must call a Hart..The third year, a Brocke. **1781** SMELLIE tr. *Buffon's Nat. Hist.* IV. 87 They take the name of knobbers till their horns lengthen into spears, and then they are called brocks or staggards. **1884** JEFFERIES *Red Deer* ii. 39 In the olden time he would have been called a brocke or brocket.

brock, *sb.*[5] (See quot.)

1770 HASTED in *Phil. Trans.* LXI. 164 In the ancient forests of Kent..remain large old chesnut stubs or brocks.

†**brock**, *v. Obs. rare.* [Identified by Mätzner with OHG. *brochôn*, mod.G. *brocken* to break into bits, crumble (bread into milk), used in Swiss in sense 'to use coarse words': but the sense-history is obscure.] *app.* To give mouth, speak querulously (*perhaps* to utter broken language).

c **1315** SHOREH. 106 Aȝe the crokkere to brokke, Wy madest thou me so. *c* **1386** CHAUCER *Millers T.* 191 He syngeth brokkynge [*so 6 texts, Harl.* crowyng] as a nyghtyngale.

brock, dial. var. of BROKE, a fragment.

brockage ('brɒkɪdʒ). [? from stem of *brok-en* + -AGE.]

1. A damaged piece in coining money, etc.

1879 *10th Rep. Master of Mint* (1880) 38 The reduced number of brockages or faulty pieces produced.

2. *Sc.* Broken or damaged stuff; broken pottery, glass, biscuits, etc.

Mod. Sc. In making these, there is always a good deal of brockage.

brocked, *a. Sc.* Also **broakit, brockit.** [Cf. Da. *broget* variegated, speckled, chequered, Sw. *brokt*, also *brokig* variegated.] 'Variegated, having a mixture of black and white' (Jamieson).

1793 *Statist. Acc. Scot.* VI. 285 (JAM.) The greatest part of them [sheep]..having black or brocked faces. **17..** *Gl. Surv. Nairn* (JAM.), The phrase, brocked oats, denotes the black and white growing promiscuously. **1818** SCOTT *Hrt. Midl.* xxxix, If Gowans, the brockit cow, has a quey.

Brocken ('brɒk(ə)n). The name of the highest of the Harz Mountains in Saxony, reputed to be the scene of witches' Walpurgis-night revels. Applied *attrib.* to a magnified shadow of the spectator thrown on a bank of cloud in high mountains when the sun is low and often encircled by rainbow-like bands (first observed on the Brocken). Also applied to a dramatic representation of the Walpurgis-night revels, and *transf.*

1801 [see SPECTRE *sb.* 3]. **1844** E. B. BROWNING *Poems* II. 45 Waved backwards (as a wind might wave a Brocken mist, and with as brave Wild roaring). **1860** [see SPIRIT *sb.* 3 *transf.*]. **1888** G. B. SHAW *How to become Mus. Critic* (1960) 136 The Brocken business, which is musically and scenically childish. **1924** —— *St. Joan* Pref. p. xvii, Brocken spectres, echoes and the like. **1951** L. MACNEICE tr. *Goethe's Faust* II. II. 202, I could essay many a Brocken-stunt But heathendom seems barred on every front. **1962** *Listener* 11 Jan. 68/1 We may conceive the divine either as an abstract entity..or else as a Brocken-spectre projection of humanity.

brocket ('brɒkɪt). Forms: 5–7 broket, 7 brockett, brochet, 6– brocket. [ad. F. *brocart*, *broquart*, f. *broque*, *broche* BROACH: see -ARD. Cf. BROCARD[2].]

1. A stag in its second year with its first horns, which are straight and single, like a small dagger. (Sometimes incorrectly a deer in its third year.)

a **1425** in *Rel. Antiq.* I. 151 The hert..the fyrst yere he is a calfe, the secunde yere a broket, the .iij. yere a spayer. **1513** DOUGLAS *Æneis* XII. Prol. 179 Heyrdis of hertis throw the thyk wod schaw, Baith the brokettis, and with brayd burnyst tyndis. **1611** COTGR., *Brocart*, a two-yeare old Deere; which if he bee a red Deere, we call a Brocket; if a fallow, a Pricket. **1881** GREENER *Gun* 510 To shoot a staggart, brocket, suckling, hind or calf is unwarrantable.

2. A genus of deer of Brazil, having only short prongs for horns.

1837 *Penny Cycl.* VIII. 361/2 The Brockets (*Les Daguets*) of the French. **1850** SWAINSON *Quadrup.* § 301 The brockets of the New World constitute the subulonine group of Major Smith.

†**3. brocket-sister**, a female deer of the second (or erron. third) year. *Obs.*

1625 in Rushw. *Hist. Coll.* (1721) III. II. App. 8 A Hind and a Brocket Suster, being then both out of Season. **1677** N. COX *Gentl. Recreations* I. (1706) 7 A Hinde..is called.. the second year a Hearse; and sometimes we say Brockets Sister. **1696** PHILLIPS s.v. *Brock*.

4. *dial.* See quots. (Probably a distinct word.)

1769 PENNANT *Tour Scotl.* 36 Sea-larks, [called] here [Farne Islands] brokets. **1867** SMYTH *Sailor's Word-bk.*, *Broket*..the sea-lark is so called at the Farne Islands.

brockett, obs. form of BRACKET *sb.*

†**'brockish**, *a. Obs. rare.* [f. BROCK *sb.*[1] (2) + -ISH.] Like a brock or badger; beastly, dirty.

1546 BALE *Eng. Votaries* I. (1550) 8 b, Those brockish boores haue gone frely foreward without checke. **1550** ——

Apol. 64 O brockyshe Gomorreane! **1553** —— *Vocacyon* in *Harl. Misc.* (Malh.) I. 351 So brockish a swine as he was.

† 'brockle, brokle, *a. Obs.* exc. *dial.* Forms: 4 brokele, 5 brokyl(l, -ylle, -el, -il, 6 brokle, brocle. [A parallel form to BRICKLE, BRUCKLE; prob. by later assimilation to *brok-en*.] Easily broken, fragile; frail.

c **1315** SHOREHAM 3 Of brokele kende is that he deithe. *c* **1325** *Metr. Hom.* 154 Fleys es brokel als wax, and neys. *c* **1430** *Hymns to Virg.* (1867) 86 A brokil poot þat freisch is and gay. **1483** *Cath. Angl.* 44 Brokylle, *vbi* brysille. **1509** FISHER *Wks.* 92 A potte that is brocle. **1552** HULOET, Bryttle, bryckle, or brokle. **1863** ATKINSON *Provinc. Danby, Bruckle, brockle*, easy to be broken, frail, brittle.

† 'brockle, *sb. Obs.* exc. *dial.* Forms: 6 brokkell, brockell, 8 brackle. [cf. prec., and BROKALY.] *collect.* Broken pieces, fragments; rubbish.

1552 HULOET s.v. *Throw*, Throw out rubbel, as mortar, stone, and such lyke brockell of olde buyldynges, *erudero.* —— s.v. *Rubbysh*, or brokkell of olde houses, or walles. **1710** A. J. *Eng. Portug. Dict.*, To carry away rubble or brackle of an old decayed house.

'brockram. *dial.* [f. stem of *brok-en*: the ending appears to have a collective force.] 'A Cumberland miners' term for a breccia' (Ure).

1855 J. PHILLIPS *Man. Geol.* 651 The word [Breccia] is Italian, and is matched by the Cumbrian term 'Brockram'. **1878** F. WILLIAMS *Midl. Railw.* 523 Not a bit of rock was found. The limestone rock and the brockram were gone.

Brock's benefit. *colloq.* [f. the name of C. T. *Brock*, maker of fireworks + BENEFIT *sb.* 4 a.] From the spectacular display of fireworks held annually at the Crystal Palace from 1865 to 1936: (*a*) fireworks; (*b*) a brilliant illumination at night, esp. in war, from searchlights, flares, artillery, etc.; (*c*) *fig.* any comparable outburst (of excitement, etc.).

1920 P. GIBBS *Realities of War* IV. vii. 188 They.. opened such a Brock's benefit that the enemy must have been shocked with surprise. **1921** 'IAN HAY' *Willing Horse* ix. 159 The Germans were furnished with bombs which exploded on impact; ours were of the Brock's Benefit type, and had to be lit with a match. **1929** *Melody Maker* Jan. 19/1 The engines puff out.., a regular Brock's Benefit of sparks. **1930** BLUNDEN *Poems* 173 Thence *Brock's Benefit* commanded endless fireworks by two nations. **1942** *New Statesman* 19 Sept. 186/2 The searchlights and anti-aircraft fire and bursting bombs are collectively referred to as.. *Brock's benefit.* **1948** *Economist* 26 June 1060 The third reading of the Representation of the People Bill produced a regular Brock's benefit of insults and expletives. **1957** *Sunday Times* 20 Oct. 13/3 The whole of the southern flank.. opened up and it looked like a real Brock's Benefit.

brocor, -our, obs. ff. BROKER.

brod (brɒd), *sb.*[1] *Obs.* exc. *dial.* Also 3 brodd, 5 brode. See also BRAD. [ME., app. a. ON. *brodd-r* spike, shaft, spike on a plant, = OE. *brord* spike, point, spire, OHG. *brort* edge, margin (cf. BRAIRD, BRERD), Goth. **brozds*:—OTeut. **brozdo-z.* There was a cognate OCeltic *brott-*, whence OIr. *brot* sting, prick, mod.Ir. and Gael. *brod*, which may be the source of some of the senses. Almost exclusively northern, and mainly Scotch. Cf. PROD.]

†**1.** A shoot or sprout. *rare.* [cf. BRAIRD.]

c **1200** ORMIN 10772 Nazaræþ bitacneþþ uss Onn Ennglissh brodd & blome. [Cf. Heb. *nêtser* shoot.]

2. A goad, prick, pointed instrument.

c **1375** ? BARBOUR *St. Paulus* 543 Saule, Saule.. it is.. hard to þe A-gane þe brod þe for to prese. *c* **1425** WYNTOUN *Cron.* VI. xiv. 70 Gyve a man wald in thame thryst A scharpe brode. **1483** *Cath. Angl.* 44 A Brod, *aculeus, stimulus, stiga.* **1548** UDALL, etc. *Erasm. Par. John* x. 75 Roddes, axes, broddes to pricke. **1661** BP. COSIN *Corr.* (Surtees) II. 311 For brod [*note*, or spit] paper at the Stationer's for the cooke. **1721** KELLY *Sc. Prov.* 168 (JAM.) He was never a good aver, that flung at the brod.

b. *fig.* An incentive, stimulus, motive.

c **1375** ? BARBOUR *St. Agnes* 370 þe wikit geste Fandit hyme.. Vith þe brodis of lichery. **1536** BELLENDEN *Cron. Scot.* II. 122 Ire and lust, quhilkis ar two maist sorrowful broddis amang wemen.

3. A prick from a goad; a PROD.

1549 *Compl. Scot.* iii. 28 Ane ox that repungnis the brod of his hird, he gettis doubil broddis.

†**4.** A prickle or thorn. *Obs. rare.*

1549 *Compl. Scot.* xvii. 148 The palme tre hes schearp broddis and pikis.

5. a. A round-headed nail made by blacksmiths. **b.** An instrument for cutting up thistles. Peacock *N.W. Linc. Gloss.*

brod, *sb.*[2] A Scotch (brɔd) variant of BOARD (see senses 1–4). Also, an escutcheon (*obs.*).

1643 *Acts Ass.* 171 (JAM.) Abuses in hinging of pensils and brods, affixing of honours and arms,—hath crept in. **1861** RAMSAY *Remin.* Ser. II. 26 As he went round with the ladle, he used to remind such members of the congregation as seemed backward in their duty, by giving them a poke with the 'brod'.

brod, *v. Obs.* exc. *dial.* [f. BROD *sb.*[1]]

†**1.** *intr.* To shoot, sprout. *Obs.*

c **1200** ORMIN 10769 To broddenn & to blomenn.

2. *trans.* To goad, prod, urge with pricks. *north. dial.* Also *fig.*

c **1450** HENRYSON *Mor. Fabl.* 73 The caller.. broded them ful sair. **1483** *Cath. Angl.* 44 To Brod, *stimulare.* **1535** STEWART *Cron. Scot.* III. 28 The stang of conscience broddit him so soir. *a* **1568** *Wife of Auchterm.*, And brodit his buttock. **1566** DRANT *Horace Sat.* v, A tyraunte forces the, and broaddes the forwarde still. **1789** R. FERGUSSON *Poems* II. 82 (JAM.) His words they brodit like a wumil, Frae ear to ear. **1877** PEACOCK *N.W. Linc. Gloss.*, *Brod*, to prick, to poke; to cut up thistles.

brod(e, obs. f. BROAD, BROOD.

brodder ('brɒdə(r)). *Sc.* and *north.* [f. BROD *v.* + -ER[1].] One who brods or uses a brod; ***rug-brodder*** (see quot. 1921).

1877 *Covenant Times* 200 This torture consisted in the free use of the 'brodder's' needles. **1885** W. ROSS *Aberdour & Inchcolme* xi. 328 'Who,' you say, 'was the Brodder?'.. His office was to settle the question, whether those accused of being witches were so or not.. by searching for the 'devil's mark' on their bodies, by 'brodding' or pricking it with a sharp needle. **1921** *Dict. Occup. Terms* (1927) §398 *Rug brodder* (Yorks. term).. makes rugs, by hand, on a canvas ground, by piercing canvas with an awl and inserting cloth cuttings.

brode, incorrect form of BRAID (sense 2).

c **1400** *Epiph.* (Turnb. 1843) 79 Ho had unnethe thes wordis sayde Bot ho yelde the gost in a brode.

brodefull: see BROODFUL.

[brodehal(f)pen(n)y: see BURGHALPENNY.]

brodel, -elle, var. of BROTHEL.

brodequin. Also 5 brodkyne, 6 brotekin, -ikin, 7 brodkin, 8 brodekin. [a. F. *brodequin* (15th c. in Littré), (for which Du Guez *c* 1532 has *brousequin*) related to Flem. *brosekin, broseken* (Kilian) buskin, also to It. *borzacchino*, Sp. *borceguí*, formerly also *boszeguí* buskin: the inter-relations of which are as yet uncertain. The mod.Du. *broos*, formerly *brôze* buskin, is according to Franck probably shortened from *broseken.* See BUSKIN.]

A high boot reaching about half-way up the calves of the legs; a buskin. Also *attrib.*

1481–90 *Howard Househ. Bks.* (1844) 345 My Lord paid for a peyer of brodkynes.. *xd.* **1535** LYNDESAY *Satyre* 3143, I can make schone, brotekins and buittis. *c* **1565** LINDESAY (Pitscottie) *Chron.* (1728) 111 A pair of brotikins on his feet to the great of his legs. **1653** URQUHART *Rabelais* II. xv, How wouldest thou defend thyself? With great buskinades or brodkin blowes.. provided thursts were forbidden. **1725** ECHARD *Hist. Eng.* II. 836 (L.) Instead of shoes and stockings, a pair of buskins or brodekins. *c* **1845** C. BRONTË *Professor* (1857) I. x. 159 Trim Parisian brodequins showed her.. feet, to complete advantage. **1850** THACKERAY *Pendennis* xxiii, From their bonnets to their brodequins. **1886** M. F. SHELDON tr. *Flaubert's Salammbô* vii. 184 He soiled his purple brodequins.

broder, -ir, -yr, obs. forms of BROTHER.

broder, -re, -ur, etc., obs. ff. BROIDER *v.*, etc.

'broderer. Also 4–5 brouderer. An earlier form of BROIDERER, retained as the name of one of the London City Companies, ranking as 34th among the City Livery Guilds.

1376 *Lett. Bk.* H. lf. xlvii. in *City Records, 50 Edw. III*, Nicholas Halley, Robert Ascombe, Brouderers. **1388** WYCLIF *Exod.* xxviii. 39 Werk of a brodere. **1398** *Test. Ebor.* (1836) I. 227 Mon vestment.. lequele je achatay de Courceray brouderer de Londres. **1488–9** *Act 4 Hen. VII*, xxii, The Wardeyn and felishipp of brouderers in your Cite of London. **1865** *Blue Bk. City of Lond. & Liv. Comp. Commission* v. 67 The Keeper or Warden and Society of the art or mistery of Broderers of the City of London. *Ibid.* The Broderers Company were known by the name of 'Imbroiderers incorporate for ever'.

‖broderie anglaise (brɔdri ɑ̃glɛz, brəʊdri: ɑ̃gleɪz). [Fr., = English embroidery.] Open embroidery on linen, cambric, etc. Also ellipt., *broderie.*

1852 *Illustr. Lond. News* 26 June 504/2 The *pardessus*,.. trimmed with *broderie Anglaise.* **1882** CAULFEILD & SAWARD *Dict. Needlework* s.v., True broderie Anglaise patterns are outlines of various sized holes, arranged so as to make floral or geometrical devices. **1905** *Westm. Gaz.* 11 May 4/2, I am perfectly charmed with these embroidered lawn and Broderie Anglaise petticoats. **1907** *Daily Chron.* 25 June 8/2 Coats in Broderie Anglaise... A plain full skirt.. finished at the hem with a band of the broderie. **1955** *Times* 8 July 10/4 The bride.. wore a gown of organdie and *broderie anglaise* and a tulle veil. **1963** *Times* 17 Jan. 12/2 Long white cotton dresses with *broderie* frills. *Ibid.*, They had *broderie anglaise* headdresses.

brodinstare, -er: see BROWDINSTER.

brodly, variant of BROTHELY, *Obs.*, fierce.

† brodmell. *Obs. Sc.* [Of doubtful origin: the form suggests *brode*, BROOD, and **mell* 'mixture, confused company', f. MELL *v.* to mix.] A litter.

1513 DOUGLAS *Æneis* III. vi. 73 All quhite brodmell About hir pappis sowkin. *Ibid.* VIII. i. 98 Hyr quhyt brodmell about hir pappis wound.

Brodrick ('brɒdrɪk). The name of the Secretary of State for War (1900–3), the Rt. Hon. W. St. J. *Brodrick*, afterwards Viscount Midleton, applied facetiously to: **a.** a soldier enlisted under the lower standard of physique introduced under his régime; more explicitly ***little Brodrick***; **b.** an army cap invented and introduced by him.

1903 *Westm. Gaz.* 19 Mar. 8/1 'Brodricks' in South Africa. **1903** *Daily Chron.* 17 Sept. 7/2 There were comparatively few so-called 'Little Brodricks' in these sturdy line battalions of the 1st Army Corps. **1905** *Westm. Gaz.* 25 May 8/2 The other half in undress uniform, with.. its fatigue jackets, its 'Brodrick' caps, and riding whips. **1915** A. D. GILLESPIE *Lett. from Flanders* (1916) 74 The soft 'Gor' bli'me' hat.. does not give such a mark as the flat-topped 'Brodrick'. **1960** E. WAUGH in *Spectator* 15 July 95/3 The officials.. wore khaki service dress and Brodrick caps.

† brodyke. *Obs. rare*[−1]. [perh. an error of some kind for *brodde.*] A prick, a goad.

1471 RIPLEY *Comp. Alch.* in Ashm. (1652) 132 Hard hyt ys with thy bare foote to spurne, Agaynst a brodyke of Iyron.

broe, variant of BROO, *Sc.*, broth.

† broft. *Obs.* Unusual form of *brocht*, BROUGHT.

1594 CAREW *Tasso* (1881) 57 Him it foretels, and scornes, nor will be broft [*rime-word* soft] To bend.

brog (brɒg), *sb. dial.* [Of uncertain origin. (Sc. also brɔg, brog) the Gaelic *brog* 'awl', must, according to Thurneysen, be an adopted word.]

1. A pricking or boring instrument: the common name in Scotland of a bradawl; also, an awl.

1808 in JAMIESON. **1861** RAMSAY *Remin.* Ser. II. 59 But oh, please tak a brog, and prod him weel, and let the wind out o' him.

2. A prick with a bradawl, etc.

1808 in JAMIESON.

3. A short stick, *esp.* one to stick in the ground; e.g. those stuck in the 'Sands' of North Lancashire, to indicate the crossing.

1781 J. HUTTON *Tour Caves* (E.D.S.) *Brogs*, small sticks. **1870** BARBER *Forness Folk* 35 in *Lanc. Gloss.* (E.D.S.) We'd gitten by t' last brog an' off t' sand. **1875** *Lanc. Gloss.*, *Brog*, a branch, a bough, a broken branch.

brog (brɒg), *v. dial.* [f. prec.]

1. *trans.* To prick, prod; to push an awl *through.*

a **1774** FERGUSSON *Election* Poems (1845) 42 Wi a muckle elshin lang He brogit Maggie's hurdies. **1818** SCOTT *Hrt. Midl.* v, 'D'ye think I was born to sit here brogging an elshin through bend-leather?' **1820** —— *Monast.* iii, 'The stony-hearted villains were brogging them on wi' their lances!'

2. To insert pointed sticks into; see quot. *dial.*

1875 *Lanc. Gloss.* (E.D.S.) 58 After obtaining a safe ford, the guides.. mark out the track by inserting branches of trees. This is called 'broggin' t' channel'.

3. *intr.* To BROGGLE for eels, to sniggle. *dial.*

1678 LITTLETON *Lat. Dict.*, To broge for Eels. **1706** PHILLIPS, *Brogue* or *Broggle*, to fish for Eels, after a particular manner, by troubling the Water. *c* **1750** J. COLLIER (Tim Bobbin) *Wks.* Gloss. s.v. *Brog*, Fishing for eels, called brogging.. by putting the hook and worm on a small stick, and thrusting it into holes where the eels lye.

Hence ***brogged staff*** (Sc.): a pointed or spiked staff as a weapon of war.

1429 *Sc. Acts Jas. I* (1597) §121 With sworde and buckler, and a gude axe, or else a brogged staffe. *a* **1550** *Peebles to Play* 9 He stert till ane broggit staff, Winchand as he were wood.

‖brogan ('brəʊgən). [Ir. and Gael. *brògan*, dim. of *bròg* shoe.] A coarse stout sort of shoe.

1846 in WORCESTER. **1864** *Morning Star* 19 Jan., Boots.. are now [during American War] only to be had for 175 dollars to 250 dollars per pair, whilst the commonest brogans bring from 30 dollars to 40 dollars per pair.

† brogetie. *Obs.* Some kind of fabric.

1610 *Histrio-m.* III. 274 What bladders swolne with pride, To strout in shreds of nitty brogetie!

† 'brogger. *Obs.* Also 5 brager, bragger, 7 broger, broggar. [App. an unexplained corruption of BROKER. Anglo-French had also *broggour* beside *brocour.* Cf. also *brogge*, BROGUE *sb.*[1]] An agent; a jobber, *esp.* a corrupt jobber of offices; a BROKER.

[**1386** *Act 10 Rich. II*, i. §2 Officers & Ministres faitz par brogage & de lour broggors & de ceux qont prise le brogage.] *c* **1460** FORTESCUE *Abs. & Lim. Mon.* xvii. (1875) 153 No man.. durst take an office.. but he ffirst had þe good will off þe said bragers [*MS.* 1532 broggers; *ed.* 1714, broggars] and engrossers of offices. **1533–4** *Act 25 Hen. VIII*, i, Euery.. grasier, fermour, breder, drouer, and brogger.. whiche.. shall haue any beoffes. **1550** *Rem. Edw. VI, Jrnl.* (Roxb.) 293 That no man shuld bie or sel the self-same thinges againe, except broggers. **1587** FLEMING *Contn. Holinshed* III. 1588/2 Broggers, and carriers of corne. **1641** BAKER *Chron.* (1679) 391/2 Broggers of Corn and Forestallers of Markets. **1682** SCARLETT *Exchanges* 8 Brogers, etc. are Persons Sworn and Authorized by the Magistrate.. to enquire of Persons that have any Monyes to remit or to draw, and to agree such persons concerning the Conditions. **1720** *Stow's Surv.* (1754) II. v. xv. 329/1 They were called Broggers in a Statute 10 Richard II—none to be Brocars in any mystery unless chosen by the same mystery.

bröggerite ('brœgəraɪt). *Min.* [ad. Sw. *bröggerit* (C. W. Blomstrand 1884, in *Geol. För. i Stockholm Förh.* VII. II. 66), f. the name of Waldemar Christopher *Brögger* (1851–1940),

Norwegian mineralogist and geologist + -ITE¹.] A thorian variety of uraninite.

1884 *Jrnl. Chem. Soc.* XLVI. 1102 The mineral, which has been named bröggerite by the author [*sc.* Blomstrand], is closely related to cleveite. **1901** *Ibid.* LXXX. II. 396 The specimen of bröggerite..from which radioactive lead was obtained..had a hardness 5·5 and a sp. gr. 9·06 at 15°. **1951** J. R. PARTINGTON *Gen. & Inorg. Chem.* (ed. 2) xxvi. 759 Cleveite and bröggerite are varieties richer in thorium and rare earths.

† **'brogging**, *vbl. sb. Obs.* = BROKING.

1592 CHETTLE *Kinde Harts Dr.* (1841) 51 There is an occupation of no long standing about London, called broking, or brogging, whether ye will; in which there is pretty jugling, especially to blind law, and bolster usury.

broggle ('brɒg(ə)l), *v. north. dial.* Also 7 braggle. [app. a frequentative f. BROG *v.*] *intr.* To continue poking with a stick or pointed instrument in a hole; also *spec.* to fish for eels, by thrusting a stick with a baited hook into the holes, and under the stones where they lie. Hence **'broggling**, also called *sniggling*.

1653 W. LAWSON *Comm. Secr. Angling* in Arb. *Garner* I. 195 A way to catch Eels by 'Braggling'..Go into some shallow place of the river among the great stones, and braggle up and down till you find holes under the stones. **1678** PHILLIPS (*App.*), *Brogle* for Eels, to fish for Eels. **1681** CHETHAM *Angler's Vade-m.* xxii. §5 (1689) 146 Brogling or Snigling. **1792** OSBALDISTONE *Brit. Sportsm.* 78/2 *Brogling*, a method of fishing for eels.

brogh, variant of BROCH, a Pictish tower.

† **brogue** (bro:g), *sb.*¹ *Obs.* exc. *Sc.* Also 6 brogge, 8 brougue. [Deriv. unknown. Cf. BROGGER.] An escheat; a cheat, fraud, trick.

1537 *St. Papers Hen. VIII*, I. 548 Ne any brogges or meanes that any of those borderers canne make, shall cause Us to altre that which We have established. **1634** JACKSON *Creed* VII. xxvii, The sacred treasury (unto which such brogues or escheats as this were by ordinary course due). **1784** BURNS *Addr. Deil* xvi, Ye [Satan] came to Paradise incog, An' play'd on man a cursed brogue. **1791** *Ep. J. Priestley* in *Poet. Register* (1808) 401 Then..[they] strive Who first a bargain with their Queen shall drive. While no mean lure her beckoning hand displays, The well-known royal brougues of better days.

brogue (brəʊg), *sb.*² Also 6 brog, 7 brouge, 7–8 broge. [a. Irish and Gael. *brōg* 'shoe, brogue, sandal' (O'Reilly):—OIr. *brōce* shoe, app.:—OCelt. *brācca*: see BREECH.

(The phonetic series *brācca, brōce, brōg*, is normal. But the sense-history is difficult: the word has in Ir. and Gael., and had even in OIr., only sense 1. Sense 2 looks as if Englishmen had confounded the Ir. *bróg* with the *mogan*, a kind of legging, covering the whole leg as well as the upper surface of the foot. Yet the etymological identity of *brōcc* with Gaulish *brācca*, would point to a covering for the legs ('barbara tegmina crurum') originally. The sense of the first quot. is doubtful.)]

1. a. A rude kind of shoe, generally made of untanned hide, worn by the inhabitants of the wilder parts of Ireland and the Scotch Highlands.

1586 J. HOOKER *Girald. Irel.* in *Holinsh.* II. 160/1 He was no sooner come home, but awaie with his English attires, and on with his brogs, his shirt, and other Irish rags. **1610** HOLLAND *Camden's Brit.* I. 123 They buckle upon their feet a pair of Broges made of raw and untanned leather up to their ankles. **1611** SHAKS. *Cymb.* IV. ii. 214, I thought, he slept, and put My clowted Brogues from off my feet. **1775** JOHNSON *Journ. West. Isl.* (1806) IX. 191 In Sky I first observed the use of brogues, a kind of artless Shoes. **1848** MACAULAY *Hist. Eng.* II. 142 Some had been so used to wear brogues that they stumbled and shuffled about strangely in their military jack boots. **1865** MAFFEI *Brigand Life* I. 258 Rough, heavy brogues which hurt our feet.

b. In full ***brogue shoe***. A strong shoe for country and sports wear, having characteristic bands of ornamental perforations.

1906 HASLUCK *Boot & Shoe Pattern Cutting* 57 Brogue Shoes.—The gentleman's brogue is always a strong shoe for shooting, golf, fishing, etc. The wing of the vamp and cap are longer..than for a lady's brogue. **1917** *Mod. Boot & Shoe Maker* III. 234 Highland Brogue Shoe... The general design is similar to a very heavy golfing brogue. **1925** *Blackw. Mag.* Jan. 35/1 An enormous pair of unlaced black brogue shoes.

†**2.** *pl.* Hose, trousers. *Obs.*

1615 G. SANDYS *Trav.* I. 48 The skirts of their [Turkish horsemen's] coates, when they ride, are gathered within long stammel broges that reach to their ancles. **1625** FLETCHER *Fair Maid* IV. ii. 45 A pair of brogs to hide thy mountainous buttocks. **1674** tr. *Scheffer's Lapland* xvii. 87 The men in summer have trouses, or brougs, reaching down to their feet. **1742** SHENSTONE *Schoolmistr.* xix, Brandishing the rod, she doth begin To loose the brogues. **1809** IRVING *Knickerb.* (Bartlett), Every man being ordered to tuck in his shirt-tail and pull up his brogues. *a* **1845** HOOD *Irish Schoolm.* xv, The scourge plies that unkindly seam In Phelim's brogues.

3. ***fishing brogues***, waterproof coverings for the feet and legs; waterproof leggings with feet.

1880 *Advt.*, Indiarubber goods, etc. Fishing brogue boots, leather soles.

4. *Comb.*, as ***brogue-maker***, ***brogue-shod***; also **brogueful**, as much as a brogue will hold; **brogue heel**, a low heel like that of a brogue shoe; **brogue vamp**, a stout vamp made like that of a brogue shoe.

1832 J. WILSON in *Blackw. Mag.* XXXI. 273 Having no.. idea of..a foot but a *brogueful of muscle. **1927** *Chambers's Jrnl.* XVII. 286/2 She'd only *brogue heels on her feet; and her..shoulders were just about on a level with his. **1795** *Statist. Acc. Scotl.* XIV. 74 A number of tailors, and a few *brogue-makers. **1812** W. TENNANT *Anster Fair* II. xxxvii, The *brogue-shod men..Plaided and breechless all. **1889** T. BROPHY *Pattern-Cutting made Easy* iv. 86 We have had boots with all sorts of..variations of design... We have had Derby and *brogue vamps fitted to elastic patterns.

brogue (brəʊg), *sb.*³ [Deriv. unknown: from the frequent mention of 'Irish brogue', it has been conjectured that this may be the same word as the prec., as if 'the speech of those who wear brogues', or 'who call their shoes *brogues*'; but of this there is no evidence.]

A strongly-marked dialectal pronunciation or accent; now particularly used of the peculiarities that generally mark the English speech of Ireland, which is treated *spec.* as ***the brogue***.

1705 *Lond. Gaz.* No. 4123/4 Charles Morgan..having much of the Irish Brogue in his Speech. **1727** DE FOE *Eng. Tradesm.* I. ix. 66 Keep the sportman's brogue upon their tongues. **1775** T. SHERIDAN *Art Reading* 146 They brought with them each their several brogues or modes of intonation. **1828** SCOTT *Review Ritson's Hist.* (1849) 345 The Doctor.. has done much for the Lowland Scottish brogue. **1843** LEVER *J. Hinton* x. (1878) 65 From the lips of a lovely woman, a little, a very little of the brogue is most seductive. **1878** BLACK *Green Past.* iii. 23 The very stones of Westminster Hall are saturated with Irish brogue.

brogue (brəʊg), *v.* [f. BROGUE *sb.*³] *trans.* To utter with a brogue. Hence **broguing** *ppl. a.*

1822 BYRON *Vis. Judg.* lix, There Paddy brogued 'By Jasus'! **1831** *Fraser's Mag.* III. 613 'How wonderful,' brogues forth a gentleman of the press, 'that, etc.'

brogued, *a.* [f. BROGUE *sb.*² + -ED.] **a.** Wearing, or fitted with, brogues.

1816 in *Q. Rev.*

b. Of a boot or shoe: made with a strong vamp like that of a brogue. Hence **broguing** ('brəʊgɪŋ) *vbl. sb.*, the manufacture of brogued shoes or brogue vamps; the vamp itself.

1894 *Standard* 11 Apr. 3/1 Strong brogued walking boots. **1894** *Queen* 17 Nov. 870/1 White kid laid under the black broguing. **1906** W. GREENFIELD in P. N. Hasluck *Boot & Shoe Pattern Cutting* i. 22 In all cases where outside fittings are to be brogued.

brogue'neer, -ineer. [f. BROGUE *sb.*³: after some such word as *buccaneer*, *cannonier*.] One who speaks with a brogue; an Irishman.

1758 MRS. DELANY *Life & Corr.* III. 503 A priest (called 'the Bishop of Down'), the quintessence of an Irish brogueneer. **1831** *Fraser's Mag.* IV. 258 The big brouguineers of Munster land. **1840** *Ibid.* XXI. 750 A place-begging, bawling broguineer of the name of Ronayne.

broguer ('brəʊgə(r)). *rare.* [f. BROGUE *sb.*² + -ER¹.] A maker of brogues.

1834 H. MILLER *Scenes & Leg.* xvii. (1857) 248 The broguer, or maker of Highland shoes.

'broguery. *nonce-wd.* [f. BROGUE *sb.*³] The speaking of a brogue: brogue-speech.

1837 *Fraser's Mag.* XV. 554 The broguery of the Tail [i.e. the followers of O'Connell]. **1839** *Ibid.* XIX. 443 By dint of swaggering, impudence, and broguery.

broguish ('brəʊgɪʃ), *a.* [f. BROGUE *sb.*³ + -ISH¹.] Inclined or tending to a brogue.

1899 *Echo* 6 July 1/5 A bright and intermittently brogueish Irishman. **1921** *Glasgow Herald* 25 Apr. 8 Fine big, broguish fellows, mostly from Ireland. **1928** *Daily Express* 11 Aug. 8/5 He has no ear at all and we all laughed at his broguish cacophonies.

† **broid**, *v.*¹ *Obs.* Also 6 broyde. [A variant of BRAID *v.*, app. owing its form to the pa. pple. BROIDEN, q.v. for the *oi.*] *trans.* To plait, intertwine, interweave.

Hence **'broided** *ppl. a.*, **'broiding** *vbl. sb.*

c **1386** CHAUCER *Knts. T.* 1051 Hir yelow heer was broyded [*So 4 MSS.*, 1 breided, 2 browded] in a tresse. *c* **1440** *Promp. Parv.* 53 Broydyn [**1499** broyded] *laqueatus*. **1530** PALSGR. 471/1, I broyde heare, or a lace, or suche like, *je tortille*. **1535** COVERDALE *Judith* x. 3 She..broyded and plated hir hayre. **1559** HEYWOOD *Seneca's Troas* (1581) 114 b, Forget henceforth thy captiue state and seemly broyd thy hayre. **1601** HOLLAND *Pliny* II. 80 Plaiting and broiding of herbes and floures. **1613** R. C. *Table Alph.* (ed. 3), *Tresses*, lockes of hayre broyded vp. **1624** BACON *New Atl.* (1677) 23 Curiously wrought with Silver and Silk of divers colours, broyding or binding in the Ivy.

† **broide**, *v.*² *Obs.* [var. of BRAID *v.*²: ? an error or due to the association of BROID *v.*¹ with BRAID *v.*¹] *trans.* To upbraid, reproach.

1562 J. HEYWOOD *Prov. & Epigr.* (1867) 56 Better dissemble it..than to broide him with it.

broiden, *pple. a. Obs.* Also 3 ibroiden, ibroyde, 5 broydyn. [A pa. pple. of BRAID *v.* (cf. ABRAID, which had also *abroiden*), and thus a doublet of BROWDEN, which was the normal form, since OE. *oȝ* became *ow, ou* in ME. But the combination was very rare before a consonant: so that evidence is wanting to show whether *oȝd* might become *oid* as well as *owd*, or whether in the case of *broiden* we have a kind of analogical variant of *broden*, somewhat on the model of *breden*, *breiden* of the infinitive. The question is the more important that the *oi* in *broiden* is apparently the source of that in BROID, BROIDER, and their derivatives, in all of which it is unexpected.

(*Littré* has Prov. *broydar*, for *brosdar* = F. *broder*, but although F. *broder*, and Eng. *broden*, were certainly confused at a later date, we cannot see how *broiden*, *abroiden* could be in any way affected by the Prov. word.)]

Woven, interwoven, plaited, braided. **b.** (More usually) *fig.* Skilfully contrived, constructed, arranged, ordered, prepared.

c **1230** *Hali Meid.* 11 Bute bruche and cleane ibroiden on himseluen. *c* **1250** *Owl & Night.* 645 Mi nest..is broiden [*v.r.* ibroyde] al abute. *a* **1300–1375** *Cursor M.* 1008 Land o blis..With blis and beild broiden [*v.r.* -in] best. *Ibid.* 13363 Bridall was þar broiden [*Gött.* ordained] an. *Ibid.* 23799 þe broiden blis to cristis dere, þe bale þat him forsakis here. *a* **1400** [see BROWDEN]. *c* **1440** *Promp. Parv.* 53/1 Broydyn *laqueatus*.

broider ('brɔɪdə(r)), *v. arch.* Forms: 5 broudre, 5–6 browdre, browder, brouder, broder, 6 brauder, 6–7 brodre, 6 brodur, brother, 7 broidre, 7– broider. [In 15th c. *broudre*, *brouder*, taken as the equivalent of F. *brode-r*, *brouder*; 'to stitch, embroider' (of which the regular Eng. repr. was *broude*, BROWD). It is not clear whether the terminal *-er* represents the F. infinitive (as in *render*, *tender*, etc.), or had some other origin. The typical forms during the 16th c. were *browder* and *broder*; *broider* (exc. as implied in BROIDERER, q.v.) is found only later; its *oi* is evidently due to the association with BROID 'to braid', so common in the 16th c.]

1. *trans.* To ornament with needle-work; to work in needlework upon cloth; to embroider. (Almost always in pa. pple.)

[**1405** *Test. Ebor.* (1836) I. 320 Unum vestimentum.. brodatum de coronis et stellis auri. *Ibid.* broudatum de stellis albis.] *c* **1450** HENRYSON *Mor. Fabl.* 45 His hude of scarlet browdered well with silke. **1455** *Test. Ebor.* (1855) II. 201 Unum lectum de sago browdered. **1513** BRADSHAW *St. Werburgh* I. xvi, Theyr noble actes..Freshly were browdred in these clothes royall. **1549** *Compl. Scot.* vii. 69 On the third part of that mantil..brodrut about al hyr tail, al sortis of cattel. **1552** *Inv. Ch. Goods* in *Norfolk Archæol.* (1865) VII. 58 Twoo tunycles of redde velvet brodred wᵗ aungells. **1825** SCOTT *Talism.* xvii, Another broidered with her own hand. **1879** SEGUIN *Black For.* viii. 120 She broidered the banners that were to carry her lover to glory.

2. *transf.* and *fig.* To adorn as with embroidery, to inlay *with* (pearl, ivory, gold, etc.). Also *fig.*

1509 HAWES *Past. Pleas.* XXVII. xxxi. 125 The pillers of yvery..With perles sette and broudred many a folde. *c* **1532** LD. BERNERS *Huon* (1883) 413 A basyn of golde broderyd with perles. **1536** *Regist. Riches* in *Antiq. Sarisb.* (1771) 189 One fair chest..broidered with Coral. **1606** *Sir G. Goosecappe* IV. ii. in Bullen *O. Pl.* (1884) IV. 64 Brodred with nothing but moone-shine ith water. **1667** MILTON *P.L.* IV. 702 The..Hyacinth with rich inlay Broiderd the ground. **1820** SCOTT *Monast.* xxix, Her converse would be broidered with..choice pearls of compliment. **1822** S. ROGERS *Italy*, *Interview* 33 A narrow glade unfolded, such as Spring Broiders with flowers.

broidered ('brɔɪdəd), *ppl. a.* Forms: see prec. [f. BROIDER *v.* + -ED.]

1. Ornamented with needlework; embroidered.

1450 etc. [see BROIDER *v.* 1]. **1562** J. HEYWOOD *Prov. & Epigr.* (1867) 182 Whens come braudered gardis? *c* **1570** *Cambyses* in Hazl. *Dodsley* IV. 175 Now may I wear the brodered guard. **1611** BIBLE *Ezek.* xvi. 13 Fine linen & silke, and broidered worke. **1633** G. HERBERT *Temple, Forerunners* iv, Thou wilt soil thy broider'd coat. **1848** LYTTON *Harold* IV. iii, All covered with broidered peacocks.

2. *fig.*

1616 W. BROWNE *Brit. Past.* II. ii, They priz'd the brodred vale. **1745** T. WARTON *Pleas. Melanch.* 27 Ye broider'd meads, adieu! **1853** RUSKIN *Stones Ven.* II. vi, Spaces of broidered field and blooming mountain.

'broiderer. *arch.* Forms: 4–6 brouderer(e, broderer(e, 5 browderere, 4, 7– broiderer. [f. *brouder*, *broder*, BROIDER *v.* + -ER¹, if not immed. a. Anglo-Fr. *brouderer*: see BRODERER.] One who works embroidery; an embroiderer.

1388 WYCLIF *2 Sam.* xxi. 19 The sone of forest, a broiderer. **1476** *Plumpton Corr.* 37 As for a broderer, I can find none. **1580** BARET *Alv.* B 1342 Broderer, *phrygio*. *a* **1755** G. WEST *Abuse Trav.*, Dancers, broiderers, slaves of luxury.

'broideress. *arch.* [f. BROIDER *v.* + -ESS. Cf. OF. *brouderesse*.] A female embroiderer.

[**1530** PALSGR. 154 *Broderesse* a woman brodurar]. **1827** HOOD *Mids. Fairies* xxxv, May, the quaint broideress.

† **'broidering**, *vbl. sb. Obs.* [f. BROIDER *v.* + -ING¹.] The act or art of adorning with needlework; embroidered work. Also *attrib.*

a **1450** *Knt. de la Tour* (1868) 168 The precious stones, wiche were on the broudryng of his sengle gowne. **1535** in Strype *Cranmer* (1694) App. 24 Of brodering work and pearls. **1546** LANGLEY *Pol. Verg. De Invent.* II. iv. 67 b, The Phrigians inuented brodring.

broidery ('brɔɪdərɪ). Now *poetic.* Forms: 4–5 brouderie, -ri, -ry, browdrye, 5 brawdrye,

broodery, broiderie, -rye, 6 broadery, 7–8 brodery, 7 broydery, 7- broidery, (9 *poet.* broidry). [a. OF. *brouderie, broderie* (14th c. in Littré), f. *brouder, broder*; see BROIDER and -ERY. The form *broidery* (for the abnormal *oi* of which see BROIDEN, BROID) was common in Purvey, and then rare till after 1600: cf. BROIDER.]

1. Ornamental needle-work wrought upon cloth; the art or practice of embroidering cloth; embroidery. Also *attrib.*, as in ***broidery work, frame.***

1382 WYCLIF *Ex.* xxxv. 33 Werkis of carpentarye, of browdrye, and of werkyng with needlis. **1388** *Ibid.* xxviii. 39 Thou schalt make also a girdil, bi werk of broideryе [*v.r.* broudery, brouderi werk]. **1490** CAXTON *Eneydos* xv. 55 A grete mauntelle of veluet cramoysin pourfylled rounde aboute wyth brawdrye, moche enryched wyth precyous stones. **1496** *Dives and Paup.* (W. de W.) I. x. 41, I suppose that sayntes in erthe were not arrayed..with clothes of broodery. **1616** W. BROWNE *Brit. Past.* II. iii, Unknown was then the Phrygian brodery. **1621** AINSWORTH *Annot. Pentat.* Gen. xlvi. 4 In shrowds of silke, or cloth of gold or broyderie. **1708** J. CHAMBERLAYNE *St. Gt. Brit.* II. III. vi. (1743) 416 No other persons wear broidery, pearls, or bullion. **1843** TENNYSON *Day-Dr.* Prol., Then take the broidery-frame, and add A crimson to the quaint Macaw. **1856** MRS. BROWNING *Aur. Leigh* III. 14 Youth's fine linen and fair broidery. **1871** R. ELLIS *Catullus* lxviii. 136.

2. *fig.*

1782 BURNEY *Hist. Mus.* II. 151 The graces, broderies, and flourishes of florid song. **1830** TENNYSON *Dirge* vi, Rare broidry of the purple clover. **1844** KINGLAKE *Eothen* iii. (1878) 46 The golden broidery of oriental praises.

broil (brɔɪl), *sb.*[1] Forms: 6 breull, bruill, 6–7 broyl(e, broile, 8–9 *Sc.* brulyie, -zie, 6- broil. [app. f. BROIL *v.*[2]: cf. It *broglio* 'hurlie burlie, confusion, mingle mangle' (Florio); the F. *brouille* is mod. and from the verb.]

1. A confused disturbance, tumult, or turmoil; a quarrel. See also BRULYIE.

1525 LD. BERNERS *Froiss.* II. 140 (R.) We shall make a great breull in Englande. **1548** HALL *Chron.* (1809) 272 The Erle of Warwickes faccion intendyng to set a bruill in the countrey. **1571** ASCHAM *Scholem.* (Arb.) 158 In the middes[t] of the broyle betwixt Cæsar and Pompeie. **1591** SHAKS. *1 Hen. VI*, I. i. 53 Prosper this Realme, keepe it from Ciuill Broyles. **1664** H. MORE *Myst. Iniq.* 439 Filling the Empire with intestine Broils. **1797** T. JEFFERSON *Writ.* (1859) IV. 173 Plunging us in all the broils of the European nations. **1813** SCOTT *Rokeby* III. xxiii, Foremost he fought in every broil. **1876** GREEN *Short Hist.* iii. §4 (1882) 130 A tavern row between scholar and townsman widens into a general broil.

†**b.** *to set in broil, on a broil. Obs.*

1577 HOLINSHED *Chron.* I. 73/1 The greeuous danger of setting things in broile. *Ibid.* IV. 204 To set things in broil ..within this hir realme of England. **1603** KNOLLES *Hist. Turkes* (1621) 839 That warre, which would set all Europe on a broile.

2. *Comb.*, as ***broil-maker.***

1561 STOW *Chron.* an. 1104 (R.) Letting out the broyle-maker into France.

broil (brɔɪl), *sb.*[2] Also 6 broyle, 9 bruil. [f. BROIL *v.*[1]]

1. A broiling, a great heat; a very hot state.

1583 BABINGTON *Commandm.* vii. 295 What broyles of scorching lust soever the minde abideth. **1821** MRS. WHEELER *Cumbld. Dial.* App. 8 My het bluid, my heart aw' in a bruil, Nor callar blasts can wear, nor drops can cuil.

2. Broiled meat; a grilled chop or steak.

1822 KITCHINER *Cook's Orac.* iv. 107 The Fat..dropping into the fire..will spoil the Broil. **1861** HUGHES *Tom Brown Oxf.* I. iii. 45 Go and get me a broil from the kitchen.

3. *Comb.*, as †**broil-iron** = *broiling-iron.*

1567 *Wills & Inv. N.C.* (1860) II. 266 One broule-Iron, vij speights, iiij pair of pottclipps.

broil, *sb.*[3], **bryle** (brɔɪl, braɪl). *Min.* (Cornwall.) Loose fragments, often of a metallic nature, found lying on the surface above a vein or lode.

1778 PRYCE *Min. Cornub.* 125 Upon the top of most Tin Lodes..is that mineralized substance, which is called the Broil or Bryle of the Lode. **1818** W. PHILLIPS *Min. & Geol.* (ed. 3) 210 Loose fragments or portions of earthy or stony substances, having generally more or less of an ochreous tinge..called the 'bryle of the load'. **1839** DE LA BECHE *Rep. Geol. Cornwall* xv. 528 The upper part of a lode is usually now termed the broil, or bryle. **1859** FORFAR *Pentowan* v, Sometimes we do discover the lode by a broil.

broil (brɔɪl), *v.*[1] Forms: 4 *Sc.* brulȝe, broilye, 4–6 brule, 5 broille, brolyyn, broylyn, broyll, 5–6 broyle, bruyle, broile, 6 brooyle, 6–7 broyl, 6- broil. [Of uncertain origin and history: the form *brule*, which is not infrequent before 1500, appears to be the F. *brûle-r* to burn (in OF. also *bruller*); but it is very doubtful what relation this *brule* bears to the general form *bruyle, broyle*; they may be distinct words, or *brule* may be a conscious assimilation to the F. *bruler*. The form *bruyle*, and Sc. *brulȝe*, appear to be the OF. *bruillir* found in Godef. in the intrans. sense of 'broil, burn' (*bruillir de soleil*); *bruyle* would become *broyle, broil.*]

†**1.** *trans.* To burn, to char with fire. *Obs.*

1375 BARBOUR *Bruce* IV. 151 Assalit Within with fyre, that thame sa brulȝeit. *c* **1375** ? —— *St. Georgis* 456 He gert brandis of fyre [til hyme] bynde, To brule it wes lewit behynde. *c* **1440** *Promp. Parv.* 53 Brolyyn or broylyn, *ustulo, ustillo, torreo.* *a* **1450** *Knt. de la Tour* (1868) 49 Ye shalle.. be broiled and brent, and sinke in the pitte of helle. **1483** CAXTON *Gold. Leg.* 280/3 That he myght be brente and bruyled. *c* **1500** *Partenay* 2289 Ther paynymes were bruled and brend entire. *a* **1533** FRITH *Disput. Purgatory* (1829) 115 He putteth them not away for broiling in purgatory. **1568** H. CHARTERIS *Pref. Lyndesay's Wks.* iij b, To bruyle and scald quha sa euer suld speik aganis thame.

2. *spec.* To cook (meat) by placing it on the fire, or on a gridiron over it; to grill.

c **1386** CHAUCER *Prol.* 383 He cowde roste, sethe, broille, and frie..and wel bake a pye. **1483** *Cath. Angl.* 45 Brule, *assare.* **1598** B. JONSON *Ev. Man Hum.* I. iv. 12 The first red herring that was broyld in Adam and Eves kitchen. **1653** WALTON *Angler* 57 Broil him [chub] upon wood-cole or char-cole. **1769** MRS. RAFFALD *Eng. Housekpr.* (1778) 71 To broil Mutton Steaks. **1835** W. IRVING *Tour Prairies* 117 An evening banquet of venison..roasted, or broiled on the coals. **1853** *Arab. Nts.* (Rtldg.) 621 Our gridiron is only fit to broil small fish.

3. To scorch; to make very hot, to heat.

1634 RAINBOW *Labour* (1635) 18 Let not his hot pursuit broyle him in an Ægyptian furnace. **1718** LADY M. W. MONTAGUE *Lett.* II. xlix. 64, I was..half broiled in the sun. **1818** BYRON *Juan* I. lxiii, That..sun..will keep..broiling, burning on. **1858** HAWTHORNE *Fr. & It. Jrnls.* I. 268 We turned back, much broiled in the hot sun.

4. *intr.* To be subjected to great heat, to be very hot. (Mainly in *to be broiling*, for *to be a-broiling.*)

1613 SHAKS. *Hen. VIII*, IV. i. 56 God saue you Sir, Where haue you bin broiling? Among the crow'd i'th' Abbey. **1642** H. MORE *Song of Soul* II. iii. IV. xxxii, One of a multitude of myriads Shall not be sav'd but broyl in scorching wo? **1748** SMOLLETT *Rod. Rand.* vii. (1804) 34 Before your age I was broiling on the coast of Guinea. **1883** *Leisure Ho.* 148/1 Don't keep us broiling here for ever!

b. *intr.* To grow hot; esp. *fig.* to become heated with excitement, anger, etc. ? *Obs.*

1561 T. NORTON tr. *Calvin's Inst.* IV. xx, If they [Magistrates] must punish..let them not broile with unappeaseable rigor. **1627** P. FLETCHER *Locusts* I. xxiv, Meantime (I burne, I broyle, I burst with spight). **1760** STERNE *Tr. Shandy* II. v, He broil'd with impatience. **1817** BYRON *Beppo* lxix, Her female friends, with envy broiling, Beheld her airs and triumph.

c. Said of passion, emotion, etc.: To burn, glow, be ardent.

1600 *Newe Metamorph.* (N.) Love broyled so Within his brest. **1709** STEELE *Tatler* No. 36 ⁋2 The secret Occasion of Envy broiled long in the Breast of Autumn.

broil, *v.*[2] Forms: 5–7 broyl, bruill, brooyl, 6–7 broile, broyle, 8 (*Sc.*) brulyie, 6- broil. [a. F. *brouille-r* 'to jumble, trouble, disorder, confound, marre by mingling together' (Cotgr.), corresp. to It. *brogliare* to stir, disorder, embroil; cf. the It. sb. *broglio* 'hurlie burlie, confusion, mingle mangle', etc. (Florio). Ulterior derivation uncertain: see Diez, Littré, Scheler.

Littré (like Diez) thinks the F. vb. identical with Pr. *bruelhar, brolhar*, Cat. *brollar* 'to bud, rise up', and connected with OF. *bruill, broel, broil*, mod.Fr. *breuil*, 'an enclosed piece of brushwood, matted underwood, or cut bushes for animals,' found in late L. in the *Capit. de Villis* (lucos nostros quos vulgus brugilos vocat), med.L. *broilus, brolius*, which is referred to the OCeltic *brog-, brogi-* territory, district (Thurneysen). But most etymologists doubt the connexion of *brouiller* with this.]

†**1.** *trans.* To mix or mingle confusedly. *Obs.*

1401 *Pol. Poems* (1859) II. 61 Thou broylist up many lesynges, ffor grounde of thin ordre. **1631** HEYWOOD *Engl. Eliz.* (1641) 187 The abundance of bloud already spilt and broiled in the land.

†**2.** To involve in confusion or disorder; to agitate, discompose (a person); to 'set by the ears', embroil. *Obs.*

1513 MORE *Rich. III* (1641) 405 He was sore moved and broyled with Melancolie and dolour. **1549** CHEKE *Hurt Sedit.* (1641) 16 Who..intende to broyle the Commonwealth with the flame of their treason [with an allusion to BROIL *v.*[1]]. **1585** JAS. I. *Ess. Poesie* (Arb.) 21 To translate it well and best, where I haue bothe euill, and worst broyled it. **1642** BP. DURHAM *Presentm. Schismatic* 4 Contentious ones..broyling the world in this manner.

3. *intr.* To be or to engage in a broil; to contend in a confused struggle, irregular fight or strife.

c **1567** TURBERVILLE *After Misadv. Good Haps* (R.) The barck that broylde in rough and churlish sease. **1592** WYRLEY *Armorie* 81 Couragious John of Gaunt Like Priams sonne strong broyling mid his foes. **1883** *Pall Mall G.* 15 Oct. 4/1 He was always broiling with his chiefs, constantly in debt.

4. *trans.* To put into a broil, to embroil.

1857 HEAVYSEGE *Saul* (1869) 243, I shall not hurry him, nor broil myself.

broiled (brɔɪld), *ppl. a.* [f. BROIL *v.*[1] + -ED.] Made very hot, scorched, charred; *spec.* grilled.

c **1440** *Promp. Parv.* 53/1 Broylyd [*K.* brolyyd], *ustulatus. Ibid.* Broylyd mete, or rostyd only on the colys. **1483** CAXTON *Gold. Leg.* 249/1 This brente and bruled laurence. **1542** BOORDE *Dyetary* xviii. (1870) 277 Bruled meat is harde of digestyon. **1586** COGAN *Haven Health* cxlviii. (1636) 146 Broyled meate is hard of digestion. **1611** BIBLE *Luke* xxiv. 42 A piece of a broyled fish. **1871** M. COLLINS *Mrq. & Merch.* I. ix. 275, I should like a broiled pheasant.

broiler[1] (ˈbrɔɪlə(r)). [f. BROIL *v.*[1] + -ER[1].]

1. a. One who or that which broils; *spec.* one who cooks by broiling; also said of a very hot day (cf. *roaster, scorcher*).

1671 J. WEBSTER *Metallogr.* ii. 31 He was a great Broyler in Gebers Kitchin. **1750** [R. PULTOCK] *Life P. Wilkins* xxxiv. (1883) 94/2 When the broilers began to throw the fish about. **1817–8** COBBETT *Resid. U.S.* (1822) 12, July 27. Fine broiler again..We spent a pleasant day; drank..of milk and water. Not more flies than in England.

b. A gridiron or similar utensil used in broiling. Now *U.S.*

1393 in *M.E.D.* **1632** SHERWOOD, A broiler, *gril.* **1828–** WEBSTER. **1907** 'O. HENRY' *Trimmed Lamp* 64 Two minutes longer on the broiler would have made this steak fit to be eaten by a gentleman. **1907** *Yesterday's Shopping* (1969) 182/2 Capt. Warren's Batchelor's Broiler, 10½ in. 2/9. **1967** *Boston Sunday Herald* 26 Mar. (Advt.), Easy dinners with non-drip cook top, smokeless broiler, and built-in aluminum griddle.

2. *spec.* A chicken for broiling. Now normally reared in close confinement in a broiler house. Also *transf.* and *attrib.*

1876 *Rep. Vermont Board Agric.* III. 244 The cockerels should be sold for broilers when large enough. **1886** *Pall Mall G.* 27 Aug. 14/1 Of these [chicks] about seventy-five per cent. live and grow to be broilers. **1952** *Daily Tel.* 4 Dec., A broiler..is a young bird, weighing about 3 lb dead weight, which has been raised on a new system. It is plump and tender enough to grill or to fry in the traditional American manner. *Ibid.*, Broiler production has been flourishing in America for the past six years. **1959** *Ibid.* 5 Mar. 11/3 The continued spread of broiler houses, the buildings for rearing chickens. **1960** *Farmer & Stockbreeder* 16 Feb. 91/3 Five batches of broilers would go through the broiler-house in the life of one steer. **1966** *New Statesman* 25 Feb. 260/1 A state of affairs which seems to be treating these old *people* [in hospitals] as if they were broiler fowls. **1970** *Times* 14 Feb. 9/6 The individual birds live a natural life in wild conditions, very unlike those of a broiler house.

broiler[2] (ˈbrɔɪlə(r)). [f. BROIL *v.*[2] + -ER[1].] One who stirs up or engages in broils or quarrels.

a **1660** HAMMOND *Wks.* IV. 544 (R.) What doth he but turn broiler and boutefeu. **1841** ORDERSON *Creol.* viii. 91 Due impression alike on the civil and the military broiler.

†**ˈbroilery.** *Obs. rare.* Forms: 6 broilerie, broylery. [a. F. *brouillerie*, f. *brouiller* to broil: see -ERY.] Dissension; strife; disturbance, disorder.

1521 MORE in Ellis *Orig. Lett.* II. 82 I. 290 The archbishop of St. Andrewis putteth all his possible power..to rere broilerie, warre, and revolution in the Realme. **1528** WRIOTHESLEY in Pocock *Rec. Ref.* I. xl. 79 To pass his promise on such sort..might..make much broylery.

broiling (ˈbrɔɪlɪŋ), *vbl. sb.*[1] [f. BROIL *v.*[1] + -ING[1].] The action or process of exposing to scorching heat; *spec.* grilling. Hence †**broiling-iron**, a kind of Dutch oven.

c **1440** *Promp. Parv.* 53 Brolyynge [*K.* broylinge], *ustulacio.* *a* **1619** DONNE *Biathan.* (1644) 140 How much [contributed] Saint Laurence to his broyling, when he called to the Tyrant, This side is enough, turne the other, and then eate? **1837** M. DONOVAN *Dom. Econ.* II. 271 Between broiling and roasting the chief difference is in the temperature. In roasting, the heat is moderate, and slow in penetrating: in broiling, it is brisk and rapid. **1562** *Richmond. Wills* (1853) 163 One brulinge iron, viijd. **1615** MARKHAM *Eng. Housew.* 70–1 Take your Broyling-iron, I do not mean a Grid-iron (though it be much used for this purpose)..but a Plate iron made with hooks and pricks, on which you may hang the meat, and set it close before the fire.

†**ˈbroiling**, *vbl. sb.*[2] *Obs. rare*[−1]. Forms: 6 brewlynge, brullynge. [f. BROIL *v.*[2] + -ING[1].] Disturbance, dissension; embroilment.

1523 LD. BERNERS *Froiss.* I. cccl. 560 The great brullynge that was than in Gaunt. *Ibid.* ccccxxxii. 759 A newe brewlynge in Flaunders.

broiling (ˈbrɔɪlɪŋ), *ppl. a.* [f. BROIL *v.*[1]]

1. That burns, scorches, makes very hot.

1555 *Fardle Facions* I. i. 24 The broyling heate. **1617** HIERON *Wks.* II. 84 Scarcely is the cup gone from his mouth, before he feeleth an increase of his broyling drought. **1820** BYRON *Blues* II. 36 To be sure it was broiling. **1865** TROLLOPE *Belton Est.* xiii. 150 There is a broiling sun.

2. That is subjected to great heat, that is very hot; *spec.* that is being grilled.

1648 GAGE *West. Ind.* i. (1655) 2 Which only can and must deliver their scorching, nay broyling souls. **1813** BYRON *Br. Abydos* II. xv, Ask the squalid peasant how His gains repay his broiling brow! **1853** KINGSLEY *Hypatia* x. 117 The savoury smell of broiling fish.

3. quasi-*adv.*, as in ***broiling hot.***

1840 HOOD *Up Rhine* 229 A broiling hot excursion up the country. **1884** Q. VICTORIA *More Leaves* 180 We stopped here about ten minutes. It was broiling hot.

ˈbroilingly, *adv.* [f. BROILING *ppl. a.* + -LY.[2]] In a broiling manner.

1885 M. BLIND *Tarant.* xiii, It was a broilingly hot day.

†**ˈbroilly**, *a. Obs. rare*[−1]. [cf. Fr. *bruilli*, pa. pple. of *bruillir* 'to be burnt' (Godef.).] ? Broiled.

c **1400** MAUNDEV. ix. (1839) 107 It is ȝit alle broylly, as tho it were half brent.

†**ˈbroilment.** *Obs. rare.* Commotion, disturbance, embroilment. See BRULYIEMENT.

ˈbroily, *a. rare*[−1]. [? f. BROIL *sb.*[1] + -Y[1].] Full of broils, tumultuous, stormy.

1594 CAREW *Tasso* (1881) 77 Stormes of broylly whistling iarre, Whom natiue caues foorth from their intrayls send.

brok, obs. form of BROCK, BROKE.

brokaded, obs. form of BROCADED.

† **'brokage, brocage.** *Obs.* Also 5 brochage, 6 broc-, brok-, broakadge, 6–7 broakage, brokeage. [In AFr. *brocage*, also *brogage*, in same sense: see BROKER.]

The following meanings are given in dictionaries, or indicated in some of the quotations: in many of the latter the exact sense cannot be fixed, so that they are not here separated. In most cases the word has an ill favour, cf. 'jobbery'.

1. a. The trade of a broker; the transaction of commercial business, as buying and selling, for other men. **b.** The premium or commission of a broker, BROKERAGE; the gain or profit derived from acting as agent, middleman, or intermediary. **c.** The corrupt farming or jobbing of offices; the price or bribe paid unlawfully for any office or place of trust; frequently mentioned as an abuse in early times. **d.** Trafficking in match-making, in the marriage of wards, etc. **e.** Procuracy in immorality, pimping. **f.** 'The trade of dealing in old things, the trade of a broker' (J.).

1377 LANGL. *P. Pl.* B. XIV. 267 A mayden þat is maried þorw brokage..bi assent of sondry partyes and syluer to bote. *c* **1383** WYCLIF *Sel. Wks.* III. 280 Symonyentis in beneficis..bi brocage maade to mene persones for to haue ony beneficis of þe chirche. *c* **1386** CHAUCER *Milleres T.* 189 He woweth hire by meenes and brocage. **1393** LANGL. *P. Pl.* C. III. 92 Vserye and Auerice, and oþer false sleithes In bargeyns and in brocages. *c* **1440** *Rom. Rose* 6973, I entremet me of brocages, I make peace and mariages. **1456** in *Rel. Ant.* II. 239 Now brocage ys made offycerys, And baratur ys made bayly. *c* **1460** FORTESCUE *Abs. & Lim. Mon.* xiv. (1885) 144 Nor thai [Suytours] shall be importunite or brocage optayne any vnresonable desires. **1555** *Fardle Facions* I. v. 50 Their women in old tyme, had all the trade of occupiying, and brokage abrode. **1584** WHETSTONE *Mirror for Mag.* 31 An other sort by brocadge bringeth him in debt. **1577** HELLOWES *Gueuara's Ep.* 125 To ryse to it by brokage or corruption. **1579** SPENSER *Sheph. Cal.* Ded., It served well Pandares purpose for the bolstering of his bawdie brocage. **1591** —— *M. Hubberd* 851 Shameles flatterie, And filthie brocage, and unseemly shifts. **1600** ROWLANDS *Lett. Humours Blood* II. 55 Vserie sure is requisite and good, And so is Brokeage, rightly vnderstood. **1603** FLORIO *Montaigne* (1634) 489 By the brokage or panderizing of the lawes. **1611** BEAUM. & FL. *Philaster* v. iii, If a man had need to use their valours, he must pay a brokage for it. **1615** G. SANDYS *Trav.* 148 Their occupations, brocage and vsury. **1618** *Barnevelt's Apol.* C iv b, Our last borrowed money is at 16, and three in the hundreth for brokeage. *a* **1618** SYLVESTER *St. Lewis* 448 That after-Judges..From Bribes and Brokeage might be warned fair. **1623** FAVINE *Theat. Hon.* VII. i. 198 By the base brokage and close contriuing of the Queene. **1644** BULWER *Chirol.* 4 Without the crafty Brocage of the Tongue. **1648** C. WALKER *Hist. & Pol. Relat.* 11 The Parliament payes 30000*l.* Broakage. **1656** J. HARRINGTON *Oceana* (1700) 110 Find better preferments without his Brocage. *a* **1680** BUTLER *Rem.* (1759) I. 428 Though the Crown is forced to pawn all its own Jewels to them for mere Brokage. **1683** D. SMITH *Constantinople* in *Misc. Cur.* (1708) III. 38 They [Jews] are of great use and service to the Turks, upon accompt of their Brocage and Merchandise. **1755** CARTE *Hist. Eng.* IV. 78 Not a fitting thing for a clergyman to be concerned in a brocage of such a nature.

2. *Comb.*, as ***brokage-money***.

1591 PERCIVALL *Sp. Dict.*, *Corretage*, broakage money.

† **'brokaly.** *Obs.* Also brocaly, brocale. A broken piece, broken pieces. (Cf. BROCKLE.)

c **1440** *Promp. Parv.* 52 Brocale, or lewynge of mete [**1499** brokaly of mete], *fragmentum. Ibid.* 428 Releef or brocaly of mete..*fragmentum.*

brokdol, erroneous f. BROCKLE, in *Promp. Parv.*

broke (brəʊk), *sb.* Forms: 1–2, 4 broc, 6–8 brok, 8–9 (*dial.*) brock, 5– broke. [OE. *broc* 'misery', and *ȝebroc* 'fragment', f. *brecan* (pa. pple. *ȝebrocen*) to BREAK. The later lengthening of the vowel may be from the inflected dissyllabic forms *broces*, *brocu*, etc.: cf. the pple. *broke*, *brōken*, formerly *brŏcen*. *Brock* remains dialectally.]

† **1.** That which breaks; affliction, trouble, misery. Only in OE.

c **888** K. ÆLFRED *Boeth.* xxxix. § 10 God nyle for his mildheortnesse nan unaberendlice broc him ansettan. **971** *Blickl. Hom.* 59 Ealle þa sar and þa brocu þe se man to ȝesceapen is. **1061** in Thorpe's *Diplom.* 389 Gefreod æghwylcere uneaþnesse ealles woroldlices broces.

† **2.** A piece of anything broken off; a fragment; e.g. of bread or food, broken meats, remains. *Obs.*

c **1160** *Hatton Gosp.* Matt. xv. 37 Þæt to lafe wæs of þam broccan [*c* **975** *Rushw. G.* ȝebroca; *c* **1000** *Ags. G.* ȝebrote], hys naman seofan wilian fulle. **1507** *Will of Bedyll* (Somerset Ho.) A parcell of a broke of woode. *a* **1568** *Wowing of Jok & Jenny* x, Bannatyne Poems 160 Quhen ye haif done, tak hame the brok. **1721** KELLY *Sc. Prov.* 211 (JAM.) I neither got stock nor brock. **1847–78** HALLIWELL, *Brock*, a piece or fragment. *West.* **1863** BARNES *Poems Dorset Dial.* Coll. III. 101 Wi' brocks an' scraps to plim well out.

† **3.** A breaking of the skin or body; a wound; a rupture. *Obs.*

c **1350** *Med. MS.* in *Archæol.* XXX. 381 Hennebane rote Of ye broc is mych bote. **1535** COVERDALE *Lev.* xxiv. 20 Broke for broke, eye for eye, tothe for tothe. *a* **1563** BECON *New Catech.* (1844) 94.

† **4.** A breach of the law; a crime. *Obs.*

1481 *Reynard* (1844) 92 Hadde I knowen my self gylty in ony feat or broke.

5. *pl.* The short-stapled wool found in certain parts of the fleece, when 'broken' or sorted. A fleece consists of two main kinds of wool distinguished by the length and strength of the fibre; the sorts which are long and suitable for combing being called 'matchings' or 'combing-sorts', the rest 'short wools' or 'brokes'. The spinning of the two sorts is by different processes. See NOILS.

1879 *Standard* 22 Apr., Wool and Worsted.—Bradford.. Noils and brokes are slow of sale. **1883** *Daily News* 3 Sept. 2/6 Noils and brokes are in rather better request. **1885** F. H. BOWMAN *Struct. Wool* 352 Gloss., *Brokes*, short locks of wool found on the edge of the fleece in the region of the neck and belly.

broke (brəʊk), *ppl. a.* Obsolescent form of BROKEN.

1. Used occasionally for BROKEN *ppl. a.*

c **1380** WYCLIF *Serm.* Sel. Wks. II. 14 Leepfullis of broke meat. **1463** *Bury Wills* (1850) 41 To recompense broke silvir I had of his. **1647** H. MORE *Song of Soul* IV. v, Bodies disjoind, broke glasses they esteem.

2. esp. in *comb.*

c **1230** *Hali Meid.* 25 Witlese beastes dumbe and broke rugget ibuhe toward te eorðe. **1362** LANGL. *P. Pl.* A. VII. 131 Blinde or broke-schonket [B. VI. 138 broke-legged]. **1440** *Promp. Parv.* 53 Broke bakkyde, *gibbosus*. **1470** HARDING *Chron.* clvii. iii, Brokebacked and bowbacked bore. **1627** MAY *Lucan* v. (R.) Broke-winded murmers, howlings, and sadd grones.

3. *slang.* **a.** In predicative use = BROKEN *ppl. a.* 7; penniless; also ***broke to the wide*** (see WIDE *sb.*) or ***broke to the world***. Freq. with qualifying word, as ***clean, dead, flat broke, stone-broke*** (see STONE *sb.* 20), ***stony broke*** (see STONY *a.* 6).

Cf. the following, which are properly instances of BREAK *v.* 11.

[**1665** PEPYS *Diary* 6 July (1895) V. 6 It seems some of his creditors have taken notice of it, and he was like to be broke yesterday in his absence. **1669** *Ibid.* 12 Mar. (1896) VIII. 258 Being newly broke by running in debt.]

1716 J. STEUART *Let.* 28 Dec. (1915) 38 Alexr. Mackpherson..is much in arear and quit broke. **1821** in *N. Carolina Hist. Comm.* I. 220 I have been broke now twelve months,..yet I move on in the old way. **1842** *Spirit of Times* 2 Apr. 58/1 Barrett, poor fellow, is dead broke. *Ibid.* 21 May 138/1 Every friend of Old Whitenose would have been flat broke! **1843** *Ibid.* 14 Jan. 544/3, I was clean broke in less than four hours. **1846** *Ibid.* 25 Apr. 101/2, I unfortunately am short of funds, flat broke, busted, collapsed. **1851** N. KINGSLEY *Diary* (1914) 173 To day men have come along 'dead broke' and have gone to work for 4 dollars pr. day. **1886** H. SMART *Outsider* vii, Well, sir, I was broke—so broke as I hope I never shall be again—'dead stoney', barely expresses it. *a* **1889** in Barrère & Leland *Dict. Slang.* s.v., Then came the *fiasco*, And Ben cried 'Carrasco! I'm bested, broke, busted—or partly!' **1889** *Pall Mall Gaz.* 14 Aug. (Farmer), I see that Sullivan made 21,000 dols. out of his fight, but as he was 'dead broke' before the battle, there won't be much of it left. **1898** 'O. THANET' *Heart of Toil* 141 Think of them boys, who are all stone-broke.., wanting to lend *me* money. **1918** W. J. LOCKE *Rough Road* iii, I believe you good people think I've come back broke to the world. **1926** J. BLACK *You can't Win* v. 53 [The landlady] wanted the rent. I told her I was broke.

b. ***go for broke***: see GO *v.* 58 h.

4. Of animals: broken to harness; = BROKEN *ppl. a.* 8. Chiefly *U.S.*

1800 *Sporting Mag.* XVI. 117/2 The grand manege consists in teaching a horse, already perfectly broke in the common way, certain artificial motions. **1833** M. A. HOLLEY *Texas* v. 97 This brutal process is repeated until the animal is thoroughly broke and rendered docile. **1850** W. MILES *Jrnl.* (1916) 12, 500 broke mules were to be in readiness. **1856** *Trans. Mich. Agric. Soc.* VII. 275 Oxen exhibited as working cattle, for their being the best broke, must be hitched to either a wagon or cart. **1893** T. ROOSEVELT *Wilderness Hunter* xx. 426 The light-hearted belief..that any animal which by main force has been saddled and ridden ..is a 'broke horse'.

5. = BROKEN *ppl. a.* 1 e. Also *ellipt.*

1888 CROSS & BEVAN *Paper-making* vi. 104 *'Broke' Paper.*—Under this head may be included all the partially formed paper which is always obtained..when a paper-machine is started, or such portions as are occasionally unavoidably damaged in its passage over the drying cylinders. *Ibid.* 105 'Broke' paper may be advantageously disintegrated by means of an edge-runner. **1954** SOUTHWARD *Mod. Printing* (ed. 7) II. xlii. 449 Broke. The third grade of imperfect paper.

broke (brəʊk), *v.* [In form the base of *broker*, *brokage*, *broking*. An AFr. vb. *abroker* occurs in *Liber Albus* (*a* 1419) 288.]

† **1.** *intr.* To bargain; to negotiate; to traffic.

1496 *Dives & Paup.* (W. de W.) VII. xxi. 308 [They] thus bargeyne & broke about the syngynge of the masse, that may not be solde ne bought, as men do in byenge & sellynge of an horse. **1601** SHAKS. *All's Well* III. v. 74 He..brokes with all that can in such a suite Corrupt the tender honour of a Maide. **1611** COTGR., *Brouillon*, one that broakes in euery thing, whereby he may get but a pennie. **1625** BACON *Riches, Ess.* (Arb.) 237 The gaines of Bargaines, are of a more doubtfull Nature; When Men shall..broake by Seruants and Instruments to draw them on.

† **2.** *trans.* To retail, traffic in. *Obs.*

1599 MARSTON *Sco. Villanie* III. xi. 227 But to retaile and broke anothers wit.

3. *intr.* To act as broker, agent, or go-between.

a **1652** BROME *City Wit* II. ii. Wks. 1873 I. 303 Prithee what art thou? or whom dost thou serve, or broke for? *a* **1666** FANSHAWE (Webster) We do want a certain necessary woman to broke between, Cupid said. **1926** G. K. CHESTERTON *Outl. Sanity* v. ii. 203 If men were not brokers, it was because they were not able to broke. **1965** 'W. HAGGARD' *Hard Sell* v. 54 I'm a stockbroker... *I* broked for Franchin.

broke, obs. form of BROOK *sb.*, *v.*

brokel, obs. form of BROCKLE *a.* brittle.

brokelempe, -hempe, obs. ff. BROOKLIME.

† **brokelet(te.** *Obs. rare.* [app. dim. of *brokel*, BROCKLE fragments.] A fragment.

1538 ELYOT *Biblioth.*, *Analectes*, he that gadereth vp brokelettes. **1563–87** FOXE *A. & M.* II. 328 Twelve maunds full of brokelets and offalls.

† **'brokeling.** *Obs. rare*⁻¹. [app. f. *brokel*, BROCKLE *a.* or *sb.* + -ING.] Fragment.

1490 CAXTON *Eneydos* xxxiv. 123 Where he sholde happe to ete the releef or brokelynges of his brode.

broken ('brəʊk(ə)n), *ppl. a.* For forms see BREAK *v.*

I. Used adjectively in many of the senses of the verb; esp. the following:

1. a. Separated forcibly into parts; in fragments; in pieces. (The resulting damaged state is often the main notion.)

[737 *Chart. Æðelhard* in *Cod. Dipl.* V. 45 To brocenan beorȝe.] **1383** WYCLIF *Isa.* xxxvi. 6 Lo! thou tristist on this brokun staf. *c* **1500** *Lancelot* 240 The tronsions of o brokine sper. **1535** COVERDALE *Ps.* xxx[i]. 12, I am become like a broken vessell. **1634** BP. HALL *Occas. Med.* cx. Wks. (1808) 203 A thin, uncovered roof..dark and broken windows. **1719** DE FOE *Crusoe* (1840) I. iv. 60 Three broken oars. **1832** DE LA BECHE *Geol. Man.* 205 Polypifers occur..rolled and broken, as on an ancient coast. **1868** J. H. BLUNT *Ref. Ch. Eng.* I. 327 A few broken walls and the roofless, unglazed churches.

b. ***broken bread, meat, victuals***, etc.: fragments of food left after a meal, etc.; by extension applied to remnants of drink, as ***broken ale, beer***.

1382 WYCLIF *Mark* viii. 20 How many leepis of brokene mete ȝe token vp? **1530** PALSGR. 201/2 Broken meat, *fragments*. **1591** PERCIVALL *Sp. Dict.*, *Escurriduras*, the dropping of a cup, broken drinke, *reliquiæ*. **1594** PLAT *Diuerse new Exper.* 13 Others doe soke chippings and other crustes of bread in broken beere. **1639** T. DE GREY *Compl. Horseman* 112 Wash the places with broken beere. **1675** HOBBES *Odyss.* 203 With broken meat and wine himself to feed. **1876** MISS BRADDON *J. Haggard's Dau.* II. 15 No sign of unwashed tea-things or broken victuals.

c. In some cases *broken* gives a specific sense to the combination, as **broken-coal**, a special size of coal; **broken granite**, granite reduced to a size fit for road-making; **broken letter** *Typogr.*, distributed type; **broken tea**, tea-siftings.

1683 MOXON *Mech. Exerc.*, *Printing* 371 By broken Letter is..meant..the breaking the orderly Succession the Letters stood in..and mingling the Letters together.

† **d.** *fig.* Dissolved. *Obs.*

1538 LATIMER *Serm. & Rem.* (1845) 397 Graciously to remember them with some piece of some broken abbey.

e. In paper-making, seriously damaged, denoting a quality of defective paper inferior to retree.

1807 [see RETREE]. **1880** J. DUNBAR *Pract. Paper-maker* 48 This method..saves broken [paper], and can be worked so near the edge that the impression is taken off at the cutter. **1907** CROSS & BEVAN *Paper-making* (ed. 3) v. 150 The fibres of the broken paper are..separated.

f. *Phonology.* Subjected to breaking (see BREAKING *vbl. sb.* 1 e).

1845 J. M. KEMBLE in *Proc. Philol. Soc.* II. 135 A tendency in the vowel to become dulled or broken when placed in particular positions. **1887** SKEAT *Princ. Etym.* 45 The symbol *ea* denotes that the vowel was, to speak technically, 'broken', i.e. was resolved into the dipthong *e-a*.

g. ***broken (over)***: in bookbinding, applied to the creasing down of a small part of an inserted print near the binding margin, for the purpose of giving support to the binding thread.

1879 ZAEHNSDORF *Art Book-binding* 169 Broken over. When plates are turned over or folded a short distance from the back edge, before they are placed in the volume, so as to facilitate their being turned easily or laid flat, they are said to be broken over. When a leaf has been turned down the paper is broken.

2. Rent, ruptured, torn, burst.

1377 LANGL. *P. Pl.* B. v. 108 Þat bar[en] awey my bolle and my broke [*v.r.* broken] schete. *Ibid.* IX. 91 He..biddeth þe begger go for his broke clothes. **1535** COVERDALE *Jer.* ii. 13 Vile and broken pittes, that holde no water. **1577** HOLINSHED *Chron.* III. 845/1 Old hosen, broken shooes. **1641** *Termes de la Ley* 43 b, Old and broken apparell. **1760** GOLDSM. *Cit. W.* xxix, His..dirty shirt, and broken silk stockings.

3. Of organic structures: **a.** Having the bone fractured; **b.** having the surface ruptured.

c **1340** *Cursor M.* 8087 (Fairf.) Wiþ crumpeled knees and brokin bak [*v.r.* boce on bak]. **1562** J. HEYWOOD *Prov. & Ep.* (1867) 113 Broken head. **1600** SHAKS. *A.Y.L.* I. i. 134 Hee that escapes me without some broken limbe. **1712** ADDISON *Spect.* No. 433 ¶6 They often came from the Council Table with broken Shins. **1753** CHAMBERS *Cycl. Supp.* s.v. *Broken*, Among horse-jockies, broken knees are a mark of a stumbler.

4. Shattered; said of water whose coherence as a mass has been destroyed by striking against an object, or whose surface is broken.

1793 SMEATON *Edystone L.* §271 Sufficiently strong to resist the falling broken water. **1804** A. DUNCAN *Mariner's Chron.* II. 77 A dreadful, hollow, broken sea. **1867** SMYTH *Sailor's Word-bk.*, *Broken Water*, the contention of currents in a narrow channel. Also, the waves breaking on and near shallows. **1875** BEDFORD *Sailor's Pocket-Bk.* VI. (ed. 2) 216 In a boat outside the broken water.

5. Crushed or exhausted by labour, etc.; with strength or power gone; enfeebled.

1490 CAXTON *Eneydos* xxxi. 117 The ladyes were sore wery and broken of theyre longe vyage. **1577** HOLINSHED *Chron.* I. 165/1 The old broken yeeres of mans life. **1615** G. SANDYS *Trav.* 118 Such a number of broken persons..by reason of their strong labour and weake foode. **1758** LADY M. W. MONTAGUE *Lett.* cvi. IV. 98 Sir Charles Williams, who I hear is much broken both in his spirits and constitution. **1864** TENNYSON *En. Ard.* 705 Enoch was so brown, so bow'd, So broken.

6. Crushed in feelings by misfortune, remorse, etc.; subdued, humbled, contrite.

1535 COVERDALE *Ps.* l[i]. 17 A broken and a contrite hert (o God) shalt thou not despise. **1642** ROGERS *Naaman* 61 Try whether..your selves grow daily lowlier, meeker, brokenner. **1652** NEEDHAM tr. *Selden's Mare Cl.* 68 The King's courage was so broken. *a* **1718** PENN *Life* Wks. I. 100 She was exceedingly broken, and took an Affectionate and Reverent Leave of us. **1831** CARLYLE *Sart. Res.* II. vii. 194 How beautiful to die of broken-heart, on Paper. **1858** ROBERTSON *Lect.* 269 Happy is the man not thoroughly broken by disappointment.

7. Reduced or shattered in worldly estate, financially ruined; having failed in business, bankrupt.

1593 SHAKS. *Rich. II*, II. i. 257 The Kings growne bankrupt like a broken man. **1602** T. FITZHERBERT *Apol.* 19 Cradock had byn a broken Merchant about Italie. **1714** ELLWOOD *Autobiog.* (1765) 257 He might thereby repair his broken fortunes. **1753** RICHARDSON *Grandison* (1781) VI. i. 7 There may be many ways..of providing for a broken tradesman. **1863** GEO. ELIOT *Romola* I. xvi. (1880) I. 225 To mend the broken fortunes of his ancient family.

8. Reduced to obedience or discipline, tamed, trained. Often with *in*.

1805 SOUTHEY *Madoc in Azt.* iii, The Elk and Bison, broken to the yoke. **1844** *Regul. & Ord. Army* 380 A Horse ..notified..to be properly broken. **1861** PALGRAVE *Gold. Treasury* 308 A language hardly yet broken in to verse.

9. broken man. *Scotch Law and Hist.* One under sentence of outlawry, or living the life of an outlaw, or depredator, chiefly in the Highlands and Border districts; **broken-clan** (see quot.).

1528 *MS. Caligula* in Tytler *Hist. Scot.* (1864) II. 348 *note*, Divers radis to be maid upon the brokin men of our realme. **1594** *Sc. Acts 13 Jas. VI* §227 Daylie heirschippes of the wicked thieues and limmers of the Clannes and surnames following..broken men of the surnames of Stewarts. *a* **1649** DRUMM. OF HAWTH. *Hist. Jas. V* Wks. (1711) 95 A thousand, all borderers and broken men. **1818** SCOTT *Rob Roy* xxvi, He..took to the brae-side, and became a broken-man. **1820** —— *Abbot* xxxiv, *Note.* A broken clan was one which had no chief able to find security for their good behaviour, a clan of outlaws. **1875** MAINE *Hist. Inst.* VI. 174 The result was probably to fill the country with 'broken men'.

10. a. Violated, transgressed, not kept intact.

1605 ARMIN *Foole upon F.* (1880) 14 A broken Uirgine, one that had had a barne. **1697** DRYDEN *Virg. Georg.* IV. 713 The sign Of Cov'nants broke. **1800–24** CAMPBELL *Lines on Poland* 84 This broken faith Has robb'd you more of Fame. *a* **1840** C. H. BATEMAN *Hymn*, *'Glory, glory, glory'*, When mercy healed the broken law. **1878** MORLEY *Diderot* I. 274 The broken oaths of old days.

b. ***broken home***, a home from which either the father or the mother of the children is absent, usu. through legal separation or divorce.

a **1846** B. R. HAYDON *Autobiogr.* (1853) I. v. 80, I left the vault, and returned to our broken home. **1919** J. C. COLCORD (*title*) Broken homes, a study of family desertion and its social treatment. **1952** M. MCCARTHY *Groves of Academe* (1953) iv. 56 The wild-haired progressive-school rejects, offspring of broken homes. **1958** *Listener* 25 Sept. 480/3 There can be no doubt that a broken home can badly affect a child. **1959** B. WOOTTON et al. *Social Sci.* x. 313 The broken home..normally means homes broken by death, desertion, separation or divorce, and often also by long absence on account of illness.

11. Having the ranks broken; routed, dispersed.

1810 SCOTT *Lady of L.* I. xxxiii, Now leader of a broken host. **1850** PRESCOTT *Peru* II. 330 The governor despised the broken followers of Almagro.

12. Having continuity or uniformity interrupted.

a. of a line: Abruptly altered in direction; turned off at an angle.

1721 BAILEY, *Broken Radiation* is the breaking of the Beams of Light, as seen through a Glass. **1753** CHAMBERS *Cycl. Supp.*, *Broken Ray*, in dioptrics, the same with ray of refraction. **1828** KIRBY & SP. *Entomol.* III. xxxii. 319 The antennæ..broken (viz. when the main body of the antenna forms an angle with the first joints).

b. of the surface of ground, etc.: Intersected with ravines or valleys; uneven. Also, broken up, ploughed, stripped of turf.

1599 HAKLUYT *Voy.* II. II. 131 Betweene them both broken ground. **1782** W. GILPIN *Wye* (1789) 21 By broken ground we mean such as hath lost it's turf, and discovers the naked soil. **1826** DISRAELI *Viv. Grey* VIII. iii, An open but broken country. **1878** BOSW. SMITH *Carthage* 112 The Carthaginian cavalry and elephants extricated themselves.. from the broken ground.

c. of states or conditions: Interrupted, disturbed.

1712 ADDISON *Spect.* No. 317 ¶21 Broken Sleep. **1848** MACAULAY *Hist. Eng.* I. 430 His rest that night was broken.

d. of weather: Unsettled, uncertain.

1793 SMEATON *Edystone L.* §275 The weather continued broken till Saturday.

e. *Hort.* Of a breeder tulip: that has developed into a striped or variegated flower. (See BREAK *v.* 32 c.)

[**1724** P. MILLER *Gardeners & Florists Dict.* II. TU 32 Some Tulips that have been already broke, or have come to stripe, do one Year abound in the dark Colours, and come finely mark'd the next Year.] **1731** —— *Gard. Dict.* 8 D/1 If one of these Flowers [*sc.* tulips] is quite broken..it will never lose its Stripes. **1824** LOUDON *Encycl. Gard.* (ed. 2) 832 Save seed from these in preference to the finest of the variegated or broken sorts [of tulips]. **1852** G. W. JOHNSON *Cottage Gardeners' Dict.* 894/2 After some years the petals of these [*sc.* tulips] become striped, and they are then said to be *broken.* **1956** *Dict. Gardening* (R. Hort. Soc.) (ed. 2) IV. 2162/1 Each group of broken Tulips..is subdivided according to the colouring and ground.

f. ***broken time***, time lost from regular employment.

1872 *Porcupine* 18 May 102/2, I..was in the category of 'broken time'. **1895** *Westm. Gaz.* 8 Nov. 1/3 The formation of a new Union on the basis of payment for 'broken-time', as it is called by courtesy. **1912** R. W. POULTON in *Life* (1919) 214 A carefully arranged payment for 'broken time' for men who are paid weekly or monthly for the hours they work.

g. ***broken line***, in cartography, ornament, etc.: = *pecked line* s.v. PECKED *ppl. a.*; also, as a road-marking.

1937 F. DEBENHAM *Exercises in Cartography* i. 9 Broken or pecked lines, and dotted lines are constantly used for boundaries, paths, shorelines, &c. **1954** *Antiquaries Jrnl.* XXXIV. 169 The broken-line ornament of D20, D24. **1956** H. WATKINSON in *Hansard Commons* 13 Dec. Writ. Answers 84/2 If the white line nearer to him [*sc.* the driver] is a broken line, he may use his judgment and cross it if he can see that the road is clear. **1959** *Highway Code* 6 A broken line does *not* mean that it is safe for you to overtake. **1976** *Milton Keynes Express* 9 July 20/3 The Public Right of Way.., shown by a double broken black line on the map.

13. a. Fragmentary, disconnected, disjointed, in patches.

1820 SCOTT *Ivanhoe* i, Here the red rays of the sun shot a broken and discoloured light. **1845** DARWIN *Voy. Nat.* xi. (1870) 249 On the two great continents in the northern hemisphere, but not in the broken land of Europe between them. **1849** RUSKIN *Sev. Lamps* vi. §1. 162 Broken masses of pine forest.

b. of time: Interrupted; 'odd'.

1621 QUARLES *Argalus & P.* (1678) Introd., The fruits of broken hours. **1667** PEPYS *Diary* 20 May, It being a broken day, did walk abroad. **1754** CHATHAM *Lett. Nephew* iii. 16 Mr. Addison's papers, to be read very frequently at broken times. **1827** HARE *Guesses* Ser. I. (1873) 162 He would have made a broken week of it.

c. of sound, voice, and the like: Uttered disjointedly, ejaculated, interrupted.

1530 PALSGR. 307/1 Brokyn as ones speche is, *abrupt.* **1609** BIBLE (Douay) *Num.* ix. 5 If the trumpeting sound in length and with a broken tune. **1719** DE FOE *Crusoe* (1840) I. xv. 260 He repeated it in the..same broken words. **1731** POPE *Ep. Boyle* 143 Light quirks of Musick, broken and uneven. **1853** *Arab. Nights* (Rtldg.) 514 Her voice much broken with sobs. **1886** STEVENSON *Dr. Jekyll* ii. 25 He spoke with a husky, whispering, and somewhat broken voice.

d. of language: Imperfectly spoken, with the syntax incomplete.

1599 SHAKS. *Hen. V*, v. ii. 265 Breake thy minde to me in broken English. **1685** *Lond. Gaz.* No. 2093/4 A Frenchman ..speaks broken English and Dutch. **1870** L'ESTRANGE *Miss Mitford* I. v. 154 Four letters of Mr. Klopstock in broken English.

14. a. Produced by breaking, severed.

c **1200** *Trin. Coll. Hom.* 93 þe brokene boȝes. **1535** COVERDALE *Acts* xxvii. 44 On broken peces of the shippe [so **1611**]. **1860** TYNDALL *Glac.* I. §9. 61 Broken fragments of rock.

b. Not whole in amount; fractional; not 'round'. ***broken number***: a fraction.

1542 RECORDE *Gr. Artes* (1575) 319 A Fraction in deede is a broken number. **1609** *MS. Acc. St. John's Hosp. Canterb.*, Rec. of the deathe of brother Barton and syster Brooke for broken wages vs. **1797** BURKE *Regic. Peace* III. Wks. VIII. 355 This new-created income of two millions will probably furnish £665,000 (I avoid broken numbers). **1868** MILMAN *St. Paul's* vii. 153 In one month..it yielded no less than £50 besides broken money.

c. Incomplete; fragmentary; imperfect.

1634 CANNE *Necess. Separ.* (1849) 169 Such broken stuff, not worthy of any answer. **1656** Burton's *Diary* (1828) I. 81 There may be a broken title. **1669** GALE *Crt. Gentiles* I. Introd. 6 Broken Traditions. **1813** BYRON *Giaour* xliii, This broken tale was all we knew.

15. Of colours: Qualified or reduced in tone by the addition of some other colour or colours.

1882 *Printing Times* 15 Feb. 35/1 Another way of regarding the tertiary colours is to contemplate them as broken hues, that is, colours degraded by the addition of their complementaries. Looked at thus, olive is a broken blue.

†**16.** Of music: **a.** Arranged for different instruments, 'part' (music); concerted. (*obs.*) Shakspere appar. played upon the phrase. **b.** Cf. sense 13 b, quot. 1731.

[Cf. **1597** MORLEY *Introd. Mus.* 97 *margin*, The plainsong of the Hymne Saluator mundi, broken in diuision, and brought in a Canon of thre parts in one, by Osbert Parsley.]

1599 SHAKS. *Hen. V*, v. ii. 263 Come your Answer in broken Musick; for thy Voyce is Musick, and thy English broken. **1600** —— *A.Y.L.* I. ii. 150 To see this broken Musicke in his sides. **1606** —— *Tr. & Cr.* III. i. 19 *Pan.* What Musique is this? *Serv.* I doe but partly know sir: it is Musicke in parts. *Ibid.* 52 Here is good broken Musicke. **1625** BACON *Masques & Tri.*, *Ess.* (Arb.) 539. **1626** —— *Sylva* §278 So likewise, in that music which we call broken-music or consort-music, some consorts of instruments are sweeter than others.

II. With adverbs: see combs. of BREAK *v.*

17. a. broken-in, broken-off, broken-up.

1837 MARRYAT *Olla Podr.* xxxiv, Broke-in horses. **1876** GEO. ELIOT *Dan. Der.* IV. lv. 131 This broken-off fragment. **1637** in *Cambridge Reg. Bk. Lands* (1896) 42, 20 ac[res] of broken upp grounde..& 25 ac[res] unbroken upp lying by it. **1684** in *Essex Inst. Hist. Coll.* (1862) IV. 68/2 He should have liberty to make use of part of ye improved & broken up ground upon ye sd ffarme. **1846** J. BAXTER *Libr. Pract. Agric.* II. 247 Winter potatoes on broken up grass land.

b. broken-down, (*a*) reduced to atoms, decomposed; (*b*) decayed, ruined; whose health, strength, character, etc. has given way; (*c*) having ceased to function (cf. BREAK *v.* 51 d).

1817 J. SCOTT *Paris Revis.* (ed. 4) 75 His poor broken-down animal. **1827** *Blackw. Mag.* Oct. 452/1 A half-drunk horse-couper, swinging to and fro..on a bit of broken-down blood. **1839–47** TODD *Cycl. Anat. & Phys.* III. 488/1 A mass of broken-down epithelium. **1840** R. DANA *Bef. Mast* xxi. 63 Broken-down politicians. **1914** MILLICENT, DUCHESS OF SUTHERLAND *Six Weeks at War* vi. 77 We saw a number of transport trains carrying broken-down auto-wagons on the trucks. **1944** AUDEN *For Time Being* (1945) 23 Where a crown Has the status of a broken-down Sofa. **1958** *Times* 9 Sept. 4/6 On three-lane highways..the problem of broken-down vehicles is less acute.

III. Combinations.

18. General comb.: chiefly parasynthetic, as ***broken-ended, -footed, -fortuned, -handed, -headed, -hipped, -hoofed, -legged, -minded, -nosed, -paced, -shanked, -spirited, -winged***, etc.

1362 LANGL. *P. Pl.* A. VII. 131 Bote heo beo blynde or broke-schonket. **1544** ASCHAM *Toxoph.* (Arb.) 83 He weueth vp many brokenended matters. *a* **1568** COVERDALE *Bk. Death* III. vii. Wks. II. 124 When he, within seven days, had lost both his sons, he was not broken-minded. **1611** BIBLE *Lev.* xxi. 19 A man that is broken footed, or broken handed. **1701** *Lond. Gaz.* No. 3693/4 A..Mare..a little broken Hoof'd before. **1741** RICHARDSON *Pamela* (1824) I. 195 The broken-fortuned peer goes into the city to marry a rich tradesman's daughter. **1824** MISS MITFORD *Village* Ser. I. (1863) 236 The widow..had a complaining broken-spirited air. **1858** HAWTHORNE *Fr. & It. Jrnls.* (1872) I. 7 A broken-nosed image.

19. Special comb.: **broken-bellied, -bodied** (*dial.*), affected with hernia, ruptured; also *fig.*; **broken-grass** (see quot.); **broken-kneed** (*Farriery*), having the knees damaged by stumbling, etc.; also *fig.*; †**broken-lended,** ruptured; **broken-mouthed** (see quot.). Also BROKEN-BACKED, BROKEN-HEARTED, BROKEN-WIND, -ED.

1634 SIR M. SANDYS *Prudence* xii. 168 Such is our *broken-bellied Age, that this Astutia is turned into Versutia. **1881** EVANS *Leicestersh. Wds.* (E.D.S.) **Broken-grass*, grass left and mown after a field has been grazed by cattle. **1702** *Lond. Gaz.* No. 3814/4 Grey Gelding..*broken Knee'd. **1822** BYRON *Juan* VI. ci, His speech grew still more broken-kneed. **1876** WHYTE MELVILLE *Katerfelto* xv. 167 He rode a broken-kneed Exmoor pony. **1483** *Cath. Angl.* 45 *Broken lendyde, *lumbifractus.* **1750** ELLIS *Country Housew.* 47 What we call *broken-mouthed sheep, that is to say, such who by age have lost most of their teeth.

broken-backed (ˈbrəʊk(ə)nˈbækt), *a.* Also 5 ˈbroke-bak, -backed.

1. Having a broken back; formerly, also, having a deformed or dislocated spine, hunch-backed. Also *transf.* and *fig.*

c **1400** *Gamelyn* 720 Broke-bak scherreue euel mot thou the! **1470** HARDING *Chron.* clvii. iii, This Edmond.. Brokebacked and bowbacked bore. **1530** PALSGR. 307/1 Broken backed, *arne.* **1883** *St. James's Gaz.* 21 Dec. 4/1 The broken-backed Government of Tewfik.

2. *Naut.* (See quot. and BREAK *v.* 7 b.)

1769 FALCONER *Dict. Marine* (1789) *Broken-backed*, the state..of a ship, which is so loosened in her frame..as to droop at each end. *c* **1850** *Rudim. Navig.* (Weale) 101 *Broken-backed or hogged.*

broken-hearted (ˈbrəʊk(ə)nˈhɑːtɪd), *a.* Having a broken heart; heart-broken; having the spirits crushed by grief or despair. See BREAK *v.* 7 c and BROKEN 6.

1526 TINDALE *Luke* iv. 18 To heale the broken harted. **1675** BAXTER *Cath. Theol.* II. x. 221 You tell men that they must not come to Christ, till they are broken-hearted. **1685** *Roxburgh Ball.* (1886) VI. 121 Say, 'the poor Shepherd he dy's broken-hearted'. **1791** BURNS *'Ae fond kiss'* iv, Had we ..Never met, or never parted, We had ne'er been broken-hearted. **1814** SCOTT *Wav.* xii, He returned from college hopeless and broken-hearted, and fell into a decline. **1848** MACAULAY *Hist. Eng.* I. 652 The broken-hearted widows and destitute orphans.

Hence **broken-ˈheartedly** *adv.*, **broken-ˈheartedness.**

1678 MANTON *20 Serm.* i. Wks. 1871 II. 178 We ought.. humbly and broken-heartedly to..accept of the grace. **1796** MORSE *Amer. Geog.* I. 98 Their chagrin and broken heartedness at the loss of their lands. **1882** J. PARKER *Apost.*

Life (1884) III. 136 He who would preach to the times must preach to the broken-heartedness of the day.

brokenly ('brəʊk(ə)nlɪ), *adv.* [f. BROKEN + -LY².]

1. In a broken manner; with frequent breaks or interruptions in the continuity or quality; abruptly, spasmodically, imperfectly, jerkily.

1591 PERCIVALL *Sp. Dict.*, *Rompidamente*, brokenly, *abruptè.* **1599** SHAKS. *Hen. V*, v. ii. 106 O faire Katherine, if you will loue me soundly with your French heart, I will be glad to heare you confesse it brokenly with your English Tongue. **1656** JEANES *Mixt. Schol. Div.* 86 These many termes express it but weakly, and brokenly. **1664-5** PEPYS *Diary* (1879) III. 110 And so to sleep, very brokenly, all night long. **1695** *Lond. Gaz.* No. 3050/4 William Peter, a Negro Man..speaks brokenly, left his Master. **1839** BAILEY *Festus* xx. (1848) 263 Even as the sun Shows brokenly on wavy waters. **1864** TENNYSON *En. Ard.* 648 And there the tale he utter'd brokenly, Scarce credited at first.

2. In a broken condition or state.

1816 BYRON *Ch. Har.* III. xxxii, The heart will break, yet brokenly live on. **1850** MRS. BROWNING *Poems* II. 27 He flapped his heavy wing all brokenly and weak. **1883** *Pall Mall G.* 6 Sept. 2/1 While some brokenly live on desolate and despairing.

brokenness ('brəʊk(ə)nnɪs). [See -NESS.]

1. The state or quality of being broken.

1666 J. SMITH *Old Age* (ed. 2) 85 Rottenness, brokenness, blackness, foulness [of the teeth]. **1757** GRAY *Wks.* (1825) II. 203 It is the brokenness, the ungrammatical position, the total subversion of the period that charms me. **1842** MRS. BROWNING *Grk. Chr. Poets* 157 His pauses frequent to brokenness. *a* **1856** H. MILLER *Rambl. Geol.* 338 As near the steep edge as the brokenness of the ground permitted.

2. *fig.* The state of being crushed or overwhelmed with sorrow, misfortune, etc.; contrition (*obs.*); prostration, despair.

1617 HIERON *Wks.* (1628) II. 371 The spirit of them both was full of contrition..Thus was their brokennesse. Now see, how pleasing it was and how accepted. **1642** ROGERS *Naaman* 133 To prepare the soule with brokennesse and emptinesse. **1655** *Life* in *Gouge's Comm. Heb.*, His confessions were accompanied with much sense of sin, broakennesse of heart, self-abhorrency. **1813** BYRON *Corsair* III. xxii, In helpless—hopeless—brokenness of heart. **1855** MACAULAY *Hist. Eng.* IV. 113 Mere stupefaction and brokenness of heart.

broken wind, broken-wind. *Farriery.* An incurable disease of the organs of respiration in horses, caused by the rupture of the air-cells, which disables them from bearing fatigue.

[**1753** CHAMBERS *Cycl. Supp.* s.v., A broken wind is discovered by a horse's blowing at the nose in the stable and his flanks beating quick, double and irregular, especially after motion.] **1838** *Penny Cycl.* XII. 311/2 Chronic cough ..often degenerating into thick wind..in a great proportion of cases terminates in broken wind. **1847** YOUATT *Horse* xii. 278 Thick-wind and broken-wind exist in various degrees.

broken-'winded, *a.* [f. prec. + -ED.]

1. *Farriery.* Affected with the disease of a broken wind (see prec.); exhaling the air from the lungs with spasmodic efforts.

1523 FITZHERB. *Husb.* §85 Broken wynded is an yll dysease, and cometh of rennynge or rydynge ouer moche.. and wyll not be mended. **1580** BARET *Alv.* s.v. *Flanke*, To moue the flanks like a broken winded horse. **1607** DEKKER *Westw. Hoe* Wks. 1873 II. 351, I shall cough like a broken winded horse. **1748** tr. *Vegetius' Distemp. Horses* 176 They are pursive or broken-winded. **1846** R. EG.-WARBURTON *Hunt. Songs, Earth Stopper* iv, Thy worn hackney, blind and broken winded. **1849-52** TODD *Cycl. Anat.* IV. 1021/2.

2. *transf.* and *fig.*

1627 MAY *Lucan* v. (R.) Broke-winded murmers, howlings, and sadd grones. **1641** MILTON *Animadv.* (1851) 190 Liberty of speaking..was girded, and straight lac'd, almost to a broken-winded tizzick. **1809** W. IRVING *Knickerb.* (1861) 244 They might as well have tried to turn a rusty weather-cock with a broken-winded bellows. **1883** *Century Mag.* XXVI. 282 Kicking a broken-winded football about the field.

broker ('brəʊkə(r)). Forms: 4-5 brocor, brokour, brocour(e, 6 brooker, brokar, 7 broaker, 5- broker. See also BROGGER. [ME. *brocor*, *-our*, *brokour*, a. AngloF. *brocour* (also *broggour*) = ONF. *brokeor* (:—L. type **broccātōrem*), nom. *brokiere* (:—L. **broccātor*) of which Godefroy has one example explained by him as 'celui qui vend du vin au broc', as to the precise sense of which see below. The Central Fr. equivalent was *brocheor*, *brochière*; and the word is the agent noun of the OFr. vb. *brochier*, ONF. *brokier* (:—L. **broccāre*) in the sense 'to broach' or 'tap' a cask. *Brocheor*, *brokeor* stand in precisely the same relation to the sb. *broche*, *broc*, and the vb. *brochier*, *brokier*, as *tapster* or rather the earlier *tapper* stand to the sb. *tap*, and vb. to *tap* in Teutonic: the *brocheor*, *brokeor*, *brokour*, or *broker*, was lit. a tapster, who retailed wine 'from the tap', and hence, by extension, any retail-dealer, one who bought to sell over again, a second-hand dealer, or who bought for another, hence a jobber, middleman, agent, etc. Cf. sense of L. *caupo*.

The Romanic vb. *broccare* was evidently f. *brocco*, *brocca* in the sense of 'spike, piercing instrument' (:—L. *broccus*, *brocca* adj.: see BROACH). But these sbs. appear to have afterwards had their sense modified from the verb, so that in the OF. *vendre à broke*, or *à broche*, in mod.F. *vendre à broc*, the sense passed from 'broach', to 'broaching, tapping', and at length to 'the quantity of wine drawn at a broaching or tapping', and hence 'the jug or vessel which held this', as in mod.F. *broc* (from 5 to 10 litres). Anglo-French had also a deriv. form *abrocour*, and there were Anglo-Latin words *abrocator*, *abrocamentum*; also *brocarius* 'proxeneta, interpres et consiliarius contractuum', and *abrocarius*. *Brocarius* appears to have been formed on the sb. (*broc(c)a*, *broc(c)us*); *abrocarius* must have been formed on the apparent analogy of *brocator*, *abrocator*.]

I. A retailer of commodities; a second-hand dealer.

†**1.** A retailer; *contemptuously*, Pedlar, petty dealer, monger. (Now sunk in sense 2.)

1393 LANGL. *P. Pl.* C. VII. 953ut am ich brocor of bakbytynge· and blame mennes ware. **1583** STANYHURST *Æneis* I. (Arb.) 33 For gould his carcasse was sold by the broker Achilles. **1598** MARSTON *Pigmal.* I. 138 But Broker of anothers wit. **1657** J. ANGIER *Elegy* in S. Purchas *Pol. Flying Ins.*, Brokers in verse condemn it. **1730** YOUNG *Ep. Pope* i. *Poems* (1757) I. 183 Millions of wits, and brokers in old song.

2. A dealer in second-hand furniture and apparel; a pawnbroker.

[**1377** LANGL. *P. Pl.* B. v. 248, I haue lent lordes and ladyes my chaffare And ben her brocour after, and bouȝte it myself.] **1583** STUBBES *Anat. Abus.* II. 39, I haue hard prisoners..declaime and crie out against brookers. For, said they..if they would not haue receiued our stollen goods, we woulde neuer haue stollen them. **1598** B. JONSON *Ev. Man in Hum.* III. v. (1616) 39 A Hounds-ditch man, sir. One of the deuils neere kinsmen, a broker. **1600** ROWLAND *Lett. Humours Blood* I. 47 Clad in the ruines of a Brokers shoppe. **1611** —— *Knave of Hrts.* in Singer *Hist. Cards* 257 Or brokers, for their buying things are stole. **1641** *Termes de la Ley* 43 b, Broker..the word is now also appropriated to them amongst us that buy and sell old and broken apparell and household-stuffe. **1766** ENTICK *London* IV. 69 Brokers, who deal in both new and old houshold goods. **1872** BLACK *Adv. Phaeton* 15 An old landscape that has lain for years in a broker's shop.

II. One who acts as a middleman in bargains.

3. 'One employed as a middleman to transact business or negotiate bargains between different merchants or individuals' (McCulloch). Formerly used more widely, including the senses of 'jobber, agent, factor, commission-agent'.

1377 LANGL. *P. Pl.* B. v. 130 Amonges Burgeyses haue I be dwellynge at Londoun, And gert bakbitinge be a brocoure [*C.* brocor] to blame mennes ware. **1410** *Will of R. Beche* (Somerset Ho.) John Houghton Brocour Artis Aurifabrorum. **1480** CAXTON *Chron. Eng.* ccv. 186 An alyen that was callyd Arnold of spayne that was a brocour of london. **1495** *Act 11 Hen. VII*, viii, [If] the seller hymself or by his broker or factour..bye the same godes. **1509** *Will of Draycot* (Somerset Ho.) Haberdassher and broker. **1570** LEVINS *Manip.* 71 A Broker, *proxeneta.* **1599** HAKLUYT *Voy.* II. 260 There are in Pegu eight Brokers..which are bound to sell your goods at the price which they be worth, and you giue them for their labour two in the hundred. **1622** MALYNES *Anc. Law-Merch.* 202 The common saying is, That a craftie Merchant needeth no Broker. **1641** *Termes de la Ley* 43 b, The true trade of a Broker..is to beat, contrive, make, and conclude Bargaines between Merchants and Tradesmen. *c* **1645** HOWELL *Lett.* vi. 24 By their profession they are for the most part Brokers. **1705** *Lond. Gaz.* No. 4131/4 John Styles, Sworn-Broker [see **1849**]. **1725** DE FOE *Voy. round World* (1840) 56 He served them for..a broker, to bargain for them with the European ships for provisions. **1849** FREESE *Comm. Class-bk.* 19 Brokers ought to be sworn by the public authorities not to transact any business on their own account, under a heavy penalty; which is the case in..London, etc. **1858** LD. ST. LEONARDS *Handy Bk. Prop. Law* XXI. 166 Never allow the money..to be retained by brokers, agents, or solicitors.

b. 'Brokers are divided into different classes; as *bill* or *exchange brokers*, STOCKBROKERS, *ship* and *insurance brokers*, PAWNBROKERS... The brokers who negotiate sales of produce between different merchants usually confine themselves to some one department or line of business' (McCulloch), as *cotton-broker*, *tea-broker*, *wool-broker*, etc.

1622 MALYNES *Anc. Law-Merch.* 64 Guided..by ignorant Brokers of Exchanges. **1769** *Junius Lett.* i. 9 A man, whose cares..have degraded the office of Commander-in-Chief into a broker of Commissions. *Ibid.* ii. 13 The dignity is depraved..into the base office of a Commission-broker. **1849** COBDEN *Speeches* 46 The cotton brokers of Liverpool, and the cotton spinners of Manchester. **1852** MCCULLOCH *Comm. Dict.* 198 Their charge as ship brokers is about 2 per cent. on the gross receipts. When they act as insurance brokers they charge 5 per cent. on the premium. *a* **1860** C. FENN *Eng. & For. Funds* (1883) 127 The members of the Stock Exchange are called *Jobbers* and *Brokers*. The broker deals with the jobber for his principal, and is remunerated by commission. **1860** *All Y. Round* No. 75. 582 Blacklegs.. the betting brokers were formerly called.

†**4.** A go-between or intermediary in love affairs; a hired match-maker, marriage-agent; also a procurer, pimp, bawd; a pander generally. *Obs.*

1377 LANGL. *P. Pl.* B. II. 65 And now worth this Mede ymaried al to a mansed schrewe..Ac fauel was þe first þat fette hire out of boure, And as a brokour brouȝte hir, to be with fals enioigned. **1393** GOWER *Conf.* II. 280 Brocours of love, that deceiven. **1514** BARCLAY *Cyt. & Uplondyshm.* (1847) 30 So many woers, baudes and brokers..that chast Penelope Coulde scant among them preserve hir chastitie. **1591** SHAKS. *Two Gent.* I. ii. 41 Now (by my modesty) a goodly Broker. **1606** —— *Tr. & Cr.* v. x. 33 *Pandarus.* But heare you? heare you? *Troylus.* Hence broker, lackie! **1621** AINSWORTH *Annot. Numb.* xv. 29 The heart and the eyes are the spies of the body, and brokers to bring it into transgression. *a* **1651** CALDERWOOD *Hist. Kirk* (1843) II. 24 Danvill..left behind him a broker betwixt him and the queene, Monsieur Chatelat. **1694** R. LESTRANGE *Fables* cxxviii. (1714) 145 This Praying Carpenter here would have made Mercury a Broker to his Knavery.

5. A middleman, intermediary, or agent generally; an interpreter, messenger, commissioner.

1530 PALSGR. 201/2 Broker that speketh many languages, *truchement* [*i.e.* dragoman]. **1576** *Tyde taryeth no man* in Collier *Illustr. E.E. Pop. Lit.* 12 Thou, Helpe, art a broker betweene man and man, Whereby much deceyte thou usest now and than. **1586** J. HOOKER in *Holinshed* II. 91/2 Thomas foorthwith sent his messengers..to his cousine the lord Butler..Wherevpon the lord Butler returned Thomas his brokers with this letter. **1593** SHAKS. *3 Hen. VI*, IV. i. 63 You shall giue me leaue To play the Broker in mine owne behalfe. **1600** HOLLAND *Livy* XXVII. xv. 639 The brocher and broker both of the treason, had brought word. **1571** HANMER *Chron. Irel.* 196 These Nuntioes were so craftv, that they needed no Brokers. **1642** T. TAYLOR *God's Judgem.* I. I. xix. 61 As Truth got ever the upper hand..so the broakers and upholders of falshood came ever to the worse. **1864** LOWELL *Study Wind.* (1886) 118 The brokers of treason in the North.

†**b.** A legal agent, a proctor. *Obs.*

1538 STARKEY *England* I. iii. §29 (1871) 83 Prokturys and brokarys of both lawys, wych rather trowbul menny causys then fynysch them justely, are to many.

†**c.** frequently with implied censure. *Obs.*

c **1510** BARCLAY *Mirr. Good Mann.* (1570) G iv, Be no towler, catchpoll nor customer, No broker nor botcher, no somner nor sergeaunt. **1562** J. HEYWOOD *Prov. & Epigr.* (1867) 135 Two false knaues neede no broker. **1586** T. B. *La Primaud. Fr. Acad.* (1594) 245 Flatterers, brokers, and such as are most wicked, carie away offices..& wastfully consume the publike treasure. **1595** SHAKS. *John* II. i. 568 That Broker, that still breakes the pate of faith, That dayly breake-vow, he that winnes of all. **1608** DEKKER *Sev. Sins* VI. (Arb.) 40 Brokers yat shaue poore men by most iewish interest.

III. 6. A person licensed to sell or appraise household furniture distrained for rent.

1818 *Act 57 Geo. III*, xciii. **1836** DICKENS *Sk. Boz* v. (1850) 16/1 'A broker's man's is not a life to be envied.. people hate and scout 'em because they're the ministers of wretchedness, like, to poor people'. **1852** MCCULLOCH *Comm. Dict.* 198 Brokers, simply so called, in their character of appraisers and sellers of goods distrained for rent, are regulated by 57 Geo. III. c. 93. *Mod.* The landlord put in the brokers yesterday, and all his furniture is gone.

7. *Comb.* **broker-between** = BROKER 3, 4; **broker-woman; broker-like** *a.*

1606 SHAKS. *Tr. & Cr.* III. ii. 211 Let all inconstant men be Troylusses, all false women Cressids, and all brokers betweene Panders. **1723** *Lond. Gaz.* No. 6217/4 Elizabeth Boden..Broker-woman. **1607** *Miseries Enf. Marr.* III. in Hazl. *Dodsley* IX. 512 What beards..gentlemenlike-beards, or brokerlike-beards?

brokerage ('brəʊkərɪdʒ). Also 7 -idge. [f. prec. + -AGE.]

1. The action or professional service of a broker; the broker's trade. Also *attrib.*

1466 *Mann. & Househ. Exp.* 361 Item [my master paid] for brokerage, ix. *d.* **1619** JER. DYKE *Counterpoison* (1620) 20 Egges of the same cockatrice, brats of the same hag, are steeple and temple brokerage. **1753** *Scots Mag.* Sept. 440/1 The trade of the Jews..was usury, brokerage, and jobbing. **1827** SCOTT *Napoleon* xxxviii, By brokerage and agiotage. **1875** POSTE *Gaius* II. (ed. 2) 213 The acquisition of Obligations..by brokerage of an independent agent. **1885** *Law Times Rep.* LI. 694/1 In ordinary brokerage transactions.

2. The commission or per-centage paid to a broker on the transactions negotiated by him.

1622 MALYNES *Anc. Law-Merch.* 196, 20 pro cent. with the Alcaualla, taken for Brokeridge to sell them. **1668** SEDLEY *Mulberry Gard.* II. ii. **1697** DAMPIER *Voy.* (1729) I. 508 An 18th part profit, by way of Brokerage for every Bargain. **1753** HANWAY *Trav.* (1762) I. v. lxxi. 323 An exorbitant brokerage of one or more per cent. **1809** R. LANGFORD *Introd. Trade* 23 The brokerage on foreign bills bought and sold is 1-10th per cent. **1884** *Manch. Exam.* 28 May 5/2 All brokerages and discounts credited to the company.

†**3.** The acting as a bawd or pimp. *Obs. rare.*

1645 PAGITT *Heresiogr.* (1665) 75 That I speak not of Brokerage, of whores, and other filthiness, too too bad.

'brokeress. [f. as prec. + -ESS.] **a.** A procuress. **b.** A female stockbroker.

1583 STANYHURST *Poems* (Arb.) 140 Now beldam brokresse must be with moonny rewarded. **1749** J. CLELAND *Mem. Woman Pleasure* II. 106 Three hundred guineas to myself, and an hundred to the brokeress. **1827** CARLYLE *Germ. Rom.* I. 32 The talking brokeress..was far from giving him a true disclosure of her blabbing. **1865** SWINBURNE *Chastelard* II. i, Yea, and she said, the Italian brokeress, She said such men were good for great queens' love. **1872** SCHELE DE VERE *Americanisms* 655 A couple of ladies having established their 'Exchange Office' in..Wall-street, they were at once spoken of in the New York papers as bankeresses or brokeresses.

'brokering, *vbl. sb.* [f. BROKER *sb.* + -ING¹.] Acting as a broker; the broker's trade.

1633 ROWLEY *Match at Midn.* I. i, I have given over brokering.

'brokering, *ppl. a.* [f. as prec. + -ING².] That is a broker, trafficking, bargain-driving.

1687 MRS. BEHN *Lucky Chance* IV. i, Griping as Hell, and as insatiable, worse than a brokering Jew.

† **'brokerly**, *a.* and *adv.* *Obs.* [f. BROKER *sb.* + -LY[1], [2].] **A.** *adj.* Of the nature of, or like a broker; pettifogging, huckstering.
1592 NASHE *P. Penilesse* (ed. 2) 9a, A certaine kind of a brokerly gentleman. 1610 B. JONSON *Alch.* IV. vii. (1616) 663 A brokerly slaue. 1611 COTGR., *Mangonne*, a Brokers wife, or brokerlie woman.
B. *adv.* By the agency of a broker.
1593 NASHE *Christ's T.* (1613) 79 Brokerly blowne vp honour, honour by antické fawning fidled vp.

'brokership. *rare.* [see -SHIP.] The office or action of a broker; intermediation.
1845 LD. CAMPBELL *Chancellors* cxxii. (1857) VI. 38 The brokership of Cottingham was at first dispensed with.

† **brokery.** *Obs.* [f. BROKER + -Y; see -ERY.]
1. The business or action of a broker.
1583 STUBBES *Anat. Abus.* II. 38 Seeing that you are ignorant of this goodly mysterie, and high profession of brokerie. *a*1593 MARLOWE *Jew of M.* II. ii, Cozening, forfeiting, and tricks belonging unto brokery. 1641 W. CARTWRIGHT *Ordinary* v. iv, She..that is So expert grown in this flesh Brokery.
2. A broker's wares; second-hand clothes; anything second-hand or stale.
1597-8 BP. HALL *Sat.* I. iii. 24 Now soouping in side robes of Royaltie, That earst did skrub in lowsie brokerie. 1611 BARREY *Ram-Alley* in *Dodsley* (1780) V. 493 Clad in old ends, and pieced with brokery. 1634 CANNE *Necess. Separ.* (1849) 262 Bringing therein nothing but his old brokery.
3. Rascally dealing or trafficking.
1597-8 BP. HALL *Sat.* (1753) 28 Busie their braines with deeper brokerie. 1602 *Life T. Cromwell* II. ii. 90 To live by falsehood or by brokery. *a*1654 ROSS *Notor. Heretics* (1675) 18 By this brokery did this crafty knave chalk out his way to that soveraign dignity.

broking ('brəʊkɪŋ), *vbl. sb.* [f. BROKE *v.*]
1. The broker's trade; acting as a broker.
1569 E. HAKE *Newes Powles Ch. Yarde* (1579) G iij, Of Brokers, they did thirtie such ordaine..To vse the trade of broking. 1864 SALA in *Temple Bar Mag.* XII, Bargaining, chaffering, broking and discounting. 1866 *Lond. Rev.* 6 Oct. 380/2 The Legislature itself must for a time abandon reform, and take to furniture broking.
†**2.** Lending of money upon pawns or pledges; dishonest or fraudulent dealing. *Obs.*
1592 CHETTLE *Kind Harts Dr.* (1841) 51 An occupation of no long standing about London, called broking, or brogging ..in which there is pretty jugling, especially to blind law, and bolster usury. 1603 BRETON *Poste w. Packet, &c.*, A crafty knave may loose by his cunning Broking. 1619 J. HEATH *House of Corr.* C iv, I told a Scriuener of his Briberie, His Broking, Forging, Cheating, Knauery.
3. *attrib.* (Difficult to separate from the *ppl. a.*)
1569 E. HAKE *Newes Powles Ch. Yarde* (1591) G iij b, Whole hundreds now doe liue by beastly broking trade. 1594 SHAKS. *Rich. III*, II. i. 293 If then we shall..Redeeme from broaking pawne the blemish'd Crowne. 1633 T. ADAMS *Exp. 2 Peter* i. 17 A usurer in his broking-house.

† **'broking,** *ppl. a.* *Obs.* [f. BROKE *v.* + -ING[2].]
1. That acts as a broker.
1592 G. HARVEY *Pierce's Super.* 175 Not such..a broking & huckstering penne [exists]. 1598 J. DICKENSON *Greene in Conc.* (1878) 155 His owne, and hir attyre, fell into the hands of brokeing Usurers. 1647 R. STAPYLTON *Juvenal* 133 A broaking usurer.
2. ? That acts as a procurer.
1599 MARSTON *Sco. Villanie* I. iii. 180 A die, a drab, and filthy broking knaues Are..all deuouring graues.
3. Base-dealing; 'peddling,' contemptible.
1592 WYRLEY *Armorie* 142 Like a broking varlet. 1594 NASHE *Unfort. Trav.* 32 This broccing duble beere oration. 1606 *Wily Beguiled* in Hazl. *Dodsley* IX. 238, I scorn that base, broking..name. 1639 J. MAYNE *City Match* in *Dodsley* (1780) IX. 379 O that I could But see that cheating rogue upon the rack: I'd..show him hell, and then recall His broking soul and give him strength to suffer His torture often.

brokke, -ing, var. forms of BROCK, -ING.

brokket, -ette, -itt, obs. ff. BROCKET.

brokle, -yl, -ylle, var. of BROCKLE.

broklembe, obs. form of BROOKLIME.

† **'brokling.** *Obs.* Also 4 brogeling. [Connected with *brokel*, BROCKLE, or with BROKEN.] Breaking off, interruption.
*c*1340 *Cursor M.* 7071 (Fairf.) þe sege lasted xxx ȝere wiþ-outen brokling [*Cott.* brogeling, *Gött.* breking, *Trin.* brekyng] of þat werre.

brokour, -ress, obs. ff. BROKER, BROKERESS.

brole, obs. form of BROIL.

brolga ('brɒlgə). [Native name.] The Australian native companion crane, *Grus rubicunda*.
1896 *Westm. Gaz.* 6 Oct. 2/1 The native companion crane, otherwise known as the brolga. 1911 BEAN *'Dreadnought' of Darling* xvii. 169 Far up one of the Darling tributaries, the brolga (native companion) and crane and ibis seemed fairly thick. 1944 A. RUSSELL *Bush Ways* xv. 75 It was a flock of native companions, or brolgas—immense birds, nearly five feet tall. 1959 J. CLEARY *Back of Sunset* 214 They..saw two brolgas, tall long-legged birds, going through their weird dance.

† **broll.** *Obs.* exc. *dial.* Forms: 4 brol, brolle, 6 brawl, 9 *dial.* browl. [Of unknown origin: The *Promp. Parv.* explains 'Breyel' as *brollus, brolla, miserculus*; but this may be merely the Eng. word latinized. It seems possible that, as *brethel* was app. reduced to *breel, brothel* may have been reduced to *brōl*, but evidence is wanting.]
Offspring, child; *contemptuously*, a brat, an 'imp', a little wretch.
*a*1325 *Lullaby* in *Rel. Ant.* II. 177 The wrech brol that is of Adams blode. 1377 LANGL. *P. Pl.* B. III. 204 þe leste brolle [*v.r.* brol] of his blode a barounes pere. *c*1380 WYCLIF *Sel. Wks.* III. 195 Fiȝtten wiþ þer wif and meyne as þei weren Sathanas brollis. 1394 *P. Pl. Crede* 745 Now mot ich soutere his sone setten to schole And ich a beggers brol on þe booke lerne. 1575 J. STILL *Gamm. Gurton* II. ii. Shall such a beggars brawl as that, thinkest thou, make me a thief? 1864 ATKINSON *Whitby Gloss.*, *Browl*, a brat, a term of displeasure towards an offending child. 'You brazen'd young browl'. 1875 F. K. ROBINSON *Whitby Gloss.* (E.D.S.), *Browl*, a 'brat', an impudent youth.

† **broll,** *v.* *Obs.* *rare*[−1]. [? by-form of BRAWL *v.*, or ? ad. Du. *brullen* to roar.] To roar, sound loud.
1660 *Engl. Monarchy Freest State* 7 Since this Rumble of a Free State and Commonwealth hath brolled in our heads.

brolly ('brɒlɪ). *colloq.* **1.** Clipped and altered form of UMBRELLA 2.
1874 HOTTEN *Slang Dict.*, *Brolly*, an umbrella. Term used at both Oxford and Cambridge Universities. 1885 *Punch* 6 June 273/2 Pair o' pattens and brolly are more in your line. 1899 KIPLING *Stalky* 209 What are you stealin' the gentleman's brolly for? 1925 *Sunday at Home* July 595/1 The lass was a clever thief who had hooked his brolly.
2. *slang.* A parachute. Also *attrib.* and *Comb.*, as **brolly-hop**, a jump made with a parachute; so ***brolly-hopping*** vbl. sb.
1934 *Daily Express* 27 June 10/4 A brolly hop is a hop into space—with a parachute! Brolly-hopping will become a commonplace to the younger generation. 1934 G. P. OLLEY *Million Miles in Air* ii. 72 Never having made what pilots refer to..as a 'brolly hop'. 1940 J. M. B. BEARD in Michie & Graebner *Their Finest Hour* xii. 180, I was floating still and peacefully with my 'brolly' canopy billowing above my head.

brolynge, obs. form of BROILING *sb.*[2]

brom-: see BROMO-.

‖ **'broma**[1]. *Obs.* [16th c. Sp. *broma*, 'a worme that eateth holes in ships' (Percivall).] A ship-worm; ? the teredo.
1555 EDEN *Decades W. Ind.* III. VI. (Arb.) 164 Of the planckes wherof, if shyppes were made, they shoulde bee safe from the woormes of the sea whiche they caule Bromas. 1599 HAKLUYT *Voy.* II. II. 22 Their ships were also in many places eaten with the wormes called Bromas or Bissas, whereof mention is made in the Decades. 1831 W. IRVING *Columbus* (1849) III. 55 As their vessels were in danger of being destroyed by the broma or worms.

‖ **broma**[2] ('brəʊmə). [a. Gr. βρῶμα food.]
1. *Med.* 'Food of any kind that is masticated and not drank' (Hooper *Med. Dict.* 1811).
2. A preparation of chocolate (so called from *theobroma*, the name of the Cacao plant).
1858 ELIZ. TWINING *Lect. Plants* x. 301 Broma is another kind of composition made from chocolate seeds.

bromal ('brəʊməl). [f. BROM-INE + AL-COHOL; cf. CHLORAL.] A compound analogous to chloral, produced by the action of bromine on alcohol.
1875 H. WOOD *Therap.* (1879) 333 Clinical experience with bromal hydrate is still wanting. 1877 WATTS *Fownes' Chem.* II. 253 Tribromaldehyde or Bromal.

bromate ('brəʊmeɪt). *Chem.* [f. BROM-IC + -ATE[4].] A salt of bromic acid.
*a*1836 *Penny Cycl.* V. 461/1 The bromates which their oxides form with bromic acid. 1854 SCOFFERN in *Orr's Circ. Sc.* Chem. 317 Must be either a nitrate..or bromate.

bromatology (brəʊmə'tɒlədʒɪ). [mod., f. Gr. βρῶμα, βρωματο- (see BROMA[2]), + -λογία -LOGY; cf. F. *bromatologie*.]
1. A discourse or treatise on food.
1811 in HOOPER *Med. Dict.*
2. 'The doctrine or consideration of food, its nature, quality, and uses' (*Syd. Soc. Lex.*).

brombille, obs. form of BRAMBLE.

brome[1] (brəʊm). *Chem.* [a. F. *brome*, f. Gr. βρῶμ-ος stink, smell.] The French name of BROMINE, formerly used in English.
1827 TURNER *Elem. Chem.* [see BROMINE]. 1836 *Penny Cycl.* V. 486/1 In case of poisoning [by caniramin], emetics may be given, and also tincture of brome or iodine. 1841 MRS. MARCET *Conv. Chem.* II. 145 Brome.. notwithstanding its high specific gravity, boils at the temperature of 160°.

brome[2] (brəʊm). *Bot.* [ad. *Bromus*, Bot. name of the genus, in Pliny *bromos*, a. Gr. βρόμος (also βρῶμος) oats.] A book-name for a genus of oat-like grasses (*Bromus*). Also **brome-grass**.
1759-91 B. STILLINGFLEET *Misc. Tracts* 371 To approach as nearly as possible to the Latin names in sound..I have called *aira* hairgrass, the *bromus* bromegrass, etc. *Ibid.* 378 Corn-Brome..*Bromus Arvensis.* 1794 MARTYN *Rousseau's Bot.* xiii. 140 The Bromes are very nearly allied to the Fescues. 1881 JEFFERIES *Wood Magic* I. vi. 136 The long brome-grass tickled his face while he was pulling.

brome, obs. form of BROOM.

Bromedgham, obs. form of BRUMMAGEM.

bromelia (brəʊ'miːlɪə). *Bot.* [Named by Linnæus after Olaus *Bromel*, a Swede.] A plant of the genus *Bromelia*, or of the family *Bromeliaceæ*, consisting of plants indigenous to S. America and W. Indies, the species of which have short stems, and generally lance-shaped leaves with spiny margins.
1822 W. J. HOOKER *Exotic Flora* I. 41 *Bromelia Pallida*, pale-flowered Bromelia. 1833 *Penny Cycl.* I. 447/1 Orchideous plants and bromelias overrun their limbs. 1963 R. P. DALES *Annelids* ix. 179 Such specialized habitats as the reservoirs of bromelias.
b. *attrib.*, as **bromelia water**, water contained in the rosette of leaves of a bromeliad.
1860 MAYNE REID *Odd People* 83 The thorny point of the *bromelia* leaf. 1908 *Smithsonian Misc. Coll.* V. 73 The species was also bred from bromelia water near Tabernilla.

bromeliaceous (brəʊ,miːlɪ'eɪʃəs), *a.* *Bot.* [see -ACEOUS.] Pertaining to the natural order *Bromeliaceæ*, which includes the pineapple.
1882 *Garden* 15 Apr. 260/1 A huge Bromeliaceous plant.

bromeliad (brəʊ'miːlɪæd). *Bot.* [f. mod.L. *Bromeliaceæ*, f. BROMELIA: see -AD.] Any plant belonging to the family *Bromeliaceæ*.
1866 LINDLEY & MOORE *Treas. Bot.* 170/1 Some of the Bromeliads grow attached to the branches of trees, and are called Air-plants. 1902 *Encycl. Brit.* XXV. 438/1 In some aerophilous Bromeliads the rosette of leaves forms a cup in which water collects. 1927 *Glasgow Herald* 23 July 4 The 'vegetable horse hair' (Tillandsia Usneoides) is a rarely flowering Bromeliad that hangs in grey festoons from the branches of the trees. 1962 *Amat. Gardening* 17 Feb. 7 Until recent years almost all bromeliads have been expensive.

bromelin ('brəʊməlɪn). *Chem.* [f. BROMEL(IA + -IN[1].] A proteolytic enzyme obtained from the juice of the pineapple.
1894 *Jrnl. Chem. Soc.* LXVI. II. 63 Bromelin..appears to be associated with a peculiar proteose-like substance. 1901 *Ibid.* LXXX. I. 355 Bromelin..readily forms leucine, tyrosine, and tryptophan, even in acid media. 1928 *Daily Express* 13 Dec. 5/5 Pineapple..contains a peculiar digestive enzyme known as bromelin.

bromellite ('brɒməlaɪt). *Min.* [ad. G. *bromellit* (G. Aminoff 1925, in *Zeitschr. f. Krystallogr.* LXII. 122), f. the name of Magnus von *Bromell* (1679–1731), Swedish physician and mineralogist + -ITE[1].] A mineral of the zincite group, consisting of beryllium oxide and occurring in white hexagonal prisms.
1926 *Chem. Abstr.* XX. 29 An analysis of an unknown mineral from Långban gave 98% BeO... It is named bromellite. 1965 *Amer. Min.* L. 22 Synthetic bromellite (BeO) is finding wide application not only in high-temperature refractory ware but also as a moderator in gas-cooled nuclear reactors and as a dielectric in electronic applications.

'bromel-worts: Lindley's English name for the *Bromeliaceæ*: see BROMELIACEOUS *a.*

bromhydrin: see BROMO-.

bromic ('brəʊmɪk), *a.* *Chem.* [f. BROM-INE + -IC.] Containing bromine in chemical combination; **bromic silver**, the native bromide of silver (AgBr), BROMYRITE; **bromic acid** ($HBrO_3$), the acid which forms bromates.
1828 WEBSTER *Chem.* (ed. 2) 109 Bromine unites with oxygen to form bromic acid. 1857 DANA *Min.* vi. (ed. 2) 328 Iodic Silver, Bromic Silver. Silver also occurs in nature united with iodine and bromine. 1878 A. HAMILTON *Nerv. Dis.* 81 The bromic salts.

Bromicham, -migham, obs. ff. BRUMMAGEM.

bromide ('brəʊmaɪd). *Chem.* [f. BROM-INE + -IDE.] **1. a.** A primary compound of bromine with an element or organic radical. Several bromides (esp. those of ammonium, iron, and potassium) are in common medicinal use.
1836 *Penny Cycl.* V. 461/1 Carbon and Bromine form a liquid bromide of carbon. 1871 B. STEWART *Heat* §58 The same law holds good for the Bromides..of ethyle and methyle. 1876 HARLEY *Mat. Med.* 204 Bromide of Iron acts as an energetic tonic. 1881 C. M. BEARD *Sea-Sickness* 36 The great value of the bromides in very large doses, as harmless and powerful sedatives.
b. *familiarly* for ***bromide of potassium*** (KBr).
1883 *Harper's Mag.* Jan. 241/1 A little bromide completed the relief that put her asleep.
c. *attrib.*
1886 FAGGE *Princ. Med.* II. 806 Bromide Rash.
2. A dose of potassium bromide taken as a sedative.
1903 *Smart Set* IX. 14/1 I'll give you a bromide when you're ready for bed.
3. *fig.* A person whose thoughts and conversation are conventional and commonplace. Also, a commonplace saying, trite remark, conventionalism; a soothing statement. *slang* (orig. *U.S.*).
[1903 *Daily Chron.* 9 May 4/5 Literature is resentful at being mistaken for bromide.] 1906 G. BURGESS (*title*) Are you a Bromide? 1909 W. RALEIGH *Lett.* (1926) II. 340

Bromides are dull partly because everyone pretends to understand them. **1924** HICHENS *After the Verdict* II. xvii, For once Mrs. Baratrie gave way to a bromide. She said: 'How good little Clive was!' **1925** *Contemp. Rev.* Oct. 469 There is the rise of slums which 'ought not to be in a new country', but which, in spite of this oft-quoted bromide, certainly existed in still earlier days. **1926** *Publishers' Weekly* 20 Feb. 563 The old bromide that poetry never sells is once again proved to be wrong. **1950** *Manch. Guardian Weekly* 29 June 2/3 The Republicans would have to fall back on the old bromide about the incurable quarrelsomeness of 'old, sick Europe'. **1961** B. FERGUSSON *Watery Maze* i. 15 These two bromides.. were quoted by the faithful.. until they were worn as thin as a Queen Victoria bun penny.

4. *Photogr.* **a.** ***bromide developer***, a developer suitable for bromide paper; ***bromide emulsion***, a gelatine emulsion impregnated with a bromide, esp. silver bromide; ***bromide paper***, a paper coated with gelatino-bromide emulsion, used for contact printing and enlargements; also ***bromide print, printer, printing*** (of or with reference to bromide paper).

1885 *Amateur Photographer* 27 Mar. 409 Britannia Bromide Paper, specially for enlargements. **1892** A. BROTHERS *Photogr.* 78 Opal glass and paper are coated with silver bromide emulsion. *Ibid.*, Bromide-Printing Process. **1902** *Bromide Monthly* Jan. 10 One well-known Bromide printer we know of makes his exposures in contact printing to the light of an ordinary candle from preference. **1904** GOODCHILD & TWENEY *Technol. & Sci. Dict.* 71/1 *Bromide Prints*.. are developed and fixed like dry plates. **1923** S. E. SHEPPARD in *Photography* 165 Characteristic Curves for Bromide Papers. **1971** *Ann. Rep. Curators Bodl. Libr. 1969–70* 46 Photography from Library material.. consisted of.. 3,544 bromide prints.

b. A reproduction or proof on bromide paper; a bromide print.

1967 F. J. M. WIJNEKUS *Elsevier's Dict. Printing* 45/2 *Bromide*, brief for bromide print. **1977** *Economist* 5 Mar. 116 Work combining original artwork, illustrations, line or screen bromides.. and type matter. **1979** *Times* 20 Nov. 4/4 Bromides, or photographic proofs, of individual reports have to be cut and pasted up in the standard way. **1983** H. EVANS *Good Times, Bad Times* ix. 182 The computer system ..was designed to translate keystrokes.. so that they emerged in the form of a photographic bromide ready for insertion.

bromidic (brəʊˈmɪdɪk), *a. slang* (orig. *U.S.*). [f. BROMIDE 3 + -IC.] Of the nature of a bromide; commonplace or conventional.

1906 G. BURGESS *Are you a Bromide?* 19 The Bromide can't possibly help being bromidic. **1911** H. S. HARRISON *Queed* xix, 'Did genius fail to burn?' he asked, employing a bromidic phrase. **1927** WILLEY *Early Ch. Portraits* 98 Athanasius did not desire the office of Bishop, in spite of the bromidic and venerable injunction of the Apostle.

‖**bromidrosis** (ˌbrəʊmɪˈdrəʊsɪs). *Med.* [mod. f. Gr. βρῶμος stench + ἱδρώς sweat.] (See quot.)

1866 HEBRA *Dis. Skin* in *N. Syd. Soc. Trans.* I. 74 The disease which is spoken of by authors as Bromidrosis. **1876** DUHRING *Dis. Skin* 129 Bromidrosis is a functional disorder of the sweat glands characterized by more or less sweating and an offensive odor.

brominated (ˈbrəʊmɪneɪtɪd), *a.* [from BROMINE + -ATE³ 7.] Charged or compounded with bromine. So **bromiˈnation**.

c **1875** THORPE *Inorg. Chem.* I. 294 The bromination of many hydro-carbons is often greatly facilitated by the presence of a small quantity of iodine in the bromine employed. **1873** FOWNES *Chem.* 555 Brominated compounds.

bromine (ˈbrəʊmɪn, -aɪn). *Chem.* [f. F. *brome*, at first also used in Eng. (f. Gr. βρῶμος stink) + -INE; after the analogy of F. *chlore, iode*, Eng. *chlorine, iodine.*] One of the non-metallic elements, discovered by Balard in 1826; in its properties and compounds closely resembling Chlorine.

Obtained as a dark reddish-black heavy liquid, with a strong irritating smell (whence its name), and highly poisonous. It freezes at −22° C. to a dark lead-grey solid, and boils at 63°. Symbol Br.

1827 TURNER *Elem. Chem.* Add. 695 The name first applied to it by its discoverer is muride; but it has since been changed to brome.. from the Greek βρῶμος signifying a strong or rank odour. This appellation may in the English language be properly converted into that of Bromine. *a* **1836** *Penny Cycl.* V. 460/2 Dr. Daubeny has detected bromine in several mineral springs in England. **1875** H. WOOD *Therap.* (1879) 575 Bromine is one of the most severe, thorough, and rapid of all the caustics. **1876** HARLEY *Mat. Med.* 84 Bromine was discovered.. in bittern, the uncrystallisable residue of sea-water.

b. *attrib.* = BROMIC; of bromine.

1869 ROSCOE *Elem. Chem.* 119 Bromine Monoxide, is not known, but the corresponding Hypobromous Acid HBrO is. **1885** tr. *Ziemssen's Skin Dis.* 469 Bromine Acne differs from Acne Simplex by attacking the hairy parts by preference.

ˈ**Bromingham**: see BRUMMAGEM.

bromism (ˈbrəʊmɪz(ə)m). *Med.* [f. BROM-INE + -ISM.] 'The condition produced by an overdose or too long continuance of bromine or a bromide' (*Syd. Soc. Lex.*); but used almost exclusively of the effects of potassium bromide.

1867 *Trousseau's Clin. Med.* in *N. Syd. Soc. Trans.* I. 101 *note*, The exhibition of large doses of Bromide of Potassium is soon followed by the marked and characteristic phenomena of Bromism. **1875** H. WOOD *Therap.* (1879) 323 When it [Bromide of Potassium] is taken with sufficient freedom to accumulate in the system, a conjunction of phenomena known as bromism arises. The cerebral symptoms are a sense of mental weakness, heaviness of intellect, failure of memory, partial aphasia, and depression of spirits.

bromite (ˈbrəʊmaɪt). *Min.* [f. (by Haidinger 1845) BROM-INE + -ITE.] = BROMYRITE.

1850 DANA *Min.* (ed. 3) 545 Bromic silver. Bromite. **1875** URE *Dict. Arts, Bromite*, native bromide of silver.

bromization (brəʊmaɪˈzeɪʃən). *Med.* [f. BROMIZE + -ATION.] Subjection to the action of bromine.

1881 G. M. BEARD *Sea-Sickness* 34 [In the use of bromides] any thing short of mild bromization is useless.

bromize, -ise (ˈbrəʊmaɪz), *v.* [f. BROM-INE + -IZE.] *trans.* To treat, compound, impregnate, or infuse with bromine; in *Photography*, to prepare (a plate) with bromine or a bromide. Hence ˈ**bromized** *ppl. a.*, ˈ**bromizing**.

1853 W. CROOKES in *Jrnl. Photogr. Soc.* 21 July 86, I have for some time past been working with bromized collodion. *c* **1865** J. WYLDE in *Circ. Sc.* I. 156/2 A similar box will be required for the bromising process. **1881** *Nature* XXIII. 260 Preparation of.. bromised derivatives of the methylic series, and especially.. bromoform. **1882** ABNEY *Instr. in Photogr.* xxv. (ed. 5) 175 The use of a highly-bromized collodion is to be recommended. *Mod.* 'It claims a first place among bromized spas'.

bromlite (ˈbrɒmlaɪt). *Min.* [Named in 1835 from *Bromley Hill*, near Alston in Cumberland + -ITE.] A double carbonate of lime and baryta: the same as ALSTONITE.

1868 DANA *Min.* 698 Most English mineralogical authors have set aside Thomson's name [*Bromlite*] although the earliest and of British origin, for Breithaupt's [*Alstonite*]. There appears to be no sufficient reason for this.

bromo- (ˈbrəʊməʊ), before a vowel **brom-**. *Chem.* Combining form of BROMINE, as in ˌ**bromaˈcetic acid**, a compound of bromine and acetic acid ($C_2H_3BrO_2$), forming salts called **broˈmacetates**; ˈ**bromanil**, the same as *tetrabromoquinone* $C_6Br_4O_2$ (see ANIL 3); **broˈmargyrite** = BROMYRITE; **bromˈhydrin**, a class of compounds 'produced by the action of tribromide or pentabromide of phosphorus on glycerin' (Watts); ˌ**bromobenˈzoic acid** $C_7H_5BrO_2$, a substitution-product of benzoic acid, forming salts called ˌ**bromo-ˈbenzoates**; ˈ**bromoform**, a compound analogous to chloroform ($CH\,Br_3$); **bromoˈphenol blue**, a dye used as an acid-base indicator; also ***bromphenol blue***; ˌ**bromoˈpicrin**, a compound of bromine and picric acid (CBr_3NO_2); etc.; ˈ**bromo-seltzer** (orig. *U.S.*), a proprietary effervescent mixture used as a sedative, etc.; also, a dose of this; ˌ**bromsulphˈthalein** [f. BROM- + SULPH- + *phenol)phthalein* (see PHENOL d)], a dye, $C_{20}H_{10}Br_4O_{10}S_2$, derived from phenolphthalein and used in a test of liver function; also ***bromsulphalein***.

1837 R. D. THOMSON *Brit. Annual* 345 Bromobenzoic acid. **1838** T. THOMSON *Chem. Org. Bodies* 314 (*heading*) Of Bromoform. **1850** DAUBENY *Atom. The.* viii. (ed. 2) 238 Bromophenisic acid. **1853** R. HUNT *Man. Photogr.* 146 The decomposition of the bromo-iodide of silver. **1862** *Catal. Internat. Exhib., Brit.* II. No. 3150, Hardwich's bromo-iodized collodion. **1873** FOWNES *Chem.* 560 Bromethine, or Bromacetylene, is produced by the action of alcoholic potash on dibromethene dibromide. *Ibid.* 592 The chlorethide or bromethide is converted by water into mercuric ethyl-hydrate. *Ibid.* 624 Bromoform is a heavy, volatile liquid. *Ibid.* 814 Bromobenzoic Acid is formed by the action of bromine on silver benzoate. **1878** KINGZETT *Anim. Chem.* 93 Acting upon an alcoholic solution of ammonia with bromacetic acid. **1881** BRAITHWAITE *Retrosp. Med.* LXXXIII. Synopsis p. xvii, Bromohydric Acid.. is useful in nervous conditions. **1883** *Athenæum* 27 Jan. 124/1 Acetylene bromiodide, boiling at 150°. **1885** REMSEN *Org. Chem.* ix. 131 Two brom-propionic acids. **1896** *Illustr. London News* 11 Jan. 63 (Advt.), Emerson's Bromo-seltzer, the most successful American Remedy... Three doses.. cure any headache. **1913** *Jrnl. Chem. Soc.* CIV. I. 1023 Two Bromo-substituted Acidyl-carbamides: Bromural and Adaline. **1916** LUBS & CLARK in *Jrnl. Washington Acad. Sci.* VI. 485 *Chemical Name*, Tetrabromphenolsulphone-phthalein. *Short Name*, Bromphenol blue. **1920** A. B. BAXTER *Parts Men Play* x. §1 Lord Durwent read the *Morning Post* as a sort of 'prairie-oyster', or 'bromoseltzer'. **1924** ROSENTHAL & WHITE in *Jrnl. Pharmac. & Exper. Therap.* Nov. 287 Dyes.. indicating hepatic injury.. Bromsulphalein appears to be the most suitable for this purpose. **1937** A. J. CRONIN *Citadel* IV. xii. 353 By introducing a small bromoform manometer close to the needle we avoid rarefaction. **1949** *New Gould Med. Dict.* 155/1 Bromophenol blue. **1955** *Sci. Amer.* Aug. 98/2 The albumin can be made more strikingly visible by labeling it with a few crystals of bromphenol blue. **1961** *Brit. Med. Dict.* 222/2 *Bromsulphthalein*,.. a non-toxic, non-irritant dye used as an indicator of liver function. **1961** *Lancet* 16 Sept. 631/2 Other flocculation tests.. and bromsulphalein retention were normal.

bromo (ˈbrəʊməʊ). *colloq.* [f. BROMO-.] (A dose of) one of the proprietary sedatives containing a bromide mixture; a bromo-seltzer. Also ***bromo-tablet***.

1916 W. OWEN *Let.* 3 Feb. (1967) 378 Would I had taken 'Bromo-Tablets', and never revived at all! **1934** J. T. FARRELL *Young Manhood* (1936) xiii. 320 You had to dope yourself with bromos, bicarbonate of soda, [etc.]. **1957** M. MILLAR *Soft Talkers* v. 46 There's some bromo in the bathroom. **1961** *Encounter* Apr. 20/2 For God's sake a Bromo!

bromography (brəʊˈmɒgrəfɪ). [f. Gr. βρωμ(ατ)ο- (see BROMATOLOGY) + -γραφία; cf. F. *bromographie.*] 'A treatise or dissertation on food' (Mayne *Exp. Lex.* 1860).

bromoil (ˈbrəʊmɔɪl). *Photogr.* [f. BROM- + OIL *sb.*¹] In full ***bromoil process***, a process in which pigment is applied to a bleached bromide print; so ***bromoil transfer***, a picture in reverse taken from a freshly pigmented print.

1909 *Westm. Gaz.* 9 Jan. 14/2 How many.. camera-users ever attempt work in gum-bichromate or in bromoil? **1909** *Amateur Photographer* 3 Aug. 108/2 Most workers in the bromoil process not only use, but advocate, smooth, platino-matt. **1952** E. O'DION *All about Photogr.* xxix. 154 The Bromoil Process. Bromoil is a 'high art' process used largely for exhibition work, mainly because of the amount of control it allows.

Brompton (ˈbrɒmptən, ˈbrʌ-). [Name of a former hamlet, now part of London, where the Brompton Park Nursery was founded in 1681.] In full ***Brompton stock***, a biennial variety of the stock (see STOCK *sb.*¹ 43).

1724 P. MILLER *Gardeners & Florists Dict.* I. GI 22 There are five Sorts of.. Stocks.. the strip'd Sort, and the large red Brompton-Stock... The Brompton Kind is esteem'd the best. **1798** C. MARSHALL *Gardening* xix. 337 Stock, Brompton, scarlet, blush, and white. **1852** G. W. JOHNSON *Cottage Gard. Dict.* 583 For the latter purpose [*sc.* spring-flowering] none [of the stocks] beats the intermediate, Queens, Bromptons, and other biennials. **1880** *Encycl. Brit.* XII. 249/2 The Brompton Stock (Matthiola incana simplicicaulis) is a robust plant, growing 3 feet high, with a long central flower stem bearing very large flowers, which are crimson, purple, or white. **1956** *Dict. Gardening* (R. Hort. Soc.) (ed. 2) IV. 2034/1 The Brompton Stocks are robust, vigorous plants.

bromstone, obs. form of BRIMSTONE.

†ˈ**bromuret**. *Chem. Obs.* [f. BROMINE + -URET.] The earlier name for a BROMIDE; now used for a compound less saturated with bromine.

1878 tr. *Ziemssen's Cycl. Med.* XVII. 313 In the Urine the Bromine appears combined with an Alkali as a bromide and ..partly also as a bromuret.

bromyrite (ˈbrəʊmɪraɪt). *Min.* [f. (by Dana 1854) BROM-INE; after *argyrite.*] The native bromide of silver, an isometric yellow, amber, or green splendent mineral, found in Mexico and Chile; also called *bromargyrite, bromic silver*.

bronc (brɒŋk). *colloq.* (orig. and chiefly *U.S.*). Also **bronch, bronk**. [Abbrev. of BRONCO.] = BRONCO, a horse. Also *attrib.* and *Comb.*

1893 T. ROOSEVELT *Wilderness Hunter* xx. 418, I saddled up the bronc' and lit out for home. **1908** MULFORD *Orphan* v, Keep it up, bronchs!.. We'll win! **1910** W. M. RAINE *B. O'Connor* 72 You're going to.. learn to stick to your saddle when the bronc and you disagree. **1911** H. QUICK *Yellowstone N.* x. 245 Old Jim Bridger was obliged to go up f'r three days on his bronk one time. **1913** MULFORD *Coming of Cassidy* 153 That's shore a long time to ride this bronc train. **1924** *Glasgow Herald* 12 June 9 The champion bronk riders, steer wrestlers, and trick horsewomen of America. *Ibid.* 4 July 9 The international bronk riding contest.. took place yesterday afternoon at the Wembley Stadium.

bronch, obs. form of BRANCH.

‖**bronchia** (ˈbrɒŋkɪə), *sb. pl. Phys.* [L. *bronchia*, a. Gr. βρόγχια (neut. pl.) the ramifications of the windpipe. Formerly sometimes treated as a sing. with a new pl. *bronchiæ.*] The branches or subdivisions of the bronchi within the lungs.

1674 GREW *Anat. Trunks* ii. §11 In an Animal, the Bronchiæ deposite the Aer into the Vesiculæ of the Lungs. **1681** tr. *T. Willis' Rem. Med. Wks.* Voc., *Bronchia*, the gristly parts about the wind-pipe. **1736** BAILEY *Househ. Dict.* 52 In humerous Asthmas and obstructions of the Bronchia. **1758** J. S. *Le Dran's Observ. Surg.* (1771) 100 Excepting a little Pus in some Branches of the Bronchiæ. **1826** KIRBY & SP. *Entomol.* IV. 57 The air vessels or bronchiæ in connection with tracheæ. **1881** MIVART *Cat* 224 The smaller tubes, into which the bronchi sub-divide within the lungs, are called bronchia.

bronchial (ˈbrɒŋkɪəl), *a.* [ad. mod.L. *bronchiālis*, f. *bronchia*; see prec. and -AL¹.] Pertaining to the bronchi or bronchia.

a **1735** ARBUTHNOT (J.) Inflammation of the lungs may happen either in the bronchial or pulmonary vessels. **1793** T. BEDDOES *Lett. Darwin* 69 Too great secretion of bronchial mucus. **1847** YOUATT *Horse* xi. 239 The air which has descended through the bronchial tubes. **1879** MISS BRADDON *Clov. Foot* III. ii. 14 He would hardly ask me to risk a bronchial attack.

Hence ˈ**bronchially** *adv.*

1885 *Kendal Merc. & Times* 13 Mar. 5/4 This ancient foe of the dyspeptic and the bronchially delicate.

bronchic ('brɒŋkɪk), *a.* [mod. f. BRONCH-US + -IC: cf. 16th c. F. *bronchique.*] = BRONCHIAL.

1731 BAILEY II, *Bronchick Muscles*, the Sternothyroides. **1758** J. S. *Le Dran's Observ. Surg.* (1771) 152 The Muscles Sterno-Mastoideus, Bronchick, and Sterno-Hyoideus.. were..larger than ordinary. [In mod. Dicts.]

‖**bronchiectasis** (ˌbrɒŋkɪ'ɛktəsɪs). *Med.* [f. Gr. βρόγχια BRONCHIA + ἔκτασις dilatation.] Dilatation of the bronchial tubes. Hence ˌ**bronchiec'tasic, -ec'tatic,** *a.* [as if ad. Gr. *ἐκτατικός.]

1877 ROBERTS *Handbk. Med.* (ed. 3) I. 376 Bronchiectasis generally arises in the course of some chronic lung disease. **1866** A. FLINT *Princ. Med.* (1880) 196 The bronchiectatic cavities are common.

bronchio- ('brɒŋkɪəʊ), before a vowel **bronchi-**. *Med.* Combining form of BRONCHIA, as in **bronchi'arctia** [L. *ar(c)tus* narrow], contraction of the bronchial tubes; BRONCHIECTASIS; **bronchio'crisis** [Gr. κρίσις crisis], 'paroxysmal attacks resembling hooping cough occurring in tabes' (*Syd. Soc. Lex.*); **bronchiopneu'monia,** inflammation of the lungs, beginning in the bronchial membrane; **bronchio-'pulmonary** *a.*, pertaining to the bronchi and lungs.

1853 BLACK in *Edin. Monthly Jrnl.* (*title*), On the Pathology of the Bronchio-Pulmonary Mucous Membrane.

bronchio'genic, *a.* [f. BRONCHIO- + -GENIC.] = *bronchogenic* adj.

a **1909** in *Buck's Handbk. Med. Sci.* IV. 356 (Cent. Dict. Suppl.). **1927** *Archives Internal Med.* XL. 347 Primary bronchiogenic carcinoma of the right lung. **1947** *Radiology* XLIX. 279/1 There is no clear-cut evidence that tumors of bronchiogenic origin occur in mice of this strain.

bronchiole ('brɒŋkɪəʊl). [ad. mod.L. **bronchiola*, dim. of *bronchia*; see -OLE.] A minute bronchial tube.

1866 A. FLINT *Princ. Med.* (1880) 160 In acute pneumonitis the inflammation is seated in the air-cells and bronchioles.

bronchiolitis (brɒŋkɪəʊ'laɪtɪs). *Path.* [f. BRONCHIOLE + -ITIS.] Inflammation of the bronchioles.

1887 VICKERY & KNAPP tr. *Strümpell's Textbk. Med.* IV. 157 Curschmann.. claims that the anatomical basis of these cases is an exudative bronchiolitis. **1961** *Lancet* 16 Sept. 660/2 When these areas are infected, bronchiolitis, or broncho-pneumonia may result.

bronchitic (brɒŋ'kɪtɪk), *a.* [f. next + -IC.] Of or pertaining to bronchitis; affected with bronchitis.

1836 TODD *Cycl. Anat. & Phys.* I. 808/1 In bronchitic affections. **1861** O. W. HOLMES *Elsie V.* 354 Some new grievance, dyspeptic, neuralgic, bronchitic, or other.

b. *absol.* as *pl.* Persons suffering from bronchitis.

1879 SALA in *Daily Tel.* 21 July, Recommended to the bronchitic and asthmatic.

bronchitis (brɒŋ'kaɪtɪs). *Med.* [mod.L. f. *bronchi, bronchia* + -ITIS (= Gr. -ῖτις), q.v. First brought into use by C. Badham *Observations on the Inflammatory Affections of the Mucous Membrane of the Bronchiae* (1808).]

a. Inflammation of the bronchial mucous membrane.

1814 J. BURNS *Princ. Midwifery* (ed. 3) x. 565 Bronchitis is far from being an uncommon disease of infants. **1830** DE QUINCEY *Ld. Carlisle on Pope* Wks. II. 25 He had no such ardour for Truth as would ever lead him to forget that wells were damp, and bronchitis alarming to a man of his constitution. **1881** *Med. Temp. Jrnl.* I. 18 He soon succumbed to an attack of acute bronchitis.

b. *attrib.*, as **bronchitis kettle,** a kettle with a long tube and a detachable medicator used for keeping the atmosphere of a room humid and for giving a medicated vapour inhalation to a patient in a case of bronchitis.

1886 *Cassell's Family Mag.* Jan. 127/2 (*heading*) New Bronchitis Kettle. **1896** *Lancet* 18 Apr. 1056/1 The unfortunate patient is kept in a room with the atmosphere saturated with moisture from a bronchitis kettle.

broncho, var. BRONCO.

broncho- ('brɒŋkəʊ), before a vowel **bronch-**. *Med.* Combining form of BRONCHUS, as in **'bronchadene** [Gr. ἀδήν a gland], one of the bronchial glands; **bron'charctia,** contraction of a bronchus (cf. *bronchiarctia* s.v. BRONCHIO-); **broncho-cavernous** *a.* (see quots.); **broncho-constriction,** stricture of the bronchi; **bronchodilator,** that which dilates the bronchi, *esp.* a drug; **bronchogenic** *a.*, of bronchial origin; **'broncholith,** a calcareous deposit in a bronchial gland (*Syd. Soc. Lex.*); ˌ**broncho-pneu'monia** = *bronchiopneumonia* (see BRONCHIO-); **broncho-pneumonic** *a.*, pertaining to broncho-pneumonia or inflammation of the bronchi and the lungs; **broncho-pulmonary** *a.*, pertaining to the bronchi and the lungs (cf. *bronchio-pulmonary*, s.v. BRONCHIO-); **broncho'rrhœa,** a kind of chronic bronchitis; **bronchospasm,** a spasm of the bronchi; **broncho-vesicular** *a.*, bronchial and vesicular. See also following words.

1890 BILLINGS *Med. Dict.*, *Broncho-cavernous respiration*, sound heard from consolidated lung surrounding a cavity. **1922** F. W. PRICE *Textbk. Pract. Med.* 905 Broncho-cavernous breathing is incomplete cavernous breathing, inspiration being bronchial, while expiration is cavernous. **1910** *Practitioner* June 859 An amount of air may be sucked through the broncho-constriction. **1903** *Jrnl. Physiol.* XIX. 164 Broncho-dilators: atropine, hyoscyamine, hyoscine, [etc.]. **1961** *Lancet* 12 Aug. 341/1 An increase in airflow resistance.. is relieved by bronchodilator substances. **1966** *Ibid.* 5 Feb. 307/2 Aerosols hold their own against oral bronchodilators. **1934** WEBSTER, Bronchogenic. **1962** *Lancet* 8 Dec. 1193/2 A bronchogenic carcinoma which was confirmed at necropsy. **1858** COPLAND *Med. Dict.* II. 769 Broncho-pneumonia very frequently intervenes in the course of Influenza. **1883** G. S. WOODHEAD *Pract. Pathol.* 249 It [*sc.* capillary bronchitis] only occurs in connection with the broncho-pneumonic process. *a* **1909** *Buck's Handbk. Med. Sci.* V. 848 (Cent. D. Suppl.), Broncho-pulmonary. **1912** OSLER & MACRAE *Princ. & Pract. Med.* (ed. 8) 636 Broncho-pulmonary hæmorrhage. **1963** *Brit. Med. Jrnl.* 7 Dec. 1425 (*heading*) Meaning of diagnostic terms in broncho-pulmonary disease. **1866** A. FLINT *Princ. Med.* (1880) 338 An abundant serous expectoration, constituting bronchorrhœa. **1877** ROBERTS *Handbk. Med.* I. 374 Bronchorrhœa is most frequent in old people. **1901** DORLAND *Med. Dict.* (ed. 2) 121/2 Bronchospasm. **1929** H. L. ALEXANDER *Bronchial Asthma* ii. 29 Bronchospasm.. stimulates the mucous gland. **1966** *Lancet* 31 Dec. 1436/1 There was evidence of bronchospasm or a clinical history of bronchial asthma. **1887** *Buck's Handbk. Med. Sci.* V. 732/2 The broncho-vesicular breathing..becomes..tubular in dyspnœa.

bronchocele ('brɒŋkəsiːl). *Med.* Also 7 **-chele.** [ad. Gr. βρογχοκήλη 'tumour in the throat', f. βρόγχος BRONCHUS + κήλη tumour; cf. F. *bronchocèle.*] A swelling of the thyroid gland; goitre.

1657 *Phys. Dict.*, Bronchochele, the rupture of the throat, a great round swelling in the throat. **1732** ARBUTHNOT *Rules of Diet* 390 A Dropsy in the forepart of the Windpipe emulating a Bronchocele. **1771** T. PROSSER (*title*), An Account and Method of cure of Bronchocele or Derby Neck. **1783** *Phil. Trans.* LXXIII. 92 The Bronchocele.. has been seen to increase to such an enormous bulk as to hang down over the breast and belly. **1878** T. BRYANT *Pract. Surg.* I. 195 Such outlying masses of thyroid gland are not rare near bronchoceles.

bron'chophonism. *Med.* = next.

1834 GOOD *Study Med.* II. 135 The bronchial respiration and cough always accompany bronchophonism.

bronchophony (brɒŋ'kɒfənɪ). *Med.* [ad. F. *bronchophonie*, f. Gr. βρόγχος BRONCHUS + -φωνία in abstr. derivs. of φωνή voice.] The sound of the voice heard in the bronchi by means of the stethoscope; *esp.* the increased vocal resonance heard in certain diseased conditions of the lungs, imitating the voice-sound heard over the healthy bronchi.

1834 J. FORBES *Laennec's Dis. Chest* 37 In persons, however, of a delicate and feeble frame.. there frequently exists.. a bronchophony very similar to the laryngophony already noticed. **1866** A. FLINT *Princ. Med.* (1880) 131 The bronchophony has sometimes a tremulous or bleating character, and is then ægophony.

Hence **broncho'phonic** *a.*

1862 H. FULLER *Dis. Lungs* 109 Not appearing to pass through the stethoscope into the ear, but concentrated as it were beneath the stethoscope (bronchophonic resonance). **1886** FAGGE *Princ. & Prac. Med.* I. 897 A bronchophonic cry.

bronchoscope ('brɒŋkəskəʊp). [f. BRONCHO- + -SCOPE.] An instrument for inspecting the interior of the bronchi.

1899 *Westm. Gaz.* 20 Dec. 10/2 Kilian's (Berlin) bronchoscope was..introduced into the trachea. **1904** *Electr. World & Engin.* 16 Jan. 140 (Cent. D. Suppl.), A bronchoscope, which consists of a tube, the inner surface of which is highly polished to serve as a reflector, with an electric lamp arranged so as to throw a strong light on the tube. **1962** H. C. WESTON *Sight, Light & Work* (ed. 2) vi. 193 The miniature lamp..is used..in cystoscopes and bronchoscopes.

So ˌ**broncho'scopic,** ˌ**broncho'scopical** *adjs.*, of or pertaining to a bronchoscope or to bronchoscopy; **bronchoscopy** (brɒŋ'kɒskəpɪ) [ad. G. *bronchoskopie* (G. Killian 1898, in *Münch. med. Wochenschr.* 5 Juli 844/2)], (the science or study of) the examination of the bronchi with a bronchoscope.

1908 *N.Y. Med. Jrnl.* 15 Aug. 293/2 Two bronchoscopical tubes of 5 and 7 mm. in diameter for upper bronchoscopy. **1910** F. W. F. ROSS tr. *Bruck's Dis. Nose*, etc., & *Larynx* IV. 381 The bronchoscopic tubes are perforated at the side, so as not to hinder respiration. **1962** *Lancet* 8 Dec. 1205/1 Prevent..lung infection, treating this (if it arises) by bronchoscopic suction and antibiotics. **1903** *Therapeutic Gaz.* Jan. 60 (Cent. D. Suppl.), Bronchoscopy allows the whole bronchial tree to be searched. **1927** *Daily Express* 6 July 9/2 The chair of bronchoscopy in the University of Pennsylvania.

bronchotome ('brɒŋkətəʊm). *Surg.* [mod. f. Gr. βρόγχος BRONCHUS + -τομος cutting, cutter; cf. F. *bronchotome.*] A knife used for bronchotomy; also, a pair of scissors for opening the bronchi in post mortem examinations.

1837 W. STOKES *Dis. Chest* (1882) 148 *note*, The lung should be dissected by means of a fine pair of scissors.. This instrument may be called a bronchotome. **1880** *Syd. Soc. Lex.*

bronchotomist (brɒŋ'kɒtəmɪst). [f. βρόγχος BRONCHUS (see next and -IST); cf. *phlebotomist.*] One who performs bronchotomy; (*humorously*) a cut-throat.

1670 G. THOMPSON *True Way Preserv. Blood*, I doubt not the time will come..that a Phlebotomist..will be looked upon little better than Bronchotomist, a cut-throat.

bronchotomy (brɒŋ'kɒtəmɪ). *Surg.* [mod. f. Gr. βρόγχος BRONCHUS + -τομία cutting.] The operation of making an incision in the wind-pipe; the generic term which includes *thyrotomy, laryngotomy,* and *tracheotomy.*

1706 in PHILLIPS. **1713** CHESELDEN *Anat.* III. xv. (1726) 259 This [nerve]..it is that we are earnestly cautioned to avoid in Bronchotomie. **1839-47** TODD *Cycl. Anat. & Phys.* III. 573/2 A peculiarly eligible spot for bronchotomy. **1879** T. BRYANT *Pract. Surg.* II. 30 Any opening made by the surgeon into the windpipe is called 'bronchotomy'.

‖**bronchus** ('brɒŋkəs). *Phys. Pl.* **bronchi** (also 8 *improperly* **bronchæ**). [mod.L., a. Gr. βρόγχος the wind-pipe.] Each of the two main branches of the trachea or wind-pipe.

1706 in PHILLIPS, *Bronchus*; hence in BAILEY 1731. **1782** A. MUNRO *Anat.* (ed. 3) 59 The water..passes betwixt the interstices of the *bronchi*, and the flap that covers them. **1769** W. BUCHAN *Dom. Med.* (1790) 175 A phthisis occasioned by a small bone sticking in the bronchæ. **1831** R. KNOX *Cloquet's Anat.* 627 The Right Bronchus is wider, shorter, and more horizontal than the left. **1881** MIVART *Cat* 223 The bronchi have the same structure as the trachea.

bronco ('brɒŋkəʊ), *sb.* (and *a.*) Also **broncho.** [ad. Sp. *bronco* rough, rude; as applied to a horse, adopted on the Mexican frontier of U.S.]

A. *sb.* **a.** An untamed or half-tamed horse, or a cross between the horse and mustang; a native horse of California or New Mexico. Also *gen.*, any horse.

1869 S. BOWLES *Our New West* v. 101 A well-broken Indian pony or a 'broncho' (a California half-breed horse). **1878** J. H. BEADLE *Western Wilds* 454 Our bronchos carried us with ease and safety. **1884** *Pall Mall G.* 22 Aug. 10/1 [He] was captured.. stripped of every bit of clothing, and bound on the back of a wild bronco, which was started off by vigorous lashing. **1924** R. CAMPBELL *Flaming Terrapin* I. 18 Bellerophon, the primal cowboy.. slewed his white-winged broncho out to sea.

b. *attrib.* and *Comb.*, as ***bronco-horse, -mule, -pony, -team***; **bronco-buster** *colloq.* (orig. *U.S.*), a breaker-in of broncos; so ***bronco-busting*** vbl. sb. and ppl. a.

1887 *Century Mag.* in Farmer *Americanisms* (1888) 89/2 An Eastern or English horse-breaker and Western *broncho-buster have so little in common with each other. **1888** T. ROOSEVELT in *Century Mag.* Feb. 507 The flash riders, or horse-breakers, always called 'bronco busters'. **1913** R. BROOKE *Let.* in *Coll. Poems* (1918) p. lxxix, A bold, bad, bearded broncho-buster. **1889** *Regina* (Sask.) *Jrnl.* 18 July 1/6 *Broncho 'busting' and base-ball are the sports most indulged in [in] these times. **1931** L. STEFFENS *Autobiogr.* I. i. 9 A gun-playing, broncho-busting vaquero. **1963** *Times* 7 June 5/7 Attend a bronco-bustin' rodeo. **1883** *Harper's Mag.* Feb. 428/1 There came rushing over the ridge-top..a ragged, tough *broncho horse. **1963** W. E. HARNEY *To Ayers Rock & Beyond* v. 48 It was a simple matter to draft the animals they required into an adjacent yard, brand them on the bronco-panel where the motor displaced the bronco-horse. **1895** *Outing* (U.S.) XXVII. 244/2 Their pack train composed of hardy little *broncho-mules. **1869** S. BOWLES *Our New West* v. 101 The mule and the Indian and '*broncho' ponies will live on the rich grasses of the country. **1892** GUNTER *Miss Dividends* 163 You can drive down in a day with a good tough *broncho-team.

B. Hence as *adj.* Wild, uncontrollable, rough. *U.S. colloq.*

1866 *Weekly New American* 21 July 1/4 The Territory did not keep fast horses and other things, and go to bronco bailes and play whiskey poker. **1887** F. FRANCIS *Saddle & Mocassin* 146 Sam's too broncho: he gets all-fired mean sometimes when he's full. **1947** *Westerners' Brand Book* 75 A man who made a false step wasn't necessarily all bad or 'broncho' as he expressed it.

brond, bronder, obs. ff. BRAND, BRANDER.

[**bronden,** a frequent error for *brouden*, BROWDEN.

a **1455** *Houlate* i. 3 (JAM.) The birth that the ground bare was brondyn in bredis.]

bronk, var. BRONC.

bronked, *a. Obs.* ? Bridled. [Cf. BRANK.]

1580 *Wills & Inv. N.C.* (Surtees) 437 Also I bequeath to Elizabethe Ironside one bronked oxe.

bronston(e, obs. form of BRIMSTONE.

†**'bronstrops.** *Obs.* [app. a further corruption of *bawstrop*, corrupt form of BAWDSTROT, q.v.] A procuress or bawd. (Frequent in Middleton.)

1617 MIDDLETON *Fair Quarr.* IV. i, I say thy sister is a bronstrops. *Ibid.* IV. iv. etc. **1661** WEBSTER *Cure for Cuckold* IV. i, A tweak or bronstrops: I learned that name in a play [i.e. in Middleton's].

bront, obs. form of BRUNT, BRAND.

Brontëan ('brɒntiːən), *a.* [See -AN.] Of, pertaining to, or characteristic of, the Brontës (esp. the sisters Charlotte (1816–55), Emily (1818–48), and Anne (1820–49)), or their literary works. So **Brontë'ana**, literature concerning the Brontës; **'Brontëism**, a quality characteristic of the Brontës (see also -ISM *suffix* 2); **Bron'tesque** *a.* = BRONTËAN *a.*

1887 *Pall Mall Gaz.* 31 Aug. 3/1 The blusterous Brontëism which..is an affliction hardly less ludicrous than Whitmania. **1900** *Daily News* 17 Aug. 6/1 'Charlotte Brontë and her Circle' seems..to have finally exhausted the vast and well-explored mines of Brontëana. **1905** *Daily Chron.* 4 Nov. 4/7 Almost Emily-Brontesque in its concentrated austerity. **1945** A. HUXLEY *Time must have Stop* vi. 69 'You mean, that I should be acting as Mrs. Gamble's companion?' The final word..took on its fullest, Brontëan significance. **1950** BLUNDEN *Reprinted Papers* 186 Some Brontesque force..in the work of the young painter-author.

‖**bron'teon.** [a. Gr. βροντεῖον 'an engine for making stage-thunder' (Liddell & Scott).]

1849 WEALE *Techn. Dict.*, *Bronteon*, in Greek architecture, brazen vessels placed under the floor of a theatre, with stones in them, to imitate thunder. [So in later Dicts.]

bronto-, comb. form of Gr. βροντή thunder, as in **brontogram** ('brɒntəʊgræm), the record made by a brontometer or brontograph; **'brontograph**, a recording brontometer; also, a chart of the phenomena recorded by that instrument; **bronto'logical** *a.*, pertaining to BRONTOLOGY; **bron'tometer**, an instrument for recording the phenomena associated with thunderstorms; **bronto'phobia**, intense dread of thunder and thunderstorms.

1888 *Symons's Monthly Meteorol. Mag.* June 71 Our German friends..were clearly the first as to thunder-storms, or rather Brontological research. *Ibid.* May 50 Messrs. Richard Frères, of Paris, are constructing for Mr. Symons a very complicated apparatus (Brontometer)..for recording the details of thunderstorms. **1905** W. G. HOLMES *Justinian & Theodora* I. iii. 298 He was affected with brontophobia in his later years.

'brontolith. *rare*$^{-0}$. [f. Gr. βροντ-ή thunder + λίθος stone.] An aerolite.

1860 in MAYNE *Exp. Lex.*; and in *Syd. Soc. Lex.*

brontology (brɒn'tɒlədʒɪ). [f. Gr. βροντ-ή thunder + -λογία discourse: see -LOGY.] The scientific treatment or doctrine of thunder; that part of Meteorology which treats of thunder.

1731 BAILEY II, *Brontology*, a treatise or discourse of thunder. [In JOHNSON, CRAIG, & later Dicts.] **1864** R. BURTON *Dahome* II. 142 Unlearned in brontology.

brontosaur ('brɒntəsɔː(r)). *Palæont.* [f. BRONTOSAUR(US.] A reptile belonging to the genus *Brontosaurus* (*Apatosaurus*); a brontosaurus; more widely, any large dinosaur.

1892 H. H. HUTCHINSON *Extinct Monsters* v. 66 The body of the Brontosaur was comparatively short. **1902** *Current Lit.* Jan. 59/1 The fossils of Gilmore's Brontosaur were loaded on board the cars at Medicine Bow. **1909** 'MARK TWAIN' *Is Shakes. Dead?* iv. 41 The colossal skeleton brontosaur. **1974** *Encycl. Brit. Micropædia* I. 258/3 A full-grown brontosaur weighed many times as much as *Allosaurus* and had a strong, whip-like tail that would have been an effective weapon. **1979** FAIRBRIDGE & JABLONSKI *Encycl. Paleontol.* 489/1 (*caption*) Cross section of thorax of brontosaur (*Diplodocus*) and elephant (*Loxodonta*).

brontosaurian (brɒntə'sɔːrɪən), *a.* Also Bronto-. [f. prec. or next + -IAN.] Of or pertaining to a brontosaurus; freq. *fig.*, antiquated; clumsy, ineffectual.

1909 'MARK TWAIN' *Is Shakes. Dead?* v. 50 Two of these cults are known as the Shakespearites and the Baconians, and I am the other one—the Brontosaurian. **1974** *Encycl. Brit. Micropædia* II. 296/2 Brontosaurian brains would seem to have been almost too small to have efficiently coordinated such a large animal. **1977** *Time* 28 Nov. 64/3 He still parks his brontosaurian 1954 Caddy behind West Hollywood's Tropicana motel.

Brontosaurus (brɒntə'sɔːrəs). *Palæont.* [mod.L., f. Gr. βροντή thunder + -O + σαῦρος lizard.] An extinct genus of dinosaurian reptiles existing on all the continents during the Jurassic and Cretaceous periods; also (with lower-case initial), a reptile belonging to this genus.

1879 O. C. MARSH in *Amer. Jrnl. Sci. & Arts* XVIII. 503 *Brontosaurus excelsus*, gen. et sp. nov. **1905** *Harper's Mag.* Dec. 73 The mighty brontosaurus came striding into camp. **1907** *Westm. Gaz.* 3 Apr. 8/1 A brontosaurus, or a chondrosteosaurus. **1924** *Public Opinion* 28 Mar. 300/3 [The Anglican Church] is going the way of the dinosaurus and the brontosaurus.

brontothere ('brɒntəʊθɪə(r)). *Palæont.* [f. Gr. βροντ-ή thunder + θηρίον wild beast.] An extinct genus of ungulate mammals, having affinities to the elephant and also to the tapir.

1877 LE CONTE *Elem. Geol.* §506 The brain of the Miocene Brontothere is larger than that of the..Dinoceros.

brontstane, obs. form of BRIMSTONE.

Bronx (brɒŋks). [f. the name of Jonas *Bronck*, a 17th-cent. landowner in New York.] **1.** The name of a borough of New York City, used *attrib.* or *absol.* of a kind of cocktail.

1906 'H. MCHUGH' *Skiddoo!* 39 Every time there was a lull in the conversation Charlie Swayne kept yelling for a Bronx cocktail. **1909** *Sat. Even. Post* 10 Apr. 37/2 The first-night death-watch..could recognize a block away a Bronx, Martini or Manhattan cocktail by its color. **1917** WYNDHAM LEWIS *Let.* 24 July (1963) 90 Then you would go to the American bar and have a Bronx or two. **1930** H. CRADDOCK *Savoy Cocktail Book* I. 37 *Bronx cocktail.* The Juice of ¼ Orange, ¼ French Vermouth, ¼ Italian Vermouth, ½ Dry Gin.

2. ***Bronx cheer***: a sound of contempt or derision made by blowing through closed lips, usually with the tongue between; = RASPBERRY 4. orig. *U.S.*

1929 *Collier's* 23 Feb. 10/4 Maxim give him a Bronx cheer. **1932** WODEHOUSE *Hot Water* i. 21 She told me..that she was through... No explanations. Just gave me the Bronx Cheer and beat it. **1955** E. HYAMS *Slaughterhouse Informer* 179 That rasping sound variously known as the raspberry or the Bronx cheer.

bronze (brɒnz), *sb.* [a. F. *bronze* (16th c. in Littré), ad. It. *bronzo* 'brass or bell-metal' (Florio); whence also Sp. *bronze, bronce.* The origin of the It. is uncertain: Muratori, cited by Diez, thinks it formed from *bruno* 'brown', through an intermediate **brunizzo*, **bruniccio*:—late L. *brunitius* 'brownish, brown-coloured'. But this is very doubtful phonetically. Diez also mentions Venetian *bronza* glowing coals, 'perh. the Ger. *brunst* fire, burning, heat', as possibly connected.]

1. a. A brown-coloured alloy of copper and tin, sometimes also containing a little zinc and lead. Formerly included under the term BRASS, q.v.; the name *bronze* was introduced for the material of ancient works of art, or perhaps rather for the works of art themselves: see sense 2.

The ratio of the constituents in ordinary bronze is about 8 or 9 parts of copper to 1 of tin; in bell-metal the proportion of tin is much greater. See BELL-METAL. (A bronze currency was introduced in Great Britain instead of copper in 1860; but from traditional habit, a bronze coin is still called familiarly 'a copper'.)

[**1617** F. MORYSON *Itin.* I. II. iii. 170 The brasen Serpent ..was of mixt mettall, vulgarly [i.e. in the vulgar Italian tongue] called *di bronzo.*] **1739** GRAY *Let.* in *Poems* (1775) 49 Nymphs and tritons, all in bronze. **1755** JOHNSON, *Bronze* (*bronze* Fr.) 1 Brass. 2 Relief or statue cast in brass. **1806** DRENNAN *Imit. Juvenal Sat.* viii. in *Poet. Register* (1806) 131 With ancestry around you plac'd In bronze, or marble, porcelain or paste. **1835** W. IRVING *Tour Prairies* 50 Like figures of monumental bronze. **1854** SCOFFERN in *Orr's Circ. Sc.* Chem. 492 Statue bronze contains only about two per cent. of tin, melted with ninety-one per cent. of copper, six per cent. of zinc, and one per cent. of lead. **1868** G. STEPHENS *Runic Mon.* I. 74 The Age of Bronze follows the Stone Age and precedes the Age of Iron. **1886** *Pall Mall G.* 13 Feb. 10/2 The prisoner..had in his possession 3*s.* 6*d.* in silver and 3*s.* 4*d.* in bronze.

b. ***aluminium bronze***: see ALUMINIUM. ***phosphor-bronze***: an alloy consisting of bronze or copper with a small proportion of phosphorus added, which increases its tenacity.

1875 URE *Dict. Arts* III. 555 Experiments on the capacity of phosphor-bronze to resist the oxidation of sea-water. **1878** *Print. Trades Jrnl.* xxv. 10 In the construction of this beautiful engine steel and phosphor-bronze are used.

c. ***bronze medal***: a medal of bronze, usu. one awarded for achieving third place in a competition or athletic contest, as in the Olympic Games (see also quot. 1984); cf. MEDAL *sb.* 2 b. Also *ellipt.* as ***bronze***.

1852, 1908 [see MEDAL *sb.* 2 b]. **1960** *Times* 5 Sept. 4/6 Italy ..gained a silver and a bronze. **1976** *All about Games* (Com. Org. des Jeux Olympiques) 20 Canada entered an official 91-member team which won three gold, three silver, and seven bronze medals. **1984** *Daily Tel.* 25 Apr. 20/4 In December Berry [*sc.* a lifeboatman] saved two more lives —and won a bronze medal.

2. (with *pl.*) A work of art, as a statue, etc., executed in bronze.

a **1721** PRIOR *Alma* III, How little gives thee joy or pain; A print, a bronze, a flower, a root. **1841** SPALDING *Italy & It. Isl.* I. 217 Its bronzes and bas-reliefs are also very important. **1871** MORLEY *Crit. Misc.* (1886) I. 67 Gay with the clocks, the bronzes, the tapestries, of the ruined court.

†**3.** *fig.* **a.** Impudence, unblushingness. (Cf. *brass.*)

1728 POPE *Dunc.* III. 199 Imbrown'd with native bronze, lo! Henley stands. **1768** GOLDSM. *Good-n. Man* II. i, *Mrs. Croaker.* 'You don't want assurance when you come to solicit for your friends.' *Lofty.* 'O, there indeed I'm in bronze.' **1823** BYRON (*title*) The Age of Bronze.

†**b.** A gull, a cheat. *Obs. slang.* Cf. BRONZE *v.* 4.

1817 *Blackw. Mag.* I. 137 This is not a 'bronze'—no story of fancy.

4. (More fully ***bronze powder***: see 7): A metallic powder (usually brass, copper, or tin) used in painting, printing, and the like.

1753 CHAMBERS *Cycl. Supp.*, *Bronze*, also denotes a colour prepared by the colourmen of Paris. **1846** *Print. Appar. Amateurs* 47 Printing in gold, silver and copper bronzes. **1854** BRANDEIS *Acc. New York Exhib.* in Ure *Dict. Arts* I. 539 Bronzes, or more correctly metallic powders resembling gold dust, were invented in 1648, by a monk, at Furth, in Bavaria. **1875** URE *Dict. Arts* I. 540 Vanadate of copper has ..been recommended as a new bronze.

5. A brown colour like that of bronze.

1817 BYRON *Beppo* xlv, The rich peasant-cheek of ruddy bronze.

6. *attrib.* or as *adj.* **a.** Made of bronze.

1839 THIRLWALL *Greece* I. 237 The first bronze statue was probably much later than the age of Homer. **1857** RUSKIN *Pol. Econ. Art* 23 Bronze crosses of honour. **1875** JEVONS *Money* (1878) 121 The bronze coinage.

b. Of the colour of bronze, bronze-coloured.

1828 STARK *Elem. Nat. Hist.* II. 274 Legs spinous, of a shining black bronze-colour. **1872** C. KING *Sierra Nev.* xiii. 276 Deep bronze foliage. **1883** *Truth* 31 May 768/2 Scarlet stockings and bronze boots.

7. *Comb.*: attrib. as ***bronze-smith***; instrumental, as ***bronze-bound, -gleaming, -shod***; adverbial, as ***bronze-golden, -purple***; parasynthetic, as ***bronze-faced, -foreheaded***; **bronze age** = *bronze-period*; **bronze-backer** *U.S.*, angler's name for the black bass; **bronze diabetes**, a disorder of iron metabolism in which hæmosiderin is deposited in the tissues and the skin becomes bronzed; also called *hæmochromatosis*; **bronze disease**, a form of corrosion affecting the surface of bronze; **bronze-founder**, one who founds or casts bronze, or fashions articles of bronze; so ***bronze founding***; **bronze-gilt**, made of bronze and covered with gilding (cf. *silver-gilt*); **bronze-liquor**, any liquor used for bronzing; **bronze man** (*Archæol.*), a man living in the bronze period; **bronze period** (*Archæol.*), the prehistoric period during which weapons, etc. were made of bronze, and which was preceded by the Stone Period, and succeeded by the Iron Period; **bronze paint** (see quot.); **bronze powder** = sense 4 above; **'bronze-wing**, a kind of pigeon (*Phaps chalcoptera*) found in Australasia; also ***bronze-wing pigeon***; **bronze-winged** (also **bronzed-winged**) **pigeon** = *bronze-wing*.

1865 LUBBOCK *Preh. Times* 31 There are four principal theories as to the *Bronze age. **1879** —— *Sci. Lect.* vi. 175 The Bronze Age..a period when the weapons were made almost entirely, and ornaments principally, of Bronze. **1888** GOODE *Amer. Fishes* 56 '*Bronze-backer' is one of its pet names among the anglers. **1894** *Outing* (U.S.) XXIV. 452/1 This old bronze-backer [*sc.* small-mouth bass] weighed.. six pounds and five ounces. [**1900** E. KLEEN *On Diabetes Mellitus* iv. 137 Bronze-colored diabetes generally appears in men between forty and sixty years old.] **1901** DUNGLISON *Dict. Med. Sci.* (ed. 22) 1214/2 **Bronze diabetes*, diabetes accompanied with pigmentation of various secretory organs and with sclerosis of the liver and pancreas. **1966** P. E. LACY in W. A. D. Anderson *Pathology* (ed. 5) II. xxix. 958/2 The term 'bronze diabetes' is sometimes used since increased pigmentation of the skin, diabetes mellitus, and cirrhosis of the liver may be present in hemochromatosis. **1925** FINK & ELDRIDGE *Restoration Anc. Bronzes* 42 The usual immediate cause of the *bronze disease is the presence of a trace of chloride, and the action is..electrolytic. **1961** *Antiquaries Jrnl.* XLI. 31 The *bucranium*..has a few spots of active copper chloride ('bronze disease'). **1896** *Godey's Mag.* Apr. 404/1 That gentle figure of contentment, *bronze-faced and white-apparelled. **1851** RUSKIN *Stones Ven.* I. App. xvii. 393 Not all the tubular bridges nor engineering of ten thousand nineteenth centuries cast into one great *bronze-foreheaded century. **1839** URE *Dict. Arts* 333 The *bronze-founder should study to obtain a rapid fusion. **1869** *Van Nostrand's Eclectic Engin. Mag.* I. 834/1 Brass and *bronze-founding is much more of a speciality in France..than it has (hitherto at least) ever been in England. **1897** *Daily News* 18 Jan. 6/4 Two works which Benvenuto Cellini wrote..on bronze founding. **1877** W. JONES *Finger-ring L.* 207 *Bronze-gilt Papal rings. **1882** *Garden* 10 June 399/2 Its *bronze-golden flowers. **1874** SAYCE *Compar. Philol.* iii. 114 The Etruscans may have been the *bronze-men of the Swiss lakes. **1875** URE *Dict. Arts* I. 539 **Bronze paint*, commonly called gold paint, is made by mixing gold-coloured bronze powder with pure turpentine. **1851** D. WILSON *Preh. Ann.* (1863) I. II. i. 319 The *Bronze Period. **1861** *Sat. Rev.* 7 Sept. 253 Belonging to the earliest or archaic bronze period. **1846** *Print. Appar. Amateurs* 47 The *bronze powder is then applied to each impression. **1880** BLACK *White Wings* xx, A strange *bronze-purple gloom. **1841** SPALDING *Italy & It. Isl.* I. 330 The guilds of tradesmen in Rome.. comprehended the goldsmiths, the *bronzesmiths, the carpenters. **1859** H. KINGSLEY *G. Hamlyn* xxvi. (D.) You've no more fight in you than a *bronsewing. **1835** T. L. MITCHELL *Jrnl.* 10 Aug. in *3 Exped. E. Australia* (1838) I. 305 The *bronze-wing pigeon was..the most numerous of that kind of bird. **1884** Bronze-wing pigeon [see PIGEON *sb.* 2 b]. **1936** F. CLUNE *Roaming round Darling* xvii. 162 There seemed an unlimited supply of bronze-wing and top-knot pigeons. **1961** *Coast to Coast 1959–60* 60 A bronze-wing pigeon, lurking in the fine sand, whirred away from almost under my feet. **1832** in Bischoff *Van Diemen's Land* ii. 31 The pigeons are by far the most beautiful birds in the island; they are called *bronze winged pigeons. **1852** MUNDY *Antipodes* xviii, I killed..a few bronzed-winged pigeons. **1897** *Daily News* 24 May 9/4 A pair of Smith's partridge bronze-winged pigeons (*Geophaps Smithi*) from Northern Queensland. **1927** M. M. BENNETT *Christison* vii. 72 A bronzewinged pigeon flew past him.

bronze (brɒnz), *v.* [f. prec. sb.; or a. F. *bronzer*, 16th c. in Littré.]

1. *trans.* To give a bronze-like surface or appearance to (metal, wood, etc.) by any mechanical or chemical process.

1645 EVELYN *Mem.* (1857) I. 196 Figures in plaster and pasteboard, which so resemble copper that..they cannot be distinguished, he has so rare an art of bronzing them. *a* **1852** MOORE *K. Crack* vi. 2 Mending their legs and new bronzing their faces. **1846** G. WRIGHT *Cream Sci. Knowl.* 61 The art of bronzing consists in painting the substance to be bronzed of a dark-green colour, and then rubbing the prominences with bronze-coloured dust.

2. *fig.* To render unfeeling or shameless; to harden, to 'steel'.

1726 D'ANVERS *Craftsm.* xvi. (ed. 3) 137 His face was bronzed over with a glare of confidence. **1742** YOUNG *Nt. Th.* v. 44 Art, cursed art! wipes off th' indebted blush From nature's cheek, and bronzes ev'ry shame. **1830** *Fraser's Mag.* I. 686 Habituation to these distressing calumnies has at length bronzed my feelings.

3. To make like bronze in colour; to brown.

1792 ROGERS *Pleas. Mem.* 51 The bald veteran..richly bronz'd by many a summer sun. **1863** LONGF. *Way-side Inn* Prel. 54 The firelight..bronzed the rafters overhead.

†**4.** To impose upon, cheat. *Obs. slang.*

1817 *Blackw. Mag.* I. 137 Beware that you are not 'bronzed'; take care that what you publish is authentic.

5. *intr.* To become like bronze, to turn brown.

1880 [see BRONZING *ppl. a.*].

bronzed (brɒnzd), *ppl. a.* [f. prec. + -ED^1.]

1. Lacquered or coated with bronze or some imitation of it; having a bronze-like lustre.

1828 STARK *Elem. Nat. Hist.* I. 270 Wings dusky, shining with bronzed-green. *c* **1865** G. GORE in *Circ. Sc.* I. 233/2 The bronzed mould may now be immersed in the..solution.

2. Bronze-coloured, browned, sunburnt.

1748 H. WALPOLE *Corr.* (1820) I. 198, I wish you could see him making squibs..and Bronzed over with a patina of gunpowder. **1847** J. WILSON *Recr. Chr. North* (1857) II. 25 The bare and bronzed Egyptian. **1865** *Daily Tel.* 12 June, The bronzed heroes of Sherman and Grant.

3. Grown shameless, feelingless; hardened.

1841 EMERSON *Misc.* 187 The most bronzed and sharpened money-catcher. **1878** BROWNING *Poets Croisic* 114 The Doctor's bronzed throat!

4. a. bronzed skin, an incurable structural disease of the supra-renal capsules, usually characterized by discolouration of the skin to a dusky brown, smoky, or olive tint, with progressive loss of strength; *supra-renal melasma*, or Addison's disease.

b. bronzed diabetes = *bronze diabetes*.

[**1886** HANOT & SCHACHMANN in *Arch. de Physiol. Normale et Pathologique* VII. 62 C'était là comme un *diabète bronzé*.] **1898** R. T. WILLIAMSON *Diabetes Mellitus* 411/2 (Index) Bronzed diabetes. **1909** *Practitioner* Feb. 194 That very rare disease called bronzed diabetes. **1966** W. A. D. ANDERSON *Path.* (ed. 5) I. iii. 70/2 Hemochromatosis is a rare disease of iron-pigment metabolism..characterized clinically by cirrhosis of the liver, diabetes mellitus, and skin pigmentation (bronzed diabetes).

bronzen ('brɒnzən), *a. rare.* [f. BRONZE *sb.* + -EN^1.] Made of bronze; resembling bronze.

1855 SINGLETON *Virgil* II. 147 The bronzen-footed [*æripedem*] hind. **1860** LD. LYTTON *Lucile* II. vi. §15. 1 One bronzen evening.

bronzer ('brɒnzə(r)). [f. BRONZE *v.* + -ER^1.] One who coats with, or colours like, bronze.

1865 *Congress. Globe* Feb. 682/1 The bronzer then [in the U.S. Treasury Department] puts the paper through his bronzing machine, and when it is all bronzed it is counted again by the man bronzing it.

bronzify ('brɒnzɪfaɪ), *v. rare*$^{-1}$. [f. BRONZE + -FY: cf. *lignify*, *ossify*.] *trans.* To turn into bronze.

1855 THACKERAY *Newcomes* xxxv. (D.) St. Michael descending upon the Fiend has been caught and bronzified, just as he lighted on the castle of St. Angelo.

'bronzine ('brɒnzɪn), *a. rare*$^{-1}$. [f. as prec. + -INE, after *crystalline*, etc.] Bronze-coloured.

1853 KANE *Grinnell Exp.* xxxvi. (1856) 333 A bronzine smoke..a peculiar russet brown smoke.

bronzing ('brɒnzɪŋ), *vbl. sb.* [f. BRONZE *v.* + -ING^1.] **a.** The action of the verb BRONZE. Also *attrib.*, as in ***bronzing liquid, machine, salt***, etc.

1758 *Monthly Rev.* 276 The various Manners of Gilding, Silvering, and Bronzing. **1865** [see BRONZER]. **1875** URE *Dict. Arts* I. 541 The best..bronzing liquid..is a solution of the chloride of patinum. **1876** DUHRING *Dis. Skin.* 339 The peculiar bronzing of the skin found in Addison's Disease. *a* **1877** KNIGHT *Dict. Mech.*, *Bronzing-machine*, a machine for bronzing wall-papers or printed sheets. *a* **1884** *Ibid.* Suppl. **1889** *Century Dict.*, *Bronzing machine*, a machine for decorating wall-papers, fabrics, labels, etc. with bronze-powder.

b. (See quots.)

1868 LEA *Photography* 42 By this time the dark shadows ought to show the greenish, almost metallic look, known as 'bronzing'. **1885** W. K. BURTON *Mod. Photogr.* (ed. 5) Index 127 Bronzing of prints. **1889** E. J. WALL *Dict. Photogr.* 23 *Bronzing*, a peculiar metallic lustre seen on looking at the shadows of some prints at a certain angle. **1903** H. R. PROCTOR *Leather Manuf.* 404 'Bronzing', the dichroic effect produced by light reflected from the surface of many colouring matters, complementary to that transmitted by them. **1968** *Gloss. Terms Offset Lithogr. Printing* (*B.S.I.*) 30 *Bronzing*, the process of dusting a metallic powder upon a wet printed base.

'bronzing, *ppl. a.* [f. as prec. + -ING^2.] Making or becoming of a bronze colour.

1880 JEFFERIES *Gt. Estate* 131 The very tips of the bronzing wheat-ears.

'bronzist. *rare*$^{-1}$. [f. BRONZE *sb.* + -IST.] A maker of bronzes, an artist in bronze.

1877 FORTNUM *Bronzes* i. 10 The sculptors and bronzists of that city.

bronzite ('brɒnzaɪt). *Min.* [f. as prec. + -ITE.] A variety of diallage, having a bronze-like lustre.

1816 P. CLEAVELAND *Min.* 341 Bronzite. Its colors are brass or bronze yellow, or tombac brown. **1879** RUTLEY *Stud. Rocks* x. 121 Some bronzite is very feebly dichroic.

bronzy ('brɒnzɪ), *a.* [f. as prec. + -Y^1.] Tinged with bronze colour; resembling bronze.

1862 DANA *Man. Geol.* 138 The brownish-black and bronzy foliated mineral hypersthene. **1876** W. MARSTON *Dram. & Poet Wks.* II. 367 Day bathed the walls of oak with bronzy gold. **1882** *Garden* 14 Jan. 18/3 The fruit..is, however, more bronzy on the sunny side. *Ibid.* 18 Nov. 451/3 The flowers are..of a bronzy red colour.

broo. *Sc.* [In 15th c. *brō*; whence regularly in mod.Sc. pronunciation, (brøː), (bryː). Of uncertain origin: perhaps a. OF. *bro*, *breu*, broth (whence dim. *brouez*, *brouet*). Often identified with BREE; but if this were correct, *broo* not *bree* would be the original, since *do*, *boots*, *shoon*, become in the north-east of Scotl. *dee*, *beets*, *sheen*, not the converse. It is hardly possible to connect the 15th c. *broo* with mod.G. *brühe* or Flem. *brui*, *bruw*.]

Broth; liquor; juice, water; = BREE *sb.*^{2} 2, 3.

c **1440** *York Myst.* xix. 135, I schall gar the leppe, And dere aby this bro. *a* **1711** *Sir Gray Steel* (1826) 2221 Good beef and mutton to be broo. **1725** RAMSAY *Gent. Sheph.* I. ii, Ae wean fa's sick, and scads itself wi' brue [*v.r.* broe, *rime-wd.* shoe]. **1786** BURNS *Brigs of Ayr* 162 A' ye douce folk I've borne aboon the broo. *a* **1800** in Leyden *Lord Soulis* Notes (Exclamation attrib. to Jas. I) 'Sorrow gin the sheriff were sodden and supped in broo!'

broo, Sc. form of BROW.

brooch (brəʊtʃ). Forms: 3-9 **broche**, 6 **brooche**, **brouche**, **brutch**, **browche**, 5-7 **bruche**, **brouch**, 7 **broch**, 8 **bruch**, ? *Sc.* **brotch(e**, 9 **broach**, 4, 6- **brooch.** [ME. *broche*; the same word as BROACH, the differentiation of spelling being only recent, and hardly yet established. Occasionally pronounced (bruːtʃ).]

1. An ornamental fastening, consisting of a safety pin, with the clasping part fashioned into a ring, boss, shield, or other device of precious metal or other material, artistically wrought, set with jewels, etc. (Cf. Fr. *broche*, 'grosse épingle à l'usage des femmes'. Littré.) Now used mainly as a (female) ornament, but always for the ostensible purpose of fastening some part of the dress.

a **1225** *Ancr. R.* 420 Ring ne broche nabbe ȝe. *c* **1385** CHAUCER *L.G.W.* 1273 Send hire letters, tokens, brooches, and rynges. ? *a* **1400** *Morte Arthure* 3257 Rebanes of golde, Bruchez and besauntez and oþer bryghte stonys. **1413** LYDG. *Pylgr. Sowle* IV. xxxiii. (1483) 81 An ouche or a broche. **1530** PALSGR. 201/1 Broche for ones cappe, *broche*. Broche with a scripture, *deuise*. **1551** ROBINSON tr. *More's Utop.* (1869) 102 With brouches and aglettes of gold vpon their cappes, which glistered ful of peerles and precious stones. **1588** SHAKS. *L.L.L.* v. ii. 620 S. Georges halfe cheeke in a brooch. **1720** *Stow's Surv.* (ed. Strype 1754) II. v. viii. 248/1 Henry VIII..wore a round flat cap..with a Bruch or Jewel and a feather. **1776** PENNANT *Tour Scotl.* II. 14 At the same time [Bruce] lost his mantle and brotche. **1877** LL. JEWITT *Half-hrs. among Eng. Antiq.* 223 The fibula in Norman times was more like an ornamental circle of jewels and stones, with a central pin; and its name 'brooch' is derived from this article, and its resemblance to a spit.

†**2.** Formerly also in a more general sense: according to Johnson 'a jewel, an ornament of jewels'. In earlier times applied to a necklace, a bracelet, and other trinkets. *Obs.*

1382 WYCLIF *Song Sol.* i. 9 Faire ben thi cheekes, as of a turtil; thi necke as brooches. *c* **1440** *Promp. Parv.* 52 Broche, juelle..*monile, armilla.* **1483** *Cath. Angl.* 45 A Broche, *firmaculum, monile.* **1533** BELLENDEN *Livy* I. (1822) 22 The Sabinis had goldin brochis of grete wecht apoun thair left arme. **1552** HULOET, Brouche or small cheyn, whiche gentlewemen do weare about their neckes. **1621** BURTON *Anat. Mel.* III. ii. III. iii, About her tender neck were costly bruches. **1676** BULLOKAR, *Brouch*, a kind of Jewel to wear appendant to a Chain.

†**b.** *fig.*; cf. *gem*, *jewel*. *Obs.*

1460 CAPGRAVE *Chron.* VI. (1858) 122 [Ethelthredus] wedded Emme, cleped 'The broche of Normandie'. **1528** MORE *Heresyes* III. (1529) lxxxviii. b, It wolde be a goodly brooche for vs to loke on our owne fawltys another whyle. **1602** SHAKS. *Ham.* IV. vii. 94 He is the Brooch indeed, And Iemme of all our Nation. **1625** B. JONSON *Staple News* III. ii, Who is The very Broch o' the Bench, Gem o' the City.

†**3.** 'A painting all in one colour'. *Obs.* (Only in Dictionaries.)

1706 in PHILLIPS. Hence in BAILEY, JOHNSON, etc.

4. *Comb.*, as ***brooch-maker***.

c **1450** *Voc.* in Wr.-Wülcker 583 *Firmacularius*, a brouche-makere. *c* **1500** *Cocke Lorell's B.* (1843) 9 Laten workers, and broche makers. **1530** PALSGR. 201/2 Broche maker, *bambelottier.*

brooch, *v. rare.* [f. prec. sb.] *trans.* To adorn as with a brooch.

1606 SHAKS. *Tr. & Cr.* IV. xv. 25 Not th' Imperious shew Of the full-Fortun'd Cæsar euer shall Be brooch'd with me. **1865** E. BURRITT *Walk Land's End* 439 Wheat-fields in their best gold brooched the broad bosom of either valley.

brooch, obs. form of BROACH.

brood (bruːd), *sb.* Forms: 1 **bród**, 3-5 **brod**, 4-5 **brode**, 5-6 **broode**, *Sc.* **brude**, 4- **brood.** [OE. *bród*, cogn. with Du. *broed* neut., MDu. *broet -d-*; also with OHG., MHG. *bruot* fem., 'heat, warmth, hatching, that which is hatched, brood', mod.G. *brut* 'hatching, brood', from Teutonic verb-root *bro-* to warm, to heat.]

1. Progeny, offspring, young.

a. *esp.* of animals that lay eggs, as birds, serpents, insects, etc. ***a brood***: a family of young hatched at once, a hatch.

c **1000** ÆLFRIC *Hom.* II. 10 þæt sind beon..of ðam huniȝe hi bredað heora brod. *a* **1250** *Owl & Night.* 1634 Ich not to hwan þu bredst þi brod. *c* **1385** CHAUCER *L.G.W.* 133 The foulere that..distroyed hadde hire brod. **1486** *Bk. St. Albans* F vj, A Brode of hennys. **1530** PALSGR. 201/2 Brood of byrdes, *couvee doiseaux.* **1611** BIBLE *Luke* xiii. 34 As a henne doeth gather her brood vnder her wings. **1697** DRYDEN *Virg. Eclog.* IV. 28 The Serpents Brood shall die. **1711** ADDISON *Spect.* No. 121 ¶1 A Hen followed by a Brood of Ducks. **1760** tr. *Keysler's Trav.* I. 356 Before the violent heats set in the first brood of [silk-] worms have finished their work. **1805** MACKINTOSH *Driffield Angler* 294 Brood of black game, or heath fowl. **1873** G. C. DAVIES *Mount. & Mere* ii. 9 A wild duck leads her brood by the rushes.

†**b.** of cattle or large animals. *Obs.*

c **1250** *Gen. & Ex.* 3712 Ful of erf and of netes brod. **1387** TREVISA *Higden* (1865) II. 201 (Mätz.) Among hem [bestes] al þe brood is liche to þe same kynde.

c. Of human beings: family, children. (Now generally somewhat *contemptuous*.)

a **1300** *Cursor M.* 1507 þar he wond ai wit his brode. *c* **1460** *Towneley Myst.* 104 A house fulle of brode. **1480** CAXTON *Descr. Brit.* 40 They prayse fast troian blode For therof come all her brode. *c* **1590** BUREL *Queens Entry Edinb.*, Thair infants sang, & bairnly brudis Quho had but new begun thair mudis. **1598** DRAYTON *Heroic. Ep.* xv. 38 Make this a meane to rayse the Nevils Brood. **1610** SHAKS. *Temp.* III. ii. 113 She will become thy bed..And bring thee forth braue brood. **1642** ROGERS *Naaman* 25 The most poore, despised..silly wench among all thy brood. **1680** OTWAY *Hist. C. Marius* 8 There's a Resemblance tells whose Brood she came of. **1876** GEO. ELIOT *Dan. Der.* 129 A widow with a brood of daughters.

†**d.** The young of fish; fry. *Obs.*

1389 *Act 13 Rich. II*, xix. §1 Le frie ou brood des salmons. **1398** TREVISA *Barth. De P.R.* XIII. xxvi. (1495) 458 Smale fysshes brynge forthe theyr brood in place wherin is but lytyll water. **1531-2** *Act 23 Hen. VIII*, xviii, Broode and frie of fisshe in the saide riuer. **1558** *Act 1 Eliz.* xvii. §1 Any young Brood, Spawn or Fry of Eels.

e. *fig.* Of things inanimate.

1597 SHAKS. *2 Hen. IV*, III. i. 86 Such things become the Hatch and Brood of Time. **1632** MILTON *Penser.* 96 The brood of Folly without father bred. **1798** FRERE *New Morality* in *Anti-Jacobin* 9 July, To drive and scatter all the brood of lies. **1863** GEO. ELIOT *Romola* I. ix. (1880) I. 136 A brood of guilty wishes.

f. Of bees and wasps: the larvæ while in the brood-cells; ***foul brood***: see FOUL *a.* 1 b.

1754 P. TEMPLEMAN *Remarks Physics* II. 82 Till all the brood have sallied forth in the form of bees. **1806** J. G. DALYELL tr. *Huber's Nat. Hist. Bees* v. 102 Another piece of comb, containing the brood of workers. **1869** *Good Words for Young* 1 Sept. 515/1 At length the first brood [of wasps] is hatched.

2. †**a.** The cherishing of the fœtus in the egg or the womb; hatching, breeding. ***to sit on brood*** or ***a-brood***: as a hen on her eggs, *fig.* to sit brooding. Cf. ABROOD. *Obs.* or *arch.*

1250-1398 [see ABROOD]. *a* **1300** *Seven Sins* in *E.E.P.* (1862) 19 A-pan is muk he sit a-brode. *c* **1420** *Pallad. on Husb.* I. 575 What woman cannot sette an hen on broode And bryng her briddes forth? *c* **1440** *Promp. Parv.* 53 Brode of byrdys, *pullificacio.* *c* **1534** tr. *Pol. Verg. Eng. Hist.* (1846) I. 182 Verie commodious for the broode and feeding of cattayle. **1602** SHAKS. *Ham.* III. i. 173 There's something in his soule O're which his Melancholly sits on brood. **1616** SURFL. & MARKH. *Countr. Farm* 80 To fat their Feasant Cockes and Hennes for Feastiuall dayes..and not for brood. **1872** BROWNING *Fifine* lix. 12 You still blew a spark at brood I' the greyest embers.

†**b.** Hence: parentage, extraction, nativity.

1596 SPENSER *F.Q.* I. III. 8 At last..Arose the virgin borne of heauenly brood. *Ibid.* v. vii. 21 They doe thy linage, and thy Lordly brood..They doe thy love forlorne in womens thraldome see.

c. *attrib.* with sense 'breeding'; as in ***brood class***; ***brood hen***, ***mare***, ***sow***, and the like, where however the words are often hyphened: see 6.

1526 *Pilgr. Perf.* (1531) 13 He..cheryssheth vs, as..the broode henne her chekyns. **1814** SCOTT *Diary* in *Lockhart* (1839) IV. 234 The brood sow making a distinguished inhabitant of the mansion. **1883** *Birmingham Weekly Post* 11 Aug. 6/3 Mares and foals shown in the brood class. **1886** *Sat. Rev.* 6 Mar. 327/2 A brood mare, one of the blue-blooded matrons of the Stud-book.

d. A state of brooding or mental contemplation, esp. ***in a brood***.

1895 HARDY *Jude* VI. vi. 469 You seem all in a brood, old man. **1941** N. MARSH *Surfeit of Lampreys* xvi. 251 We'll all have a brood over the beastly thing. **1959** *Guardian* 16 Oct. 9/1 Bill Mortlock is apt to go into a sudden brood about ethics or the rightness of Proust.

3. A race, a kind; a species of men, animals, or things, having common qualities. Now usually *contemptuous*; = 'swarm, crew, crowd'.

1581 J. BELL *Haddon's Answ. Osor.* 213 b, The secrett whisperings of Pelagius brood. **1602** CAREW *Cornwall* 22 a,

Cornish houses are most pestred with Rats, a brood very hurtful. **1706** HEARNE *Coll.* (1885) I. 208 Presbyterians and the rest of yᵗ Brood. *a* **1719** ADDISON (J.) Its tainted air and all its broods of poisons. **1867** FREEMAN *Norm. Conq.* (1876) I. iii. 96 A brood of petty despots. **1884** *Pall Mall G.* 28 June 1/1 The unclean brood of pashas and beys at present infesting London.

4. *spec.* The spat of oysters in its second year.

1862 *Macm. Mag.* Oct. 504 This brood is carefully laid down in the oyster-beds of Whitstable. **1865** *Pall Mall G.* 5 Dec. 5 The free fishermen buy not only 'brood', as the spawn is called when two years old, but oysters much nearer maturity. **1879** *Cassell's Techn. Educ.* IV. 154/1 Spat in the second year is denominated 'brood'.

5. *Min.* 'The heavier kinds of waste in tin and copper ores (*Cornwall*).' Raymond *Mining Gloss.*

1880 *W. Cornw. Gloss. Brood*, impurities mixed with ore.

6. *Comb.*, frequently with sense 'breeding, hatching', as ***brood-basket, -bed, -capsule, -comb*** (of bees), ***-goose, -mare, -oven, -oyster, -pouch, -song, -sow***; **brood-box** = *body-box* (BODY *sb.* 30); **brood-cell,** (*a*) a cell in a honeycomb, made for the reception of a larva, as distinguished from a honey-cell; (*b*) *Bot.*, an asexually produced reproductive cell (*Funk's Stand. Dict.* 1893); **brood-chamber,** (*a*) a chamber for holding the eggs or brood of an animal, etc.; (*b*) a chamber folded off from the uterus and closed around the embryo in some species of *Peripatus* (*Cent. Dict.* Suppl.); **brood-food,** a prepared food for young bees; a substance derived from pollen by digestion, and serving as a pap for a brood of bees; **brood-hen,** a breeding-hen; also an old name for the constellation of the Pleiades; **brood-lamella,** 'in crustaceans, a part of an appendage modified to form a protective cover for the eggs or young' (*Cent. Dict.* Suppl.); †**brood-man** (L. *proletarius*), a Roman citizen of the lowest class who served the republic only with his children; **brood nest,** the space inside a hive occupied by the queen and brood; **brood-space** *Anat.*, a cavity in the body of an animal, in which eggs or young are received and remain for a time; **brood spot** (see quot.).

1848 *Sketches Rur. Affairs* 236 A hen and her chickens are sometimes carried .. to the turnip-field, in a sort of basket, called a *brood-basket. **1598** SYLVESTER *Du Bartas* I. v. (1641) 45/2 The rich Merchant resolutely ventures, So soon as th' Halcyon in her *brood-bed enters. **1888** F. R. CHESHIRE *Bees & Bee-Keeping* II. 99 The section-racks .. are constructed on the general plan of the brood-chambers ..; their edges .. abut accurately upon the *brood-boxes. **1870** NICHOLSON *Zool.* (1880) 235 Instead of producing simple 'Echinococci', it [the tape-worm] may bud off numerous '*brood-capsules'. **1884** T. W. COWAN *Brit. Bee-Keeper's Guide Book* (ed. 4) ii. 11 A small portion [of pollen] is used by the mature bees .. for .. capping *brood-cells. **1888** *Brood chamber [see *brood-box* above]. **1914** GEDDES & THOMSON *Sex* iv. 90 A unique shell .. which is used as a brood-chamber for the developing ova. **1776** DEBRAW in *Phil. Trans.* LXVII. 27 The other piece of *brood-comb. *a* **1626** FLETCHER *Hum. Lieut.* II. i, They have no more burden than a *brood-goose, brother. **1526** [see 2 c] *Broode henne. **1551** RECORDE *Cast. Knowl.* 265 In Greek Pleiades, and also Atlantides: they are named in englysh the brood Henne, and the Seuen starres. **1601** HOLLAND *Pliny* I. 298 There should not be put vnder a brood-hen aboue 25 egs at one time to sit vpon. *Ibid.* II. 30 The occultation or setting of the Brood-hen. **1610** HEALEY *St. Aug. City of God* III. xvii. 133 A .. *Broodman was .. euer forborne from all offices and vses in the Cittie, beeing reserued onely to begette children. **1792** *Sporting Mag.* I. 153/2 Stallions... *Brood mares. **1878** BOSW. SMITH *Carthage* 29 Flocks and herds, and broodmares abounded in their pastures. **1875** *Encycl. Brit.* III. 494/1 In the early spring, if a clean empty piece of drone comb be put into the centre of the *brood nest, the queen will usually fill it with drone eggs. **1737** G. SMITH *Cur. Relations* I. iv. 490 *Brood-Ovens, contriv'd to breed and hatch all Sorts of Eggs. **1864** *Daily Tel.* 18 May, From *brood-oysters, whelks, shell-fish and the rest, the villages .. derive £30,000 a year. **1869** NICHOLSON *Zool.* (1880) 522 In the curious American Tree-frogs .. the females have a dorsal *brood-pouch. **1881** F. M. BALFOUR *Embryol.* II. 55 In Syngnathus the eggs are carried in a brood-pouch of the male situated behind the anus. **1840** BROWNING *Sordello* I. 279 He .. sends his soul along, With the cloud's thunder, or a dove's *brood-song. **1815** SCOTT *Guy M.* Introd. 9 Her sons .. stole a *brood-sow from their kind entertainer. **1878** BELL & LANKESTER tr. *Gegenbaur's Comp. Anat.* 268 An Egg in the *brood-space formed between the body and the mantle. **1896** KIRKALDY & POLLARD tr. *Boas' Text Bk. Zool.* 450 Usually the sitting Bird is provided with *brood spots, regions from which the feathers have fallen off, so that the eggs may come into direct contact with the warm skin.

brood (bru:d), *v.* [f. BROOD *sb.*]

I. *trans.* (mostly *arch.* or *poet.*)

1. To sit on (eggs) so as to hatch them; to incubate.

c **1440** *Promp. Parv.* 53 Brodyn, as byrdys, *foveo, fetifico.* **1626** T. H. *Caussin's Holy Crt.* 166 If the hen brood not her eggs, she hath no desire to make them disclose. **1641** J. JACKSON *True Evang. T.* iii. 179 Gods Spirit .. must incubate, and brood both, to make them fruitfull. **1816** KIRBY & SP. *Entomol.* (1843) II. 41 *note*, That the eggs .. are deposited in heaps and that the neuters brood them. **1831** CARLYLE *Sart. Res.* (1869) 88 To breed a fresh Soul, is it not like brooding a fresh (celestial) Egg?

†**b.** To produce by brooding *upon*; to breed. (Cf. *Gen.* i. 2.) *Obs.*

1649 SELDEN *Laws Eng.* II. i. (1739) 8 A Chaos capable of any form that the next daring spirit shall brood upon it.

2. To cherish (young brood) under the wings, as a hen does; often *fig.*

1571 GOLDING *Calvin on Ps.* lvii. 2 To gather in our hope unto God, that he may broode us under his winges. **1587** FLEMING *Contn. Holinshed* III. 1338/1 A hen a brooding hir chickens. **1639** HORN & ROBOTHAM *Gate Lang. Unl.* xiv. §147 They brood their broode under the covering of their wings. **1640** BP. HALL *Episc.* Ep. Ded. 3 This strange bird thus hatched by Farell .. was afterwards brooded by two more famous successors. **1675** J. SMITH *Chr. Relig. Appeal* I. 35 Those Gods, under whose wings I have been brooded.

b. ***to brood up***: = BREED *up*, to rear.

1586 WARNER *Alb. Eng.* II. xi. 49 The thriftie Earth that bringeth out and broodeth vp her breed. **1610** HEALEY *St. Aug. City of God* 94 Not able to restraine them from brooding up such desires.

3. *fig.* To breed, hatch (products or projects); to produce as it were by incubation.

1613 FLETCHER *Captain* II. i. 52 An ease that broodes Theeves and basterds onely. **1662** FULLER *Worthies* (1840) III. 362 Hell, and not the heavens, brooded that design. **1802** SOUTHEY *Thalaba* III. i, There brood the pestilence, and let The earthquake loose. **1870** LOWELL *Among my Bks.* Ser. I. (1873) 183 By the natural processes of the creative faculty, to brood those flashes of expression that transcend rhetoric.

†**4.** To cherish, nurse tenderly. *Obs.*

1618 T. ADAMS *Saints' Meeting* Wks. 1861 II. 401 Pleasures, delights, riches, are hatched and brooded by the wicked as their own. *a* **1626** FLETCHER *Woman's Prize* I. i. 97 This fellow broods his master.

b. To cherish in the mind, 'to nurse wrath (or the like) to keep it warm'; to meditate upon, contemplate with feeling. Now usually ***to brood on*** or ***over***: see sense 7.

1571 tr. *Buchanan's Detect. Mary*, She temperately broodeth good luck. **1589** WARNER *Alb. Eng.* V. xxvii. 136 The world thus brooding Vanities. **1646** FULLER *Wounded Consc.* (1841) 316 To sit moping to brood their melancholy. **1675** DRYDEN *Aurengz.* V. i. 2230 You'll sit and brood your Sorrows on a throne. **1784** JOHNSON in Boswell *Life* (1826) IV. 337, I have had no long time to brood hope. **1807** CRABBE *Village* II. 20 Their careful masters brood the painful thought. **1850** BLACKIE *Æschylus* II. 61 Such wedlock even now He blindly broods, as shall uptear his kingdom.

II. *intrans.*

5. To sit as a hen on eggs; to sit or hover with outspread cherishing wings.

1588 SHAKS. *L.L.L.* V. ii. 933 Birds sit brooding in the snow. **1629** MILTON *Nativ.* v, Birds of calm sit brooding on the charmed wave. **1667** —— *P.L.* I. 21 Thou .. with mighty wings outspread Dove-like satst brooding on the vast Abyss, And mad'st it pregnant. **1802** PALEY *Nat. Theol.* xviii. (1817) 147 A couple of sparrows .. would build their nest, and brood upon their eggs. **1852** MRS. JAMESON *Leg. Madonna* (1857) 183 [The Dove] sometimes seems to brood immediately over the head of the Virgin.

6. *fig.* To sit *on*, or hang close *over*; to hover over; with some figurative reference to the action or attitude of a brooding bird. Said esp. of ***night, darkness, silence, mist, storm-clouds***, and the like.

1697 DRYDEN *Virg. Georg.* I. 339 Perpetual Night .. In silence brooding on th' unhappy ground. **1786** S. ROGERS *Ode Superst.* I. ii, Night .. brooding, gave her shapeless shadows birth. **1810** T. PARK *Confirm. Day* in *Poet. Register* 31 The bishop's blessing broods upon their heads, (As once o'er Jordan did the dove-like form). **1855** MACAULAY *Hist. Eng.* IV. 191 Glencoe signifies the Glen of Weeping .. Mists and storms brood over it through the greater part of the finest summer. **1873** BLACK *Pr. Thule* xiii. 201 Silence brooded over the long undulations of the Park.

7. To meditate moodily, or with strong feeling, *on* or *over*; to dwell closely upon in the mind; to nurse or foster the feeling of.

1751 JOHNSON *Rambl.* No. 185 ¶6 He who has often brooded over his wrongs. **1759** FRANKLIN *Ess.* Wks. 1840 III. 364 From the 21st to the 25th .. the governor brooded over the two bills. **1805** SOUTHEY *Madoc in W.* iii, I veil'd my head, and brooded on the past. **1808** SCOTT *Marm.* VI. vi, Sit and deeply brood On dark revenge. **1822** HAZLITT *Table-t.* I. v. 98 A mind for ever brooding over itself. **1876** M. ARNOLD *Lit. & Dogma* 196 It was on this that .. their hopes brooded.

b. To meditate (*esp.* in a moody or morbid way).

1826 DISRAELI *Viv. Grey* V. iii, Their conversation allowed him no pause to brood. **1833** TENNYSON *Poems* 151 With down cast eyes we muse and brood. **1873** MORLEY *Rousseau* I. 277 The egoistic character that loves to brood, and hates to act.

8. *transf.* **a.** To breed (interest).

1678 BUTLER *Hud.* III. II. 861 Sums .. That Brooding lie in Bankers Hands.

b. To lie as a cherished nestling, a cherished thought, etc. (Cf. 4 b and 6.)

1679 DRYDEN *Tr. & Cr.* Pref., The Injury he had receiv'd .. had long been brooding in his Mind. **1812** J. WILSON *Isle of Palms* III. 659 The dovelike rest That broods within her pious breast. **1850** HAWTHORNE *Scarlet Let.* xvii, The themes that were brooding deepest in their hearts.

broode, obs. form of BROAD.

broode-axe, -exe, obs. ff. BROAD-AXE.

†**'brooded,** *ppl. a. Obs.* [f. BROOD *v.* or *sb.* + -ED[1].]

1. Incubated, hatched; also *fig.*

1674 N. FAIRFAX *Bulk & Selv.* 125 Such .. steams, as may be thought to have swarm'd from the brooding hen, and crowden into the brooded egge. *a* **1771** GRAY *Triumphs of Owen*, He nor heaps his brooded stores, Nor on all profusely pours.

2. Having a brood (chiefly in comb. as ***double-brooded***).

1857 STAINTON *Butterflies & Moths.* I. 37 *Vanessa*—all the species are single-brooded, except Urticæ, of which there appears to be a succession of broods during the summer.

¶ In the following passage, some explain 'Having a brood (to watch over)'; others, 'brooding, or occupied with brooding'. The very likely emendation of *brood-eied* = *broad-eyed* (see BROAD *a.* D 2) has also been suggested.

1595 SHAKS. *John* III. iii. 52 Then, in despight of brooded watchfull day, I would into thy bosome poure my thoughts.

brooder ('bru:də(r)). [f. BROOD *v.* + -ER[1].]

1. One who broods over things.

1869 *Daily News* 5 June, Louis Napoleon is not alone a dreamer—he is a brooder. He has brooded two whole years over the possible result of the elections.

2. A hen, etc., that broods or hatches eggs.

1599 T. M[OUFET] *Silkwormes* 26 Now what are seedes and egges of wormes or foule, But recrements of pre-existing things .. ? Yea, from themselues corruption onely springs, Vnlesse by brooders heate .. They changed be to belly, feete, or wings. **1854** *Poultry Chron.* I. 153 An anxious Brooder.

3. An apparatus for the artificial rearing of young chickens and other birds. Also *attrib.* orig. *U.S.*

1880 H. TOMLINSON *Artificial Incubation* vii. 32 [Chickens] may .. be transferred to an artificial mother, or *brooder* as the Yankees call it. **1935** AUDEN & ISHERWOOD *Dog beneath Skin* I. 19 The brooder's really excellent. I rear now 98 per cent. **1945** BETTY MACDONALD *Egg & I* (1946) 44 The brooder house was finished and the seven hundred and fifty yeeping chicks and the brooder were installed. **1959** *Times* 9 Mar. 19/4 A new heat storage chick brooder .. has been developed.

†**'broodful,** *a. Obs.* [See -FUL.] Prolific.

a **1300** *E.E. Psalter* cxliii[iv]. 13 Þair schepe brode-full .. In þar out-gang.

broodiness ('bru:dɪnɪs). [f. BROODY *a.* + -NESS.] The condition or quality of being broody.

1881 *Gard. Chron.* No. 441. 780 A change of run is almost a certain cure for broodiness [in hens].

brooding ('bru:dɪŋ), *vbl. sb.* [see -ING[1].]

1. The action of incubating or hatching.

c **1440** *Promp. Parv.* 53 Brodynge of byrdys, *focio.* **1552** HULOET, Brodyng as hennes doth to chyckens. **1656** COWLEY *Pind. Odes 25 note*, To come like an Egg that is not yet hatcht, but a brooding.

b. *fig.*

1805 SOUTHEY *Madoc in Azt.* ii, But I the while Reck'd not the brooding of the storm.

c. *attrib.*, as in ***brooding-place, -pouch, -room.***

1648 MILTON *Psalm* lxxxiv, The Swallow there .. Hath built her brooding nest. **1852** *Home Circle* Apr. 155 'Brooding-places' .. places selected by various sea-fowls, where they in common build their nests, lay their eggs, and bring up their young. **1884** ROE in *Harper's Mag.* May 930/2 The box was placed on a .. shelf in the brooding-room.

2. A cherishing in the mind; moody mental contemplation.

1873 MORLEY *Rousseau* I. 71 The morbid broodings which active life reduces to their lowest degree in most young men. **1871** R. H. HUTTON *Ess.* (ed. 2) I. Pref. 15 The brooding of man's nature .. over this .. experience.

'brooding, *ppl. a.* [f. BROOD *v.* + -ING[2].]

1. That cherishes (brood), hatches, or incubates.

1674 [see BROODED *ppl. a.*[1]]. **1802** PALEY *Nat. Theol.* (1817) 149 The question, why .. the brooding hen should look for pleasure from her chickens. **1843** HOOD *Song of Shirt* viii, Underneath the eaves The brooding swallows cling.

fig. **1667** MILTON *P.L.* VII. 235 On the watrie calme His brooding wings the Spirit of God outspred.

2. *fig.* That hovers closely around or overhangs (as a bird over her brood).

1646 CRASHAW *Steps to Temp.* 34 Darkness hovers With a sable wing, that covers Brooding horror. *a* **1725** POPE *Odyss.* XIX. 602 When nature's hush'd beneath her brooding shade. **1823** CHALMERS *Serm.* I. 346 A suppressed, but brooding storm. **1850** KINGSLEY *Alt. Locke* xxxv. (1879) 369 Lost in a brooding cloud of fog.

3. That dwells moodily upon a subject of thought.

1818 MRS. SHELLEY *Frankenst.* vi. (1865) 89 Come, Victor, not with brooding thoughts of vengeance. **1875** B. TAYLOR *Faust* II. 42 My father's was a sombre, brooding brain.

'broodingly, *adv.* [f. prec. + -LY[2].] In a brooding manner.

1840 LYTTON *Pilgr. Rhine* xxvi, Which the demon broodingly foresaw. **1854** MRS. GASKELL *North & S.* ii, The weather was sultry and broodingly still.

†**'broodious,** *a. Obs.* [f. BROOD *sb.* + -IOUS after words from Latin.] ? Prolific.

1602 WARNER *Alb. Eng.* Epit. (1612) 368 Through inter-marriages, and confederacies with Ours they grew so audatious, broodious, and powerfull in England that, etc.

'broodlet, 'broodling. *rare.* [f. BROOD *sb.* + -LET, -LING.] A young bird, a nestling.

1673 R. HEAD *Canting Academy* 21 The Hen and all Her tender Broodlings. **1866** ALGER *Solit. Nat. & Man* II. 37 The wild bird whose little heart throbs .. towards her nest and broodlets.

† **'broodly**, *adv. Obs.* = *broodily* (which was perhaps the word meant), f. BROODY.

1615 LATHAM *Falconry* (1633) 98 When you do perceiue your Hawke to sit broodly and crowching.

broody ('bru:dɪ), *a.* and *sb.* [f. BROOD *sb.* + -Y[1].]

A. *adj.* † **1.** Prolific; apt or inclined to breed. Now *dial.*

1513 DOUGLAS *Æneis* VI. xiii. 61 The quhilk ciete.. Happy and brudy of hir forcy ofspring. **1536** BELLENDEN *Cron. Scot.* I. (1821) p. xxxiv, This herbe is sa brudy, that quhair it is anis sawin.. it can nevir be distroyit. *Ibid.* I. v. (JAM.) The brudy spredyng of the Scottis. **1629** BOYD *Last Battell* 146 (JAM.) Strive to curbe your owne corruptions which are broodie within you. *a* **1639** W. WHATELEY *Prototypes* II. xxx. (1640) 97 He is broody of quarrels. **1693** J. WALLACE *Orkney* 30 The Women are very Broodie and apt for Generation. **1800** A. CARLYLE *Autobiog.* 225 His widow, being still handsome and broody, married.

2. Of fowls: Inclined to 'sit' or incubate.

1523 FITZHERB. *Husb.* §146 Whan they [hennes] waxe brodye. **1691** RAY *Creation* I. (1704) 186 The hen—while she is broody sits, and leads her chickens. **1859** DARWIN *Orig. Spec.* (1861) 236 Fowls which very rarely or never become 'broody', that is, never wish to sit on their eggs. **1875** LUBBOCK *Orig. Civiliz.* App. 498 A mongrel [fowl] that becomes broody and sits with remarkable steadiness.

3. *fig.* Of a person: contemplative, (sullenly) meditative; feeling depressed or moody. Of a woman: feeling a maternal desire to have a(nother) baby.

1851 *Gloss. Provincial Words Dorset* 3 *Broody*, sullen; cross. **1896** G. CHANTER *Witch of Withyford* iii. 31 The Squire was so broody since his trouble. **1900** H. LAWSON *Over Sliprails* 52 He.. watched my brush for a while, as if he was thinking, in a broody sort of way, of.. going in for house-painting. **1925** FRASER & GIBBONS *Soldier & Sailor Words* 37 *Broody*, lethargic. Sleepy. Slack. A frequent expression on the drill-ground by drill-sergeants to liven men up, *e.g.*, 'You there, don't get broody, get a move on.' **1961** A. VINTON *Doctor Di at Crossroads* i. 10 I'm bad-tempered and broody and going out with brash blondes. **1984** D. LESSING *Diaries of Jane Somers* II. 362 If I know nothing else it is that there are going to be weddings.. through all the departments at *Lilith*. The whole place is broody. **1986** *Times* 21 Apr. 39/4 Kate becomes broody when a colleague of hers becomes pregnant.

B. *sb.* A broody hen.

1904 *Daily Chron.* 30 July 4/7 He would.. defer putting the 'broody' on them [*sc.* the eggs] till dusk. **1923** *Daily Mail* 20 Jan. 11 Broodies of these highly developed strains are.. unreliable sitters. **1967** *Guardian* 17 May 2/5 We've no broodies left in the farmyard.

brook (brʊk), *sb.* Forms: 1 bróc, 2–3 broc, 3–4 brok, 4 bruche, 4–6 broke, 5–7 brooke, 5–6 bruke, 4– brook. [OE. *bróc* masc., corresponding in form to MDu. *broek* m., mod.Du. *broek* n., LG. *brôk* marsh, bog, OHG. *bruoh*, MHG. *bruoch* n. and m., marshy ground, morass, Ger. *bruch* m. and n., moor, marsh, bog, fen. A similar range of meaning appears in MHG. *ouwe* water, stream, watery land, island; and cf. BACHE. The ulterior derivation of the WGer. **brôka-* is uncertain; it has been doubtfully referred to *brek-an* to BREAK, as 'that which breaks or bursts forth'; cf. *spring*, 'that which springs forth'.]

1. A small stream, rivulet; *orig.* a torrent, a strong flowing stream.

c **888** K. ÆLFRED *Boeth.* vi, Hwæt eac se broc, þeah he swiþe of his rihtryne. *c* **1050** *Gloss.* in Wr.-Wülcker 178 *Fluuius*, singalflowende ea; *riuus*, rið; *latex*, burna; *torrens*, broc; *riuulus*, lytel rið. *c* **1205** LAY. 10827 Þat.. wurpen hine in ænne broc. *c* **1325** *E.E. Allit. P.* A. 1073 Vpon þe brokez brym. *c* **1450** *Merlin* xi. 167 In the brooke were wylde gees that hem dide bathe. *c* **1450** HENRYSON *Mor. Fab.* 86, I drinke beneth you far, Ergo, for mee your bruke was neuer the war. **1535** COVERDALE *Ps.* xli[i]. 1 Like as the hert desyreth the water brokes. **1538** STARKEY *England* 16 Yssue.. as Brokys out of fountaynys. **1593** SHAKS. *2 Hen. VI*, III. i. 53 Smooth runnes the Water, where the Brooke is deepe. **1600** —— *A.Y.L.* II. i. 16 This our life.. Findes tongues in trees, bookes in the running brookes, Sermons in stones. **1597** MONTGOMERIE *Cherrie & Slae* 24 Among the water broxe. **1796** MORSE *Amer. Geog.* I. 450 These rivers are fed by numberless brooks from every part of the country. **1864** TENNYSON (*title*) The Brook.

b. *transf.* A stream, a 'torrent' (*e.g.* of blood).

a **1225** *Ancr. R.* 258 Þet ilke dei þet he bledde.. brokes of ful brode & deope wunden. *c* **1240** *Ureisun* in *Lamb. Hom.* 187 Þi blod isched on þe rode.. þe large broc of þi softe side.

† **2.** The stream or 'flood' of the sea. *Obs. rare.*

c **1325** *E.E. Allit. P.* C. 145 When þe breth & þe brok & þe bote metten.

3. *attrib.* and *Comb.*, as **brook-bank**, **-side**; **brook-bounded** adj.; **brook ouzel** or **brook runner**, the water-rail (*Rallus aquaticus*).

1861 L. NOBLE *Icebergs* 161 Along the *brook-banks under the Catskills. **1839** BAILEY *Festus* xx. (1848) 238 *Brook-bounded pine spinnies. **1678** RAY *Willughby's Ornith.* 314 The Water-Rail, called by some the Bilcock or *Brook-Owzel. **1837** HAWTHORNE *Amer. Note-bks.* (1871) I. 42 Strawberries were scattered along the *brookside.

b. in plant-names, as **brook betony**, *Scrophularia aquatica*; † **brook leek**, *Arum dracunculus*; **brook mint**, the water-mint, *Mentha hirsuta*; **brook-tongue**, *Cicuta virosa*; **brook weed**, the water pimpernel, *Samolus valerandi*. (Miller *Plant-Names.*)

c **1040** *Sax. Leechd.* I. 220 Genim þysse wyrte wos þe man.. *brocminte nemneþ. **1614** MARKHAM *Cheap Husb.* I. Table Wds., Horse-mint.. is called Water-mint or Brook-mint. **1861** MISS PRATT *Flower. Pl.* IV. 245 *Brookweed or Water Pimpernel. **1863** MARG. PLUES *Wildflowers* 237 She got the brookweed too from the banks of the Fowey river.

brook (brʊk), *v.* Forms: 1 brúcan, 2 bruce(n, 2–3 bruke(n, brukien, 3–6 brouke, 4 brouk, 4–5 browke; also 3–5 broken, 3–6 broke, (4–5 brok), 5–7 brooke, 5– brook; 5–6 *Sc.* bruk(e(ü), 6 brwk, 6–8 bruik, 7 bruike. [OE. *brúcan* (pa. t. *bréac*, *brucon*, pple. *ȝebrocen*), a Com. Teut. verb, but found in the other langs. with weak conjugation: OFris. *brûka*, OS. *brûcan* (MDu. *brûken*, Du. *bruiken*), LG. *brûken*, OHG. *brûhhan* (MHG. *brûchen*, Ger. *brauchen*), Goth. *brukjan*:—OTeut. stem **bruk-* 'to make use of, have the enjoyment of, enjoy':—Aryan **bhrug-*, whence also L. *fru-i* (:—*frugv-i*), *fruct-us* in same sense. The strong pa. t. and pple. occur in OE., but no certain instance of either is known in ME.; 16th c. Scotch has the weak *brooked*, *brooket*, *bruikit*.

The phonetic history is unusual; the OE. *brúcan*, ME. *bruken*, *brouke*, would normally have given mod. *browk*; while the mod. *brook*, and Sc. *bruik* normally answer to a ME. *brōken*, found already, as a by-form, in Layamon.]

1. *trans.* To enjoy the use of, make use of, profit by; to use, enjoy, possess, hold. *Obs.* except *Sc.* in some legal phrases, and *arch.* in literature.

Beowulf 894 Þæt he beah-hordes brucan moste. *a* **1000** *Wanderer* 44 (in Sweet *Ags. Reader*) Swa he.. giefstoles breac. *c* **1175** *Lamb. Hom.* 111 Þu ane ne brukest naut þinra welena. *c* **1205** LAY. 30308 Ne scal he nauere.. kinehelme broken [*c* **1275** brouke]. *a* **1225** *St. Marher*, 19 Thu schalt aa buten ende bruken blisse. *a* **1300** *Cursor M.* 2589 To bruke þair heritage in pais. *Ibid.* 2427 (Fairf.) Take here þi wife and brok [*v.r.* brouk, -e] hir wele. *c* **1440** *Bone Flor.* 1183 Syr Emere comawndyd every man To brooke wele the tresur that they wan. **1548** *Compl. Scot.* 86 Ihone kyng of ingland.. brukit the realme tuenty ȝeirs. **1603** JAS. I in Calderwood *Hist. Kirk* 256 I, as long as I brook my life, shall maintain the same. **1637** RUTHERFORD *Lett.* cxl. (1862) I. 334 Long may He brook it! **1707** DK. ATHOL in *Vulpone* 21 To retain, enjoy or bruik and exerce all their Rights. **1828** SCOTT *F.M. Perth* xi, No man shall brook life after he has passed an affront on Douglas. *Mod. Sc.* The langest leiver bruiks a' (= the survivor has possession of everything).

† **b.** Formerly in asseverations: ***so*** (or ***as***) ***brouke I my chyn, eyes, heid***, etc: so may I (*or* as I wish to) have the use of my eyes, etc.

c **1175** *Cott. Hom.* 233 Swa ibruce ic mine rice ne scule ȝie mine mete ibite. *a* **1300** *Havelok* 311 He shal [ben] king.. So brouke I euere mi blake swire! **1384** CHAUCER *H. Fame* 273 For al-so browke I wel myn hede Ther may be vnder godelyhede Keuered many a shrewde vice. *c* **1386** —— *Nonne Pr. T.* 480 So mot I browke wel myn yen tway, Save ye, I herde never man so synge. *c* **1400** *Gamelyn* 567 Than seyde the porter, 'so brouke I my chyn, ȝe schul sey your erand er ȝe comen in'. *c* **1460** *Towneley Myst.* 12 As browke I thise two shankys, It is full sore myne unthankys. **1591** *Troub. Raigne K. John* (1611) 29 Ill may I thriue, and nothing brooke with me, If shortly I present it not to thee.

† **c.** ***to brook a name*** (***well***): to bear it appropriately, do credit to it, act consistently with it. *Obs.*

1587 HARRISON *England* II. v. (1877) 127 Would to God they might once brooke their name, *Sans reproche. a* **1600** *Robin Hood* (Ritson) II. xvi. 30 'Simon,' said the good wife, 'I wish thou mayest well brook thy name'. **1622** R. HAWKINS *Voy. S. Sea* (1847) 11 Henceforth shee should be called the Daintie; which name she brooked as well for her proportion and grace, as for the many happie voyages. **1655** FULLER *Ch. Hist.* I. i. §8 And well did he brook his Name.

† **2.** To make use of (food); in later usage, to digest, retain, or bear on the stomach.

c **950** *Lindisf. Gosp.* John iv. 32 Ic mett hafo to bruccanne ðone ȝie ne uutton. *a* **1000** ÆLFRIC *Gen.* iii. 19 On swate ðines andwlitan ðu bricst ðines hlafes. *c* **1175** *Cott. Hom.* 221 Ælra þara þing þe on paradis beoð þu most bruce. *c* **1440** *Promp. Parv.* 53 Brooke mete or drynke.. *retineo vel digerendo retinere.* **1540** RAYNALD *Byrth Man* II. ix. (1634) 142 If she refuse or cannot brooke meat. **1561** HOLLYBUSH *Hom. Apoth.* 32 Geue him a good draught of yᵉ same.. as hote as he can brouke it. **1598** W. PHILLIP *Linschoten's Trav. Ind.* in Arb. *Garner* III. 26 So fat that men can hardly brook them.

† **b.** *absol. Obs.*

1473 MARG. PASTON *Lett.* III. 79 Water of mynte.. were good for my cosyn to drynke for to make hym to browke.

c. *fig.* To digest mentally.

1548 HALL *Chron.* (1809) 178 After the letter twise redde & wisely brooked.

3. To put up with, bear with, endure, tolerate [a fig. sense of 'to stomach' in 2]. Now only in negative or preclusive constructions.

1530 PALSGR. 471/2 He can nat brooke me of all men. **1583** STUBBES *Anat. Abus.* II. 30 They cannot at any hand brooke or digest them that would counsel them to that. **1624** CAPT. SMITH *Virginia* IV. 115, I would deter such from comming here, that cannot well brooke labour. **1667** MILTON *P.L.* VI. 274 Heav'n.. Brooks not the works of violence and War. **1752** YOUNG *Brothers* II. i, Such insults are not brook'd by royal minds. *c* **1815** JANE AUSTEN *Northang. Ab.* (1833) II. xv. 208 The General could ill brook the opposition of his son. *c* **1854** STANLEY *Sinai & Pal.* v. (1858) 230 That haughty spirit that could brook no equal or superior.

† **b.** *intr.* To put up *with*. *Obs.*

1658 A. FOX tr. *Wurtz' Surg.* II. i. 49 The Wound cannot brook with the Medicine.

† **c.** To find it agreeable *to do something*. *Obs.*

1604 E. HAKE *No Gold, No G.* in Farr's *S.P.* (1848) 256 Few men brooke To helpe a man that is in need.

† **4.** ***to brook up.*** [perh. a different word.] *Obs.*

1691 RAY *S. & E.C. Wds.* 91 *To brook up*, spoken of Clouds; when they draw together and threaten rain. [Also **1721** in BAILEY.]

¶ Here probably an error for *busked*.

a **1300** *Cursor M.* 25282 Þe bodi has nede of bath to bruked be wid mete and clath.

brookable ('brʊkəb(ə)l), *a.* That may be brooked; endurable. (Chiefly *Sc.*)

c **1817** HOGG *Tales & Sk.* V. 41 The face.. gazed on him with an intensity that was hardly brookable. **1881** *Autobiog. J. Younger* xxii. 264 The idea was not brookable to the old people.

brooke, obs. pa. t. of BREAK.

brooked, *a. Sc.* Forms: 8 bruket, bruckit, 9 brooket, bruikit ('brykɪt). [Of uncertain origin: it has been taken as identical with BROCKED, but appears to be phonetically distinct.] Streaked or marked with black; soot-begrimed.

a **1796** BURNS *Wks.* (1800) IV. 85 (JAM.) The bonie bruket Lassie certainly deserves better verses. **1810** COCK *Simple Strains* 137 (JAM.) Lat me to the brooket knave. **1832–53** *Whistle-Binkie* (Sc. Songs) II. 105 To milk our bruckit cow.

† **'brooker.** *Sc. rare.* [f. BROOK *v.* + -ER[1].] One who enjoys possession *of*, a proprietor.

1721 RAMSAY *Wks.* (1848) III. 70 The loyal brooker of Belltrees [the estate of the Semples].

brooker, obs. form of BROKER.

† **'brooket.** [f. BROOK *sb.* + -ET[1].] = BROOKLET.

1538 LELAND *Itin.* I. 13 A litle withoute Welleden I passid over a Broket. **1610** HOLLAND *Camden's Brit.* I. 315 From Lewis, the river.. is fed more full with a brooket falling from Laughton.

brooking ('brʊkɪŋ), *vbl. sb.* [f. BROOK *v.*]

† **1.** The capacity to take (food); assimilation, digestion. *Obs.*

c **1440** *Promp. Parv.* 53 Brokynge of mete and drynke, *retencio.* **1626** BACON *Sylva* §61 The brooking of enormous quantity of meats.. without Surfeit.

2. Endurance, bearing. (Now chiefly gerundial.)

1624 BACON *New Atl.* iii. (1635) 42 We have ships and boats for going under water, and brooking of seas. *Mod.* After brooking such an insult.

† **'brooking,** *sb. Obs.* [f. BROOK *sb.* + -ING[1].] The maintenance or preservation of a brook.

1610 FOLKINGHAM *Art of Survey* II. ii. 50 Sometimes this Compound Boundage implies a mutuall propertie or duety participable to the Conterminants, as bancking, balking, dyking.. brooking, riuaging, foording.

brookite ('brʊkaɪt). *Min.* [Named after H. J. *Brooke*, a mineralogist.] Native titanic anhydride; Jurinite.

1879 RUTLEY *Stud. Rocks* x. 119 These plates have been referred.. to göthite, to specular iron, to brookite, etc.

brooklet ('brʊklɪt). [f. BROOK *sb.* + -LET: of very modern formation; the earlier equivalent was BROOKET.] A little brook, a rivulet, streamlet.

1813 SCOTT *Trierm.* I. v, Such lulling sounds as the brooklet sings. **1837** HAWTHORNE *Twice-told T.* (1851) II. xviii. 256 Along the brink of a freshwater brooklet. **1865** LIVINGSTONE *Zambesi* xxiv. 492 These little brooklets came down from the range on our left.

brooklime ('brʊklaɪm). Forms: [1 hleomoce, 4–5 lemoke, lemeke, lemke], 5 brokelemke, -lempk, 6 brokelem, brooklem, -lyme, 7 brokelempe, brokelhempe, 6 brooklyme, -lime. [Worn down from ME. *brok-lemok*, f. *bróc* BROOK + *lemok*:—OE. *hleomoc*, name of the plant.]

A species of Speedwell (*Veronica Beccabunga*) common on the edges of ditches; also a kindred species known as Lesser Brooklime or Narrow-leaved Water Speedwell (*V. Anagallis*).

[*c* **1000** *Sax. Leechd.* II. 92 Hleomoce hatte wyrt sio weaxeð on broce. *a* **1387** *Sinon. Barthol.* (Mowat *Anecd. Oxon.* I.) *Fabaria*, lemke [*printed* levike]. *a* **1465** *Alphita* (Mowat *Anecd. Oxon.* II.) 86 *Fabaria.. anglice* lemeke uel lemoke.] *a* **1450** *MS. Bodl.* 536 (Plant names), Brokelemke. *c* **1460** J. RUSSELL *Bk. Nurture* in *Babees Bk.* (1868) 185 Broke lempk.. is good for ache. **1548** TURNER *Names of Herbes* (1881) 25 Called in englishe Brooklem, and in Duche Bauchbung. **1551** —— *Herbal* 98 Broocklyme. **1597** GERARD *Herbal* clxxxiv. 495 Brookelime or Brooklem, hath fat, thicke stalkes. **1614** MARKHAM *Cheape Husb.* (ed. 3) 97 Take Brokelempe [ed. **1668** brooklime] the lesse, and frie it with Tallow. **1748** ANSON *Voy.* II. xii. (ed. 4) 364 Nor is there any other useful vegetable here worth mentioning except brooklime. **1794** MARTYN *Rousseau's Bot.* xii. 124. **1846** SOWERBY *Eng. Bot.* (1866) VI. 169 The leaves and young stems of the Brooklime were once in favour as an antiscorbutic.

Brooklynese (ˌbrʊklɪ'ni:z). [f. *Brooklyn* (see below) + -ESE; cf. LONDONESE *sb.*] The form of speech generally found in uncultured use in

New York City, but esp. associated with the borough of Brooklyn.

1946 *N.Y. Times Mag.* 7 July 14/1 Brooklynese is no upstart from across the tracks. **1963** *Economist* 5 Oct. 39/2 His rich Brooklynese.

brooky (ˈbrʊkɪ), *a.* [f. BROOK *sb.* + -Y[1].] Characterized by or abounding in brooks.

1757 DYER *Fleece* I. 52 Lemsters brooky tract, & airy Croft. *Ibid.* II. 208 Hermon & Seir & Hebron's brooky sides. **1882** *Three in Norway* viii. 61 The rockiest, brookiest.. country in the world.

brool (bruːl). [app. ad. Ger. *brüll* roar, roaring, f. *brüllen*, Du. *brullen* to roar (as a lion, etc.). (Cf. BRILL *v.* 2.)] A low deep humming sound; a murmur. Also *fig.* So **ˈbrooling** *vbl. sb.*

1837 CARLYLE *Fr. Rev.* (1871) I. 144 List to the brool of that royal forest-voice. **1879** *Spectator* 29 Nov. 1507 What the meaning of that multitudinous brool will be. **1884** *Ibid.* 16 Feb. 213/1 A man who could represent the ruling opinion of the hour with a brool as loud as its own. **1837** CARLYLE *Fr. Rev.* (1857) II. II. IV. iv. 14 The People also is calm.. With but a few broolings.

broom (bruːm), *sb.* Forms: 1 bróm, 2-4 brom, 3-6 brome, 5-6 brume, (6 *Sc.* broym, broume), 6 browme, 6-7 broome (7- *Sc.* brume), 5- broom. [OE. *bróm* (from WGer. *brâma-), pointing to OTeut. type *brǣmo-z: cogn. with OHG. *brâmo*, MHG. *brâme* masc. 'bramble' (whence mod.G. *brombeere*), also with Ger. *bram* 'broom', OTeut. type *brǣmon-; and OHG. *brâma*, mod.Ger. and MDu. *brame*, mod.Du. *braam* fem., bramble, thorn, (MDu. *brame* also 'broom'), OTeut. type *brǣmôn- fem.; also with BRAMBLE, q.v. The derivation of the OTeut. stem *brǣm-* is uncertain, but the earliest sense of the various forms appears to be 'thorny shrub', whence 'bramble', 'furze or gorse', and by confusion with the latter 'broom', which seems to be the only Eng. sense.]

1. A shrub, *Sarothamnus* or *Cytisus Scoparius* (N.O. *Leguminosæ*), bearing large handsome yellow papilionaceous flowers; abundant on sandy banks, pastures, and heaths in Britain, and diffused over Western Europe. Also the genus to which this belongs, and the allied genus *Genista*, including the White Broom, and Giant or Irish Broom cultivated in gardens, and many other species.

c **1000** *Sax. Leechd.* II. 32 Genim bromes ahsan. *c* **1150** *Gloss.* in Wr.-Wülcker 545 *Genesta*, brom. *c* **1384** CHAUCER *H. Fame* 1226 Lytel herde gromes That kepen bestis in the bromes. **1523** FITZHERB. *Surv.* 6 b, Yet may he.. selle all the wode, brome, gorse, fyrs, braken. **1562** TURNER *Herbal* II. 7 b, Vnder the roughe broume. **1567** MAPLET *Gr. Forest* 34 Brome.. of some is called Mirica for the bitternesse of his tast. **1620** VENNER *Via Recta* vi. 98 The young tender buds of Broome are.. gathered and preserued in pickle. **1783** COWPER *Task* VI. 170 The Broom, Yellow and bright, as bullion unalloy'd Her blossoms. **1800** WORDSW. *To Joanna*, 'Twas that delightful season when the broom, Full-flowered ..Along the copses runs in veins of gold. *c* **1854** STANLEY *Sinai & Pal.* i. (1858) 20 The Retem, or wild broom, with its high canopy and white blossoms.. is the very shrub under which.. Elijah slept in his wanderings.

2. Entering into the name of various other plants used for sweeping, or in other respects fancied to be akin to the broom proper; as BUTCHER'S BROOM, SPANISH BROOM (a kind of grass), q.v.

3. a. An implement for sweeping, a besom: originally one made of twigs of broom, heather, etc., fixed to a 'stick' or handle; now the generic name for a besom of any material. Cf. BESOM *sb.*[1] 2.

14.. *Songs Costume* 64 So many sellers of bromys, Say I never. **1481** CAXTON *Reynard* (Arb.) 15 Alle ranne.. eueryche wyth his wepen.. some with a brome. **1538** BALE *Thre Lawes* 177 Brom, brom, brom, brom, brom. Bye brom bye bye bromes for shoes and powcheryngs; botes and byskyns for newe bromes, Brom, brom, brom. **1562** J. HEYWOOD *Prov. & Epigr.* (1867) 44 The greene new brome sweepth cleene. **1590** SHAKS. *Mids. N.* v. i. 396, I am sent with broome before, To sweep the dust behinde the doore. **1664** EVELYN *Kal. Hort.* (1729) 214 Move it sometimes with a Broom or Whisk, that the Seeds clog not together. **1708** HEARNE *Coll.* (1885-6) II. 110 My chimneys with high flying broom No longer thou shalt clean. **1798** SOUTHEY *Lyric P.*, *To Spider* iii, Where is he whose broom The earth shall clean? **1829** J. W. CROKER in *Croker Papers* (1884) II. xiv. 18 As they say of a broom that it is dirty to keep other things clean.

b. *fig.* and *transf.*

1587 FLEMING *Contn. Holinshed* III. 1347/2 Thus did the broome of iustice sweepe awaie these noisome cobwebs. **1621** SANDERSON *Serm.* (1681) I. 213 Thy new broom, that now sweepeth clean all discontents from thee, will soon grow stubbed. **1855** DICKENS *Dorrit* I. xxiv, 'If he hadn't been cut short [= died] while I was a new broom'.

4. A sweeping tail of a horse; cf. *broom-tail* in 6.

1616 SURFL. & MARKH. *Country Farm* 136 There are manie wrinkles and plaits in his broome or brushing taile.

5. *Comb.* General relations: **a.** attributive, as *broom-besom*, *-blossom*, *-brush*, *-field*, *-flower*, *-grove*, *-handle*, *-head*, *-plant*, *-salve*, *-shaft*, *-shank*, *-stalk*, *-tree*, *-wood*; **b.** objective, as *broom-maker*, *-seller*.

1693 URQUHART *Rabelais* III. xvii, Three whisks of a *broom-besom. **1814** JONES in *Life Chalmers* (1851) I. 379 It is.. scrubbed off with a birch or broom besom. *c* **1314** *Guy Warw.* (1840) 292 (Halliw.) In a *brom feld ther wer hidde Thre hundred Sarrazins. **1633** AMES *Agst. Cerem.* II. 258 One instrument.. for the pastures, and another for the broome-feilds. **1595** SPENSER *Sonn.* xxvi, Sweet is the *Broome-flowre. **1846** SOWERBY *Brit. Bot.* (1864) III. 14 Henry VIII.. was wont to drinke the distilled water of Broom-flowers, against surfets and diseases thereof arising. **1610** SHAKS. *Temp.* IV. i. 66 Thy *broome-groues; Whose shadow the dismissed Batchelor loues, Being lasse-lorne. **1826** *Chron.* in *Ann. Reg.* 51/1 He entered the yard.. with a *broom-handle in one hand and a rope with a noose to it in the other. **1882** HOWELLS in *Longm. Mag.* I. 56 Wherever the piano-forte penetrates, lovely woman lifts her fingers from.. the *broom-handle, and the washboard. **1817** *Parl. Debates* 1344 Two *broom-makers, who sold their brooms in adjoining stalls. *c* **1500** *Cocke Lorell's B.* (1843) 10 Potters, *brome sellers, pedelers. **1523** FITZHERB. *Husb.* §44 *Brome salue.. to salue poore mennes shepe, that thynke terre to costely. **1764** T. BRYDGES *Homer Travest.* I. 32 Let Hector ..with his trusty *broomshaft douse ye. **1818** SCOTT *Hrt. Midl.* xviii, 'Her and the gudeman will be whirrying through the blue lift on a *broomshank'. **1646** BUCK *Rich. III*, I. 7 Geoffry Plantagenet used to weare a *Broome-stalke in his Bonnet. **1846** SOWERBY *Brit. Bot.* (1864) III. 13 *Broom-tops were often used to communicate a bitter flavour to beer. *a* **1450** WYCLIF *Jer.* xlviii. 6 (MS. E) 3ee shul be as iencian trees [*later hand* *broom trees] in desert. **1810** CAMPBELL *Poems* I. 8 A *broomwood blossom'd vale.

6. Special comb.: **broom-boy**, ? a street-sweeper or broom-seller; **broom-bush**, *Parthenium Hysterophorus*; † **broom-cat**, an old name for the hare; **broom-cod**, the seed-vessel of the broom; **broom-croft**, a croft or field in which broom grows; **broom-cypress**, *Kochia scoparia*, (see BELVEDERE 2); **broom-dasher** (*dial.*), a dealer in fagots, brooms, etc. (cf. *haberdasher*); **broom-dog** (*Sc.*), an instrument for eradicating broom (Jam.); **broom goose-foot** = *broom-cypress*; **broom-grass**, *Andropogon scoparius*; **broom-heath**, the cross-leaved heath, *Erica tetralix*; **broom-hook**, ? = *broom-dog*; **broom horse** [HORSE *sb.* 6 e] (see quot. 1921); **broom-land**, land overgrown with broom; **broom-sedge**, a species of coarse grass, ? *Spartina*; **broom-squire** (see quots.); **broom-straw** *U.S.*, the straw of broom corn; also the plant itself; **broom-tail** (of a horse), a long bushy tail (cf. 4); **broom toad-flax** = *Broom cypress*; **broom-weed**, a herbaceous plant (*Corchorus siliquosus*) of the West Indies and tropical America, from the leaves of which a drink is prepared; † **broom-wort**, a name applied by Gerard to species of Thlaspi; by others to some plant not identified (? broomrape).

1593 NASHE *Four Lett. Confut.* 127 *Broome boyes, and cornecutters. *c* **1300** *Names of Hare* in *Rel. Ant.* I. 133 The *bromkat, The purblinde, the fursecat. **1509** *Will of Lewkenor* (Somerset Ho.) A coler of gold sett with diuerse perlys & *brome codde. **1868** STANLEY *Westm. Ab.* iii. 148 The broomscods of the Plantagenets. **1871** KINGSLEY *At Last* x, Grand masses of colour.. are supplied by a heather moor, a furze or *broom-croft. **1864** *Times* 12 Dec., Heaths and plantations.. occupied by brickmakers and '*broom-dashers'. **1660** in *Select. fr. Harl. Misc.* (1793) 380 The king exchanged his woodbill for Francis Yates's *broom-hook. **1921** K. S. WOODS *Rural Industries round Oxford* II. i. 95 The broom-maker sits on a '*broom horse' which has a grip to hold one end of the band while binding the twigs. **1707** MORTIMER *Husb.* (J.), I have known sheep cured of the rot by being put into *broomlands. **1856** OLMSTED *Slave States* 9 Land.. which bore only *broom-sedge—a thin, worthless grass. **1825** D. GARROW *Hist. Lymington* 31 Besoms.. composed of heath, which grows in abundance all over the New Forest.. The manufacturers of this little useful domestic article are termed *Broom Squires. **1857** KINGSLEY *Two Y. Ago* II. xiv. 129 'Broom-squires?' 'So we call in Berkshire squatters on the moor who live by tying heath into brooms.' **1785** WASHINGTON *Diaries* (1925) II. 365 Tussics of *broom Straw. **1846** J. J. HOOPER *Simon Sugg's Adv.* (1851) iii. 38 He wont be able to step over the butt cut of a broom straw. **1684** *Lond. Gaz.* No. 1960/4 Stolen or strayed.. a Chesnut Sorrel Gelding.. with a *broom Tail. **1704** *Ibid.* No. 3981/4 A.. Mare.. with a large Brome Tail. **1786** P. BROWNE *Jamaica* 147 *Broom-weed.. is generally used in besoms by the negroes. **1614** MARKHAM *Cheap Husb.* I. (1668) Table Hard Wds., *Broomwort is an Herb with broun coloured leaves, and beareth a blew flower, and most commonly grows in Woods.

broom (bruːm), *v.* [f. prec. sb.]

1. *trans.* To sweep with a broom.

1838 J. GRANT *Sk. Lond.* 43 If he escaped being scrubbed or 'broomed' to death. **1855** THACKERAY *Newcomes* lviii. (D.), Work-people brooming away the fallen leaves. **1883** MISS BRADDON *Gold. Calf* x. 119 A feeble old woman was feebly brooming the floor.

2. To BREAM a ship. (? Only in Dicts.)

1627 CAPT. SMITH *Seaman's Gram.* ii. 13 *Broming* or *Breaming*. Breaming her, is but washing or burning of all the filth with reeds or broome. **1678** PHILLIPS, *Brooming* or *Broming* a ship: see *Breaming*. **1707** *Glossogr. Nova*, The brooming of a ship meant in old time the burning of the filth from its side. **1708-21** in KERSEY, *Brooming* or *Breaming of a Ship*. **1721-1800** in BAILEY.

ˈbroom corn. [f. (in U.S.) BROOM + (Indian) CORN.] The American name of the Common Millet, *Sorghum vulgare*, of which the panicles are made into brooms and stiff brushes; also the *Sorghum saccharatum* or Sugar Millet of the East.

1817-8 COBBETT *Resid. U.S.* (1822) 340, I have Broom-Corn and Seed-Stems enough to make fifty thousand such brushes. **1861** G. BERKELEY *Sportsm. W. Prairies* xxiv. 410 The Americans called them Broom corn. **1886** *Echo* 25 Sept. 4/2 Broom Bread.. The latest novelty.. is an American loaf made of broom corn flour. **1886** A. H. CHURCH *Food Grains Ind.* 85 Broom corn.. is cultivated in some parts of Northern India.. on account of the sugar which can be extracted from the stems.

broomer (ˈbruːmə(r)). [f. BROOM *v.*] = BROOM-MAN.

1857 *Chamb. Jrnl.* VII. 69 A company of shoe-blacks, broomers, and messengers was set on foot.

broomie (ˈbruːmɪ). *Austral.* and *N.Z.* [f. BROOM *sb.* + -IE.] A broom-hand who keeps the floor clean in a shearing shed.

1933 L. G. D. ACLAND in *Press* (Christchurch) 16 Sept. 15/7 *Broomie*, a boy who keeps the board swept of locks, etc., at shearing. **1966** G. W. TURNER *Eng. Lang. Austral. & N.Z.* vii. 147 The *broomie*, the broom-hand on the board (*on the board* is the shearer's way of saying 'in the woolshed').

broom-man (ˈbruːmmæn). [f. BROOM + MAN.] One who uses a broom; a street-sweeper.

1592 GREENE *Upst. Courtier* (1871) 27 Then Conscience was not a broom man in Kent Street but a Courtier. **1646** G. DANIEL *Poems* 1878 I. 59 Who's free? Not Broome-men, nor the baser sort, Who dress the Citie, and defile the Court. *a* **1716** SOUTH *Serm.* (1717) VI. 9 Scarce one, in Five Thousand.. knows so much as what Popery means. Only that it is.. A Word that sounds bigg and high in the Mouths of Broommen, Scavingers and Watermen, on a 5th or 17th of November.

broomrape (ˈbruːmreɪp). [A rendering of med.L. *Rapum genistæ* broom knob or tuber; f. *rapum* 'a knob or lump formed by the roots of trees', and *genista* broom. The name is therefore not of popular origin.] A large genus of parasitic herbs (*Orobanche*), which attach themselves to the roots of broom, furze, clover, and other leguminous plants, having a brownish-yellow leafless fleshy stem furnished with pointed scales or bracts. The name was first applied to *O. major*, the *Rapum genistæ* of Lobel and other early herbalists.

1578 LYTE *Dodoens* VI. vi. 664 That excrescence comming from the roote of Broome is called.. in Latine *Rapum Genistæ*, that is to say, Broome Rape. **1671** SALMON *Syn. Med.* III. xxii. 424 Broom-rape.. easeth pains in the Reins. **1711** *Phil. Trans.* XXVII. 345 A large Broom-rape with a purple Flower. **1861** MISS PRATT *Flower. Pl.* III. 120 Brown and leafless parasites, like the Broom-rapes. **1883** G. ALLEN in *Knowledge* 3 Aug. 65/1 The fat, tuberous stems of the greater broomrape.

attrib. **1863** MARG. PLUES *Wild Flowers* 240 The broom-rape order.. contains but two families, that of the broom rape and the tooth wort.

broomstaff (ˈbruːmstɑːf, -æ-). *arch.* Also **-stave** (*rare*). Pl. **-staffs, -staves.** [f. BROOM *sb.* + STAFF.] The staff or handle of a broom; a broomstick.

1613 SHAKS. *Hen. VIII*, V. iv. 57 At length they came to th' broome staffe to me, I defide 'em stil. **1711** E. WARD *Vulg. Brit.* v. 54 Rattling their Broomstaves, and their Clubs. **1712-14** PRIOR *Alma* Poems (1754) 264 Broom-staff or Poker they bestride. **1825** WATERTON *Wand. S. Amer.* II. iii. 200 The black cat and broomstaff.. considered as conductors to and from the regions of departed spirits. **1870** LOWELL *Among my Bks.* Ser. I. (1873) 117 The broomstave, which might make part of the poorest house's furniture.

broomster (ˈbruːmstə(r)). [f. as prec. + -STER.] One who wields a broom; *spec.* in *Curling*, one who sweeps the ice.

1831 *Blackw. Mag.* XXX. 972 The uncrampeted broomster, and the pilgrim with the (unboiled) peas, may go hand in hand.

broomstick (ˈbruːmstɪk). Same as BROOMSTAFF. *to marry over the broomstick*: to go through a *quasi*-marriage ceremony, in which the parties jump over a broomstick; also called 'to jump the besom'.

1683 tr. *Erasmus' Moriæ Enc.* 58 Shall take a Broom-stick for a streight-bodied woman. **1711** SHAFTESB. *Charac.* (1737) I. 148 A story of a witch upon a broomstick, & a flight in the air. **1732** POPE *Use of Riches* II. 97 The thriving plants, ignoble broomsticks made. **1824** MACAULAY *Misc. Writ.* (1860) I. 95 They were married over a broom-stick. **1841** MIALL *Nonconf.* I. 265 Not more hopeless.. the attempt to make a broomstick bud. **1881** J. HAWTHORNE *Fort. Fool* I. iv, 'There's some as think she was married over the broom-stick, if she was married at all'.

b. *comb.*

1774 *Westm. Mag.* II. 16 He had no inclination for a Broomstick-marriage. **1807** W. IRVING *Salmag.* (1824) 362 The broomstick-whirl'd hags that appear in Macbeth. **1851** MAYHEW *Lond. Labour* I. 353, I never had a wife, but I have had two or three broomstick matches, though they never turned out happy.

broomy (ˈbruːmɪ), *a.* [f. as prec. + -Y[1].]

1. Covered with or abounding in broom.

1649 BLITHE *Eng. Improv. Impr.* (1653) 132 All coarse barren Heaths, Lingy, Broomy Lands. **1679** PLOT *Staffordsh.* (1686) 110 This heathy, broomy, gorsy, barren sort of Soile. **1790** BURNS *Let. Mrs. Dunlop* Nov., The

broomy banks of Nith. **1852** D. Moir *Glen of Roslin* iii. 169 Each broomy vale..bequeaths Some old heroic tale.

†**2.** Of or pertaining to a broom or besom. *rare.*

1709 Swift *Morning* in *Tatler* No. 9 ¶1 The Youth with broomy Stumps began to trace The Kennel Edge.

3. Broom-like. Cf. *bushy. rare.*

1807 Vancouver *Agric. Devon* (1813) 253 Its leading shoot appears..to have spread into a small broomy top.

broose. *Sc.* Also **brooze, bruise, bruse.** [Sc. pron. (brøːz, bryːz): of unknown origin. The suggestion of Jamieson that the word is the same as *brose* or *brewis* is absurdly impossible; (though phonetically it might be *broos*, pl. of BROO): mod.Sc. (øː, yː), derives from OE. *ó* or Fr. *u.*] A race on horseback, or on foot, by the young men present at country weddings in the north, the course being from the place where the marriage ceremony is performed (in Scotland the bride's former home) to the bridegroom's house. Hence ***to ride, run, win the broose.*** (The prize is usually a coloured silk handkerchief.)

It is understood to be a survival from primitive marriage customs: probably the whole wedding cortège formerly conveyed the bride at full gallop to the bridegroom's house; but now the race is kept up by the young men only, the rest of the procession following at leisure. Cf. BRIDELOP, and the Teutonic synonyms there mentioned.

1786 Burns *To Auld Mare* ix, At Brooses thou had ne'er a fellow, For pith and speed. **1788** R. Galloway *Poems* 156 (Jam.) To think to ride or rin the bruise Wi' them ye name. **1845** *New Statist. Acc. Scotl.* VI. 306 The broose or contest who shall first reach the house of the bridegroom is very keenly maintained. **1863** J. Brown *Horæ Subs.* (ed. 3) 31 You know what riding the bruse means.

broose, obs. form of BRUISE.

†**broouage.** *Obs.* (See quots.)

1610 W. Folkingham *Art of Survey* I. viii. 16 Grass and plants fit for broouage, and browsage of sheepe. *Ibid.* IV. i. 80 Rents proper..may be for Landes, tenements.. Turbarie, Mastage, (of Beech, Oake, Holme, &c.) Herbage, Broouage, &c. **1688** R. Holme *Armoury* III. 333/2 Broovage or Browsage is feeding of Sheep and Goats.

brooyl, obs. form of BROIL.

Bros., commercial abbrev. of BROTHERS: see BRO.

brose (brəʊz). [mod.Sc. form of earlier *browes*, BROWIS, OFr. *broez.* Often treated as a plural, like porridge, broth, etc.; in this case partly at least from the sound of final *-s* (*-z*).] A dish made by pouring boiling water (or milk) on oatmeal (or oat-cake) seasoned with salt and butter. Hence ***brose-meal, brose-time,*** etc.

1657 Colvil *Whigs Supplic.* (1751) 21 A bag which kept his meal for brose. **1792** Burns *Deuk's dang o'er, &c.* ii, I've seen the day ye butter'd my brose. **1816** Scott *Old Mort.* xxi, 'Whiles—at brose-time', answered the..damsel. **1828** —— *F.M. Perth* xvi, The citizens had gorged themselves upon pancakes fried in lard, and brose, or brewis. **1829** Cunningham *Magic Bridle, Annivers.* 137 His favourite spring was brose and butter.

b. ***pease brose***: a similar preparation of peasemeal. ***Athole brose***: a mixture of whiskey and honey.

1818 Scott *Hrt. Midl.* xlviii, His morning draught of Athole brose. *a* **1840** *Neil Gow's Farew.*, For e'er since he wore the tartan hose He dearly liket Athole brose.

brose, obs. form of BRUISE.

Broseley, the name of a town in Shropshire, used in ***Broseley porcelain,*** a soft-paste porcelain made by Thomas Turner (1749–1809) of Caughley, near Broseley, esp. the blue transfer-printed china of Oriental design, in which the ***Broseley dragon*** was extensively used.

1836 P. Barlow in *Encycl. Metrop.* (1845) VIII. 464/2 The blue colours are supplied by the oxide of cobalt... Blue. .. Weak, (Broseley.)—Blue calc 20, flux 80. (Flint 70, nitre 9. borax 21;) or, calc 15, petuntse 85. **1878** L. Jewitt *Ceramic Art* I. 43 The white..is made of what is commonly called Brosely clay. *Ibid.* 268 The 'Broseley Blue Dragon' pattern.

brosen, brossen, brosten, dial. ff. *borsten*, obs. pa. pple. of BURST *v.*

broshe, brostle, obs. ff. BRUSH, BRISTLE.

brosier, brozier (ˈbrəʊzɪə(r), ˈbrəʊʒ(ɪ)ə(r)), *v.* [Etym. unknown.]

1. *pass.* To be bankrupt. *dial.*

1796 T. Morton *Way to get Married* I. i, I am completely brozier'd, cut down to a sixpence, and have left town.

2. *trans.* In Eton College phraseology: to attempt to exhaust the supply of food at a meal, as an expression of dissatisfaction with the fare provided; esp. in the phrase ***to brosier my dame*** or ***my tutor.***

1850 *N. & Q.* 1st Ser. II. 44/1, I well remember the phrase, 'brozier-my-dame', signifying to 'eat her out of house and home'. **1888** W. Rogers *Remin.* 15, I joined a conspiracy to 'brozier' him. There were ten or twelve of us [at breakfast], and we devoured everything within reach. **1899** C. K. Paul *Mem.* 111, If a tutor or a dame was suspected of being niggardly, it was determined to 'brosier' him or her.

brosier, brozier (ˈbrəʊzɪə(r), ˈbrəʊʒ(ɪ)ə(r)), *sb.* [Cf. prec.] **a.** A bankrupt. *dial.* **b.** A boy who has spent all his pocket-money. *Eton slang.* **c.** The custom of brosiering: see BROSIER *v.* 2.

1826 Wilbraham *Gloss. Cheshire* (ed. 2), *Brosier*, a bankrupt. It is often used by boys at play, when one of them has nothing further to stake. **1850** *N. & Q.* 1st Ser. II. 44/1 A boy at Eton was a 'brosier', when he had spent all his pocket-money. **1907** *Daily Chron.* 17 Dec. 3/4 You have heard of the Eton custom of a 'brozier'? The attempt to eat out of house and home. **1926** *Glasgow Herald* 27 Dec. 6 It was reserved for Eton..to invent the..'brozier', where eating even to beyond repletion is indulged in to gratify a sense of injury.

brosour, -ure, var. of BRUSURE, *Obs.*, wound.

brosy (ˈbrəʊzɪ), *a. Sc.* [f. BROSE + -Y[1].] Daubed with brose, brose-fed.

1789 Davidson *Seasons* 28 (Jam.) Laying the brosy weans upo' the floor Wi' dousy heght. **1823** E. Logan *St. Johnstoun* I. 240 (Jam.) A square-built, brosy-faced girl.

brotch(e, obs. or dial f. BROACH, BROOCH.

brotekin, var. of BRODEKIN, *Obs.*, a high boot.

†ˈ**brotel, brotle,** *a. Obs.* Forms: 4 brotel(l, brotil, (brutel, brutil(e), 5 brotill(e, brottyl, (brutyll), 6 brotle. [ME. *brotil, brutil*, f. *broten* broken, pa. pple. of *bréotan.* In use *brotel* appears as one of the various forms of *britil, bretil*, BRITTLE, and it may have been of later analogical formation: cf. *brickle, brockle.*]

1. Liable to break, easily broken; fragile, brittle.

1382 Wyclif *2 Cor.* iv. 7 We han this tresour in brotil [1388 britil] vesselis. *c* **1430** Lydg. *Bochas* v. vii. (1554) 127a, Fortunes fauors be made..Of brotell glasse rather than of stele. **1483** Caxton *Gold. Leg.* 324/4 Kepte in a fraylle and brutyll vessell.

b. Frail, perishable, easily destroyed, mortal.

1340 *Ayenb.* 129 Ysy hou þou art fyeble and brotel. **1362** Langl. *P. Pl.* A. IX. 37 þe Bodi þat Brutel is of kuynde. **1413** Lydg. *Pylgr. Sowle* v. xiv. (1483) 109. **1529** More *Comf. agst. Trib.* III. Wks. 1226/1 A brotle man lately made of earthe.

2. *fig.* Unstable; inconstant, fickle.

c **1315** Shoreham 5 Man is so brotel Ine his owene kende. *c* **1386** Chaucer *Parson's T.* ¶473 The commendacion of the peple is somtyme ful fals and ful brotel [*v.r.* brotil, brethil, brutile, brutel]. *a* **1420** Occleve *De Reg. Princ.* 3861 His welthe hathe but a brotille stablenesse.

Hence †ˈ**brotelhede,** frailty. *Obs.*

1340 *Ayenb.* 130 Huanne þe man..knauþ his pourhede, þe vilhede, þe brotelhede of his beringe.

†ˈ**brotelness.** *Obs.* [f. prec. + -NESS.] Frailty, fickleness; insecurity, uncertainty.

c **1386** Chaucer *Merch. T.* 35 On brutil ground thay bulde, and brutelnesse Thay fynde, whan thay wene sikernesse. *a* **1420** Occleve *De Reg. Princ.* 1 The brotilnesse of hir nature. *c* **1430** Lydg. *Bochas* II. xiii. (1554) 53a, God ..preserue your variaunt brotilnesse.

broth (brɒθ, -ɔː-), *sb.* Forms: 1–4 **broþ,** 4–6 **brothe,** 6–8 **broath,** 7 **broathe,** 3– **broth.** [Com. Teut.: OE. *broþ* = OHG. *brod, prod*, ON. *broð*:—OTeut. *broþo(m)*, f. vb.-root *brŭ-* to prepare by boiling, make a decoction: see BREW. (Cf. F. *bouillon* broth, f. *bouillir* to boil.) The OHG. word was adopted in Romanic, giving med.L. *brodum, brodium*, It. *brodo*, Sp., Pg. *brodio*, Pr. *bro*, OF. *bro, breu*, whence *broet*, BROWET, BREWIS. Irish *broth*, Gael. *brot*, are from Eng.]

1. a. The liquid in which anything has been boiled, and which is impregnated with its juice; a decoction; *esp.* that in which meat is boiled or macerated; also a thin soup made from this with the addition of vegetables, pearl barley, rice, etc., as Scotch 'broth'.

a **1000** *Colloq. Monast.* xxix. 13 (Bosw.) Fætt broþ ȝe magon habban. **1297** R. Glouc. 528 On of is men..Caste broth vp a clerc. **1398** Trevisa *Barth. De P.R.* (Tollemache MS.) XVII. lxx, Broþ of þe leues þerof [broom] abateþ swellynge of þe splene. *c* **1400** Maundev. xxiii. 250 Non other potages but the brothe of the flesche. *c* **1440** *Promp. Parv.* 53 Brothe, *brodium, liquamen.* **1530** Palsgr. 201/2 Brothe of fysshe or fleshe, *brovet.* **1535** Coverdale *Judg.* vi. 20 Take the flesh..& set it vpon the stonye rocke..and poure the broth theron. **1578** Lyte *Dodoens* I. xxxix. 57 The decoction or brothe of Agrimonie. **1580** Sidney *Arcadia* III. 281 She herself had used to make the broaths. **1611** Shaks. *Cymb.* IV. ii. 50 He..sawc'st our Brothes, as Juno had bin sicke, And he her Dieter. **1665** Gerbier *Princ.* 24 Too many Cooks spoils the Broth. **1682** N. O. *Boileau's Lutrin* I. 7 Bad 'em serve in the broath [*rime* loath]. **1712** Steele *Spect.* No. 308 ¶3, I am sure..you love Broth better than Soup. **1804** Wolcott (P. Pindar) *Gt. Cry & Litt. Wool* Wks. 1812 V. 165 The more cooks the worse broth. **1861** Ramsay *Remin.* (ed. 18) 118 She..never did more than to sup a few family broth.

b. *fig.* and *transf.* (Cf. *stew, browst*, etc.).

c **1526** Frith *Disput. Purgatory* (1829) 141 If he had thought to have gone through purgatory..there should he have had an hot broth and an heartless. *a* **1533** Ld. Berners *Huon* vi. 13 He sware he wolde purchace for the two sonnes ..suche a broth [1601 traine] that they shulde bothe dye in doloure. **1878** Seeley *Stein* III. 390 They..want to.. dissolve all civil society into a great fluid broth.

c. *Bacteriol.* A liquid (as a sterilized infusion of meat) prepared or used as a culture medium.

1885 Woodhead & Hare *Pathological Mycol.* iv. 107 To carry on cultivations with the sterile broth thus prepared, it is convenient to have it divided into small quantities. **1897** Pearmain & Moor *Appl. Bacteriol.* ii. 57 Glycerin-broth is used for the cultivation of the tubercle bacillus. **1899** G. Newman *Bacteria* i. 21 To provide peptone beef-broth, ten grains of peptone and five grains of common salt are added to every litre of acid beef-broth. **1930** *Syst. Bacteriol.* (Med. Res. Council) I. ix. 354 Old cultures in ordinary broth often yield a considerable variety of colonies when plated on agar or gelatin. **1956** R. Hare *Outl. Bacteriol. & Immunity* ii. 37 Infusion broth..consists of the extractives which go into solution when minced meat is allowed to steep in water. **1959** [see *broth culture*].

†**2.** Loosely applied to various boiled, brewed, or decocted liquors; also to the brine of ocean, melted snow (SNOW-BROTH), etc. Cf. Sc. BREE, BROO.

c **1420** *Liber Cocorum* (1862) 28 With brothe of venegur drawȝe hit withalle. **1558** Phaër *Æneid* VIII. Z iv, There went the salt sea broad with swellynge broth. **1593** *Bacchus Bountie* in *Harl. Misc.* (1809) II. 264 Bickering with the broth of bountifull Bacchus. **1633** G. Herbert *Temple, Odour* ii, This broth of smells, that feeds & fats my minde. **1691** Ray *Making of Salt* 206 If you put in too much [ale] it will make the Broth [of brine] boil over the Pan. **1765** Tucker *Lt. Nat* II. 361 A sop in the briny broth of ocean.

3. Phrases. †***to make white broth of,*** said of boiling to death (as a poisoner). ***a broth of a boy***: the essence of what a boy should be, a downright good fellow (*colloq. Irish*).

c **1645** Howell *Lett.* (1650) I. 4 She was afraid that Cook the Lord Chief Justice would have made white broth of them, but the prerogative kept them from the pot. **1822** Byron *Juan* VIII. xxiv, Juan was quite 'a broth of a boy'. **1843** Mrs. Tonna *Judah's Lion* 131 Papa says you are the broth of a boy, for taking care of me.

4. *Comb.*: **broth culture,** (the micro-organisms in) a sample of broth used as a culture medium.

1897 *Jrnl. Path. & Bacteriol.* IV. 196 To test the virulence of our bacilli we injected guinea-pigs subcutaneously with broth-cultures. **1909** *Practitioner* Nov. 596 Over the surface of the agar..pour a two-days old broth culture of bacillus prodigiosus. **1959** F. S. Stewart *Bigger's Handbk. Bacteriol.* (ed. 7) x. 190 Serial dilutions of the drug are made in broth and inoculated with the organism—the inoculum usually being a small amount of a broth culture.

†**broth, brothe,** *a. Obs.* [ME. *brōþ*:—earlier *brāþ* (north Eng. *brāth*: see BRATH):—ON. *bráð-r* hasty, rash, passionate.] Impetuous, violent, passionate, wrathful; also quasi-*sb.*

c **1200** Ormin 7172 þat he be grimme..& braþ. *c* **1325** *E.E. Allit. P.* B. 149 þat oþer burne watz abayst of his broþe wordez. *c* **1340** *Gaw. & Gr. Knt.* 2233 He..orpedly strydez, Bremly broþe on a bent. *c* **1420** *Avow. Arth.* xvi. Thus bidus that brothe.

†ˈ**brotheful,** *a. Obs.* [f. BROTHE *a.* or the cogn. BRATH *sb.* + -FUL: cf. BRATHFUL.] Violent, wrathful.

1330 R. Brunne *Chron.* 55 Bituex þam & þe messengers broþefulle wordes brak.

brothel (ˈbrɒθ(ə)l), *sb.* Also 5–7 brothell(e, 5 brodel(le. [ME. *broþel*, f. OE. *broðen* ruined, degenerate, pa. pple. of *bréoðan* to go to ruin: a variant of BRETHEL.

The modern sense arises from confusion with an entirely different word BORDEL (q.v.); the *brothel* was originally a person, the *bordel* a place. But the combinations *bordel-house* and *brothel's house* ran together in the form *brothel-house*, which being shortened to *brothel*, the personal sense of this word became obs., and it remains only as the substitute of the original *bordel.*]

†**1.** A worthless abandoned fellow, a wretch, scoundrel, scapegrace, good-for-nothing.

1393 Gower *Conf.* III. 173 Quod Achab thanne, There is one, A brothel, which Micheas hight. **1394** *P. Pl. Crede* 772 Ne bedden swiche broþels In so brode schetes. *c* **1440** *York Myst.*, xix. 265 Lorde, tokenyng hadde we none To knawe þat brothell [Christ] by. *c* **1460** *Towneley Myst.* 130, I [Herod] shall se that brodelle [Christ] bloode By hym that me has boght. *c* **1475** *Lyt. Childr. Bk.* in *Babees Bk.* (1868) 18 Fylle not thy mouth as done brothellis. **1532** More *Confut. Tindale* Wks. 514/1 The holy Lenton faste, whiche these brotheles so boldly take vpon them to breake. **1594** Carew *Tasso* (1881) 117 [They] with wrath..Enflamde, fortune vniust and brothell call.

†**2. a.** An abandoned woman, a prostitute. *Obs.*

1493 *Festivall* (W. de W. 1515) 54b, He..went agayne to a brodelles hous. **1535** Fisher *Wks.* 418 Why doeth a common brothel take no shame of hir abhomination? **1546** Langley *Pol. Verg. De Invent.* III. xii. 79b, Venus..was a common harlot & brothel of her body. **1583** Stubbes *Anat. Abus.* 58 A filthie strumpet or brothel. **1606** G. W[oodcocke] *Ivstine* 113b, A company of concubins and brothels.

†**b.** (See quot.) *Obs. rare.*

1613 R. C. *Table Alph.* (ed. 3), *Brothell*, keeper of a house of bawdry.

3. Short for *brothel's house, brothel-house* (2, 4b); taking the place of the earlier BORDEL, BORDEL-HOUSE: A house of ill fame, bawdy-house.

a **1593** H. Smith *Wks.* (1867) II. 26 Some [return] unto the taverns, and some unto the alehouses, and some unto brothels. **1605** Shaks. *Lear* III. iv. 99 Keepe thy foote out of Brothels. *a* **1704** T. Brown *Sat.* Wks. 1730 I. 56 We need not rake the brothel and the stews. **1711** Steele *Spect.* No. 190 ¶2 You understand by this time that I was left in a

Brothel. **1751** JOHNSON *Rambl.* No. 171 ¶12 Tricked up for sale by the mistress of a brothel. **1828** MACAULAY *Hallam, Ess.* (1851) I. 86 The offal of gaols and brothels.

4. *Attrib.* and *Comb.* **a.** *attrib.* or as *adj.*

1633 P. FLETCHER *Purple Isl.* I. xviii, Or Mævius chaunt his thoughts in brothell charm. *a* **1711** KEN *Hymnotheo* Wks. 1721 III. 291 With so profligate a Race, Within their Brothel-Heav'n. *a* **1856** MRS. BROWNING *Soul's Trav.* 39 The brothel shriek, and the Newgate laugh.

b. *comb.*, as ***brothel-haunting***, ***-keeper***, ***-like***, ***-master***, ***-monger***; **brothel-creeper** (shoe) *slang*, (in pl.) suède or soft-soled shoes; **brothel-house** = BROTHEL 3.

1954 G. SMITH *Flaw in Crystal* ix. 81 'Poncing about the place in those *brothel-creepers of his!'.. He always wore plush suede shoes. **1959** 'A. FRASER' *High Tension* ii. 24 He had immaculately creased grey flannel trousers and brothel-creeper shoes. **1959** H. HOBSON *Mission House Murder* iv. 31 Those ghastly suède shoes with two-inch crêpe soles and corrugated edges, known to the Edwardian *élite*..as brothel-creepers. **1969** J. FREDMAN *Fourth Agency* ix. 85 Suède brothel-creeper boots. **1692** tr. *Sallust* 17 The Rage of adulterous Lust, of *Brothel-haunting and other Bestialities. **1530** PALSGR. 201/2 *Brothelleshouse, *bordel.* **1535** COVERDALE *Ezek.* xvi. 39 [They] shal breake downe thy stewes, and destroye thy brothel houses. **1599** SHAKS. *Much Ado* I. i. 256. **1678** *Yng. Man's Call.* 273 Thou shalt be..put into the common stews & brothel-houses. **1820** T. MITCHELL *Aristoph.* I. 255 One Philostratus, a *brothel-keeper. **1803** SOUTHEY in *Ann. Rev.* I. 41 We will not transcribe Mr. Fischer's *brothel-like description. **1608** MIDDLETON *Trick to Catch, &c.*, He's a rioter, a wast-thrift, a *brothel-master. **1566** DRANT *Horace Sat.* I. iv. 113 No *brothelmonger be.

† **'brothel,** *v. Obs.* [f. prec. sb.]

1598 SYLVESTER *Du Bartas* II. i. iii. (1621) 217 Who, like Lust-greedy Goates, Brothel from bed to bed.

'brotheller. ? *Obs.* [f. prec. + -ER[1].] A frequenter of brothels, a whoremonger.

1608 MIDDLETON *Trick to Catch, &c.* II. i, What though he be a brotheller, a waste-thrift. **1784** COWPER *Task* II. 751 For Gamesters, Jockeys, Brothellers impure. **1805** SOUTHEY in *Ann. Rev.* III. 230 Not the only brotheller.

† **'brothelling.** *Obs.* [f. as prec. + -ING[1].] The frequenting of brothels, whoring. Also *attrib.*

1581 SAVILE *Tacitus' Hist.* II. §76 (1591) 97 If he had any courage..it is dulled & worne away, in tipling and brotheling houses. **1611** COTGR., *Bordelage*, brothelling, wenching, whoore-hunting.

† **'brothellous,** *a. Obs.* [see -OUS.] = next.

1583 STUBBES *Anat. Abus.* F ij, This whorish and brothellous painting and colouring of faces.

† **'brothelly,** *a. Obs.* [see -LY[1].] Whorish.

1607 TOPSELL *Serpents* 642 To play and meddle with filthy whores and brothelly queans.

† **'brothelry.** *Obs.* [f. as prec. + -RY.]

1. Lewdness; harlotry.

1546 BALE *Eng. Votaries* II. (1550) 29 He fell to the talke of as fyne brothelry, as anye craftes man in that art myght vtter. **1569** J. SANFORD *Agrippa's Van. Artes* 97 Brothelrie is the Arte of abandoninge the proper chastitie to all men. **1605** B. JONSON *Volpone* Ded. **1633** T. ADAMS *Exp. 2 Peter* ii. 14 Pestilent uses of turpitude and brothelry.

2. A place of prostitutes.

1593 MARLOWE *Lust's Domin.* I. iii, Whilst you at home suffer'd his bedchamber To be a brothelry. **1616** DEKKER *Sev. Sinnes* II. (Arb.) 22 Thou makest thy buildings a Brothelry to others.

† **'brothelsome,** *a. Obs.* [f. as prec. + -SOME.] Pertaining to a brothel, lewd, whorish.

1624 F. WHITE *Repl. Fisher* 83 The Vow of Chastitie filled all the Earth with the steame of Brothelsome impuritie.

† **'brothely,** *a.* and *adv. Obs.* Also **brodly, brothelych, brodelyche.** [ME.: in sense a., f. BROTHE *a.* + -LY[1,2]; cf. the northern form BRATHLY. Sense b. (only in *Allit. Poems*) may perhaps be a deriv. of BROTHEL.]

A. *adj.* Fierce, violent, angry.

1330 R. BRUNNE *Chron.* 166 Fulle broþely & brim he kept vp a trencheour, & kast it at Statin.

b. Vile, bad.

c **1325** *E.E. Allit. P.* B. 847 Þe worlde stynkes Of þe brych þat vpbraydez þose broþelych wordez.

B. *adv.* Quickly, hastily; violently, furiously.

c **1340** *Cursor M.* 18918 (Trin.) Brodly [*Cott.* brathli] on þat hous hit brast. *c* **1340** *Gaw. & Gr. Knt.* 2377 Þenne he ..Brayde broþely þe belt to þe burne seluen. ? *a* **1400** *Morte Arth.* 1408 Þe embuschement of Bretons brake owte at ones, Brothely at banere. *a* **1400** *Sir Perc.* 2121 Percevelle..asked wherefore and why He banned it so brothely.

b. Vilely, in ill plight.

c **1325** *E.E. Allit. P.* B. 1256 Broþely broȝt to Babyloyn þer bale to suffer. *Ibid.* C. 474 [Jonah] bluschèd to his wodbynde þat broþely watz marred.

brothen, brothin, bankrupt, broken, pa. pple. of BRETHE *v. Obs.*

brother ('brʌðə(r)), *sb.* Pl. **brothers, brethren** ('brɛðrɪn). Forms: 1 **bróðor, -ur, -er,** 2–5 **broþer,** 3– **brother** (*passim* -err, -ir, -ere, -re, -yr, broither), 4–6 **broder, -ir, -yr,** 6 **bruder;** *mod.Sc.* **brither.** *Plural*: see below. [A Common Teut., and Common Aryan word: OE. *bróðor* = OFris. *bróther, bróder*, OS. *brôthar* (MDu. and Du. *broeder*, MLG. and mod.LG. *broder*), OHG. *bruodar* (MHG. *bruoder*, Ger. *bruder*), ON. *bróðir* (Sw., Da. *broder*), Goth. *brôþar*:—OTeut. **brôþar*:—OAryan *'*bhrāter, -tor, -tr*, whence also Skr. *bhrātr*, Gr. *φράτηρ*, L. *frāter*, OSlav. *brătŭ*, OCelt. **brāter* (Ir. and Gael. *brathair*, Welsh *brawd* (from **brawdr*), Breton *breur* (formerly *breuzr*).

As in some other words in OE. long *ō*, the mod. form has undergone more than the usual vowel change, which would have left it ('bruːðər). In ME., esp. in north. dial. and Sc., the *th* was often written *d*, perhaps after *fader, moder.* The OE. dat. sing. was *bréðer*; the gen. was the same as the nom. and remained so in Scotch down to 1600, as in the connexion *broder son* (nephew), *broder bairn, broder wyfe, broder dochter*, which have often been misunderstood by modern readers. The plural has had a great variety of forms: viz. in OE. *bróðor, -ur, -er* (like the sing.), and *bróðru, -ro*, later *-ra*, also once *broeþre* (in Anglian, in Rushworth Gloss); and with collective sense, *ȝebróðer*, and *ȝebróðru, -ro, -ra.* In early ME. the *Lambeth Homilies* have *broþre, breþre*, and rarely *breþren*; the *Trin. Coll. Hom. broþren* and *breþren*; *Ormin* and *Gen. & Ex.* have always *breþre, breþere*; of *Layamon* the first text has a variety of forms, most frequently *broþ(e)ren*, frequently *breþ(e)ren*, rarely *broþ(e)re*, (never *breþre* or *breþer*), once *broþerne*, once *broþeres*; the second text has always *broþeres, broþers.* The Jesus MS. poems in *O.E. Misc.* have usually *broþren*, which is the regular form in *Ayenbite*; *broth(e)ren* occurs in many writers down nearly to 1600. In northern Eng., from the earliest distinctive specimens, the regular plural form was *breþer, brether*; often used also by non-northern writers. The standard English plural, down to 1600, was *breþ(e)ren, brethren. Brothers*, after its early appearance in Layamon, is not quoted again till the end of the 16th c., when it is used by Shakspere indiscriminately with *brethren.* In the 17th c. *brothers* became the ordinary form in the literal sense; *brethren* being retained in reference to spiritual, ecclesiastical, or professional relationship.

The original Teut. pl. nom. corresponding to Aryan *'*bhrātres*, would be **brôþriz*, whence regularly ON. *brœðr.* The corresponding OE. **bróeðer*, **bréðer* is unexpectedly wanting: but the Mercian *bróeþre*, and its ME. descendant *brethre* (see *β*) may possibly be a remnant of it. The northern *brether* (see *γ*) may actually have come down from **bróeðer*, though it may also merely be *brethre* with the final *e* dropped. The OE. *-u, -o* (*-a*) forms are difficult to explain: it has been suggested that they might be originally duals (like *sculdru* from *sculdor* masc.). They were regularly represented by ME. *brothre* (see *α*). *Brothren, brethren* exemplify the usual passage of sbs. having vowel plurals in southern early ME. into the *-en* type. The early occurrence of the modern *brothers*, as well as its subsequent non-appearance till the end of the 16th c., is notable and requires further investigation. In the genitive pl. *breðere* occurs in *Gen. & Ex.*; *breþern -e* in *St. Brandan*; *breþer, breþers* was northern; *brethren's* standard Eng., now, in ordinary use, *brothers'*.]

A. Illustrations of the plural forms.

† *α.* **plural brother, brothre:** OE. *broðor, broðru, -ro, -ra*; ME. 2–3 *broþre, -ere*, 4 *brothere*, 4–5 *-ire.*

a **1000** *Cædmon's Gen.* 2033 (Gr.) Broðor þry. *c* **1000** *Ags. Ps.* cxxi[i]. 8 For mine broðru. *c* **1000** *Ags. Gosp.* John vii. 3 His broðra [*Lindisf.* & *Rushw.*, broðro; *Hatton G.* hys broðre]. *Ibid.* John vii. 10 His ȝebroðru [*Hatton G.* broðre]. *Ibid.* Matt. xii. 47 Þin modur & þine ȝebroðra [*Hatton G.* ȝebroðre; *Lindisf.* broðra, *v.* 48 broðro; *Rushw.* broþer]. *c* **1175** *Lamb. Hom.* 5 Nu leoue broðre! *Ibid.* Leoue broðre and sustre! *c* **1205** LAY. 16120 Comen þa broðere. *c* **1275** *Passion* 626 in *O.E. Misc.* 55 Ȝe beoþ alle broþre [*rime* ych to oþre]. ? *a* **1400** *Sayn John* xix. in *Relig. Pieces fr. Thornton MS.* 94 His hyne holly and he..Become þare thi brothire [*rime* ilk one to oþer].

† *β.* **plural brethre:** OE. *bróeþre*, 2–3 *breðre, breþere*, 3 *briðere. Obs.*

c **975** *Rushw. Gl.*, Matt. i. 11 Broeþre his. *c* **1175** *Lamb. Hom.* 9, 45 Leofe breðre. *c* **1200** ORMIN 6366 Wiþþ hise breþre. *Ibid.* 8269 Arrchelawess breþre þreo. *a* **1240** *Wohunge* in *Cott. Hom.* 275 Borne breðre hauen me forwurpen. *c* **1250** *Gen. & Ex.* 1911 If he saȝ hise breðere misfaren. *Ibid.* 2213 Ðo breðere (*gen. pl.*) seckes. *Ibid.* 2271 Al ðo briðere fellen.

γ. **brether:** (3–4 *-ir, -yr, breither*, 4 *briþer*, 5 *brythir*, 4–6 *breder, -ir, -ur, -yr.*) Still in north. Eng. and Sc.

a **1300** *Cursor M.* 1210 His breþer als him-self he loued. *c* **1340** *Ibid.* 23873 (Edinb.) Al er we briþer. *c* **1340** *Gaw. & Gr. Knt.* 39 Alle þo rich breþer. **1375** BARBOUR *Bruce* III. 93 Twa brethir. *c* **1400** *Destr. Troy* 9589 His dere bredur two. *Ibid.* 13167 Bothe were þai brether. **1432–50** tr. *Higden* (1865) I. 125 The breder of Ioseph. *Ibid.* 211 Rome was made of ij. breþer, Remus and Romulus. **1473** WARKW. *Chron.* 1 His two brythir. **1513–75** *Diurn. Occurrents* (1833) 84 And vtheris his breder. **1609** SKENE *Reg. Maj.* 33 The rest of the brether or sisters. **1609** BIBLE (Douay) *Prov.* vi. 19 Our Lord hateth..him that among brether soweth discordes. **1875** *Lanc. Gloss.* (E.D.S.) *Brether*, brothers.

† *δ.* **brothren:** 3–4 *broþren, -eren* (4 *brotheryn(e*, 5 *broderen, -yrn*, 5–6 *brothern, -e*, 6 *brootherne*, Sc. (casually) *brotherand*). *Obs.*

a **1200** *Trin. Coll. Hom.* 173 Of two broðren. *c* **1205** LAY. 2759 His broðren hine cleopeden. *Ibid.* 2101 þa þreo broðeren [*c* **1275** broþers; so 5536, 6809, 10461, 11176]. *Ibid.* 3880 Beine iweren ibroðeren [*c* **1275** broþers; so 10446, 12255]. **1340** *Ayenb.* 101 We gadereþ alle oure broþren. *Ibid.* 149 Uor oure broþren. *c* **1275** *O.E. Misc.* 53 Go to myne broþren. *c* **1440** *Generydes* 2656 We are broderen. **1478** W. PASTON *Lett.* 816 III. 226 All my brodyrn and systyrs. **1483** CAXTON *Gold. Leg.* 401/2 His brothern wepte. **1533** BELLENDEN *Livy* I. (1822) 44 To haif supportit his brotherand. **1536** *Remed. Sedition* 24 b, Ye brotherne and systerne? fathers and mothers? **1555** EDEN *Decades W. Ind.* (Arb.) 50 These owre brootherne, owre flesshe & owre bones. **1567** DRANT *Horace's Epist.* II. ii. Hvj, Two brotherne.

ε. **brethren:** 2–4 *breþren, -eren*, 3– *brethren*, (3–6 *bretheren(e*, 3–5 *-in*, 4 *brithirn, -ern, -eroun*, 4–5 *-eren*, 4–7 *brethern*, 5– 6 *brederne, -urne*).

c **1175** *Lamb. Hom.* 11 Leoue breðren. *c* **1200** *Trin. Coll. Hom.* 175 Ure helende..segh þos tweie brodren and þese breðren weren on þe se. *c* **1205** LAY. 2137 Þo þa þre breðeren. *Ibid.* 4292 Þas breðren [*c* **1275** þeos broþers]. **1297** R. GLOUC. 478 The bretheren hulde al so aȝen hor fader. *c* **1300** *St. Brandan* 558 Mid oure Loverdes pans and mid oure Bretherne i-boȝt. *c* **1350** *Will. Palerne* 5304 Þe bold breþeren. *c* **1380** WYCLIF *Wks.* (1880) 284 Among here briþeren. *Ibid.* 367 Þe possessyon of her breþern. ? *a* **1400** *Morte Arth.* 4144 My faire bretherene. *c* **1450** LONELICH *Grail* lv. 52 Alle his bretheren. *Ibid.* 59 His bretherin alle. *c* **1450** *Merlin* iii. 4 The two brethern. **1489** CAXTON *Faytes of A.* IV. vii. 247 Two bretherne accused of thefte. **1535** COVERDALE *Matt.* i. 2 Iacob begat Iudas & his brethren. **1584** POWEL *Lloyd's Cambria* 68 Howel with his Bretherene. **1621** BURTON *Anat. Mel.* I. iv. I. (1676) 134 Two melancholy brethren. **1705** STANHOPE *Paraphr.* I. 49 Their Brethrens honest though mistaken Zeal. **1843** MACAULAY *Lays, Lake Regillus* ii, Unto the Great Twin Brethren We keep this solemn feast.

ζ. **brothers:** 3 *broþeres, broþres, broþers.*

c **1205** LAY. 9153 Alle his broðeres [*c* **1275** broþers] mid him. *c* **1275** *Ibid.* 12255 Broþeres hii were [*c* **1205** ibroðeren]. *Ibid.* 2101 Þe þreo broþers [*c* **1205** broðeren] alle to gadere comen. [So everywhere in the later text.] **1588** SHAKS. *Tit. A.* III. i. 30 Ah Lucius for thy brothers let me plead. **1597** —— *2 Hen. IV*, IV. iv. 23 Thou hast a better place in his Affection, Then all thy Brothers. *c* **1630** NAUNTON *Fragm. Reg.* (Arb.) 25 Being both younger Brothers. **1713** POPE *Windsor For.* 337 Around his throne the sea-born brothers stood. **1843** MACAULAY *Lays, Horatius* xxxii, The Romans were like brothers In the brave days of old.

B. Signification: **I.** as simple *sb.*

1. The word applied to a male being to express his relationship to others (male or female) as the child of the same parent or parents.

In the singular usually defined by a possessive word expressed or implied as 'my brother', 'the king's youngest brother', 'the brother of your friend', '(our) Brother Jonathan', 'come, (my) brother!'; in the plural, this may be absent, if the relationship is between the individuals themselves, as in 'they are brothers (*i.e.* to each other)'.

a. *properly.* The son of the same parents. But often extended to include one who has either parent in common with another (more strictly called *half-brother*, or *brother of the half blood*); also to a BROTHER-IN-LAW. See *brother-uterine* (in 9 d), also BROTHER-GERMAN, GOOD-BROTHER. (Also applicable to animals.)

O.E. Chron. an. 656 Min broðer is faren of þisse liue. *c* **1000** *Ags. Gosp.* Luke xii. 13 Seȝe minum breðer þæt he dæle uncer æhta wið me. —— Matt. x. 21 Soðlice broður sylð hys broður to deaðe. *c* **1160** *Hatton Gosp.* ibid., Se broðer sylleð his broðer. *c* **1200** *Trin. Coll. Hom.* 147 Þo two sustres wepen for here broðres deað. *a* **1300** *Cursor M.* 1214 Caym his aun broder slogh. **1426** AUDELAY *Poems* 15 His borne broder. *c* **1440** *Promp. Parv.* 54 Brodyr by the modyr syde onely..*germanus.* **1473** WARKW. *Chron.* 1 He create and made dukes his two brythir. **1590** SHAKS. *Com. Err.* II. ii. 154 Fie brother, how the world is chang'd with you. **1611** BIBLE *Prov.* xviii. 24 A friend that sticketh closer then a brother. **1667** MILTON *P.L.* XI. 456 His Brothers Offering found From Heav'n acceptance. **1842** TENNYSON *Dora* 15 She is my brother's daughter. **1850** —— *In Mem.* xxxi. 5 Where wert thou, brother, those four days? **1859** —— *Elaine* 40 Here two brothers..had met And fought.

b. Including more distant kin: A kinsman, as uncle, nephew, cousin. (Chiefly a Hebraism of the Bible.)

1382 WYCLIF *Gen.* xiv. 14 Loth his brother takun. *Ibid.* xxix. 12 He shewide to hir that he was the brother of hir fader. **1611** BIBLE *Gen.* xiii. 8 And Abram said vnto Lot, Let there be no strife, I pray thee, betweene mee and thee..for wee bee brethren. *Ibid.* xxix. 12 Jacob told Rachel, that hee was her fathers brother. *Ibid.* 15.

c. Said affectionately of one regarded or treated as a brother; one who fills the place of a brother.

1795 BURNS '*A man's a man*' v, Man to man, the world o'er, Shall brothers be for a' that. **1850** TENNYSON *In Mem.* ix, My friend, the brother of my love, My Arthur!

d. (i) As a familiar mode of address to a man, esp. one whose name is not known (see also quot. 1973) (*U.S.*); (ii) *int.*, a mild exclamation of annoyance, surprise, etc. (chiefly *U.S.*).

1912 *Dialect Notes* III. 572 Say, brother, can you tell me how far it is to Veedersburg? **1924** *Cosmopolitan* Dec. 68/2 'Brother, you're sitting pretty!' sighs the money-mad Hazel, enviously. **1943** *N.Y. Times* 9 May II. 5 Why, brother, all the cats cut a mean rug to that music. **1953** *Manch. Guardian Weekly* 20 Aug. 7 Never did learn to spell it. But, brother, I drank it. **1957** B. & C. EVANS *Dict. Contemp. Amer. Usage* 73/1 The singular is used a great deal in America as a semi-facetious form of address (*You said it, brother!*), as an introduction to an informal supplication (*Brother, can you spare a dime?*) and, often, just as an exclamation (*Brother! You should have seen that guy!*). **1969** *Islander* (Victoria, B.C.) 9 Nov. 6/3 Then when you think you've got used to mountain roads you hit one like the Seton-Darcy road. Oh Brother! **1973** *To Our Returned Prisoners of War* (U.S. Office of Secretary of Defense) 2 *Brother*, term mostly used by a Black man or woman to identify a Black male, and as a term of address. Also being used by Chicanos and American Indians. **1985** *Toronto Sun* 10 Oct. 42/1 And brother, when Elsie decides to 'bake' her..Cheese Cake it's a doozy of a winner.

2. A fellow-clansman, fellow-citizen, fellow-countryman (one who claims the same *patria* or father-land); in widest sense (under influence of Christianity), fellow-man, fellow-creature.

a **1000** *Ags. Ps.* cxxi[i]. 8 For mine broðru ic bidde nu. *c* **1200** *Trin. Coll. Hom.* 219 For þi beð alle man ibroþren and isustren. *a* **1300** *Cursor M.* 854 His grace it was..þat he wald bicom our broþer. **1526** *Pilgr. Perf.* (W. de W. 1531) 151 Theyr neyghbours..I meane theyr systerne and

bretherne. **1599** SHAKS. *Much Ado* II. i. 67 Adams sonnes are my brethren. **1611** BIBLE *Acts* xiii. 26 Men and brethren, children of the stocke of Abraham. **1667** MILTON *P.L.* III. 297 So Man.. Shall satisfie for Man, be judg'd and die.. and rising with him raise His Brethren. **1714** FORTESCUE-ALAND *Fortescue's Abs. & Lim. Mon.* 30 The Lombards.. Brothers and Kinsmen of the Saxons. **1789** BURNS *Capt. Grose*, Land o' Cakes and brither Scots. **1840** LONGF. *Ps. of Life* viii, Footprints, that.. A forlorn and shipwrecked brother, Seeing, shall take heart again. *a* **1860** MACKAY *Brotherhood of Nations* vi, Are ye not brothers?.. Is [God] not Father of all climes and lands? **1871** MORLEY *Voltaire* (1886) 294 An ungrateful infection, weakening and corrupting the future of his brothers.

b. ***a man and a brother***: a phrase taken from the motto on the seal of the British and Foreign Anti-Slavery Society, 'Am I not a man and a brother?' approved by a Committee of the Society on 16 Oct. 1787.

(The design, a kneeling slave in chains, uttering the words, was shortly after produced as a cameo, black on white, by Wedgwood, and became extremely popular as a personal ornament. The seal is in regular use by the philanthropic society, which still carries on the war against slavery and the slave trade.)

1791 E. DARWIN *Bot. Gard.* 101 [an engraving of the device and motto]. **1808** CLARKSON *Hist. Abolition* I. 450; II. 191. **1809** MONTGOMERY *Songs Abolition Slavery* I. ii, The Negro wakes to liberty.. Read the great charter on his brow, I am a man, a brother now.

Hence (contemptuously), ***man-and-brotherism***, the anti-slavery movement.

1865 *Pall Mall G.* 27 Mar. 3/1 Is this the principle of abolition? Are these the sentiments of man and brotherism?

3. A fellow-member of a Christian society, or of the Christian Church as a whole; a fellow-christian; a co-religionist generally. (Pl. *brethren.*)

c **1000** *Ags. Gosp.* Matt. xxiii. 8 An ys eower Lareow: ȝe synt ealle ȝebroðru [*Hatton G.* ȝebroðre; *Lindisf.* broðro]. *c* **1175** *Lamb. Hom.* 5 Leoue broðre and sustre ȝe hi hered. *Ibid.* 125 Alle we beoð ibroðran. *c* **1200** ORMIN Ded. 3 Nu, broþerr Wallterr.. broþerr min i Crisstenndom.. Icc hafe don swa summ þu badd. **1340** *Ayenb.* 101 We gadereþ alle oure broþren mid ous of adopcion. *c* **1449** PECOCK *Repr.* I. xii. 63 Thi Christen britheren and sistren. **1521** FISHER *Wks.* 329 In the epistoles of oure ryght dere broder Paule. **1552** *Bk. Com. Prayer, Morn. Pr.*, Dearly beloved brethren, the Scripture moveth us in sundry places to acknowledge and confess our manifold sins and wickedness. *Ibid. Burial Service*, The soul of our dear brother here departed. **1780** COWPER *Night. & Glow-w.* 29 Hence jarring sectaries may learn.. That brother should not war with brother. **1857** RUSKIN *Pol. Econ. Art* 20 We expect a man in a black gown, supposed to be telling us truth, to address us as brethren. **1871** MORLEY *Voltaire* (1886) 176 The Protestants.. found warm hospitality among their northern brethren.

b. ***the Brethren***: in N.T. the members of the early Christian churches; hence, sometimes adopted by (or applied ironically to) members of various Christian associations, claiming to adhere to New Testament principles; e.g. the Puritan party in the Church of England under Queen Elizabeth. Also in the adopted title or common appellation of some modern sects who reject 'orders' in the church, e.g. 'Brethren', 'Brethren in Christ', 'Christian Brethren', 'Plymouth Brethren', etc. (See the Registrar-General's *Reports.*)

1382 WYCLIF *Acts* xviii. 18 Paul.. seide fare wel to britheren. **1534** TINDALE *ibid.* Paul.. toke his leave of the brethren. **1655** FULLER *Ch. History* ix. 139 Heartned hereat the Brethren, who hitherto had no particular platforme of discipline amongst themselves.. began in a solemne Councell.. to conclude, on a certain forme, as followeth. **1886** *Whitaker's Almanac* 195/2 The Brethren, or Plymouth Brethren, have 23 places of worship in London.

c. Also in names of historical sects: e.g. ***Brethren of Alexius***: a sect of the 14th c., = Cellites. ***B. of the Free Spirit***: a sect which abounded in Western Europe in the 13th c., alleged to have derived its name from *Rom.* viii. 2–14.

1860 EDERSHEIM tr. *Kurtz's Ch. Hist.* I. §142. 457 The Brethren of the Common Life were an association of pious clergymen founded by Gerhard Groot at Deventer in the Netherlands (1384). *Ibid.* §147. 470 It is more than probable that Eccart stood in some relation to the Brothers and Sisters of the Free Spirit.

4. A fellow-member of a guild, corporation, or order; hence, by extension, one of the same profession, trade, society, or order. (Pl. *brethren.*)

1362 LANGL. *P. Pl.* A. v. 246 Dismas my broþer bi-souȝte þe of grace. **1389** *Gild of Garlekhith* in *E.E. Gilds* (1870) 3 To noriche more loue bytwene þe bretheren & sustren of þe bretherhede. *c* **1466** *Gild of Tailors, Exeter* ibid. 315 Yf any Brother of the fforsayd ffraternyte and crafte dysspyse anoder. **1609** SKENE *Reg. Maj.* 142 Gif ane man, quha is nocht ane brother of this Gilde.. leaues in legacie, any part of his gudes to this Gild: we receave him as ane of our brother. **1723** STEELE *Consc. Lovers* II. i, What shall I do for a Brother in the Case? **1805** *Med. & Phys. Jrnl.* XIV. 231 To furnish their professional brethren of the circle with a supply of recent vaccine fluid. **1824** J. JOHNSON *Typogr.* I. 559 Admitted a brother of the Stationers' Company. **1845** D. JERROLD *Curtain Lect.* xx. 49 When you were once made a 'brother' [Masonic] as you call yourself. **1848** MACAULAY *Hist. Eng.* I. 441 One physician.. assured the queen that his brethren would kill the king among them.

b. The official title of certain members of livery companies, and formerly of municipal corporations.

c. A member of Trinity House.

1602 *Return fr. Parnass.* (pt. 2) IV. v. (Arb.) 60 Two states of an incorporation, the one of the Aldermen, the other of the Brethren. **1696** *Lond. Gaz.* No. 3176/3 The Master, Wardens, Assistants and Elder Brethren of the Society of the Trinity-House at Newcastle-upon-Tyne. **1704** *Ibid.* No. 4066/3 The Mayor.. Aldermen, Brethren, and Capital Burgesses, of Your Majesty's Ancient Borough of Derby. **1766** ENTICK *London* IV. 330 This corporation [Trinity Ho.] is governed by a master, 4 wardens, 8 assistants, and 18 elder brethren. The inferior members.. are called younger brethren; into which number any master or mate, skilled in navigation, may be admitted. **1883** LD. SUDELEY in *Ho. Comm.* 19 July, The Elder Brethren of the Trinity House.

d. More vaguely: One in the same case or position; a comrade, fellow, companion, associate. (Pl. more commonly *brothers.*)

a **1300** *Cursor M.* 13086 Breþer mi dere and freinde Nu yee sal mine erand wend. **1423** JAS. I. *Kingis Q.* clxxxiv, Beseching vnto fair venus abufe, For all my brethir.. that seruandis ar to lufe. *c* **1430** *Syr Gener.* 4499 Sir, brethre we ar, both ye and I. **1611** BIBLE *Job* xxx. 29, I am a brother to dragons, and a companion to owles. —— *Prov.* xviii. 9 Hee also that is slouthfull in his worke, is brother to him that is a great waster. **1632** MASSINGER *Maid of Hon.* II. ii, I will draw my sword. Oh! for a brother! **1785** BURNS *Ep. W. Simpson* xvii, Fareweel 'my rhyme-composing brother'! **1821** SHELLEY *Prometh. Unb.* I. 663 A legioned band of linked brothers.

e. In numerous phrases indicating the kind of fellowship, as ***sworn brother***, ***brother at, in*** (*of* obs.) ***arms***, ***brother of the angle*** (= fellow-angler), ***of the blade***, ***gusset***, ***long robe***, ***quill***, etc.

c **1386** CHAUCER *Knts. T.* 302, I tolde the myn aduenture As to my cosyn, and my brother sworn. **1485** CAXTON *Paris & V.* 3 Two brethern of armes. **1596** SHAKS. *1 Hen. IV*, II. iv. 7, I am sworn brother to a leash of Drawers. **1632** MASSINGER *Maid of Hon.* v. ii, Once more brothers in arms. **1653** WALTON *Angler* i. 5, I am a Brother of the Angle. **1668** R. L'ESTRANGE *Vis. Quev.* (1708) 105 To pass for Hectors; Sons of Priam; Brothers of the Blade. **1680** *Observ.* '*Curse Ye Meroz*' 7 This Aphorism is but borrowed from another Brother of the Quill. **1814** SOUTHEY *Roderick* iv, My first sworn brother in the appointed rule. **1828** SCOTT *F.M. Perth* II. 212 That doughty burgher is Henry's brother-at-arms. **1828–41** TYTLER *Hist. Scot.* I. (1864) 144 Randolph, his friend and brother-in-arms. **1840** *Fraser's Mag.* XXI. 315 The two knights defend each other, as sworn brethren-at-arms. **1878** MORLEY *Diderot* II. 122 A chivalrous defender of poorer brethren in art.

5. *esp.* A fellow-member of a religious order (cf. *frater*, *frère*, *friar*).

Hence frequently in titles, as ***Brethren of the Sack***, ***B. of the Holy Trinity***: two fraternities of monks in the 13th c. ***B. of the Community***, and ***B. of the Observation***: laxer and stricter sects of the Franciscans. ***Little Brethren of the Poor***: the Wyclifite preachers. ***Brothers of Obedience***, ***B. of Charity***, etc.: see quots.

c **1500** *Cocke Lorell's B.* (1843) 7 The pope.. hath graunted in his byll, That euery brother may do what he wyll. **1513** BRADSHAW *St. Werburgh* (1848) 87 This kynge gaue a place.. To buylde a monastery, to relygyous brethur. **1536** *Act 27 Hen. VIII*, xlii. §2 in *Oxf. & Camb. Enactm.* 14 Scolers, Dimies, Brotherne, Chapleynes. **1552** LYNDESAY *Monarche* 5850 ȝe Brether of Religioun, In tyme leif ȝour abusioun. **1691** SOUTHERNE *Sir Ant. Love* I. i, A broken Brother of Bethlehem, with all his frippery about him. **1706** tr. *Dupin's Eccl. Hist. 16th C.* II. IV. xi. 450 The Brothers of Charity were instituted by St. John de Dieu. **1788** *Picturesque Tour thro' Europe* 19 The Brothers of Obedience.. without being obliged to go to Malta, like the rest, make the same vows. **1848** MACAULAY *Hist. Eng.* II. 61 The chief representative of the Jesuits at Whitehall was an English brother of the Order.

6. Used by sovereigns and princes to each other.

1534 K. JAS. V. to *Hen. VIII*, 5 June in *Nat. MSS.* II. xxviii, Derrest and best belouit brother and oncle.. ȝour lowynge hartly brothere and nepho James Rex. **1535** K. HEN. VIII. *ibid.* II. xxix, To be frank and playn with his saide goode Brother [of France], his Majestie woll in noo wise, directly or indirectly confesse the Bisshop of Rome to haue any Jurisdiction in princes. **1553** Q. MARY *ibid.* III. iv, Our good brothere the ffrenche king. **1711** STEELE *Spect.* No. 64 ¶1 Princes and Sovereigns.. are stiled Brothers to each other. **1848** MACAULAY *Hist. Eng.* I. 199 Lewis.. was as licentious.. as his brother of England.

7. *fig.* Said of things.

1362 LANGL. *P. Pl.* A. II. 141 Feire speche þat is feiþles is falsnes broþer. **1799** WORDSW. *Two April Mornings* vii, That April morn, Of this the very brother. **1823** LAMB *Elia* Ser. I. xxiv. (1865) 188 The art of roasting or rather broiling (which I take to be the elder brother). **1830** TENNYSON *Isabel* iii, A clear stream flowing with a muddy one, Till in its onward current it absorbs.. The vexed eddies of its wayward brother.

†**b.** ***B. of the Rose***: the five leaves of the calyx.

1611 COTGR. *Le gobelet d'vne Rose*, The fiue-leaued Cap or huske thereof; called, by some, the fiue brothers of the Rose. **1626** BACON *Sylva* §590 We see also, that the Sockets, and Supporters of Flowers, are Figured; as in the five Brethren of the Rose.

II. *attrib.* and in *Comb.*

8. *attrib.* Placed before other substantives, in the same way as *fellow-*. ***brother-man***: a man recognized as a brother, a 'man and brother'.

Often united by a hyphen, esp. in the singular, so as to make clearer the attributive relation of *brother* to the second word (contrast *brother-officer* with *brother John*); but in the plural this is sufficiently shown by the inflexion of the second word and non-inflexion of *brother*. Formerly *brother* was also made plural.

1503 *Act 19 Hen. VII*, xvii, The Mayor.. with his Brethren Aldermen. **1599** SHAKS. *Hen. V*, I. ii. 122 Your Brother Kings and Monarchs of the Earth. **1603** —— *Meas. for M.* III. ii. 219 My brother-Iustice haue I found so seuere. **1603** DEKKER, etc. *Patient Grissil* (1841) 18 Many of his brother knights. **1613** *Voy. Guiana* in *Harl. Misc.* (Malh.) III. 184 My brother-captain, Michael Harcourt. **1670** WALTON *Lives* III. 216 His Brethren Ministers of the Low Countries. **1690** LOCKE *Hum. Und.* II. xxvii. (1695) 186 To punish one Twin for what his Brother-Twin did. **1725** POPE *Odyss.* XI. 300 Two brother-heroes shall from thee be born. **1768** BOSWELL *Corsica* iii. (ed. 2) 213 Composed in praise of his brother-commander. **1820** KEATS *Hyperion* II. 160 Tell me, all ye brethren Gods, How we can war. **1837** DISRAELI *Venetia* I. xv. (1858) I. 100 An esteemed neighbour and brother magistrate. **1839** CARLYLE *Chartism* iv. 128 These wretched brother-men. **1861** *Jrnl. Sacred Lit.* 95 To recognize him as one who is our brother-man. **1871** MORLEY *Crit. Misc.* Ser. I. (1878) 220 Divorced.. from his brother men.

b. of things.

a **1822** SHELLEY *Sc. fr. Faust, Prol. Heaven*, The sun sounds.. In the song of emulation of his brother-spheres. **1873** BLACK *Pr. Thule* ii. 32 Suainabhal and his brother mountains. **1874** BOUTELL *Arms & A.* ii. 17 The substitution.. of iron, in the stead of its elder brother-metal, bronze.

c. Hence, possible parasynthetic derivatives, as **brother-'manhood**.

1864 CARLYLE *Fredk. Gt.* IV. 457 A cheery brother-manhood.

9. *Comb.* **a.** The old uninflected genitive = 'brother's', as in ***broder bairn***, ***daughter***, ***son***, ***wife***, was sometimes in later usage taken as = 'a brother's, brotherly', as in ***brother deed***, ***brother love***. **b.** objective and obj. gen., as ***brother-hater***, ***-slayer***, ***-slaughter***, ***-worship***. **c.** instrumental, as ***brother-forsaken***, etc.

a. *a* **1300** *Cursor M.* 3750 Fader, þis was na broþer dede. **1483** *Cath. Angl.* 45 A Broder doghter, *fratria*. A Broder son, *fratruus*. A Broder wyfe, *fratrissa*. **1613** SHAKS. *Hen. VIII*, v. iii. 173 With a true heart, And Brother-loue.

b. 1483 *Cath. Angl.* 45 A Broder-slaer, *fratricida*. **1561** T. NORTON *Calvin's Inst.* IV. i. (1634) 510 Did brother-slaughter seeme to the Patriarkes a lawfull thing? **1817** COLERIDGE *Lay Serm.* 387 Of many and various sorts are the brother-haters. **1864** *Chamb. Jrnl.* 31 Dec. 838 Brother-worship is natural to sisters—when young.

d. brother-consanguinean (see quot.); **brother-house**, the home of a brotherhood; †**brother-law** = BROTHER-IN-LAW; **brother-uterine**, one born of the same mother, but not of the same father. Also BROTHER-GERMAN, BROTHERWORT.

1880 MUIRHEAD *Gaius* iii. §10 Brothers born of the same father, often called *brothers-consanguinean, are each other's agnates. **1883** *Contemp. Rev.* Oct. 491 Their *brother-houses and schools.. in most of the chief cities of the Netherlands. **1677** HOBBES *Homer* 195 Your *brother-law Alcathous is kill'd. *Ibid.* 383 Hector, said she, Whom best I lov'd of all my brother-laws.

'brother, *v.* Also 6 *Sc.* bruder. [f. prec. sb.]

1. *trans.* To make a brother of; to admit to brotherhood; also, to treat or address as brother.

1573 *Sege Edinb. Castel* in *Scot. Poems 16th C.* II. 289 Thay ar bowit and bruderit in our band. **1584** FENNER *Def. Ministers* (1587) 7 Howe can you brother vs thus in euerie line, and deale so vnbrotherlie with vs in euerie sentence? **1706** FARQUHAR *Recruit. Officer* I. i, No coaxing, no brothering me 'faith. **1820** SCOTT *Ivanhoe* II. iv. 62 This same motley gentleman thou art so fond to brother. *c* **1825** BEDDOES *Sec. Brother* II. ii, Marcello is my brother, I am his, If coming of one mother brother us.

2. To be a brother to. ***to brother it***: to act or behave as a brother.

c **1600** CHAPMAN *Iliad* XIII. 692 She that brought thee forth not utterly left me Without some portion of thy spirit to make me brother thee. *a* **1648** LD. HERBERT *Life* (1826) 327 There remains now but you and I to brother it.

Hence **'brothering** *vbl. sb. rare.*

1818 SOUTHEY *Lett.* (1856) III. 97 By.. such brothering and sistering he kept up his influence among his people.

brother, obs. form of BROIDER *v.*

'brothered, *ppl. a.* [f. BROTHER *v.* + -ED.]

1. United into or by brotherhood.

1627–8 FELTHAM *Resolves* (1647) 211 When they meet a brother'd constitution they then unite. **1876** BLACKIE *Songs Relig. & Life* 3 All in brothered rays do mingle.

2. Caused by brothers; fraternal.

1850 BLACKIE *Æschylus* I. 233 Save my city From brothered strife, and from domestic brawls.

brothered, *sb.*: see BROTHERRED.

brother-german (ˌbrʌðə'dʒɜːmən). Pl. brothers-german (formerly brethren-). [f. BROTHER *sb.* + GERMAN.] A brother through both parents; a 'whole' brother.

Early writers also used it as = 'brother on the mother's side, brother-uterine'; it has been proposed in modern times to restrict it to 'brother on the father's side'.

1340 *Ayenb.* 146 Broþer germayn of uader and of moder. *c* **1450** *Merlin* viii. 122 Thei be men of high lynage, and be bretheren germain. **1480** CAXTON *Chron. Eng.* ccxxv. 230 Karoll the grete kyng of fraunce was broder germayn of Quene Isabell kynge Edwardes moder. **1530** PALSGR. 201/2 Brother germayne, *frere germain*. **1751** CHAMBERS *Cycl.* s.v. *German*, Brother German denotes a brother both by the father's and mother's side. **1882** A. MACFARLANE *Consanguinity* 8, I use the term brother-german, to denote brother on the father's side.

brotherhood (ˈbrʌðərhʊd), also †brotherhead. Forms: α. broþerhede, broiþer-, broder-, brodurhede, brethered, 4–5 bretherhede, 5 breþerheed, 4– 6 brotherheed, 5 bretherheed, britherhed(e, brodirhede, broþerhed, 5–6 bretherhed, brodered, 6 (breethreed), bretherhead, brodirhed, brotherhed, -head(e, -hedde. β. 5 broder-, broþerhode, breþerode, britherhod, 5–6 brotherode, -hode, 6 brotherhoode, 6– brotherhood. [Not in OE.: the earlier ME. form *broþerhede* was, in form, a derivative of BROTHER and *-hed*, *-hede*; but arose probably from the accession of the earlier BROTHERRED(E (which goes back to OE.) to the *-hede* class, through the intermediate *brothered(e*, the ending of which might be either *-rede* or *-hede*. This is made still more likely by the fact that the variant *brotherhode* (whence the modern *brotherhood*) is not found before the 15th c.; whereas *childhood*, *maidenhood*, *wifehood*, and other genuine derivatives in *-hood* go back to an OE. *-hád* and early ME. *-had*, later *-hōd(e*, with *-hed*, *-hede* as an occasional ME. variant. See -HEAD, -HOOD, -RED. The variant *bretherhede* was frequent from the 14th c. till about the Reformation, evidently by association with the *brether* or *brethren* of a guild or order: 'the bretheren and sustren of the bretherhede'.]

1. The relation of a brother, or of brothers mutually; fraternal tie. Also in spiritual sense.

α. *a* **1300** *Cursor M.* 1159 Felauscipe ne broiþerhede Mought te drau fra felon dede. **1526** *Pilgr. Perf.* (W. de W. 1531) 169b, Remyssyon of synnes, adopcyon of grace, brotherhed to the sone of god. **1594** CAREW *Tasso* (1881) 81 Eustace her meetes, who claymes a brother-hed In him. β. *c* **1450** *Voc.* in Wr.-Wülcker 690 *Hec fraternitas*, a brotherode. **1580** BARET *Alv.* B 1377 Brotherhood by the same father and mother, *germanitas*. **1593** SHAKS. *Rich. II*, I. ii. 9 Findes brotherhood in thee no sharper spurre? **1605** BACON *Adv. Learn.* II. 5 Nature createth Brotherhood in Families. **1860** PUSEY *Min. Proph.* 166 The brotherhood of blood was not to wear out.

2. Brotherliness, brotherly fellowship, companionship, friendly alliance.

α. *a* **1300** *Cursor M.* 3750 Þis was na broder-hede [*v.r.* broþer dede]. *c* **1386** CHAUCER *Schipm. T.* 42 Ilk of hem gan other to assure Of brotherhed [*v.r.* bretherhede, -heed, breþerode, broþerhed, -hode], whil that her lif may dure. **1535** COVERDALE *Zech.* xi. 14 That I might lowse the brother-heade betwixte Iuda and Israel.

β. **1388** WYCLIF *1 Macc.* xii. 10 To renule britherhod [**1382** bretherhed] and frenschip. **1665** MANLEY *Grotius' Low-C. Warrs* 121 He was sure of the Brother-hood of France. **1868** HAWTHORNE *Amer. Note-bks.* (1879) I. 54 We live in great harmony and brotherhood.

†**3.** The personality of a brother: in ***your brotherhood***, a dutiful mode of addressing a brother. *Obs.*

c **1400** *Apol. Loll.* 39 Eft writiþ þe pope to þe bischop, We bid to þi broþerhed, þat þu steer bisili þe clerkis of þi jurisdiccoun. **1502–3** *Plumpton Corr.* 172, I recomend me unto your mastership and brotherhode, and to my lady your wyfe. **1635** PAGITT *Christianogr.* II. vii. 84, I have opportunity to salute your brotherhood, whose face I never saw.

†**4.** The position or rank of a 'brother' in a corporation. *Obs.*

1536 *Act 27 Hen. VIII*, xlii. § 1 in *Oxf. & Camb. Enactm.* 13 Scolershippes, Dimishippees, Brotherodes. **1606** SHAKS. *Tr. & Cr.* I. iii. 104 How could.. Degrees in Schooles, and Brother-hoods in Cities.. The primogenitiue, and due of Byrth.. stand in Authentique place?

5. a. An association of brothers; a fraternity, guild, society, association of equals for mutual help, support, protection, or action. Also, the brethren of such an order collectively.

α. *c* **1340** *Gaw. & Gr. Knt.* 2516 Vche burne of þe broþerhede a bauderyk schulde haue. **1387** *E.E. Wills* (1882) 1 The Brethered of our lady of Abbechirch. **1389** in *Eng. Gilds* (1870) 3 þe bretheren & sustren of þe bretherhede. **1528** TINDALE *Doctr. Treat.* (1848) 343 The belly-brother-head of monks and friars. **1553** *Inv.* in *Ann. Dioc. Lichfield* (1863) 27 Brotherheddes, gildes, fraternities, & cumpenies.

β. **1547** *Act 1 Edw. VI*, xiv. § 1 Hospitals, Fraternities, Brotherhoods, Guilds. **1555** T. HAUKES in Foxe *A. & M.* (1631) III. xi. 260/1 There is a brotherhood of you, but I will breake it. **1653** WALTON *Angler* i. 5, I hate the Otter perfectly, even for their sakes that are of my Brotherhood. **1805** SOUTHEY *Madoc in W.* xiii, The grey brotherhood Chaunted the solemn mass. **1882** FAIRBAIRN in *Contemp. Rev.* XLII. 867 The Arab tribes.. fused into a united and enthusiastic brotherhood.

b. *fig.* A group or array of things figured as brothers.

1728 POPE *Dunc.* I. 143 Here all his suff'ring brotherhood retire, And 'scape the martyrdom of jakes and fire. **1814** WORDSW. *Excursion* I. 29 The gloom Spread by a brotherhood of lofty elms. **1843** PRESCOTT *Mexico* (1850) I. 350 This rugged brotherhood of mountains.

c. A railway trade union. *U.S.*

1883 J. D. FULTON *Sam Hobart* 83 The Brotherhood of Locomotive Engineers.. was formed in the city of Detroit in August, 1863, as the Brotherhood of the Footboard. **1959** *Economist* 6 June 947/2 The political influence of the railway brotherhoods, as the unions are called.

6. A court, convention, or meeting of a fraternity or guild; *spec.* a convention or conference of delegates from the corporations of the Cinque-Ports.

1683 *Addr. Cinque-Ports* in *Lond. Gaz.* No. 1857/2 The humble Address of the Mayors, Bayliffs, Jurats, and Commons of the Cinque-Ports.. Assembled at a Brotherhood and Guestling holden at New Romeney. **1830** *Thanet & Cinque Ports* II. 11 The annual courts anciently called Guestlings, and afterwards Brotherhoods. *Ibid.* The Brotherhood men, like members of Parliament, are privileged from arrest.

7. The fellowship or communion of Christians with one another and with Christ; also *concr.*

α. *c* **1380** WYCLIF *Serm.* Sel. Wks. II. 326 Cristen men shulden be loveris of breþerheed in Crist. **1382** —— *1 Thess.* iv. 9 Of the charite of britherhed we hadden not nede for to wryte to ȝou.

β. **1388** WYCLIF *1 Peter* ii. 17 Onoure ȝe alle men, loue ȝe brithirhod [**1382** britherhed]. **1562** D. COX in Farr's *S.P.* (1845) II. 503 Our Father, which in heauen art, And makst vs al one brotherhood. **1666** BAXTER *Call Unconverted* 238 You shall have part in the brother-hood.. of the Saints. **1865** R. W. DALE *Jewish Temp.* vii. (1877) 74 There is a brotherhood between Christ and all believers.

8. Fellowship; community of feeling uniting man and man; also *concr.* those united in such fellowship. A modern notion frequent in ***brotherhood of man***, ***universal brotherhood***, etc.

1784 COWPER *Task* III. 208 The link of brotherhood, by which One common Maker bound me to the kind. **1821** SHELLEY *Prometh. Unb.* II. ii. 95 And make the earth One brotherhood **1841** D'ISRAELI *Amen. Lit.* (1867) 581 The common brotherhood of man. **1882** FARRAR *Early Chr.* I. 107 In the Church the beautiful ideal of human brotherhood was carried into practice.

brother-in-law (ˈbrʌðərɪnˌlɔː). Also 5 **brodyr yn lawe, broder in law, broder elawe.** [App. 'in law' = *in Canon Law* (in contrast to *brother in blood* or *by nature*), with reference to the degrees of affinity within which marriage is prohibited; a brother-in-law or sister-in-law being, as regards intermarriage, treated 'in law' as a brother or sister.]

prop. The brother of one's husband or wife; the husband of one's sister. Sometimes extended to the husband of one's wife's (or husband's) sister.

c **1300** *K. Alis.* 4399 He was Daries brother in lawe. [*c* **1425** *Voc.* in Wr.-Wülcker 672 *Hic leuir, est frater in lege.*] **1483** *Cath. Angl.* 45 A Broder in law [*v.r.* Broder elawe], *leuir*. **1522** *Bury Wills* (1850) 117, I bequethe to John Bullok, my brother in law, a fetherbed. **1552** HULOET, Brotherne by mariynge the doughters of one man, called brothern in lawe. **1596** SHAKS. *1 Hen. IV*, I. iii. 80 That we at our owne charge, shall ransome straight His Brother-in-Law. **1700** TYRRELL *Hist. Eng.* II. 901 On his Brother-in-Law's behalf. **1830** MISS MITFORD *Village* Ser. iv. (1863) 273 Oakhampstead Park, the pleasant demesne of her brother-in-law, Sir Arthur Villars.

†**b.** *humorously*. The father of one's daughter-in-law or son-in-law. *Obs.*

1611 SHAKS. *Wint. T.* IV. iv. 720 Who.. is no honest man to goe about to make me the Kings Brother in Law.

Hence **'brother-in-ˌlawship**.

1840 THACKERAY *Paris Sk. Bk.* (1885) 98 The pleasures of brother-in-lawship in general.

'Brotherist. A follower of the fanatical Richard Brothers, who attracted attention 1790–1802.

1807 SOUTHEY *Espriella's Lett.* (1814) III. 199 J.'s friend saw him once at the house of one of the Brotherists.

'brotherize, *v. rare*$^{-1}$. [f. BROTHER *sb.* + -IZE.] *trans.* To provide with a brother or with brothers.

1752 MRS. DELANY *Life & Corr.* 82 It is happy for D., since she is so brotherised and sisterised, that she can make their strange and unnatural behaviour easy to her.

Brother Jonathan: see JONATHAN 1.

'brotherkin. [f. BROTHER *sb.* + -KIN.] Little brother. (After Ger. *brüderchen.*)

1827 CARLYLE *Germ. Rom.* II. 285 Brotherkin Anselmus. **1831** —— *Sart. Res.* III. vii. 289 Wert thou, my little Brotherkin, suddenly covered up within the largest imaginable glass-bell,—what a thing it were.. for the world! **1856** H. MORLEY *Corn. Agrippa* II. 59 Let this brotherkin, priest or Levite turn his heart from her.

'brotherless, *a.* Having no brother.

1460 *Pol. Rel. & L. Poems* (1866) 207 Broþerlees, spouselees, ful wrecchid y-wis. *a* **1678** MARVELL *Nymph Compl. Death Fawn*, The brotherless Heliades. **1821** BYRON *Cain* III. i. 464, I shrink from the deed which leaves thee brotherless. **1865** LADY T. LEWIS *Miss Berry's Jrnls. & Corr.* Introd. 17 She was brotherless and unmarried.

'brotherlike, *a.*, *adv.* [see -LIKE.]

A. *adj.* Like a brother; fraternal, brotherly.

1570 LEVINS *Manip.* 122 Brotherlike, *fraternus*. **1593** SHAKS. *3 Hen. VI*, V. i. 105 Welcome good Clarence, this is Brother-like. *a* **1625** E. CHALONER *Six Serm.* (1629) 19 This is a brotherlike admonition, and a friendlike expostulation.

B. *adv.* After the manner of a brother.

1837 CARLYLE *Fr. Rev.* II. III. II. viii. 212 All Patriots.. mourning brotherlike. **1859** TENNYSON *Enid* 1732 The King .. kiss'd her with all pureness, brotherlike.

brotherliness (ˈbrʌðərlɪnɪs). [f. BROTHERLY + -NESS.] The quality of being brotherly; brotherly affection or sympathy.

1532 TINDALE *Expos. Matt.* Wks. II. 86 If brotherliness will not help.. let him execute thy power. **1561** T. NORTON *Calvin's Inst.* Table Script. Quots., Honour all men, love brotherlinesse. **1618** BOLTON *Florus* (1636) 285 The brotherlinesse of the Generals drew exceeding favour to that side. **1878** T. HARDY *Return Native* II. III. ii. 85 He still cleaved to plain living.. and brotherliness with clowns.

brotherling: see BRETHELING.

brotherliwise (ˈbrʌðəlɪwaɪz), *adv.* [f. BROTHERLY *a.* + -WISE.] In brotherly fashion.

1890 KIPLING *Life's Handicap* (1891) 117 Who brotherliwise had followed his kinsman's fortune.

brotherly (ˈbrʌðəlɪ), *a.* Also 6 broderly. [f. BROTHER + -LY[1]. Cf. OE. *bróðorlic*; but no corresponding form is found in ME.]

1. Of or pertaining to a brother; also, characteristic of a brother, fraternal, kind, affectionate.

c **1000** ÆLFRIC *Gram.* vi. 15 *Fraternus*, broðorlic. **1535** COVERDALE *Amos* i. 9 They.. haue not remembred the brotherly couenaunt [WYCLIF, boond of bretheren]. **1555** EDEN *Decades W. Ind.* I. II. 72 A brotherly league. **1656** JEANES *Mixt. Schol. Div.* 152 A brotherly Saviour, and Redeemer. **1835** CARLYLE *Misc.* (1857) III. 299 The freest, brotherliest, bravest human soul.

b. Common in ***brotherly kindness***, ***love*** (sometimes, though unnecessarily, joined by a hyphen).

1526 *Pilgr. Perf.* (W. de W. 1531) 170 Fraternall charite or brotherly loue. **1611** BIBLE *2 Peter* i. 7 Adde to godlinesse, brotherly kindnesse. —— *Hebr.* xiii. 1 Let brotherly loue continue. **1667** H. MORE *Div. Dial.* v. xlii. (1713) 526 The exercise of.. Brotherly-kindness. **1856** R. VAUGHAN *Mystics* (1860) I. 199 To displace this pride by brotherly-kindness.

†**2.** Of things: Acting in harmonious conjunction.

1638 A. READ *Treat. Chirurg.* xx. 146 Two brotherly muscles, appoynted for sundry motions of the same part.

'brotherly, *adv.* [f. as prec. + -LY[2].] In the manner or spirit of a brother; fraternally.

1526 TINDALE *1 Peter* i. 22 To love brotherly withouten faynynge. **1590** H. BARROW in *Conferences* i. 1 To confer brotherly and christianly with me. **1593** SHAKS. *3 Hen. VI*, IV. iii. 38 How should you gouerne any Kingdome, That know not.. how to vse your Brothers Brotherly. **1650** S. CLARKE *Eccl. Hist.* (1654) I. 237 He exhorted them lovingly and brotherly to lay down their arms. **1805** SCOTT *Last Minstr.* II. xx, The man he had loved so brotherly.

brotherode, obs. form of BROTHERHOOD.

†**'brotherred.** *Obs.* Forms: 1 bróðorrǽden, 2–3 broþerreddene, 4 broþerrede, (5–6 brothered(e). [OE. f. *broðor* BROTHER + *-rǽden* condition, state: see -RED, and cf. *kindred*. Apparently in its later ME. form *brotherred*, *brothered*, it was merged in *brotherhed*, earlier var. of BROTHERHOOD.] = BROTHERHOOD.

(The quotations after 1400 illustrate the merging of *brotherred* in *brotherhed*.)

c **1000** ÆLFRIC *Gram.* vi. 17 *Fraternitas*, broðorræden. *c* **1175** *Lamb. Hom.* 41 Leofe breoðre haldeð broþerreddene eow bitwenen. **1340** *Ayenb.* 110 He heþ þe broþerrede and part and uelaȝrede and riȝt and ine alle þe guode dedes. *Ibid.* 146 Ane broþerhede gostlich þet is worþ betere þanne þe broþerrede ulesslich. **1464** *Mann. & Househ. Exp.* 272 The brodered of the ȝeld of Seynte Iohnes. **1513–4** *Act 5 Hen. VIII*, vii, The Felishippe and Brodered of the blessed Trinite. **1542** UDALL *Erasm. Apoph.* 340b, A certain brethreed which vsed to.. gather together at his hous.

brothership (-ʃɪp). [f. as prec. + -SHIP:—OE. *-scipe*. Only in ONorthumb. *broðerscip*, and in recent occasional use as = 'fraternity'.]

a. Brotherly fellowship, brotherliness. **b.** A fraternity or gild-brotherhood.

c **950** *Lindisf. Gosp.* Matt. xxiv. 12 Eftcoles broðerscip *vel* lufo moniȝra. **1706** FARQUAHAR *Recruit. Officer* I. i, Take your cap and your brothership back again. **1849** ROCK *Ch. of Fathers* II. vii. 337 This wish.. to be in brothership with religious houses. **1866** *Cornh. Mag.* Nov. 579 They possess trade-guilds and brotherships.

'brotherwort. [f. as prec. + WORT.] Wild Thyme, *Thymus Serpyllum*. (Britten and Holland.) (According to Halliwell, Pennyroyal.)

1387 *Sinon. Barthol.* (Anecd. Oxon.) 35 *Pulegium montanum*, brotherwort. *c* **1465** *Alphita* (Anecd. Oxon.) 81 *Herpillum, serpillum, pulegium montanum*, brothuurt. *Ibid.* 186 *Tymbra uel timbria*, brotherwrt. **1499** *Promp. Parv.* 54 Brother wort, *pulio, puleium*. **1530** PALSGR. 201/2 Brother worte herbe. **1597** in GERARD App. (Britten & Holl.).

brothery, perh. an error for *brokery*.

1638 JACKSON *Consecr. Son of God* 185 Our Saviour purged the material Temple from brothery [Wks. 1844 VIII. 359 brothelry] and merchandizing.

†**'brothfall.** *Obs.* [a. ON. **bróðfall* or **bráð-fall* 'sudden fall' (Vigf.), found in Icel. as *brotfall* epileptic fit.] Falling sickness, epilepsy.

c **1200** ORMIN 15504 And ta þatt fellen o broþþfall þeȝȝ tokenn att himm hæle.

†**brothrell,** *sb. Obs. rare*$^{-1}$. = BROTHEL 2.

1514 BARCLAY *Cyt. & Uplondyshm.* (1847) 28 Suche a brothrell hir keepeth not to one.

brothy ('brɒθɪ, -ɔː-), *a.* Also 7 **broathy.** [f. BROTH *sb.* + -Y[1].] Of, or of the nature of, broth.
1651 OGILBY *Æsop* (1665) 63 A Table in a Broathy Deluge drown'd.

brothyr, obs. form of BROTHER.

brotikin, var. BRODEKIN, *Obs.*, a high boot.

brotil(l, -tle, -ttyl, var. BROTEL *a. Obs.* brittle.

brouch(e, obs. form of BROOCH.

brouch. *Obs. rare*[−1]: perh. = BROUGH, BURR, BURROW[3], an 'orb'.
1645 G. DANIEL *Poems* Wks. 1878 II. 77 My feeble Lampe, as much Might fire Heaven's greatest Brouch.

broud(e, variant of BROWD, BROWDEN. *Obs.*

brouder, -re, etc., obs. form of BROIDER, etc.

brouderer, obs. f. BRODERER, BROIDERER.

†'**broudur,** *sb. Obs. rare.* [ad. OF. *broudure, brodeüre* (Godef.) embroidery, f. *broder* to stitch, embroider.]
Embroidered work, embroidery.
1470 HARDING *Chron.* cxciii. iii, Broudur and furres and goldsmith werke aye newe.

broues, -esse, obs. ff. BREWIS, BROSE.

brouet, var. of BROWET, *Obs.*, pottage.

brough. now *Sc.* and *north.* Also 8–9 **brugh,** 9 *dial.* **bruff.** [app. a. ON. *borg*, in sense of 'wall, enclosure': cf. the Ger. term *hof* 'yard, court, area', applied to the same phenomenon; the comparison being to the outer wall of a feudal castle. *Brough, brugh* (brʌx), now in north. Eng. dial. *bruff* (brʊf), is the northern form; southern forms are BURR, and BURROW, in *Promp. Parv. burwhe.* (The word thus appears in origin identical with BROCH, *brough* round tower.)]
1. A luminous ring or circle around a shining body, *esp.* the moon; a halo.
[*c* **1440** *Promp. Parv.* 56 Burwhe, sercle [**1499** burrowe], *orbiculus.*] **1496** *Dives & Paup.* (W. de W.) I. xxvii. 64/1 The broughe or cercle about the candell lyght is token of rayne. **1635** PERSON *Varieties* II. iv. 62 These Circles by us called broughes, are a world of way remote from the bodies of the sunne and moone. **1808** JAMIESON *Sc. Dict.* s.v. *Mone*, A brugh, or hazy circle round the moon is accounted a certain prognostic of rain. **1855** *Whitby Gloss.*, *Bruff*, the halo round the moon, when it shines through a mist or haze. **1875** ROBINSON *Whitby Gloss.* (E.D.S.) s.v. *Bruff*, 'The larger the bruff, the nearer the storm'; or, 'the bigger the bruff, the nearer the breeze'. **1882** *Standard* 26 Dec. 7/4 When round the moon there is a brugh The weather will be cold and rough.
2. *Curling*: see quot.
1857 CHAMBERS *Inform. People* II. 683/1 s.v. *Curling*, Brough—several concentric circles, varying from one to fourteen feet in diameter, drawn round each tee.

brough, variant of BROCH, round tower.

brougham, (bruːm, 'bruːəm, 'brəʊəm). [f. the name of Lord *Brougham*, of which the native northern pronunciation was ('brʊxəm) also ('brʊfɛm), and ('bruːhəm); this became in London ('bruːəm, and bruːm).
For the vehicle (bruːm) was the accepted London pronunciation, as seen in society verses, etc., and was still (1888) widely prevalent, especially among elderly people; ('bruːəm) was somewhat less frequent; but an extensive collection of evidence shows ('brəʊəm) to have been the most common in educated use in the late 19th c. (brəʊm) was heard from the vulgar.]
A one-horse closed carriage, with two or four wheels, for two or four persons.
1851 *Househ. Words* III. 567 Dukes and marquises, and people of that sort, glide away in their broughams. **1856** PATMORE *Angel in Ho.* II. Prol. i, Briggs, Factotum, Footman, Butler, Groom.. Preserv'd the rabbits, drove the brougham. **1866** MISS BRADDON *Lady's Mile* i. 2 Those dashing mail-phaetons and dainty little broughams.

brought (brɔːt), *ppl. a.* [pa. pple. of BRING *v.*] Chiefly in composition, as in *well, ill brought up* (see BRING *v.* 27 b).

brouhaha ('bruːhɑːhɑː). [a. F. *brouhaha* (15th c. in Littré).] A commotion, a to-do, a 'sensation'; hubbub, uproar.
1890 O. W. HOLMES *Over Teacups* v. 94, I enjoy the *brouhaha*.. of all this quarrelsome menagerie of noise-making machines. **1931** C. MORLEY *John Mistletoe* ii. 95 He was immediately captivated by the jargon and brouhaha of the sales department. **1937** WYNDHAM LEWIS in L. Russell *Press Gang!* 276 The peculiar esoteric *brouhaha* of the New York underworld. **1946** 'BRAHMS' & SIMON *Trottie True* vii. 186, I shall never forget the brou-ha-ha.. when Cousin Geraldine married into Trade. **1964** *Times* 24 July 16/2 Whenever there is a City brouhaha of this kind, all sorts of voices are raised for all kinds of official inquiries.

‖**brouillon** (brujɔ̃). [Fr.] A rough draft.
1678 W. TEMPLE *Let.* 19 Aug. in *Wks.* (1731) II. 492 What was signed at first was rather a *brouillon*, than any fair and formal Draught. **1735** POPE *Let.* 17 June (1956) III. 469 Your lordship has still in your custody the Brouillons of verses. **1735** *Pope's Lett.* I. 37 The first Brouillon of those Verses, and the second Copy with Corrections. **1921** *Blackw. Mag.* Feb. 251/2 'Papa Crémieux' was called in to furnish *brouillons* for letters to duchesses and authors.

brouin, obs. Sc. pa. pple. of BREW.

brouk(e, broume, obs. f. BROOK, BROOM.

broun(e, obs. f. BROWN, obs. pa. pple. of BREW.

†**brounes.** *Obs. rare*[−1]. [If this is of one syllable, it suggests as possible sing. *broune, brune*, ad. ON. *bruni* burning: but it may be a derivative in *-nes*, as taken in the later version.] ? Burning, inflammation.
1528 PAYNELL *Salerne Regim.* (1541) 61 [It] comfortethe a hotte stomake.. and repressethe his Brounes [Lat. *adustionem*; **1634** browninesse] and heate.

brount(e, obs. form of BURNT.

brous, brouse, obs. ff. BRUSH, BRUISE.

brouse, broust, obs. ff. BROWSE, BROWST.

brouster, -ar, northern ff. BREWSTER.

brout, obs. form of BRUT.

brouwys, obs. form of BREWIS, BROSE.

brow (braʊ), *sb.*[1] Forms: 1 **brú** (*pl.* **brúa**), 2 **bruw(e,** 3 **brouwe, brou, bruu,** 3–4 **brue,** 4 **brwe, brewe,** 4–7 **browe,** 5 **brouȝ, broue,** 5– **brow.** [OE. *brú* fem., inflected on the type of an OTeut. *brûâ-* str. fem., but prob. only an OE. accession to the *â-* declension of a WGer. or primitive OE. *brú* of the type of *cú, sú*:—OTeut. **brû-s* (= Skr. *bhrû-s* eye-brow, Gr. ὀφρύ-ς). The original sense appears to have been 'eye-brow', but it must have been extended at an early date from the hair over the eyes to that on the eye-lids, the 'eye-lashes', for this was the normal sense in OE., the eye-brows being distinguished as *ofer-brúa* i.e. over-eye-lashes, or otherwise contextually. From the eye-lashes, the name appears to have been transferred step by step to the eye-lids, the eye-brows, the prominences of the forehead, and finally to the forehead as a whole. See also BREE *sb.*[1], and cf. BEETLE-BROWED.
ON. *brú* fem. 'bridge' was perhaps the same word, with a transferred sense; but the ON. word actually used for 'eye-brow' was *brún*, pl. *brýnn*, conjectured to be a secondary form from *brû-* founded on the gen. pl. *brú-na.* (Cf. mod. G. *braune* brow, founded on the pl. *braun, brauen*, MHG. *brâwen*, pl. of *brâwe.*) In the other Teutonic langs. **brû-* is lost, and its place supplied by **brǣwâ-*; thus OHG. *brâwa* eye-lashes, *obarun brâwa, ubar-brâwa*, eye-brows, mod.G. *augen-braue, -braune* (see above) eye-brow, *wimper*, MHG. *wintbrâwe* eye-lash, Du. *wenkbraauw* eye-brow, all of which belong to OTeut. **brǣwâ-*, WGer. *brâw*, OE. *brǣw*; see BREE. (It appears then that the Eng. *brow* and Ger. *braue*, Du. *braauw* are not even cognate.)]
†**1.** The fringe of hair along the eye-lid, the eye-lash, L. *cilium.* Only in OE.
a **1000** *Riddles* xli. 100 (Gr.) Ne ic breaga ne bruna brucan moste. *c* **1000** ÆLFRIC *Voc.* in Wr.-Wülcker 156 *Cilia*, brua. *Ibid.* 290 Cilium, bruwa.
†**2.** The eye-lid, L. *palpebra.* Usually *pl. Obs.* (Some of the quotations are not certain.)
c **1200** *Trin. Coll. Hom.* 213 At drinche.. þere beð.. winrede bruwes. *c* **1205** LAY. 22283 [Hi] heouen up heore bruwen. *c* **1275** —— 18374 þa heng he his brouwes [*c* **1205** breowen] adun. *a* **1300** *E.E. Psalter* x[i]. 5 His brwes [*palpebræ*] askes mennes sones. *Ibid.* cxxxi[i]. 4 If I gif to min eghen slaping, And to mi browes [*palpebris*] napping. **1340** HAMPOLE *Pr. Consc.* 817 His browes heldes doun wyth-alle. *a* **1500** *Med. Receipts* in *Rel. Ant.* I. 54 Qwen his broues hildes doune.
3. a. 'The arch of hair over the eye' (J.). Usually *pl.* In later use including the super-orbital ridge, and especially the skin, on which the hair grows. Now usually EYE-BROW. ***to knit, bend one's brows***: to frown.
[*c* **1000** ÆLFRIC *Voc.* in Wr.-Wülcker 156 *Supercilia*, oferbrua. —— *Ags. Voc.* ibid. 290 *Intercilium* [cf. Gr. μεσόφρυον] betweoh bruwum.] *a* **1300** *Cursor M.* 8079 Lang and side þair brues wern And hinged all a-bout þair hern. **1398** TREVISA *Barth. De P.R.* v. ix. (1495) 114 The browes ben callyd supercilia the ouer lyddes for they ben sette aboue the eye lyddes.. The browes ben closyd with moche heere. *c* **1400** *Ywaine & Gaw.* 261 His browes was like litel buskes. **1575** J. STILL *Gamm. Gurton* v. ii, I am as true.. as skin betwene thy browes. **1593** SHAKS. *2 Hen. VI*, I. ii. 3 Why doth the Great Duke Humfrey knit his browes? **1601** CORNWALLYES *Ess.* xx, We will pull our browes, and indure any paine to imitate the fashion. **1619** R. WEST *Bk. Demeanor* 29 in *Babees Bk.* 292 Let not thy browes be backward drawn, it is a signe of pride, Exalt them not, it shewes a hart most arrogant beside. **1715** POPE *Ep. Miss T. Blount* 49 Vex'd to be still in town, I knit my brow. **1830** TENNYSON *Madeline* iii, O'er black brows drops down A sudden-curved frown. **1832** —— *Œnone* 74 The charm of married brows.
b. In the same sense as 5 b.
a **1300** *Cursor M.* 14747 To blaken þan bigan þair brous [*v.r.* bruus, brewes]. [See BLACK *v.* 1 for other instances.]
4. a. *pl.* The prominences of the forehead on either side above the eyes. Now poetically = next sense.
1588 SHAKS. *L.L.L.* v. i. 392 Helpe! hold his browes. **1601** —— *Jul. C.* v. iii. 82 Did not they Put on my Browes this wreath of Victorie? **1697** DRYDEN *Virg. Eclog.* VI. 35 Ægle.. His Brows with Berries, and his Temples dies. *a* **1725** POPE *Iliad* XI. 53 Last o'er his brows his fourfold helm he placed. **1822** W. IRVING *Braceb. Hall* xxvi. 235 The officer.. placed it [a wreath] upon the blushing brows of his mistress. **1850** TENNYSON *In Mem.* lxxxvi. 8 Fan my brows and blow The fever from my cheek.
fig. **1595** SHAKS. *John* II. i. 38 Our Cannon shall be bent Against the browes of this resisting towne.
†**b.** ? Part of a wig covering the brows. *Obs.*
c **1485** *Digby Myst.*, *Mor. Wisd.* i. *heading*, Vpon his hed a cheveler with browes.
5. a. The whole part of the face above the eyes, the forehead. (L. *frons.*)
1535 STEWART *Cron. Scot.* II. 289 With mony wound.. In breist, in brow, in bak. **1592** SHAKS. *Ven. & Ad.* 339 She kissed his brow, his cheek, his chin. **1611** BIBLE *Isa.* xlviii. 4 Thy necke is an yron sinew, and thy brow brasse. **1742** POPE *Dunciad* IV. 141 His beaver'd brow a birchen garland wears. **1789** BURNS *John Anderson* i, Your bonie brow was brent. **1872** RUSKIN *Eagle's N.* §156 The essential point in an eagle's head—the projection of the brow. **1878** B. TAYLOR *Deukalion* I. i. 21 And strong, though troubled, is her breadth of brow.
fig. **1595** SHAKS. *John* v. vi. 17 Heere walke I, in the black brow of night. **1865** GOSSE *Land & Sea* (1874) 185 The sky has settled down again in frowning gloom. A black and threatening brow it wears.
b. *esp.* as the seat of the facial expressions of joy, sorrow, shame, anxiety, resolution, etc. *poetic.*
1593 SHAKS. *Lucr.* 749 To cloak offences with a cunning brow. **1596** —— *Merch. V.* III. ii. 78 What damned error, but some sober brow will blesse it. **1667** MILTON *P.L.* IV. 886 To whom thus Satan with contemptuous brow. **1764** GOLDSM. *Trav.* 315 War in each breast, and freedom on each brow. **1802** WORDSW. *Sonn. T. l'Ouverture*, Wear rather in thy bonds a cheerful brow. **1807** CRABBE *Par. Reg.* II. 178 Joy like thy bride's, should on thy brow have sate. **1817** BYRON *Manf.* II. ii. 25 Thy calm clear brow Wherein is glass'd serenity of soul. **1843** MACAULAY *Virginia* 17 That brow of hate, that mouth of scorn.
c. *fig.* Fronting aspect, countenance. Cf. *forehead, front, face.*
1596 SHAKS. *1 Hen. IV*, IV. iii. 83 By this Face, This seeming Brow of Iustice did he winne the hearts of all. **1646** BUCK *Rich. III*, 78 His patience is deepe hypocrisie.. and his friendship meerely a Court brow. **1694** STRYPE *Cranmer* III. viii. 330 A Book writ with a Brow of Brass, so did it abound with confident Untruths. **1818** SCOTT *Hrt. Midl.* x, The old man, who had in his early youth resisted the brow of military and civil tyranny.
†**d.** *fig.* An unabashed brow; confidence, effrontery; cf. 'cheek', 'face' in slang use. *Obs.*
1642 FULLER *Holy & Prof. St.* IV. xi. 290 Men of more brow then brain. *a* **1646** J. GREGORY *Posthuma* (1649) 88 Learned men I confess, but of a strange brow, to pretend, etc. **1680** BURNET *Rochester* 172 But they have not Brow enough to say it. **1720** OZELL *Vertot's Rom. Rep.* I. II. 137 With what Brow can I.. ask him?
†**e.** Specious look or appearance. *Obs.*
1659 J. HARRINGTON *Lawgiving* III. iii. (1700) 454 Whether the threaten'd Punishments.. tho thro unacquaintance they may at first sight have som brow, would not.. expire in scorn.
f. Sc. ***to have no brow*** (***broo***) ***of***: not to like the look of, not to be favourably impressed by.
1816 SCOTT *Old Mort.* vii, 'Thir ridings and wappen-schawings.. I hae nae broo o' them ava—I can find nae warrant for them.' **1818** —— *Hrt. Midl.* xxv, 'I had never muckle broo o' my gudeman's gossips.' **1823** GALT *Entail* III. iii. 41 I hae nae brow o' sic worldly hypocrisy. **1887** *Chr. Leader* 24 Feb. 114/3 'Man', said the fisherman, 'I hae nae brew o' thae English banks ava.'
g. [= the second element in HIGHBROW, LOW-BROW, etc.] *colloq.* Level of intellectual attainment or interest. Also *attrib.*
1923 J. AGATE in *Sunday Times* 9 Sept. 4/2 There is nothing quite so abysmally boring in the theatre as your author who has got no brow at all. **1931** H. G. WELLS *Work, Wealth & Happiness* (1932) 20 That final title.. had to present a candid attractive brow to the world, broad rather than high. **1954** F. CORNFORD *Epitaph for Reviewer* in *Coll. Poems* 112, I hope to meet my Maker brow to brow And find my own the higher. **1959** *Guardian* 19 Dec. 4/4 The only differences worth noting among playwrights are their brow-levels.
6. a. The projecting edge of a cliff or hill, standing over a precipice or steep. (Arising out of sense 3: though now sometimes associated with sense 5.)
c **1435** *Torr. Portugal* 655 Bacward than be a browȝ, Twenty fote he garde hyme goo. **1604** SHAKS. *Oth.* II. i. 53 On the brow o' th' Sea Stand rankes of People. **1611** BIBLE *Luke* iv. 29, & led him vnto the brow [*marg.* edge] of the hill.. that they might cast him downe headlong. **1697** DRYDEN *Virg. Georg.* I. 159 The wary Ploughman, on the Mountain's Brow, Undams his watry Stores. *a* **1725** POPE *Odyss.* v. 614 The Wood, Whose shady horrors on a rising brow Wav'd high. **1795** SOUTHEY *Joan of Arc.* I. 286 If a traveller Appear'd at distance coming o'er the brow. **1872** JENKINSON *Guide Eng. Lakes* (1879) 200 The path.. runs along the brow of the cliff to the summit.
b. *north. dial.* A slope, an acclivity, an ascent; = Sc. *brae.* E.g. *Everton Brow, Shaw's Brow*, two steep streets in Liverpool.
1863 KINGSLEY *Water-Bab.* 38 He scrambled up.. a sandy brow.
†**7.** A projecting edge (of a pillar, wall, etc.); a ledge; a verge. ? *Obs.*
1601 HOLLAND *Pliny* II. 595 The brows of pillars and wals, to cast off rain. **1641** MILTON *Reform. in Eng.* I. Wks. 1847 6/1 The Table of Communion, now become a Table of Separation, stands like an exalted platform upon the brow of the Quire, fortify'd with bulwark and barricado.

8. *Coal-Mining.* A gallery in a coal-mine running accross the face of the coal.

9. *ellipt.* Brow-antler (see next).

1863 KINGSLEY *Water-Bab.* ii. 62 You may know.. what his rights mean, if he has them, brow, bay, tray and points.

10. *Comb.*, as ***brow-bone***, ***-pendant***; ***brow-bound***, ***-sick***, ***-wreathed*** adjs. etc.; **brow-ague**, 'strictly supra-orbital neuralgia of malarious origin; now used as synonymous with *Hemicrania* or *Megrim*' (*Syd. Soc. Lex.*); **brow-antler**, the lowest tine of the horn of a stag, the 'antler' in its original sense; **brow-band**, a band worn across the brow; *spec.* the band of a bridle, etc., which passes in front of a horse's forehead; †**brow-bending**, frowning; **brow-bent** *a.*, with bent brows, frowning (see 3); †**brow-lid**, an eye-lid; †**brow-piece** (*Arch.*), a beam over a door, a breastsummer; **brow-point**, = *brow-antler*; **brow-post** (*Arch.*), see quot.; **brow-ridge**, a superciliary ridge; **brow-snag**, **-tine** = *brow-antler*; **brow-spot**, the interocular gland of a frog or toad; **brow-stone** (cf. *brow-post*). See also BROWBEAT, etc.

1855 HOLDEN *Hum. Osteol* (1878) 65 It is this nerve which is affected in '*brow ague'. **1647** W. BROWNE *Polex.* I. 239 With two thrusts of his *brow-anclers, he was layd flat on the sand. **1596** COLSE *Penelope* (1880) 169 Brow-antlers with her Ile exchange. **1610** GUILLIM *Heraldry* III. xiv. (1660) 168 Skilfull Woodmen.. do call the Lowest Antlier the Brow Antelier. **1864** *Derby Mercury* 14 Dec., Curious articles made from the brow antler of a stag's horn. **1844** H. STEPHENS *Bk. Farm* I. 620 Brass or plated buckles and *brow-bands.. serve only to load and cover the horses when at work. **1958** J. HISLOP *From Start to Finish* 167 *Browband*: Usually called forehead-piece in racing stables; the piece of the bridle which goes round the horse's forehead, below the ears. **1542** UDALL *Erasm. Apoph.* 17b, With matrimonie commeth.. the soure *browbendyng of your wiffes kinsfolkes. **1796** COLERIDGE *To Yng. Friend* 28 His muse's witching charm Muttering *brow-bent. *c* **1450** *Voc.* in Wr.-Wülcker 675 *Hoc supercilium*, a *browbone. **1607** SHAKS. *Cor.* II. ii. 102 He.. for his meed Was *Brow-bound with the Oake. **1832** TENNYSON *Dream Fair Wom.* 128 A queen.. Brow-bound with burning gold. **1594** T. B. *La Primaud. Fr. Acad.* II. 77 One eyelid or *browlidde. **1611** COTGR., *Contrefrontail*, the *brow-peece, or vpmost post of a dore. **1877** A. B. EDWARDS *Up Nile* xix. 545 The bride.. wears a gold *brow-pendant and nose-ring. **1884** JEFFERIES *Red Deer* iv. 75 The stag.. with a blow of the formidable *brow-point, ripped the hound open. **1706** PHILLIPS, **Brow-post*, (among Carpenters) an over-thwart, or cross-Beam. **1898** *Guide Mammalia Brit. Mus.* 15 Enormous *brow-ridges give them a ferocious and savage appearance. **1927** PEAKE & FLEURE *Hunters & Artists* 60 The great frontal torus or overgrown brow-ridges of Neanderthal Man. **1964** G. B. SCHALLER *Year of Gorilla* (1965) vi. 135 The gorillas.. looked thoroughly miserable with the water dripping off their brow ridges. *a* **1641** SUCKLING *Prol. Authors* (R.) A gracious influence from you May alter nature in our *brow-sick crew. **1875** HUXLEY & MARTIN *Elem. Biol.* xiii. 187 The *browspot or inter-ocular gland. **1761** *Lond. Mag.* XXX. 17 The laying of the kennels without *brow-stones. **1880** *Geol. Mag.* 450 Distinguished.. by the presence of a *brow-tyne close to the burr.

brow (braʊ), *sb.*[2] *Naut.* [app. a. Da. or Sw. *bru*, ON. *brú* bridge.] (See quot.)

1867 SMYTH *Sailor's Wd.-bk.*, *Brow*, an inclined plane of planks, on one or both sides of a ship, to communicate internally; a stage-gangway for the accomodation of the shipwrights, in conveying plank, timber, and weighty articles on board... An old term for a gang-board. **1875** BEDFORD *Sailor's Pocket-bk.* vii. (ed. 2) 272 Plank.. to form a brow to the shore. **1882** *Standard* 20 Oct. 6/1 The horses were.. walked from deck to deck by 'brows'.. and from the deck to the wharf down a third 'brow'.

brow, *v. rare.* [f. BROW *sb.*[1]]

1. *trans.* To form a brow to, be on the brow of.

1634 MILTON *Comus* 532 The hilly crofts That brow this bottom glade. **1797** MRS. RADCLIFFE *Italian* xxii, The woods that browed the hill. **1834** J. HODGSON in J. Raine *Mem.* (1858) II. 357 Browed and hemmed with old brushwood and young plantations.

2. To face, browbeat. *Sc.*

1822 HOGG *Perils of Man* I. 21 (JAM.) I wad rather brow a' the Ha's and the Howards afore I beardit you. *Ibid.* 61 Stepping forward and browing the last speaker face to face.

brow, obs. f. of BREW.

Browallia (brəʊˈwɒlɪə). *Bot.* [Named by Linnæus after J. *Browall* (1707–55), Swedish botanist.] A plant of the genus of South American annual plants so named, bearing violet, blue, or white flowers.

1782 ABERCROMBIE *Ev. Man his own Gardener* 84 Tender Annual Flowers. The choicest kinds are.. browallia, &c. **1866** LINDLEY & MOORE *Treas. Bot.* 172/2 *Browallia*, the name of certain plants belonging to the order of linariads. **1960** *Farmer & Stockbreeder* 29 Mar. (Suppl.) 6/2 The little blue-flowered browallia with its glossy leaves.

browbeat (ˈbraʊbiːt), *v.* Pa. t. browbeat, Pa. pple. browbeaten (browbeat *obs.*). [f. BROW *sb.*[1] + BEAT *v.*; it appears from the earlier quotations (see esp. BROWBEATING *vbl. sb.*), that the *brow* in question was that of the beater, not of the beaten party; but it is not evident whether the meaning was 'to beat with one's (frowning) brows', or 'to beat (? lower) one's brows at'. Connexion with *beetle-browed* is suggested.]

1. *trans.* To bear down, discourage, or oppose, with stern, arrogant, or insolent looks or words; to snub, to bully; 'to depress with severe brows, and stern or lofty looks' (J.).

1581 [see BROWBEATING *vbl. sb.*] **1603** HOLLAND *Plutarch's Mor.* 129 We must entertaine our friends and guests, with courtesie.. and not to brow-beat them. **1662** PETTY *Taxes* 54 To be but brow-beaten by a prince or a grandee. **1706** PHILLIPS, *Brow-beat*, to look upon haughtily, or disdainfully, to snub, or keep under. **1743** FIELDING *Journey* I. xv, He browbeat the informers against us, and treated their evidence with.. little favour. **1803** JANE PORTER *Thaddeus* xxxvi. (1831) 327, I will not be browbeat and insulted. **1848** MACAULAY *Hist. Eng.* I. 663 The bar and the bench united to browbeat the unfortunate Whig. **1879** FROUDE *Cæsar* ix. 101 He was brow-beaten and threatened with violence.

b. *absol.*

1870 L'ESTRANGE *Miss Mitford* I. vi. 210 The well-fee'd lawyers have ceased to browbeat or to cajole.

2. *fig.* To present a threatening aspect to.

1860 WOOD in S. E. Dawson *Handbk. Canada* 266 One tremendous cliff.. more than 1500 feet high, and inclined forward nearly 200 feet, brow-beating all beneath it.

3. *humorously.* To beat with the brow.

1830 TENNYSON *Sonn. to J. M. K.*, While the worn-out clerk Browbeats his desk below.

browbeaten (ˈbraʊˌbiːt(ə)n), *ppl. a.* Borne down with arrogant looks; snubbed, bullied.

1747 HORSLEY *Fool* lxxii. (1748) II. 155 The browbeaten Fool.

browbeater (ˈbraʊˌbiːtə(r)). [f. BROWBEAT + -ER[1].] One who browbeats.

1670 W. SIMPSON *Hydrol. Ess.* To Rdr. 11 A magisterial browbeater. **1823** LAMB *Elia* (1860) 138 The scarecrow of his inferiors, the brow-beater of equals and superiors.

browbeating (ˈbraʊˌbiːtɪŋ), *vbl. sb.* [f. as prec. + -ING[1].] The action of the verb BROWBEAT; orig., it appears, = 'scowling, frowning'.

1581 J. BELL *Haddon's Answ. Osor.* 486b, To be afrayd of any her subjects lowring or browbeating. **1693** LOCKE *Educ.* 42 Constant Rebukes and Brow-beatings. **1765** TUCKER *Lt. Nat.* II. 611 The discouragements and browbeating of censorious.. persons. **1817** JAS. MILL *Brit. India* III. ii. 68 The brow-beating of a witness.

ˈ**browbeating**, *ppl. a.* [f. as prec. + -ING[2].] That browbeats; bullying, insolent.

1816 *Remarks Eng. Manners* 63 Browbeating insolence. **1864** MAX MÜLLER *Chips* (1880) I. vii. 147 A cross-examination by a brow-beating lawyer.

browch, obs. Sc. form of BURGH.

1566 KNOX *Hist. Ref.* Wks. 1846 I. 431 To command free Browchis to cheise Provestis and officiaris of our nameing.

browche, obs. form of BROOCH.

†**browd**, *v. Obs.* Also broud. [a. OF. *brouder*, *broder* to stitch, embroider; but, from the beginning, its pa. pple. *brouded*, *browded*, was evidently associated with the native BROWDEN, pa. pple. of BRAID *v.*, owing to contiguity of form and meaning. Cf. BRAWDE, BROID, BROIDER.

Fr. *broder* is a Common Romanic vb., Pr. *broydar*, Sp. *bordar* to embroider.]

1. *trans.* To broider, embroider. Hence ˈ**browded** *ppl. a.*

c **1385** CHAUCER *L.G.W.* 227 Silk I broudede ful of grene grevys. *c* **1386** —— *Monkes T.* 479 Alle hise clothes brouded [*v.r.* browded] vp & doun. **1430** LYDG. *Chron. Troy* I. ix, Eueryche his armes.. Brouded or bete vpon his coote armure. **1493–1503** *Ledger of A. Haliburton* in Cosmo Innes *Scotl. Mid. Ages* viii. (1860) 246 Packit in his kist at Bruges .. two pound of silk to browd with.

2. To plait, 'braid'. (Cf. next and BROIDEN.)

1386 CHAUCER *Knts. T.* 191 (Harl. MS.) Here ȝolwe heer was browdid in a tresse [*v.r.* 4 *MSS.* broyded, 1 breided, *Lansd.* browded].

†ˈ**browden**, *pa. pple. Obs.* Forms: 1 (ȝe-)broȝden, -broden, 4–7 browden, 4 broud, (4–5 browdyn, 5–6 -in, 6 broudin); 4–5 brawden, brauden. (Also 4–5 broiden, broydyn.) [OE. *broȝden*, *bróden*, pa. pple. of *breȝdan*, *brédan* to BRAID. In use almost exclusively northern. The *ow* forms are regular from **oȝ*; the *aw*, *au* forms are perhaps dial. variants of these; for the difficult *oy*, *oi* forms see BROIDEN.]

1. Twisted, plaited; intertwined, interwoven, formed of network; woven.

a **1000** *Elene* 257 (Gr.) Ðær wæs on eorle.. broȝden byrne. *c* **1325** *E.E. Allit. P.* B. 1132 Bryȝter þen þe beryl oþer browden perles. *c* **1340** *Gaw. & Gr. Knt.* 580 þe brawden bryne of bryȝt stel-ryngez. ? *a* **1400** *Morte Arth.* 1858 Thurghe brenys browdene. *a* **1400** *Cursor M.* 28016 (Cotton Galba) With bendes broud [*Cott.* broiden] and colers wide. [*c* **1440** *Promp. Parv.* 53/1 Broydyn, (**1499** broyded) *laqueatus*.]

2. (= BROWDED.) Embroidered: perh. in later usage 'emblazoned in colours'.

1375 BARBOUR *Bruce* XI. 464 Thai saw so fele browdyn baneris. *c* **1425** WYNTOUN *Cron.* VII. viii. 446 Sandalys Browdyn welle on kyngis wys. **1459** *Inv.* in *Paston Lett.* I. 477 J pece of rede satyne, brauden with *Me fauntfere.* *a* **1500** *Inv. Jewels* in Tytler *Hist. Scot.* (1864) II. 393 A covering.. browdin with thrissillis and a unicorne. **1535** STEWART *Cron. Scot.* II. 604 The baneris browdin brycht.

b. Dyed, stained.

a **1550** *Christis Kirke Gr.* xviii, His body wes with blud all browdin. **1535** STEWART *Cron. Scot.* I. 109 Blawdit and browdin in thair husbandis blude.

3. Enamoured, fond. [Perh. a distinct word, though capable of being connected with other senses, e.g. 'netted': cf. sense 1, quot. 1440.]

1597 MONTGOMERIE *Cherrie & Slae* 170 Sa was I browdin in my bow. *c* **1600** '*Lyk as Aglauros*' 24 He beheld me broudin on the bait. **1637** RUTHERFORD *Lett.* lxxvii. (1862) I. 198 We are fools to be browden and fond of a pawn in the loof of our hand. **1697** *Praise Yorkshire Ale* (JAM.) To be browden on a thing. *a* **1758** RAMSAY *Poems* (1800) I. 331 (JAM.) Less browden still on cash than verse.

browder, -re, obs. forms of BROIDER *v.*

†ˈ**browding**, *vbl. sb. Obs.* [f. BROWD *v.*] Embroidery.

c **1386** CHAUCER *Knt's. T.* 1640 So riche wrought.. Of gold-smithry, of browdying [*v.r.* broudynge], and of steel.

†ˈ**browdinster.** *Sc. Obs.* Also brodinster. = next. Hence ˈ**browdinsterschip**.

1561 *Invent. Roy Wardr.* (1815) 150 (JAM.) The browdinstaris that wrocht upoun the tapestrie. **1578** *Ibid.* 140 (JAM.) The brodinsters, quha wrocht upoun the great pece of broderie. **1592** *Act Jas. VI* (1814) 608 (JAM.) Confirmis the office of browdinsterschip.. to the said Williame.

†ˈ**browdster.** *Obs.* [f. BROWD *v.* + -STER.] An embroiderer.

1450 etc. [see BRAWDSTER]. **1530** *Lord Treas. Acc. Jas. V.* in *Chambers Jrnl.* (1833) 165 Item given John Young brodistar for stufe and broidering of sixty four pece of Crownis, James, and Thressilis. *c* **1565** LINDESAY (Pitscottie) *Chron. Scot.* 153 (JAM.) Some were.. harness-makers, tapesters, broudsters, taylors.

browe, obs. pa. t. and pple. of BREW.

browed (braʊd), *a.* [f. BROW *sb.*[1] + -ED[2].] Having a brow or brows. Chiefly in comb., as ***dark-browed***, ***low-browed***, etc.

c **1460** *Towneley Myst.* 100 She is browyd lyke a brystylle. **1483** CAXTON *Gold. Leg.* 339/2 This ymage.. was well eyed, well browed. **1526** SKELTON *Magnyf.* 1261 He frowneth fyersly, brymly browyd. **1742** R. BLAIR *Grave* 17 Low-brow'd misty vaults. **1796** SCOTT *Wild Huntsm.*, My dark-browed friend. **1888** 'L. MALET' *Counsel of Perfection* x. 233 The tall, browed, black figure in the doorway. **1899** A. WERNER *Capt. Locusts* 98 Heavily browed eyes.

browen, -in, browne, obs. pa. pples. of BREW.

browen, obs. pl. of BROW.

†**brower.** *Obs. rare*[−1]. app.: A napkin.

c **1450** *Bk. Curtasye* 663 in *Babees Bk.* (1868) 321 Browers he schalle cast þer-opon, þat þe lorde schulle clense his fyngers [on]; þe leuedy and whoseuer syttes with-inne, Alle browers schynne haue bothe more and myn.

browere, -ern: see BREWERN *Obs.*, brewhouse.

browes, -esse, obs. ff. BREWIS, BROSE.

browest, obs. form of BROWST.

†ˈ**browet.** *Obs.* Also 4–6 bruet, brewet(t. [a. F. *brouet*, *broet* (13th c. in Littré) soup made of flesh-broth, dim. of OF. *breu*, earlier *bro* (= Pr. *bro*, Sp. *brodio*, It. *brodo*, *broda*, med.L. *brodium*, *brodum*), late L. (**brodum*) or Romanic (*brodo*), ad. OHG. *brod* BROTH. The OF. nominative *brouetz*, *broez*, gave BROWIS.]

Soup or broth of the juice of boiled meat, with various thickening ingredients.

1399 LANGL. *Rich. Redeless* II. 51 ȝoure side signes, þat shente all þe browet. *c* **1420** *Liber Cocorum* (1862) 22 þese er hennes in browet. *c* **1420** *Voc.* in Wr.-Wülcker 661 *Hic garrus*, brewett. *c* **1440** *Promp. Parv.* 54 Browett, *brodiellum*. *c* **1440** *Anc. Cookery* in *Househ. Ord.* (1790) 430 Blaunche Bruet of Almayn. *c* **1460** *Towneley Myst.* 43 And broght me bruet of dere. **1495** CAXTON *Vitas Patr.* (W. de W.) I. xiii. 18a/1 He ne dranke but a lytyll browet made with meele. *a* **1500** *MS. 15th C.* in *Promp. Parv.* 54 Bruet seec, bruet salmene, and bruet sarazineys blanc.

browgh, -t, obs. Sc. form of BURGH.

browhern, var. of BREWERN, *Obs.*, brewhouse.

†**browis** (ˈbraʊɪs). *Obs.* or *dial.* Forms: 3 broys, 4 brouwys, 5 browyce, 5–6 browes, 5–7 -esse, 7– browis; see also BREWIS, BROSE. [ME. *broys*, *browes*, a. OF. *broez*, *brouetz*, nom. of *broet*, *brouet*, BROWET. Of this word *browet* is an original doublet, and *brewis*, *brose*, later variants.]

†1. = BREWIS, in both senses.

a **1300** *Havelok* 924 Make þe broys in þe led. *c* **1325** *Coer de L.* 3077 Soupyd off the brouwys a sope. *c* **1430** LYDG. *Order of Fooles* Min. Poems 165 Tendre browyce made with a mary-boon. *c* **1440** *Promp. Parv.* 53 Browesse [*v.r.* browes], *adipatum*. *c* **1450** *Knt. de la Tour* (1868) 8 She come into the warderobe to ete browesse. **1513** W. DE WORDE *Bk. Keruynge* in *Babees Bk.* (1868) 274 Potage, as wortes, Iowtes, or browes. **1562** J. HEYWOOD *Prov. & Epigr.* (1867) 72, I will eate no browesse sops. **1601** HOLLAND *Pliny* XIX. viii, A kinde of broth or browesse. **1658** R. FRANCK *North. Mem.* (1821) 209 When they kill a beast.. make a caldron of his skin, browis of his bowels.

2. A kind of BROSE; as the *browis* of the Sheffield Cutlers' Feast, a dish made by pouring

boiling water upon oat-cakes mixed with dripping, and seasoned with pepper, salt, and butter.

1839 A. BYWATER *Sheffield Dial.* (1877) 32 Nettle porridge an' brawis. **1880** *Sheff. Independent* 3 Sept., Returning to their hall, the members of the Company partook of 'browis'—a cunningly devised broth without which the installation [of the Master Cutler] would not be complete.

'browless, *a.* [f. BROW *sb.*[1] 5.] †**1.** Without shame, unabashed. Cf. *frontless. Obs.*

1615 W. HULL *Mirr. Maiestie* 81 Therefore they despite him with all illusory gestures of browlesse scorners. **1679** L. ADDISON *Life Mahomet* 84 (L.), So browless was this heretick, that he was not ashamed to tell the world, etc. *a* **1821** KEATS *Sonn. Haydon*, When men star'd at what was most divine with browless idiotism.

2. Without eyebrows.

1823 *New Monthly Mag.* VIII. 531 A composition which ..utterly destroyed the hair, and left him literally browless! **1905** E. PHILLPOTTS *Secret Woman* II. ix. 179 Browless eyes. **1906** B'NESS VON HUTTEN *What became of Pam* I. iv, The large..eyes,..so almost browless and lashless.

brown (braʊn), *a.* Forms: 1 brún, 3 brun(e, 3–4 broun, 3–6 broune, 4–7 browne, (5 browyn), 5– brown. [Common Teut.: OE. *brún* = OFris. *brûn* (MDu. *bruun*, Du. *bruin*), OHG. (MHG., MLG.) *brûn*, (mod.Ger. *braun*), ON. *brún-n* (Sw. *brun*, Da. *bruun*):—OTeut. **brûn-o-z*, **brûn-â*, corresp. to Lith. *brunas* brown:—Aryan type **bhrû-'no -s*, root **bhru-*: cf. BEAVER. Adopted in Romanic, giving med.L. *brūnus*, It., Sp., Pg. *bruno*, Pr. and F. *brun*, whence also *brunir* to BURNISH, q.v. (OHG. *brûn* meant 'glänzend' shining, as well as 'dunkel-farbig' dark-coloured.)

The shade to which the name was given was originally a dark one, as seen by sense 1; also by Johnson's sole explanation 'The name of a colour, compounded of black and any other colour'. Levins *Manip.* 1570 has 'Broune, black, *ater*; Broune *fuscus*'. *Very dark* brown is close to black, as in the so-called 'black' hair of men.]

1. a. Dusky, dark. (Now only poetic, and regarded as transf. from sense 2.)

a **1000** *Metr. Boeth.* xxvi. 58 Sio brune yð. *c* **1325** *E.E. Allit. P.* A. 536 Sone þe worlde bycom wel broun, þe sunne watz doun. *c* **1400** MAUNDEV. 160 Here colour is liche Vyolet, or more browne than the Violettes. *c* **1449** *Pol. Poems* (1859) II. 221 Oure welevette hatte, That keueryd us from mony stormys browne. **1667** MILTON *P.L.* IX. 1088 Where highest Woods..spread thir umbrage broad, And brown as Evening. *a* **1725** POPE *Odyss.* XVII. 215 Or ere brown evening spreads her chilly shade. **1792** S. ROGERS *Pleas. Mem.* I. 15 Arched with ivy's brownest shade. **1854** TENNYSON *To Maurice* iv, I watch the twilight falling brown.

b. *fig.* Gloomy, serious. See BROWN STUDY.

2. a. The proper name of a composite colour produced by a mixture of orange and black (or of red, yellow, and black), and varying greatly in shade according to the proportion of the constituents, as a red brown, yellowish brown, dark brown. Brown is the colour produced by partial charring or carbonization of starch or woody fibre, as in toasted bread or potatoes, peat, lignite, withered leaves, etc.

a **1300** *Cursor M.* 18833 His hare [was] like to þe nute brun, Quen it for ripnes fals dun. **1393** LANGL. *P. Pl. C.* IX. 330 Ale..of þe best and Brounest þat brewesters sellen. *c* **1420** *Liber Cocorum* (1862) 32 Lay hur [the gose] to fyre and rost hyr browne. *c* **1440** *Promp. Parv.* 54 Browne, *fuscus, subniger, nigellus.* **1600** SHAKS. *A.Y.L.* III. iv. 9 *Ros.* His very haire Is of the dissembling colour. *Cel.* Something browner then Iudasses. **1725** *Lond. Gaz.* No. 6381/4 With a good Stock of Pale and Brown Beer. **1708** MRS. CENTLIVRE *Busie Body* I. i. 13 My last Refuge, a brown Musquet. **1766** PENNANT *Zool.* (1768) I. 457 The head and whole upper part [of the female sparrow] are brown. **1799** SOUTHEY *Nondescr., Snuff*, Black, brown dust, From the oft reiterated pinch profuse. **1805** SCOTT *Last Minstr.* VI. ii, Land of brown heath and shaggy wood. **1859** JEPHSON *Brittany* i. 2 The brown rocky stream.

b. Used in naming varieties or species of animals, plants, minerals, etc., as *brown ant, bear, owl*; *brown willow*; *brown hæmatite*, etc.

c **1460** J. RUSSELL *Bk. Nurture* in *Babees Bk.* (1868) 183 The makyng of a bathe medicinable..Brown fenelle. **1767** G. WHITE *Selborne* xi. (1789) 31 The young of the brown owl will eat indiscriminately all that is brought. **1843** PORTLOCK *Geol.* 225 Earthy Brown Hæmatite, both compact and decomposed. **1861** MISS PRATT *Flower. Pl.* VI. 69 Brown Bent-grass. **1868** WOOD *Homes without H.* vii. 126 The most admirable subterranean architecture is perhaps that of the Brown Ant. **1882** *Garden* 28 Jan. 62/3 Lettuces ..the best of all for winter, the old Brown Cos. **1884** *St. James's Gaz.* 7 Aug. 4/2 On some estates in Scotland..a brown hare is now rarely seen.

3. Of persons: Having the skin of a brown or dusky colour: **a.** as a racial characteristic; **b.** as an individual peculiarity among 'white' races; either natural (dark-complexioned, brunette), or as an effect of exposure (sunburnt, tanned).

a **1000** *Cædmon's Ex.* 70 (Bosw.) Brune leode. *c* **1384** CHAUCER *H. Fame* 139 Vulcano That in his face was ful broune. **1398** TREVISA *Barth. De P.R.* IV. ii. (1495) 80 In hoote countrees comen forth blacke men and broun. *c* **1420** *Chron. Vilod.* 505 Þaw þ[u] be broune þ[u] art ryȝt welle shape and fere. **1589** WARNER *Alb. Eng.* V. xxvi. 127 That browne Girle of mine. **1613** SHAKS. *Hen. VIII*, III. ii. 295 When the browne Wench Lay kissing in your Armes. *a* **1763** SHENSTONE *Odes* (1765) 226 Brown exercise will lead thee where she reigns. **1764** GOLDSM. *Trav.* 416 Where..the brown Indian marks with murd'rous aim. **1834** M. G. LEWIS *Jrnl. W. Ind.* 53 The fair sex elsewhere are called the 'Brown Girls' in Jamaica. **1864** TENNYSON *En. Ard.* 704 Enoch was so brown, so bow'd, So broken.

†**4.** In reference to the sword, steel, etc., it seems to have meant: Burnished, glistening. *Obs.* [With the sense cf. MDu. *brun* 'shining' (Kalkar), and F. *brunir* to BURNISH.]

c **1325** *E. E. Allit. P.* A. 989 Brende golde bryȝt, As glemande glas burnist broun. *c* **1380** *Sir Ferumb.* 5609 Wyþ ys swerd of style broun. *c* **1460** *Lybeaus Disc.* 552 Swordes bryght and broune. *a* **1802** *Ballad 'Cospatrick'* xxii. in Child *Ballads* I. 70/2 My bonny brown sword.

5. a. *to do brown*: perhaps, 'to do thoroughly', suggested by roasting; to deceive, 'take in'. *slang.*

a **1600** *John Bon* 162 in Hazl. *E.P.P.* IV. 16 Ha! browne done! **1837** DICKENS *Pickwick* xliii, 'He goes in raythen raw, Sammy', said Mr. Weller..'and he'll come out done so exceedin' brown that his most formiliar friends won't know him'. **1840** BARHAM *Ingol. Leg., Execution*, We are all of us done so uncommonly brown!

†**b.** Cf. *round. Obs.*

1611 CHAPMAN *May Daye* Plays 1873 II. 338 You haue a whole browne dozen a suters at least.

6. *Comb.* General relations: **a.** qualifying the names of other colours: as ***brown-bay, -black, -gold, -green, -pink, -red, -rosy***; **b.** parasynthetic, as ***brown-barrelled, -bearded, -coloured, -complexioned, -edged, -eyed, -faced, -haired, -headed, -leaved (-leafed), -locked, -roofed, -sailed, -skinned, -stemmed***; **c.** ***brown-wash*** v. (nonce-wd.).

1594 BLUNDEVIL *Exerc.* v. xii. (ed. 7) 558 The other nations under the hot Zone, be of colour *browne bay, like a Chesnut. **1753** *Scots Mag.* Aug. 421/1 Thomas Hall Esq.'s brown-bay gelding. **1882** J. HAWTHORNE *Fort. Fool* I. xi, One big *brown-bearded fellow. **1849** D. CAMPBELL *Inorg. Chem.* 246 The *brown-black bisulphide. **1942** S. SPENDER *Life & Poet* 28 The field is green in summer and brown-black in winter. **1835–6** TODD *Cycl. Anat. & Phys.* I. 41/1 *note*, Eight *brown-coloured masses. **1704** in *Lond. Gaz.* No. 4034/4 John Jackson..aged near 40, *brown Complectioned. **1824–30** MISS MITFORD *Village* Ser. IV. (1863) 314 Delf, blue and white, *brown-edged and green-edged. **1865** MISS YONGE *Clever Wom.* I. iii. 56 A brown-haired, *brown-eyed child of seven. **1909** *Daily Chron.* 7 May 4/4 The sun..glittered on her *brown-gold hair. **1882** *Garden* 10 June 400/1 The downy, *brown-green young shoots. **1686** *Lond. Gaz.* No. 2100/4 A tall slender Man, *brown hair'd. **1837** CARLYLE *Fr. Rev.* III. v. iv. 279 Church Formulas seemed to flourish; a little *brown-leaved or so, but not browner than of late years. **1855** J. EDWARDS *Paint. in Oil Colours* 27 *Brown Pink..is a rich transparent olive, inclining sometimes to green, and sometimes towards the warmth of orange. **1835** HAWTHORNE *Amer. Note-bks.* (1871) I. 14 Some of the oaks are now a deep *brown red. **1926** D. H. LAWRENCE *Sun* v. 19 Ripe now, and *brown-rosy all over with the sun. **1744** MITCHELL in *Phil. Trans.* XLIII. 112 Like the Skin of many *brown-skinn'd white People. **1904** E. F. BENSON *Challoners* viii. 162 Helen's soft brown-skinned hand. **1795** SOUTHEY *Lett. fr. Spain* (1799) 106 Rubbed over, or rather *brown-washed, with clay.

7. Special combs.: **brown ale** (see quot. 1969); **brown algæ**, the algæ of seaweeds constituting the class *Phæophyceæ*, which contain a brown colouring matter in addition to chlorophyll; **brown-back** *U.S.*, (*a*) the red-breasted snipe or dowitcher in summer plumage; (*b*) the great marbled godwit, *Limosa fedoa* (Cent. Dict., 1889); †**brown baker**, a baker of brown bread; **brown-banded snake** (see quots.); †**brown bastard**, a sweet wine (see BASTARD 4); **brown belt**, the belt worn by a student of judo or karate who has attained a certain grade, usu. that next below black belt; also, a person qualified to wear such a belt; **Brown Betty** chiefly *U.S.*, a baked pudding containing apples and breadcrumbs; **brown blaze** (see quot.); **brown coal**, a name given to lignite, and to some varieties of coal intermediate between lignite and true coal; **brown earth**, a type of soil developed in temperate humid regions under deciduous forests, having a brown surface-layer rich in humus; **brown-fly**, an artificial fly used in angling; **brown-footed rat** (see quot.); **brown gannet, brown gull**, names of the booby (*Sula fusca*); **brown goods**, electrical merchandise such as radios, televisions, and hi-fi units, conventionally housed in brown casings (as distinct from the white of washing machines, cookers, etc.: cf. *white goods* s.v. WHITE *a.* 11 e); **brown gum**, 'the inspissated juice of the *Eucalyptus resinifera*' (*Syd. Soc. Lex.*); **brown-heart**, (*a*) a species of tree in Guiana; (*b*) a disease of stored apples and pears characterized by internal brown decay; (*c*) a disease of turnips and related plants in which a deficiency of boron in the soil causes internal brown decay; **brown-hen**, the female of the Black Grouse (*Tetrao tetrix*); **brown-holland** (see HOLLAND[1]); **brown house** *U.S.* = *brown-stone* house; **brown job** *slang*, a soldier; also *collect.*, the Army; **brown jolly**, West-Indian corruption of BRINJAL; **brown moth**, an artificial fly used in angling by night; **brown mould**, *Mucor mucedo* and other fungi found on decaying fruit, etc.; **brown-nose** ['from the implication that servility is tantamount to having one's nose in the anus of the person from whom advancement is sought' (Webster 1961)], chiefly *U.S. slang*, a sycophant; hence as *v. trans.* and *intr.*, to curry favour (with), to flatter; so ***brown-noser***; **brown ochre**, a variety of limonite; also the pigment prepared from it; **brown rice**, unpolished rice, with only the husk of the grain removed; **brown rot**, any of various diseases of plants and trees characterized by browning and decay; **brown rust**, a disease of wheat caused by a parasitic fungus (*Trichobasis rubigo vera*); **brown sauce**, a brown-coloured savoury sauce, *esp.* one made with browned fat and flour; also *fig.*; **brown sherry**, sweet sherry; **Brown-shirt**, a Nazi; so called from the brown shirt worn as part of the uniform; so ***brown-shirted*** ppl. a.; **brown-sleeve** *a.*, wearing brown sleeves; **brown snake**, one of several poisonous Australian snakes of the genus *Pseudonaja* (formerly included in *Demansia*); **brown-spar** (*Min.*), a variety of dolomite; also applied to varieties of the allied minerals ankerite and magnesite, and to chalybite or native ferrous carbonate; **brown-stone**, (*a*) (see quot. 1875); (*b*) *U.S.*, one or other variety of a dark-brown sandstone used for building; also *ellipt.*, a house built of brown-stone, and *attrib.* and *transf.*, designating the well-to-do; **brown stout**, a superior kind of porter; **brown sugar**, unrefined or partially refined sugar as opposed to crystallized or loaf-sugar; **brown-tail(ed) (moth)** (see quots.); **brown-thrasher**, 'the (American) Ferruginous Thrush, called also the Brown Thrush, *Turdus rufus*' (Bartlett); **brown top**, any of various pasture grasses in Australia and New Zealand (see quots.); **brown tubes** *pl.* (see quot.); **brown ware**, a common kind of pottery. See also BROWN BESS, BROWN BREAD, BROWN GEORGE, BROWN PAPER, BROWN STUDY.

1776 W. REDDINGTON *Pract. Treat. Brewing* (ed. 3) xxxi. 59 *How common *brown Ale is to be yeasted.* I understand here such ale as is intended to be drank new and mixed with stale beer. **1842** S. BAMFORD *Passages in Life of Radical* II. xlvii. 239 Our weaver lads must put up..with jannocks and barley bread, and barm dumplings, and brown ale. **1969** *Beer & Cider* (Know the Drink) 32/1 *Brown Ale*, sometimes called 'Home-brewed'. Dark and usually rather sweet. It is the bottled equivalent of mild ale and is a good mixer with it. **1902** *Encycl. Brit.* XXV. 272/1 A white efflorescence which appears on certain *Brown Algæ..when they are dried in the air. **1844** J. E. DEKAY *Zool. N.Y.* II. 255 The Dowitchee..or *Brown-back. **1872** COUES *N. Amer. Birds* 252 *Macrorhamphus. Red-breasted Snipe.* Gray Snipe. Brown-back. **1893** *Outing* (U.S.) XXII. 96/2 'Brown-back' snipe. **1528** in Turner *Sel. Records Oxford* 58 Y[e] corporation of y[e] *browne bakers. **1656** J. REEVE *Let.* in *Spirit. Epistles* (1831) Suppl., In Trinity Lane, over against a Brown Bakers. **1720** *Stow's Surv.* (ed. Strype 1754) II. v. xiv. 312/2 The Company of the Brown bakers, a Society of long standing and continuance. **1869** KREFFT *Snakes Australia* 55 The large-scaled snake..is confounded, in Victoria in particular, with the Tiger or *Brown-banded Snake (*Hoplocephalus curtus*). **1887** *Encycl. Brit.* XXII. 197/1 The Brown-banded Snake (*Hoplocephalus curtus*), with a similar distribution [throughout Australia], and also common in Tasmania, from 5 to 6 feet long. **1603** SHAKS. *Meas. for M.* III. ii. 4 We shall haue all the world drinke *browne and white bastard. **1609** *Ev. Wom. in Hum.* I. i. in Bullen *O. Pl.* IV, A Figge for Browne-bastard. **1937** J. KANO *Judo (Jujutsu)* iii. 38 A *brown belt is used from the third Kyū grade to the first Kyū grade of the senior division (adults). **1939** T. S. KUWASHIMA *Judo* p. vii, In 1916 he came to the United States as an accredited representative to teach Judo, and to confer the varying degrees of Brown Belt and Black Belt, the belts representing the degree of skill attained by the student. **1968** *N.Y. Times* 1 Apr. 66 Winners in the form divisions were Toyotaro Miyazaki of Jackson Heights, Queens, black belt; Larry Pomilio of North Miami Beach, Fla., brown belt [etc.]. **1864** *Yale Lit. Mag.* XXIX. 187 (Th.), [In training,] tea, coffee, pies, and '*brown Betty' must next be sacrificed. **1911** S. E. WHITE *Bobby Orde* (1916) x. 126 It was the season of..apple-tapioca and Brown Betty. **1948** 'J. TEY' *Franchise Aff.* xv. 164 Brown-betty with thick cream. **1854** SCOFFERN in *Orr's Circ. Sc.* Chem. 458 The first portions of volatile matter which pass over when zinc ore is distilled in contact with carbonaceous matter, and which on account of their burning with a brown flame, are called by the technical name of **brown blaze*, contain very little zinc, and are chiefly composed of arsenic and cadmium. **1833** LYELL *Princ. Geol.* III. 199 This *brown coal consists of..beds of lignite of various thickness interstratified with the clays and sands. **1878** LAWRENCE *Cotta's Rocks Class.* 321 Brown coal..differs from ordinary black coal in containing a much greater proportion of bitumen. **1932** *Forestry* VI. 27 The soil type of the dales is the '*brown earth', characterized in the vertical section (profile) by the dark brown to black colour of the top layers of the mineral soil. **1953** *Proc. Prehist. Soc.* XIX. 131 Deforestation..would in time change such a forest soil by decalcification into an ordinary brownearth. **1787** BEST *Angling* (ed. 2) 111 The *Brown-fly, or Dun-Drake..its wings are made off the feather of a Pheasant's wing, which ..exactly resembles the wing of the fly. **1884** *Encycl. Brit.* XVII. 5/2 *Mus fuscipes*, Waterh., the *Brown-footed Rat of western and southern Australia. **1976** *Brown goods [see *white goods* s.v. WHITE *a.* 11 e]. **1980** *Austral. Financial Rev.*

15 Aug. 9/1 Waltons cut retail prices by up to 50 per cent on furniture, household items and kitchenware while white and browngoods sold for cost price and less. **1984** *Times* 5 Oct. 27/1 The brown goods demand charges on. **1796** STEDMAN *Surinam* II. xxviii. 335 The *brown-heart is in hardness of the same consistency as the purple-heart, and the green-heart. **1923** F. KIDD & C. WEST in *Dept. Sci. & Ind. Res., Food Invest. Board, Spec. Rep.* XII. (*title*), Brown-heart—a functional disease of apples and pears. **1928** F. T. BROOKS *Plant Dis.* ii. 16 *Brown Heart* in apples has been shown..to be caused by asphyxiation of the fleshy part of the fruit when there is a large increase of carbon dioxide and a decrease of oxygen in the surrounding atmosphere. **1950** *N.Z. Jrnl. Agric.* May 476/3 Although the size and outward appearance of turnips or swedes affected with brown heart are quite good, when opened up they may have internal greyish or brownish markings in the flesh. **1845** S. JUDD *Margaret* II. viii. 324 The Deacon's..was a small, one story *brown house. **1861** H. B. STOWE *Pearl Orr's Isl.* I. ii. 10 Down near the end of Orr's Island..stands a brown house. **1943** HUNT & PRINGLE *Service Slang* 18 **Brown job*, the Army (R.A.F. name). **1952** SHERBROOKE-WALKER *Khaki & Blue* i. 4 Another aspect of R.A.F. dress which struck the 'brown job', as they called their brothers in the Army. **1954** 'N. BLAKE' *Whisper in Gloom* II. xvi. 230 Can you hear me, bluebottles and brown job? **1963** *Economist* 29 June 1391/3 General Delacombe was a pretty undiplomatic brown-job. **1756** P. BROWNE *Jamaica* 173 The *Brown-Jolly or Bolangena..was first imported into Jamaica by the Jews. **1814** LEENAN *Hortus Jamaic.* I. 280 Sometimes called brown jolly or mad-apple. **1837** KIRKBRIDE *Northern Angler* 48 The *Brown Moth..is made with a feather from the wing of the dark-brown owl. **1883** *Gd. Words* Nov. 732/1 In the *brown-mould quite a different arrangement prevails. **1939** *Amer. Speech* XIV. 25/1 **Brown nose, v.*, to curry favor, especially for rank; *n.*, a cadet who curries favor. **1950** HEMINGWAY *Across River* xxxiii. 208 The *brown-nosers.. and all the jerks. *Ibid.* vii. 57, I have erected the defence against brown-nosing my superiors and brown-nosing the world. **1960** J. SYMONS *Progress of Crime* xv. 91 If you don't ..get cracking on a few little jobs for this paper instead of spending your time brown-nosing Mr. Fairfield, you [etc.]. **1969** M. PUGH *Last Place Left* v. 34 It was part of the tradition to hate a Highland laird or be a brown-nose. **1823** P. NICHOLSON *Pract. Build.* 415 *Brown-Ochre is a warm brown or foul orange colour. **1855** J. EDWARDS *Paint. Oil Colours* 19 Brown Ochre..is a dark ochre of great value in landscape painting..It is of a dark brownish yellow. **1916** *Daily Colonist* (Victoria, B.C.) 20 July 11/5 The Vancouver consignment included sake, *brown rice, white rice, shoyu. **1969** *Listener* 17 July 79/3 Macrobiotics is a life science discovered in Japan by Georges Ohsawa and it's based on the two pillars of philosophy and diet—the staple food being brown rice. **1894** C. M. WEED *Fungi & Fungicides* 56 The *brown rot of stone fruit is probably familiar to every grower of plums, peaches or cherries in..the United States. **1899** G. NEWMAN *Bacteria* i. 37 Bacterial brown-rot of potatoes and tomatoes is another plant disease probably due to a bacillus. **1936** J. PERCIVAL *Agric. Bot.* (ed. 8) 816 One of the best examples of bacterial plant diseases is that known as the 'Brown Rot'..of the cabbage... The disease is caused by a bacterium named *Pseudomonas campestris*. **1968** *Gloss. Terms Timber Preservation* (*B.S.I.*) 9 *Brown rot*, a type of decay caused by fungi that attack chiefly cellulose, leaving a brown friable residue of unattacked lignin. **1723** J. NOTT *Cook's & Confectioner's Dict.* sig. H h 1 To make *brown Sauce. Toss up Cives, Parsley, Capers and Anchovies in a Sauce-pan, [etc.]. **1854** DICKENS *Hard T.* I. xvi. 125 Sweetbread..in a savoury brown sauce was her favourite supper. **1911** [see SAUCE *sb.* 1 a]. **1937** *Discovery* July 212/1 He had the courage to paint the world as he saw it, leaving out the 'brown sauce' in which, till then, most pictures had been smothered. **1986** *Daily Tel.* 10 Oct. 19/2 Caramel is an essential part of a cook's palette, used to enhance the colour of a brown sauce, gravy or any other *fond de cuisine*. **1849** THACKERAY *Pendennis* I. xxxi. 306 A pint bottle of pale ale, and some *brown sherry. **1854** E. TWISLETON *Let.* 3 Apr. (1928) x. 171 A Golden Sherry, then true Brown Sherry... The Golden was £70 the butt, the Brown..£100. **1965** *Guardian* 24 Oct. 5 Sherry..these are the main types..fino, amontillado, oloroso, cream brown. **1932** *Observer* 26 June, The concession made to Herr Hitler's *brown shirts. **1939** R. C. K. ENSOR *Who Hitler Is* 7 The heavy jack-booted hero afterwards idolized by the Brown-shirts. **1934** *Times* 16 Jan., A *brown-shirted Fascist organization which manifests strong anti-Jewish proclivities. **1840** BROWNING *Sordello* IV. 395, I Was just a *brown-sleeve brother. **1896** F. G. AFLALO *Nat. Hist. Australia* 172 The *brown snake is found all over Australia and New Guinea. **1931** R. L. DITMARS *Snakes of World* xiv. 192 The Brown Snake, *D*[*emansia*] *textilis*, broadly distributed and usually four to five feet long, is rated as highly dangerous. **1963** E. WORRELL *Reptiles of Australia* 139 Brown Snakes are fast-moving and easily aroused. **1966** 'J. HACKSTON' *Father clears Out* 163 It was the longest tiger or brown snake ever killed in the district. **1843** PORTLOCK *Geol.* 214 Bitter spar, or *Brown spar, occurs in small but well-defined crystals. [**1836** *Knickerbocker* VIII. 390 His poor remains..in one corner.. —a brown stone at his head and foot.] **1858** *Spirit of Times* 13 Feb. 377/2 A solid substantial *brown-stone front house. **1865** 'G. HAMILTON' *New Atmosphere* 32 The brown-stone friends are shocked and scandalized. **1875** tr. *Vogel's Chem. Light* xvii. 270 Hyper-oxide of manganese also named brownstone. **1909** 'O. HENRY' *Options* 22 Two old-fashioned, brownstone front residences. **1948** *Time* 8 Mar. 25/1 Nightclubs in sorry brownstones. **1957** *New Yorker* 21 Sept. 132/3 The part of Brooklyn we were riding through was..lined with old and ugly brownstones. **1803** R. C. DALLAS *Hist. Maroons* I. iv. 91 To prefer pale small beer to *brown stout. **1704** *Lond. Gaz.* No. 4032/4 Her Cargo, consisting chiefly of *Brown Sugar. **1840** BARHAM *Ingol. Leg., Wedding D.*, As 'best-refined loaf' to the coarsest 'brown sugar.' **1782** W. CURTIS *Brown-tail Moth* 10 The *Brown-tail Moth..is about two-thirds of the size of the Moth produced from the Silk-worm. **1832** J. RENNIE *Butterfl. & Moths* 42 The Brown Tail (*Porthesia Auriflua*, Stephens) appears in August. **1815** KIRBY & SPENCE *Entomol.* I. vi. 202 The *brown-tailed moth (*Bombyx phæorhæa*, F.). *a* **1847** C. MATHEWS *Wks.* 125 (Bartlett) I love the city as dearly as a *brown thrasher loves the green tree that sheltered its young. **1856** BRYANT *Rivulet* i, List the brown thrasher's vernal hymn. **1891** R. WALLACE *Rural Econ. Austral. & N.Z.* xxii. 294 *Erianthus fulvus*, Kunth. —Sugar grass or *brown top. **1902** *Encycl. Brit.* XXXII. 108/2 Some [Queensland] stockholders consider that the 'Sugar grass' or 'Brown Top' (*Pollinia fulva*) surpasses them [*sc.* the 'Mitchell grasses'] in its quickness of bursting into leaf. **1928** R. G. STAPLEDON *Tour Australia & N.Z.* viii. 53 New Zealand Chewing's fescue and New Zealand Brown top (*Agrostis vulgaris*) are at present in great demand in America. **1950** *N.Z. Jrnl. Agric.* Jan. 19/3 The dominant pasture species on this store sheep country are browntop and danthonia. **1902** *Encycl. Brit.* XXXII. 637/1 The excretory organs [of the Sipunculoidea]..serve as channels by which the reproductive cells leave the body, and they are sometimes spoken of as '*brown tubes'. **1836** *Scenes Commerce by Land & S.* 150 Common *brown ware..a superior sort is manufactured at Nottingham.

brown, *sb.* [The adj. used absol.]

1. a. Brown colour.

1607 TOPSELL *Four-f. Beasts* 435 The mingling together of black and white colours doth..produce a swart and brown, and neither of both doth appear in the brown. **1850** TENNYSON *In Mem.* ci. 3 That beech will gather brown. **1873** BLACK *Pr. Thule* i. 3 Amid the browns and greens of the heather.

b. Duskiness, gloom.

1729 M. BROWNE *Piscat. Eclog.* VIII. (1773) 111 The scatt'ring brown of night.

c. A pigment of a brown colour.

1549 in Rogers *Agric. & Prices* III. 573/2, 1 lb. Spanish brown. **1611** MARKHAM *Countr. Content.* I. x, A little Capons grease, and broun of Spain, mixt together. **1855** J. EDWARDS *Paint. Oil Colours* 25 Vandyke Brown (Bituminous Earth.) This is a rich transparent pigment.

2. *techn.* Brown or unbleached state.

1882 *Standard* 11 Sept. 6/6 Medium and fine bobbin nets in the brown.

3. a. Elliptically, for various things or parts of things of a brown colour: *e.g.* a brown butterfly, a brown fly used in angling; brown clothing, etc. Also, (a drink of) brown ale (in quot. 1862, brown sherry).

a **1300** *K. Horn* 1122 Hure horn heo leide adun, And fulde him of a brun [*Gloss.* a brown jar]. **1621** BURTON *Anat. Mel.* II. ii. I. i. (1651) 232 The burned and scorched superficies [of roast meat], the brown we call it. **1681** CHETHAM *Angler's Vade-m.* xxxiv. §26 Angle with the smallest Gnats, Browns and Duns. **1712** *Act 10 Anne* in *Lond. Gaz.* No. 5018/3 Paper called..small ordinary Brown. **1820** 'PETER CORCORAN' *Fancy* 109 *Brown*, porter.—*Heavy Brown*, stout. **1823** J. BADCOCK *Dom. Amusem.* 163 Flour or bread..as seconds, thirds, and browns. **1851** KINGSLEY *Let.* in *Life* ix, One pounder I caught to-day on the 'March brown'. **1860** GOSSE *Rom. Nat. Hist.* 4 Here, too, are the butterflies..the tawny 'browns' are dancing along the hedge-rows. **1862** DICKENS *Somebody's Luggage* in *All Yr. Round* (Christmas) 5/1 Bottle old East India Brown £0 8 0. *Ibid.* 47/1 He ordered a bottle of Old Brown. **1934** T. S. ELIOT *Rock* i. 12 Only if I 'ad a pint o' brown, I'd show you 'ow your money goes. **1959** A. SINCLAIR *Breaking of Bumbo* iii. 53 Let's go and have a brown in the NAAFI.

b. *slang.* A copper coin, a 'copper'.

1812 J. H. VAUX *Flash Dict.*, Browns and whistlers, bad halfpence and farthings. **1842** T. MARTIN in *Fraser's Mag.* Dec., 'More *browns* than *guineas* goin' vith us any day.' **1865** *Look bef. You Leap* I. 239 'There isn't a respectable boy 'ull give me browns for a sixpence.'

c. A person of brown complexion; a brunette (*obs.*). In later use, a mulatto.

c **1450** *Merlin* xxi. 373 This feire broun is sone to the kynge Belinans. **1862** *Independent* 10 Apr., The jealousy between the blacks and browns, which has done so much mischief in the West Indies, is not fostered by American people of color. **1890** H. M. FIELD *Bright Skies* 147 In Jamacia..they are distinguished as the whites and blacks and *the browns*. **1968** *Listener* 31 Oct. 57 53 A white girl found herself the only white in a class of blacks and browns.

4. ***the brown***: lit. the brown-coloured mass of a flock of game-birds; in phr. ***to fire into the brown*** (***of them***): to fire into the midst of a covey instead of singling out a bird; also *transf.*, to fire, or launch a missile, indiscriminately into a mass.

1845 J. MAYER *Sportsman's Directory* (ed. 7) 21 Always aim at one particular bird, not firing at random at the whole covey, or 'into the brown of them'. **1871** *Punch* 16 Dec. 256/2 Sportsmen, whose sport must mainly consist in 'firing into the brown'. **1885** *Ibid.* 31 Jan. 53 'Pop! Bang! Whose bird?' That's the French notion of a tag, as the husband looses off 'into the brown' of his wife's adorers. **1888** KIPLING *Phantom 'Rickshaw* (1889) 87 We three Martinis firing into the brown of the enemy. **1899** *Daily News* 4 May 8/2 The sportsman..not firing into the brown, but taking careful aim at some particular bird. **1955** C. S. FORESTER *Good Shepherd* 23 Three square miles of sea, an immense target for any torpedo fired 'into the brown'.

brown (braʊn), *v.* [f. BROWN *a.*]

1. *intr.* To become brown.

c **1300** *K. Alis.* 3293 Whan note brounith in haselrys. **1859** LEVER *Davenp. Dunn* 26 'That delicious potato-cake that I see browning..before the fire.'

2. *trans.* To make brown; to roast brown; to give (by a chemical process) a dull brown lustre to gun-barrels or other polished iron surfaces.

1570 LEVINS *Manip.* 220 To Broune, *obfuscare*. **1769** MRS. RAFFALD *Eng. Housekpr.* (1778) 133 Take off the skin and brown it. **1833** J. HOLLAND *Manuf. Metals* II. 107 The operation of browning a gun barrel. **1862** THORNBURY *Turner* II. 319 The hot Italian sun had parched and browned him.

fig. **1798** MARY WOLLSTONECR. *Posth. Wks.* III. ix. 23 To give a freshness to days browned by care.

3. [from BROWN *sb.* 4.] To fire indiscriminately at (a covey of birds or a mass of men).

1873 *Sat. Rev.* Sept. 310 We seldom did ourselves anything like justice until the coveys were out on the feed towards evening, when we were apt to brown them as they rose in little clouds. **1885** RIDER HAGGARD *K. Solomon's Mines* xiii, Good..began to fire,..industriously 'browning' the dense mass before him with a Winchester repeater. **1921** *Blackw. Mag.* Jan. 122/2 He waited till the troop was some hundred and fifty yards away, and then he 'browned' it. **1962** B. SCOTT JAMES *Asking for Trouble* xix. 145 We all shot a little wildly..one guest, a German, browned the beaters.

brown(e, obs. pa. pple. of BREW; obs. f. BRAWN.

Brown Bess. The name familiarly given in the British Army to the old flint-lock musket. (*Brown Musket* was in earlier use: both names existed long before the process of 'browning' the barrel (introduced in 1808), and apparently referred to the brown walnut stock.)

[**1708** MRS. CENTLIVRE *Busie Body* I. i 13 My last Refuge, a brown Musquet. **1754** *Connoisseur* No. 31 The ceremony is performed by a brown musket.] **1785** GROSE *Dict. Vulgar T.* s.v., *To hug brown Bess*: to carry a firelock, to serve as a private soldier. **1797** *Gent. Mag.* LXVII. 1022 'Etymologus' asks 'Can you trace the application of the term *Brown Bess* to anything *loading* or fatiguing, such as a musket to soldiers tired on a long march or to a wooden pump? Or is it.. derived from the colour of the material? Why is Bess the more favourite term than Nan or Moll? A brown musket is not an uncommon phrase, taking the part for the whole, the stock for the steel. But why is Bess brought in?' **1809** R. PORTER *Trav. Sk. Russ. & Swed.* (1813) I. xxiv. 273 A good soldier..sleeping with his hand on his musquet, his wedded wife and dear brown Bess. **1820** COMBE (Dr. Syntax) *Consol.* ii. (D.) Religion Jack did never profess, Till he had shoulder'd old Brown Bess. **1860** GEN. P. THOMPSON *Audi Alt.* III. cxix. 61 Without more danger from Enfield or Whitworth than from Brown Bess. *c* **1880** GRANT *Hist. India* I. v. 26/1 Britons with their old 'brown Besses'.

brown bill, brown-bill. [See BILL *sb.*[1] 2.] A kind of halberd painted brown, formerly used by foot-soldiers and watchmen.

1589 *Pappe w. Hatchet* C iij b, All weapons, from the taylors bodkin to the watchmans browne bil. **1678** BUTLER *Hud.* III. II. 541 Brown Bills levied in the City Made Bills to pass the Grand Committee. **1823** SCOTT *Peveril* III. ii. 38 A constable with three or four assistants, armed with the old-fashioned brown-bills. **1870** MORRIS *Earthly Par.* I. I. 316 There the porter stood, brown-bill in hand.

brown bread. 1. Any bread of a brown colour, or of a darker colour than ordinary 'white bread'. Formerly applied in England to bread made of rye or mixed rye and wheat; now *spec.* to bread made of unboulted flour, or 'whole meal', containing some of the 'bran' or outer skin of the grain as well as the fine flour. In U.S. 'a dark-colored bread made of wheat or rye, either bolted or unbolted, mixed with Indian meal, and sometimes sweetened'. (Cf. *brown baker* in BROWN *a.* 7).

c **1489** CAXTON *Sonnes of Aymon* xxi. 463 Bryng me som broun brede & water in a treen dyshe. **1530** PALSGR. 201/2 Browne bread, *pain bis*. **1577** HARRISON *England* II. vi. (1877) 154 The next sort is named browne bread, of the colour, of which we haue two sorts, one baked vp as it cometh from the mill, so that neither the bran nor the floure are anie whit diminished. **1603** SHAKS. *Meas. for M.* III. ii. 194 She smelt browne-bread and Garlicke. **1615** BEDWELL *Moham. Imp.* III. §120 We do eat broun bread which is no way so pleasing in tast. **1620** VENNER *Via Recta* i. 18 A browne houshold bread agreeable enough for labourers. **1849** *Fam. Economist* No. 19. 130 Proper brown bread is made from undressed wheat-meal. **1873** MORLEY *Rousseau* I. 65.

2. *attrib.* Of or pertaining to brown bread; †*fig.* homely, unrefined. **brown-bread ice**, ice cream made with brown-bread crumbs, popular in Victorian and Edwardian times.

a **1553** UDALL *Royster D.* I. iii, Old browne bread crustes. **1606** *Wily Beguiled* in Hawkins *Eng. Dr.* III. 313 (D.) He's a very idiot and brown-bread clown. **17..** T. HANSON in Southey *Life Wesley* (1820) II. 80, I am but a brown-bread preacher. **1846** 'A LADY' *Jewish Manual* vii. 148 The ice should be prepared in a round mould—brown-bread ice is particularly well adapted to a Juditha. **1860** L. HARCOURT *Diaries G. Rose* I. 281 The Brown-bread Act. **1875** L. TROUBRIDGE *Life among Troubridges* (1966) 117, I had a brown bread ice, which was one tiny drop of consolation. **1965** T. FITZGIBBON *Art Brit. Cooking* 201 *Brown Bread Ice Cream.* This was a most popular Edwardian ice-cream... The brown breadcrumbs give the ice a nutty flavour.

browned (braʊnd), *ppl. a.* [f. BROWN *v.* + -ED[1].] **1. a.** Made brown.

1871 *Daily News* 16 Aug., Every sort of rotten..cranky craft, is painted and varnished, literally, a whited or a browned sepulchre. **1872** BLACK *Adv. Phaeton* ii. 10 The tall, browned, big-bearded man.

†**b.** ***browned-black***. *Obs.*

c **1511** *1st Eng. Bk. Amer.* (Arb.) Introd. 28/2 They [the natives] be brounde blacke.

2. ***browned off***, bored, 'fed-up', disgusted. Hence ***browned-offness*** [-NESS], the condition of being 'browned off'. *slang.*

Partridge *Dict. Slang* (1961) states 'Regular Army since ca. 1915; adopted by the R.A.F. ca. 1929'; but pre-1938 printed evidence is lacking.

1938 J. CURTIS *They drive by Night* ii. 28 What the hell had he got to be so browned off about? He ought to be feeling proper chirpy. **1941** *Men Only* May 8 We have worked hard for success, and now that it has come we are robbed of it by this paper shortage. Believe us, we are properly browned off. **1942** W. SIMPSON *One of our Pilots* ii. 19 Most of our time was spent moping about the aerodrome getting thoroughly 'browned-off', and hoping against hope for some real action. **1943** W. ROBSON *Let.* 15 Aug. (1960) 53

Splendid things for combating the deadly browned-offness. **1958** *Observer* 9 Nov. 4/4 Medical boards were always being begged by browned-off invalids to pass them fit for active service. **1966** *Ibid.* 27 Feb. 28/7 This [programme] has got over an initial stage of browned-offness, mutiny on the knees, dumb insolence.

†**brow'netta.** *Obs.* [ad. It. *brunetta*, after BROWN: cf. BRUNETTE.] A brunette.

1582 STANYHURST *Conceites* in *Æneid* (Arb.) 141 In bodye fine fewterd, a braue Brownnetta. **1589** WARNER *Alb. Eng.* v. xxvi. 128 The next a gay Brownetta. **1598** E. GILPIN *Skial.* (1878) 19 Thou art not faire, A plaine brownetta when thou art at best.

Brown George. **1.** †**a.** A loaf of a coarse kind of brown bread (*obs.*). **b.** A hard, coarse biscuit.

1688 R. HOLME *Armoury* III. 86/1 The blackest and coarsest Bread..is..Brown Bread, or Brown-George. **1694** ECHARD *Plautus* 195 This Monarch here must dine to Day with a Brown George, and only Salt & Vinegar Sawce. **1708** MOTTEUX *Rabelais* iv. Prol. (D.) One musty crust of a brown George. **1867** SMYTH *Sailor's Word-bk.*

†**2.** A kind of wig. *Obs.*

1840 BARHAM *Ingol. Leg.*, *Jarvis's Wig* (D.) [A wig] of the colour of over-baked ginger-bread, one of the description commonly known during the latter half of the last century by the name of a brown George. **1882** *Globe* 24 July 2/1 The King [George III] wore a brown wig..known popularly a century ago as 'brown George'.

3. A brown earthenware vessel. Cf. BLACK JACK.

1861 HUGHES *Tom Brown Oxf.* xxiv. (D.) His brown George, or huge earthenware receptacle..in which his bed-maker had been washing up his tea-things. **1864** E. CAPERN *Devon Provinc.*, *Brown-George*, a chamber utensil made of red clay. **1847-78** HALLIWELL, *Brown-George*, a large earthen pitcher.

Brownian ('braʊnɪən), *a.* [f. the name of Dr. Robert *Brown*, who first described the movement in question.] ***Brownian movement***: the irregular oscillatory movement observed in microscopic particles or 'molecules' of all kinds suspended in a limpid fluid; also called *molecular movement.*

1871 BASTIAN *Orig. Lowest Organisms* 46 Bacteria..which exhibit movements resembling those known as Brownian. **1874** JONES & SIEV. *Pathol. Anat.* 28 Serum..crowded with fatty molecules, presenting an active Brownian movement. **1875** DARWIN *Insectiv. Plants* iii. 64 Small granules which exhibited Brownian movements.

brownie[1] ('braʊnɪ). Also 8 **browny**, and with capital initial. [denominative f. BROWN, with somewhat of diminutive force: cf. the ON. *svartálfar* or dark elves of the Edda. A 'wee brown man' often appears in Scottish ballads and fairy tales.] **1.** A benevolent spirit or goblin, of shaggy appearance, supposed to haunt old houses, *esp.* farmhouses, in Scotland, and sometimes to perform useful household work while the family were asleep.

1513 DOUGLAS *Æneis* VI. Prol. 18 All is bot gaistis and elriche fantasies, Of browneis and of bogillis full this buke. **1781** M. MARTIN *Descr. W. Isl.* (1716) 391 It is not long since every family of any considerable substance in these Islands [Shetland] was haunted by a Spirit they called Browny, which did several sorts of work. **1802** SCOTT *Minstr. Bord.* Introd. 41 The Brownie formed a class of beings, distinct in habit and disposition from the freakish and mischievous elves. **1847** C. BRONTË *J. Eyre* xxxvii. (D.) You talk of my being a fairy, but I am sure you are more like a brownie.

2. [Named from the colour of their uniform.] A member of the junior section of the organization known as the 'Girl Guides'. Also *attrib.*

1916 *Home Chat* 30 Sept. 558 For the younger girls who are not eleven, and therefore not old enough to become Girl Guides, the Brownie movement has been started. **1918** BADEN-POWELL *Girl Guiding* 23 In the Brownie Pack every Brownie obeys the wishes of the leader. *Ibid.* 24 When a girl has passed her test as a recruit she is admitted into her Six as a Brownie. **1959** I. & P. OPIE *Lore & Lang. Schoolch.* viii. 123 Scout's, Cub's, Guide's and Brownie's honour, are the only pledges deliberately sown by adults to have taken root.

3. Special Comb.: **Brownie point** *colloq.* (orig. *U.S.*) [prob. a development from *brown-nose* s.v. BROWN *a.* 7, but popularly associated with sense 2 above and hence freq. spelled with capital initial], a notional credit for an achievement; favour in the eyes of another, esp. gained by sycophantic or servile behaviour.

1963 *Amer. Speech* XXXVIII. 169 To curry favor with a professor: *brown nose..brownie..get *brownie points.* **1971** M. TAK *Truck Talk* 19 *Brownie points*, theoretical points gained by a trucker who goes out of his way to do a favor for a dispatcher. **1976** N. THORNBURG *Cutter & Bone* vii. 169, I said it was his big chance to make Brownie points with the old man. **1980** *Daily Tel.* 6 Sept. 19/3 Overall, the societies are considered more friendly than the banks though the banks get brownie points for speed in dealing with transactions. **1986** *Times Educ. Suppl.* 9 May 6/3 The clause would not be used to 'punish' teachers. Those who took part in extra activities would get a Brownie point, he said, but classroom effectiveness would be the prime test of a teacher's success.

brownie[2], **browny** ('braʊnɪ). [Subst. use of BROWNY *a.*] **1.** A sweet bread made with brown sugar and currants. *Austral.* and *N.Z.*

1883 J. EDGE-PARTINGTON *Random Rot* vii. 312 Each with a huge hunch of 'browny' (bread sweetened with brown sugar and currants) in one hand. **1900** H. LAWSON *On Track* 129 Pile of 'brownie' on the bare black boards at the end of the table. **1908** A. GUNN *We of Never-Never* xxiii. 331 Half the Vealer, another huge pudding, several yard of sweet currant 'brownie'. **1959** H. P. TRITTON *Time means Tucker* v. 39/1 He called us over to have a mug of tea and a hunk of brownie.

2. A small square of rich, usu. chocolate, cake containing nuts. *U.S.*

1897 *Sears, Roebuck Catal.* 17/3 *Fancy Crackers, Biscuits, Etc.*.. Brownies, in 1 lb. papers. **1954** J. STEINBECK *Sweet Thursday* xii. 80 Do you like brownies? **1968** L. J. BRAUN *Cat who turned on & off* (1969) x. 96 On her tray were chocolate brownies..frosted chocolate squares topped with walnut halves.

3. An angler's name for the trout.

1914 *Chambers's Jrnl.* July 432/2, I got him into the net at last, a thick, deep-bodied brownie of pounds weight. **1928** *Observer* 22 July 28/2 It is a difficult matter to creel a brace or so of brownies. The trout are there, but they stir not.

Brownie[3] ('braʊnɪ). The proprietary name of a simple type of camera.

1902 *Westm. Gaz.* 24 Mar. 3/2 Five shillings..is the price of the Brownie Kodak. **1906** A. BENNETT *Whom God hath Joined* viii. 285 Gater..had decided to sell his high-geared bicycle in order that he might become the possessor of a Brownie camera. **1952** P. BONNER *SPQR* (1953) xxvi. 234 Clicking our Brownies and scribbing postcards to the folks back home.

'browniness. *rare.* [f. BROWNY *a.* + -NESS.] The state of being 'browny' or somewhat brown.

1830 *Blackw. Mag.* XXVIII. 580 Fowling-pieces.. through the smooth browniness of their barrels.

¶ See also BROUNES.

browning ('braʊnɪŋ), *vbl. sb.* [f. BROWN *v.*] **1.** The action or process of making or becoming brown. (*Browning* of polished iron: see the vb.)

1791 HAMILTON *Berthollet's Dyeing* II. II. 346 To give a browning, stuff which has just been dyed must be dipped, etc. **1808** *Morn. Post* Oct. 3 The cropping of the soldiers' hair is to be followed by the browning of the hitherto bright barrel and lock of the musket. **1846** J. BAXTER *Libr. Pract. Agric.* II. 7 Shrivelling and browning of the leaves of trees. **1881** GREENER *Gun* 254 The process of browning takes from four to eight days.

2. *Cookery.* A preparation for imparting a brown colour to gravy or made dishes.

1769 MRS. RAFFALD *Eng. Housekpr.* (1778) Introd. 3 Lemon pickle and browning answers..better than cullis. **1796** MRS. GLASSE *Cookery* v. 42 Take one spoonful of red wine, half as much of browning.

'browning, *ppl. a.* [f. as prec. + -ING[2].] **a.** Becoming brown. **b.** Making brown.

1596 GOSSON *Pleas. Quippes* 98 in Hazl. *E.P.P.* IV. 254 The tallow-pale, the browning-bay, The swarthie-blacke, the grassie-greene. **1834** MARRYAT *Jac. Faithf.* v. 27 Where is the blooming cheek, ruddy with the browning air? **1884** G. C. DAVIES *Norfolk Broads* xxxviii. 290 The browning grasses quivered airily against the sky.

†**'browning,** *sb.*[1] *Obs.* Perhaps = BROWNIE[1] 1.

1601 HOLLAND *Pliny* II. 2 He..that calls for nothing else at sea but winde; and neuer rests till Browning be come. *Ibid.* Gloss., *Browning*, a term vsuall in the mouths of mariners and winnowers of corne, when they are calmed and do call for wind.

Browning ('braʊnɪŋ), *sb.*[2] The name of John M. *Browning* (1855–1926) of Ogden, Utah, U.S.A., applied *attrib.* to various weapons ranging from pistols to machine-guns, esp. automatic ones, designed by him. Also *ellipt.*

1905 *Daily Chron.* 9 Feb. 5/2 Hohental fired all the seven chambers of a Browning revolver at Herr Johnsson. **1906** *Ibid.* 6 Jan. 8/1 The party of freedom have to depend on revolvers, especially the 'Brownings'. **1906** *Westm. Gaz.* 6 Apr. 6/3 They were armed with Mauser pistols and Brownings. **1964** H. L. PETERSON *Encycl. Firearms* 68/1 Successful Browning automatic-weapon designs include the ..Browning Automatic rifle M1918, the recoil operated Browning machine guns Model 1917 and Model 1919, [etc.].

Browningesque (braʊnɪŋ'ɛsk), *a.* [f. the surname *Browning* + -ESQUE.] Of, pertaining to, or characteristic of Robert Browning or his style.

1880 G. M. HOPKINS *Let.* 23 Mar. (1935) 101 Your brother appears to admire Browning..the *Elder Brother* is quite Browningesque. **1901** *Daily Chron.* 29 June 3/1 Monologues..which trace their lineage to *Lippo Lippi* and the rest of that most Browningesque series. **1953** H. READ *True Voice of Feeling* I. vii. 128 A good deal of Browningesque swagger.

So **Browningese** (braʊnɪŋ'iːz), *a.* = prec.; *sb.* the language or style of Browning; **'Browningite**, an admirer of Browning; also *adj.* = BROWNINGESQUE *a.*

1880 G. M. HOPKINS *Let.* 26 Oct. (1935) 111 That piece is worse, indeed *it is* Browningese. *c* **1882** R. BROWNING *Lett.* (1933) 212, I am quite other than a Browningite. **1889** *Spectator* 14 Dec., [He] translated them all into Browingese forms. *Ibid.*, You never lose the Browningite manner of deliverance. **1910** H. WALKER *Lit. Vict. Era* 320 Thorold, Luria, Djabal, Valence, all speak Browningese.

brownish ('braʊnɪʃ), *a.* [f. BROWN *a.* + -ISH[1].] **1.** Somewhat brown.

1555 EDEN *Decades W. Ind.* (Arb.) 193 Eyght of their hennes..of brownyshe coloure. **1607** TOPSELL *Four-f. Beasts* 444 Hair..of colour like a Ches-nut, or brownish. **1878** HUXLEY *Physiogr.* 26 The sands of the Bagshot series.. are commonly of yellow and brownish colours.

2. *Comb.*, as ***brownish-coloured***; also with other colours, as ***brownish-black***, ***-grey***, ***-red***, etc.

1685 *Lond. Gaz.* No. 2061. 2/2 A Brownish Black Mare. **1689** *Ibid.* No. 2433/4 A middle sized Man, his Hair curled and brownish coloured. **1831** BREWSTER *Nat. Magic* ii. (1833) 23 At first..it is brownish-red.

'Brownism. [f. the surname *Brown*, *Browne.*] **1.** The system of church-government advocated *c* 1581 by Robert Brown, an English Puritan and Nonconformist. His principles, somewhat modified, became those of the Independents.

a **1617** HIERON *Wks.* II. 497 Some fall to Brownisme, some to Popery. **1642** *Compl. to Ho. Commons* 15 Schismatical men addicted to Anabaptisme and Brownisme. **1732** NEAL *Hist. Purit.* I. 595 The violence of persecution drove some of them into the extremes of Brownism.

2. The style of Sir Thomas Browne. (*nonce-use.*)

1791 BOSWELL *Johnson* (1831) I. 293 Those words which he sometimes took pleasure in adopting, in imitation of Sir Thomas Browne..In one instance only in these essays has he indulged his Brownism.

3. *Med.* The Brunonian system. See BRUNONIAN.

'Brownist. [f. as prec. (senses 1, 3) + -IST.] **1.** An adherent or follower of the ecclesiastical principles of Robert Brown. (See prec.)

1583 STUBBES *Anat. Abus.* II. 74 Diuers new phangled felows sprong vp of late, as the Brownists. **1602** WARNER *Alb. Eng.* IX. xlvi. 219 The Brownist and the Barrowist, goe hand in hand together. **1601** SHAKS. *Twel. N.* III. ii. 34, I had as liefe be a Brownist, as a Politician. **1702** C. MATHER *Magn. Chr.* I. iii. (1852) 64 Shake off the name of Brownist: it is a mere nickname, and a brand for the making of Religion odious. **1853** MARSDEN *Early Purit.* 137 The brownists and the anabaptists were the first seceders from the church of England at home.

2. *Med.* An adherent of the BRUNONIAN system.

Hence (in sense 1) **Brow'nistical** *a.*

1636 W. SAMPSON *Vow Breaker* I b, By the vertue of his good liquor hee's able to convert any Brownisticall sister. **1736** NEAL *Hist. Purit.* III. 456 Martin Mar-Prelate and the rest of the Brownistical pamphlets in the reign of Qu. Elizabeth. **1846** MACCRIE *Alex. Henderson* 35 Some persons ..tainted with Brownistical and Independent notions.

brownly ('braʊnlɪ), *adv.* [f. BROWN *a.* + -LY[2].] With a brown colour; in a brown state.

c **1825** BEDDOES *Sec. Brother* I. i, A feathered and a jewelled cap, And youthful curls to hang beside it brownly.

brownness ('braʊnnɪs). [f. as prec. + -NESS.] The quality or state of being brown.

1572 J. JONES *Bathes of Bath* III. 26 b, Blackenes or brownes of egestion. **1611** COTGR., *Rissole*, the brownenesse that is giuen to a thing in the frying thereof. **1732** DE FOE *Tour Gt. Brit.* (1769) III. 76 The Derwent is remarkable for its Brownness. **1878** HABERSHON *Dis. Abdomen* 16 Brownness of the tongue..in states of exhaustion.

'brown-out. *Chiefly Austral.* and *N. Amer.* [f. BROWN *v.*, after BLACK-OUT *sb.*] A partial black-out. Also *transf.* and *fig.*

1942 in *Amer. Speech* (1945) XX. 143/1 Brown-out..used in Australia to denote semidarkening a city as distinguished from the complete darkening of a blackout. **1943** *Ibid.* (1944) XIX. 149/1 The suggested conservation measures for electricity involve a national brownout, the extinguishing of all ornamental and display lighting and signs after 10 p.m. **1950** *N.Y. Herald* 18 Feb., New York Brownout is Ordered as Coal Dwindles. **1955** *Times* 4 May 10/4 The new 'brown-out' on information in Washington. **1969** *Daily Colonist* (Victoria, B.C.) 6 Dec. 23/1 Premier Bennett..was asked why the government found it necessary to route the transmission [line] through the park. He said:..'It is to prevent brown outs.'

brown owl. **1.** The name of any of several varieties of owl: (see BROWN *a.* 2 b and OWL *sb.* 1 b and c).

2. In the Brownie movement: (see OWL *sb.* 2 b).

brown paper.

1. A coarse stout kind of paper made of unbleached materials; chiefly used for wrapping.

1542 in Glasscock *Rec. St. Michael's Bp. Stortford* (1882) 43 Item for browne paper for the seid orgons. **1611** COTGR., *Papier marchand*, browne paper (wherein Tradesmen fould vp their Wares). **1772** *Gentl. Mag.* XLII. 192 Course brown paper, such as pedlars use. *a* **1848** MARRYAT *R. Reefer* v, [He] would..clap the vinegar and brown paper on my bruises.

2. *Comb.* and *attrib.*, as ***brown-paper parcel***, etc. **brown-paper warrant** (see quot.).

1610 *Histriom.* IV. 194 The gentlemen see into our trade, We cannot gull them with brown-paper stuff. **1691** *Lond. Gaz.* No. 2701/4 Any Brown-Paper-Maker may be furnished with what Quantity of Course Rags..they please.

1867 SMYTH *Sailor's Word-bk.* 719 Brown-paper warrants, those given by a captain, and which he can cancel. **1885** *Law Times' Rep.* LII. 736/2 [He] sent him a brown-paper parcel.

brown study. [app. originally from BROWN in sense of 'gloomy'; but this sense has been to a great extent forgotten. (The conjecture that *brown* 'might be' the Ger. *braune* 'brow' does not require serious notice.)]

A state of mental abstraction or musing: 'gloomy meditations' (J.); 'serious reverie, thoughtful absent-mindedness' (Webster); now *esp.* an idle or purposeless reverie.

1532 *Dice-Play* 6 Lack of company will soon lead a man into a brown study. **1579** LYLY *Euphues* (Arb.) 80 You are in some brown study, what colours you might best wear. **1607** TOPSELL *Serpents* 772 Nothing but sadnesse, and heavinesse of minde, brown-studies. **1693** *Oxford-Act* 2 Oft wou'd the new created Sophister Where Boy cry'd, want ye any Coffee, Sir? Start from brown-study. **1712** STEELE *Spect.* No. 286 ¶3 He often puts me into a brown Study how to answer him. **1871** BLACKIE *Four Phases* i. 13 He had been standing there in a brown study.

† **'brownswine.** *Obs. rare.* [Cf. OE. *mereswin*, Ger. *meerschwein*, Du. *meerswijn*, and the name *porpoise* itself.] A porpoise.

c **1440** *Promp. Parv.* 54 Brunswyne, or delfyne, *foca, delphinus, suillus.*

brownwort ('braʊnwɜːt). *Herb.* ? *Obs.* [perh. from its brown flowers.] A name of the Water-Betony (*Scrophularia aquatica*), and perhaps other species of *Scrophularia*.

c **1000** *Sax. Leechd.* I. 158 Genim þysse wyrte wyrttruman þe engle brunewyrt hatað. *Ibid.* 374 Wið lungen adle Genim ..& bryse wyrt & brun wyrt. *c* **1440** *Promp. Parv.* 54 Brownworte, herbe [**1499** brother wort], *pulio, peruleium* [**1499** *puleium*]. **1551** TURNER *Herbal* I. Lij, The herbe whiche we call in Englyshe water betony or brown wurt. **1673** GREW *Anat. Roots* i. §13 In Brownwort, the Basis of the Stalk sinking down by degrees .. becomes the upper part of the Root. **1884** MILLER *Plant-n.* 248 *Scrophularia aquatica*, Bishop's-leaves, Water-Betony, Brown-wort.

browny ('braʊnɪ), *a. rare.* [f. BROWN *a.* + -Y.]

1. Inclining to brown.

1582 STANYHURST *Æneid* IV. (Arb.) 164 Thee brownye lion too stalck fro the mounten he wissheth. **1597** SHAKS. *Lover's Compl.* xiii, His browny locks did hang in crooked curles. **1873** KINGSLEY *Valentine's D.*, Oh! I wish I were a tiny browny bird.

2. *Comb.*: with the name of another colour, as ***browny-green, -grey.***

1905 *Westm. Gaz.* 5 Aug. 10/2 It is a very becoming tone, that bronze browny green. **1906** *Daily Chron.* 10 Dec. 4/4 The browny-grey soldiers of Russia. **1907** *Ibid.* 12 Apr. 9/3 The browny-grey back of her sharply-pointed wings. **1945** G. MILLAR *Maquis* vii. 147 He wore a very old browny-green tweed coat and trousers.

† **'browsage.** *Obs.* [f. BROWSE *v.* + -AGE.]

1. The browsing of cattle; *concr.* that on which they browse.

1610 W. FOLKINGHAM *Art of Survey* I. viii. 16 Grasse and plants fit for broouage, and browsage of sheepe. **1688** R. HOLME *Armoury* III. 333/2 *Broovage* or *Browsage* is feeding of Sheep and Goats.

2. The right of browsing.

1611 COTGR., *Fresange*, one hog, or more, due vnto the Maister of the waters, and forrests of Aubigny (and elsewhere) by the farmers of the Mastage and brousage thereof.

browse (braʊz), *sb.*[1] Forms: 6–8 brouse, brouze, 7 brouce, brouss, 7– browze, browse. [app. a. 16th c. F. *broust* (OF. *brost*, mod.F. *brout*) 'bud, young shoot'. (But sense 3 was evidently taken from the verb in English.) The loss of the final *t* presents some difficulties: the occas. spellings *brouce, brouss* indicate an early form (bruːs), which may possibly have been a corruption of *brousts* collective pl.]

1. Young shoots and twigs of shrubs, trees, etc.

1523 FITZHERB. *Husb.* §132 If thou haue any trees to .. croppe for the fyre-wodde, croppe them in wynter that thy beastes maye eate the brouse and the mosse of the bowes and also the yues. **1558** PHAER *Æneid* VII. G iij b, This Laurel bushe ful thick of browse. **1596** SPENSER *F.Q.* III. x. 45 Their gotes upon the brouzes fedd. **1617** MARKHAM *Caval.* I. 5 Bushes, brouse, and some hie or thicke trees for shelter. **1669** WORLIDGE *Syst. Agric.* (1681) 323 Browse or brouce, or brutte, the tops of the Branches of Trees that Cattle usually feed on. **1721** DUDLEY in *Phil. Trans.* XXXI. 168 In the Winter they live upon Browse, or the tops of Bushes and young Trees. **1874** C. GEIKIE *Life Woods* vi. 118 Browse is the Canadian word for the tender twigs of trees.

2. Fodder for cattle, consisting of young shoots and twigs; that which is or can be browsed.

1552 HULOET, Browse, or meat for beastes in snow tyme, *vesca.* **1580** BARET *Alv.* B 1400 Browse made for beastes of withie bowes. **1621** FLETCHER *Thierry & Th.* I. i, Like leaves they would .. become browse for every beast. **1697** DRYDEN *Virg.* (1806) I. 261 Th' unworthy browze Of buffaloes. **1706** J. PHILIPS *Cyder* I. 108 How the Goats their shrubby Brouze Gnaw pendent. **1837** HOWITT *Rur. Life* v. ii. (1862) 367 Hollies, which were encouraged in most ancient forests for winter browze.

3. The action of browsing.

1810 CROMEK *Rem. Nithsdale Song*, All the flocks at browse. **1820** SCOTT *Abbot* iii, The cattle are even now returning from their scanty browse. **1830** W. PHILLIPS *Mt. Sinai* IV. 114 As when at browse .. A herd of deer .. disport them. **1850** LYNCH *Theo. Trin.* v. 80 [I] listened to the browse of the sheep as they cropped the grass.

Hence (or from the verb) **browse-wood.**

1598 MANWOOD *Lawes Forest* vi. §1 (1615) 51/2 The Foresters .. must prouide Browse-wood to bee cut downe for [the Deer] to feed upon. **1664** EVELYN *Sylva* 72 It is advis'd not to cut off the Browse-wood of Oaks in Copses. **1835** E. JESSE *Glean. Nat. Hist.* Ser. III. 239 Right of common for four horses, and the use of browse-wood.

browse, *sb.*[2] *Mining.* Also brouze. (See quots.)

1875 URE *Dict. Arts* I. 547 *Browse*, a metallurgical term for a variety of slag. *Ibid.* III. 59 A mass of heated fuel, mixed with partly-fused and semi-reduced ore, called *Brouze*, floating upon a stratum of melted lead.

browse, browze (braʊz), *v.* Forms: (6 brose), 6–7 brouse, 6–8 brouze, 7 browse, 7–9 browze, 6– browse. [f. BROWSE *sb.*[1], or perhaps directly from 16th c. F. *brouster*, now *brouter* (in same sense), according to Littré, f. F. *broust, brout* 'bud, young shoot'; the Eng. form being influenced by that of the sb., q.v. The pronunciation with -*z* may have begun in the verb; cf. the analogy of *grass, graze, advice, advise, use, to use*, etc. (Or if the verb was ever *broust* in Eng., we might suppose the final -*t* to have been lost, by confusion with that of the pa. t. and pa. pple.)]

1. a. *intr.* or *absol.* To feed *on* the leaves and shoots of trees and bushes; to crop the shoots or tender parts of rough plants for food: said of goats, deer, cattle. (Sometimes carelessly used for *graze*, but properly implying the cropping of scanty vegetation.)

1542 BOORDE *Dyetary* xvi. (1870) 275 At the x byt on the grasse, or brosynge on the tree. **1580** HOLLYBAND *Treas. Fr. Tong, Brouter & manger*, to brouze, to feede like an Oxe or Goate. **1593** NASHE *Christ's T.* 32 b, All the bushes and boughes .. were hewd downe and feld for men (like brute beastes) to brouze on. **1611** SHAKS. *Wint. T.* III. iii. 68. **1612** T. TAYLOR *Comm. Titus* ii. 1 (1619) 336 Cattell forsaking the .. pastures to broose vpon leaues and boughes. **1789** MRS. PIOZZI *Journ. France* I. 38 Goats .. browze upon the steeps of Snowdon. **1848** CARPENTER *Anim. Phys.* 141 The Giraffe uses its long tongue to lay hold of the young shoots on which it browzes. **1870** BRYANT *Homer* I. II. 74 The horses browsed on lotus-leaves.

b. *fig.* or *transf.*

1611 SHAKS. *Cymb.* III. vi. 38 There is cold meat i' th' Caue, we'l brouz on that. **1823** LAMB *Elia* Ser. I. xv. (1865) 119 And browsed at will upon that fair and wholesome pasturage [a good Library]. **1870** LOWELL *Among my Bks.* Ser. I. (1873) 9 We thus get a glimpse of him browsing—for .. he was always a random reader—in his father's library. **1927** J. S. HUXLEY *Religion without Revelation* iv. 127 Browsing in the public library at Colorado Springs, .. I came across some essays of Lord Morley. **1965** *Crescendo* Sept. 1/1 While browsing through a local bookshop recently I came across your excellent publication. **1968** *Listener* 22 Aug. 242/3 *Hobson-Jobson* is not of course a book to read right through but to browse in—something like, but on a vaster scale, Fowler's *Modern English Usage.*

2. *trans.* To crop and eat (leaves, twigs, etc.).

1523 FITZHERB. *Husb.* §131 Fell the vnder wodde fyrste in wynter that thy cattell or beastes maye eate & brouse the toppes. **1591** SPENSER *Virg. Gnat* 82 Others .. brouze the woodbine twigges. **1612** DRAYTON *Poly-olb.* xviii. 284. **1789** WOLCOTT (P. Pindar) *Odes* xiii. 4 Forc'd, forc'd to brouse, like goats, the lanes for food. **1859** DARWIN *Orig. Spec.* iii. (1878) 56 Little trees which had been perpetually browsed down by the cattle. **1864** *Daily Tel.* 21 May, Herds of deer have browsed all the leaves away as high as their necks could reach.

3. *causal.* To feed (cattle) *on* (twigs, etc.).

1550 [see BROWSER 1]. **1669** WORLIDGE *Syst. Agric.* vi. §2 (1681) 94 Rangers and Keepers of Parks .. brousing their Deer on it. **1876** *Rep. Vermont Board Agric.* III. 74 It was customary, in years past, when farmers were short of hay, to browse their cattle, as it was called.

browser ('braʊzə(r)). [f. BROWSE *v.* + -ER[1].]

† **1.** ? One who feeds the deer (in winter-time). Cf. BROWSE *v.* 3. *Obs.*

1550 in *Harcourt Papers* (1876) [At a survey taken 10th April 4th year of Edward VI] the jury did then present that .. the Lords of Stanton Harcourt have used and ought to find four Browsers in Woodstock Park in winter time, when any snow shall happen to fall, and tarry, lye, and abide be the space of two days, and so to feed the said Browsers there browsing soe long as the snow doth lye, every browser to have to his lodging every night one billet of wood the length of his ax-helve.

2. a. An animal which browses.

1845 MIALL in *Nonconf.* V. 312 The stupidest of the browsers of the field. **1870** YEATS *Nat. Hist. Comm.* 122 We fell a forest, and the timid browsers lose their shelter and food.

b. *fig.*; *spec.* a person who browses among books.

1863 GEO. ELIOT *Romola* I. vii. 126 Friends who were ready to praise his writings: .. amiable browsers in the Medicean park along with himself. **1937** *Atlantic Monthly* Apr. 502/1 But the perfect browser must have one possession .. a *ladder*; a library ladder. **1955** *N.Y. Times* 5 May 32/3 Conrad Library, where often the casual browser has stayed to become a serious reader. **1965** *Listener* 2 Dec. 926/2 Bookshop browsers.

browsing ('braʊzɪŋ), *vbl. sb.* [f. BROWSE *v.*]

1. a. The action of feeding upon young shoots and leaves of trees and shrubs; also *concr.* shoots and leaves; browsing-ground.

1580 BARET *Alv.* B 1401 A gathering together of leaues for beasts in winter; a browsing. *c* **1645** HOWELL *Lett.* (1650) II. 8 The park .. for groves, and browsings for the deer .. may compare with any. **1859** JEPHSON *Brittany* ix. 144 Heather and gorse, kept short by the browsing of the goats.

b. *fig.*

1899 S. A. BARNETT *Let.* in H. O. Barnett *Canon S.A.B.* (1918) II. 127 Many men owe as much to browsing as to the running... They laid hold of books to their tastes. **1902** W. RALEIGH *Let.* Aug. (1926) I. 241, I will not say that I have read it .. all through, but I found browsings to interest me. **1907** E. GODFREY *Eng. Children* xix. 309 Those early browsings in the fields of romance by no means unfitted him to become an explorer in the paths of science. **1966** *Listener* 20 Jan. 108/2 The book makes incomparable browsing.

2. *Comb.*, as ***browsing-line.***

1805 REPTON *Landsc. Gard.* 51 Stripped of their foliage to a certain height .. which I shall call the browsing line. **1828** STEUART *Planter's G.* 309 The browsing-line of the black-faced sheep seldom reaches to more than three, or three feet and a half above the surface.

'browsing, *ppl. a.* That browses.

1702 POPE *Dryope* 91 Nor let my branches feel The browzing cattle or the piercing steel. *a* **1725** POPE *Odyss.* XVII. 620 The grazing ox, and browzing goat. **1863** A. RAMSAY *Phys. Geog.* xxviii. 459 Carnivorous and browsing mammalia.

browst (braʊst). *Sc.* Forms: ? 5 browest, 6 broust, 6– browst. [f. *brow-*, pa. ppl. stem of BREW, or perh. of earlier origin, from the root *bru-*, as in OHG. *brû-hûs*; cf. also Du. *brouw-sel* 'a browst': the nature of the suffix is not clear. (Some modern writers have perverted this to BREWST.)] A brewing; a brewage. Also *fig.*

a **1500** *Burrow Lawes* xxxix. (JAM.) For the fourt browest, he [the Browster] sall giue the dewtie of ane halfe yeare. **1594** *Batt. Balrinnes* in *Scot. Poems 16th C.* II. 347 Ane bloodie broust there was brouine. **1650** ROW *Hist. Kirk* (1842) 537 Yow must cause scripture speak it, or else yow will not brew your browst well. **1816** SCOTT *Old Mort.* iv, The browst of the Howff retained .. its unrivalled reputation. **1823** —— *Q. Durward* vii, You will drink a bitter browst of your own brewing one day.

browster, -ar, northern f. BREWSTER, brewer.

a **1400** *Cov. Myst.* 132 Boutyng the browstere. *c* **1440** *Promp. Parv.* 54 Browstar or brewere. *a* **1555** LYNDESAY *Trag.* 356 Ane Browster quhilk can brew moste hoilsum aill. **1609** SKENE *Reg. Maj.* xxxix, Ane Browster. **1785** BURNS *3rd Ep. J. Lapraik* v, Browster wives and whisky stills.

browsy ('braʊzɪ), *a.* Also brousy. [f. BROWSE *v.* + -Y[1].] † **1.** Of vegetation: scanty; twiggy. *Obs.*

1738 W. ELLIS *Timber-tree* i. 6 The knotty, mossy Bodies and brousy Heads of Oaks, Ashes, and Beeches. *Ibid.* 42 These [beech sets] being of the Tree Kind .. will get a brousy, bushy Head, like the shrubby Sort.

2. Characterized by or suitable for browsing or casual reading.

1910 A. BENNETT *Jrnl.* 20 Oct. (1932) I. 388 Miscellaneous browsy reading in the evening. **1966** *Guardian* 6 May 9/3 A very quiet, wise, browsy sort of book about country life.

† **browze.** *Obs. rare*[−1]. [Corruption of F. *brou* in same sense: found earlier also as *broust*, and thus identified with the etymon of BROWSE *sb.*] The inner covering of the nutmeg.

1712 tr. *Pomet's Hist. Drugs* I. 127 The Nutmeg has three Wrappings, to wit, the Shell, the Mace and the Browze [la Coque, le Macis, et le Brou].

broyle, broyn, obs. forms of BROIL, BRINE.

broys(e, obs. f. BROWIS, and BRUISE.

brozier, var. BROSIER.

brrr (brː (brː)), *int.* Also b'rrh, brrrr. [Imitative.] An interjection expressive of shivering with cold or apprehension.

1898 R. HUGHES *Lakerim Athletic Club* vi. 109 The whirling snow hid the banks of the lake... 'Brrr!' said Tug. **1905** H. G. WELLS *Kipps* II. vii. 286 B-r-r-r. It didn't do to think of his Aunt and Uncle. **1938** O. NASH *I'm Stranger here Myself* 38 They regretfully hoist themselves up and shiver and say Brrrr! **1961** 'N. BLAKE' *Worm of Death* ii. 22 B'rrh, it's cold outside. I've swallowed about a hundred cubic feet of fog walking here.

bruart, variant of BREWARD.

bruc, variant of BRUKE, *Obs.*, a locust.

brucellosis (bruːsɛ'ləʊsɪs). *Path.* [mod.L., f. *Brucell(a*, f. the name of Sir David *Bruce*, a Scottish physician (1855–1931) + -OSIS.] A disease caused by bacteria of the genus *Brucella*; as applied to the disease in men, also called Malta fever, undulant fever, etc., and, in cattle, contagious abortion, etc.

1930 *Jrnl. Amer. Med. Assoc.* XCIV. 1905 (*title*) Brucellosis... The significance of brucella agglutinins in the blood of vegetarians. **1933** *Chem. Abstr.* XXVII. 5114 The problem of eradication of cattle brucellosis. **1936** TOPLEY & WILSON *Princ. Bacteriol.* (ed. 2) lxxii. 1333 The term brucellosis has been suggested on analogy with tuberculosis, to apply to all types of Brucella infections... We prefer ourselves to use instead the term 'Brucella infection'. **1955** *Sci. News Let.* 9 July 25/3 Brucellosis is a bacterial disease contracted in a mild but persistent form by the drinking of raw milk. **1969** *Times* 27 Jan. 10/8 Brucellosis accredited cattle only will be shown at the Surrey county show.

bruch. obs. f. BROCH, BROOCH, BROUGH, BURGH.

† **bruche**[1]. *Obs.* [OE. *bryce*, ME. *bruche* (*ü*) = OHG. *bruh*, MHG., modGer. *bruch*, MLG. *broke*, MDu. *brōke*, *bröke*, Du. *breuk*:—OTeut. **brukiz-*, from stem *bruk-* of *brek-an* to BREAK. In later ME. superseded by *breche*, BREACH.]

1. The action of breaking, fracture; *fig.* the breaking or violation of a command, engagement, etc.; transgression.

a900 *Pol. Laws Ælfred* §3 (Bosw.) Ðæs borȝes bryce. **a1000** *Guthlac* 670 (Gr.) Ne sy him banes bryce. **c1300** *Thrush & Night.* 28 Ne wes neuere bruche so strong I-broke with riȝte ne with wrong.

b. *esp.* Violation of chastity.

a1225 *Ancr. R.* 38 Wiðuten euerich bruche, mid ihol meidenhod and meidenes menske. **c1230** *Hali Meid.* 13 Vre flesch..ȝif þat ha wit hire wiðute bruche cleane.

2. A fractured or injured part; a fissure or break; = BREACH *sb.* 7.

a1225 *Leg. Kath.* 1614 Þe bruchen of hire bodi, al tobroken of þe beatinge. **a1307** in *Rel. Antiq.* II. 272 At the furmeste bruche that he fond He lep in and over he wond.

† **bruche**[2]. *Obs. rare.* Also brueche. (See quot.)

1562 TURNER *Herbal* II. 29b, Agarike is the same in a Larche tre that brueche as the Northern Englishmen call it, or as other call it, a todstole, is in a birche or a walnut tre.. It groweth..vpon the bole or body of the tre..as other thynges lyke mushrummes todestooles or bruches do.

bruchel, obs. form of BRITCHEL *a.* fragile.

† **'bruchelnesse.** [f. prec. + -NESS.] Frailty.

c1460 in *Pol. Rel. & L. Poems* (1866) 251 Ȝyue me grace to hyde and hele The blame of my bruchelnesse.

‖ **bruchus** ('bruːkəs). [L. *brūcus*, *brūchus*, a. Gr. βροῦκος, βροῦχος 'a wingless locust'.]

1. An insect; a caterpillar; = BRUKE.

1398 TREVISA *Barth. De P.R.* XI. vi. (1495) 393 Brucus is the brood of long flyes that dystroye corne and grasse. **c1475** *Bk. Found. St. Barthol. Ch.* I. vi. (1883) 52 Brucus is the issue of the buttyrflie, or he haue wynges. **1609** BIBLE (Douay) *Ps.* civ. [cv.] 34 The locust came, and the bruchus. —— *Joel* i. *comm.*, Bruchus, an other fleeing litle beast, that devoureth not only fruite but also the leaves of trees.

2. A genus of rhyncophorus beetles, of which the larvæ are destructive to pease, etc. Hence **'bruchian**, a member of the genus *Bruchus*.

1852 T. W. HARRIS *Insects New Eng.* 54 The habits of the Bruchians and their larvæ.

‖ **'brucia.** The same as BRUCINE.

1810 HENRY *Elem. Chem.* (1840) II. 304 Of Brucia. **1876** HARLEY *Mat. Med.* 513 Brucia closely resembles strychnia.

brucine ('bruːsaɪn). *Chem.* [From *Brucea antidysenterica*, the tree which was supposed to furnish false Angustura bark, now understood to be the bark of a species of Strychnos.]

A vegetable alkaloid existing in false Angustura bark, and (along with strychnine) in Nux Vomica; like strychnine it is a strong poison.

1823 J. BADCOCK *Dom. Amusem.* 148 Brucine..a new alkali is..procured..from the..*brucea anti-dysenterica*. **c1865** J. WYLDE in *Circ. Sc.* I. 416/1 Brucine may be separated from strychnine by its solubility in *cold* alcohol.

brucite ('bruːsaɪt). *Min.* [after A. *Bruce*, an American mineralogist; see -ITE.] A native hydrate of magnesia.

1868 in DANA.

bruckle ('brʌk(ə)l), *a.* Chiefly *Sc.* and *dial.* Forms: 4 brukel, 5 brukyl, 5–6 -ill, 6 -il, brukkil, -yll, brukle, brucle, 6- bruckle. [OE. *brucol* (in *scipbrucol*) f. stem *bruk-* of *brekan* to BREAK (see also BROCKLE): but in later use, perhaps phonetic variant of BRICKLE: cf. Sc. *muckle* and *mickle*.]

1. Liable to break; fragile, brittle.

1513 DOUGLAS *Æneis* XII. xii. 114 As brukkyll ice. **1562** TURNER *Herbal* II. 64a, Rootes..not brukle or easy to breke. **1589** PUTTENHAM *Eng. Poesie* (Arb.) 219 Trusting vnto a piece of bruckle wood. **a1721** KELLY *Sc. Prov.* 113 (JAM.) Lasses and glasses are bruckle ware. **1858** M. PORTEOUS *Souter Johnny* 29 In bruckle stane and lime.

2. *fig.* Frail, uncertain, precarious, 'shaky'.

c1325 *Metr. Hom* 120 Noht of brukel blod and bane. **c1425** WYNTOUN *Cron.* v. xii. 1309 Yhe Devilys war noucht wroucht of brukyl kynd. **1509** FISHER *Wks.* 91 What vessell may be more bruckle and frayle than is our body. **a1651** CALDERWOOD *Hist. Kirk* (Wodrow) III. 743 Founding them upon the bruckle authoritie of profane writers. **1814** SCOTT *Wav.* lxvii, 'My things are but in a bruckle state'. **1886** LONG *I. Wight Dial.* 8 *Bruckle*, brittle.

† **'bruckle,** *v. Obs.* or *dial.* [Related to Sc. *bruik*, to begrime (see BROOKED); prob. a frequentative: see -LE.] *trans.* To make dirty; to begrime.

Hence **'bruckled** *ppl. a.*

1648 HERRICK *Hesper.*, *Temple*, Boyes and bruckel'd children. **1661** L. GRIFFIN *Doctrine of Asse* 7 We commonly say to Dirty Children that the Gardener will sow Leeks in their faces; we may more truly tell our Bruckled Professours that the Devill will sow Tares in their Souls. **1691** RAY *N.C. Words* 11 *Bruckle*, to dirty. *Bruckled*, dirty.

† **'bruckleness.** *Obs.* exc. *dial.* [f. BRUCKLE *a.* + -NESS.] 'Bruckle' quality or condition; frailty.

1423 JAS. I *King's Q.* cxciv, Pray the reder..Of his gudnesse thy brukilnesse to knytt. **a1560** ROLLAND *Crt. Venus* II. 962 Full of brukilnes. **a1605** MONTGOMERIE *Flyting* l. 611 Fecklesse foolishnes and beastly bruklenes.

Brückner ('brʏknə(r)). *Meteorol.* The name of Professor E. *Brückner* (1862–1927), German meteorologist, used *attrib.* to designate a climatic cycle, lasting about 35 years, of alternating cold, wet periods and warm, dry periods.

1905 H. W. CLOUGH in *Astrophysical Jrnl.* XXII. 56 W. J. S. Lockyer pointed out that a cycle of about 35 years exists in the variations of the interval from one sun-spot minimum to the succeeding maximum... He considers this as the source of the Brückner cycle. **1910** *Encycl. Brit.* VI. 525/2 A somewhat longer period of slight fluctuations or oscillations of climate, known as the Brückner cycle. **1931** A. A. MILLER *Climatology* xv. 270 The best known of these is the 35-year or Brückner Cycle, found by Brückner to recur..in a variety of phenomena.

brud-, brude, obs. form of BRIDE.

bruder, obs. form of BROTHER.

brudge, obs. and dial. form of BRIDGE.

brudþing: see BRYDTHING, wedding.

brue, obs. f. BROW, BREW, and var. of BROO, *Sc.*

† **brued,** *ppl. a. Obs. rare.* In 6 brude. [Contracted from IMBRUED. (It might be from OF. *embruer*, through intermediate **abruer*.)] Imbrued.

1560 A. NEVILE *Seneca's Œdipus* 92 His eyes all bathd and brude in bloud. **1583** STANYHURST *Æneis* II. (Arb.) 49 Then they the sacred image with brude fist blooddye prophaned.

bruer, obs. form of BREWER.

brues(se, obs. form of BREWIS, BROSE.

bruet, var. of BROWET, *Obs.*, broth, soup.

bruff, dial. var. of BROUGH, a halo.

brug(e, brugg(e, obs. forms of BRIDGE.

† **Bruges.** *Obs.* Forms: 6 brigs, brug, bruges, burges, broig, brygges, 6–8 bridges, 7 birges, 8 brudges. [F. *Bruges*, Flem. *Brugge* i.e. 'bridge'.] Name of a city of Flanders, used *attrib.* in *Bruges satin*, and sometimes elliptically.

1517 T. ALLEN in Lodge *Illust. Brit. Hist.* (1838) I. 26 One black brigs hat. **1538** *Aberdeen Reg.* v. 16 (JAM.) Half ellin of Brug satine. **1545** *Lanc. Wills* (1860) II. 66 White sattin of Bridges. **1552–3** *Inv. Ch. Goods Staffords.* 17 On cope of red satin bruges. **1559** *Inv. Eccl. Vestm.* in Hay *Scotia Sacra* 189 (JAM.) Blew and yellow broig satin. **1611** *Rates* (JAM.) Threed called Birges threed. **1721** C. KING *Brit. Merch.* I. 285 Thred Sisters..Ditto Brudges. **1752** BEAWES *Lex. Mercat.* 383 Thread, called black and brown, or Bridges Outnal.

brugh, var. of BROUGH halo, and BROCH tower.

brugh, brughe, brught, obs. ff. BURGH.

brugmansia (brʊg'mænzɪə). *Bot.* [mod.L., f. the name of S. J. *Brugmans* (1763–1819), Dutch botanist: see -IA[1].] **1.** A plant of the solanaceous genus so named, native to S. America (formerly included under the genus *Datura*), the species of which have white, orange, or red tubular blossoms.

1884 LADY BRASSEY *The Trades* 352 The garden contains some..pretty 'lily-trees', as they call them here; although I should describe them as a sort of datura or brugmansia. **1961** *Amat. Gardening* 14 Oct. Suppl. 17/1 *Datura*..half-hardy plants..(also known as Brugmansias and Angels' Trumpets)..striking evergreen subjects for the cool greenhouse.

2. A plant of a genus of parasitic plants of the family Cytinaceæ, found in the Malay islands, each plant of which consists of little more than a flower.

1885 *Encycl. Brit.* XVIII. 265/2 *Rafflesia* and *Brugmansia* consists one may say of a single flower.

bruhows, obs. form of BREWHOUSE.

bruik, bruikit, Sc. forms of BROOK *v.*, BROOKED.

bruill, obs. form of BROIL.

bruilyie, bruilzie: see BRULYIE.

Bruin ('bruːɪn). In Caxton brune, brunne, bruyn. [a. MDu. *bruin* (*bruyn*, *bruun*) BROWN, the name of the bear in *Reynard the Fox*.] An appellation applied, after the manner of a proper name, to the Common or Brown Bear. (It has advanced so far in the direction of a common noun as to be often written without capital B.)

1481 CAXTON *Reynard* vii. (Arb.) 1 How bruyn the bere spedde wyth the foxe. *Ibid.* 11 The kynge..saide to brune the bere, syr brune, I wyl that ye doo this message. **1663** BUTLER *Hud.* I. III. 131 Mean while th' approach'd the place where Bruin Was now engag'd to mortal ruine. **1728** POPE *Dunc.* I. 99 So watchful Bruin forms with plastic care Each growing lump, and brings it to a Bear. **1764** T. BRYDGES *Homer Travest.* II. 89 No more each two-legg'd bruin swears. **1837** W. IRVING *Capt. Bonneville* III. 137 Promising to entrap bruin. **1867** MRS. HARVEY *Cruise Claymore* 130 During the autumn Bruin may not unfrequently be seen near the vineyards.

bruise (bruːz), *sb.* [f. the vb.]

† **1.** A breaking; a breach. *Obs.*

1441 *Plumpton Corr.* Introd. 60 In eschewing of blood-shedding and bruses of the Kings peace. **1530** PALSGR. 201/2 Brosyng or broose, *briseure*.

2. A hurt or injury to the body by a blunt or heavy instrument, causing discoloration but not laceration of the skin; a contusion.

1541 R. COPLAND *Galyen's Terap.* 2 F ij, Yf in the parties rounde about yᵉ vlcere there is eyther bruse, phlegmon, or other tumour. **1607** TOPSELL *Four-f. Beasts* 327 Wounds are most commonly made with sharp or piercing weapons, and bruises with blunt weapons. **1663–78** BUTLER *Hud.* (J.) One arm'd with metal, th' other with wood, This fit for bruise, and that for blood. **1711** ADDISON *Spect.* No. 223 ¶4 The Bruises which they often received in their Fall. **1859** TENNYSON *Elaine* 1159 His costly gift, Hard-won and hardly won with bruise and blow.

b. Of a plant, fruit, or other body.

1678 N. WANLEY *Wonders* III. xliv. §18. 226/2 He..threw it with that force against the floor that the solidest metal would have received some damage or bruise thereby. **1770** WITHERING *Brit. Plants* (1796) IV. 285 Pileus..nearly flat.. thin at the edge, turning watery on the least bruise.

c. *spec.* A contusion or injury caused by jambing; *Sc.* in form *brizz*.

Mod.Sc. His hand has got a bad brizz under the wheel.

3. *Comb.*, as **bruise-like** adj.; † **bruise-root** (see quot.); BRUISE-WORT.

1698 NEWTON *Papaver Corn.* in *Phil. Trans.* XX. 263 Or Horned Poppy, with a Yellow Flower, vulgarly called in Hampshire, Squatmore, or Bruseroot. **1839–47** TODD *Cycl. Anat. & Phys.* III. 908/1 The bruise-like swelling.

bruise (bruːz), *v.* Forms: 1 brýsan, 3–5 brisen, 3–6 brise, (4 bris), 3–7 bruse, 4–6 broose, brose, bryse, 5 brese, bresse, brysse, burse, 5–6 brisse, broyse, brouse, 6 brusse, broose, 6–7 bruze, 7, 9 bruize, 6- bruise; (also *Sc.* 4 byrs, 6 birs, 8 birze, 8- brizz; 8–9 *north. dial.* bruzz: see also BIRSE *v.*). [OE. *brýsan* to crush, bruise, with which afterwards coalesced F. *brisie-r*, *bruisier*, *bruser*, to break, smash, shatter. The latter is of uncertain origin: see Diez, Littré, and Scheler. (The Anglo-French form was *bruser*: see senses 2, 3.) The normal modern Eng. representative alike of OE. *brýse* and OF. *brise* would be *brīse* (braɪz). The early ME. *bruse* may be explained as a s.w. spelling with the usual *ü* = OE. *ȳ*; *brēse* may also be accounted for as the Kentish form with *ē* for OE. *ȳ*; but the ME. forms *brose*, *broose*, *broyse*, *brouse*, and the modern *bruize* must be from the OFr. forms, though the phonological details are obscure. The shortening of the vowel in 15th c. northern *brisse*, *brysse*, and mod.Sc. *brizz*, Eng. dial. *bruzz*, is also unusual.]

1. *trans.* 'To crush or mangle with the heavy blow of something not edged or pointed; to crush by any weight' (J.). But now chiefly in a weaker sense: To injure by a blow which discolours the skin but does not lacerate it, and breaks no bones; to contuse: **a.** (the body of men or animals).

α. Forms *brýsan*, *brise*, *brese*, *birse*, *byrse*, *briss*.

c890 K. ÆLFRED *Bæda* v. vi. (Bosw.) His preosta ænne of horse fallende and ȝebrysedne. **a1000** *Be Domes Dæȝe* 49 Ne mid swiðran his swyþe nele brysan wanhydiȝ ȝemod. **c1200** *Trin. Coll. Hom.* 61 He wile smite mid..swuerde . and brisen. **a1300** *Havelok* 1835 That he sholde him..brisen so, that wit no salue Ne sholde him helen leche non. **c1375** ? BARBOUR *St. Vincentius* 395 Sancte Vincent tormentit wes Byrsit, beft & brynt. **c1400** *Destr. Troy* 7929 My body hath þou brisit. **c1430** *Syr Tryam.* 237 Upon an olde stede, That was bresyd and blynde. **1470–85** MALORY *Arthur* (1817) I. 375 Sir kayes hors brysed hym ful sore. **1501** DOUGLAS *Pal. Hon.* III. 1924 He..brissit all my banis.

β. Form *bruse*, *bruze*.

a1375 *Joseph Arim.* 501 In þe þikkeste pres he..Breek braynes a-brod, brusede burnes. **1387** TREVISA *Higden* Rolls Ser. III. 59 þe Sabynes..brusede and ouerlay þat mayde [Tarpeia]. **1516** FABYAN *Chron.* II. 538 The erle marshall ouerthrewe his appellaunt, and so brusyd hym, yᵗ..he dyed. **1590** SPENSER *F.Q.* III. iv. 34 Least they [fishes] their finnes should bruze..upon the stony grownd. **1591** —— *Virgil's Gnat* xxxvii, And with his hand him rashly bruzing slewe. **1603** KNOLLES *Hist. Turks* (1621) 221 And thereby brused the head of the..enemie of mankinde.

γ. Form *brose*, *broyse*, *broose*, *brouse*.

1382 WYCLIF *Num.* xxii. 25 The asse ioynede hym silf to the wal, and briside [*v.r.* brosede] the foot of the sitter. **1430** LYDG. *Chron. Troy* IV. xxx, On a shelde, brosed and affrayde They bare hym home. **1494** FABYAN VI. clxiii. 140 [He] fell from his horse..whereof he was soo broysyd that he dyed. **1529** MORE *Comfort agst. Trib.* II. Wks. 1178/2 The iuste man though he fal, shall not be broosed. **1530** PALSGR. 471/2, I brose with a stroke or with a fall..I have brousyd my shoulder with fallynge downe the stayres. **c1563** *Thersites* in *4 Old Plays* (1848) 77 He wyll brose me.

δ. Form *bruise*, *bruize*.

1580 BARET *Alv.* B 1412 A wounde bruised is woorse than that is onely cut. **1598** SHAKS. *Merry W.* I. i. 294, I bruiz'd my shin th' other day. **1611** BIBLE *Gen.* iii. 15 It shal bruise thy head, and thou shalt bruise his heele. **1662** FULLER *Worthies* (1840) III. 332 He fell down, and bruised himself to death. **1709** STEELE *Tatler* No. 45 ¶7, I am bruised to Death. **1782** PRIESTLEY *Corrupt. Chr.* II. x. 261 [They] made no scruple..to beat and bruise him. **1842** TENNYSON *Two Voices* 222 Cursed and scorn'd, and bruised with

stones. **1871** MORLEY *Voltaire* 74 In England..the peasant has not his feet bruised in wooden shoes.

b. (plants, fruit).

c **1325** *E.E. Allit. P.* B. 1047 Bot quen hit [the fruit] is brused oþer broken oþer byten in twynne. **1523** FITZHERB. §129 Get as manye rotes with them as thou canste and breake them not nor bryse them. **1596** SHAKS. *1 Hen. IV*, I. i. 8 Nor bruise her Flowrets with the Armed hoofes Of hostile paces. **1633** G. HERBERT *Temple, Providence* xvii. Bees work for man; and yet they never bruise Their masters flower. **1681** BAXTER in *Bk. of Praise* (1862) 202 If death shall bruise this springing seed Before it comes to fruit.

c. To make a dent in, crush out of shape, batter (a hard surface).

1530 PALSGR. 471/2, I brose harnesse or ones flesshe, whan it synketh in with the weyghtynesse of strokes, *Jenfondre*. His heed pece was brosed with the stroke that a man myght have layed his hande in the hole. **1599** [see BRUISED *ppl. a.*] **1875** *Lanc. Gloss.* (E.D.S.) 60 Aw've bruzzed mi clog-nose wi puncin' that owd can.

d. To maul as a boxer or prize-fighter.

a **1625** FLETCHER *Nice Valour* I. i, He shall bruise three a month.

†**2.** To break (*in pieces, down*), to smash. *Obs.* [This sense was apparently from French.]

[**1292** BRITTON I. xi. §1 Ceux, qi felounousement.. brusent eglises, ou autri mesouns.] *a* **1300** *E.E. Psalter* xlv[i]. 10 Bowe shall he bris, and breke wapenes ma. **1382** WYCLIF *2 Kings* xi. 18 And thei distruyden his auters and the ymagis broosiden to gydris miȝtily. **1483** CAXTON *Gold. Leg.* 438/4 He toke breed and..brosyd and gaue it to his dyscyples. **1494** FABYAN VII. ccxxiv. 286 Kyng Phylyp.. broused or crased yᵉ castellys. *c* **1530** BERNERS *Arth. Lyt. Bryt.* (1814) 30 Not leue standyng neyther castel nor toure vp right; but I shall bruise them downe to the erth. **1535** COVERDALE *Dan.* ii. 40 As yron brusseth and breaketh all thinges. **1590** R. FERRIS *Trav. Bristowe* in Collier *Illust. E.E. Pop. Lit.* xvii, Had his foote once slipped..he would haue beene brused in peeces. **1611** *Art of Venerie* 77 Let him plash or bruse downe small twigges.

3. *fig.* (to senses 1, 2, 4) To crush, wound, disable.

[**1292** BRITTON I. xxi. §7 Qi les sequestres de nos ministres a escient eynt bruseez.] **1382** WYCLIF *Deut.* ix. 3 Fier deuowrynge and wastynge, the which brisse [*MS. E.* bruse] hem down. —— *Prov.* Prol. 1 Thurȝ long sicknesse brosid. *c* **1500** *Partenay* 3748 Peruers fortune..Which on reisith, Anothir don brise. **1594** SHAKS. *Rich. III*, v. ii. 2 Bruis'd vnderneath the yoake of Tyranny. **1600** HOLLAND *Livy* XLII. l. 1144 How they have quelled and bruised [*fregisse*] the puissance of the Carthaginians. **1667** MILTON *P.L.* v. 884 An Iron Rod to bruise and breake Thy disobedience. **1871** MORLEY *Crit. Misc.* (1886) III. 44 He feared that violent surgery which in eradicating a false opinion fatally bruises at the same time a true and wholesome feeling that may cling to it.

4. To beat small, pound, crush, bray, grind down.

1382 WYCLIF *Lev.* ii. 16 A part of the brisde corn. **1398** TREVISA *Barth. De P.R.* v. xvi. (1495) 121 The Iawes ben as it were two mylstones contynued to brose and grynde the mete. *c* **1420** *Liber Cocorum* (1862) 45 Ȝif þay [peas] ben harde..Brysse hom or strene hom. **1523** FITZHERB. *Husb.* §59 Take that grasse, and broyse it a lyttell in a morter. **1697** DRYDEN *Virg. Georg.* IV. 194 Some scatt'ring Pot-herbs.. bruis'd with Vervain. **1846** J. BAXTER *Libr. Pract. Agric.* II. 415 Bruize eight gallons of red currants with one quart of raspberries. **1847-9** TODD *Cycl. Anat. & Phys.* IV. 15/1 Larger morsels..are first seized and bruised by the dental apparatus.

†**5.** To crush by pressure, jam, squeeze. (The ordinary sense in mod. Scotch. See also BIRSE *v.*)

1614 RALEIGH *Hist. World* II. v. iii. §6 Wind bruised out of a bladder. **1725** RAMSAY *Gentle Sheph.* III. iii. Poems (1844) 38 Let my arms..brizz thy bonny breasts and lips to mine. *a* **1774** FERGUSSON *Drink Eclog.* Poems (1845) 51 The thrifty guid-wife sees Her lasses kirn, or birze the dainty cheese. *Mod.Sc.* He has briz'd his finger in the door.

6. *Naut. to bruise water*: see quots.

1867 SMYTH *Sailor's Word-bk.*, *Bruising water*, pitching heavily to a head-sea, and making but little head-way. *Bruise-water*, a ship with very bluff bows, built more for carrying than sailing. **1880** *Daily Tel.* 7 Sept., While, rail under, she is bruising her water like a barge.

7. *intr.* with *along*. To ride on recklessly, without regard to fences or crops damaged, or to sparing the horse. (Hunting slang: cf. *to pound along*.)

1865 *Dublin Univ. Mag.* II. 19 A majority of those who follow them have..no notion of hunting, but go 'bruising' along. **1872** *Anteros* xii. 110 The baron hunted his five days ..bruising along..determinedly.

8. To become bruised.

1912 W. DEEPING *Sincerity* xxii. 175 The huge mouth seemed to bruise like an over-ripe love-apple.

bruise, obs. form of BREWIS; var. of BROSE.

'bruiseable, *a. rare.* [f. BRUISE *v.* + -ABLE.]

1611 COTGR., *Friable*, bruiseable, easie to be broken.

bruised (bruːzd), *ppl. a.* [f. as prec. + -ED[1].]

1. Hurt or damaged by a heavy blow; contused; with skin crushed and discoloured. (Formerly in stronger sense.)

1388 WYCLIF *Matt.* xii. 20 A brisid [**1382** schaken] rehed he shal not breke. *c* **1450** LONELICH *Grail* xxvii. 94 A ful wery and abrosed Manne. **1573** TUSSER *Husb.* (1878) 32 Forget it not Fruit brused will rot. **1727** DE FOE *Eng. Tradesm.* (1841) I. vi. 44 Like an old invalid soldier out of the wars, maimed, bruised, and sick. **1884** G. ALLEN *Strange Stories* 85 The bruised and livid face of the old parson.

fig. **1604** SHAKS. *Oth.* I. iii. 219, I neuer yet did heare That the bruized heart was pierc'd through the eares. **1642** MILTON *Apol. Smect.* (1851) 297 The brused consciences of so many Christians.

b. Of blood: Extravasated. *Obs.* or *dial.*

1579 LANGHAM *Gard. Health* (1633) 113 Bruses and brused bloud, stampe Nep leaues with salt and apply them. *Mod.Sc.* Briz'd bluid.

2. Crushed, battered, dinted.

1590 SPENSER *F.Q.* I. xi. 14 Often bounding on the brused gras. **1599** SHAKS. *Hen. V*, v. Prol. 18 His bruised Helmet and his bended Sword. *c* **1650** in Rushw. *Hist. Coll.* III. (1692) I. 77 A bruised Ship-wrackt Vessel, full of Leaks. **1840** HOOD *Up Rhine* 44 Oh it's the beautiful brass pail.. and how it's all bruised and battered.

3. Crushed small, brayed, pounded.

1382 [see BRUISE *v.* 4]. *c* **1420** *Pallad. on Husb.* I. 679 Bresed whete and breses longe. **1664** EVELYN *Kal. Hort.* (1729) 194 Those [birds] who feed on bruised seeds.

bruiser ('bruːzə(r)). [f. BRUISE *v.* + -ER[1].]

1. One who bruises or crushes. Also, an operative who pulverizes materials.

1586 WARNER *Alb. Eng.* III. xviii. 81 The Brooser of the Serpents head. **1738** WESLEY *Hymn 'Praise by all to Christ be given'* xvi, Serpent, see in us thy Bruiser, Feel his Power. **1863** J. MURPHY *Comm. Gen.* iii. 20 The bruiser of the serpent's head. **1921** *Dict. Occup. Terms* (1927) §056 *Sample bruiser*; pulverises average sample of ore with flat-headed hammer, ready for sampler.

2. In the phraseology of the prize-ring: A professional boxer, a prize-fighter. Also *gen.*, a brawny, muscular man.

1744 H. WALPOLE *Lett. H. Mann* (1834) II. cxvi. 6 He let into the pit great numbers of bear-garden bruisers (that is the term) to knock down everybody that hissed. **1754** *Connoisseur* No. 10 (1774) I. 77 Has no more claims to heroism, than the case-hardened valour of a bruiser or prize-fighter. **1796** J. ANSTEY *Pleader's Guide* 202 A secret joy the Bruiser knows In giving and receiving blows. **1811** BYRON *Curse Min.* xi, Be all the bruisers cull'd from all St. Giles'. **1873** SYMONDS *Grk. Poets* x. 330 Polydeuces was a notable bruiser. **1907** *Daily Chron.* 11 Oct. 3/3 A 'hero' of a sufficiently 'bruiser' type to please the most athletic-minded youth. **1934** J. T. FARRELL *Young Manhood* (1936) iv. 205 Two of the bruisers were drawing close to him. He started to run.

3. *Hunting slang.* See BRUISE *v.* 7.

1830 R. EG.-WARBURTON *Hunt. Songs, Woore Country* vi, On a light thorough-bred there's a bruiser.

4. A concave tool used in grinding lenses or the specula of telescopes. Also, any machine, tool, or other implement used for bruising or crushing.

In quot. 1828 applied to a tooth.

1777 MUDGE in *Phil. Trans.* LXVII. 304 A concave tool or bruiser, with which..the brass grinder, and the hones are to be formed. *c* **1790** IMISON *Sch. Arts* II. 108 All the emery strokes are ground off from the bruiser. **1828** FLEMING *Brit. Anim.* 9 In the lower jaw [of the badger], the bruiser is small, the chewer large. **1881** OGILVIE (Annandale), *Bruiser*.., the name of various machines for bruising grain, &c., for feeding cattle.

†**'bruisewort.** *Herb. Obs.* [From supposed healing virtues.] The name of one or two different plants, *esp.* the Common Daisy. Cf. *bonewort*.

c **1000** *Sax. Leechd.* I. 374 Wið lungen adle ȝenim..and bryse wyrt and brun wyrt. *a* **1450** *Alphita* (Anecd. Oxon.) 45 *Consolida minor*..waysegle, *uel* bonwort, *uel* brosewort. *c* **1460** J. RUSSELL *Bk. Nurture* in *Babees Bk.* (1868) 184 Brese-wort..is good for ache. **1597** GERARD *Herbal* cxciii. §7. 512 The Daisie is called..in English Daisies and Bruise woort. **1611** COTGR., *Marguerite des prez*, th' ordinarie, little, white and wild Daisie, called (otherwise) Bruisewort. **1783** AINSWORTH *Lat. Dict.* (Morell) I, Bruise wort, *consolida*. **1830** WITHERING *Brit. Plants* (ed. 7) II. 537 *S[aponaria] officinalis*, Soapwort, Bruisewort.

bruising ('bruːzɪŋ), *vbl. sb.* [f. BRUISE *v.*]

1. Crushing or damaging with a heavy blow; also (*obs.*) breaking in pieces, breaking; also *fig.*

1382 WYCLIF *Ps.* cv[i]. 30 And Fynees stod and pleside; and the brosing [Vulg. *quassatio*] ceside. *c* **1460** *Towneley Myst.* 172 For bryssyng of youre bonys. **1526** *Pilgr. Perf.* (W. de W. 1531) 58 b, Kepe the rule of holy obedyence hole and sounde, without crasynge or brusynge. **1664** EVELYN *Kal. Hort.* (1729) 219 To prevent bruising by Wind-falls.. lay some Straw under your Fruit-Trees.

†**b.** *concr.* A broken piece, a fragment. *Obs.*

1382 WYCLIF *Isa.* xxx. 14 Ther shal not be founde of his brosingus [**1388** gobetis] a shord.

2. Fighting with the fists, boxing.

1780 in *Wilberforce's Life* (1838) I. 14 He is a fine fellow if you come to bruising. **1854** THACKERAY *Newcomes* I. 101 Bruising was considered a fine manly old English custom. **1881** BLACKMORE *Maid of Sk.* 163 He had held the belt for seven years, for wrestling as well as for bruising.

3. *Comb.*, as ***bruisingwise*** adv.; **bruising-match**, a boxing-match, prize-fight.

1575 BANISTER *Chyrurg.* II. (1585) 263 If it be brusingwise doone, we call it a contused wounde, or Ecchymosis. **1794** WOLCOTT (P. Pindar) *Rowl. for Oliver* Wks. II. 402 It would wear the aspect of a bruising-match.

bruising, *ppl. a.* [see -ING[2].] That bruises.

1578 LYTE *Dodoens* I. i. 3 Brusing or shyvering coldes. **1594** SHAKS. *Rich. III*, v. iii. 110 Put in their hands thy bruising Irons of wrath. **1874** BOUTELL *Arms & Arm.* vii. 121 Seriously injured by the bruising effect of the blow.

b. *Hunting slang.* See BRUISE *v.* 7.

1872 *Anteros* xvi. 142 A fair, though by no means bruising rider to hounds.

bruisse, obs. form of BREWIS.

bruit (bruːt), *sb.* Forms: 4 brout, 5 bruyt(e, 5-7 brute, 6 brewte, 6-7 bruite, 5- bruit. [a. F. *bruit* in same senses, ppl. sb. belonging to *bruire* vb. to make a noise, roar: corresp. to Pr. *bruzer, brugir*, OCat. *brogir*, It. *bruire*. According to Littré, *brugītus*, the prototype of *bruit*, occurs in late L. Diez views with favour a derivation proposed by Ménage from L. *rugīre* to roar, *rugītus* roaring, and says that *brugit* for *rugit* occurs in *Lex Alemann.* If this be so, the prefixed *b* may be due to some onomatopœic alteration.]

1. Noise, din, clamour, sound. *arch.*

c **1450** *Merlin* 211 Ther sholde ye haue herde soche bruyt and soche noyse. **1523** LD. BERNERS *Froiss.* I. xviii. 23 They made a mereuilus great brute, wᵗ blowyng of hornes. **1563** FOXE *A. & M.* I. 689/2 A brute or noise of wild Beasts. **1612** DRAYTON *Poly-olb.* xv. 240 A shrill and suddaine brute this Prothalamion brake. **1637** R. HURST tr. *Gombauld's Endim.* (1639) 202 A confused bruite of Cymballs. **1837** CARLYLE *Fr. Rev.* I. I. III. iii. 57 Testifying, as his wont is, by loud bruit. *a* **1863** MERIVALE *Rom. Emp.* (1865) V. xliii. 219 To check it with the bruit of arms.

2. Report noised abroad, rumour, tidings; matter noised abroad. *arch.*

1494 FABYAN VII. 387 Not long after yᵉ brute of this ouerthrowe of the Englysshemen came vnto the towne. **1611** BIBLE *Nahum* iii. 19 All that heare the bruit of thee, shall clap the hands ouer thee. **1671** EVELYN *Mem.* (1857) II. 66 There came an uncertain bruit from Barbadoes of some disorder there. **1748** RICHARDSON *Clarissa* (1811) III. xiv. 88 Who says Miss Clarissa Harlowe is the paragon of virtue? .. Common bruit! Is virtue to be established by common bruit only? **1864** KIRK *Chas. Bold* II. IV. iv. 483 The wildest bruits were greedily credited.

†**b.** Noising abroad, public utterance. *Obs.*

1548 UDALL, etc. *Erasm. Par. Mark* x, The bruite or preaching of the Ghospell.

†**3.** Fame, renown, celebrity, reputation. *Obs.*

c **1475** CAXTON *Jason* 51 The bruit of preu Jason augmented..from day to day. **1513** DOUGLAS *Æneis* XIII. Prol. 193 Quha evir in Latyn hes the bruit or glore. **1549-62** STERNHOLD & H. *Ps.* lxviii. 11 His people triumphes make, and purchase brute and fame. **1609** SKENE *Reg. Maj.* 20 Ane Arbitour sould be of gude brute and fame.

‖**4.** *Med.* A name for any of the sounds heard in auscultation; e.g. *bruit artériel, bruit de souffle*, etc. A French sense; sometimes used in Eng.

bruit (bruːt), *v.* Also 6-7 bruite, 6-8 brute. [f. BRUIT *sb.*]

1. *trans.* To noise, report, rumour. Often with *abroad, about*.

a **1528** SKELTON *Col. Clout* 489 With language thus poluted, Holy Churche is bruted. **1548** UDALL, etc. *Erasm. Par. John* iv. 28 The woman did bruit abrode this rumour. **1598** DRAYTON *Heroic. Ep.* XVI. 101 When Fame shall brute thy Banishment abroad. **1591** SHAKS. *1 Hen. VI*, II. iii. 68, I finde thou art no lesse then Fame hath bruited. **1682** BUNYAN *Holy War* 43 If I first bruite this, the tidings, that will come after, will all be swallowed up of this. **1837** CARLYLE *Fr. Rev.* II. III. iv. iii. 263 The country is getting up; noise of you is bruited day after day. **1840** DICKENS *Barn. Rudge* (1866) II. lxxiii. 66 This report..was bruited about with much industry.

b. with *subord. clause*, or an equivalent.

1525 LD. BERNERS *Froiss.* II. ccxxii. [ccxviii.] 691 The Frenchemen bruteth that ye wyll put out of your armes tharmes of Fraunce. **1538** LATIMER *Serm. & Rem.* (1845) 404 [Those]..which were bruited to deny the sacrament. **1651** *Proc. Parliament* No. 98. 1502 The Enemy was bruted to be upon his March towards Carlisle. **1706** ESTCOURT *Fair Examp.* IV. i. 51 To blast my Fame, and brute it to the World that you have left me. **1835** LYTTON *Rienzi* IV. i, They do bruit it that he sees visions.

c. *intr.*

1818 KEATS *Endymion* I. 791 Bronze clarions awake, and faintly bruit, Where long ago a giant battle was.

2. *trans.* To speak of, make famous, celebrate.

1553 T. WILSON *Rhet.* 11 Let Cesar, Alexander, and Hanniball be bruted for warriers. **1598** YONG *Diana* 98 Of whom Fame brutes their name in euery ground. **1641** MILTON *Ch. Govt.* v. (1851) 113 A man so much bruited for learning. **1791** COWPER *Iliad* VIII. 220 The shield of Nestor, bruited to the skies. **1816** BYRON *Ch. Har.* III. 37 Thy wild name Was ne'er more bruited in men's minds than now.

†**3.** To din. *Obs.*

1719 D'URFEY *Pills* (1872) IV. 86 Whole Towns you will bruit with a Pettifogging Suit.

bruit, -ish, obs. forms of BRUTE, BRUTISH.

bruited ('bruːtɪd), *ppl. a.* [f. BRUIT *v.* + -ED[1].] Noised abroad; rumoured, reported; famed, renowned, celebrated.

1523 SKELTON *Garl. Laurel* 395 The bruted Britons of Brutus Albion. **1630** M. GODWYN *Bp. Hereford's Ann. Eng.* I. 68 The Kings much bruited humanity. **1874** BLACKIE *Self-Cult.* 51 The most bruited..hydropathic appliances.

bruiter ('bruːtə(r)). [f. BRUIT *v.* + -ER[1].] One who spreads a report, rumour, etc.

1535 T. CROMWELL in Strype *Eccl. Mem.* I. App. lxviii, To have compressed the bruters therof to silence. **1548** UDALL, etc. *Erasm. Par. John* 50 The bruters abrode of all the thynges that he wroughte. **1638** HEYWOOD *Rape Lucr.* Wks. 1874 V. 226 Then be the bruter Of thy owne shame.

†**'bruitful**, *a. Obs.* [f. BRUIT *sb.* + -FUL.] Full of renown, renowned, famous.

1609 HEYWOOD *Brit. Troy* XIV. xxi, His bruitfull fame.

†**'bruitish**, *a. Obs.* [f. as prec. + -ISH.] Rumoured, noised abroad.

1567-8 T. HOWELL *Newe Sonets* (1879) 134 Eche bruitish broyle that forth abrode is blowne; Beleeue not lightly.

† **bruke.** *Obs.* exc. *dial.* In 4 **bruk, bruyk, bruc.** [ad. L. *brūcus, brūchus*; see BRUCHUS.]
1. 'A locust without wings'; ? the larva of the locust; a destructive caterpillar.
a **1340** HAMPOLE *Psalter* civ. 32 He sayd & the locust come and the bruyk.. *Comm.* The locust is modire of the bruyk: thai ere litill bestis, bot thai ere ful noyous. **1382** WYCLIF *Lev.* xi. 22 As is bruk [**1388** bruke] in his kynde, that is the kynde of locust er it haue wenges. —— *Jer.* li. 14 Y shal fulfille thee of men, as with bruc werm. **1609** BIBLE (Douay) *Joel* i. 4 The residue of the locust hath the bruke eaten.
2. (See quot.)
1847–78 HALLIWELL, *Bruck*, a field-cricket. *North.*

bruke, obs. f. BROOK.

bruket, -it, Sc. f. BROOKED, streaked.

brukil, -ill, -yl, obs. ff. BRUCKLE.

brule, -inge, brullynge, obs. ff. BROIL, -ING.

brulyie, brulzie, bruilzie, ('bryʎɪ, 'brylɪ). Also brully. Sc. and north. form of BROIL, a fray, disturbance. (The *z* stands for ȝ, *y*.)
1785 BURNS *Ep. W. Simpson* Postscr. xiii, We Bardies ken some better Than mind sic brulzie. **1790** —— *Election Ballad* xvii, And Hell mix'd in the brulyie. **1818** SCOTT *Hrt. Midl.* xvi, As forward in a bruilzie as their neighbours. **1826** —— in Lockhart (1839) VIII. 277 On the whole I am glad of this bruilzie. **1875** ROBINSON *Whitby Gloss.* (E.D.S.) *Brully*, a broil or squabble.
¶ See also BROIL *sb.*¹ and *v.*²

brulyiement, brulliement, Sc. and north. dial. form of BROILMENT, broil, disturbance.
1715 RAMSAY *Cont. Christ's Kirk Gr.* II. ii, And quat this brulziement at anes. **1722** HAMILTON *Wallace* 45 (JAM.) An hundred at this bruilliement were killed. **1804** R. ANDERSON *Cumbrld. Ball., Jeff & Job*, And meade a brulliment and bodder.

brum (brʌm), *v. rare*⁻¹. [cf. Ger. *brummen* to hum, murmur.] *intr.* To murmur, hum.
1844 *Blackw. Mag.* LVI. 207 Now this is the strangest well!.. always humming and brumming.

Brum. A slang contraction of BRUMMAGEM; *attrib.* 'counterfeit, not genuine'.
[**1862** *Cornh. Mag.* Nov. 648 (Hoppe) We have just touched for a rattling stake of sugar (i.e. a large stake of money) at Brum.] **1881** *Standard* 27 Sept. 2/1 The Lobster Smack, the house of call for the 'brum'—i.e. unlicensed—pilots, who are patronised by captains objecting to the higher dues charged by the regular Trinity House men at Gravesend.. Beside the fire is seated one of the 'brum' pilots.

‖**Brumaire** (brymɛr). [Fr.; f. F. *brume* fog: see BRUME.] The name adopted for the second month of the year in the calendar of the French Republic, introduced in 1793; it extended from Oct. 22 to Nov. 20.
1803 F. LATHON (*title*) The Castle of the Twileries, or a Narrative of all the events which have taken place.. from the time of its construction, to the Eighteenth Brumaire of the year VIII.

brumal ('bruːməl), *a.* Also 6 **brumaill,** 6–7 **brumall.** [ad. L. *brūmāl-is* belonging to winter, f. *brūma* contr. of **brevima*, shortest (day), winter; cf. F. *brumal.*] Belonging to winter; winter-like, wintry.
1513 DOUGLAS *Æneis* VII. Prol. 14 Thai schort days that clerkis clepe brumaill. **1646** SIR T. BROWNE *Pseud. Ep.* 129 About the brumall Solstice.. the Sea is calme, and the winds do cease. **1783** W. F. MARTYN *Geog. Mag.* II. 374 They walk barefooted, throughout the brumal season. **1870** LOWELL *Study Wind.* 32 What cheerfulness there was in brumal verse was that of Horace's.

brumby, brumbie ('brʌmbɪ). *Austral.* Also brumbee. [Origin unknown.] A wild or unbroken horse.
1880 *Australasian* 4 Dec. 712/3 (Morris), These our guide pronounced to be 'brumbies', the bush name here [Queensland] for wild horses. **1887** KIPLING *Plain Tales fr. Hills* (1890) 153 People who lost money on him [*sc.* a race-horse] called him a 'brumby'. **1899** SEMON *In Austral. Bush* 95 When one of the brumbies begins to move all the herd follow. **1916** *Anzac Book* 143 A lanky, sawny bushman who ..saddled his brumby, and rode for the nearest town. **1950** 'N. SHUTE' *Town like Alice* 90, 'I got thrown once,' he said, 'breaking in a brumby to the saddle.'
b. *attrib.*
1895 *Chambers's Jrnl.* 702/1 The Brumbie Horse of Australia.. is the descendant of runaways of imported stock. **1897** *Pall Mall Mag.* Feb. 190 And so to the unknown interior, past the points where sheep-tracks become brumby-trails. **1925** *Chambers's Jrnl.* 810/1 Wild or 'brumbie' mobs, which consisted of mares and one lord of the harem. **1926** *Brit. Weekly* 19 Aug. 412/5 An unbroken, raging devil of a brumby colt. **1967** *Sunday Mail Mag.* (Brisbane) 16 Apr. 2 Brumby hunters if they're successful, finish up with a batch of.. wild horses.

brume (bruːm). [a. F. *brume* fog:—L. *brūma* winter; see BRUMAL *a.*] Fog, mist, vapour.
1808 J. BARLOW *Columb.* I. 579 Hail, with its glassy globes, and brume congeal'd. **1863** LONGF. *Saga K. Olaf* xix. 8 Suddenly through the drifting brume The blare of the horns began to ring.

brume, obs. and Sc. form of BROOM.

†'**brument.** *Obs.* = BREVEMENT, an entry.
1523 FITZHERB. *Husb.* §152 Bokes of accompte of householde, & brumentes vpon the same.

†**brumle,** *v. Obs.*⁻¹. [app. a. Ger. *brummeln*, dim. of *brummen* to roar.] = BRIM *v.*¹
1671 *Westm. Drollery* 118 Like a Boar that runs brumling after the sows.

Brummagem ('brʌmɪdʒəm), *sb.* and *a.* Also 7 **Brom-, Brumicham, Brom-, Brim-, Brumigham, Bromedgham, Brumegeum, Brumisham, Brim-, Brumingham,** 9 **Brummejam.**
A. *sb.* **1.** A local vulgar form of the name of the town of *Birmingham*, in England. Hence (contemptuously), An article of Birmingham manufacture: *spec.* **a.** A counterfeit coin; **b.** a spur.
[**1691** G. MIEGE *New State Eng.* 235 Bromicham, particularly noted a few years ago, for the counterfeit groats made here, and from hence dispersed all over the Kingdom. **1848** MRS. GASKELL *M. Barton* (1882) 23/2 Poor babby cried ..till we got to Brummagem for the night.] **1834–43** SOUTHEY *Doctor* cxl. (D.) It proved to be a Brummejam of the coarsest and clumsiest kind. **1840** E. NAPIER *Sc. & Sports For. Lands* I. vii. 221, I tightened the reins and applied the Brummagems.
2. *Eng. Hist.* = 'Birmingham (i.e. counterfeit) Protestant' [alluding to the counterfeit groats made at Birmingham a few years before]: A nickname given to supporters of the Exclusion Bill in 1680. See BIRMINGHAM, ANTI-BIRMINGHAM.
[**1681** LUTTRELL *Brief Rel.* (1857) I. 124 The latter party have been called by the former, whigs, fanaticks, covenanteers, bromigham protestants, etc.] **1681** (Sept. 9) *Ballad, Riddle of the Round-Head*, Whigs and Brumighams, with shams and stories, Are true protestants. **1681** (Dec. 15) *Ballad, Ignoramus*, O, how they plotted! *Briminghams* voted, And all the *mobile* the holy cause promoted. **1682** *Popish Fables*, a Dialogue between Fly-blow, a Tory; Swift-heel, a Tantivy; Flash, a Brumegeum; See-well, a Whig. *Ibid.* I am a thin brass protestant silver'd over.. they call me a *Brumegeum*.. but my Sirname is *Flash*.
B. *attrib.* or *adj.* **1. a.** Made in Birmingham. **b.** With primary allusion to counterfeit groats coined there in 17th c.; but, also, with later reference to plated and lacquered wares still manufactured there: Counterfeit, sham, not genuine; of the nature of a cheap or showy imitation.
1637 *Calendar Dom. St. Papers* 105 Those swords which he.. pretends to be blades of his owne makeing are all bromedgham blades & forraine blades. **1688** T. BROWN, I coined heroes as fast as Brumingham groats. **1827** *Blackw. Mag.* XXII. Oct. 410/2 Brummagem Statesmen. **1853** LYTTON *My Novel* I. 120 (Hoppe) A work-table.. inlaid with brass.. in that peculiar taste which is vulgarly called Brummagem. **1861** A. K. H. B. *Recreat. Country Pars.* Ser. II. 47 The vulgar dandy, strutting along, with his Brummagem jewellery.
2. *Hist.* Of or pertaining to the 'Birminghams' of 1680: see A 2.
See further examples in *Birmingham Weekly Post*, 11 Dec. 1880.
1681 D'URFEY *Sir Barnaby Whig* Prol., To hear harden'd Brumicham rascals prate. **1681** (Sept. 15) *Ballad, Old Jemmy*, No mobile gay fop, With Brimigham pretences. —— (*title*) A proper New Brummigham Ballad. **1682** (Nov.) *The Cavalier Litany*, From a *Brumisham* Saint, and a serious Church Whig.. *Libera nos.* **1690** B. E. *Dict. Cant. Crew*, *Bromigham-conscience*, very bad; *Bromigham-protestants*, Dissenters or Whiggs.
Hence **Brummagemish** *a.*, **Brummagemize** *v.*, **Brummagism.**
1870 HAWTHORNE *Eng. Note-bks.* (1879) IV. 171 The country began to look Brummagemish. **1886** *Sat. Rev.* 13 Mar. 360 The reluctance of the capital to Brummagemize itself. **1858** GREENER *Gunnery* 238 As to the mechanical arrangement, to use a Brummagism, they are as if they had been pitched together.
[Of *Birmingham*, the OE. form appears to have been **Beormingahám*. The metathesis of *r*, giving *Bre-, Bri-, Bru-, Brom-*, is found as early at least as the 15th c. In No. 10 of *Edgbastonia*, 15th Feb. 1882, 140 variant forms and spellings are cited from documents. Among these may be found 1–2 (*Domesday*) Bermingeham, 3–6 Birmyngeham, 5–6 Brymyngeham, 6 Brimicham, 7 Brimingham, Brimigham, Brimmidgham, Brimisham; also 4–6 Burmyngeham, 4–7 Brum(m)ingham, Brummingsham, Brumigham, Brummidgham, Brumicham.]

Brummellian (brʌ'mɛlɪən), *a.* [f. the proper name *Brummel* + -IAN.] Of, pertaining to, or characteristic of 'Beau Brummel' (G. R. Brummell, 1778–1840), leader of fashion in London. So '**Brummelism.**
1831 CARLYLE *Misc. Ess.* (1872) IV. 26 Werterism, Byronism, even Brummelism, each has its day. **1832** *Ibid.* 127 Pharisaical Brummellean Politeness. **1908** 'LEWIS MELVILLE' *Beaux of Regency* II. 70 The last three carried on the Brummellian traditions.

brummer fly. [Obs. var. Afrikaans, Du. *brommer* blowfly, bluebottle; cf. Du. *brommen* to hum, buzz, *bromvlieg* bluebottle.] A species of blowfly generally known as the locust-fly (genus *Wohlfahrtia*).
1913 PETTMAN *Africanderisms* 92 Brummer fly, *Cynomyia pictifacies*.. An insect somewhat like the common house-fly, but considerably larger. It is useful in the destruction of locusts. **1924** *Chambers's Jrnl.* XIV. 314/2 The brummer fly (*Wolfahrtia brunis palpis*) lays its eggs in the neck of the locust.

'**brummish,** *a. low.* [f. BRUM, slang contraction of *Brummagem* + -ISH.] Of coin: Of counterfeit character, doubtfully genuine.
1805 G. COLMAN *John Bull, Brit. Theat.* 55 Two guineas ..one seems light, and t'other looks a little brummish.

Brummy ('brʌmɪ). *colloq.* Also **Brummie.** [dim. of BRUMMAGEM.] A local name for a native or inhabitant of Birmingham. Also *attrib.*
1941 G. KERSH *They die with their Boots Clean* ii. 65 You're a Brummy Boy. I can tell by your accent. **1956** *Archit. Rev.* CXX. 124/3 Now it tries hard to avoid being swamped by Birmingham—permanently, in the way of urban sprawl; temporarily, by the ebb and flow of the country-bound Brummies at week-ends. **1965** *New Statesman* 30 Apr. 670/2 He proclaims proudly, in a modulated Birmingham accent that makes him sound like a well-bred Australian: 'I'm a natural born Brummie.'

brumous ('bruːməs), *a.* [ad. F. *brumeux*, or late L. *brūmōsus* 'wintry', already in Isidore in sense of 'rainy'. See BRUMAL.] Foggy, wintry.
1850 THACKERAY *Pendennis* xxiii, The blonde misses of Albion in their brumous isle. **1859** MASSON *Milton* I. 526 In the dull brumous air.

brumstane, obs. f. BRIMSTONE.

brun(e, obs. and dial. form of BROWN, BURN.

brunch (brʌntʃ). *orig. University slang.* [A 'portmanteau' word f. BR(EAKFAST and L)UNCH.] A single meal taken late in the morning and intended to combine breakfast with lunch.
1896 *Punch* 1 Aug. 58/2 To be fashionable nowadays we must 'brunch'. Truly an excellent portmanteau word, introduced, by the way, last year, by Mr. Guy Beringer, in the now defunct *Hunter's Weekly*, and indicating a combined breakfast and lunch. **1900** G. SWIFT *Somerley* 93 Brunches (*i.e.* breakfast-cum-lunch). **1900** *Westm. Gaz.* 19 Dec. 2/3 Perish Scrambling breakfast, formal lunch! Hardened night-birds fondly cherish All the subtle charms of 'brunch'. **1924** *Blackw. Mag.* Apr. 465/1 We proposed to have a substantial 'brunch' at eleven. **1941** in Mencken *Amer. Lang.* (1963) VI. iv. 316 Sunday strollers' brunch, $1 per person, served from 11 a.m. to 3 p.m. **1967** *Boston Sunday Herald Mag.* 26 Mar. 8/2 Easter is the day when more families march forth.. to brunches and to egg hunts.
b. *attrib.*, as ***brunch-bar***; **brunch coat,** a woman's short house-coat.
1942 *N.Y. Times* 24 May 31 (Advt.), A brunch coat that's indispensable in the Summertime. **1959** *Vogue Pattern. Bk.* June–July 50 Good companion to the nightgown: short brunchcoat or dressing gown to make in a plain poplin. **1960** V. PACKARD *Status Seekers* II. v. 62 A split-level house on Long Island became 'a Georgian split, with a bi-level brunch bar in a maître d' kitchen'. **1966** *Observer* 13 Feb. (Suppl.) 28/1 Brunchbars (Have a bean-burger?) have made their appearance.

†**brune,** *sb.*¹ *Obs.* Forms: 1 **bryne, byrne, (byrn),** 2–4 **brune (y),** 4 **brene.** [OE. *bryne*:—OTeut. **bruni-z* burning, f. ablaut stem *brun-* of *brin-n-an* to burn. Cf. ON. *bruni*:—**brunon-* in same sense. The Kentish form was *brene*: *brenne* was rather a new formation on stem of ME. *brennen*, paving the way for the later *burne*, BURN *sb.*] Burning, a burn.
c **890** K. ÆLFRED *Bæda* IV. xxv. (*title*) (Bosw.) Ær ðam ðe ðæt mynster mid bryne fornumen wære. *c* **950** *Lindisf. Gosp.* Matt. xx. 12 Ðæs ðæȝes hæto *vel* byrn. *c* **1000** *Sax. Leechd.* II. 130 Wiþ bryne, ȝenim finules niþeardes. *a* **1225** *Ancr. R.* 296 Þe cwene.. þet mid one strea brouhte o brune alle hire huses. *a* **1240** *Ureisun* in *Lamb. Hom.* 203 Þer þis brune were. **1340** *Ayenb.* 264 Helle is.. Vol of brene onþolyinde. [**1523** FITZHERB. *Surv.* 28b, Catell hauynge no such brenne.]
fig. *a* **1225** *Ancr. R.* 254 Þe brune of golnesse.

brune (bryn) *sb.*² [a. F. *brune*, fem. of *brun* brown.] A dark-complexioned girl or woman, a brunette.
1865 'OUIDA' *Strathmore* I. ii. 41 Now with a blonde, and now with a brune. **1870** R. BROUGHTON *Red as Rose is She* xiii, Priscilla, a beady-eyed, brisk brune. **1894** MEREDITH *Ld. Ormont* x, Brunes are exceptional in England.

†**brunel, -elle.** *Obs.* [See quot. 1878.] The plant Self-heal (*Prunella vulgaris*).
1597 GERARD *Herbal* cxci. §1. 507 Brunell is called in English Prunell, Carpenters herbe, Selfeheale, and Hookeheale, and Sickleweort. **1611** COTGR., *Oingtereule*, Selfeheale.. Brunell, Prunell. **1878** BRITTEN & HOLLAND *Plant-n.*, *Brunel*, a modification of *Brunella*, the Latin name (now more frequently but less correctly written *Prunella*), which took its rise from the German *die Braune*, an 'infirmitie among soldiers that lie in campe' described by Gerard (p. 508); this appears to have been a kind of quinsey.. for which the *Prunella* was deemed a specific.

brunet (bruː'nɛt), *a.* and *sb.* [a. F. *brunet*, dim. of *brun* brown.] **A.** *adj.* Dark-complexioned. **B.** *sb.* A dark-complexioned person. Hence **bru'netness.**
1887 DOLE tr. *Tolstoi's Russ. Proprietor* 247 But I should like to see what sort of a man this hussar is,—whether he is brunet or blondin. **1890** T. H. HUXLEY in *19th Cent.* Nov. 757 The brunet broad-heads now met with in central France. *Ibid.* 767 The present contrast of blonds and brunets existed among them. **1899** RIPLEY *Races Eur.* 147 Our map of the distribution of brunetness. **1932** *Times Lit. Suppl.* 1 Dec. 915/1 For what reason the union of brunet-white with blackish should bring about something blacker still, is here wisely left to the biologist. **1967** T. WELLS *Dead by Light of Moon* (1968) v. 52 The boy looks like the mother, the father is brunet.

brunetta: see BURNET.

brunette (bruːˈnɛt, ‖brynɛt), *sb.* and *a.* Also 8 brunett. [a. F. *brunette* 'a nut-browne girle' (Cotgr.), fem. of *brunet*, dim. of *brun* brown.]

A. *sb.* **a.** A girl or woman of a dark complexion or with brown hair.

1713 *Guardian* No. 109 (1756) II. 108 Your fair women.. thought of this fashion to insult the Olives and the Brunetts. **1796** J. OWEN *Trav. Europe* II. 438 My landlady.. is a very pretty brunette. **1847** BARHAM *Ingol. Leg.* (1877) 12 Whether the ladies there are short or tall, Brunettes or blondes. **1859** GEO. ELIOT *A. Bede* 45 His mother, a beautiful brunette. **1908** G. WODNIL *Brunette or Blonde* 4 What shade her hair?.. Brunettes they are witty, I have heard say. **1965** T. WOLFE *Kandy-Kolored Tangerine-Flake Streamline Baby* (1966) i. 9 A pregnant brunette walks in off the street wearing black shorts.

b. A variety of the satinette pigeon.

1879 L. WRIGHT *Pract. Pigeon Keeper* 174 Brunettes are lighter Satinettes. **1891** R. WOODS *Pigeon-Culture* 138.

B. *adj.* Of dark complexion, brown-haired; nut-brown. Also *absol.* the colour.

1712 HENLEY in *Spect.* No. 396 You will excuse a Remark which this gentleman's Passion for the *Brunette* has suggested to a Brother Theorist. **1752** SIR H. BEAUMONT *Crito* 11 Raphael's most charming Madonna is a brunette Beauty. **1815** *Hist. J. Decastro* I. 180 Her complexion.. cleared up into a fine brunette. **1861** HULME tr. *Moquin-Tandon* I. v. 32 The Indian Stock.. skin brunette rather than black. **1881** G. ALLEN *Anglo-Sax. Brit.* 56 The nation which resulted.. being sometimes blonde, sometimes brunette.

Hence **bruˈnetteness** (*rare*).

1839 *Fraser's Mag.* XIX. 75 Praising.. the pretty brunetteness of a young lily-forced thing.

brung (brʌŋ), dial. pa. t. and pa. pple. of BRING *v.*

brunie, -y(e, obs. ff. BRINIE.

†**ˈbrunion.** ? *Obs.* [a. F. *brugnon* 'espèce de pêche ou de pavie à peau lisse' (Littré); cf. It. *brugna*, *prugna*, Pg. *brunho*, deriv. of L. *prunum* plum, *prunus* plum-tree.]

A smooth-skinned variety of the peach, a nectarine; sometimes described as 'a sort of fruit between a plum and a peach'.

1706 in PHILLIPS. **1736** in BAILEY; and in mod. Dicts.

brunishe, obs. form of BURNISH *v.*

brunne, obs. form of BURN.

brunneous (ˈbrʌniːəs), *a.* [f. mod.L. *brunneus*, = med.L. *brunus*, f. Teut. *brûn* BROWN.] Dark brown. (Chiefly in *Entomology*.)

1843 HUMPHREYS *Brit. Moths* I. 137 The hind wings are brunneous grey. **1847** *Proc. Berw. Nat. Club* II. No. 5. 244 Abdomen.. beneath shining brunneous or ferruginous.

Hence (from combining form **brunneo-**) **brunneo-piceous** *a.*, **brunneo-testaceous** *a.*

1847 *Proc. Berw. Nat. Club* II. No. 5. 255 Elytra.. brunneo-piceous. 256 Two lateral punctures.. brunneo-testaceous.

ˈBrunner's glands. *Anat.* [So called from their discoverer *Brunner*, a Swiss anatomist 1653–1727.] Small racemose mucous glands situated in the upper part of the small intestine in mammals and certain fishes.

1860 in MAYNE *Exp. Lex.* **1880** *Syd. Soc. Lex.*, *Brunner's glands*: duodenal glands.. They secrete a viscid fluid containing mucus.. whose purpose is not known.

Bruno (ˈbruːnəʊ). In **St. Bruno's lily**, a bulbous plant of the species *Anthericum* (*Paradisea*) *liliastrum*, cultivated for its white sweet-scented flowers, which resemble small lilies.

1760 J. LEE *Introd. Bot.* App. 325 Saint Bruno's Lily, *Hemerocallis*. **1882** *Garden* 3 June 391/3 St. Bruno's Lily is beautiful in a glass by itself.

Brunonian (bruːˈnəʊnɪən), *a. Med.* [f. *Bruno*, *Brunōn-em*, a Latinized form of the name *Brown*.]

Applied to the system or theory of medicine founded by Dr. John Brown (1735–1788), according to which physical life consists in a peculiar excitability, the normal excitement produced by all the agents which affect the body constituting the healthy condition, while all diseases arise either from deficiency or from excess of excitement, and must be treated with stimulants or sedatives.

1799 *Med. & Phys. Jrnl.* I. 124 The chief peculiarities of the Brunonian System. **1806** *Ibid.* XV. 147 The Brunonian method of preventing or curing indirect debility.

b. *sb.* One who holds this theory.

1882 *Standard* 13 Dec. 5/5 The Brunonians, of whom some adherents still linger in Italy.

brunstan, -stone, obs. or dial. ff. BRIMSTONE.

brunsvigite (ˈbrʌnzvɪgaɪt). *Min.* [ad. G. *brunsvigit* (J. Fromme 1902, in *Tschermak's min. und petrogr. Mittheil.* XXI. 171), f. Da. *Brunsvig* Brunswick + -ITE[1].] A type of oxidized chlorite occurring in gabbro in the Radauthal, Germany; *spec.* one with 5·6–6·0 per cent of silicon and six to ten percent of iron.

1902 *Jrnl. Chem. Soc.* LXXXII. II. 512 A chlorite mineral of wide distribution in the gabbro of the Radauthal, Harz, is described under the new name *brunsvigite*. **1954** *Min. Mag.* XXX. 280 The manganese-bearing chlorites include the remarkable species pennantite..; grängesite, a manganiferous brunsvigite; and manganese-pennine.

Brunswick[1] (ˈbrʌnzwɪk). [LG. *Brunswîk*, *-swyk*; Ger. *Braunschweig*.]

1. The name of a town and imperial province (formerly a duchy = *Brunswick-Wolfenbüttel*) of Germany. In earlier times Hanover constituted the electorate of Brunswick-Lüneburg, whence the name 'line of Brunswick' = 'line of Hanover' applied to the English sovereigns from George I.

2. Hence the name of an obsolete textile fabric.

1480 *Privy Purse Exp. Eliz. of York* 130 Brussell clothe dcc vij elles iij quarters: Browneswyke iiij[xx] ix elles.

3. *attrib.* **a. Brunswick black**, a black varnish made of turpentine and asphalt or lamp-black; **Brunswick green**, a green pigment consisting of oxychloride of copper (Watts *Dict. Chem.*).

b. Brunswick Club *Ir. Hist.* [f. the name of Charles, Duke (1823–31) of *Brunswick*, who founded the first club in 1828], any of a number of Irish Protestant organizations opposing the Catholic Emancipation Act of 1829.

1828 *Times* 8 Sept. 2/5 Lord Belzebub much questions whether He ever yet saw, mixed together, As 'twere in one capacious tub, Such a mess of noble silly-bub As the twenty Peers of the Brunswick Club. **1829** T. WYSE *Hist. Sketch Cath. Assoc.* II. 13 The Catholic Association on one hand, and Brunswick Clubs on the other. **1884** *Encycl. Brit.* XVII. 813/1 The Brunswick clubs.. were sprigs from the original Orange tree. **1942**, etc. [see BRUNSWICKER.]

Brunswick[2] (ˈbrʌnzwɪk). The name of Brunswick County, Virginia, used *attrib.* of a kind of stew first made there, orig. of squirrel and onion, now freq. of game or chicken and containing other vegetables.

1856 H. DAVIS *Farm Bk.* 56 Our dinner consisted of.. Soup Gumbo Brunswick stew. **1909** F. B. CALHOUN *Miss Minerva* iii. 23 Me an' Wilkes Booth Lincoln been eatin'.. Brunswick stew ever sence we's born. **1936** M. MITCHELL *Gone with Wind* vi. 93 The succulent odors of barbecue sauce and Brunswick stew. **1954** J. WALKER *Pardon my Parka* iv. 64 'That's a very good-smelling stew... What's in it?' 'Squirrel... Brunswick stew they call it.' **1983** P. B. FOSTER *Classic Amer. Cooking* iv. 130 (*heading*) Brunswick stew.

Brunswicker (ˈbrʌnzwɪkə(r)). *Ir. Hist.* [f. *Brunswick* (*Club* s.v. BRUNSWICK 3 b + -ER[1].] A member of a Brunswick Club (see BRUNSWICK[1] 3 b).

1828 *New Monthly Mag.* XXIII. 473 The opposite wing was.. occupied by the Brunswickers. **1829** D. O'CONNELL *Let.* 13 Jan. (1977) IV. 2 Afraid of a few paltry and malignant Brunswickers. **1830** *Dublin Even. Post* 11 Nov. 3/3 They are .. determined not to be *humbugged* by noisy Brunswickers. **1942** E. BOWEN *Bowen's Court* viii. 197 The 'Brunswickers' .. were the members of the Cork Brunswick Club—composed of prominent citizens and neighbouring gentlemen. **1954** J. A. REYNOLDS *Catholic Emancipation Crisis Ireland* viii. 151 The ultra-Protestants reacted more strenuously by forming Brunswick clubs... The Brunswickers displayed a fanaticism quite as violent as that of their opponents. **1980** HICKEY & DOHERTY *Dict. Irish Hist.* 47/1 *Brunswick Clubs*, Protestant clubs founded in 1828 by the Duke of Brunswick... The express purpose of such clubs was to oppose Emancipation. The members were known as 'Brunswickers'.

brunt (brʌnt), *sb.*[1] Forms: 4– brunt, 4–6 bronte, 5–6 bront, brunte, 6 brount. [First in 14th c. Origin unknown; generally sought in ON. *bruna* 'to advance with the speed of fire'; though such a formation from that is difficult to explain etymologically, and connecting links are wanting. The word may rather be an onomatopœia of Eng. itself: cf. DUNT, and various *br-* words implying sharp or smart application of force. It is possible however that some association with *burnt* (in Sc. *brunt*), as if the 'chief brunt' were 'the hottest' of the fight, has influenced sense 4.]

†**1.** A sharp blow. *Obs.*

c **1325** *E.E. Allit. P.* A. 174 Bot baysment gef myn hert a brunt. **1400** *Sowdone Bab.* 3166 He smote the bisshope withe a bronde And gaf him an evel bronte. **1470–85** MALORY *Arthur* XX. xxi. (Globe) 472/2 Sir Gawaine gave him many sad brunts and many sad strokes.

†**b.** *at a brunt*: at one blow, at once, suddenly. *Obs.* (Cf. Fr. *tout à coup, tout d'un coup.*)

c **1400** *Alexander* (Stev.) 134 All þat was bitten of the best, was at a brunt dede. *a* **1555** RIDLEY *Wks.* 53 Traditions.. at one brunt are revived. **1581** J. BELL *Haddon's Answ. Osor.* 69 Here Osorius.. uttereth all his skill at a brunt. **1609** BIBLE (Douay) *2 Kings* xxiii. 8 Which killed eight hundred at one brunt.

†**2.** An assault, charge, onset, violent attack. (Often after *bear*, *abide*, *sustain*, etc.) *Obs.*

a. of fighting men, physical agents.

1430 LYDG. *Chron. Troy* III. xxiv, The pore souldiours Which bare the bronte euer of such shoures, And the mischiefe of werre comonly. **1531** ELYOT *Gov.* (1834) 201 [He] there alone sustained the whole brunt of his enemies. **1570** LEVINS *Manip.* 189 A Brunt, *impetus*. *c* **1590** MARLOWE *Faust.* I. 93. 121 Stranger engines for the brunt of war. **1601** HOLLAND *Pliny* II. 491 Sustaining the charge and brunt of K. Porsenaes army. **1648** GAGE *West. Ind.* x. (1655) 32 At the third brunt, they made those lusty souldiers flie.

b. of sickness, temptation, persecution, etc. *Obs.* or *arch.*

1542 BOORDE *Dyetary* viii. (1870) 245 Strength maye suffre a brount. **1563** *Homilies* II. xvi. II. (1859) 461 So many and great brunts of affliction and persecution. *a* **1617** BAYNE *On Ephes.* (1658) 127 A brunt of unbelief doth not evacuate our faith. **1693** W. ROBERTSON *Phraseol. Gen.* 533 He endures sore brunts, *magnos impetus sustinet*. **1821** CLARE *Vill. Minstr.* I. 210 Wishing to despise.. Brunts of fate and scorns of men.

†**c.** *at the first brunt*: at the first charge or onset; *fig.* at starting, at first. *Obs.*

1447 BOKENHAM *Seyntys* cxlviii, Though some of his men be overthrown at the first brunt. *c* **1532** LD. BERNERS *Huon* (1883) 395 At the fyrste brounte the Almaynes were constrayned to recule abacke. **1549** COVERDALE *Erasm. Par. 1 Cor.* i. 23 A doctrine, that at the fyrste brunte seemeth base and folyshe. **1693** *Mem. Ct. Teckely* I. 44 They put them into disorder at the first brunt.

3. Shock, violence, or force (of an attack).

(This more abstract sense was at first only vaguely evolved from the preceding, which it has now superseded. Phrases like *brunt of war*, *of battle*, etc. connect 2 and 3.)

a. of war, or of any material force.

1579 FENTON *Guicciard.* II. (1599) 84 All the brunt and swaigh of that daies fight. **1614** RALEIGH *Hist. World* III. 42 Athens.. endured the hardest and worst brunt of Darius invasion. **1667** BOYLE *Orig. Formes & Qual.* 40 Neither will it [Brasse] like Gold resist the utmost brunt of the Fire. **1728** MORGAN *Algiers* II. iv. 282 Utterly averse To stand the Brunt of another Engagement. **1809** WELLINGTON *Let.* in Gurw. *Disp.* IV. 324 Bearing the first brunt of the enemy's attack. **1862** MARSH *Eng. Lang.* ii. 29 It was on the Cymry that the chief brunt of the contest fell.

b. of an immaterial force.

1573 G. HARVEY *Letter-bk.* (1884) 15, I must needes abide the brunt of his displeasure. **1662** FULLER *Worthies* (1840) II. 447 When such prisoners.. have weathered out the brunt of that disease. **1774** BURKE *Amer. Tax.* Wks. 1842 I. 175, I had rather bear the brunt of all his wit. **1827** HALLAM *Const. Hist.* (1876) I. iv. 198 Grindal.. bore the whole brunt of the queen's displeasure. **1875** JOWETT *Plato* (ed. 2) IV. 88 To avoid the brunt of their argument.

4. The chief stress or violence; crisis. (Formerly expressed by *chief brunt*, *greatest brunt*.)

1598 BARRET *Theor. Warres* I. i. 4 The first three, fiue, or seuen rankes.. do beare the chiefe brunt. **1665** MANLEY *Grotius' Low-C. Warrs* 144 It had inabled him to bear the greatest brunt of Humane Affairs.] **1769** ROBERTSON *Chas. V*, III. XI. 309 The wing of the French which stood the brunt of the combat. **1815** MOORE *Lalla R.* (1824) 93 Now comes the brunt, the crisis of the day. **1837** CARLYLE *Fr. Rev.* (1872) I. VII. ix. 239 The brunt of the danger seems past. **1855** MACAULAY *Hist. Eng.* IV. 241 But the English had borne the brunt of the fight. **1868** E. EDWARDS *Ralegh* I. vii. 110 The brunt of the defence fell on ships, not on soldiers.

†**5.** A sudden effort, strain, or outburst; a 'fit', 'spurt'. (Cf. 1 b.) *Obs.*

c **1450** *Merlin* xviii. 282 Thei spored theire horse ouer the brigge at a brunt. **1551** ROBINSON tr. *More's Utop.* (Arb.) 76 [Oxen] they graunte to be not so good as horses at a sodeyne brunte, and (as we saye) at a deade lifte. **1612** T. TAYLOR *Comm. Titus* ii. 12 It is but for a brunt of newfangledness. *a* **1626** BP. ANDREWES *Serm.* xix. (1661) 389 His vigour is not brunts only, or starts, *impetus*. **1670** R. RHODES *Flora's Vagaries* 58 It will be but one Brunt o' th' Old mans anger.

6. *Comb.*, as ***brunt-bearing*** adj.

1654 CHAPMAN *Alphonsus* Plays 1873 III. 243 Saxon lansknights and brunt-bearing Switzers.

¶ Error for *brute*, BRUIT.

c **1485** *Digby Myst.* (1882) IV. 52 Herd ye not the Exclamation And the grete brunte.. Crucyfy hym! **1523** LD. BERNERS *Froiss.* I. clxxxviii. 222 The brunt went y[t] he was chiefe heed of the prouostes treason.

†**brunt**, *sb.*[2] *Obs. rare*$^{-1}$. A bud, a 'spur' on a fruit tree.

1668 MARKHAM *Way to Wealth* No. 9 III. i. 97 You must gather your fruit clean, without leaves or brunts.. for every brunt would be a stalk for fruit to grow upon.

brunt (brʌnt), *v. rare.* [f. BRUNT *sb.*[1]]

†**1.** *intr.* To make an assault or attack. *Obs.*

c **1440** *Promp. Parv.* 54 Bruntun, or make a soden stertynge, *insilio*. **1690** W. WALKER *Idiomat. Anglo-Lat.* 74 They would brunt without a main force.

2. *trans.* To bear the brunt of, face boldly. *rare.*

1859 I. TAYLOR *Logic in Theol.* 194 Brunting the chilling fogs of a winter's afternoon, in England. **1859** G. MEREDITH *R. Feverel* iv. (1885) 29 'Do you think they'll ever suspect us?' 'What if they do? We must brunt it.'

brunt, obs. and dial. pa. t. and pple. of BURN *v.*

brurde, var. of BRERD, *Obs.*, edge.

brus, obs. form of BREWIS.

bruschalle: see BRUSHAL, *Obs.*, brushwood.

bruse, obs. form of BROOSE, BRUISE.

brusen, obs. form of *bursten*, BURST *pa. pple.*

1601 HOLLAND *Pliny* XX. v, Those who are brusen bellied, or have ruptures.

†**brusery, -ury.** *Sc. Obs.* [Cf. BRUSIT.] Embroidery.

1513 DOUGLAS *Æneis* XI. xv. 24 Hys hosing schane of wark of Barbary, In portratour of subtell brusery [*v.r.* brusury.]

brush (brʌʃ), *sb.*¹ Forms: 5 **brusche,** 6 **brushe,** 6- **brush.** [ME. *brusche*, a. OF. *brosse, broce, broche* brushwood (whence mod.F. *broussailles*: see BRUSHAL). Diez cites Pr. *brossa*, Sp. *broza*, It. *brustia*, brushwood. Du Cange has med.L. *bruscia, brocia, brossia, brozia, brucia*, all in same sense. Diez takes the late L. type as **brustia*, and refers it to OHG. *burst, bursta* bristle; cf. MHG. *bürste* brush. If his conjectures are correct, *brosse* 'brush' and *brosse* 'brushwood' were originally identical; but as their history in English shows no contact, it appears better here to treat them apart: see BRUSH *sb.*²]

1. a. Loppings of trees or hedges; cut brushwood (now in U.S.). **b.** A fagot or bavin of such brushwood. (Cf. BRASH *sb.*²)

1330 R. BRUNNE *Chron.* (Rolls Ser.) 8338 þey comaunded to al men lyk Wiþ brusch to come, & fylle þe dyk. *c* 1440 *Promp. Parv.* 54 Brusche, *bruscus.* 1530 PALSGR. 201/2 Brushe to make brushes on, *bruyère.* 1655 GURNALL *Chr. in Arm.* xiii. 218/2 One sin helps to kindle another; the less the greater, as the brush the loggs. 1690 B. E. *Dict. Cant. Crew, Brush*, a small Faggot, to light the other at Taverns. 1732 DE FOE *Tour Gt. Brit.* I. 138 (D.) Small light bavins..are called in the taverns a Brush. 1830 in W. Cobbet *Rur. Rides* (1885) II. 298 [To] supply the farm with poles and brush, and with everything wanted in the way of fuel. 1830 GALT *Lawrie T.* III. ii. (1849) 86 The two boys would be found serviceable, either in collecting the brush, or in burning off the logs. 1860 BARTLETT, *Brush, for brushwood*, is an Americanism, and..comprises also branches of trees. 1880 *W. Cornwall Gloss.* (E.D.S.), *Brush*, dried furze used for fires.

2. The small growing trees or shrubs of a wood; a thicket of small trees or underwood. (Esp. in U.S., Canada, and Australia.)

c 1440–1530 [see sense 1]. 1553 BRENDE *Q. Curtius* P j, The inhabiters of the contrey were accustumed to creape emonges the brushe like wild beastes. 1613 SYLVESTER *Elegie Sir W. Sidney*, Brush and Bryars (good for nought at all). 1702 *Eng. Theophrast.* 374 You shall never have clean underwood, but shrubs and brushes. 1766 C. BEATTY *Two Months' Tour* (1768) 35 Grown up..with small brush, or under-wood. 1789 WOLCOTT (P. Pindar) *Sir J. Banks & Emp. Morocco*, Mindless of trees, and brushes, and the brambles. 1791 in *Amer. Speech* XV. 161/2 To a white Oak & red Oak near a hollow in the Edge of Brush. 1801 *Massachusetts Spy* 23 Dec. 3/4 The imprudence of a person who set on fire a quantity of brush, &c. near Cambridge. 1820 OXLEY *N.S. Wales*, The timber standing at wide intervals, without any brush or undergrowth. *Ibid.* These plains or brushes are swamps in wet weather. 1887 I. R. *Ranche Life Montana* 8 The bright red of the brush by the river-side.

†**3.** Stubble. *Obs.* or *dial.*

1679 PLOT *Staffordsh.* (1686) 343 They sowe wheat again, upon the brush (as they call it) i.e. upon the peas stubble. 1790 MARSHALL *Midl. Counties* II. Gloss., *Brush*, stubble; as a wheat-brush.

4. *Comb.*, as ***brush-fagot, -heap, house, -pile, stable, tent, whisky U.S.***; also **brush-apple,** 'the native Australian wood of *Achras australis*' (Treas. Bot.); †**brush-bill,** a bill for cutting brushwood; **brush-bush,** a shrub (*Eucryphia pinnata*) having pinnate leaves and single white flowers; **brush-cherry,** 'the native Australian wood of *Trochocarpa laurina*' (Treas. Bot.); **brush-fire** orig. *U.S.*, a fire in brush; also *transf.*; *attrib.*, (of a war) arising suddenly and limited in scale or area; **brush-kangaroo,** a species of kangaroo inhabiting the Australian 'brush'; **brush-puller,** a machine for pulling up brushwood by the roots; **brush-scythe,** a scythe or sickle on a shaft for cutting brushwood; **brush-turkey,** an Australian bird (*Talegalla Lathami*); **brush-turnip** (see quot.); **brush wallaby** *Austral.*, several species of the genus *Wallabia*, esp. *W. rufogrisea*, found esp. in coastal brushes.

1588 R. PARKE tr. *Mendoza's China* 65 Pikes, targets, faunchers, *brushebilles, holbards. 1606 *Sir G. Goosecappe* III. i. in Bullen *O. Pl.* (1884) III. 44 She had as lieve be courted with a *brush faggot as with a Frenchman. 1767 A. YOUNG *Farmer's Lett.* 230 The fire-wood was most of it.. brush-faggots out of a wood, and but few of the small bush-faggots. 1850 L. H. GARRARD *Wah-to-yah* xix. 238 The spiral smoke..rose from the *brushfire. 1947 *Chicago Daily News* 15 May 1/3 The family outcast is stirring up a brush fire of liberal resentment against the Truman administration. 1955 *Times* 14 May 7/5 He opposed any reduction in manpower because of the risk of 'brush fire' wars. 1809 W. IRVING *Knickerb.* (1861) 141 He was a perfect *brush-heap in a blaze. 1854 B. YOUNG in *Jrnl. Discourses* I. 166 Families went there and lived in wagons and *brush houses. 1830 *Proc. R. Geog. Soc.* I. 29 These dogs..are particularly useful in catching the bandicoots, the small *brush kangaroo, and the opossum. 1865 MRS. WHITNEY *Gayworthys* II. 257 The very chickens run under the fences and the *brushpile. 1573 TUSSER *Husb.* xvii. (1878) 37 A *brush sithe and grasse sithe. 1835 *Southern Lit. Messenger* I. 581 The pony..moves homeward with accelerated velocity, leaping every obstacle in his way to his *brush stable. 1862 *Harper's Mag.* June 16/1 In the yard..were several chapadens or *brush-tents in which whisky, gin,.. and other refreshments..were for sale. 1878 J. H. BEADLE *Western Wilds* xix. 310 John A. Lee..had his wife living there in a sort of brush tent. 1799 J. ROBERTSON *Agric. Perth* 110 To sow..*brush turnips, which are not expected to produce any roots, but in the months of March and April afford an excellent food for ewes and lambs. 1847 CARPENTER *Zool.* §435 Termed..the *Brush *Turkey*, on account of the wattles with which its neck is furnished. 1852 W. BRODERIP *Note-bk. of Nat.* 139 The brush-turkey belongs to a family of birds..which never incubate, but.. leave their eggs to the genial warmth of this half-natural, half artificial mother. [1841 G. R. WATERHOUSE *Marsupialia* 221 The Walabee of New South Wales somewhat resembles the Brush Kangaroo of Van Diemen's Land.] 1896 F. G. AFLALO *Nat. Hist. Australia* II. 40 Into the specific descriptions of the rock, swamp, *brush, scrub and other *wallabies I shall not enter. 1926 LE SOUEF & BURRELL *Wild Animals of Australasia* 189 The red-necked wallaby commonly known as the scrub and in places as the brush wallaby, is found in the drier forest country of Eastern Australia. 1966 V. SERVENTY *Continent in Danger* iii. 66 The fleetness of foot of these brush wallabies led them to be hunted for sport. 1885 'C. E. CRADDOCK' *Prophet Gt. Smoky Mts.* xv. 275 The constable's heart was warmed by the *brush whiskey. 1913 M. W. MORLEY *Carolina Mts.* 66 That important beverage, variously known as..'blockade', 'brush whiskey', and..'corn whiskey'.

brush (brʌʃ), *sb.*² Forms: 4-6 **brusshe,** 5 **brusch(e,** 7 **brish,** 6- **brush.** [ME. *brusshe*, a. OF. *brosse, broisse*, identified by most French etymologists with *brosse* brushwood (see BRUSH *sb.*¹), the sense being supposed to be derived through that of 'bunch of broom or other shrub used to sweep away dust': cf. BROOM. But the history of the French words has not been satisfactorily made out: cf. MHG. *bürste* fem. 'brush', from *borste* bristle, and see Diez, Littré, Scheler, Brachet.]

I. 1. a. A utensil consisting of a piece of wood or other suitable material, set with small tufts or bunches of bristles, hair, or the like, for sweeping or scrubbing dust and dirt from a surface; and generally any utensil for brushing or sweeping.

Brushes are of many shapes and of various materials according to use; instead of bristles there may be slender wires, vegetable fibres, feathers, etc. They are named according to their use, as *clothes-brush, hat-brush, shoe-brush, blacking-brush, hair-brush, nail-brush, tooth-brush*, etc. A *hard* brush has stiff bristles; a *soft* brush fine and flexible bristles. The *chimney-sweep's brush* and *dust brush* pass into a *besom.*

1377 LANGL. *P. Pl.* B. XIV. 460 Whi he ne hadde wasshen it [a coat] or wyped it with a brusshe. 1485 *Inv.* in *Ripon Ch. Acts.* 369 Unum brusshe, 2*d.* 1519 HORMAN *Vulg.* 115 Olde men brusshed theyr dustye clothes with cowe tayles: as we do with hear brusshes. 1530 PALSGR. 182 *Vnes decrottoyres*, a rubbynge brusshe to make clene clothes with. *a* 1598 HAKLUYT *Voy.* I. 363 (R.), 100 brushes for garments (none made of swine haire). 1609 C. BUTLER *Fem. Mon.* v, Move the cluster [of bees] gently with your brush, and drive them in. The Brush is a handfull of Rosemary, Hyssop, Fennell, or other herbes; of Hazell, Withie, Plum-tree, or other boughs; or rather of boughes with hearbs, bound taper-wise together. 1619 in Pitcairn's *Crim. Trials* III. 478 Ane kame-caise, with ane brusch, with certane other necessaris. 1758 JOHNSON *Idler* No. 5 ¶11 If a coat be spotted, a lady has a brush. 1873 BLACK *Pr. Thule* xvii. 275 You want a hard brush to brush sunlight off a wall.

b. One of a pair of thin sticks set with long wire bristles with which to make a soft hissing sound on drums, cymbals, etc.; in full ***wire brush.***

1927 [implied at *brush-work*, sense 12 below]. 1955 in M. Stearns *Story of Jazz* (1957) xxiii. 288 Snare drum, sticks, brushes, [etc.]. 1961 A. BERKMAN *Singers' Gloss.* 11 *Brushes*, wire brushes used to play the drums.

2. a. An instrument consisting of a bunch of hairs attached to a straight handle, for applying moisture to a surface, moist colours in painting, colouring, and similar purposes.

These also vary greatly in size, from a small brush composed of a few fine elastic hairs of the sable, etc. fixed in a fine quill, to the large and coarse brushes of the house painter or plasterer (some of which have the hairs in distinct bunches).

1483 *Cath. Angl.* 46 A Brusch for paynterys, *celeps.* 1677 MOXON *Mech. Exerc.* (1703) 249 Brishes, of three sorts, viz. A Stock Brish, a Round Brish, and a Pencil. With these Brishes, they wet old Walls before they mend them. 1703 *Art's Improv.* I. 63 Take a fine Hogs-Hair-Brush; with this, job and beat over your Work gently, that the Gold may be pressed in close. 1792 *Gentl. Mag.* Apr. 328 Rub it over all the joints..with a painter's brush. 1804 HUDDESFORD *Wiccam. Chaplet* 136 No painter that's living can handle a brush! 1859 GULLICK & TIMBS *Paint.* 295 Brushes of brown sable are generally made by the insertion of the hair into quills; hence the size of the brush is recognised by the various names of the birds which supply the quills employed —as eagle, swan (of various sizes), goose, duck, and crow. *Ibid.* The smaller kinds of brushes are still sometimes termed 'pencils'.

b. The painter's art or professional skill. ***brother of the brush***: artist.

1687 BP. CARTWRIGHT in *Hist. Magd. Coll.* (Oxf. Hist. Soc.) 143 Pray make use of my Brother of the Brush. 1759 STERNE *Tr. Shandy* (1793) I. 133 The honourable devices which the Pentagraphic Bretheren of the brush have shewn in taking copies. 1789 WOLCOTT (P. Pindar) *Subj. for Paint.* Wks. 1812 II. 136 The world ne'er said nor thought it of thy Brush. 1833 *Byron's Wks.* (1846) 585/1 A young American brother of the brush. 1836 PRAED *Poems, Sk. Yng. Lady*, If I to-morrow Could manage just for half-an-hour Sir Joshua's brush to borrow. *Mod.* There is another picture from the same brush.

3. Any brush-like bunch or tuft.

a. generally.

1581 J. BELL *Haddon's Answ. Osor.* 258 b, Thys vayne-glorious proud pecocke is bedeckt with..glittering plumes, wrapt up together in a great brush. 1870 HOOKER *Stud. Flora* 473 *Equisetum arvense*..the barren stem terminates in an abrupt brush of branches.

b. The bushy tail, or bushy part of the tail, of an animal; *spec.* that of the fox.

1675 [see 10]. 1690 B. E. *Dict. Cant. Crew, Brush*..a Fox's Tail. 1735 SOMERVILLE *Chase* III. 145 His Brush he drags, And sweeps the Mire impure. 1774 GOLDSM. *Nat. Hist.* II. 190 His [the fox's] tail is called his brush or drag. 1784 COWPER *Task* VI. 317 The squirrel, flippant..whisks his brush. 1860 GEN. P. THOMPSON *Audi Alt.* III. cxxxix. 114 If the landed interest took the same courses in fox-hunting, it would be easy to foretell how many brushes they would bring home. 1883 J. MACKENZIE *Day-dawn in Dark Pl.* 162, I tied the brush of the tail [of the gemsbuck] to Blue-buck's saddle.

4. *Entom.* A brush-like organ on the legs of bees and other insects.

1828 STARK *Elem. Nat. Hist.* II. 201 Tarsi short, with no brush beneath. 1861 HULME tr. *Moquin-Tandon* II. III. 208 The legs of the Bee..have the first joint of the tarsus dilated ..Its inner surface is provided with several rows of stiff hairs placed transversely, which gives to this part the name of the 'brush'.

5. ***metallic brush***: 'a bundle of fine wires fixed in an insulating handle. Used for faradisation of less sensitive parts in anæsthetic conditions' (*Syd. Soc. Lex.*); also a wire hair-brush.

6. *Electricity.* **a.** A brush-like discharge of sparks. **b.** A piece of metal terminating in metallic wires, or strips of flexible metal, used for securing good metallic connexion between two portions of an electrical instrument.

1789 NICHOLSON in *Phil. Trans.* LXXIX. 275 When the intensity was greatest, brushes, of a different kind from the former, appeared. 1803 *Med. & Phys. Jrnl.* IX. 390 Somewhat like a little brush deflagration. 1842 W. GROVE *Corr. Phys. Forces* (ed. 6) 75 The electric spark, the brush, and similar phenomena. *c* 1865 J. WYLDE in *Circ. Sc.* I. 174/2 When any pointed object is presented to an electrised surface, the spark..becomes converted into a brush-like form; hence the term 'electric brush'. 1883 *Knowledge* 13 July 24/2 One of the brushes of the commutator presses the insulating piece.

7. *Optics.* Bright or dark figures accompanying certain phenomena observed in polarized light, which by their shaded and ill-defined edges combined with variations of breadth suggest the idea of brushes.

1817–45 HERSCHEL *Light* in *Encycl. Metrop.* 559. 1857 LLOYD *Wave Theory Light* 193 The dark brushes, which cross the entire system of rings. *Ibid.* 122 *Haidinger brushes* ..two brushes, of a pale orange-yellow colour, the axis of which coincides always with the track of the plane of polarization. 1878 GURNEY *Crystallog.* 111 In certain adjustments of the polariscope..two dark brushes run across the rings.

II. from BRUSH *v.*²

8. a. A brushing; an application of a brush.

1822 SCOTT *Nigel* xxxvii, He..gives his beaver a brush, and cocks it in the face of all creation. *Mod.* Give your hair a brush.

b. Short for *brush-off* (see BRUSH *v.*² 5 b). So ***brusheroo*** [-EROO].

1941 in *Amer. Speech* (1942) XVII. 12/1 That's why I'm getting the brusheroo. 1947 B. SCHULBERG *Harder they Fall* i. 27 The ones who had already made up their minds almost always got the brush. 1953 'S. RANSOME' *Drag the Dark* (1954) ii. 25 So far I had found no chance to give Goodlee the brush. 1962 E. LACY *Freeloaders* viii. 175, I told Daniele what a crawling punk her boyfriend was, and she gave him the brush.

9. A graze, *esp.* on a horse's leg. (cf. BRUSH *v.*² 6.)

1710 *Lond. Gaz.* No. 4649/4 A Grey Gelding..having.. a Brush in the right Hip.

III. *attrib.* and *Comb.*

10. *simple attrib.* Brush-like.

1675 *Lond. Gaz.* No. 1044/4 A dark brown Nag..a brush tail, if not cut since stolen. 1703 *Ibid.* No. 3895/4 Lost..a large liver-colour'd and white Spaniel, with a brush Tail. 1711 *Ibid.* No. 4900/4 A whisk Tail and brush Mane.

11. General relations: **a.** attributive, as ***brush-drop, -play, -power, -stroke***; **b.** objective, as ***brush-maker, -manufacturer***; **c.** similative and parasynthetic, as ***brush-form, -like, -shaped, -tailed.***

1878 SYMONDS *Sonn. M. Angelo* v, A rich Embroidery Bedews my face from *brush-drops thick and thin. 1872 WATTS *Dict. Chem.* II. 402 Electric discharge, especially in the *brush-form, frequently takes place in curves. 1859 TODD *Cycl. Anat. & Phys.* V. 478/2 This end of the hair is ..more or less ragged and *brush-like. 1709 *Lond. Gaz.* No. 4538/4 Joseph Wheeler, *Brushmaker by Trade. 1812 *Examiner* 12 Oct. 650/2 W. Jones..*brush manufacturer. 1884 *St. James's Gaz.* 24 Jan. 6/2 An appearance of fusion obtained by a delicate dexterity of *brush-play [in painting]. 1885 *Pall Mall G.* 10 Mar. 4/2 His *brush-power was not more remarkable than his vision. 1880 GRAY *Bot. Text-bk.* 400 *Brush-shaped..made up of numerous spreading hairs, etc. in a tuft, as the stigmas of Grasses. 1898 *Westm. Gaz.* 17 Nov. 3/1 [Gainsborough's] *brush-strokes are scarcely due to separate acts of volition. 1963 *Times* 17 Jan. 4/4 The canvas becomes a web of shimmering, delicate brushstrokes. 1853 KINGSLEY *Hypatia* xxi. 258 Four or five brace of tall *brush-tailed greyhounds.

12. Special combs.: **brush borer** = *brush driller*; **brush-burn,** an inflammation or sore caused by violent friction; **brush-colour** (see quot.); **brush discharge** *Electr.* = BRUSH *sb.*² 6 a;

brush drawer, an operative who puts in the bristles in 'drawn brushes'; **brush driller**, an operative who drills the holes in the stocks of brushes and brooms; **brush-gold** (*Painting*), gold pigment for applying with a brush; **brush-grain**, a grain produced in painting woodwork by drawing the brush over a wet coat of paint so that the under-coat is seen through the brush-marks; **brush-grass**, *Andropogon Gryllus*; **brush-hat** (see quot.); **brush-holder** (see quot. 1904); **brush-iron-ore**, **brush-ore**, an iron ore found in the Forest of Dean (see quots.); **brush-pencil**, an artist's colour brush; **brush-tail(ed) porcupine** (see quot. 1885); **brush-tea** (see quot.); **brush-tongued** *a.*, having a tongue tipped with a brush-like cluster of filaments; **brush-varnish** (see quot.); **brushware**, goods consisting of all kinds of brushes; **brush-wheel**, (*a*) a kind of friction-wheel which turns another similar wheel by means of bristles, cloth, leather, etc., fixed on their circumferences; (*b*) a circular revolving brush used for polishing, etc; **brush-work**, (*a*) painting, as distinguished from drawing; *spec.* the characteristic method (of a painter) of laying on the colours; (*b*) the use of the wire brush on percussion instruments.

1921 *Dict. Occup. Terms* (1927) §688 *Brush borer. **1845** G. DODD *Brit. Manuf.* IV. 130 Floor-cloth manufacture... A second coating of paint is laid on.. wholly with a brush... Hence it is called the '*brush-colour', to distinguish it from the first or 'trowel-colour'. **1849** NOAD *Electricity* (ed. 3) 42 The difference between the *brush discharge and the spark is, that in the former discharge begins at the root [etc.]. **1923** *Popular Wireless* 13 Oct. 11 *Brush discharge*, a discharge of high-tension electricity, which takes the form of a luminous glow. **1900** *Daily News* 6 Nov. 9/1 *Brush drawer. **1921** *Dict. Occup. Terms* (1927) §688 *Brush driller. **1861** READE *Cloister & H.* I. 13 Margaret Van Eyck gave him a little *brush-gold, and some vermilion. **1901** *N. & Q.* 9th Ser. VIII. 310/1 In the painting of wood-work, when the second coat, say of vermilion, is made to show through the third, say of brown, by passing the brush over it while the last coat is still wet, the result is spoken of as '*brush-grain'. **1968** *Gloss. Terms Offset Lithogr. Printing* (*B.S.I.*) 21 *Brush grain*, a fine grain produced by the action of abrasive brushes. **1633** GERARD *Herbal* I. xxii, *Brushgrasse. *a* **1877** KNIGHT *Dict. Mech.*, **Brush-hat*, one in which the surface is continually brushed by a hand-brush, during the process of sizing. **1894** W. P. MAYCOCK *Electric Lighting* (ed. 2) I. vi. §114. 179 Construction of *Brush-holders. **1904** GOODCHILD & TWENEY *Technol. & Sci. Dict.* 72/1 *Brush Holder*, the support or frame carrying the copper (or carbon) strips by which the current enters or leaves a motor or dynamo. **1695** WOODWARD *Nat. Hist. Earth* IV. (1723) 197 *Minera ferri Stalactica*.. called *Brush-Iron-Ore. **1678** *Phil. Trans.* XII. 932 The Iron-Ore.. is found in great abundance.. The best, which they call their *Brush-Ore, is of a Blewish colour. **1831** J. HOLLAND *Manuf. Metals* I. 33 A curious stalactite, rich in iron, and termed brush ore, from its being found hanging from the tops of caverns in striæ resembling a brush. **1703** *Art's Improv.* I. 41 With a *Brush-Pencil, Marble the thing you would Varnish. **1962** *Times* 20 Dec. 9/7 The Borneo *Brushtail Porcupine. **1885** *Encycl. Brit.* XIX. 518/2 The second genus of Old-World porcupines is *Atherura*, the *Brush-tailed Porcupines,.. with long tails tipped with bundles of peculiar flattened spines. **1953** G. DURRELL *Overloaded Ark* iv. 84 A Brush-tailed Porcupine.. about the size of a cat... He was mostly black in colour. **1813** MILBURN *Orient. Comm.* II. 525 *Brush Tea—so called from the leaves being twisted into small cords like pack-thread, about 1 ½ to 2 inches long. **1880** *St. James's Budget* 17 Sept. 12/2 Regions where humming-birds and *brush-tongued lories abound. **1875** T. SEATON *Fret Cutting* 31 Should you wish to varnish the work that has been fret cut or carved, you must do it with *brush-varnish, made with spirits of wine.. laid on with a camel-hair brush. **1923** *Glasgow Herald* 9 July 9 *Brushware and pottery. **1960** *Times* 13 Jan. 17/4 Manufacture of household and toilet brushware is generally highly mechanized. **1875** URE *Dict. Arts* I. 548 Wheels.. made to turn each other by means of bristles fixed in their circumference; these are called *brush wheels. **1868** *Illust. Lond. News* 11 Apr., There is no obtrusively pretentious *brushwork nor garish colouring. **1886** *Encycl. Brit.* XX. 218/2 Works.. wanting in the trenchant brush-work.. of subsequent productions. **1893** *Daily News* 8 Apr. 3/6 The brush work of this incomparable painter. **1927** *Melody Maker* Aug. 807/3 In this article I have discussed brush-work in conjunction with the side drum stick. **1935** *Discovery* Sept. 261/1 Flaws in the brushwork of the eyelids.

brush (brʌʃ), *sb.*³ In 5 broush, *Sc.* brwhs, 6 brous, 5-6 brusche. [? f. BRUSH *v.*¹]

1. a. A forcible rush, a hostile collision or encounter; in later use, chiefly a short but smart encounter.

a **1400** *Alexander* 783 With slik a brout & a brusche [*Dubl. MS.* broush] þe bataill a-sembild. *c* **1425** WYNTOUN *Cron.* VIII. xvi. 120 Than thai layid on dwyhs for dwyhs [= dush], Mony a rap and mony a brwhs. **1535** STEWART *Cron. Scot.* II. 51 The lansis and grit speiris with [thair] force, Maid sic ane brusche vpone the bardit horss. *Ibid.* III. 186 The feildis baith togidder thair did june, With sic ane brous quhill mony speris brak. *a* **1600** *Rob. Hood* (Ritson) II. xx. 31 His courage was flush, he'd venture a brush. **1606** SHAKS. *Tr. & Cr.* v. iii. 34 Tempt not yet the brushes of the warre. **1719** DE FOE *Crusoe* (1869) 312 Let us go and have t' other Brush with them. **1829** MARRYAT *F. Mildmay* iv, I became a scientific pugilist, and now and then took a brush with an oldster. **1860** KINGSLEY *Misc.* I. 18 A smart brush with the Spaniards.

b. Hence *at a brush, at the first brush*, †*to stand brush*; *at* or *after the first brush*: at or after the first encounter or meeting.

a **1400** *Alexander* 2133 (Dubl. MS.) þe folke of þe cite.. barred bremely at a brush þe foure brod ȝates. **1756** R. SYMMER in Ellis *Orig. Lett.* II. 460 IV. 378 The French will not carry the place at a brush. **1795** WOLCOTT (P. Pindar) *Pindariana* Wks. 1812 IV. 73 Love will stand brush against all wind and weather. **1815** SCOTT *Guy M.* lii, So you intend to give up this poor young fellow at the first brush? **1857** HUGHES *Tom Brown* II. ii, The people were.. civil to you if you were civil to them, after the first brush.

c. A rapid run or race; a contest in speed. *dial.* and *U.S.*

1841 *Spirit of Times* 16 Oct. 390/3 The third mile was a 'brush' throughout. **1860** TROLLOPE *Framley P.* xiv, Mark.. would enjoy a brush across the country quite as well as he himself. *a* **1867** H. WOODRUFF *Trotting Horse of Amer.* (1868) ix. 105 He may have a couple of brushes of a quarter of a mile each. **1906** *N.Y. Even. Post* 16 June, Apart from the annual regatta, there are endless minor 'brushes' for the 'fresh-water sailormen'.

2. *fig.* Cf. 'rub'.

1593 SHAKS. *2 Hen. VI*, v. iii. 3 Salsbury.. who in rage forgets Aged contusions, and all brush of Time. **1676** HALE *Contempl.* I. (1689) 161 Though an humble man may upon the very score of his humility and meekness, receive a brush in the world. **1800** WELLINGTON *Let.* in Gurw. *Disp.* I. 121, I have given them a brush through Colonel Pater, and have informed him that the system has not been hitherto approved.

3. ? A slight attack of illness. (Cf. BRASH.)

1733 *Swift's Corr.* II. 717, I [Dr. Sheridan] hope nothing ails her but a brush.

† **brush**, *sb.*⁴, *Obs.* A variant of BRUCHUS, BRUKE.

1382 WYCLIF *Isa.* xxxiii. 4 Gederede togidere shul be ȝoure spoiles, as is gedered brush [**1388** bruke].

brush (brʌʃ), *sb.*⁵ *Austral.* and *N.Z. slang.* [Of uncertain origin.] A girl, a young woman; freq. *derog.* Also *collect.*

1941 in BAKER *Dict. Austral. Slang.* **1945** F. SARGESON *When Wind Blows* vii. 55, I don't go looking for trouble with brushes that are under age. **1947** D. M. DAVIN *Gorse blooms Pale* 200 What comes along but an Iti bint, a real grouse brush she was. **1953** K. TENNANT *Joyful Condemned* iii. 26 To him all girls were collectively 'the brush'. **1960** N. HILLIARD *Maori Girl* III. ix. 239 It's the good-looking brush that give a man all the trouble.

brush (brʌʃ), *v.*¹ Also 4-5 brusche(n, 5 brusshe. [Perh. identical with F. *brosser* intr. 'to dash through dense underwood', said of a stag or a hunter, which Littré separates from *brosser* trans. 'to brush', and refers immediately to *brosse* 'brushwood'. But it is possible that the Eng. word is onomatopœic, or that onomatopœia has affected its use: cf. *rush* and *br-* words like *brast* (burst), *break*, *bruise*. In modern use, also affected by BRUSH *v.*², esp. in sense 4.]

† **1.** *intr.* To rush with force or speed, usually into collision. *Obs.* exc. as influenced by BRUSH *v.*²: see quot. 1863 in 4.

a **1400** *Alexander* 963 And he halis furth on hede.. Brusches doune by þe berne & bitterly wepis. ? *a* **1400** *Morte Arth.* 3681 Than brothely they bekyre with boustouse tacle, Bruschese boldlye one burde. *c* **1400** *Destr. Troy* 1192 Bothe batels on bent brusshet to-gedur. *Ibid.* 10969 Pantasilia.. brusshet into batell. **1513** DOUGLAS *Æneis* x. xiv. 192 Furth bruschit the sawle with gret stremys of blude. **1647** W. BROWNE *Polex.* I. 78 For feare to brush at the iniquity of men, betray ye the cause of the gods? *a* **1650** in Furniv. *Percy Folio* I. 388 His eares brushed out of blood.

2. †**a.** *trans.* To force, or drive with a rush. *Obs.*

c **1425** WYNTOUN *Cron.* VIII. xiii. 93 (JAM.) Wþe he stwrly bruschyd the dure, And laid it flatlyngis in the flure. *a* **1460** *Play Sacrament* 649 Brushe them hens bothe & that anon. *c* **1470** HENRY *Wallace* x. 28 Blud fra byrneis was bruschyt on the greyn.

b. To force on (*fig.*); to drive hard. *U.S.*

1755 *Connecticut Gaz.* 29 Nov. (Schele de Vere), As tending to beget ill will, and brushing a disunion in the several governments in America. **1827** J. F. COOPER *Prairie* x I have at this moment a dog brushing a deer. *a* **1867** H. WOODRUFF *Trotting Horse of Amer.* (1868) v. 70 Eight or ten days prior to the race.. brush him a half mile. **1904** *N.Y. Times* 28 Nov. 5 The drivers.. spent a couple of hours before dusk brushing their fast steppers on the upper stretch.

3. *intr.* To burst away with a rush, move off abruptly, be gone, decamp, make off.

1690 B. E. *Dict. Cant. Crew, Brush*, to Fly or Run away. **1718** PRIOR *Poems* 63 Off they brush'd, both Foot and Horse. **1728** VANBRUGH & CIB. *Prov. Husb.* II. i. 48, I believe I had as good brush off. **1730** FIELDING *Author's Farce* I. vii, Come, Sir, will you please to brush? **1820** BYRON *Morg. Mag.* lxv, He brush'd apace On to the abbey. **1833** HT. MARTINEAU *Berkeley the B.* I. viii. 154 Enoch brushed out of the door. **1842** BARHAM *Ingol. Leg.* (1877) 204 And one Sergeant Matcham had brush'd with the dibs.

¶. Blending this with BRUSH *v.*²

4. *intr.* To move briskly *by*, *through*, or *against* anything, grazing it or sweeping it aside in passing.

1674 N. FAIRFAX *Bulk & Selv.* 143 To brush through many atoms of room. **1712** ADDISON *Spect.* No. 536 ¶1 A pretty young thing.. brushing by me. **1713** *Guardian* No. 163 (1756) II. 316 The servants.. begin to brush very familiarly by me. **1821** CLARE *Vill. Minstr.* I. 13 Often brushing through the dripping grass. *a* **1845** HOOD *2 Peacocks of Belf.* ii, They brush between the Churchyard's humble walls. **1863** GEO. ELIOT *Romola* III. xxv, He brushed against a man whose face he had not stayed to recognise. **1885** BROWNING *Ferishtah* 9 Where dogs brush by thee and express contempt.

brush (brʌʃ), *v.*² Also 5 brusche, 5-6 brusshe, brushe, 7 brish. [f. BRUSH *sb.*²; or ad. F. *brosser*, similarly formed from *brosse*.]

1. a. *trans.* To pass a brush briskly across (a surface), so as to sweep off dirt, dust, or light particles, or to smooth the surface; as to brush a coat, a hat, one's hair, a person (i.e. his clothes or hair).

c **1460** J. RUSSELL *Bk. Nurture* in *Babees Bk.* (1868) 180 To brusche þem [robes] clenly. **1577** HELLOWES *Gueuara's Ep.* 162 To brushe, and lay vp their apparel. **1599** SHAKS. *Much Ado* III. ii. 41 A brushes his hat a mornings. **1664** EVELYN *Kal. Hort.* (1729) 204 Brush and cleanse them from the Dust. **1807** CRABBE *Par. Reg.* II. 160 He served the Squire, and brushed the coat he made. **1812** J. & H. SMITH *Rej. Addr.* ii. (1873) 12 Molly.. brushed it with a broom. **1837** MARRYAT *Olla Podr.* xxxii, The children could not be brushed, for the brushes were in the.. bag. *Mod.* The nurse brushes the children's hair. 'They were washing and brushing themselves in the inn.'

†**b.** *fig.* To thrash: *esp.* in *to brush one's coat for him*. *Obs.* (Cf. *to dust one's jacket*.)

1665 *Surv. Aff. Netherl.* 61 Colonel Balfour, and his English, having brushed the Spaniards, the States capitulated. **1678** BUNYAN *Pilgr.* I. 209 They had their Coats soundly brushed by them. **1783** AINSWORTH *Lat. Dict.* (Morell) II, *Converro*, to beat one, to brush his coat for him.

c. *with compl.*, as *to brush* (*a thing*) *clean*, etc., *to brush down*, etc.

1839 DICKENS *Nich. Nick.* iv, His hair.. was brushed stiffly up from a low, protruding forehead. **1858** GLENNY *Gard. Everyday Bk.* 279 Sweeping away all dead leaves, and frequently brushing down the shelves. **1879** BROWNING *Ivan Iv.* 70 His broad hands smoothed her head, as fain to brush it free From fancies.

d. *absol.* Also *to brush away*: see AWAY 7.

1854 MRS. GASKELL *North & S.* iv. She showed it by brushing away viciously at Margaret's hair. *Mod.* You brush too hard!

2. *to brush up*: to brighten up by brushing, to free from dust or cobwebs, to furbish up, rub up, renovate; also *fig.* to revive or refresh one's acquaintance with anything. (Pope associates this with using a brush in painting, but perhaps only by a word-play.) Also *absol.* (*rare*) and *intr.*

a **1600** A. SCOTT *Eagle & Robin* in *Ever Green* (1761) I. 233 Proud Pecocks.. Bruscht up thair Pens that solemn Day. **1605** CHAPMAN, etc. in *Shaks. C. Praise* 69 You should brushe vp my old Mistresse. *a* **1744** POPE (J.) You have commissioned me to paint your shop, and I have done my best to brush you up like your neighbours. **1788** LD. SHEFFIELD in *Ld. Auckland's Corr.* (1861) II. 220 Nickolls.. was happy in brushing up his acquaintance with you. **1811** *London Pract. Midwifery* (ed. 3) vi. 140 The practitioner should always be cheerful... Whenever he perceives his patient looking at him, he should brush up, and appear as cheerful as he can. **1818** KEATS *Let.* 27 Apr. (1958) I. 275 Don't you think I am brushing up in the letter way? **1832** HT. MARTINEAU *Each & All* I. 5 She must brush up her French. **1835** DICKENS *Lett.* (1965) I. 66, I felt rather tired this morning when I got up; but as I did not do so until *past eleven*, I soon brushed up again. **1840** *Knickerbocker* XVI. 162, I thought I must brush up for the occasion. **1848** C. BRONTË *J. Eyre* x, I brushed up my recollections of the map of England. **1903** *Dial* 1 Sept. (Advt.), If you wish to brush up on your English, you will find nothing better. **1904** *Hartford Courant* 5 Oct. 8 The ex-governor must brush up a bit on his ecclesiastical studies.

Hence **brush-up**, the action or process of 'brushing up'.

1897 E. TERRY *Let.* 3 July in *Ellen Terry & Bernard Shaw* (1931) 224 She looked quite nice when she'd had a nice 'wash and a brush up'. **1912** [see WASH *sb.* 1 b]. **1951** A. CHRISTIE *They came to Baghdad* xix. 192, I left her to have a wash and brush up. **1951** in M. McLuhan *Mech. Bride* 127 If your knowledge is hazy, rusty, in need of a brush-up.

3. *to brush* (*a thing*) *over*: to paint or wet its surface with a brush; to paint lightly; also *fig.*

1628 EARLE *Microcosm.* xxxiii. 72 Practise him a little in men, and brush him over with good company. **1677** MOXON *Mech. Exerc.* (1703) 249 They finish the Plastering.. by.. brishing it over with fair Water. **1762-71** H. WALPOLE *Vertue's Anecd. Paint.* (1786) III. 9 It is just brushed over for the lights and shades. **1799** G. SMITH *Laboratory* I. 39 Brush them over with brandy.

4. a. To rub softly as with a brush in passing; to graze lightly or quickly, as in passing.

1647 H. MORE *Cupid's Confl.* xxiii. 171 My mightie wings high stretch'd.. I brush the starres. **1698** DRYDEN *Æneid* IV. 839 And brush the liquid Seas with lab'ring Oars. **1725** POPE *Odyss.* IX. 569 It almost brush'd the helm. **1790** A. WILSON *Morning*, To spurn dull sleep and brush the flowery dale. **1850** BLACKIE *Æschylus* I. 31 Light with swift foot she brushed the doorstead. **1871** R. ELLIS *Catullus* lxiv. 270 Light Zephyrus even-breathing Brushes a sleeping sea.

fig. **1807-8** W. IRVING *Salmag.* (1824) 94 [They] have been brushed rather rudely by the hand of time.

b. *intr.* To come lightly *against* with the impact of a brush.

1649 SELDEN *Laws Eng.* I. lix. (1739) 111 He became so great, that his Feathers brushed against the Kings Crown.

†**c.** *trans.* To draw or pass (anything) lightly like a brush *over* (something). *Obs. rare.*

a **1700** DRYDEN (J.) A thousand nights have brush'd their balmy wings Over these eyes.

5. a. To remove (dust, etc.) with a brush, to sweep (away). Also *transf.* and *fig.* To sweep

away as with a brush, to carry off lightly in passing. (Usually with advb. or prep. adjunct.)

c **1631** MILTON *Arcades* xv. 48 From the boughs brush off the evil dew. **1697** DRYDEN *Virg. Georg.* IV. 15 The Cows and Goats.. That.. brush the Dew. **1813** BYRON *Giaour* (Orig. Draft) ii, If.. the transient breeze.. brush one blossom from the trees. **1814** SOUTHEY *Roderick* XVI, She brush'd away the dews. **1835** MARRYAT *Jacob Faithf.* xxxix, Tom passed the back of his hand across his eyes to brush away a tear. **1860** HOLLAND *Miss Gilbert* ii. 41 Brushing tears from his eyes. **1884** *Manch. Exam.* 26 Nov. 5/1 It is surely high time to brush this nonsense away. **1886** *Manch. Exam.* 8 Jan. 6/1 Brushing the snow and slush into little mounds.

b. ***to brush off***: *fig.*, to rebuff, dismiss (a person, etc.). So **brush-off**, a rebuff, dismissal. orig. *U.S.*

1941 J. R. PARKER *Attorneys at Law* i. 10 I'd have given my eye teeth to hear Forbes getting the brush-off. **1941** B. SCHULBERG *What makes Sammy Run?* vi. 132 Since Sammy was waiting for Julian the chances are he'd only brush me off. **1943** LEWIS BROWNE *See What I Mean?* i. 8 No matter where I turned, I was given the brush-off. **1944** *Amer. Speech* XIX. 310/2 The organizer of a *Brush-off-club* 'made up of mournful soldiers who were given the hemlock cup by femmes back home'. **1947** J. STEINBECK *Wayward Bus* 71 Casual kindness in a man she had found to be the preliminary to a brush-off. **1958** M. DICKENS *Man Overboard* v. 68 The bleakly familiar: 'The post has been filled', or the more courteous brush-off: 'We will keep your letter on record in case a suitable post arises'. **1969** *Listener* 31 July 131/2 The problem of the future of British sovereignty can no longer be brushed off with humorous references to accepting foreign referees' decisions in international football matches.

6. To injure or hurt by grazing; said *esp.* of a horse grazing his fetlock with the shoe or hoof of the fellow foot. Also *absol.*

1691 *Lond. Gaz.* No. 2661/4 A grey Gelding about 15 hands.. his Knees brush'd. **1868** BP. FRASER in *Life* (1887) 158 I hope he [a horse] does not 'cut' or 'brush' in his action. **1886** *Sat. Rev.* 6 Mar. 327/2 Such severe and.. unnecessary pain, as the horse [inflicts] by hitting or brushing himself behind.

7. To trim (a hedge or tree, the sides of a ditch or path). *local.*

1513 [implied in BRUSHING *vbl. sb.* 1]. **1809** *Warehorne Highway-Bk.* 29 June (E.D.D.), For brushing the footpath, 1*s.* 0*d.* **1845** *Jrnl. R. Agric. Soc.* VI. II. 479 They [*sc.* hedges] are carefully brushed, or clipped, twice a year. **1886** R. HOLLAND *Gloss. Chester* 48 *Brush*, to trim a hedge.

8. To beat (a covert). Also *intr.* in *vbl. sb.*

1876 *Coursing Cal.* 223 Our long dragging beats taking us.. round the far side by Fliskoe Forest, in proximity to which the ranges were brushed, but with no good results. **1895** W. RYE *Gloss. E. Anglia* 26 *Brush*, to beat a covert; 'a day's brushing with the governor'.

9. *Hunting.* To take the 'brush' from (a killed fox) as a trophy of the chase.

1879 *Tinsley's Mag.* XXIV. 334 As they then rode in the master 'brushed' him [*sc.* a fox], while the hounds were baying. **1893** *Field* 11 Feb. 191/3 Some twenty minutes later he had the satisfaction of brushing his fox.

10. Painting. ***to brush (in)***: to put in with the brush, to paint in.

1897 *Daily News* 16 Jan. 6/3 For flesh painting, the torso.. is so firm, so luminous; the draperies, too, are decisively brushed in. **1901** *Ibid.* 7 Mar. 6/6 These are vivid, quickly brushed impressions by an artist who has an eye for.. Italian landscape.

'brushable, *a. rare.* [f. prec. + -ABLE.] Capable of being brushed.

Mod. Everything to be readily washable and brushable.

† **brushal.** *Obs.* In 5 bruschalle, brusshayle, brushaly. [a. F. *broussaille*, f. *brosse* brushwood: see -AL^{1} 5.] Brushwood, underwood.

1430 LYDG. *Chron. Troy* v. xxxvii, He kepeth him close lo in yonder caue Amonge brusshayle. *c* **1440** *Promp. Parv.* 54 Bruschalle [*K.* brushaly], *sarmentum, ramentum, in rado, ramalia, arbustum.*

brushed (brʌʃt), *ppl. a.* Also brosshen, brusht. [f. BRUSH *v.*^{2} or *sb.*^{2} + -ED.] **1.** Swept or smoothed with a brush; grazed; furnished with a 'brush'.

c **1460** J. RUSSELL *Bk. Nurture* in *Babees Bk.* (1868) 180 Lett neuer wollyn cloth.. passe a seuenyght to be vnbrosshen and shakyn. **1580** BARET *Alv.* B. 1415 Brushed: swept.. *versus.* **1649** G. DANIEL *Trinarch., Hen. V*, st. 264 Brusht Gallants now they went. **1691** *Lond. Gaz.* No. 2627/4 A Black Roan Horse.. the near Knee brush'd. **1711** 'J. DISTAFF' *Char. Don. Sacheverellio* 11 Brush'd Beavers, and Formal Cravats. **1831** CARLYLE *Sart. Res.* I. iii, Purse-mouthed, crane-necked, clean-brushed, pacific individuals.

2. *spec.* Designating knitted or woven fabrics that have been finished with a nap.

1926 G. G. DENNY *Fabrics* (ed. 2) I. 26 *Brushed wool*, knit fabrics for sweaters, scarfs, trimmings which have been napped. Usually contain mohair fibres which make long, silky nap. **1957** M. B. PICKEN *Fashion Dict.* 37/1 *Brushed rayon*, napped rayon fabric, used for sleeping garments, sportswear, shirts. **1966** J. AIKEN *Trouble with Product X* iv. 69, I took off my brushed-nylon waist slip. **1967** *Observer* 14 May 29/6 French brushed cotton in black with pink roses.

brushed (brʌʃt), *a.* [f. BRUSH *sb.*^{1} + -ED^{2}.] Overgrown with brushwood.

1666 in *Duxbury Rec.* (Mass.) (1893) 16 A certain parcel of land,.. until you come to a low brushed swamp. **1832** *Jrnl. R. Geogr. Soc.* II. 110 The line of sight extended over a great extent of densely wooded, or brushed, land. **1888** *Century Mag.* Jan. 453/1 A cañon, liberally wooded or 'brushed' with wild plums. **1938** J. STEINBECK *Long Valley* 63 There was a draw below him.. brushed with dry struggling sage and chaparral.

brusher ('brʌʃə(r)). [f. BRUSH *v.*^{2} + -ER^{1}.] One who brushes, or uses a brush.

1598 FLORIO, *Scopatore*, a sweeper, a brusher. **1599** BRETON *Praise Vert. Ladies* (1876) 59 If he bee a good brusher, shee is a good laundrer. **1651** G. HERBERT *Jacula Prudentum* (ed. 2), Critics are like brushers of noblemen's clothes.

b. *techn.* in various trades.

1835 URE *Philos. Manuf.* 204 Operatives engaged in our woollen manufacture:—Wool-sorters.. pressers, brushers, and steamers. **1868** *Derby Mercury* 18 Feb., He was engaged as a 'brusher' to some men who were blasting.

†**c.** *slang. Obs.*

1690 B. E. *Dict. Cant. Crew, Brusher*, an exceeding full Glass.

brusheroo: see BRUSH *sb.*^{2} 8 b.

† **'brushet.** *Obs.* In 4 brusschet, 5 bruschet. [a. OF. *broissete*, **broussette*, dim. of *brosse* brushwood.] Underwood; a small thicket or covert.

c **1380** *Sir Ferumb.* 800 In þat ilke brusschet by: v. þousant of oþer and mo. *c* **1500** *Partenay* 3299 Thys bruschet made put in-to on hepe. **1645** W. HOOKE *New Eng. Sence*, Bands of Souldiers lying in ambush here under the fearn and brushet of the Wildernes.

† **'brushiness.** *Obs.* [f. BRUSHY + -NESS.] Brushy quality, shaggy roughness.

1659 H. MORE *Immort. Soul* III. xxxi. (1662) 148 Considering the brushiness and angulosity of the parts of the Air, a more than ordinary Motion.. may very well prove painful to the Soul.

brushing ('brʌʃɪŋ), *vbl. sb.* Also 6 broshyng. [f. BRUSH *v.*^{1} or *v.*^{2} + -ING^{1}.]

1. Cutting of brushwood, twigs, etc.

1513 *MS. Acc. St. John's Hosp. Canterb.*, For toppyng of xij treys & broshyng. **1886** R. HOLLAND *Gloss. Chester* 48 *Brushings*, the trimmings of hedges. **1887** DARLINGTON *Folk Speech S. Cheshire* 131 *Brushin' hook*, the hook used in *brushing* a hedge. **1969** *Gloss. Landscape Work (B.S.I.)* v. 19 *Brushing*.., clearance of light, woody growth ('brush') from rough ground by slashing.

2. Sweeping or smoothing (as) with a brush.

c **1460** J. RUSSELL *Bk. Nurture* (1868) 180 Ouer moche bruschynge werethe cloth lyghtly. **1851** H. MAYO *Pop. Superst.* (ed. 2) 151 Transverse brushings with the hand. **1858** GLENNY *Gard. Everyday Bk.* 95/1 The Lawn now requires frequent brushing, rolling, and mowing.

3. *Coal-mining.* The action of, or the work involved in, cutting or blasting down the roof, or building supporting and blocking walls in a coal mine. Also *attrib.* and *Comb.*, as ***brushing contractor***; **brushing-bed** (see quot. 1883).

1883 GRESLEY *Gloss. Coal-m., Brushers* (Scotland), men who brush the roof, build packs and stoppings, which work is called brushing. *Brushing-bed* (Scotland), the stratum brushed or ripped. **1923** *Glasgow Herald* 16 Oct. 9 The 'brushing' contractor.

4. The action or process of applying the enamel in the manufacture of enamel-ware. Also *attrib.*

1893 *Daily News* 15 Dec. 5/4 The brushing department of enamelled plate works.

5. Brush-work, as distinguished from drawing.

1896 *Daily News* 6 Apr. 6/5 No incompleteness of drawing, of brushing, or of line.

6. *attrib.*, as in ***brushing-table***; also **brushing-machine**, a name applied to various contrivances acting as brushes for smoothing, dressing flax, etc.

1575 *Richmond, Wills* (1853) 246 Brusshinge stoule, one chyste, and one chare. **1610** *Althorp MS.* in Simpkinson *Washingtons* Introd. 3 A lowe bedsted.. a brushing table. **1624** *Ibid.* 54 The nursery and brushing chamber.

'brushing, *ppl. a.* [f. BRUSH *v.*^{1}, ^{2} + -ING^{2}.]

1. That brushes (in various senses of the verb).

1513 DOUGLAS *Æneis* II. ix. (viii.) 103 The fomy rivair or flude.. with his bruscheand fairde of watter broun. **1597** DRAYTON *Mortimer.* 43 The brushing murmure stills her [Hero] like a song. **1642** H. MORE *Song of Soul* I. II. xci, Blown away with strongly brushing winds. **1854** GILFILLAN Wks. 126 The swift brushing wing of a bird.

2. Having a brushing tail.

1733 FIELDING *Quix. in Eng.* II. v, A brushing fox in yonder Wood, Secure to find we seek.

3. Rushing, brisk.

1792 OSBALDISTONE *Brit. Sportsm.* 79/2 A horse should have his brushing galop in a morning before watering. **1824** SCOTT *Redgauntlet* let. vii, I.. assured him a brushing gallop would do his favourite no harm.

brushite ('brʌʃaɪt). *Min.* [Named after Prof. Brush of Yale College, U.S.: see -ITE.] A hydrous phosphate of lime occurring in small crystals in the rock guano of Aves Island and Sombrero in the Caribbean Sea.

1880 DANA *Min.* §492 D, Guano is bone-phosphate of lime.. mixed with the hydrous phosphate, brushite.

brushless ('brʌʃlɪs), *a.* [f. BRUSH *sb.*^{2} + -LESS.]

1. Without a brush; having no brush.

1838 *Fraser's Mag.* XVIII. 484 The brilliant finish of the brushless fox.

2. Of shaving-cream: made for use without a brush.

1933 *Drug & Cosmetic Industry* July 40/2 Introducing a new shaving cream of both the brushless and lather types. **1941** JENKINS & HARTUNG *Chem. Org. Med. Products* 7 Suntan oils, brushless shaving creams, and hair tonics. **1960** H. L. LAWRENCE *Children of Light* i. 9 He.. took his Gillette and brushless shaving cream.

Hence **'brushlessness.**

1880 MISS BROUGHTON *Sec. Th.* I. vi. 81 A dressing and undressing without any toilet apparatus, an absolute brushlessness, comblessness.

brushman ('brʌʃmən). [f. BRUSH *sb.*^{2} + MAN.] One who uses a brush; a painter.

a **1819** WOLCOTT (P. Pindar) Wks. (1830) 138 (D.) How difficult in artists to allow To brother brushmen even a grain of merit!

† **'brushment.** *Obs. rare.* [f. BRUSH *sb.*^{1} + -MENT, with collective sense.] Prunings or loppings of trees; cut brushwood.

1591 RASTALL *Statutes, Chart. Forestes* §14 Those which beare vpon their backes brushment, barke, or coale to sell [Latin *buscam, corticem, vel carbonem*].

brush-off, brush-up: see BRUSH *v.*^{2} 5 b, 2.

brushwood ('brʌʃwʊd). [f. BRUSH *sb.*^{1}]

1. Cut or broken twigs or branches; small wood.

1637 *Bury Wills* (1850) 169, I owe Danyell Whitacre.. for three loades of brushe wood. **1783** COWPER *Task* IV. 381 Her scanty stock of brushwood, blazing clear. **1818** HAWTHORNE *Amer. Note-bks.* (1879) II. 44 A load of dry brushwood. *fig.* *a* **1613** OVERBURY *Newes Chimney Corn.* Wks. (1856) 199 Wit is brushwood, judgement timber: the one gives the greatest flame, the other yeelds the durablest heat. **1649** G. DANIEL *Trinarch., Hen. V*, ccxx, Lopt Royaltie, is ever to the Bold Attemptor, worth his pains; the Brush-wood's gold. **1682** DRYDEN *Relig. Laici* 269 Vain traditions stopped the gaping fence.. What safety from such brushwood helps as these?

2. Small growing trees and shrubs; thicket, underwood.

1732 BERKELEY *Alciphr.* I. §2 Land that is suffered to lie waste.. will be overspread with brush-wood, brambles, thorns. **1814** SCOTT *Wav.* xxxvi, Little dingles of stunted brushwood. **1835** W. IRVING *Tour Prairies* 235 They all three made off.. through thickets and brushwood.

attrib. **1855** RUSSELL *The War* xxviii. 250 Brushwood glades and remote dells.

brushy ('brʌʃɪ), *a.*^{1} [f. BRUSH *sb.*^{1} + -Y^{1}.] Clothed or covered with 'brush' or brushwood.

1719 LONDON & WISE *Compl. Gard.* xxix, The Elms.. must be good Brushy Trees from Top to Bottom. **1874** COUES *Birds N.-W.* 145 It frequents brushy hilltops. **1882** *Century Mag.* June 211 The wren Comes.. from its brushy den.

'brushy, *a.*^{2} [f. BRUSH *sb.*^{2} + -Y^{1}.] Brushlike; bushy, shaggy.

1673 GREW *Anat. Roots* I. i. §7 Roots.. neither Ramifi'd, nor yet Brushy, or divided at the Top into severall small Strings. **1687** *Lond. Gaz.* No. 2273/4 Lost.. Setting Dog.. a black Ear, and a long brushy Tail. **1835** *Fraser's Mag.* XI. 141 His hair was.. thick and brushy.

b. *Comb.*, as ***brushy-looking***.

1882 *Garden* 29 Apr. 286/2 Brushy-looking white blooms.

† **'brusit,** *ppl. a. Sc. Obs.* Also 6 brysit. [In form this agrees with the pa. pple. of BRUISE *v.*, but the connexion of sense is not manifest. The sense recalls med.L. *brustus, brusdus, brosdus* = *brodatus, brudatus*, Fr. *brodé*, embroidered; cf. BRUSERY.] Embroidered.

a **1450** HOLLAND *Houlate* xxxi, The said persevantis gyde was grathit I ges Brusit with ane grene tre, gudly and gay. **1513** DOUGLAS *Æneis* I. ix. 123 Ane riche garmont brysit with stif gold wire. *Ibid.* III. vii. 25 Brusit clathis, and riche wedis. *Ibid.* XI. xv. 22 Of nedill wark all brusyt was his cote.

† **brusk,** *a. Obs. Her.* An obsolete name for the colour *tawny* or *orange*.

1486 *Bk. St. Albans, Her.* A iij, An Ametist a dusketli ston, brusk hit is called in armys. **1562** LEIGH *Armory* 200 The Colour, Bruske, which is betweene Geules and tawny. **1586** FERNE *Blaz. Gentrie* 146 Tawney was named Bruske. **1688** R. HOLME *Armoury* I. 12/1 Tawny or Orange colour.. in Blazon.. is termed by some old Heraulds, Bruske.

brusk(e, obs. form of BRUSQUE.

brusket, obs. form of BRISKET.

† **'brusle,** *v. Obs.* $rare^{-1}$. [Origin uncertain: cf. BRUSTLE.] *trans.* ? To crack; to bruise a little.

1624 FLETCHER *Wife for Month* II. vi. Two broken citizens. Break 'em more; they are but brusled yet!

brusle, obs. and north. f. BIRSLE, BRISTLE.

† **bruslery.** *Obs.* [Cf. BROILERY; also BRUSTLE.] Disturbance.

1546 *St. Papers Hen. VIII*, I. 886 This pryvate cace of Reneger hath made all this bruslery.

† **bru'sole.** *Obs.* [a. F. *brussoles* 'perh. a form of *rissole* with an epenthetic *b*' (Littré).] A ragout of braised veal.

1706 PHILLIPS, *Brusoles* or *Bursoles* (Fr. in Cookery), Stakes of Veal or other Meat well season'd, in order to be laid in a Stew-pan between thin slices of Bacon, and baked between two Fires. **1724** RAMSAY *Health* 69 The collar'd veal.. Pigs *à la braise*, the tansy and *brusole*.

brusor, -our, -ure, var. of BRUSURE, *Obs.*, wound, fracture.

brusque (brʌsk, brʊsk), *a.* Also 7 brusk(e, 9 brusk. [a. F. *brusque*, according to Littré, etc., adapted in 16th c. from Italian *brusco* 'soure, tarte, eagre, briske, vnripe; also soure- or grim-looking' (Florio); cf. Sp. and Pg. *brusco* 'rude, peevish, ill-tempered, roughly hasty'. The ulterior history is uncertain: one conjecture refers it to the Celtic words mentioned under BRISK, which is hardly likely, if the Romanic word appeared first in Italian. See Diez and Littré. Commonly spelt *brusk* in the 17th c., but now usually spelt and often pronounced as French. (Cf. also BRUSSLY.)]

†**1.** Tart. (= It. *brusco.*) *Obs.*

1601 HOLLAND *Pliny* II. 152 The thin and bruske harsh wine nourisheth the body lesse. [**1752** LADY M. W. MONTAGUE *Lett.* lxxvi. IV. 23 A sort of wine they call brusco.]

2. Somewhat rough or rude in manner; blunt, 'offhand'.

1651 *Reliq. Wotton.* (1685) 582 The Scotish Gentlemen.. lately sent to that King, found..but a brusk welcome. **1757** H. WALPOLE *Corr.* (1837) I. 370 This sounds brusque, but I will explain it. **1826** DISRAELI *Viv. Grey* II. xv. 80 Yes, lively enough, but I wish her manner was less brusque. **1870** —— *Lothair* xlvi. 243 He was brusk, ungracious, scowling, and silent. **1879** MCCARTHY *Own Times* II. xxii. 123 His blunt, brusque ways of speaking and writing.

brusque (see prec.), *v.* [f. prec. adj.]

1. with impers. obj. *to brusque it*: to assume a brusque manner, to 'do it' brusquely.

1826 SCOTT *Woodst.* (1832) I. 150 I'll e'en brusque it a little..and try if I can bring him to a more intelligible mode of speaking.

2. *trans.* To treat brusquely or with scant courtesy, to treat in an off-handed way.

1836 *Fraser's Mag.* XIII. 530 Even in this first dialogue he brusques Tasso. **1839** *Ibid.* XX. 427 From the outset Blackwood domineered over and brusqued him. **1862** M. NAPIER *Life Visc. Dundee* II. 292 No disposition to slur over, or brusque the question.

'brusquely, *adv.* [f. as prec. + -LY²: see also BRUSSLY.] In a brusque manner; off-handedly.

1671 *True Non-Conf.* 85 Our Lord..doth bruskly decline, to be so much as an amicable trister. **1842** MRS. BROWNING *Grk. Chr. Poets* 15 She..rather brusquely proposes their mutual marriage. **1882** B. RAMSAY *Recoll. Mil. Serv.* II. xx. 232 The man refused most brusquely.

'brusqueness. [f. as prec. + -NESS.] The quality of being brusque or off-handed; bluntness.

1859 HELPS *Friends in C.* Ser. II. II. vii. 137 Their sensitiveness is shocked by his brusqueness. **1884** ROE in *Harper's Mag.* June 92/1 Kindness, and..girlish brusqueness were..equally blended.

‖**brusquerie** (bryskəri). [Fr., f. *brusque.*] Bluntness, abruptness of manner, brusqueness.

1752 CHESTERF. *Lett.* 275 (1792) III. 258 This most mistaken opinion gives an indelicacy, a brusquerie, and a roughness to the manners. **1817** MAR. EDGEWORTH *Ormond* lv. (1832) 172 You will lose this little brusquerie of manner ..when you have mixed a little more with mankind. **1853** RUSKIN *Stones Ven.* II. vi. §74. 204 Always quickset; erring, if at all, ever on the side of brusquerie.

brusschet, var. of BRUSHET, *Obs.*, a thicket.

brussed, obs. pa. t. and pa. pple. of BURST *v.*

Brussels ('brʌsəlz). [Name of the capital of Belgium, used *attrib.* to designate things connected, in their origin or manufacture, with that city.]

1. Short for 'Brussels carpet'.

1813 D. WORDSWORTH *Let.* in M. Moorman *W. Wordsworth* (1965) II. vii. 230 We are going to have a *Turkey*!!! carpet in the dining-room, and a Brussels in William's study. *a* **1845** HOOD *Domestic Asides* iii, What boots for my new Brussels! **1882** W. D. HOWELLS *Woman's Reason* viii, The reception-room..was respectable in threadbare brussels.

2. *Attrib.* or *Comb.*, as **Brussels carpet**, a kind of carpet having a back of stout linen thread and an upper surface of wool (see quot. 1875); **Brussels lace**, a costly kind of pillow-lace made in Brussels and its neighbourhood, noted for the thickness and evenness of its texture, and the delicate accuracy of its forms: **Brussels sprout** (almost always *pl.*), the bud-bearing Cabbage (*Brassica oleracea gemmifera*), a variety producing buds like small cabbages in the axils of its leaves.

1799 *Times* 1 June 4/2 *Brussels and Wilton carpets. **1831** CARLYLE *Sart. Res.* I. iv, A whole immensity of Brussels carpet, and pier-glasses. **1875** URE *Dict. Arts* I. 732 In the Brussels carpets the worsted yarn raised to form the pile.. is not cut. In the imperial Brussels the figure is raised above the ground, and its pile is cut, but the ground is uncut. **1748** RICHARDSON *Clarissa* iii. III. 28 Her head dress was a *Brussels lace mob. **1823** BYRON *Juan* XIV, xlvii, Sympathy ..robes sweet friendship in a Brussels lace. **1796** C. MARSHALL *Garden.* xv. (1813) 224 *Brussels sprouts are winter greens growing much like boorcole. **1861** DELAMER *Kitch. Gard.* 57 And from the bud at the root of the foot-stalk of each, will appear a miniature cabbage, which is the Brussels sprout.

brussh-: see BRUSH-.

†**'brussly**, *adv. Obs. rare*⁻¹. [This looks like a phonetic corruption of *bruskly*, BRUSQUELY: but the date presents difficulties, and further complicates the question of relation between BRISK and BRUSQUE.] ? Brusquely, roughly, harshly.

1481 CAXTON *Tulle on Friendsh.* A iv, He is well deled with all, and I more brussly deled with al than right wolde.

†**brust.** *Obs.* [OE. *byrst*: see BIRSE, BRISTLE.] A bristle.

a **1000** *Ags. Gloss.* in Wr.-Wülcker 46 *Seta*, byrst. *c* **1000** *Sax. Leechd.* I. 156 Hyre twigu beoð swylce swinen byrst. *c* **1330** *Rouland & Ver.* 861 No Jubiter, no apolin, No is worþ þe brust of a swin, In hert no in þouȝt. **1570** LEVINS *Manip.* 194 A Bruste, *seta*.

†**brust**, *a. Obs.* Also 3 **burst**. [app. pa. ppl. of a vb. **byrsten*, *bursten*, a. ON. *byrsta* to bristle, f. *burst* bristle. (Mätzner cites an ON. adj. *byrstr* bristly, maned.)] Bristled, with bristles erect, bristling; also *fig.*

a **1225** *Juliana* 68 Set þat balefule beast as an burst bar [*Bodl. MS.* iburst bar] þat grunde his tuskes. *c* **1325** *Pol. Songs* 151 Cometh the maister budel brust ase a bore.

brust, obs. form of BREAST *sb.*

brust(e, -en, -ing, etc.: see BURST.

brustel, -il, -yl(le, obs. forms of BRISTLE.

†**'brustle**, *v.*¹ *Obs.* Also 7 **brussel**. [Early ME. *brustlien*, parallel to *bræstlien*: see BRASTLE. Probably onomatopœic: expressing a duller or more muffled sound than *brastle*. Cf. *rustle*, *bustle*.]

1. *intr.* To make a crackling or rustling noise.

c **1205** LAY. 20143 Breken braden speren, Brustleden sceldes. *Ibid.* 20080 Brustlede scæftes. **1393** GOWER *Conf.* II. 93 He..brustleth as a monkes froise, Whan it is throwe into the panne. **1755** JOHNSON, *Brustle*, to crackle, to make a small noise. (*Skinner.*)

b. Of the noise of waves.

1622 FLETCHER *Sp. Curate* IV. vii, See where the sea comes, how it foams and brussels.

2. To go hastily with a rustling noise. Cf. *bustle*.

1638 H. RIDER *Horace's Odes* I. (1644) 21 The..green-skind adder brustled through a bush.

†**'brustle**, *v.*² *Obs.* Also 7 **brusle**, 8 **burstle**. [app. a variant of BRISTLE *v.*, perh. influenced in sense 3 by the prec., or by *rustle*.]

1. *intr.* To bristle as hair. See BRISTLE.

2. To bristle *up* as an excited beast, raise the mane.

1656 COWLEY *David.* I. (1669) 17 A Lyon..brustles up preparing for his feast.

3. *esp.* Of birds: To raise the feathers; hence *fig.* with reference to the turkeycock or peacock: To show off, vapour, bluster.

1648 HERRICK *Hesper.* (1859) 122 Can Yee see it brusle like a swan? **1655–60** STANLEY *Hist. Philos.* (1701) 99/2 Shewing him the Cocks of Midas brustling against those of Callias. **1657** G. STARKEY *Helmont's Vind.* 64 He vapours and brustles like Dametas in his military accoutrements. **1659** GAUDEN *Tears Ch.* 370 Like the Birds called Ruffs, ever brusling and pecking against each other. **1720** *Stow's Surv.* (ed. Strype 1754) I. v. xxviii. 486/1 A mercer in Cheapside; who had been often burstling..about this ceremony. **1721–1800** BAILEY, *Brustle*..to vapour.

†**'brustling**, *vbl. sb.*¹ *Obs.* [f. BRUSTLE *v.*¹ + -ING¹.] Rustling noise or movement.

1600 HAKLUYT *Voyages* (1810) III. 133 We fell into a great whirling and brustling of a tyde.

†**'brustling**, *vbl. sb.*² *Obs.* [f. BRUSTLE *v.*²] Raising of the feathers; vapouring, blustering.

1622 T. STOUGHTON *Chr. Sacr.* vii. 91 The Turkie cocke ..maketh a great brustling and strouting with his wings.

†**'brusure.** *Obs.* Forms: 4 brusur, 4–5 bru-, brosure, -our, 5 brissoure, brys(s)ure, broser, 6 brusor. [a. OF. *briseure*, *bruseure*, mod.F. *brisure*, f. *briser* to break.]

1. Bruising or crushing; a bruise, contusion.

c **1350** *Will. Palerne* 2461 Non schold in þat barnes bodi o brusure finde. **1382** WYCLIF *Lev.* xxiv. 20 Brusur for brusur [Vulg. *fracturam pro fractura*], eye for eye. *c* **1400** *Three Kings Cologne* 95 This bawme is good for all brusours [*v.r.* brosours, -ures] and woundes. *c* **1440** *Promp. Parv.* 52 Brisyng or brissoure [*K.* bryssynge or bryssure] *quassatio, contusio, collisio.* **1494** FABYAN VI. clxx. 165 With broser or hurte ensuynge of the wounde before taken.

2. Breaking, breach, fracture; ruin.

1382 WYCLIF *Neh.* vi. 1, I hadde bild the wal, and ther was not in it laft brosure [**1388** brekyng]. **1496** *Dives & P.* (W. de W.) VI. x. 247 Byfore brekynge & brysure gooth pryde. **1506** GUYLFORDE *Pilgr.* 36 None hole nor brusor apperyd.

brusury, var. BRUSERY *Obs.*, embroidery.

‖**brut** (bruːt), *sb.* Also 5 **brout**. [= M.Welsh *brut*, mod.W. *brud*, in the names of the Welsh chronicles of British history, as in the *Brut Gruffudd ab Arthur* of Geoffrey of Monmouth, *Brut Tysilio*, *Brut y Tywysogion*, etc. Salesbury *Dict. Eng. & Welsh* (1547) has '*Brut*, Walshe prophecies'; Davies 1632 '*Brud, brut*, historia, chronica; sumitur et pro vaticinio.' The Welsh Bible has (Dan. ii. 27) *brudwyr* 'brut-men' = soothsayers. *Brut* 'chronicle' was a transferred use of *Brut* = *Brutus*, as in *Le Roman de Brut* of Wace, and the *Brut* of Layamon, a chronicle or genealogy of the legendary Brutus and his descendants in Britain. Whether the transferred sense arose in Welsh, or was taken from a French title, as the *Brut* of Wace, or the later *Petit Brut* of Raoul de Bohon (*c* 1350), is doubtful; but the latter is more likely. For the Brutus legend, see BRUTE².]

A chronicle of British history from the mythical Brutus downward. (The ME. instance may refer to Wace, Layamon, or some Welsh *Brut.*)

c **1450** *Arth. & Merl.* (Mätz.) 2740 So ich in the brout yfinde. **1845** *Athenæum* 4 Jan. 9 A Greek version of our brute-epos. **1847** YEOWELL *Anc. Brit. Church* Pref. 7 The only other remains still extant of Ancient Welsh literature consist of Bruts, or Chronicles. **1883** H. KENNEDY *Ten Brink's E.E. Lit.* 188 A history of those who first had possession of England 'after the flood' or as a Norman would, perhaps, even then have called it, a *Brut*.

†**brut**, *v. Obs.* Also 7 **brutte**. [perh. a. F. *brouter* 'to browse': but cf. BRET, BRIT *v.*]

1. *intr.* To browse. Hence BRUTTING *vbl. sb.*

1577 [see BRUTTING *vbl. sb.*]. **1674** RAY *S. & E.C. Wds.* 60 To brutte, to browse. *Suss. Dial.* **1699** EVELYN *Acetaria* (1729) 145 Marking what the goats so greedily brutted upon.

2. *trans. dial.* To break *off* (young shoots).

Mod. Kent. Dial., Your potatoes don't come up because the young shoots were brutted off.

‖**brut** (bryt), *a.* [Fr.] Of wines: unsweetened.

1891 *Longman's Mag.* Aug. 417 An especial brand of brut champagne. *Ibid.*, Brut wines. **1896** *Pall Mall Mag.* Mar. 399 Tell my man to bring me a quail, broiled, and a pint of Piper Heidsieck, *brut*. **1932** WODEHOUSE *Louder & Funnier* 12 Washing it down with a *brut* champagne of a vintage year.

brut, obs. form of BRET, a kind of fish.

brutage, obs. form of BRATTICE.

brutal ('bruːtəl), *a.* and *sb.* Also 6 **-all**, **-ell**. [f. L. *brūt-us* (see BRUTE) + -AL¹. Cf. F. *brutal*, 16th c. in Littré.] **A.** *adj.*

1. Of or belonging to the brutes, as opposed to man; of the nature of a brute; animal. *Obs.* or *arch.*

c **1450** HENRYSON *Mor. Fab.* Prol. xii, Under the figur of sum brutal beist. **1535** STEWART *Cron. Scot.* II. 228 Lyke brutell beistis takand thair desyre. **1651** HOBBES *Govt. & Soc.* v. §5. 78 The consent of those brutall creatures is naturall, that of men by compact only. **1704** J. TRAPP *Abra-Mulé* IV. i. 1499 Hid their dazzling Forms in Brutal Shapes. **1726** GAY *Fables* (1755) II. 142 On man we brutal slaves depend. **1838** G. S. FABER *Inquiry* 95 The angel..daily infuses them into human and brutal bodies.

2. Resembling, pertaining to, or characteristic of the brutes: **a.** in want of intelligence or reasoning power.

c **1510** BARCLAY *Mirr. Good Mann.* (1570) A v, It is a brutall fury in battayle for to fight. **1541** BECON *News of Heav.* Wks. (1843) 52 He is truly too much brutal, that rejoiceth not at the hearing of them [the news]. *a* **1718** PENN *Maxims* Wks. 1726 I. 828 Inquiry is Human; Blind Obedience, Brutal. **1722** DE FOE *Plague* (1884) 120 A sort of brutal Courage..founded neither on Religion or Prudence. **1826** DISRAELI *Viv. Grey* V. iv. 182 The students affected a sort of brutal surprise.

b. in their animal or sensual nature.

1534 LD. BERNERS *Gold. Bk. M. Aurel.* xxiii. (R.) These lawes of yᵉ Lacedemonians..doth mocke thy brutall vices. *c* **1550** *Scot. Poems 16th C.* II. 193 The parish priest, that brutall beist, He polit them wantonly. *a* **1725** POPE *Odyss.* I. 175 The suitor-train, a brutal crowd, With insolence and wine, elate and loud. **1749** SMOLLETT *Regicide* V. viii, The slaves of brutal appetite. **1878** MORLEY *Diderot* II. 13 Some of it is revolting in its brutal indecency.

3. As rude or ill-mannered as a brute beast; coarse, unrefined.

1709 SHAFTESB. *Charac.* (1711) I. 129 A Man of thorow Good-Breeding..is incapable of doing a rude or brutal Action. **1742** CHESTERF. *Lett.* I. xcv. 269 There is hardly any body brutal enough..not to say, Sir, My Lord, or Madam. **1848** MACAULAY *Hist. Eng.* II. 196 His [Tyrconnel's] brutal manners made him unfit to represent the majesty of the crown.

4. Inhuman; coarsely cruel, savage, fierce.

1641 J. JACKSON *True Evang. T.* I. 5 It purporteth..the turning of fierce and brutall men..onto..calme and sociable manners. **1735–6** THOMSON *Liberty* III. 430 Brutal Marius and keen Sylla. **1836** THIRLWALL *Greece* II. xi. 53 The cruelty of a brutal master. **1840** W. HOWITT *Visits Remark. Pl.* Ser. I. 237 The brutal amusements of the bull-baiting or the cock-pit. **1878** MORLEY *Crit. Misc.* Ser. I. 268 The cruel and brutal abominations of slavery.

†**B.** *sb.* [ellipt. use of adj.] A brutal person. *Obs.*

1655 JENNINGS *Elise* 104 Should you have tormented me so much, to make me hearken to this Brutal? **1663** COWLEY *Cutter Colman St.* Pref. 10 The Honour of their Judgments (as some Brutals imagine of their Courage) consists in Quarrelling with every thing. **1676** WYCHERLEY *Pl. Dealer* I. i, The world thinks you a Mad-man, a Brutal.

brutalism (ˈbruːtəlɪz(ə)m). [f. BRUTAL *a.* + -ISM.] **1.** Brutal state, brutality.

1803 BRISTED *Pedest. Tour* I. Introd. 9 The Norman soldiery..in the systematic uniformity of their brutalism. **1831** SOUTHEY in *Q. Rev.* XLV. 439 Brought it from the lowest brutalism to the present degree of civilization. **1876** *Gentl. Mag.* 714 The fight with the brutalism of unbelief.

2. A style of art or architecture characterized by deliberate crudity of design (see quot. 1953).

1953 A. & P. SMITHSON in *Archit. Design* Dec. 342/2 House in Soho..bare concrete, brickwork and wood..would have been the first exponent of the 'new brutalism' in England, as the preamble to the specification shows: 'It is our intention in this building to have the structure exposed entirely, without internal finishes.' **1954** *Archit. Rev.* CXV. 274/2 The attitude taken by certain younger English architects and artists, and known, half satirically, as the New Brutalism. **1957** *New Yorker* 2 Nov. 95/1 This sculpture is the fulfillment of a lifetime dedicated to Constructivism..unshaken by the more popular fashions of..Brutalism, and Disintegrationism. **1962** *Observer* 1 Apr. 13/8 A style which Lady Cargill describes as 'a mild version of the "new brutalism"'.

brutalist (ˈbruːtəlɪst). [f. BRUTAL(ISM + -IST.] One who exhibits brutalism; *spec.* an exponent of brutalism in art, architecture, or literature. Also *attrib.* or as *adj.*

1934 in WEBSTER. **1937** *John o' London's* 12 Mar. 984/3 It is a good example of the modern Brutalist literature that rejoices in tearing every veil aside. **1954** *Archit. Rev.* CXV. 343/3, I understand that Paolozzi, in common with some young architects, now calls himself a 'brutalist'. **1958** *Ibid.* CXXIII. 1/3 Objects of gross physical plasticity, such as Brutalist sculptures and American cars. **1959** *Manch. Guardian* 7 Feb. 4/5 Churchill College at Cambridge will be built by a modern architect—perhaps even by a 'new brutalist'. **1960** *Observer* 17 Apr. 15/2 Furniture designs..which include..a very simple desk cum storage-cabinet on brutalist lines.

brutalitarian (bruːtælɪˈtɛərɪən). [f. BRUTALITY, after *humanitarian.*] One who practises or advocates the practice of brutality. Also as *adj.*

1904 (*title*) The Brutalitarian, a Journal for the Sane and Strong. **1909** G. K. CHESTERTON *Tremendous Trifles* 215 It is only these two types, the sentimental humanitarian and the sentimental brutalitarian, whom one hears in the modern babel. **1910** —— *Shaw* 83 And in this the brutalitarians hate him not because he is soft, but..because he is not to be softened by conventional excuses. **1960** *Spectator* 5 Feb. 171 There is obviously no point, even on the most brutalitarian of grounds, in producing weapons of more than a certain amount of destructiveness.

brutality (bruːˈtælɪtɪ). Also 7 **brutallity.** [f. as BRUTALISM + -ITY. Cf. F. *brutalité.*]

1. The state or condition of the brutes; the condition of living like a brute.

1711 ADDISON *Spect.* No. 166 ¶6 To deprave human Nature, and sink it into the Condition of Brutality. **1737** L. CLARKE *Hist. Bible* VII. (1740) 416 *note*, Nebuchadnezzar's state of brutality. **1863** J. MURPHY *Com. Gen.* iii. 1–7 The marvellous elevation from brutality to reason and speech.

2. The quality of resembling the brutes: †**a.** in want of intelligence (*obs.*); **b.** in sensuality.

1549 LATIMER *Serm. bef. Edw. VI*, Wks. I. 252 If ye will not maintain schools and universities, ye shall have a brutality. **1603** FLORIO *Montaigne* III. xii. (1632) 593 If it be so, (that the vulgar are less sensitive to pain) let us henceforth keepe a schoole of brutality. **1755** YOUNG *Centaur* VI. Wks. 1757 IV. 278 Of all brutes the most brutal is the volunteer in brutality; the brute self-made. **1836** H. COLERIDGE *North. Worthies* I. 58 The brutality of even the highest orders.

3. Coarse incivility; violent roughness of manners; sensuality.

1709 STEELE *Tatler* No. 149 ¶5 A natural Ruggedness and Brutality of Temper. **1848** MACAULAY *Hist. Eng.* II. 145 His brutality was such that many thought him mad. **1871** MORLEY *Voltaire* (1886) 46 The heavy brutality and things obscene of the court of Lewis XV.

4. Inhumanity, savage cruelty; an inhuman action.

1633 H. COGAN *Pinto's Trav.* viii. (1663) 23 They began to talk..of the Kings Brutality and Parracide. **1693** *Mem. Ct. Teckely* IV. 67 The Brutallity of the Turkish Troops. **1719** DE FOE *Crusoe* (1840) I. xii. 196 Hellish brutality. **1860** FROUDE *Hist. Eng.* VI. 390 His [Bonner's] brutality was notorious and unquestionable. **1878** MORLEY *Diderot* II. 228 The brutalities that were every day enacted.

brutalization (ˌbruːtəlaɪˈzeɪʃən). [f. next + -ATION.] **a.** The action or process of rendering or becoming brutal, or of lowering to the level of the brutes. **b.** A brutalized condition.

1797 *Monthly Rev.* XXIII. 572 It were desirable to know whether a nation which has the virtues of ignorance and poverty can preserve them without brutalization. **1863** HUXLEY *Man's Place Nat.* 110 We are told..that..the unity of origin of man and brutes involves the brutalization..of the former. **1870** *Pall Mall G.* 19 Aug. 1 A change which might be not improperly described as brutalization. **1874** H. SPENCER *Stud. Sociol.* viii. 190 A certain brutalization has to be maintained during our passing phase of civilization.

brutalize (ˈbruːtəlaɪz), *v.* [f. BRUTAL *a.* + -IZE.]

1. *intr.* To live or become like a brute.

1716 ADDISON *Freeholder* No. 5 He mixed..with his countrymen, brutalized with them in their habit and manners. **1749** WALPOLE *Lett. H. Mann* (1834) II. ccviii. 303 If possible we brutalize more and more. **1810** COLERIDGE *Friend* (1865) 152 To discuss on how much a person may vegetate or brutalize in the back settlements of the republic. *a* **1859** DE QUINCEY *Ceylon* Wks. XII. 26 Man does not brutalize, by possibility, in pure insulation.

2. *trans.* To render brutal or inhuman; to imbue with a brutal nature.

a **1704** T. BROWN *To Lumenissa* 113 Which..Were but at once to Brutalize Mankind. **1833** HT. MARTINEAU *Fr. Wines & Pol.* iv. 54 The efforts that were made to infatuate and brutalize the people. **1885** A. C. HARE *Russia* i. 23 That which does most to brutalize the lower orders in Russia is their constant habit of intemperance.

3. To treat as a brute, or brutally.

1879 STEVENSON *Trav. Cevennes* 15 God forbid..that I should brutalise this innocent creature. **1885** MRS. LINTON *Chr. Kirkland* I. 274 He would have died outright had he been brutalized in any way.

Hence **ˈbrutalized, ˈbrutalizing** *ppl. adjs.*

1800 SOUTHEY *Lett.* (1856) I. 106 The bloody and brutalising spirit of Popery. **1803** BRISTED *Pedest. Tour* I. 455 The coarse and brutalized indulgences of mere unalloyed sensuality. **1844** SIR S. ST. JOHN *Hayti* v. 183 The masses [in Hayti] are given up to this brutalising [Vaudoux] worship.

brutally (ˈbruːtəlɪ), *adv.* [f. BRUTAL *a.* + -LY[2].] In a brutal manner.

1749 CHESTERF. *Lett.* II. ccvii. 288 The animal and constitutional courage of a foot-soldier..is oftener improperly..exerted, but always brutally. **1824** W. IRVING *T. Trav.* I. 283, I have always despised the brutally vulgar. **1847** GROTE *Greece* II. xxxvi. IV. 433 He now acted still more brutally towards the Argeian priest. **1871** MORLEY *Voltaire* (1878) 123 Swift is often truculent and brutally gross.

brutaske, obs. form of BRATTICE.

brutch, obs. form of BROOCH, BROACH *sb.*[1]

brute (bruːt), *a.* and *sb.*[1] Also 7 **bruit(e.** [a. F. *brut*, fem. *brute*:—L. *brūtus* heavy, dull, irrational (Sp. *bruto*, It. *bruto* sb.). Some of the senses are probably directly from, or at least influenced by, the Latin.]

A. *adj.* (Now often an *attrib.* use of the *sb.*)

1. Of animals: Wanting in reason or understanding; chiefly in phrases ***brute beasts, the brute creation,*** = the 'lower animals'.

c **1460–70** *Bk. Quintessence* 11 Fro fleisch of alle brute beestis. **1494** FABYAN vii. ccxxii. 246 Great moreyne fell vpon brute bestes. **1580** LUPTON *Siquila* 55 More senselesse, than the senselest or brutest beast in the world. **1611** BIBLE *Pref.* 1 Bruit-beasts led with sensualitie. **1613** WITHERS *Abuses Stript* I. v. in *Juvenilia* (1633) 42 Viler than the brutest creature. **1667** MILTON *P.L.* x. 495 The brute Serpent in whose shape Man I deceav'd. **1703** ROWE *Fair Penit.* III. i, Whose bounteous Hand feeds the whole Brute Creation. **1732** BERKELEY *Alciphr.* I. §13 To degrade human-kind to a level with brute beasts. **1832** DOWNES *Lett. fr. Cont. Countries* I. 46 Not a being, human or brute, appeared. **1849** W. IRVING *Mahomed* x. (1853) 59 The very brute animals were charmed to silence.

2. a. Of human beings, their actions, and attributes: Brute-like, brutish; dull, senseless, stupid; unintelligent, unreasoning, uninstructed; sensual.

1535 T. BEDYL in Strype *Eccl. Mem.* I. II. App. lv, I suppose many of the curates to be so brute, that they would read or speake every word, as it was written. *a* **1618** SYLVESTER *Mem. Mortalitie* II. xxxix, Man (alas!) is bruter than a Brute. **1641** MILTON *Ch. Govt.* I. (1851) 100 Their owne brute inventions. **1645** —— *Tetrach.* (1851) 159 Which should preserve it in love and reason, and difference it from a brute conjugality. **1812** SOUTHEY in *Q. Rev.* VIII. 321 The deplorable doctrines of brute materialism. **1870** BOWEN *Logic* viii. 238 A black skin is not an invariable sign of a brute intellect.

b. Rough, rude, wanting in sensibilty.

1555 *Fardle Facions* II. x. 210 Their behauour was in the beginning very brute. **1645** MILTON *Colast.* Wks. (1851) 373 As to this brute Libel. *a* **1744** POPE (J.) The brute philosopher, who ne'er has proved The joy of loving or of being loved.

3. a. Of things: Not possessing or connected with reason, intelligence, or sensation; irrational, unconscious, senseless; merely material; esp. in ***brute matter, brute force.***

1540 MORYSINE tr. *Vives' Introd. Wisd.* B v b, Nature, reason, and comlynes commaunde the sayde body to be subjecte as a thynge brute, to that that dyeth never. **1611** GUILLIM *Heraldry* III. v. 97 By brute natures I understand all essences..that are meerely void of life. **1646** EVANCE *Noble Ord.* 37 Jehu, and Nebucadnezar weare but brute instruments to worke Gods purposes. **1692** BENTLEY *Boyle Lect.* viii. 259 Brute inanimate Matter. **1712** BLACKMORE *Creation* I. (1736) 6 Who..believe That the brute earth unguided should embrace The only..proper place. **1736** BUTLER *Anal.* I. iii. 82 A tendency to prevail over brute force. **1836–7** SIR W. HAMILTON *Metaph.* (1877) I. ii. 36 The necessary results of a brute mechanism. **1860** ADLER *Fauriel's Prov. Poetry* xx. 455 Our Sanctuaries are nothing but brute stone, and still they weep. **1866** KINGSLEY *Herew.* viii. 141 The land has been changed by the brute forces of nature.

†**b.** Of inarticulate sound. **c.** Of thunder: = BRUTISH 4. *Obs.*

1642 ROGERS *Naaman* 62 The workes alone are a brute sound, and have no tongue in them. **1656** COWLEY *Davideis* IV. (1669) 144 They [the curses] with brute sound, dissolv'd into the air. —— 154 *note*, *Brute*, That signified nothing. So Thunders from whence the Ancients could collect no Prognostications, were called *Brute Thunders.*

4. a. Of surfaces: Rugged; unpolished. *rare.*

1627 DRAYTON *Agincourt* (1748) 7 The shire whose surface seems most brute, Darby. **1804** SOUTHEY in *Ann. Rev.* II. 527 The value of the brute diamond. *a* **1861** T. WINTHROP *John Brent* (1883) i. 6 The precious metal was to the brute mineral in the proportion of perhaps a hundred pin-heads to the ton.

b. ***brute fact***, a crude, isolated, or unexplained fact.

1874 G. H. LEWES *Probl. Life & Mind* I. v. 296 Science looks *through* the brute fact, to contemplate the Abstraction which gives it connection, significance. **1879** W. JAMES in *Mind* IV. 329 We discriminate between brute fact and explained fact. **1926** A. E. TAYLOR *Plato* xvii. 455 Science..is always forced to retain *some* element of brute fact, the merely given, in its account of things. **1957** *Economist* 21 Sept. 931/1 He refuses to accommodate the brute facts of historical development within a convenient but artificial pattern.

B. *sb.*

1. a. One of the lower animals as distinguished from man: a brute creature.

1611 HEYWOOD *Gold. Age* I. i. Wks. 1874 III. 15 Worse then a bruit, for bruits preserue their own. **1667** MILTON *P.L.* VIII. 441 My Image not imparted to the Brute. **1712** POPE *Spect.* No. 408 ¶4 Man seems to be placed as the middle Link between Angels and Brutes. **1724** WATTS *Logic* (1736) 91 Life..attributed to Plants, to Brutes, and to Men. *a* **1876** J. H. NEWMAN *Hist. Sk.* I. I. iv. 164 Brutes..cannot invent, cannot progress.

b. The animal nature in man. (Cf. BEAST 1 c.)

1784 BURNS *Stanzas in Prosp. Death* 15 Again exalt the brute and sink the man.

2. A man resembling a brute in want of intelligence, cruelty, coarseness, sensuality, etc. Now (*colloq.*) often merely a strong term of reprobation or aversion, and sometimes extended to things.

1670 COTTON *Espernon* III. XI. 538 These Bruits incapable of Reason, were exasperated at the very name of Punishment. **1719** DE FOE *Crusoe* (1840) II. xiii. 278 The great fat brute thought it below him. **1722** —— *Relig. Courtsh.* I. iii. (1840) 117, I was a brute for living in that horrid manner. **1752** CHESTERF. *Lett.* III. ccxcii. 340 That northern Brute, the King of Sweden! **1766** ANSTEY *New Bath Guide* viii. 49 Their Husbands, those Brutes..swear they will never set Foot here again. **1876** GEO. ELIOT *Dan. Der.* I. xii. 224 The brute of a cigar required relighting. **1878** MISS BROUGHTON *Cometh up as Fl.* viii. 80 He would be a pretty brute. **1885** MRS. OLIPHANT *Madam* I. v. 67 Women can't try their husbands for being brutes.

C. *attrib.* and *comb.*, as ***brute-man, -minded, -mindedness, -shadow, -worship***; †***brute-beastish, -like*** adj. and adv.; ***brute-bastille*** (*nonce-wd.*), a menagerie; ***brute-buried*** *a.*, buried like a brute.

1845 HOOD *Monkey Mart.* v, To look around upon this *brute-bastille. **1530** PALSGR. 307/1 *Brute beestysshe..bruste. **1822** HOOD *Lycus the Cent.* 247 Let me utterly be *Brute-buried. **1813** BYRON *Giaour* 52 Man..should..trample, *brute-like, o'er each flower. **1862** LYTTON *Str. Story* II. 47 His brute-like want of sympathy with his kind. **1852** TUPPER *Proverb. Philos.* 296 Hath..the *brute-man more than instinct? **1843** CARLYLE *Past & Pr.* 271 Thou findest Ignorance, Stupidity, *Brute-mindedness, etc. **1822** HOOD *Lycus the Cent.* 123 Lest a *brute shadow should grow at my feet. **1738** WARBURTON *Div. Legat.* I. 284 The Original of *Brute-worship.

†**Brute,** *sb.*[2] *Obs.* Also 6 **bruit.** [In sense 1, a variant of *Brett* or *Britt*, influenced by the *Brutus* myth; in 2, app. = *Brut, Brutus*, itself.

From the Old Celtic (and Latin) *Britto*, BRITON, there was subsequently formed the proper name of an eponymous hero, the reputed first king and founder of Britain. His name appears in Nennius also as *Bruto*, in the Irish version as *Britus* and *Brutus.* In the latter form he was linked with classical antiquity and the tale of Troy, being made a great-grandson of Æneas. *Brutus* accordingly became the prevailing form in Latin writers; and was adapted in Welsh and OF. as *Brut.* Of this the sense was transferred through that of 'chronicle or history of Brut' to that of 'chronicle of Britain' or 'Welsh chronicle' generally: see BRUT. But its use as a proper name was not forgotten, and in the 16th c. it appears to have given rise to sense 2.]

1. A Briton, a Welshman.

1513 BRADSHAW *St. Werburgh* (1848) 152 Whyche kynge expulsed..All brutes and walshemen clere out of his londe. **1586** WARNER *Alb. Eng.* III. xvi. 73 Pledges..that Denmark it should pay Continuall Tribute to the Brutes.

2. a. The legendary Trojan Brutus, first king of Britain, and founder of 'Troynovant' or London. **b.** A 'Brutus', a hero of British, Welsh, or Arthurian story. **c.** Hence, generally, a hero, 'brave', 'gallant', 'worthy' (by some writers used quite vaguely, and apparently without any notion of the original sense).

a **1553** UDALL *Roist. D.* (Arb.) 17 Who is this? greate Goliah, Sampson, or Colbrande? No (say I) but it is a brute of the Alie lande. **1577** NORTHBROOKE *Dicing* (1843) 12 Consider..what jolly yonkers & lusty brutes these wil be when they come to be citizens. **1579** LYLY *Euphues* (Arb.) 36 A great blotte to the lynage of so noble a brute. *c* **1590** GREENE *Fr. Bacon* xiii. 78 These brave lusty Brutes, These friendly youths, did perish by thine art. **1593** PEELE *Edw. I*, Wks. 1839 I. 103 *Lluellen.* But if kind Cambria deign me good aspect, To make me chiefest Brute of western Wales. **1599** —— *Sir Clyomon* Wks. III. 83, I have given my faith and troth to such a bruit of fame As is the Knight of the Golden Shield. [**1606** DEKKER *Deadly Sinnes* (Arb.) 46 London this fairest-fac'de daughter of Brute. *Margin.* 2700 and odde yeeres since London was first builded by Brute.]

brute, obs. form of BRUIT *sb.* and *v.*

brutedom (ˈbruːtdəm). [f. BRUTE *sb.*[1] + -DOM.] Brutish nature.

1890 A. R. WALLACE in *Fortn. Rev.* Sept. 331 In proportion as men leave brutedom behind and enter into the fulness of their human heritage. **1904** *Westm. Gaz.* 29 June 2/1 The paths that lead to..the depths to which sheer brutedom may descend.

brutehood ('bru:thʊd). [f. BRUTE *sb.*[1] + -HOOD.] The condition or rank of brutes.
1852 *Fraser's Mag.* XLVI. 238 All the difference that exists..between manhood and brutehood. **1872** H. COWLES in Spurgeon *Treas. Dav.* Ps. xcii. 6 One..who has debased himself to brutehood.

brute-kind. The nature or race of brutes.
1880 VERNON LEE *Belcaro* ix. 267, I believe that mankind ..has been..evolved out of a very inferior sort of mankind or brutekind.

brutel, -il(e, -yll, var. of BROTEL *a. Obs.* brittle.

brutely ('bru:tlɪ), *adv.* [f. BRUTE *a.* + -LY[2].] **a.** Roughly, rudely; coarsely. **b.** Irrationally; mechanically.
1598 SYLVESTER *Du Bartas* II. II. i. (1621) 249 And brutely so To all that com his naked shame doth showe. **1645** MILTON *Tetrach.* (1851) 229 The vulgar expositor..rushes brutely and impetuously against all the principles..of nature. **1857** EMERSON *Poems* 109 Property will brutely draw Still to the proprietor.

bruteness ('bru:tnɪs). [f. BRUTE *a.* + -NESS.]
1. Rudeness, roughness, savageness, brutality.
1538 CDL. POLE in Strype *Eccl. Mem.* I. I. xxxviii. 457 The bruteness and danger of the thing. **1577** tr. *Bullinger's Decades* (1592) 208 Crueltie in reuenging..brutenesse in rebelling..are the thinges that in warre are worthie to be blamed. **1883** G. MACDONALD *D. Grant* III. xxix. 282 The bruteness of the life he had hitherto led.
†**2.** Unintelligence, stupidity, dullness. *Obs.*
1590 SPENSER *F.Q.* II. viii. 12 Thou dotard vile, That with thy bruteness shendst thy comely age. **1594** SYLVESTER *Paradox agst. Lib.* 591 'Tis in truth your brutenesse in misdeeming Things evill, that are good.
3. Want of consciousness, materiality. *rare.*
1836 EMERSON *Nature* 93 The immobility or bruteness of nature, is the absence of spirit.

†**bruterer.** *Obs. rare*$^{-1}$. [? variant of BRUITER; cf. *broderer, fruiterer, upholsterer.* Cf. also BRUT, in its Welsh sense of 'prophecy'.] 'A prophesier, a soothsayer' (Tindale *Table of words*).
1530 TINDALE *Deut.* xviii. 10 A bruterar or a maker of dismale dayes.

†**bruthen** (y), **brethen.** *Obs.* [OE. *bryðen* a brewing.] Brewing. **bruthen-lead** = BREWING-LEAD, vessel for brewing in.
a **1000** *Guthlac* 953 Bryðen..ðætte Adame Eue ʒebyrmde æt fruman worulde. —— *Wulfgeat's Will* (Bosw.) An bryðen mealtes. *c* **1000** *Sax. Leechd.* II. 142 Unʒehwæde mylcen oððe fild oððe bryþen. *c* **1275** *Death* 242 in *O.E. Misc.* 182 Al so beodh his eʒe puttes ase a bruthen led. *c* **1475** *Found. St. Barthol. Ch.* I. xxiii. (1881) 61 She myghte nat then, parforme the brethren [? brethen], that she hadde begunne.

brutification (ˌbru:tɪfɪ'keɪʃən). [f. BRUTIFY; see -FICATION (cf. *personification*).] The action or process of rendering or becoming brutish or brute-like; the result of the action.
1687 A. LOVELL tr. *Bergerac's Com. Hist.* II. 55 A Mate to converse with during the solitude of my Brutification. **1799** LAMB *Lett.* v. 41 One of them which had more beast than the rest..faintly resembled one of your brutifications. **1880** SWINBURNE *Stud. Shaks.* iii. (ed. 2) 194 This ultra-Circean ..brutification of spirit.

brutified ('bru:tɪfaɪd), *ppl. a.* [f. BRUTIFY *v.* + -ED.] Made brute-like or brutish.
1594 PARSONS *Confer. Succes.* I. ii. 22 A Prince ruling by affections, is lesse then a man, or a man brutified. **1683** TRYON *Way to Health* 619 Brutified things, whom they are obliged to call Husbands and Fathers. **1863** B. JERROLD *Sign. Distress* 290 He has festered..into that blurred and brutified semblance of the erect man.

brutify ('bru:tɪfaɪ), *v.* [f. L. *bruti-* (comb. form) BRUTE + -FY.]
1. *trans.* To render brute-like; to brutalize.
1668 HOWE *Bless. Righteous* Wks. (1834) 256/2 Religion doth not brutify men. **1848** MILL *Pol. Econ.* II. v. §2 Hopeless slavery effectually brutifies the intellect.
b. *absol.*
1819 *Scotsman* 9 Jan. 14/3 Their tendency..is to debase and brutify. **1848** MRS. JAMESON *Sacr. & Leg. Art* (1850) 61 Sin..degrades and brutifies.
2. *intr.* To become brute-like.
1794 MRS. PIOZZI *Synonymy* II. 19 Man unwatched by man brutified for very want of observance.
Hence '**brutifying** *vbl. sb.* and *ppl. a.*
1817 J. SCOTT *Paris Revisit.* (ed. 4) 56 Measures that were both savage and brutifying. **1831** E. CROWE *Hist. France* III. ix. 275 A course of brutifying study.

†**bru'tigenist.** *Obs. rare.* [f. L. *brūti-, brūtus* + *-gen-us* born + -IST.] One born among the brutes.
1631 R. H. *Arraignm. Whole Creature* xiv. §2. 248 The men of this world, those Brutigenists, or Terrigenists.. Earth-bred wormes. *Ibid.* 286 A dust Worme, a Brutigenist, a Terrigenist.

†'**bruting** (y), *vbl. sb.*[1] *Obs. rare*$^{-1}$. [= *bryting* or *brytning*, vbl. sb. f. OE. *bryttian, brytnian*: see BRIT, BRITTEN *v.*] Cutting in pieces; destruction.
1393 LANGL. *P. Pl.* C. XVI. 156 Ich wil hadde wynnen al Fraunce With-oute bruting of burnes.

bruting ('bru:tɪŋ), *vbl. sb.*[2] [Rendering F. *brutage*, f. *brut* rough, unworked, unformed (cf. BRUT *a.*, BRUTE *a.* 4) as in *diamant brut.*] The roughing-out of a diamond (see quots.). So **brute** *v. trans.*; '**bruter**.
1903 L. J. SPENCER tr. *M. Bauer's Precious Stones* 82 Bruting..consists in rubbing together two diamonds, each being cemented at the end of a stick or holder, until the desired form is obtained. *Ibid.* 243 The stone to be bruted is fixed to a handle. *Ibid.* 244 The three operations..are entrusted to..skilled workmen, namely cleavers, bruters, and grinders or polishers. **1906** L. CLAREMONT *Gem-cutter's Craft* iv. 41 The bruting of diamonds consists of rubbing two diamonds together in such a way that by continual friction each can be made to assume the desired shape. *Ibid.* 42 Upon the principle of 'diamond cut diamond' the stones are roughly fashioned by the bruter into whatever symmetrical form he has designed them to be when finished.

brutish ('bru:tɪʃ), *a.* Also 5-6 **brutisshe, -ysshe,** 7-8 **bruitish.** [f. BRUTE + -ISH.]
1. Of or pertaining to the brutes, or lower animals, as opposed to man.
1534 MORE *Wks.* 402 (R.) A beaste, out of whose brutishe beastely mouthe, cometh such a fylthie forme of blasphemys. **1596** SPENSER *Astroph.* 98 There his welwoven toyles..He laid the brutish nation to enwrap. **1614** T. ADAMS in Spurgeon *Treas. Dav.* lxvi. 13 The Lord takes not delight in the blood of brutish creatures. **1667** MILTON *P.L.* I. 481 Wandring Gods disguis'd in brutish forms Rather then human. **1878** BROWNING *La Saisiaz* 35 Without the want, Life, now human, would be brutish.
2. Pertaining to, resembling, or characteristic of the brutes:
a. in want of intelligence or in failure to use reason: dull, irrational, uncultured, stupid.
1555 EDEN *Decades W. Ind.* (Arb.) 50 Slowe and brutysshe wyttes. **1672** MARVELL *Reh. Transp.* I. 114 As the Opinion is brutish, so the Consequences are devilish. **1728** MORGAN *Algiers* I. i. 8 No People in the Universe, how savage and brutish soever they be, want a sufficient share of Reason. **1866** ROGERS *Agric. & Prices* I. xxix. 693 He is..dull and brutish, reckless and supine.
b. in want of control over the appetites and passions: passionate, sensual, furious.
1567 *Triall Treas.* (1850) 27 You bridled that brutishe beaste Inclination. **1615** R. C. *Times' Whis.* v. 1651, I now am come to brutish gluttonie. **1663** COWLEY *Verses & Ess.* (1669) 70 It is only a Demonstration of Brutish Madness or Diabolical Possession. **1709** STEELE *Tatler* No. 45 ¶3 The Servant of his brutish Lusts and Appetites. **1731** SWIFT *Strephon & Ch.* Misc. V. 36 How could a Nymph so chaste as Chloe..Permit a brutish Man to touch her? **1869** J. MARTINEAU *Ess.* II. 213 He scolds at [it] as a propensity absolutely brutish.
†**3.** Rough, rude; savage, brutal. ? *Obs.*
1494 FABYAN *V.* cxl. 127 To oppresse in partye theyr brutisshe blastis, I wyll bryng in here yᵉ sayinge of Guydo. **1599** GREENE *Alphons.* III, Therefore, fair maid, bridle these brutish thoughts. **1645** *Kings's Cabinet opened* in *Select. Harl. Misc.* (1793) 343 The rebels new brutish general hath refused to meddle with foreign passes. **1726** CAVALLIER *Mem.* I. 42 The Count Brollio is..fierce, haughty, cruel and brutish; having no Manner of Politeness. **1773** BURKE *Let.* Wks. IX. 135 We shall sink into surly, brutish Johns.
†**4.** = BRUTE *a.* 3. Of thunder: striking blindly, random. [after L. *brutum fulmen.*] *Obs.*
1586 C. FETHERSTONE (*title*) The Brvtish Thunderbolt: or rather Feeble Fier-Flash of Pope Sixtus the fift, against Henrie king of Navarre. **1640** G. SANDYS *Christ's Pass.* 29 (L.) Vainly we thy brutish thunder fear. —— *Notes* 100 The philosophers will have two sorts of lightning..the other brutish, that is accidental and flying at random. **1871** R. ELLIS *Catullus* lxiv. 164 Yet to the brutish winds why moan I longer unheeded?
5. quasi-*adv.*
1647 W. BROWNE *Polexander* I. 202 Bruitish bred men.

Brutish, obs. form of BRITISH.

brutishly ('bru:tɪʃlɪ), *adv.* [f. prec. + -LY[2].]
1. In a brutish manner; irrationally, sensually.
1579 FULKE *Refut. Rastel* 749 He reasoneth brutishly with putting such cases. **1674** J. B[RIAN] *Harvest Home* III. 11 Brutishly sottish, and stupidly irrational. **1720** DE FOE *Capt. Singleton* i. (1840) 8 They were so brutishly wicked. **1868** BROWNING *Ring & Bk.* x. 1701 Why not live brutishly, obey my law?
2. With brutish indifference to the feelings; coarsely, boorishly, savagely, brutally.
1580 HOLLYBAND *Treas. Fr. Tong, Mastiner*..to reuile one and vse him mastife like, brutishly, foulye. **1688** SIR J. KNATCHBULL *Diary* in *N. & Q.* III. VI. 3 They brutishly answered, Damn you..how will you endure hell-fire? *a* **1734** NORTH *Lives* (1826) II. 129 Sitting there to hear his decrees most brutishly and effrontrously arraigned, &c. **1807** G. CHALMERS *Caledonia* I. II. vi. 310 Even Iona had orchards..till the Vikingr brutishly ruined all. **1825** LD. COCKBURN *Mem.* iii. 174 A very curious edifice..was brutishly obliterated without one public murmur.

brutishness ('bru:tɪʃnɪs). [f. as prec. + -NESS.] Brutish quality or condition.
1547-64 BAULDWIN *Mor. Philos.* (Palfr.) ii. 3 The further off we shall be from the brutishnesse of beasts. **1683** CAVE *Ecclesiastici* 470 The fierceness and brutishness of the man's temper. **1850** BLACKIE *Æschylus* I. Pref. 38 What a fearful mire of brutishness.

brutism ('bru:tɪz(ə)m). [see -ISM.] The characteristic behaviour or condition of a brute.
1687 *Addr. Thanks* 7 Ingratitude that's worse than Brutism. **1691** E. TAYLOR *Behmen's Life* 429 Foolish Infatuations, Madness, and stupid Brutisms. **1845** *Blackw. Mag.* LVII. 51 He..relapses..from civism to brutism.

†'**brutist.** *Obs.* [see -IST.] One who regards or treats men as brutes.
1637 HEYWOOD *Royal King* III. iii. Wks. 1874 VI. 49 To hire one of those bruitists that make no difference between a gentleman and a beggar. **1680** BAXTER *Cath. Comm.* Pref. A ij b, The Bruitists, who prefer the Bruits, yea, the wildest before Men. **1685** BAXTER *Paraph. Acts* iv. 1 Such Brutists as the Sadducees.

†**brutize,** *v. Obs. rare.* [f. BRUTE *sb.* + -IZE.] **a.** *intr.* To become or act like a brute. **b.** *trans.* To render brutish. Hence **brutized** *ppl. a.*
1607 TOPSELL *Four-f. Beasts* 17 Brutizing in their whole life, till they taste the Roses of true science and grace. *a* **1711** KEN *Hymnoth.* Poet. Wks. 1721 III. 361 From Lands brutis'd Salvation is conceal'd.

†**bru'tologist.** *Obs. rare*$^{-1}$. [f. BRUTE or L. *brut-* (after Gr. forms in *-o*) + Gr. λόγ-ος + -IST.] One who studies the brutes.
1674 N. COX *Gentl. Recreat., Fishing* (1706) 44 If we may credit..Gesner that famous Brutologist.

†'**brutting,** *vbl. sb. Obs. rare*$^{-1}$. [f. BRUT *v.* + -ING[1].] Browsing; clippings of trees.
1577 B. GOOGE *Heresbach's Husb.* (1586) 131 b, You may give them the toppes of olive trees, lentils, or any tender brutinges, or branches of vines. **1662** EVELYN *Sylva* (1679) 22 To protect them [trees]..from the..brutting of Cattle and Sheep. **1699** —— *Acetaria* I. vi. §2 (R.) This preserves itself best from the bruttings of the deer.

Bruttische, obs. form of BRITISH.

‖**brutum fulmen** ('bru:təm 'fʌlmɛn), *phr.* Pl. **bruta fulmina.** [L., = 'senseless thunderbolt' (Pliny *N.H.* II. xliii).] A mere noise; an ineffective act or empty threat.
1603 C. HEYDON *Def. Iudic. Astrol.* 55 The Councells and decrees of the Church..prooue but *bruta fulmina*, making vaine cracks without any touch of that which I defend. *a* **1680** T. GOODWIN *Works* (1685) XI. 131 It hath been *brutum fulmen* to us, a thunderbolt of no force. **1767** J. WESLEY *Let.* 5 Mar. in *Jrnl.* (1827) III. 266 Till this is done, all you add (bitterly enough) is mere *brutum fulmen*. **1835** J. W. CROKER in *Q. Rev.* Sept. 550 This rhodomontade..was ..a mere *brutum fulmen*. **1963** *Times* 8 Mar. 5/4 No legal aid certificate in a limited form could be issued for such a limitation would be *brutum fulmen*.

Brutus ('bru:təs). More fully ***Brutus Wig***: a kind of wig. 'The rough-cropped head then fashionable was called a *Brutus* by the French, after the great hero of antiquity whom they specially reverenced'. Fairholt (ed. Dillon) I. 408.
1798 H. L. PIOZZI *Let.* 27 Mar. (1914) 152, I wonder if the pretty Misses go in *self* coloured drawers..and Brutus Heads with you as they do here. **1804** W. IRVING *Jrnls. & Notebks.* (1969) I. 464 She caught hold of his hat & it came off with his brutus wig in it. **1807** SOUTHEY *Lett. from Eng.* lxxi. 304 During one period of the French Revolution the Brutus head-dress was the mode. **1851** MAYHEW *Lond. Labour* III. 5 (Hoppe) He wore his hair with the curls arranged in a Brutus à la George the Fourth. **1857** GEO. ELIOT *Sc. Cler. Life, Janet's Rep.* II. 189 Old Mr. Crewe the curate in a brown Brutus wig.

bruvver ('brʌvə(r)). Representation of a Cockney pronunciation of BROTHER *sb.*
1898 J. D. BRAYSHAW *Slum Silhouettes* 120 Her 'big bruvver' told her..'this was the path up which the angels ran to God.' **1958** J. TOWNSEND *Young Devils* xv. 143 'My bruvver will get you,' he promised. **1966** 'S. HARVESTER' *Treacherous Road* ii. 23 We know what our 'Arold and 'is bruvvers think of us.

bruwyn, obs. form of BREW *v.*

bruxle, var. of BRIXLE *v. Obs.* to reprove.

bruyd, obs. form of BRIDE.

bruyk, variant of BRUKE, *Obs.*, a locust.

†**bruyllie.** *Obs. rare*$^{-1}$. ? = BRULYIE, or ? mistake for *cruyltie.*
1535 T. CROMWELL in Strype *Eccl. Mem.* I. App. lxviii, The French King..confessed thextreme executions, and great bruyllie of late done in his realme.

bruyse, obs. form of BREWIS.

†**bruzz,** *v. Obs.* Only in *vbl. sb.* **bruzzing.** [Imitative.] *intr.* To growl as a bear.
1693 URQUHART *Rabelais* III. xiii, The barking of Curs, bawling of Mastiffs..bruzzing of Bears.

brwe, obs. form of BROW *sb.*[1]

brwyn, obs. form of BREW *v.*

bry- in obs. words: see BRI-.

bryad, bryead, obs. forms of BREAD.

Bryanite ('braɪənaɪt). [see -ITE.] One of the sect founded by William O. *Bryan* in 1815: see BIBLE CHRISTIAN.
1882-3 SCHAFF *Encycl. Rel. Knowl.* I. 257 Bible Christians, or Bryanites, a sect closely resembling the Methodists.

†**brych.** *Obs. rare*$^{-1}$. ? (Dr. Morris suggests 'Filth, uncleanness'; cf. Ger. *sich (er-) brechen* to vomit; perhaps the word = BREACH, or BRUCHE, transgression.)
c **1325** *E.E. Allit. P.* B. 848 þe wynd, & þe weder, & þe worlde stynkes Of þe brych þat vpbraydez þose broþelych wordez.

brych(e, obs. form of BREECH.

†**bryche**, *a.* *Obs.* [OE. *bryce*:—OTeut. type **bruki-z*, f. *brek-an* to break.] Breakable, fragile; broken down.

c **1000** *Ags. Psalter* cxix. 5 Min bigengea ȝewat bryce on feor-weȝ. **1303** R. BRUNNE *Handl. Synne* 5821 Now ys Pers bycome bryche þat er was boþe stoute and ryche.

bryd-: see BRI-.

bryd(de, obs. form of BIRD *sb.*

†**brydthing**. *Obs.* Also 3 brudþing (-y-). [OE. *brýdþing*, f. *brýd-*, BRIDE- + THING.] Wedding, marriage, nuptials.

971 *Blickl. Hom.* 3 Gabriel wæs þissa brydþinga ærendwreca. *c* **1275** *Luue Ron* in *O.E. Misc.* 99 Cumen to his brudþinge heye in heouene.

brye, obs. by-form of BREEZE *sb.*[1], gadfly.

bryest, obs. form of BREAST *sb.*

brygeless, var. of BRIGUELESS *a. Obs.*

†**brygge-a-bragge**, *adv. phr. Obs.*

1509 HAWES *Past. Pleas.* 134 In a pyed cote he rode brygge a bragge.

Brygges, var. of BRUGES. *Obs.*

Brygittane, var. form of BRIDGETIN. *Obs.*

brygurdel, -gyrdyll, var. of BREECHGIRDLE.

bryk(e, obs. form of BRICK, BRIGUE.

†**bryke**, *v. Obs. rare*$^{-1}$. ? To taste, or ? to 'rise in the stomach'.

c **1315** SHOREHAM 102 Senne ys swete and lyketh, Wanne a man hi deth, And al so soure hy bryketh, Wane he venjaunce y-seth.

bryle, var. BROIL *sb.*[3]

†**bryn**[1]. *Obs.* Also **brene**. [A parallel form to *brynie*, BRINIE, perh. transp. from *byrn*:—OE. *byrne* corslet, coat of mail; cf. BURNE.] = BRINIE.

1330 R. BRUNNE 189 James of Auenue, he was verray pilgryn, He gan first remue þe croice mad on his bryn. ? *a* **1400** *Morte Arth.* 1413 Thrughe brenes and bryghte scheldes brestes they thyrle. *c* **1420** *Anturs of Arth.* xli, His brene and his basnet was busket ful bene.

bryn[2], **bryne**. *Obs.* [ME. *brȳn*, a. ON. *brýnn*, old pl. of *brún* eye-brow.] Eyebrows, eye-brow.

1330 R. BRUNNE *Chron.* 237 Maugre boþe his bryn was fayn to com to grith. *a* **1400** *Octovian* 931 A great fot was betwex hys bryn. *c* **1420** *Avow. Arth.* xv, Alle wrothe wex that sqwyne, Blu, and brayd vppe his bryne. *c* **1440** *Promp. Parv.* 51 Bryne or brow of þe eye, *supercilium*.

bryn, -ne, obs. ff. BRAN, BRINE, BURN.

brynston, bryntstane, obs. ff. BRIMSTONE.

brynt, obs. pa. t. and pple. of BURN *v.*

brynye, var. of BRINIE, *Obs.*, cuirass.

bryologist (braɪˈɒlədʒɪst). [f. as next: see -IST.] One learned in bryology.

1830 LINDLEY *Nat. Syst. Bot.* 322 The Latin words employed by Bryologists. **1863** BERKELEY *Brit. Mosses* vii. 34 The labours of British Bryologists.

bryology (braɪˈɒlədʒɪ). [f. Gr. βρύον 'a kind of mossy sea-weed', taken in modern science as = 'moss' + -λογία discourse: see -LOGY.] That branch of botany which treats of mosses. Also used for the species of mosses (collectively) of any country or place. Hence **bryoˈlogical** *a.*, **-ally** *adv.*

1863 BERKELEY *Brit. Mosses* vii. 34 Comparing the Bryology of the British Isles with that of Europe. **1881** *Nature* No. 616. 376 On the bryology of the valleys of the rivers Secchio and Magra.

†**ˈbryon**. *Obs.* [a. F. *bryon*, a. Gr. βρύον, L. *bryum*.] A kind of moss.

1579 LANGHAM *Gard. Health* (1633) 95 Bryan, stampe it and apply it three dayes to the knees that are swolne. **1601** HOLLAND *Pliny* I. 381 Ointments..made..of the odoriferous mosse Bryon.

‖**bryˈonia.** Latin form of BRYONY; familiarly used in homœopathic pharmacy.

bryonin (ˈbraɪənɪn). *Chem.* [f. BRYONY: see -IN.] 'The bitter principle of the root of the red-berried bryony (*Bryonia dioica*).' Watts.

1836 *Penny Cycl.* V. 502/2 The Wild Bryony..Its properties are apparently owing to the presence of a principle called bryonine, analogous to cathartine. **1863** WATTS *Dict. Chem.* I. 685 Bryonin acts as a drastic purgative. **1880** *Syd. Soc. Lex.*, *Bryonin*, a glucoside obtained from *Bryonia*..It is a white or slightly coloured granular substance, bitter, soluble in water and alcohol, insoluble in ether.

bryony (ˈbraɪənɪ). Also 6 brionye, bryonye, (brione), 6-7 brionie, 7-9 briony. [ad. L. *bryonia* (Pliny), a. Gr. βρυωνία (Diosc.). Cf. also Fr. *bryone*, whence Eng. *brione* in 16th c.]

1. *prop.* The English name of the plant-genus Bryonia (N.O. *Cucurbitaceæ*); and *spec.* the common wild species (*B. dioica*), sometimes called (in distinction from sense 2) red, or white Bryony.

c **1000** *Saxon Leechd.* I. 172 Genim þas wyrte ðe man bryonia..nemneð. **1552** HULOET, Bryonye or wylde vine. **1598** YONG *Diana* 302 Bryony, or the white vine, which runs winding about the bodies of trees like a snake. **1616** SURFL. & MARKH. *Country Farm* 45 Against Deafenesse..drop into your eares the iuice of..Brionie, mixed with Honey or Oyle. **1815** SHELLEY *Rev. Islam* III. 7 Drooping briony, pearled With dew..Hung, where we sate. **1832** LYTTON *Eugene A.* vi. 10 The white bryony overrunning the thicket. **1863** LONGF. *Wayside Inn, Sicilian's T.* 26 One..mended the rope with braids of briony.

2. black bryony: a name given, from similarity of habit to the prec., to an endogenous climbing plant, Lady's Seal, *Tamus communis* (N.O. *Dioscoreaceæ*), wild in the south of England.

1626 BACON *Sylva* §492 The Shrub called Our Ladies Seal, (which is a kind of Briony). **1805** *Med. & Phys. Jrnl.* XIV. 68 *T. communis*, Bryony Lady-seal. Black briony. **1872** OLIVER *Elem. Bot.* II. 271 This species..although commonly called Black Bryony, has nothing to do with the genus Bryonia. **1883** *Gd. Words* Nov. 710/2 The..red-berried bryony, and the so-called black-bryony.

3. bastard bryony: *Cissus sicyoides*.

4. *Attrib.* and *Comb.* **bryony-vine** = sense 1.

1684 BOYLE *Porousn. Anim. Bod.* iii. 18 Helmont talks much of the great vertue of white Briony root. **1842** TENNYSON *Amphion* 29 Briony-vine and ivy-wreath Ran forward to his rhyming. **1875** FORTNUM *Maiolica* ix. 84 Small vine or briony leaves and interlaced tendrils.

bryophyte (ˈbraɪəfaɪt). *Bot.* [f. mod.L. *Bryophyta* (A. Braun 1864, in P. Ascherson *Flora d. Brandenburg* I. 22), f. Gr. βρύον moss + φυτόν plant.] One of the *Bryophyta*, a group of plants comprising the liverworts and mosses. Hence ˌ**bryoˈphytic** *a.*

1878 W. R. MCNAB *Bot. Classif. Plants* i. 2 The transition from the Thallophyta to the next sub-kingdom, the Bryophyta, is not an abrupt one, hence..in the lower bryophytes the thallus is still to be met with. *Ibid.* ii. 71 The bryophytes can be divided into two classes, the Liverworts and the Mosses. **1928** *Bryologist* XXXI. 123 The hot arid conditions..are little favorable to bryophytic growths. **1958** *New Biol.* XXVII. 87 The phylum or class of bryophytes..forms the lowest group of land plants.

‖**Bryozoa** (braɪəˈzəʊə), *sb. pl. Zool.* Sing. **bryozoon** (-ˈzəʊɒn). [f. Gr. βρύον moss + ζῷα, pl. of ζῷον animal; from the appearance of some species.] The lowest class of molluscs, consisting of compound or 'colonial' animals formed by gemmation, each individual having a distinct alimentary canal. Also called *Polyzoa*. In the sing. an individual animal of this class.

1847-9 TODD *Cycl. Anat. & Phys.* IV. 50/1 The differences between a Bryozoon and an ordinary polype. **1856** GOSSE *Marine Zool.* II. 1 It has been usual [hitherto] to include the Polyzoa (or Bryozoa, as they are sometimes termed) in the class Zoophyta. **1876** BENEDEN *Anim. Parasites* 61 Many bryozoa spread themselves over marine animals. **1883** *Harper's Mag.* Dec. 107/1 The rick bryozoon..incrusts the various parts with its silvery growth.

Hence **Bryoˈzoan** *a.*, belonging to the *Bryozoa*; also as *sb.*, one of the *Bryozoa*.

1872 DANA *Corals* i. 19 The lowest tribe of Mollusks, called Bryozoans, which produce delicate corals, sometimes branching and moss-like. **1878** BELL *Gegenbauer's Comp. Anat.* 132 All the persons of a Bryozoan colony are not equally well developed.

brys-, bryt-, in obs. forms: see BRI-.

brysewort, -wyrt, var. ff. BRUISEWORT.

brysille, brysl, var. of BRISEL *a.* frail.

brys(s)ure, var. of BRUSURE, *Obs.*, a wound.

brytasqe, obs. form of BRATTICE.

bryth, obs. form of BIRTH.

bryther, -ir, obs. pl. of BROTHER.

Brython (ˈbrɪθɒn). [a. Welsh *Brython*, Briton, Britons:—OCeltic *Britton-*, BRITON. *Brython* and *Brythonic* have been introduced by Prof. Rhŷs, to avoid the misleading associations which attach to the use of 'Briton', 'British', and 'Cymric'. They are the natural correlatives of *Goidel* and *Goidelic*, applied to the Scoto-Irish or Gaelic division of the Celtic stock.] A member of that great division of the Celts of the British isles, which mainly occupied South Britain; a Briton of Wales, Cornwall, or ancient Cumbria.

Hence **Bryˈthonic**, *a.* Of or pertaining to the Brythons, or Britons of Wales, Cornwall, and Cumbria, and their kin.

1884 RHYS *Celtic Britain* 3 The other group is represented by the people of Wales and the Bretons..the national name of those speaking these dialects was that of Briton..we take the Welsh form of it, which is *Brython*, and call this group *Brythons* and *Brythonic*. —— 4 Every Celt of the United Kingdom is, so far as language is concerned, either a Goidel or a Brython. —— 208 Both the Brythonic and the Goidelic forms prove beyond doubt, etc.

brytte, variant of BRET, BRIT, a fish.

bryve, variant of BREVE *v. Obs.* to write.

brywer, obs. form of BREWER.

bryze, obs. form of BREEZE *sb.*[1], gadfly.

†**bu**, *sb.* *Obs. rare*$^{-1}$. [perh. ad. ON. *búi* dweller, **hel-búi* hell-dweller: but cf. the interj. BOO; also *bogle-bo* under BOGLE.]

c **1300** *K. Alis.* 5956 He..spaak als an helle bu.

bu, obs. or dial. f. BOW *sb.*[4], BE *v.*, BUY.

bu, Sc. form of BOO, *v.* and *int.*

Bual (ˈbjuːəl). [ad. Pg. *boal*.] A variety of wine-making grape; the madeira made from this.

1882 [see SERCIAL]. **1883** *Encycl. Brit.* XV. 178/1 (*Madeira*) Other high-class wines, known as Bual, Sercial and Malmsey. **1927** J. B. PRIESTLEY *Adam in Moonshine* vii. 134 'Old Madeira... Bual, they call it.' 'What!' cried the Baron... 'An old Bual!'

buat, var. of BOWET, *Sc.*, a lantern.

†**bub**, *sb.*[1] *Sc. Obs.* [Prob. imitating the sound of a dull blow as in *thud*: cf. BOB *sb.*[3], a firm blow.] A storm, a blast.

a **1500** Q. SHAW *Adv. to Courtier*, Thair may cum bubbis ye not suspek. **1513** DOUGLAS *Æneis* I. iii. 15 Ane blusterand bub out fra the northt braying. **1535** STEWART *Cron. Scot.* I. 124 Sum with ane bub had blawin doun hir blind.

bub (bʌb), *sb.*[2] Also 7 bubb. [? imitation of the sound of drinking; cf. BIB *v.*]

1. A slang word for drink, *esp.* strong beer.

1671-2 *Westm. Drollery* in *Roxb. Ballads* (1883) IV. 440 They..took away..their Wallets..Which brought their good Bubb. **1718** PRIOR *Poems* 193 He loves cheap Port, and double Bub. **1812** J. H. VAUX *Flash Dict.*, *Bub*, a low expression signifying drink. *c* **1840** MARRYAT *R. Reefer* lxv, Our bub and our grub. **1841** ORDERSON *Creol.* iii. 28 The gentlemen enjoyed their bub and roasted corn.

2. A mixture of meal and yeast with warm wort and water, used to promote fermentation.

1880 *Act 43 & 44 Vic.* xxiv. §33 Bub or any other composition for promoting the fermentation of wort.

†**bub**, *sb.*[3] *Obs. rare*$^{-1}$. [perh. a. F. *bube*; or suggested by BUBBLE.] A pustule.

1597 LOWE *Chirurg.* (1634) 82 Papulas..are little bubs or pustules, that breake out by themselves through the skinne.

†**bub**, *sb.*[4] *Obs. slang.* [app. short for BUBBLE *sb.* (sense 5): cf. BUB *v.*[2]]

1690 B. E. *Dict. Cant. Crew*, *Bub*, or *Bubble*, one that is Cheated.

bub, *sb.*[5] A contraction of BUBBY[1].

1860 HOTTEN *Slang Dict.* (ed. 2) 105 *Bub*, a teat, woman's breast. **1955** *Essays in Criticism* V. 123 'Breasts' are always 'bubs'. **1957** E. POUND tr. *Rimbaud* 11 The gal with the big bubs And lively eyes.

bub, *sb.*[6] *U.S. colloq.* [See BUBBY[2].] A form of familiar address to boys or men. (Cf. BUD *sb.*[3])

1839 C. F. BRIGGS *Adv. H. Franco* II. 189 'Speak louder, Bub,' said one of the vice presidents, encouragingly. **1872** 'MARK TWAIN' *Roughing It* v. 51 Well, I shall have to tear myself away from you, bub. **1896** *McClure's Mag.* VI. 485/2 She always called him 'bub' when she wanted to vex him. **1902** S. E. WHITE *Blazed Trail* xxviii, Well, bub,..blowed that stake you made out of Radway, yet? **1948** *Chicago Star* 24 Apr. 3/4 Hey bub—can I get a squint at yer uppers?

†**bub**, *v.*[1] *Obs. rare*$^{-1}$. [Cf. BUB *sb.*[1], and BUBBLE.] *trans.* To throw up in bubbles. In quot. with *up*.

1563 SACKVILLE *Mirr. Mag.* Induct. lxix, Acheron..bubs up swelth as black as hell.

†**bub**, *v.*[2] *Obs. rare*$^{-1}$. [? short for BUBBLE *v.*] ? To bribe, or ? to cheat.

1719 D'URFEY *Pills* II. 54 Another makes Racing a Trade ..And many a Crimp Match has made, By bubbing another Man's Groom.

bubal, -ale (ˈbjuːbəl). [ad. L. *būbalus* (ad. Gr. βούβαλος) an ox-like antelope; also misapplied to a kind of wild ox; cf. BUFFALO *sb.*] Used to render L. *būbalus*: **a.** (in early examples) with uncertain meaning (antelope or buffalo). **b.** (mod. *Zool.*) A species of antelope (*Antilope bubalus*) found in N. Africa.

1461-83 *Liber Niger Edw. IV.* in *Ord. R. Househ.* 17 Many fatte buballes, al maner pultry. **1483** CAXTON *Gold. Leg.* 72/2 Salomon had dayly..veneson that was taken as hertes, ghotes, bubals. **1873** TRISTRAM *Moab* ix. 168 Antelopes.. the oryx antelope and the bubale.

bubaline (ˈbjuːbəlaɪn), *a.* [ad. mod.L. *Bubalinæ*, f. *būbalus* BUBAL.] Of or pertaining to antelopes formerly grouped in a sub-family Bubalinæ or buffaloes of the genus *Bubalus*.

1827 GRIFFITH tr. *Cuvier's Anim. Kingd.* IV. 378 The Bubaline Group. **1907** *Westm. Gaz.* 2 Jan. 10/2 The Bubaline antelope is uniformly coloured bright bay.

†**buˈbbation.** [ad. L. *bubbātiōn-em*, occurring only in this passage: the readings *bullatio*, *bulbatio* have been suggested.] (See quot.)

1601 HOLLAND *Pliny* II. (1634) 515 This stone is to be found..scattered here and there in smal pieces by way of bubbation (for that is the term they vse).

†ˈ**bubber.** *Obs. slang.* [f. BUB *sb.*[2] + -ER.] (See quots.)

1673 R. HEAD *Canting Acad.* 191 A Bubber..goes to the Alehouse, and steals there the Plate. **1690** B. E. *Dict. Cant. Crew, Bubber*, a drinking Bowl; also a great Drinker, and he that used to steal Plate from Publick-houses. **1725** *New Cant. Dict.*

†**bubbing,** *vbl. sb. Obs. slang.* [f. as prec. + -ING[1].] Drinking; also in *comb.*

1678 *Poor Robin's Char. of Scold* 6 She clamours at him so long..which makes him seek blinde Bubbing-schools to hide himself in from her fury.

bubble (ˈbʌb(ə)l), *sb.* Also 5 boble, bobel, 6 bubbul, 7 buble. [orig. f. the verb: see also the earlier BURBLE *sb.* found *c* 1350. Parallel sbs. in other Teutonic langs. are Sw. *bubbla*, Da. *boble*, Du. *bobbel*, Ger. dial. *bobbel*, *bubbel*. In their development the vb. and sb. appear to have influenced each other: see sense 5.]

1. A thin globular (or hemispherical) vesicle of water or other liquid, filled with air or gas; applied alike to those produced by the agitation of a quantity of the liquid, or the uprising of gas to the surface, and to those artificially made by blowing through a tube; often = *soap-bubble*. Also a quantity of air or gas occluded within a liquid; *spec.*, the portion of air left in the spirit-level. Sometimes applied to cavities produced by occluded air in solid substances that have cooled from fusion. ***to blow bubbles***: to produce bubbles by blowing through a tube; often *fig.* to devise baseless theories, or to amuse oneself in a childish manner.

1481 CAXTON *Myrr.* II. xxi. 113 The water of those wellis sprynge vp with grete bobles. **1528** PAYNELL *Salerne Regim.* H b, Hit [wyne] hath great bubbuls and spume. **1605** SHAKS. *Macb.* I. iii. 722 The Earth hath bubbles, as the Water ha's. **1626** BACON *Sylva* §24 Bubbles, are in the form of an Hemisphere; Air within, and a little Skin of Water without. *a* **1677** HALE *True Relig.* II. (1684) 32 Boys..blow Bubbles out of a Wall-nut-shell. **1728** YOUNG *Love Fame* II. (1757) 99 What are men..But bubbles on the rapid stream of time? **1783** COWPER *Lett.* 29 Sept., One generation blows bubbles, and the next breaks them. **1831** LARDNER *Hydrostatics* iv. 75 If the bubble stand still in the middle, it proves the instrument [spirit level] to be correct. **1879** G. PRESCOTT *Sp. Telephone* Introd. 1 A bubble of hydrogen rose to the surface, as the bubble from champagne does in the wine cup.

†**2.** *transf.* **a.** A hollow globe of thin glass, produced by blowing; *spec.* one of the hollow beads of glass formerly used for testing the strength of spirits (see BEAD 7). **b.** *Hist.* Used to translate L. *bulla* a round ornament of gold or leather worn by the children of Roman freemen. *Obs.*

1647 STAPYLTON *Juvenal* v. 194 What poore man..had Hetrurian bubbles when he was a lad. *Ibid.* Comm. 154 Æmilius Lepidus..had a statue in his pretexted purple and golden bulla's (or bubbles) set up in the capitol. **1660** BOYLE *New Exp. Phys.-Mech.* II. 40 Glass bubles, such as are wont to be blown at the flame of a lamp. *Ibid.* xx. (1682) 71 Then was taken a great Glass bubble, with a long neck. **1667** PEPYS *Diary* (1877) V. 419 He..did give me a glass bubble, to try the strength of liquors with.

c. A motor-car. *U.S. colloq.* Also (in U.K.) short for *bubble car*.

1918 WODEHOUSE *Piccadilly Jim* xxiii. 209 From the direction of the street, came the roar of a starting automobile... 'Gee! He's beat it in my bubble—and it was a hired one!' **1920** —— *Coming of Bill* II. xiii. 231 I'll take you out in the bubble—the automobile, the car, the chug-chug wagon. **1958** *Economist* (Suppl.) 25 Oct. 5/1 Entirely different kinds of car: first, a standard large-sized model for the export markets..; second, some kind of 'people's car' to tap the new market of our own masses; more recently, motorised bubbles to float their way through growing traffic congestion. **1966** P. MOLONEY *Plea for Mersey* 51 Here rows of meters guard from crowding troubles, Rolls, Bentleys, Daimlers, Jaguars and Bubbles. **1967** J. B. PRIESTLEY *It's Old Country* vi. 65 Half a dozen cars, ranging from a gigantic old Rolls to a three-wheel bubble, were already parked.

d. The transparent domed canopy over the cockpit of an aeroplane. Freq. *attrib.*

1945 *Jrnl. R. Aeronaut. Soc.* XLIX. 315/2 You..showed great foresight..[with] such developments as the gyro-stabilised gun sight, bubble canopy,..gas turbine and jet power plant. **1949** *Aeronautics* Jan. 35/2 The awkward cockpit canopy has been redesigned as a 'bubble' type. **1955** *Amer. Speech* XXX. 117 *Bubble*, n., the plexiglass canopy covering the cockpit.

3. *fig.* Anything fragile, unsubstantial, empty, or worthless; a deceptive show. From 17th c. onwards often applied to delusive commercial or financial schemes, as *the Mississippi bubble*, *the South Sea bubble*.

1599 MARSTON *Sco. Villanie* II. vi. 198 To see this butterfly, This windy bubble taske my balladry. **1600** SHAKS. *A.Y.L.* II. vii. 152 Seeking the bubble Reputation Euen in the Canons mouth. *a* **1626** BACON *Ps.* in Farr's *S.P.* (1848) 301 Mortality: This bubble light, this vapour of our breath. *c* **1665** in *Roxb. Ballads* (1886) VI. 254 Why should a Woman dote on such a Bubble? **1721** SWIFT *S. Sea Proj.* Wks. 1755 III. II. 138 The nation..will find..South-sea at best a mighty bubble. **1745** DE FOE *Eng. Tradesm.* (1841) II. xliv. 157 In the good old days of trade, there were no bubbles, no stock-jobbing. **1783** COWPER *Task* III. 175 Eternity for bubbles proves at last A senseless bargain. **1858** *Sat. Rev.* 27 Nov. 524/1 We are asked..to back the luck of that gigantic bubble, the French Empire.

b. *attrib.* or *adj.*: Unsubstantial, fragile, delusive; often with reference to fraudulent commercial undertakings, as in ***bubble company, scheme.***

1635 QUARLES *Embl.* I. iv. (1718) 19 What's lighter than the mind? A thought. Than thought? This bubble world. **1726** AMHERST *Terræ Fil.* xii. 59 Several bubble-schools and academies sprung up. **1762–71** H. WALPOLE *Vertue's Anecd. Paint.* (1786) III. 119 He..was concerned in a bubble Lottery. **1798** EDGEWORTH *Pract. Educ.* (1801) II. 373 This wager would have been a bubble bet if it had been brought before the Jockey-club. *a* **1845** HOOD *Black Job* xvii, No..Bubble Company could hope to thrive.

4. The process of bubbling; the sound made by bubbling; a state of agitation. *Naut. phrase*: ***a bubble of a sea***: cf. BOBBLE.

1839 BEALE in *Sat. Mag.* 18 May 192/1 An awkward 'bubble' of a sea..began to make. **1840** MARRYAT *Poor Jack* xxiv, There was a bubble of a sea. **1874** MRS. WHITNEY *We Girls* xix. 187 There was nothing but a low, comfortable bubble in the chimney-corner to tell of..dinner.

†**5.** One who may be or is 'bubbled' (sense 5 of the verb); a dupe, a gull. *Obs.*

1668 SEDLEY *Mulb. Gard.* IV. Wks. 1722 II. 56 Are any of these Gentlemen good Bubbles, Mr. Wildish? **1702** DE FOE *Reform. Manners* I. 315 The wondring Bubbles stand amaz'd to see Their Money Mountebank'd to Mercury. **1735–8** BOLINGBR. *On Parties* 144 They were not such Bubbles as to alter, without mending, the Government. *a* **1774** GOLDSM. tr. *Scarron's Comic Rom.* (1775) I. 21 He generally dined and supped in taverns at the expence of every fool and bubble he met with. **1807** CRABBE *Par. Reg.* I. Wks. 1834 II. 151 A board, beneath a tiled retreat Allures the bubble, and maintains the cheat.

6. *Comb.* (see also 3 b), as ***bubble-blower***, ***-blowing*** ppl. adj. and vbl. sb., ***-filled*** adj.; **bubble bath**, a bath in which the water has been made to foam by a perfumed toilet preparation; such a preparation, in a liquid or crystal form; also *fig.*; **bubble car**, a miniature motor-car with a transparent domed top; **bubble chamber**, a container of super-heated liquid for the detection of ionizing particles; **bubble-dancer** *U.S.*, a woman who dances as if in the nude, covered by one or more balloons; †**bubble-glass**, glass as thin as a bubble (see also 2 a); **bubble-gum**, chewing-gum which can be blown into large bubbles; **bubble-man** (see quot.); **bubble sextant** (see quot. 1935); **bubble-shell**, a sort of mollusc; **bubble-trier**, an instrument used for testing the accuracy of the tubes of spirit-levels; **bubble-tube**, the glass tube of a spirit-level containing spirit and enclosing an air-bubble.

1949 L. CHARTERIS in *Queen's Awards* (1951) IV. 299 'I was having a *bubble bath,' said Pauline Stone. **1960** KOESTLER *Lotus & Robot* II. vi. 166 Then the lights go up, the town changes into a bubble-bath of coloured neon. **1969** *Woman* 10 May 22 Bath essence, bath oil, bubble bath, bath cubes. **1957** *Observer* 20 Oct. 3/3 The B.M.C...are not interested in *bubble cars as now known, but only in properly engineered vehicles. **1958** *Spectator* 13 June 762/1 The tiniest bubble-car I ever set eyes on. **1953** *Physical Rev.* XCI. 496/2 (*title*) A possible '*bubble chamber' for the study of ionizing events. *Ibid.* 762/1 Bubble-chamber tracks of penetrating cosmic-ray particles. **1969** *Times* 5 Feb. 13/6 The tracks are recorded by taking high-speed photographs of the tank, or bubble chamber as it is called. **1936** *Time* 11 May 28/2 *Pre-honeymoon* is concerned with the love of a U.S. Senator for a *bubble dancer. **1882** *Macm. Mag.* XLVI. 122 The iron-impregnated, *bubble-filled fountains of Schwalbach. **1591** SPENSER *Ruines of Time* 50 Why then dooth flesh, a *bubble-glas of breath, Hunt after honour? **1937** *Night & Day* 16 Sept. 28/2 *Bubble Gum..is particularly intriguing. **1958** P. MORTIMER *Daddy's gone A-Hunting* i. 7 The steady, pungent smell of bubble gum. **1862** MAYHEW *Crim. Prisons* 46 Cheats, subdivisible into ..*bubble-men, who institute annuity offices and assurance companies. **1920** *Flight* XII. 375/2 *Bubble sextant. **1935** C. G. BURGE *Compl. Bk. Aviation* 194/1 *Bubble Sextant*, a sextant employing a bubble device to provide an artificial horizon. Normally employed for determining the altitude of a celestial body. **1854** WOODWARD *Mollusca* (1856) 14 The *bubble-shell (*phyline*), itself predacious, is eaten both by star-fish and sea-anemone. *a* **1877** KNIGHT *Dict. Mech.*, **Bubble-trier*, an instrument for testing the delicacy and accuracy of the tubes for holding the spirit in leveling-instruments. **1890** W. F. STANLEY *Surveying Instr.* 88 The Bubble Trier is a bar or bed 12 to 20 inches long, with two extended feet ending in points at one end, and a micrometer screw, the point of which forms a resting foot, at the other end, thereby forming a tripod. **1888** *Lockwood's Dict. Mech. Engin.*, **Bubble Tube*, or *Spirit Glass*, the tube of a spirit-level which contains the enclosed spirit. **1890** W. F. STANLEY *Surveying Instr.* 86 Level Tubes, or Bubble Tubes as they are technically termed, are used in nearly all important surveying instruments.

bubble (ˈbʌb(ə)l), *v.* Also 5–8 buble, 6 bobyll. [Found (in the vbl. sb. BUBBLING) *a* 1400. Parallel words are Sw. *bubla*, Da. *boble*, mod.Du. and LG. *bobbelen*, mod.G. dial. *bobbelen*, *bubbelen*; all of these are modern, and it is doubtful how far they are related to each other, or are merely parallel imitative words, suggested either by the sound of bubbles forming and bursting, or by the action of the lips in making a bubble. The Eng. *bubble* can hardly be separated from the earlier BURBLE, common in the same sense from 1300; cf. *gurgle* and *guggle*. In *bubble* the verb is the source of the sb. as a whole, but sense 5 of the vb. appears to be derived from sense 3 of the sb., and in turn to have given rise to sense 5 of the latter.]

1. *intr.* To form bubbles (as boiling water, a running stream, etc.); to rise in bubbles (as gas through liquid, water from a spring, etc.; often with *out* or *up*); to emit the sounds due to the formation and bursting of bubbles.

1398 [see BUBBLING *vbl. sb.*]. **1477** NORTON *Ord. Alch.* in Ashm. iv. (1652) 47 Remember that Water will buble and boyle. **1530** PALSGR. 459/1 The potage begynneth to bobyll. **1580** H. GIFFORD *Gilloflowers* (1875) 10, I..feele certayne waters of vayne appetites to bubble vp wt in me. **1609** BIBLE (Douay) *Ex.* viii. 3 The river shal bubble with frogges. **1633** P. FLETCHER *Purple Isl.* III. xx, Water, bubbling from this fountain. **1703** MAUNDRELL *Journ. Jerus.* (1732) 63 Then bubbles up with abundance of Water. *c* **1750** SHENSTONE *Elegy* i. 4 Now hear the fountain bubbling round my cell. **1799** G. SMITH *Laboratory* I. 329 Take good acid of nitre, and fling..chalk into it, till it..ceases to bubble. **1824–29** LANDOR *Imag. Conv.* (1846) I. 3 Many bright specks bubble up along the blue Egean. **1850** TENNYSON *In Mem.* xcix, Yon swoll'n brook that bubbles fast. **1860** GEN. P. THOMPSON *Audi Alt.* III. ci. 1 The frozen notes came bubbling out together. **1871** TYNDALL *Fragm. Sc.* I. iv. 97.

2. *fig.* **a.** Of things: To arise or issue like bubbles.

1652 GAULE *Magastrom.* 228 Whence then bubble out so many and so great errors in their prognostications? **1713** BEVERIDGE *Priv. Th.* I. (1730) 94 So soon as any new Thought begins to bubble in my Soul. **1852** KINGSLEY *Androm.* 114 Feebly at last she began, while wild thoughts bubbled within her. *a* **1859** L. HUNT *To J. H.* ii, It bubbles into laughter. **1879** MCCARTHY *Own Times* II. 16 Chartism bubbled and sputtered a little yet.

b. Of persons: ***to bubble over, up*** (with merriment, anger, etc.): *fig.* from the bubbling of a pot on the fire.

1858 HAWTHORNE *Fr. & It. Jrnls.* (1872) II. 173 He bubbled and brimmed over with fun. **1860** TYNDALL *Glac.* I. §19. 133 One clergyman..appeared to bubble over with enjoyment. **1881** M. LEWIS *Two Pretty G.* III. 97 He had his views..but he never bubbled up to discuss and defend them.

c. *trans.* To send forth like bubbles. (A Hebraism.)

1611 BIBLE *Prov.* xv. 2 The mouth of the fool poureth [*marg.* bubbleth] out foolishness. —— *Ps.* xlv. 1 My heart is inditing [*marg.* boyleth or bubbleth vp] a good matter.

3. *intr.* To make a sound resembling that made by bubbles in boiling or running water. Also *trans.* (with object denoting sound). *rare.*

1602 *Metamorph. of Tobacco* (Collier) 19 Pretie waues.. Bubbled sweete Musicke with a daintie Sound. **1842** STERLING *Ess. & Tales* (1848) I. 459 Love, the name bubbled by every wave of Hippocrene. **1847** TENNYSON *Princ.* IV. 247 At mine ears Bubbled the nightingale.

4. *trans.* To cover or spread with bubbles.

1598 MARSTON *Pigmal.* IV. 151 The haile-shot drops.. onely bubble quiet Thetis face.

5. *trans.* To delude with 'bubbles' (see BUBBLE *sb.* 3); to befool, cheat, humbug. Also ***to bubble*** (any one) ***of, out of,*** or ***into*** a thing. Very common in 18th c.; now rarely used.

1675 WYCHERLEY *Countr. Wife* III. ii, He is to be bubbled of his mistress as of his money. **1702** *The Eng. Theophrast.* 37 Men are commonly bubbled when they first enter upon play. **1761** MURPHY *Citizen* II. i, And so here I am bubbled and choused out of my money. **1792** MARY WOLLSTONECR. *Rights Wom.* Introd. 2 The understanding of the sex has been so bubbled by this specious homage. **1841** HOR. SMITH *Moneyed Man* I. xi. 312 You have been preciously bubbled; ludicrously swindled and outwitted. **1880** MCCARTHY *Own Times* III. xli. 235 Some critics declared..that the French Emperor had 'bubbled' him [Mr. Cobden].

6. *Sc. and north. dial.* To blubber.

1727 WALKER *Remark. Pass.* 60 (JAM.) John Knox..left her [Q. Mary] bubbling and greeting. *Mod. Sc.* What is he bubbling about now?

7. *trans.* To make (a baby) bring up wind; = BURP *v.* 2. Also *intr.* *U.S.*

1943 L. J. HALPERN *How to raise a Healthy Baby* I. 19 During the process of belching or 'bubbling' small amounts of milk come up with the swallowed air. **1946** B. SPOCK *Common Sense Bk. Baby & Child Care* 83 You need to 'bubble' your baby in the middle of a feeding only if he swallows so much air that it stops his nursing. **1963** M. MCCARTHY *Group* x. 221 The baby belched... 'Someone should have come in to bubble him,' she said. 'He swallowed a lot of air.'

†ˈ**bubbleable,** *a. obs. rare*[−1]. [f. BUBBLE *v.* (sense 5) + -ABLE.] Capable of being duped.

1669 *Nicker Nicked* (3rd ed.) in *Harl. Misc.* II. 109 If the winner be bubbleable, they will insinuate themselves into his acquaintance.

ˌ**bubble-and-ˈsqueak.** [f. BUBBLE *v.* + SQUEAK *v.*, referring to the sounds made in cooking this dish.] **1. a.** A dish of meat and cabbage fried up together, 'cold meat fried in butter with vegetables'. Nowadays potatoes and other vegetables are often used instead of meat.

1772 T. BRIDGES *Burlesque Trans. of Homer: Iliad* XI. 507 We therefore cooked him up a dish Of lean bull-beef, with cabbage fry'd,..Bubble, they call this dish, and squeak. **1785** GROSE *Dict. Vulgar Tongue, Bubble and Squeak*, beef and cabbage fried together. **1795** WOLCOTT (P. Pindar) Wks. 1812 I. 192 What mortals Bubble call and Squeak When midst the Frying-pan in accents savage, The Beef so surly quarrels with the Cabbage. **1824** BRYON *Juan* XV. lxxi, 'Bubble and squeak' would spoil my liquid lay. **1855** BROWNING *Holy-Cr. Day*, Bubble and squeak! Blessedest

Thursday's the fat of the week. **1881** *Leicester. Gloss.* (E.D.S.) *Bubble-and-squeak*, slices of underdone beef fried and seasoned, laid on cabbage, boiled, strained, chopped, and fried in dripping. **1951** *Good Housek. Home Encycl.* 373/2 In the modern version of bubble and squeak the meat is usually omitted.

b. *transf.* and *fig.*

1927 T. E. LAWRENCE *Lett.* (1938) 509, I can make the most lovely bubble and squeak of a life for myself. **1960** *Times* 17 Sept. 9/4 The battle of the organs—British boom versus baroque bubble-and-squeak.

2. *Rhyming slang* for (*a*) BEAK *sb.*^{3}; (*b*) GREEK *sb.* 1 a; also ellipt. *bubble.*

1935 CURTIS & WALLACE *Mouthpiece* i. 16 You ought to have heard him talking to the old bubble and squeak. **1938** PARTRIDGE *Dict. Slang* Add. 983/1 *Bubble and squeak*, a Greek. **1962** R. COOK *Crust on its Uppers* I. 20 All the best Anglo-Saxon grafters come from mine [*sc.* my school], and the Bubbles and the Indians from the other. *Ibid.* Gloss., Bubble = bubble-and-squeak = Greek. **1968** L. BERG *Risinghill* 106 'Why do they call Greek children "Bubbles"?' said Mr. Colinides to me... Later it dawned on me that it was short for 'bubble-and-squeak'; rhyming slang.

† **'bubble-bow, -boy.** *Obs.* [app. f. BUBBLE *v.* 5 + BEAU as if 'beau-befooler': cf. quot. 1712.] A lady's tweezer-case.

(So explained in Pope's foot-note to quot. 1727; he remarks that the word is 'in use in this present year'. Warburton says the passage is quoted from one of Pope's own juvenile poems, in which case its date would be *c* 1704.)

[**1712** ARBUTHNOT *John Bull* (1755) 3 Charles Mather could not bubble a young beau better with a toy.]

1727 POPE, etc., *Art Sinking* 94 Lac'd in her Cosins new appear'd the Bride, A Bubble-bow and Tompion at her side. **1807** *Month. Mag.* XXIV. 550 Why was it called a bubble-boy? Probably the word is a misspelling for bauble-buoy, a support for baubles.

'bubbled ('bʌb(ə)ld), *ppl. a.* [f. BUBBLE *sb.* and *v.* + -ED.]

1. Sent forth like bubbles; full of bubbles; covered with bubbles.

1822 BEDDOES *Bride's Trag.* v. iii, What sound is that.. Harmonious as a bubbled tear? **1865** SWINBURNE *Poems & Ball., At Eleusis* 11 Smooth pitchers of pure brass Under the bubbled wells. **1871** TYNDALL *Fragm. Sc.* (ed. 6) I. vi. 224 The internal scattering common in bubbled ice.

†**2.** Befooled, cheated, deceived. *Obs.*

a **1683** OLDHAM *Wks. & Rem.* (1686) 66 Bubled Monarchs are at first beguil'd.. at last depos'd, and kill'd. **1719** D'URFEY *Pills* (1872) I. 348 A bubbled coxcomb.

bubblement ('bʌb(ə)lmənt). [f. BUBBLE *v.* + -MENT.] Effervescence (*lit.* and *fig.*).

1890 *Pall Mall Gaz.* 24 Mar. 1/2 Berlin is in a state of bubblement. **1893** *Field* 17 June 895/2 A flash, and swirl, a bubblement. **1902** J. H. SKRINE *Pastor Agnorum* 200 The wicked man.. was an etymologist and knew that zeal means bubblement, effervescence.

bubbler ('bʌblə(r)). [f. BUBBLE *v.* + -ER.^{1}]

†**1.** One who gets up bubble-companies; a swindler, cheat. *Obs.*

1720 POPE *Let. to Digby* 20 July, All the Jews, jobbers, bubblers, subscribers, etc. *c* **1778** *Conquerors* 9 Bubblers and bubbled meanly Take their stand.

2. 'A fish found in the Ohio river. Its name is derived from the singular grunting noise which it makes.' Bartlett *Dict. Amer.*

†**,bubble-the-'justice.** *Obs.* [f. BUBBLE *v.* + JUSTICE; = 'cheat the magistrate', the game being regarded as an evasion of the laws prohibiting ninepins, etc.] A game (see quot.).

1801 STRUTT *Sports & Past.* Introd. 44 The game of nine holes was revived.. with the new name of Bubble the Justice.

bubbling ('bʌblɪŋ), *vbl. sb.* [f. BUBBLE *v.*]

1. The action of the verb BUBBLE; the process of forming bubbles, rising in bubbles, etc.

1398 TREVISA *Barth. De P.R.* XI. xiv, And whan þat fyre is queynte in watry cloudes, þe bobelynge.. and crakkes of þat quenchynge is clepid þonder. **1548** THOMAS *It. Dict.* (1567) *Tocco*, the boblyng of a rennyng water, whan it retourneth from the fall out of a deepe hole. *a* **1656** BP. HALL *Occas. Medit.* (1851) 54 After some short noise, and smoke, and bubbling, the metal is quiet. **1855** MAURY *Phys. Geog. Sea* xviii. §755 (1860) 414 The bubbling made a loud noise.. heard for a long time after.

fig. **1655** GURNALL *Chr. in Arm.* xiii. (1669) 355/1 Arm us against.. bublings of our own vain hearts. **1710** PALMER *Proverbs* 237 Correct.. the bubblings of our native pride.

†**2.** Deluding, cheating (see BUBBLE *v.* 5). *Obs.*

1725 BAILEY *Erasm. Colloq.* 468 Understand the Art of Borrowing and Bubbling.

'bubbling, *ppl. a.* [f. BUBBLE *v.* + -ING^2.]

1. That bubbles, rises in bubbles, sends up bubbles, or makes a bubble-like movement.

1583 STANYHURST *Æneis* I. (Arb.) 23 Freshe bubling fountayns. **1639** HORN & ROBOTHAM *Gate Lang. Unl.* vii. (1643) §65 Out of hidden springs gush forth bubling.. fountaines. **1783** COWPER *Task* IV. 38 The bubbling.. urn Throws up a steamy column. **1829** MARRYAT *F. Mildmay* xi, The tide and the wind formed a bubbling short sea.

2. *transf.* **a.** That comes forth like bubbles; gasping, gurgling. **b.** That utters bubbling or gurgling sounds.

1819 BYRON *Juan* II. liii, At intervals there gush'd.. the bubbling cry Of some strong swimmer in his agony. **187..** BESANT & RICE *Monks of Th.* xxxi. 259 We'll make him go round like a bubbling turkey-cock. **1885** STEVENSON *Dynamiter* v. 67 There broke forth.. the bubbling.. sound of laughter.

3. That has bubbles or drops forming on it.

1621 QUARLES *Esther* (1638) 91 The Harvester with bubling brow.

†**4.** Deluding, cheating. *Obs.*

1675 WYCHERLEY *Country Wife* III. ii, Come you bubbling rogues you.

Hence **'bubblingly** *adv.*, in a bubbling manner.

1611 COTGR., *Empoulément*, swellingly, bubblingly.

bubblish ('bʌblɪʃ), *a. rare*$^{-1}$. [f. BUBBLE *sb.* 3 + -ISH.] Somewhat of the nature of a bubble.

1830 *Fraser's Mag.* II. 499 This new scheme was bubblish, and quickly blew up.

bubbly ('bʌblɪ), *a.* [f. BUBBLE *sb.* + -Y^1.] **1.** Full of bubbles. (In *Sc.* = blubbering.) ***bubbly water*** (slang), champagne; also *ellipt.* as *sb.*

1599 NASHE *Lent. Stuffe* (1871) 12 They would no more.. haue their heads washed with his bubbly spume. **1611** COTGR., *Empoulé*.. bubblie; or.. rising in bubbles. **1642** W. PRICE *Serm.* 13 Upon what slight motives from bubbly honour, fleeting riches, shadowy pleasures. **1861** C. KING *Ant. Gems* (1866) 80 The greatest part exhibited that.. bubbly texture so generally found in antique pastes. **1910** *Daily Chron.* 9 Apr. 9/3 'Too much bubbly water', so he explained, was responsible for the breach of the rules. **1920** *Chambers's Jrnl.* 346/2 It goes to the head like bubbly. **1927** *Blackw. Mag.* Feb. 231/2 [He] had finished up at dinner with some capital oysters and a bottle of bubbly. **1951** J. B. PRIESTLEY *Festival at Farbridge* III. iii. 566 Bubbly for you... Bubbly for me. George, two bubblies.

2. *fig.* Of a person: vivacious, full of high spirits.

1939 J. STEINBECK *Grapes of Wrath* xxii. 367 'Never seen you so bubbly,' Pa said. **1965** G. MCINNES *Road to Gundagai* xii. 202 They [sc. lady helps].. did vary from bubbly to bleak, but all shared a paralysing gentility. **1982** BARR & YORK *Official Sloane Ranger Handbk.* 80/2 Tudors are bubbly girls, man-chasers, 'always talking about boys' according to other schools.

'bubbly-jock ('bʌblɪdʒɒk). *Sc.* [f. prec. + *Jock* = JACK. Perh. suggested in part by the sound made by the bird; cf. the English *gobbler.*] A colloquial name for the turkey-cock; also *fig.*

1814 SCOTT *Let.* in Lockhart (1839) V. 12, I am sair halded down by the Bubbly jock. **1865** CARLYLE *Fredk. Gt.* VI. XVI. ii. 143 Oh my winged Voltaire, to what dunghill Bubbly-Jocks you do stoop with homage.

†**'bubby**^{1}. *Obs.* or *dial.* [Cf. Ger. *bübbi* teat (Grimm). Connexion with F. *poupe* teat of an animal (formerly also of a woman), Pr. *popa*, It. *poppa* teat, is very doubtful.] A woman's breast.

1686 D'URFEY *New Poems* (1690) 206 The Ladies here may without Scandal shew Face or white Bubbies, to each ogling Beau. **1712** ARBUTHNOT *John Bull* in Arb. *Garner* (1883) VI. 601 Why don't you go and suck the bubby? **1725** BRADLEY *Fam. Dict.* II. O iv b/1 If on the contrary a Woman has no occasion for Milk.. Let her put Chervil upon her Bubbies.

bubby^2. [Bartlett and Webster say a corruption of *brother*: but the word looks more like Ger. *bube, bub*, boy.] In U.S. a familiar name for a little boy.

1848–60 in BARTLETT. **1864** in WEBSTER.

bubo ('bju:bəʊ). Pl. buboes. [a. late L. *bubo*, ad. Gr. *βουβών* the groin, a swelling in the groin.] An inflamed swelling or abscess in glandular parts of the body, *esp.* the groin or arm-pits. (An ordinary symptom of the plague in the 17th c.) Also *attrib.*, as in ***bubo plague.***

1398 TREVISA *Barth. De P.R.* VII. lix. (1495) 273 Somtyme a postume comyth of ventosite and of wynde and hight Bubo. **1597** GERARD *Herbal* III. cxxxiii. (1633) 1511 Which imposthume is called Bubo by reason of his lurking in such secret places. **1658** ROWLAND *Mouffet's Theat. Ins.* 1050 A Bubo riseth on a man that he [the scorpion] stings. **1782** W. HEBERDEN *Comment.* vii. (1806) 23 These sores therefore, like pestilential buboes, point out the nature of the disorder. **1839–47** TODD *Cycl. Anat. & Phys.* III. 233/2 A bubo will originate from.. inflamed inguinal or axillary glands.

Hence **'buboed** *ppl. a.*, affected with buboes.

1824–29 LANDOR *Imag. Conv.* (1846) II. 126 They are not blotched and buboed with its pestilence.

bubonic (bju:'bɒnɪk), *a.*^{1} (*sb.*) [f. late L. *bubōn-em* (see prec.) BUBO + -IC.]

That is attended with the appearance of buboes. Also as *sb.*, short for *bubonic plague.*

1871 *Echo* 15 Aug., The bubonic disease in Khorassan. **1886** *Athenæum* 25 Sept. 405/2 A list of the dates of the appearance of the famous bubonic plague from A.D. 252 down to.. 1837. **1901** *Daily News* 11 Feb. 5/3 A native child died last night, and the post-mortem proved the existence of bubonic. **1908** KIPLING *Lett. Trav.* (1920) 121 A rot at what is called 'headquarters' may spread like bubonic, with every steamer.

bu'bonic, *a.*^{2} *nonce-wd.* [f. L. *bubōn-em* owl + -IC.] Owl-like.

1795 WOLCOTT (P. Pindar) *Lousiad* I. Wks. 1812 I. 191 With arms akimbo, and bubonic look.

bubonocele (bju:'bɒnəsi:l). [a. Gr. *βουβωνοκήλη*, f. *βουβών* the groin + *κήλη* a rupture; cf. F. *bubonocèle.*] Inguinal rupture or hernia.

1615 CROOKE *Body of Man* 91 Whence it commeth to passe, that woemen are often troubled with the Boubonocele. **1736** *Phil. Trans.* XXXIX. 329 The Cure of the Hernia.. could be obtained by no other Operation than that for the Bubonocele. **1876** GROSS *Dis. Bladder* 343 A hernia of this description is sometimes complicated with a bubonocele, or hernia of the groin.

bubu(c)kled ('bju:bʌk(ə)ld), *a. pseudo-arch.* [f. BUBUKLE (only Shakes.) + -ED^2.] Covered with 'bubukles' or large pimples.

1829 COOPER *Good's Study Med.* (ed. 3) II. 357 A welky or bubukled face. **1888** STEVENSON *Across the Plains* (1892) iv. 163 Poor bubuckled Commissary!

†**'bubukle.** *Obs.* A confusion of BUBO and CARBUNCLE (put into the mouth of Fluellen).

1599 SHAKS. *Hen. V*, III. vi. 108 His face is all bubukles and whelkes.

†**bu'bulcitate,** *v. Obs.*$^{-0}$ [f. L. *bubulcitāre, -āri*, f. *bubulcus* cowherd.] (See quots.)

1623 COCKERAM I, *Bubulcitate*, to cry like a cow boy. **1678** PHILLIPS *App. affected Wds.*, *Bubulcitate*, to do the office of a *Bubulcus* or Cowheard.

buc(c, obs. form of BUCK.

‖**'bucca.** *dial.* [Corn. *bucca* 'hobgoblin, bugbear, scarecrow', app. cogn. with mod. Welsh *bwgan* spectre.] **a.** A bogle; applied *inter alia* to the subterranean spirits supposed to frequent tin-mines (see *Philos. Trans.* vol. I.). **b.** A stupid person. The compounds ***bucca-boo*** (bugaboo), ***bucca-gwidden***, are also in dial. use (see quots.)

1865 R. HUNT *Pop. Romances W. Eng.* Ser. I. 67 The Buccas or knockers—These are the sprites of the mines, and correspond to the Kobals of the German mines. **1880** *West Cornw. Gloss.* 7 Newlyn buccas, strong as oak, Knocking 'em down at every poke. *Bucca-boo*, a ghost; a bug-bear; a black bucca. *Bucca-gwidden*, a precocious child; a simple innocent; an insane person.

buccal ('bʌkəl), *sb.* and *a.* [f. L. *bucca* cheek, mouth + -AL^1: as if ad. L. **buccālis*. With sense A, cf. Sp. *bocal* mouthpiece of a trumpet.]

†**A.** *sb.* A mouthpiece. *Obs.*

1605 CHAPMAN & MARSTON *Eastward Hoe* A ij b, You all know the deuise of the Horne, where the young fellow slippes in at the Butte end, and comes sques'd out at the Buckall.

B. *adj.* Of or pertaining to the cheek.

1831 R. KNOX *Cloquet's Anat.* 403 The buccal membrane. **1854** WOODWARD *Mollusca* (1856) 189 The buccal ganglia.

‖**bu'ccan, bu'can, bou'can,** *sb.* Also bocan. [*Boucan* is the French spelling (= bukã) of a Tupi or allied Brazilian word, conveyed by Europeans in the 16th c. to Guiana and the West Indies, and hence often set down as Carib, Haitian, etc. The modern Tupi form is *mocaém* (Pg. *moquém* = mu'kẽ): the Carib names were *ioualla* (*youlla*), *anaké*, the Haitian *barbacóa*. (E. B. Tylor.)]

1. A native South American name for a wooden framework or hurdle on which meat was roasted or smoked over a fire.

1611 E. ASTON tr. *De Lery Hist. Amer.* [The wooden grating set up on four forked posts] which in their language they call a boucan. **1751** CHAMBERS *Cycl.*, *Buccaneers*, or *Bucaneers*, a term.. properly used for a kind of savages, who prepare their meat on a grate, or hurdle made of Brazil-wood, placed in the smoke, at a good height from the fire, and called buccan. **1852** E. WARBURTON *Darien* II. 34 The buccaneers proceeded to prepare their dinner. The.. flesh was separated from the bones, cut into long strips, and laid upon the boucan. **1864** WEBSTER, *Buccan*, a grating or hurdle made of sticks. **1872** J. H. TRUMBULL *Proc. Amer. Philol. Assoc.* 13 The Virginia *barbacue* and the French *boucan* (dried meat).. were all derived from names of the high wooden gridiron or scaffolding on which Indians dried, smoked, or broiled their meats. This grill was called *boucan* by the Brazilians.

2. (in form *bocan*) = BARBECUE *sb.* 5.

1857 *Illustr. Lond. News* 28 Mar., The Bocan or building used [in West Indies] for drying and preparing.. coffee.

3. Boucaned meat. [prop. Fr.]

1860–65 CARLYLE *Fredk. Gt.* XII. xii, Bucaniers, desperate naval gentlemen living on boucan or hung beef.

‖**'buccan,** *v.* Also **boucane, bucan.** [a. F. *boucane-r*, f. *boucan*: see prec.] *trans.* To expose (meat) to the action of fire and smoke upon a *boucan* or barbecue; to barbecue. Hence **'buccaned** *ppl. a.*, **'buccaning** *vbl. sb.* (More usually spelt like the French.)

1600 tr. *Laudonnière's Hist. de la Floride* (1586) in Hakluyt III. 307 They eate all their meate broyled on the coales and dressed in the smoake, which in their language they call Boucaned. **1761** *Ann. Reg.*, *Charac.* III. 1/2 These new settlers obtained the name of Buccaneers from their custom of buccanning their beef. **1827** *Edin. Rev.* XLV. 407 Instead of always boucaning their meats.. they now often used salt. **1865** TYLOR *Early Hist. Man.* 261 The art of bucaning or barbecuing practised by the Americans. **1865** *Morning Star* 14 Feb., The very name buccaneer is derived.. from the ('jerked') beef, which was also called 'boucaned' meat.

buccaneer, -ier (bʌkə'nɪə(r)), *sb.* Also 7 buck-, 8 bac-, buc-, buchaneer, 8–9 bucanier. [a. F. *boucanier* orig. 'one who hunts wild oxen' (Littré), f. *boucan* a barbecue, *boucaner* to dry

(meat) on a barbecue, to 'jerk': see prec. (Not in Cotgr.)]

†**1.** *orig.* One who dries and smokes flesh on a *boucan* after the manner of the Indians. The name was first 'given to the French hunters of St. Domingo, who prepared the flesh of the wild oxen and boars in this way' (E. B. Tylor *Early Hist. Man.* 261). *Obs.*

1661 HICKERINGILL *Jamaica* 43 Not able..to root out a few Buckaneers or Hunting French-men. **1710** J. TAYLOR *Jrnl.* 11 There were a great many French Buchaneers there. **1753** CHAMBERS *Cycl. Supp.* s.v., The antient inhabitants of Hispaniola, and the other Caribu islands..consisted of four ranks or orders..viz. buccaneers, or bull hunters, who scoured the woods. **1761** *Ann. Reg., Charac.* III. 2/2 The Buccaneers lived..on some spots of cleared ground just large enough to..contain their buccaning houses.

2. (From the habits which these subsequently assumed:) 'A name given to piratical rovers who formerly infested the Spanish coasts in America' (Falconer *Dict. Marine* 1789).

1690 B. E. *Dict. Cant. Crew, Buckaneers,* West-Indian Pirates..also the Rude Rabble in Jamaica. **1693** LUTTRELL *Brief Rel.* (1857) III. 96 To pardon all the buccaneers that will assist in taking Martineco. **1719** DE FOE *Crusoe* (1869) 414 Having been an old Planter at Maryland, and a Buccaneer into the Bargain. **1748** ANSON *Voy.* II. i. (ed. 4) 169 The usual haunt of the buccaneers and privateers. **1767** T. HUTCHINSON *Hist. Prov. Mass.* i. 86 Bucaniers or pirates ..were very numerous. **1813** SCOTT *Rokeby* I. *note.* **1864** BURTON *Scot Abr.* II. 279 A buccaneer or pirate in the Spanish Main.

attrib. **1720** DE FOE *Capt. Singleton* xiii. (1840) 228 The captain..gave me some buccaneer words upon it.

3. By extension: A sea-rover who makes hostile incursions upon the coast, a 'filibuster'.

1846 ARNOLD *Hist. Rome* II. xl. 564 To protect the Mamertine buccaneers. **1877** GLADSTONE *Glean.* IV. xxiii. 355 Some of the less temperate of our adventurers (I must not call them buccaneers). **1883** LORD R. GOWER *Remin.* in *Glasgow Weekly Her.* 15 June 1/4 The poetic vein..was strong in that glorious old buccaneer [Garibaldi].

buccaneer (bʌkəˈnɪə(r)), *v.* [f. prec. sb.]

a. = To BUCCAN. **b.** To act as a buccaneer: cf. BUCCANEERING *vbl. sb.*

1795 WOLCOTT (P. Pindar) *Lousiad* II. Wks. 1812 I. 237 'Twould be a serious matter, we can tell ye, Were we to bucaneer it on your belly. **1828** SOUTHEY in *Q. Rev.* XXXVIII. 233 Warner would certainly.. have been roasted, buccaneered, and eaten..if he had not escaped on board an English vessel. **1853** *Blackw. Mag.* LXXIII. 493 The Indians took the snake-flesh to dry (buccaneer) it.

buccaneering (bʌkəˈnɪərɪŋ), *vbl. sb.* [f. prec. + -ING[1].] The occupation of a buccaneer; piracy. ***buccaneering piece*** (F. *fusil boucanier*): a long musket used in hunting wild oxen (Littré).

1758 H. WALPOLE *Corr.* (1837) I. 383 Lord George Sackville refused to go a-buccaneering. **1761** *Brit. Mag.* II. 612 The said Looney took up a buccaneering piece..and shot the said Captain. **1824** W. IRVING *T. Trav.* (1849) 380 Wealth, which it was whispered he had acquired by buccaneering. **1876** GREEN *Short Hist.* vii. §8 (1882) 430 A new buccaneering expedition..under Drake.

buccaˈneering, *ppl. a.* [f. as prec. + -ING[2].] That follows the occupation of a buccaneer.

1703 DE FOE *True-born Eng.* I. 186 Norwegian Pirates, Buccaneering Danes..with Norman-French compound the Breed. **1800** WEEMS *Washington* i. (1877) 8 With their buccaneering legions. **1854** H. MILLER *Sch. & Schm.* i. 12. **1868** GLADSTONE *Juv. Mundi* viii. (1870) 251 The rough manners of a sea-faring and buccaneering people.

buccaˈneerish, *a.* [f. as prec. + -ISH.] Befitting or characteristic of a buccaneer.

1812 SOUTHEY *Omniana* II. 216 From his black beard and buccaneerish sort of look, a sailor would suppose it to be Davy Jones. *c* **1850** LOWELL *Poet. Wks.* (1879) 80/2 There is a buccaneerish air About that garb outlandish.

†**bucceˈllation.** *Obs. rare*⁻⁰. [f. late L. *buccella* morsel, irreg. dim. of *bucca* cheek; cf. *buccea* mouthful, morsel. See -ATION.]

1657 *Phys. Dict., Buccellation* is dividing into gobbets, or by piece-meals. **1678** PHILLIPS, *Buccellation* (Lat.), a Chymical term, a dividing into Gobbets. Hence in BAILEY and mod. Dicts.

bucchero (bʊˈkɛərəʊ). *Archæol.* [It.] A type of pottery, characteristic of ancient Tuscany, of a uniform black, neither glazed nor painted, but decorated with figures in low relief, or, in later times, with figures moulded separately and applied to the pottery. Also *attrib.*

1889 in *Cent. Dict.* **1905** H. B. WALTERS *Anc. Pottery* II. 295 In the earlier chamber-tombs no *bucchero* is found. **1910** *Encycl. Brit.* V. 722/1 Bucchero ware—the national pottery of Etruria. **1922** *Edin. Rev.* July 54 Some goblets of finely modelled and burnished black bucchero. **1950** *Proc. Prehist. Soc.* XVI. 56 There is much to be said for correlating the Aeolic dialect with the areas that produced that grey bucchero pottery known as Grey Minyan ware.

ˈ**buccinal** (ˈbʌksɪnəl), *a.* [f. L. *buccina* a crooked trumpet + -AL[1].] Trumpet-shaped; sounding like a trumpet. Hence **bucciˈnality.**

1846 in WORCESTER.

†ˈ**buccinate,** *v. Obs. rare*⁻⁰. [f. as prec. + -ATE.] 'To blow a trumpet' (Cockeram 1623).

In BLOUNT, PHILLIPS, BAILEY, etc.

buccinator (ˈbʌksɪneɪtə(r)). *Anat.* [a. L. *buccinātor*, agent-noun f. *buccināre* to blow the crooked trumpet. So called because it is the chief muscle employed in the act of blowing.]

Name for a flat thin muscle which forms the wall of the cheek. Also *attrib.*

1671 tr. *Riolanus' Sure Guide Physick* 220 Vulgarly termed *Buccinator*, or the Trumpeter, it were more rightly called *Bucco* the Cheek driver. **1746** R. JAMES *Introd. Mouffet's Health's Improv.* 2 The Food is then applied to the double Teeth..by the various actions of the Buccinators. **1831** R. KNOX *Cloquet's Anat.* 269 The Buccinator..is much larger in glass-blowers and persons who play on wind instruments than in other individuals. **1842** *Blackw. Mag.* LI. 46 Two or three [frogs] are blowing out their buccinators.

ˈ**buccinatory,** *a.* [f. as if ad. L. *buccinātōrius.] Pertaining to a trumpeter or trumpeting.

1760 STERNE *Tr. Shandy* (1802) III. vi. 268 Directing the buccinatory muscles along his cheeks..to do their duty—he whistled Lillabullero. **1833** *Blackw. Mag.* XXXIII. 589 As if the buccinatory muscles of the cheek had not been in working condition.

buccinite (ˈbʌksɪnaɪt). *Palæont.* [f. BUCCIN-UM + -ITE.] A fossil shell allied to the buccinum.

1852 TH. ROSS *Humboldt's Trav.* I. ii. 108 Volcanic breccia, said to contain..buccinites.

buccinoid (ˈbʌksɪnɔɪd), *a. Zool.* [f. BUCCINUM + -OID.] Resembling the buccinum.

1854 WOODWARD *Mollusca* (1856) 127, *Macrocheilus*, shell thick, ventricose, buccinoid. **1875** BLAKE *Zool.* 253 The genus..forms part of the buccinoid family of the pectinibranchiate order of Gasteropods.

‖**Buccinum** (ˈbʌksɪnəm). *Zool.* [L.: from a supposed resemblance to a trumpet.] The genus of gasteropod Molluscs represented by the whelk.

1601 HOLLAND *Pliny* I. 258 The lesse shell called Buccinum, fashioned like vnto that horn or cornet..hath a round back. **1854** GOSSE *Nat. Hist. Mollusca* 182 The buccinum..was observed to perforate a small hole in the shell.

bucco- (ˈbʌkəʊ), used as comb. form (for the correct bucci-) of L. *bucca* cheek, with the meaning 'relating to the cheek (or mouth)', as ***buccocervical, -facial, -labial, -lingual, -nasal, -pharyngeal*** adjs.

1892 *Phil. Trans.* B. CLXXXIII. 98 Dastre and Morat find..that the vaso-dilator fibres for the bucco-facial region of the Dog issue by the IInd., IIIrd., IVth., and Vth. thoracic nerves. **1903** DORLAND *Med. Dict.* (ed. 3), *Buccocervical*, pertaining to the neck and the buccal surface of a tooth. *Buccolabial*, pertaining to the cheek and lip. *Buccopharyngeal*, pertaining to the mouth and pharynx. **1911** ST. CLAIR THOMSON *Dis. Nose & Throat* II. vii. 111 The bucco-nasal membrane. **1967** G. M. WYBURN et al. *Conc. Anat.* 137/2 The overlapping constrictor muscles in their sheath of buccopharyngeal fascia.

buccoon, var. of BUCKONE, *Obs.*

buccra, var. of BUCKRA.

†ˈ**bucculent,** *a. Obs. rare*⁻⁰. [a. L. *bucculentus*, f. *bucca* cheek.] 'Blub-cheeked, wide-mouth' (Blount *Glossogr.* 1656).

buce, obs. form of BUSS.

‖**bucellas** (bjuːˈsɛləs). [The name of a village near Lisbon.] A sort of Portuguese white wine.

1836 DICKENS *Sk. Boz* (C.D. ed.) 165 A bottle of sauterne, bucellas, and sherry. *a* **1845** HOOD *Public Dinner* ii, Bucellas made handy, With Cape and bad Brandy.

bucentaur (bjuːˈsɛntɔː(r), ˈbjuːsɛntɔː(r)). [ad. It. *bucentoro*, of uncertain origin; it is commonly supposed that the name was taken from the figure-head of the vessel, representing a creature half man, half ox, which may have been designated by the Gr. name *βουκένταυρος, f. Gr. βοῦς ox + κένταυρος centaur (cf. ὀνοκένταυρος ONOCENTAUR); the word is unknown to ancient mythology. The Ital. word was sometimes used unchanged.]

1. *Hist.* The state barge in which on Ascension Day the Doge of Venice went to wed the Adriatic by dropping a ring into it.

1612 W. SHUTE *Fougasse's Ven.* II. 479 The Bucentaure.. was gently towed to Venice. **1756** NUGENT *Gr. Tour Italy* III. 61 The Bucentaure..is a particular kind of vast galeasse, very much adorned with sculptures and gilding. **1818** BYRON *Ch. Har.* IV. xi, The Bucentaur lies rotting unrestored. **1866** *Punch* 27 Oct. LI. 172 She that was plight of old with Doge and Bucentaur and ring.

†**2.** *transf.* A large ship; a gaily decorated barge resembling the Bucentaur of Venice. *Obs.*

1623 COCKERAM I, *Bucentaure*, a carricke or great ship. [**1658** *Hist. Christina Q. Swedland* 83 Her Majestie continu'd her journey..towards Bruxells in a Bucentoro most richly adorn'd, and guilded within and without.]

Bucephalus (bjuːˈsɛfələs). [ad. Gr. βουκέφαλος ox-headed, f. βοῦς ox + κεφαλή head.] The name of Alexander the Great's celebrated charger; applied humorously as a name for any riding-horse.

[**1601** HOLLAND *Pliny* I. 220 Men called [him] Bucephalus ..of the marke or brand of a buls head, which was imprinted vpon his shoulder.] **1799** SHERIDAN *Pizarro* Prol., The hack Bucephalus of Rotten Row. **1814** SCOTT *Wav.* vi, The Bucephalus which he bestrode. **1818** BYRON *Mazeppa* iv, As thy Bucephalus and thou.

buch, obs. form of BUDGE and BUSH.

Buchan (ˈbʌkən). The name of a Scottish meteorologist, Alexander *Buchan* (1829–1907), used to designate certain specified periods of cold weather foretold by him as of annual occurrence.

1923 *Daily Mail* 11 May 7 The period from May 9 to 14 is known as 'Buchan's Winter'. Buchan, an old meteorologist,..50 years ago laid down six periods of which May 9–14 is the coldest. **1929** *Daily News* 17 Apr. 8/7 Is it not a fact that the proposal to fix the date of Easter will mean that this holiday will in future coincide with 'Buchan's Cold Spell' which we are at present enjoying?

Buchanite (ˈbʌkənaɪt). *Hist.* [f. the name of Mrs. Elspeth *Buchan* (1738–91), commonly known as Lucky Buchan + -ITE[1].] A member of a sect which arose in 1783, in the Relief Congregation, Irvine, Ayrshire, Scotland, and became extinct in 1848 on the death of the only surviving member.

Mrs. Buchan believed herself to be the woman of Rev. xii.

1846 J. TRAIN (*title*) The Buchanites from first to last. **1910** *Encycl. Brit.* IV. 714/1 Elspeth Buchan..founder of a Scottish religious sect known as the Buchanites.

buchch, ? obs. var. of BUNCH.

bucher, buchery, obs. ff. BUTCHER, BUTCHERY.

†**buˈchette.** *Obs. rare*⁻¹. [a. F. *bûchette*, dim. of *bûche* billet.] A piece of firewood.

1507 *Bk. Gd. Mann.* L ij, [The] Fenix..assembleth all his buchettes and styckes in the hye mountayne, and fynably the fyre enflammeth them, and the Fenix is brente.

Buchmanism (ˈbʊkmənɪz(ə)m, ˈbʌk-). [f. the name of Frank *Buchman* (1878–1961), founder of the Oxford Group + -ISM.] The theories or practice of the Oxford Group Movement. So ˈ**Buchmanite** *a.* and *sb.*

1928 *Daily Express* 29 Feb. 1/4 The disclosure in the 'Daily Express' this morning of a revival here [*sc.* in Oxford] of a movement known as Buchmanism has led to a storm of comment in the University... The Buchmanites believe that if they conceive a sudden thought, without the exercise of a process of reasoning, this is a divine revelation, and should be acted on at once. **1928** *Isis* 16 May 1/2 Buchmanism is not widespread; probably in Oxford it never will be. **1933** H. H. HENSON *Oxford Groups* 48 The Buchmanite Group reminds us irresistibly of the Russian Soviet. **1936** A. HUXLEY *Eyeless in Gaza* ii. 13 Under Guidance, as the Buchmanites would say. **1936** *New Statesman* 11 July 46/1 They tell us that Buchmanism is good business. **1961** *Times* 9 Aug. 10/3 A religious movement variously known as the Oxford Group, Moral Re-Armament, or, less politely, as Buchmanism.

bucholzite (ˈbʌkəlzaɪt). *Min.* [ad. G. *bucholzit* (R. Brandes 1819, in *Jrnl. Chem. und Physik* XXV. 125), f. the name of C. F. *Bucholz*, a German chemist: see -ITE[1].] A variety of fibrolite.

1831 *Trans. R. Soc. Edinburgh* XI. 263 The colour of Bucholzite is a greyish-white, with a very slight tinge of yellow, not recognizable in the purest specimens. **1892** *Dana's Syst. Min.* (ed. 6) 498 *Fibrolite*. Fibrous or fine columnar... Bucholzite and monrolite are here included.

bucht, Sc. form of BOUGHT, fold.

‖**buchu** (ˈbʌkuː, ˈbuːkuː). Also 9 bouchue, bucku. The name given by the natives at the Cape of Good Hope to the plant formerly termed *Diosma crenata*; now assigned in Pharmacopœias to various species of *Barosma*.

1731 MEDLEY *Kolben's Cape G. Hope* I. 150 Men and women..powder themselves all over with Buchu. **1866** *Treas. Bot.* 125 Bucku leaves are much used in medicine as a stimulant and tonic. **1875** H. WOOD *Therap.* (1879) 497 Owing to its bitter principle, buchu is perhaps slightly tonic. **1880** P. GILLMORE *On Duty* 300 He..gave me a draught of Bouchue and quinine.

buchyment, var. of BUSHMENT.

buck (bʌk), *sb.*[1] Forms: (sense 'he-goat') 1 bucca, 2–3 buc, 3–4 bucke, 4–6 bukke; (senses 'male deer', etc.) 1, 5 buc, 3–5 bok, 4–7 bukke, bucke, 5 buk, 4– buck. [Orig. two words, OE. *buc* and *bucca*, which became indistinguishable in form after 11th c. So far as the evidence goes, OE. *buc* was used for the male deer, and *bucca* for the he-goat, but the instances are so few that it is far from certain that the words were thus distinguished in meaning. OE. *buc* = MDu. *boc*, Du. *bok*, OHG. *bocch* (MHG. *boc*, mod.G. *bock*), ON. *bukkr* (Sw. *bock*, Da. *buk*), all meaning primarily 'he-goat', though in each of the mod. langs. applied to male animals of the deer kind (in Da. also to the ram):—OTeut. *bukko-z. This was adopted (only in the sense 'he-goat') in F. *bouc*, Pr., Cat. *boc*, OSp. *buco* (Diez); also, in same sense, as Welsh *bwch*, Ir., Gael. *boc*. The extended form represented by

OE. *bucca* (:—OTeut. *bukkon-) appears to exist in ON. *bokki* 'my good fellow, old buck' (Vigf.), but is otherwise peculiar to English. (With OTeut. *bukko- Fick compares Zend *bûza* he-goat, also Skr. *bukka* he-goat; but the Teutonic does not phonetically correspond to these. Franck thinks it doubtful whether the word is native Teutonic, or rather an early adoption from some other language.)]

1. The male of several animals.

†**a.** The he-goat. *Obs.* exc. *U.S.* Phrase, ***to blow the buck's horn***: to have his labour for his pains.

a **1000** ÆLFRIC *Lev.* v. 23 Gif se ealdor synȝaþ, bringaþ anne buccan to bote. *c* **1000** *Sax. Leechd.* I. 348 Firȝin buccan þæt ys wudu bucca oððe gat. *a* **1131** *O.E. Chron.* an. 1127 Ða huntes..ridone on swarte hors and on swarte bucces. *c* **1200** *Trin. Coll. Hom.* 37 Sume men leden here lif alse get oþer buckes. *c* **1386** CHAUCER *Milleres T.* 201 Absolon may blowe the bukkes horn. **1387** TREVISA *Higden* (1865) I. 265 A peple þat..beeþ i-cloþed in goot bukkes skynnes. **1551** TURNER *Herbal* I. (1568) 59 What hath a whyte fruite..to do with the lykenes of a bukkes bearde? **1869** C. L. BRACE *New West* xviii. 237 In the fall of 1861, W. Landrum obtained two bucks from a grower in the State of Georgia.

b. The male of the fallow-deer. (In early use perh. the male of any kind of deer.) ***buck of the first head, great buck*** (see quot. 1774).

a **1000** ÆLFRIC *Gloss.* in Wr.-Wülcker 119 *Ceruus* uel *eripes*, heortbuc. *a* **1240** *Cuckoo Song* 10 Bulluc sterteþ, bucke uerteþ. **1393** GOWER *Conf.* I. 45 She sigh..The buck, the doo, the hert. *c* **1440** *Promp. Parv.* 55 Buk, best, *dama*. **1588** SHAKS. *L.L.L.* IV. ii. 10 The Deare..was a Bucke of the first head. **1624** CAPT. SMITH *Virginia* I. 3 He sent vs commonly euery day a brace of Bucks. **1774** GOLDSMITH *Nat. Hist.* II. v. (1862) I. 329 The buck is called..the fifth year, a buck of the first head; and the sixth, a great buck.

c. The male of certain other animals resembling deer or goats, as the reindeer, chamois; in S. Africa (after Du. *bok*) any animal of the antelope kind. Also the male of the hare, the rabbit (the female being called the *doe*, after analogy of b), and (in quot. 1904) the ferret.

a **1674** MILTON *Hist. Mosc.* ii. (1851) 484 Being drawn on Sleds with Bucks. **1741** *Compl. Fam.-Piece* II. i. 300 They [rabbits] are distinguished by the Names of Bucks and Does; and the Males are usually call'd Jack Hares. **1879** ATCHERLEY *Boërland* 147 We..came repeatedly across large numbers of buck. **1904** *Westm. Gaz.* 11 Oct. 3/1 An old buck broken out of bounds is selfishly disposed.

d. A ram. Also *attrib. U.S.*

1812 *Niles' Reg.* II. 240/1 The product [of wool] was as follows: a Buck (*Judas*) 12 lbs. 4 oz. **1852** *Trans. Mich. Agric. Soc. 1851* III. 95 Sheep... Best buck over 2 years old. *Ibid.* 96 A lot consisting of 1 buck, 3 ewes, 10 ewe lambs and 2 buck lambs. **1948** *Daily Ardmoreite* (Okla.) 25 June 2/2 Choice native spring lambs 29.00; bucks out at 28.00.

e. A short vaulting-horse in a gymnasium. Cf. BUCK *sb.*[7]

1932 T. MCDOWELL *Vaulting* v. 23 The hands may be placed on the buck at the finish of the vault. **1952** LD. JUSTICE SINGLETON in *All England Law Rep.* II. 790 He split up the class into four parts, and the infant plaintiff was one of a party of ten who were vaulting over what is called a 'buck'. **1978** *Daily Mail* 30 Nov. 34/1 How many awful moments when once again I stuck on the top of the buck, to the loud laughter of all those lucky girls who leapfrogged so effortlessly every time.

2. *transf.* Applied to a man (in various associations).

1303 R. BRUNNE *Handl. Synne* 3212 Þese berdede buckys also..leue crystyn mennys acyse.

b. A gay, dashing fellow; a dandy, fop, 'fast' man. Used also as a form of familiar address.

In the 18th c. the word indicated rather the assumption of 'spirit' or gaiety of conduct than elegance of dress; the latter notion comes forward early in the present century, and still remains, though the word is now somewhat *arch.*

1725 *New Cant. Dict.*, *Buck*, as, *A bold Buck*, is sometimes used to signify a forward daring Person of either Sex. **1747** GRAY in Gosse *Gray* (Eng. Men Lett.) 90 The fellowcommoners—the bucks—are run mad. **1751** FIELDING *Amelia* x. ii, A large assembly of young fellows whom they call bucks. **1763** *Brit. Mag.* IV. 261 The libertine supposes it [wisdom] consists in debauchery..the buck and blood, in breaking windows. **1824** W. IRVING *T. Trav.* I. 341 The dashing young buck, driving his own equipage. **1854** THACKERAY *Newcomes* I. 82, I remember you a buck of bucks when that coat first came out to Calcutta. **1880** L. STEPHEN *Pope* i. 12 Proud..at being taken by the hand by this elderly buck.

c. *slang.* (see quot.)

1851 MAYHEW *Lond. Labour* 362 (Hoppe) The bucks are unlicensed cabdrivers who are employed by those who have a license to take charge of the cab while the regular drivers are at their meals. **1865** *Morning Star* 14 Sept., What is the prisoner? Constable: He is a 'buck', who hangs about an omnibus stand.

d. A man: applied to native Indians of S. America, and to any male Indian, Negro, or Aboriginal. So ***buck Aborigine, Indian, Maori, Negro, nigger***. Also (illogically) ***buck-woman***. Chiefly *U.S.*

1800 J. MCKENZIE *Jrnl.* 9 Apr. in L. R. Masson *Les Bourgeois* (1890) II. 385, I..kept the woman to be disposed of in the season when the Peace River bucks look out for women. **1806** PINCKARD *Notes West Indies* II. 405 The accuracy of the Bucks, in shooting with the long arrow, and in blowing the short poisoned one. **1835** *Gentleman's Vade-Mecum* (Phila.) 17 Jan. 3/6 A buck nigger is worth the slack of two or three hundred dollars. **1840** C. F. HOFFMANN *Greyslaer* II. xii. 54 There they lay on the grass, six big buck Injuns, likely fellows all. **1853** *Southern Lit. Messenger* XIX. 221/2 A big buck negro. **1857** W. CHANDLESS *Visit Salt Lake* I. 98 You could not mistake a squaw for a buck Indian. **1879** BODDAM-WHETHAM *Roraima* 123 Stepping timidly along may also be seen two or three 'bucks', as the natives of the interior are called. **1879** H. R. MIGHELS *Sage Brush Leaves* 167 The buck aborigine takes more solid comfort than the female of his tribe. **1883** *Congress. Rec.* June 4147/1, I told the boys that we wanted 20,000 'bucks', buck niggers, in Indiana this year. **1884** *Leisure H.* Jan. 63/2 'Buck' here [British Guiana] is the name for the South American Indian. **1933** F. E. BAUME *Half-Caste* 23 Four bucks from Raglan came in drunk and there was a fight. **1941** BAKER *N.Z. Slang* vi. 55 A *buck Maori*, a large well-built native (a somewhat unwarranted construction on *buck nigger*). **1951** E. MITTELHÖLZER *Shadows move among Them* i. iii. 20 His black smooth Buck hair seemed to gleam. **1958** J. CAREW *Wild Coast* xix. 234 Don't talk to me about that Buck-woman. **1964** *People* (Australia) 16 Dec. 2/1 The bucks..strike large boulders said to be the petrified forms of the dingo slayers.

3. *Comb.* **a.** appositive, indicating sex, as ***buck-fawn, -goat, -rabbit, -rat***; **b.** objective with vbl. sb., as ***buck-hunting***; **c.** parasynthetic, as ***buck-hafted*** (for *buck-horn-hafted*); **buck-ague** (also ***buck-fever***) *N. Amer.*: see quot. 1872; **buck-brush** *N. Amer.*, one or other variety of brush on which deer feed; **buck-bush** *U.S.*, 'a species of *Symphoricarpos*, also a buckbrush' (D.A.); also applied to various Australian shrubs; †**buck-hide, -hid, -hood**, the game of 'hide and seek'; **buck-pot** (cf. sense 2 d), an earthenware pot found in parts of Guyana; **buck-rake**, a large rake for farm use, freq. fixed to a vehicle (orig. *U.S.*); **buck rarebit**, a Welsh rabbit served with a poached egg on top. Also BUCK-EYE, -HORN, -HOUND, -JUMP, -SHOT, -SKIN, -TOOTH, etc.

1844 G. W. KENDALL *Santa Fé Exped.* I. 172 There is a very common disease prevalent among young and inexperienced hunters in Texas, which is known as the '*buck ague'. **1872** SCHELE DE VERE *Americanisms* 208 The *buck*..makes him speak of *buck ague*, or *buck fever* when he wishes to describe the nervous agitation of the inexperienced sportsman. **1894** *Outing* (U.S.) XXIV. 344/1 My confusion..was the direct result of buck-ague. **1933** F. B. WILLOUGHBY *Alaskans All* 146 An instant's 'buck ague', a single quiver of the arm, and there would have been a wounded beast in the boat. **1874** J. W. LONG *Amer. Wild-fowl Shooting* ix. 152 Hang up your cartridge bag on a branch of the *buck-brush. **1969** *Islander* (Victoria, B.C.) 22 June 2/3 Leather facing on both [trouser] legs keeps thorns, buck brush and thistle from drawing blood. **1911** C. E. W. BEAN *'Dreadnought' of Darling* xxix. 246 We knew it was a lake because of the line of *buck-bush—low tufted shrubs the colour and shape of big cabbages in a Chinaman's garden—that grew along the bed of it. **1918** S. S. VISHER *Geogr. S. Dakota* 93 The buck-bush, is a transition stage between grassland and woodland. **1940** A. UPFIELD *Bushranger of Skies* xi. 125 The growth of buckbush, cotton- and flannel-bush. **1859** TODD *Cycl. Anat. & Phys.* V. 517/2 At the second year the *'buck-fawn' or 'pricket' puts forth a simple 'dag'. **1841** *S. Lit. Messenger* VII. 224/2 If you see a deer..you'll be sure to git the *buck fever. **1955** C. S. FORESTER *Good Shepherd* 57 He shared the tenseness of the others... He knew that hand would tremble if he allowed it to; this was buck-fever, unmistakably. *c* **1615** CHAPMAN *Odyss.* IX. 340 Rams, and *buck-goates. **1815** KIRBY & SP. *Entomol.* (1843) I. 333 [Resembling]..even to the very handles *Buck-hafted carving knives. *c* **1450** HENRYSON *Mor. Fab.* 13 Whiles would he wink, and play with her *buk-hide. *a* **1568** in Sibbald's *Chron. Sc. Poetry* III. 237 (JAM.) Scho plaid with me bukhud. **1664** KILLIGREW *Parson's Wed.* II. ii, A *buck-hunting-nag. **1741** *Compl. Fam.-Piece* II. i. 293 The same Dogs are used in Buck-hunting. **1851** *Illustr. Catal. Gt. Exhib.* IV. I. 986/2 *Buck pot, used in preparing pepper pot. **1838** *Knickerbocker* XI. 447 Your land is so poor that a single *buck-rabbit would make a famine in your whole country. **1915** D. H. LAWRENCE *Rainbow* (1916) ii. 66 'Now my young buck-rabbit,' he said. 'Slippy!' **1893** *Funk's Stand. Dict.*, **Buck-rake*, a two-horse hay-rake having horn-like teeth projecting 6 or 8 feet in front for gathering and transferring hay to a stacker. **1958** *Times* 1 July p.i (*caption*) Tractor and buckrake cut out the heavy labour. **1927** LINDSAY & MOTTRAM *Man. Mod. Cookery* 83 **Buck rarebit*. Heat the cheese, milk, and seasoning; pour on to the hot toast. Poach the egg and serve on top of the cheese. **1959** P. BULL *I know the Face* vi. 102 Black coffee with the Buck Rarebits after that ordeal. **1877** *Gd. Words* 11/2 Fierce as a *buck-rat.

4. *ellipt.* = BUCK-SHOT 2. *U.S.*

1845 W. G. SIMMS *Wigwam & Cabin* Ser. II. 107 On using big buck, he numbered two sevens for a load; the small buck, three. **1876** *Fur, Fin & Feather* Sept. 135 The doctor soon drew a bird charge from his gun and loaded it with buck and fired. **1889** *Century Dict.*, *Buck-and-ball*, a cartridge for smooth-bore firearms containing a spherical bullet and three buckshot: now little used.

†**buck**, *sb.*[2] *Obs.* [Abbreviated from the full names BUCK-WHEAT, BUCK-MAST.]

1. = BUCK-WHEAT.

1577 B. GOOGE *Heresbach's Husb.* (1586) 40 b, As soone as your rape seede is of [= off]..you may sowe Bucke. **1610** MARKHAM *Masterp.* I. li. 107 Giuing them a certaine graine which we call bucke. **1807** VANCOUVER *Agric. Devon* (Catalog. Seeds) Buck, or French wheat.

b. ***running buck***: corn bindweed.

1580 BARET *Alv.* B 1424 Renning Bucke or binde corne, a weede so called like vnto withwinde.

2. = BUCK-MAST; beech-mast.

1664 EVELYN *Sylva* (1812) I. 138 In some parts of France they now grind the buck in mills. **1727** BRADLEY *Fam. Dict.* I. s.v. *Beech-tree*.

buck, *sb.*[3] *arch.* and *dial.* Also 6 bucke, bouke, bouck, 9 *dial.* book, bock. [In the sense of 'lye, washing', evidently belonging to BUCK *v.*[1], of which it is perh. a direct derivative. Whether sense 1 'washing-tub' (?) has the same origin, or whether the word in this sense is distinct, and to be referred to OE. *búc*, ? *buc*, 'lagena' (see BOWK) is not evident.]

†**1.** ? A washing tub, a vat in which to steep clothes in lye.

1530 PALSGR. 201/2 Bucke to wasshe clothes in, *cvuier*.

2. Lye in which linen, yarn, or cloth, is steeped or boiled as a first step in the process of buck-washing or bleaching.

[**1530** PALSGR. 200/1 Bouke of clothes, *buée*.] **1560** WHITEHORNE *Ord. Souldiours* (1588) 45 b, Take of ..ashes that haue serued in a buck.. halfe a part. **1615** MARKHAM *Eng. Housew.* II. v. (1668) 139 Give it..a couple of clean Bucks, the next fortnight following. **1721** BAILEY, *Buck*, a Lye made of Ashes. **1808–25** JAMIESON *Dict.*, *Bouk*, a lye made of cow's dung and stale urine or soapy water, in which foul linen is steeped in order to its being cleansed or whitened.

3. A quantity of clothes, cloth, or yarn, put through the process of bucking, in buckwashing or bleaching; the quantity of clothes washed at once, a 'wash'. ***to lay the buck***: to lay to steep in lye. ***to drive the buck***: to carry through the process of bucking.

1532 MORE *Confut. Tindale* Wks. (1557) 428/2 A womanne washeth a bucke of clothes. **1573** TUSSER *Husb.* (1878) 166 Maides, three a clock, knede, lay your bucks, or go brew. **1603** HARSNET *Pop. Impost.* 26 Being one day in the kitchen wringing out a Bucke of Cloathes. **1648** HERRICK *Cheap Laundress*, The laundresses, they envie her good-luck, Who can with so small charges drive the buck. **1719** D'URFEY *Pills* (1872) V. 58 A jolly brown Wench, a-washing of her Buck. **1753** CHAMBERS *Cycl. Supp.* s.v. *Bucking*, To drive a buck of yarn, they first cover the bottom of the bucking tub with fine ashes of the ash-tree, etc. **1862** BARNES *Rhymes Dorset Dial.* I. 159 She can iron up an' vwold A book o' clothes wi young or wold. **1869** BLACKMORE *Lorna D.* xxxii. (ed. 12) 198 She..pointed to the great bock of wash.

†**4.** See quot.: but cf. BUCK *v.*[5], BUCKING[4]. *Obs.*

1683 PETTUS *Fleta Min.* I. (1686) 109 It is better..that the Oars..were brought under the Buck or washing place.

5. *Comb.*, as ***buck-basket, -clothes, -sheet, -vat***; **buck-ashes**, ashes which have served for making lye, formerly used as manure; †**buck-house**, a house for 'bucking' in; **buck-lye** (see quot.) Also BUCK-WASHING.

1563 HYLL *Art Garden.* (1593) xlix, Sage is..to bee couered about with *Bucke ashes. **1598** SHAKS. *Merry W.* III. v. 86 In her inuention..they conuey'd me into a *bucke-basket. **1881** GRANT WHITE *Eng. without & w.* 186 To sprinkle clothes that lay in a large buck-basket. **1623** MABBE *Aleman's Guzman d'Alf.* II. 54, I did not goe dropping through the streets like a basket of *Buck-cloathes. **1620** *Unton Inventories* (1841) 28 In the Wash howse and Well howse one *Bouckfatt. **1738** *Belfast Newsp.* in *Antrim & Down Gloss.* (E.D.S.) 14 A good *buck-house, about 80 feet long, with a well-watered bleaching green. **1632** SHERWOOD, *Bucke-lie, *buee*. **1879** MISS JACKSON *Shropsh. Wd.-bk.*, *Buck-lee*, a lye of wood-ashes obtained from burning green 'brash' or fern, the latter being esteemed the best.

buck (bʌk), *sb.*[4] A large basket used to catch eels; on the river Thames: a wooden framework at a weir, supporting eel-baskets. Also ***eel-buck***, (EEL *sb.* 6), and *attrib.*, as in ***buck gate, -stage***.

1694 *Act 6 & 7 Will. & Mary* c. 16 *Preamble*, For the..convenience of the Navigation [of the Thames] there..are diverse Lockes Weares Buckes Winches..and other Engines. **1791** *Rep. Committees Ho. Comm.* (1803) XIV. 263/2 (*Thames & Isis*) The difficulties made by the millers and fishermen, of drawing their bucks and sluices. **1791** R. MYLNE *2nd Rep. Thames Navig.* 12 Nuneham Wear..is now used as a Fishery only, having a Tumbling, solid Wear, and two sets of Buck Gates. **1798** *Sporting Mag.* XII. 7 Having laid down our bucks in the river Loddon..we missed one. **1851** KINGSLEY *Yeast* iii. 43 The river fell over a high weir, with all its appendages of bucks and hatchways, and eel-baskets. *Ibid.* 53 Help me out along the buck-stage, said Lancelot. **1857–8** *Act 29 & 30 Vict.* lxxxix. Preamb., Certain persons..claim a Right..to fish with Nets or Bucks in Parts of the Thames. **1867** F. FRANCIS *Angling* iii. (1880) 90 Large baskets called 'bucks'. **1902** *Thames Conserv. Bye-Laws Regul. Thames* 32 No person shall without the previous consent of the Conservators erect any new buck or weir.

buck, *sb.*[5] [perh. a form of BOUK, OE. *búc* belly, body, trunk, etc.; cf. senses 1, 2 (if these are genuine, and rightly placed here). But the phonetic history is not clear, though the shortening of long *ú* is found in *suck*:—*súcan*.]

†**1.** ? The body of an animal, a carcase. *Obs.*

1592 *Acts James VI* (1814) 577 (JAM.) Sic derth is rasit in the cuntrie that ane mutton buck is deirar and far surmountis the price of ane boll of quheit.

†**2.** ? Belly. *Obs.*

1607 TOPSELL *Four-f. Beasts* 515 The ventricle [in swine] is large to receive much meat, and to concoct it perfectly, we call it vulgarly the Buck. **1691** [see sense 3].

3. The body of a cart or wagon. *dial.*

1691 RAY *S. & E. Country Wds.*, *Buck* the breast. *Suss.* It is used for the body, or the trunck of the body. 'The buck of a cart', i.e. the body of a cart. **1767** A. YOUNG *Farmer's Lett. People* 273 These waggons..should..have very stout hanging-boards..projecting, about fourteen or sixteen inches from the buck, over the wheels. **1881** EVANS *Leicestersh. Wds.* (E.D.S.) *Buck*, the front part of the body of

a cart or waggon, generally constructed with a ledge at the top called the 'fore-buck'.

4. 'A T-shaped end to the plough-beam, having notches in it for the purpose of regulating the draught of the plough. The "shackle" goes into it to which the horses are yoked.' Miss Jackson *Shropsh. Word-bk.*

1562 *Wills & Inv. N.C.* (1835) 207 J wayne heade shakle, j waynehead yoke..j bucshackill. **1688** HOLME *Armoury* III. viii. 332 The Buck [of a plow] is the iron which the Horses are tyed unto.

5. *Comb.* **buck-cart**, *U.S.*, species of vehicle; **buck-rail** *S.Afr.*, the rail of a buck-wagon; **buck-sail** *S.Afr.* [partial tr. Afrikaans *bokseil*], a large canvas or tarpaulin, esp. one used to cover a buck-wagon; **buck-wagon** *U.S.* and *S.Afr.*, a type of vehicle.

1884 *Chr. World* 7 Aug. 598/3, I have just had a ride in a *buckcart. **1896** H. A. BRYDEN *Tales S. Afr.* viii. 182 The tent I've fastened on to the *buck-rail. **1955** W. ROBERTSON *Blue Wagon* iv. 35 The wagon canted over at an angle with the buckrails below the surface [of the water]. **1882** MRS. HECKFORD *Lady Trader in Transvaal* i. 11 An open buck-waggon..with a tarpaulin, or what is here called 'a *buck-sail', thrown over it to protect the goods. **1961** *Argosy* Mar. 20 Caught in a summer storm with only a buck sail thrown over the cart to protect him from the rain. **1864** WEBSTER, *Buckwagon. **1870** in S. H. Pellissier *J. P. Pellissier van Bethulie* (1956) 662 Buckwagons, (empty,) drawn by 16 Oxen. **1877** G. MCKIERNAN *Jrnl.* 27 June (1954) 121 James' buck wagon broke the king bolt before we got off the place. **1947** H. VAUGHAN-WILLIAMS *Visit to Lobengula 1889* iv. 13 We bought two full-sized buck-wagons, half tented for sleeping in.

†**buck**, *sb.*[6] *Obs. rare.* The action of BUCK *v.*[2]

1610 GUILLIM *Heraldry* III. xiv. (1660) 166 You shall say Hart or Conie goeth to his Buck.

buck, *sb.*[7] *U.S.* [a. Du. *zaag-boc*, G. *sägebock*, or shortly *bock*; the same word as *bock* goat; so F. *chèvre*.] A frame or stand of two crotches connected by bars, serving as a rest for pieces of wood while being cross-cut; a saw-buck.

1817 J. K. PAULDING *Lett. from South* I. 189 He bought himself a buck and saw, and became a redoubtable sawyer. **1839** C. F. BRIGGS *Harry Franco* II. i. 2 There were also wood sawyers sitting listlessly on their bucks.

In *Comb.* **buck-saw**, a heavy kind of frame-saw used with a buck.

buck (bʌk), *sb.*[8] *slang* (orig. and chiefly *U.S.*). [Origin obscure.] A dollar.

1856 *Dem. State Jrnl.* (Sacramento) 3 July 3/2 Bernard, assault and battery upon Wm. Croft, mulcted in the sum of twenty bucks. **1896** ADE *Artie* xii. 106 Jimmy can afford to buy wine at four bucks a throw when he's only getting three a week out o' the job. **1921** *Blackw. Mag.* Aug. 264/2, I wonder if I've done right forking out five bucks. **1927** M. DE LA ROCHE *Jalna* xi. 116 He's afraid some of us will want to borrow a few bucks. **1953** A. BARON *Human Kind* 183 'What did you do before the war?'..'Anythin' fer a buck.' **1968** *Globe & Mail* (Toronto) (Mag.) 17 Feb. 5 If you are a supporter of the profit motive in your own life and good times, blame no one. This is strictly a matter of bucks, like selling meat.

buck (bʌk), *sb.*[9] [Origin obscure.] An article used in the game of poker; *to pass the buck* (see quot. 1887). *U.S.*

1865 *Weekly New Mexican* 14 July 1/3 They draw at the commissary, and at poker after they have passed the 'buck'. **1872** 'MARK TWAIN' *Roughing It* xlvii. 332, I reckon I can't call that hand. Ante and pass the buck. **1887** J. W. KELLER *Draw Poker* 38 They resort to the bold and ludicrous experiment of 'passing the buck'. The 'buck' is any inanimate object, usually knife or pencil, which is thrown into a jack pot and temporarily taken by the winner of the pot. Whenever the deal reaches the holder of the 'buck', a new jack pot must be made.

b. fig. *to pass the buck (to)*, to shift responsibility (to another). *colloq.* (orig. *U.S.*). Hence ***buck-passing*** vbl. sb.; ***buck-passer***, one who passes the buck. ***the buck stops here***: H. S. Truman's phrase for 'the responsibility rests here', i.e. the buck cannot be passed any further (see quot. 1952). orig. *U.S.*

1912 W. IRWIN *Red Button* 341 The Big Commissioner will get roasted by the papers and hand it to the Deputy Comish, and the Deputy will pass the buck down to me, and I'll have to report how it happened. **1932** E. WILSON *Devil take Hindmost* viii. 79 He invariably passes the buck to his subordinates. **1933** E. CUNNINGHAM *Buckaroo* 110 'Why, you lying buck-passer!' cried Dud, indignantly. **1933** *New Republic* 22 Nov. 37/1 *(heading)* Some Expert Buck-Passing. **1952** H. S. TRUMAN *Public Papers, 1952–53* (1966) 1094/2 When the decision is up before you—and on my desk I have a motto which says 'The buck stops here'—the decision has to be made. **1955** A. L. ROWSE *Expansion Eliz. Eng.* x. 404 He [*sc.* Sir Francis Vere] is very good at passing the buck. **1959** *Listener* 15 Jan. 92/1 No one is less a buck-passer than is President de Gaulle. **1963** *Times Lit. Suppl.* 24 May 365/2 A human element of buck-passing and self-exculpation. **1968** A. STORR *Human Aggression* xii. 113 Yet a recent President of the United States found it necessary to have a reminder on his desk that 'The buck stops here' as if he could not quite believe in the reality of his own ultimate responsibility. **1979** *Guardian* 2 May 28/7 Mr Callaghan sought the sympathy of the electorate..'The buck stops here.'

buck (bʌk), *sb.*[10] [f. BUCK *v.*[3]] An act of bucking; the power to buck. Cf. BUCK-JUMP.

a **1877** in *Chicago Tribune* (Bartlett), The *buck* consists of the mustang's springing forward with quick, short, plunging leaps, and coming down stiff-legged [etc.]. **1883** SWEET & KNOX *Through Texas* 69 If there had been any buck in them, it would have developed itself at an early stage in the journey. **1890** L. C. D'OYLE *Notches* 34 In two months from now the worst 'buckers' amongst them will not have a 'buck' left in them. **1908** SOMERVILLE & 'ROSS' *Further Exp. Irish R.M.* v, The white horse got over the ground in bucks like a rabbit. **1941** BAKER *Dict. Austral. Slang* 14 *Buck*, the plunge of a horse in 'bucking'.

b. A try, an attempt. *Austral.* and *N.Z. colloq.*

1913 A. BATHGATE *Sodger Sandy's Bairn* ix. 71 I've a mind to have a buck at this new rush myself. **1941** ALLEY & HALL *Farmer in N.Z.* iv. 104 Readiness to 'try anything once', or to 'give it a buck' when some innovation swims into its ken. **1941** BAKER *Dict. Austral. Slang* 14 *Give it a buck*, make an attempt at (something); to try. Also, 'have a buck at'.

buck (bʌk), *sb.*[11] *slang.* Also **bukh**. [a. Hind. *bak*, Hindi *buk buk*.] Talk, conversation; *spec.* boastful, bragging talk; insolence; esp. in phr. ***old buck***.

1895 MRS. CROKER *Village Tales* (1896) 20 Having a 'bukh' with the elders. **1912** A. NEIL LYONS *Clara* x. 99 We've 'ad enough of your old buck. **1941** *Penguin New Writing* III. 64 Nah then, none o' yer ol' buck, Ernie.

buck, *a.*[1] [The stem of BUCK *v.*[1] used *attrib.* = bucking.] Of rain: Soaking, heavy.

1759 ELLIS *Pract. Farmer* 19 in Britten *Old Country Wds.* (E.D.S.) Lest the buck rains (as the farmers call them) fall fast and harden the ground.

buck (bʌk), *a.*[2] *U.S. slang.* [Prob. f. BUCK *sb.*[1] 2.] Belonging to the lowest grade of a specific military rank.

1918 H. C. WITWER *Baseball to Boches* iii. 109 Here I am nothin' but a buck private, and I been in the army goin' on four months! **1925** FRASER & GIBBONS *Soldier & Sailor Words* 37 *Buck*,..a U.S. Army term for a Private, a smart soldier—a Buck Private. **1955** H. ROTH *Sleeper* iii. 22 He had acquired the rank of buck sergeant. **1962** *Times* 14 June 15/4 From general officer to buck private.

†**buck**, *v.*[1] *Obs.* exc. *dial.* Also 4 **bouken**, 5 **bowke**, 5–6 **bucke**, **bouck**, 9 *Sc.* **bouk**. [ME. *bouken*, *bowken*, answering to an OE. type **búcian* not found. Cognate words appear both in Teut. and Romanic; cf. OHG. **bûhhen*, MHG. *bûchen*, Ger. *bäuchen*, *beuchen*, LG. *büken*, Sw. *byka*, to steep in lye; Ger. *beuche*, Sw. *byk* lye, a wash of clothes. Also F. *buer*:—L. type **bucāre* to steep in lye, wash clothes, It. *bucata*, Sp. *bugada*, F. *buée* lye, a wash of clothes. The relation of the Teutonic and Romanic words is not settled: Kluge thinks the Teutonic may be original: see also Diez, and cf. BUCK *sb.*[3]]

1. *trans.* To steep or boil in an alkaline lye as a first process in buck-washing, or bleaching.

1377 LANGLAND *P. Plowman* B. XIV. 19 Dowel [shal] wasshen it..Dobet shal beten it and bouken it. **1413** LYDG. *Pylgr. Sowle* I. xxv. (1859) 30 She hadde bathyd, bowkid hym, and strongly wesshen hym. **1530** PALSGR. 472/1 Bucke these shyrtes, for they be to foule to be wasshed by hande. **1562** BULLEYN *Bk. Simples*, &c. 33 a, This venemous herbe ..women use to bucke their clothes with. **1615** MARKHAM *Eng. Housew.* II. v. (1668) 139 Buck it with Lie and green Hemlocks. **1720** *Stow's Surv.* (ed. Strype 1754) I. I. xxvi. 207/2 Juniper ashes to buck their clothes. **1820** *Glenfergus* III. 84 (JAM.) [They] had them [their necks and arms] boukit an' graithed.

2. *transf.* To drench, soak.

1494 FABYAN *Chron.* VII. ccxliii. 284 Fell such plente of water, yᵗ the grounde was therwith..bucked and drowned. **1619** R. HARRIS *Drunkard's Cup* 21 Our brethren..whilest they bee buckt with drinke, and then laid out to be sunn'd and scorned.

buck (bʌk), *v.*[2] [f. BUCK *sb.*[1]] To copulate with; said of male rabbits and some other animals.

1530 PALSGR. 472/1 Konyes buck every moneth. **1575** TURBERV. *Bk. Venerie* lxiii. 178 The Conie..must be bucked againe, for els she will eate vp hir Rabets. **1616** SURFL. & MARKH. *Countr. Farm* 315. **1741** *Compl. Fam.-Piece* II. i. 303.

buck (bʌk), *v.*[3] [f. BUCK *sb.*[1]] *intr.* Of a horse: To leap vertically from the ground, drawing the feet together like a deer, and arching the back. Also *trans. to buck off*, and *refl.* Cf. BUCKJUMP.

1848 H. W. HAYGARTH *Bush Life in Australia* vii. 78 Australian horses have a vicious habit known as 'buck-jumping', or as it is more familiarly called, 'bucking'. **1859** [see BUCKING *vbl. sb.*[3]]. **1880** *Blackw. Mag.* Feb. 164 When a horse bucks heavily. **1881** *Cheq. Career* 38 He bucked me off more times than I can remember. **1923** *Outward Bound* Mar. 408/2 Many ambitious young horses have bucked themselves to a finish without dislodging my cargo.

buck (bʌk), *v.*[4] *U.S.* [perh. from BUCK *sb.*[7]] *trans.* To lay across a log.

1865 *Morning Star* Oct., He also saw men bucked by order of Wirtz for attempting to escape. **1879** TOURGEE *Fool's Err.* 73 Dragging the ministers from the pulpit, bucking them across a log, and beating them.

buck (bʌk), *v.*[5] *Mining.* [Cf. Du. *boken*, *boocken* 'to beat or to strike', Hexham.] *trans.* To break ore very small with a bucker. Cf. BUCKING *vbl. sb.*[4] Also **buck-work** *v.*

1683 PETTUS *Fleta Min.* I. (1686) 243 The flinty copper Oars..may very easily..be buck'd through. **1769** *Nat. Hist.* in *Ann. Reg.* 102 *note*, To buck or buckwork the ore is a technical term among miners for beating or reducing the ore to a small sand. **1846** *Specimens Cornish Dial.* 22 [He] Trudg'd hum fram Bal fram bucking copper ore.

buck (bʌk), *v.*[6] [? corruption of *butt*, associated with BUCK *sb.*[1]] **1.** *trans.* To butt. *dial.* & *U.S.*

1750 ELLIS *Country Housew.* 174 in Britten *Old Country Wds.* (E.D.S.) Many of these kickers are very apt and prone to buck other cows..for which reasons, all cows should have wooden tips fastened to the end of their horns. **1834** M. SCOTT *Cruise Midge* (1863) 170 The pet lamb..was making believe to buck him with its head. **1848–60** in BARTLETT.

2. *intr.* Of persons. Chiefly *fig.* with *against* or *at.* orig. *U.S.*

1857 *San Fransisco Call* 21 May 3/1 They think it hardly worth while to 'buck' against the present law prohibiting the pursuit of their 'science'. **1859** BARTLETT *Dict. Amer.* (ed. 2), *To buck*, used instead of *butt*,..metaphorically of players at football and such games, pugilists, etc. **1870** in SCHELE DE VERE *Amer.* (1872) 327 You'll have to buck at it like a whole team, gentlemen, or you won't hear the whistle near your diggings for many a year. **1900** G. BONNER *Hard-Pan* ii. 41 There's no good bucking against bad luck. **1906** E. DYSON *Fact'ry 'Ands* 76 Well, if we're mostly earth t' begin with, where's ther sense in buckin' at er bit extry on the outside. **1930** J. DEVANNY *Bushman Burke* xvii. 100 The houses were terrible shacks whose shelter..a dog would 'buck at'.

3. *trans.* To butt into or against. Freq. *fig.*, to come up against, find oneself opposed to, oppose. orig. *U.S.*

1861 *Harper's Mag.* July 276/1 Mr. Fusilbury..was in a dream of philosophy, bucking a lamp-post. **1891** C. ROBERTS *Adrift Amer.* 114 There was a snow plough with two engines to it 'bucking the snow' (as the expression goes here). **1904** C. J. STEEDMAN *Bucking the Sagebrush* ii. 14 If any convert..bucked the authority of the Church, he disappeared from his 'sphere of influence'. **1929** *Publishers' Weekly* 14 May 2456/2 It is wasted time and energy to try to buck any legitimate movement, and I think it is time and energy wasted for you men to attempt to buck the book clubs. **1947** *Time* 3 Feb. 68/1 In winter months they buck four to ten foot drifts. **1959** R. COLLIER *City that wouldn't Die* vii. 101 Duty won; you didn't buck an order from the chief of the Luftwaffe.

buck, *v.*[7] *dial.* or *colloq.* [f. BUCK *sb.*[1] 2.] **1.** In ***buck up*** (*trans.*, and *intr.* for *refl.*): To dress up.

1854 DE BONELLI *Travels in Bolivia* I. 28 The young gentlemen of our party began to buck up and tried to outvie each other in doing the amiable. **1875** in *Lanc. Gloss.* (E.D.S.) 60 'Hello, Jim, what art' bucked-up for?'

2. *to buck up.* **a.** *intr.* To cheer up, be encouraged. Also *trans.* in causal sense.

1844 *Graham's Mag.* Jan. 38 'I don't see the trouble,' said Mrs Fitzgig, 'why can't a man buck up?' **1889** BARRÈRE & LELAND *Dict. Slang* s.v., (Winchester College)..to 'buck up' is to be glad. **1890** FARMER *Slang*, *Buck up*, ..(Winchester College), to be glad; pleased... The usual expression is 'Oh buck up', a phrase which at Westminster School would have a very different meaning, namely, ' exert yourself'. **1894** *Punch* 27 Oct. 193/1 Buck up, mate; you've no call to be yaller, nor a perminent bloo, heither! **1901** W. H. LAWSON et al. *Winchester Coll. Notions* 14 *Buck up*, Hurrah! The original meaning, which is still used. Hence later:—Cheer up, hurry up. **1906** B'NESS VON HUTTEN *What became of Pam* II. ix, Don't spoil it all by being weepy... Come, buck up, like a dear, and wish me joy. **1909** H. G. WELLS *Tono-Bungay* II. ii. §1 Never saw her so larky. This has bucked her up something wonderful. **1910** W. J. LOCKE *Simon the Jester* xviii, Now and again one does help a lame dog over a stile which bucks one up, you know. **1926** INGE *Lay Thoughts of a Dean* 233, I asked the medical members ..in particular whether it was impossible that microbic diseases..might be benefited by 'bucking up' the patient. **1966** 'J. HACKSTON' *Father clears Out* 37 As if to buck us up after our recent loss, he promised us poultry on the table.

b. *intr.* To make an effort, to 'brace up'; to hurry up.

1890 [see 2a]. **1909** H. G. WELLS *Tono-Bungay* I. i. §8 It was equally impossible for him to either buck-up and beat me, or give in. **1910** W. J. LOCKE *Simon the Jester* ii, You must buck up a bit, Simon, and get your name better known about the country. **1913** 'IAN HAY' *Happy-go-lucky* i, 'Hallo, you fellows—finished?' 'Yes, buck up!' commanded Rumbold.

buck (bʌk), *v.*[8] *U.S.* [Origin obscure, but cf. BUCK *sb.*[9]] **1.** *intr.* To play at a game of chance. Usu. with *against* or *at.* Also *fig.* Hence ***to buck the tiger*** (see TIGER *sb.* 9 a).

1849 *New Orleans Picayune* 18 May 1/6, I left them 'bucking' away, desiring only once more to 'get even'. **1869** BRET HARTE *Luck of Roaring Camp* (1871) 95 Why don't you say you want to buck agin' Faro? **1872** SCHELE DE VERE *Americanisms* 327 The fact that players at *Three-Card Monte* ..are said to *buck* at monte, causes the familiar phrase of *bucking* at anything. **1898** H. S. CANFIELD *Maid of Frontier* 109 The man who bucks against that kind of game is a fool.

2. *trans.* To bet or lose (money) in gambling.

1851 *Alta California* 8 July (D.A.), The money Percy took to the El Dorado, where he duly bucked it off against a faro bank. **1851** MRS. CLAPPE *Lett. from Calif.* (1922) 121 Little John was..betting, or, to speak technically, 'bucking' away large sums at monte.

buck (bʌk), *v.*[9] *N. Amer.* [f. BUCK *sb.*[7]] To cut (wood) with a buck-saw.

1870 *Philad. Press* 8 Jan., [The] Pennsylvanian does not saw wood; he 'bucks' it. **1905** *Terms Forestry & Logging* (*U.S. Dept. Agric.*) 31 *Buck*, to saw felled trees into logs (Pacific Coast Forest). **1953** *Brit. Commonw. Forest Terminol.* I. 21 *To buck*, to cut felled trees into any required lengths (Canada). **1964** *Times* 18 Sept. 13/7 One lumber executive..can still buck a log. **1969** *Islander* (Victoria, B.C.) 16 Nov. 3/3 The tree had to be bucked into seven lengths varying in size from 10 to 40 feet.

buck (bʌk), *v.*[10] *slang.* Also bukh, bukk. [Cf. BUCK *sb.*[11]] *intr.* To swagger, talk big or bumptiously, brag.

1880 G. ABERIGH-MACKAY *21 Days in India* 164 He *bucks* with a quiet, stubborn determination that would fill an American editor..with despair. **1890** KIPLING *Many Invent.* (1893) 27 You're ordered to *bukh*. **1895** MRS. CROKER *Village Tales* (1896) 157 Those who were wont to assemble..of an evening to smoke, argue, and bukh. **1899** *Daily News* 6 June 8/4 There is not much in this for Etonians to 'buck' about. **1921** *Blackw. Mag.* Apr. 517/2 Arthur and I have 'bukked' till we're hoarse.

buck-and-wing. *U.S.* [? f. BUCK *v.*[3] + WING *v.*] A dance of a lively character, usually performed by one person. Also *attrib.*

1895 *N.Y. Dram. News* 23 Nov. 13/4 Burt Jordon, an exceedingly agile buck and wing dancer. **1907** MULFORD *Bar-20* x. 110 In the centre of the room was a large man dancing a fair buck-and-wing to the time so uproariously set by his companions. *Ibid.* 112 Up by the door Bigfoot Baker, elated at winning the buck-and-wing contest, was endeavouring to learn a new step. *a* **1910** 'O. HENRY' *Rolling Stones* (1916) 192 He heard..the light, stirring staccato of a buck-and-wing dance. **1945** J. J. MATHEWS *Talking to the Moon* 45 He would get up from his chair, wave his great black hat, and do a buck-and-wing on the pine flooring.

buckaroo, buckayro. *U.S.* Also bakhara, buckeroo, buckhara, etc. [Corruption of VAQUERO.] A cowboy. Also *attrib.*

1827 W. B. DEWEES *Let.* 16 Jan. in *Lett. fr. Texas* (1852) 66 These [rancheros] are surrounded by..peons and bakharas, or herdsmen. **1889** *Century Dict.*, *Buckayro*. ..(Western U.S.). **1890** FARMER *Slang*, *Buckhara* (American), a name given in California to a cattle-driver or cowboy. **1904** *N.Y. Tribune* 17 July, He was herding a big bunch of cattle there with the help of half a dozen buckayros. **1907** S. E. WHITE *Arizona Nights* 51 If you were going to be a buckeroo, you couldn't go into harder training. **1910** J. HART *Vigilante Girl* iv. 60, I can talk what they call 'buckayro' Spanish. **1916** H. L. WILSON *Somewhere in Red Gap* iv. 129 Nothing ever did worry that buckaroo as long as his fingers wasn't too cold to roll a cigarette. **1946** MENCKEN *Amer. Lang.* (ed. 4) iv. 152 *Buckaroo* seems to have dropped out.

†ˈ**buckasie.** *Obs. Sc.* Also buckasy, bukkesy. The same as BOCASIN.

1474 *Acc. J. Bp. Glasgow* in Borthwick's *Rem. Brit. Antiq.* 131 (JAM.), 5 quarters of buckasy, for a doublate to littill Bell, 10s. **1478** *Act. Audit.* 83 (JAM.) A doublat of bukkesy. **1485** [see BOCASIN] Bokesye. **1611** *Rates* (JAM.) Buckasie, the haill peece conteining two half peeces, *xl.*

buck-bean (ˈbʌkbiːn). *Herb.* Also 6 buckes beanes. [App. a transl. by Lyte of the Flemish *bocks boonen* 'goat's beans'; cf. mod.Du. *bocksboon*, Ger. *bocksbohne* (1586 in Grimm). (Another name of the plant, of later appearance, is BOG-BEAN, which may be a rationalizing alteration of *buck-bean*, unless, like *bog nut*, *bog trefoil*, it is quite independent in origin.)]

A water plant (*Menyanthes trifoliata*) common in bogs in Britain, and widely diffused over the northern hemisphere; it bears racemes of pinkish white flowers.

1578 LYTE *Dodoens* IV. lxxviii. 542 Of Buckes Beanes—Marrishe Trefoyl..This herbe is called..in Brabant, *Bocxboonen* that is to say Bockes Beanes, bycause it is like the leaues of the common Beane. **1676** *Phil. Trans.* XI. 743 Several men cured of the Gout by a decoction of *Trifolium palustre* (Marsh-trefoil or Buck-beans). **1755** *Gentl. Mag.* 431 Two or three dishes of chocolate..or two dishes of buc-bean tea. **1794** MARTYN *Rousseau's Bot.* xvi. 176 Marsh Trefoil, Buckbean, or Bogbean. **1863** BARING GOULD *Iceland* 191 The broad leaves of the buckbean float on the red water. **1866** *Treas. Bot.* 736 The beautiful Buckbean or Marsh Trefoil..a most desirable acquisition to ornamental ponds.

ˈ**buckboard,** *sb.* orig. and chiefly *U.S.* [BUCK *sb.*[5] 5.]

1. A plank slung upon wheels, forming the body of a light vehicle.

1839 C. F. HOFFMAN *Wild Scenes* I. 10 Did he ever see a teamster riding upon a buckboard? a stout, springy plank, laid upon the bare bolsters of a waggon! **1885** *Sat. Rev.* 21 Feb. 240/1 A buckboard is a plank of well-seasoned wood..slung upon four wheels placed within two feet of either end. Across the middle of the board is a light seat holding two persons. **1947** H. VAUGHAN-WILLIAMS *Visit to Lobengual 1889* v. 23 When on the trek all cooking pots were slung on to the rails of the buckboard of the wagons.

2. A vehicle of this description. Also *Comb.*

1874 'H. CHURTON' *Toinette* (1881) iv. 45 The shivering splattered figure on the 'buck-board'. **1883** *Harper's Mag.* Aug. 390/2 The common road cart..costs $15; the fashionable buckboard, $40. **1886** *Outing* (U.S.) Oct. 57/2 For some reason or other, the buckboard driver, who usually brings us our mail, did not bring it yesterday. **1893** *Daily News* 2 May 5/4 Thence in a buckboard across Wokingham Creek..as far as Bourke..in New South Wales. **1894** C. JOHNSTONE *Winter & Summer in Canada* 64, I hired a 'rig' or 'buckboard' for 3 dollars to take me as far as Carlton. **1935** J. STEINBECK *To God Unknown* 175 He hitched up the buckboard and drove to town. **1953** A. UPFIELD *Murder must Wait* xxv. 217 A buckboard drawn by two horses.

Hence ˈ**buckboard** *v. intr.*, to ride on a buckboard.

1904 F. LYNDE *Grafters* i. 2 Two men who buckboarded in ahead of the track-layers.

buckbuck, see BOOBOOK.

ˈ**buck dance.** *U.S.* = BUCK-AND-WING. Hence *buck dancer, dancing.*

1840 *Spirit of Times* 2 May 103/2 The extra clearing in turn for the finishing buck dance. **1896** *N.Y. Dram. News* 29 Aug. 8/3 Conwell and O'Day, buck dancers, made a gigantic hit. **1897** ADE *Pink Marsh* 73, I use' to know cullud boy..'at got job on 'e stage doin' buck-dancin'. **1933** P. GODFREY *Back-Stage* xv. 187 The girls in these troupes have to undergo a hard training in widely different types of dancing: buck, ballet, tap, and acrobatic.

†**bucked,** *ppl. a.*[1] *Obs.* exc. *dial.* [f. BUCK *v.*[1] + -ED.] That has been buck-washed.

1652 URQUHART *Jewel* Wks. (1834) 230 He came out with a long gray beard and a bucked ruff.

bucked (bʌkt), *ppl. a.*[2] *colloq.* [f. BUCK *v.*[7] + -ED[1].] Cheered, encouraged, elated.

1907 *Varsity* 31 Jan. 194/3 We are very 'bucked' that he fitted in a visit this Term. **1909** SLADEN *Trag. Pyramids* i. 15 So bucked at being with you again. **1922** A. A. MILNE *Red House Myst.* vii. 61 He was unusually bucked with himself this morning. **1928** *Punch* 23 May 562/2 I am so bucked that you have asked me what to wear when you are accompanying at the concert next month. **1969** *Listener* 1 May 596/3 I'm pleased and bucked and I feel pretty good.

buckeen[1] (bʌˈkiːn). *Anglo-Irish.* [f. BUCK *sb.*[1] 2 + -EEN, dim. suffix; cf. *squireen.*] A young man belonging to the 'second-rate gentry' of Ireland, or a younger son of the poorer aristocracy, having no profession, and aping the habits of the wealthier classes.

1793 S. CRUMPE *Essay, Empl. People* 181 Those nuisances ..to every rank of society..bucks and buckeens. **1812** MAR. EDGEWORTH *Absentee* vii, Squireens..a race of men who have succeeded to the Buckeens. **1851** THACKERAY *Eng. Hum.* vi. (1858) 320 After College, he..lived for some years the life of a buckeen.

buckeen[2] (bʌˈkiːn). [ad. Guiana Du. **bokin*, fem. of *bok* goat, buck (see BUCK *sb.*[1] 2 d).] A female aboriginal Indian in Guiana.

1806 PINCKARD *Notes West Indies* II. 405 The morning was..spent..in hearing M. Heynemann relate his adventures among the Indians; whom he termed Bucks and Buckeen. **1868** W. H. BRETT *Ind. Tribes Guiana* 34 *note*, The Indian men and women were called by the Dutch 'Bucks' and 'Buckeens'. **1899** J. RODWAY *In Guiana Wilds* 39 They called her a 'buckeen'; how much prettier than the word squaw.

Buckelkeramik (ˈbʌk(ə)lkəˌræmɪk). *Archæol.* [G., lit. 'knobbed ware'.] A type of late Bronze Age pottery with protruding decorative knobs.

[**1902** W. DÖRPFELD et al. *Troja und Ilion* II. vii. 201 Für die Festsetzung der oberen Grenze ist die Zeit der..VIII. Schicht massgebend, weil die frühgeometrischen Topfwaaren und ebenso die Buckelkeramik keine genaue Datirung gestatten.] **1929** V. G. CHILDE *Danube in Prehist.* xiii. 261 *Buckelkeramik*. The commonest [Hungarian Bronze Age] pottery is the distinctive 'Tószeg wart ware' (*Buckelkeramik*, Figs. 162–3). **1937** *Amer. Jrnl. Archæol.* XLI. 46 Debris..dated by many fragments of *Buckelkeramik* to the period VII b [*i.e.* at Troy]. **1940** *Ann. Brit. Sch. Athens 1936–7* XXXVII. 11 The sudden appearance of Buckelkeramik at Troy now indicates an abrupt change in foreign contacts. **1950** H. L. LORIMER *Homer & Monum.* i. 36 Then came the intrusion from Europe of a new population, who brought with them a culture of the Lausitz type with its characteristic *Buckelkeramik*.

bucker[1] (ˈbʌkə(r)). [f. BUCK *v.*[3] + -ER[1].] A horse given to bucking.

1884 *Harper's Mag.* July 301/1 If we should..select 'a bucker', the probabilities are that we will come to grief.

ˈ**bucker**[2]. *Mining.* [f. BUCK *v.*[5]] A hammer used in bucking ore (see quot.).

1653 MANLOVE *Rhymed Chron.* 261 Break-offs, and Buckers, Randum of the Rake. **1747** HOOSON *Miner's Dict.* H ij b, A mixture of Stone..with the Ore..goes under the Bucker, and then it yeilds good Smitham. **1851** TAPPING *Gloss. Derbysh. Min. T.* (E.D.S.) *Bucker*..consists of a flat piece of iron about the size of a man's open hand; at the back of it is a broad ring, through which is thrust a piece of wood for a handle.

ˈ**bucker**[3]. *N. Amer.* [f. BUCK *v.*[9]] One who saws trees into logs.

1900 *Treasurer's Bur. Statistics* Nov. 1116, A logging crew consists of..2 swampers, 2 buckers, [etc.]. **1956** *Amer. Speech* XXXI. 149 *Bucker*, a logger who saws felled trees into log lengths. **1963** *Times* 24 Jan. 11/6 The aristocrats, the fallers and buckers, often make £15 [a day].

buckeram(e, -erom, obs. ff. BUCKRAM.

†ˈ**buckerels.** *Obs.* (See quot.)

1649 LD. HERBERT *Hen. VIII*, 68 Two Apprentices playing onely at Buckerels in the street late on May-eve. **1681** BLOUNT *Glossogr.*, *Buckerels*, a kind of play used by Boys in London Streets, in H. 8 time; now disused, and forgot.

ˈ**buckery.** *nonce-wd.* [f. BUCK *sb.*[1] + -ERY.] Bucks or swells, collectively or as a class.

1804 SOUTHEY in C. Southey *Life* II. 284 The whole mob of Park Loungers and Kensington Garden buckery.

buckesome, obs. form of BUXOM.

bucket (ˈbʌkɪt), *sb.*[1] Forms: 3–4 **bocket(t**, 4 **bukket**, 4–6 **boket(t**, 5 **buket(t**, 5–6 **buckette**, 3– **bucket**. [Etymology uncertain: app. a. OF. *buket* washing tub, milk-pail (Godef. s.v. *buquet*); cf. OE. *búc* 'lagena', BOWK.]

1. a. 'The vessel in which water is drawn out of a well.' **b.** 'The vessels in which water is carried, particularly to quench a fire.' (J.)

Buckets were formerly made of leather or wood; now of various materials, esp. metal or plastics. They are used as containers for many things. The local application of the word varies greatly: in the south-east of England and in U.S. a bucket is a round wooden pail with arched handle; in south of Scotland it is a 4-sided wooden vessel for carrying salt, coal, ashes, etc.

a **1300** *Cursor M.* 3306 Wantes vs here..Ne mele, ne bucket, ne funell. **1382** WYCLIF *Isa.* xl. 15 As a drope of a boket. **1423** JAS. I *King's Q.* 70 As Tantalus..Water to draw wᵗ buket botemles. *c* **1440** *Promp. Parv.* 42 Bokett, *situla, mergus.* **1552–3** *Inv. Ch. Goods Staffs.* 12 A pix of masten, a bokett of brasse, vj alter cloths. **1593** SHAKS. *Rich. II*, IV. i. 185 Like a deepe Well, That owes two Buckets, filling one another, The emptier euer dancing in the ayre, The other downe, vnseene, and full of Water. **1611** BIBLE *Pref.* 4 Like children at Iacobs well..without a bucket. **1720** GAY *Poems* (1745) I. 225 Fetch the leathern bucket that hangs in the belfry. **1822** SCOTT *Nigel* xxii, There are fagots and a bucket of sea-coal in the stone-chest. **1852** *Leisure Hour* 632 The blocks of stone which contain the ore are brought up in buckets. **1895** *Army & Navy Co-op. Soc. Price List* 427/1 India Rubber Bucket, Rope Handle... Canvas Bucket. **1907** *Ibid.* 181/1 Fire Buckets.., tinned steel, with iron handles, painted red and lettered. **1922** JOYCE *Ulysses* 102 A server, bearing a brass bucket with something in it, came out through a door. *Ibid.* 348 The rain falling on the rusty bucket. **1969** *Sears, Roebuck Catal.* 1269/1 Ice bucket.. made of easy-clean vinyl with a clear plastic cover.

c. Phrase, ***to give the bucket to***: to dismiss; cf. *give the bag, the sack.* ***to kick the bucket***: see BUCKET *sb.*[2].

1863 MRS. GASKELL *Sylvia's L.* II. 122 He were sore put about because Hester had gi'en him the bucket.

2. The piston of an ordinary lift-pump.

1634 BATE *Myst. Nat. & Art* 9 If you lift the sweepe, it will thrust downe the bucket upon the water. **1659** LEAK *Water-wks.* 17 The Sucker..sustains the Water when the Buckets or Suckers of the Pumps are not lifted up. **1822** IMISON *Sc. & Art* I. 183 This piston is then called the bucket.

3. a. One of the compartments on the circumference of a water-wheel, which retain the water while they descend; one of the scoops of a dredging machine; one of the series of metal cups on the endless band of a grain-elevator.

1759 SMEATON in *Phil. Trans.* LI. 133 If a stream of water falls into the bucket of an overshot wheel, it is there retained till the wheel by moving round discharges it. **1812** PLAYFAIR *Nat. Phil.* (1819) I. 217 The momentum of the water in the buckets is equal to the momentum of the resistance. **1831** LARDNER *Hydrostatics* x. 198 On the rim of the wheel..a number of cavities, called buckets, are constructed.

b. A scoop operated by power, used for hoisting coal, grain, etc., and in dredging and excavating.

a **1877** KNIGHT *Dict. Mech.*, *Bucket*, (3) The scoop of a dredging machine. **1881** [see GRAB *sb.*[2] 4]. **1902** *Encycl. Brit.* XXVII. 531/2 Grabs or buckets for dredging purposes.

4. *transf.* †**a.** A cooler over an alembic. **b.** A leathern socket or rest for the whip in driving, or for the carbine or lance as part of cavalry equipment. **c.** The socket for the stump in an artificial leg or arm. **d.** A canvas-covered frame used as a signal for boats. **e.** Applied to the 'pitcher' in certain orchids.

1594 PLAT *Jewell-ho.* II. 3 The bucket, or cooler in the head [of the Limbeck]. **1833** *Regul. Instr. Cavalry* I. 103 Draw the carbine from the bucket *Ibid.* 161 The lance is to rest with the butt-end in the bucket on the right stirrup. **1863** WHYTE MELVILLE *Ins. Bar* (ed. 12) 250, I put the whip in the bucket, and drove steadily on. **1871** TYNDALL *Fragm. Sc.* (ed. 6) II. ix. 178 A bucket, with an aperture like a spout, is formed in an orchid.

5. *Rowing.* [f. BUCKET *v.* 5.] 'A plunge forward with the body when the stroke is concluded before the arms have been straightened out, and the hands at least passed the knees' (*Encycl. Sport*).

1888 W. B. WOODGATE *Boating* iv. 70 Lateness in swing may arise *per se*, and so may a 'bucket'. **1898** R. P. P. ROWE et al. *Rowing* 35 The swing forward should be kept as slow as is reasonably possible, and a 'bucket' avoided.

6. *Comb.*, as **bucket bag**, a woman's bag, resembling a bucket in shape; **bucket chain,** (*a*) a chain linked to a bucket; (*b*) a line of persons formed to pass buckets of water or sand to a conflagration; **bucket-door**, the cover of an opening which gives access to the buckets of a pump; **bucket dredge, dredger**, a dredge that excavates by means of scoops or buckets; so ***bucket-dredging*** vbl. sb.; **bucket-elevator** [ELEVATOR 3 a], a chain of buckets for raising material or liquids to a higher level; **bucket-engine**, a machine having buckets attached to an endless chain running over sprocket-wheels, so as to utilize the power of a small stream of water with a good fall; †**bucket-fountain**, a means of raising water with buckets; **bucket-hook** (U.S.), a contrivance for attaching a bucket to the sugar-maple tree, for the purpose of catching the sap; **bucket-ladder** (see quot. 1877); **bucket-lift**, a set of iron pipes attached to a lift-

pump; **bucket-pump**, a lift-pump; **bucket-rod**, a rod carrying the piston of a lift-pump; **bucket-rope** (see quot.); **bucket-seat**, in a motor-car, aeroplane, etc., a seat partly resembling a bucket in shape; **bucket-valve**, a round valve employed in the air-pump of a steam-engine; **bucket-well**, a well from which the water is drawn by a bucket; **bucket-wheel**, an ancient contrivance for raising water, consisting of buckets fixed round a wheel, or attached to a rope passing round a wheel, which fill at the bottom and empty themselves into a trough at the top; also, an overshot or breast wheel operated by the impulse and weight of the water falling into the buckets or receptacles on its rim.

1956 'J. BELL' *Death in Retirement* iv. 49 Mrs. Weaver produced a fat envelope from her *bucket bag. **1959** *Woman* 31 Oct. 74/3 Her hand crept down to take a purse from the open bucket bag. **1911** *Daily Colonist* (Victoria, B.C.) 21 Apr. 14/3 It was expected the dredger would be ready about a week ago but the *bucket chain slipped and some time was occupied in replacing this. **1932** *Daily Express* 28 June 1/2 When one fire brigade failed, the village girls.. assisted the men in a 'bucket chain' until another brigade arrived. **1797** J. CURR *Coal Viewer* 74 Cross Bars and Bolts for *Bucket and Clack *Doors. **1907** *Jrnl. Soc. Arts* LV. 1009/1 The gold may rest in crevices, from which the *bucket dredge could not collect it. **1902** *Encycl. Brit.* XXVII. 530/2 Where it is necessary to finish off the dredging work to a uniform flat bottom.. *bucket dredgers are better adapted. **1930** *Engineering* 15 Aug. 195/3 The bucket dredger is the only type which has been uniformly successful from the time of its introduction. **1898** *Engineering Mag.* XVI. 116/1 The *bucket-dredging-apparatus. **1903** *Chambers's Jrnl.* 30 May 415/2 The grain is then lifted by a *bucket-elevator to the upper deck. **1930** *Engineering* 25 July 102/3 The function of the bucket elevators.. on the main washing plant.. will thus be understood. **1655** MRQ. WORCESTER *Cent. Inv.* Index 3 A *Bucket-fountain [How to raise water constantly with two Buckets onely—art. 21]. **1877** *Encycl. Brit.* VII. 464/2 The main feature of the machine [*sc.* steam dredger] is the *bucket-ladder... Along this ladder a series of buckets traverse which cut into the bottom.. and return loaded with the excavated material. **1902** *Ibid.* XXVII. 529/1 Bucket-Ladder Dredgers. **1627** CAPT. SMITH *Seaman's Gram.* vi. 27 The *Bucket rope that is tied to the Bucket by which you hale and draw water vp by the ships side. **1630** J. TAYLOR (Water P.) *Navy of Landships* Wks. I. 81/1 The Guestrope, Bucketrope, and Porterope.. were all of rare stuffes of great price. **1908** *Westm. Gaz.* 29 Oct. 4/1 One is fitted with a luxurious body and the other left bare with two *bucket-seats. **1943** *Jrnl. R. Aeronaut. Soc.* XLVII. Abstr. 212 The prone position is less tiring [to the pilot] than the normal bucket seat. **1958** *Vogue* June 129 Individual bucket seats are ideal since they allow drivers to adjust them to their own requirements. **1813** *Examiner*, 11 Jan. 22/1 The female was found in a *bucket well. **1797** *Encycl. Brit.* XVIII. 904/1 A *bucket-wheel has been executed lately.. of a construction entirely new. **1880** *Ibid.* XII. 523/1 When.. the supply is from 3 to 25 cubic feet per second, it is possible to construct a bucket wheel on which the water acts chiefly by its weight. **1970** *Times* 23 Feb. (Canada Suppl.) p. vi/3 (*caption*) A giant bucket-wheel excavator scooping up oil-bearing tar sands.

'bucket, *sb.*² [Perhaps a. OF. *buquet*, 'trébuchet, balance' Godef. It is uncertain whether quot. 1597, and the proverbial phrase, relate to this word or the prec.] A beam or yoke on which anything may be hung or carried.

1570 LEVINS *Manip.* 86 A Bucket, beame, *tollo.* **1597** SHAKS. *2 Hen. IV*, III. ii. 283 Swifter then hee that gibbets on the Brewers Bucket. *Mod. Newspaper.* The beam on which a pig is suspended after he has been slaughtered is called in Norfolk, even in the present day, a 'bucket'. Since he is suspended by his heels, the phrase to 'kick the bucket' came to signify to die.

Hence (perhaps) ***to kick the bucket***; (*slang*) to die.

1785 GROSE *Dict. Vulgar Tongue, To kick the bucket*, to die. **1806** WOLCOTT (P. Pindar) *Tristia* Wks. 1812 V. 242 Pitt has kicked the bucket. **1810** TANNAHILL *Poems* (1846) 57 Till time himsel' turn auld and kick the bucket. **1840** MARRYAT *Poor Jack* xxx, He drained it dry.. and 'kicked the bucket'. **1850** KINGSLEY *Alt. Locke* ii..

bucket ('bʌkɪt), *v.* [f. BUCKET *sb.*¹]

1. *trans.* To lift (water) in buckets; also with *out*, *up*. Also *fig.*

1649 *Wandering Jew, Alderman's F.* (1857) 21 Deepe wells by continuall bucketting the water out, are in the end drawne dry. **1872** A. J. ELLIS in *Philol. Soc. Trans.* (1873) 31 The Greek, that great well whence we bucket up our abstract terms.

2. a. To pour buckets of water over; to drench.

1621 BURTON *Anat. Mel.* II. ii. II. (1651) 239 He would have his patient.. to be bucketed, or have the water powred on his head. *a* **1670** HACKET *Abp. Williams* II. 194 Wo be to him whose head is bucketed with waters of a scalding bath.

b. *intr.* Of rain, etc.: to pour down heavily.

1926 *Chambers's Jrnl.* Dec. 844/1 Tramps don't walk about a marsh in bucketing rain in the midnight hours. **1970** *Woman* 21 Feb. 45/1 She stood, umbrella-less.. not even a headscarf between her and the bucketing sky.

3. *slang.* To cheat, swindle.

1812 J. H. VAUX *Flash Dict.* s.v., To bucket a person is synonymous with putting him in the well. **1828** SCOTT *Diary* in *Lockhart* (1839) IX. 253 Thurtell.. must in slang phrase have bucketed his pals.

4. To ride (a horse) hard, reckless of his fatigue; to 'pump' (take it out of him by bucketfuls). Also, to move or drive (a vehicle, etc.) roughly or jerkily. Also *intr.*

1856 [see BUCKETING *vbl. sb.* 2]. **1868** TOTTENHAM *C. Villars* I. 243 Bucketing his wretched horse home to Cambridge. **1879** L. S. WINGFIELD *My Lords of Strogue* iv, He.. was painfully alive to the possibility of finding his daughter stolen one day,.. to be bucketed about the country without a change of linen till his reluctant consent was wrung. **1904** *Westm. Gaz.* 13 Dec. 10/2 He.. was bucketed about the garrisons from the Canadas and Cape Breton to the Mediterranean. **1911** C. E. W. BEAN *'Dreadnought' of Darling* i. 10 The coach bumped and bucketed over boulders. **1921** *Blackw. Mag.* Feb. 233/1 Poor preparation.. for bucketing about the Baltic all the following day. **1922** *Chambers's Jrnl.* 437/2 The envious beggar.. buckets his old boat along for nothing. **1944** *Jrnl. R. Aeronaut. Soc.* XLVIII. 276 There is little tendency to swing or bucket. *Ibid.* 280 The aircraft can be taxied fast without danger of bucketing.

5. *Rowing. intr.* To hurry the forward swing of the body preparatory to taking the stroke; also *trans.*, as ***to bucket the recovery***; and *causally*, ***to bucket an oarsman*** or ***crew***.

1869 [see BUCKETING *ppl. a.*] **1876** BESANT & RICE *Gold. Butterfly* xv. 130 He was not so straight in the back as an Oxford stroke; and he bucketed about a good deal, but he got along. **1882** *St. James's Gaz.* 15 Mar. 6/2 Smith shows a considerable tendency to bucket the recovery. **1884** *Ibid.* 25 Jan. 6/2 Style and form are best taught to men if they are not bucketed. *Mod.* (*Oxford Coach*)—'Don't bucket your bodies'! They *bucketed* over the course: they rowed a bucketing stroke.

'bucketed, *a.* [f. BUCKET *sb.*¹] Having the form of a bucket.

1886 BRET HARTE *Snow-bound* 124 A vast niche or bucketed shelf in the hollow flank of the mountain.

bucketful ('bʌkɪtfʊl). [f. BUCKET *sb.*¹ + -FUL.] As much as a bucket will hold. Also *transf.* and quasi-*adv.*

a **1563** BECON *New Catech.* (1844) 39 All people are in comparison of him as a drop to a bucket-full. **1656** TRAPP *Comm. Matt.* vii. 11 He will pour out.. as it were by pails or buckets fuls. **1843** *Spirit of Times* 30 Sept. 366/3 The rain.. came pouring down in buckets-full. **1856** KANE *Arct. Expl.* I. xv. 165 A stove, glowing with at least a bucketful of anthracite. **1892** C. M. YONGE *That Stick* II. xxxviii. 181 She cried bucketsful. **1936** W. R. TITTERTON *G. K. Chesterton* II. iv. 145 Turning out books in buckets-full.

bucketing ('bʌkɪtɪŋ), *vbl. sb.*

1. The using of a bucket; the pouring of bucketfuls of water over a person.

1598 SYLVESTER *Du Bartas* (1608) 10 Danaides sivelike Tub.. never full for all their bucketing. **1648** HERRICK *Hesper.* I. 28 Water, Water.. come all to buckittings. **1759** B. MARTIN *Nat. Hist. Eng.* I. 85 Bucketting.. taking up the Water in Buckets, and pouring it leisurely on the Parts affected. **1863** KINGSLEY *Water-bab.* iv. 172 They.. had recourse to.. Bleedings, Bucketings with cold water.

2. a. Heavy, exhausting riding. **b.** = PUMPING; breathless exhaustion by violent exercise. **c.** Hurried and jerky rowing.

1856 WHYTE MELVILLE *Kate Coventry* xi, I had rather give Brilliant a good 'bucketting'.. over an even heath or a line of grass. **1876** BESANT & RICE *Gold. Butterfly* xv. 133 Jack's bucketing up the river. **1883** MISS BRADDON *Gold. Calf* xxi. 238 The laming of a fine horse by injudicious bucketting up hill and down hill. **1883** *Standard* 22 Feb. 3/7 Dry Remark.. had a fearful bucketting before the spin ended.

'bucketing, *ppl. a.* [f. BUCKET *v.* + -ING².] That buckets; cf. BUCKET *v.* 5.

1869 *Echo* 26 Aug., Their recovery forward is flurried and 'bucketing'. **1882** *St. James's Gaz.* 7 Mar., Smith has a hanging, bucketing recovery.

'bucket-shop. [f. BUCKET *sb.*¹ + SHOP.

The *Leeds Mercury* of Dec. 1886 says—'The market authority in Chicago, called the Board of Trade, would not allow a deal in 'options' of less than 5,000 bushels of grain. In order to catch men of small means, what was called the 'Open Board of Trade'.. commenced business in an alley under the regular Board of Trade Rooms. There was an elevator to carry the members of the board to their rooms, and occasionally a member, if trade was slack, would call out, 'I'll send down and get a bucketful pretty soon,' referring to the speculators in the 'Open Board of Trade' below. Hence the term 'bucket shop' came to be applied to all grain gambling institutions.]

1. An unauthorized office used originally for smaller gambling transactions in grain, and subsequently extended to offices for other descriptions of gambling and betting on the markets, the stocks, etc.; †also, a gin-mill, a low-class liquor-shop. orig. and chiefly *U.S.*

1875 MRS. STOWE *We & Neighbors* 380 The lowest, the most dreadful of all, was what they called the bucket shops. There the vilest of liquors are mixed in buckets and sold to the wretched, crazed people. **1880** *Bradstreet's* 1 Dec. 1/4 The failure of the 'Produce Exchanges', or bucket shops.. caused little excitement. **1881** *N. Y. Even. Post* Oct. (Th.), A 'bucket-shop' in New York is a low 'gin-mill', or 'distillery', where small quantities of spirits are dispensed in pitchers and pails (buckets). When the shops for dealing in one-share or five-share lots of stocks were opened, these dispensaries of smaller lots than could be got from regular dealers were at once named 'bucket-shops'. **1882** *Standard* 28 Dec. 6/5 A system of speculation carried on in grain in what are termed bucket-shops. **1886** *Statist* 28 Aug. 234 The 'bucket shop' is an American institution.. and it was first used for retail gambling in grain. *Ibid.* 235 Men opened offices.. and started a business in Stocks which was simply betting.. The 'bucket shop' keeper.. offered to deal at close prices and without commission.. There are 'bucket shops' and 'bucket shops'. The worst class of them are thimble and pea sharpers under a more polite name. **1886** *Boston* (Mass.) *Jrnl.* 11 Nov. 2/2 A new plan to suppress bucket-shops and restore speculative trading to former channels. **1910** *N. Y. Even. Post* 4 Apr. 4 What.. our people call a bucket-shop, is not only a gambling establishment pure and simple but is in most cases a gambling establishment which pretends to be something else. **1957** *Encycl. Brit.* IX. 703/2 'Bucket shop' means the business of a sham share broker who gambles with his customers on the rise or fall in the prices of stock exchange securities without acquiring these securities at all. **1960** *Times* 10 June 7/2 It might be said that he was conducting a bucket-shop.. except that his stock in trade was not securities but British Colonial stamps.

2. A retailer of 'cut-price' goods, aiming to undercut the market by working outside the official system; *spec.* one selling cheap airline tickets. Also *attrib.*

1973 *Times* 17 Nov. 13/1 Latest reports indicate that the introduction of ABCs has virtually driven the 'bucket shop' operators from that.. scene. **1976** *Holiday Which?* May 59/3 Bucket shops (as well as other travel firms) usually advertise in the small ads of *The Times, Time Out*, [etc.]. **1980** *Daily Tel.* 4 Dec. 6 The International Air Transport Association is being pressed to allow all air travellers a fair opportunity to buy cheap tickets at 'bucket shop' prices. **1981** *Times* 16 Dec. 16/8 One of the worst problems [for motorcycle manufacturers] was the activity of 'bucket shop' dealers who undermined the standing of official retailers. **1982** *Daily Tel.* 26 July 2/5 The meeting will seek.. co-ordinated airline action to stamp out bucket shop sales of tickets. **1985** *Times* 9 Feb. 13/2 In 1985 the public will wake up and realize that bucket shops are no longer the sole purveyors of discounted tickets.

'buckety. *Sc.* ['A corruption of *buckwheat*' (Jamieson).] Paste used by weavers in dressing their webs.

buckety ('bʌkɪtɪ), *a.* [f. BUCKET *sb.*¹ + -Y¹.] Bucket-like, clumsy.

1883 *Harper's Mag.* Jan. 177/2 Great buckety boots of Cordovan leather.

buck-eye. *U.S.* [said to be f. BUCK *sb.*¹ + EYE; see quot. 1841.]

1. *Bot.* **a.** The American Horse-chestnut (*Æsculus glabra*). Also, a tree of this species.

1763 in R. T. Durrett *Louisville* (1893) 132 Beginning at a hoop-ashe and buckeye. **1784** J. FILSON *Kentucke* 23 Here also is the buck-eye, an exceedingly soft wood, bearing a remarkable black fruit. **1789–96** MORSE *Amer. Geog.* I. 636 The buckeye.. is the horse chesnut of Europe. **1841** MRS. LOUDON *1st Bk. Bot.* (1845) 25 Called buck-eye.. from the hilum of the fruit having the appearance of a stag's eye. **1878** BRET HARTE *Man on Beach* 109 Looking down upon me through the buckeye bushes.

b. The nut or fruit of the buck-eye.

1797 in *Filson Club Hist. Q.* (1928) II. 166 Buck eye.. resembles the Chestnut, but is as large as a hickory nut of the largest Size. **1892** *Jrnl. Amer. Folk-Lore* V. 20 The negroes believe if one carries buckeyes in the pocket he will have no chills through the year. **1948** *Chicago Tribune* 28 Mar. VII. 1/3 You carry a buckeye to ward off rheumatism.

2. a. A native of Ohio, the 'Buckeye State', in which the *Æsculus glabra* abounds. *colloq.*

1822 E. JAMES *Exp. Rocky Mts.* I. 20 In allusion to this circumstance, the indigenous backwoodsman is sometimes called buck-eye. **1882** *Congress. Rec.* July 5811/1 The regenerated statesmanship of the modern Buckeye.

attrib. **1840** *Buffalo Commerc. Advertiser* 12 Sept. (Th.), Queer carryalls did these Buckeye boys construct. **1894** *Congress. Rec.* Jan., App. 79/1 The very author of the tariff plank in the Chicago platform was last fall buried beneath more than 80,000 votes in that grand old 'Buckeye' State.

b. *fig.* (as one word). Used *attrib.* and *absol.* of an inferior person or thing, esp. one of no value, poor quality, or cheap (but often showy). *colloq.*

[**1846** in C. Cist *Cincinnati Misc.* II. 97/1 The buckeye.. stood very low in the estimation of early settlers, and by a figure of speech.., it was applied to lawyers and doctors whose capacity and attainment were of a low grade.] **1906** *Atlantic Monthly* Nov. 640 The despised 'buckeye' painter who paints for department stores and cheap picture shops. **1920** S. LEWIS *Main St.* xi. 137 The walls of Mrs. Cass's parlor were plastered with.. 'buckeye' pictures. **1947** *New Yorker* 15 Feb. 59 A buckeye is a small shop in which cigars are made by hand in a back room and sold across the counter out front. **1977** *Times Lit. Suppl.* 25 Mar. 332/1 Buckeye painter—which means a painter of decorations on saloon mirrors. **1980** in S. Terkel *Amer. Dreams* 107 The place was called a buckeye, the name for a sleazy shop.

3. A type of canoe or schooner (see quots.).

1885 C. P. KUNHARDT *Small Yachts* 234 The Buckeyes.. are an exaggeration of the dugout canoe... The primitive builder bored two holes, one on each side of the stem, through which to pay out his cables. These were simply two round holes, bored with a large auger, and, when the boat was coming head on, resembled to the fancy of the negroes, the eyes of a buck. **1889** *Cent. Dict., Buckeye*... A flat-bottomed centerboard schooner of small size.. decked over, and with a cabin aft, used in oyster-fishing in Chesapeake Bay. Also called *bugeye*. **1923** *Outing* (U.S.) Jan. 187/1 The craft he suggests is one of 'those Chesapeake Bay buckeyes'.

buck-eyed, *a.* *Farriery.* Having bad or speckled eyes; said of horses.

1847 in CRAIG.

buck-horn ('bʌkhɔːn). Also buck's horn. [f. BUCK *sb.*¹ + HORN.]

†1. a. The horn of a buck. **b.** The horn of a goat used for blowing a blast. *Obs.*

1447–8 SHILLINGFORD *Lett.* (1871) 36 Whiche bukhorn was presented to my lord on Candelmasse day. **1548** *Compl. Scot.* (1801) 65 Hudit hirdis blauuand ther buc hornis.

2. The material of a buck's horn; also *attrib.* made of, or hard as buck's horn, horny.

1613 W. BROWNE *Brit. Past.* I. §5 The swarty Smith spits in his buckhorne fist. **1820** SCOTT *Monast.* xix, A large knife

hilted with buck-horn. **1881** *Macm. Mag.* XLIV. 473/1 Jacket with a..green collar, and buckshorn buttons.

3. From its hardness: Dried whiting or other fish. (Cf. early mod.Du. *bokshoren.*)

1602 CAREW *Cornwall* 35 a, Dried, as Buckhorne made of whitings. **1611** COTGR. s.v. *Merlan*, A dryed Whiting; the fish which we call Buckhorne. **1655** MOUFFET & BENNET *Health's Improv.* (1746) 262 Stock-fish, whilst it is unbeaten, is called Buckhorn. **1807** VANCOUVER *Agric. Devon* (1813) 398 Thus prepared, they..are called buckhorn.

4. In full ***buck-horn sight***: a branched form of sight of a rifle or sporting gun. *U.S.*

1877 R. I. DODGE *Hunting Grounds Gt. West* vii. 105 The very best sight, and the one almost universally in use by sportsmen and professional hunters on the plains, is the plain 'buckhorn'. *Ibid.*, Sportsmen who use the 'buck-horn' must learn to sight 'on the barrel'. **1901** S. E. WHITE *Westerners* xi. 78 He had viewed..the scout through the buck-horn sights of his long rifle.

buck-hound ('bʌkhaʊnd). [f. BUCK *sb.*^{1} + HOUND.] A smaller variety of stag-hound used for hunting bucks. ***Master of the Buckhounds***, an officer of the Royal Household.

1530 PALSGR. 201/2 Bucke hound, *limonier*. **1542** UDALL *Erasm. Apoph.* 127 b, There bee harryers, or buckehoundes. **1679–88** *Secr. Serv. M. Chas. & Jas.* (1851) 103 To John Branch, serjt of the buckhounds to King Charles 2d. **1753** HANWAY *Trav.* II. Gloss., Mir-chekarbachi..answers to our master of the buck hounds. **1875** 'STONEHENGE' *Brit. Sports* I. II. ii. §1. 153 Formerly, hounds were kept to hunt the fallow deer, called buckhounds.

Buck House (bʌk haʊs). A jocular appellation of *Buckingham Palace*, the London residence of the Sovereign.

1922 DAVID, EARL BEATTY *Let.* 28 Feb. in W. S. Chalmers *Life & Lett.* (1951) xvii. 390 A succession of very heavy solemn collections of functions at Buck House. **1954** J. B. PRIESTLEY *Magicians* i. 11 I'm told Karney plays with millions now. Pops up all over the place. Including Buck House for a Knighthood. **1962** R. JEFFRIES *Exhibit No. Thirteen* vi. 58 Come on in—the door's wide open and this isn't Buck House.

buckie ('bʌkɪ). *Sc.* Also 6 bukie. [Derivation unknown; cf. L. *buccinum* whelk. Perhaps sense 2 is a distinct word: ? f. BUCK *sb.*^{1}]

1. The whorled shell of any mollusc; e.g. whelk.

[*c* **1505** W. DUNBAR *Tua Mar. Wom. & Wedo* 276 And with a bukky in my cheik bo on him behind.] **1596** DALRYMPLE tr. *Leslie's Hist. Scot.* 57 In the space of xii. houris thay grow in fair cokilis or bukies. **1638** H. ADAMSON *Muse's Threnodie* 2 (JAM.) Triton, his trumpet of a Buckie Propin'd to him, was large and luckie. **1814** SCOTT *Diary* in *Lockhart* (1839) IV. 260 They gather shells on the shore, called Johnnie Groat's buckies. **1845** PETRIE *Eccl. Archit. Irel.* 94 Oyster shells, buckies or sea-shells.

2. A perverse or refractory person.

1719 RAMSAY *Ep. Lt. Hamilton* iii, Gin ony sourmou'd girning bucky Ca' me conceity keckling chucky. **1791** BURNS *Ep. to J. Maxwell* iii, If envious buckies view wi' sorrow Thy lengthen'd days. **1814** SCOTT *Wav.* III. 133 (JAM.) 'It was that deevil's buckie, Callum Beg'.

bucking ('bʌkɪŋ), *vbl. sb.*^{1} [f. BUCK *v.*^{1} + -ING^1.]

1. The operation of steeping or boiling yarn, cloth, or clothes in a lye of wood ashes, etc., in the old process of bleaching, or in buck-washing; the quantity of clothes, etc. so treated; app. also the lye used in the process. (Cf. *blacking*.)

1483 *Cath. Angl.* 38 A Bowkynge, *lixiuarium*. *a* **1500** DEGUILEVILLE *MS. Pilgr. Life of Manhode* 21 b, in *Cath. Angl.* 38 Of thaym I make a bowkynge for to putte in and bowke and wasche alle fylthes. **1598** SHAKS. *Merry W.* III. iii. 140 Throw fowle linnen vpon him, as if it were going to bucking. **1753** CHAMBERS *Cycl. Supp.* s.v., Bucking of cloth is the first step or degree of whitening it. **1818** HOGG *Brownie of Bodsb.* II. 161 (JAM.) Help me to the water wi' a boucking o' claes? **1822** IMISON *Sc. & Art* II. 163 This alternate bucking and exposing on the grass is the old manner of bleaching. **1875** URE *Dict. Arts* I. 364 Boiling in an alkaline lye, or, in other words, bucking or bowking.

2. *Comb.*, as ***bucking-basket***, ***-cloth***, ***-house***, ***-stoke***, ***-stool***, ***-tub***, ***-vat***. Also **bucking-ashes** = *buck-ashes* (BUCK *sb.*^{3} 5); **bucking-keir**, **-washing**, see quots.

1577 B. GOOGE *Heresbach's Husb.* (1586) 65 b, The Gardners use to lay *bucking ashes about it. **1832** SCOTT *Nigel* ii, Off with Janet in her own *bucking-basket. **1551–60** *Inv.* in H. Hall *Soc. in Elizab. Age* (1886) 152 A Bucking Tubb. A *Bucking clothe and a paile. **1615** MARKHAM *Eng. Housew.* II. v. (1668) 138 Cover the uppermost Yarn with a bucking-cloth. **1597** *Manchester Crt. Leet Records* (1885) II. 124 From the northe to the *bowking howse eight and fortie yards. **1810** HENRY *Elem. Chem.* (1826) II. 274 The goods.. are laid in a large wooden vat or *bowking keir. **1483** *Cath. Angl.* 38 A *Bowkynstoke, *lixiuatorium*. **1654** GAYTON *Fest. Notes* III. iii. (L.) No bigger than a toad upon a *bucking-stool. **1615** MARKHAM *Eng. Housew.* II. v. (1668) 138 You shall pull out the spigget of the *bucking-tub. *a* **1652** BROME *Queen's Exch.* II. ii, Their Buckets shall they bring..Their Bucking tubs, Baskets and Battledoors. **1822** IMISON *Sc. & Art* II. 163 It is then returned again into the *bucking vat. **1818** SCOTT *Hrt. Midl.* xvii, 'I'll cry up Ailie Muschat, and she and I will hae a grand *bouking-washing'. **1808–25** JAMIESON *Dict.*, *Boukin-washing*, *Boukit-washin'*, the great annual purification of the family linen, by means of bouk.

'bucking, *vbl. sb.*^{2} [f. BUCK *v.*^{2} + -ING^1.] The copulation of certain animals. Also *attrib.*

1535 COVERDALE *Gen.* xxx. 41 In the first buckynge tyme of the flockes. **1657** COLVIL *Whig's Supplic.* (1751) 122 Finmacoul..in a bucking time of year Did rout and chace a herd of deer.

bucking ('bʌkɪŋ), *vbl. sb.*^{3} [f. BUCK *v.*^{3} + -ING^1.] = Buck-jumping.

1859 H. KINGSLEY *G. Hamlyn* II. 212 That same bucking ..is just what puzzles me utterly. **1882** *Detroit Free Press* 2 Dec. 1/6 What he has just done is called bucking.

bucking ('bʌkɪŋ), *vbl. sb.*^{4} *Mining.* [f. BUCK *v.*^{5} + -ING^1.] A peculiar manner of bruising ore practised in mines in Cornwall and Derbyshire; see quot. Attrib. in ***bucking hammer***, ***iron***, ***plate***.

1875 URE *Dict. Arts* II. 85 In small mines Bucking is resorted to..This operation consists of pounding pieces of mixed ore on a slab of iron by means of a hammer or bucker. *Ibid.* I. 548 A bucking iron is a flat iron fixed on a handle, with which the ore is crushed; and a bucking plate is an iron plate on which the ore is placed to be crushed.

bucking ('bʌkɪŋ), *ppl. a.* [f. BUCK *v.*^{3}] Of a horse: That bucks or buck-jumps.

1859 H. KINGSLEY *G. Hamlyn* II. 212 [He] can sit some bucking horses which very few men will attempt to mount.

buckish ('bʌkɪʃ), *a.*^{1} [f. BUCK *sb.*^{1} + -ISH^1.]

1. Resembling or characteristic of a he-goat; lascivious; ill-smelling.

1515 BARCLAY *Egloges* IV. (1570) C vj/1 Buckishe Joly well stuffed as a ton. **1562** TURNER *Herbal* II. 62 b, Sampharitik ..hath a rammishe or buckishe styngkyng smell.

2. Of or resembling a 'buck' or dandy, foppish.

1806–7 J. BERESFORD *Miseries Hum. Life* (1826) v, Drunken hermits, Buckish magicians. **1870** *Daily News* 19 Apr., The fashionable old gentlemen who appear to flourish and look buckish to a far greater age.

Hence **'buckishly** *adv.*, **'buckishness**.

a **1822** SHELLEY *Swellfoot* II. ii, She has been putting on boots and spurs, and a hunting-cap, buckishly cocked on one side. **1803** *Pic Nic* No. 11 (1806) II. 140 Activity is fashion, honest emulation buckishness.

buckish ('bʌkɪʃ), *a.*^{2} [f. BUCK *v.*^{3} + -ISH^1.] Inclined to buck; hence, high-spirited, in good fettle (*slang*, of persons).

1911 *Scott's Last Exped.* (1913) I. xiii. 392 The ponies are very buckish and can scarcely be held in.

†**'buckism.** *Obs.* [f. BUCK *sb.*^{1} + -ISM.] The practice of a 'buck' or dandy.

1753 *Scots Mag.* May 241/1 Two gentlemen of great quality, professors of Buckism. **1798** MORTON *Secrets Worth Knowing* III. ii. (L.) I was once a delightful auctioneer—my present trade is buckism. **1804** *Miniature* (1806) II. 11 To grant licences to all professors of buckism.

'buck-jump. [f. BUCK *sb.*^{1} + JUMP.] A leap like that of a buck, *esp.* a jump from the ground made by an untamed or vicious horse, with the feet drawn together and the back arched, to unseat the rider. (Of American or Australian origin.) Hence **'buck-jump** *v.* = BUCK *v.*^{3}; also **buck-jumper**, **buck-jumping** *vbl. sb.*

1848 H. W. HAYGARTH *Bush Life in Australia* vii. 78 An expert 'buck-jumper' usually begins when his rider is in some degree off his guard. **1848** Buck-jumping [see BUCK *v.*^{3}]. **1861** *Harper's Mag.* June 8/1 The Captain..compels his animal to slide or make 'buck jumps' over the worst places. **1878** H. SMART *Play or Pay* i. (ed. 3) 18 Harlequin [a horse]..indulged in a couple of buck jumps. **1882** *Detroit Free Press* 2 Dec. 1/6 That pony is a mustang and buck-jumper. **1885** *Forman (Dakota) Item* 26 May 6/3 The majority of the horses there [in Australia] are vicious and given to the trick of buck-jumping.

bucklandite ('bʌkləndaɪt). *Min.* [f. the name of Dr. William *Buckland* (1784–1856), English geologist: see -ITE^1.] A variety of allanite or the related mineral epidote.

1824 M. LEVY in *Ann. Philos.* VII. 134 At the suggestion of Mr. Heuland, I propose to give the name of Bucklandite (in honour of the celebrated Professor of Oxford), to a mineral substance, the crystallographical characters of which I find to differ from any hitherto described. **1854** DANA *Syst. Min.* (ed. 4) II. 208 Bucklandite is from Achmatowsk, Arendal, and Lake Laach. **1910** *Encycl. Brit.* IX. 689/1 Several other names (achmatite, bucklandite, escherite,..&c.) have been applied to this species [*sc.* epidote].

buckle ('bʌk(ə)l), *sb.* Forms: 4–5 bocle, -kle, bukyll(e, 4–6 bokel(l, 5 bocul(e, -cull(e, -kull, -kyll(e, bukkel, (bogyll), 6 bucle, 5– buckle. [a. F. *boucle*:—L. *buccula* (dim. of *bucca* cheek), the recorded senses of which are 1. cheek-strap of a helmet, 2. boss of a shield. The precise relation of the Fr. senses (adopted in Eng.) to those of the L. word is obscure. Sense 1 is the only one found in ME.; the remaining senses appear to have been introduced from Fr. at much later periods.]

1. a. A rim of metal, with a hinged tongue carrying one or more spikes, for securing a belt, strap, or ribbon, which passes through the rim and is pierced by the spike or spikes. Often with defining word prefixed, as *knee-*, *shoe-buckle*.

1340 *Ayenb.* 236 þet is þe bocle of þe gerdle. **1391** *Test. Ebor.* I. 145 Un sayntour, le bukyll et le pendant de argent. *c* **1450** *Gloss.* in Wright's *Voc.* 122 *Ad plusculas*, bogyllis. *c* **1440** *Promp. Parv.* 41 Bocle or boculle [bocul *K.H.*, bokyll or bocle **1499**], *pluscula*. **1483** in ARNOLD *Chron.* (1811) 116 A purple corse..enameled in the bukkel with ij. ymagis. **1530** PALSGR. 200/1 Bocle that beareth the byt, *portemors*. **1606** SHAKS. *Tr. & Cr.* III. i. 163 His stubborne Buckles.. Shall more obey then to the edge of Steele. **1712** ADDISON *Spect.* No. 317 ¶22 Tongue of my Shoe-Buckle broke. **1777** SHERIDAN *Trip Scarb.* Prol. (1883) 281 The buckle then its modest limits knew. **1855** J. W. CROKER in *Papers* (1884) III. xxix. 329 He expected to hear next that..knee-buckles had been issued to the Highland Brigade.

b. Phrases. † ***to come to buckle and bare thong***: to be stripped of everything. † ***to turn the buckle of the girdle*** (see quots.). ***to cover the buckle***: to dance (a particular step). † ***to hold*** or ***bring*** (***bare***) ***buckle and thong together*** (in U.S., ***to make buckle and tongue meet***): to make both ends meet. *Obs.*

1562 J. HEYWOOD *Prov. & Epigr.* (1867) 73 He at length came to buckle and bare thong. **1600** *Weakest goeth to the Wall* sig E2, My benefice doth bring me in no more But what will hold bare buckle and thong together. **1603** BRETON *Post w. Packet* (1637) (N.) If you be angry, turn the buckle of your girdle behind you. **1656** CROMWELL *Sp.* 17 Sept., If any man be angry at it,—I am plain, and shall use an homely expression: Let him turn the buckle of his girdle behind him! If this were to be done again, I would do it. **1675** *Pepys Ballads* (1930) III. 12 Hold Buckle and Thong together. **1732** T. FULLER *Gnomologia* 100 He'll bring buckle and thong together. **1852** READE *Peg Woff.* viii. 131 Woffington covered the buckle in gallant style; she danced, the children danced. **1859** *Fisher's River* 249 All they cared for was 'to make buckle and tongue meet' by raising stock..and a little corn for bread. **1888** *Harper's Mag.* Apr. 703/1 Beginning without money, he had as much as he could do to make 'buckle and tongue meet', as the phrase goes.

† **c.** ***French buckle***: a ring attached to a mare, to prevent her being covered. *Obs.*

1691 *Lond. Gaz.* No. 2707/4 A Chesnut Mare..buckled up with a French Buckle.

d. An iron loop for fastening the blade to the frame of a wood-saw.

1846 HOLTZAPFFEL *Turning* II. 725 The chairmakers' saw is in general a diminutive of the ordinary pit saw, and has a central blade strained by buckles and wedges.

e. [app. f. BUCKLE *v.* 2 c.] A vigorous struggle or conflict.

1845 J. KEEGAN *Leg. & Poems* (1907) 268 Master Tom and the girls running out to..welcome me home, as if I was just returning from a buckle with the Terry Alts, or a rencontre with a scalping party of Huron Indians. **1876** *Coursing Cal.* 6 Wheatear and The Pet had a tremendous tight buckle for the lead. *Ibid.* 181 Liberator and Controversy made a tight buckle for pace.

†**2.** The drop of an ear-ring. (Fr. *boucle d'oreille.*) *Obs.*

1674 *Lond. Gaz.* No. 878/4 Lost a pair of Diamond Buckles, set Transparent in Silver, without any Gold Earrings to them.

†**3.** 'The state of the hair crisped and curled by being kept long in the same state' (J.) *Obs.*

1711 ADDISON *Spect.* No. 129 ¶7 The Wearer..lets his Wig lie in Buckle for a whole half Year. **1730** FIELDING *Tom Thumb* Wks. 1775 II. 107 What's a woman when her virtue's gone! A coat without its lace; wig out of buckle. **1732** POPE *Mor. Ess.* iii. 296 That live-long wig..Eternal buckle takes in Parian stone. **1733** CHEYNE *Eng. Malady* I. xi. §2 (1734) 100 Hair, which, with great Difficulty, receives or retains a Buckle. **1763** CHURCHILL *Ghost* III. (R.) His features too in buckle see. **1789** BURNS *Laddie's dear sel'*, An' his hair has a natural buckle an' a.

4. In *Architecture* (see quot.).

1848 RICKMAN *Archit.* xxx, A good bold corbel-table..it has been sometimes called a buckle, because some specimens resemble the tongue of a buckle. **1861** PARKER *Goth. Archit.* 131 The corbels have the ornament called a buckle or mask.

5. *Comb.*, as ***buckle-maker***, ***-manufacturer***, ***-ring***, ***-shoe***, ***-smith***, ***-tongue***; also †**buckle-chape**, the back of a buckle, over which the ribbon or strap passes; **buckle-covering**, a certain step or movement in dancing; **buckle-garter**, a garter fastened by a buckle; †**buckle-hammed**, ? having crooked legs (see BUCKLE *v.* III.); †**buckle-pit**, a child's game; **buckle-plates**: see BUCKLED 2; †**buckle-ring**, the frame of a buckle; **buckle-wig**: see BUCKLED 3.

1761 *Lond. Mag.* XXX. 233 Foreigners..can afford to give a much higher price for our *buckle-chapes than our buckle-makers can afford to do. **1859** DICKENS *Haunted H.* VIII. 48 There ensued such..*buckle-covering, and double-shuffling. **1629** GAULE *Holy Madn.* 324 *Buckle-hamm'd, Stump-legg'd, Splay-footed. *c* **1440** *Promp. Parv.* 42 *Bokulle makere, *pluscularius*. **1722** *Lond. Gaz.* No. 6088/3 A Brass Buckle-maker by Trade. **1791** *Chron.* in *Ann. Reg.* 54/1 Several respectable *buckle-manufacturers from Birmingham..waited upon H.R.H. the Prince of Wales. **1532** MORE *Confut. Tindale* Wks. (1557) 574/2 Some suche prety playes of likelyhod as chyldren be woont to playe, as cheristone, mary bone, *bokle pit, spurne poynte. **1866** *Law Reports, Com. Pleas* 163 The plaintiff is..the patentee of certain *buckle plates used for bridge flooring. **1761** *Lond. Mag.* XXX. 233 The dispute between *buckle-ring-makers and buckle-chape-makers. **1868** HOLME LEE *B. Godfrey* liv. 309 Trim *buckle-shoes. *c* **1500** *Cocke Lorell's B.* (1843) 9 *Bokell smythes, horse leches, and gold beters. **1878** *Fraser's Mag.* XVIII. 579 Men and women in..powder and *buckle wigs.

buckle ('bʌk(ə)l), *v.* [f. prec. sb.; but cf. F. *boucler*; branch III may be from the F. word, which has the sense 'to bulge' (as a wall).]

I. With reference to BUCKLE *sb.* 1.

1. a. *trans.* To fasten with a buckle. Often with prep. *on*, *to*, or adv. *on*, *up*, *together*.

c **1386** CHAUCER *Knts. T.* 1645 Nailynge the speres, and helmes bokelynge. *c* **1400** *Roland* 694 Herd bukilis his helme, and gothe out sone. **1513** DOUGLAS *Æneis* VIII. v. 17 Wyth pople tre hattis buklit on thair heid. **1597** SHAKS. *2 Hen. IV*, I. ii. 158, *Iust.* You liue in great infamy. *Fal.* He that buckles him in my belt, cannot liue in lesse. **1705** *Lond. Gaz.* No. 4156/4 Stolen..a..Mare..buckled up with a French Buckle. **1727** SWIFT *Gulliver* II. iv. 131 A servant on horseback would buckle on my box. **1805** SOUTHEY *Madoc in Azt.* xvi, Buckle this harness on. **1870** BRYANT *Iliad* I. VII. 221 About his limbs The mail was buckled.

†**b.** To fasten (*up*) in any way; also fig. *to buckle in*: to limit, enclose. *Obs.*

1460 *Quia Amore Langueo* 51 in *Pol. Rel. & L. Poems* (1866) 152 Bocled my feet, as was her wille, with scharpe naile. **1600** SHAKS. *A.Y.L.* III. ii. 140 The stretching of a span buckles in his summe of age. **1792** A. WILSON *Watty & Meg*, Up my claes and cash I buckled.

2. a. *trans.* With allusion to the fastening on of armour: To equip, prepare (for battle, an expedition, etc.). Chiefly *refl.*, and now only *fig.*: To gird oneself, apply oneself resolutely *to* (a task).

1570 LEVINS *Manip.* 185 To Buckle him, *parare se.* **1574** tr. *Marlorat's Apocalips* 31 Everie man..must buckle himselfe to a painfull kind of life. **1596** SPENSER *F.Q.* VI. viii. 12 Buckling soone himselfe, gan fiercely fly Upon that carle. **1611** W. SCLATER *Key* (1629) 326 No maruaile if Angels so desirously buckle themselues to prie hereinto. **1655** FULLER *Ch. Hist.* IX. vi. §16 Cartwright buckled himself to the employment [refuting the Rhemish Transl. of the N. Test.]. **1730** T. BOSTON *Mem.* IX. 270 Where I thought I was best buckled. **1824** DIBDIN *Libr. Comp.* 368 Now buckles himself to the uninterrupted perusal of the instructive text.

b. *intr.* (for *refl.*) in same sense.

1563 BP. SANDYS in Strype *Ann. Ref.* I. xxxv. 398 Whereat one of Sir Johns men buckled to fight with him. **1623** SANDERSON *12 Serm.* (1637) 132 Before wee either eate or drinke, or buckle about any worldly busines. **1625** BACON *Delayes, Ess.* (Arb.) 525 To teach dangers to come on, by ouer early Buckling towards them, is another Extreme. **1690** LOCKE *Hum. Und.* II. xxi. §43 The Epicure buckles to Study, when Shame..shall make him uneasy. **1757** CHESTERF. *Lett.* cccxx. IV. 90 Those who have a great deal of business must ..buckle to it. **1877** LYTTEIL *Landmarks* IV. x. 248 Their husbands and brothers must buckle to the fight.

c. *to buckle 'to*: to set to work, apply oneself vigorously. Also *to buckle down* (*to*) (orig. *U.S.*)

1712 ARBUTHNOT *John Bull* (1727) 107 'Squire South buckled too, to assist his friend Nic. **1746** BURKE *Corr.* (1844) I. 21, I have shook off idleness, and begun to buckle to. **1812** W. TAYLOR in Robberds *Mem.* II. 375, I cannot buckle to, until this business of the Museum is determined. **1865** *Atlantic Monthly* XV. 301 If he would only buckle down to serious study. **1871** BRET HARTE *Poems* 55 Chiquita Buckled right down to her work. **1884** *Pres. Addr. Philol. Soc.* 4 He buckled to at once, learned in a month or so enough Iroquois for present needs. **1934** WODEHOUSE *Right Ho, Jeeves* xxii. 280 The recollection of what this bell could do when it buckled down to it gave me pause. **1941** *N.Y. Times* 2 Oct. 28/4 The music and lyric makers [of *Best Foot Forward*] have been equally inventive, without being afraid of rhythm and melody. 'Buckle Down, Winsocki' is a song highly recommended to any school in need of such. **1949** A. MILLER *Death of Salesman* I. 40 If he doesn't buckle down he'll flunk math! **1983** E. REVELEY *In Good Faith* x. 157 But you'll really have to buckle down and cram for those exams, Moo.

3. a. *trans.* To join closely. **b.** *intr.* (for *refl.*) To close, come to close quarters; to grapple, engage. Const. *with* (an adversary); also with advbs. *together*, *in*, rarely *to*. *Obs.* or *dial.*

1535 COVERDALE *1 Macc.* iv. 14 They buckled together, and the Heithen were discomfited. **1543** GRAFTON *Contn. Harding* 455 The erle..folowed his enemyes..that..he myght fight and buckel with theim before they came to London. **1576** FLEMING tr. *Caius' Dogs* in Arb. *Garner* III. 255 Unable to buckle with the dog that would fain haue a snatch at his skin. ?**1650** *Don Bellianis* 198 A man that had been going to buckle with death. **1752** HUME *Pol. Disc.* x. 189 The whole armies were thus engag'd, and each man closely buckl'd to his antagonist.

†**c.** To adhere resolutely *to*. *Obs. rare.*

1793 ROBERTS *Looker-on* (1794) II. 338, I resolved to buckle to my tenets to the last extremity.

†**d.** *trans.* (*ellipt.*) To grapple with, engage, 'tackle'. *Obs.*

a **1605** MONTGOMERIE *Flyting* 154 Pedler, I pittie thee sa pinde To buckle him that beares the bell.

4. a. *trans.* To unite in marriage. *humorous* or *dial.* Cf. *splice*.

1724 RAMSAY *Tea-T. Misc.* (1733) I. 28 An ye wad gi's a bit land Wee'd buckle us e'en the gither. **1755** SMOLLETT *Quix.* (1803) II. 50 Our friend the licentiate, who will buckle you handsomely. **1796** MACNEILL *Will & Jean* I, Soon they loed, and soon were buckled. **1822** SCOTT *Nigel* xxvii, Dr. R. who buckles beggars for a tester and a dram of Geneva.

b. *intr.* To unite oneself in wedlock.

1693 DRYDEN *Juvenal's Sat.* vi. 37 Is this an age to buckle with a bride? **1806** TRAIN *Poet. Rev.* 64 (JAM.) Ask'd her.. Gin she wadna buckle too. **1823** LOCKHART *Reg. Dalton* III. 163 (JAM.) May..is the only month that nobody in the north country ever thinks of buckling in.

II. With reference to BUCKLE *sb.* 3.

†**5.** To fasten or retain in curl. *Obs.*

1721 BAILEY, *Buckle*..to put into buckles as hair. **1789–96** MORSE *Amer. Geog.* II. 561 Their hair..they buckle up in a very agreeable manner.

III. To bend, warp.

6. a. *trans.* To warp, crumple, bend out of its plane. Now chiefly techn.: To bend a bar or surface (under longitudinal pressure) into a double curve; as 'to buckle a saw, or the wheel of a bicycle or tricycle'. Also *fig.*

c **1525** in Thoms' *Anecdotes* (1839) 54 Ninepences are a little buckled to distinguish in their currancie. **1605** BACON *Adv. Learn.* II. 18 Reason doth buckle and bowe the mind unto the nature of things. **1658** FORD *Witch of Edm.* II. i, I am..like a bow—buckled and bent together. **1854** *N. & Q.* I. IX. 576/1 An awkward person, working incautiously with a saw, will probably..buckle it. **1868** *Daily Tel.* 3 July, It.. struck the 15-inch portion..buckling, bending, and breaking the inner bars. **1882** NARES *Seamanship* (ed. 6) 58 It would buckle the mast. **1921** *Contemp. Rev.* Mar. 291 It [*sc.* the French budget] may..for practical purposes, be considered to be 'buckled'.

b. *intr.* To bend under stress or pressure. †Of persons: To bend, stoop, double up (*obs.*).

1597 SHAKS. *2 Hen. IV*, I. i. 141 Whose Feauer-weakned ioynts, Like strengthlesse Hindges, buckle vnder life. **1637** POCKLINGTON *Altare Chr.* 154 His knees may not buckle to Baal. **1677** MOXON *Mech. Exerc.* (1703) 214 Where ever they find the Work buckle. **1700** I. BROME *Trav.* I. (1707) 38 We were enforced..to stoop, and buckle almost double. **1851** H. MELVILLE *Whale* xiii. 66 The two tall masts buckling like Indian canes in land tornadoes. *Mod.* The wheel of his tricycle has buckled.

c. *to buckle up*: to become warped and bent, to collapse. Also *fig.* (cf. 7).

1866 *Jrnl. R. Agric. Soc.* II. I. 140 Its expansion and contraction..rendering it [*sc.* plane iron] liable to 'buckle up'. **1927** *Daily Tel.* 1 Nov. 12/2 Such a man as Biquet is not given to buckling up.

†**7.** *fig.* To give way, submit; to cringe, truckle. *Obs.* exc. *dial.*

1642 ROGERS *Naaman* 260 Outwardly they..seeme to crouch and buckle. **1664** PEPYS *Diary* 17 Dec., The Dutch, as high as they seem, do begin to buckle. **1703** SAVAGE *Lett. Antients* lxxii. 212 Consider, how many great Nations..they have..forc'd to Buckle. **1864** E. CAPERN *Devon Provinc.*, 'To make him buckle' is To make him yield.

IV. *Comb.*, as †**buckle-beggar** (*Sc.*), a clergyman who performs irregular marriages, a hedge-priest; †**buckle-bosom**, a catchpoll, constable.

c **1700** LD. FOUNTAINHILL *Diary* in Larwood *Bk. Cleric. Anecd.* 294 He after turn'd a buckle-beggar, i.e. one who married without licence. **1822** SCOTT *Nigel* xvii, A hedge-parson, or buckle-beggar..sate on the Duke's left. **1623** MABBE *Aleman's Guzman d'Alf.* I. 63 Buckle-bosomes, Collar-catchers: in a word, they are Sergeants and Catchpoles.

buckled ('bʌk(ə)ld), *ppl. a.* [f. prec. + -ED.]

1. a. Fastened with a buckle. **b.** Provided with buckles. **c.** Joined closely, united.

1394 *P. Pl. Crede* 299 Nou han þei bucled schon. *c* **1420** *Anturs of Arth.* xxix. 4 Her belte was..Beten with besandus, and bocult ful bene. *c* **1460** J. RUSSELL *Bk. Nurture* 896 in *Babees Bk.* (1868) 178 His schon laced or bokelid, draw them on sure. **1876** MISS BRADDON *J. Haggard's Dau.* I. 5 He wore..stout buckled shoes.

2. Doubled or bent up, wrinkled, crumpled, knitted; bent in a double curve. *buckled plates* (*Mech.*), see quot. 1852.

1564 BAULDWIN *Mor. Philos.* (Palfr.) iii. 2 The buckled browes of majestie shall be bent against them. **1666** PEPYS *Diary* (1879) IV. 77 And took up a piece of glasse melted and buckled like parchment. **1852** *Specif. R. Mallet's Patent* No. 557 Plates of iron..bent into a peculiar convex and concave form, which I denominate 'buckled plates'.

†**3.** Crisped and curled. See BUCKLE *sb.* 3. *Obs.*

1753 RICHARDSON *Grandison* (ed. 7) I. 98 Sir Rowland.. in his full buckled wig. **1771** SMOLLETT *Humph. Cl.* (1815) 130, I have had my hair..singed, and bolstered, and buckled, in the newest fashion. **1861** WYNTER *Soc. Bees* 524 This buckled hair is..the same as that denounced by the early churchmen.

buckler ('bʌklə(r)), *sb.*[1] [f. BUCKLE *v.* + -ER[1].] One who or that which buckles; in quot. the strap of a helmet (*obs.*).

?**1650** *Don Bellianis* 184 The Emperor had the Buckler of his Helm cut.

buckler ('bʌklə(r)), *sb.*[2] Forms: 3–4 boceler, 4 bookeler, 4–5 bocler, bock-, bokeler(e, bokler, buclere, bukler, -are, 6 bouc-, buccler, 7 bucklar, 6– buckler. [a. OF. *boucler*, *bucler* (mod.F. *bouclier*), repr. a Lat. type **buccularius* adj., 'having a boss', f. *buccula*: see BUCKLE *sb.*]

1. A small round shield; in England the buckler was usually carried by a handle at the back, and 'used not so much for a shield as for a warder to catch the blow of an adversary' (Fairholt, s.v. *Buckler*), but sometimes it was larger, and fastened by straps to the arm. Sometimes wrongly applied to any kind of shield. Also *attrib.*

a **1300** *K. Alis.* 1190 Laddes, That sweord and boceleris hadde. *c* **1386** CHAUCER *Prol.* 558 A swerd and a bocler baar he by his side. *c* **1440** *Promp. Parv.* 42 Bokelere, *pelta, ancile, parma.* **1570** FLORIO *1st Fruites* 17b, What weapon is that buckler? A clownish dastardly weapon. **1611** BIBLE *1 Chron.* v. 18 Men able to beare buckler and sword. **1659** PEARSON *Creed* (1839) 280 He brought the bucklers stamped with the pictures of Cæsar into Jerusalem. **1760** GRAY *Corr.* (1843) 207 A pave..is a very large buckler..big enough to cover the tallest man. **1776** GIBBON *Decl. & Fall* I. 12 The buckler was of an oblong and concave figure, four feet in length. **1813** SCOTT *Trierm.* II. xvi, Each knight..Take buckler, spear, and brand. **1870** BRYANT *Iliad* I. VII. 222 Ajax.. upheld A buckler like a rampart.

2. *fig.* A means of defence; protection, protector.

c **1380** WYCLIF *Sel. Wks.* III. 265 þe bookeler of þis goostly fiȝt is a man to holde his pees in tyme. *c* **1449** PECOCK *Repr.* I. xiii. 71 Sufficient bokeler aȝens this assailing. **1535** COVERDALE *Ps.* xvii[i]. 1 My buckler, yᵉ horne of my health, and my proteccion. **1725** POPE *Odyss.* IV. 961 His country's buckler, and the Grecian boast. **1857** C. BRONTË *Professor* I. iii. 37 On a buckler of impenetrable indifference.

3. *Anat.* (see quots.)

[**1611** COTGR., *Bouclier de l'estomac*, The triangular gristle that grows to the bottome of the breast-bone, and from the middle thereof hangs over the stomacke.] **1541** R. COPLAND *Guydon's Quest. Chirurg.*, Commyng fro the boucler of the stomacke vnto the share bone. *a* **1648** DIGBY *Closet Open.* (1677) 126 Bones of rosted or boiled Beef..the Ribs, the Chine-bones, the buckler Plate-bone. **1706** PHILLIPS, *Buckler of beef*, a Piece cut off from the Surloin.

4. In various technical senses: **a.** (see quots.)

1674 PETTY *Disc. R. Soc.* 115 Let the same [Cylinder]..be covered with a moveable Head (such as in pressing of Pilchards they call a Buckler). **1753** CHAMBERS *Cycl. Supp.*, *Buckler of a cask* denotes a moveable head, whereby to compress the contents of it. In this sense we say, a buckler of pilchards. **1877** *Fraser's Mag.* XV. 221 Afterwards the fish are..packed in wooden hogshead casks and pressed..as closely as possible together by pressing stones and bucklers.

b. *Naut.* (see quots.)

1832 MARRYAT *N. Forster* xxxi, The cables were not yet unbent or bucklers shipped. *c* **1850** *Rudim. Navig.* (Weale) 101 *Bucklers*, pieces of elm plank barred close against the inside of the hawse-holes to prevent the water from coming in. Those used at sea, denominated Blind Bucklers, have no aperture; but those used..at anchor, and called Riding Bucklers, are made in two pieces..having a hole in the middle, large enough to admit the cable.

c. *Anat.*, *Zool.*, etc. Variously applied to the hard protective covering of parts of the body of different animals, as of the armadillo, the ganoid fishes, and some crustacea; *spec.* the anterior segment of the shell of the trilobites.

1828 STARK *Elem. Nat. Hist.* II. 171 *Alima*, Leach. The body and tail extremely elongated, as well as the shell or buckler. **1843** *Penny Cycl.* XXV. 232/1 This buckler [of the trilobites] has much analogy with the carapace of Apus. **1845** DR. BAIRD in *Proc. Berw. Nat. Club* II. xiii. 153 Copepoda..envelope consisting of a buckler, enclosing head and thorax. **1854** H. MILLER *Footpr. Creat.* iv. (1874) 43 All the ganoids of the period..have dermal bucklers placed right over their true skulls. **1855** OWEN *Skel. & Teeth* 5 In the armadillo..the trunk is protected by a large buckler of this bony armour.

†**5.** Phrases (sense 1): *to play at bucklers, at sword and buckler*: to fence; see also SWORD. *to take up the bucklers*: to enter the lists, present oneself as a champion. *to deserve to carry the buckler*: (with negative expressed or implied) to be worthy to be remotely compared with, = mod. 'to be fit to hold a candle to'. *to carry away the bucklers*: to come off winner. *to give, lay down, yield the bucklers*: to own oneself beaten. *Obs.*

a **1500** *Rel. Ant.* I. 83, iiij and xxᵗᵉ. oxon playing at the sword and bokeler. **1592** GREENE *Disput.* Wks. 1881–3 X. 222 Giuing you the bucklers at this weapon, let me haue a blow with you at another. **1593** *Tell-trothe's N.Y. Gift* 30 That could play at bucklers So soone as she was past her cradell. **1607** TOPSELL *Serpents* 644 Severus side carryed away the bucklers. **1640** BP. HALL *Episc.* I. §11. 48 When he can..prove it not Apostolike..we shall give him the Bucklers. **1649** SELDEN *Laws Eng.* I. lix. (1739) 109 The Clergy took up the Bucklers, and beat both King and Commons to a Retreat. **1642** SIR T. BROWNE *Relig. Med.* 47 One that deserves to carry the Buckler unto Sampson. **1654** GATAKER *Disc. Apol.* 3, I shal herein willinglie yeeld him the bucklers;..I confess, he hath the better of me. **1679** PRANCE *Addit. Narr. Pop. Plot* 45 After much bandying on every side, the Jesuite was fain to lay down the Bucklers. **1691** WOOD *Ath. Oxon.* II. 61 John dying before he could make a reply..Dr. Franc. White took up the bucklers. **1709** STEELE *Tatler* No. 31. ¶3 They fought at Sword and Buckler.

6. *Comb.*, as *buckler-maker*; also **buckler-beak**, a fossil ganoid with a beak-shaped upper jaw; **buckler-fern**, the genus *Aspidium*; †**buckler-hand**, the left hand; **buckler-head**, the fossil fish *Cephalaspis*; **buckler-headed**, having a head like a buckler; **buckler-mustard**, *Biscutella auriculata*; **buckler-play**, **-playing**, **-player**, fencing, a fencer; **buckler-thorn**, *Rhamnus Paliurus aculeatus*.

1882 *Proc. Berw. Nat. Club* IX. iii. 441 The *buckler ferns (*Lastrea dilatata*) of themselves forming a splendid shade. **1677** HOBBES *Homer* 238 Weari'd was thereby his *buckler-hand. **1847** CARPENTER *Zool.* §587 In the Cephalaspis (or *buckler-head). **1415** in *York Myst.* Introd. 23 *Bukler-makers. **1483** *Cath. Angl.* 36 A Bock[el]ere maker, *peltarius.* *c* **1500** *Cocke Lorell's B.* (1843) 9 Bokeler makers, dyers, and lether sellers. *a* **1560** ROLLAND *Crt. Venus* IV. 598 Bot *buklar play was thair sport most frequent. **1722** DE FOE *Hist. Plague* (1840) 47 Singing of Ballads, Buckler play, or such like causes of Assemblies of People, be utterly prohibited. **1448** SHILLINGFORD *Lett.* (1871) 68 Ever stonde yn defence as a *bokeler player. **1468** *Medulla Gram.*, *Gladiatura*, a *bokeler pleyng. **1562** TURNER *Herbal* II. 115, I knowe no Englishe name for it [Rhamnus]. But it maye be called ether Christes thorne or *buklars thorne. **1706** in PHILLIPS; hence in BAILEY, JOHNSON, etc.

buckler ('bʌklə(r)), *v.* [f. prec.]

1. *trans.* To act as a buckler to; to shield, defend, protect.

1590 MARLOWE *Edw. II*, I. iv. 579 'Tis not the king can buckler Gaveston. **1593** SHAKS. *3 Hen. VI*, III. iii. 99 Can Oxford..Now buckler Falsehood with a Pedigree? **1861** J. SHEPPARD *Fall Rome* IV. 227 These new nationalities.. bucklered the Empire against their [the Avars'] blows.

†**2.** *trans.* To ward or catch (blows).
1593 SHAKS. *3 Hen. VI*, I. iv. 50, I will..buckler with thee blowes twice two for one.

bucklered (ˈbʌklәd), *ppl. a.* [f. BUCKLER *sb.* + -ED.] Armed or furnished with bucklers.
1832 THORPE *Cædmon* 185 The bucklered warriors. **1870** BRYANT *Iliad* I. IV. 108 Bucklered warriors ranged around.

Buckley's (ˈbʌklɪz). *Austral.* and *N.Z. colloq.* [Of uncertain origin.] In full *Buckley's chance* (or *hope*, etc.): a forlorn hope, no chance at all.
1898 *Bulletin* (Sydney) 17 Dec. 31/2 'Devil shoot me!' muttered Tim..'if I see Buckley's chance of a shindy tonight.' **1903** 'T. COLLINS' *Such is Life* 339 *His* show is little better than Buckley's. **1916** C. J. DENNIS *Songs Sentim. Bloke* (1916) 118 *Buckley's (chance)*, a forlorn hope. **1918** —— *Digger Smith* 81 Doreen an' ole Mar Flood 'as got a scheme... But they've got Buckley's, as I tells me wife. **1934** *Bulletin* (Sydney) 2 May 25/1 He was especially sure..that the tourists had Buckley's hope of winning a Test. **1948** V. PALMER *Golconda* xiii. 103 Buckley's chance we have of getting our price if we're left to face the companies alone. **1955** D. NILAND *Shiralee* 216 You reckon I haven't got Buckley's?

†**'buckling**, *sb.*[1] *nonce-wd.* [f. BUCK *sb.*[1] + -LING.] A young buck; a little fop.
1778 GARRICK *Epil. to Fathers*, Ye bucks & bucklings of the age.

buckling (ˈbʌklɪŋ), *sb.*[2] Also bückling (pl. *bücklinge*). [ad. G. *bückling* bloater.] A smoked herring; a bloater (see quots.)
1909 *Cent. Dict.* Suppl., *Buckling*, a large smoked and salted herring. **1924** G. B. STERN *Tents of Israel* iv. 54 Bücklinge.., which were herrings smoked by herself according to old Maria's Viennese recipe. **1934** 'TAFFRAIL' *Seventy North* iii. 66 The 'buckling'..was a herring smoked in a special oven and cooked at the same time. **1967** M. GILBERT *Dust & Heat* I. 182 This isn't a smoked trout at all. It's a buckling.

buckling (ˈbʌklɪŋ), *vbl. sb.* [f. BUCKLE *v.*]
1. The action of fastening with a buckle; also *fig.*
1625 LAUD *Serm.* (1837) 69 A double buckling and knitting of the State together. **1808** SCOTT *Marm.* VI. xii, At buckling of the falchion belt.
b. *concr.* A brace, a fastening; that which is buckled on.
1861 SMILES *Engineers* II. 449 The main chains were to be ..secured by bucklings. **1875** BROWNING *Aristoph. Apol.* 281 Thereupon lays body bare Of bucklings.
†**2.** The action of closing *with* an enemy; engagement, onset. *Obs.*
1563 FOXE *A. & M.* 1041/2 His valiaunt buckling with two enemies. **1604** EDMONDS *Observ. Cæsar's Comm.* 98 In the buckling he might have receiued a small losse.
3. A bending, giving way; also, *techn.* the curving or crumpling of a plain surface under longitudinal pressure.
1651 tr. *Bacon's Life & Death* 56 For the buckling of their knees. **1850** E. CLARK *Britannia & C. Bridges* I. 104 No one knew, *a priori*, the resistance of plates to buckling. **1877** *Lumberman's Gaz.* 8 Dec. 362 The old 'sash-saw' was..kept strained within a frame or 'sash' to prevent its buckling or bending. **1882** *Nature* XXVI. 599 The curvature technically called buckling.
†**4.** The crisping and curling, or retaining in curl (of hair). Also *attrib. Obs.*
1713 STEELE *Guardian* No. 38 §2 It is the last time my black coat will bear scouring, or my long wig buckling. **1740** CHEYNE *Regimen* Introd. 9 The buckling upon Pipes and boiling soft broken Hair. **1846** J. TRAIN *Buchanites* in Fairholt s.v. *Buckling*, Their locks..restrained from falling ..over the back and bosom by small buckling-combs.

buckling (ˈbʌklɪŋ), *ppl. a.* [f. BUCKLE *v.* + -ING[2].] Crisply curling, waving.
18.. CRAWFURD *Classif. Races* (L.) With the European races, the hair of the head is usually, soft, silky, or buckling.

†**'buck-mast.** *Obs.* [:—OE. **bóc-mæst* mast of the beech. The name must go back to the time when the beech was still called *bóc*, *bok*, of which the latest known instance is in the 12th c. The vowel of *buck-* shows the shortening of orig. *ō* before two consonants; cf. *Buckland*:—OE. *bócland*.] Beech-mast.
a **1425** *Master of Game* (Halliw.) The bores fedyng is properliche ycleped akyr of ookys beryngе and bukmast. **1607** TOPSELL *Four-f. Beasts* 110 They will not eat Buck-mast wherewithal Hogs grow fat. **1863** PRIOR *Plant-n.* 31.

bucko (ˈbʌkәʊ). *Naut. slang.* [f. BUCK *sb.*[1] + -O[2].] **a.** A blustering, swaggering, or domineering fellow; sometimes used as a term of address. Also *attrib.* or as *adj.* = blustering, swaggering, bullying; esp. in phr. *bucko mate*. **b.** Swagger, bluster.
1883 J. F. KEANE *On Blue-Water* xv. 190 After that, no sailor will deny that a 'bucko mate' is not sometimes useful. **1899** M. ROBERTSON *Where Angels Fear* 107 Stand by here, mates. These buckoes'll kill some one yet. **1909** *Times Lit. Suppl.* 9 Sept. 325/2 Hudson was included among the victims because he was given to 'bucko' (to use a piece of sea slang). **1924** *Ibid.* 6 Nov. 712/3 Bucko skippers. **1926** *Spectator* 6 Feb. 229/2 A youngster who went to sea as apprentice and finished bucko mate of a Yankee packet. **1927** *Blackw. Mag.* Jan. 5/1 A great big bucko of a man. **1939** T. S. ELIOT *Old Possum's Practical Cats* 16 His bucko mate, Grumbuskin, long since had disappeared. **1969** *Courier-Mail* (Brisbane) 18 Aug. 5/2 The old buckos in the peaked caps..never thought they would live to see the day when Irishmen applauded the arrival of British troops.

†**bu'ckone.** *Obs.* Also buccoon. [ad. It. *boccone*, f. *bocca* mouth.] A mouthful, morsel.
1625 PURCHAS *Pilgrim* II. 1340 The Diet of the Turkes is sometimes rosted Buckones (that is, small bits or morsels of flesh). **1629** CAPT. SMITH *Trav. & Adv.* xiii. 24 The Tymor ..fed upon Pillaw..with little bits of mutton or Buckones. **1659** GAUDEN *Tears of Ch.* 673 Having purchased a good buccoon, and craving for more.

buckorome, obs. form of BUCKRAM.

‖**buckra** (ˈbʌkrә). Also **buccra, buckara, buccara, buckree, -ro.** [In negro patois of Surinam, *bakra*, master. According to J. L. Wilson, quoted in Mahn's Webster, in lang. of Calabar coast, 'demon, powerful and superior being'. H. Goldie *Dict. of Efik Lang.* (of Old Calabar) has *mbākara*, *mākara*, white man, European, f. *kara* to encompass, get round, master (a subject).]
A white man (in negro talk).
1794 *European Mag.* XXVI. 144 De noder day When Buckro no be beating. **1833** MARRYAT *P. Simple* II. x, Ah, piccaninny buccra! how you do? **1863** *20 Yrs. in W. Ind. &c.* in *Reader* 21 Feb. 189 'Buckra die hard this time' said the negroes; 'Since Gospel come buckra die hard.'

buckram (ˈbʌkrәm), *sb.* Forms: 3, 5 bukeram, (4 bougeren), 4, 6 bukram, 5 bokram, 5–6 bokeram, -ham, 6 bocram(e, -keram, bucram, -um, buckeram(e, -mme, 6–7 buckrom, -erom, -orome, 8 buchram, 6– buckram. [Found in most of the European langs. between 12th and 15th c.; cf. OF. *boquerant* (12th c.), *bouqueran*, *bouquerrant*, *bouguerant*, mod.F. *bougran*, Pr. *bocaran*, Cat. *bocaram* (Diez), Sp. *bucaran*, It. *bucherame* (in Boccaccio 14th c.), med.L. (in France) *boquerannus*, *bucaranus*, (in Italy) *buchiranus*; also MHG. *buggeram*, *buggeran*, *buckeram*, MDu. *bocraen*, *bocrael*, *bollecraen*, *boucraen*. In early continental and apparently in early Eng. use it denoted a costly and delicate fabric, sometimes of cotton and sometimes of linen; but it afterwards acquired the sense of coarse gummed linen used for linings, thus becoming synonymous with Sp. *bocací*, F. *boucassin*, BOCASIN; and this meaning it retains in modern Eng., Fr., and It. (The MHG. lexicographers state that in that lang. the word meant 'a fabric of goat's hair', but this explanation may perhaps be a conjecture founded on a supposed derivation from Ger. *bock* BUCK *sb.*[1]) As the Eng. forms generally have *m*, while all the Fr. forms have *n*, it is possible that the word may have been adopted into Eng. not from Fr. but from Italian. For the history of the word in Europe, and its probable changes of meaning, see Col. Yule's *Marco Polo* I. 46–48 and 59.
Of the ultimate etymology nothing is really known. Some refer to It. *bucherare* 'to pierce full of holes', supposing that the name was first given to a kind of muslin or net (cf. quot. 1548 in 1). Reiske (in *Constantin. Porphyrog.* ed. Niebuhr II. 530) proposes Arab *abū qirām* 'pannus cum intextis figuris', but he does not say where he found this compound; the simple *qirām* is of doubtful meaning, the native lexicographers quoted in the Qāmūs giving the various renderings 'red veil', 'striped and figured woollen cloth', 'thin veil' (Freytag, s.v.). Others suggest derivation from *Bokhara*, or from *Bulgaria*, but this does not agree with the early Fr. forms.]
†**1.** A kind of fine linen or cotton fabric. *Obs.*
1222 *Ornamenta Eccl. Sarum* in *Register S. Osmund* (1884) II. 132 Alba una de bukeram, cum parura, brodata. **1340** *Ayenb.* 258 þe queade riche þet zuo ofte ham ssredeþ ase of to zofte bougeren and of to moche of pris pourpre. **1411** *Licence to Bp. Waterford* 26 Apr. in *Close Roll*, [To export from England to Ireland, duty free], 18 pec. de Bokerham. **1463** MARG. PASTON in *Lett.* 472 II. 132, I kan gettyn non gode bokeram in this town. **1475** *Hist. MSS. Commiss., Inv. Goods* I. 555 A crosse of blue bokeram for the roode. **1548** THOMAS *Rules Italian Grammar* in *Promp. Parv.* 42 *Bucherame*, buckeramme, & some there is white, made of bombase, so thinne that a man mai see through it. **1552–3** *Inv. Ch. Goods Stafford.*, iij olde vestements, one of grene satten, the other of blewe buckeram. [**1849–53** ROCK *Ch. of Fathers* II. vi. 104 The mitre was made of..plain, fine linen ..which, during the Middle Ages, was known here in England under the name of 'buckram'.]
2. A kind of coarse linen or cloth stiffened with gum or paste. ***men in buckram***: sometimes proverbially for non-existent persons, in allusion to Falstaff's 'four rogues in buckram' (quot. 1596).
1436 *Pol. Poems* (1859) II. 171 Fustiane, and canvase, Carde, bokeram, of olde tyme thus it wase. **1549** CHEKE in Ellis *Orig. Lett. Lit. Men* (1843) 8, I lack painted bucrum to lai betweyne bokes and bordes in mi studi. **1596** SHAKS. *1 Hen. IV*, II. iv. 217 Foure Rogues in Buckrom let driue at me. **1665** BOYLE *Occas. Refl.* (1675) Pref. 21 The fashion, that now-a-days allows our Gallants to wear fine Laces upon Canvass and Buckram. **1732** BERKELEY *Alciphr.* III. §9 One of our ladies..stiffened..with hoops and whalebone and buckram. **1820** SCOTT *Abbot* xv, My stomach..is..too well bumbasted out with straw and buckram.
†**b.** A lawyer's bag; = *buckram-bag*. *Obs.*
1608 TOURNEUR *Rev. Trag.* IV. ii. 107 Yes, to looke long upon inck & black buckrom [in allusion to Attorneys' bags]. **1622** FLETCHER *Sp. Curate* IV. vii, To be..A Lawyer's Asse, to carry Bookes, and Buckrams.
3. *fig.* Stiffness; a stiff and starched manner; that which gives a man a stiff exterior.
1682 H. MORE *Annot. Glanvil's Lux O.* 55 His Style, the texture whereof is not onely Fustian, but over-often hard and stiff Buckram. **1785** CORNWALLIS *Let.* 24 May in *Corr.* (1859) I. vii. 191 A fine, good-humoured, unaffected lad, no pride or buckram. **1793** ROBERTS *Looker-on* (1794) II. 181 To endure the confinement and buckram of any formal course of habit. **1822** HAZLITT *Men & Mann.* Ser. II. x. (1869) 196 Laying aside the buckram of pedantry and pretence.
4. *attrib.* or quasi-*adj.* **a.** Of buckram, like buckram.
1537 *Bury Wills* (1850) 129, I beqwethe to Robart Payne a bocram shert, and to yonge Mr. Robt a bocram shert. **1563–87** FOXE *A. & M.* III. 623 She..took with her a Buckeram Apron. **1571** ASCHAM *Scholem.* (Arb.) 100 To clothe him selfe with nothing els, but a demie bukram cassok. **1645** MILTON *Colast.* Wks. (1851) 365 A meer petti-fogger..so hardy, as to lay aside his buckram wallet, and make himself a fool in Print. **1820** BYRON *Let. to Murray* 12 Nov., Pointing to his buckram shirt collar and inflexible cravat. **1837** CARLYLE *Fr. Rev.* I. VI. i. 263 Well may the buckram masks start together, terror-struck.
b. *fig.* Stiff, 'starched', 'stuck up'; that has a false appearance of strength.
a **1589** FULKE *Agst. Allen* 301 (L.) A few buckram bishops of Italy. **1603** H. CROSSE *Vertues Commw.* (1878) 122 Prostitute their ingenious labours to inrich such buckorome gentlemen. **1635** PAGITT *Christianogr.* II. vi. 60, 300 Buckram Bishops of the selfe same making. **1840** CARLYLE *Heroes* v. 287 A wondrous buckram style,—the best he [Johnson] could get. **1856** MISS BIRD *Englishwoman in America* 374 In America no play was ever more successful than the 'Buckram Englishman'.
5. *Comb.*, as ***buckram-maker***; also, **buckram-bag**, a lawyer's bag (sometimes = the lawyer himself); **buckram-men**, men in buckram (cf. 2).
1611 BARREY *Ram Alley* I. in *Dodsley* (1780) V. 424 The buckram-bag must trudge all weathers. *a* **1680** BUTLER *Rem.* (1759) II. 313 His Face is like a Lawyer's Buckram Bag, that has always Business in it. *c* **1644** CLEVELAND *Rupertismus* (1687) 53 The terror of whose Name can out of seven Like Falstaff's Buckram-men, make fly eleven.

buckram (ˈbʌkrәm), *v.* [f. prec.] *trans.* To pad or stiffen with buckram; to give to anything a starched pomposity or a false appearance of strength. Also with *out*, *up*. Chiefly *fig.*
1783 COWPER *Task* VI. 652 His most holy book..was never used before To buckram out the memory of a man. **1784** WARTON in Boswell *Johnson* (1831) V. 211 It may have been written by Walpole, and buckram'd by Mason. **1792** ROBERTS *Looker-on* (1794) I. 53 You pinched, buckramed, and pomatumed me up to such a degree. **1855** DE QUINCEY in H. Page *Life & Writ.* II. xviii. 111 But afterwards—he buckramed or crinolined his graceful sketch with an elaborate machinery of gnomes and sylphs.

buckramed (ˈbʌkrәmd), *ppl. a.* [f. prec. sb. or vb. + -ED.] Stiffened with buckram; clad in buckram. Also *fig.*
1793 ROBERTS *Looker-on* (1794) II. 77 Two antiquated beaux, with long buckramed accoutrements and flowing perrukes. **1813** *Examiner* 8 Feb. 88/2 It is so stiff, so buckramed, so spiritless in manners. **1850** HAWTHORNE *Scarlet L.* xx. (1879) 250 His buckramed habit of clerical decorum. **1861** SALA *Tw. round Clock* 184 The starched, buckramed..skirts of my female relatives. **1880** J. C. WATTS *Gt. Novelists* 89 Steeled and buckramed knights.

'buckramize, *v. nonce-wd.* To buckram. *fig.*
1812 G. COLMAN *Br. Grins*, *2 Parsons* xi. (1872) 201 Prigs —whose leaven Consists in buckramizing souls for heaven.

†**'buck'rams.** *Obs.* [perh. f. BUCK *sb.*[1] 1 (referring to its offensive smell) + *rams*, var. RAMSON.] Another name for Ramsons or Wild Garlic.
1578 LYTE *Dodoens* V. lxxi. 638 The thirde kinde is called ..in English, Ramsons, Buckrammes, & Beares Garlike. **1611** COTGR., *Ail d'ours*, Ramsons, Ramsies, Bucke rammes, Beares garlicke. **1783** in AINSWORTH *Lat. Dict.* (Morell) I.

bucksaree, variant of BUXERRY, *Obs.*

†**'bucks-beard.** *Obs.* [A transl. of Gr. τραγοπώγων.] A plant: Goats-beard; Salsify.
1551 TURNER *Herbal* I. (1568) 59 Dioscorides writeth no more of bukkes beard but that it is good to eat. **1578** LYTE *Dodoens* II. xvii. 167 The Spaniardes Scurzonera seemeth also to be a kinde of Tragopogon or Buckesbearde.

bucksee, buckshish, see BUKSHI, BAKSHEESH *sb.*

buck's-eye. *U.S.* (See quot.)
1883 *Leisure Hour* 476/1 Buckseye, the sweet-smelling Californian lilac (*Ceanothus*), forming a dense undergrowth.

Buck's Fizz. [f. the name of *Buck's* Club, London + FIZZ, FIZ *sb.* 3.] A cocktail drink of champagne or sparkling white wine mixed with orange juice.
1930 H. CRADDOCK *Savoy Cocktail Bk.* 194 Bucks Fizz, use long tumbler. ¼ Glass Orange Juice. Fill with Champagne. **1982** BARR & YORK *Official Sloane Ranger Handbk.* 27/2 Sainsbury's sparkling Saumur and Blanquette de Limeaux are useful for celebratory Buck's Fizzes.

buckshee (ˈbʌkʃiː, bʌkˈʃiː), *sb.* and *a. slang* (orig. Army). [Alteration of BAKSHEESH; cf. BUKSHI.]

A. *sb.* Something extra, free, or to spare; an allowance above the usual amount. **B.** *adj.* Free; spare, extra. Hence as *adv.*

1916 *Daily Mail* 1 Nov. 4/4 'Buckshee' (probably derived from back-sheesh, meaning extra rations, or anything over after an issue has been made—buckshee loaf, buckshee 'fags', etc.). **1919** *Athenæum* 1 Aug. 695/2 'Buckshee' deserves attention as probably, with 'scrounge', the most popular slang towards the end of the war. **1920** *Outward Bound* Nov. 66/2 The police help themselves freely to buckshee refreshments. **1921** *Glasgow Herald* 1 Nov. 5 To . . give the goods almost buckshee to our cut-throat friends, the tribesmen of the N.-W. Frontier of India. **1942** C. Barrett *On the Wallaby* iii. 48 The Chief of Staff . . snapped, 'Want a buckshee trip, eh?'

buck's-horn. An old name for various plants, from the shape of their leaves, or appearance of their branches. **a.** *Senebiera Coronopus*, Swine's Cress. **b.** The Virginia Sumach (*Rhus typhina*). Also **buck's horn plantain, buck's horn weld**: species of PLANTAIN, WELD.

a **1450** *MS. Bodl.* 536 (Cockayne *Leechd.* III. 316), Bukes hornes or els swynes grese (grass) and has leues slaterde as an hertys horne. **1597** Gerard *Herbal* xcvi. §1. 346 Bvckes horne . . hath long narrowe hoarie leaues. **1712** Petiver *Rare Plants* §6 in *Phil. Trans.* XXVII. 424 Virginia Sumach . . the first Branches are very soft and velvety, like the Horns of a young Deer, for which reason its call'd Buckshorn by the Country People. **1719** London & Wise *Compl. Gard.* 199 Bucks-horn Sallad is multipli'd only by Seed . . Vide Harts-Horn Sallad.

buck's-horn, var. of BUCKHORN.

buck-shot ('bʌkʃɒt). [f. BUCK *sb.*[1] + SHOT.]

†**1.** ? The distance at which a buck may be shot. *Obs. rare.*

1447-8 Shillingford *Lett.* (1871) 87 The said Cathedrall Churche stant a buc shote fro and more.

2. A coarse kind of shot, larger than *swan-shot*, used in shooting deer or other large game. Also *attrib.*, as in *buckshot-cartridge*; **buckshot-cinder** (see quot.); **buckshot-rule**, a political nickname for government (of Ireland) upheld by a constabulary with loaded rifles, which arose during the Chief-Secretaryship of Mr. W. E. Forster, and was especially associated with his name, though the order that the constabulary should load with buck-shot, instead of ball as formerly, was made under his predecessor Mr. J. Lowther.

1776 O. Schuyler in Sparks *Corr. Amer. Rev.* (1853) I. 252 Should the enemy advance . . we shall be at a loss for ball and buckshot. **1871** Napheys *Prev. & Cure Dis.* iii. iv. 740 A piece about the size of a buckshot is the ordinary dose. **1881** Parnell in *Daily News* 3 Oct. 6/3 Enemies to buckshot rule. **1881** Raymond *Mining Gloss.*, *Buckshot-cinder*, cinder from the iron blast-furnace, containing grains of iron. **1885** *Suakim* iv. 88 To be used at night pending the arrival of buckshot cartridges from England.

buckskin ('bʌkskɪn). [f. BUCK *sb.*[1] + SKIN.]

1. The skin of a buck.

1433 *Test. Ebor.* (1855) II. 31 Unum dublett coopertum cum bukskynnes. **1465** in *Ripon Ch. Acts* 159 Unam longam tunicam de bukskynnes. **1686** *Lond. Gaz.* No. 2124/4, 15 Buck-skins dry'd, not pared. **1707** *Ibid.* No. 4344/4 For Sale by the Candle . . 9000 Carolina Buck-Skins. **1809** R. Langford *Introd. Trade* 82 Buck Skins at 11*s.* 6*d.* each.

2. a. Leather made from the skin of a buck; also from sheepskin prepared in a particular way.

1804 Huddesford *Wiccam. Chaplet* 140 Bold blades in buck-skin breeched. **1828** Scott *Fair M. Perth* I. 34 Willing to see you two as closely united together, as ever needle stitched buckskin. **1846-83** R. Eg.-Warburton *Hunt. Songs* (1883) xlvi. 134 Buckskin's the only wear fit for the saddle. **1878** Black *Green Past.* xiii. 100 The suit of grey buckskin which he wore.

b. *attrib.* and *comb.*

1565 Golding *Ovid's Met.* iv. (1593) 79 In buck-skin cotes. **1660** Pepys *Diary* 1 June, The fine pair of buckskin gloves. **1710** *Tatler* No. 241 ¶9 A Pair of Buck-Skin Breeches. **1753** H. Walpole *Corr.* I. 198 A young squire booted and spurred and buckskin-breeched. **1824** Cobbett *Weekly Register* 12 June 674 Priests . . who never wear buckskin breeches, and go a fox-hunting. **1877** J. Allen *Amer. Bison* 581 The buckskin suit of the Rocky Mountain hunter.

3. Breeches made of buckskin. (In first quot. possibly gloves or boots of that material.)

1481-90 Howard *Househ. Bks.* 315 My Lord paied to his cordwaner . . for a payr bucskyns . . xviij.*d.* *a* **1658** Cleveland *News fr. Newcastle* 120 [He] . . in embroidered Buckskins blows his Nails. **1774** *Westm. Mag.* II. 657 The honest buckskin . . Our modern Nimrod turns to sattin breeches. **1851** Kingsley *Yeast* ii. 34 A red coat and white buckskins.

†**4.** A nickname of the American troops during the Revolutionary war; hence, a native American.

1787 Burns *Amer. War*, Cornwallis fought as long's he dought, An' did the buckskins claw, man. **1800** Weems *Washington* ii. (1877) 8 George Washington a buck skin! . . impossible! he was certainly an European. **1823** Thacher *Mil. Jrnl.* 72 The burlesque epithet of Yankee from one party, and that of Buckskin from the other.

5. A kind of strong twill cloth.

1894 *Tailoring* 3 Feb. 1/1 Coatings.—Black and Blue Serges, cut and covered in every size of twill, . . Buckskins, 10s. **1895** *Oracle Encycl.* I. 528/2 *Buckskin*, a strong twilled woollen fabric for trouserings. The web is usually about 27 inches wide, and when finished the pile or nap is so shorn that the texture is seen through it. **1968** J. Ironside *Fashion Alphabet* 216 Buckskin cloth . . is a closely woven woollen cloth simulating buckskin.

Hence **'buckskinned** *a.*

1829 A. Fonblanque *Eng. under Admin.* (1837) I. 240 Yorkshire buckskinned 'Squires. **1884** Joaquin Miller *Mem. & Rime* 107 A savage buckskinned delegate to Congress . . from . . Oregon.

bucksome, obs. form of BUXOM.

†**'buck-stall.** *Obs.* exc. *Hist.* [f. BUCK *sb.*[1] + STALL.] A large net for catching deer.

1503 *Act 19 Hen. VII*, xi, The greatest Destruction of Red Deer . . is with Nets called Deer-hays and Buck-stalls. **1613** W. Browne *Brit. Past.* ii. iii. (1772) II. 131 Knit thy torne Buck-stals with well-twisted threds. **1655** Fuller *Ch. Hist.* vi. 317 Sir Henry pitcht a Buckstall (wherewith he used to take Deer in the Forest) in the narrowest place of the Marsh. **1870** Edgar *Runnymede* 156 We may be dealt with as deer in a buckstall.

†**buck's tongue.** *Obs.* Some rough leaved herb; perhaps Bugloss, or Prickly Ox-tongue.

c **1450** *Alphita* (Anecd. Oxon.) 20 *Barba yrsina*, assimilatur lingue bouis, asperiora tamen habet folia; anglice *buckestonge*.

buckthorn ('bʌkθɔːn). [f. BUCK *sb.*[1] + THORN. App. Lyte's translation of the It. and mod.L. names.]

The shrub *Rhamnus catharticus*; the berries of which yield sap-green and other pigments, and were formerly used as a powerful cathartic.

1578 Lyte *Dodoens* vi. xxx. 810 The Italians do call it *Spino Merlo*, some call it *Spino ceruino* . . and of Valerius Cordus, *Cerui spina*: we may well call it in English, Bucke Thorne. **1579** Langham *Gard. Health* (1633) 99 Bvckthorne, the beries do purge downwards mightily flegme and choller. **1753** Chambers *Cycl. Supp.* s.v., Of buckthorn berries are made three several sorts of colours. **1859** W. Coleman *Woodlands* (1862) 122 On chalky or loamy soils, we may occasionally find the Buckthorn growing in considerable plenty.

'buck-tooth. [f. BUCK *sb.*[1] + TOOTH.] A large projecting tooth. Also *attrib.*

[*a* **1550** *Addicioun of Scottis Corniklis, &c.* (Th. Thomson) 3 (Jam.) Schir Thomas Boyde was slane be Alexander Stewart buktuth and his sonnes.] **1753** Hanway *Trav.* (1762) II. xvi. i. 440 He ordered a man's teeth to be pulled out, for no other reason than their being buck-teeth. **1866** Carlyle *Remin.*, *E. Irving* 99 An older . . bigger boy, with red hair, wild buck teeth, and scorched complexion.

Hence **'buck-toothed** *ppl. a.*

1863 Sir B. Burke *Viciss. Fam.* iii. 274 One shall be buck-toothed, another hair-lipped and the fourth a stammerer.

bucku: see BUCHU.

†**'buck-,washing.** *Obs.* [f. BUCK *sb.*[3] + WASH *v.*] The process of washing coarse and very dirty linen, by boiling it in an alkaline lye (BUCK *sb.*[3]), and afterwards beating and rinsing it in clear water; see *bucking-washing* in BUCKING *vbl. sb.*[1] So **buck-washer**; also dial. **buck-wash**.

1598 Shaks. *Merry W.* iii. iii. 164 You were best meddle with buck-washing. **1611** Cotgr. *Buandiere*, a laundresse, or buck-washer. **1829** Carlyle *Misc.* (1857) II. 26 His office of buckwasher, that is of verse corrector to his Majesty. **1845** —— *Cromwell's Lett. & Sp.* (1873) I. ii. 11 Such a job of buckwashing. **1879** Miss Jackson *Shropsh. Wd.-bk.* (E.D.S.) *Buch-wesh* or *weshin'*, a large wash of heavy, coarse linen . . In the buck-wesh no soap was used, but the linen was boiled in the buck-lee. It was then carried to a neighbouring stream or spring, and laid upon a smooth stone or a block . . there the linen was beaten with a 'bat-staff', after which it was well 'swilled' in the pure water.

buckwheat ('bʌkhwiːt). Also 6 **buk-, bockewheate.** [perh. immediately ad. Du. *boekweit* (*bockweydt* in Lyte) or Ger. *buchweize* 'beech-wheat' from the shape of the triquetrous seeds, whence also the botanical name *Fagopyrum*; but it was referred to as a familiar name by Turner, 30 years before Lyte professed to take it from Dutch, so that the name may have been of Eng. origin, after BUCK-MAST or BUCK *sb.*[2] Barnaby Googe app. independently called it *beech-wheat*.]

1. a. A species of *Polygonum* (*P. Fagopyrum*), a native of Central Asia, whence it was introduced into Europe by the Turks about the 13th c. The seed is in Europe used as food for horses, cattle, and poultry; in N. America its meal is made into 'buckwheat cakes', regarded as a dainty for the breakfast-table. Formerly also called BRANK.

1548 Turner *Names of Herbs* (1881) 35 Elatine is lyke wythwynde, but it hath seedes and floures lyke Buckwheate; it may be named in englishe running Buckwheate or bynde corne. **1551** [see 2]. **1577** B. Googe *Heresbach's Husb.* (1586) 31, I had rather call it Beechwheate, bicause the graine therof is threecorned, not unlike the beechmast both in color and forme. **1578** Lyte *Dodoens* iv. xiv. 468 In base Almaigne Bockweydt, after whiche name it may be englished Bock-wheat. **1597** Gerard *Herbal* i. xlvii. 89 Buckwheat nourisheth less than wheat. **1776** Adam Smith *W.N.* i. i. xi. 236 Indian Corn and buckwheat are used for feeding poultry. **1792** A. Young *Trav. France* 456 In part of Normandy and Bretagne, they live very much . . upon buck-wheat. **1859** Jephson *Brittany* ii. 20 Buckwheat is used almost exclusively for feeding pheasants.

b. *attrib.*

1865 Baring-Gould *Werewolves* 3 He was down by the hedge of his buckwheat field, and the sun had set. **1873** *Atlas of Michigan* Pref. 20 Upon a somewhat similar soil is found the 'Buckwheat' . . pine. **1881** Raymond *Mining Gloss.* s.v. *Coal*, *Buckwheat-coal* . . is the smallest size, and usually included in the dirt or culm. **1882** *Garden* 25 Mar. 191/3 To go to America for a good . . Buckwheat cake.

c. *ellipt.* A buckwheat cake. *U.S.*

1830 *Collegian* 41 (D.A.E.), Six muffins, a dozen buck-wheats. **1904** G. H. Lorimer *Old Gorgon Graham* 227 A fellow'd load up with pie and buck-wheats for breakfast, and go around wondering about his stomach-ache.

2. Applied to other species of *Polygonum*, esp. to Black Bindweed (*P. Convolvulus*) or 'Running Buckwheat', and to *P. tartaricum* 'Tartarean Buckwheat'.

1548 [see 1]. **1551** Turner *Herbal* 165, I call it runnynge bukwheate, because in thre thynges it resemblethe bukwheate. **1601** Holland *Pliny* II. 281 Running Buckwheat or Bindweed . . putteth forth smal leaues, round and hairy. **1824** Miss Mitford *Village* Ser. i. (1863) 101 The beautiful buck-wheat, whose transparent leaves and stalks are so brightly tinged with vermilion.

'buckwood. *U.S.* [BUCK *sb.*[1] i.] = BUCK-EYE i.

1787 M. Cutler in W. P. & J. P. Cutler *Life* (1888) II. 397 The more useful trees . . butternut, . . buckwood. **1810** Morse *Amer. Gazetteer* s.v. *Ohio*, Hickory, cherry, buckwood or horse chestnut, [etc.].

bucky, variant form of BUCKIE.

buclere, obs. form of BUCKLER.

bucolic (bjuː'kɒlɪk), *a.* and *sb.* Also 6 **bucolique, bucolik,** 7 **-ike, -icke,** 8 **-ick.** [ad. L. *būcolic-us*, a. Gr. βουκολικ-ός, f. βουκόλος herdsman.]

A. *adj.* **1.** Of or pertaining to herdsmen or shepherds; pastoral.

1613 R. C. *Table Alph.* (ed. 3) *Bucolike*, pertaining to beasts or heardsmen. **1750** Johnson *Rambl.* No. 37 ¶10 The Pollio of Virgil . . is a composition truly bucolick. **1803** Syd. Smith *Wks.* (1867) I. 50 He goes on, mingling bucolic details and sentimental effusions. **1863** Mary Howitt tr. *F. Bremer's Greece* II. xvii. 167 The shepherds and shepherdesses . . milk the cattle, and compose bucolic poems. **1873** Symonds *Grk. Poets* x. 308 Bucolic poetry.

2. Pertaining to country life; rural, rustic, countryfied. (Somewhat *humorous.*)

1846 Lytton *Lucretia* (1853) 247 The second [partner] had a bucolic turn. **1859** Geo. Eliot *A. Bede* 67 The keenest of bucolic minds felt a whispering awe at the sight of the gentry. **1875** A. R. Hope *Schoolboy Fr.* 308 A sturdy-looking bucolic individual. **1878** Lady Herbert *Hübner's Ramble* ii. xii. 212 In its happy, bucolic isolation.

3. *bucolic cæsura*, a cæsura after the fourth foot in a dactylic hexameter.

1887 G. M. Hopkins *Let.* 20 Feb. (1938) 130 The 'bucolic caesura' (between fourth and fifth foot, pause or no pause in sense). *Ibid.*, The rarity of spondees before the bucolic caesura. **1957** *Encycl. Brit.* XXII. 56/1 A feature in his [*sc.* Theocritus'] versification . . is the so-called bucolic caesura. The rule is that, if there is a pause at the end of the fourth foot, this foot must be a dactyl.

B. *sb.* [cf. L. *Būcolica*, Gr. βουκολικά in same use.]

1. *pl.* Pastoral poems: rarely *sing.* a single poem.

1531 Elyot *Gov.* i. x. (1883) I. 62 What thinge can be more familiar than his [Virgil's] bucolikes. *a* **1560** Rolland *Crt. Venus* iii. 103 His Georgiks and Bucolikis. **1656** Blount *Glossogr.*, *Bucolicks*, pastoral songs, or songs of Heardsmen. **1870** *Daily News* 16 Apr., The manufacture of maple sugar, of which I may sing you a bucolic when the season arrives.

2. = Bucolic poet.

1774 T. Warton *Hist. Eng. Poetry* xxxix. III. 59 Spenser, who is erroneously ranked as our earliest English bucolic.

3. A rustic, peasant. (*humorous.*)

1862 *Sat. Rev.* No. 351. 72/1 It is a satisfaction to make the personal acquaintance of so worthy a bucolic.

4. *pl.* Agricultural pursuits. *rare.*

1865 *Times* 15 Apr., A fancy farm steading . . for any special branch of bucolics that may most delight the proprietor.

bu'colical, *a.* [f. as prec. + -AL[1].] = BUCOLIC *a.*

1523 Skelton *Garl. Laurell* 327 Theocritus with his bucolycal relacyons. **1830** T. Hamilton *C. Thornton* 103 His favourite bucolical pursuits. **1881** Benham *Church Controv.* in *Macm. Mag.* XLV. 119/1 The outcry against scientific investigations has probably almost exhausted itself, except among very bucolical persons indeed.

Hence **bucolically** *adv.*

1881 *Spectator* 22 Jan. 120 Mr. Bence Jones . . will have done good work . . of which he may be bucolically proud.

bu'colican. *nonce-wd.* A rustic, a countryman.

1866 J. Banks in *Argosy* I. 171 The one characteristic of the British bucolican is his stillness and reticence.

bucolicism (bjuː'kɒlɪsɪz(ə)m). [f. BUCOLIC + -ISM.] Bucolic qualities or characteristics; the bucolic style.

1879 M. Pattison *Milton* iii. 41 This factitious bucolicism is pervaded by a pathos, which, like volcanic heat, has fused into a new compound the dilapidated débris of the Theocritean world. **1893** *Temple Bar* Jan. 63 Beer, brandy and bucolicism notwithstanding.

†**bu'colicon.** *Obs. rare.* [a. Gr. βουκολικόν, sing. of βουκολικά 'pastoral poems'.] A bucolic poem.

1640 W. Hodgson *Div. Cosmogr.* 79 His three and twentieth [Psalm] . . we may call his Bucolicon.

'bucolism. *nonce-wd.* [f. BUCOL-IC + -ISM.] A rustic phrase or characteristic.

1830 H. N. COLERIDGE *Grk. Poets* 7 The lowest 'bucolisms' of Theocritus.

bucram, -um, obs. forms of BUCKRAM.

bu'crane. *Arch.* Also bu'cranium. [F. *bucrane*, and L. *bucranium*, ad. Gr. *βουκράνιον*, f. *βοῦς* ox + *κρανίον* skull.] A sculptured ornament representing an ox-skull.

1854 FAIRHOLT *Dict. Terms in Art, Bucrania.* **1878** R. J. PLAYFAIR *Algeria* (ed. 2) 232 Over the columns and pilasters [of the Temple] are panels ornamented by bucranes.

bud (bʌd), *sb.*^{1} Forms: 4–5 bodde, 5–7 budde, (6 bood, botthe), 7 budd, 6– bud. [Late ME. *budde, bodde*; of uncertain etymology. In ME. identical in form with BUDDE.

Prof. Skeat suggests a connexion of some kind with ODu. *botte*, mod.Du. *bot* a bud, or with OF. *boter*, mod.F. *bouter* to push, put forth, whence F. *bouton* (see BUTTON *sb.*) 'bud'. (Franck refers the ODu. word to a Romanic source akin to or identical with OF. *boter*.) But such a change from *t* to *d* is anomalous.]

1. a. *Bot.* A little projection found at the axil of a leaf, composed of scales, which are small leaves, and forming the rudiment of a branch, cluster of leaves, or blossom. Hence, applied to a flower (or leaf) at any stage of growth until fully opened.

1398 TREVISA *Barth. De P.R.* XVII. lxxv, Sumtyme burgynge of boddes beþ gnawe and frete with flyes. *c* **1400** *Purif. Marie* in *Tundale's Vis.* (Turnb. 1843) 135 The comyng Of greene veer with fresch buddes new. **1526** *Pilgr. Perf.* (W. de W. 1531) 234 So longe it is called the budde of a rose, as it is not a perfyte rose. **1527** ANDREW *Brunswyke's Distyll. Waters* O ij, The best flowres ben of the rede apples . . whan the botthes begynne the blossome and to go open. **1601** SHAKS. *Twel. N.* II. iv. 114 A worme i'th budde. *a* **1682** SIR T. BROWNE *Tracts* 64 To pluck away the bearing buds, before they proceed unto flowers or fruit. **1752** JOHNSON *Rambl.* No. 207 ⁋8 The swelling bud and opening blossom. **1832** TENNYSON *Lotos-Eat.* 71 The folded leaf is woo'd from out the bud. **1842** GRAY *Struct. Bot.* i. (1880) 7 An incipient stem or branch, with its rudimentary leaves, is a Bud.

b. *Zool.* A similar growth in animals of low organization, which develops into a new individual.

1836–9 TODD *Cycl. Anat. & Phys.* II. 433/1 The new individual grows upon the parent as a bud or sprout. **1861** HULME tr. *Moquin-Tandon* II. i. 46 The creature gives off from certain parts of its body buds or gemmæ, which at a fixed period become detached, and give rise to new animals.

2. *transf.* Used of things resembling buds: as the rudiment of a horn when it begins to sprout; a nipple; a pimple in farcy, a disease of horses.

1593 NASHE *Christs T.* (1613) 145 Their breasts they embuske vp on hie, and their round Roseate buds immodestly lay forth. **1639** T. DE GREY *Compl. Horsem.* 304 This powder healeth the buds or knots of the farcin. **1641** FRENCH *Distill.* iv. (1651) 103 The young buds of Hartshorne. **1702** *Lond. Gaz.* No. 3814/4 A.. Grey Gelding.. scar'd with the Farcy Buds.

3. *fig.* **a.** Anything in an immature or undeveloped state.

1579 TOMSON *Calvin's Serm. Tim.* 238/2 Such a desire is a budde of ambition. **1592** WARNER *Alb. Eng.* VIII. xxxix. 193 Our decent Church-Rites.. Did then put forth her Braunches, and weare fruitfull in the bood. **1632** G. HERBERT *Temple, Sunday* i, The fruit of this, the next worlds bud. **1727** THOMSON *Summer* 582 The wint'ry blast of death Kills not the buds of virtue.

b. Said of children or young persons, or as a term of endearment.

1595 SHAKS. *John* III. iv. 82 Now will Canker-sorrow eat my bud [Arthur], And chase the natiue beauty from his cheeke. **1675** WYCHERLEY *Country Wife* II. i, You are my own dear bud. *Ibid.* III. ii, 'Tis no matter, no matter, bud. **1847** TENNYSON *Princ.* VI. 176 Her eye.. dwelt Full on the child; she took it: 'Pretty bud!.. half open'd bell of the woods!' **1881** *Confessions of friv. Girl* 39 This is your first party.. Yes, I am what is called a bud.

c. 'A weaned calf of the first year' (Ray *S. and E.C. Words* (1674) 60). Still in *dial.* use.

1662 *Collect. Campsey Ash* 30 in Nichols *Bibl. Top. Brit.* (1790) lii. For every gast beast and heifer, gast ware and bud [calf], three half-pence apiece. **1875** PARISH *Sussex Dial., Bud*, a calf of the first year, so called because the horns then begin to appear or bud. *Mod. dial. Kent*, There are three halfers [heifers] and two nice young buds in the yard.

d. A girl who is just 'coming out'; a débutante. Also more fully ***bud of promise***. Chiefly *U.S. colloq.*

1880 R. GRANT *Confessions of Frivolous Girl* i. 39 'This is your first party, I believe, Miss Palmer?'.. 'Yes, I am what is called a "bud".' **1888** *Charlestown Enterprise* (Farmer), The young, unmarried girl, in sport, Is called a bud of promise. **1889** *Harper's Mag.* Sept. 571/1 As dashing a belle as there was in the rooms—not a bud—a belle of some six or seven years standing. **1903** *N.Y. Tribune* 4 Oct., Among the latter [*sc.* the débutantes] will be Miss Enid Shaw, the only bud of the Cabinet circle. **1919** *Sphere* 1 Nov. 120/2 One of those dream-like young girls that only seem to happen in London during the height of the summer and winter seasons... This gilded 'bud' drove away in a cloak of warm pink panne.

4. Phr. ***in bud*** (said of plants; cf. *in leaf, in flower*): budding. ***in the bud***: not yet developed; often *fig.* = young, immature, 'in the germ'. ***to nip*** or ***crush in the bud***: *fig.* to repress or destroy (a project, etc.) in its first beginnings (see also NIP *v.*^{1} 5 b.)

1677 HORNECK *Law of Consideration* (1704) 89 If a tree does not thrive, if flowers do wither in the bud. **1746** *Rep. Cond. Sir J. Cope* 12 The crushing in the bud an Insurrection. **1844** *Mem. Babylonian P'cess.* II. 168 The plot was apparently nipped in the bud. **1847** TENNYSON *Princ.* I. 31 While life was yet in bud and blade. **1867** FREEMAN *Norm. Conq.* I. iv. 258 Promising germs of freedom were.. crushed in the bud. **1871** EARLE *Philol. Eng. Tong.* (1880) §445 A flectional word is a phrase in the bud.

5. *Comb.*, as ***bud-blighted, -crowned, -like*** adjs., ***bud-coat, -generation, -scale, -time, -variation***. Also **bud-bird** (*dial.*), the Bullfinch; †**bud-cutter**, obs. name of an insect (transl. F. *lisette* 'coupe-bourgeon', Boiste); **bud-germ** (*Zool.*) = 1 b; **bud-glue** (see quot.); **bud-graft** *v. trans.* = BUD *v.*^{1} 5; also as *sb.*, a shrub or tree grown by this process; so ***bud-grafted*** ppl. adj.; **bud-rot**, rotting of the buds of a plant or tree; a disease characterized by this; **bud-rudiment**, the cell in the embryo, from which the bud is developed; **bud-sport** [SPORT *sb.*^{1} 6 b], an abnormal variation produced from a bud; **bud-worm**, a larva that feeds upon the buds of corn, tobacco, fir-trees, etc.

1865 *Cornh. Mag.* 35 The provincial *'bud-bird' of Herefordshire, the bullfinch. **1820** SHELLEY *Prometh. Unb.* IV. i. 122 The *bud-blighted flowers of happiness. **1866** CHR. ROSSETTI *Prince's Progr. &c.* 3 Poppies.. Wrapped in *bud-coats hairy and neat. **1857** EMERSON *Poems* 50 The *bud-crowned Spring. **1693** EVELYN *De la Quint. Compl. Gard.* II. 100 To have the end of their new Shoots.. cut off by a little black round Insect, call'd *Bud-Cutter. **1880** C. & F. DARWIN *Movem. Pl.* 190 A bud may revert to the character of a former state many *bud-generations ago. **1884** BOWER & SCOTT *De Bary's Phaner. & Ferns* 99 Hanstein has termed these organs which cover the buds with a sticky secretion 'Beleimer', or Colleters, and their sticky product *bud-glue, or Blasto-colla. **1930** *Times* 26 Mar. 25/6 The yields from *bud-grafted trees will exceed those from selected seedlings. Of the 4,343 acres planted, 2,200 acres are either bud-grafted or alternate rows of bud-grafts and selected seedlings. **1936** *Economist* 18 Apr. 152/1 Those young areas.. had been budgrafted. **1839** BAILEY *Festus* (1854) 42 To watch young beauty's *budlike feelings burst And load the soul with love. **1847–9** TODD *Cycl. Anat. & Phys.* IV. 427/1 A simple canal with bud-like processes. **1906** E. J. BUTLER in *Agric. Jrnl. India* I. 310 A cocoanut palm disease known as '*bud rot'. **1946** *Nature* 14 Dec. 882/1 Bud-rot in the eastern tropics, hitherto fortunately never confused with eelworm attack, is due to *Phytophthora*. **1882** VINES *Sachs' Bot.* 297 A cell, which Pringsheim calls the *'bud-rudiment'. **1880** GRAY *Bot. Text-bk.* 400 *Bud-scales. The dry teguments which serve to protect the.. growing point within during the season of rest. **1900** B. D. JACKSON *Gloss. Bot. Terms* 38/1 *Bud sport. **1905** H. DE VRIES *Species & Varieties* xiv. 427 Bud-sports of variegated hollyhock, elms, chestnuts, beeches and others. **1956** C. AUERBACH *Genetics in Atomic Age* vi. 41 If it [*sc.* a mutated gene] is of a kind to produce a visible effect, a so-called 'bud-sport' will result, for example, a branch with white berries on a red-currant bush. **1850** *Rep. Comm. Patents 1849* (U.S.) 459 With the *bud-worm you must be more particular. **1922** W. SCHLICH *Man. Forestry* (ed. 4) I. II. 188 Financial assistance.. for the balsam bud-worm investigation.

†**bud,** *sb.*^{2} *Sc. Obs.* [prob. var. of *bod*, BODE an offering, f. ppl. stem of OE. *béodan* (see BID *v.*) to offer.] A bribe. Also in comb. ***bud-taker***.

1436 *Acts Jas. I*, clv. (JAM.) All jugeis sall gar the assysouris sweir.. that thay nouther haue tane, nor sall tak meid na buddis of ony partie. **1535** LYNDESAY *Satyre* 1616, I am ane Iudge.. Na bud nor fauour may my sicht oversyle. **1579** *Act Jas. VI* (1597) §93 The saidis Bud-takeris, to be displaced and deprived simpliciter of their offices. *a* **1651** CALDERWOOD *Hist. Kirk* (Wodrow) III. 394 They acquired wealth by taking budds from such as had sutes to him.

bud (bʌd), *sb.*^{3} *U.S. colloq.* [Childish or colloq. pronunc. of BROTHER *sb.*, or abbrev. of BUDDY *sb.* Cf. BUB *sb.*^{6}] Brother; used chiefly as a form of address.

1851 *Polly Peasblossom's Wedd.* 19 (Th.), 'An't you joking, bud?' asked Polly of her boy brother. **1889** *Harper's Mag.* Aug. 459/1 He said that his name was 'Bud' Lightwood... 'It's *brother*,' he said.. '"bud" and "sis", you know.' **1920** MULFORD *J. Nelson* iv. 46 But, say, bud, we don't have to go to Highbank at all. **1953** W. R. BURNETT *Vanity Row* i. 9 Gamblers.. would often hand him a quarter.. and say: 'Keep it, bud.'

bud (bʌd), *v.*^{1} [f. BUD *sb.*^{1}]

1. *intr.* **a.** To put forth buds, to sprout. **b.** with *out*: To come or push out, as a bud.

1398 [see BUDDING *vbl. sb.*^{1}] *c* **1440** *Promp. Parv.* 54 Buddun as trees, *gemmo*. **1535** COVERDALE *Job* xiv. 8 The stocke.. will budde. **1626** BACON *Sylva* (1677) §417 The removing of the Tree some Moneth before it Buddeth. **1684** tr. *Bonet's Merc. Compit.* VI. 206 If.. a Carbuncle bud out in the Arms or Legs. **1813** SCOTT *Rokeby* III. xxviii, The rose is budding fain. **1862** H. SPENCER *First Princ.* II. xv. §119 (1875) 336 The wings and legs of a bird.. when they bud-out from the sides of the embryo.

2. *fig.* To spring forth, as a bud; to begin to grow; to develop; also with *out, up*.

1566 KNOX *Hist. Ref.* Wks. 1846 I. 184 Thairby Goddis woord should somewhat bud. *a* **1593** H. SMITH *Serm.* (1866) II. 254 Many vices bud out of this one. **1608** GOLDING *Epit. Frossard's Chron.* II. 68 There was trouble and insurrection budding vp. **1613** SHAKS. *Hen. VIII*, I. i. 94 The sodaine breach.. is budded out, For France hath flaw'd the League. **1713** YOUNG *Last Day* III. 317 There, buds the promise of celestial worth. **1859** MERIVALE *Rom. Emp.* (1865) VIII. lxvi. 210 The camps which Agricola had planted.. budded, in the course of ages, into little towns.

3. *trans.* To put forth as buds; to produce by gemmation; also with *forth* and *out*. Also *fig.*

1591 SPENSER *Vis. Bellay* 138 This Hydra.. With seuen heads, budding monstrous crimes. **1625** *Gonsalvio's Sp. Inquis.*, It buddeth forth such pestilent blossomes. **1854** WOODWARD *Mollusca* (1856) 49 The power they [zoöphytes] possess of budding out new individuals. **1869** NICHOLSON *Zool.* lviii. (1880) 520 Within the branchial chamber [of the tadpole].. the fore-limbs are budded forth.

4. To bring into bud, cause to bud; also *fig.*

1604 DRAYTON *Owle* 3 The strength and fervour of whose pregnant ray, Buds every branch, and blossomes every spray. ? *a* **1700** *Hawthorn Tree* in Child *Ballads* I. 313 Next yere againe I will be sene To bude my branches. **1852** TUPPER *Proverb. Philos.* 403 When did the body elevate, expand, and bud the mind?

5. *Gardening.* To ingraft by inserting a bud of a shrub or tree under the bark of another 'stock', for the purpose of raising flowers or fruit different from those of the stock. Also *absol.*

1663 COWLEY *Verses & Ess.* (1669) 119 We no where Art do so triumphant see, As when it Grafs or Buds the Tree. **1664** EVELYN *Kal. Hort.* (1729) 198 You may.. bud at the end of this month. *Ibid.* Stocks to bud Oranges and Lemons on. **1725** BRADLEY *Fam. Dict.* II. s.v. *Laurel*, Grafted or budded upon black Cherry Stalks. **1853** *Blackw. Mag.* LXXIII. 131 He grafted, and budded, and hybridised. **1861** DELAMER *Fl. Gard.* 156 To be budded on the Musk Rose.

†**bud,** *v.*^{2} *Sc.* [f. BUD *sb.*^{2}.] *trans.* To bribe.

c **1565** LINDESAY (Pitscottie) *Cron. Scotl.* (1728) 148 They budded the king to bide at home. **1582–8** *Hist. Jas. VI* (1804) 198 Moirtoun.. buddit Tullybardin with the office of the Comptroller. **1636** RUTHERFORD *Lett.* lxiii. (1862) I. 169 To bud and bribe the Cross. **1657** [see BUDDING *vbl. sb.*^{2}].

bud, *v.*^{3} *Sc.* = must: see BUS *v.*

budda ('bʌdə). Also **buddah, buddha,** etc. [Native name.] An Australian myoporaceous plant, *Eremophila mitchelli*.

1890 *Sydney Mail* 14 June 1300/1, I would state that the tree known as sandalwood on the Darling and in the West generally, one of the 'Eremophylla', called 'Butha' by the natives, is not eaten by sheep. **1911** C. E. W. BEAN *'Dreadnought' of Darling* xv. 141 A feathery little bunch of light green.. which we often saw along the Darling banks; the stumpy budda. **1923** *Chambers's Jrnl.* 24/2 The air was rich with the scent of sandalwood and buddah. **1968** K. WEATHERLY *Roo Shooter* 18 The old doe and her joey camped under a thick buddha bush.

buddawong, var. BURRAWANG.

†**budde.** *Obs.* Forms: 1 budda, 5 budde (? bude, bowde): see also BOUD. [Of unknown etymology: the relation of the earlier *budda, budde*, with short *u*, to the later *bowde, boud*, with long vowel or diphthong, is also uncertain.] An insect; ? a beetle of some kind: cf. BOUD, weevil.

a **1200** *Semi-Saxon Vocab.* in Wr.-Wülcker 543 *Scarabæus*, scearnbudoa *uel* budda. *c* **1440** *Promp. Parv.* 54 Budde of a tree, *gemma*. Budde Flye. [cf. *ibid.* 46 Bowde, malte-worme [**1499** boude of malte]. *c* **1475** *Pict. Voc.* in Wr.-Wülcker 767 *Nomina Muscarum, Hec polumita* a bude, *Hic stabo* a scarbude. See BOUD.]

budded ('bʌdɪd), *ppl. a.* [f. BUD *v.*^{1} or *sb.*^{1} + -ED.] **a.** In bud, budding; furnished with buds. **b.** Subjected to the operation of budding (BUD *v.*^{1} 5). **c.** That has sprouted or put forth buds.

1552 HULOET, Budded, *gemmatus*. **1579** SPENSER *Sheph. Cal.* Feb. 36 The budded broomes. *Ibid.* May 214 His newe budded beard. **1664** EVELYN *Kal. Hort.* (1729) 195 Cut off the Heads of your budded Stocks. **1817** WORDSW. *Poems of Imag.* xvi, With songs the budded groves resounding. **1881** *Gard. Chron.* XVI. 851 The budded rose.

'budder. *rare.* [f. BUD *v.*^{1} + -ER^1.] That which buds, or is in bud.

1818 KEATS *Endym.* I. 41 Now while the early budders are just new.

Buddha ('bʊdə, 'bʊdha). Also 7–8 Buddou, 9 Booddha, Bhooddha, Boudhou, Budh, Buddh, Buddho. [a. Skr. *buddha* enlightened, awakened, pa. pple. of *budh* to awake, know, perceive.] The title given by the adherents of one of the great Asiatic religions, thence called BUDDHISM, to the founder of their faith, Śākyamuni, Gautama, or Siddârtha, who flourished in Northern India in the 5th century B.C. Śākyamuni is regarded as only the latest of a series of Buddhas or infallible religious teachers, which is hereafter to be continued indefinitely.

When applied to Śākyamuni, *Buddha* is in English use treated as a proper name, and even when used in a general sense, it is always written with a capital B.

1681 R. KNOX *Hist. Ceylon* 18 The Buddou, a great god among them. **1784** SIR W. CHAMBERS in *Asiat. Res.* (1799) I. 163 The Siamese have two orders of priests, and so have the worshippers of Buddou. **1803** MAHONY in *Asiat. Res.* VII. 32 This last Bhooddha will be born of a Braminee woman. **1844** H. H. WILSON *Brit. India* II. 87 With the acquiescence of.. the priests of Buddha. *Ibid.* III. 50 Relics of the four last Buddhas. **1853** WAYLAND *Mem. Judson* App. II. 410 A Buddh is a being who by virtue of.. certain austerities becomes the object of supreme adoration. **1858** MAX MÜLLER *Chips* (1880) I. ii. 51 The first subjective system of faith in India, the religion of Buddha.

attrib. **1784** SIR W. CHAMBERS in *Asiat. Res.* (1799) I. 163 Knox says of the Buddou Priests, etc. **1801** JOINVILLE in

Asiat. Res. VII. 421 Some prince on the continent, professing the Boudhou religion.

Hence **Buddhahood**, the condition of a Buddha; **Buddhaship**, the office of a Buddha.

1837 G. TURNOUR *Mahāwanso* I. xxviii, Prince Siddhattho attained Buddhohood, in the character of Gotamo Buddho. **1878** DODS *Moham., Buddha & C.* iii. 147 Such then was the process by which Siddartha painfully won his way to Buddhahood. **1882** SCHAFF *Encycl. Rel. Knowl.* I. 333 Gautama's Buddhaship was for five thousand years.

Buddhic (ˈbʊdɪk), *a.* [see -IC.] = BUDDHIST *a.*

1816 G. S. FABER *Orig. Pagan Idol.* I. 54 Such impieties peculiarly marked the Hermetic or Buddhic theology. **1817** —— *Eight Dissert.* (1845) I. 62 The doctrine of Buddhic Incarnation.

Buddhism (ˈbʊdɪz(ə)m). Also **Boudhism, Budhism, Booddhism.** [f. BUDDHA + -ISM.] The religious system founded by Buddha.

1801 JOINVILLE in *Asiat. Res.* VII. 400 If Boudhism could not have established itself among the Brahmins, etc. **1816** *Asiatic Jrnl.* I. 19 The name and peculiarities of Buddhism have a good deal fixed my attention. **1870** F. HALL in Wilson *Vishṇu Purāṇa* V. 376 The Hindus, with their hatred of Buddhism and everything therewith cognate.

Buddhist (ˈbʊdɪst), *sb.* and *a.* Also **Booddhist**, and (wrongly) **Bhudist, Bhudhist, Bhooddhist, Boudhist, Bauddhist.** [f. as prec. + -IST. The Sanskrit *Bauddha* 'follower of Buddha' was previously used: hence the form *Bauddhist.*]

A. *sb.* A follower of Buddha.

1801 JOINVILLE in *Asiat. Res.* VII. 398 In the opinion of the Boudhists, there has been no creation. **1803** MAHONY in *Asiat. Res.* VII. 33 The Bhooddhists speak of 26 heavens, which they divide in the following manner. **1807** WILFORD in *Asiat. Res.* IX. 88 According to the Bauddhists, the ancient Buddha..began to reign 1367 years B.C. **1810** M. GRAHAM 89 (Y.) Among the Bhuddists there are no distinct castes. **1841** H. H. WILSON *Asiat. Jrnl.* New Ser. XXXV. 44 A different class of sectarians from Buddhists or Bauddhas. **1871** ALABASTER *Wheel of the Law* 265 Buddhists are forbidden to kill animals.

B. *adj.* Relating to or connected with Buddhism.

1816 *Asiatic Jrnl.* I. 21 The harmless sacrifices of the Chinese..are obviously Buddhist. **1835** MARRYAT *Olla Podr.* xxiv. I also found..Bhudist figures. **1871** ALABASTER *Wheel of the Law* 168 My ideas on Buddhist prayer are stated in the Preface.

Buddhistic (bʊˈdɪstɪk), *a.* = BUDDHIST *a.*

1841 ANTHON *Class. Dict.* 87/1 A remnant..of an early Buddhistic system. **1860** J. MUIR *Orig. Sanskrit Texts* II. 69 In Ceylon there exists..an extensive Buddhistic literature. **1884** DK. ARGYLL *Unity of Nat.* xiii. 508 The real meaning of the Buddhistic Atheism in the mind of its original teachers.

Buddhistical (bʊˈdɪstɪkəl), *a.* [f. prec. + -AL[1].] = prec.

1837 G. TURNOUR *Mahāwanso* I. xxviii, The mystification of the Buddhistical data. **1860** J. MUIR *Orig. Sanskrit Texts* II. 68 The three pitakas, which now form the Buddhistical Scriptures.

Buddhistically (bʊˈdɪstɪkəlɪ), *adv.* Also **buddhistically.** [f. BUDDHISTICAL *a.* + -LY[2].] In a Buddhistical manner.

1920 *19th Cent.* July 59 'The Bull' makes us sympathise almost Buddhistically with the huge beast. **1921** D. H. LAWRENCE *Let.* 8 May (1962) II. 653, I suppose I buddhistically removed her beyond sorrow.

†**Buddhite** (ˈbʊdaɪt), *sb.* and *a. Obs.* Also **Buddite.** [see -ITE.] An early synonym of BUDDHIST.

1803 R. PERCIVAL *Ceylon* 200 The Brahmins prevailed, and the Buddites were compelled to take refuge in Ceylon. **1816** *Asiat. Jrnl.* I. 114 The ancient religious edifices of Java are exclusively Buddhite, and not Braminical.

budding (ˈbʌdɪŋ), *vbl. sb.*[1] [f. BUD *v.*[1] + -ING [1].]

1. The action of putting forth buds, sprouting; *concr.* buds collectively.

1398 TREVISA *Barth. De P.R.* IX. vii. (1495) 352 Harueste ..wythdrawyth the vertue of buddynge and of spryngynge. **1580** HOLLYBAND *Treas. Fr. Tong, Germement*, a budding, a sprouting. **1711** ADDISON *Spect.* No. 121 ⁋3 Before the first budding of a Horn appears. **1724** RAMSAY *Tea-T. Misc.* (1733) I. 100 Plantings..Where buddings and blossoms appear. **1878** HUXLEY *Physiogr.* xv. 252 By..budding and splitting, the corals may form masses of great size.

2. *fig.* Springing forth, beginning, 'germ'.

1601 WEEVER *Mirr. Mart.* A v, Her forward budding in the prime I blasted With wind of pride. **1677** GILPIN *Dæmonol.* (1867) 461 We must..nip it in the earliest buddings of it. **1741** WATTS *Improv. Mind* ix. (1801) 68 The young buddings of infant reason. **1822** B. CORNWALL *Let. Boccaccio* ii. 44 In budding, happiness is likest woe.

3. *Gardening.* The process of inserting a bud from one shrub or tree under the bark of another, so that adhesion takes place; inoculation.

1719 LONDON & WISE *Compl. Gard.* VII. 184 The proper time for Inoculating or Budding, is..according as the Season happens. **1861** DELAMER *Fl. Gard.* 156 Budding may be performed from June to September.

4. *attrib.*, as in *budding-knife, -time.*

1805 WORDSW. *Prel.* III. (1850) 64 A congregation in its budding time Of health. **1831–60** LOUDON *Encycl. Gard.* 656 (L.) With the budding-knife make a horizontal cut across the rind. **1839** CARLYLE *Chartism* viii. 165 There are spiritual budding-times.

†ˈ**budding**, *vbl. sb.*[2] *Sc. Obs.* [f. BUD *v.*[2] + -ING[1].] Bribery.

1640 *Pasquil* in *Bk. of Scotch Pasquils* (1868) 144 Ther was houpes for brybes and budding. **1657** COLVIL *Whigs' Supplic.* (1751) 92 It's very like, at others budding, He turn'd his coat for cake and pudding.

ˈ**budding**, *ppl. a.* [f. BUD *v.*[1] + -ING[2].]

1. That buds; in bud, sprouting.

1561 T. NORTON *Calvin's Inst.* I. xvi. (1634) 82 A budding greennesse. **1579** SPENSER *Sheph. Cal.* Feb. 58 My budding braunch. **1697** DRYDEN *Virg. Georg.* II. 765 Wanton Kids, with budding Horns. **1814** SOUTHEY *Roderick* xv, Lovely as a budding rose.

2. *fig.*

1581 SIDNEY *Apol.* (Arb.) 67 We might well want words, but neuer matter, of which..we should euer haue new budding occasions. **1648** HERRICK *Corinna's a Maying*, There's not a budding boy, or girle..But is..gone to bring in May. **1664** DRYDEN *Rival Ladies* I. i. 186, I will not.. crush a budding Virtue. **1753** SMOLLETT *Ct. Fathom* (1784) 137/2 One unlucky..circumstance blasted..the budding hopes of Melville. **1866** G. MACDONALD *Ann. Q. Neighb.* iii. (1878) 33 This gave a great help to his budding confidence.

Hence ˈ**buddingness**, budding quality or condition.

In mod. Dicts.

buddle, boodle (ˈbʌd(ə)l, ˈbuːd(ə)l), *sb.*[1] Forms: 4 **budel**, 5 **boþul(e, bothil**, 6 **bodle, boddle**, 8– **buddle**, 9 **boodle.** [Etymology unknown: the conjecture that it is a. Du. *buidel* purse, on account of its bearing *golds* (yellow flowers) is untenable.] A rural name for the Corn-marigold.

a **1400** *Names of Herbs* in MS. Sloane 5 f. 6 *Monica*, budel. *c* **1440** *Promp. Parv.* 46 Boþul [*printed* Boyul] or bothule, herbe, or cow-slope [*v.r.* bothil, boyl]. **1580** TUSSER *Husb.* li. 11 Like vnto boddle no weede there is such. **1787** MARSHALL *E. Norfolk* Gloss. (E.D.S.) *Buddle*, corn-marigold. **1830** FORBY *Voc. E. Anglia* I. 42 *Buddle*, a noxious weed among corn, *Chrysanthemum segetum.*

buddle (ˈbʌd(ə)l), *sb.*[2] *Mining.* Also 6 **buddel**, 7 **budle.** [Etymology unknown: some have compared Ger. *butteln* to shake, agitate. The word occurs in Manlove 1653 as a term used by Derbyshire lead-miners; it is still current there and in Cornwall, and also in the U.S. silver mines.]

A shallow inclined vat in which ore is washed.

1531–2 *Act 23 Hen. VIII*, viii. §1 The saide digger, owner, or wassher, shall make..sufficient hatches and ties in the ende of their buddels and cordes. **1653** MANLOVE *Rhymed Chron.* 260 Main Rakes, Cross Rakes, Brown-henns, Budles and Soughs. **1674** RAY *Smelt. Silver* 116 The Buddle which is a vessel made like to a shallow tumbrel, standing a little shelving. **1869** CHURCH in *Student* II. 402 The buddles where the ground ore is washed. **1881** RAYMOND *Mining Gloss.*, *Buddle* (Cornwall), an inclined vat or stationary or revolving platform upon which ore is concentrated by means of running water. Strictly the buddle is a shallow vat ..But general usage, particularly on the Pacific slope, makes no distinction.

Comb., as ***buddle-boy, -head, -tub.***

1860 SMILES *Self-help* iii. 62 Earning three-halfpence a day as a buddleboy at a tin mine. **1671** *Phil. Trans.* VI. 2109 A Trambling shovel..to cast up the Ore..on a long square board..which is termed the Buddle-head. **1811** *Chron.* in *Ann. Reg.* 54/1 Miner's buddle-tubs..and other materials.

†ˈ**buddle**, *v.*[1] *Obs. rare.* [? f. BUD *v.*[1] + -LE frequentative suffix; but perh. rather onomatopœic.] *intr.* ? To bud, to sprout.

1581 J. BELL *Haddon's Answ. Osor.* 268 b, More wickednes hath bene sene to buddle upp afresh [Lat. *pullulare*]. *Ibid.* 430 b, Sinnes do dayly boyle upp and buddle from without us.

buddle (ˈbʌd(ə)l), *v.*[2] *Mining.* [f. BUDDLE *sb.*[2]] *trans.* To wash (ore) by means of a buddle. Hence ˈ**buddled** *ppl. a.*; ˈ**buddler**; ˈ**buddling** *vbl. sb.*

1693 G. POOLEY in *Phil. Trans.* XVII. 675 The places where they wash, clean or buddle it, as their Term is. **1747** HOOSON *Miner's Dict.* s.v., In some places, they Buddle all their Boose. *Ibid.* I j b, The Budlers, Scrapers, and Washers. *Ibid.* X iv, Waste [is] that which is separated by the Water from the Buddled Ore, by Buddling the Boose. **1869** CHURCH in *Student* II. 402 It [ore] is separated from the accompanying rock and minerals by the process locally [Cornwall] termed buddling.

buddle, obs. f. BOODLE[1].

buddleia (ˈbʌdliːə, bʌdˈliːə). *Bot.* Also **buddlea, buddleja.** [mod.L. (Linnæus *Hortus Cliffortianus* (1737) 35), f. the name of Adam *Buddle* (died 1715), botanist: see -IA[1].] Any plant of the genus of shrubs and trees of this name of the family Loganiaceæ, natives of America, Asia, and South Africa; esp. the large deciduous shrub *B. davidii*, with mauve flowers in panicles.

1791 *Curtis's Bot. Mag.* 174 Round-headed Buddlea. **1864** GRINDON *Brit. & Garden Bot.* 415 In genial situations the Buddlea will often attain the height of 12–15 feet. **1885** *Encycl. Brit.* XVIII. 673/2 The *Buddleia*..flourishes at a height of 12,000 feet round the shores of Lake Titicaca [Peru]. **1924** *Blackw. Mag.* Apr. 446/1 Red admirals in August sunning themselves on the buddleia. **1927** *Times* (Weekly ed.) 22 Sept. 327/3 Purple buddleia. **1964** F. A. BUSH *Trees & Shrubs* viii. 109 Buddleias flourish in a deep well-drained soil in sunny but sheltered situations.

buddy (ˈbʌdɪ), *a. rare.* [f. BUD *sb.*[1] + -Y[1].]

a. Full of buds. **b.** Like a bud.

1598 FLORIO, *Fronzuto*, stalkie, buddie, spriggie. **1611** COTGR., *Fillole*, a buddie knob in a vine, like a wart. **1862** THACKERAY *Roundab. Papers* (1879) 115 Here are the scourges! choose me a nice, long, swishing, buddy one. **1871** G. MACDONALD *Roadside P.* 209 Buddy dots of light.

buddy (ˈbʌdɪ), *sb. colloq.* (orig. *U.S.*). [Possibly an alteration of BROTHER *sb.* (cf. BUD *sb.*[3]) or a variant of BUTTY.] Brother; companion, friend; freq. as form a of address. So **buddy-buddy** *sb.*, a friend; also *adj.*, friendly.

1850 'BARTON PREMIUM' *Eight Yrs. Brit. Guiana* 218 Buddy (brother) how you can fink me sha' talk so to you? **1852** WHITMORE *Diary* 25 Dec., Wrote to my folks and took a Christmas dinner with my buddy. **1858** *Harper's Mag.* Jan. 284/2 'Look, sister, see; the sky's got the measles!' 'No, buddy,' said she,..'it's only freckled.' **1927** J. BARBICAN *Confessions of Rum-Runner* ii. 24 He had a buddy [*f.n.* Chum], and they went into a liquor deal together. **1932** N. MITFORD *Christmas Pudding* iv. 51 Little Bobby Bobbin..is a great buddy of mine. **1937** *Daily Express* 17 Mar. 12/2 When I went into the night nursery to get the boys up I was greeted with a shout of 'Stick 'em up, buddy'. **1952** M. LASKI *Village* vi. 102 Those two are getting to be such buddies they can't bear to be parted. **1960** *Woman* 26 Mar. 12/3 He rather enjoyed Miss Hopkins's naïve assumption that now...he and she were buddies. **1962** L. DEIGHTON *Ipcress File* xviii. 115 This way they stopper up the information without offence to old buddy buddies. **1962** K. ORVIS *Damned & Destroyed* xxv. 184 Those two got real buddy-buddy.

Hence as *v. intr.* (U.S. colloq.), to become friendly. Usu. with *up.*

1931 G. IRWIN *Amer. Tramp & Underworld Slang* 38 'Me and Slim buddy up and take a trip'—Slim and I struck up a friendship and went for a trip together. **1948** N. ALGREN in *Penguin New Writing* XXXIV. 137 My cot was next to his, and we started buddying up.

Bude (bjuːd). [Attrib. use of the name of a place in Cornwall.] **Bude-burner**, a gas-burner invented by Sir Goldsworthy Gurney (who resided at Bude), consisting of several concentric argand rings. **Bude-light**, see quot. **Bude sand**, sand from Bude, used as a dressing for soil.

1807 VANCOUVER *Agric. Devon* (1813) 157 Old spaded and burnt moors, dressed with 100 seams of bude sand. **1835** *Mech. Mag.* XXIII. 80 The Bude Light is a name given by Mr. Gurney..to a new light..obtained by directing a stream of oxy-hydrogen gas on a quantity of pounded egg shells. **1875** URE *Dict. Arts* II. 559 The Bude burner consists of 2 or 3 concentric argand rings perforated.

†**bude**, obs. var. of BID, to announce, deliver.

c **1380** *Sir Ferumb.* 1793 þey of fraunce affore þe Amerel ȝude And Ro[land] wiþ sterne continance ys message þus gan bude.

bude, var. of BOUD.

bude = *behoved*: see BUS *v.*

budel, obs. form of BEADLE and BUDDLE *sb.*[1]

budge (bʌdʒ), *sb.*[1] Forms: 4 **bugee, -eye**, 5 **boge, bogey**, 6 **bogy, bug(g)e, buggye**, *Sc.* **buge**, 7 **budg**, 9 **boodge**, 6– **budge.** [Etymology obscure; usually identified with BUDGE *sb.*[3], BOUGE *sb.*[1], a leather bag; but the connexion of sense is not clear, and most of the early forms seem to indicate a dissyllabic etymon. If the original sense were 'kid-skin with the hair' (see quot. 1616), the OF. *bouchet, bochet* a kid, might be thought of; cf. '*budge* of court' from F. *bouche* under BOUGE *sb.*[2]]

1. A kind of fur, consisting of lamb's skin with the wool dressed outwards.

1382 *Pol. Poems* (1859) I. 265 Somme frers beren peluse aboute..Al after that thai ere..For somme bugee, and for somme byse. **1395** *Determin. Feast* in Rogers *Agric. & Prices* II. 647 De xxxix furruris pro capuciis de Bugeye. **1465** *Paston Lett.* xcix. I. 134, Ij. gounes, one furryd with bogey. **1513** DOUGLAS *Æneis* VIII. Prol. 58 Byand byssely, and bane, buge, beuir and bice. **1532–3** *Act 24 Hen. VIII*, xiii, No man, vnder the saide estates..shall weare any furre ..except foynes, genets..and Bogy. *c* **1570** THYNNE *Pride & Lowl.* (1841) 32 A gowne Of fine blacke cloth, and faced faire with budge. **1611** COTGR. s.v. *Agneau, Blanche d'agneaux*, the furre called, white Lambe, or, white Budge. **1616** BULLOKAR, *Budge*, a furre of a kinde of kid in other countries. *c* **1640** J. SMYTH *Lives Berkeleys* (1883) I. 305 Furred with Coney, lambskinne, and budge. **1721** C. KING *Brit. Merch.* I. 288 Budge and Goat Skins. *a* **1859** DE QUINCEY *Whiggism* Wks. VI. 115 *note*, Budge is a species of fur.

2. *attrib.* and *Comb.*, as in *budge-face, -fur, -gown, -skin*; **budge-bachelor**, one of a company dressed in gowns trimmed with budge, who took part in the procession on Lord Mayor's Day (see BACHELOR 2). (For *budge-doctor*, etc., see BUDGE *a.*)

1466 *Mann. & Househ. Exp.* 371 My mastyr bout of hym vj. boge scynnes prise iiij.*s.* **1526** SKELTON *Magnyf.* 1070 In the stede of a budge furre. **1599** MARSTON *Sco. Villanie* III. x. 222 Poore budge face, bowcase sleeue, but let him passe, Once furre and beard shall priuiledge an Asse. **1649** MILTON *Observ. Art. Peace* Wks. 1738 I. 355 To part freely with their own Budge-gowns. **1680** T. JORDAN *London's*

Glory 13 In the Rear of them..hastens the Foins and Budge-Batchelors together with the Gentlemen-Ushers to Guild-Hall. **1706** PHILLIPS, *Budge-Bachelers*, a Company of poor old Men Cloath'd in long Gowns, lin'd with Lambs-furr, who attend upon the Lord Mayor of the City of London, during the Solemnity of the Publick Shew.

†**budge**, *sb.*^{2} *Obs. rare*$^{-1}$. Also 6 buge. [a. OF. *bouge* 'espèce de hache d'armes, ou plutôt une grande serpe' Godef. See VOULGE.] 'A kind of bill; a warlike instrument' (Jamieson).

1513 DOUGLAS *Æneis* XI. Prol. 16 Nane vther strokis nor wapynnis had thai thar, Nother speyr, buge, pol-ax, swerd, knyfe, nor mace [*ed.* **1553** *has* budgeis].

†**budge**, *sb.*^{3} *Obs.* [Later spelling of BOUGE *sb.*^{1}, in sense 1. Cf. BUDGET *sb.*] A leather bag.

1606 HOLLAND *Sueton.* 204 To the necke of another, there was tyed a lether-bagge..with this title..But thou hast deserved a verie lether budge [*culeum*] indeed.

†**budge**, *sb.*^{4} *Obs.* [? f. BUDGE *v.*^{1}] A shove, a push.

1714 ELLWOOD *Autobiog.* (1765) 60 As for the Budge I had had it given me often in the Street but understood not the meaning of it till now; and now I found it was a Jostle, enough to throw one almost upon his Nose.

†**budge**, *sb.*^{5} *Obs. slang.* See quots. Also *attrib.*

1673 R. HEAD *Canting Acad.* 95 The *Budge*..his employment is in the dark of the Evening, to go into any door that he seeth open, and..take whatever next cometh to hand. **1676** *Warning for Housekprs.* (title), Budg and Snudg, File-lifter, Tongue-padder, The Private Theif. **1706** PHILLIPS, *Budge*, one that slips into a House, or Shop, to steal Cloaks, etc. **1751** FIELDING *Amelia* I. iii, You are some sneaking budge rascal.

budge, *sb.*^{6}, var. of BOUGE *sb.*^{2}, court rations.

†**budge**, *a.* *Obs.* Also 7 bodge, budg. [Etymology unknown: we may perhaps compare BUG *a.*, also BOG *a.* BOGGISH.

There appears to be a reference to the attrib. use of BUDGE *sb.*^{1}, as in the first quot. Possibly *budge doctor* may have originally meant one who wore budge fur.]

1. Solemn in demeanour, important-looking, pompous, stiff, formal.

1634 MILTON *Comus* 707 Those budge doctors of the Stoic fur. **1640** BROME *Sparagus Gard.* IV. v, I ha no more to zay t'yee, since you be so budge. **1676** MARVELL *Gen. Councils* Wks. 1875 IV. 119 And how budge must they look when they returned back to their diocesses. **1686** OLDHAM *Art Poetry* 66 No tutor, but the Budg Philosophers he knew. **1714** ELLWOOD *Autobiog.* (1765) 60 The Warden was a budge old man; and I looked somewhat big too: having a good gelding under me, and a good riding coat on my back. **1755** JOHNSON, *Budge*, surly, stiff, formal. **1781** COWPER *Convers.* 299 The solemn fop, significant and budge.

2. *dial.* Brisk, lively.

1691 RAY *S. & E.C. Wds.* 90 *Budge*, brisk, jocund. You are very Budge. —— *N.C. Wds.* (E.D.S.) *Crowse*, brisk, budge, lively, jolly. **1721–1800** in BAILEY.

budge (bʌdʒ), *v.*^{1} Also 6–7 bouge, (7 budg). [a. F. *bouge-r* to stir; according to Diez, prob. = Pr. *bolegar* to disturb oneself, It. *bulicare* to bubble up:—late L. **bullicare* to bubble, frequentative of *bullīre* to boil. Cf., for the sense, Pg. *bulire* to move, stir.]

1. *intr.* To stir, to move from one's place. (Almost always with negative expressed or implied, and said of that which stands firmly or stubbornly.) *to budge against*, to move against, act in hostility to, is now *obs.*

1590 GREENE *Orl. Fur.* (1599) 31 Bouge not a foot to ayd Prince Rodamant. **1603** FLORIO *Montaigne* (1634) 148 He could not be induced to bouge from his place. **1637** EARL MONM. tr. *Malvezzi's Rom. & Tarquin* 154 [He] doth not budge against his Prince. **1663** BUTLER *Hud.* I. III. 201, I thought th' hadst scorn'd to budge a step, For fear. **1768** GOLDSM. *Good-n. Man* Epil., Not a soul will budge to give him place. **1837** W. IRVING *Capt. Bonneville* (1849) 207 The trapper..refused to budge an inch. **1877** MRS. OLIPHANT *Makers Flor.* x. 252 Showing no inclination to budge.

†**b.** ? To wince, flinch, shirk (after Fr. *bouger*).

1601 SHAKS. *Jul. C.* IV. iii. 44 Must I bouge? Must I obserue you? **1607** —— *Cor.* I. vi. 44 The Mouse ne're shunn'd the Cat, as they did budge From rascals worse then they. **1630** WADSWORTH *Sp. Pilgr.* iii. 15 All are bound to bee there without budging at seuen. **1651** BAXTER *Inf. Bapt.* Apol. 10 He told them in the Pulpit, that let them budge at it how they would, it was their Hypocrisie that hindered them from receiving the truth.

c. To alter or shift from one's (predetermined) position or opinion. Usu. in negative contexts. *colloq.*

1930 N. COWARD *Private Lives* I. 20 You're as obstinate as a mule...you don't intend to budge an inch, do you? **1955** *Times* 31 Aug. 8/2 Egypt, says Colonel Sadat, will not budge from her present position that stability in the Arab world must be on the basis of United Nations resolutions. **1960** C. P. SNOW *Affair* xl. 372 Skeffington would not budge from his incorruptibility. **1982** S. BRETT *Murder Unprompted* iv. 44 Now I've argued with him about this, but he won't budge.

2. *trans.* To stir or move (a heavy inert thing).

1598 SYLVESTER *Du Bartas* II. i. IV. (1641) 106/1 A stone so huge, That in our Age three men could hardly bouge. **1853** KANE *Grinnell Exp.* xxiv. (1856) 218 Although the starboard floe..parted a six-inch hawser, it failed to budge us one inch from the icy cradle. **1883** *Harper's Mag.* Nov. 903/2 Three men were trying..and could not budge it.

†**budge**, *v.*^{2} *Obs.* [? var. of BODGE *v.*] To put together clumsily.

1628 EARLE *Microcosm.* xliv, All the actions of his life are like so many things budg'd in without any natural cadence or connection at all.

budge, var. of BOUGE *v.* *Obs.* to bilge.

1622 FLETCHER *Span. Curate* IV. v, Preach not abstinence ..'Twill budge the bottoms of their consciences.

budge-barrel. [f. BUDGE *sb.*^{3} = BOUGE *sb.*^{1}, a leather bag + BARREL *sb.*] (See quot.)

1627 CAPT. SMITH *Seaman's Gram.* xiv. 66 A Budgbarrell is a little Barrell made of Latten, filled with powder to carry from place to place for feare of fire; in the couer it hath a long necke to fill the Ladles withall without opening. **1696** PHILLIPS, *Budge-barrel*, a little Tin-barrel to carry Powder in for fear of fire. **1828** J. SPEARMAN *Brit. Gunner* s.v. *Barrel*, Budge-barrels. These barrels are employed in the service of batteries, and have leather covers drawing together like the mouth of a bag. **1862** F. GRIFFITHS *Artil. Man.* (ed. 9) 93 Budge Barrels. Weight of barrel, copper-hooped, 10 lb.

†'**budgelling.** *Obs. rare*$^{-1}$. (Dyce suggests = 'boggling', or a misprint for *budgetting*.)

a **1626** MIDDLETON *No wit, no H.* I. iii, Here is strange budgelling: I tell you, sir, Those that I put in trust were near me too.

†'**budgely**, *adv. Obs. rare.* [f. BUDGE *a.* + -LY^2.] Solemnly, stiffly, with assumed dignity.

1599 NASHE *Lent. Stuffe* in *Harl. Misc.* (1810) VI. 166 King Dionisius..saw him sit under his canopie so budgely.

'**budger.** [f. BUDGE *v.*^{1} + -ER^1.] One who budges or stirs.

1607 SHAKS. *Cor.* I. viii. 5 Let the first Budger dye the others Slaue.

budgeree ('bʌdʒərɪ), *a. Austral. colloq.* Also boojery, budger(r)y. [Native word: cf. next.] Good, excellent.

1793 J. HUNTER *Port Jackson* viii. 213 They very frequently, at the conclusion of the dance, would apply to us ..for marks of our approbation..which we never failed to give by often repeating the word *boojery*, which signifies good; or *boojery caribberie*, a good dance. **1832** T. L. MITCHELL *Jrnl.* 3 Jan. in *Three Exped. E. Australia* (1838) I. 63 In vain did Dawkins address them thus, 'What for you jerran budgerry whitefellow?' **1850** *Household Words* I. 476/2 They..spoke in a friendly strain; Budgery Master always gibit bullock along im Black fellow. **1918** *Chambers's Jrnl.* Apr. 268/1 Instead of being 'bong', he was 'budgerie' (all right). **1966** W. S. RAMSON *Austral. Eng.* vi. 105 Except, perhaps, in the north and west of Australia, *budgeree* has passed out of use.

budgerigar ('bʌdʒərɪ,gɑː(r)). Also **betcherry-gah, betshiregah, bougirigard, budgeragar, budgereg(h)ar, budgery garr, budgregore.** [Native Australian ('Port Jackson dialect', Morris *Austral English*), f. *budgeri*, *boodgeri* good + *gar* cockatoo.] A small Australian parrot, the grass or zebra parakeet, *Melopsittacus undulatus*, a popular cage-bird in Britain and elsewhere. Cf. BUDGIE.

1847 LEICHHARDT *Overland Exped.* 297 The Betshiregah (Melopsittacus undulatus, *Gould*) were very numerous. **1848** H. W. HAYGARTH *Bush Life in Australia* xii. 139 A most brilliant little parrot..about the size of a bullfinch,..called the budgery garr. **1857** W. HOWITT *Tallangetta* I. ii. 48 Young paroquets, the green leeks, and the lovely speckled budgregores. **1857** F. J. A. HORT in A. F. Hort *Life & Lett.* (1896) I. 388 A small green creature like a miniature cockatoo, called a Budgeragar. **1889** *Times* 16 Feb. 4/3 Crystal Palace Cagebird Show 1889... Two Australian budgerigars. **1922** E. V. LUCAS *Genevra's Money* xix. 132 Little foreign birds for the most part, avadavats, Java sparrows, budgerigars. **1968** K. WEATHERLY *Roo Shooter* 118 Budgerigars came in thousands, wheeling in aerial manœuvres of unbelievable intricacy.

budgerow ('bʌdʒərəʊ). *Anglo-Indian.* Also 8–9 budgero. [a. Hindī or Bengālī *bajrā*.] 'A lumbering keelless barge, formerly much used by Europeans travelling on the Ganges' (Col. Yule).

[*c* **1570** tr. *Cesare Federici* in *Hakl.* II. 358 (Y.) Their barkes be light and armed with oares..and they call these barkes Bazaras and Patuas [in Bengal].] **1727** A. HAMILTON *New Acc. E. Ind.* II. xxxiii. 12 In their Budgeroes, which is a convenient Boat, that goes swiftly with the Force of Oars. **1781** HODGES 39 (Y.) The budgerows, which both sail and row. **1834** H. CAUNTER *Scenes in Ind.* 249 Our papers..we happened luckily to have on board the budgerow.

budget ('bʌdʒɪt), *sb.* Forms: 5 bowȝette, -gett, 6 bo-, booget, bow-, bou-, boud-, budgette, (bowdshett), 6–7 bou-, bow-, boudget, 7 bugget, bu(d)git, 6– budget. [ad. F. *bougette*, dim. of *bouge* leather bag; see BOUGE *sb.*^{1}, BUDGE *sb.*^{3} Cf. BOUGET.]

†**1. a.** A pouch, bag, wallet, usually of leather. *Obs.* exc. *dial.*

1432–50 tr. *Higden* Rolls Ser. VII. 385 His bowȝettes [*manticis*] and caskettes. *c* **1530** LD. BERNERS *Arth. Lyt. Bryt.* (1814) 62 A boget wyth leteers hangyng at his sadel bow. **1542** UDALL *Erasm. Apoph.* 110b, For a pourse or a bougette. **1611** CORYAT *Crudities* 66 A certaine Pedler, hauing a budget of small wares. **1638** HEYWOOD *Wise Wom.* IV. i, You whose wealth lyes in your braines; not in your budgets. **1677** MOXON *Mech. Exerc.* (1703) 250 A Budget or Pocket to hang by their sides, to put their Nails in. **1783** JOHNSON in *Boswell* (1831) V. 116 When I landed at Billingsgate I carried my budget myself to Cornhill. **1808** SCOTT *Marm.* I. xxvii, Staff, budget, bottle, scrip, he wore. **1879** MISS JACKSON *Shropsh. Wd.-bk.*, *Budget*, a satchel of bass-matting in which workmen carry their tools.

†**b.** *fig.* Phrase, ***to open one's budget***: to speak one's mind. *Obs.* (Cf. 3.)

1548 HALL *Chron.* (1809) 100 Put it in your boget among lyes and fayned fables. **1642** ROGERS *Naaman* 139 Infinite are the subtilties which are in the bugit of this traitor. **1681** NEVILE *Plato Rediv.* 261 Most of the Wise..Men..are very silent, and will not open their Budget. **1847** A. BRONTË *Agnes Grey* III. xiv. 219 There's Matilda..and I must go and open my budget to her. **1861** TROLLOPE *Tales of all Countries* 133 At length Miss Jack was allowed to open her budget, and to make her proposition.

†**c.** ***the hangman's budget.*** *Obs.*

1589 *Pappe w. Hatchet* (1844) 37 With an Habeas Corpus to remooue them from the Shepheards tarre-boxe to the hangmans budget. **1607** DEKKER *Wh. Babylon* Wks. 1873 II. 270 A Broker and his wife that dropt out of the Hangmans budget but last day, are now eating into the Camp.

2. In various *spec.* uses:

†**a.** A leather or skin bottle. *Obs.*

1580 NORTH *Plutarch* (1676) 574 Great Leather budgets filled full of fresh Water. **1653** URQUHART *Rabelais* II. viii, The measure of twelve oyle budgets or butts of olives. **1786** tr. *Beckford's Vathek* 12 A water budget.

b. A kind of boot in a carriage, adapted for carrying luggage. ? *Obs.* Cf. BASKET 5.

1794 W. FELTON *Carriages* (1801) I. 115 Boots and budgets are mostly understood as one article..that wherein the principal difference lies, is made with a loose cover, and is properly the budget, being made convenient for trunks.

c. A leathern socket for retaining the butt of a cavalry carbine on a journey. Cf. BUCKET *sb.*^{1} 4 b.

1816 SCOTT *Old Mort.* ix, The two dragoons..have their carabines out of their budgets.

3. *transf.* The contents of a bag or wallet; a bundle, a collection or stock. Chiefly *fig.*, esp. of news; *spec.* a long letter full of news.

1597 T. MORLEY *Introd. Musicke* 157 You shall haue the hardest in all my budget. **1692** R. L'ESTRANGE *Fables* (J.) It was nature, in fine, that brought off the cat, when the fox's whole budget of inventions failed him. **1729** SWIFT *Wks.* 1841 II. 110, I read..the whole budget of papers you sent. **1784** COWPER *Task* IV. 23 But O th' important budget!.. who can say What are its tidings? **1807** C. WILMOT *Let.* 15 May in *Russ. Jrnls.* (1934) II. 241 Months have intervened since your delightful Budget reach'd these Realms. **1822** HAZLITT *Men & Mann.* Ser. II. iii. (1869) 54 His budget of general knowledge. **1852** E. RUSKIN *Let.* 16 Jan. in M. Lutyens *Effie in Venice* (1965) II. 246, I am going out to tea ..but have time to begin my weekly budget before I go. **1854** THOREAU *Walden* iv, Bed and bedstead making one budget. **1855** TROLLOPE *Warden* xii. 185 The budget of news which was prepared for her father. **1867** DE MORGAN (*title*) A Budget of Paradoxes. **1868** C. M. YONGE *Chaplet of Pearls* I. xiv. 190 He gathered up the sense of the letters.. and said, 'This is a woful budget, my poor son.' **1960** C. DAY LEWIS *Buried Day* ii. 30, I had a budget from her last week.

b. A frequent title for a journal (i.e. a budget of news, etc.): e.g. *Pall Mall Budget*, *Young Folk's Weekly Budget*.

4. a. A statement of the probable revenue and expenditure for the ensuing year, with financial proposals founded thereon, annually submitted by the Chancellor of the Exchequer, on behalf of the Ministry, for the approval of the House of Commons. Sometimes put for the condition of the national finances as disclosed in the ministerial statement; also for the financial measures proposed. Hence applied to an analogous statement made by the finance minister of any foreign country; also to a prospective estimate of receipts and expenditure, or a financial scheme, of a public body, or to the domestic accounts (of income and its manageable expenditure) of a family or individual; also, the money available for domestic spending; so ***on a budget***, with a restricted amount of money.

[The Chancellor of the Exchequer, in presenting his annual statement, was formerly said *to open the budget.* In a pamphlet entitled *The Budget Opened*, Sir R. Walpole was compared, apropos of his forthcoming Excise Bill, to a mountebank opening his wallet of quack medicines and conjuring tricks.]

1733 *Budget Opened* 8 And how is this to be done? Why by an Alteration only of the present Method of collecting the publick Revenues..So then, out it comes at last. The Budget is opened; and our State Emperick hath dispensed his packets by his Zany Couriers through all Parts of the Kingdom..I do not pretend to understand this Art of political Legerdemain. **1764** *Gent. Mag.* XXXIV. 207 The administration has condescended..to explain the *Budget* to the meanest capacity. **1771–97** H. WALPOLE *Mem. Geo. III*, I. xvii. 250 The time was now come for opening the *budget*, when it was incumbent on him to state the finances, debts, and calls of Government. **1785** *Hist. Europe* in *Ann. Reg.* 168/2 On the 30th of June Mr. Pitt opened the national accounts for the present year, or what is generally termed the Budget. **1800** PITT in G. Rose *Diaries* (1860) I. 278 Our first business..must be to prepare our budget. **1814** WELLINGTON *Let.* in Gurw. *Disp.* XII. 98 The budget has.. passed the Chamber of Deputies of the departments with trifling amendments. **1854** C. M. YONGE *Heartsease* I. I. vi. 92 Your budget? Are you good at arithmetic? *c* **1860** WRAXALL tr. *R. Houdin* xi. 143, I resolved to effect an utter reform in my budget. **1870** ROGERS Pref. to Adam Smith *W. Nat.* 20 England was crippled by foolish budgets. **1899** R. WHITEING *No. 5 John St.* iii. 18 To the Budget, then. Rent, 2s. 6d. a week; coal and candle, 6d. **1901** B. S. ROWNTREE *Poverty* p. ix, Chapter viii. deals with workmen's budgets, and especially the *diet* of the working classes. **1909** C. F. G.

MASTERMAN *Condition of England* iv. 98 The Blue Book.. analyses over a thousand 'family budgets', each giving details of how much is spent weekly on butter, tapioca, or treacle. **1932** *Listener* 4 May 630/1 Wheat occupies a much smaller place in the housewife's budget than it once did. **1955** *Oxf. Jun. Encycl.* XI. 154/1 By 1951, 11% of the weekly budget, almost as much as the rent, was being spent on milk. **1959** *Economist* 4 Apr. 46/1 Those on a budget go to Florida in spring or late autumn, the 'off seasons' when charges there are reduced.

b. *attrib.* or quasi-*adj.* Designed or suitable for someone of limited means; cheap.

1958 *Woman* 29 Nov. 6/2 This is just the drink to give party guests a glow—at a budget price. **1960** *Housewife* May 31/1 There are two restaurants catering for both luxury and budget tastes. **1969** *Woman's Own* 12 Apr. 27 Budget meals for the family.

†**5.** *Her.* = BOUGET: cf. 2a. *Obs.*

1766 PORNY *Heraldry* Gloss., Budget, v. Water-Budget.

6. (See MUM-BUDGET, a phrase enjoining silence.)

1598 SHAKS. *Merry W.* v. ii. 7, I come to her in white, and cry Mum; she cries Budget, and by that we know one another.

7. *Comb.* and *Attrib.*, as ***budget-bearer***, ***-full***, ***-maker***, ***-man***. Also **budget account**, an account opened with a department store, etc., offering the consumer revolving credit terms in return for regular payments; a charge account; **budget-bar** (see quot.); **budget-gut**, the cæcum; **budget plan**, orig. *U.S.*, a system of credit using the principles of a *budget account*; **budget-trimmer**, a man who prepares and fixes in position the leather fittings on coaches and carriages; **budget-wise**, (*a*) *adv.* (orig. *U.S.*), with reference to a budget; (*b*) *adj.*, making full use of limited resources.

1969 *Money Which?* Sept. 120/2 Other alternatives included *budget accounts in department stores. **1979** F. E. PERRY *Dict. Banking* 32/1 He gives the details of his usual outgoings to a bank which totals the annual cost, opens a budget account for the customer, and.. thereafter the bank will debit the customer's ordinary current account and credit the budget account with a monthly sum representing one-twelfth of the annual cost... Also, a system of credit-trading operated by some big department stores by which the customer pays so much each month and in return obtains credit for a multiple of the sum. **1794** W. FELTON *Carriages* (1801) I. 48 The *budget Bar.. is a straight timber, on which rests the boot or budgets. **1684** tr. *Agrippa's Van. Arts* lxii. 184 Barefooted *Budget-Bearers. **1614** *Engl. Way to Wealth* in *Harl. Misc.* (Mahl.) III. 238 Heaps and *budget-fulls in the counting-house. **1594** T. B. *La Primaud. Fr. Acad.* II. 350 The blinde gut.. is commonly called by some the sacke or *budget gut. **1553** *Act 1 Mary* 3rd Sess. viii. §2 The Currier.. *Budget-maker, and all other Artificers occupying the Craft or Mystery of Leather-buying. **1647** HAWARD *Crown Rev.* 26 Budget-maker: Fee, —6*l.* 1*s.* 8*d.* *c* **1550** *Wyll of Deuyll* (Collier) 6 To euery of these pety *Bouget men of laws.. a Bouget to put inne their sub penas. **1934** BARTLETT & REED *Methods of Instalment Selling & Collection* vi. 110 The features of the *budget plan, as explained by the salesman, make the extra sale. **1955** *Look* 4 Oct. 56/2 Under a new Certified Automotive Service Budget Plan, he borrowed $254.10 to overhaul his engine and buy two new tires. **1984** HITCHING & STONE *Understand Accounting!* x. 162 Electricity charges are covered by a monthly budget plan. **1881** *Instr. Census Clerks* (1885) 56 *Budget trimmer. **1909** *Daily Chron.* 4 Mar. 4/7 Wanted.. Budget Trimmers, accustomed to head work. **1952** T. PYLES *Words & Ways of Amer. Engish* vii. 189 Combinations with..-*wise*,..*stylewise*, **budgetwise*. **1956** A. H. COMPTON *Atomic Quest* 196 The Metallurgical Project had by now grown until it was budget-wise the major part of the University's activity. **1958** *Woman* 22 Nov. 31/1 Budget-wise dishes. Family recipes.. that are easy on the purse.

Hence **budgetism**.

1839 *Blackw. Mag.* XLVI. 105 The journalism, the budgetism, the parliamentaryism, of the 19th century.

'budget, *v.* [f. prec. sb.]

†**a.** *trans.* To put in a 'budget' or wallet; to store *up* (*obs.*). **b.** *intr.* To draw up or prepare a budget (BUDGET *sb.* 4); esp. *for* a certain supply or establishment, or *for* a particular financial result.

1618 J. TAYLOR (Water P.) *Pennilesse Pilgr.* Wks. 1630 I. 125/2 We eate a substantiall dinner, & like miserable Guests we did budget vp the reuersions. **1884** *Daily News* 9 Oct. 4/6 An army of 6,000 men and a force of 7,757 police were budgeted for in 1883. **1893** *Ibid.* 24 Mar. 5/6 Although the Government of India are most unwilling to budget for a deficit. **1900** *Westm. Gaz.* 23 Mar. 2/2 Every Chancellor of the Exchequer budgets with the fear of the Irish members before his [eyes]. **1901** *Ibid.* 4 June 2/2 When Sir Michael Hicks-Beach Budgeted for 1901-1902. **1922** G. A. GREENWOOD *England to-day* 28 There.. is the inevitable wear and tear of the home to be budgetted for. **1957** C. MORGAN *Challenge to Venus* IV. i. 197 The small professional class do worry... They budget. They keep personal accounts.

c. *trans.* To arrange (for) in a budget.

1890 *Sat. Rev.* 16 Aug. 191/1 General revenue, as budgeted for the years 1890–91, does not maintain the improvement of the previous year. **1909** D. LLOYD GEORGE in *Daily Chron.* 23 Oct. 1/1 The increment duty, which I budgetted to yield £50,000 this year. **1944** *Bath Wkly. Chron. & Herald* 24 June 3/1 (Advt.), By budgeting my points to work in with the rest of the rations, we make out very well.

Hence **'budgeting** *vbl. sb.*, the preparation of a budget; financial planning.

1945 G. WILLIAMS *Women & Work* iii. 88 Budgeting and shopping on a small income. **1951** *Good Housek. Home Encycl.* 30/2 The first essentials for budgeting are to keep weekly or monthly accounts.

budgetary ('bʌdʒɪtərɪ), *a.* [f. BUDGET *sb.* + -ARY 1 A: cf. mod.F. *budgétaire.*] Pertaining to a budget.

1879 R. H. LANG in *Macm. Mag.* Sept. 446/2 No accounts whatever, not even budgetary estimates.. have been given. **1881** *Daily News* 25 Mar. 5/4 M. Constans said such budgetary derangement was impracticable.

budgeteer (bʌdʒɪ'tɪə(r)). [f. as prec. + -EER[1].] One who makes up a budget (in sense 3 or 4).

a **1845** T. MOORE *Memor. last Week* ii, Such smooth Budgeteers have genteelly undone us. **1867** DE MORGAN *Budget of Paradoxes* in *Athenæum* 20 July 71/1 Prof. Smyth is a paradoxer; but he is one of those whom the budgeteer would place in his first class. **1880** *World* 21 Apr. 7 He has shown himself the prince of budgeteers.

budgeter ('bʌdʒɪtə(r)). [f. as prec. + -ER.] One who carries a wallet; ? a mountebank, charlatan (*obs.*); a strolling player.

1603 HARSNET *Pop. Impost.* 52 Our holy Budgetters having to deal with Devils.. doe.. provide so many to be packed up in One Patient, as except hell be drawn dry, they can never want work. **1815** C. MATHEWS *Mem.* II. 345 Never was such a thing known to a budgeter.

'budgetless, *a.* [f. as prec. + -LESS.] Without a budget; presenting no financial statement.

1865 *Morning Star* 7 Apr., Many.. Liberals suffer the present budgetless Government with the greatest patience. **1884** *Harper's Mag.* 857/1 The justification for a budgetless régime.

budgie ('bʌdʒɪ), colloq. abbrev. of BUDGERIGAR.

1936 W. WATMOUGH *Cult of Budgerigar* xv. 207 Although Budgies are so hardy.. reasonable care should.. be exercised to protect them from chills. **1959** 'A. GILBERT' *Death takes Wife* xv. 186 We've got a budgie.. that Maureen's teaching to talk.

†**'budgy**, *a.* *Obs. rare*[−1]. [f. BUDGE *sb.*[1] + -Y[1].] Of or like budge or lamb's fur.

1598 F. R. *Thule, or Virtue's Historie* R ij b, On whose furr'd chin did hang a budgie fleece.

†**'budkin.** *Obs.* [app. a variant of *bodkin*, BODIKIN.] In *God's budkin* = by the body of God: an obsolete oath.

1600 HEYWOOD *1 Edw. IV*, III. i. Wks. 1874 I. 43 Gods blue budkin! has the knaue serued me so?

'budless, *a.* [see -LESS.] Without buds.

1837 *New Monthly Mag.* LI. 115 Flowerless, bowerless, budless, and blossomless! **1849** C. BRONTË *Shirley* v. 49 Stalks budless and flowerless.

'budlet. [f. BUD *sb.*[1] + -LET.] A little bud; a secondary bud springing from another bud.

a **1864** DARWIN (in Webster) To distinguish.. the parent bud from the numerous budlets which are its offspring.

†**'budling.** *Obs. rare*[−1]. [f. BUD *sb.*[1] + -LING.] A little bud; *fig.* a young child.

1577 HOLINSHED *Chron.* III. 213 Part of these yoong ones to be taught the grammar in a faire schoole.. out of which these budlings at need from time to time to be dulie derived and drawen.

budmash, var. of BADMASH, 'bad character'.

bue, obs. form of BE *v.*, BOW *v.*

buel, obs. form of BOWEL.

buen, obs. form of *been*: see BE *v.*

‖**Buen Retiro** (bwen re'tiro). [Sp., lit. 'good retreat'.] The name of a palace near Madrid, used *attrib.* or *absol.* to designate a soft-paste porcelain made there during the reign of Charles III.

1863 W. CHAFFERS *Marks & Monogr.* 173 This monogram of Charles III is said to be found on the Buen Retiro porcelain, without the crown. **1869** LADY C. SCHREIBER *Jrnl.* (1911) I. 11 A set of Buen Retiro white (moulded) china... Figure of a man in white porcelain,.. marked Buen Retiro.

buer (bjʊə(r)). *north. dial.* and *tramps' slang.* Also 9 **bure, buor, bewer.** [Orig. unknown.] A woman, spec. one of loose character.

1807 J. STAGG *Misc. Poems* (1808) 144 A bure her neame was Meg, A winsome weel far'd body. **1886** W. NEWTON *Secrets of Tramp Life Revealed* 8 Buor, a woman. **1889** BARRÈRE & LELAND *Dict. Slang* I. 110/2 *Bewer*, (tinkers' slang), a woman... Young *bew'r*, a girl. **1938** G. GREENE *Brighton Rock* I. i. 8 'Christ,' the boy said, 'won't anybody stop that buer's mouth?' *Ibid.* VI. i. 228 That was what always happened if you took up with anything but a buer; they gave you the air.

Buerger ('bɜːgə(r)). [The surname of L. *Buerger* (1879–1943), an American physician and surgeon.] ***Buerger's disease***, inflammation and thrombosis in the small and medium-sized blood-vessels of the extremities, freq. leading to gangrene; also called *thrombo-angiitis obliterans.*

1914 *Trans. Philad. Acad. Surgery* XVI. 319 (*heading*) Thrombo-angiitis obliterans. (Buerger's disease)... The disease usually attacks Polish and Russian Jews between the ages of twenty and.. forty years. *Ibid.* 321 A man upon whom he had operated at different periods for Buerger's disease was stricken with a cerebral embolus. **1946** J. M. MURRY *Let.* 27 May (1961) 278 The condition was diagnosed eventually as a rare disease—sometimes called Buerger's disease. **1968** *Brit. Jrnl. Surgery* LV. 452/1 Many surgeons do not recognize a disease entity, Buerger's disease, and prefer to ascribe the condition to atherosclerosis.

buerne, obs. form of BERNE, BURN.

buetts, obs. form of BEWETS.

1688 R. HOLME *Armoury* II. 241/1 *Bewetts*, *Bewitts*, or *Buetts*, Boots.. to which the Bells are fastned, and are buttoned about the Hawks Legs.

bufall, var. of BUFFLE, *Obs.*, buffalo.

†**bufe.** *Obs. Cant.* [f. the sound of his bark.] A dog.

1567 HARMAN *Caveat* 84 Bufe, a dogge. **1609** DEKKER *Lanth. & Candle-L.* Wks. 1884–5 III. 199. **1688** R. HOLME *Armoury* III. iii. §68. **1725** *New Cant. Dict.*

bufet, obs. f. BUFFET.

†**buff**, *sb.*[1] *Obs.* exc. in BLIND MAN'S BUFF. Forms: 5–8 **buffe**, 6 **buf**, 6– **buff**. [perh. a. OF. *bufe*, *buffe*, a blow; cf. BUFFET *sb.*[1].] A blow, stroke, buffet. *Buff* and COUNTERBUFF seem to have been technical terms in fencing or pugilism.

c **1420** *Avow. Arth.* iv, Quo durst abide him a buffe. **1483** CAXTON *Gold. Leg.* 291/4 He gaf to her in Japyng a buffe. **1596** SPENSER *F.Q.* I. ii. 17 The Sarazin, sore daunted with the buffe. **1641** MILTON *Prel. Episc.* Wks. 1738 I. 38 Where they give the Romanists one buff, they receive two counterbuffs.

2. To this perhaps belongs the phrase **to stand buff**: to stand firm, not to flinch; to endure.

a **1680** BUTLER *Hudibras's Epitaph* (R.) For the good old cause stood buff 'Gainst many a bitter kick and cuff. **1698** VANBRUGH *Prov. Wife* V. v, The marriage-knot.. may stand buff a long, long time. **1701** COLLIER *M. Anton.* (1726) 219 To stand buff against danger and death. **1732** FIELDING *Miser* II. i, I must even stand buff, and outface him. **1827** SCOTT *Diary* in *Lockhart* (1839) IX. 146 If he does [turn on me].. it is best to stand buff to him.

buff (bʌf), *sb.*[2] Also 6–7 **buffe**. [app. ad. F. *buffle* buffalo; cf. BUFFLE.]

I. The animal.

†**1. a.** A buffalo, or other large species of wild ox.

1552 HULOET, Buffe, bugle, or wylde oxe, *bubalus.* **1577** B. GOOGE *Heresbach's Husb.* (1586) 137 Bubale, called of the common people Buffes, of Plinie Bisonte. **1582** D. INGRAM *Narrat.* in Arb. *Eng. Garner* V. 256 Buffes, which are beasts as big as two oxen. **1621** AINSWORTH *Annot. Pentat.* Deut. xiv. 5 The Buffe, Buffel, or Wilde-oxe. *a* **1674** MILTON *Moscovia* i. Wks. (1847) 569/1 Huge and desert Woods of Fir, abounding with black Wolves, Bears, Buffs. **1706** PHILLIPS, *Buff*, Buffle or Buffalo, a wild Beast.

†**b.** Used to render Pliny's *tarandus*, now usually identified with the reindeer. *Obs.*

1607 TOPSELL *Four-f. Beasts* (1658) A Buffe is called in Greek *Tarandus*.. When he is hunted or feared, he changeth his hew into whatsoever thing he seeth. **1617** MINSHEU *Ductor in Ling.* 56 A Buffe, so called because it has some likeness with the Buffle.. L. *Tarandus.*

II. Buff-skin, leather, and its uses.

†**2. a.** (More fully ***buff-leather***): *properly*, leather made of buffalo hide; but usually applied to a very stout kind of leather made of ox-hide, dressed with oil, and having a characteristic fuzzy surface, and a dull whitish-yellow colour.

1580 BARET *Alv.* B 1447 Couerings of saddles made of buffe leather. **1581** *Jrnls. Ho. Commons* 130 The Bill touching the Making of Spanish Leather and Buff within this Realm. **1613** *Voy. Guiana* in *Harl. Misc.* (Malh.) III. 190 The hide [of the Sea-cow].. will make good buff. **1711** STEELE *Spect.* No. 43 ¶10 To have Flea'd the Pict, and made Buff of his Skin. **1756** *Gentl. Mag.* XXVI. 61 Losh, or buff-leather, drest in oil, fit for the use of the army.

b. Military attire (for which buff was formerly much used); a military coat made of buff; = BUFF-COAT. Also the dress of sergeants and catch-poles. Hence, ***to wear buff***, ***be in buff.***

1590 SHAKS. *Com. Err.* IV. ii. 45 But is in a suite of buffe which rested him. **1599** BP. HALL *Sat.* IV. iv. 42 If Martius in boystrous buffes be drest. **1635** SHIRLEY *Coronat.* III. 306 To sell your glorious buffes to buy fine pumps. **1647** R. STAPYLTON *Juvenal* VI. 419 With men of Buffe and Feather [*cumque paludatis Ducibus*]. **1701** COLLIER *M. Anton.* (1726) *Life* 116 Never suffer'd to wear Buff in Italy. **1823** SCOTT *Peveril* (1865) 9 Churchmen, Presbyterians, and all, are in buff and bandoleer for King Charles. **1826** —— *Woodst.* (1832) 177 Strangled on the pulpit stairs by this man of buff and Belial.

3. *colloq.* The bare skin. ***in the buff***: naked.

[**1602** DEKKER *Satirom.* (D.) I go in stag, in buff.] **1654** CHAPMAN *Rev. for Hon.* I. i, For accoutrements you wear the buff. **1749** H. FITZCOTTON *Homer* I. 38 If you perplex me with your stuff—All that are here shan't save your buff. **1803** BRISTED *Pedest. Tour* II. 606 He had no change [of linen], consequently he slept in buff. **1872** C. KING *Sierra Nev.* viii. 176 Stripping ourselves to the buff, we hung up our steaming clothes. **1956** V. JENKINS *Lions Rampant* i. 17 They went swimming, sunbathed, did their training stripped to the buff. **1965** G. MCINNES *Road to Gundagai* ix. 153 The wizened fellow.. observed us undressing down to the buff. **1969** *Rolling Stone* 28 June 4/1 The girls call themselves the Groupies and claim they recorded their song in the buff.

4. = ***buff-stick*** or ***buff-wheel***: see 9.

1831 J. HOLLAND *Manuf. Metals* I. 292 A wheel similar to the glazer.. covered with.. buff leather, whence its name. These buffs and glazers, etc. **1884** F. BRITTEN *Watch & Clockm.* 37 Soldier's old belts make very good buffs.. Sticks coated with emery paper are also called buffs.

III. The colour, and things so coloured. [BUFF *a.*, used as *sb.*]

5. a. Buff colour; a dull light yellow. ***blue and buff*** were formerly the colours of the Whig party.

1788 DIBDIN *Musical Tour* xcvi. 394 The administration is a colour in grain, and will stand when buff and blue shall have entirely flown off. **1794** STEDMAN *Surinam* (1813) II. xxiv. 220 [The water melon's] color is..partly a very pale buff. **1818** BYRON *Juan* Ded. xvii, I still retain my 'buff and blue'. **1884** *Harper's Mag.* Feb. 349/2 A gradation of buffs and reds. *Mod.* The *Edinburgh Review*—the venerable blue-and-buff.

b. In full ***Buff Cochin***, a variety of the Cochin fowl, in which both cock and hen are of a uniform buff colour.

1855 *Poultry Chron.* III. 173 Our old friends, the Cochins, mustered pretty strong,..the buffs..were very good. **1873** L. WRIGHT *Bk. Poultry* 210 We have several shades in the Buff Cochin cock. *Ibid.* 213 The earliest and greatest breeders of Buff Cochins. **1899** NORRIS-ELYE *Brahmas & Cochins* 61 Evenness of colour is perhaps the greatest difficulty in breeding..buff Cochins.

6. a. ***the Buffs***: a popular name given, from the former colour of their facings (see BUFF *a.*), to the old 3rd regiment of the line in the British army (now the East Kent Regiment; royal assent was given to the restoration of buff facings to the East Kent Regiment on 19 August 1890). Similarly the old 78th regiment (now 2nd Battalion of Seaforth Highlanders) are called the ***Rossshire Buffs***.

1806 *Times* 10 Jan. The band of the Old Buffs playing Rule Britannia, drums muffled. **1838** *Hist. Record 3rd Regim. Foot* 157 The Men's Coats were lined and faced with buff, they also wore buff waistcoats, buff breeches and buff stockings, and were emphatically styled the Buffs. **1848** MACAULAY *Hist. Eng.* I. 295. **1883** *Harper's Mag.* Jan. 319/1 He entered the Buffs in 1817.

b. 'An enthusiast about going to fires' (Webster 1934); so called from the buff uniforms worn by volunteer firemen in New York City in former times. Hence *gen.*, an enthusiast or specialist. Chiefly *N. Amer. colloq.*

1903 *N.Y. Sun* 4 Feb. IV. 2/1 The Buffs are men and boys whose love of fires, fire-fighting and firemen is a predominant characteristic. **1907** A. M. DOWNES *Fire Fighters & Pets* xiii. 159 The 'buff' is a private citizen who is a follower, friend, and devoted admirer of the firemen. **1931** LAVINE *Third Degree* vi. 62 A dentist, known to many cops as a police buff (a person who likes to associate with members of the department and in exchange for having the run of the station house does various courtesies for the police). **1955** *Sci. Amer.* Aug. 88/3 No choo-choo buff can be without Sampson. **1962** *Listener* 1 Nov. 704/2 A neighbour of mine who is a hi-fi buff. **1963** *Economist* 20 July 244/2 The 'Pugwash' meetings between western and Russian scientists and other disarmament buffs. **1966** *New Yorker* 17 Sept. 130 For ballet buffs, Tuesday evening of last week was a great occasion. **1968** *Globe & Mail* (Toronto) 17 Feb. 37 Sports buffs will enjoy many diversions, with bicycling and camping..heading the list.

7. *Pathol.* = BUFFY COAT.

1739 HUXHAM *Fevers* (1750) 36 Blood..drawn off in high inflammatory Fevers..appears covered..with a thick glutinous coat, or Buff. **1782** DANIEL in *Med. Commun.* I. 22 *note*, The blood was covered with a buff. **1835–6** TODD *Cycl. Anat. & Phys.* I. 420/2 Louis found the blood covered by a firm thick buff at each bleeding in..cases of fatal peripneumony. **1880** *Syd. Soc. Lex.* s.v., *Inflammatory Buff*, the buffy coat of coagulated blood.

IV. *attrib.* and *comb.*

8. Obvious: as ***buff accoutrements, belt; buff-hide, -skin***; † ***buff-hard*** adj.

1599 HAKLUYT *Voy.* II. 177 Good store of Buffe Hides. **1607** TOPSELL *Four-f. Beasts* 157 His [the Rhinoceros'] more then buffe-hard skin. **1622** MALYNES *Anc. Law-Merch.* 81 The Commodities of East-land, and thereabouts ..Cables, Canuas, Buffe-hides. **1740** SOMERVILLE *Hobbinol* II. 306 His Buff Doublet, larded o'er with Fat Of slaughter'd Brutes. **1727–38** CHAMBERS *Cycl.* s.v. *Buff*, The skin of the buffalo being dressed in oil..makes..buff-skin. **1794** G. ADAMS *Nat. & Exp. Philos.* I. v. 181 A cup, furnished at bottom with a piece of buff-skin. **1813** WELLINGTON *Let.* in Gurw. *Disp.* XI. 334 Sets of buff accoutrements for the soldiers. **1831** CARLYLE *Sart. Res.* I. vii. 53 The military classes in those old times, whose buff-belts [and] complicated chains..have been bepainted in modern Romance.

9. Special comb.: **buff-jerkin**, a military jerkin of buff-leather; also *attrib.*; **buff-stick, buff-wheel**, a stick or wheel, covered with buff-leather or other soft material, used in polishing metal; †**buff-stop**, a stop on a harpsichord or spinet which produces a muffled tone by applying pieces of leather to the strings. See also BUFF-COAT.

a **1659** CLEVELAND *May Day* xiv, The *buff-fac'd Sons of War. **1596** SHAKS. *1 Hen. IV*, I. ii. 49 Is not a *Buffe Ierkin a most sweet robe of durance? **1625** FLETCHER *Elder Bro.* v. i, Among provant swords, and buff-jerkin men. **1727** SWIFT *Gulliver* I. i. 24, I had on me a buff jerkin, which they could not pierce. **1881** GREENER *Gun* 250 The..gun is then buffed over with a leather *buff stick. *a* **1819** WOLCOTT (P. Pindar) *Wks.* (1830) 122 (D.) Like the *buff-stop on harpsichords or spinnets—Muffling their pretty little tuneful throats. **1880** A. J. HIPKINS in Grove *Dict. Mus.* I. 691 A 'buff'-stop of small pieces of leather, brought into contact with the strings, damping the tone.

buff, *sb.*[3], var. of BUFFE.

†**buff,** *sb.*[4] *Obs. colloq.* [Origin uncertain: see quot. 1725, and cf. BUFFER *sb.*[4]] Fellow, 'buffer'.

1708–15 KERSEY, *Buff*..a dull Sot, or dronish Fellow. **1709** *Brit. Apollo* II. No. 8 3/2 Tell me Grave Buffs, Partly Gods, partly Men. **1725** *New Cant. Dict.* s.v., *Buff*, a Newgate Cant Word used in familiar Salutation: as, How dost do, my Buff? **1748** SMOLLETT *Rod. Rand.* (1812) I. iv. 15 Mayhap old buff has left my kinsman here his heir. **1764** BRYDGES *Homer Travest.* (1797) II. 420 You seem afraid these buffs will flinch.

buff (bʌf), *sb.*[5] and *int.* [? Onomatopœic. Cf. BUFE. Partly perhaps imitating a dog's bark (cf. BOUGH *v.*, BAFF); partly an instinctive exclamation of contempt.]

A. as *int.* In phrases **a.** † ***to say neither buff nor baff, not to say buff to a wolf's shadow*** (obs.). **b.** ***to say*** (or ***know***) ***neither buff nor stye*** (Sc.): i.e. neither one thing nor another, nothing at all.

1481 CAXTON *Reynard* K ij b, He wyste not what to saye buff ne baff. **1542** UDALL *Erasm. Apoph.* 11 b, A certain persone, beeyng of him bidden good speede, saied to hym again neither buff ne baff. **1581** N. BURNE *Disput.* 128 b (JAM.) Johann Kmnox ansuerit maist resolutlie, buf, baf, man. **1589** R. HARVEY *Pl. Perc.* (1860) 25 These toong-tide Curs that cannot barke, nor say buffe to a woulfes shadow. ? *a* **1750** *Jacobite Relics* I. 80 (JAM.) Who knew not what was right or wrong, And neither buff nor sty, sir. **1824** SCOTT *Redg.* ch. xii, 'What say you to that?'..'I say neither buff nor stye to it'.

B. *sb. Sc.* (Perh. not connected with the prec.) 'Nonsense, foolish talk' (Jamieson).

1721 RAMSAY *Addr. Town Council Edinb.* 23 It blather'd buff before them a', And aftentimes turn'd doited. **1739** A. NICOL *Poems* 84 (JAM.) Nae great ferly tho' it be Plain buff ..I'm no book-lear'd. **1790** SHIRREF *Poems* 338 (JAM.) It only gi'es him pain To read sic buff. **1813** W. BEATTIE *Poems* (1871) *Yule Feast* 1 Read: but should you think it buff, Throw't out o' sight.

buff (bʌf), *sb.*[6] A name given to the blindfold player in the game of BLIND-MAN'S BUFF. ***shadow buff***: a modern game in which one player has to guess the identity of the other players from seeing only their shadows.

1647 FANSHAWE *Pastor Fido* (1676) 78 Behold the Buff [orig. *ecco la cieca*]. **1879** HOFFMANN *Drawing-r. Amusem.* 9 Shadow Buff is a game of greater originality. The company now pass in succession before the light but behind Buff.

buff, *sb.*[7] **1.** (With capital initial.) Short for BUFFALO *sb.* 1 e. *colloq.*

1879 *The Buffalo* 16 Jan. 3/3 The great scheme of a technical university now being taken up by the City companies, was first started by Buffs. **1888** [see BUFFALO *sb.* 1 e]. **1897** *Buffalo World* Sept. 3/2 It should..be the aim of every loyal Buff..to show his desire to help on the cause for which we are fighting, viz. Progress and the Brotherhood of man. **1909** *Daily Chron.* 31 July 4/5 A..belief..that the 'Buffs', as it is generally called, originated at the Harp Tavern, in Russell-street, Drury-lane, in 1822.

2. Short for BUFFALO *sb.* senses 1 a to d. *colloq.*

1583 G. PECKHAM *True Reporte* in Hakluyt *Voy.* (1600) III. 175 He and his company did finde in one cottage aboue two hundred and fortie hides..and with this agreeth Dauid Ingram, and describeth that beast at large, supposing it to be a certaine kinde of Buffe. **1665** P. E. RADISSON *Voyages* (1885) 212 They have very handsome shoose laced very thick all over wth a peece sowen att the side of ye heele, wch was of a haire of Buff. **1884** *Bismarck Tribune* Aug., The ball struck the unsuspecting animal... But the old 'buff' took the fling as an insult. **1935** HEMINGWAY *Green Hills of Africa* (1936) II. iii. 98 I'd rather get another buff than rhino. *Ibid.* 113 Where the rhinos and the buff had come out of the reeds. **1964** C. WILLOCK *Enormous Zoo* ii. 24 When the buff was nearly up with him, the boy took off his hat and put it over the animal's eyes.

buff (bʌf), *a.* [f. BUFF *sb.*[2] 2.]

1. Of the nature or appearance of buff leather.

a **1695** MRQ. HALIFAX *On C'tess Dowager of*—— (R.) This goodly goose..did overload Her bald buff forehead with a high commode.

b. *fig.* (from BUFF *sb.*[2] 3). Naked, unrefined.

1792 W. ROBERTS *Looker-on* No. 29 (1794) I. 410 On that plain buff principle of old English hospitality.

2. Of the colour of buff leather; a light brownish yellow.

(Early quots. are doubtful, and may mean the material.)

1762–71 H. WALPOLE *Vertue's Anecd. Paint.* (1786) III. 69 *note*, The dress is that of a Cavalier about the time of the civil war, buff with blue ribbands. **1791** J. WOLCOTT (P. Pindar) *Ode to Ass* Wks. 1812 II. 462 Buff breeches too have crown'd a proud proud day. **1804** *Med. & Phys. Jrnl.* XII. 512 Pileus brown buff, darker in the centre. **1835–6** TODD *Cycl. Anat. & Phys.* I. 419/2 The buffed coat..is generally ..of a light yellow or buff colour. **1876** MISS BRADDON *J. Haggard's Dau.* I. 108 The..old-fashioned Staffordshire tea service..blue flowers on a buff ground.

3. *Comb.*, as ***buff-backed, -colour, -coloured, -orange, -washed, -yellow***; **buff-tip**, a species of moth (see quot.).

1884 J. COLBORNE *Hicks Pasha* 264 The pretty little *buff-backed heron. **1794** STEDMAN *Surinam* (1813) II. xxiv. 220 The musk [melon]..is ribbed, *buff color, orange and green. **1686** *Lond. Gaz.* No. 2106/4 A..Red Coat..with a *Buff-colour'd lining. **1882** VINES *Sachs' Bot.* 282 From dead plants [Fucaceæ] cold fresh-water extracts a buff-coloured substance. **1882** *Garden* 2 Sept. 202/1 A charming hardy Orchid..It is a *buff-orange colour. **1836** DUNCAN *Brit. Moths* 187 *Pygæra Bucephala*..named the *Buff-tip Moth, on account of a large patch of that colour on the apex of the anterior wings. **1883** MISS BRADDON *Gold. Calf* xii. 150 The walls plastered, and white-washed, or *buff-washed. **1882** *Garden* 5 Aug. 110/1 Seedling *buff-yellow Carnation.

4. Substantival uses of this adj. are for convenience treated under BUFF *sb.*[2] III.

†**buff,** *v.*[1] *Obs.* exc. *dial.* [prob. onomatopœic: cf. PUFF *v.*, and BUFF *sb.*[1], also F. *bouffer* in its various senses, and OF. *buffer* 'souffleter' (Godef.). Sense 1 has app. no connexion with 3, exc. as both may arise in different ways from some of the characteristics of a broad puff of wind, and its associated sound.] Hence '**buffing** *vbl. sb.*, and *ppl. a.*

1. *intr.* **a.** To speak with obstructed and explosive utterance, to stutter. **b.** To explode or burst into a laugh, or the like.

1297 R. GLOUC. 414 Of speche hastyf, Boffyng, & mest wanne he were in wraþþe. **1398** TREVISA *Barth. De P.R.* II. viii. (1495) 55 As I maye, though it be stamerynge and buffynge. **1611** COTGR., *Esclaffer*, to buff, or burst, out into a laughter. *Mod. Sc.* He buft out into a laugh.

2. *trans.* To cause to burst out by sudden force.

a **1637** B. JONSON *Loves Welc. at Welbeck* (R.) A shock To have buff'd out the blood From ought but a block.

3. *intr.* To act and sound as a soft inflated substance does when struck, or as the body does which strikes it.

a **1550** *Christis Kirke Gr.* xi, He hit him on the wame a wap It buft lyk ony bledder. **1881** *Leicestersh. Words* (E.D.S.) s.v., When an axe or hatchet strikes without cutting, which is sometimes the case..with unsound wood, it is said to 'buff'.

4. *intr.* and *trans.* To strike a soft inflated body (with the characteristic effect and sound).

1600 F. WALKER *Sp. Mandeville* 64 b, The furious buffing together of windes, when they meete. **1785** BURNS *Twa Herds* xiii, A chiel wha'll soundly buff our beef.

†**buff,** *v.*[2] *Sc. Obs.* [cf. F. *bouffer*.]

trans. ? To puff out. Hence **buft** *ppl. a.*

1572 *Lament. Lady Scotl.* in *Scot. Poems 16th C.* II. 252 Buft brawlit hois, coit, dowblet, sark and scho. **1573** *Sege Edinb. Castel* ibid. II. 294 That socht na tailzeours for to bufe thair breiks.

buff, *v.*[3] [f. BUFF *sb.*[2]]

1. *trans.* **a.** To polish with a buff (frequent colloq. in the metal trades). **b.** To impart the velvety surface usual in buff leather for belts, etc.

1885 *Harper's Mag.* Jan. 284/2 Sand-paper..'buffs' the grain of the leather, leaving it white and velvety.

2. To impart a buff colour to.

1897 ROTHWELL *Textile Fabrics* 237 The pieces are to be 'buffed' or 'slop-padded' with substantive dyestuffs in solutions containing soap.

buff (bʌf), *v.*[4] *slang.* [cf. BUFFER *sb.*[6]] To swear to.

1812 J. H. VAUX *Flash Dict.* s.v. *Buff*, To buff to a person or thing, is to swear to the identity of them. **1865** *Daily Tel.* 27 Feb. 6/1 What robberies are you going to 'buff' to me.. meaning 'to charge me with, or accuse me of'. **1869** *Morning Star*, 3 June, They are going to send some one to 'buff' (own) it.

buff, *v.*[5] *nonce-wd.* [Two formations: a. f. *buff* in BLINDMAN'S BUFF; b. suggested by phrase *to stand buff* (see BUFF *sb.*[1]).] In phrase ***to buff it***: **a.** to play blindman's buff (also *fig.*); **b.** to stand firm, resist.

1608 DAY *Hum. out of Br.* IV. iii. (1881) 67 Blindmans buffe? I haue bufft it fairely, and mine owne gullery grieues me not half so much as the Dukes displeasure. **1822** T. MITCHELL *Aristoph.* II. 84 Tuck yourself up, and buff it like a man.

buffal(l, var. of BUFFLE, *Obs.*, buffalo.

buffalo ('bʌfələʊ), *sb.* Forms: 6 bufalo, (7 buffolo, boufaleau, -alo, 7–8 buffelo, 8 bufolo), 7– buffalo. *Pl.* buffaloes. [a. It. *buffalo* (Florio), *bufalo, bufolo* (Baretti), or Pg. *búfalo*:—vulgar L. **būfalus*, a. Gr. βούβαλος (whence in literary L. *būbalus*), properly denoting a kind of antelope, but applied to a wild ox. Cf. BUFFLE, BUFF *sb.*[2] The early quotations suggest that the word originally came into English from Portuguese.]

1. The name of several species of Oxen; esp. **a.** *Bos bubalus*, originally a native of India, inhabiting most of Asia, southern Europe, and northern Africa. It is tamed in India, Italy, and elsewhere. **b.** *B. caffer*, the Cape Buffalo of S. Africa. **c.** Applied in popular unscientific use to the American BISON.

a. 1588 PARKE tr. *Mendoza's China* 181 They doo plough and till their ground with kine, Bufalos, and bulles. **1665** *Voy. E. India* 359 They have a Beast very large, having a smooth thick skin without hair, called a Buffelo, which gives good milk; the flesh of them is like Beef. **1682** WHELER *Journ. Greece* I. 74 Drawn..instead of Flanders Mares by a pair of Boufaleaus. **1756** NUGENT *Gr. Tour Italy* III. 214 They..make use of buffalo's in ploughing the land. **1843** MACAULAY *Lays Anc. Rome, Lake Regillus* x, The..banks of Ufens, Where..buffaloes lie wallowing Through the hot

summer's day. **1850** LAYARD *Nineveh* x. 259 The cattle were ..the buffalo and common ox.

b. **1699** CAPT. ROGERS *Descr. Natal* in *Dampier's Voy.* (1705) II. III. 109 Buffaloes and Bullocks only are kept tame. **1731** MEDLEY *Kolben's Cape G. Hope* I. 79 They could discover in them [the woods] neither Elephant nor Buffalo, **1834** PRINGLE *Afr. Sk.* viii. 269 The buffalo is a very.. powerful animal..larger than the domestic ox. **1857** LIVINGSTONE *Trav.* iii. 56 The presence of the buffalo..is a certain indication of water..within..seven or eight miles.

c. **1635** *Relat. Maryland* iii. 23 In the upper parts of the countrey there are Bufeloes, Elkes, Lions, Beares, Wolues, and Deare there are in great Store. **1705** R. BEVERLEY *Virginia* II. 39 The Elks, Buffaloes, Deer and greater Game. **1789–96** MORSE *Amer. Geog.* I. 195 This animal [bison] has generally been called the Buffalo, but very improperly. **1836** W. IRVING *Astoria* (1849) 195 Boundless wastes..animated by herds of buffalo. **1877** J. ALLEN *Amer. Bison* 456 Probably among the people generally the name buffalo will never be supplanted.

d. *collect.*

1765 G. CROGHAN *Jrnl.* (1875) 132 The country hereabouts abounds with buffalo, bears, [etc.]. **1817** S. R. BROWN *Western Gaz.* 30 The buffaloe..have lately disappeared. **1895** C. KING *Fort Frayne* xviii. 260 A deep cleft in the foothills through which the buffalo in bygone days had made their way.

e. (With capital initial.) A member of the Royal Antediluvian Order of Buffaloes, founded in 1822 for sociable and benevolent purposes. Hence '**Buffaloism**.

1869 P. EGAN *Finish Adv. Tom, Jerry, & Logic* v. 120 At the Harp, in Great Russel Street, opposite Drury Lane Theatre, the Buffalo Society was first established, in August, 1822. **1879** *The Buffalo* 16 Jan. 3/3 Bro. Barrett, the Buffalo Bootmaker of Walworth. **1881** (*title*) The Buffalo Review and Lodge Reporter. **1888** C. HINDLEY *True Hist. Tom & Jerry* 162 *Buffs—Buffaloes*—and *Buffaloism.*—A society..established in August, 1822, by an eccentric young man of the name of Joseph Lisle, an artist, in conjunction with Mr. W. Sinnett, a comedian, to perpetuate, according to their ideas upon the subject, of that hitherto neglected ballad of *We'll chase the Buffalo*! **1897** *Daily News* 16 Mar. 8/3 A room in which certain 'Buffaloes' were holding a lodge meeting. **1897** *Buffalo World* Sept. 3/1 Buffaloism can boast an existence of 300 years at least. **1970** *Sunday Times* 18 Jan. 52/3 We used to have a branch of the Buffaloes at the pub. *Ibid.*, Her family were very high up in the Buffaloes.

f. An amphibious tank.

1944 *Hutchinson's Pict. Hist. War* Oct. 139 (*caption*) British troops were carried across the Scheldt in assault craft... This 'Buffalo' assault craft is carrying back some of the prisoners taken. **1945** *Times* 1 Mar. 4/3 The generals.. rode in a 'buffalo' and inspected it minutely. **1959** *Times Lit. Suppl.* 13 Feb. 86/2 This division was also the British Army's nursery of the amphibious 'Buffaloes' of American origin.

2. 'A sort of fresh-water fish resembling the Sucker' (Bartlett).

1789–96 MORSE *Amer. Geog.* I. 636 In the rivers are plenty of buffaloe, pike and catfish. **1884** *Harper's Mag.* Mar. 516/2 The 'buffalo' and cat-fish..are not unfrequently as large as a man.

3. = *buffalo-robe*; see 4. *colloq. U.S.* & *Canada.*

1856 KANE *Arct. Expl.* I. xv. 181 Leaving all hands under their buffaloes. **1884** *Boston* (*Mass.*) *Jrnl.* 3 Sept., Asked by the groom if he would like a couple of buffaloes (robes) ..'No', replied the scientist, 'we would much prefer horses'.

4. Short for *buffalo-horn*: used by cutlers for making handles of pocket-knives; the varieties are ***black buffalo*** and ***grey*** or ***coloured buffalo***.

5. *Comb.*, as ***buffalo-hide***, ***-hunt***, ***-hunter***, ***-hunting***, ***-range***, ***-skin***; **buffalo-bag** (cf. *buffalo-robe*); **buffalo-bean**, a milk vetch of the western United States, *Astragalus crassicarpus*; **buffalo-berry**, the edible scarlet fruit of a shrub (*Shepherdia argentea*) found on the Upper Missouri; also the shrub itself; **buffalo-bird**, an insessorial bird (*Textor erythrorhynchus*) which accompanies herds of buffaloes in S. Africa; **buffalo-chips** *pl.*, the dried dung of the American bison, used as fuel; **buffalo-clover**, a species of clover (*Trifolium pennsylvanicum*) found in the prairies of N. America; **buffalo-fish** = sense 2; **buffalo fly, gnat**, a small biting insect of the genus *Simulium*; **buffalo grass**, (*a*) a kind of grass (*Buchloë dactyloides*) found in the prairies; also used generally (see quot. 1950); (*b*) any of various African grasses used for pasture and fodder; (*c*) *Austral.* and *N.Z.*, the grass *Stenotaphrum americanum*, introduced from the United States, and first noticed near Buffalo Creek in New South Wales (Webster 1911); **buffalo-horn**, (*a*) the horn of a buffalo; (*b*) an African tree, *Zizyphus mucronata*; (*c*) *U.S.* (see quot. 1887[2]); **buffalo-nut**, the fruit of a N. American shrub (*Pyrularia oleifera*), also called Oil-nut; also the shrub itself; **buffalo-robe**, a cloak or rug made of the skin of the American bison dressed with the hair on.

1856 KANE *Arct. Expl.* I. xvi. 192 Two large *buffalo-bags, each made of four skins. **1906** P. A. RYDBERG *Flora of Colorado* 202 Geoprumnon... *Buffalo Beans, Ground Plums. **1922** *Chambers's Jrnl.* 219/1, I..became acquainted with a creeping plant that grows a bean... I have since heard it called buffalo-bean. **1805** *Massachusetts Spy* 17 July 2/3 (Th.), Scions of a newly discovered berry, called the *buffaloe berry. **1856** *Gard. Chron.* 174 The felicity of tasting real Buffalo-berries. **1857** LIVINGSTONE *Trav.* xxvii. 545 *Buffalo-birds act the part of guardian spirits to the animals. *Ibid.* (1861) 357 The leader of the herd was an old cow, carrying on her withers about twenty buffalo-birds. **1840** *Picayune* 11 Oct. 2 We raised an extensive cloud of smoke from burning '*buffalo chips' to keep off the musquitos. **1859** MARCY *Prairie Trav.* 268 Buffalo-chips for fuel. **1767** in *N. Carolina Col. Rec.* VII. 1007 *Buffalow Clover was extremely thick here. **1774** D. JONES *Jrnl.* (1865) 111 Another kind of fish called *buffaloe fish, many of which are larger than our sheepshead. **1861** RUSSELL in *Times* 10 July, These..rivers are very fine for..buffalo fish to live in. **1849** CHARLES LYELL *Second Visit N. Amer.* II. 89 There were swarms of *buffalo flies to torment his horses, and sand flies to sting him and his family. **1932** *Discovery* July 210/2 The buffalo fly is another extremely serious pest, in this case of the cattle industry. **1822** J. WOODS *Eng. Prairie* 278 We had no *buffalo gnats. **1959** J. CLEGG *Freshwater Life Brit. Isles* (ed. 2) xiv. 235 The Black-flies..under such names as Buffalo Gnats..are only too well known as pests of cattle. **1784** J. FILSON *Discovery of Kentucke* 24 Where no cane grows there is abundance of wild-rye, clover, and *buffalo-grass,..affording excellent food for cattle. **1868** J. CHAPMAN *Trav. S. Afr.* II. 457 (Pettman), The Buffalo grass has a large, broad, corrugated leaf and is greedily eaten by horses and cattle. **1876** F. M. BAILEY in *Papers & Proc. R. Soc. Tasmania 1875* 132 The Buffalo grass, *Stenotaphrum Americanum*..is a very fine and desirable species. **1883** *Harper's Mag.* Nov. 943/2 The tall jointed grasses replace the short crisp buffalo-grass. **1950** *Amer. Speech* XXV. 164 The ground is covered with 'buffalo grass', which once designated a specific type but now means any tough grass that grows on the poor soil of the plains. **1703** *Lond. Gaz.* No. 3919/4 A parcel of..*Buffelo-Hides, &c. **1783** W. FLEMING in N. D. Mereness *Trav. Amer. Col.* (1916) 665 We picked up..a petrified *Buffalo horn. **1887** MOLONEY *Forestry W. Afr.* 300 'Buffalo-Horn' (*Zizyphus mucronata*, Willd.). **1887** *Scribner's Mag.* II. 507 The latter fixes his attention on the saw-like, serrated crowns, or summits, which are..typical..of true mountainous form. There are plenty of such features in the Rocky Mountains, and natives call them 'buffalo-horns'. **1810** Z. M. PIKE *Exped. Sources Mississippi* App. II. 34 Restricting (by edicts) the *buffalo hunts to certain seasons. **1824** A. ROSS *Jrnl.* 28 Mar. in *Oregon Hist. Soc. Quart.* XIV. 376 The *buffalo hunters came back today, buffalo in plenty; thirty killed. **1775** W. CALK *Jrnl.* 10 Apr. in *Filson Club Pubn.* II. 36 Some of the company went over the River a *bufelo hunting but found none. **1857** GRAY *Botany* 382 *Buffalo-nut..[is] a low straggling shrub, with..small greenish flowers. **1775** ADAIR *Hist. Amer. Indians* 118 Living very scantily, even in a *buffalo range, under a strict rule, lest by luxury their hearts should grow evil. **1804** CLARK in *Lewis & C. Exped.* (1904) I. 130 The [Sioux] Squars wore Peticoats & a white *Buffalow roabe. **1856** KANE *Arct. Expl.* I. xvi. 193 The sick ..were placed upon the bed of buffalo-robes. **1732** *S.C. Gazette* 25/1 Preparing *Buffelo, Deer, Sheep, Goat or Kid-Skins in Oil. **1835** W. IRVING *Tour Prairies* 145 We passed ..a *buffalo track, not above three days old.

'**buffalo**, *v.* *N. Amer. slang.* [f. the sb.] *trans.* To overpower, overawe, or constrain by superior force or influence; to outwit, perplex. So '**buffaloed** *ppl. a.*

1903 *Cincinnati Enquirer* 9 May 13/1 Buffaloed—Bluffed. **1904** *N.Y. Even. Post* 25 Oct. 10 All the rest [of the newspapers] were what we used to term in the Southwest 'buffaloed' by the McKinley myth—that is, silenced by the fear of incurring the resentment of a people taught to regard McKinley as a saint. **1910** W. M. RAINE *B. O'Connor* 77 O'Connor admitted that he was 'buffaloed' when he attempted an analysis of his unusual feeling. **1947** E. A. MCCOURT *Flaming Hour* 118 Jerry Potts himself would have been buffaloed.

† '**buffard**. *Obs. rare*[−1]. [? a. F. *bouffard* 'often puffing, much blowing, swelling vp, strouting out; also, swelling with anger' (Cotgr.).] ? A foolish fellow. Cf. BUFFER *sb.*[4]

c **1430** LYDG. *Min. Poems* 32 Thouhe she be yong, yet wol she wele abide, Uncoupled to a fresshe man of innesse [? iunesse], And take a buffard riche of gret vilesse.

buffat, -ed, obs. f. BUFFET *sb.*[2], footstool.

buff coat, 'buff-coat. [See BUFF *sb.*[2]]

1. A stout coat of buff leather, esp. worn by soldiers. Also *fig.*

1633 T. STAFFORD *Pac. Hib.* xi. (1821) 134 Captaine Harvy receevid..a blow with a pike..but escaped danger by the goodnesse of his Buffe Coat. **1685** W. ADAMS *Dedham Pulpit* 104 The form of religion..is a buff coat to their sins, to turn the sharpest reproofs. **1801** GROSE *Mil. Antiq.* II. 323 The buff-coat, or jerkin..originally worn under the cuirass..became frequently a substitute for it, it having been found that a good buff leather would of itself resist the stroke of a sword..Buff-coats continued to be worn by the city trained-bands till within the memory of persons now living. **1816** SCOTT *Old Mort.* ii, The jack-boots, buff coat, and other accoutrements.

2. One who wears a buff coat; a soldier.

a **1670** HACKET *Abp. Williams* I. (1692) 170 Some profane buff-coats will authorize such incendiaries. **1721** N. AMHERST *Terræ Fil.* 219 The city buff-coats, who took Liste in Bunhill-fields.

†**3.** See quot. *Obs.*

1688 R. HOLME *Armoury* III. 293/2 Buff-Coat [is] a soft Bread eaten hot with Butter. [PHILLIPS, KERSEY, & BAILEY print *bust-coat*.]

4. = BUFFY COAT.

Hence '**buff-coated** *a.*

1856 J. GRANT *Black Drag.* xlvii, The rear-guard of buff-coated and steel-capped cavalry.

buffe (bʊf). Now only *hist.* Also 6 buffie. [ad. It. *buffa* the breathing hole of a helmet.] In ancient armour, a chin piece pierced with breathing-holes, worn with the burgonet.

1598 FLORIO, *Buffa*, the buffie or breathing holes of a headpiece or helmet. **1600** HOLLAND *Livy* XLIV. xxxiv. 1192 Others furbushed their headpeeces, buffes [*bucculas*], and beavers. **1885** H. A. DILLON *Fairholt's Costume* (ed. 3) II. 102 A separate and distinct chin-piece called a *buffe* is so often associated with it [*sc.* the burgonet]. **1909** C. FFOULKES *Arm. & Weapons* iv. 83 The face-guard, when used with the burgonet, is called the Buffe. **1922** *Daily Tel.* 12 June 20/3 The 'Buffe' of French 16th century work, which belongs to the 'Colbert' casque.

buffed (bʌft), *a.* [f. BUFF *sb.*[2] + -ED.] **a.** Clad in buff. **b.** Coated or covered with buff, having a 'buffy coat'. ***buffed coat*** = BUFFY COAT.

1640 in Chambers *Bk. of Days* I. 767 This you do To a buffed captain, or perhaps unto His surly corporal. **1835–6** TODD *Cycl. Anat. & Phys.* I. 419/2 The buffed coat..is generally..of a light yellow or buff colour. *Ibid.* The specific gravity of buffed blood.

'**buffel(l**, var. of BUFFLE, *Obs.*, buffalo.

† **1. buffel duck** = BUFFLEHEAD 2. Also ***buffel's head duck***. *Obs. U.S.*

1731 CATESBY *Nat. Hist. Carolina* I. 95/1 The Buffel's Head Duck. *Ibid.*, The length and looseness of these Feathers make the Head appear bigger than it is, which seems to have given it the Name of Buffel's Head, that Animal's Head appearing very big by it's being covered with very thick long Hair. **1785** PENNANT *Arctic Zool.* II. 559 Pied and buffel duck. **1831** WILSON & BONAPARTE *Amer. Ornith.* IV. 351 Red headed buffel duck.

2. buffel grass [Du. *buffel gras*] = *buffalo grass* (b).

[**1915** R. MARLOTH *Flora S. Afr.* IV. 22 Buffelgras.] **1955** J. CLEARY *Justin Bayard* xii. 182 Between the patch of buffel grass and the grey-blue slate was a small strip of fine sand. **1958** *Austral. Encycl.* IV. 126/1 Introduced species [of].. fodder plants..from Africa, veldt..buffel (Cenchrus ciliaris)..grasses.

† '**buffen**, *a.* [? f. BUFF *sb.*[2] 2 + -EN[1].] ? Made of buff leather; or var. of BUFFIN, coarse cloth.

1621 QUARLES *Argalus & P.* (1678) 101 Beneath his arm, a Buffen-Knapsack hung.

buffen, var. of BUFFIN, *Obs.*, a coarse cloth.

† '**buffer**, *sb.*[1] *Obs.* [f. BUFF *v.*[1]] A stammerer.

1382 WYCLIF *Isa.* xxxii. 4 The tunge of bufferes [**1388** stuttynge men; **1611** stammerers] swiftli shal speke.

buffer ('bʌfə(r)), *sb.*[2] [app. f. BUFF *v.*[1] 3 + -ER (cf. BUFFING *vbl. sb.*[1]).]

1. a. *Mech.* A mechanical apparatus for deadening the force of a concussion; as a round plate or cushion (usually supported by a strong spring) fixed in pairs at the front and back of railway carriages or engines, or on the face of a terminal wall of a line of railway. Extended also to the solid projecting beam-ends of railway trucks, etc., and strong bars across sidings, which sustain without deadening the concussion. (Formerly called also *buffing apparatus*: see BUFFING *vbl. sb.*[1])

1835 *Specif. Church's Patent* No. 6791. 12 The buffers supported by metal springs *x* and air cylinder. **1841** *Penny Cycl.* XIX. 258/2 Buffers or discs of wood or metal, sometimes covered with cushions. **1860** TYNDALL *Glac.* I. §2. 9 The shock..is harmless when distributed over the interval necessary for the pushing in of the buffer. **1867** *Pall Mall G.* 27 July 9 He jumped on to a buffer of a carriage.

b. *Chem.* A substance or a mixture of substances, usu. of a weak acid or base and its salt, which stabilizes the degree of acidity or alkalinity of a solution; also, a buffer solution. Also *attrib.* in ***buffer action***, ***base***, ***salt***; **buffer solution** (see 3).

1914 *Chem. Abstr.* 3561 The action of moderators (buffers) in the shifting of the acid-base equilibrium in biological liquids... A monobasic acid shows its max. buffer reaction at a H-ion conc... The max. buffer action of all weak acids in equiv. concs. is the same. **1922** *Encycl. Brit.* XXXI. 59/1 Death will be due to acid poisoning, and the administration of what are called 'buffer salts'..is instrumental in postponing the fatal issue. **1926** TANSLEY & CHIPP *Stud. Vegetation* vii. 124 This substance acts as an acid 'buffer' to the soil solution. **1961** *Lancet* 22 July 176/1 The solvent contains 45 ml. of phosphate buffer (pH = 7·4). **1965** [see ALKALOSIS].

c. *Biol.* (See quot. 1939 and cf. BUFFER *v.* c.)

1939 H. J. MULLER in *Biol. Rev.* XIV. 271 Some 'buffers' may eventually arise—that is, genes that compensate for a change in one or more of the secondary effects of the primary gene in question. **1943** *Nature* 16 Jan. 68/2 The distinction between switch genes and buffer genes.

d. A 'memory' device in a computer (see quot. 1962); a buffer memory.

1948 *Math. Tables & other Aids to Computation* III. 289 Two 32-word delay lines, or reservoirs..are used as buffers between the main electronic part of the machine and the tape. **1956** *Control Engineering* Nov. 117/1 Input Information..is transferred to the internal memory of the computer either directly or through an external storage device or buffer. **1958** M. PHISTER *Logical Design Digital Computers* viii. 216 The buffer memory must be independent of the operation of the rest of the main memory. **1962** S. HANDEL *Dict. Electronics* 40 *Buffer*,..a memory device used to compensate for a difference in the rate of flow of information in the different parts of a computing system.

2. *fig.*; spec. used *attrib.* or quasi-*adj.* to designate a state, zone, etc., lying between two others, usu. owing allegiance to neither, and serving as a means of preventing hostilities between them.

1858 Gen. P. Thompson *Audi Alt.* I. xliv. 170 With no excuse offered as a buffer against the manifest absurdity. **1870** Lowell *Among my Bks.* Ser. II. (1873) 313 A sense of humor..may have served as a buffer against the..shock of disappointment. **1876** B. Frere in W. B. Worsfold *Sir B. Frere* (1923) 43 Using the Afghans as a 'buffer' to avoid immediate contact between our frontier and the Russian. **1883** *Daily News* 27 July 5/1 The 'buffer' State—to borrow a simile from Indo-Afghan politics—which lies between Natal and the late King's dominion. **1908** *Westm. Gaz.* 7 May 1/3 A 'buffer' zone, inhabited by independent tribes, lies between the boundaries of British India and Afghanistan. **1920** *Discovery* May 133/2 That treaty settlement of neutrality which regulated the status of Luxemburg as a buffer-duchy. **1931** A. P. Herbert *Derby Day* 27 Belgium's a buffer nation.

3. *attrib.* and *comb.*, as ***buffer-bank, -frame, -head, -plate, -rod, -spring***; **buffer amplifier** *Electr.* (see quot. 1938); **buffer-bar**, cross-piece (on an engine, etc.) carrying the buffers; **buffer-block**, (*a*) a framework of timber set up at the end of a railway line or siding; (*b*) a block on the end of a coach, which acts as a buffer; (*c*) the flat head of a buffer; **buffer-box, -case**, the case which encloses the buffer-rod and -spring; **buffer-knot**, an arrangement of two knots joining two parts of a fisherman's line in which the strain is taken by a piece of waxed silk which acts as a buffer; **buffer-plunger**, the portion of a buffer which slides in the buffer-case and carries the shock to the spring; **buffer pool** = *buffer stock*; **buffer solution** *Chem.*, a solution containing a 'buffer' (see 1 b); **buffer stock**, a stock of a commodity held in reserve so as to reduce fluctuation in prices when supplies are low; **buffer-stop** = *buffer-block* (*a*); **buffer store**, (in a computer) = sense 1 d above.

1933 J. H. Morecroft et al. *Princ. Radio Communic.* (ed. 3) vii. 727 The crystal oscillates at 2500 kc. and gives in its tank circuit about 50 volts of this frequency, and the *buffer amplifier raises this to about 400 volts at the same frequency. **1938** G. P. Harnwell *Princ. Electricity* vii. 215 Multielectrode tubes not only amplify but also isolate the plate and grid circuits, avoiding the many undesired effects of interaction; these are frequently known as *buffer amplifiers.* **1900** *Westm. Gaz.* 21 Aug. 6/1 The accident at Kent House Station, near Penge (in which a train ran into a *buffer-bank, injuring eleven people). **1889** *Century Dict.*, *Buffer-block. **1892** *Daily News* 14 Jan. 3/4 The effect was to cause the waggon furthest from the engine to mount the fixed buffer block. *a* **1877** Knight *Dict. Mech.* s.v. *Buffer*, The buffer bar or beam is attached to the framework of the car, and carries the *buffer-box, in which is the buffer-rod. **1880** *Engineering* XXX. 294 Projections h' on the *buffer case. **1883** *N.E. Railw. Specifications*, 40 Also, the fixing of 6 Buffers, and *Buffer-frames, at ends of Sidings. **1835** *Specif. Bergin's Patent* No. 6781 Within each *buffer head is a bar of iron. **1885** Treherne in Pennell et al. *Fishing* 41 Although I can lay no claim to be the inventor of the '*buffer knot', I can honestly say that I had never seen or heard of it before. **1895** 'J. Bickerdyke' et al. *Sea Fishing* 69 The buffer knot is another good one;..I learnt the way of tying it, shown in the illustration, from an Irish friend, who has greatly improved on the old original buffer. **1880** *Engineering* XXX. 294 Tijou's mode of securing *buffer plungers. **1940** *Economist* 24 Feb. 338/1 The price of the metal..had been previously pegged at the upper limit of £230 per ton under the *buffer pool scheme. **1863** *Morning Star* 13 Aug., The *buffer rod, which was..solid iron, was broken away. **1921** *Jrnl. Biol. Chem.* XLIX. 183 The use of standard *buffer solutions for colorimetric comparison. **1951** A. I. Vogel *Text-Bk. Quantitative Inorg. Analysis* i. 31 Buffer solutions usually consist of solutions containing a mixture of a weak acid or base and its salt. **1862** Smiles *Engineers* III. 282 The necessity for..preventing hard bumping of the carriage-ends..hence the contrivance of *buffer-springs. **1935** *Economist* 23 Feb. 456/1 At the end of February 7,476 tons of tin, being part of the *buffer stock held by the committee, will appear in 'visible supplies'. **1878** *Engineer* XLVI. 7 The standard *buffer stop on the London and South-Western Railway. **1962** *Gloss. Terms Automatic Data Processing* (*B.S.I.*) 64 **Buffer store*, a store used to compensate for a difference in rate of flow of data, or time of occurrence of events, when transmitting data from one device to another. **1964** F. L. Westwater *Electronic Computers* iv. 80 Buffer stores are essentially a device for gaining time or for reconciling the different time scales inherent in a computing system.

'buffer, *sb.*³ [f. buff *v.*³ to polish with a buff.] **a.** A workman or workwoman who buffs knives, plate, etc. **b.** = buff *sb.*² 4. **c.** In *Photography*, A machine used for polishing daguerreotype plates.

1854 Scoffern in *Orr's Circ. Sc.* Chem. 90 Exposing them [Daguerreotype plates] to the friction of rubbers or buffers of cotton velvet or doeskin. **1875** Ure *Dict. Arts* II. 3 The application of the highest polish by the use of a buffer. **1882** *Times* 27 June, Robert Taylor, comb buffer.

d. A farrier's shoeing tool having a blunt chisel at one end to remove clinch nails and a point at the other to punch out nails embedded in the hoof.

1902 V. Jacob *Sheep-Stealers* xiv, A smith's buffer. **1907** *Yesterday's Shopping* (1969) 706/2 Farriers' tools, set of,..containing shoeing hammer, pointing hammer, rasp, whetstone, buffer, [etc.].

'buffer, *sb.*⁴ *slang.* [Origin obscure; with sense 1 cf. bufe, bugher; with 2 and 3 cf. buffer *sb.*¹ and buffard; (but also the use of *dog* in sense 3).]

1. a. A dog. **b.** *transf.* A pistol; = barker 4.

[**1688** R. Holme *Armoury* III. iii. §68 *Cant Voc.*, *Buffar*, Dog-like.] **1812** J. H. Vaux *Flash Dict.*, *Buffer*, a dog. **1824** Scott *Redgauntlet* ch. iii, Here be a pair of buffers will bite as well as bark.

2. *Sc.* & *dial.* 'A foolish fellow' Jamieson 1808.

3. A fellow: usually expressing a slight degree of contempt.

1749 H. Fitzcotton *Homer* I. (1748) 23 You're a buffer always rear'd in The brutal pleasures of Bear-garden. **1835** Marryat *Jacob Faithf.* xxx, As the old buffer, her father, says. **1863** Miss Braddon *Lady Audley* iv. 30, I always said the old buffer would. **1876** M. Hay *Norah's Love T.*, Unless some old buffer is struck by..my sermons.

4. *Naut.* A chief boatswain's mate. Also, a petty officer.

1864 Hotten *Slang Dict.* (ed. 3) 87 *Buffer*, a navy term for a boatswain's mate, part of whose duties is to administer the 'cat'. **1916** 'Taffrail' *Stand By!* 30 It wus all I could do to stop meself larfin', 'specially when Number One sings art fur the chief buffer. **1941** *Weekly Telegraph* 25 Oct. 6/3 The 'Buffer'..is a petty officer 'go-between', his duty being that of passer-on of orders from officers to seamen.

† **buffer**, *sb.*⁵ *Obs. slang.* [? f. buff *sb.*² 2 + -er.] (See quot.)

1690 B. E. *Dict. Cant. Crew*, *Buffer*, a Rogue that kills good sound Horses, only for their Skins. **1874** J. C. Hotten *Slang Dict.* [cites *Bacchus & Venus*].

buffer, *sb.*⁶ *slang.* [f. buff *v.*⁴ + -er¹] (See quot.)

1874 J. C. Hotten *Slang Dict.*, *Buffer*, the term was once applied to those who took false oaths for a consideration.

buffer ('bʌfə(r)), *v.* [f. buffer².] *trans.* To lessen the impact of, with or as with a buffer; to act as a buffer to; freq. *fig.*

1894 *Speaker* 16 June 658/1 The crude..opinionativeness of the permanent official—which is used to being discounted and buffered by a lay chief. **1958** *Listener* 2 Jan. 32/3 Continental statesmen..saw, with a clarity which has so far eluded our more buffered countrymen. **1958** *House & Garden* Apr. 73/2 The kitchen..buffers the children's area from the main reception rooms.

b. *Chem.* To treat with a buffer (see buffer² 1 b). Also *intr.*, to act as or use a buffer.

1923 W. M. Clark *Determ. Hydrogen Ions* (ed. 2) ii. 44 Unless a solution is buffered..it is almost impossible to make an accurate electrometric determination of the pH... The failure to buffer against the effect of so-called neutral salts..may lead to gross error. **1955** *Sci. Amer.* Feb. 60/3 A thin layer of protein solution..is inserted between a pair of liquids, one acid and one alkaline, which are 'buffered' to maintain a constant pH. **1956** *Nature* 10 Mar. 478/1 The salivary glands..were incubated on a welled microscope slide in buffered substrate (pH 6·8).

c. *Biol.* To limit the effect of.

1936 J. S. Huxley in *Rep. Brit. Assoc. Advancem. Sci.* 82 Each such step is immediately *buffered* by ancillary changes in genes and gene-combinations. **1944** —— *On Living in Revol.* vi. 71 Slightly deleterious genes have been rendered harmless or even beneficial by being 'buffered'..by new combinations of other genes.

buffering ('bʌfərɪŋ), *vbl. sb.* [f. buffer² or prec. + -ing¹.] The action of bringing buffers into play; also, buffers collectively.

1898 *Times* 6 Jan. 7 The buffering up of the wagons caused one of them to tilt over. **1928** *Daily Express* 29 Dec. 9/4 The use of side buffering with screw couplings.

b. The action of buffer *v.* sense b. Also *attrib.* or as *ppl. a.*

1927 *Forestry* I. 122 Plants in which the buffering agent has a reaction of a more favourable type..counteract this acid-buffering. **1932** Fuller & Conard tr. *Braun-Blanquet's Plant Sociol.* vi. 175 Each soil has its characteristic pH value..which normally is little changed by external conditions... This property of tenaciously maintaining a 'reaction constancy' is called buffering.

c. The action of buffer *v.* sense c. Also *attrib.* or as *ppl. a.*

1936 J. S. Huxley in *Rep. Brit. Assoc. Advancem. Sci.* 82 The adjustment of such mutations..may occur entirely through recombination of existing modifiers, or, after a preliminary and partial buffering by this means, the final adjustment may have to wait. **1943** *Nature* 16 Jan. 68/2 In genetical language, the integrated genotype acts as a buffering system..to limit the variation of the organism's response to environmental fluctuations.

buffet ('bʌfɪt), *sb.*¹ Forms: 3–6 **buffett(e**, 3–5 **boffet(e**, 4 **bofet(t, -at**, 5 **bofette, bufet**, 7 **buffit**, 3– **buffet.** [app. a. OF. *buffet*, *bouffet*, a blow, dim. of *buffe* buff *sb.*¹]

a. A blow, stroke; now usually one given with the hand. †*Pl.* Fisticuffs (*rare*). ***blindman('s) buffet*** (also ***blind and buffet***) = blindman's buff.

a **1225** *Ancr. R.* 182 Nolde me tellen him alre monne dusigest, þet forsoke enne buffet, uor one speres wunde. *a* **1340** Hampole *Psalter* lxviii. 23, I suffire vnrightwisly shame in bofetis & spittyngis. *c* **1382** Wyclif *Mark* xiv. 65 And summe bigunnen for to bispitte him, and to hide his ȝȝen, and smyte him with boffatis. *c* **1450** *Merlin* xxviii. 571 Galashin..yaf hym..a buffet with his swerde. **1605** Verstegan *Dec. Intell.* ii. (1628) 32 A Hollander and a Frenchman..falling out, went to buffets. **1675** Hobbes *Odyssey* (1677) 86 How much we do all other men excel At wrestling, buffets, leaping. **1702** Pope *Wife Bath* 416, I..with one buffet fell'd him on the floor. **1783** Ainsworth *Lat. Dict.* (Morell) I. s.v. *Blind*, To play a blind and buffet, *andabatarum more pugnare.* **1805** Scott *Last Minstr.* III. x, On his cheek a buffet fell, So fierce, it stretched him on the plain. **1840** Dickens *Old C. Shop* xii, A shower of buffets rained down upon his person. **1879** O. W. Holmes *Motley* xviii. 132 The letter was like a buffet on the cheek.

b. *transf.* and *fig.* (Cf. blow, stroke.)

c **1325** *E.E. Allit. P.* B. 885 þay blwe a buffet in blande þat banned peple. **1605** Shaks. *Macb.* III. i. 109 One..Whom the vile Blowes and Buffets of the World Hath so incens'd, that, etc. **1792** S. Rogers *Pleas. Mem.* I. 326 The traveller whose altered form Has borne the buffet of the mountain storm. **1875** Hamerton *Intell. Life* v. ii. 178 The buffets of unkindly fortune.

c. *Aeronaut.* = buffeting *vbl. sb.* 2. Also *attrib.*

1951 *Jrnl. R. Aeronaut. Soc.* Oct. 629/2 With very few exceptions buffet comes from the tail. **1958** *Chambers's Techn. Dict.* 962/1 *Buffet boundary*, the maximum Mach number at which a subsonic aeroplane may be safely flown without risk of uncontrollability due to compressibility drag.

buffet ('bʌfɪt), *sb.*² Forms: 5 **bofet**, *Sc.* **buffate**, 5–7 **buffit**, 5–8 **buffett**, 6 **boffett, buffat, buffote, buffed**, 8– **buffet.** [Of unknown origin. Usually assumed to be the same word as the next, and therefore to be a. F. *buffet*; but the F. word has not this meaning, nor is there any known connexion of sense in Eng.]

1. A low stool; a footstool. Now only *Sc.* and *north. dial.* In the 15th c. described as a three-legged stool, but now denoting in north of England a low stool of any kind, and in Sc. a four-footed stool 'with sides, in form of a square table with leaves, when these are folded down' (Jamieson). The fuller **buffet-stool** occurs in the same sense from the 15th c. Also **buffet-form.**

1432 *E.E. Wills* (1882) 91, I bequethe..Idary a bofet. *c* **1440** *Promp. Parv.* 41 Bofet, thre fotyd stole [**1499** boffet stole], *tripes.* *Ibid.* 55 Buffet stole, *scabellum, tripos.* **1478** *Act. Audit.* 67 (Jam.), Ii buffate stulis. **1568** *Wills & Inv.* (1860) I. 282 in *Promp. Parv.* 42, 3 Buffett formes 3*s.*, one litle buffet stole, 6*d.* **1596** *Lanc. Wills* (1861) III. 2 Ij buffet-stooles couered for women. **1611** Cotgr., *Scabeau*, a Buffit, or ioyned, stoole to sit on. *a* **1806** A. Douglas *Poems* (Jam.) Jean brought the buffet-stool in bye. *Nursery Rime*, Little Miss Muffet sat on a buffet, Eating her curds and whey.

2. A hassock. Chiefly *dial.*

1877 E. Peacock *N.W. Lincolnsh. Gloss.* (E.D.S.) *Buffet*, a hassock. The difference between a Bass and a Buffet seems to consist in the former being covered with rush matting, and the latter with carpet. **1886** *Demos* II. 267 A couple of buffets, to supplement the number in the pew.

buffet ('bʌfɪt, 'bʊfeɪ, ‖byfɛ), *sb.*³ Also 8–9 **beaufet**; 8 **beaufette, -fait, buffette**, 9 **beauffet.** [a. mod.F. *buffet*, of unknown origin: in English, commonly spelt *beau-* in the 18th c., the cause of which is not apparent.]

1. a. ('bʌfɪt) A sideboard or side-table, often ornamental, for the disposition of china, plate, etc.

1718 Hickes & Nelson *J. Kettlewell* II. §32. 135 The Plate ..was placed upon a Table or Buffett. **1755** *Phil. Trans.* XLIX. 66 The electrical expositor stood upon a low beaufet. **1756** Colman & Thornton *Connoisseur* 15 Jan., The beaufait..embellished with a variety of China. **1814** Scott *Wav.* x, An old-fashioned beaufet. **1852** Thackeray *Esmond* I. v. (1876) 34 And with this, the intrepid father mounted the buffet with great agility. **1863** *Conf. Ticket Leave Man* 132 A magnificent beaufet in the second corridor.

b. ('bʊfeɪ) In various collocations, ***buffet meal, party, supper, table***, etc., with sense 1 extended to cover the refreshments set out on the sideboard, table, etc., and where guests or customers are usually served standing. Also *ellipt.*

1888 Mrs. Beeton *Bk. Househ. Managem.* 1443 (*caption*) Buffet Tea-Table Arranged For From Forty Guests. **1906** *Daily Colonist* (Victoria, B.C.) 30 Jan. 6/6 For the first time in Victoria, the buffet supper will be introduced, following the plans of the suppers now usually given at swell balls in Eastern cities. **1922** *Hotel World* 22 Apr. 13/1 At the close of the meeting those in attendance were tendered a buffet luncheon in the main restaurant. **1930** R. F. Wilson *How to wine & dine in Paris* v. 112 The café serves..a cold buffet lunch. **1933** E. Shanks *Enchanted Village* x. 138 The girls and young men round the buffet-table. **1937** M. Hillis *Orchids on your Budget* vi. 102 Buffet suppers are a triumphant solution of the no-maid-and-little-money party. **1951** *Good Housek. Cookery Bk.* 45 Arrange your buffet table in the most convenient place. *Ibid.*, A fair number of people will need to reach the buffet at the same time. **1951** *Good Housek. Home Encycl.* 193/2 Paper serviettes..are inexpensive and convenient..for buffet meals. *Ibid.* 582/1 Suitable food for a buffet party includes sandwiches and bridge rolls.

2. ('bʌfɪt) A cupboard in a recess for china and glasses.

a **1720** *Humourist* 116 The Cat had got into the Beaufette among the Glasses. *a* **1745** Swift *Wks.* (1841) II. 78 The beaufet letting in so much wind that it almost blows out the candles. **1751** Chambers *Cycl.*, *Beaufet*, *Buffet*, or *Bufet*, was antiently a little apartment separated from the rest of a room by slender wooden columns, for the disposing china and glass ware, etc., called also a cabinet. **1753** *Phil. Trans.* XLVIII. 92 The lightning..forced the door of a beaufet at the end of the hall. **1786** Cowper *Gratitude* 33 This china that decks the alcove Which here people call a buffet [*rime*

yet]. **1876** GWILT *Archit.* Gloss., *Buffet*, a cabinet or cupboard for plate, glass or china. Some years back it was the practice to make these small recesses very ornamental, in the form of niches, and left open in the front to display the contents.

3. a. ('bʊfeɪ, ‖ byfɛ) A refreshment bar.

1792 *Observer* 19 Feb. 3/3 At two o'clock, the buffets were opened, and the company regaled with a cold collation. *c* **1810** W. HICKEY *Mem.* (1913) I. xi. 129 The Buffets, which were numerous, were abundantly supplied with refreshments of every kind. **1869** *Daily News* 16 Dec., In the buffet of the Marseilles station.

b. buffet-car orig. *U.S.*, a railway carriage containing a refreshment bar.

1887 C. B. GEORGE *40 Yrs. on Rail* 248 Buffet,..dining and sleeping cars have all been added to meet the needs and tastes of this enterprising age. **1895** J. C. WAIT *Car-Builder's Dict.* (ed. 3) 21 *Buffet-car*, a term..applied to a style of sleeping-car or parlor-car which has an ornamental buffet where light lunches can be prepared for the passengers. **1899** *Railway Times* 11 Mar. 340/1 Five express trains will be run.., two having first and third class dining-cars attached, and one a buffet car. **1969** L. MEYNELL *Of Malicious Intent* iv. 42 A fast train back to Liverpool Street ..with a buffet car attached to it.

buffet ('bʌfɪt), *v.* Pa. t. and pple. **-eted.** [f. BUFFET *sb.*¹; but cf. OF. *buffeter* in same sense.]

1. *trans.* To beat, strike, *esp.* with the hand; to thump, cuff, knock about.

a **1225** *Ancr. R.* 106 Te Giws..buffeteden him [Christ]. **1393** LANGL. *P. Pl.* C. xxiii. 191 He boffatede me a-boute þe mouthe. **1526** *Pilgr. Perf.* (W. de W. 1531) 259 When he was buffetted & beten for vs. **1692** BENTLEY *Boyle Lect.* ii. 63 They must be bang'd and buffeted into Reason. **1748** ANSON *Voy.* I. iii. (ed. 4) 30 What we ..experienced..when buffetted by the same storms. **1826** SCOTT *Woodst.* iv, Cut a crow's wing, or break its leg, the others will buffet it to death. **1853** KANE *Grinnell Exp.* xxxvii. (1856) 337.

b. To beat back, contend with (waves, etc.).

1601 SHAKS. *Jul. C.* I. ii. 107 The Torrent roar'd, and we did buffet it With lusty Sinewes. **1791** COWPER *Odyss.* VIII. 224 Buffeting the boisterous waves. **1853** KANE *Grinnell Exp.* (1856) xxxviii. 348, I had buffeted the elements quite long enough.

c. *fig.*

a **1593** H. SMITH *Wks.* (1867) II. 212 Our sins buffet God on every side. **1678** R. BARCLAY *Apol. Quakers* II. §13. 57 [They] are continually buffeting one another with the Scripture. *a* **1884** M. PATTISON *Mem.* 49, I felt humiliated and buffeted.

2. *intr.* To deal blows, fight, contend, struggle.

1599 SHAKS. *Hen. V.*, v. ii. 146 If I might buffet for my Loue. **1839** MARRYAT *Phant. Ship* ix, She was..buffeting in a violent gale. **1847** TENNYSON *Princ.* IV. 167 Strove to buffet to land in vain. **1865** DICKENS *Mut. Fr.* xi, They buffet with opposing waves.

b. *fig.*

1824 W. IRVING *T. Trav.* I. 33 To see so delicate..a being buffet so resolutely with hardships. **1842** TENNYSON *Gold. Year* 76, I heard them blast The steep slate-quarry, and the great echo flap And buffet round the hills.

3. *trans.* To drive, force, or produce, by buffeting.

1734 WATTS *Reliq. Juv.* (1789) 118 The soul of a man..is not to be buffetted into softness. **1865** PARKMAN *Huguenots* vi. (1875) 80 He buffeted his way to riches and fame. **1872** B. HARTE *Right Eye of Commander*, He felt the salt breath of the..sea buffet a color into his smoke-dried cheeks.

4. *trans.* To muffle (bells). [Perhaps a distinct word; cf. *buff-stop* in BUFF *sb.*² 9, also BUFFER *sb.*²]

1753 *Art Ringing* 200 (L.) Buffeting the bells, that is, by tying pieces of leather, old hat, or any other thing that is pretty thick, round the ball of the clapper of each bell.

'buffeter. *rare*⁻¹. [f. prec. + -ER¹.] 'A boxer; one that buffets.' J.

1483 *Cath. Angl.* 46 A Buffetter, *alapus.* **1755** in JOHNSON; and in mod. Dicts.

'buffeting, *vbl. sb.* [f. as prec. + -ING¹.] **1.** The action of the verb BUFFET.

c **1240** *Lofsong* in *Cott. Hom.* 207 Ich bide þe..bi his spotlunge, and bufetunge. *a* **1340** HAMPOLE *Psalter* xxi. 5 In spittynge, buffetynge & pungynge with þe thornes. **1563–87** FOXE *A. & M.* in Spurgeon *Treas. Dav.* Ps. lxxxviii. 3 Sharp temptations and strong buffetings of Satan. **1788** BURNS *Let. R. Ainslie* 3 Mar., I have been..under much buffetting of the wicked one. **1826** SCOTT *Woodst.* viii. **1873** BLACK *Pr. Thule* v. 74 The buffetings of wind and rain.

2. *Aeronaut.* Irregular oscillation, caused by air eddies, of any part of an aircraft.

1931 FRAZER & DUNCAN in *Aeronaut. Res. Committee Rep. & Mem.* No. 1360 Jan. 84 The term 'buffeting' is here used to denote an irregular, and more or less severe, oscillatory movement of the organs of the tail unit. **1961** C. B. SMITH *Testing Time* x. 168 The 'buffeting' was related to a basic aerodynamic problem, the turbulence which was bound to occur when an aircraft not suitably streamlined attained to a speed approaching the speed of sound.

† **buffian.** *Obs.* [? variant of BUFFOON, suggested by *ruffian.*] = BUFFOON. Hence **buffianism,** buffoonery.

1655 *Comic. Hist. Francion* x. 13 It becometh not a man of my Learning to be so great a Buffian. **1596** NASHE *Have with you, &c.* M iv b, No buffianisme throughout his whole bookes, but they bolstered out his part with.

† **'buffin.** *Obs.* Also 6 **buffen, buffine.** 'A coarse cloth in use for the gowns of the middle classes in the time of Elizabeth' (Fairholt); a garment made of that material. Also *attrib.*

1572 *Wills & Inv. N.C.* (1860) 373 To my sonne Antonie ..a pair of Buffins wᵗʰ the slyuers to the same. **1590** *Lanc. Wills* (1860) II. 23 Unto Ellen Perpoynte a gowne of buffen. **1597** *Wills & Inv. N.C.* (1860) II. 281, Vj yds. of grene buffine 9/. **1598** FLORIO, *Gottonato*, a kinde of cotton..or buffin sarge. **1617** F. MORYSON *Itin.* I. 4 Myselfe beholding the Virgins statua..did think it had been covered with a gowne of white buffin. **1632** MASSINGER *City Mad.* IV. iv, My young ladies In buffin gowns and green aprons!

'buffing, *vbl. sb.*¹ [f. BUFF *v.*¹; cf. BUFFER *sb.*² 1.] Only in *comb.*, as ***buffing-apparatus, -block, -spring.***

1835 *Specif. Bergin's Patent* No. 6781 In order to explain the meaning of the words 'buffing apparatus.'

'buffing, *vbl. sb.*² [f. BUFF *sb.*² & *v.*³ + -ING¹.]

a. The formation of a BUFFY COAT. **b.** The process of polishing with a buff (BUFF *sb.*² 4), or with a buffer (BUFFER *sb.*³); also that of imparting a velvety surface to leather by the use of sandpaper. ***buffing-block***, in silver manufacture, a wooden block covered with leather, on which an article is rubbed to polish it.

1856 TODD & BOWMAN *Phys. Anat.* II. 295 Buffing and cupping of the blood has long attracted notice. *c* **1865** J. WYLDE in *Circ. Sc.* I. 156/2 Buffing, or rubbing the plate on some velvet fixed tightly over a piece of wood. **1885** *Harper's Mag.* Jan. 286/1 Buffing or sand-papering machine [for leather].

c. The operation of reducing the thickness of a hide by shaving off the grain surface with a currier's knife or splitting-machine; also, the thin pieces of leather so removed. Also *Comb.*, as ***buffing-machine, buffing-slicker.***

a **1884** KNIGHT *Dict. Mech.* Suppl., *Buffing* (leather), taking off thin shavings from the grain side with a buffing-slicker until the skin is very thin; the object being to make cowhide imitate calfskin. The operation is finished by whitening. **1897** C. T. DAVIS *Leather* (ed. 2) 444 The buffings which are not required for japanning are sold in russet for making stained buffings. **1920** *Chambers's Jrnl.* Sept. 622/1 Leather buffings and shavings.

buffish ('bʌfɪʃ), *a.* [f. BUFF *a.* + -ISH¹.] Somewhat buff, approaching buff in colour; also in comb. with other adjs. of colour.

1802 D. WORDSWORTH *Grasmere Jrnl.* 14 Feb. in *Jrnls.* (1941) I. 113 The snow-covered mountains were spotted with rich sunlight, a palish buffish colour. **1896** *Brit. Birds, Their Nests & Eggs* I. 3 The cheeks..are buffish white. **1902** E. GLYN *Refl. Ambrosine* 83 Terra-cotta and buffish brocade. **1910** *Westm. Gaz.* 29 Jan. 11/1 The white and buffish brown or ashy streaks..of his plumage.

buffit, obs. form of BUFFET.

† **'buffle,** *sb. Obs.* Also 6 **bulfeld?, 6–7 buffell,** *Sc.* **buffil, bufle, 7 bufall, buffel, -al(l, -ol.** [a. F. *buffle*, a common Romanic word:—vulgar L. **būfalus* (= L. *būbalus*): see BUFFALO *sb.* Cf. also BUFF *sb.*² Some of the Eng. spellings in 17th c. show influence of the It. or Sp. forms.]

1. A buffalo; = BUFFALO *sb.* 1 a, b.

c **1511** *1st Eng. Bk. Amer.* (Arb.) Introd. 29/1 There [in India] be bulfeldes [? buffelles] & coyes [? cowes] but the coyes slepe [? sleye] they not. **1532** *Victory agst. Turkes* in Dibdin's *Typog. Antiq.* (1816) III. 117 In euery place abode ..buffelles. **1623** FAVINE *Theat. Hon.* II. xiii. 223 A mouing Chariot, drawne by Oxen or Buffells. **1731** MEDLEY *Kolben's Cape G. Hope* II. 109 Buffles or Buffaloes are numerous in the Cape countries. **1738** G. SMITH *Curious Relations* II. 384 After these came a buffle and a fine horse.

b. *attrib.* (cf. BUFF *sb.*²)

1577 HARRISON *England* II. xvii. (1877) 292 Ships made of wicker and couered with buffle hides. **1611** *Bk. Rates* (JAM.) Belts called buffil belts, the dozen iiis. **1693** URQUHART *Rabelais* III. xxxvi, The death of a Buffle-ox. **1808** J. BARLOW *Columb.* v. 169 Lured o'er his lawns the buffle herds.

2. A fool; = BUFFLEHEAD 1. [After F. *buffle.*]

1655 *Comic. Hist. Francion* iv. 22 He said to the three buffles who stood with their hats in their hands, Tell me, you Waggs, etc. **1710** *Pol. Ballads* (1860) II. 90 To see the chief attorney such a buffle.

'buffle, *v.* [? Onomatopœic; connected with some sense of BUFF; or ? misprint for *bustle.* '*Buffle* to puzzle, be at a loss' in Johnson (and all subsequent Dictionaries) is a bogus word, founded on the misprint of *buffling* for *bustling.*]

1610 HEALEY *St. Aug. Citie of God* 118 The next age Silver, under Jove, then warre began to buffle. [**1730** SWIFT *Vindic. Ld. Carteret* Wks. 1778 IV. 141 That poor, angry, bustling [J. *prints* buffling] well-meaning mortal.]

bufflehead ('bʌf(ə)lhɛd). [f. BUFFLE + HEAD.] **1.** A fool, blockhead, stupid fellow.

1659 *Lady Alimony* I. ii. in Hazl. *Dodsley* XIV. 278 What a drolling bufflehead is this! **1694** ECHARD *Plautus* 48 What makes ye stare so, Bufflehead? **1718** J. FOX *Wanderer* xiv. 90 Tho' my Forehead is broad, you Bufflehead, it is not brazen. **1883** *J. Herring* III. lvi. 225, I don't want the buffle-head to be coming here.

2. A North American duck (*Bucephala albeola*), the head of which appears to be disproportionately large. *U.S.* Cf. BUFFLE-HEADED *a* 3 and BUFFEL 1.

1858 S. F. BAIRD *Birds Pacific* in *Rep. Explor. Railroad to Pacific* (U.S. War Dept.) IX. 798 The name buffle head is a corruption of buffalo head. **1870** *Amer. Naturalist* IV. 49 Buffel Head (*Bucephala albeola* Baird). **1874** J. W. LONG *Amer. Wild-fowl Shooting* Introd. 16 In the deep water varieties..I shall treat of the..buffle-head or butter-ball.

buffle-headed ('bʌf(ə)l,hɛdɪd), *a.* [f. prec. (or its elements) + -ED.]

† **1.** Having a head like a buffalo's. *Obs.*

1697 EVELYN *Numism.* ix. 293 There are remarked the Goat and Buffle-headed. **1713** C'TESS WINCHELSEA *Misc. Poems* 117 None but buffle-headed Trees.

2. *transf.* and *fig.* **a.** Large-headed. **b.** Foolish, stupid.

1654 GAYTON *Fest. Notes* III. iv. 90 So fell this buffle-headed gyant by the hand of Don Quixot. **1675** WYCHERLEY *Pl. Dealer* II. i, You know nothing, you buffle-headed stupid creature, you. *a* **1736** YALDEN *Owl & Sun*, A saucy buffle-headed owl. **1871** DIXON *Tower* IV. iv. 34 A drinking, buffle-headed fellow.

3. *U.S.* (See quots. and BUFFLE-HEAD 2)

1831 WILSON & BONAPARTE *Amer. Ornith.* III. 232 *Anas albeola*..Buffel-headed Duck. **1840** E. BLYTH et al. tr. *Cuvier's Anim. Kingd.* 264 The little Buffel-headed Garrot (*Anas albeola* Lin.), common in North America, is nearly allied [to the Golden-eyed Garrot]. **1874** J. W. LONG *Amer. Wild-fowl Shooting* 279 Buffle-headed Duck (*Fuligula alvesta*).

‖ **buffo** ('buffo), *sb.* and *a.* [a. It. *buffo* adj., comical, burlesque: see BUFFOON.]

A. *sb.* A comic actor, a singer in a comic opera. **B.** as *adj.* Belonging to or characteristic of a buffo; comic, burlesque.

1764 FOOTE *Patron* I. i, A rank impostor, the bufo of an illiberal mercenary tribe. **1789** MRS. PIOZZI *Journ. France* I. 177 They..sung a thousand buffo songs. **1821** BYRON *Juan* IV. lxxxi, The buffo of the party. **1850** L. HUNT *Autobiog.* ii. (1860) 42 Every burlesque or buffo song, of any pretension, was pretty sure to be Italian. **1851** KINGSLEY *Yeast* xiii. 237 Genial earnest buffo humour here and there.

buffol, buffolo, var. of BUFFLE, BUFFALO *sb.*

† **'buffon, -ont.** *Obs.* Also **-oon.** [a. F. *bouffante* 'espèce de guimpe gaufrée que portaient autrefois les femmes' (Littré). See BOUFFANT(E *a.*] 'A projecting covering of gauze or linen for a lady's breast.. much worn about 1750' (Fairholt).

1774 *Westm. Mag.* II. 259 Ladies in full dress still wear.. buffoons for the neck. *Ibid.* 288 Plaited tuckers and buffons for the neck. **1783** *European Mag.* III. 15 Buffonts, trimmed and plain, are in universal use still.

buffoon (bə'fuːn), *sb.* Forms: 6–7 **buffon(e, -onne, -oun, oone, bouffon, boufoon, 7– buffoon.** [a. F. *buffon, bouffon*, a. It. *buffone* buffoon, f. *buffa* a jest, connected with *buffare* to puff; Tommaseo and Bellini consider the sense of 'jest' to be developed from that of 'puff of wind', applied *fig.* to anything light and frivolous; others, e.g. Littré, refer it to the notion of puffing out the cheeks as a comic gesture. (In 17th c. accented on first syllable.)]

† **1.** A pantomime dance. *Sc. Obs. rare*⁻¹. [F. '*danser les buffons* to daunce a morris' Cotgr.]

1549 *Compl. Scot.* vi. (1872) 66 Braulis and branglis, buffons, vitht mony vthir lycht dancis.

2. 'A man whose profession is to make sport by low jests and antick postures' (J.); a comic actor, clown; a jester, fool. *arch.*

1585 JAMES I. *Ess. Poesie* (Arb.) 31 We remaine With Iuglers, buffons, and that foolish seames. **1589** PUTTENHAM *Eng. Poesie* (1869) 76 Buffons, altogether applying their wits to Scurrillities and other ridiculous matters. **1657** COLVIL *Whigs' Supplic.* (1681) 68 But how the Buffons all be outted. **1683** tr. *Erasmus' Moriæ Enc.* 2 Mountebanks, Buffoons, and Merry-Andrews. *a* **1734** NORTH *Lives* (1826) I. 411 The bey..like other voluptuous Turks, had his buffoons to divert him. **1835** LYTTON *Rienzi* I. i. 3 The stale jests of a hired buffoon. **1875** FARRAR *Seekers* I. iii. 12.

¶ Used for 'buffoonery'.

1780 COWPER *Progr. Err.* 153 Thy sabbaths will be soon Our sabbaths, closed with mummery and buffoon.

3. *transf.* A low jester; 'a man that practises indecent raillery' (J.); a wag, a joker (implying contempt or disapprobation).

1598 B. JONSON *Ev. Man. in Hum.* II. v. 8 Age was authoritie Against a buffon, and a man had, then..reverence payd unto his yeares. **1636** HEALEY *Epictetus' Man.* 73 Avoid the playing of the Buffone, and procuring of others laughter. **1680** H. MORE *Apocal. Apoc.* Pref. 14 Buffoones rather, and abusers of the Apocalypse, than serious Interpreters of it. **1750** JOHNSON *Rambl.* No. 72 ⁋8 Falstaff the cheerful companion, the loud buffoon. **1840** MACAULAY *Ess., Ranke's Hist.* (1851) II. 147 Buffoons, dressed in copes and surplices.

4. *attrib.* and *adj.* Belonging to or characteristic of a buffoon; vulgarly jocular. (Somewhat *arch.*)

1625 B. JONSON *Staple News* v. vi, With buffon licence, ieast At whatso'er is serious. **1687** DRYDEN *Hind & P.* I. 39 The buffoon Ape, as atheists use, Mimicked all sects. **1734** tr. *Rollin's Anc. Hist.* (1827) I. 102 A jumble of buffoon tales. **1762–71** H. WALPOLE *Vertue's Anecd. Paint.* (1786) III. 234 Egbert Hemskirk of Harlem, a buffoon painter. **1855** MACAULAY *Hist. Eng.* III. 469 No mean images, buffoon stories, scurrilous invectives.

5. *Comb.*, as ***buffoon-like*** adj.; **buffoon-bird.**

1611 COTGR., *Bouffonnesque*, buffoone-like. **1774** GOLDSM. *Nat. Hist.* (1862) II. VI. iv. 180 The Numidian Crane..vulgarly called by our sailors the buffoon bird.

Hence **buffoo'nesque, bu'ffoonical** *a.*; = BUFFOONISH; **bu'ffoonism** = BUFFOONERY.

1756 *Gentl. Mag.* XXVI. 254 That they should commit intellectual mendicity in buffoonesk terms. **1834** BECKFORD

Italy, &c. II. 39 The strangest, most buffoonical grimaces. *Ibid.* 169 A lay-brother, fat, round, buffoonical. **1611** COTGR., *Bouffonnerie*, bouffoonisme, ieasting. **1617** MINSHEU *Ductor in Ling.* 56 Buffoonisme..vi: jesting.

buffoon (bəˈfuːn), *v. arch.* [f. prec. sb.]

1. *trans.* To turn into ridicule, to ridicule; to burlesque.

1638 FORD *Fancies* III. i. (R.) Who, in the great dukes court, buffoons his compliment. *a* **1672** EVELYN *Mem.* (1857) II. 73 The Duke of Buckingham's..farce..buffooning all plays. **1751** J. BROWN *Shaftesb. Charac.* 371 Buffooning and disgracing Christianity, from a false representation of its material part. **1836** *Fraser's Mag.* XIV. 16 Having Polonius buffooned for him, and, to no small extent, Hamlet himself.

2. *intr.* To play the buffoon, to indulge in low jesting. Also *to* ***buffoon it.***

1672 [see BUFFOONING *vbl. sb.*] **1820** BYRON in Moore *Life* (1860) 434 Bankes and I..buffooned together very merrily. **1830** *Fraser's Mag.* II. 180 He..buffooned it up to the bent. **1832** L. HUNT *Sir R. Esher* (1850) 94 All dressed and talked and laughed and buffooned alike.

ˈbuffoon, corrupted form of BUFFON, *Obs.*

buffoonery (bəˈfuːnərɪ). Also 7 buffonnerie, 7–8 buffon-, buffoonry. [f. BUFFOON *sb.* + -ERY.] The practice of a buffoon; low jesting or ridicule, farce.

1621 BP. MOUNTAGU *Diatribæ* 450 Flatterie and Buffonrie swayed all in the Romane Senate. **1631** WEEVER *Anc. Fun. Mon.* 685 Ianglery, buffonnerie, and such other vices. **1670** G. H. *Hist. Cardinals* I. III. 81 They are the first that laugh and applaud any Buffonry. **1745** FIELDING *True Patr.* Wks. 1775 IX. 296 Power and government..have been set up as the butts of ridicule and buffoonry. **1751** JOHNSON *Rambl.* No. 125 ¶6 This conversation..degenerates too much towards buffoonery and farce. **1875** JOWETT *Plato* (ed. 2) III. 132 You may often laugh at buffoonery which you would be ashamed to utter.

buˈffooning, *vbl. sb.* [f. BUFFOON *v.* + -ING[1].] The action of playing the buffoon; low jesting, buffoonery. Also *attrib.*

a **1672** WOOD *Life* (1848) 43 Mirth..buffooning and bantering. **1811** BYRON *Let. to Mr. Dallas* 21 Aug., The two stanzas of a buffooning cast..are as well left out.

buˈffooning, *ppl. a.* [f. as prec. + -ING[2].] That plays the buffoon; coarsely jesting, mocking.

1718 MOTTEUX *Quix.* (1733) III. 101 That buffooning Devil shall never 'scape unpunished. **1763** J. BROWN *Poetry & Mus.* vii. 153 It was..as illiberal and buffooning in its Beginnings as the old Comedy had been. **1879** G. MACDONALD *Sir Gibbie* I. xix. 256 The buffooning authors of the mischief.

buffoonish (bəˈfuːnɪʃ), *a.* [f. BUFFOON *sb.* + -ISH.] Like or characteristic of a buffoon.

1672 MARVELL *Reh. Transp.* I. 312 As improper and buffoonish, as to have seen the Porter lately in the good Doctors Cassock and Girdle. **1702** *Burlesque of R. Lestrange's Quevedo* 168 This foolish, base Buffoonish throng. **1818** *Blackw. Mag.* III. 533 In one of his productions lacrymose, and in another merry, buffoonish, ludicrous.

† **ˈbuffoonize, ˈbuffonize**, *v. Obs.* [f. as prec. + -IZE.] To act the buffoon.

Hence **buffoonizing** *vbl. sb.* and *ppl. a.*

1611 COTGR., *Goguenarder*, to buffoonize it; breake iests, telle merrie tales. *Ibid.*, *Patelinage*, a buffoonizing, or acting the vice in a play. **1635** J. HAYWARD *Banish'd Virg.* 40 A buffonizing and jearing humour. **1657** COLVIL *Whig's Supplic.* (1751) 98 He can buffonize, and jest.

† **buˈffoonly**, *a. Obs.* Also buffonly. [f. as prec. + -LY[1].] = BUFFOONISH.

1607 CHAPMAN *Bussy D'Amb.* I, Your Buffonly laughters will cost yee the best blood in your bodies. **1650** R. STAPYLTON *Strada's Low-C. Warres* IX. 41 A buffoonly Calvinist, who thought himself a Wit. **1684** GOODMAN *Winter Ev. Confer.* I. (R.) Apish tricks and buffoonly discourse.

buffote, obs. form of BUFFET *sb.*[2], footstool.

buffy (ˈbʌfɪ), *a.*[1] [f. BUFF *sb.*[2] and *a.* + -Y[1].]

1. Of a colour approaching to buff.

1842 *Blackw. Mag.* LI. 678 A buffy line across the horizon. **1850** *Fraser's Mag.* XLII. 188 Tail feathers with buffy white terminations.

2. *Physiol.* Applied to blood having a 'buff' or BUFFY COAT.

1782 S. F. SIMMONS in *Med. Commun.* I. 122 A coagulum..of a firm buffy texture. **1827** ABERNETHY *Surg. Wks.* II. 11 The blood, on standing, appeared very buffy. **1835–6** TODD *Cycl. Anat. & Phys.* I. 424/2 A buffy crust is..formed on the surface of the clot.

buffy coat *Physiol.* A layer of a light buff colour forming the upper part of the clot of coagulated blood under certain conditions.

1800 *Med. & Phys. Jrnl.* III. 454 There being on the blood a slight buffy coat. **1845** TODD & BOWMAN *Phys. Anat.* 37 A yellowish white layer..called the buffy coat or inflammatory crust. **1874** JONES & SIEV. *Pathol. Anat.* 22 This layer is fibrine separated from the red corpuscles, and is commonly termed the 'buffy coat'.

buffy (ˈbʌfɪ), *a.*[2] *slang.* [Origin obscure.] Intoxicated, 'squiffy'.

1858–9 C. W. S. BROOKS *Gordian Knot* (1860) viii. 57, I must have conducted myself with extreme propriety, and not as you did at the Clissolds', when you came in buffy. **1866** E. H. YATES *Land at Last* I. vi, Flexor was fine and buffy when he came home last night. **1924** A. HUXLEY *Little Mexican* 225 She did like boasting about the amount of champagne she could put away without getting buffy.

† **ˈbuffylle.** *Obs. rare*[−0]. A leather bottle.

c **1425** *Voc.* in Wr.-Wülcker 658 *Hic uter*, buffylle.

bufle, var. of BUFFLE, *Obs.*, buffalo.

† **ˈbufo.** *Obs.* [a. L. *būfo*, lit. a toad.] 'The black tincture of the alchemists' (Gifford).

1610 B. JONSON *Alch.* II. v. (1616) 633 Both Sericon, and Bufo, shall be lost.

bufolo, obs. form of BUFFALO *sb.*

bufonite (ˈbjuːfəunaɪt). [f. L. *būfo*, *-ōnem* toad + -ITE. Cf. Fr. *bufonite.*] = TOADSTONE, q.v.

1766 PENNANT *Zool.* III. 164 (Jod.) These and the other grinding teeth are often found fossil, and in that state called bufonites, or toadstones. **1865** PAGE *Handbk. Geol. Terms*, *Bufonite* (Literally Toadstone) a name given to the fossil teeth and palatal bones of fishes belonging to the family of the Pycnodonts..in the Oolite and Chalk formations.

bufotenine (bjuːfəʊˈtɛniːn, -ɪn). *Biochem.* and *Pharm.* Also -in. [ad. F. *bufoténine* (Phisalix & Bertrand 1902, in *Compt. Rend.* 7 July 48), f. L. *būfo* toad + *ten-* (perh. repr. L. *ten-āx* holding fast (f. *ten-ēre* to hold, cf. F. *tenir*), in allusion to its 'paralysing influence') + -INE[5].] A hallucinogenic tryptamine alkaloid that produces vasoconstriction and hypertension when injected and is present in various amphibia (esp. toads), mushrooms, and tropical shrubs.

1902 *Jrnl. Chem. Soc.* LXXXII. II. 576 The toxic action [of the venom of the common toad] is due to two principal substances; one..is of resinoid nature... The other, termed bufotenin, is very soluble in both water and alcohol; it has a paralysing influence. **1936** *Jrnl. Biol. Chem.* CXVI. 91 Bufotenine has been obtained from the secretions of *Bufo bufo bufo* (*Bufo vulgaris*) and *Bufo viridis viridis.* **1966** *New Scientist* 25 Aug. 414/3 Bufotenine (5-HDMT) is the active hallucinogen in potions prepared from plants by witch-doctors in the West Indies.

bug (bʌg), *sb.*[1] *Obs.* or *dial.* Forms: 4–7 bugge, 6–8 bugg, 6– bug. [ME. *bugge*, possibly from Welsh *bwg* (= bug) 'a ghost', quoted in Lhwyd's *Archæologia Brit.* (1707) 214, from the MS. Welsh Vocabulary of Henry Salesbury (born 1561). Owen Pugh has *bwg* 'hobgoblin, scarecrow'; but the word is apparently now known chiefly in its derivatives. When *bug* became current as the name of an insect (see BUG *sb.*[2]), this sense fell into disuse, and now survives only in the compound BUGBEAR. Cf. BOGY[1], BUGABOO.

Although Salesbury's evidence takes the Welsh word back only to the latter half of the 16th c., before which there was plenty of time for its adoption from the Eng. *bugge*, *bug*, its Welsh nativity is strongly supported by a numerous family of derivatives, e.g. *bwgan* (= 'bugan) bugbear, scarer, *bwgwth* to terrify, threaten, *bwgwl* (= 'bugul) terror, terrifying, threatening, whence *bygylu* (= bʌˈgəly) to terrify, threaten, *bygwydd* (= ˈbʌgwið) hobgoblin, phantom. The S. Wales *bwci* ('buki) can however scarcely be a derivative, but looks like an adoption of ME. *bugge*, or modern *bogy*. With these Welsh words cf. Manx *boag*, *boagáne* 'bugbear, bogle, sprite' (whence *boaganach* frightful, *boagandoo* scarecrow), the Irish *bocán* hobgoblin, Gael. *bochdan* (? for *bocan*) hobgoblin (though these cannot be actually cognate with Welsh *bwgan*). Owen Pugh has also *bygel nos* 'phantom', which seems however to be an error for *bugail nos*, in Breton *buguel-nos* 'shepherd or lad of the night'.]

1. a. An object of terror, usually an imaginary one; a bugbear, hobgoblin, bogy; a scarecrow. ***to swear by no bugs***: to take a genuine oath, not a mere pretence of one.

1388 WYCLIF *Baruch* vi. 69 As a bugge, *either a man of raggis* [**1611** scarcrow] in a place where gourdis wexen. *c* **1440** *Promp. Parv.* 55 Bugge, or buglarde, *maurus, ducius.* **1529** MORE *Comfort agst. Trib.* I. Wks. (1557) 1161/2 Lest there happe to be such black bugges in dede as folke call deuilles. **1535** COVERDALE *Ps.* xc[i]. 5 Thou shalt not nede to be afrayed for eny bugges by night. **1565** JEWEL *Def. Apol.* (1611) 285 A bug meet only to fray Children. **1579** GOSSON *Sch. Abuse* 23 Caligula..bid his horse to supper..and swore by no bugs that hee would make him a Consul. **1593** SHAKS. *3 Hen. VI*, v. ii. 2 Warwicke was a Bugge that fear'd vs all. **1611** SPEED *Hist. Gt. Brit.* VII. xlii. 3. 349 Champions against the maried Clergy (for women in those dayes were great bugs in their eyes). **1681** GLANVILL *Sadducismus* II. (1726) 453 Timerous Fools that are afraid of Buggs. **1719** D'URFEY *Pills* (1872) II. 306 Let the bug Predestination Fright the Fools no better know.

b. ? A person of assumed importance. Possibly this may survive in the U.S. slang 'a big bug' for an aristocrat, 'swell', though the latter is regarded by those who use it as referring to BUG *sb.*[2]

1771 SMOLLETT *Humph. Cl.* (1815) 255 That I'm nine times as good a man as he, or e'er a bug of his country. **1827** *Harvard Reg.* Oct. 247 He who desires to be a big-Bug, rattling in a natty gig. **1843** HALIBURTON *Sam Slick Eng.* xxiv. (Bartlett), We'll go to the Lord's house..pick out the big bugs. **1892** J. NIE *Rob. Crusoe* (MS.) 21 That you're a big bug here is understood. **1932** E. WAUGH *Black Mischief* viii. 300 He seems to have been quite a big bug under the Emperor. Ran the army for him. **1939** 'G. ORWELL' *Coming Up* II. ix. 156, I saw..a big bug. You know how it is with these big business men.

2. *Comb.*, as **bug-boy** (? corruption of BUGABOO); **bug-law**, a law intended to inspire terror. Also BUGBEAR, BUG-WORD.

1601 DEACON & WALKER *Spirits & Divels* 354 The countrey hath been free from such dangerous bug-boyes. **1601** —— *Ans. to Darel* 222 Hobgoblings, Bugboies, Night-sprites, or Fairies. **1694** R. L'ESTRANGE *Fables* lxxi. (1714) 87 'Tis much the same Case betwixt the People and Bugg-Laws..that it is here betwixt the Fox and the Lyon.

bug (bʌg), *sb.*[2] [Etymology unknown. Usually supposed to be a transferred sense of prec.; but this is merely a conjecture, without actual evidence, and it has not been shown how a word meaning 'object of terror, bogle', became a generic name for beetles, grubs, etc. Sense 1 shows either connexion or confusion with the earlier *budde*; in quot. 1783 *shorn bug* appears for ME. *scearn-budde* (*-bude*):—OE. *scearn-budda* dung-beetle, and in Kent the 'stag-beetle' is still called *shawn-bug*. Cf. Cheshire '*buggin*, a louse' (Holland).]

1. A name given vaguely to various insects, esp. of the beetle kind, also to grubs, larvæ of insects, etc. Now chiefly *dial.* and in U.S.; *esp.* with defining words, as ***field bug***, ***harvest bug***, ***May bug***, ***June bug***, ***potato bug***; also **fire-bug**, in U.S. applied *colloq.* to an incendiary.

1642 ROGERS *Naaman* 74 Gods rare workmanship in the Ant, the poorest bugge that creeps. **1691** RAY *S. & E. C. Wds.*, *Bugge*: Any insect of the Scarabæi kind. It is, I suppose, a word of general use. **1710** SHAFTESB. *Charac.* II. §4 (1737) II. 314 The Bug which breeds the Butterfly. **1783** AINSWORTH *Lat. Dict.* (Morell) II, *Blatta*..a shorn bug, the chafer, or beetle. **1856** *Sat. Rev.* II. 258/1 In the field bug we have an instance, etc. **1861** EMERSON *Cond. Life* ii. 38 A good tree..will grow in spite of blight or bug. *c* **1880** WHITTIER in *Harper's Mag.* Feb. (1883) 358/1 A big black bug came flying in.

2. *spec.* **a.** The *Cimex lectularius*, more fully ***bed-bug*** or ***house-bug***, a blood-sucking hemipterous insect found in bedsteads and other furniture, of a flattened form, and emitting an offensive smell when touched. **b.** Applied to insects of the order *Hemiptera* or *Heteroptera*, to which the bed-bug belongs.

1622 MASSINGER & DEKKER *Virgin Mart.* III. iii, *Harpax.* Come, let my bosom touch you. *Spungius.* We have bugs, Sir. **1683** TRYON *Way to Health* 588 The Original of these Creatures called Bugs, is from Putrifaction. **1730** SOUTHALL *Bugs* 1 Buggs have been known to be in England above sixty Years, and every Season increasing upon us. **1798** W. HUTTON *Autobiog.* 40 The doctor visited me..and..said, 'You are as safe as a bug in a rug'. **1845** DARWIN *Voy. Nat.* xv. (1852) 330 An attack (for it deserves no other name) of the Benchuca..the great black bug of the Pampas. **1847** CARPENTER *Zool.* §721 The Geocorisæ or Land-Bugs, and the Hydrocorisæ or Water-Bugs. **1861** HULME tr. *Moquin-Tandon* II. IV. i. 219 The Cimicidæ, or Bugs, belong to the order Hemiptera. *Ibid.* II. VI. v. 304.

3. In various slang uses. **a.** A person obsessed by an idea; an enthusiast. Freq. with defining word, as *jitterbug*, *litterbug*; cf. *fire-bug* under sense 1 and *s.v.* FIRE *sb.* B 5 a. Also, an obsession, a craze. orig. *U.S.*

1841 *Congress. Globe* June 133 Mr. Alford of Georgia warned the 'tariff bugs' of the South that..he would read them out of church. **1909** 'O. HENRY' *Roads of Destiny* xiii. 208 He's got bugs. Sitting on ice and calling his best friends pseudonyms. **1911** *Daily Colonist* (Victoria, B.C.) (Magazine Section) 18 Apr. 1/2 There are no more critical people than what are generally classified as baseball 'bugs'. **1937** N. COWARD *Present Indicative* ix. 377 Bushell and Guerrier, having firmly inoculated me with the naval bug, obtained permission from their captain..for us both to travel..with them. **1946** *Penguin New Writing* XXVIII. 26 The boy's got the religious bug. **1948** 'N. SHUTE' *No Highway* xii. 303, I love being on aerodromes and seeing aeroplanes. It's a sort of bug that gets in you. **1959** *Which?* Dec. 171 A boy bitten by the railway bug.

b. A defect or fault in a machine, plan, or the like. orig. *U.S.*

1889 *Pall Mall Gaz.* 11 Mar. 1/1 Mr. Edison, I was informed, had been up the two previous nights discovering 'a bug' in his phonograph—an expression for solving a difficulty, and implying that some imaginary insect has secreted itself inside and is causing all the trouble. **1935** *Jrnl. R. Aeronaut. Soc.* XXXIX. 43 Casting, forging and riveting are processes hundreds of years old, and, to use an Americanism, 'have the bugs ironed out of them'. **1956** 'N. SHUTE' *Beyond Black Stump* v. 138 They worked..until the rig had settled down and all the bugs had been ironed out. **1958** *Engineering* 14 Mar. 336/2 The seven-and-a-half years ..was not an excessive time to..get the 'bugs' out of a new system of that kind.

c. Schoolboys' slang for 'boy'; usu. with defining word, as ***day-bug***.

1909 [see DAY *sb.* 24]. **1927** W. E. COLLINSON *Contemp. Eng.* 29 Day-bugs and boarder-bugs. **1936** A. HUXLEY *Eyeless in Gaza* vi. 63 It really wasn't right to treat New Bugs the way he did—as though they were equals. **1960** J. RAE *Custard Boys* I. i. 17 You're new, Curlew, and new bugs should be seen and not heard.

d. A microbe or germ; also, a disease. Hence in *pl.*, bacteriology or biology.

1919 W. A. FRASER *Bulldog Carney* iii. 129 'Gee! now I will get well,' he said; 'I'll beat the bug out now—I'll have heart.' **1927** W. E. COLLINSON *Contemp. Eng.* 58 Disease-germs are sometimes referred to as bugs. **1932** KIPLING *Limits & Renewals* 350 He's bugs—agar-agar—guinea-pigs —slides—slices. The microbe game. *Ibid.* 362 He used to

talk bugs to me, too. **1933** PARTRIDGE *Slang To-day & Yesterday* iii. 191 *Bugs*, according to the context, bacteria or bacteriology. **1941** J. CARY *House of Children* lxvii. 279 May I get into your bed, Harry?—I'm freezing. I won't breathe any of my bugs on you. **1943** KOESTLER *Arrival & Departure* IV. i. 128 The whole thing had probably been due to some new kind of influenza, an unknown variety of the bug. **1963** *New Society* 22 Aug. 5/2 'Bugs' may still be used for biology.

e. A burglar-alarm system. *U.S.*

1925 in PARTRIDGE *Dict. Underworld*. **1930** J. P. BURKE in *Amer. Mercury* Dec. 454/2 *Bug*, a burglar-alarm. 'The casa's bugged.' **1950** H. E. GOLDIN *Dict. Amer. Underworld* 35/2 There ain't no bug on this joint... Let's charge out (go to work).

f. A concealed microphone (see quots.). orig. *U.S.*

1946 W. L. GRESHAM *Nightmare Alley* (1947) xi. 171 That would have been a beautiful place to plant a bug if you wanted to work the waiting room gab angle. **1948** F. BROWN *Murder can be Fun* (1951) xiv. 215 There's been a bug on your phone line for three days. Man on duty in the basement. **1955** *N.Y. Times* 4 May 1/3 A telephone 'bug', or tiny microphone and wire, attached to Mr. Celler's own phone in the hearing room. **1961** A. CHRISTIE *Pale Horse* xvi. 164 Perhaps you have some idea that this office of mine might have a bug in it?

4. *Comb.*, as *bug-bite*, *-destroyer*, *-fly*, *-killer*; **bug-agaric**, *Agaricus muscarius*, 'a mushroom that used to be smeared over bedsteads to destroy bugs' (Prior *Plant-n.*); **bug-bane**, *Cimicifuga fœtida* and other allied plants, used to drive away bugs; **bug-hunter**, in various *slang* uses (see quots.); *spec.* an entomologist, a naturalist; so *bug-hunt* v. intr., *bug-hunting*; **bug-juice** *U.S. slang*, bad whisky; **bug-trap**, *Naut. slang* (see quot.); **bug-wort** = *bug-bane*.

1804 BEWICK *Brit. Birds* (1847) II. 165 It is made of..the roots of *bugbane, stalks of water lily, pond weed, and water violet. **1880** *Libr. Univ. Knowl.* III. 862 *Cimicifuga*, or bugbane, an herb of the order ranunculaceæ. **1760** GOLDSM. *Cit. W.* lxviii, One doctor who is modestly content with securing them from *bugbites. **1831** CARLYLE *Sart. Res.* I. xi. 88 Poisoned by bad cookery, blistered with bugbites. **1809** SYD. SMITH *Wks.* (1859) I. 135/1 The *bug-destroyer seizes on his bug with delight. **1711** *Phil. Trans.* XXVII. 352, 10 and 11 are *Bug-flies observed in the Woods about Hampsted Heath. **1796** GROSE *Dict. Vulgar T.* (ed. 3), **Bug-hunter*, an upholsterer. **1862** Bug-hunter [see MOOCHER 3]. **1889** M. E. BAMFORD *Up & down Brooks* 46 It seems sometimes to the bug-hunter as though there would be but very few vacant rooms to rent in Nature's house. **1962** A. WISE *Death's-Head* vii. 70 Was she one of them? I thought—a passionate bughunter? **1855** KINGSLEY *Glaucus* 7 The naturalist was looked on as a harmless enthusiast, who went '*bug-hunting', simply because he had not spirit to follow a fox. **1905** *Westm. Gaz.* 19 May 4/2 The pursuit that in schoolboy days of irreverence we used to call 'bug-hunting'. **1869** *New No. West* (Deer Lodge, Mont.) 22 Oct. 1/5 Citizens glad to see us—freedom of the city—'*bug juice', *ad lib.* **1888** FARMER *Americanisms*, *Bug-juice*, the Schlechter whiskey of the Pennsylvania Dutch—a very inferior spirit. Also called *bug-poison*. These terms are now applied to bad whiskey of all kinds. **1791** HUDDESFORD *Salmag.* 111 Shrimp-scalders and *bug-killers. **1895** *Boy's Own Paper* XVII. 427/1 Small vessels are..commonly called '*bug-traps', because they soon get filled up with cockroaches.

†**bug**, *a.* *Obs.* exc. *dial.* Also 6 bugge, byg. [Etymology unknown: cf. BIG, BOG *a.* and BUDGE *a.*] Pompous; big; proud, conceited, fine. (Still widely prevalent *dial.*)

1567 DRANT *Horace's De Arte P.* A. viij, Bugge verses which cum to the stage With waight of wordes alone. **1642** H. MORE *Song of Soul* II. III. III. lxiii, Then 'gins she [the moon] swell, and waxen bug with horn. **1682** —— *Annot. Glanvill's Lux O.* 55 A Bug and sturdy Mendicant, that pretends to be some person of Quality. **1881** *Leicestersh. Gloss.* (E.D.S.) s.v., How bug y' are o' yer new cloo'es!

bug (bʌg), *v.*[1] [f. BUG *sb.*[2]] **1. a.** *trans.* To clear (plants, etc.) of insects. **b.** *intr.* (See quot. 1889.)

1869 *Champaign Co.* (Ill.) *Gazette* 26 May 2/1 If every tree in the township was 'bugged' daily..the destruction of this little pest would be certain. **1889** *Cent. Dict.*, *Bug*.., to hunt for bugs; collect or destroy insects: chiefly in the present participle: as, to go *bugging*. **1895** *Voice* (N.Y.) 8 Aug. 7/6 While 'bugging' potatoes this season I came across a number of beetles..that I have never seen any mention of.

2. *trans.* To equip with an alarm system or a concealed microphone. (Cf. BUG *sb.*[2] 3 e, f.) Also *intr.* and in extended use. *slang* (orig. *U.S.*). So **bugged** *ppl. a.*, **bugging** *vbl. sb.* and *ppl. a.*

1919 M. ACKLOM in *Bookman* Apr. 209/1 The possibilities of the joint being bugged. **1931** *Amer. Speech* VII. 104 *Bugged*, wired to a burglar alarm. **1949** *Times* (Los Angeles) 16 Aug. I. 4/6 Cohen seemed well aware that his house was 'bugged' and that his conversations were tapped. **1955** *Newsweek* 24 Oct. 32/1 'I'll guarantee you that you're not going to do any more bugging!'.. Kalven's group had hidden microphones in Wichita, Kans., district court jury rooms and recorded the jurors' traditionally secret deliberations. **1958** J. D. MACDONALD *Executioners* (1959) v. 81 We bugged both suites. **1958** *Times* 9 July 8/6 The police..explained that 'bugging' as distinct from wire-tapping, was no crime. **1960** *News Chron.* 13 Sept. 4/8 The 'bugged' conversations of a foreign Government's leaders.

3. To annoy, irritate. *slang* (orig. and chiefly *U.S.*).

1949 *Music Library Assoc. Notes* Dec. 40/2 *Bug*, popularized by swing musicians and now much used by be-boppers: to be annoying. **1952** B. ULANOV *Hist. Jazz in Amer.* 350 *Bug*, to bewilder or irritate. **1959** J. OSBORNE *Paul Slickey* II. ix. 71 It will surely bug you when there is no man to hug... You will be bugged for ever. **1959** *Times* 31 Oct. 7/3 The heroine..inquires picturesquely of the hero 'What's bugging you?' and he replies, succinctly, 'Life.'

bug (bʌg), *v.*[2] *intr.* Of the eyes: to bulge *out*. *U.S. colloq.* Also *trans.* (*rare*).

1877 'MARK TWAIN' in *Atlantic Monthly* XL. 446 His dead-lights were bugged out like tompions; and his mouth stood..wide open. **1883** —— *Life on Mississippi* xxxvi. 346 Wouldn't their eyes bug out, to see 'em handled like that? **1929** W. FAULKNER *Sartoris* III. 225 They was..buggin' their eyes at him. **1961** D. MCN. DOUGLASS *Saba's Treasure* (1963) vi. 97 Her mouth dropped open and her eyes bugged.

bug (bʌg), *v.*[3] *slang* (chiefly *U.S.*). [Origin uncertain; perh. connected with BUG *v.*[1] or BUG *v.*[2]] *intr.* To get *out*; to leave quickly; to 'scram'.

1953 in PARTRIDGE *Dict. Slang* Suppl. (1961) 1304/2 If one were to 'swan' southward with the purpose of moving on from the enemy, the act would be called 'bugging out'. **1959** J. CHRISTOPHER *Scent of White Poppies* vii. 114 There was no sign of movement... 'Give it five minutes. If there's nothing showing by then, either he's bugged out or he's asleep.' **1969** *Daily Colonist* (Victoria, B.C.) 21 Oct. 1/7 He also said that Canada is not 'bugging out' of NATO.

bugaboo (ˈbʌgəˌbuː). Also 8 buggybow, 8– bugabo. [? f. BUG + BOO int.: cf. Cornw. *bucca-boo* under BUCCA, also BOGLE-BO, and *bug-boy* in BUG *sb.*[1] (Possibly a Celtic compound, in which case cf. OF. *Beugibus*, *Bugibus*, name of a demon.)] **1. a.** A fancied object of terror; a bogy; a bugbear.

[*c* **1200** *Aliscans* 1141 (*Anciens Poètes de la France* (1870) X. 35) Et puis d' infer iras o Bugibu, Aveuc ton Dieu Mahom[et] et Cahu.]

1740 *Xmas Entertainm.* ii, Of Hobgoblins, Rawheads, and Bloody-bones, Buggybows. **1843** POE *Premat. Burial* Wks. 1867 I. 338 No fustian about church-yards, no bugaboo tales. **1870** LOWELL *Among my Bks.* Ser. II. (1873) 128 If the sins themselves were such wretched bugaboos as he has painted.

b. *cant.* 'A sheriff's officer' (*Grose's Dict. Vulg. Tong.* 1823); 'a tally-man', a weekly creditor (*ibid.*); and similar senses.

1827 LYTTON *Pelham* lxxix. Many a mad prank..which I should not like the bugaboos and bulkies to know.

2. Loud or empty talk, nonsense, rubbish.

1897 [see GUFF[2] 2]. **1959** *Listener* 15 Jan. 121/3 So straightforward an inquiry can produce so rich a harvest of pure bugaboo.

bugan. *dial.* Also buggan(e), buggin. [See BUG *sb.*[1]] An evil spirit, hobgoblin, bogy. So ***to play the bugan***: to play the devil (with).

1839 G. C. LEWIS *Gloss. Herefordshire* 16 *To play the bugan*, to play the devil. **1872** G. M. HOPKINS *Jrnl.* 12 Aug. in *Note-Books* (1937) 165 A foolish legend of a tailor and a goblin called a Buggane. **1879** G. F. JACKSON *Shropshire Word-Bk.* 55 If yo' dunna be qweet I'll let bugan tak' yo. **1887** T. DARLINGTON *Folk-Speech S. Cheshire* 132 Ah darna go a milkin', The buggin's in the bush. **1894** HALL CAINE *Manxman* VI. i. 359 You'd have a buggane riding on your breast the night through.

bugasine, obs. form of BOCASIN, BUCKASIE.

1660 *Act 12 Chas. II*, iv. Sched. Bugasines or Calico Buckrams the half piece v.s. **1670** *Bk. Rates* (JAM.) Bugasines or callico 15 ells the piece—4s.

bugbear (ˈbʌgbɛə(r)). Forms: 6–7 buggebeare, 7– bugbear. [App. f. BUG *sb.*[1] + BEAR *sb.*[1]]

†**1.** A sort of hobgoblin (presumably in the shape of a bear) supposed to devour naughty children; hence, generally, any imaginary being invoked by nurses to frighten children. *Obs.*

1581 J. BELL *Haddon's Answ. Osor.* 10 b, Hobgoblines and Buggebeares, with whom we were never acquaynted. **1592** NASHE *P. Penilesse* (1842) 74 Meare bugge-beares to scare boyes. **1607** TOPSELL *Four-f. Beasts* 353 Certain Lamiæ.. which like Bug-bears would eat up crying boys. **1651** HOBBES *Leviath.* I. xii. 55. **1758** JOHNSON *Idler* No. 11 ¶9 To tell children of bugbears and goblins. **1842** BARHAM *Ingol. Leg.* (1877) 10 The bugbear behind him is after him still.

2. *transf.* An object of dread, esp. of needless dread; an imaginary terror. In weakened senses: an annoyance, bane, thorn in the flesh.

1580 SIDNEY *Arcadia* III. 317 At the worst it is but a bugbeare. **1642** ROGERS *Naaman* To Rdr. §2 All that thinke originall sinne a bugbeare. **1717** KENNETT in Ellis *Orig. Lett.* II. 430 IV. 306 The king of Sweden is every day a less bugbear to us. **1840** DICKENS *Old C. Shop* iii. 14 What have I done to be made a bugbear of? **1871** FREEMAN *Norm. Conq.* (1876) IV. xvii. 51 Confiscation, a word which is so frightful a bugbear to most modern ears. **1880** GEO. ELIOT *Let.* 14 Sept. (1956) VII. 322 Our only bugbear—it is a very little one—is the having to make preliminary arrangements towards settling ourselves in the new house. **1955** *Sci. Amer.* Jan. 90/1 Richness of context was their bugbear. **1966** *Observer* 10 Apr. 12/3 The great bugbear of economic management is the near impossibility of devising policies with a particular objective in view without..making it harder to attain other..desirable ends.

b. *attrib.* or as *adj.*

c **1600** *Timon* I. ii. (1842) 6 Thou shalt not fright me with thye bugbeare wordes. *a* **1734** NORTH *Exam.* III. viii. ¶25. 601 The most horrible & bug-bear Denunciations. **1853** MRS. GASKELL *Cranford* xii. 223 Indiscretion was my bugbear fault. **1930** E. SITWELL *Coll. Poems* 252 A bugbear bone that bellows white.

Hence **ˈbugˌbeardom**, bugbears collectively, needless fears; **ˈbugˌbearish** *a.*

1800 SOUTHEY in Robberds *Mem. W. Taylor* I. 35/2 Bonaparte..a name now growing more bugbearish than ever. **1862** MRS. SPEID *Last Years Ind.* 150 The assaults and tyrannies of bugbeardom.

†**ˈbugbear**, *v.* *Obs.* [f. prec. sb.] *trans.* To frighten with imaginary or needless fears.

1650 R. STAPYLTON *Strada's Low-C. Warres* I They carryed the Warre up and downe, only to bug-beare Townes and Villages. **1687** *Hist. Sir J. Hawkwood* ix. 17. **1705** S. WHATELY in W. Perry *Hist. Coll. Amer. Col. Ch.* I. 167 To be bugbear'd out of our senses by big words.

bugelet, bugelle, obs. ff. BUGLET, BUGLE *sb.*[1]

bugen, obs. form of BOW *v.*[1]

bugeye. *U.S.* [? f. BUG *sb.*[2] 1.] = BUCKEYE 3.

1881 E. INGERSOLL *Oyster Industry* 242 A bugeye is always decked over and has a cabin aft. **1889** [see BUCKEYE 3]. **1938** *Times Lit. Suppl.* 3 Sept. 574/3 She was the type of craft known as a Chesapeake 'bugeye'.

bug-eyed, *a.* orig. *U.S.* [f. BUG *v.*[2]] Having bulging eyes; esp. in phr. ***bug-eyed monster***, an extra-terrestrial monster with bulging eyes; abbrev. *B.E.M.*

1922 H. L. WILSON *Merton of Movies* xi. 193 Kind of innocent and bug-eyed the way he'd rubber at things. **1943** R. CHANDLER *Lady in Lake* (1944) viii. 47 An angular bug-eyed man with a sad sick face. **1953** KOESTLER *Trail of Dinosaur* (1955) II. 143 Young space cadets, for instance, dislike meeting Bems—for bug-eyed Monsters. **1957** P. MOORE *Science & Fiction* 45 He was no dabbler in fiction of the bug-eyed monster and ray-gun type. **1958** *New Scientist* 18 Sept. 861/3 'Space opera' and 'BEM stories' (Bug-Eyed Monsters). **1960** K. AMIS *New Maps of Hell* ii. 44 In space-opera..Indians turn up in the revised form of what are technically known as bug-eyed monsters, a phrase often abbreviated to BEMs. **1960** C. DAY LEWIS *Buried Day* viii. 165 The bug-eyed, frantic immobility of a rabbit confronted by a stoat.

‖**ˈbuggalow.** *Anglo-Ind.* Also buggala, buglah. [a. Mahratti *baglā*, *bagalā*, regarded by Col. Yule as a corruption of Pg. *baixel*, VESSEL.] 'A name commonly given on the W. coast of India to Arab vessels of the old native form' (Yule).

1842 SIR. G. ARTHUR in *Ind. Admin. of Ld. Ellenb.* 222 (Y.) Native buggalas, by which so much of the trade of this coast with Scinde, Cutch..is carried on. **1869** *Latest News* 17 Oct., There were..four vessels: two were large buglahs, each mounting about eight guns. **1884** *Times* 30 May 8 At Mocha they took passage on board an Arab buggalow.

†**ˈbuggard, buggart.** *Obs.* or *dial.* [a variant of BOGGARD, the form of which suggests formation from *bugge*, BUG *sb.*[1] (Still used in Cheshire.)] A boggard, a bogy.

1575 *Hist. Troubles Frankfort* (1642) 136 They two..may not be..such buggards to the poore if they may not beare the bagge alone. **1865** MISS LAHEE *Betty o' Yeps* 6 Railway styemers scroikin away through th' country, enew to flay a buggart eawt o'th' greawnd.

bugge, -r, obs. f. BUDGE, BUG, BUY, -ER.

bugger (ˈbʌgə(r)), *sb.*[1] Also 6 bowgard, bouguer. [a. F. *bougre*:—L. *Bulgarus* Bulgarian, a name given to a sect of heretics who came from Bulgaria in the 11th c., afterwards to other 'heretics' (to whom abominable practices were ascribed), also to usurers. See BOUGRE.]

†**1.** (With capital initial). A heretic: the name was particularly applied to the Albigenses. *Obs.* exc. *Hist.*

1340 [see BOUGRE]. **1753** CHAMBERS *Cycl. Supp.* s.v., The Buggers are mentioned by Matthew Paris..under the name of Bugares..They were strenuously refuted by Fr. Robert, a dominican, surnamed the Bugger, as having formerly made profession of this heresy.

2. One who commits buggery; a sodomite. In decent use only as a legal term.

1555 *Fardle Facions* II. x. 224 As rancke bouguers with mankinde, and with beastes, as the Saracenes are. **1587** TURBERV. *Epitaphs & Sonn.* Wks. (1837) 372 To serve his beastly lust..he will leade a bowgards life.

b. In low language a coarse term of abuse or insult; often, however, simply = 'chap', 'customer', 'fellow'. Cf. BAGGAGE 7.

So in Fr.: 'Bougre..terme de mépris et d'injure, usité dans le langage populaire le plus trivial et le plus grossier'. (Littré.)

1719 D'URFEY *Pills* I. 59 From every trench the bougers fly. **1854** M. HOLMES *Tempest & Sun.* 203 'If I'd known all you city buggers was comin' I'd a kivered my bar feet'. **1881** *Evans Leicest. Gloss.* s.v., 'Mister, can ye fit this canny little bugger wi' a cap?' said a mother to a shop-keeper of her little boy. **1929** F. MANNING *Middle Parts of Fortune* I. v. 103 Not when there are two poor buggers dead, and five more not much better. **1934** R. BLAKER *Night-Shift* xx. 261 The words that had voiced the shock at the bottom of a startled heart..were 'pore bugger'. **1955** *Times* 27 Jan., A remark of the policeman to him was: 'Don't argue, get those buggers out of here.' **1969** *Listener* 9 Jan. 53/3 Come and sit on my other side. Otherwise they will put me beside that bugger Oparin.

c. Something unpleasant or undesirable; a great nuisance. *coarse slang.*

1936 'G. ORWELL' *Let.* ? 16 Apr. (1968) I. 216 This business of class-breaking is a bugger. **1940** HARRISSON & MADGE *War begins at Home* viii. 189 Heard one old lady say, 'It's a bugger this dark!' **1942** *Penguin New Writing* XV. 28 Drilling before breakfast's a bugger, believe me.

d. = DAMN *sb.* 2. *coarse slang.*

1922 JOYCE *Ulysses* 576, I don't give a bugger who he is. **1939** DYLAN THOMAS *Let.* 2 Nov. (1966) 243, I don't care a bugger whether you won't or will. **1960** F. RAPHAEL *Limits*

of Love I. iii. 32 It'd be a wonderful thing to have a magazine that just didn't give a bugger what it said about anyone.

e. ***bugger-all***, nothing. (See ALL A. 8 f.) *coarse slang*

1937 in PARTRIDGE *Dict. Slang* 103/1. **1961** I. JEFFERIES *It wasn't Me!* v. 63 'What did they offer to give you?' 'Bugger-all.' **1967** J. CLEARY *Long Pursuit* ii. 39 Way out here in the middle of bugger-all, and you turn up!

bugger ('bʌgə(r)), *sb.*[2] orig. *U.S.* [f. BUG *v.*[1] + -ER[1].] One who installs a concealed microphone or 'bug'.

1955 H. COBURN in *Front Page Detective* June 65 Deputy Midyett, in charge of recording instruments.. was..'the chief bugger of Marin County'. **1966** *Ramparts* Nov. 5 (*heading*), I was a burglar, wiretapper, bugger, and spy for the F.B.I. **1967** R. M. BROWN *Electronic Invasion* xi. 143 The so-called 'expert' buggers more often than not are led to believe that the transistors are malfunctioning or that a circuit wire has broken loose. **1973** A. J. P. TAYLOR in *Sunday Express* 22 July 16/3 No doubt the buggers would have made a mess of it as they did at Watergate. **1983** *Daily Tel.* 31 Mar. 15/5 Chris Serle was asking himself: 'What technology is available to the bugger of today?'

'bugger, *v.* Also 7 **buggar**. [f. prec. sb.]

1. *trans.* To commit buggery with. Also *absol.*

1598 FLORIO *Worlde of Wordes* 39/1 *Bardascia*, a bardash, a buggering boy, an ingle. **1611** COTGR., s.v. *Levretée*. **1624** CAPT. SMITH *Virginia* v. 198. **1675** COTTON *Poet. Wks.* (1765) 279. **1681** *Trial S. Colledge* 42. *a* **1701** SEDLEY *Wks.* (1766) 126. **1868** *Index Expurgatorius of Martial* 49 You open your doors and bugger tall youths, Amillus. **1930** E. E. CUMMINGS *Let.* 12 Apr. (1969) 116 Hats off to thea orthodox flea who attempted to bugger a bee. **1965** *New Statesman* 30 Apr. 687/1 Her German maid, whom he buggers. **1968** *Peace News* 16 Feb. 8/3 Some were in.. for homosexuality, which is still an offence in the Army... Usually they'd have done it to get out: it was a saying, you had to bugger your way out of the Army. **1968** *Observer* 29 Sept. (Colour Mag.) 24/3 The thought of actually buggering a little boy is repulsive to me.

2. *coarse slang.* **a.** = DAMN *v.* 5.

1794 *Sessions Paper* 86/1 She said, b-st and b- gg-r your eyes, I have got none of your money. **1862** A. M'GILVRAY *Poems* (ed. 2) 21 Tho' Henderson, the sheriff-clerk, May damn, and swear, and buggar. **1867** ROSSETTI *Let.* 14 Aug. (1965) II. 628 I'm on the right side of the hedge this time, and b-g-r his drawings! **1886** BAUMANN *Londinismen* 17/2 *Bugger (you)!* geh' zum henker! **1897** *Shetland News* 22 May (E.D.D. Suppl.), 'Dat be bugger'd!' I said, 'Doo's shürly leein', Sibbie.' **1923** [see 2 b, below]. **1929** F. MANNING *Middle Parts of Fortune* I. v. 92 'Cushy be buggered,' said Minton angrily. **1936** DYLAN THOMAS *Let.* 9 Mar. (1966) 168 Whatever I do now, bugger me it's literary. **1939** JOYCE *Finnegans Wake* 522 Buggered if I know! **1953** S. BECKETT *Watt* i. 42 Bugger these buttons! *Ibid.* 45 I'll be buggered if I can understand how it could have been anything else. **1967** D. PINNER *Ritual* xix. 189 Bugger me, he thought, looking at the grin on his watch, it's three o'clock!

b. To mess *up*; to ruin, spoil. In *pass.*, to be tired out.

1923 MANCHON *Le Slang* 74 *Bugger!* or *bugger you!* merde! Salaud! *Ibid.*, *Buggered off* or *buggered up*, foutu. **1929** F. MANNING *Middle Parts of Fortune* I. ii. 31 Buggered-up by a joy-ride in the train from Rouen to Méricourt. **1934** J. O'HARA *Appointment in Samarra* (1935) iii. 77 He's probably forgotten about it, and my going there will bugger things up proper. **1942** F. WARNICK *Dialect of Garrett County, Maryland* 4 Booger up, v. phr., to treat roughly (always used in past tense) 'all buggered up'. **1947** *Coast to Coast 1946* 216 We're buggered, too—been burnin' the floor boards orf the dunny. **1953** DYLAN THOMAS *Let.* 31 Mar. (1966) 401, I hope I haven't boomily buggered the poems up. **1961** A. WILSON *Old Men at Zoo* i. 32 No hippos in their natural lovely setting of the Severn or beavers buggering up the Broads. **1968** H. C. RAE *Few Small Bones* II. i. 72 He was so utterly buggered that he had no hunger left.

c. *intr.* With *off*: to go away, depart.

1922 JOYCE *Ulysses* 586 Here bugger off, Harry. There's the cops! **1945** J. B. PRIESTLEY *Three Men in New Suits* iv. 63, I didn't come back for their bloody leavings. Bugger off! **1958** P. SCOTT *Mark of Warrior* II. 202 They sort of stared at the river a bit, then buggered off. **1969** *Private Eye* 12 Sept. 14 Let's get up to palace, pick up O.B.E.'s and bugger off 'ome, like.

d. With *about*: (see quot. 1937); also with *around*. Also *trans.*, to hound from pillar to post; to mess about with.

1929 F. MANNING *Middle Parts of Fortune* I. iii. 87 We're just 'umped an' buggered about all over.. France. **1937** PARTRIDGE *Dict. Slang* 103/1 *Bugger about*, potter about; fuss; act ineffectually; waste time on a thing, with a person. Hence *bugger about with*, to caress intimately; interfere with (person or thing). **1946** B. MARSHALL *George Brown's Schooldays* 43 Pious Aeneas went buggering about the Aegean. **1957** M. KENNEDY *Heroes of Clone* III. iii. 174 Do I then have to be buggered about by a lot of professors and critics.. asking how I rate? **1961** 'T. HINDE' *For Good of Company* v. 56 It was properly buggered around when it came back. **1968** J. WAINWRIGHT *Web of Silence* 12 Let's not bugger around being polite.

†**'buggerage.** *Obs. rare*$^{-1}$. Heresy; buggery.

1538 BALE *Thre Lawes* 671 Stodye the popes Decretals, and mixt them with buggerage.

'buggerer. [f. BUGGER *v.* + -ER[1].] = BUGGER *sb.*[1] 2.

1552 HULOET Buggerer, *Pæderastes*. *a* **1571** JEWEL *On 1 Thess.* (1611) 77 Neither fornicators, nor adulterers, nor wantons, nor buggerers shall inherit the Kingdome of Heauen. **1651** BAXTER *Inf. Bapt.* 158 He might have found these godly Reformers.. to be Ribalds, Buggerers, Sorcerers. **1704** *Faction Displ.* xi. 14 Beaus, Biters, Pathicks, B——rs and Cits.

†**buggeress.** *Obs.* A female bugger.

c **1450** *Voc.* in Wr.-Wülcker 569 *Bulgra*, bugres.

'buggerly, *adj.* and *adv.* [f. BUGGER *sb.* + -LY.] Like or pertaining to a bugger.

1545 JOYE *Exp. Dan.* vii. N vj b, Poore buggerly, beggerly fryers. **1552** HULOET, Louer of chyldren buggerly or dissolutely, *Pæderastes*. **1653** URQUHART *Rabelais* II. xxx, His great buggerly Beard.

'buggery ('bʌgərɪ). Forms: 4 bugerie, 6 buggerye, -arie, -orie, boggery, bowgery, bockery, *Sc.* bewgrye, 6–7 buggerie, 6– buggery, 8– -ary. [f. as prec.: see -ERY.] †**a.** Abominable heresy. *Obs.* **b.** Unnatural intercourse of a human being with a beast, or of men with one another, sodomy. Also used of unnatural intercourse of a man and a woman. Now mainly as a technical term in criminal law.

1330 R. BRUNNE *Chron.* 320 Þe Kyng said & did crie, þe pape was heretike.. and lyued in bugerie. **1514** FITZHERB. *Just. Peas* (1538) 125 b, It is enacted that the vice of buggorie committed with man kynd or beast be adjudged felonie. **1552** LYNDESAY *Monarche* 3473 That self Syn of Sodomye, and most abhominabyll bewgrye [*v.r.* bowgre]. **1667** CHAMBERLAYNE *St. Gt. Brit.* I. (1684) 41 The sin of Buggery brought into England by the Lombards. **1729** G. JACOB *Law-Dict.*, *Buggery*.. is defined to be *carnalis copula contra Naturam, & hoc vel per confusionem Specierum, sc.* a Man or Woman with a brute Beast; *vel Sexuum*, a Man with a Man, or Man with a Woman. **1754** EDWARDS *Freed. Will* III. vii. 187 The most horrid crimes, Adultery, Murder, Buggery, Blasphemy, &c. **1861** *Act 24 & 25 Vic.* c. §61 The abominable crime of buggery, committed either with mankind or with any animal. **1966** J. SPARROW *Controversial Ess.* 41 Lawrence weaves into his story not merely a defence but a panegyric of this practice, making *Lady Chatterley's Lover* a vehicle for conveying his belief that it is a proper, if not a necessary, element in a full sexual relationship between man and woman... The practice approved by Lawrence is that known in English law as buggery.

c. In various slang uses (see quots.) = HELL *sb.* 9; *to play buggery*: to play havoc. (Cf. 1851 *attrib.* quot. in B below)

1898 *Shetland News* 11 June (E.D.D. Suppl.), You wye 'at dey geng an' buy at private bargains outside da ring plays buggery. **1923** MANCHON *Le Slang* 74 All to buggery, foutu. **1929** F. MANNING *Middle Parts of Fortune* I. iii. 39 I saw 'im, sir; 'e were just blown to buggery. **1937** PARTRIDGE *Dict. Slang* 103/2 *Like buggery*, either vigorously, cruelly, vindictively; or, as an expletive, certainly not! **1939** DYLAN THOMAS *Let.* Mar. (1966) 228 Old stories mostly, but cut and pruned to buggery or sense. **1961** *Coast to Coast 1959/60* 83 'Pipe down, Rymill!' 'Go to *buggery*, Rymill!' **1966** 'E. LINDALL' *Time too Soon* (1967) xiii. 142 'Sah. You sick.' 'Go to buggery,' Minogue snarled. 'Yes, sah,' Basikas said, and stood aside.

B. *attrib.* or as *adj.*

1643 R. O. *Man's Mort.* vi. 49 Christ dyed not for the rationall part seperated from the materiall, nor the materiall from the rationall, if there should be such Buggery births. **1851** MAYHEW *Lond. Labour* I. 23 A buggery fool.

†**'Bugess.** *Obs.* [a. *Bugis*, 'name given by the Malays to the dominant race of the Island of Celébes' (Col. Yule).] A name formerly used in the Indian Archipelago for a native soldier in European service.

1699 DAMPIER *Voy.* II. I. 108 These Buggasses are a sort of warlike trading Malayans and mercenary soldiers of India. **1779** FORREST *Voy. N. Guinea* 213, I apprehended he was a Captain of Buggesses, in the English Company's service. **1792** —— *Voy. Mergui* 78 (Y.) The word Buggess has become amongst Europeans consonant to soldier, in the east of India, as Sepoy is in the West. **1811** *Ld. Minto in India* 279 (Y.) We had fallen in with a fleet of nine Buggese prows. [**1878** MCNAIR *Perak* 130 (Y.) The Bugis are evidently a distinct race from the Malays.]

bugget, obs. form of BUDGET *sb.*

'bugginess. [f. BUGGY *a.* + -NESS.] The state of being buggy.

1730–6 in BAILEY; thence in JOHNSON and mod. Dicts.

bugging, *vbl. sb.* and *ppl. a.*: see BUG *v.*[1] 2.

Buggins ('bʌgɪnz). [A. 'typical' proper name used generically.] **Buggins'(s turn**, the principle of assigning an appointment to persons in rotation rather than according to merit.

1901 LD. FISHER *Let.* 13 Jan. in A. J. Marder *Fear God & Dread Nought* (1952) I. 181 Favouritism was the secret of our efficiency in the old days... Going by seniority saves so much trouble. '*Buggins's turn*' has been our ruin and will be disastrous hereafter! **1917** *Let.* 8 Jan. in Ld. Fisher *Memories* (1919) iii. 39, I was sorry for Jellicoe superseding Callaghan when the war broke out, but I remembered your old saying, 'Some day the Empire will go down because it is Buggins's turn'! **1944** W. S. CHURCHILL in *Second World War* (1952) V. 616 The departmental view is no doubt opposed to long tenures and the doctrine of 'Buggin's turn' is very powerful. **1962** *Guardian* 18 Oct. 1/6 Merit, not 'Buggins's turn', was the standard. **1970** *Observer* 8 Feb. 44/4 A sort of Buggins's-turn job, with the vice-chairman automatically moving into his boss's seat.

†**'buggish,** *a. Obs. rare*$^{-1}$. [f. BUG *sb.*[1] + -ISH[1].] Like a goblin; terrifying, frightful.

1583 STANYHURST *Æneid* IV. (Arb.) 107 Mee.. with visadge buggish he [Anchises' ghost] feareth [*turbida terret imago*].

†**'buggishank.** *Obs. rare*$^{-1}$. [= *budgishank*, f. BUDGE *sb.*[1] + SHANK.] ? A kind of budge fur.

1463 *Test. Ebor.* (1855) II. 260, i. togam nigram penulatam cum buggishanke. [Cf. **1530** PALSGR. 266 Schanke of bouge, *fovrrure de cuissettes*. **1730** BAILEY *Shanks*, the skin of the leg of a kind of kid, that bears the furr called Budge.]

†**buggle-boo.** *Obs.* = BOGLE-BO.

1625 LISLE *Du Bartas* 128 Another hath his moods And like a Buggle boo straies ever through the woods.

buggy ('bʌgɪ), *sb.* [Etymology unknown: the word has been conjecturally connected with BOGIE; also with BUG (see esp. quot. 1773). There is no ground for supposing it to be of Anglo-Indian origin.]

1. a. A light one-horse (sometimes two-horse) vehicle, for one or two persons. Those in use in America have four wheels; those in England and India, two; in India there is a hood. (In recent use, esp. in U.S., India, and the colonies.)

1773 *Gentl. Mag.* XLIII. 297 Driving a post coach and four against a single horse chaise, throwing out the driver of it, and breaking the chaise to pieces.. ludicrously denominating mischief of this kind, 'Running down the Buggies'. **1778** *Ann. Reg.* 197 *The Suicide* Prol., Buggies, timwhiskies or squeezed vis-a-vis. **1782** *India Gaz.* 14 Sept. (Y.) An excellent Buggy Horse about 15 Hands high. **1794** W. FELTON *Carriages* (1801) II. 183 The Buggy is a small chaise, made to carry one person only. **1825** *Annals Sporting* vii. 59 The speed and pluck of their buggy horses. **1844** DISRAELI *Coningsby* xiv. (L.) Villebecque prevailed upon Flora to drive with him to the race in a buggy he borrowed of the steward. **1859** LANG *Wand. India* 287 We drove as far as Deobund in the buggy. **1862** B. TAYLOR *Home & Abr.* Ser. II. ii. 4. 93, I asked for a two-horse buggy and driver. **1866** GEO. ELIOT *Felix Holt* III. 166 See that somebody takes her back.. in the buggy.

b. Extended to various other vehicles or the like, as: (*a*) a perambulator (see *baby buggy*); (*b*) = CABOOSE 2; (*c*) an automobile. *slang* (orig. *U.S.*).

1890 [see BABY *sb.* B. 2]. **1894** *St. Paul's* 11 Aug. p. ii (Advt.), Safety perambulators... Coach-panel 'Buggy' mail cart,.. 33/- to 5 guineas. **1899** *Boston Globe* 18 Mar. 12/2 Estimating the total length of these [freight] cars, with the engines and buggies. **1911** *Jrnl. Amer. Med. Assoc.* LVI. XIV. p. vi/2 My use of this motor buggy has shown me that the auto is a good thing for either city or country. **1929** *Nebraska Alumnus* June 166 A doll bed and dresser and buggy with several dolls and their wardrobes. **1931** G. IRWIN *Amer. Tramp & Underworld Slang* 39 *Buggy*, an automobile; a contraction of the term 'gasoline buggy', by which the earlier automobiles were known. **1949** J. CREASEY *Battle for Insp. West* xiii. 119 'Come on,' he said, 'you're changing buggies.' Grant hesitated; rain splashed into the car. **1961** *Economist* 27 May 918/1 The green fees, he said, were a bit stiff, and the electric buggies cost $14 a day.

2. In technical uses: see quots. (Cf. BOGIE.)

1861 RAYMOND *Mining Gloss.*, *Buggy*, a small mine-wagon holding ½ ton to 1 ton of coal. **1883** *Harper's Mag.* 939/2 The men.. go out.. on the strand in a 'buggy'.. which is a board seat slung by ropes from the axis of a grooved wheel fitting and travelling on the strand.

3. *Comb.*, as **buggy-boat**, a boat made so that wheels can be fastened to it, so as to make it into a land-vehicle; **buggy-cultivator, buggy-plough**, a plough having a seat for the ploughman to ride on; **buggy-ride** orig. *U.S.*, a ride on a buggy; esp. in colloq. fig. expression of gratitude ***thanks for the buggy-ride***.

1862 G. W. WILDER *MS. Diary* 16 Jan. (D.A.E.), The officers took a buggy ride; joy go with them. **1865** *Trans. Ill. Agric. Soc. 1863* V. 255 The one on the gang plow would have a fine buggy ride. **1926–7** in *Shopper's View of Canada's Past* (1969) 261 Records.. Thanks for the Buggy Ride—Fox Trot. **1938** N. MARSH *Artists in Crime* xv. 231 When the spot of trouble comes along it's 'Thanks for the buggy ride, it was OK while it lasted'.

'buggy, *a.* [f. BUG *sb.*[2] + -Y[1].] Infested with bugs.

1714 *Phil. Trans.* XXIX. 65 With a black Speck, as buggy Peas had. **1730** SOUTHALL *Bugs* 35 When they have taken it [old Furniture] down, because it was buggy. **1854** BADHAM *Halieut.* 207 One of those provisionless Sicilian *locande*, boasting.. a thunny supper and a buggy bed.

bugh, buȝe(n, obs. inf. and pa. t. of BOW *v.*[1]; obs. form of BOUGH.

bugher. [cf. BUFFER *sb.*[4]: the vb. is still *bough, bugh* (bʌx), in Sc.] A barker, a barking dog.

1673 R. HEAD *Canting Acad.* 34 Bugher, a Dog. **1688** R. HOLME *Armoury* III. iii. §68 Bugher, a Cur Dog. **1725** *New Cant. Dict.*

'bughouse, *sb.* and *a. slang.* **A.** *sb.* **1.** [Cf. BUG *sb.*[2] 3 a.] A lunatic asylum. orig. *U.S.*

1902 O. V. LIMERICK *Billy Burgundy's Opinions* 44 Place his name upon the list of permanent guests of the county bughouse. **1907** 'O. HENRY' *Heart of West* 226, I thought he was in the bughouse. **1919** F. HURST *Humoresque* 316 It's too bad a nut from the bug-house bought the Brooklyn Bridge to-day or I'd try to sell it to you. **1940** N. MARSH *Surfeit of Lampreys* (1941) viii. 113 You're bigger bloody fools than anybody outside a bughouse.

2. [f. BUG *sb.*[2] 1.] An opprobrious term for a theatre or cinema. Cf. *flea pit* (FLEA *sb.* 6).

1946 in PARTRIDGE *Dict. Slang* Suppl. (1961) 1018/1. **1952** 'N. SHUTE' *Far Country* ix. 326 There's a little picture theatre... It's a bit of a bug-house. **1957** J. OSBORNE *Entertainer* I. iii, If there's nothing else on, I still go.. to the bug house round the corner.

B. *adj.* [Cf. sense A. 1.] Crazy; very eccentric. Chiefly *U.S.*

[**1891** *Contemp. Rev.* Aug. 255 Begging is called 'battering for chewing';..insanity, 'bug-house'.] **1895** *Century Mag.* June 291/2 How's that for bein' bughouse, eh? **1896** ADE *Artie* xvii. 161 If I don't get mine inside of a week I'll go bug-house. **1917** CONAN DOYLE *His Last Bow* viii. 292 It's enough to make a man bughouse when he has to play a part from morning to night. **1930** 'SAPPER' *Finger of Fate* 187 For a moment I thought he'd gone bughouse.

bughsom, obs. form of BUXOM.

bught, variant of BOUGHT *sb.* and *v.*
1844 W. H. MAXWELL *Sports & Adv. Scotl.* I. xv. 262 Forty-five or fifty fathoms of *tows* constitute a *bught*.

†**bugiard.** *Obs.* [ad. It. *bugiardo*.] A liar.
a **1670** HACKET *Abp. Williams* I. (1692) 71 Like an egregious bugiard here he is quite out of the truth.

Buginese (bʊgɪˈniːz, -s), *sb.* and *a.* [f. BUGIS: see -ESE.] = BUGIS *sb.* (and *a.*)
1900 J. G. FRAZER *Golden Bough* (ed. 2) II. 449 The Buginese and Macassars of Celebes. **1910** *Encycl. Brit.* V. 598/1 The Macassar language, which belongs to the Malayo-Javanese group, is spoken in many parts of the Southern peninsula; but it has a much smaller area than the Buginese, which is the language of Boni. **1948** D. DIRINGER *Alphabet* II. vii. 431 The Buginese or Bugis character is the most complete of the three varieties. **1948, 1959** [see MACASSARESE]. **1970** R. ROOLVINK in C. C. Brown tr. *Sějarah Mělayu* p. xxv, After the large infiltration of the Buginese into the Straits of Malacca..they brought a copy of this text with them to the Riau Archipelago. **1981** *Pacific Affairs* LIV. 666 Javanese, Baweanese, Sundanese, Buginese.

Bugis (ˈbuːgɪs), *sb.* (and *a.*) Pl. **Bugis.** Also **Bugi** (ˈbuːgɪ), pl. **Bugi.** [a. Mal. *Bugis* (see BUGGESS); the Buginese self-designation is *Bugi'*.] **a.** (A member of) a people of the Indonesian island of Sulawesi (formerly Celebes). **b.** The Austronesian language of this people. **c.** *attrib.* or as *adj.*
1808, etc. [see MACASSAR 2]. **1898** CONRAD *Tales of Unrest* 9 He had led his people—a scratch lot of wandering Bugis—to the conquest of the bay. *Ibid.* 15 The son of a woman who had..ruled a small Bugis state. **1909** WEBSTER, Bugi. **1921** J. RUSSELL *Where Pavement Ends* 236 For every light there hung a Bugis from the iron framework by the long hair of his head. **1932** W. L. GRAFF *Lang.* xi. 423 About eight geographical groups [of Indonesian] can be distinguished, each with a..number of dialects. A few of these are:..(2) in the *Celebes* group, *Bugi*, *Makassar*. **1948** [see BUGINESE]. **1961** P. KEMP *Alms for Oblivion* xi. 164 In addition to Sasaks and Balinese there is..an Arab colony, and a few villages of Bugi traders. **1972** M. SHEPPARD *Taman Indera* 15 The influence of Bugis warrior princes..strengthened cultural ties with the area which we now call Indonesia.

bugit, obs. form of BUDGET *sb.*

buglah, variant of BUGGALOW.

buglard = BUGGARD.
c **1440** *Promp. Parv.* 55 Bugge, or buglarde, *Maurus, Ducius.*

bugle (ˈbjuːg(ə)l), *sb.*[1] Forms: 3– **bugle**, 4 **bewgalle, -gulle**, 5 **bugelle**, 4–6 **bugull(e**, 4–7 **bugil**, 5–6 *Sc.* **bowgle**, 6 *Sc.* **bougil, bewgill**, 7 **bugill**, (8 ? **beugle**). [a. OF. *bugle*:—L. *būculus*, dim. of *bo-s bov-is* an ox.]

1. †**a.** The buffalo (= BUFFALO *sb.* 1 a) and other kinds of wild oxen. *Obs.* **b.** A young bull. *dial.*
c **1300** *K. Alis.* 5112 A thousand bugles of Ynde. **1398** TREVISA *Barth. De P.R.* XVIII. xv. (1495) 774 The Bugle..is lyke to an oxe and is a fyers beest. *c* **1400** MAUNDEV. xxvi. 269 Hornes of grete Oxen or of Bugles. **1536** BELLENDEN *Cron. Scot.* (1821) I. 47 Hornis..thikkar than ony horne of ane bewgill. **1615** E. GRIMSTONE *Hist. World* 636 Cups..made of bugles hornes. **1677** W. CHARLTON *Exerc. de Diff. et Nom. Animal.* (ed. 2) 8 *Bonasus*, the Bugle. **1881** *Isle of Wight Gloss.* (E.D.S.), *Bugle*, a young bull; the Bugle Inn at Newport.

2. *Music.* Short for BUGLE-HORN. **a.** A hunting-horn, originally made of the horn of a 'bugle' or wild ox. **b.** A military instrument of brass or copper, resembling the trumpet, but smaller; used as the signal-horn for the infantry.
c **1340** *Gaw. & Gr. Knt.* 1136 With bugle to bent felde he buskez. *c* **1435** *Torr. Portugal* 142 Terrant blewe hys bugelle bold. **1599** SHAKS. *Much Ado* I. i. 243 Hang my bugle in an inuisible baldricke. *a* **1600** A. SCOTT *Adamson & Sym* xx. in *The Ever-Green* (1761) II. 185 Be than the Bougil gan to blaw. **1623** COCKERAM, *Bugle*, a little blacke horne. *a* **1777** F. FAWKES *Virg. Æneid* VII. (R.) Stoutly Boreas his loud bugle blew. **1832** MACAULAY *Armada* 49 Bugle's note and cannon's roar The deathlike silence broke. **1877** *Field Exercise Infantry* 403 One G sounded on the Bugle will denote the right of the line.

†**3.** ? A tube. *Obs.*
1615 CROOKE *Body of Man* 180 Put your Bugle into the bladder and blow it.

4. *Comb.*, as *bugle-blast*, *-clang*; †**bugle-browed** *a.*, having horns like a wild ox; 'horned' (*fig.*); **bugle-major**, the chief bugler in a regiment; **bugle-boy, -man** = BUGLER.
a **1627** MIDDLETON *Anyth. for Q. Life* (N.) *Wife.* 'Tis for mine own credit if I forbear, not thine, thou bugle-brow'd beast thou. **1815** SCOTT *Ld. of Isles* II. xxi, A bugle-clang From the dark ocean upward rang. **1844** *Regul. & Ord. Army* 396 The Drum or Bugle-Major. **1848** J. GRANT *Advent. of Aide* lix, 'Sound!' said I to the bugle-boy. **1859** SMILES *Self-Help* 21 From the general down through all grades to the private and bugleman. **1864** BRYANT *Return of Birds* vi, There is heard the bugle-blast.

bugle (ˈbjuːg(ə)l), *sb.*[2] *Bot.* Also 5 **bugyl, -ille.** [a. F. *bugle* = It. *bugola*, Sp. *bugula*:—late L. *bugula*. The L. *bugillo*, used by Marcellus Empiricus *c* 400, seems to denote the same plant.]

1. The English name of the plants belonging to the genus *Ajuga*, esp. the common species *A. reptans*. (The names *buglossa* and *bugle* were occasionally confounded by early writers.)
c **1265** *Voc.* in Wr.-Wülcker 554 *Buglosa*, bugle. *a* **1387** *Sinon. Barthol.* (Anecd. Oxon.) 43 *Wodebroun*, bugle. *c* **1430** LYDG. *Min. Poems* (1840) 199 As bryght as bugyl or ellys bolace. **1483** *Cath. Angl.* 46 Bugille, *buglossa, lingua bouis, herba est.* **1548** TURNER *Names of Herbes* 83 *Consolida media* is called in english Bugle. **1578** LYTE *Dodoens* I. xc. 132 Bugle spreadeth and creepeth along the ground. **1616** SURFL. & MARKH. *Country Farm* 262 He that hath bugle and sanicle, will scarce vouchsafe the surgeon a bugle. **1794** MARTYN *Rousseau's Bot.* iv. 45 Plants..having little or no smell, as bugle. **1865** GOSSE *Land & Sea* 115 The..copse..is blue with the thick spikes of bugle.

2. *Comb.*, as *bugle-bloom*.
1818 KEATS *Endym.* II. 314 Velvet leaves and bugle-blooms.

bugle (ˈbjuːg(ə)l), *sb.*[3] Also 6 **buegle**, 6–7 **beau-**, 7 **beu-, bewgle.** [Etymology unknown. Of the med.L. *bugulus*, sometimes quoted as the etymon, a single instance, as the name of a 'pad', or framework for the hair, used by Italian ladies, occurs in a chapter *De moribus civium Placentiæ* 1388, in Muratori *Script. Ital.* XVI. 580; no similar word is known in Ital. or Fr. *Bugle* has a certain resemblance in form to Du. *beugel* a ring (:—MDu. *bōghil*, *bōghel*, Franck); but no connexion of meaning appears.]

1. A tube-shaped glass bead, usually black, used to ornament wearing apparel. (Formerly also collective, or as the name of material.)
1579 SPENSER *Sheph. Cal.* Feb. 66 A gyrdle..Embost with buegle. **1583** STUBBES *Anat. Abus.* (1877) 61 *note*, Thei vse to garde their clokes rounde about the skirtes with..Bugles. **1598** FLORIO, *Margaritine*, bugles or seede pearles. **1640** *Jrnl. Ho. Commons* II. 33 The sole Making and Venting of Beads and Beaugles. **1657** R. LIGON *Barbadoes* (1673) 16 Some small beads, of white Amber, or blew bugle. **1753** RICHARDSON *Grandison* (1781) I. xxii. 159 Set off with bugles and spangles. *c* **1813** MRS. SHERWOOD *Stories Ch. Catech.* xiv. 116 She would load them with presents..gloves, habit-shirts, silver spoons, bugles, brooches. **1884** 'WANDERER' *Fair Diana* xxxiii. 265 The black grapes and bugles which..decorated her bonnet.

2. *attrib.* Made of, adorned with, or resembling, bugles.
1598 SYLVESTER *Du Bartas* I. iv. (1641) 37/1 With his bristled, hoary, beaugle-beard, Comming to kisse her. **1600** SHAKS. *A.Y.L.* III. v. 47 Your inkie browes, your blacke silke haire, Your bugle eye-balls, nor your cheeke of creame. **1611** —— *Wint. T.* IV. iv. 224 Bugle-bracelet, Necke-lace Amber. **1611** BARREY *Ram Alley* IV. i, Her bugle-gown, and best-wrought smock. **1710** STEELE *Tatler* No. 245 ¶2 Adam and Eve in Bugle-Work..upon Canvas, curiously wrought. **1767** ELLIS in *Phil. Trans.* LVII. 408 The *Cellularia Salicornia*..or Bugle Coralline.

bugle, obs. form of BOGLE, hobgoblin, and BEAGLE, hound.
1555 EDEN *Decades W. Ind.* (Arb.) 206 He goeth..with a lyttle hounde or bewgle. **1696** AUBREY *Misc.* 192 (D.) They assigned it [second sight] to Bugles or Ghosts.

ˈ**bugle**, *v.* [f. BUGLE *sb.*[1] 2.] **a.** *intr.* To sound a bugle; to make a sound like a bugle. **b.** *trans.* To give forth (a sound), as a bugle; to make known with or as with a bugle; also (*nonce-use*) to summon by bugle.
1862 THACKERAY *Roundab. Papers* (1879) 89 The wind-instruments bugling the most horrible wails. **1872** DIXON *Switzers* xxxv. 362 The rank and file..who are bugled from their beds. **1876** G. M. HOPKINS *Wr. Deutschland* (1918) xi, And storms bugle his fame. **1884** COLBORNE *Hicks Pasha* 118 My friends..who trumpet, bugle, and 'tam-tam' all day long. **1890** MEREDITH *One of our Conq.* (1891) I. iv. 58 He blinked, bugled in his throat,..and smiled. **1911** W. OWEN *Let.* 7 May (1967) 72, I almost bugled forth the fact that she was addressing a B.Sc.

So ˈ**bugling** *vbl. sb.*
1847 *Infantry Man.* (1854) 93 Too much bugling..is to be avoided. **1895** *Chambers's Jrnl.* XII. 648/2 The eternal bugling on the Canea walls still continued. **1948** A. L. RAND *Mammals Eastern Rockies* 207 The bugling or whistling of the bull elk in the early autumn is the signal..that the rut is starting.

bugled (ˈbjuːg(ə)ld), *a.* Trimmed with bugles.
1881 *Daily News* 22 Aug. 3/6 Bugled..silk laces.

ˌ**bugle-**ˈ**horn.** [f. BUGLE *sb.*[1] + HORN *sb.*] The horn of a bugle or wild ox, used
†**a.** as a drinking vessel. *Obs.*
c **1386** CHAUCER *Frankl. T.* 525 Ianus..drynketh of his bugle horn the uyn. **1387** TREVISA *Higden* Rolls Ser. I. 293 ȝif þe water of þat welle is i-take in bugle horn [*in cornu bubali*]. **1519** HORMAN *Vulg.* 166 b, Preciouse cuppis be made of bugull hornys.

b. as a musical instrument, whence = BUGLE *sb.*[1] 2.
c **1300** *K. Alis.* 5282 Tweye bugle hornes, and a bowe also. **1480** CAXTON *Chron. Eng.* ccix. 192 Two squyers blewe..with ij grete bugles hornes. *c* **1630** RISDON *Surv. Devon* §222 (1810) 231 His family bare in a field Gules, a bugle horn *or*. **1808** SCOTT *Marm.* I. iii, His bugle-horn he blew. **1842** TENNYSON *Locksley H.* 2 Sound upon the bugle horn.

bugler (ˈbjuːglə(r)). [f. as prec. + -ER[1].] One who plays on a bugle; *spec.* a soldier who conveys orders by signals sounded on a bugle.
1840 H. SMITH *O. Cromwell* II. 19 The Bugler..was already handling his instrument. **1863** KINGLAKE *Crimea* II. 366 A mounted officer rode up to a bugler of the 19th Regiment, and ordered him to sound the 'retire'.

buglet (ˈbjuːglɪt). [f. as prec. + -ET[1].] A small bugle; e.g. one carried by bicyclists.
a **1803** *Douglas Trag.* iii. in Child *Ballads* I. 100/2 With a bugelet horn hung down by his side. **1838** D. MOIR *Casa's Dirge*, The wild-bee with its buglet fine. **1885** *Price-List*, A bugle having two turns will sound short calls; those with three turns will sound military calls; but the easiest to sound of all is the above Buglet, which has four turns.

ˈ**bugle-weed.** *Bot.* An American plant, *Lycopus Virginicus*, sometimes used as a remedy for hemoptysis, or spitting of blood.
1860 BARTLETT *Dict. Amer.*, *Bugle-weed*..is also known as the Virginian Water-hound.

bugling (ˈbjuːglɪŋ), *ppl. a.* [f. BUGLE *v.* + -ING[2].] That sounds a bugle.
1884 tr. *K. Bauer's Mem.* II. 50 A bugling postillion.

bugloss (ˈbjuːglɒs). *Bot.* Forms: 6–7 **buglosse**, (6 **buglose**, 8–9 **buglos**), 7– **bugloss.** [a. F. *buglosse*:—L. *būglōssa*, ad. Gr. βούγλωσσος, f. βοῦς ox + γλῶσσα tongue, from the shape and roughness of the leaves.] A name applied to several boraginaceous plants, particularly the *small*, *corn*, or *field b.* (*Lycopsis* or *Anchusa arvensis*); *viper's b.* (*Echium vulgare*), and other species of *Echium*; also by some old herbalists to *Helminthia echioides*, prickly ox-tongue.
1533 ELYOT *Cast. Helth* (1541) 11 Cynamome: Saffron..Buglosse: Borage. **1542** BOORDE *Dyetary* xix, The rootes of Borage and Buglosse soden tender..doth ingender good blode. **1605** B. JONSON *Volpone* III. iv. 61 A little muske, dri'd mints, Buglosse, and barley-meale. **1699** EVELYN *Acetaria* 14 What we now call Bugloss, was not that of the Ancients. **1783** CRABBE *Village* I. Wks. 1834 II. 77 There the blue bugloss paints the sterile soil. **1837** CAMPBELL *Dead Eagle*, Fields..blue with bugloss.

b. *Comb.* **bugloss cowslip.**
1879 PRIOR *Brit. Plant-n.*, *Bugloss-Cowslip*, the lungwort, from its having the leaves of a bugloss and the flowers of a primula. *Pulmonaria officinalis* L.

†**bu'glossate.** *Obs. rare*$^{-1}$. [f. prec. (or its source) + -ATE.] Some kind of medicine.
1727 BRADLEY *Fam. Dict.* I. s.v. *Honey*, Antidotaries..as the Buglossate made of Bugloss.

bugology (bʌˈgɒlədʒɪ). *U.S. humorous.* [f. BUG *sb.*[2] 1 + -OLOGY.] The science of 'bugs' or insects; entomology. Hence **bu'gologist**, an entomologist.
1843 'R. CARLTON' *New Purchase* II. l. 171 Chemistry, botany, anatomy, conchology, bugology. **1881** *Nat. Republican* (U.S.) 24 Feb. 2/4 Mr Riley, the eminent bugologist. **1898** *Congress. Rec.* Apr., App. 455/2 Those..acquainted with bugology know there is rather a disreputable bug that looks one way and rolls the other. **1910** *Sat. Even. Post* 2 July 49/2 Government bugologists..studied his habits.

bugong (ˈbuːgɒŋ). Also **bogong, bougong.** [Native name.] An Australian noctuid moth, *Danais limniace* or *Agrotis spina*, highly prized by the Aborigines as an article of food.
1834 G. BENNETT *Wand. N.S.W.* I. 265 It is named the 'Bugong Mountain', from the circumstance of multitudes of small moths, called Bugong by the aborigines, congregating at certain months of the year about masses of granite on this and other parts of the range. **1859** H. KINGSLEY *G. Hamlyn* xxxix, To collect and feed on the great grey moths (Bougongs) which are found on the rocks. **1878** R. B. SMYTH *Aborig. Victoria* I. 207 The Bugong moths..are greedily devoured by the natives. **1919** *Nature* CIII. 345/2 In Australia at certain seasons a 'cutworm' moth, known as the 'bogong' or 'bugong' (Agrotis infusa), swarms in myriads in many places. **1961** R. PARK *Hole in Hill* (1962) ii. 13 The big bogong moths would be coming in.

bugull(e, obs. form of BUGLE *sb.*[1]

†**bug-word, bug's-word.** *Obs.* [f. BUG *sb.*[1] + WORD. Cf. *bugbear word*.] A word meant to frighten or terrify; a word that causes dread. Usually in *pl.* Swaggering or threatening language.
1562 J. HEYWOOD *Prov. & Epigr.* (1867) 54 All be bugs woords, that I speake to spare. *a* **1600** HOOKER *Wks.* (1845) I. 277 Certaine wordes, as Nature, Reason, Will and such like which wheresoever you find named you suspect..as bugs wordes. **1632** SANDERSON *Serm.* 163 Outdared with the bigge-lookes and bug-words of those that could doe him no harme. **1668** DRYDEN *Sir M. Mar-All* I. i, I..have nothing to hope for..but death. Death is a bug-word. *a* **1734** NORTH *Exam.* I. ii. ¶105 (1740) 87 A Rebellion; O no, that's a bug Word.

bugyl, obs. f. BUGLE *sb.*[2], a plant.

buh, obs. form of BOUGH, BOW *v.*[1]

buhl (bu:l). Also Boulle, q.v. [f. *Boulle* name of a wood-carver in France in the reign of Louis XIV. (*Buhl* appears to be a modern Germanized spelling.)] Brass, tortoise-shell, or other material, worked into ornamental patterns for inlaying; work inlaid with buhl. Also *attrib.*

1823 RUTTER *Fonthill* 14 A pier table, richly ornamented with buhl. **1831** CARLYLE *Sart. Res.* III. x. 336 A wardrobe of Buhl is on the left. **1842** BARHAM *Ingol. Leg.* (1877) 185 A splendid buhl stand. **1870** *Daily News* 7 Feb., Scenes with real hangings, real buhl clocks, and other articles.

b. *Comb.*, as **buhl-saw**, a saw used in cutting out buhl-work; **buhl-work** (see quot.).

1832 BABBAGE *Econ. Manuf.* xi. (ed. 3) 96 Inlaid plates of brass and rosewood, called buhlwork. **1875** URE *Dict. Arts* s.v., Buhl-work consists of inlaid veneers; and differs from marquetry in being confined to decorative scroll-work.

buhr, var. BURR *sb.*[5]

buhrstone, variant of BURR-STONE.

buhsum, obs. f. BUXOM *a.*

buick, buik(e, obs. ff. BOOK, BOUK.

buif, obs. form of BEEF.

build (bɪld), *v.* Pa. t. and pple. built, *poet.* and *arch.* builded. Forms: *Inf.* 3-4 bulde(n, 4 bylden, bilden, (bield, byle), (4-5 belde(n, beelde), 4-6 byld(e, bild(e, 5 buylden, 5-6 buyld(e, 6 builde, (byeld, beald, *Sc.* beild), 6- build. *Pa. t.* 4 bildide, (bult), 4-5 bild(e, 5 buylde, byld, bylled, 5-6 bylded, -yd, buylded, (6 *Sc.* belt), 6- built, builded. *Pa. pple.*, 2 ȝebyld, 4 i-, y-buld, y-beld, bilde, bulde, bilt, (bilid), 5 bild, bylte, beldid, bildid, 6 bylded, bylt, (bylled, -yd), buylded, -yt, buylt, (i-bylt), (8 build), 6- built, builded. [ME. *bulden(ü), bylden, bilden*:—OE. **byldan* to build (recorded only in pa. pple. *ȝebyld*), f. *bold* a dwelling. Hence the two fundamental senses are 'to construct a dwelling' and 'to take up one's abode, dwell'. The normal modern spelling of the word would be *bild* (as it is actually pronounced); the origin of the spelling *bui-* (*buy-* in Caxton), and its retention to modern times, are difficult of explanation.

The OE. pple. *ȝebyld* might be from a compound *ȝebyldan*: but cf. the southern *bytlan* (*Gregory's Past. Care* 153, l. 9-10), later *bytlian* (see Bosw.-Toller), f. **buplo-* (whence *botl, bold*), which points to the antiquity of the vb. (Not to be confounded with OE. *byldan, ȝebyldan*, for *bieldan* to make bold: see BIELD.)]

I. To erect a building.

1. a. *trans. Orig.* To construct for a dwelling; to erect (a house), make (a nest). *Hence*, To erect, construct (any work of masonry), and by extension, To construct by fitting together of separate parts; chiefly with reference to structures of considerable size, as a ship or boat, a carriage, an organ, a steam-engine (not, e.g. a watch or a piano). Const. *of*, more rarely *from*, *out of*, *with* (the material), *on* (the foundation). In early mod. Eng. used with *up* without change of meaning; but *to build up* (in literal sense) now implies a contrast with pulling down, or with a previous state of decay, as 'to build up again'. *to build a fire*: to arrange or pile the fuel. *to build a railroad*, said in U.S., is unknown in England.

[*c* **1150** *The Grave* in Thorpe *Analecta* 142 Ðe wes bold ȝebyld er þu iboren were.] *c* **1205** LAY. 2656 He wolde bulden twa burh. **1297** R. GLOUC. 439 At Wyndelsore..þat noble stede ys, þat he let bulde hym sulf. *c* **1400** MAUNDEV. 98 [He] destroyed it [Jerico] and cursed it, and alle hem that bylled it aȝen. **1430** LYDG. *Story of Thebes* dj in *Dom. Archit.* III. 47 A porche bylte of square stons. **1480** CAXTON *Descr. Brit.* 13 He bylded Caunterbury. **1526** *Pilgr. Perf.* (W. de W. 1531) 138 b, Jerico, Hay, and Gabaon, whiche yᵉ pagans buylded. **1541** in Turner *Sel. Rec. Oxford* 164 Standyngs now made and buyldyd or hereafter to be made and buyld for the said fayre. **1562** J. HEYWOOD *Prov. & Epigr.* (1867) 168 Roome was not bylt on one day. **1601** CHESTER *Love's Mart.* cx. (1878) 27 At Mount Paladour he built his Tent. **1644** EVELYN *Mem.* (1857) I. 75 A castle builded on a very steep cliff. **1718** LADY M. W. MONTAGUE *Lett.* II. liii. 78 The houses are tolerably well built. **1794** S. WILLIAMS *Vermont* 138 When the Indian builded his house. **1861** FLOR. NIGHTINGALE *Nursing* 18 Your house must be so built as that the outer air shall find its way..to every corner of it.

b. *build up.*

c **1400** *Destr. Troy* 1535 Priam..byld vp a bygge towne of þe bare vrthe. **1490** CAXTON *Eneydos* lxv. 166 Af thys cyte ben many in doubte who buylde it vppe. **1611** BIBLE *2 Chron.* xxxii. 5 Hezekiah built up the wall that was broken. *Mod.* It is far easier to pull down than to build up.

c. *build a fire, gun, nest, organ, railroad, ship.*

1567 *Triall Treas.* (1850) 9 Synce Noe's ship Was made, and builded. **1606** SHAKS. *Ant. & Cl.* IV. xii. 4 Swallowes haue built in Cleopatra's Sailes their nests. **1651** *Proc. Parliament* No. 123. 1910 A Vessell..built at Swansey. **1789** G. WHITE *Selborne* xliii. (1853) 151 A pair of honey buzzards built them a nest. **1805** SOUTHEY *Madoc in Azt.* IV, Fires are built before the tents. **1852** SEIDEL *Organ* 21 In 1576, an organ with..a back-choir was built at Bernan. *a* **1856** LONGF. *Building Ship* 94 Thus, said he, we will build this ship! **1860** *All Y. Round* No. 73. 545 The taste of the day is for guns that are built, not cast. **1883** *Harper's Mag.* Nov. 939/1, 550 miles of railroad had been built. **1884** *Ibid.* June 127/2 He often built his own fire.

2. a. *absol.* To erect a building or buildings; 'to play the architect' (J.). Of birds or other animals: To construct nests, etc. (Possibly the earliest instances may belong rather to sense 8.)

c **1205** LAY. 29671 Al..bigunnen..to bulden bi þan watere. *c* **1340** *Gaw. & Gr. Knt.* 509 Bryddeȝ busken to bylde. **1382** WYCLIF *Esdra* iv. 2 Bilde wee vp with you. **1413** LYDG. *Pylgr. Sowle* v. xiv. (1483) 108 Yf thou..arte a maister werker, couthest thou bilde withouten mater. **1594** SHAKS. *Rich. III*, I. iii. 264 Our ayerie buildeth in the Cedars top. **1664** GERBIER *Counsel* 104 All Owners..whether they build or not. **1722** DE FOE *Plague* (1884) 294 The Ground was let out to build on. **1848** L. HUNT *Jar Honey* iii. 33 Building as if they were to live for ever. **1850** TENNYSON *In Mem.* cxv, The happy birds, that change their sky To build and brood.

b. With certain advbs., *build* forms virtual compounds founded on this sense, but used trans. with the notion 'to affect in such or such ways by building'. *to build up*: to obstruct (a doorway, window, etc.) by building. *to build in*: to immure, enclose by building; also, to construct or insert (something, esp. furniture) as an integral part of a larger unit; also *fig.*; chiefly as pa. pple. (see BUILT *ppl. a.* 1 b). *to build round*: to surround with buildings.

The advb. may either follow or precede the object.

1878 BROWNING *La Saisiaz* 6 Now built round by rock and boulder. *a* **1888** *Mod.* When we first came here, the situation was very open, but we are now completely built in. **1933** *Telegr. & Teleph. Jrnl.* XIX. 151/1 In New York telephones are 'built-in' and when you become a tenant..you 'phone as often as you like. **1956** A. H. COMPTON *Atomic Quest* 326 Better control of the amount of rubber that is built into tires. **1965** *Listener* 4 Nov. 687/1 The legacy of those years has been built in to the domestic and foreign policies of both countries.

3. *transf.* **a.** To construct by a process or with a result analogous to that of the builder. Said, e.g., of the Creator, or of natural forces, as when a crystal, an organic body, or the world, is compared to an edifice. Often said in passive of the human body, as 'His frame was strongly built' (cf. BUILD *sb.*). *Const.* as in 1. *built like a castle*: said of a horse having a strong and sturdy frame.

1598 SYLVESTER *Du Bartas* I. vi. (1641) 49/2 Beasts which thou This-Day didst build. **1699** BENTLEY *Phal.* 54 Built as it were to make a good Boxer. **1835** G. STEPHEN *Adv. Search of Horse* i, He [*sc.* a cob] was, to use the accepted phrase, 'built like a castle!' **1843** J. A. SMITH *Product. Farming* 137 Hence the reason why bodies can be nourished and built up upon food comparatively poor in nitrogen. **1860** TYNDALL *Glac.* I. §1. 2 An amethyst is a crystal built up from particles of silica. **1882** *Illustr. Sporting & Dram. News* 4 Feb. 502/1 Miss Bell's colt is built like a castle, and full of massive strength from head to heels. **1883** E. A. PARKYN *Syllabus Lect. Anim. & Pl. Life* 4 This power of building-up living from non-living matter is called Assimilation.

b. *trans.* and *intr. Tailoring.* To make (clothes).

1840 BARHAM *Ingol. Leg.* 22 [The trousers] were cleverly 'built', of a light-grey mixture. **1897** *Globe* 11 Mar. 3/4 A tailor would..have had his work cut out for him to build that..chubby creature a costume. **1897** G. DU MAURIER *Martian* iv. 183 Is it still Skinner who builds for you?

c. *to be built (that way*, etc.): to be (so) constituted or naturally disposed. *colloq.* (orig. *U.S.*).

1882 *Amer. Humorist* 12 May (Farmer), Even womankind is not built as she was a few brief years ago. **1888** *Missouri Republ.* 25 Jan. (Farmer), 'Why didn't you roll down?' 'I wasn't built that way.' **1912** A. BENNETT *Matador of Five Towns* 75 I'm not built the same way myself.

d. In card-playing: (see quot. 1901). Also *transf. U.S.*

1901 *Munsey's Mag.* XXIV. 871/2 To build down..is to place a card upon one of the next higher denomination. To build up..is to do just the opposite—that is, to place an eight on a seven. **1903** A. ADAMS *Log Cowboy* vi. 76, I built right up to him.

4. *fig.* **a.** With reference to immaterial objects: To construct, frame, raise, by gradual means (anything that is compared to an edifice, as a philosophical system, a literary work, a reputation, an empire). Often with *up*. In religious use, after N.T., *to build up* (the Church, an individual) = to EDIFY (also *absol.*). *to build up* (any one's health, strength, etc.): to establish it by gradual means.

c **1440** *Gesta Rom.* (1879) 86 All þat is ayens conscience, beldith toward helle. **1526** TINDALE *Acts* xx. 32, I commende you to God and to the worde of his grace which is able to bylde further [**1611** to build you vp]. **1526** *Pilgr. Perf.* (W. de W. 1531) 36 That..they may meryte and buylde to theyr crowne in heuen. **1589** PUTTENHAM *Eng. Poesie* II. xiii. (1811) 109 Meetres..builded with polysillables. *a* **1593** MARLOWE *Mass. at Paris* III. ii, Who will help to build religion? **1637** MILTON *Lycidas* 11 He knew Himself to sing, and build the lofty rhyme. **1646** SIR T. BROWNE *Pseud. Ep.* I. v. 18 Build our selves Men againe. **1726** WODROW *Corr.* (1843) III. 269, I rejoice that the Lord is building up your family. **1814** WORDSW. *Excurs.* IV. 1254 So build we up the Being that we are. **1842** TENNYSON *Godiva* 79 She..built herself an everlasting name. **1860** FARRAR *Orig. Lang.* i. 7 Building systems before they had collected facts. **1862** STANLEY *Jew. Ch.* (1877) I. iii. 52 His fortunes were built up. **1881** N. T. (Rev.) *2 Cor.* x. 8.

b. *to build up*: to establish or enhance the reputation or prominence of (a person, nation, etc.); to 'boost'. orig. *U.S.*

1935 S. LEWIS *It can't happen Here* ix. 86 Sarason had, as it was scientifically called, been 'building up' Senator Windrip for seven years before his nomination as President. **1939** *Ann. Reg. 1938* 262 The desire to 'build-up' the figure of the Leader (*El Caudillo*) in the approved Fascist style. **1944** A. JACOB *Traveller's War* xii. 212 Rommel had been 'built up' by the British press into a great figure. *Ibid.* 213 He set out to build himself up in the eyes of an army that had tasted defeat.

c. *to build up. trans.* and *intr.* Of an electric current, volume of sound, etc.: to increase.

1936 *Discovery* July 222/2 The sound builds up from silence to strength. *Ibid.* 223/1 The amplifier building up the sound they [*sc.* the oscillating valves] produce before it reaches the loud-speaker. **1949** *Chr. Sci. Monitor* 30 Apr. Mag. Sect. 2/4 Five relay stations..build up the signal.

d. *to build up. intr.*: to accumulate, collect; to grow.

1956 A. L. ROWSE *Early Churchills* ii. 22 Such was the spirit that was building up on either side in this deplorable war. **1962** *Which? Car Suppl.* Oct. 139/2 Some rust had built up behind the chrome strips on both front wings.

5. *lit.* and *fig.* To work up (material) *into* (a building); to join *together* so as to form a structure. Also with *up*.

1388 WYCLIF *Gen.* ii. 22 The Lord God bildide the rib..in to a womman. **1884** *Manchester Exam.* 18 Sept. 4/6 He collects the spoils of many sessions..like a skilful architect, builds them into a fair and seemly edifice.

6. *fig.* **a.** *trans.* To found (a statement, argument, hope, or confidence, etc.) *on* a basis.

1528 MORE *Dial. Heresyes* IV. Wks. 249/2 He taketh the same..for a ground therupon to byeld the distruccion of that holy sacrament of penaunce. **1658** *Whole Duty Man* Sund. x. § 1. 79, I shall..build all the particular duties..on those two general ones. **1689** LOCKE *Govt.* I. ix. 87 Sovereignty built on 'property'..comes to nothing. **1711** ADDISON *Spect.* No. 253 ¶4 The Fame that is built on Candour and Ingenuity. **1781** J. MOORE *View Soc. It.* (1790) I. vii. 70 The independence of Venice was not built on usurpation. **1837** J. H. NEWMAN *Par. Serm.* (ed. 3) I. vi. 90 A Christian's faith and obedience is built on all this.

b. *absol.* To found one's confidence, establish an argument, etc. *on*; to rely confidently *on* a person or thing (*obs.* or *arch.*).

1573 G. HARVEY *Letter-bk.* (1884) 27, I..tould him I wuld bilde uppon him. **1624** MASSINGER *Renegado* IV. iii, Heaven..will not suffer you to want a man To do that sacred office, build upon it. **1635** SWAN *Spec. M.* ii. § 3 (1643) 33, I find..little in Iosephus concerning this to build upon. **1674** tr. *Machiavelli's Prince* ix. (1883) 66 He that builds upon the people builds upon the sand. **1699** BENTLEY *Phal.* 238 One may build upon this piece of History, as a thing undeniable. **1741** RICHARDSON *Pamela* I. 144, I am deny'd..to go to Church, as I had built upon I might. **1799** *Med. & Phys. Jrnl.* II. 222 Whether or not that evidence is admissible to build upon. **1847** TENNYSON *Princ.* VII. 60 Not tho' he built upon the babe restored. **1876** E. MELLOR *Priesth.* vii. 323 The next passage upon which the Romanists and Ritualists build.

7. *quasi*-passive use of the pr. pple., as in *the house is building*, orig. *the house is a building*, where *building* was the vbl. sb., and *a* = *on*. See A *prep.*[1] 12, and BUILDING.

[**1535** COVERDALE *Ezra* v. 16 Sence that tyme hath it bene in buyldinge. *Ibid. John* ii. 20 Sixe and fourtye yeare was this temple abuyldinge. *a* **1665** J. GOODWIN *Filled w. the Spirit* (1867) 390 The wall that is a-building.] **1841** CATLIN *N. Amer. Ind.* (1844) II. xlvi. 95 A pretty little town, building up. **1860** *Merc. Mar. Mag.* VII. 300 The..lighthouse is stated to be building. **1862** THORNBURY *Turner* I. 199 Five drawings of the abbey, then building.

II. [See the etymology.]

†**8.** *intr.* To take up one's abode, to dwell. Also, To arise, form. *Obs.*

c **1340** *Gaw. & Gr. Knt.* 25 Of alle that here bult of Bretaygne kynges Ay watz Arthur þe hendest. *c* **1400** *Epiph.* (Turnb. 1843) 142 The holy goste will in the byldon. **1470** HARDING *Chron.* lxi. ii, Galerius had the este there into bylde [*v.r.* theryn hym to bylde]. **1599** GREENE *Alphons.* (1861) 241 A blister build upon that traitors tongue!

build (bɪld), *sb.* Also 4 bylde, bulde, 5 bild. [f. BUILD *v.*: cf. BUILT *sb.*]

†**1.** A building. *Obs.*

c **1325** *E.E. Allit. P.* A 726 On þe bylde. *Ibid.* 962 Bryng me to þat bygly bylde. **1387** TREVISA *Higden* Rolls Ser. II. 71 Buldes..in þe manere of Rome [*ædificia Romano more*]. **1394** *P. Pl. Crede* 157 Swich a bild bold, y-buld opon erþe heiȝte Say I nouȝt in certeine siþþe a longe tyme.

2. Building; style of construction, make: **a.** *lit.* of a ship, a carriage, etc. (rarely, if ever, of a house or other work of masonry).

1667 PEPYS *Diary* (1879) IV. 253 The difference in the build of ships now and heretofore. **1668** *Ibid.* 30 Oct., He finds most infinite fault with it [my coach]..and so I do resolve to have one of his build. **1842** DE QUINCEY *Philos. Herodotus* Wks. IX. 207 The awkwardness of their build for fast sailing.

b. *transf.* and *fig.*

1833-48 H. COLERIDGE *North. Worthies* (1852) I. 1 Andrew Marvell a patriot of the old Roman build. **1839-47** TODD *Cycl. Anat. & Phys.* III. 523/1 The build of the fibre is..of no importance. **1853** KANE *Grinnell Exp.* xxii. (1856) 175 In build he [a bear] was very solid. **1876** GREEN *Short Hist.* ii. § 3 (1882) 67 The peasant..recalls the build and features of the small English farmer.

buildable ('bɪldəb(ə)l), *a.* [f. BUILD *v.* + -ABLE.] Capable of being built (on).

1927 *Times Weekly Ed.* 10 Nov. 527/3 [A design] compact, orderly and simple—and eminently buildable. **1963** W. Holford in *Oxf. Univ. Gaz.* 23 May 1257/2 By adding a little more than a quarter of Merton Field..an extremely buildable site could be obtained. **1967** *Listener* 6 July 10/2 The megalomaniac diagrams of the late eighteenth-century French neo-classical architects were made buildable by pragmatic nineteenth-century English architects.

build-down (ˈbɪlddaʊn). *U.S. Mil.* Also unhyphened and as one word. [f. build *v.*, in contrast to build-up: cf. rundown, wind-down.] A systematic reduction of nuclear armaments, by destroying two or more for each new one deployed. Also *fig.*

1983 *N.Y. Times* 22 Mar. 25A/2 The reaction to the build-down concept has been gratifying. **1983** *Ibid.* 3 Oct. A1 This plan, referred to as a 'build down', was offered originally by Senators William S. Cohen..and Sam Nunn... Under their proposal, every time a new land-based warhead was deployed, two older ones would have to be destroyed. **1983** *Economist* 15 Oct. 48 *(heading)* Catholics and Lutherans: a theological build-down. **1984** *Miami Herald* 27 Mar. 12A/3 Hart..has backed the so-called 'build-down' plan, opposed by many nuclear freeze advocates, which would mothball two nuclear weapons for every one deployed. He abandoned this idea, however. **1985** *New Yorker* 18 Mar. 39/3 You can sit here with your finger on the pulse and say 'I like it'—and I really did like 'build-down'—and then it's gone.

builded, *ppl. a.* [f. build *v.* + -ed[1].] = built *ppl. a.* Now *poet.* or *arch.*

1563 Hyll *Art Garden.* (1593) 6 A builded inclosure. **1601** Chester *Love's Mart.* civ. (1878) 26 This famous builded Monument. **1827** Hood *Hero & L.* iii, A builded gloom shot up into the grey.

builder (ˈbɪldə(r)). [f. as prec. + -er[1].]

1. a. One who builds; the erector of a building. *spec.* One who 'builds' clothes; a tailor (see build *v.* 3b). Also *fig.*; see senses of build *v.*

As the name of a trade, *builder* now denotes the master artisan, who receives his instructions from the architect, and employs the masons, carpenters, etc., by whom the manual work is performed.

*c*1380 Wyclif *Serm.* clviii. Sel. Wks. II. 66 Þe stoon þat bilderis reproveden. **1382** Wyclif *Isa.* xlix. 17 Thi bilderes camen. *c*1420 *Pallad. on Husb.* i. 351 The bylder eke to knowe is necessarie What gravel and what lyme is profitable. **1571** Ascham *Scholem.* Pref. (Arb.) 21 As it chanceth to busie builders..the worke rose dailie higher and wider. **1596** Spenser *F.Q.* i. i. 8 The builder oake, sole king of forrests all. **1667** Milton *P.L.* iii. 466 The builders..of Babel on the Plain Of Sennaar. **1825** Hone *Every-day Bk.* I. 274 He was the..builder-up of his own greatness. **1827** Carlyle in *For. Rev. & Cont. Misc.* II. 121 Not a destroyer, but a builder up. **1845** *Ainsworth's Mag.* VIII. 214 In former days our builders of shooting jackets used to perch the buttons of the waist underneath our shoulder blades. **1851** Longf. *Gold. Leg.* 162 The builders of Cathedrals.

b. ***builder's paper***, a strong paper sheeting used in building. *U.S.*

1917 Mathewson *Sec. Base Sloan* vii. 88 Red builder's paper superseded the boards across the window frames.

c. ***builder-upper***, one who builds up (something or someone). (Cf. quots. 1825 and 1827, sense 1a above). *colloq.*

1936 *Esquire* Sept. 59/3 You, Mr. Sports Fan—it is you who plays the role of 'builder-upper' [of athletes' morale]. **1944** D. Wecter *When Johnny comes marching Home* iv. ii. 493 A strength 'that cannot be pooh-poohed even by the most agile tearer-downers nor cheapened by the most blatant builder-uppers'. **1945** L. Shelly *Hepcats Jive Talk Dict.* 22 *Builder upper*, publicity man. **1951** A. H. Cherry *Yankee R.N.* iii. 83 'Off reefers, up shirt-sleeves!' barked the Royal Navy's 'fitness and morale' builder-upper.

2. a. That part of a spinning-machine which regulates the yarn as it is wound on the bobbins.

1884 W. S. B. McLaren *Spinning* vii. 136 The lifter, or builder as it is called, moves more slowly as each layer is placed on the bobbin.

b. A substance added to soap or to a detergent to increase its efficiency.

1931 *Soap* Nov. 29/2 The various bases and salts showing alkaline reaction..are also called fillers in soap, builders, and detergents. **1958** *Spectator* 4 July 16/1 Cotton..cannot be washed so easily and it is necessary to use slightly alkaline 'builders' (sodium tripolyphosphate, etc.). **1963** A. J. Hall *Textile Sci.* vi. 284 Some soap-containing proprietary washing powders also contain mild alkalis and silicates and phosphates which are termed 'builders'.

building (ˈbɪldɪŋ), *vbl. sb.* Forms, see build *v.* [f. as prec. + -ing[1].]

1. a. The action of the verb build, *lit.* and *fig.* Freq. with *up* (also *attrib.*). †**b.** Style of construction, build (e.g. of a ship).

*c*1394 *P. Pl. Crede* 501 In beldinge of tombes þei trauaileþ. **1480** in *Bury Wills* (1850) 65 To be..applied..to the bildyng, sustentacion, and reparacion of the seid collage. **1590** Webbe *Trav.* (Arb.) 33 The houses are of a very olde building. **1604** Hieron *Wks.* I. 515 For the building vp of their soules in Christ Iesus. **1737** L. Clarke *Hist. Bible* viii. (1740) 551 In a Castle of his own Building. **1825** Hone *Every-day Book* I. 1527 This carriage..had been three years in building. **1852** Tupper *Proverb. Philos.* 37 Trifles..are levers in the building up of character. **1901** *Daily Chron.* 5 Dec. 3/4 The synthetic or building-up chemistry. **1942** W. S. Churchill *End of Beginning* (1943) 36 The steady building-up of very powerful forces and bases there.

2. That which is built; a structure, edifice: now a structure of the nature of a house built where it is to stand.

1297 R. Glouc. 271 And þer nas of olde house in þe lond non, þat he ne amendede mid som lond, oþer mid byldynge. *c*1340 *Cursor M.* 1774 Þe bildyngis fel boþe heȝe & lawe. *c*1430 *Syr Gener.* 244 This belding we made here Is for you. **1553** Eden *Treat. New Ind.* (Arb.) 14 It..hath in it very fayre byldinges. **1611** Bible *Eccles.* x. 18 By much slouthfulnesse the building decayeth. **1724** Watts *Logic* 110 A ship may be defined a large hollow building made to pass over the sea with sails. **1795** Southey *Joan of Arc* vii, Your holy buildings and your homes. **1854** Ruskin *Lect. Archit.* Add. 121 The essential thing in a building..is that it be strongly built, and fit for its uses.

†**3.** A company (of rooks), a rookery. *Obs.*

*c*1470 *Hors Shepe & G.* (1822) 30 A byldyn of rooks A clatering of chowhis. **1481** *Bk. St. Albans* f vi b, A beldyng of Rookes. [**1801** Strutt *Sports & Past.* i. ii. 33. **1883** *Standard* 26 Sept. 5/1 Every one with any pretence to be gentle-folk spoke of..a building of rooks.]

4. *Attrib.* and *Comb.*, as ***building-board***, ***building-estate***, ***-ground***, ***-land***, ***-lot***, ***-material***, ***-place***, ***-site***, ***-stone***, ***-trade***, ***-tree***; also **building-block**, (*a*) = block *sb.* 12b; also *fig.* and *attrib.*; (*b*) one of the temporary supports for a ship's keel while the ship is being built (Knight *Dict. Mech. a* 1877); **building-lease**, a lease of land on which the lessee may build; **building line**, a prescribed limit relative to the frontage beyond which a building must not extend; **building motion**, in *Cotton-spinning*, apparatus for winding and shaping uniformly the roving on the bobbins of a fly frame or the yarn of a cop on a mule; **building paper** orig. *U.S.*, a heavy paper used by builders as a covering or lining material; **building-rent** (see quot.); **building-slip**, a slip (see slip *sb.*[3] 1b) on which vessels are built; **building-society**, a society in which the members periodically contribute to a fund out of which money may be lent to any of their number for the purpose of building (or purchasing) a house (see also quot. 1965); **building-term**, the duration of a building-lease.

1846 *Boston Herald* 14 Oct. 3/1 Jewsharps, Games, *Building Blocks, Harmonicas. **1857** *Mich. Agric. Soc. Trans.* IX. 316 A dozen Patent Building Blocks. **1915** J. Webster *Dear Enemy* (1917) 152 Punch was occupying a rug..engaged with building-blocks. **1936** J. Kantor *Objective Psychol. Gram.* iii. 39 To such a building-block comparison of speech, psychological grammar is strongly opposed. **1949** *Rev. Eng. Studies* XXV. 369 *Four..pitch levels*..are the 'basic building blocks' of the tunes. **1962** F. I. Ordway et al. *Basic Astronautics* iv. 153 Some hope to learn from gravitational research more about the micro-structure of the building blocks of nature, the subatomic particle. **1969** *Times* 5 Feb. 13/7 The most successful symmetry scheme is the one in which the elusive particle, the quark, is the fundamental building block from which all the heavier particles are made. **1917** *U.S. Pat. 1,227,767* 29 May 1/2 *Building board is put in place on the outside of a house..or secured on the inside. **1959** M. S. Briggs *Conc. Encycl. Archit.* 61 *Building board*, a term covering a wide range of artificial products used internally in modern building. **1884** Sir J. C. Mathew *Law Reports 14 Queen's B. Div.* 758 The land is part of a *building estate. **1858** Ld. St. Leonards *Handy Bk. Prop. Law* vii. 48 Abutting upon *building-ground belonging to the seller. **1905** *Westm. Gaz.* 12 May 7/1 The L.C.C. purchased squares at *building-land price. **1858** Ld. St. Leonards *Handy Bk. Prop. Law* xvii. 114 Powers..to grant *building-leases. **1885** Ld. Watson 26 Feb. in *Law Rep. Appeal Cases* X. 246, I need not deal with the case of the *building line being more than fifty feet from the highway. **1891** *Laws of Missouri* 47 All cities in Missouri..may establish a building line to which all buildings and structures thereon shall conform. **1925** *Town Planning Rev.* June 185 At corners shops should be kept back to the full building line to both streets. **1971** *Reader's Digest Family Guide to Law* 98 [Planning consent is required] if the extension is beyond the original building line of the house. **1701** in *Conn. Col. Rec.* IV. 357 Pasture, *building lot, and long lott. **1881** W. O. Stoddard *E. Hardery* 15 The high prices of all building lots. **1835** C. F. Hoffman *Winter in West* I. 69 A species of yellow freestone..which, for elegance as a *building material, is not surpassed by marble itself. **1904** Goodchild & Tweney *Technol. & Sci. Dict.* 73/1 *Building motion. **1873** *Newton Kansan* 20 Feb. 3/4 *Building paper, the best substitute for plastering. **1955** G. Bowen *Wool Away!* x. 115 Building paper should be used under the iron above the shearing board. **1845** Darwin *Voy. Nat.* vii. (1870) 138 To prefer the tall trees..for its *building-place. **1776** A. Smith *W.N.* (1869) II. v. ii. 432 The *building rent is the interest or profit of the capital expended in building the house. **1848** Mill *Pol. Econ.* v. iii. §6 (1876) 501. **1871** Geo. Eliot *Middlemarch* i. iv. 52 They were driving home from an inspection of the new *building-site. **1966** D. Jenkins *Educated Society* ii. 50 Constructive forces..have no more attraction than building sites. **1846** Dodd *Brit. Manuf.* VI. 147 Every ship-yard has got one or more '*building-slips'. **1894** Building slip [see slip *sb.*[3] 1b]. **1848** H. C. Robinson *Diary* 31 Dec. (1967) 250 Miss Martineau..is now full of a prospect of forming here *building-societies for the benefit of the poor in imitation of the Birmingham societies. **1852** Geo. Eliot *Let.* 21 Oct. (1954) 62 There has been an intelligent gentleman visitor today who is interested in Miss Martineau's Building Society. **1862** Ld. St. Leonards *Vendors & Purch.* 377 The members of a building society, whose land was vested in trustees for them. **1965** J. L. Hanson *Dict. Econ.* 51/2 *Building societies*, institutions which accept deposits and then use their funds to lend on mortgage to people who wish to buy their own houses. **1790** *Pennsylv. Packet* 2 Jan. 4/4 Bourdeaux rough hewn *building stone. **1924** R. M. Ogden tr. *Koffka's Growth of Mind* v. 325 Building-stone of a peculiar shape. **1705** *Lond. Gaz.* No. 4158/4 They intend to Let to Farm a *Building Term in several Houses. **1607** Norden *Surv. Dial.* 210 The Oke, Elme and Ash..indeed are *building trees.

ˈ**building**, *ppl. a.* [f. as prec. + -ing[2].] That builds. Also in *comb.* as ***Babel-building***.

1727 De Foe *Syst. Magic* i. i. (1840) 12 That foolish Babel-building age. **1832** Tennyson *May Queen* 61 The building rook. **1843** Carlyle *Past & Pr.* (1858) 184 Building beavers.

†**buildress.** *Obs.* (or *nonce-wd.*) [f. builder + -ess.] A female builder.

1566 J. Sanford tr. *Agrippa's Van. Artes* 12b, Dido, the first buildresse of Carthage. **1650** Fuller *Pisgah* ii. ix. §8 Sherah..the greatest Buildress in the whole Bible. **1822** *Blackw. Mag.* XII. 657 Tragedianesses, sonneteeresses, or other 'buildresses of the lofty rhyme'.

build-up (ˈbɪldʌp). [f. build *v.* 4 and 5.]

a. An accumulation of favourable publicity designed to popularize a person, product, etc. Also, simply, preparatory work, preparation. Cf. build *v.* 4b. *colloq.* (orig. *U.S. slang*).

1927 *Collier's* 3 Dec. 10/4 That's the old build-up for the Patsys. **1935** *Time* 24 June 26 *One Night of Love* had a build-up unrivaled in cinema history. **1935** *Evening News* 29 June 3/2 The swindler's talk..arouses the interest and acquisitive instincts of the mug... The '*build-up*' has been made. **1936** Wodehouse *Laughing Gas* x. 103, I thought it might soften her a little if you gave the old boy a build-up. **1942** Berrey & Van den Bark *Amer. Thes. Slang* §241/1 Preparation,..build-up. *Ibid.* §489/1 *Build-up*, preparatory work for a crime. **1950** R. Chandler *Trouble is my Business* 228 The threats were a build-up for a killing. **1953** J. Pudney *Ring for Luck* 16 A big build-up for the indispensable Miss Motting, 'without whom nobody ticks in Fragos'. **1955** R. M. Lumiansky *Of Sondry Folk* viii. 85 The scene is to be understood as his careful preparation—the present-day term 'build-up' is apt here—for playing a joke on the Host. **1957** *Economist* 12 Oct. 120/2 Mr Howard gives more space for her early life—the perfect build-up for her subsequent adventures.

b. (Usu. gradual) accumulation, increase; spec. *Mil.* an accumulation of troops, weapons, etc. Also *attrib.*

1943 *Daily Tel.* 22 Apr. 1/2 The last four months' patient build up of Allied air power. **1944** *Times* 15 May 4/3 The build-up in the Eighth Army bridgehead across the River Rapido continued during the night. *Ibid.* 25 July 4/4 The build-up period lacks the excitement of the initial assaults. **1955** *Times* 14 July 4/7 The build-up of case law by the tribunal. **1958** I. Brown *Words in our Time* 29 There is now evidence of some spread in the population locally, but no evidence at present of any large build-up. **1964** *Ann. Reg. 1963* 150 On the basis of one of these reports, the Security Council noted with alarm the arms build-up in South Africa. **1969** *Times* 2 Jan. 16/1 Professor Semple's team detected a massive build-up of the bacteria in several kinds of food on the premises.

c. The gradual development or exposition of a theme, argument, work of art, etc.; artistic construction.

1942 Berrey & Van den Bark *Amer. Thes. Slang* §522/10 *Build-up*, initial plot development. **1953** A. Upfield *Murder must Wait* ix. 78 The build-up of the background against which five infants had been stolen. **1958** *Spectator* 8 Aug. 191/3 The slow build-up of *All My Sons*..is deliberate. **1959** H. Read *Concise Hist. Mod. Painting* vi. 193 The whole build-up, or orchestration, of form and colour is purposively expressive.

buile, obs. form of boil *sb.*[1]

†**built**, *sb. Obs.* [f. build *v.*; mode of formation uncertain; cf. *gilt*, f. *gild*; also build *sb.* and builth.]

1. Style of construction (of a ship, etc.), build.

*c*1615 Chapman *Odyss.* xi. 146 A sail Of foreign built. **1658** in *Hist. Glasgow* (1881) 243 Excelling the model and usual built of townhalls. **1666** Dryden *Ann. Mirab.* lx, And as the built, so different is the fight. **1764** Reid *Inquiry* vi. §20 The sailor sees the burthen, the built, and the distance of a ship at sea. **1794** W. Roberts *Looker-on* III. 408 Friendship and love require..a peculiar built of mind.

2. Action of building.

1654 G. Goddard in Burton *Diary* (1828) I. 88 *note*, A constant and continual built of ships.

built (bɪlt), *ppl. a.* [f. build *v.* q.v.]

1. a. Constructed, erected, etc.: see build *v.* Also with advbs., as ***built-over***, ***built-up***.

1570 Levins *Manip.* 130 Bilt, *aedificatus.* **1662** Gerbier *Princ.* 40 His built Banquetting House. **1851** Ruskin *Stones Ven.* I. viii. §11 The built and tower-like shaft. **1935** E. Bowen *House in Paris* ii. i. 88 A smoky built-over hill. **1954** L. MacNeice *Autumn Sequel* 131 The Roman slabs lay snug below In that built-over darkness.

b. built-in: (*a*) constructed to form an integral part of a larger unit, esp. of the fittings or appurtenances of a house; (*b*) *fig.* inherent, integral, innate.

1898 *Electrical Engin.* July 2 The first and simplest is the 'solid' or 'built-in' system, where wires, which are insulated thoroughly and thoroughly protected from mechanical disturbances, are buried in the ground. **1902** *Harper's Monthly Mag.* Jan. 302/2 A built-in refrigerator. **1929** M. Skipper *Meeting-Pool* 6 '*I* shall be waiting then,' murmured the Crocodile, snuggling his long face, with the built-in smile on it, into the warm sand. **1930** *Engineering* 7 Mar. 309/2 The employment of built-in and flange motors is also increasing. **1933** *Discovery* July 219/1 Bedrooms are small, adequate space for the storing of clothes, for a desk and so on, being found in built-in furniture. **1946** Koestler in *New Writing & Daylight* 82 Archetypes are..inherited, built-in patterns of instinct-conflicts. **1951** *Good Housek. Home Encycl.* 162/1 *Counter Unit* with..built-in storage

space underneath. **1962** *Listener* 26 July 131/1 The phrase 'built-in obsolescence'..was very fashionable, especially among cynics, about ten years ago.

Hence as *sb.*, a built-in piece of furniture, etc. Chiefly *N. Amer.*

1930 *San Antonio* (Texas) *Light* 31 Jan. 14/6 (Advt.), Houses for sale...large screened porch, cabinets, built-ins. **1963** *House & Garden* Feb. 7 (Advt.), A Moffat Built-In is a Moffat *plus*. **1970** *Globe & Mail* (Toronto) 28 Sept. 26/4 (Advt.), 3 large bedrooms, 3 washrooms, many built-ins.

c. built-up: (*a*) (see sense 1a above); (*b*) constructed of parts, esp. of parts that are separately prepared and afterwards joined or welded together; so ***built-up gun***, a gun whose parts are constructed separately and united in such a way that the elastic quality of the metal is fully utilized; (*c*) designating a locality where buildings abound, esp. in ***built-up area***. Also ***built-up butt***, a raised as distinguished from a sunken shooting-butt; ***built-up rope*** (see quot. 1908). Of a shoe: heightened.

1829 *Nat. Philos.* I. *Optics* iii. 12 (Usef. Knowl. Ser.) Dr. Brewster has contrived a built-up lens. **1853** C. BRONTE *Villette* I. x. 188 This demi-convent, secluded in the built-up core of a capital. **1865** P. BARRY *Shoeburyness & the Guns* vi. 86 The built-up system demands the same care..as the Krupp blocks. **1886** *Harper's Mag.* Oct. 786/2 The means of providing against this successive rupture of overstrained parts is found in the 'built-up gun'. **1887** *Cassell's Fam. Mag.* 509/1 A Built-up File. **1904** *Westm. Gaz.* 26 Aug. 3/1 A built-up butt. **1908** *Animal Managem.* (War Office) 143 The 'built-up' [picketing] rope, a portion of which is carried by each man. **1935** *Ann. Reg. 1934* II. 71 The recently passed Road Traffic Act..was extended shortly afterwards to all 'built-up' areas throughout the country. **1937** *Sunday Times* 10 Jan., The perils of built-up by-passes. **1946** E. JOHNSTON *Writing* xv. 255 Built-up letters are composed of compound strokes. **1950** A. L. ROWSE *England of Eliz.* v. 162 The actual built-up area grew in extent in Elizabeth's reign. **1969** T. PARKER *Twisting Lane* 19, I have to wear this special built-up shoe.

d. The simple *built* is used in the same sense as 1c (*b*) above.

1860 *All Y. Round* No. 73. 549 The Armstrong gun..is a built gun. *a* **1877** KNIGHT *Dict. Mech.*, *Built-beam*, a compound beam made up of a number of planks, or thin, deep beams, laid parallel and secured together. *Ibid.*, *Built-rib*, an arched beam made of parallel plank laid edgewise and bolted together. **1908** *Westm. Gaz.* 14 Nov. 19/2 The built all-in-one frock of lace net. **1909** *Ibid.* 20 Mar. 8/3 Three-bladed propellers of the 'built' type.

2. In comb., as ***well-built***, ***strongly built***, said of a house, body, etc.; often of a ship, denoting the style, material, or place of construction, as ***frigate-built***, ***wooden-built***, ***Clyde-built***.

1583 STANYHURST *Æneis* I. (Arb.) 17 A long buylt citty theare stood, Carthago so named. **1621** FLETCHER *Wildgoose Ch.*, They are ill-built..And weak i' the pasterns. **1663** *Act 15 Chas. II*, vii. §6 English built shipping. **1706** *Lond. Gaz.* No. 4209/4 A well-built bay Stallion. *Ibid.* No. 4691/4 A high built Gold Watch and Case. **1769** FALCONER *Dict. Marine* (1789) H 4 A ship is said to be frigate-built, galley-built. **1860** *Merc. Mar. Mag.* VII. 245 She is wooden built. **1871** M. COLLINS *Mrq. & Merch.* I. iv. 139 Several well-built girls aspired to fill the situation.

†**builth.** *Obs. rare.* [f. BUILD *v.* after *tilth*, *spilth*.] The act of building, or its cost.

1805 W. TAYLOR in *Ann. Rev.* III. 263 The builth, wear, and tear of all this needless shipping.

buine, var. of BUNE. *Obs.*

buir, buird, Sc. f. *bore* (BEAR *v.*) and BOARD.

buirdly ('bødlı), *a. Sc.* Also prob. **bierdly, bierly, beerly, boordly.** [prob. a modern perversion of the earlier Sc. *buirly*, goodly, stout, BURLY. Less prob. repr. OE. *ȝebyredlíc* suitable, seemly, meet, f. *ȝebyrian*, ONorthumb. *byra* to be pertinent, become, be becoming, with sense 'comely'.

In the latter case, the mod.Sc. *ui* would have to be explained as altered from earlier *i, ie*, which is perhaps unparalleled. (Mod.Sc. *ui*, (ø, y) normally represents OE. *ō*, ME. *ō̆*, or Fr. *u*). If = *buirly*, BURLY, we may suppose *buirdly* to be due to the ordinary popular association of the word with *buird*, BOARD, which is further seen in the anglicized form BOARDLY used by modern Scottish writers. *Bierly, bierdly* are then regular n.e. dial. forms of *buirly, buirdly*.]

'Large and well-made' (Jam.); stately; stalwart; sturdy, stout, burly.

1300–1600 See *borli, burely, buyrlie, buirlie*, under BURLY. *a* **1783** *Lady Jane* xix. in Child *Ballads* III. No. 62 (1885) 75/2 Rise up, rise up, my bierly bride. **1786** BURNS *Twa Dogs* 85 Buirdly chiels, an' clever hizzies. *a* **1800** in R. Jamieson *Pop. Ballads* (1806) II. 133 (JAM.) Out and spake the bierdly bride. **1807** R. TANNAHILL *Poems* (1846) 60 Full-grown boordly chiels like you. **1815** SCOTT *Guy M.* liii, Twelve buirdly sons and daughters.

buirlie, obs. f. BURLY.

buirn(e, variant of BERNE, *Obs.*, a warrior.

buisson ('bwi:sɔ̃). *Hort.* [Fr.] (See quots.)

1832 J. LINDLEY *Introd. Bot.* I. ii. 48 If a shrub is low, and very much branched, it is often called *dumosus*..: this kind of shrub is what the French understand by their word *buisson*. **1852** G. W. JOHNSON *Cottage Gardeners' Dict.* 159/2 Buisson, is a fruit tree on a very low stem, and with a head closely pruned. **1951** *Dict. Gardening* (R. Hort. Soc.) I. 327/2 Buisson, name given at one time to a dwarf fruit tree on a low stem, closely pruned annually.

buist, *sb.*[1] *Obs.* exc. *Sc.* Also 4 **buiste**, 5 **buyste**. [a variant of BUST(E, BOIST, box, etc.; the phonetic history is obscure.] A box, a casket = BOIST[1]; a chest.

1393 GOWER *Conf.* II. 247 To open a buist she him badde. *Ibid.* III. 292 A strong poison..Within a buist. **1451** *Act Jas. II* (1597) §33 Quhill the Wardane haue..put it [the money] in his buist. **1483** *Cath. Angl.* 49 Buyste [*v.r.* Bust], *alabastrum*. **1801** R. GILL *Tint Quey* in Chambers *Hum. Sc. Poems* 173 And frae the willow buist did scatter A tate o' meal upo' the water [*note*, Willow buist, a rustic basket, in which meal is usually held].

buist (bøst), *sb.*[2] *Sc.* Also **bust, boost.** [perhaps from BUIST *sb.*[1]: Jamieson has '*tar-buist*, the box in which the *tar* is kept with which sheep are marked'.] A mark of ownership made with tar or paint upon sheep or cattle; also *fig.*

1802 SIBBALD *Scott. Poetry* Gloss., *Bust, Boost*, tar mark upon sheep, commonly the initials of the proprietor's name. **1807** RUICKBIE *Way-side Cott.* 112 (JAM.) I'll..catch them in a net or girn Till I find out the boost or birn. **1820** SCOTT *Monast.* xxiv, He is not of the brotherhood of Saint Mary's—at least he has not the buist of these black cattle.

†**buist**, *v.*[1] *Sc. Obs.* [f. BUIST *sb.*[1]] To put in a box, or as in a box; to box, shut *up*.

c **1600** MONTGOMERIE *Sonnet R. Hudsone*, This barme and blaidry buists up all my bees.

buist, *v.*[2] *Sc. dial.* [f. BUIST *sb.*[2].]

trans. 'To mark cattle or sheep with the proprietor's distinctive mark' (Jam.). Hence ***buisting-iron***, ***-mark***.

1829 HOGG *Sheph. Cal.* I. 39 Adamson..with the buisting-iron which he held in his hand struck a dog. **1853** JOHNSTON *Nat. Hist. E. Bord.* I. 94 The sheep around recall it by their 'beesting' mark. **1864** JEFFREY *Hist. Roxburghsh.* IV. viii. 261 Tar for buisting sheep.

buisy obs. form of BUSY.

buit, buith, obs. Sc. forms of BOOTH, BOOT.

buiting, Sc. variant of BOOTING *vbl. sb.*, plunder.

1572 *Act Jas. VI.* (1597) §50 Taking and deteining of prisoners, ransounes, buitinges, raysing of taxes.

buk(e, obs. ff. BOOK, BOUK, BUCK.

†**bukenade.** *Obs.* 'A dish in ancient cookery, receipts for which are given in MS. Sloane 1201 f. 22; *Form of Cury*, 17, 107, 109' (Halliwell).

a **1425** *Anc. Cookery* in *Househ. Ord.* (1790) 429 Bukenade to Potage.

bukeram, buket(t, obs. f. BUCKRAM, BUCKET.

bukh, bukk, varr. BUCK *sb.*[11], *v.*[10]

Bukhara, see BOKHARA.

Bukharinism (bu:'kɑ:rınız(ə)m). [f. the name of N. I. *Bukharin* (1888–1938), a Russian leader and editor + -ISM.] The political principles of Bukharin. So **Bu'kharinist** *a.* and *sb.*

1937 *Times* 1 Oct. 15/6 Responsible Communist officials who are held up for public abuse as Trotskyists, Bukharinists,..and enemies of the people. **1949** I. DEUTSCHER *Stalin* ix. 384 Conspiratorial activities of the Trotskyist and Bukharinist leaders. *Ibid.* xi. 486 The evils of Trotskyism, Bukharinism, and other deviations.

bukk-, see BUCK-.

†'**bukkam.** *Obs. rare*[−1]. [Cf. Du. *bokking* red herring.] See quot.

1800 A. CARLYLE *Autobiog.* iv. (1860) 167 [We] supped on bukkam (Dutch red-herrings) and eggs.

bukler, bukram, obs. f. BUCKLER, BUCKRAM.

buksheesh, -shish, variants of BAKSHEESH *sb.*

‖**bukshi, bukshee** ('bʌkʃi:). Also 7–8 **buxy**, 8 **buxie, buxey, (bakshi, backshee)**, 9 **bucktshy, buckshee.** [a. Pers. (& Urdú) *bakhshī*, giver, paymaster, f. *bakhshīdan* to give: cf. BAKSHEESH *sb.* (But see Col. Yule's *Hobson-Jobson*.)] A high official in native Indian states, properly the Paymaster-General of the army, who often acted also as Commander-in-chief; in intercourse with the natives 'the word is still in the Anglo-Indian Army the recognised designation of a *Paymaster*' (Yule).

1615 SIR T. ROE in *Purchas* I. 541 (Y.) Hee..gave present order to the Buxy, to draw a Firma. **1753** HANWAY *Trav.* (1762) II. XIV. iii. 350 *note*, The paymaster general of the empire, whom they call bukshi. **1756** *Lett. to Court Directors* 3 (Y.) Strictly adhering to his duty during the Buxy-ship of Messrs. Bellamy and Kempe..The abuses of the post of buxy. **1763** ORME *Hist. Indostan* I. 26 (Y.) The buxey or general of the army, at the head of a select body, closed the procession. **1789** BURKE *Sp. W. Hastings* Wks. XIV. 252 A present..had been offered to him by Cheyt Sing's buxey. **1804** WELLINGTON *Let.* in Gurw. *Disp.* III. 133 The importance of his situation of buckshee of the Rajahs troops. **1858** BEVERIDGE *Hist. India* I. III. x. 572 In his capacity of buckshee or paymaster-general. **1861** MCMULLEN *Mem. on Dhar.* (Y.) Several of the witnesses..amongst these the Bukshi.

†**bul.** *Obs.* Also **bule, bull.** [app. a. OF. *boul, boule, bole* 'fraude, tromperie, astuce' (Godef.): cf. BULL *v.*[3]] ? Falsehood.

a **1300** *Cursor M.* 21270, I sal you tel, wit-vten bul [*v.r.* bule]. *Ibid.* 26371 Sais crist to ypocrites..yee ar..al ful wit wickednes, tresun, and bull.

'**bulam.** *Pathol.* 'Name given by the natives on the African coast to yellow fever' (Mayne); *attrib.*, as ***bulam fever***. Hence **bulamize** ('bju:ləmaız), *v.* (*nonce-wd.*), to affect with yellow fever.

1832 *Blackw. Mag.* XXXI. 790 [The traveller] gets a *coup de soleil*: finds his liver *Bulamized*.

bulas, bulaster, obs. f. BULLACE, BULLESTER.

bulb (bʌlb), *sb.* Also 7 **bulbe.** [ad. Lat. *bulb-us* a Gr. βολβός onion, bulbous root.]

†**1.** An onion. *Obs.*

1568 TURNER *Herbal* II. 62 The roote w[t]in is whyte rounde and knoppy after the lyknes of a bulb. **1578** LYTE *Dodoens* V. lxxvii. 644 Lyke an Onyon or Bulbe. **1601** HOLLAND *Pliny* II. 329 Asses milke warme, or sodden together with bulbe roots. *a* **1712** KING *Orpheus & E.* (Misc.) 394 Iesuit Bulbs ty'd up with Ropes.

2. *Bot.* **a.** The underground spheroidal portion of the stem of an onion, lily, or other plant of analogous mode of growth; formerly, and still in popular language, regarded as a kind of 'root', but by modern botanists defined either as 'a subterranean bud..sending off roots from below and a stem above', or as 'a very short stem, producing roots below, and leaves in the form of scales above'. Sometimes popularly applied to a solid tuber of similar external shape.

1664 EVELYN *Sylva* (1679) Advt., Bulbs, round or onion-shap'd roots. **1712** tr. *Pomet's Hist. Drugs* I. 100 Chuse such Roots or Bulbs, as are sound. **1794** MARTYN *Rousseau's Bot* i. 24 The roots are bulbs of some sort or other. **1858** CARPENTER *Veg. Phys.* §119 Bulbs..are in reality underground stems in the state of buds. **1884** BOWER & SCOTT *De Bary's Phaner. & Ferns* 142 There lies..on the outer side of the..scales of the bulb, one prismatic crystal.

b. An axillary leaf-bud of bulbous form which detaches itself from the stem, becoming an independent plant, a bulbil.

1845 LINDLEY *Sch. Bot.* x. (1858) 162 When they [leaf-buds] disarticulate from the stem..they are called bulbs. **1862** HUXLEY *Lect. Wrkg. Men* 84 A little bulb or portion of the plant drops off, detaches itself and becomes capable of growing as a separate thing.

3. *transf. Anat.* A roundish dilatation of any cylindrical organ or structure in an animal body, e.g. ***central bulb***, 'the bulbous extremity of a nerve-fibril in a corpuscle of Krause'; ***olfactory bulb***, the anterior oval termination of the olfactory tract; ***auditory bulb***, the membranous labyrinth and the cochlea together; ***bulb of the hair***, the soft enlargement of the root end of the hair; ***bulb of spinal marrow***, the medulla oblongata.

1715 *Phil. Trans.* XXIX. 327 The Bulb of the Pulmonary Vein..was extraordinarily dilated. **1758** J. S. *Le Dran's Obs. Surg.* (1771) 261 The End of the Bulb of the Urethra. **1813** J. THOMSON *Lect. Inflam.* 614 The small bulbs which surround the roots of the hair. **1870** ROLLESTON *Anim. Life* Introd. 46 The olfactory bulbs are absent.

4. a. A bulb-like dilatation of a glass tube. Also (rarely) a lump of metal of bulbous shape. In full (***electric***) ***light bulb***; the glass bulb-shaped container of the incandescent filament used for producing electric light.

1800 VINCE *Hydrostat.* x. (1806) 95 A glass tube with a bulb at the bottom. **1831** BREWSTER *Optics* x. 89 The bulb of the thermometer. **1833** J. HOLLAND *Manuf. Metals* II. 302 The metal bulb, which is moved along the graduated line of the lever, to ascertain the weight. **1856** *Enquire within on Ev.* (1862) 278 Glass water bulbs..are sold by men in the London streets at one penny each. **1856** *National Rev.* July 88 The ray of the electric bulb, so sharply defined that all beyond its pencil falls into depth of darkness. **1882** *Electric Light* 1 Sept. 70/1 Volatilized carbon being deposited on the inside of the bulb. **1884** *Daily News* 3 Sept. 3/1 The bower is illuminated by two Edison incandescent electric light bulbs. **1890** J. W. URQUHART *Electric Light Fitting* 170 It becomes a question whether it is economical to run such blackened bulbs longer after a certain percentage of light has been so cut off. **1964** NAIPAUL *Area of Darkness* v. 110 A large bulb..was attached to a stunted flexible arm..: this was the lamp.

b. ***bulb of percussion***, the convex protuberance on the fractured surface of a flint.

1872 J. EVANS *Anc. Stone Impl.* xii. 247 Where a splinter of flint is struck off by a blow, there will be a bulb or projection, of a more or less conical form, at the end where the blow was administered... This projection is usually known as the 'bulb of percussion'. **1923** *Discovery* Dec. 316/2 Even the bulb of percussion which arises when a flint is broken by a violent blow, owing to the elasticity of its substance, can be produced by [natural] forces.

c. A pneumatic rubber bulb-shaped device on syringes, camera-mechanisms, etc.

1885 *Army & Navy Co-op. Soc. Price List* 874 The bulb can be disconnected, and fitted to any of the pipes as an Injection Bottle. **1911** *Encycl. Brit.* XXI. 514/2 J. Cadett's system of pneumatic pressure, applied by means of a compressible rubber bulb and tube, which may drive a piston acting on the lever holding the shutter. **1966** *McGraw-Hill Encycl. Sci. & Technol.* II. 431/2 Arrangements are made for keeping the shutter open for

long times if needed (bulb and time or B and T). **1968** *Listener* 19 Dec. 811/3 He took from his pocket..a small glass instrument with a rubber bulb at the end. With this bulb he sucked some of the whisky into the tube.

5. *Comb.*, as ***bulb-like*** adj.; also **bulb-fin, bulb-keel**, a keel of a yacht having a cigar-shaped attachment which in section presents a bulb-like appearance; also *ellipt.* a yacht having such an attachment; **bulb-iron, angle-iron** (*Mech.*), a bulbed iron or angle-iron used to strengthen joints or angles in the framework of ships; **bulb-scales** (see quot.); **bulb-tube**, a tube terminating in a bulb.

1894 E. R. SULLIVAN et al. *Yachting* I. 91 She was very deficient in stability when the lead slab forming the keel was recast in the form of a bulb on the bottom of the plate, the completed design simply forming one of our modern *bulb fin keels. **1895** *Outing* (U.S.) Sept. 481/1 The great bulb-fins *Jubilee* and *Pilgrim*. **1869** SIR E. REED *Ship Build.* i. 10 To introduce separate straps for the *bulb-irons. *Ibid.* viii. 138 A bulb angle-iron has been used for the deck beam. **1893** *bulb keel [see FIN *sb.*[1] 6]. **1927** R. A. FREEMAN *Certain Dr. Thorndyke* I. ix. 136 Spoon-bows and bulb keels were things as yet undreamed of. **1836-9** TODD *Cycl. Anat. & Phys.* II. 962/1 A soft *bulb-like extremity. **1882** VINES *Sachs' Bot.* 714 The *bulb-scales of the Tulip. **1839-47** TODD *Cycl. Anat. & Phys.* III. 818/2 The contents of the *bulb-tube are emptied into a small evaporating dish.

bulb (bʌlb), *v.* [f. prec.] *intr.* **a.** To swell into a bulb-like or rounded form. **b.** To form a bulb-shaped root.

1681 COTTON *Wond. Peak* (ed. 4) 11 Bulbing out in figure of a sphere. **1846** HANNAM in *Jrnl. R. Agric. Soc.* VII. II. 589 The turnips did not bulb well. **1886** *Dagonet the Jester* ii. 73 How sweetly bulbeth out the figure of Psyche as she looks into the lamp.

bul'baceous, *a.* [f. L. *bulbāceus*, f. *bulbus*: see -ACEOUS.] = BULBOUS; producing bulbs.

1731 BAILEY II, *Bulbaceous*, full of little round heads in the root.

bulbar ('bʌlbə(r)), *a.* [f. BULB *sb.* + -AR[1].] Of or pertaining to a bulb; *esp.* to the bulb of the spinal cord.

1878 A. HAMILTON *Nerv. Dis.* 339 Bulbar Paralysis is one of middle age, and attacks men more often than women.

bulbed (bʌlbd), *ppl. a.* [f. BULB *sb.* or *v.* + -ED.] **a.** Bulb-shaped. **b.** Having a bulb or bulbs.

1597 GERARD *Herbal* I. lxxiii. 102 These bulbed Flur de luces. **1611** COTGR., *Bulbe*..a bulbed, or onion, root..the bulbed roots of all Daffodils. **1836-9** TODD *Cycl. Anat. & Phys.* II. 961/2 They exhibit no bulbed extremity. **1854** J. SCOFFERN in *Orr's Circ. Sc.* Chem. 111 The aperture..is fitted up with a bulbed glass and stem. **1858** W. ELLIS *Visits Madagasc.* xvi. 436 A large bulbed plant.

bulbel, var. of BULBIL.

†**bulberie.** *Obs. rare.* (See quot.)

a **1450** *Alphita* (Anecd. Oxon.) 22 Berberies sunt fructus cuiusdam arboris, *angl.* bulberies uel berberies.

bulberry ('bʊlbərɪ). *U.S.* Also **bulberry, bull berry.** [? f. BULL *sb.*[1]] The buffalo-berry. Also *attrib.*

1841 T. J. FARNHAM *Trav. West. Prairies* 121 A fruit called bullberry. **1880** *Libr. Univ. Knowl.* (N.Y.) X. 159 Bulberries, which resemble red currants, grow by the rivers [in Montana]. **1888** ROOSEVELT in *Century Mag.* XXXVI. 45/2 A great patch of bulberry bushes. **1946** E. B. THOMPSON *Amer. Daughter* 190, I..went bullberry-picking down in the sharp ravines.

bulbiferous (bʌl'bɪfərəs), *a.* [ad. mod.L. *bulbifer*, f. *bulb-us* BULB *sb.* + *-fer*, see -FEROUS.] Bulb-bearing; producing bulbs.

1807 G. GREGORY *Dict. Arts* I. 251/3 Cauline [bulbs]..in some species of onion..called bulbiferous..produced at the origin of the umbel of flowers. **1816** KIRBY & SP. *Entomol.* (1843) I. 227 The bulbiferous egg that produced it. **1861** MISS PRATT *Flower. Pl.* V. 268 Bulbiferous Great Round-Garlic. **1870** HOOKER *Stud. Flora* 382 Head globose usually bulbiferous.

bulbiform ('bʌlbɪfɔːm), *a.* [ad. mod.L. *bulbiform-is*, see BULB *sb.* and -FORM.] Bulb-shaped.

1847-9 TODD *Cycl. Anat. & Phys.* IV. 449/1 The blood-vessels..form a rete around the bulbiform cæca. **1884** *Athenæum* 20 Sept. 376/2 The comet, losing the bulbiform figure, assumed the appearance usual with these bodies.

bulbil ('bʌlbɪl). Also **bulbel.** [ad. mod.L. *bulbillus* dim. of *bulb-us*.] **a.** A small bulb formed at the side of an old one. **b.** A small solid or scaly bud, which detaches itself from the stem, becoming an independent plant.

1831 MACGILLIVRAY tr. *Richard's Bot.* 110. **1848** FORBES *Brit. Medusae* 86 The buds..are thrown off like the bulbels of certain plants. **1863** OLIVER *Less. Bot.* (1873) 138 The axillary bulbels of Bulbiferous Toothcress. **1884** J. E. TAYLOR *Sagacity & Mor. Plants* 190 Whenever excess of food-materials have been elaborated we get bulbils (or buds from the bulbs).

†**'bulbine.** *Obs.* Also 6 **bulbyne.** [L. *bulbinē*, Gr. βολβίνη.] A bulbous plant mentioned by Pliny; applied by Turner to *Gagea lutea.*

1548 TURNER *Names of Herbes* (1881) 21 Bulbine called in Duche hundes vllich maye be called in englishe dogges Leike. **1568** —— *Herbal* I. G v a, Of bulbine or wylde leeke. **1601** HOLLAND *Pliny* II. 52 An herb which the Greekes call bulbine, with a red bulbous root. **1611** COTGR., *Oignon sauvage*, Bulbine, wild Bulbus, Corne Leeke.

†**'bulbitate.** *Obs. rare*—⁰. [ad. L. *bulbitare* (Festus), f. Gr. βόλβιτον cow-dung.] 'To befilth one's breech.'

1623 in COCKERAM.

bulbless ('bʌlblɪs), *a.* [f. BULB *sb.* + -LESS.] Without a bulb or bulbous root.

1883 G. ALLEN *Col. Clout's Gard.* vii. 43 It is a bulbless annual.

bulblet ('bʌlblɪt). [f. BULB *sb.* + -LET.] **a.** = BULBIL b.

1842 GRAY *Struct. Bot.* iii. §3 (1880) 63 Bulblets are small aerial buds..which arise in the axils of the leaves of several plants. **1870** BENTLEY *Bot.* 111 Called Aerial bulbs..or from their small size, bulbils or bulblets.

b. = BULBIL a.

1890 in WEBSTER. **1904** *Daily Chron.* 7 Oct. 8/1 By-and-by little bulblets begin to form—sometimes as many as thirty.. growing from the one source. **1933** *Jrnl. R. Hort. Soc.* LVIII. 16 Clusters of bulblets formed round the base of the parent bulb.

'bulbo-, comb. form (used also in mod.L.) of L. *bulbus*, BULB, forming principally adjs. used in physiology; sometimes *spec.* of the bulb of the urethra, as in ***bulbo-cavernous, -membranous, -rectal***, pertaining to the bulb of the urethra and to the 'cavernous bodies', the membrane, the rectum; sometimes as in ***bulbo-medullary, -urethral***, etc., pertaining to the bulb of the spinal marrow, of the urethra, etc.; also **bulbo-tuber** = CORM.

1836-9 TODD *Cycl. Anat. & Phys.* II. 836/1 The perineal artery..gives..a branch to the *bulbo-cavernous. **1881** *Nature* XXV. 72 The grey substance of the *bulbo-medullary nerve-centres. **1836** TODD *Cycl. Anat. & Phys.* I. 179/2 The *bulbo-rectal hollow, will now become distinct. **1836** *Penny Cycl.* V. 252/1 **Bulbotuber*, a short, roundish, underground stem resembling a bulb. **1880** GRAY *Bot. Text-bk.* 400 Bulbo-tuber: Synonym of Corm. **1839-48** TODD *Cycl. Anat. & Phys.* III. 928/2 This nerve (the *bulbo-urethral of Cruveilhier).

bulbonach, var. of BOLBANAC. *Obs.*

bulbose (bʌl'bəʊs), *a.* [ad. L. *bulbōs-us*, f. *bulbus*.] = BULBOUS. Also comb. ***bulbose-rooted.***

1747 CATESBY in *Phil. Trans.* XLIV. 602 Bulbose Roots. —— *Ibid.* This bulbose-rooted Plant.

bulbosity (bʌl'bɒsɪtɪ). [f. BULBOUS *a.*: see -ITY, -OSITY.] The condition or quality of being bulbous or bulb-shaped.

1901 'G. DOUGLAS' *House with Green Shutters* 209 He had ..a body of such bulging bulbosity, that all the droppings of his spoon..were caught on his..waistcoat. **1963** G. F. KANTOROWICZ et al. *Inlays, Crowns & Bridges* ix. 107 Other areas..present bulbosity.

bulbous ('bʌlbəs), *a.* Also 6-7 **bulbus.** [f. L. *bulb-us* BULB *sb.* + -OUS, cf. F. *bulbeux.*]

1. Of, pertaining to, or of the nature of, a bulb.

1578 LYTE *Dodoens* liv. 215 The roote is white and bulbus. —— 216 White bulbus violet. **1616** SURFL. & MARKH. *Country Farm* 210 A bulbous and whitish root, of a sharpe tast. **1719** LONDON & WISE *Compl. Gard.* IX. 298 The Bulbous Roots of Flowers must now be put into the Earth again. **1807** J. E. SMITH *Phys. Bot.* 113 Fleshy roots, whether of a tuberous or bulbous nature, must..powerfully resist drought.

2. Having bulbous or bulb-like roots.

1578 LYTE *Dodoens* II. xl. 198 *Bulbosa Iris*..We may call it Bulbus Ireos in English. **1610** FOLKINGHAM *Art of Survey* I. viii. 18 The little white bulbous Crow-toes. **1861** MISS PRATT *Flower. Pl.* III. 91 It has several rustic names as Glory-less, Bulbous Fumitory. **1879** WALLACE *Australas.* iii. 43 Lovely bulbous plants.

3. Bulb-shaped; swollen.

1783 T. HUTCHINS in *Phil. Trans.* LXXIII. 320 As much quicksilver..as..just filled the bulbous part of the cylinder. **1807** SOUTHEY *Espriella's Lett.* (1814) II. 203 A..fellow, with a bottle belly and a bulbous nose. **1809** W. IRVING *Knickerb.* (1861) 50 The worthy in question was a burly, bulbous man. **1836** TODD *Cycl. Anat. & Phys.* I. 635/2 The cilia were bulbous at the root. **1866** *Cornh. Mag.* Dec. 760 The bulbous minarets of Garben's new Kursaal.

†**4.** In concentric layers, like coats of an onion.

1677 PLOT *Oxfordsh.* 55 The Earth is here..I think I may say of a bulbous nature, several folds of divers colours.

5. *Comb.*, as ***bulbous-rooted***; also **bulbous-headed; bulbous-shoed** (*humorous*).

1860 HAWTHORNE *Marb. Faun* (1878) II. xxiv. 269 He looked at each..*bulbous-headed monster. **1611** COTGR., *Satyrion*..*Bulbous-rooted..hearbs. **1807** J. E. SMITH *Phys. Bot.* 41 Bulbous-rooted grasses. **1852** DICKENS *Bleak Ho.* I. i. 16 Blue-nosed, *bulbous-shoed old benchers.

bulbul ('bʊlbʊl). [a. (through Pers.) Arab. *bulbul.*]

1. A bird: a species of the genus *Pycnonotus*, belonging to the Thrush family, much admired in the East for its song; hence sometimes called the 'nightingale' of the East.

1784 SIR W. JONES in *Memoirs* II. 37 (Y.) We..cease to wonder that the Bulbul, with a thousand tales, makes such a figure in Persian poetry. **1797** *Gentl. Mag.* LXVII. II. 947 The fighting Bulbul, a kind of nightingale, said to be enamoured of the rose. **1830** TENNYSON *Recoll. Arab. Nts.* 70 The living airs of middle night Died round the bulbul as he sung. **1871** DARWIN *Desc. Man* I. II. xiii, The Bulbuls (*Pycnonotus hæmorrhous*) which fight with great spirit. **1878** C. R. CONDER *Tent Wk. Pal.* II. 136 Among these thickets ..the bulbuls, and hopping thrushes, were the only living things visible.

2. *transf.* A sweet singer; also *attrib.*

1848 THACKERAY *Van. Fair* lxii, You must belong to the Bulbul faction. **1865** *Lond. Rev.* 30 Dec. 685/2 The Irish bulbul [T. Moore] records..how his oriental songs opened the west-end drawing-rooms.

bulbule ('bʌlbjuːl). [ad. L. *bulbulus*, dim. of *bulbus* BULB.] A little bulb.

1836-61 HENSLOW in WEBSTER.

bulbus obs. f. of BULBOUS.

bulby ('bʌlbɪ), *a.* [f. BULB *sb.* + -Y[1].] Characterised by bulbs.

1880 *Scribner's Mag.* Feb. 507 Bulby stalks of golden-rod.

†**'bulcard.** *dial.* A local name (Cornwall, etc.) of the smooth Blenny (*Pholis lævis*).

1674 RAY *Fishes* 101 The Bulcard. **1753** CHAMBERS *Cycl. Supp.*, *Bulcard*..a small sea-fish caught among the rocks on the Cornish and other shores.

†**bulch**, *sb.*[1] *Obs.* [prob. a variant of BULGE: perh. influenced by BUNCH, BOTCH.] A hump or swelling. Cf. BULGE *sb.*[2]

c **1300** *Body & Soul* in *Map's Poems* (Wright) 34 They were ragged, roue, and tayled, with brode bulches [*c* **1325** bunches] on here bak. **1600** DARRELL *True Narr.* 11 A foul ugly man with a white beard and a great Bulch on his brest. **1634** BRERETON *Trav.* (1844) I, Dromedaries are ugly creatures, bulches behind and before. **1747** HOOSON *Miner's Dict.* M ij, Ore, growing out on Knobs and Bulches.

†**bulch**, *sb.*[2] *Obs. rare*—¹. = BULCHIN. A term of endearment.

c **1622** FORD *Witch Edm.* v. i, So that my bulch Shew but his swarth cheek to me, let earth cleave..I care not.

†**bulch**, *v. Obs.* [prob. a variant of BULGE *v.* See BULCH *sb.*[1], also BOUGE *v.*, BILGE *v.*]

1. *trans.* To stave in (a ship); = BULGE *v.* 1.

1583 STANYHURST *Æneis* I. (Arb.) 21 Wher Ilionus was shipt..And what vessel Abas possest..Were bulcht by billows. **1586** J. HOOKER *Girald. Irel.* in *Holinshed* II. 94/2 He might..bulch the..ships if they durst anerre the coast.

2. *intr.* To swell out; BULGE *v.* 3.

1611 COTGR., *Piece poictreuse*, a peece of coyne that rises, bulches, or beares out in the middle.

†**bulchin.** *Obs.* or *dial.* Also 4 **bulchyn**, 6-8 **bulching.** [Variant of BULKIN; cf. BULCH *sb.*[2]]

1. A bull-calf.

1330 R. BRUNNE *Chron.* 174 For ten mark men sold a litille bulchyn. **1573** TUSSER *Husb.* xxxiii. (1878) 74 Lamb, bulchin, and pig, geld vnder the big. **1637** HEYWOOD *Jup. & Io* Wks. 1874 VI. 272 Wouldst thou not haue some Bulchin from the herd? **1727** BRADLEY *Fam. Dict.* I, *Bulching*, a word used in some Counties for a Calf.

2. Used as a term of contempt or reproach.

1617 MIDDLETON & ROWLEY *Fair Quarr.* IV. iv, The bulchins will use the Irish captain with respect. **1638** FORD *Fancies* III. iii, Roguery, brokage and roguery, or call me bulchin.

3. Used as a term of endearment.

1633 SHIRLEY *Gamester* IV. i, How is't, Bulchins? Would you had been with us. **1690** B. E. *Dict. Cant. Crew*, *Bulchim*, a Chubbingly Boy or Lad. **1725** *New Cant. Dict.*

bulck(e, bulcking, obs. f. BULK, BULKIN.

buld(e, obs. f. BUILD *v.* and *sb.*

bulderston(e, obs. form of BOULDER-STONE.

bule, obs. form of BOIL *sb.*, tumour, swelling; BUL, *Obs.*, falsehood; BULL *sb.*[1]

bule, dial. var. of, BULLE, BOUL.

Bulgar ('bʌlgɑː(r)), *sb.* [ad. med.L. *Bulgarus* (F. *Bulgare*, G. *Bulgar*), ad. OBulg. *Blŭgarinŭ* (Bulg. *Bălgarin*, Russ. *Bolgáry̆* pl., *Bolgárin* sing.).] Any member of an ancient Finnish tribe who conquered the Slavs of Mœsia in the seventh century A.D. and settled what is now Bulgaria, becoming Slavonic in language; a native or inhabitant of Bulgaria. Also *attrib.* or as *adj.*, Bulgarian.

1759 *Mod. Part Universal Hist.* IV. IV. i. 498 Bulgars. **1886** *Encycl. Brit.* XXI. 78/2 The Bulgars, whose origin still remains doubtful. **1902** *Ibid.* XXX. 395/1 The Bulgar *millet* comprises the Bulgarians who accept the rule of the exarchate. **1920** *Q. Rev.* Jan. 63 Basil II, whom the Greeks of to-day still admire as the 'Bulgar-slayer'. **1921** S. GRAHAM *Europe—Whither Bound?* 27 The Bulgars have certainly hit on a novelty. *Ibid.* 33 Refugee Bulgars from the lost Bulgar territories. **1965** H. M. SMYSER in Bessinger & Creed *Medieval & Linguistic Stud.* 93 The Bulgars and.. the so-called Jewish Khazars, about whom Ibn Faḍlān learned from his Bulgar hosts.

Hence **'Bulgarize** *v. trans.*, to make Bulgarian in character; so **,Bulgari'zation.**

1869 TOZER *Highl. Turkey* I. 183 They become denationalized and Bulgarized. *Ibid.*, The Bulgarians are endeavouring the ecclesiastical superiority over them, and.. will bring about their Bulgarisation. **1903** *Daily Chron.* 9 Nov., The Bulgarisation of race-divided Macedonia. **1925** *Glasgow Herald* 2 Oct. 5 Fully Bulgarised Macedonians.

bulgar, var. BULGUR.

Bulgarian (bʌl'gɛərɪən), *a.* and *sb.* [f. med.L. *Bulgaria*, f. *Bulgarus*: see prec. and -IAN.] **A.** *adj.* Of or pertaining to the ancient Bulgars or to Bulgaria, a country in the Balkans. **B.** *sb.* **a.** Any member of the Bulgarian people; a native of Bulgaria; a Bulgar. **b.** The language of Bulgaria. ***Old Bulgarian***: the oldest extant form of the Slavonic group of languages, also called Old Slavonic, Church Slavic or Slavonic (G. *kirchslavisch*).

1555 R. EDEN tr. *P. Martyr's Decades* f. 289ᵛ The Slauon tounge..vsed of..the Mysians, Seruians, Bulgarians. **1797** *Encycl. Brit.* III. 769/1 The Bulgarians anciently inhabited the plains of Sarmatia that extended along the banks of the Volga. *Ibid.*, Bulgarian Language, the same with the Sclavonic. **1861** *Chambers's Encycl.* II. 418/2 The Bulgarian Language is divided into two dialects—Old Bulgarian and New Bulgarian; the former, the richest and best of the Slavonic dialects. **1869** TOZER *Highl. Turkey* I. 182 Even the priest, a Bulgarian, did not know a word of Greek. *Ibid.* 199 Children are taught to read and write both Greek and Bulgarian. **1959** J. CHAPIN tr. *Giovannetti's We Have a Pope* ii. 33 He delivered part of his Christmas sermon in Bulgarian. **1964** P. F. ANSON *Bishops at Large* x. 469 Brother Michael, Bulgarian-born superior of the White Brotherhood.

So **Bulgaric** (bʌl'gærɪk), *a.*, of or pertaining to the ancient Bulgars or their modern representatives; *sb.*, the language of the ancient Bulgars. **'Bulgaro-**, comb. form of BULGAR, *Bulgaria*, or BULGARIAN, as in *Bulgaro-Wallachian* adj., **Bulgarophil(e, -philism, -phobe**.

1880 *Encycl. Brit.* XI. 119/1 The Bulgaro-Wallachian kingdom. **1888** *Ibid.* XXIV. 269/2 The Bulgaro-Vlach Empire. **1917** *Observer* 15 Apr. 4/2 The war of 1912 made us Bulgarophil; the war of today makes us—with much better reason—Bulgarophobe. **1921** *Glasgow Herald* 30 Dec. 6 His passionate Bulgarophilism. **1931** *Times Lit. Suppl.* 19 Mar. 218/3 Bulgarophil, pro-Turk or Serbophil. **1949** I. DEUTSCHER *Stalin* vii. 243 An aristocratic revolutionary Bulgaro-Rumanian family.

bulge (bʌldʒ), *sb.* Also 7 bouldge, buldge. [ME. *bulge*, a. OF. *boulge* (also *bouge*), or ad. L. *bulga* leathern knapsack, bag, of Gaulish origin. Sense 2, in which there is a variant BULCH, may have been influenced by BOTCH *sb.*[1], BOUCH *sb.*; sense 3 seems to be a recent formation from the verb. Sense 4 = BILGE, still belongs to the Fr. *bouge*, but the history of its introduction into English is not known.]

†**1.** A wallet or bag, *esp.* one made of hide; a skin-bottle, a pouch, a purse; = BOUGE *sb.*[1] 1. *Obs.*

c **1230** *Hali Meid.* 35 þe bitte þat beoreð forð as a water bulge. **1623** FAVINE *Theat. Hon.* III. xiii. 523 The Crownes Reuennues..wherewith she would fill her owne Bouldges.

†**2.** A hump. Cf. BULCH, BOTCH, BOUCH. *Obs.*

c **1400** *Ywaine & Gaw.* 260 A ful grete bulge opon his bak.

3. a. A bulging, an irregularly rounded protuberance.

1741 MONRO *Anatomy* 131 A large Tuberosity, or Bulge of the Bone appears. **1856** KANE *Arct. Exp.* xxix. 396 They have the characteristic bulge of the carbonate-of-lime stalactite. **1861** WRIGHT *Ess. Archæol.* I. iv. 50 A bulge in the wall. **1879** LE CONTE *Elem. Geol.* 240 A mountain-chain consists of a great plateau or bulge of the earth's surface.

b. *fig.* Usu. with *the*: the advantage or upper hand; the superior position; esp. in phr. ***to have the bulge on***: to have the advantage over. *slang* (orig. *U.S.*).

1841 *Spirit of Times* 18 Dec. 498/3 Kate got the bulge on her at the start. **1872** 'MARK TWAIN' *Innoc. at Home* in *Roughing It* (1873) xlvii. 332 Well, you've ruther got the bulge on me. Or maybe we've both got the bulge, somehow. **1899** E. W. HORNUNG *Amat. Cracksman* 197 We had the bulge before; he has it now. **1963** WODEHOUSE *Stiff Upper Lip, Jeeves* xv. 120 The Assyrians had the bulge on him.

c. A slight swell made on the surface by a fish moving through water as it feeds on flies, etc.

1878 C. HALLOCK *Hallock's Amer. Club List* p. ii, *Bulge*, the swirl made by a salmon rising to the surface. **1889** F. M. HALFORD *Dry-fly Fishing* vi. 122 [The angler] knows only too well that the apparent rises are bulges. **1892** *Field* 16 July 104/2 The rises, splashes, and bulges of burly brown fish.

d. A rise in prices or shares. *U.S. colloq.*

1890 BIFF HALL *Turnover Club* 208 There is quite a bulge on June cocktails, and I fear a corner. **1908** G. H. LORIMER *J. Spurlock* xi. 272 The city house which the Bonsalls had occupied just before the big bulge in Southern Pacific landed them on top.

e. *Mil.* A bulging part of a military front; a salient.

1927 W. S. CHURCHILL *World Crisis 1916–18* II. xviii. 433 The German line formed a salient or bulge fifteen kilometers deep and sixty-four wide in the original British positions. **1942** *Daily Tel.* 28 Jan., The Russian officers I met around the Smolensk bulge.

f. *colloq.* A temporary increase in volume or numbers; *spec.* the increased number of children of school age resulting from the rise in the birth-rate at the end of the 1914–18 and 1939–45 wars. Also *attrib.*

1930 *Times Educ. Suppl.* 26 Apr. 186/2 Accommodation would have to be provided which would not be required when the 'bulge' years had passed. **1933** *Planning* I. XIII. 9 The impending flood of excess juvenile labour (the post-war bulge). **1935** *Economist* 23 Feb. 426/2 A temporary phenomenon, which corrected a 'bulge' in the curve without affecting its main upward trend. **1956** *Times* 2 June 7/7 The school population 'bulge' is moving up toward the 11–15 ages.

4. a. The bottom of a ship's hull. (Now generally superseded by BILGE.)

1622 R. HAWKINS *Voy. S. Sea* (1847) 135 Shippes have beene put in danger..by a hole made in the bulge. **1689** *Lond. Gaz.* No. 2168/4 The *Turkey Merchant* was..driven ashore, where she stav'd in her Buldge. *c* **1850** *Rudim. Navig.* (Weale) 101 *Bulge* or *Bilge*, that part of the ship which she bears on most when not afloat.

b. A protuberance on the hull of a ship to increase stability or to protect against under-water attack (cf. BLISTER *sb.* 2 c).

1919 *Chambers's Jrnl.* Aug. 543/1 Immunity from the evil effects of torpedoes and mines is sought by the provision of a swelling, commonly called a 'bulge' or a 'blister', below the water-line on each side. **1920** *Glasgow Herald* 10 Sept. 8 The modified 'bulge' for the protection against under-water attack.

5. bulge-water, -ways. = BILGE-WATER, -WAYS.

1735 DESAGULIERS in *Phil. Trans.* XXXIX. 48 The Stench and foul Air from the Surface of the Bulge-Water. **1777** W. WRIGHT *ibid.* LXVII. 508 By some called the bulge-water tree. *c* **1850** *Rudim. Navig.* (Weale) 116 The heel..is cleated on the bulgeways.

bulge (bʌldʒ), *v.* Also 6 boulge. [f. BULGE *sb.*; see the variants BILGE, BOUGE, BULCH *vbs.*]

I. † **1. a.** *trans.* To stave in the bottom of a ship, cause her to spring a leak; = BILGE *v.* 1. *Obs.*

1563–87 FOXE *A. & M.* 281/1 In which fight..were three of the Genowaies ships both boulged and soonke. **1686** W. DE BRITAINE *Hum. Prud.* §9. 46 Labouring to buoy up a sunk Ship of anothers, [he] bulged his own Vessel. **1782** in Nicolas *Disp. Nelson* (1846) VII, Add. iv, Fearing, from the great swell..it [the wreck] might bulge the ship. **1821** BYRON *To Murray* 7 Feb., Falconer's *ship* was bulged upon them.

b. *transf.*

1827 HONE *Every-day bk.* II. 1341 It was not a fair fall, as only one shoulder had bulged the ground.

†**2. a.** *refl.* and *intr.* Of a ship: To suffer fracture in the bilge; to strike (*on* or *against*) so as to damage the bilge. *Obs.*

1581 J. BELL *Haddon's Answ. Osor.* 452 b, So doe they also in the same shyppe bulge themselves most of all. **1595** SIR A. PRESTON in *Hakluyt's Voy.* III. 579 The rest bulged themselves. **1611** BEAUM. & FL. *Scornf. Lady* III. i, Forc'd by a tyrant storm, our beaten bark Bulg'd under us. **1695** LUTTRELL *Brief Rel.* (1857) III. 508 The Henry..bulg'd upon a rock, and lost all her cargo. **1774** GOLDSM. *Hist. Greece* I. 275 Their vessels..bulged furiously one against the other. **1796–7** COLERIDGE *Poems* (1862) 13 It bulged on a rock, and the waves rushed in fast. **1807** ROBINSON *Archæol. Græca* IV. xviii. 403 The ship received no damage by bulging against rocks.

b. *transf.*

1677 HALE *Prim. Orig. Man.* 348 If..Planetary Bodies should bulge and fall foul one upon the other.

II. Connected with BULGE *sb.* 2, 3, protuberance.

3. a. *intr.* To form a protuberance, to swell out; *esp.* in an irregular, clumsy, or faulty manner; e.g. as a wall of which the surface projects beyond the top and bottom.

1677 MOXON *Mech. Exerc.* (L.), The side of a wall..that bulges from its bottom or foundation, is said to batter. **1703** MAUNDRELL *Journ. Jerus.* (1721) Add. 10 The thin crust of Salt upon the surface bulged up. **1787** G. WHITE *Selborne* ii. 6 An oak..bulged out into a large excrescence about the middle of the stem. **1833** I. TAYLOR *Fanat.* vi. 165 If the dyke of despotism had not bulged and gaped. **1868** LOCKYER *Heavens* (ed. 3) 211 The globe of Mars..bulges, like our Earth, at the equator.

b. Of a fish: to make a bulge (see prec. 3 c). Hence **'bulger, 'bulging** *vbl. sb.* and *ppl. a.*

1889 F. M. HALFORD *Dry-fly Fishing* vi. 116 A fish taking caddis, shrimp, or snails is said to be tailing, from its tail appearing at intervals above water,..when feeding on larvæ or nymphæ it is described as bulging, from its motion through the water. *Ibid.* 123 A bulging fish is feeding and looking out for food. *Ibid.* 124 At times trout bulge at shrimp, snail, and caddis. **1889** *Sat. Rev.* 18 May 612/2 Mr. Halford..mentions a short way with bulgers, which he condemns as unsportsmanlike. **1892** *Field* 4 June 838/2 The fish were smutting or bulging on the shallows. **1904** *Westm. Gaz.* 13 Dec. 4/2 The question of herrings 'bulging', as it is called.

4. *trans.* To make protuberant.

1865 SIR J. HERSCHEL in *Intell. Observ.* No. 46. 248 By bulging them upwards. **1866** *Morning Star* 22 July A purse bulged with Austrian florin notes.

5. *intr.* To rush *in*, make a rush *for*. Also *trans.* (causative). To cause to rush *off*. *U.S. colloq.*

1834 CROCKETT *Narr. Life* xiv. 96 My dogs..bulged in, and in an instant the bear followed them out. *Ibid.* xvi. 105 As soon as we struck, I bulged for my hatchway. *a* **1867** H. WOODRUFF *Trotting Horse Amer.* (1868) xxii. 207 Brooks and Harry Jones bulged them [*sc.* the horses] off in the lead at such a rate I was forced to let them take the pole on the turn. **1884** 'MARK TWAIN' *Huck. Finn* 372 Here comes a couple of the hounds bulging in from under Jim's bed.

bulged (bʌldʒd), *ppl. a.* Also 5 bolgit. [f. BULGE *v.* + -ED[1].]

1. Forced into a protuberance; swollen.

1436 *Pol. Poems* (1859) II. 155 They com..With bolgit schipis ful craftly. **1821** CLARE *Vill. Minstr.* I. 213 The crack'd wall, bulg'd and bow'd. **1872** RUSKIN *Eagle's N.* §86 The wood-carvers..adopted this bulged form.

†**2.** Of a ship: With the bottom or sides stove in.

1618 BOLTON *Florus* (1636) 315 The huge Armada, bulged, and split in the fight. **1730–6** BAILEY, *Bulged* [spoken of a ship] when she has struck off some of her Timber upon a Rock. **1790** BEATSON *Nav. & Mil. Mem.* I. 276 As she was bulged he could not bring her off.

bulger ('bʌldʒə(r)). [f. BULGE *v.* + -ER[1].] **1.** (See quot. 1872.) *U.S. slang.*

1835 CROCKETT *Tour* 37 We.. soon came in sight of the great city of New York, and a bulger of a place it is. **1872** SCHELE DE VERE *Americanisms* 587 *Bulger*,..in the United States generally designates anything very large. 'That's a bulger of a story.'

2. *Golf.* A wooden club with a convex face. (Disused.)

1889 *Sat. Rev.* 25 May 622/2 In golf there is little to note beyond the apparition of the Bulger. This club is the invention of a fresh and scientific mind. **1890** W. PARK, Jun. in *Golf* 17 Oct. 70/1, I know for a fact, which I can prove, that I invented the bulger..; and I am undoubtedly entitled to the honour of producing the first bulger cleek [*read* club]. **1907** *Westm. Gaz.* 15 Feb. 4/2 The 'bulger'..that club with the round face which was designed as an aid to straightness of hitting, but has now..been quite discarded.

3. (See BULGE *v.* 3 b.)

† **'bulget.** *Sc. Obs.* [a. OF. *boulgette*. Cf. BUDGET *sb.*] A pouch.

c **1550** BALFOUR *Practicks* (1754) 235 (JAM.) Ane pair of bulgettis, ane barrow. **1562** in Keith *Hist.* 217 (JAM.) Coffenis, bulzettis, fardellis.

bulghur, var. BULGUR.

bulgily ('bʌldʒɪlɪ), *adv.* [f. BULGY *a.* + -LY[2].] In a bulgy manner.

1891 V. C. COTES *Two Girls on Barge* 156 Settling down bulgily, much as the robins do before they go to sleep.

bulginess ('bʌldʒɪnɪs). [f. BULGY + -NESS.] The quality of being bulgy.

1883 *Sat. Rev.* LV. 497 [Umbrellas] rolled up tight and not brought into use and bulginess.

bulging ('bʌldʒɪŋ), *vbl. sb.* [f. BULGE *v.*]

†**1.** The staving in of the bottom or sides of a ship. *Obs.*

1611 COTGR., *Enfoncement*, a sinking, a bulging. **1648** HERRICK *Hesper.* I. 31 Nor wrack or bulging thou hast cause to feare. **1755** MAGENS *Insurances* II. 17 When a Ship..is in danger of bulging.

2. A becoming protuberant, swelling out.

1753 HOGARTH *Anal. Beauty* ix. 49 By their bulging too much in their curvature. **1847–9** TODD *Cycl. Anat. & Phys.* IV. 246/1 The appearance of bulging presented by the distended capsule. **1882** VINES *Sachs' Bot.* 393 Ramification takes place by the bulging out of lateral cells.

3. *concr.* A protuberance; a swelling.

1831 R. KNOX *Cloquet's Anat.* 425 This bulging is named the Additamentum pedum Hippocampi. **1854** WOODWARD *Mollusca* (1856) 152 Animal with..eyes on bulgings at the outer bases of the tentacles.

'bulging, *ppl. a.* [f. BULGE *v.* + -ING[2].] That bulges or swells out; bending outward, projecting, protuberant, swelling; baggy.

1812 WOODHOUSE *Astron.* x. 80 The bulging equatorial parts of the terrestrial spheroid. **1851** KINGSLEY *Yeast* iii. 45 He was dressed in a..fustian jacket..with bulging, greasy pockets. **1859** R. BURTON *Centr. Afr.* in *Jrnl. R.G.S.* XXIX. 101 Irregular bulging lines of rolling hill.

bulgingly ('bʌldʒɪŋlɪ), *adv.* [f. BULGING *ppl. a.* + -LY[2].] In a bulging manner; *fig.*, prominently.

1896 *Daily News* 25 Feb. 4/7 They only offend persons in whom the moral sense is so bulgingly hypertrophied as to prompt them to yell 'Plagiarist!'

‖ **bulgur** ('bʊlgə(r)). Also **bulgar, bulghur.** [Turk.] A cereal food consisting of whole wheat partially boiled and then dried and crushed. Also *attrib.* Cf. BURGOO.

Principally eaten as a staple element of diet in Turkey and neighbouring regions, but also available commercially in the West.

1934 in WEBSTER. **1961** *Economist* 23 Dec. 1220/2 'Survival biscuits' made of bulgar, a specially treated wheatmeal. **1967** V. MEHTA *Portrait of India* 349 Volunteers staffed soup kitchens dispensing rations of three ounces of bulgur or crushed wheat, per person every three days. **1977** *New Yorker* 27 June 59/1 On these he set shelves for their pinto beans and bulgur. **1980** E. & W. ESKO *Macrobiotic Cooking for Everyone* 107 Bulghur is a form of whole wheat that is partially boiled and then dried. **1982** L. CHAMBERLAIN *Food & Cooking of Russia* (1983) 15 Armenian cooking..provided ways of cooking bulghur wheat.

bulgy ('bʌldʒɪ), *a.* [f. BULGE *sb.* + -Y[1].] Swollen, clumsily or unduly protuberant.

1848 DICKENS *Dombey* 290 A man with bulgy legs. **1859** SALA *Tw. round Clock* (1861) 61 Third-class umbrellas are dubious in colour..bulgy in the body. **1879** BROWNING *Martin Relph* 74 The bulgy nose and the blood-shot eyes.

bulimarexia (bjuːlɪmə'rɛksɪə, bʊ-, -ˌliː-). *Med.* (chiefly *U.S.*). [f. BULIM(IA + A(NO)REXIA.] = *bulimia nervosa* s.v. BULIMY 1.

1976 M. BOSKIND-LOHDAHL in *Signs* Winter 355 Since anorexia nervosa and bulimarexia are appearing with greater frequency, I can only hope that..women suffering from these syndromes can avail themselves of a humane therapy. **1977** *Psychol. Today* Mar. 50 The distinguishing feature of bulimarexia is its *regular* binges, its orgies of eating followed

by ritual purification. **1978** *Jrnl. Amer. College Health Assoc.* Oct. 84 (*heading*) The definition and treatment of bulimarexia in college women. **1984** M. B. & W. C. White (*title*) Bulimarexia: the binge/purge cycle. **1985** *Anorexic Aid Mag.* June 8 They have treated more than 2,000 women suffering from Bulimarexia.

Hence **bulima'rexic** *sb.* and *a.* = BULIMIC *a.* 2 and *sb.*

1976 M. Boskind-Lohdahl in *Signs* Winter 343 Relating anorexia to bulimia, it may also help to stimulate successful therapies for young women whom I shall describe as 'bulimarexics'. **1977** *Psychol. Today* Mar. 50/2 Many of the bulimarexic women who joined our therapy group expressed immense relief at finding other women with the same awful secret. **1982** *Jrnl. Psychosomatic Res.* XXVI. 403 (*heading*) Bulimia nervosa: sex role attitude, sex role behavior, and sex role related locus of control in bulimarexic women. **1985** *Anorexic Aid Mag.* June 8 For me and possibly the same type of Bulimarexic, this book was like 'coming home'.

‖**bu'limia**, mod.L. form of BULIMY, q.v.

bulimic (bjuːˈlɪmɪk), *a.* and *sb.* [f. prec. + -IC.]

A. *adj.* **1.** Symptomatic of bulimy; voracious.

2. *spec.* Suffering from or characteristic of bulimia nervosa.

1977 *Behavior Therapy* VIII. 258 None of the patients in the studies cited were bulimic anorexics. **1981** *Canad. Jrnl. Psychiatry* XXVI. 229/1 The very powerful oral drive which manifests itself so clearly during the bulimic phase. **1983** *Oxf. Textbk. Med.* I. VIII. 54 It is uncertain why the bulimic patient should crave for food and suffer bouts of overeating.

B. *sb.* One who suffers from bulimia nervosa.

1980 *Washington Post* 1 Aug. c5 Bulimics may not exhibit the outward signs of starvation that are the hallmark of the anorexic. **1982** *Woman's Own* 28 Aug. 22/1 The risk of suicide among bulimics is high. **1984** *Daily Tel.* 18 May 19/5 Both anorectics and bulimics are often unhappy in their predicament in which everything in life is subjected to the twin obsessions with food and shape. **1985** *Listener* 28 Feb. 20/2 In the main, group 'contacts' are recovered anorectics/bulimics, who thus understand only too well the feelings of despair and isolation.

So **bu'limious** (bjuːˈlɪmɪəs), *a.* [*see* -OUS], having a voracious appetite.

1854 Badham *Halieut.* 130 The bulimic propensities of the callionymus. **1885** F. Hall in *N.Y. Nation* 4 June 466 The bulimious Doctor [Johnson] would not have transacted his feeding so porcinely and perspiringly.

bulimong, variant of BULLIMONG.

‖**Bulimus** (bjuːˈlaɪməs). Pl. bulimi. [mod.Lat., a. Gr. βουλῖμός, occurring only as a sb. (see BULIMY), but perh. regarded as an adj. with sense 'having a voracious appetite'.] The scientific name of a genus of terrestrial gasteropods. Hence **bulimiform** (bjuːˈlɪmɪfɔːm), *a.*

1830 Lyell *Princ. Geol.* I. 384 Terrestrial shells, chiefly helices and spiral bulimi. **1854** Woodward *Mollusca* II. 165 *Achatina Variegata*..shell imperforate, bulimiform. **1866** Tate *Brit. Mollusks* iv. 164 The animal is bulimus-like.

bulimy (ˈbjuːlɪmɪ). Forms: 7 **boulimie**, 7–8 **boulimy**, (8 **boulomee**, 9 **bullimy**), 7– **bulimy**. See also etymology. [ad. Gr. βουλῑμία, f. βου- intensive prefix (properly combining form of βοῦς ox) + λῑμός hunger; sometimes adopted as *boulimia*. The synonymous Gr. βουλῖμός was adopted in med.L. in the incorrect form *bolismus*, whence OF. *bolisme*, both used by Trevisa; and in 17th c. appears as *boulime* and as *boulimos*. The mod.Lat. form *bulimia* is now generally used in medical works, though *bulimus* also occurs.]

1. *Med.* 'A morbid hunger, chiefly occurring in idiots and maniacs..the so-called canine hunger' (*Syd. Soc. Lex.*). *spec.* (more fully ***bulimia nervosa***), an emotional disorder (occurring chiefly in young women) in which 'binges' of extreme overeating alternate with depression and self-induced vomiting, purging, or fasting, and there is a persistent over-concern with body shape and weight.

1398 Trevisa *Barth. de. P.R.* VII. xlv. (1495) 258 Bolismus is inmoderate and vnmesurable as it were an houndes appetyte. *Ibid.* XVIII. xxvii. 786 Houndes haue contynuall Bolisme, that is inmoderat appetyte. **1598** Sylvester *Du Bartas* (1608) 210 One while the boulime, then the anorexie ..rage with monstrous ryot. **1651** Fuller *Abel Rediv.* (1867) I. 222 He fell into a most devouring and unsatiable bulimy. **1661** Lovell *Hist. Anim. & Min.* 365 The boulimos and dog like appetite. **1679** Plot *Staffordsh.* (1686) 301 A strange Boulimy..seized one Brian Careswell ..who would knaw and eat both Linnen and Woollen. **1720** W. Gibson *Dispens.* VI. III. (1734) 155 Continuing too long in them..may cause a Bulimy or Dog-appetite. **1751** R. Brooke *Gen. Practice Physic* (ed. 3) II. 193 A Bulimus is a Disease..wherein the Patient is affected with an insatiable and perpetual Desire of Eating. **1780** Beckford *Biog. Mem. Painters* 19 Hemmeline, who had long been troubled with a boulomee, or voracious appetite. **1880** Beale *Slight Ailm.* 74 Boulimia..may be due to a very irritable state of the nerves of the stomach. **1976** *Sci. Amer.* Apr. 80/3 After about two years a second phase [of anorexia], called bulimia, usually develops, in which the victim alternately fasts and gorges herself. **1978** *Jrnl. Amer. Med. Assoc.* 23 June 2688 Self-induced vomiting has been associated with the psychiatric diagnosis of anorexia nervosa and a newly proposed disorder named bulimia. **1979** *Psychol. Med.* IX. 429 (*heading*) Bulimia nervosa: an ominous variant of anorexia nervosa. **1982** [see BULIMAREXIC *a.*]. **1983** *Oxf. Textbk. Med.* I. VIII. 54 A minority of patients with anorexia nervosa do not recover but enter a chronic phase of the illness with altered clinical picture. This is called bulimia nervosa because one of its main features is the recurrence of gross overeating. **1985** *Woman's Own* 22 June 10/2 She developed another slimmer's disease—bulimia nervosa. 'For four months I stuffed myself with food then purged myself with laxatives.'

2. *fig.*

1654 Fuller *Comm. Ruth* (1868) 135 The boulimie of all-consuming Time. **1696** *Monthly Mercury* VII. 83 The French King has had..such a Bulimy after Money. **1705** Hickeringill *Priest-Cr.* II. iv. 44 There is enough left to glut..any that has not..an Ecclesiastick Boulimy. **1833** Hood *Wks.* (1862) II. 440 Novel reading is to some constitutions a sort of literary bullimy, or unnatural appetite. **1834** Southey *Doctor* xvii, First cousins of the moth who labour under a bulimy for black-letter. **1853** H. Rogers *Ecl. Faith* 144 One incessant bulimia for idolatry.

bulis, Sc. pl. form of BOUL *sb. Obs.*

bulk (bʌlk), *sb.*[1] Forms: 5 **bolk(e**, 5–7 **bulke**, 6 **bulcke**, **boulke**, **bowlke**, (5–6, 9 *Sc.* **bowk**, see BOUK), 7 **bulck**, (**boak**), 6– **bulk**. [Of complicated etymology. The coincidence in meaning with ON. **bulki*, Icel. *búlki* 'heap, cargo of a ship' (Vigf.), Da. *bulk* lump, clod (cf. mod.Icel. *búlka-st* to be bulky), suggests that the word, though not recorded before 15th c., may (in the senses 'heap', 'cargo') be of Scandinavian origin. Within a few years of its first appearance, *bulk* occurs in the senses 'belly, trunk of the body', due app. to confusion with BOUK, which word it has entirely superseded in literary English. (Cf. however, the Flemish *bulck* 'thorax' in Kilian.) The sense of 'size' (branch III) seems to have been evolved chiefly from the notion of 'body', though it may be partly due to that of 'heap' or 'cargo'. The form *boak*, used by N. Fairfax 1674 indiscriminately with *bulk* in the sense of 'magnitude', is apparently:—ME. *bolk*.]

I. Heap, cargo.

1. a. A heap; *spec.* the pile in which fish are laid for salting; a pile of tobacco made up to undergo sweating. *U.S.*

c **1440** *Promp. Parv.* 43 Bolke, or hepe, *cumulus.* **1602** Carew *Cornwall* 33 a, Pilchards are first salted & piled vp.. vntil the superfluous moysture of the bloud & salt be soked from them: which accomplished, they rip the bulk & saue the residue of the salt. **1725** De Foe *Voy. round World* (1840) 297 All the gold they found..should be put together in a bulk every night. **1784** J. Smyth *Tour U.S.* II. 135 When the tobacco house is quite full,..all that is within the house is..carefully placed in bulks, or regular rows one upon another. **1850** *Rep. Comm. Patents 1849* (U.S.) 322 Two rows or bundles are put in a bulk. **1902** *U.S. Dept. Agric., Farmers' Bulletin* No. 60. 14 Before the sweat is completed the bulk is pulled down and built up eight or ten times.

attrib. **1693** in *Cal. Virginia St. Papers* (1875) I. 48 An answer to a former message of yours relating to the Act of Ports & Bulke Tobacco.

b. The cargo of a ship; a cargo as a whole; the whole lot (of a commodity). Phrase, *to break bulk* (see BREAK *v.* 43).

1575 in *Hist. Glasgow* (1881) 117 Breking bowk [of a cargo]. **1626** Sir R. Boyle in *Lismore Papers* (1886) II. 190 To keep them from breaking Bulck, and from selling their goods at an vndervallue. **1776** T. Paine *Com. Sense* (1791) 58 The premiums to be in proportion to the loss of bulk to the merchants. **1884** *Harper's Mag.* June 51/2 Until this is done the bulk of his cargo can not be broken. *a* **1888** *Mod.* The bulk is not equal to sample.

c. ***in bulk*** (of fish, etc.): lying loose in heaps, without package; (*gen.*) in large quantities. ***to load*** (a ship) ***in bulk***: to put the cargo in loose, when it consists of wheat, salt, or the like. ***to sell in bulk***: to sell the cargo as it is in the hold; to sell in large quantities.

1678 *New Castle* (Del.) *Court Rec.* (1904) 253 Tobacco which was struck & Lay in bulke. **1727** De Foe *Eng. Tradesm.* xx. (1841) I. 195 There was an old office erected in the city of London for searching & viewing all the goods which were sold in bulk. **1769** Falconer *Dict. Marine* (1789), She is to be laden in-bulk; as with corn, salt, etc. **1848** C. Johns *Wk. at Lizard* 53 This process is continued until the pile is several feet high..The fish are now said to be 'in bulk'. **1866** Rogers *Agric. & Prices* I. xxiv. 619 Wine ..sold either in bulk or by retail. **1908** *Mod. Business* II. II. 165/1 It is possible for traders to effect a considerable saving by buying in bulk. **1928** [see COUPON 2].

II. Senses belonging to BOUK.

†**2. a.** = BOUK 1, 2. The belly; also the trunk, the body generally. *Obs.*

c **1460** J. Russell *Bk. Nurture* in *Babees Bk.* (1868) 145 þen ley bulke, chyne, & sides, to-gedire. **1533** Elyot *Cast. Helth* (1541) 89 The boulke, called in latyn *thorax*, whiche conteyneth the brest, the sides, the stomake, and entrayles. **1570** Levins *Manip.* 187 Ye Bulke, *thorax.* **1575** Turberv. *Bk. Venerie* 215 They kill and smoother them, or breake their bulckes with the force. **1594** Shaks. *Lucr.* 467 His hand..May feele her heart..Beating her bulke. **1632** Heywood *Iron Age* II. III. i. Wks. 1874 III. 392 My sword through Priams bulke shall flie. **1697** Dryden *Virg. Georg.* III. 782 His Bulk too weighty for his Thighs is grown. **1718** Pope *Iliad* XI. 458 His arm and knee his sinking bulk sustain.

†**b.** A dead body, carcase. *Obs.*

1575 Turberv. *Bk. Venerie* 175 Lette the huntesman take out of his wallet..small morsels, and put them into the Bulke of the hare. **1612** Heywood *Apol. Actors* (1841) 20 See a Hector..trampling upon the bulkes of Kinges. **1637** Rutherford *Lett.* No. 141 (1862) I. 336 Christ shall..mow down His enemies & lay bulks..on the green.

c. With some notion of 4: A body of great proportions, a huge frame (chiefly with adj. implying large size); also *fig.*

1587 Greene *Poems* (1861) 285 Trees Whose stately bulks do fame th' Arabian groves. **1606** Shaks. *Tr. & Cr.* IV. iv. 130 Though the great bulke Achilles be thy guard. **1624** Heywood *Captives* II. ii. in Bullen *O. Pl.* IV, That grand maister Of mechall lusts, that bulke of brothelree. **1718** Pope *Iliad* XVII. 837 Behold the bulk of Ajax stands, And breaks the torrent of the rushing bands. **1821** Shelley *Adonais* ii, He had adorned and hid the coming bulk of death. **1850** Tennyson *In Mem.* lxx. 11 Dark bulks that tumble half alive.

†**3.** *transf.* **a.** The hull or hold of a ship; cf. Ger. *bauch.* **b.** = BOUK 2 b; ? the main body or nave of a church; cf. BODY *sb.* 8 a. (Possibly the sense may be 'crypt', cf. It. *buca*, Tommaseo's Dict.). **c.** The part of a vehicle fitted to receive the load; cf. BODY *sb.* 8 g, BUCK *sb.*[5] 3.

c **1450** Lonelich *Grail* xxviii. 189 Thanne to þe bowk of þe schippe gan he gon. **1518** *Will of Selwode* (Somerset Ho.), Bowlke of the same churche. **1546** Strype *Eccl. Mem.* II. App. A. 9 And so was it [the corpse] reverently setled in the bulk of the chariot. **1611** Cotgr., *Vaisseau d'un navire*, the bulke, bellie, or bodie of a ship. **1652** Needham tr. *Selden's Mare Cl.* 191 The rest of the bulk of their Vessels..was cover'd with Hides. **1678** *Lond. Gaz.* No. 1269/3 Her Bulke is still kept entire.

III. Size: cf. 1 and 2 c.

4. a. Magnitude in three dimensions; volume.

c **1449** Pecock *Repr.* V. xv. 565 To make this book..eny ouer greet bolk. **1674** N. Fairfax *Bulk & Selv.* To Rdr., To another thing that was earlyer and Bulkier, and to somwhat still that was more betimes and more of Boak. **1736** Butler *Anal.* I. i. 27 What is the certain bulk of the living being each man calls himself. **1795** Southey *Vis. Maid Orleans* 291 Below, the vault dilates Its ample bulk. **1816** Scott *Antiq.* xxv, 'I hope it's bowk eneugh to haud a' the gear'. **1825** McCulloch *Pol. Econ.* II. ii. 141 They [gold and silver] possess great value in small bulk. **1878** Huxley *Physiogr.* 57 Sea water is denser or heavier, bulk for bulk, than fresh water.

b. *esp.* Great or considerable volume. Also *fig.*

1626 Bacon *Sylva* §771 Rather thin and small than of Bulk. **1669** Penn *No Cross* xi. §3 Wks. 1726 I. 332 'Tis Vanity..for a man of Bulk and Character, to despise another of Less Size in the World. **1798** Ferriar *Illustr. Sterne* iii. 58 The bulk of his materials generally overwhelms him. **1855** Macaulay *Hist. Eng.* III. 457 The facility and assiduity with which he wrote are proved by the bulk..of his works.

c. *Paper-making.* The thickness of paper (see quots.).

1903 C. Beadle in C. F. Cross et al. *Paper Testing* i. 9 The simplest numerical expression of 'bulk', (*i.e.*, the bulking qualities of the fibres composing the paper). **1906** R. W. Sindall *Paper Technology* ix. 100 The bulk of a paper may be expressed in terms of the thickness of a single sheet or the thickness of a ream. **1920** H. A. Bromley *Paper & its Constituents* III. ii. 161 Bulk in its most correct sense may be defined as the ratio of fibre volume to total volume. **1969** *Brit. Printer* June 65/2 In the field of book papers..one can still obtain a ton or two, tailor-made to a particular requirement of shade, bulk and finish.

d. *spec.* The thickness of a book without its covers.

1906 L. L. Walton in F. H. Hitchcock *Building of Book* 27 The bulk or thickness that the book must be, to make a volume of proper proportions, is determined. **1960** G. A. Glaister *Gloss. Book* 48/1 *Bulk*, the thickness of a book without its covers. The bulk will be less after binding than before.

e. = ROUGHAGE 2.

1940 G. Bourne *Nutrition & War* i. 8 This necessity for bulk in food is one reason why we are not likely to have all our food requirements reduced to one small pill. **1950** *N.Z. Jrnl. Agric.* May 485/2 There are three groups of crops suitable for feeding to pigs: Concentrates, semi-bulk foods, and bulk foods. **1962** *Which?* Jan. 25/1 These are all harmless laxatives, useful if your normal diet produces insufficient bulk. *Ibid.* 26/2 All preparations used as laxatives are effective by acting as bulk-suppliers, or irritants, or lubricants.

5. A mass; the collective mass of any object. Often *esp.* a large mass.

1641 J. Jackson *True Evang. T.* III. 203 The last Use of redargution did not lie..against the whole bulk of Popery. **1658–9** Col. Briscoe in Burton's *Diary* (1828) IV. 204, I was as much against confirming the laws in a bulk as any man. **1658** Ussher *Ann.* VI. 153 Locking their ships close together, and making one bulke of them. *a* **1718** Penn *Tracts* in *Wks.* (1726) I. 815 Those who distinguish the Tree in the Bulk, cannot with the like Ease discern every Branch. **1842** Tennyson *Edw. Morris* 11 A Tudor-chimnied bulk Of mellow brickwork. **1853** Kane *Grinnell Exp.* xxx. (1856) 260 A similar bulk of lamp oil, denuded of the staves, stood [frozen] like a yellow sandstone roller.

6. Greater part, or, in relation to number, the majority; the main body. (Sc. *bouk*; cf. BODY *sb.* 9.)

[**1662** Gerbier *Princ.* 37 As for the main bulk of Palaces, its true some have a greatness in plainness.] **1711** Addison *Spect.* No. 124 ¶3 Prints..calculated to diffuse good sense through the Bulk of a People. **1752** Hume *Pol. Disc.* I. 4 The bulk of every state may be divided into husbandmen and manufacturers. **1837** Ht. Martineau *Soc. Amer.* III. 279 The bulk of the Presbyterian clergy are as fierce as the slave-holders against the abolitionists. **1866** Bright *Sp. Irel.* 30 Oct. (1876) 188 The bulk of his land has only been brought under cultivated.

7. *attrib.* **a.** = in bulk, as ***bulk-buying***, ***-purchasing***, ***supply***, etc.

1693 [see sense 1 a.] **1848** *Rep. Comm. Patents 1847* (U.S.) 527 Bulk pork is that which is intended for immediate use or

smoking. **1892** *Daily News* 13 May 5/8 Bulk transport threatens 'danger to the security, safety, and freedom from interruption of the Suez Canal'. **1906** *Daily Chron.* 3 Mar. 4/4 Bulk power generation. *Ibid.* 13 June 4/6 A monopoly of the bulk supply [of electricity]. **1930** *Economist* 19 July 107/1 The question of import boards for bulk purchases. *Ibid.* 9 Aug. 272/1 The project of setting up bulk-purchasing import boards. **1932** *Times Lit. Suppl.* 10 Nov. 824/3 Not only is it impossible for the potentialities of bulk-buying.. to be exploited, [etc.]. **1940** 'M. INNES' *Secret Vanguard* xix. 209 Let us worry rather about petrol and bulk wheat. **1949** *Hansard Commons* CDLXV. 1453, 50 per cent.. of the total imports of the country are bulk-purchased by the Government. *Ibid.* 1558 When we talk about bulk buying, we obviously mean three or four different things. We mean an ordinary large single purchase; we mean centralised buying; and, of course, we mean State trading.

b. bulk barrel, a barrel of 36 gallons of wort or beer without regard to specific gravity (as distinguished from *standard barrel*); so ***bulk gallon***; **bulk carrier**, a ship that carries cargo in bulk; **bulk eraser** (see quot. 1959); **bulk modulus** *Math.* (see quots.).

1905 *Daily Chron.* 29 July 4/5 The discrepancy between the number of 'standard' barrels of beer upon which duty is paid and the number of 'bulk' barrels actually brewed. **1909** *Ibid.* 12 May 1/4 The bulk barrel may be of any specific gravity. The average is, I should say, about 1·053. **1909** W. S. TOWER *Story of Oil* vi. 100 Before long tank steamers were also added to the fleet of bulk carriers. **1954** *Shipping World* 7 July 20/1 The bulk carrier *Sunrip*, a turbine steamship of about 12,700 tons deadweight.. was launched on June 21. **1984** *Financial Times* 17 Apr. 22 Reduction in the number of.. tankers and the introduction of highly efficient.. bulk carriers. **1956** R. E. B. HICKMAN *Magnetic Recording Handbk.* v. 120 A tape may be cleaned more rapidly by the use of a bulk eraser. **1959** W. S. SHARPS *Dict. Cinematogr.* 82/1 *Bulk eraser*, a device designed to pass a high intensity alternating current through wound reels of magnetic tape such that the recorded magnetic patterns are completely erased in a matter of seconds. **1889** in G. Birch *Handbk. Gauging* (1894) 67 When the deduction for tenths reduces bulk gallons to less than those of next lower inch. **1908** E. S. ANDREWS *Theory & Design of Structures* i. 9 There is an additional modulus called the *bulk* or *volume modulus* (K), which represents the ratio between the unital change in volume and the intensity of pressure or tension on a cube of material subjected to pressure or tension on all faces. **1935** C. G. BURGE *Compl. Bk. Aviation* 194/1 The bulk modulus is that which expresses the relation between stress and change in unit volume when a body is subjected to equal stresses on all faces, such as when a body is under pressure.

bulk (bʌlk), *sb.*[2] [Not recorded before late 16th c. Etymology doubtful: Prof. Skeat suggests ON. *bálk-r*, *bǫ́lk-r* beam (= BALK), which might perhaps give ME. **bolk*, and mod.Eng. *bulk*; there is also an OE. *bolca* 'gangway of a ship', supposed to be a parallel form to *bealca*, BALK. Cf. '*Bulkar*.. a Beam or Rafter, Lincolnsh.' (Bailey.)]

A framework projecting from the front of a shop; a stall.

1586 *Praise of Musicke* 44 The tailor on his bulk, the shomaker at his last. **1607** SHAKS. *Cor.* II. i. 226 Stalls, Bulkes, Windowes, Are smother'd vp. **1680** *Vind. Conform. Clergy* (ed. 2) 50 Leave him under a Bulk whetting his crooked Knife. **1771** SMOLLETT *Humph. Cl.* (1815) 156 During the heats of summer, he commonly took his repose upon a bulk. **1875** HAMERTON *Intell. Life* XI. ii. 406 A cobbler in his bulk was out-and-out his master.

† **bulk**, *sb.*[3] *Obs. slang.* [cf. BULKER.] (See quots.)

1673 R. HEAD *Canting Acad.* 35 *Bulk and File.* The one jostles you whilst the other picks your pocket. **1721** in BAILEY. **1725** *New Cant. Dict.*, *Bulk*, an Assistant to a *File* or Pickpocket, who jostles a Person up against the Wall, while the other picks his Pocket.

bulk (bʌlk), *v.*[1] [f. BULK *sb.*[1], giving a number of unconnected or loosely connected senses.]

1. *intr.* To be of bulk; to present an appearance of size; to be of weight or importance. *lit.* and *fig.*

1672 W. CARSTARES in Story *Life* 27 Other things would be so far from bulking in our eyes that they would evanish and disappear. **1725** WODROW *Corr.* (1843) III. 211 Your loss.. bulks not with me in comparison of that of the public. **1832** CARLYLE in *Fraser's Mag.* V. 384 Any one of whom bulked much larger in the world's eye than Johnson ever did. **1859** G. WILSON *E. Forbes* iv. 91 For us.. of this generation, the years between 1831 and 1855 must bulk large.

2. *to bulk* (*up*): to swell *up*, rise in bulk or mass.

1551 RECORDE *Pathw. Knowl.* I. Def., The middle partes nother bulke vp, nother shrink down more then the bothe endes. **1601** BP. BARLOW *Defence* 116 That corne hath bulkt into a stemme, and branched out into armes.. I neuer heard or read. **1883** J. PARKER in *Homil. Month.* Oct. 18 A few coins.. shall bulk up into quite a surprising offering.

†**3.** *trans. to bulk out*: to swell out, stuff out. (In quot. 1553 the word may be = BOLK, belch.)

1540 HYRDE *Vives' Instr. Chr. Wom.* (1592) F vi, One of Sathans officers, that usest.. so many chosen meats at the ful, bulking out Capons. **1553** BRENDE *Q. Curtius* R. iij, Which violence of toung and rashenes of wordes, bulked out .. was nothing elles but a declaration and token of his trayterous haste. *a* **1641** BP. MOUNTAGU *Acts & Mon.* (1642) 457 The most ancient Churches.. were.. like some kinde of ships.. bulked out upon both sides in the midst.

4. To pile in heaps, as fish for salting. Cf. BULK *sb.*[1] 1. Also, to pile (tobacco) in the course of preparing it for use (*U.S.*).

1822 G. WOODLEY *Scilly Isl.* I. vi. 154 Pilchards are said to be bulked, when they are piled up in layers, on the pavement of the cellars. **1850** *Rep. Comm. Patents 1849* (U.S.) 322 Stripping should never be done in drying.. weather, unless the tobacco is bulked up almost as fast as it is stript. **1863** *Ret. Agric. Soc. Maine* 163 When the weather again becomes moist,.. take it [*sc.* tobacco] down and carefully bulk it away as before directed. *Ibid.*, Care must be taken that the tobacco does not.. get too high in case before it is bulked. **1881** *Scotsman* 12 Apr. 3/1 Sometimes when seals are found in great abundance, they are 'bulked'. **1902** *U.S. Dept. Agric., Farmer's Bulletin* No. 60. 17 These are tied up into hands and bulked down for a short time.

5. *Comm.* **a.** To ascertain the bulk of.

1883 *Times* 24 Mar. 6 Indian teas are 'bulked' by Her Majesty's Customs—that is to say, each chest is opened and emptied, in order to ascertain the exact weight of the tea and of the package. *Ibid.* The Customs are not to blame for the bulking of Indian tea.

b. (See quot.)

1931 C. MAUGHAN *Markets of London* xxix. 104 Most of the descriptions of coffee.. are poured out from the bags on to special floors, where they are 'bulked', or mixed, in order to ensure that the contents of all the bags are of uniform quality, and they are then rebagged.

6. *trans.* To put together (two or more consignments of goods) for transport as one. Also *absol.*

1908 *Modern Business* Sept. 164/2 Had they been 'bulked' —*i.e.* sent as one consignment, from one consignee to an agent to deliver—the company would have had no alternative but to charge the lower rate. *Ibid.* 165/1 If a merchant can, by bulking several parcels, get them through at a much lower rate. **1928** *Daily Express* 10 Mar. 9/4 Bulking means.. that two or more consignments for different consignees in one town, forwarded at one and the same time, can be charged together as one lot.

7. To enlarge a book by adding to the number or thickness of its leaves; esp. to make a book look big by printing it on paper of abnormally loose texture. Also *intr.*, to have a specified bulk (see BULK *sb.*[1] 4 c).

1920 CROSS & BEVAN *Textbk. Paper-Making* (ed. 5) xiv. 403 A paper either 'bulks high' or 'bulks low' in relation to its 'substance'. **1932** B. BLACKWELL *World of Books* 41 Setting their faces against the artificial bulking of books. **1937** E. J. LABARRE *Dict. Paper* 114/1 Light and 'bulky' papers, the opposite of which are heavy or dense, have 'bulking' qualities, and papers are said to 'bulk well'. **1957** *Times Lit. Suppl.* 27 Dec. 787/2 For this deterioration publishers are in part to blame in their demand for 'bulking' properties.

† **bulk**, *v.*[2] *Obs.* Also 4 **bolk.** [Origin unknown.] *intr.* ? To beat.

a **1300** *Cursor M.* 18511 A-pon þair breistes can þai bulk [*Fairf.* gon they bolk].

bulk(e, var. of BOLK *Obs.*, to belch.

bulked (bʌlkt), *ppl. a.* Also 5 **(y)bolked.** [f. BULK *sb.*[1] + -ED[2].] **a.** Having bulk, bulky; esp. in comb. ***big-bulked***.

c **1420** *Pallad. on Husb.* IV. 891 A stalon asse ybolked, brawny. **1583** STANYHURST *Descr. Liparen, Æneis* (Arb.) 137 In this caue the rakehels yrne bars, biggen bulcked, ar hamring. **1623** LISLE *Ælfric on O. & N. T.* Ded. xxvii, How this bulked world unto thee bowes. *a* **1843** SOUTHEY *Comm.-pl. Bk.* Ser. II. 325 Big bulked volumes of physic.

b. Having its bulk increased; *spec.* of books (cf. BULK *v.*[1] 7) and of yarn (see quot. 1957).

1954 J. H. KENNEDY in *Textile World* Oct. 80/2 Pioneering in the field of bulked-Orlon yarns from tow. **1957** *Times Lit. Suppl.* 27 Dec. 787/2 Max Reinhardt should ask public librarians for their view of 'bulked' books. **1957** *Textile Terms & Defs.* (ed. 3) 30 *Bulked yarns*, yarns which have been treated physically or chemically so as to have a notably greater 'apparent volume' or bulk.

† **'bulker**[1]. *Obs. slang.* [Perh. f. BULK *sb.*[2] + -ER[1], with the meaning 'one who sleeps on a bulk', 'one who steals from a bulk'; cf. Johnson *Savage* Wks. (1787) III. 325 'On a bulk, in a cellar, or in a glass-house, among thieves and beggars, was to be found the Author of *The Wanderer*'.]

A low-lived person; a petty thief; a street-walker, prostitute. Also = BULK *sb.*[3]

1673 R. HEAD *Canting Acad.* 99 The Bulker jostles them up, and the File doth the work. **1678** *Four for Penny* in *Harl. Misc.* IV. 147 (D.) He is.. the common fender of all bulkers and shop lifts in the town. **1690** B. E. *Dict. Cant. Crew*, *Bulker*, one that lodges all Night on Shop-windows and Bulkheads. **1690** SHADWELL *Am. Bigot* III. 265 Her mother sells fish, and she is little better than a bulker. *a* **1705** T. BROWN in J. Ashton *Soc. Life in Q. Anne's Reign* 83 In comparison of whom the common Bulkers, and Pickpockets, are a very honest Society. **1790** BAILEY, *Bulker*, one that would lie down on a Bulk to any one; a common Jilt; a whore.

bulker[2] ('bʌlkə(r)). [f. BULK *v.* (sense 6) + -ER[1].]

1. (See quot.)

1867 SMYTH *Sailor's Word-bk.*, *Bulker*, a person employed to measure goods, and ascertain the amount of freight with which they are chargeable.

2. One who makes up tobacco into piles for curing. *U.S.*

1863 *Ret. Agric. Soc. Maine* 163 This [bulking] is done by lapping the bundles over each course.. the bulker having his knees upon the bulk. *Ibid.*, Under the pressure of the bulker's knee.

bulker[3] ('bʌlkə(r)). [f. BULK *sb.*[1] + -ER[1].] = *bulk carrier* s.v. BULK *sb.*[1] 7 b.

1975 *Marine Week* 27 June 15 (*heading*) Icebreaker bulker. **1979** *Cape Times* 11 July 13 The world's increasing need for additional grain shipments to stave off hunger in Asia inevitably represents immediate business for bulkers. **1983** *Financial Times* 14 Nov. 4/4 The volume of purchase interests.., shown for second-hand bulkers of all sizes, was another pointer to next year's possible level of activity.

bulkhead ('bʌlkhɛd). Also 7 **bulkeshead.** [App. f. BULK *sb.*[2] (or its etymon) + HEAD; 1 and 2 may however be f. BULK *sb.*[1] in some sense.]

1. a. One of the upright partitions serving to form the cabins in a ship or to divide the hold into distinct water-tight compartments, for safety in case of collision or other damage. ***collision bulkhead***: the foremost bulkhead in a vessel.

1496 *Naval Accts. Henry VII* (1896) 167 Amendyng of the Bulke hede for Couching of Bere. **1626** CAPT. SMITH *Accid. Yng. Seamen* 11 A quarter decke, the bulke, the bulkeshead. **1691** T. HALE *Acc. New Invent.* 120 The Hull.. shall be subdivided by other Decks and Bulk-heads. **1805** NELSON in Nicolas *Disp.* VI. 354 Ever since we have been prepared for Battle: not a Bulk-head up in the Fleet. **1884** *Pall Mall G.* 25 Aug. 8/2 She had a collision bulkhead and a bulkhead fore and aft.

b. *transf.*

1880 HUXLEY *Cray-Fish* iv. 157 The curious pillars and bulkheads which enter into the composition of the Endophragmal system.

c. A similar partition in an airship, an aeroplane, or a train.

1921 *Discovery* II. 97/1 The fuselage [*sc.* of the airship].. consists of riveted sheet duralumin, kept rigid by a series of internal duralumin girder bulkheads. **1935** C. G. BURGE *Compl. Bk. Aviation* 306/2 The main precaution against fire is the inclusion of a fireproof bulkhead between the engine compartment and the rest of the aeroplane. **1948** 'N. SHUTE' *No Highway* iii. 80 You must.. sit down on the floor facing to the tail, with your back against the forward bulkhead. **1952** *Railway Age* 24 Nov. 10 (Advt.), Bulkheads and partitions in this luxury car are 73% lighter than standard steel construction.

d. In a motor-car: the partition dividing the engine from the body. Cf. SCUTTLE *sb.*[2] 1 d.

1958 F. J. CAMM *Practical Motorist's Encycl.* (ed. 9) 473/2 Holes are drilled in the metal bulkhead or scuttle, and the holder fixed. **1962** *Which?* (*Car Suppl.*) Oct. 138/2 The mounting bracket for the accelerator linkage came adrift from the bulkhead.

2. *Mining.* (See quot.)

1881 RAYMOND *Mining Gloss.*, *Bulkhead*, 1. A tight partition or stopping in a mine for protection against water, fire, gas. 2. The end of a flume, whence water is carried in iron pipes to hydraulic workings.

3. The roof of a bulk or projecting stall; also the stall itself. Cf. BULK *sb.*[2]

1722 DE FOE *Col. Jack* (1840) 59 Resting his hand.. upon the bulkhead of a ship. **1823** SCOTT *Peveril* III. xii. 213 Suddenly placing him on the bulk-head, that is to say, the flat wooden roof of the cutler's projecting booth. **1837** DICKENS *Pickw.* xx, A small bulk-head beneath the taproom window, in size and shape not unlike a sedan-chair, being underlet to a mender of shoes. **1865** THOREAU *Cape Cod* v. 73 An old woman came out and fastened the door of her bulkhead.

Hence **'bulk,headed** *ppl. a.*, furnished with bulkheads; partitioned off by bulkheads.

1814 *Ann. Reg.* 79/2 The vessel was bulk-headed up fore and aft. **1856** KANE *Arct. Expl.* II. 311 A single apartment was bulkheaded off amidships as a dormitory. **1884** *Pall Mall G.* 29 Oct. 2/1 The armed and bulkheaded merchant steamer giving a good account of the French man-of-war.. is an enticing picture, and has been much petted and cackled about in some quarters.

bulkily ('bʌlkɪlɪ), *adv.* [f. BULKY *a.* + -LY[2].] In a bulky manner.

1886 STEVENSON *Pr. Otto* II. xiv, He grovelled bulkily upon the floor.

† **'bulkin.** *Obs.* [app. f. BULL *sb.*[1] + -KIN; perh. after Du. or LG. Sense b (= BULCH[2], BULCHIN 2) may be a distinct word, cf. MDu. *boelekijn*, darling (Verwijs and Verdam); also BULLY *sb.* The form of the variants *Bulch*, *Bulchin* may possibly be due to the pronunciation of the Du. suffix indicated by its later spelling *-tje(n*. No other instance is known in Eng. of *-chin* as a variant of -KIN.] **a.** A bull calf; a young bull. **b.** Used as a term of endearment.

1583 STANYHURST *Æneis* I. (Arb.) 39 My sweete choise bulcking, my force and my power onlye. **1601** HOLLAND *Pliny* XXVIII. xii, A young white bulkin or steere. **1616** SURFL. & MARKH. *Country Farm* 31 Bore-Pigs, Rammes, Bull-Calues, or Bulkins.

bulkiness ('bʌlkɪnɪs). [f. BULKY *a.* + -NESS.] The quality of being bulky; largeness of volume. Used by Fairfax for 'extension'.

1674 N. FAIRFAX *Bulk & Selv.* 29 A thing being cleave some, not from its bulkiness, but inward emptiness mingled. **1691** LOCKE *Money* Wks. 1727 II. 24 Wheat.. cannot serve instead of money; because of its Bulkiness. **1740** GRAY *Let.* in Poems (1775) 100 The Gothic character and bulkiness of those volumes. **1848** MILL *Pol. Econ.* III. xix. §2 (1876) 368 The expense of transport.. is much affected by the bulkiness of the goods.

bulking (ˈbʌlkɪŋ), *vbl. sb.* [f. BULK *v.*[1] + -ING[1].]

1. The action or process of laying in heaps, or piling without package: also *attrib.* Cf. BULK *v.*[1] 5.

1602 CAREW *Cornwall* 33 a, Pilchards..are first salted & piled vp..in square heapes..which they terme Bulking. **1881** *Scotsman* 12 Apr. 3/1 Complaints..made by those interested in the seal fishery against the bulking system.

†**2.** = BULGING, swelling *out*. Cf. BULK *v.*[1] 3.

1599 MINSHEU *Sp. Dict.* (1623), *Turma de tierra*..[The root] is found out by the bulking out of the earth.

†ˈ**bulking**, *ppl. a. Obs. rare*[−1]. [cf. BULKER[1].] Sleeping out on bulks; street-walking.

1676 D'URFEY *Mad. Fickle* v. i, Now will this damm'd bulking Quean be too witty for me.

†ˈ**bulkish**, *a. Obs. rare*[−1]. [f. BULK *sb.*[1] + -ISH[1].] Of considerable bulk, big.

c **1660** *Hist. Europe* 434 in *Burton's Diary* (1828) III. 547 He was a knight of the new order already, & grown very bulkish & considerable.

†ˈ**bulksome**, *a. Obs. rare.* [f. BULK *sb.*[1] + -SOME; cf. BOUKSOME.] Occupying space, bulky. Hence †ˈ**bulksomeness**, magnitude, extension; BULKINESS b.

1674 N. FAIRFAX *Bulk & Selv.* 56 An Immensity, or a being boundless in its bulksomness. **1708** M. BRUCE *Lect. & Serm.* 33 (JAM.) Where Christ grows ay bulksomer in the bosom.

bulky (ˈbʌlkɪ), *sb. slang.* A policeman.

1827 LYTTON *Pelham* lxxix, The bugaboos and bulkies. **1841** —— *Nt. & Morn.* v. ii, Inquiries about your respectability would soon bring the bulkies about me.

bulky (ˈbʌlkɪ), *a.* Also 7 boaky, bulkey, -ie. [f. BULK *sb.*[1] + -Y[1].]

1. Of large bulk, voluminous; occupying much space (*esp.* with a notion of excess).

1687 T. BROWN *Saints in Upr.* Wks. 1730 I. 73 Will bang half a dozen such bulky fellows. **1774** JOHNSON in *Boswell* (1831) III. 115 If anything is too bulky for the post, let me have it by the carrier. **1879** GLADSTONE *Glean.* II. v. 213 This is a large but not a bulky biography. For the word *bulky* insinuates the idea of size in excess of pith and meaning.

†**2.** Having extension, occupying space. *Obs.*

1674 N. FAIRFAX *Bulk & Selv.* 84 Suppose a being that is bulkie, and nothing about it that is so, or two beings that are bulky and nothing between them that is so. *Ibid.* 138 Body being a..boaky unthroughfaresom thing.

†**3.** ? Pompous, 'big', self-important. *Obs.*

1672 MARVELL *Reh. Transp.* I. 7 A bulky Dutchman diverted it quite from its first Institution. **1673** *Ibid.* II. (1674) 245 One of your bulkie Princes, who had the Trumpet ready to sound whensoever he hit the Ball at Tennis.

bull (bʊl), *sb.*[1] Forms: 3–4 bule, (3–4 *pl.* bulles, 4–5 -is), 5 bulle, 6–7 bul, 6– bull; also 3–5 bole, 4 bol, 4–5 boole, (5 bolle), (8 *Sc. dial.* bill). [ME. *bole* (*bool(e)*, app. a. ON. *bole, boli*; cf. MLG. *bulle* (whence mod.G.), MDu. *bulle* (*bolle*), Du. *bul, bol.* There may have been an OE. **bulla*, whence the deriv. *bulluc* 'bullock', as the source of the ME. *bule, bulle*, and the modern *bull*, which do not fit phonetically the *bole* forms. Outside Teutonic, cf. Lithuanian *bullus.* Prob. from a verb-stem found in some German dialects, as *büllen, bullen* to roar, perh. related by ablaut to *bellen*: see BELL *v.*[4].]

I. Of animals.

1. The male of any bovine animal; most commonly applied to the male of the domestic species (*Bos Taurus*); also of the buffalo, etc.

c **1200** ORMIN 990 Þe33re lac wass bule, & lamb, & buckess twa togeddre. *a* **1300** *Cursor M.* 10395 Þe bulles [*v.r.* bolys] tuelue he offrid sua. *c* **1325** *E.E. Allit. P.* B. 1682 A best þat he be, a bol oþer an oxe. *c* **1380** WYCLIF *Serm.* li. Sel. Wks. I. 150 A bole þat shal be kild goiþ in corn at his wille. **1413** LYDG. *Pylgr. Sowle* v. xi. (1483) 102 The cruell horned boole. **1474** CAXTON *Chesse* 112 A grete bole is suffisid with right a litil pasture. *a* **1528** SKELTON *Image Hypocr.* IV. 114 As gredy as a gull And ranke as any bull. **1587** *Censure loyall Subj.* (Collier) 54 When the Captain could no longer withstand the Kings importunities, he drank buls blood, and died. *a* **1649** DRUMM. OF HAWTH. *Hist. Scot.* (1655) 42 The head of a Bull (a sign of present Death in these times) is set down before him. **1733** POPE *Hor. Sat.* I. i. 86 Bulls aim their horns, and Asses lift their heels. **1786** BURNS *Addr. Deil* x, An' dawtit, twal-pint Hawkie's gaen As yell's the Bill. **1818** in Knight *Once upon a Time* II. 249 A bull is to be baited on Monday next.

b. ***bulls of brass, brazen bulls***, as those that guarded the golden fleece, and Phalaris' bull (proverbial as an engine of torture).

c **1385** CHAUCER *L.G.W.* 1428 Two bolys makid all of bras. **1611** BEAUM. & FL. *Philaster* III. i, The points of swords, tortures, nor bulls of brass, Should draw it from me. **1621** BURTON *Anat. Mel.* I. i. I. i, All manner of tortures, brazen bulls, racks, wheels. **1724** SWIFT *Wks.* (1841) II. 4 To torment people, by putting them into a bull of brass with fire under it.

c. In phrases (mostly proverbial): † ***he may bear a bull that hath borne a calf***, in allusion to the story of Milo of Crotona (see quot.). ***a bull in a china shop***: the symbol of one who produces reckless destruction. ***to take the bull by the horns***: to meet a difficulty with courage. ***to show the bull-horn***: to make a show of resistance. (***like a***) ***bull at a*** (***five-barred***) ***gate***: with direct violence or impetuosity; so ***bull-at-a-gate***, used attrib. to describe a direct and vigorous attack.

1539 TAVERNER *Erasm. Prov.* (1552) 10 He that hath borne a calfe, shall also beare a bull, He that accustometh hym selfe to lytle thynges, by lytle and lytle shal be able to go a waye with greater thynges. **1711** SWIFT *Conduct of Allies* 58 To engage with France, was to take a bull by the Horns. **1816** SCOTT *Old Mort.* in *Tales of my Landlord* III. xii. 258 He had not, as the phrase goes, taken the bull by the horns, or advanced in front of the enemie's fire. **1833** GALT in *Fraser's Mag.* VIII. 655 He shewed, when he durst, the bull-horn. **1841** MARRYAT *Jac. Faithf.* xv, I'm like a bull in a china-shop. **1873** TRISTRAM *Moab* vi. 107 Determined to take the bull by the horns..I stepped forward. **1896** *Westm. Gaz.* 14 Oct. 5/3 [He] cross-examined in his usual blusterous bull-at-a-gate sort of fashion. **1957** *Times* 11 May 7/3 If the whole scheme is to be rushed through, bull at a gate, there is bound to be some initial chaos. **1963** *Ibid* 2 Mar. 3/4 Blair has always possessed cover and straight drives of the purest quality, but has usually adopted bull-at-a-gate tactics.

†**d.** ***hell bull.*** Applied to Belial. *Obs.*

a **1225** *Juliana* 54 He þe kingene king helle bule haueð ouercumen te dei belial baldest of helle.

†**e.** ***bull's head*** (Sc.): 'a signal of condemnation, and prelude of immediate execution, said to have been anciently used in Scotland' (Jam.).

1565 LINDESAY (Pitscottie) *Chron. Scotl.* (1728) 17 (JAM.) The chancellor presentit the bullis head befoir the earle of Douglas. **1649** [see 1]. *a* **1800** in Scott *Minstr. Scot. Bord.* (1803) II. 399 (JAM.) If the bull's ill-omen'd head Appear to grace the feast, Your whingers..Plunge in each neighbour's breast.

2. The male of certain other large animals, as the elephant, alligator, whale, etc. † ***bull of the river***: see quot. (*obs.*).

1615 G. SANDYS *Trav.* 99 [The Nilus produceth] Buls of the Riuer (so they write) not much vnlike to those of the land, but no bigger than a calfe of halfe a yeare old. **1725** DUDLEY in *Phil. Trans.* XXXIII. 260 They [whales] generate much like to our neat Cattle, and therefore they are termed Bull, Cow, and Calf. **1857** CHAMBERS *Inform. People* I. 716 Fights usually take place when male whales or bulls..meet with rivals. **1886** GUILLEMARD *Cruise Marchesa* I. 198 The attitude of the bulls [seals] towards each other becomes more peaceable.

3. *Astron.* The constellation and sign Taurus.

1509 HAWES *Past. Pleas.* xv. ii, The golden rayes..Of radyant Phebus..Right in the Bull. **1607** TOPSELL *Serpents* 755 Diana..translated him into heaven, close by the constellation of the Bull. **1728** THOMSON *Spring* 27 From Aries rolls the bounteous Sun, And the bright Bull receives him. **1868** LOCKYER *Heavens* (ed. 3) 323 Aldebaran, the most beautiful star in the constellation of the Bull.

II. Transf. senses of diverse origin.

†**4.** = BULL-HEAD, BULL-TOUR. *Obs. slang.*

1690 B. E. *Dict. Cant. Crew, Bull*..false Hair worn (formerly much) by Women.

5. *Mining.* An iron rod used in the process of blasting. **b.** = *Clay-iron.* Raymond *Mining Gloss.*

1851 *Coal-tr. Terms, Northumbld. & Durh.* 12 Filling a drill hole in wet stone with strong clay, and then driving a round iron rod (called a bull), nearly the size of the hole, to its far end.

6. ? *dial.* See quot.

1884 *Leisure Hour* Sept. 530/1 A huge whistle..attached by pipes to a steam boiler..is familiarly styled the 'bull'.

7. *slang.* **a.** A crown piece. (cf. BULL'S-EYE 11.)

1812 J. H. VAUX *Flash Dict., Bull*, a crown or five shillings. **1852** DICKENS *Bleak Ho.* xlvii, 'Four halfbulls, wot you may call halfcrowns'.

b. A locomotive. *U.S. slang.*

a **1889** *On the Trail* (Barrère & Leland), Had just touched a bloke's leather as the bull bellowed for the last time. **1889** FARMER *Americanisms, Bull* (Cant), a locomotive; the word is sometimes lengthened into Bullgine.

c. A policeman. *U.S. slang.*

[**1859** G. W. MATSELL *Vocabulum* 15 *Bull-traps*, rogues who personate [police] officers for the purposes of extorting money.] **1893** J. FLYNT in *Century Mag.* Nov. 103/2, I have seldom met a hobo who was very angry with a New York 'bull'. **1909** J. LONDON in *Contemp. Rev.* June 699, I noticed the bull, a strapping policeman in a grey suit... I never dreamed that bull was after me. **1959** 'A. GILBERT' *Death takes Wife* xvii. 217 Sam putting the bulls on you.

III. 8. *Stock-Exchange* [see BEAR *sb.*[1] 8]. One who endeavours by speculative purchases, or otherwise, to raise the price of stocks. *Bulls* and *Bears*, the two different classes of speculators. *Bull* was originally a speculative purchase for a rise.

1714 C. JOHNSON *Country Lasses* I. i, You deal in Bears and Bulls. **1721** CIBBER *Refusal* I, And all this out of Change-Alley? Every Shilling, Sir; all out of Stocks, Tuts, Bulls, Rams, Bears, and Bubbles. **1761** *Brit. Mag.* II. 278 The cow turned into 'Change-alley, which frighted not a little not only all the bulls, but the bears too. **1818** SCOTT *Rob Roy* iv, The hum and bustle which his approach was wont to produce among the bulls, bears, and brokers of Stock-alley. **1880** F. HALL in *19th Cent.* Sept. 437 *note*, Can Mr. Bryant really have supposed financial bulls and bears to be peculiar to Wall-street, New York?

b. *attrib.* **bull point** *colloq.*, a point of advantage or superiority, a great 'score'.

1851 *Illust. Lond. News* 14 The bull party will not be able to carry on much longer. **1881** *Chicago Times* 1 June, The surrounding influences were..favorable to the 'bull' movement. **1881** *Mark Lane Express* 8 Aug. 1085 The speculative movement which has..exerted a 'bull' influence on the maize market. **1900** *Westm. Gaz.* 27 Sept. 9/3, I am afraid that Lord Lansdowne has proved anything but a bull point to the House. **1923** *Daily Mail* 12 Oct. 7/2 The great bull point of our manufactures is their reputation for quality. **1961** *Times* 14 Apr. 5/4 It is a bull point in his favour that the visitors..found him eminently satisfactory.

IV. *Attrib.* and *Comb.*

9. *attrib.* **a.** In sense of 'male'. (Sometimes hyphened.)

a **1300** *Cursor M.* 10386 (Gött.), To godd he gaue þe lambis to lottis, And to þe pore men þe bole stottis [*printed* stostis]. **1462** *Test. Ebor.* (1855) II. 254 Et xxx bull-stirkus. **1596** SHAKS. *1 Hen. IV*, II. iv. 287 Falstaffe, you..roared for mercy..as euer I heard Bull-Calfe. **1825** ADAMS *Compl. Serv.* 77 The meat of the bull-calf is generally firmest. **1861** DU CHAILLU *Equat. Afr.* xii. 170 We saw..a..bull-elephant. **1863** *Spring in Lapland* 185 Certainly a bull elk is an awkward customer when brought to bay. **1880** *Daily News* 8 Dec. 6/7 One bull whale..measured 48 ft.

b. Of or pertaining to a bull, bull-like.

1814 SIR R. WILSON *Diary* II. 336 Butting his head with bull rage and closed eyes. **1830** MARRYAT *King's Own* xxvi, You've such a bull neck. **1837** CARLYLE *Fr. Rev.* II. IV. xi. 190 A doom proclaimed, audible in bull voice, towards the four winds.

10. Simple combinations: **a.** attributive, belonging to (or resembling what belongs to) a bull, as ***bull-hide, -house, -meat, -skin, -team***; **b.** similative and parasynthetic, as ***bull-bragging, -browed, -face(d, -fronted, -like, -mouthed, -necked, -throated, -voiced***, adjs.; **c.** objective with vbl. sb. or ppl. adj., as ***bull-bearing***.

1606 SHAKS. *Tr. & Cr.* II. iii. 258 *Bull-bearing Milo. **1563-87** FOXE *A. & M.* (1596) 1170/2 The doltish braines of these *Bull bragging bedlems. **1631** R. BYFIELD *Doctr. Sabb.* 174 His *bul-browd-forlorne-downe-cast haire covering all his forehead. **1795** WOLCOTT (P. Pindar) *Hair Powder* Wks. 1812 III. 298 Let..*bull-face Brudenell roar. **1775** *Phil. Trans.* LXVI. 102 The sea-lyon and lyoness are *bull-faced, with long shaggy hair. **1837** CARLYLE *Fr. Rev.* II. II. v. 106 He is of indomitable *bull-heart; and also, unfortunately, of thick *bull-head. *c* **1205** LAY. 14187 Swa muchel lond . swa wule anes *bule hude . ælches weies ouer-spræden. **1297** R. GLOUC. 116 Þo carf he a bole hyde small al to a þong. *c* **1300** *St. Brandan* 93 With bole huden stronge y-nou y-nailed therto faste. **1718** POPE *Iliad* VII. 268 With seven thick folds o'ercast, Of tough bull-hides. **1878** H. STANLEY *Dark Cont.* I. xvi. 439 Well wrapped in bull-hides. **1807** VANCOUVER *Agric. Devon* 473 *Bull-house, with two pens in it for bull calves. **1859** R. BURTON *Centr. Afr.* in *Jrnl. R.G.S.* XXIX. 321 The neck is *bull-like, short, heavy, and broad. **1673** DRYDEN *Love in Nunnery* I. II. i, When the Place falls, you shall be *Bull-master-General at Court. **1812** R. STUART *Narratives* (1935) 160 Poor *Bull meat or Buck Antelope. **1859** R. B. SAGE *Rocky Mountain Life* 64 Bull-meat at this time..is unprecedentedly tough, strong-tasted, and poor. **1893** KIPLING *Seven Seas* (1896) 22 When the *bull-mouthed breakers flee. ? *a* **1400** *Morte Arth.* 1094 *Bullenekkyde was þat bierne. **1647** CLEVELAND *Char. Lond. Diurn. Maker* (1677) 107 A Bull-neck'd Presbyter. **1818** SCOTT *Rob Roy* vi, Rashleigh, though strong in person, was bull-necked and cross-made. *c* **1400** *Ywaine & Gaw.* 2440 Al the armure he was yn Was noght bot of a *bull-skyn. **1855** *Golden Era* (San Francisco) 1 Apr. 4/2 The humbler occupation of swaying a *bull-team. **1888** *San Francisco Weekly Exam.* 23 Feb. (Farmer), I gave instructions to the wagon boss, and the long bull-team moved away. **1888** KIPLING *Departm. Ditties*, etc. (ed. 4, 1890) 69 Hans the blue-eyed Dane, *Bull-throated, bare of arm. **1928** *Daily Express* 12 Sept. 8 Bull-throated foremen bawled for more and yet more labour. **1837** CARLYLE *Fr. Rev.* I. VII. vii. 325 The *bull-voiced Marquis Saint-Huruge.

11. Special comb.: **bull and cow**, rhyming slang for ROW *sb.*[2]; **bulls and cows** (see quot.); **bull-ant** = BULL-DOG 4 b; † **bull-back** = PIGGY-BACK; **bull-bat**, the American Goatsucker (*Caprimulgus Americanus*); **bull-beef**, the flesh of bulls, also †a term of abuse; esp. in ***to bluster like bull-beef, as big as bull-beef***, etc.; **bull-bird** = BULLFINCH; **bull-boat**, a boat made of hides stretched on a wooden frame; **bull-comber**, a dung-beetle (*Typhœus vulgaris*); **bull-dance** (see quot.); **bull dust** *Austral.*, (*a*) a coarse dust; (*b*) nonsense, rubbish (*slang*); **bull-feast**, a bull-baiting (Eng.); a bull-fight (Sp.); **bull-fiddle** *U.S. colloq.*, a bass-viol or double-bass; hence ***bull-fiddler***; **bull-flesh**, *fig.* brag, swagger; † **bull-fly**, a stag-beetle; **bull-foot** (*Bot.*) Colt's-foot (*Tussilago*); **bull-god**, a god worshipped under the form of a bull; **bull-holder** (see quot. 1940); **bull-hoof**, *Bot.* (see quot.); **bull-horn**, a megaphone; **bull-kelp**, any of several varieties of large seaweed found in Pacific and Antarctic waters; cf. *bull-head kelp* (KELP[1] 1 a); **bull-man**, a monster half bull half man; **bullmanship** (*nonce-wd.*), the art of fighting with bulls; **bull-nose**, (*a*) = *bull's nose* (see 11 b); (*b*) see quots.; also *attrib.*; so **bull-nosed** *a.* (see quots.); **bull oak** *Austral.*, a name given to several species of *Casuarina*, esp. *C. luehmanni* (cf. OAK 3 b); **bull-of-the-bog**, the bittern, from its booming cry; **bull-poll**, the Turfy Hair-grass (*Aira cæspitosa*); **bull-pout** *U.S.*, a fish, ? = BIB *sb.*[2]; **bull-pump** (see quot.); **bull-puncher**, (*a*) *Austral.*, a bullock-driver; (*b*) *U.S.*, a cowboy, cow-puncher; so ***bull-punching***; **bull-pup**, a young bull-dog; **bull-ring**, the arena for a bull-fight (Sp.); the place where bulls were baited (Eng.); the ring to which a bull was fastened; also *transf.* (*slang*) a military training-ground; **bull-roarer**,

spec. used by Australian Aborigines in certain (religious) ceremonies; **bull-rope** (see quot.); **bull-run**, **bull-running**, a race after a bull or bull-baiting (e.g. the famous one at Stamford); † **bull-seg** (*dial.*) = *bull-stag*; **bull-snake** *U.S.*, a large North American snake (*Pityophis melanoleucus*); the pine-snake; **bull-stag**, a bull gelded when past his prime; **bull-sticker** (see quots.); **bull-strong** *a. U.S.*, strong enough to resist a bull; **bull's wool**, **bullswool**, (*a*) *Army slang*, coarse woollen cloth or yarn; (*b*) *Austral.* and *N.Z. colloq.* = BULL *sb.*⁴ 3; see also quot. 1898; **bull-toad**, ? = BULL-FROG; **bull-tongue (plough)** *U.S.*, a simple form of plough; **bull-ward**, the keeper of a bull; **bull-week** (see quot.); **bull-whack** *sb. U.S.* (see quot.); **bull-whack** *v. trans.* and *intr.* (*U.S.*), to drive (cattle); **bull-whacker** (*U.S.*), (*a*) a bullock driver in the Western states; (*b*) = *bull-whack* sb.; **bull-wheel** (see quot.); **bull-whip** *U.S.*, a whip with a long heavy lash, used for driving cattle. Also BULL-BAIT, -BAITING, etc.

1859 HOTTEN *Slang Dict.* 142 *Bull and cow, a row. **1962** 'A. GILBERT' *No Dust in Attic* xi. 138 The murder might have been the result of a private bull-and-cow. **1863** PRIOR *Pop. Names Brit. Plants* 34 *Bulls and Cows, more commonly called Lords and Ladies, the purple and the pale spadices, respectively, of Arum maculatum. **1900** *Daily News* 26 May 3/5 As eager for fight as a *bull ant on a hot plate. **1908** *Westm. Gaz.* 10 Dec. 1/3 His first bite from an Australian 'bull-ant'. **1948** B. JAMES in *Coast to Coast 1947* 162 But Tommy could fight—game as a bull-ant. *c* **1600** *Rob. Hood* (Ritson) II. i. 183 Some were on *bull-back, some dancing a morris. **1838** P. H. GOSSE *Lett.* (1859) 62 The common people here generally call these birds by the name of *bull-bats. **1883** *Macm. Mag.* '*Old Virg. Gentl.*', The 'bull-bats' or night-hawks, in the air above us. **1572** GASCOIGNE *Voy. Holland* in Southey *Comm.-pl. Bk.* Ser. II. (1849) 311 Methinks they be a race of *bull-beef born. *c* **1618** FLETCHER *Doubl. Marr.* III. i, Down with the bul-beefes. **1690** W. WALKER *Idiomat. Anglo-Lat.* 57 He looks as big as bull-beef. **1785** WOLCOTT (P. Pindar) *Ode III to R. A.* Wks. 1812 I. 83 Thou may'st bluster like Bull-beef so big. **1837** W. IRVING *Capt. Bonneville* III. 109 We have the crew of the little *bull boat complete. **1841** CATLIN *N. Amer. Ind.* (1844) I. xxiv. 195 A skin-canoe—more familiarly called in this country a bull-boat. **1802** BINGLEY *Anim. Biog.* III. 111 The *bull-comber, clock beetle, and spring beetle. **1855** *Whitby Gloss.*, **Bull-Dance*, rustic merriment connected with cattle-show feasts. **1867** SMYTH *Sailor's Word-bk.*, *Bull-dance*, at sea it is performed by men only, when without women. It is sometimes called a stag-dance. **1943** BAKER *Dict. Austral. Slang* 16 **Bull dust*..bullsh. **1943** W. E. HARNEY *Taboo* 127 The gypsum crumbles into copi or bulldust. **1954** B. MILES *Stars my Blanket* xvi. 105 We found the track..to be inches deep in bull dust—a soft, powdery dust that seeps through into everything. **1967** J. HAMILTON *Man with Brown Paper Face* iv. 50 I'm not in the mood for any of your bulldust. Where have you been all night? **1688** *Lond. Gaz.* No. 2364/2 Bilboa, July 12..To morrow there will be a *Bull Feast. **1768** EARL MALMESBURY *Diaries & Corr.* (1844) I. 42 The amusements of this town ..are, the bull-feast, two play-houses, and, during the carnival, masquerades. **1824** J. MCCULLOCH *Highlands Scotl.* I. 367 Some squire is born, and there is a bull-feast at Grantham or Chirk. **1883** *Sunday Mag.* Sept. 574/2 The bull-ring, or, as it is called, the bull-feast. **1880** G. A. SALA *Amer. Revisited* 209/1 A '*bull-fiddle' which is American for violoncello. **1941** STEINBECK & RICKETTS *Sea of Cortez* (1951) iv. 30 A deep and yet penetrating tone like the lowest string of an incredible bull-fiddle. **1957** W. C. HANDY *Father of Blues* xvii. 237 As usual the bull-fiddler sawed away in G. **1820** T. MITCHELL *Aristoph.* I. 220 What! shall a little *bull-flesh gain the day? **1583** J. HIGINS *Junius' Nomenclator* (N.) *Cerf volant*, a *bullflie, or hornet. **1611** COTGR., *Cerf volant*, the great horned beetle, or bull-flie. **1706** PHILLIPS, *Bull-fly* or *Bull-bee*, an Insect. **1562** TURNER *Herbal* II. 158 *Tussilago* is named..in Englishe Horse houe or *Bullfoote. **1816** G. S. FABER *Orig. Pag. Idol.* I. 433 The *bull-god of Phenicia. **1871** ROSSETTI *Burden Nineveh* xviii, That Bull-god once did stand And watched the burial-clouds of sand. **1940** *Chambers's Techn. Dict.* 119/2 **Bull-holder*, forceps for grasping the nasal septum of cattle as a means of restraint. **1756** P. BROWNE *Jamaica* 328 The *Bull-hoof or Dutchman's Laudanum..a climber, whose fruit is..about the size of a large olive. **1866** *Treas. Bot.*, Bull-hoof, *Murucuja ocellata*. **1955** C. S. FORESTER *Good Shepherd* ii. 38 Her captain shouting himself hoarse through his *bull-horn at the laggards. **1959** *Ottawa Citizen* 24 Sept. 48/6 Mr. Garst tried to explain something to reporters through an electric bull-horn. *c* **1929** W. MARTIN *N.Z. Nature Book* II. i, The Giant *Bull Kelp (*Durvillea utilis*) is a truly Antarctic sea-weed. **1954** *New Biol.* XVII. 96 The genera vary in size from the great bull-kelps..to a small parasite. **1816** G. S. FABER *Orig. Pag. Idol.* I. 232 That being was succeeded by a second *bull-man. **1821** *New Monthly Mag.* II. 340 To her [Seville's] school of *bullmanship that art owes all its refinements. **1858** *Skyring's Builders' Prices* 41 Circular styles to *bull-nose corners. *a* **1884** KNIGHT *Dict. Mech.* Suppl., *Bull-nose Rabbet Plane*, a plane with the bit at the end, in order to enable it to work up close into corners. **1895** *Funk's Standard Dict.* s.v. *Nose*, *Bull-nose*, a front coupler on a locomotive: named from its shape; a bull-nose coupler. **1904** GOODCHILD & TWENEY *Technol. & Sci. Dict.* 75/2 *Bullnosed bricks*, bricks having one angle on the end rounded off. *Bullnosed step*, a step with a rounded end. **1933** *Archit. Rev.* LXXIII. 198/2 It could be chiselled with a bull-nosed chisel. **1952** 'W. COOPER' *Struggles of Albert Woods* II. ii. 83 Albert pointed his bull-nosed Morris Cowley in the direction of Islip. **1884** A. NILSON *Timber Trees N.S.W.* 7 The most widely-distributed and best-known species are..'Pine' or 'Cypress Pine'..'She Oak', 'He Oak', '*Bull Oak'. **1963** W. E. HARNEY *To Ayers Rock & Beyond* ii. 23 The famous 'Drunk's-seat', beneath a shady bull-oak tree. **1815** SCOTT *Guy M.* i, The deep cry of the bog-blitter, or *bull-of-the-bog. **1880** JEFFERIES *Gt. Estate* 36 Some bulrushes and great bunches of *bullpolls..The bullpoll sends up tall slender stalks with graceful feathery heads. **1823** F. COOPER *Pioneer* xxiii. (1869) 101/1 'Away with you, you varmint!' said Billy Kirby, plucking a *bull-pout from the meshes. **1881** RAYMOND *Gloss.*, **Bull-pump* (Cornwall), a direct single-acting pump..The steam lifts piston and pump-rods, and the weight of these makes the down-stroke. **1872** C. H. EDEN *My Wife & I in Queensland* ii. 49 The '*bull-puncher', as bullock-drivers are familiarly called. **1874** *Chambers's Jrnl.* 543/2 Commissariat beeves, guarded by the commissariat 'bull-punchers'. **1887** M. ROBERTS *Western Avernus* ii. 19 He followed the profession of a 'bull-puncher', that is, he went in charge of the cattle destined for slaughter and canning in the distant North, and made money at it. *Ibid.* 20, I found this bull-punching a very wearisome and dangerous business. **1917** 'H. H. RICHARDSON' *Fortunes R. Mahony* I. v. 39 Stock-riders and bull-punchers rubbed shoulders with elegants in skirted coats. **1883** *Congregationalist* July 585 Toying with a tiny, toddling *bull-pup. **1609** D. ROGERS in *Digby Myst.* (1882) Introd. 26 He caused..The *bull ringe..to be taken vp. **1802** SOUTHEY *King Ramiro* viii, Let me be led to your bull-ring..And let me be set upon a stone. **1828** SCOTT *F.M. Perth* Introd., A poor mastiff that had misbehaved in the bull-ring. **1928** BLUNDEN *Undertones of War* i. 3, I associate it [Étaples], as millions do, with 'The Bull-Ring', that thirsty, savage, interminable training-ground. **1949** E. DE MAUNY *Huntsman in Career* I. i. 13 Drawing equipment at the Q.M., drilling on the bull-ring. **1881** *Academy* 9 Apr. 263/3 A flat slip of wood a few inches long, narrowing to one or both ends, and fastened by one end to a thong for whirling it round, when it gives an intermittent whirring or roaring noise, heard a long way off..it is known as a country boy's plaything in Europe, called in England a 'whizzer' or '*bull-roarer'. **1898** *Daily News* 23 July 6/1 Among Australian blacks, the bullroarer is associated with tales of a deluge. **1943** W. E. HARNEY *Taboo* 43 In this ritual the lads are taken away from the women, initiated into the secrets of the 'bullroarer' and..live as outcasts. **1882** NARES *Seamanship* (ed. 6) 173 A *bull-rope..is a hawser let through a block on the bow-sprit end to the buoy, to keep the buoy clear of the stem. **1864** CHAMBERS *Bk. of Days* 13 Nov. II. 575/2 As..there could be no *bull-run without a bull. **1656** J. HARRINGTON *Oceana* 196 There is a solemnity of the Pipers, and Fidlers of this Nation..call'd the *Bull-running, and he that catcheth and holdeth the Bull, is the annuall and Supream Magistrate of that Comitia, or Congregation, called King-Piper. **1861** SMILES *Engineers* I. v. i. 310 If there was a bull-running within twenty miles, he was sure to be there. **1641** BEST *Farm. Bks.* (1856) 141 Makinge a *bullsegge of a bull that is two or three yeares olde. **1820** SCOTT *Monastery* iv, 'Roaring like bullsegs, to frighten the leddy'. **1784** J. FILSON *Kentucke* 27 The *bull, the horned and the mockason snakes. **1791** W. BARTRAM *Travels* 276 The pine or bull snake is very large. **1878** J. H. BEADLE *Western Wilds* ix. 133 The 'bull-snake'..an immense thing of four or five feet in length, which gets its name from its blunt head and thick clumsy body. **1680** *Lond. Gaz.* No. 1482/4 One red *Bull Stag with the same Mark. **1776** *Chron.* in *Ann. Reg.* 149/1 Good ox beef, instead of which he had substituted bull beef and bull stag beef. **1933** *Discovery* Oct. 319/2 Numerous varieties of burins called by such pleasant names as spitstickers, *bullstickers, [etc.]. **1958** J. R. BIGGS *Woodcuts* 49 The bull-sticker..is virtually a spitstick with bulging sides. The line it makes will therefore have a very rapid 'spread'. **1859** *Harper's Mag.* Oct. 712/2 A fence that is *bull strong, horse high, and pig tight! **1850** 'Two MOUNTED SENTRIES' *Horse Guards* 70 The 'sealed pattern' [of cloth] provided for the British soldier, and familiarly known among the men by the euphonious cognomen of '*bull's wool'. **1893** KIPLING *Many Inventions* 268 If iver you feel that you've got a felt sole in your boot instid av a Government bull's-wool, come to me. **1898** MORRIS *Austral. Eng.* 64/1 *Bulls-wool*, colloquial name for the inner portion of the covering of the Stringybark-tree. **1911** E. M. CLOWES *On Wallaby* ix. 247 To build one's fire, kindling it surely and quickly with what is called 'bull's-wool', the thick, dry fibre, like fine cocoa-nut matting, which forms the hair shirt of the gum-tree between the white skin and the cream and green and madder-tinted bark. **1933** *Bulletin* (Sydney) 13 Dec. 40/1 'And I'm dropping fifteen!' 'Bullswool!' declared Tommy. 'What you'd drop it'd take a bloke with a microscope to find.' **1950** G. MEEK in A. E. Woodhouse *N.Z. Farm & Station Verse* 153 Don't think that it's all bullswool. **1957** I. CROSS *God Boy* (1958) ix. 67 That last bit was bulls-wool of course, but I had to be careful. **1806** MOORE *Poems* 166 Let the *bull-toad taint him over. **1831** M. A. HOLLEY *Texas* (1833) 139 Many farmers use the coulter and *bull-tongue plough. **1837** in N. E. Eliason *Tarheel Talk* (1956) 262, 25¢ for making a bul tung. **1886** *Harper's Mag.* June 58/2 Ploughing is commonly done with a 'bull-tongue', an implement hardly more than a sharpened stick with a metal rim. **1614** HORNBY *Sco. Drunk.* (1859) 19 It is a cage of all base villany..*Bul-wards and beare-wards with like company. **1878** HALLIWELL, **Bull-week*, the week before Christmas, in which the work-people at Sheffield push their strength to the utmost. **1869** A. K. MCCLURE *Rocky Mts.* 102 You will often find some graduate of Yale '*bull-whacking' his own team from the river to his mines. **1885** C. L. NORTON in *Mag. Amer. Hist.* XIII. 98 In Texas and western Louisiana the 'bull-whack' is a terrible whip with a long and very heavy lash and a short handle. It is used by drovers to intimidate refractory animals. **1906** *Dialect Notes* III. 129 He's a bull-whackin'. **1858** *Valley Tan* (Salt Lake City) 17 Dec. 2/2 An example that will make the blush of shame mantle upon the cheek of the *bull-whacker. **1878** BLACK *Green Past.* xiii. 106 Not even the stoutest bull-whacker who ever crossed the plains. **1887** E. B. CUSTER *Tenting on Plains* (1888) vii. 229 There is no sound like the snap of the lash of a 'bull-whacker'. **1883** *Century Mag.* July 329/2 Attached to the derrick is also a big windlass, called the '*bull-wheel', which hoists the drilling apparatus out of the [oil] well. **1852** *Southern Lit. Messenger* XVIII. 749/2 An overseer..omitted..laying down at once his *bull-whip for the yard-stick. **1935** J. STEINBECK *To God Unknown* xxii. 205 Romas snapped his bull-whip and the popper spat up the dirt like an explosion.

b. Comb. with gen. *bull's*: **bull's blood**, a full-bodied red wine made in and around the village of Eger in Hungary; † **bull's feather**, a horn, the mark of cuckoldry; **bull's-noon**, midnight (*dial.*); **bull's-nose** (see quot.); **bull's-pizzle**, the penis of the bull, formerly a much-used instrument of flagellation.

1926 P. M. SHAND *Bk. Wine* ix. 242 An almost black wine called..'*Bulls' Blood Wine' used to be made here [*sc.* Eger] by a very protracted process of fermentation. **1967** A. LICHINE *Encycl. Wines* 294/1 Bull's blood of Eger is a blend of three kinds of grapes. *a* **1700** *Bull's Feather* (N.) There's many an honest man hath worn the *bull's feather. **1748** RICHARDSON *Clarissa* V. 295 (D.) They may very probably adorn, as well as bestow the bull's feather. **18..** *Northampton dial.* If I go on at this rate I shan't be done at *bull's-noon. **1839** C. CLARK *John Noakes, &c.* 17 No bull's noon hours I'll ha' ya keep. **1842** GWILT *Archit.* (1875) Gloss., **Bull's Nose*, the external or other angle of a polygon, or of any two lines meeting at an obtuse angle. **1599** HAKLUYT *Voy.* II. 187 The Boteswaine..walked abaft the Maste, and his Mate afore the Maste..eche of them a *bulls pissell dried in their handes. **1664** BUTLER *Hud.* II. I. 879 Th' illustrious Bassa..with Bull's-pizzle..Was taw'd as gentle as a Glove. **1737** tr. (anon.) *Gil Blas* vi. 1771 I. 26 I felt on my shoulders half a dozen lusty bangs of a bull's pizzle.

bull (bʊl), *sb.*² Also 3–6 bulle, 6 bul. [ad. L. *bulla*, denoting various globular objects.]

1. A seal attached to an official document; *esp.* the leaden seal attached to the Pope's edicts.

1340 *Ayenb.* 62 Me ualseþ þe kinges sel oþer þe popes bulle. **1480** CAXTON *Chron. Eng.* cxci. 167 The pope sente a general sentence vnder his bulles of lede vnto the archebisshop. **1555** EDEN *Decades W. Ind.* I. III. (Arb.) 74 The byshop of Rome..graunted to the Kynge of Spayne by thauctoritie of his leaden bulles. **1643** PRYNNE *Open. Gt. Seal* 4 Now the French Kings long before his dayes, used to seale their charters with golden Bulls. **1726** AYLIFFE *Parerg.* 132 These Letters are not said to be expedited till that Bull is annex'd to them. **1727–51** CHAMBERS *Cycl.* s.v.

2. A papal or episcopal edict or mandate.

1297 R. GLOUC. 494 The king vorbed ek in this lond al the popes playdinge Of bullen. **1362** LANGL. *P. Pl.* A. Prol. 66 And brouȝt vp a Bulle with bisshopes seles. *c* **1380** WYCLIF *Grete Sentence* xvi. Sel. Wks. III. 308 þei magnyfien þe popis bulle more þan þe gospel. **1483** CAXTON *Gold. Leg.* 108/1 And after..toke away hys bullys and wrytynges. **1561** DAUS tr. *Bullinger on Apoc.* (1573) 209 The Popes Bulles..may well be called Buls, since they be more vayne then bubbles or bladders in the water. **1583** STUBBES *Anat. Abus.* II. 5 How often hath he sent foorth his roring buls against hir Maiestie. **1667** MILTON *P.L.* III. 492 Then might ye see..Indulgences, Dispenses, Pardons, Bulls, The sport of Winds. **1827** HALLAM *Const. Hist.* (1876) I. iii. 134 Pius V ..now (1570) published his celebrated bull, excommunicating and deposing Elizabeth. **1873** MORLEY *Rousseau* II. 63 The bull Unigenitus, which had been..an infraction of French liberties.

3. Applied to a non-ecclesiastical edict. ***the Golden Bull*** (Lat. *Aurea Bulla*), a decree issued by the emperor Charles IV in 1356 to regulate the election and coronation of an emperor.

1696 PHILLIPS. **1751** CHAMBERS *Cycl.*, s.v. *Bull*, The Golden Bull..on the backside of it there are several knots of black and yellow silk; to which hangs a bull, or seal of gold. **1789–96** MORSE *Amer. Geog.* II. 222.

4. *Comb.* † **bull-driver** (see quot.); † **bull-founder**, one that issues bulls or edicts (perhaps with reference to founding or casting the leaden seals); † **bullman**, issuer of bulls, said of the Pope; † **bull-office**, the office for issuing Papal bulls.

1649 SELDEN *Laws Eng.* II. vi. (1739) 33 These *Bull-drivers or Summoners to the Romish Court were no late upstarts. **1563–87** FOXE *A. & M.* (1596) 1173/2 If these *Bull founders doe charge me with any other thing besides in this article. **1588** *Holy Bull & Crusade Rome* 29 All the holines of this Romish *Bulman consisteth onely in externall ceremonies. **1736** J. SERCES *Popery Enemy to Script.* 112 Before Henry VIII, England paid more into the *Bull-office than all the Roman Catholic Countries put together.

† **bull**, *sb.*³ *Obs. rare.* [a. F. *bulle*:—L. *bulla*.] A bubble.

1561 [see BULL *sb.*² 2]. **1563** NOWELL *Homily* in *Liturg. Serv. Q. Eliz.* (1847) 501 This life is..a vapour..as a bull rising on the water.

bull (bʊl), *sb.*⁴ [Of unknown origin; cf. OF. *boul*, *boule*, *bole* fraud, deceit, trickery; mod.Icel. *bull* 'nonsense'; also ME. *bull* BUL 'falsehood', and BULL *v.*³, to befool, mock, cheat.

(No foundation appears for the guess that the word originated in 'a contemptuous allusion to papal edicts', nor for the assertion of the 'British Apollo' (No. 22. 1708) that 'it became a Proverb from the repeated Blunders of one Obadiah Bull, a Lawyer of London, who liv'd in the Reign of K. Henry the Seventh'.)]

† **1.** A ludicrous jest (cf. BULL *v.*³). *Obs.*

1630 J. TAYLOR (Water P.) *J. Garret's Ghost* Ded., Wit and Mirth..Made vp, and fashioned into Clinches, Bulls, Quirkes, Yerkes, Quips, and Ierkes. **1652** URQUHART *Jewel* Wks. (1834) 229 He had all the jeers, squibs, flouts, buls, quips, taunts, etc. *a* **1695** A. À WOOD in *Oxoniana* II. 23 Every one in order was to..make a jest or bull, or speake some eloquent nonsense, to make the company laugh.

2. A self-contradictory proposition; in mod. use, an expression containing a manifest contradiction in terms or involving a ludicrous inconsistency unperceived by the speaker. Now often with epithet *Irish*; but the word had been long in use before it came to be associated with Irishmen.

1640 BROME *Antip.* v. iv. 323 Dumbe Speaker! that's a Bull. Thou wert the Bull Then, in the Play. Would I had seene thee rore. *Bla.* That's a Bull too, as wise as you are, Bab. **1649** SELDEN *Laws Eng.* II. xi. (1739) 63 It is no Bull,

to speak of a common Peace, in the place of War. **1673** MILTON *True Relig.* 5 Whereas the Papist boasts himself to be a Roman Catholick, it is a meer contradiction, one of the Popes Bulls. **1702** *Let. fr. Soldier to Ho. Commons* 17 These Gentlemen seem to me to have copied the Bull of their Countryman, who said his Mother was barren. **1711** POPE *Lett. to J. C.* Wks. 1736 V. 174, I confess it what the English call a Bull, in the expression, tho' the sense be manifest enough. **1802** EDGEWORTH (*title*) Essay on Irish Bulls. **1803** SYD. SMITH *Wks.* (1867) I. 69 A bull is an apparent congruity, and real incongruity of ideas, suddenly discovered.

b. A bad blunder. *U.S.*

1846 D. CORCORAN *Pickings* 13 When we speak of 'Irish Evenings' in New Orleans, we are guilty of neither bull nor blunder. **1855** 'P. PAXTON' *Capt. Priest* 226, I had committed a bull myself, by intruding where I evidently was *de trop.* **1904** *N.Y. Times* 4 July 3 They are going to nominate Parker, and they are going to make a bull by doing it. **1934** J. T. FARRELL *Young Manhood* (1936) xviii. 379 It was bull number one for him, [a] bad way to start the evening off.

3. Trivial, insincere, or untruthful talk or writing; nonsense. *slang* (orig. *U.S.*).

Popularly associated with BULLSHIT 1.

1914 *Dialect Notes* IV. 162 *Bull*, talk which is not to the purpose; 'hot air'. **1925** WODEHOUSE *Sam the Sudden* xx. 160 You threw a lot of bull about being the brains of the concern. **1932** *Times Lit. Suppl.* 8 Dec. 933/3 'Bull' is the slang term for a combination of bluff, bravado, 'hot-air', and what we used to call in the Army 'Kidding the troops'. **1946** G. GIBSON *Enemy Coast Ahead* xii. 159, I have never heard such a line of bull in all my life. **1952** M. MCCARTHY *Groves of Academe* (1953) vi. 116, I never thought I'd be listening to that old bull slung at Jocelyn.

b. *attrib.*, esp. in **bull session** (orig. and chiefly *U.S.*), an informal conversation or discussion, esp. of a group of males.

1920 T. WOLFE *Let.* 26 Nov. (1956) 11 With no more delightful 'bull sessions', I have turned to work. **1924** P. MARKS *Plastic Age* x. 77 Religion and sex, the favorite topics for 'bull sessions'. *Ibid.* xxxiv. 286 The monthly meetings were nothing but 'bull fests'. **1931** 'DEAN STIFF' *Milk & Honey Route* 201 *Bull artist*, a hobo with the gift of gab. **1960** *Guardian* 8 Dec. 12/3 The kind of college 'bull session' that is common among English students.

4. Unnecessary routine tasks or ceremonial; excessive discipline or 'spit-and-polish'; = RED-TAPE b. Cf. BULLSHIT 2. orig. *Services' slang.*

1941 *New Statesman* 30 Aug. 218/3 *Bull*, discipline. **1942** I. GLEED *Arise to Conquer* vi. 51 The Squadron..felt very bolshie about all the bull that was flying around the station. **1953** A. BARON *Human Kind* xxiv. 178 Them turning out the guard for us, us marching past eyes right, all that sort of bull. **1958** *Economist* 8 Feb. 470/1 The drudgery and 'bull' in an MP's life.

bull (bʊl), *sb.*[5] [Etymology unknown.] One of the main bars of a harrow. Also *attrib.*

1523 FITZHERB. *Husb.* §15 The horse-harrowe is made of fyue bulles, and passe not an elne of lengthe. **1649** BLITHE *Eng. Impr. Improv.* (1652) 220 As little & light a harrow, which may contain three little buls & about five Tines in a Bull. **1677** PLOT *Oxfordsh.* 247 The great square Bull harrow, drawn by the second bull on the near side of the harrow. **1799** J. ROBERTSON *Agric. Perth* 97 General Robertson of Lawers uses five bulls, having five teeth in each bull. **1843** B. ALMACK in *Jrnl. Agric. Soc.* IV. I. 61 The bulls or parts to contain the teeth, were made of dry foreign pine.

bull (bʊl), *sb.*[6] Drink made by putting water into an empty spirit cask, or over a sugar-mat, to catch some of the flavour.

1830 MARRYAT *King's Own* xx, I'll pass the bottle, and you may make a bull of it. **1835** —— *Jac. Faithf.* xx, A *bull* means putting a quart or two of water into a cask which has had spirits in it. **1859** *All Y. Round* No. 4. 78 He would.. have abdicated his sovereignty for an old sugar mat, wherewith to make 'bull'.

bull, *sb.*[7] Ellipt. for BULL-DOG 1 a.

1827 PIERCE EGAN *Anecdotes of Turf* 107 Turk was a thorough-bred bull, and the other two were half-bred between a bull and a mastiff. **1939** T. WOLFE *Web & Rock* (1947) 17 The little bull..had his fierce teeth buried..in the great throat of the larger dog.

Hence **bull-mastiff, bullmastiff,** a dog of a cross-breed between a bull-dog and a mastiff.

1871 *Field* 29 Apr. 343/2 The fight which took place in the earlier part of this century between Wombwell's two lions and bull-mastiffs. **1948** D. J. NASH in B. Vesey-Fitzgerald *Book of Dog* 384 In 1795 an advertisement appeared for a lost Bullmastiff. **1959** *Country Life* 10 Dec. 1139/1 When the bull-mastiff or bull mastiff graduated from the gamekeeper's kennel..to the show-ring and a place in the Kennel Club register, the breed became known as the bullmastiff.

bull (bʊl), *sb.*[8] [Origin obscure.] A game resembling quoits. Also *attrib.*

1864 TREVELYAN *Compet. Wallah* 16 In search of sport these join the circle full That smokes and lounges round the game of 'Bull'. **1889** *Pall Mall Gaz.* 22 June 3/2 We tried to help on the dreary time with..a game called 'bull'—a kind of sea-quoits. **1928** *Blackw. Mag.* Mar. 418/2 Indifferent to the call of the 'Bull-board' or the deck-quoit. **1963** M. MALIM *Pagoda Tree* xiii. 77 She was good at bull-board—a matter of lobbing little sacks of sand into numbered squares upon an inclined board.

bull, *sb.*[9] Short for BULL'S-EYE 7; also, a shot hitting the bull's-eye.

1900 *Westm. Gaz.* 13 June 5/2 Able to hit a two-foot bull five times out of ten at 500 yards. **1932** A. J. WORRALL *Eng. Idioms* 3 He scored seven bulls in eight shots. **1955** *Times* 11 Aug. 8/4 The uninitiated..soon learn to refer to a 'gold', and not to a 'bull' or an 'inner'.

Bull *sb.*[10] Short for JOHN BULL. Hence 'Bullism = JOHN BULLISM.

1825 CARLYLE *Early Lett.* (Norton) II. 295 Bull himself, again, though a frank, beef-loving, joyous kind of person, is excessively stupid. **1843** SYD. SMITH *Wks.* (1867) II. 331 Bull is naturally disposed to love you, but he loves nobody who does not pay him. **1821** *Blackw. Mag.* X. 89 English jurors have been lately so bepreached out of bullism by him.

bull (bʊl), *v.*[1] [f. BULL *sb.*[1]]

†**1. a.** *trans.* Said of a bull: To gender with (the cow). **b.** *intr.* Of the cow: To take the bull, to desire the bull. Also *to go a bulling. Obs.*

1398 TREVISA *Barth. de P.R.* XVIII. cix. (1495) 850 Kene lowe whan they be a bullynge. **1523** FITZHERB. *Husb.* §66 The damme of the calfe shall bull agayne. **1601** HOLLAND *Pliny* I. 224 Kine commonly..seeke the fellow, and goe a bulling againe. **1659** HOWELL *Lex. Tetraglotton*, He that bulls the Cow must keep the Calf. **1675** COTTON *Poet. Wks.* (1765) 182 Unless I had a Spell, To bull my Cow invisible. **1736** in BAILEY.

2. *Stock-Exchange.* To try to raise the price of (stocks, etc.); to speculate for the rise.

a **1842** [see BEAR *v.*[2]]. *c* **1880** BESANT & RICE *Harp. & Cr.* xix. 196 Men who bull and bear the stock market. **1881** *Chicago Times* 4 June, If we succeed in bulling silver we shall also succeed in bearing gold to the same extent.

b. *intr.* To advance in price; *fig.* to be in the ascendant.

1928 S. VINES *Humours Unreconciled* 252 Music was 'bulling' in Japan and the Conservatory crammed to bursting point.

3. To behave or move like a bull; to act with violence in the manner of a bull. Also *refl. U.S. slang.*

1884 'MARK TWAIN' *Huck. Finn* xvi. 144 Up-stream boats ..bull right up the channel. *Ibid.* xxvii. 276 The old fool he bulled right along. **1947** A. MILLER *All my Sons* 11, Don't come bulling in here. If you've got something to say, be civilized about it. *Ibid.* 111, You can't bull yourself through this one, Joe, you better be smart now. **1956** *Time* 10 Sept. 30/1 A mob of about 400 Texans bulled about the school grounds.

†**bull,** *v.*[2] *Obs.* [f. BULL *sb.*[2]] *trans.* To insert or publish (a matter, or a name) in a Papal bull; to affix the Papal seal to (a document).

1563-87 FOXE *A. & M.* (1684) I. 325/2 Shortly after the Pope sent M. Martin with blanks, being bulled for contribution of 10000 Marks. *a* **1670** HACKET *Abp. Williams* I. (1692) 130 As soon as the Dispensation was Bulled.

bull, *v.*[3] [Cf. ME. *bul* falsehood, OF. *boler, bouller* to deceive.] **1.** To make a fool of, to mock; to cheat (*out of*).

1532 [see BULLING *vbl. sb.*[3]]. **1609** *Man in Moone* (1849) 38 Never laugh in your sleeve how you have gulled, or bulled, your husband. **1645** *Sacred Decretal* in Prynne *Discov. New Blazing-Stars* 12 Wherefore being thus jeer'd and bul'd, we Decree and Ordaine, etc. **1674** R. GODFREY *Inj. & Ab. Physic* 207 'Tis admirable the World is so stupid to be thus bull'd out of their Moneys. **1927** J. BARBICAN *Confessions of Rum-Runner* xxiii. 256, I thought he was trying to bull me.

2. *intr.* To talk emptily or boastfully (cf. BULL *sb.*[4] 3).

1850 T. M. GARRETT *Diary* in *Amer. Speech* (1951) XXVI. 182 Elaborate bulling about a point that has been exploded for years. **1941** BAKER *Dict. Austral. Slang* 14 *To bull*, to brag, talk nonsense.

3. *trans.* To polish (equipment, etc.) in order to meet excessive standards of neatness. Hence **bulled** *ppl. a.*[3] Cf. BULL *sb.*[4] 4. *Services' slang.*

1957 *Times* 4 Oct. 13/5 Those army recruits who spend so much time 'bulling' their boots with a hot spoon. **1967** 'M. HUNTER' *Cambridgeshire Disaster* v. 32 The bed..collapsed, spilling equipment haberdashery over the bulled-up floor. **1969** D. CLARK *Nobody's Perfect* ii. 35 His shoes were bulled so that the toecaps gleamed like patent leather.

bull (bʊl), *v.*[4] [f. BULL *sb.*[6]] See quot.

1824 J. D. COCHRANE *Journ. Russia & Tartary* 225, I could do nothing but bull the barrel, that is, put a little water into it, and so preserve at least the appearance of vodkey.

bull-. [prob. in most cases = BULL *sb.*[1]; but *bull-weed* has the alternative form *boll-weed*, see BOLL *sb.*[1], which may be the etymon in some of the words. (The suggestion that *bull-* in some plant names may be a corruption of *pool*, is quite baseless.)]

A prefix occurring in certain names of plants, as **bull-brier** *U.S.*, see quot.; **bull-oak** (see quot.); **bull-plum**, a sloe (*Prunus spinosa*), cf. however BULLACE; **bull-sedge** (see quot.); **bull-weed**, *Centaurea nigra*, = *boll-weed*; **bull-wort**, *Ammi majus*, also called Bishop-weed.

1860 BARTLETT *Dict. Amer.*, *Bull Briar, a large briar.. the root of which contains a farinaceous substance from which the Indians make bread. **1830** J. G. STRUTT *Sylva Brit.* 22 *Bull-Oaks..are thus denominated from the.. circumstance of bulls taking shelter within them; which they effect..by retreating backwards into the cavity. **1770** FOOTE *Lame Lover* III. (D.) A plum-tree indeed, but not..a damascen plum; our proofs say loudly a *bull plum. **1879** PRIOR *Plant-names*, *Bull-segg or sedge, the reed-mace. *a* **1450** *Alphita.* (Anecd Oxon) 83 Iacea nigra..*Bulwed uel hardaw. **1597** GERARD *Herbal* ccxcix. §1. 703 Harts ease is named..in English, Knapweede, Bull weede. **1598** FLORIO, *Ammi.* the..herbe William, *bulwoort or bishops weede.

‖**bulla** ('bʊlə, 'bʌlə). Pl. **bullæ**. [L. = bubble.]

1. *Pathol.* A vesicle containing watery humour and causing an elevation of the skin.

1876 DUHRING *Dis. Skin* 44 Bullæ are irregularly-shaped elevations of the epidermis, varying in size from a split pea to a goose-egg, containing a clear or opaque fluid.

b. *Physiol.* 'The tympanic element of the temporal bone, when, as in the dog, it forms a large bubble-like appearance.' *Syd. Soc. Lex.*

1872 MIVART *Elem. Anat.* 106 In many Mammals..it forms a large inflated structure termed a bulla. **1881** —— *Cat* 62 The posterior surface of the auditory bulla.

2. *Zool.* A genus of molluscs, with thin and fragile shells, inhabiting deep water.

1847 CARPENTER *Zool.* §917 The Bulla and Bullæa..have a small calcareous shell in which the spiral form begins to manifest itself. **1851** MARY ROBERTS *Mollusca* 201 The fragile shell of the solitary bulla is utterly inadequate to contend with either winds or waves.

bullace ('bʊlɪs). Forms: 4-5 bolace, 5 bolys, -ysse, 5-6 bolas, bulas, 6 bulles, -ase, -asse, 7 bullas, 6-7 bulloes, bullies, -eis, 9 (*dial.* bulloe, -y), 6- bullace. *Pl.* 4 bolaces, bolas, 6 bullises, bulleys, -aze, boollesse, 6-7 bullies, bullase, 7 bullis, -eis, -aise, -ice, -ices, -ises, -asis, 7- bullace, -aces, (*Sc.* bullees, *Devon.* bullens.) [app. connected with OF. *beloce* of same meaning (13th c., Littré); but its precise relation to the OF. word, and the etymology of the latter, are not ascertained.

The Ir. *bulistair*, Ga. *bulaistear*, sometimes accepted as the etymon, appear to be adopted from ME. *bolaster* = *bullace-tree*. Legonidec gives a Breton *polos, bolos* 'prune sauvage', and Florio 1611 has an It. *bulloi* 'bulloes, slowne, or skegs', which may possibly be ultimately connected.]

1. A wild plum (*Prunus insititia*) larger than the sloe; there are two varieties, the black (or dark-blue) and the white; also well-known as a semi-cultivated fruit.

c **1350** *Will. Palerne* (1809) 66 Gete vs..bolaces & blakeberies þat on breres growen. *c* **1400** *Rom. Rose* 1377 Notes, aleys, and bolas. *c* **1430** LYDG. *Min. Poems* (1840) 199 As bryght as bugyl or ellys bolace. **1483** *Cath. Angl.* 47 A Bulas, *pepulum.* **1523** FITZHERB. *Husb.* §140 Bulleys plummes and suche other, may be sette of stones. **1573** TUSSER *Husb.* (1878) 76 Boollesse, black and white. **1599** A. M. tr. *Gabelhouer's Bk. Physick* 183/2 Take whyt bullises pounded to pappe. **1629** PARKINSON *Orchard* xiii. 578 The black Bulleis also are those..that they call French Prunes. **1655** MOUFFET & BENNET *Health's Improv.* (1746) 293 Bullices likewise, both white, speckled and black, are of the like Nature. **1664** COTTON *Scarron.* IV. (1741) 137 So have I seen in Forest tall..Bullace tumble from the Tree. **1741** *Compl. Fam.-Piece* II. iii. 394 Damasines, and Bullace. **1762** SMOLLETT *Sir L. Greaves* iii. (D.) Dick and I be come hither to pick haws and bullies. **1769** MRS. RAFFALD *Eng. Housekpr.* (1778) 236 To make Bullace Cheese. Take your bullace when they are full ripe, etc. **1830** SCOTT *Demonol.* viii. 248 While gathering bullees..he saw two greyhounds. **1837** HOOD *Mem. T. H.* (1860) I. 263 Our landlady.. comforted her inside with a mess of dried bullaces in sour wine! **1875** *Lanc. Gloss.* (E.D.S.) 61 *Bulloe*, the sloe or wild plum.

b. Applied fancifully to a black eye.

a **1659** CLEVELAND *Wks.* (1687) 256 The sparkling Bullies of her Eyes Like two eclipsed Suns did rise.

2. The tree bearing the plum.

1616 SURFL. & MARKH. *Countr. Farm* 670 You shall also by no meanes alongst your pale walke plant fruit trees, blacke-thorne, or bullies. **1688** R. HOLME *Armoury* II. 119/3 Spinous or thorny Shrubs whose Fruit may be eaten, as.. Bullas. **1859** W. COLEMAN *Woodlands* (1862) 119 The Bullace Plum..a variety of the common Sloe, from which it chiefly differs in the superior size of all its parts, especially the fruit.

3. *Attrib.* and *Comb.*, as ***bullace-fruit, -plum***; †**bullace-bay** *a.*, of a particular dark-bay colour (said of a horse); **bullace-tree** (see also BULLESTER).

c **1440** *Promp. Parv.* 42 Bolas tre, *pepulus.* **1530** PALSGR. 199/2 Bolas frute, *prunelle.* **1608** TOPSELL *Serpents* 768 Their egges..are round..in quantity as big as bullies plums. **1684** *Bucaniers Amer.* (1699) 19 Yaco..bears a fruit like our Bullace or Damson plums. **1690** *Lond. Gaz.* No. 2576/4 The other [Gelding] a dark Bullace-Bay. **1848** W. GARDINER *Flora of Forfar.* 54 *P. insititia*, Wild Bullace-tree.

bullamacow ('bʊləməkaʊ). Also bulli-. [Fiji combination of *bull* and *cow.*] **a.** Cattle. **b.** Corned beef; bully beef.

1887 W. B. CHURCHWARD *My Consulate in Samoa* xxiii. 277 'Bulli-ma-cou', applicable both to the meat and the animal... On the first animals being landed the natives.. were told that the beasts they saw before them were a bull and a cow; so combining the two English words they made one of their own. **1902** *Westm. Gaz.* 30 July 2/1 Their supper of rice and bullmacow [*sic*]. **1925** *Chambers's Jrnl.* Feb. 87/2 If they wanted *bullamacow*..he would readily provide that food. **1927** *Observer* 6 Feb. 19/5 The Fijians had no words for bull or cow and now have only one portmanteau word, 'bulumacau'. **1952** A. GRIMBLE *Pattern of Islands* 80 We never entertained one whose face brightened perceptibly when bullimacow and beetroot were placed before him.

bullantic, *a. rare*[−1]. [ad. F. *bullantique*, used by Fournier in the original passage of which the quot. from Fry is a translation. The Fr. dictionaries have *bullatique* (f. *bulla* Papal bull) in this sense; *bullantique* is perh. due to association with *antique.*] (See quot.)

1799 E. FRY *Pantogr.* 23 *Bullantic*, capital ornamented letters in use for the dispatch of the Apostolic Bulls.

†**bullard.** *Obs.* [Contracted form of *bull-ward*, or perhaps rather of *bull-herd*; cf. *cow-herd, neat-*

herd, and *bearard* for BEARHERD.] One who keeps a bull, or who takes part in bull-running. Cf. *bull-run* s.v. BULL *sb.*[1] II.

1825 LOWE in Hone *Every-day Bk.* I. 1484 Every bullard [at Stamford]..ought to drink on that day. **1830** *Champion of East* 12 Jan. 14 The bullards of Stamford intended yesterday..to have had another day's sport. **1864** CHAMBERS *Bk. of Days* 13 Nov. II. 574/2 The *bullards*, a name given to the admirers and supporters of bull-running [at Stamford].

bullary (ˈbʊlərɪ). Also 7 **-ery**. [ad. med.L. *bullārium* f. *bulla* papal bull: see -ARY, -ARIUM. Cf. F. *bullaire*. Also used in L. form *Bullarium*.] A collection of papal bulls.

a **1674** CLARENDON *Surv. Leviath.* 153 Their whole Bullarium..abounds in Canonizations. **1679** T. BARLOW *Popery* 78 Many more such impious Bulls there are in that Roman Bullary. *c* **1690** SOUTH *Serm.* V. v. (R.) The whole bull is extant in the bullery of Laertius Cherubinus. **1726** AYLIFFE *Parerg.* xxvi, Out of these Registers there were afterwards compil'd these several Bullariums. **1745–1836** A. BUTLER *Lives of Saints* II. 936 *note*, Parts of the latest bullaries of Clement XII. and Benedict XIV. **1881** *Philadelphia Press* XXXV. 12 Aug. 4 Which in itself was compiled from the Bullarium and decretals of the Popes.

bullary, var. of BULLERY. *Obs.*

bullase, -asse, obs. ff. BULLACE.

†ˈ**bullate**, *sb. Obs. rare*$^{-1}$. A kind of metal; ? = *bullet-iron* (see BULLET *sb.*[1] 8).

1591 G. FLETCHER *Russe Commw.* (1856) 93 They [the Tartars]..preferre brasse and steele before other mettals, specially bullate, which they use for swords, knives, and other necessaries.

bullate (ˈbʊleɪt, ˈbʌleɪt), *a.* [ad. Lat. *bullāt-us*, having bubbles.]

1. *Bot.* Having blisters; inflated: said of leaves, in which the surface rises in a convexity between the veins.

1819 *Pantologia*, s.v. *Bullate leaf*, in botany, when the substance rises high above the veins, so as to appear like blisters. **1870** HOOKER *Stud. Flora* 465 Clothed with large bullate acuminate pale scales.

2. *Phys.* Having *bullæ* or puffy excrescences on the surface.

1872 MIVART *Elem. Anat.* 111 The pterygoid may be swollen and bullate, as in the Mole. **1877** HUXLEY *Anat. Inv. An.* vi. 293 This is principally composed of a large bullate labium.

ˈ**bullated**, *ppl. a.* [f. as prec. + -ED.]

†**1.** *Rom. Ant.* Furnished with a *bulla*, or gold ornament worn round the neck. *Obs.*

1698 W. KING *Journ. Lond.* 222, I could never meet with a statue in London but what was clothed with a Toga pura and no representation of a Bullated one.

2. = BULLATE.

1707 SLOANE *Jamaica* I. 261 The stalks..had leaves set on them..rough and bullated, or like the leaves of wild sage. **1822** BURROWES *Cycl.* s.v. *Rana*, The toes are bullated at the ends.

bu'llation. *Bot.* [as if ad. L. *bullatio*; cf. BULLATE and -ATION.] A bullate formation.

1882 *Gard. Chron.* XVIII. 71 The bullations depressed around the insertion of the petiole.

bull-bait (ˈbʊlbeɪt). *Obs.* or *arch.* [f. BULL *sb.*[1] + BAIT *sb.*[1] III.] = BULL-BAITING.

1656 W. WEBB in *Digby Myst.* (1882) Introd. 28 This Maior..would not suffer any..Bull-bait. **1818** in Knight *Once upon Time* (1859) 485 Whenever a bull-bait has taken place here. **1876** BANCROFT *Hist. U.S.* II. xxiv. 124 Bull-baits and cock-fights, were prohibited.

fig. **17..** *Douglas Trag.* iv. in Child *Ballads* I. 103/2 'O hold your hand, sweet William', she said, 'Your bull baits are wondrous sair'.

bull-baiter (ˈbʊlbeɪtə(r)). [f. BULL *sb.*[1] + BAITER.] One who baits bulls.

1802 *Hist. Europe* in *Ann. Reg.* 169/1 He doubted whether a bull-baiter..had ever distinguished himself in disaffection.

bull-baiting (ˈbʊlbeɪtɪŋ), *vbl. sb.* [f. BULL *sb.*[1] + BAITING.] The action of baiting a bull with dogs. (Cf. BULL-DOG *sb.*)

1580 BARET *Alv.* B 1478 Bulbaitinges. **1583** BABINGTON *Commandm.* iv. (1637) 36 Gadding to this Ale or that, to this Bearbaiting and that bulbaiting. **1652** *Let. fr. Madrid* in *Proc. Parl.* No. 170 The next day there was Bull-beating. **1711** ADDISON *Spect.* No. 31 ⁋2 The bull-baiting..cannot possibly be exhibited in the theatre, by reason of the lowness of the roof. **1802** *Hist. Europe* in *Ann. Reg.* 168/2 The practise of bull-baiting was dying away of itself.

†ˈ**bull-bear.** *Obs.* [App. f. BULL *sb.*[1] + BEAR *sb.*[1]; but, to account for the sense, it has been conjectured that the first element may be BOLL *sb.*[3], or BOGLE. Cf. BUGBEAR (of which also it is not impossible that this is a corruption); also Du. *bulle-man* 'larva, spectrum', *bulle-back* 'lemures' (Kilian 1642). See next.] A spectre, bogy; a scare-crow; a bugbear, or object of groundless terror.

1561 T. NORTON *Calvin's Inst.* III. v. (1634) 319 They saw themselves to be openly and uncolourably scorned of the Pope and his Bulbeares. **1581** J. BELL *Haddon's Answ. Osor.* 423/2 Such as be alyve now should dreadd any Bull-beares of Purgatory. **1592** G. HARVEY *Four Lett.* (1815) 21 That Fleeting (imprisonment in the Fleet) also proved like the other a silly bullbeare.

†ˈ**bull-beggar.** *Obs.* [See prec. As the obvious combination *bull* + *beggar* does not appear to yield a suitable sense, it is generally assumed that there must have been some alteration under the influence of 'popular etymology', e.g. that it is a (further) alteration of *bull-bear*; or that the second element has been altered from *boggard*, *buggart* 'bogle'. But evidence is entirely wanting. The word was sometimes (see b.) used with a punning allusion to the Papal BULL, and to BEGGAR.] = prec. Hence ˈ**bull-begging** *ppl. a.* (*nonce-wd.*), that operates as a terror.

1584 R. SCOT *Discov. Witchcr.* VII. xv. 122 They have so fraied us with bull beggers, spirits, witches..that we are afraid of our own Shadowes. **1588** J. HARVEY *Disc. Probl.* 73 And beggers will needes be somewaies bulbeggers. **1592** G. HARVEY *Four Lett.*, Her redoutable Bull-begging Knight. **1601** DENT *Path-w. Heauen* 109 A mother, when her child is wayward..scareth it with some pocar, or bull-begger. **1634** J. TAYLOR (Water P.) *Gt. Eater Kent* Wks. I. 147/2 The name of Good-friday affrights him like a Bulbegger. **1673** MARVELL *Reh. transp.* II. 250 Private Conscience is..a Bul-begger to fright children. **1813** HOBHOUSE *Journ.* 32 Looking altogether, as to his garments, like what we call a bull-beggar. **1851** S. JUDD *Margaret* v. (1871) 20 The haunt of bulbeggars, witches, spirits.

b. *a* **1625** BOYS *Wks.* (1630) 550 The Popes Bullbegger Cardinall Bellarmeni. **1726** AYLIFFE *Parerg.* 132 These Fulminations from the Vatican..were called Bull-Beggars.

bullberry, bull berry: see BULBERRY.

bull-bitch. The female of the bull-dog.

1681 *Lond. Gaz.* No. 1632/4 The most part of her Head Black, shaped like a Bull-Bitch. **1885** *Bazaar* 30 Mar. 1258/2 Nell, bull bitch..game to death at anything breathing.

bull-dike (ˈbʊldaɪk). *slang.* Also **bull-diker, -dyke(r.** [Origin unknown. Cf. DIKE *sb.*[3]] A lesbian with masculine tendencies.

1926 C. VAN VECHTEN *Nigger Heaven* 285 *Bulldiker*, Lesbian. **1942** BERREY & VAN DEN BARK *Amer. Thes. Slang* §405/3 Masculine woman, *boy*, *bulldike*, *bulldyke*, *bulldiker*. **1964** J. RECHY *City of Night* 174 On the dance-floor, too, lesbians—the masculine ones, the bulldikes—dance with hugely effeminate queens.

bull-dog, *sb.* (Also 6 **bold-dogge**.) Often without hyphen (as one word) *esp.* in *transf.* uses. [f. BULL *sb.*[1] + DOG; because used in bull-baiting, or ? from the shape of the head.

With the oldest spelling *bolddogge*, compare 'Hic molossus, a *bonddoge*', *a* **1500** in Wr.-Wülcker 758.]

1. a. A dog of a bold and fierce breed, with large bull-head, short muzzle, strong muscular body of medium height, and short smooth hair, formerly much used for bull-baiting.

c **1500** *Cocke Lorelles B.* 2 Than came one wᵗ two bold-dogges at his tayle. **1752** HUME *Ess. & Treat.* (1777) I. 216 The courage of bull-dogs and game-cocks seems peculiar to England. **1828** SCOTT *F.M. Perth* II. 279 What are the useful properties of this fellow Bonthron? Those of a bull-dog..he worries without barking. **1863** KINGSLEY *Water-bab.* i. 5 He would be..a master sweep..and keep a white bull-dog with one grey ear.

b. *attrib.* and *quasi-adj.*, as *bull-dog breed*.

1855 MACAULAY *Hist. Eng.* IV. 588 That bulldog courage which flinches from no danger. **1857** C. KINGSLEY *Two Years Ago* II. iv. 67 Knowing him to be of the original British bull-dog breed, which, once stroked against the hair, shows his teeth at you for ever afterwards. **1871** *Standard* 18 Jan., Can Paris wait even until the bull-dog spirit of this hard-dying chief is able once more to show itself? **1897** F. MCGLENNON *Sons of Sea* 4 Sons of the Sea! All British born!..boys of the bull-dog breed Who made old England's name. **1940** 'G. ORWELL' *Inside Whale* 40 The typical English boasting, the..'bulldog breed'..style of talk.

c. *transf.* Applied to persons: One that possesses the obstinate courage of the bulldog. Hence ˈ**bulldoggy** *a.*, and ˈ**bulldogism** (*nonce-wds.*).

1863 KINGSLEY *Water-bab.* iv. 138 Tom was always a brave, determined little English bull-dog, who never knew when he was beaten. **1858** *Chamb. Jrnl.* X. 20 Tom..was an English youth of about my own age, but a great deal more bulldoggy. **1852** SAVAGE *R. Medlicott* II. vi. (D.) He possessed the element of bulldogism also.

d. Stock Exchange jargon. *bulldog bond*, a sterling bond issued by an overseas borrower. Also *bulldog issue*, *market*, etc., and *absol.*

1980 *Financial Weekly* 1 Aug. 23/5 Denmark's £75m sterling bond..is the first 'bulldog' bond (domestic sterling issue for a foreign borrower) to be made since 1962. **1981** *Times* 27 Apr. 17/1 The World Bank is expected to announce a £100m bond issue this week on the domestic sterling market, the first such 'bulldog' issue by the bank in a decade. **1981** *Daily Tel.* 9 June 19 Some 'bulldogs', like those issued by the World Bank.., have held up relatively well in the recent shake-out. **1982** *Financial Times* 22 Mar. 1/6 This will be the second time the World Bank has tapped what is known as the bulldog market—the domestic sterling bond sector open to foreign borrowers. **1983** *Times* 9 Apr. 14/3 Neither corporate bonds nor bulldogs seem to be in the offing. The last bulldog issued, that for Sweden, is now at a premium of £8¼. **1984** *Daily Tel.* 27 Mar. 17/3 Finland is making its second venture into the domestic sterling bond market with a £50 million 25-year partly paid 'bulldog' issue which is priced to yield about 11.75 p.c. to redemption.

2. †A sheriff's officer (*obs.*); one of the Proctors' attendants at the Universities of Oxford and Cambridge. *colloq.*

1698 FARQUHAR *Love & Bottle* iii. 2 He would have put me off, so I sent for a couple of bull-dogs, and arrested him. **1823** LOCKHART *Reg. Dalton* I. x. (1842) 59 Long forgotten stories about proctors bit, and bull-dogs baffled. **1884** G. ALLEN *Str. Stories* 289 It was quite a fortnight before I [senior proctor] could face my own bulldogs unabashed.

3. *transf.* Applied humorously to a cannon or other firearm; in mod. use, a particular kind of revolver. Cf. BARKER. Also *attrib.*

1700 FARQUHAR *Const. Couple* III. i, He whips out his Stiletto and I whips out my bull-dog. **1820** SCOTT *Abbot* xvi, A plague..on cannon and demi-cannon, and all the barking bulldogs whom they halloo against stone and lime in these our days! **1824** —— *St. Ronan's W.* II. 191 (D.), 'I have always a brace of bull-dogs about me'..so saying he exhibited a very handsome, highly finished..pair of pistols. **1867** SMYTH *Sailor's Wd-bk.*, *Bull-dog* or *Muzzled Bull-dog*, the great gun which stands 'housed' in the officer's ward-room cabin. General term for main-deck guns. **1881** *Daily News* 27 Oct. 6/2 Revolver cartridges of the ordinary 'bulldog' pattern.

4. An insect: **a.** A kind of gad-fly (American). In full *bull-dog fly*. **b.** A kind of ant; also *bulldog ant* (Australian).

1792 P. TURNOR *Jrnl.* (1934) 488 A kind of fly..called bull dogs. **1848** R. M. BALLANTYNE *Hudson's Bay* (ed. 2) vii. 147 The whole room was filled with mosquitoes and bull-dog flies. **1853** E. CLACY *Gold Diggings Austr.* xvi. 249 The largest [ants] are called by the old colonists, 'bull-dogs', and formidable creatures they are. **1860** W. B. CLARKE *Res. S. Gold Fields N.S.W.* vii. 120 It was difficult to find a spot on which to lay our blankets, on account of the 'Bull Dog Ants'. **1865** VIS. MILTON & W. CHEADLE *Northw. Passage* 219 The 'bull-dog' or tabanus, is a large fly..with a long body, banded with yellow..and its mouth is armed with a formidable cutting apparatus of four lancets. **1881** *Cheq. Career* 324 The 'bull-dog' ant and the 'soldier' are about on a par as regards venom. **1883** *St. James' Gaz.* 19 Apr., 'Bull-dogs' (a large horse-fly) render existence almost unendurable.

5. In *Iron-works.* See quot.; also in comb. **bulldog-burner**.

1881 RAYMOND *Mining Gloss.*, *Bulldog*, a refractory material used as furnace-lining, got by calcining mill-cinder, and containing silica and ferric oxide. **1884** *Times* 8 Jan., The 'bulldog burner'..is one of the hands in ironworks whose duty it is to roast the refuse cinder (called 'bulldog') which is necessary for the fettling of the puddling furnace.

6. *pl.* An old name of the Snap-dragon (*Antirrhinum*).

1861 MISS PRATT *Flower. Pl.* IV. 124 Great Snapdragon.. Bull-dogs, Lion's-snap..are also old names of the plant.

7. a. *bulldog forceps.* 'Forceps with a spring catch..the extremity of one blade pointed, of the other notched, for the reception of the point'. *Syd. Soc. Lex.*

1880 MACCORMAC *Antisept. Surg.* 166 He was led from the use of the old 'bull-dogs' to the convenient and powerful clamp forceps he has now employed.

b. Used (freq. *attrib.*) of a clip or other fastening having a strong closure.

1908 *Sears, Roebuck Catal.* 204/3 Bull Dog Wire Grip. The more you pull the tighter it grips. **1923** *Man. Seamanship* II. 307 Special screw clamps, after the fashion of bull-dog grips. **1943** *Trade Marks Jrnl.* 26 May No. 3400 224/2 (*heading*) *Bulldog*, B 620,897 metal clips being articles of stationery..6th Nov. 1942 [date of registration]. **1944** 'N. SHUTE' *Pastoral* ii. 28 Messages and signal forms in bulldog clips. **1969** D. CLARK *Nobody's Perfect* v. 153 Her invoices hung in large bulldog clips from hooks on the walls.

8. *slang.* A sugar-loaf.

1812 J. H. VAUX *Flash Dict.*, *Bull-dog*, a sugar-loaf.

9. In full *bull-dog pipe*. A short tobacco-pipe of brier-wood.

1885 A. EDWARDES *Girton Girl* I. iv. 84 The pipe was a black, ferociously Bohemian-looking 'bulldog'. **1900** W. C. MORROW *Bohemian Paris* 306 Three-days-in-Paris English tourists wearing knickerbockers and golf-caps, and always smoking bulldog pipes. **1966** L. J. BRAUN *Cat who could read Backwards* (1967) v. 56 'I use a pipe.' Qwilleran searched for his quarter-bend bulldog and his tobacco pouch.

10. *bull-dog edition*, the earliest edition of a daily or Sunday newspaper. *U.S.*

1926 *Nation* 13 Oct. 342/2 This story got into the bull-dog edition of one of the papers before he could finish his midnight rounds. **1934** D. WILKIE *Amer. Secret Service Agent* iii. 33 That night I took the bulldog edition with my spread to a restaurant where the newspaper men congregated.

bull-dog, *v.* Chiefly *U.S.* [f. the sb.] *trans.* To attack like a bull-dog; to assail or treat roughly; *spec.* to wrestle with and throw (a steer or other animal). Hence ˈ**bull-ˌdogger**, ˈ**bull-ˌdogging**.

1842 *Congress. Globe* 29 Apr. 457/3 Mr. Whitney had not been 'dogged' to the door of the committee-room, but, when inside, he had been 'bull-dogged' with a vengeance. *Ibid.* 4 May 478/1, I made the reply about bull-dogging for the gentleman from Virginia. **1883** MEREDITH *Let.* 20 July (1970) II. 706 Greenwood..is bull-dogging France. **1907** *Outing* (U.S.) Dec. 329/1 'No more necked calves,' they announced, 'catch 'em by the hind legs, or bull-dog 'em yourself.' **1907** S. E. WHITE *Arizona Nights* I. viii. 148 The two 'bull-doggers' immediately pounced upon the victim. *Ibid.* 151 One of the men..reached well over the animal's [*sc.* a calf's] back to get a slack of the loose hide next the belly, lifted strongly, and tripped. This is called 'bull-dogging'. **1953** R. CAMPBELL *Mamba's Precipice* viii. 94 He wasn't as good as Antonio..in bulldogging them by the horns and throwing them on their sides. **1963** *Times* 7 Mar.

9/4 A wonderful exhibition of.. bulldogging (leaping from a horse and throwing a running bull to the ground).

bull-dogged ('bʊldɒgd), *a.* [f. BULL-DOG *sb.*] Characteristic of or like that of a bull-dog.

1904 *Daily Chron.* 4 Jan. 9/1 The face has become pushed back, or 'bull-dogged'. **1921** GALSWORTHY *To Let* III. II. xi, All that was bull-dogged in Soames stared for a moment out of his grey eyes.

bull-dose, -doze ('bʊldəʊz), *sb.* and *v.* orig. *U.S. colloq.* [According to U.S. newspapers, f. BULL *sb.*[1] + DOSE.]

A. *sb.* ? A severe dose (of flogging).

1876 *American Newspr.*, If a negro is invited to join it [a society called 'The Stop'], and refuses, he is taken to the woods and whipped. This whipping is called a 'bull-doze', or doze fit for a bull. **1881** *Sat. Rev.* 9 July 40/2 A 'bull-dose' means a large efficient dose of any sort of medicine or punishment.

B. *vb.* (The usual spelling, influenced by BULLDOZER 2 a, is now *bulldoze.*) **1. a.** ? To flog severely. **b.** To coerce by violence, intimidate.

1880 C. B. BERRY *Other Side* 155 They.. pull him out of bed with a revolver to his head.. That's called 'bull-dosing' a man. **1881** *Sat. Rev.* 9 July 40/2 To 'bull-dose' a negro in the Southern States means to flog him to death, or nearly to death. **1884** H. GEORGE *Social Prob.* 16 Large Employers regularly 'bulldose' their hands into voting as *they* wish. **1897** E. A. BARTLETT *Battlefields of Thessaly* iii. 53 There is a remarkable resemblance.. between the way in which English public opinion has been 'bulldozed' and misled in both cases. **1916** J. B. COOPER *Coo-oo-ee!* viii. 104 Debenham backed Danvers up by.. pointing out to Hawley the folly of handing a loaded revolver to Boder to examine. They simply bull-dozed Hawley. **1941** G. G. SCHOLEM *Major Trends in Jewish Mysticism* viii. 320 The philosophers who tried to bulldoze us into accepting the God of Aristotle as the God of Religion. **1954** *Encounter* July 31/1 The men .. were.. trying to bulldoze the creative Czech artist.. into conformity with the precepts of Socialist Realism.

2. a. *intr.* To use a bulldozer (BULLDOZER 2 a); also, to push *one's way* by means of a bulldozer. Also *trans.*, to move, clear, or level by means of a bulldozer.

1942 *Interpretation Aerial Photographs* (U.S. War Dept., Techn. Man. TM5-246) 188 The road was constructed by bulldozing the earth and painting the edges with asphalt paint. **1944** *Reader's Digest* Aug. 93 Men were coming out of the sea continually and starting to work—digging, hammering, bulldozing. **1946** *Spectator* 12 Apr. 372/1 Americans had to bulldoze their way through the rubble. **1948** *Time* 5 July 19/3 Trucks were lumbering.. up a goat path, newly bulldozed.

b. *transf.* and *fig.*

1948 *Sat. Rev. Lit.* 21 Feb. 26 She bulldozed her way through her songs. **1950** G. BARKER *News of World* 37 The juggernauts Go bulldozing through my thoughts. **1963** *Rev. Eng. Studies* XIV. 319 The second edition of 1934.. has been bulldozed away and a new edifice constructed.

So **'bulldozed** *ppl. a.*, **'bulldozing** *vbl. sb.* and *ppl. a.*

1876 *American Newspr.*, The application of the bull-doze was for the purpose of making Tilden voters; hence we hear of the 'bull-dozed' parishes. **1937** *Geogr. Jrnl.* XC. 369 'Bull-dozing', in which the vertical walls at the head of a gully are destroyed and a sloping surface constructed. **1949** *Good Housekeeping* June 76/2 Every panacea-pamphlet that pours from the bull-dozing pens of doctrinaire Utopians. **1953** *Proc. Prehist. Soc.* XIX. 232 The destruction of many of the downland earthworks by bulldozing and deep ploughing.

bulldozer ('bʊldəʊzə(r)). orig. *U.S.* Also bull-doser, bull-dozer. [f. BULL-DOSE, -DOZE *v.*]

1. a. One who 'bull-dozes'. **b.** A large pistol.

1876 in *Congress. Rec.* (1877) 9 Jan. 500/1 A band of bulldozers came into Saint Francisville. **1878** *N. Amer. Rev.* CXXVII. 426 The great 'Bulldozer' of Europe. **1881** *Sat. Rev.* 9 July 40/2 A Californian bull-doser is a pistol which carries a bullet heavy enough to destroy human life with certainty. **1882** *New York Tribune* 3 May, The hotel where he was staying was visited.. by a mob of bull-dozers. **1899** M. KINGSLEY *Let.* 19 Mar. in S. Gwynn *Life of M. K.* (1933) 210 They leave that to the bulldozers, and the present system mistakes these bulldozers for representative men.

2. A heavy caterpillar tractor fitted with a broad steel blade in front, used for removing obstacles, levelling uneven surfaces, etc.

1930 *Water Works & Sewerage* (U.S.) June 262/3 The bulldozer is built for heavy duty. **1941** *N. & Q.* CLXXXI. 119/1 If they can bring in American machinery, why can't they bring in bull-dozers? **1942** *Times* 9 Oct. 2/2 There are .. machines for levelling—motor-propelled scrapers—tractors, dumpers, angle-dozers and bull-dozers.

b. *fig.* (Also *attrib.*)

1945 R. J. OAKES in *Coast to Coast 1944* 100 The fourth man was a gunner, a bulldozer of a man. **1952** *Sat. Rev.* 9 Aug. 12 The bulldozer determination with which he plowed through confused happenings. **1955** *Times* 21 June 9/4 Such spotters can.. obtain 'bulldozer' rights for a patrol on a hot scent to pass through the areas of other units without being shot in error. **1959** *Times Lit. Suppl.* 20 Feb. 102/1 The bulldozer detective tactics of Inspector Evans.

† **bulle, bule.** *obs.* exc. *dial.* [A variant spelling of BOUL, q.v.] A semicircular or bowed handle, as of a pail, a door, etc.

1483 *Cath. Angl.* 47 A Bulle (Bwylle) of a dore, *grapa.* **1747** HOOSON *Miner's Dict.* F. 1 b, In the Bottom [of the Corfe] near the ends of it are two Holes bored, in which the bended Bule is put. **1790** W. MARSHALL *Midl. Counties* (E.D.S.) *Bule*, the bow-handle of a pail. **1875** *Lanc. Gloss.* (E.D.S.) *Bule*, the handle of a pot, pan, or other utensil. **1881** *Leicestersh. Words* (E.D.S.) *Bule*, semicircular handle of a bucket, pot-lid, etc.

bulle, obs. form of BULL.

† **'bulled,** *ppl. a.*[1] *Obs.* [f. BULL *sb.*[2] or *v.*[2] + -ED.] Having a bull or seal attached.

1330 R. BRUNNE *Chron.* 265 Þe pape Celestyn.. With letter bulled fyn assoyled to Scotlond sent. **1610** BP. CARLETON *Jurisd.* 268 He threw away the Popes bulled Letters.

† **bulled,** *ppl. a.*[2] *rare*⁻¹. ? = BOLLED *ppl. a.*[1] 1.

1637 B. JONSON *Sad Sheph.* I. iii, Hang the bulled Nosegaies 'bove their heads.

bullee, -eis, obs. and Sc. forms of BULLACE.

† **'bullen.** *Obs.* or ? *dial.* 'Hemp-stalks peeled'.

1674 in RAY. **1681** in WORLIDGE. **1706** in PHILLIPS; in BAILEY, HALLIWELL, etc. **1876** KNIGHT *Pract. Dict. Mech.*, *Bullen*, the awn or chaff from flax or hemp.

bullen, obs. form of BULLION.

['**bullenger,** erroneous form of BALINGER. (In the AF. passage (*Rot. Parl. 2 Hen. IV*, 22) referred to by Blount the printed ed. reads *balyngers.*)

1670 in BLOUNT *Law Dict.* **1678** in PHILLIPS, etc.]

bullen-nail. [? corruption of *bullion-nail*; see quot. 1707 in BULLION[1] 1.]

1842-76 GWILT *Archit.* Gloss., *Bullen nails*, such as have round heads with short shanks turned and lacquered. They are principally used in the hangings of rooms. **1847** in CRAIG; and in mod. Dicts.

† **'buller,** *sb.*[1] *Obs.* [f. BULL *sb.*[2] + -ER[1].] **a.** One who issues or publishes a bull. **b.** A deceiver, cheat. [perh. a distinct word, cf. BULL *v.*[3], OF. *bouleur* 'trompeur' Godef.]

a **1300** *Cursor M.* 29306 Fals bulleres þat þam makes and þam furth beres, or els þat falses þe papes sele. *c* **1460** *Towneley Myst.* 242 (Mätz.) Thise dysars and thise hullars, Thise cokkers and thise bollars.

buller ('bʊlə(r)), *sb.*[2] *Sc.* Also 6 bullyer. [cf. Sw. *buller* noise, roar, Da. *bulder* tumbling noise. But influence of *boil* is manifest.]

1. A roaring noise (of waves or flood); the boiling of an eddy or torrent.

1513 DOUGLAS *Æneis* x. vi. 13 Calmyt all is But stowr or bullyer, murmour or moving.

b. ***the Buller(s) of Buchan***, a rocky recess on the Aberdeenshire coast, near Peterhead, open at the top; the sea, constantly raging in it, gives it the appearance of a boiling pot or caldron.

1769 PENNANT *Tour Scotl.* 145 (JAM.) The famous Bullers of Buchan lying about a mile North of Bowness. **1774** JOHNSON *West. Isl.* Wks. 1787 X. 334 We.. turned our eyes to the Buller.. of Buchan. **1836** *Penny Cycl.* V. 508/1 The Bullers of Buchan, a nearly round basin about 30 yards wide.

2. *fig.*

1851 WILSON *Tales of Borders* XX. 23 This new cause of sorrow increased my paroxysm to a perfect buller.

buller ('bʊlə(r)), *sb.*[3] [f. BULL *sb.*[1] + -ER[1].] (See quots.)

1858 *Jrnl. R. Agric. Soc.* XIX. 151 The cow.. became what is called a 'perpetual buller', that is, always in a state to take the bull. **1901-3** *Rep. Kansas State Board Agric.* 253 (*Cent. Dict.* Suppl.), *Buller*, in *stock-raising*, a cow of irregular reproductive habit. **1953** S. J. BAKER *Australia Speaks* II. iii. 76 From dairy farm folk have come.. *buller*, a cow on heat.

buller ('bʊlə(r)), *sb.*[4] *University slang.* [See -ER.[6]] = BULL-DOG 2.

1906 *'Varsity* 1 Feb. 165/3 There's a buller over there. Wonder if he's waiting to spot anyone. **1919** *Isis* 5 Nov. 7/2 The Proctor.. on a motor-scooter, accompanied by a couple of attendant 'bullers' on a push-bike. **1937** *Evening News* 5 May 10/3 A 'buller' was sent round to their house to collect the fines of 13/4 each.

buller ('bʊlə(r)), *v.*[1] *Sc.* Also 6 bullir. [f. BULLER *sb.*[2]; cf. Sw. *bullr-a*, Da. *buldre* to roar, make a noise.] To make a noise, to roar, to bellow.

1530 LYNDESAY *Test. Papyngo* 95 Blait lyke ane hog, and buller lyke ane bull. **1549** *Compl. Scot.* (1872) 39 The bullis began to bullir, quhen the scheip began to blait. **1663** SPALDING *Troub. Chas. I.* (1829) 33 It.. would duck under water, snorting and bullering. **1818** SCOTT *Hrt. Midl.* xv, Screeching and bullering like a Bull of Bashan.

† **'buller,** *v.*[2] *Obs. Sc.* Also buler. [Perh. the same word as prec., but influenced in sense by OF. *bullir* to BOIL.]

1. a. *intr.* To boil, to foam; to rush foaming. **b.** *trans.* To wash up in foaming waves.

1513 DOUGLAS *Æneis* I. iii. 26 The stowr wp bullerit sand as it war wind. *Ibid.* I. iii. 50 Salt watter stremis Fast bullerand in at every rift. *Ibid.* XI. xi. 34 Amasenus, that river.. Abuf the brais bulryt as it war wod.

2. *intr.* To make bubbles or foam.

1535 STEWART *Cron. Scot.* II. 259 Full mony berne lay bulrand in his blude. **1536** BELLENDEN *Cron. Scot.* (1821) I. 231 The king was liand bullerand in his blude. *a* **1555** LYNDESAY *Trag.* 338 Quhow I laye bulrand, baithit in my blude.

Hence **bullering** *ppl. a.*

1533 BELLENDEN *Livy* v. (1822) 457 Thay sank doun and perist in the depe bullerand stremes. **1537** LYNDESAY *Deplor. Q. Magd.* 45 So did this prince [swim] throw bulryng stremis wode. **1552** —— *Monarche* 1553 The gret Occiane.. did nocht spred sic bulryng strandis As it dois now.

† **'bullery.** *Obs.* Also 6 bullary. = BOILERY.

1542 HEN. VIII in Rymer *Fœdera* (1710) XIV. 748 Foure Bullaryes of Salte Water. **1704** *Lond. Gaz.* No. 4071/4 The Salt-Works or Bullery of Salt.. are to be Sold.

bullery: see BULLARY.

bullescence (bʊ'lɛsəns). *Bot.* [as if ad. Lat. **bullescentia* f. pres. pple. of *bullesc-ĕre* to bubble.] A term applied to the condition occurring in leaves when the inter-venous structure rises above the veins, as in the Savoy cabbage. Cf. BULLATE.

1880 in *Syd. Soc. Lex.*

bullesse, obs. form of BULLACE.

† **'bullester.** *Obs.* Also 6 bolaster, 7 bulaster. App. a phonetically reduced form of *bullestre*, *bullace-tree* (see BULLACE). Also ***bullester-tree***.

1500 *Ort. Voc.* in *Promp. Parv.* 42 *Pepulus*, a bolaster. **1562** TURNER *Herbal* II. 103 b, The one [kind of plum] is called the bulles tre or the bullestertre. *a* **1700** D. CAMPBELL *Let.* in C. Innes *Sk. Early Sc. Hist.* 432 *note*, I send you the wrack of all my plumes damsones and bulasters.

bullet ('bʊlɪt), *sb.*[1] Also 6 bollet(te, boolet, boullette, bullot, *Sc.* bullat. [a. F. *boulette* (in 16th c. *boullette*) dim. of *boule* ball; cf. F. *boulet* = 2.]

1. (In mod. use this sense is *transf.* from 3.) **a.** A small round ball.

1578 LYTE *Dodoens* I. viii. 15 Upon the braunches [of the burdock] there groweth small bullets or rounde balles. *Ibid.* IV. lv. 515 It [the Reed Grass] bringeth foorth his boullettes, or prickley knoppes in August. **1664** H. MORE *Myst. Iniq.* 241 If a Beast were made of little wax bullets sticking together. **1851** D. WILSON *Preh. Ann.* (1863) II. IV. iii. 261 Small gold bullets.. seem to have been the current coin.

b. *pl.* Beans or peas. *slang.*

1929 *Papers Michigan Acad. Sci., Arts & Lett.* X. 282/2 *Bullets*, beans. **1943** HUNT & PRINGLE *Service Slang* 18 *Bullets*, peas. **1963** *Daily Mail* 26 Aug. 4/3 He [*sc.* a schoolboy] calls peas 'bullets'.

†**2.** A cannon-ball (of metal or stone); sometimes ***cannon-bullet***. *Obs.* exc. *Hist.*

1557 RECORDE *Whetst.* P iv b, A Gonne.. doeth shotte a bollet of twentiepound weighte. **1560** WHITEHORNE *Certaine Wayes* (1573) 33 a, If the boolet of a peese of ordinaunce waighe xxi. pounde. **1561** STOW *Chron.* an. 1557 (R.) A ship before Greenwich.. shot off her ordnance, one piece being charged with a bullet of stone. **1605** *1st Pt. Jeronimo* in *Dodsley* (1780) III. 98 Raise spleens big as a cannon-bullet Within your bosoms. **1703** *Lond. Gaz.* No. 3914/5 Their Forces.. fired several Red-hot Bullets into the Town. **1882** SHORTHOUSE *J. Inglesant* II. 378 More than once a cannon bullet burst into the Minster.

3. a. A ball of lead or other metal, used in firearms of small calibre; now often conical. Formerly also collective (cf. BALL *sb.*[1] 5 b).

1579 GOSSON *Sch. Abuse* (Arb.) 38 The souldier is sooner killed with a little Bullet then a large Swoorde. **1652** *Proc. Parliament* No. 134 Ammunition.. found in the Castle of Bradock.. 700 weight of Musket Bullet. **1758** JOHNSON *Idler* No. 10 ¶4 The man was not hurt by the bullet. **1839** tr. *Lamartine's Trav. East* 48/1 Beschir.. precipitated himself from the top of it under a shower of bullets.

fig. **1599** SHAKS. *Much Ado* II. iii. 249 Shall quips and sentences, and these paper bullets of the braine awe a man from the careere of his humour?

b. *fig.* Notice to quit, the 'sack'. *slang.*

1841 SAVAGE *Dict. Art Printing* s.v., When a workman, at case or press, either for neglect, want of punctuality, or for gross misconduct, is discharged *instanter*, and the usual notice of 'a fortnight' is not given, it is said, *He has got the Bullet.* **1868** T. WRIGHT *Great Unwashed* 254 [One] who has .. got 'the bullet', as the formal note intimating that, 'owing to a reduction of our establishment your services will no longer be required', is called among working men. **1874** HOTTEN *Slang Dict.* s.v., To shake the bullet at any one, is to threaten him with 'the sack', but not to give him actual notice to leave. **1887** *Punch* 17 Sept. 126/1, I have just got the 'bullet', Mate—sacked without notice. **1929** *Melody Maker* Jan. 9/1 You and your band are getting the bullet, Bert Ambrose is taking over the Savoy in your place. **1960** H. PINTER *Caretaker* I. 10 The guvnor give me the bullet. Making too much commotion, he says. **1967** *Crescendo* Oct. 14/1 It was only the boss's inherent good nature that saved me from the bullet.

4. a. Formerly, The missile from a sling; also *attrib.* **b.** The angler's plumb or sinker.

1587 TURBERV. *Trag. T.* (1837) 175 The arrowes flewe from side to side, The bullot stones did walke. **1633** T. STAFFORD *Pac. Hib.* viii. (1821) 574 Captaine Roger Harvie, receevid severall bruises with stones and Iron bullets, flung upon them. **1807** ROBINSON *Archæol. Græca* IV. iii. 349 In slinging, they whirled it twice or thrice about the head, and then cast the bullet. **1847** GROTE *Greece* (1862) VI. II. lxx. 262 The Greeks.. obtained.. lead for bullets to be used by the slingers. **1867** F. FRANCIS *Angling* i. (1880) 47 It is not desirable to plunge.. the bullet into the water.

5. *pl. Sc.* The game of bowls. [Cf. OF. *boulete* in same sense.]

1843 *Proc. Berw. Nat. Club* II. No. 11. 58 In the eastern district of Berwickshire the game was called *bowls* or *bullets*.

6. An ace in the game of brag or poker; esp in phr. ***two bullets and a bragger*** (see BRAGGER 2): a winning hand; also *fig. U.S.*

1807 W. IRVING *Salmag.* (1824) 354 One of them.. exclaimed triumphantly, 'Two bullets and a bragger!' and swept all the money into his pocket. **1841** *Spirit of Times* (N.Y.) 23 Oct. 402 Zenith, Magnate, and Jim Bell are 'two bullets and a bragger' that Kentucky can 'travel on' and 'pay

expenses'. **1878** F. H. HART *Sazerac Lying Club* 151 'Here's four bullets,' said Brown, as he reached for the pot. **1889** BARRÈRE & LELAND *Dict. Slang* I. 196/1 The highest hand in the game is three white (or real) aces, the next highest is 'two bullets and a bragger'.

7. Phrases. †*every bullet has its lighting place. every bullet has its billet* (see BILLET *sb.*[1] 4). †*full bullet*: of full size. †*bullet in mouth*: ready for action (cf. BOUCHE *sb.*[1] 2). *to bite* (*on*) *the bullet*: see BITE *v.* 16.

c **1575** GASCOIGNE *Fruites Warre* lxvii, Every bullet hath a lighting place. **1649** G. DANIEL *Trinarch., Hen. IV*, cxxv, Some Minds are cast Full Bullett to the widest mouth of Sin. **1692** *Siege Lymerick* 31 The said Garrison to march out.. with Arms.. Bullet in Mouth, Colours flying. **1837** DICKENS *Pickw.* xix, It is an established axiom that 'every bullet has its billet'.

8. *Comb.* and *Attrib.*, as ***bullet-bag, -boy, -buttons, -gun, -hole, -maker, -mould, -pouch***; and ***bullet-less, -like, -proof, -riddled, -swept*** adjs.; also †**bullet-bore**, a tool for finishing the interior of a bullet-mould; **bullet-bush** (see quot.); **bullet-drawer**, an instrument for extracting bullets from wounds; †**bullet-iron** (see quot.); **bullet-money** (see quot.); **bullet-shell**, a shell used with small arms. Also BULLET-HEAD.

1598 BARRET *Theor. Warres* III. i. 34 On his right side a *Bullet bagge or purse of canuas.. for bullets. **1652** *Proc. Parliament* No. 170 Behind the hangings were found 66 Muskets.. and the bullet bagges filled with new cast bullets. **1677** MOXON *Mech. Exerc.* (1703) 55 The *Bullet-bore, is a Shank of Steel, having a Steel Globe or Bullet at one end, just of your intended Bullet size. **1876** *Daily News* 18 Oct. 3/6 A *bullet boy in the Royal Arsenal, was brought up from Maidstone gaol. **1731** MORTIMER in *Phil. Trans.* XXXVII. 177 *Prunus Buxi folio cordato, fructu nigro rotundo.* The *Bullet-Bush. **1823** F. COOPER *Pioneer* v. 24/1 A frock of bottle-green with *bullet buttons. **1749** in *Phil. Trans.* XLVI. 85 The Extraction of it.. by the *Bullet-drawers. **1703** MAUNDRELL *Journ. Jerus.* (1721) Add. 3 A long *bullet-gun could not shoot a ball over it. **1869** 'MARK TWAIN' *Sk. New & Old* (1875) 49 Freckles me with *bullet-holes. **1917** 'CONTACT' *Airman's Outings* 246 We land.. and count the bullet-holes on the machines. **1679** PLOT *Staffordsh.* (1686) 374 Spanish or Swedish barrs, here called *bullet-Iron. **1876** E. CLARK *Life Japan* 185 Throwing volley after volley of *bulletless smoke into the stubborn ranks of the enemy. **1874** LUBBOCK *Orig. & Met. Ins.* i. 10 The species making the *bullet-like galls. **1644** PRYNNE & WALKER *Fiennes's Trial* 17 The said Governour.. had.. A Match-make[r], a *Bullet-maker. **1677** MOXON *Mech. Exerc.* (1703) 52 The making of *Bullet molds. **1879** H. PHILLIPS *Notes Coins* 13 The *'bullet-money' of Siam is formed by bringing together the ends of oval pieces of silver. **1757** LOUDOUN & LYMAN *Gen. Orders* (1899) 65 The Deficiency of Powder Horns & *Bullet Pouches. **1849** PARKMAN *Calif. & Oregon Trail* 20 His bullet-pouch and powder-horn hung at his side. **1856** J. GRANT *Black Drag.* xxxvi, Others.. believed in *bulletproof men, and put in a silver coin with their bullets. **1905** *Daily Chron.* 10 Jan. 4/5 The head of the drum was so *bullet-riddled that it resembled a sieve. **1897** *Westm. Gaz.* 3 June 2/2 The *bullet-swept square. **1901** 'LINESMAN' *Words by Eyewitness* (1902) 33 The bullet-swept hills above Ladysmith.

†**'bullet**, *sb.*[2] *Obs. rare.* [Ultimately identical with BILLET *sb.*[1]: in sense 1 perh. a mere corruption of that word; in sense 2 ad. It. *bulletta.*]

1. = BILLET *sb.*[1] 4.

1612 *Passenger of Benvenuto* (N.) There is a bullet for the warrant of your lodging.

2. A slip of paper on which the voter wrote the name of the candidate he supported. Cf. BULLETIN.

1615 G. SANDYS *Travels* 230 Elected by the Great Master and his Knights, who giue their voices by bullets, as do the Venetians.

'bullet, *v. nonce-wd.* [f. BULLET *sb.*[1]] *trans.* To shoot with a bullet.

1884 GILBART-SMITH *Log o' the 'Norseman'* 135 A veritable stuffed pig, born, bred, and bulleted in Albania.

bulleted ('bʊlɪtɪd), *ppl. a.* [f. BULLET *sb.*[1] + -ED.] **a.** Bullet-shaped. **b.** Furnished with bullets.

a **1583** STANYHURST *Conceites* (Arb.) 143 A leshe of bulleted hard stoans. **1858** in Greener *Gunnery* Advt. 12 Manufacturer of Powder.. Saloon Pistols, Bulleted Caps, etc.

bullet-head. [f. BULLET *sb.*[1] + HEAD.] **a.** A head round like a bullet. **b.** A person with such a head; in U.S., *fig.* a 'pig-headed', obstinate person. *Hence* **'bullet-ˌheaded, -'headedness.**

1690 B. E. *Dict. Cant. Crew, Bullet-headed*, a dull silly Fellow. **1722** DE. FOE *Col. Jack* (1840) 142 He would have whipped the poor bullet-head, so they called the negro. **1793** HOLCROFT *Lavater's Physiog.* xx. 102 Savages, by being distorted, acquired the appellation of bowl- or bullet-head. **1848** LOWELL *Biglow P.* ix. 129 He aint No more 'n a tough old bullethead. *a* **1849** POE *Marginalia* lxxiv, The disgusting sternness, captiousness, and bullet-headedness of her husband. **1857** E. BEADLE *To Nebraska* (1923) 19 A clever bullet-headed Kentuckyan. **1872** F. W. ROBINSON *Tito's Troub.* in *Wrayford's Ward*, I was a thin, gawky, bullet-headed youth. **1875** BUCKLAND *Log-Bk.* 25 Popped his bullet head.. round from the Curtain. **1947** AUDEN *Age of Anxiety* (1948) ii. 54 Bullet-headed bandit.

bulletin ('bʊlɪtɪn). Also 7 bolletine, -ettine. [In 17th c. ad. It. *bullettino, bollettino* dim. of *bulletta* = BULLET *sb.*[1]; but the mod. word (senses 2, 3), first recorded in latter half of 18th c., appears to be a. Fr. *bulletin.*]

†**1. a.** A short note or memorandum. **b.** An official certificate; a warrant of appointment to an office. *Obs.*

[**1645** EVELYN *Mem.* (1819) I. 181 We went now towards Ferrara, carrying with us a Bulletino or bill of health.] **1651** tr. *Life Father Sarpi* (1676) 46 He.. kept under Key.. even to the least bolletines and short notes that he made. **1673** RAY *Journ. Low C., Venice* 178 The sealing of bollettines for them that are to undertake any new office, etc.

2. a. A short account or report of public news or events, issued by authority; applied *esp.*, *c* 1800, to a report sent from the seat of war by a commander for publication at home.

1791 BURKE *Appeal Whigs* (R.) The pithy and sententious brevity of these bulletins of ancient rebellion. **1792** LD. SPENCER in *Ld. Auckland's Corr.* (1861) II. 474 They brought me.. a bulletin, for which I am much obliged to you. **1813** WELLINGTON *Let.* in Gurw. *Disp.* X. 410 There is at Lisbon a newspaper of the 13th containing the French bulletin of their action. **1840** CARLYLE *Heroes* vi, 374 'False as a bulletin' became a proverb in Napoleon's time. **1880** *Daily News* 29 Oct., Daily bulletins of the weather are despatched to subscribers.

b. A broadcast report of news, weather, etc. Also *fig.*

1925 *Times* 23 July 8/3 The news given out as a bulletin on a very recent Sunday from the London Station must have made many listeners pause. *Ibid.* 3 Aug. 5/5 The news bulletins are broadcast in the exact terms in which they are received from the news agencies. **1938** AUDEN & ISHERWOOD *On Frontier* 7 The drums tap out sensational bulletins; Frantic the efforts of the violins. **1938** WODEHOUSE *Summer Moonshine* i. 7 The weather-bulletin announcer of the British Broadcasting Corporation.

3. An official statement as to the health of an invalid.

1765 H. WALPOLE *Corr.* (1817) II. 312 The dauphin is at the point of death. Every morning the physicians frame an account of him, and happy is he or she who can produce a copy of this lie, called a bulletin. **1836** DICKENS *Sk. Boz* 5 Verbal bulletins of the state of his health were circulated throughout the parish half-a-dozen times a day. **1870** DISRAELI *Lothair* lix, Lothair, after having heard the first.. bulletin of the surgeon, had been obliged to leave the convent.

4. *attrib.*, esp. in **bulletin-board**, (*a*) *U.S.*, a notice-board; (*b*) a computer-based system giving users access from remote terminals to text and programs contributed by one another and stored centrally.

1831 *Boston Transcript* 5 July 2/4 From the City Hall Bulletin Board. **1869** 'MARK TWAIN' *Innoc. Abr.* 333 A great public bulletin-board in Pompeii. **1897** —— *Following Equator* iv. 75 To-day per the bulletin-board at the head of the companionway, it is September 10. **1949** *Lisle* (Ill.) *Eagle* 10 Mar. 5/1 With the new scroll placed on the bulletin board all may see who made the honor roll this time. **1979** *Byte* Dec. 103 Computerized bulletin board systems are multiplying like rabbits! These systems, which allow people to communicate with others via terminal modems and personal computer systems, are skyrocketing in popularity. **1984** *Times* 21 Sept. 12/4 He put out the challenge through the network of personal computer 'bulletin boards' which have sprung up in Britain.

Hence **'bulletin** *v. trans.* To make known by bulletin.

1838 JERROLD *Men of Char., J. Pippins* vii, Job again and again bulletined his convalescence. **1884** *Reading* (*Pa.*) *Herald* 3 Apr., Mr. L—— has made arrangements to have all.. championship games bulletined.

†**'bulleting**, *vbl. sb. Obs. rare*$^{-1}$. [f. BULLET *sb.*[1] + -ING[1].] The firing of bullets. Also *attrib.*

1635 SWAN *Spec. M.* v. §2 (1643) 167 In a bloudie bulleting fight, the aire is forced and stirred.

bullet tree, var. of BULLY TREE: see BULLY *sb.*[4]

bullet-wood. [Cf. F. *bois de balle* and *boulet de canon.*] The wood of the bully tree (BULLY *sb.*[4]).

1843 HOLTZAPFFEL *Turning* I. 77 Bullet-wood, from the Virgin Isles, West Indies. *Ibid.*, Bullet-wood, another species so called, is supposed to come from Berbice; its colour is hazel brown..; it is.. well adapted to general and to eccentric turning. **1858** [see BALATA 1].

bullety ('bʊlɪtɪ), *a.* [f. BULLET *sb.*[1] + -Y[1].] Shaped like a bullet.

1846 POE *Wks.* (1864) III. 111 His forehead is.. what is termed bullety. **1857** *Tait's Mag.* XXIV. 174 It covered a round, bullety head.

†**bulleyn**, var. of BOLLEN *sb. Obs.*, seed-pod.

1578 LYTE *Dodoens* I. lxxxiii. 123 Ye shall finde in the huskes wherein they stood littell long bulleyns wherein the seede is contayned.

bulleys, obs. form of BULLACE.

'bull-fight. [Of recent introduction, having superseded *bull-feast* (see BULL *sb.*[1] 11), which is found in Ash and Bailey, while neither they nor Johnson give *bull-fight.*] A sport practised in Spain, in which a bull is first attacked by horsemen called *toreadores*, and footmen called *picadores*, and finally slain by a swordsman called *matador*. Hence **bull-fighter, -ing** *vbl. sb.*

1753 CHAMBERS *Cycl. Supp.* s.v. *Bull*, Bull-fighting, a sport or exercise much in vogue among the Spaniards and Portugueze. **1788** LD. AUCKLAND *Diary* in *Corr.* II. 63 All the gentlemen.. went for the first time to the bull-fight. **1846** *Byron's Wks.* 13/1 *note*, The professional bull-fighter gave.. lessons. **1862** *Sat. Rev.* XIV. 219/2 If we go on in this way, we shall be ready for bull-fights and gladiators. **1883** *Sunday Mag.* 575/1 Ferdinand VII founded at Seville a university for.. education.. in the art of bull-fighting.

b. ? = BULL-BAITING.

1824 J. MCCULLOCH *Highlands Scotl.* I. 367 If there is not a bull-fight at Wrexham or Stamford, some squire is born, and there is a bull-feast at Grantham or Chirk.

bullfinch[1] ('bʊlfɪnʃ). Also bulfinch. [f. BULL *sb.*[1] + FINCH. The reason for the name is uncertain: some have suggested that it was given on account of the thickness of the bird's neck.]

One of a genus of birds (*Pyrrhula*), allied to the Grosbeaks, having handsome plumage and a short, hard, rounded beak; well known for its aptness to be trained as a singing bird.

1570 LEVINS *Manip.* 134/4 A Bulfinche, bird, *ribicilla.* **1609** N. F. *Fruiterers Secrets* 2 A Bulfinch will eate [cherries] stones and all. **1655** MOUFFET & BENNET *Health's Improv.* (1746) 188 Bulfinches feed.. upon Hemp-seed, and the Blossoms of Pear, plum, and Apple-trees. **1789** G. WHITE *Selborne* xxxix. (1853) 134 Bullfinches when fed on hempseed often become wholly black. **1835** MARRYAT *Olla Podr.* xiv, The piping bullfinch.. must have a good memory. **1847** *Gard. Chron.* 118 The bill of the bulfinch is a most suspicious-looking instrument.

b. *Comb.*, as ***bullfinch plover, bullfinch trainer.***

1864 ATKINSON *Provinc. names Birds, Bullfinch Plover*, Prov. name for Turnstone, *Strepsilas interpres.* **1857** MAYHEW *Lond. Labour* II. 59 This tuition among professional bullfinch-trainers, is systematic.

bullfinch[2] ('bʊlfɪnʃ). [Evans *Leicestersh. Gloss.* (1881) suggests a corruption of *bull-fence.* If it was so, the origin must have been forgotten before *bull-finch fence* was said.] A kind of hedge (see quot.).

1832 *Quart. Rev.* Mar. 226 The bull-finch fence.. is a quickset hedge of perhaps fifty years' growth with a ditch on one side or the other, and so high and strong that [one] cannot clear it. **1857** KINGSLEY in *Life* xvi. (1879) II. 56 Race at the brook, Then smash at the bullfinch. **1880** *Times* 2 Nov. 4/5 Double-stitched shooting coats, that will stand the ordeal of 'bull-finches' and brambles.

Hence **'bullfinch** *v. intr.*, to leap a horse through such a hedge.

1837 *Gambler's Dream* III. 208 A fox hunter who must bullfinch out [of] a field in Northamptonshire, looks out for a little daylight between the twigs.

bullfincher. = prec.

1862 *Sat. Rev.* XIV. 219/2 A man exhibits his skill over a bullfincher for his own amusement.

†**'bullfist.** *Obs.* exc. *dial.* [f. BULL *sb.*[1] + FIST *sb.*[2] 'flatus ventris'.] The fungus called puff-ball (*Lycoperdon bovista*). 'Still in use in Suffolk' Britten and Holland.

1611 COTGR., *Pissaulict*, a fuss-ball.. puffiste, or bullfiste. **1755** *Gentl. Mag.* XXV. 124 The remarkable quality of the Lycoperdon, Puff-ball, or Bul-fist for stopping hæmorrhages.

'bull-ˌfrog. [f. BULL *sb.*[1] + FROG.] The name given to certain large American frogs, esp. *Rana pipiens*, a species 6 or 8 inches long, which has a voice not unlike that of a bull.

1738 MORTIMER *Nat. Hist. Carolina* in *Phil. Trans.* XL. 348 The Bull-Frog. This hath its English Name from its Noise, which seems not unlike the Bellowing of a Bull at a Distance. **1795** WOLCOTT (P. Pindar) *Lousiad* III. Wks. 1812 I. 248 The Bull-frog's snore. **1824** W. IRVING *T. Trav.* (1849) 384 The bull-frog croaked dolefully from a neighboring pool. **1855** LONGF. *Hiaw.* IX. 118 And the bull-frog, the Dahinda, Thrust his head into the moonlight.

bullgine ('bʊldʒaɪn). *colloq.* (orig. *U.S.*). Also **bulgine, bulljine.** [f. BULL *sb.*[1] + EN)GINE *sb.*] A locomotive or steam-engine.

1848 F. A. DURIVAGE *Stray Subjects* 38 [He made] himself agreeable to his officers by.. imitating the 'bullgine'. **1848** in *Amer. Speech* (1946) XXI. 116/1 Going ober to Hobuc, in de steamboat, De bulgine busted and we all got afloat! *Ibid.*, Clar de track, de bullgine's coming. **1889** [see BULL *sb.*[1] 7 b]. **1922** JOYCE *Ulysses* 395 The men of the island.. let the bullgine run.. and put to sea. **1927** in J. Sampson *Seven Seas Shanty Book* 32 So clear the track let the Bullgine run.

'bullˌhead. Also 6 bullyhead.

1. A small freshwater fish with a large head (*Aspidophorus cataphractes*); the *Miller's Thumb.*

c **1450** *Voc.* in Wr.-Wülcker 704 *Hic capito*, a bulhede. **1558** *Act 1 Eliz.* xvii, Places where Smelts, Loches, Minnies, Bulheads, etc... have been used to be taken. **1653** WALTON *Angler* 232 The Miller's thumb or Bull-head is a fish of no pleasing shape. **1841** H. MILLER *O.R. Sandst.* iii. 77 The river bull-head, when attacked by an enemy, or immediately as it feels the hook in its jaws, erects its two spines at nearly right angles with the plates of the head.

b. Any of various North American fresh-water fish of the genus *Amiurus* or allied genera, esp. the bull-pout or horned pout (*Amiurus nebulosus*).

1674 J. JOSSELYN *Two Voy.* 113 Blew-fish, Bull-head, Bur-fish. **1758** J. WILLIAMS *Redeemed Captive* (ed. 3) 18 There seven of us supped on the Fish, called Bull-head or Pout. **1814** MITCHILL *Fishes N.Y.* 380 Eighteen-spined Bullhead, *Cottus octodecem-spinosus.* **1997** *Sports Afield* (U.S.) Feb. 21/2 Our lake is full of bullheads.

2. A tadpole. Now only *dial.*

1611 COTGR., *Cavesot*, a Pole-head, or Bull-head; the little black vermine whereof toads and frogs do come. **1883** *Lane. Gloss.* (E.D.S.) *Bull-heads, Bull-Jones*, tadpoles.

†**3.** A mass of curled or frizzled hair worn over the forehead; called also BULL-TOUR. *Obs.*

1672 MARVELL *Reh. Transp.* I. 3 To trick up the good old Bishop in a yellow Coif and a Bulls-head, that he may.. appear in Fashion. **1673** R. LEIGH *Transpr. Rehears'd* 140 The Glories of her Yellow Hood and Bull-head. **1688** R. HOLME *Armoury* II. xvii. §119 Some term this curled Forehead from the French word *Taure*, a Bull-head. This was the fashion of Women to wear Bull-heads, or Bull-like foreheads, anno 1674.

4. 'A stupid fellow; a blockhead.' J. Also *attrib.*

1624 *Essex's Ghost* in *Harl. Misc.* III. 514 Why should this bull head bishop.. against me roar with brazen bull? **1840** W. G. SIMMS *Border Beagles* 487 We've time enough to scud and run to-night, and to-morrow we can turn upon that bullhead, Rawling.

5. A brick wider at one end than the other, used for arches.

1862 *Catal. Internat. Exhib. Industr. Dept. Brit. Div.* II. x. 27/1 Common fire-bricks, of various forms, arch bricks, bull-heads, pin bricks, soap bricks &c.

bullheaded (ˈbʊlˌhɛdɪd), *a.* Having a massive head, broadheaded; *fig.* blindly impetuous, blockheaded. Hence ˌ**bullˈheadedness**.

1818 SCOTT *Hrt. Midl.* xviii, They.. flourish with their bull-headed obstinacy. **1846** *Comic Jack Giant Kill.* (ed. 3) 7 This beef-eating, bull-headed, 'son-of-a-gun'. **1884** F. BRITTEN *Watch & Clockm.* 153 See that the pivots are.. neither bull headed nor taper. **1858** CARLYLE *Fredk. Gt.* I. IV. viii. 465 Rough and stiff as natural bull-headedness helped by Prussian pipeclay can make it.

bullhood (ˈbʊlhʊd). [f. BULL *sb.*[1] + -HOOD.] The condition of being a bull.

1845 FORD *Hand-bk. Spain* I. 290 The priest.. selected a bull and christened him;.. but.. on the morrow he relapsed into his former bullhood and brutality. **1885** *Fortnight in Waggonette* 92 He was destined never to reach the full maturity of bullhood.

Bulli (ˈbʊlaɪ). *Austral.* The name of *Bulli*, a town south of Sydney, New South Wales, used (chiefly *attrib.*) to designate a type of soil used esp. for cricket pitches.

1904 *Westm. Gaz.* 18 Apr. 3/1 This Bulli soil is wonderful in its resistance to wet... The wet does not run through the Bulli. **1907** *Daily Chron.* 19 Dec. 4/7 The famous rain-resisting 'Bulli soil' of which the pitch on the Sydney Cricket Ground is composed. **1929** CONAN DOYLE *Maracot Deep* 244 The perfect Bulli-earth wicket, so far as England could supply that commodity, reminded our visitors of their native conditions. **1963** *Guardian* 4 May 4/6 The flawless bulli soil and merry creek pitches which were the terror of all bowlers half a century ago.

bullied (ˈbʊlɪd), *ppl. a.* [f. BULLY *v.*[1] + -ED[1].] Roughly treated; cowed by a bully.

1851 SIR F. PALGRAVE *Norm. & Eng.* (1864) IV. 67 The story of Flambard's mother enlivened the chansons of some bullied minstrel. *a* **1863** THACKERAY *Song of Cane* viii, That cringing, bullied lout Had once a generous soul.

†ˈ**bullient**, *a. Obs. rare.* [a. L. *bullient-em*, pr. pple. of *bullīre* to BOIL.] Boiling, bubbling.

1669 BOYLE *Contn. New Exp.* II. (1682) 141 Bullient Spirit of Wine.. The murmer of the bullient water was heard.

bullies, obs. form of BULLACE.

†ˈ**bullifant.** *Obs. rare*[−1].

a **1528** SKELTON *Elynour Rummyng* 520 Necked lyke an olyfant, It was a bullyfant, A greedy cormorant.

bullimong (ˈbʊlɪmʌŋ). Forms: 4, 9 buli-, 5–7, 9 boly-, 6 bul-, 7 bally-, 8 bollimong, (6 bullimoong, 7 -mung, 8 -mond), 6– bullimong. (7–8 Dicts. have bulli-, bolli-, bullmony.) [Of obscure composition: the second element is app. IMONG:—OE. *ʒemang*, *-mǫng*, mixture.]

1. A mixture of various kinds of grain sown together (as oats, pease, and vetches) for feeding cattle. Cf. DREDGE, MESLIN, and L. *farrago.*

1313 etc. in Rogers *Agric. & Prices* II. 174/4 etc. **1494** *Will of Fyche, Essex* (Somerset Ho.), Frumenti et duo quarteria de Bolymong. **1552** HULOET, Bolymonge whyche is a kynd of myxture of corne and grayne, *farrago.* **1577** HARRISON *Descr. Brit.* I. xviii, Of mixed corne, as.. tares and otes (which they call bulmong).. here is no place to speake. **1601** HOLLAND *Pliny* I. 557 Grain which.. is sown for beasts .. which they call dredge or ballimong. **1639** HORN & ROBOTHAM *Gate Lang. Unl.* xii. §130 Bullimong [mixt provender] is sowne for cattell. **1706** in PHILLIPS [see 2]. **1753** CHAMBERS *Cycl. Supp.*, Bullimony, bullimong, bollimony, etc. **1844** BAKER in *Jrnl. R.A.S.* V. I. 4 Peas.. are frequently sown with oats.. This crop is denominated bullimong.

b. *attrib.*

1615 T. ADAMS *Sacrifice of Thankf.* Wks. 1861 I. 127 They are full of farraginous and bullimong mixtures. **1647** WARD *Simp. Cobler* 24 If any man mislikes a bully mong drassock more then I, let him take her for all mee.

†**2.** = BUCKWHEAT. *Obs.*

1578 LYTE *Dodoens* III. liii. 393 The seede is blacke and triangled.. like to the seede of Bockweyde or Bolymong. **1598** GERARD *Herbal* I. lx. ¶4. 83 Buckwheat is called.. in English.. Bullimong. **1706** PHILLIPS, *Bollimong* or *Bollmong*, Buck-wheat, a kind of Grain: Also a Medley of several sorts of Grain together, otherwise call'd Mastin, or Mong-corn.

ˈ**bulling**, *vbl. sb.*[1] See BULL *v.*[1] Also *attrib.*

1398 [see BULL *v.*[1]]. **1607** TOPSELL *Four-f. Beasts* 57 The signes of their Bulling (as it is termed) are their cries, and disorderly forsaking their fellows. **1624** FLETCHER *Rule a Wife, &c.* v. **1725** BRADLEY *Fam. Dict.* I. s.v. *Cow*, The Advantages of their bulling at that Time is, that they will calve in ten Months. **1950** J. G. DAVIS *Dict. Dairying* 84 *Bulling heifer*, a heifer which is the right age and size for being served. **1960** *Times* 9 May 3/3 The calfhood vaccination scheme allowed animals to be vaccinated up to the age of bulling.

ˈ**bulling**, *vbl. sb.*[2] [f. BULL *v.*[1], or nonce-vb. f. BULL *sb.*[1], + -ING[1].] (*nonce-use*) = BULL-BAITING.

c **1645** HOWELL *Lett.* (1713) 124 The Pope hath sent divers Bulls against this Sport of bullings.

†ˈ**bulling**, *vbl. sb.*[3] *Obs.* [f. BULL *v.*[3] to deceive; cf. BULLER *sb.*[1] b.] ? Fraudulent scheming.

1532 MORE *Confut. Barnes* VIII. Wks. (1557) 736/1 Hys asseheded exclamacions, and all hys busy bulling.

†ˈ**bulling**, *vbl. sb.*[4] *Obs.*[−0]. [Cf. F. *bouillir* and L. *bullīre* to BOIL.] The action of water issuing from a spring; bubbling.

1552 HULOET, Bullyng, bollynge, or bubblyng of water out of a sprynge.

†ˈ**bulling,** *ppl. a. Obs. rare*[−1]. [f. BULL *v.*[2]] That issues (papal) bulls.

1624 *Essex's Ghost* in *Harl. Misc.* (Malh.) III. 515 This bulling Pius.

†ˈ**bullion**[1]. *Obs.* Also 5 **bolyon.** [a. F. *bouillon*, f. *bouillir* to BOIL.] **a.** A boiling, a quantity (of salt, etc.) boiled at one time (OF. *boullon de sel*, med.L. *bullio* 'mensura salinaria' Du Cange); cf. mod. 'a boil of soap'. **b.** A certain quantity of quicksilver; cf. 'un bouillon de vif argent xxv livres pesant' (Carpentier s.v. *Bullionum*).

1453 *Weighing Charges* in Heath *Grocers' Comp.* (1869) 422 Argent Vyff, ye bolyon.. iiijd. **1610** HOLLAND *Camden's Brit.* 575 (D.) In Wich the King and Earle have eight salt pits, which.. yeelded on the Friday sixteene Bullions.

bullion[2] (ˈbʊlɪən). Forms: 5 bullioun(e, (*Sc.* bulʒeon), 6 bolion, -lyon, bulloyn, 6–7 bullyon, 7 bulloin, -oigne, (bullen, bulline), 5– **bullion.** [Of obscure etymology. First recorded as AF. *bullion* (see quot. 1336 in 1); the form appears to point to identity with F. *bouillon*, med.L. *bullio* 'boiling' (cf. prec.), but it does not appear that the word ever had, except in England, any of the senses defined below. If this etymology be correct, the sense of 'boiling' must have undergone a purely English development into those of 'melting', 'melted mass of metal'; the applications quoted under the preceding sb. (which are common to OF. and Eng.) probably furnished the suggestion for this extension of meaning. In MDu. *boelioen* seems to have had the sense of alloyed gold or silver (cf. 3, 4); see Verwijs & Verdam, who however identify the word with *billioen*, a. Fr. *billon.* The conjecture that *bullion* is in some way derived from L. *bulla* in the sense of seal or stamp appears to fail both with regard to form and meaning. The Fr. *billon* base metal (see BILLON) is unconnected in origin, but it seems to have influenced sense 4 of the present word; on the other hand, some obs. senses of Fr. *billon* seem to have been imitated from those of Eng. *bullion.*]

I. 1. ? Melting-house or mint; but the 16th c. legal antiquaries understood it as 'place of exchange'. (App. only in the Anglo-French Statutes, or the translations of them.)

1336 *Act 9 Edw. III*, ii. §2 Puissent sauvement porter a les eschanges ou bullion.. argent en plate, vessel d'argent, etc. **1354** *Act 27 Edw. III*, ii. §14 Puissent savement porter.. plate d'argent, billetes d'or et tut autre maner d'or et toutz moneys d'or et d'argent a nostre bullione ou a nos eschanges. **1632** *transl.* That all Merchants.. may safely carie and bring ..all money of gold and siluer to our bullion or to our exchanges which we shall cause to be ordeyned at our said Staples. **1641** *Termes de la Ley* 43 Bullion.. is the place where gold is tryed. **1670** BLOUNT *Law Dict.*, *Bullion*.. signifies.. sometimes the Kings Exchange, or place, whither such Gold in the lump is brought to be tryed or exchanged. **1725** SWIFT *Drapier's Lett.* Wks. 1755 V. II. 21 The third part of all the money of silver plate, which shall be brought to the bullion, shall be made into half-pence and farthings.

II. Precious metal in the mass.

2. Gold or silver in the lump, as distinguished from coin or manufactured articles; also applied to coined or manufactured gold or silver when considered simply with reference to its value as raw material.

1451 *Sc. Acts Jas. II* (1597) §34 Na man haue out of the Realme, gold, siluer, nor Bulʒeon. *c* **1460** FORTESCUE *Abs. & Lim. Mon.* (1714) 115 How Bullion may be brought into this Land. [**1477** *Act. 17 Edw. IV*, i, Toutz gentz en quelecon*q*e Roialme puissent porter a leschaungez come bullion tout maner de bon monoie dargent, de quelecon*q*e value *q*e fuisse.] **1488** *Invent.* in Tytler *Hist. Scot.* (1864) II. 393 Item twa braid pecis of brynt silver bullioune. **1580** NORTH *Plutarch* 865 Bringing with him all his plate, both Gold and Silver, unto the Mint-master, he gave it him to put into bullion, and so to be converted into currant coin. **1633** T. STAFFORD *Pac. Hib.* iv. (1821) 267 All such Moneys be.. esteemed for Bullion onely. **1651** HOWELL *Venice* 17 Their charge is to look to all sorts of bullions and coines, that they be not embasd and adulterated. *a* **1674** CLARENDON *Hist. Reb.* I. I. 59 The Bullion of neighbour Kingdoms brought to receive a Stamp from the Mint of England. **1688** R. HOLME *Armoury* II. 39/1 Mettal.. which is unwrought is called.. of some a Wedge or Bulline. **1725** SWIFT *Drapier's Lett.* Wks. 1755 V. II. 22 All silver money should be taken only as bullion. **1863** FAWCETT *Pol. Econ.* III. v. (1876) 361 It is unprofitable to melt down our silver coinage, and sell it as bullion. **1868** ROGERS *Pol. Econ.* iv. (1876) 6 The sum.. retained by the Bank of England as bullion.

b. *fig.*

1635 QUARLES *Embl.* II. xiii. (1718) 114, I cannot serve my God and bullion too. **1832** DOWNES *Lett. Cont. Countries* I. 91 It was tough work for foreign lips to coin the Swiss-German bullion into a circulating medium of communication.

c. Solid gold or silver (as opposed to mere showy imitations.) Often *fig.* Also *attrib.*

1596 SPENSER *F.Q.* III. i. 32 All of purest bullion framed were. **1779** JOHNSON *L.P.* Wks. 1816 X. 160 The spangles of wit which he could afford he knew how to polish; but he wanted the bullion of his master. **1822** SCOTT *Nigel* xiv, Broidery and bullion buttons make bare pouches. *a* **1834** COLERIDGE *Lit. Rem.* (1836) II. 361 There is.. weighty bullion Sense in this book. **1850** THACKERAY *Pendennis* xlvi, A red neckcloth.. with a large pin of bullion or other metal.

†**3.** Impure gold or silver; also *fig.* and *attrib.*

1616 BULLOKAR, *Bullion*, silver unrefined, not yet made into money. **1641** MILTON *Ch. Discip.* II. (1851) 50 To extract heaps of gold and silver out of the drossie Bullion of the Peoples sinnes. **1667** —— *P.L.* I. 704 A second multitude ..scum'd the Bullion dross. **1820** HAZLITT *Lect. Dram. Lit.* 264 The coarse, heavy, dirty, unwieldy bullion of books, is driven out of the market of learning.

III. Applied to other metals.

4. †**a.** Any metal in the lump (*obs.*). †**b.** Base metal; = BILLON (*obs.*). **c.** ***base bullion***: formerly = b; mod. in *Mining* (see quot. 1881).

c **1590** MARLOWE *Hero & L.* I, Base bullion for the stamps sake we allow. **1598** SYLVESTER *Du Bartas* II. II. ii. (1621) 261 And those [words], which Elds strict doom did disallow, And damn for bullion, go for current now. **1601** HOLLAND *Pliny* II. 462 (Æris grauis) that is to say.. brasse Bullion, or in Masse. **1632** SHERWOOD *Dict.*, Bullion, *Billon.* **1881** RAYMOND *Mining Gloss.*, *Base bullion* (Pacific), is pig lead containing silver and some gold, which are separated by refining.

IV. 5. *Comb.* (sense 2), as ***bullion-dealer***; also **bullion-coal**, local name of a particular seam; †**bullion-heretic** (*nonce-wd.*, see quot.).

1881 E. HULL *Coal-fields Gt. Brit.* (ed. 4) 204 Amongst the strata overlying the 'Upper-foot', or '*Bullion-coal', marine fossils occur. **1861** *N. Brit. Rev.* Nov. 358 Will *bullion-dealers refuse to buy gold for us abroad? **1869** ROGERS in *Adam Smith's W.N.* I. Pref. 40 The military chests of Napoleon were supplied by.. British bullion dealers. **1662** THORNDIKE *Just Weights* vii. §2 They are *bullion-heretics ..though not stamped by conviction, and contumacy succeeding, and the declaration of the church upon that.

†ˈ**bullion**[3]. *Obs.* Also 5 **bolyon, -en,** 6 **bulion, bullyon.** [app. a. F. *boulon* (spelt *bouillon* in Cotgr.), f. *boule* ball; assimilated in form to prec.]

†**1.** A knob or boss of metal; a convex ornament on a book, girdle, harness, or ring. Also *attrib. Obs.*

1463 in *Bury Wills* (1850) 36, I beqwethe to Anne Smyth a ryng of gold with bolyonys. **1464** *Mann. & Househ. Exp.* 254 My mastyr payd to Martyn Goldsmythe, for bolyons gyldynge, ij.*s.* **1517** in Glasscock *Rec. St. Michaels, Bp. Stortford* (1882) 35 Item pd for x bolyens and claspis, viij*d.* **1523** SKELTON *Garl. Laurel* 1165 The claspis and bullyons were worth a thousande pounde. **1538–48** ELYOT *Dict.*, *Bulla*, a bullion sette on the cover of a booke, or other thynge. **1562** PHAËR *Æneid* IX. Bbijb, Bulions broad of gold, and girdling girthes miraclose fyne. **1611** COTGR., *Bossette*.. a bosse or bullion set on a booke. **1706** PHILLIPS, *Bullion* of Copper is Copper-plates set on the Breast-leathers, or Bridles of Horses for ornament. **1707** EARL BINDON in *Lond. Gaz.* No. 4339/3 To Prohibit.. all Coachmakers.. that they do not use Varnish'd Bullion-Nails.

2. Bull's eye in glass.

1834 *Specif. Hartley's Patent* No. 6702. 2 When the table of glass is complete there are.. more or less waved lines for some inches round the 'bullion' or the centre of the table of glass, which lessens the value. **1881** *Spons' Encycl. Industr. Arts* 1064 Pressing this lump upon an iron point, so as to give it the form of a little cup, he fits it, when thus shaped, on to the bullion-point, to which it soon becomes firmly attached. The lump thus formed is called the 'bull's-eye' or 'bullion' of the developed plate. **1885** *Spons' Mech. Own Bk.* 630 'Roundels' and 'bullions' are small discs of glass, some made with a knob in the centre, and used in fretwork with cathedral glass.

†**3.** = *bolien*, BOLLEN *sb.*, BULLEYN. *Obs.*

1589 FLEMING *Virg. Georg.* I. 9 She [the pine] beareth balls or bullions of chesnut colour.

4. *Comb.*: **bullion-bar**, the bar on or against which the end of the sphere of glass is pressed in blowing crown glass; **bullion embroidery** (see quot. 1968); **bullion knot** = *bullion stitch*; **bullion-point**, the point or end of a bulb that is being worked on a blow-pipe; also, the thick centre of a disc of blown glass, the bull's-eye; **bullion-rod** = *bullion-bar*; **bullion stitch** (see quot. 1968).

a **1854** TOMLINSON *Cycl. Usef. Arts* I. 773/2 In again blowing out the bulb, the man supports it on a horizontal

smooth iron rod, called the bullion-bar. **1882** CAULFEILD & SAWARD *Dict. Needlework* 55 Bullion embroidery, when used for letters and large pieces, is applied to the material, as in appliqué. **1968** J. IRONSIDE *Fashion Alphabet* iii. 82 Bullion embroidery is an ancient embroidery done with gold wires instead of threads. **1882** CAULFEILD & SAWARD *Dict. Needlework* 55 *Bullion knot*, useful in crewel and silk embroideries, and largely employed in ancient embroideries for the foliage of trees and shrubs, and the hair of figures. **1881** Bullion-point [see above]. *a* **1884** KNIGHT *Dict. Mech.* Suppl., *Bullion Point* (glass), the thick portion at the center of a disk of crown glass. **1890** W. J. GORDON *Foundry* 143 The globe is heated and again blown, and becomes a Florence flask, the 'bullion-point', the apex of the old cone, being still conspicuous. **1862** *Chambers's Encycl.* IV. 780/1 The workman..next ma[r]vers it, without, however, using the bullion-rod. *c* **1890** tr. *T. de Dillmont's Encycl. Needlework* 231 For bullion stitch, select a needle, a little thicker towards the handle, and finer than you would use for any other crochet stitch. **1968** J. IRONSIDE *Fashion Alphabet* iii. 82 *Bullion-stitch*, a decorative stitch formed by twisting the thread several times round the needle before inserting it.

bullion[4] (ˈbʊlɪən). [prob. a. F. *bouillon* (see BULLION[1]) in senses derived from that of 'bubble': 'I. Plis bouffants qu'on fait à certains vêtements; 2. Fil d'or ou d'argent tourné en rond' (Littré).]

†**1.** More fully ***bullion-hose***: Trunk-hose, puffed out at the upper part, in several folds. *Obs.* Cf. BOUILLON 4.

1594 *Gesta Gray.* in Nichols *Progr. Q. Eliz.* III. 341 A bullion-hose is best to goe a woeinge in; for 'tis full of promisinge promontories. **1616** B. JONSON *Devil an Ass* III. iii, Not, While you doe eate, and lie, about the towne, here; And coozen i'your bullions. **1622** FLETCHER *Beggar's Bush* IV. iv, His baster'd bullions In a long stock ty'd up. **1632** MASSINGER & FIELD *Fatal Dow.* II. ii, You shall see him..at noon in the bullion, in the evening in Quirpo.

2. a. An ornamental fringe made of twists of gold or silver thread. **b.** A single twist of such fringe. Also *attrib.* [Prob. now often associated with BULLION[2] precious metal.]

1662 FULLER *Worthies* I. 247 Bullion, like other Lace, costing nothing safe a little thread. **1702** J. CHAMBERLAYNE *St. Gt. Brit.* II. III. vi. (1743) 416 None might wear silk or costly furring..without license from the king, nor no other persons wear broidery, pearls, or bullion. **1854** THACKERAY *Newcomes* I. 277 All in a blaze of scarlet and bullion and steel. **1879** *Uniform Reg.* in *Navy List* July (1882) 488/2 Epaulettes.—Bullions to be two and three-quarter inches in length and one and one-eighth inch in circumference. **1832** *Athenæum* No. 221. 42 Richly trimmed with embroidery and bullion fringes.

bullioned (ˈbʊlɪənd), *a.* [f. BULLION[4] 2 + -ED[2].] Ornamented with bullion.

1902 *Daily Chron.* 1 Feb. 8/3 Of clear white muslin..heavily bullioned up the centre breadth. **1905** *Westm. Gaz.* 13 July 5/1 The well-known ball dress of the British Navy, with its heavily bullioned epaulettes.

†**ˈbullioner.** *Obs.* [f. BULLION[2] + -ER[1].] A dealer in bullion.

1662 PETTY *Taxes* 77 To save it [money] from being melted down by goldsmiths and bullioners. **1675** R. VAUGHAN *Coinage* 30 (L.) Base money..melted down by the bullioners.

bullionist (ˈbʊlɪənɪst). [f. as prec. + -IST.] One who advocates a metallic currency.

1811 SOUTHEY *Ess.* (1832) I. 58 The vaunted discoveries of the bullionists and of the new political economists. **1828** TAYLOR *Money Syst. Eng.* 110 The bullionists were opposed by Mr. Vansittart, on the part of the ministry. *a* **1852** WEBSTER *Wks.* (1877) I. 374, I profess to be a bullionist in the usual and acceptable sense of the word. I am for a solid specie basis for our circulation. **1878** *N. Amer. Rev.* CXXVII. 106 Ricardo, the high-priest of the bullionists.

bullionless (ˈbʊlɪənlɪs), *a. nonce-wd.* [f. as prec. + -LESS.] Without bullion.

1854 *Fraser's Mag.* L. 351 From the bullionless bank.

bullir, bullis, obs. ff. BULLER, BULLACE.

bullish (ˈbʊlɪʃ), *a.*[1] [f. BULL *sb.*[1] + -ISH[1].]

1. Of or pertaining to a bull; resembling or having the nature of a bull.

1566 NUCE *Seneca's Octavia* (1581) 166 b, Cuckoldes bullysh badge. *a* **1722** LISLE *Husb.* (1752) 314 His bullish nature will be ploughed out in three years. **1830** *Fraser's Mag.* II. 610 They are bullish, they are unmanageable, vindictive and irreconcileable.

2. *Stock-Exchange*, etc. Tending to or aiming at a rise in the price of stocks or of merchandise.

1882 *Pall Mall G.* 5 July 5/2 We want to..make prices higher that Paris may see how 'bullish' we are. **1884** *Manch. Exam.* 11 June 4/4 In this market..a great majority are 'bullish' about cotton.

†**ˈbullish,** *a.*[2] *nonce-wd.* [f. BULL *sb.*[2] + -ISH[1].] Of or pertaining to papal bulls.

1546 BALE *Eng. Votaries* II. 36 Thys baudy bulle maker and hys other bullish begles.

†**bullish,** *a.*[3] *Obs. rare.* [f. BULL *sb.*[4] + -ISH[1].] Having the nature of a 'bull' or grotesque blunder; laughably erroneous.

1641 MILTON *Animadv.* (1851) 191 A toothlesse Satyr is as improper as a toothed sleekstone, and as bullish. **1660** S. FISHER *Rusticks Alarm* Wks. (1679) 149 That Bullish Title of works but imperfectly good.

bullishly (ˈbʊlɪʃlɪ), *adv.* [f. BULLISH *a.*[1] + -LY[2].] After the manner of a bull.

c **1827** LAMB in *Sel. Bernard Barton* (1849) 131 Making me, ever and anon, roar bullishly.

bullishness (ˈbʊlɪʃnɪs). *Stock Exchange.* [f. BULLISH *a.*[1] + -NESS.] The quality or condition of being bullish.

1895 *Daily News* 9 Feb. 8/4 'Bullishness' is a thing almost unknown. **1903** *Westm. Gaz.* 3 Jan. 7/1 The Kaffir Circus has come to a pause in its rakish career of bullishness. **1922** *Daily Mail* 1 Nov. 10 American Futures closed steady after recent bullishness.

bullism (ˈbʊlɪz(ə)m). [f. BULL *sb.*[4] + -ISM.] The making of 'bulls' or absurd blunders.

1835 MARRYAT *Jac. Faithf.* i, This lighter was manned (an expression amounting to bullism) by my father, my mother, and your humble servant.

†**ˈbullist.** [f. BULL *sb.*[2] + -IST.] A drawer up of papal bulls.

1587 HARMAR tr. *Beza's Serm.* 134 (L.) Proctors in the court ecclesiastical, dataries, bullists, copyists. **1653** URQUHART *Rabelais* II. vii. 213.

†**buˈllition.** *Obs.* [as if ad. L. **bullītiōn-em*, n. of action f. *bullīre* to BOIL.] The action of bubbling or boiling; ebullition.

c **1620** BACON *Physiol. Rem.* Wks. 1857 III. 809 The effects are..the bullition..the precipitation to the bottom. **1651** BIGGS *New Disp.* ¶296. 219 Many things by their first bullition depone their pristine vertues. **1791** E. DARWIN *Bot. Gard.* I. 206 With sudden flash the fierce bullitions rise.

bullmony, obs. form of BULLIMONG.

bullock (ˈbʊlək), *sb.* Forms: 1–3 bulluc, 5 bullok, 6 bolok, 6–7 bullocke, 6– bullock. [OE. *bulluc*; see BULL *sb.*[1], and cf. *ballock, hassock*. (The alleged form *bulluca* is spurious.)]

1. Orig. a young bull, or bull calf; but afterwards, and in later times always, a castrated bull, an ox.

a **1000** *Interlinear Gloss. on the Liber Scintillarum* liv. (*MS. Reg.* 7. C. iv.) To bulluce [Lat. *ad vitulum*]. *a* **1240** *Cuckoo Song* in Ritson *Anc. Songs* 3 Bulluc sterteþ. bucke uerteþ. *c* **1440** *Promp. Parv.* 55 Bullok, *boculus, vitulus.* **1521** *Bury Wills* (1850) 122 Item, delyuerid the boloks, vj, acordyng after yᵉ will. *a* **1553** UDALL *Royster D.* I. iv, I know that, but my mind was on bullockes and steeres. **1599** SHAKS. *Much Ado* II. i. 202 Why that's spoken like an honest Drouier, so they sel Bullockes. **1611** BIBLE *Ps.* li. 19 Then shall they offer bullockes vpon thine altar. **1720** GAY *Poems* (1745) I. 178 Here lowing bullocks raise their horned head. **1815** ELPHINSTONE *Acc. Caubul* (1842) II. 135 Bullocks are..more used to plough than camels.

†**2.** Applied loosely to a bull, or bovine beast generally. *Obs.* exc. *dial.*

1535 COVERDALE *Job* xxi. 10 Their bullock gendreth, and that not out of tyme. **1787** MARSHALL *Norfolk Gloss.* (E.D.S.) *Bullocks*, a general term, in Norfolk, for all kinds of cattle at turneps, etc.; whether they be oxen, steers, heifers, or cows. **1875** PARISH *Sussex Dial.*, *Bullock*, a fat beast of either sex..'Yes, she's a purty cow..one of these days she'll make a nice bullock.'

†**3.** Jestingly used for: A papal *bull*. *Obs.*

1537 LATIMER *Serm. & Rem.* (1845) 378, I send you here a bullock which I did find amongst my bulls. **1589** WARNER *Alb. Eng.* v. xxiv. 121 Some egge vs sla the Prince and shewe a Bullocke fra the Pope.

4. A slang term applied in Australian cities to a countryman or bushman.

5. In the names of various plants, as **bullock's eye**, the common Houseleek, *Sempervivum tectorum*; **bullock's heart**, the fruit of *Anona reticulata*; **bullock's lungwort**, the Great Mullein, *Verbascum Thapsus* L.

1597 GERARD *Herbal* cclvi. 630 The countrey people..in Kent, doe giue their cattell the leaues to drinke against the cough of the lungs..whereupon they do call it Bullocks Longwoort. **1861** MISS PRATT *Flower. Pl.* IV. 135 Great Mullein..was..Bullock's Lungwort. **1861** MRS. LANKESTER *Wild Flowers* 57 House-leek..is frequently called Jupiter's Eye, Bullock's Eye, or Jupiter's Beard. **1866** *Treas. Bot.*, *Bullock's Heart*, a name given to the fruit of *Anona reticulata*, a kind of custard apple.

6. *Comb.* and *Attrib.* **a.** simple attrib., as ***bullock-bell, -car, -carriage, -cart, -chariot, -dray, -gear, -hump, -land, -load, -pasture, -shed, -ship, -train, -turnip, -vessel, -wagon, -wainster***; **b.** objective genitive, as ***bullock-driver, -teasing***; also **bullock-leech**, a cattle-doctor; **bullock-puncher** (*Australian* and *N.Z.*) = *bullock-driver*; hence ***bullock-punching***. **bullock's-eye** (see quot.; cf. BULL'S-EYE); also see 5; **bullock-trunk**, a trunk suited for carriage in a bullock-cart, or on bullock-back.

1911 C. E. W. BEAN *'Dreadnought' of Darling* v. 48, I fancy there is a *bullock-bell somewhere, Joe. **1928** 'BRENT OF BIN BIN' *Up Country* viii. 126 The bullock bells added to the orchestra of frogs and the millions of crickets. **1830** W. S. MOORSOM *Lett. fr. Nova Scotia* 241 The Portuguese *bullock-car of Peninsular memory. **1903** *Daily Chron.* 11 Mar. 8/2 Mr. Chamberlain..subsequently proceeded to Mount Church, partly by municipal bullock-car. **1839** J. C. MAITLAND *Lett. fr. Madras* (1843) 299 All the poor widows, with their palanquins and *bullock-carriages covered with black cloth. **1858** *Merc. Mar. Mag.* V. 47 The difference..is 48 hours by *bullock-carts. **1837** CARLYLE *Fr. Rev.* II. v. xii. 316 *Bullock-chariots, and goadsmen in Roman Costume. **1857** WESTGARTH *Victoria, &c.* xi. 251 Carriage by *bullock-drays from Melbourne. **1792** *Gentl. Mag.* LXII. I. 175 We lost..about 600 privates, besides pack-horse and *bullock-drivers. **1862** LLOYD *Tasmania* xix. 480 Shepherds, Bullock drivers, and other servants were seized with the desire to turn diggers of gold. **1848** HAYGARTH *Bush Life Australia* ii. 19 Every sort of saddlery, *bullock-gear, and harness of every description. **1849–52** TODD *Cycl. Anat. & Phys.* IV. 1355 The *bullock-hump..is not by any means so characteristic of this race. **1881** *Daily News* 31 Aug. 2/2 The excellent *bullock land..would meet ready purchasers. **1774** LAMBERT in *Phil. Trans.* LXVI. 498 A farrier and *bullock-leach. **1803** WELLLINGTON *Let.* in Gurw. *Disp.* II. 567 We have not lost a *bullock-load of any thing during the war. **1856** W. H. S. ROBERTS *Diary* 19 Sept. in H. Beattie *Early Runholding in Otago* (1947) I. vi. 43 The whip..was a powerful flagellator in the hands of an experienced '*bullock-puncher'. **1921** H. GUTHRIE-SMITH *Tutira* xxxviii. 382 Owners and employees had worked shoulder to shoulder as..bullock-punchers. **1891** G. CHAMIER *Philosopher Dick* II. xv. 411 He soon got charge of a team, and was loud in expatiating on the art of *bullock-punching. **1751** CHAMBERS *Cycl.* s.v. *Eye*, **Bullock's Eye, Oeil de bœuf*, denotes a little sky-light in the covering, or roof, intended to illumine a granary, or the like. **1865** *Cornh. Mag.* XI. 105 The filthy quarters allotted me in an old *bullock-shed..exhausted all endurance. **1858** W. ELLIS *Vis. Madagascar* ii. 21 Mr. Jeffreys..died during a voyage from Madagascar to Mauritius in the miserable hold of a *bullock ship. **1879** DOWDEN *Southey* iii. 47 The sorry spectacle of *bullock-teasing made a slighter impression on him. **1859** LANG *Wand. India* 182 The Government has a *bullock-train for the conveyance of stores. **1845** STOCQUELER *Handbk. Brit. India* (1854) 78 *Bullock-trunks..are preferable, as they are permanently useful. **1884** *Whitby Gaz.* 9 Aug. 2/5 The crop of..*bullock turnips must now be sown. **1863** KINGLAKE *Crimea* II. 179 There were some Tartar peasants passing..with small *bullock-waggons. **1883** *Gd. Words* July 420/1 The *bullock-wainster who dared to hinder his progress.

ˈbullock, *v.* [f. prec.] †**1.** *trans.* and *intr.* = BULLY *v.*[1] *Obs.* exc. *dial.*

1716 [Implied in BULLOCKING *ppl. a.* below]. **1749** FIELDING *Tom Jones* II. vi, You have charged me with bullocking you into owning the truth. **1764** FOOTE *Mayor of G.* II. i, She shan't think to bullock and domineer over me. **1875** *Lanc. Gloss.* (E.D.S.) 61 Fair play! yo munnot bullock him.

2. *intr.* To work like a bullock, *i.e.* strenuously without intermission. *Austral.* and *N.Z. colloq.*

1888, 1900 [Implied in BULLOCKING below]. **1900** H. LAWSON *Over Sliprails* 19 We've..come down to have a bit of a holiday before going back to bullock for another six months or a year. **1946** K. TENNANT *Lost Haven* (1947) 52 If he had not 'bullocked' and sweated and driven himself.

3. ***to bullock one's way***: to make one's way with heavy violence.

1909 *Westm. Gaz.* 1 June 1/2 Sir William has frequently been referred to as 'bullocking' his way through Parliament. **1921** *Public Opinion* 10 June 538/2 To bullock his way through a British Amateur Championship. **1930** V. PALMER *Passage* i. 15 Fred was tough as tarred canvas, able to bullock his way anywhere. **1965** *Economist* 31 July 416/2 They picked, by a narrow majority, the man they reckoned most likely to bullock their way back into power.

Hence **ˈbullocking** *vbl. sb.* and *ppl. a.*

1716 M. DAVIES *Ath. Brit.* I. 272 Upon the Evidence of that bullocking Fryar Campanella. **1888** 'R. BOLDREWOOD' *Robbery under Arms* vii, It would have paid us better if we'd read a little more and put the 'bullocking' on one side. **1900** H. LAWSON *Over Sliprails* 12 You'll never make money, except by hard graft—hard, bullocking nigger-driving graft.

bullocker (ˈbʊləkə(r)). [f. BULLOCK *sb.* + -ER[1].]

1. A bullock-driver. *Austral.* and *N.Z.*

1889 BARRÈRE & LELAND *Dict. Slang.* s.v. *Bullocky*, Bullock[e]rs in Australia are as proverbial as bargees or Billingsgate fishwives in England for the forcibleness of their language. **1894** J. K. ARTHUR *Kangaroo & Kauri* II. ii. 91, I once saw..a bullocker who was working along with his team.

2. A ship used for carrying cattle.

1915 J. SIBREE *Naturalist in Madagascar* ii. 20 'Bullockers'..were still considered good enough to convey from two to three hundred oxen from Tamatave to Port Louis or Réunion.

ˈbullocky, *a.* and *sb.* [f. BULLOCK *sb.* + -Y[1].]

A. *adj.* **1.** Of the nature of or relating to bullocks.

1881 GRANT *Bush Life Queensl.* I. iii. 29 As a rule the conversation was very horsey or bullocky.

2. Having to do with driving bullocks or managing cattle. *Austral.*

1885 T. L. WORK in *Australasian Printers' Keepsake* 16 'When you *make* Mokepilly,' quoth one of the sunburnt bullocky men, 'keep on the brush fence...' **1890** 'R. BOLDREWOOD' *Col. Reformer* xii. 121 By George, Jack, you're a regular bullocky boy.

3. Resembling a bullock.

1890 *Temple Bar* Jan. 118 With more enthusiasm than persons of his bullocky conformation commonly exhibit. **1892** *Illustr. Sporting & Dram. News* 27 Aug. 862/3 Deer get bullocky if fed on ordinary cattle rations. **1954** E. C. STUDHOLME *Te Waimate* (ed. 2) xx. 179 The swine made a bullocky rush for home.

B. *sb.* **a.** A bullock-driver. *Austral.* and *N.Z. colloq.*

1889 in BARRÈRE & LELAND *Dict. Slang.* **1891** G. CHAMIER *Philosopher Dick* II. xii. 335 'And as for them bullockies,' said she, [etc.]. **1900** H. LAWSON *On Track* 49 The party had been increased by Jimmy Nowlett, the bullocky. **1934** T. WOOD *Cobbers* vi. 82 He was a bullocky, one of a race which speaks straight and spares none, like the bargees. **1966** 'J. HACKSTON' *Father clears Out* 92 A red-bearded, six-foot bullocky, known everywhere for his cleverness with his whip.

b. Language of the sort used by bullock-drivers; swearing. *Austral.* and *N.Z. slang.*

1916 *Anzac Bk.* 103/2 We heard fragments of language, of the category known in Australia as 'bullocky'. **1941** BAKER *N.Z. Slang* v. 47 The noun *bullocky* has even been evolved to describe the language used by such men.

c. ***bullocky's*** (or ***bullockys'***) ***joy***: treacle or golden syrup. *Austral.* and *N.Z. slang.*

1918 R. H. KNYVETT *Over There* IV. xvii. 158 This last is merely molasses or 'golden syrup' called 'bullocky's joy'.. because it is the chief covering for slices of bread with the bullock-driver. **1929** A. RUSSELL *Diary* 6 Mar. in *Tramp-Royal* (1934) xxxi. 202 Damper and 'bullockys' joy' (treacle) take the place of porridge. **1946** L. R. C. MACFARLANE *Amuri* III. 109 Out in camp he lived on hard bread, meat and bullockey's joy (treacle).

bulloe(s), obs. and dial. form of BULLACE.

bulloigne, -oin, -oyn, obs. ff. BULLION[2].

bullous ('bʊləs), *a. Path.* [f. BULL(A + -OUS.] Characterized by the presence of bullæ; resembling a bulla.

1833 P. RAYER *Treat. Dis. Skin* i. 49 Bullous inflammations of the skin. **1876** J. S. BRISTOWE *Treat. Theory & Pract. Med.* II. ii. 318 Herpes and pemphigus are vesicular or bullous affections. **1917** M. B. HARTZELL *Dis. Skin* viii. 286 The bullous syphiloderm.. occurs as pea- to nut-sized blebs. **1961** *Lancet* 2 Sept. 550/2 She developed a bullous skin eruption. **1974** PASSMORE & ROBSON *Compan. Med. Stud.* III. II. xxxi. 29 Vesicular and bullous diseases constitute a group of eruptions of widely varying aetiology and prognosis but all share the common feature of blister formation within or below the epidermis. **1984** TIGHE & DAVIES *Pathology* (ed. 4) xv. 132 The virus causes bullous lesions in the oral mucosa.

bull-pen. [f. BULL *sb.*[1] + PEN *sb.*[1]]

1. A pen or enclosure for bulls; *spec.* a square enclosure made of logs, freq. used in early times as a place of confinement; hence, a lock-up or prison. Also *transf.*, any enclosure or enclosed area. orig. and chiefly *U.S.*

1809 M. L. WEEMS *Life F. Marion* xxv. 214 The tories were all.. confined together under a centinel, in what was called a *bull pen*, made of pine trees. **1820** in *Pubn. Col. Soc. Mass.* (1906) VIII. 391 A circumscribed valley within the mountains, called the Bull-pen. **1865** *Nation* I. 15 A guardhouse.. which appears to have gone by the name of the 'Bull-pen'. **1912** *N.Y. Even. Post* 5 Sept. 2/5 Rioting convicts who broke out of 'bull pens' here are gathered in the prison yard, considering further steps. **1926** J. BLACK *You can't Win* vii. 76, I was taken downstairs and locked in a cell; I saw no more of the 'bull pen' where I spent the night. **1931** *Amer. Speech* VII. Oct. 49 [Lumberjacks'] 'free-for-all' when the 'shanty men' join the 'bull pen boys' around the box stove. **1933** *Jrnl. R. Aeronaut. Soc.* XXXVII. 14 To erect in front of the terminal building a semi-circular fence enclosing an area colloquially known as the 'bull pen'.

b. In baseball, a place outside the playing limits where pitchers are exercised for possible use during a game. *N. Amer.*

1924 *Chicago Tribune* 5 Oct. II. 1/1 Blake was rushed from the battlefield and Rip Wheeler from the bullpen. **1957** O. NASH *You can't get there from Here* 93 The pitcher too unrenowned, Who is always in the bull pen, But never reaches the mound.

2. A schoolboys' ball game, played by two groups, one group outlining the sides of a square enclosure, called the 'bull-pen', within which are the opposing players. *U.S.*

1857 *Spirit of Times* 19 Dec. 241/1 Some playing—the boys at bull-pen, the girls at jumping the rope. **1944** DUNCAN & NICKOLS *Mentor Graham* 99 Sometimes he joined the boys at 'bull pen'.

'bull's-eye. The eye of a bull (cf. F. *œil de bœuf*); hence **I.** Of glass.

1. A boss of glass, or the central protuberance formed in making a sheet of blown glass. Hence **bull's-eyed** *ppl. a.*, containing a bull's-eye.

1832 BABBAGE *Econ. Manuf.* iv. (ed. 2) 36 The centre [of a sheet of glass] presents the appearance of a thick boss or prominence, called the 'Bull's-eye'. **1863** *Reader* 28 Nov. 624 A window of small panes with the bull's-eyes in them. **1869** SALA *Ship-Chand.* (L.) Dingy bull's-eyed panes. **1878** BESANT & RICE *Chaplain of Fl.* iv. 34 Every other pane being those bull's-eye panes.

2. *Naut.* A hemispherical piece or thick disc of glass inserted in the side or deck of a ship, or elsewhere, to light the interior.

1825 H. GASCOIGNE *Nav. Fame* 64 Here a Bulls-eye gives a feeble light. **1843** *Commissioner* 342 A 'bull's-eye'.. that is a thick, green, half sphere of ground glass. **1882** NARES *Seamansh.* (ed. 6) 96 A light room outside, with a bull's-eye between it and the magazine.

3. A lens, hemispherical or plano-convex.

1839-47 TODD *Cycl. Anat. & Phys.* III. 354/1 The condenser.. should be a bull's eye or hemispherical lens. **1879** *Cassell's Techn. Educ.* IV. 258/1 The condensers in ordinary use are, The common 'bull's-eye' or plano-convex.

4. A glass of similar shape inserted in the side of a lantern; the lantern itself; also *attrib.*

1851 MAYHEW *Lond. Labour* I. 25, 2 or 3 Policemen, with their Bull's-eyes and.. truncheons speedily restored order. **1853** HERSCHEL *Pop. Lect. Sc.* VI. vi. (1873) 224 In a thick fog the bull's-eye of a lanthorn seems to throw out a broad diverging luminous cone. **1861** ANDERSSON *Okabango Riv.* xxv. 264 We then tried, bull's-eye lanthorn in hand, to obtain a glimpse of his retreating spoor. **1883** *Harper's Mag.* July 204/1 One.. was dazzled.. with opening bull's-eyes, and captured.

II. A circular hole, or an object containing one.

5. *Naut.* Also ***bull's eye cringle*** (see quots.).

1769 FALCONER *Dict. Marine* (1789) *Bull's-eye*, a small pulley in the form of a ring, having a rope round the outer edge.. and a.. hole in the middle for another rope to slide in. **1833** MARRYAT *P. Simple* vi, Pass that brace through the *bull's eye*. **1860** *Merc. Mar. Mag.* VII. 113 A leach-line is.. carried.. through a bull's-eye. **1867** SMYTH *Sailor's Word-bk.*, *Bull's-eye cringle*, a piece of wood in the form of a ring, which answers the purpose of an iron thimble; it is seldom used by English seamen, and then only for the fore and main bowline-bridles.

6. *Arch.* A small circular opening or window.

1865 *Athenæum* No. 1978. 412/3 The plate-tracery, or bull's-eyes, of the transept ends. **1875** GWILT *Archit.* Gloss., *Bull's eye*, any small circular aperture for the admission of light or air.

III. Other uses.

7. a. The centre of a target.

1833 *Regul. Instr. Cavalry* I. 32 A bull's eye of eight inches diameter. **1840** DICKENS *Old C. Shop* 256 This is wide of the bull's-eye. **1860** G. H. K. *Vacation Tour* 121 The house.. stands clear and white on the brown moor, like a target, with a black window for a bull's-eye.

b. A shot that hits the bull's-eye of a target; *fig.* a 'shot' that hits the mark.

1857 J. BLACKWOOD *Let.* 30 Jan. in G. S. Haight *G. Eliot Lett.* (1954) II. 290 The public is a very curious animal and.. how difficult it is to tell what will hit the bull's eye. **1887**, **1891** [see INNER B. *sb.*]. **1894** [see MAGPIE 7]. **1951** *Essays in Criticism* I. 1. 6 Some of his observations.. seem also to be very just—especially his opinion of Amiel, which is a bulls-eye.

8. A circular ornament of gold lace.

1879 *Uniform Reg.* in *Navy List* July (1882) 497/1 Gold lace, to form bull's eyes at the bottom of each back seam.

9. A sweetmeat so called from its globular shape.

1825 HONE *Every-day Bk.* I. 51 Hard-bake, brandy-balls, and bulls'-eyes. **1857** HUGHES *Tom Brown* I. iii, Where huge bull's-eyes, and unctuous toffy might be procured.

10. *Naut.* 'A little dark cloud, reddish in the middle, chiefly appearing about the Cape of Good Hope' (Chambers *Cycl. Supp.* 1753), supposed to portend a storm; hence the storm itself.

1849 D. P. THOMSON *Meteorol.* 406 (L.) The ox-eye or bull's-eye is a wind similar to the tornado.

11. *slang.* A crown-piece. (Cf. BULL *sb.*[1] 7.)

1690 B. E. *Dict. Cant. Crew.* **1714** in *Mem. J. Hall* 11 Bull's-Eye, a Crown. **1725** *New Cant. Dict.*

12. A hole in cheese, the result of imperfect manufacture. *dial.*

1879 MISS JACKSON *Shropsh. Word-bk.* s.v., I dunna like this cheese, it's got too many bulls' eyes in for me.

13. An old-fashioned type of watch, with the case partly enclosing the glass. Also *attrib. U.S.*

1833 J. NEAL *Down-Easters* I. 78 Lugging out a heavy silver watch,.. a genuine bull's eye. **1854** B. P. SHILLABER *Mrs. Partington* 26 The old bull's-eye watch on the nail over the mantel-piece.

14. A fish of New South Wales, *Priacanthus macracanthus*, excellent for the table.

1883 E. P. RAMSAY *Food Fishes N.S.W.* 9 The 'bull's-eye', a beautiful salmon-red fish with small scales. **1966** T. C. MARSHALL *Trop. Fishes Gt. Barrier Reef* 181 Family Priacanthidae: Bulls-eyes or Big-eyes.

bullsh (bʊlʃ). *coarse slang.* Abbrev. of next.

1919 DOWNING *Digger Dialects* 14 *Bullsh*, (1) insincerity; (2) an incorrect or insincere thing; (3) flattery; (4) praise. **1948** J. B. PRIESTLEY *Linden Tree* 33 Look—I'm talking too much—and most of it bullsh, I suppose.

bullshit ('bʊlʃɪt). *coarse slang.* [f. BULL *sb.*[1] + SHIT *sb.*] **1.** Rubbish, nonsense; = BULL *sb.*[4] 3.

c **1915** WYNDHAM LEWIS *Let.* (1963) 66 Eliot has sent me Bullshit and the Ballad for Big Louise. They are excellent bits of scholarly ribaldry. **1928** E. E. CUMMINGS *Enormous Room* vii. 194 When we asked him once what he thought about the war, he replied, 'I t'ink lotta bullsh—t.' **1953** G. LAMMING *In Castle of Skin* vi. 135 Some say they had no time for all that bullshit. **1961** R. KEE *Refugee World* xii. 130 'What do you think of the criticisms..?' 'Sheer bullshit, frankly.' **1969** P. ROTH *Portnoy's Complaint* 97, I swear to you, this is not bullshit or a screen memory, these are the very words these women use.

2. = BULL *sb.*[4] 4.

1930 T. E. LAWRENCE *Let.* 8 Jan. (1938) 677, I would like to know (1) Guards or Fire Pickets? (2) Drill Parades? (3) Equipment..? When worn? (4) Bullshit generally? **1957** R. HOGGART *Uses of Literacy* iv. 93 The world of special parades in the Services, of 'blanco and bullshit'.

Hence as *v. trans.* and *intr.*, to talk nonsense (to); = BULL *v.*[3]; also, to bluff *one's way through* (something) by talking nonsense.

1942 BERREY & VAN DEN BARK *Amer. Thes. Slang* §151/6 Talk nonsense,.. *bull-shit.* **1949** E. POUND *Pisan Cantos* lxxiv. 12 Wot are the books ov the bible? Name 'em, don't bullshit ME. **1967** E. AMBLER *Dirty Story* I. iii. 25 Never tell a lie when you can bullshit your way through. **1969** P. ROTH *Portnoy's Complaint* 105 Please, let us not bullshit one another about 'love' and its duration.

ˌbull-'terrier. A dog of a cross breed between a bull-dog and a terrier.

1848 THACKERAY *Van. Fair* xxxiv, Come down with me to Tom Corduroy's.. I'll show you such a bull-terrier. **1857** HUGHES *Tom Brown* iv, As dogged as a bull-terrier. **1871** M. COLLINS *Mrq. & Merch.* II. x. 289 A.. bull-terrier.. snarled.

†**bull-tour.** *Obs.* [App. f. BULL *sb.*[1] 4 + TOUR. R. Holme (cf. BULL-HEAD 3, quot. 1688) referred it to 'F. *taure*, a bull', but see Littré s.v. *tour*.]

A mass of frizzled hair worn (by a woman) on the forehead; a frowze, or 'frizz'.

1724 LITTLETON *Lat. Dict.* s.v. *Anthiæ*, Bull-tour, a woman's forelock, frouze.

'bull-ˌtrout. [f. BULL *sb.*[1] + TROUT; the name probably refers to the large size of this species.] A fish of the Salmon tribe (*Salmo eriox*) of considerable size, found in some British rivers.

1653 WALTON *Angler* 88 There is also in Northumberland, a *Trout*, called a *Bull Trout*, of a much greater length and bigness then any in these Southern parts. **1769** PENNANT *Zool.* III. 249 This species is in some places called the bull trout from the thickness and shortness of its head. **1799** J. ROBERTSON *Agric. Perth* 461 Loch-Rannoch.. has bull-trouts of 24 lb. weight. **1842** *Proc. Berw. Nat. Club* II. 4 Specimens of the fry of both Bull-trout.

bullule ('bʌljuːl). *Med.* [ad. L. *bullula* dim. of *bulla*.] A watery vesicle; a small bubble.

1707 FLOYER *Pulse-Watch* 429 The Motion or Rarifaction of the red Bullule in the Blood. **1880** *Syd. Soc. Lex.*, Bullule, a small bleb or blister.

bully ('bʊlɪ), *sb.*[1] Also 6 bullye. [Etymology obscure: possibly ad. Du. *boel* 'lover (of either sex)', also 'brother' (Verwijs & Verdam); cf. MHG. *buole*, mod.Ger. *buhle* 'lover', earlier also 'friend, kinsman'. Bailey 1721 has *boolie* 'beloved' as an 'old word'. *Bully* can hardly be identical with Sc. BILLIE, brother, but the dial. sense 2 seems to have been influenced by that word. There does not appear to be sufficient reason for supposing that the senses under branch II. are of distinct etymology: the sense of 'hired ruffian' may be a development of that of 'fine fellow, gallant' (cf. *bravo*); or the notion of 'lover' may have given rise to that of 'protector of a prostitute', and this to the more general sense. In the popular etymological consciousness the word is perhaps now associated with BULL *sb.*[1]; cf. BULLOCK *v.*]

I. † **1. a.** A term of endearment and familiarity, orig. applied to either sex: sweetheart, darling. Later applied to men only, implying friendly admiration: good friend, fine fellow, 'gallant'. Often prefixed as a sort of title to the name or designation of the person addressed, as in Shaks., 'bully Bottom', 'bully doctor'. *Obs.* exc. *arch.*

1538 BALE *Thre Lawes* 475 Though she be sumwhat olde It is myne owne swete bullye My muskyne and my mullye. **1590** SHAKS. *Mids. N.* III. i. 8 What saist thou, bully Bottome? **1598** —— *Merry W.* II. iii. 18 'Blesse thee, bully-Doctor. **1599** —— *Hen. V*, IV. i. 48 From heartstring I loue the louely Bully. **1610** —— *Temp.* v. i. 258 Coragio Bully-Monster Corasio. **1688** A. PULTON *Refl. Missioner's Arts* 8 A Band of Bully Scholars, marching under ground with their Black-Bills. **1754** RICHARDSON *Grandison* IV. xv. 115, I haue promised to be with the sweet Bully early in the morning of her important day.

b. *attrib.*, as in ***bully-boy***.

1609 T. RAVENSCROFT *Deuterom.*, He that is a bully boy, Come pledge me on the ground. *a* **1687** COTTON *Æn. Burlesqued* (1692) 53 From each part runs yon bully rustick, To take advantage of the first kick. **1809** W. IRVING *Knickerb.* (1861) 143 The bully-boys of the Helderberg. **1818** SCOTT *Rob Roy* viii, You are not the first bully-boy that has said stand to a true man. **1880** WEBB *Goethe's Faust* I. ii. 53 My over jolly bully-boy, let be.

2. *dial.* Brother, companion, 'mate'.

1825 BROCKETT *North Country Gloss.* 32 Now generally used among keelmen and pitmen to designate their brothers, as bully Jack, bully Bob, etc. Probably derived from the obsolete word *boulie*, beloved. **1860** FORDYCE *Hist. Coal, &c.* 60 They [the keelmen] are remarkably friendly to each other, being all 'keel bullies', or keel brothers. **1862** SMILES *Engineers* III. 12 'Bully'.. an appellation still in familiar use amongst brother workers in the coal districts. **1863** *Tyneside Songs* 61 Marrows, cries a bully, aw've an idea.. We'll find Sir John Franklin.

II. 3. a. A blustering 'gallant'; a bravo, hector, or 'swash-buckler'; now, *esp.* a tyrannical coward who makes himself a terror to the weak.

1688 SHADWELL *Bury F.* IV. Wks. (1720) 193 A lady is no more to be accounted a Beauty, till she has killed her man, than the bullies think one a fine gentleman, till he has kill'd his. **1692** WASHINGTON tr. *Milton's Def. Pop.* Pref. (1851) 10 Those furious Hectors we value not of a rush. We have been accustomed to rout such Bullies [L. *istos minaces*] in the Field. **1732** POPE *Ep. Bathurst* 340 Where London's column, pointing at the skies Like a tall bully, lifts the head, and lyes. **1780** DUNCAN *Mariner's Chron.* (1804) II. 296 The most swaggering, swearing bullies in fine weather, were the most pitiful wretches on earth, when death appeared before them. **1863** DICEY *Federal St.* II. 245 A low-minded, unscrupulous bully, notorious for his pro-Slavery sympathies.

b. A ruffian hired for purposes of violence or intimidation. *arch.*

1730 FIELDING *Tom Thumb* II. i, Were he.. a bully, a highway-man, or prize-fighter, I'd nab him. **1813** SHELLEY *Q. Mab.* IX. 179 These are the hired bravos who defend The tyrant's throne—the bullies of his fear. **1848** MACAULAY *Hist. Eng.* I. 204 A gang of bullies was secretly sent to slit the nose of the offender.

4. *spec.* **a.** The 'gallant' or protector of a prostitute; one who lives by protecting prostitutes.

1706 De Foe *Jure Div.* I. 8 Mars the Celestial Bully they adore, And Venus for an Everlasting Whore. **1707** Farquhar *Beaux' Strat.* III. iii. 37, *Sull.* What! Murther your Husband to defend your Bully. *Mrs. Sull.* Bully! for shame.. Bullies wear long Swords. **1711** Swift *Lett.* (1767) III. 249 A bully that will fight for a whore, and run away in an army. **1749** Chesterf. *Lett.* (1792) II. ccxii. 312 Shew yourself.. the advocate, the friend, but not the bully of Virtue. **1750** Johnson *Rambl.* No. 107 ¶ 12 The bully and the bawd, who fatten on their misery. **1817** M. Bennet in *Parl. Deb.* 861 Would he be less the bully of a brothel?

5. *attrib.* and *comb.*, as **bully-critic, -fop, -killer, -rake, -royster, -ruffian, -swordsman**; also †**bully-back,** a bully who supports another person; hence †**bully-back** *v.*; **bully-boy,** (*a*) (see sense 1 b); (*b*) a young ruffian; a 'tough'; esp. = sense 3 b; †**bully-cock** *sb.*, †**bully-cocked** *a.*, (a hat) worn as a bully wears it (cf. BILLY-COCK); †**bully-huff,** a boaster who is also a bully; †**bully-scribbler,** a writer who bullies.

1726 Amherst *Terræ Fil.* xxxiii. 179 They have spiritual bravoes on their side, and old lecherous *bully-backs to revenge their cause. **1759** Dilworth *Pope* 43 Supported and *bully-backed by that blind hector impudence. **1932** B. de Voto *Mark Twain's America* iii. 60 Or pulled at the end of ropes which the *bully-boys lugged through swamp and mire. **1952** S. Kauffmann *Philanderer* (1953) xii. 197 Typical of this whole generation of bully-boy, movie-tough-guy, Hemingway idolaters. **1963** *New Statesman* 30 Aug. 245/1 Tenants.. told one how Rachman's bully-boys had beaten them up. **1726** Amherst *Terræ Fil.* xlvi. 255 A broad *bully-cock'd hat, or a square cap of above twice the usual size. **1882** *Daily News* (Leader) 3 Feb., In a 'bowler' hat, or in the form which our ancestors called a 'bully-cock'. **1690** B. E. *Dict. Cant. Crew,* **Bully-fop*, a Maggot-pated, huffing, silly ratling Fellow. **1680** Cotton in Singer *Hist. Cards* 334 They will rarely adventure on the attempt, unless they are backed with some *bully-huffs. **1690** B. E. *Dict. Cant. Crew, Bully-huff*, a poor sorry Rogue that haunts Bawdy-houses, and pretends to get Money out of Gentlemen. **1815** Scott *Guy M.* xxviii, 'Here mother,.. never mind that bully-huff'. **1837** Carlyle *Fr. Rev.* II. III. iii. 145 M. Boyer.. is at the head of Fifty Spadassinicides, or *Bully-killers. **1711** E. Ward *Quix.* I. 33 He combats like that *Bully-Rake That only fights for Fighting's sake. **1687** T. Brown *Saints in Upr.* Wks. 1730 I. 74 Why, how now, *bully Royster! what's the meaning of this outrage in the face of Justice? **1653** Urquhart *Rabelais* I. xi, Pick-lock, Pioneer, *Bully-ruffin, Smell-smock. **1671** Dryden *Mock Astrol.* III. i, Snatch the Money like a Bully-Ruffin. **1809** W. Irving *Knickerb.* (1861) 233 Peter.. strode up to the brawling bully-ruffian. *a* **1715** Wycherley *Posth. Wks.* 5 (Jod.) The *bully scribbler.. is beat out of his bravadoes only for assuming them. **1837** Carlyle *Fr. Rev.* II. III. iii. 142 *Bully-swordsmen, 'Spadassins' of that party, go swaggering.

bully (ˈbʊlɪ), *sb.*[2] **1.** *Eton foot-ball.* A mêlée, a scrimmage.

1865 W. L. C. *Etoniana* xv. 213 Knees put out in the fierce football bully. **1873** M. Collins *Sqr. Silchester* II. xvii. 213 A youngster who has held his own in a football bully.

2. *Hockey.* The procedure of putting the ball in play by two players, one from each side, who strike with their sticks, first the ground then their opponent's stick, three times, after which the ball is in play. Also *bully-off*.

1883 *Boy's Own Paper* 13 Oct. 30/1 The game shall be commenced and renewed by a bully in the centre of the ground. **1895** Battersby *Hockey* 92 From the bully off until his opponents' 'twenty-five' is invaded. **1897** *Encycl. Sport* I. 516/2 A penalty bully is given for deliberately unfair play by the defending side in their own circle. **1901** *Daily News* 28 Feb. 7/5 The Oxford centre-forward got away directly after the bully-off. **1963** *Times* 18 Feb. 3/7 West's centre forward put the ball into the net almost before South had moved from the bully.

†**ˈbully,** *sb.*[3] *Obs.* Also bullie. [Cf. BOOLY.] A cottage, hut.

1598 Florio, *Tugurio*, a shepherds cottage, bully or shead. **1611** Cotgr., *Tugure*.. a shepheards shed, or bullie.

ˈbully, *sb.*[4] Also 8 bullet. [Etymology uncertain: variously referred to Eng. *bully*, dial. form of BULLACE (cf. the 2nd quot.), and to F. *boulet de canon* (lit. cannon-ball) 'fruit d'un arbre de la Guiane' (Boiste). The form *bullet* occurs only late, and the F. name may be due to popular etymology.]

attrib. in **bully bay, bully-berry tree, bully tree,** names for certain genera of the order *Sapotaceæ*, also for a species of *Mimusops* (all natives of the W. Indies and of Guiana).

1657 R. Ligon *Barbadoes* (1673) 14 Lofty trees, as the Palmeto, Royal.. Bully, Redwood. *Ibid.* 73 The Bully tree .. bears a fruit like a Bullis in England. **1693** *Phil. Trans.* XVII. 621 The Sope-Berry.. Indian Damozen, and the Bully Bay. **1725** Sloane *Jamaica* II. 124 When old it had a great many sulci not unlike the Bully tree. **1750** G. Hughes *Barbados* 177 The Bully-Berry tree.. a very durable timber tree. **1796** Stedman *Surinam* II. xxviii. 335 The bullet-tree .. the bark is grey and smooth, the timber brown, variegated or powdered with white specks. **1866** *Treas. Bot., Bully* or *Bullet Tree*.. a species of Mimusops.

bully (ˈbʊlɪ), *sb.*[5] [? f. BULL, or corruption of F. *bouilli* boiled meat.] Pickled or tinned beef. Also as *bully beef*.

1753 Smollett *Ct. Fathom* I. xxiv. 160, I could get no eatables upon the ruoad, but what they called Bully, which looks like the flesh of Pharaoh's lean kine stewed into rags and tatters. **1788** J. Woodforde *Diary* 18 Sept. (1927) III. 47 We had for Dinner some Hare Soup, a Couple of Chicken boiled and Ham—Some Beef Bulley, Stewed Pork—Partridges,.. &c. **1883** Clark Russell in *Longm. Mag.* III. 2, I have been shipmates with a man who grew white-haired at thirty on soup and bully. **1884** J. Macdonald in *19th Cent.* June 1002 The colonel.. was.. quietly consuming.. his luncheon of 'bully beef' and whiskey.

ˈbully, *sb.*[6] A pattern of miner's hammer, varying from '*broad bully*' to '*narrow bully*'. Raymond *Mining Gloss.*

bully, *sb.*[7] **a.** Dial. name for some kind of fish; cf. BULL-HEAD. (Also short for BULLFINCH[1].)

1857 Kingsley *Two Y. Ago* ii. (D.) Turning the stones for 'shannies' and 'bullies', and other.. fish left by the tide.

b. Abbrev. of COCKABULLY. *N.Z.*

1912 B. E. Baughan *Brown Bread fr. Colonial Oven* 2 The beloved creek where bullies wait the hook. **1943** G. E. Mannering *80 Years in N.Z.* xxi. 158 In the North Island the bully run follows the whitebait.

bully (ˈbʊlɪ), *a.*[1] [f. BULLY *sb.*[1]]

I. [Orig. BULLY *sb.*[1] I., used *attrib.*; cf. *brother*.]

1. Of persons: Worthy, 'jolly', admirable.

1681 Chetham *Angler's Vade-m.* (1689) Pref., From such Bully fishers, this Book expects no other reception. **1852** Hood *Lamia* v. 231 Here, bully mates, These, lady, are my friends.

2. a. *U.S.* and *Colonies.* Capital, first-rate, 'crack'. Also *spec.* in the earlier *bully-boat* (*U.S.*).

1844 *Scribblings & Sk.* 181 (Th.), A two days' race with bully-boats combines every sort of pleasing excitement. It were well to inform you that a bully-boat means a boat that beats everything on those [Mississippi] waters. **1847** W. T. Porter *Quarter Race Kentucky* 126 (Th.), Our 'bully' boat sped away like a bird. **1855** Wm. Carleton *Willy Reilly* v, The cook will give you a bully dinner. *a* **1860** *Cairo City Times* (Bartlett) The bully 'Crystal Palace' passed up to St. Louis on Monday. **1865** *Daily Tel.* 20 July, The citizens of New York, who were aware that the celebration would be more 'bully' than usual. **1870** Meade *New Zeal.* 331, The roof fell in, there was a 'bully' blaze. **1875** *N. Amer. Rev.* CXX. 128 'That's bully!' exclaimed Tweed.

b. as an exclamation, *esp.* in phrase 'Bully for you!' = bravo! well done!

1864 *Sanatory Commiss. U.S. Army* 133 *note*, Others would say 'good', and others would use the very expressive phrase 'bully'! **1864** *Daily Tel.* 18 Nov., The freckles have vanished, and bully for you. **1883** *Punch* 28 July, Lady Dufferin—bully for her, mate!

II. 3. Resembling a bully or ruffian; characteristic of a bully.

1727 Swift *City Shower* Wks. 1755 III. II. 40 Those bully Greeks, who, as the moderns do, Instead of paying chairmen, run them through. **1749** (*title*) Considerations on the Establishment of the French Strolers; the Behaviour of their Bully Champions. **1885** G. Meredith *Diana Crossw.* I. iv. 94 A bully imposition of sheer physical ascendancy.

bully (ˈbʊlɪ), *a.*[2] [f. BULL *sb.*[1] + -Y[1].] Resembling a bull-dog.

1884 Miss Braddon *Phant. Fort.* vii. 47 Angelina is bully about the muzzle.

bully (ˈbʊlɪ), *v.*[1] [f. BULLY *sb.*[1]]

1. *trans.* To act the bully towards; to treat in an overbearing manner; to intimidate, overawe.

1710 Palmer *Proverbs* 69 His poor neighbour is bully'd by his big appearance. **1747** *Gentl. Mag.*, The French observing that we were not to be bullied by their 17 sail, etc. **1802** Mar. Edgeworth *Moral T.* (1816) I. xii. 96 He saw, that he had no chance of bullying the servant. **1874** Greville *Mem. Geo. IV* (1875) III. xxi. 8 For the purpose of bullying the House of Lords, who would not be bullied.

b. To overweigh, overbalance.

1883 *Harper's Mag.* Aug. 449/1 A light displacement being bullied by large sails.

2. To drive or force by bullying; to frighten into a certain course; with *away, into, out of, to.*

1723 De Foe *Col. Jack* (1840) 27 What ails you, to bully away our customers so? **1748** Richardson *Clarissa* II. xxxviii. 258 They are in the right not to be bullied out of their child. **1817** Jas. Mill *Brit. India* II. v. iv. 444 They are bullied by the Plenipotentiaries to support him. **1854** Bright *Sp., Russia* 31 Mar. (1876) 227, I have no belief that Russia.. would have been bullied into any change of policy.

3. *intr.* and *absol.* To bluster, use violent threats; to swagger.

a **1744** Bramston (L.), So Britain's monarch once uncover'd sat, While Bradshaw bullied in a broad-brimm'd hat. **1783** Johnson *Lett.* II. ccci. 272, I bullied and bounced .. and compelled the apothecary to make his salve according to the Edinburgh Dispensatory. **1833** Marryat *P. Simple* (1863) 143 The officer.. mounted a small horse, galloping up and down.. bullying, swearing.

bully (ˈbʊlɪ), *v.*[2] *Hockey.* [f. BULLY *sb.*[2] 2.] *trans.* To put (the ball) in play by a bully. Also *intr.*, usu. with *off*, to start play in this manner.

1886 *Rules of Game of Hockey* 11 The game shall be started by one player of each side bullying the ball in the centre of the ground. **1909** *Westm. Gaz.* 30 Mar. 12/2 When two players are bullying-off they stand perfectly square. **1967** J. Potter *Foul Play* vi. 77 The two centre forwards bullied. *Ibid.* ix. 110 Julian bent over the ball to bully-off with a stocky, close-cropped French student.

bullyable, bulliable (ˈbʊlɪəb(ə)l), *a. rare.* [f. BULLY *v.*[1] + -ABLE.] Capable of being bullied.

1868 H. Kingsley *Silcote of Sil.* II. xii. 148 Silcote was in a bullyable mood.

bullydom (ˈbʊlɪdəm). *nonce-wd.* [f. BULLY *sb.*[1] or *v.*[1] + -DOM.] The state dominated by bullies.

1856 Lever *Martins of Cro' M.* 599 The fellow.. has been through all the phases of 'bulleydom'.

bullyer, obs. form of BULLER *sb.*

bully-head, variant of BULL-HEAD.

bullying (ˈbʊlɪɪŋ), *vbl. sb.* [f. BULLY *v.*[1] + -ING[1].] The action of the verb to BULLY: overbearing insolence; personal intimidation; petty tyranny. Often used with reference to schoolboy life. Also *attrib.*

1802 G. Rose *Diaries* (1860) I. 484 It is ridiculous to suppose she will mind our bullying when we cannot strike. **1829** *Censor* 131 The bullying system.. a system tending to brutalize the kindest natures. **1838** Dickens *O. Twist* (1850) 187/2 Mr. Bumble.. had a decided propensity for bullying .. and, consequently, was (it is needless to say) a coward.

bullying (ˈbʊlɪɪŋ), *ppl. a.* [f. BULLY *v.*[1] + -ING[2].] That bullies or acts like a bully; domineering, menacing.

1746 W. Horsley *Fool* No. 22 (1748) I. 153 A Rock which .. bids the bullying Sea-God Defiance. **1812** *Examiner* 24 Aug. 541/1 The bullying intolerance of William Cobbett. **1831** Scott *Diary* in Lockhart (1839) X. 50 No bullying Mirabeau to assail, no eloquent Maury to defend.

bullyism (ˈbʊlɪɪz(ə)m). [f. BULLY *sb.* + -ISM.] The conduct or practice of a bully.

a **1849** Poe *Longf. &c.* Wks. 1864 III. 320 The Outises who practice this species of bullyism are as a matter of course anonymous. **1886** *All Y. Round* 27 Feb. 35 The spirit of 'bullyism'.. peculiarly prevalent in the Northern States.

bullymong, bullyon, obs. forms of BULLIMONG, BULLION.

bullyrag (ˈbʊlɪræg), *v. dial.* or *colloq.* Also **balrag, balla-, balli-, ballyrag** (ˈbælɪræg). [Etymology unknown: connexion with BULLY *sb.* or *v.* is unlikely, as forms with *bal-*, *bally-* are widely diffused in the dialects.]

a. To overawe, intimidate. Also, to scold, harass, badger. Hence **bullyragging** *ppl. a.* **b.** To assail with abusive language.

a **1790** T. Warton *Poet. Wks.* (1802) II. 210 You vainly thought to ballarag us With your fine squadron off Cape Lagos. **1823** Carlyle in Froude *Life* I. 203, I bullyrag the sluttish harlots of the place. **1864** Atkinson *Whitby Gloss.*, To *Balrag* or *Bullyrag*, to abuse ferociously with a foul tongue, to bully. **1869** H. Kingsley *Stretton* II. 3 He asked .. whether a fellow was to be bullyragged out of his very bed. **1879** *Spectator* 14 June 757 Irish tenantry engaged in what may be called bullyragging their Member. **1888** G. M. Hopkins *Let.* 30 Nov. (1938) 50, I am afraid this ballyragging will make you gloomy. **1889** Barrère & Leland *Dict. Slang* s.v., To *ballyrag* a man [at Oxford] is to mob him and play practical jokes upon him, to hustle him. To *ballyrág* a man's rooms is to turn them upside down, to make 'hay' of them. **1935** Wodehouse *Blandings Castle* vi. 148, I won't have her ballyragged. Understand that! **1958** B. Hamilton *Too Much of Water* v. 121, I like *Samson* too... Don't be bullyragged out of it.

Hence **bullyragging** *ppl.a.* and *vbl. sb.*

1820 M. Wilmot *Let.* 5 Aug. (1935) 76 What a Ballyragging foulmouthed son of a gun art thou. **1863** H. Kingsley *A. Elliot* I. 225 The pair on 'em should have the bullying and ballyragging of nine thousand a year. **1880** Mrs. Parr *Adam & E.* xxi. 292 There'll be more set to the score o' my coaxin' than ever 'all be to Adam's bully-raggin'.

†**bully-rock, bully-rook.** *Obs.* [Of uncertain origin; if not f. BULLY *sb.*[1] + ROOK, the form and some of the senses must be due to popular etymology. Cf. *bully-rake* in BULLY *sb.*[1] 5.]

1. = BULLY *sb.*[1] 1; jolly comrade, boon companion.

1598 Shaks. *Merry W.* I. iii. 2 What saies my Bully Rooke? **1697** *Praise of Yorksh. Ale*, My Bully Rocks, I've been experienced long In most of Liquors.

2. = BULLY *sb.*[1] 3; a bravo, hired ruffian. (In quot. 1673 app. a bully who is also a *rook* or sharper.)

1653 Urquhart *Rabelais* I. liv, Ye Bully-rocks, And rogues. **1673** *Char. Coffee House* in *Harl. Misc.* (1810) I. 469 The bully-rook makes it his bubbling pond, where he angles for fops. **1685** Cotton tr. *Montaigne* III. 7 It properly belongs to Kings only to.. laugh at those bully-rocks. **1827** Carlyle *Germ. Romance* III. 44 A stout swordsman and hector as spiritual relative and bully-rock so to speak.

bulmong, obs. form of BULLIMONG.

buln-buln (bʊln bʊln). *Austral.* Also bullen-bullen. [Imitative.] An Aboriginal name for the lyre-bird.

1857 D. Bunce *Australasiatic Remin.* xi. 70 The ground had been torn or scratched up... This was the work of the Bullen Bullen, or lyre bird, in its search for large worms, its favorite food. **1871** *Athenæum* 27 May 660/3 The Gipps Land and Murray districts have been divided into the following counties:.. Buln Buln (name of Lyre bird), [etc.]. **1965** *Austral. Encycl.* V. 393 Very few aboriginal names for the lyrebird have been recorded. The best-known one is *bullen-bullen*, or *buln-buln*, a term based on one of the bird's calls.

bulrush (ˈbʊlrʌʃ). Also 5 bolroysche, 5–6 bul(l)-rysche, -rissh, -rysshe, 6–8 bullrush. [f. *bull* of uncertain origin (identified by some with BOLE[1],

cf. *bulaxe*, BOLE-AXE; by others supposed to be an attrib. use of BULL *sb.*[1]) + RUSH. (The suggestion '*pool-rush*' is baseless.)] A name applied in books to *Scirpus lacustris*, a tall rush growing in or near water; but in modern popular use, more usually, to *Typha latifolia*, the 'Cat's Tail' or 'Reed-mace'. In the Bible applied to the Papyrus of Egypt.

c **1440** *Promp. Parv.* 244 Holrysche or bulrysche, *papirus.* *c* **1475** *Voc.* in Wr.-Wülcker 785 *Hec papirus*, bolroysche. **1483** *Act 1 Rich. III*, viii. Preamb., Dyers..upon the Lists of the same Clothes festen and sowe great Risshes, called Bullrisshes. **1611** BIBLE *Ex.* ii. 3 She tooke for him an arke of bul-rushes. **1652** CULPEPPER *Eng. Physic.* 191 The Bulrushes and others of the soft and smooth kindes. **1794** MARTYN *Rousseau's Bot.* xiii. 153 There are many plants nearly allied to the grasses; as..Club-rush or Bulrush. **1821** CLARE *Vill. Minstr.* I. 46 Nodding bulrush down its drowk head hings. **1867** PARKMAN *Jesuits N. Amer.* xvi. (1875) 215 A dense growth of tall bulrushes.

2. *fig.* In allusion to the fragility of the bulrush, or its delusive appearance of strength.

1646 J. HALL *Horae Vac.* 37 We leane on the bulrush of our oune merits. **1672** BRAMHALL *Vind. Grotius* i, Compare those..Fellows, and Scholars, who were turned out of our Universities, with those bulrushes in comparison, whom for the most part they introduced. **1861** MOTLEY *Dutch Rep.* II. 250 To wield so slight a bulrush against a man who had just been girded with the consecrated sword of the Pope.

3. Phrases. ***to bow the head like a bulrush***, in allusion to Isaiah lviii. 8. †***to seek (find) a knot in a bulrush***, Lat. *nodum in scirpo quærere*, to find difficulties where there are none. So sarcastically, †***to take away every knot in the bulrush.***

1581 J. BELL *Haddon's Answ. Osor.* 436 Myne opposed adversary will seeke after a knott in a Bullrush as the Proverbe is. **1611** BIBLE *Isa.* lviii. 8 Is it to bow down his head as a bulrush? **1662** CHANDLER *Van Helmont's Oriat.* 199 The Schools did presume to have taken away every knot in the Bulrush. **1767** FORDYCE *Serm. Yng. Wom.* II. xi. 162 Do we wish you..to hang your heads like a bulrush?

4. *Comb.* and *attrib.*, as ***bulrush-bed, -bridge, -cradle, -fetter, -hurdle***; also ***bulrush-like*** adj.

1675 HOBBES *Odyss.* (1677) 66 Then on a *bulrush-bed himself he laid. **1842** TENNYSON *Morte D' Arth.* 135 Sir Bedivere..plunged Among the bulrush-beds, and clutch'd the sword. **1706** PHILLIPS, **Bulrush Bridge* (in the Art of War) a Bridge made of many bundles of Bullrushes bound together and cover'd with Planks. **1627** N. CARPENTER *Achitophel* (1629) 27 Whence could Moses haue better deriued his greatnesse..than from the *bulrush cradle? **1655** H. VAUGHAN *Silex Scint.* (1858) 108 Shall straw and *bul-rush-fetters temper his short hour? **1658** ROWLAND *Mouffet's Theat. Ins.* 916 They then dry it [the wax] on a *bul-rush hurdle by day and by night in the open air. **1628** WITHER *Brit. Rememb.* I. 1250 To shake the head, or hang it *Bul-rush-like.

bulrushy ('bʊlrʌʃɪ), *a.* [f. prec. + -Y[1].] 'Made of bulrushes', also 'full of bulrushes' (Huloet, ed. 1672). In Todd 1827 and some mod. Dicts.

bulse (bʌls), *arch.* [ad. Pg. *bolsa* = Sp. *bolsa*, It. *borsa*:—med.L. *bursa* a purse. Cf. BURSE.] A package of diamonds or gold-dust.

1708 *Lond. Gaz.* No. 4499/4 There was brought from India, in the Ship Albemarle..Three Bulses of Diamonds. **1779** FORREST *Voy. N. Guinea* 283 Amongst other things, was a bulse of gold dust. **1787** WOLCOTT (P. Pindar) *Ode upon Ode* Wks. 1812 I. 409 And tweak'd a Bulse of Jewels from the nose Of Dames in India. **1813** MILBURN *Orient. Commerce* II. 79 These gems [diamonds] are generally imported..in small parcels called bulses, neatly secured in muslin and sealed by the merchant. **1855** MACAULAY *Hist. Eng.* III. xviii.

†**bulstare.** *Obs.* [? for *bultare.*] = BOLTER *sb.*[1] 2.

c **1440** *Promp. Parv.* 55 Bulte pooke, or bulstare, *taratantarare.*

bult (bʊlt, ‖bœlt). *S. Afr.* [Afrikaans, a. Du. *bult* hump, hunch.] A hillock, ridge.

1852 C. BARTER *Dorp & Veld* vii. 96 They [*sc.* the lions] retreated slowly up the *bult.* **1864** T. BAINES *Explor. S.W. Afr.* xii. 371 We crossed the seringa bult at a narrower place. **1901** TURNBULL *Tales from Natal* 149 Hidden from view by a slight bult he was then ascending. **1926** *Blackw. Mag.* May 638/1 Dairy cows grazing on a rise or 'bult' (as these are called locally). **1946** M. WILMAN *Check List Fl. Plants Griqualand W.* 320 A sturdy, decumbent plant on lime bults.

†**bult**, variant of BOLT *sb.*[3], *Obs.*, a flour-sieve. Hence (or from stem of *bult*, BOLT *v.*[1]), †**bultpele**, ? a shovel for putting meal into the bolter.

c **1475** *Voc.* in Wr.-Wülcker 808 *Hoc pollentridium*, a bultpele. *Polenduare*, a bult.

bult, -e, bulter, obs. ff. of BOLT *v.* and BOLTER[1].

bult, -e, obs. pa. t. of BUILD *v.*

bultell(e, var. of BOULTEL, *Obs.*, a sieve, sieve-cloth.

(Owing to a misunderstanding of the passage in *Act 51 Hen. III.* (quoted s.v. BOULTEL) the word *bultel* was explained in Blount *Law Dict.* 1670 as 'the refuse of the Meal after it is dressed by the Baker'. This erroneous definition was repeated with some differences of expression by Phillips and Bailey, and appears in many recent Dicts.)

bulter, bultey ('bʌltə(r), 'bʌltɪ). [A word belonging to the Cornish fisheries, also called *bolter*, BOULTER; of unknown derivation.] See quots.

1769 PENNANT *Zool.* III. 117 Bulters..are strong lines five hundred feet long, with sixty hooks, each eight feet asunder baited with pilchards or mackrel. **1865** COUCH *Brit. Fishes* III. 89 Another and more successful method (sc. of fishing for ling) is with the long line or bultey.

bultong, var. BILTONG.

1883 OLIVE SCHREINER *Afr. Farm* I. ii, Did not Tant' Sannie keep in the loft 'bultongs', and nice smoked sausages?

bultow ('bʊltəʊ). [Mahn says 'f. BULL large, and TOW'; but the word looks like an alteration of BULTER, BULTEY, under the influence of 'popular etymology'. (Du. *bulletouw*, 'a name applied to several ropes about a ship', has also been suggested.)] (See quots.)

1858 P. L. SIMMONDS *Comm. Dict.*, *Bultow*, a mode of fishing practised in the [Newfoundland] Bank fisheries by stringing a number of hooks on one line. **1883** *Standard* 13 Sept. 5/4 The 'bultow' is..a set line, called in some places a 'trawl line'.

bulwark ('bʊlwək), *sb.* Forms: 5 **bulwerke**, 5–6 **bul-, bullwork(e**, 6 **bolwark, (bulwarge)**, 6–7 **bulwarke, (7 burwarke)**, 9 **bullwark**, 6– **bulwark.** [Cf. Du., MHG. *bolwerk*, mod.G. *bollwerk*, Da. *bulværk*, Sw. *bolverk*; the word is not recorded in ON., and the Da. and Sw. forms may be of German origin. Prof. Skeat, regarding the word as ultimately Scandinavian, derives it from the words represented in Eng. by BOLE and WORK, in which case the primitive sense would be 'a work constructed of tree-trunks'. Others would connect the first element with the MHG. verb *boln* to throw, on the ground that the MHG. word seems in some cases to have meant a machine for throwing large stones. Both etymologies are found in early mod. German authors. The Teut. word was borrowed in French as *boullewerc*, *bollewerc*, whence *boulever*, mod. BOULEVARD.]

1. A substantial defensive work of earth, or other material; a rampart, a fortification. Now only *arch.* or *poet.*

c **1418** *Gesta Hen. V* (1850) 17 Unum forte fortalitium quod nos 'barbican' sui communis ' bulwerke' appellamus. **1430** LYDG. *Chron. Troy* II. xi, Barbycans and also bulworkes huge Afore the towne made for hyghe refuge. **1494** FABYAN VII. 517 Syr John de Pyguygny..wan within the bulwerkys of the same [Amyas]. **1535** COVERDALE *Habak.* ii. 1 Set me vpon my bulworke, to loke & se what he wolde saye. **1611** BIBLE *Deut.* xx. 20 Thou shalt build bulwarkes against the city that maketh warre with thee. **1692** BENTLEY *Boyle Lect.* viii. 294 They have not the Form of a regular Bulwark. **1791** COWPER *Odyss.* VI. 11 With bulwarks strong their city he enclosed. **1813** SCOTT *Trierm.* III. iii, Bulwarks and battlement and spire In the red gulf we spy.

b. A breakwater, mole, sea-wall; an embankment confining the bed of a river. Also *fig.*

1555 EDEN *Decades W. Ind.* II. VII. (Arb.) 133 The famous ryuer of Padus..hath the greate mountaynes cauled Alpes ..lyinge at the backe therof as it were bulwarges full of moysture. **1586** T. B. *La Primaud. Fr. Acad.* (1589) 320 Men provide bulwarks and banks against a river that useth to overflow. **1677** PLOT *Oxfordsh.* 11 At Magdalen College, in the water-walks, near the Bull-work called Dover Peer. **1861** MOTLEY *Dutch Rep.* II. 271 The Hand-bos, a bulwark formed of oaken piles, was snapped like pack thread. **1865** GEIKIE *Scen. & Geol. Scot.* iii. 57 To check the further ravages of the waves a stone bulwark was erected.

2. *transf.* and *fig.* A powerful defence or safeguard. Sometimes applied to persons.

1577 HOLINSHED *Chron.* III. 900/2 The citie and Ile of Rhodes, one of the principall bulworkes of christendome. **1614** RALEIGH *Hist. World* II. 247 Fortescue, that notable Bulwarke of our Lawes. *a* **1674** CLARENDON *Hist. Reb.* III. XIII. 357 To destroy their Fleete: which..are their Walls and Bulwarks. **1718** POPE *Iliad* VII. 258 He stood, the bulwark of the Grecian band. **1789** BELSHAM *Ess.* I. xvi. 297 England..appeared..the great bulwark of the common liberties of Europe. **1837–39** HALLAM *Hist. Lit.* I. v. I. 342 Melanchthon..perceived the necessity of preserving human learning as a bulwark to theology.

3. The raised woodwork running along the sides of a vessel above the level of the deck. (Not in Bailey, Ash, or Johnson.) Usually *pl.*

1804 DUNCAN *Mariner's Chron.* II. 274 The guns on the quarter-deck tearing away the bulwark. **1825** H. GASCOIGNE *Nav. Fame* 60 Along the side a yellow streak extends Between his Bullwark and the varnish'd Bends. **1840** R. DANA *Bef. Mast* xxxi. 112 Our ship had uncommonly high bulwarks and rail. **1866** NEALE *Seq. & Hymns* 36 Dashed upon our labouring bulwarks that fierce wind Euroclydon.

bulwark ('bʊlwək), *v.* [f. prec.]

1. a. *trans.* To furnish with bulwarks. **b.** *intr.* To throw up bulwarks. *lit.* and *fig.*

1450 *Charter Jas. II* in *Hist. Edin* II. (1753) 137 Licence to fosse, bullwark, wall, toure and turote the said Burgh. *c* **1530** LD. BERNERS *Arth. Lyt. Bryt.* (1814) 187 They espyed..a hous..wel bolwarked and fausbrayed. **1545** JOYE *Exp. Dan.* iv. 7 The angel of the Lord bulworketh round about the godly. **1598** SYLVESTER *Du Bartas* I. vi. 557 The Lord hath Bulwarkt them about. **1657** MAY *Satir. Puppy* 33 Commits the protection of his whole Body to his Eielids, and bullwarks it with closing them.

2. *trans.* To serve as a bulwark to; to defend, protect, shelter.

1610 *Chester's Tri., Rumor's Sp.* 14 A hideous Dragon—whose thick scales, Like shields..Did bulwarke him. **1630** J. TAYLOR (Water P.) *Penn. Pilgr.* Wks. I. 123/2 Well bulwarked by a hedge from raine and winde. **1746** W. HORSLEY *Fool* No. 21 (1748) I. 146 A General..who.. bulwarks Europe against the common Enemy. **1873** BROWNING *Red Cott. Night-C.* 1170 Friends bulwarked him about From infancy to boyhood.

bulwarked ('bʊlwəkt), *ppl. a.* [f. prec. + -ED.] Furnished with, protected by, bulwarks.

c **1530** [see BULWARK *v.* 1]. **1612** DRAYTON *Poly-olb.* xviii. 289 Before her bulwarkt gates the Burgesses hee tooke. **1791** COWPER *Iliad* II. 398 Wide-bulwark'd Troy. **1884** *Pall Mall G.* 2 Aug. 4/1 To wander along the dear old granite bulwarked cliffs.

†**bulyiement**, *Sc.* variant of BILIMENT.

1768 ROSS *Helenore* 121 (JAM.) Gird on their bulyiement and come alang.

bum (bʌm), *sb.*[1] Not in polite use. Forms: 4 **bom**, 6 **bumbe**, 6–7 **bumme, bomm(e**, 7–8 **bumb**, 6– **bum.** [Origin uncertain.

Probably onomatopœic, to be compared with other words of similar sound and with the general sense of 'protuberance, swelling', e.g. BUMP *sb.*, BUMB a pimple, mod.Icel. *bumba* belly of a cask or other vessel, Fr. *bombe* BOMB. Cf. also BUM *v.*[1] (The guess that *bum* is 'a mere contraction of bottom', besides its phonetic difficulties, is at variance with the historical fact that 'bottom' in this sense is found only from the 18th c.)]

1. 'The buttocks, the part on which we sit' (J.); the posteriors.

1387 TREVISA *Higden* Rolls Ser. VI. 357 It semeþ þat his bom is oute þat haþ þat euel [*ficus*, i.e. piles]. *c* **1530** REDFORDE *Play Wit & Sc.* (1848) 20, I woold thy mother had kyst thy bum! **1550** CROWLEY *Epigr.* 1317 A bumbe lyke a barrell wyth whoopes at the skyrte. **1590** SHAKS. *Mids. N.* II. i. 53. **1638** A. READ *Treat. Chirurg.* xii. 97 To pull the feathers from the bummes of hens or cocks. **1708** *Lond. Gaz.* No. 4441/4 A Sorrel Gelding, with..some white Hairs on his Bumb. **1785** BURNS *Jolly Beggars* 42 Many a tatter'd rag hanging over my bum. **1816** KIRBY & SP. *Entomol.* (1828) II. xxiii. 329 Heating their bums or tails against them as they creep along.

2. Applied opprobriously to a person. Cf. BATIEBUM and BUMBLE *sb.*[2]

1540 LINDESAY *Satyre* 2772 Quhair Devil gat we this ill-fairde blaitie bum? **1572** [see BATIE-BUM.] **1825** JAMIESON. *Bum*, a lazy, dirty, tawdry, careless woman.

3. *colloq.* Short for BUM-BAILIFF; (like the F. *cul* for *pousse-cul.*)

[**1663** BUTLER *Hud.* I. I. 372 It had appeared with Courage bolder Then Sergeant Bum, invading shoulder.] **1691** *Long Vacation* 1 The Bums press hard on Poor Debtor. **1790** COWPER *Wks.* (1836) VI. 315 Threatened with attorneys and bums. *a* **1845** BARHAM *Ingol. Leg.* (1877) 307 Serjeant Barham with his bums and tip staves.

4. *Comb.* (mostly obs. or nonce-words), as ***bum-delighting, -grown, -proof***, †***-thin***; also †**bum-barrel** (? = *bum-roll*), some protuberant part of a woman's dress; †**bum-beating** *vbl. sb.* (used in quot. for jostling, pushing others off the pavement); †**bum-blade**, a large sword; †**bum-brusher**, humorous for a flogging schoolmaster; †**bum-creeper**, ? one who walks bent almost double; †**bum-dagger**, cf. *bum-blade*; †**bum-fodder**, L. *anitergium*, hence, worthless literature; **bum-freezer**, **-perisher**, **-shaver**, **-starver** (*slang*), a short jacket, coat, etc.; †**bum-rolls**, 'stuffed cushions worn by women about the hips' (Halliw.); **bum-sucker** *slang* = SYCOPHANT *sb.* 3; hence **bum-suck** *v. intr.*, to toady; **bum-sucking** *vbl. sb.*, toadying; †**bum-trap** (*slang*), a bailiff, a sheriff's officer (cf. BUMBAILIFF).

1609 *Ev. Wom. in Hum.* I. i. in Bullen *O. Pl.* IV, Ile have no soping, no puffs, nor no Cobwebs, no busks nor *bumbarrels. **1616** BEAUM. & FL. *Wit without M.* III. i, Can there be aught in this but pride of show, lady, And pride of *bum-beating? **1632** MASSINGER *City Madam* I. ii, Draw! my little rapier against your *bumb blades! *a* **1704** T. BROWN *Wks.* (1760) II. 86 (D.), I [Dionysius] was forced to turn *bum-brusher. **1832** *Blackw. Mag.* Oct. 426 To protract existence..in the shape of bumbrushers, and so forth, after the fashion of the exalted emigrés of 1792? *a* **1652** BROME *Eng. Moor* III. iii. (1873) II. 48 All alike to me ..from the huckle back'd *Bum-creeper, To the streight spiny Shop-maid of St. Martins. **1600** ROWLANDS *Lett. Humours Blood* iii. 57 The huge *bum Dagger at his backe. **1782** WOLCOTT (P. Pindar) *Ode 1 to R.A.'s* Wks. 1812 I. 17 That easy *bum-delighting thing Rid by the Chancellor, yclep'd a Sack. **1653** URQUHART *Rabelais* I. xiii, Torcheculs, arsewisps *bumfodders. **1753** *Scots Mag.* Apr. 208/1 (*title*) Bum fodder for the ladies. **1932** L. GOLDING *Magnolia St.* I. iii. 58 He wore..an Eton coat, or '*bum-freezer', as they termed it in Magnolia Street. **1943** G. GREENE *Ministry of Fear* I. vi. 98 The tight little blue trousers and the bum-freezer jacket. **1955** H. SPRING *These Lovers fled Away* 73 A nice little Eton suit—what Greg inevitably called my bum-freezer. **1611** COTGR., *Hancher*, Big haunched, well *bumme-growne. **1889** BARRÈRE & LELAND *Dict. Slang* s.v., **Bum perisher*, or *shaver*, a short-tailed coat. **1780–6** WOLCOTT (P. Pindar) *Ode R.A.'s* Wks. 1790 I. 58 *Bump-proof to all the flogging of the schools. **1663** KILLIGREW *Parson's Wed.* III. v, Those virtues raised her from the flat petticoat and kercher, to the gorget and *bumroll. **1936** E. WAUGH *Waugh in Abyssinia* 121 A gloomy, uniform row in white *bum-shavers. **1930** O. ONIONS *Open Secret* i. 15 'Is

it at Eton they wear toppers?' 'Yes.' '*And bum-starvers?' **1930** in PARTRIDGE *Dict. Slang* (1937) 107/1 *Bum-suck v. **1953** D. PARRY *Going up—Going Down* iv. 132 He crawls round bum-sucking to the Press. **1960** L. COOPER *Accomplices* III. i. 151 He bumsucked to all the rich men. **1877** SWINBURNE *Let.* 7 Sept. (1960) IV. 18 Mr. *Bumsucker Walford (excuse the Rabelaisian term current at our universities to define a sycophant). **1943** 'G. ORWELL' in Comfort & Bayliss *New Road* 156 The lords of property and their hired liars and bumsuckers. **1949** PARTRIDGE *Dict. Slang* (ed. 3) 1003/2 **Bum-sucking*, arse-crawling. **1963** C. MACKENZIE *My Life & Times* II. 21 Being accused of sucking up, or even of bum-sucking. **1602** WARNER *Alb. Eng.* IX. xlvii, 220 Supporters, Pooters, Fardingales above the Loynes to waire, That be she near so *bombe-thin, yet she crosse-like seems foure-square. **1749** FIELDING *Tom Jones* (1775) 300 The noble *bumtrap..into the hands of the jailer resolves to deliver his miserable prey.

bum, *sb.*[2] and *int.* [Imitative. Cf. BUMBO[1].]

†**a.** A child's word for drink (cf. BUM *v.*[1]). *Obs.* **b.** Sc. ***to say neither ba nor bum***: not to say a word (cf. BAFF).

1552 HULOET, *Bua*, the terme or voyce of infantes, askynge drynke, englyshed yf ye wyll, Bumme. **1570** LEVINS *Manip.* 187 Bum, drinke, *potus.* **1598** *Tom Tytler & W.* (1661) 4 Tipple (arriving with liquor)..here is good bum, I dare boldly say. **1861** RAMSAY *Remin.* iv. (ed. 18) 75 They neither said ba nor bum.

†**bum**, *sb.*[3] *Obs. rare*[—0].

1570 LEVINS *Manip.* 188 Bum of a pipe, *oblonga fistula.*

bum (bʌm), *sb.*[4] *slang* (orig. and chiefly *U.S.*). [Prob. short for BUMMER[3]; cf. BUM *sb.*[1] 2.]

1. A lazy and dissolute person; an habitual loafer or tramp; = BUMMER[3]. See also quot. 1933.

1864 *Gold Hill* (Nevada) *News* 15 Apr. 5/1 The policemen say that even their old, regular and reliable 'bums' appear to have reformed. **1891** C. ROBERTS *Adrift Amer.* 68, I don't believe in feeding professional bums. **1926** J. BLACK *You can't Win* ix. 104 A thoroughgoing bum from the road. The term 'bum' is not used here in any cheap or disparaging sense. In those days it meant any kind of a traveling thief. **1931** E. LINKLATER *Juan in Amer.* II. iii. 75, I'll fix the dirty bum that framed me! **1933** *Observer* 2 Apr., 'Bum', a term of affectionate obloquy which young American friends have applied to me..means not merely a fool, but a droning fool. **1941** A. L. ROWSE *Poems of Decade* 103 Lord, how he pontificates, Lays down the law to these poor bums. **1958** *Punch* 5 Feb. 218/2 The bums in the dosshouse have reached bottom.

b. ***bum's rush***: forcible ejection.

1925 L. O'FLAHERTY *Informer* iii. 46 They might give him 'the bum's rush', breaking his neck silently like a rabbit's neck. **1931** E. LINKLATER *Juan in Amer.* II. xv. 167, I told him I'd give him the bum's rush if he tried to pull that stuff on me. **1959** M. CUMBERLAND *Murmurs in Rue Morgue* xxxi. 176 Chotin was being given what the vulgar term the 'bum's rush'. He was down the steps..through the gate and flat on his back on the pavement.

2. A debauch or spree.

1871 L. H. BAGG *At Yale* 153 Aside from the annual convention on Commencement night, there are two other 'bums' held during the year. **1885** E. CUSTER *Boots & Saddles* xx. 193, I intend to celebrate their return by going on a tremendous 'bum'.

3. ***on the bum***: (*a*) vagrant; begging (cf. BUMMEL *sb.* and *v.*); (*b*) in a state of disorder.

1895 *Century Mag.* Oct. 941/2 Plans are made also for going 'on the bum' the moment they are free. **1896** ADE *Artie* iii. 28, I sized it up that the house was on the bum and she didn't want me to see it. **1931** D. RUNYON *Guys & Dolls* (1932) ix. 185 Trade is strictly on the bum. **1932** J. T. FARRELL *Young Lonigan* (1936) vi. 141 He vowed he'd blow the place, and go on the bum.

†**bum**, *v.*[1] *Obs.* Also bom. [? Onomatopœic, imitating the motion of the lips in drinking; cf. BUM *sb.*-] *intr.* To taste (drink); to drink.

1362 LANGL. *P. Pl.* A. VII. 139 He abydeþ wel þe bet · þat Bommeþ not to ofte. **1393** *Ibid.* C. VII. 229 Who so bommede [A. v. 137 bummede] þer-of · he bouht yt [ale] þer-after.

†**bum**, *v.*[2] *Obs.* exc. *dial.* Also bumb. [Var. of BOOM *v.*[1]; of echoic origin.]

1. *intr.* To hum loudly; to boom.

c **1450** CHAUCER *Wyf Bathes T.* 116 (Camb. MS.) As a bitore bumbith [*v.r.* bombleth] in þe myre. **1499** *Promp. Parv.* 55 Bummyn or bumbyn [*v.r.* bombon], *bombizo.* **1688** R. HOLME *Armoury* II. ix. 191 The Wasp and Hornet Bumbeth. **1722** HAMILTON *Wallace* x. 253 (JAM.) English men bum there [Stirling] as thick as bees. **1785** BURNS *To W. Simpson*, Let the busy, grumbling hive Bum owre their treasure. **1821** SCOTT *Kenilw*, You shall hear the bittern bumb. **1864** TENNYSON *North. Farmer* 18, I..'eerd un a bummin' awaäy loike a buzzard-clock. *Mod. Sc.* The stones came bumming past my head.

2. *trans. Sc.* **a.** To throw or hurl a missile with vibrating or booming effect, as 'to bum stones at anything'. **b.** To pelt with missiles, as 'to bum one with stones'. Cf. also '*bumb* sb., the game of bandy' (Halliwell).

†**bum**, *v.*[3] *Obs.* [perh. f. BUM *sb.*[1] (cf. BUMBASTE), though the sense 'flog on the breech' is not distinctly evidenced. Or it may belong to prec. word, cf. sense 2 b.]

trans. (or *absol.*) To strike, beat, thump.

1579 STUDLEY *Seneca's Hippolytus* (1581) 64 b, To scratch and cuffe, to boxe and bum. **1598** GREENE *Jas. IV* (1861) 203 Sirrah, hold your hand, lest I bum you. **1608** MIDDLETON *Fam. Love* IV. iii, Sirrah, you would be bummed for your roguery. **1622** DEKKER & MASS. *Virg. Mart.* IV. ii.

†**bum**, *v.*[4] *nonce-wd.* [f. BUM *sb.*[1]]

1. *trans.* To pad or make a projection about the posteriors.

1605 CAMDEN *Rem.* (1637) 197 Women bummed themselves with foxe tailes under their garments.

2. *intr.* To project, form a protuberance.

1633 ROWLEY *Match at Midn.* I. i. in Hazl. *Dodsley* XIII. 8 What have you bumming out there, goodman File?

bum, *v.*[5] To act as a bum-boat woman.

1833 MARRYAT *P. Simple* lxi, He's dead and I'm bumming. *Ibid.* lvii, To see his wife go a bumming.

bum, *v.*[6] *slang* (orig. and chiefly *U.S.*). [? back-formation from BUMMER[3]. Cf. BUM *sb.*[4]] **1.** *intr.* To wander *around*, to loaf; to go 'on the bum'; to act as a 'bum'. Also with *it.*

1863 *Boston Herald* 2 Aug. 2/5 They are just fit to..read the News and Express, bum round rum-shops [etc.]. **1876** *Wheatland* (California) *Free Press* 4 Mar. 2/2 The Professor is readier..to 'flunk' the student, who spent his time 'bumming' the night before. **1883** C. S. KEENE in Layard *Life & Lett.* (1892) 350 I've been bumming around all day ..and haven't caught a darned fish. **1890** L. C. D'OYLE *Notches* 168 Qualifications which eminently fitted a man to 'bum it' on such a community. **1897** KIPLING *Capt. Cour.* 72 You ought to hev more sense than to bum araound on deck this weather. **1942** P. ABRAHAMS *Dark Testament* I. xiv. 75 Dinnie was the fellow with whom I went bumming in Vrededorp when I was a kid. **1950** *Manch. Guardian Weekly* 12 Jan. 7 The unshaven months he spent bumming around New York.

2. *trans.* To beg; to obtain by begging; to cadge.

1863 *Unionville* (Nevada) *Humboldt Reg.* 4 July 2/1 He offered to pay, and didn't undertake to bum a puff out. **1931** W. FAULKNER *Sanctuary* ii. 14, I have been walking and bumming rides ever since. **1931** 'DEAN STIFF' *Milk & Honey Route* p. v, Nobody knows where the hobo..bums his feeds. **1941** L. A. G. STRONG *Bay* 279 An odd sort of bloke..bummed a light and a fill of tobacco off me.

b. To travel on (a train) without a ticket.

1896 *Pop. Sci. Monthly* L. 254 Several of the 'lads' had been 'pulled' at the Rapids for 'bumming the freights'.

c. To beg (a person) *for* (something); to cadge from.

1923 H. L. FOSTER *Beachcomber in Orient* i. 2 Then he bummed me for the price of a 'square meal'. **1931** 'DEAN STIFF' *Milk & Honey Route* 191 He had bummed every guy up in Portland, And they all came across with the goods.

d. ***to bum one's way***: to make one's way by begging; to hitch-hike.

1925 F. SCOTT FITZGERALD *Great Gatsby* (1926) vii. 154 He was probably bumming his way home. **1932** E. WILSON *Devil Take Hindmost* ii. 8 Some will bum their way—others will have their transportation provided.

bum, *a. slang* (orig. *U.S.*). [Cf. BUM *sb.*[4]] Of poor, wretched, or miserable quality; spec. ***bum steer***, false or poor information or advice.

1859 in *Pacific N.W. Quart.* (1940) XXXI. 292 Bum River Ferry. **1888** *Nation* (N.Y.) 31 May 439/2 One of them.. heard B. called a 'bum actor'. **1896** ADE *Artie* xii. 109 He didn't have a sou markee except what was tied up in a bum little grocery store. **1911** H. QUICK *Yellowstone N.* vii. 190 A stranger that had seen better days and had a bum lung. **1924** G. C. HENDERSON *Keys to Crookdom* 399 Bum steer, poor advice. **1931** A. POWELL *Afternoon Men* I. iii. 40 This is a bum party. **1934** J. M. CAIN *Postman always rings Twice* ix. 87 If I told a bum story first. **1957** W. H. WHYTE *Organization Man* 137 The muddy-headed way so many of us do [= talk] gives young men a bum steer.

†**bum**, *Obs.* Colloq. contraction for *by my.*

1571 R. EDWARDES *Damon & Pith.* in Hazl. *Dodsley* IV. 73 Bum troth, but few such roisters come to my years. **1578** WHETSTONE *Promos & Cass.* in Reed *Dodsley* IV. 7 (N.) Nay, bum-ladie, I will not.

bum-: see BOM-.

bumaloe, bumaree: see BUMM-.

†**bumb.** *Obs.* [Cf. BUB *sb.*[3], BUMP *sb.*[1]] A pimple.

1598 FLORIO, *Quosi*, red pimples, bumbs or pearles in ones face.

bumb, var. of BUM *v.*[2], *Obs.*, to hum.

†**bumbail.** Apparently shortened f. next.

1696 *Growth of Deism* 22 Where [at the altar, under the Test Acts] Men were capacitated to be Bumbails, keep Gaming-houses and sell Ale.

bumbailiff ('bʌm'beɪlɪf). Forms: 7 bumbaylie, 7, 9 *dial.* -baily, 7 -bayliff(e, 7- -bailiff. [app. f. BUM *sb.*[1] + BAILIFF: i.e. the bailiff that is close at the debtor's back, or that catches him in the rear. Cf. the F. equivalent *pousse-cul*, colloquially shortened to *cul*, precisely like the Eng. BUM.] A contemptuous synonym of BAILIFF 2: 'A bailiff of the meanest kind; one that is employed in arrests' (J.).

1601 SHAKS. *Twel. N.* III. iv. 194 Scout mee for him at the corner of the Orchard like a bum-Baylie. **1638** G. M. *Ess. & Char. Prison & Pr.* 30 The very offscum of the rascall multitude, as..Decoyes, Bum-bayliffes, disgraced Pursevants..and a rabble of such stinkardly companions. **1650** J. JONES *Judges Judg.* 34 [Debtors] taken..from their Ploughs, which are their Livelihood..by vagrant Bum-baylies, and imprisoned. **1768–78** TUCKER *Lt. Nat.* II. 528 The two necessary ministers of justice, a bum-bailiff and a Jack Ketch. **1809** W. IRVING *Knickerb.* III. ii. (1849) 148, I have a mortal antipathy to catchpolls, bumbailiffs and little great men. **1859** THACKERAY *Virgin.* i, A confounded pettifogging bum-bailiff.

bumbalo, variant of BUMMALO.

†**bumbard, -art**, *sb.* and *a. Obs.* Also 6 bombard. [f. BUM *bumb*, *v.*[2] + -ARD. Cf. also BOWBERT in a similar sense.]

A. *sb.* A bumble-bee, a drone; also *fig.* a droning person, a driveller. Cf. BUMBLE *sb.*[1] 2.

c **1505** DUNBAR *Twa Mariit Wem. & Wedo* 91 Ane bumbart, ane dron bee, ane bag full of flewme. *Ibid. Quhome to sall I complene* 24 Cairlis of nobillis hes the cure, And bumbardis brukis the benifyiss. *a* **1614** J. MELVILL *Mem. MS.* 129 (JAM.) Like adercope webs, that takes the silly flies, but the bombards breaks through them. **1614** J. COOKE in Dodsley I. 93 Your Spaniard is a mere Bumbard to him.

B. *a.* Lazy, indolent, drivelling.

c **1505** DUNBAR *Dance Sev. Deidly Synnis* 70 Mony sweir bumbard [*v.r.* lumbard] belly huddroun.

bumbard, obs. form of BOMBARD.

bumbaree, variant of BUMMAREE.

bumbarge ('bʌmbɑːdʒ). [? Perversion of BUMBOAT, after BARGE.]

1839 CARLYLE *Chartism* viii. 163 What ship Argo..was other than a foolish bumbarge in comparison? **1885** *Pall Mall G.* 20 June 3 A torpedo boat is not as tough as a bumbarge.

†**bumbass.** *Obs. rare*[—1]. [? f. *bomb-* in BOMBARD.] ? A large projectile to be thrown from a bombard.

1655 MRQ. WORCESTER *Cent. Inv.* No. 24 A Spring..to shoot Bumbasses and Bullets of an hundred pound weight a Steeple height.

bumbast, -er, -ic, etc., var. of BOMBAST, etc.

†**bumbaste**, *v. Obs.* exc. *dial.* Also 6–7 bumbast, bombast(e. [app. f. BUM *sb.*[1] + BASTE *v.*[3]: but *bum* might be a meaningless intensive or reduplicative prefix; cf. next.] *trans.* To beat on the posteriors; hence, to flog, beat soundly, thrash.

1571 R. EDWARDES *Damon & P.* in *Dodsley* IV. 60, I shall bombast you, you mocking knave. **1616** SURFL. & MARKH. *Countr. Farm* I. xxviii. 146 You must bumbast his buttocks with a good long sticke. **1657** TOMLINSON *Renou's Disp.* 50 We use..to smite and bombaste them (vipers) with rods. **1682** *New News fr. Bedlam* 56, I am resolved to bumbast him as soon as you are gone. **1731** BAILEY II, *To bumbaste* [of bum and baste, i.e. to beat] to beat or bang. **1847–78** HALLIWELL, *Bumbaste.* To beat, or flog. *East.*

b. ? To finish *off*, 'dispose of' (a can of liquor).

1640 GLAPTHORNE *Wit. in Constab.* v. ii, Here let's canvass This quart and then we'll bumbaste off another.

Hence **bumbasting** *ppl. a.*, 'thumping', violent.

1598 FLORIO, *Rugione*, a good drie bumbasting blow.

bumbaze (bʌm'beɪz), *v.* Chiefly *Sc.* Also 8 bombaze, -base, 9 bumbaize. [app. a kind of intensive form of BAZE *v.*; but cf. also BAMBOOZLE.] To confound, perplex, bamboozle.

1725 RAMSAY *Gentle Sheph.* I. i, She..gars me look bombaz'd and unco blate. *Ibid.* IV. ii, Then oft by night, bombase hare-hearted fools. **1824** SCOTT *Redgaunt.* II. iv, How the scoundrel redcoats must have been bumbazed. **1840** BARHAM *Ingol. Leg.* 117 Clear bumbaized, and amazed, and fixed all the room stick. **1882** *Gd. Words* 100 The mother..poor body, looked a good deal bumbazed.

'bum-'bee. *Sc.* [f. BUM *v.*[2] hum + BEE *sb.*[1]] = BUMBLE-BEE. With quot. 1653 cf. BUM-BAILIFF.

1653 URQUHART *Rabelais* II. xi. The Swissers, who had assembled themselves to the full number of the Bum-bees, and Myrmidons. **1718** RAMSAY *Contin. Christ's Kirk* III. xix, Spawn'd out..Wi' mony an unco skirl and shout, Like bumbees frae their bykes. **1789** DAVIDSON *Seasons* 5 (JAM.) Auld farnyear stories come athwart their minds, Of bumbee bykes. **1826** J. WILSON *Noct. Ambr.* Wks. 1855 I. 153 Caterpillars and bumbees and a' the rest o' the insect world. **1862** D. CAMPBELL *Language, &c. Highl. Clans*, The inexpressive notes..made by three unfortunate bumbees.

'bumbelo, 'bumbolo. [a. It. *bombola* 'sort of glass vessel for holding wine', etc. (Tommaseo and Bellini).] A glass flask for subliming camphor.

1854 TOMLINSON *Cycl. Usef. Arts* (1866) I. 286 Spheroidal vessels called bomboloes. They are made of thin flint glass..and measure about 12 inches across.

bumbeloe, variant of BUMMALO.

†**'bumbis.** ? Meaningless. See quot.

1622 FLETCHER *Beggars' Bush* III. i, Sa, sa, flim, flam, tara-dumbis! East, West, North, South, now fly like Jack with a bumbis!

'bumble, *sb.*[1] Also 6 *Sc.* bombill, 8 *Sc.* bummil, bummle. [f. BUMBLE *v.*[1]]

1. ? A humming noise; bluster. *Sc.*

1597 MONTGOMERIE *Flyting* 105 for all ȝour bombill.

2. a. A bumble-bee. **b.** 'A provincial name for the Common Bittern' (Atkinson *Prov. Names of Birds* 1864).

1638 WHITING *Albino & Bell.* (N.) Yon tender webs.. Through which with ease the lusty bumbles break. **1789**

DAVIDSON *Seasons* 63 (JAM.) Up the howes the bummles fly in troops.

c. An angler's artificial fly.

1873 H. ST. J. DICK *Flies & Fly Fishing* ix. 138 *The Bumble.* This is a Derbyshire grayling fly used in that part of the country nearly all the season. *Ibid.* 39 It is, I suppose, meant for some water insect, but the local fishermen have spring, summer, and autum bumbles, all dressed differently. **1889** F. M. HALFORD *Dry-Fly Fishing* vi. 123 An *orange bumble*, floated occasionally over the feeding fish, may be successful.

†'**bumble**, *sb.*^{2} *Obs.* exc. *dial.* [onomatopœic, cf. BUNGLE, JUMBLE, FUMBLE.]

1. A confusion, jumble.

1648 JENKYN *Blind Guide* i. 15 A bumble of musty reasons. **1660** S. FISHER *Rusticks Alarm* Wks. (1679) 427 With many more Bumbles of their Senses, Meanings, Opinions. **1690** B. E. *Dict. Cant. Crew, Bumble*, Cloaths setting in a heap, or ruck. **1847–78** HALLIWELL, *Bumble*, a confused heap. *North.*

2. A bumbler or blunderer; an idler. (Cf. *batie-bummil*, BATIE-BUM; also BUMBLE *sb.*^{1} 2 a.)

1786 BURNS *Sc. Bard gone W. Ind.* iv, Some drowsy bummle, Wha can do nought but fyke an' fumble. **1789** DAVIDSON *Seasons* 181 (JAM.) The Muse..ca'd me bumble.

3. [The name of the beadle in Dicken's *Oliver Twist* (see BUMBLEDOM)] A beadle; a member of a municipal corporation, parish council, or the like, to whom official pomposity and fussy stupidity are attributed; a consequential jack-in-office; sometimes used *attrib.*

1856 *Sat. Rev.* II. 416/2 It will..be useless to impress upon the great Bumble mind, etc. **1865** HOTTEN *Slang Dict.*, *Bumble*, a beadle. *a* **1889** *Punch* (Barrère & Leland), The apish antics of a bumble crew. **1890** FARMER *Slang* s.v., *Bumble-Crew*, a collective name for corporations, vestries, and other official bodies. **1895** MORRIS in Mackail *W.M.* (1899) II. 308, I hope we shall beat our Bumbles.

4. *attrib.* and *comb.*, as **bumble-bath, bumble-broth**, ? a mess, 'pickle, soapsuds'; also with sense of 'clumsy, unwieldy': **bumble-foot**, a club foot; (also) a disease of the feet of domestic fowls, etc.; **bumble-footed**, club-footed.

1661 K. W. *Conf. Charac.* (1860) 56 A hog in armour, just such another bumble-arst furfact piece of mortality. **1595** *Marocous Ext.* (1843) 17 Such carrion as lies there in their bumble baths. **1602** DEKKER *Satirom.* Wks. 1873 I. 218 If I might ha my wil, thou shouldst not put thy spoone into that bumble-broth. **1630** J. TAYLOR (Water P.) *Praise Clean Linn.* Wks. II. 169/1 Laundresses are testy..When they are lathering in their bumble broth. **1854** *Poultry Chron.* I. 105 Bumble-foot comes from the ball of the foot. **1861** H. KINGSLEY *Ravenshoe* xli. (D.) She died mostly along of Mr. Malone's bumble foot..he being drunk and bumble-footed too. **1886** J. W. HILL *Dis. Poultry* 87 Occasionally the sole of the foot becomes the seat of a thick corn-like growth, which ultimately festers and exposes a ragged ulcerated wound. Such a condition is commonly termed 'Bumble-Foot'.

bumble, *sb.*^{3} *dial.* See quot.

1694 WESTMACOTT *Script. Herb.* 32 Bull-Rushes..in some Countries..are called Bumbles. **1877** PEACOCK *N.W. Lincoln. Gloss.* (E.D.S.) *Bumbles*, such as are used for chair-bottoms.

bumble ('bʌmb(ə)l), *sb.*^{4} *dial.* 'A small round stone. *West.*' (Halliwell.)

1839 MURCHISON *Silur. System* I. xxxi. 413 Small concretions, which..alternate with beds of solid limestone. The former..are here known under the name of bumbles.

†'**bumble**, *sb.*^{5} *Obs. rare*$^{-1}$. A bandage for blindfolding. 'A kind of blinkers. *North.*' (Halliw.)

1623 LISLE *Ælfric on O. & N.T.* Pref. 14 Hood-winked with his implicite faith, as with a bumble on his head. **1863** *Gloss.* in Morton *Cycl. Agric., Bumbles*, covers for horses' eyes.

bumble, *v.*^{1} Also 4–6 bomble. [f. BOOM *v.*^{1}, BUM *v.*^{2} + frequentative suffix -LE.]

1. a. *intr.* To boom, as a bittern; to buzz, as a fly. Also *transf.*

c **1386** CHAUCER *Wife's T.* 116 As a Bitore bombleth in the Myre [*v.r.* bumbith, bumliþ]. **1556–1693** [see BUMBLING *vbl. sb.*]. **1868** ATKINSON *Cleveland Gloss.* 78 *Bumble*, to hum or buzz. **1908** 'IAN HAY' *Right Stuff* II. iii. 198 The bees were bumbling in the heather. **1925** C. DODD *Farthing Spinster* 240 Grasshoppers sang, bees bumbled. **1941** WYNDHAM LEWIS *Let.* 10 Aug. (1963) 296 How can people read books with war-planes incessantly bumbling away over their heads.

b. To speak ramblingly, to drone *on* (in some examples influenced by BUMBLE *v.*^{2}).

1958 *Listener* 2 Jan. 36/1 To doze contentedly over my set, bumbling on about the good fortune of my colleague. **1958** *Punch* 29 Jan. 181/2 His style of oratory is peculiar, as he bumbles along like a metaphysical farmer. **1969** *Sunday Times* (Colour Suppl.) 9 Nov. 80/3 You can quite happily bumble on without too much trouble if that's what you want.

†**2.** *trans.* To grumble at, blame, take to task. *Obs.*

1675 DUFFETT *Mock Temp.* III. i, Be bumbled, and jumbl'd, and grumbl'd at. **1781** COWPER *Corr.* (1824) I. 201, I shall not bumble Johnson for finding fault with Friendship.

'**bumble**, *v.*^{2} Also 6 bomble, 8–9 *Sc.* bummil, -el. [See BUMBLE *sb.*^{2}]

a. *intr.* To blunder, flounder. See BUMBLING *vbl. sb.* and cf. BUMBLING *ppl. a.* **b.** *trans.* To bungle over; to do in a bungling manner.

1532 MORE *Confut. Tindale* Wks. (1557) 693/1 The thinge wher about he hath bombled all thys while. *Ibid.* 734/2 Which argument Tindall hath all thys while bumbled aboute to soyle. **1719** RAMSAY *Epist. Hamilton* ii, 'Tis ne'er be me Shall..say ye bummil Ye'r poetrie. **1807** STAGG *Poems* 145 As for a bang he bummel'd..An' down the warrior tumel'd. **1876** *Coursing Cal.* 212 Merry Girl beat Unknown in good style, the latter bumbling very much at his fences. **1926** *Chambers's Jrnl.* 87/1 Ploughmen of thirty learning to hold a pen and 'bummel through the Single Carritch'. **1959** E. POUND *Thrones* xcvii. 32 The artigianato bumbles into technology.

bumble-bee ('bʌmb(ə)l'biː). [f. stem of BUMBLE *v.*^{1} + BEE^{1}; cf. BUMBLE *sb.*^{1}] A large bee of the genus *Bombus*; a humble-bee.

1530 PALSGR. 460/1, I bomme, as a bombyll bee dothe. **1678** H. MORE *Lett.* 25 May in Glanvil *Sadduc.* (1681) Hunting of Butter-flies and Bumble-bees. **1794** S. WILLIAMS *Vermont* 129 There is a species called with us the bumble bee. **1881** *Proc. Berw. Nat. Club* IX. No. 3. 571 A most unusual number of wasps and bumble bees.

bumbledom ('bʌmb(ə)ldəm). [f. *Bumble*, name of the beadle in Dickens's *Oliver Twist* + -DOM.] Fussy official pomposity and stupidity, especially as displayed by the officers of petty corporations, vestries, etc.; beadledom in its glory.

1856 *Sat. Rev.* II. 12/1 The collective Bumbledom of Westminster. **1865** *Spectator* 22 Apr. 427 There spoke the true spirit of parish Bumbledom. **1880** *Daily Tel.* 8 Oct., The uncomplimentary epithet applied to municipal bureaucracy, 'Bumbledom'.

'**bumblekite.** *dial.* Also bummel-kite. A blackberry.

1691 RAY *N.C. Wds.*, *Bumblekites*: Bramble-Berries. *Yorkshire.* **1789–96** MORSE *Amer. Geog.* I. 188 Sowteat blackberry or Bumblekites. **1824** *Craven Dial.* 15 To pike.. some shoups, bummlekites, an hindberries. **1883** *Hampsh. Gloss., Bummell* or *Bumble-kite*..a bramble or blackberry.

'**bumblepupper.** [f. BUMBLE-PUPPY + -ER^{1}.] One who plays unscientific whist. So '**bumblepuppist**.

1880 'PEMBRIDGE' *Whist*, etc. 2 The Bumblepuppist only admires his own eccentricities. **1891** *Daily News* 30 Sept. 5/1 The careless Bumblepupper dreads the expert.

bumble-puppy ('bʌmb(ə)lpʌpɪ). [Derivation unknown. Cf. BUMBLE *v.*^{2}]

a. An old game resembling bagatelle, but played out of doors with marbles or 'dumps' of lead; nine-holes. **b.** Applied humorously to whist played unscientifically. Also of bridge. Also *attrib.*

1801 STRUTT *Sports & Past.* III. vii. 242 *note.* **1884** *Sat. Rev.* 25 Oct. 520 'Bumble puppy' or domestic whist at shilling points. **1885** *Longm. Mag.* VI. 597 A common form of home whist—called by Pembridge, Bumblepuppy. **1936** E. CULBERTSON *Contract Bridge Complete* i. 34 Persons who claim they 'play no conventions' either play bumble-puppy Bridge or do play conventions that are tacitly understood. **1947** W. S. MAUGHAM *Creatures of Circumstance* 104 Templeton isn't the sort of chap to play bumble-puppy bridge with a girl like that unless he's getting something out of it.

c. A game in which a ball slung to a post is struck with a racket by each player in opposite directions, the object being to wind the string entirely round the post; also, the post so used.

1900 L. B. WALFORD *One of Ourselves* xiv, They had had a great game of 'bumble-puppy'. *a* **1918** J. T. B. MCCUDDEN *Five Yrs. R.F.C.* (1919) xii. 227 We had a wonderful game called 'Bumble-puppy', which one played with tennis rackets. **1940** M. SADLEIR *Fanny by Gaslight* I. 43 One of the boys seized a chance to occupy the bumble-puppy... It was great fun hitting the ball in its string-bag so that it wound tightly round the pole.

'**bumbler.** *dial.* [f. BUMBLE *v.*^{1} and *v.*^{2} + -ER^{1}.]

a. A bumble-bee. (Applied to the Tyneside artilleryman.) **b.** A blunderer.

1847–78 HALLIWELL, *Bumbler.* A humble bee. *North.* **1863** ROBSON *Bards of Tyne* 108 You'll fight your battles o'er your pipe..You blue tail bumbler. **1881** MRS. L. LINTON *My Love* III. 244 He is a bit of a bumbler when all is said and done.

'**bumbling**, *vbl. sb.* [f. BUMBLE *v.*^{1} and *v.*^{2} + -ING^{1}.]

a. Blundering. **b.** Buzzing, humming.

1533 MORE *Answ. Poyson. Bk.* Wks. (1557) 1088/2 Tyndall dydde..make some bumlyng aboute a colour for the matter. **1556** J. HEYWOOD *Spider & Fl.* lxiv. 71 Much bumbling among them all [flies]: there was. **1693** URQUHART *Rabelais* III. xiii, Bumbling of Bees. **1952** *Essays in Criticism* II. 11 The incongruity between Emma's high-flown sentiments and Charles's pedestrian bumblings.

'**bumbling**, *ppl. a.* [f. BUMBLE *v.*^{2} + -ING^{2}.] Awkward, blundering.

1886 MRS. LYNN LINTON *Paston Carew* ix, The rector's only son, a big bumbling young fellow. **1954** N. BALCHIN *Last Recoll. Uncle Charles* iv. 60 There must be some people about who'd like to have a really fine car and not some bumbling old cab. **1955** *Amer. Dial. Soc. Pubn.* XXIV. 40 Every pickpocket has to believe that he is good,..even if he is the most bumbling of operators.

'**bumbo**^{1}. Also bumboo, bombo. [Cf. It. *bombo* a child's word for drink (Tommaseo and Bellini).] 'A liquor composed of rum, sugar, water, and nutmeg' (Note to *Rod. Random*); also other alcoholic mixtures.

1748 SMOLLETT *Rod. Rand.* xxxiv, A table well stored with bumbo and wine. **1756** T. TURNER *Diary* 28 Apr. in Parish *Sussex Gloss.* s.v., One bowl of punch and two muggs of bumboo. **1867** SMYTH *Sailor's Word-bk.*, *Bombo*, weak cold punch. *a* **1886** *Northumb Song* in *N. & Q.* 6 Mar. 195 The pitmen and the keelman..drink bumbo made of gin.

bumbo^{2} ('bʌmbəʊ). Also bombo, bumboo, bungo. [Native name.] A fabaceous tree, *Daniellia thurifera*, of Sierra Leone, yielding a fragrant resin; also ***bumbo-*** or ***bungo-tree***. Also, the gum or resin obtainable from this tree.

1874 LINDLEY & MOORE *Treas. Bot.* Suppl. s.v. *Daniellia.* **1916** C. E. LANE-POOLE *Trees of Sierra Leone* 32 *Daniella* [*sic*] *thurifera*. Bennett... The Frankincense Tree... Creole: Bungbo. **1965** G. KUNKEL *Trees of Liberia* 88 *Daniellia thurifera* Benn... Names: Daniellia, Copal Tree, Bungo, Bumbo, Faro, Gum Copal.

bumboat ('bʌmbəʊt). Also 8 bomb-boat. [app. f. BUM *sb.*^{1} + BOAT *sb.* (Cf. *bumbay* 'a quagmire from stagnating water, dung, etc., such as is often seen in farm-yards' *Suffolk Words* from Cullum *Hist. Hawsted* 1815; also Ray *S. & E.C. Words.*)]

†**1.** A scavenger's boat, employed to remove 'filth' from ships lying in the Thames, as prescribed by the Trinity House Bye Laws of 1685. (These 'dirt-boats' used also to bring vegetables etc. for sale on board the ships, whence sense 2.)

1671 *Proclam. Chas. II*, 6 Apr., Whereas several Dirt-Boats, and Bum-Boats..under pretence of Fetching Dirt, and Furnishing necessary Provisions on Board such Ships as are in the River, do commit divers Thefts and Robberies. **1685** *By-Laws Trinity House* No. 6 Dirtboats, otherwise called Bumboats.

2. 'A boat employed to carry provisions, vegetables, and small merchandise for sale to ships, either in port or lying at a distance from the shore.' Smyth *Sailor's Word-bk.*

1769 FALCONER *Dict. Marine* (1789) *Bumboat*, a small boat used to sell vegetables, etc. to ships lying at a distance from the shore. **1833** MARRYAT *P. Simple* (1863) 407 All the bumboats were very anxious to supply the ship. **1863** *Life Man-of-War* in *Cornh. Mag.* Feb., The bumboat has come alongside..with oranges and grapes, loaf-bread..herrings, and similar dainties.

3. *attrib.*, as ***bumboat act, man, people, woman.***

1714 *Lond. Gaz.* No. 5245/3 John Daniel, an Alehouse-keeper and Bomb-boat Man at Woolwich. **1820** BRODERIP & BINGHAM *Rep.* I. 433 The vessel..was seized..under the Bum-boat act (2 Geo. III. *c.* 28). **1835** MARRYAT *Jac. Faithf.* xxxvii, We purchased some sheets of paper from the bumboat people. **1884** *Littell's Living Age* 700 Fruits from ..the bumboat-woman at a seaport.

Hence **bumboating** *vbl. sb.*

1841 MARRYAT *Poacher* xxxvii, It was only bumboating on a large scale.

bumby(e, *adv. dial.* [var. BIMEBY *adv.*] By and by; presently.

1786 *Boston Exchange Advertiser* 19 Oct. (Th.), [Negro talk.] Oh! he say, land dear now, bumbye buy him five dollars nacre. **1839** C. CLARK *J. Noakes* 15 John Noakes, bum-by, come up he ded, When Mary seem'd more settled. **1872** 'THE VILLAGE SCHOOLMASTER' *Giles's Trip to London* v. 51 But bum-by I woke up.

†**bum-card.** *Obs.* Also bun-, bumbe-, bumme-card. [Of uncertain origin.] A raised or otherwise marked card used for cheating at play; also *fig.*

1577 NORTHBROOKE *Dicing* (1843) 142 A bumbe carde finely vnder, ouer, or in the middes, &c. and what not to deceyue? **1589** *Pappe w. Hatchet* C ij, Hee'le cog the die of deceipt, and cutte at the bumme-carde of his conscience. **1611** FLORIO, *Rinterzata carta*, a bun-card. **1631** BRATHWAIT *Whimzies Gamester* 42 The more generous professants have by this discarded him for a bum-card.

bum-clock. *Sc.* and *north. dial.* [f. BUM *v.*^{2} to hum + CLOCK beetle.] A drone-beetle.

1786 BURNS *Twa Dogs* 33 The bum-clock humm'd wi' lazy drone. **1875** ROBINSON *Whitby Gloss.*, *Bumclock*, the humming beetle.

†**bum-court.** *Obs.* [Etymol. uncertain: app. f. BUM *sb.*^{1} (cf. the first quot.).] Apparently, a vulgar nick-name for the Ecclesiastical Court.

1544 *Suppl. to Hen. VIII*, 28 The hearing of testamenterye causes..of sclaunders, of leachery, adultery, and punyshement of bawedrye; and suche other bumme courte matters. **1580** FULKE *Stapl. & Mart. Confuted* 128 These quarrels sir Bachiler, are more meet for the bomme-courts, in which perhaps you are a prating proctor, than for the schools of divinity. **1583** —— *Brief Confut.* 33 In this saying, if the term of bumcourts seem too light, I yield unto the censure of grave and godly men.

†**bumdockdousse.** *Obs.* [f. BUM *sb.*^{1} + DOCK rump + DOUSE *v.* beat, thump.] Urquhart's word for *pimpompet*, 'a kinde of game wherein

three hit each other on the bumme with one of their feet' (Cotgrave).

1653 URQUHART *Rabelais* I. xxii, At the leek, at Bumdockdousse.

bumf (bʌmf). *slang.* Also **bumph.** [Short for *bum-fodder* (see BUM *sb.*^{1} 4).] Toilet-paper; hence, paper (esp. with contemptuous implication), documents collectively. Also *attrib.*

1889 BARRÈRE & LELAND *Dict. Slang*, *Bumf* (schoolboys), paper... A *bumf*-hunt is a paper-chase. 1912 V. WOOLF *Let.* 16 Nov. in *Woolf & Strachey Lett.* (1956) 46 Is this letter written upon Bumf? It looks like it. 1930 WYNDHAM LEWIS *Apes of God* (1932) v. 161 Low-lid fodder or high-brow bumph! 1930 E. RAYMOND *Jesting Army* I. vi. 90 The Brigadier pushed back the mess accounts to me and said, 'You'll keep all that bumf till next time, won't you, padre?' 1938 E. WAUGH *Scoop* II. iv. 211, I shall get a daily pile of bumf from the Ministry of Mines. 1957 M. K. JOSEPH *I'll soldier no More* (1958) 21 Matthews is bringing the bumf... He says be sure and type it on Army Form A2.

† **bum'feage, bum'feagle, bum'feg,** *vbs. Obs.* [cf. BUM *v.*^{3}] Humorous synonyms for to flog, thrash. (Nashe apparently regarded the word as a coinage of 'Martin Marprelate'.)

1589 *Hay any Work* 6 Ise so bumfeg the Cooper. 1589 NASHE *Almond for Parrat* 7 b, You.. neuer knewe what his Bumfeging ment. 1589 —— *Martin's Month's M.* F 1 b, I wil so bumfeage him. 1598 FLORIO, *Scardassare*.. to beate, bumbaste.. or bumfeagle.

† **bum'fiddle,** *sb.* = BUM *sb.*^{1}

1675 COTTON *Burlesque* in *Poet. Wks.* (1765) 231 So her Bum-fiddle I had clapp'd. *c*1810 W. HICKEY *Mem.* (1960) xix. 311, I, of course, shall pay, and they may kiss my bum fiddle. 1825 H. WILSON *Mem.* I. 91, I am puzzled to guess .. how, you came to shew me, an utter stranger, your bum-fiddle!

bum'fiddle *v.*, see quots.; also **bum'fiddler.**

*c*1560 *Trag. Rich. II* (1870) 42 To say I will teare this paper.. or fowler words than that, as to say I will bumfidle your paper. 1611 DAVIES *Scourge Folly* in Wright *Dict. Obs. & Prov. Eng.*, A busie-body hardly she abides; Yet she's well-pleased with all bumfidlers. 1618 FLETCHER *Chances* I. vi, And am I now bumfidl'd with a Bastard? 1815 SOUTHEY *Lett.* (1856) II. 399 [An ode] too good to be fiddled; so I sent them a second, which was fit to be bum-fiddled.

bumkin, bumpkin ('bʌmkɪn). *Naut.* Also 8–9 boomkin. [f. BOOM *sb.*^{2} + -KIN; possibly the Du. *boomken* may formerly have been used in this special sense. The spelling *bumpkin* is now more usual.] 'A short boom projecting from each bow of a ship, to extend the lower edge of the foresail to windward.' Falconer *Dict. Marine*, 1769. Also applied to similar booms for extending the mainsail and the mizen.

1632 SHERWOOD, Bumkin (in a ship), *chicambault.* 1769 FALCONER *Dict. Marine* (1789) *Bumkin*, or *Boomkin*, a short boom. 1799 *Naval Chron.* I. 258 Carrying away her bumpkin. 1825 H. GASCOIGNE *Nav. Fame* 75 Dragg'd to the Bumpkin the Foretack is found. 1840 R. DANA *Bef. Mast* xv. 41 Breaking off her larboard bumpkin.

attrib. 1794 *Rigging & Seamanship* I. 231 *Boomkin-Shrouds*, to support the boomkins, have their after ends hooked to eye-bolts.

† **bumkin^{2}.** *Obs. rare.* See quot.

1697 DAMPIER *Voy.* (1729) I. 2 Another Canoa which had been sawn asunder in the middle, in order to have made Bumkins, or Vessels for carrying water.

† **'bumkin^{3}.** [f. BUM *sb.*^{1} + -KIN.] 'A burlesque term for the posteriors'. Nares, q.v.

bumkin(g, obs. form of BUMPKIN.

† **'bumleaf,** *Obs. rare.* [Cf. BUM-CARD.] A leaf of paper with a slip projecting from the edge (in a book used for a conjuring trick); it served a similar purpose to that of the 'bum-card', being intended to enable the conjuror to open the book, as if by accident, at the right places.

1584 R. SCOT *Discov. Witchcr.* XIII. xxxiii. 283 Each Bumleafe or high inch of paper.. rest your thombe upon anie of those Bumleaves, or high inches.

‖ **bummalo.** Also bumbeloe, bumbalo, bumaloe. [Yule quotes *bombil* or *bombila* from Molesworth's *Mahratti Dict.*] A small fish (*Harpodon nehereus*) found off the coasts of Southern Asia, used, when dried, as a relish.

1673 FRYER *E. India & P.* 67 (Y.) Massigoung.. notable for a fish called Bumbelow, the Sustenance of the Poorer sort. 1787 *Archaeologia* VIII. 262 (D.) Dried fish, which in this country [India] are called bumbeloes. 1813 J. FORBES *Oriental Mem.* I. 53 The Bumbalo, a small fish extremely nutritive. 1845 STOCQUELER *Handbk. Brit. India* (1854) 283 Skate, sword-fish, bumaloe, cockup, crabs, lobsters. 1885 BALFOUR *Cycl. India* (ed. 3) 512 *Bummalo*, a small fish, salted and dried; also called Bombay Duck.

bummaree (bʌmə'riː). Also 8–9 bomaree, 9 bumbaree, bommeree. [Origin unknown. Cf. BUMMERY.] **1.** A middleman in the fish trade at Billingsgate.

[1707 *Lond. Gaz.* No. 4330/7 Run away.. a Negro Boy.. called Hermitage or Bumaree.] 1786 *Rep. Committee of City of Lond. on Price Provisions* 31 The Bomarees will buy up half the fish the Salesmen have, and sell to the Fish-mongers. 1851 MAYHEW *Lond. Labour* I. 67 In Billingsgate the 'forestallers' or middlemen are known as 'bummarees'.. The bummarree is the jobber or speculator on the fish-exchange. 1859 SALA *Tw. round Clock* (1861) 17 Stands are erected at different parts of the market for 'bumbarees'.

2. Also **bummeree.** A licensed porter at Smithfield meat-market in London. Also *attrib.*

1954 *Meat Marketing* 29 Sept. 44/1 There are adequate bummeree or middle porters already. 1955 *Times* 1 Dec. 7/6 A 'test case' as to whether or not a retail butcher was entitled to remove meat purchased at Smithfield Market by himself or his full-time employees, or whether he had to employ porters known as 'bummarees'. 1968 M. C. BORER *England's Markets* 19 There are about a hundred and thirty 'bummarees' at Smithfield, and they are all self-employed.

Hence **bumma'reeing** *vbl. sb.* The acting as a bummaree.

1859 SALA *Tw. round Clock* 21 The process of bumbareeing is very simple.

bumme, obs. f. BUM *sb.*^{1}

† **bummed,** *a. Obs.* Also 6 bumbd. [f. BUM *sb.*^{1} and *v*^{4} + -ED.] **a.** Of garments: Padded out, made to project. **b.** Having a bum (only in *comb.*).

1588 W. AVERELL *Comb. Contrarieties* B ij, This yeere bumbd like a Barrell, the next shottend like a Herring. 1611 COTGR., *Fessé*.. Fat-bumd.

bummel ('bʊməl, 'bʌməl), *sb.* and *v.* [a. G. *bummel* a stroll, *bummeln* to stroll; cf. BUMMER^{3}.] **A.** *sb.* A leisurely stroll or journey. **B.** *v. intr.* To stroll or wander in a leisurely fashion. Hence **'bummelling** *vbl. sb.*, wandering, sauntering.

[1891 *Pall Mall Gaz.* 29 Aug. 3/2 The verb to 'bummeln', apparently an equivalent of the French 'flâner'. *Ibid.*, We do not 'bummeln' so much or so thoroughly as the Germans.] 1900 J. K. JEROME (*title*) Three Men on the Bummel. *Ibid.* xiii. 284 He.. lays out his time bummelling, beer drinking, and fighting. *Ibid.* xiv. 327 A 'Bummel'.. I should describe as a journey, long or short, without an end. 1909 *Daily Chron.* 24 July 6/4 Hitherto it has been the proud prerogative of males [in Berlin] to 'bummel' (loaf). 1947 F. SMYTHE *Again Switzerland* x. 187 It is an easy mountain.. a ski runner's 'bummel'. 1952 H. W. TILMAN *Nepal Himalaya* II. xviii. 212, I had already been 'bummeling' about Nepal for five months.

bummel, -il, Sc. ff. of BUMBLE *v.*^{2}

† **'bummer^{1}.** *Obs.* = BUMBAILIFF.

1675 CROWNE *Country Wit* III. 40 I'le go get the writ and bailiffs.. my Bummers shall have her in bed.

bummer^{2}. *Sc.* [f. BUM *v.*^{2} + -ER^{1}.] That which hums or buzzes; *spec.* a toy (see quot. 1821).

1821 *Blackw. Mag.* Aug. 35 (JAM.) Bummers—a thin piece of wood swung round by a cord. 1862 HISLOP *Prov. Scot.* 185 The loudest bummer's no the best bee.

bummer^{3} ('bʌmə(r)). *U.S. slang.* [cf. Ger. *bummler* in same sense.] An idler, lounger, loafer. See also quots. Hence **bummerish** *a.*

1855 *Oregonian* (Portland) 27 Jan. 1/4 Come, clear out, you trunken loafer! Ve don't vant no *bummers* here! 1856 *San Francisco Call* 25 Dec. (Th.), 'Pon my word I'm no bummer. I never ate a lunch in all my life without taking a square drink. 1865 MAJ. NICHOLLS *Gt. March* in *Pall Mall G.* 23 Sept. 11/2 If it be asked what a 'bummer' is, the reply is easy. He is a raider on his own account—a man who temporarily deserts his place in the ranks.. and starts out upon an independent foraging expedition. 1865 *Atlantic Monthly* Mar. 286 The brain.. a lazy bummer, that lived at the stomach's expense. 1872 C. KING *Sierra Nev.* ii. 36 Indians.. lying off with that peculiar bummerish ease. 1878 BLACK *Green Past.* (ed. 2) III. 83 A system of local government controlled by 30,000 bummers, loafers, and dead-beats.

bummer^{4} ('bʌmə(r)). (See quot.)

1905 *Terms Forestry & Logging* 32 *Bummer*, a small truck with two low wheels and a long pole, used in skidding logs. Syn.: drag cart, skidder.

† **'bummery.** *Obs.* [a. Du. *bommerye* (Hexham), *bodmerij*; see BOTTOMRY *sb.*] = BOTTOMRY.

1663 PEPYS *Diary* 25 Nov. He advised me in things I desired, about bummary, and other ways of putting out money as in parts of ships. 1668 CHILD *Disc. Trade* (1698) 144 Bills of Bottomry or Bumery. *a*1734 NORTH *Lives* II. 33 A bummery bond. 1836 *Penny Cycl.* V. 263/1 Bottomry, Bottomree, or Bummaree.

'bumming, *ppl. a.* [f. BUM *v.*^{2} + -ING^{2}.] **a.** Buzzing, humming. **b.** † ***bumming sound*** (obs.): Something of note, or worth listening to.

1599 MARSTON *Sco. Villanie* I. iv. 188 Hath rak't together some four thousand pound, To make his smug gurle beare a bumming sound In a young merchants eare. 1616 *Pasquil & Kath.* III. 182 A thousand pound a yeere! B'ar Ladie, that's a bumming sound. 1821 CLARE *Vill. Minstr.* I. 131 Bumming gad-flies ceased to tease.

'bumming, *vbl. sb. U.S. slang.* The action of BUM *v.*^{6}

1857 *San Francisco Call* 9 Jan. 1/2 The 'Bumming and Gassing Company' were out in full strength, the novelty of labor being a new experience in their existence. 1860 *Yale Lit. Mag.* XXV. 398 (Th.), Another great sham connected with our social life is that of spreeing or 'bumming'. 1891 C. ROBERTS *Adrift Amer.* 66 The idea of begging or 'bumming' as it is popularly called out there, went strongly against my stomach.

† **'bummock, 'bummack.** *Sc.* [Etymology unknown: presumably ON.]

1. A large brewing of ale for a merry meeting; the ale itself. (In Caithness.) (Jam.)

1693 WALLACE *Orkney* 30 The Tennant will not fail to have.. strong Ale (which they call Bummocks) in readiness. 1822 SCOTT *Pirate* III. 200 (JAM.) The mickle bicker of Scapa.. was always offered to the Bishop of Orkney brimful of the best bummock.

2. A Christmas entertainment in Orkney given by tenants to their landlords.

1795 *Statist. Acc. Orkney* XV. 393 *note* (JAM.) These entertainments, called Bummacks, strengthened.. the bonds of mutual confidence.. The Christmas Bummacks are almost universally discontinued.

bump (bʌmp), *sb.*^{1} [Belongs to BUMP *v.*^{1} Onomatopœic: the *vb.* and *sb.* of action being probably coeval. App. the order was *bump* v. to knock, and *bump* sb. a knock; hence as *sb.* a swelling protuberance caused by a blow, and as *vb.* to swell or rise in a protuberance; but the historical record is not very complete. Cf. BOUNCE, THUMP, etc. Also as a parallel instance of an onomatopœia combining the two senses 'sudden blow' and 'swelling' cf. BUNCH.]

I. 1. a. A blow somewhat heavy, but rather dull in sound; a sudden collision, more or less violent. So ***with a bump*** (*fig.*), abruptly, with a shock.

1611 COTGR., *Adot*, a blow, bumpe, or thumpe. 1768–78 TUCKER *Lt. Nat.* II. 149 An unlucky bump upon the head [might have] rendered him stupid. 1862 SMILES *Engineers* III. 10 When the pump descends, there is heard a plunge, a heavy sigh, and a loud bump. 1882 *Lett.* in *Royal Acad. Catal.* (1883) 95 It went into the ditch with a bump. 1920 O. W. HOLMES *Let.* 6 Apr. in *Holmes-Laski Lett.* (1953) I. 259, I must go in 5 minutes to a conference of the JJ and therefore run down with a bump. 1935 W. G. HARDY *Father Abraham* I. viii. 111 His mood of exaltation fell with a bump into the trough of melancholy. 1955 E. HILLARY *High Adventure* ix. 171, I came back to full consciousness with a bump.

b. (See quots.)

1883 GRESLEY *Gloss. Coal-m.*, *Bump*, a very sudden breaking, sometimes accompanied by a settling down, or upheaval of, the strata, during the working away of the mineral, accompanied by a loud report or bumping noise heard in the mine. 1893 *Trans. Fed. Instit. Mining Eng.* V. 381 A bump (or earth explosion) occurred on November 5th, 1892. 1960 *Times* (S. Afr. Suppl.) 31 May p. xviii/1 That was a 'bump', a subterranean movement caused mainly by the settling of strata disturbed by mining activity.

c. *Cricket.* The rise of a ball from the pitch to a greater height than is usual. Cf. BUMP *v.*^{1} 2 b.

1901 R. H. LYTTELTON *Out-door Games* i. 31 A man who plays fairly straight,.. and can meet the ball with the bat when it comes on straight with no hang or bump.

d. *Aeronaut.* An air-pocket.

1914 ROSHER *In R.N.A.S.* (1916) 15 While flying at 200 feet, the machine suddenly bumped [*note*, met an airwave]. .. These bumps are due to the sun's action on the air and are called 'sun bumps'. 1918 E. M. ROBERTS *Flying Fighter* 279 When correcting bumps or small erratic air currents one has often to resort to his inclinometer.

e. *slang.* Usu. in *pl.* An uneven landing of an aeroplane.

1943 HUNT & PRINGLE *Service Slang* 19 *Bumps*, the touching down of the aircraft during landing due to uneven ground or bad handling. 1958 'N. SHUTE' *Rainbow & Rose* v. 207 Rather than keep him at the dreary round of circuits and bumps I had been teaching him aerobatics.

f. The action of thrusting forward the abdomen or hips in a dance or the like. (Cf. GRIND *sb.*^{1} 5.) *slang* (orig. *U.S.*).

1946 MEZZROW & WOLFE *Really the Blues* vi. 75 She [a dancer] went through her whole routine, bumps and grinds and shakes and breaks. 1964 *Punch* 26 Aug. 295/2 Sing a song.. and do a bump-and-grind routine.

2. *Boating.* The impact of the stem of a boat against the stern or side of another boat in front of it: in boat-racing at the English Universities, the making of a 'bump' is the technical proof of one boat's overtaking and beating another.

1861 HUGHES *Tom Brown Oxf.* I. xiv. 282 A bump now and no mistake; the bow of the St. Ambrose boat jams the oar of the Oriel stroke. 1884 *Sat. Rev.*, *College Life* 12 July 47/1 An unexpected bump in May.

II. Swelling.

3. A protuberance such as is caused by a blow or collision; a swelling, an irregular prominence.

1592 SHAKS. *Rom. & Jul.* I. iii. 53 It had upon it brow, a bumpe as big as a young Cockrels stone; a perilous knock. 1611 COTGR., *Angonailles*, botches, (pockie) bumps or sores. *Ibid. Bigne*, a bumpe, knob, rising, or swelling after a knocke. *a*1700 DRYDEN (J.) Not though.. in bumps his forehead rise. 1825–7 HONE *Every-day Bk.* II. 1016, I sat upon a small knoll, surrounded by curves and bumps.

4. *transf.* One of the prominences on the cranium associated by phrenologists with special mental faculties and propensities; sometimes used for the faculties, etc., themselves. (*colloq.*)

1815 *Edin. Rev.* XXV. 251 The aforesaid bumps on the head are.. signs of peculiar energy, in some of the special faculties. 1863 KINGSLEY *Water-bab.* iv. 165 She felt his bumps, and cast his nativity. *Mod.* I never knew anyone so deficient in the bump of locality.

5. Phr. ***like a bump on a log***: stupidly silent or inarticulate. *colloq.* (orig. and chiefly *U.S.*).

1863 'MARK TWAIN' *Mark Twain of Enterprise* (1957) II. xvi. 103 You have been sitting there for thirty days like a bump on a log, and you never rightly understand anything. **1922** S. LEWIS *Babbitt* xviii. 226 With that he drove on and left the fellow standing there in the road like a bump on a log! **1935** N. L. MCCLUNG *Clearing in West* xxxii. 280 You couldn't expect her to sit there like a bump on a log, Mrs. Mooney.

III. *Comb.*, as **bump-ball** *Cricket*, a ball hit hard upon the ground close to the bat, coming with a long hop to the fieldsman, and having the specious appearance of a catch; also (erron.) *bum(-ball)*; **bump-car** = DODGEM; **bump-stick**, a tool used by shoe-makers for smoothing soles (= *sleek-stick*); **bump-supper**, a supper given to celebrate the making of a 'bump' by a college boat (see 2); **bump-up**, a sudden increase (cf. BUMP *v.*[1] 1 d).

1867 *Australasian* 9 Mar. 300/4 The apparent sincerity of a..wicket-keeper, when appealing for a 'leg before', or a 'bum'. **1870** *Marlburian* 8 June 58/2 Woollcombe..was caught off what appeared to be a 'bum ball'. **1877** C. BOX *Eng. Game Cricket* 444 *Bump ball*, a ball caught after it has bounded from the ground. **1963** *Times* 18 Feb. 10/2 When an appeal was made the umpire ruled that it was a bump ball. **1937** HULL & WHITLOCK *Far-distant Oxus* xx. 276 The six wandered off to have turns on the bump cars. **1725** BRADLEY *Fam. Dict.* s.v. *Box*, It [Boxwood] makes also..Bump-Sticks and Dressers for Shoemakers. **1853** 'C. BEDE' *Adv. Verdant Green* x. 94 A Bump-supper,—that is,..a supper to commemorate the fact of the boat of one college having, in the annual races, bumped, or touched the boat of another college. **1940** J. BUCHAN *Memory Hold-the-Door* iii. 61 Raymond [Asquith] wrote the poem,..On a Viscount who died on the Morrow of a Bump Supper. **1958** *Economist* 13 Sept. 819/1 They are excited because of the bump-up in their support and by-election votes this year.

bump, *sb.*[2] [f. BUMP *v.*[2]] The cry of the bittern.

a **1528** SKELTON *Poems* 227 (L.) The bitter with his bump, The crane with his trump.

bump (bʌmp), *sb.*[3] [Origin unknown.] **a.** A kind of matting used for covering floors. **b.** A material composed of cotton threads loosely twisted together (formerly also refuse flax) used for candlewicks, also woven for making coarse sheets; *attrib.* in ***bump-sheet***, also **bump-mill**, a factory where this fabric is manufactured.

1881 *Instr. Census Clerks* (1885) 68 Bump Mill Worker. **1921** *Dict. Occup. Terms* (1927) §36 5 *Spinner, bump mill*.. spins candle wick yarn from coarse cotton waste.

bump, *v.*[1] [see BUMP *sb.*[1]]

I. To strike heavily or firmly.

1. *trans.* †**a.** *generally*. To strike heavily, knock, thump. *Obs.* **b.** To impinge heavily upon; of persons, to push (a heavy body) violently *against*, or *on* any object; to hurt (one's head, one's knee, etc.) by knocking against a hard object (sometimes const. *against*, *on*); to strike or knock with anything heavy and bulky; to seize (a person) by the arms and legs, and strike his posteriors against a wall, tree, etc. *spec.* in *Services' slang*: to explode (a mine or mine-field); to shell.

1611 COTGR., *Baculer*, to bumpe on the Posteriorums with a Bat. **1768** TUCKER *Lt. Nat.* I. 471 That antagonist, whom he bumps and pummels so furiously. **1815** SCOTT *Guy M.* iv, We bumped ashore a hundred kegs. **1842** TENNYSON *Epic* 12, I bump'd the ice into three several stars. *a* **1888** *Mod.* I bumped my head on the low ceiling. Several boys were 'bumped' against this wall at the beating of the bounds. **1915** 'BARTIMEUS' *Tall Ship* ix. 160 We haven't bumped a mine-field. *Ibid.* 168 The chance of 'bumping a mine'. **1919** *Athenæum* 1 Aug. 695/2 An artilleryman speaks of having 'bumped' a certain town or spot, meaning shelled.

c. ***to bump off***: to remove by violence; to kill. Also ellipt., *to bump*. *slang* (orig. *U.S.*).

1910 W. M. RAINE *B. O'Connor* 117 I've got several good reasons why I don't aim to get bumped off just yet. **1914** JACKSON & HELLYER *Vocab. Criminal Slang* 21 He copped a cuter and got bumped making a get-away. **1927** *Cleveland Press* 29 Jan., Senator Thomas J. Heflin..informed his colleagues that a thug had threatened to 'bump him off'. **1927** C. F. COE *Me—Gangster* iii. 52 Who bumped that poor chump that was drivin' the car? **1930** *Punch* 16 Apr. 442 Jimmy is duly bumped off. **1932** E. WAUGH *Black Mischief* vii. 266 They had two shots at bumping me off yesterday. **1943** P. CHEYNEY *You can always Duck* xii. 186 You didn't want him..to know you had bumped Clemensky. **1958** HAYWARD & HARARI tr. *Pasternak's Dr. Zhivago* I. vii. 212 A few were bumped off by way of example.

d. ***to bump up***: to increase or raise (prices, etc.) suddenly. *colloq.*

1940 N. MITFORD *Pigeon Pie* xii. 192 Olga bumps up his allowance every time he horsewhips anybody for making a pass at her. **1958** *Spectator* 10 Jan. 42/2 It is wise at night to look out for places which bump up the prices without warning.

2. a. *intr.* To strike solidly, to come with a bump or violent jolt *against*; to move with a bump or a succession of bumps. *Naut.* see quot. 1844.

a **1843** SOUTHEY *Lodore* 94 Thumping and flumping and bumping and jumping. **1844** MRS. HOUSTON *Yacht Voy. Texas* II. 150 The extremely heavy swell on the bar, which ..materially increases the chance of a vessel's 'bumping'; a term the Americans use for touching on the sand banks. **1857** HOLLAND *Bay Path* xxv. 301 His heart bumped So heavily against the walls of his chest. **1860** *Merc. Mar. Mag.* VII. 305 She bumped several times..losing her false keel. **1885** M. D. CHALMERS *Law Times* LXXX. 191/1 Due to the cask bumping against the cellar wall.

b. *Cricket.* Of a ball: to rise abruptly to an unusual height.

1863 *Baily's Mag.* June 257 At one time the ball would hit a batsman on the ribs, another time bump up and fly yards over his head. **1871** *Ibid.* June 172 There was an ugly place where the ball bumped near the north wicket. **1882** PARDON *Australians in England* 173 Bates was caught, a bumping ball from Spofforth going off the shoulder of his bat. **1888** W. G. GRACE in Steel & Lyttelton *Cricket* 310 Emmett was in his glory, his bowling bumping and kicking up as I have never seen it since. **1891** —— *Cricket* 130 The first ball..bumped and hit him on the head. **1929** *Times* 24 May 6/1 A pitch which, apart from the fact that two or three balls bumped in the afternoon, was beautifully easy.

c. *Chem.* 'To give off vapour intermittently and with almost explosive violence' (Cent. Dict. 1889). Cf. BUMPING *vbl. sb.* 2.

1883 *Encycl. Brit.* XVI. 32/2 Mercury 'bumps' badly on boiling. *Ibid.* 195/2 Methyl-alcohol has quite a characteristic tendency to 'bump' badly on distillation. **1950** P. J. DURRANT *Org. Chem.* iii. 64 As the pressure of a boiling liquid is lowered, the tendency to 'bump' is greatly increased.

d. *Aeronaut.* To move irregularly owing to an inequality of air pressure.

1914 [see BUMP *sb.*[1] 1 d].

e. ***to bump into***: to meet (a person) by chance, to run into (a person). *colloq.*

[**1886** 'P. PERKINS' *Fam. Lett.* 22 Went down those old stairs lickety-wallup, and bumped into that old party who was evidently running for the..station.] **1953** W. P. MCGIVERN *Big Heat* ii. 24 We just bumped into each other on Market Street. **1958** E. DUNDY *Dud Avocado* I. v. 82 What a *mad* coincidence bumping into John.

3. *trans. Boat-racing.* To overtake and impinge on (the boat in front). Also *absol.* = 'make a bump': see BUMP *sb.*[1] 2. (In the boat-races at the English Universities, a boat which bumps another changes place with it in the order of boats on the river.)

1826 *Lit. Lounger* 222 in *Oxf. Mag.* [Extra No.] 18 May 1887, 2/2 Christ Church bumps her. *Ibid.* 3/1, I never thought of her bumping the Exeter. **1850** KINGSLEY *Alt. Locke* xiii. 105 Having, as he informed me, 'bumped the first Trinity'. **1861** HUGHES *Tom Brown Oxf.* I. xiv. 276 Colleges, whose boats have no chance of bumping or being bumped.

4. a. To dismiss from a position; to take the position of another, *spec.* by exercising the right to displace a less senior member of an organization (e.g. after being displaced from one's own job). *U.S.*

[**1915** *Dialect Notes* IV. 224 *Bump, v.t.*, to reject; esp., in college slang, to reject a fraternity's 'bid'.] **1918** *Ibid.* V. 23 *To bump*, vb. t., to dismiss from service. General. **1941** *Boston Daily Globe* 3 Jan. 20 Joe Begin is working on the section for the C.P.R. here, having bumped Romeo Lavallee. Romeo then bumped Henri Carrier, who was working at Camp 12, and Henri, having no one to bump, is out of work pro temps. **1943** *Amer. Speech* XVIII. 163/1 When a crew is deprived of its assignment, as when a train is removed from the timetable, its members select the jobs they wish among those held by others with less seniority —this is called bumping. **1972** *Fortune* Jan. 148/1 Agreement has also been reached with the unions to cut down on the costly practice of unqualified workers 'bumping' experienced employees in different job classifications who have lower seniority. **1980** *Washington Star* 20 Jan. G1 Has Iowa bumped New Hampshire as the first state to say which way the wind is blowing in the presidential election?

b. To deprive (a passenger) of a reserved place on an airline flight, esp. after deliberate overbooking. Also *transf.* Freq. in *pass.* orig. *U.S.*

1947 *Funk & Wagnalls New College Stand. Dict.* 157/1 *Bump*.., to deprive (a passenger) of airplane transportation in favor of a later but more important traveler. **1969** *Daily Colonist* (Victoria, B.C.) 11 Mar. 6/2 No bumping—arbitrary cancellation by senior authority of someone's reservation—is allowed 'except in emergencies or exceptional circumstances'. **1978** *Observer* 30 July 3/1 They were blandly told that their flight was full. In other words, they had been 'bumped'. **1984** *Daily Tel.* 4 May 18/1 Fifty passengers were turned away (or 'bumped') at Barbados this week by British Airways. **1986** *Flight* 27 Dec. 15/4 Engle was bumped off the crew [of Apollo 17] by geologist Jack Schmitt.

II. To bulge out.

†**5.** *intr.* To rise in protuberances, to bulge out, to be convex. *Obs.*

1566 [see BUMPING *ppl. a.*]. **1579** STUDLEY *Seneca's Hippolytus* (1581) 71 His..necke With..knobby curnels hie out bumping big do swell. **1597** GERARD *Herbal* (1633) 1299 (L.) Long fruite..with kernels bumping out. **1603** HOLLAND *Plutarch's Mor.* 1021 Of the round line that part which is..without doth bumpe and bunch.

†**6.** *trans.* To make protuberant, cause to swell *up*.

1662 J. BARGRAVE *Pope Alex. VII* (1867) 120 Another triangular, unequilateral, bumped-up, large loadstone. **1719** D'URFEY *Pills* I. 187 He bumpt up our Bellies.

7. *trans. Printing.* ***to bump out***: To spread out the matter of a book, article, or the like (by wide spacing, arrangement of page, etc.), so as to make it fill the desired number of pages.

1885 *Bookseller* 6 July 49/1 The text had been so ingeniously bumped out by the publishers that it filled twice the number of pages it should have done.

III. 8. *Watchmaking*: see quot.

1884 F. BRITTEN *Watch & Clockm.* 246 'Bumping' wheels, i.e. altering the plane of the teeth with relation to the hole.

IV. 9. The verb stem used adverbially = With a bump, with sudden collision; ***bump, bump***, with repeated shocks of contact on the part of a heavy moving body.

1806 BLOOMFIELD *Wild Flowers* Poems (1845) 217 Bump in his hat the shillings tumbled. **1863** KINGSLEY *Water-bab.* i. 47 As he came bump, stump, jump, down the steep. *Mod.* The carriage went bump, bump, over the sleepers.

bump, *v.*[2] [Of echoic origin: cf. BOOM *v.*] A word used to express the cry of the bittern.

1646 SIR T. BROWNE *Pseud. Ep.* 173 A Bittor maketh that mugient noyse, or as we terme it Bumping. *a* **1700** DRYDEN *Wife of Bath* 194 As a bittour bumps within a reed.

†'**bumped**, *ppl. a. Obs.* [f. BUMP *sb.*[1] and *v.*[1] + -ED.] Covered with bumps; swelled out in bumps.

1611 COTGR., *Bossé*..knobbie, bulked, or bumped out. **1662** [see BUMP *v.*[1] 6] Bumped up. **1776** tr. *Da Costa's Conchol.* 177 (Jod.) The two ends or extremes, on the upper part are very bumped and prominent.

bumper ('bʌmpə(r)), *sb.*[1] [perh. from BUMP *sb.*[1] or *v.*[1]: with notion of a 'bumping', i.e. large, 'thumping' glass.]

1. a. A cup or glass of wine, etc., filled to the brim, *esp.* when drunk as a toast.

1676 D'URFEY *Mad. Fickle* v. i. (1677) 52 Full Bumpers crown our Blisses. **1774** GOLDSM. *Retal.* 127 He cherish'd his friend, and he relish'd a bumper. **1856** KANE *Arct. Exp.* I. xiii. 151 A dinner of marled beef..and a bumper of champagne all round.

b. *Comb.*, as ***bumper-dram, -toast***.

1818 SCOTT *Hrt. Midl.* iv, Drinking their meridian (a bumper-dram of brandy). **1839** LOCKHART *Ballantyne-humbug* Few will doubt that he did..pledge, with hearty zeal, many a bumper-toast.

2. *slang.* Anything unusually large or abundant. (Cf. *whopper*, *whacker*, *thumper*, etc.) Esp. freq. in attrib. use = exceptionally abundant or good (see also quot. 1864). Cf. sense 3.

1759 *Gentl. Mag.* XXIX. 271/2 In some of the midland counties, anything large is called *a bumper*, as a large apple or pear. **1859** LANG *Wand. India* 9 Tellwell and Long..have just lost a bumper—twenty-seven gold mohurs. **1864** G. BERKELEY *My Life & Recoll.* I. 182 The country was immensely deep and the brook a bumper. **1864** HOTTEN *Slang Dict.* 89 A match at quoits, bowls, &c., may end in a 'bumper game', if the play and score be all on one side. **1885** *Times* (Weekly ed.) 2 Oct. 5/3 The floods will have the effect of giving a 'bumper' rubbee crop. **1898** *Westm. Gaz.* 18 Nov. 8/1 The past fortnight's bumper traffic. **1908** *Daily Chron.* 8 Jan. 4/4 So far as the foreign trade of this country is concerned, 1907 was a bumper year. **1955** *Times* 22 June 9/6 Instead of an expected crop of 600,000 bags there was a bumper crop of 1,400,000 bags.

3. *Theatr. slang.* A crowded 'house' at a theatre.

1789 J. B. WATSON *Let.* 25 Aug. in L. Sumbel *Mem.* (1811) III. 144 Her benefit, at Gloster, which, if a bumper, in every and the truest sense will be no more than I most cordially wish it. **1795** TATE WILKINSON *Wand. Patentee* IV. 36 A bumper of a house. **1839** DICKENS *Nich. Nick.* xxiv, This charming actress will be greeted with a bumper. **1886** *Pall Mall G.* 2 Aug. 3/2, I have heard a crowded house on a benefit night called 'a bumper'.

4. In *Whist* and other games: see quots.

1876 A. CAMPBELL-WALKER *Correct Card* (1880) Gloss. 11 *Bumper.* Winning two games—i.e. eight points—before your adversaries have scored. **1880** BESANT & RICE *Seamy Side* xxxii. 282 After seeing a double bumper fooled away, his partner rose in silent dignity, and left the house.

5. a. [f. sense 1 of the verb.] The buffer of a railway carriage (*U.S.*).

1839 *Jrnl. Franklin Institute* XXIV. 156 The bumpers or elastic cushions are to be attached..to the front and rear draw-bar. **1864** *Sanatory Commission U.S. Army* 110 *note*, The Bumper is surrounded by a stiff spring, which prevents the communication of the jar.

b. (See quot.)

1868 FAIRLEY *Gloss. Coal-Mining* II. 5 A massive piece of iron, so heavy that when the cage is at the bottom of the cut, it will draw it empty to the top, and when the cage at the top is laden, it will act as a balance as the cage descends: this piece of iron is called the bumper.

c. A log, bar, etc., serving as a fender or shock-absorber; *spec.* a metal bar attached to either end of a motor vehicle to lessen the shock in a collision. Also *attrib.* and *Comb.*, as **bumper-to-bumper** *adv.* and *a.*, (of cars) travelling very close together.

1867 SMYTH *Sailor's Word-Bk.* 144 *Bumpers*, logs of wood placed over a ship's side to keep off ice. **1883** GRESLEY *Gloss. Coal-Mining* 38 *Bumpers*,..projecting blocks of wood attached to pump spears for preventing damage in case of a break down. **1889** *Cent. Dict.*, *Bumper-timber*, in some locomotives, a timber to which the cow-catcher or pilot is fastened, designed to receive the shock or blow of a collision. **1901** *Law Times* 11 May 29/2 An elevator car..passed downward until it struck the bumpers at the bottom of the shaft. **1926** *Morris Owner* Feb. 1600/2 The front face of the bumper bar is attractively finished in bright nickel plate. **1928** *Punch* 25 Apr. p. xxxiii (Advt.), 'The Bumper with the Leaf Spring Buffer.' This unique and ingenious feature evenly distributes and reduces the shock of an impact. **1938** 'ELLERY QUEEN' *Four of Hearts* (1939) v. 75 Los Feliz Boulevard was jammed with cars crawling bumper to bumper. **1959** *Manch. Guardian* 18 May 1/1 A bumper-to-bumper traffic jam on roads. **1959** *Motor* 21 Oct. 346/2

Lights..repositioned behind the front bumper. **1967** G. LEGMAN *Fake Revolt* 16 The bumpersticker approach to hallucinatory drugs and sex technique.

6. a. One who or a thing that bumps; spec. *Bookbinding* = SMASHER[1] 3.

1881 *Instr. Census Clerks* (1885) 43 Rocker or Bumper. **1887** C. C. RHYS *Minora Carmina* 267 Up at Oxford by eights on the Isis, The gloom of bumpees and of bumpers the glow. **1921** *Dict. Occup. Terms* (1927) §279 *Bumper* (tin boxes, etc.), packs into bundles, scrap tinplate left from stamping or cutting, by shovelling it into iron box, ramming or bumping it into compact shape with long-handled iron ram. *Ibid.* §409 *Bumper*, a planker who operates a bumping machine; places felt forms in a sort of trough, sets machine in motion, so that forms are bumped about against arms of machine. **1951** S. JENNETT *Making Books* xi. 171 The machine appropriately called the smasher or the bumper.. is in effect an automatic clamp.

b. *Cricket.* A bumping ball (see BUMP *v.*[1] 2 b).

1855 *Bell's Life in London* 19 Aug. 8/3 From the fact of the ground not being a good wearing one, the 'bumpers' of Lillywhite could not be mastered. **1904** *Westm. Gaz.* 24 May 3/2 With the likelihood of..an occasional 'bumper' even such great batsmen..might have failed. **1955** *Times* 30 Aug. 3/2 Heine bowled a number of rude, honest bumpers.

c. *bumper car* = DODGEM.

[**1949** M. LASKI *Little Boy Lost* III. xiv. 195 'We'll go in the bumpy-cars,' he said, and climbed into a bright blue car.] **1959** P. BROWN *As far as Singapore* vi. 124 They are big amusement parks... They have bumper cars. **1960** *New Left Rev.* Jan.–Feb. 52/1 Going to a fair to ride on the bumper cars.

bumper, *sb.*[2] [f. BUMP *v.*[2] and *sb.*[2]] In comb. ***bog-bumper*** = BITTERN.

1866 *Inverness Cour.* 4 Jan., The bog-bumper. **1887** JESSOPP *Arcady* 56 'Were there any bitterns here?' 'Why, you must mean Bog Bumpers.'

'bumper, *sb.*[3] *colloq.* [-ER[6].] A bumping-race.

1906 D. COKE *Bending of Twig* x. 157 The Bumpers, to give them their familiar name, are split in such a way that a day of rest is allowed in the middle of the four days' racing. **1910** H. W. CHAUNDRY *Rec. Rowing Club S. Philip & S. James', Oxf.* 13 Each of its two crews secured four bumps in the City 'Bumpers'.

'bumper, *sb.*[4] *Austral.* and *N.Z. slang.* [App. telescoped form of BUTT *sb.*[3] and STUMP *sb.*[1] 3 + -ER[1] 3.] A cigarette end.

1916 *Anzac Book* 47/2 While we was standin' to arms 'e lights up a bumper. **1945** *Salt* 2 July 43/2 Tom is busily engaged searching in the dust for enough bumpers to roll a smoke. **1958** R. STOW *To Islands* ii. 42 Galumbu, resigning it, requested 'Bumper, bodj,' and Heriot, after stubbing it placed the butt in the open mouth. **1967** *Southerly* XXVII. 212 He patted the bare mattress..where a bumper had burned a hole sometime in the past.

'bumper, *v.*[1] [f. BUMPER *sb.*[1]] **a.** *trans.* To fill (a drinking-vessel) to the brim. **b.** *trans.* To toast in a bumper. **c.** *intr.* (and with object *it*) to drink bumpers or toasts.

Hence **bumpering** *vbl. sb.* (*attrib.* in quot.).

1696 W. MOUNTAGUE *Delights Holland* 40 They [the Dutch] Bumper it but seldom. **1789** BURNS *Whistle* viii, I'll ..bumper his horn with him twenty times o'er. **1795** WOLCOTT (P. Pindar) *Hair Powd.* Wks. 1812 III. 301 Ye bumper it in England's cause. **1808** *Cumbrian Ballads* No. 75. 175 Come, bumper the Cummerlan lasses. **1859** M. SCOTT *Tom Cringle* xviii. 510 We all sang and bumpered away.

'bumper, *v.*[2] [? connected with BUMP *v.*[1] or *sb.*[1]] *intr.* Frequentative and dim. of *bump*: to make or receive slight bumps; to cause jolts.

1822 *Blackw. Mag.* XI. 159 A hand-gallop, in which I trust you will think that Peggy [i.e. Pegasus] has bumpered very seldom.

†**'bumperize,** *v. nonce-wd.* [f. BUMPER *sb.*[1] + -IZE.] To drink bumpers.

a **1794** GIBBON *Mem.* in *Misc. Wks.* (1814) I. 141 We kept bumperizing till after roll-calling.

bumpety, bumpity ('bʌmpɪtɪ), *adv.* A childish form of BUMP *v.*[1] 9; ***bumpety-bump***, with repeated bumps. Also *attrib.* and as *v. intr.*

1874 HARDY *Far fr. Madding Crowd* lvii, Souls alive, what news! It makes my heart go quite bumpity-bump! **1894** B. PAIN *Kindn. Celestial* 190 You could almost fancy that you heard the man going bumpety-bump down the stairs. **1902** W. DE LA MARE *Songs of Childh.* 10 A bumpity ride in a wagon of hay. **1958** *Spectator* 14 Feb. 194/3 His plane bumpety-bumps to a standstill. **1967** K. GILES *Death in Diamonds* vi. 99 My heart went bumpity because it seemed she looked right at me.

bumph, var. BUMF.

'bumpiness. BUMPY state or condition.

1817 *Blackw. Mag.* I. 38 A modification in the shape or bumpiness of its [the heart's] apex. **1886** *Bicycling News* 17 Sept. 748/2 Its bumpiness excelled any other wood-pavement bumpiness in London.

'bumping, *vbl. sb.* [f. BUMP *v.*[1] + -ING[1].]

1. The action of the verb to BUMP. **a.** *intr.* Sudden (usually repeated) collision or knocking. **b.** *trans.* Striking heavily, thrashing. **c.** Banging the posteriors of a person against a post or wall.

1842 *Fraser's Mag.* Dec., A very tedious passage..Four days of..bumping about. *a* **1848** MARRYAT *R. Reefer* ix, The bumping of obnoxious ushers, and the 'barring out' of tyrannical masters. **1862** WHYTE MELVILLE *Ins. Bar* vi. (ed. 12) 298 Sundry bumpings and thumpings on the stairs.

2. (See quot.)

1883 W. M. WILLIAMS in *Knowledge* 18 Aug. 99/1 What the practical chemist calls 'bumping', or the sudden formation of a big bubble of steam.

3. *Comb.*, as ***bumping-race*** (see BUMP *v.*[1] 3). **bumping-post, bumping-table** (see quots.).

1871 PROCTOR *Light Science* 298 A closely contested bumping-race. *a* **1877** KNIGHT *Dict. Mech.*, *Bumping-post* (Railway Engineering), a timber or set of timbers at the termination of a railroad track, to limit the motion of the train in that direction. **1889** P. MILFORD *Dict. Mining Terms* (ed. 2) 13 A bumping-table is an appliance used in a stamp-mill for treating tailings. It consists of an inclined table, which is given a bumping or jerking motion which serves to force upwards by each successive bump the mineral or heavier portion of the slimes, while the lighter portion is washed off the lower end of the table. **1902** *Encycl. Brit.* XXXI. 371/2 *Bumping Tables.*—Rittinger's table is a rectangular gently-sloping plane surface which by a bumping motion throws the heavy particles to one side while the current of water washes down the quartz to another.

bumping, *ppl. a.* [f. BUMP *v.*[1] + -ING[2].] Huge, great; 'thumping'.

1566 NUCE *Seneca's Octavia* (1581) 172 b, All the bumping bignes it doth beare. **1712** ARBUTHNOT *John Bull* IV. vi, Thou shalt have a bumping pennyworth.

'bumpingly, *adv.* [f. *bumping* pr. pple. of BUMP *v.*[1] + -LY.] In a bumping or jolting manner.

1854 *Chamb. Jrnl.* I. 242 The carriage goes bumpingly.

bumpkin ('bʌmpkɪn). Forms: 6 **bunkin**, 7–8 **bumkin**, (7 **bumking**), 7– **bumpkin**. [The curious gloss in the first quot. suggests that *bunkin* (presumably the same word) was a humorous appellation for a Dutchman, and meant a man with short stumpy figure. The word may be a. Du. *boomken* 'little tree' (Hexham); cf. BUMKIN *sb.*[1] It may however be ad. MDu. *bommekijn* 'little barrel', or f. BUM *sb.*[1] + -KIN.]

1. An awkward country fellow, a clown.

1570 LEVINS *Manip.* 133 A Bunkin, felow, *Batavus, strigo.* **1658** LD. WINDSOR in *Hatton Corresp.* (1878) 15 That I may not looke more lyke a bumking than the rest. **1713** STEELE in *Englishman* No. 40. 258 A Northamptonshire Bumpkin would disdain to gather in such a Crop. **1774** CHESTERF. *Lett.* I. No. 44. 141 A country bumpkin is ashamed when he comes into good company. **1820** IRVING *Sketch Bk.* II. 357 The more bashful country bumpkins hung sheepishly back. **1862** *Comm. Pl. Philosopher* 369.

2. ? Some kind of dance.

1823 LOCKHART *Reg. Dalton* I. xii. (1842) 74, I danced a bumpkin with the boy.

Hence **bumpkinet**, a little bumpkin. **bumpkinish, bumpkinly** *adjs.*, like a bumpkin, clownish, rustic. **bumpkinship** (*humorous*), the personality of a bumpkin.

1774 J. LANGHORNE *Country Just.* 122 Shall Bumpkin come, and bumpkinets be born! **1881** *Times* 12 Jan. 4/1 Peggy..was a little, vulgar, country bumpkinet. **1778** MISS BURNEY *Evelina* (1794) I. 73, I had been brought up in the country, which..had given me a very bumpkinish air. **1861** *Court Life Naples* 140 Our heroine..had the bumpkinish taste to love every person and thing connected with her home. **1697** VANBRUGH *Relapse* IV. v, A pax of these bumkinly people! **1823** SCOTT *Peveril* (1831) II. 265 A bumpkinly, clod-compelling sort of look. **1872** MISS BRADDON *R. Ainsleigh* I. xiii. 223 A man of the world..to be ousted and cheated by your bumpkinship.

bumpkin, another form of BUMKIN[1] (in a ship).

bum'pologist. *humorous.* [f. BUMP *sb.*[1] 4 + -OLOGIST.] One who is learned in bumpology. So **bumpo'logically** *adv.*

1824 *Blackw. Mag.* XVI. 237 He you recollect is one, not of the Bumpologists, but of the Fistologists. **1837** *Southern Lit. Messenger* III. 107, I once had my head examined—bumpologically—in a regular way. **1848** J. RICHARDSON *Trav. Sahara* I. vi. 166 This afternoon examined phrenologically, *bump*ologically, the heads of many children. **1899** *Westm. Gaz.* 3 Jan. 8/2 It is not only porters who patronise the bumpologist.

bum'pology. *Humorous.* [f. BUMP *sb.*[1] 4, after words in *-ology.*] The (alleged) science of bumps; 'phrenology'. So **bum'posopher** [after *philosopher*], one who is learned in bumps.

1834 GEN. P. THOMPSON *Exerc.* (1842) III. 414 The argument is a specimen of the same defective bumpology. **1841** *Englishman's Mag.* 1 Feb. 20 The general principles of bumpology. **1886** *Pall Mall G.* 23 Aug. 4/2 Phrenology, viewed as bumpology, has ceased to occupy the minds of the scientific. **1836** *Blackw. Mag.* XL. 33 The most redoubtable bumposopher that ever discoursed.

†**bumpsy,** *a. Obs.* exc. *dial.* Also bumsie. [? f. BUMP *sb.*[1] or *vb.*[1]] Tipsy, intoxicated.

1611 TARLETON *Jests* (1844) 8, I being a carousing, drunk so long to the watermen that one of them was bumpsie. **1630** J. TAYLOR (Water P.) *Epigr. Wks.* II. 264/2 Strait staggers by a Porter or a Carman, As bumsie as a fox'd flapdragon German.

bumptious ('bʌmpʃəs), *a.* [A humorous formation, suggested perh. by BUMP *sb.*[1] or *v.*[1], and words in *-tious*, like *fractious*. (Not in Craig 1847, nor in any earlier Dict.)] Offensively self-conceited; self-assertive. (*colloq.* and *undignified.*)

1803 MAD. D'ARBLAY *Diary & Lett.* VI. 324 No my dearest Padre, bumptious! no I deny the charge in toto. **1821** CLARE *Vill. Minstr.* I. 36 The bumptious serjeant struts before his men..And look as big as if King George himsen. **1847–78** HALLIWELL, *Bumptious*, proud, arrogant. *Var. dial.* **1857** C. MAXWELL *Lett.* in *Life* x. (1882) 295 Buckle's History of Civilisation—a bumptious book, strong positivism, emancipation from exploded notions, and that style of thing.

Hence **'bumptiously** *adv.*, **'bumptiousness.**

1871 M. COLLINS *Mrq. & Merch.* I. i. 17 That long-legged isosceles triangle that bumptiously bestrides the asses' bridge. **1857** HUGHES *Tom Brown* I. v, Tom, notwithstanding his bumptiousness, felt friends with him at once. **1881** *Macm. Mag.* XLV. 169 The bumptiousness of minor British officialism.

bumpy ('bʌmpɪ), *a.* [f. BUMP *sb.*[1] or *vb.*[1] + -Y[1].]

a. Full of bumps or protuberances; of a road, etc., jolty, uneven; causing bumps or jolts.

1865 E. BURRITT *Walk Land's E.* 239 A wall of brown, brambly, humpy, bumpy heatherland. **1884** C. GURDON in Lillywhite *Crick. Comp.* 49 On a bumpy wicket a dangerous bowler.

b. *Cricket.* Of a ball: that rises abruptly from the pitch; of bowling: using or characterized by 'bumpers' (see BUMPER *sb.*[1] 6 b).

1867 *Australasian* 9 Mar. 300/3 The batsmen seemed afraid to look at him, especially after the first bumpy over. **1871** 'THOMSONBY' *Cricketers in Council* 28 Balls too high to strike the wicket, and too 'bumpy' to be hit down. **1906** *Westm. Gaz.* 8 May 2/1 He delivers a very fast bumpy ball.

c. *Aeronaut.* Full of bumps (see BUMP *sb.*[1] 1 d); uneven because of bumps.

1911 H. R. P. REYNOLDS in A. E. Berriman *Aviation* (1913) 166, I scarcely moved my control lever until I got to Bletchley, where it [the air] began to get rather 'bumpy'. **1918** *Punch* 3 Apr. 222/3 Weather looks dud—you're going to have it bumpy in the morning, if you're on a pup. **1959** *Times* 13 June 9/6 It was a nightmare journey for pilot and navigator alike. Conditions were very bumpy. **1963** V. GIELGUD *Goggle-Box Affair* xxii. 249 He was..suffering from the after-effects of a bumpy flight.

bumsie, var. of BUMPSY, *Obs.*, tipsy.

†**bun** (bʌn), *sb.*[1] *Obs.* exc. *dial.* Forms: 1 **bune**, 4 **bon(e**, 5–6 **bunne**, 6– **bun**; see also BOON *sb.*[2] [OE. *bune*, origin unknown.]

1. A hollow stem, *esp.* of an umbelliferous plant; a kex.

a **1000** *Gloss.* in Wr.-Wülcker 198 *Canna, harundo, calamus*, bune. *c* **1440** *Promp. Parv.* 277 Kyx or bunne or dry weed. **1523** FITZHERB. *Husb.* §70 The..lowe places, and all the holowe bunnes and pypes that grow therin. **1875** *Whitby Gloss.*, *Buns*, or *Bunnons*, the hollow stems of the hog-weed or cow-parsnep.

2. The stalk or stalky part of flax or hemp.

1388 [see BOON *sb.*]. *c* **1400** ARDERNE *Chirurgica* in *MS. Sloane* 56 f. 3 a, *Chanyuot*, bunes. **1601** HOLLAND *Pliny* XIX. i, The spinning of this fine Flax..what shall be done with all the hard refuse, the long buns? **1704** WORLIDGE *Dict. Rust. et Urb.* s.v. *Drying*, The dry Bun or kexe of the Hempe or Flax. **1877** PEACOCK *N.W. Lincoln. Gloss.* (E.D.S.) *Bun*.. The stalk of flax or hemp.

3. *Comb.*, as †**bun-wand**. Obs. Sc. = 1.

1588 A. HUME *Trium. of the Lord*, Thair speirs lyk bun-wands brak. *a* **1605** MONTGOMERIE *Flyting* 276 Some buckled on a bunwand, and some on a been.

bun (bʌn), *sb.*[2] Forms: 4–7 **bunne**, 5 **bonn(e**, 8–9 **bunn**, 5– **bun**. [Etymology doubtful. The mod. provincial Fr. *bugne* is said by Burguy and by Boiste (1840), to be used at Lyons for a sort of fritter; the word is not recorded in OF. with this sense, but *bugne, beugne* (= mod. *bigne*) occurs with the sense of 'swelling produced by a blow'; the dim. *bugnete* is found in OF. with the sense of 'fritter', and *bugnets* given by Cotgr. (1611) as a synonym of *bignets* (now *beignets*), explained by him as 'little round loaves, or lumpes made of fine meale, oyle or butter, and reasons; bunnes, Lenten loaves'. (Cf. Sp. *buñuelo* bun, fritter.) It is conjectured that OF. *bugne*, originally 'swelling' may have had the unrecorded sense of 'puffed loaf' (= *bugnet*), and may have been adopted into English as *bun*. But the existence of this sense in OF. is at present hypothetical, and it is questionable whether such a derivation would account for the form of the Eng. word.]

1. a. A sort of cake: the use differs greatly in different localities, but the word generally denotes in England a sweet cake (usually round) not too large to be held in the hand while being eaten. In Scotland it usually means a very rich description of cake, the substance of which is almost entirely composed of fruit and spice; the richest kind of currant bread. In some places, as in the north of Ireland, it means a round loaf of ordinary bread. In the earliest examples the meaning is doubtful, the context merely indicating some kind of loaf or cake. (See CROSS-BUN.) Slang phrases: ***to take the bun***, to take the cake (see CAKE *sb.* 7); ***a bun in the oven***, a child conceived; ***to do one's bun*** (N.Z. slang), to lose one's temper.

1371 *Assisa Panis* in Riley *Munim. Gildhall* III. 423 Cum uno pane albo, vocato 'bunne', de obolo. *c* **1440** *Promp. Parv.* 55 Bunne, brede, *placenta*. *c* **1460** J. RUSSELL *Bk. Nurture* in *Babees Bk.* (1868) 133, viij loves or bonnes. **1506** *Churchw. Acc. St. Mary hill, Lond.* (1797) 104 Two dozen de white Bunnys for pore pepyll. **1572** J. JONES *Bathes Buckstone* 9b, Simnels, Cracknels, and Buns. **1630** J. TAYLOR (Water P.) *Jacke-a-L.* Wks. I. 118/1 The light puft vp foure-corner'd Bun. *a* **1640** J. DAY *Peregr. Schol.* (1881) 44 Give em such a buttered bun to breakfast. **1714** GRAY *Sheph. Week* v. 96 Sweeter.. Than.. Bunns and Sugar to the Damsel's Tooth. **1783** AINSWORTH *Lat. Dict.* (Morell) II, *Collyra*, a little loaf of bread, a bun, a cracknell. **1825** HONE *Every-day Bk.* I. 403 One-a-penny, two-a-penny, hot-cross-buns! *Ibid.* 405 Hot-cross-buns are.. consecrated loaves, bestowed in the church as alms, and to those who.. could not receive the host,.. made from the dough from whence the host itself is taken. **1845** HOOD *Numb. One* viii, As brown as any bun. **1867** JEAN INGELOW *Gladys* 135 The round plump buns they gave me.

1887 in *Amer. Speech* (1950) XXV. 31/1 But 'the pale and yellow babe of her white sister' takes the bun. **1896** *Dialect Notes* I. 414 'That takes the bun', that's very good... Also *yanks the bun*. **1901** KIPLING *Kim* xii. 315 You take the bally bun, by Jove! It was splendid. **1934** L. VAN DER POST *In a Province* I. xiii. 140, I've seen many dressed-up niggers, but that one takes the bun. **1944** *Korero* II. no. xix. 24 The most important of Army slang expressions, however, has been 'doing the scone' with its variant 'doing the bun', used for losing one's temper. **1949** 'THE SARGE' *Excuse my Feet* xii. 128 'O.K.! O.K.! don't do your bun,' he answered. **1951** N. MONSARRAT *Cruel Sea* II. vi. 105, 'I bet you left a bun in the oven, both of you,' said Bennett thickly... Lockhart explained.. the reference to pregnancy. **1958** A. SILLITOE *Sat. Night & Sun. Morning* v. 69 Brenda on the tub, up the stick, with a bun in the oven. **1960** B. CRUMP *Good Keen Man* 76 Jock did his bun properly, 'So my money's not good enough, eh mate?' he snarled at the driver.

b. *transf.* Hair coiled at the back of the head in a shape suggesting a bun. Also *attrib.*

1894 *Daily News* 26 May 6/4 The fashionable ladies to be seen in the Park with their bun-chignons. **1894** *Cassell's Fam. Mag.* Dec. 73/1 The days of the 'bun' coiffures are over. **1921** *Chambers's Jrnl.* Dec. 782/1 His chief glory was, however, his head, the hair of which was dressed in a large 'bun'. **1929** *Church Times* 19 Apr. 400/3 Victorian fashion, with hats perched on the head, permitted a free view of chignon, 'bun', or curls.

c. In full *bun hat*. A bowler hat. *N.Z. slang.*

1941 BAKER *N.Z. Slang* vi. 52 A bowler hat has become a *bun* in colloquial speech. **1950** *Landfall* IV. 21 He was thin .. and was wearing an old bun hat.

2. *Comb.*, as ***bun-and-milk*** attrib., †***bun-bread, -house, -pan, -seller, -shop***; **bun-face**, a face resembling a bun; hence **bun-faced** *a.* (also *fig.*); **bun-fight**, a jocular expression for a tea-party (cf. *tea-fight*); **bun foot**, of furniture (see quot. 1952); **bun-loaf** (Lanc. and Yorks.), rich currant-bread; **bun-penny** [sense 1 b], a penny showing the head of Queen Victoria with her hair worn in a bun; **bun-struggle, -worry** = *bun-fight*.

1906 B'NESS VON HUTTEN *What became of Pam* I. v, The bun-and-milk establishments. **1494** *Will of Hagis* (Somerset Ho.) In pane vocato Bun-brede. **1913** R. BROOKE *Let.* 1 Dec. (1968) 546 Fijians swinging along half naked with bun-faces. **1927** W. DEEPING *Kitty* xx. 254 A local decorator, a little bun-faced man with bright eyes. **1966** *Listener* 2 June 806/3 The novelist-farceur is a serious man; and the bun-faced academic is a frivolous one. **1928** R. CAMPBELL *Wayzgoose* 7 It [the wayzgoose] combines the functions of a bun-fight, an Eisteddfod and an Olympic contest. **1904** P. MACQUOID *Hist. Eng. Furniture* IV. 115 The solid back is a modern addition, as are the bun feet on which the buffet stands. **1952** J. GLOAG *Dict. Furniture* 154 *Bun foot*, a foot in the form of a bun-like, flattened sphere, used on chairs, tables, [etc.].. during the latter part of the 17th century. *a* **1845** SYD. SMITH *Wks.* (1859) I. 329/1 Let us seize a little grammar boy.. throw over him a delicate puff-paste, and bake him in a bun-pan. **1958** S. HYLAND *Who goes Hang!* xxxix. 187 The Victorian 'bun-penny' was first minted in the year 1860. **1653** URQUHART *Rabelais* I. xxv, The Bunsellers or Cake-bakers were in nothing inclinable to their request. **1889** *Dramatic Notes 1888* 145 An innocent flirtation in a bun-shop. **1903** *Daily Chron.* 25 May 3/3 Bun-shop waitress. **1889** BARRÈRE & LELAND *Dict. Slang*, *Bun-struggle* or *worry* (army), a tea meeting; an entertainment [for] soldiers in a garrison. **1899** R. WHITEING *No. 5 John St.* vi. 53 She wants yer to show up at a sort o' bun-struggle in 'er room.. kind of a tea-fight. **1911** W. DE MORGAN *Likely Story* 224 Madeline.. had been going to a Bun-worry.

bun, *sb.*^{3} *Sc.* and *north. dial.* Also 6 (*Sc.* **bwn**), **bunn**. [Derivation unknown: the Gael. *bun*, 'stump, root', has been compared.] The tail of a hare; in Sc. also *transf.* of human beings. (Cf. *tail*.) See also BUNT *sb.*^{4}

c **1538** LYNDESAY *Supplic. anent Tailles* 56, I lauch best to se ane Nwn, Gar beir hir taill abone hir bwn. *a* **1578** *Gude & Godly Ballates* 'Hay trix' (1868) 179 The seily Nunnis Keist up their bunnis. **1789** DAVIDSON *Seasons* 27 (JAM.) Poor maukin.. scudding cocks Her bun. **1805** A. SCOTT *Poems* 50 (JAM.) We British frogs.. bathe our buns amang the stanks. **1847–78** HALLIW., *Bun*, the tail of a hare. *North.*

bun (bʌn), *sb.*^{4} [Etymology unknown: connexion with the prec. is not very likely. Cf. BUNNY.] A name given sportively **a.** to the squirrel, **b.** to the rabbit (*dial.*). **c.** Also used as a term of endearment.

1587 CHURCHYARD *Worth. Wales* (1876) 57 Her Squirrell lept away.. she sought to stay The little pretie Bun. *c* **1614** DRAYTON *Moon Calf* Wks. (1748) 178 She was wont to call him.. her pretty bun. **1847–78** HALLIW., *Bun*, a rabbit. *Var. dial.* **1857** EMERSON *Poems* 155 The mountain and the squirrel Had a quarrel; And the former called the latter 'Little Prig'; Bun replied, 'You are doubtless very big'.

bun, *sb.*^{5} *slang.* [Origin unknown.] A drunken condition, esp. in ***to get, have, tie a bun on***: to become drunk.

1901 'H. MCHUGH' *John Henry* i. 16 You've got another bun on! How dare you trail into my flat with your tide high enough to float a battleship? **1914** W. L. GEORGE *Making of Englishman* II. v. 306 You've had four now, and I'm not stayin' here for you to get a bun on. **1954** J. VAN DRUTEN *I am a Camera* I. ii, We'll celebrate tonight, if you do. And if you don't, well, then we'll tie a bun on anyway, just to forget it all.

bun, obs. dial. f. *buen*, *ben*, pl. pres. ind., and inf. of BE *v.*

1415 *E.E. Wills* (1882) 20 Halfe to the pores nedy folk that bun yn Marcle paryssh. *Ibid.* 24 The londe rentes that ȝe bun feoffed In.

bun, obs. f. BOON *sb.*^{1}; obs. f. BOUND *ppl. a.*^{1,2}.

buna, Buna ('bjuːnə). [a. G. *Buna*, f. BU(TADIENE + NA(TRIUM.] A synthetic rubber first developed in Germany, made by the polymerization of butadiene.

1936 *Chem. Abstr.* XXX. 7384 The new German synthetic (Buna) rubber. **1938** *Encycl. Brit. Bk. of Yr. 1938* 282/2 Buna, or synthetic rubber,.. was awarded the Grand Prix at the Paris Exhibition for 1937. **1940** GRAVES & HODGE *Long Week-end* xxiii. 394 German Buna car-tyres were said to last half as long again. **1943** H. M. LANGTON in R. S. Morrell *Synthetic Resins* (ed. 2) i. 40 Buna 85 is a pure butadiene polymer, Buna S a mixed polymer of butadiene and styrene.

Bunbury ('bʌnbərɪ). The name of an imaginary person used as a fictitious excuse for visiting a place or avoiding obligations (see quot. 1899). Hence used allusively in various formations (see quots.).

1899 WILDE *Importance of being Earnest* I. 14, I have Bunburyed all over Shropshire on two separate occasions. *Ibid.* 16, I have invented an invaluable permanent invalid called Bunbury, in order that I may be able to go down into the country whenever I choose. *Ibid.* 17 Now that I know you to be a confirmed Bunburyist I naturally want to talk to you about Bunburying. **1959** *Listener* 12 Feb. 300/3 He may even be able to kill the faint hope in many hearts that the former has merely gone Bunburying. **1960** *Times* 27 Apr. 10/1 The perils of Bunburying—to use the classical term for the creation of a spurious alibi—increase in proportion to the complexity of the story told. **1965** P. MOYES *Johnny under Ground* ix. 117 I've evolved this rather attractive *alter ego*—Mr. Reginald Derbyshire-Bentinck. Quite Bunburyish, in his own little way. **1969** *Listener* 5 June 794/3 For he who lives more lives than one More deaths than one must die... At least the words are an apt motto for a Bunburyist.

bunce (bʌns). *slang.* [Of unknown origin: it has been plausibly conjectured to be a corruption of *bonus*. On the other hand, the modern variant *bunts* is treated as a plural of BUNT (q.v.), but the latter may be an erroneous form.] Money; gains; extra profit or gain, bonus; something to the good.

1719 D'URFEY *Pills* 278 If Cards came no better.. Oh! oh! I shall lose all my *Buns*. **1812** J. H. VAUX *Flash Dict.*, *Bunce*, money. **1851** [see BUNT *sb.*^{7}]. **1865** *Morning Star* 27 Jan. [Witness said] That there were 100 bags of rice.. removed after the fire.. and that they were 'bunce'. [Explained as 'overs for the firm'.] **1879** JAMIESON, *Bunce.* An exclamation used by boys at the High School of Edinburgh. When one finds anything, he who cries *Bunce!* has a claim to the half of it. *Stick up for your bunce*, 'stand to it, claim your dividend'. **1880** *Antrim & Down Gloss.* (E.D.S.) *Bunce*, a consideration in the way of commission given to persons who bring together buyer and seller at a flax market. Perhaps a corruption of bonus. **1962** *Guardian* 19 Nov. 7/5 You make your 'bunce' (big profit) in the summer. **1968** C. DRUMMOND *Death & Leaping Ladies* viii. 194 They take the place for a fee and pocket any bunce.

bunch (bʌnʃ), *sb.*^{1} Forms: 5 bonche, 5–6 bunche, bounche, 6–7 bounch, (7 bunsh), 6– bunch. [Of uncertain origin; prob. onomatopœic; cf. the synonymous BULCH, also *hunch*, *lunch* (dial.).

As to the relation between BUNCH *sb.*^{1}, *v.*^{2}, and BUNCH *sb.*^{2}, *v.*^{1}, cf. BUMP. See also BOUCHE *sb.*^{2}; possibly the *bouch(e* of the *Cursor M.* should be read *bonch(e*, and identified with the present word.]

1. a. A protuberance, *esp.* on the body of an animal; a hump on the back (of a human being, a camel, etc.); a goitre; a swelling, tumour.

c **1325** *Body & Soul* in *Map's Poems* (1841) 344 Summe were ragged and tayled Mid brode bunches on heore bak. **1398** TREVISA *Barth. De P.R.* XVIII. xix. (1495) 778 A camell of Arabia hathe two bonches in the backe. **1543** TRAHERON *Vigo's Chirurg.* I. x. 9 The gibbosyte or bounch of the liver. **1598** GERARD *Herbal* I. xl. 60 The leauen made of Wheate.. openeth all swellings, bunches, tumors and felons. **1688** R. HOLME *Armoury* II. 86/1 Bunch, or bunched eminencies. are knots in sprouts or shoots above others in the.. Lance. **1728** MORGAN *Algiers* I. iv. 100 The rider sits behind the Bunch or Hump. **1816** KEITH *Phys. Bot.* II. 378 Bunches.. on the branches of the Birch-tree.. known.. by the name of witches' knots. **1826** F. COOPER *Mohicans* (1829) I. i. 18. **1874** *Rep. Vermont Board Agric.* II. 428 Their bite is poisonous to a certain extent, as bunches can be felt around their bites.

†**b.** In *plur.* A disease of horses. ? *Obs.*

1706 PHILLIPS, *Bunches*, Knobs, Warts and Wens, are Diseases in Horses. **1715** in KERSEY. **1721–90** in BAILEY. **1753** CHAMBERS *Cycl. Supp.*, *Bunches*, in horses called also knobs, warts, and wens, are diseases arising from foul meat, bruises, hard labour, or the like; whereby the blood becoming putrefied and foul, occasions such excrescences. **1775** in ASH.

†**c.** 'The horn of a young stag.' *Obs.*

1710 BLOME *Gentl. Recreat.* 79 [referred to by Halliwell].

d. See quot.

1884 *Pall Mall G.* 17 May 4 A cigar consists of three parts, the wrapper, the bunch, and the filler.

†**2. a.** A bundle (of straw). *Obs.* Also a bundle of reeds, or teasels, containing a definite quantity. *dial.*

c **1450** HENRYSON *Test. Cres.*, For thy bed tak now a bunche of stro. **1863** MORTON *Cycl. Agric.* (E.D.S.), *Bunch* (*Camb.*), of oziers, a bundle 45 inches round at the band; of reeds, a bundle 28 inches round, formerly an ell. (*Ess.*) of teazles, 25 heads, otherwise a glean. (*Glouc.*), of teazles, 20; a glen; of king's teazles, 10. (*Yks.*, *N.R.*), of teazles, 10.

b. A certain quantity fastened together for sale, as a bundle of flax.

a **1877** KNIGHT *Dict. Mech.*, *Bunch*.. (Flax-manufacture), three bundles, or 180,000 yards, of linen yarn. **1882** P. SHARP *Flax, Tow & Jute* 145 The bunch generally weighs about 40 lbs., the number of hanks depending on the size of the yarn.

3. A collection or cluster of things of the same kind, either growing together (as a bunch of grapes), or fastened closely together in any way (as a bunch of flowers, a bunch of keys); also a portion of a dress gathered together in irregular folds.

1570 LEVINS *Manip.* 188 A bunche of flowers, *floretum*. **1590** SPENSER *F.Q.* I. ii. xi. On his craven crest A bounch of heares discolourd diversly. **1597** SHAKS. *2 Hen. IV*, I. ii. 44 Bunches of Keyes at their girdles. **1610** —— *Temp.* IV. 112 Vines, with clustring bunches growing. **1719** DE FOE *Crusoe* (1840) I. xiv. 244, I gave him.. a bunch of raisins. **1821** BYRON in Moore *Life* (1838) 490 The old woman.. brought me two bunches of violets. **1842** TENNYSON *Day-Dr.* 64 Grapes with bunches red as blood. **1873** SIR J. HERSCHEL *Pop. Lect. Sc.* III. §32. 119 That comet.. was a mere bunch of vapours.

4. *fig.* A collection, 'lot'. Also, a company or group of persons.

1622 JACKSON *Judah* 76 See what persons God hath picked out of all the bunch of the Patriarches, Prophets, Judges, and Kings. **1633** SANDERSON *Serm.* II. 39 Though.. he do but only name it [charity] in the bunch among other duties. **1687** W. SHERWIN in *Hist. Magd. Coll.* (Oxf. Hist. Soc.) 79 As very a rascal as any in the Bunch. *a* **1784** JOHNSON in *Boswell* (1816) IV. 151, I am glad the Ministry is removed. Such a bunch of imbecility never disgraced a country. **1832** *Athenæum* No. 243. 355 Two friars are bargaining for a bunch of cherubs. **1840** C. F. HOFFMAN *Greyslaer* I. v. 92 You'll find them pretty much here and there, in bunches, helping one another. *a* **1888** *Mod.* She's the best of the bunch. **1893** W. S. GILBERT *Utopia* I. 11 Because we are, By furlongs far The best of all the bunch. **1909** G. B. SHAW *Lett. to Granville Barker* (1956) 156 He will be the best of the bunch, like all new converts. **1936** D. POWELL *Turn, Magic Wheel* I. 37 He liked knowing the 'Greenwich Village Bunch'.

5. *spec.* †**a.** A pack of cards (*obs.*) **b.** A flock of waterfowl. **c.** (*U.S.*) A herd of cattle.

1563 FOXE in *Latimer's Serm. & Rem.* (1845) Introd. 12 The best coat card.. in the bunch. **1608** MIDDLETON *Trick to Catch*, *&c.* II. i, The best card in all the bunch. **1612** DRAYTON *Poly-olb.* xxv. (1748) 366 The lesser dibbling teale In bunches. **1835** E. JESSE *Glean. Nat. Hist.* Ser. III. 146 They [ducks] come in what are called bunches.. sometimes .. 150 ducks in a bunch. **1884** *Harper's Mag.* July 294/2 The expence of herding a 'bunch' of cattle.

d. *bunch of fives*: see FIVE *sb.* 3 b.

6. *Mining.* A small isolated body of ore, etc.

1815 W. PHILLIPS *Outl. Min. & Geol.* (1818) 160 The ores both of copper and tin principally occur in quantities which .. occupy.. but a small comparative portion of the vein, and are.. termed bunches. **1865** I. T. F. TURNER *Slate Quarries* 20 It took seven years to reach a good bunch of slate.

7. *Comb.*, as †**bunch-back**, a back with a 'bunch' or hump; †**bunch-backed** *a.*, hump-backed; **bunch-bean** *U.S.*, a dwarf kidney-bean, also called *bush-bean*; **bunch-berry**, the dwarf cornel, *Cornus canadensis*, or its fruit; **bunch flower**, a liliaceous plant of N. America, *Melanthium virginicum*; **bunch-grass**, *Festuca scabrella*, of N. America; any of various grasses, chiefly of western North America, characterized by growing in clumps; **bunch greens**, greens sold by the bunch; **bunch-knot**, a knot joining broken ends of yarn; **bunch-oyster**, a wild oyster which grows in clusters; **bunch pink**, a name for the sweet-william; **bunch-word** (*rare*), a word formed by agglutination.

1618 HOLYDAY *Juvenal* 191 Virginia would exchange her grace Of shape for Rutila's *bunch-back. **1677** W. CHARLETON *Exercit. de diff. et nom. Animal.* (ed. 2) 8 The little Scythian Ox with a bunch-back. **1519** HORMAN *Vulg.* 31 No man shulde rebuke and scorne a blereyied man or gogylyed.. or blabberlypped, or *bounchebacked. **1650** FULLER *Pisgah* IV. vi. 115 Who.. affirme all Jews to be crooked, or bunch-backed. **1787** WASHINGTON *Diaries* (1925) III. 212 The *bunch Nomeny bean. **1805** R. PARKINSON *Tour in Amer.* 341 The bunch-bean.. produces abundantly. **1860** DARLINGTON *Amer. Weeds* 107 The.. Dwarf or Bunch Bean. **1845** S. JUDD *Margaret* I. xiv. 106 She got boxberry flowers and fruit, *bunch-berry and star-of-Bethlehem flowers. **1969** *Islander* (Victoria, B.C.) 31 Aug. 11/1 The bunch-berries, I thought, were loveliest of all. **1818** A. EATON *Man. Bot.* (ed. 2) 316 *Melanthium racemosum* *bunch flower. **1899** T. W. SANDERS *Encycl. Gardening* (ed. 3), *Melanthium* (American Bunch-flower). **1837** W. IRVING *Capt. Bonneville* I. xii. 203 The upland *bunch grass.. retained its nutritious properties.. in the

autumn. **1866** *Intell. Observ.* No. 53. 324 Thickly clothed with bunch-grass. **1878** J. H. BEADLE *Western Wilds* viii. 125 One may ride all day through good bunch-grass pasture. **1959** MCLINTOCK *Descr. Atlas N.Z.* 24 Tussock (bunch grass) grasslands, generally with species of *Poa* and *Festuca* dominant. **1884** W. S. B. MCLAREN *Spinning* xi. 238 When one end of yarn breaks or runs out, the other must be broken too, and what is called a *bunch-knot tied. **1881** E. INGERSOLL *Oyster Industry* 242 **Bunch oysters*, those growing in clusters (South). **1857** GRAY *Botany* 54 Sweet William or *Bunch Pink. **1877** *Rep. Vermont Board Agric.* IV. 99 Bunch pinks and candytufts coming from self-sown seeds. **1725** DUDLEY in *Phil. Trans.* XXXIII. 258 The *Bunch or humpback Whale. **1862** D. WILSON *Pre-hist. Man* II. xix. 136 Like the *bunch-words, as they have been called, of the American languages, compounded of a number of parts.

†**bunch**, *sb.*^{2} *Obs.* [f. BUNCH *v.*^{1}] A punch, a thump.

1642 ROGERS *Naaman* 193 The Angell gave him [Peter] a bunch on the to-side.

†**bunch** (bʌnʃ), *v.*^{1} *Obs.* exc. *dial.* Forms: 4–5 bonch, 5 bunche, 5–6 bounch(e, 5– bunch. [Etymology obscure: perh. onomatopœic; cf. BOUNCE *v.* and PUNCH *v.*, both which are closely parallel in sense to this word. The Du. *bonken* to beat, thrash, has been compared, but relationship between it and the Eng. word is very doubtful.]

a. *trans.* To strike, thump; to bruise flax, etc., by beating it.

1362 LANGL. *P. Pl.* A. Prol. 71 He bonchede [*v.r.* bunched] hem with his Breuet. *c* **1440** *Promp. Parv.* 55 Bunchon', *tundo.* **1496** *Dives & Paup.* (W. de W.) I. iii. 34/2 Men..bounche or knocke theyr brestis. **1577** HARRISON *England* I. II. vi. (1877) 147 A fall..might peradventure bunch or batter it. **1601** CORNWALLYES *Seneca* (1631) 74, I will reele, and bunch hempe. **1611** CHARENTE *Let. Customs Mauritania* 49 These golden Apples, especially the biggest, bunched in several places with the blows of Musket bullets. **1840** SPURDENS *Suppl. Voc. E. Anglia* (E.D.S.) *Bunch*, to beat hemp. **1877** PEACOCK *N.W. Lincoln. Gloss.* (E.D.S.) Cauves bunch their mother's bags as they can stan'.

b. To kick. (Yorksh., Lincolnsh., etc.)

1647 *Depos. York Cast.* 10 in Peacock *N.W. Lincoln. Gloss.* (E.D.S.) He actually saw him bunching an old man. **1665** R. SELLAR in *Abstr. Quakers' Sufferings* iii. (1738) 176 They bunched me with their Feet that I fell backwards into a Tub. **1825** *Gentl. Mag.* XCI. I. 397. **1864** ATKINSON *Whitby Gloss.*, He bunch'd me.

Hence **bunchclot**, a farmer; a clodhopper.

1877 *Holderness Gloss.* (E.D.S.).

bunch (bʌnʃ), *v.*^{2} [f. BUNCH *sb.*^{1}]

†**1.** *intr.* **a.** To bulge (*out*), protrude, stick out. **b.** To form bunches or clusters. *Obs.*

1398 TREVISA *Barth. De P.R.* XVIII. xxi. (1495) 780 Camelion..his rydgebonys bonchyth vpwarde as it were a fysshe. **1572** BOSSEWELL *Armorie* II. 52b, Hys [the Cameleon's]..ridge bones bounche upward. **1601** HOLLAND *Pliny* XVI. xxxiv, Big berries growing thick together, and bunching round in manner of grapes. **1603** —— *Plutarch's Mor.* 1021 Of the round line that part which is..without doth bumpe and bunch. **1622** MABBE tr. *Aleman's Guzman d'Alf.* II. 342 Which made the wheales to bunch out vpon their backs. **1638** A. READ *Treat. Chirurg.* xxiii. 167 If the eyes of the patient..bunch out. **1728** WOODWARD *Fossils* (R.) Bunching out into a large round knob. **1806–7** J. BERESFORD *Miseries Hum. Life* (1826) III. No. 10 Winding up a top badly grooved, so that the string bunches down over the peg.

c. To crowd together in a body. Also with *up*.

1873 BEADLE *Undevel. West* 60 Buffalo grass and gama grass..show a tendency to bunch together, leaving large portions of the surface bare. **1887** F. FRANCIS JR. *Saddle & Mocassin* vii. 124 They had got scared, and had bunched up like a bevy of quail. **1909** *Westm. Gaz.* 23 Dec. 12/3 The result..is to force the opposing defences back to their own goal and so bunch. **1924** GALSWORTHY *White Monkey* I. ii, The really big people don't talk—and don't bunch—they paddle their own canoes in what seem backwaters. **1959** I. & P. OPIE *Lore & Lang. Schoolch.* xii. 269 Guisers usually 'bunch up in groups of three or four'.

d. *Mining.* Of a vein or lode of ore: to form an irregular mass. Cf. BUNCH *sb.*^{1} 6.

1883 BARING-GOULD *J. Herring* III. xlviii. 102 The vein 'bunched', and the bunch of nearly pure metal was before him. **1889** *Temple Bar* LXXXV. 26 The lode ran under Orleigh gardens and promised freely to 'bunch' under the mansion.

2. a. *trans.* To make into a bunch; to gather (a dress) into folds; to group (animals) (*U.S.*). Also *absol.* (see quot. 1887). Also with *up*.

1828 WEBSTER, *Bunch*, v.t., to form or tie in a bunch or bunches. **1869** A. K. MCCLURE *Rocky Mountains* 99 The horses..have been 'bunched' at either end of the hostile country. **1873** 'MARK TWAIN' & WARNER *Gilded Age* (1903) i. 16 The speaker bunched his thick lips together like the stem end of a tomato. **1881** *Chicago Times* 16 Apr., When trees are bunched together..they are scrubs. **1883** *Chamb. Jrnl.* 690 Her hair rudely bunched into an uncomely heap. **1883** *Cassell's Family Mag.* Aug. 561 Gathering and 'bunching' flowers. **1884** *Bazaar* 22 Dec. 664/2 An over-dress of chintz, much bunched up on hips and at back. **1885** *Milnor* (*Dak.*) *Free Press* 18 Aug. 3/5 They [hogs] stand bunched around at the root of the tree. **1887** *Overland Monthly* (Farmer), Two men often bunch on the march, *i.e.* unite their herds for convenience in driving. **1893** G. B. SHAW *Let.* 27 Apr. (1965) 392 The way you..bunch up your back.

b. In technical use (see quots.). In *Baseball*, to secure (hits) in close succession. Chiefly *U.S.*

1883 *Chicago Tribune* 3 July 6/5 Detroit played a wretched muffing game today and failed to bunch hits. **1905** *Terms Forestry & Logging* 32 To *bunch load*, to encircle several logs with a chain and load them at once, by steam or horse-power. To *bunch logs*, to collect logs in one place for loading. **1909** WEBSTER s.v., To bunch..shots (in target practice).

3. To present (a woman) with a bunch of flowers. Also *transf.*

1901 *Daily Chron.* 7 Dec. 8/3 The King's gift of a bouquet to Miss Brodrick upon her wedding morning, it is hoped will revive the charming old fashion of 'bunching' young beauties, a very modish practice, that only languished a few years ago. **1959** N. MARSH *Singing in Shrouds* iv. 59 Captain Bannerman felt that in a way he would be bunching Mrs. Dillington-Blick by presenting her with a No. I Personality. **1961** G. EGMONT *Art of Egmontese* v. 99 Send flowers next day with a brief thank-you note. The older the hostess, the more she will like being 'bunched'.

bunched (bʌnʃt), *ppl. a.* [f. BUNCH *sb.*^{1} and *v.*^{2} + -ED.] †**a.** Having or forming a protuberance; covered with swellings; humped; bulging, protuberant. ***bunched line***, use by Guillim for: A waved line. *Obs.* **b.** ***bunched up, out***: (of a dress) gathered into a bunch; also of other things than a dress. †**c. buncht-back** *adj.* = *bunch-backed. Obs.*

1519 HORMAN *Vulg.* 31 His nase was bounchyd aboue, and flat downeward. **1578** BANISTER *Hist. Man* I. 20 The vse of the swelled or bounched parte of the first Vertebre. **1603** HOLLAND *Plutarch's Mor.* 34 Those disciples who counterfeited to be..buncht backe like their master Plato. **1610** GUILLIM *Heraldry* II. iii. (1660) 54 A Bunched Line is that which is carried with round reflections or bowings up and down. **1791** COWPER *Odyss.* XIX. 307 His back was bunch'd. **1883** *Harper's Mag.* Mar. 532/1 Children with bunched-out gowns. **1917** D. H. LAWRENCE *Look! We have come Through!* 62 A bunched-up deer, its four little feet Clustered dead. **1934** *Burlington Mag.* Mar. 128/1 A wild movement of bunched-up draperies. **1959** D. DAVIE *Forests of Lithuania* iv. 42 And a knot Of bunched-up mosses.

d. *Bot.* Having convex protuberances.

1776 J. LEE *Introd. Bot.* (ed. 3) 378 *Fascicularis*, bunched. **1900** B. D. JACKSON *Gloss. Bot. Terms*, *Bunched*, gibbous.

e. Clustered, gathered into a bunch or bunches. Cf. BUNCH *v.*^{2} 2.

1904 R. J. FARRER *Garden Asia* 42 The ground is thick with the bunched stars of a wee blue gentian. **1964** *Economist* 14 Nov. 737/2 'Bunched gains'—heavy realisations coming together in one year that would jack up the applicable rate of tax.

buncher ('bʌntʃə(r)). [f. BUNCH *sb.*^{1} or *v.*^{2} + -ER^{1}.]

1. One who or that which bunches; *spec.* a machine for forming bunches or collecting things in bunches.

1881 *Instr. Census Clerks* (1885) 74 Straw Plait Buncher. **1909** WEBSTER s.v., An asparagus buncher. **1921** *Dict. Occup. Terms* (1927) §399 *Buncher, yarn buncher*; (i) ties several hanks of yarn into bunches, in readiness for succeeding processes, bleaching, etc.; (ii) [=] crofter. **1930** C. S. JOHNSON *Negro in Amer. Civilization* (1931) v. 64 The lowest median weekly earners were..Tobacco bunchers $1.85. **1939** M. SPRING RICE *Working-Class Wives* vii. 164 She worked as a 'buncher' in flower gardens.

2. A device that modulates a beam of charged particles and causes them to collect together in 'bunches' or groups. Also *attrib.*

1939 R. H. & S. F. VARIAN in *Jrnl. Appl. Physics* X. 324/1 The rhumbatron in which the electrons are given their first modulation of speed is called the 'buncher', and the one into which the bunches 'break' is called the 'catcher'. **1948** J. B. H. KUPER in D. R. Hamilton et al. *Klystrons & Microwave Triodes* i. 11 The velocity of each electron depends on the instant at which it crossed the buncher gap. **1955** *Science* CXXII. 1131/3 The ion beam passes through the buncher, which applies a 24-megacycle ripple of 5 to 7 kev to the beam. **1962** LIVINGSTON & BLEWETT *Particle Accelerators* x. 333 The buncher..is merely a section of accelerator in which the phase velocity is matched to the particle velocity.

'**bunchiness.** [f. BUNCHY *a.* + -NESS.] Quality of being bunchy, protuberance.

1594 CAREW *Huarte's Exam. Wits* iii. (1596) 25 There will remaine..the forehead and the nape with a little bunchinesse. **1611** COTGR., *Gibbosité*, bunchinesse. **1922** JOYCE *Ulysses* 501 Those pannier pockets of the skirt and slightly pegtop effect are devised to suggest bunchiness of hip.

'**bunching,** *vbl. sb.* [f. BUNCH *v.*^{1} and ^{2} + -ING^{1}.] The action of the verbs to BUNCH: †**a.** Thumping, beating (*obs.*). †**b.** Bulging, protuberance (*obs.*). **c.** Making into bunches.

1398 TREVISA *Barth. De P.R.* XII. xi, [The swan] haþ a byl with a maner bonchinge [**1535** bounchynge; **1582** bounching] þat distingueþ þe syȝte fro smel and taste. *c* **1440** *Promp. Parv.* 55 Bunchynge, *tuncio.* **1668** CULPEPPER & COLE *Barthol. Anat.* I. ix. 20 [The stomach] hath two bunchings. *c* **1720** W. GIBSON *Farrier's Guide* I. vi. (1738) 81 The Protuberances or Bunchings of the Cerebellum. **1883** *Cassell's Family Mag.* Aug. 561 Flower-picking, bunching, and selling. **1901** L. M. WATERHOUSE *Conduit Wiring* 51 The system of bunching which, with wood casing, is objectionable from a fire insurance point of view. **1906** DEWAR *Faery Year* 27 Bunching up of the cress for local retail business. **1967** *Economist* 7 Jan. 4/1 The negative attitude of London bus drivers to their work, e.g., bunching, largely stems from their low wages.

d. The action of a buncher (see BUNCHER 2). Also *attrib.*

1939 R. H. & S. F. VARIAN in *Jrnl. Appl. Physics* X. 326/2 A large bunching distance increases the difficulty of getting a large fraction of the beam into the catcher. **1946** *Electronic Engin.* XVIII. 153 Another method..makes use of the klystron bunching principle.

†'**bunching,** *ppl. a. Obs.* [f. BUNCH *v.*^{2} + -ING^{2}.] Protuberant, bulging.

1398 TREVISA *Barth. De P.R.* V. xxvi. (1495) 135 The bones of þe sholdres that ben holowe wythin and bounchynge wythout. **1677** MOXON *Mech. Exerc.* (1703) 11 Your Punch will print a bunching mark. **1668** CULPEPPER & COLE *Barthol. Anat.* I. viii. 17 The bunching part of the Spleen. **1813** W. BEATTIE *Yule Feast* 11 Twa bunching megs.

bunchy ('bʌnʃɪ), *a.* [f. BUNCH *sb.*^{1} + -Y^{1}.]

1. Bulging, protuberant; full of protuberances or swellings; humped.

1398 TREVISA *Barth De P.R.* VII. lxiv. (1495) 280 The nayles ben boystouse and bounche [**1582** bounchye] as they were scabbed. **1543** TRAHERON *Vigo's Chirurg.* I. x. 9 The lyver is hollowe in the inwarde parte..and bounchye wythout. **1562** PHAËR *Æneid.* IX. C civ, An vnshapen bunchy speare [*rudem nodis hastam*]. **1607** TOPSELL *Four-f. Beasts* 76 The fat in their [camels] bunchy back. **1873** BESANT & RICE *Little Girl* II. xx. 185 Augustine, the fat, the bunchy, the smiling. *Mod.* Who is that with the bunchy skirts?

2. a. Like a bunch; having bunches or clusters.

1824 MISS MITFORD *Village* Ser. I. (1863) 213 So as to hang..in a sort of bunchy festoon. **1833** TENNYSON *Poems* 72 Bowers Trellised with bunchy vine. **1852** ROCK *Ch. Fathers* III. I. 111 Those leaf-like bunchy finials..seem all too soft and light to be of stone.

b. *Mining.* (See quots.)

1778 PRYCE *Min. Cornub.* 88 The Ore in this nidus is bunchy and uncertain. **1796** KIRWAN *Elem. Min.* (ed. 2) II. 173 The surface often uneven and bunchy. **1849** J. WEALE *Dict. Terms Archit.* s.v. *Bunch*, A mine that is sometimes rich and at other times poor, is said to be bunchy. **1867** *Ure's Dict. Arts* (ed. 6) 504 s.v. *Bunch*, A lode is said to be bunchy when the metalliferous ore is found in irregular and sparsely distributed masses.

c. ***bunchy top***, a virus disease of plants (esp. bananas) in which the leaves are crowded at the tip of the stem.

1919 *Agric. Gaz. N.S. Wales* XXX. 809, I lately visited the Tweed River district..to investigate the disease known as 'Bunchy Top' in bananas. **1930** *Discovery* June 196/1 Other important virus diseases of plants include, bunchy top of bananas, [etc.]. **1935** *Union S. Afr. Dept. Agric. Sci. Bull.* CXXXIX. 46 (*title*) Further investigations on the bunchy-top disease of tomato. **1951** *New Biol.* XI. 76 Bunchy Top Disease, a virus disease, transmitted by the banana aphid, *Pentalonia nigronervosa*.

bunco ('bʌŋkəʊ), *sb. U.S. slang.* Also **banco, bunko.** [Said to be ad. Sp. *banca*, a card-game similar to monte.] A swindle perpetrated by means of card-sharping or some form of confidence trick. Freq. *attrib.* or as *adj.*; esp. **bunco-steerer**, a swindler; so ***bunco-steering*** vbl. sb. and ppl. a.

1872 *Chicago Tribune* 18 Oct. 8/4 A quintet of bunco thieves were tried by jury. **1875** *Ibid.* 30 Sept. 4/2 The criminal classes..proceeded to introduce the business of 'bunko-steering'. *Ibid.* 1 Oct. 4/3 A 'bunko-steerer' seems to be a subordinate confidence-man. *Ibid.* 8 Dec. 12/3 This marriage was merely a 'confidence' or 'bunko' game on both sides. **1883** *Philada. Times* No. 2892. 2 Tom's method of bunko was the well-known lottery game. *Ibid.*, There is not a smoother-tongued fellow in the great army of bunko-steerers. **1883** *Standard* 1 Dec. 2/4 'Bunko men', and swindlers..pick up a very good living. **1901** S. E. WHITE *Westerners* xiii. 94 Bunco men can clean him out in a gambling joint. **1920** H. CRANE *Let.* 24 Feb. (1965) 33 It's the old bunko stuff about 'working from the bottom up'. **1929** *Atlantic Monthly* Sept. 378/2 I'm glad we got Aggie by a bunco-steering trick. **1963** *Spectator* 5 July 9 The bunco-artists from the lunatic fringe of the Democratic party.

'**bunco,** *v. U.S. slang.* Also **bunko.** [f. prec.] *trans.* To swindle or cheat.

1875 *Chicago Tribune* 6 July 8/1 The fugitive is the same person who bunkoed a stranger out of $75 recently. **1883** *Philada. Times* No. 2892. 2 A Reading banker bunkoed. **1892** *Congress Rec.* Mar. 2651/2 The farmer is always buncoed by the three-card monte, green-goods protection shouter. **1926** J. BLACK *You can't Win* xiii. 174 The way to sell a brass brick is to bunko yourself first into the belief that your brick is solid gold.

buncombe, bunkum (bʌŋkəm). [f. *Buncombe*, name of a county in N. Carolina, U.S. The use of the word originated near the close of the debate on the 'Missouri Question' in the 16th congress, when the member from this district rose to speak, while the house was impatiently calling for the 'Question'. Several members gathered round him, begging him to desist; he persevered, however, for a while, declaring that the people of his district expected it, and that he was bound to *make a speech for Buncombe*. (See Bartlett, *Amer. Dict.*)]

1. *in U.S. use* (see above):

a. In phrases, such as, ***to talk*** or ***speak for*** or ***to Buncombe, to pass*** a measure ***for buncombe*** (i.e. to please or gull a constituency), ***a bid for buncombe*** (i.e. for the favourable notice of the electors), and the like. **b.** Political speaking or action not from conviction, but in order to gain the favour of electors, or make a show of patriotism, or zeal; political clap-trap.

a. **1828** [See CANTLY *adv.*^{2}]. **1857** S. G. GOODRICH *Remin.* I. 101 (Bartlett), Congresses of crows, clamorous as if talking to buncombe. **1857** *N. York Tribune* 2 Mar. (Bartlett) The House of Representatives broke down upon the corruption committee's bill, having first passed it for

buncombe. **1859** *N. York Her.* 12 Mar., The bill was another bid for buncombe. **1863** W. PHILLIPS *Speeches* ix. 234 They sometimes talked for Buncombe.

b. **1850** *Times* 24 Jan. 4/3 Conventions, rights of independence, caucuses, agitation, and whatever else may be implied by the American expression 'bunkum'. **1856** *Sat. Rev.* II. 372/1 Rather meant as a piece of bunkum for his countrymen, than as a serious exposition of policy. **1857** KINGSLEY *Two Y. Ago* xxv, Talk plain truth, and leave bunkum for right honourables who keep their places thereby. **1880** JOHNSON *W. Lloyd Garrison & Times* 245 To take some sort of action that would *seem* to be anti-slavery ..[but] amount to little or nothing—in short, mere buncombe.

2. Empty clap-trap oratory; 'tall talk'; humbug.

1862 *Sat. Rev.* 15 Mar. 299 Did it [the Volunteer movement] signify business or 'bunkum'? **1865** *Pall Mall G.* 8 Sept. 11/2 The philosopher is tempted to talk a good deal of what we may call scientific 'buncombe'. **1884** *Congregationalist* June 456 This appeal to the 'splendid history and the roll of saints' is bunkum, or something worse.

3. *attrib.*

1863 DICEY *Federal St.* II. 317 General Butler's 'bunkum' proclamation. **1864** SALA in *Daily Tel.* 9 Aug. A most amusing deduction of bunkum logic. **1868** *Temple Bar* Dec. 42 A buncombe story relating to his ring.

Hence **buncomize** *v.*, to talk 'bunkum'; **bunkumite**, one who talks 'bunkum'.

1864 *Morning Star* 13 Sept., Dispel the mist raised by the petty breath of journalistic bunkumites. **1871** *Daily News* 15 Mar., He either gammons you [an 'interviewer'] intentionally, buncomises, or is reticent.

‖**bund** (bʌnd), *sb.*[1] *Anglo-Indian.* [Hindustani *band*; of Persian origin.] In India: 'Any artificial embankment, a dam, dyke, or causeway.' In the Anglo-Chinese ports, 'applied specially to the embanked quay along the shore'. (Col. Yule.)

1813 WILLIAMSON *East-Indian Vade Mec.* II. 279 (Y.) The great bund or dyke. **1834** MEDWIN *Angler in Wales* II. xx. 72 The 'bund' is a colossal piece of masonry, consisting of massy walls, the interspace filled up by earth. **1839** THIRLWALL *Greece* VII. 83 To remove the dykes, or bunds, by which the ancient kings of Persia or Assyria had obstructed the navigation. **1865** RAWLINSON *Anc. Mon.* III. i. 267 A bund or dam thrown across it.

Bund, bund (bʊnt), *sb.*[2] [G.; related to BAND *sb.*[2], BIND *v.*] A league, confederacy, or association; *spec.* (*a*) the confederation of German states; (*b*) a Jewish Social Democratic workers' organization in Eastern Europe, founded in 1897; (*c*) *U.S.*, an American pro-Nazi organization founded in 1936. Hence '**Bundist** *sb.*

1850 *Ann. Reg. 1849* 363/2 The Governments of Prussia, Saxony, and Hanover have therefore agreed, according to the 11th Article of the Act of Confederation, to enter into a union (*bund*) that has for its object the mutual protection of its members. *Ibid.* 364/1 The Government is required to join this *bund* called into existence by the danger of the moment. **1851** *Fraser's Mag.* Feb. 144/2 The new 'Bund', with all the motley crew of his fifteen nationalities. **1903** *Forest & Stream* 24 Jan. 78/3 The institution of revolver shooting is regarded likely to create much interest, as many members of the bunds favor this sort of work. **1905** *Westm. Gaz.* 4 July 4/1 After the massacre at Kischineff, after the bloodshed at Homel, the idea of self-defence took root.. and the 'Bund' was organised. **1907** I. ZANGWILL *Ghetto Comedies* 357 Our *Bund* is the soul of the Russian revolution; our self-defence bands are bringing back the days of Judas Maccabæus. *Ibid.* 398 'A Bundist!'.. From the bravest revolutionary party in Russia he could surely cull a recruit or two. **1918** C. G. ROBERTSON *Bismarck* ii. 81 German Liberalism called for the abolition of the Bund and the Diet. **1939** *Life* 27 Nov. 69 German American Bund. **1940** G. MARX *Let.* 12 June (1967) 21 I'm not able to sleep... I see Bund members dropping down my chimney, Commies under my bed. **1947** C. MORGAN *Judge's Story* xiv. 91 Pressure-groups, leagues, bunds, confederations. **1956** F. CASTLE *Violent Hours* (1966) vi. 61 But I don't think he'd dare approach any of the Bundists he once used. *Ibid.* vii. 72 Did you ever do any work on the German-American Bund? **1968** *Guardian* 25 Oct. 8/6 Anti-Zionism of the Left began with the 'Bund', the Russian movement of the 1890s representing Marxist Jews in the revolutionary struggle.

bund (bʌnd), *v.* [f. BUND *sb.*] *trans.* To embank.

1883 F. DAY *Indian Fish* 41 Rivers which can be easily bunded. **1917** R. DOLLAR *Mem.* xiv. 141 The river front had been substantially *bunded*.

So '**bunding** *vbl. sb.*, embanking; embankment.

1939 *Geogr. Jrnl.* XCIII. 136 The more common forms [of soil conservation] include silt pits, contour terracing (or bunding), and contour drains. **1950** E. M. HOUGH *Co-operative Movement in India* (ed. 2) iii. 170 The bunding of fields to prevent erosion.

bund, bunden, -in, obs. forms of BOUND *ppl. a.*[2], and *pa. pple.* of BIND.

‖**bunder** ('bʌndə(r)). *Anglo-Indian.* [Hindustani *bandar*; a Pers. word.]

1. 'A landing-place or quay; a seaport; a harbour; (sometimes a custom-house)' (Col. Yule).

1673 FRYER *Acc. E. India & P.* (1698) 115 (Y.) We.. have Bunders or Docks for our Vessels. **1727** A. HAMILTON *New Acc. E. Ind.* I. xviii. 209 The King granted us a Piece of Ground for a Bunder to repair our Ships and Vessels. **1809** MAR. GRAHAM *Jrnl. Resid. India* 11 (Y.) The new bunder, or pier.

2. *Comb.* **bunder-boat**, 'a boat in use on the Bombay coast for communicating with ships at anchor, and also.. employed.. in going up and down the coast' (Col. Yule).

1825 BP. HEBER *Journ. Upper Prov. India* (1828) II. 172 We crossed over.. in a stout boat called here a bundur boat, I suppose from 'bundur' a harbour. **1845** STOCQUELER *Hand-bk. Brit. India* (1854) 112 Bunder-boats are obtainable at the piers.

bunder, var. BANDAR.

Bundesrat ('bʊndəsraːt). Formerly **-rath**. [G., f. gen. of *bund* BUND *sb.*[2] + *rat(h* council.] A federal council; *spec.* (*a*) the upper house of the German or Austrian parliament; (*b*) the federal council of Switzerland.

1872 *Ann. Reg. 1871* I. 239 This Bill was adopted by the Reichstag; but the *Bundesrath*, or Federal Council, refused to pass it. **1879** *Encycl. Brit.* IX. 62/1 Delegates of the various confederated Governments form the Bundesrath. *Ibid.* 62/2 The emperor.. has power, with consent of the Bundesrath, to declare war in name of the empire. **1887** *Ibid.* XXII. 795/2 The [Swiss] federal council or executive (Bundesrath) consisted of seven members elected by the federal assembly. **1950** *Ann. Reg. 1949* 233 The.. Constitution for the 'Federal Republic of Germany'.. provided for.. two Chambers, the *Bundestag* (or Lower House), elected for 4 years according to a mixed electoral system,.. and the *Bundesrat* (or Upper House), representing the constituent confederate Länder and consisting of members of their Governments appointed by them.

Bundestag ('bʊndəstaːk). [f. as prec. + *-tag*, prob. f. G. *tagen* to meet, sit in conference, f. *tag* (see DAY).] An assembly of representatives of a league, confederacy, etc.; *spec.* (since 1949) the lower house of parliament of the Federal Republic of Germany.

1879 *Encycl. Brit.* X. 468/1 A few men-of-war.. were sold, the German bundestag (federal council) not being in sympathy with the aspirations of the nation. **1950** [see prec.].

'**bunding** ('bʌndɪŋ), *sb. Mining.* Also 7-8 **bunning**. 'A staging of boards on *stulls* or *stemples*, to carry *deads*.' Raymond *Mining Gloss.* Hence **bunding** *v.*, to furnish with a bunding.

1653 MANLOVE *Lead-Mines* (E.D.S.) 257 Bunnings, Polings, Stemples. **1747** HOOSON *Miner's Dict.* Divb, Shafts are likewise Bunding'd over when the Miner has done with them. *Ibid.* Tiv, The use of these are to Climbe by, or for making Bundings. **1795** MILNES in *Phil. Trans.* LXXXVI. 359 Expecting that the whole mass of bunnings above them, which contains many hundred tons weight of rubbish, had given way.

bundle ('bʌnd(ə)l), *sb.* Forms: 4-7 **bundel**, 5 **bondel(l**, 5-6 **bundelle, boundell**, (6 **byndle**), 6-7 **bundell**, 7- **bundle**. [Proximate derivation obscure; ultimately f. ****bund-*** pa. pple. stem of OTeut. **bind-an* to BIND; the precise form of the suffix is uncertain. Cf. MDu. *bondel* (mod. *bundel*), mod.G. *bündel*; also OHG. *gibuntilî, -lîn* neut., MHG. *gebündel*, and OE. *byndele* wk. fem. 'act of binding' (only in *Laws of Ælfred* xxxv.); but these forms are not exactly parallel. The OE. *byndele*, or the OE. equivalent of any of the continental words quoted, would have yielded mod.Eng. **bindle*, so that the form of the existing word seems to point to adoption from Du. or LG., or else to analogy with the pple. *bund*, 'bound'.]

†**1.** That which binds; a bandage. *Obs. rare.*

1382 WYCLIF *Jer.* ii. 32 Whether forȝete shal.. the womman spouse of hir brest bundel [**1388** brest girdil, COVERD. stomacher; Vulg. *fasciae pectoralis*]?

2. a. A collection of things bound or otherwise fastened together; a bunch; a package, parcel.

In some spec. uses now superseded by *bunch*; e.g. we no longer speak of 'a *bundle* of keys, of flowers'; but we still say 'a *bundle* of sticks', etc., not 'a *bunch*'. The most frequent application of the word, when not followed by *of*, is to denote a parcel tied up in a handkerchief.

1388 WYCLIF *Song of Sol.* i. 12 My derlyng is a bundel of myrre to me. **1398** TREVISA *Barth. De P.R.* XVII. xcvii, [Flax] bounde in praty nytches & boundel. *c* **1440** *Promp. Parv.* 55 Bundelle, *fasciculus*. **1474** CAXTON *Chesse* 110 On his gurdel a bondel of keyes. **1534** MORE *On Passion* Wks. (1557) 1297/1 A boundell of the lowe growing herbe of Ysope. **1577** DEE *Relat. Spir.* I. (1659) 133 He appeareth now all in violet Silk like a Cloke, and on his head a bundel wreathed of the same. **1636** HEALEY *Theophrast.* 26 In his hand a bundle of papers. **1716-18** LADY M. W. MONTAGUE *Lett.* I. xxiii. 71 How may I send a large bundle to you? **1796** MRS. GLASSE *Cookery* v. 81 Put in some good broth or gravy, and a bundle of sweet herbs. **1802** MAR. EDGEWORTH *Moral T.* (1816) I. viii. 63 Tied up a.. bundle of linen. **1831** BREWSTER *Optics* xx. 181 A bundle of glass plates.

b. *Animal Phys.* A set of muscular or nervous fibres bound closely together. ***fibro-vascular*** (or ***vascular***) ***bundle*** (Veg. Phys.): one of the collections of fibres, vessels, and cells, which constitute the fibro-vascular tissue.

1732 ARBUTHNOT *Rules of Diet* 283 The bundle of Fibres which constitute the Muscle may be small. **1802** *Med. & Phys. Jrnl.* VIII. 368 The Mollusca.. have all the remainder of the common bundle of nerves.. contained in the same cavity with the other viscera. **1866** HUXLEY *Phys.* xi. (1869) 4 Delicate bundles of nervous filaments, the roots of the spinal nerves. **1884** BOWER & SCOTT *De Bary's Phaner. & Ferns* 232.

c. *Law*, in *pl.* (see quots.).

1678 PHILLIPS, *Bundles*, a sort of Records of Chancery, lying in the office of the Rolls; as, the Files of Bills, and Answers in *Chancery*, the Files of *Corpus cum Causa*, all writs of *Certiorari*, with their Certificates, and divers others. **1715** in KERSEY. **1721-90** in BAILEY.

d. Twenty hanks, or 60,000 yards, of linen yarn.

1875 URE *Dict. Arts* II. 450 These packages.. consist of from quarter of a bundle to five or six bundles.

e. *Iron work.* A 'fagot' of iron or steel rods for welding together and working into a mass of greater toughness.

1831 J. HOLLAND *Manuf. Metals* I. 98 The whole mass was bound together by collars driven on tight, or by strips of iron wrapped firmly about the bundle. Several of these faggots being thus prepared, were placed in a furnace and brought to a welding heat.

f. Two reams of printing or brown paper, a quantity fixed by statute.

1724 *Act 11 Geo.* I. c. 7 p. 367/1 Brown Paper, the Bundle containing 40 Quire.. 3*s.* 4*d.*

g. *dial.* or *slang.* A woman, esp. a fat one. Cf. BAGGAGE 6 and 7.

1830 R. FORBY *Vocab. E. Anglia* I. 46 *Bundle*, an opprobrious term applied to females, equivalent to baggage, which perhaps means strictly, a follower of the camp. *a* **1841** T. SHARP *Gloss. Words Warwicksh.* (1865) 11 *Bundle*, a large fat woman. **1922** JOYCE *Ulysses* 753 The ironmould mark the stupid old bundle burned on them.

h. (See quot. 1922.) So in phr. ***to go a*** (or ***the***) ***bundle on***: to bet much money on; *fig.* to be very fond of. *slang* (orig. *U.S.*).

[**1899** J. FLYNT *Tramping with Tramps* (1900) IV. 392 *Bundle*, plunder from a robbery.] **1905** 'H. MCHUGH' *You can search Me* 15 Did they sting you for the whole bundle? **1922** *N. & Q.* 12th Ser. XI. 206/2 *Packet, parcel,* and *bundle*, a considerable sum of money. To say a person 'won a packet', &c., or 'had a parcel (or bundle) on a horse', infers that a considerabale sum has been won or laid. **1938** D. RUNYON *Take it Easy* ii. 45 So he goes for his entire bundle on Apparition. **1942** H. C. BAILEY *Dead Man's Shoes* xxx. 116 Brewing black, pungent liquor, Bryony said he went the bundle on tea himself. **1957** P. WILDEBLOOD *Main Chance* xi. 197 'I go a bundle on you,' he said. **1968** A. DIMENT *Bang Bang Birds* I. v. 60, I don't go a bundle on being told I'm a pro. **1969** *Northern Territory News* 11 July 18/2 (Dog Racing) Brindle Louvre.. backed for bundles.

i. *slang.* A fight or scrap.

1936 J. CURTIS *Gilt Kid* xii. 124 If there was going to be a bundle, he was not going to be bashed sitting down. **1963** 'A. GARVE' *Sea Monks* iii. 88 None o'them ain't goin' to start a bundle if he knows his mate's goin' to get shot for it.

3. a. *fig.* A collection, 'lot' (of things material or immaterial); usually either with contemptuous implication, or with allusion to a figurative 'tying together'. †***to be bound in the bundle of life*** (a Hebraism derived from the Bible): to be foreordained to continued life.

1535 COVERDALE *1 Sam.* xxv. 29 Then shal the soule of my lorde be bounde in the bundell of yͤ lyuynge [**1611** bound in the bundle of life] euen with the Lorde thy God. **1564** GRINDAL *Rem.* (1843) 11 A bundle of the principal nobility of the christian world. **1646** SIR T. BROWNE *Pseud Ep.* I. ii. (1686) 5 A bundle of calumnies. **1768-78** TUCKER *Lt. Nat.* II. 336 A bundle of superstitions and gross absurdities. **1785** REID *Int. Powers* 186 A bundle of sensations. **1863** E. NEALE *Anal. Th. & Nat.* 40 The thought of any object is not that of a mere bundle of qualities. **1864** BURTON *Scot. Abr.* I. i. 25 The King and Queen of France, the King of Navarre, and the royal dukes in a bundle.

b. ***to drop one's bundle***: to give up hope, surrender, resist or compete no further. *Austral.* and *N.Z. slang.*

1915 C. J. DENNIS *Songs Sentim. Bloke* (1916) 119 *To drop the bundle*, to surrender; to give up hope. **1928** *Bulletin* (Sydney) 7 Mar. 39/1 'E [a dog] wouldn't chase the '*are*. 'E dropped 'is bundle. **1947** P. NEWTON *Wayleggo* (1949) x. 115 My confidence immediately disappeared. However, I could not 'drop my bundle', so into the jungle I went.

c. Colloq. phr. (***to be***) ***a bundle of nerves***: (see quot. 1940). (Cf. quot. 1802 for sense 2 b.)

1940 PARTRIDGE *Dict. Clichés* 35 *Bundle of nerves, to be a*, to be in an extremely nervous condition; to start at every noise, show irritation at every mishap or hindrance and fear at every alarm. **1946** F. SARGESON *That Summer* 110, I was just a bundle of nerves. **1965** J. FLEMING *Nothing is the Number* II. viii. 116, I am haunted, shadowed. 'A bundle of nerves' is the English idiom, is it not?

4. *Attrib.* and *Comb.*, as ***bundle handkerchief***: **bundle-man** *Naut. slang*, a married seaman (see quot. 1925); **bundle pillar** (see quot.); **bundle-ring**, ring of fibro-vascular bundles; so **bundle-system, -tube**; **bundle-sheath**, the sheath investing each fibro-vascular bundle, the endodermis; **bundle-wood**, firewood made up into bundles; **bundle-yarn**, yarn made up in bundles (see sense 2 d).

1884 *Pall Mall G.* 11 Sept. 4/2 Crowds.. with huge carpet bags, tin boxes and *bundle handkerchiefs. **1895** *United Service Mag.* 518 If one of the officers is on the sick list it is well to have a spare room in the *bundle-man's house. **1925** FRASER & GIBBONS *Soldier & Sailor Words* 39 *Bundle-man*, *a*, a Lower Deck phrase for a married man, apparently suggested by the small bundle tied up with a blue handkerchief which married seamen.. usually take ashore with them when going on leave. **1876** GWILT *Archit.* Gloss., **Bundle Pillar*, in Gothic architecture, a column consisting of a number of small pillars around its circumference. **1884** BOWER & SCOTT *De Bary's Phaner. & Ferns* 258 In the internode of Nepenthes there is found an inner typical

*bundle-ring. **1882** Vines *Sachs' Bot.* 123 Masses of tissue accompany the separate fibro-vascular bundles as.. envelopes or sheaths; these I term generally *Bundle-sheaths. **1884** Bower & Scott *De Bary's Phaner. & Ferns* 248 A..number of Dicotyledons..differ in their *bundle-system from that which characterises their allies. **1879** *Good Words* 781/1 These great yards are the storage ground of the '*bundle' fire-wood trade. *Ibid.* 781/2 The bundle wood coming into his own household. **1883** *Daily News* 3 Oct. 2/6 The market for *bundle yarns.

'bundle, *v.* [f. prec. sb.]

1. *trans.* To tie in, or make *up* into, a bundle. **1649** *Apparitions at Woodstock*, in Hone *Every-day Bk.* II. 584 The..oak..they had..bundled up into faggots. **1756** Lady M. W. Montague *Lett.* xcvi. IV. 76, I bundle up all your letters. **1783** Cowper *Task* iv. 668 Flow'rs..bundled close to fill some crowded vase. **1828** Steuart *Planter's G.* 249 Care must be taken to bundle up all the flexible parts of the roots. **1859** M. Scott *Tom Cringle* x. 204 The cape.. was bundled..into a round heap. **1862** Miss Yonge *C'tess Kate* vi. 63 She..bundled up her hair as best she might.

b. To 'fagot' bar iron for the purpose of welding it together.

1831 J. Holland *Manuf. Metals* I. 98 To cause bar iron ..to be closely fagotted or bundled together.

c. To wrap in warm, heavy, or cumbersome clothing, etc. Usu. in *pass.* and with *up*.

1893 in *Funk Stand. Dict.* **1923** R. Macaulay *Told by Idiot* II. vi. 85 The two children were bundled up in bear-skin coats. **1949** N. Mitford *Love in Cold Climate* I. xiii. 135 Lady Montdore was hardly visible, bundled up in her corner. **1957** E. Eager *Magic by Lake* iv. 85 The four children found themselves seated in the middle of it, suitably bundled up and befurred. **1967** W. Styron *Confessions of Nat Turner* I. 32 Men and women bundled against the cold had commenced to hurry up the road. **1976** A. Haley *Roots* (1977) cii. 548 He saw the usually bedridden Uncle Pompey sitting outside his cabin in an old cane chair, bundled in a heavy quilt.

†**2.** *fig.* To collect, to gather into a mass. (Usually with *up* or *together*.) *Obs.*

a **1628** F. Greville *Sidney* (1652) 235 The former recited particulars, howsoever improperly..bundled up together. **1633** Bp. Hall *Hard Texts* 541, I have bundled up all his sins together..for a meet day of punishment. **1690** Locke *Hum. Und.* III. v. (1695) 243 Under one Term, bundle together a great variety of..Ideas.

3. *intr.* To pack up one's effects in preparation for a journey; hence, to go with all one's luggage or incumbrances. Of a number of persons: To go precipitately and in disorder, 'all in a bundle' (cf. 4): chiefly with *in*, *off*, *out*; also used with sing. subj. and in extended use.

1787 Burns *Prose Wks.* 25 The devil's bagpiper will touch him off 'Bundle and go!' **1802** G. Colman *Poor Gentl.* v. iii. (L.) Is your ladyship's honour bundling off then? **1845** Kinglake *Eothen* xviii. 282 He made both his wives bundle out. **1847** J. O. Halliwell *Dict. Archaic & Provinc. Words* I. 219/1 *Bundle*... To set off in a hurry. *a* **1863** Whately in Miss Whately *Life & Corr.* (1866) II. 428 'Curates, rectors, archdeacons, deans, bundle in, bundle in!' **1879** Browning *Ivan Iv.* 109 So in we bundled—I and those God gave me once. **1954** D. Abse *Ash on Young Man's Sleeve* 152 Leo bundled out of the train. **1984** W. Golding *Paper Men* i. 10, I bundled into my dressing gown, shoved on my slippers.

4. *trans.* To put or send (persons or things) *away*, *in*, *off*, *out*, etc., hurriedly and unceremoniously. Cf. 'pack off', 'send packing'.

1823 Scott *Peveril* (1865) 63, I will bundle away her rags to the Hall. **1830** De Quincey *Bentley* Wks. VII. 39 When he and his are all bundled off to Hades. **1857** Livingstone *Trav.* xvi. 300 She..bundled him into the hut. **1876** E. Jenkins *Blot on Queen's H.* 5 They were bundled out pretty quick. **1878** C. Bethell in *Law Rep.* (1887) 18/1, I have been bundled off to the Cape for a year.

5. *intr.* To sleep in one's clothes on the same bed or couch *with* (as was formerly customary with persons of opposite sexes, in Wales and New England).

1781 S. Peters *Gen. Hist. Connecticut* (Bartlett) It is thought but a piece of civility to ask [a lady] to bundle. **1809** W. Irving *Knickerb.* (Bartlett) Van Corlear stopped occasionally in the villages to..dance at country frolics, and bundle with the Yankee lasses. **1842–78** [see bundling *vbl. sb.*].

bundled ('bʌnd(ə)ld), *ppl. a.* [f. prec. + -ed¹.] Made into bundles, collected in bundles; wrought (as iron) by welding bundles of rods or bars.

1796 Withering *Brit. Plants* III. 316 Root small, fibrous, bundled, a little woolly. **1831** J. Holland *Manuf. Metals* I. 98 Those [anchors] which are forged from bundled or scrap iron. **1854** S. Thomson *Wild Fl.* I. (ed. 4) 29 The fasciculated or bundled [root] we see in the bird's-nest orchis. **1868** Browning *Ring & Bk.* ix. 1052 Beds of bundled straw.

bundler ('bʌndlə(r)). [f. bundle *v.* + -er¹.]

1. One who makes up (goods) in bundles. In *comb.*, as ***wood-bundler***.

1869 *Daily News* 21 May, Bootblacks, wood-bundlers. **1879** *Good Words* 781/2 Children, working shifts as half-timers, 'pile' for the bundler. **1881** *Instr. Census Clerks* (1885) 70 Flax, Linen Mill:..Drying and Bundling: Dryer. Bundler. **1921** *Dict. Occup. Terms* (1927) §399 *Bundler, waste*, makes waste from various departments of mill up into bundles.

2. One who bundles: see bundle *v.* 5.

†**'bundlet.** *Obs. rare.* [f. bundle *sb.* + dim. suffix -et¹.] A small bundle, a fascicle.

1382 Wyclif *Song of Sol.* i. 12 A bundelet of myrre my lemman is to me. **1774** T. West *Antiq. Furness* App. xiii, Two Shields..suspended by Bundlets of Nightshade.

bundling ('bʌndlɪŋ), *vbl. sb.* [f. bundle *v.* + -ing¹.] The action of the verb to bundle, in various senses.

1650 Fuller *Pisgah* II. v. 129 Haran..and Eden and Sheba..all near one another (as appeares by their bundling up together). **1705** Hickeringill *Priest-cr.* iv. (1721) 242 That know no other Test of Holy Writ, but the Book-binders bundling them into one Volume. **1807** *Edin. Rev.* X. 109 An amusement in New England..called bundling. **1842** C. Masson *Jrnl. Balochistan, &c.* III. 287 Many of the Afghan tribes have a custom in wooing, similar to what in Wales is known as bundling-up. **1851** H. Melville *Whale* I. 58 A speechlessly quick..bundling of a man into Eternity. **1878** C. Wake *Evol. Moral.* I. 401 The custom of bundling ..among Celtic peoples.

attrib. **1831** J. Holland *Manuf. Metals* I. 145 These are at the forge made up into faggots on the bundling bench. **1875** Ure *Dict. Arts* II. 450 It is..better to employ a bundling press than an ordinary table, as the yarn can then be made up more solidly. **1887** *Scotsman* 19 Mar. *Advt.*, Bundling and packing machinery.

bundly ('bʌndlɪ), *a.* [f. bundle *sb.* + -y¹.] Like a bundle.

1895 *Westm. Gaz.* 21 Mar. 7/3 The clothes were all loose. Were they bundly? Perhaps. **1925** D. H. Lawrence *Let.* 21 Apr. (1962) II. 838 We look such a bundly Mexican outfit.

‖**bundobust, bandobast** ('bʌndəbʌst). *India.* Also banda-, bando-, bunda-, bunder-, bundo-, bundoo-; -bast, -bust, -bustt. [Hind. (Pers.) *band-o-bast* tying and binding.] An arrangement, organization; preparations.

1776 *Trial Jos. Fowke, Depositions* 17/2 In the year 1180.. when the Bundobustt of the farms took place. **1813** *Gloss. 5th Rep. Sel. Comm. E. India Co.* 10/1 Bundoobust... A settlement of the amount of revenue to be paid or collected. **1880** G. Aberigh-Mackay *Twenty-one Days India* 181 This unhappy creature whose mind is a perfect blank regarding *Faujdari* and *Bandobast*..will..actually presume to discuss Indian subjects with you. **1896** A. Forbes *Camps, Quarters, & Casual Places* 270 George Martell did not make quite so bad a *bandobast* after all. **1920** *Blackw. Mag.* Sept. 319/2 'Sahib, what *bundobast* fer dinner?' asked Khuda Bux. **1925** E. F. Norton *Fight for Everest 1924* 163 [We] set off with a minimum bandobast to penetrate as far down into Nepal as we could. **1927** *Blackw. Mag.* Aug. 327/2 An Indian regiment whose water *bundobust* had somehow gone wrong. **1963** M. Malim *Pagoda Tree* xxiii. 157 A great one for rushing about with a tremendous air of determination 'making *bundobusts*' right, left and centre.

bundook ('bʌndu:k). *India.* [Hind. *bandūq*, a. Pers. *bunduq* filbert nut, musket or cannon ball, firearm, ad. Gr. Ποντικόν (sc. κάρυον hazel nut) pontic *a.*¹] A musket or matchlock; a rifle.

1886 in Yule & Burnell *Hobson-Jobson*. **1916** 'Sapper' *Men, Women & Guns* v. 156, I had words with a sentry at the frontier, but I put it across him with his own bundook. **1923** *Blackw. Mag.* May 574/2 Those old *bundooks* were a source of perpetual nerves to us. **1926** *Ibid.* Nov. 664/2 Fortunately bundooks..do not shoot very straight.

bundu ('bʊndu:). *Southern Afr.* [Bantu.] An uncivilized rural region; wilds. Also *attrib.*

1946 *Cape Times* 22 Oct. 6/7 The King is expected to wear a bush shirt and shorts and, while he is in Rhodesia, a bundu hat. **1947** L. Hastings *Dragons are Extra* vii. 133 Life in the bundu. **1950** *Cape Argus* 27 May 4/6 He..finds time to go into the bundu after big game. **1958** N. Gordimer *World of Strangers* ii. 54 It's absolutely in the bundu, of course, forty-three miles from Neksburg.

†**'bundwork.** *Obs. rare*⁻¹. [? ad. Du. *bontwerk* fur, peltry; cf. Ger. *buntwerk* (written *bundwerk* by Luther) 'pelzwerk', Grimm.]

1663 *Inv. Ld. J. Gordon's Furniture*, A chapell bed all of bundwork with two peice of hingings and pan.

†**'bundy.** *Obs.* ? *north. dial.* ? A kind of horse.

1591 *Wills & Inv. N.C.* II. (1860) 193 Baie Williamson and soard bundy, coltes, 3*l.* 6/8*d.*.. An old gray bundy and j crooked mare 20/-.

†**bune.** *Obs.* Also 3 buine. [perh. worn down f. OE. *bycȝen* sb. 'buying', f. *bycȝan* to buy; cf. ME. *buð* for *buggeð* (3rd pers. sing. pres. of the verb).] Buying, purchase. (In the last quot. a pa. pple. seems required.)

c **1175** *Lamb. Hom.* 18 Min ihesu..þu beadest us þin elming [? *read* elnung] al wiþ uten bune. *a* **1225** *Ancr. R.* 362 (MSS. C. & T.) Me ne mei nout..two þongede schone habben wiðuten bune [MS. N. buggunge]. *Ibid.* 368 (MS. N.) Þauh clennesse ne beo nout buine [MS. C. bune] ed God.

bunewand, var. of bunwand; see bun *sb.*¹

bunfyte, obs. form of benefit.

bung (bʌŋ), *sb.*¹ Also 5 bunge, 6 boung(e. [Cf. MDu. *bonghe* in same sense, said by Franck to be a regular dial. form for *bonde, whence the recorded MDu. *bonne*, mod.Du. *bom*.

The Du. word corresponds to MHG. *punt*, *punte*; the synonymous F. *bonde* is supposed to be adopted from some Teut. lang. It has been conjectured that the source of all these words is the L. *puncta* in the sense of 'hole', and that the synonymous OHG., MHG. *spunt*, mod.G. *spund*, Du. *spon* are originally the same word.]

1. A stopper; *spec.* a large cork stopper for the 'mouth' of a cask, i.e. the hole in the bulge by which it is filled.

c **1440** *Promp. Parv.* 55 Bunge of a wesselle, as a tonne, barelle, botelle, or other lyke. **1530** Palsgr. 202/1 Bung of a tonne or pype. **1669** Worlidge *Syst. Agric.* iv. §7 (1681) 54 Put into a vessel, and stopt with a Bung and Rag. **1769** Mrs. Raffald *Eng. Housekpr.* (1778) 329 Take out the bung. **1830** M. Donovan *Dom. Econ.* I. 279. *c* **1860** H. Stuart *Seaman's Catech.* 64 They are stowed bung up.

2. *transf.* The 'mouth' of a cask; the bung-hole. (Still *dial.*)

1571 Digges *Pantom.* III. xiii. S i b, Take youre rodde.. and let it descende perpendicularly downe thorough the bung. **1684** tr. *Bonet's Merc. Compit.* VIII. 274 Stopping the bung of the Vessel. **1775** *Phil. Trans.* LXV. 103 A small cask of rum, with a large bung.

3. a. *Naut.* A nickname for the master's assistant who superintends the serving of the grog. [Cf. *bung-starter*.]

1863 *Man-of-War* in *Cornh. Mag.* Feb., To..see the grog served out..the discharge of which [duty] has invested them..with the title of Bungs. **1865** *Pall Mall G.* 19 May 1 The second master and master's assistant..are, or used to be..known as 'bungs' in the service.

b. A brewer, or landlord of a public house. Also, the brewing interest (as in politics); hence *attrib.* or as *adj.*, favouring the brewers or their interests in politics.

1860 Hotten *Dict. Slang* (ed. 2), *Bung*, the landlord of a public-house. **1884** *Graphic* 23 Feb. 170/1 That Sir Wilfrid Lawson had turned 'Bung', and applied for a spirit licence. *a* **1889** *Truth* (Barrère & Leland), Within the last few years several bungs have been made Peers. **1891** *Pall Mall Gaz.* 31 Aug. 2/3 It is true that the temperance organizations rendered yeoman service, but as a consequence the 'bung' party put forth its full strength on the other side. **1910** *Daily Chron.* 1 Feb. 1/4 Since the power of 'Bung' has been so demonstrated in this constituency. **1969** C. Drummond *Odds on Death* viii. 169 There's a pub in North London which might help: the bung is named Scoot.

4. [Perh. not the same word.] **a.** A bundle of hemp-stalks. **b.** *Pottery*: A pile of 'seggars' or clay cases in which fine stoneware is baked.

1704 Worlidge *Dict. Rust. et Urb.* s.v. *Watering*, To lay the Bungs (which are bundles of Stalks) in Water. **1832** G. Porter *Porcelain* 57 Each of these piles [of seggars] as it stands, is called a bung. **1875** Ure *Dict. Arts* III. 614 The 'setters' for china plates..are 'reared' in the oven in 'bungs'.

†**5.** = bum *sb.*¹ *Obs. rare.*

1691 *New Disc. Old Intreague* xxviii. 6.

6. *Comb.*, as ***bung-cloth***; **bung eye** *Austral.*, a form of ophthalmia caused by flies; **bung-hole**, the hole in a cask, which is closed with the bung; †*transf.* the anus (*obs.*); **bung-knife**, ? a knife for cutting bungs; **bung-starter**, 'a stave shaped like a bat, which, applied to either side of the bung, causes it to start out; also a soubriquet for the captain of the hold; also a name given to the master's assistant serving his apprenticeship for hold duties' (Smyth *Sailor's Word-bk.*); **bung-stave**, that stave of a cask in which is the bung-hole.

1882 Nares *Seamansh.* (ed. 6) 146 Bungs and *bung cloths. **1933** *Bulletin* (Sydney) 13 Sept. 23/2 Epidemic ophthalmia (or 'pink eye' or '*bung eye'), an acute inflammation of the eyelids lasts only a few weeks. **1966** 'J. Hackston' *Father clears Out* 98 The ordinary fly.. arranged, with punctilious regularity, that the school received its full summer quota of bung eyes. **1571** Digges *Pantom.* III. xii. S b, The diagonall..lynes from the *bung holes to the..lowest parte of either base. **1611** Cotgr., *Cul de cheval*, a small and ouglie fish, or excrescence of the Sea, resembling a mans bung-hole, and called the red Nettle [= Sea Anemone]. **1871** Tyndall *Fragm. Sc.* (ed. 6) II. xii. 255 A cask with a very large bunghole. **1592** Greene *Upst. Courtier* (1871) 40 By his side a skein like a brewers *boung-knife. **1860** H. Stuart *Seaman's Catech.* 64 The *bung stave is known by the rivets of the hoops being on that stave. **1867** Smyth *Sailor's Word-bk.* 144 Its bung-stave is uppermost.

†**bung,** *sb.*² *Thieves' Cant. Obs.* Also 6 bong, boong, 6–7 boung. [Origin unknown: the resemblance to OE. *pung* purse (also Fris. *pung* 'purse' in Koolman), is worthy of notice. Cf. quot. 1592 in bung *v.* 3.]

a. A purse. **b.** A pick-pocket. Also in *comb.*, as **bung-nipper**, a pick-pocket.

1567 Harman *Caveat* 83/1 Bunge, a pursse. **1592** *Def. Coneycatching* (1859) 4 Some..would venture all the byte in their boung at dice. **1597** Shaks. *2 Hen. IV*, II. iv. 138 You Cut-purse Rascall, you filthy Bung. **1611** Dekker *Roar. Girle* Wks. 1873 III. 217 Shal you and I nip a bung? shall you and I cut a purse? *a* **1658** Cleveland *Cl. Vind.* (1677) 96 An Authentick Gypsie, that nips your Bung with a Canting Ordinance. **1659** *Caterpillers of Nat. Anat., Bung-Nibber*, or Cut-purse = a pickpocket. **1725** *New Cant. Dict., Bung*, a Purse, Pocket, or Fob... Bung-nippers, Cut-purses.

bung, *sb.*³ *slang.* A lie, falsehood.

1882 A. M. Brookfield *Autob. Thomas Allen* I. v. 61 'And for having told a bung,' said Fisher. 'A beastly bung,' cried all the judges. **1913** M. Baring *Lost Diaries* 8 Mac reported him for telling bungs.

bung, *sb.*⁴ *Criminals' slang.* [Origin unknown.] A bribe. Cf. bung *v.*³

1958 F. Norman *Bang to Rights* III. 149 'Is'nt it a coinsidence that Stanley Golsberg's shop was screwed the other day, and a load of cloth was nicked?' 'Alright so how much is the bung?' Asked Solie. 'Well lets say a fifty and we

did'nt see a thing.' **1966** J. ASHFORD *Consider Evidence* vii. 67 What's the matter? Not being offered enough bung?

bung, *a.*[1] *Sc.* 'Tipsy, fuddled; a low word' (Jam.)

1721 RAMSAY *Epistle to R.H.B.* Wks. 1848 III. 62 When with wine he's bung. *a* **1758** —— *Poems* (1844) 84 She.. chang'd her mind, whan bung.

bung, *a.*[2] *Austral.* and *N.Z. slang.* Also formerly **bong**. [Austral. Aboriginal word.]

a. Dead. **b.** Bankrupt. **c.** Ruined, useless. Also in phr. ***to go bung***, to die; to fail; to go bankrupt.

[**1847** J. D. LANG *Cooksland* x. 430 A place called *Umpie Bung*, or the dead houses.] **1882** W. A. J. BOYD *Old Colonials* 73 Just afore you hands 'im [*sc.* the horse] over and gets the money, he goes bong on you [i.e. he dies]. **1885** *Austral. Printers' Keepsake* 40 His musical talent had 'gone bung'. **1885** H. FINCH-HATTON *Adv. Australia* x. 142 Directly me bung (die) me jump up white feller. **1893** *Argus* 15 Apr. 13/2 (Morris), All flesh is grass, says the preacher,.. And we gaze on a bank in the evening, and lo, in the morn 'tis bung. **1893** *Melbourne Herald* 25 Apr. 2/4 (Morris), One member of the mischief-making brotherhood wrote the words 'gone bung' under a notice on the Government Savings Bank. **1902** W. SATCHELL *Land of Lost* vii. 47 The merchant princes who have gone bung, and the geniuses who have gone bunger. **1930** A. GROOM *Merry Christmas* xxvi. 209 The telephone line's been mostly bung and broke since, but I got through. **1948** L. MACFARLANE *This N.Z.* xiv. 137 We were bung, completely down and out. **1952** G. WILSON *Julien Ware* viii. 68 'Why aren't you playing?'..'Got a bung ankle. Don't want to hurt it again.'

bung (bʌŋ), *v.*[1] [f. BUNG *sb.*[1]] *trans.*

1. To stop with a bung; also with *down*, *up*.

1616 SURFL. & MARKH. *Countr. Farm* 431 You must bung it vp very close. **1741** HANBURY in *Phil. Trans.* XLI. 674 Unctuous Clay, such as Brewers use to bong their Vessels. **1835** MARRYAT *Pacha* ii, I had bunged up the cask. **1836** *Penny Cycl.* V. 405/1 The beer [should be] well flattened before bunging down in the casks.

2. *transf.* and *fig.* To stop, close; to shut up. Now chiefly in pugilistic slang, ***to bung up the eyes***.

1589 *Pappe w. Hatchet* A iiij, These mutiners.. must haue their mouthes bungd with iests. **1622** MABBE tr. *Aleman's Guzman d'Alf.* II. 294 My mouth was bung'd vp, I durst not speake. **1655** GURNALL *Chr. in Arm.* xii. §3 (1669) 356/2 Resolve to bung up thine ear from all by-discourse. **1755** *Connoisseur* No. 53 (1774) II. 139 In the vulgar idiom Bunging your eye. **1829** MARRYAT *F. Mildmay* v, With his eyes bunged up and his face.. swollen.

3. To shut *up*, enclose, as in a bunged cask.

1592 NASHE *P. Penilesse* (ed. 2) 23 a, Bung vp all the welth of the Land in their snap-haunce bags. **1775** GARRICK in Colman *Posth. Lett.* (1820) 308 Henderson play'd Regulus; & you would have wish'd him bung'd up with his nails, before yᵉ End of yᵉ 3ᵈ act. **1794** J. WOLCOTT (P. Pindar) *Celebration* Wks. III. 419 Chain'd be the tempests, and well bung'd the rain.

bung, *v.*[2] *slang* (orig. *dial.*). [Echoic.] *trans.* To throw (violently); to send; to put forcibly. Also with *in*. Also *fig.*

1825 JAMIESON, To *bung*, to throw with violence, Aberd. **1835** *Sessions' Paper Cent. Criminal Court* May 37, I heard one say to the other, '*Bill, bung 'em*,' and one of them *chucked* the beads down. **1839** *Ibid.* Mar. 889 The policeman says that '*bung* it' means 'Put it back'. **1903** *Daily Chron.* 8 Dec. 9/2 'We are police officers. What have you in that parcel?' Stevens replied, 'I don't know; I have just had it bunged on to me.' **1913** C. MACKENZIE *Sinister St.* I. II. ii. 174 Let's bung these sticks into the sea. **1923** *Glasgow Herald* 29 Oct. 12 The cinema.. can.. take the skeletons of 'Macbeth', [etc.] and make very entertaining films of them with.. a good deal of photographed natural scenery bunged in. **1933** WODEHOUSE *Mulliner Nights* iv. 139 Telling the butler to bung Mr. Mulliner into the drawing-room and lock up all the silver. **1944** R. LEHMANN *Ballad & Source* 222 We've torn them in pieces and bunged them into a giant's stew-pot.

bung, *v.*[3] *Criminals' slang.* [Origin unknown; perh. f. prec.] *trans.* To bribe; to pay; to tip. Cf. BUNG *sb.*[4]

1950 P. TEMPEST *Lag's Lexicon* 27 'Did he bung you?' = did he give you a tip? 'I will let you have some grub if you will bung me' = I will let you have some food if you will pay me. **1963** T. & P. MORRIS *Pentonville* 378 To 'bung' a person is to give him a fixed amount of tobacco each week to bring regular supplies—of anything. **1966** J. ASHFORD *Consider Evidence* i. 5 He needed it [*sc.* the money].. for bunging the cozzpots if anything went wrong. **1967** J. BURKE *Till Death us do Part* i. 24 Don't forget the solicitors.. They'll want bunging.

bung, *adv.* [Cf. BUNG *v.*[2] and BANG *v.*[1] 8.] In or into the very middle of things; = SMACK *v.*[2] 7 b.

1899 KIPLING *Stalky & Co.* 132 They have babies and teething and measles and all that sort of thing right bung *in* the school. *Ibid.* 154, I used to go bung off to sleep on a form sometimes. **1940** 'N. SHUTE' *Landfall* 25 'Where was the ship, anyway?' 'Bung in the middle of Matheson's zone.'

bungaloid ('bʌŋgəlɔɪd), *a.* [f. BUNGALO(W + -OID after *fungoid*.] Having the appearance or style of a bungalow or bungalows; characterized by the presence of bungalows. Also *sb.*, a bungaloid building.

1927 *Daily Express* 22 Nov. 1/3 Hideous allotments and bungaloid growths make the approaches to any city repulsive. **1928** *Sunday Dispatch* 30 Sept. 11/2 Mr. Shaw designates our modern urban communities 'bungaloid promiscuities', and refuses them the more dignified term of civilisations. **1929** *Morning Post* 4 May 1/3 Will somebody.. pay reasonable cash price for freehold and preserve its beauty from bungaloids. **1968** A. SMITHSON in B. S. Johnson *Evacuees* 249 Now it's a tatty bungaloid estate or worse.

bungalow ('bʌŋgələʊ). orig. *Anglo-Indian*. Also 7 **bungale**, 8 **bungula**, **bungelow**, **bungilo**, 8–9 **bungalo** (*pl.* **-oes**), 9 **bungallow**. [a. Hindustani *banglā*, understood to be identical with the adj. of same form, meaning 'belonging to Bengal'.]

Orig., a one-storied house (or temporary building, e.g. a summer-house), lightly built, usually with a thatched roof. In modern use, any one-storied house. Also *attrib.* and *Comb.* **dāk bungalow**: see DĀK.

1676 STREYNSHAM MASTER *MS. Diary* (India Office) 25 Nov., It was thought fitt.. to sett up Bungales or Hovells.. for all such English in the Company's Service as belong to their Sloopes & Vessells. **1711** [? THORNTON] *Engl. Pilot* III. 54 All along the Hughley Shore.. almost as far as the Dutch Bungelow. **1754** E. THOMPSON *Sailor's Lett.* (1766) I. xii. 90 In an evening.. we swing to the Bread and cheese Bungula in our palanquins. **1809** MAR. GRAHAM *Journ. Resid. India* 10 (Y.) We came to a small bungalo or garden-house. *a* **1847** MRS. SHERWOOD *Lady of Manor* III. xxi. 239 The bungalows in India.. are, for the most part.. built of unbaked bricks and covered with thatch, having in the centre a hall.. the whole being encompassed by an open verandah. **1875** F. HALL in *Lippincott's Mag.* XV. 338/1 Every day I stopped once or twice at a travellers' bungalow, or rest-house. **1886** W. RALEIGH *Let.* May (1926) I. 72 Ten marches with a bungalow rest house of some description to stop at. **1903** *Arch. & Contr. Reporter* 24 Apr. 272/2 The buildings have been designed in a bungalow type. **1906** *Daily Chron.* 9 Mar. 8/3 The bungalow village. **1907** *Westm. Gaz.* 8 Apr. 9/1 The meeting of bungalow-holders. **1936** *Discovery* Feb. 42/1 The permitting of extensive uncontrolled camping and of inferior-type bungalow-towns.

bungarum ('bʌŋgərəm). Also **bungarus**, **bungar**, **bongar**. [Bengali (Skr., neut. sing. of *bhangura* bent, curled (sb. bend of a river), f. *bhanj* to break, bend).] Any of the venomous snakes of the genus *Bungarus*; esp. the krait of India.

1835 *Encycl. Metrop.* XXIII. 640/1 *P*[*seudoboa*] *Fasciata*. ..A native of India. In Bengal is called *Bungarum Pamah* and *Sackeenee*. **1869** GILLMORE tr. *Figuier's Reptiles & Birds* (1870) ii. 71 According to Cantor, the Bungarums are capable of darting nearly the anterior half of the body. **1887** *Encycl. Brit.* XXII. 196/2 The fangs of the bungarums are shorter than those of the cobras. **1921** F. WALL *Snakes of Ceylon* 435 The Telugu word 'bungarum', gold.. is applied by the Telugus to the banded krait.

bungee. = PONGEE.

1760 GOLDSMITH *Cit. W.* lxxvii, I know these [silks].. to be no better than your mere flimsy bungees.

bungell, obs. form of BUNGLE.

bunger, bungie, bungy, varr. PUNGA.

†'**bungerly**, *a.* and *adv. Obs.* Also 7 **bungarly**. [f. **bunger* (? for BUNGLER) + -LY.]

A. *adj.* Unworkmanlike, bungling, slovenly. **B.** *adv.* Clumsily. Hence '**bungerliness**.

1580 BARET *Alv.* B 1498 Bungerly done, *infabre*. **1584** STANYHURST *Descr. Irel.* in *Holinshed* VI. Ep. Ded., Bungerlie to botch up a rich garment, by clouting it with patches of sundrie colours. **1596** NASHE *Have with you, &c.* 91 The bungerliest vearses.. that euer were scande. **1598** FLORIO, *Grossolaneria*, clownishnes.. grosnes, bungerlines. **1615** T. ADAMS *Black Dev.* 18 The more shallow in Knowledge, the more bungerly in wickednesse. **1618** BOLTON *Florus* III. x. 199 The Enemies Ships.. were bungerly made.

bung-ho (bʌŋ'həʊ), *int.* Also **bung-o, -oh**. An exclamation used at parting or as a drinking toast.

1925 *Springfield Union* 20 Nov., They now say 'Bungo!' instead of 'Here's how!' over cocktails. **1926** HEMINGWAY *Fiesta* (1927) II. xviii. 258 'Well, bung-o,' Mike said. 'Get some sleep, old Jake.' **1928** D. L. SAYERS *Unpl. Bellona Club* i. 8 'Dry Martini,' said Wimsey.. 'Bung-ho!' **1935** N. MARSH *Enter a Murderer* xi. 142 'Bung-oh,' said Wakeford genially, and went his ways. **1961** L. PAYNE *Nose on my Face* xvii. 257 'Bung ho!' I.. had a long and refreshing drink.

bungie, bungy ('bʌndʒɪ). *slang.* Also **bunje(e, bunjie, bunjy**. [Origin unknown.]

a. India-rubber; a rubber. **b.** (A nickname for) a Naval physical-training instructor.

1915 'BARTIMEUS' *Tall Ship* iv. 75 'Bunje,' said the First Lieutenant, 'come to the club and have tea and play "pills" afterwards?' The Indiarubber Man shook his head. **1928** E. SCOTT *War among Ladies* I. ii. 24 Where's my rubber? Joan, have you pinched my bunjy? **1934** *N. & Q.* CLXVII. 441/2 In the schoolroom fifty years ago, the piece of india-rubber for erasing purposes was referred to as 'india-bungie' or 'bungie'—pronounced with the *g* soft, *bunjie*. **1958** *Listener* 6 Nov. 722/2 Any bits and pieces of pencil, string, bungy, and odd nibs.

†'**bungie-bird.** *Obs. rare*[−1]. [app. related to the name 'Friar Bungay' or 'Bungy'. See Ward's *Friar Bacon and Friar Bungay*: Notes 195.] Contemptuous designation for a (? Franciscan) friar.

1591 *Troub. Raigne K. John* (1611) 50 Bald and barefoot Bungie birds.

bungle ('bʌŋg(ə)l), *v.* Also 6 **bongyll, boungle**, 7 **bungell**. [App. onomatopœic; cf. BUMBLE, BRANGLE, BOGGLE *v.*

(Prof. Skeat compares Sw. dial. *bangla* to work ineffectually (Rietz), and OSw. *bunga* to strike (Ihre).]

1. *trans.* To do or make in a clumsy or unskilful manner; formerly often with *up*, *out*. Now, usually, To spoil by unskilful workmanship. Cf. BOTCH *v.*[1]

1530 PALSGR. 627/2 A man may bongyll it up in a senyght. **1570** LEVINS *Manip.* 189 To Bungle, *infabre facere*.. **1579** G. HARVEY *Letter-bk.* (1884) 59 They were hudlid and.. bunglid upp in more haste then good speede. **1649** BLITHE *Eng. Improv. Impr.* (1653) 52 He either wholly spoils it, or at least bungles out a half work. **1791** SCOTT *Let.* in *Lockhart* (1839) I. 247 Never was an affair more completely bungled. **1845** E. HOLMES *Mozart* 260 The oratorio.. some may expect to be patched or bungled.

2. *intr.* To work or act unskilfully or clumsily; to blunder.

1549 OLDE *Erasm. Par. Ephes.* Prol., Bunglyng at the thyng that is ferre aboue my capacitie. **1647** H. MORE *Song of Soul* Notes 139/2 Physis or Nature is sometimes puzzeld and bungells in ill disposed matter. **1791–1824** D'ISRAELI *Cur. Lit.* (1859) II. 498 Shenstone.. found that his engraver ..had sadly bungled with the poet's ideal. **1862** MAURICE *Mor. & Met. Philos.* IV. iv. §29. 118 Very likely Luther bungled in his arguments.

'**bungle**, *sb.* [f. prec. vb.] A clumsy or unskilful piece of work; a botch, blunder, muddle. Hence **bungle-headed** *a.*

1656 H. MORE *Antid. Atheism* (1662) 84 The most enormous slip or bungle she could commit. **1678** CUDWORTH *Intell. Syst.* 150 Those ἁμαρτήματα (as Aristotle calls them) those Errors and Bungles. **1833** MARRYAT *P. Simple* (1863) 231 The second figure commenced, and I made a sad bungle.. for I had never danced a cotillon. **1865** *Leeds Mercury* 15 Apr., This dear old bungle-headed commercial man.

bungled ('bʌŋg(ə)ld), *ppl. a.* [f. as prec. + -ED[1].] Done or made clumsily or unskilfully.

1618 BOLTON *Florus* III. viii. 194 They ventured forth to Sea in bungled Boats. **1787** T. JEFFERSON *Writ.* (1859) II. 310 Spoiling all his plans by a bungled execution. **1825** WATERTON *Wand. S. Amer.* III. ii. (1879) 316 On the ground he [the sloth] appeared.. a bungled composition.

bungler ('bʌŋglə(r)). Also 6 **bongler**, 7 **bunglar**. [f. as prec. + -ER[1].] One who bungles; a clumsy unskilful worker.

1533 MORE *Answ. Poyson. Bk.* Wks. (1557) 1089/1 He is euen but a very bungler. **1642** MILTON *Apol. Smect.* Wks. 1738 I. 127 If any Carpenter, Smith, or Weaver, were such a bungler in his Trade. **1820** IRVING *Sketch Bk.* II. 326 A bungler at all.. sports that required.. patience or adroitness. **1858** HAWTHORNE *Fr. & It. Jrnls.* I. 292 The greatest bungler that ever botched a block of marble.

Hence **bungler-like** *a.* and *adv.*

1603 FLORIO *Montaigne* (1634) 491 That Painter.. having bungler-like drawn.. some Cockes. **1613** COTGR., *Rudement* ..ruggedly, harshly, bunglarlike.

'**bunglery.** *rare*[−1]. [f. prec. + -Y[3].] = BUNGLING *vbl. sb.*

1837 *Fraser's Mag.* XVI. 656 The deficit of Rice; the bunglery Of protocolling Cupid.

'**bunglesome**, *a. U.S.* [f. BUNGLE *v.*] Awkward to handle, bungling and troublesome.

1889 in *Century Dict.* **1897** *Congress Rec.* Feb., App. 55/1 An inexcusable and bunglesome fraud or mistake on the part of some one handling [the ballots]. **1915** MRS. STRATTON-PORTER *M. O'Halloran* xv. 337 But this sheet is going to be rather bunglesome. Ma, could you do anything about it?

bungling ('bʌŋglɪŋ), *vbl. sb.* [f. BUNGLE *v.*]

1. The action of the verb to BUNGLE; unskilful or clumsy working or action.

1663 BUTLER *Hud.* I. II. 330 To prophane a thing So Sacred, with vile Bungling. **1692** BENTLEY *Boyle Lect.* 24 To believe that.. the whole universe is meer bungling & blundring. **1845** LD. CAMPBELL *Chancellors* (1857) V. cxvi. 290 Losing all patience at his bungling.

†**2.** ? Used (for the sake of rime) for *bundling*.

1593 BARNES *Elegies* in Arb. *Garner* V. 412 The viper's youngling.. can[not] endure the bongling Within the viper's belly.

'**bungling**, *ppl. a.* [f. as prec. + -ING[2].]

1. That bungles; unskilful and clumsy in working.

1589 NASHE in Greene *Menaph.* Ded. (Arb.) 12 Such bungling practitioners in principles. **1699** BENTLEY *Phal.* Pref. 75 A Bungling Tinker, that makes two Holes, while he mends one. **1747** COSTARD in *Phil. Trans.* XLIV. 483 Such Notions.. demonstrate them to be very bungling Astronomers. **1875** T. HILL *True Ord. Studies* 66 Danger of a bungling teacher's extinguishing the child's thirst for knowledge.

2. Of actions: Showing unskilfulness, clumsy.

1598 FLORIO, *Abbozzamento*, a.. bungling peece of worke. **1634** T. JOHNSON *Parey's Chirurg.* XI. xviii. (1678) 291 It is a shameful and bungling part to do more harm with your hand than the Iron [of an Arrow] hath done. **1773** BURKE *Corr.* (1844) I. 439 Done in an awkward bungling manner. **1867** FREEMAN *Norm. Conq.* (1876) I. App. 644 The bungling attempt of a compiler.

bunglingly ('bʌŋglɪŋlɪ), *adv.* [f. prec. + -LY[2].] In a bungling manner; unskilfully, clumsily.

1611 FLORIO, *Acciarpa*, botchinglie, bunglinglie. **1655** FULLER *Ch. Hist.* VI. 330 When done so bunglingly, that it is detected. **1720** DE FOE *Capt. Singleton* iii. (1840) 47 They

did it but bunglingly. **1864** MRS. WOOD *Trev. Hold.* I. iii. 37 So bunglingly did she execute her commission.

‖**bungo** ('bʌŋgəʊ). A kind of boat used in the Southern States and in Central America.

1854 J. STEPHENS *Centr. Amer.* 2 Sundry schooners, bungoes, canoes, and a steamboat, were riding at anchor. *Ibid.* 246 The bungo was about forty feet long, dug out of the trunk of a Guanacaste tree.

bungo, var. BUMBO[2].

'**Bungtown.** *U.S.* Also with lower-case initial. [App. a fictitious local name, associated with Rehoboth in Massachusetts (Schele de Vere *Americanisms* 587).] ***Bungtown copper*** or ***cent***, a counterfeit English halfpenny or other spurious copper coin. Also *ellipt.*

1787 *Newport Mercury* 13 Aug. in *Mag. Amer. Hist.* (1885) XIII. 206 We are informed that all Coppers by law, in New York, except Bungtowns, are fixed at 160 for a Dollar. **1840** *Knickerbocker* XV. 385 [He took] a five cent piece and two bungtown coppers out of the till. **1853** *Oregonian* 13 Aug. (Th.), What is the currency of the U.S.? —Coppers, bogus, Bungtown cents, pennies, fips, [etc.].

†'**bungy**, *a. Obs. rare.* [Cf. BULGY, BUNCHY.] ? Puffed out, protuberant.

1634 SIR T. HERBERT *Trav.* 146 Great roules of Calico.. somewhat higher and not so bungy as the Turkish Tulipants. **1638** *Ibid.* 170 His shash or turbant was white and bungie. *Ibid.* 346 The tree is not high nor bungie.

bungy ('bʌŋgi), *sb. India.* Also **bungheea.** [Hind. *bhangī.*] In Bombay, a member of the low caste of sweepers.

1823 *Trans. Lit. Soc. Bombay* III. 374 *Bungheea*, the sweeper, particularly of filth. **1886** YULE & BURNELL *Hobson-Jobson* s.v., The colloquial application of the term *bungy* to such servants is.. peculiar to Bombay.

bungy, bunje, etc. See BUNGIE.

bunion ('bʌnjən). Also 8 **bunnian**, 9 **bunnion, bunyan, bunyon.** [Of obscure etymology; prob. connected with BUNNY[1]. Prof. Skeat regards it as a. It. *bugnone* 'a push, a bile, a blane, a botch' (Florio 1598), f. *bugno* = OF. *bugne* (? whence *bunny*); this suits the form, but the word was until recently so rare in literary use that derivation from Italian seems very unlikely.] An inflamed swelling on the foot, *esp.* of the bursa mucosa at the inside of the ball of the great toe; see quot. 1878.

a **1718** ROWE *Tonson & Congr.*, Warm my bunnians [*footnote*, Jacob's name for his corns] at your fire. **1821** GALT *Ayrsh. Legat.* 198 (JAM.) Miss Mally had an orthodox corn, or bunyan. **1863** C. M. SMITH *Deadlock* 248 His bunions never mar his quiet pilgrimage. **1878** T. BRYANT *Pract. Surg.* I. 176 When from excessive pressure a bursa forms over one of the tarsal or metatarsal articulations, a bunion is said to be present.

bunjara, -jarrah, -jarree, var. of BRINJARRY.

bunk (bʌŋk), *sb.*[1] [Of unknown etymology; possibly related to BANK: cf. BUNKER *sb.*[1]. Skeat compares OSw. *bunke* boarding to protect the cargo of a ship from the weather (Ihre). Cf. also BULK *sb.*[2]]

1. a. A box or recess in a ship's cabin, railway-carriage, lodging-house, etc., serving for a bed; a sleeping-berth. Freq. one of two or more beds arranged in a tier.

1758 L. LYON in A. Tomlinson *Mil. Jrnls.* (1855) 37 We made us up 2 straw bunks for 4 of us to lay in. **1780** W. HEATH *Let.* 2 Feb. in *Mass. Hist. Soc. Coll.* (1905) V. 28 The bunks and lineing of the bomb proof were taken out. **1810** *Deb. Congress* (1853) XXI. App. 2448, 20 bunks at $3.50 each [among expenses in military hospital, New Orleans]. **1815** *Chron.* in *Ann. Reg.* 58/2 He suddenly fell back upon his bunk. **1859** R. BURTON *Centr. Afr.* in *Jrnl. Geog. Soc.* XXIX. 47 Some houses have a second story like a ship's bunk. **1862** B. TAYLOR *Home & Abr.* Ser. II. IV. 363 The Summit House.. where travellers can pass the night in comfortable bunks. **1866** *Harvard Mem. Biog., Peabody* I. 165 At the end of the train, a blue car.. one end of which is decorated with bunks and shelves, which serve as sleeping apartments. **1879** DIXON *Brit. Cyprus* ix. 79, I am lying in a bunk, on board the flag-ship.

b. *attrib.*, as ***bunk-car, -room***; **bunk-bed**, a piece of furniture comprising two bunks; **bunk-house**, a house where workmen, etc., are lodged.

1951 *Catal. Exhibits, Festival of Britain* 127/2 Bunk beds. **1967** *Observer* 21 May 30/7 Bunk beds that split into single beds. **1894** P. L. FORD *P. Stirling* xl. 236 By the light, one of the superintendents found the bunk cars gone. **1877** R. W. RAYMOND *8th Rep. Mines* 332 Bunk-house. **1901** S. E. WHITE *Claim Jumpers* xxii. 274 The old 'bunk house' now accomodated a good-sized gang of miners. **1952** H. INNES *Campbell's Kingdom* I. iii. 50 This is bunkhouse for men working on road. **1848** BAKER *Glance at N.Y.* 24 De way de boys laid out of de old bunk-room was sinful. **1957** J. MASTERS *Far, Far Mountain Peak* 110 Someone was scratching at the door of the women's bunkroom.

c. *spec.* The lodging of a student at St. Andrews university. Hence *attrib.* in ***bunk-wife***, the (or a) keeper of a 'bunk'; landlady.

1891 R. F. MURRAY *Scarlet Gown* 58 Though rents be heavy and bunks be few.. Never take rooms in a corner house. **1936** *St. Andrews Cit.* 5 Sept. 12/4 Quiet bunk required by student. **1937** *Ibid.* 27 Feb. 7/3 Those bunk-wives who refuse students any concession.

2. 'A piece of wood placed on a lumberman's sled to enable it to sustain the end of heavy pieces of timber. *Maine* (*U.S.*).' Bartlett.

1770 M. PATTEN *Diary* (1903) 238, I hewed a bunk and a Slat for my brors loging Sled. **1902** S. E. WHITE *Blazed Trail* 72 These sleighs, with.. bunks nine feet in width for the reception of logs.

†**bunk**, *sb.*[2] *Obs.* Also **bunken, bunkins.** [Cf. *bunk* 'nascaptha, an odoriferous root', given as Arabic in Johnson's Pers.-Ar.-Eng. Dict., 1852; not in Freytag or Lane.]

A plant (or root) yielding a drug.

1660 *Act 12 Chas. II*, iv. Sched., Bunkins, Holliwortles, or pistolachia. **1753** CHAMBERS *Cycl. Supp.*, *Bunk*, or *Bunken*, a word frequently occurring in the writings of the Arabian physicians.. it was an aromatic root used in cardiac, stomachic, and carminative compositions. **1775** ASH *Bunk, Bunken* (in medicine), the leucacantha.

bunk, *sb.*[3] [f. BUNK *v.*[2]] In slang phr. ***to do a bunk***: to make an escape; to depart hurriedly.

c **1870** *Broadside Ball., 'Peck's Bad Boy'* (Farmer), The keeper tried to catch him, but the bad boy did a bunk. **1905** E. CANDLER *Unveiling of Lhasa* xiii. 256 The old bloke's done a bunk. **1919** J. B. MORTON *Barber of Putney* ix, 'All right, son,' said Curly. 'They [*sc.* Germans] done a bunk.' **1921** G. B. SHAW *Back to Methuselah* IV. III. 199 If my legs would support me I'd just do a bunk straight for the ship.

bunk, *sb.*[4] *slang* (orig. *U.S.*). [Abbrev. of BUNKUM.] Humbug, nonsense.

1900 ADE *More Fables* 15 He surmised that the Bunk was about to be Handed to him. **1916** H. FORD in *Chicago Tribune* 25 May 10/1 History is more or less bunk. **1930** *Punch* 5 Mar. 265/3 No tempting blurb, no critics' bunk Can animate this mass of junk. **1932** W. S. MAUGHAM *For Services Rendered* III. 70 It's all bunk what they're saying to you, about honour and patriotism and glory, bunk, bunk, bunk.

bunk, *v.*[1] [f. BUNK *sb.*[1]] *intr.* To sleep in a bunk; *hence*, to occupy rough sleeping quarters, camp out. Also, ***to bunk it.*** (*colloq.*, chiefly U.S.) Also ***to bunk down***: to go to bed, retire to bed.

1840 R. H. DANA *Bef. Mast* viii, We turned in to bunk and mess with the crew forward. **1850** H. C. WATSON *Camp-Fires Revol.* 250 It's about time for us to bunk. **1861** C. ANDERSON *Okavango Riv.* xxvii. 317 They would not let us .. sleep in their huts; we had to bunk it out on the sand. **1884** J. G. BOURKE *Snake Dance* v. 53 My comrade and myself bunked together in the double bed. **1885** *Pall Mall G.* 29 Aug. 61 The Orientals are a 'bunking' people. **1940** *War Illustr.* 2 Feb. 59/2, I.. was snugly bunked down when the explosion happened. **1965** M. SHADBOLT *Among Cinders* ii. 9, I was wondering if this might be a decent place to bunk down for the night.

bunk (bʌŋk), *v.*[2] *colloq.* and *slang.*

1. To be off. Also const. *about.*

1877 E. PEACOCK *N.W. Lincoln. Gloss.* (E.D.S.), *Bunk*, to run away, to make off. **1880** BESANT & RICE *Seamy Side* ix. 67 Mark my words, Bunk it is. **1881** *Leicestersh. Gloss.* (E.D.S.), *Bunk*.. budge! be off! *apage!* **1949** R. ALDINGTON *Strange Life of C. Waterton* xiii. 160 A schoolboy prefers to bunk about the fields.. rather than work in class.

2. *trans.* To expel from school. So **bunked** *ppl. a.*, expelled.

1890 FARMER *Slang* I. 385/2 *Bunk*, (Wellington College) —To expel (from the school). *c* **1898** WYNDHAM LEWIS *Lett.* (1963) 6 A sixth (form boy) has been bunked (expelled) for stealing out of the shop in town. **1902** W. S. MAUGHAM *Mrs. Craddock* xxviii. 283, I was bunked from Rugby. Well, that wasn't my fault.. . I'm blowed if I was worse than anybody else. **1923** H. WALPOLE *Jeremy & Hamlet* i. 21 A chap called Bates got bunked for stealing.

bunked (bʌŋkt), *a.* [f. BUNK *sb.*[1] + -ED[2].] Furnished with or having a bunk or bunks.

1892 STEVENSON & OSBOURNE *Wrecker* xiii. 209 A double bunked division for the cook.. and second mate. **1940** *Economist* 9 Nov. 575/2 A survey is being taken of private basement shelters, much of which will be bunked.

bunker ('bʌŋkə(r)), *sb.*[1] Also 9 **bunkart.** [Etymology uncertain; cf. BUNK and BANKER[4].]

1. A seat or bench ('serving also for a chest' Jamieson). *Sc.*

a **1758** RAMSAY *Poems* (1844) 91 Ithers frae aff the bunkers sank. **1790** BURNS *Tam o' Shanter* 119 At winnock-bunker.. sat auld Nick. **1818** SCOTT *Hrt. Midl.* ix, No seat accommodated him so well as the 'bunker' at Woodend. *attrib.* **1831** *Hone's Year-book* 1127 Upon the bunker seat of the window they found three bottles.

2. An earthen seat or bank in the fields. *dial.*

1805 *Leslie of Powis, &c.* (JAM.) The fishers.. built an open bunkart or seat. **1880** *Antrim & Down Gloss.* (E.D.S.), *Bunker*, a low bank at a road side, a road side channel.

3. a. A receptacle for coal on board ship; sometimes also on land.

1839 *Parl. Report Steam Vessel Accid.* 74 Neither the bunkers nor the coal-hold were cleared out so often as they should be. **1851** *Illust. Lond. News* 24 Bunkers to hold 890 tons of coal. **1864** *Times* 10 Dec., The Cadmus has.. her bunkers filled with upwards of 200 tons of coal. **1876** DAVIS *Polaris Exp.* xviii. 450 The bunkers and bulkheads below deck were torn down. **1921** *Dict. Occup. Terms* (1927) §279 *Bunkerman*.. tips wagons to discharge coal or iron into bunkers at ironworks. **1930** *Engineering* 16 May 629/3 This conveyor distributes the coal to three bunkers.

b. *pl.* = *bunker coal* (see 5 below).

1883 GRESLEY *Gloss. Coal-m.*, *Bunkers*, steam coal consumed on board ship. **1898** *Daily News* 18 Apr. 11/5 More money has to be paid for steam, bunkers, and gas coals. **1935** *Economist* 5 Jan. 48/2 Prime unscreened bunkers, 13s. 6d.

c. = *bunker-man* (see 5 below).

1921 *Dict. Occup. Terms* (1927) §744 *Bunker*, tips coal from baskets or trucks into coal bins or bunkers as they are lowered by hoist... *Collier*.. includes bunker, trimmer, loader.

4. a. *Golf*: 'A sandy hollow formed by the wearing away of the turf on the "links"' (*Sc.*). Now, an artificial sand-hole with a built-up face; also, any natural obstruction (as water, long grass, etc.) on a golf-course.

1824 SCOTT *Redgauntlet* Let. x, They sat cosily niched into what you might call a *bunker*, a little sand-pit. **1857** CHAMBERS *Inform. People* II. 693/2 This club is useful too for elevating a ball.. over.. bunkers, whins, etc. **1857** H. B. FARNIE in J. L. Stewart *Golfiana Miscellanea* (1887) 119 The surface is dotted over at frequent intervals with sandy holes, technically called bunkers, from two to six feet deep, of irregular forms and sizes. **1867** *Cornh. Mag.* Apr. 496 A fellow who puts you into a whin or a bunker every other stroke. **1893** H. G. HUTCHINSON *Golfing* 60 Sometimes you may be driven to invent hazards, by throwing up banks, cutting bunkers or planting bushes. **1897** *Encycl. Sport* I. 458/1 Between the teeing-ground and the putting-green should be found, whether they be natural or artificially formed, various 'hazards' in the shape of sand-pits or 'bunkers'. *Ibid.* 472/1 *Bunker*, originally a natural sand hole on the golf course. Now used also of artificially made hazards with built-up faces. **1955** *Times* 17 May 5/6 Mrs. Smith cut her second shot into the rough and put her recovery into a bunker on the right.

b. *fig.*

1900 A. BIRRELL in *Cornhill Mag.* Mar. 313 If you want to find the natural man at work you must look for him in the bunkers of life. **1905** *Westm. Gaz.* 28 Oct. 16/1 The Princess frock is a bunker not to be cleared by any economies or adaptations.

c. A military dug-out; a reinforced concrete shelter.

1939 *War Pictorial* 13 Oct. 29/2 A Nazi field gun hidden in a cemented 'bunker' on the Western front. **1945** *Over-All Report* (U.S. Strategic Bombing Survey, Europ. War) 30 Sept. 104/1 Germany promised its people 'bombproof' shelters for all, and planned the construction of extensive above-ground concrete structures known as 'bunkers'. **1947** H. TREVOR-ROPER *Last Days of Hitler* iv. 117 A curved stair led downwards to a still deeper and slightly larger bunker. This was.. Hitler's own bunker, the stage on which the last act of the Nazi melodrama was played out. **1949** F. MACLEAN *Eastern Approaches* III. iv. 354 The turf-covered 'bunkers' in which the Germans and Ustaše had made their last stand.

5. *attrib.* and *Comb.* (See also sense 1.) Also (sense 4) ***bunker-iron***; **bunker coal**, *spec.* steam coal; also, coal carried by a steamer for its own use and not as cargo; **bunker-man** (see quot. 1921).

1885 *Pall Mall G.* 19 Dec. 9/1 Calling.. to embark bunker coals for use on the voyage. **1888** *Daily News* 10 July 5/2 The exports of 'bunker' coal.. show an improvement. **1857** H. B. FARNIE in J. L. Stewart *Golfiana Miscellanea* (1887) 142 Some bunker irons of the old make are round bottomed. **1886** A. LANG in *Longman's Mag.* July 332 The iron head makes it more like a bunker iron than a play club. **1921** *Dict. Occup. Terms* (1927) §089 *Bunker-man*, in charge of bunkers at coke ovens where coal is stored. *Ibid.* §279 [see sense 3 a above]. **1882** *Harper's Mag.* 594 The trail of smoke from that bunker steamer.

'**bunker**, *sb.*[2] *local U.S.* Short for MOSSBUNKER.

1842 J. E. DEKAY *Zool. N. Y.* IV. 260 The Mossbonker... At the east end of the island, they are called Skippangs or Bunkers. **1888** [see MOSSBUNKER].

'**bunker**, *v.* [f. BUNKER *sb.*[1]]

1. *trans.* To fill the bunkers of (a steamer) with coal or oil for its own consumption. Also with the coal or oil as object.

1891 *Pall Mall Gaz.* 19 Jan. 4/1 Many.. of the great steamship companies of Liverpool were simply begging for coal to either bunker or cargo their steamers. **1893** *Times* 11 July 3/6 The ordinary rate of bunkering coal by manual labour. **1925** *Blackw. Mag.* June 836/1 She was bunkered for the twenty-nine days' run to Batavia.

b. *intr.* To take in a supply of coal or oil for consumption on a voyage.

1893 *Whitby Gaz.* 3 Feb. 2/6 The foreign coaling clause in the outward coal charter bound them to bunker with the agents of the charterers. **1895** *Ibid.* 11 Apr. 3/2 We bunkered at Malta at four o'clock in the morning. **1925** *Chambers's Jrnl.* Dec. 778/2 There was some delay at Durban, where she bunkered.

2. *Golf. pass.* **a.** Of the ball: to be hit into a bunker. Of a player: to have one's ball in a bunker.

1886 H. G. HUTCHINSON *Hints Game Golf* 40 Your adversary is badly bunkered. **1891** —— *Famous Golf Links* v. 56 His ball lofted on Mr. Maitland's, knocked it out of the hazard, and lay bunkered in its place. **1903** *Punch* 22 Apr. 283 On.. the Golf Links.. watching the Colonel, who has been bunkered for the last ten minutes. **1955** *Times* 19 May 4/7 She was bunkered at the 18th.

b. To be furnished with a bunker or bunkers.

1907 *Daily Chron.* 17 Aug. 7/2 The point of controversy.. is as to how such a hole should be bunkered, or rather as to whether it should be bunkered at all.

c. *fig.* (*colloq.*) To be placed in a situation from which it is difficult to extricate oneself. Also, to place in such a situation.

1894 BARON RIBBLESDALE in *Westm. Gaz.* 6 Sept. 4/2 The Liberal peers were powerless. To use a golfing simile, they were bunkered. **1899** *Geogr. Jrnl.* May 474 In the long narrow ice-bound valleys which lead up from the Hindu Kush to the Pamirs.. we were once, to use a familiar term, fairly bunkered. **1905** *Westm. Gaz.* 27 Dec. 1/3 The truth is that Mr. Balfour is bunkered by his own record. **1917** H. A.

VACHELL *Fishpingle* ix, 'Perhaps you regard golf as a sort of epitome of life?'..'I suppose I do.' 'If you found yourself "bunkered", you would not lose heart?' **1930** G. B. SHAW *Apple Cart* I. 18 *Balbus.* Thatll do it. He couldnt face that. *Crassus.* Yes: thatll bunker him.

bunkering ('bʌŋkərɪŋ), *vbl. sb.* [f. BUNKER *v.*]
1. The action of filling a ship's bunkers with coal or oil. Also *attrib.*
1899 *Westm. Gaz.* 7 Nov. 9/3 It is thought that the North country coal will be used by transports for bunkering. **1920** *Act 10 & 11 Geo. V* c. 50 §3 Regulating the export of coal and the supply of coal for the bunkering of vessels. **1922** *Daily Mail* 9 Nov. 3 A group of foreign bunkering depots. **1958** *Times Rev. Industry* May 51/3 The bunkering trade has increased in proportion to output and Kuwait now delivers well over one million tons of bunker oils a year to ocean-going vessels.
2. The action of furnishing (a golf course) with bunkers.
1909 *Westm. Gaz.* 8 Mar. 12/2 The final bunkering of the course.

bunkery ('bʌŋkərɪ), *a.* [f. BUNKER *sb.*[1] 4 + -Y[1].] Full of or abounding in bunkers.
1890 *Sat. Rev.* 31 May 665/2 That mountainous range of bunkery sandhills. **1894** *Blackw. Mag.* Oct. 561 The sand was..strewed in a thick bunkery mattress over all the ladies' links.

'bunkie, 'bunky. *U.S. colloq.* [f. BUNK *sb.*[1] 1 + -Y[6].] One who shares a bunk with another.
1858 VIELÉ *Following the Drum* 218 Which triumph over paternal love I rewarded by giving him Jack for his 'bunkie'. **1903** *N.Y. Even. Post* 10 Oct., In a logging camp in Maine a lanky Yankee had been unburdening himself of his past life for the entertainment of his 'bunky'. **1910** W. M. RAINE *B. O'Connor* 58 If it is certain that my old bunkie came to his death foully. **1948** *Southwest Rev.* Winter 29/2 The next morning Bud's 'bunkie' sat watching him shave.

bunkin, obs. variant of BUMPKIN.

'bunkin. Var. of, or misreading for, BUNTING[1].
1570 LEVINS *Manip.* 133 A Bunkin, bird, *terraneola.*

bunko. Variant form of BUNCO *sb.* and *v.*

bunkum, etc.: see BUNCOMBE, etc.

bunk-up, *sb.* [Cf. BUNT *sb.*[8] and E.D.D. 'a bunt up' (1888).] A lifting-up.
1919 DOWNING *Digger Dialects* 14 *Bunk-up*, a lifting up. **1938** F. D. SHARPE *S. of Flying Squad* v. 51, I was given a bunk up, and..got through the wire. **1951** A. BARON *Rosie Hogarth* II. iii. 103 'Here,' he appealed, 'give us a bunk-up, someone.'

bunn(e, obs. f. BOUND *sb.*[1] limit, and BUN.

bunned (bʌnd), *a.* [f. BUN *sb.*[2] 1 b + -ED[2].] Of hair: coiled into a bun.
1944 *Penguin New Writing* XXI. 77 Hair straggled and bunned. **1951** W. SANSOM *Face of Innocence* iv. 59 Her tweeds and her efficiently bunned hair.

†**'bunnell.** *Obs.* exc. *dial.* A beverage made from the crushed apples or pears, after nearly all the juice has been expressed for the cider or perry.
1594 BARNFIELD *Affect. Sheph.* II. xii, Bunnell and Perry I haue for thee. **1693** W. ROBERTSON *Phraseol. Gen.* 1327 A drink much like our Bunnel, in the Perry-countrey.

bunnet, obs. variant of BONNET.

bunnia ('bʌnjə). *India.* Also buneeya, bunia, -ar; bunneah, bunniah, bunnya; bania, -(i)ya. [Hind. *banyā*, a. Gujarati *vāniya* (see BANIAN).] A trader or merchant. Also *attrib.*
The usual form now is *bania.*
1794 MORSE *Amer. Geogr.* 687 The tribe of Beise, who are chiefly merchants, bankers, and banias or shopkeepers. **1829** *Encycl. Metrop.* XX. 33/2 Some of the Banyás are Awaks, or seceders from the Brahmanical faith. **1879** MRS. A. E. JAMES *Ind. Househ. Managem.* 77 The native *bunniahs*..do not give long credit. **1880** *Encycl. Brit.* XII. 760/1 In the interior of the Bombay Presidency, business is mainly divided between two classes, the Baniyas of Guzerat and the Marwaris from Rajputana. **1926** *Blackw. Mag.* Dec. 799/1 The Hindu Bunia in remote villages is still bullied by the wealthy zamindar of the neighbourhood. **1936** J. NEHRU *Autobiogr.* liii. 432 The *bania* civilisation of the capitalist West. **1945** 'P. WOODRUFF' *Call Next Witness* I. 30 Banias reckoning the day's gains.

†**'bunnikin.** *Obs. rare*$^{-1}$. Some early flower.
1657 PURCHAS *Pol. Flying Ins.* I. xv. 94 Bees gather these flowers following..in March... Bunnikin.

bunning, obs. variant of BUNDING.

†**'bunny**[1]. *Obs.* Forms: 5 bony, 6 bounny, 7 bonny, 6–7 bunnye, 6 bunny. [perh. a. OF. *bugne, beugne*, var. forms of *bigne*, a swelling caused by a blow; cf. *boine* (dial.) under BOIN *v.*; also BUNION.] A lump, hump, or swelling; *spec.* a soft watery swelling on the joints of animals.
c **1440** *Promp. Parv.* 43/2 Bony, or hurtynge Fleumon. *Ibid.* 44/1 Bony, or grete knobbe..*gibbus.* **1552** HULOET Bownche or bunnye, *gibba.* **1597** GERARD *Herbal* II. cclxxix. (1633) 793 Continual bunnies and looseness of certain joints. **1610** MARKHAM *Masterp.* II. lxxvi. 347 The Hough bonny is a round swelling like a Paris ball. **1667** N. FAIRFAX in *Phil. Trans.* II. 482 In some places his head bled; in others Bunnyes arose. **1784** SIR J. CULLUM *Hist. Hawsted* 170 A Bunny, a swelling from a blow.

bunny[2] ('bʌnɪ). [f. BUN *sb.*[4] + -Y.]
1. a. A pet name for a rabbit. †**b.** A term of endearment applied to women and children (*obs.*).
1690 B. E. *Dict. Cant. Crew*, *Bunny*, a Rabbit. **1719** D'URFEY *Pills* IV. 74 Downy as any Bunny. **1863** FR. KEMBLE *Resid. Georg.* 258 Rabbits..slightly different from our English bunnies. **1873** G. DAVIES *Mount. & Mere* vi. 46 Bunny gave a flick of his white tail.
1606 *Wily Beguil.* in Hazl. *Dodsley* IX. 252 Sweet Peg..my honey, my bunny, my duck, my dear. **1691** RAY *S. & E. Country Wds.*, *Bunny* is also used as a flattering word to children.
c. Rabbit-fur. *colloq.*
1950 H. MCCLOY *Through Glass Darkly* (1951) v. 44 Girls in wolf or bunny that looked almost like fox or ermine. **1955** M. LASKI *Apologies* 59 You know bunny wears just as well.
d. In full ***bunny girl.*** A night-club hostess, or the like, dressed in a costume which is partly imitative of a rabbit. Also ***attrib.***
1960 *Playboy* Aug. 42/1 The girls are called Bunnies and they're invitingly attired in brightly coloured rabbit costumes, complete to the ears and white cotton tails. *Ibid.*, Proportions..as remarkable as those of the Bunny Girls. **1963** *Listener* 7 Feb. 260/3 American Bunny Clubs, with their Freudian fantasy-tease hostesses. **1963** *Daily Mail* 16 Feb. 6/6 These bunnies are the newest import to London night-club life from America. *Ibid.* 6/7 The bunny costumes with their stylised unreality somehow defuse the provocation of the dress. **1966** 'E. E. SUMNER' *Second-hand Death* vii. 131 The girl..worked as a night club Bunny. **1967** J. GARDNER *Madrigal* i. 12 A fallen Bunny girl, with strange fetishes.
2. Bunny Mouth: the Common Snapdragon. *Antirrhinum majus.* Also called Rabbit's Mouth.
1846 SOWERBY *Brit. Bot.* **1847–78** in HALLIWELL.

'bunny[3]. '*In Mining.* A pipe of ore or a mass —not a vein or lode.' Ure *Dict. Arts.*

bunny[4] ('bʌnɪ). *dial.* 'A small ravine opening through the cliff line to the sea; as in Chewton Bunny, Beckton Bunny. Also any small drain, culvert,' etc. Cope *Hampsh. Gloss.* (E.D.S.) 1883.
1873 BLACKMORE *Cradock N.* xxxi. (1883) 180 The little village of Rushford was happy enough in its bunny. *Ibid.* 181 A boat house at the bottom of the bunny.

'bunny ˌhug. [f. BUNNY[2] 1 a + HUG *sb.*] A dance in ragtime rhythm, esp. popular in the early part of the 20th century. Hence **'bunny-ˌhugger, -ˌhugging.**
1912 *Daily Mirror* 6 Jan. 7/1 Fashionable society in New York..is fighting upon the great question as to whether ..'The Bunny Hug'..shall be..allowed. **1914** *Art* (U.S.) 290 It is not in the souls of the bunny-huggers that the new ferment is potent. **1916** *Daily Colonist* (Victoria, B.C.) 11 July 3/7 Such dances should not be classed with fox-trotting, bunny-hugging, Wilson gliding, [etc.]. **1926** GALSWORTHY *Silver Spoon* II. vi. 158 What is there to give up—bunny-hugging? **1937** *Evening News* 26 Jan. 9/4 Some time ago many people were dancing the bunny hug. **1954** DANNETT & RACHEL *Down Memory Lane* 70 The bunny hug survived its contemporaries and made the transition to jazz.

bunodont ('bju:nədɒnt), *a.* and *sb.* [f. Gr. βουνός mound + ὀδοντ-, ὀδούς tooth.] **A.** *adj.* Designating molar teeth whose crowns are elevated into tubercles; having tuberculate molars. **B.** *sb.* A mammal with teeth of this pattern.
1874 E. D. COPE in *Jrnl. Acad. Nat. Sci.* VIII. 72 Bunodont type; crown supporting tubercles. *Ibid.* 73 The Bunodonts, except some *Carnivora*, are all of the former or isognathous type. **1883** *Encycl. Brit.* XV. 429/2 The grinding surfaces of the molar teeth either of a distinctly tubercular (bunodont) or of a crescentic ridged (selenodont) form. **1902** *Nature* 25 Sept. 523 A series of six cheek-teeth, distinct and bunodont in type. **1969** *Ibid.* 22 Nov. 821/2 The Nagri suids..are low-skulled, with bunodont dentitions.

‖**bunraku** ('bunraku). [Jap.] A kind of traditional Japanese puppetry practised at the Bunraku-za marionette theatre by its company; also, a contracted name for this company; hence, the Japanese puppet theatre in general. Also *attrib.*
1920 B. KURE *Hist. Devel. Marionette Theatre Japan* 30 There are two schools in the marionette art: Yuki School, which manipulates the dolls by strings and Bunraku School, which makes the dolls act by holding them. **1936** *Travel in Japan* II. 24 Even on a stage of Bunraku's pretention, only puppets in important roles are handled by three manipulators. **1955** A. C. SCOTT *Kabuki Theatre of Japan* iv. 56 If ever there was a case for State support it is that of the Bunraku. *Ibid.*, The title Bunraku has now come to mean the doll theatre as a whole. **1959** *Listener* 12 Feb. 299/1 Like puppets in the Bunraku doll-theatre.

Bunsen ('bʊnsən, 'bʌnsən). Attributive use of the name of Professor R. W. E. Bunsen of Heidelberg, denoting appliances invented by him: **Bunsen('s) burner, lamp**, a kind of gas-burner used for heating and for blowpipe work, in which air is burnt along with gas. **Bunsen('s) battery**, a voltaic battery in which the elements are carbon and zinc, and in which nitric and sulphuric acids, or solution of bichromate of potash and sulphuric acid, are employed. **Bunsen cell**, one of the cells of which a Bunsen battery is composed.
1879 NOAD *Electricity* (ed. Preece) 179 Bunsen's battery has the cylindrical form of Daniell's. **1870** TYNDALL *Heat* ii. §54 As in the case of Bunsen's burner. **1870** *Eng. Mech.* 11 Feb. 525/1 [He] describes..a Bunsen cell modified by him.

bunsenite ('bʊnsənaɪt). *Min.* [f. BUNSEN, the name of the discoverer, + -ITE.] A native protoxide of nickel.
1868 DANA *Min.* 134.

bunt (bʌnt), *sb.*[1] Chiefly *Naut.* [Etymology unknown. Some have compared Da. *bundt*, Sw. *bunt* a bundle (which seem to be merely a. Ger. *bund*).] *gen.* A swelling, a pouch- or bag-shaped part of a net, sail, etc.
1. The cavity or bagging part of a fishing-net; also of a napkin or the like when folded or tied so as to form a bag; the funnel or bottom of an eel-trap.
1602 CAREW *Cornwall* 30 a, The Weare is a frith..hauing in it a bunt or cod. *a* **1648** DIGBY *Closet Open.* (1677) 216 That the whey may run..through the bunt of the napkin. **1861** COUCH *Brit. Fishes* II. 73 The sean for Mackarel is.. nine fathoms in depth at the middle or bunt. **1880** *Harper's Mag.* LX. 852 As the bunt of the seine nears the shore, silence prevails. **1883** *Fisheries Exhib. Catal.* 367 Apparatus ..to be fixed at the end of the bunt of an Eel Trap.
2. 'The middle part of a sail, formed designedly into a bag or cavity, that the sail may gather more wind. In "handed" or "furled" sails, the bunt is the middle gathering which is tossed up on the centre of the yard' (Smyth *Sailor's Word-bk.*). **b.** The middle part of a yard: the *Slings.*
c **1582** *Cotton MS. App.* xlvii. (Halliw.) Flying fyshes to break ther noses agaynst the bunt of the sayle. **1611** COTGR., *Bourser*,..to bunt, or leaue a bunt in a sayle. **1627** [see BUNTLINE]. **1678–96** PHILLIPS, *Bunt*, the hollowness which is allowed in making of Sails. **1706** —— *Bunt*, (Sea-term) the Bag, Pouch, or middle Part of a Sail, which serves to catch and keep the wind; as The Bunt holds much Leeward Wind, i.e. the Bunt hangs too much to the Leeward. **1794** *Rigging & Seamanship* I. 86 *Bunt*, the middle-part of the foot of square sails, and the foremost leech of staysails cut with a nock. **1881** CLARK RUSSELL *Ocean Fr.-Lance* ii. 31 The bunt of the top-gallant sail. **1882** NARES *Seamanship* (ed. 6) 10 *Slings* or *Bunt*, the middle of a yard where the rigging is placed.
3. *Comb.*, as ***bunt-gasket, -whip***; **bunt-jigger**, 'a small gun-tackle purchase..used in large vessels for bowsing up the bunt of a sail when furling' (*Sailor's Word-bk.*). Also BUNTLINE.
1860 H. STUART *Seaman's Catech.* 18 Bunt lines, bow-lines, and bunt jiggers. *Ibid.* 46 The sail loosers..overhaul the buntlines and bunt whip.
b. ***bunt fair***, adv. phr.: 'Before the wind' (Smyth *Sailor's Word-bk.*).
1653 URQUHART *Rabelais* II. i, Spooming with a full Sail, bunt fair before the Wind.

bunt (bʌnt), *sb.*[2] *Bot.* [Origin unknown.]
†**1.** The Puffball (*Lycoperdon bovista*). Now *dial.*
1601 HOLLAND *Pliny* XVI. xl. I. 490 Tinder, made..of bunts and withered leaues. **1609** C. BUTLER *Fem. Mon.* VII. (1623) Q iij, Smother them with Brimstone or Bunt, as you kill Bees. **1878** BRITTEN & HOLLAND *Plant-n.*, Bunt, *Lycoperdon Bovista*, Nhamp.
2. A parasitic fungoid, *Tilletia caries*, which attacks wheat, filling the grain with black fetid powder; also the disease caused by it.
1797 *Ann. Reg.* 409/2 Wheat..very much injured by smut-balls or bunts. **1847** BERKELEY *Jrnl. Horticult. Soc. London* II. 108 The principal diseases of plants, such as rust, bunt, mildew, etc., are of vegetable origin. **1865** Carter's *Gard. & Farmer's Vade-M.* II. 124 Bunt..results in a swollen discoloured seed..On the kernel being broken, it is found to be full of a black stinking powder. **1882** A. CAREY *Princ. Agricult.* xix. 164 Bunt, or Smut-ball, the most formidable disease, perhaps, to which wheat is subject.

bunt, *sb.*[3] *rare*$^{-1}$. [perh. related to BUN *sb.*[1]] ? A portion of the stem or rachis of corn.
1775 *Specif. Rawlinsons Patent* No. 1099 A coarse try [sieve] to convey the bunts from the chaff and corn.

bunt, *sb.*[4] ? *Obs.* [f. BUNT *v.*[3]] **a.** An instrument for sifting meal. **b.** in *comb.* **bunt-mill**, a machine for cleaning corn.
1794 STEDMAN *Surinam* (1813) II. xxvi. 298 Their dancing music..is not unlike that of a baker's bunt, when he separates the flour from the bran. *Ibid.* xxix. 369 Separated from the chaff through a bunt-mill.

bunt (bʌnt), *sb.*[5] *Sc.* and *dial.* [Var. and perh. more original form of BUN *sb.*[3]] The tail of a hare or rabbit.
1805 A. SCOTT *Hare's Compl.* in *Poems* 79 (JAM.) A strolling hound Had near hand catched me by the bunt. **1877** E. PEACOCK *N.W. Lincoln. Gloss. Bunt*, the tail of a rabbit.

bunt, *sb.*[6] *local.* A medium quality of fagot.
'There are three classes of fagots for household use in Sussex, 1. brish fagots or kiln fagots, 2. seconds, spray fagots, lordings, or bunts, 3. house-fagots (the best quality).' —Rev. W. D. Parish.
1884 *West Sussex G.* 25 Sept. *Advt.*, Clearance Stock of Agricultural Drain Tiles, Pipes, Bricks, etc., and a quantity of Bunts, Faggots, Mare, Pony, and other stock.

bunt, *sb.*^{7} *cant.* [Of unknown origin: cf. BUNCE.] An extra profit or gain; something to the good. (See quot.)

1851 MAYHEW *Lond. Labour* I, 33 'Boys' deputed to sell a man's goods for a certain sum, all over that amount being the boy's profit or bunts [on p. 470 spelt *bunse*]. **1881** *Cheq. Career* 270 In the stable..in livery-stables, there is a box into which all tips are placed. This is called 'Bunt'.

bunt, *sb.*^{8} *dial.* **1.** The action of BUNT *v.*^{2}

1767 *Boston Gaz.* 19 Jan. (Th.), [The black ram] will sometimes come behind a great Weather..and give him a paultry Bunt at unawares. **1875** PARISH *Sussex Dial.* s.v., A bunt is described to me as a push with a knock in it, or a knock with a push in it.

2. *Baseball.* An act of stopping the ball with the bat without striking. Also *bunt-hit. U.S.*

1889 *Chicago Tribune* 8 Aug. 6/1 Connor got around on bases on balls given himself and Richardson, Ward's bunt toward third..and a wild pitch. **1896** KNOWLES & MORTON *Baseball* 114 A bunt hit is a deliberate attempt on the part of the batsmen to hit a ball slowly within the infield so that it cannot be fielded by any fielder in time to retire the batsman. **1917** MATHEWSON *Sec. Base Sloan* ii. 169 Despaigne started out poorly enough, trickling a bunt to third. **1968** *Washington Post* 4 July C 1/8 With Rich Reese looking for a bunt and charging in from first base, Azcue punched his game-winning hit into right field.

bunt, *sb.*^{9} *Aeronaut.* [perh. f. BUNT *v.*^{2}] A manœuvre in aerobatics involving half an outside loop followed by a half roll.

1932 *Techn. Rep. Aeronaut. Research Comm. 1930–1931* I. 47 Load factors one half that of normal flight would be adequate to cover the manoeuvre known as the bunt. **1935** C. G. BURGE *Compl. Bk. Aviation* 89/2 Like most aerobatic manoeuvres the bunt was first done by Pégoud.

bunt, *v.*^{1} *Naut.* [f. BUNT *sb.*^{1}]

1. *trans.* 'To haul up the middle part of (a sail) in furling' (Smyth *Sailor's Word-bk.*).

1611 COTGR., *Bourser*, to bunt, or leaue a bunt in a sayle. **1756** *Gentl. Mag.* XXVI. 449 Haul'd up my courses, bunted my main sail.

2. *intr.* Of a sail: To swell, to belly.

1681 [see BUNTING *vbl. sb.*^{1}]. **1755** in JOHNSON, and in mod. Dicts. (Not in SMYTH *Sailor's Word-bk.*)

bunt, *v.*^{2} Chiefly *dial.* [cf. BUTT *v.*; also BUNCH, BOUNCE; Breton has *bounta* in same sense, but connexion is scarcely possible.]

1. *trans.* and *intr.* To strike, knock, push, butt.

1825 *Wiltsh. Gloss.*, *Bunt*, to strike with the head, as a young animal pushes the udder of its dam. **1867** BUSHNELL *Mor. Uses Dark Th.* 203 When the gusty shocks of broad-side pressure bunt upon the house. **1875** PARISH *Sussex Dial.*, *Bunt*, to rock a cradle with the foot; to push or butt.

2. *Baseball.* To stop (the ball) with the bat without swinging the latter. Also *absol.* So **'bunted** *ppl. a.*, **'bunting** *vbl. sb.*^{2}

1889 *Reach's Base Ball Guide* 144 Bunted Ball. **1892** *Courier-Journal* 2 Oct. 13/5 There is not a man in his team that can bunt. **1896** *Spalding's Base Ball Guide* 77 The 'bunting' of the ball, so as to cause it to drop to the ground almost dead. **1912** MATHEWSON *Pitching* ii. 23 Doyle bunted and was safe, filling the bases. *Ibid.* xiii. 298 Once, ..McGraw planned a bunting game against Overall. **1967** *Boston Sunday Herald* (This Week Mag.) 9 Apr. 5/2 Don't wait till after a pitch is thrown to decide whether the batter will bunt or try for the hit-and-run.

bunt, *v.*^{3} *dial.* [Etymology unknown: goes with BUNT *sb.*^{4} (In the 13th c. quot. we might read *boutep*, as a possible variant of *bultep*, from BOLT *v.*^{1}; but the spelling with *ou* does not otherwise occur until 15th c., and is peculiarly northern.)] *trans.* To sift (meal).

1340 *Ayenb.* 93 Ase þe ilke þet bonteþ þet mele, þet to-delþ þet flour uram þe bren. **1880** MISS COURTNEY *W. Cornw. Gloss.*, *Bunting*, sifting flour. **1883** *Hampsh. Gloss.* (E.D.S.) *Bunt*, to sift meal.

buntal ('bʌntəl). [Philippine name. See also BALIBUNTAL.] A straw prepared from the fibres of the petioles, or leaf-stems, of the talipot or buri palm (*Corypha umbraculifera*), used for the manufacture of hats in the Philippine Islands. Also *attrib.*

1910 H. H. MILLER *Philippine Hats* 38 Very lately, buntal straw has been imported into Baliwag and there woven into very beautiful hats in the Baliwag weave. **1911** C. B. ROBINSON in *Philippine Jrnl. Science* June 114 Until the beginning of 1909, all buntal hats were made in one weave, that of Lucban, Tayabas. **1926** *Commerce & Industry Jrnl.* (Manila, P.I.) Nov. 11 The hat manufacturers of China.. are making hats out of buntal fibers from the Philippines.

bunted ('bʌntɪd), *ppl. a.* [f. BUNT *sb.*^{2} 2 + -ED^{2}.] Of wheat: Infected with bunt.

1857 BERKELEY *Cryptog. Bot.* 318 Bunted wheat often forms a large proportion in flour, and is used more particularly for the manufacture of gingerbread.

†**bunter**^{1} ('bʌntə(r)). *Obs.* exc. *dial.* [Etymology unknown.] 'A cant word for a woman who picks up rags about the street; and used, by way of contempt, for any low vulgar woman.' J. (Also see quots.) Also *attrib.*

1707 E. WARD *Hudibras Rediv.* II. II. ii. (1715) 25 Punks, Strolers, Market Dames, and Bunters. **1721** BAILEY, *Bunter*, a gatherer of Rags in the Streets for the making of Paper. **1758** *Monthly Rev.* 184 A nasty bunter or stinking dirty fish drab. **1759** H. WALPOLE *Par. Register* in A. Dobson *Fielding* v. 118 There Fielding met his bunter muse. **1763** *Brit. Mag.* IV. 542, I heard a bunter at the Horse-guards last Friday evening swear she would not venture into the Park. **1819** *Abeillard & Hel.* 344 Complete fox-hunters and much addicted to the bunters. *a* **1852** MAYHEW *Lond. Labour* (1861) II. 142/1 Old women alone gathered the substance [dogs' dung], and they were known by the name of 'bunters', which signifies properly gatherers of rags. **1861** *Ibid.* Extra vol. (1862) 223/1 There is a class of women technically known as 'bunters', who take lodgings, and after staying some time run away without paying their rent. **1891** C. WORDSWORTH *Rutland Words* 5 *Bunter*, a disreputable woman. 'She stood at the gate and called me a *bunter*.'

‖**bunter**^{2} ('bʊntər). *Geol.* Short for *bunter Sandstein*, i.e. 'mottled sandstone', German name for the New Red Sandstone.

[**1830** LYELL *Princ. Geol.* xiii. (1850) 187 The Muschelkalk, Keuper, and Bunter Sandstein.] **1874** —— *Elem. Geol.* xxii. (1885) 331 The basement beds of the Keuper rest with a slight unconformability, upon an eroded surface of the Bunter. **1881** J. E. LEE *Note-bk. Amat. Geol.* 72 The bone-bed has evidently filled cracks or hollows in the 'bunter'.

'bunter^{3}. *dial.* [f. BUNT *v.*^{3}] 'An old-fashioned machine for cleaning corn.' Parish *Sussex Dial.* 1875.

bunting ('bʌntɪŋ), *sb.*^{1} Also 4 **bountyng**, 5 **buntynge**; cf. the variants BUNKIN, BUNTYLE, BUNTLIN. [Origin unknown: Skeat suggests comparison with BUNT *v.*^{2}, Sc. *buntin* short and thick, plump (see 3), BUNT *sb.*^{5}, Welsh *bontin* the rump, *bontinog* large-buttocked.]

1. a. The English name of a group of insessorial birds, the *Emberizinæ*, a sub-family of *Fringillidæ* allied to the larks. The chief species are the **common b.** (*E. miliaris*), also called **corn b.**; **yellow b.** (*E. citrinella*) = YELLOW-HAMMER; **black-headed b.**; **reed b.** (*E. schœniclus*); **snow b.** (*Plectrophanes nivalis*), a bird inhabiting the arctic regions, and visiting Britain in the winter; **rice b.** (*Dolichonyx oryzivorus*) = BOBOLINK. See also CIRL, ORTOLAN 2 a, REED-BUNTING, SNOW-BUNTING.

c **1300** in Wright *Lyric P.* XI. ix. 40 Ich wold ich were a threstelcok, A bountyng other a lavercok. *c* **1440** *Promp. Parv.* 56 Buntynge, byrde, *pratellus.* **1601** SHAKS. *All's Well* II. v. 7, I tooke this Larke for a bunting. **1655** MOUFFET & BENN. *Health's Improv.* (1746) 188 Buntings feed chiefly upon little Worms. **1789** G. WHITE *Selborne* xiii. (1853) 57 The bunting does not leave this country in the winter. **1878** MARKHAM *Gt. Frozen Sea* xxiv. Great excitement was caused by the appearance of a snow bunting.

b. Applied by extension to any bird of the bunting subfamily, and to similar birds of other families. *U.S.*

1831 WILSON & BONAPARTE *Amer. Ornith.* II. 242 Black-throated Bunting... In their shape and manners they very much resemble the yellow-hammer of Britain. *Ibid.* 245 *Fringilla Graminea*,..*Emberiza Graminea*..Bay-winged Bunting. **1893** NEWTON *Dict. Birds* 459 Indigo-bird,..a well-known North-American species,..American ornithologists give full accounts of the habits of this bird, together with those of..the still more gaudy Painted Bunting. **1964** A. L. THOMSON *New Dict. Birds* 112/1 The buntings (Emberizinae) are predominantly terrestrial.

2. The grey shrimp (*Crangon vulgaris*).

1836 *Scenes Comm. by Land & S.* 92 Red shrimps, white shrimps, and buntings, or grey shrimps, of which the last are most esteemed for their flavour.

3. A term of endearment: in 'baby bunting', the meaning (if there be any at all) may possibly be as in Jamieson's '*buntin*, short and thick, as a buntin brat, a plump child'.

1665 DAVENANT *Wits* III. i, Bunting [to the speaker's wife] in very deed, You are to blame. *Nursery Rime.* Bye, baby bunting, Father's gone a hunting.

4. *attrib.*, esp. **bunting lark**, the corn bunting; also *bunting-lark fly*, an angler's fly.

1802 MONTAGU *Ornith. Dict.* I, Bunting-lark. **1837** KIRKBRIDE *Northern Angler* 25 The Bunting Lark Fly. **1876** *Encycl. Brit.* IV. 525/2 The true Bunting (or Corn-Bunting, or Bunting-Lark, as it is called in some districts). **1884** COUES *N. Amer. Birds* (ed. 2) 356 Bill very small and truly conic, well exhibiting 'emberizine' or 'bunting' characters.

'bunting, *sb.*^{2} Also 8–9 **buntine**. [Origin uncertain: it has been conjecturally derived from BUNT *v.*^{3} to sift, bolt. The analogy of the Fr. *étamine*, which means both bolting-cloth and bunting, supports this derivation, although there is no evidence that *bunting* was ever actually used for 'bolting-cloth'. The fact mentioned in quot. 1836 would suggest connexion with Ger. *bunt*, Du. *bont* parti-coloured. (The word is not in Beawes *Lex Mercatoria Rediviva* 1752, which has always *estamina*, *-as*).]

a. 'An open-made worsted stuff, used for making flags' (Ure *Dict. Arts*); also in general, a flag, or flags collectively.

1742 *Navy Board Letter to L.C.A.* 24 Sept. (MS. in Pub. Rec. O.) The French and Spanish colours allowed his Majesty's Ships are of bunting, whereas those used by the French and Spanish are of linen. **1755** JOHNSON, *Bunting*, the stuff of which a ship's colours are made. **1769** FALCONER *Dict. Marine* (1789) *Buntine*, a thin woollen stuff, of which the colours and signals of a ship are usually formed. **1832** MARRYAT *N. Forster* xxxvi, Up goes her bunting. **1836** *Scenes Comm. by Land & S.* 235 Buntine is a thin open sort of woollen stuff..it is woven in stripes, blue, white, red. **1845** DARWIN *Voy. Nat.* viii. (1879) 161 A net made of bunting. **1871** PITMAN *Phonogr.* 7 Bunting, streaming from the masthead.

b. *attrib.* **bunting-tosser** *Naval slang*, a signaller.

1905 *Daily Chron.* 23 Jan. 3/1 From which breathless catalogue it will be gathered that the path of the 'bunting-tosser' is not an easy one! **1909** in J. R. WARE *Passing Eng.*

'bunting, *vbl. sb.*^{1} [f. BUNT *v.*^{1} + -ING^{1}.] The bellying, bulging, or swelling of a sail, a net, etc.

1681 *Phil. Collect.* XII. No. 3. 62 Without any bellying, bunting, or curvity in the superficies thereof.

bunting *vbl. sb.*^{2}: see BUNT *v.*^{2}

bunting ('bʌntɪŋ), *ppl. a.* [Of various origin: senses 1, 2, f. BUNT *v.*^{1} + -ING^{2}.]

1. Of a sail: Bellying, swelling.

a **1702** R. HOOKE in *Phil. Trans.* LXXIII. 141 To prefer bellying or bunting sails to such as were hauled taught.

2. Swelling, plump; filled out, rounded, short and thick. (But *bunting lamb* may be from BUNT *v.*^{2})

1584 PEELE *Arraignm. Paris* I. i, I have brought a twagger for the nones, A bunting lamb. **1613** MARKHAM *Eng. Husbandman* I. I. xvii. (1635) 108 Barley for your seede.. elect that which is whitest, fullest, and roundest, being as the Plough-man calles it, a full bunting Corne. **1808–25** JAMIESON *Dict.*, *Buntin*, short and thick; as a buntin brat, a plump child, Roxb.

3. ? Resembling a rabbit's bunt: short and cocked.

1688 R. HOLME *Armoury* II. 259/2 The stork..hath but a short bunting Tail.

4. ? Untidy, tawdry.

1759 *Compl. Lett.-Writer* (ed. 6) 224 A large Pattern embroider'd Gown..which..was unfashionable and bunting. **1839** C. CLARK *J. Noakes* 13 When yow saa Mary drest, Nought she had on look'd bunting.

bunting crow ('bʌntɪŋ 'krəʊ). [Du. *bonte-kraai*, f. *bont* parti-coloured + *kraai* crow; infl. by BUNTING *sb.*^{1}] The Hooded Crow (*Corvus cornix*).

[**1658** HEXHAM *Dutch Dict.*, *Bonte-kraaye*, a Pide Crowe, or a Roiston crowe.] **1802** G. MONTAGU *Ornith. Dict.* (1833) 62 Bunting crow—a name for the Crow.

'buntlin. *Sc.* **a.** = BUNTING *sb.*^{1} 1.

17.. *Hynde Etin* in Child's *Ballads* I. 296 We'll shoot the laverock in the lift, The buntlin on the tree.

buntline ('bʌnt,laɪn). *Naut.* [f. BUNT *sb.*^{1} + LINE.]

1. A rope fastened to the foot-rope of a sail and passing in front of the canvas, so as to prevent it from 'bellying' when being furled.

1627 CAPT. SMITH *Seaman's Gram.* v. 22 Bunt lines is..a small rope..to trice or draw vp the Bunt of the saile, when you farthell or make it vp. **1748** ANSON *Voy.* I. x. (ed. 4) 139 Endeavouring to hand the top-sails, the clew-lines and bunt-lines broke. **1840** R. DANA *Bef. Mast* xxiii. 70 The jigger was bent on to the slack of the buntlines.

2. *Comb.*, as *buntline-cringle*; **buntline-cloth**, **buntline-span** (see quots.).

1794 *Rigging & Seamanship* I. 86 *Buntline Cloth*, the lining sewed up the sail, in the direction of the buntline, to prevent the sail being chafed. **1882** NARES *Seamansh.* (ed. 6) 80 A buntline span is a short piece of rope, with a thimble spliced into one end, through which the buntline is rove; they are used to keep the sail, when hauled up by the buntlines, from being blown away from the yard.

buntons ('bʌntənz). [orig. in sing. *bunting*, a piece of squared timber, of obscure etym.

1633 *Gateshead Church Bks.* in Heslop *Northumb. Words* (1892) s.v., It. p^{d} for one bunting and two sparres to a yeat and the makeing it, 4s. 4d.]

Strong balks of timber placed crosswise in the shaft of a mine serving to divide it into compartments and to support the guides on which the cages run, etc. (Rarely *sing.*)

1839 URE *Dict. Arts* 971 In quadrant shafts the buntons cross each other towards the middle of the pit. *Ibid.* 986 The compartment intended for the upcast is made air-tight at top, by placing strong buntons or beams across it. **1860** *Eng. & For. Mining Gloss.* (ed. 2) 51 *Buntons*, strong balks of timber. **1883** *Encycl. Brit.* XVI. 450/2 Pieces of timber parallel to the end-pieces (buntons or dividings) are fixed across the shaft, and serve to stay the wall-plates. **1888** GREENWELL *Gloss. Coal Trade Northumb. & Durh.* (ed. 3) 81 A cistern which stands on a strong oak bunton. **1967** *Gloss. Mining Terms* (*B.S.I.*) IX. 6 *Bunton*, one of a series of horizontal beams set at intervals across a shaft to support rigid guides, cables and pipes and, in rectangular shafts, to act as struts.

bunty, *a.* [f. BUNT *sb.*^{2} + -Y^{1}.] Of grain: infected with bunt.

1855 MORTON *Cycl. Agric.* I. 363/2 A year or two since, we saw a very bunty crop in the fields of a first rate farmer. **1896** *Chron.* 19 Dec. (E.D.D.), If he sowed bunty seed he should expect to reap bunty crop.

†**'buntyle**, obs. var. of BUNTING *sb.*^{1}

c **1450** *Gloss.* in Wr.-Wülcker 702 *Hic pratellus*, a buntyle.

bunwand: see BUN *sb.*^{1}

bunweed (ˈbʌnwiːd). *Herb.* [Another form of BENWEED, occurring also as *binweed, bindweed*: etymological form and derivation uncertain.] A Scotch name of the Ragweed (*Senecio Jacobæa*).

a **1455** HOLLAND *Houlate* xxvii. 12 Bot a blak bunwede. **1812** J. WILSON *Renfrewsh.* 136 (JAM.) Prevailing weeds in meadows and grass lands are rag-wort or bindweed, *Senecio jacobea.* **1820** *Blackw. Mag.* June 266 The Scottish witches always went by air on broomsticks and bunweeds. **1847** J. WILSON *Chr. North* (1857) II. 22 Sitting among the binweeds and thistles.

bunya (ˈbʌnjə). Also **bunya-bunya.** [Native name.] An Australian tree, *Araucaria bidwillii*, which bears a cone of great size yielding a nutritious vegetable pulp. Also *attrib.*

1843 L. LEICHHARDT *Let.* in J. D. Lang *Cooksland* (1847) 82 The bunya-bunya tree is noble and gigantic. **1844** *Ibid.* 89 The kernel of the Bunya fruit. **1844** *Port Phillip Patriot* 25 July 4/4 The Bunya Bunya or *Araucaria* on the seeds of which numerous tribes of blacks are accustomed to feed. **1875** *Encycl. Brit.* II. 310/2 The Bunya-Bunya pine, found on the mountains of Eastern Australia. **1885** R. C. PRAED *Head Station* 179 In dense scrub..where the stately bunya-branches drooped. **1887** J. MATHEW in Curr *Austral. Race* III. 161 In laying up a store of bunyas, the Blacks exhibited an unusual foresight. **1934** T. WOOD *Cobbers* xvi. 191 Orange groves and bunya nuts. **1957** P. WHITE *Voss* iii. 60 They had gone..as far as the elbow and the bunya bunya.

Bunyanesque (bʌnjəˈnɛsk), *a.* [f. *Bunyan* (see below) + -ESQUE.] Of, pertaining to, or characteristic of either (*a*) John Bunyan (1628–88), the English writer, or (*b*) Paul Bunyan, the legendary American hero.

a. 1888 F. THOMPSON in *Merry England* Nov. 6 A rustic alehouse bench, upholstered with cushions by a daring flight of Bunyanesque fancy. **1965** M. DRABBLE *Millstone* 19 Their eye-for-an-eye and Bunyanesque attention to the detail of offence.

b. 1952 D. HOFFMAN *Paul Bunyan* v. 149 Mr. Steven's Bunyanesque maxims for business executives. **1961** B. MALAMUD *New Life* (1962) 59 Enormous leaves..he had thought, until the old woman told him..that they were from some Bunyanesque species of maple tree.

bunyip (ˈbʌnjɪp). Also **bunyup. 1.** The Aboriginal name of a fabulous monster inhabiting the rushy swamps and lagoons in the interior of Australia. Also *attrib.*

1848 W. WESTGARTH *Australia Felix* 391 Certain large fossil bones..have been referred by the natives..to a huge animal of extraordinary appearance, called in some districts the Bunyup, in others the Kianpraty, which they assert to be still alive. **1888** *Athenæum* 14 Jan. 47/2 There are plenty of sea-gods, little better than salt-water kelpies or marine bunyips. **1891** *Coo-ee* 275 When a black fellow disappears, it is generally understood that the Bunyip has got hold of him. **1894** A. ROBERTSON *Nuggets*, etc. 61 A weird boom, from bittern or bunyip, came from the swamp. **1916** J. B. COOPER *Coo-oo-ee!* xiv. 199 Were not chivalrous men in these venal days as extinct as the bunyip? **1936** M. FRANKLIN *All that Swagger* i. 7 The wild Murrumbidgee sinking into the Bunyip Hole..would dissolve.

2. An impostor. Hence *attrib. Obs.*

1852 MUNDY *Antipodes* (1858) ix. 215 Bunyip became, and remains a Sydney synonyme for *impostor, pretender, humbug*, and the like. **1853** W. C. WENTWORTH in H. Parkes *Fifty Years Austral. Hist.* (1892) I. 41 A mushroom, a Brummagem, a bunyip aristocracy.

‖**buon fresco** (bwon ˈfresko). [It., lit. 'good fresco'.] = FRESCO *sb.* 2 a.

1874 *Amer. Cycl.* VII. 483/1 Painting designs in colors ground in water and mixed with lime upon the freshly laid plaster..was called by the Italians *buon fresco*, or the true fresco. **1957** *Encycl. Brit.* IX. 835/2 In the 15th century, Italian painters distinguished between *fresco secco*—the pigments being mixed with egg as a medium, and *buon fresco*—the pigments being mixed with water and laid on the fresh wet plaster.

buoy (bɔɪ, bwɔɪ), *sb.* Forms: 5–7 **boye**, 6 **bwoy**, (**buie, buy**), 6–8 **boy**, (7 **bouye, buye, boigh, bowie, boa**, *pl.* **boes**), 7– **buoy.** [15th c. *boye* corresponds to OF. *boye* (Diez), *boyee* (Palsgr.), modF. *bouée*, Norm. *boie* (Littré), Sp. *boya*, Pg. *boia* 'buoy'; Du. *boei*, MDu. *boeie* 'buoy', and 'fetter'; the same word as OF. *boie, buie, boe, bue, beue*, Pr. *boia*, OSp. *boya* fetter, chain:—L. *boia* halter, fetter (cf. BOY *sb.*[2]); applied to a buoy because of its being fettered to a spot. It is not clear whether the Eng. was originally from OF., or MDu. The pronunciation (bwɔɪ), indicated already in Hakluyt, is recognized by all orthoepists British and American; but (bɔɪ) is universal among sailors, and now prevalent in England: Annandale's *Imperial Dictionary*, 1885, has (bɔɪ or bwɔɪ), Cassell's *Encyclopædic Dict.*, 1879, says '*u* silent'. Some orthoepists give (buɪ).]

1. a. A floating object fastened in a particular place to point out the position of things under the water (as anchors, shoals, rocks), or the course which ships have to take; or to float a cable in a rocky anchorage to prevent its chafing against the rocks (= *cable-buoy, mooring-buoy*). ***bell-buoy***, a buoy fitted with a bell, to ring with the agitation of the water, and so give warning of danger. See also CAN-BUOY, NUN-BUOY. **b.** Something adapted to buoy up or keep afloat a person in the water (= *life-buoy*).

1466 *Mann. & Househ. Exp.* 325 Kabeles, and an hawser, and ij. boyes. **1530** PALSGR. 199/1 Boy of an ancre, *boyee.* **1584** R. NORMAN *Safeguard of Sailers* 6 The markes of the southern Buie. *Ibid.* 10 The Buy upon the Nes. **1600** HAKLUYT *Voy.* (1810) III. 490 Marking..how ur bwoy floated vpon the water. **1634** BRERETON *Trav.* (1844) 4 The Flats..where buoys are placed, 'twixt which all ships are to sail. **1677** YARRANTON *Engl. Improv.* 41 An Harbour..where a Boy and a Cord two Inches Diameter will be sufficient to a hold a Ship. **1802** SOUTHEY *Inchcape Rock*, That bell on the Inchcape Rock; On a buoy in the storm it floated and swung, And over the waves its warning rung. **1840** HOOD *Up Rhine* 25 The Buoys which mark the entrance into the Maas. **1884** G. C. DAVIES *Norfolk Broads* xl. 315 The melancholy cadence of the bell-buoy.

2. *fig.* Something which marks out a course, indicates danger, or keeps one afloat.

a **1603** T. CARTWRIGHT *Confut. Rhem. N.T.* (1618) Pref. 10 Which haue waded so farre..as the Bowies and markes of holy Scriptures doe teach them. **1660** Z. CROFTON *Fasten. St. Peter's Fett.* To Rdr. 7 Reformed Churches [are made] our lanched boighs to detect our dangers. *a* **1770** G. WHITEFIELD *Serm.* xxxii. Wks. (1772) VI. 16 Love..is a..buoy against the tempests of this boisterous world. **1803** BRISTED *Pedest. Tour* I. 149 Having no intellectual buoy by which to steer his course.

3. *attrib.* (See also BUOY-ROPE.)

1668 WILKINS *Real Char.* II. vii. §6. 186 Cone with Cone: having Base to Base..Buoy figure. **1870** *Chambers's Jrnl.* 15 Jan. 34/2 This 'buoy-shifting' is a duty which calls forth all the skill and energy of the officers and men. **1872** BAKER *Nile Tribut.* xiii. 225 The buoy end is carried in the left hand. **1846** MCCULLOCH *Acc. Brit. Empire* (1854) II. 167 Masters in the buoy or light service. *a* **1877** KNIGHT *Dict. Mech.*, *Buoy-safe*, a metallic body divided into compartments, by which it is braced, and having water-tight doors opening to the inside. **1921** *Dict. Occup. Terms* (1927) §731 Buoy master.

buoy (bɔɪ, bwɔɪ), *v.* Also 7 **boy, bouy.** [In senses 1–3 app. adapted from some foreign source: cf. Sp. *boyar* to float (f. *boya* BUOY sb.), and see BUOYANT; in sense 4 from the sb.]

†**1.** *intr.* To rise to, or float on, the surface of a liquid; to rise, swell (as the sea). *Obs.*

1605 SHAKS. *Lear* III. vii. 60 The Sea, with such a storme..would haue buoy'd vp And quench'd the Stelled fires. **1625** PURCHAS *Pilgrimes* II. 1617 Our Wine wee saued which boyed to the shoare. **1674** N. FAIRFAX *Bulk & Selv.* 73 Which will not allow an heavy body left to itself within a flowsom one that is lighter, to buoy up.

†**b.** *fig. Obs.*

1709 POPE *Ess. Crit.* 463 Rising merit will buoy up at last. **1716–8** —— in *Lady M. W. Montague's Lett.* I. viii. 24 Folly..will buoy up..in spite of all our art to keep it down. **1742** YOUNG *Nt. Th.* VI. 251 When the great Soul buoys up to this high Point.

2. *trans.* To keep from sinking (in a fluid), to keep afloat; *transf.* to keep up, support, sustain. (Usually with *up.*)

1651 T. BARKER *Art Angling* (1653) 8 The menow may swim..being buoyed up with a Cork or Quill. **1774** BURKE *Corr.* (1844) I. 490 It is as hard to sink a cork, as to buoy up a lump of lead. **1782** A. MONRO *Compar. Anat.* (ed. 3) 3 The bat and flying squirrel..have wings to buoy themselves up in the air. **1809** W. IRVING *Knickerb.* II. v. (1849) 113 Thus buoyed up, he floated on the waves.

b. To raise to the surface of a liquid; to bring afloat (e.g. a sunken ship).

1616 BEAUM. & FL. *Cust. Country* I. i, I will descend to thee, And buoy thee up. **1667** *Lond. Gaz.* No. 196/3 She sunk, with a Lighter..Great care is taking to Buoy them up with all the speed that may be. **1756** C. LUCAS *Ess. Waters* III. 297 They..buoy up some particles of the iron & carry it to the surface.

3. *fig.* To keep up, keep from sinking, support, sustain, (persons, courage, hope, heart, spirits, etc.). (Usually with *up.*)

1645 in Rushw. *Hist. Coll.* IV. I. 136 Lord Byron buoy'd up with continual hopes. **1681** DRYDEN *Abs. & Achit.* 821 Brave to buoy the State. *a* **1797** H. WALPOLE *Mem. Geo. III*, (1845) I. ix. 135 France had been buoyed up by the ambition..of Spain. **1836** MARRYAT *Japhet* xliii, The hopes which had been..buoying me up.

b. To raise, lift, cause to rise (the heart, spirits, etc.). (Usually with *up.*)

1652 J. WADSWORTH tr. *Sandoval's Civ. Wars Spain* 181 They ought to..boüy them up out of that gulf of miserie whereinto they were plunged. **1662** FULLER *Worthies* I. 262 Hearts sunk down are not to be boyed up. *a* **1796** BURKE *Regic. Peace* i. Wks. VIII. 86 Buoyed up to the highest point of practical vigour. *a* **1850** ROSSETTI *Dante & Circ.* I. (1874) 185 The spirits of thy life depart Daily to heaven with her—they so are buoy'd With their desire.

4. To furnish or mark with a buoy or buoys; to mark as with a buoy (rarely with *out*).

1596 RALEIGH *Discov. Guiana* 36 Which shold [= shoal] John Douglas boyed and bekonned for them before. **1707** *Lond. Gaz.* No. 4350/3 They have..lately buoy'd a new Chanel..with 3 Black Buoys. **1710** in Picton *L'pool Munic. Rec.* (1886) II. 49 The buoying out of Formby Channell. **1772–84** COOK *Voy.* (1790) I. 215 The captain sounded and buoyed the bar. **1883** DK. ARGYLL *Sp. Ho. Lords* 19 July, Rocks on the [Scotch] west coast are not sufficiently buoyed and beaconed.

buoyage (ˈbɔɪɪdʒ, bwɔɪ-). [f. BUOY *v.* and *sb.* + -AGE.] The providing of (or with) buoys; buoys collectively, a series of buoys which mark out a channel.

1855 in OGILVIE Suppl. **1858** *Merc. Mar. Mag.* V. 29 Buoyage of the River Tees. **1863** *Standard* 5 Sept. 3/1 Charged equally by law with the buoyage, beaconage, and lights of the river. **1883** *Chamb. Jrnl.* 8 Dec. 769/1 Proposal for a uniform system of buoyage.

buoyance (ˈbɔɪəns, bwɔɪ-). [f. BUOYANT: see -ANCE.]

1. = BUOYANCY. (*poet.* or *rhetorical.*)

1821 LOCKHART *Valerino* III. iii. 86 The words..produced I know not what of buoyance and of emotion. **1833** H. COLERIDGE *To Nautilus* in *Q. Rev.* XLIX. 520 Leap along with gladsome buoyance.

2. A contrivance for imparting buoyancy to boats.

1883 *Fisheries Exhib. Catal.* 39 The side buoyance can be taken out and repaired..Punt, fitted with buoyance, if swamped not to sink.

buoyancy (ˈbɔɪənsɪ, bwɔɪ-). Also 8 **boyancy.** [f. BUOYANT: see -ANCY.] The quality of being buoyant.

1. a. Power of floating (on liquid or fluid); tendency to float. **b.** As an attribute of the liquid: Power of supporting a floating body (*rare*). **c.** *Hydrostatics*: Loss of weight due to immersion in a liquid; the vertical upward pressure of a liquid on an immersed or floating body, which is equal to the weight of displaced liquid; also of the lower layers of a liquid on those above.

1713 DERHAM *Phys. Theol.* 9 All the winged Tribes owe their Flight and Boyancy hereunto. **1765** WILKINSON in *Phil. Trans.* LV. 97 The cork had not..lost any force of buoyancy. **1793** SMEATON *Edystone L.* §248 When the stone was got up to the surface of the water..becoming heavier by losing its buoyancy. **1831** LARDNER *Hydrostat.* v. 97 The support, whether partial or total, which a solid receives from a liquid..is expressed by the term buoyancy. **1868** WRIGHT *Ocean World* i. 19 The saltness of sea water increases its density, and at the same time its buoyancy.

2. *fig.* Elasticity of spirit, lightheartedness; capacity for recovering after depression.

1819 *Blackw. Mag.* Aug., The reckless buoyancy of young blood. **1824** DIBDIN *Libr. Comp.* 516 There is neither fancy, nor brilliancy, nor buoyancy, about him. **1866** DICKENS *Lett.* (1880) II. 249, I have noticed..a decided change in my buoyancy and hopefulness. **1886** MORLEY *Crit. Misc.* III. 102 To the last he retained his extraordinary buoyancy.

3. Tendency to rise (in the price of stocks and shares), in the national revenue, etc.

1883 *Manch. Exam.* 14 Dec. 4/1 Considerable buoyancy was developed owing to a smart recovery on the Paris Bourse.

4. *attrib.*, as ***buoyancy chamber, garment, tank.***

1930 *Engineering* 17 Jan. 69/1 The buoyancy chamber..is divided by a longitudinal watertight bulkhead along the centre line. **1959** A. HARDY *Fish & Fisheries* i. 1 Many of the fish are swollen..as their air-bladders (buoyancy chambers) are violently distended. **1962** *B.S.I. News* May 9/2 Buoyancy garments are being used in increasing numbers by yachtsmen, canoeists and other 'weekend' sailors. **1928** C. F. S. GAMBLE *Story of North Sea Air Station* xviii. 309 In order to dive a submarine her commander fills the buoyancy tanks with sea-water.

buoyant (ˈbɔɪənt, bwɔɪ-), *a.* Also 6 **boyent**, 7 **boyant.** [perhaps ad. Sp. *boyante* in same sense, or OF. *bouyant* (app. also synonymous, though explained differently in Godef.); in Eng. it is app. older than BUOY *v.* See -ANT[1].]

1. Having the power of floating, tending to float; floating.

1578 W. BOURNE *Treas. for Trav.* IV. x, The syde [of a ship] being rounde and full, it is the more boyenter a great deale. **1713** DERHAM *Phys. Theol.* 442 *note*, The Air-Bladder [of a fish] makes the Body more or less buoyant. **1765** WILKINSON in *Phil. Trans.* LV. 98 The buoyant power of cork in fresh water. **1792** *Gentl. Mag.* Mar. 210 Produced from seed buoyant in the atmosphere. **1835–6** TODD *Cycl. Anat. & Phys.* I. 40/2 Filled with air, which renders the whole animal so buoyant that it floats on the surface.

b. Lightly elastic.

1835–6 TODD *Cycl. Anat. & Phys.* I. 70/1 The quick and buoyant motions of the lively child.

c. *fig.* Tending to rise or keep up.

c **1661** *Mrq. Argyle's Will, &c.* in *Harl. Misc.* (1746) VIII. 30/2 His Vices were most notorious and boyant. **1808** SYD. SMITH *Wks.* (1869) 112 Religion is so noble and powerful a consideration—it is so buoyant and so unsubmergible. **1868** ROGERS *Pol. Econ.* xxi. (ed. 3) 282 That part of the public revenue is most buoyant.

2. Of liquid: Having the power of keeping bodies afloat on its surface.

1692 DRYDEN *Eleonora* Ded. (Globe), The water under me was buoyant. **1813** BYRON *Br. Abydos* II. iii, These limbs that buoyant wave hath borne. **1873** MORLEY *Rousseau* I. 324 The buoyant waters of emotion and sentiment.

3. *fig.* Of the spirits: Easily recovering from depression, elastic, light. Of persons: Light-hearted, cheerful, hopeful.

a **1748** THOMSON *Wks.* (1766) I. 130 Nerves..full of buoyant spirit. **1770** LANGHORNE *Plutarch* (1879) I. 211/1 A man of buoyant and animated valour. **1824** W. IRVING *T. Trav.* I. 338 My spirits were most buoyant after a temporary prostration. **1843** PRESCOTT *Mexico* (1850) I. 198 His buoyant spirits were continually breaking out in troublesome frolics. **1845** S. AUSTIN *Ranke's Hist. Ref.* I. I. 105 The buoyant confidence of youth.

4. *Comb.*, as ***buoyant-minded*** adj.

1833 HT. MARTINEAU *Charm. Sea* iii. 27 One or two of the..more buoyant-minded of the party.

'buoyantly, *adv.* In a buoyant manner.

1854 BADHAM *Halieut.* 24 We might fail to carry him buoyantly over. **1873** HOLLAND *A. Bonnic.* xiv. 225, I could not have been more buoyantly expectant. **1883** *Knowledge* 22 June 370/2 Shares went up buoyantly.

†**'buoyantness.** *Obs. rare.* = BUOYANCY.

1668 *Proc. Royal Soc.* III. 395 (L.), The lightness and buoyantness of the rope. **1716** J. PERRY *State of Russ.* 121 The Air being..without that Strength of Elasticity or Buoyantness that is occasioned by the Heat of the Sun.

buoyed (bɔɪd, bwɔɪd), *ppl. a.* [f. BUOY *v.*]

1. Kept afloat, supported, etc.: see BUOY *v.*

2. Furnished with a buoy or buoys.

1881 *Philada. Record.* No. 3438. 2 The best lighted and buoyed river in the world. **1881** *Echo* 28 June 3/1 The buoyed end of the new American cable.

buoy-rope ('b(w)ɔɪrəʊp). [f. BUOY *sb.* + ROPE.] The rope by which the buoy is fastened to the anchor. †Also *transf.* (quot. 1562 used for a woman's pig-tail).

1562 J. HEYWOOD *Prov. & Epigr.* (1867) 64 Except hir maide shewe a fayre paire of heeles, She haleth her by the boy rope, tyll her braines ake. **1630** J. TAYLOR (Water P.) *Wks.* III. 65 a/2 Cleere, cleere the boighrope, steddy, well steered. **1723** *Ibid.* No. 6129/3 Twelve Fathom of a Buoy Rope of six Inches and an half. **1860** H. STUART *Seaman's Catech.* 56 If the cable should be slipped or parted, the buoy-rope is used for weighing.

buphthalmos (bʊf'θælmɒs). *Ophthalm.* [ad. Gr. βούφθαλμον ox-eye, f. βοῦς ox + ὀφθαλμός eye.] Gross enlargement of the eyeball owing to increased intra-ocular pressure; now *spec.* (as a sign of) congenital glaucoma.

1821 G. C. MONTEATH tr. *Beer & Weller's Man. Dis. Eye* II. 39 In the third species of Dropsy of the Eye, where both the vitreous and the aqueous humour is unnaturally accumulated..the eyeball..not unfrequently attains an enormous size, projects from the orbit, and produces that which many oculists have called the Ox's Eye, Buphthalmos. **1879** *Ophthalmic Hosp. Rep.* IX. 200 In the buphthalmos cases, enlargement of the chamber of the aqueous is the most prominent symptom. **1902** *Lancet* 27 Sept. 867/1 Buphthalmos..in these cases, is a congenital disease... Clinical observers..consider the disease to be glaucoma but occurring in young subjects. **1954** S. DUKE-ELDER *Parsons' Dis. Eye* (ed. 12) xii. 200 Keratoglobus..differs from buphthalmos..in that the intra-ocular pressure is normal, the cornea clear, the angle of the anterior chamber normal, and there is no cupping of the disc. **1974** PASSMORE & ROBSON *Compan. Med. Stud.* III. II. xxxiii. 21 The high intraocular pressure distends the soft infantile sclera causing gross enlargement of the eye, hence the term buphthalmos or ox-eye. **1983** *Radiology* CXLVI. 113/2 Buphthalmos was present in five patients.

Hence **buph'thalmic** *a.*, characterized by or affected with buphthalmos.

1896 *Trans. Ophthalmol. Soc. U.K.* XVI. 349 Mr Devereux Marshall showed a specimen of a buphthalmic eye from a boy aged five years. **1964** S. DUKE-ELDER *Syst. Ophthalm.* III. xiv. 551 The picture presented by the buphthalmic eye is characteristic.

buplever (b(j)uː'plɛvə(r)). *Bot.* [a. F. *buplèvre*:—L. *būpleurum*, a. Gr. βούπλευρον, f. βου- ox + πλευρόν rib.] The plant Hare's-ear or Thorough-wax. 'An English name adapted from the French, proposed by Bentham' (*Treas. Bot.*).

1881 G. ALLEN in *Cornh. Mag.* June 706 The narrow buplever flowers only at Torquay and in Jersey and Guernsey. *Ibid.* 716 Torquay..shares a southern buplever with the Channel Islands.

‖**buprestis** (b(j)uː'prɛstɪs). [L. *buprestis*, a. Gr. βούπρηστις, lit. 'ox-burner'.]

1. An unidentified insect of the ancients, very harmful to cattle; 'perhaps of the genus Mylabris' (Kirby and Spence).

1398 TREVISA *Barth. De P.R.* XVIII. xiii. (1495) 773 This Burestes lyeth amonge herbes and grasse: and the oxe swalowyth this beste, and whan this Burestes is swalowed he chaufeth sodenly the lyuour of the oxe and makyth hym breke with grete payne and sorowe. **1601** HOLLAND *Pliny* II. 377 There is a kind of insect or flie called Buprestis..kine and oxen catch much harme by this flie. [**1658** ROWLAND *Mouffet's Theat. Ins.* 1001, I have seen about Heidelberg two Buprestes like Scarabees.]

2. *Zool.* A genus of beetles, natives of the tropics, remarkable for brilliant colouring. Hence the family *Buprestidæ*, rarely anglicized as **bu'prestidans**.

1835 KIRBY *Hab. & Inst. Anim.* II. xx. 364 The most splendid and brilliant of the whole Order, the Buprestidans.

bur, burr (bɜː(r)), *sb.* Forms: 4 borre, 4–7 burre, 6– bur, 7– burr. [app. identical or cogn. with Da. *borre* bur, burdock, Sw. *borre* sea-urchin, and in comb. *kard-borre* burdock, though the word is not found in ON., nor in Eng. before the 14th c. A derivation from F. *bourre* 'rough hair, flock of wool', labours under the difficulty that the F. word is not found ever to have had the sense which Eng. *bur* shares with Da. and Sw. *borre*; nor does the Eng. word show the wider sense of F. *bourre*.

The spelling of this and various other words or senses of words, phonetically and perhaps even etymologically identical with it, is very unsettled: in nearly all *burr* is an earlier spelling, but in the present word *bur* is now usual. See further under BURR.]

1. a. Any rough or prickly seed-vessel or flower-head of a plant: *esp.* the flower-head of the Burdock (*Arctium lappa*); also, the small seed-vessel of the Goose-grass (*Galium aparine*) and other plants; the husk of the chestnut.

c **1330** *Arth. & Merl.* 8290 Togider thai cleued..So with other doth the burre. *c* **1440** *Promp. Parv.* 56 Burre, *lappa, glis.* *a* **1547** J. HEYWOOD *Four P's* in Dodsley (1780) I. 87 Hys eares as ruged as burres. **1600** SHAKS. *A.Y.L.* I. iii. 13 They are but burs, Cosen, throwne vpon thee in holiday foolerie..our very petty-coates will catch them. **1684** R. WALLER *Nat. Exper.* 87 Like the Burre or Husk of a Chestnut. **1779** MRS. DELANY *Lett.* Ser. II. II. 425 Goose grass or cleavers..does not bear burrs (which are the seed vessels) till after the time of its flowring. *c* **1817** HOGG *Tales & Sk.* III. 316 The burr of a Scots thistle. **1861** MISS PRATT *Flower. Pl.* III. 87 Fruits, beset with prickles, are truly burs, clinging very readily to any object. **1874** ROE *Open. Chestnut Burr* xiii, She took the burr from his hand and plucking out the chestnut tossed the burr away.

b. Phr. *to stick* (*cleave, cling*, etc.) *like a bur.*

c **1330** [see above]. **1514** BARCLAY *Cyt. & Uplondyshm.* (1847) 43 Together they cleve more fast then do burres. **1603** SHAKS. *Meas. for M.* I. iii. 189, I am a kind of Burre, I shal sticke. **1712** ARBUTHNOT *John Bull* (1727) 59 When a fellow stuck like a bur, that there was no shaking him off. **1810** CRABBE *Borough* v, Friends who will hang like burs upon his coat. **1865** MERIVALE *Rom. Emp.* VIII. lxiv. 81 It fastens itself like a burr on the memory.

c. The female catkin or 'cone' of the hop before fertilization. [Possibly a different word: in Fr. the vine when coming into bud is said to be *en bourre*; cf. 5.]

1846 J. BAXTER *Libr. Pract. Agric.* I. 396 The male hop has its..pollen previously perfected, so as to impregnate the stigma or bur of the female. *Ibid.* 403 About the middle of this month [July] the hop..begins to put forth bloom, which is called 'coming out into bur'. **1881** WHITEHEAD *Hops* 51 It is worse than useless to wash the plants after they are in burr, or blossom.

2. Any plant which produces burs, esp. *Arctium lappa* (the Burdock), and the genus *Xanthium.*

1480 *Cath. Angl.* 48 A Burre..*paliurus.* **1562** BULLEYN *Bk. Simples* 38 a, The great Burre, which is more commonly known then commended. **1585** LLOYD *Treas. Health* F viij, The rote of a little burre sodden in Vinegar. **1634** MILTON *Comus* 350 Where may she wander now..amongst rude burs and thistles? **1815** ELPHINSTONE *Acc. Caubul* (1845) I. 33 We found ourselves..among sand-hills, stunted bushes, burs, and phoke. **1842** TENNYSON *Day-Dr.* 66 Bur and brake and briar.

3. *fig.* That which clings like a bur; a thing or person difficult to get rid of or 'shake off'.

1590 SHAKS. *Mids. N.* III. ii. 260 Hang off thou cat, thou bur. **1633** HEYWOOD *Eng. Trav.* III. Wks. 1874 IV. 51 This burre will still cleaue to me; what, no meanes To shake him off? **1690** B. E. *Dict. Cant. Crew, Burre*, a Hanger on, or Dependant. **1826** J. WILSON *Noct. Ambr.* Wks. 1855 I. 119 The burr has a pawky expression that's no canny.

4. *fig.* 'Bur in the throat': anything that appears to stick in the throat or that produces a choking sensation, accumulation of phlegm, huskiness; 'a lump in the throat'.

1393 LANGL. *P. Pl.* C. xx. 306 Smoke and smorþre..Til he be bler-eyed oþer blynde · and þe borre [*v.r.* burre] in hus þrote. **1609** *Ev. Wom. in Hum.* II. ii. in Bullen *O. Pl.* IV, Theres hemming indeede, like a Cat..with a burre in her throate. **1641** MILTON *Ch. Govt.* Wks. 1738 I. 74 Their honest..natures coming to the Universities..were sent home again with..a scholastical Bur in their throats. **1749** CHESTERF. *Lett.* II. ccxiii. 319, I hemm'd once or twice (for it gave me a bur in my throat).

5. a. A knob or knot in a tree; also, one of the 'buds' or pimples characteristic of the farcy. [Perhaps a distinct word: cf. F. *bourre* vine-bud (see 1 c) *bourrelet* 'round swelling on a tree'.]

1725 BRADLEY *Fam. Dict.* II. s.v. *Maple*, That which is fullest of Knots and Burs is of greatest Value. **1725** *Lond. Gaz.* No. 6397/2 Several Burs, Remains of the Farcy. **1869** MASTERS *Veg. Terat.* 347 The large 'gnaurs' or 'burrs', met with in elms, etc., also in certain varieties of apples.

b. An ornamental veneering wood or veneer, esp. of walnut, containing knots. Also *attrib.*, as *burr-walnut.* Cf. BURL *sb.*[1] 4 b.

1885 *Spons' Mech. Own Bk.* 357 Walnut burrs are best cut with scissors. **1901** *Tradesman's Catal.* 1 Bedroom Suite, in solid American Walnut and Burr. **1908** *Daily Report* 5 Sept. 8/2 A burr-walnut armoire. **1923** *Daily Mail* 23 Jan. 1 Sideboard in oak..with finely figured panels of burr walnut. **1938** *Times* 17 Oct. 8/5 The cabinet work is in two shades of burr walnut.

6. a. The rounded knob forming the base of a deer's horn. [Cf. BURL, bud of a deer's horn.]

1575 TURBERV. *Bk. Venerie* 236 The round roll of pyrled horne that is next to the head of an harte is called the Burre. **1677** N. COX *Gentl. Recreat.* (1706) 65 The Bur is next the Head; and that which is about the Bur, is called Pearles. **1736** DALE in *Phil. Trans.* XXXIX. 386 The Moose hath a branched Brow-Antler between the Burr and the Palm. **1828** STARK *Elem. Nat. Hist.* I. 148 Horns..with a branch above the burr pointing forward.

b. (See quot.)

1753 CHAMBERS *Cycl. Supp.* s.v., Burrs denote bits of flesh adjoining to the horns of a beef's hide, cut off by poor women after it is brought to market.

7. *dial.* See quots. [? from sense 1.]

1863 ATKINSON *Danby Provinc., N. Riding Yorksh., Bur*, the stone or other obstacle placed behind the wheel. **1875** *Whitby Gloss.* (E.D.S.), *Bur*, (1) an impediment; an annoyance; (2) the drag-chain and shoe for fastening up a carriage wheel when going down a hill.

8. *Comb.*, as **bur-breeding**, **-head**, **-leaf-**, **-root**; **bur-bark**, the fibrous bark of *Triumfetta semitriloba*, a tropical shrub bearing prickly fruits or burs; **bur-flag** = *bur-reed*; **bur-grass**, *Sc.* ? a species of Carex; **bur-knot** = BUR 6: **bur-marigold**, popular name of the genus *Bidens*; †**bur-nettle**, perhaps *Urtica pilulifera*; **bur-oak**, *Quercus macrocarpa* of N. America; **bur-parsley**, the genus *Caucalis*, esp. *C. daucoides*, an umbelliferous weed with prickly fruit; **bur-reed**, common name of the genus *Sparganium*; **bur-thistle**, *Carduus lanceolatus*, also called Spear-thistle; **bur-weed**, *Xanthium strumarium*; also other plants producing burs, as *Galium aparine* (Goose-grass), *Caucalis nodosa*, and the genus *Triumfetta*. See also BURDOCK.

1756 P. BROWNE *Jamaica* 233 The *Bur-Bark. The plant is common in Jamaica. **1630** DRAYTON *Muses Elysium* III. (R.) By the rough *bur breeding docks Ranker than the oldest fox. **1834** *Brit. Husb.* I. xxix. 463 A coarse kind of grass called *'bur-grass'. **1840** BROWNING *Sordello* v. 412 'Spear-heads for battle, *burr-heads for the joust.' **1483** *Cath. Angl.* 48 A *Burre hylle, *lappetum, est locus vbi crescunt lappe.* **1615** LAWSON *Orch. & Gard.* III. vii. (1668) 15 A *bur-knot..taken from an Apple-tree. **1634** BP. HALL *Occas. Med.* cxiii. Wks. (1808) 204 On a *bur-leaf. **1833** in *Proc. Berw. Nat. Club* I. No. 1. 29. **1879** PRIOR *Plant-n.*, **Bur Marigold*, a composite flower allied to the marigold, with seeds that adhere to the clothes like burrs. **1713** PETIVER in *Phil. Trans.* XXVIII. 36 Common *Bur-Nettle. **1815** D. DRAKE *Cincinnati* ii. 82 The most valuable timber trees are the..*bur oaks. **1876** *Encycl. Brit.* IV. 704/2 The bur oak (*Q. lobata*). **1888** *Ibid.* XXIII. 808/1 The burr oak (*Q. macrocarpa*) has almost as wide a range as the white oak. **1962** *Victoria & Albert Museum Internat. Art Treasures Exhib.* 55/1 A Louis XV Tortoiseshell Casket on burr oak. **1865** C. A. JOHNS in *Treas. Bot.* I. 241 The *Bur Parsley..is a British plant, growing in corn-fields in a chalky soil. **1597** GERARD *Herbal* I. xxx. §2. 41 These plants of some are called Sparganium..I rather call them *Burre Reede. **1769** SIR J. HILL *Fam. Herbal* (1789) 98 *Bur-Reed*, a common water-plant, with rough heads of seeds. **1883** G. C. DAVIES in *Pall Mall G.* 26 Oct. 4/2 The eye to see beauty in bur-reeds and sweet-sedges. **1650** tr. *Bacon's Life & Death* 43 Asparagus, pith of Artichokes and *Burre-roots boiled. **1787** BURNS *Ep. Miss Scott* ii, The rough *burr-thistle, spreading wide. **1783** AINSWORTH *Lat. Dict.* (Morell) I. s.v. Burr, *Burrweed, *Sparganium ramosum.* **1882** G. ALLEN *Colours of Fl.* iv. 84 Unless..like..*Xanthium strumarium*, burweed, they have declined as far as colourless or green florets.

¶ See also BURR *sb.* in all senses.

bur, *v.*[1] [f. prec.: cf. also BURR *sb.*[6]] *trans.* To remove burs from (wool): see BURRING.

bur, *v.*[2] *dial.* [f. BUR *sb.* 5.] *trans.* (See quots.).

1863 ATKINSON *Danby Provinc., N. Riding Yorksh., Bur*, to block or stop the wheel of a waggon or cart..by..a stone. **1876** *Mid-Yorksh. Gloss.* (E.D.S.) *Bur*, to maintain an object in position by blockage or leverage, as..a partially raised weight is burred up from the ground with a crowbar.

bur, obs. f. BIRR, BOWER *sb.*[1]

†**burail.** *Obs.* [Fr. = 'Silke rash' Cotgr.] A stuff half silk and half worsted.

1714 *Fr. Bk. Rates* 36 Burail-Stuff per 100 Weight, 07 00.

buran ('buːrɑːn). [a. Russ. *burán*, ad. Turki *boran.*] In the steppes, a snowstorm, esp. one accompanied by high winds; a blizzard.

1886 *Encycl. Brit.* XXI. 76 Gales with snow (*burans, myatels*), lasting from two to three days..are especially dangerous to man and beast. **1898** J. T. BEALBY tr. *Hedin's Through Asia* I. viii. 99 These burans or snow-hurricanes come on with startling suddenness. **1936** P. FLEMING *News from Tartary* VI. xi. 305 When we went on the evening sky was overcast and presently the *buran* hit us.

Burano (buː'rɑːnəʊ). The name of an island near Venice, used attrib. in *Burano* (*point*) *lace*, a needle-made lace having a net ground, resembling Alençon and Brussels lace.

1865 MRS. B. PALLISER *Hist. Lace* iv. 54 (*caption*) Burano. **1869** *Ibid.* (ed. 2) iv. 50 (*caption*) Burano Point. **1874** *Queen Lace Book* viii. 22 In the latest specimens of Burano Point, the ground is a heavy fabric formed of square meshes. **1934** *Discovery* Sept. 255/2 Her sleeve ruffles are of the finest Burano point lace.

‖**bu'rat, bu'rato.** *Obs.* [OF. *burat*, Sp. *burato.*] The same as BORATO, q.v.

1588 R. PARKE tr. *Mendoza's Hist. China* 350 Shippes laden with..calles of networke, Buratos, Espumillas. *c* **1601** J. KEYMER *Dutch Fishing* in *Phenix* I. 226 Velvets, Buratoes, Rash, Fustians. **1750** BEAWES *Lex Mercat.* (1752) 816..Camblets..Burats (a coarse woollen stuff).

buratite ('bjʊərətaɪt). *Min.* [f. the mineralogist Burat + -ITE.] A variety of aurichalcite.

1863–79 WATTS *Dict. Chem.* I. 686 Buratite..is very variable in composition, and is probably a mixture of several minerals. **1868** DANA *Min.* 712 Buratite or the so-called lime aurichalcite.

Burberry ('bɜːbərɪ). The registered trade mark (in form *Burberrys*) distinctive of cloth or clothing made by the firm of Burberrys Ltd.; *spec.* a raincoat made by this firm.

1903 *Burberry Yarn Proofs* 3 Burberry Yarn Proof Coatings. **1909** *Trade Marks Jrnl.* 13 Oct. 1717 *Burberrys.*

Cloths and Stuffs of Wool, Worsted and Hair. The Firm trading as Burberrys, 30 to 33 Haymarket..Outfitters. **1915** T. CASSELS *Men Knotted Heart* iii. 37 Somebody presented to him once a Burberry. **1919** C. ORR *Glorious Thing* iii, She was clad in a drooping burberry coat. **1944** A. CHRISTIE *Towards Zero* 89 'It's raining, you know.' 'I know, I've got a Burberry.'

burbet, obs. form of BURBOT.

'burble, *sb.*[1] Forms: 4 burbel, 5 burbulle, -byl(l(e, 6 burbul, 5–7 burble. [f. BURBLE *v.*: cf. BUBBLE *sb.* With sense 2 cf. the use of OF. *bubette* in the two senses of pimple, swelling, and 'bulle d'air dans l'eau' (Godef.).]

†**1.** *Obs.* **a.** A bubble, bubbling.

c **1350** *Legendae Catholicae, Marie Maud.* 239 A litel child ..The se it was comen tille Therwith it made michel gale With gret stones and with smale And playd with burbels of the water. **1483** *Cath. Angl.* 47 A Burbylle in yᵉ water. *bulla.* **1530** PALSGR. 202/1 Burble in the water, *bubette.* **1547** BOORDE *Brev. Health* lxxiii. 21 b, A wyndy spume the which is full of burbles.

b. quasi-*adj.* Bubbling.

c **1430** LYDG. *Chorle & Birde* (1818) 3 The burbill [*v.r.* burbly] wawes in their up boyllyng.

†**2.** A pimple; a boil. *Obs.*

1555 EDEN *Decades W. Ind.* (Arb.) 266 Certeine pimples or burbuls. **1610** BARROUGH *Meth. Physick* VII. iv. (1639) 387 As often as burbles are broken in the bowels. **1622** MALYNES *Anc. Law-Merch.* 77 Iacinths..have commonly pimples or burbles in them.

3. A murmurous flow of words.

1898 G. W. STEEVENS *With Kitchener to Khartum* 33 An inarticulate burble more like the sound of a distant railway train than any known form of human speech. **1909** J. H. SKRINE *Pastor Ovium* 140 What I listened to was a burble of platitudes in a honeyed voice. **1923** *Blackw. Mag.* Dec. 767/1 The low burble of petition-reading and the murmurous flow of false evidence were still proceeding.

4. *attrib.*, as **burble point**, the point at which the smooth flow of air over an airfoil is broken up.

1918 COWLEY & LEVY *Aeronautics in Theory & Experiment* ii. 25 At the burble point the lifting force drops sharply and just as quickly rises again. **1918** W. E. DOMMETT *Dict. Aircraft* 11 *Burble point*, that point on the lift curve of a wing which is reached when the angle of incidence has become so great that the stream lines change from a steady to a fluctuating and eddying state, causing the lift to fade and the drag to increase. **1920** *Conquest* I. 439/2 The angle at which the loss of lift is first noticed is called the 'critical angle' or 'burble point'.

burble, *sb.*[2] *Sc. dial.* [see BURBLE *v.*[2]] 'Trouble, perplexity, disorder' (Jam.).

1812 *Case, Moffat* 45 (JAM.) He always made burbles, by which the deponent understood trouble. **1836** CARLYLE in Froude *Life* (1885) I. 78 Much that was a burble will begin to unravel itself.

†**'burble,** *v.*[1] *Obs.* Also 4 burbull, (5 brobill), 6 burbyll, -bul. [Found *c* 1300. There are several similar forms in Romanic: It. *borbogliare* to make a rumbling or grumbling noise, Pg. *borbulhar*, Sp. *borbollar* to bubble forth, also mod. Picard *borbouller* to murmur (Diez); all apparently imitative words, though Diez thinks the Sp. and Pg. possibly formed on L. *bulla* bubble. The Eng. word can hardly have any actual connexion with these, exc. as a parallel onomatopœia, expressing the sound made by the agitation, issuing forth, or flowing of a liquid mixed with vesicles of air or gas. Of this the later BUBBLE appears to have been either a simple variant or a conscious modification. In the later use of *burble* there is more of the notion of flowing than in *bubble*, as though *burble* combined the notions of *bubble* and *purl*; but the sb. *burble* was in 14–16th c. exactly = L. *bulla* 'bubble'.]

1. a. *intr.* To form vesicles or bubbles like boiling water; to rise in bubbles; to flow in or with bubbles, or with bubbling sound.

1303 R. BRUNNE *Handl. Synne* 10207 As þoȝ here yȝen shulde burble out. *c* **1440** *Promp. Parv.* 56 Burblon [**1499** burbelyn], as ale or oþer lykore, *bullo.* **1470–85** MALORY *Arthur* x. ii, A fayre welle, with clere water burbelynge. **1530** PALSGR. 459/2 To boyle up or burbyll up as a water dothe in a spring, *bouilloner.* **1577** W. VALLANS *Two Swannes* in *Leland's Itin.* (1759) V. 10 To Whitwell short, whereof doth burbling rise The spring, that makes this little river runne.

b. To form bubbles in water, etc., to gurgle; cf. BURL *v.*[2]

c **1400** *Destr. Troy* 5760 Hom was leuer..be brittnet in batell, þen burbull in the flod. *c* **1440** *MS. Lincoln* A. i. 17 f. 115 (Halliw.) Many a balde manne laye there swykede, Brobillande in his blode.

2. a. To speak murmurously; to 'ramble' *on.* **b.** *trans.* To say (something) murmurously or in a rambling manner. Also *transf.*

[**1871** 'LEWIS CARROLL' *Through Looking-Glass* i. 22 The Jabberwock..Came whiffling through the tulgey wood, And burbled as it came!] **1891** KIPLING *Light that Failed* viii, You only burble and call me names. **1906** B'NESS VON HUTTEN *What became of Pam* III. iv, Miss Wantage..began to burble, and then to roar. **1920** MULFORD *J. Nelson* vii. 67 'Forty feet of rope an' a sycamore tree,' burbled Smitty. **1921** *Blackw. Mag.* July 31/2 A sleepy dinner it was. We burbled a few plans for next day, and fell asleep by the fire. **1934** T. E. LAWRENCE *Let.* 6 Aug. (1938) 813 You send me a sensible working-man of a letter..and I burble back in this unconscionable way. **1965** *Parade* 15 May, 'I think they just called our flight number,' burbled Carter.

Hence **'burbler** *sb.*; **'burbling** *vbl. sb.* and *ppl. a.*

a **1528** SKELTON *Replyc.*, These..friscairly yonkerkyns.. basked and baththed in their..burblyng and boyling blode. **1555** EDEN *Decades W. Ind.* II. II. (Arb.) 113 The burbulinge of the sande declared the sea to bee..shalowe. **1609** *Ev. Wom. in Hum.* II. i. in Bullen *O. Pl.* IV, The Meridian Sol Discern'd a dauncing in the burbling brook. **1622** J. HAGTHORPE in Farr's *S.P.* (1848) 346 Burbling streames. **1920** *Blackw. Mag.* July 44/2 They..hold his answering burblings to be the divine voice of Kali. **1923** KIPLING *Land & Sea Tales* 139 Now are you satisfied, you burbler? **1934** *Punch* 7 Mar. 280/2 *Lady Placidia* was a confirmed burbler, and if at times she is in danger of exceeding her burbling allowance, she remains entirely lovable and amusing.

'burble, *v.*[2] *Sc. dial.* [Cf. F. *barbouiller* 'to jumble, confound, huddle, or mingle ill-fauouredly' (Cotgr.), and its cognates: cf. esp. Catalan *borbollar* to perplex, bewilder. But actual connexion between these and the Sc. word is not evidenced. Cf. BARBULYE.]

trans. To perplex, confuse, muddle.

1843 MRS. CARLYLE *Lett.* (1883) I. 244 His external life fallen into a horribly burbled state.

† **'burbly,** *a. Obs.* [f. BURBLE *sb.*[1] + -Y[1].] Full of bubbles, bubbling.

c **1430** LYDG. *Min. Poems* 181 The burbly [*v.r.* burbill] wawes in [their] up boyling.

burbolt, -boulte, obs. forms of BIRD-BOLT.

1575 G. HARVEY *Letter-bk.* (1884) 90 Owte of the quiver of good likinge, On burboulte of truste, worthe the shootinge.

burbot ('bɜːbət). Forms: 5 borbot (6 borbotha), 7 burbott, -bate, -bout, 8–9 burbolt, (7–8 bird-bolt), 7– burbot, (9 burbet, barbott). [a. F. *bourbotte* (Littré), *bourbete* (Godef.), *bourbette* (Cotgr.); the usual mod.F. form is *barbote*, *barbotte*; cf. *bourboter*, *barbotter*, to dabble or wallow in mud. (The variant *bird-bolt* appears to be due merely to popular etymology.)]

A fresh-water fish (*Lota vulgaris*) of the family *Gadidæ*, somewhat like an eel, but with a flat head, having two small 'beards' on the nose and one on the chin. Also called *Eel-pout* or *Coney-fish.*

a **1475** in *Rel. Ant.* I. 85 The borbottus and the stykyl-bakys. *c* **1520** ANDREW *Noble Lyfe* in *Babees Bk.* (1868) 231 Borbotha be fisshes very slepery, somewhat lyke an ele hauinge wyde mouthes & great hedes, it is a swete mete. **1605** in *Archæologia* (1800) XIII. 348 These Fishe bee nowe in seasone..Burbott. **1679** PLOT *Staffordsh.* (1686) 241 In Staffordshire..it is call'd a Burbot or bird-bolt, perhaps from that sort of Arrow rounded at head, somewhat like this fishes. **1769** PENNANT *Zool.* III. 163 Burbot or Bird-bolt. **1772** FORSTER in *Phil. Trans.* LXIII. 150 The four kinds of Hudson's Bay fish are the Sturgeon, the Burbot, the Gwyniad..the Sucker. **1865** KINGSLEY *Herew.* xxix, The knights think scorn of any thing worse than smelts and burbot. **1883** *Fisheries Exhib. Catal.* (ed. 4) 106 Barbott (or Eelpout).

burbreach, obs. form of *borough-breach*: see BOROUGH 7.

burcer, obs. form of BURSAR.

burch, obs. form of BOROUGH, BURGH.

burchin, obs. form of BIRCHEN.

† **burd.** *Obs.* (exc. in ballad poetry). Forms: 3–4 burde, bird, 4–5 berd(e, birde, buyrde, buirde, byrd(e, (5 byurde), 5 beerde, 8, 9 bird, 5– burd. [A word of obscure origin, found in the earliest ME. in form *burde*, frequent in Layamon, but afterwards chiefly in northern, or north midl. writers, and in alliterative verse.

Burd has been variously identified with BIRD *sb.*, and with BRIDE. Although its later spelling is identical with the mod.Sc. form of *bird*, and it has been sometimes treated as merely a fig. use of this word, the earlier forms of both show them to be quite distinct. The identification with *bride* has somewhat more plausibility; but even if we take as the basis the Da. *brud* instead of the OE. *brýd*, the phonetic difficulties are many and serious. The various ME. spellings seem to indicate that the vowel was *ü* = OE. *y*; some of them also favour a dissyllabic form. The OE. adj. *byrde* 'wealthy', or perhaps 'well-born, noble' answers phonetically, and the sense 'well-born' or 'wealthy *lady*', would apparently make it a suitable companion-word to *beorn.* But the rarity of the OE. adj. (found once, *Oros.* I. i. 15, and there masc., *se byrdesta* 'the wealthiest man') presents obvious difficulties.]

A poetic word for 'woman, lady', corresponding to the masculine BERNE; in later use chiefly = 'young lady, maiden'. (See BIRD *sb.* 1 d.)

c **1205** LAY. 19271 Æfter Arður wes iboren þeo ædie burde [*c* **1275** maide] Æne. *a* **1225** *St. Marher.* 21 Cum nu forð burde to þi brudgume..alre burde brihtest. *c* **1325** *E.E. Allit. P.* B. 80 Boþe burnez & burdez. *c* **1340** *Cursor M.* 12305 (Trin.) Ioseph went also soone Wiþ him marie þat burde [*v.r.* bird] bolde. **1377** LANGL. *P. Pl.* B. XIX. 131 The berdes þo songe *Saul interfecit mille, et dauid decem milia.* **1393** *Ibid.* C. XXII. 135 The buyrdes [þo] songen. *c* **1400** *Destr. Troy* 12037 Fro bale deth þe burd [Helen] for to saue. *c* **1430** *Hymns Virg.* (1867) 13 Heil þou blessid beerde in whom [crist] was piȝt. *c* **1440** *York Myst.* xli. 209 But Mary byrde, thowe neyd not soo. *a* **1560** ROLLAND *Crt. Venus* IV. 418 Thay wald Venus make content Be sum new burd. ? *a* **1600** *Ballad* in D. Wilson *Mem. Edinb.* 33 My birde ladie in Halyroode. **17..** *Fair Helen* II. in Scott *Minstr. Sc. B.* 103 When in my arms burd Helen dropt. **1858** MORRIS *Welland Riv.* 229 'It is some burd', the fair dame said..'Has come to see your bonny face'.

burd, obs. and Sc. form of BIRD *sb.*, BOARD.

1596 SPENSER *F.Q.* IV. ii. 35 Tunes of beasts and burds.

burd alisander, var. of BORD ALEXANDER, *Obs.*, a kind of striped silk.

† **burd-alone,** *a. Obs. Sc.* (a rare archaism in mod. poet.) Also **burd-alane, bird-.** [Origin of *burd* obscure; perh. = BIRD *sb.*, 'like a sparrow alone upon the house tops', *Ps.* cii. 7. Jamieson says the word 'is used to denote one who is the only child left in a family', but the examples show a much more general sense.] As a solitary person or being; entirely alone, 'all alone'.

1572 *Lament. Lady Scotl.* in *Scot. Poems 16th C.* II. 251 Tak ȝe ane, We must not leif the vther bird alane. *a* **1600** *Auld Maitland* Introd. in Scott *Minstr. Sc. B.*, Burd-allane, his only son and air. **17..** *Gallant Grahams, ibid.* And Newton Gordon, burd-alone, And Dalgatie both stout and keen. **1717** RAMSAY *Lucky Wood* in *Poems* (1800) I. 228 She's dead and gane, Left us and Willie burd alane, To bleer and greet. *a* **1800** *Sir Roland* x. in Chambers *Sc. Ballads* (1829) 259 He was riding burd-alane. *a* **1800** *King Henrie* in Scott *Minstr. Sc. B.*, And this was seen o' King Henrie For he lay burd alane. **1870** MORRIS *Earthly Par.* III. IV. 32 When thou a maiden burd-alone, Hadst eighteen summers!

† **bur'dash.** *Obs.* Also **berdash.** [Derivation uncertain. Possibly the same as BARDASH (as sometimes also spelt), on the ground that the article of apparel was considered to be of effeminate charater, and a foppery for men to be ashamed of. Connexion with HABERDASH is also suggested, though at present unsupported by any evidence.]

An article of personal adornment worn in the time of Queen Anne and George I; 'the fringed sash worn round the waist by gentlemen' (Fairholt); 'it would seem a kind of cravat' (Hare *Fragm.* 1873).

1713 STEELE *Guardian* No. 10 ¶5, I have prepared a treatise against the Cravat and Berdash [*other edd.* bardash]. **1721** MRS. CENTLIVRE *Plat. Lady* Epil. 190 Yet tell me, Sire, don't you as nice appear [as the woman] With your false Calves, Burdash, and Fav'rites [*i.e.* curls on the temples. *Stage direction* 'Pointing to her head']. **1730** *Female Parson* (in Fairholt *s.v.*) A modern beau..Cane, ruffles, sword-knot, burdash, hat, and feather.

burde, obs. f. BEARD, BOARD; var. of BIRDE (birth), BOURD (jest).

burde, pa. t. of BIR, BUR *v. Obs.* to behove.

c **1400** *Rowland & Ot.* 1253 A nobill suerde the burde not wolde.

Burdeaux, obs. f. BORDEAUX.

Burdekin ('bɜːdɪkɪn). The name of a river in the eastern part of Queensland, Australia; used attrib. in ***Burdekin plum***, an Australian timber tree (see quots.); ***Burdekin vine***, an Australian vine, *Vitis* (*Cissus*) *opaca*, bearing large edible tubers, also called *round yam.*

1889 J. H. MAIDEN *Useful Native Plants Austral.* 67 *Vitis Opaca*, 'Burdekin Vine', 'Round Yam'. *Ibid.* 599 *Spondias pleiogyna*, 'Sweet Plum', or 'Burdekin Plum'. **1902** *Encycl. Brit.* XXXII. 108/1 Other orders..furnish equally serviceable, large-sized timber, particularly the following: ..'Burdekin Plum' (*Pleiogynium Solandri*), [etc.]. **1963** *Austral. Encycl.* I. 174/2 Burdekin plum (*Pleiogynium cerasiferum*) is a very common tree in coastal Queensland from about the Burnett River northwards.

burdell, var. BORDEL, BORDELLO, *Obs.* brothel.

burden, burthen ('bɜːd(ə)n, 'bɜːð(ə)n), *sb.* Forms: α. 1 berðen, 2 byrðen, **-þan**, 3–4 byr-, birþin(e, -then(e, -thun, (borþon), 4 burþen, -on, 4–5 berthen, 5 birthan, byrthyn, borhtyn, 5– burthen. β. 2 byrden, 3 birden, -in, 4 byrdoun, 5 byrdune, -dyn(g, bir-, burdyne, 6 bordone, bir-, burding, burdayne, -eyne, -un, bourdon, *Sc.* buirdin, 2– burden. [OE. *byrðen* str. fem. = OS. *burthinnia*:—WGer. type **burþinnja*, an extension (with suffix *-innja* as in OE. *rǣden*) of **burþi-* (see BIRTH), f. stem. *bur-* of **ber-an* to BEAR. The synonymous OHG. *burdîn*, Goth. *baurþei*, differ only in the suffix. The Eng. forms with *d*, which began to appear early in 12th c., may be compared with *murder* for *murther*, and dial. *farden*, *furder*, for *farthing*, *further*. The prevalent form is now *burden*, but *burthen* is still often retained for 'capacity of a ship', and also as a poet. or rhetorical archaism in other senses. Of the senses in Branch IV, some are derived from the Romanic BOURDON[2], influenced by the Eng. *burden*; others belong to the native word with more or less influence from *bourdon.* The fusion

of the two words is so complete that it is not possible to treat Branch IV as an independent sb.]

I. That which is borne.

1. A load.

α. *a* **1000** ÆLFRIC *Gloss.* in Wr.-Wülcker 106 *Sarcina*, seam *uel* berðen. **1154** *O.E. Chron.* (Laud MS.) an. 1135 Wua sua bare his byrþen gold & syluer. *c* **1205** LAY. 25970 He bar uppen his rugge burðene [**1275** borþone] grete. *a* **1300** *Havelok* 807 Gladlike I wile the paniers bere.. They ther be inne a birthene gret. **1382** WYCLIF *Numb.* iv. 47 Berthens to be bore [**1388** To bere chargis]. **1398** TREVISA *Barth. De P.R.* VIII. xxv, Bereris of heuy burþones. **1566** T. STAPLETON *Ret. Untr. Jewell* I. 4, I trust the burthen will sone be disburdened. **1703** MAUNDRELL *Journ. Jerus.* (1732) 45 All Ships, that take in their Burthen here. **1827** KEBLE *Chr. Y.* 4 Oh! by Thine own sad burthen, borne So meekly.

β. *c* **1160** *Hatton Gosp.* Matt. xxiii. 4 Hyo bindeð hefiȝe byrdene þe man abere ne mæȝ. *c* **1175** *Lamb. Hom.* 5 Ne ber hit nes nefre nane burdene. *a* **1300** *Cursor M.* 6830 If þu find of þin ill-willand vnder birdin his best ligand. *c* **1440** *York Myst.* xxxii. 114 Bring on his bak a burdeyne of golde. *c* **1470** HENRY *Wallace* XI. 29 A Churll yai had, yat felloune byrdyngs bar. **1595** SHAKS. *John* II. i. 92 With burden of our armor heere we sweat. **1733** POPE *Ess. Man* III. 203 Did here the trees with ruddier burdens bend. **1850** PRESCOTT *Peru* II. 98 A light burden..was laid on his back.

2. *fig.* **a.** A load of labour, duty, responsibility, blame, sin, sorrow, etc. ***the white man's burden***: a rhetorical expression for the responsibility of the white for the coloured races.

α. *c* **971** *Blickl. Hom.* 75 Swa sæt þonne seo unaræfnedlice byrþen synna on eallum þysum menniscan cynne. *c* **1000** *Ags. Gosp.* Matt. xi. 30 Soðlice min ȝeoc is wynsum, and min byrðyn [*v.r.* byrðen, *Hatton* berðene] is leoht. *a* **1300** *Cursor M.* 17338 Late us and urs þe birthen ber. **1594** SHAKS. *Rich. III*, IV. iv. 167 A greeuous burthen was thy Birth to me. **1744** BERKELEY *Siris* §119 Wks. 1871 II. 408 A nervous colic, which rendered my life a burthen. **1748** SMOLLETT *Rod. Rand.* (1812) I. 34 The folly of laying the burthen at my door. **1812** J. WILSON *Isle of Palms* IV. 221 Hath she no friend whose heart may share With her the burthen of despair?

β. **1303** R. BRUNNE *Handl. Synne* 11959 For heuy byrdoun þat y of hem [sins] bere Y am confoundede. *c* **1374** CHAUCER *Boeth.* 101 þe burden of my sorwe. **1661** *Sir H. Vanes Politicks* 13 The burden of an injury. **1885** GLADSTONE (in *Christian World* 15 Jan. 37/2 Sovereignty has been relieved by our modern institutions of some of its burdens. **1899** KIPLING *White Man's Burden* vi, Take up the White Man's burden—Ye dare not stoop to less. **1911** H. G. WELLS *New Machiavelli* I. iv. 128 We were all..Imperialists also, and professed a vivid sense of the 'White Man's Burden'. **1922** JOAD *Common-Sense Theology* 135 Little nationalised Jingoes who are ready enough to adopt any parrot cry such as 'The White Man's Burden', or 'The Kultur of the Fatherland'. **1966** *Observer* 17 Apr. 10/6 In the seventies we can and should lay down the White Man's Burden with a clear conscience.

b. ***burden of proof***, etc.: (*onus probandi* in Roman Law) the obligation to prove a controversial assertion, falling upon the person who makes it.

1593 HOOKER *Eccl. Pol.* IV. iv. §2 Wks. 1841 I. 360 The burden of proving doth rest on them. **1780** BURKE *Sp. Econ. Ref.* Wks. III. 313 The burthen of proof rests upon me, that so many pensions..are necessary for the publick service. **1848** MACAULAY *Hist. Eng.* II. 152 The Roman Catholic divines took on themselves the burden of the proof.

c. An obligatory expense, whether due on private account or as a contribution to national funds; often with the additional notion of pressing heavily upon industry and restraining freedom of action.

1661 MARVELL *Corr.* xxi. Wks. 1872–5 II. 55 In the matter of your two companyes, if they be of any charge or burthen to you, he is willing to indulge you. **1741** MIDDLETON *Cicero* I. ii. 62 Without any burthen on the Province. **1769** ROBERTSON *Chas. V*, V. IV. 392 The addition of such a load to their former burdens, drove them to despair. **1813** WELLINGTON *Let.* in Gurw. *Disp.* X. 110 The burdens imposed shall be imposed with equality. **1863** FAWCETT *Pol. Econ.* III. vi. 369 The burden of any fixed money payment. **1876** FREEMAN *Norm. Conq.* V. xxiv. 373 The King lays certain feudal burthens on his tenants in chief.

3. A 'load' (whether of man, animal, vehicle, etc.) considered as a measure of quantity. Now only applied to the carrying capacity of a ship, stated as a certain number of tons. Cf. 7.

α. **1388** WYCLIF *2 Kings* v. 17 Graunte thou to me..that Y take of the lond the birthun of twei burdones. *c* **1449** PECOCK *Repr.* II. iv. 155 A man which stale sumtyme a birthan of thornis was sett in to the moone. **1560** in *Etoniana* ii. 32 Fyve burthens of rushes to straw Mr. Durstons chamber. **1601** SHAKS. *All's Well* II. iii. 215 A vessell of too great a burthen. **1813** WELLINGTON *Let.* in Gurw. *Disp.* XI. 505 Vessels of from fifteen to thirty tons burthen.

β. **1515** *MS. Acc. St. John's Hosp., Canterb.*, Payd for ij bordones off thornis for a hows. **1555** EDEN *Decades W. Ind.* (Arb.) 379 A shyppe of the burden of seuen score toonne. **1630** WADSWORTH *Sp. Pilgr.* iv. 33 This ship was of an 100 Tunne burden. **1871** J. Q. ADAMS in C. Davies *Metr. Syst.* III. 168 The burden of a ship, as a weight, is ascertained by the depth of the water she draws.

†**4. a.** That which is borne in the womb; a child.

c **1489** CAXTON *Sonnes of Aymon* (1885) 131, I see my ryche burden go to exyle. **1594** T. B. *La Primaud. Fr. Acad.* II. 397 The veines whereby the burthen is nourished, may well be likened to small rootes, whereby plants are cherished. **1595** SHAKS. *John* III. i. 90 Let wiues with childe Pray that their burthens may not fall this day. **1628** GAULE *Pract. The.* (1629) 112 Mary's burden and vnweildinesse, might well haue excused her absence. **1667** MILTON *P.L.* II. 767 That my womb conceiv'd A growing burden.

†**b.** ***at one burden***: at one birth. *Obs.*

c **1250** *Gen. & Ex.* 1467 At on burdene ȝhe under-stod two ðe weren hire sibbe blod. **1387** TREVISA *Higden* (Rolls Ser.) III. 43 Sche bare tweie children at oon burþen. **1548** UDALL, etc. *Erasm. Par. Matt.* i. 3 Further Judas had two children at a burden. **1572** BOSSEWELL *Armorie* II. 83 b, Where many children are borne at one burdeyne. *a* **1639** W. WHATELEY *Prototypes* I. iv. (1640) 17 Some are of opinion that Evah at every burden bare twinnes.

†**5.** What is borne by the soil; produce, crop.

1523 FITZHERB. *Husb.* §12 Good grounde wylle haue the burthen of corne or of wede. **1669** WORLIDGE *Syst. Agric.* (1681) 11 It furnisheth the Owners thereof with a greater burthen of Corn, Pulse, or whatever is sown thereon.

6. In *Mining* and *Metallurgy*. (See quot.)

1825 J. NICHOLSON *Operat. Mechanic* 329 In proportion to the quantity of lime and ore that is added to the standard quantity of the coke, the furnace is said to carry a greater or less burthen. **1881** RAYMOND *Mining Gloss.*, *Burden* (Cornw.) 1. The tops or heads of stream-work, which lie over the stream of tin. 2. The proportion of ore and flux to fuel in the charge of a blast-furnace. **1944** *Jrnl. Iron & Steel Inst.* CL. 419 We are operating at present on a burden of 60% brown Northampton ore and 30% carbonate ore. **1952** *Gloss. Welding & Cutting Metals* (*B.S.I.*) 43 *Burden*, the layer of melt and fused metal above the welding zone in submerged-arc welding.

II. 7. The bearing of loads, as in ***beast of burden***, ***ship of burden*** (= merchant-ship).

α. *a* **1300** *Cursor M.* 5520 Halds þam..In birtþin, bath to bere and drau. **1697** DRYDEN *Virg. Georg.* III. 557 Which before Tall Ships of Burthen on its Bosom bore. **1740** JOHNSON *Sir F. Drake* Wks. IV. 440 Peruvian sheep, which are the beasts of burthen in that country. **1803** WELLINGTON in Gurw. *Disp.* II. 199 Every animal..of the description of a beast of burthen.

β. **1653** URQUHART *Rabelais* I. l, With nine thousand and thirty eight great ships of burden. **1789** MRS. PIOZZI *Journ. France* II. 385 Dogs drawing in carts as beasts of burden. **1863** GEO. ELIOT *Romola* II. xxx. (1880) I. 370 To do the work that was most like that of a beast of burden.

III. 8. Used in the Eng. Bible (like *onus* in the Vulgate) to render Heb. *massā*, which Gesenius would translate 'lifting up (of the voice), utterance, oracle'; the Septuagint has ῥῆμα, λῆμμα, ὅραμα. But it is generally taken in English to mean a 'burdensome or heavy lot or fate'.

α. **1388** WYCLIF *Zech.* xii. 1 The birthun [**1382** charge] of the word of the Lord on Israel. **1535** COVERDALE *Zech.* xii, The heuy burthen which the Lorde hath deuysed for Israel.

β. **1611** BIBLE *Isa.* xiii. 1 The burden of Babylon, which Isaiah the sonne of Amoz did see. **1865** SWINBURNE *Ballad of Burd.* 1 The burden of fair women.

IV. Senses showing confusion with BOURDON².

[The earliest quotation for BOURDON² shows that word already confused with this. Apparently the notion was that the bass or undersong was 'heavier' than the air. The *bourdon* usually continued when the singer of the air paused at the end of a stanza, and (when vocal) was usually sung to words forming a refrain, being often taken up in chorus; hence sense 10. As the refrain often expresses the pervading sentiment or thought of a poem, this use became coloured by the notion of 'that which is carried' by the poem; its 'gist' or essential contents.]

†**9.** The bass, 'undersong', or accompaniment: = BOURDON² 1. *Obs.*

α. **1593** SHAKS. *Lucr.* 1133 Burthen-wise I'll hum on Tarquin still, While thou on Tereus descant'st. **1600** —— *A.Y.L.* III. ii. 261, I would sing my song without a burthen, thou bring'st me out of tune. **1833** I. TAYLOR *Fanat.* ii. 46 The burthen of the dull echoes that shake the damps from the roof of his cavern.

β. **1591** SHAKS. *Two Gent.* I. ii. 85 Heauy? belike it hath some burden then? *Lu.* I: and melodious were it, would you sing it. *c* **1840** LONGF. *Terrest. Paradise* vi, Foliage that made monotonous burden to their [birds'] rhymes.

10. The refrain or chorus of a song; a set of words recurring at the end of each verse.

α. **1598** BACON *Sacred. Medit.* x. 123 As it were a burthen or verse of returne to all his other discourses. **1610** SHAKS. *Temp.* I. ii. 380 Foote it featly heere and there, and sweete Sprights beare the burthen. *Burthen dispersedly*, Harke, harke, bowgh wawgh. **1659** HAMMOND *On Ps.* cvii. *heading* 543 Having a double burthen, or intercalary verse oft recurring. **1774** T. WARTON *Eng. Poetry* I. 26 It has a burthen or chorus. **1838** E. GUEST *Eng. Rhythms* II. 290 Burthen..the return of the same words at the close of each stave.

β. **1777** SIR W. JONES *Poems* Pref. 13 A lively burden at the end of each stanza. **1801** STRUTT *Sports & Past.* IV. iii. 304 At intervals, in place of a burden, they imitated the braying of an ass. **1868** HELPS *Realmah* vii. (1876) 167 Realmah had joined in the burden of the Ainah's song.

11. *fig.* The chief theme; leading idea; prevailing sentiment.

1649 BLITHE *Eng. Improv. Impr.* (1653) 121 What is the Burden of my Song, and is the onely sure Cure. **1793** BURKE *Observ. Cond. Minority* Wks. VII. 247 This was the burthen of all his song—'Every thing which we could reasonably hope from war, would be obtained from treaty.' **1847** L. HUNT *Men, Wom. & Bks.* I. xi. 199 The burden or leading idea of every couplet was the same. **1862** STANLEY *Jew. Ch.* (1877) I. xx. 386 Mercy and justice..is the burden of the whole Prophetic Teaching. **1879** FROUDE *Cæsar* xi. 126 The burden of what he said was to defend enthusiastically the conservative aristocracy.

V. 12. *attrib.* and *Comb.*, as in ***burden-band***, ***-bearer***, ***-bearing***, ***-board***, ***-carrying***, ***ship***.

1855 *Whitby Gloss.*, **Burdenband*, a hempen hayband. **1580** HOLLYBAND *Treas. Fr. Tong.*, *Crocheteur*..a *burthen bearer. **1833** HT. MARTINEAU *Charm. Sea* iv. 45 The burden-bearers must find their account in..a medium of exchange. **1793** HOLCROFT tr. *Lavater's Physiog.* xl. 209 Nothing but *burden-bearing patience in the eyes [of the camel and dromedary]. **1768** TUCKER *Lt. Nat.* I. 475 Ale-drinking, *burthen-carrying, fish-selling rhetoricians. **1658** USSHER *Ann.* VI. 424, 50 *burden-ships of their friends shut in by the beaked ships of Eumenes.

VI. 13. *pl.* The floor boards of a rowing boat; ***side burdens***, the side seats in a rowing boat.

1857 P. COLQUHOUN *Comp.* '*Oarsman's Guide*' 29 The flooring is termed *burthens*. *Ibid.* 31 *Side burthens* are extra thwarts laid in provisionally to carry sitters: *burthens* are the bottom boards. **1898** ANSTED *Dict. Sea Terms* 37 In boats the burdens are the footwalings.

burden, burthen (ˈbɜːd(ə)n, -ð(ə)n), *v.* Forms: *α.* 6– burthen. *β.* 6 burdon, bourdain, 6– burden. [f. prec. sb.]

1. *trans.* To lay a (material) burden on; to load.

1570 LEVINS *Manip.* 61 To burden, *onerare*. **1592** SHAKS. *Ven. & Ad.* 419 The colt that's backed and burthened being young. **1621** BARGRAVE *Serm. Selfe-Policy* (1624) 2 Coffers burdned with the aboundance of silver and gold. **1830** LYELL *Geol.* I. 299 Glaciers..burdened with alluvial debris.

b. *fig.* To load, encumber, oppress, lay a burden on, tax (memory, conscience, resources, etc.).

1541 ELYOT *Image Gov.* 153 b, Bourdainyng theim with continuall labours. **1610** SHAKS. *Temp.* V. i. 199 Let vs not burthen our remembrances, with A heauinesse that's gon. **1637** *Sc. Prayer Bk.*, *Ceremonies*, Which..did burden mens consciences without any cause. **1727** SWIFT *Gulliver* IV. ix. 316 Without burthening their memories. **1832** HT. MARTINEAU *Homes Abr.* ii. 34 Without burthening the parish. **1868** E. EDWARDS *Ralegh* I. xxi. 459 Burdened with variety of pursuits and duties.

†**2.** To charge (a person) *with* (an accusation); to lay as a charge *upon* (a person). *Obs.* or *arch.*

1559 *Declar. of Doctrine* in Strype *Ann. Ref.* I. i. viii. 114 Elias the prophet was burthened with false doctrine, and to be a disturber of the commonwealth. **1577** HOLINSHED *Chron.* II. 14 Manie writers burthen King William for the procuring of Stigand his deprivation. **1580** NORTH *Plutarch* 721 One of the Tribunes..burdened him [Clodius] that he had prophaned the holy Ceremonies. **1581** J. BELL *Haddon's Answ. Osor.* 276 b, You must..convince all these patcheries to be falsly burdened upon your Church. **1590** SHAKS. *Com. Err.* V. i. 209 This is false he burthens me with-all. [**1779** JOHNSON *L.P.* Wks. 1816 X. 21 Too studious of truth to have them burdened with a false charge.]

†**3.** ***to burden out***: to outweigh. *Obs. rare.*

1668 CULPEPPER & COLE *Barthol. Anat.* 375 Whether.. they have in them any weight, wherewith to burthen out Opinion.

Hence ˈ**burdening** *vbl. sb.* and *ppl. a.*

1591 SHAKS. *1 Hen. VI*, II. v. 10 Weake Shoulders, ouer-borne with burthening Griefe. **1641** R. BROOKE *Eng. Episc.* II. v. 82 A Synod hath a commanding and burdening Power.

†ˈ**burdenable**, *a.* *Obs.* [f. BURDEN *sb.* + -ABLE.] **a.** Capable of bearing a burden; **b.** burdensome, chargeable, causing expense.

1632 W. LITHGOW *Totall Disc.* 362 Without Ordonance, munition, and a burdenable ship. **1663** SPALDING *Troub. Chas. I* (1792) I. 291 (JAM.) They were but silly poor naked bodies, burdenable to the country and not fit for soldiers.

burdened, burthened (ˈbɜːd(ə)nd, ˈbɜːð(ə)nd), *ppl. a.* [f. BURDEN *sb.* and *v.* + -ED.] †**a.** Imposed as a burden (*obs.*). **b.** Heavily loaded, encumbered, oppressed.

1594 SHAKS. *Rich. III*, IV. iv. 111 Thy proud Necke, beares halfe my burthen'd yoke. **1697** DRYDEN *Virg. Past.* IX. 41 May thy Cows their burden'd Bags distend. **1725** POPE *Odyss.* XVII. 413 Constrained to wield..the scythe along the burthened field. **1818** *Parl. Deb.* 1409 The present burdened state of the country.

burdener (ˈbɜːd(ə)nə(r)). One who burdens.

1552 HULOET, Burdener, *onerator*. **1604** HIERON *Wks.* I. 488 An vnnecessary burdener of mankind.

ˈ**burdenless**, *a.* [f. BURDEN *sb.* + -LESS.] Without a burden.

1858 J. THOMSON *Vane's Story, &c.* (1881) 177 Now thine heart is burdenless.

†ˈ**burdenous**, ˈ**burthenous**, *a.* *Obs.* Forms: *α.* 6 burthyn-, burthenouse, 7 bourthenous, 6–7 burthenous. *β.* 6 bourdenous, -dynous, -daynouse, burdeinous, -deynous(e, 6–7 burdnous, 6– burdenous. [f. BURDEN *sb.* + -OUS, after words from Latin; cf. *onerous*.]

1. Constituting a burden, burdensome. **a.** *lit.* Heavy, ponderous.

1529 MORE *Dial. Heresyes* II. Wks. (1557) 188/2 Aungels ..vncharged of all bourdynous fleshe and bones. **1576** FLEMING tr. *Caius' Dogs* in Arb. *Garner* III. 256 A wheel which they [dogs] turn..by the moving of their burthenous bodies. **1616** SURFL. & MARKH. *Countr. Farm* 9 Anie burthenous weight. **1632** BROME *North. Lasse* I. vii, When you groan beneath your burdenous charge.

b. *fig.* Onerous, cumbersome; oppressive.

1534 MORE *Comf. agst. Trib.* I. Wks. 1150/2 Job..in..his dispicions with his burdenous comforters. **1567** DRANT *Horace's Epist.* I. xiii, If that my booke be burthenouse. **1593** SHAKS. *Rich. II*, II. i. 260 His burthenous taxations. **1657** COKAINE *Obstin. Lady* Poems (1669) 341 The burthenous draught Of misery. **1671** MILTON *Samson* 567 To sit idle on the household hearth, A burdenous drone.

†**2.** Burdened, oppressed. *rare.*

1614 R. TAILOR *Hog hath lost Pearl* IV. in *Dodsley* (1780) VI. 421 My burthenous conscience was so fraught with Sin. **1812** W. TENNANT *Anster F.* VI. xiii, The burdenous and bustling multitude.

Hence ˈ**burdenously** *adv.*

1556 J. HEYWOOD *Spider & Flie* xci. 25 Ye finalli, burdenuslie, Burdend the flie.

burdensak, variant of BYRTHYNSAK.

burdensome, burthensome ('bɜːd(ə)nsəm, 'bɜːð(ə)n-), *a.* [f. BURDEN *sb.* + -SOME.]

1. a. Of the nature of a burden; onerous, cumbersome, oppressive, troublesome, wearisome.

1578 *Chr. Prayers* in *Priv. Prayers* (1851) 459 Considering how burthensome crowns and sceptres are. **1611** BIBLE *Zech.* xii. 3 In that day will I make Ierusalem a burdensome stone. **1712** F. H. T. *Shorthand* p. iv, Not at all burdensome to the memory. **1838** SIR W. HAMILTON *Logic* xxiv. (1866) II. 20 A long definition is..burthensome to the memory. **1863** FAWCETT *Pol. Econ.* I. iv. (1876) 39 The tax becomes burdensome.

b. as quasi-*sb.* Burdensomeness.

1645 MILTON *Tetrach.* (1851) 204 If our Saviour tooke away ought of law, it was the burdensome of it.

2. Capable of carrying a good burden. *U.S. Obs.*

1763 *Boston Even. Post* 9 May (Th.), A very good and burthensome Schooner for sale. **1834** M. SCOTT *Cruise Midge* (1836) II. vi. 210 'Pull under the stern of that large ship.'.. 'A fine burdensome craft that, sir.' **1834** HOFFMAN *Winter in West* (1835) II. xxvii. 74 The burthensome steam-boats from New-Orleans reach here at the lowest stage of the river.

'burdensomely, 'burthen-, *adv.* [f. prec. + -LY².] In a burdensome manner.

1611 COTGR., *Poisamment*, heauily, weightily, burthensomely. **1848** J. S. MILL *Pol. Econ.* II. v. vi. §3. 425 That as few employments as possible may be burthensomely and vexatiously interfered with.

'burdensomeness, 'burthen-. [f. as prec. + -NESS.] The quality of being burdensome.

1574 WHITGIFT *Def. Aunsw.* II. Wks. 1851 I. 242 Defending the multitude or burdensomeness of ceremonies. **1607** *Schol. Disc. agst. Antichr.* I. ii. 86. **1865** *Spectator* 14 Jan. 34 The..burdensomeness of the legislation of last year.

† **'burdet, 'burdit.** *Obs.* [Cf. F. *bordat*, 'petite étoffe d'Egypte': also *burat* in Godef.] Some kind of cotton fabric.

1710 *Lond. Gaz.* No. 4787/4 A blue Burdit Mantua and Petticoat. **1720** *Proclam.*, *ibid.* No. 5880/1 Camblets, Burdets, or other Manufactures of Silk and Cotton. **1783** W. F. MARTYN *Geog. Mag.* I. 42 Carpets, dimities, burdets.

Burdeux, obs. f. BORDEAUX.

'burdican, ? for BAUDEKIN; cf. also BURRACAN.

1498 *Will of Muschampe* (Somerset Ho.) A testoʳ of Burdycan.

† **'burdie.** *Sc.* = BIRDIE *sb.*, little bird.

1790 BURNS *Tam O'Shanter*, The bonie burdies.

burding, obs. f. BURDEN *sb.*

burding, var. of BOURDING *vbl. sb. Obs.*

burdis, var. of BOURDIS *sb. Obs.* tilting; BOURDISE *v.* to joust.

burdly, var. of BUIRDLY *a. Sc.*

burdnous, var. of BURDENOUS.

burdock ('bɜːdɒk). *Bot.* [f. BUR *sb.*¹ + DOCK *sb.*]

1. A coarse weedy plant (*Arctium Lappa*, and kindred species) common on waste ground, bearing prickly flower-heads called burs, and large leaves like those of the dock.

1597 GERARD *Herbal* cclxxvi. §1. 664 The great Burre is called..Great Burre, Burre Docke, or Clot Burre. **1605** TIMME *Quersit.* III. 181 Take..of the seedes..of the bur-dock. **1794** MARTYN *Rousseau's Bot.* xxvi. 383 The Bur-dock, whose heads sometimes fasten themselves to your clothes as you pass. **1859** TENNYSON *Holy Grail* 570 A bed-mate of the snail and eft and snake, In grass and burdock. **1860** *All Y. Round* No. 48. 510 The hooks of the burdock cling to the passing animal, and are carried..miles away.

b. Rarely applied to *Xanthium strumarium* (Small Burdock or BURWEED). **c.** *prairie burdock*, of N. America (*Silphium terebinthinaceum*), having leaves like those of the burdock.

2. *attrib.*, as in *burdock-leaf, -root.*

1607 TOPSELL *Four-f. Beasts* 281 Take a handful of Sorrel, and lay it in a Bur-dock leaf. **1764** GALE in *Phil. Trans.* LV. 245 *note*, A pultice of burdock-root pounded. **1872** BLACK *Adv. Phaeton* xix. 268 The mighty burdock-leaves.. beloved of painters.

† **burdon.** *Obs.* Also 4 burdown. [a. L. *burdōnem.*] A mule between a horse and she-ass; a hinny. Also *attrib.*

1382 WYCLIF *2 Kings* v. 17 Graunte to me..that I take two burdowns [**1388** burdones] charge fro the lond. **1607** TOPSELL *Four-f. Beasts* 433 The Burdon is begotten betwixt a Horse, and a shee-ass.

† **burdoun**¹. *Obs.* Common early spelling of BOURDON *sb.*¹ and ².

† **burdoun**². *Obs.* [Cf. OF. *bourdon* 'clou à grosse tête?' (Godef.).] A stud on the boards of a book.

c **1440** *Promp. Parv.* 56 Burdon of a boke, *burdo.* **1483** *Cath. Angl.* 48 A Burdun of a buke; *clauillus.*

burdour(e, var. of BOURDER, *Obs.*, jester.

burdyn, var. of BOARDEN *a. Obs.* made of boards.

burdyn(e, -dyng, obs. forms of BURDEN *sb.*

bure¹. [Fr.: see BUREL.] A coarse woollen stuff.

1585 *Edinb. Test.* XIV. 230b (D.O.S.T.), Ane steik of buir. **1591** *Ibid.* XXIII. 298 Of braid claytht for cloiking callit bure. **1714** *Fr. Bk. of Rates* 64 Bures Stuff white per Piece. **1853** C. BRONTË *Villette* III. xxx. 23 He wished to counsel me, whenever I wore it [*sc.* a coloured dress] to do so..as if its material were 'bure'. **1909** *Westm. Gaz.* 4 Sept. 15/2 A favourite material with some of the best French designers is the coarse sacking of which nuns make their dresses... It is called bure; the finer makes of it are combined with velvet. *Ibid.* 9 Oct. 15/1 The fabric of the season is undoubtedly the coarse bure which takes its name from the stuff used for the costumes of monks in the Middle Ages.

‖ **bure**² ('bjuːreɪ). [Fijian.] A Fijian house.

1843 T. WILLIAMS *Jrnl.* 21 Jan. (1931) I. 140 He was sitting in a *bure* with some of the 'old ones' whilst his yang-gona was being prepared. **1963** A. BURNS *Fiji* 6 There are typical Fijian houses, the *bure*, with thatched roofs and sides. **1970** *Observer* (Colour Suppl.) 15 Feb. 24/1 When you've gotten your bearings in Nadi Town head out to native *bures* (thatched huts).

bure, obs. Sc. f. *bore*, pa. t. of BEAR *v.*¹; obs. f. BIRR, BOWER *sb.*¹

bure, var. BUER.

bureall, obs. f. BERYL.

bureau (bjuː'rəʊ, 'bjʊərəʊ); pl. **-x, -s** (-əʊz). [a. F. *bureau* writing-desk, office, from *bureau* coarse woollen stuff, baize (for covering writing-desks); see BUREL. (In sense 2 formerly treated as Fr. and pronounced (byro).) In Great Britain the stress was orig. on the final syllable; Webster gives it only on the first.]

1. a. 'A chest of drawers with a writing-board' (J.): a writing-desk with drawers for papers, etc. ***bureau-bed*** = BOX-BED.

1742 RICHARDSON *Pamela* IV. 79 My Diamond Buckle.. Miss Nancy will find in the inner Till of my Bureau. **1764** FOOTE *Patron* II. i, I suppose..my memory or mind to be a chest of drawers, a kind of bureau. **1818** CRUISE *Digest* vi. 66 After the testator's death both sheets of paper were found in his bureau. **1875** MISS BRADDON *Str. World* II. i. 3 A heavy old bureau, brass handled and brass clamped.

b. A chest of drawers. *U.S.*

1819 *St. Louis Enquirer* 15 Sept. (Th.), Look in the bureaus and trunks of modern men of fashion and see the number of coats, waistcoats, pantaloons, &c. **1837** *Southern Lit. Messenger* III. 333 The only bureau and the only rocking-chair were in Charlotte's room. **1890** MRS. CUSTER *Following Guidon* 253 Our *bureaus* were always called *bureaus*; but they were in fact packing boxes.

c. *attrib.*

1843 'R. CARLTON' *New Purchase* I. 199 The bureau-top was consecrated to Bibles and Hymn-Books. **1854** M. J. HOLMES *Tempest & Sunshine* xxiii. 328 Safely stowed away at the bottom of her bureau-drawer..was a big daguerreo-type. **1867** MRS. WHITNEY *L. Goldthwaite* vi, Bits of most delicate ferns..filled a great shallow Indian china dish upon her bureau-top. **1939** T. S. ELIOT *Old Possum's Pract. Cats* 18 He likes to lie in the bureau drawer. **1969** R. JAFFE *Fame Game* xii. 184 When she was out of the house her mother went through her bureau drawers.

2. An office, *esp.* for the transaction of public business; a department of public administration. *spec.* In modern use, an office or business with a specified function; an agency for the co-ordination of related activities, the distribution of information, etc.

In this sense the word is chiefly employed when foreign countries are referred to. In the U.S. it occurs in the official titles of certain government offices, whence also in very recent official use in England, as in 'Emigration Bureau', 'Labour Bureau'.

1720 *Lond. Gaz.* 5835/3 The Bank having opened a Bureau for buying and selling Actions. **1789-96** MORSE *Amer. Geog.* II. 463 The department of the treasury..is divided into twelve bureaux. **1813** SIR R. WILSON *Priv. Diary* II. 433 The counsels which have..emanated from the Austrian bureaux. **1856** EMERSON *Eng. Traits* Wks. 1874 II. 41 They have made London a shop, a law-court, a record office, and scientific bureau. **1880** E. KIRKE *Garfield* 43 What can a bureau do, with the whole weight of congressional influence pressing for the appointment of men because they are our friends. **1926** Information bureau [see INFORMATION 8]. **1932** L. GOLDING *Magnolia St.* II. xi. 417 The family was to make all arrangements at Garden's Travel Bureau. **1962** WODEHOUSE *Service with a Smile* v. 70 A typewriting bureau, eh?.. One of those places full of machines and girls hammering away at them like a lot of dashed riveters.

Hence **bu'reauism**, officialism, 'red-tape-ism'.

1871 *Daily News* 9 Feb., The Ministry..with all its routine of tape, wax, seals, and bureauism.

bureaucracy (bjuː'rəʊkrəsɪ, -'ɒkrəsɪ). Also † **bureaucratie, bureau-ocracy.** [a. F. *bureaucratie*, f. *bureau* (see prec.) + Gr. -κρατία rule (cf. *aristocracy*).] **a.** Government by bureaux; usually officialism. **b.** Government officials collectively.

1818 LADY MORGAN *Florence Macarthy* II. i. 35 Mr. Commisioner..represented the *Bureaucratie*, or office tyranny, by which Ireland has been so long governed. **1834** *Tait's Mag.* I. 180 The trade-ocracy and bureau-ocracy must now..prepare themselves. **1837** J. S. MILL in *Westm. Rev.* XXVIII. 71 That vast net-work of administrative tyranny..that system of *bureaucracy*, which leaves no free agent in all France, except the man at Paris who pulls the wires. **1843** R. R. MADDEN *United Irishmen* II. xvii. 367 This 'bureau-cracy' was an inveterate evil of Ireland, in the early part of Earl Grey's administration. **1848** MILL *Pol. Econ.* II. 529 The..inexpediency of concentrating in a dominant bureaucracy..all the power of organized action.. in the community. **1850** CARLYLE *Latter-d. Pamph.* iv. (1872) 121 The Continental nuisance called 'Bureaucracy'. **1858** *Merc. Mar. Mag.* V. 43 The brigand bureaucracy of China. **1860** MILL *Repr. Govt.* 40/1 The work of government has been in the hands of governors by profession; which is the essence and meaning of bureaucracy.

bureaucrat ('bjʊərəʊkræt). [a. F. *bureaucrate*, f. as prec.: cf. *aristocrat.*] An official who endeavours to concentrate administrative power in his bureau; a member of a bureaucracy; sometimes = *bureaucratist.*

1842 MOTLEY *Let.* 10 Jan. (1889) I. 94, I don't know whether I have ever described to you the great bureaucrat [Count Nesselrode] of the great autocrat [Emperor of Russia]. **1850** KINGSLEY *Alt. Locke* xx. (D.) He had..done dirty work for Dublin Castle bureaucrats. *Ibid.* xli. (D.) The tyrants of the earth..the plutocrats and bureaucrats. **1870** *Daily News* 3 Nov., That bureaucrat love of classification which is the curse of France. **1883** *Harper's Mag.* June 107/1 A great centralizer and bureaucrat.

bureaucratic (bjʊərəʊ'krætɪk), *a.* [Cf. F. *bureaucratique*, and prec.] Of or pertaining to bureaucracy.

So **bureau'cratically** *adv.*, in a bureaucratic manner; **bu'reaucratism**, a bureaucratic system; **bu'reaucratist**, a supporter or advocate of bureaucrats and bureaucracy.

1836 *Blackw. Mag.* XL. 587 They are given usually through a bureaucratic influence. **1877** A. B. EDWARDS *Up Nile* xv. 401 We find an elaborate bureaucratic system in full operation. **1863** *Sat. Rev.* XV. 265/1 A people.. bureaucratically governed, yet jealous of office. **1880** *Athenæum* 11 Sept. 336/2 Thanks to Russian bureaucratism. **1883** *19th Cent.* Dec. 740 The intelligent but stern central bureaucratism of Germany. **1836** *Foreign Q. Rev.* XVII. 255 As a 'bureaucratist' at home, or as a diplomatist abroad. **1854** *Blackw. Mag.* LXXVI. 134 German bureaucratists.. and Muscovite diplomatists.

bureaucratize (bjʊə'rɒkrətaɪz), *v.* [f. BUREAUCRATIC + -IZE.] *trans.* To govern by, or transform into, a bureaucratic administration or system.

So **bu,reaucrati'zation; bu'reaucratized** *ppl. a.*; **bu'reaucratizing** *vbl. sb.*

1892 A. C. MORANT tr. *Schäffle's Impossibility Soc. Democr.* 39, I do not by any means contemplate the bureaucratizing and nationalization of industry. **1916** *Trans. Soc. Engineers* 112 It is essential to guard against the bureaucratization of science. **1920** *Times Lit. Suppl.* 2 Sept. 559/2 The centralization of power..was..accompanied by a progressive system of bureaucratization. **1920** *Contemp. Rev.* Dec. 882 It proved itself to be a mere bureaucratization of distribution. **1945** 'G. ORWELL' in *New Saxon Pamphlets* III. 39 The radio was bureaucratised so early in its career that the relationship between broadcasting and literature has never been thought out. **1961** B. R. WILSON *Sects & Society* I. ii. 39 The bureaucratisation of the movement had begun. **1966** *Economist* 22 Oct. 377/2 American life has become too bureaucratised, too centralised.

† **'buredely, burethely,** *adv. Obs. rare.* [Of doubtful etymology and meaning: the form suggests OE. *ȝebyredlíce* 'as it behoves, duly, conveniently', but it is not easy to connect this sense with first quot.] ? At random, heedlessly.

1387 TREVISA *Higden* Rolls Ser. VII. 427 In the whiche cytees Robert wente burethely up and doun [*passim vagabatur*]. *c* **1440** *Gaw. & Galoran* ii. 21 (JAM.) Als wounded as he was, Sone buredely he ras.

buregh, bureh, obs. ff. BOROUGH.

bureȝen, var. of BERGH *v. Obs.* to protect.

bureit, obs. pa. t. and pple. of BURY *v.*

† **burel**¹. *Obs.* exc. *Hist.* Forms: ? 3, 4-5 borel, 4-7 burel, 5 borelle, burell, 6-7 burrell, 8 burail. [a. OF. *burel* (now *bureau*), a kind of cloth, dim. of *bure*, fem. 'coarse (? brown) woollen cloth, bay, baize', of uncertain origin, referred by Diez, Littré, and others to an adj. which appears in OF. as *buire* 'dark brown':—late L. **burreus*, **burrius*, f. L. *burrus* red, commonly taken as ad. Gr. πυῤῥός red. Cognate words to F. *bure, buire*, are Lomb. *bur*, It. *bujo* dark; to *burel*, Sp. *buriel*, Pr. *burel*, red-brown; also Sp. *buriel*, Pg., Pr. *burel*, coarse woollen cloth. See BUREAU.]

A coarse woollen cloth (prob. originally of brown colour: cf. BAIZE); frieze; a garment of this fabric; (plain) clothing.

c **1300** *K. Alis.* 5475 The kyng..dooth on a borel of a squyer. *c* **1300** *Pol. Songs* 221 In a curtel of burel. *c* **1386** CHAUCER *Wife's Prol.* 356 If I be gay sire shrewe, I wol renne out, my borel [*in 6 MSS.*, *Petw.* burel] for to shewe. **1483** CAXTON *G. de la Tour* E ij, Of the valewe of one of her gownes .I. poure peple had had .I. ellys of burell or fryse. **1600** *Queen's Wardr.* in Nichols *Progr. Q. Eliz.* III. 511 Item, towe remnants of blacke burrell, conteyninge both together 12 yeardes. **1720** *Stow's Surv.* (ed. Strype 1754) I.

III. v. 579/1 Burels, or Cloth-listed, according to the Constitution made for Breadth of cloth. *Ibid.* II. v. x. 286/2 Cloth ought to have been two Ells wide from List to List which was called Burrells. [**1876** ROCK *Text. Fabr.* vi. 65.]

b. *attrib.*

a **1400** *Eng. Gilds* 351 Non ne shal make burelle werk, but ȝif he be of þe ffraunchyse of the town.

†**'burel²**. *Obs. rare*⁻¹. A spoke of a wheel.

c **1325** *Gloss W. de Biblesw.* in Wright *Voc.* 167 Mes les rays [bureles] de la charette En les moyaus [in the nawes] untreceyte.

burel(l, var. of BORREL *a. Obs.* lay, rude.

burely, obs. f. BURLY.

†**buret**. *Obs.* [Cf. F. *burat* 'stuff that's halfe silke, and halfe worsted' (Cotgr.); but this may be a dim. of *bure*.] (See quot.)

1714 *Fr. Bk. of Rates* 36 Bures and Burets Stuff, per 100 Weight.

burette (bjʊ'rɛt). Also in 5 **buret, buyret.** [a. F. *burette* small vase, dim. of *buire* vase for liquors. (In sense 2 of recent adoption.)]

†**1.** 'A small cruet, violl, or bottle for oyle, or vinegar' (Cotgr.).

1483 CAXTON *Gold. Leg.* 198/1 Beryng a buyret of oyle.

2. A graduated glass tube for measuring small quantities of liquid.

1836 *Penny Cycl.* VI. 25 Burette, an instrument in chemistry, invented by M. Gay-Lussac. *Ibid.* The burette .. is a very useful instrument .. where the value .. of acids, alkalies .. etc. has to be quickly and correctly ascertained. **1882** VINES *Sachs' Bot.* 686 A glass tube bent downwards, which .. terminates in a burette. **1945** E. A. BRECHT in R. A. Lyman *Amer. Pharmacy* I. i. 20/2 Burets are used for the very accurate measurement of volumes, as in volumetric analysis. **1964** R. J. HENRY *Clinical Chem.* vi. 115 Micro burets fall into two general classes. The first is the Rehberg Buret.

3. A cruet used for the wine or the water at the Eucharist.

1856 J. C. ROBINSON *Invent. Objects Mus. Ornamental Art* 57 Plated Flagon or Burette. *Ibid.* App. 11 Pair of Sacramental Cruets, or 'Burettes'. **1871** O. SHIPLEY *Gloss. Eccl. Terms* 79/1.

‖**burg** (bʊrg, bʊəg, also bɜːg). [WGer. *burg* (whence late L. *burgus*), an earlier form of the word which has become *borough* in English.]

1. Occasionally applied by historians to a fortress (BOROUGH 1) or a walled town (BOROUGH 2) of early and mediæval times, so as to exclude the later notions connected with *burgh, borough*. See BOROUGH 3. Also *comb.* **burg-ward** (see quot.)

1753 CHAMBERS *Cycl. Supp.*, *Burgward* .. in middle age writers, the same with bulwark. The name is also extended to the town, and even the country about such a fortress. **1859** MERIVALE *Rom. Emp.* (1865) VII. lvi. 104 The fierce warriors of the north, Romans only in name .. now fell without remorse on the burgs and colonies. **1864** KINGSLEY *Rom. & Teut.* 219 The monk who guarded the relics of the saint within the walled burg. **1876** MORRIS *Sigurd* III. 172 And there is the burg of Brynhild, the white-walled house and long.

2. A town or city. (Also **berg, burgh.**) *U.S. colloq.*

1843 *Spirit of Times* 25 Mar. 43/1 Two 'individs' in this 'burg' will give our friend Greer 'the run of his teeth' whenever he visits New York. **1846** S. SMITH *Theatr. Apprent.* 151 The stranger .. also disembarked at the same burgh. **1888** *Battle Creek Weekly Jrnl.* 8 Feb., If successful, it will make a lively burg in the next few years. **1901** 'J. FLYNT' *World of Graft* ii. 30 All cities where fakirs show up strong in the streets and tramps have a quarter of their own, are recognized by grafters in general as 'open bergs'. **1903** A. ADAMS *Log Cowboy* vi. 71 The wagon and a number of the boys went into the burg. **1944** D. RUNYON *Runyon à la Carte* (1946) vi. 92 There are no more opportunities for you in this burg.

burg, obs. f. BOROUGH; var. of BROCH.

burgade, obs. form of BOURGADE.

burgage ('bɜːgɪdʒ). *Law.* Also 4 **borgage**. [ad. med.L. *burgāgium* (OF. *bourgage*), f. *burg-us* (see prec. and BOROUGH) + *-agium*.]

1. A tenure whereby lands or tenements in cities and towns were held of the king or other lord, for a certain yearly rent.

In Scotland, that tenure by which the property in royal burghs is held under the crown, proprietors being liable to the (nominal) service of watching and warding; or, as it is commonly termed, 'service of burgh, used and wont'.

1502 *Gt. Charter* in *Arnold's Chron.* (1811) 219 Yf ani holde of vs bi feeferme or bi socage or burgage. **1602** FULBECKE *1st Pt. Parallel* 21 Burgage is where the tenants of an auncient borough, do hold lands within the Borough of the King or some other person. **1676** B. W[ILLIS] *Man. Goldsm.* 71 The said Tenements and Rents be held of Us in Free Burgage. **1768** BLACKSTONE *Comm.* II. 82 Tenure in burgage is .. where the king or other person is lord of an antient borough, in which the tenements are held by a rent certain. **1863** H. COX *Instit.* I. viii. 94 The more ancient [boroughs] hold their lands in burgage.

b. *ellipt.* = in burgage.

1868 *Act 31 & 32 Vict.* ci. §102 (Referring to Scotland) Seised in any lands held burgage.

†**2.** A freehold property in a borough; also, a house or other property held by burgage tenure.

[**1292** BRITTON III. ii. §10 Bourgage est tenement de cité ou de bourg, ou de autre lu privilegie par nous.] **1362** LANGL. *P. Pl.* A. III. 77 Þei timbrede not so hye, Ne bouȝte none Borgages. **1538** LELAND *Itin.* IV. 117 A. B. of Lichfield gave .. certaine Free Burgages in the Towne for to sett this House on. **1609** SKENE *Reg. Maj.* 121 Gif ane bond man of ane Earle .. comes to ane burgh, and buyes to himselfe, ane burgage, and dwelles in that burgage ane zeare. **1827** HALLAM *Const. Hist.* (1876) III. xiii. 40 The right [to the elective franchise] sprang from the tenure of certain freehold lands or burgages within the borough.

3. *Attrib.* and *Comb.*, as ***burgage-holder, -holding, -house, -land, -tenant, -tenement, -tenure.***

1835 *Blackw. Mag.* XXXV. 975 A check to the abuses of the *burgage aristocracy. **1748** *Lond. Mag.* 32 The two Representatives [of Aldborough, Suffolk] are chosen by the Majority of the *Burgage-holders. **1754** ERSKINE *Princ. Sc. Law* (1809) 151 *Burgage-holding is that by which boroughs-royal hold of the sovereign. **1710** *Lond. Gaz.* No. 4700/4 Two *Burgage Houses or Tenements. **1586** FERNE *Blaz. Gentrie* 107 If he were possessed .. of *burgage lands. **1819** MACKINTOSH *Parl. Suffrage* Wks. 1846 III. 213 In the reign of Edward the First .. the members .. for cities and towns [were chosen] by freemen, *burgage tenants, householders or freeholders. **1876** DIGBY *Real Prop.* I. ii. §3. 48 An important class of socage tenants .. who held lands of lords by this tenure in towns .. had obtained the distinctive name of burgage tenants. **1828** SCOTT *F.M. Perth* III. 321, I will change .. thy *burgage tenement for an hundred-pound-land to maintain thy rank withal. **1523** FITZHERB. *Surv.* 12 Dyuers tenures .. as .. escuage, socage .. *burgage tenures. **1810** in *Risdon's Surv. Devon* 402 The borough .. is held .. in burgage tenure.

†**burgaine**. *Obs. rare*⁻¹. = BARGAIN *sb.*²

1608 NORDEN *Surv. Dial.* 208 The fruite .. haue made in some little Farmes (or as they call them in those parts [S. & W.]) Burgaines, a tunne, two, three, foure, of Syder.

burgal, obs. f. BURGHAL.

burgall ('bɜːgɔːl). [Cf. BERGLE.] (See quot.)

1860 BARTLETT *Dict. Amer.*, *Burgall* (*Ctenolabrus ceruleus*), a small fish very common in New York .. The usual length is about six inches .. Other names .. are Nibbler, from its nibbling off the bait when thrown for other fishes, Blue Perch and Conner.

burgamot, obs. form of BERGAMOT.

burganet, var. of BURGONET.

burgar, burgas, obs. ff. BURGHER, BURGESS.

burgard, obs. form of BOURGADE.

‖**burgau** (byrgo). [Fr.] 'The name of several univalve nacreous shells' (Littré).

1753 CHAMBERS *Cycl. Supp.*, *Burgau* in natural history, the name of a large species of sea snail, of the lunar or round-mouthed kind; it is very beautifully lined with a coat, of the nature of the mother of pearl, and the artificers take this out, to use under the name of mother of pearl, though some call it after the name of the shell they take it from, burgaudine. **1865** *Morning Star* May 20, Cormorants, with wings of mother of pearl and burgau.

‖**burgaudine**. [Fr.; 'the Academy has *burgandine*; the other Dicts. *burgaudine*' (Littré).] Mother-of-pearl made from the burgau shell.

1753 [see BURGAU].

†**burge**, *v. Obs.* Shortened form of BURGEON *v.* Hence **'burging** *vbl. sb.* and *ppl. a.*

1387 TREVISA *Higden* Rolls Ser. V. 263 Germania comeþ of Germinare, þat is for to burge and bringe forþ. **1398** —— *Barth. De. P.R.* XVII. lxxv, Burgynge þat firste brekeþ oute of þe rote of an herbe .. is calde 'Germen'. **1483** CAXTON *Gold. Leg.* 40/1 A braunche of an olyue tree burgyng. **1523** FITZHERB. *Husb.* §135 It burges out of many braunches.

burgean(t, -gen, -gyon, obs. ff. BURGEON *sb.*

burgee (bɜː'dʒiː). Also **burgie**. [Etymology unknown: senses 1 and 2 may be unconnected.]

1. A small tapered flag or pennant, three-cornered (or swallow-tailed), used by cutters, yachts, etc., generally as a distinguishing flag.

1848 *Blackw. Mag.* LXIII. 87 She allowed her burgee to droop listlessly, flapping it against her mast. **1862** *Lond. Rev.* 16 Aug. 139 The Commodore 'makes' eight o'clock, and up go all the ensigns and burgees. **1884** G. C. DAVIES *Norfolk Broads* xxxix. 294 A pretty burgee was selected as a distinguishing flag.

2. A kind of small coal suitable for burning in the furnaces of engines.

1867 SIMMONDS *Commercial Dict.*, Burgie [also in sense 1].

burgeis, -emott, obs. ff. BURGESS, BERGAMOT.

burgenet, obs. form of BURGONET.

burgeois, -se, -sie, obs. forms of BOURGEOIS, BURGESS, and BURGESSY.

burgeon ('bɜːdʒən), *sb.* Forms: 3 **burjon**, 4 **bor-, burioun, -ion, -ioyn, -gean, borgun**, 4-7 **burgen**, 5 **bergyng, burgyon**, 6 **burgeant, -gine, burryon**, 7-9 **bourgeon**, 4- **burgeon**. [ME. *borioun, burioun, -jon*, a. OFr. *bor-, burjon*, mod.Fr. *bourgeon*, of uncertain etymology. (Diez suggests its derivation from OHG. *burjan* to raise, to hold up.) The sb. and its derived vb. seem to have died out in ordinary and even in poetic use before the 18th c., but to have survived as technical terms in gardening. In the 19th c. they have been revived in poetry; the use of the sb. in *Zool.* corresponds to that of mod.F. *bourgeon*.]

1. A swelling bud, a young shoot of a plant. Now only *poet.* **b.** *Zool.* A 'bud' or reproductive germ of a zoophyte.

a **1300** *Cursor M.* 10735 Quilk o þaim þat bar burjon [*Gött.* burioun] Suld spus þat mai. **1375** BARBOUR *Bruce* v. 10 The treis begouth to ma Burgeonys. *c* **1430** LYDG. *Min. Poems* (1840) 56 To se burgyons on a dede drye stok. **1577** B. GOOGE *Heresbach's Husb.* (1586) 81 The sette must be .. full of knottes and jointes, and many little burgeons. **1601** HOLLAND *Pliny* I. 476 The Vine in her eies and burgeons. **1753** CHAMBERS *Cycl. Supp.*, *Burgeon*, in gardening a knot or button put forth by the branch of a tree in the spring. **1836** TODD *Cycl. Anat. & Phys.* I. 129/2 The parent .. throws out burgeons or buds from its surface. **1876** SWINBURNE *Erechth.* 1170 Bounteous with .. burgeon of birth.

2. *fig.*

a **1340** HAMPOLE *Psalter* 513 My lare .. make to be grene in ȝou the burioyns of vertus. **1577** HARRISON *England* III. xiv. (1878) II. 91 Nascad originall burgeant of the kings of Essex. **1655-60** STANLEY *Hist. Chaldaick Philos.* (1701) 11/2 The bourgeons even of ill matter are beneficial and good.

†**3.** *transf.* A slight swelling or pimple. *Obs.*

1597 LOWE *Chirurg.* (1634) 83 Furuncle is a tumor procreate of the like humor, as the burgens of the face.

burgeon ('bɜːdʒən), *v.* Forms: 4 **borgoune, burioune, -wne**, 4-5 **burion**, 4-6 **burgone, -own, -oyne, -yn(e**, 5 **burryn**, 6 **borgeon**, 4-7 **burgen(e**, 5-7 **burgein(e** (also *poet.* in 9), **-in(e, -inne, -ion(e, bourgen(e**, 7-9 **bourgeon**, 4- **burgeon**. [f. prec. sb. Cf. F. *bourgeonner*.]

1. *intr.* To bud or sprout; to begin to grow.

c **1325** *E.E. Allit. P.* B. 1042 Þay borgounez & beres blomez ful fayre. **1382** WYCLIF *Numb.* xvii. 8 The ȝerde of Aaron .. hadde buriowned. **1483** CAXTON *Gold. Leg.* 391/3 To burgene and brynge forth fruyte more plenteously. **1584** PEELE *Arraignm. Paris* I. iii. (1829) 10 The watery flowers burgen all in ranks. **1650** BP. HALL *Balm. Gil.* 79 When the Sun returnes .. it burgens out afresh. **1721** BAILEY, *Burgeon*, to grow big about or gross, to bud forth. **1775** ASH, *Burgein*, *Burgeon* (v. intr. obsolete). **1810** SCOTT *Lady of L.* II. xix, Earth lend it sap anew, Gaily to bourgeon, and broadly to grow. **1814** CARY *Dante* (Chandos) 209 Our plants then burgein. **1850** TENNYSON *In Mem.* cxv. 2.

b. *transf.* Of the limbs or appendages of animals. Formerly also of animals and diseases.

1382 WYCLIF *Lev.* xiii. 29 Man or womman, in whos heed or beerde borioneth a lepre. **1536** BELLENDEN *Cron. Scot.* (1821) II. 326 Thir eddaris .. burgeon with mair plentuous nowmer than evir was sene. **1566** ADLINGTON *Apuleius* 31, I perceaved a plume feathers did burgen out. **1774** GOLDSMITH *Nat. Hist.* (1862) II. I. ii. 380 Two small feet are seen beginning to bourgeon near the tail. **1827** SCOTT *Napoleon* (1835) II. 390 A hydra whose heads bourgeoned .. as fast as they were cut off.

c. *fig.* To bud, burst forth; to grow, flourish.

1382 WYCLIF *Prov.* xiv. 11 The tabernaclis of riȝtwis men shal burioune. **1531** ELYOT *Gov.* I. xiii. (1883) I. 132 Learning .. sowen in a childe .. springeth and burgeneth. **1641** MILTON *Animadv.* (1851) 195 The Prelatism of Episcopacy .. began then to burgeon. **1848** KINGSLEY *Saint's Trag.* III. i. 33 Beneath whose fragrant dews all tender thoughts Might bud and burgeon.

2. *trans.* To shoot out, put forth as buds. Also with *out, forth.* Also *transf.* and *fig.*

1382 WYCLIF *Gen.* iii. 18 It shal buriown to thee thornes and brembles. *c* **1400** *Beryn* 692 The busshis burgyn out blosomis, & flouris. **1596** LODGE *Marg. Amer.* 22 Love .. had newe burgend his wings. *c* **1820** SURTEES in Taylor *Life* (1852) 288 This goodly graft .. bourgeon'd forth its flowers and leaf.

burgeoned ('bɜːdʒənd), *ppl. a.* [f. BURGEON *sb.* + -ED².] Furnished or covered with buds.

burgeoning ('bɜːdʒənɪŋ), *vbl. sb.* [f. BURGEON *v.* + -ING¹.]

1. The action of budding or sprouting: also *fig.*

c **1400** *Primer* in Maskell *Mon. Rit.* II. 24 Thou ȝeldist with hooly buriownynge. **1616** MARKHAM *Countr. Farm* III. xlvi. 401 It keepeth the tree from growing and rising, which is the same that we call bourgening. **1878** B. TAYLOR *Deukalion* II. v. 91 April burgeoning of sunny locks.

†**2.** *concr.* A bud, a growing shoot, a branch; also *transf.* offspring. *Obs.*

a **1340** HAMPOLE *Psalter* 513 As rayne on herbe, and as droppis on burionyngis. **1382** WYCLIF *Matt.* xxiii. 33 Зee .. fruytis, *or buriownyngus*, of eddris. **1618** *Sheph. Kal.* (1656) xlvii, Thou ugly beast, Which of the Wines the burgenings doth eat.

'burgeoning, *ppl. a.* [f. BURGEON *v.* + -ING².] That buds or sprouts.

1382 WYCLIF *Wisd.* xix. 7 A buriounende feeld. **1635** HEYWOOD *Hierarch.* III. 150 It is still greene and burgeoning. **1886** *Standard* 17 May, Sitting on bench and chair under the burgeoning trees.

burger ('bɜːgə(r)). A familiar shortening of HAMBURGER. Also used as a terminal element, e.g. in ***beefburger, porkburger***, etc., usu. denoting a roll, sandwich, etc., containing the foodstuff specified in the first element. orig. *U.S.*

1939 *Amer. Speech* XIV. 154. **1941** *Word Study* Nov. 7/1 A favorite broth of the word-brewers .. forms like *-burger*, *-krieg*, *-teria*. **1946** *Amer. Speech* XXI. 88 *Burger*, hamburger sandwich. 'Burger steak' is hamburger steak.

1960 *Observer* 28 Feb. 13/4 Recently the Hamburger has become just a 'burger', and there are 'beefburgers', 'chefburgers', 'cheeseburgers', 'eggburgers' and even 'kingburgers'. **1960** *Guardian* 10 Dec. 6/6 Lines of frozen food, such as fish, vegetables, steakburgers. **1966** T. CAPOTE *In Cold Blood* ii. 72 'Perry, baby,' Dick said, 'you don't want that burger. I'll take it.' Perry shoved the plate across the table.

burger, -ship: see BURGHER, -SHIP.

burgermeester, -meister = BURGOMASTER.

† **'burgery.** *Obs. rare.* = BURGAGE or BURGHAL.
1832 T. ALLEN *Hist. Yorksh.* III. 8 The sum fixed.. continued to be paid..under the designation of burgery rents.

burges, burgeship: see BRUGES, BURGESS-SHIP.

burgesie, -eosie, obs. ff. BURGESSY.

burgess ('bɜːdʒɪs), *sb.* Forms: 3-5 **burgeis, -eys, borgeis, -eys, -es**, 3-7 **burges**, (4 **burgas(e, buries, -eys, ? boryeis**), 4-5 **bourgeis, -eys**, (**burias, -jase, -iays**, 5 **burgens, bergeys**), 5-6 **burgeois(e**, 5- **burgess**. In ME. the pl. was generally the same as the sing., as still in F. *bourgeois*. [ME. *burgeis*, a. OF. *burgeis*:—late L. *burgēnsis*: see BOURGEOIS.]

1. An inhabitant of a borough; *strictly*, one possessing full municipal rights; a citizen, freeman of a borough.
a **1225** *Ancr. R.* 168 Hit is beggares rihte uorte beren bagge on bac: & burgeises for to beren purses. **1297** R. GLOUC. 540 The borgeis anon The ȝates made aȝen him. *c* **1340** *Ayenb.* 162 Ane yongne boryeis and ane newene kniȝt ..þe borgeys wylneþ to chapfari. *c* **1380** *Sir Ferumb.* 444 At Perigot ich was y-bore: a borgeys dude me gete. *c* **1420** *Sir Amadace* xxv, Mony a riche burias. *c* **1532** LD. BERNERS *Huon* 560 He logyd in a notable burgesse howse. **1571** *Jrnls. Ho. Commons* I. 84 The Bill for the Validity of Burgesses non resiant. **1651** BAXTER *Inf. Bapt.* 243 Every Burgess at age..hath power to trade, and bear office, in the City. **1727** SWIFT *Poison. E. Curll* Wks. 1755 III. I. 150 All persons of honour, lords spiritual and temporal, gentry, burgesses and commonalty. **1862** *Municip. Corp. Act* 45-6 *Vict.* l. §7 In this Act Burgess includes Citizen. **1876** GRANT *Burgh. Sch. Scot.* II. ix. 288 In every burgh of Scotland, schools have been founded for instructing the children of Burgesses.

b. *spec.* One elected to represent his fellow-citizens in parliament; the member of parliament for a borough, corporate town, or university. Now only technical and *Hist.* The same term was used in some of the American colonies (as Virginia) to denote the representatives sent by the towns to the legislative body, which was called the 'House of Burgesses'.
1472 J. PASTON in *Lett.* 701 III. 55 Ther be a doseyn townys in Inglond that chesse no bergeys, whyche ought to do. **1554** *Jrnls. Ho. Commons* I. 29 Examine the case of Mr. Foster, Burgess elect. **1648** *Art. Peace* xvii. in *Milton's Wks.* (1851) II, The said Citizens..shall be enabled..to choose and return Burgesses into the same Parliament. **1697** BLAIR in Perry *Hist. Coll. Amer. Col. Ch.* I. 18 In Elections of Burgesses for the General Assembly, or in the choosing a speaker for the House of Burgesses. **1702** *Lond. Gaz.* No. 3840/1 One of the Burgesses for the University. **1863** H. COX *Instit.* I. iii. 13 Writs addressed..to cities and boroughs for sending burgesses.

† **2.** *spec.* A magistrate or member of the governing body of a town. Used as an official title (with varying signification) in certain English boroughs before the Municipal Reform Act of 1835.
a **1300** *Cursor M.* 16060 Pilat satt, and him a-butte þe burges [*v.r.* burgeises] o þe tun. **1483** CAXTON *Gold. Leg.* 113/1 The burgeyses that were in their gownes and mantellis ..called their seruantes. **1591** LAMBARDE *Arch.* (1635) 38 Sheriffes, Coroners, Hundreders, Burgesses, Serjeants, and Beadles, have their Courts within every their particular limits. **1613** R. C. *Table Alph.* (ed. 3) *Burgesse*, a head man of a towne. **1766** ENTICK *London* IV. 401 There are also 16 burgesses and their assistants, whose office..resembles that of an alderman's deputy in London. **1796** MORSE *Amer. Geog.* II. 205 Belfast..is..governed by a Sovereign and 12 Burgesses. **1855** MACAULAY *Hist. Eng.* xvi. III. 616 He was welcomed at the North Gate [of Belfast, in 1690] by the magistrates and burgesses in their robes of office.

† **3.** *transf.* and *fig.* Said of a man or animal: Freeman, free denizen (*of*). *Obs.*
1580 SIDNEY *Arcadia* (1622) 368 No other companions then the wild burgesses of the forrest. **1616** BEAUM. & FL. *Cust. Country* (L.) Twenty years have I lived A burgess of the sea. *c* **1630** in Risdon *Surv. Devon* §308 (1810) 315 The deer securely stood, And walk'd a burgess of the wood.

4. a. *attrib.*
1836 *Penny Cycl.* V. 207/2 An alphabetical list, to be called 'The Burgess List'. *Ibid.* 197/2 The watchword of the burgess population. **1881** MACGREGOR *Hist. Glasgow* xi. 97 The burgess class was subdivided into merchants and craftsmen.

b. *Comb.*, as † ***burgess-man, -wife***; also **burgess-roll**, the register or official list of burgesses in a borough; † **burgess-ticket**, a certificate of burgess-ship: † **burgess-town** (see quot.).
1540 SIR W. EURE in Hone *Every-day Bk.* II. 15 A king, a bushop, a *burges man, armed in harness. **1836** *Penny Cycl.* V. 208/1 To cause the *burgess-roll to be made out in alphabetical lists of the burgesses. **1657** COLVIL *Whig's Supplic.* (1751) 56 Beside her loss of *burgess ticket. **1682** WHELER *Journ. Greece* VI. 448 [It] was reckoned one of the ..*Burgess-Towns of the Athenians. **1483** CAXTON *Cato* B vij, A good *burgeys wyf and wel beloued of her husband. *c* **1550** *Scot. Poems 16th C.* II. 192 With burges wifes they led their liues.

'burgess, *v. Sc.* [f. prec.] To make a burgess, to admit to the freedom of a borough or burgh. Also ludicrously applied to rough practices symbolizing this. (See Jamieson.)

burgessdom ('bɜːdʒɪsdəm). [f. BURGESS *sb.* + -DOM.] The body of burgesses; burgess-ship.
1668 in Smyth *Rom. Family Coins* (1856) 288 Robert Paulin having come to be sworn off the burgessdom. **1885** J. BROWN *Bunyan* 329 Fifty-three persons were at one stroke admitted to the burgessdom of the town.

† **'burgessing**, *ppl. a. Obs. rare.* [f. as prec. + -ING[2].] That lives as a burgess; indwelling.
1663 SIR G. MACKENZIE *Relig. Stoic* xiv. (1685) 133 [Influence] no more sure than the Case hath upon the Watch, or the Heavens upon its burgessing Angels.

burgess-ship ('bɜːdʒɪsʃɪp). [see -SHIP.]
1. The status and privileges of a burgess; the 'freedom' of a borough, citizenship.
1467 *Eng. Gilds* 390 That no prentice haue his freedom of Burgesshippe. **1580** NORTH *Plutarch* 971 To some [of the Towns] he gave the right of Burgesship of Rome. **1662** PEPYS *Diary* 30 Apr., The Mayor and burgesses did desire my acceptance of a burgess-ship. **1752** CARTE *Hist. Eng.* III. 333 A right of burgessship in that place. **1873** MORLEY *Rousseau* I. 9 The position of burgess-ship.

b. *fig.* a rendering of πολίτευμα in Phil. iii. 20.
1612 R. CARPENTER *Soules Sent.* 91 Your Burgeship is in heauen. **1656** TRAPP *Comm. Phil.* iii. 20 Our civil conversation, or our burgess-ship, while we live by heaven's laws.

† **2.** ? The position of 'burgess' or member of parliament for a borough. *Obs.*
1673 VILLIERS (Dk. Buckhm.) *Wks.* (1705) II. 71 In the Election of his Lordship to the same Burgesship before. **1695** in Sir J. Picton *L'pool Munic. Rec.* (1883) I. 261 A vacancy was then here in the said Burgesship.

† **'burgessy.** *Obs.* Forms: 4 **borgeysye**, 6-7 **burgesie, -eosie, -eoise, -eoisie**, 7 **bourgessy**, 8 **burghesie**. [a. OF. *borgeisie* (mod.F. *bourgeoisie*), f. *borgeis* BOURGEOIS, BURGESS.] = prec.
1340 *Ayenb.* 161 Mannes lyf ine þe erþe is ase borgeysye. **1586** T. B. *La Primaud. Fr. Acad.* (1589) 544 Policie.. somtime signifieth a Burgesie..the participation and enjoying of the rights and privileges of a towne. **1636** E. DACRES tr. *Machiavel's Disc. Livy* II. xxiii. 381 They.. honourd them [the Privernates] with all the priviledges of their Bourgessie. **1700** SOUTHERNE *Fate Capua* I. i, The citizens of Rome and Capua Enjoying common rights of burghesie.

burgeys, obs. form of BURGESS.

† **'burgeyse.** *Obs.* Also 5 **buriays, burioyse, burgoyze, -oise.** [a. OF. *burgeise*, fem. of *burgeis*: see BURGESS.] The wife of a burgess; a female citizen.
c **1450** *Knt. de la Tour* (1868) 12 A worthi burgoyze, a good woman. *Ibid.* 138 A burioyse, a riche woman. **1483** CAXTON *Cato* C iv, The husbond of the sayd burgeyse.

burgh ('bʌrə). *Sc.* Forms: 4 **burch**, 5 **bwrch**, 6 **bruch, brughe, browght, burcht**, 7 **bourgh, burrow, brught**, 8-9 **brugh**, 6- **burgh**. [Var. of BOROUGH; obs. in ordinary Eng. use since 17th c., but continued in Scotland, and now always used instead of *borough* when a Scotch town is referred to. The form *brugh* is found in Burns and other writers of rustic dialect.]

1. Originally = BOROUGH; now restricted to denote a town in Scotland possessing a charter. (The earlier English instances will be found under BOROUGH; the examples given here are all Scottish.)

There are three classes of burghs, viz. ***royal burghs***, the charter of which is derived from the king, ***burgh of regality*** and ***burgh of barony***, having their charters respectively from a lord of regality and from a baron. Originally only the royal burghs sent representatives to Parliament.

1375 BARBOUR *Bruce* IV. 213 In burch I wist weill I suld de. *c* **1425** WYNTOUN *Cron.* VI. xi. 31 Þe Bwrch of Jerusalem. *c* **1505** DUNBAR *Flyting* 201 Thow held the burcht lang with ane borrowit goun. **1566** KNOX *Hist. Ref.* Wks. 1846 I. 99 The Commissionaris of browghtis. **1597** *Acts James VI* (1814) 148 (JAM.) To erect ane vniuersitie within the said brughe. **1609** SKENE *Reg. Maj.* 119 The Lawes and Constitvtions of Bvrghs. *a* **1670** SPALDING *Troub. Chas. I* (1829) 74 The body of puritan ministers of the burrows of Scotland. **1732-69** DE FOE, etc. *Tour Gt. Brit.* IV. 45 There are three Sorts of Burghs; viz. Burghs Royal, Burghs of Regality, and Burghs of Barony. **1785** BURNS *Author's Earnest Cry and Pr.* i, Ye Knights an' Squires, Wha represent our brughs an' shires. **1828** SCOTT *F.M. Perth* I. 60 The right of hunting and sporting over the lands of the burgh. **1846** MCCULLOCH *Acc. Brit. Empire* (1854) II. 371 In burghs, there is often a separate school for classics.

b. ***burgh and land***: town and country. *Sc.*
1513-75 *Diurnal of Occurr.* (1833) 81 Chargeing all our soueranes liegis alsweill to burgh as to land, regalitie as to royalitie, to address thame to come to Edinburgh. **1540** LYNDESAY *Satyre* 1795 Baith in bruch and land. **1634-46** Row *Hist. Kirk* (1842) 74 [The] whole body of this Realme both in brught and land. **1818** SCOTT *Hrt. Midl.* xxix, I glance like the wildfire through brugh and through land. **1827** —— *Surg. Dau.* i, Within burgh, and not landward.

2. Used for *borough*: **a.** by Scotch writers in speaking of foreign towns; **b.** as an archaism, either *poet.* or *Hist.* (see BOROUGH 6 a, BURG).
1798 CANNING *New Moral.* 434 in *Anti-Jacobin* 9 July (1852) 219 Till each fair burgh, numerically free Shall choose its members by the *Rule of Three*. **1816** J. SCOTT *Vis. Paris* (ed. 5) 274 The wars of the Normans..made the inhabitants [of Paris] feel the necessity of an enclosure to preserve their burghs from the invasion. **1828** CARLYLE *For. Rev. & Cont. Misc.* II. 118 The mere earthly burgh of Stratford-on-Avon.

3. *attrib.* and *comb.*, as ***burgh-moor, -school***; † **burgh-lands**, † **burgh-roods**, lands in a burgh or held by burgage tenure.
c **1505** DUNBAR *Tua Mariit Wem.* 338 And gottin his biggingis to my barne, & hie *burrow landis. **1513-75** *Diurnal of Occurr.* (1833) 296 Mr. Archibald Grahmes hous ..in the *burrowmure. *c* **1570** *Leg. Bp. St. Andrews* in *Scot. Poems 16th C.* II. 317 Save tua pure aikers of *borrow ruddis. **1864** A. MCKAY *Hist. Kilmarnock* 137 Such was the origin of the *burgh-school. **1876** GRANT (*title*) History of the Burgh Schools in Scotland.

burgh, obs. form of BARROW *sb.*[1], BOROUGH, BURR *sb.*[1]; var. of BROCH.

burgh, var. BURG 2.

burghal ('bɜːgəl), *a.* Also **burgal**. [f. BURGH + -AL[1].] Of or pertaining to a burgh, borough, or municipal corporation; † **burghal division**, a portion (of land) of size suitable for a burgage tenement; cf. BOROUGH 4.
1591 *Charter of Jas. VI*, in A. MCKay *Hist. Kilmarnock* (1864) 300 To assign his lands..in whole or in part, into burghal divisions, for buildings or houses to be erected on the same. **1839** W. CHAMBERS *Tour Holland* 33/1 These times of Amsterdam's burgal glory. **1847** *National Cycl.* 691 The burgh warrant is a burghal or civic proceeding directed against foreign debtors. **1864** BURTON *Scot Abr.* II. 282 That old burghal community..the Hanse Towns.

† **'burghal-,penny.** *Obs. English Law.* Forms: 2 **boreghal-, borghalpani**, 4 **burghal-penni**, 5 **borthalpeni.** (Spurious forms only *Hist.* and in Dicts.: 7 **brodehalpeny, -halfpeny, broodhalpeny, -halfepeny, broadhalfepenny, bordhalpeny, -halfpeny**, 8-9 **bordhalfpenny.**) [Of uncertain form and meaning; perh. f. *burghal*, or some other deriv. of BOROUGH, + PENNY.]

A municipal tax of some kind; in ancient charters certain monasteries are exempted from paying it.

Cowell's guess (quot. 1607) adopted by later writers, appears to be founded on an erroneous derivation. Apparently the word became obs. early in 15th c.; perhaps even long before that time, as the examples in the later charters may be merely repetitions of a conventional formula.

c **1177** *Charter Hen. II* (Waltham Abbey) in Dugdale *Monasticon* II. 14 Warda & Wardpani & Boreghalpani. *c* **1190** *Charter Rich. I* (Waltham Abbey) *ibid.* II. 16 Warpani & borghalpani. **1355** *Charter Edw. III* (Pulton Priory) *ibid.* II. 827 Wardepenny & Burghalpenny. **1414** *Charter Hen. V* (Shene Priory) *ibid.* I. 976 Averpeny, Hundredpeny, & Borthalpeny [*error for* Borȝhalpeny].

[**1607** COWELL *Interpreter, Brodehalpeny* commeth of the three Saxon words (*bret* a boord) and (*halve*) that is, for this or that cause..and (*penning*) it signifieth a tolle or custom for setting up of tables or boords in a Faire or Market. **1641** *Termes de la Ley* 42 Broodhalpeny, in some Copies Broodhalfepeny, that is, to be quit of a certaine custome, exacted for setting up of Tables or Boords in Faires..At this day the freedome it selfe..is called by the name of Broadhalfepenny. **1656** BLOUNT *Glossogr., Brodehalfpeny.* **1664** SPELMAN *Gloss., Bordhalpeny.* **1670** BLOUNT *Law Dict., Bord-halfpeny.* **1706** PHILLIPS, *Bord-halfpenny*: so in BAILEY, and mod. Dicts.]

† **'burghen, -ȝen, -hen**, *v. Obs.* [app. in form a var. of BERGH *v.* (cf. *bureȝen* there quoted), but perhaps influenced in sense by BORROW *v.*[1]] *trans.* To protect, save.
c **1205** LAY. 8713 Cassibellaune wurhte ful swiðe to burȝen his liue. *a* **1225** *Juliana* 26 Ȝet tu maht ȝef þu wult burhen þe seoluen.

burgh-english, obs. f. BOROUGH-ENGLISH.

burgher ('bɜːgə(r)), *sb.* Also 6-7 **burger, -ar, -or.** [In 16th c. *burger*, a. early mod.G. or Du. *burger* citizen of a *burg* or fortified town; afterwards assimilated to Eng. *burgh*, BOROUGH.]

1. a. An inhabitant of a burgh, borough, or corporate town; a citizen. Chiefly used of continental towns, but also of English boroughs, in a sense less technical than *burgess*. Now somewhat *archaic*.
1568 [see BURGHERSHIP]. **1590** MARLOWE *2nd Pt. Tamburl.* v. i. 160 Go now, and bind the burghers, hand and foot. **1600** SHAKS. *Merch. V.* I. i. 10 Your Argosies..Like Signiors and rich Burgers on the flood. **1660** R. COKE *Power & Subj.* 186 A Burger who hath..half a mark, let him pay a Peter-peny. **1698** in R. Holmes *Bk. of Entries of Pontefract Corp.* 233 The most able and sufficient Burgesse or Burgor inhabiting and residing in the said town. **1727** DE FOE *Eng. Tradesm.* xxvi. (1841) I. 265 The burgher's wives of Horsham, go as fine as they do in other places. **1824** W. IRVING *T. Trav.* I. 56 A rich burgher of Antwerp..in a broad Flemish hat. *a* **1842** MACAULAY *Armada* 74 And the red glare on Skiddaw roused the burghers of Carlisle. **1867** FREEMAN *Norm. Conq.* (1876) I. v. 288 The valiant burghers had already learned to grapple with the Dane.

fig. **1619** DRAYTON *Man Moon* (R.) As those great burghers of the forest wild, The hart, the goat.

b. *attrib.* and *comb.*

1818 SCOTT *Hrt. Midl.* xviii, 'I do not understand,' answered the burgher-magistrate, 'that the young man Butler's zeal is of so inflammable a character.' **1837** CARLYLE *Fr. Rev.* II. I. viii. 56 Mark that queenlike burgher-woman. **1841** SPALDING *Italy & It. Isl.* II. 170 Contests, in which one club of burgher-oligarchs successively displaced another. **1855** MOTLEY *Dutch Rep.* (1861) I. 38 The burgher class controlled the government. **1873** DIXON *Two Queens* III. XIII. iv. 20 Springing from a burgher stock. **1878** SIMPSON *Sch. Shaks.* i. 154 To show the inferiority of a burgher militia to professional soldiers in war.

2. A member of that section of the Scottish Secession Church, which upheld the lawfulness of the burgess oath: also *attrib.* See ANTIBURGHER.

1766 J. BROWN *Hist. Seceders* 67 The Anti-burghers.. persecuted their Burgher brethren with deposition and excommunication. **1773** J. SMITH *Hist. Sk. Relief Ch.* 41 The Burgher clergy maintained that it [the Synod] remained in their society, while the Antiburghers endeavoured to prove that they carried it away with them to Mr. Gibb's manse. **1861** RAMSAY *Remin.* (ed. 18) 18 John Brown, Burgher minister at Whitburn. **1881** MASSON *Carlyle* in *Macm. Mag.* XLV. 74 That Nonconforming communion, called the Burgher Seceders.

3. In Ceylon; see quot.

1807 CORDINER *Ceylon* (Y.) Admitted by the Dutch to all the privileges of citizens under the denomination of Burghers. **1836** *Penny Cycl.* VI. 457/1 The descendants of Europeans of unmixed blood, and that race which has sprung from the intercourse of Europeans with the natives, are called Burghers.

4. *S. Afr.* A citizen of the Cape Colony, the Natal or Transvaal Republics, or the Orange Free State before the advent of British rule. Also *attrib.*

1879 B. FRERE et al. *Speech Cape Town* 24 To encourage the brave Burghers and Southey's Volunteers to do their best to put an end to the war on the northern border of the Colony. **1879** (*title*) Interview between.. Sir Bartle Frere, and the Deputation from the Boer Committee, At the Burgher Camp, April, 1879. **1881** F. R. STATHAM *Blacks, Boers, & British* iii. 43 To save them from annihilation at the hands of the Free State burghers, the Basutos were, in 1868, taken under British protection. **1898** KRUGER in *South Africa* 1 Jan. 11/1 Burghers and fellow-countrymen, the times are such that a wise and judicious development of our sources of aid requires the most earnest consideration. **1958** L. VAN DER POST *Lost World of Kalahari* iii. 56 Every burgher was permitted, if not actually enjoined, to shoot a Bushman on sight.

Hence **'burgherage**, **'burgherdom**, **'burgherhood**, the body of burghers or citizens collectively.

1858 CARLYLE *Fredk. Gt.* I. III. iii. 210 Baronage, Burgherage, they were German mostly by blood, and by culture were wholly German. **1884** *19th Cent.* July 121 Voss the poet of burgherdom. **1885** *Harper's Mag.* Feb. 413/2 As the burgherhood enlarged, the assembly became a huge mob.

'burgher, *v. Sc.* [f. the sb.] = BURGESS *v.*

1825 LD. COCKBURN *Mem.* i. 70 Being 'Burghered' or made to 'ride the Stang'.

burgheress ('bɜːgərɪs). [f. BURGHER *sb.* + -ESS[1].] A female burgher.

1901 *Westm. Gaz.* 7 May 2/2 Stout German burgheresses patrolling the streets in whaleboned uniforms. **1912** R. BROUGHTON *Between Two Stools* ix, A tender-hearted burgher-ess of Catterwell.

[**burgheristh.** An incorrect spelling of *burhriht* 'borough-right,' in Domesday (Taunton).

In Domesday there are several instances of *st* for OE. *ht*, as in *radchenistres* for *rādcnihtas*. Spelman conjectured that it might be = *burgh-breche* burglary, and the word appears with erroneous explanation in many Law Dicts.]

burgherly ('bɜːgəlɪ), *a.* [f. BURGHER *sb.* + -LY[1].] Of, belonging to, or characteristic of a burgher.

1762 P. MURDOCH tr. *Büsching's Syst. Geogr.* IV. 445 The town consists of what are called free and burgherly houses, as also of free and burgherly inhabitants, and of the garrison. **1906** *Daily Chron.* 19 Feb. 3 There met in Bruges.. a princely and burgherly splendour. **1969** *Daily Tel.* (Colour Suppl.) 16 May 40/2 The quietly smiling creators of such burgherly tosh.

burghermaster ('bɜːrgə,mɑːstə(r)). *rare.* [Cf. Ger. *bürgermeister*.] = BURGOMASTER.

1676 *Lond. Gaz.* No. 1089/3 The Burghermasters have empowred several Burghers and Merchants to raise a Sum of Money among themselves. **1738** G. SMITH *Curious Relat.* II. 445 All the Birds that are found here [in Greenland] can swim except one sort.. called Burgher masters. **1845** S. AUSTIN *Ranke's Hist. Ref.* II. 523 A post we sometimes find occupied by a burghermaster.

burghership ('bɜːgəʃɪp). [f. BURGHER + -SHIP.] The rights and privileges of a burgher.

1725 tr. *Dupin's Eccl. Hist. 16th C.* I. v. 188 Who had lost their Burghership for some great Crimes. **1871** FREEMAN *Norm. Conq.* IV. xviii. 209 The rights both of burghership and clanship were strictly enforced.

b. *fig.* (cf. BURGESS-SHIP 1 b).

1568 COVERDALE *Bk. Death* ('transl. out of High Dutch') xvi. (1579) 69 Our conuersation and burgership is in heauen.

burghesy, variant of BURGESSY, *Obs.*

burghmaster, obs. form of BOROUGH-MASTER.

burghmaster, incorrect spelling for *berghmaster*, BARMASTER. In mod. Dicts.

‖**burg(h)ul** ('burgul). Also **bourg(h)ol**, **burgle**, etc. [Pers. *burghul* 'blé mondé, gruau'. Zenker. Cf. BULGUR, BURGOO.] In the Middle East: wheat which has been cooked, dried, and then crushed; cracked wheat.

1764 HARMER *Observ.* VII. iv. 147 Burgle is wheat boiled, then bruised by a mill, so as to take the husk off, then dryed and kept for use. **1822** J. L. BURCKHARDT *Travels in Syria & Holy Land* 24 The host gives the traveller a supper, consisting of milk, bread, and Borgul, and if rich and liberal, feeds his mule or mare also. *Ibid.* 638 Their usual fare is Burgoul; this dish is made of wheat boiled, and afterwards dried in the sun in sufficient quantity for a year's consumption: the grain is re-boiled with butter or oil, and affords a very palateable nourishment; it is a favourite dish all over Syria. **1920** *Handbk. Syria* 278 *Burghul* is wheat which is boiled before being milled. **1923** G. BELL *Let.* 7 Nov. (1927) II. xxiii. 674 Ragout, sour curds and burghul, a sort of crushed wheat. **1934** in WEBSTER. **1954** M. WALDO *Compl. Round-World Cookbk.* 198 Lamb and cracked wheat. .. 4 pounds lamb, 2 pounds *bourghol* (cracked wheat), [etc.]. **1955** P. SMOUKA *Middle Eastern Cooking* 14 *Bourgol*, with which *kebaebas* are made, are the husks of wheat. **1960** KHAYAT & KEATING *Lebanon* vii. 90 All *burghul* used to be crushed at home by a miller who brought his rotary cracking machine to the house. **1984** HUSSAINI & SAKR *Islamic Dietary Laws & Practices* (ed. 2) 149 Bulgur (or Burgul) can be found in all stores that handle Greek, Indian and Arab foods.

burgine, -gione, obs. forms of BURGEON.

burglar ('bɜːglə(r)), *sb.* Also 6 **burglour, burghlar, burgleyer**, 7 **burglare, -layer.** [Found in AFr. in 16th c.: ad. Anglo-Lat. *burglator* (13th c.), *burgulator* (16th c.), altered form of *burgator* (13th c.), perhaps f. the first element of *burgh-breche*, the native Eng. term for burglary. The Anglo-Lat. verb *burgulare* (*quasi* 'to burgle') is recorded in 1354 (*Assis.* 27 Edw. III, quoted in Reeves *Hist. Eng. Law* ed. Finlason II. 419). The 13th c. AF. word for 'burglar', *burgesour, burgeysour*, is of obscure formation, but of the same ultimate origin. The related BURGLARY is in legal AF. *burglarie*, in Anglo-Lat. *burgaria, burgeria* (early 13th c.), for which *burglaria* is found in 16th c. The origin of the intrusive *l*, in *burglator, burglaria*, and the corresponding Eng. forms, is not clear; but the notion of Lambarde (1581) and later writers that the ending *-lar* represents AF. *ler-s, laroun* (:—L. *'latro, la'trōnem*) thief, is contrary to the evidence. A 'burglator' or 'burgesour' was not necessarily a 'latro'; his object might be something else than plunder.

No corresponding words are known in continental OF. or med.L.; the rare OF. *burger* 'saccager, piller' (Godef.), occurring in Garnier's *Vie de Saint Thomas*, is unconnected, unless perhaps this sense of the word may be due to AF. influence.]

1. One who is guilty of burglary.

[*a* **1268** BRACTON *De Legibus* (Rolls ed.) II. 234 fo. 115 b, Murdritores & robbatores & burglatores. *c* **1287** *Fleta* I. xvi. (ed. 1685 p. 15) Tempus autem discernit prædonem a fure & a Burgatore. **1292** BRITTON I. xi, De Burgeysours... Tenoms a burgesours trestouz ceux, qi felounousement en tens de pes brusent eglises, ou autri mesouns, ou murs ou portes de nos citez ou de nos burgs. **1516** in Fitzherbert *Graunde Abridgement* 268 b, Burglers sont ceux que entrent mesons ou eglises al entent de inbloier beins.] **1541** tr. *Fitzherbert's New Bk. Justyces* 125 b, Burglours are properly such as felonously in yᵉ tyme of peace breke any house, church, etc. **1581** LAMBARDE *Eiren.* I. xxi. 221 A Burglour whom Britton calleth a Burgessor.. that by night breaketh into a house, wyth intent to Robbe, Kill or doe other Felonie [ed. **1582** has *burglour, burglar*; **1588** *burghlar* passim]. **1599** *Broughton's Lett.* v. 15 In Moses law he that had slaine a Burgleyer by night had been guiltles. **1603** FLORIO *Montaigne* II. xv. 358 A common burglayer will passe by quietly things that lie open. **1682** *Lond. Gaz.* No. 1768/4 This day were apprehended.. two persons suspected to be notorious Burglars and Robbers. **1769** BLACKSTONE *Comm.* IV. 224 The definition of a burglar, as given us by sir Edward Coke, is, 'he that by night breaketh and entreth into a mansion-house, with intent to commit a felony'. **1860** G. K. *Vacat. Tour* 140 Still the thing looks well, and might.. prevent a particularly conscientious burglar from breaking in.

2. *Comb.*, as ***burglar-alarm***, ***-season***; also ***burglar-proof*** adj., also *attrib.*

1840 in M. D. Leggett *Index Pat. Inventions* (1874) 173 *Burglar-alarm, L. E. Denison, Saybrook, Conn., Oct. 22, 1840, 1,835. **1877** *Telegraphic Jrnl.* V. 19/1 The application of the magneto-electric current for.. burglar alarms. **1884** *Health Exhib. Catal.* 93/2 Bells, Burglar Alarms, Lightning Conductors. **1889** *Cent. Dict.*, *Burglar-alarm lock*, a lock having an attachment which when set will sound an alarm if the bolt is improperly moved. **1963** *B.S.I. News* Apr. 10/1 Bad news for burglars is BSI's decision to give burglar alarm systems some close attention. **1856** *Spirit of Times* 13 Dec. 247/3 Manufacturers of..*Burglar Proof Safes for stores and dwelling houses. **1882** *Daily News* 24 May 7/6 Stock of second-hand Fire-and-Burglar-proof Safes. **1886** *Pall Mall G.* 4 Sept. 3/2 The *burglar season has set in.

burglar ('bɜːglə(r)), *v.* [f. the sb.] **a.** *trans.* To steal (goods) or rob (a place) as a burglar. **b.** *intr.* To commit a burglary. Cf. BURGLE *v.* Hence **'burglared, 'burglaring** *ppl. adjs.*

1890 MRS. HUNGERFORD *Born Coquette* II. xiii. 128 He certainly burglared Nan. He broke into the house.. and stole her away. **1890** *Mercury* (Tasmania) 27 Dec., A news agency.. was burglared yesterday morning. **1896** 'MARK TWAIN' in *Harper's Mag.* Aug. 345/2 They used to hear about him robbing and burglaring now and then. **1909** *Daily Chron.* 31 Aug. 1/2 'Raffles' remains a more endeared and far more possible character than the burglaring 'Duke'. **1919** W. T. GRENFELL *Labrador Doctor* (1920) iv. 76 He.. got alarmed when busy burglaring. **1928** *Sunday Dispatch* 22 July 12/4 The burglared shop.

†**'burglarer.** *Obs.* Also 7 **burglerer.** [f. BURGLAR-Y + -ER[1].] = BURGLAR *sb.*

1598 KITCHIN *Courts Leet* (1675) 17 Burglarers are those, which in time of Peace break Houses, etc. **1606** EARL NORTHAMPTON in *True and Perf. Relat.* G gij a, Certaine Burglerers that robbed his owne house. **1664** BUTLER *Hud.* II. i. 417 Love is a Burglarer, a Felon. **1704** LUTTRELL *Brief Rel.* (1857) V. 499 A reward for apprehending burglarers.

†**'burglarily**, *adv. Obs.* [f. BURGLARY + -LY[2].] After the manner of burglary; burglariously.

1533 *Act 24 Hen. VIII*, v, Euill disposed person or persons, attempting to murder, rob, or burglarily to breake mansion houses.

burglarious (bɜː'glɛərɪəs), *a.* [f. BURGLARY + -OUS. Cf. *felonious*.]

1. Of or pertaining to burglary; addicted to burglary; involving the guilt of burglary.

1769 BLACKSTONE *Comm.* IV. 226 All these entries have been adjudged burglarious, though there was no actual breaking. **1807** SYD. SMITH *Plymley's Lett.* iv, The larcenous and burglarious world. **1822** BYRON *Werner* II. i. 26 This burglarious, larcenous felony.

2. Burglar-like.

1859 THACKERAY *Virgin.* lxxxix, The daring and burglarious capture of two forts of which he forced the doors. **1865** DICKENS *Mut. Fr.* I A burglarious stream of fog creeping in.. through the key-hole.

Hence **bur'glariously** *adv.*

1807 OPIE *Lect. Art* III. (1848) 311 Burglariously entered the Temple of Fame by the window. **1883** *Law Rep.* XI. *Queen's B.* 588 The plaintiff's dwelling-house.. was burglariously entered.

burglarize ('bɜːgləraɪz), *v. U.S.* [f. BURGLAR *sb.* + -IZE.] *trans.* To rob burglariously; to break into by violence for the purpose of theft. Also *intr.*

1871 *Southern Mag.* Apr. (Schele de Vere), The Yankeeisms donated, collided, and burglarized, have been badly used up by an English magazine-writer. **1876** *Congress Rec.* July 4419/2, I found that the house of a lady moving in good society had been burglarized. **1883** TALMAGE in *Chr. Globe* 13 Sept. 829/2 The man who had a contempt for a petty theft will burglarise the wheat-bin of a nation. **1884** *Boston* (Mass.) *Jrnl.* 7 Feb. 1 The house of John Fuller was burglarized on Wednesday night. **1926** J. BLACK *You can't Win* xi. 142 It was built to be burglarized. **1947** *Jrnl. Crim. Law & Criminol.* Nov.-Dec. 319, I tried to resist the urge to get outside and burglarize.

Hence **'burglarizing** *vbl. sb.*

1872 SCHELE DE VERE *Americanisms* 655 In like manner the burglar's occupation has been designated as burglarizing. **1888** *Merchant Traveler* (Farmer), 'What have you been doing for a living lately?'.. 'Burglarizing.'

†**'burglarly**, *adv. Obs.* In 5–6 **burgularlie**, 6 **burghlarlie.** [f. BURGLAR *sb.* + -LY[2].] After the manner of a burglar.

[**1495** *Act 11 Hen. VII*, lix. Pream., Intendyng burgularie [-lie] and feloniously to have broken the hous of your seid Subget]. **1532-3** *Act 24 Hen. VIII*, v, Their dwellynge house, whiche the same euyl doers shuld attempt burgularlie to break by night. **1581** LAMBARDE *Eiren.* II. vii. (1588) 291 He robbeth him Burghlarlie in the night season.

burglary[1] ('bɜːglərɪ). Also 6 **burgulary**, 6–7 **burglarie, burghlarie.** [see BURGLAR *sb.*]

The crime of breaking (formerly by night) into a house with intent to commit felony. Now, a statutory crime of entering a building by day or night with the intention of committing a theft or other serious offence. Also *attrib.*

The legal definition of burglary in the U.K. differs slightly from that of the U.S. and elsewhere (see quots. for certain distinctions).

[**1199–1216** *Assize K. John* in *Placit. Abbrev.* 68 De burgaria & aliis latrociniis.. De Burgeria & de ligatura & aliis latrociniis. **1516** in Fitzherbert *Graunde Abridgement* 268 b, Que il vient a son meson de faire burglarie.] **1532–3** *Act 24 Hen. VIII*, v, Any suche persoune, so attemptinge to committe suche murder or burgulary. **1581** LAMBARDE *Eiren.* II. vii. (1588) 262 Burghlarie is the theft done by entrie into a dwelling house. *a* **1603** T. CARTWRIGHT *Confut. Rhem. N.T.* (1618) 558 How like burglary theeues they break open all dores. **1649** SELDEN *Laws Eng.* I. xl. (1739) 63 Burning of woods was finable.. but Burglary was Felony. **1679** *Jesuites Ghostly Ways* 3 Wounded his creditor, Hugh Hare, a Gentleman of the Temple, by committing burglary. **1768** BLACKSTONE *Comm.* IV. xvi. 226 Neither can burglary be committed in a tent or booth erected in a market or fair. *a* **1843** SOUTHEY *Nondescr.* vi, There is a maggot there.. it is his house, His castle.. oh commit not burglary! **1855** WHARTON *Crim. Law U.S.* 598 Burglary is the breaking and entering the dwelling-house of another in the night. *Ibid.* 611 The breaking and entering must be in the night. **1968** *Hansard Lords* 15 Feb. 217 Clauses 9 and 10 deal with burglary. They replace the complicated 'breaking and entering offences'... The concept of 'breaking' is itself unsatisfactory... This Bill draws no distinction between different kinds of building or between night and day; the

concept of breaking disappears and is replaced by the concept of entering as a trespasser. **1974** *Encycl. Brit. Micropædia* IX. 928/3 Housebreaking originally covered daytime entries, whereas burglary was limited to nighttime thefts; but burglary has been extended to cover all hours of the day and to cover buildings other than houses, as well as automobiles. **1975** A. D. HECHTMAN in *McKinney's Consolidated Laws N.Y.* 35 Burglary in the third degree is committed when a person knowingly enters or remains unlawfully in a building with intent to commit a crime therein. If such a building happens to be a dwelling, and the invasion occurs in the night time,..the intruder is..guilty of the more serious crime of burglary in the second degree [etc.]. **1976** *Times Lit. Suppl.* 6 Aug. 998/2 He sticks rigidly to burglary three—breaking into empty apartments in the daytime—since this carries a much less severe rap than burglary one or two. **1985** *Financial Times* 29 May I. 3 One of the more unusual of Budapest's 1,700 burglaries last year was by a skilled labourer who drove to work in a Mercedes.

b. As an act: A felonious breaking into a house.

1609 W. BARLOW *Answ. Nameless Cath.* 308 The second comming of Christ is resembled to a theeues burghlarie. **1712** in Maidment's *Sc. Pasquils* 438 Like fearful women in burglaries they generally add bloodshed to theft. *Mod.* The season for burglaries has commenced.

c. *fig.*

1636 FITZ-GEFFREY *Blessed Birthday* (1881) 155 To breake into Gods sealed secresie, This is..bold burglary. *a* **1677** BARROW *Serm.* I. xxi. (R.) To break open the closet of a man's breast..may well be deemed a worse sort of burglary ..than to break open doors.

† **'burglary**[2]. *Obs.* [As if ad. L. *burglārius*, ad. AF. *burgler.*] = BURGLAR *sb.*

1533-4 *Act 24 Hen. VIII*, iii, Diuers and many great arrant robbers, murderers, bulglaries [*sic*] and felons. **1624** T. TAYLOR *Two Serm.* ii. 9 With what severity are the lawes executed upon Burglaries, that breake into mens houses, to rob and spoile? **1651** W. G. tr. *Cowel's Inst.* 88 Murderers, Robbers, or Burglaries.

Hence † **'burglary** *v. Obs.*

1598 FLORIO, *Robbachiare*, to filch, to pilfer..to burglarie.

burglayer, obs. form of BURGLAR *sb.*

burgle ('bɜːg(ə)l), *sb.* [f. BURGLE *v.*] An act of burgling; a burglary.

1889 *Punch* 26 Jan. 37/2 The Burgle Song. **1898** *Tit-Bits* 26 Feb. 418/1 This afternoon we did a little burgle on our own account.

burgle ('bɜːg(ə)l), *v.* orig. *colloq.* or *humorous.* [A back-formation from BURGLAR *sb.*, of very recent appearance, though English law-Latin (1354) had a verb *burgulāre* of same meaning.]

a. *intr.* To follow the occupation of a burglar. **b.** *trans.* To break feloniously into the house of; to steal or rob burglariously.

1872 M. COLLINS *Pr. Clarice* I. iv. 63 The burglar who attempted to enter that room would never burgle again. **1874** *Standard* 14 Nov. 3 New words with which the American vocabulary has lately been enriched; 'to burgle', meaning to injure a person by breaking into his or her house. **1884** *Blackw. Mag.* 513/2, I burgled myself again in the night.

Hence **'burgled** *ppl. a.*, and **'burgling** *vbl. sb.* and *ppl. a.*

1880 *Daily News* 28 Oct. 5/3 Treachery seems to have been developed even in burgling circles. **1884** C. DICKENS *Dict. Lond.* 28/3 A gentleman of the burgling persuasion. **1885** *Graphic* 14 Feb. 151/1 After the 'burgling' is completed. **1886** PHELPS *Burglars in Par.* vii. 117 'Oh', said the mistress of the burgled cottage..to the policeman.

burgle, var. BURG(H)UL.

burgleyer, obs. form of BURGLAR *sb.*

burgomaske, variant of BERGOMASK.

burgomaster ('bɜːgəʊ,mɑːstə(r)). Also 6-7 **bourgomaster.** [ad. Du. *burgemeester*, after Eng. MASTER; see also BURGHER-, BOROUGH-MASTER.]

1. The chief magistrate of a Dutch or Flemish town, nearly corresponding to the *mayor* in England. Often used loosely for any member of the governing body of a foreign municipality. Also for BOROUGH-MASTER, as an official title in certain English boroughs.

1592 NASHE *P. Penilesse* (1842) 69 The beare beeing chiefe burgomaster of all the beastes vnder the lyon. **1596** SHAKS. *1 Hen. IV*, II. i. 84, I am ioyned with..Burgomasters, and great Oneyers, such as can holde in. *a* **1598** HAKLUYT *Voy.* I. 157 Euery of the foresayd cities sent one of their burgomasters vnto the towne of Hage in Holland. **1707** *Lond. Gaz.* No. 4350/1 The..Freeholders, Burgomasters, and other Inhabitants, of the ancient Borough of Cricklade. *c* **1710** ADDISON (J.) They chuse their councils and burgomasters out of the burgeois, as in the other governments of Switzerland. **1779** JOHNSON *Boerhaave* Wks. IV. 356 The only daughter of a burgo-master of Leyden. **1864** KIRK *Chas. Bold* II. IV. i. 220 The Burgo-masters were..employed in strengthening the defences.

2. A species of gull (*Larus glaucus*).

1678 RAY *Willughby's Ornith.* 349 The Great grey Gull.. called at Amsterdam the Burgomaster of Groenland. **1753** CHAMBERS *Cycl. Supp.*, *Burgomaster* of Greenland..a whimsical name given by the Dutch sailors to a species of.. sea gull. **1853** KANE *Grinnell Exp.* xvi. (1856) 124 The birds, too, were back with us..the Ivory gull, the Burgomaster, and the tern. **1883** tr. *Nordenskiöld's Voy. Vega* 43.

'burgo,mastership. [-SHIP.] The office of burgomaster.

1896 *Daily News* 28 Apr. 3/5 Dr. Lüger..proceeded to the Town Hall and communicated his renunciation of the Burgomastership. **1909** *Daily Chron.* 25 May 6/7 The burgomastership of Breslau.

burgone, obs. form of BURGEON.

† **burgonet** ('bɜːgənɛt). *Obs.* exc. *Hist.* Also 6 **burguenet, (burgant),** 6-7 **burgenet,** 6-9 **burganet,** 9 **bourginot, -goinette.** [ad. OF. *bourguignotte*, app. f. *Bourgogne* Burgundy.]

a. A very light casque, or steel cap, for the use of the infantry, especially pikemen. **b.** A helmet with a visor, so fitted to the gorget or neck-piece, that the head could be turned without exposing the neck.

[**1598** BARRET *Theor. Warres* Gloss. 249 *Burgonet*, a French word, is a certaine kind of head-peece, either for foote or horsemen, couering the head, and part of the face and cheeke.]

1563-87 FOXE *A. & M.* (1596) 1083/1 I was page to a foot-man, carying after him his pike and burganet. **1570-87** HOLINSHED *Scot. Chron.* (1806) II. 255 His burguenet beaten into his head. **1592** GREENE *Upst. Court.* Wks. (Grosart) XI. 235 With Burgants to resist the stroke of a Battleaxe. **1611** SPEED *Hist. Gt. Brit.* VIII. v. (1632) 407 On their heads they all wore guilt Burgenets. **1796** SOUTHEY *Joan* VII. 296 A massy burgonet..helming his head. **1825** WIFFEN *Tasso* VII. xc, The glistening burganet that veils His brows. **1834** PLANCHÉ *Brit. Costume* 280 A morion and bourginot of the same period. **1852** D. MOIR *Tomb de Bruce* v, In the hall hung the target and burgonet rusting.

fig. **1606** SHAKS. *Ant. & Cl.* I. v. 24 [Antony] The demy Atlas of this Earth, the Arme And Burganet of men.

burgoo (bɜː'guː). Also **burgou(t).** [ad. Arab. *burġul* cooked, parched, and crushed wheat, ultimately ad. Turk. *bulgur*: see BULGUR, BURG(H)UL.]

1. A thick oatmeal gruel or porridge used chiefly by seamen; loblolly.

1750 ELLIS *Country Housew.* 206 (E.D.S.) Whole greets (grits) boiled in water till they burst, and then mixt with butter, and so eaten with spoons, which [was] formerly called loblolly, now burgoo. **1753** CHAMBERS *Cycl. Supp. Burgoo*, a sea-faring dish. **1825** KNAPP & BALDW. *Newgate Cal.* III. 489/1 Burgoo of as good a quality as the barley. **1863** SALA *Capt. Dang.* II. i. 15 [He] had the best Beef and Burgoo at the Skipper's table.

comb. **1833** MARRYAT *P. Simple* xxxiii, Mark my words, you burgoo-eating..trowsers-scrubbing son of a bitch!

2. A soup or stew made with a variety of meat and vegetables, used especially at outdoor feasts. *N. Amer.*

1743 J. ISHAM in *Publ. Hudson's Bay Rec. Soc.* (1949) XII. 132 There is a Sort of mawse which grows upon the Rocks, which is of a Brownish Colour, which the Indians Eats frequent, they wash itt clean, then Boil itt for a considerable time till itts tender, then mixing it with Ruhiggan Burgoe or other Victuals, and Reckon itt Good Eating. **1853** J. L. MCCONNEL *Western Char.* 363 Around a burgou pot..he shone in meridian splendor. *Note.* A kind of soup, made by boiling all sorts of game with corn, onions, tomatoes, and a variety of other vegetables. **1906** *Washington Post* 16 June 6 Who, excepting Kentuckians and their favored Southern friends and kinsmen, has ever really known the bliss of genuine burgoo? **1906** H. D. PITTMAN *Belle of Bluegrass C.* xix. 272 The old timers smacked their lips as they,..in fancy,..tasted the burgout. **1966** *Times Lit. Suppl.* 22 Sept. 879/4 Burgoo..is traditionally served at a barbecue for thousands of Kentucky colonels during the weekend of the Kentucky Derby.

burgor, var. of BURGHER.

burgown, burgoyn, obs. ff. of BURGEON.

burgoyze, var. form of BURGEYSE, *Obs.*

burgrave, burggrave ('bɜːgreɪv). Also 6 **burgreve.** [ad. Ger. *burggraf*, f. *burg* town, castle + *graf* count.] The governor of a town or castle; later, a noble ruling by hereditary right a town or castle, with the adjacent domain.

1550 BALE *Eng. Votaries* II. 13 Foure dukes, four marquesses, four landgraues, four burgraues..were appoynted. **1576** LAMBARDE *Peramb. Kent* (1826) 435 They of the lowe and high Germanie..cal one ruler, Burgreve, another Margreve. **1684** *Scanderbeg Rediv.* ii. 23 The Burgraves of each City. **1818** HALLAM *Mid. Ages* (1841) IV. v. 459 The burgraves of Nuremburg. **1879** BARING-GOULD *Germany* II. 247 The majority of gentry did not occupy their own castles, but lived in those of the princes, as burggraves or stewards.

Hence **bur'graviate**, the rank or office of burgrave.

1762 tr. *Busching's Syst. Geogr.* IV. 50 The imperial land-judicatory of the burgraviate of Nurenberg.

burgularie, -arlie, obs. ff. BURGLARY, -LARLY.

† **bur'gullian.** *nonce-wd.* [According to Nares 'Conjectured to be a term of contempt, invented upon the overthrow of the Bastard of Burgundy in a contest with Anthony Woodville, in Smithfield 1467'; but this, in absence of evidence, is very improbable.] A braggadocio, bully.

1598 B. JONSON *Ev. Man in Hum.* IV. iv, Bobadill..that rogue, that foist, that fencing Burgullian?

Burgundian (bɜː'gʌndɪən), *a.* and *sb.* Also 6-7 **burgonian.** [f. the territorial name *Burgundy* (L. *Burgundia*, F. *Bourgogne*) + -AN.]

A. *adj.* Belonging to Burgundy (in any of the senses of the name). † ***Burgonian cross*** = *St. Andrew's cross* (see ANDREW). ***Burgundian hay***: = *Burgundy Hay*, see BURGUNDY 4. ***Burgundian pear***: an old variety of pear of globular shape and delicate flavour.

1578 LYTE *Dodoens* III. xiii. 334 The leaves are set togyther, standing lyke to a Burgonian Crosse. **1607** TOPSELL *Serpents* 666 As it were in form of a Burgonian crosse, or of the letter X. **1664** EVELYN *Kal. Hort.* (1727) 234 Burgundian Grape. **1671** GREW *Anat. Plants* vi. §10 Amongst Pears, the Burgundian. **1712** tr. *Pomet's Hist. Drugs* I. 12 Burgundian Hay..is a Species of Trefoil, or Saintfoin. **1832** DOWNES *Lett. fr. Cont. Count.* I. 527 Some traces of Burgundian times, still extant here.

B. *sb.* **1.** An inhabitant of Burgundy; also used for one of the Teutonic nation of the Burgunds, from whom Burgundy received its name.

†**2.** (In form *Burgonian.*) A kind of ship; perh. merely a ship built in the Burgundian dominions, which in the 15th c. included the Netherlands.

1601 HOLLAND *Pliny* I. 86 The Vindili, part of whom be the Burgundians. **1618** *Perkin Warb.* in *Select. Harl. Misc.* (1793) 60 A conference he had once with a Burgonian. **1627** DRAYTON *Agincourt* 110 Foure Burgonians excellently man'd.

Burgundy ('bɜːgəndɪ). [ad. med.L. *Burgundia*, F. *Bourgogne.* (Swift rimed it with *Sunday.*)]

1. The name of a kingdom, and afterwards a duchy of the Western Empire, subsequently giving its name to a province of France. Used *attrib.*, as in ***Burgundy Wine.***

1697 W. POPE *Old Man's Wish*, With Monte Fiascone or Burgundy wine.

2. a. Hence *ellipt.* Wine made in Burgundy. Generally understood to apply to the red wines of that province, unless otherwise stated.

1672 WYCHERLEY *Love in Wood* I. ii, I hate his impertinent Chat more than he does the honest Burgundy. **1728** SWIFT *Ladies at Sot's H.* Wks. 1755 IV. I. 92 At the *Rose* on Sunday, I'll treat you with burgundy. **1797** HOLCROFT *Stolberg's Trav.* (ed. 2) III. lxxxiv. 351 That kind of red burgundy which the French call *petit Burgogne.* **1848** THACKERAY *Van. Fair* ix, The cellars were filled with burgundy then.

b. *attrib.*

1672 WYCHERLEY *Love in Wood* V. ii, No Burgundy man or drunken scourer will reel my way.

c. A red wine resembling the Burgundy of France, made in other wine-growing districts, esp. Australian and Californian 'Burgundy'.

1886 *Catal. Colonial & Ind. Exhibition, W. Australian Court* 53 One dozen Burgundy, vintage 1882. *Ibid.*, *S. Australian Court* 36/2 Number of gallons manufactured last vintage 18,000; of Burgundy type. **1888** *W. & A. Gilbey's Wine List* 11 Australian Wines—..Burgundy Red. **1894** C. F. OLDHAM *California Wines* 8 Of natural dry red wines, the Burgundy types are perhaps the best. **1907** *Daily Chron.* 12 Oct. 9/4 You find 'Burgundy' imported into this country from Australia, California, Spain, Italy and Hungary.

d. A shade of red of the colour of Burgundy wine.

1881 *Household Words* 9 July 215/2 New colours in gloves are steel and burgundy. **1891** *Daily News* 30 Dec. 2/2 Every tone of red, from brilliant military scarlet to the deep claret and burgundy tones. **1942** R. CHANDLER *High Window* (1943) i. 5 A big solid cool-looking house with burgundy brick walls.

†**3.** A sort of head-dress for women; = BOURGOIGNE. *Obs.* (See *bourgogne* in Littré *Supp.*)

1700 FARQUHAR *Const. Couple* II. I. i, Running to..the French milliner, for a new Burgundy for my Lady's head.

4. Burgundy hay, B. trefoil [F. *burgogne*, *foin de bourgogne*]: applied by English writers to the plant Lucerne, *Medicago sativa*: but in French originally to Sainfoin, *Onobrychis sativa.* (The two were formerly confused: see SAINFOIN).

1616 SURFL. & MARKH. *Countr. Farm* 698 in Britten and Holl. s.v., *Burgundy Hay*..Because the Burgundians have been alwaies very carefull for the sowing and tilling of this herbe. **1834** BAXTER *Phænog. Bot.*, Burgundy Trefoil.

5. Burgundy pitch. [The substance is still chiefly obtained from the neighbourhood of Neufchâtel, which was once Burgundian territory. So F. *poix de Bourgogne.*] The resinous juice of the Spruce-fir (*Abies excelsa*); sometimes called *white pitch*, though its colour is reddish brown or whitish yellow. See also quot. 1875. Also *attrib.*

1678 SALMON *Pharmacop. Londin.* I. viii. 170 Burgundy Pitch..is the Rosin of the Pitch-Tree. *Ibid.* 225, Burgundy pitch plaster applied between the shoulders. **1769** W. BUCHAN *Dom. Med.* xxix. (1845) 227 Burgundy pitch may be spread thin upon a piece of soft leather. **1875** URE *Dict. Arts* I. 550 Burgundy pitch, when genuine, is made by melting frankincense..in water and straining it through a coarse cloth. The substance usually sold as Burgundy pitch is, however, common resin incorporated with water and coloured with palm-oil.

6. ***Burgundy mixture***, a preparation of soda and copper sulphate used for spraying potato-tops to destroy fungi.

1894 *Board of Agric. & Fisheries, Leaflet No. 23* By the use of Bordeaux or Burgundy mixture, the spores of the fungus are prevented from germinating. **1951** *Dict. Gardening* (R. Hort. Soc.) II. 849/2 Burgundy mixture is made like Bordeaux mixture but washing soda is used instead of lime.

burgyn(e, burgyon, obs. ff. BURGEON.

burh, OE. form of BOROUGH, BURGH, q.v.

burhel, var. BHARAL.

buri ('buəri). [Tagalog.] The talipot palm. Also *attrib.*

1890 J. FOREMAN *Philippine Isl.* xxii. 404 Tall *buri* palms. *Ibid.* 423 The canoe..was gaily decked out with festoons of *buri*. **1911** C. B. ROBINSON in *Philippine Jrnl. Science* June 106 Three different parts of the leaves of the buri palm are used for hats. **1926** *Commerce & Industry Jrnl.* (Manila, P.I.) Nov. 6 In the trade, 'buri hats' refer only to those made of the bleached buri leaf, as distinguished from those made from the unbleached leaves which are known as the 'Arayat hats'.

buriable ('bɛrɪəb(ə)l), *a.* [f. BURY *v.* + -ABLE.] Capable of being buried. *lit.* and *fig.*

1598 FLORIO, *Sepellibile*, buriable, that may be buried. **1841** GEN. P. THOMPSON *Exerc.* (1842) VI. 296 A buriable corpse. **1858-65** CARLYLE *Fredk. Gt.* XII. i. IV. 120, I notice, as not yet entirely buriable, Three Epochs.

burial ('bɛrɪəl). Forms: 3 biriel, 4-6 bery-, beri-, buryel, -ell, -elle, -all, -alle, 5-6 byryall, -ele, -elle, 6 bereall, 6-7 buriall, 6- burial. [ME. *buryel*, *biriel*, incorrectly formed as a sing. of *byriels*, BURIELS, q.v.; in later times associated with sbs. in *-al* from Fr., such as *espousal-s*.]

†**1.** A burying place, grave, or tomb. *Obs.*

c **1250** *Gen. & Ex.* 2488 Ðor is ðat liche in biriele don. **1388** WYCLIF *2 Kings* xxiii. 17 And the kyng seide, What is this biriel, which Y se? **1398** TREVISA *Barth. de P.R.* XII. xxviii. (1495) 430 The nyghte owle hauntyth and dwellyth in buryels. *c* **1450** tr. *Higden* (1865) I. 415 There is a maruellous berielle..in Weste Wales. **1535** COVERDALE *Neh.* ii. 5, I beseke the sende me..vnto yᵉ cite of my fathers buryall [**1611** sepulchres]. **1612** *Acts Jas. VI* (1814) 499 (JAM.) And thairfore the said Revestrie was disponit to Schir James Dundas of Arnestoun knycht to be ane buriall for him and his posteritie.

fig. **1596** SHAKS. *Merch. V.* I. i. 29 Vailing her high top lower then her ribs To kisse her buriall.

2. a. The act of burying; interment; funeral.

1453 *Test. Ebor.* (1855) II. 171 To the kyrk-wark for my beriall, xxs. **1467** *Ibid.* II. 278 The day of my beriall. **1549** *Bk. Com. Prayer*, The Order for the Burial of the Dead. **1602** SHAKS. *Ham.* v. i. 2 Is she to be buried in Christian buriall, that wilfully seekes her owne saluation. **1611** BIBLE *Jer.* xxii. 19 He shall be buried with the buriall of an asse. **1647** F. BLAND *Souldiers March Salv.* 35 To commend his body to due burials. **1753** CHAMBERS *Cycl. Supp.* s.v., *Christian Burial*, that performed in holy ground, and with the usual service or ceremonies of the church. *Burial of an ass*, *Asini sepultura*, an ignominious kind of burial, out of holy ground, under the gallows, or in a high way, where several roads meet, and performed by public hangmen. Such is that of suicides, excommunicated persons, etc., sometimes denoted *canine burial*, or *burial of a dog*. **1867** FREEMAN *Norm. Conq.* I. vi. 513 The body received a second burial.

b. *transf.* and *fig.*

1603 DRAYTON *Bar. Warres* VI. xcvi, Which in this Bosom shall their Buriall have. **1878** MORLEY *Diderot* II. 50 The burial of men and women alive in the cloister.

c. *pl.* Formerly in computations, etc. of mortality, which were based on the entries of burials: = Deaths.

a **1687** PETTY *Pol. Arith.* 1 The Medium of the Burials at London in the three last years..was 22337. **1753** CHAMBERS *Cycl. Supp.* s.v., Burials, in computations of mortality, denote deaths, and stand opposed to births. **1782** BURKE *Sk. Negro Code* Wks. IX. 305 Every Minister shall keep a register of births, burials and marriages. **1803** *Med. Jrnl.* X. 408 During the same months of the year 1803, the burials amounted to 238.

3. The depositing of anything under earth or water, or enclosing it in some other substance.

a **1626** BACON *New Atlantis* (1635) 33 We have great lakes, both salt and fresh; we use them for burials of some natural bodies. **1753** CHAMBERS *Cycl. Supp.* s.v., Some commend burials in the earth, others in wheat, to season timber when first felled, and make it of more durable use.

4. *Comb.* and *Attrib.*, as ***burial-cake***, ***-chamber***, ***-cloth***, ***-clothes***, ***-feast***, ***-field***, ***-law***, ***-office***, ***-procession***, ***-torch***, ***-truce***, ***-urn***, ***-vault***.

1864 A. MCKAY *Hist. Kilmarnock* 194 He ordered twelve dozen of *burial-cakes. **1871** ALGER *Future Life* 94 Along the sides of the *burial-chamber were ranged massive stone shelves. **1570-1** *Old City Acc. Bk.* (Archæol. Jrnl. XLIII.) Rd. for the *bwryall cloth of mr. peke, xvjd. **1876** GEO. ELIOT *Dan. Der.* II. xxii. 75, I had better put my *burial-clothes in my portmanteau and set off at once. **1579** FULKE *Refut. Rastel* 798 They called together the people..to their *buriall feastes. **1592** SHAKS. *Rom. & Jul.* IV. v. 87 Our wedding cheare, to a sad buriall Feast. **1742** R. BLAIR *Grave* 484 What is this world? What but a spacious *burial-field unwall'd! **1880** *Burial Law Amendment Act. **1871** ALGER *Future Life* 93 Perceiving their [Etruscans'] *burial-processions and funeral festivals. **1709** STEELE *Tatler* No. 109 ¶1 Three Men with *Burial Torches. **1862** GROTE *Greece* V. II. lvi. 76 Granting the customary *burial-truce to the defeated enemy. **1766** ENTICK *London* IV. 76 A *burial-vault the whole length of the church.

5. Special Comb.: **burial-aisle**, an aisle in a religious building used for interments, also *fig.*; **burial-board**, a body of persons appointed by public authority to regulate burials; **burial-case** *U.S.*, a shaped coffin, made to close air-tight, for the preservation of a corpse; **burial club** = *burial-society*; **burial-hill**, **-mound**, a mound erected over a grave, a tumulus, barrow; **burial permit** *U.S.*, a certificate authorizing the burial of a deceased person; **burial-service**, a religious service accompanying a burial; a form of words prescribed by ecclesiastical authority to be used at funerals; *esp.* that used in the Church of England; **burial-society**, an insurance society for providing money for the expenses of burial; **burial-stone**, a stone on a grave, a tomb-stone; **burial-yard**, burial-ground, grave-yard. Also BURIAL-GROUND, -PLACE.

1820 SCOTT *Abbot* xxxviii, To send his body and his heart to be buried in Avenel *burial-aisle. **1831** CARLYLE *Sart. Res.* I. xi. 88 Looks he also wistfully into the long burial-aisle of the Past. **1851** C. CIST *Cincinnati* 191 Every possible variety in which iron can be cast, from a butt hinge to a *burial case. **1870** 'MARK TWAIN' in *Wks.* (1900) XIX. 259, I am talking about your high-toned, silver mounted burial-case. **1848** MRS. GASKELL *Mary Barton* I. vi. 109 The town must bury him; he had paid to a *burial club..but by a few weeks' omission, he had forfeited his claim. **1910** A. BENNETT *Clayhanger* I. x. 76 To be an established subscriber to the Burial Club was evidence of good character and social spirit. *c* **1600** NORDEN *Spec. Brit.* Cornw. (1728) 70 He was a digging a borowe or *buriall hill. **1854** H. MILLER *Sch. & Schm.* 210 Stumbling among *burial-mounds and tombstones, he had toppled into an open grave. **1865** LUBBOCK *Preh. Times* 63 The tumuli or ancient burial-mounds. **1888** *St. Louis Globe Democrat* (Farmer), Yesterday's *Burial Permits. **1908** *Daily Chron.* 22 May 1/3 The case..has developed sensational features through the refusal of the authorities to grant a burial permit. **1726** AYLIFFE *Parerg.* 132 If it be not..prohibited..by a Rubrick of the *Burial-Service. **1838** DICKENS *O. Twist* v, The reverend gentleman..read as much of the burial-service as could be compressed into four minutes. **1857** GEO. ELIOT *Cleric. Life* xxxvii. 329 The faces were not hard at this funeral; the burial-service was not a hollow form. **1812** in C. S. Davies *Hist. Macclesfield* (1961) IV. 180 Sick and *burial societies which are the germ of revolution. **1850** *Rep. Extramural Sepulture* 63 in *Parl. Papers* XXI. 575 Mr. George Downing, a mechanic and secretary to a burial society,..represents the sentiments prevalent among persons of his own class on this subject. *c* **1475** *Pict. Voc.* in Wr.-Wülcker 756 *Hoc poliandrum*, a *byryelston. **1864** SKEAT *Uhland's Poems* 117 Engraven on this burial-stone Two hands together clasped you view. **1842** MIALL in *Nonconf.* II. 33 The same authority demands a *burial-yard rate.

6. As second element in comb. with sbs., as ***house-***, ***ship-***, ***tree-***, ***urn-burial***, etc.: see under the first element.

Hence '**burialer**, one who assists at a burial.

1832 HOGG in *Fraser's Mag.* VI. 166 The burialers..were lying powerless..beside the corpse of their dead relative.

burial-ground. A piece of ground set apart as devoted to the regular interment of the dead; a burying-ground, cemetery.

1803 *Ann. Rev.* I. 98 The account of the burial-grounds furnishes the most interesting description in this work. **1842** LONGF. *God's Acre* i, I like that ancient Saxon phrase, which calls The burial ground God's acre! **1845** DARWIN *Voy. Nat.* viii, It was the burial-ground of all the goats in the island. **1850** LYELL *2nd Visit U.S.* II. 325 That burial-ground commands a beautiful view.

buriall, obs. form of BERYL.

1552 LYNDESAY *Monarche* 6203 The Heuinnis, brycht lyke buriall.

burial-place. A place of burial; a place, as a vault, church, piece of ground, etc., set apart for the interment of the dead; a burying-place.

1633 BP. HALL *Hard Texts* 482 The graves of his Companies and Complices are set in the sides of the Buriall place. **1715** *Lond. Gaz.* No. 5375/2 They broke into the Burial-Place of the Family of Rothes. **1753** CHAMBERS *Cycl. Supp.* s.v. *Burial*, Westminster Abbey is the burial-place of most of our English kings. **1867** FREEMAN *Norm. Conq.* I. vi. 513 The population..had a burial place of their own. **1875** HIGGINSON *Hist. U.S.* vi. 42 Cabot gave England a continent—and no one knows his burial-place.

†'**burian.** *Obs.* exc. *Sc.* Forms in sense 1: 1 byrʒen, 2 berien, burien. [OE. *byrʒen* str. fem. has no parallel forms in the other Teut. langs., but represents a WGer. *burginnja, f. ablaut-stem *burg-* (*borg-*) of *berg-an BERGH to protect + *innja* (cf. BURDEN *sb.*). But evidence is wanting as to the identity of this with the local Sc. *burian*, which is not associated with it in sense.]

†**1.** A tomb, sepulchre. *Obs.*

a **1000** *Elene* (Gr.) 186 þy þriddan dæʒe of byrʒenne beorna wuldor of deaðe aras. *c* **1000** *Ags. Gosp.* Matt. xxiii. 20 Wa eow..forðam ʒe synt ʒelice hwitum byrʒenum. *c* **1160** *Hatton G.* ibid., ʒelic hwite beriene. *c* **1175** *Lamb. Hom.* 111 [He forðfarene] mon fereð to buriene.

2. *Sc.* 'A mound, a tumulus; or, a kind of fortification' (Jamieson). Usually applied in south of Scotland to a prehistoric 'camp' or hill-fort.

1792 *Stat. Acc. Scotl.* IV. 522 (Kirkpatrick-Juxta) There are a great number of Cairns or burians. **1794** *Ibid.* XI. 528 (Westerkirk) There is a great number of burians in this parish. These are all of a circular form, and are from 36 to 50 yards diameter. They are supposed by some to be remains of Pictish encampments. **1794** *Ibid.* XIII. 599 Burians are to be seen in different places, whether British towns or asylums for cattle. **1805** R. FORSYTH *Beaut. Scotl.* II. 285.

burias, -ayse, -es, -eys, -oyse, obs. forms of BURGESS, BURGEYSE.

Buriat ('buːrɪət). Also **Buryat**. A member of a Mongolian people inhabiting the borders of Lake Baikal, Siberia; their language. Also *attrib.* or *adj.* = **Buri'atic** *a.*, belonging to the Buriat people.

1836 *Penny Cycl.* VI. 29 The Buriates constitute one of the three great divisions of nations into which the Mongols are divided. **1888** *Encycl. Brit.* XXIV. 1/2 *Ural-Altaic languages*..*Mongolic*..*Buriat* or *Siberian Mongolian*, east and west of Lake Baikal. **1895** *Westm. Gaz.* 23 Nov. 7/1 The thirty Mongolian Buriats who, on the Emperor's initiative, have been brought to St. Petersburg for their education. **1902** *Ibid.* 28 Feb. 2/1 Disguised as a Buryat, and accompanied by one Buryatic Cossack..I set off. **1903** *Daily Chron.* 18 Nov. 3/2 He made the experiment..in disguise as a Buriat Lama. **1947** D. DIRINGER *Alphabet* II. v. 318 The three principal [Mongolian] dialects, Khalkha, Kalmuck and Buriat, do not differ much. **1957** *Encycl. Brit.* IV. 410/2 *Buriat* (*Buryat*) *Mongol Republic*, an autonomous Soviet Socialist Republic in Asiatic Russia, created as a region in Jan. 1922, and as a republic in Sept. 1923.

burie, obs. form of BERRY, BOROUGH, BURY.

buried ('bɛrɪd), *ppl. a.* [f. BURY *v.*]

1. a. Laid in a grave, interred. **b.** Laid, sunk, or concealed under ground. ***buried treasure***; also *fig.* and *attrib.*

c **1440** *Promp. Parv.* 37 Byryyde [**1499** biryed], *sepultus*. **1579** SPENSER *Sheph. Cal.* Nov. 159 That did her buried body hould. **1715** POPE *Ep. Addison* 16 Some bury'd marble half preserves a Name. **1801** SOUTHEY *Thalaba* III. i, Some open rocks and mountains, and lay bare Their buried treasures. **1844** TUPPER *Proverb. Philos.* 388 In company of buried kindred. **1851** (*title*) Buried treasures. Part I. The law of liberty: a letter on toleration, by John Locke. Part II. Milton 'on the civil power in ecclesiastical causes'. **1863** LYELL *Antiq. Man.* 9 A flint instrument from below a buried trunk of one of these pines. **1886** A. SYMONS *Introd. Browning* Pref., Criticism is..a hazel-switch for the discovery of buried treasure. **1896** H. JAMES in *Cosmopolis* I. 390 Vereker's secret..the string the pearls were strung on, the buried treasure. **1904** E. NESBIT *Phoenix & Carpet* ii. 42 'I believe it *is* a buried treasure,' he cried... I wonder what you would say if you suddenly came upon a buried treasure? **1964** *Times* 11 Feb. 12/7 Catalogues..have a buried-treasure charm.

2. *transf.* and *fig.*

1812 BYRON *To Thyrza, 'And thou art dead'* 71 More thy buried love endears Than aught, except its living years. **1844** LINGARD *Anglo-Sax. Ch.* (1858) I. i. 48 How they, buried in an obscure corner of the earth, dared to oppose. **1850** TENNYSON *In Mem.* cxx, Sad Hesper [watches] o'er the buried sun.

3. *Comb.*, as ***buried-alive*** (also *fig.*).

1851 H. MELVILLE *Moby Dick* II. xxxvi. 244 Poor, buried-alive Tashtego. **1871** GEO. ELIOT *Let.* 6 June in J. W. Cross *Life* (1885) III. xvi. 131 A resurrection of a buried-alive friendship.

buried, obs. form of BERRIED, threshed.

†'**buriels.** *Obs.* Forms: 1 byrʒels, byriels, birʒels, 2, 5 berieles, 3-4 biriʒeles, -ieles, -iles, 3-5 buryels, -iels, -ieles, -ielles, 5 beryels. [OE. *byrʒels* str. masc., cogn. w. OSax. *burgisli* neut., f. *burg-* ablaut-stem of *bergan* BERGH to protect + suffix *-isli-*; cf. OE. *græfels* quarry, *fætels* purse, etc. See also BURY *v.* and BURIAL.]

1. A burying-place; a sepulchre, tomb.

854 *Chart. Æthelwulf of Wessex* in *Cod. Dipl.* V. 107 Of ðære holan pannan up on Icenhilde weʒ on ðæne hæðenan byriels. *c* **1000** ÆLFRIC *Gen.* xxiii. 9 Ðæt he him sealde..þæt twyfælde scræf..to birʒelse. *c* **1175** *Cott. Hom.* 229 Deade men he arerde of hare berieles to life. **1297** R. GLOUC. 204 Þo vond he..An buryels al nywe ymad. **1393** LANGL. *P. Pl.* C. XXII. 146 Prophetes hem tolde That þat blessed body of buriels sholde aryse. *a* **1450** *Knt. de la Tour* 12 In alle mennis sight her berieles began to smoke. **1483** CAXTON *Gold. Leg.* 151/2 Upon the buryels grewe a right fayr flour-delis.

2. An interment, funeral.

c **1250** *Gen. & Ex.* 2474 So woren forð .x. wukes gon, ʒet adde Iacob biriʒeles non.

burier ('bɛrɪə(r)). Also 1 byrʒere, 4 by-, birier, 6 buriar, 6-9 buryer. [OE. *byrʒere*, f. *byriʒ-an* to BURY + *-ere*, -ER[1].] **a.** One who buries; †**b.** a grave-digger; also ***dead-burier***.

c **1050** *Voc.* in Wr-Wülcker 468 *Per uispellones* þurh byrʒeras. **1382** WYCLIF *Ezek.* xxxix. 15 Thei shuln sette a title..bisidis it [a boon of man] til that byriers byrye it. **1535** COVERDALE *Amos* vi. 10 The deed buriers shall take them, and cary awaye their bones. **1598** FLORIO, *Sepellitore*, a burier, a digger of graues to burie the dead. **1642** ROGERS *Naaman* 32 The buriers and mourners gape for him. **1722** DE FOE *Plague* (1884) 51 The..buryers of the Dead..were ..terrify'd. **1798** *Monthly Rev.* XXVII. 496 Amid the carcases wander Slowly the buriers. **1876** BLACKMORE *Cripps* I. ii. 27 Secret buryers.

†**buriller, burriller.** *Obs.* Of doubtful sense: see quots. App. identical with BURLER; but possibly a maker of BUREL.

[*c* **1226** in Herbert *Livery Comp.* (1837) I. 25 [quoting Strype] Non vexantur propter Burillos, vel pannos Burillatos.] **1837** HERBERT *Livery Comp.* I. 26 The matter was referred to the arbitration of three of the burillers' gild.

1875 Stubbs *Const. Hist.* III. xxi. 573 They persecuted the guild of burrillers, a sort of clothworkers.

burin ('bjʊərɪn). Also 7, 9 burine. [a. Fr. *burin*, cogn. w. It. *bolino, borino*, Sp. and Pg. *buril*, OSp. *boril*, perh. f. OHG. *bora* boring-tool. The It. form *bolino* was occas. used in 17th c.]

1. a. A graver; the tool used by an engraver on copper; also *attrib.*

1662 Evelyn *Chalcogr.* (1769) 57 [The utmost efforts and excellency of the bolino]. *Ibid.* xi. (1805) 262 Whither wrought with the burin.. or with aqua fortis. **1674** *Govt. Tongue* vii. §2. 140 Like the gravers burine upon copper. **1762–71** H. Walpole *Vertue's Anecd. Paint.* (1786) III. 227 Several of his designs.. were afterwards retouched with the burin by his disciple. **1865** Carlyle *Fredk. Gt.* III. x. vi. 266 The Text itself engraved; all by the exquisite burin of Pine. **1880** Hamerton in *Daily News* 13 Apr. 3/6 Painters of the present day consider etchings at least equal to burin engravings.. a burin engraver can only plod patiently to a foreseen result.

b. The style or manner of using the graver.

1824 Dibdin *Libr. Comp.* 507 'Tis a fine specimen of Loggan's bold burin.

2. A triangular tool used by marble-workers.

3. *Archæol.* A flint tool with a point like that of a chisel.

1916 H. F. Osborn *Men of Old Stone Age* iv. 308 The primitive graving-tool, or *burin*.. which we know was designed by the Crô-Magnon artists for their early engravings on stone. **1921** M. C. Burkitt *Prehist.* iv. 69 Gravers or *burins* fall into two main groups, the difference being determined by an observation of the working edge. In one variety this is straight like a screw-driver,.. the other variety, being curved like a gouge, is known as the gouge type. **1939** W. B. Wright *Tools & Man* ii. 15 The burin or graver of flint. **1957** *Encycl. Brit.* II. 239/2 *Aurignacian*.. The tool types include various kinds of steep-ended scrapers,.. busked gravers or burins and split-base bone points.

Hence **'burinist**, an engraver.

[**1796** Pegge *Anonym.* (1809) 187 We.. might not improperly, as we use a tool called a burin, be called Burinators, and the Art, Burining.] *a* **1864** *For. Q. Rev.* No. 1 (L.) Many expert burinists. **1882** *American* V. 124 All the great original burinists did not invent, but reproduced with the burin.

†**'buriness.** *Obs.* Forms: 1 byriȝnes, 2 buri-, burienesse, 3 burinæsse, -isse, 4–5 berenes, berynes(s. [OE. *byriȝnes*, f. stem of OE. *byriȝan* to bury + -ness.] **a.** A burying, burial, sepulture. **b.** A burial-place; a grave, tomb.

c **890** K. Ælfred *Bæda* iv. xi, Ða wæs mycel uneþelicnes ȝeworden be his byriȝnesse [Lat. *facta difficultate tumulandi*]. **1175** *Lamb. Hom.* 35 Ga to þine feder burinesse oðer þer eni of þine cunne lið in. *c* **1205** Lay. 25852 Sæt and biheold æuere: ænne burinæsse [**1250** burinisse]. **1375** Barbour *Bruce* iv. 334 He deit.. And syne wes brocht to berynes. *c* **1400** *Destr. Troy* 12160 The grekes.. broght hir to berenes, as hom best þoght. *c* **1470** Henry *Wallace* iv. 498 Fyfe off hys awne to beryness he gart leid.

buringe, obs. form of burying.

burion, -ioun, -iown, -jon, obs. ff. burgeon.

burk(e, var. berk.

burka[1] ('bɜːkə). Also burqa, boorka, bourkha, burko. [Hind. (from Arabic) *burqa'*.] A long enveloping garment worn in public places by Muslim women to screen them from the view of men and strangers.

1836 E. W. Lane *Manners Mod. Egyptians* I. i. 51 The *boor'ko'*, or face-veil, which is a long strip of white muslin, concealing the whole of the face except the eyes, and reaching nearly to the feet. **1884** Kipling *Plain Tales* (1888) 149 He went.. clad in a *boorka*, which cloaks a man as well as a woman. **1905** Holman Hunt *Pre-Raphaelitism* I. 386 His pleadings to be allowed to satisfy his eyes as to the features hidden under the black *burko*. **1905** *Daily Chron.* 16 Nov. 5/4 The Begum was clothed in strictest purdah costume, and wore a burka. **1927** *Blackw. Mag.* May 755/1 A burka with netted eyeholes. **1929** *Daily Express* 15 Jan. 1/1 The Queen [of Afghanistan] is wearing the boorka—a heavy shapeless garment which effectually hides her beauty. **1955** G. Band *Road to Rakaposhi* x. 119 Their gay red and yellow burqas, which cover the wearer from head to foot and permit only a latticed window before the eyes, made a brilliant patch of colour. **1959** *Times* 21 Sept. 13/4 The bourkhas which veiled the students from top to toe.

burka[2] ('bɜːkə). Also burkha, boorka, burqa. [Russ.] A long Caucasian cloak of felt or goat's hair.

1898 J. T. Bealby tr. *Hedin's Through Asia* I. viii. 103 A Caucasian *burkha* (cloak or mantle). **1916** J. Y. Simpson *Self-Discov. Russia* 138 Caucasian Cossack officers with.. black burka sweeping behind them. **1924** *Blackw. Mag.* Feb. 180/2 The ample folds of the ankle-long burqa. **1927** *Ibid.* Sept. 299/1 Broad-built men, like giants in their hairy boorkas and astrakhan caps.

burke (bɜːk), *v.* [f. *Burke*, the name of a notorious criminal executed at Edinburgh in 1829, for smothering many persons in order to sell their bodies for dissection.]

1. *trans.* To murder, in the same manner or for the same purpose as Burke did; to kill secretly by suffocation or strangulation, or for the purpose of selling the victim's body for dissection.

1829 *Times* 2 Feb. 3/5 As soon as the executioner proceeded to his duty, the cries of 'Burke him, Burke him —give him no rope'.. were vociferated.. 'Burke Hare too!' **1830** Lamb *Last Ess.* (Chandos) 489 Positively burking you under pretence of cleansing. **1833** T. Hook *Parson's Dau.* ii. i. 172 Perhaps he is Burked, and his body sold for nine pounds. *a* **1845** Barham *Ingol. Leg.*, *The Tragedy* ad. fin., The rest of the rascals jump'd on him and Burk'd him.

2. *fig.* To smother, 'hush up', suppress quietly. Also, to evade, to shirk, to avoid.

1835 J. A. Roebuck *Dorchester Labourers* 6/1 (*note*), The reporters *left it out*... Those who spoke in favour of the poor men, were what the reporters call *burked*. **1840** Hood *Up Rhine* Introd. iv, The Age of Chivalry is Burked by Time. **1848** Ld. G. Bentinck in *Croker Papers* (1884) III. xxv. 165 [Disraeli's] last speech, altogether burked in the Times, but pretty well given in the 'Post'. **1860** Gen. P. Thompson *Audi Alt.* III. cxxxviii. 111 Permitting a minister to burke the parliamentary conscience. **1880** *Oracle & Corr.* No. 55 A book suppressed before issue is popularly said to have been burked. **1921** *Daily Colonist* (Victoria, B.C.) 3 Apr. 32/1 He had before him a clear issue—and he burked it. **1931** *Economist* 4 July 25/1 The problem, as it concerns the investor, of the holding company and its accounts is one which it is not wise to burke. **1953** R. Graves *Poems* 4 Socrates and Plato burked the issue.

Hence **'burker, 'burkism.**

1831 Southey in *Q. Rev.* XLIV. 314 We can tell them that there are travelling Burkers in the land. **1859** Worcester, s.v. *Burkism* cites *Westm. Rev.*

Burke (bɜːk), *sb.* A colloquial designation of 'A General and Heraldic Dictionary of the Peerage and Baronetage of the United Kingdom', the first edition of which, issued in 1826, was compiled by John Burke (1787–1848). Also *transf.*

1848 Thackeray *Van. Fair* li. 451 Her ladyship is of the Kingstreet family, see Debrett and Burke. **1901** F. H. Burnett *Making of Marchioness* i. iii. 41 'If we were not in Debrett and Burke, one might be reserved about such matters,' poor Lady Claraway wrote. **1966** D. Francis *Flying Finish* i. 7 Bastard I was not: not with parents joined by bishop with half Debrett and Burke in the pews.

burking ('bɜːkɪŋ), *vbl. sb.* [f. burke *v.* + -ing[1].] **a.** The action of murdering in Burke's fashion. **b.** *fig.* The action of stifling or quietly but effectively suppressing.

1831 Southey *Lett.* (1856) IV. 252 The burking must make every one see the necessity of this. **1831** Sir J. Scarlett in *Trial of T. B. Hodgson* 373 As bad as those who have been lately convicted of burking. **1880** A. Forbes in *19th Cent.* 195 The despotism of burking is not to be tholed.

Burkite ('bɜːkaɪt). [f. the proper name *Burke* + -ite.] **a.** A political follower of Edmund Burke. **b.** An imitator of Burke the murderer.

1807 *Ann. Rev.* V. 164 To reverse the policy of the Burkites or Antijacobins. **1830** *Fraser's Mag.* I. 289 Save as a thief, a murderer, or a Burkite.

‖**burkundaz, -auze** ('bɜːkən,dɔːz). Also burkendoss. [Arabo-Pers. *barq-andāz* lightning-darter.] 'A matchlock man, but commonly applied to a native of Hindustan, armed with a sword and shield, who acts as doorkeeper, watchman, guard, or escort' (H. H. Wilson *Gloss. Judicial Terms*).

1781 *Ann. Reg.* 14/1 He.. prepared 500 cavalry and 500 burkendosses.. for this purpose. **1845** Stocqueler *Handbk. Brit. India* (1854) 68 The force is sufficiently large, consisting.. of thousands of thannadars, chokeedars, burkundauzes, pykes, etc. **1848** G. Wyatt *Revel. of Orderly* (1849) 20 A poor devil of a burkundaz.

burl (bɜːl), *sb.*[1] [a. OF. *bourle* tuft of wool; cf. Sp. *borla* tuft, tassel, and burr.]

1. A small knot or lump in wool or cloth.

c **1440** *Promp. Parv.* 56 Burle of clothe, *tumentum*. **1870** Slater *Colours* 39 These spots or 'burls' arise from portions of cotton intermixed with the wool. **1879** in *Cassell's Techn. Educ.* IV. 342/1 The burler.. carefully removes any knots or burls.

†**2.** *transf.* A small lump or rising in the skin; a pimple or pustule. *Obs.* (Cf. bur *sb.* 5.)

1607 Topsell *Four-f. Beasts* (1658) 220 The powder of the Hedge-hogs skin, being mingled with oil by anointment, taketh away the burles in the face. **1651** Culpepper *Astrol. Judgem. Dis.* (1658) 82 The Sun causeth Pimples and Burles in the Face.

†**3.** The rudiment or bud of a red deer's horn; see quot. *Obs.* (Cf. bur *sb.* 6.)

1611 Cotgr. s.v. *Bosse*, Our wood-men call [the bump], if it bee a red deeres, the burle or seale, and, if a fallow deeres, the button.

4. a. A knot in wood (U.S.).

1886 E. S. Morse *Japan. Homes* iii. 133 If it is gnarled or tortuous in grain, or if it presents knots or burls, it is all the more desirable. **1887** *Advance* (*Chicago*) 10 Mar. 145/1 From each ragged wound grew a burl.

b. An overgrown knot or excrescence in walnut and other woods, used in veneering; also, a log or piece of timber containing such a knot; also, a veneer made with this wood. Cf. bur, burr, *sb.* 5 b.

1885 *Spons' Mech. Own Bk.* 356 French walnut burls. *Ibid.*, The ash burls.. avoid the necessity of a stay log by having a sufficient part of the trunk on which the burl grew left to serve for this purpose.

burl (bɜːl), *sb.*[2] [App. var. north. dial. *birl* a whirring sound, a rapid twist or turn, etc. (see *E.D.D.* and *Sc. Nat. Dict.*); cf. birl *v.* to revolve, rotate.]

1. ? Roundness, fullness. *poet.*

1876 G. M. Hopkins *Wr. Deutschland* (1918) st. 16 The burl of the fountains of air. **1883** —— *Serm. & Writings* (1959) 154 Therefore in that 'cleave' of being which each of his creatures shews to God's eyes alone (or in its 'burl' of being|uncleven) God can choose countless points in the strain (or countless cleaves of the 'burl') where the creature has consented, does consent, to God's will in the way above shewn.

2. Also birl. An attempt, a try, a test; esp. in phr. ***to give it a burl***, to make an attempt. *Austral.* and *N.Z. colloq.*

1917 *N.Z.E.F. Chrons.* 16 May 137/2 So up they [pennies] went and spinning well And betters cried, 'Fair "burl"!' **1933** *Bulletin* (Sydney) 8 Nov. 20/4 He [a whale] decided to give the launch a birl. He butted it frequently with his nose. **1939** K. Tennant *Foveaux* iv. i. 348 How about giving it a burl? **1947** D. M. Davin *For Rest of Lives* xlv. 227, I thought I'd give it a burl. And I made it, got clean away. **1955** D. Niland *Shiralee* 108, I'm going to give Eucla a birl. Want to get there as soon as I can. **1969** *Private Eye* 23 May 14 Might as well give this mead another burl.

burl (bɜːl), *v.*[1] [f. the sb. There was a med.L. *burillāre*: see buriller.]

1. *trans.* To dress (cloth), *esp.* by removing knots and lumps; 'to dress cloth as fullers do' (J).

1483 *Cath. Angl.* 48 To Burle clothe, *extuberare*. **1552** *Act 5 & 6 Edw. VI*, vi. §27 If.. Cloth.. happen to be evil burled or wasted in the Mill. **1611** Markham *Countr. Content.* ii. v. (1668) 128 That the Cloth-worker or Sheer-man burle and dress it sufficiently. **1706** Phillips, *Burl*, to dress Cloath as Fullers do. **1730–6** Bailey, *Burl*, to pick out the Straws or Threads of Cloth which have not taken the Dye, as Cloth-drawers do. **1882** Beck *Draper's Dict.*, *Burl*, to pick the burls from the surface of woollen cloths.

2. To pick out, remove (a lock or flock of wool).

1650 Charleton *Paradoxes* 26 The.. Priest burles a small lock of wooll, from the.. upper garment of the Saint. **1863** Morton *Cycl. Agric.* Gloss. (E.D.S.), *Burl*, to cut away the dirty wool from the hind parts of a sheep.

†**3.** To remove 'burls' from the face. *nonce-use* (see burl *sb.*[1] 2). *Obs.*

1648 Herrick *Hesper.* (1869) 226 Of pushes Spalt has such a knottie race, He needs a tucker for to burle his face.

†**burl**, *v.*[2] *Obs.* [Stratmann and Mätzner compare LG. *burreln* 'sprudeln'; cf. also burble, purl.] *intr.* To bubble, as a spring or fountain out of which water flows gently.

c **1440** *Bone Flor.* 1639 Betres lay burlyng in hur blode. *c* **1450** *Erle of Tolous* 99 Many a bolde baron.. Lay burland yn hys own blode.

burl, burler, dial. forms of birl, birler.

†**burlace, burlake, burlet**, corruptions of *Bourdelais*, name of a variety of grape, cultivated in the 17th c., which long ago dropped out of cultivation, and its name along with it.

1629 Parkinson *Orchard* vi. 663 The Burlet is a very great white Grape. **1664** Evelyn *Kal. Hort.* (1729) 234 A Catalogue of.. excellent Fruit Trees; Vines, Raisin, Bursa-robe, Burlet. **1688** Ray *Hist. Plant.* II. 1615 The Burlet Grape. **1737** Miller *Gard. Dict.* (ed. 3) s.v. *Vitis*, The Burdelais, vulgarly called Burlake. [**1797** *Ibid.* The Claret Grape, Bourdelais or Verjuice Grape.] **1755** Johnson, *Burlace*; (whence in all subseq. Dicts.).

burlady: see byrlady: By our Lady!

burlap ('bɜːlæp), *sb.* Also 7–8 borelaps, -lapps. [Etymology uncertain. (Cf. Du. *boenlap* 'rubbing-clout, linen' Calisch; the first component may have been confused with *boer* peasant.)]

Originally perhaps a sort of holland; now a coarse canvas made of jute or hemp, used for bagging; also, a finer material used for curtains.

1695–6 *Act 7 & 8 Will. III*, x. §16 Course Linnens commonly called Borelapps. **1696** J. F. *Merchants Wareho.* 2, I shall begin with Bore-laps; because that for Shifts or Shirts is counted and known to be a very strong Cloth. **1871** Napheys *Prev. & Cure Dis.* iii. iv. 725 Pack them in large burlaps. **1880** N. H. Bishop *4 Months in Sneak-Box* 15 Captain George Bogart.. affectionately sewed her [the duck boat] up in a covering of burlap.

'burlap, *v.* [f. the sb.] *trans.* To wrap round with burlap. So **'burlapped** *ppl. a.*

1908 *Sears, Roebuck Catal.* 415 Each article.. is securely wrapped, burlapped or crated. **1927** *Ladies' Home Jrnl.* Dec. 109/2 Evergreens should be balled and burlapped, if they are to be successfully transplanted. *Ibid.*, Insist on carefully balled and burlapped stock.

burlaw, obs. variant of byrlaw.

†**burle**, *Obs.* [Cf. burly *sb.*, burr *sb.*[5]] Disturbance, confused noise.

1563 *Mirr. Mag.*, *Somerset* xxxvii, After this burle the kyng was fayne to flee. *a* **1684** Leighton *Rem.* (1875) VI. 102 The noise of gain makes such a burle in their ears, that there is no remedy.

†**'burled**, *ppl. a.*[1] *Obs.* [Cf. F. *burelé* bearing fesses of different tinctures (*Heraldry*).] Striped.

c **1500** *Partenay* 2809 With siluer and asure the tail burlid was.

†**burled**, *ppl. a.*² *Obs. rare*⁻¹. [Cf. BIRL *v.*¹]
1451 *Acts Jas. II* (1597) xxxiii, Na man sall take the said money, fra it be burled and clypped, bot at his awin lyking.

†**burled**, *ppl. a.*³ *Obs. rare*⁻⁰. Armed. (A dictionary word of very questionable authenticity.)
1616–76 in BULLOKAR. **1678** in PHILLIPS. **1721** in BAILEY.

burler ('bɜːlə(r)). Also 6 borler, 7 buriler. [f. BURL *v.*¹ + -ER¹. The form *borler* doubtfully belongs here: see also BURILLER.] One who dresses cloth by removing knots and extraneous particles.
1483 *Cath. Angl.* 48 A burler, *extuberarius*. *c* **1500** *Cocke Lorell's B.* (1843) 9 Borlers, tapstry workemakers and dyers. **1565** J. HALLE *Hist. Expost.* 8 One Thomas Lufkyn..a fuller, and burler of clothe. **1720** *Stow's Surv.* (ed. Strype 1754) II. v. x. 286/2 The..sheriffs caused to appear before them the Dyers, Taylors, Burilers..and fullers. **1757** DYER *Fleece* (1807) 96 The clothier's shears And burler's thistle skim the surface sheen. **1875** URE *Dict. Arts* I. 550 *Burlers*, women are so called who are engaged in removing from woollen cloths, with tweezers, all irregular threads or hair.

burler, variant of BIRLER.

burlesque (bɜː'lɛsk), *a.* and *sb.* [a. F. *burlesque*, ad. It. *burlesco* f. *burla* ridicule, mockery.]
A. *adj.*
†**1.** Droll in look, manner or speech; jocular; odd, grotesque. *Obs.*
1656 BLOUNT *Glossogr.*, *Burlesque* (Ital.) drolish, merry, pleasant. **1684** *Bucaniers Amer.* I. (ed. 2) 2 On his head he put a sutable cap which was made very burlesque. **1762–71** H. WALPOLE *Vertue's Anecd. Paint.* (1786) III. 8 Graham speaks of Fuller as extravagant and burlesque in his manners. **1848** W. K. KELLY tr. *L. Blanc's Hist. Ten Y.* II. 299 Such was the burlesque origin of the ministry of three days.
2. Of the nature of derisive imitation; ironically bombastic, mock-heroic or mock-pathetic; now chiefly said of literary or oratorical compositions and dramatic representations; formerly (quot. 1712) also of pictorial caricatures. In ***burlesque author, poet, actor*** = a writer of burlesque literature, an actor of burlesque parts, there is a mixture of the *attrib.* use of the sb. in B.
a **1700** *Sc. Pasquils* (1868) 285, I shall not here, with burlesque penners, Carp at her beauty. **1712** HUGHES in *Spect.* No. 537 ¶2 Those burlesque Pictures, which the Italians call Caracatura's. **1714** *Ibid.* No. 616 ¶2 Our little burlesque authors, who are the delight of ordinary readers. **1756** J. WARTON *Ess. Pope* (1782) I. IV. 255 Our nation can boast..poems of the burlesque kind. **1814** SCOTT *Wav.* xxiii, Cathleen sang..a little Gaelic song, the burlesque elegy of a countryman on the loss of his cow. **1840** MACAULAY *Ranke's Hist.*, *Ess.* (1854) II. 552 Burlesque romances in the sweetest Tuscan.
b. quasi-*sb.*
1742 FIELDING *J. Andrews* Pref., No two species of writing can differ more widely than the comic and the burlesque. **1779** JOHNSON *L.P.*, *Cowley* 43 A..pleasing specimen of the familiar descending to the burlesque. **1821** CRAIG *Lect. Drawing* I. 52 This..borders..on the burlesque in representation.
B. *sb.*
1. That species of literary composition, or of dramatic representation, which aims at exciting laughter by caricature of the manner or spirit of serious works, or by ludicrous treatment of their subjects; a literary or dramatic work of this kind. Also *attrib.*
1667 SIR W. TEMPLE in *Four C. Eng. Lett.* 123, I hear Mr. Waller is turned to burlesque among them, while he is alive. **1709** *Tatler* No. 63 ¶2 The Burlesque of Virgil himself has passed, among Men of little Taste, for Wit. **1768** TUCKER *Lt. Nat.* II. 130 Witty burlesques of the noblest performances. **1867** MISS BRADDON *Rupert Godw.* ii. 24/2 The..night..on which the new burlesque was to be performed. **1869** *Daily News* 7 Jan., For the last fifteen years, burlesque has been driving pantomime off the stage.
2. Grotesque imitation of what is, or is intended to be, dignified or pathetic, in action, speech, or manner; *concr.* an action or performance which casts ridicule on that which it imitates, or is itself ridiculous as an unsuccessful attempt at serious impressiveness; a mockery.
1753 HOGARTH *Anal. Beauty* vi. 31 Were it [the wig] to be worn as large again, it would become a burlesque. **1772** WESLEY *Jrnl.* 3 May, Why is such a burlesque upon public worship suffered? **1846** MᶜCULLOCH *Acc. Brit. Empire* (1854) II. 213 The representative system..established in Scotland previously to the Reform Act, was..a burlesque of all principle.
3. a. The concluding portion of a Negro minstrel entertainment, containing dialogue and sketches. *U.S.*
1857 *Porter's Spirit of Times* I. 344/3 The nightly concert which precedes the burlesque. *c* **1864** *Corsican Twins* t-p. (D.A.E.), An Ethiopian Burlesque..As performed by Griffin & Christy's Minstrels. **1957** *Oxf. Compan. Theatre* (ed. 2) 556/1 The third part [*sc.* of a Negro minstrel show] consisted of after-pieces—farces, comic opera, or burlesque.
b. A variety show, frequently featuring strip-tease. Also *attrib.* orig. and chiefly *U.S.*
1870 T. A. BROWN *Hist. Amer. Stage* 66/2 She..reappeared during the winter of 1868, at the Fifth Avenue Opera House, New York, in burlesque. **1870** O. LOGAN *Bef. Footlights* 563 There are numberless people..who are utterly unable to see any difference between the dancing of a ballet-girl and the caperings of a jigging burlesque woman. **1887** 'M. CORELLI' *Thelma* II. II. iv. 217 You'd better not go to the Brilliant Theatre to-night—it's only a burlesque, and is sure to be vulgar and noisy. **1895** *N.Y. Dramatic News* 12 Oct. 5/3 The only burlesque show in town [*sc.* Chicago]. **1930** C. WITTKE *Tambo & Bones* iv. 158 Cheap burlesque 'girl' shows. **1956** *N.Y. Times* 10 Dec. 33/6 [The License Commissioner] felt burlesque was 'synonymous with the strip tease and the dialogue of unvarnished salaciousness'.

burlesque (bɜː'lɛsk), *v.* [f. prec.] *trans.* To turn into ridicule by grotesque parody or imitation; to caricature, travesty.
1676 'A. RIVETUS JUN.' *Mr. Smirke* i, It seem'd a piece of Wit..to Burlesque them in earnest. *a* **1764** LLOYD *Ep. Mr. Colman* Poet. Wks. 1774 I. 167 Ere I burlesqu'd the rural cit. **1804–6** SYD. SMITH *Sk. Moral Philos.* XI. 136 Cervantes has burlesqued the old romances. **1855** MACAULAY *Hist. Eng.* IV. 600 Prior burlesqued..the bombastic verses in which Boileau had celebrated the first taking of Namur.
b. *intr.*
1680 *Du Moulin's Adv. Ch. Eng. towards Rome* 31 (L.) Dr. Patrick joins hands with them in burlesquing upon the doctrine. **1683** tr. *Erasmus' Moriæ Enc.* 27 The Poet shall be burlesqu'd upon with his own doggrel rythms.

burlesqued (bɜː'lɛskt), *ppl. a.* [f. as BURLESQUE *v.* + -ED.] Caricatured; made ridiculous; travestied.
1766 GOLDSM. *Vic. W.* (1857) xxvi, Groans of contrition burlesqued. **1784** *New Spectator* XIX. 4/1 A..burlesqued procession of the disappointed constituents.

burlesquely (bɜː'lɛsklɪ), *adv.* [f. BURLESQUE, *a.* + -LY.] In a burlesque manner.
1817 COLERIDGE *Biog. Lit.* 221 We seem to sink most abruptly, not to say burlesquely. **1833** *Q. Rev.* XLIX. 41 [He] had ventured to assume the title, burlesquely ferocious, of Attorney-General to the Lantern.

burlesquer (bɜː'lɛskə(r)). [f. BURLESQUE *v.* and *sb.* + -ER¹.] **a.** One who burlesques. **b.** An actor in burlesque dramas.
1657 COLVIL *Whigs Supplic.* (1751) 95 Fifteen poetasters, Half fools, half beggars, half burlesquers. **1751** SHENSTONE *Wks. & Lett.* III. 187, I wish the burlesquers of such ingenuous profusions could be punished. **1869** *Daily News* 26 Nov., It was at this theatre that Mr. Henderson's troupe of English burlesquers appeared.

burlesquing (bɜː'lɛskɪŋ), *vbl. sb.* [f. as prec. + -ING¹.] Ridiculing by grotesque imitation or travestying. (Chiefly *gerundial.*)
1677 W. SHERLOCK *Answ. Pamph. by T. Danson* 70. **1699** FARQUHAR *Love & Bottle* I. i, His imitation was downright burlesquing it. **1873** SYMONDS *Gk. Poets* viii. 247 Burlesquing the gods was always a capital resource of the comic poets.

burlesquing (bɜː'lɛskɪŋ), *ppl. a.* [f. as prec. + -ING.²] That burlesques.
1688 W. DARREL *St. Ignatius no Phanatick* 19 Vent your Burlesquing Vein till Dooms-Day. **1884** *Pall Mall G.* 31 Mar. 5/1 In sarcastic and yet burlesquing mood.

†'**burlet.** *Obs.* Also 6 byrlet, 7 bourlet, 7–8 birlet. [a. Fr. *bourlet* or *bourrelet*.] A padded roll of cloth for a woman's head; a coif or hood; also, a similar roll serving as a support for a ruff.
1490 *Coventry Acc.* in T. Sharp *Dissert. Pageants* (1825) 17 *note*, Item twoo Burlettis. **1552** HULOET, Byrlet or tyrynge for women, *calantica callotte en champ*[*agne*]. **1578** in *Collect. Inventories* (1815) 219 A lang taillit gowne of layn ..with burlettis. **1611** COTGR., *Le grand papillon*, a high Bourlet or Hood. **1678** PHILLIPS, *Birlet*, (old word) a Coife, or Hood. [Whence in BAILEY.]

burlet: see BURLACE.

†**bur'letta.** *Obs.* [a. It. *burletta*, dim. f. *burla* fun.] A comic opera; a musical farce.
1748 H. WALPOLE *Corr.* (ed. 5) II. cxcv. 243 The burlettas are begun; I think not decisively liked or condemned yet. **1813** *Examiner* 15 Feb. 106/2 A revived Olio, calling itself the burletta of Poor Vulcan. **1879** PLANCHÉ *Extravag.* I. 13 A more appropriate name than 'Burletta', which disappeared from the play-bills on the emancipation of the minor theatres from their legal fetters in 1844.
b. *attrib.*
1762 *Lond. Mag.* XXXI. 674 She then sings a very pretty song of Arne's in the Burletta taste. **1831** *Lincoln Herald* 6 May, The best buffo and burletta singer.

†'**burley**¹. *Obs. rare*⁻¹. [cf. F. *bourrelet*, and BURR *sb.*¹ 2.] 'The butt end of a lance' (Halliwell).
1548 HALL *Chron.* 12 One company had the plackard, the rest the port, the burley, the tasses..al gylte.

burley², **-lie**, **-ly.** *Sc.* and *north. Eng.* A corrupted form of BYRLAW, q.v., used in comb. **burleyman**, also **burleybailie**, an officer of a *byrlaw-court*; see quot. 1879.
[**1599** SKENE *Verb. Signif.* (JAM.) Laws of Burlaw are maid & determined be consent of neichtbors..quhilk..ar commonly called Byrlaw-man.] **1750** C. CAMPBELL in *Stewart's Trial App.* 146, I..think it's quite right to have burliemen..You will therefore appoint two discreet honest men for that purpose of the tenants; and..be sure you swear them to fidelity in their office. *a* **1758** RAMSAY *Poems* (1800) II. 536 Jude took him for a burlie-bailie. **1864** A. MᶜKAY *Hist. Kilmarnock* 108 Twelve young men, with such a number of the burliemen in town. **1875** *Lanc. Gloss.* (E.D.S.) 62 *Burly-man.* **1879** *Athenæum* 26 July 115 Burleymen are still appointed at the Courts Leet and Courts Baron. Men of agricultural experience are always chosen, and their duty is to value damages, e.g. to crops from cattle straying.

Burley, burley³ ('bɜːlɪ). *U.S.* [? Personal name.] An American tobacco, of which there are two varieties, red and white. Also *attrib.*
1881 *Southern Planter* in B. W. Arnold *Tobacco Ind.* (1897) 35 The White Burley produced in the west has now thoroughly substituted our dark grades. **1900** *Yearbk. U.S. Dept. Agric.* 435 The White Burley is entirely air cured, except in exceedingly damp weather, when wood fires may be used. **1909** *Westm. Gaz.* 10 Feb. 5/2 From the Blue Grass also comes most of what is called the Burley, another fine quality, which is made into chewing tobacco for the American and German. **1952** *Economist* 29 Nov., Over 155,000 growers of burley tobacco voted on whether they wished to continue..price support for their 1953 crop.

burley, var. BERLEY.

burlily ('bɜːlɪlɪ), *adv.* [f. BURLY *a.* + -LY².] In a pompous or swaggering manner.
1863 LYTTON *Caxtoniana* I. 70 Polysperchon called in person, and said, burlily, 'Why do you refuse my invitation?'

burliness ('bɜːlɪnɪs). [f. BURLY + -NESS.] Burly state; fullness of figure; stoutness, bigness.
1612 DRAYTON *Poly-olb.* VIII. 119 Into a lesser roomth thy burlinesse to bring. **1832** L. HUNT *Sir R. Esher* (1850) 128 In the rest of his face..a kind of bloated prominence, or rather burliness. **1859** SALA *Tw. round Clock* (1861) 143 Who shall tell..the pitchy burliness of their bulging sides.

'**burling**, *sb. Obs.* exc. *dial.* A yearling heifer.
1503 *Will of Etton, Lincoln* (Somerset Ho.) A kowe & a burlyng. **1863** MORTON *Cycl. Agric.* (E.D.S.) *Burling* (Linc.), a yearling heifer.

burling ('bɜːlɪŋ), *vbl. sb.*¹ Also 6 byrling. [f. BURL *v.*¹ + -ING¹.]
1. The dressing of cloth, *esp.* by removing knots.
1530 PALSGR. 198/2 Byrling of clothe, *pinsure*. **1552** *Act 5 & 6 Edw. VI*, xxii, Mills called Gig-Mills, for the perching and burling of Cloth. **1601** HOLLAND *Pliny* II. 560 They fall anone to burling of it with Cimolia. **1836** URE *Philos. Manuf.* 187 Burling is..a process, in which the dried cloth is examined minutely in every part, freed from knots or uneven threads, and repaired by sewing any little rents.
†**b.** (contemptuously.)
1548 HOOPER *Commandm.* x. Wks. (1843–52) 377 Other sort..are a-dilling and burling of their hair.
2. *attrib.*, as in ***burling-comb***, ***-machine***; also **burling-iron**, a pair of tweezers or small pincers for extracting the knots from wool.
1530 PALSGR. 198/2 Byrlyng yron, *unes espinces*. **1603** HOLLAND *Plutarch's Mor.* 1231 He..all to beclawed and mangled him with tuckers cards, and burling combs. **1648** HERRICK *Hesp.*, *To Painter*, Then for an easie fansie, place A burling iron for his face. **1730–6** BAILEY, *Burling-iron*, a Sort of Pinchers or Nippers for that Use.
3. *concr.* See quot., and cf. BURL *v.*¹ 2.
1847–78 HALLIWELL, *Burlings*, pieces of dirty wool.

†**burling**, *vbl. sb.*² *Obs.* Cf. BURLY *sb.*, BURLE.
c **1530** BERNERS *Arth. Lyt. Bryt.* (1814) 240 There began muche hurlynge and burlynge in the courte.

burling ('bɜːlɪŋ), *vbl. sb.*³ and *ppl. a. poet.* [f. *burl* vb., var. BIRL *v.* to revolve, rotate.] Whirling, rotating.
1874 G. M. HOPKINS *Jrnls. & Papers* 11 Aug. (1959) 251, I marked the bole, the burling and roundness of the world. **1886** —— *Poems* (1918) 72 Ringlet-race on burling Barrow brown.

'**burlow-'beanie.** See quot. 1884.
a **1650** *K. Arthur & K. Cornwall* in Child *Ballads* (1857) I. 361, I coniure thee, thou Burlow-beanie, The powder-box thou feitch me. *Ibid.*, Forth is gone Burlow-beanie, As fast as he cold hie. **1884** CHILD *Ballads* II. §30. 279/2 A Burlow-Beanie, or Billy-Blin, a seven-headed, fire-breathing fiend whom he has in his service.

burly, *sb.*, and **burly-hurly**, early var. of HURLY-BURLY.
1876 example in sense 'bluster'.
1835 *Blackw. Mag.* XXXVIII. 310 Let him fancy the burly—the contention—the claims and counterclaims. **1876** G. M. HOPKINS *Wt. Deutschland* (1918) st. 27 In wind's burly and beat of endragonèd seas. **1563** GOLDING *Cæsar* (1565) 31 Againe of late in Italy at the burlyhurly of the bondmen.

burly ('bɜːlɪ), *a.* and *adv.* Forms: 3 borli, 4–5 borelich, burlich, -lych(e, (*north.*) burely, 6 boorelie, -lye, bourlie, -ly, *Sc.* 5 buyrlie, 6 buirlie, 7 borely, 4– burly. (See also BOWERLY, BUIRDLY.) [ME. *borlich*, northern *burli*. Usually identified with OHG. *burlîh*, MHG. *burlîch* exalted, lofty, stately, f. **bur-* cogn. w. OHG. *burjan* to lift up + *-lîh* = -LY. If this be so, the word must have existed in OE. or ON.; but it is unrecorded, and no plausible etymon for the first element has yet been found in either of those langs. The phonology is also difficult, for the ME. *borli*, *borelych*, 16th c. *borely*, *boorelye*, northern 15th c. *burly*, Sc. *buyrlie*, *buirlie*, require a ME. **bōrli*, OE. type **bórlíc*, whence the later ('burlɪ, 'bʌrlɪ) comes by shortening the vowel before two consonants as in *turn*, *month*. The spelling *burly*

was originally only northern. The dial. BOWERLY would seem from the sense to be a variant, but it is difficult to reconcile phonologically with the ME. forms.]

A. *adj.*

†**1.** Stately, dignified, of noble or imposing presence or appearance. *Obs.*

a **1300** *Cursor M.* 8541 Salamon Was king sittand in his fader tron, He was a borli [*v.r.* burli] bachelere. *c* **1375** BARBOUR *Troy-bk.* I. 295 þe commowns hade gret ferly Of sa buyrly a companye. ? *a* **1400** *Morte Arth.* 2191 Grete wele my ladye þe qwene..And alle þe burliche birdes þat to hir boure lengez. **1664** *Floddan F.* I. 8 A Talbot brave, a borely tike. *Ibid.* III. 25 A burly band Of warlike wights.

absol. *c* **1420** *Anturs of Arth.* l, He..bede the burlyche his brand, that burneschit was briȝt.

†**b.** *poet.* Of things: Goodly, excellent, noble. *Obs.* (As an epithet of *spear*, *brand*, the meaning may have been 'stout': cf. BOISTEROUS.)

c **1325** *E.E. Allit. P.* B. 1488 With mony a borlych best al of brende golde. *c* **1340** *Gaw. & Gr. Knt.* 2224 A denez ax nwe dyȝt, þe dynt with [t]o ȝelde With a borelych bytte. *c* **1420** *Anturs of Arth.* xliii, Greselle..wos the burlokke[st] blonke, ther euyr bote brede. *c* **1450** *Rauf Coilȝear* 190 Within that burelie bygging. *Ibid.* 266 Ane burely bed was wrocht in that wane, Closit with Courtingis, and cumlie cled. **1535** STEWART *Cron. Scot.* (1858) I. 7 He semit weill to weir ane buirlie brand. **1873** SYMONDS *Grk. Poets* v. 124 My wealth's a burly spear and brand.

2. Stout, sturdy, massively built, corpulent; of large body or trunk.

c **1340** *Gaw. & Gr. Knt.* 766 A won in a mote..loken vnder boȝez, Of mony borelych bole. *c* **1400** *Destr. Troy* 3769 Tantelus..was a tulke hoge, Borly of brede. **1513** MORE *Hist. Rich. III*, Wks. 36/2 Sommewhat corpulente and boorelye, and nathelesse not vncomelye. **1596** SPENSER *Astrophel* Elegy 7 There might you see the burly Beare. **1709** ADDISON *Tatler* No. 116 ¶1 She had a Mind to look as big and burly as other Persons of her Quality. **1856** MRS. BROWNING *Aur. Leigh* I. 596 Burly oaks projecting from the line. **1866** KINGSLEY *Herew.* vii. 133 He singled out the burliest knight he saw.

†**b.** Of a garment, or wool: Thick, heavy. *Obs.* (Cf. BURL *sb.*[1])

1651 *Mercurius Politicus* 1153 Casting his Eye upon the Executioner, he [Earl of Derby] said Thy Coat is so burly, thou will never hit right. **1805** LUCCOCK *Nat. Wool* 88 The sheep of England, when transported to Jamaica, yield the same kind of 'burly fleece'.

3. 'Big'; domineering, bluff. *arch.*

1592 SYLVESTER *Triumph Faith* II. 25 The Circumsised Crew Of Cabalists and burly Talmudists. **1645** MILTON *Tetrach.* (1851) 180 Erasmus..was wrote against by som burly standard Divine. **1648** JOS. BEAUMONT *Psyche* 224 (L.) When a burly tempest rolls his pride About the world. **1864** J. H. NEWMAN *Apol.* (1885) Pref. 16 They [Englishmen] are as generous as they are hasty and burly.

4. *Comb.*, as ***burly-boned***, ***-headed***, adjs.

1590 *Almond for Parrat* (1845) 12 These are nothing in comparison of his auncient burlibond adiunctes. **1592** NASHE *P. Penilesse* 25 Unweildie burliboand soldiery. **1593** SHAKS. *2 Hen. VI*, IV. x. 60 Cut..out the burly bon'd Clowne in chines of Beefe. **1837** CARLYLE *Fr. Rev.* I. I. iv. iv. 108 Destiny has work for that swart burly-headed Mirabeau.

B. *adv.* Sturdily, stoutly.

c **1400** *Destr. Troy* 11059 So burly þo big brusshit togedur.

†**'burly**, *v.* *Obs.* *rare*[−1]. [f. the adj.] *trans.* with *out*: To make burly; to puff out.

1635 QUARLES *Embl.* I. xii. (1718) 49 Think'st thou that paunch that burlies out thy coat Is thriving fat.

burm, var. form of BORM or BARM.

Burma. In full *Burma cheroot.* A kind of cheroot manufactured in Burma and with a peculiar aroma.

1891 KIPLING *City Dreadf. Night* iv. 26 'Honest Bombay Jack' supplies nothing but Burma cheroots and whisky. **1899** —— *From Sea to Sea* I. xxi. 422 He should bring with him thousands of cheroots... Singapur is the last place on the line where you can buy Burmas. **1969** *Fine Cigars* (Harrods Ltd.) 7 Burma cheroots.

burmaiden, obs. f. of BOWERMAIDEN.

Burman ('bɜːmən), *a.* and *sb.* Also †**Birman**, **Burmhan.** [f. *Burma* + -AN.] Of or belonging to, a native of, Burma; also, (of) the Burman language.

1800 M. SYMES *Embassy to Ava* 7 The Birmans..became masters of Ava. **1814** F. CAREY *Gram. Burman Lang.* 1 The Burman alphabet consists of forty-five letters. *Ibid.* 39 This mark (ʺ) is the only stop the Burmans have. **1821** HIRAM COX (*title*) Journal of a Residence in the Burmhan Empire. **1826** *Mod. Traveller: Birmah* 1 The vast region of Asia..comprehending the Birman empire, the kingdoms of Siam and Anam. *Ibid.* 10 The Birman, which is spoken in Ava and Arracan. **1835** *Penny Cycl.* IV. 439 Among the vegetable productions of the Birman forests the teak holds the first place. **1883** A. P. PHAYRE *Hist. Burma* 1 The Burman people ..were formed into a nation by the union of Mongoloid tribes. **1965** B. SWEET-ESCOTT *Baker St. Irreg.* viii. 243 The Burmans, or the peoples of the Irrawaddy delta and the great central plain of Burma. *Ibid.*, The Burma Defence Army under the command of a number of young Burman officers trained by the Japanese in Japan.

Burmese (bɜː'miːz), *a.* and *sb.* Also †**Birmese.** [f. *Burma* + -ESE.]

A. *adj.* Of or pertaining to Burma or its inhabitants or their language.

1823 A. JUDSON in F. Wayland *Mem.* (1853) I. 256 Translated from the Burmese original. **1827** H. G. BELL in *Constable's Misc.* IX. (*title*) A Narrative of the Late Military and Political Operations in the Birmese Empire. **1842** A. JUDSON *Burmese Lang.* 5 The Burmese alphabet consists of ten vowels..and thirty two consonants. **1876** *Encycl. Brit.* IV. 551 The Burmese empire with its present limits contains no maritime districts. **1920** *Blackw. Mag.* Oct. 519/2 Adorable Burmese babies. **1965** [see sense B. 2].

b. In the specific names of minerals, fauna, etc., found in Burma, as ***Burmese naphtha***; **Burmese cat**, a breed of domestic cat (see quots.); also *ellipt.*; **Burmese squirrel**, a squirrel native to Burma and Tenasserim, closely allied to *Sciurus caniceps*; **Burmese worm**, a mulberry-feeding silkworm found domesticated in India.

1939 I. M. MELLEN *Pract. Cat Book* i. 3 Various long-haired cats of the Orient, Persian, Angora, Russian, Burmese, etc. *Ibid.* i. 26 The Burmese Cat..is of medium size, muscular, with slim legs, the hind legs being long and tilting the body slightly downward. **1962** *House & Garden* Dec. 6/3 The fashionable Burmese, which..combine the fluffy coat of the Persian with Siamese colouring and eyes. **1858** FOWNES *Man. Chem.* (ed. 7) 655 The Burmese naphtha (Rangoon tar)..consists principally of liquid homologues of marsh gas, associated with small quantities of hydrocarbons of the benzol-series, [etc.]. **1887** *Encycl. Brit.* XXII. 60 *Bombyx arracanensis*, the Burmese worm. *Ibid.* 438 Burmese squirrel.

B. *sb.* **1.** A native of Burma; also *collect.*

1824 T. EVANS *Disp.* 11 Oct. in W. James *Naval Hist. Gt. Brit.* (1837) VI. 465 The Burmese jumping overboard to save themselves. **1842** A. JUDSON *Burmese Lang.* 9 The character °..is reckoned among the consonants, by the Burmese. **1876** *Encycl. Brit.* IV. 551 The sugar cane appears to have been long known to the Burmese. *Ibid.* 552 The Burmese in person have the Mongoloid characteristics. **1876** 'J. BRADLEY' *Trav. & Sport* ii. 29 These people, like all other Burmese, were vivacious and noisy. **1885** G. C. WHITWORTH *Anglo-Ind. Dict.* 54/2 *Burman*, a native of Burma, a Burmese. **1937** C. V. WARREN *Burmese Interlude* xxi. 141 The 'victories' claimed by the Burmese in their riots during 1930 against the Chinese and Indians.

2. The language of Burma.

1842 A. JUDSON *Burmese Lang.* 6 The pronunciation of the cerebrals and the dentals, though different in the Sungskrit, is the same in the Burmese. **1894** R. F. ST. JOHN *Burmese Reader* Pref., It is a great mistake to suppose that Burmese ..can be learnt properly from a phrase-book. **1965** B. SWEET-ESCOTT *Baker St. Irreg.* viii. 246 None of us could speak Burmese, but..he proposed to read us the Burmese text of a letter he had received.

burmite ('bɜːmaɪt). [f. *Burma* + -ITE[1].] A variety of amber found in Burma, used by the Chinese in the manufacture of objects of art.

1893 BRUHL tr. *Helm's Note on Burmite* in *Rec. Geol. Surv. India* XXVI. 62 My researches..have rendered it evident, that we have to deal with a remarkable fossil resin, which differs essentially from all other fossil resins known hitherto, and to which I have given the name of Burmite. **1893** F. NOETLING *Ibid.* 31 The Burmese amber is totally different from..amber (Succinite)... In concordance with Dr Helm's suggestion, the name of Burmite is adopted for the new fossil resin. **1932** *Times Lit. Suppl.* 12 May 343/2 The deep-red opalescent Burmite from Burmah.

burn (bɜːn), *sb.*[1] Forms: 1 **burna, burne, burn,** 2–6 **burne,** (4 **bourne, buerne**), 4–5 **brynne,** 3– **burn.** See also BOURNE *sb.*[1] [Common Teut.: the OE. *burna* wk. masc., *burne* wk. fem., *burn* str. fem. (apparently not distinguished in sense) correspond to OFris. *burna* masc., MDu. *borne* masc., Du. *born*, MLG. *borne*, *born* masc., mod.G. (*poet.*) *born* masc., which are metathetic forms of the words appearing as OHG. *brunno*, Goth. *brunna* wk. masc., Du *bron* masc., ON. *brunn-r* str. masc., repr. OTeut. types **brunnon-*, **brunno-z*. The primitive and prevailing sense of the Teut. word is 'spring, fountain', of which there are some traces in OE., the word being used to render Lat. *fons* of the Vulgate.

A connexion is often assumed with *brunn-* ablaut-stem of OTeut. **brin-n-an* BURN *v.*[1], on the supposition that that root had originally the wider sense 'well up, be in commotion', applicable to water as well as to fire; but of this there is no actual evidence. Curtius and others have regarded the sb. as cogn. w. Gr. φρέαρ a well, supposing the root to be the same with that of L. *fervēre* to boil up; but the form of the Teut. word does not permit this explanation.]

1. In OE.: A spring, fountain; a stream or river. In later use: A small stream or brook. Now (exc. in the form BOURNE *sb.*[1]) chiefly *north.*

c **1000** *Ags. Gosp.* John xviii. 1 þa eode he ofer ðа burnan Cedron. *a* **1250** *Moral Ode* in *Lamb. Hom.* 175 Weter..of þe burne. *a* **1250** *Owl & Night.* 916 An ydel wel, That springeth bi burne thar is suel. **1375** BARBOUR *Bruce* VII. 78 At that burn eschapit the king. *a* **1400** *Cov. Myst.* (1841) 162 By bankys and brynnys browne. **1535** STEWART *Cron. Scot.* II. 611 Thair blude like burnis rynnand on the grene. **1641** *Nth. Riding Records* IV. 206 Presentment for nonpayment of assessment..for Whitby-burne [*previously always* beck]. **1753** *Stewart's Trial* 191 Allan Breck..was fishing in a burn near the deponent's house. **1839** STONEHOUSE *Axholme* 311 Well watered by a beck or burn. **1855** BROWNING *Last Ride together* viii, Yonder girl that fords the burn. **1878** BLACK *Macleod of D.* I. 176 Munching the young grass, and drinking out of the burn.

2. (*a*) Water from a fountain or well. (*b*) 'Warm water used in brewing or washing' (Jamieson).

a **800** *Corpus Gloss.* (O.E. Texts) 1185 *Latex*, burne. *c* **1000** ÆLFRIC *Voc. Suppl.* in Wr.-Wülcker 177 *Latex*, burna. *c* **1565** LYNDESAY *Satyre* 4140 To mak thin aill they think na falt Of mekill burne and lytill malt. *a* **1806** *Allan o' Maut* in Jamieson *Pop. Ballads* II. 239 (JAM.) They..put the burn untill the gleed.

b. Said poet. like *flood*, of the sea. Cf. BROOK.

c **1400** *Destr. Troy* 12523 Thretty and two [shippes] There were brent on the buerne with the breme low.

†**c.** ***to make one's burn***: to 'make water'. *Obs.*

1788 PICKEN *Poems* 118 (JAM.) Or stap the very haly sang To mak his burn.

3. *attrib.* and in *comb.*, as ***burn-brae***, ***-fishing***, ***-foot***, ***-head***, ***-mouth***, ***-trout***; also **burn-gate**, a small water-course; **burn-side**, the side of a brook, the strip of ground alongside of it.

1724 RAMSAY *Tea-T. Misc.* (1733) I. 57 They bigg'd a bower on yon *burn-brae. **1873** G. C. DAVIES *Mount. & Mere* xiii. 104 Good sport for *burn fishing. **1832** CARLYLE *Remin.* I. 36 Every dell and *burngate..he had traversed. **1875** J. VEITCH *Tweed* 30 The depths of glen that fold The *Burn-heads. *c* **1400** *Destr. Troy* 5768 All borne were þai backe to þe *buerne syde. **1789** BURNS *A waukrife Minnie* ii, By yon burnside..wi' my minnie. **1849** W. IRVING *Crayon Misc.* 255 The green shaws and burnsides of Scotland. **1805** R. FORSYTH *Beauties Scotl.* II. 360 Pike are..caught with..lines baited with *burn-trouts or frogs.

†**burn**, *sb.*[2] *Obs.* exc. *dial.* Also 4 **byrne,** 5–7 **burne,** 8 *Sc.* **birn.** Contracted form of BURDEN *sb.*

c **1375** BARBOUR *St. Thadea* 231 Al my synnis ful & sere I band as it a byrne hade bene. ? *a* **1400** *Chester Pl.* I. (1843) 65 Isaake..taketh a burne of stickes and beareth after his father. **1595** B. CHAPPELL in Farr's *S.P.* (1845) II. 465 The earth of late hath shakt herself, As wearie of her sin-full burne. **1614** *Scourge of Venus* (1876) 40 Weeping much her burne to beare. *a* **1774** FERGUSSON *Farmer's Ingle* in *Poems* (1845) 38 How big a birn maun lie on Bassie's back. **1855** E. WAUGH in *Lanc. Sk.* 50 Gathering..'a burn o' nettles' to put in their broth. **1880** *West. Cornw. Gloss.* (E.D.S.) *Burn*, twenty-one hakes (probably a burden).

Hence **burn-rope**, a rope for carrying a burden.

burn (bɜːn), *sb.*[3] Forms: 4–6 **brenne,** 6–7 **burne,** 7– **burn,** *Sc.* 6– **birn** (in sense 2). [f. BURN *v.*[1] The earlier *brenne* derives from the ME. form *brennen* of the vb.: it took the place of the orig. sb. *bryne*, *brene*, BRUNE, q.v.]

1. a. The act or effect of burning; *esp.* an injury to the body caused by burning, a burnt place.

[*a* **1300** *Havelok* 1239 Hwan he..the fir brouth on brenne.] **1594** PLAT *Chem. Conclus.* 20 It is commended especiallie in a burne. **1601** HOLLAND *Pliny* XX. viii. (R.) [It] healeth any burne or scalding. *a* **1691** BOYLE (J.) A very effectual remedy against burns. **1813** J. THOMSON *Inflamm.* 137 An external injury, as a blow, a wound, or a burn.

b. *spec.* An instance of burning the vegetation on land as a means of clearing it for cultivation. (Cf. BURNING *vbl. sb.* 8 a and e.) **c.** A place where the trees or brush have been burned; a clearing in the woods made in this way. *N. Amer.*, *Austral.*, and *N.Z.*

1792 J. BELKNAP *Hist. New Hampshire* III. 132 Much depends on getting what is called a *good burn*, to prepare the ground for planting. **1834** S. MOODIE *Jrnl.* 28 Apr. in *Six Years in Bush* (1838) 92 [Canada] A great burn, during which the wind rose so high as to endanger my shanty. **1839** E. HOLMES *Rep. Explor. Aroostook River* 69 Very little ploughing is as yet done, since most of the crops are raised on a 'burn'. **1854** J. M. RICHMOND *Let.* 19 Feb. in *Richmond-Atkinson Papers* (1960) I. 143 He wants to preserve a magnificent red pine..that a good burn would probably have killed. **1868** *Amer. Naturalist* Oct. 468 They [*sc.* deer] resort always to a recent burn, when grass and weeds are just shooting again and are soft. **1905** W. BAUCKE in D. M. Davin *N.Z. Short Stories* (1953) 85 Suddenly..where one had looked for fresh wonders of forest beauty, spread a settler's recent burn! **1950** *N.Z. Jrnl. Agric.* Sept. 215/3 In places where a good primary burn was not obtained stumps and tree trunks [still] litter the ground.

d. A manifestation of anger or frustration; usu. in phr. ***slow burn***, a display of slowly-mounting anger; the act or state of gradually becoming enraged. *colloq.* (orig. *U.S.*).

1938 *Daily News* (Los Angeles) 2 Aug. 18 The saga of the Slow Burn Man, or 'Killer' [Edgar] Kennedy. **1951** 'J. TEY' *Daughter of Time* xiv. 184 Just a nice polite reasonable Act for him to swallow and like it. I bet he did a slow burn about that one. **1969** H. CARVIC *Miss Seeton draws Line* v. 93 A slow burn began inside Bob.

e. A 'smoke'; tobacco, esp. a cigarette; ***to have a burn***: to smoke a cigarette. *slang.*

1941 G. JEFFERY in *Penguin New Writing* II. 89, I just sat there, having a burn, dressed to go home. **1943** BAKER *Dict. Austral. Slang* (ed. 3) 17 *Burn*, a cigarette. 'To twist a burn', to roll a cigarette. **1956** A. THORNE *Baby & Battleship* II. 89 Rolling cigarettes for 'a quiet burn'. **1964** *Times* 26 June 14/6 To a non-smoker [in prison] it is..an advantage to acquire a steady income of 'burn'.

f. The provision of thrust by the engine of a spacecraft. Also *attrib.*

1965 K. W. GATLAND *Spacecraft & Boosters* II. 266/2 First stage thrust, 172,000 lb, burn time 146 sec; second stage thrust, 7,500 lb, burn time, 165 sec. **1968** *Radio Times* 19 Dec. 41/1 The rocket burn that takes Apollo away from Earth orbit. **1969** *Guardian* 8 Mar. 1/1 Relieved ground controllers heard that the burn had gone as planned.

2. a. A mark made by burning, a brand.

[**1523** FITZHERB. *Surv.* 28 b, If any of these sayde officers fynde any maner of catell hauynge no suche brenne.] **1563** *Sc. Acts Mary* (1597) §85 That all bestiall, slane to land-wart and Burgh..bring with them in all times cumming their hide, skin, and birne, vnder the paine of confiscation. **1661** *Sc. Acts Chas. II.* xxxiii. (Jam.) That no barrel be sooner made and blown, but the coupers birn be set thereon. **1703**

Lond. Gaz. No. 3947/4 A Burn on the near Shoulder with the Letters R. C. **1820** SCOTT *Monast.* ix, A fat bullock.. somewhat kenspeckle, and marked both with cut and birn.

b. '*skin and birn*, a common phrase, denoting the whole of anything, or of any number of persons and things.' Jamieson, s.v. *Birn.* (Cf. quot. 1563 above.)

1718 RAMSAY *Christ's Kirk* III. xv, The smith's wife.. fand him skin and birn. **1806** A. DOUGLAS *Poems* 143 (JAM.) Now a' thegither, skin an' birn, They're round the..table.

c. A branding iron, brand.

1641 BEST *Farm. Bks.* (1856) 71 When yow marke..dippe in the very bottome of the burne and botte, and then it maketh a cleaner and better impression.

d. *attrib.*

1705 *Lond. Gaz.* No. 4179/4 An X burn mark on the near Buttock. **1879** *Shropshire Word-bk., Burn-mark*, (1) the mark on an animal's hide made by the brand-iron, *obs.*; (2) the stamp of the brand-iron on tools and implements.

3. a. Heat, 'hot haste', velocity. *rare.*

1835 L. HUNT *Capt. Sword* VI. 75 Lo! the earth went round To the burn of their speed with a golden sound.

b. *slang.* A race, ride, or drive in a motor car, etc., at high speed; = *burn-up* (b) s.v. BURN-.

1966 *Telegraph* (Brisbane) 19 Oct. 14/7 A youth had told police after a car chase, 'I thought you were a mate and I was going to give you a burn'. **1969** *Sunday Truth* (Brisbane) 14 Sept. 12/5 Garry..was invited to go in it for a drive. They said they were going for a burn. **1977** *Rolling Stone* 13 Jan. 45/3 The nonstop, trans-Texas burn was 800 miles and Aykroyd took it in 16 hours.

burn (bɜːn), *v.*[1] *Pa. t.* and *pple.* burned (bɜːnd), burnt (bɜːnt). Forms: *α. Inf.* 1 beornan, (bearnan, bernan), 2–3 beornen, birnen, 2–4 berne(n, 4–6 birne, byrne, 5–7 burne, (6 bourne), 6– burn. *Pa. t., str.* 1 bearn, (barn), *pl.* burnon, 3 born, *pl.* burnen; *weak* 3–4 bernde, 5 byrnyd, 6 byrned, 7– burnt, 9 burned. *Pa. pple.* 1 bornen; *weak* 6– burnt, burned. *β. Inf.* 1 brinnan, 2–3 brinnen, 3–4 brinne, brin, 4–6 brynne, bryn. *Pa. t.* (1 bran), 3–5 brint, (3 brind), 4 brinde, 4–5 brynt, 5 brynnede, 5– *Sc.* brunt, (6 brint). *Pa. pple.* 3–6 brint, 3–4 brind, 5–6 brynt, 6– *Sc.* brunt, (6 brount). *γ. Inf.* 1 bærnan, 2–3 bærnen, barnen, 3 bearnen, *Orm.* bærnenn. *Pa. t.* 1 bærnde, 3 barnde, bearnde. *Pa. pple.* 1 bærned. *δ. Inf.* 3–4 brennen, 3–6 brenne, bren, brene, 8–9 *north. dial.* bren. *Pa. t.* 3 *Orm.* brennde, 3–5 brende, 3–6 brente, 4–5 brennede, -yde, (5 brend), 4–6 brenned, 4–7 brent. *Pa. pple.* 3–6 (*dial.* 6–) brent, (-te, -tte), 3–6 brend, (-de), 6 (9 *dial.*) brenned, (7 brended). [The modern verb represents two earlier verbs, viz. (1) the intransitive strong vb., Goth. *brinnan*, (*brann, brunnum*; *brunnans*), ON. *brinnan* (later *brennan*), OS., OHG., MHG. *brinnan*, OE. *brinnan*, by metathesis **birnan, bernan, beornan*, (*bran, barn, born, bearn*; *burnon, bornen*) 'ardere'; and (2) the derived factitive weak vb., Goth. *brannjan* (*brannida, brannips*), ON. *brenna*, OS., OHG. *brenn(i)an*, (MHG. and Ger. *brennen*), OE. *bærnan* (by metathesis for *brennan*), *bærnde*, 'urere'. *Beornan* and *bærnan* were still distinct in OE., but ran together early in the ME. period. ME. had four types of the present stem, *bern-, brin(n-, barn-, bren(n-*, the two former of which appear to represent the intr., and the third the trans. OE. verb; *bren(n-* appears to be mainly the ON. *brenna*, but may partly have originated by metathesis from *bern-*. Of the original strong verb, the strong pa. t. does not appear later than Layamon, and the distinction of transitive and intransitive was soon lost, the different types being used indiscriminately as to sense, though with dialectal preferences. *Brenne, brent* was the most common type in late ME., and even down to the 16th c., when it was somewhat abruptly dispossessed by *burn, burnt*, app. the descendant of the earlier *bern-, birn-*, though the continuity is not very clearly made out, as, between the 13th and 16th c., this type is scarcely recorded in Sc. writers.

In the Teut. *brinn-an* it is considered that only *brin-* (:—Aryan **bhren*) belongs to the root, the second *n* being originally a present suffix: cf. OE. *bryne*:—OTeut. **bruni-z* burning. The root does not appear outside Teutonic: the comparisons often made rest on the untenable assumption that the *n* of *brin-* is not radical.

The distinction in usage between the two modern forms of the pa. t. and pa. pple. is difficult to state with precision. *Burnt* is now the prevailing form, and its use is always permissible; *burned* is slightly archaic, and somewhat more formal in effect; it occurs more frequently as pa. t., or in combination with the auxiliary *have* than as ppl. adj.]

I. Intransitive senses.

1. a. Of fire, a furnace, or conflagration: To be in the state of activity characteristic of fire; to be in the state of combustion. Sometimes the prominent notion is that of intense heat (whence also *transf.* of a fever, etc.): sometimes that of the visible flaming or blazing.

α. c **1000** [see BURNING *ppl. a.*]. *c* **1175** *Lamb. Hom.* 97 Ic walde sendan fur on eorðan, and ic wile þat hit berne. *c* **1205** LAY. 289 In þere temple he lette beornen enne blase of fure. **1535** COVERDALE *Isa.* lxv. 5 Smoke and fyre, that shal burne for euer. **1590** SHAKS. *Mids. N.* III. i. 113 Sometime a fire [Ile be]..and burne. **1665** in *Phil. Trans.* I. 80 The Air enters to make the Fire burn. **1864** TENNYSON *En. Ard.* 72 A still and sacred fire, That burn'd as on an altar.

β. a **1400** *Syr Perc.* 440 A bryghte fire..Brynnande therby. *c* **1530** *Pol. Rel. & L. Poems* (1866) 29 A gret fyre brynnyng vp-an a houce.

γ. c **1200** ORMIN 10452 Haliȝ Gast iss haliȝ fir, þatt bærneþþ i þatt herrte. *a* **1250** *Moral Ode* 125 in *E.E.P.* (1862) 30 þer is fur þat eure barnð.

δ. **1382** WYCLIF *Isa.* lxv. 5 Fyr brennende all dai. *c* **1400** MAUNDEV. vi. (1839) 69 As the fyre began to brenne. **1534** LD. BERNERS *Gold. Bk. M. Aurel.* (1546) P vj, The fire that brenneth in mount Ethna.

b. *fig.* Of the passions, as love, wrath, etc.; also *poet.* of a battle: To be fierce, furious; to glow, rage.

α. c **825** *Vespasian Psalter* ii. 12 Ðonne beorneð in scortnisse eorre his. **1591** SHAKS. *Two Gent.* II. vii. 23 Quench your Loues hot fire..Lest it should burne aboue the bounds of reason. **1611** BIBLE *Gen.* xliv. 18 Let not thine anger burne against thy seruant. **1718** POPE *Iliad* XIII. 313 This said, he rushes where the combat burns. **1844** *Mem. Babylonian P'cess* II. 313 The grace of the Holy Spirit.. burns in his heart. **1876** GREEN *Short Hist.* i. §2 (1882) 12 The rage of the conquerors burnt fiercest against the clergy.

δ. c **1385** CHAUCER *L.G.W.* 1747 Desyr That in his herte brende as any fer. *a* **1541** WYATT *Lovers Case* 41 Abroad needs must it [love] glide, That brens so hot within.

2. a. Of matter: To be in process of consumption by fire; to be on fire; to be enveloped in flames.

α. c **1000** ÆLFRIC *Deut.* v. 23 Ȝe ȝehirdon his word & ȝesawon þone munt birnan. *a* **1225** *Ancr. R.* 306 Ȝe schulen ..bernen mid him iðe eche fure of helle. **1375** BARBOUR *Bruce* XVII. 619 Thai flaggatis byrnand in a baill. **1423** JAS. I. *King's Q.* clxviii, The fyre In quhich I birn. **1526** *Pilgr. Perf.* (W. de W. 1531) 48 b, Chyppes, hey, or hardes, mater apte to burne. **1593** SHAKS. *Rich. II*, v. v. 109 That hand shall burne in neuer-quenching fire. **1678** BUNYAN *Pilgr.* I. 7 A place that burns with Fire and Brimstone. **1728** POPE *Dunc.* III. 105 Padua with sighs beholds her Livy burn. **1810** HENRY *Elem. Chem.* (1826) I. 406 It then burns with a pale yellow flame. **1864** TENNYSON *Ringlet* 53 Burn, you glossy heretic.

β. a **1300** *Cursor M.* 5742 (Gött.) Ʒon tre..þat brinand semis as on ferre. **15..** in Hazl. *E.P.P.* III. 15 Though he deserve To brynne and stewe In the infernal glede.

γ. c **1270** *Saints' Lives* (Laud MS.) (1887) 229 þe more þat þe þorn barnde, þe grenore þe leues were.

δ. c **1300** *St. Brandan* 511 So stronge brende the mountayne. **1377** LANGL. *P. Pl.* B. XVII. 326 Brynge in better wode · or blowe it till it brende. ? *a* **1400** *Chester Pl.* II. (1847) 148 The fourth daie after then Sea and watter all shall brene.

b. *fig.* Of persons, of the heart, etc.: To be on fire (with desire, lust, passion, wrath); to glow, pant. Often followed by infinitive of purpose: To desire ardently.

α. c **1000** *Ags. Gosp.* Luke xxiv. 32 Næs uncer heorte byrnende [**950** *Lindisf.* bernende; **975** *Rushw.* biornende; **1160** *Hatton* beornende] þa he on weȝe wið unc spæc. *c* **1175** *Lamb. Hom.* 95 þe halia gast..dude þet heo weren birn-ende on godes willan. **1552** LYNDESAY *Monarche* 4875 That law.. Causyng ȝoung Clerkis byrne in lustis rage. **1579** FENTON *Guicciard.* (1618) 181 Burning in desire to be reuenged of the Gibelins. **1611** BIBLE *Rom.* i. 27 Men..burned in their lust one towards another. **1720** OZELL *Vertot's Rom. Rep.* I. v. 297 Virginius burnt with Impatience to revenge himself of Appius. **1885** STEVENSON *Dynamiter* xiii. 195 You cannot conceive How I burn to see you on the gallows.

β. a **1300** *Cursor M.* 23271 þai war won to brin in catel wit couetise to win. *c* **1386** CHAUCER *Wife's Prol.* 52 Bet is to be wedded than to brynne. **1513** DOUGLAS *Æneis* II. iii.[ii.] 84 Than haistit we, and brint to heir him say.

γ. a **1225** *Leg. Kath.* 1362 Bearninde al as he was of grome and of teone.

δ. c **1320** R. BRUNNE *Medit.* 201 þyn herte shulde brenne for grete loue. **1430** LYDG. *Chron. Troy* I. v, For him I brenne as doth the glede. *a* **1547** EARL SURREY *Aeneid* II. 403 To throng out..our hartes brent with desire.

c. *lit.* and *fig.* With certain modifying adverbs. ***to burn out, forth***: to burst out in flame (*arch.*). ***to burn out***, also (quasi-*refl.* and *pass.*) ***to burn itself out, to be burnt out***: to burn until extinguished by want of fuel; spec. (*a*) of an electrical valve, fuse, etc.; (*b*) of a space rocket. Also, ***to burn oneself out***: to exhaust one's strength (by over-exertion) (1937 in PARTRIDGE *Dict. Slang* s.v.). ***to burn down, burn low***: to burn until it becomes feeble from want of fuel. ***to burn up***: to take strong hold of the combustible material, get fairly alight. Also with certain adjs. denoting the colours or quality of the flame, as *to burn red, blue, bright*, etc.

1382 WYCLIF *Wisd.* xvi. 19 Fyr brende out on either side. **1593** SHAKS. *Rich. II*, II. i. 34 Violent fires soone burne out themselues. **1814** *Lett. fr. England* I. viii. 92 Till the lights were burnt out. **1816** SOUTHEY *Ess.* (1832) I. 336 In the tenth year of the war, the spirit of Jacobinism was burnt out in France. **1831** CARLYLE *Sart. Res.* II. ix. 214 Till it burn forth, in our conduct, a visible, acted Gospel. *a* **1887** *Mod.* Do not let the fire burn out. It is burnt out already. His zeal will soon burn itself out. The fire has burnt down to a spark. Do not go before the fire has burnt up. **1931** *Boys' Mag.* XIV. 171/1 To operate the valve with increase of voltage does not solve the problem, for this means that the valve (which is already partially ruined) will soon cease to function, or in other words 'burn out'. **1955** R. BANNISTER *First Four Minutes* iv. 48, $7\frac{1}{2}$ miles is much too far for me —I want to be a miler and I shall burn myself out. **1958** *Listener* 11 Dec. 992/1 The American rocket..burns out over the Sahara Desert.

¶ *Phys.* Occasionally used (with conscious metaphor) for: To undergo the same kind of chemical change (oxidation) as in burning, accompanied by more or less evolution of heat.

1885 HUXLEY *Phys.* 17 All parts of the body are continually being oxidized, or, in other words, are continually burning.

d. Of nuclear fuel: to undergo fission or fusion. Also const. *up*.

1958 *Times Lit. Suppl.* 20 June 337/2 When a uranium pile burns—physicists use the word habitually and correctly—useful energy is released under control. **1959** *New Scientist* 29 Jan. 242/2 So that the element will not buckle as it burns up, a metal frame is welded around it to brace it in the middle.

3. a. *gen.* To become or be violently hot; said of solids or gases (not of liquids). Also of persons: To have a sensation like that arising from exposure to fire; often of the face, as an effect of shame or anger; also (*colloq.*) of the ears, in allusion to the superstition that a person's ears feel hot when he is spoken of in his absence.

c **1000** ÆLFRIC *Hom.* in Sweet *Ags. Read.* 92 His [Herod's] lichama barn wiðutan mid langsumere hætan. *c* **1563** *Jack Juggler* s. B2v., I feel a vengeable burning in my left ere. **1607** W. S. *Puritaine* I. s. B4v., I warrant my Kinsman's talking of me, for my left eare burnes most tyrannically. **1727** DE FOE *Syst. Magic* I. ii. (1840) 59 If you put it [lime] into water, it would burn. **1738** SWIFT *Polite Conv.* i. 70 Miss, didn't your Left Ear burn last Night?.. Because.. you were extoll'd to the Skies. **1868** DICKENS *Let.* 25 May (1938) III. 651, I dine with Dolby..and if your ears do not burn from six to nine this evening, then the Atlantic is a non-conductor. **1881** *Oxfordsh. Gloss.* Suppl. (E.D.S.) If it be my own true love, burn, cheek, burn. **1967** G. FALLON *Rendezvous in Rio* xvii. 146 'Richard! We were just talking about you!'.. 'Is that so? No wonder my ears were burning!'

†**b.** To be inflamed, suffer from inflammatory disease. *spec.* Of a horse: To suffer from glanders. *Obs.* or *dial.*

1611 BIBLE *Lev.* xiii. 24 If..the quicke flesh that burneth haue a white bright spot. **1686** *Lond. Gaz.* No. 2155/4 A dark bay Nag..commonly burning at the left Nostril.

c. fig. ***the money, etc., burns in one's pocket***, meaning that the owner is eager to take it out, or spend it. (The same notion is expressed by other constructions of the verb; e.g. *to burn one's pocket, a hole in one's pocket*, cf. 16; more rarely the pocket is said *to be burning out with* its contents.)

1740 MRS. DELANY *Autobiog. & Corr.* (1861) II. 165 The post brought me your letter, which burnt in my pocket. **1768** TUCKER *Lt. Nat.* I. 152 Children..cannot rest till they get rid of their money, or, as we say, it burns in their pockets. **1849** COBDEN *Speeches* 82 Your pockets are burning out at the bottom with railway shares. **1885** *Harper's Mag.* Feb. 361/1 The thousand dollars was burning in her pocket-book.

d. In certain games: of a person approaching so near to a concealed object sought, that he would feel it very warm or hot, if it were fire. (Cf. WARM.) Hence *fig.* To approach near to the truth. [Cf. Fr. 'nous brûlons, comme on dit au jeu de pincette'.]

1821 *Blackw. Mag.* Jan. 355 (JAM.) As children say at hide-and-seek..I do flatter myself that I burn in the conclusion of this paper. **1871** F. HALL *Mod. English* (1873) 339 As children say at play, Mr. White burns here.

e. Said *poet.* or rhetorically of water: To be in violent agitation. *rare.*

1692 RAY *Disc.* iii. (1732) 18 The whole Sea boiled and burned. **1728** POPE *Dunc.* II. 184 His [Eridanus'] rapid waters in their passage burn.

4. a. Of candles, lamps, etc.: To be in process of combustion so as to give light; hence, to flame, give light, shine. Also *transf.* of the sun, stars, or any other luminary.

α. a **1000** *Cædmon's Ex.* (Gr.) 115 Heofon candel barn. *c* **1000** *Ags. Gosp.* Luke xii. 35 Sin eower lendenn begyrde & leohtfatu byrnende [**950** *Lindisf.* bernendo; **975** *Rushw.* be-rende; **1160** *Hatton* bearnende]. *c* **1200** *Trin. Coll. Hom.* 47 We oȝen..on ure honde beren candele berninde. *c* **1300** *St. Brandan* 337 Hou this tapres berneth thus. **1562** J. HEYWOOD *Prov. & Epigr.* (1867) 104 This candell burnth dim. **1601** SHAKS. *Jul. C.* IV. iii. 275 How ill this taper burns. **1717** POPE *Eloisa* 258 The torch of Venus burns not for the dead. **1871** MORLEY *Voltaire* (1886) 24 So clearly does that light burn for many even now.

β. c **1420** *Chron. Vilod.* 318 þe cerge þ[t] stode bryngnyng þ[t] auter by.

δ. c **1300** *St. Brandan* 335 This tapres brende longe y-nouȝ. *c* **1420** *Sir Amadace* (1842) 29 Candils ther were brennyng toe. **1526** *Pilgr. Perf.* (W. de W. 1531) 40 A lampe that brenned contynually.

b. Of other objects: To appear as if on fire, glow with light or colour.

1423 JAS. I. *King's Q.* xlviii, A ruby..Semyt birnyng vpon hir quhyte throte. *c* **1435** *Torr. Portugal* 555 On the tayle an hed ther wase, That byrnyd bryght as anny glase. **1530** PALSGR. 460/2 His eyes burned in his heed, as lyght as a candell. **1606** SHAKS. *Ant. & Cl.* II. ii. 197 The Barge she sat in, like a burnisht Throne, Burnt on the water. **1667** MILTON *P.L.* II. 538 With feats of Arms From either end of Heaven the welkin burns. *a* **1718** ROWE (J.) Oh! prince, oh! wherefore burn your eyes? **1832** TENNYSON *Pal. Art* 48 The light aërial gallery, golden-rail'd, Burnt like a fringe of fire. **1872** BLACK *Adv. Phaeton* xix. 265 The earth-banks of the railway-line burned crimson under the darkening sky.

†**c.** Of the sea: To be phosphorescent. Cf. BURNING *vbl. sb.* 3.

1667 in *Phil. Trans.* II. 497 At East and South winds it [the sea] burned most.

d. Of the engine of a spacecraft: to consume fuel and provide thrust. (Cf. sense 2 c.)

1964 K. W. Gatland *Spacecraft & Boosters* I. 278/2 The Thor first stage burned for approximately 160 sec, propelling the vehicle to an altitude of 41 miles. **1969** *Daily Tel.* 8 Mar. 1/2 The ascent stage's engine will burn and place the two returning astronauts..back into orbit round the moon.

e. Of a motor car, etc.: to travel at speed. *slang.*

1942 Berrey & Van den Bark *Amer. Thes. Slang* §58/5 *Depart, esp. hurriedly,*..burn, chase along, [etc.]. **1972** *Sunday Mail* (Brisbane) 11 June 2/5 In burns a police car... Out jumps a senior sergeant.

5. a. To suffer destruction, injury, change of structure or properties from contact with fire; to be reduced *to* ashes, a cinder, etc., by fire; to be scorched, charred, etc. Often said of food spoiled by too great or prolonged exposure to heat in roasting or baking. ***to burn to*** (the inside of a vessel): to adhere to by burning; also with *to* (absol. as adv.). ***to burn away***: to be gradually dissipated or consumed by burning (also quasi-*refl.* ***to burn itself away***). Sometimes with adjs. denoting the result, as *to burn black, brown, hard*, etc.

α. *a* **1225** *Ancr. R.* 242 Hwo ber euer fur wiðinnen hire þet heo ne bernde? **1590** Shaks. *Com. Err.* I. ii. 44 The Capon burnes, the Pig fals from the spit. **1677** Moxon *Mech. Exerc.* (1703) 10 You must take special Care that your Iron burn not in the Fire. **1709** *Brit. Apollo* II. No. 69. 3/2 The Pudding burnt unto the Pot. **1725** Bradley *Fam. Dict.* II. s.v. *Syrup*, Boil it [sugar] to a Caramel, and take great care it does not burn to. **1830** M. Donovan *Dom. Econ.* II. 267 The meat would inevitably burn, and become hard and tasteless.

β., δ. *a* **1300** *Cursor M.* 22704 þis midel erth..Al to noght sal brin awai. *c* **1440** *Anc. Cookery* in *Househ. Ord.* (1790) 439 Boyle hom togedur with esy fire, that hit brenne not. *a* **1520** *Myrr. Our Ladye* 296 A busshe al on fyre. & yet it brente not.

†**b.** *transf.* Of crops, etc.: To be withered by the sun's heat; to suffer decay in such a manner as to present the appearance of being scorched.

1523 Fitzherb. *Husb.* §23 If drye wether come, it [the grass] wyll drye and burne vpon the grounde, and waste away. **1750** Ellis *Mod. Husbandm.* II. II. v. 42 The Crop [of turnips] would set, or what we call *burn* or *spoil*, if it was not houghed in due Time.

6. To suffer death by fire. Now somewhat *arch.*, the usual modern expression being *to be burnt.*

1600 Fairfax *Tasso* II. liii. 30 With him content Was she to liue, that would with her haue brent. *c* **1604** J. C. in *Shaks. C. Praise* 63 They should all burne for their vilde heresie. **1779** Forrest *Voy. N. Guinea* 170 Here..women often kill themselves, or burn with their deceased husbands; but men also burn in honour of their deceased masters. **1878** Tennyson *Q. Mary* I. i. 7, I can't argue upon it; but I and my old woman 'ud burn upon it.

7. ***to burn into*** (of fire, a caustic, etc.): to eat its way into (a thing or substance). Usually *fig.* of an event, a conviction, etc.; to make an indelible impression upon (a person's mind).

1823 Lamb *Elia* Ser. II. Pref. (1865) 238 The impressions of infancy had burnt into him. **1861** Hughes *Tom Brown Oxf.* I. xvi. 318 The scenes of the last few hours..burnt into his soul. **1878** Morley *Crit. Misc.* Ser. I. 213 Deeply and bitterly the spectacle of this injustice burnt into his soul.

II. Transitive senses.

* *to consume by fire.*

8. a. Of fire: To destroy, consume (any combustible object). Of persons: To cause to be destroyed or consumed by fire; to set on fire, commit to the flames. Also *absol.*

α. *c* **1200** *Trin. Coll. Hom.* 61 He wile smite..mid orde. and pilten and bernen. *c* **1205** Lay. 14000 þurh þi lond heo ærneð & hærʒieð & berneð. **1375** Barbour *Bruce* xv. 438 Of his menʒhe sum send he For till burne townys twa or thre. *c* **1511** *1st Eng. Bk. Amer.* (Arb.) Introd. 28/2 The towne Bombassa, that they also byrned and robbed. **1535** Coverdale *Rev.* viii. 7 The thyrd parte of trees was burnt, and all grene grasse was brent. **1662** Stillingfl. *Orig. Sacr.* I. iii. §4 Nabonasser did burn and destroy all the antient records of the Chaldæans. **1717** Lady M. W. Montague *Lett.* II. xlvi. 38 This letter..you may burn it when you have read enough. *a* **1843** Southey *Roprecht* iii, They were for burning the body outright.

β. *a* **1300** *Cursor M.* 12219 Fur i wat him mai noght brin. **1375** Barbour *Bruce* XIII. 737 [He] brynt houss and tuk the pray. *c* **1400** *Melayne* 27 [He] Brynnede tham in a fire. **1552** Lyndesay *Monarche* 3476 Quhen all wes brynt,—flesche, blud and bonis. **1609** Skene *Reg. Maj.* 94 Gif ane alledges that ane other hes brunt his house.

γ. *a* **1000** *Sal. & Sat.* (Gr.) 412 Briceð and bærneð bold ʒetimbru. *c* **1200** Ormin 1529 þatt illke chaff þatt helle fir shall bærnenn. **1297** R. Glouc. 511 Hii barnde hous & other god, & defoulede louerd & hine.

δ. **1154** *O.E. Chron.* (Laud MS.) an. 1137. §3 þa ræueden hi & brendon alle þe tunes. *c* **1325** *E.E. Allit. P.* B. 916 þe brath of his breth þat brennez alle þinkez. *c* **1400** *Destr. Troy* 11931 The knightes..brentyn and betyn doun all the big houses. **1507** *Bk. Gd. Mann.* (W. de W.) L. ij, The Fenix is brente in the myddes of theym. **1528** More *Heresyes* II. Wks. 179/1 The bookes also bee gone and loste, whan there was no law made yet to brenne them. **1657** Howell *Londinop.* 120 Beat them to their houses, and brent them therein. [**1796** F. Leighton *MS. Let. to J. Boucher* Feb., I heard yesterday from a Shropshire Farmer the old verb bren and its participle brent for burn burnt.]

b. With advbs. or complementary phrases. ***to burn up***: to consume entirely by burning; *fig.*, to irritate, to upset, to enrage (*U.S. slang.*); also (*U.S. colloq.*) to travel through or along at speed. Also *fig.* ***to burn away***: to consume or dissipate gradually by burning. ***to burn out***: to consume the contents and interior of (a building). So also ***to burn to, into*** (formerly also ***in***) ***ashes, powder***, etc.; and ***to burn*** (a building) ***down, to the ground.***

α. *c* **1305** in *E.E.P.* (1862) 4 þe fire sal berne vp sinful man þat haþ misdo. *c* **1511** *1st Eng. Bk. Amer.* (Arb.) Introd. 33/1 Thonder & lytenynge shall..bourne theym all in po[w]der. **1611** Bible *Job* i. 16 The fire of God..hath burnt vp the sheepe. **1858** Ld. St. Leonards *Handy Bk. Prop. Law* xv. 101 Although the house should be burned down, yet the tenant must continue to pay the rent. *a* **1887** *Mod. Newspaper.* The first and second floors of the front building were burned out, roofs off. **1909** *Chicago Daily Tribune* 21 Aug. 7/1 Barney [Oldfield] started to burn up the track and opened a big gap, leading the first lap. **1923** H. C. Witwer *Fighting Blood* i. 23, I certainly burnt Ajariah Stubbs up that day... I fell asleep..and I give a guy pepsin bismuth and a stiff argument, when all he says he asked for was a plain chocolate soda. **1931** D. Runyon *Guys & Dolls* (1932) ii. 34 Naturally this crack burns Handsome Jack up quite some. **1934** J. O'Hara *Appointment in Samarra* (1935) vii. 211 Ed is plenty burned up, and, my God, I don't blame him. **1935** S. Lewis *It can't happen Here* xiii. 124 What burns me up is the fact that..7 per cent of all the families in the country earned $500 a year or less. **1937** C. Odets *Golden Boy* III. ii. 214 We'll drive through the night... That's what speed's for, an easy way to live! Lorna darling, we'll burn up the night. **1943** P. Cheyney *You can always Duck* ii. 39, I told him the story, an' was he burned up!

β. *a* **1300** *Cursor M.* 13237 And al to pouder þai it brint. **1548** *Compl. Scot.* 21 Vas it [Carthage] nocht brynt in puldir ande asse.

δ. *c* **1200** Ormin 1468, & brenn itt all till asskess þær. **1382** Wyclif *Lev.* vi. 10 The asken, the which the fier vowrynge brent out. —— *Ecclus.* xlix. 8 Thei brenden vp the chosen cite of hoelynesse. **1549** Latimer *Serm. bef. Edw. VI*, III. (Arb.) 98 God..brente theym all vp wyth brymstone. **1596** Spenser *F.Q.* I. ix. 10 The fire which them to ashes brent. **1863** Mrs. Gaskell *Sylvia's L.* II. 176 It were a good job it were brenned down.

c. Used in the imperative as an imprecation.

1711 Swift *Lett.* (1767) III. 287 The box at Chester; oh, burn that box, and hang that Sterne. **1838** Dickens *O. Twist* xxxix, 'Why, burn my body!' said the man.

d. To spend or use freely; esp. ***to have*** (money, etc.) ***to burn***, to have in abundance or to spare. orig. *U.S.*

1896 Ade *Artie* 106 Two years ago he was on his uppers and now he's got money to burn. **1897** *Congress. Rec.* Mar. 400/1 Mr. Simpson:—You have plenty of time. Mr. Payne:—No; I have not got time to burn. **1904** *Louisville Courier Jrnl.* 2 July 5 She has..already had literary experience to burn. **1909** 'O. Henry' *Options* (1916) 76 The gentleman of the family had owned plantations and had slaves to burn. **1910** W. M. Raine *B. O'Connor* 39 We'll keep an eye on the gambling hells and see who is burning up money. **1911** H. Quick *Yellowstone N.* ix. 240 The gall of my swearing against these big men that had money to burn. **1915** 'Ian Hay' *First Hundred Thous.* xvi. 220 You will get baccy and cigarettes to burn out there. **1917** H. A. Vachell *Fishpingle* x, Why not? I have money to burn. **1928** *Sunday Express* 6 May 6 People in the States have 'money to burn'.

9. Specific uses of sense 8.

a. To make a burnt-offering of (incense, a victim) *to* a deity. Also *absol.* (with incense as implied object).

1535 Coverdale *Ezek.* xliii. 21 Thou shalt take the bullock..and burne him in a seuerall place. **1667** Milton *P.L.* I. 474 One [altar] of Syrian mode, whereon to burn His odious offerings. **1718** Pope *Iliad* I. 607 The priest..burns the offering with his holy hands. **1839** Thirlwall *Greece* II. 232 He burnt a great pile of precious incense on the altar. **1883** *Harper's Mag.* Nov. 877/2 These altruistic servants of 'society'..burn the lamp of sacrifice before this modern shrine.

β. *a* **1300** *Cursor M.* 1098 He to brin his tend bigan.

δ. *c* **1200** Ormin 1745 þatt recless..te bisscopp þær Beforenn allterr brennde. **1382** Wyclif *Lev.* vi. 12 He shal brenne the talwʒ of the pesible thingis. **1526** Tindale *Luke* i. 9 His lott was to bren odoures. *a* **1556** Cranmer *Wks.* (Parker Soc.) I. 85 He..made him carry the same wood wherewith he should be brent.

†**b.** With metonymy of the object; ***to burn a country***: i.e. to set fire to all objects on the surface of the ground. *Obs.* ***to burn the earth*** or ***wind***: to go at full speed. *U.S.*

c **1205** Lay. 6139 Mine kene men..al þis lond bearneð. *c* **1350** *Will. Palerne* 2646 þei hadde luþerli here lond brend and destrued. **1470** Harding *Chron.* (1543) 165 Into Fiffes he went, and brent it clene. **1470–85** Malory *Arthur* I. xiii, They lete brenne and destroye alle the contrey afore them. **1571** Campion *Hist. Irel.* XI. vii. (1633) 94 He spoyled Arthur Mac Murrough, brent his country. [**1881** G. W. Romspert *Western Echo* 164 The first day the mustangs will burn the prairie.] **1891** 'O. Thanet' *Otto the Knight* 219 An' we all ayfter 'im... Didn't he burn the wind, though! **1903** A. Adams *Log Cowboy* iii. 37, I was half a mile in the lead burning the earth like a canned dog. **1910** W. M. Raine *B. O'Connor* 20 So burn the wind, and go through the car on the jump. *Ibid.* 57 When he finds out how the horse he's after is burning the wind, his suspicions grow stronger.

c. *fig.* ***to burn one's boats***: to cut oneself off from all chance of retreat. ***to burn the Thames***: to perform some startling prodigy, 'set the Thames on fire'. ***to burn the mill*** (in allusion to letting the millstones become red-hot by friction from want of grist). ***to burn one's bridges***: see bridge *sb.*[1] 1 e.

1719 D'Urfey *Pills* (1719) II. 24 His Measure too so scanty, she fear'd 'twould burn her Mill. **1787** Wolcott (P. Pindar) *Sir J. Banks & Emp. of Mor.* 6 Whose modest wisdom..never aims To find the longitude, or burn the Thames. **1886** *Manch. Guard.* 23 Feb. 5 The sooner Mr. Goschen burns the boats in which he quitted the shores of Opposition, etc.

10. To put to death by fire, *esp.* as a judicial punishment. Now often ***to burn alive, to death.***

a **1300** *Cursor M.* 21235 Barnabas..bath for-draun and brint [*v.r.* brend] wit feir. **1547** *Homilies* I. *Faith* II. (1859) 41 Some have been..beheaded, some brent without mercy. **1552** Lyndesay *Monarche* 5103 Sum hangit..Sum brynt; sum soddin in to leiddis. **1591** Shaks. *1 Hen. VI*, v. iv. 33 O burne her, burne her, hanging is too good. **1635** Pagitt *Christianogr.* III. (1636) 112 He was brent for an hereticke. **1685** *Lond. Gaz.* No. 2080/4 Elizabeth Gaunt likewise Convicted of High Treason was burnt at Tyburn. **1753** *Scots Mag.* Apr. 200/2 Anne Williams was burnt at a stake at Gloucester, Apr. 13, for poisoning her husband. **1855** Browning *Heretic's Trag., Men & Wom.* II. 199 They bring him now to be burned alive.

11. a. To consume for artificial warming or lighting; to keep (a candle, a lamp) alight.

1712 Addison *Spect.* No. 488 ¶3 Let a family burn but a candle a-night less. **1866** Wilson *Chem.* 128 Fuel of any kind should never be burned in rooms, unless in fireplaces provided with chimneys. *Mod.* I do not burn gas in my bedroom.

¶ *Phys.* Sometimes used for: To consume by oxidation with evolution of heat (cf. 2 ¶).

Mod. A large portion of our food does not go to form tissue, but is simply burnt as fuel for the production of heat.

b. In fig. phrases: ***to burn daylight***: to burn candles in the daytime, also to waste or consume the daylight. So †***to burn seasonable weather***: to fail to turn it to advantage, consume, waste (*obs.*). ***to burn the*** (or ***one's***) ***candle at both ends***; see candle.

1592 Shaks. *Rom. & Jul.* I. iv. 43 (Qo. 1) *Merc.* We burne daylight here. *Rom.* Nay thats not so. *Merc.* I meane sir in delay, We burne our lights by night, like Lampes by day. **1618** Raleigh *Son to Father* in *Rem.* (1661) 120 It is a strange piece of Art..to lie idely at the road, burning so seasonable weather. *c* **1620** Z. Boyd *Zion's Flowers* (1855) 92 Why burne wee day light? wee have time and place. *a* **1643** W. Cartwright *Ordinary* I. ii. (D.) Her nose the candle.. Put out your nose, good lady, you burn daylight. **1682** N. O. *Boileau's Lutrin* III. 100 They burn the day in game, and sport the faster. **1738** Swift *Polite Conv.* III. (D) No candles yet..don't let us burn daylight. **1820** Scott *Ivanhoe* xliii, Burn not daylight about it; we have short time to spare.

†**c.** fig. ***to burn it blue***: ? to act outrageously. *Obs. slang.* (See blue.)

1731 Swift *Strephon & Ch.* Wks. 1755 IV. I. 153 Miss Moll the jade will burn it blue.

12. *fig.* **a.** To inflame with desire, love, passion, etc.

a **1300** *Cursor M.* 4315 First to brin [*v.r.* bren] þin hert wit-in. **1513** Douglas *Æneis* I. x. 11 Of cruell Juno the dreid brynt hir inwart. *a* **1528** Skelton *Bk. Fooles* I. 202 Thou brennest the desyres. **1697** Dryden *Virg. Georg.* III. 333 With two fair Eyes his Mistress burns his Breast.

b. To anger, infuriate, or incense. *U.S. slang.*

1935 G. & S. Lorimer *Heart Specialist* v. 144 'The way I feel now I wish I could..retire for the rest of my life.' 'Well, wouldn't that burn you!' Davy howled. **1940** J. O'Hara *Pal Joey* 37, I was plenty burned. **1967** L. J. Braun *Cat who ate Danish Modern* iii. 32 That burns me... A man like Tait can squander millions on teapots, and I have trouble paying my milk bill. **1977** *Amer. Speech* 1975 L. 56 She burned her date by going home with Bill. **1986** *New Yorker* 26 May 98/2 George Schultz..continues to resent Syria's backing off from a peace agreement with Israel...'George still feels burned by that', one of his friends says.

** *to affect by burning.*

13. a. Of fire, or any heating agency: To produce the characteristic effects of combustion upon; to calcine, char, scorch, discolour, or mark by burning; to spoil food in cooking from such a cause; to alter in chemical composition (by oxidation, volatilization of a constituent, etc.), or in appearance, physical structure or properties, by intense heat. (Not used when the effect is merely that of melting or softening.) Of persons: To expose (something) to the action of fire so as to produce these results; *esp.* to treat with fire for a specific purpose, e.g. *to burn wood* (for charcoal), *clay* (for bricks or pottery), *the soil* (as an agricultural process). Also with adjs. denoting the result, as ***to burn hard, red, black, clean.***

1519 *Interl. Elem.* in Hazl. *Dodsley* I. 31 Great riches might come thereby, Both pitch and tar, and soap ashes..By brenning thereof only. **1669** Worlidge *Syst. Agric.* viii. §1 (1681) 146 If your land be to cold..the best way is..to burn it. **1719** D'Urfey *Pills* V. 142 'Till Pudding and Dumpling are burnt to Pot. **1726** *Lond. Gaz.* No. 6438/2 Supposed to be employed in burning Ground in Nottinghamshire. **1846** J. Baxter *Libr. Pract. Agric.* II. 25 When bones are burned in the open fire, the animal matter..disappears. *Ibid.* 186 It is difficult to burn the earth.

b. Hence, To produce (charcoal, bricks, lime, etc.) by burning.

1205 Lay. 15466 Lim heo gunnen bærnen. **1635** J. Babington *Pyrotechn.* 7 Take good dry coale, well burnt, and beat it to dust. **1663** Gerbier *Counsel* D ij a, To burn more Lime in twenty four hours time. **1716** *Lond. Gaz.* No. 5446/9 All [bricks?] that are samel, or under burnt, to be excluded. **1719** De Foe *Crusoe* (1840) I. ix. 146 These [earthen vessels] I burnt in the fire. **1727** —— *Eng. Tradesm.* iii. (1841) I. 20 The bricks would not be so good..when they were burnt.

c. *to burn* (metals) *together*: to join them by melting their adjacent edges, or heating the adjacent edges and running some molten metal of the same kind into the intermediate space. *to burn on*: to add (a part) to an injured or incomplete casting by running in a stream of molten metal.

1888 *Lockwood's Dict. Terms Mech. Engin.* 53 A sand mould of the portion to be burned on is made and placed in proper juxtaposition to the old casting in the bed of the foundry floor.

d. *transf.* To produce on (anything) an effect resembling that of burning; e.g. (of the sun) to wither, dry up (vegetation), to parch, dry up (the ground); to freckle, embrown, or discolour (the skin), cf. SUNBURNT. Sometimes said of cold, and of certain manures and crops, to express their effect on vegetation or on the soil. †*poet.* Of cattle: *to burn* (the ground) *bare*: to crop it close.

a **1300** *Cursor M.* 6025 Haile and fir was menged samen . . þe gresse it brint. *c* **1374** CHAUCER *Compl. Mars* 88 Phebus cam to bren [*v.r.* birn] hem with his hete. *c* **1425** *Three Kings Cologne* 44 Hit wexeþ liche eerys of corn þat were brent with þe wedir. *c* **1511** *1st Eng. Bk. Amer.* (Arb.) Introd. 29/2 Lest that the soon shuld burne hym. **1591** SPENSER *Bellay's Ruines of R.* xvii, Scortching sunne had brent His wings. **1607** TOPSELL *Four-f. Beasts* 527 Vines also are burned therewithal [swine's dung]. **1697** DRYDEN *Virg. Georg.* II. 271 Goats . . graze the Field, and burn it bare.

e. fig. *to burn the planks*: to remain long sitting.

1843 CARLYLE *Past & Pr.* (1858) 208 Sit obstinately burning the planks.

f. *to burn off*: to clear (land) for cultivation by burning the vegetation; to burn dry or rank vegetation (tussock, etc.). Also *absol.* (Cf. BURN *sb.*³ 1 b and BURNING *vbl. sb.* 8 a and e.) *N. Amer.*, *Austral.*, and *N.Z.*

1843 C. A. DILLON *Let.* 16 Jan. (1954) 17 The fern was all burnt off by the surveyors. **1852** S. MOODIE *Roughing It* 90 Moodie and Jacob had chopped eight acres during the winter, but these had to be burnt off and logged-up before we could put in a crop of wheat. **1860** G. DUPPA in S. S. Crawford *Sheep & Sheepmen of Canterbury* (1949) v. 46 Burn off portions of the run for winter feed to destroy tuft grass. **1932** K. S. PRICHARD in Murdoch & Drake-Brockman *Austral. Short Stories* (1951) 189 He cleared and grubbed, burnt off, and cultivated his land. **1959** A. MCLINTOCK *Descr. Atlas N.Z.* 39/1 The Maoris had long been aware that much of the bush country was more fertile [than the open country], for they burned off patches for cultivation. **1966** 'J. HACKSTON' *Father clears Out* 87 The men started burning off opposite and the heavy clouds of smoke hid the tree for a while.

g. To vulcanize (india-rubber) by mixing it with sulphur or metallic sulphides and heating it.

1900 SADTLER *Handbk. Indust. Chem.* (ed. 3) 106 In vulcanizing by the first process, that of 'burning', as it is termed, the crude caoutchouc is mixed with varying amounts of sulphur.

h. To utilize the nuclear energy of (uranium, etc.).

1946 *Rep. Internat. Control Atomic Energy* (Dept. of State, U.S.) III. i. 35 Such power reactors would 'burn' the active materials and require replenishing from time to time. **1949** *Britannica Bk. Year 1948* 686/2 *Burn*, to utilize the atomic energy of (nuclear fuel). **1957** *Encycl. Brit.* II. 649/2 Some losses could be tolerated and still leave a neutron to initiate another fission of uranium, thus producing a chain reaction which would continue to burn uranium. *Ibid.* 651/2 It is also possible to burn plutonium in the presence of U-238 and make more plutonium. **1962** *Newnes Concise Encycl. Nuclear Energy* 278/1 To achieve power balance, it is necessary also that at least about 1 per cent of the fuel is 'burned' before being lost from the system.

14. a. To wound or to cause pain to (a person, animal, or part of the body) by the contact of fire or of something intensely heated: said both of the fire or heated body itself, and of the person who applies it. Often *refl.* (of persons, with approach to the passive sense); also in expressions such as *to burn one's fingers, one's foot* = to suffer injury in those members by burning. Also *absol.*

a **1300** *Cursor M.* 7224 Man aght to dred þe brand þat brint [*v.r.* brende] him forwit in his hand. **1382** WYCLIF *Isa.* xliii. 2 Whan thou shalt go in fyr, thou shalt not be brent. *a* **1420** OCCLEVE *De Reg. Princ.* 2382 He that is brent, men seithe, dredethe the fire. *a* **1520** *Myrr. Our Ladye* 43 Yt brennyth hym, and woundeth hym so sore. **1596** DRAYTON *Leg.* II. 280 Warm'd with the Fire, that unawares might burne Mee. **1713** BERKELEY *Hylas & P.* I. Wks. 1871 I. 270 When a coal burns your finger. **1875** JOWETT *Plato* (ed. 2) I. 28 The power of heat to burn.

b. In fig. phrase, *to burn one's* (*own*) *fingers*: to sustain damage through meddling with something; rarely *to burn* (*another's*) *fingers*.

1710 PALMER *Proverbs* 356 The busiebody burns his own fingers. **1713** *Guardian* No. 108, I do not care for burning my fingers in a quarrel. **1865** HOLLAND *Plain T.* IV. 126 Strove to overreach each other, and burn the fingers of unsuspicious outsiders. **1877** *Punch* 26 May 130 Without burning its fingers with Clerical Fellowships, etc.

c. To cauterize, as a surgical operation; to brand with the mark of a criminal. *to burn out*: to destroy (the eyes, etc.) by burning.

1483 *Cath. Angl.* 32 To Birne with yrne; *cauteriare, incauteriare.* **1486** *Bk. St. Albans* C. vj b, Brynne the narellis [of a hawk] thourogh owte. **1570–87** HOLINSHED *Scot. Chron.* (1806) II. 203 Him that is brunt in the hand. **1595** SHAKS. *John* IV. i. 59 These eyes . . with hot Irons must I burne them out. **1655** BAXTER *Quaker's Catech.* 3, I dare no more accuse them . . for persecution who shall burn a Thief in the hand. **1715** *Lond. Gaz.* No. 5329/4 He . . was burnt in the Hand last Assizes at Worcester. **1722** DE FOE *Col. Jack* (1840) 128 Transported felons . . burnt in the hand.

d. *transf.* Said of a caustic, acrid, or irritating substance (as vitriol, a blister, etc.); sometimes of intense cold, the effect produced by which resembles that caused by burning: To wound or cause local pain to, in a manner resembling the effect of contact with fire. Also *absol.*

1509 FISHER *Wks.* I. (E.E.T.) 31 Teres . . shall scalde and brenne our bodyes. **1562** TURNER *Baths* 6 b, If any entring into the bath . . thynke . . that he is burned. **1607** TOPSELL *Four-f. Beasts* 212 The snow burneth the Dogs nose. **1667** MILTON *P.L.* II. 595 The parching air Burns froze, and cold performs th' effect of Fire. **1696** *Lond. Gaz.* No. 3240/4 His face burnt or scalded by some Humor. **1865** J. H. NEWMAN *Gerontius* Ice which blisters may be said to burn.

†**e.** To infect with sores; *esp.* with venereal disease. Cf. 3 b. *Obs.*

1529 S. FISH *Supplic. Begg.* (Arb.) 7 These be they . . that be brent wyth one woman, and bere it to another. *c* **1556** BALE in Chambers *Cycl.* s.v. *Burning*, He [leacherous Weston] not long ago brent a beggar of St. Botolphs parish. **1590** SHAKS. *Com. Err.* IV. iii. 58 Light wenches will burne, come not neere her.

f. To swindle. (See *Sc. Nat. Dict.*)

In quot. 1655 the sense may be 'to suffer'.

1655 R. BAILLIE *Let.* (1842) III. 290 Our people were so ill-burnt, that they had no stomach for any farder medling. [*a* **1700** B. E. *Dict. Cant. Crew*, Burnt the Town, when the Soldiers leave the Place without paying their Quarters.] **1808** JAMIESON, *Burn*, to deceive, to cheat in a bargain. **1844** *Philad. Spirit of Times* 19 Aug. (Th.), Two negro burners were arrested in the act of trying to burn two Pottsville boatmen with a plated chain worth about fifteen cents. **1926** J. BLACK *You can't Win* ix. 106 If you'd burnt Shorty for his end of that coin, you'd have been here just the same. **1969** *Sunday Truth* (Brisbane) 16 Mar. 39/2, I figured I'd burn the guy for a thousand.

15. To drive (a person or animal) *out of* a place by heat, or by the burning of his dwelling. Phrase, *to burn out of house and home.*

1710 *Lond. Gaz.* No. 4702/3 [He] was formerly burnt out of the Fountain Tavern in the Strand. **1780** PITT in Earl Stanhope's *Life* (1861) I. 43 Thanks to the sun . . I was burnt out of my bed this morning before seven o'clock. **1851** C. CIST *Cincinnati* 250 Henry Albro, who was burnt out some months since, on Front street, has recently put up new veneer and saw mills. *a* **1861** T. WINTHROP *John Brent* (1883) i. 7 They had been burnt out, they had been cleaned out, they had been drowned out.

16. To make (a mark) *on* or *in*, (a hole) *in* or *through*, anything, by burning. Also *fig.* to make (a recollection, a conviction) indelible *in* a person's mind. *to burn in*: to render indelible (the painting upon pottery, etc.) by exposure to fire. *to burn a hole in one's pocket.*

a **1840** MOORE in *Sheridaniana* 61 They [some verses] bear, burnt into every line, the marks of personal feeling. **1857** TROLLOPE *Three Clerks* II. ix. 198 How was she to give him the purse? It was burning a hole in her pocket till she could do so. **1860** GOSSE *Rom. Nat. Hist.* 172 A power which . . burnt-in the image of each in his remembrance. **1863** GEO. ELIOT *Romola* I. xvii. (1880) I. 244 Her brother's words . . had burnt themselves into her memory. *c* **1865** J. WYLDE in *Circ. Sc.* I. 389/1 They are 'burnt in' on the surface of the ware. **1883** *Harper's Mag.* Mar. 538/1 Cash burning holes in our pockets.

17. *to burn the water*: to spear salmon by torchlight. Also, *to burn a bowl, a curling stone*, etc.: to displace it accidentally.

1805 SKENE in Lockhart *Scott* (1839) II. 265 This amusement of burning the water . . was not without some hazard. **1884** *Pall Mall G.* 19 Aug. 5/1 Water-bailiffs are sent up the rivers at certain times to prevent 'burning the water'.

18. *to burn out*: to fuse by means of an electric current. Cf. *burn-out* b, s.v. BURN- 3.

1924 *Discovery* June 83/2 The Germans were using some objectionable form of frightfulness that burnt out the magnetos of French planes flying across German zones.

19. *slang.* To smoke (tobacco). Cf. BURN *sb.*³ 1 e.

1929 F. C. BOWEN *Sea Slang* 20 *Burning*, smoking in the training ships. **1958** F. NORMAN *Bang to Rights* III. 82 The more [tobacco] we got the more we used to burn.

☛*Phrase-key*:—To *burn* alive, 10; *b* away, 5, 8 b; *b* black, 5, 13; *b* blue, 2 c; *b* boats, 9 c; *b* a bowl, 17; *b* the breast, 12; *b* bricks, 13 b; *b* brown, 5; *b* a candle, 4, 11; *b* candle at both ends, 11 b; *b* charcoal, 13 b; *b* clay, 13; *b* a country, 9 b; *b* a curling-stone, 17; *b* daylight, 11 b; *b* down, 2 c, 8 b; *b* ears *b*, 3; *b* one's fingers, 14, 14 b; *b* forth, 2 c; *b* ground, 13; *b* hard, 5, 13; horse *b*, 3 b; *b* in, 16; *b* incense, 9; *b* into, 7, 16; *b* into ashes, 8 b; *b* it blue, 11 c; *b* lamp, 4, 11; *b* lime, 13 b; *b* low, 2 c; *b* the mill, 9 c; *b* offering, 9; *b* out, 2 c, 8 b, 14 c, 15; *b* the planks, 13 e; *b* one's pocket, 3 c; *b* red, 2 c, 13; sea *b*, 4 c; *b* seasonable weather, 11 b; *b* soil, 13; *b* the Thames, 9 c; *b* to, 5; *b* to ashes, 8 b; *b* to death, 10; *b* to the ground, 8 b; *b* together, 13 c; *b* up, 2 c, 8 b; *b* the water, 17; *b* wood, 13.

burn-. The verb or verb-stem in composition forming sbs. or adjs.

1. With verb + object, as *burn-grain* adj.; †**burn-cow**, transl. Gr. βούπρηστις (an insect, also a herb, injurious to cattle), cf. *burst-cow*, BUPRESTIS; **burn-grange** (*Sc.*), one who sets fire to barns; **burn-the-wind, burnewin**, a Sc. designation for a blacksmith.

1658 ROWLAND *Mouffet's Theat. Ins.* 1000 The Latines retain the Greek name of Bupestris . . But I . . do adventure to call it by a new name in English, *Burncow, or Burstcow. **1783** AINSWORTH *Lat. Dict.* (Morell) II, Also a sort of herb which kills cattle; the burncow. **1598** SYLVESTER *Du Bartas* II. i. *Furies* 165 (D.) Turning our seed-wheat-kernel To *burn-grain thistle. *a* **1500** *Colkelbie Sow* I. v. 92 (JAM.) Ane ypocreit in haly kirk, A *burn-grenge in the dirk. **1785** BURNS *Scotch Drink* x, Then *Burnewin comes on like death. **1828** SCOTT *F.M. Perth* I. ii. 57 Thou hast had a quarrel with some Edinburgh Burn-the-wind.

2. With the verb used *attrib.* = *burning*; as †*burn-coal*, †*-wood*; also **burn-fire** (*dial.*), perversion of BONFIRE; **burn-iron**, *Sc.* **burn-airn**, a branding-iron; **burn-stick** (see quot.); **burn-weed** = THORN-APPLE, *Datura stramonium*.

1597 *Sc. Acts, Jas. VI*, §253 (title) Great *burne Coale, suld not be transported furth of this realm. **1609** SKENE *Reg. Maj.* 152 Burne coalis. **1708** W. KING *Cookery* 37 Not to make his *burnfire at the upper end of Ludgate street. *c* **1750** J. NELSON *Jrnl.* (1836) 96 Monday being a rejoicing day, they had burn-fires in the market place. **1485** *Inv.* in *Ripon Ch. Acts* 373 Ij *birne iron et j markyng iron 4*d.* **1675** COTTON *Poet. Wks.* (1765) 202 I'll make a *Burn-mark with a T. **1847–78** HALLIWELL *Dict.*, **Burn-stick*, a crooked stick, on which a large piece of coal is daily carried from the pit by each working collier over his shoulder for his own private use. **1756** P. BROWNE *Jamaica*, The Thorn-apple or *Burn-weed. All the parts of this plant are remarkably narcotic. **1701** BRAND *Zetland* 92 (JAM.) The inhabitants make use of the wrack [of ships] for *burn-wood.

3. With the verb + adv., as **burn-off** (cf. BURN *v.*¹ 13 f); **burn-out**, (*a*) a complete destruction by fire; also = BURN *sb.*³ 1 c; (*b*) *Electr.*, the fusing of a wire or other electric conductor by excess of electric current; also *attrib.*, as *burn-out fuse, alloy*, one that melts at a comparatively low temperature and serves as a safeguard against damage by excess of current; (*c*) (the moment of) final consumption of fuel by a space rocket, etc.; also *attrib.*; (*d*) orig. *U.S.*, physical or emotional exhaustion, esp. caused by stress at work; depression, disillusionment; cf. *to burn oneself out* s.v. BURN *v.*¹ 2 c; **burn-up**, (*a*) the consumption of fuel in a nuclear reactor; (*b*) *slang*, a ride on a motor-cycle, etc., at an extremely high speed (cf. SCORCH *v.*¹ 3).

1861 W. MORGAN *Jrnl.* 27 Feb. (1963) iii. 28 Not an over excellent *burn off—there having been of late a good deal of wet. **1869** J. MAY *May's Guide to Farming in N.Z.* 18 In due time we fired it [the bush], and had the satisfaction of having a clean burn-off. **1933** *Bulletin* (Sydney) 6 Dec. 28/2 A good burn-off gets rid of a lot of rubbish in the form of insects and other pests, but it also destroys the organic matter (*i.e.*, humus) without which no soil can be cropped successfully. **1903** *Daily Chron.* 29 June 7/5 It has been a *burn-out of three floors and roof destroyed. **1907** *Installation News* Mar. 4/1 Incipient fires and burnouts, due to the earthing of high voltage systems on building fronts, etc. **1940** W. STEGNER in *Atlantic Monthly* June 774/1 Even without shoes he would have run across burnouts, over stretches so undermined with gopher holes that sometimes he broke through to the ankle. **1941** —— in *Harper's Mag.* Jan. 160/1 The topless Ford lurched, one wheel at a time, through the deep burnout. **1952** *Jrnl. Brit. Interplan. Soc.* XI. 10 Ideal performance of multi-stage vehicles is secured if . . the burnout weights of each stage form a geometric progression. **1953** *Time* 14 Sept. 89/2 The three tons of fuel lasted less than three minutes. At 'burnout', Carl was at 79,000 ft. **1957** *Spaceflight* I. 64/2 Four wings provide the lift necessary for controlled flight and four small fins at the rear are used for steering after burn-out. **1975** H. J. FREUDENBERGER in *Psychotherapy* XII. 73/1 Some years ago, a few of us who had been working intensively in the free clinic movement began to talk of a concept which we referred to as 'burn-out'. **1978** *Hospital & Community Psychiatry* XXIX. 233 (*heading*) Characteristics of staff burnout in mental health settings. **1986** *Sun* 3 Nov. 19/4 It has happened so often, it is now known in medical circles as 'AIDS burnout'. **1954** R. STEPHENSON *Introd. Nucl. Engineering* vii. 276 As a reactor continues to operate, the fissionable material is gradually used up and the reactivity may decrease accordingly. This is known as fuel depletion, or *burnup. **1959** *New Scientist* 29 Jan. 239/1 A major aim is to obtain a large 'burn up'—in other words to use up as large a proportion of the fuel as possible between refuelling operations. **1961** *Guardian* 18 Mar. 2/3 If I was going for a real burn-up, you wouldn't have caught me. **1963** A. PRIOR *Z Cars Again* iii. 26 Ton-up boys were doing early morning burn-ups at the Turntable Roundabout.

†**burn**, *v.*² *Obs.* 5 boorn-, born-, bourn-en. Chiefly in *pa. pple.* burned: see BURNED *ppl. a.*² [a. OF. *burnir*, var. of *brunir* to BURNISH, originally to brown, f. *brun* BROWN.] = BURNISH *v.*¹

c **1374** CHAUCER *Troylus* I. 327 (*Harl. MS.* 1239) Al feynith he in lust that he sojournith, And al his speche and chere he bournith [*Harl. MS.* 3943 vnournith]. **1393** GOWER *Conf.* II. 231 An harneis . . which burned was as silver bright. *c* **1430** LYDG. *Bochas* IV. ii. (1554) 112 a, A chaire . . of gold boorned bryght. *c* **1440** *Promp. Parv.* 44 Bormyn or pulchyn [*v.r.* bornyn, boornyn], *polio.*

burn(e, variant of BERNE, *Obs.*, a man.

burnable ('bɜːnəb(ə)l), *a.* [f. BURN *v.*¹ + -ABLE.] Capable of being burnt or consumed by fire.

1611 COTGR., *Adustible*, burnable. **1678** R. RUSSELL *Geber* III. II. 2. ii. 174 Ignible (or burnable by Fire). **1721–90** BAILEY, *Adustible*, burnable. **1861** *All Y. Round* 23 Feb. 465 Not to rear houses of frail burnable plank.

b. quasi-*sb.*: A combustible. (*rare.*)

1825 HONE *Every-day Bk.* I. 1430 Burnables are deemed lawful prize.

'burn-bake, -beak, obs. var. of next. Hence **'burn-baking** *vbl. sb.*, **burn-beaked** *ppl. a.*

1803 A. HUNTER *Georgical Ess.* I. 35 What happens after the operation of Burn-baking. *a* 1722 LISLE *Husb.* (1752) 163 He is very much against feeding burn-beaked wheat.

'burn-beat, *v.* Also **-bait, -bate.** [f. BURN *v.* + BEAT *sb.*³ or *v.*²: the latter part is inflected; pr. pple. *burnbeating* pa. pple. *burnbeat.*] *trans.* To pare off and burn the rough turf or sod of moorland or fallow ground in order to improve it. Hence **'burn-baited** *ppl. a.*; **'burnbeating** *vbl. sb.*

1669 WORLIDGE *Syst. Agric.* (1681) 37 The best way..to improve and reduce these Lands into Tillage, is to Burn-Beat, or Denshire them. 1676 —— *Cider* (1691) 74 The ground being turfie..may be burn-beat in June or July. 1681 —— *Kal. Rust.* Nov., Wheat may yet be sown.. especially on burn-baited Land. 1727 ABP. BOULTER *Lett.* I. 221 The tenant shall not be able to burnbeat any ground in virtue of this act. 1808 J. WALKER *Hist. Hebrides & Highl. Scotl.* I. 176 The practice of..Burnbaiting, or sod burning.

burnderthe, var. BRANDRETH, *Obs.*, gridiron.

c 1425 *Voc.* in Wr.-Wülcker 660 *Hec tripes*, burnderthe.

†**burne.** *Obs.* [Early ME. *burne* (ü):—OE. *byrne* 'cuirass, corslet': the later form of this would have been **byrn*, **birn*, whence the metathetized forms BRYN, *brene*, q.v. Cf. the parallel dissyllabic *brynie*, *brunie*, BRINIE, from ON., and its metathetized form BYRNIE.] = BRINIE.

c 1050 *Gloss.* in Wr.-Wülcker 434 *Lorica anata*, hringedu byrne. *c* 1175 *Lamb. Hom.* 155 Nimeð gode ileue to burne. *c* 1205 LAY. 21123 Cnihtes mid burnen [*c* 1275 brunie] wel idihten. *Ibid.* 21129 þa dude he on his burne [*c* 1275 brunie].

burned (bɜːnd), *ppl. a.*¹ See BURNT.

†**'burned,** *ppl. a.*² *Obs.* Forms: 4-6 borned, burned, 5 bourned, boorned. [f. BURN *v.*² + -ED.] Burnished; brilliant; often said of gold or silver. (In later instances perh. confused with prec.)

c 1384 CHAUCER *H. Fame* 1387 As burned gold hyt shoon to see. *c* 1386 —— *Doctor's T.* 38 Phebus deyed hadde hire tresses..I-lyk to þe stremes of his borned hete. *c* 1430 LYDG. *Min. Poems* (1840) 65 They have espyed..i-graven, in lettris of bourned gold, Maria. *c* 1530 LD. BERNERS *Arth. Lyt. Brit.* (1814) 156 And in the toppe therof stode an egle of borned golde. 1577-87 HOLINSHED *Chron.* III. 801/1 Their horsses trapped in burned silver.

Burne-Jones ('bɜːn 'dʒəʊnz). The name of E. C. *Burne-Jones* (1833-98), English artist and designer, used *attrib.* to designate art or a type of beauty suggestive of or characteristic of the work of Burne-Jones.

1892 E. LYTTON *Let.* 15 Nov. in E. Lutyens *Blessed Girl* (1953) ix. 172 Lady Grandby is a beauty of the Burne-Jones type. 1958 J. CANNAN *And be a Villain* i. 25 Her Burne-Jones beauty. 1967 *Vogue* June 78 The Burne-Jones type was pale and lissom and romantic, hollow-cheeked and with haunted eyes.

Hence **Burne-'Jonesian** *a.* and *sb.*

1895 G. B. SHAW *Theatres in Nineties* (1932) I. 17 He has a beautiful costume, mostly of plate-armor of Burne-Jonesian design. 1908 D. H. LAWRENCE *Let.* 26 Oct. (1962) I. 32 Shall I make her longer or shorter, fatter or frailer, a Burne-Jonesian or a Moore? 1925 W. DEEPING *Sorrell & Son* xxv. 241 His sisters, pale, sweet, Burne-Jonesian. 1965 G. MCINNES *Road to Gundagai* ix. 139 The injection of a few rich commercial corpuscles into our pale Burne-Jonesian fluid.

burner ('bɜːnə(r)). Also 4-6 **brenner, -ar,** 6 **borner.** [f. BURN *v.*¹ + -ER¹.]

1. a. One who burns, or consumes with fire.

c 1380 WYCLIF *Sel. Wks.* III. 329 Alle brenneris of houses and cornes ben cursed opynly in parische chirches. 1502 ARNOLDE *Chron.* 176 Brenners of houses & chirches. 1563 *Homilies* II. *Wilful Rebell.* I. (1859) 558 The burners of their villages. 1702 C. MATHER *Magn. Chr.* VII. vi. (1852) 569 Weymouth also suffered from these burners no little damage. 1871 MORLEY *Voltaire* (1886) 14 The burner of books and the tormentor of those who wrote them.

b. *fig.*

1872 SPURGEON *Treas. Dav.* Ps. lix. 12 Persecutors in talk, burners and stabbers with the tongue.

c. A swindler. *U.S.* ? *Obs.* (Cf. BURN *v.*¹ 14 f.)

1838 *Lexington Observer & Reporter* 3 Nov., He pulls out his pocket book, it is seized by the burner who makes off with it. 1842 *Philad. Spirit of Times* 15 Jan. (Th.), The burners make better plots than most of our dramatists. 1844 [see BURN *v.*¹ 14 f]. 1845 *Congress. Globe* 6 Jan. App. 118/1 The Empire Club [of New York]..consisted of gamblers, pickpockets, droppers, burners, thimble-riggers and the like.

2. One who prepares or produces by burning. Chiefly in comb., as ***brick-, charcoal-, lime-burner.***

1463 *Mann. & Househ. Exp.* (1790) 154 To pay to a lyme brenner ffor lyme vis. viiid. *c* 1500 *Cocke Lorell's B.* (1843) 10 Parys plasterers, daubers, and lyme borners. 1562 *Act 5 Eliz.* iv. §30 The Art or Occupation of a..Lime burner, Brickmaker..Burner of Oare and Wood-Ashes. 1703 *Art's Improv.* p. xiv, The Trades of Brick-burners, etc. 1825 *Bro. Jonathan* II. 71, I mistook them at first for charcoal-burners. 1874 *Linc. Chron.* 4 Dec. in Peacock *N.W. Linc. Gloss.* (E.D.S.) To brickyard hands: wanted two steady men as burners.

3. A vessel to hold something that is burning.

1856 T. HOOK *G. Gurney* I. vi. (L) To put three or four of the pastilles into a burner on the chimney-piece.

4. a. That part of an illuminating apparatus from which the flame comes; in a lamp the wick-holder; in a gas-light the part containing the hole or holes through which the gas passes before combustion. Often with defining words, as ***Argand, batwing, Bunsen, cockspur, fish-tail burner.***

1790 ROY in *Phil. Trans.* LXXX. 162 A simple Argand's burner. 1808 MURDOCH in *Phil. Trans.* XCVIII. 125 The burners..are connected with the mains, by short tubes. 1828 MISS MITFORD *Village* (1863) 113 The luminary..had four burners, which never..were all in action together. 1886 *Harper's Mag.* LXXII. 463/2 From the centre of the dome a large chandelier was suspended, furnished with four electric burners.

b. ***Welsbach incandescent gas burner,*** a burner devised by Auer von Welsbach for producing an incandescent light by means of a mantle (see MANTLE *sb.* 5 g) and Bunsen burner. Also called the ***Auer, incandescent,*** or ***Welsbach burner.***

1894 [see INCANDESCENT *a.* 1 d]. 1902 *Encycl. Brit.* XXX. 260/2 Incandescent Burners. The invention of the Welsbach mantle places at the disposal of lighthouse authorities the means of producing a light of high intensity.

c. In a gas cooker, the part containing the hole or holes through which the gas passes before combustion. See also COOK *v.*¹ 1 b.

1885 *Army & Navy Co-op. Soc. Price List* Jan. 368 *Gas stove*.., lever taps to hot-plate, and extra simmering burner in centre of ring burner, with brass handle tap. 1963 *Good Housek. Setting Up Home* viii. 113 A cooker with four burners and a grill is the usual choice for family cooking. *Ibid.*, Oven burners may be arranged at the sides or back.

†**'burnet,** *a.* and *sb.*¹ *Obs.* [a. OFr. *burnete*, *brunette* in same sense, dim. of *brun*, BROWN.]

A. *adj.* **a.** Of a dark brown colour.

c 1200 *Trin. Coll. Hom.* 163 Hire mentel grene oðer burnet. *c* 1440 *Promp. Parv.* 56 Burnet colowre, *burnetum.* *a* 1500 *Voc.* in Wr.-Wülcker 569 *Burnetus*, burnet, *color quidam est.* 1513 DOUGLAS *Æneis* XII. Prol. 106 Sa mony diuers hew, Sum pers, sum paill, sum burnet, and sum blew.

b. *absol.*

a 1450 *Syr Peny* v. in *Rel. Ant.* II. 108 He may gar them trayle syde In burnet and in grene. 1605 CAMDEN *Rem.* (1637) 194 The roabes..of Greene or Burnet.

B. *sb.* A wool-dyed cloth of superior quality, orig. of dark brown colour.

1284 in Rogers *Agric. & Prices.* II. 536/3. *c* 1325 *Love song* in *Rel. Ant.* II. 19 Of a blak bornet al wos hir wede. *c* 1400 *Rom. Rose* 4759 As well be amourettes In mourning blak, as bright burnettes. 1753 CHAMBERS *Cycl. Supp.*, *Burnet*, in middle age writers, denotes brown cloth made of dyed wool.

attrib. *c* 1400 *Rom. Rose* 226 A burnet cote henge therwithalle.

¶ See quot.

1616 BULLOKAR, *Burnet*, a hood, or attire for the head. 1623 in COCKERAM. 1678 in PHILLIPS.

burnet ('bɜːrnɪt), *sb.*² [f. prec. from the dark brown colour of its flowers.]

1. The popular name of plants belonging to the genera *Sanguisorba* and *Poterium* (N.O. *Rosaceæ*), of which the Great or Common Burnet (*Sanguisorba officinalis*) is common in meadows, and the Lesser or Salad Burnet (*Poterium Sanguisorba*) on the Chalk. The old herbalists confounded with these the Burnet Saxifrage *Pimpinella Saxifraga*, an umbelliferous plant resembling the Burnets in foliage.

[*c* 1265 *Anglo-Norm. Voc.* in Wr.-Wülcker 557 *Burneta*, sprungwurt.] *c* 1400 *MS. Sloane* 2457, f. 6 (Halliw.) Pympurnolle..Englysch y-called is burnet. *c* 1450 *Alphita* (Anecd. Oxon.) 25 Burnete [*uel* burnette]. 1527 ANDREW *Brunswyke's Distyll. Waters* Cj, The other is named the greate Pympinella or burnet. 1579 LANGHAM *Gard. Health* (1633) 109 Byrnet openeth the stoppings of the liuer..and helpeth the Jaundies. 1599 SHAKS. *Hen. V*, v. ii. 49 The euen Meade, that erst brought sweetly forth The freckled Cowslip, Burnet, and greene Clouer. 1693 EVELYN *De la Quint. Compl. Gard.* II. 188 Burnet, called in French *Pimprenelle* or *Pimpernelle*, is a very common and ordinary Sallet furniture. 1757 DYER *Fleece* I. 695 Mix'd with the greens of burnet, mint & thyme. 1796 C. MARSHALL *Garden.* XII. (1813) 264 Burnet is a warm perennial sallad herb, used also in cool tankards. 1882 *Proc. Berw. Nat. Club* IX. No. 3. 461 By the waysides..the common burnet was growing.

2. *Comb.*, as **burnet blood-wort,** *Sanguisorba officinalis*; **burnet-buttons,** the flower-heads of Burnet; **burnet-fly, -moth** (*Anthrocera* or *Zygæna filipendulæ*), a greenish black moth, with crimson spots on its wings; **burnet-rose,** the Scotch Rose (*Rosa spinosissima*); **burnet saxifrage,** *Pimpinella Saxifraga* (cf. 1); **burnet-sphinx** = *burnet-moth.*

1776 WITHERING *Bot. Arrangem.* (1801) II. 197 *Burnet Blood-wort, a hard woody plant with winged leaves and a 4-cleft blossom. 1821 CLARE *Vill. Minstr.* I. 124 On the pismire's castle hill While the *burnet-buttons quak'd. 1885 *Pall Mall G.* 1 June 5/1 A good *burnett fly, and some harelips hovering overhead. 1842 *Penny Cycl.* XXII. 345/2 The six-spotted *Burnet moth (*Anthrocera Filipendulæ*).. has six red spots on the superior wings. 1884 WORSLEY-BENISON in *Evang. Mag.* June 251 The little *Burnet-Rose of our chalk-hills and sandy shores..has white flowers. 1668 WILKINS *Real Char.* II. iv. §4 *Burnet saxifrage. 1794 MARTYN *Rousseau's Bot.* v. 57 Most of them have their little flowers white as..burnet-saxifrage. 1870 J. CLIFFORD in *Eng. Mech.* 21 Jan. 449 3 In February..the caterpillars of the Six Spotted *Burnet Sphinx (*Zygæna Filipendulæ*).

3. In the names of species of moths belonging to the genus *Zygæna*; cf. *burnet-moth* in 2.

1775 M. HARRIS *Engl. Lepidoptera..Catal. Moths & Butterflies* 15 English Names... Burnet, sphinx..six spots of scarlet, inferiors scarlet. Burnet, companion... Brown clouded, inferior yellow vein'd with brown. 1832 J. RENNIE *Butterfl. & Moths* 22 The Melilot Burnet... The Trefoil Burnet... The Five Spot Burnet. 1921 *19th Cent.* Feb. 273 The Zygaenidae, or Burnets. 1961 R. SOUTH *Moths* 334 The Six-spot Burnet..is the most generally common of our Burnets.

Burnettize ('bɜːnətaɪz), *v.* [f. the name of Sir William Burnett, who in 1837 patented the process.] (See quot.) Hence **'Burnettizing** *vbl. sb.*

1867 SMYTH *Sailor's Word-bk.* 147 *Burnetize*, to impregnate canvas, timber, or cordage, with Sir William Burnett's fluid, a solution of chloride of zinc. 1885 CULLEY *Handbk. Pract. Telegraphy* (ed. 8) 112 Burnettising or steeping in a solution of Chloride of Zinc.

†**burneux.** *Obs.* A sauce made of butter, pepper, salt, etc. (Halliwell).

1430-50 GREGORY *Chron.* (1876) 141 Braune with mustarde, elys in burneus. 1494 FABYAN VII. 586 For the firste course—Brawne and mustarde. Ded ellys in burneux.

†**burn-grace.** Corruption of BONGRACE.

1654 GAYTON *Fest. Notes* III. xi. 148 Burn-graces in Summer to save childrens Faces.

Burnham ('bɜːnəm). The name of Harry Lawson Webster Levy-Lawson, first Viscount *Burnham* (1862-1933), who was chairman of the Standing Joint Committee of Education Authorities and Teachers, set up on the 12th Sept. 1919; hence applied to the scale of salaries, etc., recommended by this committee and periodically revised.

1920 *Jrnl. Education* Jan. 18 The notable modesty of the proposals of the Burnham Committee on Salaries. 1921 *Ibid.* July 426 The Burnham scale of salaries. 1923 *Daily Mail* 7 June 7 The National Union of Teachers..at South Shields is demanding the Burnham scale 3 in place of the lower scale paid by the local education committee. 1945 *Educ. Syst. Eng. & W.* (H.M.S.O.) 57 *Burnham scales*, scales of salaries payable to all teachers in publicly maintained schools and institutions. So called because they are fixed by the Burnham committees, consisting of representatives of L.E.A.s and teachers.

burnie ('bɜːnɪ). *Sc.* [dim. of BURN *sb.*¹ See -Y⁴.] A small burn; a brooklet.

1724 RAMSAY *Tea-T. Misc.* (1733) I. 100 By burnies sae clear We wander for pleasure. *a* 1854 J. WILSON *Trees.* The little waterfall of the wimpling burnie.

†**burnikat,** *a. Obs.* [ad. OF. *bruniquet* in 'safren bruniquet' (see Godef.); prob. some sort of dim. of *brun* BROWN.] A kind of saffron.

1502 ARNOLDE *Chron.* (1811) 234 (*List of Spicery*), Burnijkat safraen.

burning ('bɜːnɪŋ), *vbl. sb.* Forms: see BURN *v.*¹ [f. BURN *v.*¹ + -ING¹.] The action of the verb BURN in its various senses.

I. Connected with the *intr.* senses of the verb.

1. a. The condition of being on fire; the action of sending up flames; hence *concr.* flame. Cf. 5 b.

a 1300 *Cursor M.* 2875 þe fire it haldes þar stedfast, thoru brennyng of þe brinstane. *c* 1449 PECOCK *Repr.* 358 Brennyng of Laumpis. 1526 *Pilgr. Perf.* (W. de W. 1531) 39 Flamynge in fyre as though all the kechyn had ben in brennynge. 1592 SHAKS. *Rom. & Jul.* I. ii. 45 Tut, man! one fire burnes out anothers burning. 1695 BLACKMORE *Pr. Arthur* III. 711 The troubled whirlpool belches Burnings out. 1805 WORDSW. *Waggoner* I. 169 A burning of portentous red.

b. *fig.* The intensity of passion; the state of being inflamed with grief, rage, desire, etc. Also in *comb.*, as ***heart-burning.***

1398 TREVISA *Barth. De P.R.* II. vii. (1495) 33 Seraphin passyth other angels in brennynge of loue. *a* 1400 *Relig. Pieces fr. Thornton MS.* (1867) 22 All þat kyndills þi lykynge in brynnynge of charite. 1633 P. FLETCHER *Poet. Misc.* 80 All his verses turning Onely fann'd his poore hearts burning. 1643 MILTON *Divorce* I. iv, That burning mentioned by St. Paul, wherof Marriage ought to be the remedy. 1822 SCOTT *Nigel* i, While these heart-burnings were at their highest.

2. Heat, glowing warmth.

1513 DOUGLAS *Æneis* XIII. Prol. 23 The recent dew begynnis doun to scaill To meys the byrnyng quhar the son had schine. 1592 SHAKS. *Ven. & Ad.* 50 She with her teares Doth quench the maiden burning of his cheekes.

3. Phosphorescence of the sea; = BRIMING. Cf. also BRINY *a.* 2

1667 H. STUBBE in *Phil. Trans.* II. 497 As to the Burning of the Sea, I could never observe so great a Light, as to perceive Fishes in the Sea. 1753 CHAMBERS *Cycl. Supp.* s.v., The burning of sea water..its yielding a brisk light.

†**4.** Heat attendant upon disease or a serpent's bite; the disease itself; *esp.* erysipelas or St. Anthony's fire, and venereal disease. *Obs.*

1382 WYCLIF *Levit.* xiii. 28 And therfor it shal be clensid, for a fel wounde of brennyng it is. *c* 1390 *MS.* quoted in *Phil. Trans.* XXX. 845 A Receipt for Brenning of the Pyntyl, yat men clepe ye Apegalle. 1398 TREVISA *Barth. De*

P.R. XVIII. ix. (1495) 759 The serpent Ophites hath as many manere of brennynges and greuynges as he hath speckles and colours. *c* **1430** *MS.* quoted in *Phil. Trans.* XXX. 842 That no Stew-holder keep noo Woman wythin his Hous that hath any Sycknesse of Brenning. **1547** BOORDE *Breuyary*, The 19th Chapiter doth shew of Burning of an Harlotte. **1552** HULOET, Burning or ytche in the skynne, *vredo.* *a* **1571** JEWEL *On Thess.* ii. (1583) 346 Ech Saint was assigned..to his sundry charge..Antonie, for the burning **1751** CHAMBERS *Cycl.* s.v. **1753** —— *Cycl. Supp.*, *Burning* is more particularly used for..erysipelas. **1860** MAYNE *Exp. Lex.*, *Burning*, an old English name for Gonorrhœa.

II. Connected with the *trans.* senses of the verb.

5. a. The action of consuming or injuring by fire.

c **1250** *Gen. & Ex.* 3653 Brenninge he [Moyses] calde ðat stede. *c* **1386** CHAUCER *Knts. T.* 138 At the brennynge [*v.r.* berneynge] Of the bodies. **1594** WEST *Symbol.* II. §201 Burning of a barne adioyning to a dwelling house by night. **1648** *Art. Peace* xxii. in *Milton's Wks.* 1851 II, The other [Act] prohibiting the Burning of Oats in the Straw. **1865** *Reader* 25 Feb. 221/2 Whether Omar really ordered the burning of the Alexandrian library or not.

b. *concr.* A conflagration, a fire.

c **1425** WYNTOUN *Cron.* VII. ix. 509 Of þat brynnyn Schyre Willame De Besat bare þan girt defame. **1543-4** *Act 35 Hen. VIII*, xii, The same Scottes..make..spoyles burnynges, murders..and depopulations in this his realme. **1611** BIBLE *Amos* iv. 11 And yee were as a firebrand pluckt out of the burning. **1700** TYRRELL *Hist. Eng.* II. 792 There were cruel Plunderings and Burnings committed in that Province. **1758** HAYWARD *Serm.* xvi. 485 Sentenced to everlasting burnings.

6. The infliction of capital punishment by burning.

c **1375** WYCLIF *Antecrist* 119 Martyres han suffrid many dyvers kyndis of peynes as..drenchyng, brennyng & many oþer. *c* **1450** *Merlin* i. 21 He hadde delyuered his moder fro brennynge be gode reson. **1526** *Pilgr. Perf.* (1531) 205 b, All maner of outwarde paynes, as burnynge, drownynge, or suche other. **1812** L. HUNT in *Examiner* 28 Dec. 819/2 The burnings of Queen Mary might have been excused because there was a burning under Edward the Sixth.

†**7.** A sore caused by fire or heat; a burn. *Obs.*

1542-3 *Act 34 & 35 Hen. VIII*, viii. §1 Scaldinges, burninges, sore mouthes..& such other like diseases. **1616** SURFL. & MARKH. *Countr. Farm* 75 A Cataplasme made of the yolke and white of an egge..applyed vnto burnings, doth quench..them.

8. The treatment of any substance with fire for a specific purpose. **a.** = BURNBEATING.

1669 WORLIDGE *Syst. Agric.* v. §1. 62 This Art of Burning of Land..is not applicable or necessary to all sorts of Land. **1751** CHAMBERS *Cycl.*, *Burning* of land, called also burn beating. **1814** SIR H. DAVY *Agric. Chem.* 344 The improvement of sterile lands by burning was known to the Romans. **1842** LANCE *Cott. Farm.* 7.

b. The preparation of lime, bricks, pottery, etc. by the use of fire; also the ***burning on*** or fixing of colours by the application of fire. Also, the quantity of bricks burnt at one operation.

1559 MORWYNG *Evonym.* 214 Men thinke them to be..les smelling of any fyrines and brenning. **1663** GERBIER *Counsel* 57 The burning of lime in China..being as followeth. **1719** DE FOE *Crusoe* (1840) I. ix. 146 Tiles of my own making and burning. **1784** WEDGWOOD in *Phil. Trans.* LXXIV. 366 The burning-on of enamel colours upon earthen ware. **1881** RAYMOND *Mining Gloss.*, *Burning*, see Calcining. **1901** *Pall Mall Gaz.* 9 Dec. 8/2 No two burnings (a burning is a kiln full of bricks) have exactly the same shade of colour.

c. *Surg.* Cautery.

1636 HEALEY *Epictetus' Man.* 163 To live, of itselfe, is neither good nor evill, no more then cutting or burning. *a* **1677** BARROW *Serm.* II. iv. (R.), To endure cuttings and burnings.

d. See BURN *v.* 13 c.

1688 R. HOLME *Armoury* III. vii. §144 Yet there is another way of joining the two edges together in one, and yet not sodder them, but melt the edges by running hot Lead along it; which is termed the Burning of a joint.

e. burning off. *Austral.* and *N.Z.* See BURN *v.*[1] 13 f.

1800 P. G. KING in *Hist. Rec. N.S.W.* (1896) IV. 188 For falling, burning off, and breaking up an acre of ground. **1844** C. CHAPMAN *Let.* 30 Nov. in A. Drummond *Married & Gone to N.Z.* (1960) iv. 69 Xmas is the time for burning off. **1860** in A. F. Ridgway *Voices from Auckland* 73 The burning off should be driven as late in the season as it is safe to do so. **1891** R. WALLACE *Rural Econ. Austral. & N.Z.* xv. 232 Falling [of the bush] is done in winter, and burning off in the middle or end of summer, when everything is withered and the weather dry. **1949** D. WALKER *We went to Australia* 201 This was the hot season and all 'burning off' strictly forbidden.

†**9. a.** Lighting up; illumination. *Obs.*

1466 in *Past. Lett.* 549 II. 267 For brinnyng of the Abbes [? Abbey] with the torches xxd.

b. The illumination of a river by torches for the gaffing of salmon.

1844 W. H. MAXWELL *Sports & Adv. Scotl.* xxix. (1855) 235, I look upon sunning and burning as the acts of privileged poachers.

10. *Comb.*, as (sense 5) ***burning-lens, -mirror, -speculum***; **burning-ghat**: see GHAUT, GHAT 4; †**burning-point**, the focus of a lens (*obs.*); ***burning-fluid, -oil, -wood***; (sense 8) ***burning-house, -iron***. Also BURNING-GLASS.

1849 WEALE *Dict. Terms*, **Burning-house*, the furnace in which tin ores are calcined. **1865** *Morning Star* 3 May, There was a large burning-house, that evolved arsenical vapour. **1483** *Cath. Angl.* 32 A *Birnynge yrne..*cauterium.* **1503** *Mem. Ripon* (Surtees) III. 167 De proficuo ferri Sancti Wilfridi vocati Seintwilfride burningeyron. **1523** FITZHERB. *Surv.* 286 Euery townshyppe..ought to haue a dyuers brennynge yron. **1651** C. CARTWRIGHT *Cert. Relig.* I. 96 For which last he was..branded on the shoulder with a hot borning iron. **1831** BREWSTER *Optics* xxxviii. §164 By means of this powerful *burning lens platina..quartz, garnet.. were melted in a few seconds. **1751** CHAMBERS *Cycl.* s.v. *Burning-glass*, Every concave mirrour..is..a *burning mirrour. **1698** A. VAN LEEUWENHOEK in *Phil. Trans.* XX. 171 The *burning Point of the Magnifying Glass. **1807** HUTTON *Course Math.* II. 120 All rays parallel to the axis, are reflected to the focus, or burning point. **1837** WHEWELL *Hist. Induct. Sc.* (1857) I. 367 Remarkable inventions—as ..*burning specula. **1642** *MS. Acc. St. John's Hosp. Canterb.*, For fellinge..ashes and other *burning wood vjs.

burning ('bɜːnɪŋ), *ppl. a.* For forms see the verb. [f. BURN *v.*[1] + -ING[2].] That burns (in the various senses of the verb).

I. Connected with the *intr.* senses of the verb.

1. In a state of active heat, glowing, flaming.

c **1000** ÆLFRIC *on O.T.* in Sweet *Ags. Reader* (1879) 68 Ðas þri cnihtas het se cyning awurpan into byrnendum ofne. *c* **1175** *Lamb. Hom.* 41 On berninde fure. *c* **1270** *Saints' Lives* (Laud MS. 1887) 234 For in þe brennynde hulle..Mi ri3te is to brennen Inne. *c* **1430** *Life St. Katharine* (1884) 41 Among þe flaumes of þat brennyng fyre. **1517** TORKINGTON *Pilgr.* (1884) 37 In the likenesse of brennyng tongis. **1713** YOUNG *Last Day* III. 209 Bound to the bottom of the burning pool.

b. *transf.* Of fever, thirst, etc.: Characterized by great heat, raging, violent.

1393 LANGL. *P. Pl.* C. xx. 83 Byles and bocches and brennyng agues. **1661** LOVELL *Hist. Anim. & Min.* 518 A feaver, burning, tertian, and exquisite, requireth a liquid consistence. **1753** CHAMBERS *Cycl. Supp.* s.v., On account of a sensation of heat..we say a burning fever. **1857** LIVINGSTONE *Trav.* ii. 52 In a state of burning thirst.

c. *fig.* Of the passions: Ardent, glowing; vehement, excited.

a **1300** *Cursor M.*, *Resurrection* 264, p. 988 With brennand luf scho dwelled. *a* **1450** *Knt. de la Tour* (1868) 164 So brenninge plesaunce that they wol neuer eschew thaire synne. **1552** LYNDESAY *Monarche* 2570 Thare byrnand yre. **1709** STEELE *Tatler* No. 81 ⁋3 A burning Desire to join that glorious Company. **1814** SOUTHEY *Roderick* xxiv, With copious tears Of burning anger. **1862** STANLEY *Jew. Ch.* (1877) I. xiii. 260 A burning enthusiasm. **1871** R. ELLIS *Catullus* lxiv. 226 This burning sorrow within me.

d. *fig.* In ***burning shame, disgrace***, etc., the prevailing idea is now perhaps 'flagrant, flaming, conspicuous'; but there is often a mixture of notions derived from other senses, such as those of branding, stigmatizing; torturing as an inward fire; causing the cheeks to glow, etc.

1605 SHAKS. *Lear* IV. iii. 48 Burning shame Detains him from Cordelia. **1709** STEELE *Tatler* No. 44 ⁋5 It is really a burning shame this Man should be tolerated. **1817** CHALMERS *Astron. Disc.* VI. 202 [To] sit down in patient endurance under the burning disgrace of such a violation.

2. On fire, as a combustible; in process of being destroyed by fire; enveloped in flames. spec. ***burning mountain*** (now *arch.*), a volcano.

c **1000** ÆLFRIC *Deut.* ix. 15 þa ic nyþereode of þam byrnendan munte. *c* **1175** *Lamb. Hom.* 37 He mahte iseon ane berninde glede. *c* **1380** *Sir Ferumb.* 2236 Lucafer þanne tok op an-haste þe brennyngest bronde a couþe. *a* **1502** ARNOLDE *Chron.* (1811) p. xx, Bering burning coles. **1598** BARRET *Theor. Warres* IV. ii. 107 The Sentinell..ought to cock his burning match. **1667** MILTON *P.L.* I. 69 A fiery deluge, fed With ever-burning Sulphur unconsum'd. **1690** [see VOLCANO 1 a β]. **1712** ADDISON *Spect.* No. 281 ⁋13 A Pan of burning Coals. **1797** *Encycl. Brit.* XVIII. 686/1 Thus.. the foundation of the burning mountain would be laid in the bottom of the sea. **1804** M. LEWIS in *Lewis & Clark Exped.* (1905) VI. v. 163, I can hear of no burning mountain in the neighbourhood of the Missouri. **1867** FREEMAN *Norm. Conq.* (ed. 3) I. v. 324 They were hardly clear of the burning town. **1937** C. S. FORESTER *Happy Return* i. 22 He heard young Clay bellowing from the masthead, where presumably Gerard had sent him with a glass. 'Looks like a burning mountain, sir. Two burning mountains. Volcanoes, sir'. **1944** A. HOLMES *Princ. Physical Geol.* xx. 444 These 'fiery' and 'smoky' appearances, together with the glare reflected from the glowing lavas beneath, were responsible for the formerly popular idea that volcanoes are 'burning mountains'.

b. *fig.* ***burning matter, burning question*** (cf. F. *question brûlante*, Ger. *brennende Frage*): one that is under hot discussion, or about which the public are excited.

1865 M. ARNOLD *Ess. Crit.* i. (1875) 42 Where these burning matters [politics and religion] are in question, it [criticism] is most likely to go astray. **1873** DISRAELI in *St. James's Gaz.* (Feb. 1882), Those institutions..in due time will become great and burning questions. *a* **1883** MAX MÜLLER *India, What Can It Teach Us?* i. (1883) 32 Take any of the burning questions of the day.

c. *fig.* That is on fire with feeling and passion, or that glows with vehemence; ardent, fiery.

a **1340** HAMPOLE *Psalter* xxiii. 6 þa ere þai þat ere brennandere in luf. **1508** FISHER *Wks.* I. (E.E.T.) 182 Shynynge in fayth..brennynge in charyte. *a* **1560** ROLLAND *Crt. Venus* Prol. 68 Bauld and birnand in rancour and malice. **1819** BYRON *Juan* III. lxxxvi, The isles of Greece! Where burning Sappho lov'd and sung. **1873** G. C. DAVIES *Mount. & Mere* xiv. 117, I had prepared a most burning and eloquent address.

3. In a highly heated state; exceedingly hot. †***burning line***: the equator (*obs.*). ***burning zone***: the torrid zone (*poet.*).

1483 CAXTON *G. de la Tour* C iij b, The devil..dyde put brennyng nedles through her browes. **1553** EDEN *Treat. New Ind.* (Arb.) 10 Vnder the Equinoctial or burninge lyne. **1661** LOVELL *Hist. Anim. & Min.*, Engendring cholerick humours, and burning bloud. **1697** DRYDEN *Virg. Georg.* III. 390 In the Desart Land Of Libya travels, o'er the burning Sand. **1713** ADDISON *Cato* I. iii. 31 Lord of half the burning Zone. **1807** CRABBE *Library* 318 We trace In dens and burning plains, her savage race.

b. ***burning scent***: strong, very 'warm' scent; ***burning chase***: hot, uninterrupted, pursued without a check.

a **1700** DRYDEN (J.), He shot by me Like a young hound upon a burning scent. **1755** YOUNG *Centaur* Wks. 1762 IV. 182 Ye staunch pursuers of Pleasure Opening full cry on its burning Scent. **1854** R. MASSIE in *Bk. Praise* IV. No. 358 (1862) 384 The hart..Heated in the burning chace. **1859** *Art Taming Horses* xii. 200 *Burning scent*, when hounds go so fast, from the goodness of the scent, they have no breath to spare, and run almost mute.

4. That burns luminously; giving light, shining; *transf.* glowing as if incandescent.

c **1000** *Ags. Gosp.* John v. 35 He wæs byrnende leoht-fæt and lyhtende. **1297** R. GLOUC. 534 The bissops amansede alle..Mid berninde taperes. **1398** TREVISA *Barth. De P.R.* XVIII. ix. (1495) 759 The serpent Ophites is paynted wyth brennyng speckles. *c* **1430** LYDG. *Bochas* VI. I. (1554) 143 Brenning eyen sparkling of their light. **1564** BECON *Gen. Pref.* in *Wks.* (1843) 18 They are..like unto a brenning candle. **1596** SPENSER *F.Q.* I. v. 6 Burning blades about their heades [they] doe blesse. **1821** SHELLEY *Prometh. Unb.* II. i. 22 The burning threads of woven cloud unravel.

II. Connected with the *trans.* senses of the verb.

5. Affecting with heat; scorching, withering.

1382 WYCLIF *Gen.* xli. 23 Other seuen [eeris], thinne and smytun with a brennynge blaste. *c* **1620** Z. BOYD *Zion's Flowers* (1855) 38 The burning ray, That from the sun comes. **1718** POPE *Iliad* I. 90 Phoebus [shall] dart his burning shafts no more. **1805** WORDSW. *Waggoner* I. 1 'Tis spent—this burning day of June!

b. Causing a sensation like that of contact with fire. †***burning water*** = ardent spirit (*obs.*).

1460-70 *Bk. Quintessence* 2 Oure quinta essencia..hath .iij. names..brennynge watir, þe soule in þe spirit of wyn, and watir of lijf. **1528** PAYNELL *Salerne Regim.* F iv b, Wyne citrine is not so burnynge as redde claret. **1559** MORWYNG *Evonym.* 8 Brenning water..doth..make hoat and dry mens bodies. **1578** LYTE *Dodoens* I. lxxxvii. 129 The small burning Nettell. **1878** BRITTEN & HOLLAND *Plant-n.*, Burning Nettle, *Urtica urens*, L.

c. That resembles heat in its effects.

1697 DRYDEN *Virg. Georg.* III. 675 Burning Isicles are lodg'd within. **1821** SHELLEY *Prometh. Unb.* I. 33 The bright chains Eat with their burning cold into my bones.

6. quasi-*adv.*, as in ***burning hot***.

1475 *Bk. Noblesse* (1860) 6 Now at erst the irnesse be brennyng hote in the fire. **1549** *Compl. Scot.* vi. 52 Ther tua symmyrs ar vondir birnand heyt. *Mod.* It was a burning hot day in July.

7. In parasynthetic combinations.

1597 DRAYTON *Mortimer.* 145 His Cradell Phalaris burning-bellyed Bull.

burning bush. a. 'The bush that burned and was not consumed' mentioned in Exod. iii., and assumed as an ensign by the Presbyterian churches of Scotland, in memory of the persecution of the 17th c. **b.** A name applied to various shrubs or plants, as the Artillery plant, *Pilea Serpylliflora*, the *Dictamnus Fraxinella*, and (U.S.) the *Euonymus atropurpureus* and *E. Americanus.*

1866 *Treas. Bot.*, *Burning Bush*, sometimes applied in gardens to the Artillery plant. **1878** BRITTEN & HOLL. *Plant-n.*, Burning Bush, *Dictamnus Fraxinella*, L. (in gardens). It is said that the plant gives off so large a quantity of essential oil that the air around it becomes inflammable, and will ignite if a light be brought near. **1883** *Harper's Mag.* Apr. 726/1 The euonymus, or burning-bush, clothed in the autumn with its brilliant scarlet berries.

burning-glass ('bɜːnɪŋ glɑːs, -æ-). A lens, by which the rays of the sun may be concentrated on an object, so as to burn it if combustible.

1570 DEE *Math. Pref.* 35 Archimedes..with his Burning Glasses..fired their other Shippes a far off. **1598** SHAKS. *Merry W.* I. iii. 74 The appetite of her eye did seeme to scorch me vp like a burning-glasse. **1643** CARYL *Sacr. Covt.* 33 The fiery beames of Gods wrath are contracted into this burning-Glasse. **1727** SWIFT *Gulliver* III. i. 180, I had about me my flint, steel, match, and burning-glass. **1768** TUCKER *Lt. Nat.* II. 426 Not unlike the virtuoso's scheme, who would needs try to make a burning-glass of ice. **1878** *Masque Poets* 213 Beauty is a burning-glass that brings The soft, diffusive sunshine to a focus.

b. A concave mirror, by the use of which the same effect may be produced.

1675 BAXTER *Cath. Theol.* I. III. 11 The Spirits effect on the soul to come by reflection..as Light and Heat from the Sun by a Speculum or Burning-Glass. **1751** CHAMBERS *Cycl.* s.v., The second..are concave; very improperly called burning-glasses, being usually made of metal. **1760** tr. *Keysler's Travels* I. 428 A concave burning-glass reflects.. the solar rays into one focus.

burningly ('bɜːnɪŋlɪ), *adv.* [f. prec. + -LY[2].]

1. In a burning manner, with burning effect.

c **1386** CHAUCER *Knts. T.* 707 Loue hath his firy dart so brennyngly Ystiked thurgh my..herte. **1853** F. W. NEWMAN *Odes of Horace* 76 Nor clung more burningly the fatal boon on huge Alcides' shoulders. **1855** BROWNING *Ch. Roland*, Burningly it came on me all at once. **1876** G. MEREDITH *Beauch. Career* II. xv. 276 She sat over the portrait blushing burningly.

2. *fig.* With ardour; hotly; ardently; eagerly.

1340 *Ayenb.* 31 Oure Lhord..he ssolde lovye bernindeliche. **1382** WYCLIF *1 Kings* xi. 1 Kyng Salomon to brennyngly lovede many hethen wymmen. **1506** *Ord. Crysten Men* (W. de W.) II. xi. 116 In getynge to moche

brennyngely, in retaynynge to straytely. **1866** ALGER *Solit. Nat. & Man* III. 134 Hopelessly separated from the world by their vows..yet burningly attached to it by the passions.

burnish (ˈbɜːnɪʃ), *sb. rare.* [f. BURNISH *v.*[1]] Burnishing; a burnishing; *spec.* anything laid over a surface to give a bright and glossy look.

c **1647** CRASHAW *Poems* 135 Blushes, that bin The burnish of no sin. **1728** RAMSAY *Ep. Friends Ireland*, Giving ilka verse a burnish. **1781** SMEATHMAN in *Phil. Trans.* LXXI. 179 The lacquer or burnish with which the brasswork was covered was totally spoiled. **1871** *Daily News* 6 Sept., The burnish..was..no subtraction from efficiency.

burnish (ˈbɜːnɪʃ), *v.*[1] Forms: 4–5 **burnissh, -essh, -yssch, bornyssh,** 4–6 **burnyssh, -isch, bornysch,** 5 **bornysh, burnesh, -esch, -eyssh,** 5–6 **burnysh,** 6 **burnech, bournysh, -yssh, byrnysh,** 6– **burnish.** *Pa. pple.*: also 4 **bur-, bornyst(e,** 5 **burnysyd, byrnyst,** 6 **bur-, birneist.** [f. OF. *burniss-* stem of *burnir*, var. of *brunir*; cf. Pr. *bornir*; see BURN *v.*[2]]

1. *trans.* To make (metal) shining by friction; to furbish; to polish (a surface) by rubbing with a hard and smooth tool.

c **1325** *E.E. Allit. P.* 554 Þe beryl bornyst byhouez be clene. **1375** BARBOUR *Bruce* VIII. 225 Thair basnetis burnyst var all brycht. **1460** *Pol. Rel. & L. Poems* (1866) 102 Off clothes of gold burneysshed bright. **1556** *Chron. Gr. Friars* (1852) 36 The standert new payntyd..the crosse new burnechyd. **1652** NEEDHAM tr. *Selden's Mare Cl.* 192 They ..burnish the hilts of their swords with the teeth of such great Animals as swim in the sea. **1837** THIRLWALL *Greece* IV. xxxiii. 291 Their shields were burnished for the occasion. **1875** URE *Dict. Arts* I. 424 Gold-leaf is laid upon the edges, and is then burnished with a polishing tool, tipped with agate.

b. *fig.* (Of things non-material.)

1526 *Pilgr. Perf.* (1531) 61 b, Hye walles & noble, all bournysshed and polysshed with charite. **1589** PUTTENHAM *Eng. Poesie* (Arb.) 155 Figuratiue speaches [are] the instrument wherewith we burnish our language. **1606** DEKKER *Sev. Sins* II. (Arb.) 21 If a Lye..be not smooth enough, there is no instrument to burnish it, but an oath. **1728** YOUNG *Love Fame* VII. (1757) 166 Pursuit of fame.. into coxcombs burnishes our fools.

†**c.** *in extended nonce-use.*

1596 SPENSER *F.Q.* V. viii. 29 So forth he came all in a cote of plate Burnisht with bloudie rust.

2. *transf.* To make bright and glossy; to overspread with lustre.

c **1325** *E.E. Allit. P.* B. 1085 Þenne watz her blyþe barne burnyst so clene. **1658** T. MAYERNE *Archimag. Anglo-Gall.* xix. 17 You may burnish your pye or pasty and..put it to the Oven. **1667** MILTON *P.L.* IV. 249 Fruit burnisht with Golden Rind, Hung amiable. **1753** HOGARTH *Anal. Beauty* xii. 94 As he proceeds in burnishing the lights. **1833** HT. MARTINEAU *Cinn. & Pearls* iv. 74 A mild sunshine burnished the scene.

b. *absol.* for *refl.* To make oneself shine.

1701 D'URFEY *Pills* II. (1719) 104 A..flashy Fop..Who if he is not burnishing thinks he all's Time does lose.

3. Of a stag: To rub the dead 'velvet' or skin from his horns [cf. Fr. *brunir* in same sense]; applied loosely to the annual renewal of the horns, perhaps by confusion with BURNISH *v.*[2]

1616 BULLOKAR, *Burnish*, is also a terme among hunters when Harts spread their hornes after they be fraied. **1677** N. COX *Gentl. Recreat.* (1706) 64 All Stags as they are burnish'd, beat their Heads dry against some Tree or other. **1693** W. ROBERTSON *Phraseol. Gen.* 289 The Deer burnisheth his head. **1751** CHAMBERS *Cycl.* s.v. *Burnishing*, Deer are said to burnish their heads, when rubbing off a white downy skin from their horns against a tree, they thrust them..into a reddish earth, to give them a new colour and lustre. **1792** OSBALDISTONE *Brit. Sportsm.* 83/1.

4. *intr.* To become bright or glossy; to shine, gleam. Also *fig.*

1624 FLETCHER *Rule a Wife* I, How you itch, Michael! how you burnish! **1713** SWIFT *Salamander* Wks. 1755 III. II. 77 I've seen a snake..Burnish, and make a gaudy show. **1763** C. SMART *Song David* 61 The crocus burnishes alive Upon the snow-clad earth. *a* **1834** LAMB *Wks.* 491 With Churchill's compliment still burnishing upon her..lips.

5. *trans.* To fix *into* (a setting) by pressing down the metal rim with a burnisher.

1793 SIR G. SHUCKBURGH in *Phil. Trans.* LXXXIII. 109 Upon the cell, into which the glass is burnished, and also upon the tube of the telescope, into which the cell is screwed.

†**ˈburnish,** *v.*[2] *Obs.* except *dial.* Also 4 and 9 *dial.* **barnish.** [Etymology unknown; connexion with senses 3 or 4 of prec. seems hardly possible, and is also opposed by the early s.w. and still dial. form *barnish.* East Anglian dial. uses *furnish* in same sense.]

1. *intr.* Of the human frame: To grow plump, or stout, to spread out; to increase in breadth.

1398 TREVISA *Barth De P.R.* VI. i, This age is calde adolescencia, for it is full age to gete children, and able to barnisch [**1535** burnyshe]. *c* **1430** *Syr Generides* 780 The childe..began to burnesh and sprede. **1601** HOLLAND *Pliny* I. 345 A man Groweth in height..vntill hee be one and twentie yeares of age: then beginnes he to spread and burnish in squarenesse. **1640** FULLER *Joseph's Coat* (1867) 101 We must not all run up in height, like a hop-pole, but also burnish and spread in breadth. **1684** DRYDEN *Davenant's Circe* Prol. 398 A slender Poet must have time to grow, And spread and burnish as his Brothers do. **1847–78** HALLIWELL, *Barnish*, to increase in strength or vigour; to fatten; look ruddy and sleek. **1875** PARISH *Sussex Dial.* s.v., 'You burnish nicely', meaning, 'You look well'.

b. *transf.*

1624 WOTTON *Archit.* in *Reliq. Wotton.* (1685) 68 Whether the Fabrick be of a beautiful Stature; whether for the breadth it appear well burnished. **1662** FULLER *Worthies* II. 190 [London] will be found to Burnish round about, to every point of the compasse.

ˈburnishable, *a. rare*[−0]. [f. BURNISH *v.*[1] + -ABLE.] Capable of being burnished.

1611 COTGR., *Pollissable*, polishable, burnishable.

burnished (ˈbɜːnɪʃt), *ppl. a.* [f. BURNISH *v.*[1]]

1. Made bright and shining as by friction, polished.

c **1325** *E.E. Allit. P.* A. 77 As bornyst syluer þe lef onslydez. **1413** LYDG. *Pilgr. Sowle* V. v, Bryght bornyshed gold. *c* **1470** HENRY *Wallace* II. 130 Hys byrnyst brand he byrstyt at ye last. **1606** SHAKS. *Ant. & Cl.* II. ii. 196 The Barge..like a burnisht Throne Burnt on the water. *a* **1775** POPE *Odyss.* IV. 66. **1789** WORDSW. *Even. Walk*, The whole wide lake..like a burnished mirror glows.

b. *fig.*

1853 (3 June) BRIGHT *Sp. India* (1876) 11 The glossed and burnished statement.

2. *transf.* Having the appearance of polished metal; bright, shining, glossy.

c **1325** *E.E. Allit. P.* A. 220 Bornyste quyte watz hyr uesture. **1596** SHAKS. *Merch. V.* II. i. 2 The shadowed liuerie of the burnisht sunne. **1667** MILTON *P.L.* IX. 501 Serpent ..With burnisht Neck of verdant Gold. **1827** KEBLE *Chr. Y., Burial of Dead* iii, Let some graceful arch be there.. With burnish'd ivy for its screen.

b. Of deer: (see the vb.)

1649 G. DANIEL *Trinarch., Hen. V*, 232 Chase Whole Burnish't Herds. **1697** DRYDEN *Virg. Georg.* IV. 422 A Steer ..whose Head..with burnish'd Horns begins to spread.

burnisher (ˈbɜːnɪʃə(r)). [f. BURNISH *v.*[1] + -ER[1].]

1. One who burnishes.

c **1450** *Voc.* in Wr.-Wülcker 604 *Pollictor*, a bornyshour. **1580** HOLLYBAND *Treas. Fr. Tong*, *Enlumineur de livres*, a burnisher of books. **1664** PEPYS *Diary* (1879) III. 65 By and by the flaggon finished at the burnisher's. **1708** *Brit. Apollo* 13 Feb. 8 Mrs. Wills Burnisher of Plate, at the Iron Anchor. **1884** *Birmingham Daily Post* 23 Feb. 3/4 Chandelier Trade. —Wanted, Burnisher used to best work.

2. A tool for smoothing surfaces or for burnishing or polishing articles. It differs in material and shape according to the purpose and trade.

1598 FLORIO *Frugatore*..a burnisher [**1611** a rubbing cloth, a rubber, a burnishing toole, a burnisher]. **1662** EVELYN *Chalcogr.* (1769) 21 Burnisher, (another tool used by Chalcographers). **1751** CHAMBERS *Cycl.*, *Burnishers* for gold or silver are commonly made of a dog's or wolf's tooth, set in the end of an iron or wooden handle. Of late, agates and pebbles have been introduced. **1837** WHITTOCK *Bk. Trades, Engraver* (1842) 214 The burnisher is..formed of hard steel, rounded and polished.

burnishing (ˈbɜːnɪʃɪŋ), *vbl. sb.* [BURNISH *v.*[1]]

1. The action of brightening or polishing (chiefly metallic surfaces); also *attrib.*

1552 HULOET, Bournyshyng or poolyshyng. **1598** FLORIO, *Frugatoio*, a burnishing toole. **1644** MILTON *Educ.* Wks. (1847) 98/2 As it were the burnishing of many studious & contemplative years. **1764** HARMER *Observ.* IV. vii. 320 The burnishing of gold. **1879** in *Cassell's Techn. Educ.* IV. 299/2 The next process is burnishing—Steel tools are used.

b. *fig.* **c.** *concr.* Metallic polish, lustre.

1780 BURKE *Election Sp. Bristol* Wks. III. 372 That our disgrace might want no sort of brightening and burnishing. **1851** RUSKIN *Stones Venice* I. App. xvii. 393 You cannot perfectly see the form of a humming-bird, on account of its burnishing.

2. *transf.* Of deer. Cf. BURNISH *v.*[1] 3.

1611 COTGR., *Frayouër*, a Deeres burnishing of his head. **1859** TODD *Cycl. Anat. & Phys.* V. 518/2 The animals.. rubbing them [i.e. the horns] against any hard substances.. this action is termed 'burnishing'.

burnishment (ˈbɜːnɪʃmənt). *rare.* [f. BURNISH *v.*[1]] Metallic polish, lustrous adornment.

1862 CHRISTINA ROSSETTI *My Dream* in *Goblin Market, etc.* 63 But special burnishment adorned his mail.

‖**burnous, burnouse** (bɜːˈnuːs, -ˈnuːz). Also 7 **bernou, -noo, -nooe,** 9 **ber-, bornouse, boornoos, bournous, burnoos(e.** [a. F. *burnous*, a. Arab. *burnus.* On account of the final *-s*, the word has often been treated in Eng. as a plural.]

1. A mantle or cloak with a hood, an upper garment extensively worn by Arabs and Moors.

1695 MOTTEUX *St. Olon's Morocco* 81 The black Caps and Bernous they are oblig'd to wear. *Ibid.* 91 A Bernooe, or kind of Stuff or Cloath Cloak, edg'd with a Fringe, whence there hangs a kind of a Cowle behind with a Tuft at the end on't. *Ibid.* 92 The Alcaydes..have a Bernoo of Scarlet, or black Cloth, without a Cowle. *Ibid.* 93 The King's Blacks are seldom seen to wear Bernoos. **1811** *Ann. Reg.* 568/1 A cloak, or Bernouse as it is called. **1832** LANDER *Exped. Niger* II. xiv. 277 Dressed in a full bornouse, or Arab cloak. **1841** MARRYAT *Poacher* (Rtldg.) 279 Their white bournous.. waving in the wind. **1863** KINGLAKE *Crimea* I. 289 The burnous..is his [the Arab's] garment by day and by night. **1875** J. BENNET *Winter Medit.* I. ix. 263 The inhabitants of Algiers..wear..thick woollen bournous with hoods.

2. A kind of cloak or mantle worn by women, resembling the Arabian garment.

1859 SALA *Tw. round Clock* 111 The Burnouse cloaks, and the Llama shawls. **1863** —— *Capt. Dang.* III. viii. 254 The folds of her White Burnouse. **1876** GEO. ELIOT *Dan. Der.* I. xi. 219, I want to put on my burnous.

burˈnoused, *ppl. a.* [f. prec. + -ED[2].] Wearing a burnous.

1846 *Blackw. Mag.* LX. 337 Burnoused warriors. **1864** SALA in *Daily Tel.* 20 Apr., The burnoused Kabyle and the kilted Highlander. **1868** *Daily Tel.* 22 May, The lovely.. ladies of Genoa..turned out..shawled and burnoused.

Burnsian (ˈbɜːnzɪən), *a.* and *sb.* [f. the name of Robert *Burns* (1759–96), Scottish poet + -IAN.] **A.** *adj.* Of or relating to Burns, his works, or his style. **B.** *sb.* An admirer of Burns or his works. So **Burnsiˈana** [-ANA], things connected with Burns; **ˈBurnsite** = BURNSIAN *sb.*

[**1866** J. MACKIE (*title*) Bibliotheca Burnsiana. Life and works of Burns: title pages and imprints of the various editions in the private library of James M'Kie, Kilmarnock.] **1874** J. GIBSON (*title*) The Burns calendar: a manual of Burnsiana; relating events in the poet's history, names associated with his life and writings, a concise bibliography, and a record of Burns relics. **1904** *Daily Chron.* 22 Aug. 3/1 The accumulating literature of Burnsian topography. **1905** *Westm. Gaz.* 13 Apr. 12/1 Collectors of Burnsiana. **1909** *Daily Chron.* 14 Aug. 3/1 All Burnsites—common or peculiar. *Ibid.*, Devotees of the Burnsian cult. **1920** *Glasgow Herald* 28 July 6 A representative gathering of Scottish Burnsians.

Burnside, burnside (ˈbɜːnsaɪd). *U.S.* [f. the proper name: see below.] 'A style of beard such as that affected by General Burnside (1824–81), consisting of a mustache, whiskers, and a clean-shaven chin' (*Cent. Dict.* Suppl. 1909). Freq. *pl.* Also *attrib.* Cf. *side-burn* (SIDE *sb.*[1] 27).

1875 *Cincinnati Enquirer* 6 July 2/1 His whisker was of the Burnside type, consisting of mustache and 'muttonchop', the chin being perfectly clean. **1881** I. M. RITTENHOUSE *Jrnl.* in *Maud* (1939) i. 36 The older one has *lovely* burnsides. **1907** *Outing* (U.S.) L. 279 Such various patterns of ornamental whiskers as the 'Piccadilly Weeper' (No. 2), the 'Burnside', etc. **1930** *Publishers' Weekly* 8 Feb. 679 In the days of copper-toed boots and burnsides..our grandfathers were buying this book.

burnt, burned (bɜːrnt, bɜːnd), *ppl. a.* For forms see the vb. [f. BURN *v.*[1]]

1. Set on fire, consumed with fire.

1382 WYCLIF *Isa.* xiii. 9 Brent faces [Vulg. *facies combustæ*]. **1535** COVERDALE *Jer.* li. 25 A brente hill. *a* **1547** SURREY *Æneid* II. 1015 Reft from the brent Temples of Troy. **1591** SPENSER *Ruines of Time* 19 Th' auncient Genius of that Citie brent. **1611** BIBLE *Jer.* li. 25, I wil..make thee a burnt mountaine. *Mod.* Many objects of value were discovered amid the ruins of the burnt houses.

b. *fig.* Fired with passion; inflamed, excited.

a **1564** BECON *Humble Supplic.* in *Prayers, &c.* (1844) 247 Brent with a fervent and unfeigned zeal. **1859** TENNYSON *Enid* 560 All his face Glow'd..So burnt he was with passion.

2. ***burnt out***: **a.** extinct after entire consumption of the fuel; sometimes *fig.*; **b.** driven out by a conflagration; cf. BURN *v.* 15.

1837 CARLYLE *Fr. Rev.* I. VII. ii. 302 Burnt-out Seigneurs, rally round your Queen! **1837** DE QUINCEY *Lake Poets &c.* Wks. II. 108 It was a burnt-out volcano. **1887** *Manch. Guardian* 31 May 5 The burned-out company of the Opéra Comique. **1908** HARDY *Dynasts* III. VII. ix. 347 This is my burnt-out hour. **1917** T. S. ELIOT *Prufrock* 24 The burnt-out ends of smoky days. **1919** F. HURST *Humoresque* 256 She looked up at him with a tired, a burned-out, an ashamed smile. **1926** E. BOWEN *Ann Lee's* 93 Mrs Pym was a fair, burnt-out young woman of twenty-five. **1969** *Listener* 3 Apr. 472/1 Joss Ackland as Danton, the not entirely burnt-out volcano.

c. Of a leper: cured (see quot. 1959), esp. in *burnt-out case.* Also *fig.* (freq. with influence of sense 2 a).

1959 G. GREENE *Congo Jrnl.* 10 Feb. (1961) 42 Leprosy cures where disease has been arrested and cured only after the loss of fingers or toes are known as burnt-out cases. **1961** —— (*title*) A burnt-out case. **1961** *New Statesman* 24 Feb. 318/1 Yet had this priest not burned at the stake in 1634, he could be discovered in the Congo as a nobler but still walking 'burnt-out case'. **1961** *Encounter* XVI. 70 The burnt-out leper is not too obtrusive. **1961** *Times Lit. Suppl.* 2 June 340/2 His constitution 'seemed to have broken down, and no career in life lay open' to him. A burnt-out case. **1968** R. HARRIS *Nice Girl's Story* ii. 18 He was probably a burnt-out case—perhaps his wife had perished in the gas chambers. His interest in life, except to get through it somehow, might be dead.

3. a. Affected or damaged by fire or excessive heat, scorched. †***burnt line***: the equator. †***burnt zone***: the torrid zone. In †***burnt planet***, †***burnt way***, = COMBUST (*Astrol.*).

1393 GOWER *Conf.* II. 375 They destruied king and all And leften but the brente wall. **1552** HULOET, Burned rostemeate on the spyt. **1555** EDEN *Decades W. Ind.* (Arb.) 59 The marchaunt..passeth to Inde, By the burnte line or Equinoctiall. **1614** RALEIGH *Hist. World* I. 142 Being under the burnt Zone, it was held uninhabitable. **1667** PEPYS *Diary* (1879) IV. 442 The ground was everywhere so burned and dry. **1862** MARY E. ROGERS *Dom. Life Palestine* 17 Cattle were browsing on the scanty burnt-up pasture.

b. Of persons: That has suffered injury or pain from fire, or agencies resembling fire; *esp.* in proverb, ***the burnt child dreads the fire.***

c **1400** *Rom. Rose* 1820 Brent child of fier hath mych drede. **1562** J. HEYWOOD *Prov. & Epigr.* (1867) 45 Burnt childe fyre dredth. **1674** DUKE OF LAUDERD. in *Lauderd. Papers* (1885) III. xxxii. 53 A burn'd Child dreads the fire.

†**c.** *Med.* Adust. ***burnt choler***: 'choler adust'.

1578 LYTE *Dodoens* I. xv. 24 Hoate, cholerique, burnte, and pernicious humors. **1585** LLOYD *Treas. Health* Y iv, Against a quartaine of burnt coler in haruest, take yᵉ rote of fennel, parcely, of bochers brome, sperage, cinkfoyle.

4. That has been treated with fire for a specific purpose: **a.** Said of earth that has been burn-beated; of clay, bricks, tiles, etc. Also **burnt-iron** (see quot. 1881).

1387 TREVISA *Higden* (1865) I. 97 þe walles were i-made of brend tile and of glewe in stede of morter. **1616** SURFL. & MARKH. *Countr. Farm* 687 Harts doe run ouerthwart the burned ground where the dogges can haue no sent. **1834** *Brit. Husb.* xvii. I. 367 Part of the field was dressed with burned clay. **1881** RAYMOND *Mining Gloss., Burnt iron*, in the Bessemer and open-hearth processes, iron which has been exposed to oxidation until all its carbon is gone.

b. Of gold and silver: Molten, refined by fire.

c **1325** *E.E. Allit. P.* A. 988 þe borȝ watz al of brende golde bryȝt. *c* **1386** CHAUCER *Knts. T.* 1304 His sadel was of brend gold newe ybete. *c* **1420** *Anturs of Arth.* xxx, A bordur a-boute alle of brent gold. **1488** *Inv. Jewels of Jas. III* in Tytler *Hist. Scot.* (1864) II. 393 Item twa braid pecis of brynt silver bullioune.

c. Calcined or treated by fire for use as a drug, pigment, etc., as ***burnt alum, carmine, ochre, sienna, sponge, umber***, etc. (see ALUM *sb.*, CARMINE, etc.); † **burnt-brass**, obs. name for copper sulphate; † **burnt copper**, copper oxide; † **burnt lead**, lead sulphide.

1661 LOVELL *Hist. Anim. & Min.* 459 *Cathereticks*, burnt pumice-stone, burnt alum, burnt vitriol, burnt antimony or crocus metallorum..*Causticks*, live lime, burnt-brasse, sublimat mercury. **1751** CHAMBERS *Cycl.* s.v. *Lead*, Burnt Lead, *plumbum ustum*, is..lead melted in a pot with sulphur, and reduced by fire into a brown powder. **1790** RICHARDSON *Chem. Princ. Metallic Arts* 124 When it [copper] is exposed to a red heat..it separates in scales, which are called burnt copper. **1800** *Med. Jrnl.* IV. 412 To medical practitioners in general, burnt sponge is known to be the basis of the Coventry remedy. **1844** THACKERAY *May Gambols* in *Wks.* (1899) XIII. 441, I have so often wandered before with burnt-sienna plough-boys. **1846** DICKENS *Pict. from Italy* 41 Two burnt-sienna natives. **1946** R. LEHMANN *Gipsy's Baby* 78 The expanses of burnt sienna mud.

d. Impressed by burning or branding; branded.

1652 *Advt.* in *Proc. Parliament* No. 163 A Browne bay Mare..a burned O upon each hip.

e. ***burnt taste, flavour***, etc.: a taste, etc., resembling that of something that has been burnt; ***burnt cream*** = *crème brûlée.*

1723 J. NOTT *Cook's & Confectioner's Dict.* C. 209 Burnt Cream. Take Yolks of four or five Eggs, beat them well in a Stew-pan. Set the Cream on the Furnace [etc.]. **1969** *Observer* 12 Jan. 32/8 *Burnt Cream* (layers of custard and clotted cream covered with sugar and browned).

5. Of wine, etc.: 'Made hot' (J.); see quot. 1876; the precise early sense is doubtful. (Now only *dial.*) ***burnt brandy***: that from which part of the spirit has been removed by burning.

1583 STUBBES *Anat. Abus.* 120 Commyng to..a tavern, called for burnt-wine, sacke, malmesie, hipocras and what not. **1598** SHAKS. *Merry W.* II. i. 222 Ile giue you a pottle of burn'd sacke. **1661** PEPYS *Diary* 15 Jan., A cupp of burnt wine at the taverne. **1709** STEELE *Tatler* No. 36 ¶5 I'll lay Ten to Three, I drink Three Pints of burnt Claret at your Funeral. **1876** F. ROBINSON *Whitby Gloss.* Pref. 9 'Burnt wine from a silver flagon' was handed..being a heated preparation of port wine with spices and sugar. **1880** *Barman's Man.* 55 Burnt brandy..one glass of Cognac and half a table-spoonful of white sugar, burnt in a saucer.

6. Affected as with burning.

a. Of grain: Affected by smut, ergot, etc.; cf. 7.

1597 GERARD *Herbal* I. lvii. 77 Burnt Rie hath no one good property. **1806** R. ANDREWS in Young *Agric. Essex* I. 295, Ears of smut, or what we call burnt wheat.

b. Affected by venereal disease.

1693 W. ROBERTSON *Phraseol. Gen.* 289 A burnt whore.

c. (See quot.)

1909 *Daily Chron.* 23 Feb. 7/2 The buyer should beware of..burnt furs. Such furs have been over-dyed, and the hair will soon become rusty and fall out.

7. *Comb.*, as **burnt almond**, an almond enclosed in burnt sugar; hence, a fashion shade of brown; † **burnt-cat** [F. *chat brûlé*], a sort of pear; **burnt cork**, cork that has been burnt so that it can be used for blackening the face, hands, etc.; freq. *attrib.*, as ***burnt-cork artist***, a Negro minstrel (see NEGRO 3); **burnt-cork** *v. trans.*, to blacken with burnt cork; **burnt-corked** *a.*, blackened with burnt cork; **burnt-ear**, a disease in corn, in which, owing to the growth of a minute fungus *Uredo segetum*, the ear appears covered with blackened powder; **burnt feed** *Austral.* (see quot.); † **burnt-marked** *a.*, branded; **burnt stuff** *Austral.* (see quot. 1945).

1850 *Family Friend* III. 327/1 Put a *burnt almond..in the centre. **1892** *Encycl. Pract. Cookery* 14/2 Pound the Burnt Almonds..in a mortar. **1895** *Cassell's Fam. Mag.* June 554/1 [A bonnet] of burnt-almond straw. **1913** 'ASCOTT R. HOPE' *Half & Half Trag.* 121 Treating me to twopence worth of 'burned almonds'. **1690** W. WALKER *Idiomat. Anglo-Lat.* 80 The Pot calls the Pan *burnt-arse. **1676** WORLIDGE *Cyder* (1691) 216 *Burnt-cat, Lady-pear, Ice-pear..are all very good winter-pears. *c* **1800** C. MATHEWS in Mrs. Mathews *Mem. C. M.* (1838) I. xv. 305 Camel's hair pencils, hare's feet, whiting, *burnt corks. **1840** Burnt Cork [see CORK *sb.*[1] I]. **1869** *Porcupine* 3 July 123/1 The Theatre Royal has within the last week or two been usurped by a company of the 'burnt cork' professors. **1873** 'ASCOTT R. HOPE' *Night before Holidays* (1874) 98 We had one very fine false beard,..and there was plenty of burned cork to be had. **1880** E. JAMES *Amat. Negro Minstrel's Guide* 10 A pair of legs such as Nelse Seymour had ..are great attractions in a burnt-cork artist. **1893** P. H. EMERSON (*title*) Signor Lippo, burnt-cork artiste. **1884** *Liverpool Daily Post* 2 Jan. 4/7 Their *burnt-corked faces. **1885** JEROME *On the Stage* 3 We..burnt-corked our hands and faces. **1898** *Daily News* 6 May 2/6 For money-making it is necessary to wear masks or to burnt-cork the face. *a* **1722** LISLE *Husb.* 150 (E.D.S.) *Burnt-ear, *Ustilago* in corn. **1835** *Penny Cycl.* III. 465/2 Diseases to which barley is subject..the smut, the burnt ear, blight. **1848** H. W. HAYGARTH *Bush Life Australia* vii. 73 A patch of '*burnt feed' (as the young herbage is called which springs up..where the old grass has been set on fire). **1705** in *Lond. Gaz.* No. 4163/4 A..Mare..*burnt-marked on the near Hip with H. **1852** J. BONWICK *Notes Gold Digger* 9 Some neighbouring bearded digger turns round and condescendingly remarks, that it is only the '*burnt stuff'. **1945** BAKER *Austral. Lang.* v. 94 *Burnt stuff*, a stratum of iron-hard rock or compacted clay and rock encountered during digging.

8. ***burnt*** (***colour***), a deep shade of yellowish brown; so ***burnt-coloured*** adj.

1896 *Daily News* 2 July 8/7 Hats of 'burnt' straw, this being the technical name of a deep shade of yellowish brown. **1899** *Westm. Gaz.* 20 Apr. 3/3 Burnt-coloured straw. **1923** *Weekly Dispatch* 25 Feb. 14 Colours: Navy,..Nut, Mastic and Burnt.

b. Of a colour or shade of colour: having the appearance of darkening by scorching.

1897 *Sears, Roebuck Catal.* 360/3 Colors for Artists... Burnt Roman Ochre—Burnt Sienna—Burnt Terre Verte. **1923** *Daily Mail* 19 Feb. 5 Coloured Shantung... In a full range of new colourings, including..Rose, Burnt Orange, Almond, [etc.]. *Ibid.* 19 Mar. 1 Burnt Gold.

† **'burntish**, *a. Obs.* [f. BURNT + -ISH.] Having symptoms of burning, somewhat burnt.

1662 J. CHANDLER *Van Helmont's Oriat.* 227 Thirst ariseth in Fevers by reason of burntish putrefactions. **1674** R. GODFREY *Inj. & Ab. Physic* 70 Burntish and stinking belchings..plainly attest it.

† **'burntness.** *Obs. rare*⁻¹. In 6 **brentness.** [f. BURNT + -NESS.] Burnt quality.

1559 MORWYNG *Evonym.* 23 Destill it..with a soft fire; least the waters stink or savour of brentnes.

burnt 'offering, burnt-'offering. A sacrifice offered to a deity by burning. (As the word is chiefly familiar in Scriptural use, it naturally suggests in the first place the animal sacrifices of the Jews.) So also **burnt-sacrifice**.

1382 WYCLIF *Mark* xii. 33 More than alle brend offringis [*v.r.* sacrifices] and sacrificis. **1535** COVERDALE *Job* i. 5 Job..offred for every one a brentofferinge. **1751** CHAMBERS *Cycl.* s.v. *Sacrifice*, When the victim was slain, they flayed him, if it was not a burnt-offering (for then they burnt skin and all). **1852** GROTE *Greece* II. lxxi. IX. 236 Have you ever sacrificed to him with entire burnt-offerings as we used to do together at Athens?

1382 WYCLIF *Ex.* xx. 24 ȝe shulen offre vpon it ȝoure brent sacrifices. **1588** A. KING *Canisius' Catech.* 21, I offer my self to this mornyng in ane brounte sacrifice. **1611** BIBLE *2 Kings* xvi. 15 Burne..the Kings burnt sacrifice.

burnwood ('bɜːnwʊd). A species of sumac, *Rhus metopium*, found in the West Indies and southern Florida.

1874 LINDLEY & MOORE *Treas. Bot.* Suppl., Burnwood of the West Indian negroes. *Rhus Metopium.* **1926** FAWCETT & RENDLE *Flora of Jamaica* V. 9 R[hus] Metopium... Jamaica Sumach. Burn Wood.

buroo (bə'ruː, bruː). *slang* (chiefly *Sc.*). Also brew, broo, b'roo. [Repr. regional (esp. *Sc.*) pronunc. of BUREAU (sense 2).] The Labour 'Bureau' or employment exchange; hence, unemployment benefit, esp. in phr. ***on the buroo.***

1934 D. ALLAN *Hunger March* I. vi. 76 'What are you, signor?' 'What indeed? A "moocher"? A supporter of the "buroo"?' **1937** PARTRIDGE *Dict. Slang* 111/2 *Buroo* or *brew*, an employment-exchange. Public Works' coll.: from ca. 1924. **1937** in *Sc. Nat. Dict.* s.v., Weel, weel, this is the b'roo day, nuvver mind the fushin'. Come on for oor b'roo. **1969** M. PUGH *Last Place Left* iv. 22 'You'll be on the broo as well.' She meant that I would soon be unemployed. Nell was..inclined to use dated Scottish slang. **1969** N. NICHOLSON in *English* XVIII. 19 The Market Square is busy as the men file by To sign on at the 'Brew'. **1978** J. GALWAY *Autobiogr.* vii. 78 The 'buroo' (a Belfast corruption of 'Unemployment Bureau') was all right, because by working and paying for your stamps, you had earned that. **1983** *Listener* 9 June 18/3, I can remember as a child 60 years ago hearing the unemployed..saying they were 'on the buroo'. This was in Plumstead, London SE 18.

burough, -row, obs. ff. BOROUGH.

burp (bɜːp), *v. slang* (orig. *U.S.*). [Imitative.]

1. *intr.* To belch. Hence **'burping** *vbl. sb.* and *ppl. a.*, belching or making a similar sound.

1932 *Amer. Speech* VII. 330 *Burp*, to belch. **1934** *Etude* Aug. 456/3 Saxophonists also go in for this slapping effect; when done by the larger members of the family, it bears a ludicrous resemblance to the 'burping' of a frog. **1939** I. BAIRD *Waste Heritage* xii. 150 Charlie settled back on the burping springs. **1953** W. R. BURNETT *Vanity Row* xvii. 131 He belched, 'It's an old Arab custom... You no like food—no burp—host insulted.' **1958** *Spectator* 6 June 726/3 At the hot springs the mud bubbles and burps.

2. *trans.* To cause to belch or bring up wind.

1940 in *Amer. Speech* (1941) XVI. 145/2 Chronic air swallowers should be 'burped' three or four times..during each feeding. **1950** *Lancet* 4 Feb. 218/1 In the U.S.A. babies are 'burped' during and at the end of feeds. **1968** 'G. BAGBY' *Another Day* ii. 28 'What would you do with a baby?' I asked. 'Feed it, diaper it, and burp it,' she said.

burp (bɜːp), *sb. slang* (orig. *U.S.*). [f. the vb.]

1. A belch. Also *transf.* and *fig.*

1932 *Amer. Speech* VII. 330 *Burp*, sound made when belching. **1946** P. KESTEN *Radio Alphabet* 18 *Burp*, an interloping noise on transmitting or receiving stations. **1951** J. MASTERS *Nightrunners of Bengal* v. 64 He forced a small musical burp and giggled. **1957** *Observer* 3 Nov. 19/7 Hollywood gives vent to one of its periodic burps of sentiment over an entertainer whose sorrows drove him to the bottle. **1962** V. NABOKOV *Pale Fire* 22 A comfortable burp told me he had a flask of brandy concealed about his warmly coated person.

2. ***burp gun*** (see quot. 1946). *Army slang.*

1945 *Finito! Po Valley Campaign* 41 The whirr of burp guns. **1946** *Amer. Speech* XXI. 246 Practically any type of German automatic or semi-automatic small arm was apt to be described as a *burp gun*, presumably from the resemblance of shots or short bursts of fire to hiccoughs; but I have been told by a combat infantryman that the name is properly applicable only to the Schmeisser machine pistol.

burqa, var. BURKA[1] and [2].

burr, bur (bɜː(r)), *sb.*[1] Also 7 **burgh**, 6–7 **burre.** [Derivation obscure: nor is it at all clear whether the senses under II and III ought not to be treated as separate words. But the co-existence of the form BURROW *sb.*[5] (q.v.) with BURR sense 5, and its explanation as 'a circle about the moon', seem to identify this with the *burwhe, burrowe* of the Promptorium, the phonetic variants being analogous to *fur, furrow*; while the form *burgh*, besides *burre*, as well as the sense of II, appears equally to point back to the same ME. forms. For the source of the ME. see BROUGH.]

I. 1. General sense: A circle.

c **1440** *Promp. Parv.* 56 Burwhe, sercle [**1499** burrowe], *orbiculus.*

II. A (? protecting) ring, etc.

† **2.** A broad iron ring on a tilting spear just behind the place for the hand. *Obs.*

c **1530** LD. BERNERS *Arth. Lyt. Bryt.* (1814) 327 Squyers and varlettes were..knockynge on hedes and burres on myghtye speres. **1603** FLORIO *Montaigne* II. xxxvii. (1632) 427 Burre, or yron of a launce, etc. **1611** DEKKER & MIDDLETON *Roar. Girl* II. i, I'll try one spear..though it prove too short by the burgh. **1610** GUILLIM *Heraldry* IV. xiv. (1660) 338 The Burre..is a broad ring of Iron behind the..place made for the hand, which Burre is brought unto the Rest when the Tilter chargeth his Speare or Staffe.

3. A washer placed on the small end of a rivet before the end is swaged down; also (*Gunnery*) see quot. 1802.

1627 FELTHAM *Resolves* II. xxix. Wks. (1677) 218 A brawl ..which with all the burrs of silence should have still stood firmly riveted. **1802** C. JAMES *Mil. Dict., Bur* [in *Gunnery*], a round iron ring, which serves to rivet the end of the bolt, so as to form a round head. **1851** *Ord. & Regul. Roy. Engineers* §11. 51 Leather Pipes, joined by Copper Rivets and Burs. **1860** H. STUART *Seaman's Catech.* 5 Bolt and burr.

4. (See BURR-PUMP.)

III. 5. A circle of light round the moon (or a star); a BROUGH. The original sense seems to have been merely 'circle, halo'; but in modern use there is usually the notion of a nebulous or nimbous disc of light enfolding the luminary; as if modified by association with BUR *sb.*

1631 BRATHWAIT *Whimzies, Xantipp.* 104 A burre about the moone is..a presage of a tempest. **1794** G. ADAMS *Nat. & Exp. Philos.* IV. lii. 463 The stars seem..surrounded with a sort of burs. **1802** HERSCHEL in *Phil. Trans.* XCII. 499 Of Stars with Burs, or Stellar Nebulæ. **1851** NICHOL *Archit. Heav.* 128 The halo itself gradually sinking into a bur, or an atmosphere around a star.

burr, bur (bɜː(r)), *sb.*[2] [Origin unknown.] The sweet-bread of a calf, sheep, etc.

1573 *Art of Limning* 10 To take grease out of parchement or paper: Take shepes burres and burne them to pouder, etc. **1730–6** BAILEY s.v., The Bur of a Beef, etc., the sweet bread. **1752** *Hist. Pompey the Litt.* 125 Sitting down to a breast of veal..raving at the landlord, because the bur was gone. **1834** ESTHER COPLEY *Housekpr's. Guide* v. 107 A sweet-bread (or burr)..boiled.

burr, bur, *sb.*[3] [Etymol. uncertain. Though the sense approaches that of BORE *sb.*[1], connexion with that appears to be phonetically impossible. Mr. E. B. Poulton suggests that the general notion is that of 'a roughness or scar, which looks artificial or as if resulting from accident—the look presented by an ear (beyond any other organ of special sense) in birds, and other animals which have not the external pinna possessed by mammals'. This would connect it with the following word, or even with BUR *sb.*]

The external meatus of the ear, the opening leading to the tympanum.

(This is clear in quot. 1688, since hawks have nothing but an opening; so practically the cropt-eared dog in quot. 1677; quot. 1573 refers to the secretion of wax in the meatus of the ear, and (as was formerly supposed) in the parotid glands or 'kernels of the ears' (though it might be read as identifying the 'burres' with the 'kirnels'). Dr. Johnson's explanation 'the lobe or lap of the ear' was an unfortunate guess, servilely followed by later dictionaries.)

1573 COOPER *Thesaurus, Parotis*..an impostume behinde the eares comming of a matter distilling from the heade into the burres or kirnels of the eares. **1677** *Lond. Gaz.* No. 1203/4 A Little White Shock Bitch..cropt ears..red above

the burrs of her ears. **1688** R. HOLME *Armoury* II. 237/1 *Names of the parts of a Falcon*—Of the Head.. The Burrs, or Ear burs, are the Ears. **1730-6** BAILEY, *Burr*, the round Knob of Horn next a Deer's Head; also the Burr of the Ear. [Hence in JOHNSON.] **1857** P. CARTWRIGHT *Autob.* (1858) viii. 46, I struck a sudden blow in the burr of the ear and dropped him to the earth. **1928** P. GREEN *In Valley* 121, I whammed him in the burr of the ear and piled him. **1954** C. L. B. HUBBARD *Compl. Dog Breeders' Man.* xxxvi. 318 *Burr*, the irregular formation inside the ear.

burr, bur (bɜː(r)), *sb.*[4] [app. the same word as BUR *sb.*; at least having some notion of roughness derived from it: but usually spelt *burr*, and therefore here treated apart.]

1. A rough ridge or edge left on metal or other substance after cutting, punching, etc.; e.g. the roughness produced on a copper-plate by the graver; the rough neck left on a bullet in casting; the ridge produced on paper, etc., by puncture.

1611 FLORIO, *Bocchina*..that stalke or necke of a bullet which in the casting remaines in the necke of the mould, called of our Gunners the bur of the bullet. **1784** E. DARWIN in *Phil. Trans.* LXXV. 5 A bur made by forcing a bodkin through several parallel sheets of paper. **1837** WHITTOCK *Bk. Trades* (1842) 214 The scraper..for rubbing off the burr or barb raised by the graver on the copper plate. **1846** *Print. Appar. Amateurs* 13 [In type-founding] when the waste piece of metal called the 'break' is broken off, the burr that is left is planed away. **1876** *Athenæum* 25 Nov. 693/3 Burr.. is caused by the tearing up of the copper by the needle or burin. A ragged edge is left which holds the ink and gives a rich velvety effect. **1879** *Cassell's Techn. Educ.* IV. 117/2 A burr left at the hinder end of the thread [of a screw] which 'ragged' the wood.

2. Technical senses of obscure origin. [? With notion of 'something rough', or of 'tool for removing roughness'.] **a.** short for *burr-chisel*, *burr-drill* (also, a similar instrument used for surgical operations on the bones), *burr-saw*: see 3. Hence ***burr-hole***, a hole made by such an instrument. **b.** (See quot.).

1794 *Rigging & Seamanship* I. 150 *Burr*, a triangular hollow chissel, used to clear the corners of mortises. **1833** J. HOLLAND *Manuf. Metals* II. 145 In the making of screws.. workmen..use what they call a burr, or burring tool..The burr is a square piece of steel..having in the centre a hole screwed as accurately as possible with a square thread or worm. **1859** J. TAFT *Pract. Treat. Operative Dentistry* iv. 99 The burs and drills may be made of pieces of wire..and fitted to a socket handle. **1881** C. A. HARRIS *Princ. & Pract. Dentistry* (ed. 10) III. ii. 305 Dr. Forbes has adapted to enamel burrs, chisels and gouges an ingenious handle. **1899** C. TRUAX *Mech. Surgery* xviii. 392 *Surgical burrs*..may be either olive shaped or in cylindrical form, the former being generally preferred. **1939** PARFITT & HERBERT *Oper. Dental Surg.* (ed. 4) ix. 125 The introduction of diamond burs in recent years has almost revolutionized cavity cutting. **1948** E. H. BOTTERELL in *Brit. Surg. Practice* II. 379 Bilateral burr holes are made in the mid-temporal region.

3. *Comb.* **burr-chisel**, a three-edged chisel used to clear the corners of mortises; **burr-cutter, burr-nipper**, nippers for cutting away the burr from a leaden bullet; **burr-drill**, a dentist's drill with a serrated or file-cut knob or head; **burr-gauge**, a plate perforated with holes of graduated sizes, for determining the sizes of burr-drills; **burr-saw**, a small circular saw used in turning.

[**1850** C. A. HARRIS *Dental Surg.* (ed. 4) III. iii. 290 The flat and burr-headed drills are very useful for enlarging the opening into the cavity.] **1859** J. TAFT *Pract. Treat. Operative Dentistry* iv. 96 *Bur Drills*..should be manufactured of the best steel, and wrought with the greatest care.

burr, bur (bɜː(r)), *sb.*[5] Also buhr. [Origin uncertain: possibly identical with BUR *sb.*, being so called from its roughness.]

1. a. Siliceous rock capable of being employed for millstones. **b.** A whetstone.

1721 C. KING *Brit. Merch.* I. 288 Burrs for Mill-Stones. **1816** W. SMITH *Strata Ident.* 12 Burs, or scythe stones. **1834** *Amer. Jrnl. Sci.* XXV. 233 Millstones equal to the best French buhrs. **1879** *Shropsh. Word-bk.*, *Bur*..a whetstone for scythes. **1880** JEFFERIES *Gt. Estate* 168 The French burrs ..come over in fragments.

2. A siliceous boss or rock occurring among calcareous, or other softer, formations; a harder part in any freestone.

1839 MURCHISON *Silur. Syst.* I. iv. 49 Upright bands of hard sandstone, termed 'Burrs', which cut through the strata. **1865** I. TURNER *Slate Quarries* 16 Circular saws..are ..unable to cut through 'burrs'..and other hard places.

3. *spec.* A term applied by quarrymen in Dorsetshire to a soft sandy limestone, with hard silicified bosses, above the 'Dirt bed' in the Lower Purbeck series. Also to a harder sandy limestone chiefly made up of comminuted shells, in the Upper Purbeck beds.

1829 T. WEBSTER *Observ. Purb. & Portland Beds, Trans. Geol. Soc.* Ser. II. II, Below this is another mass of calcareous stone, considerably softer..it is divided into two by a slaty bed, the upper being called aish, and the lower the soft burr. **1882** *Cornh. Mag.* 728 Above this we get the soft burr, a lake sediment. **1883** T. BOND *Corfe Castle* 51 The stone..locally known by the name of Bur, is perhaps the most durable building stone in England.

4. A partly fused mass of brick; a clinker.

1823 P. NICHOLSON *Pract. Build.* 344 Burrs or Clinkers are such as are so much over-burnt as to vitrify, and run two or three together. **1864** *Daily Tel.* 2 June, The advisability of sinking brick burrs in different parts of the river. **1876** GWILT *Encycl. Archit.* §1824 Burrs and clinkers are such bricks as have been violently burnt, or masses of several bricks run together in the clamp or kiln.

5. *attrib.*: see BURR-STONE. ***burr millstone*** (U.S.).

1771 WASHINGTON *Writings* (1931) III. 63 A pair of French burr millstones. **1829** S. CUMINGS *Western Pilot* 23 This..is famous for its quarries of stone; from which are manufactured burr mill stones. **1851** C. CIST *Cincinnati* 182 James Bradford & Co...manufacture yearly seventy-five pairs burr millstones. **1883** *Specif. N.E. Railw. (Alnwick & Cornh. Branch)* 58 Price of Dry or Burr Walling.

burr (bɜː(r), bʌrr), *sb.*[6] Also burrh. [app. imitative of the sound; though probably associated in idea with the roughness of a bur; cf. BUR *sb.*, esp. sense 4, *bur* in the throat.]

1. A rough sounding of the letter *r*; *spec.* the rough uvular trill (= French *r grasseyé*) characteristic of the county of Northumberland, and found elsewhere as an individual peculiarity. (Writers ignorant of phonology often confuse the Northumberland *burr* with the entirely different Scotch *r*, which is a lingual trill: see quots. 1835, 1873.)

1760 FOOTE *Minor* (1781) Introd. 9 An Aunt just come from the North, with the true NewCastle bur in her throat. **1805** R. FORSYTH *Beauties Scotl.* II. 57 From [the Tweed], southward as far as Yorkshire, universally all persons annex a guttural sound to the letter *r*; a practice which in some places receives the appellation of the Berwick *burrh.* **1835** W. IRVING *Crayon Misc.* (1849) 240 He spoke with a Scottish accent, and with somewhat of the Northumbrian 'burr'. **1873** J. A. H. MURRAY *Dial. S. Scotl.* 86 The northern limits of the *burr* are very sharply defined, there being no transitional sound between it and the Scotch *r*. Along the line of the Cheviots, the Scotch *r* has driven the *burr* a few miles back, perhaps because many of the farmers and shepherds are of Scotch origin. **1876** GREEN *Short Hist.* i. §3 (1882) 25 The rough Northumbrian burr.

b. Hence, *loosely*, A rough or dialectal pronunciation, a peculiarity of utterance.

1849 C. BRONTË *Shirley* iv. 39 'A Yorkshire burr..was.. much better than a cockney's lisp.' *Ibid.* III. ii. 41 Your accent..has no rugged burr. **1867** A. J. ELLIS *E.E. Pronunc.* I. i. 19 Each district has its burr or brogue. **1874** FARRAR *Christ* II. lix. 348 Betrayed by his Galilæan burr.

2. [= BIRR *sb.* 3.] Whirr, vibratory or rushing noise.

1818 KEATS *Endym.* II. 138 Holding his forehead, to keep off the burr Of smothering fancies. **1825** COLERIDGE *Lett.* xl. in *Lett. Convers., &c.* II. 177 Put the whole working hive of my thoughts in a whirl and a bur. **1856** MISS MULOCH *J. Halifax* i. 2 The open house-doors..through which came the drowsy burr of many a stocking-loom. **1860** *All Y. Round* No. 57. 159 The burr of working wheels and cranks.

burr, bur (bɜː(r)), *sb.*[7] [a. F. *bourre* 'padding', also 'refuse of raw silk'. Cf. BURL *sb.*[1]]

1. A sort of pad for a saddle.

1688 R. HOLME *Armoury* III. 345/1 The French Pad Saddle..the Burs of it come wholly round the seat. **1725** BRADLEY *Fam. Dict.* II. 6 a/2 Pad Saddle, of which there are Two sorts, some being made with Burrs before the Seat, others with Bolsters under the Thighs.

2. The refuse of raw silk.

1798 W. HUTTON *Autobiog.* 117 To take out the burs and uneven parts [of a thread of silk]. **1812** SMYTH *Pract. Customs* 185 Waste silk is what surrounds the cocoon..This burr is proper to stuff quilts.

‖**burr, bur,** *sb.*[8] [Hind. *bar*:—Skr. *vaṭa*.] The Banyan-tree (*Ficus indica*); also *attrib.*

1813 J. FORBES *Orient. Mem.* III. 14 A sacred Burr, or pipal tree. **1849** SOUTHEY *Comm.-Pl. Bk.* Ser. II. 407 A remarkable banian or burr tree. **1845** STOCQUELER *Handbk. Brit. India* (1854) 141 The bur, the largest of trees.

†**burr,** *v.*[1] *Obs. rare*—[1]. [f. BURR *sb.*[1]] *intr.* To spread *out* like a burr round the moon.

1660 H. MORE *Myst. Godl.* III. vi. 71 The Rayes of things, burring out from all Bodies that act at a distance.

burr (bɜː(r)), *v.*[2] [f. BURR *sb.*[1] 3.] *trans.* To fashion into a *burr* or rivet-head.

1880 *Times* 27 Dec. 9/4 A tool having a screw and triple clip, which grasps the gas check and burrs it over a projection at the base of the shell.

burr, *v.*[3] [f. BURR *sb.*[6]]

1. *intr.* To pronounce a strong uvular *r* (instead of a trilled *r*), as is done in Northumberland. Also, *loosely*, to speak with a rough articulation; to speak inarticulately or indistinctly, to utter the syllable *burr* or something like it.

1798 WORDSW. *Idiot Boy* xxii, Burr, burr—now Johnny's lips they burr, As loud as any mill, or near it. **1816** *Monthly Mag.* XLI. 527 There let them burr and oy. **1866** CARLYLE *Remin.* (1881) II. 126 He..burred with his *r*.

2. *trans.* To pronounce (*r*) with a 'burr' (or, *loosely*, with a trill).

1868 H. KINGSLEY *Mathilde* II. 268 There were plenty of r's in it, and he burred them. *Mod.* You cannot speak French like a Parisian, until you have learnt to burr your r's.

3. *intr.* To make a whirring noise.

1838 AUDUBON *Ornith. Biogr.* IV. 555 We..saw the males [*sc.* humming birds] in numbers, darting, burring, and squeaking. **1886** [see BURRING *ppl. a.*]. **1946** K. TENNANT *Lost Haven* (1968) xviii. 311 She hated moths. Let it stay there burring and fluttering. **1959** G. USHER *Death in Bag* xvi. 167 The telephone clacked and burred at length.

burr (bɜː(r)), *v.*[4] [f. BURR *sb.*[4]] **a.** *intr.* To use a burr. **b.** *trans.* To excavate (a tooth) with a burr. Hence 'burring *vbl. sb.* used *attrib.*, as **burring-engine**, a dentist's machine for driving a burr-drill, etc.; **burring tool** (see BURR *sb.*[4] 2 b).

1875 *Dental Cosmos* XVII. 510 With the burring-engine I ground off enough of the cusp.

†**burracan.** *Obs.* [a. F. *bouracan* 'gros camelot' (Littré).] A coarse kind of cloth.

1588 *Lanc. Wills* (1861) III. 135 The same hanginges of redd and yelowe burracan.

burracho, var. BORACHIO, *Obs.*, leather bottle.

burrage, obs. form of BORAGE.

burral, burrel ('bʌrəl). *Sc.* See quot.

1796 *Statist. Acc. Scotl.* XVII. 404 That partial kind [of cultivation] called balk and burral. **1811** *Agr. Surv. Aberd.* 235 (JAM.) The inferior land, besides the outfields..was called..burrel ley, where there was only a narrow ridge ploughed, and a large stripe or baulk of barren land between every ridge.

burramundi, -munda, see BARRAMUNDI.

burranet. *Obs.* exc. *dial.* [app. repr. an OE. **beorh-ened* (= Du. *berg-eend* BERGANDER), f. *beorh* BURROW *sb.*[2] + *ened* duck; cf. BURROW-DUCK.] The Sheldrake.

1602 CAREW *Cornwall* 35 a, Widgeon, Burranets, Shags, Duck and Mallard. **1759** B. MARTIN *Nat. Hist. Eng.* I. *Dorset* 39 Geese, Galls, Burranets, Woodcocks. **1882** JAGO *Cornish Gloss.* 125 *Burranet*, the Shell-drake.

burras, obs. form of BORAX.

burra sahib ('bʌrə'sɑːɪb). *India.* Also with capital initials. [Hind. *barā* great, *çāhib* master (see SAHIB).] A title of respect used by Indians in referring to the head of a family, the chief officer in a station, the head of a department, etc. Also *transf.* So **burra beebee** or **mem(-sahib)**, a similar title for a lady.

1807 G. ELLIOTT *Let.* 20 Sept. in *Lord Minto in India* (1880) ii. 29 The Burro Bebee, or lady of the highest rank. *c* **1810** W. HICKEY *Memoirs* (1918) II. x. 136 The Governor-General, Mr. Wheler, General Stibbert, Mr. Barwell, and in fact all the *Burra Sahibs* (great men) of Calcutta. **1848** J. H. STOCQUELER *Oriental Interpreter* 44 *Burra-beebee*, or *burra-mem*, a great lady; the appellation bestowed upon the female head of a house, or the wife of the principal personage at a station or presidency of India. **1863** TREVELYAN *Dawk Bungalow* 1, Chota Sahib one rupee give. Burra Sahib two rupee. **1885** LADY DUFFERIN *Viceregal Life India* (1889) I. 57 The great lords and Ladies (Burra Sahib and Burra Mem Sahib). **1922** *Blackw. Mag.* Sept. 283/2, I made my way to the burra Police Sahib. **1922** *Outward Bound* Nov. 137/2 Part of the headdress or person of a *burra-mem.* **1928** *Chamber's Jrnl.* Feb. 180/2 The Hindu..announced it to be the habitation of a very *burra* (high in station) sahib. **1934** 'G. ORWELL' *Burmese Days* xxv. 371 The position for which Nature had designed her from the first, that of a burra memsahib. **1936** R. W. CHAPMAN *Names, Designations & Appellations* 240 The societies of industry, commerce..are commonly divisible into three grades... Members of A say '*Smith*' to each other (..but a Burra Sahib may be '*Sir*'). **1963** M. MALIM *Pagoda Tree* xxii. 145 The gathering throng of eminently decorous knights, *burra sahibs* and *burra mems* gathering on the lamplit lawn below.

burras-pipe. ? *Obs.* [f. *burras*, obs. form of BORAX (see quot. 1688).] See quots.

1676 J. COOKE *Marrow of Surg.* (ed. 4) 2 Those [Instruments] needful to be carried about are..Incision-knife, Burras-Pipe and Stitching-Quill both in one. **1678** PHILLIPS, *Burras-pipe*, a certain Instrument derived originally from the Goldsmiths, and now also used in Chyrurgery, to keep corroding Powders in, as Vitriol, burnt Allum, Præcipitate, etc. [**1688** R. HOLME *Armoury* III. 259/2 Terms of Art used by the Gold-smiths. *Charging*, is to lay on the place to be soldered both Soder and Burras. *Ibid.* III. 308/2 Founders Tools. The Borax Box; of some termed a Borace Box; but more vulgarly a Burras Box, is a Brass or Copper Box with a Pipe in the side, in which bruised Borax is put, to scratch it by little and little out of the Knobbed Pipe, on the place intended to be Soddered.] **1753** CHAMBERS *Cycl. Supp.*, *Burras-pipe*, an instrument used by goldsmiths, consisting of a copper box, with a spout, having teeth like a saw; sometimes also used by surgeons for the application of certain solid medicines by inspersion. **1721-1800** in BAILEY as in PHILLIPS; hence in JOHNSON and mod. Dicts.

burrass. [a. F. *bourras* (same sense).] Coarse hempen cloth. Cf. BARRAS[1], and *barras* sb.[2] in Eng. Dial. Dict.

1770 C. CARROLL *Let.* 24 Oct. in *Maryland Hist. Mag.* (1918) XIII. 66 Pray write for 6 strong matrasses..strongly Quilted & Covered with Burras or a Coarse strong Canvass. **1807** VANCOUVER *Agric. Devon* (1813) 241 The dregs are.. filtered through brown burrass bags.

†**burratine.** *Obs. rare*—[1]. [ad. It. *burattino* 'quel fantoccio di cenci o di legno, con molti de' quali il burattinajo rappresenta commedie e farse' (Tommaseo and Bellini).] A puppet; 'a sillie gull in a Comedie' (Florio).

1617 B. JONSON *Vis. of Delight* 19 A she monster delivered of sixe Burratines, that dance with sixe Pantalones.

burrawang (ˈbʌrəwæŋ). *Austral.* Also buddawong, burrawong, burrowan, burwan. [f. the name of Mt. *Budawang*, New South Wales.] An Australian palm-like tree, *Macrozamia spiralis*; the nut produced by this tree.

1826 J. ATKINSON *Agric. & Grazing N.S.W.* 19 The burwan is a plant with leaves very much like the cocoa nut. **1851** J. HENDERSON *Excurs. N.S. Wales* II. 238 The Burrowan, which grows in a sandy soil. **1877** E. A. HERON *Balance Pain* 108 A Buddawong seed-nut fell to earth. **1889** J. H. MAIDEN *Usef. Native Plants Australia* 41 'Burrawang Nut', so called because they used to be, and are to some extent now, very common about Burrawang, N.S.W. **1934** *Bulletin* (Sydney) 3 Oct. 21/1 The burrawang is another slow grower. **1956** *Landfall* X. 122 Straight-trunked burrawong trees.

burreau, var. of BURRIO, *Sc. Obs.*, hangman.

burred (bɜːd), *a.* [f. BUR *sb.* + -ED[2].] Rough and prickly like a burr.

1906 *Westm. Gaz.* 8 Sept. 2/3 He falls furiously on the ball..until it is hopelessly burred and gashed. **1924** *Glasgow Herald* 4 Apr. 8 The burred fruits are accounted for by their clinging to the feathers of birds.

‖ **ˈburred**, another form of BARRAD.

1823 *New Monthly Mag.* VII. 232 His long hair was.. surmounted by a burred or conical woollen cap.

† **buˈrree.** *Obs.* [a. F. *beurré* (lit. 'buttered') 'espèce de poire fondante' (Littré).] See quot.

1719 LONDON & WISE *Compl. Gard.* 52 [Page headed *La Burree*] The Burree..call'd the Butter Pear, because of its smooth, delicious, melting soft pulp.

‖ **burrel.** [ad. Hindi *bharal* (Col. Yule).] The blue wild sheep of the Himālaya.

1860 GOSSE *Rom. Nat. Hist.* 54 The burrell, or wild sheep, of the Himalaya Peaks..The burrell is considered as the first of Himalayan game animals.

burrel, app. misprint for BURREE.

1706 in PHILLIPS (with explanation nearly as in BURREE above). **1721–1800** in BAILEY; hence in JOHNSON, etc.

burrel-fly. [Derivation unknown: cf. F. *bourreler* to torment.] The gadfly.

1658 [see WHAME *sb.*]. **1678** PHILLIPS (App.), *Burrel-fly*, the same as Gad-fly. **1713** DERHAM *Phys.-Theol.* (L.) The whame, or burrel-fly, is vexatious to horses in summer. **1721** BAILEY, *Burrel-fly*, an Insect very troublesome to working Cattle. Hence in JOHNSON and mod. Dicts. **1829** [see WHAME *sb.*]. **1951** COLYER & HAMMOND *Flies Brit. Isles* vi. 102 Various names have been bestowed upon Tabanidae, including burrel-flies, gad flies..horse flies [etc.].

† **burrell.** *Obs. rare.* (Cf. BURR *sb.*[1] sense 2.)

1548 W. PATTEN *Exped. Scotl.* in Arb. *Garner* III. 118 They brake and bare away the nether end of the staff [of a standard] to the burrell.

burrell, var. of BORREL, BUREL. *Obs.*

burrell, burrhal, burrhel, varr. BHARAL.

burrel-shot. See quot.

1706 PHILLIPS, *Burrel-shot* = Case-shot. **1730–6** BAILEY, *Burrel Shot* (with Gunners) small Bullets, Nails, Stones, Pieces of old Iron, etc. put into Cases, to be discharged out of the Ordnance or murdering Pieces; Case shot. Hence in JOHNSON and mod. Dicts.

† **burret.** *Obs. rare.* [a. F. *bouret*, *buret*, used to render L. *murex*, also *conchylium*, in Du Pinet's transl. of Pliny 1566, whence Holland may have obtained the word.] Used to render L. *murex*, a kind of shell-fish yielding a dye.

1601 HOLLAND *Pliny* IX. xxxvi. 258 The Murex or Burret. **1745** tr. *Columella's Husb.* VIII. xvi. 373 Conchyls, burrets, oysters, and others of the purple kind [Lat. *conchyliis, muricibus, et ostreis*]. *Ibid.* 374 *footnote*, The murex, which some call a burret.

burrh-stone, variant of BURR-STONE.

burridge, burrie, obs. ff. BORAGE, BURRY.

burring (ˈbɜːrɪŋ), *vbl. sb.*[1] [f. BUR *v.*[1] + -ING[1].] The removing of burs and other foreign bodies from wool or cotton in the process of manufacture. Hence ***burring-machine***, ***-saw***, ***-wheel***. **burring rollers** *pl.*, an apparatus for removing the burrs from wool in preparing it for carding.

1879 in *Cassell's Techn. Educ.* IV. 340/1 To clean the wool of these troublesome seeds, the burring machine was brought into requisition. **1884** W. S. B. MCLAREN *Spinning* v. 83 The burrs..lie along the fibres of wool... To clear them off, burring rollers are fixed on the top of two of the lickers-in. **1888** *Encycl. Brit.* XXIV. 658 The swift as it travels round is met by a series of three burring rollers rotating in an opposite direction.

burring (ˈbɜːrɪŋ), *ppl. a.* [f. BURR *v.*[3] + -ING[2].] **a.** That burrs in speech; **b.** whirring.

1883 *Mag. Art* Sept. 470/2 What a funny burring patois. **1886** E. HODDER *Life Earl Shaftesbury* I. iii. 139 Amidst the burring din of machinery.

† **burrio, burio.** *Sc. Obs.* Also 7 burreo; see also BOURREAU. [a. F. *bourreau*, earlier *boreau*, *borel*.] A hangman, an executioner.

1536 BELLENDEN *Cron. Scot.* (1821) I. 201 He was burio to himself mair schamefully than we micht devise. **1567** *Declar. Lordis Quarr.* in Dalyell *Scot. Poems 16th C.* II. 274 Syne with his Burrio [she] band ane new mariage. **1634–46** Row *Hist. Kirk* (1842) 322 Should ye be burrioes to your brethren? [**1830** SCOTT *Demonol.* 324 The Devil..had made her associates..to be their own burrioes.]

fig. *a* **1600** MONTGOMERIE *Sonn.* lix, Lovers..Thoght they persaivd that Burrio Death to bost within [hir] eyis.

† **burriour, burior.** *Sc. Obs.* Also 7 burrier. [An adaptation of prec., after agent nouns in *-our*, *-or*.] = prec.

c **1550** *Clariodus* (JAM.) Sum burriouris ye sall gar come yow to. *a* **1600** BURELL *Pilgr.* in Watson *Coll. Poems* (1706) II. 40 (JAM.) Thir catiff miscreants I mene, As buriors has euer bene. **1676** W. ROW *Contn. Blair's Autobiog.* xii. (1848) 456 To be his executioners and burriers against ministers.

‖ **burrito** (bəˈriːtəʊ). Chiefly *U.S.* [Amer. Sp., dim. of *burro* BURRO, ass.] A Mexican dish consisting of a maize-flour tortilla rolled round a savoury filling (of beef, chicken, refried beans, etc.).

1934 E. FERGUSSON *Mexican Cookbk.* 33 Burritos (*Little Burros*). Mix tortillas..but mold them thicker than usual. Make a depression in the middle of each and fill with chicharrones. **1962** MULVEY & ALVAREZ *Good Food from Mexico* (rev. ed.) iii. 81 Burritos in the northern part of Mexico and in the southwestern part of the United States are quite different. Now a popular dish in many restaurants and taco stands in California and Texas are northern burritos, which are made by folding a flour tortilla around a mound of re-fried beans, seasoned to taste with chili. **1971** *Sunset* Jan. 85/1 A burrito party is an excellent way to entertain a few guests. **1978** J. WAMBAUGH *Black Marble* iv. 35, I got a victim who'll I.D. anybody I show him. Owns the burrito stand over on Western. **1984** *Miami Herald* 30 Mar. 14A/3 She ate three tacos and a burrito at lunch.

‖ **burro** (ˈburo). [Sp.] A donkey. Now esp. *U.S.* (common in Western states).

1800 SOUTHEY in *Life* (1850) II. 119 The easy pace and sure step of the John burros. **1800** —— *Lett.* (1856) I. 129 By the aid of a burro and the good baiting-places in the way. [Frequent in Southey.] **1845** T. J. GREEN *Jrnl. Texian Exped.* xii. 166 The sick were permitted to ride upon 'burros' (jack-asses). **1882** *Rep. Prec. Met.* (U.S. Bureau of Mint) 569 With these attached a burro or horse runs the machine. **1884** *Harper's Mag.* Oct. 750/2 Even pottery and singing-birds, are..brought burro-back, packed in..crates. **1932** E. WILSON *Devil take Hindmost* xviii. 197 One of the burros is laden with wooden casks.

burrock (ˈbʌrək). [Apparently in its origin a mere dictionary word, though perh. it may have found its way into actual use; ad. mod. or med.L. *burrochium*, ad. OF. *bourroiche*, explained by Littré and Godef. as an apparatus made of wickerwork for catching fish.]

1701 *Cowell's Interpreter* (ed. Kennet), *Burrochium*, a Burrock or small Wear, where Wheels [i.e. weels] are lay'd in a River, for the taking of Fish. **1706** in PHILLIPS; hence in BAILEY, JOHNSON, and mod. Dicts.

burrough, ordinary f. BOROUGH in 16–18th c.

† **burrough-gate.** *Obs.* [ad. OE. *burh-ȝeat* gate of a castle.]

a **1000** THORPE *Laws* I. 190 Gif ceorl hæfde fif hida aȝenes landes, cirican and cycenan, bellhus, & burhȝeat-setl & sunder note on cynȝes healle. **1680** *Jani Anglorum Fac. Nova* 32 What in Ancient time made a Churl..become a Theyn or Noble..was five hides of his own Land, a Church and a Kitchin, a Bell-house and a Burrough-gate.

burrow (ˈbʌrəʊ), *sb.*[1] Forms: 4 borwȝ, 4–6 borow, 6 boroughe, 6–7 borough, burrowe, bury, 7 burrough(e, 7– burrow, (9 ? *dial.* bury, burry). See also BERRY *sb.*[3] [Of somewhat obscure origin. The forms are identical with those of BOROUGH, of which the word is commonly regarded as a variant; but the sense is not known to have belonged to OE. *burh*, ON. *borg*, or to the parallel form in any Teut. lang. Possibly it may be a special use of BOROUGH 1, stronghold; or else a derivative (unrecorded in OE. and ON.) of *burg- ablaut-stem of OTeut. *bergan to shelter, protect; cf. BURY *v.*, BURIELS. The forms *bury*, BERRY *sb.*[3] may perhaps be connected with BERGH *sb.* protection, shelter.]

1. A hole or excavation made in the ground for a dwelling-place by rabbits, foxes and the like.

c **1360** *Will. Palerne* 9 By-side þe borwȝ þere þe barn was inne. **1382** WYCLIF *Matt.* viii. 20 Foxis han dichis, or borowis, and briddis of the eir han nestis. **1538** LELAND *Itin.* V. 59 There is nothing now but a Fox borow. **1540** *Act 32 Hen. VIII*, xi, Rabettes, in or vpon any bury. **1616** SURFL. & MARKH. *Countr. Farm* 504 The wood Torteise..maketh her borough in the woods. **1669** WORLIDGE *Syst. Agric.* (1681) 173 Leaving places on the sides for the Coneys to draw and make their Stops or Buries. **1759** JOHNSON *Rasselas* 35 The conies which the rain had driven from their burrows. **1832** HT. MARTINEAU *Ella of Gar.* iii. 37 To hunt the puffins out of their burrows in the rock. **1849** MURCHISON *Siluria* iii. 40 The burrows..made by Crustaceans. **1879** JEFFERIES *Wild Life in S.C.* 38 In heavy rain..they [rabbits] generally remain within their buries.

† **b.** A burrowing; any small tubular excavation, or underground passage. *Obs.*

1615 CROOKE *Body of Man* 607 The burroughes [of the internal ear] in their inward superficies are inuested with a very soft and fine membrane. **1662** J. CHANDLER *Van Helmont's Oriat.* 82 Fiery Mines or Burroughs.

2. *transf.* and *fig.* A secluded or small hole-like dwelling-place, or place of retreat; a 'hole'.

1650 WELDON *Crt. Jas. I* (1651) 44 This fellow knew his Burrough well enough. **1790** BOSWELL *Johnson* (1816) III. 409 The chief advantage of London is, that a man is always so near his burrow. **1835** SIR J. ROSS *N.-W. Pass.* xxix. 408 A fresh breeze made our burrow colder than was agreeable. **1848** MACAULAY *Hist. Eng.* II. 130 Within a few miles of Dublin, the traveller..saw..the miserable burrows out of which squalid..barbarians stared wildly.

3. *Comb.*, as † **burrow-headed** *a.*, ? given to searching things out, inquisitive, curious (*obs.*).

1650 B. *Discolliminium* 17 Over-brain'd Burrow-headed Men, restlesse in studying new things.

ˈburrow, *sb.*[2] *dial.* or *techn.* Forms: 5 boroughe, burgh, 7 borough, 7– burrow. See also BARROW *sb.*[1] [The form taken in some parts of Engl., esp. Cornwall, by the OE. *beorȝ*, ME. *berȝ*, *berw*, *borȝ*, *borw*, *burgh* hill, of which the more general representative is BARROW *sb.*[1], and a by-form BERRY *sb.*[2], q.v.]

A heap or mound; in earlier use a hillock; now, *esp.* a heap of refuse made in mining or beat-burning. See *beat-borough* under BEAT *sb.*[3]

885–1393 [see BARROW *sb.*[1]]. **1480** *Robt. Devyll* 20 Farre from boroughe or hyll. **1483** CAXTON *Gold. Leg.* 314/1 This holy man sawe upon the burgh on the ground the deuyls makyng joye. **1602** CAREW *Cornwall* 19 b, Before ploughing time, they scatter abroad those Beat-boroughs..upon the ground. *Ibid.* (1723) 148 a, One Gidly..digged downe a little hillocke, or Borough. **1663** CHARLETON *Chor. Gigant.* 39 Those Tumuli, or (as we call them) Burrows. **1696** C. MERRET in *Phil. Trans.* XIX. 351 Hills..called Burrows.. supposed to be Sepulchral Monuments. **1784** TWAMLEY *Dairying* 125 Prepare a burrow of soil..from old Turf. **1875** URE *Dict. Arts* I. 550 *Burrow*, a miner's term for a heap of rubbish. **1880** *East Cornw. Gloss.* (E.D.S.) *Burrow*, a mound or heap; a sepulchral tumulus. *Beat-burrow*, a heap of burnt turves.

ˈburrow, *sb.*[3] *dial.* [:—OE. *beorȝ*, *beorh* fem. (only in compounds), *ȝebeorh* neut. ME. *bergh*, shelter, f. *beorȝan* to shelter, BERGH.] Shelter.

1577 HARRISON *England* I. II. xxiv. 358 Enclosed burrowes where their legions accustomed..to winter. *Ibid.* 360 The boroughs or buries were certeine plots of ground, whereon the Roman souldiers did use to lie, when they kept in the open field. **1609** HOLLAND *Amm. Marcell.* XVIII. vi. 114 Flat levell and plaine fields not able to affoord us..any borough to shelter us [*latibula præbere sufficiens*]. **1867** *Leisure Hour* 352 Where there has been convenient shelter or burrow, as it is called in Oxfordshire, from the wind.

† **ˈburrow**, *sb.*[4] *Obs.* Another form of BOROUGH, BURGH. Used also in plural for the Burgesses, or representatives of the Burghs or 'Commonalty' in the Scottish parliament. Cf. BURGESS.

1634–46 Row *Hist. Kirk* (1842) 135 Many commissioners being assembled, they were parted in three, barrons, burrowes, ministers. **1642** *Declar. Lords & Comm. to Gen. Ass. Ch. Scot., Lond.* 10 The Nobility, Gentry, Burrowes, Ministers and Commons. **1650** Row (son) *Hist. Kirk* (1842) 486 The gentrie by themselves, the burrows by themselves.

† **ˈburrow**, *sb.*[5] *Obs.* Another form of BURR *sb.*[1], BROUGH; a circle of light about the moon.

1499 *Promp. Parv.*, Burrowe [**1440** Burwhe, sercle], *orbiculus*. **1656** DUGARD *Gate Lang. Unl.* vi. (1659) §64 A circle (Burrow) about the moon foresheweth wet..weather.

burrow (ˈbʌrəʊ), *v.*[1] [f. BURROW *sb.*[1]]

1. *intr.* Of animals: To make a burrow or small excavation, *esp.* as a hiding- or dwelling-place.

1771 BARRINGTON in *Phil. Trans.* LXII. 10 They.. burrow under ground. **1796** MORSE *Amer. Geog.* I. 218 Their dens which they [alligators] form by burrowing far under ground. **1828** STARK *Elem. Nat. Hist.* II. 307 The larvæ burrow in the wood. **1831** SOUTHEY *Lit. Bk. in Green & G.* Wks. X. 380 Worms..Burrowing safely in thy side.

b. *fig.* To lodge as in a burrow, hide oneself.

1614 T. ADAMS *Divell's Banq.* 47 These Monsters are in the Wildernesse! No they borough in Sion. **1640** BASTWICK *Lord Bps.* vi. F ij, These Lordly Prelates..will not suffer any one..to burrow within their Diocese. *a* **1848** MARRYAT *R. Reefer* vii, We were forced to burrow in mean lodgings. **1884** W. C. SMITH *Kildrostan* 95 Some dim cave where he [an anchorite] had burrowed With bats and owls.

c. *fig.* To bore, penetrate, or make one's way under the surface; also ***to burrow one's way***.

1804 ABERNETHY *Surg. Observ.* 169, I have known many diseases which burrow. **1831** BREWSTER *Newton* (1855) II. xxiv. 340 To burrow for heresy among the obscurities of thought. **1836–9** TODD *Cycl. Anat. & Phys.* II. 637/1 The ulcer..as it burrows deeply..may perforate the muscular wall. **1851** GLADSTONE *Glean.* VI. xliii. 29 Each local body has to find, I should say rather to burrow its own way. **1859** HAWTHORNE *Fr. & It. Jrnls.* II. 260 We were burrowing through its bewildering passages.

2. a. *refl.* with *passive pple.*: To hide away in, or as in, a burrow.

1602 WARNER *Alb. Eng.* IX. li. 233 These lie burrowed, safe from skath. **1807** CRABBE *Par. Reg.* I. 221 An infant.. Left by neglect, and burrowed in that bed. **1837** CARLYLE *Fr. Rev.* II. v. v. 282 A blustering Effervescence, of brawlers and spouters, which, at the flash of chivalrous broadswords ..will burrow itself in dens.

b. *trans.* With *into*. To sink or 'bury' (one's head, etc.) in. Cf. BURY *v.* 4 a.

1915 J. BUCHAN *39 Steps* iii. 61 He swung his heels up on the seat, and burrowed a frowsy head into the cushions. **1982** T. KENEALLY *Schindler's Ark* ii. 53 The other Jews in the office bowed their heads and burrowed their eyes into worksheets.

3. *trans.* To construct by burrowing, to excavate.

1831 *Q. Rev.* XLIV. 357 Most of their habitations were wretched cabins..burrowed in the sides of the mountains.

†**'burrow**, *v.*² *Obs. rare*⁻¹. [f. BURROW *sb.*³, or var. of BERGH *v.*] *trans.* To protect, to shelter.

1657 AUSTEN *Fruit Trees* I. 116 Hills, houses or such like, to burrow or shelter it from the North..winds.

burrow-duck. [f. BURROW *sb.*¹ (or ? possibly *sb.*², in sense 'sand-hill'; cf. BURRANET) + DUCK. The bird makes its nest in rabbit-burrows or in sand-hills on the sea-shore.] The Sheldrake or Bergander, *Anas tadorna.*

1678 RAY *Willughby's Ornith.* 363 They are called by some, Burrow-Ducks, because they build in Coney-burroughs. **1709** DERHAM in *Phil. Trans.* XXVI. 466 The Sheldrake, or Burrough-Duck. **1841** *Penny Cycl.* XXI. 371/1 Sheldrake..called in different parts of Britain Bargander, St. George's Duck, Burrow Duck, and Burrough Duck, etc.

burrower ('bʌrəʊə(r)). [f. BURROW *v.*¹ + -ER¹.] An animal or person that burrows. (*lit.* and *fig.*)

1854 WOODWARD *Mollusca* (1856) 241 The boring shell-fish have been distinguished from the mere burrowers. **1862** *Lond. Rev.* 16 Aug. 142 The shrewdest burrower after facts. **1874** LUBBOCK *Orig. & Met. Ins.* ii. 29 The larvæ of Sirex being wood-burrowers. **1883** G. ALLEN in *Knowledge* 22 June 367/2 [Shrews and moles] are..most of them burrowers.

burrowing ('bʌrəʊɪŋ), *vbl. sb.* [f. as prec. + -ING¹.] The action of BURROW *v.*¹ Also *attrib.*

1771 BARRINGTON in *Phil. Trans.* LXII. 4 Its property of burrowing. **1836–9** TODD *Cycl. Anat. & Phys.* II. 161/2 With reference to its burrowing habits.

'burrowing, *ppl. a.* [f. as prec. + -ING².] That burrows. **burrowing owl**, an American species of owl (*Noctua cunicularia*) dwelling in burrows made by itself, or by other animals.

1757 DYER *Fleece* I. 36 Where the burrowing rabbit turns the dust. **1808** HOME in *Phil. Trans.* XCVIII. 307 The mole, or other burrowing animals. **1842** *Penny Cycl.* XXIII. 121/2 The well-known burrowing little owl. **1870** HOOKER *Stud. Flora* 40 *Crambe maritima*..Rootstock..burrowing.

†**'burrow-mail.** *Sc. Obs.* [f. BURROW⁴ + MAIL tribute.] 'The annual duty payable to the sovereign by a burgh for the enjoyment of certain rights' (Jamieson).

1424 *Sc. Acts Jas. I* (1597) §8 All the greate and smal customes, and burrow-mailles of the Realme, abide and remaine with the King till his living. *c* **1550** SIR J. BALFOUR *Practicks* (1754) 46 He sall faithfullie pay to the King his burrow-maill. **1617** *Sc. Acts Jas. VI.* (1816) 579 (JAM.) His Majesties burgh off Abirdene..doted with ampill priuiledges and immunityes for the yeirlie payment of the soume of tua hundereth threttene pundis sex schillingis aucht pennyes of borrow maill.

burrows-town ('bʌrəstaʊn). Only *Sc.* exc. in Ormin. Forms: 3 (*Orm.*) **burrȝhess tun**, 4 **burwis toun**, 5–8 **borrows-town**, 6 **burous-toun**, **borous-, borroustoun**, **burrowistown**, 9 **burrows-town** (cf. proper name *Borrowston-ness* or *Bo'ness*). = BOROUGH-TOWN. Also *attrib.*

c **1200** ORMIN 6538 þatt illke burrȝhess tun þatt Crist wass borenn inne. *c* **1325** *Metr. Hom.* 107 Burwis tounes war tharinne. *c* **1450** HENRYSON *Twa Mice*, The elder dwelt in borrows town. **1548** *Compl. Scot.* 87 ȝour feildis, villagis and buroustounis. *a* **1649** *Sc. Acts Charles I* (1814) VI. 142 (JAM.) Borrowstoun kirks being alwayes excepted. **1724** RAMSAY *Tea-T. Misc.* (1733) I. 92 The brawest beau in borrows-town. **1816** SCOTT *Antiq.* xxvi, 'Ou ay, hinny—thae's your landward and burrows-town notions'.

'burr-pump, 'bur-pump. *Naut.* [f. BUR, or BURR *sb.*¹ + PUMP.] A form of bilge-pump with the piston so constructed as not to require a valve: see quot.

1627 CAPT. SMITH *Seaman's Gram.* ii. 8 A Bur Pump. The Dutch men vse a Burre pumpe..wherein is onely a long staffe with a Burre at the end, like a Gunners spunge, to pumpe vp the Billage water that..cannot come to the well. **1688** R. HOLME *Armoury* III. 297/2 The Bur-Pump, or Bildge-Pump..The maner of these are to have a staffe 6, 7 or 8 foot long with a Bur of wood, where unto the Leather is nailed, this serveth in stead of a Box. And so two men standing over the Pump do thrust down this staffe, to the middle whereof is fastned a rope 6, 8, or 10 to hale by, and so they pull it up and down. **1678–1706** in PHILLIPS. **1721–90** in BAILEY. **1755** JOHNSON, *Burr Pump.* **1867** SMYTH *Sailor's Word-bk.*, *Burr-pump*, a name for the bilge-pump. **1874** KNIGHT *Dict. Mech.* I. 412 *Burr-pump*,..in which a cup-shaped cone of leather is nailed by a disk (burr) on the end of a pump-rod, the cone collapsing as it is depressed, and expanding by the weight of the column of water as it is raised.

burr-stone ('bɜːstəʊn). Also buhr-, burrh-, bur-. [f. BURR *sb.*⁵ + STONE.] A siliceous rock of coarse cellular texture, found chiefly in France and N. America, and used for millstones; a piece of this rock.

1690 *Lond. Gaz.* No. 2538/4 Her Loading, consisting of about 750 Burr Stones. **1708** *Ibid.* 4501/4 A Pink..with her Cargo, consisting in Burstone, Lime, and Glasses for Windows. **1821** *Edin. Philos. Jrnl.* IV. 246 Particular account of the recently discovered Buhrstone. **1840** HUMBLE *Dict. Geol. & Min.* (1843) 35 The substance of burrh-stone, or mill-stone, when unmixed is pure silex. **1850** LYELL *2nd Visit U.S.* II. 9 This burr-stone..constitutes one of the members of the Eocene group.

burru ('buru). *Jamaica.* Also buro. [Perh. ad. Twi *búru* filthiness, sluttishness or Yoruba *buru* wicked.] A kind of vigorous, popular, and sometimes indecent, dance; the music, esp. drumming, used to accompany this.

1929 C. MCKAY *Banjo* II. ix. 105 They played the 'beguin,' which was just a Martinique variant of the 'jelly-roll' or the Jamaican 'burru' or the Senegalese 'bombé.' **1940**, etc. in Cassidy & Le Page *Dict. Jamaican Eng.* (1980). **1983** DAVIS & SIMON *Reggae Internat.* ii. 26 (*caption*) Ras Michael and the Sons of Negus, legatees of the ancient burru drumming tradition.

burry ('bɜːrɪ), *a.*¹ [f. BUR *sb.* + -Y¹.]

1. a. Full of burs (see BUR *sb.*). **b.** Of the nature of a bur; rough, prickly.

1468 *Medulla Gram.* in *Cath. Angl.* 48 *Lappetum*, a burry place. **1597** GERARD *Herbal* I. xxx. §2. 41 They bring foorth their burrie bullets..in August. **1676** T. GLOVER in *Phil. Trans.* II. 629 Another [nut]..like a Chesnut, with a Burry husk. **1737** MILLER *Gard. Dict.* (1768) I. 4 Seeds armed with three burry prickles. **1865** *Times* 13 Feb., Wool..gray, 2½*d.* to 5*d.*, burry and refuse, ½*d.* to 6*d.*

†**2.** Shaggy, rough. *Obs.*

c **1450** HENRYSON in *Bannatyne Poems* 109 (JAM.) That he [the sheep]..heir quhat burry Dog wald say him till.

burry ('bɜːrɪ), *a.*² [f. BURR *sb.*⁶ + -Y¹.] Characterized by a burr or uvular trill.

1866 *Chamb. Jrnl.* 793 Their language was..so extra burry as to be nearly unintelligible.

burry, dial. form of BURROW *sb.*¹

burryn, -yon, obs. ff. of BURGEON.

‖**bursa** ('bɜːsə). Pl. **bursæ**. [med.L. *bursa* bag, purse, a. Gr. βύρσα hide, wine-skin.]

1. *Phys.* (more fully ***bursa mucosa***): 'A synovial sac of discoidal form interposed between muscles, tendons, or skin, and bony prominences, for the purpose of lessening friction'. *Syd. Soc. Lex.* 1880. Some of these are constant, some only occasional.

1803 *Med. Jrnl.* X. 69 While engaged in dissecting the bursæ mucosæ of the human body, I discovered two new bursæ on the knee. **1811** HOOPER *Med. Dict.* 131/2 A bursa of the superior oblique muscle of the eye. **1878** T. BRYANT *Pract. Surg.* I. 175 When a bursa has formed it may inflame or suppurate. **1880** *Syd. Soc. Lex.* s.v., The occasional bursæ are generally developed as the result of unusual friction.

2. See quot. (Cf. BURSE 7.)

1852 SIR W. HAMILTON *Discuss.* 407 In Germany..the name of Bursa was given to houses inhabited by students, under the superintendence of a Graduate in Arts.

bursal ('bɜːsəl), *a.* [f. prec. + -AL¹.]

1. *Phys.* Pertaining to, or of the nature of, a bursa (see BURSA 1).

1751 *Phil. Trans.* XLVII. xxxvii. 261 The bursal and crucial ligaments..were..in their natural order. **1878** T. BRYANT *Pract. Surg.* I. 176 Bursal swellings.

2. (See BURSA 2.)

[**1753** CHAMBERS *Cycl. Supp.* s.v., Bursa is more particularly used in middle age writers for a little college or hall in an university, for the residence of students, called bursales, or bursarii.] **1852** SIR W. HAMILTON *Discuss.* (1853) 24 *note*, Occupiers of the same bursal room.

3. Pertaining to the public revenue.

1837 CARLYLE *Fr. Rev.* I. I. III. iv. 64 Quite another sort of Edicts, namely 'bursal' or fiscal ones.

bur'salogy. More correctly bursology. [f. BURSA + Gr. -λογία (see -LOGY).] The doctrine or consideration of the *bursae mucosae.*

1811 HOOPER *Med. Dict.* **1860** MAYNE *Exp. Lex.*

bursar ('bɜːsə(r)). Forms: 6 bursor, 6–8 burser, 8 bourser, boursar, 7– bursar. [ad. med.L. *bursārius*, f. BURSA; cf. F. *boursier* used in senses 1 and 2.]

1. A treasurer, *esp.* of a college.

1587 HARRISON *England* II. iii. 82 In ech of these [colleges]..they haue one or moe thresurers whom they call Bursarios or bursers. **1587** FLEMING *Contn. Holinshed* III. 1361/2 A bursor or paiemaster for those wars. **1695** KENNETT *Par. Antiq.* Gloss. s.v. *Bursaria*, The conventual bursar was to deliver up his accounts yearly on the day after Michael-mas. **1706** HEARNE *Collect.* (1885) I. 198 He..continu'd Bourser of yᵉ College several years together. **1868** M. PATTISON *Academ. Org.* iv. 109 Each college has one or more bursars who administer the finances.

2. In Scotch universities and schools: A student or scholar who holds a bursary, an exhibitioner.

1567 *Sc. Acts Jas. VI* (1597) §12 Al Patronis hauand Provestries, or Prebendaries of Colleges, Alterages or Chaplaneries, at their giftis and dispositioun, may..present the samin to Bursaris, quhom they pleise to name, to studie vertew & letteris, within ane College of ony of the Vniuersiteis of this Realme. **1634–46** ROW *Hist. Kirk* (1842) Introd. 20 Quhairby a burser might be intertened at the New Colledge of Santandrous. **1787** BEATTIE *Scotticisms* 16. **1856** J. GRANT *Black Drag.* xxxii, A bursar fresh from Glasgow College. **1876** GRANT *Burgh Sch. Scotl.* II. 497 Three bursaries..at the grammar School of Banff, each bursar receiving free education and £2 10 0 yearly for maintenance.

3. A student in a 'bursa' (see BURSA 2).

1852 SIR W. HAMILTON *Discuss.* 408 The rector..repeated with his bursars their public lessons.

bursarial (bɜː'sɛərɪəl), *a.* [f. med.L. *bursāri-us* + -AL¹.] Belonging to a bursar or a bursary.

1862 *Sat. Rev.* XIV. 255/2 Careful in all bursarial and presidential matters. **1882** *Oxford under Purit.* in *Q. Rev.* Oct. 492 The Fellow being engaged in tutorial or bursarial work. **1886** *Athenæum* 17 July 80/1 A central bursarial power.

bursarship ('bɜːsəʃɪp). [f. BURSAR + -SHIP.] **a.** The office of a bursar. **b.** = BURSARY 3.

a **1656** HALES *Gold. Rem.* 276 (L.) Not the plotting of an headship..but the contriving of a bursership of twenty nobles a year. **1864** *Athenæum* No. 1921. 244/3 A few bursarships. **1878** LECKY *England in 18th Cent.* II. v. 35 Burnet..showed his gratitude by founding eight bursarships in his will.

bursary ('bɜːsərɪ). [ad. med.L. *bursārius* treasurer, *bursāria* treasurer's room; see BURSAR.]

†**1.** ? = BURSAR 1. *Obs.*

1538 LELAND *Itin.* III. 68 Certen Bursaries, Ministers and Choristes.

2. A treasury; the bursar's room in a college, etc.

1695 KENNETT *Par. Antiq.* Gloss. s.v. *Bursaria*, The bursary, or place of receiving and paying money and rents by the *bursarii*, bursars, or officers of account in religious houses. **1732** DE FOE *Tour Gt. Brit.* (1769) II. 244 In the Bursary [of New College, Oxford] is shewn the Crosier of the Founder. **1736** NEAL *Hist. Purit.* III. 429 The Bursaries were emptied of the public money.

3. (orig. in Scotland.) An endowment given to a student in a university or school, an exhibition. Also, in extended use, an endowment to persons other than students.

1733 P. LINDSAY *Interest Scot.* 124 To procure a Bursary for this hopeful Boy. **1800** A. CARLYLE *Autobiog.* 62 The bursaries given..to students in divinity to pass two winters in Glasgow College, and a third in some foreign university. **1850** DE QUINCEY in H. Page *De Quincey* (1877) II. xvii. 74 Such small 'bursaries' or 'exhibitions,' as the Scottish college system offers. **1907** *Act 7 Edward VII* c. 43 §11 The powers and duties of a local education authority..shall include a power to aid by scholarships or bursaries the instruction in public elementary schools of scholars from the age of twelve up to the limit of age fixed. **1910** *Encycl. Brit.* IV. 863/1 *Bursar*..is also applied to the holder of 'a bursary'..in England a scholarship or exhibition enabling a pupil of an elementary school to continue his education at a secondary school. **1943** *Hansard* (Canada) 1 Mar. 787/1 A third field to which the committee should give some consideration is that of providing federal bursaries and scholarships at both secondary school and university levels. **1955** *Times* 10 May 12/4 This bursary has been awarded to a playwright or producer in order to enable him to make a study of the theatre.

‖**bursch** (bʊrʃ). Pl. burschen. [Ger. *bursch, bursche*, fellow-student, young fellow:—MHG. *burse*, a. L. *bursa* = BURSA 2, whence the sense passed in university slang to a student living in a bursa. See Grimm, Kluge.] A student in a German university. Hence **burschenism**, *nonce-wd.*, the manner and customs of the burschen.

1830 CARLYLE *Richter, Misc.* (1857) II. 138 *note*, Burschenism is not without its meaning, more than Oxfordism or Cambridgeism. The Bursch strives to say in the strongest language he can: 'See! I am an unmoneyed scholar, and a free man'.

burse (bɜːs). Also 6 burss(e, (6–7 buss), 7 burs, burze, byrse. [a. F. *bourse* purse, wallet:—med.L. *bursa*, a. Gr. βύρσα hide, wine-skin. The history of sense 3, and its F. form *bourse*, is doubtful, but apparently it did *not* originate in any reference to the money business there transacted.]

I. 1. A purse: now the designation of one of the official insignia of the Lord High Chancellor of England.

1570 LEVINS *Manip.* 191 A Burse, *bursa.* **1863** BARING-GOULD *Iceland* 239 An ancient crimson velvet burse.

b. *Eccl.* A receptacle for the 'corporal' or linen cloth used to cover the elements in the Eucharist.

1844 LINGARD *Anglo-Saxon Ch.* (1858) II. ix. 70 A burse to hold the linen for the altar. **1866** *Direct. Angl.* (ed. 3) 352 Burse, the case for the corporal.

†**2.** A purse-like sac or covering. *Obs.*

1601 HOLLAND *Pliny* I. 395 The burse or cod wherin this woollie substance lyes. *Ibid.* XXXII. ii. (R.) A twofold burse or skin, which no living creature hath besides.

II. In commerce.

†**3.** A meeting-place of merchants for transaction of business; an Exchange. *Obs.* (See BOURSE.)

[According to Guicciardini and Catel (quoted in Chambers *Cycl. Supp.* 1753), the name arose at Bruges, from the sign of a purse, or three purses, on the front of the house which the merchants there bought to meet in: some say this was the arms of the former owners, the family *Bursa* or *de la Bourse*. Others assign the circumstance to Antwerp. See Chambers *Cycl. Supp.* 1753, Littré (*Supp.*, and *Additions*), *Notes & Queries* 1st Ser. I. 74, etc. All the accounts agree as to the sign of a purse or purses.]

1553 EDEN *Treat. New Ind.* 25 Whether the marchauntes..haue their continual recourse as to yᵉ burse or strete. **1580** LYLY *Euphues* 434 It [London] hath..a gorgious Burse which they call the Ryoll Exchaung. **1598** BARCKLEY *Felic. Man* v. (1603) 540 Socrates walking in the Bursse or Market

place. **1638** L. ROBERTS *Merch. Map Commerce* clxxxi, This citie [Bruges] hath an eminent market place with a publicke house for the meeting of all Marchants..called the Burse, of ..the extinct familie Bursa, bearing three purses for their armes, ingraven upon their houses, from whence these meeting places to this day are called Burses. **1721–33** STRYPE *Eccl. Mem.* II. I. 327 In the burse of Antwerp money was never so scanty. **1732** DE FOE *Tour Gt. Brit.* (1769) II. 110 The Royal Exchange is the greatest Burse in the World.

†**b.** ***the Burse***: (spec.) the Royal Exchange in London, built by Sir Thomas Gresham in 1566. ***Britain's Burse***: the New Exchange in the Strand, built by the Earl of Salisbury in 1609, afterwards known as Exeter 'Change, on the site of the present Exeter Hall. In both of these there were shops, allusions to which are frequent. *Obs.*

1570 *Churchw. Acc. St. Margarets, Westminister* (Nicholls 1797) 18 When the Queens Majesty went to the Bursse. **1597** J. PAYNE *Royal Exch.* 12 Our soueraigne Ladie in abolishing the fyrst title (Buss)..had prudent consideration to tearme yt the exchange. **1611** DEKKER & MIDDLETON *Roar. Girl* Wks. 1873 III. 196 She says, she went to the burse for patterns. **1625** *Diff. East. & West Churches*, Title-page, To be sold at the signe of the Windmill in Britain's Burse. **1632** MASSINGER *City Madam* III. i. (Nares) A coach ..To hurry me to the Burse, or Old Exchange. **1640** GLAPTHORNE *Wit in Constab.* I, She has been at Britain's burse a buying pins and needles. **1653** A. WILSON *Jas. I*, 48 A goodly Fabrick, Rival to the Old Exchange which the King..dignified with the name of Britain's Burse. **1720** *Stow's Surv.* (ed. Strype 1754) II. VI. i. 577/2 It pleased his Majesty..to intitle it Britain's Burse or Buss.

†**c.** *fig. Obs.*

1617 COLLINS *Def. Bp. Ely* II. x. 441 The whores factors would faine drawe customers to her burse of bawderies. **1634** J. TAYLOR (Water-P.) *Gt. Eater Kent* 11 His guts are the rendezvous or meeting-place or burse for the beasts of the fields, the fowles of the ayre, and fishes of the sea. **1636** FITZGEFFREY *Blessed Birthd.* (1881) 150 O royall change for vs, o blessed Burse, Where man the blessing gets, God takes the curse!

†**4.** ? A shop. *Obs.*

a **1661** HOLYDAY *Juvenal* 4 Five burses [*tabernæ*] which I let, adde to my store Four hundred sesterces.

III. In French and Scotch universities.

†**5.** A fund or foundation to provide bursaries.

1695 KENNETT *Par. Antiq.* Gloss. s.v. *Bursaria*, Formerly all exhibitioners..at Paris were called bursars, as they lived on the burs, or fund, or endowment of founders and benefactors..Which *bursarii* were most properly those novices or young scholars, who were sent to the university, and maintained by the religious out of their public burs, or stock. **1753** CHAMBERS *Cycl. Supp.*, *Bursa, Burse*, or *Bourse*, in the French universities, still denotes a foundation for the maintenance of poor scholars in their studies.

6. = BURSARY 3.

1560 *1st Bk. Discipl.* v. (1836) 34 They must have the priviledges in schooles, and bursis in colledges. **1579** *Sc. Acts Jas. VI* (1814) 179 (JAM.) Nane sall bruik ane burss in ony facultie bot for the space of foure yeiris. **1677** in Spottiswood *Hist. Ch. Scotl.* App. 26 Inviting young Scholars to come and dispute for a Burse, (which is their maintenance at the Colledge). **1779** in Grant *Burgh Sch. Scotl.* II. v. 210 In 1779 the council of Aberdeen enacted that no boy who has..competed for a 'burse', shall receive premium.

7. A college, or academic hall. See BURSA 2.

1577 tr. *Bullinger's Decades* (1592) 1114 Samuel..was gouernour and principal of Naioth, that is to say ye Burse (as they terme it) or College of Prophetes. *c* **1840** SIR W. HAMILTON *Log.* App. II. 374 *note*, The..Masters Regent in the Burse (or College) of St. Lawrence, in Cologne.

burser, -or, obs. forms of BURSAR.

†**burseu, bursew.** *Obs.* A dish in cookery.

c **1400** *Forme of Cury* 5 Burseu [Warner *Antiq. Culin.* prints *bursen*]..Take noumbles of swyne, and parboyle hem in broth and wyne, etc. *Ibid.* 32 (Mätz.) *Bursews*, Take pork, seeth it, and grynde it smale, etc.

bursiculate (bɜːˈsɪkjʊlət), *a. Bot.* and *Anat.* [ad. mod.L. *bursiculatus*, f. *bursicula*, dim. of L. *bursa* purse.] Resembling a purse or pouch; bursiform.

1880 in WEBSTER Suppl. **1957** SNELL & DICK *Gloss. Mycology* 23/1 Bursiculate, purselike; pouchlike.

bursiform (ˈbɜːsɪfɔːm), *a.* [ad. mod.L. *bursiformis*, f. BURSA purse: see -FORM.] Purse-shaped.

1836 TODD *Cycl. Anat. & Phys.* I. 518/1 *note*, The Cephalopods of the Foraminiferous Order have a bursiform body. **1872** NICHOLSON *Palæont.* 119 Cup-shaped, pyriform, bursiform, or discoidal.

bursitis (bɜːˈsaɪtɪs). *Path.* [mod.L., f. BURSA + -ITIS.] Inflammation of a bursa.

1857 DUNGLISON *Med. Lex.*, *Synovitis*... When it affects the bursæ it is sometimes called Bursitis. **1908** *Practitioner* June 865 Myositis, phlebitis, bursitis. **1950** R. A. WILLIS *Princ. Path.* xii. 138 The traumatic pre-patellar bursitis known as 'housemaid's knee'.

burst (bɜːst), *v.* Pa. t. and pple. burst. Forms: α. (type *berst, burst*) 1 berstan, 3 bersten, (bursten), 4–5 berst(e, 5–6 barst, 6– burst. β. (type *brest, brast, brust*) 3–5 bresten, 4–5 breste, 4–6 brest, briste, (4 brusten), 5 bruste, 5–6 brust, bryste, brast, 6 braste, 9 *dial.* and *arch.* brast. *Pa. t.* α. 1 bærst, 3 bearst, 4 berst, 3 barste, 5–6 barst, 6– burst, (8–9 *incorrectly* bursted). β. 3–7 brast, 4–6 braste, brest, 5 breste, (6 brust, brusted), 9 *dial.* and *arch.* brast. *pl.* α. 1 burston, 2–4 burste(n, 4–5 borsten, 5–6 barst, 6– burst. *Pa. pple.* α. 1 borsten, 4–5 borsten, -un, 5 burstyn, (borsen, 6 *Sc.* bursin), 6–8 bursten, 6– burst, (8–9 *incorrectly* bursted, 9 *Sc.* bursen). β. 4–5 brosten, brusten, (4 brost, brast), 6 brasten, 6–7 brast, brust, 9 *arch.* brast, (9 *north. dial.* brossen, brosen). [(1) A Common Teut. strong vb.: OE. *berstan* (pa. t. *bærst, burston*, pple. *borsten*) = OFris. *bersta*, OS. *brestan* (*brast, bruston*; *brostan*), (MDu., Du. *berstan, barsten*, LG. *barsten, basten*), OHG. *brestan* (MHG. *brestan*, Ger. *bersten* from LG.), ON. *bresta*, (*brast, brustum*; *brostinn*), (Sw. *brista*, Da. *briste*):—OTeut. **brestan*, possibly from **brek-st-an*, a derivative (intensive) of *brek-an* to BREAK[2].

(2) The earlier *brest-* of WGer. became by metathesis *berst-* in OE., Frisian, Du., and LG. (whence also it has passed into mod.Ger. in place of MHG. *brest-*). In Eng. this *berst-* mostly again became *brest-* in ME., partly perh. under Norse influence, whence the pa. pple. *brosten* still, in north. dial.; but this has since the 16th c. gone back to *berst*, changed by the disturbing influence of *r* to *burst*. So that we have the alternate series OTeut. and WGer. *brest-*, OE. *berst-*, ME. *brest*, mod.Eng. *berst, burst*. But the 15–16th c. had often *brust* and *brast, barst* in the present; and the north. dial. had *brist, bryst*, as in Danish.

(3) The original strong conjugation survived during the ME. period, with the typical forms, after metathesis, *bresten, brast, brosten*, but with much disturbance and mixture of forms in 14–15th c. In the 16th c. a very common form was *brast* for all the principal parts; but about the end of that century, *burst* (for all the parts) began to gain the ascendancy which it has since maintained, though the pa. t. was frequently *brast* in 17th and the pa. pple. *bursten* till 18th c. Various old forms survive dialectally, and in U.S. the pa. t. and pple. are frequently *bursted*, vulgarly *busted*.]

I. *intr.* To break or be broken suddenly.

†**1. a.** To break suddenly, snap, crack, under violent pressure, strain, or concussion. Chiefly said of things possessing considerable capacity for resistance and breaking with loud noise; often of cords, etc., snapping under tension; also of spears, swords, etc., shivered in battle. *Obs.*

α. *a* **1000** *Beowulf* 818 Burston ban locan. *a* **1000** *Byrhtnoð* 284 (Gr.) Bærst bordes lærig. **1297** R. GLOUC. 460 Atte laste þoru stronge duntes hys suerd berst atuo. **1413** LYDG. *Pylgr. Sowle* v. xi. (1483) 102 Then enforcid hym soo sore to the weyght tyll the cordys borsten of the balaunce. *a* **1593** MARLOWE *Dido* IV. iv, Was it not you [the tacklings of a ship] that hoised up these sails? Why burst you not? **1718** POPE *Iliad* XV. 545 As the tough string he drew, Struck by an arm unseen, it burst in two.

β. **1340** HAMPOLE *Pr. Consc.* 7014 Als smyths strykes on þe yren fast, Swa þat it brekes and brestes at þe last. *c* **1430** *Syr Generides* 44 8 The helm went of also, The laces brast even a twoo. **1566** ADLINGTON *Apuleius* 7 The rope being olde & rotten brast in the middle & I fell down. **1577** HOLINSHED *Chron.* III. 809/1 There was good running and manie a speare brast. **1803** W. ROSE *Amadis* 136 Brast each strong lance.

†**b.** Of ships: To go to pieces. *Obs.*

1513 BRADSHAW *St. Werburgh* (1848) 193 Incontinently the ship barst all in sondre. **1523** LD. BERNERS *Froiss.* I. ccclvi. 574 Thre of their shyppes brast and went to wrake.

†**c.** Of persons, in fig. phrase 'it is better to bow than to burst'. Also: To perish (by hunger).

a **1440** *Ipomydon* 1722 Thoughe he shulde for hungre brest. *c* **1450** in *Babees Bk.* (1868) 34 Often tyme it is betere to bowe þan to berst. *c* **1450** HENRYSON *Mor. Fab.* 65 To bow at bidding, and bide not while thou brest.

†**d.** *fig.* To cease, come to an end. Also (in OE.) said of an oath: To be broken. *Obs.*

a **1100** *Laws of K. Edw.* §3 Ʒif þæt ʒeswutelod wære oþþe him að burste.

2. a. Now chiefly of a surface or thing with extended surface: To break suddenly when in a state of tension, to fly asunder or in pieces; to be broken by expansion of the contents. Of persons or animals: often as an imagined consequence of excess in eating or drinking, or of violent exertion. Also *fig.* (chiefly with allusion to the bursting of a bubble); now often colloq. with *up*.

α. **1535** COVERDALE *Bel.* i. 27 This he put in ye Dragons mouth and so ye dragon barst in sonder. **1562** J. HEYWOOD *Prov. & Epigr.* (1867) 90 Thus drinke we..tyll we burst. *a* **1600** HOOKER *Eccl. Pol.* VII. xx. §5 Lest the very entrails of some..should thereat haply burst in sunder. **1709** STEELE *Tatler* No. 40 ¶10 By an Accident of Firing a Piece of Ordnance, it burst, and kill'd 15 or 16 Men. **1713** ADDISON *Guardian* No. 159 His breast heaved as if it would have bursted. **1732** POPE *Ess. Man* I. 90 And now a bubble burst, and now a World! **1774** J. BRYANT *Mythol.* II. 406 If I burst I don't care. I drink with a good will and a safe conscience. **1881** *Daily News* 1 Sept. 3/5 The boilers had not burst.

β. *a* **1300** *Cursor M.* 16505 He brest in tua his buels all, vte at his wambe þai wrang. *c* **1340** *Gaw. & Gr. Knt.* 1166 With such a crakkande kry, as klyffes haden brusten. *a* **1400** *Cov. Myst.* (1841) 232 Myn hed doth ake, as it xolde brest. **1430** LYDG. *Chron. Troy* I. vi, This Bufo ryght anone Through myght ther of brusteth euen a twain. **1526** SKELTON *Magnyf.* 2186 For laughter I am lyke to brast. **1558** KNOX *First Blast* (Arb.) 40 Let them blowe til they brust. **1591** SPENSER *Bellay's Vis.* vi, Poyson..Made him to swell, that nigh his bowells brust. **1865** B. BRIERLEY *Irkdale* I. 12 Bring me another pint afore I brast wi' thinking. **1865** SWINBURNE *Masque Q. Bersabe* 16 He [a bird]..suddenly woxe big and brast.

b. Said of boils, tumours etc.: To break the outer covering and discharge the matter. Of a bud: To break the envelope, open out. Of a cloud: To disperse in heavy rain (often *fig.*).

c **1000** *Sax. Leechd.* I. 272 [Leʒe þysse wyrte leaf] to þam sare hyt sceal berstan and halian. **1547–64** BAULDWIN *Mor. Philos.* (Palfr.) x. 5 Stop the beginning, so shalt thou be sure All doubtfull diseases to swage and to cure: But if thou be carelesse and suffer them brast, Too late commeth plaister. **1776** WITHERING *Bot. Arrangem.* (1796) I. 360 Two stamens of the *Bryum extinctorium*..one ready to burst. **1807** *Med. Jrnl.* XVII. 9 The sac would go on increasing until it would burst. **1855** TENNYSON *Maud* II. i. 42 The heavens..should burst and drown in deluging storms The feeble vassals of wine and anger and lust. **1885** *Daily News* 16 July 5/2 When the cloud bursts.

†**c.** To break up explosively. *Obs. rare.*

c **1432–50** tr. *Higden* (1865) I. 319 White salte, contrary to the nature of other salte, whiche, beenge soluble in the fyre, brestethe and brekethe in the water.

d. With *up.* To become 'broken' or bankrupt. Cf. BUST *v.*[2] c.

1848 W. ARMSTRONG *Stocks* 9 If any firm or individual does not fulfill his obligations..he is unable to do so, or,.. he has 'burst up'. **1865** DICKENS *Mut. Fr.* III. xii, Then you think, Mrs. Lammle, that if Lammle got time, he wouldn't burst up?—To use an expression..which is adopted in the Money Market.

3. a. Said *hyperbolically*, as a strong expression for 'to be exuberantly full' (cf. 12). Also with *out*.

1563 *Homilies* II. *Serm. Rogation Wk.* (1859) 499 And thy presses shall burst with new wine. **1611** BIBLE *Prov.* iii. 10 Thy presses shall burst out with new wine.

b. Of persons: To be unable to contain oneself. Chiefly in fut., or in phrases ***to be ready to burst, to be bursting***. Const. *with* (information, envy, delight, etc.); also with inf. as 'to be bursting to tell a secret', i.e. with desire to tell it. Cf. 3.

1633 FORD *Broken H.* IV. ii. (1811) 305 Ere I speak a word I will look on and burst. **1649** JER. TAYLOR *Gt. Exemp.* II. xii. 45 The Pharisees could hold no longer, being ready to burst with envy. **1712** STEELE *Spect.* No. 533 ¶2 Ready to burst with shame and indignation. **1732** BERKELEY *Alciphr.* v. §13 One of these tame bullies ready to burst with pride and ill-humour. **1789** WOLCOTT (P. Pindar) *Subj. for Paint.* 65 She bursted with th' important secret soon. **1867** FROUDE *Short Stud.* (1872) I. 2 Most of us when we have hit on something ..original, feel as if we should burst with it. **1884** *West. Morning News* 11 Sept. 4/4 Sir Richard..had been bursting ..to let the news be known.

†**4.** *fig.* Of the heart: To 'break' by the shock or pressure of grief, or by the swelling of emotion.

α. *a* **1225** *Ancr. R.* 80 Hu stout ham þæt beoð..wiðuten hope of vtcome, and heorte ne mei bersten. **1393** GOWER *Conf.* III. 311 Ha, herte, why ne wolt thou berst. **1593** SHAKS. *3 Hen. VI*, V. v. 59 No, no, my heart will burst, and if I speake.

β. *a* **1300** *Cursor M.* 15956 Quen he himself it vnderstod, Almast his hert can brest. *c* **1386** CHAUCER *Frankl. T.* 31 Have here my trouthe, til that myn herte bruste. **1535** FISHER *Wks.* I. 404 Hir harte..for very payne it myght haue brast. **1578** T. PROCTOR *Gorg. Gallery, Lover in Distress, &c.*, O heauy hart..If thou shouldest brast..Then should I dye without reward.

5. Said of a door. Now usually ***to burst open***: to fly open suddenly.

1596 SPENSER *F.Q.* I. viii. 4 No gate so strong, no locke so firme and fast, But with that piercing noise flew open quite, or brast. *Mod.* The door burst open, and a man rushed into the room.

II. intrans. *fig.* (With adverbial extension expressing the nature of the action.)

6. To break forth into sudden activity, or manifestation of an inward force. Of persons: To break out into sudden action or forcible expression of feeling. Usually with *out, forth.*

a. Const. *in, with* (a speech, a cry, or other mode of expression); also *simply*.

α. **1682** DRYDEN *Mac Fl.* 138 Long he stood..At length burst out in this prophetick mood. **1711** ADDISON *Spect.* No. 164 ¶5 She burst out in Tears. **1842** TENNYSON *Dora* 155 And all at once the old man burst in sobs. **1848** W. K. KELLY tr. *L. Blanc's Hist. Ten Y.* I. 560 M. Henri Baud..burst out enthusiastically: 'My father was a common man'.

β. *c* **1450** LONELICH *Grail* lv. 317 Thanne with a swerd he owt braste, that in his hond he held wel faste. **1562** PILKINGTON *On Abdias* 284 They will brast out and declare their faith. **1596** SPENSER *F.Q.* III. iii. 19 The wisard.. brusting forth in laughter, to her sayd. **1869** WAUGH *Yeth-Bobs* ii. 33 He brast eawt again, as if his heart wur breighkin.

b. Formerly with *on*. Often with vbl. sb., ***to burst*** (***out, forth***) ***on weeping***. Afterwards replaced by *a*, as ***to burst out*** (***on***) ***a-laughing, a-crying*** (now *dial.* or *arch.*); the prep. is now omitted in general use: ***to burst out laughing, crying***, etc.

c **1370** *Robt. K. Cicyle* 53 He smote hym..That mowthe and nose braste on blode. **1485** CAXTON *Chas. Gt.* 44 Hys nose breste a blood habundauntly. **1564** HAWARD *Eutropius* VI. 57 Cesar..braste forthe on weepinge to beholde the

heade of so worthye a manne. **1711** Addison *Spect.* No. 90 ¶7 One of the Ladies burst out a laughing. **1825** *Bro. Jonathan* III. 315 He burst out a-crying. **1836** Marryat *Japhet* xxxiii, The remembrance .. made us both burst out a laughing. **1863** H. E. P. Spofford *Amber Gods* 126 The other girls burst out crying at the sight of the coffin. **1875** Jowett *Plato* (ed. 2) I. 84 The crew of his own trireme also burst out laughing.

c. Const. *into*; also, formerly, with infinitive. Often with *out, forth*, e.g. †*to burst* (*out, forth*) *to weep*. In same sense, ***to burst into tears*** (influenced by some notion of 2). So ***to burst*** (*out*) ***into laughter, song, speech***; ***to burst*** (*out*) ***into flame***; of plants, ***to burst*** (*out*) ***into blossom***, etc.

α. **1630** [see 16]. **1637** Milton *Lycidas* 74 When .. we .. think to burst out into sudden blaze. **1709** Steele *Tatler* No. 58 ¶1 The Father burst into the following Words. **1716–8** Lady M. W. Montague *Lett.* I. xxxi. 105 She could not forbear bursting into tears. **1727** Swift *Gulliver* II. viii. 163 Bursting at the same time into a flood of tears. **1802** Bloomfield *Soldier's Home* ii, I .. rose at once, and bursted into tears. **1832** Tennyson *Fatima* v, My heart .. Bursts into blossom in his sight. **1853** *Arab. Nts.* (Rtldg.) 661 The courtiers .. could not avoid bursting into a violent fit of laughter. **1878** Huxley *Physiogr.* 78 The taper will burst again into full flame.

β. *c* **1385** Chaucer *L.G.W.* 1031 With that word he brast out for to wepe. *c* **1400** *Destr. Troy* 9425 Deffibus .. For bale of his brother brest out to wepe. **1528** More *Heresyes* IV. Wks. (1557) 255/2 Thei brast out in vyrulent and venimouse wordes. **1578** Timme *Calvine on Gen.* 132 They bruste forth into manifest rage. **1611** Speed *Hist. Gt. Brit.* IX. viii. (1632) 555 Heart-burnings betwixt the King and his Clergy, which .. brast forth into a more fearfull flame. **1637** *Valentine & O.* 13 He .. brast out into these speeches.

III. Transitive (causative). Not in OE.

†**7. a.** To break, snap, shatter suddenly. *Obs.* in general sense.

α. **1297** R. Glouc. 437 Þe suerde hii nome .. & barste mony a sselde. **1362** Langl. *P. Pl.* A. VII. 165 He beot so þe Boyes he barst neih heore Ribbes. **1590** Marlowe *2nd Pt. Tamburl.* v. i. 71 Whose chariot-wheels have burst the Assyrians' bones. **1596** Shaks. *Tam. Shr.* I. Induct. 8 You will not pay for the glasses you haue burst. **1715** in *Sc. Pasquils* (1868) 393 Dee'l knock, Dee'l sink, Dee'l ryve and burst him.

β. **1340** Hampole *Pr. Consc.* 1787 Alle thyng it brestes in sonder. *c* **1385** Chaucer *L.G.W.* 2413 And with a wawe brostyn was his stere. **1480** *Robt. Devyll* 16 Tenne noble stedes backes he dyd brust. **1508** Fisher *Wks.* I. 60 Whan he is ones fallen to the grounde he is brasten all to peces. **1509** Barclay *Ship of Fooles* (1570) 170 God .. geueth thee not his beard to draw and brast. **1563–87** Foxe *A. & M.* (1684) II. 85 He .. brast them [the images] all down in pieces. **1855** Singleton *Virgil* I. 192 Drear winter with its cold would brast the rocks. *a* **1881** Rossetti *Ballads & Sonn.* 130 All the locks Had the traitor riven and brast.

†**b.** ***to burst down***: to break down violently.

c **1440** [see bursting *vbl. sb.*].

†**c.** *fig.* To break or violate (a law, a principle). *Obs. rare.*

1600 Fairfax *Tasso* v. lv. 85 If Rinaldo .. haue the sacred lore of war so brust.

d. *poet.* To interrupt, put a sudden end to.

1842 Tennyson *St. Sim. Stylites* 175 With hoggish whine they burst my prayer. **1859** —— *Enid* 1120 Many a .. heel against the pavement echoing burst their drowse.

8. a. To disrupt, shatter, cause to fly to pieces (a surface, or thing having extended surface).

In mod. use the tendency is to restrict the word to cases in which a containing envelope is ruptured by the expansion (or the too great size) of the contents.

1382 Wyclif *Dan.* xiv. 26 He made gobettis, and ȝaue in to mouthe of the dragoun, and the dragoun is borstun. **1535** Coverdale *Luke* v. 37 Yᵉ new wyne barsteth yᵉ vessels and runneth out. **1591** Shaks. *1 Hen. VI*, I. i. 64 The losse of those great Townes Will make him burst his Lead, and rise from death. **1736** Butler *Anal.* I. i. Wks. 1874 I. 14 Birds and insects bursting the shell their habitation. **1775** Haffenden in *Phil. Trans.* LXV. 340 The place where the leaden pipe is bursten. **1791** Smeaton *Edystone L.* §174 Nothing .. but .. gun-powder, could have burst and dispersed the materials of the spire in the manner it had done. **1817–8** Cobbett *Resid. U.S.* (1822) 42 The buds of a Lilac .. are almost *bursted*, which is a great deal better than to say, 'almost *burst*'.

b. To rupture (something) by internal force, or by pressure, a blow, etc., upon it when inflated or distended. ***to burst a blood-vessel***: to cause its rupture by exertion, etc., or simply to suffer the rupture of a vessel. ***to burst one's sides***: imagined as a result of excessive laughter. ***to burst one's buttons*** (through over-feeding or exertion).

1712 Arbuthnot *John Bull* (1755) 47 You would have burst your sides to hear him talk of politicks. **1796** Pegge *Anonym.* (1809) 354 We were ready to burst our sides. **1863** Kingsley *Water-bab.* v. 185 He .. played leap-frog with the town-clerk till he burst his buttons. **1865** Miss Lahee *Billy o' Yeps T.* 10 Lads laughin' fit to brast their soides. *Mod.* Take care you do not burst your gun.

†**c.** *fig.* ***to burst up***: to shatter, destroy. *Obs.*

1597 Daniel *Civ. Wares* VII. ii, Who else had burst-up Right to come t' his right.

†**d.** To ruin financially = break *v.* 11. *Obs.*

1712 Arbuthnot *John Bull* II. iv, I therefore hold it advisable that you continue the Lawsuit, and burst him at once.

e. To spend (money) extravagantly; *esp.* to spend it 'on the burst' or 'on the spree'. *slang.*

1892 J. Murdoch *From Australia & Japan* 151 It sounds odd to be told that a fellow's conscientious scruples are lax enough to permit him to 'burst' $6 50c. on the very much off-chance of ever seeing a cent of his investment again. **1908** *Westm. Gaz.* 31 Mar. 10/3 Two natives .. returned to visit their old relatives at home, and burst a little money on the spree.

9. a. ***to burst bonds, barriers***, etc. Now said only of the person or thing confined within; formerly with wider meaning as in 7. Now chiefly *fig.*

α. *c* **1325** *E.E. Allit. P.* B. 963 Þe grete barrez of þe abyme he barst vp at onez. **1535** Coverdale *Jer.* v. 5 These .. haue .. bursten the bondes in sonder. **1824–9** Landor *Imag. Conv.* (1846) II. 3 My madness .. would burst asunder the strong swathes. **18..** *Hymns Anc. & Mod.* '*Come see the place*' ii, Who burst the bands of death and hell.

β. *c* **1340** *Cursor M.* 7203 (Fairf.) His bandis al he brest in twa. *c* **1440** *York Myst.* xxxvii. 196 And brosten are alle our bandis of bras. **1548** Udall, etc. *Erasm. Par. Mark* v. 4 To braste all his chaynes and fetters in pieces. **1596** Spenser *F.Q.* I. v. 31 Furies which their chaines have brast.

b. Of a river or water: ***to burst its banks***.

1860 Tyndall *Glac.* I. §8. 58 A subglacial lake had burst its boundary.

†**c.** *transf.* To force one's way across (a frontier) *Obs.*; also, ***to burst*** (the enemy's) ***ranks***. *poet.* or *rhetorical.*

1652 C. Stapylton *Herodian* VIII. 67 The Frontiers they had brast. **1847** Tennyson *Princ.* IV. 483 Clad in iron, burst the ranks of war.

d. To separate (continuous stationery) into its constituent sheets, esp. automatically.

1966 R. R. Arnold et al. *Introd. Data Processing* v. 82/2 The machine bursts the one-part form into individual units. **1967** *Oxford Computer Explained* 36 Documents may, if required, be burst on a high-speed unit. **1982** *What's New in Computing* Nov. 90/2 It is the only machine in its price category that will burst a 7 part printout. **1985** *Neat Ideas Catal.* Spring 3/1 The PNK 610 can burst forms from a width of 4" (102 mm) to 15" (382mm).

†**10.** ***to burst the heart***: said of grief or violent emotions. Also of persons, ***to burst one's heart***. So ***to burst one's brain***: to take or occasion excessive thought. *Obs.*

c **1385** Chaucer *L.G.W.* 1298 Ffor which methynkyth brostyn is myn herte. **1555** *Let.* in Strype *Eccl. Mem.* III. App. I. 162 Though thou wouldest brast thine heart about it. **1587** Golding *De Mornay* xxiv. 373 Bookes which busteth not our braines about Mooneshine in the water. **1591** Spenser *Ruines of T.* 518 Nigh with griefe .. my heart was brust.

11. a. To cause (the body) to swell till it bursts. Chiefly as an imagined result of over-feeding or violent exertion; often *refl.*

1530 Palsgr. 757/1, I thruste out ones guttes, or burste one. *Je accreue.* **1667** Milton *P.L.* x. 635 Cramm'd and gorged, right burst With suck'd and glutted offal. **1719** De Foe *Crusoe* (1840) I. xiii. 227 Water, with which .. he would have burst himself. **1839** *Cumberl. & Westmoreland Dial.* 31 He hed welly brosen his sel wie runnin.

b. *causatively.*

a **1802** '*Broomfield Hill*' xiv. in Child *Ballads* II. (1884) 394/2 Ye need na burst your gude white steed Wi racing oer the howm. *a* **1822** '*Fair Marjory*' xvii. *ibid.* III. 121/2 It's first he burst the bonny black, An syne the bonny broun.

12. *hyperbolically.* To fill to overflowing.

1697 Dryden *Virg. Georg.* I. 74 That Crop .. bursts the crowded Barns.

13. ***to burst a door, gate***, etc.: to force it open by a violent thrust, so as to break the door or its fastenings. Also ***burst open***.

1591 Shaks. *1 Hen. VI*, I. iii. 28 Open the Gates .. Or wee'le burst them open. *a* **1700** Dryden *Desp. Lover* Misc. Wks. 1760 II. 118 The bounce burst ope the door. **1721** De Foe *Mem. Cavalier* (1840) 113 They burst open the gate. **1847** Tennyson *Princ.* VI. 59 She spoke, and .. Descending, burst the great bronze valves. **1864** —— *Boadicea* 64 Burst the gates and burn the palaces.

†**14.** To cause to burst *out, abroad. Obs.*

c **1400** *Destr. Troy* 865 Sho brast out bright water at hir brode een. *a* **1593** Marlowe *Mass. at Paris* I. ii, To burst abroad those never-dying flames.

IV. Intransitive senses implying movement accompanied by the bursting of barriers.

These uses mostly correspond with those of break, branch VII, but express more strongly the notion of sudden violence.

15. a. To issue forth suddenly and copiously by breaking an enclosure, or by overcoming resistance. Usually with *out, forth*, or other *adv.*

a **1300** *Cursor M.* 11704 Vnder þe rote a well vte-brast. **1375** Barbour *Bruce* xv. 481 Blude brist out at voundis vyde. **1480** Caxton *Chron. Eng.* ccxxii. 216 One of hem .. smote the same hugh vpon the hede that the brayn brest out. **1563** Foxe *A. & M.* (1684) I. 259/1 The blood brast incontinent out of the Nose of the King. **1578** Timme *Calvine on Gen.* 199 The waters under the earth braste not up, nor the waters aboue the Heauens fall down upon us. **1847** Tennyson *Princ.* IV. 453 A river level with the dam Ready to burst and fill the world with foam. **1852** —— *Elaine* 516 Half his blood burst forth.

b. *transf.* and *fig.* Of tears, cries, etc.: To issue suddenly in spite of repressive effort. Of light, sounds, etc.: To issue suddenly *from* a source; to become visible or audible with startling suddenness and clearness; often const. *on* (the eye, ear, etc.). Of the sun: ***to burst from, through*** (the clouds); often with *out, forth*. Also of news, events, sights, truths, etc.: ***to burst upon*** (a person): to be revealed with overwhelming suddenness to.

c **1250** *Gen. & Ex.* 1808 Get held he wið ðis angel fast, Til ðe dauing up it brast. *a* **1300** *Cursor M.* 18916 Þar come a sune Vte o þe air al bristand dune. *c* **1386** Chaucer *Doctor's T.* 234 The teeres brast out of hir eyghen tuo. **1508** Fisher *Wks.* I. 165 The sounde of a grete trumpe braste out. **1591** Spenser *Petrarch's Vis.* iii, Sudden flash of heavens fire out brast. **1678** Bunyan *Pilgr.* I. 73 What sighs and groans brast from Christians heart. **1826** F. Cooper *Mohicans* xvii, Such a yell .. as seldom bursted from human lips before. **1867** Lady Herbert *Cradle L.* vii. 168 On turning a sharp corner, Hebron burst upon them.

¶ ***to burst upon a view***. (rare.)

c **1854** Stanley *Sinai & Pal.* i. 69 The Israelites, coming down through that very valley, burst upon that very view.

c. *fig.* Of thoughts, emotions, latent forces, etc.: To find utterance or manifestation suddenly, *esp.* after long repression or concealment. Usually with *out, forth*; const. *into* (the result).

1542 Becon *Christm. Banq.*, Wks. (1843) 81 Charity .. brasteth out into good works whensoever it seeth an occasion given. **1591** Shaks. *1 Hen. VI*, IV. i. 183 Had the passions of thy heart burst out .. we should haue seene decipher'd there .. rancorous spight. *a* **1603** in *Liturg. Services Q. Eliz.* (1847) 680 Defections in Ireland .. in the end brast out into open rebellion. **1810** Scott *Lady of L.* II. xxxiv, Anguish of despair Burst, in fierce jealousy, to air.

†**d.** Of an eruptive disease. Also of the body affected by it: To break out into sores or pimples.

The latter sense appears to have existed in OE., where however it probably originated from 1 or 2. Cf. quot. *a* 1000 under bursting *ppl. a.*

1552 Huloet *Breake oute*, or braste oute, as a mannes face doth with heate. *a* **1593** H. Smith *Wks.* (1866) I. 301 The leprosy which brast out of the forehead.

e. To spring forth, as a plant, shoot, etc. (Usually implying the overcoming of restraint.)

a **1300** *Cursor M.* 10723 Bath flour and frut suld þar-of brest [*v.r.* briste]. **1578** Banister *Hist. Man* IV. 60 The fift [Muscle] likewise brusteth forth of Fibula. **1835–6** Todd *Cycl. Anat. & Phys.* I. 120/2 The radicle that bursts from the fecundated seed of a plant.

†**f.** To emanate, originate *from. Obs.*

a **1300** *Cursor M.* 10059 But o þe grace þat of hir brestes, Of al þis werld bett er þe brestes. **1567** Jewel *Def. Apol.* (1611) 409 All these mischiefes brast out first from the High Throne of the Pope of Rome.

16. Of a tempest, conflagration, disease, or the like. Chiefly with *out, forth.*

1542 Henry VIII *Declar. Scots* 192 Things of suche enormitie do brest out and appere. **1546** Langley *Pol. Verg. De Invent.* I. xvi. 29 a, Diseases, that brest furthe on euery syde. **1579** Tomson *Calvin Serm. Tim.* 250/2 We do but heap vp wood, and the wrath of God brasteth out at a blow. **1630** Lord *Banians* 87 The windes in the bowels of the earth .. brast forth into eruptions. **1792** *Anecd. W. Pitt* I. x. 203 The flame of war .. was preparing to burst out in Europe. **1808** R. Porter *Trav. Sk. Russ. & Swed.* (1813) I. i. 11 War burst around him, and he fell in combat. **1848** Macaulay *Hist. Eng.* I. 665 A tempest burst forth, such as had not been known since that great hurricane.

17. To make a sudden overwhelming assault *on*; to rush violently and suddenly *over*.

a **1300** *Cursor M.* 21400 Brathli on his fas he brast. **1862** Stanley *Jew. Ch.* (1877) I. ix. 180 Immense swarms of hornets burst upon the country with unusual force.

18. *poet.* ***to burst away***: to rush away impetuously. Also (of a bird) ***to burst on the wing***: to start off into flight.

1809 Campbell *Gert. Wyom.* III. iii, Wild bird bursting on the wing. **1859** Tennyson *Elaine* 1237 The wild Queen .. burst away to weep. **1864** —— *En. Ard.* 635 A crew that landing burst away In search of stream or fount.

19. To force a passage impetuously *through* (a barrier, physical or moral, the ememy's ranks, a crowd of people).

a **1300** *Cursor M.* 12872 Opin he sau þe liftes seuen, þe fader steuen þar thoru it brast. **1837** Newman *Par. Serm.* (ed. 3) I. xx. 305 There are times when a thankful heart bursts through all Forms of prayer. **1853** Kingsley *Hypatia* xxii. 288 Bursting desperately through the women who surrounded him, the monk vanished.

20. To break forcibly *into*, come suddenly and impetuously *into* (a room, a country, etc.); also with adv. *in*. Similarly ***to burst up*** (from below).

1563 Foxe *A. & M.* (1684) I. 397/1 Thorow windows and doors .. they brast in to the Pope. **1600** Fairfax *Tasso* II. xxvii. 25 He broke the throng, and into presence brast. **1742** Richardson *Pamela* III. 128 In burst the pert Slut, with an Air of Assurance. **1798** Coleridge *Anc. Mar.* II. v, We were the first that ever burst Into that silent sea. **1813** Mar. Edgeworth *Patron.* I. v. 98 The flames burst in from the burning trellis. **1835** Marryat *Jacob Faithf.* i, My father burst up from the cabin.

☛*Phrase-key*:—To *burst* abroad, 14; *b* away, 18; *b* banks, 9b; *b* a blood-vessel, 8b; *b* bonds, 9; *b* one's brains, 10; bud *b*, 2b; *b* one's buttons, 8b; cloud *b*, 2b; *b* a door, 13; *b* down, 7b; *b* forth, 6b, 6c, 15, 15b, 15c, 16; *b* from, 15b, 15f; *b* a frontier, 9c; *b* the heart, 10; *b* for hunger, 1c; *b* into, 6c, 15, 20; *b* on, 6b, 15b, 17; *b* on the wing, 18; *b* open, 5, 13; *b* out, 3, 6b, 6c, 14, 15, 15b, 15d, 16; *b* ranks, 9c; *b* one's sides, 8b; *b* through, 15b, 19; *b* up, 2, 8c, 20; *b* upon, 15b; *b* with, 6a.

burst (bɜːst), *sb.* Forms: 1 byrst, 1–4 berst, birst, 5 byrst, 3– burst. [In sense 1 repr. OE. *byrst* (*berst*) = OHG. *brust*:—OTeut. **brusti-z*, f. pa. pple. stem of *brestan* to burst. This seems to have become obs. about the middle of 14th c.; the modern sb. was apparently f. the verb. in 16th c. Cf. the parallel brest, brist.]

I. †**1.** Damage, injury, harm; loss. *Obs.*

c **1000** Ælfric *Ex.* xxii. 6 Ȝilde þone byrst þe þæt fyr ontende. *c* **1205** Lay. 1347 Brutus at bræc al buten burstan [*c* **1275** harme]. *Ibid.* 1610 Þe king Goffar iseih his burst

[*c* **1275** lure]. *c* **1300** in Wright *Lyric P.* iv. 24 That burst shal bete for hem bo. *c* **1320** *Syr Bevis* 1929 A-dede hire ete al ther ferst That she ne dede him no berst. *c* **1420** *Chron. Vilod.* 330 þen in all þe toþer worldelyche burste. *c* **1430** *How Gd. Wyf tauȝte Dau.* in *Babees Bk.* (1868) 45 The more nede hyt make or the grettyr byrst.

II. Senses formed anew from the verb.

2. a. An act of bursting; the result of this action.

1611 SHAKS. *Cymb.* IV. ii. 106 The snatches in his voice And bursts of speaking were as his. **1836** MACGILLIVRAY *Humboldt's Trav.* iii. 52 The Peak of Teneriffe exhibited a lateral burst, preceded by tremendous earthquakes. **1885** G. MEREDITH *Diana of Crossw.* I. iv. 107 When beech-buds were near the burst.

b. fig. ***burst-up***: the failure, collapse, of an organization or scheme.

1879 *Daily News* 22 Sept. 2/1 A speedy burst-up of the whole agricultural system.

c. House-breaking, burglary. *slang.*

1857 'DUCANGE ANGLICUS' *Vulg. Tongue* 3 *Burst*, burglary. **1863** *Sessions' Paper* Apr. 786, I asked Simpson where they had done the *burst*—that is what is commonly called house-breaking.

3. a. A sudden and violent issuing forth. Chiefly of light and sounds. So also ***a burst of flame, a burst of fish*** (in local use).

1610 SHAKS. *Temp.* II. i. 311 We heard a hollow burst of bellowing Like Buls. **1671** MILTON *Samson* 1651 Down they came, and drew The whole roof after them, with burst of thunder, Upon the heads of all. **1816** SOUTHEY *Lay of Laur.*, *Dream* vi, Burst after burst the innocuous thunders brake. **1854** BREWSTER *More Worlds* ii. 17 The gloomy landscape whose varied beauties a burst of sun-light has revealed. **1857** *National Mag.* II. 197 Terminating in a glorious burst of acclamatory harmony.

b. A sudden opening on the view.

1798 COLERIDGE *Tears in Solit.* 215 This burst of prospect. **1814** JANE AUSTEN *Mansf. P.* viii. (D.) Here is a fine burst of country. **1875** BROWNING *Inn Album* 4 Not so the burst of landscape surging in.

4. a. An explosion, eruption, outbreak.

1649 MILTON *Eikon.* Wks. 1738 I. 403 He..kept them up, the only Army in his three Kingdoms, till the very burst of that Rebellion. *a* **1719** ADDISON (J.) Imprison'd fires, in the close dungeons pent, Roar to get loose, and struggle for a vent..Till with a mighty burst whole mountains fall. **1790** WEDGWOOD in *Phil. Trans.* LXXX. 309 As often as the heat was at or near the boiling point of the acid, frequent..bursts or explosions happened. **1870** *Pall Mall. G.* 17 Nov. 12 Out of 8,245 shells and shrapnel fired with this fuze..there were 128 premature bursts.

b. *spec.* Of gunfire, esp. from an automatic weapon.

1893 in *Funk's Stand. Dict.* **1902** *Times Hist. War in S. Afr. 1899–1902* II. 159 The effect of this sudden burst—the first experience of the massed fire of modern rifles in the war—did not stay the advance. **1916** *King's Roy. Rifle Corps Chron. 1915* 41 The Companies in the trenches fired short bursts of rapid fire. **1942** T. RATTIGAN *Flare Path* III. 158 O.K., Kyle. Shoot. Give us the five-second burst. **1964** *Times* 21 Aug. 8/1 A Soviet sentry fired..a second burst as the car was leaving the area.

c. *Physics.* (See quot. 1960.)

1933 *Physical Rev.* XLIV. 779/1 The time intervals between the occurrence of bursts of ionization..were measured. **1942** J. D. STRANATHAN *Particles* xii. 509 The cosmic ray phenomenon responsible for..excessive momentary ionizations is referred to as a burst. *Ibid.* 519 It has been remarked that the cosmic ray burst is probably identical with the shower. **1949** *Austral. Jrnl. Sci. Res.* A. II. 214 (*title*) Bursts of solar radiation at metre wavelengths. **1960** COOKE & MARKUS *Electronics & Nucleonics Dict.* 59/1 *Burst.* 1. A sudden increase in the strength of a signal being received from beyond line-of-sight range. It is believed due to meteors passing through the upper atmosphere and momentarily affecting the ionized layers that reflect radio waves back to earth. 2. An exceptionally large pulse observed in an ionization chamber, signifying the arrival of several ionizing particles simultaneously. It may be caused by a cosmic-ray shower.

5. A vehement outbreak (of emotion or its expression).

1751 JOHNSON *Rambl.* No. 141 ⁋10 A mistake which had given rise to a burst of merriment. **1775** BURKE *Amer. Tax.* Wks. II. 408 From the whole of that grave multitude there arose an involuntary burst of gratitude and transport. **1838** THIRLWALL *Greece* V. xliv. 370 A burst of ill humour, which it would have been wiser to suppress. *Mod.* The statement was received with a burst of laughter.

6. a. A great and sudden exertion of activity, a vigorous display of energy; a 'spurt'. Phrase, ***at a (one) burst.***

1862 ABP. TRENCH *Eng. Past & Pr.* III. 97 With Chaucer English literature had made a burst, which it was not able to maintain. **1865** M. ARNOLD *Ess. Crit.* I. (1875) 8 The burst of creative activity in our literature. **1876** GREEN *Short Hist.* vii. §5 (1882) 393 The great poetic burst for which this intellectual advance was paving the way.

b. *Horsemanship.* A hard run, a gallop without a check.

1789 *Loiterer* 14 Feb. 6 Pompous accounts of *sharp bursts*, and long chaces. **1810** SCOTT *Lady of L.* I. iv, So shrewdly, on the mountainside, Had the bold burst their metal tried. **1852** THACKERAY *Esmond* I. iv. (1876) 29 During a burst over the Downs after a hare. **1868** R. EG.-WARBURTON *Hunt. Songs* lvi. (1883) 155 How keen their emulation in the bustle of the burst, When side by side the foremost ride.

c. Hence, in other sports; *spec.* a short spurt, etc., at greater speed than that employed for the remainder of the course.

1824 *Mirror* III. 290/2 The dogs..pursue it..with great impetuosity, which sportsmen term a burst. **1925** 'IAN HAY' *Paid with Thanks* xvi. 211 They..proceeded to row courses, half courses..and short bursts. **1957** DUNCAN & BONE *Oxf. Pkt. Bk. Athletic Training* (ed. 2) iii. 22 *Bursts*, a sprint put into the middle of a period of striding or jogging.

7. *colloq.* A prolonged bout of drunkenness, a 'spree'. Also a big feed, a 'blow out'. (See also BUST *sb.*[3])

1849 T. T. JOHNSON *Sights in Gold Region* xix. 183 Bill and Gus had come over from the Middle Fork for a particular, general and universal 'burst'. **1881** MRS. PRAED *Policy & Pass.* I. 288 When..his men go on the burst. **1881** *Cheq. Career* 356 A good week's burst.

burst (bɜːst), *ppl. a.* Also *arch.* **brast.** [pa. pple. of BURST *v.*; see BURSTEN *ppl. a.*]

1. See senses of BURST *v.* **†a.** Shattered, broken, *Obs.* **b.** Rent by force when in a state of tension; exploded, torn open. Also with advs., as ***burst-out, burst-up.***

1812 BYRON *Ch. Har.* I. lxxviii, Clinging darts, and lances brast. **1824** MISS MITFORD *Village* Ser. I. (1863) 138 Working over the weak irregular burst-out button-hole. **1885** STEVENSON *Dynamiter* 190 You behold me sitting here like a burst drum. **1900** *Engineering Mag.* XIX. 746/1 The burst-up condition of the decks..showing..the behaviour of the lyddite shells.

†2. *spec.* Ruptured, suffering from hernia. Also as quasi-*sb. Obs.*

1580 BARET *Alv.* B. 1569 He that is burst, or hath his bowels fallen down into his coddes. **1611** COTGR., s.v. *Bergamasque*, a trusse for a burst man. **1631** R. BYFIELD *Doctr. Sabb.* 14 [It] appeares also by the example of the burst, and of the bastard.

burstable (ˈbɜːstəb(ə)l), *a. rare.* [f. BURST *v.* + -ABLE.] Capable of being burst.

1611 COTGR., *Rompable*, burstable, breakable.

†burst-cow. *Obs.* [f. BURST *v.* + COW.] = *burn-cow*, an old name for the BUPRESTIS, q.v.

1646 SIR. T. BROWNE *Pseud. Ep.* 177 [Insects] pernicious unto cattell, as the Buprestis or burstcow. **1658** ROWLAND *Mouffet's Theat. Ins.* 1000, I..adventure to call it by a new name in English, Burncow, or Burstcow. **1706** PHILLIPS, s.v. *Bupestris*, the Burn-cow, Burst-cow, or Blain-worm.

bursted (ˈbɜːstɪd), *ppl. a.* Also 6 **brested, brasted, brysted.** [Weak pa. pple. of BURST *v.* + -ED.] = BURST *ppl. a.* Now *dial.*

1527 ANDREW *Brunswyke's Distyll. Waters* L i b, Membres whiche be frosen, and brested or wounded of the frost. **1561** *Newe Enterl. Q. Hester* (1873) 23, I wote not how they were brysted. *a* **1600** HOOKER *Serm.* iii. (1845) III. 760 It causeth their brasted hearts to rejoice. *a* **1649** DRUMM. OF HAWTH. *Poems* Wks. (1711) 25 The long-since dead from bursted graves arise. **1728** T. SHERIDAN *Persius* v. 83 The Dangers portended you from a bursted Egg.

bursten (ˈbɜːst(ə)n), *ppl. a.* [Obs. pa. pple. of BURST *v.*; like many other strong pples. in *-en*, it is still sometimes used attrib., esp. in poetical or rhetorical language.] = BURST *ppl. a.*

c **1440** *Anc. Cookery* in *Housh. Ord.* (1790) 462 Take qwete streyned, that is for to say brosten. *c* **1440** *Promp. Parv.* 53 Brostyn man, *herniosus.* **1544** PHAËR *Regim. Lyfe* (1560) U iij b, A drynke for one that is brusten. *c* **1620** CHAPMAN *Batrachom.* Ep. Ded. (1858) 38 Even bursten profusion. **1638** MYNSHUL *Ess. Prison* 44 In prisons, Gentlemen, and bursten Citizens meet as upon the Exchange. **1712** STEELE *Spect.* No. 444 ⁋4 A Doctor for the Cure of bursten Children. **1762** tr. *Duhamel's Husb.* III. xii. (ed. 2) 414 All rotten or bursten grapes. **1843** CARLYLE *Past & Pr.* (1858) 111 Now grown quite corpulent, bursten, superfluous. **1879** FARRAR *St. Paul* (1883) 544 The worn-out and bursten condition of the old bottles.

†b. *Comb.*, as ***bursten-bellied, -gutted.*** *Obs.*

1601 HOLLAND *Pliny* II. 263 To cure those that be bursten bellied. **1661** K. W. *Conf. Charact.* (1860) 47 A..clubfooted burstengutted, longneck't..hircocerous. *a* **1722** LISLE *Husb.* 477 Whether it was usual for pigs to be bursten-bellied.

†burstened, *ppl. a. Obs.* [incorrectly f. prec.] Filled to bursting.

1697 *Snake in Grass* (ed. 2) 37 A very Night-Bird, and Vagrant, Bursten'd with Folly and Revenge.

†ˈburstenness. *Obs.* Also 5 **brostynes,** 6 **burstiness,** 7 **bursunesse;** see also BURSTNESS. [f. BURSTEN *ppl. a.* + -NESS.] Burst state or quality; *spec.* rupture, hernia.

1483 *Cath. Angl.* 45 A Brostynes, *hernia.* **1528** PAYNELL *Salerne Regim.* X iij, Specially when the burstennes cometh by ventosite. **1615** MARKHAM *Eng. Housew.* II. i. (1668) 29 For the rupture or burstennesse in men.

burster (ˈbɜːstə(r)). [f. BURST *v.* + -ER[1].]

1. a. He who, or that which, bursts; *spec.* (*Artill.*) a charge of gunpowder for bursting a shell, or the bag containing it. Hence **burster-bag.**

1611 COTGR., *Rompeur*, a burster, a breaker. **1862** F. GRIFFITHS *Artil. Man.* (ed. 9) 193 The segment shells..are each charged with a burster, containing powder. **1876** *Daily News* 22 Sept. 3/5 The Palliser shells will have capacity for a 25 lbs. burster.

b. *fig.* ? An exhausting piece of exercise, something which 'takes the wind out' of one.

1851 *Illustr. Lond. News* 99 A pace that would have been a burster to many a fresh man.

c. ? *Racing slang.* A heavy fall; a 'cropper'.

1863 *Even. Standard* 24 Apr., Benedict came down a burster, and was out of the race.

d. A machine or device for bursting stationery (see BURST *v.* 9 d).

1950 *Mod. Office Appliances* (Office Appliance Trade Assoc.) (ed. 4) III. 330 (*caption*) Burster unit for single-ply forms. **1962** *Mode* Apr. 14 After the customer's continuous stationery has been decollated on either of these machines, it is fed into a burster for separating into single forms. **1980** *Daily Tel.* 23 Apr. 3 (*Advt.*), Products include..filing cabinets,..bursters, decollators and forms handling equipment. **1895** *Neat Ideas Catal.* Spring 3/1 The new burster PNK610 separates continuous form stationery into separate sheets and stacks them into an adjustable size stacker tray.

2. In *Australia* and *N.Z.*: see quot. (Usually BUSTER.)

1851 *Austral. & N.Z. Gaz.* 29 Nov. 483 The order of the day has been for some time past, rain, rainbows, and southerly bursters. **1879** WALLACE *Australas.* ii. 31 The well-known southerly 'bursters' are violent storms of wind occurring in summer. **1922** W. G. KENDREW *Climates of Continents* xlvii. 364 On the east coast of the continent..cold winds from the south, known as Southerly Bursters. *Ibid.* 365 A striking roll of cumulus cloud may accompany the Burster, and there is usually heavy rain.

3. *Astr.* = *x-ray burster* s.v. X RAYS *sb. pl.* 5 b; an emitter of other electromagnetic radiation with analogous intermittent emission.

1976 *Nature* 17 June 562/2 A new type of time variability of cosmic X-ray sources ('bursters') was discovered from Astronomical Netherlands Satellite..observations. **1977** *Daily Tel.* 30 Apr. 8/4 The explosions have been nicknamed 'bursters' since they consist of violent bursts of X-rays and are not associated with the more familiar 'novae' and 'supernovae' explosions of stars. **1978** PASACHOFF & KUTNER *University Astron.* xxv. 632 Some two dozen bursters are now known; only a handful are in globular clusters. **1982** *Sci. Amer.* Mar. 62/3 Of the objects in space that defy the slow rhythms of the stars by emitting short pulses of intense electromagnetic radiation, the ones most recently discovered are the gamma-ray bursters.

bursting (ˈbɜːstɪŋ), *vbl. sb.* [f. BURST *v.*]

1. a. The process or action of breaking suddenly and violently, as under tension.

1375 BARBOUR *Bruce* XVI. 158 Thar wes of speris sic bristing. **1575** J. STILL *Gamm. Gurton* I. iii, We would not greatly care For bursting of her huckle-bone. *c* **1600** *Rob. Hood* (Ritson) I. iv. 47 And it were not for bursting of my bowe, John, I thy head wold breake. **1611** BIBLE *Isa.* xxx. 14 There shall not be found in the bursting of it, a sheard.

b. *spec.* by internal force or pressure.

1526 *Pilgr. Perf.* (W. de W. 1531) 291 b, The body is not able to receyue it all, without feare of brastynge. **1600** SHAKS. *A.Y.L.* II. i. 38 The wretched annimall heau'd forth such groanes That their discharge did stretch his leatherne coat Almost to bursting. **1885** *Manchester Exam.* 22 Sept. 5/2 The damage caused by the bursting of an embankment.

†2. *spec.* Rupture; hernia. *Obs.*

1544 PHAËR *Regim. Lyfe* (1560) U viij b, To remove the swelling of the coddes proceding of ventositie, or of anye other cause (except brustyng).

†3. Explosion, explosive noise. *Obs.*

1771 SMOLLETT *Humph. Cl.* (1793) II. 34 The bursting, belching, and brattling of the French horns in the passage.

4. Rushing impetuously from restraint or rest.

1871 R. ELLIS *Catullus* lxiii. 86 The lion..With a step, a roar, a bursting unarrested of any brake.

5. *comb.* with various advbs. (cf. the vb)

c **1440** *Promp. Parv.* 50 Brestynge downe, *prostracio.* **1552** HULOET *Aposthume*, or brasting out. **1712** STEELE *Spect.* No. 474 ⁋2 The occasional burstings out into laughter.

6. *attrib.* **bursting charge,** the charge of powder required for bursting a shell or case-shot; a small charge of fine powder placed in contact with a charge of coarser powder to ensure the ignition of the latter; **bursting point,** the internal pressure at which an enclosed vessel will explode; usu. *transf.*

1858 GREENER *Gunnery* 134 The bursting charge is very small, but it suffices to break the shell into about 30 pieces. **1862** F. GRIFFITHS *Artil. Man.* (ed. 9) 194 Loaded shells should never be fired with less than the authorized bursting charge. **1902** W. JAMES *Varieties Relig. Exp.* x. 236 The tension of subliminal memories reaching the bursting-point. **1931** E. LINKLATER *Juan in Amer.* II. iv. 81 Their columns had been stuffed to bursting-point with superlatives. **1933** D. L. SAYERS *Murder must Advertise* i. 9 A small, inconvenient cubicle, crowded at the moment to bursting-point. **1944** R. LEHMANN *Ballad & Source* III. 168 There came the bursting point of a complexity of hideous fears and pressures.

bursting (ˈbɜːstɪŋ), *ppl. a.* [f. BURST *v.* + -ING[2].] That bursts (see senses of the verb).

a **1000** *Sax. Leechd.* I. 272 Untrumnissa ðæs lichoman þæt is berstende lic. **1667** MILTON *P.L.* IX. 98 Bursting passion. **1714** YOUNG *Force Relig.* II. 210 Afar his bursting groans were heard. **1777** SIR W. JONES *Palace of Fort.* 15 As distant thunder breaks the bursting cloud. **1847** LONGF. *Evan.* I. ii. 99 From our bursting barns they would feed. **1863** KINGLAKE *Crimea* V. i. (1877) 245 Fragments..from a bursting shell.

burstle, var. of BRISTLE *v.*[2], BRUSTLE *v.*[2]

burstness (ˈbɜːstnɪs). Also 6 **brastnes;** and see BURSTENNESS. [f. BURST *ppl. a.* + -NESS.] The state of being burst; rupture; hernia.

1552 HULOET, *Brastnes*, or rupture of a man. **1607** TOPSELL *Four-f. Beasts* 204 The Ointment..healeth burstness. *Ibid.* (1658) 64 The skin of the feet and nose of an Ox..helpeth..burstness very much. **1725** BRADLEY *Fam. Dict.* II., *Rupture*..burstness; a distemper in a horse.

†ˈburstning, *vbl. sb. Obs.* Incorrect form = BURSTING; rupture, hernia.

1607 TOPSELL *Four-f. Beasts* 504 Arnoldus commendeth a plaister made of a Rams skin for burstning. **1635** SWAN

Spec. M. (1670) 220 Sulphur-wort..is used with good success against the ruptures and burstnings of young children.

bur-stone, variant of BURR-STONE.

†**burst-wort.** *Obs.* [f. BURST *sb.* + WORT.] An old name for *Herniaria glabra*, a herb formerly thought helpful for curing ruptures.

1597 GERARD *Herbal* clxiii. 455 [Herniaria] is called..in English Rupture woort, and Burstwoort. **1661** LOVELL *Hist. Anim. & Min.* 448 Leaves, of burst-wort, marsh-mallows.

burstyll, obs. form of BRISTLE.

†**burt**, *v. Obs.* Also 5 burt-on, 6 burte. *Pa. t.* and *pa. pple.* burt. [Cf. BUTT *v.*]

1. *trans.* and *absol.* To push or thrust, as with horns; to butt.

c **1440** *Promp. Parv.* 56 Burton', as hornyd bestys, *cornupeto.* **1552** HULOET, *Burt* lyke a ramme, *arieto.* **1556** ABP. PARKER *Psalter* cxxviii. 44 Our hornes shall burte them downe.

2. To pierce, gore.

1597 MONTGOMERIE *Cherrie & Sl.* 165 Than furth I drew that deadlie dairt..It hurt me, it burt me, The ofter I it handill. *a* **1605** —— *In Prais of Maistres*, Quhais beutie has me burt? Quhais beutie healls my hurt?

3. To indent, dint (as a tin-kettle). *Somerset.* Hence **burter**, **burting** vbl. sb.

c **1440** *Promp. Parv.* 56 Burtare, beste [**1499** burter], *cornupeta. Ibid.* Burtynge, *cornupetus.*

burt(e, burth-e: see BIRT, BIRTH.

burthen, etc.: see BURDEN *sb.*

burton[1] ('bɜːt(ə)n). Also **barton**.

a. A small tackle consisting of two or three blocks or pulleys used to set up or tighten rigging, or to shift heavy bodies. There are several varieties, as ***Spanish burton***, ***top burton***.

1704 in HARRIS *Lex. Technicum.* **1769** FALCONER *Dict. Marine* (1789) *Burton*, a..small tackle, formed by two blocks or pulleys..generally employed to tighten the shrouds of the top-masts. **1794** *Rigging & Seamanship* I. 199 *Burton-Pendents* are..placed over the topmast-head, that the thimbles may hang on each side, to hook the burton-tackles in. **1841** *Penny Cycl.* XIX. 118/1 The Spanish barton consists of two moveable wheels and one fixed wheel. **1860** H. STUART *Seaman's Catech.* 35 The top burtons are hooked to the burton pendants.

b. A term denoting the thwartship stowage of casks, bags, etc. Also **a-burton** (see quots. 1846, 1867).

1846 A. YOUNG *Naut. Dict.* s.v. *A-burton*, Casks are said to be stowed a-burton, when placed athwartships in the hold. **1867** SMYTH *Sailor's Word-bk.*, *A-burton*, the situation of casks when they are stowed in the hold athwart ship, or in a line with the beam. **1928** *Observer* 22 July 10/7 Terms as used by stevedores... 'Burton' to describe the thwart-ship stowage of bags, as against the fore and aft method. *Ibid.* 29 July 7/3, I have..both stowed and worked out 'Burtons' many scores of times during the twenty-five years I spent along the East End waterside.

Burton[2] ('bɜːt(ə)n). The name of a town in Staffordshire (in full ***Burton-on-Trent***) used *attrib.* and *absol.* to designate a type of ale: (*a*) = BASS *sb.*[6]; (*b*) (see quot. 1953).

1738 in *Westm. Gaz.* (1902) 24 Feb. 2/3 Genuine Burton Ale, Brew'd to the Greatest Perfection for Keeping by Sea and Land. **1843** TIZARD *Brewing* 88 The Burton ales principally owe their superior qualities and uniform permanency to the nature of the water there used. **1861** *Let.* 3 Aug. in C. Tovey *Wines & Wine Countries* (1862) iv. 171 The workman takes..'Bitter Beer', instead of his Burton. **1882** E. G. HOOPER *Man. Brewing* (ed. 2) 118 The Burton beer has been long noted for its high character. **1896** H. G. WELLS *Wheels of Chance* vi, Burton and biscuit and cheese he had, which indeed, is Burton in its proper company. **1953** *Word for Word* (*Whitbread & Co.*) 15/1 *Burton*, a strong ale, dark in colour, made with a proportion of highly dried or roasted malts. It is not necessarily brewed in Burton, and the term is in general use for all varieties of 'strong' or 'old' ales.

burton[3] ('bɜːt(ə)n). Also **Burton**. [Origin unknown; perh. connected with prec.] In slang phr. ***to go for a burton***, (of an airman) to be killed; (of a person or thing) to be missing, ruined, destroyed.

None of the several colourful explanations of the origin of the expression is authenticated by contemporary printed evidence.

1941 *New Statesman* 30 Aug. 218/3 *Go for a Burton*, crash. **1943** C. H. WARD-JACKSON *Piece of Cake* 32 *Gone for a Burton*, killed, dead. **1946** E. ROBERTS in Raymond & Langdon *Slipstream* 38, I can see those flowers going for a burton. **1947** 'N. SHUTE' *Chequer Board* iii. 49 He went for a Burton over France last year. **1957** J. BRAINE *Room at Top* xx. 176 We noncoms used to say *got the chopper*. Going for a Burton was journalist's talk.

Burtonize ('bɜːt(ə)naɪz), *v.* [f. BURTON[2] + -IZE.] *trans.* To harden (water for brewing) by treatment with the sulphate and chloride of magnesium and calcium or other salts.

1882 E. G. HOOPER *Man. Brewing* (ed. 2) 120 Burtonising. .. A hardening mixture giving solids similar to those of the Burton water may be made as follows:—Four parts of gypsum [etc.]. **1892** H. E. WRIGHT *Handy Bk. Brewers* 116 The presence of bicarbonates or carbonates may explain certain negative..results which sometimes attend the so-called 'Burtonising' of brewing water. **1940** H. L. HIND *Brewing* II. xxiv. 589 The fall in p_H from its original value of 5·6–5·8, which are normal figures with liquors that contain 10–12 parts per 100,000 of carbonates and little or no gypsum, or rather lower values if 'Burtonizing' is adopted, is very slight.

Hence **Burtonizer** ('bɜːt(ə)naɪzə(r)): see quot.

1908 *Daily Chron.* 12 Nov. 1/2 Burtonisers..are chiefly sulphates and chlorides of calcium and magnesium.

†**'burton-wood.** *Obs.* A shrub found in Campeachy and in the Galápagos islands.

1697 DAMPIER *Voy.* I. 101 Bushes of Burton-wood, which is very good firing. **1699** *Ibid.* II. II. 57 We..harden the Steels of our Fire-Arms..in a Logwood-fire [or else]..with Burton wood or the Grape-tree.

bur-tree, var. of BOURTREE, elder; see also BURR *sb.*[8], banyan-tree.

burwan, var. BURRAWANG.

burwarke, obs. form of BULWARK.

burwe, **burwgh**, **burwhe**, obs. ff. BOROUGH, BURROW.

†**'bury**, *sb. Obs.* Also 6 bery, 7 berry. [Originally dative of *burh*: see BOROUGH 1 b.] A manor-house, or large farm; a specialization of the OE. *burh*, *byriȝ* 'an enclosed or fortified place' which still survives in many local names.

1175–1576 [see BOROUGH 1 b]. **1598** STOW *Surv.* xxxiii. (1603) 294 The name of Aldermans burie (which is to say a Court) there kept in their Bery or Court-hall. **1654** GAYTON *Fest. Notes* III. vi. 106 They went untill they came to a Bury. **1656** BLOUNT *Glossogr.*, *Berry*..The chief house of a Manor, or the Lords seat is so called..to this day; especially in Herefordshire, where there are the Berries of Luston, Stockton, etc.

bury ('bɛrɪ), *v.* Forms: 1 byrȝ(e)an, byriȝan, 2 byrien, 3 birrȝenn (Orm.), 3–5 burien, byry(en, birien, 4 birin, 5 byryyn, byryn, beryyn, berry, 3–5 biry, beri(e, 4–6 bery, byry, (6 byrry, byrrey, burrey, burry, burye, bewry, 7 buerie, bure), 4 burye, 4–7 burie, 4– bury. Also Sc. 5 beryss, 6 berisch. [OE. *byrȝan* wk. v.:—WGer. **burgjan* (of which the only other trace is the OS. derivative *burgisli* sb. = BURIELS), app. f. *burg-* ablaut-stem of OTeut. **berg-an* str. v. to protect, cover: see BERGH *v.* The Scotch forms *beryss*, *berisch*, appear to follow the analogy of words from French like *peryss*, *perisch*.]

1. a. To deposit (a corpse) in the ground, in a tomb; to inter. Hence to commit (a corpse) to the sea, with appropriate funeral rites.

a **1000** *Hymns* (Gr.) x. 29 þone ȝeomormod Josep byriȝde. **1154** *O.E. Chron.* (Laud MS.) an. 1137. §7, & sythen byrieden him. *c* **1250** *Gen. & Ex.* 2520 Hise oðre breðere.. Woren ybiried at ebron. **1375** BARBOUR *Bruce* x. 489 He deit soyn, and beryit was. *c* **1400** *Destr. Troy* 13674 Ascatus.. Gert bryng hom to burgh, birit hom faire. *c* **1440** *York Myst.* xvii. 285 Sen thy body beryed shalbe, This mirre will I giffe to þi grauyng. **1552** ABP. HAMILTON *Catech.* 51 Thame that will nocht berisch or erde the bodis of thair freindis on the North part of the kirk yard. **1593** SHAKS. *Rich. II*, III. iii. 155 Ile be buryed in the Kings high-way. **1635** *Tom a Lincolne* II. in Thoms' *E.E. Prose Rom.* (1858) II. 344 Buring him inhumanly upon a dunghill. **1852** TENNYSON *Ode on Wellington* 1 Let us bury the Great Duke.

b. Said of the surviving relatives: hence, *to **have buried*** (one's relatives) = to have lost them by death.

1710 STEELE *Tatler* No. 215 ¶4 My elder Sister buried her Husband about Six Months ago. **1723** S. MORLAND *Spec. Lat. Dict.* 11 To Bury, as one buries his Relations when he survives them, *Efferre.*

c. Said of the religious functionary who celebrates the rites which accompany interment.

c **1400** *Apol. Loll.* 51 So no þing be askid..for dead to be byried. **1401** *Pol. Poems & Songs* (1859) II. 87 Whi..wil we not..birien the pore as wel as the riche? *Mod.* 'I never object to bury a dissenter; indeed I should be most happy to bury them all.'

d. *absol.*

1552–3 *Inv. Ch. Goods Staffs.* in *Ann. Diocese Lichfield* IV. 46, Xls. peyd to the bysshope for his laysance to byrrey. **1854** CDL. WISEMAN *Fabiola* II. xi. 145 There is no evidence of the Christians having buried anywhere, anteriorly to the construction of catacombs.

e. *fig.*

c **1175** *Lamb. Hom.* 51 Hwenne þu scrift underuongest þenne buriest þu þine sunnen. **1382** WYCLIF *Rom.* vi. 4 We ben to gidere biried with him bi cristendom in to deeth. *a* **1555** LYNDESAY *Trag.* 427 3e Prencis and Prelatis..Sall bureit be in hell. **1594** SHAKS. *Rich. III*, IV. iv. 423 Thou didst kil my Children. But in your daughters wombe I bury them. **1850** MERIVALE *Rom. Emp.* (1865) I. iii. 119 His first care must have been to bury the evidence in the graves of his associates. **1875** JOWETT *Plato*, *Gorgias* (ed. 2) II. 393 He would bury you under a mountain of words.

2. a. To put under ground for the same purposes as a corpse, e.g. *to **bury*** a person ***alive***; to consign to the ground any carcase, decaying organized matter, rubbish, etc.; also, other things, in sign of their final abandonment or abrogation. ***to bury the hatchet***: to put away strife, settle a quarrel, in allusion to the American-Indian ceremony of burying a tomahawk on the conclusion of a peace.

1535 COVERDALE *Jer.* xxii. 19 As an Asse shall he be buried. **1610** SHAKS. *Temp.* v. i. 55 I'le breake my staffe, Bury it certaine fadomes in the earth. [**1680** S. SEWALL in *New England Hist. & Genealogical Reg.* (1870) XXIV. 121 Meeting wth y[e] Sachem the[y] came to an agreemt and buried two Axes in y[e] Ground;..which ceremony to them is more significant & binding than all Articles of Peace the Hatchet being a principal weapon wth y[m].] **1754** in *Mass. Hist. Soc. Coll.* (1836) 3rd Ser. V. 10 We have ordered..our Governor of New York to hold an interview with them [*sc.* the Six Nations] for delivering those presents, [and] for burying the hatchet. **1796** 'P. PINDAR' *Wks.* IV. 485 Gentle Reader, Wouldst thou not have imagined that the war hatchet was buried for ever? **1794**, etc. [see HATCHET *sb.* 2]. **1884** *Harper's Mag.* Feb. 412/2 She buried the hatchet. **1954** I. MURDOCH *Under Net* xiv. 189 It is possible to break the ice without burying the hatchet.

b. *fig.* To consign to oblivion, put out of the way, abandon and forget.

1593 SHAKS. *3 Hen. VI*, IV. i. 55 In your Bride you bury Brotherhood. **1601** —— *Jul. C.* IV. iii. 159 Giue me a bowl of wine, In this I bury all vnkindnesse Cassius. **1670** J. LAW *Let.* in *Lauderdale Papers* (1885) III. App. i. 234 To burie presbiterian government with their oun consent. **1712** *Addr. Cambridge* in *Lond. Gaz.* No. 5027/5 May Faction be buried. **1885** A. B. ELLIS *W. Afric. Isl.* xi. 263 The natives ..had buried their own differences and united to repel the invaders.

c. To consign to a position of obscurity, inaccessibility, or inaction; often *refl.* and *pass.*

1711 *Vind. Sacheverell* 74 It would be a pity to bury so promising a young Gentleman in such a place. **1722** DE FOE *Col. Jack* (1840) 186, I looked upon myself as one buried alive in a remote part of the world. **1751** JOHNSON *Rambl.* No. 100 ¶1 Many well disposed persons..are so unfortunate as to be totally buried in the country. **1782** COWPER *Truth* 443 Sorrow might..Bury herself in solitude profound. **1828** SCOTT *F.M. Perth* (1860) 5 To retire from the world and bury herself in the recesses of the cloister.

3. a. Without restriction of purpose: To deposit or hide under ground; to cover up with earth or other material.

c **1340** *Cursor M.* 16919 (Fairf.) þe Iewis..beried [tho crossis] fro Crysten men in a preuy stede. **1530** PALSGR. 451/1 It is the propertye of a dogge to burye his meate in the grounde. **1542** BOORDE *Dyetary* xviii. (1870) 277 Bake meate ..is buryd in paast. **1626** BACON *Sylva* §378 A Bottle of Beer, buried in like manner as before, became more lively. **1697** DRYDEN *Virg. Georg.* III. 547 The frozen Earth lyes buried there, below A hilly Heap, seven Cubits deep in Snow. **1753** CHAMBERS *Cycl. Supp.* s.v. *Burial*, Chemists sometimes bury their cements. **1841** LANE *Arab. Nts.* 53 So I took the money..and buried 3000 pieces of gold.

b. Of things: To cover over out of sight, to submerge.

1737 MILLER *Gard. Dict.* (1759) s.v. *Cedrus*, This wood.. resisting gun shots, and burying the shot without splintering. **1791** SMEATON *Edystone L.* §272 The seas that are said..in a manner to bury the house in time of storms. *Ibid.* §273 The two stones together would compleatly..bury the cramps.

4. a. To plunge or sink deep *in*, so as to cover from view; to put out of sight; also in phrases, ***to bury one's face in one's hands***, ***one's hands in one's pockets***, etc.

1601 HOLLAND *Pliny* I. 45 The riuer that is buried vnder the earth, twentie miles off appeareth againe. **1710** ADDISON *Whig-Exam.* No. 4 ¶1 As well assault an army that is buried in intrenchments. **1815** BYRON *Heb. Melodies*, *Song of Saul* i, Bury your steel in the bosoms of Gath. **1850** MRS. STOWE *Uncle Tom's C.* xxxiii. 299 Taking a pin..he buried it to the head in her flesh. **1853** KINGSLEY *Hypatia* xxv. 312 Hypatia sat still in her chamber, her face buried in her hands.

b. *intr.* for *refl.* or *pass.* To burrow; also *Mech.* to lie embedded or enclosed. Of a vessel: to plunge the bows under water. Also *trans.*

1841 JOHNSTON in *Proc. Berw. Nat. Club* I. No. 9. 266 The animal buries in sand. *c* **1850** *Rudim. Navig.* (Weale) 124 Those ends of the planks which bury in the rabbets. **1866** 'ARGONAUT' *Arts Rowing & Training* I. iv. 28 The oar will be feathered under water, and thus the boat will be buried. **1886** *Outing* (U.S.) Nov. 117/1 It was asserted that she [*sc.* the keel schooner] was too fine forward,..that she would bury in driving hard. **1888** W. B. WOODGATE *Boating* x. 128 The aspirant to sculling honours had better..take his first lesson in a gig... A dingey buries too much on the stroke, and spoils style.

c. *fig.*

c **1449** PECOCK *Repr.* I. viii. 39 The inward book of lawe of kinde, biried in mannis soule and herte. **1712** BERKELEY *Pass. Obed.* §9 Wks. 1871 III. 113 Every man's particular rule is buried in his own breast. **1855** H. REED *Lect. Eng. Hist.* ii. 61 The truth, that now is buried beneath the mass of the old British legends.

5. *pass.* To be profoundly absorbed or engrossed *in* a habit or practice.

c **1380** WYCLIF *Tracts* xviii. Wks. (1880) 271 Prelatis & peynted religious beried in here olde synne. **1603** KNOLLES *Hist. Turkes* (1621) 654 Charles the emperour resolved..to passe over into Affricke, whilest Solyman was yet buried in the Persian wars. **1868** TENNYSON *Lucretius* 9 His mind Half buried in some weightier argument.

bury, obs. form of BURROW.

Buryat: see BURIAT.

buryer, obs. form of BURIER.

burying ('bɛrɪɪŋ), *vbl. sb.* (Forms: see the verb.) [f. BURY *v.* + -ING[1].]

1. a. The action of entombing a dead body or anything similarly treated; burial, interment.

1297 R. GLOUC. 382 Henry, hys 3onge sone, was at hys buryng. *c* **1300** *K. Alis.* 8013 N'uste mon never hethen kyng Have so riche a buryeng. **1388** WYCLIF *Jer.* xxii. 19 He schal

be biried with the biriyng of an asse. *c* **1420** *Sir Amadace* xxiv, I schalle..Bringe his bodi to Cristun beriinge. **1608** SHAKS. *Per.* III. ii. 72 Who finds her, give her burying. **1753** CHAMBERS *Cycl. Supp.* s.v., Burying alive, was the punishment of a Vestal who had violated her vow of virginity. **1772** JOHNSON in *Phil. Trans.* LXIII. 144 An axe ..imports war: the taking it up, being a declaration of war; and the burying it, a token of peace. *Mod.* The day after the battle was devoted to the burying of the dead.

† **b.** *concr.* A funeral, a burial. *Obs.* or *dial.*

1681 E. MURPHY *State Irel.* §31 He..tarried a while in the ..place ere the Burying came. **1750** WESLEY *Wks.* (1872) II. 192 There being a great burying in the afternoon. **1787** WOLCOTT (P. Pindar) *Ode upon O.* Wks. 1812 I. 433 Palls that grace a burying.

2. The action of depositing under ground, covering over with earth or other material; also *fig.*

1626 BACON *Sylva* §315 The Burying of Bottles of Drink well stopped. *Mod.* The burying of his talent by the unprofitable servant.

3. *Comb.* and *Attrib.*, as ***burying-bell***, ***-day***, ***-grave***, ***-party***; also † **burying-light**, ? the tapers used at a funeral service; † **burying-ticket**, ? a funeral card.

1552 in *Church Goods of Berks.* 8 A *buriennge bell, a sakeringe bell. **1602** *Return fr. Parnass.* III. v. (Arb.) 47 From our first birth, vntil our *burying day. **1592** SHAKS. *Rom. & Jul.* II. iii. 10 What is her *burying graue that is her wombe. **1887** H. R. HAGGARD xxxi. *Jess* in *Cornhill Mag.* Mar. 321 You are likely to meet a *burying party. *a* **1918** W. OWEN *Poems* (1920) 19 The burying-party, picks and shovels in their shaking grasp. **1522** *Bk. Founder's Comp.* in *N. & Q.* III. IX. 62 Payd to the Wax Chaundler for the *beryin lycht at Sen Markytts. **1712** STEELE *Spect.* No. 431. ⁋3, I then nibbled all the red Wax of our last Ball-Tickets, and three Weeks after the black Wax from the *Burying-Tickets of the old Gentleman.

'burying, *ppl. a.* [f. as prec. + -ING².] Interring; enclosing, whelming.

1762–9 FALCONER *Shipwr.* III. 590 The burying waters close around their head. **1855** TENNYSON *Maud* II. v. 12 Never an end to the stream of passing feet, Driving, hurrying, marrying, burying.

Hence **burying-beetle**, **-sylph**, a clavicorn beetle, which excavates the ground beneath the dead bodies of mice, moles, and other small quadrupeds, so as to bury them as a nidus for its larvæ.

1802 BINGLEY *Anim. Biog.* (1813) III. 126 The burying sylph..Synonyms. Silpha vespillo. Linn.—Scarabæus silphoides? **1818** KIRBY & SPENCE *Entomol.* I. ix. 258 The burying-beetle (*Necrophorus Vespillo*, F.) inters the bodies of small animals. **1883** WOOD in *Gd. Words* Dec. 762/1 Burying Beetles, with their orange and black-banded bodies.

'burying-ground. A place for burial; a churchyard, graveyard, cemetery.

1711 *Lond. Gaz.* 4911/4 They intend to let by Lease the Burying-ground in Bunhill-field. **1814** *Q. Rev.* II. 83 A Moravian burying-ground. **1854** H. MILLER *Sch. & Schm.* 210 Getting out, just as a party of unscrupulous resurrectionists were in the act of entering the burying-ground. **1872** MARK TWAIN *Innoc. Abr.* xv. 99 Père la Chaise, the national burying-ground of France.

'burying-place. A place of burial, a tomb; now usually = prec.

1382 WYCLIF *Gen.* xxiii. 4 Gif ȝe to me ryȝt of a biryyng place with ȝow. *c* **1450** MERLIN iii. 57 Uter..lete write vpon eche beryinge place his name that lay vnder. **1561** T. NORTON *Calvin's Inst.* III. 330 Burying places were called *Cæmeteria*, Sleping places. **1611** BIBLE *Gen.* xlix. 30 The caue..which Abraham bought..for a possession of a burying place. **1726** AYLIFFE *Parerg.* 132 Every Person may have a Burying-place in his own Estate. **1870** F. WILSON *Ch. Lindisf.* 65 The burying-place around it has been used within memory.

buryt, obs. form of BORITH, soapwort.

† **bus**, *sb.*¹ *Obs.* Also 6 bowse. [a. Du *bus*, MDu. *buis* 'gun', a specialized sense of *bus*, *buis* box: cf. Ger. *büchse*, and see HARQUEBUS.] A harquebus.

1549 *Compl. Scot.* (1801) Mak reddy your cannons bastardis, falcons..busis, doggis, doubil busis, hagbuttis of croche, half haggis. **1556** *Chron. Gr. Friars* 42 [see BOWZE].

bus, 'bus (bʌs), *sb.*² Occas. buss. **1. a.** A familiar shortening of OMNIBUS.

1832 HT. MARTINEAU *Weal & Woe* i. 14 If the station offers me a place in a buss. **1837** *Fraser's Mag.* XVI. 680 Another Buss came up. *a* **1845** BARHAM *Ingol. Leg.* Ser. III. (1858) 445 There was no taking refuge too then, as with us, On a slip-sloppy day, in a cab or a 'bus. **1851** *Belgravia* 73 Whilst thundering down Hundreds of busses scour the trembling town. **1887** *Punch* 12 Mar. 130/2 She is left without a penny to pay for tram or bus.

b. Phr. ***to miss the bus*** (fig.): to lose an opportunity; to fail in an undertaking. *slang.*

[**1886** J. MORLEY *Miscell.* III. 147 Though he [*sc.* Mark Pattison] appeared..as much a Catholic at heart as Newman ..it was probably his constitutional incapacity for heroic and decisive courses that made him, according to the Oxford legend, miss the omnibus.] **1915** C. J. DENNIS *Sentimental Bloke* 118 The deeds and words of some un'appy bloke Who's missed the bus. **1922** *Daily Mail* 28 Oct. 8/3 The Prime Minister has 'missed the 'bus'... He has thrown away the greatest opportunity ever offered..to any statesman. **1940** *Manch. Guardian Weekly* 10 May 357 He [*sc.* Mr. Chamberlain]..boasted that Hitler has 'missed the bus'.

2. a. Short for *bus-bar* (see 3) (*Cent. Dict.* Suppl. 1909). *spec.* (also buss) a major path along which signals are transferred from one part of a computer system to another; = HIGHWAY 2 c.

1930 *Proc. Inst. Radio Engin.* XVIII. 438 A panel voltmeter is connected to the filament bus to facilitate the adjustment of the bus voltage. **1946** *Ann. Computation Lab. Harvard Univ.* I. 12 All units in the machine are connected to the central distribution buss over which numbers are transferred from one unit to another with the aid of timed electrical impulses. **1949** [see HIGHWAY 2 c]. **1969** *U.S. Patent 3,480,769*, Control signals are encoded and routed over single wire busses and decoded at each analog computer circuit so that the signal on a single buss can provide any one of a fairly large number of operating conditions. **1972** *IEEE Trans. Nuclear Sci.* XIX. 674/1 The general data bus consists of a controller on the computer 1-0 bus and a bidirectional 16-bit parallel data bus with six additional control lines. **1977** *Sci. Amer.* Sept. 88/1 An organizational principle of almost all microprocessors is that the various parts of the machine communicate with one another through a system of conductors called a bus. **1985** *Personal Computer World* Feb. 183 (Advt.), Range of host interfaces for popular buses.

b. *colloq.* (*a*) an aeroplane; (*b*) a motor car; (*c*) a motor cycle.

1910 *Flight* 13 Aug. 648 (*caption*) A Blériot 'Bus' being Built. *Ibid.*, M. *Blériot*..has nearly completed a four-seater monoplane... The day of the aerial 'bus will soon be with us. **1916** C. WINCHESTER *Flying Men* 213 We were about 2500 feet above the "buses'. **1921** *Times Lit. Suppl.* 24 Feb. 113/4 Cadets..marching in their companies and battalions or gadgeting with 'buses on Port Meadow. **1924** J. BUCHAN *Three Hostages* xii. 179 Got here last night after a clinkin' journey, with the bus [*sc.* an aeroplane] behavin' like a lamb. **1927** D. L. SAYERS *Unnat. Death* xi. 131 'Excuse me,' said.. a youth in motor-cycling kit, 'but could you give me a hand with my 'bus?'

3. *attrib.* and *Comb.*, as ***bus company***, ***conductor*** (CONDUCTOR 7), ***conductress***, ***crew***, ***driver***, ***load***, ***queue*** (QUEUE *sb.* 3), ***ride***, ***route***, ***station***, ***terminal***, ***ticket***, ***time-table***, ***top***; ***bus-riding*** adj.; **bus-bar**, **-conductor** *Electr.*, a system of conductors in a generating station on which all the power of all the generators is collected for distribution or, in a receiving station, on which the power from the generating station is received for distribution; also *attrib.* (cf. OMNIBUS *a.* 2 c); **bus-boy** orig. *U.S.* = OMNIBUS *sb.* 4; **busman**, the driver of a bus; so **busman's holiday**, leisure time spent in occupations of the same nature as those in which one engages for a living; **bus-rod** = *bus-bar*; **bus-shelter**, a roadside structure affording protection from the weather to passengers intending to travel by bus; **bus-stop**, a place at which a bus makes a regular halt.

1893 SLOANE *Stand. Elect. Dict.*, *Bus Rod*... *Synonyms* —Omnibus Rod, Wire or Bar—Bus Bar, or Wire. **1897** *Daily News* 9 Dec. 10/3 The currents of electricity generated at these dynamos are led to one common conductor called 'the bus-bar'. **1911** *Engineer* 10 Mar. 238/3 The busbar voltage suddenly dropped. **1948** *Electronic Engin.* XX. 38 Two cores of magnetic material linked the busbar so that the current caused them to be magnetically saturated. **1913** *Industrial Worker* (Spokane, Washington) 12 June 4/2 They are cooks, bus boys, dishwashers. **1947** AUDEN *Age of Anxiety* (1948) ii. 36 A bus-boy brushing a table. **1965** R. HOWARD tr. *S. de Beauvoir's Force of Circumstance* x. 477 After a difficult adolescence, he had been a sailor, then a busboy in a London restaurant, and I don't know what else. **1899** R. WHITEING *No. 5 John St.* xi. 107 My Samaritan gave me the letter to the 'bus company. **1905** *Times* 9 Mar. 13/4 The London and District Motor Bus Company. **1846** *Chambers's Jrnl.* V. 28/2 The only cry heard would be that of the 'bus-conductor for Paddington and Holloway. **1886** *Punch* 27 Nov. 254/1 Bus Conductor (shouting from the Foot-board), Wes'minister! **1902** WEBSTER Suppl. s.v. *Bus*, Bus..conductor, etc. (*Elec.*). **1919** *Manch. Guardian* 22 Oct. 8/6 Women 'bus conductors. **1935** *Discovery* Feb. 58/2 London bus-conductors on the new 'Q' type motor-buses are having a busy time. **1916** *Sphere* 30 Dec. 237 His [*sc.* a soldier's] sister in the garb of a 'bus conductress, an employment which she has taken up in her brother's absence. **1939** *Daily Mail* 13 Sept. 3/3 The first women bus conductresses appeared in Manchester yesterday. **1958** *New Statesman* 7 June 713/2 The admittedly underpaid bus crews. **1870** D. J. KIRWAN *Palace & Hovel* (1963) xi. 98 The cabbies are to the buss drivers a sort of gypsies. **1905** G. B. SHAW in *Shaw on Shakespeare* (1962) 149 Beatrice.. saying things that a flower-girl would spare a busdriver as if they were gems of delicate intuition. **1888** G. & W. GROSSMITH *Diary of Nobody* (1892) iii. 42 All our 'bus-load ..seemed to be going in. **1959** I. & P. OPIE *Lore & Lang. Schoolchildren* xvi. 359 Bus-loads of youngsters come in from the surrounding villages. **1851** MAYHEW *Lond. Labour* III. 348 As the busmen call them. **1887** *Pall Mall G.* 25 July 6/1 Tale of the 'bus men's woes..the private 'buses. **1893** *Eng. Illustr. Mag.* 488/2, I shall indeed take a holiday soon, ..but it will be a 'Busman's Holiday'. **1921** *Times* (weekly ed.) 19 Aug., The proverbial 'busman's holiday' is nothing to that of the man who retires from business. **1927** *Observer* 21 Aug. 13/2 The U.S.A. Secretary for War..said..'No, I did not go to see the military manœuvres. Busmen's holidays do not give me any delight.' **1938** R. FINLAYSON *Brown Man's Burden* 31 He was lucky to get safely back to the village at all! A friendly bus-man put him off at the right place. **1950** 'R. CROMPTON' *William—the Bold* ii. 58 You'd think it was a treat to stand in a bus queue. **1908** KIPLING *Lett. Travel* (1920) 199 A 'bus-ride down the Strand. **1952** M. LASKI *Village* xii. 175 It would save the bus-ride. **1898** *Daily News* 14 Apr. 7/2 The 'bus riding public. **1898** A. BENNETT *Man fr. North* vii. 44 Cab-fares, bus-routes, and local railways. **1936** *Discovery* Sept. 299/2 *Birds of the Green Belt* contains a useful transport guide of train and bus routes. **1945** *City of Oxf. Council Rep.* 16 Feb. 240 It is recommended that..the principle of the provision by Council of roadside bus shelters be accepted. **1960** C. WILSON *Ritual in Dark* II. ii. 212 An old man, crouched in a bus shelter. **1952** M. LASKI *Village* vii. 120 The big mock-marble cinema opposite the bus-station. **1916** E. POUND *Lustra* 25 You loiter at the corners and bus-stops. **1930** *City of Oxf. Council Rep.* 20 Feb. 241 That notices 'Bus Stop' be marked on the road at the usual stopping places at Carfax. **1947** M. LOWRY *Under Volcano* ix. 254 Had not Geoffrey met her at the Bus Terminal? **1949** *Granta* Christmas No. 43 Punctopapyrists (bus ticket collectors to you). **1928** R. KNOX *Footsteps at Lock* xiv. 138 He asked for a railway guide and a 'bus time-table. **1905** *Westm. Gaz.* 31 May 10/2 'The Delights of London', introducing various amusing 'imitations'—in a tea-shop, on a 'bus-top, and so forth. **1927** *Glasgow Herald* 18 Aug. 9 The most interesting 'bus-top ride which London can offer.

bus (bɪz), *sb.*³ Colloq. abbrev. of BUSINESS 20.

1864 HOTTEN *Slang Dict.* (ed. 3) 90 *Bus*, business (of which it is a contraction) or action, on the stage. **1933** AUDEN *Dance of Death* 10 *A.* Shall I show you? *B.* Please. [*Bus.*] **1949** WODEHOUSE *Mating Season* ix. 90 'Throughout the script the word "*bus*" in brackets occurs... Can you explain it?' 'It's short for "*business*". That's where you hit Mike with your umbrella. To show the audience that there has been a joke.'

bus, *v.* (*3rd sing.*) *north. dial.* Also buse, bos, bose, boes, (boost). *Pa. t.* bud(e, bute, bood, boot, boud, bode. *Pres. Subj.* bove. [Contracted f. *behoves*, *behoved*, chiefly used impersonally. Transition forms in pa. t. were *byhod*, *behode*: see BEHOVE. The pa. t. *bud*, *bid*, is still used in Sc. of moral or logical necessity: it is no longer impersonal.]

† **1.** *impersonally.* (It) behoves, is obligatory upon, is necessary for. *Obs.*

a **1300** *Cursor M.* 9870 Of a womman bos him be born. *Ibid.* 10639 þan bus þis may be clene and bright. *Ibid. Resurrection* 68. p. 986 þat day..bode man again be boght. **1352** MINOT *Poems* (1887) ix. 28 At the Nevil-cros, nedes bud tham knele. *c* **1386** CHAUCER *Reeve's T.* 107 (Ellesm.) Him boes [*v.r.* bihoues, byhoueþ, falles, he muste] serue hym selne that has na swayn. *c* **1400** *Ywaine & Gaw.* 3022 With both at ones bihoves him fight, So bus the do. *c* **1400** *Destr. Troy* 5115, I bid þerfore barly, þat he bove herchyn. *c* **1440** *York Myst.* viii. 148 Nowe bus me wende. *c* **1500** *Poem on Death* in Halliwell *Nugæ P.* 40 To rekkenynge buse us ryse.

2. *mod.Sc. Pa. tense* also as *pres.*, with subject: Must, ought.

a **1774** FERGUSON *Election*, For tricks ye buit be tryin'. **1786** BURNS *Dream* vi, I fear, that wi' the geese, I shortly boost to pasture I' the craft some day. **1790** SHIRREF *Poems* 43 (JAM.) A' he said boot just be to the point. **1818** SUS. FERRIER *Marriage* II. 123 'An' ye bute to hae an English wife tu.' **1866** *Cornh. Mag.* XIII. 359 They bude to meet again. **1868** G. MACDONALD *R. Falconer* I. 67, 'I bude to speik whan I was spoken till.'

bus, *v.*² **1.** *intr.* To travel by bus; also in phr. *to bus it. colloq.*

1838 *New Monthly Mag.* LIII. 93 A little too bad..that you and I..should be compelled to 'buss it. **1860** *Chamb. Jrnl.* XIV. 116 We may 'cab' it..we may 'bus it; or we may go by boat. **1889** *Punch* 2 Mar. 107/1 'Bus'-ing on the cheap. **1936** J. B. PRIESTLEY *They walk in City* viii. 220 He had plenty of time to walk, bus, walk again. **1963** *Times* 11 Mar. 13/3 Mother now wins the car for termtime and the foreseeable future, and father has to bus it or bicycle.

2. *trans.* To transport (people) by bus from one place to another, esp. in order to encourage or achieve racial integration. Hence **'bus(s)ed** *ppl. a. U.S.*

1961 WEBSTER s.v., The children were bussed to school. **1969** *New Yorker* 31 May 86/3 Nine thousand children are now bused—about half as many as would have to be bused in the final stage of integration. **1969** *Ibid.* 29 Nov. 151/1 What had been a restless gathering of bused-in teenagers turned into a rapt adoring cult as soon as Dayan began to speak.

Hence **'bus(s)ing** *vbl. sb.*, travelling or transportation by bus; (*Mil.*) boarding a bus.

1888 G. & W. GROSSMITH *Diary of Nobody* (1892) v. 76 'We had better get into this blue 'bus.'.. 'No blue-bussing for me.' **1889** [see above]. **1923** KIPLING *Irish Guards* I. 108 They were instructed in march-discipline..as well as in bussing and debussing against time into motor-buses. **1965** *Economist* 19 June 1405/1 Local authorities should adopt the policy known in the United States as 'bussing'—that is to say, spreading immigrants' children around over a wide area. **1969** *Guardian* 18 Dec. 2/1 Southern Senators made a strong attempt today to prevent the integration of schools in the South by the bringing of black children from Negro areas to..schools in predominantly white areas. This controversial practice has become known simply as busing.

bus, Sc. form of BUSH.

busard, obs. form of BUZZARD¹.

‖ **busaun** (buːˈzaʊn). [G.] = POSAUNE.

1776 [see POSAUNE 1]. **1876** STAINER & BARRETT *Dict. Mus. Terms* 65/2 *Busaun. Busain. Buzain.* A reed-stop on the organ.

busbied (ˈbʌzbɪd). *a.* [f. BUSBY 2 + -ED².] Wearing a busby.

1914 G. LLOYD *Englishwoman's Adventures* 13 Four busbied officers. **1960** D. POTTER *Glittering Coffin* ii. 24 The busbied guards are on parade.

busby (ˈbʌzbɪ). [Derivation unknown.

Busby is the name of an English village, and also a personal surname of some antiquity, well known as that of Dr. Richard Busby, Head Master of Westminster School 1640–1695.]

†**1.** A kind of large bushy wig. *Obs.*

1764 T. BRYDGES *Homer Travest.* (1797) II. 144 But I'm afraid we cannot get him A busby large enough to fit him. **1882** *Globe* 24 July 2/1 This 'Busby', so often used colloquially when a large bushy wig is meant, most probably took its origin, not..from Dr. Busby, the famous head master of Westminster School, but from the wig denominated a 'Buzz', from being frizzled and bushy.

2. A tall fur cap, with or without a plume, having a bag (generally of cloth, and of the colour of the facings of the regiment) hanging out of the top, on the right side; worn by hussars, artillerymen, and engineers; hence, one who wears a busby. Also ***busby-bag***.

1807 (25 Dec.) in Malet *Hist. Rec. 18th Hussars* (1869) 16 Permission received to be clothed as Hussars—jackets light blue, silver lace; busby-bags blue. **1853** in Duncan *Hist. Royal Regt. Artill.* (1873) II. 44 Sealskin busbies were substituted for bearskin. **1854** in Kinglake *Crimea* V. i. 271 The Busby-bags taking it coolly. **1870** *Daily News* 27 July 5 They wore the handsome and characteristic jacket which our Hussars have discarded for the tunic, and retained their busby. **1885** ANNANDALE *Impl. Dict.* s.v., The bag appears to be a relic of a Hungarian head-dress from which a long padded bag hung over, and was attached to the right shoulder as a defence against sword-cuts.

buscage, obs. form of BOSCAGE = thicket.

buscarl ('bʌskɑːl). *Hist.* A modernized form of the 11th c. *butsecarl*, a. ON. *buzukarl*, meaning 'seaman, sailor, mariner' [cf. BUSS *sb.*[1]]. Found in the 17th c. legal antiquaries, and occasionally used by modern historical writers in this or the original form.

a **1121** *O.E. Chron.* an. 1066 (Laud MS.) þa butsecarlas hine forsocan. [**1664** SPELMAN cites the forms *buzecarl* (Domesday), *butsecarl*, *buthsecarl*, buzsecarl, bucecarl. **1678** BLOUNT has *Buzcarles*, *Buscarles*, Mariners or Seamen. **1730–6** BAILEY *Butsecarl*, *Butescarl*, a Boatswain or Mariner.] **1864** SIR F. PALGRAVE *Norm. & Eng.* III. 176 Sturdy knights, active squires, weather-beaten butsecarles ..assembled at Fécamp. **1866** KINGSLEY *Herew.* i. 53 Out and away aboard a ship among the buscarles. *Ibid.* vi. 118 The broad hats of peaceful buscarles.

buscaylle, obs. form of BUSHAILE.

†**busch**, *v. northern. Obs.* Also bossh. [app. onomatopœic: cf. *brush*, *rush*, *gush*; also BASH, etc.] *trans.* To flow with a rush, to gush; to rush with force.

c **1325** *E.E. Allit. P.* C. 143 þe wawes & efte busched to þe abyme þat breed fysches. *c* **1350** *Will. Palerne* 173 Til hit big was & bold to buschen on felde. *c* **1400** *Destr. Troy* 11120 Myche blode of his body bosshet out after. **1535** STEWART *Cron. Scot.* III. 368 And all the bowellis buschit out.

busch-, earlier spelling of BUSH-.

busch(e, buscie, obs. forms of BUSS.

busch(en, var. of BUSK *v. Obs.*

†**buschbome**. *Sc. Obs.* [a. Flem. *busboom*, i.e. *box-beam*, *box-tree*: see BOX *sb.*[1]] Boxwood, box.

1513 DOUGLAS *Æneis* IX. x. 67 Bos schawmys of turnyt buschboun [ed. **1553** buschbome] tre.

buschie, early equivalent of BUSHMAN.

1731 MEDLEY *Kolben's Cape G. Hope* I. 89 A sort of Hottentot Banditti infests all the nations about the Cape.. They are called Buschies or High-way men. *Ibid.* 269 The honest Hottentots abhor these Buschies as they do their devil.

buschop(e, obs. form of BISHOP.

buscom, obs. form of BUXOM.

buscy, obs. form of BUSS *sb.*[1]

†**buse**, *v. rare.* Aphetic form of ABUSE.

1589 WARNER *Alb. Eng.* VI. xxx. (1612) 151 My wife.. Shall not ywis be bused by the squandring Pollo.

buse, obs. = BOOSE, cattle-stall; BUS *v.* behoves.

busemare, var. BISMER, *Obs.*, shame, reproach.

buser ('bʌsə(r)). (Disused.) Also **busser**. [f. BUS *sb.*[2] + -ER[1].] A bus horse.

1894 *Daily Tel.* 10 Nov. 10/5 [For sale] By order of the Star Omnibus Company, six useful busers. **1900** *Ibid.* 5 Sept. 7/2 The English 'bussers'..performed their part admirably as heavy artillery horses. **1901** *Morn. Post* 9 Apr. 8/1 Active short-legged bussers. All warranted quiet in harness.

buserde, obs. form of BUZZARD[1].

bush (bʊʃ), *sb.*[1] Forms: 3–7 **busk**, 4–7 **buske**; 4 **bos(s)ch(e, bossh(e, buss(e, (also bousch(e, boysch, buysch(e)**, 4–5 **busch(e, bussch(e**, 4–6 **bussh(e**, 5 **boshe**, 6 **bushe, buszhe**, 5– **bush**; *Sc.* 6– **bus, buss**. [ME. *busk*, a. ON. *busk-r* (Da. *busk*, Sw. *buske*), cogn. w. OHG. *bush* (MHG. *busch*, *bosch*, Ger. *busch*), MDu. *busc*, *bosc* (Du. *bosch*, *bos*), all ad. Rom. *bosco* or late L. *boscum*, *boscus* wood, of which the ulterior source is unknown. Cf. BOSCAGE, BOSK. The form *busk* is still found in northern dial., but in Sc. is reduced to *bus*, *buss*; the *buss* of the Ayenbite was only Dan Michel's way of spelling *bush* with *ss* for *sh*.]

1. a. A shrub, particularly one with close branches arising from or near the ground; a small clump of shrubs apparently forming one plant.

α. Form *busk*. *Obs.* exc. *dial.*

c **1250** *Gen. & Ex.* 2779 Vt of ðat busk..God sente an steuene. **1377** LANGL. *P. Pl.* B. XI. 136 Briddes..þat in buskes [**1393** C. XIV. 156 bosshes, bussches, busches] made nestes. *c* **1440** *Promp. Parv.* 56 Buske or busshe, *rubus*, *dumus*. **1549** *Compl. Scot.* 37 Birdis hoppand fra busk to tuist. **1601** YARINGTON *Two Lament. Traj.* III. ii. in Bullen *O. Pl.* IV, Thickets full of buskes. **1670** RAY. *Eng. Prov.* (1678) 54 Lads' love's a busk of broom. **1863** LD. LYTTON *Ring Amasis* II. 211 The old straight carriage-drives..now wind in and out among the busks and thickets. **1855** *Whitby Gloss.*, *Busks*, bushes.

β. Form *bush*.

c **1315** SHOREHAM 131 Thou art the bosche of Synay. **1340** *Ayenb.* 28 Ne in gerse, ne in busse, ne in trauwe. **1382** WYCLIF *Luke* vi. 44 A boysch [**1388** buysche] of breris. **1398** TREVISA *Barth. De P.R.* XVII. cxl. (1495) 696 A bussche hyghte Rubus. *c* **1420** *Pallad. on Husb.* I. 87 As plummes boshes are. **1543** *Act 35 Hen. VIII*, xvii. §4 Over-grown with Bushes or Under-wood. **1667** MILTON *P.L.* IV. 176 The undergrowth Of shrubs and tangling bushes. **1864** TENNYSON *Grandmother* 40 In the bush beside me chirrupt the nightingale.

γ. Form *bus* (*Sc.*).

1528 LYNDESAY *Dreme* 62 And flemit Flora frome euery bank and bus. **1768** ROSS *Helenore* 26 (JAM.) Upon the busses birdies sweetly sung. **1813** PICKEN *Poems* 163 (JAM.) I like our hills an' heathery braes, Ilk burdie, buss, an' burnie. *Sc. Proverbs*, Better a wee buss than nae beild. Ye maun bow to the buss ye get bield frae.

b. Phr. ***to beat the bush***: (*lit.*) in bat-fowling, to rouse the birds that they may fly into the net held by some one else; (*fig.*) to expend labour of which the fruit is not gained by oneself. (Cf. BEAT *v.* 26.) ***to beat*** (formerly also ***go, wend, seek***) ***about the bush***: to go indirectly and tentatively towards an object, to avoid coming to the point. Cf. BEAT *v.* 26 C.)

c **1440** *Generydes* 4524 Some bete the bussh and some the byrdes take. **1520** WHITTINTON *Vulg.* (1527) 1 A longe betynge aboute the busshe and losse of tyme to a yonge begynner. **1553** T. WILSON *Rhet.* 1 b, If he utter his mind in plain wordes: and tell it orderly, without goynge about the bushe. **1561** T. NORTON *Calvin's Inst.* I. 12 That we shuld not seke about the bush for an vncertaine Godhead. **1658–9** in Burton *Diary* (1828) III. 528 We have beaten the bush, and not come plainly to the point. **1705** VANBRUGH *Confeder.* III. ii, I went round the bush, and round the bush, before I came to the matter. **1819** *Blackw. Mag.* IV. 621 He never goes about the bush for a phrase. **1822** HAZLITT *Table-t.* II. ix. 212 He does not beat about the bush for difficulties or excuses. **1837** CARLYLE *Fr. Rev.* (1871) II. I. iii. 18 Benighted fowls, when you beat their bushes, rush towards any light.

c. *Proverbs.*

1599 SANDYS *Europæ Spec.* (1632) 123 Thus hath every gap his bush, each suspition his prevention. **1600** HOLLAND *Livy* XXIII. iii. 474 Therefore with one bush (as they say) ye are to stop two gaps, and to do both at once. **1638** SANDERSON *Serm.* II. 97 This common usage of the phrase, as it well preserveth the sence, so doth it also (that I may stop two gaps with one bush) justifie the truth of this charge in my text. *c* **1689** *Popish Pol. Unmaskt* 84 in *3rd Coll. Poems* (1689) 23/2 With them one Bird in Hand's worth two i' th' Bush. **1875** JEVONS *Money* (1878) 247 The..chance of receiving gold which is still like the bird in the bush.

2. In northern dialects extended to sub-shrubs as *heather*, or herbaceous plants growing in a clump, as *nettles*, *ferns*, *rushes*.

1529 LYNDESAY *Complaynt* 408 Ihone Vpeland bene full blyith, I trow, Because the rysche bus kepis his kow. **1570** *Trag.* in *Scot. Poems 16th C.* II. 232 Than mycht the Rasche bus keip ky on the bordour. **1570–87** HOLINSHED *Scot. Chron.* (1806) II. 96 Caused the rash bush to keep the cow. **1818** SCOTT *Rob Roy* xxv, The oppressors that hae driven me to tak the heather-bush for a bield.

†**3.** *collectively.* A clump of shrubs, a thicket; bushy ground. (Cf. BOSK 2.) *Obs.* exc. as reintroduced in sense 9.

1523 FITZHERB. *Surv.* 2 b, Highe grounde and drie is moost conuenyent for shepe, wode grounde and busshe for beestes. **1580** NORTH *Plutarch* (1676) 4 She had hidden herself in a grove..But Theseus finding her, called her.. Upon which..she came out of the bush. *a* **1639** SPOTTISWOOD *Hist. Ch. Scot.* v. (1677) 261 The rest betook them to a little bush of wood, where being environed on all sides, they yielded.

†**4. a.** A clump of shrubs used as a place of concealment; = AM-BUSH, q.v. So ***to take a bush, to thrust*** or ***run one's head in a bush***. *Obs.*

c **1330** *Arth. & Merl.* 8432 In on busse thou the hide. **1375** BARBOUR *Bruce* VII. 71 [He] stud in-till a busk lurkand. *c* **1380** *Sir Ferumb.* 2887 þan schullaþ our men of hem be-war: & breken out of þe bossche. *c* **1386** CHAUCER *Knt's T.* 659 This Palamon Was in a bussh that no man myghte hym se. *a* **1553** UDALL *Royster D.* I. iv. (Arb.) 28 As the beast passed by, he start out of a buske. **1631** J. BURGES *Answ. Rejoined* 52 Hee againe takes a bush, and hides himselfe vnder the ambiguous terme of Religious Ceremonies. **1655** GURNALL *Chr. in Arm.* i. (1669) 21/1 Instead of confessing their sins, they run their head in a bush, and by their good will would not come where God is.

b. ***beggar's-bush***: see BEGGAR 8.

1600 SHAKS. *A.Y.L.* III. iii. 85 And wil you (being a man of your breeding), be married vnder a bush like a begger?

5. a. A branch or bunch of ivy (perhaps as the plant sacred to Bacchus) hung up as a vintner's sign; *hence*, the sign-board of a tavern.

1532 MORE *Confut. Tindale* Wks. (1557) 642/1 Set vp for a bare signe, as a tauerners bush or tapsters ale stake. **1591** FLORIO *2nd Frutes* 185 Womens beauty..is like vnto an Iuy bush, that cals men to the tauern, but hangs itselfe withoute to winde and wether. **1612** DEKKER *If not good Play* Wks. 1873 III. 280 As a drawer in a new Tauern, first day the bush is hung vp. *c* **1613** ROWLANDS *More Knaues Yet* 36 At next bush and signe Calling for clarret. **1644** EVELYN *Mem.* (1857) I. 97 Wicker bottles dangling over even the chief entrance..serving for a vintner's bush. **1692** in *Capt. Smith's Seaman's Gram.* II. xxxi. 150 You may bind two of them across, like a Tavern-Bush. **1753** CHAMBERS *Cycl. Supp.*, *Bush*, also denotes a coronated frame of wood hung out as a sign at taverns..antiently, signs where wine was sold were bushes. **1788** H. WALPOLE *Remin.* ix. 71 How should people know where wine is sold, unless a bush is hung out?

b. Hence, the tavern itself.

a **1625** BEAUM. & FL. (O.) Twenty to one you find him at the bush. **1631** HEYWOOD *Maid of West* II. v. Wks. 1874 II. 415 Then will I go home to the bush Where I drew wine.

c. Proverb. ***good wine needs no bush***.

1600 SHAKS. *A.Y.L.* Epil., If it be true that good wine needs no bush, 'tis true, that a good play needes no Epilogue. **1611** COTGR. s.v. *Bon*, Good wine draws customers without any help of an iuy-bush. **1674** R. GODFREY *Inj. & Ab. Physic* 168 As good Wine needs no Bush, no more do good Medicines a printed Bill. **1845** FORD *Handbk. Spain* I. 30 Good wine needs neither bush, herald, nor crier. **1861** W. THORNBURY in *Gd. Words* 432 Faded boughs—the bush that good wine does not need—rustle over the door.

d. *fig.* as ***to hang out bushes***.

1616 BEAUM. & FL. *Cust. Countr.* III. ii, Young women in the old world were not wont, Sir, To hang out gaudy bushes for their beauties. **1643** SIR T. BROWNE *Relig. Med.* II. §2 In every one of them, some outward figures, which hang as signes or bushes of their inward formes.

e. *fig.* Boasting, bluster, 'tall talk'. *U.S. dial.*

1837 HALIBURTON *Clockm.* (1862) 450 You Maine folks have been talkin' a leetle too fast lately, a leetle too much bush.

†**6.** *transf.* **a.** Anything resembling a bush; a bushy mass of foliage, feathers, etc.; a bunch. *Obs.* or *dial.*

1513 DOUGLAS *Æneis* VII. xii. 77 Amyd a bus of speris in rayd thai. **1530** PALSGR. 202/1 Busshe of oystrisshe fethers, *plumart*. **1542** UDALL *Erasm. Apophth.* 296 a, The cypres tree..growyng sharpe with a bushe greate beneth and smal aboue of a trymme facion. **1611** SPEED *Hist. Gt. Brit.* IX. iii. (1632) 464 In the ninth of his Raigne a blazing Starre appeared with two bushes. **1648** GAGE *West Ind.* xi. (1655) 40 They put on all their bravery..and bushes of feathers.

b. A signalling instrument used in Cornish pilchard fishing. *local.*

1880 in M. A. COURTNEY *W. Cornw. Gloss.* **1892** *Graphic* 13 Aug. 194/1 The huers on land making signals to the boatmen with two instruments called 'bushes', which are hoops crossing each other, and covered with a white bag, and fastened to the end of short rods.

c. The cat-o'-nine-tails. *slang.*

1895 *Daily News* 13 Sept. 7/6 They might give him twenty years, and he should not care, so long as they did not order him the bush.

7. a. *esp.* A bushy head of hair. (Very common in 16th c.: *of hair* is now expressed.)

1509 BARCLAY *Ship of Fooles* (1570) 232 To hyre the bush of one that late is dead, Therewith to disguise his fooles doting head. **1530** PALSGR. 762 Trymme my busshe, barber. **1609** BIBLE (Douay) *2 Kings* xiv. 26 Once a yeare he was polled, because his bush did burden him. **1640** SANDERSON *Serm.* 147 A bush of hair will do it, where it groweth. **1719** D'URFEY *Pills* I. 57 He who wears a long bush, All powder'd down from his Pericrane. *a* **1845** BARHAM *Ingold. Leg.* Ser. III. (1858) 508 A continued tuft of coarse, wiry hair.. swelled out in a greyish-looking bush above the occiput. **1880** *Chamb. Jrnl.* 774 Their heads..covered with great bushes of wool.

b. occas. of a bushy beard, or eyebrows.

[*c* **1400** *Ywaine & Gaw.* 261 His browes war like litel buskes.] **1647** S. SHEPPARD *2d pt. Committee-Man. Curr.* I. ii. 2 His chin has no bush, save a little downe. **1859** TENNYSON *Vivien* 669 He dragg'd his eyebrow bushes down, and made A snowy penthouse for his hollow eyes.

c. (A bushy growth of) pubic hair. *slang.*

1922 JOYCE *Ulysses* 85 He..saw the dark tangled curls of his bush floating, floating hair of the stream around the limp father of thousands. **1959** M. RICHLER *Apprenticeship Duddy Kravitz* I. ix. 50 Milty ran off crying... 'What is it, pussy-lamb?' 'I'm never going to grow a bush, Mummy.' **1968** J. UPDIKE *Couples* i. 9 Her throat, wrists, and triangular bush appeared the pivots for some undeniable effort of flight. **1973** A. POWELL *Temporary Kings* ii. 72 He insisted on taking a cutting from my bush—said he always did that after having anyone for the first time.

†**8.** A bushy tail, *esp.* of a fox; = BRUSH *sb.*[2] 3 b.

1575 TURBERV. *Bk. Venerie* 241 The tayle of a foxe is called his Bush. **1577** DEE *Relat. Spir.* I. (1659) 113 It seemeth to be a dead Lion; for it hath a long tail with a bush at the end. **1610** GUILLIM *Heraldry* III. xiv. (1660) 166 Termes of the Tayle, That of a Fox is termed his Bush.

9. a. (Recent, and probably a direct adoption of the Dutch *bosch*, in colonies originally Dutch.) Woodland, country more or less covered with natural wood: applied to the uncleared or untilled districts in the British Colonies which are still in a state of nature, or largely so, even though not wooded; and by extension to the *country* as opposed to the *towns*. For U.S. examples see *D.A.*, *D.A.E.*

1780 [cf. *bush-cat* in 11]. **1826** J. ATKINSON *Agric. & Grazing N.S.W.* iv. 64 When any person finds himself overstocked..they go into the interior, or *bush*, as it is

termed, beyond the occupied parts of the country. **1828** SCOTT *Tapestr. Chamber*, When I was in the Bush, as the Virginians call it. **1836** W. B. MARSHALL *Two Visits N.Z.* 152 They [*sc.* the interpreters] took to the bush for shelter by day. **1837** J. LANG *N.S. Wales* I. 253 His house was well enough for the bush, as the country is generally termed in the colony. **1837** CARLYLE *Fr. Rev.* (1871) II. v. iv. 187 The Black man loves the Bush. **1851** N. J. MERRIMAN *Jrnl.* 21 Sept. in *Kafir, Hottentot, & Frontier Farmer* (1854) 121 His mother and sister had escaped into the bush for refuge. **1857** R. B. PAUL *Lett. fr. Canterbury* iv. 65 A pleasant walk of three hours through the bush. **1873** TROLLOPE *Australia* I. 299 Nearly every place beyond the influences of the big towns is called 'bush' even though there should be not a tree to be seen. **1874** GEIKIE *Life Woods* ii. 21 Every thing being much cheaper in Toronto than away in the bush. **1886** *New Zealand Herald* 1 June 2/4 There is a bush upon it of 63 acres. **1888** *Castle Line Guide to S. Afr.* 69 (Pettman), The soil..having been covered to a large extent by a thick forest of trees (usually termed *bush*). **1953** A. PATON *Too Late the Phalarope* vii. 52 The kloof was wooded, not with forest, but with what we in South Africa call the bush. **1968** K. WEATHERLY *Roo Shooter* 27 He's been in the bush so long he's started to look like a roo.

b. *to take to the bush.*

1837 J. LANG *N.S. Wales* II. 15 Four of them immediately take to the bush, i.e. become bush-rangers, or run-away convicts, subsisting on plunder.

†**c.** A clump of trees. *N.Z. Obs.*

1856 T. TANCRED in *Edin. New Phil. Jrnl.* III. 7 Over these tracts are scattered some small 'bushes', or woods. **1857** R. B. PAUL *Lett. fr. Canterbury* vi. 94 You should try to have a bush on or near your section. **1867** LADY BARKER *Station Life N.Z.* (1870) x. 62 Most stations have a bush near the homestead.

d. *pl.* = sense 9a. *U.S.*

1879 TOURGÉE *Fool's Err.* xxii. 130 That refuge of free thought at the South, the woods (or 'the bushes', as the scraggly growth is more generally termed). **1912** C. MATHEWSON *Pitching* x. 210 The youngsters, who have come from the bushes and realize that this is their..chance to make good.

e. *to go bush*, to go into the country; to leave the city; to disappear from one's usual surroundings. Also *transf.*, to run wild, to go berserk. orig. and chiefly *Austral.*

1908 A. GUNN *We of Never-Never* 8 *She* went bush with me when I'd nothing but a skeeto net and a quart-pot to share with her. **1933** *Bulletin* (Sydney) 8 Feb. 20 It is rare for this fellow [*sc.* a dog] to go bush, but it has been recorded. **1934** A. RUSSELL *Tramp-Royal* x. 78 Milbuka had fled, 'gone bush' that morning, and could not be found. **1946** F. DAVISON *Dusty* xiv. 156 From the fact that separate killings [of sheep] were reported it was natural to conclude that they were the work of a sheep dog gone bush. **1953** V. BARTLETT *Struggle for Africa* i. 24 An African may do the same job day after day for months or years, and then suddenly 'go bush', omit some vital part of his routine, even say or do things which he himself cannot remember or explain when the mood is over. **1958** R. STOW *To Islands* 118 Brother Heriot has disappeared. He's gone bush somewhere and he might never come back. **1964** *Economist* 30 May 1000/1 To take refuge from [Australian] urban problems by 'going bush'.

10. *Attrib.* and general *Comb.*: **a.** in sense 1, as ***bush-fagot, -fruit, -ground, -planting, -tuft; bush-clad, -covered, -fringed, -grown, -like, -skirted*** adjs.; **b.** in senses 7 and 8, as ***bush-beard, -hair, -head, -tail, -wig***; so ***bush-bearded, -haired, -headed, -tailed*** adjs.; **c.** in sense 9 (= 'in the Bush'), as ***bush-country, -farm, -farming, -fire, -flat, -girl, -hand, -hut, -inn, -land, -life, -line, -range, -rider, -school, -shanty, -tea, -track, -walking*** (so ***-walk, -walker***), ***-work, -worker***, BUSH-RANGER.

1606 *Sir G. Goosecappe* I. i. in *O. Pl.* (1884) III. 11 He weares a *bush beard. **1662** GREENHALGH in Ellis *Orig. Lett.* II. 309. IV. 8 A learned Jew with a mighty bush-beard. **1615** A. STAFFORD *Heav. Dogge* 59 An austere *bushbearded Philosopher. **1876** G. MEREDITH *Beauch. Career* II. i. 13 He was a fair, huge, bush-bearded man. **1909** *Westm. Gaz.* 4 June 5/3 The *bush-clad plains of the North-Eastern Transvaal. **1855** W. G. SIMMS *Forayers* 544 Who would have thought of any fellow being such a..booby as to bring a bathing-tub..into..*bush country? **1859** J. ROCHFORT in *Jrnl. R. Geogr. Soc.* (1862) XXXII. 297 In looking across this lake you perceive a flat bush-country. **1954** J. COLLIN-SMITH *Scorpion on Stone* xx. 291 The lightening landscape of uninhabited scrub and bush-country. **1873** J. H. H. ST. JOHN *Pakeha Rambles through Maori Lands* v. 67 The dark *bush-covered hills of the Hunua. **1901** 'LINESMAN' *Words Eye-witness* (1902) 81 The rocky bush-covered foot of Schwartz Kop. **1843** *Jrnl. R. Agric. Soc.* IV. II. 292 Two rows of *bush-faggots are laid for perhaps 50 yards in advance on the mud at low water. **1851** *Househ. Wds.* II. 490 He had been down to the port from his *Bush-farm to sell his stuff. **1866** MARK LEMON *Wait for End.* x. 131 His log-house and his *bush-farming. **1845** L. LEICHHARDT *Jrnl. Exped. Austral.* 12 Feb. (1847) v. 147 The smoke of extensive *bush-fires was observed under Lord's Table Range. **1868** DILKE *Greater Brit.* II. III. iii. 32 The smoke from these bush-fires sometimes extends for hundreds of miles to sea. **1847** *N.Z. Jrnl.* VII. cxc. 90 The Ma-Whera river, another very considerable stream running through fine *bush flats. **1960** B. CRUMP *Good Keen Man* 136 Four deer and three hours later we came to a long bush-flat where the trees were enormous. **1891** 'J. EVELYN' *Baffled Vengeance* 47 The river between its *bush-fringed banks. **1884** *Pall Mall Budget* 22 Aug. 11/1 *Bush fruit, including gooseberries..raspberries, nuts, &c. **1822** *New Monthly Mag.* Sept. 414/2 She was, in fact, the prettiest young *Bush-girl I had yet seen. **1963** W. SOYINKA *Lion & Jewel* 9 Bush-girl you are, bush-girl you'll always be; Uncivilized and primitive—bush-girl! **1523** FITZHERB. *Surv.* 34b, Howe moche wode grounde or *busshe grounde, heythe, lyng, or suche other. **1837** HAWTHORNE *Amer. Note-bks.* (1871) I. 51 A deep dell, wooded and *bush grown. **1884** M. PATTISON *Mem.* (1885) 32 The little bush-grown beck which bounded our parish. **1692** *Lond. Gaz.* No. 2809/4 Another..Man.. with small grey Eyes, brown *bush Hair. **1530** PALSGR. 307/1 *Busshe heered, *crespelleux*. **1863** S. BUTLER *First Year Canterbury Settlement* x. 147 How many hands shall you want? We will say a couple of good *bush hands, who will put up your hut and yards and wool-shed. **1867** LADY BARKER *Station Life N.Z.* (1870) xxi. 183 First came two of the most experienced 'bush-hands'. *a* **1603** T. CARTWRIGHT *Confut. Rhem. N.T.* (1618) 196 Your puppet being lifted aboue the Priests *bush head. **1552** HULOET, *Bussh hedded, or he that hath a good bussh of heare. **1775** S. THAYER *Jrnl.* (1867) 12 Our troops..had not the satisfaction ..to build..a *Bush hut to pass the tedious night in. **1867** LADY BARKER *Station Life N.Z.* (1870) xxi. 181 The mistress of this charming bush-hut insisted on our having some hot coffee. **1885** MRS. PRAED *Australian Life* iii. 73 The usual bush hut of slabs and bark. **1881** MRS. PRAED *Policy & P.* I. 59 The driver paused before a *bush inn. **1881** GRANT *Bush Life Queensl.* I. viii. 96 Holding the long sweeping tail, tangled in a huge *bush-knot. **1842** C. HEAPHY *Narr. Residence* N.Z. viii. 103 The *bush land will be cleared with less..expense than at Wellington. **1862** LYTTON *St. Story* lxxxvii, All the Bush-land..was on fire. **1868** DILKE *Greater Brit.* II. III. ii. 14 Tropical bush-lands in which sheep-farming is impossible. **1849** LYTTON *Caxtons* II. XVII. ci, The memory of that wild *Bush-life. **1878** OGLE *Flowers & Unb. Guests* iv. 37 Great *bush-like plants of Senecio. **1889** R. PAULIN *Wild West Coast N.Z.* xiv. 119 Fresh snow ..came down to within 2000 feet of sea level—*i.e.*, considerably below the *bush-line. **1955** J. K. BAXTER *Fire & Anvil* iii. 58 A hut above the bush-line of the Southern Alps. **1879** T. W. GUDGEON *Reminisc. War N.Z.* xii. 70 Allowing the Hauhaus to erect a strong pah in the *bush-ranges. **1883** *Field* 10 Feb. 199 The tremendous stock whips of the Australian *bush-riders. **1852** G. C. MUNDY *Our Antipodes* III. ii. 61 The humble hedge-school—or rather *bush-school..and a crowd of flaxen..children rushing from its porch. **1896** H. LAWSON *While Billy Boils* 3 You remember when we hurried home from the old bush school. **1936** G. GREENE *Journey without Maps* II. 97 Even in the Sierra Leone Protectorate..most natives..will attend a bush school. **1942** J. S. HUXLEY in *Political Q.* XIII. 395 Over most of Africa..not 10 per cent of the schools are anything but the most primitive sub-elementary bush-schools, confining themselves to hymn-singing, the catechism, and the rudiments of the three R's. **1857** S. H. HAMMOND *Wild Northern Scenes* 169 Crop crept close alongside of me, in our *bush-shanty. **1888** 'R. BOLDREWOOD' *Robbery under Arms* III. xi. 161 Like a man in ..a bush shanty, not likely to wake before sunrise. **1924** H. T. GIBSON *That Gibbie Galoot* 66 Most bush shanties possess such a butt. **1858** H. MILLER *Sch. & Schm.* 313 This woody, *bush-skirted walk. **1606** *Wily Beguiled* in Hazl. *Dodsley* IX. 290, I might have turned my fair *bushtail to you instead of your father. **1708** *Lond. Gaz.* No. 4453/3 A.. Danish Bitch, with a Black Muzzle, and a long Bush Tail. **1872** W. F. BUTLER *Gt. Lone Land* xxi. (1875) 339 The *bush-tailed..clean-legged animals. **1891** R. WALLACE *Rural Econ. Austral. & N.Z.* ii. 43 *Bush tea is..boiled in a can. **1832** *N.S.W. Cal. & G.P.O. Directory* 51 Several *bush tracks lead to the farms. **1916** J. B. COOPER *Coo-oo-ee* i. 17 He..catches his father's favourite mare..and drives like mad over the five miles of rough bush track. **1968** K. WEATHERLY *Roo Shooter* 12 It was the shooter going to work, following a bush track that skirted the box flat. **1586** WEBBE *Eng. Poetrie* (Arb.) 77 Fro the sun beames safe lie lyzardes vnder a *bushtufte. **1956** S. HOPE *Diggers' Paradise* 196 Nothing deters young hikers from going bare-legged on *bushwalks. **1955** *Times* 21 June 9/5 Four hundred soldiers, police and *bush-walkers..are searching 5,000 ft Mount Baw Baw for Mihran Haig. **1853** in *Richmond-Atkinson Papers* (1960) I. 133 Beyond it there are two miles of *bush walking along what is called 'a line'. **1957** *Times* 2 Dec. 9/6 Four members of a bushwalking club who were burnt to death when trapped by a bush fire in the Blue Mountains yesterday. **1959** *Ibid.* 23 Sept. 1/4 Experience in out-door life such as skiing..bushwalking. **1805** *Miniature* (1806) No. 34 II. 175 Sober whist is by no means below the dignity of a *bush-wig. **1830** GALT *Laurie T.* II. xi. (1849) 78, I knew as little of *bush-work as any other store-keeper or mechanic. **1852** *Fraser's Mag.* XLV. 240 The sort of service that fits..for the bush-work of the Cape. **1936** I. L. IDRIESS *Cattle King* v. 41 He found a fair sale from travelling *bush-workers.

d. (Extended use of sense 9, passing into *adj.*) Crude; rough and ready; without the formal training or qualifications usually considered necessary for an occupation.

1851 E. J. WAKEFIELD *Let. to Sir G. Grey* 31 The stock-owner, though brought up as a gentleman, if he lives long in the 'bush', learns first to be proud of the 'bush' manners, and then becomes unfit for any but 'bush' society. **1870** R. P. WHITWORTH *Martin's Bay Settlement* 48/2, I found..tied to a stick (a bush candlestick), about two inches of candle. **1873** LADY BARKER *Station Amusem. N.Z.* vi. 101 He was what is called a bush-carpenter: *i.e.* a wandering carpenter, who travels from station to station, doing any little odd jobs wanted. *Ibid.* ix. 150 A bush doctor..was likely to be round by Simmons', cos o' his missus. **1891** G. CHAMIER *Philosopher Dick* I. vi. 141 The table was laid in regular bush style, with tin plates and pannikins, iron forks and spoons. **1916** J. B. COOPER *Coo-oo-ee!* ix. 115 Pilkins' gate, a skilful piece of rough bush carpentry, swinging on a wooden pivot. **1933** E. JONES *Autobiogr. Early Settler* xi. 52 As it was too far to get a tradesman up for any repairs, we were all, what was called, 'Bush Carpenters'. **1944** *Return to Attack* (Army Board, N.Z.) 9/2 Any available timber was turned into ingenious bush furniture. **1960** B. CRUMP *Good Keen Man* 114, I..put nine stitches in his [*sc.* the dog's] side with a pack-needle and string... He recovered..from both the wound and the bush surgery.

11. Spec. combs.: †**bush adder** (see quot., and cf. *boske addre* s.v. BOSK); **bush antelope**, ? = BUSH-BUCK; **bush-baby**, an African lemur of the species *Galago senegalensis*; **bush baptist** *slang* (chiefly *Austral.* and *N.Z.*) (see quot. 1959); **bush basil**, *Ocymum minimum*; **bush-bean**, the American name for the Kidney-bean (*Phaseolus vulgaris*); †**bush-bill**, ? a bill-hook; **bushboy**, a native Australian or South African bushman; **Bush Brotherhood**, a society of missionaries, clerical and lay, established to evangelize the inhabitants of the Australian bush; hence ***Bush Brother***; **bush burn** *N.Z.*, the burning of bush on cultivable land; land so cleared; so ***bush-burning*** vbl. sb.; **bush canary**, the popular name of various birds in Australia and New Zealand (see quots.); **bush-car** (see quot. 1926); **bush-cat**, the Serval or Tiger-cat of South Africa; **bush-chat**, a bird, one of the Chats or Saxicolæ; **bush cow**, (*a*) a wild cow of the bush; (*b*) the tapir; **bushcraft**, skill in matters pertaining to life in the bush; **bush-creepers**, a group of tropical birds belonging to the family of the Warblers; **bush dassie**, a S. African hyrax, *Dendrohyrax arboreus arboreus*; also *attrib.*; **bush deer**, in W. Africa, a gazelle; **bush dog** (see quot.); **bush-draining**, the draining of land by trenches filled with brushwood; **bush-dray** *Austral.* (see quot.); **bush-drive**, a drive of game in the South African bush; **bush eel** (see quots.); **bush-faller**, one who cuts down timber in the Bush; **bush-falling**, the felling of trees in the bush; **bush flea**, a variety of *Pulex* so called in Natal; **bush-fly**, an Australian blow-fly of the family *Calliphoridæ*; **bush-goat** = BUSH-BUCK; a S. African warbler, *Camaroptera brachyura*; **bush gourd**, the squash gourd, *Cucurbita melopepo*; **bush-grass**, *Calamagrostis epigejos*; **bush-hawk**, the New Zealand falcon, *Falco novæseelandiæ*; **bush-hen** *N.Z.*, the weka, *Gallirallus australis*; **bush-hog**, a wild pig of South Africa, the *bosch-vaark* of the colonists; **bush-hook**, a bill-hook (*U.S.*); **bush-house**, a house or hut in the bush; in Australia, also one in a (suburban) garden; **bush jacket**, a belted cotton jacket; **bush-lawyer**, (*a*) the New Zealand Bramble (*Rubus australis*); (*b*) *Austral.* and *N.Z.*, a layman who fancies he has a knowledge of law; an argumentative person; see also quot. 1874; **bush-magpie**, an Australian crow-shrike of the genus *Gymnorhina*; **bush-master**, a very venomous South American snake; **bush nurse**, a qualified nurse who is 'on call' in the remote districts of Australia; **bush-pig**, (*a*) a species of S. African swine, *Potamochœrus porcus koiropotamus*; (*b*) *N.Z.*, a wild pig; **bush pilot**, the pilot of an aeroplane which flies over sparsely inhabited country (chiefly *N. Amer.*); **bush poppy**, an evergreen Californian shrub, *Dendromecon rigida*; **bush-quail**, (*a*) a HEMIPOD; (*b*) an Indian bird of the genus *Perdicula* (Funk's Stand. Dict. 1893); **bush-rat**, a popular name for many small rodents; **bush road**, a road through the Bush; **bush robin**, the popular name esp. in Africa of various small birds; **bush-scythe**, a bill-hook; **bush-sheep** *U.S.* (see quot.); **bush shirt**, a loose-fitting light shirt worn by men in hot climates; **bush-shrike**, the English name of the *Thamnophilinæ*, a sub-family of the Shrikes; any of various birds belonging to the African subfamily Malaconotinæ; **bush-sickness** (see quots.); so *bush-sick* adj.; **bush-sparrow**, an American name for a kind of sparrow (see quot.); **bush-spider**, a large spider of S. America; **bush-syrup** (see quot.); **bush tea**, tea made from the leaves of certain shrubs, esp. those of species of *Cyclopia*, *Borbonia*, etc., dried and used medicinally in S. Africa; **bush telegraph** orig. *Austral.*, bush-rangers' confederates who disseminated information as to the movements of the police; *transf.*, rapid spreading of information, or of a rumour, etc.; the 'grapevine'; **bush-tick** (see quot. 1886); also *attrib.* in **bush-tick berry**, the fruit of *Osteospermum moniliferum*; **bush-tit**, a bird of the genus *Psaltriparus* (Cent. Dict. 1889); **bush-titmouse** *U.S.* (see quot.); **bush-track** = *bush-road*; †**bush-tree**, the Box (*Buxus sempervirens*); **bush vetch**, *Vicia sepium*; **bush-warbler**, any of several genera of warblers belonging to the family Sylviidæ, found in Asia, Australasia, and Africa; **bush-water**, rain water that collects in the low-lying parts of tropical forests; **bush willow**, in S. Africa, a plant of either of the species *Combretum erythrophyllum* or *C. salicifolium*; **bushwoman**, a woman living in the Australian or African bush; **bush-wood**, underwood, brushwood; **bush-worm** (see quot.); **bush-wren**, the New Zealand name for a bird of the species *Xenicus longipes*; see also BUSH-BUCK, -FIGHTER, etc.

1611 COTGR., *Anguille de bois*.. the *bush Adder, or wood snake. **1834** *Penny Cycl.* II. 81/1 The *Bush Antelope (*A. silvicultrix*), called bush-goat by the English residents at Sierra Leone. **1901** A. R. R. TURNBULL *Tales fr. Natal* 81 The occasional cry of a *bush-baby alone broke the awful silence. **1928** *Daily Tel.* 15 May 14/3 Two bush babies, the pets of Baroness de Tuyll. **1902** J. MILNE *Epistles of Atkins* i. 18 Nothing is left to the imagination by the corporal who ranks himself among '*Bush Baptists and other fancy religions', in order to evade Sunday Service. **1959** BAKER *Drum* 97 *Bush Baptist*, a person of dubious religious persuasion or one who has no religious persuasion at all. Rare. **1597** GERARD *Herbal* ccxii. §3. 547 *Bush Basill, or fine Basill, is a low and base plant. **1821** *Plough Boy* II. 358/3 An opinion prevails here (Columbus, Ohio) that our soil is *too rich*, for the profitable culture of the **bush bean*, (called, I believe, at the eastward, the *fisher bean*). **1865** *Trans. Ill. Agric. Soc. 1862* V. 518 We usually plant bush beans in garden drills. **1631** GOUGE *God's Arrows* v. §11. 421 Such men are more fit.. to carrie a *bush-bill rather then a battell-axe. *a* **1834** T. PRINGLE *Poet. Wks.* (1839) 8 Afar in the Desert I love to ride, With the silent *Bush-boy alone by my side. **1850** R. G. CUMMING *Hunter's Life S. Afr.* (1902) 32/1, I found a funny little fellow in the shape of the Bushboy before alluded to, awaiting my arrival. **1899** J. MILNE *Romance Proconsul* xiv. 149 He would.. shoulder his rifle, and start off, with a couple of bush-boys for gillies. **1930** *Bulletin* (Sydney) 26 Mar. 31/2 The *Bush Brother turned out to be a woman, born in Queensland. **1950** 'N. SHUTE' *Town like Alice* 315 They were married by a travelling Church of England priest, one of the Bush Brothers. **1903** *Daily Chron.* 7 Nov. 5/5 Founding a *Bush Brotherhood under the direction of the Bishop. **1861** W. MORGAN *Jrnl.* 27 Apr. (1963) iii. 29 Last week sowed some grass seed on *bush burn. **1900** J. G. WILSON in *Rep. Agric. Societies N.Z.* 132 On bush-burns, if sown at the rate of a few pounds per acre [cocksfoot] rapidly takes possession. **1950** *N.Z. Jrnl. Agric.* Dec. 508/3 Thousands of acres were ploughed (much of it after a bush burn). **1964** *Weekly News* (Auckland) 22 Jan. 39/2 To burn everything cleanly but the heavy trunks is so important to the success of a bush burn. **1898** J. BELL *In Shadow of Bush* xxx. 198 The season promised to be a good one for *bush-burning. **1904** HUTTON & DRUMMOND *Animals N.Z.* II. 91 *The *Bush Canary. Mohua ochrocephala*... The New Zealand Canary has a sharp, strident call, and its movements are quick and active. **1918** *Bulletin* (Sydney) 14 Feb. Red Page 4 *White-throated Flyeater* (Bush Canary) and other members of the genus *Gerygone*. **1936** H. GUTHRIE-SMITH *Sorrows & Joys N.Z. Naturalist* viii. 67 The rain-forests beloved of the Bush Canary. **1946** J. C. ANDERSEN in *Jrnl. Polynesian Soc.* June 154 *Mohua*, a gregarious bird (*Mohoua ochrocephala*), South Island form of the bush-canary, the North Island form (*Mohoua albicilla*) being upokotea. **1921** *United Free Ch. Mission Rec.* Apr. 116/1 She left at midday in a *bush-car. **1926** *Ibid.* May 227/1 The bush-car is an arm-chair placed high above one wheel, excellent for the narrow paths and high grass of Africa. **1780** FORSTER in *Phil. Trans.* LXXI. 2 The common *Bush-cat of the Cape. *Ibid.* 3 Kolbe.. speaks of a Tyger Bush-cat, which he describes as the largest of all the Wild Cats of the Cape-countries. **1847** 'A. HARRIS' *Settlers & Convicts* xiv. 287 On a new farm.. the stockyard .. is necessary for milking *bush cows. **1851** W. H. BRETT *Indian Missions Guiana* 37 The tapir or maipuri, called the bush-cow by the settlers. **1897** M. KINGSLEY *W. Africa* 734 The bush cow came on, and drove its horns through his thigh. **1871** C. L. MONEY *Knocking about in N.Z.* iii. 29 He gave me my first lessons in *bushcraft such as a knowledge of edible roots, modes of crossing rivers, snaring birds. **1897** *Westm. Gaz.* 22 July 4/2 Leichardt perished.. because he lacked the rudiments of bushcraft. **1911** C. E. W. BEAN *'Dreadnought' of Darling* xxxvi. 324 Real scouting and bush-craft will always be part of the station life. **1911** *East London Dispatch* 20 Dec. 5 (Pettman), *Bush dassie flesh was the staple food for the Hottentots. **1897** M. KINGSLEY *W. Africa* 734 He.. put his net into the forest, and caught *bush deer (gazelles). **1883** *Encycl. Brit.* XV. 438/2 *Icticyon*, with one small species, *Canis venaticus*, the *Bush Dog, from Guiana and Brazil. **1732** DE FOE *Tour Gt. Brit.* (1769) II. 179 These last cold and wet Lands have been.. greatly improved, by draining off the Rain-water.. an Invention, called *Bush-draining. **1848** HAYGARTH *Bush Life Australia* v. 48 The *bush-dray, the only vehicle used in New South Wales for the conveyance of wool and other produce, is open and low, more resembling a brewer's dray than any other description of dray known in England. **1899** *Proc. Zool. Soc. Lond.* 831 At the *bush-drives so common in the [Cape] Colony, Blue-buck are seldom turned out. **1828** HONE *Table-book* II. 224 At this season when persons, at inns in Lincolnshire, ask for 'eel pie', they are presently provided with '*bush eels'; namely snakes, caught for that purpose in the bushes. **1965** R. & D. MORRIS *Men & Snakes* vii. 160 In hard times the grass snake and other species were eaten as 'hedge eels' or 'bush eels'. **1882** *Pall Mall G.* 29 June 2/1 A broken-down, deserted shanty, inhabited once, perhaps, by rail-splitters, or *bush-fallers. **1882** W. D. HAY *Brighter Britain!* I. 184 We worked steadily at *bush-falling. **1921** H. GUTHRIE-SMITH *Tutira* xxii. 203 Bush-falling had barely been started. **1899** G. RUSSELL *Old Durban* 503 The *Bush Flea.. is quite content to share your camp blanket if you do not resent his liberty of action. **1934** A. RUSSELL *Tramp-Royal* xxvii. 172 No sooner were the *bush-flies at rest than plagues of sand-flies would rise up to take their places. **1952** M. BOYD *Cardboard Crown* v. 85 The room.. was thick with the buzzing of bush-flies, a species of blow-fly. **1865** *Athenæum* No. 1948. 279/1 A new species of *Bush-goat. **1908** HAAGNER & IVY *Sk. S. Afr. Birdlife* 79 This Warbler is called the Bush-goat on account of the plaintive goat-like call to which the bird gives utterance. **1842** *Bush gourd [see *squash-melon pumpkin* s.v. SQUASH *sb.*[2] 4]. **1882** W. BULLER *Man. Birds N.Z.* 2 The *Bush-Hawk is generally met with on the outskirts of the woods. **1939** J. MULGAN *Man Alone* 80 *Bush-hens were calling across the valley. **1854** *Chamb. Jrnl.* I. 66 By good luck we came on a *bush-hog. **1883** *Harper's Mag.* Dec. 44/1 Shrubs that.. had run the gauntlet of the *bush-hook. **1834** C. A. DAVIS *Lett. J. Downing* 367 Saratogue, for politicians, is just like the *bush-houses for killing pigeons. **1901** F. CAMPBELL *Love, the Atonement* ix. 133 Let us have ices in the bush-house. **1902** W. SATCHELL *Land of Lost* xviii. 164 'Come around to the bush-house.'.. They seated themselves together on a rustic seat among the ferns. **1939** J. CARY *Mister Johnson* 11 The station.. consists of six old bush houses, with blackened thatch reaching almost to the ground. **1959** M. NEVILLE *Sweet Night for Murder* xviii. 175 The bush-house.. was made of brushwood and housed seed boxes.. indoor plants, and bulbs under sacks waiting for planting. **1939** M. B. PICKEN *Lang. of Fashion* 16/1 **Bush jacket* or *coat*, belted, hip-length jacket. **1959** 'M. DERBY' *Tigress* ii. 62 He took the plastic flask from his bush-jacket pocket. **1961** *Listener* 24 Aug. 292/2 The familiar picture of Fidel Castro with beard, bush-jacket and peak-cap. **1853** *Fraser's Mag.* XLVIII. 258 Half dead with their long struggle against the '*bush-lawyer', a tough and tangled bramble. **1874** A. BATHGATE *Colonial Exper.* xvi. 225 The bush lawyers, or mining agents, which is the name they accept,.. are of great use to the diggers. **1908** E. J. BANFIELD *Confessions of Beachcomber* I. i. 13 A 'bush' carpenter is a very admirable person, when he is not also a bush lawyer. **1926** J. DOONE *Timely Tips New Australians* Gloss., *Bush-lawyer*, a man who gratuitously voices legal opinions although possessing no qualifications for doing so. **1933** N. SCANLAN *Tides of Youth* viii. 91 You're a regular bush-lawyer. **1948** B. JAMES in *Coast to Coast 1947* 168 Mrs. Bolton loved the touch of legality, being a good deal of a bush lawyer. **1948** V. PALMER *Golconda* iv. 29 It's easier to find a bush-lawyer than a man who's bent his back at all sorts of jobs. **1890** E. E. MORRIS *Cassell's Picturesque Australasia* II. 235 The College precincts are sacred to the classic muse and the omnipresent *bush-magpie. **1826** *Edin. Rev.* XLIII. 300 The most venomous of reptiles, and known by the name of the *bush-master. **1860** GOSSE *Rom. Nat. Hist.* 267 The couni-couchi, or bush-master, is the most dreaded of all the South American snakes. **1933** *Bulletin* (Sydney) 28 June 20/4 He was under the *bush nurse for a fortnight. **1840** J. S. POLACK *Manners & Customs N.Z.* II. 270 The narrator had been hunting the *cochon maron* or *bush-pig. **1844** J. BACKHOUSE *Narr. Mauritius & S. Afr.* 213 The Bosch Vark, *Bush Pig*. **1907** W. H. KOEBEL *Return of Joe* 20 Mutton down to the price of bush-pig. **1910** J. BUCHAN *Prester John* xiv, I was inclined to think him a very large bush-pig. **1936** *Beaver* Mar. 52/2 The northern *bush pilot is dependent solely on his own good judgement, resourcefulness and initiative. **1948** 'N. SHUTE' *No Highway* ix. 243 The pilot was to be a civilian bush-pilot called Hennessey, a thick-set tough who knew that country [*sc.* Labrador] intimately. **1948** *Shell Aviation News* cxxv. 2/1 The small aircraft, usually single-engined, flown by the bush pilot. **1869** J. MUIR *First Summer in Sierra* (1911) 51 A marked plant is the *bush poppy (*Dendromecon rigidum*). **1900** W. D. DRURY *Bk. Gardening* 281 Californian Bush Poppy. **1893** H. A. BRYDEN *Gun & Camera in S. Afr.* 158 Tiny *bush-quail (*Turnix lepurana*), dainty creatures, scarcely bigger than sparrows. **1964** A. L. THOMSON *New Dict. Birds* 625/1 The so-called 'bush quails' of India (*Perdicula*) are dwarf partridges. **1867** *Amer. Naturalist* I. 399 The *Bush Rat (*Neotoma Mexicana*) is abundant throughout the territory [*sc.* Arizona]. **1889** *Trans. N.Z. Inst.* XXII. 301 On the habits of the New Zealand Bush-rat (*Mus maorium*). **1947** I. L. IDRIESS *Isles of Despair* xxxii. 213 There were bush rats and water rats. **1966** *Southerly* XXVI. 93 You, long-dead entomologist Sidney, like this bush rat, have found the crumbling edge cave in. **1827** P. CUNNINGHAM *Two Years N.S.W.* I. 123 A *made* *bush-road is one where the brushes have been cleared, banks of rivers and gullies levelled, [etc.].. ; while a *natural* bush-road signifies one to which nothing has been done except notching the trees, the carts simply following each other's track. **1857** W. WESTGARTH *Victoria & Austr. Gold Mines* xi. 250 The gloomy antithesis of good bush-rangers and bad bush-roads. **1916** J. B. COOPER *Coo-oo-ee* i. 2 Along the side of the Ironbark ranges was a bush road, leading to the hamlet. **1966** *Weekly News* (N.Z.) 1 June 43/2 In the area that we visited, which is already served by the bush road, we saw isolated kauri trees more than five feet in diameter. **1901** A. C. STARK *Birds S. Afr.* II. 217 Tarsiger stellatus. White-starred *Bush Robin. *Ibid.* 219 Tarsiger silens. Silent Bush Robin. **1932** *Discovery* July 231/2 No bird calls but the bush-robin with chrome-yellow underparts and silver stars on his slate-blue forehead. **1552** HULOET, Byl called a forest bil, or *bush-sithe. **1856** *Trans. Mich. Agric. Soc.* VII. 54 D. O. and W. S. Perry ..[exhibited] three bush scythes. **1874** *Rep. Vermont Board Agric.* II. 194 It is possible to subdue them.. by cutting them off near the ground with a bush-scythe. **1869** *Trans. Ill. Agric. Soc. 1867-8* VII. 457 Sheep shipped in for sale because they 'didn't flourish' on prairie grass. These '*bush sheep', as they are called, have been in abundant supply. **1909** M. S. KISCH *Let. Nigeria* (1910) xii. 169 This is the kind of costume I go about in; a *bush shirt.. and long native-made boots. **1953** D. LESSING *Five* iii. 144 Now he strode fast over the ground, his loose bush-shirt flying around him. **1893** NEWTON *Dict. Birds* 21 The large genus *Thamnophilus*, containing upwards of 50 species, is one of the most important of the so-called '*Bush-Shrikes'. **1932** *Discovery* Jan. 25/2 A wonderful new black-breasted bush-shrike.. an entirely new species.. christened *Chlorophoneus nigrescens*. **1953** R. CAMPBELL *Mamba's Precipice* iv. 40 A pretty bush-robin came out.. followed by a lovely bush-shrike with a bright green back, a yellow stomach, and a brilliant crimson chest. **1950** *N.Z. Jrnl. Agric.* Jan. 31/1 The amount of cobaltised fertiliser used.. in 1949.. would be sufficient to correct cobalt deficiency in 940,000 acres of *bush-sick pasture. **1929** *Times* 1 July 15/6 Lack of minerals in pastures causes innumerable diseases, such as.. '*bush-sickness'.. in New Zealand. *Ibid.* 16/2 Able to.. identify 'Nakuruitis' as similar to 'bush-sickness' in New Zealand. **1950** *N.Z. Jrnl. Agric.* July 67/3 As a result of research in both New Zealand and Australia, the cause of bush sickness was found in 1935 to be a deficiency of cobalt. **1869** J. BURROUGHS in *Galaxy Mag.* Aug., A favourite sparrow of my own.. is the wood, or *bush-sparrow, usually called *spizella pusilla*. **1796** STEDMAN *Surinam* II. xx. 93 A *bush-spider of such magnitude, that putting him into a case-bottle above eight inches high, he.. reached the surface with some of his hideous claws. **1866** *Treas. Bot.* s.v., **Bush Syrup*, a saccharine fluid obtained from the flowers of *Protea mellifera*, in the Cape Colony. **1768** *Holyoke Diaries* (1911) 30 Began to take *Bush Tea. **1838** J. E. ALEXANDER *Exped. Interior Afr.* I. 141 He regaled Mr. Schmelen and myself on boiled salt beef and bush tea. **1858** SIMMONDS *Dict. Trade*, *Bush Tea*, the leaflets of a species of *Cyclopia*, probably *C. latifolia*,.. supposed to possess expectorant and restorative properties. **1902** 'X. C.' *Everyday Life in Cape Colony* ix. 122 In most of these Colonial stores 'bush' tea can be bought. **1946** *Cape Argus* 27 Feb. 6/9 In the country districts bushtea has many names—honey tea, boer tea, rooibos and so on. **1878** *Australian* I. 507 (Morris), The police are baffled by.. the number and activity of the *bush telegraphs. **1893** J. A. K. MACKAY *Out Back* v, A hint dropped in this town set the bush telegraphs riding in all directions. **1934** *Bulletin* (Sydney) 21 Nov. 21/1 The bush telegraph sends tidings to and fro. **1946** U. KRIGE *Way Out* x. 121 We had heard too many 'latrinograms' now to be unduly impressed by the particular form of bush-telegraph .. practised by the Italian peasants. **1951** 'N. SHUTE' *Round the Bend* 208 'How did the Imam get to know about it?'.. 'The bush telegraph works very well, here in Bahrein.' **1954** L. P. HARTLEY *White Wand* i. 12 'How did he know that I was here?' I asked—a silly question from someone who knew the workings of the Venetian bush-telegraph as well as I did. **1856** C. J. ANDERSSON *Lake Ngami* ii. 20 Besides myriads of fleas, our encampment swarmed with a species of *bush-tick. **1865** HARVEY & SONDER *Flora Capensis* III. 436 A large bush.. the Colonial name is Bush-tick Berry. **1886** *Pall Mall Gaz.* 22 July 4/1 The *carrapato*, or bush-tick.. is a degenerate spider. **1893** NEWTON *Dict. Birds* 83 *Chamæa*. .. '*Bush-Tit' and 'Ground-Wren'. **1881** *Amer. Naturalist* XV. 213 That diminutive little bird, the least *bush titmouse (*Psaltriparus minimus*). **1864** *Reader* 2 Apr. 420/1 The roads from the nascent metropolis still partook mainly of the random character of *'bush tracks'. **1595** DUNCAN *Append. Etym.* (E.D.S.) *Buxus*, the *bush-tree. **1599** HAKLUYT *Voy.* II. II. 127 A litle way off was a great high bush-tree as though it had no leaues. **1898** MORRIS *Austral Eng.*, *Gerygone*... In New Zealand they are called *Bush-warblers. **1808** *Ann. Reg. 1806* 856 Some were cutting wood for firing—Some collecting *bush-water with a calabash. **1871** J. E. JENKINS *Coolie* ix. 120 That strange ebonised 'bush-water', which.. anon curls and eddies round us like the smiles on a Negro's face. **1891** *Eng. Illustr. Mag.* Feb. 383 The plantations.. were surrounded by four dams or embankments;.. one behind to exclude the 'bush water', the accumulated rain of the interior. **1917** R. MARLOTH *Dict. Common Names of Plants* 89 The so-called 'Bushveld [Willow]' or '*Bush [Willow]' is *Combretum salicifolium*. **1863** LYELL *Antiq. Man* 484 The human brain here given.. is that of an African *bushwoman. **1874** W. M. BAINES *Narr. E. Crewe* viii. 192 The white bushwoman—creatures of a mature age, hideous to look upon. **1905** *Daily Chron.* 16 Dec. 4/7 Bushmen and bushwomen within a radius of forty or fifty miles ride to these functions. **1768** WALES in *Phil. Trans.* LX. 119 It is entirely covered with low *bush-wood. **1852** LYTTON *My Novel* in *Blackw. Mag.* LXXI. 184, I perceived the form of a man seated amongst the bushwood. **1796** STEDMAN *Surinam* II. xxiii. 183, I had now extracted out of my right arm two dreadful insects.. These are called in Surinam the *bush-worms, and are the shape and size of the aurelia of the common butterfly, with a pointed tail and black head. **1887** W. L. BULLER *Birds N.Z.* I. 115 *Bush-wren [*Xenicus longipes*].. is generally met with singly or in pairs.

bush (bʊʃ), *sb.*[2] [app. a. MDu. *busse*, (mod.Du. *bus*) Box, bush of a wheel; cf. G. *büchse*, *radbüchse*, Sw. *hjul-bössa* 'wheel-bush'. Cf., for the form, early forms of BLUNDERBUSS, HARQUEBUS, in *-bush*. As to connexion with BOUCHE, see BUSH *v.*[3]]

1. The metal lining of the axle-hole of a wheel; hence, the metal (or wooden) case in which the journal of a shaft revolves. (Cf. BOX *sb.*[2] 16.) **b.** A cylindrical metal lining of an orifice; a perforated plug, cylinder, or disk; *esp.* a drilled plug inserted in the touch-hole of a gun, or in a bearing of a watch when worn (cf. BOUCHE).

1566 in *Collect. Invent.* (1815) 169 Item, fyve buscheis of found for cannonis and batterd quheillis. **1578** *Ibid.* 250 Garnist with yron werk and bousches of fonte. **1625** *Invent.* in *Shropshire Word-bk.* (E.D.S.) One paire of bushes.. one paire of bushes soles. **1688** R. HOLME *Acad. Armory* III. viii. 332 The Busshes are Irons within the hole of the Nave to keep it from wearing. **1770** J. FERGUSON *Lect.* (1805) I. 82 The upper part of the spindle turns in a wooden bush fixt into the nether millstone. **1797** A. CUMMING *Commun. Board of Agric.* II. 365 The nave is commonly lined with metal, which lining is called the box or bush. **1865** LD. ELCHO in *Times* 9 Mar., What are ordinarily known as front aperture sights, i.e. solid discs or bushes pierced in the centre. **1884** F. BRITTEN *Watch & Clockm.* 95 The hole is tapped at one end to receive a bush.

2. *Comb.* **bush-metal**, an alloy of copper and tin used for journals.

bush (bʊʃ), *v.*[1] For forms see sb. [f. BUSH *sb.*[1]]

†**1.** *trans.* To set in a bush or thicket as a place of concealment, to place in ambush; *intr.* (for *refl.*) to hide in a bush, lie in ambush. (Cf. BUSH *sb.*[1] 4.) *Obs.*

1330 R. BRUNNE *Chron.* 187 Saladyn priuely was bussed beside þe flom. *c* **1400** *Destr. Troy* 1168 Lurkyt vnder lefe-sals loget with vines, Busket vndur bankes on bourders with-oute. *c* **1440** *York Myst.* XIII. 8, I may nowder buske ne belde But owther in frith or felde. **1480** CAXTON *Chron. Eng.* II. (1520) 11 Coryn sholde go out and busshe hym in a wode. **1535** STEWART *Cron. Scot.* (1858) I. 263 The Pechtis than wes buschit neir hand by. **1623** DANIEL *Hymen's Tri.* II. i, Being closely bush'd a pretty Distance off.

2. To protect (trees, etc.) with bushes or cut brushwood set round about; to support with bushes.

1647 *MS. Acc. St. John's Hosp. Canterb.*, Paid for bushes to bush the ashes in the meadowe vjd. **1676** WORLIDGE *Cider* (1691) 34 Care must be taken to bush them, so that cattel may not rub against them. **1741** *Compl. Fam.-Piece* III. 416 Let the Sets be bushed about for some time, to prevent their being injured. **1884** [see BUSHED 2 b].

3. To protect (land or game) from net-poachers by placing bushes or branches at intervals in the preserved ground, so as to interrupt the sweep of a net. Also *absol.*

1843 CARLYLE *Past & Pr.* 288 Assist us still better to bush the partridges. *Ibid.* IV. viii. (1872) 254 Game-preserving Aristocracies, let them 'bush' never so effectually, cannot escape the Subtle Fowler. **1860** *Chamb. Jrnl.* XIV. 274 As for netting by night, bush your fields closely. **1883** J. PURVES in *Contemp. Rev.* Sept. 355 They know the fields to avoid for net-work, those that have been bushed—i.e. irregularly dotted with posts driven upright into the ground.

4. To bush-harrow (ground, etc.); to cover *in* (seed) with a bush-harrow.

1787 WINTER *Syst. Husb.* 313 Sow the clover seed, which bush in, by the horses walking in the furrows. **1848** *Jrnl. R. Agric. Soc.* IX. I. 10 By attention to the spreading and bushing the field the whole surface becomes..changed.

5. See quot.; cf. *bush-draining* in BUSH *sb.*[1] 11.

1838 *New Monthly Mag.* LIII. 32 They might hae thocht of bushing the tent-pegs..This is done, on the approach of heavy rain, by digging a hole near each tent-peg, and filling it with brushwood, to act as a sort of drain and prevent the water from saturating the ground, and making the pegs draw.

6. To tether a horse by burying the knotted end of the head-rope in the ground.

1871 *Daily News* 11 Sept., The system of 'bushing', by which the officers' horses of the 9th Lancers are now fastened.

7. a. *intr.* To be bushy, to grow thick like a bush.

1562 TURNER *Herbal* II. 133 a, It [wilde Thyme] busheth largely, and groweth somthyng asyde. **1667** MILTON *P.L.* IX. 426 So thick the Roses bushing round About her glowd. **1809** PARKINS *Culpepper's Eng. Physic. Enl.* 257 Greyish or whitish leaves..many bushing together at a joint.

b. *transf.* of hair. Also with *out.*

1509 BARCLAY *Ship of Fooles* (1570) 159 Their heare out bushing as a foxes tayle. **1526** SKELTON *Magnyf.* 844 My heyr bussheth So plesauntlie. **1575** TURBERV. *Bk. Falconrie* 369 The dogge becommes more beautifull by cutting the toppe of his sterne: for then will it bushe out verie gallantly.

†**c.** of the 'tail' of a comet. *Obs.*

1587 FLEMING *Contn. Holinshed* III. 1314/1 There appeared a blasing star in the south, bushing toward the east.

†**8.** ***to bush about*** or ***out***: ? to beat or hunt about *for* (as for game). Cf. BUSK *v.*[2] 2.

1686 (3 June) *MS. Let. from Job Charnock & Council of Húgli to Council at Balasore*, Wee take notice that you can Procure us about 20[mds] [maunds] of Wax, pray bushe out for some more. *a* **1734** NORTH *Life Ld. Guilford* (1742) 201 They are forced to bush about for ways and means to pay their rent and charges.

†**9.** To camp in the bush. Usu. with *it. Austral.* and *N.Z. Obs.*

1827 W. J. DUMARESQ *Let.* in G. Mackaness *Fourteen Journeys* (1950–1) 99 Not being provided for *bushing* it, in these early frosts, we made up our minds to return. **1846** *N.Z. Jrnl.* VI. 166/1, I passed the night under a pine-tree.. and awoke, after my first experience of 'bushing it', exceedingly refreshed. **1853** MRS. C. CLACY *Visit to Gold Diggings Australia* 245 If this fails, you must just bush it for the night. **1862** J. GOLDIE *Jrnl.* 5 May in H. Beattie *Pioneers explore Otago* (1947) 98, I resolved to scramble along the side of the lake..even although we had to 'bush it' for a night or two. **1868** *People's Mag.* II. 365/2, I have 'bushed' it many a rough night in Australia.

†**bush,** *v.*[2] *Obs.* exc. *dial.* Forms: 4 busche, 4–5 bussh(e, 5 boyssh(e, 6 bush. [Deriv. uncertain: cf. OF. *buschier* 'frapper, heurter', MDu. *buusschen* (= MHG. *biuschen*) to knock, beat; also PUSH.] *intr.* To butt with the head; to push.

1387 TREVISA *Higden* Rolls Ser. II. 191 He may busche aȝenst men and horshedes and breke strong dores wiþ his heed. **1398** —— *Barth. De P.R.* XVIII. iii. (1495) 749 The ramme is excyted and busshyth full strongely. **1515** *Scot. Field* 439 Then full boldlie on the brode hills, we bushed with our standarts. **1590** GREENE *Mourn. Garm.* 33 If he bush not at beautie. **1864** E. CAPERN *Devon Provinc.*, *To Bush*, to butt or strike with the head.

Hence **'bushing** *vbl. sb.*

1398 TREVISA *Barth. De P.R.* VII. lix. (1495) 273 A postume comyth..of brekynge and brusinge and boysshynge and hurtelynge. **1399** LANGL. *Rich. Redeless* I. 99 þey made ȝou to leue þat regne ȝe ne myȝte, Withoute busshinge adoune of best ȝoure ffrendis.

bush (bʊʃ), *v.*[3] [f. BUSH *sb.*[2]; originally said of wheels; with the extension of the word to the vent of muskets, etc., it appears to have been erroneously associated with F. *bouche* mouth, *boucher* to stop up (see next), or *bouchon* cork, plug; whence the frequent later BOUCHE *v.*]

1. *trans.* To furnish with a bush; to line (an orifice) with metal.

1566 *Invent.* 168 (JAM.) Item, ane pair of new cannone quheillis buschit with brass. **1675** COTTON *Burlesque upon B.* 233 (D.) [He] Bushes the Naves, clouts th' Axle-trees. **1781** THOMPSON in *Phil. Trans.* LXXI. 264 The vent of a musket is very soon enlarged by firing, and..it is found necessary to stop it up with a solid screw, through the center of which a new vent is made of the proper dimensions. This operation is called bushing, or rather bouching the piece. **1882** *Field* 16 Sept. 410 A 12-gauge gun that I had bushed on my system.

2. *transf.*

1881 C. A. EDWARDS *Organs* 69 The front pin is bushed by two or three thicknesses of baize..to avoid rattling.

†**bush,** *v.*[4] *Obs.* [a. F. *boucher* to shut an aperture; of doubtful derivation: see Littré.] To stop a hole, opening, or passage.

a **1659** OSBORN *Observ. Turks* (1673) 315 Eyeing Christians with a high disdain, for..bushing the way to Heaven with Purgatory and other Bugbears. *a* **1693** URQUHART *Rabelais* III. ix. II. 279 If..all the holes in the world be not shut up, stopped, closed, and bushed.

bush(e, obs. form of BUSS.

busha ('bʊʃə). The manager or overseer of an estate in Jamaica.

1832 M. SCOTT in *Blackw. Mag.* XXXI. 902 The Overseer, or Busha, to give him his Jamaica name, looked at me. **1834** —— *Cruise Midge* xii, Gangs of negroes..waiting to receive busha's orders for the morrow. **1866** *Morning Star* 17 Mar., The magistrates and bushas, or overseers.

†**bushaile.** *Obs.* Also in 5 busshaile, buscayl(l)e, -kayle, boschayle. [a. OF. *boschaille* (Godef.) a wood = It. *boscaglia*:—low Lat. *boscalia* (Du Cange), pl. of *boscāle*, f. late L. *boscum* a wood.] A copse or thicket; often as a place of concealment, an ambush.

? *a* **1400** *Morte Arthur* 895 On blonkez by ȝone buscayle. *Ibid.* 1634 They buskede theme..In the buskayle of his waye. *a* **1400** *Octouian* 1607 Besyde Acrys, yn a boschayle They token rest. *c* **1430** *Syr Gener.* 9189 Thei..come out of here busshaile Streight forto bede hem bataile.

b. *collect.* Brushwood, underwood.

c **1400** MAUNDEV. xxvii. 271 A gret yle fulle of Trees and Buscaylle. *Ibid.* Buscaylle & Thornes & Breres & grene Grasse.

bush-buck ('bʊʃbʌk). [ad. Du. *bosch-bok*; see BOSCH[1].] A small species of African antelope, also called the Bush-goat.

1852 *Blackw. Mag.* LXXI. 294 A shot at an ostrich or bushbuck. **1865** LIVINGSTONE *Zambesi* 343 In the mornings and evenings the pretty little bush-buck (*Tragelaphus sylvatica*) ventures..out of the mangroves, to feed.

bushed (bʊʃt), *ppl. a.*[1] [f. BUSH *sb.*[1], *v.*[1] + -ED.]

†**1.** Of plants or shrubs: Formed into a bush.

1573 TUSSER *Husb.* (1878) 95 Bassel, fine and busht, sowe in May. **1597** GERARD *Herbal* xxxiv. §1. 239 Leaues.. bushed or braunched at the top.

2. a. Covered with bushes or 'bush'.

1868 DILKE *Greater Brit.* II. III. vi. 62 The coastlands.. are exhausted, densely bushed, and uninhabited. **1883** MISS BROUGHTON *Belinda* III. III. vii. 22 The homely loveliness of bushed bank.

b. Protected with bushes. (Cf. BUSH *v.*[1] 2.)

1884 *Illust. Lond. News* 29 Nov. 539 It matters but little what the fence may be—a bushed or unbushed one.

3. *transf.* **a.** Having a bushy head of hair.

1494 FABYAN VII. ccxxiv. 251 For that tyme clerkes vsed busshed and brayded hedys. **1552** HULOET, Boye with a bushed heade, *comatulus.* **1623** FAVINE *Theat. Hon.* XI. xiii. 235 A great head, thickly bushed and tufted with haire. **1849** LYTTON *K. Arthur* VI. cxxxi, Hideous visage bush'd with tawny hair.

b. Of the hair: Spreading like a bush, bushy; also ***bushed out, up.***

1535 COVERDALE *Song of Sol.* v. 11 The lockes of his hayre are buszshed, browne as the euenynge. **1779** FORREST *Voy. N. Guinea* 95 The hair of the women was bushed out also. **1842** PRICHARD *Nat. Hist. Man* 24 Frizzling hair..bushed out round their heads.

4. *slang.* At 'Beggar's Bush'. ? *Obs.*

1812 J. H. VAUX *Flash Dict.*, *Bush'd*, poor; without money.

5. a. Lost in the bush (*sb.*[1] 9). Cf. *bogged.*

1856 *Tait's Mag.* XXIII. 740, I narrowly escaped being 'bushed'. **1881** A. C. GRANT *Bush Life Queensl.* II. xxxi. 154 John feared that he might get bushed.

b. *transf.* and *fig.* Lost as in the bush. *Austral.* and *N.Z. colloq.*

1885 MRS. PRAED *Australian Life* 29, I get quite bushed in these streets. **1898** *Westm. Gaz.* 29 Sept. 3/2 He tangled himself up and got 'bushed', and frantically implored.. everybody..to help him with his contract. **1900** H. LAWSON *Over Sliprails* 1 The deeper you read..about things that end in ism..the more likely you are to get bushed. **1916** *Anzac Book* 144/1 To be 'bushed' in the heart of London became a common experience with him. **1944** J. H. FULLARTON *Troop Target* v. 45 We're bushed behind the enemy lines about a hundred miles from nowhere. **1953** 'N. SHUTE' *In Wet* ii. 39 It is a very easy country to get bushed in; the sense of direction can be easily lost.

c. Tired, exhausted. *N. Amer.*

1870 *Nation* July 57/1 To be 'bushed' was to be tired. **1910** W. A. FRASER *Red Meekins* 266, I was that danged near bushed, toward the last that I was feared I might go right on sleepin'. **1958** 'CASTLE' & HAILEY *Flight into Danger* x. 132 You thought you'd reached the end then—completely bushed, with not another ounce left in you. **1966** *Oxford Mail* 4 June 1/1 Astronaut Eugene Cernan's..spacewalk was postponed..because he and the Gemini-9 command pilot..were 'pretty well bushed' from their exertions in space.

d. Suffering from the effects of isolation (see quots.). *Canada.*

1952 J. MARSHALL in R. Weaver *Canadian Short Stories* (1960) 289 'You had three years here alone,' she began. 'I have never been bushed,' Toddy interrupted. **1959** *Maclean's Mag.* 14 Feb. 40/2 It was geographically isolated, and its inhabitants were cut off in separate buildings by the cold and by storms, and often..psychologically isolated—that is, bushed.

bushed (bʊʃt), *ppl. a.*[2] [f. BUSH *v.*[3] + -ED[1].] Fitted with a bush or lining; lined.

1907 *Installation News* May 11/1 Bushed outlets. **1909** *Ibid.* III. 121 These..boxes are provided with bushed holes.

bushel ('bʊʃəl), *sb.*[1] Forms: 4 bus(s)chel, buisshel, buysshel, boussel, boyschel, 4–5 buyschel, 4–6 busshel(le, 5 bu-, byschelle, buscel, bysshel, 5–6 bowsshell(e, 6 buszshel, buszhell, bushylle, bousshell, beyschell, 5–7 bushell, 4– bushel. [ME. *boyschel*, *buyschel*, a. OF. *boissiel*, *-el*, *buissiel* (mod.F. *boisseau*, dial. *boisteau*), according to Diez dim. of *boiste* (Pr. *bostea* and *boissa*) box. This explanation is supported by the med.L. form *bustellus*, beside *bussellus*, *bissellus*. Du Cange took the word as a dim. of OF. *boise* = med.L. *buza*, *buta* BUTT.]

1. A measure of capacity used for corn, fruit, etc., containing four pecks or eight gallons.

The ***imperial bushel***, legally established in Great Britain in 1826, contains 2218.192 cubic inches, or 80 pounds of distilled water weighed in air at 62° Fah. The ***Winchester bushel***, much used from the time of Henry VIII, was somewhat smaller, containing 2150.42 cubic inches or 77.627413 pounds of distilled water; it is still generally used in United States and Canada. The bushel had a great variety of other values, now abolished by law, though often, in local use, varying not only from place to place, but in the same place according to the kind or quality of the commodity in question. Frequently it was no longer a measure, but a *weight* of so many (30, 40, 45, 50, 56, 60, 70, 75, 80, 90, 93, 220) pounds of flour, wheat, oats, potatoes, etc. A full account of these local values is given in *Old Country & Farming Words* (Eng. Dial. Soc.) 169.

c **1300** *Battle Abb. Custumals* (1887) 67 Habebit iiij bussellos de bericorn. *c* **1330** *Poem on Times Edw. II*, 393 in *Pol. Songs* (1839) 341 A bussel of whete was at foure shillinges or more. **1382** WYCLIF *Gen.* xviii. 6 Mynge to gidre thre half buysshelis of clene floure. **1497** *Act 12 Hen. VII*, v, That the measure of a Bushell containe viii. gallons of Wheat. **1523** FITZHERB. *Husb.* §12 An acre of grounde.. may be metelye well sowen with two London busshelles of pease. **1596** SHAKS. *Merch. V.* I. i. 116 His reasons are two graines of wheate hid in two bushels of chaffe. **1710** SWIFT *Lett.* (1767) III. 55, I have my coals by half a bushel at a time, I'll assure you. **1787** WINTER *Syst. Husb.* 146 This wheat weighed sixty-six pounds ten ounces per bushel, of nine gallons. **1872** E. ROBERTSON *Hist. Ess.* I. i. 1 An English Imperial bushel contains 60 lbs. of average wheat or 80 lbs. liquid measure.

†**b.** ? A liquid measure. *Obs.*

1483 *Cath. Angl.* 49 A Buschelle; *batulus liquidorum est, bacus.*

†**c.** Sometimes used without *of. Obs.*

c **1374** CHAUCER *Boeth.* I. iv. 15 Who so bouȝt[e] a busshel corn. *c* **1386** —— *Reves T.* 392 Hir cake Of half a busshel flour.

d. *loosely.* A large quantity or number.

c **1374** CHAUCER *Troylus* III. 976 And would a bushel of venim al excusen For that a grane of love is on it shove. **1680** *Answ. Stillingfleet's Serm.* 33 Who have Benefices and Honours by Heaps, and by the Bushel. **1683** TRYON *Way to Health* 579 He..has got a Bushel of Money by his Practice. **1718** LADY M. W. MONTAGUE *Lett.* liii. II. 78 An old beau..with a bushel of curled hair on his head. **1873** MISS BROUGHTON *Nancy* III. 187 Bushels of girls..there always are bushels of girls somehow; here they come.

2. A vessel used as a bushel measure.

1382 WYCLIF *Luke* xi. 33 No man liȝtneth a lanterne, and puttith in hidlis, other vndir a boyschel [**1388** buyschel], but on a candel sticke. **1489** CAXTON *Faytes of A.* I. viii. 20 Thre mues or busshellis all full of rynges of gold. *a* **1565** HEYWOOD *Four P's* in *Dodsley* (1780) I. 87 Rolynge his eyes as rounde as two bushels. **1607** TOPSELL *Four-f. Beasts* 154 Their feet..are as broad as a bushel. **1677** HALE *Prim. Orig. Man.* I. i. 22 The Sense represents the Sun no bigger than a Bushel. **1724** WATTS *Logic* 152 The apples will fill a bushel.

b. *fig.* (with ref. to Matt. v. 15). 'To hide one's light under a bushel.'

1557 *Tottell's Misc.* (Arb.) 244 Trouth vnder bushell is faine to crepe. **1627** SANDERSON *Serm.* I. 267 The light of Gods word, hid from them under two bushels for sureness: under the bushel of a tyrannous clergy..and under the bushel of an unknown tongue. **1644** Z. BOYD *Gard. Zion* in *Zion's Flowers* (1855) App. 7/2 From under the Bushell of ignorance. **1868** FREEMAN *Norm. Conq.* (1876) II. App. 540 The light of those saintly ladies should in no case be hidden under a bushel.

c. Phrase. ***to measure other people's corn by one's own bushel***: to apply one's own standard to others, to judge others by oneself.

1636 HENSHAW *Horæ subc.* 279 Men usually measure others by their own bushels: they that are ill themselves, are commonly apt to think ill of others. **1801** HUNTINGTON *Bank of Faith* 35 We must not measure every body's corn by our own bushel.

3. *attrib.* and *comb.*: **a.** of a bushel, as ***bushel-bag, -basket, -measure,*** †***-poke***; **b.** resembling or as wide as a bushel-measure, as ***bushel-breeches, -wig***; also **bushel-iron,** ? (old) iron sold by the bushel.

1529 in Rogers *Agric. & Prices* III. 567/3, 1 *bushel basket. **1850** *Jrnl. R. Agric. Soc.* XI. I. 202 The food.. carried in bushel-baskets. **1831** CARLYLE *Sart. Res.* I. vii, Bell-girdles, *bushel-breeches, cornuted shoes, or other the like phenomena. **1831** J. HOLLAND *Manuf. Metals* I. 144 *Bushel-iron, or the fragments of old hoops, and all pieces of similar size. **1851** *Ord. & Regul. Royal Engineers* xvi. 66 All Bushel or Scrap Iron, and Waste in conversion. **1530** PALSGR. 200/2 *Bousshell measure, *boisseau.* **1523** FITZHERB. *Husb.* §141 Bagges, wallettes, or *busshell-pokes. **1794** WOLCOTT (P. Pindar) *Rowl. for Oliver* Wks. II. 344 What gives them consequence, I trow, Is nothing but a *bushel wig.

bushel, *sb.*[2] [cf. BUSH *sb.*[2]] The bush or box of a wheel. ? *Obs.*

1433 in Rogers *Agric. & Prices* III. 550/4 New bushel, /8; Iron to do., 1/-. **1730–36** BAILEY, *Bushels* [of a Cart wheel] certain Irons within the Hole of the Nave, to preserve it from Wearing. [So JOHNSON.] **1864** WEBSTER, *Bushel*, the circle of iron in the nave of a wheel.

bushel ('bʊʃəl), *v.*[1] *rare.* [f. BUSHEL *sb.*[1]] To hide under a bushel. *fig.* (see BUSHEL *sb.*[1] 2 b.)

1650 T. VAUGHAN *Anima Mag. Abscond.* 56, I have not Busheld my Light, nor buried my Talent in the Ground. **1653** JENKYN *On Jude* (1845) 82 Not bushel the candle of Scripture discovery. **1882** H. MERIVALE *Faucit of B.* II. I. xxiv. 105 The agricole..thinks that he is wasting his days and bushelling his light out of London.

bushel ('bʊʃəl), *v.*[2] *U.S.* [perh. f. G. *bosseln* to do odd jobs, to do poor work.] *trans.* and *intr.* To repair (garments). So **'bushelman, -woman**, a man or woman employed in repair tailoring.

1864 WEBSTER 177/3 Bushelman. **1877** BARTLETT *Dict. Amer.* 777 *To bushel*,..to repair garments. **1889** *Cent. Dict.*, *Bushelwoman*, a woman who assists a tailor in repairing garments. **1909** 'O. HENRY' *Options* (1916) 92 You would say he had been brought up a bushelman in Essex Street.

'bushelage ('bʊʃəlɪdʒ). [f. as BUSHEL *v.*[1] + -AGE; prob. after OFr. *boisselage, boesselage* a species of 'droit'.] Duty payable by the bushel on measurable commodities.

1818 in TODD; and in mod. Dicts.

busheler, busheller ('bʊʃələ(r)). *U.S. local.* [Cf. Ger. *bossler* (Sanders) f. *bosseln* to do odd jobs of repairing.] One who repairs garments for tailors: also called **bushelman**.

1847 in WORCESTER; and in later Dicts.

'bushelful. [see -FUL.] As much as fills a bushel; *fig.* a large quantity.

c **1449** PECOCK *Repr.* IV. ix. 474 Worth..a buyschel ful of gold. **1600–12** J. M. in *Shaks. C. Praise* 98 Lovers will tell a bushell-full of Lyes! **1818** SCOTT *Rob Roy* v, Nature has given him a mouthful of common sense, and the priest has added a bushelful of learning. **1861** *Temple-bar Mag.* I. 188 A bushelful of gold pieces would scarcely have sufficed.

†**'bushet.** *Obs.* [f. BUSH *sb.*[1] + -ET[1].] A small shrub or bush; a small thicket. Cf. BUSKET.

1573 TUSSER *Husb.* (1878) 90 So haue you good feeding, in bushets and lease. **1662** RAY *Three Itin.* II. 139 We rode through a bushet, or common called Rodwell Hake.

bush-fighter ('bʊʃ,faɪtə(r)). An irregular combatant or skirmisher, accustomed to fight in the bush; one who fires from among the bushes.

1760 WESLEY *Jrnl.* 22 Nov. (1827) III. 27 If it should happen, that any one of these silly bush-fighters steps out into the plain. **1825** *Blackw. Mag.* XVII. 343 Cornwallis and Burgoyne had been over-reached by the despicable bush-fighters opposed to them. **1857** MAYNE REID in *Chamb. Jrnl.* VII. 363 Not so much with the eye of a soldier, as with that of a hunter and bush-fighter.

bush-fighting ('bʊʃ,faɪtɪŋ), *vbl. sb.* Guerilla-warfare in the bush. Also *fig.*

1760 in Wesley *Jrnl.* 22 Nov. (1827) III. 26 You may keep up..a little bush-fighting in controversy; you may skirmish awhile. **1795** BURKE *Regic. Peace* iv, Pray let us leave this bush-fighting. **1830** *Fraser's Mag.* I. 189 Accustomed to bush-fighting in his own country. **1837** W. IRVING *Capt. Bonneville* (1849) 76 The very Indian allies, though accustomed to bush-fighting, regarded it as..full of frightful danger.

'bush-hammer. *U.S.* [prob. ad. Ger. *bosz-hammer*, in same sense, f. *boszen* to beat.] A mason's large breaking hammer, often having square ends cut into pyramidal points; also a hammer for dressing millstones, usually having detachable steel-bits in the dressing face.

1885 *Harper's Mag.* Mar. 558/1 They took the bush-hammer out..that the ladies might see the varieties with five, six, eight, and ten edges, which gave the granite the slightly lined or ridged appearance.

Hence **bush-hammer**, *v.* To strike or dress with the bush-hammer.

1884 KNIGHT *Dict. Mech.* Supp. s.v., Rough-pointing, tooth-axing, bush-hammering. *Ibid.* Sandstone is seldom bush-hammered, as the stunning makes it scale.

bush-harrow ('bʊʃ,hærəʊ), *sb.* An agricultural implement for harrowing grass land or 'bushing in' seed, consisting of a heavy frame with bars in which bushes are interwoven underneath.

1770–4 A. HUNTER *Georgical Ess.* (1803) I. 372 We constantly employ a heavy bush-harrow to spread the dung. **1877** BLACKMORE *Erema* I. ix. 101 As a bush-harrow jumps on the clods of the field.

'bush-,harrow, *v.* [from prec.] *trans.* To use the bush-harrow upon (ground). Also *absol.*

1834 *Brit. Husb.* I. 486 After the cattle are removed, the land is bush-harrowed and rolled. **1839** HT. MARTINEAU *Deerbrook* II. xi. 211 A man beside his horse, bush-harrowing in a distant green field. **1862** H. KINGSLEY *Ravenshoe* xxxii. 188 The meadows were all bush-harrowed, rolled, and laid up for hay.

Hence **'bush-,harrowing** *vbl. sb.*

1834 *Brit. Husb.* I. 481 The subsequent operation of cross bush-harrowing. **1866** ROGERS *Agric. & Prices* I. xxi. 540 The ordinary means by which our forefathers covered their seed was by bush-harrowing.

bushido ('buːʃiːdəʊ). [Jap.: see quot. 1900.] In feudal Japan, the ethical code of the Samurai or military knighthood.

1898 *Trans. Asiatic Soc. Japan* Dec. 149 The knowledge of *Bushidō*, or 'Way of *Samurai*', is absolutely necessary for any one desirous of knowing something about the Japanese people. **1900** I. NITOBÉ *Bushido* 3 *Bu-shi-do* means literally Military-knight-ways—the ways which fighting nobles should observe in their daily life as well as in their vocation. **1902** *Encycl. Brit.* XXIX. 709 It is essential to know something of the ethical code of the *samurai*, the *bushi-do* ('way of the warrior') as it was called. **1923** *19th Cent.* Jan. 133 The old samurai spirit of *bushido* will prove equal to stemming the tide of radicalism. **1961** R. SETH *Anat. Spying* iv. 70 They [*sc.* the Japanese] brought espionage within the scope of *bushido*, their extremely strict and elevated code of morals and conduct.

bushie, var. BUSHY *sb.*

bushily ('bʊʃɪlɪ), *adv.* In a bushy manner.

1857 G. LAWRENCE *Guy Liv.* x, She wore her hair bushily on each side of her small face.

bushiness ('bʊʃɪnɪs). Bushy state or quality.

1730–6 in BAILEY; hence in JOHNSON. **1790** BEWICK *Hist. Quadrupeds* (1807) 277 The bushiness of its hair. **1851** GLENNY *Handbk. Fl. Gard.* 210 Bushiness and compactness of growth. **1875** MASSON *Wordsw. &c.* 175 The bushiness of his [Scott's] eyebrows.

bushing ('bʊʃɪŋ), *vbl. sb.*[1] [f. BUSH *v.*[1]]

1. Training on bushes (*obs.*), setting with bushes.

c **1420** *Pallad. on Husb.* XI. 33 Trailyng, repairyng, bosshyng vyne clene. **1843** CARLYLE *Past & Pr.* II. iii. (1872) 46 We hear not..by what methods he preserved his game, whether by 'bushing' or how. **1875** 'STONEHENGE' *Brit. Sports* I. I. i. §5. 7 Bushing the stubbles interferes with the drag-net.

2. Growing bushy; forming a bush.

1597 GERARD *Herbal* 739 The goodly shadowe which they make with their thicke bushing and clyming. **1610** FOLKINGHAM *Art of Survey* I. iii. 6 The braunching and bearing of Plants, Bushing of Shrubs.

bushing ('bʊʃɪŋ), *vbl. sb.*[2] [f. BUSH *sb.*[2] and *v.*[3] + -ING[1].]

1. The operation of fitting a hole with a bush. Also *concr.* = BUSH *sb.*[2] I. *spec.* in *Electr.*, an insulating device.

1794 *Rigging & Seamanship* I. 154 *Bushing* is letting through the middle of a sheave a cylindrical piece of metal, with a hole through its centre, to admit the pin..on which the sheave turns. **1839** R. S. ROBINSON *Naut. Steam Eng.* 81 The brass bushing of the strap. **1864** WEBSTER, *Bushing*, a thimble; sometimes called a *bush*. **1896** R. ROBB *Electric Wiring* v. 151 Where the cord enters the socket there is gradual wear of the insulation by abrasion unless the hole is bushed with an 'insulating bushing'. **1934** *Times* 28 Feb. 8/6 The failure was caused by a flash-over on a transformer bushing at Croydon sub-station. **1943** *Electronic Engin.* XV. 410 Components like bushings..where metal parts have to be affixed to the porcelain insulator. **1957** *New Scientist* 23 May 24/1 The glass thus formed flows into the forehearth and then into platinum bushings, which are heated electrically to keep the glass fluid.

2. *Watchmaking.* See BOUCHON.

bushing ('bʊʃɪŋ), *ppl. a.* [f. BUSH *v.*[1] + -ING[2].] Growing or spreading like a bush.

1608 TOURNEUR *Rev. Traj.* v. iii, That bushing-staring star. **1688** R. HOLME *Armoury* II. 89/2 Fine leaves, bushing and spreading over the ground. **1725** POPE *Odyss.* IX. 164 The bushing alders form'd a shady scene.

bushless ('bʊʃlɪs), *a.* Devoid of bushes.

1830 TENNYSON *Ode to Mem.* 96 The high field on the bushless Pike. **1872** W. F. BUTLER *Gt. Lone Land* xvi. (1875) 247 A rough and bushless plateau.

bushlet ('bʊʃlɪt). *rare.* [f. BUSH *sb.*[1] + -LET.] A diminutive or tiny bush.

1822 *New Monthly Mag.* V. 4 Birds as they flutter from bushlet to tree.

'bushling. *rare.* [see -LING.] A little bush.

1562 TURNER *Herbal* II. 64 a, Nardus celtica..is a litle bushlyng. *Ibid.* 96 a, A bushlyng, a spanne long.

Bushman, bushman. ('bʊʃmən). [f. BUSH *sb.*[1] 9 + MAN, app. orig. after Du. *boschjesman* applied by the Dutch colonists in S. Africa to the natives living in the 'bush'; and since extended in application.]

1. a. A member of an aboriginal people of Southern Africa; = SAN[2] a. The Du. forms *Bosjesman, Boschjesman*, also occur as ethnic names.

1785 SPARRMAN *Voy. Cape G. Hope* I. v. 197 There is another species of Hottentots, who have got the name of Boshees-men, from dwelling in woody or mountainous places. **1824** BURCHELL *Trav.* I. 64 For our mutual safety and defence..against the Bushmen. **1842** PRICHARD *Nat. Hist. Man* 513 Considering the Bushmen, or Bosjesmen, of South Africa as the most degraded and miserable of all nations. **1845** *Foreign Quart. Rev.* XXXIV. 421 Stunted representatives of humanity..under the name of Bushmen.

b. ***Bushman grass***, in S. Africa any of various grasses, esp. species of *Aristida* and *Stipa*.

[**1789** W. PATERSON *Narr. Journeys Country of Hottentots* 63 Here I found many new species of Gramina, particularly that which the Dutch call Boshman's Grass, from the use made of it by that people, who eat the seed of it.] **1857** A. WYLEY *Rep. Min. Struct. Namaqualand* App. 44 There the various kinds of Bushman grass prevail, almost to the exclusion of every other plant. **1886** G. A. FARINI *Through Kalahari Desert* 448 Bushman grass, the best that grows on the Kalahari. **1915** R. MARLOTH *Flora S. Afr.* IV. 19 *Stipa* (bushman grass).

2. A dweller or traveller in the Australian 'bush'; a bush-farmer; a station-hand; a teamster who carries stores to the stations. Also, one who fells timber.

1846 *N.Z. Jrnl.* VI. 274/1 E Kehu, our guide, is thus a perfect bushman, and is of very great service on an expedition. **1848** T. BRUNNER *Jrnl. Exped. Middle Isl.* 360, I have now acquired the two greatest requisites for bushmen in New Zealand, viz., the capability of walking barefoot, and the proper method of cooking and eating fern root. **1849** S. C. BREES *Guide & Descr. N.Z.* 29 This tree [*sc.* Titoki] is tall ..and the wood..is prized by the bushmen for axe-handles. **1852** *Blackw. Mag.* LXXII. 522 Where the wild bushman eats his loathly fare. **1856** *Tait's Mag.* XXIII. 742 An experienced bushman and well mounted. **1867** LADY BARKER *Station Life N.Z.* (1870) xxi. 180 The 'bushmen'—as the men who had bought 20 acre sections and settled in the bush are called—had scattered English grass-seed. **1880** *Chamb. Jrnl.* 4 Dec. 774 Crowds of Bushmen, as those who live in the interior are called by their brethren of the coast. **1916** G. THORNTON *Wowser* xii. 189 These bushmen..lead a very different life from that of the woodcutters and sawyers (although they too are called bushmen) employed at a saw-mill. **1961** B. CRUMP *Hang on a Minute* (1963) 32 Just find out if he wants a couple of experienced bushmen.

3. The language of the aboriginal bushmen of South Africa; = SAN[2] b.

1869 BLEEK in R. Noble *Cape & its People* 277 Many nouns in Bushman vary in their terminations according to their position or use. *Ibid.* 278 The Bushman nouns do not appear to possess any representative parts. **1874** J. M. ORPEN in *Folklore* (1919) XXX. 146 Then he sent another bird, the tinktinki..—qinqininyq in Bushman. **1960** *Times* (S. Afr. Suppl.) 31 May p. xv/4 Afrikaans also borrowed from..the Hottentot and Bushman tongues.

Bushmanoid ('bʊʃmənɔɪd), *a.* [f. BUSHMAN I + -OID.] Of a Bushman type.

1940 *Jrnl. R. Anthrop. Inst.* 15 The Bushmanoid races are not negroid stock. **1959** J. D. CLARK *Prehist. S. Afr.* iv. 99 Or else both represent parallel specializations from an ancestral proto-Bushmanoid stock.

'bushmanship. [f. prec., sense 2.] The practice of working, etc., in the bush; bush-farming.

1880 *Blackw. Mag.* Feb. 169 *Bush-Life. Queensl.* His intimate knowledge of bushmanship. **1922** *Times Lit. Suppl.* 28 Dec. 869/3 He made his way back to South Africa and.. found himself serving in the Intelligence Department, for which the knowledge of bushmanship and native customs obtained in lion-hunting specially recommended him. **1931** T. A. HARPER *Windy Island* II. v. 146 A friendship based on bushmanship. **1968** K. WEATHERLY *Roo Shooter* 56 The first rule of bushmanship is 'Don't cross a fence or go through a gate when you're bushed'.

bushment ('bʊʃmənt). Forms: 4 bussche-, busse-, buysche-, buche-, buchy-, 4–6 busch(e)-, busshe-, (5 bussh-), 5–6 bushe-, 6 bus-, 5– bushment. [In senses 1–3, an aphetic form of ABUSHMENT, AMBUSHMENT, q.v. In some early quotations it is difficult to know whether *abushment* or *a bushment* was intended. In sense 4, cf. BUSH *sb.*[1] + -MENT.]

1. = AMBUSHMENT I. *arch.*

1375 BARBOUR *Bruce* VIII. 442 A buschement slely maid he thair. **1393** GOWER *Conf.* I. 349 And of his men a great partie He made in bussheme̵nt abide. *c* **1440** *Generydes* II. 5977 In a buschement he layde his men eche on. **1485** CAXTON *Chas. Gt.* 133 Your peple that shal be hydde in the bussheme̵nt. **1553** BRENDE *Q. Curtius* III. D ij, For feare the enemyes should lye there in busshement. **1592** WYRLEY *Armorie* 86 Two Gascoin Lords warie bushment make. **1870** MORRIS *Earthly Par.* I. I. 54 The barbarous folk Once and again from bushments on us broke.

†**2.** = AMBUSHMENT 2. *Obs.*

c **1400** *Destr. Troy* 13014 A bussheme̵nt of bold men breke hym vpon. *c* **1465** *Eng. Chron.* (1856) 48 In the way as he sholde go, lay a greet busshement of Frenssheme̵nne to take him. *a* **1550** *Christis Kirke Gr.* xix, The buschment haill about him brak, An bickert him with bows.

†**3.** A surprise party; = AMBUSHMENT 3. *Obs.*

1513 MORE *Rich. III* (1557) 64/2 A bushement of the dukes seruantes..began sodainely at mannes backes to crye owte as lowde as their throtes would gyve: King Rycharde. **1536** BELLENDEN *Cron. Scot.* I. 144 Galdus assemblit ane army..and dividit the same in divers buschementis. **1549** LATIMER *Serm. bef. Edw. VI* (Arb.) 187 Iudas also when he came wyth bushementes to take his maister Christe.

4. 'A thicket, a cluster of bushes' (J.); a mass of bushes. ? *Obs.*

1586 J. HOOKER *Girald. Irel.* II. 169/2 The sides are full of great and mightie trees vpon the sides of the hils, and full of bushments and vnderwoods. **1614** RALEIGH *Hist. World* I. viii. §2. 111 These our grounds would..be covered, either with Woods, or with other offensive Thickets and Bushments. **1619** W. SCLATER *Expos. 1 Thess.* (1630) 62 These thickets of bushment. **1762** DUNN in *Phil. Trans.* LII. 466 The most distant trees and bushments.

†**b.** A bushy formation (of plumage). *Obs.*

1555 EDEN *Decades W. Ind.* (Arb.) 224 These byrdes.. haue a much greater bushement of fethers.

bushop(e, -hopp(e, obs. ff. BISHOP.

bush-ranger ('bʊʃ,reɪndʒə(r)). [f. BUSH[1] 9 + RANGER.] An escaped convict who took refuge in the Australian 'bush'; a criminal living in the bush, and subsisting by robbery with violence.

1817 *Sydney Gazette* 25 Jan., Robberies by the banditti of bush-rangers on Van Dieman's Land. **1826** *Gentl. Mag.* July XCVI. II. 69/2 Van Diemen's Land papers and private letters are full of details of atrocities by the bush-rangers (escaped convicts). **1852** WEST *Tasmania* II. 130 The bushrangers at first were absentees [convicts] who were soon allured or driven to theft and violence; so early as 1808 by systematic robbery they had excited feelings of alarm. **1869**

PARKMAN *Discov. Gt. West* xxvii. (1875) 389 His little garrison of bush-rangers greeted them with a salute of musketry.

bush-ranging (ˈbʊʃˌreɪndʒɪŋ), *vbl. sb.* Also -'rangering. [see prec.] The practice of the bush-ranger; the attacking and robbing of travellers or settlers in the bush. Also *attrib.*

1832 HT. MARTINEAU *Homes Abr.* v. 72 As long as any convicts were disposed to bush-ranging..he could not for his part feel very secure. **1863** *Guardian* 23 Dec., Bush-ranging has obtained such a head in New South Wales, that the Government have offered a reward of £2500 for the capture of a gang of five. **1864** SALA in *Daily Tel.* 9 Aug., Bushranging broils between Federal dragoons and half-naked guerillas. **1853** *Fraser's Mag.* XLVIII. 662 What has bushrangering and the police come to?

bush-rope (ˈbʊʃrəʊp). [f. BUSH *sb.*[1] 9.] A name given to certain climbing shrubs in tropical forests, *esp.* to species of *Cissus* or Wild Vine.

1814 *Q. Rev.* XI. 70 They are in many places so closely interwoven with rattan and bush-rope that they seem to be spun together. **1825** WATERTON *Wand. S. Amer.* I. i. 91 A vine called the Bush-rope by the wood cutters, on account of its use in hauling out the heaviest timber. **1826** SYD. SMITH *Wks.* (1859) II. 74 The bush-rope joins tree and tree, so as to render the forest impervious.

bushveld (ˈbʊʃfɛlt, -vɛlt). Also **bush veldt.** [ad. Afrikaans *bosveld*: see BUSH *sb.*[1] and VELD.] **a.** Veld composed largely of bush. **b.** (Usu. with capital initial.) The wooded region of north-western, northern, and eastern Transvaal, the low-lying portion of which is called the Lowveld or Low Country.

1879 *Chambers's Jrnl.* 1 Mar. 134/2 For big game, the low country and Bushveld is that part of the Transvaal which the hunter must seek. **1887** *Atalanta* Nov. 80/1 The roar of a lion..in the solemn bush veldt. **1887** A. A. ANDERSON *Twenty-five Yrs. in Waggon* (1888) 153 The Notuane River, in what is termed the Bush Veldt. **1901** *Contemp. Rev.* Mar. 333 An efficient guide, whose knowledge of the dense bushveld proved of great value. **1903** KIPLING *Five Nations* 205 The Low Bush-veldt that sends men stragglin' unaware. **1903** 'INDICUS' *Labour S. Africa* 19 Their farm is of about 5,000 acres in extent, on the lower or Bush Veldt. **1907** P. FITZPATRICK *Jock of Bushveld* 14 Between the goldfields and the nearest port lay the Bushveld. **1940** V. POHL *Bushveld Adv.* i. 41 My family had moved to the Bushveld of the Northern Transvaal. **1958** L. VAN DER POST *Lost World of Kalahari* (1961) vii. 126 Soon the main stream carried us away from the bush-veld banks.

bushwa, -wah (ˈbʊʃwɑː). *N. Amer. slang.* Also **booshwa(h), bushwha.** [app. a euphemism for BULLSHIT.] Rubbish, nonsense. Also *attrib.*

1920 in WENTWORTH *Amer. Dial. Dict.* **1921** J. DOS PASSOS *Three Soldiers* (1922) IV. 215 Can't do anything without getting a general order about it. Looks to me like it's all bushwa. **1924** *Chicago Tribune* 1 Oct. 25/8 The Bull, the Glad Hand, the Old Oil, and Il Bushwa. **1932** *Amer. Speech* VII. 329 *Booshwah*, nonsense. **1932** J. DOS PASSOS *1919* 162 They said this war-talk was a lot of bushwa propaganda. **1934** J. O'HARA *Appt. Samarra* (1935) vi. 164 'Oh, bushwah on you,' said Irma. **1936** MENCKEN *Amer. Lang.* (ed. 4) vi. 301 The college boys and girls launched *bushwah*..and a number of other thinly disguised shockers. **1949** E. F. RUSSELL in E. Crispin *Best SF* (1962) 205 'Certain of them may have secret knowledge...' 'Bushwa!' defined Queth, unhesitatingly. **1959** 'J. R. MACDONALD' *Galton Case* (1960) x. 83 If you're a detective, what was all that bushwa about Hollywood and Sunset Boulevard?

'bushwhack, *v. U.S.* [f. BUSH + WHACK *v.* to beat; prob. after BUSHWHACKER.] To act as a bushwhacker; to beat the bush; to attack or kill in the manner of a bushwhacker (sense 2).

1837 *Fraser's Mag.* XVI. 613 The Colonel had begun to make a speech, or, as he phrases it, 'to bushwhack in the most approved style'. **1866** J. E. SKINNER *After Storm* I. 234 While peaceable citizens were robbed with impunity and government officers were bushwhacked. **1877** G. FLEMING *Mirage* III. viii. 212 A good many men were missing, shot or bushwhacked, we did not know which.

bushwhacker (ˈbʊʃˌhwækə(r)). *U.S.* [f. BUSH *sb.*[1] + WHACKER, one who 'whacks' or beats. (Cf. also Du. *bosch-wachter*, forest-keeper.)]

lit. One who whacks or beats bushes; hence, **1.** One accustomed to beat about or make his way through bushes; a backwoodsman, a bush-ranger.

1809 W. IRVING *Knickerb.* VI. v. (1849) 342 They were gallant bush-whackers and hunters of racoons by moonlight.

2. Applied in the American Civil War to irregular combatants who took to the woods, and were variously regarded as patriot guerillas, or as bush-rangers and banditti; a bush-fighter.

1862 *Macm. Mag.* June 141 Of banditti, or bush-whackers ..we say nothing. **1866** J. E. SKINNER *After Storm* I. 240 Neither bushwhackers or slaves were seen in the streets.

3. A scythe or other implement used to cut away brushwood.

1858 J. DOW *Serm.* I. (Bartlett) The victim soon destined to fall before the keen-edged bush-whacker of Time. **1870** EMERSON *Soc. & Solit.* iv. 81 He is a graduate of the plough, and the stub-hoe, and the bushwhacker.

4. One who clears the land of bush, esp. an axeman engaged in cutting timber. *N.Z.*

1898 J. BELL *In Shadow of Bush* iv. 18 Davie isn't qualified as a bush whacker yet. **1907** W. H. KOEBEL *Return of Joe* 257 The most skilful bush-whacker in the district. **1948** R. FINLAYSON *Tidal Creek* II. v. 149 How nice after Uncle Ted's bushwhacker style to see a table with a crisp white cloth.

Hence **bushwhackerism.**

1883 *American* VI. 356 The 'border ruffianism' and the 'bushwhackerism' which disgraced Missouri.

bushwhacking (ˈbʊʃˌhwækɪŋ), *vbl. sb. U.S.*

1. Making one's way through bushes; *esp.* the pulling of a boat by means of the bushes along the margin of a stream.

1826 T. FLINT *Recoll. Miss. Valley* 86 A process, which, in the technics of the boatmen [of the Mississippi] is called bush-whacking. **1828** —— *Hist. & Geog. Miss. Valley* (Bartlett) The propelling power of the keel-boat is by oars, sails, setting-poles, the cordelle, and..bush-whacking, or pulling up by the bushes.

2. The making of the woods a basis of operations for fighting or deeds of violence; bush-fighting.

1864 *Daily Tel.* 23 Aug. An unimportant bushwhacking foray. **1880** *Scribner's Monthly* XXI. Dec. 301 Forbes underwent four months of bushwhacking with the Carlists.

3. Felling or clearing bush (with an axe). *N.Z.*

1906 E. W. ELKINGTON *Adrift in N.Z.* xvi. 262 Bush-felling, or, as it is termed, bush-whacking was a favourite pastime of mine. **1907** W. H. KOEBEL *Return of Joe* 287 You new chums cuttin' good terbacker as if you was bush-wackin'. **1930** W. SMYTH *Wooden Rails* iii. 39 Don't you like saw-mills and bush whacking and all that?

'bushˌwhacking, *ppl. a.* That bushwhacks.

1883 *American* VI. 92 The scouting, bushwhacking Unionist, Fortner.

bushy (ˈbʊʃɪ), *a.* [f. BUSH *sb.*[1] + -Y.]

1. Abounding in bushes; overgrown with shrubs or underwood.

1382 WYCLIF *Isa.* vii. 19 In alle busshi places. **1552** HULOET, Busshy places, *Vespices.* **1575** TURBERV. *Bk. Venerie* Pref. Seruants such as beat the bushie woods To make their masters sport. **1641** MILTON *Ch. Discip.* I. (1851) 32 They seek the dark, the bushie, the tangled Forrest. **1725** DE FOE *Voy. round World* (1840) 305 The country being.. something more bushy, and here and there a few trees. **1885** *Manch. Examiner* 15 May 5/2 The enemy still occupied the bushy ravine running down to the river.

2. Growing like a bush; shrub-like.

1567 MAPLET *Gr. Forest* 44 Fumitorie..is a bushie or shrublike Herbe, like to Coreander. **1579** SPENSER *Sheph. Cal.* Dec. 2 All in the shadowe of a bushye brere. **1667** MILTON *P.L.* IV. 696 Each odorous bushie shrub. **1719** DE FOE *Crusoe* (1840) I. iii. 54 A thick bushy tree like a fir. **1814** WORDSW. *White Doe of Ryl.* I. 96 The spread Of the elder's bushy head. **1861** PRATT *Flower. Pl.* IV. 111.

3. a. Of hair: Growing thick like a bush.

1611 BIBLE *Song of Sol.* v. 11 His locks are bushy. *a* **1613** J. DENNYS in Arb. *Garner* I. 150 Some lusty horse..Whose bushy tail upon the ground doth track. **1652** GAULE *Magastrom.* 305 A bushy head of haire. **1843** CARLYLE *Past. & Pr.* II. x. (1872) 78 A man with eminent nose, bushy brows and clear-flashing eyes. **1873** BLACK *Pr. Thule* i. 1 The gusts of wind that blew about his bushy grey beard.

†**b.** Of persons: With long thick hair; also quasi-*sb. Obs.*

1615 P. SMALL *Man's May* in Farr's *S.P.* (1848) 331 Time still describ'd in poets thus we finde, Bushy before, but very bald behinde. **1650** BULWER *Anthropomet.* II. 56 He does that which is ridiculous..who is..a Bushie among those who are Poled.

c. *Ent.* Of antennæ: covered with long, erect hairs (Cent. Dict. 1889).

4. Puffed out like a bush.

1756 NUGENT *Gr. Tour, Germany* II. 298 They wear pointed hats, and monstrous bushy ruffs. **1832** *Fraser's Mag.* VI. 386 All..had taken more stuff than necessary for their clothes..It is as if the women could not be bushy enough, the men not puffy enough, to please themselves.

†**5.** Dwelling among the bushes. *rare.*

1563 T. HOWELL *Arb. Amitie* (1879) 83 The Nightingal.. gettes the peerlesse prayse, The bushie birdes among.

6. *Comb.*, as *bushy-browed, -tailed, -whiskered, -wigged*, adjs. **bushy stunt**, a virus disease of tomato plants (see quot. 1956).

1912 W. OWEN *Let.* 2 July (1967) 148 A bushy-browed and horny-fisted *blacksmith's assistant.* **1965** G. MCINNES *Road to Gundagai* x. 176 The crinkly lines round his bushy browed eyes were thoughtful. **1812** J. H. VAUX *Flash Dict.*, A man who is poor is said to be 'at Bushy park', or 'in the park'. [Cf. BUSHED.]. **1936** G. C. AINSWORTH in *Jrnl. Min. Agric.* XLIII. 266 It is proposed to call this disease of tomato, 'Bushy Stunt'. **1939** *Ann. Reg. 1938* 376 The virus of bushy stunt of tomato was obtained in a fully crystalline state. **1956** *Dict. Gardening (R.H.S.)* IV. 2124/1 Another virus disease [of tomato plants] is Bushy Stunt, in which there is enormous production of secondary shoots with a resulting bushy appearance in the plant. **1868** *Amer. Naturalist* II. 535 It seems widely separated..in habits from its nearest relative *Nycteris occidentalis*, or bushy-tailed Bat. **1947** J. STEVENSON-HAMILTON *Wild Life S. Afr.* xxv. 207 The bushy-tailed meercat (*Bdeogale crassicaude*). **1837** CARLYLE *Fr. Rev.* (1871) II. I. ix. 40 Impassioned bushy-whiskered youth threatening suicide. **1832** —— in *Fraser's Mag.* V. 402 Old sedentary bushy-wigged Cave.

7. Concerned with the (Australian) bush.

1900 H. LAWSON *On Track* 37 The foreman was a bushman; his sympathies were bushy. **1904** *Daily Chron.* 19 Apr. 3/5 Her stories are of the bush bushy.

bushy (ˈbʊʃɪ), *sb. Austral.* and *N.Z.* Also **bushie.** [f. BUSH *sb.*[1] + -Y[6].] A dweller in the bush; a bushman as distinguished from a townsman.

1896 H. LAWSON *While Billy Boils* 144 Bushies don't generally carry their swags out of pubs in their sleep. **1899** *Bulletin* (Sydney) 7 Jan. 14/1 The usual summer query—Why won't the bushy wear straw hats? **1924** H. T. GIBSON *That Gibbie Galoot* xvii. 66 The unlucky 'bushie' whose mannerisms or objectionable traits attract overmuch attention from his mates. **1934** *Bulletin* (Sydney) 19 Dec. 20/1 The sweet test of a bushie! He looks round for a rail to lean his elbows on, while the townie negligently leans up against a post. **1968** K. WEATHERLY *Roo Shooter* 21 The bushie spoke for the first time.

bushylle, obs. form of BUSHEL.

busied (ˈbɪzɪd), *ppl. a.* For forms see BUSY *v.* [f. BUSY *v.* + -ED.] Attentively occupied, engaged, actively employed. (The attrib. use is rare; for the use as predicate see BUSY *v.* 1 c.)

1611 FLORIO, *Affacendato*, busied, full of affaires. **1659** *Land-Mark betwixt Prince & People* 2 Our..too much busied forefathers. **1669** WOODHEAD *St. Teresa* II. vii. 55 That the busied Monk was tempted but with one Devil.

busily (ˈbɪzɪlɪ), *adv.* Forms: 3 **busiliche,** (*sup.* **bisilukest**), 3–5 **bisiliche,** 4 **bysely, bysily, bisili, bisyly, besaly, besiliche,** (*comp.* **bisiloker**), 4–5 **bysyly, bisily, besily,** 4–6 **besyly,** 4–7 **besely,** 5 **besele, besylyche, bysiliche, bysylyche,** (*comp.* **besilier**), 6 **bisilye, buisyly(e, busely(e, busilie,** 4, 6– **busily.** [f. BUSY *a.* + -LY[2].]

†**1.** With fixed attention; carefully, heedfully; attentively, intently; with attention to details; particularly, minutely, 'curiously'. *Obs.*

c **1205** LAY. 4473 His cnihtes..laien bi þan brimme and bisilichen [*c* **1275** busiliche] hit wisten. ? *a* **1300** *Cato Major* IV. 35 Let not o Bok bisiliche Beo lernynge euer-more. *c* **1325** *E.E. Allit. P.* B. 1446 Wyth besten blod busily anoynted. **1382** WYCLIF *Matt.* ii. 7, 8 Than Herode, bisily lernyde of hem the tyme of the sterre..And he..saide, Go ȝee, and axe ȝee bisily of the chyld. *c* **1386** CHAUCER *Man of Lawes T.* 997 He loked besily Upon the child. **1483** CAXTON *Gold. Leg.* C ij/2 He demanded more besilier after hym. *a* **1520** *Myrr. Our Ladye* 225 How besely she was to kepe her tongue. **1577** tr. *Bullinger's Decades* (1592) 344 It is in the 3. of Kings, very busily set downe.

†**b.** Anxiously, solicitously. *Obs.*

c **1400** in *Pol. Rel. & L. Poems* (1866) 234 Here we liue bisiliche wit strong sorwe & care.

†**2.** Earnestly, fervently, eagerly, importunately.

c **1340** *Cursor M.* 17710 (Trin.) Bisili to god preyonde. *c* **1375** *Lay-Folks Mass-Bk.* B. 14 We blesse þe bisyly. *c* **1460** *Towneley Myst.* 26 Pray for me besele. **1534** LD. BERNERS *Gold. Bk. M. Aurel.* (1546) B b ij, My wife..busily praied me to kepe it. **1621** BOLTON *Stat. Irel.* (11 *Eliz.*) 316 Dermot Mac Morche..went..to the said king Henry, and him besely besought of succour.

3. So as to be fully occupied: diligently, industriously, assiduously, energetically.

1340 HAMPOLE *Pr. Consc.* 1067 About worldisshe thynges þai here travaile Ful bysily. **1447–8** J. SHILLINGFORD *Lett.* (1871) 3 Have full bisily labored to make an answere to the articulys. **1508** FISHER *Wks.* I. (E.E.T.) 58 He shoulde haue resysted..more besyly. **1596** SHAKS. *1 Hen. IV*, v. v. 38 Northumberland, and the Prelate Scroope..are busily in Armes. **1736** BUTLER *Anal.* vii. 142 This little scene of human life, in which we are so busily engaged. **1798** SOUTHEY *To Spider*, Busily our needful food to win, We work. **1866** KINGSLEY *Herew.* x, The old Lapp nurse sat.. sewing busily.

b. Actively, briskly.

1513 BRADSHAW *St. Werburge* (1848) 1 Byrdes besely syngynge. **1843** CARLYLE *Past & Pr.* II. vii. (1872) 65 St. Edmundsbury..is a busily fermenting place. **1860** TYNDALL *Glac.* I. §11. 72 The stars..twinkled busily.

business (ˈbɪznɪs). Forms: 1 *North.* **bisiȝnis,** 3 **bisenes,** 3–4 **bisines,** 4 **bisy-, bysi-, bissynes, bissinesse,** 4–5 **besines(se, besenes, bisy-, bysynesse,** 4–6 **besynes(se, bysy-, busynes,** 4–7 **busynesse,** 5 **besiness, bessynes, byse-, bisinesse,** 6 **besyness, busenes(s, buysines,** 6–7 **busines, -nesse,** (7 **bius'ness, busynese),** 7– **business.** [OE. (North.) *bisiȝnis*, f. BUSY *a.*, or stem of BUSY *v.*; see -NESS. Shortened to a dissyllable, since it ceased to be a noun of state. The plural *businesses* (formerly also *business*) is used only in a few senses, chiefly 14, 15.]

I. State or quality of being busy. (Cf. the adj.)

(These senses are all obs., but some of them occur as nonce-words with special spelling BUSYNESS, and trisyllabic pronunciation.)

†**1. a.** The state of being busily engaged in anything. **b.** Industry, diligence. *Obs.*

c **1350** *Cursor M.* 28748 (Cott. Galba MS.) Fasting and gude bisines Gers a man fle lustes of fless. *c* **1380** WYCLIF *Wks.* (1880) 60 Cristis bysynesse in prechynge. *c* **1440** *Promp. Parv.* 37 Bysynesse, *assiduitas, diligencia.* **1549** *Compl. Scot.* 2 Distitute of..al verteus bysynes of body ande saul. **1611** BIBLE *Rom.* xii. 11 Not slouthfull in busines [**1881** *Rev. Vers.* in diligence not slothful]. **1696** STILLINGFL. *12 Serm.* VIII. 349 Apprehensive..not so much from the business of our enemies. *a* **1713** in *Guardian* No. 35 §12 Behold the raptures which a writer knows..Behold his business while he works the mine.

†**2.** Activity, briskness. *Obs.*

1423 JAS. I. *King's Q.* clv, The lytill squerell, full of besynesse. **1616** SURFL. & MARKH. *Countr. Farm* 681 The businesse of his [a dog's] taile. **1674** N. FAIRFAX *Bulk & Selv.* 11 The bulkiness of the world, the business of motion.

†**3.** Mischievous or impertinent activity, officiousness. *Obs.*

1466 *Paston Lett.* No. 543 II. 263 Al by her awne bessynes of her tunge. **1528** MORE *Dial. Heresyes* III. Wks. 212/1 Faccious wayes full of busynes. **1580** SIDNEY *Arcadia* 315 O

noble sisters..now you be gone what is left in that sex, but babling and businesse?

†**4.** Eagerness, earnestness, importunity. *Obs.*

? *a* **1300** *Cato Major* II. xvii, Envye wiþ gret bisinesse Beoþenk þe forte fleo. **1398** Trevisa *Barth. De P.R.* XII. Introd., Males secheþ females with besinesse. *c* **1400** *Lay-Folks Mass-Bk.* App. iii. 122 þorouȝ besynesse of preyers. **1543** *Prymer* ibid. 86 Make me accordyng to my busynes Partaker of thy..glory endles.

†**5.** Anxiety, solicitude, care; distress, uneasiness. (The earliest cited sense.) *Obs.*

c **950** *Lindisf. Gosp.* Matt., Table Contents xx, Ne bisiȝnisse mettes & woedes hæbende [Lat. *nec solicitudinem escæ et vestis habendam*]. *a* **1300** *Cursor M.* 14105 'Martha, Martha'..'In mikel bisenes ert þou'. **1382** Wyclif *Ezek.* xii. 19 Thei shulen eete her breed in bisynes [*solicitudine*]. **1475** *Bk. Noblesse* 3 Put away thoughte and gret pensifnes..and besinesse. **1526** Tindale *Gal.* v. 17 From hence forth, let no man put me to busynes [so in Coverdale, Cranmer, *Geneva*]. **1577** *St. Augustine's Man.* (ed. Longman) 90 Leave of thine own businesses..and withdrawe thy selfe from thy troublesome thoughtes.

†**6.** Care, attention, observance. *Obs.*

1382 Wyclif *Ecclus.* xli. 15 Haue thou bisynesse [*curam habe*] of a good name. **1398** Trevisa *Barth. De P.R.* v. xxxvi. (1495) 148 The herte hyghte *cor*..of *cura* besynesse, for therin is all besynesse and cause of witte and of knowinge. **1503–4** *Act 19 Hen. VII*, xxxii. §5 Takyng uppon theym the charge and besynes for the assessyng of the seid somme. **1540** Hyrde *Vives Instr. Chr. Wom.* (1592) CC ij, All these busines, & keeping of the corce.

†**7. a.** Trouble, difficulty; ado. Cf. busy *a.* 3. *Obs.*

c **1374** Chaucer *Anel. & Arc.* 102 Ful mychell besynesse had he or þat he myght his lady wynne. **1387** Trevisa *Higden* Rolls Ser. III. 449 [He] aleyde þis sorwe unneþe wiþ grete besynesse. **1528** Tindale *Obedience Chr. Man* Wks. I. 310 What business had he to pacify his children. *a* **1599** R. Bodenham in Arb. *Garner* I. 34, I had no small business to cause my mariners to venture. **1693** Locke *Educ.* §157 His learning to read should be made as little Trouble or Business to him as might be.

†**b.** Ado, disturbance, commotion. *Obs.*

1494 Fabyan vii. 684 For whose goodes was besynesse by-twen the Kynges amner and the sheryffe. **1514** Ld. Mountjoy in Strype *Eccl. Mem.* I. I. 9 He feared that if they had not their pardons in likewise, they would either make business or they would avoid. **1526** Tindale *Matt.* xxvii. 24 When Pilate sawe..that moare busenes [**1611** a tumult] was made. **1560** Daus *Sleidane's Comm.* 343a, One of the Sergeaunts..made a busines with him as though he would haue caried him to pryson. **1570–87** Holinshed *Sc. Chron.* (1806) 110 Argadus sent foorth..with a power to appease that businesse.

†**8.** Diligent labour, exertion, pains. Phrases. ***to do*** (***one's***) ***business***, ***give business***: to take pains, do one's endeavour (L. *dare operam*).

1340 Hampole *Pr. Consc.* 1068 Wald þai do half swilk bysines About goddes of heven. *c* **1380** Wyclif *Wks.* (1880) 373 He wol þat þai ȝeue bissynes to þe londe. *c* **1400** Maundev. xxiii. 251 Thei..alle weys don here besynes, to destroyen hire enemyes. **1422** *E.E. Wills* (1882) 51 They will do her besynesse to fulfyll goddes will. **1509** Hawes *Past. Pleas.* xiv. xiv, In vayne they spende their besynes.

†**II. 9.** A company of flies, also of ferrets. *Obs.*

c **1470** *Hors, Shepe, & G.* (1822) 31 A besynes of flyes. **1486** *Bk. St. Albans* f vi a, A Besynes of ferettis.

III. That about which one is busy.

†**10.** The object of anxiety or serious effort; a serious purpose or aim. *Obs.*

c **1392** Chaucer *Compl. Venus* 20 Me to serue is al his besynesse. **1413** Lydg. *Pylgr. Sowle* III. iii. (1483) 51 Alle youre study and besinesse hath ben to defame tho that were better than ye. ? *c* **1530** *Prov. Howsolde-kepyng* in *Pol. Rel. & L. Poems* (1866) 29 Peyse wisely the besynes & the purpose of them wich ammynyster thy goodes.

11. a. A task appointed or undertaken; a person's official duty, part or province; function, occupation. Phr. ***to make it one's business***: to undertake as a self-appointed task (*to* do something).

c **1385** Chaucer *L.G.W.* 1719 Bad hire seruauntis don hire besynesse. *a* **1533** Ld. Berners *Huon* lviii. 199 It behoueth vs shortely to determyne oure besynes..I shall shew you what is best for vs ii to do. **1611** Bible *Gen.* xxxix. 11 Ioseph went in to the house, to doe his busines. **1642** Fuller *Holy & Prof. St.* I. x. 25 Though going abroad sometimes about her businesse, She never makes it her businesse to go abroad. *a* **1680** Butler *Rem.* (1759) I. 95 Love's Business is to love, and to enjoy. **1709** Steele *Tatler* No. 18 ⁋1 Because a Thing is every Body's Business, it is no Body's Business. **1723** G. P[arry] tr. *Cicero's De Orat.* II. 134 When, as you said, I had first made it my Business not to examine but to aggravate. **1735** Berkeley *Defence Free-Thinking in Maths.* 54 And since the publication thereof, I have myself freely conversed with Mathematicians of all ranks, and some of the ablest Professors, as well as made it my business to be informed of the Opinions of others. **1802** Mar. Edgeworth *Mor. T.* (1816) I. xvii. 141 It is our business to keep the room aired and swept. **1878** Huxley *Physiogr.* 183 The great business of the sea is..eating away the margin of the coast. **1946** 'P. Wentworth' *Clock strikes Twelve* ix. 43 'I don't know how she knew.' 'She's the sort of woman who makes it her business to know.'

b. That on which one is engaged, or with which one is concerned, at the time; often *spec.* the errand on which one comes.

1596 Shaks. *Tam. Shr.* III. ii. 193 If you knew my businesse, You would intreat me rather goe then stay. **1684** Bunyan *Pilgr.* II. 72 What is your business here so late to Night? **1697** Dryden *Virg. Georg.* IV. 644 What Buis'ness brought thee to my dark abode? **1740** J. Clarke *Educ. Youth* (ed. 3) 15 His Business will have no Difficulty in it. *Mod.* I asked him his business. What business brings you here?

12. a. A person's official or professional duties as a whole; stated occupation, profession, or trade.

1477 Earl Rivers *Dictes* (Caxton) 106 He that wele & dyligently vnderstondith to his bysenesse. **1549** Latimer *Serm. on the Ploughers* (Arb.) 29 Lette euerie man do his owne busines, and folow his callyng. **1694** R. L'Estrange *Fables* ccclxv. (ed. 6) 385 They make Fooling their Business and their Livelihood. **1732** Law *Serious C.* ii. (ed. 2) 19 His every day business, will be a course of wise and reasonable actions. **1745** Chesterf. *Lett.* I. c. 278 To apply yourself seriously to your business. **1882** Beecher in *Homiletic Monthly* (*N.Y.*) Apr. 381 One whose business it is to preach.

†**b.** Official or public engagements generally, active life. *Obs.* See also *man of business*: 22 a.

1750 Chesterf. *Lett.* III. ccxxiv. 15 Your German..will be of great use to you when you come into business. **1779** Johnson *Pope* Wks. IV. 6 Sir William Trumbal, who had been..secretary of state, when he retired from business, fixed his residence in the neighbourhood of Binfield.

c. Phr. ***business as usual***: things proceeding normally in spite of disturbing circumstances.

1884 *Punch* 12 Apr. 178/2 The true way she could show respect to Her Majesty was by letting her shopmen carry on 'business as usual' for the benefit of Her Majesty's subjects. **1914** Wilson & Hammerton *Great War* I. 84 'Business as usual' was the motto of London. **1944** J. S. Huxley *On Living in Rev.* iii. 38 The subordination of the profit motive and all ideas of 'business as usual' to the non-economic motive of success in war. **1969** *Times* 25 Nov. 21/7 We can never expect it to be a case of, after the squeeze, business as usual.

13. a. In general sense: action which occupies time, demands attention and labour; *esp.* serious occupation, work, as opposed to pleasure or recreation.

c **1400** *Apol. Loll.* 3 Hatyng to be enpliȝed wiþ seculer bisines. **1532** More *Confut. Tindale* Wks. 826/1 Occupied in honorable businesse. **1600** C. Percy in *Shaks. C. Praise* 38 Pestred with contrie businesse. **1653** Walton *Angler* Ep. Ded. 3 To give rest to your mind, and devest your self of your more serious business. **1796** Southey *Occas. Pieces* v, The business of the day is done. **1857** Heavysege *Saul* (1869) 141 Business still should alternate with pleasure.

†**b.** Work done by beasts. *Obs. rare.*

1737 H. Bracken *Farriery Impr.* (1756) II. v. 104 A Horse which eats only a moderate Quantity of Food, will do as much Business..[as] one that eats continually.

c. Phrases. ***to mean business***: to be in earnest (*colloq.*). ***on business***: with an errand or purpose relating to business.

1857 Hughes *Tom Brown* I. ix, I tells 'ee I means business, and you'd better keep on your own side. *Mod.* No admittance except on business.

d. ***a person's business***: work to be done or matters to be attended to in his service or on his behalf. ***to do*** (***a person's***) ***business***: to 'do for', ruin, or kill him. Also *fig.*

1535 Coverdale *2 Macc.* xv. 5 To perfourme the kynges busynesse. **1611** Bible *Luke* ii. 49 Wist ye not that I must be about my Father's business? **1667** Pepys *Diary* 16 Nov., Lord Vaughan, that is so great against the Chancellor..was heard to swear he would do my Lord Clarendon's business. **1694** Luttrell *Brief Rel.* (1857) III. 349 They would now doe the queens businesse, if she were not immortall. **1773** Goldsmith *Stoops to Conq.* v, Oh, Tony, I'm killed!..That last jolt, that laid us against the quickset hedge, has done my business. **1816** Jane Austen *Emma* I. viii. 122 Her visit to Abbey Mill..seems to have done his business. He is desperately in love. **1883** J. Greenwood *Odd People in Odd Places* 7 It was the bricks and mortar that did *his* business, poor chap. **1891** J. M. Dixon *Dict. Idiom. Eng. Phr.* 47 His last imprudent exposure of himself to the night air did the business for him.

14. a. (With *plural.*) A pursuit or occupation demanding time and attention; a serious employment as distinguished from a pastime.

c **1400** *Apol. Loll.* 77 Now al most is no worldly bysines þat ministres of þe auter are not inplied in. **1458** *MS. of Christ's Hosp. Abingdon* in *Dom. Archit.* III. 41 Another blissed besines is brigges to make. **1535** Coverdale *2 Tim.* ii. 4 No man that warreth tangleth him selfe with worldly busynesses. **1727** De Foe *Eng. Tradesm.* v. (1841) I. 33 Trade ought to be followed as one of the great businesses of life. **1853** A. J. Morris *Relig. & Business*, Title-page, Wherever religion is a business, there will business be a religion. **1848** Macaulay *Hist. Eng.* II. 54

b. *spec.* A particular occupation; a trade or profession.

1827 Carlyle *Transl.* (1874) 217, I wished to be a fisherman, and tried that business for a time. **1852** McCulloch *Taxation* I. ii. (ed. 2) 74 Taxes on the profits of particular businesses. **1856** Froude *Hist. Eng.* (1858) I. i. 51 Not allowing any man to work at a business for which he was unfit. **1878** Jevons *Primer Pol. Econ.* 58 A good butcher makes high wages, because his business is a greasy one, besides being thought to be cruel. *Mod.* Which of these businesses is to be preferred?

15. a. A particular matter demanding attention; a piece of work, a job. (The plur. is now unusual.)

1557 North *Gueuara's Diall Pr.* (1582) 424b, The continuall buysines they haue do vex them. **1590** Shaks. *Mids. N.* III. i. 395 We may effect this businesse, yet ere day. **1595** —— *John* IV. iii. 158 A thousand businesses are briefe in hand. **1611** Bible *Pref.* 11 In a businesse of moment a man feareth not the blame of conuenient slacknesse. **1647** W. Browne *Polex.* I. 66 During all these great businesse. **1718** Pope *Iliad* xix. 152 What I act, survey, And learn from thence the business of the day. **1851** Carlyle *Sterling* II. vi. (1872) 139 On these businesses..he was often running up to London. **1881** *Daily Tel.* 27 Dec., Attention was paid to the business of the evening.

b. Elliptically for: A difficult matter (*colloq.*).

1843 Carlyle *Past & Pr.* II. xii. (1872) 90 If he had known what a business it was to govern the Abbey.

c. ***to do one's business***: 'to ease oneself'.

1645 *Sacr. Decretal* 3 Have a..care..that..no birds build, chatter, or do their businesse, or sing there.

d. ***letters of business***: a royal letter authorizing Convocation to transact business.

[**1839** Cardwell *Doc. Ann. Ch. Eng.* II. 359 No business can be undertaken in convocation, unless it has been specially proposed to them by royal license. **1842** Lathbury *Hist. Convocation* 350 Parliament was summoned in February, 1713: and the convocation met on the 16th... On the 17th, the convocation was authorized, by a royal letter, to proceed to business.] **1873** Phillimore *Eccles. Law* 1934 In 1713, convocation had royal letters of business, and considered various subjects,—penance, excommunication, forms for the visitation of prisoners. **1906** *Convocations Cant. & York* in *Parl. Papers* LXXXIV. 805 You may see your way to advise His Majesty the King to direct that Letters of Business be issued.

16. a. A matter that concerns or relates to a particular person or thing; const. *of*, or genitive case.

1525 Ld. Berners *Froiss.* II. xxi. 43 It is longe now sith I made any mencion of the busynesses of farre countreis. **1526** Tindale *Phil.* 12, That my busynes [τὰ κατ' ἐμὲ] is happened unto the gretter furtherynge off the gospell. **1875** Jowett *Plato* (ed. 2) V. 32 Virtue is the business of the legislator.

b. Concern, the fact of being concerned *with.*

1759 Johnson *Rasselas* xxix. (1787) 85 My business is with man. **1837** Carlyle *Fr. Rev.* (1871) II. I. i. 4 Madame, your business is with the children.

c. *colloq.* A matter with which one has the right to meddle. Also, justifying motive or right of action or interference, 'anything to do' (*with*). Almost always with negative expressed or implied. Const. usually *with*, or infinitive.

c **1690** R. L'Estrange (J.), What business has a tortoise among the clouds? **1761** Sheridan *Mem. Miss Sidney Bidulph* II. 308 She has no business to go into her own lonely house again; it would be enough to kill her. **1849** Ruskin *Sev. Lamps* iv. §13. 105 Such kind of architecture has no business with rich ornament. *a* **1859** Kingsley *Misc.* II. 311 That is no business of ours. **1878** H. Smart *Play or Pay* ix. (ed. 3) 177 A Captain of Dragoons has no business with a wife; but then we're always doing what we've no business to do.

d. ***to mind one's own business***: to attend to one's own affairs, to refrain from meddling with what does not concern one. Now *colloq.*

1625 Bacon, *Envy, Ess.* (Arb.) 512 Neither can he, that mindeth but his own Businesse, finde much matter for Envy. **1711** Addison *Spect.* No. 16 ⁋7, I..have nothing to do but to mind my own Business. **1749** Fielding *Tom Jones* (1836) I. I. ii. 27, I must desire all those critics to mind their own business. **1882** Besant *All Sorts* 40 'Mind your own business,' growled his uncle.

e. ***to go about one's business***: to go and attend to one's own affairs, to go away; in *imperative* used as a formula of impatient dismissal. So ***to send about one's business***: to dismiss unceremoniously, to 'send packing'.

1687 *Magd. Coll. & Jas. II* (Oxf. Hist. Soc.) 210 He was a pert..man..and..might go about his business. **1702** *Lond. Gaz.* No. 3801/6 They advised him to go about his business. **1712** Arbuthnot *John Bull* 70 Shall I leave all this matter to thy management..and go about my business? **1749** Fielding *Tom Jones* xvi. v. (1840) 236/2 Go about your business, I hate the sight of you. **1768** Blackstone *Comm.* III. 423 The basha..sends them about their business. **1878** Jevons *Prim. Pol. Econ.* 62 He would..be told to go about his business.

f. ***like nobody's business***, beyond the normal range (of a person's capacity); in no ordinary way; 'like anything'. Hence also ***nobody's business***, an extraordinary affair. *colloq.*

1931 E. Linklater *Juan in America* 242 'How I love you is just nobody's business,' she said. **1938** Wodehouse *Code of Woosters* vii. 163 The fount of memory spouting like nobody's business. **1941** 'N. Blake' *Abominable Snowman* xii. 132 Plays the piano like nobody's business. **1957** H. Croome *Forgotten Place* vii. 92 My head this morning is nobody's business.

†**17.** A subject or topic of consideration or discussion; the subject of a book, etc. *Obs.* (common in 17th c.)

1622 Sparrow *Bk. Com. Prayer* (1661) 128 This Sunday ..the Epistle and Gospel treat about the same businesse, the birth of Christ. **1640–4** in Rushw. *Hist. Coll.* III. (1692) I. 42 When a Business was begun and in debate. **1652** *Proc. Parliament* No. 133. 2073 Resolved..That..the House doe only take into consideration publique businesses, and no private businesses. **1660** Stanley *Hist. Philos.* (1701) 379/1 The Pythagoreans..were studiously addicted to the business of Numbers. **1699** Bentley *Phal.* 480 The very Matter and Business of the Letters sufficiently discovers them to be an Imposture.

18. a. *vaguely*, An affair, concern, matter. (Now usually indicating some degree of contempt or impatience, *esp.* when preceded by a sb. in attrib. relation.) Frequent in colloquial phrases like 'a bad business', 'a queer business'.

1605 Shaks. *Macb.* II. i. 24 We would spend [an houre] in some words vpon that Businesse. **1658–9** Knightley in Burton *Diary* (1828) IV. 75 Their officer expostulated the business with me. **1675** Traherne *Chr. Ethics* xxvii. 433 It is a poor business for a man to be secure that has nothing to lose. **1706** *Lond. Gaz.* No. 4012/1 A Business has lately happened which may..engage us in new Disputes. **1805** *Med. Jrnl.* XIV. 354 The vaccinator should..see his patient at least four times during the progress of the business. **1813** Southey *Nelson* II. 177 This boat business..might be part of a great plan of invasion. **1863** Geo. Eliot *Romola* I. iii.

(1880) I. 40. **1868** H. KINGSLEY *Silcote of S.* III. v. 73, I am getting so sick of the whole business.

†**b.** Affectedly used for an 'affair of honour', a duel. *Obs.*

a **1637** B. JONSON *Masque of Merc.* Wks. V. 431 (N.) For that's the word of tincture, the business. Let me alone with the business. I will carry the business. I do understand the business. I do find an affront in the business.

c. *colloq.* Used with intentional indefiniteness of material objects. (Cf. *affair*, *concern*.)

1654 EVELYN *Diary* (Chandos) 228 Sir Thos. Fowler's aviarie..is a poor businesse. **1697** tr. *C'tess D' Aunoy's Trav.* (1706) 231 Some Pastry business, which burns the Mouth, it is so excessively peppered. **1847** L. HUNT *Men, Wom. & Bks.* I. i. 10 A business of screws and iron wheels.

19. a. Dealings, intercourse (*with*). *arch.*

1611 BIBLE *Judges* xviii. 7 They..had no businesse with any man. **1843** CARLYLE *Past & Pr.* IV. vi. (1872) 245 What a shallow delusion is this..That any man..can keep himself apart from men, have 'no business' with them, except a cash-account 'business'.

†**b.** Euphemism for 'sexual intercourse'. *Obs.*

1630 TAYLOR (N.), Lais of Corinth, ask'd Demosthenes One hundred crownes for one nights businesse. **1654** *Wits Recreations* (N.), He does no business of thy wives, not he, He does thy business (Coracine) for thee.

20. *Theat.* Action as distinguished from dialogue. (Formerly used more widely.) Also in phr. ***business of the stage***.

1671 VILLIERS (Dk. Buckhm.) *Rehearsal* III. ii. (Arb.) 83, 'I see here is a great deal of Plot, Mr. Bayes.' *Bayes.* 'Yes, now it begins to break; but we shall have a world of more business anon.' **1763** GARRICK *Let.* 10 Aug. (1831) I. 163 If you mean by the *warmth of temper* you have accused me of to Mr. Johnson, a certain anxiety for the business of the stage, your accusation was well founded. **1779** SHERIDAN *Critic* II. ii, The carpenters say, that unless there is some business put in here..they shan't have time to clear away the fort. **1833** LAMB *Elia* (1860) 264 He carried the same rigid exclusiveness of attention to the stage business. **1849** *Theatrical Programme* 4 June 13/1 Mr. Hurlstone is not sufficiently alive to the business of the stage to make a figure among professionals. **1860** *Cornh. Mag.* II. 749 They give the literary composition the almost contemptuous title of 'words', while they dignify the movements of the actors with the name of 'business'. **1893** I. ZANGWILL *Children of Ghetto* (ed. 3) xiii. 123 An actor who knows all the 'business' elaborated by his predecessors. **1923** WODEHOUSE *Adv. Sally* vi. 78 'Bit o' business,' she announced, at length. 'What do you mean, a bit of business?' 'Character stuff,' explained Miss Winch... 'Thought it out myself. Maids chew gum, you know.' **1949** [see BUS *sb.*[3]].

21. a. *spec.* (from 13 and 19): Trade, commercial transactions or engagements.

1727 DE FOE *Eng. Tradesm.* iv. (1841) I. 30 The merchants' exchange, where they manage, negotiate, and frequently indeed beget business with one another. *Ibid.* If they do not get money, they gain knowledge in business. **1823** LAMB *Elia* (1860) 3 To open a book of business, or bill of lading. **1862** BURTON *Bk-hunter* I. 84 [People] who wanted to do a stroke of business with some old volume. **1884** *Times* (weekly ed.) 12 Sept. 7/3 They are evidently doing a very brisk business.

fig. **1847** DE QUINCEY *Secret Soc.* Wks. VI. 256 It has done business as a swindle through thirty generations. *Ibid.* 258 The goddess and her establishment of hoaxers at Eleusis did a vast 'stroke of business' for more than six centuries.

b. ***place of business***: usually in *spec.* sense, a shop, office, warehouse, commercial establishment; so also ***house of business***. ***hours of business***, ***business hours***: the hours in the day during which commercial or other business is transacted.

c. The audience or attendance at a theatre; a 'house'. Also, the total of box-office receipts.

1755 MRS. C. CHARKE *Life* 130 Business continuing very shocking. **1811** C. MATHEWS *Let.* 5 Dec. in Mrs. Mathews *Mem. C.M.* (1838) II. viii. 173 They may promise a salary, and I am sure they would pay it; but can they promise business? **1837** in W. R. Alger *Life E. Forrest* (1877) I. 324 Will conclude with her benefit on Friday evening when she will probably have between $900 and $1,000... This is considered a very handsome business. **1895** *N.Y. Dramatic News* 12 Oct. 5/2 Hanlon brothers' Superba has played to 'banner' business.

d. *Bridge.* Calling for the purpose of gaining a penalty. Freq. *attrib.*

1925 A. E. M. FOSTER *Auction Bridge* 46 The two players with the better cards are going to get the contract, or they are going to force the others into a bid when a real 'business' double for penalties can be made... A double of four or more is always a 'business' double. *Ibid.* 51 The Business Redouble is seldom sound business. **1927** *Observer* 6 Mar. 25 This Business Pass is one of the most formidable weapons. It converts the Informatory Double into a Business Double. **1959** *Listener* 23 July 154/3 It is standard practice to regard a double as primarily for business.

22. ***man of business***. †**a.** One engaged in public affairs (*obs.*). **b.** One engaged in mercantile transactions. **c.** A man of business-like habits, one skilled in business. **d.** The professional agent who transacts a person's legal business, an attorney.

1670 BURNET *Let. to Brisbane*, I am..resolved never to have anything to do more with men of business, particularly with any in opposition to the Court. **1712** STEELE *Spect.* No. 466 ¶3, I am a Man of Business, and obliged to be much abroad. **1727** DE FOE *Eng. Tradesm.* iv. (1841) I. 30 Men of business are companions for men of business. **1752** HUME *Ess. & Treat.* (1777) I. 113 *note*, Pericles, a man of business, & a man of sense. **1787** 'GAMBADO' (H. Bunbury) *Acad. Horsem.* (1809) 30 By a man of business is not meant a Lord of the Treasury, or a Commissioner of Accounts, but what is called on the road, a rider, a bag-man, or bagster. **1857** BUCKLE *Civiliz.* I. xi. 629 If we were all men of business our mental pleasures would be abridged. **1861** RAMSAY *Remin.* vi. (ed. 18) 232 In Scotland it is usual to term the law-agent or man of business of any party his 'doer'.

23. A commercial enterprise regarded as a 'going concern'; a commercial establishment with all its 'trade', liabilities, etc.

a **1888** *Mod.* (*Heading of Advt. column*) Businesses, etc., to be disposed of.

24. *attrib.* and in *Comb.*, as ***business agent***, ***centre***, ***college***, ***committee***, ***efficiency***, ***girl***, ***habits***, ***hours***, ***house***, ***letter***, ***life***, ***proposition***, ***school***, ***suit***, ***transaction***, ***woman***, etc.; also, **business card**, a card of a tradesman, manufacturer, commercial traveller, etc., with his address and various particulars as to the nature of his business, used for advertising purposes; **business doctor** (see quot. 1909); **business edge**, cf. *business end*; **business end** (used humorously, see quot.); *colloq.*, the operative part; **business-looking** *a.*, having an appearance suggestive of business; **business lunch(eon)**, a luncheon at which commercial transactions are discussed; **business man** = *man of business*; see 22 b, c; **business manager**, a manager of the business or commercial side of an enterprise; hence ***business-manage*** vb. trans.; **business part**, the sphere of business (also *concr.* = *business end*).

1849 C. LANMAN *Alleghany Mts.* xi. 85 The 'guide, counsellor, and friend' of the Indians, as well as their *business agent. **1901** MERWIN & WEBSTER *Calumet 'K'* i. 15 All that remained was to wait until the business agent made the next move. **1840** *Boston* (Mass.) *Almanac* 119 *Business cards printed in the most expeditious manner. **1865** DICKENS *Mut. Fr.* I. 317 (Hoppe) Bland strangers with business-cards meeting the servants in the streets. **1959** T. S. ELIOT *Elder Statesman* III. 102 Here's my business card With the full address. **1851** C. CIST *Cincinnati* 278 *Business centre. **1888** J. KIRKLAND *McVeys* 4 In the 'business centre' one might see an occasional tall, narrow, straight-sided brick structure. **1865** *Indianapolis Daily Jrnl.* 14 Sept. 2/4 Students in Bryant's *Business College. **1903** A. D. MCFAUL *Ike Glidden* xvi. 124 He had just graduated from a business college, and claimed to know how to do business 'in a business like manner'. **1838** W. L. GARRISON in Garrison & Jackson *Life* (1885) II. 227 A *business committee was then appointed. **1901** *Daily Express* 6 Aug. 6/2 A very novel profession has been lately started in the City. It may be called that of the *business doctor. **1909** *Modern Business* Jan. 606/1 In America..there exists a body of men who are known as 'Business Doctors', men who are called in to give advice upon the proper conduct of business. **1935** *Antiquity* IX. 211 The *business edge of the chisel-ended arrow. **1926** A. HUXLEY *Jesting Pilate* IV. 316 Reduced to an Indian diet, Americans would be a good deal less interested than they actually are in *business efficiency, uplift and the Charleston. **1953** D. PARRY *Going Up* iv. 154, I was supposed to be a business-efficiency expert, one of those menaces who crawl round doing time-and-motion studies. **1878** HOLBROOK *Hyg. Brain* 56 The *business end of a carpet-tack. **1936** 'R. CROMPTON' *Sweet William* ix. 227 The business end of a geometrical compass was jabbed into Douglas's arm. **1955** *Sci. Amer.* Sept. 197/1 The business end of the coronagraph is the quartz polarizing monochromator. **1962** *Sunday Express* 25 Feb. 16/2 The business end of a rifle barrel. **1888** C. M. YONGE *Beechcroft at Rockstone* I. ix. 167, I..mixed her up with the ordinary class of *business girls. **1958** BETJEMAN *Coll. Poems* 215 (*title*) Business girls. **1839** DICKENS *Nickleby* xl. 390 You will be surprised..to witness this, in *business hours. **1881** *Daily Tel.* 31 Jan., What are they to do after business hours? **1766** J. ROSE *Let.* 8 Apr. in A. & H. Tayler *Lord Fife* (1925) ii. 31, I will have *business letters also to write. **1914** W. OWEN *Let.* 6 Mar. (1967) 237, I make money for this by doing a few translations..of business letters. **1941** T. S. ELIOT *Dry Salvages* iii. 12 The passengers are settled To fruit, periodicals and business letters. **1868** W. COLLINS *Moonstone* II. v. 148 Female Boards..drew the breath of their *business-life through the nostrils of Mr. Godfrey. **1951** M. MCLUHAN *Mech. Bride* 137/2 People..could maintain an intimate link with ordinary social and business life. **1839** DICKENS *Nich. Nick.* ii, A business-looking table, and several *business-looking people. **1926** S. LEWIS *Mantrap* xxv. 289, I don't really know a soul..except for meeting them at *business lunches. **1954** L. MACNEICE *Autumn Sequel* XII. 76 The foregone Conclusion of a business lunch. **1963** P. MOYES *Murder à la Mode* v. 83 He knew enough of the protocol of business luncheons..not to be surprised..that Goring studiously avoided all reference to the matter in hand until the coffee arrived. **1826** H. C. ROBINSON *Diary* 9 June (1967) 91 Watts is a *business man and is editor and publisher on his own account. **1832** *Congress. Globe* 30 Jan. 1511 Having been in the practice of the law..and somewhat conversant with business men. **1843** DICKENS *Chr. Carol* iv. 124 One little group of business men. **1860** O. W. HOLMES *Prof. Breakf.-t.* i. 16 People of cultivation, of pure character, shrewd business-men, men of science [etc.]. **1878** *N. Amer. Rev.* CXXVII. 109 The mass of business men. **1901** R. LORAINE in W. Loraine *R.L.* (1938) I. iv. 79 Mr. Frohman would finance the enterprise and *business manage it entirely. **1852** *Chambers's Edin. Jrnl.* XVII. 306/2 Clerks, book-keepers, foremen, *business-managers. **1906** B. STOKER *Pers. Remin. H. Irving* II. lxxiii. §3. 319, I was Sir Henry Irving's business manager. **1838** J. S. MILL in *Westm. Rev.* Apr.–Aug. XXIX. 490 He [*sc.* Bentham] committed the mistake of supposing that the *business part of human affairs was the whole of them. **1910** T. E. LAWRENCE *Let.* 29 Aug. (1938) 86 The business part of the log with which you are going to block your staircase. **1901** S. E. WHITE *Claim Jumpers* v. 70, I have a plain *business proposition to make. You and I are going to be great friends. **1909** 'O. HENRY' *Options* (1916) 11 He had been used to having his business propositions heard of. **1916** *Nat. Educ. Assoc. U.S. Addresses & Proc. 1915* 325 (*heading*) The service of *business schools at the close of the Great War. **1966** 'N. BLAKE' *Morning after Death* i. 19 'What do you actually do in the Business School?' 'There are courses in economics, management, salesmanship, commercial history, theory of exchange, the ethical aspect of business—all that kind of thing.' **1840** CARLYLE *Heroes* I. 36 Snorro..almost in a brief *business style, writes down, etc. **1870** *Harper's Bazaar* 5 Nov. 707 *Business suits. **1882** *Advt.* in *W. Burnot's Mother Goose* (Elephant & Castle Theatre) 30 Business Suits—21s. **1932** E. WILSON *Devil take Hindmost* iv. 30 A prosaic, gray business suit. **1871** MARKBY *Elem. Law* (1874) §472 Nearly all *business transactions have reference..to the ownership of property. **1862** BURTON *Bk-hunter* I. 38 Persons who might take a purely *business view of such transactions. **1850** CLOUGH *Dipsychus* II. i. 49 Men's *business-wits the only sane things. **1844** *Southern Lit. Messenger* X. 486 Reputation of being a '*business woman'. **1958** BETJEMAN *Coll. Poems* 215 A thousand business women Having baths in Camden Town.

ˈbusinessless, *a. nonce-wd.* Without business.

1881 *Argosy* XXXI. 375 His 'Hegira' from the businessless chambers to which he objected.

ˈbusiness-like, *a.* Of persons and things: Suitable for business, befitting business; apt for business, practical, methodical, systematic. Hence **ˈbusiness,like-ness**.

1791 BURKE *Corr.* (1844) III. 349 They are steady, sensible, and have business-like heads. **1804** G. ROSE *Diaries* (1860) II. 157 His Lordship..had hardly ever anything businesslike to say. **1875** STUBBS *Const. Hist.* I. ii. 18 Inveterate and business-like gamblers. **1886** *Pall Mall Budg.* 8 July 28/2 The essence of businesslikeness.

busk (bʌsk), *sb.*[1] Also 6–7 **buske**. [a. F. *busc*, of uncertain origin. Scheler regards it as a doublet of F. *bois* wood:—late L. *boscum* (see BUSH *sb.*[1]); cf. the related F. *bûche*, OF. *busche* fem., splinter of wood. In Fr. as in Eng. the word was formerly sometimes used for the whole corset, and Littré considers it cognate with It. *busto* (see BUST); but this is unsatisfactory with regard to both sense and form.]

A strip of wood, whalebone, steel, or other rigid material passed down the front of a corset, and used to stiffen and support it. Formerly and still *dial.* applied also to the whole corset.

1592 WARNER *Alb. Eng.* VII. xxxvi. 175 Her face was Maskt..her bodie pent with buske. **1611** COTGR., *Buc*, a buske, plated bodie, or other quilted thing, worne to make, or keepe, the bodie straight. **1688** R. HOLME *Armoury* III. 94/2 A Busk..is a strong peece of Wood, or Whalebone thrust down the middle of the Stomacker **1755** MRS. C. CLARKE *Autobiog.* (1827) 64 The want of which latter instrument of death [a dagger] I once saw supplied with a lady's busk; who had just presence of mind sufficient to draw it from her stays. **1786** *Misc. Ess.* in *Ann. Reg.* 125/2 Whale bone and busks, which martyr European girls, they know not. **1824** *Craven Dial.* 15, I lost my hollin busk, finely flower'd. **1862** MAYHEW *Crim. Prisons* 40 Bundles of wooden busks, and little bits of whalebone.

Hence †**busk-point**. 'The lace, with its tag, which secured the end of the busk' (Nares). *Obs.*

1599 MARSTON *Sc. Villanie* II. viii. 213, I saw him court his Mistresse looking-glasse, Worship a busk-point. **1612** CHAPMAN *Widdowes T.* Plays 1873 III. 43 Certaine morall disguises of coinesse..ye borrow of art to couer your buske points. *a* **1667** WITHER *Passion of Love*, He..doth crave her To grant him but a busk-point for a favour.

†**busk**, *sb.*[2] *Obs.* Some kind of linen fabric.

1458 in Rogers *Agric. & Prices* III. 478/2 Busk for table linen 24½ ells @ /4. **1480** *Acc. Edw. IV* in *Privy P. Exp. Eliz. of York* 124 For washing of divers old peces of busk and of a paillet vjd.

†**busk**, *sb.*[3] *Obs. Sc.* [f. BUSK *v.*[1]; cf. BUSKRY.] Attire, dress, decoration.

1723 M'WARD *Contendings* 356 (JAM.) Cloathed and adorned with the busk and bravery of beautiful and big words.

busk, *v.*[1] *Obs.* exc. *Sc.* and *north. dial.* Also 4–5 bosk, 4–7 buske, (4 busky). See also BUSS *v.*[2] [Generally thought to be a. ON. *búa-sk*, refl. of *búa* to prepare (see BOUN *ppl. a.*), the refl. pron. having been agglutinated to the stem, as in *bask*.

(The *trans.*, *intr.* and *refl.* constructions are all found in the earliest northern specimens of ME., so that no evidence is available for their development: the order here followed is purely provisional. But for the presumed derivation, it would be more in accordance with the history of other verbs, to start with the *trans.*, including the *refl.*, and take the *intr.* as the usual elliptical construction of the latter.)]

I. *intr.* **1.** To prepare oneself, get ready.

a **1300** *Cursor M.* 11585 (Cott.) Rise vp, iosep, and busk [*Gött.* busk þe] and ga. *c* **1340** *Gaw. & Gr. Knt.* 509 Bryddez busken to bylde. **1375** BARBOUR *Bruce* VIII. 409 The king buskit and maid him ȝar. *c* **1400** *Destr. Troy* 2568, I bid þat ye buske, and no bode make. *c* **1440** *York Myst.* xxx. 87 Nowe wiffe, þan ye bythely be buskand.

b. *spec.* To attire or deck oneself; to dress.

1795 MACNEILL *Will & J.* Poems (1844) 72 Jean..loo'd to busk aye In her hame-spun thrifty work. **1875** in *Lanc. Gloss.* (E.D.S.) 62 Come busk up, an' let's be off.

c. *transf.* To essay, attempt.

c **1340** *Alex. & Dind.* 135 Whan þer buskede a burn a bow for to touche.

2. To set out, go (chiefly with notion of speed); to hie, hurry, haste.

a **1300** *Cursor M.* 4309 Quen þou seis him busk to þe, þou do þe stallworthli to flei. *c* **1350** *Leg. Cathol., Pope Greg.* 12 Thai bosked to the biriing. *a* **1375** *Joseph Arim.* 202 þe kyng ..to his bed buskes. **1375** BARBOUR *Bruce* x. 404 Ane of the vachis..buskit thiddirward but baid. *c* **1440** *Gaw. & Gol.* i.

24 (JAM.) He maid his offering; Syne buskit hame the samyne way. **1583** STANYHURST *Æneid* IV. (Arb.) 102 Flee my sun, and busk on. **1876** ROBINSON *Mid. Yorksh. Gloss.* (E.D.S.) 'Now, come busk' be off!

3. *to busk up*: to get up, rise.

c **1340** *Gaw. & Gr. Knt.* 1128 Þay busken vp bilyue, blonkkez to sadel. *c* **1360** *Know Thyself* in *E.E.P.* (1862) 133 Þe morwe he buskeþ vp to rise.

II. *trans.*

4. To prepare, make, or get ready; to set in order, fit out. Still in *Sc.* (Sometimes with *up.*)

a **1300** *Cursor M.* 11710 Apon þe morn þai were busked to þair wai. *c* **1325** *E.E. Allit. P.* C. 437 Þer he busked hym a bour. *c* **1450** *Erle of Tolous* 232 [We] were buskyd yare, On owre jurney for to fare. **1460** *Lybeaus Disc.* 822 Buske her and make her boun. **1663** SPALDING *Troub. Chas. I* (1792) I. 108 (JAM.) The covenanters..busked the yard dykes very commodiously. **1828** SCOTT *F.M. Perth* v, It were hard to deny thee time to busk thy body-clothes. **1839** *Blackw. Mag.* XLV. 179 Heaven help us..if the good lady's specs are not 'busked' and ready in the case!

5. To dress, attire, accoutre, adorn, dress *up*; = 'to dress' in its widest sense. Still in *Sc.*

c **1325** *E.E. Allit. P.* B. 142 Þou burne for no brydale art busked in wedez! *a* **1440** *Sire Degrev.* 1427 Hyt was buskyd above With besauntus ful bry3th. **1535** STEWART *Cron. Scot.* II. 390 King Bredus buskit in armour brycht. **1663** SPALDING *Troub. Chas. I* (1829) 7 The lady Frendraught.. busked in a white plaid..came weeping and mourning to the Bog. **1787** BURNS *Burlesq. Lament* ii, But now they'll busk her like a fright. **1800–24** CAMPBELL *Cora Linn* iii, Hedges, busk'd in bravery, Look'd rich that sunny morn.

b. *spec.* To dress a fishing-hook.

1814 SCOTT *Wav.* I. ix. 123 He has done nothing..unless trimming the laird's fishing-wand or busking his flies. **1819** *Blackw. Mag.* V. 124 His daughter..we have sometimes seen 'busking hooks'. **1823** SCOTT *Quentin D.* xii, I..use not to gulp the angler's hook because it is busked up with a feather called honour.

c. *fig.*

1656 TRAPP *Comm. Rev.* xvii. 3 His head only before was busked with the blasphemy..now his whole body. **1827** POLLOK *Course of Time* VI, The frothy orator, who busked his tales In quackish pomp of noisy words.

6. To dispatch, hurry, hasten.

1413 LYDG. *Pylgr. Sowle* I. xxii. (1859) 25 Deth spareth no persone..but buskyth you vnto pyttes brynke. **1877** PEACOCK *N.W. Linc. Gloss.* (E.D.S.) *Busk*, to hasten, to hurry forward. 'Noo busk thee sen off, an' doant stan gawmin' there for a week.' 'I liv'd sarvant wi' her for a bit, but she buskt me aboot while I couldn't bide it.'

III. *refl.*

7. To prepare or equip (oneself), get ready; now *esp. Sc.* to dress, clothe, or deck (oneself).

a **1300** *Cursor M.* 10556 Anna busked hir and yede. *c* **1325** *Pol. Songs* 239 Hue bosketh huem with botouns, Ase hit were a brude. *c* **1440** *Bone Flor.* 276 My lord will buske hym to ryde. **1515** *Scott. Field* 83 in *Chetham Misc.* (1856) II, He bid buske and bowne him, to go on his message. **1600** FAIRFAX *Tasso* VII. xxxvii. 124 The noble Baron..buskt him boldly to the dreadfull fight. **1863** BARING-GOULD *Iceland* 125 Grettir busked himself for a cold ride.

8. To betake oneself; to hie one.

c **1350** *Will. Palerne* 2477 Þei busked hem homward. **1377** LANGL. *P. Pl.* B. IX. 133 Buske 3ow to þat bote and bideth 3e þer-inne. **1558** PHAËR *Æneid* IV. Kj *marg. note*, Mercury busketh him forward. **1571** CAMPION *Hist. Irel.* ix. (1633) 27 Gathelus and his wife..were faine to buske them, with all their traine into Europe. **1877** [see 6].

busk, *v.*² *Naut.* [app. a. obs. F. *busquer* 'to shift, filch; prowle, catch by hook or crook; *busquer fortune* to go seek his fortune' (Cotgr.), ad. It. *buscare* 'to filch, to prowl, to shift for' (Florio), or Sp. *buscar*, OSp. *boscar* to seek; perh. orig. 'to hunt', or 'to beat a wood', f. *bosco* wood.]

1. a. *intr.* Of a ship: To beat or cruise about; to beat to windward, tack: with adv. *about, to and again*. Also *to busk it out*: to weather a storm by tacking about.

1665 *Lond. Gaz.* No. 9/2 A Ship from Longsound, who hath been busking too and again this Fortnight. **1678** WYCHERLEY *Pl.-Dealer* III. i. 33 Go, busk about, and run thyself into the next great Man's Lobby. **1713** C. JOHNSON *Successf. Pirate* I. i (D.) The ship was found busking on the seas without a mast or rudder. *a* **1734** NORTH *Lives* II. 316 Sometimes a-try and sometimes a-hull we busked it out.

b. 'To cruise as a pirate'. [Perh. the original sense: cf. It. *buscare*, F. *busquer* (above).]

1867 SMYTH *Sailor's Word-bk.*, *Busking*, piratical cruising.

c. trans. *to busk the seas*: ? = to scour the seas.

1747 J. LIND *Lett. Navy* i. (1757) 29 Three deck'd ships are too large and unweildy to busk the seas, as they call it.

2. *fig.* To go about seeking *for*, to seek *after*.

a **1734** NORTH *Exam.* I. iii. ¶123. 203 The Parties would be less industrious to busk about for any other [defence]. —— *Lives* II. 122 My Lord Rochester..was inclined..to busk for some other way to raise the supply. *Ibid.* III. 54 Running up and down and through the city..perpetually busking after one thing or other.

3. a. *slang.* See quots. (But perhaps this is a distinct word.) Hence **'busking** *vbl. sb.* and *ppl. a.* Now usu., to play music or entertain in the streets, etc.

1851 MAYHEW *Lond. Labour* I. 215 Obtain a livelihood by 'busking', as it is technically termed, or, in other words, by offering their goods for sale only at the bars and in the taprooms and parlours of taverns. *Ibid.* (ed. 2) III. 216 Busking is going into public houses and playing and singing and dancing. *Ibid.* 222 Busking, that is going into public houses and cutting likenesses of the company. **1860** *Cornh. Mag.* II. 334 Thieves' words and phrases..selling obscene songs—busking. **1874** *Sunday Mag.* Xmas No. 1 Chair-caners, 'busking vocalists', musicians and acrobats. **1897** *Daily News* 21 Sept. 8/3 A highly-accomplished lady..begs for a dress in which to go busking. Busking is the jargon for wandering minstrels—folk who play the perambulating pianos we see in the streets or on the sands—folk who sing from morning till midnight. **1905** *Evening News* 12 Aug. 5/3 We are all 'busking' this year. It would surprise the public if they knew who constituted many of the troupes of pierrots and mysterious minstrels that are performing at the various holiday resorts. **1934** P. ALLINGHAM *Cheapjack* 318 *Busk*, to perform in the street.

b. *trans.* and *intr.* To improvise (jazz or similar music). *Musicians' slang.*

1934 S. R. NELSON *All about Jazz* ii. 51 The drummer can still busk his part, and except for roughly glancing at the score, that is what the best drummers do today. **1966** *Crescendo* Feb. 35/1 Many drummers are with small groups or busking outfits and therefore never see a drum part.

busk, *v.*³ [Origin unknown; if not identical with prec.] *intr.* Of fowls: To move or shift about restlessly or uneasily.

1567 TURBERV. *Passions* in Chalmers *Epitaphs, &c.*, Birds will alway buske and bate and scape the fowlers trap. **1575** —— *Bk. Falconrie* 4 This sorte of hawkes do never use to plume or tyre uppon the foul whom they have seazed untill such time as they percieve it to leave busking and bating. **1835** MARRYAT *Olla Podr.* v, A hole..as large as if a covey of partridges had been busking in it.

†**busk**, *v.*⁴ ? *Obs. rare*⁻¹. [? f. *busk*, var. of *bush*: cf. BUSH *v.*¹ But possibly, an application of BUSK *v.*²] *intr.*

1653 W. LAUSON in Arb. *Eng. Garner* I. 104 This fly.. among wood or close by a bush, moved in the crust of the water is deadly in an evening..This is called 'Busking for Trout'.

busk(e, obs. form of BUSH.

buskayle, var. of BUSHAILE, *Obs.*

†**'buskboard.** *Obs.* [? f. BUSK *sb.*¹ (or ? *v.*¹) + BOARD.] A part of the apparatus for hanging the clapper of a bell. See BALDRIC 4.

1857 W. C. LUKIS *Ch. Bells* 24 The great object in suspending a clapper. The ancient mode with bawdrick and buskboard, was clumsy and expensive.

busked (bʌskt), *ppl. a.*¹ In mod.Sc. buskit. [f. BUSK *v.*¹ + -ED.] Dressed, attired; decked.

1787 BURNS *Burlesq. Lament* i. Nae joy her bonie buskit nest Can yield ava.

busked, *ppl. a.*² [f. BUSK *sb.*¹ + -ED².] Provided with or wearing a busk.

1876 MISS BROUGHTON *Joan* iv, Mrs. Moberly's is not that tight, compact, well-busked fat.

buskel(l, busken, obs. ff. BUSKLE, BUSKIN.

busker¹ ('bʌskə(r)). [f. BUSK *v.*¹ + -ER¹.] One that prepares, attires, dresses, etc.

1568 SIR F. KNOLLYS in *Cornh. Mag.* (1867) 48 She praysed Mystres Marye Ceaton for being the fynest busker, that is to say, the fynest dresser of a womans heade or heare, that is to be seen in any countrye. **1819** *Blackw. Mag.* V. 233 His enumeration of the famous fly-buskers of Auld Reekie?

busker² ('bʌskə(r)). [f. BUSK *v.*² + -ER¹.] One who 'busks'; an itinerant entertainer or musician.

1857 *National Mag.* II. 167/1 (*heading*) The Busker..His avocation is strictly peripatetic; and hence he takes his title from the short boot, or 'buskin', which has been a common article of stage-apparel..ever since the earliest days of the drama. **1859** HOTTEN *Dict. Slang*, *Busker*, a man who sings or performs in a public house. *Scotch.* **1908** *Daily Chron.* 1 Sept. 7/4 'Buskers'..can be counted as belonging to the most genuine of the professional vagrant fraternity. **1951** L. MACNEICE tr. *Goethe's Faust* I. 33 Leave me not here a hopeless busker!

†**'busket.** *Obs. rare.* [f. *busk*, var. of BUSH *sb.*¹ + -ET¹, or ad. Fr. *bosquet*: cf. also BUSHET, BOSKET.]

1. (See quot.)

1579 SPENSER *Sheph. Cal.* May 10 To gather May buskets [Gloss. *Buskets*, a diminutive, little bushes of hauthorne].

2. = BOSKET.

1803 W. ROSE *Amadis* 127 Wend thy way Thro' yonder buskets.

buskey, -ie, obs. forms of BUSHY, BUSKY *a.*

buskill, var. of BUSKLE, *v. Obs.*

buskin ('bʌskɪn). Also 6 **buskyn(g, busken**, 6–7 **buskine, busgin.** [A word existing in many European langs.: known in Eng. since 16th c. Cf. Fr. *brousequin* (16th c.), early mod.Du. *brōzeken* (now *broosken*), Sp. *borceguí*, formerly also *boszegui*, Pg. *borzeguim* (Dozy cites as earlier forms *morsequill*, *mosequin*), It. *borzacchino*; the synonymous Fr. *brodequin*, BRODEKIN, q.v., is doubtless related, but the phonetic relations are obscure. The special source of the Eng. is uncertain: the early mention of 'Spanish buskin' might suggest that it was adopted from Spain, a view in some degree supported by the fact that OSp. *boszeguí* (Minsheu) is the only continental form without the *r*. (The Sp. word appears to have originally had a final *n*: cf. *borceguinero* buskin maker.) But it is not impossible that the Eng. word was corrupted from Fr. or Du.

The ultimate etymology is unknown. Diez regarded the Romanic words as a. Du. *brōzeken*, and this as a dim. of *brōze*, supposed by him to be ultimately ad. late L. *byrsa* leather. But the wide diffusion of the word in Romanic and its late appearance in Du. are inconsistent with this hypothesis, which Dutch etymologists decisively reject (see BRODEKIN); and the Romanic forms do not admit of derivation from *byrsa*. The appearance of the Sp. and Pg. words suggests an oriental origin, but the Arabic etymology proposed by Dozy is far-fetched and untenable. The OF. *broissequin, brusquin*, the name of a woollen fabric, is prob. unconnected; Godef. says that the material was so called from its colour: cf. BRUSK.]

1. A covering for the foot and leg reaching to the calf, or to the knee; a half-boot.

1503 *Privy P. Exp. Eliz. York* (1830) 86 Twoo payre of buskins for the Quenes grace at..iiijs. the payre. **1530** PALSGR. 202/1 Buskyng, *brodequin*. *Ibid.* 907 The buskyns, *les brousequins*. *c* **1550** *Wyll of Deuyll* (Collier) 9, I geue to euery Ruffian..a payre of chayned buskens. **1579** *Lanc. Wills* (1860) II. 178 My Spanishe buskins furred. **1596** SPENSER *F.Q.* I. vi. 16 Sometimes Diana he her takes to be; But misseth bow and shaftes, and buskins to her knee. **1671** F. PHILLIPS *Reg. Necess.* 28 They..put on Furre Buskins of white Leather. **1683** CHALKHILL *Thealma & Cl.* 51 White Buskins lac'd with ribbanding they wore. **1781** GIBBON *Decl. & F.* III. lxiii. 583 He assumed the royal privilege of red shoes or buskins. **1860** MISS YONGE *Stokesley Secr.* i. (1880) 186 A..shrewd-looking labourer in..high buskins and old wide-awake.

2. *spec.* The high thick-soled boot (*cothurnus*) worn by the actors in ancient Athenian tragedy; frequently contrasted with the 'sock' (*soccus*), or low shoe worn by comedians.

1570 LEVINS *Manip.* 133 A Buskin, *cothurnus*. **1597** BP. HALL *Sat.* I. i. 19 Trumpet, and reeds, and socks, and buskins fine. **1663** BP. PATRICK *Parab. Pilgr.* xxxiv. (1668) 262 The Play is ended, and the high-heel'd Buskins are pull'd off. **1763** J. BROWN *Poetry & Mus.* vi. 119 The Buskin ..hightened the Stature. **1871** MORLEY *Crit. Misc.* (1886) I. 127 Doff the buskin or the sock, wash away the paint from their cheeks, and gravely sit down to meat.

b. Hence *fig.* and *transf.* The style or spirit of this class of drama; the tragic vein; tragedy. *to put on the buskins*: to assume a tragic style; to write tragedy.

1579 SPENSER *Sheph. Cal.* Oct. 113 How I could reare the Muse on stately stage, And teache her tread aloft in bus-kin fine. [*Gloss.*, the buskin in poetrie is vsed for tragical matter.] **1679** DRYDEN *Tr. & Cr.* Pref. B ij, I doubt to smell a little too strongly of the Buskin. **1711** H. CROMWELL *Let. to Pope* 7 Dec. 1736 V. 114 Mr. Wilks..has express'd a furious ambition to swell in your buskins. **1817** BYRON *Beppo* xxxi, He was a critic upon operas, too, And knew all niceties of the sock and buskin. **1860** A. WINDSOR *Ethica* iii. 171 Our English dramatists combine the office of comedy and tragedy writers in one and the same person.. Aristophanes, Plautus, and Terence never put on the buskin.

c. *attrib.* = Tragic.

1602 *Return fr. Parnass.* I. ii. (Arb.) 12 Marlowe was happy in his buskine muse. **1709** STEELE *Tatler* No. 47 ¶5 Gentlemen who write in the Buskin Style. **1747** W. HORSLEY *Fool* (1748) II. 187 The Stile..has something of the Buskin Vaunt.

3. *Attrib.* and *Comb.*, as *buskin-maker*; **buskin-wise** *adv.*, after the manner of a buskin.

1591 PERCIVALL *Sp. Dict.*, *Borzoguineria* a buskin makers shop, *Cothurnaria sutrina*. **1637** BRIAN *Pisse-Proph.* (1679) 47 This messenger..is a very plain fellow in his Holy-day Jacket, and his busking Hose. **1725** BRADLEY *Fam. Dict.* II. s.v. *Knee*, Wrap the Knees in Oil Cloth, Buskinwise.

'buskin, *v. nonce-wd.* [f. prec. sb.] *trans.* To cover as with a buskin.

1795 *Monthly Rev.* XVIII. 542 Her population..had zoned every hill with vines..and buskined its foot with the various species of corn.

†**buski'nade.** *nonce-wd.* [f. BUSKIN *sb.* + -ADE, on analogy of *bastinade* (*-ado*), *blockade*, etc.] A blow with a buskin.

1653 URQUHART *Rabelais* II. xv, How wouldest thou defend thyself? With great buskinades or brodkin blows, answered he.

buskined ('bʌskɪnd), *ppl. a.* [f. BUSKIN *sb.* + -ED².]

1. Shod or covered with buskins.

1590 SHAKS. *Mids. N.* II. i. 71 The bouncing Amazon Your buskin'd Mistresse. **1704** POPE *Windsor For.* 168 Her buskin'd Virgins. **1877** MRS. OLIPHANT *Makers Flor.* iv. 104 A brown peasant boy of ten, with buskined legs.

2. *spec.* Wearing the buskins of tragedy; *fig.* and *transf.*, concerned with or belonging to tragedy.

1626 MASSINGER *Rom. Actor* I. i, The Greeks, to whom we owe the first invention Both of the buskined scene & humble sock. **1742** YOUNG *Nt. Th.* VI. 349 See the buskin'd chief Unshod..Reduc'd to his own Stature. **1820** HAZLITT *Lect. Dram. Lit.* 135 They would be ranted on the stage by some buskined hero or tragedy queen.

b. Tragic; dignified, elevated, lofty.

1595 MARKHAM *Sir R. Grinuile* lxxi, Rich buskin'd Seneca. **1632** BROME *Court Begg.* III. i. Wks. 1873 I. 220 Petra[r]k's buskin'd stile. *a* **1771** GRAY *Poems* (1775) 35 In buskin'd measures move Pale Grief, and pleasing Pain. **1838–9** HALLAM *Hist. Lit.* III. III. vi. §98 The interest serious, but not always of buskined dignity. **1841** DE QUINCEY *Homer & H.* Wks. VI. 393 To speak in a sort of stilted, or at least buskined language.

† **'busking**, *vbl. sb.*[1] *Sc. Obs.* [f. BUSK *v.*[1] + -ING[1].]

1. Fitting out, attiring; *concr.* attire.

c **1320** *Sir Tristr.* 92 Bliþe was his bosking. **1619** Z. BOYD *Last Battell* 961 (JAM.) Too curious busking is the mother of lusting lookes. **1632** RUTHERFORD *Lett.* xxiii. (1862) I. 90 The wooer's busking and bravery..are in vain. **1638** *Relat. Accidents* in *Harl. Misc.* (Malh.) IV. 289 Some [had]..their outward buskings not one thread singed.

fig. **1637** RUTHERFORD *Letters* 70 Godliness is more than the outside and this world's passments and their buskings.

†**b.** *spec.* The dressing of the head; head-dress.

1571 ASCHAM *Scholem.* (Arb.) 54 Either a slouinglie busking, or an ouerstaring frounced hed. **1621** *Sc. Act. Jas. VI*, xxv. §3 That none weare upon their Heads, or Buskings, any Feathers.

†**2.** Setting out, departure. *Obs.*

a **1300** *Cursor M.* 3245 Bun was he made til his buskyng, Wit tresur grette and riche ring.

'busking, *vbl. sb.*[2] [f. BUSK *v.*[2]] 'Piratical cruising; also, used generally, for beating to windward along a coast, or cruising off and on' (Smyth *Sailor's Word-bk.*). Also *fig.* (see quot.).

1841 *Fraser's Mag.* XXIII. 310 This practice..for which they had a technical term of reproach, viz. 'going a-busking'. [The practice was to pawn property not his own, shift his quarters and disappear.]

busking, *vbl. sb.* and *ppl. a.*: see BUSK *v.*[2] 3.

† **'buskle**, *v. Obs.* Also 6 buskel, buskill, 7 buskell. [app. a frequentative of BUSK *v.*[1]; the senses correspond closely to senses of *busk*, and both verbs are in the early examples often accompanied by the ppl. adj. *boun*. See BUSTLE *v.*]

1. *trans.* To 'busk', prepare, equip, attire. (Chiefly *refl.*)

a **1555** BRADFORD *Wks.* 445 Buskel thyself, and make thee bowne to turn to the Lord. **1585** PILKINGTON *Exp. Nehem.* Wks. (1848) 352 They buskle and bowne themselves to this work. **1594** CAREW *Tasso* (1881) 117 Buskled in armes.. them readie make The ten knights.

2. *intr.* To prepare oneself; *hence*, to set out, start on a journey, address oneself *to* a task; to set to work (*esp.* hastily or promptly).

a **1535** MORE *Wks.* (1557) 81 In what place..ye stand whan ye buskle forward. **1583** STANYHURST *Æneid* III. (Arb.) 81 King Helenus..From towne to us buskling. **1594** CAREW *Tasso* (1881) 53 The Campe to armes which buskelled. **1602** WARNER *Alb. Eng.* XII. lxxvii. 313 Then buskling to his Sword cride Theeues.

3. *intr.* To hurry about; to be in agitation or commotion, to bustle.

1545 JOYE *Exp. Dan.* ii. (R.) Now began the bisshopes to busskle and bere rule. **1561** AWDELAY *Frat. Vacab.* 15 This slouthfull knave wyll buskill and scratch when he is called in the morning. **1586** W. WARNER *Alb. Eng.* I. vi. 22 In buskling vp and downe In Plutoes Pallace, to her ioy, Proserpine he found. **1642** ROGERS *Naaman* 174 He buskells and takes on like a mad man.

4. *trans.* To agitate, shake, toss; L. *jactare*. (Cf. BRUSTLE *v.*[2] 2, and BUSTLE *v.* 5.)

1581 STUDLEY *Seneca's Hercules Œt.* 189 He buskling vp his burning Mane, doth dry the dropping south.

† **'buskling**, *vbl. sb. Obs.* [f. prec. vb. + -ING[1].] Eager activity, bustling; scuffling, agitation.

1548 THOMAS *Ital. Gram., Dimenamento*, buskelyng or shakyng. **1563–87** FOXE *A. & M.* (1596) 309/1 The princes seruants..hearing the buskling, came with great hast. **1571** GOLDING *Calvin on Ps.* lv. 2 A shufling or buskling suche as is wont to bee in a great preace of people **1600** HOLLAND *Livy* II. xlix. 78 Suddainly, at the very first buskling [*primam trepidationem*].

† **'buskry.** *Sc. Obs.* [f. BUSK *sb.*[3] + -RY.] Attire.

1723 M'WARD *Contendings* 324 (JAM.) We must not be pleased or put off with the buskry or bravery of words.

busky ('bʌskɪ), *a.* [f. *busk*, var. of BUSH *sb.*[1] + -Y; cf. BUSHY, BOSKY.] Bosky, bushy.

1570 LEVINS *Manip.* 99 Buskye, *dumosus.* **1596** SHAKS. *I Hen. IV*, v. i. 2 The Sunne begins to peere Aboue yon busky hill. **1600** TOURNEUR *Transf. Met.* xlviii. Wks. II. 206 And sometimes nibble on the buskie root. **1606** J. RAYNOLDS *Dolarnys Prim.* (1880) 71 Huge Tmolus..with buskey haire. *c* **1800** K. WHITE *Clift Gr.* 272 Yon busky dingle.

busle, busling, obs. ff. BUSTLE, BUSTLING.

busmar, variant of BISMER, *Obs.*, shame.

busment, obs. form of BUSHMENT.

buss (bʌs), *sb.*[1] Forms: 4–7 busse, 5 busch, 6 busche, 7 buce, buscie, (brisse, burse), bushe, 8 buche, bush, 7– buss. [A word found in many European langs.: OF. *busse*, OSp. *buce*, *buzo*, Pr. *bus*, med.L. (12th c.) *bucia*, *bussa*; also OHG. (rare) *buzo*, MHG. *buze*, ON. *buza*, OE. *butse(-carlas)* in OE. Chron. A.D. 1066, Du. *buis*, whence app. mod.G. *büse*, F. *buse*, and sense 2 below. In sense 1 the word probably came into English from OF. The remoter etymology is unknown; the OF. *busse* cask, is usually assumed to be identical.]

†**1.** A vessel of burden; perh. similar in build and rig to 2. *Obs.* exc. *Hist.*, or as in 2.

1330 R. BRUNNE *Chron.* 153 Busses þritti Charged with vitaile, with gode men & douhti. *Ibid.* 169 þei sauh fer in þe se A grete busse & gay. **1538** *Aberd. Regist.* V. 16 (JAM.) Ane busche quhilk was takin be the Franchemen. **1611** SPEED *Hist. Gt. Brit.* IX. vii. 25 Thirteene Buces or Buscies, which had each of them three course of Sailes. **1865** *Cornh. Mag.* XII. 375 Richard's fleet..with its heavy busses and dromons for carrying horses and provisions.

2. *spec.* A two- or three-masted vessel of various sizes, used esp. in the Dutch herring-fishery; in 1794 identified with a 'fly-boat'.

1471 *Sc. Acts Jas. III* (1597) §48 That Lordes, Barronnes, and Burrowes gar make Schippes, Busches, and greate Pinck-boates with nettes. **1601** J. KEYMER *Dutch Fishing* in *Phenix* I. 223 The 2000 Busses..are employ'd only to take Herrings about Baughamness in Scotland, etc. **1668** CHILD *Disc. Trade* (1698) 56 A Dutchman will be content to employ a stock of 5 or 10000*l.* in burses. **1706** DE FOE *Jure Div.* I. 10 Neptune..In Holland's Buss for Herrings Fish'd. **1749** *Wealth Gt. Brit.* 37 The vessels that go upon this fishery, are buches, or busses, of the burthen of 70 to 100 tons. **1776** FALCONER *Dict. Marine, Buss*, a ship of two masts, used by the English and Dutch in their herring fisheries. It is generally from 50 to 70 tons burthen. **1794** *Rigging & Seamanship* I. 239 *Buss*, a Dutch fishing-vessel with three short masts, each in one piece. On each is carried a square-sail, and sometimes a topsail above the mainsail. [A plate is given.] **1867** *Q. Rev.* Apr. 317 The..fishery has seen year by year the number of its busses decrease.

b. *attrib.* and in *comb.* See also BUS-CARL.

1580 in Wadley *Bristol Wills* (1886) 226 The busse chest in the Alarie. **1615** *Trades Incr.* in *Harl. Misc.* (Malh.) III. 308 Buss-fishing is more easy than any other kind of fishing. **1667** DENHAM *Direct. Paint.* IV. v. 12 Buss-Skippers.. stamp to think Their Catching-craft is over. **1776** ADAM SMITH *W.N.* (1869) II. IV. v. 94 Two-thirds of the buss-caught herrings are exported. *Ibid.* 95 The great encouragement which a bounty..gives to the buss fishery. *Ibid.* The establishment of the buss bounty.

buss (bʌs), *sb.*[2] Now *arch.* and *dial.* Also 6–7 busse. [app. an alteration of the earlier BASS *sb.*[3]; cf. also Sp. *buz*, Ger. dial. *buss*, which however may be only parallel onomatopœias.] A kiss, a smack.

1570 TURBERV. *Ladie Venus, &c.* He that brings him home agaıne, A busse? yet not a busse alone doubtlesse shall haue. **1596** SPENSER *F.Q.* III. x. 46 Every satyre first did give a busse To Hellenore. **1634** J. LEVETT *Order. Bees* Pref. Poems, The winged Citizens of mount Hymete..harmless busses gave him [Plato]. **1706** FARQUHAR *Recruit. Offic.* v. ii, My dear Plume give me a buss. **1749** FIELDING *Tom Jones* VII. xiii. (1840) 100/1 He gave Jones a hearty buss. **1859** E. WAUGH *Lanc. Songs* in *Lanc. Gloss.* (E.D.S.) 63 Let mammy have a buss. **1863** *Sat. Rev.* 368 Giving him a hearty buss upon each cheek. **1882** TENNYSON *Prom. May* II. (1886) 117 Gi'e us a buss fust, lass.

b. Kissing.

1708 PRIOR *Mice*, After much buss and great grimace Much chat arose.

buss (bʌs), *v.*[1] *arch.* and *dial.* Also 6–7 busse, 7 boss (*dial.*); pa. t. 6 bust. [Belongs to BUSS *sb.*[2]]

1. *trans.* To kiss. (See quot. 1648.)

1571 R. EDWARDS *Damon & P.* in Hazl. *Dodsley* IV. 82 Your wife now will buss you. **1595** SHAKS. *John* III. iv. 35, I will thinke thou smil'st, And busse thee as thy wife. **1648** HERRICK *Hesper.* (1823) I. 266 Kissing and bussing differ both in this, We busse our wantons, but our wives we kisse. **1719** D'URFEY *Pills* (1872) V. 95 To every one that I did meet, I bravely bussed my Hand. **1847** TENNYSON *Princ.* v. 213 You..Nor burnt the grange, nor buss'd the milking-maid. **1866** G. MEREDITH *Vittoria* xxix. (1886) 300 Up with your red lips, and buss me a Napoleon salute.

b. *fig.*

1606 SHAKS. *Tr. & Cr.* IV. v. 220 Yond Towers, whose wanton tops do busse the clouds, Must kisse their owne feet. **1607** —— *Cor.* III. ii. 75 Thy knee bussing the stones.

2. *absol.*

1635 QUARLES *Embl.* II. viii. (1718) 93 Come buss and friends, my lamb. **1741** RICHARDSON *Pamela* (1824) I. 69, I now forgive you heartily; let's buss and be friends. **1879** BROWNING *Ned Bratts* 265 So blubbered we, and bussed, and went to bed.

buss, *v.*[2], Sc. form of BUSK *v.*[1] To attire, dress, dress up, deck, adorn; to dress (a fishing hook).

(In Hawick, before the annual Common-riding, the ancient 'colour' or town's standard is ceremoniously *bussed* for the occasion with ribbons, etc.)

c **1570** *Leg. Bp. St. Andrews* in *Scot. Poems 16th C.* II. 331 A cowe [i.e. scarecrow] bust in a biscops place. **1805** A. SCOTT *Poems* (1811) 18 (JAM.) Wi' fly-buss'd hook, an' fishing rod. **1818** *Edin. Mag.* 327 (JAM.) I'll buss my hair wi' the gowden brume. **1882** *Proc. Berw. Nat. Club* IX. No. 3. 562 Only the feathers to 'buss flies'.

buss, variant of BUS *sb.*[2], omnibus.

buss, obs. form of BURSE, BUSH.

bussard, -erd, -ly, obs. forms of BUZZARD, -LY.

busschel, -chop(e, obs. ff. BUSHEL, BISHOP.

busse, obs. form of BUSS, BUZZ.

bussel(l, obs. form of BUSTLE.

† **'bussell, busshell.** *Obs.* Var. of BOSSELL, the 'print' of a mazer or drinking-bowl.

c **1530** in Gutch *Coll. Cur.* II. 314 The mending of a Bason ..and the makyng of thamell and the bussell withe my Lordis Armes. **1625** in Rymer *Fœdera* XVIII. 236 The bason enamelled about the busshell and brymme.

busser, var. BUSER.

bussh-, obs. spelling of BUSH-.

† **busshe.** *Obs.* [Cf. *bush-tree* in BUSH *sb.*[1] 11.] Boxwood.

1430 *Test. Ebor.* II. 8 Pecten de busshe.

bussing ('bʌsɪŋ), *vbl. sb.*[1] Also bossing (*dial.*). [f. BUSS *v.*[1] + -ING[1].] Kissing.

1577 NORTHBROOKE *Dicing* (1843) 166 A very kindling of lechery, whereto serveth all that bussing. **1656** DUGARD *Gate Lat. Unl.* §626 All lechery, uncomly bussings..are unchastitie and defile the mind. **1691** RAY *N.C. Wds.* s.v. *Osse*, Ossing comes to bossing. Prov. Chesh. **1882** TENNYSON *Prom. May* II. (1886) 117 Wasn't thou and me a-bussin' o' one another t'other side o' the haäycock?

† **bussing**, *vbl. sb.*[2] *Sc. Obs.* [f. BUSS *v.*[2]]

1. = BUSKING *vbl. sb.*[1]

? *c* **1600** *Reid Squair* xv. in *Evergreen* II. 230 To put the Bussing on thair Theis.

2. 'A linen cap or hood, worn by old women, much the same as Toy' (Jamieson).

1788 PICKEN *Poems* 59 (JAM.) Witches..Wi long-tailed bussins, ty'd behin'.

bussle, obs. or Sc. form of BUSTLE.

† **'bussle-headed**, *a. dial.* ? *Obs.* See quot.

a **1722** LISLE *Husb.* (1757 4to.) 183 The ears [of wheat] being long and heavy were bussle-headed, that is, did hang their heads downward into the sheaf.

‖ **bussu.** A South American name for a species of palm (*Manicaria saccifera*), the spathes of which supply a kind of coarse strong cloth. Hence ***bussu palm, bussu cloth.***

1858 HOGG *Veg. Kingd.* 754 Manicaria saccifera is a native of Brazil..where it is called Bussu. **1858** *Ibid.* 755 Between layers of the smooth Bussu cloth. **1866** *Treas. Bot.* II. 717/2. **1885** LADY BRASSEY *In Trades* 166 The delicate brown net-work that covers the spathe of the Bussu palm.

bussyn(n)e, var. of BUYSINE, *Obs.*, trumpet.

bust (bʌst), *sb.*[1] [a. F. *buste* (of which Littré gives no examples earlier than 17th c.), ad. It. *busto* = Sp., Pg. *busto*, Pr. *bustz* (rare). The primary sense in It., and the only sense in Pr., is 'trunk or upper portion of the body'. The origin of the Romanic word has not been satisfactorily ascertained; see Diez, Scheler, Littré]

1. A piece of sculpture representing the head, shoulders, and breast of a person. Cf. BUSTO.

1691 WOOD *Ath. Oxon.* I. 264 Over his grave was..the Statua or Bust..to the middle part of his body. **1768** EARL CARLISLE in *G. Selwyn & Contemp.* II. 311, I have this morning been sitting for my bust, which is to be done in marble. **1816** BYRON *Ch. Har.* III. lxvi, Their tomb was simple, and without a bust. **1821** —— *Juan* III. viii, Romances paint at full length people's wooings, But only give a bust of marriages. **1839** THIRLWALL *Greece* III. 3 The reward..consisted in three stone busts of Hermes.

¶ ? Influenced by L. *bustum* sepulchral monument.

1735 POPE *Epist. Lady* 139 But die, and she'll adore you —then the bust And temple rise—then fall again to dust. *a* **1761** CAWTHORN *Elegy Capt. Hughes*, Nature! 'tis thine.. To teach..The dirge to murmur, and the bust to rise. *a* **1771** GRAY (1775) *Poems*, Can storied urn or animated bust Back to its mansion call the fleeting breath?

2. a. The upper front part of the human body; the bosom (esp. of a woman).

1727–51 CHAMBERS *Cycl.* s.v., In speaking of an antique, we say the head is marble, and the bust porphyry, or bronze, that is, the stomach and shoulders. **1819** BYRON *Juan* II. cxix, There was an Irish lady, to whose bust I ne'er saw justice done. **1835** W. IRVING *Tour Prairies* 32 His naked bust would have furnished a model for a statuary. **1886** MISS CLEVELAND in *Pall Mall G.* 13 Mar. 13/2, I do not approve of any dress which shows the bust.

b. The measurement around a woman's body at the level of her bust, usually measured in inches. So ***bust measure, measurement, size.***

1895 *Montgomery Ward Catal.* 36/3 Unlaundered Waists. Sizes 32 to 42 inches bust measure. **1961** M. DICKENS *Heart of London* i. 14 Beautiful model offers her services. Anything considered. Bust 40. Waist 20. Hips 37. **1969** *Woman* 4 Oct. 34/2 Her bust measurement had never been more than 38 in. **1969** *Woman's Own* 11 Jan. 26/2 *Flower-printed red dress*... In bust sizes 32–36 ins. **1970** *Woman* 7 Mar. 19/1 Dress and coat... Sizes 32 in. to 42 in. bust.

†**3.** *transf.* A swelling or protuberance. *Obs.*

1653 URQUHART *Rabelais* I. viii, It [i.e. a necklace] reached down to the very bust of the rising of his belly [Fr. à la boucque du petit ventre.]

4. *attrib.* and *Comb.*, as ***bust bodice, -costume, -improver, -line, -maker; bust-like*** adj.

1903 in C. W. Cunnington *Eng. Women's Clothing* (1952) ii. 59 Patent bust bodice worn above the corset. **1961** M. SPARK *Prime of Miss Jean Brodie* iii. 73 Her chest was a slight bulge flattened by a bust bodice. **1910** *Maggs' Catal.* No. 255, 85 Etchings, Illustrating the Head-Dress and Bust-Costume Worn by Ladies during the Early 17th Century. **1849** in C. W. Cunnington *Fem. Attitudes* (1935) 312 The Registered Bust Improver. For the purpose of..giving an elegant figure and appearance to the wearer. **1905** *Daily Chron.* 1 July 4/5 Many artificial aids have been devised, such as hip pads, bust improvers. **1826** *Blackw. Mag.* XIX. 393 Her lips were not wont to be so cold and white..not so moveless and bustlike her bosom. **1939** *Ottawa Jrnl.* 24 June 10/6 The brief bra top is an uplift and is webbed to cling below the bustline. **1969** *Woman* 4 Oct. 34/3 Slim, happy and confident with a 36 in. bustline. **1860** HAWTHORNE *Marb. Faun* I. i. 5 You never chiselled..a more vivid likeness than this, cunning bust-maker as you think

yourself. **1837** CARLYLE *Fr. Rev.* I. v. iv. 217 Will the Bust-Procession pass that way?

bust, *sb.*² A box: see BUSTE.

bust, *sb.*³ *colloq.* and *U.S.* [dial. var. of BURST *sb.*] = BURST *sb. spec.* 'a frolic; a spree' (Bartlett); cf. BURST *sb.* 7. Phrs. *to go on the bust*, *to go a bust*.

1764 in *Essex Inst. Hist. Coll.* XLIX. 284 Stray'd or stolen ..a Bay mare, with a cut main, and a Bust on the near Side of the Hind Flank. **1840** *American Joe Miller* 116 Away with the expense..when a fellow is on a bust. *a* **1860** *California Song* (Bartlett), When we get our pockets full Of this bright, shinin' dust We'll..spend it on a bust. **1890** 'R. BOLDREWOOD' *Col. Reformer* vii, There would be a slight probability of some of the party going 'on the bust' after three or four months' teetotalism. **1909** *Westm. Gaz.* 4 Sept. 2/3 We wish to go on the bust mildly. **1912** BEERBOHM *Christmas Garland* 17 Wot'll 'e do then poor devil? Go a bust on 'is conduc' money. **1963** L. MEYNELL *Virgin Luck* vi. 127, I was in pocket now. So I decided to go a bust and back a number.

b. A sudden failure or collapse of trade, etc. (cf. *burst-up* s.v. BURST *sb.*² 2 b); *spec.* opp. BOOM *sb.*³ 1.

1842 *Knickerbocker* XX. 99 'A mistake!' exclaimed the other; 'not a bit of it! It's a reg'lar built bu'st!' **1942** H. A. WALLACE *Cent. of Common Man* 28 Dec. (1944) 41 We cannot afford either a speculative boom or its inevitable bust. **1947** *Chr. Sci. Monitor* 24 Jan. 1/1 We had an agricultural 'boom and bust' after the other World War. **1969** *Times* (Suppl.) 5 May p. ii/2 The general reasoning is that it is better to have a slowdown now than a bust later. At least that is the thinking of many economists and politicos.

c. A person, etc., who is a failure; *spec.* in *Poker*, a busted flush or straight (see BUSTED *ppl. a.*); hence, a bad hand at cards.

1928 *Amer. Speech* III. 218 *Bust*..Sometimes the word is used to mean failure... 'The Theta dance sure was a bust'. **1931** D. RUNYON *Guys & Dolls* (1932) vi. 134 As Cupid I am a total bust. **1932** *Amer. Speech* VII. 330 *Bust*, a very poor bridge hand. *Ibid.* 435 A worthless hand [at poker] is called ..a 'bust'. **1934** M. ELLINGER *Poker* 166 *Bust*, a hand which the player has endeavoured and failed to make into a straight or a flush. **1957** WODEHOUSE *Over Seventy* iv. 54 At the age of ten I was a social bust. **1959** H. O. YARDLEY *Education of Poker Player* II. i. 86 A bust is a useless hand.

d. = BURST *sb.* 2 c.

1859 in G. W. MATSELL *Vocabulum* 16. **1887** J. W. HORSLEY *Jottings fr. Jail* i. 23 'Rem for a bust'.. means.. remanded for a burglary. **1947** *Sci. News* IV. 50 The back of a pub where you and a 'screwer'..had decided to 'do a bust'.

e. A blow with the fist.

1925 H. LEVERAGE in *Flynn's* III. 693/2 *Bust*, a blow; a stroke (in the face). **1962** J. F. POWERS *Morte d'Urban* viii. 176 How'd you like a bust in the nose?

f. A police raid or arrest. *slang* (orig. *U.S.*). Cf. BUST *v.*² e.

1938 *New Yorker* 12 Mar. 38/3 'One whiff [of marijuana]' said Chappy, 'and we get a bust.' ('Bust' is Harlem for a police raid.) **1959** W. BURROUGHS *Naked Lunch* 15 Provident junkies..keep stashes against a bust. **1969** *It* 10–23 Oct. 10/1 At the moment, there are over a hundred of our kids in nick as a result of the busts at 144 Piccadilly & Endell Street.

†**bust**, *v.*¹ *Obs.* exc. ? *dial.* [Origin unknown: cf. BASTE *v.*³, also Sw. dial. *bysta* (Rietz), OF. *boster* (rare, ? var. of *bouter*) to knock at a door, MDu. *buust* cudgel, f. *buusschen* to beat.] *trans.* To beat, thrash.

a **1225** *Juliana* 24 Speche þu maht spillen ant ne speden nawiht þah þu me buste and beate. *c* **1230** *Hali Meid.* 31 Beateð þe & busteð þe as his ibohte þrel. *c* **1400** *Alexius* (Laud MS. 463) 331 Ofte þei him bete and buste (*rime-wd.* niste). [**1808–25** JAMIESON, *To bust*, to beat, Aberd.]

bust, *v.*² *colloq.* and *U.S.* [dial. var. of BURST *v.*] To burst; to break.

1806 M. LEWIS in *Lewis & Clark Exped.* (1905) V. 137 Windsor busted his rifle near the muzzle. **1839** DICKENS *Nickleby* lvii, His genius would have busted all bonds. **1843** —— *Mart. Chuz.* xvi, Keep cool, Jefferson... Don't bust! **1844** *Ibid.* xxxiv, If the biler of this vessel was Toe bust, Sir. **1885** *Advt.* in *Lisbon* (Dakota) *Star* 3 Apr. 6/7 N.P. Express Monopoly Busted. **1891** G. CHAMIER *Philosopher Dick* I. ix. 249 We must have a spell anyhow. Nobody has ever *bust* himself as I have for the old man. **1915** A. D. GILLESPIE *Let.* 3 Mar. (1916) 30 The shells make a scraping sound... When they 'bust' in the distance, I see a bright flash. **1918** H. C. WITWER *Baseball to Boches* vii. 249, I oughta bust you in the nose! **1919** WODEHOUSE *Damsel in Distress* iii, I shall infallibly bust you one on the jaw. **1930** *Diary Public Sch. Girl* (ed. 2) 25 Quite a decent game. Bust my crosse though. **1942** T. RATTIGAN *Flare Path* I, Caught us bending proper this time. Group must be fair busting their stays with laughter. **1953** M. SCOTT *Breakfast at Six* xxii. 181 It's yours. Have a good time with it [*sc.* £15]. Bust it any way you like. **1963** *Listener* 28 Mar. 568/3 Protocol would hardly permit him to..bust his interviewer one on that earnest Canadian snoot of his.

b. *spec.* To break (a horse). Cf. BUSTER 4.

1891 *Harper's Mag.* July 208/2 The whole secret of 'busting'..lies in completely exhausting the bronco at the first lesson. *Ibid.* 210/1 Two rides will usually bust a bronco so that the average cow-puncher can use him. **1941** *Nat. Geogr. Mag.* Mar. 300/1 He's too old now to..bust a bronco.

c. *trans.* To reduce to insolvency (cf. BURST *v.* 8 d). Also *intr.*, to go bankrupt.

1829 R. C. SANDS *Writings* (1834) II. 153 The Aigle Bank was *bussted*. **1837** *Knickerbocker* X. 329 Can it truly be That 'Providence, which oft afflicts the just', Has fore-ordain'd that all the banks should *bu'st*? *a* **1860** J. C. NEAL *Dolly Jones* (Bartlett), I was soon fotch'd up in the victualling line—and I busted, for the benefit of my creditors. **1880** *Harper's Mag.* Oct. 729/1 After the fate of the town, be it to 'boom' or 'bust', has been decided. **1909** H. G. WELLS *Ann Veronica* vi. 124 Gives you a right to hang on to the old man until he busts—practically. **1923** H. CRANE *Let.* 15 Feb. (1965) 123 *Broom*, by the way, has busted; N.Y. office closed last Saturday. **1923** T. E. LAWRENCE *Let.* 22 Sept. (1938) 431, 300 copies could be produced, with the fifty or sixty portraits I've bust myself upon, for £10 a copy.

d. To break into (a house, etc.). Cf. BUST *sb.*³ d.

1859 in G. W. MATSELL *Vocabulum* 16. **1879** *Sessions' Papers* 29 May 184 *Busting* means burglary or house-breaking. **1927** E. WALLACE *Feathered Serpent* ix. 110 There's a little house just outside of Thatcham..me and Harry..thought we might 'bust' it and get a few warm clothes. **1948** WODEHOUSE *Spring Fever* xiv. 143 What! You're asking me to bust a pete?

e. Usu. in pa. pple. *busted*: dismissed, demoted; arrested, jailed.

1918 R. W. LARDNER *Treat 'Em Rough* 81 His captain.. busted him and I don't mean he cracked him in the jaw but when a man gets busted in the army it means you get reduced to a private. **1930** *Amer. Speech* V. 382 *Busted, to be*, to be demoted. **1943** HUNT & PRINGLE *Service Slang* 19 *Bust*, to reduce to the ranks or a lower rank; to deprive an N.C.O. of his stripes. **1953** W. R. BURNETT *Vanity Row* v. 40 Roy showed his [police] badge. 'You'll get busted for this,' shouted the man. **1958** *Landfall* XII. 115 The little man came out of his cell... 'This your first time busted?'

f. *intr.* In vingt-et-un, to exceed the score of twenty-one, and so lose one's stake. Also *to go bust*.

1939 PHILLIPS & WESTALL *Complete Bk. Card Games* 195 When each of the players has had the cards he wants (those who are 'busted' having disclosed the fact), the Dealer turns up his two cards. *Ibid.*, Players who have gone 'bust', i.e. exceeded 21, will have forfeited their stakes automatically. **1945** A. A. OSTROW *Complete Card Player* 39 If a player's total count passes 21..he has 'gone over', 'gone overboard' or 'busted'. Banker collects the bet. **1950** *Chambers's Encycl.* XIV. 326/2 Each of the players may..have cards 'twisted'.. until such time as he either 'sticks' on the hand he has, or 'busts' (i.e. exceeds 21).

Hence **bust-head** *a.*

1864 SALA in *Daily Tel.* 19 Oct., Irresistible proclivities towards 'bust-head' whisky, 'red-eye' rum, and loafing generally.

bust, *ppl. a.* = BUSTED *ppl. a.* Also *bust-up*.

1913 R. BROOKE *Let.* Aug. (1968) 499 *The Blue Review* has gone bust, through lack of support. **1915** J. BUCHAN *39 Steps* vi. 140 A bust-up motor-car. **1921** WODEHOUSE *Jill the Reckless* viii. 121 Jill Mariner had gone completely bust. **1928** D. L. SAYERS *Unpl. Bellona Club* xiv. 165 Well, it's all gone bust—but it was a darn' good stunt while it lasted. **1952** KOESTLER *Arrow in Blue* xxv. 350, I woke up in the morning ..financially broke, and with a bust-up car. **1964** *Observer* 26 July 8/2 Companies do go bust. *Ibid.* 8/5 The firm..is noted for its history of winding up bust companies.

†'**bustal**, *a. Obs.*⁻⁰ [f. L. *bust-um* a tomb + -AL¹.] Of or pertaining to burial or the grave.

1730–6 in BAILEY.

'**bustamite.** *Min.* [Named after the discoverer *Bustamente*.] A greyish-red calciferous variety of Rhodonite, a bisilicate of manganese and lime.

bu'stangee, obs. form of BOSTANGI.

1686 *Lond. Gaz.* No. 2196/1 The Grand Signior.. doubled his Guard of Bustangees.

bustard ('bʌstəd). Forms: 5–6 **bustarde**, 4– **bustard**; also, 6 **bistarda**, **bistarde**, **bystarde**, 7 **bistard**. [The form *bustard* in 15th c. appears to be exclusively English, and looks like a mixture of the two OF. forms *bistarde* and *oustarde*, both going back to L. *avis tarda*, the name given to the bird, according to Pliny, in Spain. This name, if purely Latin, would mean 'slow bird', but 'the application of the epithet is not understood' (Prof. Newton), as the bird is remarkably swift on foot, and, though averse to flight, capable of great speed when compelled to take wing. Prof. Newton suggests that *tarda* may have been a sb.; perh. *avis tarda* is a mere etymologizing alteration of a non-Latin name. Hence Pg. *abetarda*, *betarda*, Sp. *avutarda*, It. *ottarda*, Pr. *austarda*. The Eng. form *bistard* was of later appearance, taken directly from Fr.]

1. A genus of birds (*Otis*) presenting affinities both to the *Cursores* and the *Grallatores* or waders; remarkable for their great size and running powers. The great bustard (*Otis tarda*) is the largest European bird, and was formerly common in England, though now extinct, or found only as a rare visitant.

[**1391** *Test. Ebor.* (1836) I. 155 Lego Elisotæ, uxori Ricardi Bustard.] *c* **1460** J. RUSSELL *Bk. Nurture* in *Babees Bk.* (1868) 144 Pecok, Stork, Bustarde, & Shovellewre. **1486** *Bk. St. Albans* D iij b, The symplest of theis will slee..a Bustarde. **1514** FITZHERB. *Just. Peas* (1538) 126 b, To forfayt for every egge of crane, or bustarde so distroyed.. twenty pens. *c* **1520** L. ANDREW *Noble Lyfe* L ij b in *Babees Bk.* (1868) 218 The Bistarda is a birde as great as an egle. **1597** BP. HALL *Sat.*, *Def. Envie* 20 Nor lowly bustard dreads the distant rayes. **1655** MOUFET & BENNET *Health's Improv.* (1746) 174 Bistards or Bustards, so called for their slow Pace and heavy flying; or as the Scots term them, Gusestards; that is to say, Slow Geese. **1732** FIELDING *Miser* III. iii, A bustard, which, I believe, may be bought for a guinea. **1794** WORDSW. *Guilt & Sorr.*, The bustard..Forced hard against the wind a thick unwieldy flight. **1836** *Penny Cycl.* VI. 57/1 Bustards have been heard of within the last few years in the neighbourhood of Bury St. Edmund's. **1864** *Times* 19 Nov., A specimen of the Great Bustard, long an extinct British bird, was picked up in the sea..off Burlington Quay about a week ago.

fig. **1831** CARLYLE *Sart. Res.* I. vii. 56 By what strange chances do we live in History..Milo by a bullock; Henry Darnley, an unfledged booby and bustard, by his limbs.

2. Applied to other related birds: in America to the Canada goose, *Bernicla Canadensis* (Prof. Newton in *Encycl. Brit.*). *thick-kneed bustard*: the stone curlew (*Œdicnemus crepitans*).

3. Local var. BUZZARD, applied to large moths.

1886 M. G. WATKINS in *Academy* 14 Aug. 101/3 There are some capital chapters on 'bustard' fishing (that is, fishing during the night with a large artificial moth).

bust-coat, mistake for BUFF-COAT 3.

1706 in PHILLIPS. **1721–1800** in BAILEY.

†**buste, bust.** *Obs.* Also 4 *Sc.* bouste. [var. of BOIST *sb.*] A box, esp. for containing ointments, drugs, confectionery, etc. Cf. BOIST, BOOST, BUIST.

a **1225** *Ancr. R.* 226 He haueð so monie bustes ful of his letuaries. *c* **1375** ? BARBOUR *St. Magdalena* 111 A bouste of precius vngument. *c* **1450** HENRYSON *Mor. Fab.* 30 Out of his buste ane bill can hee braid. **1483** *Cath. Angl.* 49/1 A Buyste [*v.r.* Bust]. **1566** KNOX *Hist. Ref.* Wks. 1846 I. 264 The Lord James..had (by all appearance) lyked of the same bust that dispatched the rest.

busted ('bʌstɪd), *a.* [f. BUST *sb.*¹ + -ED².] Having a bust, or breast; chiefly in *comb.*

1864 TENNYSON *En. Ard.* 539 Her full-busted figure-head Stared o'er the ripple feathering from her bows.

'**busted**, *ppl. a. colloq.* (orig. *U.S.*). [f. BUST *v.*² to burst.] Burst, broken; bankrupt or ruined; *spec.* in *Poker* denoting a flush or straight that one fails to complete (also *fig.*). Also *busted-up*.

1837 *Knickerbocker* X. 170 He was a busted man. **1860** *Harper's Mag.* July 278/2 Having lost all he had..on a 'busted' bank at a game of poker. **1868** M. M. POMEROY *Nonsense* xx. 185 Now I'm a gone nutmeg, a busted what-do-you-call-it. **1909** 'O. HENRY' *Roads of Destiny* vi. 97 The precarious busted flush. *Ibid.* xiii. 212 There was a buck coon who had drifted down there from a busted-up colored colony. **1919** W. S. MAUGHAM *Moon & Sixpence* xlvii. 198 Busted?.. I'll get you some breakfast. **1920** MULFORD *J. Nelson* vi. 58 They took him over to th' SV to set Ol' Arnold's busted laig. **1953** A. UPFIELD *Murder must Wait* xviii. 161 Damn this busted leg. **1956** 'N. SHUTE' *Beyond Black Stump* 205 There's no goddam oil here. This is a dry hole, a busted flush.

‖**bustee** ('bʌstiː). Also busti. [Hindustani *bastī* dwelling.] A village: 'applied in Calcutta to the separate groups of huts in the humbler native quarters' (Yule).

1883 *Sat. Rev.* 8 Sept. 301/2 Collections of huts, which are known as 'Bustees'. **1885** *Daily Tel.* 25 Dec., No cases of cholera were found in the squalid bustees round several tanks. **1907** *Westm. Gaz.* 16 Sept. 8/3 A large tiger..lurking among the 'bustis'. **1960** 'S. HARVESTER' *Chinese Hammer* xxv. 202 Bustee hovels and sugar-cake temples..Calcutta. **1963** *Times* 30 May 13/6 In *bustees*—as the shanty towns where 25 per cent of the population live are called—..fresh, clean water is never available.

bustel, obs. form of BUSTLE.

busteous, -ious, variants of BOISTOUS *a. Obs.*

buster ('bʌstə(r)). [dial. var. of BURSTER.]

1. = BURSTER (in unknown sense).

1839 *New Monthly Mag.* LVI. 358 We can..buy a two-penny buster at a baker's-shop.

2. *slang* (chiefly U.S.). **a.** 'Something great' (W.); something that 'takes one's breath away'; something that provokes excessive admiration or amusement. **b.** A roistering blade, a dashing fellow. Also used as a slang form of address, usu. friendly or slightly disrespectful; 'mate', fellow; *old buster*: an affectionate or disrespectful designation for an elderly man. **c.** A frolic; a spree.

1850 MRS. STOWE *Uncle Tom's C.* iv. 23 Mas'r George.. declared decidedly that Mose was a buster. *a* **1860** THORPE *Big Bear Arkansas* (Bartlett), I went on, larning something every day, until I was reckened a buster, and allowed to be the best bar-hunter in my district. **1867** F. LUDLOW *Fleeing to Tarshish* 176 The rector's growing reputation for preaching busters, which is the Missourian for pulpit eloquence. **1905** H. A. VACHELL *Hill* vi. 137 You funny old buster. **1919** WODEHOUSE *My Man Jeeves* 79 An extremely wealthy old buster. **1931** M. A. VON ARNIM *Father* ix. 213 Shall you be all right, shut up alone with that old buster? **1948** A. SEAGER *Inheritance* 174 'Hi-ya, buster. What's new?' he heard a woman's coarse voice say. **1962** A. SHEPARD in *Into Orbit* 101 'OK, Buster,' I said to myself, 'you volunteered for this thing.' **1965** P. ARROWSMITH *Jericho* xix. 199 If you go on accusing me of attacking you lot, buster, you'll have the police to answer to.

3. *Australia.* **a.** A violent southern gale prevalent at Sydney. Also, any violent gale (usage not confined to Australia).

1848 BARTLETT *Dict. Amer.* 57 'This is a buster,' i.e. a powerful or heavy wind. **1863** F. FOWLER *Let.* in *Athenæum* 21 Feb., The brick-fielder is..the cold wind or southerly buster, which..carries a thick cloud of dust..across the city. **1883** *Times* 27 Sept. 9 The port is exposed to sudden gales, known as 'southerly busters'. **1886** COWAN *Charcoal*

Sk., The buster and brick-fielder: Austral red-dust blizzard and red-hot simoom. **1852** G. C. MUNDY *Our Antipodes* I. ii. 83 The Brickfielder, or, as the Port Jackson boatmen call it, the Sûtherly Bûster! **1888** *Longman's Mag.* Apr. 630 In New Zealand there are the *Southerly Busters*, following the dry hot 'nor'-wester'. **1935** 'L. LUARD' *Conquering Seas* xvii. 231 Flamers in sky. Northerly buster, I'm thinking. **1952** A. GRIMBLE *Pattern of Islands* v. 107 If the northerly buster takes your mainsail aback close-hauled to the south-easter. **1953** F. ROBB *Sea Hunters* vi. 59 Whatever was on the way would be no normal line squall—no summer 'buster'! **1956** S. HOPE *Diggers' Paradise* viii. 71 Sometimes the south wind or a 'south-westerly buster' puts a chill on the city [*sc.* Sydney].

b. = BURSTER 1 c. ***to come a buster***: to be thrown from a horse, 'to come a cropper'. Also *fig.*

1928 'BRENT OF BIN BIN' *Up Country* xi. 184 The fancy riding resulted in 'busters' galore to skilled and unskilled. **1952** D. NILAND in *Coast to Coast 1951–2* 198 She doesn't look like having a buster. **1968** *Sunday Truth* (Brisbane) 30 June 20 The Australian Government has come an incredible double buster on the design for its Vietnam campaign medal.

4. A horse-breaker. (Cf. *bronco-buster* s.v. BRONCO.) *U.S.*

1891 *Harper's Mag.* July 208/2 The buster must be careful to keep well away from sheds and timber. **1903** *Wide World Mag.* Apr. 545 On a large ranch which employs many cowboys, there is much rivalry among them as to who is the best rider or buster.

-buster. As the second element of an objective compound, as in *bronco-buster*; in familiar designations of guns, bombs, etc., as in *block-buster*.

†**'bustian.** *Obs.* Forms: 5 busteyn, 6 bustiane, bustion, bustyon, -yan, borstyan, 7 bustiam, 8 bustine, 6–8 bustian. [Derivation uncertain; cf. OF. *bustanne, -ane, buttenne*, 'sorte d'étoffe fabriquée à Valenciennes' (Godef.); It. *bottana* 'specie di tela bambagina', mentioned along with *fustagno* fustian (Tommaseo and Bellini); F. *boutanes* 'toile de coton de Chypre', *boutane* 'étoffe qui se fait à Montpellier' (Boiste).]

A cotton fabric of foreign manufacture, used for waistcoats and for certain church vestments; sometimes described as a species of fustian, but sometimes mentioned as distinct from it.

1463 in *Bury Wills* (1850) 18, I wele haue anothir vestement made of white busteyn. **1566** *Eng. Ch. Furniture* (Peacock, 1866) 43 A cope and a vestment of Bustian defaced. **1571** *Wills & Inv. N.C.* (1835) 362 j yeard & ½ of whit borstyan xviij*d.* **1578** *Richmond. Wills* (1853) 276, Viij yeards and a quarter of bustion at xiiij*d.* a yeard..v yeards of whit holme fustion at xij*d.* a yeard. **1598** FLORIO, *Restagno*, a kinde of stuffe like bustian, such as they make waste-cotes of. **1611** COTGR., *Fustaine à grain d'orge*, bustian. **1611** *Rates* (JAM.), Bustians or woven tweill stuff, the single peece not above fifteen elnes. **1622** MALYNES *Anc. Law-Merch.* 229 The commodities which are not made at all, or but in small quantitie in England, and may be practised, are manie, as Buckrams, Tapistrie, Bustians, Cambrickes. **1720** STOW *Surv.* (ed. Strype, 1754) II. v. xviii. 382/1 All..Fustians and Bustians made in England and Wales shall pay for each horse-pack, 8*d.* **1725** RAMSAY *Gentl. Sheph.* I. i, Neat, neat she was, in bustine waistcoat clean.

bustle ('bʌs(ə)l), *sb.*^{1} Also 7–8 **bussle**. [f. BUSTLE *v.*^{1}]

1. Activity with excitement, noise, and commotion; stir, tumult, disturbance, fuss, ado.

1634 MILTON *Comus* 379 Feathers..That, in the various bustle of resort, Were all to-ruffled. **1692** LOCKE *Educ.* §167 (1880) 143 All his Bustle and Pother will be to little or no purpose. **1733** FIELDING *Intr. Chamberm.* I. x, What was the occasion of this bustle? **1758** JOHNSON *Idler* No. 19 ¶3 Many..pass their lives..in bustle without business. **1822** BYRON *Juan* VIII. xxxix, He..could be very busy without bustle. **1853** KANE *Grinnell Exp.* xxix. (1856) 249 In the bustle of preparation. **1875** JEVONS *Money* (1878) 266 The bustle and turmoil..grow to a climax at four o'clock.

b. *transf.* The agitation or 'working' in the process of fermentation.

1674 N. FAIRFAX *Bulk & Selv.* 128 Fermentation or bustle of the vvorking or leavening particles. **1713** *Lond. & Countr. Brew.* IV. (1743) 331 Now the greater the Vessel is, the more Parts may arise and sink down; and..the more must be the Bustle.

2. The commotion of conflict; *concr.* a conflict, struggle, scuffle, fray. *arch.*

1622–62 HEYLIN *Cosmogr.* II. (1682) 188 The Bustle betwixt Athens and Lacedæmon. **1678** BUTLER *Hud.* III. III. 363 Caligula..Engag'd his Legions in fierce Bustles, With Periwinkles, Prawns and Muscles. **1693** LUTTRELL *Brief Rel.* (1857) III. 51 Divers were killed in the bustle. **1721** DE FOE *Mem. Cavalier* (1840) 286 We had a small bustle with some of the..troops of horse. **1769** *Junius Lett.* xxx. 136 His escape he attempts..a bustle ensues. **1865** KINGSLEY *Herew.* xli. (1877) 503 There was a bustle, a heavy fall.

3. *Thieves' cant.* (See quots.)

1812 J. H. VAUX *Flash Dict.*, *Bustle*, a cant term for money. *Ibid.* s.v. *Bustle*, Any object effected very suddenly, or in a hurry, is said to be done upon the bustle. **1830** LYTTON *P. Clifford* 56 He who surreptitiously accumulates bustle, is, in fact, nothing better than a buzz gloak.

'bustle, *sb.*^{2} [Perh. the same word as prec.: in the earlier examples it seems to denote rather the projecting portion of the dress itself than the means employed to produce the projection; cf. quot. 1826 in BUSTLING *ppl. a.*]

A stuffed pad or cushion, or small wire framework, worn beneath the skirt of a woman's dress, for the purpose of expanding and supporting it behind; a 'dress-improver'.

1788 T. MONRO in *Olla Podrida* No. 40 Such locks the nymphs now wear (in silks who rustle,) In rich luxuriance reaching to the bustle. **1830** MISS MITFORD *Village* Ser. IV. (1863) 177 A waist like a wasp, a magnificent bustle, and petticoats..puffed out round the bottom. **1838** *New Month. Mag.* LIV. 207 It caught the bustle—the projecting mass of muslin, silk, or cotton, as might be. **1865** *Daily Tel.* 12 Apr. 7 Originally the 'bustle' was merely a species of pillow, which was tied round the waist.

bustle ('bʌs(ə)l), *v.*^{1} Forms: 4 **bustelen**, 6 **bustel, bussel**, 6–7 **bussle, bussell**, 7 **busle**, 6– **bustle**. [ME. *bustelen*, used (once only) by Langland, is perh. onomatopœic, suggested by BLUSTER and by the sound of the alliterative words in the line. The mod. verb differs in sense, and has not been found earlier than the middle of the 16th c.; possibly it may be a phonetic variant of BUSKLE, from which in early use it is scarcely distinguishable in sense; cf. also *hustle, rustle*, etc. The resemblance in sound to mod.Icel. *bustl* a splash, as of a fish in water, *að bustla* to make a splash, to bustle, is noteworthy, but evidence of historical connexion is wanting.]

I. in ME. †**1.** *intr.* ? To wander blindly or stupidly; = BLUSTER *v.* 1. *Obs. rare*$^{-1}$.

1362 LANGL. *P. Pl.* A. VI. 4 Ther were fewe men so wys that couthe the wei thider, Bote bustelyng [**1377** B. v. 521 blustreden; **1393** C. VIII. 159 blostrede] forþ as bestes ouer valeyes and hulles.

II. The mod. word.

2. a. *intr.* To bestir oneself or display activity with a certain amount of noise or agitation, to be fussily active: usually implying excessive or obtrusive show of energy. Often with advs. *about, along, up and down.* (Cf. BUSKLE *v.* 2, 3.)

1580 NORTH *Plutarch* 123 Some..for fear to be taken tardy did bustle up at this noise. **1594** SHAKS. *Rich. III*, I. i. 152 God..leaue the world for me to bussle in. **1621** BURTON *Anat. Mel.* II. iii. VI. (1651) 349, I was once..mad to bussell abroad. **1628** WITHER *Brit. Rememb.* II. 1759 How they trudg'd, and busled up and downe. **1632** SANDERSON *Serm.* I. 312 Many servants..will..bustle at it..so long as their masters eye is upon them. **1633** BP. HALL *Hard Texts* 315 All shall be glad to bustle into armes for their defence. **1672** VILLIERS (Dk. Buckhm.) *Rehearsal* V. i. 113 Busie, busie, busie, busie, we bustle along. **1711** STEELE *Spect.* No. 6 ¶6 The good Man bustled through the Crowd. **1781** COWPER *Convers.* 215 We bustle up with unsuccessful speed. **1818** BYRON *Juan* I. clix, Antonia bustled round the ransack'd room. **1838** DICKENS *O. Twist* xxxix, Get up, and bustle about. **1844** KINGSLEY *Lett.* (1878) I. 122 We bustle and God works. **1857** EMERSON *Poems* 37 Let the great world bustle on.

b. as *imper.* = Bestir yourself! Make haste!

1594 SHAKS. *Rich. III*, V. iii. 289 Come, bustle, bustle. Caparison my horse. **1822** BYRON *Werner* I. i. 258 What, ho, there! bustle! **1837** DICKENS *Pickw.* vi, 'Bustle', said the old gentleman. **1869** LD. LYTTON *Orval* 98 Run to the Apothecary! Bustle, wench!

†**c.** To come *down* with commotion. *Obs.*

a **1611** CHAPMAN *Iliad* XII. 369 Down he bustled like an oak..Hewn down for shipwood.

d. Of a place: to be full of activity or bustle; to be alive *with*.

1880 *All Year Round* 9 Oct. 514 Transports..bustling with sailors. **1905** F. TREVES *Other Side of Lantern* x. 85 Those who walk along its empty terraces..see it as it was when it bustled with men and women three centuries ago.

†**3.** *intr.* To struggle, scuffle, contend; to elbow one's way through a crowd. ***to bustle it out***: = to fight it out. *Obs.* (Cf. *hustle*.)

c **1600** *Timon* III. i. (1842) 42 The foure windes doe bussle in my heade. **1610** HOLLAND *Camden's Brit.* I. 261 Edward the Third..and Philip Valois bustled for the very kingdome of France. **1647** W. BROWNE *Polex.* II. 321 'Tis in vaine..to bustle with my resolution. **1712** ARBUTHNOT *John Bull* (1755) 52 Peg's lads bustled pretty hard for that.

4. *trans.* and *refl.* To bestir, stir, rouse: also with *up*. Now *rare*.

1579 A. MUNDAY in Arb. *Garner* V. 209 Bustling themselves to dress up the galleys. **1584** LYLY *Campaspe* IV. i, My master bustels himself to flie. **1610** *Histriom.* VI. 251 Bustle up Your drouping spirits. **1880** *Daily Tel.* 12 Oct., We spend a couple of hours in bustling up the denizens of the big wood.

5. *trans.* (and *refl.*) **a.** To cause to move precipitately and in disorder; to hurry (a person or thing) in a fussy or over-energetic manner. Const. with preps. or advs. **b.** To make (hot, etc.) by bustling.

1563–87 FOXE *A. & M.* III. 771 The Bishop..bustleth himself with all speed possible to the Church. **1833** *Blackw. Mag.* XXXIII. 281 A man who bustled himself into importance with the mob. **1849** *Ibid.* LXV. 695 Old Thomas had to bustle on his coat. **1855** KINGSLEY *Westw. Ho* ii, The churchwardens and sidesmen..have bustled themselves hot and red. *Ibid.* v. 92 The jolly old man bustled them out of the house. **1883** *Standard* 8 Sept., If a stroke oar spurted at every two hundred yards, and then eased when he was striking fast, he would 'bustle' his men into utter confusion.

'bustle, *v.*^{2} *rare*. [f. BUSTLE *sb.*^{2}] *intr.* To stick out, project, as if supported by a bustle.

1853 DICKENS *Lett.* (1881) III. 157 A clinging flounced black silk dress, which wouldn't drape, or bustle, or fall.

bustled ('bʌs(ə)ld), *ppl. a.* [f. BUSTLE *sb.*^{2} + -ED^{2}.] Wearing a bustle.

1832 CARRICK in *Whistle-Binkie* (Sc. Songs) Ser. I. 38 The bustled beauty may engage, The dandy in his corset. **1837** *New Month. Mag.* LI. 27 Furbelowed and bustled in the extravagance of the mode.

†**'bustlepate.** *Obs. rare*$^{-1}$. [f. BUSTLE *v.*^{1} + PATE.] ? A bustling person.

a **1652** BROME *Queenes Exch.* V. Wks. 1873 III. 539 Did he so put thee to't, my little Bustlepate?

bustler ('bʌslə(r)). [f. BUSTLE *v.*^{1} + -ER^{1}.] One who bustles or displays fussy activity.

a **1680** BUTLER *Rem.* (1759) II. 393 An Hypocrite..is a great Bustler in Reformation. **1784** COWPER *Task* VI. 951 Thou bustler in concerns Of little worth. **1852** HAWTHORNE *Blithed. Rom.* I. v. 81 The little sphere..in which we were the prattlers and bustlers of a moment.

bustless ('bʌstlɪs), *a.* [f. BUST *sb.*^{1} + -LESS.] Without a (developed) bust.

1870 MISS BROUGHTON *Red as Rose* I. 122 Their little, bustless, waistless, hipless figures.

bustling ('bʌslɪŋ). *vbl. sb.* [f. BUSTLE *v.*^{1} + -ING^{1}.] The action of the verb BUSTLE.

1589 R. HARVEY *Pl. Perc.* 7 Let the yoouth..not continew such bustling, backbiting, with facing and defacing one another. **1625** K. LONG tr. *Barclay's Argenis* (1636) 681 The shore resounded at..the bustling of the Cables. **1628** EARLE *Microcosm.* (Arb.) 88 An eager bustling, that rather keepes adoe, than do's any thing. **1651** HOBBES *Leviath.* II. xviii. 91 The most sudden, and rough busling in of a new Truth.. does never breake the Peace. **1662** FULLER *Worthies* III. 109 In his time was much busling in the University, about an Apocrypha Book. **1674** BURNET *Royal Martyr &c.* (1710) 41 This doth..discharge all busling and fighting on the pretence of Religion. **1843** CARLYLE *Past & Pr.* (1858) 167 His life is but a bustling and a justling. **1865** KINGSLEY *Herew.* xv. (1877) 186 There was bustling to and fro of her and her maids.

'bustling, *ppl. a.* [f. as prec. + -ING^{2}.] That bustles; full of bustle or agitation.

1597 DRAYTON *Mortimer.* 25 A bustling tempests rouzing blasts. *a* **1611** CHAPMAN *Iliad* XIII. 312 From hollow bustling winds engendered storms arise. **1647** CLARENDON *Hist. Reb.* II. (1843) 49/2 Sir Harry Vane was a busy and a bustling man. **1823** SYD. SMITH *Wks.* (1859) II. 14/2 A little merry bustling clergyman. **1826** MISS MITFORD *Village* Ser. II. (1863) 357 *note*, The rustling bustling silk gown, redolent in every fold of clerical dignity. **1881** J. HAWTHORNE *Fort. Fool* I. xiv, The bustling period of the day.

Hence **'bustlingly** *adv.*

1822 SCOTT *Nigel* xvii, Reginald Lowestoffe was bustlingly officious and good-natured. **1885** D. C. MURRAY *Rainb. Gold* II. III. iii. 78 He searched bustlingly for his hat.

†**'busto.** *Obs.* Pl. **-os**, (**-oes, o's**). [a. It. *busto*: see BUST.] = BUST *sb.*^{1} 1.

1662 J. BARGRAVE *Pope Alex. VII* (1867) 117 An handsome ancient busto (as called at Rome) of Augustus —that is, the head and shoulders—in brass. **1732** DE FOE *Tour Gt. Brit.* (1769) II. 143 A fine busto of Dr. Harvey. **1754** RICHARDSON *Grandison* VII. v. 20 It is ornamented with pictures..statues, bustoes, bronzes. *c* **1800** K. WHITE *My Study* 68 Nor think it aught of a misnomer To christen Chaucer's busto Homer. **1863** SALA *Capt. Dang.* I. iii. 64 Bustos, pictures, and prints cut in brass.

†**'bustuary**, *a.* and *sb.* *Obs.* [ad. L. *bustuārius* pertaining to burning or the funeral-pyre.]

A. *adj.* Of or belonging to the funeral pile; funereal. *rare*.

1693 URQUHART *Rabelais* III. lii, Ashes, into which the fuel of the funeral and bustuary fire hath been converted.

B. *sb.* An incendiary.

1607 J. KING *Serm.* (Nov.) 25 The disloiall broode of Ignatius Loiola, the notorious Incendiaries, Bustuaries, of christian states. *c* **1633** T. ADAMS *Wks.* (1862) II. 32 (D.) They are the firebrands and bustuaries of kingdoms. *Ibid.* 157 (D.) Satan..is the great bustuary himself.

bust-up ('bʌstʌp). [See BUST *sb.*^{3}] = *burst-up* (see BURST *sb.* 2 b): an explosion (*lit.* and *fig.*); a flare-up, an altercation; excitement.

1846 *Knickerbocker* XXVIII. 313 The houdaciousest bust-up I ever seed. **1899** KIPLING *Stalky & Co.* 133 Then there's a big bust-up and a row that gets into the papers. **1908** W. DE MORGAN *Somehow Good* xi, There are hundreds of English equivalents for *éclaircissement*. There's bust-up. **1914** *English Rev.* Sept. 250 It [*sc.* this war] is the 'bust-up' of materialism. **1945** A. L. ROWSE *West-Country Stories* 148 They were having a tremendous bust-up with the railway porters about their belongings.

bustuus, bustwys, var. BOISTOUS *a. Obs.*

'busty. Rare corruption of BUST *sb.*^{1} or BUSTO.

1684 *1st Dk. Beaufort's Progr.* 113 A busty representing him down to the waste.

busty ('bʌstɪ), *a.* [f. BUST *sb.*^{1} + -Y^{1}.] Having a prominent bust.

1944 S. J. PERELMAN *Crazy like a Fox* (1945) 117 The leitmotiv of the campaign was a busty Polynesian hussy. **1954** K. AMIS *Lucky Jim* viii. 91 Bertrand's blonde and busty Callaghan piece.

bustyan, -yon, var. BUSTIAN, *Obs.*, a cloth.

busum, obs. form of BUXOM.

† '**busy**, *sb.*[1] *Obs.* [OE. *bisȝu*, *bysȝu* str. fem. abstr., f. *bisiȝ* BUSY *a.*; also *bisiȝ*, *bysiȝ*, neut. of the adj. used as sb. (only in pl. *bisȝu*).] Occupation, business; state of being actively employed.

a **1000** *Proem to Ælfred's Boeth.*, Ða bisȝu us sint swiþe earfoþrime [and see BUSY *v.*[1] 1]. ? *a* **1400** *Morte Arth.* 3631 The bolde kynge es in a barge and a-bowtte rowes, Alle bare-hevvede for besye. *a* **1400** *Octouian* 340 Nother of hem myght fram other ascape, For besy of fyght.

busy ('bɪzɪ), *sb.*[2] *slang.* [f. BUSY *a.*] A detective.

1904 *Daily Chron.* 17 Sept. 6/6 We had better slide; he looks like a 'busy'. **1928** *Sunday Dispatch* 2 Sept. 3/1 A porter.. replied: 'Not to-night, sir... You see, we've had the "blow" that the "Busies" are coming.' **1948** M. ALLINGHAM *More Work Undertaker* (1949) xiv. 179, I don't know 'ow long we've got before the busies come trampin' in.

busy ('bɪzɪ), *a.* *Compared* busier, -iest. Forms: 1 bysiȝ, 3 biseȝ, bese, busi, 3–4 bisi, bise, 3–6 besy, bisie, 4 bisaie, bysi(e, bisye, 4–5 bysy, bessy, bissy, (buysy), 4–6 bisy, besye, 5 besie, 5–8 busie, 6 busye, buisie, 7–8 buisy, 8 *Sc.* bizzie, -y, 5– busy. [OE. *bisiȝ*, later *bysiȝ*, = ODu. *bezich* (mod.Du. *bezig*), LG. *besig*; no cognate words are known in any other Teut. or Aryan lang. The ME. typical form was *bisi*, *bisy*, *bysy*: the form *busi* (with *ü* = OE. *y*) occurs in the later text of Layamon, but otherwise the *u* form is not found before the 15th c.: its prevalence in modern spelling, while the pronunciation is with *i*, as in ME., is difficult to account for.]

1. a. Occupied with constant attention; actively engaged; doing something that engrosses the attention. Said of persons; also of the mind, the hands, a mental faculty, or the like. (Rare in attrib. use.) *to get busy*: to become active; to begin to act (*colloq.* (orig. *U.S.*)).

In the earlier examples (esp. those under b and d) this sense is often not to be distinguished from that of 'careful, eager, anxious'. The latter notion has now disappeared, though a trace of it is found in Johnson's definition, 'employed with earnestness', which does not quite agree with the present usage.

a **1225** *Ancr. R.* 182 So þe sicnesse is more, se þe gold-smið is biseȝure. *c* **1300** *K. Alis.* 3906 Whan he Alisaunder besy seoth. *c* **1400** *Destr. Troy* 6047 Bise was the buerne all the bare night. **1570** LEVINS *Manip.* 108 Busie, *satagens*, *intentus*. **1596** SHAKS. *Tam. Shr.* v. ii. 81 She is busie, and she cannot come. **1611** BIBLE *1 Kings* xx. 40 As thy seruant was busie here and there. **1690** W. WALKER *Idiomat. Anglo-Lat.* 74 You are as busie as a bee. **1752** JOHNSON *Rambl.* No. 201 ¶12 Time slips.. away, while he is either idle or busy. **1802** SOUTHEY *Thalaba* IV. xiv, The youth, whose busy mind Dwelt on Lobabu's.. words. **1843** CARLYLE *Past & Pr.* III. xii. (1872) 178 A People energetically busy; heaving, struggling, all shoulders at the wheel. **1883** FROUDE *Short Stud.* IV. II. i. 170 His children knew him as a continually busy, useful man of the world. *a* **1888** *Mod.* Don't interrupt me, I'm busy. **1904** *Louisville Courier-Jrnl.* 27 Sept. 3 It was necessary to call upon the sergeant-at-arms... When that functionary got busy there came near being a riot. **1906** 'O. HENRY' *Four Million* 121 'Ikey,' said he,.. 'get busy with your ear. It's drugs for me if you've got the line I need.'

b. Const. *about*, †*after*, †*of*, *on*, *upon*, *over*, *with* (an object of attention).

a **1000** *Sal. & Sat.* (Gr.) 61 Bysiȝ æfter bocum. *a* **1225** *Ancr. R.* 142 Bisi abuten gostliche biȝete. *c* **1340** *Cursor M.* 192 (App. iii. Laud MS.) Of martha also that buysy [*v.r.* bysy, bisy, bessy] was abowte cryst þo. *c* **1380** WYCLIF *Rule St. Francis* ii. (1880) 40 þat þei be not bisi of here temporal goodis. **1599** SHAKS. *Much Ado* I. ii. 3 He is verie busie about it. **1712** ADDISON *Spect.* No. 329 ¶1 He had been very busy.. upon Baker's Chronicle. **1719** DE FOE *Crusoe* (1840) I. xvi. 285 He was so busy about his father. **1823** LAMB *Elia* Ser. I. ii. (1865) 15 Busy as a moth over some rotten archive. **1876** GREEN *Short Hist.* v. §3 (1882) 231 Busy with the cares of political office.

c. Const. *in* (an employment). Often with vbl. sb.; in which construction the prep. is now commonly omitted, so that the vbl. sb. becomes indistinguishable from the pr. pple.

a **1225** *Ancr. R.* 84 þus ha beoð bisie i þisse fule mester. *a* **1500** *Knt. & Wife* (Halliw.) Be bessy in Godis servys. **1663** SIR C. LYTTELTON in *Hatton Corr.* (1878) 30, I am soe buisy.. in the dispatch of a fleete. *c* **1680** BEVERIDGE *Serm.* (1729) I. 430 Busie in providing a suitable entertainment. **1702** ROWE *Amb. Step-Moth.* I. i. 235 So busie were my faculties in thought. **1713** ADDISON *Guardian* No. 112 ¶1 Busy in finding out the art of flying. *Mod.* I found him busy packing his trunk.

†**d.** Const. *for*. Also with *inf.* *Obs.*

1340 HAMPOLE *Pr. Consc.* 5489 þe devels.. þat to tempte men.. ay er bysy. *c* **1380** WYCLIF *Serm.* xv. Sel. Wks. I. 36 Men.. shulden be bisye for blisse. *c* **1440** *Gesta Rom.* (1879) 245 Late vs be euer besye to plese god. **1533** MORE *Answ. Poyson. Bk.* Wks. (1557) 1036/1 The leche that.. sytteth by the sicke man busye aboute to cure hym. **1629** *S'hertogenbosh* 21 The English were busie to fill the ditch. **1726** *Life of Penn* in *Wks.* I. 138 Busie for Forms.

†**e.** *euphemistic.* *to be busy with*: to have to do with (sexually). *Obs.*

1612 *Pasquil's Night-cap* (N.) Thou hast beene too busy with a man, And art with child. **1687** DRYDEN *Hind & P.* III. xiii. 7 The Wolf has been too busie in your bed. **1728** VANBR. & CIB. *Prov. Husb.* II. i, You would have the Impudence to Sup, and be busy with her.

2. a. Said of things; *fig.* of passions, etc.

a **1000** *Byrhtnoth* (Gr.) 110 Boȝan wæron bysiȝe. *c* **1750** SHENSTONE *Ruin'd Ab.* 15 Birds.. With busy pinion skim the.. wave. **1813** SCOTT *Rokeby* I. iii, Grief was busy in his breast. **1827** CARLYLE *Transl.*, *Libussa* (1874) 63 The screeching of the busy saw. **1855** H. REED *Lect. Eng. Lit.* iv. (1878) 143 Time is busy in the work of change. **1863** KINGLAKE *Crimea* (1876) I. vii. 104 For many days rumour was busy. **1876** GREEN *Short Hist.* vi. §3 (1882) 290 Busy as was Caxton's printing-press.

b. Of a telephone line: engaged; *busy tone*: the signal indicating that a line is engaged.

1893 KEENAN & RILEY *Transmitted Word* iv. 69 In this way.. the operator.. knows if the line is 'busy'. **1894** *Jrnl. Electr. Engin.* XXIII. 58 The operator has rarely to say, 'Wire engaged', or 'Busy', which is the common expression. *Ibid.* 63 False busy signals were frequently received. Now a third wire and an automatic restoring indicator has made the busy test reliable. **1914** W. ATKINS *Princ. Automatic Teleph.* 27 If all the lines are engaged the wipers will rotate to this busy-tone circuit. **1921** *Conquest* II. 127/2 The 'busy tone' is sent back to the calling subscriber if the line he wants is busy.

†**3.** Occupied to the full or to the limit of one's powers: in phrase *to be busy to do* (a thing): to be fully occupied with it alone, to have enough to do *to*... Obs. (Cf. ALBYSI.)

c **1386** CHAUCER *Knts. T.* 1584 Swich strif.. Bitwixe Venus.. And Mars.. That Iuppiter was bisy it to stente. **1387** TREVISA *Higden* Rolls Ser. IV. 453 þe Est ȝate.. was so hevy of sound bras þat twenty men were besy i-now for to tende it. *c* **1400** *Destr. Troy* 10388 þe kyng.. harmyt hym sore, þat bisi was þe buerne to bide in his sadill.

4. a. Constantly or habitually occupied; full of business, always employed. Also of things: Constantly in motion or activity.

c **1205** LAY. 2837 He wes a swiðe bisi [**1275** busi] mon. *c* **1386** CHAUCER *Knts. T.* 633 (Harl. MS. 7334) The busy [*v.r.* bisy, besye, besy, bysy, besi] larke, messager of daye. **1548** LATIMER *Serm. Ploughers* (Arb.) 38 No Lordelie loyterer.. but a busie ploughe man. **1628** EARLE *Microcosm.* (Arb.) 34 The busie mans recreation, the idle mans businesse. **1642** T. TAYLOR *God's Judgem.* I. I. xv. 42 A busie-doer in setting up stakes for the burning of poore Martyrs. **1702** ROWE *Amb. Step-Moth.* I. i. 220 The Etherial Energy That busie restless Principle. **1814** SCOTT *Wav.* I. viii. 102 Curiosity, the busiest passion of the idle. **1831** CARLYLE *Sart. Res.* I. iii. (1871) 10 A most busy brain. *Mod.* How can so busy a man find time for visiting?

†**b.** Devoted to business; diligent, active, industrious. *Obs.*

c **1470** HENRY *Wallace* III. 390 He in wer was besy, wycht and wyss. *c* **1500** *Lancelot* 2449 He was bissy and was deligent.

5. In bad sense: Active in what does not concern one; prying, inquisitive, meddlesome, officious; restless, fussy, importunate. Cf. BUSYBODY.

c **1400** MAUNDEV. xxix. 295 Thei asked him [Alisandre], whi he was so proud and so fierce and so besy. *c* **1475** *Lerne or be L.* 2 in *Babees Bk.* (1868) 9 To Bolde, ne to Besy, ne Bourde nat to large. **1530** PALSGR. 306/1 Besy, malapert or medlyng in maters, *entremetteux*. **1580** BARET *Alv.* B 1585 A Busie man: a medler in all matters. **1679** *Trials Green, etc. for Murder of Sir E. Godfrey* 14 He was a busie man, and.. would do a great deal of mischief. **1740–61** MRS. DELANY *Life & Corr.* (1862) III. 299 That little busy, mischievous fiend, jealousy. **1809–10** COLERIDGE *Friend* (1865) 55 A busy and inquisitorial tyranny.

†**6. a.** Solicitous, anxious, uneasy; careful, attentive (see note under 1). Of desires, prayers, etc.: Earnest, eager, importunate. *Obs.*

c **1380** WYCLIF *Wks.* (1880) 362 Bissy study and contemplacyon. *c* **1391** CHAUCER *Astrol.* Prol., Thy bisi preyere.. to lerne the tretis of the astrelabie. **1406** OCCLEVE *Misrule* 25 My grief and bisy smert. **1413** LYDG. *Pylgr. Sowle* IV. xxiv. 70 Besy entendement to that that she techeth. **1483** *Cath. Angl.* 29/1 To make besy, *solicitare*.

†**b.** phr. *to do one's busy pain* (*diligence*, *cure*): to exert oneself diligently, to do what one can. *Obs.* Cf. BUSINESS 8.

c **1387** CHAUCER *Truth* 108 Do your bysy peyne To wasshe away our cloudeful offense. *c* **1460** J. RUSSELL *Bk. Nurture* in *Babees Bk.* (1868) 199 My copy.. whiche to drawe out [I] haue do my besy diligence. **1502** ARNOLDE *Chron.* (1811) 238 This lytil yle.. For to repayre, do ay thy besy cure.

7. Of actions, employments, conditions, etc.: Energetically carried on; pursued with vigour; active; that keeps one constantly occupied.

1548 LATIMER *Serm. Ploughers* (Arb.) 24 Right prelatynge is busye labourynge. **1718** POPE *Iliad* XVI. 778 On every side the busy combat grows. **1815** L. HUNT *Notes on Feast of Poets* 33 Engaged in the busier pursuits. **1837** HT. MARTINEAU *Soc. in Amer.* II. 338 The busiest.. concerns of life. *a* **1875** KINGSLEY *Lit. & Gen. Ess.* xii. (1880) 353 Here and there a stray gleam of sunlight.. awoke into busy life the denizens of the water. **1872** YEATS *Growth Comm.* 143 A busy trade in timber.

†**8. a.** Of things: Involving much work or trouble; elaborate, intricate, 'curious.' *Obs.*

1441 *Lett. patent Hen. VI re Eton Coll.* in *Liber Cantabrig.* (1855) 390 Curious works of entayle and busie mouldings. **1536** J. HUSCE in *Lisle Papers* XII. 53 It [cushion to be worked] shall be very busy because of diversity of colours. **1542** UDALL *Erasm. Apoph.* 230 b, Alexander perceiuyng the [Gordian] knotte to bee ouer busie to bee vn-dooen with his handes. *Ibid.* 51 b, Buisie and sumptuous buildynges. **1577** tr. *Bullinger's Decades* (1592) 332 The manner of consecrating them, is far more large and busie. **1615** CROOKE *Body of Man* 925 The History of the Bones is a busie piece of Worke.

b. Of ornamentation: full of detail. Of a picture, photograph, etc.: having much or excessive background detail.

1903 *Burlington Mag.* III. 86/1 The decoration, in dealers' language, being too 'busy' for broad effects. **1909** *Athenæum* 1 May 535/3 His pictures.. look a little 'busy', and ask to be displayed.. with.. reasonable relief of bare space. **1909** MRS. H. WARD *Daphne* v. 99 The ceilings spoilt, the decorations 'busy', pretentious, overdone.

9. Of times and places: Full of business, stir, or activity.

1697 DRYDEN *Virg. Georg.* IV. 26 For thy Bees a quiet Station find.. And plant.. Wild Olive Trees.. before the busie Shop. **1814** BYRON *Lara* I. i, Bright faces in the busy hall. **1832** MACAULAY *Armada* 36 That time of slumber was as bright and busy as the day. **1871** MORLEY *Crit. Misc.* Ser. I. (1878) 215 The busy world of men.

10. That indicates activity or business.

1632 MILTON *Allegro* 118 The busy hum of men. **1702** ROWE *Amb. Step-Moth.* I. i. 299 Each busie face we meet. **1716** LADY M. W. MONTAGUE *Lett.* I. i. 8 People, with.. busy faces. *Mod.* We were surprised at the busy aspect of the village.

11. *Comb.*, as ***busy-brained***, ***-fingered***, ***-headed***, ***-tongued***, adjs. (often in unfavourable sense). Also †**busy-head** = BUSYBODY; **busy-idle** *a.*, busily employed about trifles (so ***busy idleness***); **busy-idler**, a person so employed; **busy Lizzie**, any of various house plants of the family Balsamaceæ, *Impatiens sultani* or *I. holstii* or hybrids of these two species.

1572 J. MAITLAND *Agst. Sklanderous Toungs*, Gif *bissie-branit bodeis yow bakbyte. **1579** TOMSON *Calvin's Serm. Tim.* 658/2 If wee be more busie brained then we shoulde be. *a* **1577** SIR T. SMITH *Commonw. Eng.* (1633) 217 For what will not *busie-heads and lovers of trouble.. invent? **1603** DAVIES *Microcosm.* 57 (D.) Many a busie-head.. Put in their heads how they may compasse crownes. **1583** STUBBES *Anat. Abus.* II. 60 These *busie heded astronomers, and curious serching astrologers. **1633** *Costlie Whore* IV. ii. in Bullen *O. Plays* IV, A plague upon this busie-headed rabble! **1823** LAMB *Elia* Ser. I. xx. (1865) 159 These *busy-idle diversions. **1880** BERTHA THOMAS *Violin-Player* I. ii. 45 He amused himself in carving wooden figures.. and other busy-idle ways. **1822** T. MITCHELL *Aristoph.* II. 18 A sort of ennuyé, triste, pitiable *busy-idler. **1956** X. FIELD *House Plants* 79 *Impatiens*.. gathered nicknames, and among them were Patient Lucy, Patience Plant or just *Busy Lizzie. **1970** *Woman's Own* 21 Mar. 23/1 The table where the variegated busy lizzie fought for living-space with the telephone. **1878** BOSW. SMITH *Carthage* 255 *Busy-tongued rumour passed from mouth to mouth.

busy ('bɪzɪ), *v.* Forms: 1 **bysȝian**, **bisȝian**, **bysiȝan**, 4 **besien**, **bisien**, **bisie**, **bysi**, **bisy**, 4–6 **besy**, 5 **besye**, 5–6 **busye**, 5–7 **busie**, 6 **bussy**, **bysye**, 5– **busy**. [OE. *bisȝian*, *bysȝian*, f. *bisiȝ* BUSY *a.*]

1. *trans.* To employ with constant attention; to engage or occupy assiduously; to keep busy (persons, employments, or objects of attention).

a **1000** *Proem to Ælfred's Boeth.*, For þæm.. maniȝfealdum weoruldbisȝum þe hine.. bisȝodan. **1530** PALSGR. 451/2, I besy, I set aworke or I put in busynesse. *Ibid.* 455/2, I bysye my body. **1587** GOLDING *De Mornay* i. 7 Thou.. busiest all thy wits about it. *a* **1698** TEMPLE *Ess. Poetry* Wks. 1731 I. 241 Before the Discourses.. of Philosophers began to busy.. the Grecian Wits. **1724** SWIFT *Drapier's Lett.* Wks. 1755 V. II. 95 To busy my head and my hands to the loss of my time. **1871** R. ELLIS *Catullus* xl. 5 Wouldst thou busy the breath of half the people?

b. *refl.* (The most usual construction.) Const. *inf.* (*obs.*), *with*, *in*, *about*.

c **1000** *O.E. Hom.* (Thorpe) II. 406 (Bosw.) Se man biþ heriȝendlic, ðe mid godum weorcum hine sylfne bysȝaþ. *c* **1340** *Cursor M.* 23048 (Trin.) þei.. bisieden hem to pleisen hym. *c* **1400** *Destr. Troy* 9306 Achilles.. to bryng hit aboute besit hym sore. **1530** PALSGR. 895 My self.. whiche.. have besyed me.. to teche.. many.. princes and princesses. **1655** FULLER *Ch. Hist.* II. ii. §97 He busied himself in Toyes and Trifles. **1736** BUTLER *Anal.* II. vii. 353 To how little purpose those persons busy themselves. **1851** HELPS *Comp. Solit.* iii. (1874) 46 He busied himself about many worldly things. **1856** KANE *Arct. Expl.* II. ii. 33 Petersen began.. to busy himself with his wardrobe. **1876** GREEN *Short Hist.* ii. §5 (1882) 79 The King.. busied himself in the erection of numerous castles. **1878** BROWNING *La Saisiaz* 64 Busy thee for ill or good.

c. in *passive*. Const. as in b.

c **1000** *Colloq. Monast.* (Thorpe) 18 (Bosw.) Ic eom bysȝod on sange. **1526** *Pilgr. Perf.* W. de W. (1531) 58 Be thou neuer more than nedeth.. busyed or troubled in the defautes or offences of other. **1623** BINGHAM *Xenophon* 85 That the enemie might be busied on all sides. **1758** JOHNSON *Idler* No. 4 ¶7 Every tongue is busied in solicitation. **1868** E. EDWARDS *Ralegh* I. xviii. 361 Ralegh was busied.. with his official duties.

d. *trans.* To occupy (time) fully. *rare.*

1629 FORD *Lover's Mel.* I. i. (1811) 125 Him.. whose study Had busied many hours. **1802** W. TAYLOR in Robberds *Mem.* I. 431 Two elections.. which busied time and idea.

†**2.** To trouble the body (only in OE.) or mind; to afflict, worry, disturb, perplex. *Obs.*

a **1000** *Metr. Boeth.* xxii. 30 (Gr.) þæs lichoman leahtras and hefiȝnes.. oft bysiȝen monna modsefan. *c* **1000** *Whale* (Gr.) 51 Hine hungor bysȝaþ. *c* **1000** *Sax. Leechd.* I. 82 Gif se lichoma hwær mid hefiȝlicre hæto sy gebysȝod. *c* **1325** *E.E. Allit. P.* A. 268, & busyez þe aboute a raysoun bref. *c* **1380** WYCLIF *Serm.* v. Sel. Wks. I. 13 It is no nede to bisie us what hiȝt Tobies hound. **1591** *Troub. Raigne K. John* (1611) 61 That were to busie men with doubts.

†**b.** To disturb, agitate (a material object). *Obs.*

c **1374** CHAUCER *Boeth.* (1868) 8 The causes whennes þe sounyng wyndes.. bisien þe smoþe water of the see.

3. *intr.* (? for *refl.*). To be busy, occupy oneself, take trouble (now *rare*).

c **1340** *Gaw. & Gr. Knt.* 1066 Naf I now to busy, bot bare þre dayez. **1382** WYCLIF *Luke* x. 40 Martha bisyede aboute moche seruyce. *c* **1450** *Merlin* xiii. (1877) 201 Oon part

bisied for the rescew. **1573** G. Harvey *Letter-bk.* (1884) 132 Chaos, whereon I bussid over longe. **1582** Batman *Barth. De P.R.* 201 b/2 Euery part [of the earth]..busieth with his owne weight to come to the middle of yᵉ earth. **1878** Besant & Rice *Celia's Arb.* III. xiv. 218 She..fell to busying about my pillows.

busybody (ˈbɪzɪˌbɒdɪ). [f. busy *a.* 5 + body *sb.*]

a. An officious or meddlesome person; one who is improperly busy in other people's affairs.

1526 Tindale 1 *Pet.* iv. 15 Se that none of you suffre..as a busybody in other mens matters. **1530** Palsgr. 423/2 He his a busye body, *il est entre-metteux.* **1570** Dee *Math. Pref.* 46 Vaine pratling busie bodies. **1679** Prance *Addit. Narr. Pop. Plot* 40 The Jesuites, who are the great *Polypragmons*, or Busie-bodies. **1710** Palmer *Proverbs* 356 A busiebody burns his own fingers. **1847** Disraeli *Tancred* vi. xi. 480 The most energetic men in Europe are mere busybodies. **1875** Jowett *Plato* (ed. 2) III. 56 The habit of being a busybody and of doing another man's business.

b. *transf.* A mirror attached to a building, reflecting a view of the street, etc. *U.S.*

1892 *Outing* (U.S.) Mar. 487/1 Only a 'tell-tale mirror'—otherwise 'a busybody'—set at a tantalizing angle outside the window. **1942** C. Morley *Thorofare* xxxv. 159 One of those telltale mirrors called 'busybodies' projecting from a three-sided bay upstairs.

Hence **busybody** *v.*, (*a*) *intr.*, to be or behave like a busybody, to interfere, also with *about*; (*b*) *trans.*, to meddle in, concern oneself improperly in (*rare*); **busybodied** *a.*, of the nature of a busybody, meddlesome (*rare*); **busybodying**, *vbl. sb.*, acting the busybody; *ppl. a.* acting as a busybody; **busybodyish**; **busybodyism**; **busybodyness**.

1655 Fuller *Ch. Hist.* ii. iv. §23 It is not out of Curiosity, or Busybodinesse, to be medling in other mens Lines. **1812** G. Colman *Br. Grins, Lady of Wr.* ii. xvii, The busybodied, brainless knight. **1828** J. Wilson in *Blackw. Mag.* XXIII. 129 Curiosity..and a habit of busybodyism. *a* **1849** Poe *Myst. Marie Roget* Wks. (1872) 226 Romantic busybodyism. **1857** *Chamb. Jrnl.* XX. 427 The whole system of busy-bodying and scandal-mongering. **1863** Mrs. C. Clarke *Shaks. Char.* vi. 160 A fussy, busy-bodying old woman. **1865** Carlyle *Fredk. Gt.* III. x. ii. 234 A rather impudent busybodyish fellow. **1882** *Fraser's Mag.* XXVI. 53 Merely the result of..a sort of intellectual busybodyness. **1920** G. Bell *Let.* 29 Nov. (1927) II. xix. 576 All the busybodies come in to say what they're busybodying and have to be listened to. **1939** A. Thirkell *Brandons* xi. 306 Lady Norton is always busybodying about her nieces. **1966** 'M. Innes' *Bloody Wood* i. vii. 58 'Did I see you trying to get some sense out of Diana Page?'.. 'I did have a slight impulse to busybody.' **1978** I. Murdoch *Sea* 270 Gilbert, bursting with curiosity, was longing to busybody about. **1978** *Washington Post* 16 Jan. A20 Some critics..have expressed anxiety that the federal government will..once again be..busybodying people's lives.

†ˈ**busyful**, *a. Obs.* In 5 bisi-. [? f. *bisi*, busy *sb.*¹ + -ful.] Elaborate, made with much work.

1340 *Ayenb.* 226 Loȝe cloþinge naȝt proud ne bisiuol.

†ˈ**busyhede.** *Obs.* In 4 bisi-, bisy-, bysy-, bysihed, -hede. [f. busy *a.* + -head.] **a.** State or quality of being busy; occupation, labour; care, anxiety. **b.** Curiosity, inquisitiveness. **c.** Elaborateness, 'curiousness'.

(Frequent in Ayenb.; scarcely found elsewhere.)

c **1300** *K. Alis.* 3 Bisyhed, care, and sorowe, Is with mony uche a-morowe. **1340** *Ayenb.* 55 Þe bysihede of glotuns þet ne zecheþ bote to þe delit of hare zuelȝ. *Ibid.* 164 Alle þe bisyhedes and þe greate niedes of þe wordle. *Ibid.* 228 Non ne wolde..zeche uairhede ne bisihede of robes..bote yef he ne wende to by yzoȝe of þe uolke. *Ibid.* 231 Ydele bysyhede of ziȝþe of hyerþe and of speche.

busying (ˈbɪzɪɪŋ), *vbl. sb.* and *ppl. a.* [f. busy *v.* + -ing.] **A.** *vbl. sb.* The action of the verb busy. **B.** *ppl. a.* That makes busy.

1398 Trevisa *Barth. De P.R.* xiv. ii. (1495) 215 a/2 Þᵗ besyeng and Inclynacon of partyes. **1656** S. H. *Gold. Law* 58 A world of other busying performances.

busyish (ˈbɪzɪɪʃ), *a.* [f. busy *a.* + -ish¹.] Somewhat busy.

1861 Clough *Poems & Prose Rem.* (1869) I. 268 Cauterets ..is a busyish water-place.

[**busyless**, *a.* (A conjectural reading of Theobald 1726 in Shaks. *Tempest* iii. i. 15 where the folio of 1623 has 'busie lest'.)]

busyn, var. of buysine, *Obs.*, trumpet.

busyness (ˈbɪzɪnɪs). [f. busy *a.* + -ness: a modern formation on *busy*, the already existing word *business* having acquired different meaning and pronunciation.] Busy state or quality; = business I, and next.

1849 Thoreau *Week* 380 Behind every man's busy-ness there should be a level of undisturbed serenity. **1868** Mrs. Whitney *P. Strong* vii, The bright brisk busy-ness of the squirrel. **1868** G. Macdonald *Seaboard Par.* I. xi. 164 In the midst of the world of light and busy-ness. **1880** *Macm. Mag.* May 53 An interesting example of the busyness of rumour. **1929** J. Buchan *Courts of Morning* iii. 351 It was a week of desperate busyness. **1961** A. Wilson *Old Men at Zoo* vii. 323 Nothing could chill the warmth I generated in my cocoon of busyness.

†ˈ**busyship.** *Obs.* In 3 bisi-, 4 besi-. [f. busy *a.* + -ship.] Busy state or quality; business, activity, exercise; = prec.

a **1225** *Ancr. R.* 384 *Exercitatio corporis ad modicum ualet* ..Licomliche bisischipe is to lutel wurð. **1393** Gower *Conf.* II. 39 What hast thou done of besiship To love.

†ˈ**busyty.** *Obs. rare*⁻¹. In 6 besyte. [f. busy + -ty; after words from F. and L. like *veri-ty*, *jolli-ty*.] Officiousness, fussiness.

c **1511** Colet *Serm. Conf. & Ref.* in *Phenix* (1708) II. 4 The Besyte and Wantonness of Officials.

ˈ**busywork.** orig. and chiefly *U.S.* Also busy-work, busy work. [f. busy *a.* + work *sb.*] Work performed simply to keep (oneself) occupied; repetitive or routine activity.

1910 *Primary Educ.* Feb. 82/1 (*heading*) Practical busy work. **1930** *Grade Teacher* Sept. 30/1 The old term 'busy work,' now an expression in bad repute, was a quite honest label of what was too often seat work of this character. **1944** L. Mumford *Condition of Man* ix. 307 The utilitarians took too much pride in their limitations, and buried too many ultimate problems in the mere routine of busy work. **1960** C. Geertz *Relig. Java* vi. 72 The detailed busy-work of the funeral, the politely formal social intercourse with the neighbors pressing in from all sides..are supposed to carry one through the grief process evenly and without severe emotional disturbance. **1963** B. Friedan *Feminine Mystique* x. 245 The time-filling busywork of suburban house and community. **1974** H. L. Foster *Ribbin'* vi. 243 Their students are controlled and supposedly educated with worksheets, notes for copying, and other fruitless forms of 'busy-work'.

but (bʌt), *prep.*, *conj.*, *adv.* Forms: 1 be-útan (only as *prep.* or *adv.*), bútan, -on, -un, búta, búte, 2–3 buten, 2–4 bute, (2–3 boten, 2–4 bote, 3–7 *Sc.* bot), 3– but. [The OE. adv. and prep. *be-útan*, *bútan*, *búta*, 'on the outside, without', of which the strong form regularly became in ME. *bouten*, *boute*, bout, as adv. and prep., was phonetically weakened to *bŭten*, *bŭte*, *but*, as a conjunction, with uses arising immediately out of the prepositional sense. In some of these uses, the conjunction is, even in modern English, not distinctly separated from the preposition: the want of inflexions in substantives, and the colloquial use of *me*, *us*, for *I*, *we*, etc., as complemental nominatives in the pronouns, making it uncertain whether *but* is to be taken as governing a case. In other words 'nobody else went but me (or I)' is variously analysed as = 'nobody else went except me' and 'nobody else went except (that) I (went)', and as these mean precisely the same thing, both are pronounced grammatically correct. (See Latham, *Eng. Lang.* ed. 1850, p. 483; also F. Hall, *Modern English* 104, 303, *notes*.) In colloquial use *me*, *us*, etc., are more common than *I*, *we*, etc.; in literary use, the point is usually avoided by substituting *except*, *save*, or otherwise altering the phraseology. In certain phrases the conjunctional *but* develops, by ellipsis of a preceding negative, the adverbial sense 'only': see C. 6 below. Otherwise the modern use of *but* as a preposition or adverb is only Scotch; the form bout which was the regular ME. repr. of OE. *bútan* as prep. and adv. having become obsolete by 1500.]

A. *prep.* †**1.** Outside of, without.

Only in OE. (see bout), exc. in mod.Sc. in such phrases as *but the house*: see but *adv.* 1 e.

2. Without, apart from, unprovided with, void of. (Used in Sc. since 14th c. but now obsolescent. The ME. was *boute*, bout, q.v.

[**894–1500** see bout.] **1375** Barbour *Bruce* v. 91 Till the toun soyn cumin ar thai Sa preuely, bot noyss making. **1423** Jas. I *King's Q.* viii, And doun I lay bot ony tarying. **1497** *Minute Town-Counc. Edinb.* in *Phil. Trans.* XLII. 421 Thai sall be banist but favors. **1533** Bellenden *Livy* iv. (1822) 321 The samin wes done but ony respect to juris or lawe. *a* **1644** Laud *Serm.* (1847) 127 They..joy in their very tears to see they cannot call but crying. **1724** Ramsay *Tea-t. Misc.* (1733) II. 163 I'd tak my Katie but a gown Bare-footed in her little coatie. **1794** Burns *Auld Man* ii, My trunk of eild, but buss or bield Sinks in time's wintry rage. **1810** Tannahill *Poems* (1846) 21 Safe but skaith or scar.

3. Leaving out, barring, with the exception of, except, save. Distinctly a preposition in OE.

979–82 *O.E. Chron.* (MS. Cott. Tib. A iii) Þa feng Eadmund to..and heold seofoðe healf ȝear butan ii nihtum. *a* **1000** *Menolog.* 87 (Gr.) Ymb first wucan butan anre niht.

In later times, the original prepositional and later conjunctional uses are so inseparable that the whole are treated under C.

B. *adv.* **1.** Without, outside.

†**a.** in general sense, with forms *bútan*, *búta*, *bute*, *boute*: see bout.

b. spec. in *Sc.* with sense: Outside the house (of motion as well as rest); in *mod.Sc.* in or into the outer or more public apartment of the house, in the ante-room or kitchen: opposed to ben, q.v. (Now less common than *ben*.)

c **1450** Henryson *Mor. Fab.* 14 Her den..Full beenlie stuffed both butte and ben, Of Beines and Nuttes, Pease, Rye and Wheat. **1513** Douglas *Æneis* iv. xii. 53 Flambe.. Spreding fra thak to thak, baith but and ben. **1568** *Wife of Aucht.* iv. in *Bannatyne Poems* (1770) 216 Aye as ye gang but and ben. *a* **1646** A. Henderson *Let. Chas. I*, Wks. 160 It cannot be brought But, that is not the Ben. **1787** Burns *Lett.* lii. Wks. (Globe) 334, I can hardly stoiter but and ben. **1827** J. Wilson *Noct. Ambr.* Wks. 1855 I. 357 Bring but a bottle o' primrose wine. *Mod.Sc.* Gae but, and wait while I am ready.

c. as *adj.* Outside, outer, exterior: as in ***but end***.

1619 Sir R. Boyle in *Lismore Papers* (1886) I. 219 The but end of a great stone howse that was never fynished. **1862** R. H. Story in *Athenæum* 30 Aug. 270 He conducted me to the but end of the mansion.

d. as *sb.* The outer room of a house, into which the outer door opens. A ***but-and-ben***: a house having an outer and an inner apartment; a two-roomed house.

1724 Ramsay *Tea-T. Misc.* (1733) I. 29 A house is butt and benn. **1786** Burns *Calf* iv, Some kind, connubial dear, Your but-and-ben adorns. **1859** R. Burton *Centr. Afr.* in *Jrnl. R.G.S.* XXIX. 134 Each house has two rooms, a 'but' and a 'ben' separated by a screen of corn-canes..The but, used as parlour, kitchen, and dormitory, opens upon the central square; the ben..serves for sleeping and for a storeroom. **1861** Ramsay *Remin.* iii. (ed. 18) 60 A cosy but, and a canty ben. *c* **1870** R. Buchanan *Sutherland's Pansies* iii, I found him settled in this but and ben.

e. As *prep.*

1768 Ross *Helenore* 74 (Jam.) Lindy..looking butt the floor, Sees Bydby standing just within the door. *Mod.Sc.* Gang but the house and see who is there, and come ben again and tell me. The mistress happened to be but the house [*i.e.* out in the kitchen] at the time.

2. In sense: Only. An elliptic development of the conjunction: see C. 6.

C. *conj.*

General Scheme. I. In a simple sentence. II. In a complex sentence. III. In a compound sentence, or introducing a consequent sentence. IV. In phrases.

I. In a simple sentence; introducing a word or phrase (rarely a clause) which is excepted from the general statement: Without, with the exception of, except, save.

1. After universal statements with *all*, *every*, *any*.

†**a.** In OE. construed as a *prep.* with dative. (See A. 3.)

a **1000** *Beowulf* 705 (Z.) Ealle buton anum. *c* **1000** Ælfric *Job* (Ettm.) iv. 15 Ealle þa þing..buton þam anum.

b. In ME. and modern use weakened to a conjunction, as in 3 and 4.

(*a*) This is shown before a nominative pronoun.

c **1460** *Towneley Myst.* 23 Alle shalle be slayn but oonely we. *a* **1835** Mrs. Hemans *Casabianca* 2 The boy stood on the burning deck, Whence all but he had fled. **1872** J. H. Newman *Disc. & Arguments* 6, I am one among a thousand; all of them wrong but I. [*Colloq.* also, 'but me'.]

(*b*) Otherwise, on account of the levelling of inflexions, the case is not shown, or may be independent of *but* (quot. *a* 1000), or *but* introduces a phrase.

a **1000** *Panther* 16 (Gr.) Se is æthwam freond butan dracan anum. *a* **1300** *Cursor M.* 763 Sua do we [ete] Of al þe tres bot of an. **1423** Jas. I *King's Q.* 94 With wingis bright, all plumyt, bot his face. **1596** *Edw. III*, ii. i. 13 Wisdom is foolishness, but in her tongue. **1599** Nashe *Christ's T.* 57 b, If wee did imitate ought but the imperfections of Beastes. *a* **1618** Raleigh *Verses* (Mildmay MS.) Love all eaten out but in outward showe. **1681** Dryden *Abs. & Achit.* 56 And thought that all but Savages were Slaves. **1802** Mar. Edgeworth *Moral T.* (1816) I. ix. 68, I can bear any thing but contempt. **1838** Thirlwall *Greece* V. xxxix. 81 It [an oath] was taken..by all but the Eleans. *Mod.* Anything but that! Any one but a fool would understand. Anywhere but in England. At any time but the present. Everybody but you has signed.

c. ***all but***: everything short of. Hence, *advb.* Almost, very nearly, well nigh: see all A. 8 b.

2. After *only*, or a superlative. Const. as in 1 b.

1580 North *Plutarch* 672 The first time that ever the two Kings were of one House but then. *Mod.* The only person I have met but you. He is last but one in the class.

3. After interrogatives (*who*, *what*, etc.) *but* was already in OE. construed as a conjunction, not affecting the case of the following sb. or pronoun, which depends upon the expansion of its own clause. This appears to have been universal in ME., and is regular now. Only rarely in modern times is *but* treated as a preposition governing the word.

a. With pronouns showing the case.

a **1000** *Crist* 695 (Gr.) Hwæt sindon þa ȝimmas butan god sylfe. *c* **1380** Wyclif *Serm.* Sel. Wks. I. 279 Who shulde be dampned but þou? **1782** Cowper *Gilpin* 113 Away went Gilpin—who but he? **1777** Sheridan *Sch. Scand.* 3. 181 Come—for, but thee, who seeks the Muse? *Mod.* Is there any one in the house but she? (*or* but her?) Who could have done it but he? (*or* but him?).

b. Otherwise the case is not shown, or is objective independently of *but*.

c **1300** *Cato Major* iv. v, What prou may þi catel do But hele wol with þe dele? *c* **1440** *Gesta Rom.* (1878) 123 What dude he but yede, and purveyde him of iij. cautils. **1576** Gascoigne *Steel Gl.* (Arb.) 60 What causeth this, but

greedy golde to get? **1601** WEEVER in *Shaks. C. Praise* 42 Who but Brutus then was vicious? **1790** BURKE *Fr. Rev.* 339 Who but the most desperate adventurers . . could at all have thought of [it]. **1872** BLACK *Adv. Phaeton* xxiv. 336 What must she do but immediately turn to the Lieutenant? *Mod.* Whom could he mean but me? Why have they come but to annoy us?

4. So after a negative, expressed or implied. (Here *but* regularly translates L. *nisi*, and may be explained as 'unless, if not'. It has been treated as a conjunction from the earliest times.)

†**a.** With sb. or pron. as compl. to *be*: see 6 a.

c **893** K. ÆLFRED *Oros.* I. i, þær næran butan twegen dælas. *a* **1225** *Leg. Kath.* 282 þer nis bot a Godd. *c* **1240** *Ureisun* in *Lamb. Hom.* 185 Aȝein hwam þe sunne nis boten a schadwe. **1340** *Ayenb.* 258 þe ssredinge þet ne ssolde by bote a tokne . . of þe ssame of his vader. **1393** LANGL. *P. Pl.* C. I. 205 Ther þe cat nys bote a kyton. *Ibid.* xx. 149 Alle þre nys bote o god.

b. With a sb. or pronoun whose case depends on its own clause. (*a*) The case is now shown only in a personal pronoun.

a **1000** *Phœnix* (Gr.) 358 Ne wat ænig butan metod ana. *a* **1000** *Seafarer* (Gr.) 18 Ic ne gehyrde butan hlimman sæ. *c* **1000** *Ags. Gosp.* Matt. xi. 27 Nan mann ne can þone sunu butun fædyr [*Lind.* buta ðe fæder; *Hatt.* buto se fader; Vulg. *nisi pater*]. *c* **1230** *Hali Meid.* 21 Ne moten nane bute heo hoppen ne singen. **1330** R. BRUNNE *Chron.* 183 No body bot he alone vnto þe Cristen cam. ? *c* **1370** *Robt. K. Cicyle* 61 There was lefte noon but he allone. *c* **1380** WYCLIF *Sel. Wks.* III. 45 Othir God is noon but I. *c* **1430** *Syr. Tryam.* 1166 Ther schalle no man fyght but y. **1560** A. L. tr. *Calvin's Foure Serm.* (1574) 48 There is none but he alone to save us. **1615** tr. *De Montfart's Surv. E. Indies* 26 None but he and his men can tell, what is become of them. *a* **1842** ARNOLD *Fragm. on Church* (1845) 223 None but they . . have a right to rule in the Church.

(*b*) Otherwise, on account of the levelling of inflexions, the case is not shown, or would be objective independently of *but* (as in quot. 1300, 1599, 1808).

1154 *O.E. Chron.* (Laud MS.) an. 1135 Durste nan man sei to him naht bute god. *c* **1200** *Moral Ode* in *Trin. Coll. Hom.* 223 Non ne cnoweð hine alse wel buten one drihte. *a* **1300** *Cursor M.* 961, I wat bot þe haf i na frend. *c* **1380** WYCLIF *Sel. Wks.* I. 94 Love we God . . and drede we noo thing but hym. **1599** GREENE *George a Gr.* (1861) 256 He is the man and she will none but him. **1618** J. TAYLOR (Water P.) *Penniless Pilgr.* (1883) 23 Nothing, (but my weary self) was bad. **1627** PERKINS *Prof. Bk.* ii. §158 (1642) 71 None speakes the same but their principall. *a* **1711** KEN *Hymnotheo* Poet. Wks. 1721 III. 7 For I Nothing but Ants about this Hill descry. **1802** MAR. EDGEWORTH *Moral T.* (1816) I. iii. 17 He wants nothing but a little common sense. **1808** J. BARLOW *Columb.* I. 30 Invoke no miracle, no Muse but thee. **1821** SHELLEY *Hellas*, Nought is but that which feels itself to be.

¶(*c*) The nominative occurs erroneously, where the construction requires the objective.

c **1430** *Syr Gener.* 902 This child hath no modre but I. **1607** TOPSELL *Four-f. Beasts* 111 They have no other King but he. *a* **1866** in Engel *Nat. Mus.* ix. 358 And I had nae mair bot hee, O.

c. With a prepositional, adverbial, infinitive, or other phrase (rarely expanded to a clause).

971 *Blickl. Hom.* 33 Nolde he him na andswerian buton mid monþwærnesse. *a* **1300** *Cursor M.* 455 He þat noght hadd bot of him. **1303** R. BRUNNE *Handl. Synne* 7939 þey do nat wrong,—but al day. **1398** TREVISA *Barth. De P.R.* III. xxi. (1495) 69 He erryth not but by happe. *c* **1400** *Rom. Rose* 292 She ne lokide but awrie, Or overthart, alle baggyngly. **1448** SHILLINGFORD *Lett.* (1871) 66 We wolde noght aggre bot to have power to arreste chanons men servants. **1609** SKENE *Reg. Maj.*, *Burrow Lawes* 129 No man sould presume to buy fish . . in any other place, bot in the Kings market. **1701** WOTTON *Hist. Rome* 401 He never us'd any Linnen or other Clothes but once. **1743** J. MORRIS *Serm.* ii. 49 Faith and hope have no aptitude to make us happy, but as they incline us to love. **1779** FORREST *Voy. N. Guinea* 246 In the streets, women seldom speak but to women. **1843** RUSKIN *Mod. Paint.* (1851) I. I. I. i. 2 No man can be really appreciated but by his equal or superior. **1884** W. C. SMITH *Kildrostan* 77 You have no choice but marry Doris now.

†**d.** *But* was strengthened by *only*. *Obs.*

c **1230** *Hali Meid.* 5 Ha nawiht ne þarf of oðer þing þenchen bute an of hire leofmon. *c* **1460** FORTESCUE *Abs. & Lim. Mon.* (1714) 42 It nedith not to . . purvey, but only for the Kyngs Hous. **1602** L. LLOYD *Confer. Lawes* 27 There was no God but onely his maister. **1682** WHELER *Journ. Greece* I. 2 No Appeal can be made, but only to the Senate. **1715** BURNET *Own Time* II. 242 They took little care of it, but only to find men who would bear the charge.

5. Negative and interrogative sentences containing a comparative (esp. *more*) were formerly followed by *but*; they now usually take *than*, or else the comparative is omitted and *but* retained; modern idiom preferring sometimes one, sometimes the other.

1440 J. SHIRLEY *Dethe K. James* (1818) 12 There be no mo kynges yn this reume bot ye and I. *c* **1500** *Rob. Hood* (Ritson) I. i. 155, I have no more but ten shillings. **1523** LD. BERNERS *Froiss.* I. cxi. 134 They . . toke their horses, wherof they had no mo but sixe. **1530** —— *Gold. Bk. M. Aurel.* Nnij b, What greatter correction shuld I haue of thy wyckednes . . but to be certain that all the lovyng ladis of Rome ar sory of thy life. **1583** GOLDING *Calvin on Deut.* xlv. 266 To bestow it vpon men which are no better but dung. **1606** G. W[ODDCOCKE] *Hist. Ivstine* 97 a, They were no better but a ragged sort of shepheards. **1644** CHILLINGWORTH *Serm.* 32 Our whole lives (if sincerely examined) would appeare, I feare, little lesse but a perpetuall lye. **1686** *Papist not Misrepr.* 21 The difference . . is no more but this. **1713** STEELE *Guardian* No. 143 ⁋5 There needed no more but to advance one step. *Mod.* There remains no more but to thank you for your courteous attention.

b. So with similar sentences containing *other*, *otherwise*, *else*; in which *but* is still sometimes retained, *esp.* after *else*, as 'Who else but he?'

971 *Blickl. Hom.* 39 Hwylc beren mænde he þonne elles buton heofona rice? *Ibid.* Hwæt mænde he þonne elles, buton þæt we gefyllon þæs þearfan wambe mid urum godum? **1495** *Act. 11 Hen. VII*, ii. § 1 Ther to have noon other sustenaunce but brede and water. **1589** PUTTENHAM *Eng. Poesie* III. xix. (Arb.) 207 What els is man but his minde? **1611** BIBLE *Pref.* 1 For none other fault but for seeking to reduce their Countrey-men to good order. **1689** SELDEN *Table T.* (1847) 149 Pleasure is nothing else but the intermission of Pain. **1713** STEELE *Guardian* No. 143 ⁋5 Had no other fault, but that of being too short. *Mod.* It is nothing else but laziness!

†**c.** After *unlike*. *Obs. rare.*

1652 ASHMOLE *Theatr. Chem.* Prol. 7 Not unlike, but the Wall-nut-Tree which . . grew in Glastenbury-Church-yard.

6. By the omission of the negative accompanying the preceding verb (see 4 a), *but* passes into the adverbial sense of: Nought but, no more than, only, merely. (Thus the earlier 'he nis but a child' is now 'he is but a child'; here north. dialects use NOBBUT = nought but, not but, 'he is nobbut a child'.)

a **1300** *Cursor M.* 4322 Bettur . . þan folu þi prai þat es bot tint. **1393** LANGL. *P. Pl.* C. XVII. 359 He comeþ but selde. *c* **1400** MAUNDEV. 157 The folk . . han but litille appetyt to mete. *c* **1440** *Anc. Cookery* in *Househ. Ord.* (1790) 465 Take rys, and gif hom but a boyle. **1512** *Act 3 Hen. VIII*, vi. Preamb., The forsaid penaltie expressed in the said Statute is but xxs. **1617** S. COLLINS *Epphata to F.T.* (1628) 239 It was impious . . but euen to touch the bodies of Saints dead. **1647** COWLEY *Mistr.*, *Spring* ii, Could they remember but last year. **1732** BERKELEY *Alciphr.* I. §3 Wks. 1871 II. 29 Do but consider this. **1766** GOLDSM. *Vic. W.* iii, Premature consolation is but the remembrancer of sorrow. **1794** BURNS (*title*) My love she's but a lassie yet. **1876** GREEN *Short Hist.* i. §3 (1882) 30 In arms the kingdom had but a single rival.

†**b.** In obsolete or dialectal use in various connected senses: Neither more nor less than, absolutely, actually, just, even. (Sometimes *but* seems merely expletive.) ***but now*** = just now, only this moment.

c **1430** *Syr Tryam.* 596 For welle y wot that y am but dede. *c* **1530** LD. BERNERS *Arth. Lyt. Bryt.* 79 Yf thei se him, they are but lost for ever. **1594** NASHE *Unfort. Trav.* 39 He tolde me but euerie thing that she and he agreed of. **1622** MABBE tr. *Aleman's Guzman d'Alf.* I. 248 He is heere (Sir) about the house, I saw him but now. **1665** BOYLE *Occas. Refl.* (1675) 37 A but plausible Argument, dress'd up in fine Similitudes. **1844** F. PAGET *Tales Village Childr.* Ser. II. (1858) 16 My poor legs how they do but tremble. **1859** BARNES *Rhymes in Dorset Dial.* II. 7 Back here, but now, the jobber John Come by.

†**c.** Formerly strengthened with *only*, which now would be used alone.

1477 EARL RIVERS *Dictes* 9, Another litil flode whiche drowned but the contre of Egipte onely. *c* **1532** LD. BERNERS *Huon* lxxxviii. 280, I had but alonely my swerde in my hande. **1598** BARNFIELD *Poems* (Arb.) 112 They are indeed but onely meere Illusions. **1605** SHAKS. *Macb.* v. viii. 40 He onely liu'd but till he was a man. **1644** MILTON *Areop.* (Arb.) 36, I find but only two sorts of writings.

7. *elliptically*: Any but, aught but, anything else than, other than, otherwise than. (Often after *ever*, *never*.)

1523 LD. BERNERS *Froiss.* I. xviii. 20 Fewe had slepte but lytle, and yet they had sore traualed the daye before. **1596** *Edw. III*, IV. i. 50 Never to be but Edwards faithful friend. **1610** SHAKS. *Temp.* I. ii. 118, I should sinne To thinke but Noblie of my Grand-mother. **1644** MILTON *Areop.* (Arb.) 56 It cannot be but a dishonour and derogation to the author. **1794** BURNS *How long & dreary is the night*, How can I be but eerie? **1832** *Blackw. Mag.* XXXII. 166 He never took but one voyage. **1864** R. PAUL *Let.* in *Mem.* (1872) xviii. 273 You say you are tied hand and foot. You will never be but that in London.

b. After *cannot choose*. 'I cannot choose but speak' = 'I cannot help speaking'. So interrogative 'Who could choose but . . ?' (Here the infinitive phrase was sometimes expanded into a sub-ordinate clause (cf. 16); esp. after the passive *it cannot be chosen but*.)

1557 NORTH *Gueuara's Diall Pr.* (1582) 402 It cannot be chosen but wee must come before these judges, etc. *Ibid.* 412 He cannot chose but he must falle downe flat to the grounde. **1619** W. SCLATER *Exp. 1 Thess.* (1630) 295 Canst thou chuse now but say, God is in vs, of a truth? **1622** MABBE *Aleman's Guzman d'Alf.* II. 296 We could not choose but be weary with our last night's ill rest. **1676** HOBBES *Iliad* II. 240 He could not chuse but laugh. **1742** RICHARDSON *Pamela* III. 70, I could not chuse but to forgive her! **1854** LADY LYTTON *Behind Sc.* I. Pref. 12 They cannot choose but echo them.

c. After *cannot, could not, dare not*, etc., and the interrogative *who could*, etc., with ellipsis of *do*, *be*, etc. (Lat. *non possum non*.)

1549 *Bk. Com. Prayer* Coll. 15th Sund. after Tr., The frailty of man without thee cannot but fall. **1579** GOSSON *Sch. Abuse* (Arb.) 19, I cannot but commende his wisedome. **1619** W. SCLATER *Expos. 1 Thess.* (1638) 166 What Atheist dares but yield attention? **1628** BP. DAVENANT *Serm.* 35 If hee bid it stand still . . it dares not but stand. **1644** MILTON *Areop.* (Arb.) 32 It could not but much redound to the lustre of your milde and equall Government. **1705** ADDISON *Italy* Ded., It can't but be obvious to them. **1777** WATSON *Philip II* (1793) I. II. 26 Such power, and . . resources could not but appear formidable. **1812** T. JEFFERSON *Writ.* (1830) IV. 180, I cannot but be gratified by the assurance. **1832** HT. MARTINEAU *Each & All* ii. 23 He could not but try.

II. In a complex sentence; introducing the subordinate clause.

* With general sense 'except that'; the full expression being *but that*, often reduced to *but*.

†**8.** ***but that*** = Except (that), save (that). *Obs.*

a **1000** *Cædmon's Gen.* 1403 (Gr.) Egorhere eall acwealde buton þæt earce bord heold heofona frea. *c* **1000** *Ags. Gosp.* Matt. v. 13 Ne mæg [þæt sealt] to nahte, buton þæt hit sy utaworpen. *c* **1205** LAY. 31186 He wolde al þis kinelond setten an heore hond, bute þat he icleoped were king.

b. with omission of *that*.

1701 W. WOTTON *Hist. Rome* 316 Nothing would serve him, but he must imitate Alexander. **1713** STEELE *Guardian* No. 146 ⁋4 Nothing would satisfy Sir George . . but he must go into the den. **1820** H. MATTHEWS *Diary Invalid* 174 Nothing would please him but I must try on his mitres.

9. ***but that***, introducing a consideration or reason to the contrary: Except for the fact that, were it not that. (Formerly *that* was occas. omitted.)

a **1400** *Cov. Myst.* 43 (Mätz.) Myn handwerk to sle sore grevyth me, but that here synne here deth doth brewe. ? *a* **1400** *Morte Arth.* 44 Nere for joye she swounyd swythe, But as that he her helde vp ryght. **1611** SHAKS. *Cymb.* v. v. 41 And but she spoke it dying, I would not Beleeue her lips. **1628** EARLE *Microcosm.* xlvi. (Arb.) 66 Hee would be wholy a Christian, but that he is something of an Atheist. **1682** WHELER *Journ. Greece* I. 78 We had not staid here long, but the Wind expected proved a brisque South-wind. **1726** AMHERST *Terræ Fil.* xiv. 71, I need not have put the case so far, but that I was willing to shew, etc. **1795** SOUTHEY *Joan of Arc* I. 359, I too should be content to dwell in peace . . But that my country calls. **1850** SIR H. TAYLOR *Sicilian Sum.* II. iii, Each by the other would have done the like But that they lack'd the courage.

** With general sense 'if not'.

10. Introducing a condition: If not, unless, except. *arch.*

c **888** K. ÆLFRED *Boeth.* xli. §2 Ðu segst þæt Nan þing wyrþe, bute hit God wille. *c* **1000** *Ags. Ps.* vii. 12 Bute ge to him gecyrren, se deofol cweð his sweord to eow. *c* **1175** *Lamb. Hom.* 147 Ne mei na Mon me folȝen, bute he forlete al. *c* **1250** *Gen. & Ex.* 3616 Ðat folc on him ne miȝte sen But a veil wore hem bi-twen. **1388** WYCLIF *Matt.* v. 20 That but [**1382** but ȝif] ȝour riȝtfulnesse be more plenteuouse than of scribis . . ȝe schulen not entre into the kyngdom of heuenes. ? **1461** *Paston Lett.* II. 79 But I maye have helpe of my mayster and of yow, I am but lost. **1534** LD. BERNERS *Gold Bk. M. Aurel.* S vij b, He is of an yll inclinacion, but he be forced. **1721** *St. German's Doctor & Stud.* 278 No man may take the man, but he have authority from the Sheriff.

†**b.** Expanded into ***but if***. Obs. (Very common from 14th to 16th c.)

c **1200** ORMIN 1662 þatt nohht ne maȝȝ ben don . . But iff itt bee wiþþ witt. *c* **1325** *E.E. Allit. P.* B. 1110 Hov schulde þou com to his kyth bot-if þou clene were? **1393** LANGL. *P. Pl.* C. II. 184 Feith . . ys . . ded as a dore-nayle · bote yf þe dede folwe. *a* **1450** *Knt. de la Tour* ix. 13 But yef thei amende hem, the citee and the peple shulde be perysshed. **1580** SIDNEY *Arcadia* (1613) 115 He did not like that maides should once stir out of their fathers houses, but if it were to milke a cow. **1596** SPENSER *F.Q.* III. iii. 16 But if remedee Thou her afford, full shortly I her dead shall see.

11. Hence **a.** With 'It shall go hard' and phrases of the nature of a threat. 'I'd burn the house down but I'd find it', *i.e.* if I did not find it (without doing so) = even though I should have to burn the house down, I'd find it.

1530 LD. BERNERS *Arth. Lyt. Bryt.* 102, I wyll abyde here this seven yere but I will wynne it. **1628** EARLE *Microcosm.* xxxi. (Arb.) 53 It shall goe hard but he will wind in his opportunity. **1643** *Answ. Observ. W. Bridges conc. War.* 21 Hee will worke wonders but he will doe it. **1725** DE FOE *Voy. round World* (1840) 307 They would go quite up to the Andes but they would find them. **1727** —— *Secrets Invis. World* (1840) 300 I'd burn the house down but I'd find it. **1793** BURNS *Scots, wha hae* v, We will drain our dearest veins, But they shall be free! **1839** *New Monthly Mag.* LVI. 513 It shall go hard but we shall damage the theory.

b. After *it is marvel* (obs.); *it is odds*; *it is ten to one*, and the like.

1583 FULKE *Defence* (1843) 124 It is marvel but you will say, a dead body is not altogether void of strength. **1627** H. BURTON *Bait. Pope's Bull* To Rdr. 3 A thousand to one, but he will breake loosse. **1663** BP. PATRICK *Parab. Pilgr.* viii. (1668) 35 It is a thousand to one but they will find the means. **1712** *Spectator* No. 457 ⁋3 It is ten to one but my friend Peter is among them. **1713** STEELE *Guardian* No. 14 ⁋1 It is odds but you lose. **1815** *Scribbleomania* 261 It is odds but he miscarries in his suit. **1864** MISS YONGE *Trial* I. xii. 238 Ten to one but the police have got them.

c. With an asseveration after an imprecation: If . . not. *arch.* 'Beshrew me, but I shall go' = if I shall not go.

1596 SHAKS. *Merch. V.* II. vi. 52 Beshrew me but I loue her heartily. **1691** J. WILSON *Belphegor* I. iii, Beshrew me, but I should have broken my heart. **1766** GOLDSMITH *Vic. W.* vii, May this glass suffocate me, but a fine girl is worth all the priestcraft in the creation. **1775** BICKERSTAFF *Sultan* II. i, Let me die but I believe it is their dinner.

*** With general sense 'that not', L. *quin*. After negative and questioning constructions.

12. In a simple attributive clause belonging to a sb. or pronoun in the main sentence: That . . not.

c **1500** *Cocke Lorelles B.* (1843) 12 There was non that there was But he had an offyce more or lasse. **1535** COVERDALE *2 Kings* xx. 15 There is nothynge in my treasures but I haue shewed it them. **1662** H. MORE *Immort. Soul* 66 We cannot conceive of any portion of matter but it is either hard or soft. *c* **1846** SPEDDING *Even. with Rev.* (1881) Hardly a man passes by but he must add a wreath to it. **1880** *Daily Tel.* 11 Dec., There never was a reform yet propounded . . but some one pronounced it forthwith to be chimerical, extravagant, and Utopian.

b. With omission of the pronominal subject or object of the dependent sentence, so that *but* acts as a negative relative: That . . not, who . . not. (L. *quin*.)

[**1523** LD. BERNERS *Froiss.* I. cxli. 170 There departed none agayne, but that had great gyftes gyuen them.] **1556** J. HEYWOOD *Spider & F.* lii. 4 No kind of flie a liue, but was there that day. **1587** CHURCHYARD in *Mirr. Mag.* (1815) II. 490 Not one of these but gave his maister thanke. **1628** EARLE *Microcosm.* (Arb.) 71 There is no man of worth but has a piece of singularity. **1689** SELDEN *Table T.* (1847) 210 There is no Prince in Christendom but is directly a Tradesman. **1723** DE FOE *Col. Jack* (1840) 290 There was scarce a plantation near me but had some of them. **1760** GOLDSM. *Cit. W.* l, There is no work whatsoever but he can criticize. **1820** KEATS *Lamia* 665 Not a man but felt the terror in his hair. **1866** KINGSLEY *Herew.* xli. (1877) 495 Hardly one of the Frenchmen round, but . . looked on Hereward as a barbarian Englishman.

c. *But what* is sometimes erron. put for *but*: see 30.

13. Following an adjective qualified by *not so*. Cf. '*So* brave *that* he ventured', and '*not so* brave *but* (*that*) he hesitated'.

1534 LD. BERNERS *Gold. Bk. M. Aurel.* (1546) C vj b, There is nothyng that is so loste but that there is hope of recoveryng. **1579** GOSSON *Sch. Abuse* (Arb.) 50 There was neuer fort so strong, but it might be battered. **1621** BURTON *Anat. Mel.* II. 538 No garden so well tilled but some noxious weeds grow up in it. **1711** ADDISON *Spect.* No. 203 ¶6 It is impossible . . to make them so fast, but a cat . . will find a way through them. **1814** CARY *Dante* (Chandos ed.) 79 Yet 'scap'd they not so covertly, but well I mark'd Sciancato. **1883** E. GOSSE *17th Cent. Studies* 10 Lodge was not so vagrant a person but that he had married by this time.

14. Introducing an inevitable accompanying circumstance or result: So that . . not. Now generally expressed by *without* and gerund: 'you cannot look but you will see it', *i.e.* without seeing it. Formerly sometimes *but that*.

a **1400** *Cursor M.* 9654 (Laud. MS.) He may not scape where he go But him assaieþ euyr his fo. *c* **1400** MAUNDEV. 40 No Straungere comethe before him, but that he makethe him sum Promys. **1534** LD. BERNERS *Gold. Bk. M. Aurel.* (1546) M iv b, One unhappynes chaunceth not, but an nother foloweth. **1644** HEYLIN *Stumbling-bl.* in *Hist. & Misc. Tracts* 653 The Magistrate cannot be resisted, but that God is resisted, also. **1686** GOAD *Celest. Bodies* II. i. 123 You cannot dip into a Diary but you will find it. **1758** JOHNSON *Idler* No. 12 ¶4 Scarce any couple comes together, but the nuptials are declared in the newspapers with encomiums on each party. **1796** MRS. INCHBALD *Nat. & Art* xxxiii, Nor did she ever weep, but he wept too. **1835** LYTTON *Rienzi* x. vi. 422 He had never confided but he had been betrayed. *Prov.* It never rains but it pours.

†**15. a.** After *no sooner*, where modern use requires *than*. (Also *but that*.) *Obs.*

1580 SIDNEY *Arcadia* (1613) 69 Philoclea no sooner espied the lyon but that . . she leapt up, and ran to the lodge-ward. **1597** T. BEARD *Theat. God's Judgem.* (1612) 194 It was no sooner said but done. **1749** FIELDING *Tom Jones* VI. v. (1840) 72/1 No sooner acquainted my brother, but he immediately wanted to propose it. *a* **1774** GOLDSM. *Hist. Greece* (1774) I. 265 Which Nicias had no sooner notice of, but he embarked his troops.

†**b.** After *scarce, scarcely*; *not half*; *not long, not far*, and the like; where modern use requires *when* or *before*. *Obs.*

1523 LD. BERNERS *Froiss.* I. 230 They were scant entred, but that the frenchmen came thyder. **1563** SACKVILLE in *Mirr. Mag.* R iij b, We had not long furth past, but that we sawe Blacke Cerberus. **1587** TURBERV. *Trag. T.* (1837) 32 He scarcely spake the worde, but by and by . . unto her flankes they flewe. **1681** H. MORE *Exp. Dan.* II. 35 He had scarce rub'd his eyes . . but Darius fled. **1713** ADDISON *Cato* IV. iv, Scarce had I left my father, but I met him. **1725** DE FOE *Voy. round World* (1840) 208 Nor had we received him on board half an hour, but . . we put out to sea. **1727** —— *Secrets Invis. World* (1840) 236 He had not gone many steps more, but he saw his brother. **1800** COLERIDGE *Piccol.* I. ix, Scarce have I arrived . . But there is brought to me from your equerry A splendid richly plated hunting dress.

†**c.** After *it was not long after*, where modern use requires *that*.

1525 LD. BERNERS *Froiss.* II. 156 It was not longe after but that the duke of Lancastre, etc. **1563–87** FOXE *A. & M.* (1596) 182/2 It was not long after, but Eustace sonne to King Stephan . . made war on duke Henrie.

16. After *it cannot be, it is impossible, it is not possible, is it possible?* More fully ***but that***.

1539 CRANMER *Bible* Luke xvii. 1 It can not be but offences wyl come [WYCLIF, It is impossible that sclaundris come not; **1526** TINDALE, It can not be avoyded but that offences will come; **1582** *Rhem.*, It is impossible that scandale should not come; **1611** BIBLE, It is impossible but that offences will come]. **1557** NORTH *Gueuara's Diall Pr.* (1582) 185 It cannot be but that the writings of such a woman . . were very lively. **1621** BURTON *Anat. Mel.* (1806) I. 161 How is it possible but that we should be discontent? **1650** R. STAPYLTON *Strada's Low-C. Warres* VIII. 7 She said it was not possible but she must be in great anxiety. **1724** DE FOE *Mem. Cavalier* (1840) 160 It was impossible but he should see it. **1792** MARY WOLLSTONECR. *Rights Wom.* Ded. 5, I think it scarcely possible but that some of the enlarged minds . . will coincide with me. **1880** T. SPALDING *Eliz. Demonol.* 41 It can hardly be but that the 'thousand noses' are intended as a satirical hit.

¶**b.** Erroneously for *that*, after *it is not impossible, not improbable, not unlikely*, etc. (Cf. 21.)

1665 J. WILSON *Projectors* III, 'Tis not impossible but I may make my party good. **1680** *Vind. Conform. Clergy* (ed. 2) 38 It is not unlikely but somebody may know. **1684** N. S. *Crit. Eng. Edit. Bible* xviii. 184 It is not improbable but that Origen . . marked the various reading. **1711** *Medley* No. 33 It is not impossible, but such a day as this may come, etc. **1780** MADAN *Thelyph.* I. 3 It is not impossible but that the light of that great reformer had remained hidden under the bushel of monkery.

17. After (*'tis*) *pity*.

1573 *New Custom* II. iii. in Hazl. *Dodsley* III. 34 It were pity but thou were hanged before. **1598** BARNFIELD *Poems* (Arb.) 121 Pity but hee were a King. **1667** H. MORE *Div. Dial.* I. 64 It's pitty but what you say should be true. **1852** MISS YONGE *Cameos* II. xviii. 194 Pity but we knew more of the one loyal man of his time!

18. ***not but*** (***that***), elliptically = 'it is not but that'; or perh. sometimes 'not to say but that'; cf. next.

1642 R. BROOKE *Eng. Episc.* 67 Not but that they were most worthy men. **1704** POPE *Disc. Past. Poetry* §10 Not but he [Spenser] may be thought imperfect on some few points. **1768** BICKERSTAFF *Lionel & Cl.* I. i, Not but your father had good qualities. *Mod.* Not but that I should have gone if I had had the chance.

**** After various verbs in negative or interrogative construction, with same general sense as in prec. series (12–18). In all cases *but that* is a possible variant.

19. After *not say, think, conceive, conclude, believe, know, see, be sure, persuade*, and the like.

a **1400** *Against Miracle Plays* in *Rel. Ant.* II. 56 Peraventure ye seyen that no man schal make ȝou to byleven but that is good. **1534** LD. BERNERS *Gold. Bk. M. Aurel.* (1546) E e v b, Thinke not but it dooeth brenne my heart. **1581** STYWARD *Martial Discip.* I. 28 He maie not say but that hee was forewarned. **1656** S. H. *Gold. Law* 89, I see not but that . . one or both are undone. **1686** GOAD *Celest. Bodies* I. ix. 33 Who knows but that Light and Cold may have kindness one for the other. **1760** GOLDSM. *Cit. W.* xxxii, Who knows but we may see a lord holding the bowl to a minister. **1847** *Blackw. Mag.* LXI. 220 How could he tell but that Mildred might do the same? **1884** *Times* (weekly ed.) 5 Sept. 3/4, I am not sure but that there is a state of facts by which . . the Constitution would be in some danger.

¶**b.** So formerly after *deny*, where *that* is now used.

1547 *Homilies* I. *Fruitf. Exhort.* II. (1859) 11 Yet no man can deny, but this is the chiefe. **1575** GASCOIGNE *Notes of Instr.* (Arb.) 32, I will not denie but this may seeme a preposterous ordre. **1663** BP. PATRICK *Parab. Pilgr.* viii. (1668) 33, I will not deny but that it is a difficult thing. **1790** PALEY *Horæ Paul.* I. 5, I cannot deny but that it would be easy.

20. After *fear* and equivalent verbs.

1556 J. HEYWOOD *Spider & F.* lxvii. 31 Feare not: but I, Wyll fauer and forder your sute. **1641** T. EDWARDS *Reasons agst. Indep.* 20, I doe not feare but that these few Souldiers will be able to returne againe. **1820** *Blackw. Mag.* VI. 684, I do not fear but that my grandfather will recover. **1879** MRS. OLIPHANT *Within Prec.* xvii. 15 Never fear but I'll go.

21. After *doubt, despair, make no question, scruple*, and the like. (Cf. L. *non dubito quin*.) Here *that* is now considered more logical.

c **1340** *Cursor M.* 12322 (Trin.) She . . douted nouȝt But goddes wille wolde be wrouȝt. *a* **1400** *Against Miracle Plays* in *Rel. Ant.* II. 51 No dowte but that it is deadly synne. **1548** LATIMER *Serm. Ploughers* (Arb.) 37, I dout not but there were many blanchers in the olde time. **1600** O. E. (? M. SUTCLIFFE) *Repl. Libel* I. i. 23, I make no question, but they do farre excell them. **1656** *Artif. Handsomeness* 73 Who . . scruples, but that they may lawfully be pluckt out? *a* **1661** FULLER *Triana* iii, Sabina's friends despair not but . . to mould him. **1701** W. WOTTON *Hist. Rome* 482 They questioned not but to stike terror into the Romans. **1764** REID *Inquiry* iii. Wks. I. 116/2 Nor is it to be doubted, but smells . . would appear to have as great variety. **1832** CARLYLE in *Fraser's Mag.* V. 399 Who doubted but the catastrophe was over? **1857** LIVINGSTONE *Trav.* i. 19 We . . have no doubt but it will yet spring up. **1870** RUSKIN *Lect. on Art* (1875) 87, I do not doubt but that you are surprised.

†**22.** After *prevent* (*let*), *hinder, restrain*, etc.; now expressed by *from* with the gerund, or the gerund alone. (Cf. L. *nihil impedit quin* or *quominus*.) Also after *fail, miss, hold, forbear*, and the like, where various constructions are now used, for which see those verbs.

An infinitive phrase often took the place of the clause.

1528 PERKINS *Prof. Bk.* ii. §156 (1642) 69 These words . . shall not bind him but that hee may enter. **1553** T. WILSON *Rhet.* 81 b, If you loke in the boke . . you shal not faile but find them. **1588** R. PARKE *Hist. China* 23 He cannot let but haue in his shop men that must worke of his occupation. **1589** PUTTENHAM *Eng. Poesie* III. xxv. (Arb.) 308 Our maker may not be in all cases restrayned, but that he may . . manifest his arte. **1610** MARKHAM *Masterp.* II. clxxii. 482 You shall not faile but . . you shall spet in his mouth. **1626** G. HAKEWILL *Comparison* 29 He could not hold but let fall teares at the sight thereof. **1653** *Cloria & Narcissus* I. 294 Cloria . . could not forbeare but plainly to tell him her thoughts. **1656** *Artif. Handsomeness* 70 What . . hinders . . but that we may study to adorn our lookes? **1713** ADDISON *Cato* III. vii. 18 What hinders then, but that thou find her out? **1737** WHISTON *Josephus* x. x. §2 It could not be avoided but their . . colours must be changed. **1844** F. PAGET *Tales Village Childr.* Ser. II. (1858) 96 She cannot miss but see us.

†**b.** After *I see not* or *no cause* = I see nothing to prevent. Also after *there wanted but little*; cf. L. *parum abfuit quin*. *Obs.*

1589 PUTTENHAM *Eng. Poesie* III. xxi, I see not but the reste . . may be borne with. **1600** O. E. (? M. SUTCLIFFE) *Repl. Libel* I. ix. 236, I see no cause . . but that the Spaniardes should rather feare vs. **1658** USSHER *Ann.* 624 There wanted but little, but that the people had killed the Judges.

c. After *God forbid*, and the like.

1393 LANGL. *P. Pl.* C. IV. 149 Lord it me for-bede Bote ich be holly at þyn heste. **1596** SHAKS. *1 Hen. IV*, IV. iii. 38 Heauen defend, but still I should stand so.

III. In a compound sentence, connecting the two co-ordinate members; or introducing an independent sentence connected in sense, though not in form, with the preceding. In a compound sentence the second member is often greatly contracted, as in 'Thou hast not lied unto men, but (thou hast lied) unto God'.

* In a compound sentence.

23. As adversative conjunction, appending a statement contrary to, or incompatible with, one that is negatived:

On the contrary. = Ger. *sondern*.

897 *O.E. Chron.*, Nawðer ne on Fresisc ȝescæpene ne on Denisc, bute swa him selfum ðuhte þæt hie nytwyrðoste beon meahten. *a* **1300** *Cursor M.* 8598 Þai had na credel ne wit to bij Bot did þair childer bi þam lij. **1393** LANGL. *P. Pl.* C. I. 36 Þat wollen neyþer swynke ne swete bote swery grete oþes. **1593** HOOKER *Eccl. Pol.* II. v. §7 Wks. 1841 I. 250 Neither the matter . . was arbitrary, but necessary. **1610** HEALEY *St. Aug. City of God* 581 Monkeyes, and Babiounes, were not men but beasts. **1681** DRYDEN *Abs. & Achit.* 567 He left not Faction, but of That was left. **1751** JOHNSON *Rambl.* No. 141 ¶10 A reply, not to what the lady had said, but to what it was convenient for me to hear.

24. Appending a statement which is not contrary to, but is not fully consonant with, or is contrasted with, that already made:

Nevertheless, yet, however. = Ger. *aber*.

1535 COVERDALE *Isa.* lxiii. 16 Abraham knoweth vs not . . But thou Lorde art oure father. **1691** NORRIS *Pract. Disc.* To Rdr. 5 Now we Discourse better, but we live worse. *a* **1703** BURKITT *On N.T.* Mark iv. 29 The care and endeavour is ours, but the blessing and success is God's. **1711** STEELE *Spect.* No. 144 ¶8 Her face speaks a Vestal, but her Heart a Messalina. **1766** GOLDSM. *Vic. W.* x, That pride which I had laid asleep, but not removed. **1821** SHELLEY *Hellas*, Life may change, but it may flie not; Hope may vanish, but can die not. **1839** THIRLWALL *Greece* I. 351 The hopes of the Messenians sank, but not their courage.

b. After *not only, not merely* (sometimes strengthened by the addition of *also*).

1382 WYCLIF *Petition King. &c.* in *Sel. Wks.* III. 511 Nott oonli . . medful, butt moost medeful. **1589** PUTTENHAM *Eng. Poesie* I. xxiii. (Arb.) 60 It is not only allowable, but also necessary. **1682** WHELER *Journ. Greece* I. 18 We had time not only to see the Town, but the places circumjacent also. **1727** SWIFT *Gulliver* IV. vii, I was not only endowed with the faculty of speech, but likewise with some rudiments of reason. **1848** MACAULAY *Hist. Eng.* I. 232 The ally . . was not only a Roman Catholic, but a persecutor of the reformed Churches. **1866** KINGSLEY *Herew.* Prel. (1877) 15 Leofric was not merely Lord of Bourne, but Earl of Mercia. **1875** JOWETT *Plato* (ed. 2) III. 29 They not only tell lies but bad lies.

** In a distinct member of a compound sentence (usually after a semicolon or colon); or at the beginning of a following sentence.

25. Introducing a statement of the nature of an exception, objection, limitation, or contrast to what has gone before; sometimes, in its weakest form, merely expressing disconnexion, or emphasizing the introduction of a distinct or independent fact, as the minor premiss of a syllogism: However, on the other hand, moreover, yet. In OE. *ac*, Ger. *aber*, L. *autem*.

c **1205** LAY. 8263 Al hit þuncð him wel idon . . bute nele he þe nauere Euelin mid ærhðe bi-tæchen. *a* **1240** *Wohunge of ure L.* in *Cott. Hom.* 277 Poure þu wunden was in a beastes cribbe; Bote swa þu eldere wex, swa þu pourere was. *a* **1300** *K. Horn* 1113 Alle dronken of þe ber Bute horn alone Nadde þerof no mone. *c* **1300** *Beket* 43 Gilbert . . seide he was al to hire wille: bote he moste bithenche. *c* **1380** WYCLIF *Sel. Wks.* III. 220 3if ȝe axen ony þing in my name, he schal ȝeve it to ȝow. But we axen in the name of Jesus, whanne we, etc. *c* **1400** *Ywaine & Gaw.* 788 (Mätz.) Now must I ga, bot drede the noght. **1548** LATIMER *Serm. Ploughers* (Arb.) 19 But now you wyll aske me whom I cal a prelate. **1611** BIBLE *John* xix. 9 But Iesus gave him no answer. **1626** DONNE *Serm.* iv. 36 He saw it; but with the Eye of Hope. **1690** LOCKE *Hum. Und.* III. vii. §5 All Animals have Sense; But a Dog is an Animal. Here *but* signifies little more, but that the latter Proposition is join'd to the former, as the Minor of a Syllogism. **1724** SWIFT *Corr.* Wks. 1841 II. 570 We are here preparing for your reception . . but whether you approve the manner I can only guess. **1816** J. WILSON *City of Plague* I. i. 414 Fare ye well. But list! sweet youths, where'er you go, beware. **1848** MACAULAY *Hist. Eng.* I. 615 Feversham passed for a good-natured man: but he was a foreigner. *Mod.* 'Get money; honestly, if you can: but, get money!'

†**26.** Introducing a reply to a question: cf. the modern unemphatic *why*. Cf. Fr. *mais*, Gr. ἀλλά.

a **1300** *Cursor M.* 19622 Quat art þou, lauerd, sua vnsen? Bot i hatt iesus nazaren. *c* **1320** *Cast. Loue* 809 And whuche beoþ [þe] þreo bayles ȝet . . Bote þe inemaste bayle, I wot, Bi-tokenþ hire holy maidenhod.

27. After an interjection or exclamation, as ***yes! but, aye! but, nay! but, ah! but, I say! but***, expressing some degree of opposition, objection, or protest; but also colloquially, mere surprise or recognition of something unexpected.

1846 LANDOR *Wks.* I. 347 God forgive me! but I think him as worthy as the best of the saints. *Mod.* Ah! but he knows better than to go there. I say! but you had a narrow escape! Eh! but that's a queer story! Whew! but I am tired! Faith! but that's a poser! Come! but that's drawing it rather strong. Excuse me! but your coat is dusty. Beg pardon! but have you found a scarf on the road?

b. Also with preceding exclamation occasionally omitted, esp. as a gallicism (cf. F. *mais oui, mais énormément*, etc.), used to give

emphasis to a following word or statement, and with the sense of 'indeed'.

1887 M. CORELLI *Thelma* II. II. ii. 156 'I believe you would do it if I asked you!' he said. 'But, of course!' **1941** B. SCHULBERG *What makes Sammy Run?* viii. 153 Now you've really bitched yourself up. But good. **1960** L. COOPER *Accomplices* II. ii. 84 If the other.. looks like getting in the way it must be turned out, but quick. **1965** I. FLEMING *Man with Golden Gun* vi. 81 I'm goin' fix that man, but good.

c. Introducing an emphatic repetition.

1920 R. MACAULAY *Potterism* VI. iv. 239 A weekly, and it promised to sell better than any other weekly on the market, but far better. **1921** 'K. MANSFIELD' *Coll. Stories* (1945) 422 She knew what it was to be in love, but-in-love! **1928** D. H. LAWRENCE *Lady Chatt.* xiv. 240 And about *everything* I talked to her: but everything. **1950** S. ERTZ *Prodigal Heart* iv. 68 They're very gay, and entertain a lot and I feel years older than they are. But years older. **1958** B. NICHOLS *Sweet & Twenties* iv. 59 He sold enormously—but enormously. *Ibid.* x. 132 There is nothing, but nothing, to be said for the female knee.

IV. *Phrases and casual collocations.*

28. ***but and*** = but also, and also: see AND. *Obs.* exc. *Sc.*

1375 BARBOUR *Bruce* v. 595, I haf a bow, bot and a vyre. **1382** WYCLIF *Wisd.* xi. 2 Not onli the hurting.. but and the looking bi drede slen. But and withoute these with o spirit, thei myȝten ben slayn. *c* **1450** HENRYSON *Bludy Serk*, Meik, bot and debonair. **1724** RAMSAY *Tea-T. Misc.* (1733) II. 181 A kame but and a kamingstock. **1832–53** *Whistle-Binkie* (Sc. Songs) Ser. II. 75 In height an ell but an' a span.

†**b.** ***but and, but and if*** = but if: see AND C.

c **1385** CHAUCER *L.G.W.* 1786 But and thow crye, or noyse make. **1535** COVERDALE *Matt.* v. 13 But and yf the salt haue lost his saltnes. **1540** HYRDE *Vives' Instr. Chr. Wom.* (1592) G ij, But and thou array thy body sumptuously.. thou canst not be excused as chast in mind.

29. ***but for*** = except for, were it not for: see sense 1.

c **1205** LAY. 31446 Hit likede wel þan kinge, buten for ane þinge. **1592** SHAKS. *Ven. & Ad.* 504 These mine eyes.. But for thy piteous lips no more had seen. **1667** PEPYS *Diary* (1879) IV. 351 Several of the Council.. would come but for their attending the King. **1885** *Law Rep.* XXIX. Ch. Div. 291 But for the concurrent jurisdiction, the decision.. would have been the other way.

†**b.** ***but for***: but because, but since: see FOR.

1398 TREVISA *Barth. De P.R.* v. i. (1495) 101 That is no wonder but for it is selden seen. **1563–87** FOXE *A. & M.* (1684) I. 462/1 But for thy shepheards wolden be excused. *a* **1593** MARLOWE *Massacr. Paris* II. v, But for you know our quarrel is no more.

but if: see sense 10b.

but that: see senses 8–9, 13–22, in some of which *that* is now obs., while in others *but that* is still the better form, and *but* is familiar or colloquial.

30. ***but what*** often occurs for *but that* in various senses, and is still *dial.* and *colloq.*

1662 H. MORE *Immort. Soul* 96 We cannot discover any immediate operation of any kind of soul.. but what it first works upon, etc. **1711** *Medley* No. 24, I don't know one Politician but what Drunkenness wou'd make a Sot of. **1761** FRANCES SHERIDAN *Miss Bidulph* I. 45 There are not many masters of eminence but what have a hundred originals palmed upon them more than ever they painted in their lives. *Ibid.* (1767) V. 45 There is not a circumstance but what is worthy to be writ in letters of gold. **1862** TROLLOPE *N. Amer.* I. 47 Nor am I yet so old but what I can rough it still. **1868** MISS BRADDON *Birds of Prey* VI. ii. 313 Not but what his head is as clear as ever it was. **1884** *Standard* 22 Dec. 5/2 Not but what the picture has its darker side. [See many modern instances in F. HALL, *Mod. English* 262.]

D. quasi-*sb.* [The adv. used *ellipt.*] The outer room of a house; see BUT *adv.* 1 d.

E. quasi-*adj.* [The adv. used *attrib.*] Out, outer, exterior; see B. 1 c.

F. quasi-*pron.* The negative of *who*, = Lat. *quin*: see 12b.

but, *sb.*[1] The conjunction *but* (sense 25), used as a name for itself; *hence*, a verbal objection presented.

1571 *Sempill Ballates* (1872) 137 ȝit botis & hummis declairis ȝow quhat I mene. **1614** T. ADAMS *Divell's Banq.* 139 There is a corrective But, a *veruntamen*, spoyles all in the vp-shot.. here is a But that shipwrackes all. **1682** T. GOODWIN *Wks.* (1864) IX. 485 The grants of grace run without ifs and ands and buts. **1752** A. STEWART in *Scots Mag.* (1753) Sept. 446/2 He was a sufficient *but* himself for all the sum. **1816** SCOTT *Antiq.* xi, 'I heartily wish I could, but'—'Nay, but me no buts—I have set my heart upon it.' **1872** MINTO *Eng. Lit.* 108 We are.. jerked back with a 'but'.

†**but,** *sb.*[2] *Obs.* [cf. PUT *v.* (which occurs in the context), also OF. *bout* 'coup', *boute* 'coup porté en boutant' (Godef.).] 'Putting' the stone.

a **1300** *Havelok* 1040 He maden mikel strout Abouten the altherbeste but.

but (bʌt), *v. arch.* [f. BUT *sb.*[1]; cf. *to thou.*] *intr.* To say or use 'but'; also quasi-*trans.* in phrase 'but me no buts'.

1553 [see BUTTING *vbl. sb.*[4]]. *a* **1625** FLETCHER *Hum. Lieut.* I. v, *Phys.* Yes, you may live; but—. *Leo.* Finely butted, doctor. **1708** MRS. CENTLIVRE *Busie Bod.* II. i. 28 *Cha.* Sir, I obey: But—. *Sir Fran.* But me no Buts. **1816** SCOTT *Antiq.* [see BUT *sb.*[1] above].

butadiene (ˌbjuːtəˈdaiːn). *Chem.* [f. BUTA(NE + DI-[2] + -ENE.] Either of the two isomeric hydrocarbons $CH_3{\cdot}CH{:}CH{\cdot}CH_3$ (also called *methylallene*) and $CH_2{:}CH{\cdot}CH{:}CH_2$ (also called *erythrene*), the latter being used as a constituent of various artificial rubbers (cf. BUNA). Also *attrib.* and *Comb.*, as ***butadiene-acrylonitrile, -styrene.***

1900 *Jrnl. Chem. Soc.* LXXVIII. I. 2 According to the author's theory of unsaturated compounds, butadiene.. should yield an αδ-dibromide on direct addition of bromine. **1911** *Chem. Abstr.* V. 3519 Hydrocarbons of the Butadiene Series and Artificial Caoutchoucs. **1937** *Discovery* Aug. 247/1 The real raw material of synthetic rubber—a product known as butadiene. **1959** *Times* 13 Mar. 10/1 (Advt.), Cariflex general purpose butadiene-styrene rubber. **1959** *Times* (Suppl.) 27 Apr. vi/7 For oil and fuel resistance the butadiene-acrylonitrile type rubbers are in common use.

butane (ˈbjuːteɪn). *Chem.* [f. BUT(YL + -ANE 2b.] Butyl hydride, C_4H_{10}; = TETRANE. Also *attrib.* and *Comb.*

1875 *Jrnl. Chem. Soc.* XXVIII. 561 The simplest saturated hydrocarbons which afford substitution-products belonging to all the three groups of primary, secondary, and tertiary nitro-compounds, are the two isomeric butanes. **1877** *Fownes' Chem.* (ed. 12) 47 Normal Butane, Diethyl, or Methyl-propyl. **1918** COLVER *High Explosives* 60 The propane, butane, and pentane hydrocarbons in the form of gases and vapours which can only be condensed with difficulty. **1935** *Discovery* Dec. 361/1 The allied gas, butane, compressed similarly in cylinders, is now in frequent use for gas-cookers etc. **1953** *Ann. Reg. 1952* 74 The experimental use of butane-air mixture [for gas supplies] at Whitland. **1958** *Engineering* 7 Feb. 192/3 A butane burning blowlamp is now marketed in Britain.

butanol (ˈbjuːtənɒl). *Chem.* [G., f. BUTAN(E + -OL.] Butyl alcohol, esp. the normal isomer.

1894 G. M'GOWAN tr. *Bernthsen's Text-bk. Org. Chem.* (ed. 2) 93 Normal butyl alcohol. [*Note*] 1-Butanol. *Ibid.*, Secondary butyl alcohol. [*Note*] 2-Butanol. **1957** *Encycl. Brit.* IV. 472/2 Normal butyl alcohol (butanol) is made commercially by the fermentation of corn or molasses and also from acetylene. **1964** BODEN & KAMPA in *Oceanogr. & Marine Biol.* II. 351 Considerable purification has been obtained with butanol extraction.

butanone (ˈbjuːtənəʊn). *Chem.* [f. BUTAN(E + -ONE.] Methyl ethyl ketone, $CH_3{\cdot}CH_2{\cdot}CO{\cdot}CH_3$, an ethereal liquid used industrially.

1905 *Jrnl. Chem. Soc.* LXXXVIII. I. 355 *cyclo* Butanone.. prepared by brominating tetramethylenecarboxylic acid and treating the bromo-anhydride thus obtained with ammonia. **1964** N. G. CLARK *Mod. Org. Chem.* x. 194 *Butanone*.. also known as methyl ethyl ketone.. is largely used as a solvent for cellulose nitrate.. and vinyl resins.

butargo, obs. form of BOTARGO.

†**butch,** *v. Obs.* exc. *dial.* [incorrect back-formation from BUTCHER *sb.*]

†**a.** *trans.* To cut up, hack (*obs.*). **b.** *intr.* (*north. dial.*) To follow the trade of a butcher.

1785 [see BUTCHING]. **1834** SIR H. TAYLOR *Artevelde* II. III. i, I shall be butching thee from nape to rump. **1846** J. T. BROCKETT *Gloss. N. Count. Wds.* (ed. 3) I. 75 Butch, to practice the trade of a butcher, to kill. **1875** *Lanc. Gloss.* (E.D.S.) 63 He use't to be a farmer, but he butches neaw.

Hence **butch-knife** = *butcher's knife.*

a **1849** POE *Wks.* (1864) III. 172 White throats sweetly jagged With a ragged butch-knife dull.

butch (bʊtʃ), *sb.*[1] *slang* (orig. *U.S.*). [Origin unknown, but perh. = next.] A tough youth or man; a lesbian of masculine appearance or behaviour. Also *attrib.* or as *adj.* In the U.S. also applied to a type of short haircut, crew-cut.

[**1902** *Pinkerton's Nat. Detective Agency Circular* 3 Feb., George Parker, alias 'Butch' Cassidy, alias George Cassidy. **1930** D. RUNYON *Guys & Dolls* (1932) 71 (*title*) Butch minds the baby.] **1941** AUDEN *New Year Let.* III. 72 And culture on all fours to greet A butch and criminal élite. **1947** *Cromwellian* May 35 *Butch*, a strongly-built person. **1949** W. R. BURNETT *Asphalt Jungle* (1950) v. 30 His white-blond hair disfigured by a butch haircut. **1950** *Neurotica* Spring 37, I no longer remotely resembled a 'butch' fairy. **1954** *News* (San Francisco) 10 Sept. 1 Then some of the girls began wearing mannish clothing. They called themselves 'Butches'. **1954** *Observer* 26 Sept. 9/2 The homosexual Stoics with their crew-cuts and 'butch' behaviour. **1965** *New Statesman* 26 Mar. 493/1 This rejection of the female role is very common among the 'butch' type of lesbian. **1966** *Ibid.* 13 May 696/3 One of the femmes, secure in the loving protection of her butch. **1967** W. MURRAY *Sweet Ride* ix. 148 Three burly men with butch haircuts.

butch, *sb.*[2] Colloq. abbrev. of BUTCHER *sb.* (see quots.).

1919 DOWNING *Digger Dialects* 14 Butch, doctor. **1942** W. FAULKNER *Go Down, Moses* 164 Boon bought.. a bottle of beer from the news butch. **1960** WENTWORTH & FLEXNER *Dict. Amer. Slang* 80/2 *Butch*,.. a vendor.

butcher (ˈbʊtʃə(r)), *sb.* Forms: [3 boucher], 3–6 bocher, 4–6 boucher, 4–7 bowcher, 5 bochere, -or, -our, -eyr, *Sc.* bowchour, (bochyer), 5–7 bucher(e, 6 *Sc.* boucheour, (boscher, bochsar), 6– butcher. [ME. *bocher, boucher*, Anglo-Fr. form of OF. *bochier, bouchier* (mod.F. *boucher*) = Pr. *bochier*; f. OF., Pr. *boc* BUCK *sb.*[1] he-goat. The literal sense is thus 'dealer in goat's flesh'; cf. It. *beccaio* butcher, f. *becco* he-goat.]

1. a. One whose trade is the slaughtering of large tame animals for food; one who kills such animals and sells their flesh; in mod. use it sometimes denotes a tradesman who merely deals in meat.

[**1292** BRITTON I. xxi. §11 De tannours, qi se fount tannours et bouchers qi vendent chars par peces.] *a* **1300** *K. Alis.* 2832 He is to-hewe.. so the bocher doth the oxe. **1387** TREVISA *Higden* (Rolls Ser.) I. 285 A woman þat was quene of Fraunce by eritage wedded a bocher for his fairenesse. *c* **1440** *Gesta Rom.* (1879) 370 The mayster sente for the buchere.. for to sle the hogges. **1525** *Old City Acc. Bk.* in *Archæol. Jrnl.* XLIII, Itm payd to the Bochsar for a greyt serlyn xvjd. **1593** SHAKS. *2 Hen. VI*, III. i. 210 As the Butcher takes away the Calfe. **1726** GAY *Fables* I. ix, Beneath a butcher train'd, Whose hands with cruelty are stain'd. **1873** MORLEY *Rousseau* II. 44 The butcher pays himself in live cattle. *Mod.* To pay his butcher's bill.

b. *fig.* One who slaughters men indiscriminately or brutally; a 'man of blood'; a brutal murderer.

1529 RASTELL *Pastyme, Hist. Brit.* (1811) 282 Erle of Worcester whiche for his crueltye was called the bocher of Englande. **1592** SHAKS. *Ven. & Ad.* 766 A mischiefe worse then.. Butcher sire, that reaues his sonne of life. **1595** —— *John* IV. ii. 259 To be butcher of an innocent childe. **1621** BURTON *Anat. Mel.* To Rdr. (1849) 31 Bloody butchers, wicked destroyers.. common executioners of the human kind. **1720** OZELL *Vertot's Rom. Rep.* II. IX. 158 The Murderer of Caius, the Butcher of three Thousand of his Fellow-Citizens. **1837** CARLYLE *Fr. Rev.* (1871) II. v. iii. 182 With wild yell, with cries of 'Cut the Butcher down!'

†**2. a.** An executioner; one who inflicts capital punishment or torture; also *attrib. Obs.*

c **1450** HENRYSON *Mor. Fab.* 38 The Ape was boucher, and.. hanged him. **1483** CAXTON *Gold. Leg.* 85/3 He.. unclad hym and gaf hys clothys unto the bochyers. *Ibid.* 121/3 The bochyers toke combes of yron and began to kembe hym on the sides within the flesshe. **1494** FABYAN VII. (1811) 572 When yᵉ bysshop came vnto his place of execucion, he prayed the bowcher to gyue to hym v. strokes in the worshyp of Cristes fyue woundes.

†**b.** *fig. Obs.*

1579 TOMSON *Calvin's Serm. Tim.* 474/1 Their conscience is their boucher. *Ibid.* 591/2 They shal need no other butcher.. but they shal haue as it were an hote yron always burning within themselues.

3. a. A kind of artificial fly used by anglers for salmon. [Cf. BAKER 3.]

1860 C. M. YONGE *Hopes & Fears* I. II. iv. 229 The doctor the butcher, the duchess, and all her other fabrications of.. feathers. **1867** F. FRANCIS *Angling* x. (1880) 345 The Butcher.. kills almost wherever there are salmon. **1884** M. G. WATKINS in *Longm. Mag.* June 177 What fly had been used..'The Butcher'? Yes; but he did not care much for that lure.

b. A vendor of sweets, fruit, etc., in a railway train, a theatre, etc. *U.S. colloq.*

1882 J. J. JENNINGS *Theatrical & Circus Life* 513 In the spring ye 'candy-butcher' shows confections old and tough. **1883** G. W. PECK *Peck's Bad Boy* 54 They never prayed in circus, 'cept the lemonade butchers. *a* **1889** *Detroit Free Press* (Barrère & Leland), On a Michigan central train the other day as the butcher came into the car with a basket of oranges [etc.]. **1924** W. M. RAINE *Troubled Waters* vii. 70 From the train butcher he bought a magazine and settled himself for a long ride.

c. Short for *butcher('s) blue.*

1922 *Daily Mail* 13 Dec. 1 (Advt.), Strong Cotton *Dresses.* In plain Butcher, Navy, Brown, [etc.]. **1923** *Ibid.* 30 May 4 (Advt.), Mauve, Pink or Butcher on White ground. **1952** 'P. WENTWORTH' *Brading Coll.* xv. 93 Most of the time she wore blue... Navy, or butcher.

d. A glass or measure of beer (see quots.). *Austral. slang.*

1898 MORRIS *Austral Eng.* 73/1 *Butcher*, South Australian slang for a long drink of beer, so-called (it is said) because the men of a certain butchery in Adelaide used this refreshment regularly. **1934** *Bulletin* (Sydney) 7 Mar. 10/3 A 'butcher'.. is identical in volume with the fourpenny glass of the other capitals. **1945** BAKER *Austral. Lang.* ix. 168 *Butcher* is Adelaide slang; in the early days it was used for a glass containing about two-thirds of a pint. In modern times the size has dropped to about half a pint.

4. General combinations: **a.** attrib. and similative (sense 1b), as ***butcher-like*** adj. and adv., †***-wise*** adv., ***-work.*** **b.** syntactical (genitival), as ***butcher's-block, -boy, -cleaver, -hook, -shop, -tray.***

1587 TURBERV. *Trag. T.* (1837) 35 *Butcherlike to rippe her downe the raynes. **1625** HART *Anat. Ur.* II. xi. 127 By.. his butcherlike boldnesse he cast many into.. laskes. **1687** SETTLE *Refl. Dryden* 3 The Butcher-like discords that arose. **1852** *Blackw. Mag.* LXXI. 231 A butcher-like assistant.. creeps up, and pierces the spinal marrow. **1558** PHAËR *Æneid* VI. Q ivb, There.. Priams son he sawe all *boucherwise Bemanglid. **1808** SCOTT *Marm.* II. xxxii, To tell The *butcher-work that there befel.

1842 DICKENS *Amer. Notes* (1850) 110/2 Great unsightly stumps, like earthy *butchers'-blocks. **1725** *Lond. Gaz.* No. 6345/2 A *Butcher's Hook with a little Notch upon the End of the flat Part. **1533** MORE *Answ. Poyson. Bk.* Wks. (1557) 1059/1 As men bye bief, or moten out of the *bouchers shoppes. **1812** H. & J. SMITH *Rej. Addr.* 1, Who fills the butchers' shops with large blue flies? **1859** W. COLEMAN *Woodlands* (1862) 76 Wooden vessels, such as bowls, platters, *butchers' trays, etc.

5. Special comb.: **butcher blue** = *butcher's blue*; **butcher-boots** *pl.*, high boots without tops (see TOP *sb.*[1] 10); **butcher-crow**, a crow-shrike (Funk's Stand. Dict. 1893); **butcher-fly**, ? a kind of blow-fly; †**butcherman**, a butcher (*obs.*); **butcher's bill**, sometimes used sarcastically for the list of killed in a battle (less frequently for the money cost of a war); **butcher's blue**, a dressmaker's name for a particular shade of dark blue like the colour of a

butcher's apron; **butcher's** or †**butcher-dog**, app. formerly a breed of dog (*obs.* in *spec.* sense); **butcher's grip**, a particular method of clasping the hands; **butcher's knife**, also **butcher-knife**, a particular kind of knife used by butchers; also, any large, strong-bladed knife of many uses; **butcher's sleeves**, short sleeves covering the forearm from elbow to wrist, worn by butchers as a protection against soiling the sleeves of their ordinary clothes. Also BUTCHER-BIRD, -ROW, BUTCHER'S BROOM, -MEAT.

1909 D. LEVITT *Woman & Car* ii. 28 Indispensable to the motoriste..is the over-all. This should be made of *butcher blue or brown linen. **1923** R. MACAULAY *Told by an Idiot* III. vi. 199 The girl in a short butcher-blue cotton frock. **1960** *Times* 18 Jan. 15/2 Dresses in linens, such as one in butcher blue. **1861** WHYTE MELVILLE *Market Harb.* v, My friend sharing with me a strong prejudice against what have been termed '*Butcher-boots'. **1886** *Eng. Illustr. Mag.* Mar. 414/1 A man in a round hat and butcher-boots is as out of place at a hunt as a man in a tweed suit at a ball. **1897** *Badminton Mag.* IV. 397 Men in cords and butcher boots, tweeds and gaiters. **1941** *Manch. Guardian Weekly* 17 Jan. 45 Butcher boots are de luxe knee-boots used by officers. **1663** T. JAMES *Voyage* 81 Butterflyes, *Butchers-flyes, Horseflyes. **1821** *New Monthly Mag.* I. 568 The butcher-fly fastens by instinct..upon those parts only that are defective and disgusting. **1867** F. FRANCIS *Angling* xi. (1880) 430 The Butcher Fly..is not the fly known elsewhere as 'The Butcher'. **1481–90** *Howard Househ. Bks.* 60 Item, to Watkyn, *bocherman iij *li.* **1881** SULLIVAN *July Annivers.* in *Macm. Mag.* XLIV. 343 There may be politicians who would prefer the anniversaries kept in the good old style, however heavy the '*butcher's bill'. **1883** *Daily News* 17 May 6/1 Even Venus must have mislaid some of her charm if arrayed in '*butcher's blue' or 'rotten orange'. **1576** FLEMING tr. *Caius' Dogs* iv. in Arb. *Garner* III. 255 In Latin, *Canis Laniarius*, in English, the *Butcher Dog. **1597** *Return Parnass.* Pt. 2. II. v. 871 All kinde of dogges..Butchers dogs, Bloud-hounds, Dunghill dogges. **1755** *Phil. Trans.* XLIX. 260, I procured six puppies, of the butcher-dog-kind. **1882** *Standard* 26 Aug. 2/2 The men linking hands with the *butcher's grip. **1714** *Boston News-Let.* 1–8 Mar. 2/2 *Butchers knives. **1766** H. BROOKE *Fool of Qual.* II. 591 Pulling out his butcher's knife from a sheath in his side-pocket, he..made a stab at my heart. **1822** *Massachusetts Spy* 25 Dec. (Th.), Her foot slipt, and she fell upon a large butcher-knife which she had in her hand. **1878** J. H. BEADLE *Western Wilds* xviii. 294 We fell to with our..butcher-knives and dug several holes. **1856** *Household Words* XIII. 206/2 After a long delay the doctor came in, with scientific *butcher's sleeves on his arms, and an apron tied round his portly waist.

6. ***butcher's***, short for *butcher's hook*, rhyming slang for 'look'.

1936 J. CURTIS *Gilt Kid* ii. 23 And while he's there he takes a butchers. **1960** K. AMIS *Take Girl like You* xxvii. 311 Have a butcher's at the *News of the World*.

b. *Austral.* and *N.Z. rhyming slang.* (See quots.)

1941 BAKER *Dict. Austral. Slang* 16 *To be butcher's*, to be angry, annoyed (about something). Often 'go butchers at' (i.e., 'go butcher's hook' or crook). **1943** J. A. W. BENNETT in *Amer. Speech* XVIII. 90 *To go crook* is to show anger or annoyance, to 'sling off at'; and *to go butcher's hook* is presumably a development of this in rhyming slang [in New Zealand]. **1951** D. STIVENS *Jimmy Brockett* 126 As soon as Sadie came in I went butcher's hook. 'What's this bloody nonsense about a studio, Sadie?' I said, going straight to the point.

butcher ('bʊtʃə(r)), *v.* [f. prec. sb.]

1. a. *trans.* To slaughter in the manner of a butcher, or in a brutal and indiscriminate manner.

1562 *Compl. of Church* (Collier) 8 You, as sheep, were butchard doun. **1594** SHAKS. *Rich. III*, I. ii. 67 Thou dost swallow vp this good Kings blood, Which his Hell-gouern'd arme hath butchered. **1621** BURTON *Anat. Mel.* Democr. 29 So many myriads..were butchered up with sword, famine, war. **1680** OTWAY *Caius Marius* 57 Matrons with Infants in their Arms are butcher'd. **1716** ADDISON *Freeholder* No. 10 (1751) 60 A couple of Moors, whom he had been butchering with his own Imperial Hands. **1818** BYRON *Ch. Har.* IV. cxli, He, their sire, Butcher'd to make a Roman holiday. **1850** PRESCOTT *Mexico* I. 138.

b. *fig.* To 'murder' a reputation, an author's language by blundering delivery, etc.

1647 BIRKENHEAD *Assembly-Man* (1662–3) 16 He Butcher's a Text. **1677** in Maidment *Sc. Pasquils* (1868) 244 For pelf Butcher'd thy fame estate, and last thyself. **1761** CHURCHILL *Rosciad* Poems (1763) I. 28 Could authors butcher'd give an actor grace. **1827** CARLYLE *Transl., Melechsala* (1874) 113 As a modern critic butchers the defenceless rabble..who venture..into the literary tilt-yard. **1850** WHIPPLE *Ess. & Rev.* (ed. 3) II. 60 The text is not butchered by misprinting.

2. To torment, inflict torture upon (cf. *sb.* 2).

1642 T. TAYLOR *God's Judgem.* I. I. lii. 410 Turmoyled and butchered with their owne guilty consciences.

3. Peculiarly used with *out*.

1611 TOURNEUR *Ath. Trag.* v. ii. 151 I'll butcher out the passage of his soule That dares attempt to interrupt the blow. **1848** G. F. RUXTON in *Blackw. Mag.* LXIII. 718.

4. To cut up or divide (an animal or flesh) after the manner of a butcher; to cut *off* or *from* in this fashion. *U.S.*

1822 J. FOWLER *Jrnl.* (1898) 121 The former killed two Elk, and left the latter to butcher them. *a* **1848** RUXTON *Life Far West* (1849) iv. 118 The..body of one of the Indian squaws, with a large portion of the flesh butchered from it. *Ibid.* 160 Bill..called to him..to butcher off a piece of meat and put it in the pot. **1855** MAYNE REID *Hunters' Feast* xxxix, The fat cows only were 'butchered'. The bulls were left where they had fallen, to become the food of wolves.

5. *intr.* To do butchering. *U.S.*

1865 *Atlantic Monthly* XV. 454 If it isn't about time to butcher: we butchered last year [etc.]. **1896** *Scribner's Mag.* VI. 484/1 'Don't butcher next week. Friday is Christmas day.'..'Well, we always butcher Christmas week, don't we?'

'butcher-ˌbird. [f. BUTCHER *sb.* + BIRD *sb.* (see quot. 1802): Cf. F. *bouchari* 'un des noms vulgaires de la pie-grièche.' Littré.] A name given to several species of shrike (*Laniadæ*): *Lanius excubitor*, *L. tertius*, *L. cinereus*, etc.

1668 WILKINS *Real Char.* 146 Lanius or Butcher bird, is of three several kinds. **1674** RAY *Eng. Birds* Coll. 82 The great Butcher-bird called in the Peak of Derbyshire Wirrangle, *Lanius cinereus major.* **1679** PLOT *Staffordsh.* (1686) 229 The Butcher-bird or Wierangel, here called the Shreek or French-Pye. **1802** PALEY *Nat. Theol.* xii. 109 The butcher-bird transfixes its prey upon the spike of a thorn, whilst it picks its bones. **1846** *Gard. Chron.* 517 The red-backed shrike or butcher-bird.

butcherdom ('bʊtʃədəm). [f. BUTCHER *sb.* + -DOM.] Butchers collectively, or their trade.

1889 in *Cent. Dict.* **1904** H. HAWKINS *Remin.* II. 109 The butcher's slander was one that seemed to shake the very foundations of butcherdom throughout the world.

butchered ('bʊtʃəd), *ppl. a.* [f. BUTCHER *v.* + -ED[1].] Killed by a butcher; killed remorselessly, brutally, or in cold blood.

1594 SHAKS. *Rich. III*, v. iii. 123 The wronged Soules Of butcher'd Princes, fight in thy behalfe. **1837** W. IRVING *Capt. Bonneville* I. 191 The remains of their butchered leader. **1859** LANG *Wand. India* 70 Ellen..buried her butchered husband.

butcherer ('bʊtʃərə(r)). [f. BUTCHER *v.* + -ER[1].] One who butchers.

1646 EARL MONM. tr. *Biondi's Civ. Warres Eng.* II. 66 'Twas thought he should be the Butcherer of Edwards sons. **1689** *Defence Liberty agst. Tyrants* 16 Nero, that inhuman Butcherer of Christians. **1757** *Herald* No. 14 (1758) I. 235 The paracidical butcherer of the Roman constitution.

butcheress ('bʊtʃərɪs). [f. BUTCHER *sb.* + -ESS.] A female butcher; also (*humorously*) a butcher's wife or daughter.

1833 *Fraser's Mag.* VII. 500 Why need these fair butcheresses [butcher's daughters] torment themselves. **1854** *Chamb. Jrnl.* I. 226 Almost every man..has a wife who is groceress, linen-draperess, butcheress, or confectioner.

'butchering, *vbl. sb.* [f. BUTCHER *v.* + -ING[1].]

1. The trade or occupation of a butcher.

1860 O. W. HOLMES *Elsie Venner* (1887) 28 A great, hulking fellow, who had been bred to butchering.

2. The action of killing in the manner of a butcher. *lit.* and *fig.* Also *attrib.*

1604 J. WILLIAMS *Ballads fr. MSS.* I. 53 Thexecutioners playde there butchringe partes. **1613** BP. HALL *Holy Panegyr.* 79 Here hath been..no Bonner-ing or Butchering of Gods Saints. **1831** CARLYLE *Sart. Res.* II. iii. 125 The Soldier wears openly, and even parades, his butchering-tool. **1865** BUSHNELL *Vicar. Sacr.* IV. i. 395 Every woman, every child, looked on at the butchering.

3. The slaughtering of cattle. Also *attrib.*, as ***butchering cow***.

1773 in *Maryland Hist. Mag.* (1920) XV. 63, I expect one more steer from the Island; the last we had from thence was ..miserably mangled in the butchering. **1900** *Daily News* 10 Apr. 8/6 Fat butchering cows.

'butchering, *ppl. a.* [f. as prec. + -ING[2].] That butchers; that kills wantonly or in cold blood.

1775 WARREN in *Harper's Mag.* Oct. (1883) 736/1 The butchering hands of an inhuman soldiery. **1816** SOUTHEY *Poet's Pilgr.* IV. xliii, From butchering strife Deliver'd.

'butcherly, *a.* and *adv.* [f. BUTCHER *sb.* + -LY.]

A. as *adj.* Like or characteristic of a butcher. Said of persons or their actions. *lit.* and *fig.*

1513 MORE *Hist. Rich. III*, 37 He..would haue appointed that bocherly office to some other then his owne borne brother. **1528** ROY *Sat.* (1845) To croutche Before this butcherly sloutche. **1683** EVELYN *Mem.* (1857) III. 192 Lord Russell was beheaded..the executioner giving him three butcherly strokes. **1720** DE FOE *Capt. Singleton* viii. (1840) 145 The man..came to be so butcherly and rude, as to shoot at our men. **1826** SOUTHEY *Lett.* (1856) III. 537 The ..consequence would be division, anarchy, and butcherly civil wars.

¶ Of or connected with physical torture.

1571 ASCHAM *Scholem.* I. (Arb.) 26 Take wholly away this butcherlie feare in making of latines. *Ibid.* 101 That boocherlie feare.

†**B.** as *adv.* In the manner of a butcher; brutally, cruelly, grossly. *Obs.*

1563–87 FOXE *A. & M.* II. 363 They..understood him butcherly—that he would cut out lumps..out of his body. *a* **1603** T. CARTWRIGHT *Confut. Rhem. N.T.* (1618) 421 Our brethren whose bloud you haue butcherly shed. **1678** N. WANLEY *Wonders* II. xx. §5. 126/1 He found his Wife most butcherly mangled.

Hence **'butcherliness.**

1755 in JOHNSON; and in mod. Dicts.

†**'butcherous,** *a. Obs.* Also 6 bou(t)cherus. [f. BUTCHER *sb.* + -OUS.] Butcherly, murderous.

1583 STANYHURST *Æneis* II. 51 Thee missing boucherus hatchet. **1620** SHELTON *Don Quix.* IV. xxvii. 213 Ye murderous Polymeans, ye butcherous Lions.

†**'butcher-row.** *Obs.* Also 6 bucherow, 8 butcherow. [f. BUTCHER *sb.* + ROW *sb.*; cf. *Packers' Row*, *Saddlers' Row*, names of streets in midland towns.] A shambles, meat-market.

1581 J. BELL *Haddon's Answ.* 268 The Bucherow and shambles of Christian Bloud. **1658** ROWLAND *Mouffet's Theat. Ins.* 934 At Toletum in the open Butcher-row. **1702** W. J. *Bruyn's Voy. Levant* xxxviii. 152 In the City and Suburbs there are reckoned to be nine Publick Butcherows.

'butcher's 'broom. [See quot. 1847.] Common name of *Ruscus aculeatus* (N.O. *Liliaceæ*, tribe *Asparageæ*), also called Knee Holly, a curious low-growing shrubby evergreen, with rigid branched stems, and coriaceous spiny leaves, or more strictly phyllodes, bearing on their disk the flower and fruit. It is found in the south of England, and is the only native endogenous shrub.

1562 TURNER *Herbal* II. 60 The wild myrte tre..is called in Englishe bochers brome. **1578** LYTE *Dodoens* VI. xiii. 674 In Shoppes it is called Ruscus; in English Kneeholme, Kneehul, Butchers Broome and Petigree. **1718** QUINCY *Compl. Disp.* 131 Butchers broom..is of an austere and bitterish Taste. **1847** *Rural Cycl.* I. 550 The whole plant is gathered by butchers, and made into besoms for sweeping their blocks and shops; and hence it obtained the name of butcher's broom. **1859** W. COLEMAN *Woodlands* (1862) 133 Botanically speaking, the Butcher's Broom is only a half-shrubby plant.

'butcher's ˌmeat, 'butcher-ˌmeat. Meat sold by butchers (beef, mutton, veal, or lamb) as distinguished from poultry, game, fish, etc.

1632 MASSINGER *City Madam* I. i, I fear it will be spent in poultry: Butcher's meat will not go down. **1769** BURKE *Pres. St. Nat.* Wks. II. 88 Corn, hay, meal, butchers-meat, fish, fowls, every thing [is excised]. **1799** J. ROBERTSON *Agric. Perth* 322 Butcher meat of all kinds has risen in the same proportion. **1846** MCCULLOCH *Acc. Brit. Empire* (1854) II. 515 The consumption of butchers' meat in the metropolis. **1862** R. PATTERSON *Ess. Hist. & Art* 302 No people.. consume so little butcher-meat as the Chinese.

butchery ('bʊtʃərɪ), *sb.* Forms: 4 bocherie, 5 bocheri, 5–6 bochery(e, buchery, 6 boucherie, bouchery(e, bochery, butcherie, 6– butchery. [a. F. *boucherie* (13th c. in Littré): see BUTCHER *sb.* and -Y[3].]

1. A slaughter-house, shambles; a butcher's shop or stall; also *attrib.* (Now chiefly applied to the slaughterhouses in public establishments, as barracks, etc., in a camp, or on shipboard.)

c **1340** *Ayenb.* 64 Þise him tobrekeþ smaller þanne me deþ þet zuyn ine bocherie. **1382** WYCLIF *1 Cor.* x. 25 Al thing that cometh in the bocherie, ete ȝe. **1494** FABYAN VII. 495 He was..hanged vpon a tree lyke as an oxe is hanged in the bochery. **1555** EDEN *Decades W. Ind.* (Arb.) 189 A streame of congeled blud as thoughe it had runne from a bouchery. **1792** A. YOUNG *Trav. France* 299 Five shepherds were conducting eight hundred sheep to the butcheries at Marseilles. **1870** *Daily News* 23 Sept., The bakery, the butchery, the magazines are all models of cleanliness. **1882** *Standard* 11 Sept. 2/1 Employed in connection with the bakery and butchery train.

b. *fig.*

1587 GOLDING *De Mornay* xxxi. 501 What shall all Hierusalem be but a verie Slaughterhouse and Butcherie? **1600** SHAKS. *A.Y.L.* II. iii. 27 This house is but a butcherie: Abhorre it, feare it, doe not enter it. **1646** SIR J. TEMPLE *Irish Rebell.* 94 The whole County, as it were, a common Butchery.

2. The trade or craft of a butcher. Now only *attrib.*, as in ***butchery business***.

c **1449** PECOCK *Repr.* I. x. 49 Tailour craft..sadeler craft.. bocheri..masonrie. **1551** ROBINSON tr. *More's Utop.* 112 They counte huntynge..the vyleste..part of boucherie. **1725** BRADLEY *Fam. Dict.* II. s.v. *Sweetbread*, A Butchery and Culinary Term. **1886** *Auckland Even. Star* 25 June 3/4 Butchery Business for Sale.

†**3.** Butchers collectively or as a community. *Obs.*

c **1475** *Bk. Found. St. Barthol. Ch.* (1886) Introd. 70 Whan this was dyvulgate, by all the bocherie, for a wurthy myracle..it was toke. **1525** LD. BERNERS *Froiss.* II. xviii. 35 Jaques Dandenboure founde all tho of the bochery well enclyned.

†**4.** Place of torture or torment: L. *carnificīna*, F. *boucherie*, applied to a horrible prison. *Obs.*

1533 BELLENDEN *Livy* II. (1822) 140 He wes nocht condampnit to service, bot erar to presoun and bouchery.

5. Cruel and wanton slaughter, carnage. Also *fig.*

1561 T. NORTON *Calvin's Inst.* Pref., The doctrine..is a deadly butcherie of soules. **1602** WARNER *Alb. Eng.* x. lvii. (1612) 251 The ciuill Warres and Butcheries in France. **1866** KINGSLEY *Herew.* iii. 77 He began boasting of his fights, his cruelties and his butcheries.

†**b.** Torture, torment. *Obs.*

1592 tr. *Junius on Rev.* xvi. 2 That torture of butcherie of conscience.

†**'butchery,** *a. Obs.* = BUTCHERLY.

1626 T. H. *Caussin's Holy Crt.* 65 He would find out other wayes to dye..then by this Butchery frenzy.

butching ('bʊtʃɪŋ), *vbl. sb. dial.* [f. BUTCH *v.* + -ING[1].] = BUTCHERING *vbl. sb.*

1785 BURNS *Death & Dr. Hornb.* xiii, Sax thousand years are near hand fled, Sin' I was to the butching bred.

† **bute**, Sc. form of BOOT *sb.*[2] booty, and *v.*[2] to make booty of, to share or divide as booty. Hence **buteing** *vbl. sb.* (cf. BOOTING, BUTIN).
c **1550** BALFOUR *Practicks* (1754) 636 (JAM.) To bute and part the prizes takin. —— 640 Gif it beis mair, it sall remane to bute and parting. —— 640 Of all pillage, the Capitane.. gettis na part nor buteing.

bute, var. of BUTTE, a hill; obs. form of BOOT, BUTT; obs. pa. t. of BEAT *v.*

bute(n, early form of BOUT *adv.*, BUT *prep.*

bute, var. BEAUT. *U.S.*
1903 A. H. LEWIS *The Boss* 272, I know that gang of card sharps,.. an' they're a bunch of butes at that!

butea ('bjuːtiːə). [mod.L. (W. Roxburgh 1792, in *Asiatick Researches* III. 469), named after John Stuart, Earl of *Bute* (1713–92).] A member of a genus of Indian or Chinese trees or climbers so named, belonging to the family Leguminosæ; esp. *Butea frondosa*, the dhak or palas of India. Also the resin of these trees (in full ***butea gum***).
1792 W. ROXBURGH in *Asiatick Researches* III. 469 (*title*) A Description of the Plant Butea. *a* **1815** —— *Flora Indica* III. 236 Here it [*sc.* the gum of *Pterocarpus marsupium*] differs from Butea gum. **1866** LINDLEY & MOORE *Treas. Bot.* 183 Butea kino or gum butea. **1879** WATTS *Dict. Chem.* I. 686 Butea gum. Bengal kino—The juice of *Butea frondosa*, Roxb., often sent into the market instead of genuine kino. **1921** R. S. TROUP *Silvicult. Indian Trees* I. 261 The *Butea* seedlings suffered greatly from the attacks of porcupines.

buteler(e, obs. f. BUTLER *sb.*

butene ('bjuːtiːn). *Chem.* [f. BUT-YL + -ENE.] The olefine of the BUTYL series C_4H_8, also called BUTYLENE.

butenyl ('bjuːtiːnɪl). *Chem.* [f. BUTEN(E + -YL.] Any of the three isomeric forms of the radical C_4H_7—, of which the two normal butylenes are hydrides.
1881 *Jrnl. Chem. Soc.* XL. 711 A liquid is obtained, which, on evaporating, leaves butenylglycerol as a thick yellow liquid. **1884** ROSCOE & SCHORLEMMER *Treat. Chem.* III. II. 377 Butenyl Alcohol, $C_4H_7(OH)_3$. **1957** T. S. STEVENS in E. H. Rodd *Chem. Carbon Compounds* IVA. iii. 228, 2-Butenylthiophen yields 95% of thionaphthen when passed over kieselguhr-P_2O_5 at 600°.

buteonine (bjuː'tiːənaɪn), *a.* [f. L. *būteōn-em* hawk or buzzard + -INE; cf. L. *leōnīnus* LEONINE.] Of, pertaining to, or resembling the Buzzard.
1865 *Athenæum* No. 1987. 732/3 Raptorial bird.. somewhat buteonine. **1874** COUES *Birds N.-W.* 356 The only buteonine species observed.

butere, buterie, obs. ff. BUTTER, BUTTERY.

buthe, obs. form of BOOTH.

† **butin.** *Obs.* Also 5–6 butyn, 6 butyne, -en, -ine, -iene, 7 bootyn, *Sc.* 6–7 buiting, but(e)ing. [a. F. *butin* 'booty'; according to Littré, from ON. *býti* 'exchange, barter' (cf. MG. *bûten*, mod.Ger. *beute*), though the actual form in Fr. does not appear to be explained. Cf. BOOTY.]
Spoil, prey, or plunder, taken in common; booty.
1474 CAXTON *Chesse* 39 He that abode behynde by maladye or sekenes shold haue as moche part of the butyn. **1475** —— *Jason* 31 b, Whan they had departed their gayn and butin. **1530** PALSGR. 653, I parte a butyne, or a pray taken in the warre. **1531** ELYOT *Gov.* II. i. (1557) 86 It is no buten or praie. **1573** *Sege Edin. Cast.* in *Scot. Poems 16th C.* II. 294 Sum gat ane butiene for thair being thair. **1597** MONTGOMERIE *Cherrie & Slae* 208 Quha bringis hame the buiting? **1635** J. HAYWARD tr. *Biondi's Banish'd Virgin* 196 Good store of bootyn. **1646** H. LAWRENCE *Comm. Angels* 169 Captaines, when they harrang their Souldiers, tell them of the butin, of the prey.

butine ('bjuːtaɪn, -iːn). *Chem.* [ad. G. *butin*, f. L. *būt-yrum* BUTTER *sb.*[1] + -INE[5].] † **1.** The name given by W. Heintz (*Ann. der Physik und Chem.* (1853) XC. 151) to a substance present in butter. *Obs.*
1867 BLOXAM *Chem.* 582 Butter.. contains also butine, which yields glycerine and butic acid ($HO.C_{40}H_{39}O_3$) when saponified.
2. Orig., any of the four unsaturated unbranched hydrocarbons with the formula C_4H_6; later restricted to the two isomers that have a triple bond, those with two double bonds being called BUTADIENE.
The word is now obsolescent, being replaced by BUTYNE.
1884 ROSCOE & SCHORLEMMER *Treat. Chem.* III. II. 463 Butine, $C=H_2CH.CH=CH_2$. When erythrite, $C_4H_6(OH)_4$, is heated with concentrated formic acid to 230°, butine is formed. **1888** *Amer. Chem. Jrnl.* X. 431 The fourth butine, methylisoallylene, was the subject of this investigation. **1889** G. M'GOWAN tr. *Bernthsen's Text-bk. Org. Chem.* 57 Crotonylene or Butine, $CH_2=CH-CH=CH_2$, is contained in illuminating gas. *Ibid.*, Pyrrolylene, C_4H_6, from pyrrolidine, is probably identical with the butine from erythrite. **1895** THOMSON & BLOXAM *Bloxam's Chem.* (ed. 8) 524 The hydrocarbon C_4H_6 (butine) can exist in two forms, each of which will have a pair of trebly-linked carbon atoms. **1934** *Chem. Abstr.* XXVIII. 2321 EtI and NaC⋮CH in liquid NH_3 at −45° give 78% of 1-butine.

‖ **bu'tizia.** *Obs.* [The sense suits Sp. *botija*; cf. BOTOZIO.] Some kind of earthen jar.
a **1622** R. HAWKINS *Voy. S. Sea* (1847) 156 The butizias, in which the wine was, which were found in Balparizo, had many sparkes of gold shining in them.

† **'butkin.** *Obs.* [? dim. of BUTT *sb.*[2]] A small fish.
1526 *Househ. Exp. Sir T. Le Strange, Addit. MS. B.M.* 27448. 31 b, In butkyns, sandlyngs and lityll playce, iiij*d*.

butler ('bʌtlə(r)). *sb.* Forms: 3 butuler, botyler, 3–4 buteler, 3–5 boteler, 4–5 -ere, 4 botoler, bottelar, 4–5 botelar, botil(l)er(e, botyller, botler(e, 5 buteler(e, butiller, buttiler, -are, bouteler, 5–6 butteler, buttler, 6 botteler, buttelar, butlar, 5– butler. [a. AF. *butuiller* = OF. *bouteillier*:—med.L. *buticulārius*, f. *buticula* BOTTLE *sb.*[1]]
1. a. A servant who has charge of the wine-cellar and dispenses the liquor. Formerly also, one who hands round wine, a cup-bearer. He is now usually the head-servant of a household, who keeps the plate, etc.
c **1250** *Gen. & Ex.* 2092 Ðis buteler Ioseph sone for-gat [cf. *Gen.* xl.]. *a* **1300** *Cursor M.* 4497 Þe bottelar was lesed þat ilk dai. *c* **1300** *K. Alis.* 834 Som to marchal, and to botileris, To knyght, to page, and to jogoleris. **1387** TREVISA *Higden* (Rolls Ser.) V. 269 [Rowena] schulde serve hym instede of his boteler. *c* **1440** *Promp. Parv.* 45 Botlere [**1499** boteler]. *c* **1460** *Bk. Curtasye* 423 in *Babees Bk.* 312 Botler shalle sett for yche a messe, A pot, a lofe. **1589** *True Coppie of Disc.* (1881) 50 Though any man.. doo locke up their drinke and set buttlers upon it. **1598** STOW *Surv.* xi. (1603) 96 These Citizens did minister wine, as Botelers. **1616** *Pasquil & Kath.* v. 228 Bid the Butler broch fresh wine. **1727** SWIFT *Gulliver* I. ii. 33 He ordered his cooks and butlers.. to give me victuals and drink. **1842** TENNYSON *Day-dr.* 45. **1859** GEO. ELIOT *A. Bede* 9 A man who had been butler 'to the family' for fifteen years.
b. *fig.*
1387 TREVISA *Higden* (Rolls Ser.) I. 273 Þere is the faire floure þe citee of Parys norice of þewes, botiller of lettres [*pincerna litterarum*]. *c* **1420** *Pallad. on Husb.* III. 696 And gladde be thai to stande aboute a welle That humour euer may thaire boteler be. **1594** *Mirr. Policie* (1599) 265 Saint Hierom calleth it [the S. wind] the butler or pourer forth of water, because it commonly bringeth raine.
† **c.** phr. ***with butler's grace***: ? with a drink.
1609 MELTON *Sixefolde Polit.* 33 (N.) Fidlers, who are regarded but for a baudy song.. and when they haue done, are commonly sent away with Butlers grace.
2. An officer who originally had charge of the wine for the royal table; hence the title of an official of high rank nominally connected with the supply, importation, etc., of wine, but having different duties in different countries and at various times. (Cf. *marshall, lord chamberlain*, etc.)
1297 R. GLOUC. 438 Boþe Wyllam & Rychard hys sones adrentte were, And hys panyter & hys chamberleyn, & hys boteler also. *c* **1330** *Amis & Amil.* 188 Sir Amis, as ye may here, He made his chef botelere, In his court for to be. **1495** *Act 11 Hen. VII*, lxii. §1 Item of the Chief Buttler of England *Cli.* **1587** J. HIGINS *Mirr. Mag.* (1610) 482 (*title*) How.. Sir Nicholas Burdel, Chiefe Butler of Normandie, was slaine at Pontoise. **1611** COTGR., *Grand bouteillier*, the great Butler of France; an honourable officer, but out of date euer since Charles the seuenths time. **1667** J. CHAMBERLAYNE *St. Gt. Brit.* I. III. iii. (1743) 161 Edward Fitz-Theobald being long ago made Butler of Ireland, the Duke of Ormond.. took the sirname of Butler. **1887** *Burke's Peerage* 1068 James 7th Earl of Ormonde and 7th Butler had (1328) a renewed grant of the prisage of wines (which had been resumed by the crown).
3. *Comb.*, as ***butler-like*** adj.; † **butler's box**, ? a box into which players put a portion of their winnings at Christmas-time as a 'Christmas-box' for the butler (cf. BOX *sb.*[2] 5); **butler's pantry**, a pantry where the plate, glass, etc., are kept.
1880 MRS. EILOART *Dean's Wife* III. ii. 16 Then his eye met that of the respectable *butler-like man opposite. *a* **1593** H. SMITH *Serm.* (1866) II. 240 The law is like a *butlers-box, play still on till all come to the candlestick. **1597** *Return Parnass.* Pt. 2 Prol. 44 The Pilgrimage to Pernassus, and the returne from Pernassus haue.. hindred the buttlers box, and emptied the Colledge barrells. **1621** *Tract agst. Usurie* (N.) The old comparison, which compares usury to the butler's boxe, deserves to be remembred. Whilest men are at play, they feele not what they give to the boxe, but at the end of Christmas it makes all or neere all gamesters loosers. **1660** JER. TAYLOR *Duct. Dubit.* III. iii. vii. §3 Whoever lost, signor *papa*, like the butler's-box, was sure to get. **1816** JANE AUSTEN *Emma* II. vi. 113 A bad *butler's pantry. **1885** *Harper's Mag.* Mar. 544/1 A.. cousin.. was discovered.. in the butler's pantry.

butler ('bʌtlə(r)), *v.* [f. prec. sb.] In various nonce-uses: **a.** *trans.* To take charge of and serve (liquor); also *absol.* to act as butler; **b.** *pass.* To be served by a butler. Hence **'butlering** *vbl. sb.*
1742 JARVIS *Quix.* II. IV. vii. (D.) The calling he is of allows of no catering nor butlering. **1826** *Blackw. Mag.* XIX. 587 We have consigned the flasks.. to the safe custody of Ambrose, till they can be butlered by Hogg. **1855** DICKENS *Dorrit* (Househ. ed.) 317/1 As nations are made to be taxed, so families are made to be butlered.

butlerage ('bʌtlərɪdʒ). Forms: 5 botelarage, 6 butlarage, 7 butlaridge, buttleradge, 8 butleridge. [f. as prec. + -AGE.]
† **1.** A duty formerly payable to the king's butler on every cargo of wine imported (? by merchant-strangers); called also *prisage*. *Obs.* exc. *Hist.*
1491 in Arnolde *Chron.* (1811) 112 For all maner other dutees, botelarage, costis and chargis.. concernyng the said wynes. **1509** *Act 1 Hen. VIII*, v. §6 Any other being free of Prisage or Butlarage of Wines. **1654** in Sir J. Picton *L'pool Munic. Rec.* (1883) I. 180, 22 tunnes of Wyne.. to pay for y[e] butlerage the somme of tenn pounds. **1768** BLACKSTONE *Comm.* I. 315 Prisage was a right of taking two tons of wine from every ship importing into England twenty tons or more; which by Edward I was exchanged into a duty of 2*s.* for every ton imported by merchant-strangers, and called butlerage, because paid to the king's butler.
† **2.** The office or dignity of king's butler; the department over which he had charge. *Obs.*
1615 *MS. of Dk. Northumbld.* in *3rd Rep. Commiss. Hist. MSS.* (1872) 62/1 Officers of the mint, of the works, of the great wardrobe, of the butlaridge. **1736** CARTE *Ormonde* II. 219 A perquisite or appendage of the butlerage of Ireland.
3. That part of the household management and expenses which pertains to the butler or the butlery.
1815 *Misc.* in *Ann. Reg.* 554/1 For providing.. things in the Butlerage department. **1853** *Fraser's Mag.* XLVII. 414 An exact account of the cost of washing, lighting, firing, of kitchen, of butlerage, of cellarage.

butlerdom ('bʌtlədəm). *nonce-wd.* [f. as prec. + -DOM.] The class or estate of butlers.
1861 *Sat. Rev.* 21 Dec. 633 Butlerdom is a serious obstacle to the felicity of a wealthy establishment.

'butleress. [see -ESS.] A female butler.
c **1615** CHAPMAN *Odyss.* III. 530 His sweet-wine cup.. Which now the butleresse had leaue t'employ. **1860** *Sat. Rev.* 7 Jan. 13 Is the porter to be a daughter of the plough? What of the committee, the stewardess, and the butleress?

butlerian (bʌt'lɪərɪən), *a. nonce-wd.* [f. as prec. + -IAN.] Of or pertaining to a butler.
1882 E. C. CLAYTON (Mrs. Needham) *Girl's Destiny* I. iv. 61 Obtrusive, in his strict attention to his butlerian duties.

butlerish ('bʌtlərɪʃ), *a.* [f. BUTLER *sb.* + -ISH[1].] Belonging to or characteristic of a butler.
1923 A. HUXLEY *Antic Hay* iii. 45 He moved with a certain pomp, a butlerish gravity.

butlership ('bʌtləʃɪp). [f. BUTLER *sb.* + -SHIP.] The office of butler.
1535 COVERDALE *Gen.* xl. 21 And restored the chefe butlar to his butlarshipe agayne. **1587** J. HIGINS *Mirr. Mag.* (1610) 482 Chief butlership of Normandy unto me fell. **1612** *Caius Coll. MS.* in *Gentl. Mag.* (1883) Oct. 384 [Plate] spoyled and battered at the going out of Sir Utting out of his buttlership. **1621** BOLTON *Stat. Irel.* 399 (an. 28 Eliz.) Any Patentee or Patentees of any the office or offices of Collectorship.. or of the Butlership, or price Wines. **1829** HEATH *Grocers' Comp.* (1869) 182 The Mayor's claim to the chief butlership. **1840** MRS. GORE in *New Monthly Mag.* LX. 54 The clodpole she has disciplined into butlership.

butlery ('bʌtlərɪ). In 3, 5 botelerye, 5 botelary. [ME. *botelerye*, a. F. *bouteillerie* (13th c. in Littré) 'lieu où l'on conserve le vin', f. *bouteille* BOTTLE; but in mod. use prob. directly f. BUTLER *sb.* + -Y[3].] A butler's room or pantry; a buttery.
1297 *R. Glouc.* 191 Bedwer þe botyler, kyng of Normandye, Nom also in ys half a uayr companye.. vorto seruy of þe botelerye. *c* **1425** *Gloss.* in Wr.-Wülcker 670 *Hec botelaria*, botelary. **1480** CAXTON *Chron. Eng.* cxcvi. 172 A knyght that the Erle hadde brought vp of nought and hadde norisshed hym in his botelerye. **1822** J. PLATTS *Bk. Curios.* lxii. 628 He should go into the butlery of the king's palace there, and draw.. as much wine as should be needful for making a pitcher of claret. **1868** MILMAN *St. Paul's* iii. 69 It is the full inventory of his plate.. his kitchen, his butlery.

butling: see BUTTLE *v.*

butment ('bʌtmənt). [f. BUTT *v.*[2] + -MENT; cf. ABUTMENT and Fr. *boutée* 'ouvrage qui soutient la poussée d'une voute'.]
1. *Arch.* The supporter of an arch; = ABUTMENT 3.
1624 WOTTON *Archit.* (1672) 31 The Supporters or Butments (as they are termed) of the said Arch. **1773** *Gentl. Mag.* XLIII. 164 One of the main pillars or arch butments seems to tremble at the sound of a certain bell. **1806** T. PAINE *Yellow Fever* Misc. Wks. II. 184 Arches joining each other lengthways, serve as butments to each other.
b. butment cheeks: see quot.
1876 GWILT *Archit.* Gloss., *Butment cheeks*, the two solid sides of a mortise. The thickness of each cheek is usually equal to the thickness of the mortise.
2. An out-standing mass (of rock or masonry).
1865 E. BURRITT *Walk Land's E.* 168 It stood on the southern battlement or butment of the bluff.
3. A piece of ground abutting on a larger piece.
1677 MOXON *Mech. Exerc.* (1703) 158 The piece of Ground in the Yard.. is a Butment from the rest of the Ground-plot. **1751** CHAMBERS *Cycl.* s.v., The name butment is also given to little places taken out of the yard, or the ground-plot of an house, for butteries, sculleries, etc.

butning, obs. form of BUTTONING.

butor, etc., obs. forms of BITTERN.

Butskellism (ˈbʌtskɪlɪz(ə)m). *Pol.* [Blend of the names of Richard Austen *Butler*, Conservative Chancellor of the Exchequer (1951–55) and Hugh Todd Naylor *Gaitskell*, Labour Chancellor of the Exchequer (1950–51) and subsequently Shadow Chancellor + -ISM.] The economic policy of Butler, regarded as largely undifferentiable from that of his predecessor and Shadow Chancellor Gaitskell; advocacy of this policy. Also in extended use, esp. the centrist attitudes and policies which, according to many commentators, influenced both Labour and Conservative parties during the post-war period, leading to a previously unexpected measure of agreement on such matters as law, education, social policy, and defence.

'Yes, he [*sc.* Richard Fort MP] *did* invent 'Butskellism'. It was over lunch at the Reform; Norman McRae (our host) completed the trio... We were having a general discussion about the political-cum-economic situation, and it is our recollection that Richard coined the actual word. Norman then went off and wrote the Economist leader.' — Sir I. Trethowan, in private letter to Sir E. W. Playfair (1987).

[**1954** *Economist* 13 Feb. 440/1 Mr Butskell is already a well-known figure in dinner table conversations in both Westminster and Whitehall, and the time has come to introduce him to a wider audience. He is a composite of the present Chancellor and the previous one.] *Ibid.* 441/2 The next few weeks will show whether the Opposition will seize this chance of golden silence; or whether, in a Brown fury, it is going to throw the opportunity for constructive Butskellism away. **1969** H. MACMILLAN *Tides of Fortune* xx. 691 Gaitskell..no doubt wishing to avoid the stigma of 'Butskellism', made an unusually violent speech. **1972** *Daily Tel.* 24 Oct. 16 These [policies] differed radically from the consensus policy of 'Butskellism' which had been pursued by the Tories during the Macmillan era. **1978** R. MAUDLING *Mem.* i. 28 In politics it may be called the Middle Way, Butskellism, or consensus. **1981** *Economist* 21 Feb. 15 The heirs of Butskellism, the centrist Tory policies of the 1950s and 1960s, are not ready to see the real value of pensions cut.

Hence **'Butskellite** *a.*, that is or resembles Butskellism; also as *sb.*, an adherent of Butskellism. Also (*rare*) **'Butskellist** *sb.*

1956 *Economist* 31 Mar. 669/1 The Butskellite policies of 1951–55. **1959** F. MACLEAN *Back to Bokhara* i. 58 There is certainly much in the Soviet Government's lavish use of incentives..that would shock our own old-time Butskellists. **1964** *Economist* 11 Apr. 115/1 A bunch of Butskellites. **1977** *Financial Times* 25 Feb. 31/8 Nor is it too difficult to piece together a perfectly sensible eclectic programme of measures on the leftward side of a central moderate consensus. One could concoct a modern Butskellite programme of this kind. **1982** *Times* 12 Feb. 4/3 The prevailing mood in the church is 'Butskellite', whatever may have happened to Parliament.

butt (bʌt), *sb.*[1] Also 4–6 butte. [cogn. w. Sw. *butta* turbot, mod.G. *butte*, Du. *bot*, flounder; of obscure origin: perh. from the blunt shape of the head (cf. Da. *but* stumpy, and BUTT *sb.*[3]). See HALIBUT.]

A name applied variously in different places to kinds of flat fish, as sole, fluke, plaice, turbot, etc.

Hence **butt-woman**, who sells these, a fish-wife.

a **1300** *Havelok* 759 He tok..Hering, and the makerel, The butte, the schulle, the thornebake. *c* **1440** *Promp. Parv.* 56 But, fysche, *pecten.* **1530** PALSGR. 202/1 Butte fysshe, *plye.* **1599** NASHE *Lent. Stuffe* (1871) 79 The plaice and the butt..for their mocking have wry mouths ever since. **1655** MOUFET & BENNET *Health's Improv.* (1746) 266 Whilst they [Turbots] be young..they are called Butts. **1776** COWPER *Corr.* (1824) I. 30 Whatever fish are likely..butts, plaice, flounder, or any other. **1886** R. C. LESLIE *Seapainter's Log* x. 192 The butt or sole, the turbot, the halibut..all belong to that strange family of fish.

1620 MELTON *Astrolog.* 37 Sell their good Fortunes to Oyster-wives and Butte-women for greasie Two-pences.

butt (bʌt), *sb.*[2] Also 5–6 butte, 5–6 but. [app. first adopted in 15th c. (the ME. *butte(ü)* belongs to BIT *sb.*[3] of the same ultimate origin); a common Romanic word, F. *botte, boute*, Sp., Pg. *bota*, It. *botte*, late L. *butta, buttis* cask, wine-skin, of unknown origin: not connected with BOOT *sb.*[3]

With 'butt of malmsey' cf. It. *botte di malvasia.*]

1. a. A cask for wine or ale, of capacity varying from 108 to 140 gallons. (Earlier the size was app. much smaller; see quot. 1443; cf. also 1462 in b.) Afterwards also as a measure of capacity = 2 hogsheads, i.e. usually in ale measure 108 gallons, in wine measure 126 gallons; but these standards were not always precisely adhered to.

1443 in Rogers *Agric. & Prices* III. 511/1 [Rhenish 1 butt = 36 gals.]. **1483** *Act 1 Rich. III*, xiii, [The preamble recites that the butt of malmsey formerly held sometimes seven score gallons, and never less than six score; but that through the dishonesty of the merchant strangers it has come to contain 'scantly five score eight gallons'.] **1500** in Rogers *Agric. & Prices* III. 514/2 [Malmsey 5 butts]. **1513** MORE *Hist. Rich. III*, Hastely drouned in a Butte of Malmesey. **1593** NASHE *Christ's T.* 32 a, Buts of Sack and Muscadine. **1610** SHAKS. *Temp.* II. ii. 126, I escap'd vpon a But of Sacke, which the Saylors heaued o'reboord. **1727** BRADLEY *Fam. Dict.* I, *Butt*, or Pipe, a Liquid Measure, whereof two Hogsheads make a Butt or Pipe, as two Pipes or Butts make one Tun. **1731** BAILEY II. *Butt*, a large Vessel for Liquids, 120 Gallons of Wine. **1836** H. COLERIDGE *North. Worthies* (1852) I. 22 Did not Joseph Hume graciously receive a butt of cyder?

†**b.** A cask for fish, fruit, etc., of a capacity varying according to the contents and locality. *Obs.*

1423 *Act 2 Hen. VI*, [xi.] xiv, Buttes de Samon..serroient de..iiij^xx & iiij galons pleinement pakkez [*transl.* Butts of Salmon..should be of..lxxxiv Gallons fully packed]. **1462** in Rogers *Agric. & Prices* III. 315/4 [Salmon (Pershore) 2 pipes at 60/-, 2 butts at 30/-]. **1481–90** *Howard Househ. Bks.* 120, xv. buttes. Schrempes viijd. ijd. **1540** *Act 32 Hen. VIII*, xiv, For a butte of currantes, iiis. iiiid. **1649** THORPE *Charge York Assiz.* 28 In a Butt of Salmon four-score and four gallons. **1751** CHAMBERS *Cycl.* s.v., A butt of currans is from fifteen to twenty-two hundred weight. **1753** MAITLAND *Edinburgh* v. 327 For ilk Bale of Madder or Butt of Prunes, 1/-.

c. *fig.*

1831 GALT in *Fraser's Mag.* II. 708 This single fact speaks more than butts and tons of declamation.

2. In wider sense: A cask, barrel.

1626 T. HAWKINS *Caussin's Holy Crt.* 343 He liueth like a But, which doth nothing, but leake, and roule vp, and downe. **1823** J. BADCOCK *Dom. Amusem.* 80 To the end which projected overboard, was suspended a water-butt. *a* **1859** L. HUNT *Rob. Hood* II. xxviii, As in a leathern butt of wine Stuck that arrow with a dump.

3. *Comb.*, chiefly *attrib.*, as *butt-beer, -cooper, -sling*; **butt-beaker** *Archæol.*, a butt-shaped beaker; **butt-howel**, a howelling-adze used by coopers (Knight *Dict. Mech.* 1874); **butt-keeping** *a.*, suitable to be kept in butts; **butt-shaped** *a.*, shaped like a butt or cask; spec. *Archæol.* applied to a type of Belgic pottery.

1933 *Antiquity* VII. 29 There are no butt-beakers, no imported Italic wares. **1941** *Proc. Prehist. Soc.* VII. 140 Butt-beaker of sandy, biscuit-coloured ware. **1713** *Lond. & Countr. Brew.* I. (1742) 13 Fine Ales and Butt-beers. **1771** SMOLLETT *Humph. Cl.* II. 8 June, Whom he treats with.. Calvert's entire butt beer. **1837** WHITTOCK *Bk. Trades* (1842) 161 The Butt-cooper is confined to working for brewers or distillers. **1713** *Lond. & Countr. Brew.* I. (1742) 13 Many thousand Quarterns of this Malt have been..used ..for brewing the Butt-keeping Beers. **1916** T. MAY *Pottery at Silchester* 168 Tall 'butt-shaped vase'. *Ibid.*, This is a still later development of the 'butt-shaped' beaker. **1930** —— *Catal. Rom. Pottery in Colchester & Essex Museum* 12 'Butt-shaped' beaker. **1836** *Fraser's Mag.* XIV. 477 A pair of butt-slings, strong enough to have held up the cupola of St. Paul's.

butt (bʌt), *sb.*[3] Forms: 5 bott, butte, 5–8 but, 7– butt. [First appears in 15th c., but must be much older if BUTTOCK (13th c.) be a dim. of it. Of obscure etymology: words apparently cognate are ON. *butt-r* ('short' Vigf.; but occurring only as a nickname); Da., LG. *but*, Du. *bot*, blunt, short, thickset, stumpy; Sp., Pg. *boto* blunt, F. *bot* in *pied-bot* (club foot). Cf. further ON. *bút-r* (*but-r*, Fritzner) log of wood, Sw. *but* clod, stump, MHG. *butze* clod, mod.G. *butze(n* 'log, piece cut from a tree-trunk' (Sanders) = sense 2 below, also 'core of apples, catkin or bud of shrubs and trees' (Grimm) = sense 4.

F. *bout* end (OF. also *bot, but*) is apparently not connected with these words. It has naturally been thought of as the source of the Eng. word, but it does not appear to be recorded in the specific sense of 'thick end'. But cf. BUTT *sb.*[7]]

1. a. The thicker end of anything, *esp.* of a tool or weapon, the part by which it is held or on which it rests; e.g. the lower end of a spear-shaft, whip-handle, fishing-rod, the broad end of the stock of a gun or pistol.

1470–85 MALORY *Arthur* x. ii, Sir Tristram awaked hym with the but of his spere. **1548** HALL *Chron.*, *10 Hen. V*, 82 Round about the charet rode ccccc men of armes..with the but of their speres vpward. **1814** SCOTT *Wav.* II. xiii. 205 The pedlar, snatching a musket..bestowed the butt of it.. on the head of his late instructor. **1872** BAKER *Nile Tribut.* x. 158 My only way of working him [a fish] was to project the butt of the rod in the usual manner. **1873** BENNETT & CAVENDISH *Billiards* 25 The cues should taper gradually from a diameter of two and a half inches at the butt. **1871** KINGSLEY *At Last* II. xiii. 214 Three eyes in the monkey's face, as the children call it, at the butt of the nut.

b. Angling. *to give* (a fish when hooked) *the butt*: to turn the bottom of the rod towards him, so as to get a more rigid hold upon the line; also *fig.*

1828 J. WILSON in *Blackw. Mag.* XXIV. 275 Give her [a fish] the butt—or she is gone for ever. **1835** *Ibid.* XXXVIII. 121 He writes like a man who could give the butt. **1872** BAKER *Nile Tribut.* ix. 150 Giving him the butt, I held him by main force.

2. The trunk of a tree, *esp.* the thickest part just above the root.

1601 HOLLAND *Pliny* XXIV. i. (R.) Trees..prove harder to be hewed..if a man touch them with his hand before hee set the edge of the ax to their butt. **1735** SOMERVILLE *Chase* III. 234 Then in the midst a Column high is rear'd, The But of some fair Tree. **1787** WINTER *Syst. Husb.* 103 The tops and buts of ash and oak are more advantageous for burning into charcoal than if sold for firing. **1807** VANCOUVER *Agric. Devon* (1813) 52 An oak..which squared 15 inches at the butt. **1881** JEFFERIES *Wood Magic* I. i. 4 A round wooden box ..hollowed out from the sawn butt of an elm.

3. A buttock. Chiefly *dial.* and *colloq.* in *U.S.*

c **1450** *Nominale* in Wr.-Wülcker 737 *Hic lumbus*, a bott. *c* **1450** *Bk. Cookery* in *Holkham Coll.* (1882) 58 Tak Buttes of pork and smyt them to peces. **1486** *Bk. St. Albans* A v, The marow of hogges that is in the bone of the butte of porke. **1601** HOLLAND *Pliny* I. 344 A Lion likewise hath but very little [marrow], to wit, in some few bones of his thighes & buts behind. **1860** BARTLETT *Dict. Amer.* 61 *Butt*..the buttocks. The word is used in the West in such phrases as, 'I fell on my butt,' 'He kick'd my butt'. **1884** *Harper's Mag.* July 299/1 Rump butts, strips, rounds, and canning beef.

4. a. The foot or base of a leaf-stalk; the end or tip of a branch; also *Sc.* a catkin. [cf. *botthe*, BUD *sb.*[1]]

1807–10 TANNAHILL in *Autobiog. Beggar-boy* (1859) 191 Siller saughs wi' downy buts. *a* **1835** COBBETT *Eng. Gard.* (1845) 127 Horse-Radish. The butts of the leaves will grow, if put into the ground. **1870** KINGSLEY in *Gd. Words* 390/1 It is all jagged with the brown butts of its old fallen leaves.

b. *transf.* (see quot.)

1862 ANSTED *Channel Isl.* II. ix. (ed. 2) 238 The creature when deprived of food, throwing off part after part, till nothing remains but a little spherical butt.

5. *Iron-work.* (see quot.)

1831 J. HOLLAND *Manuf. Metals* I. 89 The blocks out of which iron anvils are formed..consist of what are known to the trade by the appellation of butts.

6. *Comb.*, as **butt-head** = BUTT-END *sb.* q.v.; **butt-hole**, a blind hole, a cul-de-sac; **butt-log** (cf. BUTTER[5]); **butt-piece**; **butt-sheath**, a leather case for holding a mounted soldier's carbine.

c **1634** in *Harper's Mag.* (1883) Apr. 720/2 One might thrust a pike down to the *butt-head. **1905** *Westm. Gaz.* 3 Mar. 3/2 The old dog's got him [*sc.* a badger] in a *butt hole. **1879** *Lumberman's Gaz.* 15 Oct., If, in sawing a *butt log, one end of the stick is set out from the standard, our Dog will reach it and hold it firmly in its place. **1863** *National (U.S.) Bank Act* (1882) 21 The Comptroller of the Currency shall cause to be examined, each year, the plates, dies, *butt-pieces, etc. **1848** W. K. KELLY tr. *L. Blanc's Hist. Ten Years* II. 47 Their pistols were in their holsters, and their carbines in the *butt-sheaths.

7. The piece of the inner margin of a single leaf of a book, which projects as a narrow strip beyond the sewing or other fastening when the book is bound.

1921 A. ESDAILE in *Library* Dec. 185 The last leaf of B.. is a single leaf, whose butt is visible after B. 1.

8. The fag-end of a cigar or of a cigarette.

1847 W. H. GREGORY *Paddiana* I. 235 Will yer honor give me the butt? **1888** KIPLING *Departm. Ditties* (1890) 106 Like the butt of a dead cigar. **1918** WODEHOUSE *Piccadilly Jim* i. 5 'Smoking cigarettes.'.. 'There are two butts in the ash-tray.' **1940** DYLAN THOMAS *Portr. Artist* 117, I cupped a match..I puffed my last butt. **1958** S. ELLIN *Eighth Circle* (1959) II. v. 62 A litter of used paper cups and cigarette butts.

¶ See also BUTT *sb.*[7], BUTT *sb.*[11]

butt (bʌt), *sb.*[4] Also 5 botte, 5–7 butte, 5–9 but. [a. F. *but* goal, shooting-target (see Diez s.v. *Bozza*, and Littré); the cognate *butte* in early instances is closely associated in meaning (see next).

Cf. the senses of L. *meta*. Sense 1 may have been influenced by ABUT and BUTT *v.*[2]]

†**I. 1.** A terminal point; a boundary-mark, *esp.* in phr. *butts and bounds*; a goal; often *fig.* *Obs.* exc. *dial.* and *U.S.*

From quot. 1592 in BUTT *v.*[2] 1 it appears that a *butt* was understood to refer to the *end* of a piece of ground, and a *bound* to its side.

c **1475** *Bk. Found. St. Barthol. Ch.* II. iii. (1886) 84 We be come for oure synnys to the butte & terme or marke of vniuersale kynde of man. **1557** *Order of Hospitalls* F viij, A Booke of all the Lands and Tenements..of their Buts and boundes. **1572** R. H. *Lavaterus' Ghostes* (1596) 91 The bounds of countries and buts of lands. **1604** SHAKS. *Oth.* v. ii. 267 Heere is my journies end, heere is my butt. **1726** DE FOE *Hist. Devil* I. v. (1840) 62 The butts and bounds of Parnassus are not yet ascertained. **1838** W. HOLLOWAY *Dict. Provinc.* 23 *Butts and Bounds*, the borders of a person's estate. *E. Sussex.* **1903** MCFAUL *Ike Glidden* vii. 44 Have you any documents for reference in order to fix the butts and bounds?

II. A mark for shooting.

2. a. A mark for archery practice; properly a mound or other erection on which the target is set up. Hence in mod. use a mound or embankment in front of which the targets are placed for artillery, musketry, or rifle practice.

For the purposes of archery there were usually two butts, one at each extremity of the range; hence the frequent mention of *a pair of butts*, and the use of *the butts* for 'the archery-ground' (Jam.).

a **1400** *Octouian* 899 Ther na's nother..That myght the ston to hys but bryng. *c* **1440** *Promp. Parv.* 56 But or bertel or bysselle, *meta.* **1477** EARL RIVERS (Caxton) *Dictes* 89 An archier to faile of the butte is no wonder, but to hytte the pryke is a greet maistrie. **1526** SKELTON *Magnyf.* 297 Ye wante but a wylde flyeng bolte to shote at the buttes. **1620** J. WILKINSON *Courts Leet* 117 There ought to be buts made in every Tything, Village, and Hamlet. **1642** BP. REYNOLDS *Israel's Petit.* 13 The arrow sticks in the Butt unto which the marke is fastned. **1678** A. LITTLETON *Lat. Dict.*, A butt, or bank to shoot at, *agger.* **1697** DRYDEN *Virg. Georg.* II. 773 The Groom his Fellow-Groom at Buts defies. **1857** KINGSLEY *Gt. Cities* in *Misc.* (1859) II. 324 There were the butts..where..lads ran and wrestled, and pitched the bar.. and practised with the long-bow. **1867** *Leisure Hour* 477 We ..see..solid mounds of earth..These are the butts for the rifleman's practice. **1873** *Act 36 & 37 Vict.* lxxvii. §29 Any butt or target belonging to..any naval artillery volunteer corps.

b. *transf* and *fig.* with conscious reference to prec.

1534 MORE *Comf. agst. Trib.* II. Wks. (1557) 1199/2 Ye proude man..hath no..butte, or pricke vpon erth, wherat he determineth to shoote. **1593** SHAKS. *3 Hen. VI*. I. iv. 29 Come bloody Clifford..I am your Butt, and I abide your Shot. **1628** EARLE *Microcosm*. iii. (Arb.) 24 Hee shoots all his meditations at one Butt. **1679** *Establ. Test*. 26 The Crown.. and..the Church, the two butts against which he levels all the arrows of his poisoned quiver. **1870** SPURGEON *Treas. Dav. Ps*. xliv. 14 They were the common butts of every fool's arrow.

c. In grouse-shooting, a position either sunken or on the level ground, protected by a wall or bank of earth behind which the sportsman may stand and fire unobserved by the game.

1885 W. S. STANHOPE *Let*. 28 Nov. in Walsingham & Payne-Gallwey *Shooting: Moor & Marsh* (1886) i. 11, I began to shoot grouse in 1841; we had our regular drives then, but without butts. **1897** *Encycl. Sport* I. 489/2 The butts, or batteries, as they are indifferently called. **1935** *Encycl. Sports* 322/2 A semi-circular, or..almost circular wall of peat or turf, covered with heather..is the usual form of butt. **1955** *Times* 13 May 12/6 The butts all ready set up for the grouse-shooting.

†**3.** The distance between the two butts; the length of the shooting-range. Also as a measure of distance (cf. *bow-shot*); in same senses ***a pair of butts, a butt('s) length***, Sc. a ***butelang***. *Obs.*

1544 ASCHAM *Toxoph*. (Arb.) 129 At a short but..ye Pecock fether doth seldome kepe vp ye shaft. **1562** J. HEYWOOD *Prov. & Epigr*. (1867) 144 Thy braine lacketh strength To beare a pinte of wine a payre of buttes length. **1600** *Sc. Acts Jas. VI* (1814) 203 Within tua pair of butelangis to the towne of Perth. **1611** RALEIGH in Arb. *Garner* I. 72 When two armies are within a distance of a butt's length. **1696** *Let*. in Aubrey *Misc*. (1721) 209 E're we were two pair of Butts past the House.

4. a. That towards which one's efforts are directed; an end, aim, object.

1594 R. PARSONS *Confer. Success*. I. iv. 66 For enioying of Iustice were Kings appointed..but if they be bound to no iustice at al..then is this end and butte of..al royal authority, vtterly frustrat. **1599** SHAKS. *Hen. V*, I. ii. 187 To which is fixed as an ayme or butt, Obedience. **1624** *Brief Inform. Aff. Palatinate* 29 His principall Butt and Marke was..to reuenge himselfe. **1710** NORRIS *Chr. Prud*. iii. 114 Which he makes the great scope and butt of his Life. **1869** GOULBURN *Purs. Holiness* vi. 46 Love is represented..as the mark or butt to which every precept is directed.

†**b.** A model, pattern. *Obs.*

1654 GAYTON *Fest. Notes* III. vii. 115 A Fashion to be whistled into a Tailors head without Butts or Patternes.

5. An object at which ridicule, scorn, or abuse, is aimed; from 18th c. often *absol.*, a person who is habitually the object of derisive jokes. (Cf. 1 b).

1616 BEAUM & FL. *Cust. Countr*. v. i, Let me stand the butt of thy fell malice. **1628** WITHER *Brit. Rememb*. I. 1443 Oh; make them not the Butt of thy displeasure. **1711** ADDISON *Spect*. No. 47 ¶ 10 A Man is not qualified for a Butt who has not a good deal of Wit and Vivacity..A stupid Butt is only fit for the Conversation of ordinary People. **1833** COLERIDGE *Table-t*. 16 Aug., He could not make a fool of me, as he did of Godwin and some other of his butts. **1852** GLADSTONE *Glean*. IV. 128 He was the butt and byword of liberalism. **1880** L. STEPHEN *Pope* v. 114 A taste for fossils ..was at that time regarded as a fair butt for unsparing ridicule.

6. a. *Attrib.* and *Comb.*, as ***butt-bow, -mark, -shaft, -shot***; †**butt-bolt**, 'the strong unbarbed arrow used by citizens in shooting at the butt' (Gifford); **butt-garden**, an archery ground.

1467 *Mann. & Househ. Exp*. 427 My mastyr paid to Fraykok for iij flytes ij *bottebolts and ij byres, xvij.*d.* ?**1623** FORD, &c. *Witch of Edmonton* II. i, I saw a little devil fly out of her eye like a but-bolt [*v.r.* bur-bolt]. *a***1693** URQUHART *Rabelais* III. li. 415 The *Butt and Rover-bows. **1855** KINGSLEY *Westw. Ho* x. (1879) 184 What could he do but lounge down to the *butt-garden to show off his fine black coat? **1653** URQUHART *Rabelais* I. xxiii, He..shot at *butt-marks. **1588** SHAKS. *L.L.L.* I. ii. 181 Cupids *Butshaft is too hard for Hercules Clubbe. **1884** *Longm. Mag*. Feb. 378 They were thought to be safe from the blind boy's butt-shaft. **1538** LELAND *Itin*. I. 96 Another feld a good *But shot of. **1622** R. HAWKINS *Voy. S. Sea* (1847) 88 A standing water..neare a butt-shot from the sea shore.

butt (bʌt), *sb.*[5] *Obs.* exc. *dial.* [? a. F. *butte* mound, hillock: a parallel formation to *but*: see prec. Cf. also BUTTE.] A hillock, mound.

1693 EVELYN *De la Quint. Compl. Gard*. I. 7 It will not be improper to make a little But or Hillock over those Roots. **1862** BARNES *Rhymes Dorset Dial*. I. 166, I used to hop The emmet-buts, vrom top to top. *Ibid*. II. 197 [He] broke The nut o' the wheel at a butt. [**1877** PEACOCK *N.W. Linc. Gloss*. (E.D.S.) *Butt-hills*.]

butt *sb.*[6] [Of uncertain derivation. In med. Anglo-Lat. *butta, buttis*; Du Cange identifies *butta terræ* with F. *bout de terre*. If this be correct, the word is = F. *bout* 'end, terminal part, small remaining part' as in *bouts de chandelle* 'candle-ends'. This would make sense 2 the original, but the history is not clear, and it is not impossible that sense 1 should be referred to BUTT *sb.*[5]]

1. One of the parallel divisions of a ploughed field contained between two parallel furrows, called also a 'ridge', 'rig', 'land', or 'selion'.

*c***1450** *Gloss*. in Wr.-Wülcker 737 *Hic selio*..a butt. *c***1475** *Ibid*. 796 *Hec amsages* [sic], a but of lond. **1589** *Wills & Inv. N.C.* (1860) 167, I give to..my servantt, thre buttes or rigges of land. **1681** *Sc. Acts Chas. II* (1814) VIII. 295 (JAM) That other rigg or butt of the samen lyand in the ffield called the Gallowbank. **1885** A. N. PALMER *Anc. Ten. Marches N. Wales* 9 'Butts' are the parallel ridges of land in a ploughed field that lie between the 'gutters' or 'reens'.

†**b.** ? A measure of land; cf. *selion*. *Obs.*

1552 HULOET, *Butte* of a lande, *jugus*. **1570** LEVINS *Manip*. 195 A Butte of land, *iugerum*. **1688** R. HOLME *Armoury* II. ii. §32 Smaller parcells according to that quantity of ground it containeth, both for length and breadth..3 Ridges, Butts, Flats, Stitches or small Butts, Pikes.

2. Such a ridge when short of its full length owing to the irregular shape of the boundary of the field. (This may be the original and proper sense.) Jamieson says 'A piece of ground which in ploughing does not form a proper ridge [i.e. rig], but is excluded as an angle'.

1523 FITZHERB. *Surv*. 39 If it be lasse than a rodde than call it a but. **1649** BLITHE *Eng. Improv. Impr*. (1653) 137, I had about fifteen or sixteen little short Lands, or Buts. **1787** WINTER *Syst. Husb*. 276 A few buts or short ridges, which were planted with a proportion of one bushel to an acre. **1803** REES *Cycl.*, *Butt*, a provincial term applied to such ridges or portions of arable land as run out short at the sides or other parts of the field. **1883** SEEBOHM *Eng. Vill. Comm*. 6 Where the strips abruptly meet others, or abut upon a boundary at right angles, they are sometimes called *butts*.

3. *dial.* 'A small piece of ground disjoined in whatever manner from the adjacent lands. In this sense, a small parcel of land is often called "the butts".' Jam.

1699 *N. Riding Records* IV. 171 Certain closes known as Long Coverdale Close and the Butts thereunto belonging. **1875** *Whitby Gloss*. (E.D.S.) *Butts*..uneven shaped portions of waste sward. **1881** *I. of Wight Gloss*. (E.D.S.) *Butt*, a small enclosure of land, as the church butt at Shanklin. [Ibid. *Batts*, short ridges, odd corners of fields.]

butt (bʌt), *sb.*[7] Also 8 but. [perh. a. F. *bout* end, vbl. sb. from *bouter* to push out, project; but possibly a sense of BUTT *sb.*[3], or f. BUTT *v.*[2] II.]

1. *Naut.* **a.** More fully **butt-end, butt-head**: The end of a plank or plate in a vessel's side which joins or butts on to the end of the next; the plane of juncture of two such planks, etc.

A vessel is said to 'start' or 'spring' a butt when a plank is loosened at the end; so a butt is said to 'start'. '*butt and butt*, a term denoting that the butt ends of two planks come together, but do not overlay each other. *hook and butt*, the scarphing or laying two ends of planks over each other'; Smyth *Sailor's Word-bk*.

1627 CAPT. SMITH *Seaman's Gram*. ii. 3 Now all those plankes under water..the fore-end is called the Butt-end.. if one of those ends should spring, or give way it would be a great troublesome danger to stop such a leake. *a***1642** SIR W. MONSON *Naval Tracts* iii. (1704) 345/1 Buts-end. **1644** SIR H. MANWAYRING *Sea-man's Dict*. s.v., A Butt is properly the end of a plancke, joyning to an other. To spring a Butt, that is, when a planke is loose at one end, and therefore they bolt all the Butt-heads: by Butt-heads, is meant the end of the plancks. **1691** T. H[ALE] *Acc. New Invent*. 26 Starting of a But-head in a Ship's side. **1769** FALCONER *Dict. Marine* (1789) *Butt* [as in Manwayring]. **1783** in Nicolas *Disp. Nelson* (1846) VII. Add. 6 Found a but at the starboard bow to have started, from which the Ship made much water. **1802** *Naval Chron*. VII. 177 A..hoy.. sprung a butt end, and foundered. **1859** *Merc. Mar. Mag*. (1860) VII. 15 Some of the paint had cracked at the joining of the butts..amidships. **1860** H. STUART *Seaman's Catech*. 70 Any place where two outside planks come together are called butt ends. **1867** SMYTH *Sailor's Word-bk.*, Butt-heads are the same with butt-ends.

b. *Comb.* **butt-strap**, a strip of metal riveted over the joining of two plates in an iron ship, whence **butt-strapped** *a.*

1869 SIR E. REED *Ship-build*. ii. 35 The gutter-plate is also strapped by double butt-straps. *Ibid*. ii. 33 The keel angle-irons..are properly butt-strapped. **1883** NARES *Constr. Ironclad* 3 A strip of iron called a *butt-strap* is laid over the two ends.

2. The sb. (or else the stem of BUTT *v.*[2]) occurs in comb. implying the close contact of two plane ends or edges without overlapping, as in **butt-chain** (see quot.); **butt-hinge**, a form of hinge, also in shortened form *butt*; **butt-joint**, in *Ironwork*, a joint in which the pieces to be joined are placed end to end, the juncture forming a plane surface at right angles to the length; so in *Carpentry* (= *butting-joint*); **butt-joint** *v. trans.*, to join with a butt-joint; **butt-riveting**, riveting in which a butt-strap is used; **butt-strip** = *butt-strap* sb.; **butt-weld** *sb.*, a butt-joint made by welding; *v. trans.*, to join with a butt-weld (Webster 1909); **butt-welded** *a.*, joined with a butt-weld; so ***butt-welding***.

1881 *Mechanic* §816 The window must then be attached to the frame by a pair of hinges, 2½ in. or 3 in. common iron butts being the most suitable. *a***1877** KNIGHT *Dict. Mech.*, *Butt-chain* (Saddlery), a short chain which reaches from the leather tug to the single-tree, to each of which it is hooked. **1823** P. NICHOLSON *Pract. Build*. 199 If each joint be in a plane perpendicular to one of the arrises, the joint is called a butt-joint. **1869** *Eng. Mech*. 19 Mar. 577/1 Mr. Bourne.. recommends the butt-joint in boiler construction as opposed to the lap. **1885** *Spons' Mechanics' Own Bk*. 361 There are 3 or 4 ways of butt-jointing curbs. **1904** GOODCHILD & TWENEY *Technol. & Sci. Dict*. 77/2 *Butt riveting*, a riveted joint where the plates touch at the edge only, and a strip overlaps and is riveted to both of them. *Ibid*., *Butt strip*, the strip of plate used to cover a butt joint. **1864** WEBSTER s.v. *Weld*, Butt-weld, or jump-weld. **1944** *Jrnl. Iron & Steel Inst*. CL. 50A The abrupt change in section at the edge of the reinforcement of a butt weld is a serious stress raiser. **1927** *Glasgow Herald* 27 Aug. 12 Butt-welded tubes. **1962** *B.S.I. News* Feb. 10/1 Storage tanks (vertical mild steel welded with butt-welded shells). **1925** *Jrnl. Iron & Steel Inst*. CXII. 463 Butt welding and its application to joining wires.

3. a. *Coal-min.* 'A surface [of coal] exposed at right-angles to the face' (Raymond *Mining Gloss.*).

b. A place where the stratum of rock to be quarried is cut off by other rock.

1900 *Coal & Metal Miners' Pocket Bk*. (ed. 6) 576 The butt of a slate quarry is where the overlying rock comes into contact with an inclined stratum of slate rock.

†**butt**, *sb.*[8] *Obs.* exc. in local names, as *The Butt of Lewis*. [? f. BUTT *v.*[1] 4, to jut out.] A headland, promontory.

1598 FLORIO, *Capo*..a cape or but of any lands end.

butt (bʌt), *sb.*[9] [f. BUTT *v.*[1]; cf. F. *botte* a thrust in fencing.] A push or thrust with the head or with the horns of horned animals.

1647 H. MORE *Poems* 58 The fiercest but of Ram no'te make them [the walls] fall. **1824** MISS MITFORD *Village* Ser. I. (1863) 80 [One of the ewes] has selected her own [lamb] and given her a gentle butt. **1869** BLACKMORE *Lorna D*. xlii. (1879) 261 Then fighting Tom [a sheep] jumped up at once, and made a little butt at Watch.

b. A thrust or stroke in fencing. *rare.*

*a***1721** PRIOR *Alma* I. 199 If disputes arise..To prove who gave the fairer butt, John shows the chalk on Robert's coat.

†**butt**, *sb.*[10] *Obs.* [? a. F. *botte* bundle.]

1. ? A bundle, pack.

1598 W. PHILLIPS *Linschoten's Trav. Ind*. (1864) 224 Coming to the things which the elephants are to draw, they bind the But or Packe with a rope that he may feel the weight thereof. **1705** *Lond. Gaz*. No. 4109/4 A But, cont. 75 Pieces of English Dyed Linen, making 1500 Yards.

2. *dial.* 'A hassock. *Devon*' (Halliwell). Hence **butt-woman** (see quots.).

1862 MARG. GOODMAN *Exper. Eng. Sister of Mercy* 25 The pew-opener or 'butt-woman'. **1878** *Free & Open Ch. Advoc*. 1 June (D.) A buttwoman is one who cleans the church, and ..assists the verger or pew-opener in shewing persons into seats..In the west of England butt is an old word for hassock.

butt (bʌt), *sb.*[11] [Perh. a special use of BUTT *sb.*[3] in sense 1 (the notion of 'thick end' being extended into 'thickest part'), or in sense 3 'buttock'.]

The thicker or hinder part of a hide or skin, as ***horse-butts, calf-butts, kip-butts, shoe-butts***; *esp.* the hide of the back and flanks of an ox or cow reduced to a rough rectangle by 'rounding' (see BEND *sb.*[2] 4); the thick leather made from this part; sole-leather.

1661 *Act 14 Chas. II*, 141 Whereas divers Tanners do shave cut and rake..the necks of their backs, and buts, to the great impairing thereof. **1686** *Lond. Gaz*. No. 2124/4 Stolen ..about 350 of the best Kids..writ in the Butt of the Skins. **1776** *Excise-book* in *Dorset County Chron*. (1881) 2 June [Kinds of hides] sheep and lamb, butts and backs, calves and kips. **1822** IMISON *Sc. & Art* II. 202 Butts are generally made from the stoutest and heaviest ox hides. **1886** *Leeds Mercury* 4 Mar., English butts and bends have been quietly dealt in. **1887** *Daily News* 31 Aug. 6/7 (Leather) English butt of stout substance..and heavy English bellies.

butt, *sb.*[12] Now *dial.* [Origin unknown: cf. BUCK *sb.*[4]] ? A kind of basket-net for catching fish. Also, a kind of basket. Cf. PUTT[2].

1533-4 *Act 25 Hen. VIII*, vii, No..person..shal..take.. in or by meanes of any wele, butte, net..the yonge frie..of any kinde of salmon. **1556** *Act 1 Eliz*. xvii. §1 Any..Net, Weele, But, Taining, Kepper. **1869** J. JENNINGS *Dial. W. Eng*. 124 A knaw'd well how ta make buts. **1883** F. SEEBOHM *Eng. Village Community* 152 These baskets are called putts or butts. **1983** *Country Life* 3 Mar. 538 To the big, bell-shaped hazel kype, with a mouth diameter of 8ft, is joined the 4ft osier butt, a secondary basket of finer weave.

butt (bʌt), *sb.*[13] *dial.* (See quots.)

1796 MARSHALL *W. England* I. Gloss. (E.D.S.) *Butt*, a close-bodied cart; as dung-butt..gurry-butt..ox-butt, etc. *Butt-load*, about six seams. **1807** VANCOUVER *Agric. Devon* (1813) 125 One-horse carts, or butts, are also generally made use of. **1875** BLACKMORE *C. Vaughan* xiii. (ed. 3) 44 A vehicle called a 'butt'..a short and rudely made cart. **1880** MISS COURTNEY *West Cornw. Gloss*. (E.D.S.) *Butt*, a heavy, two-wheeled cart, with timber and yoked oxen.

butt (bʌt), *sb.*[14] *dial.* Also but. A shoemaker's knife. In full ***butt-knife***.

1847 HALLIWELL, *But*, a shoemaker's knife. *North*. **1905** *Daily Chron*. 7 Feb. 3/1 Butt-knives..of French and Swedish makes.

butt (bʌt), *v.*[1] [a. OF. *bote-r, buter* (mod.F. *bouter*) to strike, thrust, project. But senses 3 and 4 have been influenced by association with BUTT *v.*[2]; and quotations occur of which it is difficult to say to which verb they mainly belong.]

1. a. *intr.* To strike, thrust, shove. Now almost always to strike or push with the head or horns, or with allusion to that sense. Const. *at, against*.

*c***1200** ORMIN 2810 Min child tatt i min wambe liþ.. bigann forrþrihht anan To stirenn & to buttenn. *c***1300** *Havelok* 2323 Buttinge with sharpe speres..Wrastling with laddes, putting of ston. **1579** SPENSER *Sheph. Cal*. Sept. 125 That with theyr hornes butten. **1748** RICHARDSON *Clarissa* (1811) II. xxiii. 150 Whenever he has the power, depend

upon it, he will butt at one as valiantly as the other. **1853** KANE *Grinnell Exp.* xliv. (1856) 406 We have butted several times rudely against projecting floes. **1858** DORAN *Crt. Fools* 72 Amused by .. a couple of rams butting at each other.

b. *fig.*

1832 *Blackw. Mag.* XXXI. 117 It [Reform Bill] will butt forcefully against the ramparts of aristocracy. **1859** TENNYSON *Enid* 1525 Amazed am I, Beholding how you butt against my wish.

c. To pitch or dive head-foremost. *rare.*

c **1330** *Arth. & Merl.* 5175 The knight donward gan butten Amidward the hors gutten. **1884** J. COLBORNE *Hicks Pasha* 160 As they came within our zone of fire, they butted forward, hit to death.

d. ***to butt in***: to thrust oneself unceremoniously and uninvited into an affair, discussion, etc.; to intrude, interfere without good reason. orig. *U.S.*

1900 G. ADE *Fables in Slang* 106 One Student .. whose people butt into the Society Column with Sickening Regularity. **1904** *Philad. Even. Telegraph* 8 June 8 To the victors belong the spoils, and not to those who butted in when the smoke of the battle had cleared away. **1915** W. J. LOCKE *Jaffery* viii, If a man loves a woman .. he ought to know what to do with the guy that butted in, without being told. **1920** R. MACAULAY *Potterism* IV. i. §2 I've not gone there or written, or anything yet, because I didn't want to butt in. **1922** [see BUTTINSKY]. **1928** R. CAMPBELL *Wayzgoose* ii. 53 And what if total strangers butted in? **1957** E. EAGER *Magic by Lake* 65 'I'm sorry,' he said, 'butting in like this, but I've got to tell you something.'

2. *trans.* To strike, *esp.* with the head or horns; to drive or push *away*, *out*, etc., by blows with the head or horns.

1590 GREENE *Neuer too late* (1600) 99 The eaw was coy and butted him. **1607** SHAKS. *Cor.* IV. i. 2 The beast With many heads butts me away. **1630** DRAYTON *Muses Eliz. Nymphal* (R.), I have a lamb .. Into laughter 'twill put you To see how prettily 'twill butt you. **1826** SCOTT *Woodst.* iv. 191 The very deer there will butt a sick or wounded buck from the herd. **1848** KINGSLEY *Yeast* in *Fraser's Mag.* XXXVIII. 206 That horrid gazelle has butted him in, and he'll be drowned. **1853** KANE *Grinnell Exp.* x. (1856) 73.

3. To come or strike 'dead' against. Of the teeth of wheels: to come in contact at their crowns so as to stop each other.

1875 BEDFORD *Sailor's Pocket-bk.* v. (ed. 2) 190 In winding up chronometers, the turns of the key should .. be counted, and the last turn made gently .. until it is felt to butt. **1884** F. BRITTEN *Watch & Clockm.* 37 The tendency of pinion leaves to butt the wheel teeth.

4. a. *intr.* To run out, project as an end, jut. Sometimes quasi-*refl.* with *out*, *into*.

1523 FITZHERB. *Surv.* 40 b, The long dolez yt butte fro the said northe felde to the said broke. **1535** COVERDALE *Jer.* xlviii. 32 The braunches off Iazer but vnto the see. **1611** CORYAT *Crudities* 184 A little square gallery butting out from the Tower. **1644** DIGBY *Nat. Bodies* xx. (1658) 228 The nose of a weathercock butteth it self into the wind. **1664** POWER *Exp. Philos.* I. 40 The Cone, or obtuse Tip of this Capsula butts or shoots itself into the basis of the Liver. **1715** DESAGULIERS *Fires Impr.* 118 Leave a small part butting forward into the opening.

†**b.** ***to butt on, to, over against***: to jut out towards, to be opposite to. *Obs.*

c **1534** tr. *Pol. Verg. Eng. Hist.* (1846) I. 1, Britaine .. beinge an Ilonde in the ocean sea buttinge over agaynste the Frenche shore. **1571** CAMPION *Hist. Irel.* i. 4 Leinster butteth upon England. **1624** HEYWOODE *Gunaik.* II. 92 That part .. which butted upon the west. **1647** LILLY *Chr. Astrol.* xxv. 154 A Ground .. butting or lying to that quarter of Heaven, as is formerly directed.

¶**5.** With association of BUTT *sb.*^{4} **a.** *trans.* To aim a missile. **b.** *intr.* To aim.

a **1593** MARLOWE *Dido* III. iv, Whenas he butts his beams on Flora's bed. **1652** URQUHART *Jewel* Wks. (1834) 271 The meer scope thereof, and end whereat it buts.

6. The verb stem (sense 1) is used adverbially with some verbs of motion (as *go*, *meet*, *run*), often with the intensifying adv. *full*, implying 'point-blank' meeting or violent collision. [Cf. OF. *de plain bout* (Godef. s.v. *Bot*).]

?*a* **1400** *Morte Arth.* 1112 Ffulle butt in þe frunt the fromonde he hittez. *c* **1430** *Syr Gener.* 4587 He .. smote Darel In middes of the sheld ful butt. **1600** HOLLAND *Livy* II. xix. 56 Tarquinius Superbus .. ran full butt against him. **1673** R. HEAD *Canting Acad.* 30, I .. met full-but with my Comrade. **1752** FIELDING *Amelia* VIII. i, Before he arrived at the shop, a gentleman stopt him full butt. **1832** M. SCOTT in *Blackw. Mag.* XXXII. 474 They .. ran butt at each other like ram-goats. **1837** MARRYAT *Dog-fiend* vi, The corporal .. ran full butt at the lieutenant.

butt (bʌt), *v.*^{2} [Partly f. BUTT *sb.*^{4} 1; partly aphetic f. ABUT.]

I. †**1. a.** To fix or mark (*out*) the limits of (land, etc.) lengthwise, to bound or delimitate as to length; to terminate; to limit, bound. Chiefly in the *passive*, and *esp.* in the Conveyancing phrase '*to be butted and bounded*'. Obs.

1523 FITZHERB. *Surv.* Prol., It is necessarye to be knowen howe all these maners .. shulde be extended, surueyed, butted, bounded and valued. **1592** WEST *Symbol.* C j b, Butting it at thends and bounding it at the sides. *a* **1642** SIR W. MONSON *Naval Tracts* iv. (1704) 393/1 By the Eastern Discovery the length of Africk is butted out .. to the Southward. **1657** HOWELL *Londinop.* 342 A handsome new Street butted out, and fairly built by the Company of Goldsmiths. *c* **1688** *5th Coll. Papers Pres. Juncture* 18 The Scripture supposes .. Mens Lands to be already butted and bounded, when it forbids removing the Ancient Landmarks. **1727** DE FOE *Eng. Tradesm.* I. xxv. 248 We have gained nothing by war and encroachment, we are butted and bounded just where we were in Queen Elizabeth's time. **1816** U. BROWN *Jrnl.* in *Maryland Hist. Mag.* (1915) X. 361 This [40,000 acres] is butted and bounded and described directly as the grant is from the Commonwealth of Virginia. *Ibid.* 367 This John Hall .. Butted and Bounded of the 2 first lines with our 70,000 Acre tract.

†**b.** *fig. Obs.*

1659 C. NOBLE *Inexped. Expedient* 14 The Humble Petition .. hath butted and bounded our Interests. **1680** C. NESS *Ch. Hist.* 447 Antichrist and his Auxiliaries .. are so Butted and Bounded by the great God. **1694** S. JOHNSON *Notes on Past. Lett. Bp. Burnet* I. 22 They are butted and bounded by Law.

†**2.** *absol.* To mark out limits (in surveying). *Obs.*

1523 FITZHERB. *Surv.* 38 b, And he must stande in the myddes of the flatte whan he shall butte truely.

II. †**3. a.** *intr.* To abut *on*, *upon*, *against*; to touch with the end (cf. BOUND *v.*^{1} 3); to adjoin; = ABUT *v.* 2, 3. Also *fig. Obs.*

1523 FITZHERB. *Surv.* 38 b, The southe endes butteth vpon the hall orcharde .. and the northe endes but vpon ryhyll. **1570** LEVINS *Manip.* 195 To Butte, *adiacere.* **1565** GOLDING *Ovid's Met.* XIII. (1593) 321 She gat her to a hill That butted on the sea. **1581** SAVILE *Agric.* (1622) 188 The neerest [Britons] to France likewise resemble the French .. because .. that in countries butting together the same aspects of the heauens doe yeeld the same complexions of bodies. **1601** HOLLAND *Pliny* XVIII. vi, Cn. Pompeius .. never .. would purchase any ground that butted or bordered upon his owne. **1682** BUNYAN *Holy War* (R.T.S.) 314 The remote parts of their country .. do both butt and bound upon Hell-gate hill. **1685** H. MORE *Paralip. Prophet.* 127 The expiration of the sixty-nine Weeks of Daniel which butt vpon the Manifestation of the Messias. **1720** *Stow's Surv.* (ed. Strype 1754) II. vi. iv. 650/1 Burleigh Street buts against Exeter Street. **1798** W. HUTTON *Autobiog.* 25 The bedstead, whose head butted against their bedside. **1853** P. P. KENNEDY *Blackwater Chron.* i. 6 A large spur—apparently the Backbone itself—keeps straight to the south, and butts down on the Cheat.

b. To border *on*, go along the margin of.

1594 CAREW *Tasso* (1881) 24 He euer butting on the salt-sea waue, By wayes directest doth conduct his hoast.

†**4.** ***to butt on, upon***: (of a line) to end in (a point); (of a road) to issue or lead into. (Cf. Fr. *aboutir à*, and ABUT 3). Also *fig. Obs.*

1634 CANNE *Necess. Separ.* (1849) 171 Their practice butteth full upon the others' unreasonable and unsound resoning. **1656** TRAPP *Comm. Matt.* xxiii. 18 All the worldling's ploughing, sailing, building, buying, buts upon commodity, he knows no other duty. **1673** NEWTON in Rigaud *Corr. Sci. Men* (1841) II. 355 Draw AK and BK butting on the eye-glass at F. **1678** BUNYAN *Pilgr.* I. 37 There are many ways butt down upon this. **1720** [see in 3].

5. *intr.* chiefly *techn.* of beams, parts of machinery, etc.: To come with one end flat *against*, *on*; usually implying that the contiguous surfaces are planes at right angles to the length of beam, etc.

1670 COTTON *Espernon* I. IV. 182 A great Beam that butted upon the Chimney of the Chamber. **1769** FALCONER *Dict. Marine* (1789) s.v. *Scarf*, When the ends of the two pieces are cut square, and put together, they are said to *butt* to one another. **1791** SMEATON *Edystone L.* §56 A lantern, that was raised upon eight fir Balks, which butted upon the solid. **1875** 'STONEHENGE' *Brit. Sports* II. VIII. ii. §1. 640 From the handle to a little beyond the rowlock most sculls are square, with an oblong leather button .. butting against the inside of the thowle.

6. *trans.* To place (timber, etc.) with its end resting *against* a plane surface at right angles to its length; to join (iron plates, beams, etc.) end to end, with a flat transverse juncture.

1785 ROY in *Phil. Trans.* LXXV. 460 What may have been lost by constantly butting one rod against the other. **1881** *Mechanic* §1323. 608 The back has not been let in under the brickwork at F, but is merely butted against it.

¶ See also prec. vb., senses 3, 4.

butt (bʌt), *v.*^{3} [f. BUTT *sb.*^{3}]

1. *Angling.* (*trans.*) To give the butt to (see BUTT *sb.*^{3} 1 b).

1867 F. FRANCIS *Angling* ix. (1880) 332 If it becomes necessary to butt a fish.

2. *U.S.* To cut off the rough ends of logs or boards.

1774 M. PATTEN *Diary* (1903) 331, I cut of 9 Rail cuts and butted 8. **1850** S. JUDD *R. Edney* 41 Richard took an axe and very neatly proceeded to 'butt' a log; that is, to cut the end of it square off. **1880** *Northw. Lumberman* Jan. 24 If we were buying the logs, we should try to get enough off the scale to pay for the butting, or rather for manufacturing the timber into logs.

†**'buttal**, *sb. Obs.* Forms: 6 buttel(l, buttelle, 6–7 buttal(l, 7 buttle, butel. [? f. BUTT *v.*^{2} + -AL^1 2; cf. ABUTTAL.] A bound or boundary.

1552 HULOET, Buttel, or bound of land, *meta.* **1577** *Test. 12 Patriarchs* (1604) 85, I have not .. removed the bounds and buttles of lands. **1598** YONG *Diana* 23 Busines about the buttals of certaine pastures. **1636** HEALEY *Theophrast.* x. 42 Every day he surveighs his grounds and the buttals thereof, lest there be any incroaching.

b. *transf.* ? A measured piece (of land). Cf. BUTT *sb.*^{6} 1 b.

1620 BRATHWAIT *Five Senses*, To purchase a buttall of land from his neighbour.

†**'buttal, buttel**, *v. Obs.* [f. prec. sb.]

1. *trans.* To bound or limit, to set boundaries to; to mete *out*. Hence **'butteling** *vbl. sb.*

1571 GOLDING *Calvin on Ps.* lxxiv. 2 Inasmuch as they were wont to buttel out grounds with metepoles. *Ibid.* Yt God (by ye secret buttelling of his own good pleasure, as it were by a tenfoote rod) bounded out Israel from the other nacions. **1583** —— *Calvin on Deut.* clxxxi. 1124 Some Geometrician that should haue butteled and bounded the whole world.

2. To abut, be bounded. Const. *of*.

1642 in T. Gardner *Hist. Dunwich* (1754) 166 A Porch-Houst that stound in the South Street, buteling of Robart Barfot on the North Syd, butel of South Fisher-Way on South; butel East latle Houses; butel on West upon latly caled Maynfeld.

buttal, obs. dial. form of BITTERN.

1691 RAY *S. & E.C. Wds.* Coll. 91 A Buttal; a Bittern.

†**buttall.**

1552 in Peacock *Eng. Ch. Furniture* (1866) 219 Item tooe blew Curtens for the alter end. Item iiij buttall Clothes.

buttargo, obs. f. BOTARGO.

'butt-cut. *U.S.* [BUTT *sb.*^{3} 2.] **a.** The first portion of a tree cut off above the stump. Also *fig.*, an important or a heavy man. **b.** The section of tan-bark taken from the butt of a tree before felling it for further peeling (*Terms Forestry & Logging* 1905).

1830 *Northern Watchman* (Troy, N.Y.) 19 Oct. (Th.), [He] weighs little short of 450 lbs. and is familiarly known as the But-cut. **1840** J. P. KENNEDY *Quodlibet* 172 Nebuchadnezzar couldn't beat him at a speech. He's the Butt cut of democracy. **1878** J. H. BEADLE *Western Wilds* x. 143 The 'butt cut' of the tree lies as it fell, the top reached by means of a ladder. **1948** *Country Gentleman* May 177/1, I rived enough boards to kiver it from the butt-cuts.

butte (bjuːt). *U.S.* Also bute. [a. F. *butte* a hillock or rising ground; cf. BUTT *sb.*^{5}]

In Western U.S.: An isolated hill or peak rising abruptly (see quot. 1845).

1838 PARKER *Rocky Mts.* 70 Red Bute, which is a high bluff. **1845** FRÉMONT *Rocky Mount.* 145 (Bartlett) It [the word *butte*] is applied to the detached hills and ridges which rise abruptly, and reach too high to be called hills or ridges, and not high enough to be called mountains. *Knob*, as applied in the Western States, is their most descriptive term in English. **1880** *Century Mag.* xxiv. 510 Everything in the way of hill, rock, mountain, or clay-heap is called a butte in Montana. **1881** GEIKIE *In Wyoming* in *Macm. Mag.* XLIV. 236 Here and there isolated flat-topped eminences or 'buttes', as they are styled .. rise from the plain.

attrib. **1880** *Scribner's Mag.* July 454 Broken down among the rocks of a stony bit of butte-road.

butted ('bʌtɪd), *ppl. a.* [f. BUTT *sb.*^{3} + -ED^2.] Furnished with a butt; used chiefly in parasynthetic comb., as ***brass-butted***, ***stiff-butted***, etc.

1866 KINGSLEY *Herew.* i. (1877) 54 The handle was .. butted with narwhal ivory. **1858** MAYNE REID in *Chamb. Jrnl.* IX. 266 From the huge brass-butted holsters. **1886** *Q. Rev.* CLXIII. 345 The stiff-butted Kelso [fishing] rods.

buttel(le, var. of BUTTAL.

butteler, butten, obs. ff. BUTLER *sb.*, BUTTON.

butt-end ('bʌt 'ɛnd), *sb.* [f. BUTT *sb.*^{3}, ^{7} + END.]

1. a. = BUTT *sb.*^{3} (and now more frequent).

1580 NORTH *Plutarch* (1676) 955 Leptines .. took a Halbard .. and with the butt end of it drew on the ground that which he would. **1611** CHAPMAN *May Day* Wks. 1873 II. 339 The butt end of a shoemakers horn. **1677** HOBBES *Homer* 141 The butt-ends of their spears fixt in the ground. **1792** *Munchausen's Trav.* ii. 8 The butt-end of my whip. **1833** *Regul. Instr. Cavalry* I. 34 The butt-end of the carbine. **1855** MACAULAY *Hist. Eng.* III. 244 His brains would have been knocked out with the but end of a musket.

b. *fig.* The mere concluding part; the 'fag end'.

1594 SHAKS. *Rich. III*, II. ii. 110 The butt-end of a Mothers blessing. **1676** *Adv. Men of Shaftesbury* 36 The Dear Bag was gone, the Butt-end of all his hopes. **1820** *Edin. Rev.* XXXIII. 207 Added to a Deposition the but-end of an Indictment. **1825** *Blackw. Mag.* XVIII. 162 Their rhapsodies only recall the butt-end of an ancient cavalier song.

†**2.** The thickest part of the trunk of a tree, just above the root. *Obs.*

1677 HUBBARD *Narr.* 66 He nimbly got behind the butt-end of a tree newly turned up by the roots. **1760** WINTHROP in *Phil. Trans.* LII. 10 A great tree, 2½ feet in diameter at the butt-end.

3. *Naut.* See BUTT *sb.*^{7}

4. *Hockey* and *Lacrosse.* A jab or thrust with the handle end of a hockey-stick. Chiefly *Canadian.*

1963 A. O'BRIEN *Headline Hockey* 79 Blair told Ted O'Connor to hand No. 11 of the Swedish national team a butt-end. **1965** *Globe & Mail* (Toronto) 9 Apr. 38/1 Nobody ever gave you a better butt-end.

butt-end, *v. nonce-wd.* [f. prec.] **1.** To use the butt-end (e.g. of a gun).

1859 M. THOMSON *Cawnpore* 48 (Hoppe) For destructive aggression, battering, and butt-ending, the palm must be awarded to the privates of —— Regiment.

2. *Hockey* and *Lacrosse.* To jab or thrust at (an opponent's body) with the handle end of the stick. Chiefly *Canadian.*

1955 *Telegram* (Toronto) 21 Apr. 6/8 A hockey coach says even youngsters playing hockey are taught kneeing and butt-ending. **1965** *Globe & Mail* (Toronto) 9 Apr. 38/1 The art of butt-ending is almost an obsolete illegality in hockey. So **butt-ending** *vbl. sb.*

1859, etc. [see above].

ˈbutt-ended, *a.* [f. BUTT-END *sb.* + -ED².] Having a blunt end; having ends that butt or come flat, the one against the other.

1897 KIPLING *Capt. Cour.* v. 124 *Standez awayez*, you butt-ended *mucho bono!* **1898** *Cycling* 72 A hopeless single-tube tyre may be slit open at the valve and a butt-ended air-tube inserted.

butter (ˈbʌtə(r)), *sb.*¹ Forms: 1-3 butere, 3 buttere, 4 boter(e, botter, butre, 4-5 buttur, 5 butture, buttir, buttyr, botyr, boture, bottre, 7 butyr, 4- butter. [OE. *butere* wk. fem. (in compounds *buttor-*); ad. L. *butyrum*, ad. Gr. *βούτυρον*. So OFris. *butera, botera*, MDu. *bōter(e, botre*, Du. *boter*, MLG. *botter*, late OHG. (10th or 11th c.) *butera*, MHG., mod.G. *butter*, all from Latin.

The Gr. is usually supposed to be f. *βοῦς* ox or cow + *τυρός* cheese, but is perhaps of Scythian or other barbarous origin.]

I. 1. a. The fatty substance obtained from cream by churning. It is chiefly used for spreading on bread (see BREAD AND BUTTER), and in cookery.

c **1000** *Sax. Leechd.* I. 194 Wið ȝeswell, ȝenim þas ylcan wyrte myllefolium mid buteran ȝecnucode. *c* **1250** *Gen. & Ex.* 1014 Bred, kalues fleis, and flures bred, And buttere. *a* **1300** *Havelok* 643 Bred an chese, butere and milk. **1377** LANGL. *P. Pl.* B. v. 444 Bothe bred and ale · butter, melke, and chese. *c* **1440** *Promp. Parv.* 56 Buttyr or botyr [*K.* butture], *buturum*. **1562** J. HEYWOOD *Prov. & Epigr.* (1867) 71 Euery promise that thou therin dost vtter, Is as sure as it were sealed with butter. **1596** SHAKS. *1 Hen. IV*, II. iv. 560 A grosse fat man.—As fat as Butter. **1601** HOLLAND *Pliny* II. 318 The fattest Butyr is made of Ewes milke. **1722** DE FOE *Plague* (1884) 105, I laid in..Salt-butter and Cheshire Cheese. *a* **1867** BUCKLE *Misc. Wks.* (1872) I. 307 The Greeks were acquainted with butter, but never ate it.

b. *to make butter and cheese of*: ? to confound, bamboozle. (Cf. Gr. *τυρεύειν*.)

1642 *Tract conc. Schisme* 11 They made butter and cheese one of another.

c. (*to look*) *as if butter would not melt in one's mouth*: said contemptuously of persons of excessively demure appearance.

1530 PALSGR. 620/1 He maketh as thoughe butter wolde nat melte in his mouthe. **1552** LATIMER *Serm. Lord's Prayer* v. II. 79 These fellows..can speak so finely, that a man would think butter should scant melt in their mouths. **1738** SWIFT *Pol. Conv.* I. (D.) She looks as if butter would not melt in her mouth, but I warrant cheese won't choak her. **1850** THACKERAY *Pendennis* lx. (1885) 595 She smiles and languishes, you'd think that butter would not melt in her mouth.

d. *melted butter*: butter melted with water, flour, etc., used as a sauce. *clarified* or *run butter*: butter melted and potted for culinary use.

1709 ADDISON *Tatler* No. 192 ¶ 1 A Plate of Butter which had not been melted to his Mind. **1807** WINDHAM *Parl. Sp.* (1812) III. 46 It was the sort of poverty of conception, reproached by some foreigner to English cookery, that we had but one sauce, and that that sauce was melted butter. **1833** MARRYAT *P. Simple* i. 7 I've thickened the butter. **1879** M. C. TYREE *Housekpng. Virginia* 102 Dish, and serve with drawn butter and parsley.

e. formerly used as an unguent; *esp.* in the preparation called *May butter* (see quots.).

1643 J. STEER tr. *Exp. Chyrurg.* viii. 34 Let him apply the ..Ointment of Sweet Butter thereto. **1718** QUINCY *Dispens.* III. xi. 476 *Butyrum Majale, May Butter.* This is made by melting fresh Butter that has been made up without any Salt, in the Sun; which is to be repeated until it grows of a whitish Colour. This is a very trifling Medicine, and of no use but as any simple Unguent, or plain Lard may be. **1753** CHAMBERS *Cycl. Supp.* s.v.

f. *fig.* Unctuous flattery. (Cf. BUTTER *v.*) *colloq.*

1823 *Blackw. Mag.* XIV. 309 You have been daubed over by the dirty butter of his applause. **1880** *World* 13 Oct., A lavish interchange of compliments, the butter being laid on pretty thick.

†**2.** ? A dish or confection made with butter. *Obs.*

c **1600** DAY *Begg. Bednall Gr.* v. (1881) 114 The old woman my Mother..could have taught thee how to a made butters and flap-jacks.

3. *transf.* **a.** As a name for various substances resembling butter in appearance or consistence, as **butter of almonds** = ALMOND-BUTTER; **butter of cacao**, a white unctuous substance obtained from the seeds of the cacao: so **butter of mace**, **shea butter** (the substance which exudes from the African butter-tree), and similar products, called generically ***vegetable butters***; **butter of wax**, a butyraceous oil, obtained from wax by distillation, **rock butter**, a mineral composed of alum combined with iron, which exudes as a soft butter-like paste from certain aluminiferous rocks [see quot. 1811 and cf. Ger. *berg-butter*].

c **1440** *Anc. Cookery* in *Househ. Ord.* (1790) 447 Botyr of Almondes. Take almonde mylke, and let hit boyle, and in the boylinge cast therto a lytel wyn or vynegur. **1672** GREW *Phil. Hist. Plants* §51 No Oyl which remained liquid; but instead of that a Butyr, almost of the Consistence and Colour of the Oyl of Mace. **1752** CHAMBERS *Cycl.* s.v. *Wax*, By chemistry, wax yields a white thick oil, resembling butter; whence the chemists call it butter of wax. **1811** PINKERTON *Petral.* I. 117 The *kamennoie maslo*, or rock butter, a fat yellowish substance of a penetrating smell, being a mixture of alum and fluid bitumen. **1836** *Penny Cycl.* VI. 68/2 The most important vegetable butters are produced by the *Bassia butyracea*..and certain palms, such as the *Cocos butyracea* and the *Elæis Guineensis*. **1861** *Our English Home* 151 Almonds..were boiled until the liquor became a delicious cream, from which was made the famous butter of almonds. **1866** *Treas. Bot.* s.v. *Myristica*, [The fixed oil of nutmegs] is extracted by pressure, and forms what is called butter of mace.

b. *esp.* in *Chem.*, an old name of several anhydrous chlorides, as **butter of antimony, arsenic, bismuth, tin, zinc**.

1641 FRENCH *Distill.* iii. (1651) 71 Oil or Butter of Antimony. **1802** CHEVENIX in *Phil. Trans.* XCII. 164 The muriatic salts, formerly known by the strange name of butters of the metals. **1812** SIR H. DAVY *Chem. Philos.* 407 The only known compound, bismuth and chlorine..called butter of bismuth. *Ibid.* 377 Butter of zinc. **1876** HARLEY *Mat. Med.* 260 Butter of Antimony is an energetic caustic.

c. A perfumed fat obtained by inflowering or maceration with a heated fat.

1885 *Encycl. Brit.* XVIII. 526 For the manufacture of perfumes for the handkerchief the greases now known as pomades, butters, or philocomes are treated with rectified spirit of wine..which practically completely abstracts the odour.

II. *Comb.* and *Attrib.*

4. General comb.: **a.** attributive, as ***butter-cart, -cask, -churn, -crock, -dairy, -dealer, -dew, -dish, -firkin***, †***-kit, -merchant***, †***-monger, -pot, -shop*** (also *fig.*), †***-skep, -tub***; **b.** objective gen., as ***butter-maker, -making***; **c.** similative, as ***butter-bright, -colour, -coloured, -like, -smooth***, adjs.

1868 G. M. HOPKINS 17 July in *Jrnls. & Papers* (1959) 176 The sun coming out..with a *butter-bright lustre. **1828** MISS MITFORD *Village* (1863) 129 [They] would run to meet the *butter-cart as if it were a carriage and four. **1706** *Lond. Gaz.* No. 4383/1 An Act..for Amending of the Law, in relation to *Butter-Casks. **1847** MOIR in *Rural Cycl.* I. 592 The lime is pre-eminently suited for the manufacture of butter-casks. **1589** in H. Hall *Soc. in Elizabethan Age* (1886) 201 A *butter-churn, 3*s.* **1865** TYLOR *Early Hist. Man.* ix. 240 In modern India, butter churns are worked with a cord. **1877** LITTLEDALE in *Academy* 24 Feb. 158 There are at least six shades of *butter-colour. **1894** *Daily News* 20 Mar. 3/2 A deep frill of *butter-coloured lace. **1784** TWAMLEY *Dairying* 81 A near relation of mine, who kept a *Butter Dairy. **1780** *British Topogr.* II. 777 Mr. Van's account of *butter-dew that fell in the provinces of Munster and Leinster. **1572** *Wills & Inv. N.C.* (1835) 349, xxxix *butter Dishes. **1861** MRS. BEETON *Househ. Managem.* 814 An ornamental butter-dish. **1640** *Debate* in Rushw. *Hist. Coll.* III. (1692) I. 151 The..marking of *Butter-Firkins. **1567** *Richmond Wills* (1853) 209, Ij *butterkitts. **1700** W. SALMON tr. *Bate's Pharm. Bat.* (ed. 2) 380/2 A *butter-like oil. **1802** PALEY *Nat. Theol.* xiii, A small nipple, yielding upon pressure a butter-like substance. **1964** M. HYNES *Med. Bacteriol.* (ed. 8) xi. 157 To give a butter-like flavour to margarine. **1859** GEO. ELIOT *A. Bede* 111 He actually dared not look at this little *buttermaker for the first minute or two. **1751** LADY M. W. MONTAGUE *Lett.* III. 102, I expect immortality from the science of *butter-making. **1859** GEO. ELIOT *A. Bede* 70 The linen butter-making apron, with its bib. **1813** VANCOUVER *Agric. Devon* 231 The *butter-merchants in London. **1720** *Lond. Gaz.* No. 5879/4 William Dixon..*Buttermonger. *a* **1693** URQUHART *Rabelais* III. xvii. 139 A great *Butter-pot full of fresh Cheese. **1865** E. METEYARD *J. Wedgwood* I. 125 The butter-pot was a coarse cylindrical vessel..formed of clay. **1773** *Gentl. Mag.* XLIII. 579 The poor man, who keeps a *butter-shop in Newgate-market. **1831** *Blackw. Mag.* 55 He has carefully collected, preserved, published, and transmitted to the butter-shops, all the hyperbolical bombast. **1572** *Wills & Inv. N.C.* (1835) 249 One *butter-skepp. **1920** GALSWORTHY *In Chancery* II. v. 170 His grandfather's first gold hunter watch, *butter-smooth with age. **1969** *Observer* (Colour Suppl.) 23 Mar. 27/2 (Advt.), There isn't even a clutch pedal. Just a Selective-Automatic transmission. With butter-smooth gears. **1570** *Wills & Inv. N.C.* (1835) 318 *Buttertubbes, scuttles and other stuff. **1741** *Compl. Fam.-Piece* I. i. 95 Take a Butter-tub.

5. Special comb.: †**butter-ale** = *buttered ale* (see ALE 4); **butter-and-egg man** *U.S. slang*, a wealthy, unsophisticated man who spends money freely; **butter and eggs**, a popular name for several flowers which are of two shades of yellow, *esp.* Toadflax (*Linaria vulgaris*) and varieties of *Narcissus*; **butter and tallow tree** (see quot.); **butter-back**, a kind of wild duck (*U.S.*); **butter-badger** (*dial.*), an itinerant butter-factor; †**butter-bag**, a contemptuous epithet for a Dutchman (cf. BUTTER-BOX); **butter-bake**, *Sc.*, a butter biscuit; **butter-barrel** = *butter-cask* in 4; also *dial.* a barrel-churn; **butter-basher, butter-boy** *slang*, a new driver of a taxi-cab; **butter-bird**, a name for the Bobolink (*U.S.*); †**butter-bitten**, *a.*, ? given to biting butter (cf. BITTEN *ppl. a.* 4); **butter-boat**, a vessel for serving melted butter in; used *fig.* of lavish adulation (*colloq.*); **butter-bush**, an Australian tree, *Pittosporum phyllirææoides*, of which the wood is used for turnery and the leaves as fodder; **butter-cake**, a rich cake usu. containing butter, sugar, flour, and eggs; **butter cloth**, a thin loosely-woven cloth with a fine mesh used primarily as a wrapping for butter; **butter colour**, (*a*) the colour of butter; (*b*) a preparation used to give a good colour to butter and butter substitutes (Cent. Dict. 1889); **butter-cooler**, a vessel for keeping butter cool when brought on the table; **butter cream**, a creamed mixture of butter and sugar, etc., used as filling or topping for cake; **butter cross**, a market-cross near which butter is sold; **butter-cutter**, the name of an insect (? corruption of *bud-cutter*; see BUD *sb.*¹ 5); **butter-dock** (see quot.); **butter-duck** *U.S.* (see quot.); **butter-factor**, a tradesman who buys butter from the farmers to sell wholesale; **butter fat**, the essential fats of pure butter; also *attrib.*; **butter-flip**, a local name of the Avocet; **butter-jags**, a dial. name for *Lotus corniculatus*, also for *Medicago falcata*; **butter-knife**, a blunt knife used for cutting butter at table; **butter-lamp**, a lamp fed with butter instead of oil; **butter-leaves**, a name for *Atriplex hortensis* and *Rumex alpinus*; **butter letter**, a letter issued on ecclesiastical authority giving permission to eat butter in Lent; **butter-man**, a man who makes or sells butter; also *Naut.* a schooner rigged in a particular way; †**butter-mark** = BUTTER-PRINT 1; **butter-mould** (see quot.); **butter-mouth** *attrib.*, a contemptuous epithet for a Dutchman = *butter-bag*; **butter muslin** = *butter cloth*; **butter oil**, that part of refined cotton-seed oil which is used in making oleomargarine; **butter paper**, a semi-transparent waterproof wrapping-paper for butter, cream cheese, etc.; **butter-pat**, a small piece of butter rolled or shaped into some ornamental form for the table; **butter-pear** = BEURRÉ; **butter-plate**, a plate for holding butter; also, a name for *Ranunculus flammula*; †**butter-quean** = *butter-whore*; **butter-rigged** *a. Naut.* (see quot. 1885, and cf. *butter-man*); †**butter-root** = BUTTERWORT; **butter salt**, fine common salt in small crystals obtained by rapid evaporation of brine, used in salting butter; **butter scoop** (see quot. 1902); **butter-scotch** (also dial. *butterscot*), a kind of toffee, chiefly composed of sugar and butter; **butter-slide**, a slide (SLIDE *sb.* 9) made of butter or ice; also *fig.*; **butter spade**, a wooden spatula used in cutting butter from a firkin or other vessel, or used (as one of a pair) for making up butter; **butter stamp** = BUTTER-PRINT 1; **butter-stick**, a wooden implement used in working butter; **butter substitute**, a substance used as a substitute for butter in food; **butter-toast** (more commonly *buttered toast*), toast spread with butter; **butter tongs** (see quot).; **butter-tree**, name of *Bassia butyracea* and *Bassia Parkii*; **butter trier** *U.S.*, a segment of a tube used to pierce a firkin of butter for sample; **butter-weed**, a name for *Erigeron canadensis* and *Senecio lobatus*; **butter week** (see quots.); **butter-weight**, formerly 18 or more ounces to the pound; hence, *fig.* for 'good measure' (*obs.*); †**butter-whore**, a scolding butter-woman; †**butter-wife, butter-woman**, a woman who makes or sells butter; **butter-worker**, a contrivance for pressing the butter-milk out of butter; **butter-working**, the moulding of butter into rolls, prints, pats, etc., for sale; **butter yellow**, a coal-tar dye formerly used for colouring butter, oils, etc. See also BUTTER-BOX, -BUR, -CUP, -FLY, -WORT, etc.

1666 PEPYS *Diary* 17 Mar., Home, having a great cold: so to bed, drinking *butter-ale. **1776** WITHERING *Bot. Arrangem.* (1796) III. 552 Toadflax, Snap dragon, *Butter and Eggs. **1880** JEFFERIES *Gt. Estate* 83 In shady woodlands the toadflax or butter-and-eggs is often pale,—a sulphur colour. **1926** H. C. WITWER *Roughly Speaking* 229 A couple of big *butter and egg men from Verona, New Jersey. **1927** *Daily Express* 31 Aug. 8/7 'Butter and egg man' is an American slang expression practically equal to our term 'greenhorn', that is, a man of money who spends lavishly and is an easy prey of the gold-digger and other unscrupulous persons. **1948** *Antioch Rev.* Spring 105 The 'butter-and-egg' man who startles the foreign lecturer with blunt questions. **1830** LINDLEY *Nat. Syst. Bot.* 46 The *Butter and Tallow-tree of Sierra Leone, which owes its name (*Pentadesma butyracea*) to the yellow greasy juice its fruit yields when cut. **1796** MORSE *Amer. Geog.* I. 213 Little black and white duck, called *Butter Back (*Anas minor picta*). **1857** *Fraser's Mag.* LVI. 355 His father was..a *butter-badger. *c* **1645** HOWELL *Lett.* II. xi, The *butterbag Hollander. **1828** *Blackw. Mag.* XXIV. 910 He..thumped *butter-bakes with his elbows to some purpose. **1862** BARNES *Rhymes Dorset Dial.* I. 6 The *butter-barrel An' cheese wring. **1939** H. HODGE *Cab, Sir?* xv. 216 Contemptuous cabmen, therefore, called these blacklegs '*Butter-bashers'. **1883** *Standard* 26 Dec., They [bobolinks]..grow so fat that they receive the name of '*butter birds'. *a* **1577** GASCOIGNE *Voy. Hollande* (1831) 221 The Dutche with *butterbitten iawes. **1787** *Gentl. Mag.* Sept. 821/2 His mustard-glass and *butter-boat were overturned. **1807** BYRON *To Miss Pigot* 5 July, Upset a butter-boat in the lap of a lady. **1865** *Sat. Rev.* 7 Jan. 16/2 That kind of praise which feels like the butter-boat down one's back. **1866** J. H. SKINNER *After Storm* I. 181 He praised some things and gave advice about others, using the butter-boat less freely than is customary at volunteer inspections. **1939** H. HODGE *Cab, Sir* x. 134 During my

'*butter-boy' period. *Ibid.* xv. 215 The new driver is called a 'Butter-Boy'. **1960** C. RAY *Merry England* 26 [The] owner-driver..is called a 'butter-boy' when he first appears on the rank, taking the butter from the older hands' bread, they say. **1885** *Outing* (U.S.) Nov. 180/2 A thick hedge of *butter-bush. **1936** I. L. IDRIESS *Cattle King* xxviii. 252 The rabbits had killed all the white wood, apple-bush and butter-bush. **1747** H. GLASSE *Art of Cookery* xv. 139 (*heading*) To make a *Butter Cake. **1897** G. DU MAURIER *Martian* II. 53 Scotch butter-cake. **1963** *Times* 11 Mar. 13/5 Irish butter cakes... Serve hot or cold. **1885** WILDE *Lett.* (1962) 172 My wife has a huge bill against you—for your meat-safe and the *buttercloth. **1894** *Daily News* 20 Mar. 3/1 Yellowish cream-colour, called *butter-colour by the modistes. **1895** *Montgomery Ward Catal.* 573/1 Improved Butter Color... 1 Gallon Cans. **1790** *Pennsylvania Packet* 7 Dec. 3/3 *Butter coolers. **1875** G. H. LEWES *Problems Life & Mind* II. 135 The china service and glass butter-cooler. **1884** *Health Exhib. Catal.* 112/1 Ice Jugs and Butter Coolers. **1937** FOWLER & WEST *Food for Fifty* 121 *Butter cream,..1 lb. sugar, powdered, 5 Eggs [etc.]. **1950** W. H. EVANS *Spoth's Cake Making & Decoration* 195 Butter cream (smooth) for icing and decorating birthday cakes. *c* **1983** *McDougalls Better Baking* 22/2 When cold, cut in two and sandwich with coffee butter cream. **1883** FLOR. MARRYAT *Moment Madness &c.* III. 170 Their old-world institutions and buildings—their *butter crosses and market steps. **1719** LONDON & WISE *Compl. Gard.* 178 The end of their new Shoots intirely cut off by a little black round Insect, called *Buttercutter. **1863** PRIOR *Plant-n.* 36 **Butter-dock*, from its leaves being used for lapping butter, whence the Scotch name of it, Smair-dock, *Rumex obtusifolius*. **1857** J. G. SWAN *Northwest Coast* 357 The Colonel saw a '*butter-duck' in a shallow creek... These ducks are the black surf-duck (*Fuligula perspicillata*). **1813** VANCOUVER *Agric. Devon* 230 The *butter-factors at Honiton. **1889** in A. Davis *Package & Print* (1967) Pl. 69 Powdered milk without *butter fat. **1899** *Daily News* 17 Feb. 8/3 The sample..afforded no evidence of the presence of fat other than butter fat. **1906** *Macmillan's Mag.* June 612 If wanting in butter-fat, it [*sc.* milk] was not fit for the purpose for which it had been sold. **1946** *Nature* 12 Oct. 522/1 The obvious technique for assessing levels of performance is milk and butter-fat recording. **1802** G. MONTAGU *Ornith. Dict.* (1833) 66 **Butterflip*, a name for the Avoset. **1691** RAY *N.C. Wds.* Coll. 12 **Butter-jags*, the Flowers of the *Trifolium siliqua cornuta*. **1776** WITHERING *Bot. Arrangem.* (1796) VI. 659 Yellow Medick, Butterjags. **1850** DICKENS *Dav. Copp.* lxi. 602 Fish-slices, *butter-knives, and sugar-tongs. **1884** GILMOUR *Mongols* 91 The altar on which a *butter-lamp was then burning. **1789** MARSHALL *Glocester* (E.D.S.) *Butter-leaves, the leaves of the *Atriplex hortensis*, or garden orach; which dairywomen in general sow in their gardens, annually, [for packing butter in]. **1893** *Westm. Gaz.* 25 Feb. 5/3 In Italy, butter is prohibited [in Lent]... The Northerners, however,..would have none of this, and special '*butter-letters' were consequently dispatched to them from the obliging Vatican. **1802** *Edin. Rev.* I. 51 *Butter-men..are scarcely ever attacked by the plague. **1885** *Daily Tel.* 26 Nov. (on *Rigs*), He believed that this name [butter-man] was given in consequence of numbers of this kind of craft trading to Holland for butter. **1483** *Cath. Angl.* 50 *Buttir marke. **1861** MRS. BEETON *Househ. Managem.* 814 *Butter-moulds, or wooden stamps for moulding fresh butter. **1547** BOORDE *Introd. Knowl.* 147, I am a Flemyng, what for all that?.. '*Buttermouth Flemyng', men doth me call. **1902** *Connoisseur* II. No. 8. p. xvii, Frilled *Butter Muslin. **1903** TISDALE & ROBINSON *Soft Cheesemaking* 34 Instead of paper, the cheese is done up in butter muslin. **1906** —— *Buttermaking* 55 Place a damp butter-muslin over the roller and butter-board. **1951** *Good Housek. Home Encycl.* 193/1 The coarser muslins, such as butter muslin, are used for household purposes, for example, straining liquids. **1894** *Dairy Rev.* Aug. 46/2 Some makers used to prepare the annatto in *butter oil. **1895** *Montgomery Ward Catal.* 573/1 Waxed *Butter Paper, grease proof. **1844** *Ainsworth's Mag.* VI. 547 The two oars appeared to be playing the parts of *butter-pats with him. **1953** DYLAN THOMAS *Under Milk Wood* (1954) 30 My crisp toast-fingers, my home-made plum and butterpat. **1616** SURFL. & MARKH. *Countr. Farm* 417 Garden tender or delicate pear such as *Butter peare. **1719** LONDON & WISE *Compl. Gard.* 52 The Burree..It's call'd the Butter Pear, because of its smooth, delicious, melting soft Pulp. **1753** H. WALPOLE *Corr.* (1837) I. 203 The *butter-plate is not exactly what you ordered, but I flatter myself you will like it as well. **1853** G. JOHNSTON *Nat. Hist. E. Bord.* I. 26 *Ranunculus Flammula*, the Butter-Plate, a name expressive of the comparative flatness of the corolla. **1650** H. MORE in *Enthus. Tri.* (1656) 106 You..scold more bitterly than any *Butter-quean. **1881** W. C. RUSSELL *Ocean Free L.* III. iv. 121 The little wooden cabin of a *butter-rigged schooner. **1885** *Daily Tel.* 26 Nov. (on *Rigs*), A butter-rigged schooner's a vessel that sets her top-gallant sail flying. The yard comes down on the top-sail yard, and the sails is furled together. **1597** GERARD *Herbal* cclxiii. §4. 645 In Yorkshire..it is called Butter-woorts, *Butter roote, and white roote. **1884** R. HOLLAND *Gloss. Wds. Chester*, **Butter salt*, salt-making term. A fine boiled salt, not stoved, used specially for making up butter. **1892** *Cornhill Mag.* Sept. 264 The unmoulded salt—locally termed 'butter-salt'—is sent away in trucks. **1872** O. W. HOLMES *Poet Breakf.-t.* i. 2 As the market people run a *butter-scoop through a firkin. **1902** *Encycl. Brit.* XXVII. 358 The butter-scoop is of wood, and is sometimes perforated; it is used for taking the butter out of the churn. **1855** *Whitby Gloss.*, **Butterscot*, treacle ball, with an amalgamation of butter in it. **1865** MISS BRADDON *Sir Jasper* XXVI. 260 The vendors of toothsome *butterscotch were blithe and busy. **1887** WILDE in *Court & Soc. Rev.* 2 Mar. 207/2 He met with a severe fall, through treading on a *butter-slide, which the twins had constructed. **1927** W. E. COLLINSON *Contemp. Eng.* 20 Ice to make slides (if very slippery sometimes called a *butterslide*). **1928** *Observer* 1 Apr. 22 It will do us all the good in the world to slip on a mental butter-slide now and again. **1895** *Montgomery Ward Catal.* 572/2 Wooden *Butter Spades and Ladles. **1906** *Chambers's Jrnl.* Jan. 119/1 An old Dublin butter-spade with ivory handle. **1881** OGILVIE (Annandale) **Butter-stamp*, a piece of carved wood used to mark cakes of butter. **1836** *Southern Lit. Messenger* II. 480 To beat the collected ends of the fingers with an implement..made like a *butterstick. **1888** *Butter substitute [see SUBSTITUTE *sb.* 6 b]. **1906** *Macmillan's Mag.* June 607 What are termed 'butter-substitutes',—in other words, fraudulent adulterants. **1908** *Westm. Gaz.* 5 Aug. 2/2 Vegetarians use very extensively a butter substitute derived from the fat of nuts. **1826** POLWHELE *Trad. & Recoll.* II. 381, I found time to..treat him with *butter-toast for his supper, and butter-toast for his breakfast. *a* **1877** KNIGHT *Dict. Mech.*, **Butter-tongs*, an implement for cutting and transferring pieces of butter. **1830** LINDLEY *Nat. Syst. Bot.* 181 The *Butter Tree of Mungo Park was also a species of Bassia. **1866** *Treas. Bot.*, *Bassia butyracea*, the Indian Butter tree. **1878** H. STANLEY *Dark Cont.* II. xiii. 365 The Bassia Parkii, or Shea butter-tree..exudes a yellowish-white sticky matter. **1886** *N. & Q.* 30 Jan. 98 The Shea tree or butter tree of Africa. **1868** *Rep. Comm. Patents 1867* (U.S.) II. 1218/1 **Butter Tryer*... The scraper fits the trough of the gouge to remove the butter therefrom. **1762** P. MURDOCH tr. *Busching's Syst. Geogr.* I. 384 The *Butter-week..when eating of flesh is forbidden and butter is allowed, is the week immediately preceding the great Fast of Lent. **1923** *Daily Mail* 3 Mar. 10 Maslenitza, or Butter Week, as the Russians call the fortnight preceding Lent, is always celebrated with feasting and drinking in Russia. **1733** SWIFT *On Poetry* 540 Yet why should we be lac'd so strait? I'll give my monarch *butter-weight. **1807** VANCOUVER *Agric. Devon* (1813) 231 This salting in some measure accounts for the enlarged customary butter-weight in this country. **1593** NASHE *Four Lett. Confut.* 49 Thou arrant *butterwhore, thou cotqueane, & scrattop of scoldes. **1764** T. BRYDGES *Homer Travest.* (1797) I. 249 You..scolded like a butter-whore. **1542** BRINKLOW *Complaynt* vi. (1874) 19 Not so moch as the poore *butter-wife but she is spoyled. **1601** SHAKS. *All's Well* IV. i. 245, Tongue, I must put you into a *Butter-womans mouth..if you prattle mee into these perilles. **1883** *Punch* 24 Feb. 87 The five Royal Commissioners in their butterwoman's cloaks. **1854** *Rep. Comm. Patents 1853* (U.S.) 247 Improvement in *Butter Workers. **1908** *Daily Chron.* 16 Nov. 7/1 Churns, cream separators, and butter-workers are turned out by the million in Stockholm. **1906** *Ibid.* 25 Sept. 2/6 One is reluctantly obliged to conclude that *butter-working is a lost art amongst grocers' assistants. **1909** *Cent. Dict. Suppl.*, *Butter Yellow. **1956** *Nature* 24 Mar. 576/2 Rat liver tumours induced by butter yellow.

†'butter, *sb.*[2] *Obs.* [a. F. *boutoir* 'a Farriers Buttresse' (Cotgr.).] = BUTTERIS.

1483 *Cath. Angl.* 50 A Buttyr, *scalprum.* **1607** TOPSELL *Four-f. Beasts* (1673) 311 The humor lies in the foot, for the which you must search with your Butter, paring all the soles of the fore-feet. *Ibid.* 323 Pull off the shooe, and then open the place grieved with a Butter or Drawer.

†'butter, *sb.*[3] *Obs.* (? *nonce-wd.*) [app. a. MDu. or Flem. *botter* 'aleator improbus et præuaricator' (Kilian).] One who cheats at play.

1474 CAXTON *Chesse* 127 Players at dyse, ribauldes and butters.

butter ('bʌtə(r)), *sb.*[4] [f. BUTT *v.*[1] + -ER[1].] An animal that butts.

1611 COTGR., *Cousseur*, a butter or iurrer. **1883** *Fifesh. Jrnl.* 10 May 3/6 The goat is a hard butter.

butter ('bʌtə(r)), *sb.*[5] [f. BUTT *sb.*[3] (or the derived *v.*[3]) + ER[1].] A machine for sawing off the ends of legs or boards, to render them square.

1874 KNIGHT *Dict. Mech.* s.v., In the large saw-mills of the lumber regions double butters are used.

butter, obs. form of BITTERN.

1600 *Sc. Acts 16 Jas. VI*, xxiii, Skaildraik, Herron, Butter, or any sic kynde of fowlles. **1620** J. MASON *Newfoundl.* 4 Butters, blacke Birds with red breastes.

butter ('bʌtə(r)), *v.* [f. BUTTER *sb.*[1]]

1. a. *trans.* To smear or spread with butter. Also, To cook or dish up with butter (see BUTTERED 2).

1496 [see BUTTERED *ppl. a.*]. **1528** TINDALE *Obed. Chr. Man* in *Doctr. Treatises* (1848) 277 They think that, if the bishop butter the child in the forehead, that it is safe. **1589** *Darrell's Accts.* in H. Hall *Soc. in Elizabeth. Age* (1886) 213 For..buttering ij cold chickens, *vd.* **1598** SHAKS. *Merry W.* III. v. 8 If I be seru'd such another tricke, Ile haue my braines tane out and butter'd. **1608** —— *Lear* II. iv. 127 'Twas her Brother, that in pure kindnesse to his Horse buttered his Hay. **1796** MRS. GLASSE *Cookery* v. 53 Butter the paper and also the gridiron. **1883** JAGO in *Knowledge* 24 Aug. 120/2 Ship-biscuits..soaked in hot coffee and then buttered.

b. To close *up* with butter.

1807 SYD. SMITH *Plymley's Lett.* Wks. 1859 II. 163/1 An Irish peasant fills the barrel of his gun full of tow dipped in oil, butters up the lock, buries it in a bog.

c. in proverbial expressions, as ***fine words butter no parsnips***. ***to know on which side one's bread is buttered***: see BREAD 2 f. ***to butter one's bread on both sides***: to be wasteful or luxurious. ***to have one's bread buttered for life***: to be well provided for. †***to butter the cony***: see quot. 1611.

1611 COTGR. s.v. *Ambezatz*, *Ayant faict Ambezatz*, having buttered the connie; hauing had that chance that no wise man would nicke. **1645** *Sacred Decretal* 5 Fair words butter no fish. **1821** BYRON *Vis. Judgm.* xcvi, His bread, Of which he buttered both sides. **1870** LOWELL *Among my Bks.* Ser. I. (1873) 358 Fine words, says our homely old proverb, butter no parsnips. **1885** D. C. MURRAY *First Pers. Sing.* xx. (1886) 152 He told himself that in any case his bread was buttered for life.

2. *fig.* **†a.** See quot. 1725. **b.** To flatter lavishly, to bedaub with fulsome praise or compliment. Now usu. with *up*. Hence **buttering-up** *vbl. sb.*

1700 CONGREVE *Way World* Prol. (1866) 259 The squire that's butter'd still is sure to be undone. **1725** *New Cant. Dict.*, *To butter*, signifies also, to cheat or defraud in a smooth or plausible Manner. **1816** SCOTT *Antiq.* xxxvii. 257 Butter him with some warlike terms—praise his dress and address. **1819** T. MOORE *Tom Crib's Memorial* 40 This *buttering-up*, against the grain, We thought was *curs'd* genteel in Bob. **1832** LYTTON *Eugene A.* II. II. viii. 42 Your honour should see how they fawns and flatters, and butters up a man. *a* **1845** HOOD *Public Dinner* ii, Long speeches are stutter'd, And toasts are well butter'd. **1884** *Sat. Rev.* 5 July 27/1 The Lord Chief Justice of England made a tour through America and generously buttered the natives. **1924** E. M. FORSTER *Passage to India* ix. 106 'This is a great relief to us, it is very good of you to call, Doctor Sahib,' said Hamidullah, buttering him up a bit. **1943** H. PEARSON *Conan Doyle* iii. 42 The little country practitioner who had been buttering them up for a quarter of a century found that he might as well put up his shutters.

†3. *slang.* 'To increase the stakes every throw or every game' J. *Obs.*

1690 B. E. *Dict. Cant. Crew*, *Butter*, to double or treble the Bet or Wager to recover all Losses. *a* **1719** ADDISON *Freeholder* No. 40 Wks. (1821) 505 One of Mr. Congreve's prologues, which compares a writer to a buttering gamester, that stakes all his winning upon one cast; so that if he loses the last throw, he is sure to be undone.

butte'raceous, *a. nonce-wd.* = BUTYRACEOUS.

1837 LOCKHART *Scott* vii. (Chandos) 159 Our butteraceous friend at the Cross.

butteras, obs. f. BUTTRESS.

'butter-ball. 1. A ball of butter; butter moulded into a ball.

1892 J. C. HARRIS *Plantation Printer* 58 She wur a fine cow too, ez fat ez a butter-ball. **1901** GREENOUGH & KITTREDGE *Words* (1902) 177 Thus we have butterball, a ball that consists of butter. **1952** L. MACNEICE *Ten Burnt Offerings* IX. 85 One minute quicksilver, next minute butterballs.

2. The buffle-head or buffle-headed duck, *Clangula albeola*, of North America, so called from its exceeding fatness in autumn. *U.S.*

a **1813** WILSON *Amer. Ornith.* (1814) VIII. 51 Buffel-headed Duck...usually known by the name of the Butter-box, or Butter-ball. **1874** [see BUFFLEHEAD 2]. **1895** *Outing* (U.S.) XXVII. 212/1 Over me they went, so close that I could tell that they were butter balls. **1902** S. E. WHITE *Blazed Trail* xiii. 85 Butterballs and scoters paddled up at his approach.

'butter-bean. A variety of the French bean, *Phaseolus vulgaris*, with almost white pods, or the dried seeds of the Lima bean, *P. limensis*.

1819 W. COBBETT *Amer. Gardener* (1821) iv. §197 The *Lima*-bean..is sometimes called the *butter*-bean. **1884** MILLER *Plant-n.* s.v. *Bean*, Butter Bean, a tender-podded variety of *Phaseolus vulgaris*. **1906** *Macmillan's Mag.* July 676 Butterbeans somewhat resemble white fish in colour and the task of turning out a butter-bean fritter..to look like a fried sole would not be a difficult one. **1951** *Dict. Gardening* (R. Hort. Soc.) I. 244/1 Pods without green colouring...are known as waxpod or Butter Beans, but they are not to be confused with the Butter Beans of the grocer. *Ibid.* 244/2 The seeds [of Lima Beans] vary considerably in colour and size, the white varieties being best for use as dry seeds, constituting the Butter Beans of the grocer.

†'butterbore. *Obs.* [Possibly f. BUTTER *sb.*[1] (the implement being compared in form to a 'cheese-taster') + BORE *sb.*[1] 5; but cf. Fr. *bouterot*, *boutereau*, *bouterolle*, denoting pointed instruments for punching or boring.] (See quot.)

1679 PLOT *Staffordsh.* (1686) 109 Who if he have ground to suspect any of the pots, tryes them with an instrument of Iron made like a Cheese-Taster, only much larger and longer, called an Auger or Butterboare, with which he makes proof (thrusting it in obliquely) to the bottom of the pot.

†'butter-bowzy, *a. Obs.* [f. Du. *boterbus* butter-box.] Of the nature of a BUTTER-BOX 2.

1719 D'URFEY *Pills* I. 252 The Italian and the butterbowzy *Hogan Mogan*.

'butter-box.

1. a. A box for holding butter.

1756 NUGENT *Gr. Tour* I. 44 The common people seldom go upon a journey without a butter-box in their pockets. **1874** *Contemp. Rev.* XXIV. 698 The wits declared that Denmark had sent a hundred thousand herrings, Holland a hundred thousand butter-boxes.

b. *transf.* A vessel or vehicle resembling a butter-box. Also *attrib.*

1840 DANA *Bef. Mast* ix, She was the *Loriotte*,..and was engaged in the hide and tallow trade. She was a lump of a thing, what the sailors call a butter-box. **1851** H. MELVILLE *Moby Dick* I. xvi. 110 You may have seen many a quaint craft in your day,..butter-box galliots, and what not. **1893** CLARK RUSSELL *List, ye Landsmen* ix, Why the deuce don't the shipwrights ease off when they come aft, instead of holding on with the square run of the butter-box to the very lap of the taffrail? **1909** *N. Y. Even. Post* 28 Jan. (Th.), What New York youngster ever heard of a butterbox? This is the name applied [in the country] to the spring wagons of farmer and grocer, divested of wheels and set up on runners for the winter season.

2. Contemptuous designation for a Dutchman. Cf. also *butter bag*, *-mouth* (BUTTER *sb.*[1] 5). *Obs.* exc. in Naut. slang. Also, a Dutch ship.

1600 DEKKER *Gentle Craft* Wks. 1873 I. 21 We have not men enow, but wee must entertaine every butterbox. **1624** MASSINGER *Renegado* II. v, Some low country butterbox. **1672** H. STUBBE *Justif. Dutch War* 79 The World is coming to a fine pass when these Butter-boxes presume to teach all Europe Civility. **1811** *Dict. Buckish Slang*, *Butter Box*, a Dutchman, from the great quantity of butter eaten by the

people of that country. **1867** SMYTH *Sailor's Word-Bk.* 148 *Butter-box*..A cant term for a Dutchman. **1929** F. BOWEN *Sea Slang* 21 *Butter Box*..Dutch ship or seaman.

3. = BUTTER-BALL 2. *U.S.*

1806 W. CLARK in *Lewis & Clark Exped.* (1905) IV. 50 The same species of duck..called the butterbox. *a* **1813** [see BUTTER-BALL 2]. **1874** J. W. LONG *Amer. Wild-fowl Shooting* xxix. 281 Local names [of the buffle-headed duck]: butter-box, butter-ball, and little whistler.

butter-bump, bitter-bump. [f. *butter, bitter*, earlier forms of BITTERN + BUMP *v.*[2]] Local name of the Bittern; Phillips 1678 makes it a different bird, but prob. in error.

1671 in SKINNER. **1678** PHILLIPS (App.), *Butterbump*, a sort of Bird which some call Onocrotalus..Others think this bird rather than the Bittern (which they call *Ardea Stellaris*) to be that which is called in Latin *Buteo.* **1678** H. MORE *Glanvill's Sadducismus* Postsc. (1681) 30 And does she not..put her Neb also into it sometimes, as into a Reed..and cry like a Butterbump? **1864** TENNYSON *North. Farmer* (*Old Style*) viii, Moäst loike a butter-bump, fur I 'eerd 'um aboot an' aboot. **1871** E. PEACOCK *Ralf Skirl.* II. 111 We got ten couple..besides two butter-bumps and a heronsew.

butterbur ('bʌtəbɜː(r)). Also 7 -burn. [f. BUTTER *sb.*[1] + BUR *sb.* Conjectured to be so named because its leaves were used for wrapping butter in; cf. *butter-dock, butter-leaves* in BUTTER *sb.*[1] 5. See, however, quot. 1651, which suggests a different explanation.] A plant, *Petasites vulgaris*, with large soft leaves, growing in wet land; sometimes made the English name of the genus.

1548 TURNER *Names Herbes* s.v., Petasites is called in the South partes of Englande a Butter bur. **1597** GERARD *Herbal* cclxxviii. §1. 667 Bvtter Burre doth..bring foorth flowers before the leaues, as doth Coltesfoot. **1651** N. BIGGS *New Dispens.* 43 ¶79 From Butter-burre floweth Gum, from Chameleon bird-lime. **1673** RAY *Trav.* (1738) II. 192 The leaves thereof are rough and round, as big very near as those of Petasites, call'd Butterburn in our language. **1794** MARTYN *Rousseau's Bot.* xxvi. 389 Butter-bur has vast leaves shaped like those of the Colts-foot; many..flowers collected into an ovate thyrse. **1857** KINGSLEY *Two Y. Ago* II. 269 A long bar of gravel, covered with giant 'butterbur' leaves. **1880** *Encycl. Brit.* XI. 634/1 What..is sometimes called 'winter heliotrope', is the fragrant 'butterbur', or sweet-scented coltsfoot, *Petasites* (*Tussilago*) *fragrans.*

¶ Erroneously: the Burdock (*Arctium lappa*).

1861 S. THOMSON *Wild Flowers* III. (ed. 4) 306 The butter-bur (*Arctium lappa*) has a repute in malignant fevers.

buttercup ('bʌtəkʌp).

†**1.** A cup for holding butter. *Obs.*

1512 *Will E. Grantham* (Somerset Ho.) My buttercuppis of silver.

2. A name popularly applied to species of Ranunculus bearing yellow cup-shaped flowers, esp. *R. bulbosus, R. acris*, and *R. repens*; and usually taken as the English name of the genus.

[The name, which seems to be first recorded in the course of 18th c., may be regarded as a mixture of the older names for these plants, viz. BUTTERFLOWER and *gold-cups* or *king-cups*. In the earlier instances it is always *buttercups*.]

1777 LIGHTFOOT *Fl. Scot.* (1789) I. 292 *Ranunculus bulbosus*, Bulbous Crowfoot, or Butter-cups, *Anglis*; *R. acris*, Upright Meadow Crowfoot. **1792** MARTYN *Flora Rust.* I. 30 These three Crowfoots are confounded by persons ignorant of Botany under the names of Butter-flowers, Butter-cups, King-Cups, Gold-cups and Gold-knops. **1797** MILLER *Gard. Dict.*, It..is confounded vulgarly with the *repens* and *bulbosus* under the name of Butterflower or Butter-cups; under the notion that the yellow colour of butter is owing to these plants. **1803** WORDSW. *Small Celandine* 51 Wks. (1869) 120 Buttercups, that will be seen, Whether we will see or no. **1817** REES *Cycl.* s.v., *Ranunculus bulbosus*, Bulbous Crow-foot, or Buttercups. **1821** CLARE *Vill. Minstr.* II. 173 Feather-headed grasses..And yellow buttercup. **1872** OLIVER *Elem. Bot.* II. §2. 123 Thus, we refer all the species of Buttercup to the genus *Ranunculus.*

b. Applied (with distinctive epithets) to other plants bearing flowers of similar appearance, **water buttercup** (*Caltha palustris* and *Ranunculus aquatilis*), **white buttercups** (*Parnassia palustris*). (Britten and Holland.)

3. *attrib.* (in late use, referring to the bright golden-yellow colour of the flower).

1875 MISS BRADDON *Str. World* i. 1 In buttercup-time, just when May..melts into tender June. **1883** *Truth* 31 May 760/2 Smartly dressed in a short buttercup satin skirt...The boots were of the buttercup shade of the satin skirt.

buttercupped ('bʌtəkʌpt), *a.* [f. BUTTERCUP + -ED[2].] Abounding in or covered with buttercups.

1872 C. S. CALVERLEY *Fly Leaves* 89 Looking far over buttercupped leas. **1888** MRS. H. WARD *R. Elsmere* xliv, A wavering rainy light played..over the buttercupped river meadows. **1924** *Public Opinion* 9 May 400/1 Banks all buttercup'd and burning.

So **buttercuppy** ('bʌtəkʌpɪ), *a.*

1871 W. MORRIS in Mackail *Life* (1899) I. 237 The fields are all butter-cuppy. **1958** BETJEMAN *Coll. Poems* 259 That burning buttercuppy day.

buttered ('bʌtəd), *ppl. a.* [f. BUTTER *v.*[1]]

1. Smeared or spread with butter.

1496 *Bk. St. Albans, Fysshynge* 30 Browne breede tostyd wyth hony in lyknesse of a butteryd loof. *a* **1680** ROCHESTER in D'Urfey *Pills* (1719) 343 With greasy painted Faces drest, With butter'd Hair. **1769** MRS. RAFFALD *Eng. Housekpr.* (1778) 181 Tie it close up in a cloth well buttered. **1812** L. HUNT in *Examiner* 7 Dec. 796/1 The urn and the buttered toast. **1847** BARHAM *Ingol. Leg.* Ser. III. (1858) 474 A round and a half of some hot butter'd toast.

†**2. a.** Cooked with butter; served up with melted butter. *Obs.*

1567 *Triall Treas.* (1850) 6, I would you had a dishe of buttered peason. **1596** NASHE *Saffron Walden* O iv, Trotters, sheepes porknells, and buttered rootes. **1627** CAPT. SMITH *Seaman's Gram.* xv. 75 A dish of buttered Rice with a little Cynamon. **1678** B. R. *Let. Pop. Friends* 4 Butter'd Codfish. **1785** BURNS *Halloween* xxviii, Butter'd sow'ns.

†**b.** ***buttered ale*** (*beer*): see ALE 4.

1547 BOORDE *Breu. Health* (1552) 120, A remedy [for hoarseness]..drynke buttered Ale or buttered beere. **1764** T. BRIDGES *Homer Travest.* II. 213 Good old wives shall tell the tale O'er roasted eggs and butter'd ale. **1789** J. O'DONNEL in *Med. Commun.* II. 292 He desired to have some buttered ale for his supper.

c. ***buttered eggs***: eggs beaten up and cooked with butter; now applied to the dish otherwise called *scrambled eggs.*

c **1410** *Master of Game* (MS. Digby 182) xii, Buttured egges doth hem moche goode. **1865** MRS. BEETON *Dict. Everyday Cookery* 113/1 Buttered Eggs. Ingredients.—4 new-laid eggs, 2 oz. of butter.

3. a. *fig.*

1625 HART *Anat. Ur.* II. i. 56 If faire buttered speeches..could cure diseases. **1793** J. BERESFORD in *Looker-on* No. 80 (1794) III. 275 Well-buttered blasphemies, stolen, through the medium of the foot-boy, from his master's table. **1822** C. SWAN *Heir of Foiz* 246 At this poetic shop they sell..Best buttered sentiments in rhyme.

†**b.** ***buttered bun***(*s* (*slang*). A harlot, a mistress. (Cf. B. E. *Dict. Cant. Crew* 1690).

1679 *Cullen w. Flock of Court Misses* in *Roxb. Ballads* (1884) V. 126 This is the day..that sets our Monarch free From butter'd Buns [*i.e.* Louise de Quérouaille] and Slavery.

butteress(**e**, obs. f. BUTTRESS.

'**butter-,fingered**, *a.* That takes hold of things with a loose slippery grasp, as if with fingers greased with butter; apt to let things fall or slip through one's fingers. Also *fig.* (*colloq.*)

The dial. sense is often 'unable to handle anything hot'.

1615 MARKHAM *Eng. Housew.* II. ii. (1668) 51 She must not be butter-fingred, sweet-toothed, nor faint-hearted; for the first will let everything fall, etc. **1841** *Fraser's Mag.* XXIII. 671 Butterfingered at a catch. **1884** *Chr. Commw.* 14 Feb. 428/3 A discreet Christian meets with few rebuffs; a blundering butter-fingered one with many.

butter-fingers ('bʌtə,fɪŋgəz). A butter-fingered person; *esp.* one who lets slip through his fingers a cricket-ball that he ought to catch or stop. (*colloq.*, chiefly in vocative.)

1837 DICKENS *Pickw.* vii, At every bad attempt to catch, and every failure to stop the ball, he launched his personal displeasure at the head of the devoted individual in such denunciations as..now, butter-fingers, muff, humbug, and so forth. **1840** THACKERAY *Misc.* (1857) II. 375 When the executioner had come to the last of the heads, he lifted it up, but, by some clumsiness, allowed it to drop; at this the crowd yelled out, 'Ah, Butter-fingers!' **1868** H. KINGSLEY *Silcote of S.* III. vii. 123, I never was a butter-fingers, though a bad batter.

So **butter-finger**, *attrib.* (*rare.*)

1851 *Fraser's Mag.* XLIV. 279 His 'butterfinger' fashion of taking hold of things.

'**butter-fish.** Any of several fishes having a slippery coating of mucus, esp. the Gunnel found in British waters; the Murray perch, *Oligorus mitchelli*, a fresh-water fish of Australia; the kelp fish of New Zealand (see quot. 1880); the dollar-fish, *Stromateus* or *Poronotus triacanthus*, a food-fish of the eastern U.S.

1674 RAY (*Sea*) *Fishes, Coll.* 104, 56 Butter-Fish. **1740** R. BROOKES *Art Angling* II. xviii. 123 The Butter-Fish or Gunnel..sometimes attains the Length of six Inches..is taken frequently on the Cornish Coast. **1842** J. E. DEKAY *Zool. N.Y.* IV. 153 The American Butter-fish, *Gunnellus mucronatus.* **1850** J. B. CLUTTERBUCK *Port Phillip* iii. 44 In the bay are large quantities of..butter-fish. **1880** GÜNTHER *Fishes* 533 The 'butter-fish', or 'Kelp-fish' of the colonists of New Zealand (*C*[*oridodax*] *pullus*), is prized as food. **1883** E. P. RAMSAY *Food Fishes N.S. Wales* 12 *H*[*aplodactylus*] *obscurus*,..known to our southern fishermen as the 'butter-fish', is highly esteemed. **1883** *Fisheries Exhib. Catal.* (ed. 4) 179 The Butter-fish is an excellent and delicate morsel. **1888** G. B. GOODE *Amer. Fishes* 221 The 'Butter-fish' of Massachusetts and New York, *Stromateus triacanthus. Ibid.* 232 [*Selene setipinnis*] is a frequent summer visitor all along the coast as far north as Woods Holl, Mass., where it has a peculiar name,..the 'Hump-backed Butterfish'. **1946** K. TENNANT *Lost Haven* (1968) xxii. 393 One of them little butter-fish, all fins and flaps. **1962** K. F. LAGLER et al. *Ichthyology* xiv. 443 Among the many other fishes of the neritic zone are the..butter-fishes (Stromateidae).

†'**butter-flower.** *Obs.* [cf. Ger. *butterblume*: perh. from colour of the flower, but see quots. 1607 and 1762; the notion expressed in the latter is common both in England and Germany, but is unfounded, as cows do not eat the buttercup.]

1. An older name of the BUTTERCUP, q.v.

1578 LYTE *Dodoens* III. lxxiv. 422 Some do also name it..in Englishe Goldcuppes, Goldknoppes, and Butterflowers. **1607** TOPSELL *Four-f. Beasts* (1673) 56 There is an herb much like crow-foot, called of the Germans 'Butter-bloumen', and in English 'butter-flower', which is used to colour butter. **1692** *Poems in Burlesque* 9 New Rigg'd and gay, As Beaux or Butter-flowers in May. **1748** RICHARDSON *Clarissa* (1811) VIII. 54 A verdant field overspread with butter-flowers, and daisies. **1762** B. STILLINGFL. *Nat. Hist.* in *Misc. Tracts* 359 It is a notion that prevails commonly that cows eat the crow-foot..and that this occasions the butter to be yellow, from whence I suppose it is generally known by the name of the butter-flower. But this I believe is all a mistake. **1792** [see BUTTERCUP 2]. **1829** LOUDON *Encycl.* IV. 724 Butter-flower or Butter-cup is a species of Crowfoot. **1839** HOOPER *Med. Dict.* 290.

2. ***blue butterflower***: some unknown plant.

1599 A. M. *Gabelhouer's Bk. Physic* 201/1 Take blewe butterflowers.

butterfly ('bʌtəflaɪ), *sb.* Forms: 1 buttorfleoȝe, 3 buterfliȝe, 4 boterfleȝe, -flye, botter-, bottir-, botyrflye, (-flie), 4–6 butterflye, -flie, 5 botur-, botir-, buttur-, buttyrflye, (-flie), butter-, buttyrfle(e, botirfley, 7 butterflee, 7- butterfly. [f. BUTTER *sb.*[1] + FLY *sb.*; with OE. *buttorfléoȝe* cf. Du. *botervlieg*, earlier *botervlieghe*, mod.G. *butterfliege*. The reason of the name is unknown: Wedgwood points out a Du. synonym *boterschijte* in Kilian, which suggests that the insect was so called from the appearance of its excrement.]

I. 1. An insect belonging to any of those diurnal species of lepidoptera, or scaly-winged flies, which have knobbed antennæ, and carry their wings erect when at rest.

a **1000** ÆLFRIC *Voc.* in Wr.-Wülcker 121 *Papilio*, buttorfleoȝe. *a* **1300** *Floriz & Bl.* 473 þer fliste ut a buterfliȝe Are ihc wiste on min iȝe. *c* **1386** CHAUCER *Nonne Prestes Prol.* 24 Swich talkyng is nat worth a boterflye. *c* **1440** *Promp. Parv.* 46 Boturflye, *papilio. c* **1440** HYLTON *Scala Perf.* (W. de W.) III. xxv, Lyke to children þat renneth after butter flyes. **1548** LATIMER *Serm. Ploughers* (Arb.) 22 The butterflye glorieth not in hyr owne dedes. **1606** SHAKS. *Tr. & Cr.* III. iii. 78 Men like butter-flies, Shew not their mealie wings, but to the Summer. **1626** BACON *Sylva* §696 As Butterflies quicken with heat, which were benummed with cold. **1726** GAY *Fables* I. xxiv. 41 And what's a Butterfly? At best He's but a caterpillar, drest. **1845** DARWIN *Nat. Voy.* ii. 33 This [*Papilio feronia*] is the only butterfly which I have ever seen, that uses its legs for running. **1856** MRS. BROWNING *Aur. Leigh* 312 Butterflies that bear Upon their blue wings such red embers round.

2. *fig.* **a.** A vain, gaudily attired person (e.g. a courtier who flutters about the court); a light-headed, inconstant person; a giddy trifler.

1605 SHAKS. *Lear* v. iii. 13 Wee'l..tell old tales, and laugh At gilded Butterflies. **1649** DRUMM. OF HAWTH. *Fam. Ep.* Wks. (1711) 142 Long since I learned not to esteem of any golden butterflies there [at court], but as of counters. **1767** FORDYCE *Serm. Yng. Wom.* (ed. 4) I. ii. 76 Nor will you be in danger of appearing butterflies one day, and slatterns the next. **1841** *Blackw. Mag.* L. 63 Coroneted carriages abound: the butterflies of fashion are abroad. **1885** M. G. WATKINS in *Academy* 5 Dec. 379/1 Sufficiently interesting to captivate that butterfly, the 'general reader'.

b. Applied to something flimsy, like a butterfly's wings.

a **1603** T. CARTWRIGHT *Confut. Rhem. N.T.* (1618) 407 Those Churches which used unleavened bread, used no such butterflies as you doe; but had a great Cake which was sufficient for the whole congregation to communicate in.

c. Phr. ***to break a butterfly on a wheel***, to use unnecessary force in destroying something fragile. Also *ellipt.*

1735 [see BREAK *v.* 7 b]. **1874** TROLLOPE *Way we live Now* I. ix. 70 One doesn't want to break a butterfly on the wheel. **1931** W. HOLTBY *Poor Caroline* vi. 213, I can't bear to see a woman in the dock—butterfly on the wheel. **1951** N. ANNAN *L. Stephen* 292 Why break a butterfly on the wheel of scholarship?

d. Applied to persons whose periods of work or occupation of a place are transitory or seasonal.

1890 *Chambers's Jrnl.* 10 May 289/2 A 'butterfly' man rests for a moment to wipe his streaming brow, when the warder's stern voice bids him proceed with his work. **1891** *Daily News* 29 Dec. 6/4 The 'butterfly man', who is given cabs by the proprietors in the height of the season. **1895** *Westm. Gaz.* 8 Mar. 3/1 Those cabbies who come upon the streets in the fine days and disappear with the autumn leaves are called 'butterflies'. **1902** *Daily Chron.* 2 June 7/1 Chelsea will welcome the return of the truant 'butterfly' to a region always to be associated with his artistic fame. **1912** *Standard* 15 Apr. 6/7 It was stated..that the word 'butterflies' was a 'technical term' for painters and decorators who worked upon bank holidays.

e. A fanciful name (usu. *pl.*) used of the fluttering sensations felt before any formidable venture, esp. in phr. ***butterflies in the stomach, tummy***, etc. Also *attrib.*

1908 F. CONVERSE *House of Prayer* iv. 43 The three o'clock train going down the valley..gave him a sad feeling, as if he had a butterfly in his stomach. **1943** *Word Study* Oct. 6/1 The expression some aviators use to describe their condition before taking off. They have 'butterfly stomach', they say, so marked is the fluttering in the Department of the Interior. **1944** H. CROOME *You've gone Astray* v. 52 There was no electrical response to the movement of that firmly gentle hand, no butterflies on the backbone. **1955** J. CANNAN *Long Shadows* viii. 132 With butterflies in her stomach..she ascended the pretentious flight of dirty marble steps. **1958** *Woman* 20 Sept. 69/3, I still have 'butterflies' even now when I hear the Tiger Moth plane throttling back, which is my signal to prepare for the jump. **1959** *Sunday Times* 25 Jan. 15/5 'I always have butterflies when I open Parliament,' she [*sc.* Queen Elizabeth II] remarked.

†**3.** Humorous designation for: ? Some sort of legal summons or paper. *Obs.*

1583 STUBBES *Anat. Abus.* (1836) 140 If the poore manne haue not where with to pay..out goe butterflies and writtes as thick as haile.

4. a. The guide for the reins on the front of a hansom cab, named from a fancied resemblance to a butterfly with extended wings.

1883 *Standard* 6 Mar. 6/3 The box covered the whole roof of the cab, preventing him [the cabman] from seeing the 'butterfly'. **1885** *Specif. Rowley & Wheeler's Patent* No. 14398 The butterfly, or bracket, is screwed to the top of the Hansom cab.

b. In full ***butterfly bow***, a bow made up or tied with the loop and end on each side spread apart like the expanded wings of a butterfly. So ***butterfly tie***.

1870 *Young Ladies' Jrnl.* 1 Mar. 138/2 The butterfly bow ..is of black or coloured velvet. **1887** E. B. CUSTER *Tenting on Plains* (1889) xv. 502 It was then the fashion for men to wear a tiny neck-bow, called a butterfly tie. **1888** *Cassell's Fam. Mag.* Feb. 182/1 A bonnet à la Folle, with a tricoloured butterfly bow at the top. **1914** G. K. CHESTERTON *Wisdom Fr. Brown* xi. 264 A very young gentleman with..a black butterfly tie. **1920** *Punch* 4 Aug. 97/2 The wearing of a butterfly bow with a double event collar was a solecism past forgiveness.

c. *Swimming*. (See quot. 1957.) Also *attrib.*

1936 *N.Y. Times* 15 Aug. 8/2 The men's 200-metre breast-stroke..seemed to prove that the butterfly stroke is not all that some..think it is. *Ibid.* 15 Aug. 8/2 Higgins.. used the butterfly only at the beginning and end [of the race]. **1937** *Off. Rep. XIth Olympiad 1936* 168 The breast stroke swimmers used the butterfly style, which was a failure. **1938** *Times* 10 Aug. 6 The butterfly, it may be explained, is made by recovering both arms at once out of the water. *Ibid.* 15 Aug. 5 A proposal will be made that the Butterfly stroke be abolished from international competitions. **1957** *Encycl. Brit.* XXI. 665/2 The butterfly is a competitive style only... In the butterfly the arms pull under the body all the way to the thighs, then emerge and fling forward above surface in circular motion.

5. *Coal-mining*. ? A set of catches which open out so as to prevent the falling of the cage. Also *attrib.*, as ***butterfly apparatus***, ***catch***.

1882 in *West. Morn. News* 25 Nov. 5/6 The ascending cage was hurled into the headgear, smashing the butterflies and breaking the engine rope, and had it not been for the remaining butterflies the cage must have fallen to the bottom. **1887** *Daily News* 11 Jan. 2/7 The butterfly apparatus..had acted, but..the bolts..were torn away. **1909** *Daily Chron.* 8 Jan. 5/3 When the winding rope was detached the safety 'butterfly' catches failed to act.

II. *attrib.* and *comb.*

6. *attrib.* Of, pertaining to, or resembling a butterfly; *fig.* vain, giddy, inconstant, frivolous.

1673 R. HEAD *Canting Acad.* 103 The Bawd furnisheth them with Butterfly Garments. **1728** MRS. PENDARVES in *Mrs. Delany's Corr.* 165 All the butterfly men were at court last night. **1837** *Fraser's Mag.* XV. 239 Mr. Bailey was a dandy of the butterfly order. **1847–9** TODD *Cycl. Anat. & Phys.* IV. 171/2 The butterfly movement of the wings being most commonly resorted to. **1855** C. BRONTË *Villette* i. 3 He is fond of science..a thing his butterfly wife could not endure.

7. Simple combinations, as ***butterfly-brained***, ***-catching***, ***-hunting***, ***-like***.

1878 BROWNING *Poets Croisic* 53 The bard born to bask Butterfly-like in shine which kings and queens And baby-dauphins shed. **1881** J. PAYN *Grape fr. Thorn* I. ii. 29 His only exercise (he was an entomologist) being butterfly-catching. **1881** GRANT ALLEN *Vignettes Nat.* iv. 31 The date when flower-hunting and butterfly-hunting both begin. **1961** *Times* 6 Dec. 17/3 The butterfly-brained society hostess.

8. Special comb.: **butterfly blenny** = *butterfly-fish*; **butterfly-block**, *Naut.*, a small block consisting of two wings containing rollers for a chain to pass over; **butterfly bomb** (see quot.); **butterfly clack**, **-cock** = *butterfly-valve*; **butterfly-fish**, the Ocellated Blenny (*Blennius ocellaris*): **butterfly-flower**, the genus *Schizanthus*; **butterfly kiss** (see quots.); **butterfly lily** = MARIPOSA LILY; **butterfly lobster**, a marine crustacean, *Ibacus incisus*, found in Tasmanian waters; **butterfly lupus**, lupus of the nose and cheeks; **butterfly-net**, a net used for catching butterflies; **butterfly nose**, a dog's nose when spotted or mottled; **butterfly nut** (*Mech.*), a nut provided with wings so as to be turned by the thumb and finger = *thumb-nut*; **butterfly orchis**, a book-name for *Habenaria chlorantha* and *H. bifolia*; **butterfly-pea**: see PEA[1] 3; **butterfly plant**, the name of two Orchids, *Oncidium papilio* and *Phalænopsis amabilis*; also (quot. 1882) = *butterfly flower*; **butterfly ray**, an Australian sting-ray, *Gymnura tentaculata*; **butterfly screw** (*Mech.*), a screw with a thumb-piece, a thumb-screw; **butterfly-shaped** *a. Bot.* = PAPILIONACEOUS; **butterfly-shell**, the popular name of the genus *Voluta* of testaceous molluscs; **butterfly snail**, a mollusc of the sub-class *Pteropoda*, a sea-butterfly; **butterfly tulip** = MARIPOSA LILY; **butterfly-valve**, a kind of double clack-valve, so called from its resemblance, when open, to a butterfly's wings; **butterfly-weed**, a name of various American plants, esp. *Asclepias tuberosa*.

1897 MCINTOSH & MASTERMAN *Life-Hist. Brit. Marine Food-Fishes* vii. 205 (*heading*) *Butterfly Blenny. **1959** A. HARDY *Fish & Fisheries* x. 213 The beautiful little butterfly blenny..which is not uncommon to the south west. **1882** NARES *Seamanship* (ed. 6) 41 Rollers or *butterfly-blocks are fitted to bands round the yard. **1944** *Sci. News Let.* 14 Oct. 247/2 Recently they developed a '*butterfly bomb', with wings that open up as soon as the bomb is released, and act like a parachute to slow its descent. **1861** N. RANKINE *Steam Engine* 123 A pair of flap valves placed hinge to hinge (usually made of one piece of leather fastened down in the middle) constitutes a '*butterfly-clack'. **1740** R. BROOKES *Art Angling* II. vi. 187 The *Butterfly-Fish is often exposed to sale at Venice among other small Fish. **1762** B. STILLINGFL. *Econ. Nat.* in *Misc. Tracts* 84 The butterfly fish ..brings forth its fœtus alive. **1881** F. DARWIN in *Nature* XXIII. 334 It seems impossible to believe that a *butterfly-flower could be developed under such circumstances. **1871** GEO. ELIOT *Middlem.* I. i. v. 73 Celia knelt down..and gave her little *butterfly kiss. **1932** E. WAUGH *Black Mischief* ii. 58 'I've invented a new way of kissing. You do it with your eye-lashes.' 'I've known that for years. It's called a butterfly kiss.' **1945** G. ENDORE *Methinks the Lady* (1947) iii. 47 Don't you know what a butterfly kiss is?.. You flutter your eyelashes against his cheek, and then he flutters his against yours. **1902** V. K. CHESNUT *Plants used by Indians Calif.* 323 Calochortus venustus..the commonest species of the Mariposa or *butterfly lilies. **1880** L. A. MEREDITH *Tasmanian Friends & Foes* 248 '*Butterfly lobsters'..the shell of the head and body..expands into something like wing-forms. **1913** DORLAND *Med. Dict.* (ed. 7) s.v. *Lupus*, *Butterfly lupus. **1827** M. WILMOT *Jrnl.* 25 July in *More Lett.* (1935) 278 Edmund and Wilmot amused themselves with their *butterfly nets. **1939** T. S. ELIOT *Fam. Reunion* II. i. 77 The day I lost my butterfly net. **1883** W. G. STABLES *Our Friend Dog* vii. 59 **Butterfly nose*, a nostril with white spots in it. **1869** SIR E. REED *Shipbuild.* xi. 233 When the door is closed, the clamp-screws or *butterfly nuts which are hinged to the frame, are turned back from the doorway. **1597** GERARDE *Herball* 165 (*caption*) *Ornithophora Candida*, *Butter-flie Orchis. **1629** PARKINSON *Parad.* xxii. 192 *Orchis Hermaphroditica candida*, the white Butter-flie Orchis. **1898** C. M. YONGE *J. Keble's Parishes* xiv. 155 Butterfly or honey-suckle orchis, *Habenaria*. **1963** *Times* 25 Apr. 14/6 A solitary exquisite butterfly-orchis. **1882** *Garden* 11 Feb. 91/2 *Butterfly plants (*Schizanthus*) are a charming class of annuals. **1931** J. R. NORMAN *Hist. Fishes* xvi. 325 The *Butterfly Rays (*Pteroplatea*). **1876** *S. Kens. Mus. Catal.* No. 1146 A milled headed screw works this lift, and an adjacent *butterfly screw. **1776** WITHERING *Bot. Arrangem.* 1796 I. 306 Blossoms *butterfly-shaped, unequal. **1890** *Chambers's Encycl.* V. 110/2 The yet more closely allied '*butterfly-snails' or Pteropods. **1886** J. M. HUTCHINGS *In Heart Sierras* 92 The charming Mariposa, or '*Butterfly Tulip'. **1896** T. W. SANDERS *Encycl. Gardening* (ed. 2) 47 *Calochortus* (Butterfly Tulip). *c* **1865** LETHEBY in *Circ. Sc.* I. 129/1 In this tube there is placed a *butterfly-valve. **1830** LINDLEY *Nat. Syst. Bot.* 213 *Butterfly weed is a popular remedy in the United States for a variety of disorders.

Hence **'butterflydom**, **-ism**, *nonce-wds.*

1882 H. MERIVALE *Faucit of B.* II. II. vii. 240 The world in all its aspects bore the pleasant face of butterflydom. **1866** S. G. OSBORNE *Lett. Educ. Yng. Children* 25 That great amount of butterflyism of which we see so much in after-life.

'butterfly, *v.* [f. prec. sb.]

a. *intr.* To flutter or flit like a butterfly.

1875 HOWELLS *Foregone Concl.* viii, Gaming, sonneteering, and butterflying about generally. **1880** *Time* II. 448 Who are those young gentlemen at that side seat, who butterfly round that smiling lily?

b. *fig.* To flirt or philander.

1893 *Chambers's Jrnl.* 12 Aug. 504/2 The young graduate was only butterflying after all. **1906** B'NESS VON HUTTEN *What became of Pam* III. ix, 'What about Wantage?'.. 'He is still butterflying.'

† **'butter-ham.** *Obs. rare.* [app. ad. Du. *boterham* 'slice of bread-and-butter', used in a slang or humorous sense.] ? A partial lining to a cloak.

[**1863** *Good Words* 868 [A Dutchman says] 'Give me a butterham with flesh and a half-bottle wine'.] **1716** MRS. BEHN *Dutch Lov.* III. ii. 189 A Cloak..not through lin'd, but fac'd as far as 'twas turn'd back, with a pair of frugal *Butter-hams.

butteridge, obs. form of BUTTRESS.

butterie, obs. form of BUTTERY.

butterine ('bʌtəriːn). [f. BUTTER *sb.*[1] + -INE.] An imitation butter manufactured from oleomargarine (one of the constituents of animal fat) churned up with milk. (By *Act 50 & 51 Vict.* xxix. 'all substances, whether compound or otherwise, prepared in imitation of butter' must after 1 Jan. 1888, be offered for sale under the name of *Margarine*.)

1874 [advertised in 'The Grocer' in March.] **1878** PARKES *Man. Pract. Hygiene* (ed. De Chaumont) 270 *note*, A substance from New York has lately made its appearance in the market under the name of butterine. **1881** *Times* 5 Apr. 10/1 A substance which is called 'butterine' in commerce and oleo-margarine in laboratories. **1882** in *Nature* XXV. 270 Oleo-margarine..is made into butterine by adding 10 per cent. of milk to it, and churning the mixture. **1887** *Newspaper* 14 July, The dairy farmers scored heavily against the butterinists by securing the substitution of the word 'margarine' for 'butterine' in the bill for regulating the sale of imitation butter.

butteriness ('bʌtərɪnɪs). [f. BUTTERY *a.* + -NESS.] Buttery quality or state.

1528 PAYNELL *Salerne's Regim.* E, Mylke..washeth the entrayles with it wattrishenes, and hit mundifieth with hit buttrines. **1882** *Spectator* No. 2805 The unromantic butteriness of her little brother's kisses.

buttering ('bʌtərɪŋ), *vbl. sb.* and *ppl. a.* [f. BUTTER *v.* + -ING.] **A.** *sb.* Flattery. *Sc.* Jamieson. **B.** *a.* That butters.

a **1719** [see BUTTER *v.* 3.]

butteris[1] ('bʌtərɪs). Forms: 6 buttris, 6, 8 buttrice, 7 buttresse, butterys(se, 7–8 buttress, 7– butteris. [Cf. BUTTER *sb.*[2], F. *boutoir*; also F. *boutereau*, *bouterolle*, names of instruments used in various trades for punching or boring. The precise formation of the Eng. word is unknown.] A farrier's tool for paring a horse's hoofs.

1573 TUSSER *Husb.* (1878) 36 A buttrice and pincers, a hammer and naile. **1591** PERCIVALL *Sp. Dict.*, *Pujavante*, a smithes buttris, *scaber*. **1617** MARKHAM *Caval.* IV. 9 With a fine sharpe Butteris or pairing knife, pare the hoofe of the Foale. **1611** COTGR., *Boutoir*, a Farriers Buttresse. **1781** P. BECKFORD *Hunting* (1802) 348 *note*, That destructive instrument called the butteris..should be banished for ever. **1831** YOUATT *Horse* (1853) 120 The formidable butteris is still often found in the smithy of the country farrier, although it is banished from the practice of every respectable operator.

† **butteris**[2], **-esse**, *sb. Obs.* In 6 butteris, -esse. ? An obsolete measure used for coals.

1635 *Althorp MS.* in Simpkinson *Washingtons* Introd. 73, 28 butteris of pitt coales brought by the waynes at 6*s.* 4*d.* the butteresse.

† **'butterish**, *a. Obs.* [f. BUTTER *sb.*[1] + -ISH[1].] Of the nature of butter, buttery.

1542 BOORDE *Dyetary* xiii. (1870) 265 Euery thyng that is vnctious, that is to say, butterysshe. **1594** CAREW *Huarte's Exam. Wits* (1616) 330 This [meat]..was the butterish part of the milke eaten with honnie. **1661** LOVELL *Hist. of Animals & Minerals*, If they [curds] be equally mixed with the butterish part, the cheese made thereof is wholsome.

butterless ('bʌtəlɪs), *a.* Without butter.

1859 MRS. GASKELL *Round Sofa* 229 Sally had had her butterless tea. **1860** H. MARRYAT *Resid. Jutland* I. i. 13 The milk-woman is no more to be found, or you breakfast butterless. **1883** *Harper's Mag.* Feb. 442/1 She hated her breakfast of butterless rye bread.

buttermilk ('bʌtəmɪlk). [cf. Ger. *buttermilch*.]

a. The acidulous milk which remains after the butter has been churned out.

1528 PAYNELL *Salerne's Regim.* G b, Butter mylke.. Nothynge nourisheth more than this mylke whan hit is newe sopped vp with newe hotte breadde. **1586** COGAN *Haven Health* cxcvi. (1636) 181 Of the making of Butter is left a kinde of whey, which they commonly call Butter milke, or soure milke. **1611** COTGR., *Laict esburré*, butter-milke, churnd milke. *a* **1674** CLARENDON *Hist. Reb.* III. XIII. 322 The poor Man had nothing for him to eat, but promised him good Butter-milk. **1727** SWIFT *State Irel.* V. II. 167 The families of farmers, who pay great rents, living in filth and nastiness upon buttermilk and potatoes. **1861** HULME tr. *Moquin-Tandon*, II. II. 190 Butter-milk..contains all the elements of the milk, but only a very little caseum, and a large proportion of butyric acid.

b. *fig.*

1719 D'URFEY *Pills* III. 47 So many Blades now rant in Silk, At first did spring from Butter-milk, Their Ancestors worth nothing. **1794** J. WOLCOTT (P. Pindar) Wks. III. 188 Whose soul is butter-milk, and song is love.

c. *attrib.* Also quasi-*adj.* in ***buttermilk land*** U.S.

1616 *Wily Beguiled* in Hazl. *Dodsl.* IX. 285 But he has such a butter-milk face, that she'll never have him. **1633** MASSINGER *New Way*, &c. II. iii, This most incredible lie would call up one [blush] On thy buttermilk cheeks. **1843** 'R. CARLTON' *New Purchase* ix. 58 They had been sufficiently fortunate as to get a taste of 'buttermilk land' —'spouty land'. **1918** J. GALSWORTHY *Let.* 9 Aug. in E. V. Lucas *Post-Bag Div.* (1934) 70 Do you think..that this shows..that I ate too much of Mrs. Endacott's butter-milk bread?

butter-nut ('bʌtənʌt). [f. BUTTER *sb.*[1] + NUT.]

1. A large oily nut, the fruit of the *Juglans cinerea* or White Walnut-tree of N. America.

1753 CHAMBERS *Cycl. Supp.* s.v., *Butter-nut*, a fruit in New England, whose kernel yields a great quantity of sweet oil. **1882** *Garden* 11 Nov. 433/3 The Butter Nut..strongly resembles the Walnut both in shape and flavour. **1883** AYER in *Harper's Mag.* Feb. 365/1 That is where the children used to crack the hickory and butter nuts.

b. The tree itself. (More fully ***butternut-tree***.)

1783 DR. RUSH *Let.* in *Mem. J. C. Lettsom* III. 188 The Butter-nut pill..is made by boiling the inner bark of a species of the Walnut in water. **1856** BRYANT *Fountain* vii, The dark fruit That falls from the gray butternut's long boughs. **1877** J. HAWTHORNE *Garth* III. x. lxxxiv. 270 Butternut trees flung their black shadows.

2. Name of the genus *Caryocar* of S. America (esp. *C. nuciferum*) and its fruit.

1845 DON *Hortus Cantabrigiensis* 373. **1866** *Treas. Bot.* s.v. *Caryocar*, *C. nuciferum*, which produces the Souari or Butter-nuts, occasionally met with in English fruit-shops.

3. *attrib.* and quasi-*adj.* Of the colour of the butter-nut (sense 1), i.e. of a brownish-grey. This was the colour of the Southern uniform in the American War of Secession.

1861 MRS. STOWE *Pearl Orr's Isl.* 9 His coarse butter-nut-coloured coat-flaps fluttering..in the breeze. **1863** LUDLOW in *Daily News* 5 Oct. /5 The..atrocious murder of 20 fugitive negroes by guerillas wearing the butternut uniform. **1864** SALA in *Daily Tel.* 7 Apr., The 'butternut' hue, I was informed, is a kind of warm grey. **1882** WOOLSON *For the Major* iii. in *Harper's Mag.* Dec. 104/2 He was attired in a coat of..black, with butternut trousers.

b. Hence *absol.* (sb. omitted).

1863 *Cornh. Mag.* Jan. 102 The regiments in homespun grey and butternut that trail dustily through the high-streets [of Richmond]. **1863** *Times* 6 Mar., A 'Butternut' is one who sympathizes with the South—one, in fact, who wears the uniform or livery of the Southern army. **1864** *Nasby Papers* xi, The benevelent old butternut.

butter-print ('bʌtəprɪnt).

1. A stamp of carved wood for marking butter-pats; the impression of such a stamp.

1632 BROME *North. Lasse* II. i. 23 A thumb-Ring with his Grandsirs Sheep-mark, or Grannams butter-print on't. *a* **1704** LOCKE *Posth. Wks.* (1706) 157 An infinite Butter-print, in which was ingraven Figures of all sorts and Sizes. **1822** *Blackw. Mag.* XII. 659 Much pastoral poetry now wore the semblance of very tasteful butter-prints.

comb. **1829** SOUTHEY *Sir T. More* II. 67 The various trades of Taylor, Clogger, and Butter-print maker.

†**2.** *fig.* A child. *Obs. slang.*

1616 BEAUM. & FL. *Wit without Money* v. iv, I hope she has brought me no butter-print along with her to lay to my charge. **1618** FLETCHER *Chances* I. v, You will be wiser one day, when you have purchased A bevy of these butter-prints. **1709** *Brit. Apollo* II. No. 46. 3/2 Her Girl and her Boy, For Patterns employ, To make little Butter-Prints by.

3. The Indian mallow, *Abutilon theophrasti*, bearing a round seed-capsule marked with radiating furrows.

1872 *Illinois Dept. Agric. Trans. 1871* p. ix, The Indian Mallow (*Abutilon Avicennae*) is.. known as.. 'butter print'. **1899** *Mem. Amer. Folk-Lore Soc.* VII. 120 *Abutilon Avicennae* is called 'butter-print'.. because its pods are used to stamp butter.

†'**butter-tooth.** *Obs.* [f. BUTTER *sb.*[1] + TOOTH: cf. Du. *boter-tand* 'an incisor tooth, esp. when broad and large' (Bomhoff). The reason for the name is uncertain.] Originally perh. a front tooth; later app. = BUCK-TOOTH.

1571 R. EDWARDS *Damon & P.* in *Dodsl.* IV. 79 Father, you have good butter-teeth full seen. **1622** MASSINGER *Old Law* III. ii, I'd had.. my two butter-teeth Thrust down my throat. **1736** BAILEY, *Butter-Teeth*, great, broad Foreteeth. **1782** A. MONRO *Anat.* 121 Whence come *butter* or *buck* teeth?

Hence '**butter-toothed** *ppl. a.*

1688 R. HOLME *Armoury* II. 427/1 Butter Toothed is to have broad and great teeth before.

butterwort ('bʌtəwɜːt). In 6 also **-worts.** [f. BUTTER *sb.*[1] + WORT; cf. quot. 1597.] A plant with yellowish-green fleshy leaves (*Pinguicula vulgaris*) common on boggy ground; also the English name of the genus *Pinguicula*.

1597 GERARD *Herbal* cclxiii. §4. 645 Called Pinguicula, of the fatnes or fulnes of the leafe, or of fatning; in Yorkshire ..it is called Butterwoorts, Butter roote, and white roote. **1794** MARTYN *Rousseau's Bot.* xii. 124 Pinguicula or Butterwort has a personate flower. **1848** C. A. JOHNS *Week Lizard* 289 *Pinguicula lusitanica*, Pale Butterwort. **1863** KINGSLEY *Water-bab.* v. 195 The little pink butterwort of Devon, and the great blue butterwort of Ireland.

buttery ('bʌtərɪ), *sb.* Forms: 4 boteri, 5 boterie, botrie, botre, butry, 5–6 botry(e, 5–7 botery, 6 bottrye, buttrie, buttre, buttrye, 6–7 butterie, 6–8 buttry, 7 bottery, boutery, but(t)ery(e, buterie, buttrey, 6– buttery. [app. a. OF. *boterie* = *bouteillerie* (Godef.):—late L. *botāria*, f. *bota*, var. of *butta* cask, bottle; see BUTT *sb.*[5] The transition from the sense of 'store-room for liquor' to that of 'store-room for provisions generally' is in accordance with analogy, but may have been helped by association with BUTTER *sb.*[1]]

1. A place for storing liquor; but the name was also, from an early period, extended to 'the room where provisions are laid up' (J.).

1389 in *Eng. Gilds* (1870) 98 Whoso entre into ye boteri yer ye ale lytz. **1411** *E.E. Wills* (1882) 18 Botrie. *a* **1440** *Ipomydon* 316 And to the botery he went anon.. He toke the cuppe of the botelere. *c* **1440** *Promp. Parv.* 45 Boterye, *celarium, boteria, pincernaculum.* **1484** MARG. PASTON in *Lett.* 881 III. 314 Some man.. to kepe your botry, for the mane that ye lefte.. seyth he hath not usyd to geve a rekenyng nothyr of bred nor alle tyll at the wekys end. **1530** PALSGR. 200/1 Bottrye, *despence.* **1570** LEVINS *Manip.* 103 A Butterie, *promptuarium.* **1586** J. HOOKER *Girald. Irel.* in *Holinshed* II. 138/1 His cellar doore was neuer shut, and his butterie alwaies open, to all commers of anie credit. **1596** SHAKS. *Tam. Shr.* I. i. 102 Take them to the Butterie, And giue them friendly welcome euerie one. **1608** ARMIN *Nest Ninn.* 8 [He] giues them each one a hand, and so takes them into the buttry to drinke. **1665** PEPYS *Diary* (1879) III. 212 Then down to the buttery, and eat a piece of cold venison pie. **1755** SMOLLETT tr. *Quix.* (1803) I. 158 For in their bags they had lost their whole buttery and provision. **1832** SCOTT *Woodstock* 180 When the pantry has no bread and the buttery no ale. **1875** STUBBS *Const. Hist.* III. xxi. 531 Regular officers of the buttery, the kitchen.. and the like.

b. In the colleges at Oxford and Cambridge: The place where ale and bread, butter, etc., are kept. (The 'residence' of members of the college is recorded by the appearance of their names in the buttery-books.)

1684 *Lond. Gaz.* No. 1910. 4 Whoever gives notice of him either at the Buttery of Christchurch to the Butler, etc. **1688** SWIFT *Wks.* (1841) II. 56 But [the College Steward is] always sworn brother in iniquity to the clerks of the buttery. **1710** PALMER *Proverbs* 210 To converse in the world requir'd somewhat more than to have heard a little talk about Aristotle and Cartes, or to have ones name in the butteries. **1850** KINGSLEY *Alt. Locke* xii. (1876) 141 I'll send you in a luncheon as I go through the butteries. **1869** ROGERS in *Adam Smith's W.N.* I. Pref. 7 During this time he drew his commons from the college buttery.

†**c.** *the spirit of the buttery*: a 16th c. phrase for 'the spirit of wine'.

1530 PALSGR. 591, I wene he be inspyred with the spyrites of the buttery. **1547** BOORDE *Breu. Health* clxxxiii. 64 b, I shulde haue sayde afrayd of the spirite of the buttry, whiche be perylous beastes, for such spirites doth trouble a man so sore that he can not dyuers times stande vpon his legges. **1592** G. HARVEY *Pierces Super.* 15 His frisking penne began to play the sprite of the buttry.

2. *Comb.*, as ***buttery-door***; **buttery-bar**, a board or ledge on the top of the buttery-hatch, on which to rest tankards, etc.; **buttery-book** (at the Universities), the book in which are entered the names of the members of a college, and the account of their commons; **buttery-hatch**, the half-door over which the buttery provisions are served; **buttery-worn** *a. nonce-wd.* (see quot.).

1577–87 HOLINSHED *Chron.* III. 933/2 The maior of Oxford kept the *buttrie bar. **1601** SHAKS. *Twel. N.* I. iii. 74, I pray you bring your hand to'th Buttry barre, and let it drinke. **1820** SCOTT *Abbot* xviii, 'Mend your draught'.. 'I know the way to the buttery-bar.' *a* **1672** WOOD *Life* (1848) 34 Munday he was entred into the *buttery-book.. by Mr. Edw. Copley, fellow of that house. **1709** STEELE *Tatler* No. 19 ⁋2 There are of the Middle-Temple, including all in the Buttery Books, and in the Lists of the House, 5000. **1726** AMHERST *Terræ Fil.* xxxix. 214 The Master of the college sent his servitor to the buttery-book to sconce him five shillings. **1832** CARLYLE *Misc.* (1857) III. 73 Weekly accounts in the buttery-books. **1562** HEYWOOD *Prov. & Epigr.* (1867) 99 Thy *buttry doore I here not creake. **1857** HUGHES *Tom Brown* I. vi, Bill pounced on the big table, and began to rattle it away to its place outside the buttery-door. **1614** T. ADAMS *Divell's Banq.* 207 Hee will turne out of his cast Seruitours.. from the *Buttry-hatch to the Pulpit. **1845** DISRAELI *Sybil* (1863) 37 A hall.. with the dais, the screen, the gallery, and the buttery-hatch all perfect. **1885** *Macm. Mag.* Nov. 28/1 Old scouts.. battered *buttery-worn bodies.

buttery ('bʌtərɪ), *a.* [f. BUTTER *sb.*[1] + -Y[1].]

1. Of the nature of butter; containing butter.

1398 TREVISA *Barth. De P.R.* XIX. lxv. (1495) 433 Cowe mylke is.. less sharpe, & more buttry. **1586** COGAN *Haven Health* cxciv. (1636) 178 Because it is buttery, it.. is good against pricking paynes of the Lungs. **1615** CROOKE *Body of Man* 418 His fatty and buttery part is hotter then the whole body of the milke. **1859** TODD *Cycl. Anat. & Phys.* V. 392/2 To increase the buttery constituent.

2. Resembling butter in consistence.

1719 LONDON & WISE *Compl. Gard.* 61 Its Pulp tender, but not buttery. **1802** FORSYTH *Fruit Trees* vii. (1824) 170 The flesh melting, delicate, and very buttery. **1847** CLARKE in *Jrnl. Roy. Agric. Soc.* VIII. I. 91 The same buttery clay may be found above a stratum of moor. *c* **1865** LETHEBY in *Circ. Sc.* I. 95/1 The oil has a buttery consistence.

b. *fig.* Soft.

1868 F. PAGET *Lucretia* 281 His buttery heart.

3. Smeared with butter.

1796 MRS. GLASSE *Cookery* iii. 19 Rub it over with a buttery cloth.

4. *fig.* Given to fulsome flattery (cf. the *sb.*).

1842 *Tait's Mag.* IX. 725 With the Germans and Italians she is charitable, liberal, indulgent, honeyed; nay, with very particular noble favourites, buttery.

5. *Comb.*, as ***buttery-fingered*** = BUTTER-FINGERED.

1852 READE *Peg Woff.* i. (1868) 23 All the ladies and gentlemen.. whom the buttery-fingered author could not keep in hand until the fall of the curtain.

6. '**buttery** '**Benjie.** In the Scottish Universities a humorous synonym for BEJAN.

1854 *Blackw. Mag.* LXXVI. 433.

butterys, buttiler, obs. ff. BUTTRESS, BUTLER *sb.*

'**butt-**ˌ**head:** see BUTT *sb.*[3], [7].

butt-in. *U.S.* One who butts in (see BUTT *v.*[1] 1 d); an intruder. So **butt-iner.**

1906 H. GREEN *Actors' Boarding House* 97 Gettee 'way... No want flesh butt-ins round! *a* **1910** 'O. HENRY' *Rolling Stones* (1916) 198 Any of the Flat bush or Hackensack Meadow kind of butt-iners. **1911** J. C. LINCOLN *Cap'n Warren's Wards* viii. 124 If I had my way the old butt-in should understand exactly what I think of him. **1930** *Liberty Mag.* 1 Nov. 43/1 She [*sc.* a gangster's moll] may be just a butt-in.

†'**butting,** *sb. Obs.* Apparently some term of endearment.

a **1528** SKELTON *Agst. Garnesche* Wks. 1843 I. 127 Ye haue a fantasy to Fanchyrche strete, With Lumbardes lemmans for to mete, With, Bas me, buttyng, praty Cys!

butting ('bʌtɪŋ), *vbl. sb.*[1] [f. BUTT *v.*[1] + -ING[1].]

1. The action of thrusting or striking violently with the head or horns; also *attrib.*

1661 LOVELL *Hist. Anim. & Min.* 115 Rams.. may be made to leave off their butting. **1858** GEO. ELIOT *Cleric. Life* 214 Mr. Dempster.. poked his head forward with a butting motion by way of bow.

2. *dial.* (see quot.)

1602 CAREW *Cornwall* 73 b, Hee that is once possessed of the ball [in 'hurling'], hath his contrary male waiting.. The other thrusteth him in the breast, with his closed fist to keepe him off: which they call Butting.

†'**butting,** *vbl. sb.*[2] *Obs.* [f. BUTT *v.*[2] or *sb.*[7] + -ING[1].]

1. Bounding, boundary, limit, confine; also *fig.*

1552 HULOET, Bowndynge or buttynge of thre fieldes ioynynge together, *trifinium.* **1616** SURFL. & MARKH. *Countr. Farm* 522 Setting downe in writing the lying, buttings, and contents of the said peece of ground. **1706** DE FOE *Jure Div.* v. 23 Nature has its Buttings and Boundings. **1750** G. HUGHES *Barbados* 6 The buttings and boundings of several tenements.

2. The making of butt-joints.

c **1850** *Rudim. Nav.* (Weale) 116 *Ekeing*, making good a deficiency in the length.. by scarphing or butting.

3. 'Two wheels touching on the points of the teeth, when entering into action with each other.' Britten (1884) 37.

1881 F. BRITTEN *Watch & Clockm.* 132 Butting is generally indicative of a pinion too large. *Ibid.* If [the engaging contact] is on the roundings of the teeth a butting action ensues.

†**4.** A projection. *Obs.*

1677 MOXON *Mech. Exerc.* (1703) 94 The Stock of the Piercer by reason of.. a Sholder, or Butting out upon the work will not turn about.

butting ('bʌtɪŋ), *vbl. sb.*[3] [f. BUT *v.* + -ING[1].] The making use of 'buts', i.e. objections or qualifying statements.

1553 T. WILSON *Rhet.* 72 b, What is geven to one by commendyng, the same is streight taken away by buttyng.

butting ('bʌtɪŋ), *vbl. sb.*[4] In the game of Curling: see quot.

1831 *Blackw. Mag.* XXX. 971 Butting, or chap and guard, is to put up a stone, and lie guard upon it.

butting ('bʌtɪŋ), *ppl. a.* [f. BUTT *v.*[1] + -ING[2].]

†**a.** That projects or juts out. **b.** That pushes or strikes violently with the head or horns.

1447–8 SHILLINGFORD *Lett.* (1871) 102 The which postren dores.. oughte to stande.. in the saide buttyng wall. **1697** DRYDEN *Virg. Past.* III. 135 A Bull.. With spurning Heels, and with a butting Head.

butting, obs. f. BUTIN, booty.

butting-joint. *Carp.* [see BUTT *v.*[2]] A joint 'formed by the surfaces of two pieces of wood whereof one is perpendicular to the fibres, and the other in their direction, or making an oblique angle with them, as for example the joints made by the struts and braces with the post' (Gwilt).

1837 WHITTOCK *Bk. Trades* (1842) 105 Butting-joints are fixed together with bolts. **1850** *Jrnl. Roy. Agric. Soc.* XI. II. 569 Notching or cocking down, butting joints, scarfing [etc.] .. are the principal combinations of timbers in trusses.

buttinsky (bə'tɪnskɪ). *slang* (orig. *U.S.*). Also **buttinski.** [Jocular, f. *butt in* (see BUTT *v.*[1] 1 d) + *-sky*, final element in many Slavonic names.] = BUTT-IN. So (nonce-wd.) **butte'rinsky.**

1902 ADE *Girl Proposition* 70 The Friend belonged to the Buttinsky Family and refused to stay on the Far Side of the Room. **1903** *Cincinnati Enquirer* 9 May 13/2 Piker.. a cheap grafter; a noser; a butterinsky. **1922** S. LEWIS *Babbitt* xx. 252 If you think I'm a buttinsky, then I'll just butt in. **1933** D. L. SAYERS *Murder must Advertise* iv. 69, I never.. met with such a bunch of buttinskis... Nothing is sacred to you. **1960** WODEHOUSE *Jeeves in Offing* v. 50 It is never pleasant for a man of sensibility to find himself regarded as a buttinski and a trailing arbutus.

buttir, obs. form of BITTERN, BUTTER *sb.*[1]

buttle ('bʌt(ə)l), *v. dial.* [Back-formation from BUTLER *sb.*] **a.** To pour out (drink).

1867 B. BRIERLEY *Marlocks Merriton* 5 in *Lanc. Gloss.* (E.D.S.) 60 The broad village green buttled round its cheap delights. **1875** E. WAUGH *Old Cronies* iii. 34 *ibid.*, 'Buttle out, free!' cried Giles to the servants.

b. To do a butler's work. *jocular.*

1918 MRS. H. WARD *War & Elizabeth* iii, The under-housemaid 'buttles' for him like a lamb. **1923** F. H. KITCHIN *Diversions of Dawson* 292 Nobody could buttle like James who had not been born in a pantry and taken pap out of silver spoons. **1929** W. J. LOCKE *Ancestor Jorico* xvi, Peters —the head steward—is a fat fool... Seems he buttled for decaying noble families. **1954** R. FULLER *Fantasy & Fugue* iv. 91 He valeted him as well as buttled. **1968** J. C. HOLMES *Nothing More to Declare* 98 Eric Blore spluttered and buttled like a paranoid chipmunk.

Hence '**buttling,** '**butling** *vbl. sbs.*

1918 WODEHOUSE *Piccadilly Jim* xix. 185 How on earth did you come to be here? What's the idea? Why the buttling? **1945** A. L. ROWSE *West-Country Stories* 37 The baronet did his own butling. **1968** A. DIMENT *Gt. Spy Race* x. 177 Petite was there, dressed in his butling clothes.

buttless ('bʌtlɪs), *a. nonce-wd.* [f. BUTT *sb.*[3] + -LESS.] Without a butt.

1828 J. WILSON in *Blackw. Mag.* XXIV. 300 Butless, lockless.. though thou [a gun] be'st.

buttock ('bʌtək), *sb.* Forms: 3, 6 buttoke, 4–5 buttok, 5–7 buttocke, 7 buttoc, 5– buttock. [app. f. BUTT *sb.*[3] + -OCK.]

1. a. One of the two protuberances of the rump (of men and beasts). Usually in *pl.* the rump, posteriors.

a **1300** *Fragm. Pop. Sc.* (Wright) 320 The heles atte buttokes, the kneon in aither eye. *c* **1305** in *E.E.P.* (1862) 75 A strong rop.. fram þe schuldre ido To his buttok. *c* **1386**

CHAUCER *Reeves T.* 55 Buttokkes brode, and brestes round and hye. *c* **1489** CAXTON *Sonnes Aymon* x. 259 He righted hymself vpon his buttocke. **1523** FITZHERB. *Husb.* §76 The .ix. propertyes of an hare..the .viii. to haue shorte buttockes. **1601** SHAKS. *All's Well* II. ii. 17 A Barbers chaire that fits all buttockes. **1650** BULWER *Anthropomet.* xxii. 240 To whip their Buttocks and Loins with Rods. **1704** ADDISON *Italy* (1733) 54 Set..with his bare Buttocks on this Stone. **1846** D. JERROLD *Chron. Clovernook* Wks. 1864 IV. 393 Their tails have been bitten short to the buttock.

†**b.** *pl.* used as a *sing.*

c **1590** MARLOWE *Faustus* 850 My horse..has a buttocks as slick as an eel.

2. As a joint of meat.

1623 *Althorp MS.* xlvi, A buttocke, 2 necks, and a rond of beef. **1791** BOSWELL *Johnson* (1831) I. 482 The outside cut of a salt buttock of beef. **1817** SCOTT *Rob Roy* iv, As prime a buttock of beef as e'er hungry mon stuck fork in.

†**3.** *buttocks of the brain*: transl. of Galen's γλούτια, 'certain medullary tubercles near the pineal gland' (Liddell and Scott). *Obs. rare.*

1615 CROOKE *Body of Man* 431 The fourth Ventricle where the Glandule or Kernell called κονάριον is seated, at each side of which do adioyne the Buttockes of the Braine.

4. *Naut.* 'The breadth of the ship astern from the tuck upwards.' 'That part abaft the after body, which is bounded by the fashion pieces, and by the wing transom, and the upper or second water-line' (Smyth *Sailor's Word-bk.*). (Cf. Fr. *les fesses d'un navire.*)

1627 CAPT. SMITH *Seaman's Gram.* ii. 4 According there to her breadth or narrownesse, we say she hath a narrow or broad buttocke. **1769** FALCONER *Dict. Marine* (1789), *Buttock*, the convexity of a ship behind, under the stern. *c* **1850** *Rudim. Nav.* (Weale) 102.

†**5.** *slang.* A common strumpet. (Fielding's sense is obscure.) *Obs.*

1673 R. HEAD *Canting Acad.* 105 The Bawds and the Buttocks that lived there round. **1688** SHADWELL *Sqr. Alsatia* I. Wks. 1720 IV. 17 What ogling there will be between thee and the Blowings!..every Buttock shall fall down before thee. **1690** B. E. *Dict. Cant. Crew, Buttock and File*, both whore and pickpocket.

1743 FIELDING *J. Wild* I. v. (D.) The..capacity which qualifies a mill-ben, a bridle-call, or a buttock and file to arrive at any degree of eminence in his profession.

6. [f. BUTTOCK *v.*] A certain manœuvre in wrestling (see the verb); varieties mentioned are the ***cross-buttock***, ***running-buttock***, etc.

1688 R. HOLME *Armoury* III. v. §64 Running Buttock, is when..he turns his Buttock on his adversary, and lifts him up on his side. **1714** SIR T. PARKYNS *Inn-Play* (ed. 2) 47 Then you are ready for the In-lock backwards or forwards, Buttock, or to return to the Trip with a draught. *Ibid.* 50 At the same time take the cross Buttock from the Under Hold. **1826** SCOTT *Woodstock* II. vii. 178 One of their..saints had given the devil..a cross-buttock. **1881** *Sportsm. Year Bk.* 314 Frears gaining two falls in succession, the first with a back heel and the second with a splendid buttock.

7. *Comb.*, as ***buttock-beef***, ***-bone***, ***-hump***; †**buttock-ball**, ? a ball attended by prostitutes; †**buttock-banqueting**, harlotry; **buttock-lines**, 'in ship-building, the longitudinal curves at the rounding part of the after body in a vertical section' (Smyth *Sailor's Word-bk.*); †**buttock-mail** (*Sc.*), ludicrous term for a fine imposed for fornication.

1687 T. BROWN *Lib. Consc.* in *Dk. Buckingham's Wks.* (1705) II. 131 Why not into a Bibbing-House, as well as a Dancing School, a *Buttoc Ball, or the like? **1555** *Fardle Facions* II. viii. 167 Whiche [wiues] maie neuerthelesse vse *buttoke banquetyng abrode. *a* **1652** BROME *Queene's Exch.* II. iii, I would I had but this Fellows weight in *buttock Beef. **1594** T. B. *La Primaud. Fr. Acad.* II. 48 The *buttocke bones and the flesh wherewith they are covered..are unto him in stead of a stoole and a cushion. **1849–52** TODD *Cycl. Anat. & Phys.* IV. 1355/b The *buttock-hump..is not..so characteristic of this race as has been imagined. **1833** RICHARDSON *Merc. Mar. Arch.* 34 Perpendicular sections, called also *buttock lines. **1535** LYNDESAY *Sat.* 3353, I gat gude payment of my Temporall lands, My *buttock-maill, my coattis, & my offrands. **1814** SCOTT *Wav.* II. vii. 122 'D'ye think the lads wi' the kilts will care for yere synods and yere presbyteries, and yere buttock-mail, and yere stool o' repentance?'

8. *Coal-mining.* The portion of the working-face of coal to be broken out next. Hence **buttocker**, a man who works at the buttock.

1883 in GRESLEY *Gloss. Coal Mining.* **1912** BULMAN & REDMAYNE *Colliery Working* (ed. 3) 294 *Buttocker*, one who breaks down the coal which has been undercut by the 'holers'. A 'getter'. **1967** *Gloss. Mining Terms (B.S.I.)* VIII. 8 *Buttock*, in some longwall faces, a short step in the line of face, and substantially at right angles to it, from which coal can be more conveniently worked.

ˈbuttock, *v. trans.* [f. prec. sb.]

†**1.** In horse-racing: To overtake (a horse).

1617 MARKHAM *Caval.* VI. 43 Say you come in that twelue score [yards] to buttocke him, you shall then finde, etc.

2. In wrestling: To throw (an adversary) by a manœuvre in which the buttock or the hip is used.

1883 *Standard* 24 Mar. 3/7 Simpson buttocked Carradyce.

buttocked (ˈbʌtəkt), *a.* [f. BUTTOCK *sb.* + -ED².] Having buttocks; always with defining words, as ***broad-***, ***great-***, † ***pin-buttocked.***

1548 THOMAS *Ital. Gram.*, *Natichuta*, well buttocked. **1580** BARET *Alv.* B 1606 Great buttocked, *lumbosus.* **1580** BLUNDEVILL *Horsemanship* i. (1609) 3 The horses of Greece ..bee..not [wel made] backward, because they are pin buttocked. **1634** HEYWOOD *Witches Lanc.* IV. Wks. IV. 223 Broad buttock'd and full flanck'd. **1709** *Brit. Apollo* No. 29. 3/1 This is no Pin-buttock'd Wench.

buttocker (ˈbʌtəkə(r)). *Wrestling.* [f. BUTTOCK + -ER.] **a.** A wrestler who 'buttocks'. **b.** = BUTTOCK *sb.* 6.

1823 *Blackw. Mag.* XIV. 709 The first of whom we have any authentic records of excelling as a buttocker. *Ibid.* 715 Thrown clean..by a vigorous and judicious buttocker.

button (ˈbʌt(ə)n), *sb.* Forms: 4 **botoun, botone,** (sense 2) **bothum, -eum, -om, 5 botwn, -un, -onne,** *Sc.* **bwttowne, 6 boton, botton, buttoun, -one, 7–8 butten, 5– button.** [a. OF. *boton* (mod.F. *bouton*) bud, knob, button; a common Romanic word = Pr., Sp. *boton*, Pg. *botão*, It. *bottone*:—late L. **bottōn-em*, app. connected with late L. **bottare*, *buttare*, to thrust, put forth (whence OF. *boter*, F. *bouter*, Sp. *botar*, It. *bottare*); the ultimate etymology is commonly supposed to be Teutonic; for conjectures see Diez, Scheler, Littré.

Sense 2 'bud' appears to be the original sense in Romanic, but we have no instance of it in Eng. before 16th c., exc. as used (with peculiar spelling) in the *Romaunt of the Rose.*]

Generally. A small knob or stud attached to any object for use or ornament. *spec.*

1. a. A knob or stud of metal or other material sewn by a shank or neck to articles of dress, usually for the purpose of fastening one part of the dress to another by passing through a *button-hole*, but often merely for ornament: in process of use, the name has passed from the connotation of the shape to that of the purpose, and been extended to all appliances of the kind, a common type being a disc, quite flat, or slightly convex or concave, of metal, bone, glass, mother of pearl, paste, etc., perforated or otherwise adapted to be sewn on by its central part. (This specific application is now regarded as the primary sense, all the other meanings, whatever their historical origin, being understood as merely *transf.*)

c **1340** *Gaw. & Gr. Knt.* 220 On botounz of þe bryȝt grene brayden ful ryche. **1377** LANGL. *P. Pl.* B. xv. 121 A ballok-knyf · with botones ouergylte. *c* **1440** *Promp. Parv.* 45/2 Botwn, *boto, fibula, nodulus.* **1483** *Cath. Angl.* 50/1 A Button, *fibula, nodulus, bulla.* **1525** LD. BERNERS *Froiss.* II. cci. [cxcvii.] 618 My booke..was..couered with crymson veluet, with ten botons of syluer and gylte. **1591** FLORIO *Sec. Fruites* 5 There Lacks I know not how many buttons. Set them on then. **1605** SHAKS. *Lear* V. iii. 309 Pray you vndo this Button. **1647** *Husbandman's Plea agst. Tithes* 75 It hath no buttons, nor hooks upon it. **1695** BLACKMORE *Pr. Arth.* IX. 296 Fast with Golden Buttons held. **1716** *Lond. Gaz.* No. 5435/4 Suits of Cloaths with Cloth Buttons. **1725** *Ibid.* No. 6402/2 A Wastcoat, with Glass Buttons set in Brass. **1753** HANWAY *Trav.* (1762) I. v. lxix. 314 The new fashion of metal buttons. **1814** SCOTT *Wav.* xli, My short green coat, with silver lace and silver buttons. **1841** CATLIN *N. Amer. Ind.* (1844) II. lv. 198 A fine linen shirt with studs and sleeve buttons.

b. As a type of anything of very small value.

c **1320** *Sir Beues* 1004 Hauberk ne scheld ne actoun Ne vailede him nouȝt worþ a botoun. **1340** *Ayenb.* 86 Hi ne prayseþ þe wordle bote ane botoun. **1480** CAXTON *Chron. Eng.* clxxviii. 159 To haue of me as moche helpe as the value of a botonne. **1549** COVERDALE *Erasm. Par. Gal.* II. 21 A button therfore for all worldely differences. **1577** tr. *Bullinger's Decades* (1592) 146 They set not a button by his commaundements. **1672** VILLIERS (Dk. Buckhm.) *Rehearsal* III. ii. (Arb.) 79, I would not give a button for my Play. **1713** *Guardian* No. 84 (1756) II. 13 Not..a button the worse for it. **1861** GEO. ELIOT *Silas M.* 27 He did not care a button for cock-fighting.

c. Playfully used *transf.*

1855 *Househ. Words* XII. 258 Screwing up its red little button of a mouth.

d. ***boy in buttons***: a boy servant in livery, a 'page'. So ***to put into buttons***: to make a page of. Cf. BUTTONS.

1848 THACKERAY *Bk. Snobs* xxxix, We don't put the latter into buttons. **1855** —— *Newcomes* xi, Boys in buttons (pages who minister to female grace).

e. Phrases. ***to take by the button***, etc.: to detain in conversation, to BUTTONHOLE; also *fig.* †***it is in his buttons***: ? = he has fortune at his command, is sure to succeed. ***dash my buttons***: an exclamation indicating surprise and vexation (*colloq.*). ***to have a soul above buttons***: said of persons who consider their actual employment unworthy of their talents (see quot. 1795). In phrases expressing weakness of intellect, as: ***not to have*** (***got***) ***all his buttons on, to be a button short.*** Similarly ***he has all his buttons*** (***on***): he is sound in intellect, 'all there'.

1598 SHAKS. *Merry W.* III. ii. 71 'Tis in his buttons, he will carry't. **1716** *Lond. Gaz.* No. 5459/2 The King was talking with him, and had hold of one of his Coat-Buttons **1768** GOLDSM. *Good-n. Man* II. i, I take my friend by the button. **1795** G. COLMAN *Sylv. Daggerwood* i. (1808) 10 My father was an eminent Button-Maker..but I had a soul above buttons..I panted for a liberal profession. **1828** SCOTT *F.M. Perth* I. 48 His fingers upon every one's button, and his mouth in every man's ear. **1833** MARRYAT *P. Simple* i, My father..had..a 'soul above buttons'. **1833** HT. MARTINEAU *Manch. Strike* i. 2 Caught him by the button and detained him in consultation. **1846** *Comic Jack Giant K.* III. xiv. 18 'Dash my buttons', he cried, 'I have lost my way!' **1860** HOTTEN *Dict. Slang* (ed. 2) 109 *Not to have all one's buttons*, to be deficient in intellect. **1864** LOWELL *Biglow P.* Wks. (1879) 314 Fame..is..privileged to take the world by the button. **1890** *Daily News* 21 May 6/3 He is 83 years of age, but as we say hereabouts, has all his buttons on. **1892** *Leeds Merc. Suppl.* 23 Jan. (E.D.D.), In Wilsden, one lacking full mental capacities has 'some of his buttons off'. **1893** MRS. A. KENNARD *Diogenes' Sandals* xi, They said..he had not 'got all his buttons', meaning that he was not 'all there'. **1961** *Times* 16 Jan. 4/5 But East Midlands, too, had all their buttons on.

f. *Naut.* ***button and loop***: see quot.

1794 *Rigging & Seamanship* I. 163 *Button and Loop*, a short piece of rope, having at one end a walnut knot, crowned, and at the other end an eye. It is used as a becket to confine ropes in.

g. *spec.* A knob on the top of a cap (in the case of a Chinese mandarin indicating by its material the degree of his rank).

1602 SHAKS. *Ham.* II. ii. 233 On Fortunes Cap, we are not the very Button. **1834** *Fraser's Mag.* X. 225 A mandarin of any considerable button.

h. A button of a particular colour, or bearing a distinctive design, worn as a party badge.

1895 *Montgomery Ward Catal.* 180 Emblem Pins and Buttons..Masonic..Odd Fellows..Eastern Star. **1900** *Daily News* 5 Nov. 7/1 Another feature of an American Presidential campaign is the lavish display of political 'buttons'. **1915** V. WOOLF *Voyage Out* xix. 314 The parti-coloured button of a suffrage society. **1970** *Times* 14 Mar. 5/6 One [demonstrator] wore a Mao button.

2. a. A bud; also used of various other parts of plants of a similar shape, as the protuberant receptacle of the rose; the small round flower-head of some *Compositæ*; a small sort of fig; a small round seed-vessel.

c **1400** *Rom. Rose* 1790 The roser, where that grewe The freysshe bothum so bright of hewe. **1513** DOUGLAS *Æneis* XII. Prol. 101 The lowkyt buttonis on the gemmyt treis. **1578** LYTE *Dodoens* I. i. 4 Alongst the braunches [of wormewood] groweth little yellow buttons. **1665–76** RAY *Flora* 26 The button under the rose being bigger than that of any other. *a* **1682** SIR T. BROWNE *Misc. Tracts* (1684) 70 The Buttons, or small sort of Figgs. **1682** WHELER *Journ. Greece* III. 219 A Yellow Flower..succeeded with a Button, full of downy Seeds. **1727** BRADLEY *Fam. Dict.* I. s.v. *Hop Gard.*, About August the Hop will begin to be in the bell or Button. **1852** AIRD in *Blackw. Mag.* LXXI. 237 The simple flowerets..open their infant buttons.

b. *spec.* The 'head' of a mushroom in its unexpanded state. Also applied *dial.* to a fossil.

1743 PICKERING in *Phil. Trans.* XLII. 598 The Head of the Mushroom..while it is, what is commonly called, a Button. **1839** ALFORD in *Life* (1873) 11 Bright bronzed ammonites..other sparkling nondescripts, known as mushrooms and buttons. **1882** JEFFERIES *Bevis* II. xviii. 280 'Buttons,' full grown mushrooms, and overgrown ketchup ones.

†**c.** *transf.* The knob or 'bud' which forms the beginning of a stag's horn. *Obs.*

1575 TURBERV. *Venerie* 47 Hartes..beginne in..March and Apryll to thrust out their Buttones. **1623** COCKERAM s.v. *Pollard*, Butten is the first part in putting vp a Stagges head.

3. Used (chiefly in *pl.* form) as the popular name of many different plants having button-like flowers or seed-vessels: see *bachelor's*, *beggar's buttons* under BACHELOR, BEGGAR. ***Barbary buttons*** (formerly also *button*), *Medicago scutellata*. ***gentlemen's buttons***, *Scabiosa succisa* (Britten and Holland). ***London buttons*** (see quots.).

1598 FLORIO, *Baccara*, an hearbe, whose roote is very sweete..called our ladies gloues, or London buttons. **1611** COTGR., *Gantelée*, the hearbe called Fox-gloues, our Ladies gloues..and London buttons. **1665–76** RAY *Flora* 190 Snails or Button..The vessels..in some are like a Snail's house..in some like small Buttons. **1711** PETIVER in *Phil. Trans.* XXVII. 386 Round Snails or Barbary Buttons.

4. a. *transf.* from 1. Applied to various productions of art resembling a button in shape or function; a knob, handle, catch; the knob or disc of an electric bell. *spec.* An oblong piece of wood or metal, turning on a screw fixed through its centre, used to fasten doors, etc.

1607 TOPSELL *Four-f. Beasts* 396 The button of the [mouse-] trap. **1787** WINTER *Syst. Husb.* 301 Covered with buttons or sliders to prevent dirt or dust falling into the holes. **1801** W. FELTON *Carriages* Gloss., *Buttons*, nails or screws with large brass heads for the purpose of hitching on the straps. **1852** SEIDEL *Organ* 35 A number of handles or buttons..called stops. **1862** *All Y. Round* VII. 381 There are buttons on window-sashes, and buttons on drawer handles. **1867** E. YATES *Forl. Hope* iii. 28 Untwist the button on the door. **1871** LE FANU *Checkm.* I. xiv. 197 Mr. Davies turned the button of his old-fashioned window. **1880** J. HAWTHORNE *Ellice Quent.* II. 261 By turning a button attached to the pipe that supplied the lights, they were at once extinguished. **1884** F. BRITTEN *Watch & Clockm.* 134 By means of the winding button the contrate wheel is turned to the right.

b. Phr. ***to press the button***: to push back a disc, pin, knob, or the like and thus produce the required result by completing an electric circuit, operating the shutter of a camera, etc. Often *fig.* in colloquial use, to perform an action that automatically brings about the required state of affairs.

1860 *Nat. Mag.* VIII. 278/2 By pressing a button..the light can be given in flashes. **1865** *Mech. Mag.* 10 Mar. 155/1 On pressing one of these buttons with the finger, the bell..

is rung loudly. **1893** *Cassell's Fam. Mag.* Mar. 318/1 Then he pressed the button of the camera. **1893** *Jrnl. Soc. Arts* XLI. 629/2 President Cleveland..pressed the button which started all the..machinery... The button..was of ivory. **1893** [see PRESS *v.*[1] 1 a]. **1905** *Minister's Gaz. Fashion* July 138/1 Pressing the Button. A Plea for Modern Methods... When the art of cutting will be reduced to a mechanical science. **1914** E. GREY in *Europ. Crisis, Corr.* (Parlt. Papers Cl) 46 Mediation was ready to come into operation..if only Germany would 'press the button' in the interests of peace. E. GOSCHEN *Ibid.* 59 The Chancellor told me last night that he was 'pressing the button' as hard as he could. **1962** WODEHOUSE *Service with Smile* i. 12 Thinking..that the ideal way of opening Parliament would be to put a bomb under it and press the button.

Also ***to press button A*** or ***B***: of a former type of telephone coin-box; *button A* completed the connection after the called subscriber had answered; *button B* actuated a mechanism to return the coins if there was no answer or if the required number was engaged.

1934 *Discovery* Mar. 58/2 Distinguishing between buttons A and B, deciding when to press either or both. **1935** G. GREENE *England made Me* I. 17, I rang up four times from a box..and I remembered three times to press Button B and get my money back. **1942** J. D. CARR *Seat of Scornful* xiii. 188 Unless you put the money in, you couldn't press Button A and the connection wouldn't work. **1961** 'T. HINDE' *For Good of Company* i. 16 Tony seized the phone and held it out of the box towards him. 'Press Button A,' he shouted.

c. The leather projection on an oar, by which it is kept in position in the rowlock.

1866 'ARGONAUT' *Arts Rowing & Training* ii. 11 Both [oars and sculls] are kept in their proper place in the rowlock by a circular button of a peculiar shape, on the leather, which plays against the inner side of the thowl. **1888** W. B. WOODGATE *Boating* iii. 63 If the body swings true, the oar will keep home to the rowlock; there should be just sufficient fraction of weight pressed against the button to keep it home. **1963** *Times* 18 Feb. 3/7 Mead was pulling his button away from the rowlock, almost clear of the leather.

d. In an organ, a round piece of leather that keeps the tracker from jumping out of place.

1876 STAINER & BARRETT *Dict. Mus. Terms* s.v. *Organ*, A tracker, a strip of light wood provided with a tap wire and leather button at the end. **1877** STAINER *Organ* 17 The little wire passing from the end of the tracker into the hole in the backfall is made like a screw,..so, where it appears below the backfall, a little leather button can be screwed on to it.

e. Each of the keys of an accordion.

1876 STAINER & BARRETT *Dict. Mus. Terms* s.v. *Accordion*, The first instruments had only four buttons, or keys, each of which acted on two reeds.

5. a. Any small rounded body; a knob, globule, disc, etc. *Obs.* exc. as in spec. senses following.

a **1603** T. CARTWRIGHT *Confut. Rhem. N.T.* (1618) 127 The clots or buttons of bloud in the garden [of Gethsemane]. **1684** R. WALLER *Nat. Exper.* 54 An hollow Button of Glass.

b. *Chem.* A globule of metal remaining in the cupel or crucible after fusion. [So Fr. *bouton.*]

1801 CHENEVIX in *Phil. Trans.* XCI. 221 He..obtained a metallic button, which was found to be Copper. **1812** SIR H. DAVY *Chem. Philos.* 379 A button of pure tin will be found at the bottom of the crucible. **1854** SCOFFERN in *Orr's Circ. Sc.* Chem. 509 The result..is a button of gold mixed with silver.

c. *Anat.* and *Surg.* In various applications.

1748 HARTLEY *Observ. Man* I. ii. § 4. ¶ 55 The Button of the Optic Nerve. **1835-6** TODD *Cycl. Anat.* I. 321/1 At the parts of the gizzard opposite the *musculi laterales* two callous buttons are..formed. **1885** *Harper's Mag.* Mar. 633/1 The removal of a button of bone from the skull.

d. *pl.* The testes of an animal.

e. A knob or disc fixed on the point of a fencing foil. [So in Fr.: *bouton d' un fleuret.*]

[**1615** (see BUTTON *v.* 1 b).] *a* **1649** DRUMM. OF HAWTH. *Challenge of Knts. Err.* Wks. (1711) 232 They would have most willingly taken the buttons off the foils. **1824** CARLYLE *W. Meister* (1874) I. II. xiv. 121 We can rub the buttons of them with a piece of chalk. **1868** HELPS *Realmah* xv. (1876) 410 The buttons are on their foils.

f. *Naut.* (See quot.)

1794 *Rigging & Seamanship* I. 163 *Buttons*, small pieces of thick leather under the heads of nails that are driven through ropes.

g. The point of the chin. *U.S. slang.*

1921 H. C. WITWER *Leather Pushers* 48 The Kid..floored him with a right cross to the button of the jaw. **1931** D. RUNYON *Guys & Dolls* (1932) 278, I never saw a more accurate puncher than Rusty Charley, because he always connects with that old button. **1936** WODEHOUSE *Laughing Gas* ii. 27 He soaked him on the button, don't you know.

6. An ornamental terminal knob, as on a handle, staff, or sceptre. *spec.* The knob of metal at the breech end of a piece of ordnance; also *attrib.* in ***button astragal***, the raised moulding encircling the button. [Fr. *bouton.*]

1685 *Lond. Gaz.* No. 2030/4 The Button of His Majesty's Scepter. **1769** FALCONER *Dict. Marine* (1789) I iij, The breech..and it's button, or cascabel. **1859** F. GRIFFITHS *Artil. Man. Plate* (1862) 50 *S* Button, *a b* Button Astragal.

7. A ring of leather through which the reins of the bridle pass, and which may be moved along so as to tighten up and restrain the horse's head (see Littré). Also *fig.* cf. *serrer le bouton à*, 'to restraine,..beare a hard hand ouer' (Cotgr.).

1586 T. B. *La Primaud. Fr. Acad.* (1594) 504 They must ..let downe the button, and holde them hard in with the bridle.

8. (See quot.)

1850 *Jrnl. R. Agric. Soc.* XI. I. 140 [The hay is] then made into button or small cock.

9. *slang.* A person who acts as a decoy; the accomplice of a thimble-rigger; a sham-buyer at an auction employed to bid and raise the price of articles.

1851 MAYHEW *Lond. Labour* I. 328 To..act as a button (a decoy), to purchase the first lot of goods put up. **1877** BESANT & RICE *Son of Vulc.* ix, The 'Button', that is, the confederate who egged on the flats.

10. *pl.* The dung of sheep, etc. Hence in obs. phrase meaning 'to be in great terror'.

1749 W. ELLIS *Shep. Guide* 148. **1778** *Exmoor Scolding* Gloss., *Buttons*..sometimes us'd to express Sheeps Dung, and other Buttons of that kind. **1847-78** in HALLIWELL. **1598** FLORIO 198 *Il culo gli fa lappe*, his taile makes buttons, his buttocks goes a twitter twatter. **1690** W. WALKER *Idiom. Anglo-Lat.* 78. **1702** *Mouse grown Rat* 23 My Breech began to make Buttons; I dream't of nothing but Impeachments, Attainders, Poll-Axes and Gibbets. **1808** AINSWORTH *Lat. Dict.* I. s.v. *Button*, His tail maketh buttons, *valde trepidat.*

†**11. a.** A swelling, pimple [Fr. *bouton*]; cf. *button-farcy* (below). ***buttons of Naples***: 'syphilitic buboes' (Nares).

? *a* **1600** in Nares s.v., The Frenchmen at that siege got the buttons of Naples (as we terme them) which doth much annoy them at this day.

b. ***Aleppo button***: cutaneous leishmaniasis (oriental sore), a form of the disease endemic in parts of Asia and Africa and caused by infection with *Leishmania tropica*; also, the local lesion characteristic of this infection. So also ***Baghdad***, ***Biskra button*** (also *boil*), etc.

The F. form *bouton* was formerly also used.

1874 *Med. Times & Gaz.* 24 Jan. 94/2 It is generally believed that the Aleppo Button takes about a year before it heals: hence the name of the *year pimple*, given to it by the natives. **1876** *Brit. Med. Jrnl.* 19 Feb. 225/2 (*heading*) Aleppo boil or 'Biskra bouton'. **1897** *Daily News* 18 Sept. 6/2 The 'Bagdad button' (a painful species of boil). **1911** T. E. LAWRENCE *Home Lett.* (1954) 138 The Aleppo button is the effect of a fly. **1969** KURBAN & CHAGLASSIAN in Simons & Marshall *Ess. Trop. Dermatol.* 187 Various synonyms are used for oriental sore, depending on the region in which it is found, *e.g.*, Aleppo boil, Baghdad boil, Delhi boil, Biskra button, Jericho boil and many others.

c. *Med.* Any small, rounded elevation on the cutaneous or mucous surface. (Cf. prec. sense.)

[**1876** *Brit. Med. Jrnl.* 19 Feb. 226/1 Villemin mentions that the 'boutons on the feet are sometimes multiple, simulating syphilitic ulcers'.] **1888** C. M. DOUGHTY *Trav. Arabia Deserta* II. xv. 452, I washed the wound..but a red button remained. **1900** *Jrnl. Exper. Med.* 15 Dec. 259 More characteristic lesions..are the so-called 'buttons'.

12. a. *attrib.* and *Comb.*, as ***button-cap***, ***-end***, ***-farcy***, ***-lac***, ***-like*** adj., ***-maker***, ***-making***, ***-seller***, ***-shank***, ***-shaped*** adj., ***-stamper***, ***-suit***, ***-top***, ***-tuft***, ***-worker***; **button-ball**, *Platanus occidentalis* (= *button-wood*); **button-blank**, a disc of metal, bone, or other material, to be formed into a button; **button-board**, pasteboard used for making button-moulds; **button-boot**, a boot fastened with buttons; **button-boy**, a page (cf. 1 d); **button-brace**, a brace (see BRACE *sb.*[2] 6) used in the manufacture of buttons; **button brass**, (*a*) (see quot. 1884); (*b*) a strip of brass slipped under a metal button to shield the garment while the button is being cleaned; **button bud**, a bud resembling a button; **button-bur** (see quot.); **button-bush**, a North American shrub (*Cephalanthus occidentalis*), so called from its globular flower-heads; **button-down** *a.* (orig. *U.S.*), applied to a collar the points of which are buttoned to the shirt; **button ear**, an ear, of a dog, that laps over and hides the inside; hence ***button-eared*** adj.; **button fastener**, (*a*) a spring loop, the free ends of which are passed through the shank of the button to keep it in place; (*b*) (see quot. 1884); **button-fish**, the sea-urchin (*Echinus*); **button-flower**, the genus *Gomphia* of tropical trees or shrubs; **button-grass** *Austral.* (see quot. 1898); **button-hanger** (see quot.); **button-hook**, a hook for pulling buttons (of boots and gloves) through the button-holes; †**button-iron**, an iron instrument with a knob at the end, used for cauterizing; **button key** = *button fastener* (a); **button-mould**, a disc of wood or other material to be covered with cloth to form a button; **button-mushroom**, a young mushroom (= BUTTON 2 b); **button-nosed** *a.*, having a small roundish nose; **button-pointed** *a.*, having a button or knob at the point; **button-quail** (see quots.); **button-regal**, an obsolete reed stop on an organ; **button-scar**, a scar drawn up into button-shape, used for ornamentation of the body by some African peoples; **button shell**, a small marine univalve of the genus *Rotella*, with a lenticular polished shell (*Funk's Stand. Dict.* 1893); **button-stick**, a soldier's appliance for use in button-polishing (= *button brass* b, but usu. made of wood); **button-tree**, the genus *Conocarpus*, 'consisting of trees and shrubs from tropical America and Western Africa' (*Treas. Bot.*); **button-turn** (see quot.); **button-weed**, the genera *Spermacoce* and *Diodia* of tropical *Cinchonaceæ*; also a local name for the Knapweed, *Centaurea nigra*; **button-wood**, an American name for the Occidental Plane-tree (*Platanus occidentalis*); also = *button-bush*; also = *button-tree*. See also BUTTON-HOLD, -HOLDER, BUTTON-HOLE, -HOLER.

1882 *Century Mag.* XXII. 760 Beneath the *button-ball at the gate. **1851** *Illust. Lond. News* 16 Paper of any description, or *button board, millboard, etc. **1875** URE *Dict. Arts* I. 556 A circular disc of button-board suitable for forming the core of a button. **1883** *Daily News* 14 Feb. 3/4 A long overcoat, *button boots, and cloth cap. **1877** MISS BROUGHTON *Joan* xii. (1881) 120 The *button-boy never would answer her bell. **1884** LOCK *Workshop Rec.* Ser. III. 16/2 For *button brass, an alloy of 8 parts of copper and 5 of zinc is commonly used by the Birmingham makers, under the name of 'platin'. **1899** *Daily News* 27 Dec. 8/3 The 'button brass'... This little plate tucked under the button with its shank in the slit enables the button to be well rubbed without mischief. **1869** BLACKMORE *Lorna D.* xvii, The opening cones were struck with brown, in between the *button buds. **1634** T. JOHNSON *Merc. Bot.*, **Button Bur*, Xanthium Strumarium. **1754** J. ELIOT *Ess. Field-Husb.* (1760) v. 124 There was not the same Success attending the cutting these *Button Bushes. **1880** *Scribner's Mag.* Feb. 510 In thickets of button-bushes. **1606** T. WHETENHALL *Disc. Abuses Ch. of Christ* 162 Som [weare] round cappes, som hattes, som *button cappes. **1934** J. O'HARA *Appt. Samarra* (1935) v. 151 Soft white shirt with *button-down collar. **1960** *Guardian* 9 June 1/1 The egg-head in the button-down collar..an American type. **1883** W. G. STABLES *Our Friend Dog* vii. 59 **Button-ear*, an ear that falls in front, entirely concealing the inside. **1952** R. LEIGHTON *Complete Bk. Dog* 73 Unfortunately, within the last few years the 'button' and 'semi-tulip' ear have been rather prevalent. **1607** TOPSELL *Four-f. Beasts* 279 A hole..made with the *button end of your drawing Iron. **1674** N. COX *Gentl. Recreat.* (1706) v. 97 Commonly divided into these kinds; the *Button or Knotted Farcy, the Running Farcy, the Water Farcy, and the Pocky Farcy. **1867** MRS. WHITNEY *L. Goldthwaite* x, She had hooks and eyes, and *button-fasteners, when these gave out. *a* **1877** [see *button key*]. *a* **1884** KNIGHT *Dict. Mech.* Suppl., *Button Fastener*, a clasp which hooks over the eye of a shoe button and is then clinched to the shoe. **1740** HUMPHREYS *La Pluche's Nature Displ.* xxii. 148 Sea-Urchins or *Button-Fishes. **1898** MORRIS *Austral Eng.*, *Button-grass, *Schœnus sphærocephalus*, Poiret, N.O. *Cyperaceæ*... So called from the round shaped flower (capitate inflorescence), on a thin stalk four or five feet long, like a button on the end of a foil. **1927** *Blackw. Mag.* Oct. 470/1 A steep razor-backed hill, covered with ragged clumps of button-grass and dwarfed ti-tree. **1958** 'N. SHUTE' *Rainbow & Rose* i. 6 Button-grass plains where no feed grows that will sustain a horse. **1801** FELTON *Carriages* Gloss., **Button-hangers*, small ornamental tassels, which are placed on the fringe. **1870** MISS BRIDGMAN *R. Lynne* II. v. 116 Tweezers, *button-hooks, and corkscrews. **1607** TOPSELL *Four-f. Beasts* 285 With a *button iron of an inch about, burn at each end a hole. *a* **1877** KNIGHT *Dict. Mech.*, **Button Key or Fastener*, a spring loop..to..keep the button in place. **1883** *Cassell's Fam. Mag.* CVII. 686/2 Lac is exported almost exclusively in the manufactured state as dye, shell-lac, and *button-lac. **1874** WYVILLE THOMSON in *Gd. Words* 747 *Button-like heads of yellow flowers. *a* **1613** OVERBURY *A Wife* (1638) 181 A *Button-maker of Amsterdam. **1863** *Reader* 21 Feb. 188 The prodigal..marries the daughter of a deceased buttonmaker. **1687** *Royal Proclam.* in *Lond. Gaz.* No. 2297/1 The Trade of *Button-making. **1621** *Hist. T. Thumbe* in *Halliwell's Shaks.* (1850) VI. 192 The wheeles [of Tom Thumb's coach] were made of foure *button-mouldes. **1801** MAR. EDGEWORTH *Early Less.* II. *Harry & L.*, A large wafer..and a wooden button mould of the same size. **1865** *Cornh. Mag.* XII. 627 Produced like *button-mushrooms in a hot-bed. **1909** H. G. WELLS *Tono-Bungay* III. ii, *Button-nosed, pink-and-white Aunt Susan. **1885** *Harper's Mag.* Jan. 280/1 The upper is found to consist..in the case of a button boot, of a 'vamp'..a large and small 'quarter'..and a *button piece to fasten the shoe around the foot. **1835-6** TODD *Cycl. Anat.* I. 183/1 A *button-pointed bistoury. **1885** *Encycl. Brit.* XVIII. 46/1 The Hemipodes or *Button-Quails. **1893** Button quail [see HEMIPOD]. **1947** J. STEVENSON-HAMILTON *Wild Life S. Afr.* xxxii. 276 Button quail or riet kwartel (*Turnicidæ*).—Three species of Hemipodes, or button quail, exist in South Africa. They are smaller than true quail and lack a hind toe. **1852** SEIDEL *Organ* 84 The obsolete registers; bear's pipe, and Apple, or *button-regal, were stopped reed-registers. **1897** A. J. BUTLER tr. *Ratzel's Hist. Mank.* II. 394 In the so-called '*button-scars', a row of button-shaped warty scars runs from the edge of the forehead to the tip of the nose; this is found both on the Congo and on the Zambesi. **1687** *Lond. Gaz.* No. 2220/4 Mr. Edward Miller, *Button-seller. **1862** *All Y. Round* VII. 378 Down upon his knees grubbing for buttons and *button-shanks. **1880** L. WINGFIELD *In her Maj. Keeping* II. I. xii. 51 It don't matter to me a buttonshank. **1849-52** TODD *Cycl. Anat.* IV. 1213/1 *Button-shaped, dilated suckers. **1883** *Birmingham Daily Post* 11 Oct., *Button-stamper, for Brace and Shell-work. **1890** KIPLING *Barrack-r. Ballads* (1892) 20 I've a head like a concertina: I've a tongue like a *button-stick. **1969** E. H. PINTO *Treen* 150 Button sticks..were used for cleaning uniform buttons. **1848** THACKERAY *Bk. Snobs* xxxvii, Tummus's *button-suit was worn. **1840** *Blackw. Mag.* XLVIII. 305 A result which..nobody would think worth a decent-looking *button-top. **1725** SLOANE *Jamaica* II. 18 *Button Tree. This tree..grows near the sea-side..among the mangroves. **1756** P. BROWNE *Jamaica* 159 Button-tree or Button-wood. These trees..grow luxuriantly in all the low sandy bays and marshes. **1884** F. BRITTEN *Watch & Clockm.* 37 [A] *Button Turn [is] a brass block pivotted in the index arm and covering the curb-pin. **1878** BRITTEN & HOLLAND *Plant-n.*, **Button Weed*, Centaurea nigra, L.—Suss. **1698** PETIVER in *Phil. Trans.* XX. 401 Lignum Fibularium (i.e.) *Button-wood *nostratibus dicta*. **1837** *Fraser's Mag.* 686 The cool shade of some spreading buttonwood-tree. **1852** HAWTHORNE *Blithed. Rom.* xvii, Besieging the button-wood tree. **1883** *Century Mag.* Aug. 547/2 The long lane, shaded by button-woods. **1856** KANE *Arct. Expl.* II. iv. 50 [It]

would find a ready sale among the *button-workers of England.

b. *attrib.* with qualifying numeral; having (so many) buttons, as in ***ten-button gloves***.

1884 HOWELLS in *Harper's Mag.* Dec. 117/1 What if he should bring a ten-button instead of an eight!

button ('bʌt(ə)n), *v.* Forms: 4–5 **boten,** 5 **bothon,** 6–7 **butten,** 5– **button.** [f. BUTTON *sb.*; cf. F. *boutonner*.]

1. a. *trans.* To furnish or adorn with buttons or knobs. (Usually in pa. pple.)

c **1380** *Sir Ferumb.* 166 Gloues..þat with gold ibotened were. **1394** *P. Pl. Crede* 296 A cote..queyntly y-botend. **1480** CAXTON *Chron. Eng.* ccxxvi. 233 Short clothes..on euery syde slatered and botened. **1658** USSHER *Ann.* 742 A purple robe buttoned with precious stones. **1831** CARLYLE *Sart. Res.* I. viii, Without vestments, till he buy or steal such, and..sew and button them.

b. To fit (a fencing foil) with a button (see BUTTON *sb.* 5 e).

1615 G. SANDYS *Trav.* 168 A sticke..buttoned at the end with leather, in manner of a foile. **1662** FULLER *Worthies* (1840) III. 17 To have fenced with rebated rapiers and swords buttoned up.

†**c.** To raise knobs or pimples on. *Obs.*

1598 SYLVESTER *Du Bartas* II. i. III. (1606) 345 Humour which..within Their bodies boyling butt'neth all their Skin.

2. a. To fasten (a garment) with buttons; to secure or close by means of a button or buttons. Often with *up*.

c **1440** *Promp. Parv.* 46 Bothon clothys, *botono, fibulo.* **1555** EDEN *Decades W. Ind.* (Arb.) 320 These the Christians vse to butten on the right syde: and the Tartars butten them on the lefte syde. **1695** BLACKMORE *Pr. Arth.* x. 484 Elia.. buttoned on his rich embroider'd Vest. **1701** *Lond. Gaz.* No. 3701/4 A Beaver Hat buttoned up. **1827** CARLYLE *Transl.* (1874) 41 He..buttoned-up his scissor-pouch. **1828** SCOTT *F.M. Perth* xv, He buttoned his doublet anew. **1840** CARLYLE *Heroes* v. 274 Something he can button in his pocket. **1864** *Mag. for Young* Sept. 290 Jack had got Euclid buttoned up inside his jacket.

b. To fasten the clothes of (a person) with buttons. Usually *refl.*; also *absol.* (for *refl.*).

1662 R. MATHEW *Unl. Alch.* §20 He could not button himself, nor put on his clothes. **1855** *Chamb. Jrnl.* IV. 187, I had to button up against a succession of short summer showers. **1862** H. KINGSLEY *Ravenshoe* xxxiv. 201 Old gentlemen buttoned up across the chest. **1879** STEVENSON *Trav. Cevennes* 66, I buttoned myself into my coat.

c. To fasten (a door) with a BUTTON (*sb.* 4).

1837 *New Monthly Mag.* L. 397 [She]..buttoned the door. **1882** BLACKMORE *Christowell* I. xvi. 249 To keep one pew buttoned on a Sunday.

3. *fig.* To close tightly, fasten, confine, keep under restraint, etc. Often with *up*. ***to button*** (a person's) ***mouth***: to silence (a person); ***to button (up) one's lip, face*** (slang): to be silent; also *ellipt.*

1590 SHAKS. *Com. Err.* IV. ii. 34 On[e] whose hard heart is button'd vp with steele. **1598** GRENEWEY *Tacitus' Ann.* XI. ix. (1622) 151 The Princes eares would be buttened and deafe. **1647** J. TRAPP *Comment. Four Evang.* 526 How easily can God button up the mouths of our busiest adversaries. **1823** LAMB *Elia* Ser. I. xi, Buttoned up in the straitest non-conformity. **1837** CARLYLE *Fr. Rev.* (1871) II. iv. iii. 136 Thoughts—which he must button close up. **1840** W. IRVING *Wolfert's R.* (1855) 151 Shy and solitary, and, as it were, buttoned up, body and soul. **1868** *N. & Q.* I. 603 At school, it was thought quite an accomplishment in the young gentlemen who were fast of tongue to be able to silence a talkative comrade with the phrase 'button your lip'. **1936** A. HUXLEY *Eyeless in Gaza* xxv. 352 Mr. Beavis..began to describe his researches into modern American slang..Horse feathers, dish the dope, button up your face—delicious! **1945** L. SHELLY *Hepcats Jive Talk Dict.* 22/2 *Button up your lip*, don't talk. **1962** K. ORVIS *Damned & Destroyed* ix. 61 If the little pusher chose to button up now, I would be left helpless.

4. *intr.* (for *refl.*) Of garments: To be, or be capable of being, fastened (*up*) with buttons. Hence **button-through** *a.*, applied to a garment fastened with buttons from top to bottom; **button-up** *a.*, that buttons up; also *absol.* as *sb.*

1777 SHERIDAN *Trip Scarb.* I. ii, If it had been tighter, 'twould neither have hooked nor buttoned. **1839** *New Monthly Mag.* LV. 483 A jacket that buttons up close to the neck. **1875** BESANT & RICE *Harp & Cr.* II. iii. 66 It [the coat] buttons across the chest. **1920** *Ware-Pratt Co. Stylebook* Nov., It is a double-breasted, button-through model with long rolling lapels, narrow gorge and velvet collar. **1952** C. W. CUNNINGTON *Eng. Women's Clothing* viii. 275 Wool housecoat in button-through style. **1962** L. DEIGHTON *Ipcress File* xxxi. 198 A new round-necked, sleeveless, button-through dress. **1943** K. TENNANT *Ride on Stranger* ii. 13 Anyway there would be trouble..over the soggy state of her button-up boots. **1951** J. FRAME *Lagoon* 62 To have button-up shoes instead of lace-ups. *Ibid.* 67 O for button-ups! O for a dress with a cape collar! **1956** A. MILLER *Memory Two Mondays* (1958) 360 He wears a blue button-up sweater.

†**5. a.** *intr.* Of plants: To bud, put forth buds. Of fruits: To assume the globular shape.

1669 WOODHEAD *St. Teresa* I. xiv. 88 These Trees begin to button, and bud out towards flouring. **1772–84** COOK *Voy.* (1790) III. 899 Some [fruit] just beginning to button.

b. Of broccoli and cauliflowers: To come to a head prematurely.

1852 [see BUTTONING *vbl. sb.*]. **1882** *Garden* 18 Mar. 187/3 The crop..showing no tendency either to button or run to seed. **1884** *Field* 12 July 67 Cauliflowers button at an early stage, and are useless.

6. *trans.* In fencing: To touch with the button of the foil.

1842 *Blackw. Mag.* LII. 566, I should have buttoned them ten times for every twice they touched me.

buttoned ('bʌt(ə)nd), *ppl. a.* [f. BUTTON *sb.* and *v.* + -ED.]

1. a. Having buttons, adorned with buttons; usually with defining words, as ***silver-, eight-buttoned***.

1534 MORE *On the Passion* Wks. 1272/2 A bearewarde with his syluer buttened bawdrike. **1597** SIR R. CECIL in Ellis *Orig. Lett.* II. 234 III. 43 A longe robe of black velvett, well jeweld and buttond. **1713** *Guardian* No. 113 (1756) II. 121 My silver-button'd coat. **1862** MAYHEW *Crim. Prisons* 61 A custom-house officer in his brass-buttoned jacket. **1883** *Truth* 31 May 768/1 [Gloves] were all to be eight-buttoned.

b. Of persons: Wearing buttons.

1813 MOORE *Post Bag* vi. 64 This buttoned nation. **1882** T. HARDY *Two on Tower* I. xiv. 232 The buttoned boy.

c. Of a stick or a fencing-foil: Having a 'button' or knob at the end.

1648 HERRICK *Hesper.* I. 204 No black-bearded vigil from thy doore Beats with a button'd-staffe the poore. **1838** *Fraser's Mag.* XVII. 307 Safe and well-buttoned foils.

2. a. Fastened with buttons; with one's clothes fastened with buttons. Also with *up*.

1826 MISS MITFORD *Village* Ser. II. (1863) 298 The buttoned-up crosses. **1837** CARLYLE *Fr. Rev.* (1871) II. IV. vii. 153 National Guards rank themselves, half-buttoned. **1863** THORNBURY *True as Steel* III. 292 With a buttoned velvet cap drawn over his ears.

b. *fig.* With *up*, spec. of persons: reserved, uncommunicative. Cf. BUTTON *v.* 3.

1936 R. LEHMANN *Weather in Streets* I. v. 92 Plump, buttoned-up face. **1946** M. DICKENS *Happy Prisoner* viii. 158 Why is she so quiet and buttoned up? **1957** *Economist* 2 Nov. 393/1 The British are notoriously bad..at human relationships; buttoned-up, standoffish.

c. *fig.* With *up*. Of a plan, etc.: successfully arranged. *slang.*

1940 'N. SHUTE' *Old Captivity* vi. 197, I was thinking about this photography. But I believe we've got that buttoned up now. **1942** *Gen* 1 Sept. 12/2 When army things are under control they are 'buttoned up'.

buttoner ('bʌt(ə)nə(r)). [f. as prec. -ER.]

1. One who or that which buttons (see BUTTON *v.* 2); a button-hook.

1611 COTGR., *Boutonneur*, a Buttoner; or an instrument wherewith buttons are pulled through their ouer-strait holes. **1881** *Confess. frivolous Girl* 68 Silver glove-buttoners.

b. *fig.* That which fastens or knits tightly.

1885 WINGFIELD *Barb. Philpot* III. i. 17 Gratitude is a buttoner of hearts.

2. One who sews buttons on garments.

1886 *Pall Mall G.* 2 Aug. 6/2, 2*s.* 6*d.* for the aforesaid dozen shirts, which sum has to be divided between machinist, finisher, buttonholer, buttoner, ironer and folder.

3. *Thieves' cant.* = BUTTON *sb.* 9.

1841 *Blackw. Mag.* L. 202 Buttoners are those accomplices of thimbleriggers..whose duty it is to act as flat-catchers or decoys, by personating flats. **1860** *Cornh. Mag.* II. 334 Enticer of another to play—buttoner.

'button-hold, *v.* [f. BUTTON *sb.* + HOLD *v.*, or rather, deduced immediately from *button-hold-er*.]

trans. To take hold of (a person) by a button, and detain him in conversation against his will. Hence **'button-ˌholding** *vbl. sb.* and *ppl. a.*

1834 S. R. MAITLAND *Volunt. Syst.* (1837) 192 Forwardness, impudence, and button-holding perseverance. **1841** HOR. SMITH *Moneyed Man* III. x. 278 Welford, button-held by Mr. Curling. **1858** GLADSTONE *Homer* I. i. iii. 27 Patroclus..is (to use the modern phrase) button-held by Nestor. **1860** *Cornh. Mag.* II. 97 Barricade your door..against the button-holding world. **1880** *Home Jrnl.* (*N.Y.*) 21 Jan., Charles Lamb, being button-held one day by Coleridge..cut off the button.

'button-ˌholder. [f. BUTTON *sb.* + HOLDER.]

1. One who takes hold of a man by a button of his coat, so as to detain him in conversation.

1806–7 J. BERESFORD *Miseries Hum. Life* (1826) I. i, While attending a button-holder to your gate. *a* **1850** ROSSETTI *Dante & Circ.* I. (1874) 28 The buttonholders of learned Italy, who will not let one go on one's way.

2. A case for holding buttons.

1870 DICKENS *E. Drood* 12 My mother-of-pearl button-holder.

button-hole ('bʌt(ə)nhəʊl), *sb.*

1. a. The hole or slit through which a button passes.

1561 SIR T. HOBY tr. *Castiglione's Courtier* (1577) M iij a, Thou shalt one daye be the botton, and the haulter shal be the buttonhole. **1580** BARET *Alv.* B 1608 A button hole, *ansula.* **1685** *Lond. Gaz.* No. 2094/4 One sad-coloured Cloth Sute with Gold Buttons and Button-holes. **1791** BOSWELL *Johnson* III. 339 With an ink-horn and pen in his button-hole.

b. colloq. phrase. ***to take one down a button-hole*** or ***a button-hole lower***: to humiliate or take the conceit out of him. (Cf. *to take one down a peg.*)

1588 SHAKS. *L.L.L.* v. ii. 706 Master, let me take you a button hole lower. **1593** PEELE *Edw. I*, On my word, I'll take you down a button-hole. **1655** HEYWOOD *Fort. by Land, &c.* II. ii. Wks. 1874 VI. 387 You are taken a button-hole lower. **1850** MRS. STOWE *Uncle Tom* iv. 21 Better mind yerselves, or I'll take ye down a button-hole lower.

c. *spec.* one in the lapel of a coat.

1842 *Knickerbocker* XIX. 44 A bud and two leaves..at his buttonhole. **1847** DICKENS *Dombey* xxxi, The Major..wears a white geranium in his button-hole. **1863** KINGSLEY *Water-bab.* 5 With a..flower in his button-hole. **1929** EDINGTON *Studio Murder Myst.* xvii, The white gardenia in his buttonhole.

2. a. *transf.* An opening like a button-hole.

1599 NASHE *Lent. Stuffe* (1871) 74 The raveled button-holes of her blear eyes. **1862** *Temple Bar Mag.* IV. 419 The little red button-hole of a mouth.

b. *Surg.* A small straight opening in an organ or part.

1884 B. BRAMWELL *Dis. Heart & Thoracic Aorta* v. 478 In cases of this description, the orifice, when seen from above, looks like a narrow slit, hence the term button-hole mitral which has been applied to it. **1907** *Practitioner* Oct. 526 Without making a 'button-hole' through the mucoperichondrium. **1946** H. T. HYMAN *Integrated Pract. Med.* III. XIX. cxxxvii. 2971 Metacarpal shaft driven through joint capsule between flexor tendons (button-hole dislocation).

3. *colloq.* Short for *button-hole flower, bouquet*.

1879 E. H. MARSHALL in *My Sunday Friend* Mar. 19 The little girl who sold him a button-hole. **1881** M. C. HAY *Missing* III. 239 A dainty little buttonhole of tinted leaves. **1883** in *Harper's Mag.* Nov. 840/2 A button-hole of hyacinths.

4. *attrib.*, as in ***button gimp, hand, -hole cutter, -hole flower, scissors, stitch, twist***; **button-hole globe, light**, an electric bulb to be fastened in one's button-hole as a reading light.

1852 *Blackw. Mag.* LXXI. 341 Button-hole eyes and upright eyelids. **1869** *Rep. U.S. Commissioner Agric. 1868* 289 Button-hole twist is the same, with a tighter twist. **1873** *Young Englishwoman* Mar. 147/2 Cutting-out scissors, small scissors, and button-hole scissors. **1875** *Chamb. Jrnl.* 67 Traffic in button-hole flowers. *a* **1877** KNIGHT *Dict. Mech.*, Button-hole Cutter. **1884** *Harper's Mag.* 286/1 A wine-glass containing a button-hole bouquet. **1887** *Mag. Art* Mar. 152 These threads were worked over with close button-hole stitch. **1890** *Daily News* 27 Jan. 3/1 The apparatus is about the same as that of the buttonhole light, only that instead of a buttonhole globe at the end of a thread there is a fine, minute drill. **1899** in A. Adburgham *Shops & Shopping* (1964) xxii. 261 Button hole gimp and twist. **1908** *Daily Chron.* 13 June 9/6 Tailoring.—Wanted button-hole hand for coats and vests. **1964** *McCall's Sewing* v. 62/1 *Buttonhole scissors*, a handy item if you make a lot of garments with machine-made buttonholes, these are designed to cut open buttonholes accurately.

'button-hole, *v.* [f. prec. sb.: in sense 2 app. altered from BUTTON-HOLD. which it has almost superseded.]

1. a. *intr.* To sew button-holes. **b.** *trans.* To sew with button-hole stitch.

1828 [see BUTTON-HOLING below]. **1868** HOLME LEE *B. Godfrey* xli. 224 Whether button-holing and embroidering or not. **1882** *Cassell's Fam. Mag.* XCVII. 44 Penwipers.. button-holed round with silk.

c. To make button-hole openings in.

1908 *Practitioner* Oct. 522 The hand is kept in that position..by long strips of adhesive plaster..; these are button-holed over the knuckles to adapt themselves to them.

d. *Surg.* To make (esp. accidentally) a button-hole incision in.

1907 *Practitioner* Oct. 530 It may seem impossible to strip off the muco-chondrium without buttonholing it. **1964** S. DUKE-ELDER *Parsons' Dis. Eye* (ed. 14) xxvii. 423 The dissection is made by sharp-pointed scissors in the sub-conjunctival tissue..care being taken to avoid button-holing the flap.

2. *trans.* = BUTTON-HOLD.

1862 *All Y. Round* VII. 381 The man who is button-holed, or held..and must listen to half an hour's harangue about nothing interesting. **1868** H. KINGSLEY *Mathilde* II. 140 He went about button-holing and boring every one. **1951** 'A. GARVE' *Murder in Moscow* iii. 48 Jeff..had buttonholed a Russian who spoke a few words of English. **1953** *Encounter* Oct. 58/2 Scientists were free to..publish their findings, talk about them to colleagues (or to anyone else they could buttonhole).

Hence **'button-ˌholing** *vbl. sb.*: also **button-holeing**, and as *ppl. a.*

1828 MISS MITFORD *Village* Ser. III. (1863) 7 The.. mysteries of stitching and button-holing. **1862** in Sperber & Trittschuh *Amer. Pol. Terms* (1962) 68/2 Quarreling, fighting, button-holeing. **1873** *Daily News* 7 Nov. 5/5 They were subjected to a good deal of button-holing. **1883** *Standard* 6 Nov. 2/2 After buttonholing, the uniform goes into the hands of the 'finishers'. **1894** *Athenæum* 10 Feb. 176/1 The reticence of Mr. Maartens..contrasts vividly enough with the buttonholing familiarity of his English model. **1909** H. G. WELLS *Tono-Bungay* II. iii. 179 That alluring, button-holeing..style of newspaper advertisement. **1963** *Times* 13 June 15/5 His book is a button-holing chronicle of daring theft and boudoir hanky-panky.

'button-ˌholer. [f. BUTTON-HOLE + -ER.]

1. a. One who makes button-holes.

1883 *Standard* 6 Nov. 2/2 The garment next goes to the 'button-holers'. **1884** *Graphic* 16 Aug. 166 The skirt-hands get twelve shillings a week..the button-holers fifteen.

b. (Also as one word.) An attachment to a sewing-machine, for making buttonholes.

1958 *Clothing Machine Engineer* Feb. 11 (Advt.), For the home moneymaker The Stitchmaster Automatic Button-holer. **1964** *McCall's Sewing* v. 73/1 The buttonholer is easy to operate and works well on most fabrics. **1978** *Detroit Free Press* 5 Mar. B14 (Advt.), Futura II machine with the exclusive Singer..buttonholer. **1984** *Sears Catal.* *1985* Spring/Summer 968 This 12-stitch machine gives you a built-in buttonholer for bartack buttonholes.

2. One who 'button-holes'; = BUTTON-HOLDER 1.

1874 E. GOSSE in *Academy* 447 The two great button-holers, John Gower and Thomas Heywood. **1883** —— *17th Cent. Stud.* 286 Malagene, Otway's tiresome button-holer.

3. *colloq.* A button-hole flower.

1884 *Punch* 29 Nov. 257/1 Any young clerk who.. contemplates buying a 'button-holer', or sending a Valentine.

buttoning ('bʌt(ə)nɪŋ), *vbl. sb.* [f. BUTTON *v.* + -ING[1].] The action of the verb BUTTON, in different senses. †*concr.* A fastening, button (*obs.*).

1579 J. JONES *Preserv. Body & Soul* I. x. 21 The Persian, Spanish, or Italian working of silks, as spinning, twisting.. purling, buttoning, etc. **1647** W. BROWNE *Polex.* II. 263 A long vestment.. fastned with buttonings of diamonds. **1693** *Lond. Gaz.* No. 2832/4 A black Hat, the buttening commonly behind. **1826** SCOTT *Woodstock* II. 233 Albert.. undid the coarse buttonings of his leathern gamashes. **1852** J. H. KNIGHT *Midl. Florist* vi. 108 The prevention of premature heading, or buttoning [in broccoli]. **1873** *Sunday Mag.* June 622 A funny little buttoning of her lips.

buttonless ('bʌt(ə)nlɪs), *a.* [f. BUTTON *sb.* + -LESS.] Without buttons. Hence **'buttonlessness**.

1655 *Francion* I. iii. 73 My Doublet was Buttenlesse. **1820** *Blackw. Mag.* VIII. 276 Ungartered stockings—buttonless array. **1846** D. JERROLD *Chron. Clovernook* Wks. IV. 380 The buttonless man remonstrates with his laundress. **1861** WYNTER *Soc. Bees* 464 A man in a state of utter buttonlessness.

'buttons. [pl. of BUTTON *sb.* used as a sing.]

1. A boy in buttons, a page. *colloq.*

1848 THACKERAY *Dinner at Timmins's* I. ii. More than fourteen years older than little Buttons. **1855** *Fraser's Mag.* LI. 433 He was a tiger—'a buttons'. **1879** *Daily News* 6 Mar. 5/6 The variety of domestic known as a 'Buttons'.

2. A popular name for the tansy and other plants: see BUTTON *sb.* 3.

buttony ('bʌt(ə)nɪ), *a.* [f. BUTTON *sb.* + -Y[1].]

1. Resembling a button.

1597 GERARD *Herbal* I. x. §2. 12 The buttonie flowers of Sea wormwood. **1862** *All Y. Round* VII. 381 Buttony mushrooms.

2. Abounding in buttons.

1848 THACKERAY *Van. Fair* lx, The buttony page. **1856** —— *Christm. Bks.* (1872) 57 The buttoniest page in all the street. **1861** O. W. HOLMES *Elsie V.* vii. 65 The small youth .. in a new jacket and trousers, buttony in front.

†**buttrelle.** *rare*[−1]. ? Mistake for BUTTAL.

1546 LANGLEY *Pol. Verg. De Invent.* I. xv. 28 a, The meeres and buttrelles with whiche they desseuered theyr porcions of lande.

buttress ('bʌtrɪs), *sb.* Forms: 4 butres, 5 boterace, boteras, butras, botrass, boterasse, (bountrace), botrase, 6 buttereis, butteras, bottras, butrese, butteresse, 6–7 buttresse, 7 buttrise, buttrice, boutrisse, 8 butteress, butteridge, 7– buttress. [perh. a. OF. *bouterez* nom. sing. (or ? pl.) of *bouteret*, 'flying-buttress', 'arc-boutant' (Godef.); app. f. *bouter* to push, bear against.]

1. a. A structure of wood, stone, or brick built against a wall or building to strengthen or support it.

1388 WYCLIF *Ezek.* xli. 15 He mat the boteraces on euer either side of an hundrid cubitis. **1393** *Test. Ebor.* (1836) I. 185 My body to be graven in the mynster-garth be-for the butres at the charnell. *c* **1440** *Promp. Parv.* 45 Boteras of a walle, *machinis, muripula.* **1487** *Churchw. Acc. Wigtoft, Lincolnsh.* (Nicholls 1797) 82 Lyme for mendyng and stoppyng of the Botrasses. **1501** DOUGLAS *Pal. Hon.* 1437 Subtile muldrie wrocht mony day agone, On buttereis, jalme, pillaris. **1530** PALSGR. 432/2 This pyller within the churche answereth to this butteras without forthe. **1570** LEVINS *Manip.* 84 A Buttresse, *fulcimentum.* **1605** SHAKS. *Macb.* I. vi. 7 No Jutty frieze, Buttrice, nor Coigne of Vantage. **1682** WHELER *Journ. Greece* IV. 296 The Pilaster.. is propped on both sides with Buttrices. **1789** SMYTH tr. *Aldrich's Archit.* (1818) 84 He proposes to erect brick buttresses at the angles. **1849** FREEMAN *Archit.* 157 A long dead wall, unbroken by porch or buttress.

b. *fig.*

1436 *Pol. Poems* (1859) II. 187 Wyth alle youre myghte take hede To kepe Yrelond.. Ffor it is a boterasse and a poste Undre Englond. **1550** BALE *Image both Ch.* F viij. **1639** FULLER *Holy War* v. xxv. (1840) 287 Though his title was builded on a bad foundation, yet it had strong buttresses. **1702** *Eng. Theoph.* 300 To transform those into butteresses of reputation, who threaten'd to ruin the same.

2. *loosely*, A prop, support; a pier or abutment.

1609 HOLLAND *Amm. Marcell.* XXIII. iv. 222 Under which piece of wood there lyeth a huge great boutrisse or supporter [*fulmentum*], even hayre-cloth stuffed full of, etc. **1745** tr. *Columella's Husb.* I. v, The foundations.. will.. serve as a butteridge and underpropping. **1850** PRESCOTT *Mexico* I. 155 An aqueduct that was carried over hill and valley.. on huge buttresses of masonry.

3. A projecting portion of a hill or mountain looking like the buttress of a building.

1682 WHELER *Journ. Greece* VI. 453 It is.. situated as it were between the two Buttrices of the Mountain. **1814** CARY *Dante* (1871) 145 We.. stood Upon the second buttress of that mount. **1879** F. MALLESON in *Lett. to Clergy* 51 The mountain and its opposing buttress the Dow Crags.

4. *Phys.* **a.** Used as a translation of the F. *éperon*; **b.** a bony process or protuberance.

1836–9 TODD *Cycl. Anat.* II. 749/2 And between them [i.e. two portions of the bowel] is that double partition termed 'eperon' or buttress by Dupuytren. **1849–52** *Ibid.* IV. 894/2 Triangular plates of bone forming a zig-zag buttress. **1859** *Ibid.* V. 139/1 The pelvis presents two lateral curved thickened buttresses or columns.

c. *Bot.* = buttress-root. (See quots.) Cf. *buttress-root*.

1900 B. D. JACKSON *Gloss. Bot. Terms* 39/1 *Buttress*, the knee-like growths of trunk or roots in certain trees. **1969** *Gloss. Landscape Work* (*B.S.I.*) v. 27 *Buttress*, a projecting growth linking the trunk of a tree to a major root.

5. *Fortification.* (See quot.)

1802 JAMES *Mil. Dict.*, *Fortification*, Counter-forts.. are by some called buttresses; they are solids of masonry, built behind walls, and joined to them at 18 feet distance from center to center, in order to strengthen them.

6. *Comb.*, as ***buttress-less***, ***-like*** adjs. **buttress-root**, = *plank-buttress* (see PLANK *sb.* 7); **buttress thread**, a screw-thread having one face at right angles to the axis of the bolt or shaft. See also FLYING-BUTTRESS.

1882 *Athenæum* 1 Apr. 408/2 The buttressless tower of St. Stephen's. **1853** KANE *Grinnell Exp.* xxxi, These escarped masses became more buttress-like and monumental. **1914** M. DRUMMOND tr. *Haberlandt's Physiol. Plant Anat.* iv. 188 This complex condition is exemplified by the stilt- or buttress-roots which occur in the genus *Pandanus* [etc.]. **1930** *Discovery* Nov. 381/1 Buttress roots [of trees] resemble thick planks and are often four or five feet in height at the trunk. **1964** J. P. CLARK *Three Plays* 8 The burden was voided and buried In the crook of twin buttress roots. **1887** D. A. LOW *Introd. Machine Drawing* iii. 15 The Buttress thread.. is designed to combine the advantages of the v and square threads. **1930** *Engineering* 6 June 721/2 In asymmetrical threads, such as.. certain buttress threads.

'buttress, *v.* Also 5 boterace, boterase, 6 butteras, 7 buttresse. [f. BUTTRESS *sb.*]

1. To furnish, sustain, or strengthen with a buttress or support.

1377 [cf. b.]. **1530** PALSGR. 473/1 This buylding is butterassed very wel. **1843** CARLYLE *Past & Pr.* II. iii. (1872) 49 Stately masonries.. buttress it. **1886** *Athenæum* 30 Oct. 574/1 The walls were buttressed with pillars.

b. *fig.* Also with *up*.

1377 LANGL. *P. Pl.* B. v. 598 Þe wallis ben.. Boterased [A. VI. 79 brutaget] with bileue-so-or-þow-beest-nouȝte-ysaued. **1611** SPEED *Hist. Gt. Brit.* IX. xx. (1632) 960 Arguments concurring to buttresse this affirmation. **1769** BURKE *Corr.* (1844) I. 174 The plan of the court, would be .. to buttress it [the ministry] up with the Grenvilles. **1882** CAR. FOX *Mem.* II. xv. 115 Some of the facts concerning America.. buttressed their arguments.

2. To conceal by a buttress *from. rare.*

1820 KEATS *St. Agnes* ix, Beside the portal doors, Buttress'd from moonlight, stands he.

Hence **'buttressing** *vbl. sb.* and *ppl. a.*

1851 RUSKIN *Stones Ven.* I. xv. §11 The tiny buttressings look as if they carried the superstructure on the points of their pinnacles. **1881** *Fifeshire Jrnl.* 13 Jan. 4/3 Mr. Gladstone and.. his buttressing factions.

buttresse(e, obs. form of BUTTERIS.

buttressed ('bʌtrɪst), *ppl. a.* [f. prec. + -ED.] Furnished with a buttress or buttresses; strengthened, supported, or stayed by a buttress.

1813 SCOTT *Trierm.* III. iii, Fain would he hope the rocks 'gan change To buttress'd walls their shapeless range. **1853** RUSKIN *Stones Ven.* II. vi. §77. 206 The.. shadowed niche, and buttressed pier. **1860** RUSKIN *Mod. Paint.* V. IX. ix. 296 A religion towering over all the city—many buttressed. **1881** GEIKIE in *Macm. Mag.* XLIV. 238 The isolated peaks and ranges of buttressed cliffs. **1886** G. ALLEN *Life Darwin* x. 170 A.. powerfully buttressed theory.

buttrice, -ise, obs. ff. BUTTERIS, BUTTRESS.

butt-woman: see BUTT *sb.*[1], [10].

butty[1] ('bʌtɪ). *dial.* [In sense 1 perh. a corruption of BOOTY *a.* It is not clear whether sense 2 is the same word, but its identity seems not improbable; cf. similar use of *gaffer*.]

1. A confederate, companion, 'mate'.

[**1802** J. WILSON (Congleton) *MS. Let.* 17 Apr. to *J. Boucher*, Butty, going Halves, *Chesh. Staff.*] **1865** [see BUTTY-LARK]. **1875** *Lanc. Gloss.* 63 *Butty*, a confederate.

2. A middleman between proprietors of mines and workmen, who engages to work the mine and raise coal or ore at so much per ton.

1845 DISRAELI *Sybil* (1863) 116 A Butty in the mining districts is a middleman: a Doggy is his manager. **1873** *Echo* 22 Sept. 2/2 'Butties'.. can make £3 a week without difficulty. **1886** *Law Times* LXXX. 166/2 The butties who had a contract with Earl Granville to raise and get the ironstone from the mine at 4*s.* 10*d.* per ton.

3. *Comb.* and *Attrib.*, as ***butty-collier***, ***-system***; also **butty-gang**, a gang of men to whom a portion of the work in some large engineering enterprise is allotted, and who divide the proceeds equally among themselves.

1845 *Penny Cycl.* 1st Supp. I. 380/2 The miners entertain a bitter dislike to the 'butty' system. **1848** *Fraser's Mag.* XXXVII. 383 A sort of middlemanship, somewhat of the nature of the 'butty' system carried on in Staffordshire. **1881** GOLDW. SMITH *Lett. & Ess.* 164 He [Mr. Brassey] favoured the butty-gang system, that of letting work to a gang of a dozen men, who divide the pay, allowing something extra to the head of the gang.

4. In full ***butty-boat***, a second barge or freight-boat in tow by a first.

1909 QUILLER COUCH *True Tilda* ix, With two horses hauling at the first [barge], and the second (which Sam called a butty-boat) towed astern. **1923** *Blackw. Mag.* Nov. 663/2, I overhauled two barges, the foremost with its little steam-engine towing the second or 'butty'. **1946** *Archit. Rev.* C. 161/1 They [*sc.* barges] go in pairs, a diesel-engined motor boat and a butty boat towed behind.. The cabin of the butty is down into the bottom of the boat.

'butty[2]. *north. dial.* Also buttie. [f. BUTT(ER *sb.*[1] + -Y[6].] A slice of bread and butter.

1855 MRS. GASKELL *North & South* II. xi. 142 He's always mithering me for 'daddy' and 'butty'; and I ha' no butties to give him, and daddy's away. **1927** W. E. COLLINSON *Contemp. Eng.* 121 Buttie, general in North for a piece of bread and butter (together with jam-buttie). **1959** I. & P. OPIE *Lore & Lang. Schoolchildren* ix. 162 Spread it on the butty nice and thick. **1965** *Oxford Mail* 17 Nov. 11/5 The biggest jam butty in the world.

'butty-lark. *dial.* [f. BUTTY[1] 1 + LARK.] The tit-lark; see quot.

1865 *Cornh. Mag.* July 36 In the South the tit-lark is known as the 'butty-lark', or companion lark, because the cuckoo so frequently lays its eggs in that bird's nest.

†**'buttyly,** *adv. Obs.*[−1]. ? Beautifully.

a **1528** ? SKELTON *Epitaph Dk. Bedford* 44 He that of late regnyd in glory, With grete glosse, buttyly glased, Now low under fete doth he ly.

†**'butward, buteward,** *a.* or *adv. Obs.* [Aphetic f. *abuteward*, ABOUTWARD, q.v.] Striving, using influence; busied about, going.

a **1300** *Cursor M.* 27696 If þou.. buteward was to lette his thrift, of this behoues þe mak þi scrift. *Ibid.* 28540, I ha bene butward for to lett tuix man and wijf þair childer gett.

†**'butwin(e, -wink.** *Obs.*[−0] [Origin and correct form unknown: for the second element cf. OE. *hléapwince* LAPWING.] Some unknown bird.

1570 LEVINS *Manip.* 133 A Butwin, bird, *capella.* **1678** PHILLIPS (App.), *Butt-wine*, a sort of bird which some think to be the same which Rider calls Capella avis. **1721–1800** BAILEY, *Butwink, Butwin*, a Bird.

buty, butyful, obs. ff. BOOTY, BEAUTIFUL.

butyl ('bjuːtɪl). *Chem.* [f. BUT-YRIC (f. L. *butyrum* butter) + -YL. So called from its relation to *butyric acid*, q.v.]

1. The monatomic alcohol radical of the tetracarbon series, C_4H_9, called by its discoverer Corbet *Valyl*, and by later chemists also *Tetryl*, and *Quartyl*.

(There are four isomeric modifications of TETRYL, $CH_3CH_2CH_2CH_2$, $(CH_3)_2.CHCH_2$, $C_2H_5.CH.CH_3$, $(CH_3)_3.C$, of which the second or *Isobutyl* is the butyl of Wurtz, 'a colourless oily liquid, having a faint but agreeable odour, and a slight taste with burning after-taste' (Watts).

1868–77 WATTS *Dict. Chem.* (1879) V. 731 Tetryl or butyl. *Ibid.* VI. 373 With sodium it gives off.. but little butyl. **1870** TYNDALL *Heat* xv. §750 It is called nitrite of butyl.

2. *attrib.* Of butyl, butylic, tetrylic: as in ***butyl compounds***, ***group***, ***series***; also ***butyl acetate***, ***aldehyde***, ***chloride***, ***oxide***, ***sulphide***, etc.; and esp. in **butyl alcohol**, $C_4H_{10}O$, of which there are four isomers, 1. ***normal butyl alcohol*** or *propyl carbinol* (which yields butyric acid), 2. ***fermentation*** or ***isobutyl alcohol*** or ***isopropyl*** *carbinol*, 3. ***secondary butyl alcohol***, or *methyl-ethyl carbinol*, 4. ***tertiary butyl alcohol*** or *trimethyl carbinol*; **butyl hydride** = *quartane*, a volatile hydro-carbon C_4H_{10}, the lightest of all known liquids; **butyl aldehyde**, the same as *butyric aldehyde*; **butyl rubber**, a type of synthetic rubber made from isobutylene; also *ellipt.* So many other combinations as ***butyl carbinol***, ***butyl benzene***, etc.

1869 ROSCOE *Elem. Chem.* (1874) 330 Butyl hydride.. is the lightest of all known liquids. *Ibid.* 331 This [normal butyl alcohol] is the primary alcohol, as it yields on oxidation butyl aldehyde and butyric acid. **1869–71** WATTS *Dict. Chem.* (1879) VI. 373 *Isopropyl-carbinol* or *isoprimary-butylic Alcohol* constitutes the butylic alcohol of Wurtz, which was extracted from fusel-oil. For a long time it was the only butyl alcohol known to chemists. **1873** FOWNES *Chem.* 599 Butyl-carbinol is prepared from normal butyl alcohol in the same manner as the latter from normal propyl alcohol. **1880** *Med. Temp. Jrnl.* July 167 He found that butyl and propyl alcohols were possessed of strong toxic properties. **1940** *Economist* 20 July 100/1 The Standard Oil Company of New Jersey has evolved an entirely new product, which it calls 'butyl'. **1940** R. M. THOMAS et al. in *Ind. & Engin. Chem.* XXXIII. 1283 (*title*) Butyl Rubber: A new hydrocarbon Product. *Ibid.* 1284/2 The designation 'butyl rubber' must be considered a generic term. **1957** *Encycl. Brit.* IV. 459/2 Isobutylene.. polymerizes to a spongelike material called butyl rubber, which is used for the production of high-grade tire tubings. **1962** *Times* 6 Mar. 15/7 Butyl-rubber tyres.

3. Hence derivatives in **butyl-**: **buty'lactic**, in ***butylactic acid***: the monobasic acid, $C_4H_8O_3$, derived from Butyl glycol; the tetracarbon or Butylene member of the Lactic series. **butylamide**, a less correct name for BUTYRAMIDE. **'butyla,mine**, an AMINE, or compound ammonia of the butyl series. **'butylene**, the diatomic hydrocarbon or olefine

of the butyl series, C_4H_8, also called *butene* and *tetrene*, of which there are several isomeric modifications; in comb. as ***butylene alcohol***, etc. **buty'lenic** *a.*, of or pertaining to Butylene. **butylic** (bjuː'tɪlɪk) *a.*, of or pertaining to Butyl, as in ***butylic alcohol, butylic ether***, etc.

1863–72 WATTS *Dict. Chem.* I. 688 Butylactic acid bears to butyric acid the same relation that lactic acid bears to propionic acid. *Ibid.* (1877) V. 733 Tetrylic or butylic alcohol of fermentation is a primary alcohol. **1866** H. E. ROSCOE *Elem. Chem.* xxxi. 279 *Primary Monoamines*.. Butylamine. **1877** —— *Fownes' Chem.* II. 57 Butene or Butylene—of this hydro-carbon there are three modifications.. *Normal butene, Pseudo-butene, Isobutene.* **1964** N. G. CLARK *Mod. Org. Chem.* xii. 245 The *butylamines* and *pentylamines* are obtained by the action of ammonia on the corresponding chlorides.

butyne ('bjuːtaɪn). *Chem.* [altered form of BUTINE: see -YNE.] Either of the two isomers $CH_3{\cdot}CH_2{\cdot}C{\vdots}CH$ and $CH_3{\cdot}C{\vdots}C{\cdot}CH_3$ (also called *crotonylene*) of the hydrocarbon C_4H_6. (Formerly called BUTINE.)

1935 *Proc. Indiana Acad. Sci.* XLIV. 148 Ethyl sulphate reacts vigorously with calcium acetylide in ammonia and gives a theoretical yield of pure butyne-1. **1951** A. W. JOHNSON in E. H. Rodd *Chem. Carbon Compounds* IA. ii. 264 The acetylenic hydrocarbons are isomeric with the corresponding diolefines, e.g. propyne (allylene).. is isomeric with allene and butyne with butadiene.

butyr. *Chem.* An adaptation of L. *butyrum* BUTTER, sometimes used in technical senses.

1840 H. CLEEVE in *Jrnl. Agric. Soc.* I. III. 321 Butyr, (or, as it is commonly called, butter) of antimony. **1882** *Chemist & Drug.* XXIV. 56/1 Butyr of antimony, oil of vitriol, etc.

butyr-, a formative of the names of chemical compounds belonging to or derived from the butyric series, and of some minerals. (Cf. BUTYRO-.)

butyra'cetic acid, an acid having the composition of a combination of butyric and acetic acid, $C_2H_4O_2.C_4H_8O_2$, also called *pseudo-acetic acid*; its salts are **butyracetates**. **'butyral, butyraldehyde**, two isomeric compounds, C_4H_8O, aldehydes of the butyric series. **'butyra,mide**, the amide of the butyric series, $C_4H_7O.NH_2$, crystallizing in snow-white nacreous tables. **'butyrate**, a salt of butyric acid. **buty'rellite**, *Min.*, Dana's name for the natural fatty substance, *bog-butter*. **'butyrin**, an oily liquid analogous to the acetins, obtained by the direct action of butyric acid on glycerin. **'butyrite a.** *Chem.*, a compound formed from butyric acid and mannite (Watts); **b.** *Min.*, another name for *Butyrellite*. **'butyrone**, the ketone of the butyric series, also called dipropyl ketone $CO.(C_3H_7)_2$. **'butyryl**, C_4H_7O, the radical of butyric acid.

1826 HENRY *Chem.* II. 446 This oil [butter], according to Chevreul, is resolvable into two; the one.. he calls butirine, because it contains butyric acid or its elements. **1839–47** TODD *Cycl. Anat.* III. 359/1 Butter may be regarded as composed of.. stearine, elain, and butyrine. **1873** FOWNES *Chem.* 547 Several of the paraffins are produced by the dry .. distillation of butyrates. **1853** *Pharmaceut. Jrnl.* XIII. 72 The Chloride of Butyryle is.. liquid. **1869–71** WATTS *Dict. Chem.* (1879) VI. 380 Butyryl.. is an aromatic oil, slightly soluble or insoluble in water.

butyraceous (bjuːtɪ'reɪʃəs), *a.* [f. L. *butyr-um* butter + -ACEOUS: cf. F. *butyracé*.]

1. Of the nature of butter; buttery.

1668 *Phil. Trans.* III. 887 Milk.. whence, and from the three parts whereof, viz. Butyraceous, Serous, and Caseous .. he would deduce the different nature of the Humors and Spirits composing the blood. **1778** *Anat. Dialogues* 6 An oleaginous or butyraceous matter. **1844** T. GRAHAM *Dom. Med.* 174 Whey is the watery saccharine part of milk, freed in a great measure from the butyraceous and caseous matters.

fig. **1870** LOWELL *Study Wind.* 249 If repugnance for having fine phrases take the place of butyraceous principle.

2. Producing or containing butter.

1863 R. BURTON *Abeokuta* I. 324 The varieties of butyraceous nuts are almost wholly unknown. **1876** —— *Gorilla L.* I. 220 The Nje or Njeve, a towering butyraceous tree.

butyric (bjuː'tɪrɪk), *a. Chem.* [f. as prec. + -IC.] Of or pertaining to butter, *esp.* in reference to its chemical constitution and formation. Hence:

1. ***butyric acid***, the monatomic, monobasic, fatty acid of the BUTYL series, $C_4H_8O_2$, of which there are two modifications, *normal butyric* and *isobutyric* acid; the former occurring in butter, cod-liver oil, and other substances, is a colourless viscous liquid, with a smell suggestive of both vinegar and rancid butter. Its salts are *butyrates*.

1826 [see BUTYR-]. **1839–47** TODD *Cycl. Anat.* III. 359/1 Chevreul.. has named them the butyric, caproic, and capric acids. **1845** G. DAY *Simon's Anim. Chem.* I. 78 By.. fermentation butyric acid may be obtained from sugar.. the fermentation, at first viscous, subsequently lactic, gradually becomes butyric. **1871** TYNDALL *Fragm. Sc.* (ed. 6) II. xii. 275 Air.. is according to Pasteur, absolutely deadly to the vibrios which provoke the butyric acid fermentation.

2. ***butyric series***: the series of compound bodies related to butyric acid, or containing the radical BUTYRYL, C_4H_7O; as ***butyric aldehyde***, C_4H_8O; ***butyric ether*** or *ethyl butyrate*, $C_2H_5{\cdot}C_4H_7O_2$, a colourless oily liquid, having a pleasant fruity odour; ***butyric anhydride*** or ***oxide*** $(C_4H_7O)_2O$.

1854 SCOFFERN in *Orr's Circ. Sc.* Chem. 109 Butyric ether and butyric methyl ether. **1863** WATTS *Dict. Chem.* (1879) I. 695 To the presence of small quantities of butyric ether, the peculiar flavour of pine-apples, melons, and some other fruits is due. *Ibid.* Butyric anhydride is a colourless, very mobile, and highly refracting liquid.

Hence **bu'tyrically** *adv.*

1876 tr. *Schutzenberger's Ferment.* 209 A great number of compounds are susceptible of fermenting butyrically.

butyro- ('bjuːtɪrəʊ), comb. form of L. *butyrum*, used in technical, chiefly chemical words, as ***butyro-acetic***, combining butyric and acetic. Cf. BUTYR-.

c **1865** *Circ. Sc.* I. 336/2 The chemist calls these butyric, butyro-acetic, and formic acids.

butyrometer (bjuːtɪ'rɒmɪtə(r)). [f. BUTYRO- + -METER.] An instrument for estimating the percentage of butter-fat in milk. Cf. *lacto-butyrometer* s.v. LACTO-.

[**1863** *Jrnl. R. Agric. Soc.* XXIV. II. 315 Marchand's lacto-butyrometer.] **1902** *Encycl. Brit.* XXVII. 360/1 The butyrometer is extremely useful, alike for measuring periodically the fat-producing capacity of individual cows in a herd, for rapidly ascertaining the percentage of fat in milk delivered to factories [etc.]. **1961** *B.S.I. News* Sept. 13/1 Milk hydrometers, butyrometers, [etc.].

butyrous ('bjuːtɪrəs), *a.* [f. L. *butyr-um* + -OUS, corresp. to F. *butyreux*.] Of the quality or nature of butter; butyraceous, buttery.

1669 BOYLE *Contn. new Exp.* II. (1682) 117 To separate the Butyrous from the Caseous part. **1689** G. HARVEY *Curing Dis. by Expect.* vi. 39. **1774** A. HUNTER *Georgic. Ess.* (1803) III. 257 The cream was of a thick butyrous consistence.

Hence **'butyrousness**, buttery quality.

1662 H. STUBBE *Ind. Nectar* iii. 42 You may easily perceive in a rich nut.. an extraordinary butyrousness.

† **'buvable**, *a. Obs. rare*$^{-1}$. [a. F. *buvable*, f. *buv-* stem of *boire* to drink.] Drinkable.

1480 CAXTON *Ovid's Met.* xv. iv, Hypanis, whyche somtyme was sweet & buvable, & now is salt and bitter.

buve(n, var. of BOVE *prep. Obs.*

‖ **buvette** (byvɛt). [a. F. *buvette* tavern, road-side inn.] A tavern, small inn; a refreshment bar or room.

1753 in Chambers *Cycl. Supp.* **1866** *Cornh. Mag.* Oct. 505 They passed little roadside inns and buvettes. **1885** *Cornhill Mag.* June 597 We.. went into the stove-stifling heat of the little buvette of the station to keep ourselves warm.

buwe(n, obs. form of BOW *v.*

buxam, obs. form of BUXOM.

buxees, obs. form of BAKSHEESH *sb.*

1686 *MS. Let. Job Charnock to Council of Balasore* 3 June, If the peons come in five days give them 4 annas buxees.

buxeous ('bʌksɪəs), *a.* [f. L. *buxe-us*, f. *buxus* box-tree + -OUS.] Of or pertaining to box or the box tree.

1731 in BAILEY vol. II. **1847** in CRAIG; and in mod. Dicts.

† **'buxerry.** *Obs.* exc. *Hist.* Also **bucksaree, -ry, buxarry.** [Of uncertain etymology; Col. Yule (Appendix) suggests that it may be Hind. *baksārī* 'native of Buxar'.] A matchlock-man.

1757 CLIVE in Grant *Hist. India* I. ix. 52/2 Leaving only a few Europeans with 200 new-raised Bucksarees to guard our camp. **1778** E. LONG *Jamaica* I (Y.) Having sent Ensign McKion with.. 150 buxerries. **1850** BROOME *Rise & Progr. Bengal Army* (Y.) Buxarries were nothing more than Burkandaz, armed and equipped in the usual native manner. *c* **1880** GRANT *Hist. India* I. viii. 45/1, 1,500 Bucksaries, or native matchlockmen.

buxey, var. of BUKSHI.

buxhome, -humnesse, obs. ff. BUXOM, -NESS.

buxia, buxie, var. ff. BUXINE, BAKSHEESH *sb.*

bu'xiferous, *a. rare*$^{-0}$. [f. L. *buxifer* box-bearing + -OUS.] Bearing or producing box-trees.

1656 in BLOUNT *Glossogr.* **1721–1800** in BAILEY.

buxine ('bʌksaɪn). Also **buxin(a, buxia.** [mod. f. L. *bux-us* box + -INE[4].] A vegetable alkaloid obtained from the box-tree, said to be identical with bebeerine (see BEBEERU).

1836 *Penny Cycl.* VI. 73/1 Buxina.. has generally the appearance of a translucid deep brown-coloured mass. **1863** WATTS *Dict. Chem.* (1879) I. 699 Buxine has a bitter taste and excites sneezing. **1875** H. WOOD *Therap.* (1879) 56 Bebeeria, or.. buxia, is whitish, amorphous, inodorous.

[**buxion**, misreading of *burion*, BURGEON.

c **1400** *Test. Love.* II (1560) 290 b/1 A sere tree, without buxioning or fruite. *Ibid.* III. 299 b/1 Though.. the braunches [be] seere, and no buxions shew. *Ibid.* Thy braunches must buxionen. **1736** BAILEY, *Buxionen*, to Bud. *Chauc.*]

buxom ('bʌksəm), *a.* Forms: **ibuhsum, ibucsum, 2–3 buhsum(m, 3 bocsum, -om, 3–8 buxum, 4 boȝsam, boghsom, bousum, -om,** (?) **busum, boxsom(e, bouxsome, bowxom, buxsom, 4–5 bowsom, boxsum, buxsum, 4–6 bouxom(e, boxom(e, -um, 4–7 bughsom, bowsum, buxome, 5 bouxum, buxhum, 5–6 buxume, buxsome, -home,** (?) **buscom, 6 bowsome, buxam, buckesom(e, 6–8 bucksome, 7–8 bucksom,** (9 **bucksome**), 4– **buxom.** [early ME. *buhsum, ibucsum* (perh.:—OE. **búhsum*, **ȝebúhsum*), f. stem of *búȝan* (*ȝebúȝan*) BOW *v.*[1] + -SOME; cf. MDu. *boochsaem*, Du. *buigzaam*, Ger. *biegsam* flexible, pliant. Branch II seems to have arisen from sense 1 c; the development of sense 3 being precisely the same as in BLITHE, that of 4 as in Fr. *joli* from 'blithe' to 'comely'.]

I. Easily bowed or bent. **1.** Morally.

† **a.** Obedient; pliant; compliant, tractable (*to*). *Obs.* (exc. as a rare archaism.)

c **1175** *Lamb. Hom.* 57 Beo buhsum toward gode. *Ibid.* 75 Beon him ibucsum ouer alle þing. *c* **1200** ORMIN 6176 þin laferrd birrþ þe buhsumm beon. *c* **1250** *Gen. & Ex.* 980 An angel.. bad hire.. to hire leuedi buxum ben. **1340** HAMPOLE *Pr. Consc.* 8148 Alle men.. þat meke of hert er here, and bowsom. *c* **1380** WYCLIF *Sel. Wks.* III. 49 Oure Ladi Marye .. was.. buxumer to his bidding þan ony hond-mayde. *c* **1440** *Generydes* 2505, Thanne came ther in.. The buscommest folk. *c* **1450** LONELICH *Grail* lii. 1006, I schal.. maken hem buxom to ȝowre hond. **1496** *Dives & Paup.* (W. de W.) IV. i. 160/1 We ben.. to them buxom and meke. **1523** FITZHERB. *Surv.* (1539) 15, I shall be buxome and obedient to justyces. **1581** J. BELL *Haddon's Answ. Osor.* 287 b, The Consuls should.. sweare faythfully to become bonnaire and buxome to the Pope. **1591** SPENSER *M. Hubberd* 626 So wilde a beast.. buxome to his bands, is ioy to see. *c* **1684** *MS. Let. Corporation of Kirkby to Judge Jeffreys*, Your Lordship was pleased to give us.. your oath to become a buxome and beneficial member of this corporation. [**1843** BORROW *Bible in Spain* xliii, To be buxom and obedient to the customs and laws of the republic. **1867** THIRLWALL *Lett. Friend* (1881) 88 In the hope that you will be buxom and good, I conclude now my New Year's Lecture.]

† **b.** Submissive, humble, meek. *Obs.*

a **1300** *Cursor M.* 8356 þat lauedi til hir lauerd lute Wit buxum reuerence and dute. *Ibid.* 29009 Oure praier aw euer for to be bowsum. **1340** *Ayenb.* 59 Hi.. ziggeþ.. þet hi byeþ zuo kueade and zuo zenful.. vor þet me ham hereþ and hyealde uor wel boȝsam. *c* **1440** *Promp. Parv.* 57 Buxum, or lowly or make, *humilis, pius, mansuetus.* *c* **1440** *York Myst.* xxiv. 141 His sisteres praye with bowsom beede. *a* **1455** HOLLAND *Houlate* xxxiv. 12 Bowsum obeysance.

† **c.** Gracious, indulgent, favourable; obliging, amiable, courteous, affable, kindly. *Obs.*

1362 LANGL. *P. Pl.* A. VI. 56 Bouweþ forþ bi a brok beo-boxum-of-speche. **1393** *Ibid.* C. IV. 421 God hym-self hoteþ To be boxome at my bidding. *c* **1460** *Towneley Myst.* Annunc. 79 (*Angel to Joseph*) Meek and buxom looke thou be, And with her dwelle. **1536** BELLENDEN *Cron. Scot.* (1821) I. 18 To mak the reders more bowsum and attent. *Ibid.* 108 Ilk story be thi self is separat, To mak thaim bowsome to thine audience.

† **d.** with *inf.*: Easily moved, prone, ready. *Obs.*

a **1300** *Cursor M.* 25208 þan suld we be.. bowsom his bidinges to fullfill. **1340** HAMPOLE *Pr. Consc.* 50 The creatours þat er dom.. er bughsom To lof hym. **1377** LANGL. *P. Pl.* B. VI. 197 Many a beggere for benes buxome was to swynke. *c* **1440** *Gesta Rom.* (1879) 22 þe flesh is euer lewid, and buxom to do Evil.

† **2.** Physically: Flexible, pliant. Yielding to pressure, unresisting (*poet.*). *Obs.*

1596 SPENSER *F.Q.* I. xi. 37 Then gan he.. scourge the buxome aire so sore That to his force to yielden it was faine. **1599** A. M. *Gabelhouer's Bk. Physicke* 278/2 The Pockes.. are verye buxume. **1615** CROOKE *Body of Man* 1111 Their substance is.. flexible or buxome that they should not breake but giue way to violence. **1667** MILTON *P.L.* II. 842 Wing silently the buxom Air. *a* **1700** DRYDEN *Palamon & Arc.* II. 519 Her turtles fann'd the buxom air above.

II. Blithe, jolly, well-favoured.

3. Blithe, gladsome, bright, lively, gay. *arch.* (The explanation in Bailey and Johnson, 'amorous, wanton', is apparently only contextual.)

1590 GREENE *Never too late* A iv, Grey and buxome were his eyne. **1598** FLORIO, *Vago*.. blithe.. buckesome, full of glee. **1599** SHAKS. *Hen. V*, III. vi. 28 A Souldier firme and sound of heart, and of buxome valour. **1620** SHELTON *Quix.* IV. xxx. 229 He went on his Journey.. most glad and bucksome. **1658** LENNARD tr. *Charron's Wisd.* Pref., Philosophy, such as this Book teacheth, is altogether pleasant, free, bucksome, and if I may so say, wanton too. **1675** COTTON *Poet. Wks.* (1765) 267 A fine Miss.. as free, Buxom, and amorous as He. **1678** MARVELL *Def. J. Howe* Wks. 1875 IV. 196, I could not but remark here of The Discourse.. how jovial It is and bucksom. **1827** HEBER *Europe* 312 Freedom's buxom blast. **1848** LYTTON *Harold* I. i, That buxom month.

4. Full of health, vigour, and good temper; well-favoured, plump and comely, 'jolly', comfortable-looking (in person). (Chiefly of women.)

1589 GREENE *Menaph.* (Arb.) 43 A bonny prety one, As bright, buxsome and as sheene As was shee. **1608** MIDDLETON *Fam. Love* III. vii, Those ribs shall not enfold thy buxom limbs. **1611** COTGR. s.v. *Matineux*, An earlie man is buxome. **1681** HICKERINGILL *Vind. Naked Truth* II. 22 Those lazy and bucksome Abby-Lubbers. **1683** tr. *Erasmus' Moriæ Enc.* 16 My followers are smooth, plump, and bucksom. **1742** GRAY *Ode Eton Coll.*, Theirs buxom health of rosy hue. **1779** JOHNSON *Gray* Wks. 1787 IV. 303 His

epithet *buxom health* is not elegant; he seems not to understand the word. **1823** SCOTT *Peveril* xxi, She was a buxom dame about thirty. **1828** —— *F.M. Perth* iii, A buxom priest. **1843** CARLYLE *Past. & Pr.* III. viii. (1872) 153 Fresh buxom countenances. **1873** *S. Sea Bubbles* i. 4 A slight gathering in of her dress..to exhibit her buxom figure to full perfection.

5. *Comb.*, as ***buxom-looking***.

1840 BARHAM *Ingol. Leg.* (1858) 77 He..followed a buxom-looking handmaiden into the breakfast parlour.

†**'buxom,** *v. Obs. rare*⁻¹. [f. prec. adj.] With *to*: To yield *to*, obey.

c **1305** *Edmund Conf.* 467 in *E.E.P.* (1862) 83 Þe bischop ..him bet atte laste þat he scholde not bileue godes wille to do To buxom to holi churche. [Query, *read* To be buxom.]

†**buxomly** ('bʌksəmlɪ), *adv. Obs.* [f. prec. adj. (which see for Forms) + -LY².] Obediently, humbly, meekly; courteously, willingly.

a **1240** *Lofsong* in *Cott. Hom.* 215 Ich buhsumliche biseche þe louerd..ðet þu beo mi red nu. *a* **1300** *Cursor M.* 21351 We agh to buxumli it ber. *c* **1320** *Seuyn Sages* 3459 He bowed him ful bowsumly. **1340** *Ayenb.* 70 He ssel herye god and him boȝsamliche þonky, þet him beþ yloked. **1393** LANGL. *P. Pl.* C. XVIII. 283 Eueriche busshope, by þe lawe sholde buxumliche wende..þorgh hus prouynce. *c* **1400** MAUNDEV. viii. 82 He commanded..to all his subgettes.. buxomly to resceyve me. **1513** DOUGLAS *Æneis* VIII. vi. 124 Amang small geyr now entris bowsumly. **1540** HYRDE *Vives' Instr. Chr. Wom.* (1592) X. iv, That they do their duty diligently, meekly, and buxomly. **1678** A. LITTLETON *Lat. Dict.* s.v., Buxomly, *clementer, obedienter.*

buxomness ('bʌksəmnɪs). [f. BUXOM *a.* (which see for Forms); see -NESS.]

†**1.** Obedience, submissiveness; lowliness, humility. *Obs.*

c **1175** *Lamb. Hom.* 73 Bi-spreng me lauerd mid buhsumnesse. *c* **1230** *Hali Meid.* 41 Þu schalt..teamen.. Simplete of semblaunt and buhsumnesse and stilðe. **1297** R. GLOUC. 318 He bygan ys herte in bocsumnesse amende. *a* **1300** *Cursor M.* 25135 We sall..knaw with bowsumnes þat no gude dede of oure self es. **1340** HAMPOLE *Pr. Consc.* 7848 Þare es lowtyng and reverence, And boghsomnes and obedience [in heaven]. **1362** LANGL. *P. Pl.* A. I. 111 He brak Boxumnes þorw bost of him-seluen. *a* **1420** OCCLEVE *De Reg. Princ.* 3575 God toke upone hym humble buxomnesse. **1613** R. C. *Table Alph.* (ed. 3) *Buxomnesse*, plyablenesse, or humble stooping, in signe of obedience. **1678** A. LITTLETON *Lat. Dict.* s.v., Buxomness or meekness, *obsequium*. **1721** in BAILEY.

†**2.** Graciousness, kindly disposition; courtesy, complaisance. *Obs.*

14.. *Gold. Litany* in Maskell *Mon. Rit.* II. 245 By thy infinite buxomnes: haue mercy on vs. **1483** *Cath. Angl.* 50 A Buxumnes, *clemencia*. **1502** ARNOLDE *Chron.* 162 Moost blessed fader Primate..whom Almighty God by hys ineffable buxumnes..hath creat and erecte. **1577** STANYHURST *Descr. Irel.* in *Holinshed* VI. 22 You should never marke him or his bedfellow (such was their buxomnesse)..once make a sowre face at anie ghest.

3. Blitheness, gaiety. *arch.*

1598 FLORIO, *Gaiezza*..blithnes, iolitie, buckesomnes. **1620** SHELTON *Quix.* IV. xix. 159 The Beauty, Spirit and Bucksomeness of the wench mislik'd him not. **1814** CARY *Dante* (1871) 317 In him are summed, Whate'er of buxomness and free delight May be in spirit.

4. *modern.* Comely plumpness.

1875 BESANT & R. *Harp & Cr.* II. viii. 196 She is fat, she is fair..she has still many summers of buxomness before her.

buy (baɪ), *v.* Forms: 1 byczan, -can, (biczan), 2–5 buggen, biggen, bugge, bigge, 4 byȝe, 4–5 bygge(n, begge(n), 5 byche. Also 3 biȝen, 3–7 buye, 3–5 bien, 3–6 bie, 4–5 byen, 4–6 bye, by, (4 byi, biy, bii, bij, bi, byȝe, biȝe, byye, 4–5 be, 5 byin, -yn), 5 beye(n, bey, 6–7 buie, 7– buy; *3rd sing.* 1 byȝ(e)þ, 2 bihð, 3 bu(e)ð, 4 (Ayenb.) bayþ, buyeþ, 5 bieth.

Imper. 1 byze, 3 bu(e), 4 bye, by, *pl.* 1 byczað.

Pa. t. 1–3 bohte, (2–3 bouchte), 3–4 bouhte, 3–5 boȝte, bouȝte, (3 bochte), 4 boȝt, (bohut), 4–5 bouȝt, boght, boughte, (5 bout), 5– bought, *Sc.* bocht, (6 bowth).

Pa. pple. 1 (ȝe)boht, 2 iboht, 3 boht, 3–4 bohut, (i-, y-)bouȝt, 3–4, 7 boght, 3–5 boȝt, 4 yboht, bowght, (bout), 4–5 boghte, boȝte, (y-)bouȝte, (5 ybouȝht), 5–6 boughte, (6 bouht, bowte, beyght), 5– bought, *Sc.* bocht. [OE. *bycȝ(e)an, bohte, ȝeboht*, corresp. to OS. *buggjan, *bohta, giboht*, Goth. *bugjan, bauhta, bauhts*; of unknown origin, not found outside Teut., and not to be connected, so far as can be seen, with the stem *bug-* BOW. The inflexion was imper. *byȝe, bycȝað*; ind. pres. *bycȝe, byȝest, byȝeþ*, pl. *bycȝað*; subj. pres. *bycȝe, bycȝen*; whence ME. s.w. *buye, buggeþ*; *bugge, buyest, buyeþ, buggeþ*; *bugge, -en*; levelled before 1500 to *buy-* all through, whence the modern spelling. The forms in *begge, bey-* were Kentish; *bigge, bie, by*, midland and north.; in the latter the levelling to *bie, by*, took place as early as 1300. Cf. the comp. ABY, ABYE.

In the pa. t. of this vb., the terminations were added without connecting vowel: WGer. *boh-ta* has the regular OTeut. *o* for *u* before an *a-* vowel, as in *worhta*, from *wurkjan*, OE. *wyrcan* to WORK.]

I. 1. a. *trans.* To get possession of by giving an equivalent, usually in money; to obtain by paying a price; to purchase. (Correlative to *sell.*) Const. *of, from*, †*at* (the seller), *for, with* (the price).

c **1000** *Ags. Gosp.* Matt. xxvii. 7 Þa ȝebohten hiȝ ænne æcyr, mid þam feo. *Ibid.* John iv. 8 His leorning-cnihtas ferdon þa to þære ceastre woldon him mete bicȝan. **1154** *O.E. Chron.* (Laud MS.) an. 1137 Þe Judeus of Noruuic bohten an Christen cild. *a* **1240** *Ureisun* in *Cott. Hom.* 185 Nis he fol chapmon þe buþ deore a wac þing. **1297** R. GLOUC. 390 Bu a peyre [hose] of a marc. *a* **1300** *Cursor M.* 4764 Þai moght noght find to bi þam bred. **1340** *Ayenb.* 36 To begge..corn..lesse be þe haluedele, þanne hit his worþ. *c* **1380** WYCLIF *Serm.* lviii. Sel. Wks. I. 177 Men shulden not bie þis office. **1393** LANGL. *P. Pl.* C. IX. 304 Ich haue no peny ..polettes for to bigge. *c* **1400** MAUNDEV. ii. 12 A kyng of Fraunce boughte theise Relikes..of the Jewes. *c* **1400** *Apol. Loll.* 9 Wan I by meit for money, I selle þe money þat þe toþer man bieth. *c* **1420** *Pallad* I. 1065 To bey thi been [i.e. bees] beholde hem riche and fulle. *c* **1430** *Freemasonry* 358 Pay wele every mon algate, That thou hast ybowȝht any vytayles ate. *c* **1440** AGNES PASTON in *Lett.* xxv. I. 39 Gif ye wolde byin her a goune. *c* **1449** PECOCK *Repr.* 493 It was not leeful that men ete fleisch which was offrid to idols neither bigge thilk fleisch. **1476** *Plumpton Corr.* 37 Under a hundred shillings I can by non. **1502–3** in *Comm.-Place Bk. 15th Cent.* (1886) 173 Item bowte of Roger Cawthaw..v cumbe berly. **1545** BRINKLOW *Lament.* (1874) 99 No man will bye their ware any more. **1580** BARET *Alv.* B 1000 Be the price neuer so great it is well bought that a man must needes haue. **1597** SHAKS. *2 Hen. IV*, I. ii. 56, I bought him in Paules, and hee'l buy mee a horse in Smithfield. **1714** LADY M. W. MONTAGUE *Lett.* xc. 146 To..buy some little Cornish borough. **1790** BURKE *Fr. Rev.* Wks. V. 346 With you a man can neither earn nor buy his dinner, without a speculation. **1855** TENNYSON *Brook* 222 We bought the farm we tenanted before.

b. *absol.* (Often coupled with *sell.*)

c **1000** *Ags. Gosp.* Matt. xxv. 10 Þa hiȝ ferdun and woldon bycȝean, þa com se bryd-guma *c* **1200** *Trin. Coll. Hom.* 213 Þat is ure alre wune, þe biggeð and silleð. **1340** HAMPOLE *Pr. Consc.* 4399 Nan sal bye with þam ne selle. *c* **1386** CHAUCER *Schipm. T.* 304 This marchaund..bieth, and creaunceth. **1483** *Cath. Angl.* 30/1 To by and selle, *auccionari*. *c* **1538** STARKEY *England* II. i. 175 He that Byth dere, may sel dere. **1755** SMOLLETT *Quix.* (1803) I. 233 He that buys and denies, his own purse belies. **1863** MRS. C. CLARKE *Shaks. Char.* xiv. 360 Pestering her swain to buy for her.

c. *intr. to buy into* (earlier also *in*, prep.): to buy a commission in (a regiment); to purchase stock in (the public funds), shares in (a trading company).

1681 *Treat. East-India Trade* 11, I..had rather buy in this Stock..at 300*l.* for 100*l.* then come into any New Stock at even Money. **1849** *Blackw. Mag.* LXVI. 671 The man who buys into a public stock.

d. *trans.* Of things: To be an equivalent price for; to be the means of purchasing.

1599 SHAKS. *Much Ado* I. i. 183 Can the world buie such a jewell? **1622** MALYNES *Anc. Law.-Merch.* 87 A London mingled colour cloth, would haue bought at Lisborne two chests of Sugar. **1691** LOCKE *Wks.* (1727) II. 67 If one Ounce of Silver will buy, i.e. is of equal Value to one Bushel of Wheat. *Mod.* Health is a treasure that gold cannot buy. It was his wife's money that bought the farm.

2. *fig.* To obtain, gain, procure, in exchange for something else, or by making some sacrifice.

c **1175** *Lamb. Hom.* 137 Ðenne bið þes monnes wile ibeht mid þere elmisse. *a* **1225** *Ancr. R.* 190 Worldliche men buggeð deorre helle, þen ȝe doð heuene. *c* **1250** *Moral Ode* 65 in *Cott. Hom.* 163 Ech mon mid þet he hauet mei buggen houene riche. *a* **1307** *Prov. Hendyng* xxix, Dere is boþt þe hony þat is licked of þe þorne, quoþ Hendyng. **1430** LYDG. *Chron. Troy* I. vi, No honor may be wonne, But that I muste with my deth it beye. **1513** DOUGLAS *Æneis* X. viii. 157 Desyrand he mycht by for mekill thing That he had nevyr tuichit Pallas ȝing. **1571** ASCHAM *Scholem.* (Arb.) 155 B[u]ying witte at the dearest hand, that is, by long experience of the hurt and shame that cummeth of mischeif. **1667** MILTON *P.L.* IV. 102 Short intermission bought with double smart. **1813** SCOTT *Rokeby* I. x, Forced the embarrassed host to buy By query close, direct reply. **1866** KINGSLEY *Herew.* xviii. (1877) 222 A war which could buy them neither spoil nor land.

†**3. a.** To pay the penalty of, suffer the consequences of, 'pay for'; to expiate, atone for; = ABY *v.* 2 (of which it was probably an aphetic form: cf. BYE *v.*). Often with *dear*; sometimes with *bitter, sore*; and in phrase, *to buy the bargain*.

c **1250** *Gen. & Ex.* 3683 Ðat gruching hauen he derre boȝt. *a* **1300** *Cursor M.* 1115 And [god] will þat he bii þe vttrage. **1330** R. BRUNNE *Chron.* 61 Griffyn..was proued traitoure fals, & þat bouht he fulle dere. **1393** LANGL. *P. Pl.* C. XVI. 304 Now he buyeþ hit ful bitere. ? *a* **1400** *Morte Arth.* (Roxb.) 66 His dedis shall be bought full sore. *c* **1400** MAUNDEV. vii. 76 In tokene that the Synnes of Adam scholde ben boughte in that same place. **1530** PALSGR. 455/1, I bye the bargayne, or I fele the hurte or displeasure of a thyng. *a* **1553** UDALL *Royster D.* (Arb.) 72 Let them the bargaine bie. **1556** J. HEYWOOD *Spider & F.* lvii. 87 Then is that bitter beyght. **1587** TURBERV. *Trag. T.* (1837) 154 Whether they Did buie their marriage deare. **1599** GREENE *George a Gr.* (1861) 263, I will make thee by this treason dear. *c* **1615** CHAPMAN *Odyss.* IV. 664 'Twill not long be.. Before thou buy this curious skill with tears.

†**b.** In *pass.* Of an offence: To be expiated or 'visited' *upon* (the offender). *Obs. rare.*

a **1300** *Cursor M.* 13849 And qua þis couenand haldes noght þat it be dere apon him boght.

†**4.** To set free by paying a price; to redeem, ransom; *esp. fig.* in *Theol.* to redeem (from sin, hell, etc.). *Obs.* exc. in theological use, and in that now rather a conscious metaphor from 1; *redeem* being the ordinary word for this sense.

c **1175** *Lamb. Hom.* 19 Þet þet ear us bohte deore. *a* **1300** *Hymn to God* in *Trin. Coll. Hom.* 258 He vs bouchte wið his blod of þe feondes swiche. *a* **1300** *E.E. Psalter* cxxix. [cxxx.] 8 And he sal bie [*v.r.* bien] Irael of alle his wicednesses. *Ibid.* xxv[i]. 11 Bye me, and of me have merci. *a* **1300** *Cursor M.* 152 He com his folk to bij. *Ibid.* 6173 Mans barn wit pris he boght. *Ibid.* 9598 For to bij his prisun vte. **1375** BARBOUR *Bruce* XVII. 336 Mary, That bare the byrth that all can by. **1377** LANGL. *P. Pl.* B. XI. 202 *Redemptor* was his name, And we his bretheren, þourgh hym ybouȝt. *c* **1400** MAUNDEV. Prol. 2 To bye and to delyvere us from Peynes of Helle. **1413** LYDG. *Pylgr. Sowle* IV. xiii. (1483) 63 He that hath mysdone hath no thynge wherwith to beyen hym seluen. **1534** MORE *On the Passion* Wks. 1325/1 By hys payne to..bye our soules from payne. **1552** ABP. HAMILTON *Catech.* 95 Quhilk hais bocht us with his precious blude. **1633** P. FLETCHER *Purple Isl.* I. xxxii, Who bought'st man, whom man (though God) did sell. **1709** WATTS *Hymn*, '*I [We] give immortal praise*', God the Son..who bought us with his blood. **1836** J. GILBERT *Chr. Atonem.* VI. (1852) 172 So far from mercy having been properly purchased for us, mercy herself buys us.

5. To gain over, engage (a person) by money or otherwise (*to* or *to do* something); usually in bad sense, to hire. *arch.* (Cf. *buy off*, 7 a; *buy over*, 9.)

1652 *Free State comp. Monarchy* 1, [I] did..lay out..the poore Talent God intrusted me with, to buy them to the waies of Peace. **1655–60** STANLEY *Hist. Philos.* (1701) 88/1 One that for a Drachm might be bought into any thing. **1697** DRYDEN *Virg. Georg.* IV. 573 Nor is [he] with Pray'rs, or Bribes, or Flatt'ry bought. **1713** ADDISON *Cato* II. ii. 57 Millions of worlds Should never buy me to be like that Cæsar. **1878** MORLEY *Diderot* II. 121 She did her best..to buy the author.

II. Phrases and combinations.

* Combined with adverbs.

6. buy in.

a. *trans.* To collect a stock of (commodities) by purchase; often in expressed or implied opposition to *sell out*. Often *absol.*

1622 E. MISSELDEN *Free Trade* 71 Some..few..doe ioine ..to engrosse and buy in a Commodity, and sell it out againe at their owne price. **1628** SANDERSON *Two Serm. at St. Paul's* I. 36 To buy in provision for his house. **1861** *Times* 16 Oct., Many farmers buy in ewes in autumn.

b. To buy back for the owner, *esp.* at an auction when no sufficient price has been offered.

1642 SIR E. DERING *Sp. on Relig.* 161 Impropriations may be bought in. **1770** WILKES *Corr.* (1805) IV. 31 Mrs. Macauley bought-in herself the house in Berners-street. *a* **1845** HOOD *Sniff. Birthday* xvi, Let Robins advertise..My 'Man's Estate', I'm sure enough I shall not buy it in.

c. (*absol.* from 1 c.) To buy a commission in a regiment; to purchase stock or shares.

1826 DISRAELI *Viv. Grey* III. viii. 124 Young Premium, the son of the celebrated loan-monger, has bought in. **1840** *Fraser's Mag.* XL. 606 The..capitalist reappeared on the Bourse; buying in cautiously for the rise.

7. buy off.

a. *trans.* To induce (a person) by payment, to relinquish a claim, a course of action, etc.; to get rid of (a claim, a person's opposition or interference) by paying money to the claimant or opponent. Often *fig.*

1629 EARLE *Microcosm.* lxvii. (Arb.) 91 One whom no rate can buy off from the least piece of his freedom. **1851** HT. MARTINEAU *Hist. Eng.* I. iv. (1878) 89 Buying off the Prince's claim for the revenues of the Duchy of Cornwall. **1865** TRENCH *Gust. Adolphus* ii. 65 To buy off the presence of troops by enormous gifts to their captains. **1868** FREEMAN *Norm. Conq.* (1876) II. ix. 408 Gruffydd was perhaps bought off in this way.

b. To release from military service by payment.

Mod. He has enlisted, but his friends will buy him off.

8. buy out.

†**a.** *trans.* To ransom, redeem. *Obs.*

1297 R. GLOUC. 496 Her maistres hom out bouȝte. *c* **1440** *Gesta Rom.* (1879) 306 This yong man wrote to his fadir, praying him to bey him out [of prison]. **1590** SHAKS. *Com. Err.* I. ii. 5 Not being able to buy out his life. **1633** BP. HALL *Hard Texts* 291 By whom wee are..bought out from the bondage of sin.

b. To purchase a person's estate, or share in any concern, and so to turn (him) out of it.

[**1297** R. GLOUC. 379 So þat hii þat bode meste broȝt out monyon...me boȝte [*v.r.* broute] ys out wyþ woȝ]. **1644** J. GOODWIN *Danger Fight. agst. God* 26 By buying out some Inhabitant, or by purchasing ground. **1840** BARHAM *Ingol. Leg.* Ser. I. (1858) 77 A Yeoman of Kent, With his yearly rent, Will buy them out all three! **1885** *Spectator* 25 July 967/1 In so far as the landlords are bought out.

c. To get rid of or remove (any kind of liability) by a money payment.

1595 SHAKS. *John* III. i. 164 Dreading the curse that money may buy out. **1596** SHAKS. *1 Hen. IV*, IV. ii. 24 They haue bought out their seruices. **1828** LD. GRENVILLE *Sink. Fund* 42 A landed proprietor..buys out..a rent-charge with which it [his estate] is burthened. **1885** *Law Reports 14 Queen's B. Div.* 875 Money paid in order to buy out the execution.

9. buy over.

trans. To gain over by a payment or bribe.

1848 *Blackw. Mag.* LXIV. 630 Attempting to buy over their chiefs? **1860** FREER *Henry IV*, I. i. 9 [He] had bought the soldiers over to a man. **1877** MISS BRADDON *Weavers & W.* 328 He..bought over the lodging-house keeper to his interest.

10. buy up [cf. *heap up, scrape up*].

To purchase with the aim of amassing in one's own hands or taking up out of the market (a stock, or the *whole* of any commodity).

1533-4 *Act 25 Hen. VIII*, iv, They bie vp all maner of fishe thither brought. **1542** UDALL *Erasm. Apoph.* 250b, Augustus..meruaillyng at the same thyng in a pye, bought hir vp also. **1593** NASHE *Christ's T.* (1613) 107 Them..that would buy them vp by the whole sale, and make them away againe by retaile. **1622** E. MISSELDEN *Free Trade* 56 Another who bought vp all the Iron in Sicilia. **1624** GEE *Foot out of Snare* 48 The most of these Books..were bought-vp by Papists. **1667** PEPYS *Diary* (1879) IV. 269 Buying up of goods in case there should be war. **1701** W. WOTTON *Hist. Rome* 214 Cleander had bought up all the Corn. **1867** R. PATTERSON in *Fortn. Rev.* July 77 An..appeal to the State to buy up all the railways in the kingdom. **1874** STUBBS *Const. Hist.* I. xiii. 630 John..was buying up help on every side.

** Phrases.

11. †**a.** ***to buy and sell***: to barter, traffic with (in bad sense). *Obs.* or *arch.*

1613 SHAKS. *Hen. VIII*, I. i. 192 The Cardinall Does buy and sell his Honour as he pleases.

b. ***to be bought and sold***: often *fig.*, chiefly in sense To be betrayed for a bribe. *arch.*

a **1300** *Cursor M.* 142 How þat ioseph was boght and sald. **1426** AUDELAY *Poems* 4 Sche schal be boȝt and sold. **1594** SHAKS. *Rich. III*, v. iii. 305 Dickon thy maister is bought and sold. **1791** BURNS *Such a Parcel of Rogues, &c.* iii, We're bought and sold for English gold. **1864** TENNYSON *Ringlet* 33 She that gave you's bought and sold.

12. ***to buy a pig*** (in Scotl. ***a cat***) ***in a poke***: (Fr. *acheter chat en poche*) to purchase something which one has not examined; *hence*, to enter into an engagement in ignorance of the responsibilities incurred.

1562 J. HEYWOOD *Prov. & Epigr.* (1867) 80 Ye loue not to bye the pyg in the poke. **1573** TUSSER *Husb.* (1878) 16. **1611** COTGR. s.v. *Sac*, To buy a Pig in a poake (say we); to bargaine vnaduisedly or hand ouer head. **1821** SOUTHEY *Lett.* (1856) III. 252. **1882** *The Garden* 7 Oct. 313/2 Timidly buying..a pig-in-a-poke cheap collection.

13. ***to buy over a person's head***: to buy for a higher price, to outbid.

1682 WHELER *Journ. Greece* II. 195 The Bishops are always buying it over one anothers Heads.

14. ***to buy a brush***: = BRUSH *v.*[1] 3. (*slang.*)

1699 B. E. *Dict. Cant. Crew, Let's buy a Brush*, let us scour off. **1725** in *New Cant. Dict.*

15. ***to buy money***: see quot. 1922. *Racing slang.*

1906 FOX-DAVIES *Dangerville Inheritance* vii. 99 The public had left off buying money, and the wagering had become slack. **1922** *N. & Q.* 12th Ser. XI. 206/2 *Buying money*, laying heavy odds on a favourite. **1928** *Daily Express* 12 July 12/2 Backers..had to buy money over On Avon and Rainbow Bridge.

16. In slang use.

a. To suffer some mishap or reverse; *spec.* to be wounded; to get killed, to die; (of an airman) to be shot down. Freq. with *it*.

1825 W. N. GLASCOCK *Naval Sketch-Bk.* (1826) I. 30 Never mind, in closing with *Crappo*, if we didn't buy it with his raking broadsides. **1920** W. NOBLE *With Bristol Fighter Squadron* v. 70 The wings and fuselage, with fifty-three bullet holes, caused us to realize on our return how near we had been to 'buying it'. **1925** FRASER & GIBBONS *Soldier & Sailor Words* 41 *To buy*, to have something not desired, such as a job, thrust on one unexpectedly, *e.g.*, 'Just as he was going out, he ran into the Corporal and bought a fatigue.'.. Another meaning: to be scored off or victimized. Of a man getting an answer to a question which made him ridiculous: 'He bought it that time.' **1943** HUNT & PRINGLE *Service Slang* 39 *He bought it*, he was shot down. **1943** C. H. WARD-JACKSON *Piece of Cake* 16 *He's bought it*, he is dead—that is, he has paid with his life. **1944** J. E. MORPURGO in *Penguin New Writing* XXII. 11 I'm afraid we want you elsewhere... Jim Barton bought it, and you'll have to take on his troop. **1953** R. LEHMANN *Echoing Grove* 261 He'd lived in London before the war, but the whole street where he'd hung out had bought it in the blitz.

b. To believe; to accept, to approve. Chiefly *U.S.*

1926 E. WALLACE *More Educ. Evans* vi. 139 'It's rather early in the day for fairy-tales,' he said, 'but I'll buy this one.' **1944** *Amer. Speech* XIX. 72/1 If the work is perfect, the inspector *buys* it... In the drilling departments, one might hear a worker say, 'I am waiting for the company to buy this hole.' **1949** *Time* 2 May 8/1 After talking it over with the President..Secretary Johnson bought the Air Force point of view. **1951** I. SHAW *Troubled Air* xiii. 213 People feel that the best way to prove how loyal they are is to be as nasty..as they know how, and I'm not buying any of that. **1952** M. MCCARTHY *Groves of Academe* (1953) ix. 182 It doesn't seem to me likely that they cooked it up between them... More likely she half guessed and he told her. I'm willing to buy that for what it's worth.

c. ***I'll buy it*** (in reply to a question or riddle): I give it up (as an invitation to reveal the answer), I don't know, I'll accept your answer.

1930 E. WALLACE *White Face* xvi. 248 'You thinking, too?' growled Mason. 'All right, I'll buy it.' **1932** D. L. SAYERS *Have his Carcase* xi. 128, I'll buy it, Inspector. *What* did he do with it? **1957** P. FRANKAU *Bridge* 136 'Confession coming,' he said. 'I'll buy it. Something that happened last night?'

buy (baɪ), *sb.* orig. *U.S.* [f. BUY *v.*] A purchase; ***best buy***, the most worth-while purchase or bargain. Also *fig.* Phr. ***on the buy***: actively buying.

1879 F. A. BUCK *Yankee Trader* (1930) 274, I believe the Mammoth Mine here to be the best buy in the lot. **1890** VAN DYKE *Millionaires of Day* 134 Biggest buy in town. **1903** *Longman's Mag.* Mar. 444 What do you think of my new buy? **1911** H. QUICK *Yellowstone N.* vii. 191, I believe it's a good buy! **1929** *Star* 21 Aug. 18/2 His clients are 'on the buy'. **1952** J. PINCKNEY *My Son & Foe* ii. 14 Knowing the intrinsic quality of the goods, what the best buys are that life puts out on the counter. **1957** *Times* 21 Oct. 13/1 Among the best 'buys' from these departments are the deceptively simple models that..bear an unmistakable *chic*. **1964** *Which?* Feb. 43/2 Because each of these prams had some drawbacks, we do not choose a Best Buy.

buy, buȝe, var. of BEY *v. Obs.*, to bend.

buyable ('baɪəb(ə)l), *a.* That can be bought.

1483 *Cath. Angl.* 31 Byabylle, *empticius*. **1837** CARLYLE *Fr. Rev.* II. I. ii. 11 The spiritual fire which is in that man ..is not buyable or saleable. **1848** *Tait's Mag.* XV. 351 Flagrantly venal—buyable, saleable, for any purpose.

† **'buyal.** *Obs. rare*[−1]. [f. BUY *v.* + -AL[2]; cf. *trial*, etc.] Act of buying, purchase.

1612 SHELTON *Quix.* III. xiii, Not the Buyal of the Horses, but that of his Delights..had moved Don Ferdinando.

buyer ('baɪə(r)). Forms: 3 beger, beggere, 3–5 biere, 3–6 bier, 4 byȝer, -ar, begger, byggere, 4–5 bigger, bugger(e, byar, 5 byare, 5–7 byer, 6 buier, 6– buyer. [f. BUY *v.* + -ER[1].]

1. a. One who buys, a purchaser.

c **1200** *Trin. Coll. Hom.* 213 þe sullere loueð his þing dere ..Ðe beger bet litel þar fore. *a* **1300** *Cursor M.* 14730 Bath best and bier vte he beft. *a* **1400** *E.E. Gilds* 359 To don trewleche þe assys to þe sellere and to þe byggere. **1480** CAXTON *Descr. Brit.* 13 The byars and sellars that ben at london. **1577** HOLINSHED *Chron.* II. 35/1 He came here as a bier, not as a beggar. **1855** MACAULAY *Hist. Eng.* (1876) III. ix. 223 A market place swarming with buyers and sellers. **1872** YEATS *Growth Comm.* 99 The towns of Lombardy were active buyers of Eastern commodities.

b. *spec.* One employed by a mercantile house to conduct the purchase of goods.

1884 *Manch. Exam.* 18 Sept. 5/3 He was a buyer under this firm. **1885** *Ibid.* 20 May 4/7 The prisoner represented himself as buyer to Messrs. Huntley and Palmer.

†**2.** = *redeemer*. *Obs.*

a **1300** *E.E. Psalter* xviii. [xix.] 15 Laverd..mi bier un-to blisse. *c* **1380** WYCLIF *Sel. Wks.* III. 12 Jesus Crist, bier of mankynde.

3. ***buyers' market***: one in which goods are plentiful and low prices favour buyers.

1926 *Textile World* 11 Dec. 91 (*heading*) Buyers' market. **1930** *Economist* 13 Dec. 1105/1 The problem..is the marketing of about 300 million bushels of Canadian grain at adequate prices in what is obviously a buyers' market. **1959** *Times Rev. Industry* Feb. 18/3 The Board now has to face heavy losses in fighting back on a buyers' market.

buying ('baɪɪŋ), *vbl. sb.* [f. BUY *v.* + -ING[1].]

1. a. The action of the verb BUY; purchase.

a **1225** *Ancr. R.* 362 Me ne mei..nout two þongede scheon habben, wiðuten buggunge. *c* **1380** WYCLIF *Wks.* (1880) 25 þei han desceyued hem in byynge of here catel. **1509–10** *Act 1 Hen. VIII*, xx. §1 That they coste at the firste byeng or achate. **1528** in Turner *Sel. Rec. Oxford* 60 Buyings and sellings by retaile. **1713** *Guardian* No. 76 ¶12 We never have so good a revenue by buying as by lending. **1816** JANE AUSTEN *Emma* II. iii. 150 Going on with their buyings.

b. *attrib.*

c **1440** *Promp. Parv.* 36 Byynge place, or place of byynge, *emptorium*. **1727** DE FOE *Eng. Tradesm.* (1841) I. viii. 58 His buying-part requires..a good judgment. **1883** *Pall Mall G.* 30 Nov. 5/2 Buying orders were received.

†**2.** *Theol.* Redemption. *Obs.*

a **1300** *E.E. Psalter* cxxix[xxx]. 7 At Laverd it es merci, Fulli bying at him. *c* **1325** *Metr. Hom.* (1862) 22 Your bi-ing ..Ful ner cumen tilward you es. *c* **1380** WYCLIF *Serm.* xxvii. Sel. Wks. I. 69 Youre bigginge is nyȝe. *c* **1410** N. LOVE *Bonaventure's Life Christ* lxii. (Gibbs MS. f. 119) He suffrede for our redempcioun and byynge.

3. The purchasing of shares on the stock exchange. ***buying-in day***, the day on which, owing to non-delivery within the appointed time of shares bought, the buyer may purchase the shares on the market; ***buying-in rule***, the rule with regard to buying-in day.

1900 *Westm. Gaz.* 24 Mar. 7/1 'Buying-in Day.'.. He immediately delivers the shares, usually on the day after the buying-in takes place. **1902** *Encycl. Brit.* XXXII. 865 The 'corner' in Northern Pacific common shares produced..the suspension for two or three weeks of the 'buying in' rule.

buyl, obs. form of BOIL *sb.*

buyld(e, obs. form of BUILD.

buy-out, buyout ('baɪaʊt). [f. vbl. phr. *to buy out*: see BUY *v.* 8.] The purchase of a controlling share in a company. ***management buy-out***: see MANAGEMENT 7.

1976 *Mergers & Acquisitions* Spring 9/2 Federal funds are another possible source of financing for employee buy-outs when conventional credit sources are unavailable. **1979** *Time* 7 May 60 At the end of 1978, Time Inc. completed a buyout of A.T.C. for a total price of $175.6 million. **1981** *Observer* 21 June 20/3 A buy-out by a management-led consortium of staff. **1982** *Economist* 17 Apr. 51/3 Buy-outs by employees of bust and heavily trade-unionised businesses. **1986** *Daily Tel.* 7 Oct. 9 (Advt.), Our commitment can perhaps best be measured by the £1 billion that represents the value of the buyouts in which we've invested.

buyrne, variant of BERNE, *Obs.*, hero, man.

buysch, buyschel, obs. ff. BUSH, BUSHEL.

† **buysine.** *Obs.* Also 4 bosyne, 5 buys(s)yne, 5–6 bussyne, 6 bussynne, busyn. [a. OF. *bosine*, *buisine* trumpet, clarion, ad. L. *buccina*.] A trumpet.

1340 *Ayenb.* 137 þe ilke orible bosyne him went to þe yeare: 'com to þine dome'. **1475** CAXTON *Jason* 29 Jason did do sowne..cornes sarasins, buysines and other instruments. **1490** —— *Eneydos* xlviii. 141 Thenne beganne the bussynes and the trompettes for to blowe. *c* **1530** LD. BERNERS *Arth. Lyt. Bryt.* (1814) 232 Than began hornes and bussynnes to blowe. *c* **1532** —— *Huon* 472 The noyse of hornes and busyns.

buyste, var. of BUIST, *Obs.*, a box.

buysy, obs. form of BUSY.

buz, var. of BUZZ in various senses.

buze (bju:z). *rare*[−0]. [a. F. *buse* of same meaning.] A wooden or leaden pipe to convey air into mines.

1823 in CRABB *Techn. Dict.* **1881** in WORCESTER.

‖**buzkashi** (bʊʃkə'ʃi:). Also **bushkashee**, **Buz(-)kashi**. [Pers., f. *buz* goat + *kašī* drawing, f. *kashīdan* to draw, extract.] An Afghan sport played by teams on horseback competing for the carcass of a goat (see quots.).

1956 D. N. WILBER *Afghanistan* xxiii. 441 *Boz Kashi* or Goat Wrestling..is described as very dangerous. A goat is beheaded and the body thrown into a ditch, from which it is to be taken to the goal by any one of several hundreds of swift-riding horsemen competing for the honor. **1959** E. HUNTER *Past Present* 111 Although *bushkashee* is referred to as Afghanistan's national game, actually it is regional, for it is not played in the south and south-west. **1962** *Listener* 15 Feb. 312/2 Buz-Kashi is a vigorous sport of the nomad horsemen of central Asia, bearing something of the relation to polo that real tennis does to lawn tennis. **1973** J. BRONOWSKI *Ascent of Man* (1976) ii. 82 There is played to this day in Afghanistan a game called Buz Kashi which comes from the kind of competitive riding that was carried on by the Mongols. **1984** *Times* 16 June 10/1 Buzkashi is a basic kind of game: between two posts set two miles apart, a dead goat is buried in the centre of a circle 10 yards across. The object is to rescue the goat, carry it round first one post and then the second, and finally to fling the carcass back into the circle.

buzz (bʌz), *sb.*[1] Also 7 buzze, 8 *Sc.* bizz, 7– buz. [f. BUZZ *v.*[1]]

1. a. A sibilant hum, such as is made by bees, flies, and other winged insects.

1645 MILTON *Colast.* Wks. (1851) 348 A Reply to the buzze of such a Drones nest. **1787** WOLCOTT (P. Pindar) *Sir T. Banks & Emp. Morocco* 20 Prodigious was the buz about his ears. **1808** ALLEN & PEPYS in *Phil. Trans.* XCVIII. 262 That buzz in the ears which is noticed in breathing nitrous oxide. **1878** GILDER *Poet & Master* 17 The honey bees Swarm by with buzz and boom.

b. *Phonetics.* A voiced hiss (see HISS *sb.* 1 b).

1877 SWEET *Handbk. Phonetics* 79 The voiced buzzes admit of more variety than the voiced stops. **1887** *Encycl. Brit.* XXII. 383 A hiss (s), followed without a positional glide by the buzz (z). **1888** SWEET *Hist. Eng. Sounds* 24 Some consonants..are pronounced with..a complete absence of buzz. **1908** —— *Sounds of English* 43 The English r is vowellike in sound, being quite free from buzz.

c. A round game in which each player in turn utters a number in numerical order, with the exception that 'buz(z)' must be substituted for 7 and multiples of 7.

1864 HOTTEN *Slang Dict.* 91 *Buz*, a well-known flash game. **1868** L. M. ALCOTT *Little Women* iii, They..were in the midst of a quiet game of 'buzz'.

d. *spec.* The buzzing sound made by a telephone. Hence *slang*, a telephone call.

1913 G. B. SHAW *Let.* 14 July (1952) 132, I rang a second time, but the answer was buzz, buzz. **1930** *Punch* 26 Feb. 236 One of the cops..directed another to beat it to his desk and give headquarters a buzz. **1938** E. BOWEN *Death of Heart* I. ii. 38 The Quaynes had a room-to-room telephone, which, instead of ringing, let out a piercing buzz. **1959** G. USHER *Death in Bag* xi. 128 Shall I give him a buzz?

2. *transf.* **a.** The confused or mingled sound made by a number of people talking or busily occupied; busy talk, 'hum'; *hence*, a condition of busy activity, stir, ferment.

1627 FELTHAM *Resolves* I. xv. Wks. (1677) 23 The frothy buzze of the world. **1629** FORD *Lover's Mel.* IV. ii. (1839) 17 The buzz of drugs, and minerals and simples. **1647** COWLEY *Mistr.* i. (1669) 22 The Crowd, and Buz, and Murmurings Of this great Hive, the City. **1678** RYMER *Trag. Last Age Consid.* 13 All the buz in Athens was now about vertue. **1712** ADDISON *Spect.* No. 403 ¶3, I found the whole..Room in a Buz of Politicks. **1760** MRS. DELANY *Autobiog.* (1861) III. 604 The buz and bustle of unpacking. **1805** SOUTHEY *Madoc in W.* viii, The clamour and the buz Ceased. **1824** CARLYLE *W. Meister* (1874) I. II. xi. 111 A buzz of joyful approbation. **1855** MACAULAY *Hist. Eng.* IV. 549 A buzz of conversation. **1875** BLACKMORE *Maid of Sk.* lvii. 388 My brain was in a buzz.

b. A feeling of excitement or euphoria, esp. one induced by a stimulant; a thrill, a 'kick'. *slang* (orig. *U.S.*).

1942 BERREY & VAN DEN BARK *Amer. Thes. Slang* §277/2 *Thrill*; '*kick*'. (As in 'get a kick out of'.)..buzz. **1952** *Amer. Speech* XXVII. 24 *Buzz*, the effect of a drug; the feeling under the influence of drug. **1962** J. BALDWIN *Another Country* I. i. 26 He felt..on top of everything, and he had a mild buzz on. **1967** M. M. GLATT et al. *Drug Scene* iii. 39 Unable to get a buzz from the drugs George began to get a kick from the acts necessary for injecting the drugs. **1976** *New Musical Express* 17 Apr. 19/6 It must be a real buzz for the musicians who're playing with Wings to be playing with an ex-Beatle. **1978** J. KRANTZ *Scruples* vi. 166 She walked up

Rodeo or down Camden, feeling a sexual buzz as she searched the windows for new merchandise. **1983** *Times* 7 Mar. 3/1 Some players get a 'buzz' from the game [of Space Invaders] and that might explain why they become addicted.

3. *fig.* **a.** A groundless fancy, whim, 'fad': (cf. BEE[1] 5.) *Obs.* **b.** A busy rumour.

1605 SHAKS. *Lear* I. iv. 348 On euerie dreame, Each buz, each fancie. **1612** CHAPMAN *Widowes T.* Wks. 1873 III. 24 'Twas but a buzz devised by him. **1639** FULLER *Holy War* II. xli. (1840) 106 This suspicion..though at first but a buzz, soon got a sting in the king's head. **1646** BUCK *Rich. III*, III. 103 Buzes and quaint devises, to amaze the people. **1656** FINETT *For. Ambass.* 13 Some new buz gotten into his Braine. **1825** COBBETT *Rur. Rides* 23 A sort of buz got about. **1892** LUGARD *Diary* 8 June (1959) III. viii. 290 Juma.. asked him if he had heard of this. He said *Yes*, but not from any responsible chief, merely a buzz through the country. **1919** 'ETIENNE' *Strange Tales fr. Fleet* 135 There's a buzz floating round that we are slipping off at 8 p.m. **1962** B. KNOX *Little Drops of Blood* iii. 62 There's a strong buzz on the go that his team are building some new engine.

4. Short for *buzz-saw*; see 5.

1823 *Mechanic's Mag.* No. 7. 108 The Shakers sometimes made use of what he called a buzz to cut iron. He made a circular plate of soft sheet-iron, and put it in his lathe, which gave it a very rapid rotary motion.

5. *Comb.*, as **buzz-bomb** *colloq.* = *flying bomb*; **buzz-box** *slang* = *buzz-wagon*; **buzz-fly**, a fly that buzzes, ? a bluebottle; **buzz-planer**, a small wood-planing machine (Knight *Dict. Mech.* Suppl. *a* 1884); **buzz-saw**, a circular saw; **buzz-wagon** *slang*, a motorcar; **buzzword** (orig. and chiefly U.S.), a keyword; a catchword or expression currently fashionable; a term used more to impress than to inform, esp. a technical or jargon term; also *buzz-phrase*.

1944 in *News Rev.* 10 May (1945) 7/1 The Germans sent over 11 pilotless planes or 'Buzz-bombs'. **1946** *Amer. Speech* XXI. 246 The V-1 was in the U.S. and British official parlance a *flying bomb*... The troops, however, generally called it a *buzz bomb*, probably because it normally came in at rather low altitude, reminiscent of an airplane buzzing the ground. **1920** 'SAPPER' *Bull-dog Drummond* x. 264 How long will it take me to get the old buzz-box to Laidley Towers? **1934** *Passing Show* 12 May 10/1 Ring up Mason's yard..and ask 'em to send round the old buzz-box. **1848** E. LEATHAM *Charmione* (1858) I. 250 A great greedy buzzfly. **1868** *Pall Mall G.* 1843/2 The only food for buzz-flies. **1977** *Canadian* 12 Nov. 19/2 For a lot of us, Affirmative Action was very much an IWY buzz-phrase like Total Fulfillment, Consciousness raising or even that tired old tease Why-Not! **1858** *Varieties* (San Francisco) 17 July 3/1 'Any taste for music?' 'Strong. Buzz and buck saws in the day time, and wolf howling and cat fighting nights.' **1886** *Sat. Rev.* 31 July 142 The characteristic and picturesque Americanism for a circular saw—'a buzz saw'. **1897** 'MARK TWAIN' *Following Equator* xxxiv. 313 Whizzing green Ballarat flies..with.. stunning buzz-saw noise. **1914** *Dial. Notes* IV. 104 *Buzz-wagon*, automobile. **1918** WODEHOUSE *Piccadilly Jim* xxi. 197 Dere's a buzz-waggon outside, waitin'. **1923** 'IAN HAY' *Lucky Number* ix. 253 Let's go to the stable and start up your little friend's buzz-wagon. **1946** *Amer. Speech* XXI. 263/1 Students at the Graduate School of Business Administration at Harvard University use a specialized vocabulary known as 'buzz words' to describe the key to any particular course or situation. **1968** *Scottish Daily Mail* 7 Aug. 6 The possibilities of a send-up were spotted by the First National City Bank of America which gives its customers what it calls the Instant Buzzword Generator. 'Technology', it says, 'has created a new type of jargon that is nearly as incomprehensible as it is sophisticated.' With the card 'you can generate an almost endless variety of intelligent-sounding technical terms'. **1980** *Time* 28 Jan. 90/1 The air is thick with devalued buzz words, including 'buzz words'.

buzz, *sb.*[2] [perh. onomatopoeic, with the general sense of 'loose down', 'flocky substance': cf. FUZZ, and BUZZY *a*[2]. In sense 1 the dialectical *buzz* may really be for *burs*: cf. the s.w. *vuzzes*, *vuzzen*, pl. of *vuzz* = *furze*, in OE. and ME. *fyrs*.]

1. The rough setose or pilose seed-vessel of a plant, a bur. 'In Suffolk the seeds of certain plants which are easily detached and stick to clothes are universally called *buzzes*; "bur" not being in popular use'. F. Hall. (So in the east and south of England generally.) In quot. 1612 it has been explained as the globular seeding head of the dandelion and similar plants.

1612 FIELD *Wom. is Weathercock* II. i. in Hazl. *Dodsley* II. 37 All your virtues Are like the buzzes growing in the fields. **1877** *Holderness Gloss.* (E.D.S.) *Buzzes*, the burrs of the teazel.

2. a. A downy land-beetle (*Rhizotrogus solstitialis* Latr.) used as bait; the artificial 'fly' made in imitation of it.

1760 *Compleat Angler*, App. 121 *Marlow Buzz*. **1799** G. SMITH *Laborat.* II. 311 Buzz-brown. Dubbing, of the light brown hair of a cur. **1851** H. NEWLAND *Erne* 205 Black and red buzzes. **1867** F. FRANCIS *Angling* (1876) 267 The best land-beetles are the..Marlow buzz, or fern-webb.

b. quasi-*adv.* With or like a 'buzz'. Also quasi-*adj.* of an artificial fly (see quot. 1877).

1867 F. FRANCIS *Angling* vi. (1880) 207 All buzz dressed flies. *Ibid.* 216 To dress the fly hackle fashion, or buzz, as it is termed. **1877** HALLOCK *Sportsman's Gazetteer* 599 A fly is said to be buz when the hackle is wrapped on thick and it looks 'bushy' as we Americans would term it. **1889** F. M. HALFORD *Dry-Fly Fishing* ix. 205 Arguments in favour of dressing spinners hackle or buzz fashion.

buzz (bʌz), *sb.*[3] Only *attrib.* [? Short f. BUSBY; or related to prec.; cf. *bush*, *fuzz*, and 'Sergeant Buzfuz' in Pickwick.]

1. Epithet of a large bushy wig. Also in comb. *buzz-wig*, a person wearing such a wig; 'a bigwig'.

1798 [see 2]. **1816** SCOTT *Antiq.* xvii, The reverend gentleman was equipped in a buzz wig. **1826** MISS MITFORD *Village* Ser. II. (1863) 357 *note*, The full swelling burly buzz wig. **1854** DE QUINCEY *Sp. Mil. Nun* Wks. III. 69 Whom the old Spanish buzwigs doated on. **1859** W. IRVING in *Life* IV. 283 Old Dr. Rodgers with his buzz wig.

2. *transf.* (See quot.)

1798 *Anti Jacobin* 22 Jan. (1852) 47 Parr's buzz prose. *Footnote*, This is an elegant metonymy..Buzz is an epithet usually applied to a large wig. It is here used for swelling, burly, bombastic writing.

buzz (bʌz), *v.*[1] Forms: 6-7 busse, buzze, 6- buz, 7- buzz, *Sc.* bizz. [From the sound.]

1. *intr.* To make the humming sibilant sound characteristic of bees and other insects; to fly *out*, *in*, etc. with such a sound.

1398 [see BUZZING *vbl. sb.*[1]] . **1530** PALSGR. 473/1 Harke how this fleshe flye busseth. **1556** J. HEYWOOD *Spider & F.* lvii. 241 As if ten milions of flies had ben buzzing. **1604** T. WRIGHT *Passions* VI. 334 Winds do buzze about it. **1613** SHAKS. *Hen. VIII*, III. ii. 55 Waspes that buz about his Nose. **1709** SWIFT *Tritical Ess.* Wks. 1755 II. I. 142 Flies..buz.. about the candle, till they burn their wings. **1790** BURNS *Tam O'Shanter*, As bees bizz out wi' angry fyke. **1820** W. IRVING *Sketch Book* II. 280 A fly cannot buzz..without startling his repose. **1833** M. SCOTT *Tom Cringle* xviii, The water was buzzing under our bows. **1879** JEFFERIES *Wild Life in S.C.* 202 If a humble-bee buzzes in at the window.

2. a. *fig.* To flutter or hover (*about*, *along*, *over* (*a*)*round*). like a buzzing insect; to move about busily.

1650 T. GOODWIN *Wks.* (1862) IV. 200 Terrors of conscience would buz about a man. **1696** *View Crt. St. Germain* in *Select. fr. Harl. Misc.* (1793) 556 The priest was always buzzing about him. **1710-11** SWIFT *Lett.* (1767) III. 81 Boys and wenches buzzing about the cake-shops like flies. **1712** ADDISON *Spect.* No. 439 ¶2 Those voluntary Informers that are buzzing about the Ears of a great Man. **1748** RICHARDSON *Clarissa* (1811) I. xvii. 122 While this man ..buzzes about you. **1923** WODEHOUSE *Inimit. Jeeves* ii. 20 Anyhow, things seemed to be buzzing along quite satisfactorily. **1924** —— *Leave it to Psmith* i. 36 Greatest mistake go buzzing about to different dentists. **1925** T. DREISER *Amer. Tragedy* (1926) II. i. 165 Too many youths and men were already buzzing around. **1959** T. S. ELIOT *Elder Statesman* I. 10 To have the waiters All buzzing round you.

b. *slang.* To go (quickly). *to buzz off*: to go off or away quickly. Also *to buzz in*: to come in (quickly), to enter.

1914 E. PUGH *Cockney at Home* 144 'Here you!' to the Cub, 'you'd better buzz off—quick!' **1925** A. HUXLEY *Those Barren Leaves* IV. v. 313 So I buzzed after you till I saw old Ernest wiv ve car. **1931** L. ROBINSON *Far-Off Hills* I, Are you buzzing too? You're very short and sweet. **1938** E. BOWEN *Death of Heart* II. iii. 232, I asked Daphne who you were the moment you buzzed in. *Ibid.* iv. 241 We may buzz back here for tea. **1948** C. DAY LEWIS *Otterbury Incident* ii. 19 We were just about to buzz, when the yard door opened.

3. a. To speak indistinctly, mutter, murmur busily. (Usually somewhat contemptuous.) *arch.*

1555 *Fardle Facions* I. vi. 93 They..sieme rather to busse or churre betwene the tiethe then to speak. **1586** FERNE *Blaz. Gentrie* 22 Bussing like a preacher. **1588** SHAKS. *Tit. A.* IV. iv. 7 How euer these disturbers of our peace Buz in the peoples eares. *c* **1645** HOWELL *Lett.* (1650) II. *The Vote*, My Muse..Did softly buz: 'Then let me somthing bring,' etc. **1886** *Tinsley's Mag.* Sept. 227 [He] sat by my side and buzzed in my ear.

b. To make the indistinct murmuring sound or 'hum' produced by a large number of people talking; to talk busily. (Also said of the place in which such talking is going on.)

1832 L. HUNT *Sir R. Esher* (1850) 98 The court buzzed like gnats in the sunshine. **1855** BROWNING *Old Pict. in Flor.*, vii, The Michaels and Rafaels, you hum and buzz Round the works of. **1879** FARRAR *St. Paul* (1883) 385 The Agora buzzed with inquiring chatter.

c. Said of the sound or words so uttered.

1848 LYTTON *Harold* III. iii, A murmur buzzed through the hall. **1879** DIXON *Windsor* II. viii. 85 A whisper buzzed about the Castle that an ugly deed was likely to be done.

4. *trans.* To tell in a low murmur or whisper, to communicate privately and busily. (Occas. with noun-sentence as obj., introduced by *that*.) *arch.*

1583 STUBBES *Anat. Abus.* (1877) 36 Having buzzed his venemous suggestions into their eares. **1609** SIR G. PAULE *Abp. Whitgift* 9 Buzzing these conceipts into the heads of diuers young preachers. **1625** FLETCHER *Noble Gent.* I. i, To undermine me And buz love into me. **1748** RICHARDSON *Clarissa* I. xxxvi. 242 My brother continually buzzing in my father's ears that my cousin would soon arrive. **1879** FARRAR *St. Paul* (1883) 278 Buzzing their envenomed slanders into the ears of these country people.

5. To spread as a rumour, with whispering or busy talk.

1616 PURCHAS *Pilgr., Descr. India* (1864) 30 Buzzing the neerenesse and Greatnesse of the Kings power. **1639** FULLER *Holy War* IV. xx. (1840) 216 A bruit constantly buzzed. **1723** STEELE *Consc. Lovers* I. i, I soon heard it buzz'd about, she was the daughter of a famous Sea-Officer. **1752** FIELDING *Amelia* II. iii, Our amour had already been buzzed all over the town. **1859** J. LANG *Wand. India* 403 It was very soon 'buzzed about' who was the artist. **1863** GEO. ELIOT *Romola* I. xvi. (1880) I. 234 Stories..beginning to be buzzed about.

6. a. To utter with buzzing; to express by buzzing.

1763 *Brit. Mag.* IV. 548 All..buz the same insipid strain. **1854** THACKERAY *Newcomes* I. 9 The professional gentlemen hummed and buzzed a sincere applause. **1855** LONGF. *Hiaw.* xvii. 8 He buzzed and muttered words of anger. **1863** MRS. OLIPHANT *Salem Ch.* 107 The deacons buzzed approbation.

b. *Phonetics.* To pronounce as or with a buzz. Cf. BUZZ *sb.*[1] 1 b.

1877 SWEET *Handbk. Phonetics* 37 (j) in N[orth] G[erman] is often distinctly buzzed. *Ibid.*, Buzzed (j) is the ordinary G. *g* in 'liegen', 'regen'.

†**7.** With person as obj.: To whisper to, suggest to, tell privately; to incite by suggestions. *Obs.*

1637 BASTWICK *Litany* II. 27 They all buzze Nobles and Princes in the eare, that, etc. **1665** *Surv. Aff. Netherl.* 162 The nicities of Priviledges and Liberty..shall buzze the people..to Mutinies. **1692** WAGSTAFFE *Vind. Carol.* xii. 83 They..buzze the people, that it was done with the Kings Privity.

8. a. To assail, din, or molest by buzzing. In extended use: to fly (an aircraft) fast and close to. Also *buzzing* vbl. sb. Also *transf.*

1679 DRYDEN *Tr. & Cr.* I. i, Having his Ears buzz'd with his noisy Fame. **1683** BARNARD *Heylin* 30 That swarm like Gnats and Flyes to buz the Head. **1884** A. A. PUTNAM 10 *Yrs. Police Judge* xiii. 155 He has..been badgered, buzzed, and besieged. **1941** *Amer. Speech* XVI. 164/1 *Buzzing a town*..in Air Corps, to fly over it. **1942** *Time* 14 Dec. 82/2 They said he could buzz the camouflage off the top of a hangar without touching it. **1948** in BERG *Dict. New Words* (1953) 49/2 Two fighters buzzed a Bristol Wayfarer. **1958** *Daily Mail* 18 July 1/4 The reported 'buzzing' of British air transports by Israeli fighters as they crossed the coast. **1959** *Times* 23 May 6/4 The commander said that the Chaplet.. circled and 'buzzed' the Odinn before hitting her in the stern. **1969** *Daily Tel.* 17 Dec. 10/6 It can be a frightening experience to be shadowed, or 'buzzed' by a heavy lorry in fog.

b. To move with buzzing; to cause to buzz.

1820 KEATS *Lamia* II. 13 Love..Hover'd and buzz'd his wings. **1865** G. MEREDITH *Farina* 74 The stranger buzzed his moustache in a pause of cool pity.

9. To telephone or signal (a call or message) by the 'buzzer'. *to buzz off*: to ring off on the telephone. Also *intr.* of a message: to come *in* by the 'buzzer'. Hence (*slang*) to telephone (a person) (cf. BUZZ *sb.*[1] 1 d).

1914 *Pears' Christmas Ann.* 20/2 Are you the *Bainbridge*? Then buzz off!.. You there—have you had a call from the *Bainbridge*? **1916** 'BOYD CABLE' *Action Front* 173 The telephonists..'buzzed' even more monotonous strings of longs and shorts on the buzzer. *Ibid.*, The messages that had just 'buzzed' in over their wires. *Ibid.* 183 It's bad enough ..to get all these messages through by voice. I haven't a dog's chance of doing it if I have to buzz each one. **1929** 'E. QUEEN' *Roman Hat Myst.* viii. 117, I wouldn't have buzzed you so early in the morning except that Ritter just phoned. **1956** R. HEINLEIN *Double Star* (1958) vi. 101 He's gone to his room. I'm buzzing him.

10. To cut (wood) with a buzz-saw. *U.S.*

1925 *British Weekly* 5 Mar. 554/5 His home-built contraption for 'buzzin'' wood.

11. To throw swiftly or forcibly. *colloq.*

1890 KIPLING *Many Invent.* (1893) 35 Dennis buzzed his carbine after him, and it caught him on the back of his head. *a* **1917** E. A. MACKINTOSH *War, the Liberator* (1918) 113 If we cannae throw a live We can aye buzz a dud. **1948** C. DAY LEWIS *Otterbury Incident* i. 10 The Prune buzzed a half-brick at Ted.

buzz (bʌz), *v.*[2] Also buzza, buz.

trans. To finish to the last drop in the bottle.

1785 GROSE *Dict. Vulgar Tong.* s.v. *Buzza*, To Buzza one, is to challenge him to pour out all the wine in the bottle into his glass, undertaking to drink it, should it prove more than the glass would hold. **1817** PEACOCK *Melincourt* II. 28 Buz the bottle..The Baronet has a most mathematical eye.. buzzed to a drop. **1848** THACKERAY *Van. Fair* xxxiv, Get some more port..whilst I buzz this bottle. **1848** *Blackw. Mag.* LXIII. 366 Buzza that jug..and touch the bell for another.

buzz, *v.*[3] *Thieves' cant.* Cf. BUZZER[2], BUZZING *vbl. sb.*[2].

1812 J. H. VAUX *Flash Dict.*, *Buz*, to buz a person is to pick his pocket.

†**buzz**, *int. Obs.* Also buz, buzze.

a. Said in the Variorum Shakspere (1803) to have been a common exclamation (of impatience or contempt) when any one was telling a well-known story; Schmidt and others say 'a sound to command silence'. **b.** Attributed to conjurors = 'hey, presto', etc.

1602 SHAKS. *Ham.* II. ii. 412 *Pol.* The Actors are come hither my Lord. *Ham.* Buzze, buzze. **1608** MIDDLETON *Mad World* v. i. 93 She was married yesterday. *Sir B.* Buz! **1610** B. JONSON *Alch.* I. ii, Cry hum, Thrise; and then buz, as often. *a* **1654** SELDEN *Table-T.*, *Witches* (Arb.) 117 If one should professe that by turning his Hat thrice, and crying Buz; he could take away a man's life. **1830** SCOTT *Demonol.* 226 Wave his hat and cry Buzz!

buzza, var. of BUZZ *v.*[2]

buzzar, obs. form of BAZAAR.

buzzard, *sb.*[1] ('bʌzəd). Forms: 3 busard, 4-6 bosarde, 5 bosard, buserde, (busherde), busserd,

5–7 bussard, 6 busarde, bussarde, (bousarde, basert), buzarde, buzzarde, 6–7 buzard, 7 busard, 7– buzzard, (*Sc.* 6 bissart, 8 bizzard, 9 buzzart, *dial.* buzzert). [a. OF. *busart* = Pr. *buzart*; cf. the synonymous Pr. *buzac*, It. *bozzago*, *-agro*, *abuzzago*, F. *buse* (16th c. in Littré). The mutual relation of these words is unknown; they are commonly assumed to be derived from L. *buteōn-em* of same meaning, but the process of formation is not evident.]

1. a. Name for the genus *Buteo* of birds of the falcon family, esp. *B. vulgaris*. Applied also, with defining words, to other birds belonging to the *Falconidæ*: as **bald buzzard**, the Osprey, *Pandion haliaëtus*; **honey buzzard**, *Pernis apivorus*; **moor buzzard**, *Circus æruginosus*.

The buzzard was an inferior kind of hawk, useless for falconry; hence app. sense 2. Cf. Fr. *buse* buzzard, also 'sot, ignorant, stupide', Boiste; 'imbecille' Littré. (The chronology appears to make it impossible to connect this sense with the next word.)

c **1300** *K. Alis.* 3049 Nultou never..No faucon mak of busard, No hardy knyght mak of coward. *c* **1400** *Rom. Rose* 4033 Man may for no dauntyng Make a sperhauke of a bosarde. **1486** *Bk. St. Albans* B ij, An hauke that is broght vp vnder a Bussard or a Puttocke. **1533** *Act 25 Hen. VIII*, xi. §6 Crowes, choughes, rauons, and bosardes. **1594** SHAKS. *Rich. III*, I. i. 133 That the Eagles should be mew'd, Whiles Kites and Buzards play at liberty. **1616** SURFL. & MARKH. *Countr. Farm* 715 The short winged hawkes are, etc...some intrude the Bauld Buzzard. *a* **1734** NORTH *Exam.* III. viii. ¶70. 638 An Historian and a Libeller are as different as Hawk and Buzzard. **1789** G. WHITE *Selborne* II. xli. (1853) 267 Kites and buzzards sail round in circles. **1839** STONEHOUSE *Axholme* 66 The moor buzzard still frequents the waste which surrounds Lindholme.

b. ***between hawk and buzzard***: (see quot. 1662).

1636 ABP. WILLIAMS *Holy Table* (1637) 226 [To] awake him thus between Hawk and Buzzard. **1662** *Janua Ling.* §146 (N.) *Between hawk and buzzard*, means between a good thing and a bad of the same kind: the hawk being the true sporting bird, the buzzard a heavy lazy fowl of the same species. **1775** N. CRESSWELL *Jrnl.* (1924) 147 We are between Hawk and Buzzard. **1832** [see HAWK sb.¹ 1 c]. **1895** E. C. BREWER *Dict. Phr. & Fable* 193 *Between hawk and buzzard*. Not quite a lady or gentleman, nor quite a servant. Applied to tutors in private houses [etc.]. **1904** *Courier-Jrnl.* (Louisville, Ky.) 12 July 4 The intelligence of the Commonwealth found itself literally between hawk and buzzard. It hovered in the balance.

2. *fig.* A worthless, stupid, or ignorant person. Often with the adj. *blind*; also used *euphem.* = BASTARD *sb.* 1 c.

1377 LANGL. *P. Pl.* B. x. 266, I rede eche a blynde bosarde do bote to hym-selue. **1401** *Pol. Poems* (1859) II. 98 Thou blundyrst As a blynde buserde. **1549** LATIMER *Serm. bef. Edw. VI* (Arb.) 36 Wo worth such counsellers, bishops, nay rather bussardes. **1571** ASCHAM *Scholem.* (Arb.) 111 Those blind bussardes, who..would neyther learne themselues, nor could teach others. **1652** GATAKER *Antinom.* 31 A company of..blind blundering bussards. *a* **1774** GOLDSM. *Nat. Hist.* (1862) II. II. v. 49 It is common to a proverb, to call one who cannot be taught, or continues obstinately ignorant, a buzzard. **1807** W. IRVING *Salmag.* (1824) 101 That unlucky passage of Shakspeare which..has..puzzled ..many a somniferous buzzard. **1822** SCOTT *Nigel* ii. **1889** BARRÈRE & LELAND *Dict. Slang*, *Buzzard* (American), an oppressive, arrogant person, jealous of rivalry, and vindictive. **1918** MULFORD *Man fr. Bar-20* viii. 77 'Pop', he said, sharply, 'who is this buzzard?' *Ibid.* xi. 108 You two buzzards are about as cheerful an' pleasant as a rattler in August. **1939** A. HUXLEY *After Many a Summer* I. v. 57 Not that he was doing anything spectacular with the old buzzard at the moment. **1960** J. WAIN *Nuncle* 163, I could never have accused the old buzzard of caring excessively for me as a person.

3. *attrib.* or as *adj.* **a.** Of a buzzard; resembling a buzzard's...

1878 TENNYSON *Q. Mary* I. iv. 29 His buzzard beak and deep-incavern'd eyes Half fright me.

b. Senseless, stupid, 'blind'.

1592 CONSTABLE *Poems* v. (1859) 34 Lowe on the ground with buzzard Cupids wings. **1649** MILTON *Eikon.* i. Wks. (1847) 280/1 A buzzard idol. **1844** CARLYLE *Misc.* (1857) IV. 314 Ignorance and buzzard stupidity.

4. *Comb.*, as ***buzzard-blind***, ***-like***, adjs.

1581 J. BELL *Haddon's Answ. Osor.* 179 Compare with this blynd Philosophy of Cicero, the Divinitie of Osorius in all respectes as bussardlyke. **1590** C. S. *Right Relig.* 9 Is anie man so buzzardlike, or so blockishly blind? **1619** FLETCHER *M. Thomas* III. i, Do not anger me, For by this hand I'le beat the buzard blind then.

ˈbuzzard, *sb.*² *dial.* [f. BUZZ *v.*¹ + -ARD.]

1. A name applied to various insects that fly by night, e.g. large moths and cockchafers. (Undoubted instances of its use in earlier times are wanting. Cf. BUZZER¹.)

[Cf. SHAKS. *Tam. Shr.* II. 209, where there is perh. a play on this sense. Also, the following among other passages: **1654** GAYTON *Fest. Notes* 188 (N.) O owle! hast thou only kept company with bats, buzzards, and beetles in this long retirement in the desert.]

1825 HOOD *Ode to Graham*, They are wise that choose the near, A few small buzzards in the ear, To organs ages hence. **1875** *Lanc. Gloss.* (E.D.S.) 64 He's olez after buzzerts and things.

2. = BUZZER¹ 3.

1878 GROSART in *H. More's Poems* Index 211/1 The steam-whistle for calling the mill-operatives to work is named 'buzzard' in Lancashire (Blackburn).

Comb. **buzzard-clock**, a cockchafer.

1864 TENNYSON *North. Farm.* 18 An' [I] 'eerd un a bummin' awaäy loike a buzzard-clock ower my yeäd. **1877** E. PEACOCK *N.-W. Lincoln. Gloss.* (E.D.S.) *Buzzard-clock*, a kind of beetle; a cockchafer.

†**ˈbuzzard**, *v. Obs.* [cf. BUZZARD *sb.*¹ 2.] ? To make a 'buzzard' of, puzzle completely, nonplus.

1624 MOUNTAGU *Immed. Addresse* 185 Baronius is plainely buzzarded in the point, and wisely concealing that which hee could not reconcile, passeth it ouer as in a dreame.

buzzardet. [f. BUZZARD¹ + -ET¹.] A hawk, resembling the buzzard, but having rather longer legs.

1784 PENNANT *Arctic Zool.* II. No. 109.

ˈbuzzardism. *nonce-word.* Conduct resembling that of the buzzard; cowardice.

1659 *Lady Alimony* v. ii. in Hazl. *Dodsley* XIV. 357 All that puisne pen-feathered aerie of buzzardism and stanielry.

†**ˈbuzzardly**, *a.* and *adv. Obs.* Also 6 **bussardly**, **buzardly**, 7 **-lie**. [f. BUZZARD¹ + -LY.] Like a buzzard; stupid(ly), senseless(ly).

1561 DAUS tr. *Bullinger on Apoc.* (1573) 132b, Which thing..the bussardly Anabaptistes will not vnderstand. **1581** J. BELL *Haddon's Answ. Osor.* 24b, So captious and bussardly a Sophister? *Ibid.* 405b, So superstitious and bussardly blinde. **1654** GATAKER *Disc. Apol.* 96 My clumsie Annotation, and buzzardlie Vindication.

buzzart, Sc. and dial. form of BUZZARD¹.

buzzed (bʌzd), *ppl. a.* [f. BUZZ *v.*¹ + -ED¹.] Uttered with a buzz; rumoured about.

1820 KEATS *St. Agnes* x, Let no buzz'd whisper tell. **1877** SWEET *Handbk. Phonetics* cix. 38 Buzzed (r) is..allied to the sibilants.

buzzer¹ (ˈbʌzə(r)). [f. BUZZ *v.*¹ + -ER¹.]

1. An insect that buzzes. Also *fig.*

1606 SYLVESTER *Du Bartas* II. III. i. (1623) 311 Swarms of busie Buzzers. **1611** COTGR., *Bourdonneur*, a hummer, a buzzer. **1834** WILSON in *Blackw. Mag.* XXXV. 1006 To keep the buzzers from settling round his eyes. **1847** *Fraser's Mag.* XXXVI. 524 Greek and Latin literature have been blown upon by the buzzers of metre.

†**2.** A private obtruder of tales. *Obs.*

1602 SHAKS. *Ham.* IV. v. 90 Her Brother..wants not Buzzers to infect his eare With pestilent Speeches of his Fathers death.

3. A steam apparatus for making a loud buzzing noise as a signal; cf. *hummer*, *hooter*.

1870 *Echo* 17 Jan., Two..steam alarm whistles or 'buzzers' were fixed on Saturday. **1872** JEANS *West. Worthies* 95 No sounds of the ponderous hammer or screeching 'buzzer' are to be heard. **1885** *Daily News* 2 Oct. 2/1.

4. a. An electric mechanism for producing an intermittent current and a buzzing sound or series of sounds; used chiefly as a call or signal. Also *attrib.*

a **1884** KNIGHT *Dict. Mech.* Suppl., *Buzzer*, a telegraphic call in which a vibrating hammer strikes a sounding piece and gives out a buzzing sound, which, in certain cases, is preferable to a bell. **1901** 'LINESMAN' *Words Eyewitness* (1902) 203 The little station, with its brave air of business, its stationmaster, and its electric 'buzzer'. **1916** 'BOYD CABLE' *Action Front* 183 He could hear the morse signals on the buzzer plain enough. *a* **1917** E. A. MACKINTOSH *War, the Liberator* (1918) 99 If..his bloody barrage-fire's Broken all your buzzer wires Don't get flurried. **1920** *Conquest* June 404/1 There is a local buzzer-circuit in the call box. **1943** HUNT & PRINGLE *Service Slang* 20 *The Buzzer*, another name for the telephone, and particularly the modern 'buzz' boxes or house-phone systems. **1968** *Globe & Mail* (Toronto) 5 Feb. 17/5 Oakland's Ted Hampson and Minnesota's Mike McMahon..scuffled after the final buzzer [in ice hockey].

fig. **1930** H. NICOLSON *Swinburne* i. 11 Although, so to speak, this obstructon exists only on one line of communication, yet it acts as a buzzer which disturbs the rest.

b. Hence (*Services' slang*), a signaller.

1915 'IAN HAY' *First Hundred Thousand* vii. 55 One of the Battalion signallers—or 'buzzers', as the vernacular has it, in imitation of the buzzing of the Morse instrument. **1917** 'TAFFRAIL' *Off Shore* 1 His friends..refer to him as 'Buzzer' ..because the instruments of which he is the custodian.. emit buzzing and humming sounds.

c. A door-bell. *colloq.* (orig. *U.S.*).

1934 R. STOUT *Fer-de-lance* xvii. 295 Fritz, the buzzer, attend the front door, please. **1959** 'J. WELCOME' *Stop at Nothing* viii. 132 The door buzzer sounded in the hall... She..pressed the button that freed the lock.

5. *Electr.* The trembler of an induction coil.

1882 W. H. PREECE in J. J. Fahie *Hist. Wireless Telegr.* (1899) 138 *Buzzers*, little instruments that make and break the current very rapidly with a buzzing sound. **1888** *Chambers's Jrnl.* 14 Jan. 25 It is called a 'buzzer'. .. It is a rapid current-breaker.

ˈbuzzer². *Thieves' cant.* [f. BUZZ *v.*³ + -ER¹.] A pickpocket. (See quot.)

1862 MAYHEW *Crim. Prisons* 46 'Buzzers' who pick gentlemen's pockets, and 'wires' who pick ladies' pockets.

buzzert, var. of BUZZARD².

buzzgloak. *Thieves' cant.* Also buzgloak. [f. BUZZ *v.*³] A pickpocket.

1812 J. H. VAUX *Flash Dict.*, *Buz-cove* or *Buz-gloak*, a pickpocket; a person who is clever at this practice, is said to be a *good buz.* **1830** LYTTON *P. Clifford* 56 He is nothing better than a buzz gloak. **1859** SALA *Tw. round Clock* 175 These copper captains and cozening bugzloaks.

buzzing (ˈbʌzɪŋ), *vbl. sb.*¹ [f. BUZZ *v.*¹ + -ING¹.] The action of the verb BUZZ.

1. A sibilant humming.

1398 TREVISA *Barth. De P.R.* XVIII. xii. (1495) 768 Tyll one bee wake them all with twyes bussyng or thryes. *c* **1540** *Pilgrym's Tale* 66 in *Thynne's Animadv.* (1865) 79, I herde a bussinge..I thought yt had beyn the dran be. **1657** S. PURCHAS *Pol. Flying Ins.* I. v. 12 Two or three loud buzzings. **1865** BLACKMORE *Maid of Sk.* xxvi. 155 He had..a kind of a buzzing in one ear. **1869** RUSKIN *Q. of Air* §35 The buzzing of the fly [is] produced..by a constant current of air through the trachea.

2. Confused or mingled utterance; busy murmuring, muttering; murmur, busy talk, rumour.

1532 MORE *Confut. Tindale* Wks. (1557) 408/2 The.. obseruaunces of the churche, which he calleth..howling, buzsing, and crying oute. **1613** SHAKS. *Hen. VIII*, II. i. 148 A buzzing of a Separation Betweene the King and Katherine. **1827** CARLYLE *Libussa, Transl.* (1874) 94 The hum of the multitude, the whispering and buzzing. **1882** H. MERIVALE *Faucit of B.* II. II. i. 151 The buzzings of the Agnostics.

ˈbuzzing, *vbl. sb.*² *Thieves' cant.* [f. BUZZ *v.*³ + -ING¹.] Pocket-picking.

1819 J. H. VAUX *Mem.* I. xii. 140, I had not been accustomed to buzzing. **1884** *Pall Mall G.* 29 Dec. 4/2 Descending somewhat in the scale of crime, we come to simple 'buzzing', or the picking of pockets.

ˈbuzzing, *ppl. a.* [f. BUZZ *v.*¹ + -ING².]

1. Making, or characterized by, a sibilant humming.

1556 J. HEYWOOD *Spider & F.* ii. 13 What is this buzzynge blumberinge trow we: thunder? **1600** *Maydes Metam.* I. in *O. Pl.* (1882) I. 113 Bees..Whose buzing musick..shall her sences greet. **1697** DRYDEN *Virg. Georg.* III. 239 A fierce loud buzzing Breez. **1727** THOMSON *Summer* 231 In a corner of the buzzing shade. **1827–8** LAMB in *Poems* (Chandos) 559. **1843** MACAULAY *Lays, Virginia* 25 Where'er ye shed the honey, the buzzing flies will crowd.

b. Said of sounds.

1635 SWAN *Spec. M.* v. §2 (1643) 117 A kind of buzzing noise. **1844** DUFTON *Deafness* 85 Pains over the forehead.. succeeded by a buzzing noise.

2. Whispering, muttering; busily talking, full of busy talk.

1577 HOLINSHED *Chron.* III. 840/1 A companie of bussing monks. **1618** *Barnevelt's Apol.* B iv, Buzzing whisperer, tell mee, etc. **1735** SOMERVILLE *Chase* II. 306 The buzzing Multitudes. **1818** BYRON *Ch. Har.* IV. cxlii, Where buzzing nations choked the ways.

Hence **ˈbuzzingly** *adv.*

1861 DICKENS *Gt. Expect.* x, The pupils..buzzingly passed a ragged book from hand to hand.

†**ˈbuzzle**, *v. Obs.* [? onomatopœic; cf. *bustle*, *puzzle*.]

1. *trans.* ? To distend, fill out. [cf. BUSTLE *sb.*²]

? *a* **1600** *Masque Twelve Months* (N.) Ile take my perche upon Some citty head-attire..(Buzzell'd with bone-lace).

2. *intr.* ? To contend; to be emulous, envious. Hence **ˈbuzzling** *ppl. a.*

a **1639** W. WHATELEY *Prototypes* I. xix. (1640) 226 Have you not these kind of vying buzling thoughts in you? **1638** N. W[HITING] *Albino & Bell.* 65 Distracted were her thoughts in silence tyde Till love and honour buzzled, then she cryde.

3. = PUZZLE. ? Hence **ˈbuzzle-ˌheaded** (but cf. BUSSLE-HEADED).

1671 J. WEBSTER *Metallogr.* xxiii. 305 They may well buzzle the brains of a person reasonably well versed in their terms. *a* **1644** QUARLES *Virg. Widow* 32 Ye..addle-pated, buzzle-headed, splatter-footed Moon-calf.

ˈbuzzman. *Thieves' cant.* [f. BUZZ *v.*³ + MAN.] A pickpocket.

1832 *Fraser's Mag.* VI. 460.

ˈbuzznack. *dial.* and ? *nautical.* ? = BUSK *v.*²

1864 ATKINSON *Whitby Gloss.* s.v., In and out, buzznacking about. **1868** RUSSELL *Adv. Dr. Brady* I. 172 Some of our cruisers from Halifax might be knocking about ..bussnacking for something or other.

buzzy (ˈbʌzɪ), *a.*¹ [f. BUZZ *sb.*¹ + -Y¹.] Full of buzzing; buzzing.

1871 G. MACDONALD *Poems for Childr.* in *Wks. Fancy & Imag.* III. 227 The buzzy bees. **1877** BLACKIE *Wise Men* 101 A buzzy army of mosquitos.

buzzy (ˈbʌzɪ), *a.*² [cf. BUZZ *sb.*², ³.] ? Rough and hairy; fuzzy.

1836 *New Month. Mag.* XLVI. 80 The long judicial cloak and buzzy wig. **1858** KINGSLEY *Chalk-Str. Stud.* Misc. (1859) I. 213 The 'buzzy' look of the fly.

B.V.D. (biːviːˈdiː). Chiefly *U.S.* Also **beeveedee**, **BVD**. [Acronym f. the initial letters of the name of its manufacturers, *B*radley, *V*oorhees & *D*ay: the widely-held belief that *B.V.D.* stood for 'babies' ventilated diapers' is mistaken.] A proprietary name for a type of lightweight, long underwear for men, popular in the first half of the twentieth century. Usu. in *pl.* Also *fig.*

1893 *Official Gaz.* (U.S. Patent Office) 6 June 1528/1 Suspenders, belts, shirts, and drawers. Lyman H. Day. New York... *B.V.D.*... Used since September 1, 1876. **1906** *Ibid.* 2 Jan. 308/2 Undershirts and underdrawers. Erlanger Bros., New York... B.V.D. **1908** *Sat. Even. Post*

4 July 1/1 All B.V.D. Garments are made of thoroughly tested woven materials selected for their *cooling* and *wearing* qualities. **1923** *Trade Marks Jrnl.* 13 June 1230 B.V.D... Shirts, Drawers for Wear, Sleeping Garments and Union Suits for Men and Women. The B.V.D. Company Incorporated..519, West Pratt Street, Baltimore.. Maryland, United States..Manufacturers. **1935** J. T. FARRELL *Judgment Day* xiv. 305 Studs entered the parlor, wearing old trousers over his B.V.D.'s. **1947** *Sooner Mag.* Nov. 14/1 The 'frosh' started a 'back to nature' movement but compromised on 'beeveedees'. **1953** R. MAIS *Hills were Joyful Together* I. x. 82 Surjue sat in his BVD's, shuffled the worn pack of playing cards. **1959** *Tamarack Rev.* XII. 22 The most brilliant lawyer and financier in Montreal getting trimmed down to his BVD's by a couple of snot-nosed kids! **1977** H. FAST *Immigrants* III. 189 His BVDs were the most ridiculous garment ever invented.

bwana ('bwɑːnə). Also **Bwana**. [Swahili.] A term of respectful address or reverence (formerly used) in East Africa, equivalent to '(the) master', 'Mr.', or 'Sir'.

1878 H. M. STANLEY *Dark Cont.* I. iii. 59 Bwana, you see these scars. *Ibid.* II. xvii. 478 It is Bwana Stanley's expedition that has returned. **1887** E. C. DAWSON *James Hannington* 212 The cries of 'Run, bwana, run!' were accentuated by a double roar. **1921** *Blackw. Mag.* Jan. 119/1 He had not been able to tell his Bwana about the bustard. **1963** *Punch* 24 July 113/1 An African moving..on to his ex-*bwana's* farm.

bwy, obs. Sc. form of BOUGH.

b'w'y, b'w'ye: see GOOD-BYE.

†**by**, *sb.*[1] *Obs.* Forms: 1- by, 4 bi, bii, bij, bie, 9 bye. [north. OE. *bý*, prob. a. ON. *bœ-r, bý-r* (Sw. and Da. *by*) habitation, village, town, f. *búa* to dwell; cf. BIG *v.* Retained in place-names, as *Whitby, Grimsby, Derby.*]

a. A place of habitation; a village or town. Also, an instance of a place-name in *-by*.

c **950** *Lindisf. Gosp.* Mark v. 3 Se ðe hus *vel* lytelo by hæfde in byrȝennum. *a* **1300** *Cursor M.* 19511 To preche he come intil a bi þat men cleped samari. *c* **1314** *Guy Warw.* (1840) 267 Balder bern was non in bi. [**1803** R. ANDERSON *Cumbrld. Ballads* xxxiii. 71 There's Oughterby and Souterby, And bys beath far and weyde.] **1884** *Pall Mall Gaz.* 20 Feb. 5/1 Dr. Taylor..had already taught us to recognize the general tokens of Scandinavian settlement in the..*bys* where they [*sc.* the pirates] made their solitary..homesteads. **1908** W. G. COLLINGWOOD *Scandinavian Brit.* 113 'Thorpes' indicating villages as opposed to 'byes' or isolated farmsteads..are found.

b. *Comb.*, as *by-mill* 'town-mill', *by-well*.

1456 in *Ripon Ch. Acts* Add 383 Juxta Byemyllne. *Note.* The village well at North Kelsey, in Lincolnshire, is still called the Bye well.

by, *sb.*[2] Forms: (6 buy), 6- by, bye. [Ellipt. use of the adj. (or adv.), when *by* is contrasted with *main*, some such word as *object, road, course, part*, etc., or *stake, throw*, being understood; the earliest quots. suggest that the subst. use had its origin in dicing phraseology. Rarely used except with prep. preceding. Often also written BYE *sb.*, q.v.]

†**1.** A secondary or subsidiary object, course, or undertaking; a side issue; something of minor importance: chiefly contrasted with *main*; whence phr. ***to bar by and main***: to prevent entirely, stop altogether. *Obs.*

1567 TURBERV. *Ovid's Epist.* 13 b, Refuseth me and all the wealth, and barres me by and maine. **1580** LYLY *Euphues* (Arb.) 430 Alwayes haue an eye to the mayne, what so ever thou art chaunced at the buy. **1598** BARCKLEY *Felic. Man* (1631) Pref., Dice players, that gaine more by the bye than by the maine. **1603** *St. Trials* (R.) You are fools, you are on the bye, Raleigh and I are on the main; we mean to take away the king and his cubs. **1610** FOLKINGHAM *Art of Survey* II. v. 55 Extend from some fewe Maine Angles Base lines for Boundaries..and from conuenient distances in the same, distantiate euery By. **1639** SIR R. BAKER in Spurgeon *Treas. Dav.* Ps. cxliii. 3 These are but the bye; the main of his aim is at the soul. *a* **1734** NORTH *Lives* II. 188 Neither was the main let fall, nor time lost, upon the by. **1791-1824** D'ISRAELI *Cur. Lit.* (1866) 433/1 This critic was right in the main, but not by the by; in the general, not in the particular.

2. Phrases with a preposition: †**a.** ***at the by*** (see quot.). ***of the by***: of secondary or subsidiary importance. *Obs.*

1611 FLORIO, *Massare*, to play or cast at the by, at hazard or gresco. *a* **1619** DANIEL *Coll. Hist. Eng.* (1626) Pref. 3 These things being but of the By. *a* **1639** W. WHATELEY *Prototypes* II. xxxiv. (1640) 159 Religion is made of the by, it serveth some other Mistresse.

b. by the by (earlier ***by a by, on*** or ***upon the by***): by a side way, on a side issue; as a matter of secondary or subsidiary importance, incidentally, casually, in passing. *Obs.* or *arch.* Also in predicative or complemental use (quasi-*adj.*): Off the main track, away from the point at issue, of secondary importance, incidental.

1615 W. HULL *Mirr. Maiestie* 98 Not intentionally, but accidentally (as we say) vpon the bye. *c* **1620** Z. BOYD *Zion's Flowers* (1855) 85 Who ever he be that in adultery, Begets a child, he stealeth by a by. **1627** HAKEWILL *Apol.* Pref. 10 It led them some other way, thwarting and upon the by, not directly. **1642** FULLER *Holy & Prof. St.* v. v. 377 They had something..in the favour of Friers, though brought in only by the by. *a* **1661** HOLYDAY *Juvenal* (1673) 149 If he be ask'd, though but by chance, and on the by. **1678** BUTLER *Hud.* III. I. 605 All he does upon the By, She is not bound to Justifie. **1740** J. CLARKE *Educ. Youth* (ed. 3) 66 Let it be done sparingly, and by the bye. **1794** G. ADAMS *Nat. & Exp. Philos.* IV. xlvi. 259 [Chemists] hunt, perhaps, after chimeras..and find something really valuable by the bye.

1621 BP. MOUNTAGU *Diatribe* 9 You are much upon the by, to bring in your Philologicall observations. **1649** CROMWELL *Lett.* 13 Aug., As for the pleasures of this life, and outward business, let that be upon the bye. **1661** J. STEPHENS *Procurations* 67 Little else than a τὸ παρεργον a work by the by. **1705** STANHOPE *Paraphr.* II. 222 They would not make Religion a thing by the by. **1831** SIR W. HAMILTON *Discuss.* (1853) 416 Tuition..lightly viewed and undertaken, as a matter of convenience, a business by the by. **1872** GEO. ELIOT *Middlem.* II. IV. 240 All these matters were by the by.

c. ***by the by*** is used parenthetically, with the omission of some phrase, such as 'it may be remarked'. So ***by the way***: see WAY.

1708 SWIFT *Bickerstaff Detect.* Wks. 1755 II. I. 164 My wife's voice, (which by the by, is pretty distinguishable). **1762** T. JEFFERSON *Corr.* Wks. 1859 I. 183 As brother Job says, (who, by-the-bye..began to whine a little under his afflictions,) 'Are not my days few?' **1847** BARHAM *Ingol. Leg.* (1877) 269 A line that's not mine but Tom Moore's, by-the-by. **1866** KINGSLEY *Herew.* i, By-the-by, Martin—any message from my lady mother?

3. ? A by-current, side current.

1877 BLACKMORE *Erema* III. liv. 229 By running the byes of the wind, and craftily hugging the corners.

See also BYE *sb.*

by (baɪ), *prep.*, *adv.* [OE. *bí* (*biȝ*) accented; *bĭ, be* unaccented, = OFris., OS., MDu., *bî, be*, (Du. *bij, be-*), OHG. *bî, bi, bi-* (MHG. *bî, be-*, Ger. *bei, be-*), Goth. *bi, bi-* 'about, by':—OTeut. **bi*, prob. cognate with L. *am-bi-* prefix, Gr. ἀμφί, prep. and prefix 'about'. (For the disappearance of *am-* in Teut., cf. OTeut. *bo-*, with L. *am-bo-*, Gr. ἀμ-φο- both.) Originally an adverbial particle of place; when prefixed to a verb it generally coalesced with the latter, and was treated as a prefix; when construed with substantives (in the dative or accusative, according as the relation was that of *being* near, or *moving* near *to*), it became, like other adverbs, a preposition. Cf. the series: 'þæt folc bí stód (bi-stód)', 'þæt folc him bí stod (him bi-stód)', 'þæt folc stód him bí', 'the folk stood by him', and the mod.English, 'to stand by, stand by him, be a bystander'.

The single form *bi* of OTeut. was subsequently, under the influence of the stress, differentiated into the strong or accented *bí, bī* (*by, bij, bei*), and the weak or stressless *bĭ*, later *bĕ*. The strong form was used for the adverb, the accented prefix of nouns, and a stressed preposition; the weak form for the stressless prefix of verbs, and a stressless preposition. The influence of levelling, however, tended at length to make *bî* (*by*, etc.) the separate form in all cases, and to leave *be-* as the weak prefix; thus, while in OE. the prep. was both *be* and *bi*, in ME. it was usually written *bi, by*, and modern Eng. makes the preposition, like the adverb, *by*, in all positions and senses, and has *be-* only as a stressless prefix. The same is true of mod.Ger. *bei, be-*, and Du. *bij, be-*. But in pronunciation there was a weak and a strong form in ME. (cf. forms like *be-sides, be-times, bum troth, bum Lady, byrlady*), as is still usual in the dialects. In modern Sc. *bĕ* is the ordinary form of the preposition unaccented, or in a weakened sense, as in 'sit be the fire', 'written be a clerk', 'ane be ane', *by* the form of the adverb and strong preposition, as in 'stand by', 'to pass *by* a place *be* the railway'. This use of *be* as preposition has been uniform in the northern dialect since the earliest preserved ME. specimens.]

A. *prep.* Forms: 1-2 be, 1-5 bi, 1 bi (biȝ), 3- by, (4 bie, 5 bye, *north.* 3- be). (Formerly often placed after the governed word, which may still be done in verse).

General scheme of signification. I. Of position in space: (1) Position or action near, including notions of comparison by juxtaposition; (2) Direction and vague localization. II. Of motion in space: (1) Motion alongside, along, or over a course; (2) Motion up to; (3) Motion alongside and beyond, including notions of distance to reach, and of excess, short-coming, or inferiority. III. Of time. IV. Of mental or ideal proximity. V. Of medium, means, instrumentality, agency. VI. Of circumstance, condition, manner, cause. VII. In phrases.

I. Of position in space.

* *Of position or action near or adjacent to.*

1. a. At the side or edge of; in the vicinity of; near, close to, beside.

898 *O.E. Chron.* an. 894 §2 On Defna scire be þære norþ sæ. **971** *Blickl. Hom.* 15 þa sæt þær sum blind þearfa be ðon weȝe. *c* **1000** *Whale* (poem) 18 Ceolas stondað bi staðe fæste. **1160** *Hatton G.* Matt. xiii. 40 Hyo..sæten be þam strande. *c* **1200** ORMIN 3340 þat engel..stod hemm bi. *c* **1330** *Assump. Virg.* 368 To kepe þee & by þee by [?be thee by, *or* by thee be]. **1375** BARBOUR *Bruce* VI. 667 The Kyng lukyt hym by. *c* **1400** *Destr. Troy* 11569 To be..laid by hir legis, þat the lond aght. *c* **1485** *Digby Myst.* (1882) IV. 658 Com sit me bye. **1513** DOUGLAS *Æneis* IX. ix. 138 Hys scheild syne by hym lais. **1682** WHELER *Journ. Greece* I. 4 Hard by this Island..is Ruigna. **1764** REID *Inquiry* ii. § 10. 174 The clock may strike by us without being heard. **1832** W. IRVING *Alhambra* II. 125 A sword by his side. **1860** DICKENS *Uncomm. Trav.* xx, Down by the Docks they 'board seamen' at the eating houses. **1881** SAINTSBURY *Dryden* 179 In Poets' Corner, where he has been buried by Chaucer and Cowley.

b. In names of places, introducing the name of a place better known, or of a natural feature, which serves as a distinction, as in *Bromley-by-Bow, Stoke-by-Nayland, St. Stephen's-by-Saltash, Stanton-by-Bridge, St. Leonard's-by-Sea.* Also in postal addresses of subordinate offices, where *by* introduces the name of the chief office, as *Coniston by Ambleside*, and the like.

c. after such verbs as *abide, stick, stand*, q.v.

1508 FISHER *Wks.* I. 221 His commaundement must nedes be..abyden by. **1736** CIBBER *School-Boy* II. i, You'll stand by me upon Occasion. **1742** H. WALPOLE *Corr.* (1857) I. 193 They have given Mrs. Pulteney an admirable name and one that will stick by her. **1818** MOORE *Fudge Fam. Paris* vi. 4 We Fudges stand by one another. **1865** CARLYLE *Fredk. Gt.* (1873) V. 271 Let us stick by our excerpting. **1885** SIR W. BRETT in *Law Rep.* 15 *Queen's B. Div.* 189 He was willing to abide by the event of such a trial.

†**d.** ***by the sight of, by view of***: under the supervision of. *Obs.*

a **1500** tr. *Magna Charta* in Arnolde *Chron.* (1811) 217 Be the sight of holy church, his goodis shalbe destribute. **1601** F. TATE *Househ. Ord. Edw. II*, §15. 13 Serve the house-hold bi view of the same clark.

2. a. In forms of swearing or adjuration.

Here *bi* is the original prep. in Teutonic (Goth., OHG., OS.), and must have had a local sense, 'in presence of', or perhaps 'in touch of' some sacred object: in ON. where *bi* was entirely lost, *at* appears, and must have been local. But in OE. literature the prep. was ordinarily *þurh*, perhaps after L. *per*; though *be* occurs in one place in the Rushw. Gloss. and may represent native usage. It is thus not certain how far the ME. use of *by* was native, or how far it was a translation of F. *par*, of instrumentality. To modern apprehension there is apparently no notion of place, but one approaching that of instrumentality or medium. See SWEAR. Cf. BEFORE 6.

c **975** *Rushw. Gl.* Matt. xxiii. 22 Seþe sweraþ be heofune swerat be sedle godes, and in ðæm seþe siteþ on him. *c* **1205** LAY. 3447 Heo swor..bi al heuenliche main. *a* **1300** *Cursor M.* 7934 Bi godd o-liue he suor his ath. *c* **1435** *Torr. Portugal* 52 Tho he sware be hevyn kyng, Ther wase told hym a wondyr thyng. **1586** WARNER *Alb. Eng.* I. ii. 5 Sworne-by Stix and wreakfull Mars at periuries repine. **1611** BIBLE *Matt.* v. 36 Neither shalt thou sweare by thy head. **1751** JORTIN *Serm.* (1771) V. iii. 56 They took up a custom of swearing not by the Lord, but by other things. **1875** JOWETT *Plato* (ed. 2) I. 354 And I swear to you Athenians, by the dog I swear! **1884** *St. James's Gaz.* 20 June 6/1 The farmers.. swear 'by'r Leddie' and 'by Jings'.

b. So in ellipt. phrases, ***by God, by our Lady, by my life***, etc., without mention of the verb *swear*.

1297 R. GLOUC. 25 þou ne schalt (bi hym þat made me) of scapie so lyȝte. *a* **1300** *Cursor M.* 13593 'A prophet,' said he, 'be mi lai.' *a* **1330** *Otuel* 476 Bisengeme [= By Saint James] ihc habbe i-fouȝt Otuwel. **1393** LANGL. *P. Pl.* C. IV. 285 By Cryst, at my knowynge, Mede ys worthy, me þynkeþ, þe maistrye to haue. *c* **1440** *Generydes* 2445, I take hir for my owen, sir, be the rode. **1519** *Interl. Elem.* in Hazl. *Dodsley* I. 33 Of all meats in the world that be, By this light, I love best drink. **1653** URQUHART *Rabelais* I. xlii, By's death, I would plume them. **1672** DAVENANT *Siege* (1673) 69 By this Light, you eat nimbly. **1841-4** EMERSON *Ess., Poet* Wks. (Bohn) I. 170 By God, it is in me, and must go forth of me. **1875** JOWETT *Plato* (ed. 2) I. 33 By the dog of Egypt, I said, there I agree with you.

3. a. In the presence of (*obs.*); at the house of (*obs.*); beside, with, in possession of, about (a person).

a **1300** *Fragm. Pop. Sc.* (Wright) 134 Whan a man is an urthe ded, and his soule bi God. **1509** HAWES *Past. Pleas.* XII. ii, Accordynge as by hym is audyence. **1535** COVERDALE *Acts* ix. 43 He taried..at Joppa by one Simon which was a tanner. **1541** BARNES *Wks.* (1573) 347/2 We haue an aduocate by the father, Christ Iesus. **1661** BOYLE *Scep. Chem.* I. (1680) 73 What I have yet lying by me of that anomalous Salt. **1712** HENLEY *Spect.* No. 396 ¶1, I have kept it [a letter] by me some Months. **1800** COLERIDGE *Wallenst.* I. viii. 17 This plot he has long had in writing by him From the emperor.

†**b.** In the writings of, in (a specified passage).

c **1460** *Towneley Myst.* 145 (Mätz.) We rede thus by I say. **1579** TOMSON *Calvin's Serm. Tim.* 15/2 S. Paules mind is by this place, that no man take vppon him to teach otherwise then he taught.

†**c.** With, having about one. *Obs.*

a **1225** *Ancren R.* 420 3if ȝe muwen beon wimpel-leas, beoð bi warme keppen.

4. a. ***by oneself*** (***himself, themselves***, etc.): in one's own company, to the exclusion of any one else; *hence*, apart from others, without companion; alone, singly, in isolation.

c **1200** ORMIN 821 Sone summ he cuþe ben Himm ane bi himm selfenn. **1297** R. GLOUC. 104 þo heo were al bi hem selue.. He slow þe kyng. *a* **1300** *Cursor M.* 12834 He fand his cosin Ion, In wildernes bi him allan. *c* **1440** *Promp. Parv.* 35 By thy selfe, *seorsum*. **1559** BP. COX in Strype *Ann. Ref.* I. vi. 99 Weigh this matter by your self. **1611** SHAKS. *Cymb.* III. i. 13 Britaine's a world By it selfe. **1711** ADDISON *Spect.* No. 26 ⁋1, I very often walk by myself in Westminster Abbey. **1712** STEELE *ibid.* No. 302 ⁋11 My husband and I were sitting all alone by our selves. **1813** JANE AUSTEN *Pride & Prej.* (1846) 301 We may as well leave them by themselves. **1884** G. DENMAN *Law Reports*, 29 *Chanc. Div.* 467 Look at each statement by itself without regard to the other statements.

b. This blends with other senses (esp. 33) in ***by oneself***: by one's own power, without assistance, independently; of one's own motion or authority, spontaneously.

a **1000** *Ags. Gosp.* John vii. 17 Hwæðer þe ic be me sylfum spece. **1393** LANGL. *P. Pl.* C. xx. 140 The paume.. haþ power by hym-self, Oþer-wise þan þe wrythen fust. *c* **1400** MAUNDEV. 194 ȝif thei abyden to dyen be hem self, as nature wolde. *c* **1450** *Merlin* i. 14 Tyll she be stronge to goo by her-self. **1711** *Lond. Gaz.* No. 4794/2 The Battalions.. charg'd by their own selves. **1744** BERKELEY *Siris* §233 Going like a clock or a machine by itself.

5. By the side of; *hence*, in addition to, beside. ***by and beside***: over and above. *Sc.* or *north.* Cf. FORBYE.

1330 R. BRUNNE *Chron.* 149 We þre haf.. þe schippes of Kyng Richard to keep & ȝow þam bie. *c* **1425** WYNTOUN *Cron.* IX. xxvii. 331 By his awyn war Baneris five Dysplayt. **1535** STEWART *Cron. Scot.* III. 230 Nocht be the clething on oure bak. **1600** J. MELVILL *Diary* (1842) 146 By and besyde the inward hand of my God, I haid twa utward speciall comforts. **1722** DE FOE *Col. Jack* (1840) 95 We will have a lift, if we don't get the horse by the bargain. **1816** SCOTT *Antiq.* xxi, 'Few folks ken o' this place.. there's just twa living by mysell.'

†**6. a.** In comparison with, in proportion to (*i.e.* placed beside, for the sake of comparison or correlation); after verbs of *distinguishing* = from. *Obs.* exc. *Sc.*

1340 *Ayenb.* 249 Amang þe bestes man heþ þane leste mouþ be þe bodie. **1393** LANGL. *P. Pl.* C. XVIII. 104 Noþer þei knoweþ ne conneþ o cours by a-noþer. *c* **1489** CAXTON *Sonnes of Aymon* ix. 224 The four sones of Aymon were good to knowe by thother. *c* **1515** *Elegy on Henry VIII's Fool* in Halliw. *Nugæ P.* 45 Many folys by the thynke themselfe none. **1578** in *Scot. Poems 16th C.* II. 126, I gaif thee ressoun, quhereby thou might Haue knawin the day by the dark night. **1729** *Let.* in *Wodrow Corr.* (1843) III. 448 Twenty-six years ago.. we were in a pleasant situation.. by what we are at present. **1768** GOLDSM. *Good-n. Man* I, Compare that part of life which is to come by that which we have passed. *Mod. Sc.* So dark that one could not tell a house by a hay-stack.

b. ***to set*** or ***let*** (obs.) ***little, nought,*** etc. ***by***: to put little, nothing, etc. in comparison with; to value, esteem little, etc.; also absol. ***to set by*** (obs.): to esteem highly. See SET and LET.

1362 LANGL. *P. Pl.* A. XI. 29 Luytel is he loued or leten bi. **1393** *Ibid.* C. VI. 3 Cloþed as a lollere, And lytel y-lete by. *c* **1382** WYCLIF *Isa.* liii. 3 Wherfore ne wee setteden by hym. *c* **1400** MAUNDEV. xxvii. 272 Thei sette not.. by Caw-teles. **1407** *Songs Costume* (1849) 57 Ye be so lewyd your selfe there setteth no man you bye. *c* **1430** *How Wise man tauȝt Son* 126 in *Babees Bk.* (1868) 52 Bi oþir richesse sette no greet price. *c* **1440** *York Myst.* xxxi. 105 Sette I noght be hym. **1549** *Psalm* xv. 4 (Prayer Bk.) He that setteth not by himself, but is lowly in his own eyes. **1637** BASTWICK *Litany* III. 13 That booke was highly set by and commended. **1729** BUTLER *Serm.* 540 In all lowliness of mind we set lightly by ourselves. **1839** KEIGHTLEY *Hist. Eng.* I. 102. He also set by the hares, and they must go free.

7. More than, beyond, in preference to. †***by and beside***; outside of, without. ***by common, by ordinary*** (used adjectively): unusual, extraordinary. All *Sc.*

1567 *Test. H. Stewart* in *Scot. Poems 16th C.* II. 257 Lancit with luif, sho luid me by all wycht. **1603** *Philotus* cx, Our Parents hes opprest, And by all dew thair Dochters drest. *a* **1657** SIR J. BALFOUR *Ann. Scotl.* (1824–5) II. 182 The motione.. is made by and besyde the knouledge and conscience of the kirke of this land. **1822** GALT *Entail* II. ii. 13 He's mair than weel enough. He's by common. **1824** SCOTT *Redgaunt.* let. xi, There was something in it by ordinar. **1832–53** *Whistle-Binkie* (Sc. Songs) Ser. II. 27 He courts a' the lasses.. Yet for nane by anither cares bauld braxy Tam. **1851** MRS. OLIPHANT *Marg. Maitland* i, My father was a man of bye-ordinary mildness.

†**8. a.** Beyond (= L. *præter*); *hence*, contrary to, (a limiting decree or authority); in spite of, against. *Obs.* exc. *Sc.*

1460–70 *Compl. Abbot of Arbroath* in C. Innes *E. Scot. Hist.* App. (1861) 506 [He] has gart eyre and saw owr said landis by all resoun or apperans of ony clame thartyll. **1513** DOUGLAS *Æneis* VII. x. 109 The hevynnis hie To wytnes drew he, all was by his wyll. **1650** ROW *Hist. Kirk* (1842) 366 By the expectation of many.. the Parliament did ryde and end upon Fryday. **1668** PEPYS *Diary* 24 Feb., I could not deny him, but was forced, by myself, to give. *Mod.Sc.* That's by belief.

†**b.** Apart from, away from. ***by oneself***: beside oneself, out of one's wits. *Sc.*

1600 *Gowrie's Conspir.* in *Harl. Misc.* (Malh.) II. 339 The young gentleman.. was become somewhat by himselfe, which his Maiestie conjectured.. by his.. vncouth stairing. **1785** BURNS *Halloween* xvi, He monie a day was by himsel, He was sae sairly frighted. **1832** *Blackw. Mag.* XXXII. 644 Surely we're by ourselves, to speak this open blasphemy.

** *Of direction or vague localization.*

9. a. In the region or general direction of, towards. ***by the head*** (Naut.): deeper in the water forward than abaft; the opposite of which is ***by the stern***. ***by the board***: see BOARD *sb.* 12. ***by the wind***: (see quot. 1867).

(Hence in many adverbs and prepositions; as *be-east, be-fore, be-half, be-hind, be-low, be-north, be-side, be-south, be-west*; †*be-mong*, etc.)

c **893** K. ÆLFRED *Oros.* I. i. §7 Caucasus se beorȝ is be norþan and Indus seo ea be westan, and seo Reade Sæ be suþan. *a* **1225** *Leg. Kath.* 591 þe alre wiseste þe wuneð bi westen. *c* **1340** *Cursor M.* 12131 (Trin.) Who herde euer suche ferly Of any mon bi norþ or souþ. **1393** LANGL. *P. Pl.* C. II. 117 Hit is sykerer by southe þer þe sonne regneth þan in þe north. **1556** J. HEYWOOD *Spider & F.* lx. 101 One sort by east, an other by west, did rise. **1627** CAPT. SMITH *Seaman's Gram.* ix. (1692) 43 Lay the Ship by the Lee to trie the Dep-sea Line. **1628** DIGBY *Voy. Medit.* (1868) 46 In smooth water, and by a wind, was her best way. **1664** BUSHNELL *Shipwright* 7 The most Ships saile by the Sterne. **1849** *Blackw. Mag.* LXVI. 196 She's too much by the head. **1867** SMYTH *Sailor's Word-bk.*, *By the wind* is when a ship sails as nearly to the direction of the wind as possible.

b. *spec.* used in the names of the sixteen smallest points of the compass, viz. North by East, North-east by North, North-east by East, East by North, etc., indicating one point towards the east, west, north, or south of N., NE., E., SE., S. SW., W., NW. respectively.

The point midway between N. and E. is NE.; that midway between N. and NE. is NNE.: the intermediate point between N. and NNE. is N. by E., that between NE. and NNE. is NE. by N.

1682 WHELER *Journ. Greece* VI. 481, I observed Corinth to lie South-East by South off us. **1719** DE FOE *Crusoe* (1840) I. ii. 26, I.. steered directly south and by east. **1837** *Fraser's Mag.* XVI. 48 We steered S.E. by E. **1849** *Ibid.* XL. 666 Cape Trafalgar bore east by south.

†**c.** In compound preps. of direction, as ***by-hither*** on this side of, ***by west*** to the west of, etc.; which are also used substantively. *Obs.* More commonly BE-EAST, BE-NORTH, BEHITHER, etc., q.v.

c **893** K. ÆLFRED *Oros.* I. i. §6 Be norþam þæm porte. *c* **1420** *Avow. Arth.* xlvii, He.. was comun fro bi-southe. **1577** HOLINSHED *Chron.* III. 961/2 The whole armie was landed two miles by west the towne of Lith. **1612** DAVIES *Why Ireland, &c.* (1787) 177 They dwelt by west the law, which dwelt beyond the river of the Barrow. **1614** RALEIGH *Hist. World* v. ii. §8. 354 Like as they called Cisalpines, or bi-hither the Alpes, those who dwelt between them and the Mountaines. **1716** *Let.* in *Wodrow Corr.* (1843) II. 119 The places in Fife, by-east Dunfermline.

†**10.** On (vaguely and indefinitely), in the region or domain of. *Obs.* exc. in phr. ***by land***, etc. Cf. 11 c.

c **1205** LAY. 10511 þa vt-laȝes beoð swa stronge bi watere & bi londe. *c* **1314** *Guy Warw.* (A.) 830 Who so winneþ þe turnament al Bi aiþer half, þe priis haue schal. *c* **1325** *Coer de L.* 1849 By the water-half ye them assail, And we will by land saunsfayl. **1578** LYTE *Dodoens* III. lxv. 407 The whiche leaves are playne by one side. **1770** LANGHORNE *Plutarch* (1879) I. 241/2 They commonly commanded both by sea and land. **1866** KINGSLEY *Herew.* i, I never saw one yet, by flood or field.

II. Of motion.

* *Of motion alongside, along, or over a course.*

11. a. Alongside of, along, down over, up over.

(In *by a way, path, road*, this touches the sense of *means.*)

c **888** K. ÆLFRED *Boeth.* xl. §5 ȝif ic þe læde be þam weȝe. *c* **1175** *Lamb. Hom.* 79 þer com a prost bi þe weie. *a* **1250** *Owl & Night.* 506 þe heisugge þat flihþ bi grunde a mong þe stubbe. *c* **1300** *K. Alis.* 1767 Hom heo wendith by doune and dale. *a* **1300** *Cursor M.* 14285 þe teres bi þair chekes þon ran. **1486** *Bk. St. Albans* D j b, And comyth low bi the grounde. **1534** LD. BERNERS *Gold. Bk. M. Aurel.* (1546) C. iij, To goo by the stretes as vacabundes. **1682** WHELER *Journ. Greece* I. 47 It fell to the Hollanders share to come by our Lee. **1712** PARNELL *Spect.* No. 460 ⁋6 The way by which we ascended. **1816** J. WILSON *City of Plague* I. i. 187 Moving by the river side, Came on a ghost. **1885** *Act* 48 & 49 *Vic.* liv. §14 The churches.. are within four miles of one another by the nearest road.

¶**b.** *By* is sometimes elliptically omitted.

1768 WESLEY *Jrnl.* 23 Sept., Nor could I get to my lodgings the foot way. *Mod.* We came back the same way. You went a roundabout way to get there.

c. blended with some sense of means of transit; cf. 30 b.

c **1205** LAY. 31195 Comen.. bi sæ & bi londe feole cunne leoden. **1382** WYCLIF *Acts* xx. 13 Makinge journey bi lond. *c* **1450** *Merlin* iii. 41 The shippes comynge by the see. **1630** M. GODWYN *Bp. Hereford's Ann. Eng.* 82 Hee went by water to Greenwich. **1712** BUDGELL *Spect.* No. 425 ⁋1 You descend at first by twelve Stone Steps. **1851** KINGSLEY *Yeast* 216 Why not send a parcel by rail?

12. a. In passing along: said of incidents happening on a journey, etc.; chiefly in phr. ***by the way***.

c **1000** ÆLFRIC *Gen.* xlv. 24 Ne forlæte ȝe nan þing be weȝe. *c* **1340** *Cursor M.* 18378 (Trin.) Amen alleluya songen þei And honoured him euer bi þe wey. **1526** *Pilgr. Perf.* (W. de W. 1531) 5 b, But the sayd rychesse holpe them well by the waye. **1530** TINDALE *Exp.* (1849) 330 If a woman should find a man-child by the streets. **1611** SHAKS. *Wint. T.* IV. iii. 253, I was cozen'd by the way, and lost all my money. **1760** GOLDSM. *Cit. World* xcix, They always grow young by the way. *Mod.* And by the way I dropped it.

b. Hence fig. ***by the way, by the by***: (*a*) in passing, incidentally, as a chance idea in speech or writing; (*b*) *ellipt.*, omitting words like 'it may be remarked'. See BY *sb.*², WAY.

(*a*) **1548** LATIMER *Serm. Ploughers* (Arb.) 21 Here haue I an occasion by the way somwhat to say vnto you. **1642** FULLER *Holy & Prof. St.* v. 377 They had something.. in the favour of Friers, though brought in only by the by. **1677** MOXON *Mech. Exerc.* (1703) 202 And by the way you may take notice, that, etc. **1830** *Blackw. Mag.* XXVIII. 247 All this is by the way. **1832** J. C. HARE *Philol. Museum* I. 254 This question.. merely came in by the by.

(*b*) **1574** tr. *Marlorat's Apocalyps* 41 By the waye, thys place teacheth vs, that, etc. **1631** GOUGE *God's Arrows* IV. xv. 396 Here by the way, the Providence of God.. is remarkable. **1711** STEELE *Spect.* No. 32 ⁋3 One of the Seniors (whom by the by Mr. President had taken all this Pains to bring over) sat still. **1818** BYRON *Juan* I. lvi, Her blood was not all Spanish, by the by. **1882** *Knowledge* No. 39. 144 Artificial irrigation, which, by-the-way, is now being extensively developed in Australia, etc.

†**13.** Through the extent of, throughout. *Obs.*

a **1225** *St. Marher.* 9 þe fuheles þe fleon bi ðe lufte. *c* **1380** WYCLIF *Wks.* (1880) 41 Hou freris schullen go bi þe world. **1502** tr. *Magna Charta* in Arnolde *Chron.* (1811) 220 To.. dwell & goo bi England. **1647** W. BROWNE *Polex.* P ij a, By the whole extent of her Territories.

14. Through, or so as to pass (in one's course); also expanded into ***by way of***.

c **1340** *Cursor M.* 11529 (Fairf.) An angill come & hem forbad To wend by hym [Herod] eny way. **1382** WYCLIF *John* x. 1 He that cometh not in by the dore. *c* **1400** *Epiph.* (Turnb. 1843) 108 They returned by Jerusalem. *c* **1485** *Digby Myst.* (1882) I. 37 The thre kynges.. promysed kyng herowde.. To come a-geyn by him. **1553** EDEN *Treat. New Ind.* (Arb.) 8 The passage.. by the strayghtes of Magellanus. **1625** K. LONG *Barclay's Argenis* IV. ix. 270 Faithful Sicambes was conveyed in by a backe chamber. **1633** FEATLEY in P. Fletcher *Purple Isl.* Introd., The Way to God is by ourselves. **1719** DE FOE *Crusoe* (1848) 357 The place was inaccessible, except by such windings, &c., as they themselves only who made them could find. **1885** SIR J. HANNEN in *Law Rep.* 15 *Queen's B. Div.* 140 Leaving the building by a side door.

1701 W. WOTTON *Hist. Rome* 481 He went by the way of Illyricum. **1865** *Cornh. Mag.* XI. 595 It invaded France by way of Avignon.

** *Of motion into a position beside, or within reach.*

15. Near to, close up, into the presence of: chiefly in ***to come by***, for the phraseological and fig. uses of which see COME *v.*

c **1175** *Lamb. Hom.* 83 He [Christ] com bi þis forwundede mon. **1330** R. BRUNNE *Chron.* 296 Alle þat he mot com bie, he robbed. *c* **1350** *Will. Palerne* 220 By-þan he com by þat barn. **1535** COVERDALE *Tobit* iv. 20 Seke some meanes, how thou mayest come by him. **1607** SHAKS. *Cor.* II. iii. 46 We are not to stay altogether, but to come by him where he stands. *Mod.* Come close by me, and tell me what is the matter.

*** *Of motion alongside and beyond.*

16. a. On alongside of, into the vicinity of and on beyond, past. Originally the *nearness in passing* was emphasized; in later use 'by' is more frequently distinguished from 'through' or other word, and expresses *passing without stopping or contact*, and thus *avoidance, aloofness*; but often the notion is merely that of getting beyond, or to the other side of, and *pass by, go by* merely = *pass*.

c **1380** *Sir. Ferumb.* 1108 By hilles & roches swyþe horrible on hur cors þay wente. **1393** GOWER *Conf.* I. 227 To hem that passen all day by me. **1509** HAWES *Examp. Virtue* vi. 78 That came vs by and very nere, Ascendynge vp into her hyghe sete. **1632** RUTHERFORD *Lett.* xxiii. (1862) I. 91 Your jealous Husband will not be content that ye look by Him to another. **1660** PEPYS *Diary* 2 Nov., I.. got as far as Ludgate by all the bonfires. **1732** BERKELEY *Alciphr.* v. §1 We saw a fox run by the foot of our mount. **1786** BURNS *Twa Dogs* 92 They gang as saucy by poor folk, As I wad by a stinking brock. **1820** KEATS *Lamia* 315 She saw him as once she pass'd him by.

b. The notion of avoidance, disregard, omission, neglect, is especially present in fig. uses of GO BY, PASS BY and the like: see the verbs. Cf. 8.

c **1385** CHAUCER *Man of Law's T.* 1026 But I lete all his storie passen by. **1535** STEWART *Cron Scot.* II 639 Foull appetyte.. causis thame oft till go by the rycht. **1552** ABP. HAMILTON *Catech.* (1884) 31 Cursit ar thai quhilk gangis by the commandis of God. **1667** PEPYS *Diary* (1877) V. 470 The king hath.. passed by the thing and pardoned it already. **1673** MARVELL *Reh. Transp.* II. 346, I am content to go by the loss. **1869** J. MARTINEAU *Ess.* II. 76 Instances may be accumulated.. which legislation passes by in silence.

c. So in ***to put*** or ***set*** (anyone) ***by*** (an aim, purpose, duty, etc.): to cause him to miss or omit it; to deprive, disappoint, or cheat of, do out of. *arch.* and *dial.*

1580 NORTH *Plutarch* 798 The King.. did put Tiribazus by his Wife. **1596** SPENSER *Astroph. Elegy* 174 Perhaps this may a suter be, To set Mars by his deitie. **1643** PRYNNE *Power Parl.* I. (ed. 2) 53 Maude the Empresse.. was put by the Crowne by the Prelates and Barons. **1647** W. BROWNE *Polexander* II. 329 We met with a storme, which put us by our course. **1726** AMHERST *Terræ Fil.* xliii. 236 He can put him by his degree for a whole year. **1768** JOHNSON *Lett.* I. xiv. 17, I have been oddly put by my purpose. *Mod. dial.* The child has been put by his sleep.

d. *dial.* transferred to the idea of time.

1863 ATKINSON *Danby Provinc.*, *By the time*, beyond or past the time. They're a lang way by their tahm.

17. Defining the space passed over, or to be passed over, in order to reach a point: At, to, or within the distance of.

c **1230** *Hali Meid.* 23 Loke.. bi hu moni degrez ha falleð duneward. **1393** LANGL. *P. Pl.* C. xx. 58 Wolde nat neyhle him by nyne londes lengthe. *c* **1489** CAXTON *Sonnes of Aymon* 227 There is nother castell nor towne by xx myles nyghe aboute it. **1551** R. ROBINSON tr. *More's Utop.* (Arb.)

77 By all that space..the water ebbeth and floweth. **1682** WHELER *Journ. Greece* IV. 291 No Ship..can come near them by four or five Miles. **1880** MCCARTHY *Own Times* III. xlv. 386 The Conservative miss by a foot was as good..as a miss by a mile.

18. Expressing, as the result of comparison, the amount of excess or increase, inferiority or diminution, in length, duration, weight, or quantity: **a.** definitely.

c **1200** *Trin. Coll. Hom.* 169 þe þridde biwist..was bi twifold more þane þe forme. **1375** BARBOUR *Bruce* II. 230 Thar fayis war may then thai Be xv. c. **1556** J. HEYWOOD *Spider & F.* lx. 38, I thought him to young to haue winges, by a yeare. **1585** JAS. I. *Ess. Poesie* (Arb.) 61 Gif ȝe place thame in the begynning of a lyne, they are shorter be a fute, nor they are, gif ȝe place thame hinmest in the lyne. **1614** B. JONSON *Barth. Fair* I. i, He is taller than either of you by the head. **1753** CHAMBERS *Cycl. Supp.* s.v. *Account*, Balance of an Account is the sum by which the debt exceeds the credit, or vice versa. **1777** SHERIDAN *Sch. Scand.* IV. iii, He is too moral by half. **1815** *Scribbleomania* 261 Selwyn..missed it only by seven votes out of 7000. **1884** *Manch. Exam.* 21 May 4/7 The M.C.C. winning by an innings and four runs.

b. in phrases ***by far, by much, by so much***, etc.

c **1230** *Hali Meid.* 23 Bi hu muchel þe an passeð þe oðre. *c* **1375** WYCLIF *Antecrist* (Todd) 117 By hou myche þei shul be more merueilous to men, bi so myche þe hooli men..shulen be dispised. **1393** LANGL. *P. Pl.* C. XXIII. 314 More of fisik by fer. **1423** JAS. I. *Kingis Q.* cxxxi, The werk that first is foundit sure..langere sall endure Be monyfald. **1450** MYRC 1629 A-bregge hys penaunce þen by myche. **1595** BARNFIELD *Poems* (Arb.) 43 By how much the lesse I am able to expresse it, by so much the more it is infinite. **1677** MOXON *Mech. Exerc.* (1703) 35 By so much as Brass is a weaker Mettal than Iron. **1808** SCOTT *Marmion* V. xii, 'Twere better by far To have matched our fair cousin with young Lochinvar.

III. Of time.

†**19. a.** In the course of, at, in, on (the time or date of an action or event). *Obs.* exc. as in b.

a **1000** *Laws of Eadgar* I. 4 (Mätz.) Sy ælc heorðpening agyfen be Petres mæssedæg. *c* **1200** *Trin. Coll. Hom.* 47 Swich þeu wes bi þan dagen. *c* **1300** *Beket* 2494 This was bi a Tywesdai. *c* **1380** WYCLIF *De Eccles.* Sel. Wks. III. 350 Crist techiþ..þat men shulden snybbe her briþeren bi þre tymes. **1393** LANGL. *P. Pl.* C. II. 102 Dauid by hus daies dobbede knyȝtes. **1488** CAXTON *Chast. Goddes Chyldr.* 42 Men haue dwellid stably in wyldernesse by hemselfe by olde tyme. **1543** LD. BERNERS *Gold. Bk. M. Aurel.* (1546) F vij, His sonnes in lawe, that he hadde chose by his lifetyme. *a* **1687** H. MORE in R. Ward *Life* (1710) 352, I wish you would resolve to see Cambridge once by the year at least. **1797** *Philanthrope* No. 23. 177 Where he used to wander many a morning by sun-rise, and many an evening by moonlight.

b. esp. ***by day*** (L. *interdiu*), ***by night*** (L. *noctu*). Here the statement of time approaches very nearly to the indication of the physical conditions, as in 'by day-light': see 34.

OE. used in this sense the adverbial genitive *dæȝes and nihtes*, or *on* with the dative *on dæȝ(e) and on niht(e)*; the early ME. examples show a mixture of these and the modern form with *by*.

c **1200** ORMIN 11332 Heold Crist hiss fasste..Bi daȝhess & bi nahhtess. *a* **1250** *Owl & Night.* 241 Bi daie þu art stareblind. *c* **1380** *Sir Ferumb.* 4265 þe Ameral be-segeþ hymen þer-yn..Be niȝtes & be daye. *c* **1440** *Partonope* 1632 He come to Pountyff by the day. **1697** DRYDEN *Virg. Georg.* III. 405 Alone, by Night, his watery way he took. **1855** MACAULAY *Hist. Eng.* III. 232 The breaches made by day were repaired by night with indefatigable activity.

†**20.** During, for (a space of time). *Obs.* exc. in arch. ***by the space of.*** (Now expressed by *for*.)

c **1460** *Towneley Myst.* 274 (Mätz.) He ded shuld be, And ly in erthe by dayes thre. **1503-4** *Act 19 Hen. VII*, xxxvi. Preamb., [He] lay both at Surgery and fesyk..by the space of ij yeres and more. **1509** HAWES *Past. Pleas.* I viii, Thus stode I musynge myselfe all alone By right long tyme. **1611** BIBLE *Acts* xx. 31. By the space of three yeeres, I ceased not to warne euery one. **1623-4** *Act 21 Jas. I*, xx. § 1 The Offender..shall..be set in the Stocks by three whole Hours. **1841** G. S. FABER *Provinc. Lett.* (1844) I. 221 Wholly given to..idolatry by the space of above eight hundred years.

21. a. Marking the completion of the time required or assigned for the performance of an action: On or before, not later than; †within (a space of time). Cf. BETIMES.

c **1350** *Will. Palerne* 2683 But hire fader com bi þe fourteniȝtes hende. *c* **1380** WYCLIF *Sel. Wks.* III. 346 He bryngiþ in newe [servants] þat done werse bi litil tyme. *c* **1500** *Lancelot* 30 Be the morow set I was a-fyre. **1616** W. FORDE *Serm.* 25 Learne by time how to die. **1682** WHELER *Journ. Greece* I. 24 We parted and came by noon to Lesina. **1712** STEELE *Spect.* No. 503 ¶2 By this time the best of the Congregation was at the Church-door. **1768** STERNE *Sent. Journ.* (1778) II. 32 Ready at the door of the hotel by nine in the morning. **1867** FREEMAN *Norm. Conq.* (1876) I. v. 349 By midwinter they came back to their ships.

b. Hence, with omission of sb.: ***by this, by that***; also ***by now, by then***, etc.

a **1300** *Cursor M.* 3007 Bi þis come sarra to þe tide O birth sco moght not ouerbide. *Ibid.* 2827 (Trin.) Bi þenne bigan þe liȝt of day. ? *a* **1400** *Morte Arth.* (1847) 19 By that was Launcelot hole and fere. *c* **1500** *Lancelot* 774 Be this the word wes to king arthur gone. *c* **1565** R. LINDESAY (Pitscottie) *Chron. Scot.* (1728) 62 There are other ambassadors..directed by-now from the pope. **1671** MILTON *Samson* 262 Had Judah that day joined..They had by this possessed the towers of Gath. **1795** SOUTHEY *Joan of Arc* I. cxxxii, By this Dunois Had arm'd. **1864** ATKINSON *Whitby Gloss.* s.v., They must have sailed by now.

c. In the conjunctive phrase ***by the time (that)***; also formerly, ***by then (that), by that.***

a **1300** *Floriz & Bl.* 151 Biþat hit was middai hiȝ Floriz was þe brigge niȝ. *a* **1300** *Cursor M.* 2839 Bi þe time þat þe sune ras, Strang cri in þa tounes was. ? *a* **1400** *Morte Arth.* (1847) 99 By than that endyd was the fight, The fals were feld. *c* **1435** *Torr. Portugal* 19 Be tyme he was xviij yer old, Of deddes of armys he wase bold. **1470-85** MALORY *Arthur* I. x, By than they were redy on horsbak there were vii C knyghtes. **1523** LD. BERNERS *Froiss.* I. xlvi. 64 By yᵗ it was day in the mornyng, they were before Courtray. **1575-85** ABP. SANDYS *Serm.* (1841) 300 They cannot tell what is said: it is forgotten by that it is spoken. **1684** BUNYAN *Pilgr.* II. 82 By that these Pilgrims had been at this place a week, Mercy had a Visitor. **1701** W. WOTTON *Hist. Rome* 356 By that time he had overtaken the poor flying Emperor, he was almost equal to him. **1854** THOREAU *Walden* iv. (1886) 111 By the time the villagers had broken their fast. **1868** MORRIS *Jason* III. 503 Now was it eve by then that Orpheus came Into the hall.

†**d.** whence *by* as quasi-*conj.* in same sense: By the time that, when, after. *Obs.* exc. *Sc.*

1297 R. GLOUC. 369 Be hii aryse..Wolues dede hii nymeþ vorþ. *a* **1440** *Sir Degrev.* 961 That lady was glad By sche that chartur had rad. *c* **1565** LINDESAY (Pitscottie) *Chron.* 31 (JAM.) By thir words were said, his men were so enraged. *c* **1644** *MS. Hist. Somerville Family*, Be this execution was done, the prince returned from the persuite. **1724** RAMSAY *Tea-t. Misc.* (1733) I. 103 By you've drunk a dozen bumpers, Bacchus will begin to prove..Drinking better is than love. *Mod.Sc.* It was done be (or bӯ) we came home.

IV. Of mental or ideal proximity. (*fig.* from I. 1.)

* *Of accordance to a model, rule, or standard.*

22. In imitation of, after; with verbs of *calling* or *naming*. Cf. 29.

c **893** K. ÆLFRED *Oros.* III. ix. § 14 Oþer [byriȝ] wæs hatenu be his horse Bucefal, oþer Nicea. *a* **1593** MARLOWE *Dido* V. i, Let it be term'd Aenea, by your name. *Serg.* Rather Ascania, by your little son. **1682** WHELER *Journ. Greece* I. 24 The Town is called by the name of the Isle.

23. According to, in accordance with, in conformity or harmony with: **a.** a command, law, rule, will, or any standard of action. So in phrases ***by book***, †***by course*** (= in turn), ***by heart, by rote***, †***by row*** (= in order). (See the sbs.)

a **1000** *O.E. Chron.* (Laud MS.) an. 634 Se Birinus com þider be Honorius wordum. *c* **1000** ÆLFRIC *Gen.* xxiv. 10 Ferde to þam lande be his hlafordes hæse. *c* **1175** *Lamb. Hom.* 97 Todelende u wilchen bi þan þet him iwurð. *a* **1300** *Cursor M.* 13052 þi broþer wijf þat þou agh not to haf be lau. *Ibid.* 9589 Mercy þou owest to haue be riȝt. **1463** *Bury Wills* (1850) 16, I will that they be revardyd..by the discrecion of my executours. **1556** *Chron. Gr. Friars* (1852) 11 To be songe solemply be note. **1663** BUTLER *Hud.* I. i. 86 And tell what Rules he did it by. **1712** ADDISON *Spect.* No. 409 ¶7 In examining Æneas his Voyage by the Map. **1848** MACAULAY *Hist. Eng.* II. 665 The right by which freeholders chose knights of the shire. **1859** F. GRIFFITHS *Artil. Man.* (1862) 14 By the left.—Quick march. By the right.—Quick march. **1866** KINGSLEY *Herew.* v. 109 They had timed their journey by the tides. **1884** W. C. SMITH *Kildrostan* 46 We judge a stranger by our home-bred ways. **1470-85** MALORY *Arthur* (1816) I. 52 The barons..assayed all by row, but none might speed. **1551-6** R. ROBINSON tr. *More's Utop.* (Arb.) 93 The women of euery family by course haue the office..of cookerie. **1552** HULOET By herte, *memoriter*. *c* **1579** G. HARVEY in *Athenæum* 789/1 His œconomicks..every on hath by rote. **1709** ADD. & STEELE *Tatler* No. 93 ¶4, I am therefore obliged to learn by book. *a* **1834** COLERIDGE *Table T.* (1874) 91 In Germany, the hymns are known by heart by every peasant.

b. *ellipt.* with persons: According to the words or instructions of (*obs.*); *now* only in ***take example, pattern,*** or ***warning by***, i.e. by the case of.

c **1300** *K. Alis.* 3089 No doth nought by Dalmadas. *c* **1550** *Scot. Poems 16th C.* II. 133 Euer liue in charity Be Christ Iesu. **1643** *Parables on Times* 12, I will take warning by the Eagle. **1866** KINGSLEY *Herew.* iv. (1877) 96 Take example by Alcinous. **1882** *Athenæum* 18 Mar. 339 He has taken pattern by Goethe.

c. in ***by your leave, by consent***, etc.

c **1250** *Gen. & Ex.* 2865 God..of israel, ðe bode sente ..ðat bi ði leve, hise folc vt-fare. *c* **1386** CHAUCER *Reeve's Prol.* 62 By youre leue I shal him quite anoon. **1470** HARDING *Chron.* xxvii. iii, His heire to been by their bothes assent. **1558** Q. ELIZ. in Strype *Ann. Ref.* I. App. i, Elizabeth, by the grace of God, queen of England, Fraunce and Ireland. **1593** HOOKER *Eccl. Pol.* Pref. vi. §2 Given by authority. **1754** RICHARDSON *Grandison* (1811) IV. iii. 22 By the doctor's allowance, I enclose it to you. **1848** MACAULAY *Hist. Eng.* I. 153 The old civil polity was, therefore, by the general consent of both the great parties, re-established.

†**d.** ***by so, by so that***: if only, provided that.

1393 LANGL. *P. Pl.* C. V. 98 So alle myne claymes ben quyt by so þe kynge asente. *Ibid.* XVII. 209 By so þat no man were a-greued. *Ibid.* XXIII. 221 Ich counte conscience no more by so ich cacche seluer.

e. = 'Judging by or from', 'judged by'.

1597 SHAKS. *2 Hen. VI*, IV. i. 21 By the ground they hide, I iudge their number..thirtie thousand. **1768** ELIZ. CARTER *Lett.* (1809) III. 164 By what I have heard of his character, I fear it affords no very comfortable prospects for our poor Princess. **1879** L. STEPHEN *Hours in Libr.* III. vii. 294 He [Macaulay] ought, by all his intellectual sympathies, to be a utilitarian.

24. According to: **a.** estimation or measurement of any kind. Whence the phrases ***by the great*** (obs.) = ***by wholesale, by piecemeal(s, by retail***, etc.

c **1000** ÆLFRIC *Lev.* xxvi. 26 And ȝe etaþ hlaf be ȝewihte. *c* **1205** LAY. 27607 Fif hundred bi tale fusden to-somne. *c* **1400** *Destr. Troy* 1291 Seuyn thousand be sowme all of sure knightes. **1609** BIBLE (Douay) *Lament.* iii. 16 And he hath broken my teeth by number. **1611** BIBLE *Josh.* iii. 4 A space..about two thousand cubites by measure. **1682** WHELER *Journ. Greece* II. 203 They sell it by weight. **1697** DRYDEN *Virg. Georg.* IV. 212 For ev'ry Bloom..An Autumn Apple was by tale restor'd. **1886** *Law Times* LXXX. 166/2 A miner..paid by piecework.

1598 W. PHILIPS *Linschoten's Trav. Ind.* (1864) 189 By means of their Brokers they buy by the great, and sell them againe by the piece. **1691** *Reply Vind. Disc. Unreasonableness of New Separ.* 14, I have Englished your Latin by Piecemeal. **1748** ANSON *Voy.* III viii. (ed. 4) 485 The Carpenters went on board to agree for all the work by the great. **1842** *Blackw. Mag.* LII. 279 The..people are 'perishing by wholesale'.

b. a definite standard or unit of measurement.

1494 *Act 1. 1 Hen. VII*, xxiii, No such Merchant..should put any Herring to Sale by Barrel, Demy-Barrel, or Firkin. **1600** O.E. *Repl. Libel* I. viii. 210 The rest ate bread by the ounce, and drunke water by the quart. **1728** YOUNG *Love Fame* II. 64 'Tis hard That Science should be purchased by the yard. **1885** *Manch. Exam.* 2 May 6/2 Roses..may be gathered by the basketful.

c. *distributively*, For each, for every, a; see A *adj.*² 4. (Cf. *per cent., per annum, per pound*; F. *par jour*, etc.)

a **1300** *Cursor M.* 8833 To wijt hu þat it [be tre] gru be yere. **1495** HEN. VII. in Ellis *Orig. Lett.* I. 11 I. 21 For..an archer or bille on horsback viij*d.* by the day. **1570** ASCHAM *Scholem.* (Arb.) 38 A stipend of 200 crounes by yeare. **1647** *Husbandman's Plea agst. Tithes* 35 Arable land at 6*s.* 8*d.* by the Acre. **1781** *Phil. Trans.* LXXI. 305 The common price ..is just two shillings by the pound. **1797** *Philanthrope* No. 4. 22 He..had now several thousands by year. **1815** *Scribbleomania* 30 A public accustomed to quartos of original poetry by the month.

25. Succession of numerical groups or quantities, *later* of individuals, of the same class is indicated by *by*: **a.** followed by the sb. of quantity repeated with *and* between, as ***by two and two, by little and little.*** *arch.*

c **1205** LAY. 16128 Heo droȝen ut of þan wuden bi sixti & bi sixti. *c* **1300** *K. Alis.* 548 By threo, by foure, with his taile, To the ground he smot. **1413** LYDG. *Pylgr. Sowle* III. viii. (1483) 55 They..bounden them to geders by ten and by twelue. **1483** *Cath. Angl.* 31/2 By lytylle and lytylle, *sensim, paulatim.* **1556** J. HEYWOOD *Spider & F.* lxix. 2 Streight these twelue a rose By foure, four, and foure. **1593** SHAKS. *Rich. II*, III. ii. 198, I play the Torturer by small and small To lengthen out the worst. **1682** WHELER *Journ. Greece* IV. 321 Which, by little and little, enlargeth it self. **1710** STEELE *Tatler* No. 225 ¶2 A Set of Wags..appear generally by Two and Two. **1820** KEATS *St. Agnes* xli, By one and one the bolts full easy slide.

b. followed by the sb. of quantity in *pl.*, as ***by hundreds, by inches, by files, by degrees***; also ***by times, by turns*** (obs.), = 'time after time, turn after turn'.

a **1300** *Cursor M.* 4710 Togider þei flocked in þat lond Bi hundrides & bi þousond. **1535** COVERDALE *Habak.* i. 8 Their horsmen come by greate heapes from farre. **1578** LYTE *Dodoens* IV. lviii. 519 The roote is..full of joyntes by spaces. **1593** HOOKER *Eccl. Pol.* I. vi. §1 They grow by degrees. **1607** SHAKS. *Cor.* II. iii. 47 We are..to come..by ones, by twoes, & by threes. **1635** QUARLES *Embl.* I. (1818) 42 One..rends hair by handfuls. **1645** *City Alarum* 11 We do worse then stand still, in doing things by halves. **1686** GOAD *Celest. Bodies* II. iii. 191 To win our Ground by Inches. **1704** POPE *Spring* 41 Then sing by turns, by turns the Muses sing. **1728** —— *Dunciad* III. 89 The North by myriads pours her mighty sons. **1817** J. GILCHRIST *Intell. Patrimony* 71 Raving, perchance, by times, concerning religion and morality. **1843** BARHAM *Ingol. Leg., Nurse's Story*, Hand in hand The murderers stand, By one, by two, by three. **1869** FREEMAN *Norm. Conq.* (1876) III. xii. 146 By twenties, by hundreds, by thousands, the force gathered.

c. preceded and followed by the sb. or word of quantity, as ***man by man, little by little.***

c **1392** CHAUCER *Compl. Venus* 81 To folowe word by word the Curiosite of Graunson. **1393** LANGL. *P. Pl.* C. XIII. 11 And praye for þe, pol by pol, yf þow be pecunyous. *c* **1449** PECOCK *Repr.* II. iiij. 144 Ouer long to be rehercid word bi word here. *c* **1500** *Cocke Lorelles B.* (1843) 8, I wyll..reken them one by one. **1630** WADSWORTH *Sp. Pilgr.* iii. 15 They go downe two by two. **1709** *Tatler* No. 42 ¶14 Draw out Company by Company, and Troop by Troop. **1812** KEATS *Lamia* 663 A deadly silence step by step increased. **1830** TENNYSON *Poems* 66 The thick snow falls on her flake by flake.

d. To this may perhaps be referred the arithmetical phrases, ***to multiply, divide by*** (although *by* is now associated with the agent or factor); also the ellipt. *by* = 'multiplied by' in measurements of surface or content.

c **1391** CHAUCER *Astrol.* II. §41 a, Multiplie þat be 12. *Ibid.* §42 b, ȝif þou deuide 144 be 3. **1581** STYWARD *Mart. Discip.* I. 23 Then deuide the product by 1000. **1614** T. BEDWELL *Nat. Geom. Numbers* iv. 65, I square the quotient 2, that is, I multiply it by it selfe. **1753** CHAMBERS *Cycl. Supp.* s.v. *Multiplication*, It is easy to conceive a quantity of any kind multiplied by a number. **1859** BARN. SMITH *Arith. & Algebra* (ed. 6) 194 The former of these quantities is to be divided by the latter.

1731 SWIFT *Corr.* II. 690 Adjoining the kitchen may be made one room of 18 feet by 18. **1771** GOLDSM. *Haunch of Ven.* 68 A chair-lumber'd closet, just twelve feet by nine. **1865** *Cornh. Mag.* XI. 60 An open water sixteen miles long by three broad.

** *Of relation to an object about which physical or mental activity is engaged.*

26. About, concerning, with respect to, in regard to, as concerns: **a.** after verbs of action, as *do, act, deal.* Phr. ***do as you would be done by***: see DO *v.* 37.

c **1175** *Lamb. Hom.* 51 Þenne do we bi ure sunne al swa me deað bi þe deade. *a* **1225** *Ancr. R.* 122 Þauh me dude so bi þe, me dude þe eorðe riht. *c* **1380** *Sir Ferumb.* 5855 Doþ now syre by thys man As it is þy wille. **1579** SPENSER *Sheph. Cal.* May 171 Such faitors..Will doe as did the Foxe by the Kidde. **1621** BURTON *Anat. Mel.* II. i. I. i, As the Spanish Marques is said to have done by one of his slaves. **1769**

GOLDSM. *Roman Hist.* (1786) I. 332 He murdered Hiempsal .. and attempted the same by Adherbal. **1812** JANE AUSTEN *Mansf. Pk.* v, He will consider it a right thing by Mrs. Grant, as well as by Fanny. **1869** MRS. NORTON *Old Sir Douglas* xxx. 178 That Kenneth should do his duty by his mother. **1872** YEATS *Growth Comm.* 32 Neither side acting unfairly by the other.

b. after neuter impersonal verbs, as *be*, *fall*, *fare*: With. *Obs.* or *dial.*

a **1250** *Owl & Night.* 1373 Al swa hit is bi mine songe. *c* **1280** *Commandm.* 31 in *E.E.P.* (1862) 16 Hit falliþ bi children þat beþ quede, as fariþ bi been in hiue. **1393** LANGL. *P. Pl.* C. XXI. 236 So shal hit fare by þis folke. **1523** LD. BERNERS *Froiss.* I. ccccxi. 717 Bycause they rode forth lyke foles, so it came by them.

†**c.** after verbs of thinking, saying, etc.: About, of. *Obs.*

a **1000** *Elene* 562 Witȝan sungon .. be godes bearne. *a* **1121** *O.E. Chron.* (Laud MS.) an. 1036 Sume men sædon be Harolde þæt he wære Cnute sunu cynges. *c* **1175** *Lamb. Hom.* 7 þis he witeȝede bi drihtene þurh þene halie gast. *a* **1250** *Owl & Night.* 46 Hu thincthe nu bi mine songe? *c* **1320** *Cast. Loue* 495 Be vs foure þis I telle. *c* **1460** *Towneley Myst.* 188 How thynk the, sir Pilate, Bi this brodelle. **1556** J. HEYWOOD *Spider & F.* xliv. 9 What dishonestie know you by flies, sur? More then flies know by spiders. **1601** SHAKS. *All's Well* v. III. 237 By him and by this woman heere, what know you? **1645** T. HILL *Olive Branch* (1648) 12 God knows more good and evil by us, then we know by our selves. **1752** FIELDING *Amelia* VIII. ii, I always love to speak by people as I find.

†**d.** with pejorative force: Against. *Obs.* exc. *dial.*

c **1300** *Beket* 871 Bi the Bischop of Londone thulke word he sede. *c* **1530** LD. BERNERS *Arth. Lyt. Bryt.* 23 Arthur wolde fayne fynde some cause by her. **1611** BIBLE *1 Cor.* iv. 4, I know nothing by myself [*Revised* against]. **1678** *Yng. Man's Call.* 351 He never knew any thing by her to be worthy of the least suspicion. **1879** MISS JACKSON *Shropsh. Wd.-bk.* (E.D.S.), 'E's a tidy mon, leastways I know nuthin' by 'im.

*** *Of relation to a circumstance.*

27. With respect to, in the matter of, as concerns (name, trade, age; also birth, blood, nature, etc., in which there is prob. some notion of instrumentality also).

c **1380** *Sir Ferumb.* 1131 A knyȝt of fraunce, Be name ne know y noȝt wat he was. **1606** G. W[OODCOCKE] *Justine* 96 By age but a boy. **1622–62** HEYLIN *Cosmogr.* III. (1673) 58/1 The People .. were by composition of a middle stature. **1711** ADDISON *Spect.* No. 47 ¶7 A Neighbour of mine, who is a Haberdasher by Trade. **1712** *Ibid.* No. 69 ¶2 A Merchant .. who just knows me by sight. **1848** MACAULAY *Hist. Eng.* I. 529 Allowed to associate .. with him as with a brother by blood. **1864** *Cornh. Mag.* X. 175 Frenchmen by blood as well as by birth and estate.

V. Of medium, means, instrumentality, agency. (A *fig.* development of the notion of *way* in II. 11.)

28. a. Indicating the part which serves as the medium of application or direct point and means whereby an action is applied to the whole.

a **1000** *Beowulf* 3298 þa wæs be feaxe on flet boren Grendles heafod. *c* **1000** ÆLFRIC *Gen.* xxxix. 12 Heo teh hine be his claþum. *a* **1154** *O.E. Chron.* an. 1137 Me henged up bi the fet. **1393** LANGL. *P. Pl.* C. IV. 10 Corteisliche þe clerk þenne .. Toke mede by þe myddel. **1526** *Pilgr. Perf.* (W. de W. 1531) 272 b, An hande sent downe toke me by the heer of my heed. **1547** BOORDE *Introd. Knowl.* 131 Pediculus other whyle do byte me by the backe. **1667** PEPYS *Diary* 13 July, I did give her a pull by the nose, and some ill words. **1711** ADDISON *Spect.* No. 12 ¶2 Her little boy offers to pull me by the coat. **1798** GOUV. MORRIS in Sparks *Life & Writ.* (1832) III. 109 The new peace hangs by a very slender thread. **1830** TENNYSON *Ode to Mem.* 30 Thou leddest by the hand thine infant Hope.

b. *by the roots*; *by the ground*: (? orig. = from the foundation), completely.

c **1420** *Pallad. on Husb.* I. 1132 Floure of lyme in oil, yf thou confounde And helde it in, upheleth it by grounde. **1713** BERKELEY *Hylas & P.* ii, If I were to .. tear up a tree by the roots. **1833** HT. MARTINEAU *Briery Creek* ii. 26 They could pull up a tall tree by the roots.

c. *to set by the ears*: to set quarrelling. *to be, fall, go by the ears* (Sc. *lugs*): to quarrel.

1556 J. HEYWOOD *Spider & F.* lvi. 18, I thought they wold all haue gone by thears theare. **1600** O. E. *Repl. Libel* I. i. 32 We must needes fall by the eares together. **1650** A. B. *Mutat. Polemo* 8 Set the Cavaleer and Presbyter together by the ears. **1702** DE FOE *Ref. Manners* I. 306 To set the Town together by the Ears. **1822** SCOTT *Nigel* x, The King, and the Prince, and the Duke have been by the lugs about ye.

29. a. After verbs of *knowing*, *perceiving*, *calling*, etc.; introducing that which serves as a sign or means of identification. Also with omission of the verb. Phr. *by the name of*: see NAME *sb.* 13.

c **1000** *Ags. Gosp.* Matt. vii. 20 Be hyra wæstmum ȝe hiȝ oncnawað. *c* **1200** ORMIN 479 þatt ta bi name nemmnedd wass Abyuþþ. **1393** LANGL. *P. Pl.* C. XVIII. 98 Shephurdes by the seuen sterres Wisten .. whenne hit shoude reynen. *a* **1400** *Cov. Myst.* 297 (Mätz.) Be thi face wel we may the ken. **1562** J. HEYWOOD *Prov. & Epigr.* (1867) 202, I here by the hounds, the hare is a foote. **1596** SPENSER *F.Q.* VI. iii. 1 The gentle minde by gentle deeds is knowne. **1611** BIBLE *Luke* i. 61 There is none of thy kinred that is called by this name. **1682** WHELER *Journ. Greece* v. 341 The Athenians .. would never more have any Governour by the Name or Title of King. **1796** GOUV. MORRIS in Sparks *Life & Writ.* (1832) III. 98 That anarchy which goes by the name of the German Empire. **1867** FREEMAN *Norm. Conq.* (1876) I. App. 692 Cnut was baptized by the name of Lambert. **1869** J. T. COLERIDGE *Mem. Keble* 217 Dialogues, in which a mason by that name [*sc.* Richard Nelson] bears a principal part.

b. In *to understand by*, *mean by*: see these verbs.

1382 WYCLIF *Prol. Bible* xiv. 54 Bi Salamon here is vndirstonden God himself. **1692** BP. ELY *Answ. Touchstone* 49 He .. by the way understands that narrow way which he taught.

30. a. Introducing the means or instrumentality: = by means of. (OE. more usually employed *fram*, *thurh*, *of*). (The material instrument or tool is usually introduced by *with*: 'to cut with a knife'.)

a **1000** *Scopes Widsið* 100 Ic be songe secȝan sceolde. *c* **1205** LAY. 28337 Ich wuste bi mine sweuene whæt sorȝen me weoren ȝeneðe. *c* **1300** *K. Alis.* 2941 That Y have by lettre yow saide. *c* **1340** *Cursor M.* 15986 (Trin.) He shal neuer rise aȝeyn truly bi no myȝt. *c* **1380** WYCLIF *Sel. Wks.* III. 302 þes feyned religious .. amortisen many grete lordischipis bi fals title. *c* **1450** *Merlin* x. 156 Thei remounted Gifflet be fyn force a-monge his enmyes. **1548** LATIMER *Serm. Ploughers* (Arb.) 34 Christe .. draweth soules unto hym by his bloudy sacrifice. **1548** UDALL, etc. *Erasm. Par., Mark* i. 14 The firste teachyng by mouthe of Christes religion. **1573** G. HARVEY *Letter-bk.* (1884) 13 Nether to be allurid by prommissis nor persuadid bi wurds. **1628** EARLE *Microcosm.* iii. (Arb.) 4 Hee instructs men to dye by his example. **1769** GOLDSM. *Roman Hist.* (1786) II. 475 He .. at last died either by poison or madness. **1855** KINGSLEY *Glaucus* (1878) 167 The bird's foot star .. you may see crawling by its thousand sucking feet. **1866** —— *Herew.* Prel. 6 Trying to expiate by justice and mercy the dark deeds of his bloodstained youth.

b. In *by coach*, *by ship*, *by rail*, the idea of motion blends with that of means; cf. 11 c.

c **1440** *Partonope* 383 Be shipp come merchandyse to the town. **1535** COVERDALE *Deut.* ii. 28 Onely let me go thorow by fote. **1866** *Cornh. Mag.* XIII. 348 To go by coach in that direction is a sort of tempting of fortune.

c. *by no ways* (obs.), *by no means*: in no possible way, in no respect, in no degree. *by all means*: in every way possible. (These have gradually come to be used as strong expressions respectively of negation and affirmation.)

c **1340** *Cursor M.* 12908 (Fairf.) þat is na ferly be na wayes. *c* **1430** *Freemasonry* 626 ȝef thou wolt not thyselve pray, Latte non other mon by no way. *c* **1489** CAXTON *Sonnes of Aymon* 235 By no wyse we maye not scape. **1593** HOOKER *Eccl. Pol.* Pref. ii. §7 To argue and by all means to reason for it. **1713** *Guardian* No. 140 (1756) II. 224, I can by no means consent to spoil the skin of my pretty country-women. **1768** GRAY in *Corr. w. Nicholls* (1843) 85, I would wish by all means to oblige and serve Temple. **1813** JANE AUSTEN *Pride & Prej.* (1846) 29 Jane was by no means better.

d. in numerous phrases, see 38.

31. With *live*: introducing both the food and the means of obtaining it. Also *fig.*

971 *Blickl. Hom.* 57 þa gastlican lare .. þe ure saul biȝ leofaþ. *a* **1000** *Guthlac* 244 Bi hwon scealt þu lifȝan, þeah þu lond aȝe? *c* **1205** LAY. 467 Leouere heom his to libben bi þan wode-roten. *c* **1300** *K. Alis.* 4971 Hy .. libben by the wylde goot. **1393** LANGL. *P. Pl.* C. VII. 292 ȝut were me leuere .. lyue by well-carses. **1583** STUBBES *Anat. Abus.* II. 89 The most of them .. attempt .. vnlawfull meanes to liue by. **1600** SHAKS. *A.Y.L.* II. vii. 14 As I do liue by foode, I met a foole. **1611** BIBLE *Matt.* iv. 4 Man shall not liue by bread alone. **1815** *Scribbleomania* 217 Each pestle's displayer who living by drugs, proves humanity's slayer. **1880** CHURCH *Spenser* iii. 52 No one in those days could live by poetry.

32. a. Introducing the intermediate or subordinate agent viewed as the medium or channel of action; = L. *per*, OE. *þurh*.

c **1300** *K. Alis.* 4304 Darie hit wot by a spye. *c* **1325** *Coer de L.* 1522 Sche greetes the wel by me. **1382** WYCLIF *John* i. 3 Alle þingis ben maad bi [Gr. διά, L. *per*] him. **1393** LANGL. *P. Pl.* C. IV. 417 God sente to saul by samuel þe prophete. *c* **1450** *Merlin* i. 23 Thow hast herde be my moder the trauayle that they hadden. **1622** T. STOUGHTON *Chr. Sacrif.* xvii. 239 Hath he more benefit by his horse then by his Minister? **1711** STEELE *Spect.* No. 118 ¶2 The Lady is addressed to, presented and flattered, only by Proxy, in her Woman. **1785** HENRY *Hist. Gt. Brit.* V. v. xxxviii. 382 The King could not .. administer justice to his subjects in person, but only by his judges. **1833** *Fraser's Mag.* VIII. 312 Send check by bearer. **1866** ROGERS *Agric. & Prices* I. xxi. 527 The lord was present either in person or by a deputy.

b. in extended phrase *by the hands of*.

1411 *E. E. Wills* (1882) 17 Whiche somme ys owynge to me, to be payd .. by þe handes of my lady lovell. *a* **1500** tr. *Magna Charta* in Arnolde *Chron.* 217 By the handis of his kynnes folk .. his goodis shalbe destribute. **1534** *Old City Acc. Bk.* in *Archæol. Jrnl.* XLIII, Resuyd of mʳ grayn by the hands of mʳ hoxton v wrytyngs. **1866** *Cornh. Mag.* XIII. 692 The Doctor will kill him, by my hands.

c. In phrases *to have children by*, *to be pregnant by*, and the like.

a **1000** *Cædmon's Gen.* 2326 (Gr.) þu scealt sunu aȝan, bearn be bryde þinre. *c* **1000** ÆLFRIC *Gen.* xxxviii. 25 Be þam men ic eom mid childe. *c* **1205** LAY. 19249 Ygærne wes mid childe bi Uther. **1297** R. GLOUC. 23 Brut .. sones hadde þre By hys wyf. **1393** LANGL. *P. Pl.* C. XI. 144 And haþ fyue faire sones by hus furste wyf. **1576** GASCOIGNE *Steel Gl.* (Arb.) 50 He begat me by Simplycitie. **1631** GOUGE *God's Arrows* III. ii. 183 Amalek was the sonne of Esaus sonne by a concubine. **1750** JOHNSON *Rambl.* No. 22 ¶1 Wit and learning were the children of Apollo, by different mothers. **1788** J. POWELL *Devises* (1827) II. 351 The testator .. had had several children by a native woman. **1805** EAST *Reports* V. 234 A bastard child .. which a young woman had had by the defendant. *c* **1812** JANE AUSTEN *Sense & Sens.* (1846) 1 By a former marriage, Dashwood had one son.

33. a. Introducing the principal agent.

This, which has now become a main use of *by*, is hardly found before 15th c.; OE. used *of*, *fram*, ME. commonly *of*, which is still poetical, esp. with non-material verbs, as 'he was beloved of all'. Cf. Fr. use of *de* and *par*.

c **1400** MAUNDEV. iii. 15 That Cytee was destroyed by hem of Grece. **1461** J. PASTON *Lett.* 384 II. 3 Assigned be the commissioners. **1570–87** HOLINSHED *Scot. Chron.* II. 52 Slaine miserablie in prison be .. the duke Albanie. **1593** HOOKER *Eccl. Pol.* I. iii. §2 A law natural to be observed by creatures. **1682** WHELER *Journ. Greece* I. 26 The Walls of it were built by Diocletian. **1785** REID *Let.* Wks. I. 66/1 A malefactor is not hanged by the law, but according to the law, by the executioner. **1848** MACAULAY *Hist. Eng.* I. 31 It was among the articles which John was compelled by the Barons to sign. *Mod.* By whom was the book written?

b. So with personal qualities and attributes, natural agencies, etc., treated as principal agents.

For usage as to *by* after particular verbs, see these.

1549 *Bk. Com. Prayer* Pref., There was never anything by the wit of man so well devised .. which hath not been corrupted. **1712** ADDISON *Spect.* No. 333 ¶5 This is followed by the tearing up of mountains and promontories. **1757** JOHNSON *Rambl.* No. 165 ¶2 Truth finds an easy entrance into the Mind when she is introduced by desire, and attended by pleasure. **1816** J. WILSON *City of Plague* I. i. 255 Swallow'd up in a moment by the heedless earth. **1844** *Punch* 13 Jan. 27 Pipes and alcoholic liquors are superseded by matrimony. **1848** MACAULAY *Hist. Eng.* II. 263 Such a demand .. was not authorised by the existing treaties. **1875** BROWNING *Aristoph. Apol.* 99 Demonstrable By time, that tries things.

c. Used for: written, painted, executed by (an author, painter, sculptor, etc.).

1570 (*title*) The Scholemaster .. ¶By Roger Ascham. **1595** (*title*) Colin Clovts Come home againe. By Ed. Spencer. **1673** (*title*) Poems, &c. upon Several Occasions. By Mr. John Milton: Both English and Latin, &c. Composed at several times. **1779** *Mirror* No. 24 Can the representations of moon-light, even by Homer, Milton, and Shakespeare, be more exquisitely finished? **1832** DISRAELI *Cont. Fleming* II. xiv, I must get 'Manstein' directly, if it be by young Moskoffsky. **1901** *Lincoln City & Cathedral* 154 The latter [window], by a Nuremburg executant, is poor and feeble. **1966** *Observer* 23 Oct. 22/2 (Advt.), Lady Windermere's Fan. Directed by Anthony Quayle. Scenery & costumes by Cecil Beaton.

d. Of a public house, etc.: kept or managed by (as licensee).

1840 DICKENS *Old C. Shop* xxix, This is the Valiant Soldier, by James Groves. **1885** HENLEY & STEVENSON *Macaire* I. iii, *Auberge des Adrets*, by John Paul Dumont. **1919** MASEFIELD *Reynard the Fox* 2 The meet was at 'The Cock and Pye By Charles and Martha Enderby'.

e. Followed by a personal pronoun or personal name in expressions indicating agreement: with, as far as I (etc.) am concerned. *colloq.* (orig. *U.S.*).

1930 *Amer. Mercury* Dec. 456 Five skins is jake by me. **1940** 'N. SHUTE' *Old Captivity* i. 37 If it pleases you to think like that, it's O.K. by me. **1956** —— *Beyond Black Stump* vi. 167 I'd like to go on .. if that's all right by you. **1960** *New York Times Bk. Rev.* 30 Apr. 8 He is regarded as a youngish-type people's critic .. and this is fine by Mr. Fiedler.

VI. Of circumstance, condition, manner, cause, reason. (Chiefly developments or weakenings of earlier senses.)

34. a. The physical circumstances of an action often become conditions more or less contributory or essential to its performance, and hence pass into the notion of aid or *means*, cf. 'to walk by moonlight', 'read by moonlight', 'read by candle-light'.

(*by day light* closely approaches *by day*: see 19 b.)

a **1000** *Riddles* xxviii. 17 (Gr.) Ic .. on eorðan swa esnas binde dole æfter dyntum be dæȝes leohte. **1154** *O.E. Chron.* (Laud MS.) an. 1138 §2 Me lihtede candles to æten bi. *a* **1300** *Cursor M.* 14195 God es to go bi light o dai. ? *a* **1400** *Chester Pl.* (1843) I. 4 Those wise Kinges three .. by the starre that did shine, Sought the sighte of the Saviour. **1701** J. CUNNINGHAM in *Phil. Trans.* XXIII. 1201 The Weather so favouring us, that we never but by our Topsails. **1712** ADDISON *Spect.* No. 409 ¶6 Seeing an Object by the Light of a Taper. **1872** MARK TWAIN *Innoc. Abr.* xii. 85 No gas to read by.

b. From, after, according to (a model).

a **1650** E. NORGATE *Miniatura* (1919) 84 When the Italians have not the Life to draw by, they make use off Models. *Ibid.* 86 By these and such others they draw. **1654** H. VAUGHAN tr. *Nieremberg's Discourses* 88 Pictures that have not so much as an ayre of those faces they were drawn by.

35. a. The sense of 'means' often passes into that of 'attendant circumstances', and so approaches or reaches that of *manner*.

c **1340** *Cursor M.* 18323 (Laud MS.), Alle that þou seidist by prophecy Thou hast fulle-fillid. **1483** CAXTON *G. de la Tour* I ij, Thenne wente shee and told it to hym by .. fayre and attemperate language. *c* **1489** —— *Sonnes of Aymon* 32 Reynawde .. thwerled his swerde by grete fyers-nesse. **1509** HAWES *Examp. Virt.* ix. 161 Where byrdys sange by grete melody. **1523** LD. BERNERS *Froiss.* I. clxxvi. 214 By this manere was the stronge castell of Eureux won agayne. **1589** PUTTENHAM *Eng. Poesie* III. xxii. (Arb.) 257 Wordes .. written by wrong ortographie. **1677** MOXON *Mech. Exerc.* (1703) 241 A great part of its increase goes away by a kind of Glass. **1765** *Act 5 Geo. III*, xxvi. Preamb., To hold to the said John .. by liege homage. **1840** DANA *Bef. Mast.* xi. 25 The halyards were at this moment let go by the run. **1875** JOWETT *Plato* (ed. 2) I. 350 The cause when heard went by default.

b. esp. in phrase *to begin by*, *end by*, etc., with gerund. (See further under these verbs.)

1684 *Scanderbeg Rediv.* vi. 150 The next Considerable Exploit of his Majesty .. was, by taking of Zytchin. **1827** HALLAM *Const. Hist.* (1842) I. 151 Ministers who employ spies .. are sure to .. end by the most violent injustice and tyranny. **1839** THIRLWALL *Greece* II. 76 He began by

banishing 700 families. **1887** GLADSTONE in *Ho. Comm.* 12 Sept., The right hon. gentleman the Secretary for Ireland sat down by saying that, etc. *Mod.* He finished by putting them all in the fire.

c. In *by way of*: as an instance of, as something tending or amounting to, somewhat under the form of. For full illustration see WAY *sb.*[1] 32 d.

c **1400** MAUNDEV. 199 The king ȝeveth leve to pore men.. to gadre hem precyous stones and perles, be weye of ælmesse. **1762** HUME *Hist. Eng.* (1806) V. lxx. 235 By way of pleasantry he [Jefferies] used to call them [the soldiers] his lambs.

36. a. The sense of 'means' sometimes approaches or passes into that of 'cause' or 'reason': Because of, on account of, in consequence of, through; in virtue of, on the ground of. † *by so, by that*: therefore.

1398 TREVISA *Barth. De P.R.* IV. ix. (1495) 93 Though flewme of hymself be thicke and vnsauery by strengthe of heete. **1483** CAXTON *G. de la Tour* H iij, Soone after by this synne he fylle. —— *Cato* G iv, And by so thou oughtest to be contente. **1540** HYRDE *Vives' Instr. Chr. Wom.* (1592) F v, He would haue women of his country to be regarded by their virtue. **1557** N. T. (Geneva) *Matt.* xxvi. 31 Al ye shalbe offended by me this nyght. **1593** SHAKS. *3 Hen. VI*, IV. iv. 12 Warwickes Brother, and by that our Foe. **1627** FELTHAM *Resolves* I. xxix. Wks. (1677) 49 A Hill almost unascendable, by the roughness of a craggy way. **1667** PEPYS *Diary* 27 Aug., By the growth of his beard and gray hairs, I did not know him. **1771** GOLDSM. *Hist. Eng.* III. 240 The press.. swarmed with productions, dangerous by their sedition and calumny, more than by their eloquence or style. **1839** THIRLWALL *Greece* IV. 263 In his house Protagoras was said to have read one of his works by which he incurred a charge of atheism.

b. in the conjunctive phrases ***be þam þe, by that, by reason that, by reason***: inasmuch as, because, since. Now only in full form ***by reason that.***

c **1175** *Cott. Hom.* 235 Be þam þe he fader is and laford he him self cwed be þe witie, *Si ego*, etc. *a* **1536** TINDALE *Exp. Matt.* Wks. II. 128 By that they prophesied.. and by that they cast out devils.. it is plain that they be false prophets. **1558** KENNEDY *Compend. Tract.* in *Wodr. Soc. Misc.* (1844) 101 Be ressoun the Kirk.. can nevir be gatherit togidder. **1601** F. TATE *Househ. Ord. Edw II*, §10 He shal have no more, bi reson that he shal have cariage. **1606** EARL NORTHAMPTON in *True & Perf. Relation* (1606) R r 4 b, By that hee cals him virum mortis, I may lawfully conclude, etc. **1682** WHELER *Journ. Greece* II. 203 Wine is scarce, by reason that it is prohibited. **1711** STEELE *Spect* No. 2 ⁋1 He keeps himself a Batchelor by reason he was crossed in Love.

37. In *Book-keeping*, placed before Credit entries; the person or account being made creditor *by* the amount entered.

1695 E. HATTON *Merch. Mag.* 140 By all the Cash you receive, and deliver nothing for the same; as By Money received with an Apprentice; By Rebate for paying a Summ before due. *Ibid.* 169 By stock, £150. **1751** CHAMBERS *Cycl.* s.v. *Book*, Ledger Book. By Cash for his remittance on James £1900. **1838** R. LANGFORD *Introd. Trade* 79, 1837 July 10 By remittance per W. Jackson £1000.

VII. In phrases.

38. *By* enters into a great number of phrases, which originated in one or other of the preceding uses, but are now used without analysis, and sometimes with such modification of meaning as to obliterate or obscure the force of the preposition. Such are **a.** *adverbial*, † ***by cas, by chance, by force, by guess, by hook or by crook, by might***; and others for which an adverb might easily be substituted, as ***by consequence***, † ***by cover*** (= covertly), † ***by matter in deed*** (? = as an actual fact), ***by metaphor***, † ***by name*** (= especially), † ***by occasion***, † ***by particular, by stealth.*** [Here Fr. has usually *par.*] See the various substantives.

1297 R. GLOUC. 490 He vel of is palefrey, & brec is fot bi cas. *c* **1340** *Cursor M.* 10700 (Laud MS.) Vow that is made by right, Ow no man to breke by might. **1475** *Bk. Noblesse* 31 Provided that.. no man take vitaile beforce. **1544** PHAËR *Regim. Lyfe* (1560) R vij, Hitherto have I declined by occasion. **1565** in Sir J. Picton *L'pool Munic. Rec.* (1883) I. 113 That no.. person.. succour by cover or operte, any apprentice. **1583** STUBBES *Anat. Abus.* II. 22 Either by hooke or crooke, by night or day. *a* **1586** *Answ. Cartwright* 17 He alleadgeth another proofe by peraduenture. *a* **1610** BABINGTON *Wks.* (1622) 257 This Manna followed the Israelites whatsoeuer the earth was: and by name in the wilderness. **1620** J. WILKINSON *Courts Leet* 117 These persons by particular are said to be by the statute rogues. **1660** FULLER *Mixt Contemp.* (1841) 171 Ponderous, and by consequence probable to settle.. on the earth. **1697** DRYDEN *Virg. Georg.* IV. 745 Some prying Churl had.. thence, By Stealth, convey'd th' unfeather'd Innocence. **1711** STEELE *Spect.* No. 145 ⁋6 He snatches Kisses by Surprise. **1721** *St. German's Doctor & Stud.* 338 It is alledged in the indictment by matter in deed that he had such weapon. **1751** JORTIN *Serm.* (1771) V. v. 90 They might not imagine that the world was.. made by chance. **1836** LANDOR *Pericles & Asp.* Wks. 1846 II. 394/1, I am not speaking by metaphor and Asiatically. **1848** MACAULAY *Hist. Eng.* II. 649 *note*, I have therefore been forced to arrange them [the events] by guess.

b. *prepositional*, † ***by cause of, by chesun of, by colour of, by dint of, by the hands of, by means of, by reason of, by virtue of, by way of***, etc. See under the various substantives.

c **1380** WYCLIF *Last Age Ch.* (1840) 25 Bi resoun of whiche þe þridde tribulacioun schal entre into Cristis Chirche. *c* **1420** *Avow. Arth.* xxxii, Ther to-gedur faȝte we Be chesun of this lady fre. **1535** COVERDALE *Tobit* xi. 18 By reason of all the good that God had shewed vnto him. *c* **1555** *Songs & Ball., Ph. & Mary* (1860) 3 He hathe us up lyfft By the means of hys sonne callyd Emanuell. **1593** SHAKS. *Rich. III*, I. iii. 78 Our Brother is imprison'd by your meanes. **1597** —— *2 Hen. IV*, IV. i. 128 All.. That.. by dint of Sword, Haue since miscarryed vnder Bullingbrooke. **1621** ELSING *Debates Ho. Lords* (1870) 127 The Parlement is adjourned by virtue thereof [the Comission]. **1664** BUTLER *Hud.* II. ii. 736 Vict'ry gotten without Blows, By dint of sharp hard words. **1710** in *Select. fr. Harl. Misc.* (1793) 561 Edward Whitacre.. hath, by colour of his employment received the sum of twenty-five thousand pounds. **1712** ADDISON *Spect.* No. 523 ⁋6 By virtue of that spectatorial authority with which I stand invested. **1728** MORGAN *Algiers* I. iii. 32 Jugurtha.. by Dint of Money, corrupted many of the Senators. **1737** L. CLARKE *Hist. Bible* VIII. (1740) 496 By means thereof he took the City. **1864** BRYCE *Holy Rom. Emp.* 99 It was chiefly by means of the Papacy that this came to pass. **1876** BLACKMORE *Cripps* I. ii. 23 Quite out of sight.. by reason of the bend of the hollow. **1881** R. BUCHANAN *God & Man* I. 111 The widow—by dint of strict parsimony, had saved a trifle.

39. Phrases occurring under preceding senses: *by and beside* 5, 7; *by common, by ordinar* 7; *by day*, etc. 19 b; *by no means, ways* 30 c; *by one's self* 4, 8 b; *by so, by that* 23 d, 36; *by that, by reason that* 36 b; *by the by, by the way* 12 b; *by wholesale, degrees*, etc. 24, 25.

B. *adv.*

Forms: [1 bí, biȝ], 4 bi, (4–6 bie, 5–8, 9 (*dial.*) bye, 4– by. In OE. the instances of the adv. may all be treated (from the modern point of view) either as prefixes to a verb, or as prepositions following their object.

1. a. Of position: Near, close at hand, in another's presence or immediate neighbourhood; occas. after verbal sbs., as in ***dweller by, stander by***, Naut. phr. ***stand by!*** = be ready. See BY- in *comb.* 2 a.

[*c* **993** *Battle of Maldon* 182 Beȝen ða beornas þe him biȝ stodon.] *c* **1340** *Cursor M.* 14282 (Trin.) Men say hir þat bi stood Rennonde. *c* **1425** WYNTOUN *Cron.* VIII. xl. 93 Oþir Lordis, þat war by. **1463** *Bury Wills* (1850) 35 If any bedrede man or woman ly by. **1526** TINDALE *John* xi. 42 Because of the people that stonde by I sayde it. **1606** *Return fr. Parnass.* III. iii. (Arb.) 43 He thinkes hee hath gulld the standers by sufficiently. **1623** MASSINGER *Dk. of Milan* II. i, My brother being not by now to protect her. **1732** BERKELEY *Alciphr.* I. §15 Methinks you sit by very tamely. **1834** MARRYAT *P. Simple* III. 101 Stand by to haul over the boom-sheet when she pays off. **1861** FLOR. NIGHTINGALE *Nursing* 39 Patients are often accused of being able to 'do much more when nobody is by'. **1867** SMYTH *Sailor's Word-bk., Stand by!* the order to be prepared.

b. preceded by *fast, hard, near.* Also transferred to the idea of time.

c **1400** MAUNDEV. viii. 93 Faste by, is ȝit the Tree of Eldre, that Judas henge him self upon. **1580** BARET *Alv.* B 631 Here is a little towne or village harde bie to flie vnto. **1795** SOUTHEY *Joan of Arc* I. cliv, Domremi's cottages Gleam'd in the sun hard by. **1866** KINGSLEY *Herew.* i. (1877) 20 He founded Boston near by.

c **1385** CHAUCER *L.G.W.* 2604 The aray is wrought, the tyme is faste by. **1535** COVERDALE *Isa.* li. 5 It is hard by, that my health and my rightuousness shal go forth.

c. following a sb. in sense *lying, living, situate* close or hard by. Not now used alone. Also in *fig.* expressions.

c **1470** HENRY *Wallace* I. 50 Bruce [clamyt as] fyrst male of the secund gre by. **1475** CAXTON *Jason* 41 b, Thauncient knight that was loggid in that other bedde by might not slepe. *Ibid.* 52 Alle the nobles.. of the countrees by and adjacent. **1588** SHAKS. *L.L.L.* v. ii. 94, I stole into a neighbour thicket by. **1627** J. CARTER *Expos.* 54 Dead in trespasses and sinnes, or next doore by.

d. Naut. *by and large*: see as main entry. ***full and by***: sailing close-hauled to the wind. (Adm. Smyth.)

1627 CAPT. SMITH *Seaman's Gram.* ix. (1692) 42 Fill the Sails, keep full, full and by. **1628** DIGBY *Voy. Medit.* (1868) 83 Your chace goeth best before the wind, and.. you can outbeare her, by. **1881** W. C. RUSSELL *Ocean Free-L.* I. vi. 265 They held on after us nevertheless, sailing full and bye.

2. a. Aside, out of the way; out of use or consideration. ***to put, set*** or ***lay by***: to put aside from use, set aside, discard; (*more recently*) to put aside from present use, so as to reserve for the future. ***to put by***: also (*obs.*) to turn from one's purpose; cf. A. 16 c.

c **1425** WYNTOUN *Cron.* VIII. iv. 253 For Custwme approwyd oft by drawys Of Canon and Cyvyle bath the Lawys. **1535** STEWART *Cron. Scot.* II. 222 This ȝoung Arthure.. Tha crownit king and put the richt air bye. *Ibid.* 339 All kynd of armour in that place cast by. *a* **1586** *Answ. Cartwright* 6 He must.. laye by his proofe as vntrue. **1595** SHAKS. *John* IV. iii. 95 Stand by, or I shall gaul you Faulconbridge. **1614** W. B. *Philos. Banquet* (ed. 2) 3 Age might be kept backe, and sicknesse kept bye. **1634** BAYNE *On Coloss.* 344 What a Pride is it, for some ignorant Schollar to put by the direction of his Tutor. **1655** L'ESTRANGE *Chas. I*, 125 Some thing or other ever came travers.. and put him by. **1721** DE FOE *Mem. Cavalier* (1840) 311 They had set by the lords for not agreeing to it. **1731** SWIFT *Corr.* II. 701 These things can lie by till you come to carp at them. **1766** GOLDSM. *Vic. W.* xx, Vile things that nature designed should be thrown by into her lumber room. **1807** WINDHAM *Speeches Parl.* (1812) III. 19 Laying something by for a rainy day. **1867** FROUDE *Short Stud.* (ed. 2) 161 Neither party is entitled to say.. 'Stand by, I am holier than thou'.

b. Naut. *to lie (lay) by*: (*a*) to come almost to a stand, either by backing sail or by leaving only enough sail to keep the vessel's head straight; = modern phrase *lie to*; also *transf.*; (*b*) to dodge under small sail under the land (Adm. Smyth).

1613 SHAKS. *Hen. VIII*, III. i. 11 The Billowes of the Sea, Hung their heads, and then lay by. **1674** PETTY *Disc. bef. Royal Soc.* 102 To stop Leaks afore, the Ship must stop its motion, lye by, or bear up. **1704** *Lond. Gaz.* No. 4054/1 We lay by all day.. repairing our Defects. **1753** HANWAY *Trav.* I. II. xvi. 72 We were obliged to lay-by in the night.

3. Of motion: Past a certain point, beyond. Also transferred to time; cf. BY- in *comb.* 2 b.

[*c* **950** *Lindisf. Gosp.* Mark xv. 21 Geneddon bi geongende [*Rushw.* bigongende]. ? *a* **1400** *Morte Arth.* (1847) 233 Ffloridas with a swerde, as he by glenttys, Alle the flesche of the flanke he flappes in sondyre. *c* **1425** WYNTOUN *Cron.* VIII. xviii. 186 Thai persawyd by gangand A man. **1535** COVERDALE *2 Sam.* xvi. 1 Dauid was gone a lytle by from the toppe of the mount. **1606** B. JONSON *Barriers* Wks. 1870 III. 34 They marched by in pairs. **1766** GOLDSM. *Vic. W.* xxi, A stage coach happening to pass by. **1844** DISRAELI *Coningsby* I. iii. 14 The days are gone by for senates to have their beards plucked in the forum.

†**4.** In addition, besides, also. *Obs.* (Cf. Sc. *for-by*.) ***by (and) attour***, see ATOUR.

1436 *Pol. Poems* (1859) II. 185 Thys coloure.. muste be seyde alofte, And by declared of the grete fulle ofte. *a* **1440** *Sir Degrev.* 223 Tene score knythis.. And iii hondred archerus by. **1600** in Farr's *S.P.* (1845) II. 435 Onlesse my seruice be employed by. **1653** HOLCROFT *Procopius*, He might spend less wood, and wages upon bakers, and by gain the weight. **1763** C. JOHNSTON *Reverie* I. 143 For a guinea by. **1804** *Illust. Lond. News* 21 Aug. (1886) 194 The Gallant and Spirited Race run.. for 500 guineas, and 1000 guineas bye, between Mrs. Thornton and Mr. Flint.

5. a. Over in duration, finished, at an end. Of time: past, gone by. Also ***by with.*** Sc. and *north.*

1784 BURNS *Ep. Rankine* x, As soon 's the clocking-time is buy, And the wee pouts begun to cry. **1846** ALEX. LAING *Wayside Flowers* 20 Whan the buryin' was bye, an' relations a' gane. **1896** CROCKETT *Grey Man* xii, The days of curses are by with.

b. Of a person: done for, ruined, dead: esp. in *to be by with it. Sc.* and *north.*

1890 SERVICE *Notandums* vi. 34 When the dykes are broken you're bye, ye ken,—ouay! fairly bye! **1893** STEVENSON *Catriona* xxx, You're by with it, James More. You can never show your face again. **1900** KIPLING in *Daily Express* 26 June 4/6 I'll not call it farmin'—up yonder, but ye're by with that even.

by, bye, *a.* Forms: 5–9 bye, 6– by; also 6 bi, 7 bie. [Attrib. use of prec. *by-* in adv., as in *out patient*, etc. Not separated by any clear line from *by* combinations: see BY- III. (In modern use the spelling *bye* seems to be preferred when the word is treated as an adj.)]

Generally. The opposite of *main.*

1. Situated to one side, as a door, or out of the way, as a place; running in a side direction, or out of the way, as a path. Also *fig.* See BY- in *comb.* 3 a, b, and BY-PATH, BY-WAY, etc.

c **1330**, etc. [see BY-WAY, BY-DOOR]. **1485** CAXTON *St. Wenefr.* 2 By a bye dore of the chamber she wente oute. **1582** BENTLEY *Mon. Matrones* 39 Seeking manie crooked and biwaies. **1583** STANYHURST *Æneis* III. (Arb.) 73 Soom bye place of resting graunt vs. **1655** GOUGE *Comm. Heb.* x. 20 There are so many bie broad pathes. **1706** *Lond. Gaz.* No. 4259/4 The Man that is supposed to have robb'd.. a bye Hackney Coach.. upon the Forest of Sherwood. **1748** RICHARDSON *Clarissa* (1811) II. xli. 307 Nothing can be more bye and unfrequented. **1796** MORSE *Amer. Geog.* I. 335 Hospitals erected.. in bye places. **1830** SOUTHEY in *For. Rev. & Cont. Misc.* V. 278 The mule preferred the high road to the bye one. **1880** *W. Cornw. Gloss.* (E.D.S.) *Bye*, lonely. Our house is rather bye.

2. *fig.* **a.** Away from the main purpose, occurring 'by the way', incidental, casual; **b.** of secondary importance; **c.** privy, clandestine, secret, underhand; cf. BY- in *comb.* 3 c, d, 4, 5: often coupled with another epithet, as *by and sinister, familiar and by*, etc. See BY-MATTER, BY-WORD, etc.

c **1050**, etc. [see BY-WORD, BY-MATTER]. **1562** COOPER *Answ. Priv. Masse* (1850) 168 You have brought out of them all but a few bye sentences. **1599** B. JONSON *Ev. Man out of Hum., The Stage*, Entertain this troop With some familiar and by-conference. **1632** D. LUPTON *London Carbon.* 105 He.. hopes to haue.. some by preferment. **1633** FOSBROOKE *Warre or Confl.* 9 Done either in hypocrisie or for some by and sinister respect. *a* **1652** BROME *Crt. Beggar* II. i, Have we spent all this while in by and idle talke? **1674** [Z. CAWDREY] *Catholicon* 16 Those whom they have gained in their concealed and by-trade as Undertakers. **1802** PALEY *Nat. Theol.* xxvi. (1819) 455 The bye effect may be unfavourable. **1842** MIALL *Nonconf.* II. 393 Some trivial bye consideration being unsound will vitiate our whole conclusion. **1849** RUSKIN *Sev. Lamps* iv. §3. 96 Far too serious a work to be undertaken in a bye way. **1857** GEN. P. THOMPSON *Audi Alt.* I. ii. 5 A bye debate.. arose on a motion by Lord Claud Hamilton.

by, obs. f. BE, BEE, BUY; also of *been* pa. pple. of BE *v.*

by- in composition.

A. A ME. variant spelling of the prefix BI-, BE-, under which see most of the words, as, under BE-, *bycause, bydene, bydryve, byfall, byfore, byget, bygynne, bygile*, etc.; under BI-, *byreusy, byweve*, etc. Those words only are given under BY- for which no forms with *be-* or *bi-* have been met with.

B. by- (sometimes bye-): the preposition, adverb, or adjective BY in combination, either in words already formed in OE. with the accented form of the prefix, bi-, biȝ-, or in words of later formation, especially those in which by has an attributive sense, and cannot be separated by any clear line from BY adj., since the use of the hyphen is very uncertain. All the principal words so formed are treated as main words in their alphabetical places; the less important and more obvious combinations here follow, under the various uses and senses of the prefix.

I. 1. Compounds in which by- is a prep., as **by-rote** a. See also by-hither, by-south (BY prep. 9 c), by-ordinary, by-common, etc. (BY prep. 7), and BYHAND.

1669 PENN No Cross xx. §23 That a little By-rote Babble shall serve your Turn at the Great Day?

II. Compounds in which by- has an advb. force.

2. a. with nouns of agent or action, with senses 'beside, past'; as by-inhabitant, -seer, -sitter, -stroller; †**by-lier**, a neutral; †**by-coming**, passing; †**by-settel**, a lodger; so BY-DWELLER, BY-STANDER, etc.

1600 Gowrie's Conspir. in Select. fr. Harl. Misc. (1793) 195 Which [doore]..he had lokked in his *bycomming. **1658** W. BURTON Itin. Anton. 135 Ruins of Walls, which the *by-inhabitants call, The old Work of Wrockcester. **a 1572** KNOX Hist. Ref. 222 (JAM.) In caise it beis inquyred of all *By-lyars. **1642** T. HILL Trade of Truth 45 Many are aposcopi, rather then Episcopi..*by-seers, rather then over-seers. **1612** N. Riding Record Soc. I. 264 These persons following for reteyning of inmates or *by-settells. **1837** HAWTHORNE Amer. Note-bks. (1871) I. 63 Others of the ..*by-sitters put various questions. **1859** SALA Tw. round Clock 12 Yawing..on the *bye-strollers.

b. with sense 'aside, SIDE-'; as by-glance, glancing, -leap, -start, -step, etc.; also indicating movement astray, or in a wrong direction, as by-fantasy, -lusting, -regard, -thought, -wishing; also BY-VIEW, etc. **by(e)-child, -son**, a bastard. dial. Cf. BY-BLOW 3.

1873 Lett. from Jamaica 81 Concubinage is a universal institution, and bears with it no disgrace. The offspring of such connexions—'*bye-children', 'out-children', or 'love-children', as they are called,—generally follow the mother. **1894** HALL CAINE Manxman III. xvi, You'd be hearing of the by-child, it's like? **1609** R. BARNERD Faithf. Shepheard 14 Interrupted with wauering thoughts and *by-fantasies. **a 1659** CLEVELAND Committee 2 No packing, I beseech you, no *by-glance. **1598** GRENEWEY Tacitus, Ann. XIV. iii. (1622) 203 By a *by-glancing at Claudius raigne. **1571** GOLDING Calvin on Ps. xi. 2 The fearfull bird, was fayne to make dyverse *byleapes. **1583** —— Calvin on Deut. cxxxvi. 835 He forbiddeth vs also to haue any *by lusting. **1623** LISLE Ælfric on O. & N.T. Pref. 11 They for divers *by-regards, may hide..the truth. **1887** A. E. BARR Border Shepherdess xii, 'That play-acting *by-son o' the Graeme.' 'He was no by-son.' **1542** UDALL Erasm. Apoph. 280 b, His soudiours in gooyng foorthward..made *by stertes out of their waye, and did muche oppression. **1567** DRANT Horace's Epist. To Rdr. 4 To speake according to the man, (which is a *bystep from the pathe of diuinitye). **1652** BENLOWES Theoph. XIII. cxvi. 251 Pardon the by-steps that my soul has trod. **1561** T. NORTON Calvin's Inst. III. 279 No man can be so bente to praye, but that he shall fele many *bythoughts to crepe vpon him. **1601** DENT Pathw. Heauen 322, I demand of you, whether you neuer had any by-thoughts in your praiers. **1571** GOLDING Calvin on Ps. xxxv. 14 To some it seemeth a *by-wishing.

c. with a sense akin to that of side-blow, side-stroke; and often fig. of allusions in speech or writing: 'Indirect'; as by-fling, -hint, -quip, -stroke; **by-wipe** (= side-stroke).

1651 BAXTER Inf. Bapt. Apol. 8 Many told him of my *by-flings at him. **1853** KINGSLEY Hypatia II. vi. 163 *By-hints, and unexpected hits at one and the other. **1855** —— Westw. Ho xiii, Some *bye-quip, perhaps, at the character of her most dainty captain. **1679** BEDLOE Popish Plot A b, I shall say nothing of their Politick *By-strooks. **1641** MILTON Animadv. (1851) 187 Wherefore that conceit of Legion with a *by-wipe?

d. with pples., as by-flown, by-travelling, -wandering; **by-advanced**, already past; †**by-come**, past; **by-peeping**, looking aside; BYGONE, BY-PAST, etc.

1827 CARLYLE Richter, Misc. (1869) 20 In thy steeples, behind the *by-advanced great midnight it struck half-past two. **1592** WARNER Alb. Eng. VII. xxxvi. (1612) 173 His happiest daies *by come or to be past. **1884** H. S. WILSON Stud. Hist. 171 Mere names, vaguely realised through the mists of a *by-flown time. **1611** SHAKS. Cymb. I. vi. 108 *By peeping in an eye Base and illustrious. **1610** GUILLIM Heraldry VI. vi, Lampen..took name from the *by-travailing River. **1567** Pilgr. Parnass. I. 114 Keepe mee from devious and *by-wandringe wayes.

III. Combinations in which by has an adjectival force.

(Here the senses so pass one into another, that it is not possible to classify them distinctly; different senses also often blend in the same combination. The following arrangement aims only at presenting the more obvious combinations under their predominating sense.)

3. With a notion of local position or direction and usually equivalent to SIDE.

a. in the sense 'Placed beside, at one side, aside, or off at the side', hence 'out-of-the-way'; generally with relation to a main or principal thing of the same kind, and thus often involving some notion of 'subsidiary' or 'subordinate' (see 5): as in †by-board (= side-table), -chamber, -chapel, -cliff, -closet, -dish, -door, -gulf, -hole, -nook, †-note (= side or marginal note), -paper, -part, -settle (= side seat or bench), -slade, †-stall, -station, -tail, -town, -vale, -window; also BY-PLACE, BY-ROOM, BY-TABLE, etc.

1637 RUTHERFORD Lett. lxxvii. (1862) I. 198 A sufferer for Christ..will be fain to eat with the bairns and to take the *by-board. **1853** KINGSLEY Hypatia II. xii. 312 Where was he now? In a little *by chamber. **1562** COOPER Answ. Priv. Masse (1850) 99 To creep in corners or *by-chapels as a sign of separation. **1596** FITZ-GEFFRAY Sir F. Drake (1881) 88 O now descend my ever mourning Muse Downe from the *by-cliffe of thy sisters mount. **1696** WHISTON Th. Earth Introd. 57 Will a wise Builder bestow twice as much time in decking ..of one *Bycloset of inferior use? **1599** H. BUTTES Diet's Dry Dinner in James I's Counterbl. (Arb.) 92, I haue put into a *by-dish (like Eg-shelles in a Saucer) what worthily may breed offence. **1545** BRINKLOW Lament. (1874) 94 They may also forsake their *bydores, and clyminge in at the windowes. **1639** FULLER Holy War II. xxxi. (1840) 90 He, like a *by-gulf, devoured her affection, which should flow to her children. **1664** H. MORE Myst. Iniq. 565 They..seek for Inspirations and Revelations in *by-holes amongst the squallid Sepulchers of the dead. **1862** Country Gentl. II. 145 Odd corners, and little *by-nooks. **1579** G. HARVEY Letter-bk. (1884) 78, I have once in my life bestowid uppon the a *Byenote for thy lerninge. **a 1603** T. CARTWRIGHT Confut. Rhem. N.T. (1618) 581 This reliefe, whereof your by-note in the margent tatleth. **1659** Instruct. Oratory 108 A memorandum being made of it in a *by-paper as you are writing. **1707** J. STEPHENS Quevedo's Com. Wks. (1709) 54 Apple-street..is a *by-part of the Town. **1602** ROWLANDS Greene's Ghost (1860) 26 A cloake vpon a *by-settle. **1635** J. HAYWARD Banish'd Virg. 126 They found, in an uncouth *by-slad, a slender Barge. **1682** MS. Ord. Crt. of Sewers, Alford, Lincolnsh., The breaches of the New Sea Banke & *Bystall lately broken. **1864** Times 24 Dec., A goods train is timed to be shunted at a *by-station. **1879** MISS JACKSON Shropsh. Word-bk., *By-tail, the right handle of a plough; it is fastened to the 'shell-board'. **1683** Royal Procl. in Lond. Gaz. No. 1856/2 A Settled Post in or near particular *By-Towns, or Places lying on the Post Road. **1686** GOAD Celest. Bodies I. iv. 10 Dayes wherein Fog..chooses to nestle in a *by-Vale. **1611** BARREY Ram Alley IV, She is shewing..rare faces In a *by-window.

b. in the sense 'Running along-side and apart', whence 'devious, circuitous', and again 'little used, unfrequented'; as in by-alley, -conduit, -course, -court, -cut, -ditch, -journey, -rill, -river, -route, -shoot, -stream, -track, -turning, -water; also **bygang** (dial.), a by-path; **by-gate** (dial.), a by-way; **by-lead** = by-wash; **by-sprouting**, a side-shoot; **by-wash** (see quot.); also BY-CHANNEL, BY-STREET, BY-WALK, etc.

1667 PRIMATT City & C. Build. 148 The Statute..for *By-Alleys, Lanes, By-Courts, and such places. **1631** Celestina IV. 50 Glory and quietnesse run from the rich by other *by-conduits and gutters of subtilty and deceit. **1626** Impeach. Dk. Buckhm. in Rushw. Hist. Coll. (1659) I. 305 Irregular running into all *by-courses of the Planets. **1753** World No. 52 Returning home through a *by-court. **1883** Pall Mall G. 10 Nov. 8/2 Clearing the Regent's Canal and the *by-cut at Haggerston. **1650** FULLER Pisgah I. x. 32 The *by-ditches of Dan and Bethel, did not so drain the peoples devotion. **1855** Whitby Gloss., *By-gang, a by-path. **c 1330** R. BRUNNE Chron. (Rolls Ser.) 10145 *Bigate [see BYWAY]. **1573** J. TYRIE Refut. Knox's Answ. Pref. 7 (JAM.) Euer seikand refugis and by-gets. **1596** DALRYMPLE tr. Leslie's Hist. Scot. 102 Thay take the pray, be bout-gates alanerlie & bygates. **1808** MAYNE Siller Gun 31 (JAM.) By a' the bye-gates..crowds were flocking down. **1673** RAY Journ. Low C. 38 Before we left Leyden we made a *by-journey to Sevenbuys. **a 1711** KEN Hymnotheo Poet. Wks. 1721 III. 243 Sin with *by-rills devaricates the Stream. **1577–87** HARRISON Descr. Brit. I. xvi. 107 A verie few *by-rivers. **1855** Chamb. Jrnl. IV. 37 We return to the city by a *by-route little frequented. **1669** WORLIDGE Syst. Agric. viii. §3 (1681) 161 Take away about blossoming time, all the *by-shots. **1562** TURNER Herbal II. 84 a, Peony..hath many *bysproutynges. **1615** CROOKE Body of Man 550 Learned men..may repaire to those fountaines from whence we haue drawne our *by-streame. **1834** M. SCOTT Cruise Midge (1863) 39 We encountered in another small *by-tracke.. three others. **1581** SIDNEY Def. Poesie (Arb.) 39 The many *by-turnings that may diuert you from your way. **1885** OGILVIE, *Bye-wash, By-lead, a channel cut to convey the surplus water from a reservoir or aqueduct, and prevent overflow. **1864** H. W. BATES Nat. Amazon vi. 150 An extensive lake..which..has therefore the appearance of a *by-water or an old channel of the river.

c. transferred to matters, action, etc., collateral with the main matter or action: 'aside, SIDE-', as in by-battle, -concernment, -consideration, -dialogue, -discourse, -disputation, -history, -interest, -issue, -object, -point, -question, -touch; also BY-PLAY.

1842 DE QUINCEY Cicero Wks. VI. 207 The *by-battle with the Cilician pirates is more obscure. **1667** DRYDEN Ess. Dram. Poesie Wks. 1725 I. 51 Our Plays, besides the main design, have Under Plots, or *By-Concernments. **1691** NORRIS Pract. Disc. 60 We are not determined..but by some other *By-consideration. **1818** SCOTT Rob Roy xxx, This *by-dialogue prevented my hearing what passed between the prisoner and Captain Thornton. **1655–60** STANLEY Hist. Philos. (1701) 557/2 It is fit to premise, and put, as a *By discourse, a Treatise concerning Divine Nature. **1580** G. HARVEY 3 Wittie Lett. 33 But to let this *by-disputation passe. **1697** Verdicts conc. Virg. & Homer iii. 6 The marshalling..of the Episodes or *by-Histories. **1801** T. JEFFERSON Writ. (1830) III. 484 They have so many other *by-interests of greater weight. **1768** TUCKER Lt. Nat. II. 503 A thousand *by-objects soliciting on all sides. **1610** BP. CARLETON Jurisd. 160 Not spending time in the examination of *by-points. **1886** Pall Mall G. 14 Sept. 5/2 But this is a by-point; and in its main line..Mr. Montague's work could hardly be improved upon. **1603** SIR C. HEYDON Jud. Astrol. xviii. 385 To digresse from the matter in hand to *by-questions. **1832** J. C. HARE Philol. Museum I. 469 The value of the poems is independent of these *by-touches.

d. The sense 'aside', develops that of 'private, privy, covert'; also connoting 'indirect, underhand, or sinister' dealing, as by-aim, -babbling, -conference, -contrivement, -design, -errand, -intent, -interest, -motive, -payment, -practice, -purpose, -trick, -warning, -wit.

1702 Case of Schedule Stated 7 [He] might have other *By-aims, and Collateral Views, in what he did. **1614** J. ROBINSON Relig. Commun. 64 His *by-bablings, and revyleings. **1625** K. LONG tr. Barclay's Argenis II. xii. 103 Amongst other *by-conference, hee learned much.. touching the Queenes affaires. **1657** REEVE God's Plea Ep. Ded. 12 All *by-contrivments are but sinister drifts and bents. **1622–62** HEYLIN Cosmogr. (1674) To Rdr. A ij, Without any *by-design to abuse the Reader. **1706** Reflex. upon Ridicules 116 With a by-design to be paid by them in the same coin. **1673** CAVE Prim. Chr. III. i. 228 To go to Court upon *by-errands and private designs of their own. **1619** LUSHINGTON Repetit.-Serm. in Phenix (1708) II. 483 Had they any *By-intent, they would have been very forward to report and spread the Fame. **1692** LOCKE Toleration III. viii, A Pretence made use of to cover some other *By-Interest. **1849** GROTE Greece (1854) I. 434 With the certainty of..counterworking sinister *by-motives. **1820** SHELLEY Œdipus Tyr. II. i, The patronage, and pensions, and *by-payments. **1913** C. READ in Eng. Hist. Rev. Jan. 48 Walsingham believed that his [sc. Burghley's] *by-practice through Hunsdon with Arran was influenced by these considerations. **1826** E. IRVING Babylon II. 444 If ye carry any *by-purposes in your breast..woe unto you! **1818** HAZLITT Eng. Poets iii. (1870) 85 To support his argument by the *by-tricks of a hump and cloven foot. **1542** UDALL Erasm. Apoph. **vj a, Aristotle..gaue a *bywarnyng with this verse of the poete Homere. **1605** BRETON Soul's Immort. Crowne i. (D.) She is of a more heuenly nature, Than with such *by-wit to abuse a creature.

e. Sometimes the sense appears to be 'wrested from the right, distorted, erroneous'.

1670 BAXTER Cure Ch.-div. 174 He will make but an engine of his *by-opinions, to destroy true Piety. **1782** J. TRUMBULL M'Fingal III. (1795) 68 Liberty in your own *by-sense Is but for crimes a patent license. **1581** J. BELL Haddon's Answ. Osor. A vii b, Sondry deformed *byshapes of doctrine are fostered upp in the Church. **1651** Mr. Love's Case 33 Not wont to pervert or wrest words into *by-significations.

¶ See also 2 b., c., for combinations which lie on the border between the adverbial and adjective uses of by.

4. Occurring or done out of the ordinary course, or in the intervals between main occasions, or main engagements; apart from the main purpose; occurring by the way, incidental, casual, as by-accident, -betting, -bit, -business, -day, -drinking, -drop, -employment, -goodness, -hour, -job, -letter, -match, -production (= Gr. πάρεργον), -service, -sess, -vote, -wager; †**by-acquist**, an incidental gain; **by-charge**, a casual expense; † **by-clap**, ? an interlude; also BY-TIME, BY-WORK, etc.

1648 BP. HALL Select Th. §24 Whatever *by-accidents I may meet withal besides. **1661** BOYLE Style of H. Script. 48 Our *By-acquists do richly recompence our frustrated pains. **1886** H. SMART Outsider II. i. 2 On no race of late years had there been so much *bye-betting, that is to say, wagers in which one horse was backed against one other. **1818** SCOTT Br. Lamm. iv, A *by bit between meals. **1653** HOLCROFT Procopius II. 49 Those Romans finding Petra in their way, attempted the Castle as a *by-businesse. **a 1677** BARROW Serm. (1840) II. 403 A παρεργον, a diversion or by-business of our lives. **1525** LD. BERNERS Froiss. II. ccxxiv. [ccxx.] 702 To paye the erles *by charges. **1661** R. DAVENPORT City Nt.-Cap IV. in Dodsley (1780) XI. 332 No mask but a *by-clap. **1637** LAUD Sp. Star-Chamb. 14 June 18 Upon those *by-dayes [i.e. days when there is no sermon] to runne to other Churches. **1857** Guy Livingstone 32 (Hoppe) Being park-hack in the summer, and cover-hack in the winter, with a bye-day now and then when the country's light. **1596** SHAKS. 1 Hen. IV, III. iii. 84 You owe Money ..for your Dyet, and *by-Drinkings. **1824** Blackw. Mag. XVI. 662 The whole expense, by-drinkings included, might be defrayed for four pounds. **1647** FULLER Good Th. in Worse T. (1841) 95, I..sprinkle some *by-drops for the instruction of the people. **a 1617** HIERON Wks. II. 84 To deceiue their inward anguish, by I know not what *by-imployments. **a 1679** T. GOODWIN Wks. (1861) I. 417 There is a proper goodness, and there is an accidental, a *by-goodness. **1639** SALTMARSHE Policy 278 The best opportunities are meale times, and some other *by-houres of relaxation. **1867** SMILES Huguenots Eng. xiv. (1880) 247 His chief delight in his bye-hours was to shut himself up with Le Gendre's arithmetic. **1773** GRAVES Spir. Quix. II. ii. (D.) He could secrete a tester for some *bye-job. **1685** Royal Procl. in Lond. Gaz. No. 2068/2 The Post-Master General..to take effectual Care for the Conveyance of all *By-Letters. **1758** JOHNSON Idler No. 62 ¶ 10 A chesnut horse..who won ..ten *by-matches. **1870** LOWELL Study Wind. 110 The *by-productions of a busy man. **1639** FULLER Holy War III. xviii. (1840) 146 Employing the army of pilgrims in *by-services. **1650** Overseers' Acc. Holy Cross, Canterb., Sixe *By Sesses made within the yeare. **1880** H. E. MANNING in 19th Cent. Aug. 181 But Parliament has not yet confirmed that *by-vote. Ibid. A by-vote like that which shut the door of the House of Commons against Horne Tooke because he was a clergyman. **1886** H. SMART Outsider Others.. who had laid these heavy *bye-wagers, looking upon the horse as

having no possible chance, had never taken the trouble to secure themselves.

5. Of *character*, *relative standing*, or *importance*: Additional, extra, subsidiary, secondary, minor, of less importance. Contrasted with MAIN. As *by-art*, *-assembly*, *-authority*, *-bill*, *-book*, *-cause*, *-ceremony*, *-character*, *-crop*, *-dependency*, *-feature*, *-help*, *-ingredient*, *-knife*, *-meaning*, *-meter*, *-ornament*, *-part*, *-root*, *-rule*, *-saint's-day*, *-stamp*, *-taste*, *-tone*, *-world*, *-writer*, etc., etc. Also **by-bootings** (? *boltings*), 'the finest kind of bran' (Halliw.); **by-faith**, a secondary article of belief; **by-form**, a collateral and sometimes less frequent form; *spec.* in *Philology*; **by-foundation**, a second endowment or benefaction; **by-founder**, the bestower of such an endowment; †**by-leman**, a second lover or gallant (see quots.); **by-member**, an additional limb; **by-stake**, each of the short intermediate stakes used in basket-making; hence **by-stake** *v.*, to furnish with by-stakes; **by-staking** *vbl. sb.*; **by-tack** (see quot.).

a **1643** W. CARTWRIGHT *On death of Mrs. Ashford* (R.) What others now count qualities and parts She thought but complements, and meer *by-arts. **1673** SIR L. JENKINS *Let.* in W. Wynne *Life* I. 121 Encouraging a kind of *by-assembly here of the best affected princes of Germany. **1622** F. MARKHAM *Bk. War* IV. ix. §6. 156 Many other *by-authorities are transferred vpon these officers, as distribution of victuals. **1732** *Acc. Workhouses* 148 The weekly payments to the poor were 3*l.* 5*s.* or thereabouts, besides *By-bills, as they are called. **1663-4** PEPYS *Diary* 24 Jan., I..fell on entering, out of a *bye-book, part of my second journall-book. **1593** *Munic. Acc. Newcastle* (1848) 29 Keepeinge the by-booke of the rente of Gateshead. **1614** B. JONSON *Barth. Fair* III. i, I, the said Adam, was one cause (a *by-cause) why the purse was lost. **1633** AMES *Agst. Cerem.* II. 122 He..doeth now..admit such *by-Ceremonies. **1884** W. G. WILLS in *Pall Mall G.* 28 July 4/2 The *by-characters..support and feed the situations chiefly occupied by an impression full-length. **1880** *Academy* 24 July 61 Jute is only a *by-crop, like turnips and beans in this country. **1611** SHAKS. *Cymb.* V. v. 390 All the other *by-dependancies, From chance to chance. *a* **1679** T. GOODWIN *Wks.* (1864) VIII. 487 The Jews sought it [i.e. righteousness] but as a *by-faith. *c* **1683** DRYDEN *Vind. Dk. of Guise* Wks. 1725 V. 318 There is..no Dash of a Pen to make any *By-feature resemble him to any other Man. **1887** tr. *Hehn's Wanderings Pl. & Anim.* 461 Some Teutonic languages have a *by-form in which the Latin *n* is retained. **1905** *Science* 26 May 802/2 The English masque is a by-form of the English drama. **1934** PRIEBSCH & COLLINSON *German Lang.* II. ii. 172 The plural *Dinge* has a pejorative bye-form in *Dinger*. **1655** FULLER *Ch. Hist.* III. 75 There is a *By-Foundation of Postmasters in this House, (a kinde of Colledg in the Colledg). —— *Hist. Camb.* (1840) 216 The bounty of sir Francis Clark..justly entitled him to be a *by-founder. **1571** GOLDING *Calvin on Ps.* lxxiii. 25 They truste to theire owne riches and other *byhelpes. **1882** T. G. PINCHES in *Trans. Philol. Soc.* I. 99 We have, in these tongues, a valuable by-help in the Science of Semitic philology. **1645** J. GOODWIN *Innoc. & Truth Tri.* To Rdr. 2 Did not the God of Truth..put many a *by ingredient into his providence. *c* **1570** *Leg. Bp. St. Andrews* in *Scot. Poems 16th C.* II. 323 With y[t] his *byknife forth hes tane. *c* **1650** in C. Innes *Sk. Scot. Hist.* (1861) 431 He had a dirk and a 'by knife' for Highland expeditions. *c* **1400** *Lay le Freine* 103 Yif ich say ich hadde a *bi-leman. *a* **1400** *Octouian* (W.) 119 Thy yonge wyyf: Sche hathd a by-leman. **1836-7** SIR W. HAMILTON *Metaph.* iii. (1859) I. 54 Discharge from your minds the *by-meaning accidentally associated with the word *empiric*. **1509** HAWES *Past. Pleas.* XXIII. iii, A *bye membre she [nature] wyll than more devyse. **1851** MAYHEW *Lond. Labour* III. 270 (Hoppe) There were formerly several *bye-meters (for coal), chosen by the merchants from their own men, as they pleased. **1639** MASSINGER *Unnat. Comb.* Ded., When such *by-ornaments were not advanced above the fabric of the whole work. **1612** WOODALL *Surg. Mate* Wks. (1653) 19 A *by-part of Surgery not common. **1578** *Chr. Prayers* in *Priv. Prayers* (1851) 527 To weaken the principal root, that the *byroots..may lose all their power. **1862** POPE *Dubois on People Ind.* III. vi. (ed. 2) 336 *note*, The *bye-rule that no one shall engage in the same employment as his neighbour. **1624** GEE *Foot out of Snare* 79 When he preacheth vpon any *By-Saints-day. **1912** T. OKEY *Art of Basket-making* viii. 84 It is usual to supplement the stakes with *bye-stakes..which are inserted in the waling of the upsett between the pairs of stakes. This is termed half bye-staking. Square work is full bye-staked. **1960** E. LEGG *Country Baskets* 43 Double stakes—this is side stakes and long bye-stakes. **1884** *Law Times Rep.* LI. 221/2 They registered such name in Sweden as a *bye-stamp in addition to such mark. **1836** J. DOWNES *Mount. Decameron* III. 74 Didn't my father put his father into a *bye tack of our farm? **1847-78** HALLIW., *Bytack*, a farm taken in addition to another farm, and on which the tenant does not reside. *Herefordsh.* **1879** MISS JACKSON *Shropsh. Word-bk.* s.v., One 'afe o' the farms bin let bytack. **1799** J. ROBERTSON *Agric. Perth* 183 Persons of a nice palate loathe the milk on account of a *by-taste, which the turnips give it. **1852** SEIDEL *Organ* 87 The higher the fundamental tone is, the quicker the *by-tones follow each other. **1711** SHAFTESB. *Charac.* (1737) II. 298 'Tis only a separate *by-world, of which perhaps there are, in the wide waste, millions besides. **1872** LYTTON *Parisians* VII. iii, She..did enjoy that ideal by-world. **1577-87** HARRISON *Descr. Brit.* I. ix. 23 Let us see what Fortunatus hath written..and afterward what is to be found of other *by-writers.

6. in the sense of Counterfeit, mock, *pseudo-*, as †**by-fruit**, a gall or other excrescence simulating a fruit; †**by-gold**, imitation gold, tinsel; cf. BI-GOLD; ***by-teacher***.

1679 PLOT *Staffordsh.* (1686) 224 That *by-fruit that grows on the leaves of the Oak, which we call Galls. **1682** LISTER in *Phil. Coll.* XII. 166 By-fruits or Wens which Insects raise upon Vegetables. **1611** COTGR., *Orpel*, silver and *by-gold; a kind of leafe-tinne. **1633** AMES *Agst. Cerem.* II. 210 He maketh shew of a distinction, betwixt an authentique teacher, and another..*by-teacher.

-by (bɪ) *suffix*, forming

1. names of places (in the north of England), from BY *sb.*[1], as in *Grimsby*, *Netherby*, *Kirkby*, *Ormesby*, *Rugby*, *Whitby*.

2. descriptive personal appellations, playful or derisive, as ***idleby***, ***idlesby*** (= idler, Mr. Idleness), ***lewdsby***, ***litherby***, ***rudesby***, ***sneaksby***, ***sureby***, ***suresby***, ***wigsby*** (wearer of a wig), etc., especially frequent in 17th c. Perhaps formed in imitation of the place-names, or rather of personal surnames derived from these, such as *Crosby*, *Littleby*, *Slingsby*, *Spilsby*, *Thoresby*, some of which readily lent themselves to paronomasia. Cf. also such appellations as *Chatterbox*, *Butterfingers*, *Lazybones*, *Slyboots*. Some have suggested identity with *-boy*.

byabylle, obs. form of BUYABLE.

by-alde, obs. form of BEHOLD *v.*

byally, variant of BIALLY *a. Obs. Her.*

by-altar (ˈbaɪˌɔːltə(r)). [f. BY- 3 a + ALTAR.] A side altar; a secondary, as distinguished from the high, altar.

1882 SCHAFF *Relig. Encycl.* I. 67 Wherever the Reformation became victorious, all the by-altars were generally broken down.

by and by (ˈbaɪ ənd ˈbaɪ, ˈbaɪ ən ˈbaɪ), *advb. phr.* (and *sb.*) [originating app. in the use of BY *prep.* to denote succession (see BY *prep.* 25).]

†**1.** Of a succession of (persons or things): One by one, one after another, in order: **a.** in place.

1330 R. BRUNNE *Chron.* 267 He slouh tuenti, þer hedes quyte & clene, he laid þam bi & bi. *c* **1385** CHAUCER *L.G.W.* 304 Ffyrst sat the god of loue..And sithyn al the remenant by and by As they were of degre. *c* **1440** *Partonope* 1929 Wyth Rybyes and Saphires by and by. *c* **1485** in *E.E. Misc.* (1855) 4 The towres shal be of every [= ivory] Clene corvene by and by.

†**b.** in order or succession. *Obs.*

c **1330** *Assump. Virg.* (1866) 85 Vp ros oure swete ladi And kist þe apostles bi & bi. **1330** R. BRUNNE *Chron.* 73 Whan William..had taken homage of barons bi & bi. *c* **1400** *Rom. Rose* 4581 These were his wordis by and by [*mot à mot*]. *c* **1485** *Digby Myst.* (1882) III. 1911, I have gon þe stacyounes by and by.

†**2.** On and on, continuously. *Obs.*

c **1314** *Guy Warw.* (A.) 4828 Gij..souȝt þat maiden bi & bi: Op and doun he ȝede hir secheinde. *c* **1340** *Cursor M.* 15194 (Fairf.) Folowes forþ þat ilk man al-way bi & by. *c* **1430** *Syr Gener.* 4836 The knightes..So thei bare hem by and by That the host without began to fleen. *c* **1620** Z. BOYD *Zion's Flowers* (1855) 83 The Ivie bush the Oak claspes by and by.

3. Of sequence of events: †**a.** Straightway, immediately, directly, at once. *Obs.*

1407 *W. of Thorpe's Exam.* in Arb. *Garner* VI. 110 Some counselled the Archbishop to burn me by and by. **1526** TINDALE *Mark* i. 31 By and by [COVERDALE, immediatly] the fever left her. **1586** COGAN *Haven Health* ccxiv. (1636) 224 Ill seeds..shew not themselves by and by, but yet in processe of time they bud forth. **1611** BIBLE *Luke* xxi. 9 The end is not by and by. **1690** W. WALKER *Idiom. Anglo-Lat.* 390 They say he will be here by and by (even now).

4. [With the same development of sense as in *anon*, *presently*, and F. *bientôt*]: Before long, presently, soon, shortly. (The usual current sense; in U.S. vulgarly *by'm-by*.)

1526 *Pilgr. Perf.* (W. de W. 1531) 164 Innocentius counseyleth us to say it by & by. **1549** OLDE *Erasm. Par. Thess.* ii. 15 To haue slayne the Prophetes before, and byanby Christ after the Prophetes. **1596** SHAKS. *1 Hen. IV*, V. iv. 109 Imbowell'd will I see thee by and by, Till then, in blood, by Noble Percie lye. **1627** SANDERSON *12 Serm.* (1637) 554 Restraining Grace may tie us now, and bye and by unloose us. **1711** STEELE *Spect.* No. 132 ¶4 Thee and I are to part by and by. **1825** *Bro. Jonathan* I. 106 Bym by, naiteral enough, there they go! **1862** HUXLEY *Lect. Wrkg. Men* 93 You may by-and-by convert single flowers into double flowers. **1884** *Harper's Mag.* Feb. 410/2 Byme-by he ..gave up goin' to see the..girls.

†**5.** Of logical sequence: For that reason, therefore, as a consequence; = L. *continuo*. *Obs.*

1565-73 COOPER *Thesaur.* s.v. *Continuo*, If he did speake foolishly, will you by and by doe more foolishly? **1581** J. BELL *Haddon's Answ. Osor.* 263 b, As though y[t] whatsoever were unlike unto Ciceroes phrase, were by & by barbarous. **1621-31** LAUD *Sev. Serm.* (1847) 96 All 'heats' are not by and by a furnace.

B. Used as *sb.* **1. a.** Procrastination; **b.** Time coming.

1591 FLORIO *Sec. Fruites* 95 Neuer giue credite..to the by and by of England, nor to the warrant you of Scotland. **1719** OZELL tr. *Misson's Mem.* 120 Negligences (the French call them by and by's). **1792** ROBERTS *Looker-on* No. 1 Husbanding up wise resolutions to be executed by and by. This by-and-by is a sort of phantom which seduces us on till we drop into old age. **1869** *Daily News* 4 Feb., By the road of Bye-and-bye one arrives at the town of Never. **18..** S. F. BENNETT, '*There's a land that is fairer than day*,' In the sweet by-and-by We shall meet on that beautiful shore.

2. The name by which cannon were known to some African tribes.

1857 J. SHOOTER *Kafirs of Natal* 112 They believe that the fearful *by-and-bye* eats up everything. **1893** B. MITFORD *Gun-Runner* xxiv, We laugh at their *baï-nbaï*. What are guns, big or small, against the broad shields and devouring spears of the ever-conquering Amazulu? **1894** C. H. W. DONOVAN *With Wilson in Matabeleland* x. 234 They used to call common shells 'by-and-byes', because they could see the smoke, and by and by a shell would explode in their midst.

by and large, *advb. phr.* **1.** *Naut.* To the wind (within six points; cf. BY *prep.* 9) and off it.

1669 STURMY *Mariner's Mag.* 17 Thus you see the ship handled in fair weather and foul, by and learge. **1833** *Fraser's Mag.* VIII. 158 They soon find out one another's rate of sailing, by and large. **1961** F. H. BURGESS *Dict. Sailing* 42 *By and large*, with the wind near the beam.

2. In one direction and another, all ways; now esp., in a general aspect, without entering into details, on the whole.

1706 [see LARGE *adv.* 7 b]. **1769** in *Southern Lit. Mess.* XVII. 183/2 Miss Betsey, a charming frigate, that will do honour to our country, if you take her by and large. **1833** J. NEAL *Down-Easters* I. 23 A man who feels rather perplexed on the whole, take it by and large. **1869** 'MARK TWAIN' *Innoc. Abr.* v. 47 Taking it 'by and large', as the sailors say, we had a pleasant..run. **1929** WODEHOUSE *Mr. Mulliner Speaking* viii. 248 Taking it by and large—Australia seemed to him a pretty good egg. **1955** *Times* 23 May 9/2 The virtue of sound broadcasting was that, by and large, the content mattered more than anything else.

byar, obs. form of BUYER, BYRE.

byard (ˈbaɪəd). *Mining.* A leather strap crossing the breast, used by the men who drag wagons in coal-mines.

1847 in CRAIG; and in mod. Dicts.

byas(s, byasnesse, obs. ff. BIAS, -NESS.

by-battle, etc.: see BY- 3 c.

†**bybbey.** *Obs.* Some kind of herb.

? *a* **1400** *Chester Pl.* (Shaks. Soc.) 119 Bybbey [*Bodl. MS.* tibbie] raydishe and egremounde Which be my erbes.

bybell-babbel, obs. f. BIBBLE-BABBLE *sb.*

†ˈ**by-bet.** *Obs.* [The general sense is evident from the context, but the analysis is doubtful.]

a **1627** MIDDLETON & ROWLEY *Changeling* IV. i, The gold Is but a by-bet to wedge in the honour.

ˈ**bybidder.** [see BY- 3 c.] 'A person at an auction who bids with the object of raising the prices' Mrs. Toogood *Yorksh. Dial.* 1863. So ˈ**by-bidding.**

1880 *Libr. Univ. Knowl.* III. 238 By-bidding, at auctions where the bidder may be employed by the owner, and really bidding to enhance the price, not meaning to purchase.

bybill, -ylle, etc., obs. ff. BIBLE.

bybloemen (ˈbaɪbluːmən). [? Du., f. *bij* BY + *bloem* (pl. *bloemen*) BLOOM, flower.] One of the main varieties of the Garden Tulip.

1843 *Penny Cycl.* XXV. 343/2 The varieties of the latter tulip [*T. Gesneriana*]..are divided into..Bizarres, Bybloemens, Roses, and Selfs. **1846** MRS. LOUDON *Ladies' Comp. Flower-Gard.* 303 The Bybloemens..are white, shaded with violet or dark purple.

by-blow (ˈbaɪbləʊ). Also 8–9 **bye-**. [f. BY- 2 b, c, 4.]

1. A side-blow or side-stroke: *lit.* and *fig.*

1594 BARNFIELD *Helen's Rape* 67 In such a Ladie's lappe, at such a slipperie by-blow [cf. sense 3]. **1611** DEKKER *Roar. Girle* I. Wks. 1873 III. 145 How finely like a fencer my father fetches his by-blowes to hit me. **1645** MILTON *Colast.* Wks. (1851) 343 Now and then a by-blow from the Pulpit. **1808** *Edin. Rev.* XII. 52 Juvenal deals his by-blows to less prominent..characters.

†**2.** *fig.* A calamity or disaster not in the main course. *Obs.*

1600 HOLLAND *Livy* XXV. xxii. 564 So long as the Consuls, in whom rested the maine chaunce..sped well, they were the lesse troubled at these by-blowes. *a* **1677** BARROW *Serm. on Duty to Poor*, Inequality and private interest in things.. were the by-blows of our fall.

3. One who comes into the world by a side stroke; an illegitimate child, a bastard. Also *fig.*

1595 *Eng. Tripe-wife* (1881) 152 Not your wifes daughter, but a by-blowe..of your predecessours. **1658** USSHER *Ann.* 499 Ptolemei Apion, a By-blow by a Harlot. **1673** [R. LEIGH] *Transp. Reh.* 8 Had not his brain been delivered of this By-blow. **1708** MOTTEUX *Rabelais* IV. lxii, Kind Venus cur'd her beloved By-blow Æneas. **1749** FIELDING *Tom Jones* VIII. iv. (1840) 108/2, I thought he was a gentleman's son, thof he was a by-blow. **1868** BROWNING *Ring & Bk.* IV. 612 A drab's brat, A beggar's bye-blow.

†**4.** A blow that goes by, or misses its aim. *Obs.*

1639 J. CLARKE *Parœmiologia* s.v. *Crudelitas*, He would have made a good butcher, but for the by-blow. **1684** BUNYAN *Pilgr.* II. 103 Now also with their by-blows, they did split the very Stones in pieces.

byblus, var. spelling of BIBLUS, papyrus.

by-board, etc.: see BY- 3.

†ˈ**by-boat.** *Obs.* Also 8 **bye-boat.** [f. BY- + BOAT *sb.*] ? A supplementary or extra boat. Used esp. of the Newfoundland fishery; also *attrib.* in **by-boat-keeper**.

1698–9 *Stat. Admiralty, Shipping, &c.* (1810) Every Master of a By-boat or By-boats shall carry with him at least Two fresh Men in Six. *Ibid.* 26 Persons..that shall go over with their Servants to Newfoundland, to keep Boats on a Fishing Voyage, commonly called By-boat Keepers. **1708** *Royal Procl.* in *Lond. Gaz.* No. 4452/1 No By-Boat-Keepers should meddle with any..Cook-Room, Train Fat, or other Conveniency. **1796** *Campaigns* 1793–4 I. I. i. 1 Others were obliged to follow the transports in packets and bye boats.

by-business, etc.: see BY- 4.

bycal, -calle, obs. forms of BECALL.

†**bycapped**, *pa. pple. Obs. rare*⁻¹. [f. *by-* = BE- *pref.*: for the root cf. CAP *v.*; also L. *captus* and *bycaȝt*, pa. pple. of BECATCH.] ? Taken, attracted, captivated.

1387 TREVISA *Higden* Rolls Ser. VII. 331 Lanfrank was bycapped [*v.r.* cappet, ycapped; L. *captus*] by þe pouert and religioun of þat place [Bec].

bycaught, pa. pple. of BECATCH *v. Obs.*

bycause, byccer, obs. ff. BECAUSE, BICKER.

byce, bych(e, obs. ff. BICE, BITCH.

by-chamber, -chapel, etc.: see BY- 3.

by-channel (ˈbaɪˌtʃænəl). [f. BY- 3 b + CHANNEL.] A side-stream apart from the main channel; *fig.* a collateral branch (of a family).

1628 EARLE *Microcosm.* (Arb.) 71 Not a by-Channell or bastard escapes him. **1864** BATES *Nat. Amazon* Pref. 6 The network of by-channels and lakes which everywhere accompanies its [the Amazon's] course.

†ˈ**by-chop**. *Obs.* [see BY-, BY-SLIP.] A bastard. Cf. BY-BLOW.

1632 B. JONSON *Magn. Lady* IV. ii, I have sent By-chop away; the cause gone, the fame ceaseth.

byclag, byclappe, etc.: see BECLOG, BECLAP.

†**bycoket**. *Obs.* Also 5–6 **byekoket, bycokett, bicokett**; also *erron.* 6 **abocket, -ed, abococke**, 7 **abacoc**, 7–9 **abacot**. [a. OF. *bicoquet, bicocquet, biquoquet*, cap, casque, head-dress, 'capuce, casaque à capuchon; habituellement, coiffure militaire; quelquefois parure de femme, chaperon' (Godef.); dim. of F. *bicoque* = It. *bicocca* little castle on a hill, Sp. *bicoca* a lookout; probably the original meaning, as in the diminutives and derivatives, was some kind of cap, whence transf. to a structure, topping or 'crowning' a height. App. f. *bi-* twice + *cocca* as in *cocca del capo* 'crown of the head' (Florio). Cf. also Sp. *bicoquin* a cap with two peaks, *bicoquete* a peasant's cap, Piedm. *bicochin* a priest's cap (Diez).]

A kind of cap or head-dress (peaked before and behind): **a.** as a military head-dress, a casque; **b.** as an ornamental cap or head-dress, worn by men and women.

(The two crowns [? of England and France] with which the bycoket of Henry VI was 'garnished' or 'embroidered', were, of course, no part of the ordinary bycoket.)

1464 *Mann. & Househ. Exp.* 243 The man that browt the byekoket [of Henry VI, taken at Hexham] ffro Syre Robart Chaumbreleyn. **1488** in Leland *Brit. Coll.* (1770) IV. 225 Having a mannes hede in a Bycokett of silver. **1494** FABYAN VII. 654 The lorde John of Mountagu..chasyd Henry so nere, that he wan from hym..his bycoket, garnysshed with .ii. crownes of golde, and fret with perle and ryche stone. **1513** in *Archæol.* XXVI. 398 A nother paire of hostynge harness..wyth a bycoket. **1819–49** LINGARD *Hist. Eng.* (1855) IV. ii. 74 His bycoket or cap of state, embroidered with two crowns of gold, and ornamented with pearls.

¶ Through a remarkable series of blunders and ignorant reproductions of error, this word appears in modern dictionaries as ABACOT. In Hall's Chron. *a bicocket* appears to have been misprinted *abococket*, which was copied by Grafton, altered by Holinshed to *abococke*, and finally 'improved' by Abraham Fleming to *abacot* (perhaps through an intermediate *abacoc*); hence it was again copied by Baker, inserted in his *Glossarium* by Spelman, and thence copied by Phillips, and so handed down through Bailey, Ash, Todd, etc., to 19th century dictionaries (some of which provide a picture of the 'abacot'), and even inserted in dictionaries of English and foreign languages.

1548 HALL *Chron. Edw. IV* an. 2 One of them had on his hed the said Kyng Henrie's helmet (some say his high cap of estate), called abococked [*ed.* **1550** abococket], garnished with two riche Crownes. **1568** GRAFTON *Chron.* II. 661 His high Cap of estate, called Abococket. **1577** HOLINSHED *Chron.* 1314 His highe cappe of estate, called abococke. **1587** *Ibid.* (ed. Fleming) called Abacot. **1664** SPELMAN *Gloss., Abacot*: pileus augustalis Regum Anglorum 2 coronis insignitum *V. Chron.* An. 1463, Ed. 4, pag. 666, col. 2, l. 27 [*i.e.* Holinshed]. **1696** PHILLIPS, *Abacoc* [**1706** *Abacot*], the Regal Cap of Maintenance of the Kings of England adorn'd with two Crowns. **1721** BAILEY, *Abacot*, a Cap of State, made like a double Crown, worn anciently by the Kings of England. **1775** in ASH. **1810** *New Dict. Germ. Lang., Abacot*, die Staatsmütze, der Hauptschmuck der alten Engl. Könige. **1818** in TODD. **1882** LASCARIDES *Eng. Grk. Lex., Abacot*, τῆς κεφαλῆς κάλυμμα.

by-common, *a.* unusual: see BY *prep.* 7.

by-concernment, -consideration, etc.: see BY- 3 c.

†**bycorne**. *Obs.*

1. An early spelling of BICORN(E.

2. Given by Lydgate as the proper name of a fabulous beast represented in an old satire as feeding on patient husbands, and being always fat from the abundance of the diet, whilst his spouse *chicheface* or CHICHEVACHE (q.v.) fed upon patient wives and was always lean.

[The French form of the name (which does not appear before the 15th c.) was *Bigorne*, which does not appear to be the same as *bicorne* 'two horned'; the oldest Fr. version of the poem has a portrait of the creature, which has no horns.]

c **1430** LYDG. *Bycorne & Chichevache, Min. Poems* (1840) 130 Of Bycornoys I am bycorne fful fatte and rounde here as I stonde And in mariage bounde and sworne To Chi[che]vache as hir husbonde. *Ibid.* 131 For we, for oure humylite Of Bycorne shal devoured be.

by-corner (ˈbaɪˌkɔːnə(r)). [f. BY- 3 a + CORNER.] An odd or out-of-the-way corner.

1565 GOLDING *Ovid's Met.* v. (1593) 125 Sinking into blind By-corners. **1655** FULLER *Ch. Hist.* I. i. 2 Britain being a by-Corner, out of the Road of the World. **1792** *Anecd. W. Pitt* I. v. 127 Ready money..locked up in iron chests or hid in bye-corners. **1857** GEO. ELIOT *Sc. Cleric. Life* II. 198 No longer a nuisance existing merely in by-corners.

byd(de, byde, obs. forms of BID, BIDE.

bydeene, bydene, var. BEDENE *adv. Obs.*

bydel(le, obs. form of BEADLE.

bydelve, -dolve(n, etc.; see BEDELVE *v. Obs.*

by-dependency: see BY- 5.

by-design, -drinking: see BY- 3 d, 4.

by-dish, -door, etc.: see BY- 3.

by-doing (ˈbaɪˌduːɪŋ). *rare.* [f. BY- 4 + DOING.] †**a.** An additional or extra act. **b.** A casual by-work, *parergon*.

1496 *Dives & Paup.* (W. de W.) IV. xx. 185/2, Yf he were bounde to all suche bydoynges. **1842** J. H. NEWMAN *Ch. of Fathers* 86 The by doings of this man are more precious..than what others do with labour.

bydrive, var. of BEDRIVE *v. Obs.*

†ˈ**by-ˌdweller**. *Obs.* [f. BY- 2 a + DWELLER.] One who dwells close by or near; a neighbour.

1611 SPEED *Hist. Gt. Brit.* IX. xxii. 32 Artillery brought them in abundance by the By-dwellers. **1658** W. BURTON *Itin. Anton.* 144 Called Mading-bower..by the By-dwellers.

bye (baɪ), *sb.* [Variant spelling of BY *prep.* in its subst. use.]

1. A term used in various games and sports: **a.** *Cricket.* A run scored for a ball which passes the batsman, and which the wicket-keeper and long-stop fail to stop. ***to steal a bye***: to make a run for a ball by starting the instant it passes the wicket-keeper. ***leg-bye***: a run obtained for a ball diverted by grazing the batsman's person.

1746 in 'Bat' *Cricket Manual* (1850) 80, Byes..3. **1857** T. HUGHES *Tom Brown* II. viii, He has stolen three byes in the first ten minutes. *Ibid.* The ball..rises fast, catching Jack on the outside of the thigh, and bounding away as if from india-rubber, while they run two for a leg-bye amidst great applause. **1880** *Times* 28 Sept. 11/5 When a bye was obtained stumps were drawn.

b. in *Tennis, Boxing, Coursing, Cockfighting*, etc.: The position of an individual, who, in consequence of the numbers being odd, is left without a competitor after the rest have been drawn in pairs. Hence the phrases ***to draw a bye, to run a bye***, etc.

1883 *Field* 22 Dec. 863 To do away with byes in the penultimate and final rounds of [lawn-tennis] matches. **1887** *Daily News* 23 Feb. 3/7 The latter had had the benefit of drawing the bye in the second round. **1848** CRAIG s.v. *Bye*, In Coursing, a dog is said to 'run a bye' when it runs a course against another *not* in the match—thus equalising its runnings to the other dogs *in* the match. **1883** *Field* 22 Dec. 857 Sabrina then ran her bye, which she won.

c. in *Assoc. Football, Lacrosse*, etc.: A goal; a starting line. Also ***bye-line***, the line extending the alignment of the goal-posts.

1841 CATLIN *N. Amer. Ind.* (1844) II. xlix. 124 Erecting the 'byes' or goals which were to guide the play. **1847–78** HALLIW., *By*, the point or mark from which boys emit the marbles or taws. *Yorksh.* **1928** *Sunday Express* 16 Dec. 21/1 There was scarcely one who was not positive that the ball had passed the bye-line. **1959** *Times* 23 Feb. 3/2 Viollet pulled his pass back from the by-line. **1962** *Times* 6 Feb. 4/6 As is usual at the universities nowadays, the game [lacrosse] was played with side-lines and bye-lines.

d. A by-match or 'event'; one not in the programme. esp. in *Cockfighting*: in full ***bye-battle*** (also *transf.* and *fig.*), as distinguished from the 'main': see MAIN *sb.*³ 3.

1716 [see MAIN *sb.*³ 3]. **1754** *Connoisseur* 22 Aug. I. 178 Our present race of spindle-shanked beaux had rather close with an orange wench at the playhouse, than engage in a bye battle at Tottenham Court. **1859** LENNOX *Picts. Sporting Life* I. 175 Eleven a-head on the main and byes seven. *Ibid.*, On the usual fighting night..at the same pit, for bye-battles. **1882** R. CALDECOTT *'Graphic' Picts.* I. 13/1 There were carpet-dances on off-nights by way of byes. **1884** *L'pool Daily Post* 30 June 6/5 [Cockfighting] Some byes afterwards took place.

e. *Golf.* The hole or holes of the stipulated course that are unplayed when the match is finished.

1887 *Golfing* 92 *Bye.* Any hole or holes that remain to be played after the match is finished, are played for singly; unless the sides agree to make another match of them. **1890** *Sat. Rev.* 31 May 666/1 Prestwick golfers of to-day do not play for such stakes as a soul on the round and a nose on the bye.

2. The name of a plot against the government of James I. (So called in opposition to the *Main* plot: the relation between the two is one of the disputed points in English history. Cf. BY *sb.*² 1.)

1603 *St. Trials*, You are fools, you are on the bye, Raleigh and I are on the main; we mean to take away the king and his cubs. [**1885** LOW & PULLING *Dict. Eng. Hist.* s.v. *Bye Plot.* It is certain that the Bye Plot had no connection with the Main or Raleigh's Plot.] **1886** C. E. DOBLE in Hearne *Collect.* (1886) II. 436 Wm. Clarke was executed at Winchester, for his participation in 'the Bye', Nov. 29, 1603.

3. = BYWATER.

1928 J. R. SUTTON *Diamond* 34 Yellow Diamond... Fine White. White. First Cape... First Bye.

†**bye, by**, *v. Obs.* [Aphetic f. ABY, ABYE *v.*, but in sense 1 not separable from BUY *v.*]

1. *trans.* To pay for, atone for, make amends for; = ABY *v.* 2, BUY *v.* 3.

c **1340** *Cursor M.* 1146 (Fairf.) Þou sal bye [*Cott.* bi] hit selcouþ dere. **1561** NORTON & SACKV. *Gorboduc* (R.) Thou, Porrex, thou, shalt dearly bye the same. [See BUY *v.* 3, for other examples.]

2. *absol.* To pay the penalty, suffer; = ABY *v.* 4.

c **1440** *Sir Degrev.* xlvii. 737 Sche said, Tratur, thou shalt bye! Why were thou so hardye To do me this vylanye?

3. *intr.* To remain, stay, abide; = ABY *v.* 5 (confused with ABIDE).

c **1425** *Seven Sag.* (P.) 1202 The fyve were out wente, And the twa at home thay byeth, For to do that he thaym bydeth. **1594** *True Trag. Rich. III*, 57 Captain Blunt, Peter Landoyse and you Shall by in quarters.

bye, var. of BY.

bye, obs. form of BEE², ring; also of BUY.

bye, obs. form of BOY.

c **1440** *Promp. Parv.* 35 Bye or boye, *bostio.*

bye, var. of BEY *v. Obs.* to bend.

c **1305** *Edmund Conf.* 167 in *E.E.P.* (1862) 75 Vneþe he miȝte bye his rug: oþer lokie to þe grounde.

bye-bye¹ (ˈbaɪˌbaɪ). Also **by-by**, and simply **bye**. A sound used to lull a child to sleep; *hence*, a childish name for 'sleep' or 'bed'.

a **1500** *Carol* in *Rel. Ant.* II. 76 By, by, lulley...By and lulley. **1636** N. WALLINGTON in *Ann. Dubrensia* (1877) 32 Pug sang By-babie, with delightfull charmes. **1689** in *Gazophyl. Angl.* **1721–1800** BAILEY, *By by*..commonly Sung by Nurses to cause their Nurslings to fall asleep. **1867** MISS BROUGHTON *Cometh up as Fl.* xxii, Go to bye bye. **1885** BOUGHTON *Sk. Rambl. Holland* x. 144 Various strange 'by-by's' that he has gone to in his time. *Nursery Rime.* Bye, baby bunting.

bye-bye² (ˈbaɪˈbaɪ). Also **by-by(e, bye bye**, 8 **b'uy b'uy** and simply **b'y**. A colloquial and nursery variant of GOOD-BYE.

1709 *Tatler* No. 2, For Hat and Sword He'd call, Then, after a faint Kiss,—cry, B'y, Dear Moll: Supper and Friends expect me. **1736** BAILEY, *By by*, us'd familiarly, and chiefly to Children, instead of *Good b'y* or *God be with you.* *a* **1745** SWIFT *Wks.* (1768) VI. 320 B'uy, B'uy, Nic, not one poor smile at parting. **1777** SHERIDAN *Sch. Scand.* III. i, I shall..interrupt you—so bye! bye! **1872** LEVER *Ld. Kilgobbin* xiv. (1875) 95 'By-by!' said Atlee, carelessly, and he strolled away.

byefþe, var. BIHOFTH(E, *Obs.*, behoof.

byekoket, obs. form of BYCOKET.

byeld, byelle, obs. ff. BUILD, BOIL *sb.*

by-election. [f. BY- 4 + ELECTION *sb.* 1 b.] The choice of a parliamentary representative at a time other than that of a General Election. Also *attrib.*

1880 SIR W. HART DYKE in *Standard* 29 Nov., As a rule we do not apply money to bye-elections. **1897** *Daily News* 6 Jan. 4/5 Very actively engaged in by-election work. **1957** *Times* 11 May 7/2 In the borough elections the leftward movement seen in national by-elections has been repeated.

Hence **by-electioneering** *vbl. sb.* and *ppl. a.*, (the) contesting (of) a by-election. Also **by-electioneer**, a (successful) candidate at a by-election.

1897 *Westm. Gaz.* 25 Oct. 2/2 By-electioneering exigencies. **1938** *Times* 28 Apr. 15/4 By-electioneering will not be added to the work of Ministers with special responsibilities. **1962** *Punch* 4 July 25/1 Three by-electioneers had to take their seats.

So **by-eˈlectoral** *a.*, of, belonging to, or characteristic of a by-election.

1892 *Pall Mall Gaz.* 6 July 2/2 The Liberals are deprived of their by-electoral successes.

Byelorussian, var. BELORUSSIAN.

byen, obs. form of BE, BUY.

by-end (ˈbaɪɛnd). Also 7–8 bye-end. [f. BY- 3 c, d + END.] An object lying aside from the main one; a subordinate end or aim; *esp.* a secret selfish purpose, a covert purpose of private advantage. Hence †**by-ended** *ppl. a.*, having by-ends.

c **1610** SIR J. MELVIL *Mem.* (1683) 104 He took better with these of my hands, who he knew had no by-end. **1633** SANDERSON *3 Serm. ad Aul.* (1681) II. 38 If we do.. serviceable offices to our Brethren, out of any By-end or Sinister respect. **1651** J. ROCKET *Chr. Subject* vii. (1658) 96 Tyranny..consists in the..arbitrarie..immoderate, and by-ended exercise of power. **1678** BUNYAN *Pilgr. Progr.* 140 *marg.*, How By-ends got his name. **1760** LAW *Spirit of Prayer* II. 110 Love is quite pure; it hath no by-ends. **1869** GOULBURN *Purs. Holiness* xiii. 120 A man with a double aim or by-end.

†**byental**. *Obs.* (See quot.)

1708–21 KERSEY, *Byental*, the Yard of a Horse.

byer, obs. form of BIER; also of BUYER, BYRE.

1387 TREVISA *Higden* (1527) v. xiii, A byer [L. *feretrum*] of a wonder werke is yet seen at Dorchester aboue the place of his fyrste graue.

byern(e, variant form of BAIRN, BERNE.

byeth, obs. f. 3rd sing. and pl. pres. t. of BE.

†**ˈbyfall**. *Obs.* [see BY- 4.] An incidental accessory or accretion.

1571 GOLDING *Calvin on Ps.* xl. 9 The ceremonies are as it were an income or a byfall.

†**by-fellow**. *Obs.* [see BY- 5.] A fellow of a college (in the University of Cambridge) not on the foundation, and having inferior privileges to a foundation fellow. Hence **by-fellowship**.

1856–7 *Act 19 & 20 Vict.* lxxxviii. §50 in *Oxf. & Camb. Enactm.* 239 All actual Bye-Fellows excepted. **1589** in R. Potts *Liber Cantabrig.* (1855) 209[Andrew Perne D.D., formerly Master of the College, founded] two Bye-fellowships. **1846** MCCULLOCH *Acc. Brit. Empire* (1854) II. 355 Queens' College has nineteen fellowships, one by-fellowship, and numerous scholarships. Its head is styled president.

byffe, obs. form of BEEF.

†**by-ˈfleke**, obs. corrupt f. BEFLEE *v.*

c **1315** SHOREHAM 36 He that by-fleke wel lecherye Bi-vlekth foule continaunce.

byfore, byforne, obs. forms of BEFORE.

†**byˈfrap**, *v. Obs. rare*$^{-1}$. [f. BY- = BE- 2 + FRAP *v.*, a. OF. *frape-r* to strike.] *trans.* To beat about, thrash.

c **1380** *Sir Ferumb.* 2987 Þat company was so by-fraped among þes frenschemen.

by-fruit, mock fruit: see BY- 6.

byg, byge, obs. forms of BIG.

bygane, obs. form of BYGONE.

†**bygate**, var. form of BEGET *sb. Obs.* gain.

c **1300** *K. Alis.* 2136 Ye schul have, after bataile, Alle the bygates, saun faile; Y kepe nought, bote honour Al the bygate schal beo your.

byger, obs. form of BICKER *v.*

bygg(e, -en, -ere, obs. ff. BIG(G, BUY(ER.

byȝe, byȝer, -ar, byȝt, obs. ff. BEE², BUYER, BIGHT.

†**ˈby-ˌgirdle**. *Obs.* Forms: 1 biȝ-, bígyrdel, 2 bygerdel, 3–4 bi-, bygurdel, bygirdel, 5 bygirdylle, 6 bygyrdell, -yll. [OE. *bígyrdel* (= OFris. *bígerdel*, OHG. *bígurtil*, MHG. *bígürtel*), f. same elements as *begyrdan* to BEGIRD, with accented form of the prefix: for the suffix, cf. *gyrdel* GIRDLE.]

That which begirds; a girdle or belt; also, from the use of this, a purse, money-bag.

c **1000** *Ags. Gosp.* Matt. x. 9 Næbbe ȝe gold..on eowrum bigyrdlum [**1160** *Hatton G.* bygerdlen]. *c* **1000** ÆLFRIC *Gloss.* in Wr.-Wülcker 117 *Fiscus, uel saccus publicus*, biȝ-gyrdel. *a* **1225** *Ancr. R.* 124 Ane monne þet wurpe up on him a bigurdel ful of ponewes. **1362** LANGL. *P. Pl.* A. IX. 79 Þe Bagges and þe Bigurdeles [*v.r.* bygirdles] he haþ broken hem alle. **1393** *Ibid.* C. XI. 85 Þe bygurdeles. **1483** *Cath. Angl.* 31 A Bygirdylle, *marsupium, renale.* **1532** *Ort. Voc.*, *Renale*, a bygyrdyll, *est zona circa renes.*

bygo, -gon, -gone, pa. pple. of BEGO *v. Obs.*

bygoing (ˈbaɪˌɡəʊɪŋ), *vbl. sb.* Also 9 *Sc.* byganging, by-gaun. [f. BY- 2 a.] The action of passing by; esp. in phr. ***in the bygoing***: in passing, incidentally, by the way.

1637 RUTHERFORD *Lett.* cxxii. (1862) I. 303 A smell in the by-going is sufficient. **1818** SCOTT *Rob Roy* xxxv, Your beasts had been taking a rug of..moorland grass in the by-ganging. **1833** M. SCOTT *Tom Cringle* xv. (1859) 358 Timotheus I may state in the bygoing was not a Dutchman.

by-gold, mock gold, tinsel: see BY- 6.

bygone, by-gone (ˈbaɪɡɒn, -ɔː-), *ppl. a.* and *sb.* Also *Sc.* 5–8 bygan(e, 6 bygo, -gonne; and 6 begonne, 7–9 byegone. [f. BY- 2 d + GONE, pa. pple. of GO. Cf. *above-named* s.v. ABOVE D. 'A Scotch word' (J.); but used by Shakspere in sense 1.]

A. *ppl. a.* (In earlier quots. following the sb.)

1. a. That has gone by, past, (of time) elapsed; that has happened or existed in past time; former.

1424 *Sc. Acts Jas. I* (1597) §30 Gif onie [leagues] hes bene maid in time by-gane. **1452** EARL DOUGLAS in Tytler *Hist. Scot.* (1864) II. 387 Any actions, causes or querrels bygane. **1552** ABP. HAMILTON *Catech.* 224 To thoil temporal payne for our synnis by gane. **1611** SHAKS. *Wint. T.* I. ii. 32 This satisfaction, The by-gone-day proclaym'd, say this to him. **1788** J. POWELL *Devises* (1827) II. 315 A child subsequently born was entitled to a share in the by-gone income. **1824** CARLYLE *W. Meister* (1874) I. II. i. 64 The scenes of his by-gone happiness. **1826** J. WILSON *Noct. Ambr.* Wks. 1855 I. 168, I have not smoked a cigar for some months bygone.

†**b.** = AGO.

a **1745** SWIFT *Wks.* (1841) II. 47 About five or six and forty years bygone there were certain brass tokens current.

2. a. Of human beings: Gone out of life, deceased, departed. Also *transf.* of plants.

1513 DOUGLAS *Æneis* X. v. 168 The worthy actis of ȝour eldaris bygane. **1535** STEWART *Cron. Scot.* II. 669 Herald.. The eldest sone of Godowyn bygo. **1832** DE LA BECHE *Geol. Man.* 195 The roots..of the by-gone annuals..are matted together. **1856** KANE *Arct. Expl.* II. xv. 159 These evidences of a bygone generation of their fathers.

b. Belonging to past times.

1869 DICKENS *Lett.* (1880) II. 413, I hate the sight of the bygone assembly-rooms.

B. *sb.* [the ppl. adj. used ellipt.]

1. a. *pl.* Things that are past; *esp.* past offences.

1568 Q. MARY in H. Campbell *Love-lett. Mary Q. Scots* App. 29 For good amitie, as well for bygonnes as to come, betwixt them and all our obedient subjects. **1649** BP. GUTHRIE *Mem.* (1702) 75 That bygones on both sides should be passed by. **1790** MORRISON *Poems* 135 (JAM.) All byganes are forgot and gone, And Arthur views her as his own. [See also c.]

b. Payments overdue; arrears.

1663 SPALDING *Troub. Chas. I* (1829) 25 [They] compelled the tenants..to produce their last acquittances and pay them bygones. **1721** WODROW *Hist. Ch. Scot.* II. 256 (JAM.) He could have no warrant for bygones [of his stipend], unless he would..conform to the established church.

c. *esp.* in phr. ***bygones are bygones***, ***let bygones be bygones***, etc. (Rarely in *collect. sing.*)

1636 RUTHERFORD *Lett.* lxii. (1862) I. 166 Pray..that byegones betwixt me and my Lord may be byegones. **1648** NETHERSOLE *Parables* 5 Let bygans be bygans. **1758** CHESTERF. *Lett.* (1792) IV. 147 By-gones are by-gones, as Chartres, when he was dying, said of his sins. **1837** CARLYLE *Fr. Rev.* (1871) II. v. i. 166 Bygone shall be bygone; the new Era shall begin! **1847** TENNYSON *Princ.* IV. 51 Nor is it Wiser to weep a true occasion lost, But trim our sails, and let old bygones be. **1864** BURTON *Scot. Abr.* I. iii. 118 The truce.. was cordially ratified; bygones were counted bygones.

d. *sing.* A person or thing of the past; *spec.* a domestic, industrial, etc., artefact of a disused kind.

1857 MELVILLE *Confidence-Man* xxii. 161 The working or serving man, shall be a buried by-gone, a superseded fossil. **1891** HARDY *Tess* III. xlv. 89 Bygones would never be complete bygones until she was a bygone herself. **1897** *Westm. Gaz.* 24 July 4/2 We would let the bygone of the Rae Mine, whatever its case, be a bygone. **1935** *Burlington Mag.* Feb. p. xiii/2 These diverse dispersals should give a real spurt to the collecting of so-called 'by-gones'. **1940** *Ibid.* Dec. 173/2 Italian Maiolica, pottery and porcelain of other lands, curious and entertaining 'bygones' of many kinds. **1960** H. HAYWARD *Antique Coll.* 52/1 *Bygones*, any objects no longer in use, such as obsolete agricultural implements, old-fashioned spits [etc.].

2. Past time; the past: *rare.*

1872 W. F. BUTLER *Gt. Lone Land* iii. (1875) 24 Bunker has long passed into the bygone. **1887** SALA in *Illust. Lond. News* 19 Mar. 306 Dealings with booksellers in the bygone.

†**ˈby-ground**. *Obs.* [f. BY- 3 a, 5 + GROUND.] **a.** A piece of ground lying out of the way. **b.** *fig.* A secondary ground or cause.

a **1603** T. CARTWRIGHT *Confut. Rhem. N.T.* (1618) 499 Augustine esteemed it but of custome, and other by-grounds, that in one Church there should bee but one onely Bishop. **1611** SPEED *Hist. Gt. Brit.* VI. xvi. 96 Many remnants [of causeways] remaine, especially in pastures, or by-grounds out of the rode way.

bygyn(ne, obs. ff. BEGIN, BEGUINE.

by-hand (ˈbaɪhænd), *adv. Sc.* [f. BY- 1 + HAND.] **a.** Out of hand, aside, out of the way. **b.** Incidentally.

1636 RUTHERFORD *Lett.* lxxii. (1862) I. 187 Cast them by-hand as we do old clothes. **1834** GALT in *Fraser's Mag.* X. 160 She was far advanced when it was by-hand noticed.

†**ˈby-ˌhanger**. *Obs.* [f. BY- 2 a + HANGER.] **a.** A hanger-on, a parasite. **b.** An appendage.

1581 J. BELL *Haddon's Answ. Osor.* 275 b, How many byhangers do you couple to this uniforme & common creed? **1591** HORSEY *Trav.* (1857) 216 Sir Jerom Bowes offers to prove it by one Finch, a by-hanger of his.

byhede(n, -heede, obs. ff. BEHEAD *v.*

†**byˈhirne**, *v. Obs. rare*$^{-1}$. [f. BY- = BE- 6 + *hirne*, HERNE, corner.] *trans.* To hide in a corner.

1394 *P. Pl. Crede* 642 Þat þei may henten, þey holden; by-hirneþ it sone.

byhod, obs. f. *behoved*, pa. t. of BEHOVE.

byhofþe, -ofthe, var. BIHOFTH(E, *Obs.*, behoof.

†**byˈhore**, *v. Obs.* [f. BY- = BE- *pref.* 6 + WHORE *v.*] To commit adultery against. See BEWHORE.

c **1440** (*Erle Toulous*) *Lincoln MS.* A. i. 17 f. 120 (Halliw.) For thou haste byhorede my lorde.

byhynde(n, obs. form of BEHIND.

byhyng, byil, obs. ff. BUYING, BOIL *sb.*

by-intent, -interest: see BY- 3 d.

byk(e, byik, variants of BIKE *dial.*, bees' nest.

†**byke**, *v. Obs. Sc.* [? f. BIKE *sb.*¹] *trans.* ? To crowd *in* (as with a swarm).

1606 BIRNIE *Kirk-Burial* (1833) 22 We may be laid, not in the Kirk, but in a competent Kirk-ile or yarde..not byked in with the belly-god beastes that blinds the world with buriall in Kirk.

byker, obs. form of BEAKER, BICKER.

bylad, -aft, -eft, pa. pples. of BELEAD, -LEAVE.

†**ˈbyland**. *Obs.* Also biland. [See quot. 1577: *by-* seems to have been taken by Harrison in the sense of 'off at the side'.] A peninsula.

1577–87 HARRISON *Descr. Brit.* x. 30 The How, which is not an Iland..but almost an Iland, which parcels the Latins call *Peninsulas*, and I do English a *Byland*. **1610** HOLLAND *Camden's Brit.* (1637) 22 The Biland Taurica Chersonesus. **1622–62** HEYLIN *Cosmogr.* III. (1673) 163/2 This Biland or Demy-Island. *c* **1630** RISDON *Surv. Devon* (1714) II. 302 [The river] Tamer..leaveth Cornwall, as it were a Peninsula, or By-land.

bylander, obs. form of BILANDER.

by-lane (ˈbaɪˌleɪn). Also 6 bie-, 9 bye-lane. [f. BY- 3 b + LANE.] A lane lying off from the main street or road; *also*, a side passage in a mine.

1587 FLEMING *Contn. Holinshed* III. 1350/1 The citizens ..set vpon them..by the bylanes. **1666** EVELYN *Diary* 7 Sept., The bie lanes..were..fill'd up with rubbish. **1697** E. LHWYD in *Phil. Trans.* XXVII. 467 They make their By-lanes (as in other Pits) as the Vein requires. **1762** HUME *Hist. Eng.* (1806) V. lxix. 189 Through by-lanes and cross the fields, to make their escape. **1858** BRIGHT *For. Policy, Sp.* (1876) 468 Turning fertilizing rivulets into every bye-lane and alley.

bylaucte, pa. t. of BILAUH *v. Obs.* to laugh at.

bylaue, var. of BELEAVE *v. Obs.*

by-law, bye-law (ˈbaɪlɔː). Also 4 bilage, 4–6 bilawe, 6–7 by-lawe. [In sense 1 apparently (from the identity of meaning, and the identification of *bylaw-man* (see below) with *byrlaw-man*) a doublet of BYRLAW. The difference of form would be explained by the derivation of *bylaw* from the stem instead of the genitive case of ON. *bý-r*, Sw. and Da. *by*, 'dwelling-place, farm, village, township, town': cf. the Dan. *bylag*, Sw. *byalag*, *bylag*, mentioned below. It is less probable that *bylaw* might be formed in England itself from the same elements: cf. BY *sb.*¹; but it might be a corruption of *byr-law* either phonetic, or due to confusion with the adverbial prefix BY-. The earliest examples of the word refer to Kent: the difficulty of assigning a Scandinavian etymology to the local name of a Kentish custom is obvious, but cf. quot. 1292 under BYRLAW from an assize held in Devonshire, and quot. 1370 for the general use of *bylaw* in sense 2. Sense 3 however shows that the word was in the 16th c. used as if f. BY *adv.* + LAW, analogous to *by-name*, *by-path*, *by-way*; and this is the way in which sense 2 is now understood and used. This may have been, in its origin, merely a mistaken interpretation, but it is also possible that a word may have been formed independently from these elements, without influence of the Scandinavian word, although naturally falling together with it in the general sense of subsidiary or side-law.

The compounds actually found in the Scandinavian langs. are Da. *bylag*, explained by Molbech as 'Forening imellem alle eller endeel Bönder i en Landsby, Bymenighed', i.e. 'association between all or some of the farmers in a rural township, *bymenighed*', the latter being further said to be 'the community of citizens in a town, of farmers in a rural township, etc.'; also Sw. *byalag*, *bylag*, village community. In ON. *lag* had, among other senses, that of 'fellowship'; the pl. *lög* those of 'law', 'law-community or association', and 'law-district' (cf. the *Dena-lagu* or *Dane-law*). The sing. has given Sw. and Dan. *lag-et*; the pl. Sw. *lag-en*, Da. *lov-en* 'law'. The word *belagines*, alleged by Jordanis to be Gothic

for 'written law', has sometimes been referred to in this connexion; but it can have no relation to the Eng. word.]

† **1.** Apparently the same as BYRLAW: occurring in the 13th c. as the name of a custom (in Kent) according to which disputes concerning boundaries were settled outside the law courts, on the testimony of neighbours, by official or specially deputed arbitrators. *Obs.*

1283 in W. Thorn *Chronica* (Twysden p. 1936) [Abbas Nicholaus ordinavit] Item si contingat quæstionem moveri inter nos [monks of St. Augustine, Canterbury] & archiepiscopum vel ejus tenentes de subtractionibus, purpresturis, dampnis seu aliis injuriis hinc inde factis, quod consuetudo illa quæ dicitur *bilage* observetur. **1303** *ibid.* Ad sextum articulum petitur, quid intelligitur per hanc dictionem Bilage. 'Dicunt quod quidam usus vel consuetudo, qui Bilage in partibus Kantiæ vulgaliter appellatur, sic se habere consuevit: quod cum contentio vel controversia aliqua suborta fuerit inter aliquos super finibus, seu limitibus, debent seneschalli seu ballivi partium, vel aliæ personæ fide dignæ, ad hoc per partes specialiter deputatæ, in loco de quo est contentio convenire, remque oculis subicere, informationeque per viros vicinos fide dignos habita, absque strepitu judiciali, & figura judicii, mox totam dirimere quæstionem.

b. Often specially applied to ordinances made by common assent in a Court-leet or Court-baron. Cf. BYLAW-MAN.

1607 COWELL *Interpr.*, *Bilawes* [*ed. 16 adds* ' or rather *By-laws*, that is Laws made *obiter* or by the *By*'] are orders made in court leets or court Barons by common assent, for the good of those that make them, farder then the publique law doth binde. These in Scotland are called (burlawe) or (birlawe) Skene *de Verb. Sign.* verbo *Burlawe.* **1622** CALLIS *Stat. Sewers* (1647) 230 Also Ordinances may be made by the power of a Court, as in a Court Baron to make Orders, or by the Inhabitants of a Town by Custom.. And these are more properly by-Laws then Laws. **1642** *N. Riding Rec.* IV. 225 A Barmeby gent. presented for not paying the sum in which he was assessed according to an ancient custom of the inhabitants called a Bylaw. **1676** COLES, *Bylaw, Burlaw* or *Byrlaw*, laws determined by persons elected by common consent of neighbours. **1689** SELDEN *Table Talk*, *Convocation* §2 A Court-Leet, where they have a power to make By-Laws, as they call them. **1875** STUBBS *Const. Hist.* I. v. 91 In the courts of the manor are transacted the other remaining portions of the old township jurisdiction; the enforcing of pains and penalties on the breakers of by-laws, etc.

c. In Old Danish, *bylag* had also the sense 'Payment or contribution in order to receive citizenship or the freedom of the *by*' (see Kalkar); the following quotation applies the name to a proportional charge or assessment made for a local purpose: cf. 1642 in b.

1691 BLOUNT *Law Dict.* s.v. *Bi-scot*, 9 Edw. 3, At a Session of Sewers held at Wigenhale in Norfolk, it was decreed, That if any one in those parts of Marchland, should not repair his proportion of the Banks, Ditches and Causeys, by a day assigned, xii*d.* for every Perch unrepaired (which is called a Bilaw) should be levied upon him.

2. A 'law' or ordinance dealing with matters of local or internal regulation, made by a local authority, or by the members of a corporation or association. More particularly: An ordinance made by the members of a corporation for the better government of their own body, or for the regulation of their dealings with the public; in modern times most commonly (as by railway companies) in the exercise of powers expressly conferred by the Legislature.

a. of a town or local authority.

1370 *Yearbook 44 Edw. III*, 19 Inhabitants dun ville, sauns ascun custome poient fayre ordinaunces ou Bilawes pur reparation del Eglise, ou dun haut voy, ou dascun tiel chose, que est pur le bien publique generalment, & in tiel case le greinderpart liera touts sauns ascun custome. **1622** BACON *Hen. VII*, Wks. (Bohn) 459 There was likewise a law to restrain the by-laws, or ordinances of corporations. **1628** COKE *On Litt.* 110b, An vpland Towne may alledge a Custome..to make By-lawes for the reparations of the Church, the well ordering of the Commons, etc. **1732** (*title*) City Liberties..and Bye Laws, relating to Carts, Coaches, Fire-cocks, Fairs, etc. **1815** SCOTT *Guy M.* xxiii, A by-law of the corporation of Newcastle.

b. of a society or corporation.

1366–80 WYCLIF *Wks.* (1880) 276 þat þe ordre of presthod ..be holden..sikerer þan ony newe secte wiþ bilawes, customes, obseruancis founden of synful men. **1523** in Turner *Sel. Records Oxford* 40 By lawes wch the..Schollers ..have made. **1681** *Trial S. Colledge* 98, I heard a man was in trouble..upon a By-Law in the Stationers Company. **1694** LUTTRELL *Brief Rel.* (1857) III. 355 The new bank.. have appointed a committee of 15 to make by laws. **1876** BANCROFT *Hist. U.S.* III. xi. 450 The power of making by-laws, subject to parliamentary control. *Mod.* Prosecuted for a breach of the Company's Bye-Laws.

3. A secondary, subordinate, or accessory law.

1541 COVERDALE *Old Faith* vi. Wks. 1844 I. 41 As for all the laws and ordinances which afterward were added unto these two tables, they were not joined thereunto as principal laws, but as by-laws. *a* **1680** BUTLER *Rem.* (1759) I. 209 Great Philosophers..proudly think t' unriddle ev'ry Cause, That Nature uses, by their own By-laws. *a* **1719** ADDISON (J.) In the beginning..is inserted the law or institution; to which are added two by-laws, as a comment upon the general law. **1780** SIR J. REYNOLDS *Disc.* x. (1876) 13 In detail, or what may be called the by-laws of each art.

Hence **bylaw-man** = BYRLAW-MAN.

1552–84 *Court-leet Rec. Manchester* in *Athenæum* 2 Aug. (1879) 146 Byrlamen; birlamen; **1590** bylawmen; **1593** berlawmen. **1591** *Acc. Feoffees of Comm. Lands Rotherham*, ibid. 9 Aug., To the byer law-men for casting open closes. **1620** —— Bye-lawe men with the rest of the neabors..The multitude of pore people which follow the Bye-law men. **1622** —— Ale and bread which was bestowed on the Bylaw-men. *a* **1800** *Form of Bylawmen's Oath*, formerly used in the Cholmley Courts (MS. communicated by Rev. J. C. Atkinson) 'You shall well and truly execute the office of Bylawman for the year ensuing for the Township of ——, and you shall take care that the commons and common fields be broken at the usual time, that the common gates, fences, and bridges be duly made and repaired, and the bylaws be duly kept and observed, etc.' **1875** STUBBS *Const. Hist.* I. v. 91 *note*, The officers elected [at Aldborough, Yorksh.] in the ninth of Charles I were four by-lawmen or *plebiscitarii*, two constables, etc.

bylboes, bylbres, obs. pl. form of BILBO².

byld(e, obs. f. BUILD *v.*; obs. pa. t. BUILD *v.*

bylders, var. of BILDERS, narrow-leaved water-parsnip; in Ireland water-cress.

byle, obs. form of BOIL *sb.* and *v.*

† **byles**, *sb. pl. Obs.* Also 6 bilis, bylis. [Prob. (although the phonetic correspondence is not quite clear) a. F. *bille* 'ball', also 'a piece of wood'. In French *jeu de billes* has been the name of three distinct games: (1) a game with balls, identified by some with billiards, (2) a game like 'knur and spell' or 'tipcat', (3) skittles: see Littré s.v. *bille*, and Charpentier s.v. *billa*.]

An obsolete game with bowls, mentioned chiefly as Scotch.

1530 PALSGR. 200/2 Bowle to playe at the byles, *bille.* *c* **1565** in Chalmers *Life Mary* (1818) I. 133 (JAM.), I had the honour..to play a party at a game called the Bilis. **1565** *Aberdeen Reg.* V. 26 (JAM.) Cartis, dyiss, tabillis, goif, kylis, bylis, & sic wther playis.

bylet, byllet, obs. forms of BILLET².

byleue, -leve, -liue, obs. ff. BELIEF, -LIEVE, -LEAVE, -LIVE.

bylike, -lyke, obs. ff. BELIKE.

‖ **bylina** (bəˈliːnə). Pl. byliny, bylinas. [Russ.] A Russian traditional heroic poem.

1886 I. F. HAPGOOD *Epic Songs Russia* 1 Amid the vast swamps and forests of Northern Russia the *bylinas* are sung to-day by scores of peasants. **1902** L. WIENER *Anthol. Russ. Lit.* I. 10 The bylinas of the Vladimir cycle, the last and most numerous of all that are preserved, point to an old poetic tradition. **1932** N. K. CHADWICK *Russ. Heroic Poetry* 2 Even in the province of Olonets on Lake Onega, the district in which the great majority of the *byliny* have been collected, the practice of singing *byliny* has for long been restricted to a limited area.

by-line (ˈbaɪlaɪn). [f. BY- + LINE *sb.*²]

1. A line giving the name of the writer of an article in a newspaper or magazine. orig. *U.S.*

1926 HEMINGWAY *Fiesta* (1927) ii. 19, I sorted out the carbons, stamped on a by-line. **1928** *Sat. Even. Post* 12 May 36/2 The term 'by-line' means the signature of the writer. **1938** I. KUHN *Assigned to Adv.* iii. 26 The thing I wanted most was a by-line—that magic inch of print above a story I had written which would identify me as the author of the gem. **1963** *Punch* 14 Aug. 238/3 To win a by-line is..the rising newspaperman's dream.

2. A secondary line; a side-line.

1936 *Scrutiny* V. June 16 But when we think of Johnson and Crabbe..then Gray, Thomson..and the rest belong plainly to a by-line.

Hence as *v.*, to print a by-line. So ***by-lined*** ppl. a.; **by-liner**, one who writes under a by-line.

1944 *Birmingham* (U.S.) *News* 7 Apr. 9 He discovered a young writer and launched him in the newspaper business, where he soon became a popular sports by-liner. **1958** 'E. A. ROBERTSON' *Justice of Heart* iii. 35 It's my business to decide whether I by-line the stuff on my page or not! **1959** I. Ross *Image Merchants* (1960) viii. 126 He..soon had a by-lined column on science. **1961** *Guardian* 30 Sept. 12/6 The ace byliners found their stories on the back page. **1970** G. LORD *Marshmallow* xv. 129 He would swap two years of by-lined cuttings for one book on the shelf with his name on the spine.

† **ˈbylive, ˈbylif(e.** *Obs.* Also 1 biȝ-, bic-, bileofa, bilifen, 1–3 biliue, 3 bileue, -leoue, -lif, 4 bylyf, -lyue. [OE. *biȝleofa*, f. *biȝ*, *bí*, BY + *lif* life, *-leofa* living.] That which one lives by; living, sustenance.

c **1000** ÆLFRIC *Gen.* vi. 21 Of eallum mettum..þæt hiȝ beon æȝþer ȝe ðe ȝe him to biȝleofan. *c* **1000** *O.E. Gloss.* in Wr.Wülcker 492 *Pulmentum*, bilifen. *c* **1200** *Trin. Coll. Hom.* 99 He let hem reine manne to bi-liue. *a* **1225** *Ancr. R.* 168 Kinges & kaiseres habbeð hore bileoue of oure large relef. *c* **1275** *Prov. Alfred* 96 in *O.E. Misc.* 109 His medis to mowen, his plouis to drivin to ure alre bilif. **1377** LANGL. *P. Pl.* B. xix. 230 With sellyng and buggynge her bylyf to wynne. **1393** *Ibid.* II. 18 He het þe elementes..brynge forth ȝoure bylyue.

byllament, var. of BILIMENT. *Obs.*

bylle(n, obs. form of BILL *v.*

bylled, bylt(e, obs. pa. t. and pple. of BUILD *v.*

byllerne, obs. form of BILDERS.

bylly, obs. form of BELLY.

byloke, var. BELOUKE *v.*, to shut up, keep close.

c **1380** *Sir Ferumb.* 2127 Fyrum[bras]..bad me kepe þys & faste hit her by-loke.

bylowȝ, pa. t. of BILAUH *v. Obs.* to laugh at.

bylynne, -lyve, var. BLIN, BELIVE.

by-matter (ˈbaɪˌmætə(r)). [f. BY- 3c, 5 + MATTER.] Something beside the main business; a side incident; a trivial, unimportant matter.

1552 T. BARNABE in Ellis *Orig. Lett.* II. No. 145 II. 197 Few men..was sente soe manye tymes to the Counsell privylye, for bye matters as I was. **1580** NORTH *Plutarch* 286 His Accusers..running into other by-matters, left the chief matter. **1674** *Consid. Peace & Goodw. Prot.* 8 Dissenters and Scruplers in by-matters. **1685** MANTON *Christ's Tempt.* vi. Wks. 1870 I. 314 Christ answereth to the main point, not to by-matters. **1755** in JOHNSON. **1852** SMITH *Eng. & Fr. Dict.*, By-matter, *incident.*

bymeby, var. BIMEBY *adv.*

bymene, obs. form of BEMOAN.

† **byˈmodered**, *ppl. a. Obs.* [f. BY- = BE- *pref.*; cf. Du. *modder*, Ger. *moder* mud.] Besmeared with mud, bemired.

a **1307** *Pol. Songs* 158 Ant heo cometh by-modered ase a mor-hen.

bymolen: see BEMOLE in BE- *pref.* 6.

bymoorne, -mowe, obs. ff. BEMOURN, BEMOW.

byn, -ne, obs. ff. BIN, BEEN; = *are* (see BE *v.*).

byname, by-name (ˈbaɪneɪm), *sb.* Also 9 bye-name. [f. BY- 5 + NAME.]

1. A name other than the principal or main one; a subsidiary name or appellation; *esp.* a cognomen or surname; a sobriquet.

c **1374** CHAUCER *Boeth.* III. ix. 84 Suffisaunce, power, noblesse, reuerence, and gladnesse ben only dyuerse bynames [of happiness], but hir substance haþ no diuersite. **1631** WEEVER *Anc. Fun. Mon.* 644 Lions-heart, is..the by-name of K. Richard. **1655** FULLER *Ch. Hist.* III. ii. §52 Some of these by-names..remained many years after to them, and theirs; amongst which Plantagenist was entailed on the Royal bloud of England. **1865** MERIVALE *Rom. Emp.* VIII. lviii. 16 Eutropius..gives him the additional name of Crinitus, perhaps a by-name of his family.

2. A nickname given in sport or ridicule.

1580 NORTH *Plutarch* 975 Pleasant by-Names against Augustus, Livia, and their familiars, whereat every one of them laughed. **1589** PUTTENHAM *Eng. Poesie* (Arb.) 212 A by-name geuen in sport..As, Tiberius the Emperor, because he was a great drinker of wine, they called him.. Caldius Biberius Mero, in steade of Claudius Tiberius Nero. **1601** HOLLAND *Pliny* II. 504 Callimachus is the workeman of greatest note, in regard of a by-name giuen vnto him, and that was Cacizotechnos. **1705** HICKERINGILL *Priest-Cr* II. vii. 70 No By-names of Whig or Tory, Highflyers or Dissenters. **1862** EARL STANHOPE *Pitt* I. 67 Mr. Welbore Ellis..the butt of Junius, under the by-name of Grildrig.

byname (ˈbaɪneɪm), *v.* ? *Obs.* [f. prec. sb.] *trans.* To surname, to nickname.

1570–87 HOLINSHED *Scot. Chron.* (1806) II. 442 The Scots in like manner bynamed a parliament..and called the same a running parliament. **1611** SPEED *Hist. Gt. Brit.* IX. xii. 20 Edward, by-named (not of his colour, but of his dreaded acts in battle) the Black Prince. **1632** BROME *Novella* Dram. Pers., Paulo, By-named Burgio. **1755** in JOHNSON; and in mod. Dicts.

byname, -nemme, -nom, etc.: see BENIM.

bynd, bynte, obs. ff. BIND, BOUND.

bynempt, pa. t. of BENAME *v. Obs.*

bynethe(n, -neithe, etc., obs. ff. BENEATH.

bynfet, byngger: see BENEFIT, BENGER(E.

bynge, bynk(e, obs. ff. BINGE, BINK.

† **by-ˈnight.** *Obs. rare*⁻¹. [f. BY *prep.* + NIGHT.] ? A letter dispatched by the night post.

1766 ENTICK *London* IV. 295 There is..a clerk of the by-nights, and his assistant.

† **bynny-pepper.** *Obs.* A kind of pepper.

1603–4 *Act 1 Jas I*, xix. §1 All Spices..and other Merchandises garbleable..Long-pepper..Coliander seeds, Bynny-pepper.

bynym, obs. f. BENIM *v.*

ˈby-office. [f. BY- 4, 5 + OFFICE.] **a.** An office other than the main one. **b.** A form of religious service for by-occasions.

1577 VAUTROULLIER *Luther's Ep. Gal.* 185 It is not the proper office of Christ..to teach the law, but an accidentall or a byoffice. **1680** BAXTER *Cath. Commun.* (1684) 12 Not medling..with the Discipline, By-offices, etc. **1689** *Myst. Iniq.* 40 Exceptions some may have against some Things in the By-Offices, and Occasional Service.

byofþe, var. BIHOFTH(E, *Obs.*, behoof.

byon (bjəʊn). [ad. Burmese *brun* refuse, as of grain, peas, etc., the matrix earth of rubies and the rejected stones; app. related to *prun*, *phrun* to be worn out or exhausted.] The ruby-bearing

clay of the ruby mines district of Upper Burma; also *attrib.*

1892 E. W. STREETER *Prec. Stones* (ed. 5) 153 A brown or yellowish clay, known locally as *Byon*, seems to be the typical Ruby-bearing earth. **1895** *Standard* 24 July, The valley byon beds of Mogok, Tagoungnandine, and Loodah. **1922** *Chambers's Jrnl.* July 447/1 Coolies will still..be required to take the 'byon' to the sluice.

by ordinar, extraordinary: see BY *prep.*7.

by-pass ('baɪpɑːs, -æ-), *sb.* Also formerly **bye-pass.** [f. BY- B. 3 b + PASS *sb.*]

1. A secondary pipe issuing from the main or service pipe below a stop-tap or cock, allowing the free passage of a small supply of gas, steam, etc., when the main supply is shut off; *esp.* the small tube and pilot light of a gas-jet, which remains alight when the jet is turned off. Also *attrib.*

1848 W. POLE tr. *Alban's Steam Engine* 264 It is a sort of by-pass to allow the steam to travel freely from the upper into the lower box. **1876** *Amer. Gas-L. Jrnl.* 3 July 20 (Knight *a* 1884), Farmer's hydraulic main, with dip-pipe and bye-pass. **1888** *Morning Post* 12 Jan. 2/3 The only service from the stage supply that was open being one half inch bye-pass for the pilot light of auditorium sun burner. **1895** *Daily News* 10 Oct. 6/4 The innovation..consists of a little 'by-pass' arrangement by which a tiny flame is always kept going. **1901** [see ACCELERATOR c]. **1959** *Times* 25 July 9/4 An external by-pass valve.

2. *Electr.* A circuit or element providing an alternative path for the flow of current. Also *attrib.*

1914 R. A. PHILIP in H. Pender *Amer. Handbk. for Electr. Engineers* 364 To avoid the excessively high voltage which would occur when the circuit opened..an automatic by-pass is provided in multiple with the lamps. **1930** *Engineering* 9 May 600/1 The sides of these two switches, which are remote from the transformer, being connected together to form a 'by-pass' connection. **1931** *Answers* 10 Oct. 36/2 It might be found advantageous to connect a by-pass condenser across the telephones in the case of short-wave sets. **1964** R. F. FICCHI *Electrical Interference* v. 49 A typical bypass filter made up of a capacitor component.

3. A road diverging from and re-entering a main road, *esp.* one constructed as an alternative route to relieve congestion of traffic in a town. Also *attrib.*

1922 *Daily Mail* 2 Dec. 5 New roads and by-passes, which should remove some of these danger spots. **1923** *Times* (*Weekly Ed.*) 25 Jan., The Kingston by-pass will begin at the Robin Hood gate. **1929** *Times* 13 Nov. 9/4 It was recommended that the proposal to make a by-pass road be dropped. **1937** [see BY-PASS *v.* 1 b]. **1955** *Times* 13 June 5/3 Before they considered secondary roads..the trust should urge..the completion of the by-passes. **1966** J. BETJEMAN *High & Low* 70 This had to happen at the corner where the by-pass Comes into Egham out of Staines.

4. *transf.* and *fig.*

1928 T. E. LAWRENCE *Let.* 15 Mar. (1938) 579 They will come to you, round about through the parcel mail... I sent them by an official by-pass, for safety. **1957** *Listener* 18 July 102/3 To overstress Crashaw's capacity for writing hypnotic poetry would be a dangerous simplification, a crude bypass for those who want to dodge the implications of his belief.

5. *Aeronaut.* Applied to a type of jet engine (see quot. 1955).

1948 *Jrnl. R. Aeronaut. Soc.* LII. 714/1 One stage on towards eliminating the propeller, the ducted fan or 'by-pass' engine offers interesting possibilities. **1955** *Times* 26 Aug. 4/5 In a conventional jet engine all the air is compressed and then heated by the injection of burning fuel, expanded through the turbine, and finally ejected at high velocity. In a by-pass engine only a proportion of the air is compressed and heated; the remainder by-passes the combustion system and turbine and rejoins the heated gases in the jet pipe, to mix with them and lower their temperature before the whole mixture is ejected at a lower speed than that in the 'simple' jet engine.

6. An alternative passage for the circulation of blood during a surgical operation (on the heart). Also *attrib.*

1957 *Times* 1 Nov. 11/7 The circulating blood may have to be diverted and oxygenated through a by-pass circuit while the heart is opened, so that a defect within it may be rectified. **1961** *Lancet* 22 July 182/2 The patient was on bypass for eighty-one minutes. *Ibid.*, The first open repair on the heart, using a cardiopulmonary bypass, was carried out by Cooley et al. (1958).

by-pass ('baɪpɑːs, -æ-), *v.* [f. prec.]

1. *trans.* To furnish with a by-pass.

1886 *Sci. Amer.* Suppl. 4 Dec. 9099/3, I next by-passed the outlet valve with a one inch pipe. **1929** *Times* 28 May 17/4 Schemes are on foot for by-passing both Leatherhead and Dorking.

b. To take an indirect route around, to avoid (a locality, military position, etc.).

1928 *Even. Standard* 12 Mar. 6/2 King's Langley and Tring by passing Bushey and Watford. **1937** *Times* 13 July 10/4 The scheme has been referred to as 'the Selborne by-pass', but it does not by-pass Selborne at all. **1942** *Hutchinson's Pict. Hist. War* 10 June–1 Sept. 72/1 German armoured divisions which had by-passed our positions west of Mersa Matruh. **1959** *Listener* 15 Jan. 115/2 We had to by-pass Tippaburra.

c. *fig.*

1941 *Spectator* 10 Oct. 358/1 Congress is only one party in India, but by general consent it is the largest one, and it's no good trying to by-pass it. **1949** KOESTLER *Promise & Fulf.* vii. 70 Conditioned during the course of a whole generation to bypass the law. **1959** *Listener* 4 June 971/1 Whenever he was at odds with his Secretary of State he simply by-passed him.

2. To conduct (liquid, gas, etc.) by means of a by-pass.

1909 in *Cent. Dict.* Suppl. **1922** *Encycl. Brit.* XXX. 41/1 A valve for bypassing the whole or part of the exhaust gas directly into the atmosphere is provided to enable the output from the blower to be regulated. **1924** *Glasgow Herald* 6 Nov. 9 A small portion of the gas..is by-passed to a boiler.

'by-passage. [f. BY- 3 b, c, 5 + PASSAGE.] **a.** A side passage or alley. **b.** A casual and incidental passage in a book or document.

1674 HICKMAN *Hist. Quinquart.* (ed. 2) 232 What need I contend about by-passages relating to the Recantation? **1697** DRYDEN *Virg. Life* (1721) I. 61 When People crouded to see him, he [Virgil] would slip into the next Shop, or By-passage to avoid them. **1864** in WEBSTER.

by-passer ('baɪˌpɑːsə(r)). [cf. BY- 2 a.] One who passes by, a passer by.

1566 GASCOIGNE *Supposes* Wks. (1587) 32 No blazer of her beauty..at the dore for the bypassers. **1807** SOUTHEY *Espriella's Lett.* I. 156 Each window has blinds, to prevent the by-passers from looking in. **1862** *Times* 23 Dec., Appealing with mute looks to the sympathy of the by-passers.

† **'by-ˌpassing,** *vbl. sb. Obs.* [f. BY- 2 a.] The action of going past: said both of the movements of a person and of the lapse of time.

1526 *Pilgr. Perf.* (1531) 3 The great mystery of this by passynge of god. **1621** *Sc. Acts Jas. VI*, iii. ¶1 If they fayle therein at the by-passing of every one of the sayde Tearmes.

'by-passing, *pr. pple. rare.* Passing, surpassing.

1839 BAILEY *Festus* x. (1848) 107 By-passing all night's constellated chart.

bypast, by-past ('baɪˌpɑːst, -æ-), *ppl. a.* Also 6 **bi-, bepast, byepassed,** 7 **biepast** (all *Sc.*); 9 **bypassed.** [f. BY- 2 d + PAST. In earlier use often following the sb.; cf. BYGONE A 1.]

1. That has passed or gone by, (of time) elapsed; that has happened or existed in past time; former.

1452 EARL DOUGLAS in Tytler *Hist. Scot.* (1864) II. 387 Before the xxii day of the moneth of July last bypast. **1535** COVERDALE *Job* xxix. 2 O yᵗ I were as I was in the monethes bypast. **1609** *Act agst. Libels, &c.* in Maidment *Sc. Pasquils* 422 Ancient grudges borne in tyme of biepast troubles. **1705** SIR E. WALKER *Hist. Disc.* v. 364 They had promised..to clear His by-past Actions. **1804** KNOX & JEBB *Corr.* I. 142 The ecclesiastical history of Britain, during the by-past century. **1852** D. MOIR *Angler* iii, The twilight labyrinth Of bypast things.

†**b.** That has passed out of life; deceased, departed. *Obs.*

1425 in Entick *London* (1766) IV. 354 Shal pray..for al the now being alive, and also for the by-past, to God. **1535** STEWART *Cron. Scot.* II. 74 To be revengit of the skaith Is done to ws, and oure eldaris bipast.

†**c.** Overdue, in arrear; cf. BYGONE *sb. Obs.*

1693 *Apol. Clergy Scot.* 21 Had not the Clergy as good right to their by-past Stipends?

bypath, by-path ('baɪpɑːθ, -æ-). Also 4–5 **bi path(e,** 4–6 **bypathe,** 8 **bye path.** [f. BY- 3 b + PATH.] A side path, as opposed to the highroad; a private, retired, or unfrequented path.

c **1374** CHAUCER *Troylus* III. 1706 Tho swifte stedis thre, Which that drawyn forth the Sunnis chare, Hath go some bi path in despite of me, That makith hit so sone day to be. **1481** CAXTON *Reynard* (Arb.) 12 Brune..cam in a derke wode..were as reynard had a bypath whan he was hunted. *a* **1520** *Myrr. Our Ladye* 140 There ys a dyfference bytwyxte an hyghe waye and a bypathe. **1684** BUNYAN *Pilgr.* II. 70 The Travellers have been made..to walk thorough by-Paths. **1786** tr. *Beckford's Vathek* (1868) 70 Nouronihar..coming to the turn of a little bye path, stopped. **1814** SCOTT *Wav.* lx, By following by-paths, known to the young farmer, they hoped to escape.

b. *fig.* (Formerly often in a bad sense.)

c **1400** *Test. Love* I. (1560) 275/2 The bypathes to heaven. **1413** LYDG. *Pylgr. Sowle* I. xiii. (1859) 10 Bypathes of synne and al vnthryftynes. **1528** MORE *Heresyes* II. Wks. 202/2 Such euil persons as..led his flocke out of the right way in a bypath to helward. **1597** SHAKS. *2 Hen. IV*, IV. v. 185 By what by-pathes, and indirect crook'd-wayes I met this Crowne. **1779** JOHNSON *Butler* Wks. II. 188 The bye-paths of literature. **1858** FROUDE *Hist. Eng.* III. 142 Shining on the bypaths of history like a rare rich flower.

Hence † **'bypathed** *ppl. a.*

1641 J. JOHNSON *Acad. of Love* 3, I found a by-pathed gate, which led me into Loves pleasant garden.

by-place ('baɪpleɪs). [f. BY- 3 a + PLACE.] A place situated aside, an out-of-the-way spot; an odd corner; also *fig.*

1580 HOLLYBAND *Treas. Fr. Tong, Lieux destournez*, by-places. **1603** DRAYTON *Bar. Wars* IV, Till in the castle, in an odd by-place, It casts the foul mask from its dusky face. **1685** BOYLE *Salubr. Air* Pref. 5, I found it laid in a by-place. **1714** ELLWOOD *Autobiog.* (1765) 256 She lived at a Farm called Whites, a By-place in the Parish of Beconsfield. **1835** HAWTHORNE *Tales & Sk., O. Woman's T.*, Traditions lurking in the corners and by-places of my mind.

by-play ('baɪpleɪ). Also **bye-.** [f. BY- 3 c + PLAY.]

1. Chiefly on the stage: Action carried on aside, and commonly in dumb-show, while the main action proceeds.

1812 L. HUNT in *Examiner* 21 Dec. 803/1 We need not point out these delicacies of bye-play. **1822** *Blackw. Mag.* XI. 536 If Mr. Kean were to fill up the intervals of his bye-play in tragedy by leaping through the back-scene. **1844** H. ROGERS *Ess.* I. II. 80 His opponent often has a byplay of malignity even when bestowing commendations. **1850** BLACKIE *Æschylus* I. Pref. 46 They probably neglected anything like by-play or making points, which are so effective on the English stage.

2. *transf.* Play or action apart from the main action in any acceptation.

1816 *Edin. Rev.* XXVI. 310 He is certainly most happy..in the by-play of his fictions. **1871** EARLE *Philol. Eng. Tong.* (1880) §629 The various kinds of by-play in poetry, such as alliteration, rhyme, and assonance. **1878** BOSW. SMITH *Carthage* 269 The tide of invasion..is broken up into a number of smaller currents, which..are often in the nature of by-play rather than have any direct bearing on the main issues of the war.

by-plot ('baɪplɒt). Also **bye-.** [f. BY- 3 a, c, d + PLOT.]

†**1.** An outlying plot of ground. *Obs.*

1577–87 HARRISON *Descr. Brit.* xix. 114 Ech surveior amendeth such by-plots and lanes as seeme best for his own commoditie.

2. A subordinate plot by the side of the main one; a plot within a plot.

1850 MERIVALE *Rom. Emp.* (1865) III. xxiv. 93 In an era of revolution there are always by-plots..parallel..with the main action of the drama. **1859** KINGSLEY *Misc.* II. 121 This bye-plot runs through the play.

† **'by-post.** *Obs.* Also 8 **bye-.** [f. BY- 3 a, 4, 5 + POST.]

1. In a building: A side post, a door post.

1535 COVERDALE *Ezek.* xli. 21 The bypostes of the temple were foure squared.

2. Service of horses for travelling on cross-roads. Dispatch of letters by cross-roads, or by a post subsidiary to the regular mail.

1593 in *Municipal Acc. Newcastle* (1848) 29 Paide to John Carr, post, for keeping horses for by-poste, 2*s.* 8*d.* **1720** *Lond. Gaz.* No. 5910/3 The Dispatch of the Bye-Post between Chester and York. **1766** WILKES *Corr.* (1805) III. 174, I have now, by the bye-post, an opportunity of just saying that I am well.

by-product ('baɪˌprɒdʌkt). Also **bye-.** [f. BY- 4, 5 + PRODUCT.] **a.** A secondary product; a substance of more or less value obtained in the course of a specific process, though not its primary object.

1857 ELIZA ACTON *Eng. Bread-bk.* II. 95 German yeast..in many distilleries forms an important by-product. **1876** M. FOSTER *Physiol.* (1879) App. 663 When any proteid is digested with pepsin..a bye-product makes its appearance. **1882** *Standard* 24 Aug., By-products of gas manufacture.

b. *attrib.* and *transf.*

1905 *Daily Report* 9 Dec. iv/1 By-product coke ovens. **1926** FOWLER *Mod. Eng. Usage* 304/1 But a regrettable by-product of their activities has been a relapse into primitive methods of soliciting attention. **1952** S. KAUFFMANN *Philanderer* (1953) ii. 23, I was going to say the principal thing is that you're here. But that's a by-product. The principal thing..is that you know me. **1969** *Nature* 27 Dec. 1297/2 By-product gypsum formed during the wet process manufacture of phosphoric acid contains various impurities.

byqu-; see BEQU-.

† **byr,** *v. Obs.* [The same as BIR *v.*, q.v. for etymology.]

1. *impers.* It belongs to, behoves; see BIR *v.*

2. with personal subject: To owe, ought. [Cf. BEHOVE.]

c **1200** ORMIN 4028 þat alle þa..Well ȝeorne birrdenn clennsenn hemm I bodiȝ & i sawle. *c* **1325** *E.E. Allit. P.* C. 507 þe sor of suche a swete place burde synk to my hert. *c* **1330** R. BRUNNE *Chron.* 76 þat vengeance burd be don.

byr, etc.: see BIR.

byr(e, byrre, obs. ff. BIRR *sb.*

byrad, pa. pple. of BEREDE *v. Obs.*

byraft, obs. f. BEREFT.

byral(l, obs. f. BERYL.

Byram, obs. form of BAIRAM.

1656 in BLOUNT *Glossogr.* **1678** in PHILLIPS. **1708** in KERSEY. **1721–1790** in BAILEY.

byrayn(e, -reyn, var. BERAIN *v. Obs.*

byrch(e, byrd, obs. ff. BIRCH, BIRD.

byrden, -oun, -yng, obs. ff. BURDEN.

byre[1] (baɪə(r)). Forms: 1– byre; also 6 bire, 6–9 byer, 8 byar. [OE. *býre*, found only in vocabularies and hence of doubtful gender and declension; but perh.:—OTeut. type **bûrjo(m*, deriv. of **bûro(m*, OE. *búr*, cottage, dwelling, 'bower', f. **bû-* to dwell: see BOWER. Not the same word as ON. *bý-r, bœ-r*, Icel. *bær* str. masc. 'farm house', etc. (in which the final *r* is merely the nom. ending:—**bûi-z*, **bôi-z*); although from the same root.]

1. A cow-house. Perh. in OE. times, more generally, 'a shed'. ***to muck the byre*** (Sc.): to take out the dung and cleanse the byre.

a **800** *Corpus Gl.*, *Wr.-Wülcker* 32 Magalia, byre. *c* **1050** *Supp. Ælfric's Gloss.* ibid. 185 *Magalia*, uel *capanna*, byre, *uel* sceapheorden. *c* **1440** *Gaw. & Gol.* i. 3 (JAM.) The king

farith with his folk our firthis and fellis, Withoutin beilding of blis, of bern, or of byre. **1521** in *Archæol.* XVII. 203 Ther is a bire made for oxen. **1535** STEWART *Cron. Scot.* III. 420 Bayth hall and chalmer, bakhous, barne and byre. **1570** LEVINS *Manip.* 143 A Byre, cowhouse, *bouile.* **1724** RAMSAY *Tea-t. Misc.* (1733) I. 76, I ha' a good ha' house, a barn and a byer. *a* **1775** *Jacobite Song*, 'The mucking o' Geordie's byre.' **1805** WORDSW. *Prel.* VIII. (1851) 169 Long ere heat of noon, From byre or field the kine were brought. **1847** BARHAM *Ingol. Leg.* Ser. III. (1858) 440 He had beeves in the byre, he had flocks in the fold.

¶ Misused (from a mistaken notion as to the etymology) to english the Icelandic *bær* (ON. *bœr*, *býr*): 'A farmyard and buildings, including the farm-house', called in Scotland a 'farm-toun'.

1863 BARING-GOULD *Iceland* 137 He set about erecting a byre with a great hall one hundred feet long.

2. *attrib.*, as in *byre-door*, *-dung*, *-loft*, *-man*, *-woman*; and in *comb.*, as **byre-mucker**, one who 'mucks' or cleanses a byre; **byrewards** *adv.*, towards the byre.

1883 *Gd. Words* Aug. 495/2 From the *byre door, he watched the birds. **1833** *Act 3 & 4 Will. IV*, xlvi. §3 Stable and *byre dung. **1822** BEWICK *Mem.* 19, I always took up my abode for the night in the *byer-loft. **1814** *Edinb. Corresp.* 4 June (JAM.) Mr. Heriot's byreman .. was found .. dreadfully bruised. **1790** BURNS *Let. to Dr. Moore* 14 July As ill-spelt as country John's billet-doux, or as unsightly a scrawl as Betty *Byremucker's answer to it. **1880** MRS. C. READE *Brown Hand & Wh.* I. Prol. 30 The goat and kid now being driven *byrewards by a boy. **1820** SCOTT *Monast.* xxviii, 'There is na ane fit to do a turn but the *byre-woman and myself'.

byre[2]. ? Obs. form of BIER.

1467 *Mann. & Househ. Exp.* 427 For iij. flytes, ij. bottebolts and ij. byres, xvij.*d.*

byred, ? pa. pple. of BEREDE *v. Obs.* to advise.

1620 *Hist. Fryer Bacon* in Thoms *E.E. Prose Rom.* I. 223 You are byred reasonable well already.

byrelaw(e, **byrele**, var. ff. BYRLAW, BIRLE.

† **'by-re,spect.** *Obs.* Also 7 bie-. [f. BY- 3 c, d + RESPECT *sb.*] Regard to something other than the ostensible main object; a side aim or motive; a by-consideration.

1585 ABP. SANDYS *Serm.* (1841) 341 Nor any other by-respect in the world was able to stay them. **1655** GOUGE *Comm. Heb.* iii. 12. 362 Many make profession on bie-respects .. to serue their own turns. **1703** BURKITT *On N.T.* John vi. 27 How natural it is for men to seek Christ for sinister ends and by-respects. **1755** in JOHNSON; and in mod. Dicts.

byriels, var. of BURIELS. *Obs.*

byrk(e, **byrkyn**, obs. ff. BIRCH, BREAK.

byr'lady, *int.* Still *dial.* Forms: 6 byrladye, ber-, burlady, byr lady, 6–7 bir lady, ber-, birladie, barlady, 7 birlady, b'ar ladie, 9 *dial.* by'r leddie, by-leddy, 6– byrlady, by'rlady. Contraction of *by our Lady*, used as an oath, form of adjuration, or expletive.

1570 *Play Wit & Sc.* (1848) 18 Byrladye, not thou wench, I judge you. **1592** CHETTLE *Kind-Harts Dr.* (1841) 35 Byr lady, this would be lookt into. **1592** SHAKS. *Rom. & Jul.* I. v. 35 Berlady thirtie yeares. **1616** *Pasquil & Kath.* III. 182 B'ar Ladie, that's a bumming sound. **1632** BROME *North. Lasse* IV. iv, Birladie a competent modern portion. **1821** COLERIDGE *Lett. Convers.*, *&c.* I. 221 Very late, or, by'r lady, it might be early in the morning. **1884** *St. James's Gaz.* 20 June 6/1 The farmers [near Ludlow, Shropshire], although none of them are Roman Catholics, swear 'by'r Leddie'.

† **byr'lakin.** *Obs.* Also 6 bylakyn, belakin, byrlakyn, berlaken, 7 birlakin. A contraction of *by our Ladykin*; cf. prec.

a **1528** SKELTON *Magnyf.* 341 By lakyn, Sir, it hath cost. **1548** *Warrikin Fair* in *Gentl. Mag.* (1740) Sept., 'Belakin' quo hee, 'but I connau tel'. **1570** *Play Wit & Sc.* (1848) 52 Byrlakyn! Syr. **1590** SHAKS. *Mids. N.* III. i. 14 Berlaken, a parlous feare. *a* **1625** FLETCHER *Nice Val.* III. i, Birlakin sir, the difference of long taggs Has cost many a man's life.

'byrlaw. *arch.* or *dial.* Forms: 3 birelage, birlawe, (birelegia), 5–7 byrelaw(e, 6 byerlaw, 6–7 berlaw, burlaw, 7–8 birlaw, 9 bourlaw, *dial.* byar law, 6– byrlaw; also corrupted, esp. in comb., into 6 byerley, byrla, birla, 7 birlay, burlie, 7–8 birley, 8–9 birlie, 9 burley; see BIRLEY, BOURLAW, BURLEY, BY-LAW. [app. a. ON. **býjar-lög*, f. *býjar* gen. case of *bý-r* (= BY *sb.*), dial. variant of *bœ́r* (*bær*) village, town, farm + *lög* (pl. of *lag*) law, 'law community, communion, also a law district' (Vigf.); cf. BY-LAW.

(The existence of **byjar-*, *bǽjar-lög* in ON. is scarcely proved by the occurrence of *bæjar-lögmaðr* 'a town justice' in *Diplomat. Norvegicum* of 13–14th c. (Vigf.), as a 'by' might have its own *lögmaðr* 'lawman' without having its own special law.]

1. The local custom or 'law' of a township, manor, or rural district, whereby disputes as to boundaries, trespass of cattle, etc., were settled without going into the law courts; a law or custom established in such a district by common consent of all who held land therein, and having binding force within its limits. Hence ***byrlaw-court*** and BYRLAW-MAN, -GRAYVE, q.v.

These laws regulated such matters as the dates of ploughing, the turning out of cattle, the number of cattle turned out by each tenant of common land, the fines for trespass and damage done to fences, etc., the keeping up of fences, sea banks, the pound, the 'balks' in fields, and the like.

1257 *Composition betw. Convent & W. de Furness*, in *Coucher Bk. of Furness Abbey* (1887) 458 Si contingat averia ipsius Abbatis vel succ. suorum dampnum facere in bladis vel pratis ipsius Willelmi, .. [or *vice versa*] .. emendabitur ex utraque parte secundum Birelag' absque placito. **1412** *Tabula Sententialis*, ibid. 84 Ex utraque parte fient emendæ secundum Birelegia absque placito. **1292** *Assize 20 Edw. I* (Devon) *Abbreviatio Plac.* 286 b, Quod quidem factum [destruction of the parson's crops] manifeste est injuriosum et non per aliquod Birlawe sustinendum, consideratum est quod, etc. *a* **1400** GLANVILLE *Reg. Maj.*, Exceptis burlawis [SKENE *tr.* Birlaw Courts] que per consensum vicinorum concurrunt. **1483** *Cath. Angl.* 32 A Byrelawe, *agraria, plebiscitum.* **1500** *Ortus Voc.* in *Cath. Angl.* 32 *note*, *Plebiscitum, statutum populi; anglice*, a byrelawe. **1597** SKENE *Verb. Sign.*, Laws of Burlaw ar maid & determined be consent of neichtbors, elected and chosen be common consent, in the courts called the Byrlaw courts. In the quhilk cognition is taken of complaintes, betuixt nichtbour & nichtbour. The quhilk men sa chosen, as judges & arbitrators to the effect foresaid, ar commonly called Byrlaw-men. **1609** HUME *Admon.* in *Wodrow Soc. Misc.* (1844) 587 Comparing them to Birlay Courtis, where is much jangling. **1883** D. GRAHAM *Wks.* II. 102 *note*, This birley-court consisted of certain parties in the barony who looked after local affairs. **1881** W. DICKINSON *Cumbrld. Gloss.* 2nd Supp. (E.D.S.) *Byar law, Byr law*, a custom or law established in a township or village. **1876** *Mid-Yorksh. Gloss.* (E.D.S.) [The bellman at Tollerton used to say] 'Away to t' Bahlaw' [*i.e.* to a parish meeting].

2. *transf.* A district having its own byrlaw court, or local law.

In the form *Bierlow* this word is common as an appendage to place-names in Yorkshire: *Brampton Bierlow*, *Ecclesall Bierlow*, *Brightside Bierlow*. These are the names of somewhat extensive parishes; it is to be presumed that the various hamlets forming each were originally connected by their resort to a district court of justice.

1850 *N. & Q.* Ser. I. II. 92/2 The above are the four byerlaws or divisions of the parish, and the Churchwardens used separately to collect in their respective byerlaws.

'byrlawman. Also byerlaw-, birlaw-, berlaw-, byrelaw-, and BURLEY-, q.v. [f. prec. + MAN: cf. the Norse form there cited.]

An officer appointed at a Court-leet for various local duties, as the framing and execution of byrlaws, looking after nuisances, administration of justice in minor matters, arbitration in agricultural disputes, etc. etc. Also occas. called **bierlaw-grayves** (see GREAVE).

This still survives locally in Scotland and the north of England under various forms, e.g. BOURLAWMAN, BURLEYMAN (also *burlie bailie*), BIRLEYMAN, q.v. for further examples.

1432 *Ingleby Arncliff Manor Court Rolls* (per Rev. J. C. Atkinson) Juratores elegerunt in officium de Birlawmen John North et Rob. Phelipson. **1477–8** *Ibid.* Elegerunt Joh. Hardwyke et Joh. Jacson Bierlaw-grayves [explan. in Latin *custodes plebisciti*] pro anno futuro, et jurati sunt. **1521** *Ibid.* That no bruester shall sell anie aile but according to the price of the cuntrie, and at the sight of the Bierlaymen. **1588** *Ibid.* That euerie one shall comme to the byerleys & other common workes after warning be gyven them eyther by constable or byerley men vpon payne of euerie defawte ivd. **1552–1584** *Manch. Court-leet Rec.* in *Athenæum* 2 Aug. (1879) 146 Byrlamen, birlamen. **1595** *Ibid.*, Berlawmen [fined for suffering swine to go up and down the street unyoked]. **1591** *Acc. Common Lands Rotherham* ibid. 9 Aug., To the byer law-men for casting open closes according to our custome, 2*s.* **1799** J. ROBERTSON *Agric. Perth* 40 Sworn appraisers or valuers (called Byrelawmen) .. are called mutually by each party, to settle disputes between landlord and tenants, or between one tenant and another. **1875** *Lanc. Gloss.* (E.D.S.) 62 *Burly-man*, an officer appointed at a court-leet to examine and determine respecting disputed fences.

byrle(r, **-let**, obs. forms of BIRLE(R, BURLET.

byrn(e, obs. f. BURN; var. BERNE, *Obs.*, warrior.

byrnacle, **-akille**, obs. forms of BARNACLE.

† **'byrnie.** *Obs.* exc. *Hist.* Forms: 4 (9 *Hist.*) byrny, 4–6 (9 *Hist.*) byrnie, 6 birny(e. [Sc. variant of ME. *brynie*, BRINIE, with metathesis of *r*. The word was thus brought nearer to OE. *byrne*, from which however it could not directly come, as this gave only the monosyllabic **byrn*, BURNE, BRYN.]

A cuirass, corslet, coat of mail; = BRINIE.

1375 BARBOUR *Bruce* II. 352 The blud owt at thar byrnys brest. *c* **1470** HENRY *Wallace* II. 106 Into yᵉ byrneis [*v.r.* birny] yᵉ formast can he ber. **1513** DOUGLAS *Æneis* VII. xi. 95 His breistplayt strang and his byrnie. **1535** STEWART *Cron. Scot.* I. 140 With breistplait, birny, as the buriall brycht. **1864** SIR G. DASENT *Jest & Earn.* (1873) II. 273 He had armed himself in two byrnies or shirts of mail. **1870** MAGNUSSON & MORRIS *Volsungs* xi. 37 No shield or byrny might hold against him.

byrnstone, obs. form of BRIMSTONE.

byrnysh, **byrnyst**, obs. ff. BURNISH, -ED.

by-road ('baɪrəʊd). Also 8–9 bye-. [f. BY- 3 b, + ROAD.] A road which is not a main road; a side road which does not form the highway between towns or places of importance; an out-of-the-way, little-frequented road.

1673 R. HEAD *Canting Acad.* 91 Choose when you travel, the By-Roads. **1709** STEELE *Tatler* No. 45 ¶1 Strolling wherever Chance led me, I was insensibly carried into a By-Road. **1742** R. BLAIR *Grave* 691 There's no bye-road To bliss. **1848** MACAULAY *Hist. Eng.* I. 377 On byroads .. goods were carried by long trains of pack-horses.

Byronic (baɪ'rɒnɪk), *a.* [f. the name of the poet Lord Byron; see -IC, and cf. *Miltonic*.]

1. Characteristic of, or after the manner of Byron or his poetry. Also *absol.*

1823 *Blackw. Mag.* XIII. 511 His Byronic muse procured for him the hand of one of our fair countrywomen. **1830** *Diary of Nun* II. 35 A Byronic contempt for our fellow creatures. **1856** *Chamb. Jrnl.* VI. 228 A Byronic youth in a turn-down collar. **1875** MASSON *Wordsw.*, *&c.* 35 The Byronic in poetry is, in some respects, the contradictory of the Wordsworthian. **1879** FROUDE *Cæsar* viii. 83 No sentimental passion .. no Byronic mock heroics.

2. quasi-*sb. pl.* [after *philippics*.] Declamatory utterances or invectives in the style of Byron.

1850 WHIPPLE *Ess. & Rev.* II. 394 Vociferating impotent Byronics against conventional morality.

Byronism ('baɪərənɪz(ə)m). [f. as prec. + -ISM.] **a.** The characteristics of Byron or his poetry. **b.** Imitation of Byron.

1817 W. S. WALKER *Poet. Rem.* (1852) Introd. 38 Lord Byron's drama of Manfred is .. the perfection of Byronism. **1857** *Fraser's Mag.* LVI. 66 When Byronism was at its height, when .. you could not be interesting unless you were miserable and vicious. **1870** SWINBURNE *Ess. & Stud.* (1875) 307 One of his [de Musset's] decoctions of watered Byronism.

So also **By'roniad** (-'əʊnɪəd), [see -AD 1 c], ? the epic of a Byronian hero. **By'ronian** *a.*, of or pertaining to Byron, resembling Byron; also *sb.*, an admirer or imitator of Byron. **By'ro nical** *a.*, **'Byronish** *a.*, = BYRONIAN; **By'ronically** *adv.*; **'Byronist**, **'Byronite** [see -IST, -ITE], a follower or imitator of Byron. **'Byronize** *v.* [*see* -IZE], (*a*) *trans.* to invest with the characteristics of Byron; (*b*) *intr.* to affect or play the Byron.

1819 *Literary Gaz.* 546 The prose *Byroniads which infest the times. **1822** *Blackw. Mag.* XII. 753 Old-established freeholders on the *Byronian Parnassus. **1883** *Athenæum* 17 Mar. 340/1 Alfred de Musset and the French *Byronians. **1871** MORLEY *Crit. Misc.* (1878) 225 Silly *Byronical votaries, who only half understood their idol. **1839** *Blackw. Mag.* XLV. 356 Wearing his shirt collar *Byronically tied in front with a slip of black ribbon. **1830** WILSON *ibid.* XXVII. 674 An exceedingly neat small *Byronish hand. **1830** CAMPBELL in *Fraser's Mag.* I. 485 If the *Byronists were to face the savage ordeal. **1884** SWINBURNE in *19th Cent.* Apr. 587 The smallest perceptible *Byronite or Wordsworthian. **1823** *Blackw. Mag.* XIII. 267 *Byronized Cockneys. **1836** *Edin. Rev.* LXII. 299 His gentleness and devoutness would have Byronized but ill. **1847** *Blackw. Mag.* LXI. 430 Let others .. fling their curls back from their brows, unbutton their shirt-collars, and, thus Byronised, begin.

'by-room. [f. BY- 3 a + ROOM.] A side or private room; a smaller room opening out of another.

1596 SHAKS. *1 Hen. IV*, II. iv. 32 Doe thou stand in some by-roome, while I question my puny Drawer. *c* **1615** CHAPMAN *Odyss.* III. 545 Himself lay in a by-room, far above. **1727** BRADLEY *Fam. Dict.* I. s.v. *Cabbage*, Lay them in some Cellar or by-room. **1755** in JOHNSON; and in mod. Dicts.

byrral(l, obs. form of BERYL.

‖ **byrsa** ('bɜːsə). *Med.* [L.; a. Gr. *βύρσα* hide.]

1811 HOOPER *Med. Dict.*, *Byrsa*, a leather skin, to spread plaisters upon. **1881** in *Syd. Soc. Lex.* (citing Quincy).

byrse, obs. form of BURSE.

byrselle, var. BERCEL, *Obs.*, archer's butt.

byrsle, **byrst**, obs. ff. BIRSLE, BURST.

byrt(e, **byrth(e**, **-yn**, obs. ff. BIRT, BIRTH, BURDEN.

† **'byrthynsak.** *Sc. Law. Obs.* Forms: 2–3 berthynsak, 3 byrthynsak, berthinsak, (6–7 byrthinsak, berthinsek, birdinsek, burdingseck, burdensack). [Derived by Skene (1609) from BURDEN *sb.* + SACK, and explained accordingly; but no reference to a 'sack' appears in the original passages in the *Assisæ* of William the Lion (and its vernacular version), or in the *Regiam Majestatem*. The early vernacular form *byrthynsak*, *berthinsak*, appears to be f. OE. *byrðen* burthen + *sacu* legal process, action at law, jurisdiction. But the latinized forms *iburþenenseca*, *yburþananseca*, present features not easily explained.] (See quots.)

? **1177** *Assise Regis Willelmi* xiii [earliest MS. *a* 1300], De Iburþenenseca seu Berthynsak id est de furto vituli vel arietis vel quantum quis supra dorsum suum portare poterit. 15th c. *transl.* Of byrthynsak þat is to say of þe thyft of a calf or of a ram or how mekil as a man may ber on his bak þar is na court to be haldyn. *a* **1400** *Reg. Maj.* (1844) iv. 12 De

berthinsak seu yburþananseca. **1609** SKENE *Reg. Maj.* [*Scotch transl.*] 68 Table, Bvrdingseck, be the Law of burdingseck, na man sould be hanged for sa meikill of stollen meat, as he may beare in ane seck vpon his back: as for ane scheepe or ane calfe. **1658** in PHILLIPS.

† **'by-run,** *sb.*, *pa. pple.*, *ppl. a. Obs.* [f. BY- 2 a + RUN *sb.* and *pple.*]

A. *sb.* Running by, course, current.

1674 N. FAIRFAX *Bulk & Selv.* 143 Time all the while holding on its even by-run.

B. *pa. pple.* and *ppl. a.* Also 6 *Sc.* **byrunnyn.**

1. Past, elapsed; (of payments) in arrear, overdue.

1513 DOUGLAS *Æneis* V. xi. 54 Lo, sen the fall of Troy.. Byrunnyn is the sevint somer. **1536** BELLENDEN *Cron. Scot.* (1821) I. 241 The day byrunne, all Scottis war exilit. *a* **1639** SPOTTISWOOD *Hist. Ch. Scotl.* VI. (1677) 325 The by-run profits intrometted by the Thesaurer. **1653** in *Z. Boyd's Zion's Flowers* (1855) Introd. 41 Byrun stipends owing by the toun.

2. As *sb. pl.* Arrears (of rent, etc.). Cf. BY-GONE B. 1 b.

1573 *Sc. Acts Jas VI* (1597) §58 For the by-runes awand them. **1613** SKENE *Reg. Maj.* Index s.v. *Maister* (JAM.) The byrunis of his ferms.

† **'by-running,** *pr. pple.* and *vbl. sb. Obs.* [f. BY- 2 a + RUNNING.]

A. *pr. pple.* Going by, passing, current. **B.** *vbl. sb.* The action of going by or passing.

1674 N. FAIRFAX *Bulk & Selv.* 18 The very existence of God, with an outward badge or denomination from time by-running. *Ibid.* 201 There were framed, the sundry ages or by-runnings and wheelings about of things in this world.

byryall, -ele, -ell, obs. ff. BURIAL.

byryne, byryyde, obs. ff. BERAIN, BURIED.

byrynnyn, pa. pple. of BERUN, to encompass.

by's, by't = by his, by it; see HE, IT.

bys(e, obs. and var. ff. BICE, BYSE, BYSS.

bysale, -ayeul, var. BESAIEL, great-grandfather.

Bysantin, obs. form of BYZANTINE.

† **'bysawe.** *Obs.* Also 3 **bisawe.** [early ME. *bisawe*, f. *bi-*, BY + *sawe*, SAW, saying; cf. BY-WORD.] A current saying; a proverb.

a **1225** *Ancr. R.* 88 Me seið ine bisawe—'Vrom mulne & from cheping.. me tiðinge bringeð'. **1387** TREVISA *Higden* Rolls Ser. V. 461 Hit is a bysawe, 'God have mercy of soules, quoth Oswalde, and fil to þe grounde'.

bysb, var. of BISP, *Obs.*, bishop.

† **'by-scape.** *Obs. rare*⁻¹. [f. BY- 2 b + *scape*, aphet. f. ESCAPE.] A bastard; cf. BY-BLOW, -SLIP.

1646 EARL MONM. *Biondi's Hist.* VI-IX. 197 For his being God-son to her Brother, and.. for that (being very fair) she thought him a by-scape of his.

byschelle, -schop(e, obs. ff. BUSHEL, BISHOP.

† **by'scorn,** *v. Obs.* [= BESCORN; see BE- *pref.* 2.] *trans.* To cover with scorn.

a **1300** *Cursor M.* 16611 þe riche men bi-scornd him. *c* **1386** CHAUCER *Pers. T.* ¶204 Thanne was he bescorned [*v.r.* by-scorned, bi-scorned].

† **byscorn,** *sb. Obs. rare*⁻¹. In 4 **byskorne.** [f. prec. vb.] Contempt, scorn.

1387 TREVISA *Higden* (1865) I. 179 Ymages of false goddes ..he broȝte to byskorne and bysmere.

byscute, obs. form of BISCUIT.

† **byse.** *Obs.* Also 3 **bise,** 5 **bys, besshe,** 6 **bice.** [Origin unknown: possibly F. *bis* dark brown. The suggestion that it is the same as BISSE, OF. *bisse, bisce, biche* 'female deer', hardly suits the sense, and the forms do not agree.]

Some kind of (? brown) fur, much used in the 15th c. for trimming gowns, etc.

c **1280** *A Sarmun* 11 in *E.E.P.* (1862) 2 Silk no sendale nis þer none no bise no no meniuer. **1407** *Will of Escryk* (Somerset Ho.), Furrata cum Bys. **1422** *E.E. Wills* (1882) 50 A gown furred with Besshe. **1483** CAXTON *Gold. Leg.* 50/3 A double stole furryd with byse. **1513** DOUGLAS *Æneis* VIII. Prol. 57 Byand byssely.. beuir and bice.

byse(e, bysege, obs. ff. BESEE, BESIEGE.

† **'bysen,** *sb. Obs.* exc. *Sc.* and *north. dial.* Forms: 1 **býsen, bisine,** 1-4 **bisen,** 2-3 **bisne,** 3 **bisin,** 4 **bysine, -yne,** 5 **bysyn (bysynt),** 6-7 **bysin,** 9 **bison, byzen, bysen.** [partly OE. *býsen* example; but the later use is exclusively northern, and apparently from the cognate ON. *býsn* wonder, portentous thing. See also BYSYM.]

I. 1. An example, a pattern.

c **950** *Lindisf. Gosp.* John xiii. 15 Bisen [*Rushw.* bisine] forðon ic salde iuh. *c* **1175** *Lamb Hom.* 5 Godalmihti.. sette us bisne. *c* **1230** *Hali Meid.* 45 After þe bisne of þat eadi meiden. *a* **1240** *Sawles Warde* in *Cott. Hom.* 245 Ure lauerd ..teacheð us þurh a bisne. **1340** HAMPOLE *Pr. Consc.* 1027 þe bodys of þe world.. Shewes us for bisens.. How we suld serve God.

II. 2. Something monstrous or portentous; a shocking sight, sorry spectacle, disgraceful thing.

a **1455** HOLLAND *Houlate* ix, I am nytherit ane Owll.. Bysyn of all birdis that euer body bure. *a* **1600** MONTGOMERIE *Sonn.* xxxiv, Fy, lothsome lyfe! Fy, death, that dou not [serve me] Bot quik and dedd a bysin thow must [preserve me]. **1803** R. ANDERSON *Cumberld. Ball.* 63 She's a shem and a byzen to aw the heale town. **1874** WAUGH *Jannock* ii. 13 in *Lanc. Gloss.* (E.D.S.), It'll be a sham an' a bizen, if we cannot find him a menseful of a dinner.

3. *attrib.* or as *adj.* Monstrous, shocking, conspicuously bad or disgraceful.

c **1375** ? BARBOUR *St. Mathias* 29 He sal be a bysyne mane For his ill to al þat spek cane. —— *St. Catherine* 945, & mak a bysine wyf of þe. *c* **1425** WYNTOUN *Cron.* VI. xiii. 59 (JAM.) Eftyre that he wes broucht on bere Til a bysynt best all lyke. **1863** ROBSON *Bards of Tyne* 504 A bison sight.. The warst that e'er you saw.

† **'bysen,** *v. Obs.* [OE. *býsenian, býsnian*, f. *býsen*; see prec. Cf. also ON. *býsna* to portend, bode.] *trans.*

1. a. To set an example to; only in OE. **b.** To afford an example or type of, typify, betoken.

a **1000** K. ÆLFRED *Boeth.* xxxiii. §4 Ne bisnode þe nan man, forþam ðe nan ær þe næs. *Ibid.* xxxix. §11 Ða bisnodon hiora aftergengum. *c* **1325** *Metr. Hom.* 111 Þik that cleues quen it is tan, Bisens deling wit wik man, For his sin clefes on god men. *Ibid.* 124 Water bisenes sin and pliht.

2. To liken, compare.

c **1325** *Metr. Hom.* 37 Mani man mai bisend be Unto the rede.

bysene, obs. form of BESEE *v.*

† **'bysening,** *vbl. sb. Obs.* [f. prec. + -ING[1].] The action of setting an example; *concr.* a pattern, example, symbol, type.

c **1175** *Lamb. Hom.* 93 Efter þissere bisnunge weren arerede munechene lif mid. *a* **1300** *Cursor M.* 21718 Of croice in þe ald testament was mani bisning [*v.r.* bisening]. *c* **1325** *Metr. Hom.* 138 Forthi wil I schaw other thinges, That er apert biseninges.

† **'bysening, bysning,** *ppl. a. Obs.* [f. BYSEN *v.* (in sense of ON. *býsna* to portend) + -ING[2].] Ill-boding, portentous, monstrous, frightful; also quasi-*sb.* a monster.

c **1375** ? BARBOUR *St. Pelagia* 268 To mak hethinge Of me as of a bysninge thinge. —— *St. Ninian* 645 Sa wes it borne a bysnynge.. For a-gane kynd wes it sa þat bak-wart stud hele & ta. **1501** DOUGLAS *Pal. Hon.* 625 Ilk wicht hes sum weilfair.. Saif me bysning. *Ibid.* 740 In till sum bysning beist transfigurat me.

byset, obs. pa. t. of BUSY *v.*

bysext, variant of BISSEXT, *Obs.*

byshehopp(e, byshop, obs. forms of BISHOP.

bysi(e, bysily, -nes, obs. ff. BUSY, -ILY, -INESS.

byside, obs. f. BESIDE; obs. pa. t. of BUSY *v.*

bysket, obs. form of BISCUIT, BRISKET.

† **'by-slip.** *Obs.* [f. BY- 2 b + SLIP *sb.*]

1. A casual or trivial fault.

1612 CHAPMAN *Widow's T.* v, Might it not concur with.. your office.. to wink a little at a by-slip or so?

2. *transf.* A bastard. Cf. BY-SCAPE.

a **1670** HACKET *Abp. Williams* II. (1692) 37 As Pope Paul the third carried himself to his ungracious by-slips (an Incubus could not have begot worse).

byslober, obs. form of BESLOBBER *v.*

† **bysm(e,** aphetic form of ABYSM (cf. BISME).

1483 CAXTON *Gold. Leg.* 94/3 He was a bysme or swolowe by cause he deserued to perse the depnes of dyuynyte.

bysm-, bysn-, obs. forms of BESM-, BESN-.

bysmalith ('bɪzməlɪθ). *Geol.* [f. Gr. βύσμα plug + λίθος stone: see -LITH.] A large roughly cylindrical body of igneous rock which, when it was forced upward, lifted up the overlying rock.

1898 J. P. IDDINGS in *Jrnl. Geol.* VI. 706 By this mode of intrusion, the vertical dimension of the intruded mass becomes still greater as compared with the lateral dimensions, so that its shape is more that of a plug or core. Such an intruded plug of igneous rock may be termed a *bysmalith*. **1905** CHAMBERLIN & SALISBURY *Geol.* I. 477 Between the bysmalith and the laccolith there are various gradations.

Hence **bysma'lithic** *a.*, characteristic of a bysmalith.

1933 R. A. DALY *Igneous Rocks & Depths of Earth* vii. 132 We have no direct evidence that the intracrustal space occupied by a typical batholith was gained principally through a laccolithic or bysmalithic lifting of the roof.

bysom(e, byson(e, bysount: see BESOM, BISON, BISSON.

† **by'sondre,** *adv. Obs. rare*⁻¹. [f. BY-, BE- *pref.* + A-SUNDER, after pairs like *afore, before, alow, below*, etc.] Apart, asunder.

1496 *Dives & Paup.* (W. de W.) I. liv. 96/1 Men dwelle in many dyuerse londes many a thousande myles bysondre.

bysouth: see BY *prep.* 9, and BE-SOUTH.

† **by'sparkit,** *ppl. a. Sc. Obs.* [f. BY- = BE- *pref.* + SPARK.] Bespattered, spotted.

1513 DOUGLAS *Æneis* VII. x. 74 Wyth blude bysparkit vyssage heyd and hals.

† **'by-speech.** *Obs.* [see BY- 2 c, 3 c.] An incidental or casual speech: an indirect utterance or allusion; an *obiter dictum*; an 'aside'.

1594 HOOKER *Eccl. Pol.* III. (1632) 135 Their common practice is to quote by-speeches in some historicall narration. **1625** K. LONG *Barclay's Argenis* II. vii. 83 His wife.. would many times cast out by-speeches of Arsidas.

† **'byspel, 'bispel.** *Obs.* or ? *dial.* Also 9 *Sc.* and *north.* **byspale.** [ME. *bispell*, OE. *'bíspell, 'bíȝspell*, f. *bí*, BY + SPELL tale, story, narration; cogn. w. MHG. *bîspel, bîspil* 'instance, example', MDu. *bispel, byspel* (Kilian). As in other nominal compounds, the prefix had the strong accented form, and appears to retain the sound of *by* (baɪ) in the dialects in which the word lingers; but it was perhaps shortened to ('bɪspɛl) in ME.]

1. A parable.

c **950** *Lindisf. Gosp.* Matt. xxi. 33 Oðero bispell heres ȝe. *c* **1000** *Ags. Gosp.* ibid., Gehyrað me oðer biȝspel. *c* **1160** *Hatton G.* ibid., Geherað nu oðer byspel. *c* **1175** *Cott. Hom.* 233 Gode menn, understandeð þis bispel.

2. A proverb.

c **1000** ÆLFRIC *Deut.* xxviii. 37 And ȝe forwurþaþ þurh biȝspell [WYCLIF & **1611** proverb] and biȝcwidas. *a* **1250** *Owl & Night.* 127 Her-bi men segget a bi-spel. **1656** BLOUNT *Glossogr.* s.v. *Gospel, Bigspell* (*Deut.* 28. 37) signifies a by-word or Proverb; or (as it is used in the North) *By-spell.*

3. *dial.* One whose worthlessness is proverbial, who becomes a byword.

1691 NICHOLSON in Ray *N.C. Words* (E.D.S.), Bispel, nequam, q.d. Qui adeo insignis est Nebulo ut jam in proverbium abiit. **1709** T. HEARNE *Collect.* (1886) II. 281 By-spel, *homo nihili*: Ita Angli Boreales. **1808** JAMIESON s.v., 'He's just a byspale.' 'He's nae byspel mair than me.' **1811** WILLAN *Gloss. West R. Yorksh.* (E.D.S.), *Byspelt.*

4. An illegitimate child, a bastard. Cf. BY-BLOW.

1781 J. HUTTON *Tour Caves* Gloss. (E.D.S.), *Byspel*, a bastard, or an outcast in a family. **1808** JAMIESON *By-spel*, an illegitimate child.

† **byss,** *sb.*[1] *Obs.* Forms: 3-6 **bise,** 4 **bies, biis, bijs, biys, bijce,** 4-6 **bis, bys,** 4-7 **byse, bisse,** 5-7 **bysse,** 6 **biss,** 7 **byss.** [a. OF. *bysse*, ad. L. *byssus*: see BYSSUS.] = BYSSUS 1; Fine linen. The word was to English writers often a mere name to which they attached no certain meaning, except that of fineness and value; in the versions of the Bible it is variously rendered; the version of 1611 has 'fine linen'.

c **1314** *Guy Warw.* (A.) 2835 Gode clothes of.. purper and biis. **1382** WYCLIF *Luke* xvi. 19 Clothid in purpur, and biys, *ether whit silk* [TINDALE fyne bysse; CRANMER fyne whyte; *Genev.* fyne lynnen; *Rhem.* silke; **1611** fine linnen]. —— *Rev.* xix. 8 With whijte bijce shijnynge [**1388** white bissyn schynynge; TINDALE, CRANMER pure and goodly raynes; *Genev.* pure fyne lynen cloth and shining; *Rhem.* silke glittering and vvhite; **1611** fine linnen, cleane and white]. **1460** *Lybeaus Disc.* 2071 A robe of purpure bys. **1593** PEELE *Ord. of Garter* Wks. II. 228 A canopy of crimson bysse Spangled with gold. **1635** HEYWOOD *Hierarch.* v. 286 Costly robes of sundry colour'd Bisse. **1648** BP. HALL *Sel. Thoughts* §13 The rich glutton.. clothed in purple & byss.

† **byss,** *sb.*[2] *Obs.* [formed by removing the privative ἀ from *abyss*, Gr. ἄ-βυσσος; cf. Gr. βυσσός 'depth of the sea, bottom'.] In the philosophy of Boehme: The opposite of abyss or void; *plenum*, substance, ground of attributes.

1649 tr. *Behmen's Epist.* ii. (1886) 8 I saw.. the Being of all Beings, the Byss (the ground or original foundation), and Abyss. **1662** SPARROW tr. *Behme's Rem. Wks.*, *Apol. Perfection* 63 Here is.. neither place nor Limit, but the Manifestation of the Abysse in a Bysse or Ground. **1691** E. TAYLOR *Behmen's Theos. Philos.* 42 A Byss or Ground, whence come Forms or Properties. *Ibid.* 346 It.. is the greatest substance in the Deity; drawing Abyss into Byss.

† **byss,** *v. Obs.* Also 5 **byszyn, bissyn,** 6 **bis.** [onomatopœic.]

1. *trans.* To sing or hum (children) to sleep. Hence **'byssing** *vbl. sb.* and *ppl. a.*

1440 *Promp. Parv.* 37/1 Byszyn chyldur, *sopio, nenior.* Byssynge of chyldyrne, *sopicio.* Byssynge songys, *fascinnina.*

2. *intr.* To hiss, fizz (as in the fire).

1513 DOUGLAS *Æneis* VIII. vii. 119 The irne lumpis.. Can byss and quhisyll. *c* **1550** *Fyre of Purgat.* iii. in *Gude & Godlie Ball.* 163 Thay.. lat the saulis burn and bis Of all thair Foundatouris.

byssaceous (bɪ'seɪʃəs), *a. Bot.* [f. BYSS-US; see -ACEOUS.] 'Composed of fine entangled threads' (*Treas. Bot.* 1866).

1835 LINDLEY *Introd. Bot.* II. 362 *Byssaceous*, divided into very fine pieces, like wool, as the roots of some agarics.

byssal ('bɪsəl), *a.* [f. BYSS-US + -AL[1].] Of or belonging to the byssus of molluscs.

1854 WOODWARD *Mollusca* (1856) 204 The posterior, byssal foramen of the bivalve. **1866** *Intell. Observ.* No. 49. 54 The byssal threads.

bysse, obs. and var. form of BICE, BYSS.

bysshell, bysshope, obs. ff. BUSHEL, BISHOP.

byssiferous (bɪˈsɪfərəs), *a. Zool.* [f. BYSS-US + -(I)FEROUS.] Furnished (as a shell-fish) with a byssus (sense 3).
1835-6 TODD *Cycl. Anat.* I. 702/1 The group of byssiferous Dimyaria. **1875** BLAKE *Zool.* 269 The foot is cylindrical, grooved and byssiferous.

byssine (ˈbɪsɪn), *a.* In 4 bissyn, bijcen. [ad. L. *byssin-us*, a. Gr. βύσσινος made of byssus.]
1. Made of byssus or fine linen.
1656 BLOUNT *Glossogr.*, *Byssine*, silken, or which is made of fine flax or cloth. **1715** tr. *Pancirollus' Rerum Mem.* I. I. v. 14 That delicate Down..which sticks to a certain kind of Shell-fish..whence are made a sort of Garments called Byssine. **1849** KINGSLEY *Misc.* (1859) II. 173 The East sent to Rome 2000 years ago its 'byssine garments'. **1877** PLUMPTRE *Sophocles* 407 Æneas..on his shoulders bears his sire, Who lets his byssine mantle fall in folds.
2. quasi-*sb.* [L. *byssinum.*] = BYSS *sb.*[1]
1382 WYCLIF *Rev.* xix. 8 And it is ȝouun to hir, that she couere hir with whijte bijce [**1388** bissyn] shijnynge; forsothe bijcen [**1388** bissyn, Vulg. *byssinum*] ben the iustifiynges of seyntis. **1821** LOCKHART *Valerius* II. iii. 106 Perhaps a yellow byssine would suit me better.

byssinosis (bɪsɪˈnəʊsɪs). *Path.* [mod.L., f. Gr. βύσσινος made of byssus (see BYSSINE) + -OSIS.] A chronic disease of the lungs caused by the inhalation of fine particles of textile fibres, esp. cotton dust, over a long period.
1881 *Jrnl. Anat. & Physiol.* XV. 395 Other forms, such as byssinosis (or the disease produced by the inhalation of cotton fibre) do not differ from the ordinary forms of phthisis. **1890** BILLINGS *Med. Dict.* I. 203/2 *Byssinosis*, production of lung disease by inhalation of cotton-fibres. **1948** *Lancet* 14 Feb. 253/1 Byssinosis develops after long and continuous exposure to cotton dust. **1958** *Times* 20 June 11/7 A worker [at Calder Hall] is apparently a good deal healthier than one in a Lancashire cotton mill where byssinosis has not yet been eradicated.
Hence **byssiˈnotic** *a.*, affected with, characteristic of byssinosis; also as *sb.*, a byssinotic person.
1952 *Brit. Jrnl. Industr. Med.* IX. 138/2 Prausnitz..stated that byssinotics were hypersensitive..to a substance which could be extracted from cotton dust. *Ibid.* 195/1 The skin testing of byssinotic persons with cotton dust extracts fails to distinguish them from their symptomless fellow workers. **1964** *Lancet* 19 Sept. 609/2 The most severe attacks of byssinotic symptoms are after the annual holidays.

ˈbysso-ark. Anglicized form of *bysso-arca*, a sub-genus of molluscs, having a byssus.
[**1836** *Penny Cycl.* VI. 80/2 Byssoarca.] **1854** WOODWARD *Mollusca* (1856) 267 The Bysso-arks secrete themselves under stones at low-water.

byssogenous (bɪˈsɒdʒɪnəs), *a.* [f. BYSS-US + -GEN 2 + -OUS.] That (normally) produces a byssus.
1886 *Ann. Rep. Smithsonian Inst. 1885* I. 777 Lamellibranchs generally exhibit more or less well marked traces of this byssogenous apparatus. **1895** *Camb. Nat. Hist.* III. 453 Foot with byssogenous slit, but no byssus.

byssoid (ˈbɪsɔɪd), *a. Bot.* [f. BYSS-US + -OID.] Like a byssus; having a fringed structure with threads of unequal lengths.
1857 BERKELEY *Cryptog. Bot.* §160. 185 Nucleus surrounded by a whorl of byssoid branchlets. **1861** H. MACMILLAN *Footnotes Page Nat.* 140 The yellow hyaline filaments found at the bottom of wine bottles..their byssoid nature.

byssolite (ˈbɪsəlaɪt). [f. Gr. βύσσος + -LITE.] An olive-green fibrous mineral, a variety of AMPHIBOLE; the same as ASBESTOID.
1847 in CRAIG. **1869** *Daily News* 8 Oct., Columns of Oriental byssolite. **1879** RUTLEY *Stud. Rocks* x. 131 Byssolite is more compact in aggregation.

byssop, -ryche, obs. ff. BISHOP, -RIC.

byssus (ˈbɪsəs). Also 5-7 bissus. [a. L. *byssus*, a. Gr. βύσσος 'a fine yellowish flax, and the linen made from it, but in later writers taken for *cotton*, also *silk*, which was supposed to be a kind of cotton' (Liddell & Scott), ad. Heb. *bûts*, applied to 'the finest and most precious stuffs, as worn by kings, priests, and persons of high rank or honour' (Gesenius), transl. in Bible of 1611 'fine linen', f. root **bûts*, Arab. *bāḍ* to be white, to surpass in whiteness. Originally therefore a fibre or fabric distinguished for its whiteness.]
1. An exceedingly fine and valuable textile fibre and fabric known to the ancients; apparently the word was used, or misused, of various substances, linen, cotton, and silk, but it denoted properly (as shown by recent microscopic examination of mummy-cloths, which according to Herodotus were made of βύσσος) a kind of flax, and hence is appropriately translated in the English Bible 'fine linen'.
1398 TREVISA *Barth De P.R.* XVII. xcvii. (1495) 664 Therbe many manere flexe. but the fayrest of al growyth in Egypte: for therof is Bissus made ryght fayre and whyte as snowe. **1605** CAMDEN *Rem.* (1637) 194 Bissus was a plante or kinde of silke grasse. **1715** tr. *Pancirollus' Rerum Mem.* I. I. v. 13 Byssus was a fine sort of Flax, which grew in Greece. **1828** DE QUINCEY *Toilette Hebr. Lady* Wks. XII. 117 For wool and flax was often substituted the finest byssus or other silky substance. **1866** FELTON *Anc. & Mod.Gr.* I. vi. 38 Hair-nets made of golden thread or silk or byssus.
†**2.** A name formerly given to filamentous fungoid growths of different kinds, which are now more accurately classified. *Obs.*
1753 CHAMBERS *Cycl. Supp.*, *Byssus*..a genus of mosses the most imperfect of the whole class of vegetables. **1770** WITHERING *Brit. Plants* (1796) IV. 143 Cryptogamia. Algæ. Byssus, substance like fine down or velvet, simple or feathered. **1838** *Econ. of Vegetation* 152 The mouse-skin byssus may be seen attached to the roof of the vault in wine cellars.
3. *Zool.* The tuft of fine silky filaments by which molluscs of the genus *Pinna* and various mussels attach themselves to the surface of rocks; it is secreted by the *byssus-gland* in the foot.
'These filaments have been spun, and made into small articles of apparel..Their colour is brilliant, and ranges from a beautiful golden yellow to a rich brown; they also are very durable..The fabric is so thin that a pair of stockings may be put in an ordinary-sized snuff-box' (BECK *Draper's Dict.* 39).
1836 TODD *Cycl. Anat.* I. 702 The byssus is a bundle of horny or silky filaments. **1838** *New Monthly Mag.* LIII. 546 They..moor themselves to rocks and stones by the tiny cables of their byssus. **1879** *Cassell's Techn. Educ.* IV. 199 Mussels are used at Bideford to fix, by means of their byssus, the stones of a bridge, which is difficult to keep in repair, owing to the rapidity of the tide.
4. *Bot.* 'The thread-like stipe of some fungi'. *Syd. Soc. Lex.* 1881.
1866 *Treas. Bot.* s.v.
†**5.** A name formerly given to ASBESTOS.
1864 WEBSTER cites NICHOLSON.

byst, for *biddest* = prayest: see BID *v.* 7 b.

bystade, obs. form of BESTED.

bystander (ˈbaɪˌstændə(r)). Also 8-9 byestander. [f. BY- 2 a + STANDER.] One who is standing by; one who is present without taking part in what is going on; a passive spectator.
a **1619** DONNE *Biathan.* (1644) 137 Such an act, either in Executioner or by-stander, is no way justifiable. **1665** MANLEY tr. *Grotius' Low-C. Wars* 439 The Gunpowder..being by chance fired, destroyed many of the by-standers. **1713** SWIFT *Salaman.* Wks. 1755 III. II. 77 Then I'll appeal to each by-stander, If this be not a Salamander? **1822** IMISON *Sc. & Art* I. 269 A bye-stander will see nothing of the image. **1848** MACAULAY *Hist. Eng.* I. 366 Bystanders whom His Majesty recognised. **1875** JOWETT *Plato* (ed. 2) V. 154 Let the bystander inform the rulers.

ˈby-standing, *ppl. a.* [f. BY- 2 a + STANDING.] That stands by or near.
1622 SPARROW *Bk. Com. Prayer* (1661) 250 A by-standing Table called the Table of Proposition. **1884** A. A. PUTNAM *10 Yrs. Judge* xii. 85 Money..forthcoming from the pockets of by-standing friends.

bystarde, obs. form of BUSTARD.

bystole, bystorye: see BESTEAL, BISTOURY.

†**ˈbystour.** *Sc. Obs.* Also 7 boystour, boisture. [The variant *boistour* suggests identity with BOASTER; and the earlier senses of BOAST (in Sc. *boist*) give a suitable meaning; but the form *bystour* is not explained.]
A loud rude talker; a braggart, bully.
1535 LYNDESAY *Satyre* 2991 That bystour salbe brunt incontinent. *a* **1600** MONTGOMERIE *Flyting* 125 Bleird, babling, bystour-baird, obey. *Ibid.* 215 Ridand like boistures all beshitten. *Ibid.* 655 Beshitten boystour [ed. **1688** by-stour].

by-street (ˈbaɪstriːt). Also 8-9 bye-street. [f. BY- 3 b + STREET.] A street out of the main thoroughfare; a side street, lying out of the way, and hence less frequented.
1672 DRYDEN *Prol. Women* (Globe) 412 In sum by-street To take a lodging. **1704** *Lond. Gaz.* No. 4029/2 They were to watch him at the turning of a certain By-street. **1780** COXE *Russ. Discov.* 216 It has two principal streets..with two by-streets running South. **1880** BROWNING *Dram. Idyls, Pietro* 38 Padua's blackest blindest bye-street.

by-stroke: see BY- 2 c.

bystrow, bystryde: see BESTREW, BESTRIDE.

†**byˈsulp**, *v. Obs. rare*$^{-1}$. [f. BY- = BE- *pref.* 2 + SULP *v.* to sully.] *trans.* To besully, befoul.
c **1325** *E.E. Allit. P.* B. 575 Þe vylanye..þat by-sulpez mannez saule in vnsounde hert.

†**ˈbyˈswelt**, *v. Obs. rare*$^{-1}$. Pa. pple. in 5 byswult. [f. BY- = BE- *pref.* 2 + SWELT.] *trans.* To burn, scorch.
c **1420** *Chron. Vilod.* 329 How hurre clothus lye..Among þe gledys alle by swulte.

†**byˈswenke**, *v. Obs. rare*$^{-1}$. [properly *byswinke*, f. BY- = BE- intensive + SWINK *v.* to labour, toil.] *intr.* To work hard, exert oneself, labour.
? *a* **1400** *Morte Arth.* 1128 Fulle swythe he byswenkez, Swappez in with the swerde þat it þe swange brystedd.

bysy, -nes(se, obs. forms of BUSY, BUSINESS.

†**by-sybbe.** *Obs.* [f. BY- + *sybbe* SIB.] Related, a relative.
[*c* **1315** SHOREHAM 70 And thet ine the selve degre That hy beth here by sybbe.] *c* **1440** *Voc.* in Wr.-Wülcker 562 *Affinis*, by sybbe.

†**bysym.** *Sc. Obs.* [Apparently a corrupt form of BYSEN.] = BYSEN 2.
c **1445** HOLLAND *Houlate* lxxiv. (Bannatyne MS.) Allace, I am lost, lathest of all, Bysym [*v.r.* bysyn] in bale beft. [Cf. i. 6 Quhame sall I bleme in this breth, a besum [*v.r.* bysyn] that I be?]

bysyne, bysynt: see BISEN, -ING.

byszyn, var. of BYSS *v. Obs.*

byt, etc.: see BIT.

byt = biddeth: see BID *v.*

†**ˈby-table.** *Obs.* [f. BY- 3 a + TABLE.] A side-table; one which is not the main table in a room.
1550 RIDLEY in Strype *Eccl. Mem.* II. I. xxx. 256 To take down and abolish all other by-tables and altars. **1625** K. LONG tr. *Barclay's Argenis* III. xxiv. 229 He had seen a Box of most curious worke, upon a by-table. *a* **1805** A. CARLYLE *Autobiog.* 488 His companions [sat] at a by-table.

bytaken, obs. form of BETOKEN *v.*

†**ˈby-tale.** *Obs.* Also 4 bitale, 6 bytaile. [f. *bi-*, BY- + TALE.] **a.** A parable; cf. BYSPEL 1. **b.** An irrelevant tale, a tale by the way.
a **1300** *Life of Jesus* (Horstm.) 242 (Mätz.) Ore louerd prechede þat folk..And seide heom þar to ane bitale. **1553** T. WILSON *Rhet.* 48 Tel me no bytailes, such as are to no purpose.

by-talk (ˈbaɪtɔːk). Also 9 bye-. [f. BY- 3 c + TALK *sb.*]
1. Talk aside; incidental talk away from the main business, or at by-times; irrelevant speech, small talk, tittle-tattle.
1563 FOXE *A. & M.* 820/1 The sayde bishops bytalke..was not muche materiall. **1580** NORTH *Plutarch* 730 Demosthenes..sought occasions in his by-talk to shew men that he was excellently well learned. **1653** *Lilburn Tryed & Cast* 126 He knew, by such by-talk and impertinencies..how to take away..their reason. **1815** SCOTT *Guy Mannering* iii, 'O troth, Laird,' continued they, during this by-talk, 'it's but,' etc.
†**2.** The object or butt of such talk; a BYWORD.
1579 TOMSON *Calvin's Serm. Tim.* 292/1 He shalbe made a mocking stock, & a bytalk in euery mans mouth.

bytaught, etc.: see BETAUGHT.

bytch(e, byte, obs. forms of BITCH, BITE.

byte (baɪt). *Computers.* [Arbitrary, prob. influenced by BIT *sb.*[4] and BITE *sb.*] A group of eight consecutive bits operated on as a unit in a computer.
1964 BLAAUW & BROOKS in *IBM Systems Jrnl.* III. 122 An 8-bit unit of information is fundamental to most of the formats [of the System/360]. A consecutive group of *n* such units constitutes a field of length *n*. Fixed-length fields of length one, two, four, and eight are termed bytes, halfwords, words, and double words respectively. **1964** *IBM Jrnl. Res. & Develop.* VIII. 97/1 When a byte of data appears from an I/O device, the CPU is seized, dumped, used and restored. **1967** P. A. STARK *Digital Computer Programming* xix. 351 The normal operations in fixed point are done on four bytes at a time. **1968** *Dataweek* 24 Jan. 1/1 Tape reading and writing is at from 34,160 to 192,000 bytes per second.

byteche, var. of BETEACH *v. Obs.*

bytell, -ylle, byttil, obs. forms of BEETLE.

byten, bytone, obs. forms of BETONY.

by-term (ˈbaɪtɜːm). Also 6 bye-tearme. [f. BY- 4, 5 + TERM.]
†**1.** A by-name, a nickname. *Obs.*
1579 TWYNE *Phisicke agst. Fort.* I. xlii. 60 b, Oftentymes great infamie groweth vppon small causes, and vile bye tearmes, vppon honourable names.
2. In University of Cambridge: A term which is not the main one for entering or for taking degrees.
(The degree of B.A. can be taken after residing for a certain number of terms; but to make this fit with the annual examination for honours, a student must enter at the beginning of the October term.)
1883 *Athenæum* 15 Dec. 770 Bulwer took his degree at a by-term, and did not try for honours.

by the by: see BY *prep.* 12 b, BY *sb.*[2] 2 b, c.

bythenche, -thenke, obs. ff. BETHINK.

by-the-way, *sb.* [f. phr. *by the way*: see BY *prep.* 12 b.] An incidental remark.
1896 *Punch* 1 Feb. 52/1, I think I may indulge myself with a short by-the-way on the subject of hampers. **1907** *Daily Chron.* 2 Oct. 3/3 Here are two 'by-the-ways' from her pages of observation.

by-thing (ˈbaɪθɪŋ). [f. BY- 4, 5 + THING.] That which is not the main thing; a matter by the way, or for by-times.

1721 STRYPE *Eccl. Mem.* I. I. xxiv. 174 Not [content to swear] to the whole act, some by-things in it not agreeing to their judgments. **1859** G. WILSON *E. Forbes* x. (1861) 318 Only..as a kind of by-thing could he find time for zoological ..pursuits. **1884** TENNYSON *Becket* III. iii. 132 These are by-things In the great cause.

†**by'thinne, by'thout.** Also **biþinne, biþute, bythowte, bethout.** Altered forms [app. produced by the substitution of *by* for *wi'*, in *with*] of WITHIN, WITHOUT (cf. BEDENE).

a **1300** *Floriz & Bl.* 218 Seue hundred tures and two Beoþ in þe burȝ biþute mo. *Ibid.* 244 Ef þer comeþ eni man Biþinne þilke barbecan. *a* **1400** *Usages of Winchester* in *Eng. Gilds* 354 Euerych defawte by-þinne þe amountaunce of þre shyllynges. *Ibid.* 363 Lese þe tenaunt by-þowte rekenerynge. **1589** *Marprel. Epit.* (1843) 15 Tell me then bethout dissimblation. **1879** JAMIESON, *Bethout*, without. *Fife.*

bythwind, obs. f. WITHWIND, a plant. (cf. prec.)

1647 LILLY *Chr. Astrol.* viii. 59 He [Saturn] governeth.. Nightshade, Bythwind, Angelica, Sage.

bytide, bytimes: see BETIDE, BETIMES.

by-time (ˈbaɪtaɪm). Also 9 bye-. [f. BY- 4 + TIME.] Time not occupied by one's main work or pursuits; spare time, odd hours.

1609 C. BUTLER *Fem. Mon.* Pref. (1823) 3 To spend some by-time for my recreation in searching out their [bees'] nature. **1775** JOHNSON *Lett.* I. cxxiv. 267, I, therefore, step over at by-times, and of by-times I have enough. **1865** DICKENS *Mut. Fr.* II. v, In bye-times, as on this holiday.

bytoken(e, bytore, obs. ff. BETOKEN, BITTERN.

bytownite (ˈbaɪtaʊnaɪt). *Min.* [f. *Bytown*, (now Ottawa) in Canada, where it occurs + -ITE.] A variety of ANORTHITE.

1868 DANA *Min.* 340.

bytr-: see BETR-.

byttel, -ell, -il, -ylle, obs. forms of BEETLE.

byttour, -ur(e, -yr, obs. forms of BITTERN.

bytumen, obs. form of BITUMEN.

by-turning, a turning, leading aside: see BY- 3 b.

†**'by-verse.** *Obs.* [f. BY *a.* + VERSE: cf. BYWORD.] A verse that passes current, a rimed saw or maxim.

1655 MOUFET & BENN. *Health's Improv.* (1746) 218 The Dutchmen have a By-verse amongst them to this Effect.

'by-view. ? *Obs.* Also 8 bye-. [f. BY- 2 b, 3 c, d + VIEW *sb.*] **a.** A side glance, or glimpse; a look directed to an object not immediately before the eye. **b.** A private, unavowed, or self-interested aim; cf. BY-END.

a **1731** ATTERBURY (J.) No by views of his own shall mislead him. **1753** *Gray's Inn Jrnl.* No. 30 (1756) I. 193 Every Reader of Taste must have been greatly delighted with these Bye-views.

by-walk (ˈbaɪwɔːk). Also 6 **biwalk.** [f. BY- 3 b + WALK *sb.*] A private or sequestered walk; a by-path. *lit.* and *fig.*

1549 LATIMER *Serm. bef. Edw. VI*, i. (Arb.) 36 Let vs not take any biwalkes, but let gods word directe vs. **1672** WYCHERLEY *Love in Wood* III. iii, Have I found you in your by-walks? **1725** POPE *Odyss.* XIII. 510 *note*, There should be by-walks to retire into sometimes for our ease. **1852** SMITH *Eng. & Fr. Dict.*, By-walk, *promenade écartée.*

So **'by-walker**, one who frequents by-paths, one who strays from the highway or right way; *lit.* and *fig.*; also **'by-walking** *vbl. sb.*

1549 LATIMER *Serm. bef. Edw. VI*, iii. (Arb.) 78 Excytinge my audience to beware of by-walkynges. *Ibid.* iv. 112 Absalon David's son was a bywalker. **1575–85** ABP. SANDYS *Serm.* (1841) 118 St. Paul noteth other by-walkers.

byward (ˈbaɪwɔːd), *sb.* [f. BY- 3, 5 + WARD.] A ward or guard which is not the main one; as in the *Byward Tower* in the Tower of London.

1840 AINSWORTH *Tower of Lond.* iv, A large drawbridge then led to another portal forming the principal entrance to the outer ward, and called the By-ward or Gate Tower.

†**'byward, 'bywards,** *adv. Obs.* [f. BY *adv.* + -WARD(S.] Sideways.

(In first quot. *ward* perh. = 'confinement, custody'.)

1556 J. HEYWOOD *Spider & Fl.* iv. 28 In eche weake place is wouen a weauing cast, By warde, in warde, to warde the flie more fast. **1674** N. FAIRFAX *Bulk & Selv.* 75 The spring ..would only be pusht forwards or by-wards.

bywater (ˈbaɪwɔːtə(r)). [f. BY- B 5 + WATER *sb.* 20.] A diamond of inferior water, yellowish in colour; also *attrib.*

1878 [see OFF COLOUR 2]. **1895** *Westm. Gaz.* 1 Oct. 2/1, I ..woke up to consider two fresh lots of treasure, 'whites' and 'by-waters', so termed from their colour. **1916** F. B. WADE *Diamonds* 25 Yellows, or by-waters.

by-way (ˈbaɪweɪ). Forms: 4 **biwei**, 5 **bye-waye**, 6 **bie-, by-waie**, 9 **bye-way**, 5– **by-way.** [f. BY- 3 b + WAY.]

1. A way other than the highway; a side road; a secluded, private, obscure, or unfrequented way.

1330 R. BRUNNE *Chron.* 10145 (Rolls Ser.) By a bywey [*v.r.* bigate] to Totenes lay, Cador & hyse toke þat way. *c* **1425** WYNTOUN *Cron.* VIII. xxxii. 65 Ðat kennyd þame a by way. **1596** SPENSER *F.Q.* I. i. 28 That path he kept, which beaten was most plaine, Ne ever would to any by-way bend. **1611** BIBLE *Judg.* v. 6 In the dayes of Iael..the traueilers walked thorow by-wayes. **1708** MOTTEUX *Rabelais* V. xxvi. (1737) 114 Highways, Crossways, and Byways. **1860** ADLER *Fauriel's Prov. Poetry* xi. 239 Totally unacquainted with the by-ways of the forest.

2. *transf.* or *fig.*; often depreciatively.

1488 CAXTON *Chast. Goddes Chyldr.* 23 Suche a man cometh lightly in to a byewaye and for many errours he slideth ful folyly. **1535** COVERDALE *Isa.* lvii. 17 He turneth him self, and foloweth yᵉ bywaye of his owne hert. **1697** DRYDEN *Virg., Ess. Georg.* (1721) I. 203 A Precept that enters it [the Understanding] as it were thro' a By-way. **1768–78** TUCKER *Lt. Nat.* II. 611 Children drawn into the world through this by-way are looked upon as a burden. **1846** D. JERROLD *Chron. Clovernook* Wks. IV. 439 The by-ways and short-cuts to wealth. **1848** MRS. JAMESON *Sacr. & Leg. Art* (1850) 195 A friend, learned in all the byways..of Italian literature.

3. *attrib.*

1661 HICKERINGILL *Jamaica* 84 Undisputed Titles need not..by-way stratagems to ensure their Negotiations. **1720** *Lond. Gaz.* No. 5910/4 All Bye-Way and Cross-Road Letters are to be paid for.

4. *advb. genitive* (cf. *crossways*) or ? *plural cognate object*: with quot. 1725 cf. BY *a.* 1.

1549 LATIMER *Serm. bef. Edw. VI*, ii. (Arb.) 56 The Iewes ..take vpon them to breke lawes and to go by wayes. *a* **1674** CLARENDON *Hist. Reb.* (1703) II. VIII. 410 Marching by-ways..they likewise passed over the Thames. **1725** DE FOE *Voy. round World* (1840) 311 Carrying them by-ways and unfrequented.

bywelde, obs. f. BEWIELD.

†**by'went,** *ppl. a. Sc. Obs.* [f. BY- 2 d + *went*, pa. pple. of WEND.] Bygone, past.

1513 DOUGLAS *Æneis* VI. xii. 40 For thair inveterat vicis ald bywent, By pvnycioun satisfactioun to mak. **1533** BELLENDEN *Livy* (1822) Introd. 6 Considder of Romanis, in all thare time bywent.

bywepe, obs. form of BEWEEP *v.*

by-west: see BY *prep.* 9 c.

byweuen, -ven, var. of BIWEVE *v.*[1] *Obs.*

†**by'whopen.** Also **by-woopen, -wopen.** ? Irregular str. pa. pple. of BEWHAPE *v. Obs.* (It does not appear where Phillips found the word.)

1676 PHILLIPS (App.) *By-woopen* [**1678** bywopen], (old word) made senseless. **1775** ASH, *By whopen* (obsolete), stupified, made senseless.

by-wipe, side-stroke: see BY- 2 c.

bywoner (ˈbaɪwəʊnə(r), ˈbeɪvoːnər). *S.Afr.* Also (corruptly) **beiwoner, bywonner.** [Afrikaans, f. *by* with + *woon* live + *-er*, pers. suff.] A poor tenant farmer who lives on the farm of another man to whom he renders certain services (with or without payment in produce or money), being allowed to carry on some farming on his own account. Also *attrib.*

1886 J. J. AUBERTIN *Six Months in Cape Colony & Natal* ix. 235 Then there is what are called the Baywhoner [*sic*] tribe among the Dutch..that live upon the landowners, their friends. **1889** H. A. BRYDEN *Kloof & Karroo* 253 A beiwoner (a sort of sub-farmer on the estate of a richer farmer, who is expected to perform certain duties for the privilege of running his stock). **1901** *Daily News* 22 Mar. 4/7 Steyn and De Wet and their following of 'bywoners'. **1916** F. E. MILLS YOUNG (*title*) The Bywonner. **1955** L. G. GREEN *Karoo* i. 15 Farmers lived on biltong and brak water, and their bywoners ate dead donkeys.

byword (ˈbaɪwɜːd). Forms: 1–2 **biwyrde, -word**, 4–6 **by-worde, bie-word**, 6–9 **bye-word(e**, 6– **by-word.** [f. BY *a.* 2 + WORD.]

1. A proverb, proverbial saying.

c **1050** *Gloss.* in Wr-Wülcker 470 *Prouerbium*, biwyrde. *a* **1131** *O.E. Chron.* an. 1130 Oc man seið to biworde, hæge sitteð þa aceres dæleth. *c* **1374** CHAUCER *Troylus* IV. 769 For which ful oft a by worde here I seye, That rooteles mot grene soone deye. *c* **1400** *Beryn* 2243 There is a comyn by word.. Wele sellith he his peny that the pound therby savith. **1579** LYLY *Euphues* (Arb.) 48 Is it not a by word, like will to like. **1741** RICHARDSON *Pamela* (1824) I. 99 As honest as goodman Andrews, was a bye-word. **1849** *Blackw. Mag.* 686 An old byword, which says more people know Tom Fool than Tom Fool knows.

†**b.** A parable. *Obs.*

c **1550** CHEKE *Matt.* xiii. 3 He spaak vnto yem much in biwordes and said.

2. A person or thing who becomes proverbial, as a type of specified characteristics; an object of scorn or contempt.

1535 COVERDALE *Deut.* xxviii. 37 Thou shalt go to waist, and become a byworde, and a laughinge stocke amonge all nacions. **1575–85** ABP. SANDYS *Serm.* (1841) 349 Marked like Cain..to be a bye-word, and an example of Gods justice to all the world. **1611** BIBLE *1 Kings* ix. 7 Israel shall bee a prouerbe, and a by-word among all people. **1748** RICHARDSON *Clarissa* II. 277, I am the talk and the bye-word of half the county. **1776** ADAM SMITH *W. Nat.* I. I. x. 116 Apothecaries' profit is become a bye-word. **1867** FROUDE *Short Stud.* (1883) IV. II. vi. 252 The Church courts were a byword for iniquity in every country in Europe.

b. A nickname, byname, epithet of scorn.

1598 DRAYTON *Heroic. Epist.* xiii. 104 Give a thousand by-words to my Name, And call me Beldam, Gib, Witch, Nightmare, Trot. **1672** MARVELL *Reh. Transp.* I. 70 These Doctrines which he traduces under that by-word [*i.e.* Calvinism]. **1818** BYRON *Ch. Har.* IV. xiv, Her [Venice's] very byword sprung from victory, The 'Planter of the Lion'.

†**3.** A word or phrase of frequent occurrence in speech, esp. in the mouth of a particular individual; a trick of speech, pet phrase. *Obs.*

1563–87 FOXE *A. & M.* (1631) III. x. 106/1 [Bonner] saying, as his by word was, Before God thou art a knaue. **1575** GASCOIGNE *Philomene* (Arb.) 111 This byword *phy* betokneth bad, And things to cast away. **1651** *Proc. Parliament* No. 104. 1612 Broke his brain with thinking there was some-thing in it, some 'whatchecal e', which is his by-word. **1710** STEELE *Tatler* No. 241 ¶8 His By-Words (as they call a Sentence a Man particularly affects).

†**b.** A watchword, signal. *Obs.*

1494 FABYAN V. lxxxix. 66 He gaue to theym this watche or by worde, 'Nempnyth your Sexis'.

†**4.** (cf. BY-TALK and BY- III): A casual word, a hint; a word beside the matter in hand. *Obs.*

1542 UDALL *Erasm. Apoph.* 18 b, He saied emong his frendes; I would haue bought a robe, if I had had money. He craued nothyng, but did onely after a maidenly sorte geue a bywoorde of his greate penurie. **1572** FORREST *Theophil.* 540 What though a bye worde, unwares, doe owte starte. *a* **1652** BROME *City Wit* III. ii. 322 There is no woman, though she use never so many bywords, but yet in the end she will come to the point. **1658** *Whole Duty Man* iv. §13. 41 In idle by-words.

by-work (ˈbaɪwɜːk). Also 9 bye-. [f. BY- 3 d, e, 4, 5 + WORK.]

1. Work done by the way, in intervals of leisure, as opposed to one's main business; = Gr. πάρεργον; also depreciatively, work done with ulterior or interested motives.

1587 GOLDING *De Mornay* xvi. (1617) 281 Which of vs doth it [good] not as a by-worke for some other things sake. **1607** T. WALKINGTON *Optic Glass* 159 To make a by-worke a worke, is to make our worke a by-worke. **1647** H. MORE *Infinity of Worlds* lvi, The appearance of the nightly starres Is but the by-work of each neighbour sun. **1710** NORRIS *Chr. Prud.* viii. 385 To make Religion the great business and concern of their Lives, and not as most do a By-work. **1873** H. ROGERS *Orig. Bible* ii. 82 Which are but the bye-work of her beneficence. **1885** G. ALLEN *Darwin* 128 The by-work with which he filled up one of the intervals between his greater and more comprehensive treatises.

2. An accessory and subsidiary work. ? *Obs.*

1587 GOLDING *De Mornay* xi. 154 Nailes, pinnes, Riuets, Buttons & such, I haue thought them to be but byworkes. **1601** HOLLAND *Pliny* II. 550 He deuised another by-worke to expresse the same.

†**3.** A work done awry or amiss. *Obs.*

1615 CROOKE *Body of Man* 271 Wherefore Aristotle thinketh..that the female is a bye worke or preuarication, yea the first monster in Nature.

byyond(e, obs. form of BEYOND.

by your leave, *sb.* [f. phr. *by your leave*: see LEAVE *sb.* 1.] An expression of apology for not having asked permission; the asking of permission.

1914 H. R. MARTIN *Barnabetta* xii. 106 She was sportively handling huge sums like this without a By-Your-Leave. **1924** W. M. RAINE *Troubled Waters* i. 13 'With not even a by your leave. You're a claim jumper,' she said. **1936** *Scrutiny* V. 38 Jung, indeed, insists that he is a bold man nowadays who would roundly declare, without so much as by-your-leave from the doctor, that he is altogether free of it [*sc.* neurosis]. **1948** 'J. TEY' *Franchise Affair* viii. 90 He picked Robert's glass out of his hand without a by-your-leave and rose to fill it.

byzant, var. spelling of BEZANT.

Byzantian (bɪˈzænʃ(ɪ)ən), *a.* and *sb.* Also 7 biz-. [f. L. *Byzantius* belonging to Byzantium: see -AN.] = next.

a **1619** FOTHERBY *Atheom.* I. vi. §2 (1622) 44 Doest thou sweare, like a Bizantian, by their yron pence? **1861** LYTTON *Str. Story* xxxv, This casket..of ancient Byzantian workmanship. **1879** SIR G. SCOTT *Recollect.* v. 210 Byzantine in all forms but those used by the Byzantians.

Byzantine (bɪˈzæntaɪn, ˈbɪzəntaɪn), *a.* and *sb.* Also 6 **Byzantin**, 6–7 **Bi-, Bezantin(e**, 7 **Bysantin.** [ad. L. *Byzantīnus*, f. *Byzantium*: see BEZANT and -INE; cf. F. *byzantin*. Byron has the first pronunciation, which the derivatives also follow; the second is frequent with classical scholars.]

A. *adj.* **a.** Belonging to Byzantium or Constantinople; also, reminiscent of the manner, style, or spirit of Byzantine politics. Hence, intricate, complicated; inflexible, rigid, unyielding. ***Byzantine historians***: those who lived in the Eastern Empire from the 6th to the 15th c.

1794 Martyn *Rousseau's Bot.* xxviii. 442 The Byzantine or Spanish-nut. **1817** Byron *Manfred* II. ii. 183 From the Byzantine maid's unsleeping spirit. **1876** Bancroft *Hist. U.S.* V. l. 95 The throne of the Byzantine Cæsars. **1937** Koestler *Spanish Testament* iv. 75 In the old days people often smiled at the Byzantine structure of the Spanish Army. **1965** *Economist* 25 Dec. 1404/3 From the byzantine procedural caution of the approach work [to the Common Market] on both sides, it seems that substantive issues are still beyond the diplomats' grasp. **1966** G. Steiner *Lang. Silence* (1967) 399 It was precisely on this occasion that Stalin struck the new ominous note of the cult of personality, of the Byzantine homage to the leader. **1966** *Listener* 26 May 765/1 To hint that one does not quite catch the drift of their byzantine prose .. pierces to the heart of their intellectual pride.

b. *spec.* Pertaining to the style of art, esp. of architecture, developed in the Eastern division of the Roman Empire. The Byzantine architecture is distinguished by its use of the round arch, cross, circle, dome, and rich mosaic ornamentation.

1848 Mrs. Jameson *Sacr. & Leg. Art* (1850) 88 Those of the Greek or Byzantine school. **1879** Sir G. Scott *Lect. Archit.* I. 10 The earliest style that may fairly be called Christian is the Byzantine.

B. *sb.* **1.** An inhabitant of Byzantium.

1836 *Penny Cycl.* VI. 84/2 The Byzantines at one time had 500 ships. **1875** Jevons *Money* xiv. 195 The iron money of the Byzantines .. was token representative money.

2. = BEZANT 1.

1599 Hakluyt *Voy.* II. 109 A Bizantin, which is .. six pence sterling. **1610** Holland *Camden's Brit.* I. 421 Bizantines of silver valued at two shillings anciently. **1695** Kennett *Par. Antiq.* ix. 97 Gave .. one bezantine to his wife. **1862** H. Marryat *Year in Sweden* II. 248 *note*, Byzantines also, of gold and silver, are constantly disinterred.

† **3.** = BEZANT 2.

1605 Camden *Rem.* 236 The piece of gold valued at £15 which the king was antiently accustomed to offer on high festival days was called a Bizantine.

† **4.** Old name of some herb. *Obs.*

1621 Burton *Anat. Mel.* II. iv. I. v, Syrup of Borage .. of .. Fumitory, Maiden-hair, Bizantine, etc. **1661** Lovell *Hist. Anim. & Min.* 451 Syrups, of the confiture of citron peel, and byzantine.

So also **By,zanti'nesque** *a.* [see -ESQUE], in the Byzantine style of art; **By'zantinize** *v. trans.*, to make Byzantine.

1879 Sir G. Scott *Recollect.* iv. 193 The Byzantinesque [design]. **1855** Milman *Lat. Chr.* (1864) IX. xiv. x. 321 Either in Constantinople or in the Byzantinised parts of the west.

By'zantinism. [f. prec. + -ISM.] The style and methods of art (esp. of architecture) developed in the Byzantine empire. Also *fig.*

1855 Milman *Lat. Chr.* (1864) IX. xiv. x. 331 Italian painting .. threw off with Giotto the last trammels of Byzantinism. **1945** Koestler *Yogi & Commissar* III. iii. 225 The antidote to Eastern Byzantinism is Western revolutionary humanism. **1963** *Times* 21 Feb. 15/2 The Byzantinism of much academic criticism in America. **1967** *Economist* 18 Mar. p. xxxix/3 The only way to cut through the dead wood is often to peddle influence in Rome... In the end it only aggravates the tendency to confuse political byzantinism with energetic administration.

Byzantinist (baɪ-, bɪ'zæntɪnɪst). [f. BYZANTINE + -IST.] A student of or an expert in Byzantine matters.

1892 *Nation* (N.Y.) 21 Apr. 306/1 The collaboration of Greek, English, and Italian 'Byzantinists' is already pledged to support it. **1927** *Observer* 24 Apr. 20/3 The Congress of Byzantinists has concluded its work. **1958** *Times Lit. Suppl.* 21 Mar. 148/3 Viewed through the eyes of a distinguished and enthusiastic Byzantinist.

byzen, -on: see BYSEN, etc.

C

C (siː), the third letter of the Roman alphabet, was originally identical with the Greek *Gamma*, *Γ*, and Semitic *Gimel*, whence it derived its form through the successive types Γ, ⟨, C. The Greek *Kappa*, *K*, being from the first little used by the Romans, C functioned in earlier Latin both as (g) and (k); the latter sound being the more frequent came to be viewed as the more appropriate to C, and about 300–230 B.C., a modified character, G or G, was introduced for the (g) sound, and C itself retained for the (k) sound. Hence, in the classical period and after, G was treated as the phonetic representative of Gamma, and C as the equivalent of Kappa, in the transliteration of Greek words into Roman spelling, as in *ΚΑΔΜΟΣ*, *ΚΥΡΟΣ*, *ΦΩΚΙΣ*, in Roman letters CADMVS, CYRVS, PHOCIS.

When the Roman alphabet was introduced into Britain, C had only the sound (k); and this value of the letter has been retained by all the insular Celts: in Welsh, Irish, Gaelic, C, c, is still only = (k). The Old English or 'Anglo-Saxon' writing was learned from the Celts, apparently of Ireland; hence C, c, in Old English, was also originally = (k): the words *kin*, *break*, *broken*, *thick*, *seek*, were in OE. written *cyn*, *brecan*, *brocen*, *þicc*, *séoc*. But during the course of the OE. period, the k-sound before *e* and *i* became palatalized, and had by the 10th c. advanced nearly or quite to the sound of (tʃ), though still written c, as in *cir(i)ce*, *wrecc(e)a*. On the continent, meanwhile, a similar phonetic change had also been going on. Original Latin C (= k) before *e*, *i*, had by palatalization advanced in Italy to the sound of (tʃ), and in France still further to that of (ts). Yet for these new sounds the old character C, c, was still retained before *e* and *i*, the letter thus acquiring two distinct values. Moreover the sound (k) also occurred in French before *e* and *i* (chiefly as a representative of Latin *qu*); this was now expressed in Northern French by the Greek letter *K*, k; so that the sound (k) had two symbols, k and c, while the symbol c had two sounds (k and ts). These French inconsistencies as to C and K were, after the Norman Conquest, applied to the writing of English, which caused a considerable re-spelling of the Old English words. Thus while OE. *candel*, *clif*, *corn*, *crop*, *cú*, remained unchanged, *Cent*, *cǽȝ* (*céȝ*), *cyng*, *brece*, *séoce*, were now (without any change of sound) spelt *Kent*, *keȝ*, *kyng*, *breke*, *seoke*; even *cniht* was subsequently spelt *kniht*, *knight*, and *þic*, *picc*, became *thik*, *thikk*, *thick*. The OE. *cw-* was also at length (very unnecessarily) displaced by the Fr. *qw*, *qu*, so that the OE. *cwén*, *cwic*, became ME. *qwen*, *quen*, *qwik*, *quik*, now *queen*, *quick*. The sound (tʃ) to which OE. palatalized c had advanced, also occurred in French, chiefly (in Central French) from Latin *c* before *a*. In French it was represented by *ch*, as in *champ*, *cher*:—L. *camp-um*, *cār-um*; and this spelling was now introduced into English: the Hatton Gospels, written about 1160, have in Matt. i–iii, *child*, *chyld*, *riche*, *mychel*, for the *cild*, *rice*, *mycel*, of the OE. version whence they were copied: this was, phonetically, an improvement. In these cases, the OE. *c* gave place to *k*, *qu*, *ch*; but, on the other hand, *c* in its new value of (ts) came in largely in Fr. words like *processiun*, *emperice*, *grace*, and was also substituted for *ts* in a few OE. words, as *miltse*, *bletsien*, in early ME. *milce*, *blecien*. By the end of the 13th c. both in France and England, this sound (ts) was reduced to simple (s); and from that date c before *e*, *i*, *y*, has been, phonetically, a duplicate or subsidiary letter to s; used either for 'etymological' reasons, as in *lance*, *cent*, or (in defiance of etymology) to avoid the ambiguity due to the 'etymological' use of s for (z), as in *ace*, *mice*, *once*, *pence*, *defence*.

Thus, on the plea of showing the etymology, we write *advise*, *devise*, instead of *advize*, *devize*, which obliges us to write *advice*, *device*, *dice*, *ice*, *mice*, *twice*, etc., in defiance of the etymology; bad example has extended this to *hence*, *pence*, *defence*, etc., where there is no plea whatever for *c*. Former generations also wrote *sence* for *sense*.

Hence, in modern English, C has (1) the 'hard' sound (k) before *a*, *o*, *u*, before a consonant (except *h*), and when final, as in *cab*, *cot*, *cut*, *claw*, *crow*, *acme*, *cycle*, *sac*, *tic*, *epic*; (2) before *e*, *i*, *y*, it has the 'soft' sound (s). In all words from Old English or Old French, final *c* is avoided: the (k) sound being written *k* or *ck*, as in *beak*, *meek*, *oak*, *book*, *bark*, *balk*, *bank*, *pack*, *peck*, *pick*, *rock*. This is probably due to the claims of derivatives like *meeker*, *oaken*, *barking*, *rocky*, where *c* could not be used. Final *c* however is written in modern words from Latin, Greek, or other languages, and (of late) in the ending *-ic*, as in *sac*, *tic*, *epic*, *critic*, *music*, *picnic*. In the rare cases in which this *c* is followed in inflexion by *e* or *i*, it is necessary to change it to *ck*, as in *physicking*, *mimicking*, *frolicking*, *trafficker*, *picnicker*. When the (s) sound is final, it must be written *-ce*, as in *trace*, *ice*, *thrice*, and this final *e* must be retained in composition before *a*, *o*, *u*, as in *trace-able*, *peace-able*. (3) *Ci* (rarely *ce*) preceding another vowel has frequently the sound of (ʃ), esp. in the endings *-cious*, *-cial*, *-cion*, as *atrocious*, *glacial*, *coercion* (*ocean*). This sound (which is also taken by *t* in the same position) has been developed in comparatively modern times by palatalization of (s).

In a few words from foreign languages, *c* retains the foreign pronunciation, as in It. *cicerone* (tʃitʃe'rone).

The combination CH virtually constitutes a distinct letter, having a history and sound of its own, and as such it receives a separate place in the alphabet of some languages, e.g. Spanish, Welsh. In English it is not so treated, and the ch- words are placed in Dictionaries and alphabetical lists between ce- and ci-. This inclusion of ch in the middle of C is one reason why the latter occupies so large a space in the Dictionary: C is virtually two letters in one, since beside the series *ca-*, *ce-*, *ci-*, *cl-*, etc., there is the parallel series *cha-*, *che-*, *chi-*, *chl-*, etc. For the history and sounds of ch, see before the beginning of the ch- words.

c **1000** ÆLFRIC *Gram.* iii. (Z.) 6 *B*, *c*, *d*, *g*, *p*, *t*, ȝeendjað on *e*. **1588** J. MELLIS *Briefe Instr.* D vij, Goe to your Calender to the letter C. and there enter Chyst. *a* **1682** SIR T. BROWNE *Tracts* 126 The long poem of Hugbaldus the Monk, wherein every word beginneth with a C. **1885** GOSCHEN in *Pall Mall G.* 5 Nov. 6/1 The 'Three C's' of Foreign Policy.. cleanhandedness, continuity, and courage. **1887** *Spectator* 19 Mar. 395/1 [He] writes Corinthians now with a 'C', as Professor Jowett writes it.

2. *C springs*: see CEE (springs). *C-scroll*: a decorative scroll shaped like the letter C.

1904 P. MACQUOID *Hist. Eng. Furniture* iii. 63 A strap-work of C scrolls and cocksheaded arabesques.

II. 1. a. Used like the other letters of the alphabet (see A, B) to denote serial order, with the value of *third*, as quire C, the third 'quire' or sheet of a book, 'Horse Artillery, B Brigade, B and C Batteries, Woolwich'. So with the subdivisions of the longer articles in this Dictionary.

b. C 3: the lowest grade in the scale of physical fitness for military service employed in the classification of recruits conscripted under the Military Service Act, 1916; hence *fig.* of the lowest grade, of grossly inferior status or quality.

1918 D. LLOYD GEORGE in *Times* 13 Sept. 8/2 You cannot maintain an A1 Empire with a C3 population. **1923** *Daily Mail* 1 Mar. 7 He would agree prisoner's left arm would be a C3 left arm. *Ibid.* 11 July 13 Sunshine all the way, no C3 affair but a magnificent blaze of light. **1924** GALSWORTHY *White Monkey* I. viii, Eight years her senior and C3 during the war!

2. *spec.* **a.** in *Music*: The name of the first note, or key-note, of the 'natural' major scale; called also C in Germany, in France *Ut*, in Italy *Do*. Also, the scale or key which has that note for its tonic. Applied to a tenor saxophone in C; also *ellipt.*

1596 SHAKS. *Tam. Shr.* III. i. 76 C fa vt, that loues with all affection. **1782** BURNEY *Hist. Music* II. 13 The sounds belonging to the key of C. natural. **1864** BROWNING *Abt Vogler* XII, For my resting-place is found, The C Major of this life. **1879** GROVE *Dict. Mus.* I. 205 The famous Quartet in C, dedicated to Haydn. **1932** B. DAVIS *Saxophone* xxx. 154 Because it is not necessary to change the key when reading for the C Melody, this instrument has come to be regarded as non-transposing, in order to differentiate it from those for which it *is* necessary to change key. **1955** L. FEATHER *Encycl. Jazz* i. 20 Frank Trumbauer with his C-Melody saxophone.

b. In *abstract reasoning*, *hypothetical argumentation*, *law*, etc. C is put for a third person or thing. (Cf. A II. 4.)

1864 BOWEN *Logic* (1870) 243 If *B is A* and *B is C*, the two conclusions *A is C*, or *C is A* are equally competent.

3. In *Algebra*: (see A II. 5). In the higher mathematics, *c* is especially used to denote a constant, as distinguished from a variable quantity.

4. Designating a range of international standard paper sizes (as *C1*, *C2*, etc.), used mainly for envelopes and folders: see A 9.

1937 [see B 2 (iv)]. **1962** F. T. DAY *Introd. Paper* vii. 77 The C sizes are not now looked upon as paper sizes but as sizes for envelopes or folders suitable for enclosing the A series of stationery. **1986** *Neat Ideas Catal.* Apr. 15 Business envelopes.. pocket C5 9″ × 6⅜″.

III. Abbreviations.

1. a. C, now rarely c., = L. *centum* a hundred; the common sign for 100 in Roman numerals, as in dates, numbering of books or chapters; so CC = 200, CCCC or CD = 400; formerly written ii.c., etc. Also formerly = hundredweight, now cwt.

1420 *E.E. Wills* (1882) 46 Also iij.c of ledyn wyȝtis. **1509** HAWES *Past. Pleas.* xix. xxii, The shyp was great fyve c. tonne to charge. **1535** COVERDALE *2 Sam.* xxi. 16 Thre C. weight of brasse. —— *Judg.* xvi. 5 So wyll we geue the euery man a M. and an C. syluerlinges. **1709** *Lond. Gaz.* No. 4509/3 About 2*s.* per C. *Mod.* The year of our Lord MCMLXXXVIII.

b. c = CENTI-, as in *cg*, centigram(s); *cl*, centilitre(s); *cm*, centimetre(s).

1892 G. COLLAR *Notes on Metric System* 7, 10 milligrammes (mg.) make 1 centigramme (cg.). **1983** J. V. DRAZIL *Quantities & Units of Measurement* 43 *cg*, centigram. **1892** Cl. [see M 5 d]. **1983** J. V. DRAZIL *Quantities & Units of Measurement* 45 *cl*, *cL*, centilitre. **1874** J. P. PUTNAM *Metric System Weights & Measures* 39, 1 cu. cm. of water weighs 1g. **1923** [see ULTRASONIC *a.* 1 b]. **1982** cm [see TWEETER].

2. *Music.* 'As a sign of time C stands for common time, 4 crotchets in a bar; and ₵ for allabreve time, with 2 or 4 minims in a bar' (Grove *Dict. Music*). C = Counter-tenor, or Contralto; C.F. = *canto fermo*.

3. (Abbreviations cited here with full stops are frequently used without them.) **C.** = various proper names, as Charles, Caius; **C** (*Chem.*), Carbon; **C.**, Cardinal (*obs.*); **C.**, Celsius, Centigrade (temperature); **C**, cocaine; **C** (*Electricity*), current; **C** (*U.S.*), $100; **c.** (*Cricket*), caught; also **c. and b.**, caught and bowled; **c.**, chapter; **c.**, century; **c.**, cubic, as in *c.c.*, cubic centimetre; *c.* (in a dental formula in Zoology), canine teeth; *c.* (before a date) = Lat. *circa* about; ©, copyright (followed by the name or other indication of the owner of the copyright); **C.A.** Chartered Accountant (Scotland); **CAMRA** ('kæmrə), Campaign for Real Ale [orig. Campaign for the Revitalization of Ale]; **C. & W.**, **c. & w.**, country-and-western (music); **C.A.P.**, Common Agricultural Policy (of the European Economic Community); **C.A.T.**, College of Advanced Technology; **C.B.** Companion of the Bath; **C.B.**, confined to barracks, as a punishment in the army; **C.B.E.**, Commander of the Order of the British Empire; **C.B.I.**, Confederation of British Industry; formerly, *F.B.I.*: see F III. 3; **C.B.S.**, Columbia Broadcasting System; **C.B.(W.)**, chemical and biological (warfare); **C.C.**, County Council(lor); **C.C.**, Cricket Club; **c.c.**, carbon copy or copies (followed by a list of others to whom correspondence is to be copied); **C.D.**, compact disc; **C.D.**, corps diplomatique; **CD ROM** (ˌsiːdiː'rɒm), a compact disc on which text or data is stored and which is used as a read-only memory; **C.E.**, Civil Engineer; **C.E.**, **C.Æ.**, Common Era; occas., Christian Era; **C.E.G.B.**, Central Electricity Generating Board; **C.E.M.A.**, Council for the Encouragement of Music and the Arts; **C.E.R.N.**, **Cern** (sɜːn) [F. *Conseil Européen pour la Recherche Nucléaire*], European Council for Nuclear Research; **C.F.**, Chaplain to the Forces; **cf.**, L. *confer* 'compare' (cf. CONFER *v.* 4); **C.G.M.**, Conspicuous Gallantry Medal; **C.G.S.**, centimetre-gramme-

second; **C.G.S.**, Chief of the General Staff (cf. *C.I.G.S.* below); **C.H.**, Companion of Honour; **C.I.A.** (*U.S.*), Central Intelligence Agency; **C.I.D.**, Committee of Imperial Defence; **C.I.D.**, Criminal Investigation Department; **C.I.E.**, Companion of the Order of the Indian Empire; **C.I.F.**, **c.i.f.**, Cost, Insurance, plus Freight; †**C.I.G.S.**, Chief of the Imperial General Staff (now C.G.S.); **C. in C.**, Commander in Chief; **C.K.D.**, completely knocked down; **C.Litt.**, Companion of Literature; **C.M.** Master of Surgery; **C.M.**, (in *Hymns*) common metre; **C.M.G.**, Companion of the Order of St. Michael and St. George; **C.N.A.A.**, Council for National Academic Awards; **C.N.D.**, Campaign for Nuclear Disarmament; **C.N.S.**, central nervous system; **C.O.**, Commanding Officer; **C.O.**, conscientious objector; **c/o**, care of (CARE *sb.*[1] 4a); **C.O.D.**, see separate entry; **C. of A.**, Certificate of Airworthiness; **C. of E.**, Church of England; **C.O.R.E.** *U.S.*, Congress of Racial Equality; **C.O.S.**, Charity Organization Society (*Cent. Dict.* Suppl. 1909); **C.P.**, Communist Party; **C.P.**, 'convicted poacher'; **cp.** = L. *compara* 'compare'; **Cpl.**, Corporal; **C.P.O.**, Chief Petty Officer; **c.p.s.**, cycles per second; (*Computing*) characters per second; **C.P.R.**, Canadian Pacific Railway; **CPU** (*Computing*), central processing unit; **C.Q.D.**, in wireless telegraphy, the signal formerly used by ships in distress, consisting of C.Q., the international sign for 'all stations', followed by D indicating 'urgent'; after 1908 superseded by S.O.S.; **C.R.T.**, **c.r.t.**, cathode-ray tube; **C.S.**, Civil Service; **CS** [the initials of B. B. *C*orson (b. 1896) and R. W. *S*toughton (1906–57), American chemists who discovered its properties in 1928], a designation of *o*-chlorobenzalmalononitrile, $ClC_6H_4CH{:}C(CN)_2$, a substance that causes irritation of the skin, lachrymation, coughing, etc., and is used in the form of a finely divided solid as a quick-acting irritant for riot control and other purposes; so ***CS gas***, etc.; **c/s**, cycles per second; **C.S.E.**, Certificate of Secondary Education; **C.S.I.R.O.**, Commonwealth [of Australia] Scientific and Industrial Research Organization (replacing the Council for Scientific and Industrial Research); **CT** (*Med.*), computed (or computerized) tomography; freq. *attrib.* as ***CT scan***, etc. (= *CAT scan*: see CAT *sb.*[5]); **ct.**, carat, cent; **c.v.** = *curriculum vitæ* s.v. CURRICULUM; **C.V.O.**, Commander of the Royal Victorian Order. See also C.B. as separate entry.

1855 OWEN *Skel. & Teeth* 304 The homologies of the typical formula may be signified by *i* 1, *i* 2; **c*; *p* 3, *p* 4; *m* 1, *m* 2, *m* 3. **1744** in J. Nyren *Young Cricketer's Tutor* (1833) 111 Smith o *C by Bartrum. **1810** in Alverstone & Alcock *Surrey Cricket* (1902) ii. 54 Lord F. Beauclerck..c. & b. Lambert 21. **1882** *Daily News* 30 May 3/7 G. B. Studd was missed twice—first by Palmer from an easy chance of 'c and b.' **1884** Lillywhite's *Cricket Ann.* 76 C. R. Seymour c Chester b Barratt 34. **1842** E. TURNER *Elem. Chem.* II. ii. 179 Carbon *C...it is much to be wished that these symbols, being now generally known, should be rigorously adhered to. Berzelius has properly selected them from Latin names, as being known to all civilized nations. **1549** LATIMER *Serm. bef. Edw. VI*, v. (Arb.) 133 M. Latimer lamentes the defection of *C. Pole. *a* **1888** *Mod.* Water boils at 100° *C. **1922** E. F. MURPHY *Black Candle* II. xi. 212, I cried and made a fuss when I could not get enough ' M' or '*C', so we moved to a house where no one would hear me. **1959** W. BURROUGHS *Naked Lunch* 29 The craving for C lasts only a few hours, as long as the C channels are stimulated. **1881** THOMPSON *Electr. & Magn.* vi. 307 The number of webers per second of current flowing through a circuit is equal to the number of volts of electromotive-force divided by the number of ohms of resistance in the entire circuit. $*C = \frac{E}{R}$. **1839** *Spirit of Times* 13 Apr. 66/3, I had no idea of betting more than an 'L', or a '*C'. **1930** *Liberty* 11 Oct. 30/3 We gave him five C notes and two tens, or 10 per cent [of $5,200] to make the payoff. **1946** *Science Digest* Aug. 23/2 A goodly supply of crisp C-notes. **1955** 'H. ROBBINS' *Stone for Danny Fisher* II. xiii. 159 My biggest worry was somebody's clipping the five C's from my trousers back there in the dressing room. **1947** *U.S. Congress, Statutes* c. 391 §19 The notice of copyright..shall consist either of the word 'Copyright' or the abbreviation 'Copr.', accompanied by the name of the copyright proprietor... In the case..of copies of works specified in subsections (f) to (k)..the notice may consist of the letter C enclosed within a circle, thus *©, accompanied by the initials, monogram, mark, or symbol of the copyright proprietor. **1957** *Encycl. Brit.* VI. 429/1 The form of notice, which is required for literary, musical and dramatic works and may be used on any other works, consists of the word 'Copyright' or the abbreviation 'Copr.' or the symbol ©, accompanied by the name of the copyright owner and the year in which the copyright was secured; e.g. '© 19— by John Doe'. **1972** *Brewers' Guardian* Aug. 23/3 Yet another organisation has been formed to 'protect the British drinker against the adulteration of his pint'.. Campaign for the Revitalisation of Ale (*CAMRA!!). **1973** [see REAL *a.*[2] 4b]. **1984** *Financial Times* 16 July 18/1 Mr Christopher Hutt, managing director of the small chain of free houses, insists that 'We have not moved away from the CAMRA ideals'. **1953** *Downbeat* 6 May 29/1 Today many of the biggest selling records and most popular hit tunes come from the *c & w side of the tracks. *Ibid.* 29 July 19/5 *Mexican Joe* started slow, but after a few weeks it skyrocketed to the top position in the C & W field. **1981** *Variety* 15 July 67/1 (*heading*) Gilley's Picnic, Rose Bowl C & W Event fall below break-even. **1965** *Acronyms & Initialisms Dict.* (Gale Research Co.) 155 **CAP*, Common Agricultural Policy (Common Market). **1979** H. WILSON *Final Term* v. 95 The CAP issues would have to be settled by those 'fighting-cocks', the Ministers of Agriculture. **1957** *Technology* July 167/2 (*caption*) *CAT for North. **1964** *Economist* 27 June 1485/1 Universities, CATs and the professional social work institutions. **1888** KIPLING *Soldiers Three* 11 Now, I put ut to you, Sorr, *is* ten days' *C.B. a fit an' a proper tratement for a man who has behaved as me? **1892** —— *Barrack-room Ball.* 20 O it's pack-drill for me and a fortnight's C.B. For 'drunk and resisting the Guard'! **1919** *War Slang* in *Athenæum* 8 Aug. 787/2 When doing C.B...he [*sc.* the soldier] was doing 'jankers' or 'Paddy Doyle'. **1928** W. EMPSON in *Granta* 2 Nov. 74/2 We would have put the cooks in C.B...if they'd served up this cat's food. **1917** *Illustr. London News* 30 June 759/1 The five classes of the Order [of the British Empire] are..3. Commanders (*C.B.E.) **1985** *Church Times* 4 Jan. 1/4 Also made CBEs are the Rev. Professor C. F. D. Moule..(for services to theology); the Rev. John Brian Smethurst..(for political and public services), [etc.]. **1965** *Guardian* 2 Aug. 2/8 (*heading*) Royal charter turns FBI into *CBI. **1985** *Daily Tel.* 24 Jan. 21/7 The CBI is on well trodden ground in arguing that the increase in allowances will improve the incentive to work. **1930** *What's on Air* Mar. 12/2 He will call his agency and say, 'Go up to NBC or *CBS and insist they change our hour.' **1985** *Daily Tel.* 19 Feb. 17/3 The settlement of General Westmoreland's £10 million libel suit against CBS has ended a long and expensive legal battle for the American media giant. [**1949** T. ROSEBURY *Peace or Pestilence* ix. 99 In its modern form BW has never been used in a military operation. **1960** M. STUBBS in *Advances in Chem.* XXVI. 36 A growing awareness of the potential threat of a CW-BW attack.] **1964** *Bull. Atomic Sci.* XX. Oct. 35/1 More attention to *CB weapons is required. *Ibid.*, In 1961, the budget for Army expenditures for CBW research, development, and procurement was somewhat over 100 million dollars per year. **1966** *New Scientist* 29 Sept. 717/1 The employment of any one CB weapon weakens the barriers to the use of others. **1967** *Times* 29 May 4/4 John H. Hoskins..denied all charges that Yale was in any way engaged in classified research on C.B.W. **1936** L. I. HUTCHINSON *Stand. Handbk. Secretaries* 287 The carbon copy notation, '*c.c.', should be the last notation. **1969** M. PUGH *Last Place Left* iv. 22 Have you seen the letter?.. It says c.c. to you. Carbon copy. **1982** *Computerworld* 23 Aug. 33/3 You may sometimes want to keep others informed of what you are asking a person or group to do. In that case, indicate it as a 'carbon copy' (CC) on the bottom of the memo. **1902** *Manch. Faces & Places* XIII. 10 (*heading*) Mr. W. J. Crossley, J.P., *C.C. **1906** E. COLLYNS *Typists' Man.* (ed. 6) 218 *C.C.*, County Council. **1985** *Westmorland Gaz.* 28 June 15/2 It was agreed that the clerk contact Cumbria CC about this matter. **1862** *C.C. [see *M.C.C.* s.v. *M II. 5]. **1895** *Badminton Mag.* I. 211 (*heading*) The Best Eleven by the Secretaries of M.C.C. and Surrey C.C. **1980** *Guinness Bk. Records* (ed. 26) 261/1 Playing for Gentlemen of Leicestershire C.C. *v.* Free Foresters, at Oakham, Rutland, on 19 Aug. 1963, Ian H. S. Balfour batted for 100 min without adding to his score of five runs. [**1866** J. J. GRIFFIN *Chem. Handicraft* 298 Graduated for Centimetre Cubes..1 *cc. 6d.] **1899** EDSER *Heat for Adv. Students* iv. 64, 1 c.c. will possess a mass of m/v grams. **1955** *Times* 18 July 12/6 The meeting opened with a 17-lap race for 500 c.c. cars. **1979** *New Scientist* 22 Mar. 948/1 Although the Compact Disc (*CD) system indubitably works as claimed and could offer an attractive alternative to today's grooved records..CD is sure to receive far hotter competition from Japan than the compact cassette. **1984** *What Video?* Aug. 24/1 My musical examples came from what is still one of the best examples of CD recording around. **1942** PARTRIDGE *Dict. Abbrev.* 23/1 **CD*, *Corps Diplomatique*..On, e.g., motor-cars and letters. **1955** G. GREENE *Quiet American* II. ii. 104 Along the route to Tanyin flowed a fast stream of staff and C.D. cars. **1961** *Guardian* 4 May 2/5 Lord Lansdowne..said in the Lords..that the 'CD' plate did not..afford the occupant of a car any privilege or immunity. **1983** *Electronics* 20 Oct. 102/2 The *CD ROM, which is expected to hit the market next year, can hold 525 megabytes of formatted data. **1984** *Byte* Dec. 10 NAPC's Philips Subsystems and Peripherals Inc...will offer its CM 100 Compact Disc Read-Only-Memory (CD ROM) unit to other manufacturers. **1986** S. P. HARTER *Online Information Retrieval* ix. 226 Databases are now being offered on CD-ROM and videodisk, for use on personal information retrieval systems. **1986** *Bookseller* 10 Oct. 1501/2 There was an increase in the prominence of CD-ROM technology at this year's Frankfurt Book Fair. **1838** E. H. LINDO *Jewish Calendar* (title-p.), Tables for continuing the calendar to A.M. 6000–2240 *C.Æ. *Ibid.* 111 (*heading*) 3760 C.Æ. Commencement of the Christian Æra. **1886** K. MAGNUS (*title*) Outlines of Jewish History from B.C. 586 to C.E. 1885. **1957** *Economist* 21 Dec. 1076/2 The *CEGB estimate..might mean that about 53 million tons of coal a year would be used for electricity by 1965. **1960** *Times Rev. Industry* May 49/1 *C.E.G.B.*, Central Electricity Generating Board. **1985** *Financial Times* 16 Mar. 28/5 The indications of possible new PWR sites..underlines the CEGB's hope that the PWR proposal will be authorised. **1940** *Times* 15 June 7/4 The *C.E.M.A. has one expert representative of each art on its Council. **1958** *Ibid.* 4 June 11/3 In 1946 C.E.M.A. was incorporated by royal charter and given the name Arts Council. **1955** *Ibid.* 13 June 6/7 The juridical agreement between the Swiss Government and the European Organization for Nuclear Research (known as *C.E.R.N.). **1967** *Economist* 29 Apr. 492/2 It [*sc.* a Russian particle accelerator] is rather more than twice the power of the biggest now operating, at the international Cern centre in Geneva. **1985** *Christian Sci. Monitor* 23 Jan. 16/2 In the international ball game of physics, recent innings have gone to CERN. **1909** *Cent. Dict.* Suppl., **C.F.* Chaplain to the Forces. **1850** *N. & Q.* 2 Nov. 373/1 *Shakspeare and George Herbert*... *Cf. *Hamlet*, III. 4. **1982** K. J. LEYSER *Medieval Germany* ii. 30 Ekivrid's shield.. lacked the ' umbo', the metal-boss of Waltharius's. (Cf. lines 772 and 776.) **1916** *Admiralty Weekly Orders* 30 June 5 (*heading*) *C.G.M. **1983** *Navy News* June 7/1 Do soldiers holding the MM, DCM, CGM, QGM etc feel they have been discriminated against? **1873** *C.G.S. [see *absolute unit*]. **1875** J. D. EVERETT (*title*) Illustrations of the Centimetre-Gramme-Second (C.G.S.) System of Units. **1962** CORSON & LORRAIN *Introd. Electromagn. Fields* ii. 29 In the c.g.s. system of units, K is made unity by choosing appropriate units for these quantities. **1904** *Min. Proc. Army Council* 12 Aug. (Publ. Rec. Office, Kew WO 163/9, 1905) 46 The *C.G.S. was requested to report upon the necessity for the retention of the Fortress Company, R.E., in Egypt. **1982** S. RAVEN *Shadows on Grass* xi. 223 Lieutenant-Colonel John Mogg (later C.G.S.). **1918** *Whitaker's Almanack* 143 (*heading*) Order of the Companions of Honour (1917)—*C.H. **1984** *Ann. Reg. 1983* 499/1 Boult, Sir Adrian, CH (b. 1889), British conductor. **1951** *Sat. Even. Post* 17 Mar. 71 The *CIA, or Central Intelligence Agency, which deals with the war capabilities of an enemy. **1910** E. H. RICHARDSON *War, Police & Watch Dogs* iii. 56 Detective F. H. Carr of the *C.I.D. **1914** W. S. CHURCHILL *World Crisis* (1923) xii. 267 The situation..is entirely different from those which have been discussed in the Invasion Committee of the C.I.D. **1960** *Times* 3 Oct. 13/6 Every C.I.D. man must start as a uniform constable. **1886** KIPLING *Departm. Ditties* (ed. 2) 8 Then the Birthday Honours came... Stood against the Rajah's name nothing more than **C.I.E.* **1937** *Discovery* Jan. 6/1 Dr. J. H. Hutton, C.I.E. **1902** *Times* 7 July 3/3, 90 per cent. f.o.b. invoice on the basis of 52s. 6d. *c.i.f. sawn pitch pine 35 cubic feet average Blaenavon. **1907** *Westm. Gaz.* 7 May 2/2 The United Kingdom figures are c.i.f. at the ports of arrival. **1958** *Times Rev. Industry* June 63/1 Redwood deals and battens have dropped from £88 to £84 c.i.f. **1909** *War Office Memo. 601* (Publ. Rec. Office WO32/6469) 26 Nov. 7 By an Order in Council of the 22nd November, 1909, the title of the Chief of the General Staff has been changed to that of Chief of the Imperial General Staff. In future minutes will be addressed, and papers transited, to *C.I.G.S. **1917** LD. DERBY *Let.* 15 Aug. in M. Gilbert *Winston S. Churchill* (1977) IV. Compan. I. 132 Dear CIGS. **1942** G. CUNNINGHAM *Diary* 23 Aug. in N. Mitchell *Sir G. Cunningham* (1968) v. 99 Claude thinks it is largely the P.M.'s own brain wave, and that Brooke (C.I.G.S.) has weakly acquiesced. **1981** *Dict. Nat. Biogr. 1961–1970* 148/1 Junior officers were always struck by the considerable awe in which their seniors held the CIGS—the man [*sc.* Brooke], not just the office. **1889** BARRÈRE & LELAND *Dict. Slang* I. 3/2 **C. in C.*, Commander-in-Chief. **1951** L. MACNEICE tr. *Goethe's Faust* II. IV. 256 No, you shall win it, believe you me. It's you to-day are C.-in-C. **1937** *Times* 13 Apr. iv/1 The successful working at Wellington, New Zealand, of a *C.K.D.—'Completely Knocked Down'—plant for the manufacture of the same make of car. **1961** *Times* 19 Apr. 13/3 The new 'literary honour'..is to be distributed by the Royal Society of Literature to not more than ten holders at any one time and the first batch of five living British writers ..become 'Companions of Literature' and free to put '*C.Litt.' after their names from May 10. **1903** *Encycl. Brit.* XXXV. 1060/1 Aston, William George, *C.M.G., M.A., D.Litt. **1985** *Library Assoc. Rec.* Feb. 63/2 The term Companion... Its use is..confined to awards of honours in the various degrees of chivalry, eg CB, CMG, etc. **1964** *Internat. Assoc. of Universities Bull.* XII. 296/2 The *CNAA will have the power to approve appropriate colleges in which these subjects can be studied to degree level. **1985** *Daily Tel.* 22 Apr. 11/3 The CNAA is also responsible for maintaining poly standards. **1958** C. JUDD in C. Driver *Disarmers* (1964) ii. 47 There are major points in the policy of the *CND which UNA cannot support. **1961** *Times* 8 May 17/3 The C.N.D. has ceased to be a movement of moral protest..and has become a political organization. **1932** J. S. HUXLEY *Probl. Relative Growth* vi. 186 In organs where, to use Hammett's phrase, the work-growth ratio is high, as in glands, heart, etc.,..the growth-function will be more seriously impaired than in organs such as *C.N.S. or skeleton, where the work-growth ratio is low. **1974** D. & M. WEBSTER *Compar. Vertebr. Morphol.* ix. 191 Knowledge of which central nervous structures are involved in particular reflexes is a valuable diagnostic tool in delineating damage to the CNS. **1889** *Cent. Dict.* I. 1065/3 **c.o.*, an abbreviation of *care of*, common in addressing letters, etc. Often written *c/o*. **1910** *Dalton's Weekly Advertiser* 24 Dec. 6/2 F., c/o 'Housekeeper', 5 Fenchurch Street, London. **1985** *Church Times* 1 Feb. 15/4 Application forms..can be obtained from: The Headmaster, c/o School House, 201, Park Road. **1889** BARRÈRE & LELAND *Dict. Slang* I. 3/2 **C.-O.*, Commanding-Officer. **1890** KIPLING *Many Inv.* (1893) 29 'Who was your C.O.?' said Boileau. **1915** F. H. LAWRENCE in *Home Lett. T.E. Lawrence* (1954) 701 One officer was C.O., and the other four company commanders. **1916** *Tribunal* 23 Mar. 4/1 (*heading*) Treatment of *C.O.'s. **1919** J. BUCHAN *Mr. Standfast* i. 30 'Launcelot's a C.O., you know,' said Miss Doria... I remembered that the letters stood..for 'Conscientious Objector'. **1968** *War Resistance* II. XXIV. 27 Nazarene leaders have made petitions to Marshal Tito for the release of the COs. **1932** *Flight* 15 Apr. 318/1 This is in excess of the normal *C. of A. gross weight of 5,400 lb. **1913** W. T. ROGERS *Dict. Abbrev.* 41/2 **C. of E.*, Church of England. **1954** J. BETJEMAN *Poems in Porch*, Still it gives the chance to me To praise our dear old C. of E. **1962** in *Amer. Speech* (1963) XXXVIII. 229 An official of the Congress of Racial Equality (*CORE). **1968** *Chicago Tribune* 9 July I. 21/1 (*heading*) Chapters in 3 cities drop out of C.O.R.E. **1910** CHESTERTON *What's Wrong with World* IV. xiii. 248, I do not expect the schoolmaster to hate hospitals and *C.O.S. centres so much as the schoolboy's father. **1936** J. CURTIS *Gilt Kid* iii. 29, 'I want to talk to you about joining.' 'About joining the *C.P.?' **1969** *Listener* 9 Jan. 54/2 One of the few commendable features of the CP is that, at that time, its outlook on many issues was seldom more than a year behind enlightened opinion. *a* **1848** MARRYAT *R. Reefer* xxxii, The fellow was put on board with '*C.P.' before his name. **1889** R. L. OTTLEY in C. Gore *Lux Mundi* xii. 482 (*note*) See Bengel *in loc.* and *cp. S. Luke xvii. 10. **1950** *Classica & Mediævalia* XI. 228 Extensive use of Latin abbreviations is a regular feature of English printing, other examples..being..*cf.* (confer), *cp.* (compara), *id.* (idem), *ib.* (ibidem), *et seqq.* (et sequentia). **1901** *Army & Navy Gaz.* 19 Jan. 68/1 Near Heilbron, Jan. 3... Killed:..*Cpl. 22212 Stephan. **1977** *R.A.F. News* 22 June–5 July 10 (*caption*) Right centre: Cpl Dave Lowe, Cpl Pat Jones, Jnr Tech Ben Timms (on wing). **1907** *Army & Navy Gaz.* 8 June 535/1 Foil v. Foil—*C.P.O. Smeaton, R.N. **1985** *Navy News* Feb. 4/5 Vacancies now exist for Submarine senior ratings to

qualify as Escape Instructors (CPOs) and Assistant instructors (POs) in the Submarine Escape Training Tank ..in HMS Dolphin. **1892** KIPLING *Lett. Travel* (1920) 80 The traveller is on the *C.P.R. train at Vancouver. **1968** *Globe & Mail* (Toronto) 3 Feb. 1/8 A CPR right-of-way in Eastview. **1940** *Chambers's Techn. Dict.* 206/1 **C.P.S., cps.*, ..abbrevs. for cycles per second, the usual measure of frequency. **1957** [see UNSMOOTHED *ppl. a.*]. **1964** *Honeywell Gloss. Data Processing* 16/2 *CPS*, abbreviation for both 'characters per second' and 'cycles per second'. **1976** *New Scientist* 4 Nov. 281 (Advt.), Our new 30 and 60 cps terminal printers. **1982** *Which Computer?* June 95/2 Capable of coping with 80-column paper, the MT 100 prints at 160 cps. **1962** *IBM Systems Jrnl.* Sept. 65 It was calculated..that.. increasing the *CPU speed by a factor of fifty would increase the throughput by a factor of only two. **1970** *Daily Tel.* 24 Apr. 25 (Advt.), Have you..the experience of large files accessed by several programs and/or CPU's? **1983** *Mini-Micro Systems* Feb. 84/1 Plexus manufactures a sister computer system..that uses a Zilog z8000 as the CPU. **1909** *Daily Chron.* 17 Feb. 3/5 Among the ships responding to the '*C.Q.D.' message were the Lucania, [etc.]. **1928** *Manchester Guardian Weekly* 7 Dec. 450/3 That..when his ship took a list..[he] should have sent out a peremptory C.Q. call. **1941** *Rev. Sci. Instruments* XII. 298/2 The connection of the lower deflecting plate of the **CRT* is incorrect. **1946** *Electronic Engin.* May 149/1 The c.r.t. is an essential part of radar equipment. **1969** *Computers & Humanities* IV. 79 A CRT screen with only ten lines of 40 characters each cannot completely replace a printed page. **1960** *Armed Forces Chem. Jrnl.* Nov.–Dec. 27/1 *CS is an Army chemical symbol for an agent that causes burning and watering of the eyes. **1961** *Techn. Man.* (U.S. Dept. of Army) 3-215, change 2, 25 Sept. 4 CS..a white crystalline solid..has a pungent, pepperlike odor. **1969** *Listener* 4 Sept. 297/1 The effects of the CS chemical contained in this gas are now the subject of an inquiry. **1970** *Daily Tel.* 7 Apr. 2/7 CS gas has been used by British troops during peace-keeping operations in Ulster, and by American forces in Vietnam. **1940** *Chambers's Techn. Dict.* 206/1 **C/s.*, cycles per second. **1943** C. L. BOLTZ *Basic Radio* ix. 147 The range of frequencies making audible sound is approximately from 20c/s to 20000c/s. **1968** *Radio Communication Handbk.* (ed. 4) v. 32/1 The oscillator..may be..frequency modulated by 50 c/s if the bottom end of the grid leak is connected to the live 6·3 volt heater supply. **1963** *Daily Tel.* 1 Oct. 1/7 In three or four years' time the *CSE examination may be taken by as many as 300,000 candidates. **1966** *New Statesman* 10 June 859/3 Mathematics on sound traditional lines is taken to CSE, 'O' and 'A' levels. **1949** *1st Ann. Rep. Commonwealth Sci. & Industr. Research Organization 1948–49* 8 *C.S.I.R.O. is working in conjunction with the State Department of Agriculture and Stock on the agricultural aspects of crops and pasture production in the irrigable areas. **1984** *Nature* 19 Jan. (Advt.), CSIRO Research Scientist... CSIRO conducts scientific and technological research in Laboratories throughout Australia and employs about 7,500 staff. **1865** H. EMANUEL *Diamonds & Precious Stones* 92–93 (in figure) 1*c^t. **1985** *Exchange & Mart* 25 Apr. 34/1 (Advt.), Wholesale 9 ct gold jewellery. *a* **1875** in M. Johnson *Amer. Advertising* (1960), Its marvelously low price *Only 25*cts. a year!* **1878** W. WHITMAN *Daybks. & Notebks.* (1978) I. 80 N Y Sun—Dec. 23—at 5 cts a copy. **1974** *Radiology* CX. 109/1 So dramatic is this advance in neuroradiological capability and so important is the developing impact of computerized axial tomography (*CT scanning)..that we believe an early report of our experience to be mandatory. *Ibid.* 118/2 CT scans were clearly positive. **1975** *Jrnl. Amer. Med. Assoc.* 20 Oct. 316/1 The brain, an immobile structure of relatively homogeneous density is ideal for CT. **1983** *Oxf. Textbk. Med.* I. XII. 10/1 Infiltration of liver by fat or iron causes a dramatic change in liver density which can be well shown on CT. **1984** S. D. SHORON *Epilepsy* 18/2 It could be argued that all patients with epilepsy should have a CT scan, but in over 80% it will be normal. **1971** I. D. MACHORTON *How to get Better Job in Managem.* iv. 36 When a prospect has read your *CV he should know all there is to know about you. **1985** *Economist* 2 Feb. ('Survey Wales' Suppl.) 18/2 They resent Welsh being regarded as a plus on anybody's cv. **1896** *London Gaz.* 6 Aug. 4498 The Count Moltke, G.C.V.O., Captain Bull, *C.V.O.,..the Gentlemen in Attendance on His Royal Highness the Crown Prince of Denmark. **1972** *Times* 6 May 16/7 His services to the history of the Royal Family were fittingly commemorated on his retirement by the award of the CVO.

ca, obs. form of KAE, a jackdaw.

ca, ca', Sc. form of CALF.

ca', mod.Sc. form of CALL *sb.* and *v.* call, drive.

‖**Caaba** ('kɑːəbə). Also **Kaaba, Kaabeh.** [Arab. *kaʿbah* square (or cubical) house.]

The sacred edifice at Mecca, which contains the venerated 'black stone', and is the 'Holy of Holies' of Islam. (See quot. 1883, and a photographic view in the work cited.)

1734 SALE *Koran* 16 This is the Caaba, which is usually called, by way of eminence, *the House*. **1781** GIBBON *Decl. & F.* l. **1798** in *Wellesley's Desp.* 82 The illustrious Kaaba is the object of veneration to the followers of truth. **1855** MILMAN *Lat. Chr.* (1864) II. IV. i. 180 The temple of the Caaba was at once the centre of the commerce and of the religion of Arabia. **1856** EMERSON *Eng. Traits* viii. Wks. (Bohn) II. 59 Every cell of the Inquisition, every Turkish caaba, every Holy of holies. **1883** *Sunday at Home* 11 The Káabeh..is a plain unornamented oblong of massive masonry, 38 feet by 30 square, and 40 feet high, covered with a heavy black cloth, of a fabric of mixed silk and cotton, which has a richly embroidered band worked in bullion, about two and a half feet deep, encircling it about ten feet from the top, with the Kalumna, the Moslem profession of faith, wrought in gold letters.

caa'ing whale, var. CA'ING-WHALE.

caal, caas, obs. forms of CALL, CASE.

caam (kɑːm). Also **calm.** [By Jamieson identified with CALM *sb.*^{2} a mould, or frame; but this is doubtful.] The HEDDLES of a loom. Hence **caaming** *vbl. sb.*

1792 ADAM *Rom. Antiq.* 523 The principal part of the machinery of a loom, vulgarly called the *Caam* or *Hiddles*, composed of *eyed* or *hooked* threads through which the warp passes, and which, being alternately raised and depressed by the motion of the feet on the *Treadles*, raises or depresses the warp, and makes the *shed* for transmitting the shuttle with the weft, seems also to have been called *Licia*. **1808** JAMIESON s.v. *Calm*. **1874** KNIGHT *Dict. Mech.*, *Caam*, the weaver's *reed*. The *sley* or *slaie*. *Caaming*, the setting of the reed by the disposing of the warp-threads.

caama, var. KAAMA.

caatinga ('kɑːtɪŋgə). Also **catinga.** [Tupi, f. *caa* natural vegetation, forest + *tinga* white.] In Brazil, a forest consisting of thorny shrubs and stunted trees.

1846 G. GARDNER *Trav. Brazil* 166 Woods..consisting of low trees and shrubs..called by the inhabitants *Catingas*. **1869** BURTON *Explor. Highl. Brazil* I. 61 Low woods known in Brazil as Caatingas and Carrascos. **1927** KENDREW *Climates of Continents* (ed. 2) 328 A region of caatinga or dry thornwood. **1944** S. PUTNAM tr. *da Cunha's Rebellion in Backlands* II. i. 30 The caatinga..repulses him with its thorns and prickly leaves, its twigs sharp as lances.

‖**cab** (kæb), *sb.*^{1} Also **kab.** [Heb. *qab*, prop. hollow or concave vessel, f. *qbb* to curve, hollow out.] A Hebrew dry measure, according to the Rabbins the sixth part of a seah; about $2\frac{5}{6}$ imperial pints.

1535 COVERDALE *2 Kings* vi. 25 The fourth parte of a Cab of doues donge worth fyue syluer pens. **1611** *ibid.* kab. **1631** R. H. *Arraignm. Whole Creat.* iv. 29 Worse meate than huskes..yea old Shooes and leather..yea, Cabs, and Doves dung. **1710** PALMER *Proverbs* 364 In two cabs of dates there is one cab of stones.

†**Cab**, *sb.*^{2} *Obs.* An abridged and corrupted form of *cavalier* (or Sp. *caballero*), in the 17th c.

1650 A. B. *Mutat. Polemo* 16 The poor Cabbs had been all surprised, if not surrendred to our Parliament Army. *Ibid.* 18 A convention of the Scots States in Parliament which puts the Cabs..into a shrewd fright.

cab (kæb), *sb.*^{3}

1. a. A shortened form of CABRIOLET, applied not only to the original vehicle so named and its improved successor the 'hansom', but also to four-wheeled carriages shaped like broughams; thus, a public carriage with two or four wheels, drawn by one horse, and seating two or four persons, of which various types are used in different towns. Applied also to motor-driven vehicles (see TAXI-CAB). **b.** for CABMAN.

1827 HONE *Every-day Bk.* II. 461 Some [were] in gigs, some in cabs, some in drags. **1831** MACAULAY *Letter* 28 May, I dressed, called a cab, and was whisked away to Hill Street. **1832** B. HALL *Fragm. Voy. & Trav.* Ser. II. V. 115 Off I hurried in a cab, or more probably in a chariot, for this was some years before the glorious era of cabs. **1858** LYTTON *What will he do, &c.* VI. i, My cab is waiting yonder. **1868** *Daily News* 30 Dec. 5 Cabs—or cabriolets, as they were first called—were not known to us until 1820. **1850** THACKERAY *Pendennis* xlvi, 'Drive to Shepherd's Inn, Cab'. **1899** *Westm. Gaz.* 15 Nov. 4/3 The cab-without-a-horse. **1954** [see BUMBLING *ppl. a.*].

2. A small erection, somewhat like the head of a cabriolet, serving as a shelter to the drivers of locomotive engines, lorries, or cranes.

1864 in WEBSTER s.v. *Locomotive*. **1877** M. REYNOLDS *Locom. Engine Driving* (1882) 47 The cab, or covering for the engine-driver and stoker, is erected over the foot plate. **1883** *Harper's Mag.* Jan. 198/2 There is no cab, or place to put one. **1973** [see *truck-driver* s.v. TRUCK *sb.*^{2} 5].

3. *attrib.* and in *Comb.*, as ***cab-body, -door, -driver, -driving, -hire, -hirer, -master, -minder, -owner, -proprietor, -trade, -user, -washer, wheel***; **cab-box**, the driver's seat on a cab; **cab-boy**, a boy in livery who attends his master when driving to hold the horse, etc., a 'tiger'; **cab-car**, a larger vehicle than a cab (see quot.); **cab-horse**, a horse that draws a cab; **cab-rank**, a row of cabs on a stand; also *transf.* (see quots.), esp. a line of aircraft waiting in readiness; also *attrib.*; **cab-runner, cab-tout**, one who makes a living by calling cabs; **cab-shelter**, a shelter for cabmen; **cab-stand**, a place where cabs are authorized to stand while waiting for hire; **cab-yard**, a yard where cabs are kept when off duty. Also CABMAN, etc.

1908 *Westm. Gaz.* 30 Mar. 5/2 All Humber *cab-bodies are interchangeable. **1868** *Once a Week* 11 Apr. 322 Planted upon a London *cab-box. **1827** LYTTON *Pelham* xlv, I sent my *cab-boy (vulgò Tiger) to inquire of the groom whether the horse was to be sold, and to whom it belonged. **1882** *Daily News* 14 Jan. 31/4 The cab..is termed a '*cab-car'.. the weight..is balanced upon the two hind wheels. The cab, which will contain five or six persons, is entered from the front. **1888** A. C. GUNTER *Mr. Potter of Texas* xxii. 261 He ..opens the *cab door. **1842** T. MARTIN in *Fraser's Mag.* Dec., A dozen or two of *cab-drivers. **1860** LD. LYTTON *Lucile* II. IV. iv. 7 The complaint of a much disappointed cab-driver. **1860** *All Y. Round* No. 44. 416 The business and trials of *cab-driving. **1885** *Law Times* LXXIX. 328/2 The cabdriving class. **1840** THACKERAY *Paris Sk. Bk.* (1885) 134 A prancing *cab-horse. **1858** LYTTON *What will he do, &c.* (1860) III. VII. vii. 58 The finest cab-horse in London. **1864** *Soc. Science Rev.* I. 407 The relations of *cab-masters and cab-men..*cab-owners and *cab-hirers. **1898** *Daily News* 16 Nov. 5/4 C. B...described as a *cab minder. **1884** *St. James's Gaz.* 25 Jan. 5/2 Madness may be more common on the *cab-rank than is suspected. **1919** DOWNING *Digger Dial.* 15 *Cab-rank*, transport lines. **1939** H. HODGE *Cab, Sir?* 268 Cab-ranks are appointed by the Commissioner of Police. **1945** *Times* 1 Mar. 5/7 A 'cab-rank' has been maintained over the bridgehead. *Ibid.* 6 Mar. 5/6 'Cab-rank' fighter bombers have been overhead continuously. **1946** L. E. O. CHARLTON *Britain at War* IV. 275 R.A.F. Typhoons ..came in time to develop..the 'cab rank' technique. Based on their own special air strips,..they there awaited a wireless summons. **1883** *St. James's Gaz.* 1 June, The *cab-runner..is a very undesirable addition to modern civilization. **1936** E. M. FORSTER *Abinger Harvest* I. 17, I heard profanity in the *cab-shelter. **1848** THACKERAY *Van. Fair* liv. 484 The people joked at the *cabstand about his appearance, as he took a carriage there. **1860** TRISTRAM *Gt. Sahara* i. 4 Place Mahon, now merely the cab-stand of Algiers. **1863** LD. LYTTON *Ring Amasis* I. I. II. viii. 190 Order a carriage from the nearest cabstand. **1883** *Daily News* 6 June 5/2 When the cab reaches its goal the *cab-tout makes himself busy in unlading the luggage. **1894** *Westm. Gaz.* 22 May 5/3 The ins and outs of the matter are but imperfectly understood by the mass of *cab-users. **1897** *Daily News* 19 Oct. 2/3 The death of C. W...a *cabwasher. **1862** GEO. ELIOT *Let.* 12 Mar. (1956) IV. 21 The sound of *cab wheels.

cab (kæb), *sb.*^{4} *slang.* [short for CABBAGE *sb.*^{2}] A translation clandestinely used by a student in getting up his lessons; a crib.

1876 *Academy* 4 Nov. 448/2 The use of translations, 'cribs' or 'cabs', as boys call them, must at some time or other engage the serious attention of school-masters.

cab, *sb.*^{5} *dial.* [short for CABAL.] 'A small number of persons secretly united in the performance of some undertaking'. Parish *Sussex Dial.*

cab (kæb), *v.*^{1} *colloq.* [f. CAB *sb.*^{3}] **1.** *intr.* (Also *to cab it*). To travel or go in a cab.

1835 DICKENS *Let.* ? 29 Oct. (1965) I. 84 Worth your while to walk or Cab so far East. **1845** W. C. MACREADY *Diary* 1 Aug. (1912) II. 300 Walked and cabbed down to Forster. **1858** BAILEY *Age* 30 Cabbing from Hyde Park Corner to the Tower. **1860** *Chamb. Jrnl.* XIV. 116 We may 'cab' it.. we may 'bus it; or we may go by boat. **1866** C. H. ROBINSON *Diary* III. 520, I cabbed it home. **1882** *Blackw. Mag.* Feb. 238/1 He..cabs off to take advice.

2. To drive a cab. Cf. CABBING *vbl. sb.*

1887 A. CONAN DOYLE *Study in Scarlet* (1888) II. vi. 160, I went on cabbing it for a day or so. **1939** H. HODGE *Cab, Sir?* 19 When a man first starts cabbing, he usually rubs his neck sore with this constant turning of his head.

cab, *v.*^{2} *slang.* [? short for CABBAGE: cf. CAB *sb.*^{4}] To pilfer, snatch dishonestly or meanly; to 'crib'.

Mod. Schoolboy slang. You've cabbed that apple on your way up.

caba. *U.S.* Also 9 **cabas.** [ad. F. *cabas* basket, panier.] A small satchel or hand-bag. (See also quot. 1865).

1833 LADY MORGAN *Dram. Scenes* II. 74 Bring me down my *cabas*. I must have something to toss these things in. *c* **1845** C. BRONTË *Professor* (1857) I. x. 171 Day-pupils, tearing down their cloaks, bonnets, and cabas from the wooden pegs. *Ibid.* xiii. 229 She proceeded..to open her cabas, to take out her books. **1865** WEBSTER, *Cabas*, a flat basket..for figs, &c.; hence, a lady's flat work-basket or reticule;—often written *caba*. **1877** H. RUEDE *Sod-House Days* (1937) 27 The pump..furnished the liquor and the caba furnished the solids for the meal. **1885** *Boston (Mass.) Jrnl.* 7 Sept. 2/4 The origin of the word 'caba' applying to the small hand-bag or satchel..The French cabas, a frail basket, hand basket, etc., was used upon ladies' work-boxes imported thirty years ago.

‖**cabaan, caban** (kə'bɑːn). [a. Arab. and Pers. *qabāʾ* a man's outer tunic.]

A white cloth worn by Arabs over their shoulders.

1693 RAY *Trav.* (1705) II. 13 Sitting..with a delicate white turbant, and a long red lined caban. **1863** KINGLAKE *Crimea* (1877) II. xii. 158 The gleam of his epaulettes, half hidden and half revealed by the graceful white cabaan.

cabache, -a(d)ge, obs. ff. CABBAGE, CABOCHE.

‖**caback** (kə'bæk). [Russ. *ka'bak*, dram-shop.] A Russian dram-shop or pot-house.

1591 G. FLETCHER *Russe Commw.* (1836) 58 In every great towne of his realme he hath a caback or drinking house, where is sold..mead, beere, etc. **1678** in PHILLIPS.

†**cabage**, *v.* *Obs.*$^{-0}$ [? var. of CABOCHE.]

1570 LEVINS *Manip.* 11 To cabage, *mactare*.

†'**cabaging.** *Obs.* (See CABBAGE *sb.*^{1} 4, and CABOCHE *v.*)

1575 TURBERV. *Bk. Venerie* xliii. 130 The huntsman.. shall take the cabaging of the heade, and the heart of the Deare to reward his bloud hound first.

cabal (kə'bæl), *sb.*^{1} Also 7–8 **caball, cabbal.** [a. F. *cabale* (16th c. in Littré), used in all the English senses, ad. med.L. *cab(b)ala* (It., Sp., Pg. *cabala*), CABBALA, q.v. In 17th c. at first pronounced '*cabal* (whence the abridged CAB

sb.[5]); the current pronunciation was evidently reintroduced from Fr., perh. with sense 5 or 6.]

†**1.** = CABBALA 1: The Jewish tradition as to the interpretation of the Old Testament. *Obs.*

1616 BULLOKAR, *Cabal*, the tradition of the Jewes doctrine of religion. **1660** HOWELL *Lex. Tetragl.*, Words do involve the deepest Mysteries, By them the Jew into his Caball pries. **1663** BUTLER *Hud.* I. i. 530 For Mystick Learning, wondrous able In Magick, Talisman, and Cabal.

†**2.** = CABBALA 2: **a.** Any tradition or special private interpretation. **b.** A secret. *Obs.*

a **1637** B. JONSON (O.) The measuring of the temple, a cabal found out but lately. **1635** PERSON *Varieties* I. Introd. 3 An insight in the Cabals and secrets of Nature. **1660–3** J. SPENCER *Prodigies* (1665) 344 If the truth..had been still reserved as a Cabbal amongst men. **1663** J. HEATH *Flagellum or O. Cromwell* 192 How the whole mystery and cabal of this business was managed by the..Committee. *a* **1763** SHENSTONE *Ess.* 220 To suppose that He will regulate His government according to the cabals of human wisdom.

3. A secret or private intrigue of a sinister character formed by a small body of persons; 'something less than conspiracy' (J.).

1646–7 CLARENDON *Hist. Reb.* (1702) I. v. 439 The King ..asked him, whether he were engaged in any Cabal concerning the army? **1663** J. HEATH *Flagellum or O. Cromwell*, He was no sooner rid of the danger of this but he was puzzled with Lambert's cabal. **1707** FREIND *Peterboro's Cond. Sp.* 171 The contrivances and cabals of others have too often prevail'd. **1824** W. IRVING *T. Trav.* II. 30 There were cabals breaking out in the company. **1876** BANCROFT *Hist. U.S.* VI. xlvi. 299 The cabal against Washington found supporters exclusively in the north.

b. as a species of action; = CABALLING.

1734 tr. *Rollin's Anc. Hist.* (1827) III. 22 To advance themselves..by cabal, treachery and violence. **1791** BURKE *Th. on Fr. Affairs* VII. 74 Centres of cabal. **1876** BANCROFT *Hist. U.S.* III. 261 Restless activity and the arts of cabal.

4. A secret or private meeting, esp. of intriguers or of a faction. *arch.* or *Obs.*

1649 BP. GUTHRIE *Mem.* (1702) 23 The Supplicants..met again at their several Caballs. **1656–7** CROMWELL in Burton *Diary* (1828) I. 382 He had never been at any cabal about the same. **1715** BENTLEY *Serm.* x. 356 A mercenary conclave and nocturnal Cabal of Cardinals. **1738** WARBURTON *Div. Legat.* I. 169 Celebrate the Mysteries in a private Cabal. **1822** W. IRVING *Braceb. Hall* iii. 23 To tell the anecdote..at those little cabals, that will occasionally take place among the most orderly servants.

b. phrase. *in cabal. arch.* or *Obs.*

a **1678** MARVELL *Poems* Wks. I. Pref. 8 Is he in caball in his cabinett sett. **1725** DE FOE *Voy. round World* (1840) 28 The gunner and second mate were in a close cabal together. **1807** CRABBE *Par. Reg.* I. (1810) 55 Here, in cabal, a disputatious crew Each evening meet.

5. A small body of persons engaged in secret or private machination or intrigue; a junto, clique, côterie, party, faction.

1660 *Trial Regic.* 175 You were..of the cabal. **1670** MARVELL *Corr.* cxlvii. Wks. 1872–5 II. 326 The governing *cabal* are Buckingham, Lauderdale, Ashly, Orery, and Trevor. Not but the other cabal [Arlington, Clifford, and their party] too have seemingly sometimes their turn. **1732** BERKELEY *Alciphr.* v. §21 A gentleman who has been idle at college, and kept idle company, will judge a whole university by his own cabal. **1767** G. CANNING *Poet. Wks.* (1827) 56 Should Fat Jack and his Cabal Cry 'Rob us the Exchequer, Hal!' **1859** GULLICK & TIMBS *Paint.* 183 In Naples, where a cabal of artists was formed.

6. Applied in the reign of Charles II to the small committee or junto of the Privy Council, otherwise called the 'Committee for Foreign Affairs', which had the chief management of the course of government, and was the precursor of the modern *cabinet.*

1665 PEPYS *Diary* 14 Oct., It being read before the King, Duke, and the Caball, with complete applause. **1667** *Ibid.* 31 Mar., Walked to my Lord Treasurer's, where the King, Duke of York, and the Cabal, and much company withal. **1667** *Ibid.* (1877) V. 128 The Cabal at present, being as he says the King, and the Duke of Buckingham, and Lord Keeper, the Duke of Albemarle and privy seale.

b. in *Hist.* applied *spec.* to the five ministers of Charles II, who signed the Treaty of Alliance with France for war against Holland in 1672: these were Clifford, Arlington, Buckingham, Ashley (Earl of Shaftesbury), and Lauderdale, the initials of whose names thus arranged chanced to spell the word *cabal*.

This was merely a witticism referring to sense 6; in point of fact these five men did not constitute the whole 'Cabal', or Committee for Foreign Affairs; nor were they so closely united in policy as to constitute a 'cabal' in sense 5, where quot. 1670 shows that three of them belonged to one 'cabal' or clique, and two to another. The name seems to have been first given to the five ministers in the pamphlet of 1673 'England's Appeal from the private Cabal at White-hall to the Great Council of the nation..by a true lover of his country.' Modern historians often write loosely of the Buckingham-Arlington administration from the fall of Clarendon in 1667 to 1673 as the *Cabal Cabinet* or *Cabal Ministry*.

1673 *England's Appeal* 18 The safest way not to wrong neither the cabal nor the truth is to take a short survey of the carriage of the chief promoters of this war. **1689** *Mem. God's 29 Years Wonders* §25. 72 The great Ahitophel, the chiefest head-piece..of all the Cabal. **1715** BURNET *Own Time* (1766) I. 430 This junta..being called the cabal, it was observed that *cabal* proved a technical word, every letter in it being the first letter of those five, Clifford, Ashley, Buckingham, Arlington and Lauderdale. *a* **1734** NORTH *Exam.* III. vi. ¶41. 453 The..Promoters of Popery, supposed to rise by the Misfortunes of the Earl of Clarendon, were the famous CABAL. **1762** HUME *Hist. Eng.* (1806) V. lxix. 163 When the Cabal entered into the mysterious alliance with France. **1848** MACAULAY *Hist. Eng.* (1864) I. 101 It happened by a whimsical coincidence that, in 1671, the Cabinet consisted of five persons the initial letters of whose names made up the word Cabal..These ministers were therefore emphatically called the Cabal; and they soon made that appellation so infamous that it has never since their time been used except as a term of reproach.

7. *attrib.* or in obvious *comb.*

1673 R. LEIGH *Transp. Reh.* 36 By this time, the Politick Cabal-men were most of 'um set. **1674** R. LAW *Mem.* (1818) 61 The parliament was jealous of their caball lords. **1678** *Trans Crt. Spain* 189 They maintain themselves only by a Cabal-genius, without any foundation of justice or fidelity. **1700** CONGREVE *Way of W.* I. i, Last night was one of their cabal nights. **1871** W. CHRISTIE *Life Shaftesbury* II. xii. 81 The heavy indictment of History against the so-called Cabal Ministry.

†**cabal**, *sb.*[2] *Obs.* (See quot.)

1613 PURCHAS *Pilgr.* I. v. xiv. (1617) 517 The Cabal is a wilde Beast in this Island [Java] whose bones doe restraine the blood from issuing in wounded parties.

cabal (kə'bæl), *v.* [a. F. *cabale-r*, f. *cabale* sb.; or ? f. the Eng. sb.]

1. *intr.* To combine (*together*) for some secret or private end. (Usually in a bad sense.)

a **1680** [see CABALLING *vbl. sb.*]. **1725** DE FOE *Voy. round World* (1840) 46 Time to club and cabal together. **1814** D'ISRAELI *Quarrels Auth.* (1867) 409 A club of wits caballed and produced a collection of short poems. **1885** *Manch. Exam.* 16 June 5/1 Caballing together for their private ends.

2. *intr.* To intrigue privately (*against*).

1680 SIR W. SOAME *Art Poetry* (Dryden) iv, Base rivals.. Caballing still against it. **1725** DE FOE *Voy. round World* (1840) 28 They would be..caballing and making an interest among the men. **1757** BURKE *Abridgm. Eng. Hist.* Wks. 1842 II. 535 Elfrida caballed in favour of her son. **1789** T. JEFFERSON *Writ.* (1859) III. 116 Time has been given..to cabal, to sow dissensions, etc. **1818** HALLAM *Mid. Ages* (1872) I. 494 The barons..began to cabal against his succession.

3. *refl.* To bring *oneself* by caballing.

1790 BURKE *Fr. Rev.* Wks. V. 340 In this time he may cabal himself into a superiority over the wisest.

cabala, a common variant of CABBALA; also = CABAL (*rare*).

1671 H. STUBBE *Reply unto Letter, &c.* 13 Though an entire cabala of the R.S. did consult upon this responsory letter.

cabalatar, var. of CABULATOR, *Obs.*

‖**cabaletta** (kæbə'lɛtə). *Mus.* Pl. -ette, -ettas. [It., prob. ad. *coboletta*, dim. of *cobola* stanza, couplet, L. *copula*: see COUPLE *sb.*]

a. A short aria in simple style with a repetitive rhythm. **b.** The final section of an aria, marked by a quick, uniform rhythm. Also *transf.*

1842 J. F. WARNER *Dict. Mus. Terms* 16/2 *Cabaletta*, (frequently also *Cabbaletta*, better, perhaps *Cavaletta*). This term is applied in the fashionable musical language of the Italians to a very particularly musical, agreeable and soothing passage occurring..in an air (aria). It not unfrequently happens that an Italian audience..listen to a whole air simply for the purpose of being entertained by the *cavaletta*. **1896** G. B. SHAW *Our Theatres in Nineties* (1932) II. 133 Old-fashioned arias with florid cabalettas at the ends of them. **1947** A. EINSTEIN *Music in Romantic Era* xvi. 276 The lyric *cabalette* or shortened arias introduced by Rossini. **1947** AUDEN *Age of Anxiety* (1948) iii. 82 And a chronic chorus of cascades and birds Cuts loose in a wild cabaletta. **1960** *Times* 29 Aug. 12/6 In the closing *cabaletta*..*fioritura* was most perfectly dissolved into the vocal line itself.

cabalic(al, -ism, -ist, -ize, etc.: see CABBAL-.

†**cabalie.** *Obs.* = CABBALISM.

1652 GAULE *Magastrom.* 238 The cabalie is an art..very ancient.

†**cabalist.** *Obs.* [The same word as CABBALIST, (which was formerly spelt with one *b*); but affiliated by sense to CABAL, and perhaps pronounced in 1660 *ca'ballist*.]

One who cabals, or adheres to any cabal; a secret intriguer or plotter.

[**1569** J. SANFORD *Agrippa's Van. Artes* 2 b, A disloial Cabalist.] **1642** CHAS. I. *Answ. 19 Proposals Parlt.* 1 The Cabalists of this businesse have with great Prudence reserved themselves. **1660** *Trial Regic.* (title-page), Dark and Horrid Decrees of those Caballists. **1670** in Somers *Tracts* I. 17 General Essex began now to appear to the private Cabalists somewhat wresty.

†'**caball.** *Obs.* Also 5 cabylle, 6 cable, cabill. [ad. L. *caball-us* horse, or rather an assimilation of the word CAPLE, *capul*, *capil* (which was in much earlier use, and is still dialectal) to the original L. form.] A horse.

c **1450** *Voc.* in Wr.-Wülcker 697 *Hic caballus*, a cabylle. **1515** BARCLAY *Eglogues* (1570) C iij/4 But the stronge Caball standeth at the racke. **1518** *Rental Bk. Earl Kildare* in *Trans. Kilkenny Archæol. Soc.* Ser. II. IV. 123 Every howse hawing a cabill to draw to Dublyn quarterly. **1538–48** ELYOT *Lat. Dict.*, *Caballus*, a horse; yet in some partes of England they do call an horse a cable. **1570** LEVINS *Manip.* 1 A cable, horse, *caballus*. A caple, *idem*. **1623** COCKERAM, *Caball*, a little horse, a jade. **1650** T. BAYLY *Herba Parietis* 73 This cavalliers caball was unwilling to clime.

caballada (kæbə'lɑːdə). *U.S.* Also caballado, cavallado, cavayado. [Sp., f. *caballo* horse. Cf. CAVALLARD.] A herd or train of horses (or mules, etc.).

1841 W. L. MCCALLA *Adventures in Texas* 57 (Bentley), Fifty or sixty horses.., forty of which were from one caballado. **1844** J. GREGG *Commerce of Prairies* I. 27 [The Indians] drove off the entire *caballada* of near five hundred head of horses, mules, and asses. **1844** G. W. KENDALL *Santa Fé Exped.* (1855) I. 97 Nothing can exceed the grandeur of the scene when a large cavallada, or drove of horses, takes a 'scare'. **1900** SMITHWICK *Evol. State* 22 He had his caballada driven in for us to choose from. **1901** in *Kansas Hist. Coll.* (1902) VII. 52, I was driving a cavayado. .. The Mexicans always drove their cavayado in front of their trains.

caballer (kə'bælə(r)). [f. CABAL *v.* + -ER[1].] One who cabals or intrigues.

1686 in Ellis *Orig. Lett.* II. 332 IV. 115 From Holland the Amsterdam caballers have sent spies. **1796** BURKE *Regic. Peace* Wks. 1842 II. 315 As courts are the field for caballers, the publick is the theatre for mountebanks and impostors. **1882** *Times* 8 Dec. 4 A mere puppet in the hands of Palace caballers.

‖**caballero** (ˌkaba'ʎero). [Sp. *caballero* knight, gentleman = F. *chevalier*, It. *cavaliere*:—L. *caballārius* horseman, f. *caball-us* horse.] A (Spanish) gentleman. See also CAVALIER *sb.*

[**1749** FIELDING *Tom Jones* x. ii, This gentleman was one of those whom the Irish call a calabalaro, or cavalier.] **1835** R. M. BIRD *Infidel* I. 217 He has invited all my caballeros on this paper. **1868** GEO. ELIOT *Sp. Gypsy* I. 11 A goodly knight, A noble caballero. **1877** KINGSTON *Yng. Llanero* 122 Now go, young caballero, and bring him here. **1878** LADY HERBERT *Hübner's Ramble* I. xii. 192 He is a mixture of a caballero and an ascetic Castilian.

caballine ('kæbəlaɪn), *a.* [ad. L. *caballīn-us*, f. *caballus* horse.] Of or belonging to horses; equine. *caballine aloes* (see quot.). *caballine fountain* = L. *fons caballinus*, the fountain Hippocrene of Greek poetry, fabled to have been produced by a stroke of the foot of Pegasus the winged horse of the Muses; hence = 'fountain of inspiration'.

1430 LYDG. *Chron. Troy* Prol. 13 In Cirrha by Helycon the welle..called..the fountayne Caballyn. *a* **1560** ROLLAND *Crt. Venus* III. 899 The font Caballine, Quhair all vertew dois flurische with fusioun. *a* **1616** BEAUMONT *Ex-ale-tation of Ale* (R.) Having washed their throat With the caballine spring of a pot of good ale. **1712** tr. *Pomet's Hist. Drugs* I. 220 The Aloes is divided into three Kinds, the Succotrine, the Hepatick, and the Caballine. **1725** BRADLEY *Fam. Dict.* I. s.v. *Aloes*, The Cabaline Aloes..call'd Cabaline, because it's given to diseased Horses. **1803** 'C. CAUSTIC' *Terr. Tractor.* III. 101 *note*, For his services to the caballine race. **1878** J. THOMSON *Plenip. Key* 9 This bottle; it's my true and only Helicon; it's my caballine fountain.

caballing (kə'bælɪŋ), *vbl. sb.* [cf. CABAL *v.* + -ING[1].] Petty plotting, intriguing.

a **1680** BUTLER *Rem.* (1759) I. 425 Their caballing is the same thing exactly with packing of Cards. **1714** MANDEVILLE *Fab. Bees* (1733) II. 34 The court of Rome is ..the best school to learn the art of caballing. **1722** *Minute-Bk.* in A. McKay *Hist. Kilmarnock* (1864) 36 To prevent cabbawlling..by the servants. **1866** *Cornh. Mag.* Oct. 435 That petty partisanship and caballing which are the curse of convents.

ca'balling, *ppl. a.* [f. as prec. + -ING[2].] That cabals or intrigues.

a **1700** DRYDEN (J.) What those caballing captains may design. **1831** LYTTON *Godolph.* xviii, A sordid and caballing faction.

cabalmute, var. form of CAPILMUTE.

caban, cabane, earliest forms of CABIN *sb.* Still sometimes used for the sake of local colouring (French or Canadian).

1866 W. R. KING *Sportsm. & Nat. Canada* xii. 316 Huts or *cabans* are built for this purpose on the frozen surface of the river. **1866** *Cornh. Mag.* Nov. 533 He could sit contentedly talking for hours in his cabane.

‖**cabana**[1] (kə'bɑːnə). A cigar, so called from the name of a Spanish exporting house.

1840 W. G. SIMMS *Border Beagles* 65 I'll go a quart and a dozen cabanas upon it. **1864** SALA in *Daily Tel.* 23 Aug., To order champagne cocktails and fifty cent cabanas. **1865** MISS BRADDON *Only a Clod* i. 5 The last of a case of choice cabanas.

cabana[2] (kə'bɑːnə, -njə). Chiefly *U.S.* [Sp., see CABIN *sb.*] A cabin; esp. a hut or shelter at a beach or swimming-pool.

1898 *Land of Sunshine* (Los Angeles) Jan. 61 Though not lacking a certain picturesqueness, what the *cabana* means, and what it stands for, is a large thing. **1931** N. COWARD *Coll. Sk. & Lyrics* 191 The scene is the Lido Beach... In the foreground a row of cabanas with coloured striped awnings. **1953** W. R. BURNETT *Vanity Row* x. 74 A swimming-pool with cabanas. **1957** 'F. RICHARDS' *Practise to Deceive* (1959) xiii. 185 He asked why Lane had gone into the bath-house cabaña. **1959** *Encounter* Sept. 50/2 The physical stage.. looks like a beach cabana. **1967** *London* (Ontario) *Free Press* 21 June 7/2 Cabana sets with matching beach jacket & bathing suit.

cabane (kə'bɑːn). *Aeronaut.* [a. F. *cabane* CABIN.] A pyramidal structure supporting the wings of an aircraft.

1913 A. E. BERRIMAN *Aviation* iii. 33 Each spar is supported at intervals by wires that run overhead to a mast or *cabane* above the pilot's seat. **1914** *Aeronaut. Jrnl.* Oct.

315 *Cabane*, a French word to denote the mast structure projecting above the body to which the top load wires of a monoplane are attached. **1930** *Flight* 12 Sept. 1015/2 The framework of the wing cellule comprises a central 'cabane' supported by four streamlined struts.

cabanet, earlier form of CABINET *sb.*

||**cabaret**[1] ('kæbəreɪ, formerly ||kabarɛ). Also 7 -ett. [F.: of unknown origin: see Littré and Scheler.]

†**1.** A wooden dwelling, a booth, shed; = L. *taberna*. [Here perh. used on account of the connexion of *taberna* and *tavern*: but perh. an error of some kind for *cabanet*.] *Obs.*

1632 SIR T. HAWKINS *Unhap. Prosper.* 261 The greatest houses were heretofore but Cabarets, the Capitoll was at first covered with thatch.

2. a. A drinking house, a pot-house. (Now almost exclusively an alien word referring to France, etc.; but formerly somewhat naturalized.)

1655 BP. BRAMHALL *Agst. Hobbes* (J.) Suppose this servant passing by some cabaret, or tennis court, where his comrades were drinking or playing. **1662** PEPYS *Diary* 23 Sept., In most cabaretts in France they have writ upon the walls..'*Dieu te regarde*'. **1673** DRYDEN *Marr. à la Mode* v. i. 328 Sung two or three years ago in cabarets. **1682** WHELER *Journ. Greece* II. 203 At Gallata are some Christian Cabarets; but the Wine is dear. **1858** DE QUINCEY *Autobiog. Sk.* Wks. II. iv. 197 The little homely cabaret, which had been the scene of her brief romance.

b. A restaurant or night-club in which entertainment is provided as an accompaniment to a meal; also, the entertainment so provided, a floor-show. Also *attrib.*

1912 W. IRWIN *Red Button* 42 He spends most of his extra money at pool parlors, Austrian villages and cabaret shows. **1915** T. BURKE *Nights in Town* 254 Those melancholy places, the night clubs and cabarets. **1920** F. SCOTT FITZGERALD *This Side of Paradise* (1921) II. ii. 211 A famous cabaret star was at the next table. **1922** *Daily Mail* 13 Nov. 7 Cabaret, as exemplified by the Midnight Follies at the Hotel Metropole, also broke all records... This cabaret form of entertainment is very popular just now. *Ibid.* 25 Nov. 13 The new cabaret show which was to have been started on Tuesday has been rehearsed for a fortnight. **1923** *Westm. Gaz.* 22 May, There is to be a super cabaret at the Hotel Metropole on Friday evening. **1938** G. GREENE *Brighton Rock* II. i. 68 The floor was cleared for the last cabaret of the evening.

3. A porcelain tea, coffee, etc., service sometimes accompanied by a small table or tray.

1856 J. C. ROBINSON *Invent. Mus. Ornamental Art* 32 Old Sèvres porcelain... 'Cabaret', rose du Barry ground..the set consisting of four pieces. **1904** *Daily Chron.* 9 June 3/2 A cabaret, painted with flowers, fruit, and trophies..by Lene père. **1968** R. H. R. SMITHIES *Shoplifter* (1969) v. 98 A cabaret tray of Swansea porcelain.

||**cabaret**[2]. *Obs.* [Fr.: Littré gives a conjecture of Saumaise that it represents L. *combretum* or *cobretum* 'a kind of rush': but there is no approach in sense.] A plant: the Asarabacca (*Asarum Europæum*).

1580 BARET *Alv.* H 208 An hearbe called Haselwort, or Cabaret, *Perpensa*..*Bacchar.* **1678** A. LITTLETON *Lat. Dict.*, *Cabarick*, or hazlewort, *Perpensa.* **1712** tr. *Pomet's Hist. Drugs* I. 50 Cabaret or Wild Spikenard, grows in most parts of the Levant.

||**cabarr, -e.** *Obs.* [F. *cabarre*, var. *gabare*.] A lighter.

a **1670** SPALDING *Troub. Chas. I*, I. 59 They sent down six barks or cabarrs full of ammunition.

cabas, see CABA.

†'**cabasset.** *Obs. rare.* [Fr.; dim. of *cabas* basket, panier, etc.] A kind of small helmet.

1622 PEACHAM *Compl. Gentl.* III. (1634) 150 Keyes, lockes, buckles, cabassets or morians, helmets and the like. **1874** BOUTELL *Arms & Arm.* ix. 162.

cabazed, obs. form of CABOCHED *ppl. a.*

cabback, variant of KEBBUCK, *Sc.*, cheese.

cabbage ('kæbɪdʒ), *sb.*[1] Forms: 5 **caboche, cabache,** 5-6 **cabage,** 6 **cabbysshe, cabish,** 6-7 **cabidge,** 7 **cabige, cabadge, cabbadge, cabbach, cabbish,** 7- **cabbage.** [ME. *caboche*, a. F. *caboche* head (in the Channel Islands 'cabbage') = It. *capocchia*, a derivative of It. *capo*:—L. *caput* head. But the actual Fr. name is *choux cabus*, lit. 'great-headed cole, cabbage cole': F. *cabus*, fem. *cabusse* = It. *capuccio*:—L. type **capūceum*, **capūteum*, f. *caput* head.

Cf. also Du. *kabuis(-kool)* cabbage(-cole), f. F. *cabus*: OHG. *chabuz, chapuz*, MHG. *kappaz, kappûs, kabez*, mod.G. *kappes, kappus* 'cabbage', is taken by Grimm and Kluge as a direct adoption of L. *caput* itself, though no use of this in the required sense is known. It is possible that the Eng. *cabbage-cole* was really an adaptation of the Du. *kabuis-kool* influenced by F. *caboche*.]

1. a. A well-known culinary vegetable: a plane-leaved cultivated variety of *Brassica oleracea*, the unexpanded leaves of which form a compact globular heart or head. Originally the 'cabbage' was the head thus formed (cf. *cabbage-head* in 5), the plant being apparently called *cabbage-cole* or *colewort*; now the name 'cabbage' is sometimes extended to the whole species or genus, whether hearting or not, as in ***Savoy cabbage, wild cabbage, Isle of Man cabbage*** (*Brassica Monensis*).

c **1440** *Anc. Cookery* in *Househ. Ord.* (1790) 426 Take cabaches and cut hom on foure..and let hit boyle. **1495** CAXTON *Vitas Patr.* 118 He laboured the gardins, sewe the seedes for cabochis, and colewortes. **1570** LEVINS *Manip.* 11 A cabage, herbe. **1580** BARET *Alv.* Cabage, or colewoort, *brassica.* Cabage, or cole cabege, *brassica capitata.* **1580** LYLY *Euphues* (Arb.) 373 As little agreement..as is betwixt the Vine and the Cabish. **1598** SHAKS. *Merry W.* I. i. 124 Good worts? good Cabidge. **1620** VENNER *Via Recta* vii. 135 The great, hard, and compacted heads of Cole, commonly called Cabbage. **1624** CAPT. SMITH *Virginia* vi. 220 Those that sow..Carrats, Cabidge, and such like. **1658** SIR T. BROWNE *Hydriot.* Ded., Cato seemed to dote upon Cabbadge. **1670** G. H. *Hist. Cardinals* III. III. 307 They.. knew how to save both their Goat and their Cabbadge. **1688** R. HOLME *Armoury* II. 64/2 The Colewort is the same to the Cabbach. **1699** EVELYN *Acetaria* §11 'Tis scarce a hundred years since we first had cabbages out of Holland. **1719** LOUDON & WISE *Compl. Gard.* 199 Pancaliers, or Millan-Cabbages, which produce small headed Cabbages for Winter. **1852** HAWTHORNE *Blithedale Rom.* vii. (1885) 79 Unless it be a Savoy cabbage. **1875** JOWETT *Plato* (ed. 2) III. 243 Cabbages or any other vegetables which are fit for boiling.

b. As a term of endearment: ***my cabbage*** [tr. F. *mon chou*], my dear, darling.

1840 THACKERAY *Miscellanies* (1855) I. 488 Oui, mon chou, mon ange; yase, my angel, my cabbage, quite right. **1896** C. M. YONGE *Release* I. vii. 71 'Ah, my dear little cabbage,' she began, 'I fear they will never forgive you!' **1924** J. M. BARRIE *Mary Rose* I, This wasn't the drawing-room, my cabbage; at least not in my time. **1968** 'J. T. MCINTOSH' *Take a Pair of Private Eyes* iii. 41 Ambrose drew her close and murmured menacingly: 'But I'm completely merciless, my little French cabbage.'

c. = CHOU 2. Also *attrib.*

1888 *Daily News* 21 Sept. 5/6 A large 'cabbage' bow of surah in the same colour. **1895** *Ibid.* 19 Oct. 6/3 The toque worn with this had a large green velvet 'cabbage' at either side. **1896** *Ibid.* 14 Nov. 6/5 Folds of black satin, held down by 'cabbage' knots. **1899** *Ibid.* 3 June 8/3 The inevitable chou, or cabbage-bow, of black or dark green velvet.

d. *fig.* = ***cabbage-head.*** So ***cabbage-looking*** adj., stupid, 'green'.

1870 'MARK TWAIN' *Writings* (1922) VII. 1 All this human cabbage could see was that the watch was four minutes slow. **1898** *Westm. Gaz.* 3 Nov. 4/1, I said I knew 'ow many beans made 5..and if I wor cabbage-looking I woren't green. **1922** JOYCE *Ulysses* 307 Gob, he's not as green as he's cabbagelooking. **1928** R. CAMPBELL *Wayzgoose* i. 9 What wonder if..any cabbage win the critics' praise Who wears his own green leaves instead of bays! **1969** *Guardian* 5 Mar. 7/3, I stayed at home for nearly a year. It was awful. I became a cabbage.

e. Money. *slang* (chiefly *N. Amer.*).

1926 J. BLACK *You can't Win* xv. 213 'You carry this head of cabbage, Kid,' passing me a pack of greenbacks. **1960** *Observer* 24 Jan. 5/1 The white, crinkle, cabbage, poppy, lolly, in other words cash.

2. Transferred with epithets to various other plants: **Arkansas cabbage**, *Streplanthus obtusifolius*; **Chinese cabbage**, *Brassica chinensis*; **dog's c.**, *Thelygonum Cynocrambe*, a succulent herb of the Mediterranean; **Kerguelen's Land c.**, *Pringlea antiscorbutica*; **meadow** or **skunk c.**, *Symplocarpus fœtidus*, a North American plant with a garlic odour; **St. Patrick's c.** = LONDON PRIDE; **sea cabbage** = SEA KALE, *Crambe maritima*; **sea-otter's c.**, a remarkable sea-weed, *Nereocystis*, found in the North Pacific. (*Treas. Bot.*, and Miller *Eng. Names of Plants.*)

3. The tender unexpanded centre or terminal bud of palm trees, which is in most species edible, and is often eaten, though its removal kills the tree. See CABBAGE-TREE.

1638 T. VERNEY in *Verney Papers* (1853) 195 Cabiges, that grows on trees, some an hundred foot high. **1697** DAMPIER *Voy.* I. 166 The Cabbage itself when it is taken out of the Leaves..is as white as Milk, and as sweet as a Nut if eaten raw. **1756** P. BROWNE *Jamaica* (1789) 342 The Coco-Nut Tree..The tender shoots at the top afford a pleasant green or cabbage. **1832** *Veg. Subst. Food* 175 The cabbage..is white..two feet long..thick as a man's arm. **1860** TENNENT *Ceylon* I. 109 *note*, The cabbage, or cluster of unexpanded leaves, for pickles and preserves.

†**4.** The burr whence spring the horns of a deer; also = CABAGING.

c **1550** LACY *Bucke's Test.*, My cabage I wyll the hounde for strife. **1611** COTGR., *Meule*..the cabbadge of a Deeres head.

5. Comb. **a.** Simple: of cabbage or cabbages, as ***cabbage-bed, -blade, -eater, -flower, -garden, -garth, -ground, -grower, -leaf, -patch*** (also *fig.*), ***-seed, -stalk, -stock, -stump***; like a cabbage in shape, as †***cabbage-ruff***, †***-shoe-string.*** **b.** Special, as **cabbage bark**, the narcotic and anthelmintic bark of the **cabbage-bark tree** or CABBAGE-TREE, *Andira inermis* (N.O. *Leguminosæ*); **cabbage beetle** = *cabbage flea*; **cabbage butterfly**, the Large White butterfly of English gardens and fields, *Pieris Brassicæ*, sometimes also the Small White (*P. Rapæ*); **cabbage-cole** = CABBAGE 1; **cabbage-daisy**, a local name of the Globe-flower (*Trollius*); **cabbage-flea**, a minute leaping beetle, *Haltica consobrina*, the larvæ of which destroy cabbage plants; **cabbage-fly**, a two-winged fly (*Anthomyia Brassicæ*), the grubs of which destroy the roots of cabbage; **cabbage-head**, the head formed by the unexpanded leaves of a cabbage; also *fig.* a brainless fellow, a thickhead; **cabbage-leaf hat** = *cabbage-tree hat* (see CABBAGE-TREE 3); **cabbage-lettuce**, a variety of lettuce, with leaves forming a cabbage-like head; **cabbage-moth**, one of the Noctuina (*Mamestra Brassicæ*), the caterpillar of which infests the cabbage; **cabbage-net**, a small net to boil cabbage in; **cabbage-palm**, (*a*) *Areca oleracea*, a native of the West Indies, etc.: see CABBAGE-TREE; (*b*) = next; **cabbage palm-tree** *Austral.* = CABBAGE-TREE 1 e; **cabbage-palmetto**, the West Indian cabbage-tree; **cabbage-plant**, a young plant or seedling of the cabbage; **cabbage-rose**, a double red rose, with large round compact flower (*Rosa centifolia*); **cabbage-wood**, (*a*) the wood of the cabbage-tree, (*b*) *Eriodendron anfractuosum*, a tree related to *Bombax*; **cabbage-worm**, any larva which devours cabbage, esp. that of the Large White butterfly, called in Scotland *kailworm*; also the CABBAGE-TREE worm.

1777 WRIGHT in *Phil. Trans.* LXVII. 507 The *Cabbage-bark tree, or Worm-bark tree, grows in..Jamaica. *Ibid.* 508 Fresh cabbage-bark tastes mucilaginous. **1866** *Treas. Bot.* 63 The bark is known as Bastard Cabbage Bark or Worm Bark; its use is now obsolete. **1816** JANE AUSTEN *Emma* III. vi. 84 *Cabbage-beds would have been enough to tempt the lady. **1816** KIRBY & SP. *Entomol.* (1843) II. 383 The larva of the *cabbage-butterfly (*Pontia Brassicæ*). **1848** *Proc. Berw. Nat. Club* II. No. 6. 328 The caterpillar of the Common White Cabbage Butterfly..is often injurious to the Swedish ..turnip. **1865** *Intell. Observ.* No. 47. 396 The small white cabbage-butterfly (*Pieris Rapæ*). **1579** LANGHAM *Gard. Health* (1633) 151 *Cabbage cole boyled, is very good with beefe. **1620** VENNER *Via Recta* vii. 135 Coleworts or Cole are much vsed to be eaten, especially the Cabbage-Cole. **1861** MRS. LANKESTER *Wild Flowers* 20 Globe-flower..In Scotland..called Lucken Gowan, or *Cabbage-daisy. **1882** *Garden* 4 Mar. 147/1 The root-eating fly, or *Cabbage fly. **1790** BURKE *Fr. Rev.* 224 The tenant-right of a *cabbage-garden..the very shadow of a constructive property. **1887** J. K. LAUGHTON in *Dict. Nat. Biog.* IX. 435/2 During Smith O'Brien's 'cabbage-garden' rebellion. **1863** *N. & Q.* Ser. III. III. 344 The old 'Shandy' garden..is staked out into three *cabbage-garths. **1884** *Athenæum* 6 Dec. 725/2 The eyes of those poor *cabbage-growers down there. **1682** MRS. BEHN *False Count* (1724) III. 146 Thou foul filthy *cabbage-head. **1865** *Nation* (N.Y.) I. 369 We hear persons whose talents are rather of the solid than the brilliant order familiarly spoken of as 'cabbage heads'. **1880** J. R. LOWELL *Biglow Papers* II. 164 When all's come an' past, The kebbige-heads'll cair the day et last. **1688** R. HOLME *Armoury* II. 194/1 The green Caterpiller worm..feeds on *Cabbish-leaves. **1753** HANWAY *Trav.* (1762) I. III. xlii. 196 They also use..a cabbage-leaf under their hats. **1849** LYTTON *Caxtons* III. XVII. i. 199 A cabbage-leaf hat shading a face rarely seen in the Bush. **1562** TURNER *Herbal* II. 26 a, Called..*Cabbage lettes, because it goeth all into one heade, as cabbage cole dothe. **1741** *Compl. Fam.-Piece* I. ii. 175 The largest and hardest Cabbage-Lettuce you can get. **1848** *Proc. Berw. Nat. Club* II. No. 6. 329 Caterpillars of..the *Cabbage Moth. **1721** C. KING *Brit. Merch.* II. 136 The Unshorn Dozens, the *Cabbage-Net Bays, and other sorry Woollen Manufactures of the French Nation. **1742** SHENSTONE *Schoolmistr.* xxxiii. 291 Apples with Cabbage-net y' cover'd o'er. **1833** MARRYAT *P. Simple* xiv, Officers who boil their 'tators in a cabbage-net hanging in the ship's coppers. **1772–84** COOK *Voy.* (1790) I. 199 A few plants, gathered from the *cabbage-palm, which had been mistaken for the cocoa-tree. **1847** LEICHHARDT *Jrnl.* iii. 72 My companions suffered by eating too much of the cabbage-palm. **1852** MUNDY *Antipodes* III. ii. 46 The cabbage palm-tree..[is] becoming scarce. **1853** TH. ROSS *Humboldt's Trav.* III. xxx. 211 The cylinders of palmetto, improperly called 'the cabbage palm', three feet long, and five to six inches thick. **1802** J. DRAYTON *S. Carolina* 66 *Cabbage palmetto. **1850** *Rep. Comm. Patents 1849* (U.S.) 250 Adaptation of the branches of the cabbage palmetto tree to the manufacture of brooms. **1862** R. H. NEWELL *Orpheus C. Kerr Papers* I. 227 How often does man, after making something his particular forte, discover at last that it is only a *cabbage-patch. **1923** Cabbage patch [see BEYONDNESS]. **1923** W. J. LOCKE *Moordius & Co.* xv. 201 Moordius spoke as one does to a child doubtful of the stork or cabbage-patch theory of babies. **1646** EVELYN *Kal. Hort.* (1729) 193 Plant forth your *Cabbage-Plants. **1741** *Compl. Fam.-Piece* II. iii. 355 Transplant some Cabbage-plants of the Sugar-loaf kind. **1795** WOLCOTT (P. Pindar) *Pindariana* Wks. 1812 IV. 183 With *Cabbage-roses loaded, glaring, vast. **1838** *Visitor*, The cabbage rose has been known as the hundred-leaved rose since the time of Pliny. **1613** ROWLANDS *Four Knaves, Paire of Spy*, His *cabage ruffe, of the outrageouse size, Starched in colour to beholders eyes. **1751** J. ELIOT *Field-Husb.* (1760) iii. 51 Millet..is a small grain..of the bigness of Turnip or *Cabbage Seed. **1840** J. C. LOUDON *Cottager's Man.* 44 When the first cabbage-seed is sown. **1613** ROWLANDS *Four Knaves, Paire of Spy* (1843) 48 Let us have standing collers, in the fashion..great *cabbage-shooestrings, (pray you bigge enough). **1844** DISRAELI *Coningsby* v. iii, The interruption of a *cabbage-stalk was represented as a question from some intelligent individual in the crowd. **1851** MAYHEW *Lond. Labour* I. 339, I picked out of the gutter, and eat like a dog—orange-peel and old *cabbage-stumps. **1843** WATERSTON *Cycl. Commerce* v, *Cabbagewood..is sometimes used in ornamental furniture. **1885** A. B. ELLIS *W. Afr. Isl.* i. 9 Tree-ferns and cabbage-wood grow luxuriantly on the main ridge of mountains [in St. Helena]. **1688** R. HOLME *Armoury* II.

204/1 The *Cabbach or Lettice Worm.. turns into a Butterfly all white.

cabbage ('kæbɪdʒ), *sb.*[2] [This and the accompanying CABBAGE *v.*[2] appear in the 17th c. Herrick (1648) uses *garbage* and *carbage*, apparently for 'shreds and patches used as padding'. If this was a genuine use at the time, *carbage* may easily have been further corrupted to *cabbage*.

HERRICK *Hesper.* (Hazl.) I. 79 *Upon some Women*, Pieces, patches, ropes of haire, In-laid garbage ev'rywhere. II. 325 *Upon Lupes*, His credit cannot get the inward carbage for his cloathes as yet.

(Among other guesses as to its origin, are that it is, in some unexplained way, identical with CABBAGE *sb.*[1]; or to be referred to OF. *cabuse* imposture, trick, *cabuser* to deceive, cheat; or to F. *cabas* rush-basket, Sp. *cabacho*, also OF. *cabas* cheating, theft, F. *cabasser* to pack up, to cheat, steal, *cabasseur* deceiver, thief; but evidence is wanting.)]

1. Shreds (or larger pieces) of cloth cut off by tailors in the process of cutting out clothes, and appropriated by them as a perquisite.

1663 *Hudibras* (Spurious) II. 56 (L.) For as tailors preserve their cabbage, So squires take care of bag and baggage. **1719** D'URFEY *Pills* (1872) IV. 50 The Taylor we know he is loth To take any Cabbage at all. **1812** SOUTHEY *Omniana* II. 37 Those philosophers who have a taylorlike propensity for cabbage. **1831** CARLYLE *Sart. Res.* III. xi, Living on Cabbage.

†**2.** *slang.* A tailor. *Obs.*

1690 B. E. *Dict. Cant. Crew*, *Cabbage*, a Taylor, and what they pinch from the Cloaths they make up. **1708** MOTTEUX *Rabelais* IV. lii. (1737) 212 Poor Cabbage's Hair grows through his Hood. **1725** *New Cant. Dict.*, *Cabbage*; Taylors are so called, because of their.. Love of that Vegetable. The Cloth they steal and purloin.. is also called *Cabbage*.

3. *Schoolboy slang.* A 'crib' or key whence a pupil surreptitiously copies his exercise; a 'cab'.

†**'cabbage**, *sb.*[3] *Obs. rare.* Also 6 **cabage**. [app. related to CABIN *sb.* (*caban*, *cabane*, *cabbin*), in sense 'den or lair of a beast'.] A den or lair.

1567 MAPLET *Gr. Forest* 92 He hath his cabbage in the yearth with two contrary wayes vndermined to enter into it, or to run out of it at his pleasure: verie wide at the comming in, but as narrow and straight about the mid cabbage. **1570** LEVINS *Manip.* 11 A cabage, bedde, *stega*.

'cabbage, *v.*[1] [f. CABBAGE *sb.*[1]; or ad. F. *cabusser* 'to cabbadge, to grow to a head' (Cotgr.).]

†**1.** *intr.* **a.** To grow or come to a head, as the horns of a deer. *Obs.*

a **1528** SKELTON *Sp. Parrot* 481 So bygge a bulke of brow auntlers cabagyd that yere.

b. To form a head, as a cabbage or lettuce.

1601 HOLLAND *Pliny* XIX. viii. II. 25 To make them cabbage the better and grow faire and big. **1616** SURFL. & MARKH. *Countr. Farm* 163 The sooner you remove your Lettuce.. the sooner it will Cabbage. **1843** KIRBY & SP. *Entomol.* I. 155 Destroying the plant before it cabbages.

2. *trans.* See CABOCHE *v.*

1530 PALSGR. 596/1, I kabage a deere, *je cabaiche*.. I wyll cabage my dere, and go with you. **1819** SCOTT *Br. Lamm.* ix, The head of the stag should be cabbaged in order to reward them.

'cabbage, *v.*[2] [see CABBAGE *sb.*[2]] *trans.* (and *absol.*) To pilfer, to appropriate surreptitiously: **a.** *orig.* said of a tailor appropriating part of the cloth given to him to make up into garments.

1712 ARBUTHNOT *John Bull* (1755) 14 Your taylor instead of shreds, cabages whole yards of cloath. **1793** W. ROBERTS *Looker-on* (1794) III. 388 Ben Bodkin, who had cabbaged most notoriously in the making of Sam Spruce's new coat. **1830** *Blackw. Mag.* XXVII. 117 Our Tailor says, 'I like not the charge of plagiarism.' Nevertheless, he cabbages. **1873** H. SPENCER *Stud. Soc.* vi. 137 The tailor 'cabbaged' the cloth he used.

b. *transf.* **c.** In Schoolboy slang = To crib, cab.

1837 GEN. P. THOMPSON *Exerc.* (1842) IV. 234 A speech, which.. had been what schoolboys call 'cabbaged', from some of the forms of oration.. published by way of caricature. **1862** H. MARRYAT *Year in Sweden* II. 387 Steelyards.. sent by Gustaf Wasa as checks upon country dealers, who cabbaged, giving short weight.

'cabbaged, *ppl. a.*[1] [f. CABBAGE *v.*[1] (or *sb.*[1]) + -ED.] Grown cabbage-fashion, formed into or having a head like a cabbage.

1577 B. GOOGE *Heresbach's Husb.* (1586) 25 Cabegged rape sowen after rie. **1616** SURFL. & MARKH. *Countr. Farm* 167 The cabbaged Lettuce. **1656** DUGARD *Gate Lat. Unl.* §88. 29 Colewort, which.. becometh cabbaged. **1725** BRADLEY *Fam. Dict.* II. s.v. *May*, If any of the Imperial Lettices are cabbaged.

'cabbaged, *ppl. a.*[2] [f. CABBAGE *v.*[2]] Pilfered, as shreds by a tailor.

1729 COFFEY *Beggar's Wed.* I. i, I shall convert his cabbaged shreads into a stone Doublet.

cabbage-palm = next: see CABBAGE *sb.*[1] 5.

'cabbage-tree. [f. CABBAGE *sb.*[1] 1, 2.]

1. A name given to several palm trees, whose central unexpanded mass of leaves or terminal bud is eaten like the head of a cabbage; *esp.*

a. The West Indian tree, *Areca* or *Oreodoxa oleracea*, also called *cabbage-palm* and *Palmetto Royal*, growing to a height of 150 or 200 feet. **b.** *Chamærops Palmetto* of the Southern U.S. **c.** *Euterpe oleracea* of Brazil and ? W. Indies. **d.** *Livistona inermis* of Northern Australia. **e.** *Corypha australis* of Australia, the leaves of which are made into baskets, hats, etc.

1725 SLOANE *Jamaica* II. 110 This is most evident in the top of that called the Cabbage tree. **1756** P. BROWNE *Jamaica* 342 The Barbadoes Cabbage Tree.. is the most beautiful tree I have ever seen, and may be esteemed the queen of the woods. **1779** FORREST *Voy. N. Guinea* 123 We.. saw many aneebong or cabbage trees growing on the island. **1796** MORSE *Amer. Geog.* I. 677 (S. Carolina) The palmetto or cabbage tree, the utility of which, in the construction of forts was experienced during the late war.

2. Other trees and plants, so called for various trivial reasons, as the cabbage-bark tree, *Andira inermis* of the West Indies; a palm-like liliaceous plant of New Zealand, *Cordyline indivisa*, bearing a head of narrow leaves. **bastard** or **black c. t.**, *Andira inermis* (see above);—of St. Helena: *Melanodendron integrifolium*;—of South America: the leguminous genus *Geoffroya*. **Canary Island c. t.**, *Cacolia kleinia nervifolia*, a composite plant. **small umbelled c. t.**, *Commidendron spurium*. (Miller *Plant Names*, 1884.)

1796 STEDMAN *Surinam* II. xxiii. 164 The black-cabbage tree, the wood of which.. is in high estimation among carpenters and joiners. **1848** T. ARNOLD *Let.* 26 Apr. (1966) 41 There is a certain stiffness in the appearance of a New Zealand forest.. but some of the trees and shrubs are very beautiful... There is the cabbage-tree [etc.]. **1884** GORDON-CUMMING in *Century Mag.* XXVII. 920 The settlers with strange perversity have dubbed this the cabbage-tree. **1905** W. B. *Where White Man Treads* 145 Then the engine would.. show off its paces to an admiring cluster of ancient cabbage trees. **1930** L. G. D. ACLAND *Early Canterbury Runs* iv. 65 Cabbage trees only grow thick on good land. **1935** 'J. GUTHRIE' *Little Country* xxvii. 390 In the clump of cabbage trees.. one palm, alas, had been blown down by the fierce southerly gale. **1967** *N.Z. Listener* 29 Sept. 10/1 A New Zealand play without sentimentality, brashness or cabbage trees.

3. *attrib.*, as in ***cabbage-tree hat*** (ellipt., *cabbage-tree*); **cabbage-tree worm**, a fat grub found in the decaying cabbage tree eaten in Guiana.

1880 *Blackw. Mag.* Feb. 167 The chin-straps of their cabbage-tree hats. *Ibid.* 171 Raising his cabbage-tree, allowed the chin-strap to drop to its place. **1796** STEDMAN *Surinam* II. 23 Groe-groe, or cabbage-tree worms, as they are called in Surinam.. In taste they partake of all the spices of India.. these worms are produced in all the palm-trees, when beginning to rot. **1905** W. B. *Where White Man Treads* 297 A hurrying woman in a man's soiled cabbage-tree hat. **1908** E. J. BANFIELD *Confessions of Beach-Comber* II. iii. 314 A stock-rider.. in a.. cabbage-tree hat. **1928** 'BRENT OF BIN BIN' *Up Country* i. 2 He flung off his streaming oilskin and shook the water from his wide-brimmed cabbage-tree hat, with its bobbing corklets attached as fly chasers.

'cabbaging, *vbl. sb.*[1] [f. CABBAGE *v.*[1]] The growth or formation of a head (by a cabbage, etc.).

1737 MILLER *Gard. Dict.* s.v. *Brassica*. **1741** *Compl. Fam.-Piece* II. iii. 364 Transplant Lettuce for Cabbaging.

'cabbaging, *vbl. sb.*[2] [f. CABBAGE *v.*[2] + -ING[1].] Pilfering, purloining. Also *attrib.*

1768 EARL CARLISLE in *Selwyn & Contemp.* II. 312 You had better come to Spa; it is an excellent cabbaging place.

'cabbagy, *a.* Also **cabbagey**. [see -Y[1].] Having the characteristics of a cabbage; cabbage-like.

1861 G. DU MAURIER *Let.* Aug. (1951) 60, I got your jolly letter this morning and it imparted quite a delicious flavour to a very cabbagey German citizen. **1883** LADY BLOOMFIELD *Remin. Court & Diplom. Life* I. iii. 65 The very cabbagy green of summer. **1957** C. MACINNES *City of Spades* II. iii. 123 Muriel was cooking something cabbagey. **1960** A. BURGESS *Right to Answer* xi. 144 The whole damp cabbagy essence of winter England.

‖**cabbala** (kə'bɑːlə, 'kæbələ). Also 6– **cabala** (7 **caballa**, 9 **kabbala**). [a. med.L. *cabbala*, ad. Rabbinical Heb. *qabbālāh* 'tradition', f. (the biblical) *qbl* (in Piel) *qibbēl* 'to receive, accept, admit'.]

1. The name given in post-biblical Hebrew to the oral tradition handed down from Moses to the Rabbis of the Mishnah and the Talmud. **b.** Towards the beginning of the thirteenth century A.D. applied to the pretended tradition of the mystical interpretation of the Old Testament.

1521 FISHER *Wks.* (1876) 332 Cabala.. is derived fro man to man by mouth only and not by wrytynge. *Ibid.* 336 Also theyr Cabala that is to say their secrete erudycyons not wryten in the byble. **1653** MORE *Conject. Cabbal.* (1713) Pref. i, The Jewish Cabbala is conceived to be a Traditional doctrine or exposition of the Pentateuch, which Moses received from the mouth of God. **1693** *Phil. Trans.* XVII. 801 The real Cabala they make Two-fold, i.e. The Doctrine of Sephiroth, and the Doctrine of the Four Worlds. **1837–9** HALLAM *Hist. Lit.* (1847) I. iii. §93. 202 In the class of traditional theology.. we must place the Jewish Cabbala.

2. *gen.* †**a.** An unwritten tradition. *Obs.*

1641 J. JACKSON *True Evang. T.* I. 47 H[enry] 8. of whom a Cabala or tradition goes, that on his death-bed, he confessed, hee had never spared man in his wrath, nor woman in his lust. **1662** STILLINGFL. *Orig. Sacr.* II. iv. §4 Though the Jews would fain make the gift of Prophecy to be a kind of Cabala too, and conveyed in a constant succession from one Prophet to another. **1692** BENTLEY *Boyle Lect.* viii. 274 Without the benefit of letters, the whole Gospel would be a mere tradition and old cabbala.

b. Mystery, secret or esoteric doctrine or art.

1665 GLANVILL *Sceps. Sci.* Addr. 13 Branches of a dangerous Cabbala. **1678** NORRIS *Coll. Misc.* (1699) 59 Nor is it He to whom kind Heaven A secret cabala has given. **1795** BURKE *Let.* Wks. 1842 II. 241 Magisterial rabbins and doctors in the cabala of political science. **1810** SCOTT *Lady of L.* III. vi, Eager he read whatever tells Of magic, cabala, and spells. **1851** D. WILSON *Preh. Ann.* II. IV. ii. 226 Visible signs of some native cabbala.

†**3.** ***of cabbala with***: in the secrets of. *Obs.*

1646 SIR T. BROWNE *Pseud. Ep.* I. iii. 11 Astrologers, which pretend to be of Caballa with the starres.

ca'bbalic, *a.* [ad. med.L. *cabbalic-us.*] Of or pertaining to the Cabbala.

1684 N. S. *Crit. Enq. Edit. Bible* xii. 94 He rebukes the Cabbalick Doctors. **1753** CHAMBERS *Cycl. Supp.*, *Cabbalic art*, *Ars caballica*, is used by some writers for *ars palæstrica*, or the art of wrestling.

cabbalism ('kæbəlɪz(ə)m). Also **cabalism**. [f. CABBALA + -ISM: or ad. med.L. *cabbalism-us.*]

1. The system or manner of the Jewish Cabbala.

1614 WILKINS *Mercury* viii. (1707) 33 Which kind of Cabalism is six Times repeated in the History of the Creation. **1652** J. SMITH *Sel. Disc.* VI. 200 Sailing between Cabbalism and Platonism. **1854** KINGSLEY *Alexandria* IV. 156 The cabbalism of the old Rabbis.

2. Mystic or occult doctrine; mystery.

1590 GREENE *Fr. Bacon* (1630) 8 Sore he doubts of Bacons Cabalisme. **1641** *Vind. Smectymnuus* xiii. 141 What Cabalisme have we here? **1660–3** J. SPENCER *Prodigies* (1665) 287 Pretty allegories, parables, cabbalisms.

3. ? (Cf. CABAL, CABALIST.)

1847 EMERSON *Repres. Men* Wks. (Bohn) I. 284 They are the exceptions which we want, where all grows alike. A foreign greatness is the antidote for cabalism. **1856** —— *Eng. Traits* xiii. Wks. 1874 II. 99, I do not know that there is more Cabalism in the Anglican, than in other Churches.

cabbalist ('kæbəlɪst). Also **cabalist**. [ad. med.L. *cabbalista*: see -IST. Cf. also F. *cabaliste*.]

1. One who professes acquaintance with and faith in the Jewish Cabbala.

c **1533** DEWES *Introd. Fr.* in *Palsgr.* 1058 Of the whiche knowlege the cabalystes doth make fyftie gates. **1646** SIR T. BROWNE *Pseud. Ep.* (1650) 212 The doctrine of the Cabalists, who in each of the four banners inscribe a letter of the Tetragrammaton. **1794** SULLIVAN *View Nat.* II. 236 The Masorites and Cabbalists. **1878** *N. Amer. Rev.* 468 The cabalists and Talmudists are responsible for him [Adam].

2. One skilled in mystic arts or learning.

a **1592** GREENE *Dram. Wks.* (1831) I. 182 The cabalists that write of magic spells. **1704** SWIFT *T. Tub* v. (1709) 76 As eminent a Cabalist as his Disciples would represent him. **1847** EMERSON *Poems, Initial Love*, Cupid is a casuist, A mystic, and a cabalist. **1850** MAURICE *Mor. & Met. Philos.* I. 157 Plato felt the temptation to be a cabbalist.

3. See CABALIST.

cabbalistic (kæbə'lɪstɪk), *a.* Also **cabal-**. [f. prec. + -IC, or direct ad. F. *cabalistique*, or med.L. *cabbalistic-us.*] Pertaining to, of the nature of, or like the Cabbala or cabbalists; having a private or mystic sense; mysterious.

1624 MIDDLETON *Game Chess* IV. ii, Out of that cabalistic bloody riddle. **1665** J. SPENCER *Prophecies* 97 The Cabbalistick sense of Scripture. **1684** N. S. *Crit. Enq. Edit. Bible* xii. 95 The Cabbalistick, and Allegorical Doctors. **1724** A. COLLINS *Gr. Chr. Relig.* 258 The Revelation.. being written.. in the Cabalistick style. **1865** TYLOR *Early Hist. Man.* vi. 129 Certain figures and cabalistic signs upon the skull.

cabba'listical, *a.* Also **cabal-**. [f. as prec. + -AL[1].] Of or pertaining to what is cabbalistic; also = CABBALISTIC.

a **1593** H. SMITH *Wks.* (1867) II. 382 By art cabalistical. **1723** MATHER *Vind. Bible* 300 A Cabalistical explanation of Deut. iv. 4. **1830** SCOTT *Demonol.* VI. 189 To show the extent of his cabalistical knowledge. **1838–9** HALLAM *Hist. Lit.* I. I. iii. §96. 208 His famous 900 theses logical, ethical.. and cabbalistical.

cabba'listically, *adv.* [f. prec. + -LY[2].] In a cabbalistic manner; according to the Cabbala.

1634 SIR T. HERBERT *Trav.* 123 (T.) Rabbi Elias, from the first verse of the first chapter of Genesis, where the letter aleph is six times found, cabalistically concludes that the world shall endure just six thousand years. **1693** W. FREKE *Sel. Ess.* iv. 23 Who but a Madman would think the Number Five Cabalistically sanctified, because a Man has Five Fingers, Five Toes, etc. **1856** R. VAUGHAN *Mystics* (1860) II. 107 How to pronounce cabbalistically the potent name.

cabbalistico- *in comb.* Cabbalistically.

1831 CARLYLE *Sart. R.* I. v, Disquisitions of a cabalistico-sartorial and quite antediluvian cast.

†**'cabbalize**, *v. Obs.* Also **cabal-**. [ad. F. *cabalise-r* (16th c. in Littrè), or med.L. *cabbalizāre*: see -IZE.] *intr.* To use or affect the manner of the cabbalists; to speak mystically.

1660 H. MORE *Myst. Godl.* I. viii. 23 Here St. John seems to cabbalize, as in several places of the Apocalypse, that is, to speak in the language of the Learned of the Jews.

†'**cabbalizer.** *Obs.* Also cabal-. One who cabbalizes; one who interprets by cabbala.
1593 NASHE *Christ's T.* (1613) 77 Not all thy seuenty Esdrean Cabalizers, who traditionately from Moyses receiued the Laws interpretation.

cabban, -ane, -aine, -en, early ff. CABIN *sb.*

cabber ('kæbə(r)). *colloq.* [f. CAB *sb.*[3] + -ER[1].] A cab-horse.
1884 *Times* 27 Oct. 2/4 Sixteen short-legged, active, clever, Young Cabbers.

cabbie ('kæbɪ). *Obs.* or *dial.* 'A sort of box made of laths, which claps close to a horse's side, narrow at the top so as to prevent the grain in it from being spilled' (Jam.). Also 'a small barrow or box with two wheels used for drawing' *ibid.*
1795 *Statist. Acc. Scot.* XVI. 187 The other implements of husbandry are harrows..cabbies, crook-saddles, creels.

cabbin, -ine, cabbinet: see CABIN *sb.*, CABINET *sb.*

'**cabbing,** *vbl. sb.* [f. CAB *v.*] Cab-driving, cab-letting. (Also *attrib.*)
1870 *Pall Mall G.* 24 Oct. 11 The cabbing interest has suffered from the war. **1939** H. HODGE *Cab, Sir?* 13 During my cabbing life I have worked at all hours. *Ibid.* 219 'Cabology', of course, is the art or science of cabbing. **1939** *John o' London's* XLI. 299/1 Let no one laugh at cabmen until he's tried cabbing.

cabble ('kæb(ə)l), *v. Iron-smelting.* To break up flat pieces of partially finished iron for fagotting. (See quots.) Hence **cabbler, cabbling.**
1849 WEALE *Dict. Terms* s.v., The process..which in Gloucestershire is called 'scabbling' or more correctly 'cabbling' ..is simply breaking up this flat iron into small pieces. Men are especially allocated for this operation, and are named 'cabblers'. **1874** KNIGHT *Dict. Mech.* 418/1 The pig iron is..4. *Tilted*; making a flat, oval plate. 5. *Cabbled*; that is, broken up into pieces. 6. *Fagoted.* **1875** URE *Dict. Arts* I. 558 Finery iron is smelted with charcoal, and when a soft mass of about two hundredweight is formed it is hammered out into a flat oval from two to four inches in thickness; this is allowed to cool, and is then broken up into small pieces, which is the process of cabbling or scabbling.

cabbon, cabbonet, early ff. CABIN *sb.*, CABINET *sb.*

cabborne, obs. var. of *cabbon, cabon,* CABIN *sb.*
1556 ABP. PARKER *Psalter* cxxxii. 385 Be it my shame: if I go in My Cabborne house: in rest to lygh.

†'**cabby**[1]. *Obs.* ? A garden pick or hoe.
1653 URQUHART *Rabelais* I. xxiii, With little Mattocks, Pickaxes, Grubbing-hooks, Cabbies [*bèches*], Pruning-knives, and other Instruments requisit for gardning.

cabby[2] ('kæbɪ). *colloq.* [f. CAB *sb.*[3] + -Y[4].] A cab-driver.
1859 *All Y. Round* No. 34. 177 Call the cabby up for my trunk and hat-box. **1881** *Times* 19 Jan. 10/2 Such 'cabbies' as were about, turned a deaf ear to any one who hailed them.

cabbyn, obs. form of CABIN *sb.*

cabbysshe, obs. form of CABBAGE.

'**cabdom.** *nonce wd.* [f. CAB *sb.*[3] + -DOM.] That part of the community specially interested in cabs, as owners or drivers.
1868 *Morn. Her.* 25 Aug., Cabdom is furious against the railway companies.

‖**cabeer** (kə'bɪə(r)). [Arab. *kabīr*, lit. 'big, *gros*'.]
1752 BEAWES *Lex Mercat.* 911 Cabeer, a Money used for accounts at Mocha, of which 80 may be reckoned to a French Crown. *Ibid.* 913 Caveers.

cabel, -ell, -elle, obs. forms of CABLE.

caben, early form of CABIN *sb.*

caber ('keɪbə(r)). *Sc.* Also 6 cabir, **kabar, kebber, kebbre.** [a. Gaelic *cabar* pole, spar, rafter = Irish *cabar* lath, Welsh *ceibr* beam, rafter, Corn. *ceber, keber* rafter, beam, Breton 9th c. in Luxemb. fol. 'tignæ, *cepriou*'.]

1. A pole, or spar, usually consisting of the stem of a young pine or fir-tree, used in house-carpentry, scaffolding, etc.
1513 DOUGLAS *Æneis* XII. v. 186 His schaft that was als rude and squair, As it had beyn a cabyr or a spar. **1718** A. RAMSAY *Christ's Kirk* III. xviii, They frae a barn a kabar raught. **1756** MRS. CALDERWOOD *Jrnl.* (1884) 162 To every plant they give a pole, which is a tree, like the smallest sort of what we call cabers. **1860** G. H. K. *Vac. Tour* 164 They hung them [trouts] on the cabers of their wigwams.

2. *esp.* as used in the Highland athletic exercise of ***throwing*** or ***tossing the caber.***
1862 *Standard* 16 July, Tossing the caber. **1872** *Daily News* 26 July, Caber Throwing. **1881** *Boys' Newspaper* 6 July, The caber is simply a roughly hewn pine trunk denuded of its branches..To toss this skilfully the athlete poises the smaller end against his breast, in an upright position, and, suddenly raising it by sheer force to a level with his shoulder, throws it from him in such a manner that the thick end touches the ground first, and the trunk falls away from him.

cabern, obs. form of CABIN *sb.* (of a ship).

Cabernet (kabɛrne). Formerly also **Carbenet, Carbonet.** [Fr.] Any of a family of vines, esp. ***Cabernet Sauvignon*** (see SAUVIGNON 1 b), yielding grapes used in wine-making; the grape of these vines. Also, wine made from Cabernet grapes.
1833 C. REDDING *Hist. Mod. Wines* v. 146 The *carbenet, carmenet*,..and *verdot*, are the plants most cultivated in the plain of Medoc. **1846** C. COCKS *Bordeaux & its Wines* 140 The *Carmenère*, or grosse *Vidure*, called also *grand Carmenet, Carbonet*, or *Sauvignon*, has larger berries than the former. **1888** *Encycl. Brit.* XXIV. 604/2 The vines of the Cabernet species, although producing excellent grapes, are especially susceptible to damage from weather at flowering time. **1911** *Ibid.* XXVIII. 721/1 The principal vines grown in the Médoc are the Cabernet-Sauvignon, which is the most important, the Gros Cabernet, [etc.]. **1924** H. W. ALLEN *Wines of France* ii. 75 The king of the vines from which red Bordeaux is derived is the *cabernet-sauvignon.* **1946** A. L. SIMON *Conc. Encycl. Gastron.* VIII. 35/2 *Cabernet*, one of the most extensively grown wine-making grapes for red table wines, the best of the many different Cabernet grapes being the Cabernet Sauvignon. **1961** WEBSTER, *Cabernet*, a dry red California table wine like claret with medium body and fruity flavor. **1970** *Guardian* 13 Feb. 9/2 A Bulgarian or Chilean Cabernet (13s to 14s). **1985** *N.Y. Times* 17 Feb. XI. 23/3 Some worthwhile red wine selections under $20 include..cabernet sauvignon from Umbria ($18).

cabful ('kæbfʊl). [f. CAB *sb.*[3] + -FUL.] As much or as many as a cab will hold.
1856 MACAULAY in *Life & Lett.* (1880) II. 432 Took a cabfull of books to Westbourne Terrace.

‖**cabiai** ('kɑːbɪaɪ). [Fr., a. Galibi (or Carib of French Guiana). Martius *Brasil-Sprachen.*] A native name of the Capybara (*Hydrochœrus Capybara*), sometimes used by naturalists.
1774 GOLDSM. *Nat. Hist.* (1862) I. xiv. 239 Animals which seem..to make each a distinct species in itself..the Cabiai. *Ibid.* III. vi. (JOD.) The capibara, or cabiai; it is a native of South America, and is chiefly seen in frequenting the borders of lakes and rivers like an otter.

cabidge, -ige, obs. forms of CABBAGE.

cabil(le, obs. form of CABLE.

‖**cabildo** (ka'bildo). [Sp., f. late L. *capitulum* chapter-house: see CHAPTER *sb.*] **1.** A town hall or town council.
1824 J. R. POINSETT *Notes on Mexico* (1825) iv. 53 Opposite to it stands the cabildo, or town house. *Ibid.* x. 156 The *ayuntamientos*, or *cabildos*, were, and still are, an important branch of the government of Spanish America. **1934** A. HUXLEY *Beyond Mexique Bay* 140 The little plaza between the church and the *cabildo*, or municipality. **1960** H. S. FERNS *Britain & Argentina in 19th Cent.* i. 29 All purchases..would be at moderate prices fixed by the *cabildo* or municipal government.

2. (Usu. with capital initial.) The chapterhouse of a cathedral or collegiate church, or the chapter itself.
1880 G. W. CABLE *Grandissimes* xli. 320 He saw his clerks ..standing idle and shabby in the arcade of the Cabildo. **1924** L. HEARN *Amer. Miscellany* lxviii, I wish to thank those who did this service for me..at the Cabildo, in New Orleans.

cabill, var. form of CABALL, a horse.

‖**cabilliau, cabeliau** (kabijo, 'kabiljau). Also **kabbelow.** [a. F. *cabillaud, cabliau*, Du. *kabeljauw*, a name used (according to Franck) by all the coast Germans since the 14th c.; MLG. *kabelaw*, Ger. *kabliau, kabeljau*, Sw. *kabeljo*, Da. *kabeljau*, med.L. *cabellauwus* (A.D. 1133 in Carpentier's Du Cange). It has been generally regarded as a transposed form of *bakeljauw, bakkeljau*, BACALAO, which is however not compatible with the history of that word, q.v.] Cod-fish; 'codfish which has been salted and hung for a few days, but not thoroughly dried; also, a dish of cod mashed' (Smyth *Sailor's Word-bk.*).
1696 W. MOUNTAGUE *Delights Holland* 36 A good Dish of Cabilliau, Cod-Fish, of which the Dutch in general are great Admirers. **1731** MEDLEY *Kolben's Cape of G. Hope* II. 188 At the Cape there are several sorts of the fish call'd Cabeliau. **1867** SMYTH *Sailor's Word-bk., Kabbelow.*

cabin ('kæbɪn), *sb.* Forms: 4-7 cabane, 5-8 caban, 5 kaban, 5-7 cabon, 6 cabban, -ane, -aine, -on, -yn, caben, 6-8 cabbin, 7 cabben, cabbine, cabine, cabern, 7- cabin. [ME. *cabane*, a. F. *cabane* (= Pr., Pg. *cabana*, Sp. *cabaña*, Cat. *cabanya*, It. *capanna*):—late L. *capanna*, in Isidore, 'tugurium parva casa est; hoc rustici capanna vocant'; in Reichenau glosses 8th cent. *cabanna*. Mod.F. has *cabine* from Eng. in sense 5.]

†**1. a.** A temporary shelter of slight materials; a tent, booth, temporary hut. *Obs.*
?*a* **1400** *Morte Arth.* 3099 Cabanes coverede for kynges anoyntede With clothes of clere golde for knyghtez and oþer. **1581** MARBECK *Bk. of Notes* 148 They made with pretie boughs and twigs of trees, such little pretie lodgings as we call Cabens or Boothes. **1601** SHAKS. *Twel. N.* I. v. 287 Make me a willow Cabine at your gate. *a* **1649** DRUMM. OF HAWTH. *Hist. Jam. IV*, Wks. (1711) 76 Cabanes raised of boughs of trees and reeds. **1857-69** HEAVYSEGE *Saul* 237 From the wilderness there comes a blast, That casts my cabin of assurance down.

†**b.** *spec.* A soldier's tent or temporary shelter.
?*a* **1400** *Morte Arth.* 733 Tentez and othire toylez, and targez fulle ryche, Cabanes and clathe sokkes. **1553** BRENDE *Q. Curtius* B b j, There fell sodainlie a great storme..within their cabbaines, which so moche afflicted the Souldiours.. that, etc. **1598** B. JONSON *Ev. Man in Hum.* III. vii, The Courts of Princes..the Cabbins of Soldiers. **1653** HOLCROFT *Procopius* II. 67 The Persians..fell among their Cabbins, and were rifling the camp.

2. a. A permanent human habitation of rude construction. Applied esp. to the mud or turf-built hovels of slaves or impoverished peasantry, as distinguished from the more comfortable 'cottage' of working men, or from the 'hut' of the savage, or temporary 'hut' of travellers, explorers, etc.
c **1440** *Promp. Parv.* 57 Caban, lytylle howse, *pretoriolum, capana.* **1566** PAINTER *Pal. Pleas.* I. 98 He dwelt alone in a little cabane in the fieldes not farre from Athenes. **1570** LEVINS *Manip.* 163 A cabbon, *gurgustium.* **1587** FLEMING *Contn. Holinshed* III. 1356/1 Being taken in his cabbin by one of the Irishrie. **1618** SIR R. BOYLE in *Lismore Papers* (1886) I. 196 To give her a Room to bwyld her a cabben in. **1670** G. H. *Hist. Cardinals* I. iii. 65 Not a Mendicant..could be perswaded to leave his Cabane. **1691** PETTY *Pol. Anat.* 9 There be [in Ireland] 160,000 Cabins without Chimneys. **1729** SHELVOCKE *Artillery* IV. 255 The Cabbin of Romulus was only thatched with Straw. *a* **1745** SWIFT *Wks.* (1841) II. 78 The wretches are forced to pay for a filthy cabin and two ridges of potatoes treble the worth. **1794** SULLIVAN *View Nat.* II. 369 An extensive country covered with cabans. **1832** HT. MARTINEAU *Ireland* i. 1 A mud cabin here and there is the only vestige of human habitation. **1850** MRS. STOWE (*title*) Uncle Tom's Cabin.

b. Used rhetorically for 'poor dwelling'.
1598 B. JONSON *Ev. Man in Hum.* I. v. (1616) 16 Possesse no gentlemen of our acquaintance, with notice of my lodging ..Not that I need care who know it, for the Cabin is conuenient. **1607** DEKKER *Sir T. Wyatt* Wks. 1873 III. 101 A simple Cabin, for so great a Prince.

†**3. a.** A cell: e.g. of an anchorite or hermit, in a convent or prison; a cell of a honeycomb. *Obs.*
1362 LANGL. *P. Pl.* A. XII. 35 Clergy in to a caban crepte. **1387** TREVISA *Higden* Rolls Ser. I. 221 In the theatre.. cabans and dennes [*cellulæ mansionum*]. **1480** CAXTON *Chron. Eng.* ccliv. 329 They put hym in a Cabon and his chapelyne for to shryue hym. *c* **1530** MORE *De quat. Noviss.* Wks. 84/2 The gailor..thrusteth your blode into some other caban. **1571** HANMER *Chron. Irel.* (1633) 57 Hee went into France, and made them Cabanes, after the Irish manner, in stead of Monasteries. **1611** BIBLE *Jer.* xxxvii. 16 When Ieremiah was entred into the dungeon, and into the cabbins. **1616** SURFL. & MARKH. *Countr. Farm* 322 [Bees] busie in making Combes, and building of little Cabbins.

†**b.** A small room, a bedroom, a boudoir. *Obs.*
1594 CAREW *Tasso* (1881) 38 Gay clothing, and close cabbanes eke she flyes. **1607** R. WILKINSON *Merchant-roy.* 30 She that riseth to dinner..& for every fit of an idle feuer betakes her straight to her cabbin againe. **1614** RALEIGH *Hist. World* I. 83 Thou shalt make Cabines in the Arke. *c* **1620** Z. BOYD *Zion's Flowers* (1855) 71 She steek't her cabin doore.

†**4.** A natural cave or grotto; the den or hole of a wild beast. *Obs.*
1377 LANGL. *P. Pl.* B. III. 190 Ac þow..crope in to a kaban for colde of þi nailes. **1583** STANYHURST *Aeneis* I. (Arb.) 23 A cel or a cabban by nature formed, is vnder. **1589** *Gold. Mirr.* (1851) 5 Cabbins and caues in England and in Wales. *Ibid.* 14 The beastly belling bull, lay coucht in cabbin closse. **1601** HOLLAND *Pliny* I. 358 It might resemble a very cabbin and caue indeed. **1794** S. WILLIAMS *Vermont* 98 The beavers..build cabins, or houses for themselves.

5. a. A room or compartment in a vessel for sleeping or eating in. An apartment or small room in a ship for officers or passengers. Also in an aircraft or spacecraft.
1382 WYCLIF *Ezek.* xxvii. 6 Thi seetis of rowers..and thi litil cabans. **1483** *Cath. Angl.* 50 A Caban of cuke (coke A.); *capana.* **1530** PALSGR. 202/1 Cabbyn in a shyppe, *cabain.* **1555** EDEN *Decades W. Ind.* I. v. (Arb.) 86 Beholdinge..the toppe castell..the cabens, the keele. **1610** SHAKS. *Temp.* I. i. 15 Keepe your Cabines: you do assist the storme. **1626** CAPT. SMITH *Accid. Yng. Seamen* 10 The Captaines Cabben or great Cabben. **1718** LADY M. W. MONTAGUE *Lett.* II. lvi. 85 An English lady..desired me to let her go over with me in my cabin. **1748** ANSON *Voy.* I. iii. (ed. 4) 41 Orellana.. drew towards the great cabbin. **1835** SIR J. ROSS *N.-W. Pass.* xvii. 259 They were taken into the cabin. **1908** H. G. WELLS *War in Air* VII. 214 There followed upon these things a long, deep swaying of the airship, and then Bert began a struggle to get back to his cabin. **1913** C. GRAHAME-WHITE *Aviation* 214 The pilot and his passenger are provided with a completely covered body, which they enter through a small door. This cabin, which has a roof, walls, and floor,.. is equipped with celluloid windows. **1921** M. CORELLI *Secret Power* viii. 87 The steering cabin and accommodation for the pilot and observer. **1962** J. GLENN in *Into Orbit* 41 You have one large handle for repressurizing the cabin with oxygen in case of a bad leak.

†**b.** A berth (in a ship). ***hanging cabin:*** a hammock, cot. *Obs.*
1598 W. PHILLIPS *Linschoten's Trav. Ind.* in Arb. *Garner* III. 20 Each man his cabin to sleep in. **1626** CAPT. SMITH *Accid. Yng. Seamen* 11 A cabben, a hanging cabben, a Hamacke. **1697** DAMPIER *Voy.* (1729) III. I. 191 Captain Davis..was thrown out of his Cabbin. **1732** LEDIARD *Sethos* II. VII. 120 Cabbins hung upon palm-trees. **1769** FALCONER *Dict. Marine, Cajutes*, the cabins or bed-places..for the common sailors.

†**6.** A litter. *Obs.*

1577 HOLINSHED *Chron.* II. 770 People flocking..some with beires, some with cabbins, some with carts..to fetch awaie the dead and the wounded. *a* 1631 DONNE *Poems* (1650) 143 Some coffin'd in their cabbins lie.

†7. A (political) CABINET: hence ***cabin council, counsellor, signet.*** *Obs.*

1636 FEATLY *Clavis Myst.* xiv. 193 They are made of the Cabin Councell, and become leaders in our vestries. 1643 *True Informer* 2 Their Majesties Letters under the cabine Signet. 1644 MILTON *Areop.* Wks. 1738 I. 142 Haughtiness of Prelates and cabin Counsellors that usurp'd of late. 1649 —— *Eikon.* iv. (1851) 364 Putting off such wholesome acts and councels, as the politic Cabin at Whitehall had no mind to. *Ibid.* xi. 425 To vindicate and restore the Rights of Parlament invaded by Cabin councels. 1676 W. ROW *Contn. Blair's Autobiog.* xii. (1848) 430 A close cabin council plotting and contriving all things.

8. *Comb.* Chiefly in sense 5, as ***cabin-keeper, -passage, -passenger, -scuttle, -stairs, -window***, etc.; ***cabin-parloured*** (having a parlour no bigger than a ship's cabin); †**cabin-bed**, a berth; **cabin class**, the designation of a type of accommodation in a passenger ship (cf. *first, tourist class*); also *attrib.*; **cabin crew**, the crew members of an aircraft whose principal duty is the care of passengers (or cargo); the flight attendants on an aeroplane; **cabin cruiser**, a cruiser with a cabin for living in (in quot. 1921, a flying-boat); **cabin fever** *N. Amer. colloq.*, lassitude, restlessness, irritability, or aggressiveness resulting from being confined for too long with few or no companions; **cabin ship**, a vessel carrying only one class of cabin passengers. Also CABIN-BOY, -MATE.

1719 DE FOE *Crusoe* (1840) II. ii. 31 He lay in a *cabin-bed. 1929 *Evening News* 18 Nov. 5/5 The plans for the *cabin-class vessels. 1936 *Times* 3 Feb. 17/5 There are four agreements in the North Atlantic passenger route—*i.e.* first-class, cabin, tourist, and third-class. 1954 *Aviation Week* 25 Jan. 39/1 Another film..shows how the *cabin crew, by assuming roles as hosts and hostesses, work together to satisfy the customer. 1986 *Daily Tel.* 17 Feb. 11/7 For would-be air cabin crew the news is discouraging. BA now run a bank of trained part-time stewards/stewardesses, willing to be 'on call' for specified tours of duty. 1921 *Aircraft Year Book* 187 Practical experimental work..was also carried on with the Dayton Wright K.T. '*Cabin Cruiser'. 1928 *Vanity Fair* Aug. 73/1 Among the standard craft..is the 38-foot single cabin cruiser. 1959 *Manchester Guardian* 15 Aug. 5/2 Everywhere in the United States the outboard motor, the cabin cruiser..are to be seen. 1918 'B. M. BOWER' *Cabin Fever* i. 1 The mind fed too long upon monotony succumbs to the insidious mental ailment which the West calls '*cabin fever'. 1924 E. SHEPHARD *Paul Bunyan* 135 But that year they got the spring-fever or cabin-fever or somethin', and got lazy and laid down on their jobs. 1953 E. MUNSTERHJELM *Wind & Caribou* 128 Cabin fever..is an insidious disease which creeps unnoticed upon people who are forced to live together for a long time in cramped quarters. 1980 *Hunting Ann. 1981* 42/2 At first, I figured the post-Christmas grouse forays would be only a cure for the almost terminal case of cabin fever I suffer each winter. 1807 VANCOUVER *Agric. Devon* (1813) 389 *Cabin keepers to shipwrights. 1802 W. TAYLOR in Robberds *Mem.* I. 410 The squeezed, *cabin-parloured houselets of Dover. 1830 GALT *Laurie T.* VII. i. (1849) 300, I took my passage in her —a *cabin-passage. 1760 WESLEY *Jrnl.* 24 Aug., Half..were *cabin passengers. 1851 H. MELVILLE *Whale* xxix. 138 The silent steersman would watch the *cabin-scuttle. 1926 *Daily Colonist* (Victoria, B.C.) 3 July 7/6 (Advt.), Fine Scotch *cabin ships to the old country, and real Scotch hospitality. 1958 B. HAMILTON *Too much of Water* i. 9 What used to be called a cabin ship, with accommodation in a single class. 1743 FIELDING *J. Wild* III. vii. 323 Falling down the *cabbin stairs he dislocated his shoulder.

cabin ('kæbɪn), *v.* [f. the sb., q.v. for Forms.]

1. *intr.* To dwell, lodge, take shelter, in, or as in, a cabin (senses 1–4).

1586 FERNE *Blaz. Gentrie* 49 Flying from their houses, and cabaning in woods and caues. 1588 SHAKS. *Tit. A.* IV. ii. 179 And sucke the Goate, And cabbin in a Caue. 1602 FULBECKE *Pandectes* 32 Vnder the shadow of Scipio the Citie, the Ladie of the world did cabbon. 1611 HEYWOOD *Gold. Age* I. i. Wks. 1874 III. 15 Perpetuall care shall cabin in my heart. 1865 PARKMAN *Champlain* ix. (1875) 298 Bands of Indians cabined along the borders of the cove.

2. *trans.* To lodge, entertain, or shelter, as in a cabin.

1602 FULBECKE *2nd Pt. Parall.* 74 Chast learning cabboned with frugall contentment. 1745 W. THOMPSON *Sickness* p. iv, Rock'd by the blast, and cabin'd in the storm.

3. *trans.* To shut up or confine within narrow and hampering bounds. (Mostly after Shakspere.)

1605 SHAKS. *Macb.* III. iv. 24 Now I am cabin'd, crib'd, confin'd, bound in. 1818 BYRON *Ch. Har.* IV. cxxvi, The faculty divine Is chain'd and tortured—cabin'd, cribb'd, confined. 1846 LYTTON *Lucretia* (1853) 253 [One who] had the authority to cabin his mind in the walls of form. 1871 FREEMAN *Norm. Conq.* (1876) IV. xvii. 58 The newer foundation was cabined, cribbed, and confined in a very narrow space between the Cathedral Church and the buildings of the City.

b. with *in.*

1780 BURKE *Sp. Bristol* Wks. III. 417 They imagine that their souls are cooped and cabined in, unless they have some man..dependent on their mercy.

4. *trans.* To partition *off* into small apartments.

1815 *Hist. J. Decastro* I. 79 The inside of it..is..cabbined off into small apartments.

'**cabin boy.** [f. CABIN *sb.* 5 + BOY.] A boy who waits on the officers and passengers on board.

1726 AMHERST *Terræ Fil.* xiii. 67, I was sent to Oxford, scholar of a college, and my elder brother a cabbin boy to the West-Indies. 1773 *Gentl. Mag.* XLIII. 467 Every soul on board perished, except the cabbin-boy. 1848 MACAULAY *Hist. Eng.* I. iii. 303 Sir Christopher Mings..entered the service as a cabin boy..His cabin boy was Sir John Narborough, and the cabin boy of Sir John Narborough was Sir Cloudesley Shovel.

cabined ('kæbɪnd), *ppl. a.* [f. CABIN *sb.* and *v.* + -ED.] **a.** Made like a cabin; furnished with a cabin. **b.** Confined in narrow space. **c.** *fig.* Cramped, hampered, confined in action, thought, etc.

1592 WYRLEY *Armorie* 146 Cabbind lodgings. 1634 MILTON *Comus* 140 From her cabined loophole peep. 18.. BP. D. WILSON in *Life* (1860) II. xiv. 41, I am in a bholeah or cabined boat. 1854 M. ARNOLD *Poems* (1877) I. 23 Her cabin'd ample spirit. 1863 W. PHILLIPS *Speeches* xii. 266 Cabined American civilization.

cabinet ('kæbɪnɪt), *sb.* Forms: 6–7 **cabanet, cabbonet, cabonet,** 6– **cabinet,** (7 **cabbinet**). [app. Eng. dim. of CABIN *sb.*, as seen by the earlier forms *cabanet, cabonet*, which go with the earlier forms of *cabin*; but in senses 3–6 largely influenced by F. *cabinet*, which according to Scheler and Brachet is not a direct derivative of F. *cabane*, but ad. It. *gabinetto* (= Sp. *gabinete*) 'closet, press, chest of drawers', app. a dialectal It. word going back to the same origin as CABIN *sb.*]

I. A little cabin, room, repository. (Senses 1–3 run parallel to those of BOWER 1–3.)

†**1. a.** A little cabin, hut, soldier's tent; a rustic cottage; a dwelling, lodging, tabernacle; a den or hole of a beast. *Obs.*

1572 DIGGES *Stratiot.* (1579) 120 The Lance Knights encamp always in the field very strongly, two or three to a Cabbonet. 1597 LYLY *Wom. in Moone* IV. i. 194 He hath thrust me from his cabanet. 1607 TOPSELL *Four-f. Beasts* 105 A flock of..four-footed beasts, came about their cabanet.

β. 1579 FENTON *Guicciard.* IV. (1599) 178 The whole campe was constrained..to pitch their Cabinets within the ditches. 1591 SPENSER *Daphn.* 558, I him desyrde sith daie was overcast..To turne aside unto my cabinet, And staie with me. 1592 SHAKS. *Ven. & Ad.* 853 The gentle larke..From his moyst cabinet mounts vp on hie. *a* 1640 DAY *Peregr. Schol.* (1881) 54 Where snakes..and half-starvd crocodiles made them sommer beds and winter cabbinets.

†**b.** *fig.* 'Tabernacle'. *Obs.*

1614 T. ADAMS *Devill's Banq.* 205 Whereas the Soule might dwell in the body..shee findes it a crazy, sickish, rotten cabinet. 1630 BRATHWAIT *Eng. Gentl.* (1641) 413/1 Their bodies..were too fraile Cabonets for such rich eminences to lodge in.

†**2.** A summer-house or bower in a garden. *Obs.*

1579 SPENSER *Sheph. Cal.* Dec. 17 The greene cabinet. 1590 —— *F.Q.* II. xii. 83 Their Gardens did deface, Their Arbers spoyld, their Cabinets suppresse. 1610 FOLKINGHAM *Art of Survey* I. xii. 44 Externall, as Groues, Arbours, Bowers, Cabinets, Allies, Ambulatories. 1737 MILLER *Gard. Dict., Cabinet*, in a Garden, is a Conveniency which differs from an Arbour, in this; that an Arbour..is of a great Length..but a Cabinet is either square, circular, or in Cants, making a kind of a Salon.

3. A small chamber or room; a private apartment, a boudoir. *arch.* or *Obs.*

1565 EARL BEDFORD in Ellis *Orig. Lett.* I. 186 II. 210 Ther is a cabinet abowte xii footes square, in the same a lyttle lowe reposinge bedde, and a table, at the which ther were syttinge at the supper the Quene..and David [Rizzio]. 1603 HOLLAND *Plutarch's Mor.* 1133 Sending us unto womens chambers and cabinets. 1609 BIBLE (Douay) *Gen.* vi. 14 Cabinets shalt thou make in the arke. 1727 SWIFT *Gulliver* II. iii. 118 The king, who was then retired to his cabinet. 1814 SCOTT *Wav.* I. ii. 20 The stained window of the gloomy cabinet in which they were seated. 1822 W. IRVING *Braceb. Hall* ii. 9 A small cabinet which he calls his study.

†**4.** A room devoted to the arrangement or display of works of art and objects of vertu; a museum, picture-gallery, etc. *Obs.* or *arch.*

1676 HOBBES *Iliad* (1686) Pref. 7 Which [a painting]..will not be worthy to be plac'd in a Cabinet. 1727 POPE, etc. *Art Sinking* 101 A curious person in a cabinet of antique statues, etc. 1796 J. OWEN *Trav. Europe* II. 124 The Musæum at Portici is the most interesting cabinet in Europe, to a man not professedly scientific. The generality of cabinets are schools of study, rather than exhibitions.

5. A case for the safe custody of jewels, or other valuables, letters, documents, etc.; and thus, a repository or case, often itself forming an ornamental piece of furniture, fitted with compartments, drawers, shelves, etc., for the proper preservation and display of a collection of specimens. Also, one containing a radio or television receiver or the like.

c 1550 in *Our Eng. Home* (1861) 164 Fayre large cabonett, covered with crimson vellet..with the Kings armes crowned. *a* 1631 DONNE *Select.* (1840) 24 The best jewel in the best cabinet. 1680 SIR C. LYTTELTON in *Hatton Corr.* (1878) 232 Tother day, in shifting of a cabinet..I found abundance of y^r letters. 1742 CHESTERF. *Lett.* I. lxxxix. 250 That fine wood, of which you see screens, cabinets, and tea-tables. 1839 THIRLWALL *Greece* III. 129 Papers had been found in Alexander's cabinet, containing the outlines of some vast projects. 1875 JEVONS *Money* (1878) 44 In innumerable cabinets may be found series of tin coins. 1934 WEBSTER, *Console*..a cabinet, often decorated, for a radio receiving set, and designed to be placed against a wall. 1962 A. NISBETT *Technique Sound Studio* 245 Many people..'like a loudspeaker to sound like a loudspeaker', i.e., to exhibit cone and cabinet resonances. *Ibid.* 251 *Enclosure*, a loudspeaker cabinet.

†**6.** *fig.* A secret receptacle, treasure-chamber, store-house; *arcanum*, etc. *Obs.*

1549 *Compl. Scot.* (1873) 7, I socht all the secreit corneris of my gazophile..vitht in the cabinet of my interior thochtis. 1634 SANDERSON *Serm.* II. 312 That counsel of His, which is lockt up in the cabinet of His secret will. 1660 *Trial Regic.* 173, I look upon the Nation as the Cabinet of the world. 1667 OLDENBURG in *Phil. Trans.* II. 411 By Anatomy we have sometimes enter'd into the Chambers and Cabinets of Animal Functions.

¶ Short for *cabinet photograph* (11, 14).

II. In politics.

7. a. As a specific use of 3: The private room in which the confidential advisers of the sovereign or chief ministers of a country meet; the council-chamber. Originally in the literal sense; now taken chiefly for what goes on or is transacted there, i.e. political consultation and action, as 'the field' is taken for 'fighting, warlike action'.

1607–12 [see 8 a]. 1625 W. YONGE *Diary* (1848) 83 The King made choice of six of the nobility for his Council of the Cabinet. 1692 DRYDEN *St. Euremont's Ess.* 90 Weak, unactive, and purely for the Cabinet. 1693 *Mem. Ct. Teckely* II. 117 Neither a Man of the Cabinet, nor of the War. 1700 DRYDEN *Fabl.* Ded., You began in the Cabinet what you afterwards practis'd in the Camp. 1804 WELLINGTON *Let.* in Gurw. *Disp.* III. 145 Equally great in the cabinet as in the field. 1860 TROLLOPE *Framley P.* i. 12 Harold in early life had intended himself for the cabinet.

b. The body of persons who meet in such a cabinet; that limited number of the ministers of the sovereign or head of the state who are in a more confidential position and have, in effect, with the head of the state, the determination and administration of affairs.

Formerly called more fully the *Cabinet Council*, as distinguished from the *Privy Council*, and as meeting in the cabinet; the later abbreviation is like the use of 'the House', 'the field', for those who fill or frequent it, and would be encouraged by such expressions as 'he is of the cabinet' used of Vane by Roe, 1630. ***member of the cabinet*** is later.

1644 *Mercurius Brit.* 44. 347 According to..the practice of your Cabinet or Junto; but our State Committee know better. 1692 DRYDEN *St. Euremont's Ess.* 108 Every thing was then managed by the jealousie of her Mysterious Cabinet. *a* 1734 NORTH *Lives* I. 380 As for his lordship's being taken into the cabinet. 1796 MORSE *Amer. Geog.* II. 6 The cabinets of Europe..have endeavoured to keep up a constant equilibrium between the different states. 1844 H. H. WILSON *Brit. India* II. i, He had been authorised by the Prince Regent to attempt the formation of a cabinet. 1848 MACAULAY *Hist. Eng.* I. 211 Few things in our history are more curious than the origin and growth of the power now possessed by the Cabinet. 1874 BANCROFT *Footpr. Time* iii. 236 The members of the President's Cabinet.

†**c.** A meeting of this body. Now called a 'Cabinet council', or 'meeting of the Cabinet'.

(What is now called 'the Cabinet' was formerly 'the Cabinet Council', and what is now 'a Cabinet Council' was formerly termed 'a Cabinet'.)

1711 SWIFT *Lett.* (1768) III. 195 To day the duke was forced to go to the race while the cabinet was held. 1788–9 DK. LEEDS *Polit. Mem.* (1884) 140 There was a Cabinet at my office. 1805 PITT in Ld. Stanhope *Life* III. 318 A Cabinet is summoned for twelve to-morrow.

8. Cabinet Council: **a.** the earlier appellation of the body now styled ***the Cabinet***: see 7 b.

Apparently introduced, at the accession of Charles I, in 1625; but the expression ***cabinet counsel*** = counsel given privately or secretly in the cabinet or private apartment, occurs earlier and, from the confusion of *counsel* and *council*, was prob. a factor in the name: see *Cabinet Counsellor* in 9.

[1607–12 BACON *Counsel, Ess.* (Arb.) 318 For which inconveniences the doctrine of Italy, and practize of Fraunce, [ed. 1625 in some Kings times] hath introduced Cabanett Councelles [ed. 1612 Cabanet counsels; 1625 Cabinet counsels], a remedy worse than the disease. 1623 MASSINGER *Dk. Milan* II. i. 10 No, those are cabinet councils, And not to be communicated, but To such as are his own, and sure.]

1632 MASSINGER *Maid of Hon.* I. i. 6 Though a counsellor of state, I am not of the cabinet council. 1646–7 CLARENDON *Hist. Reb.* (1702) I. II. 117 These persons made up the Committee of State (which was reproachfully after call'd the Juncto, and enviously then in the Court the Cabinet Council). *Ibid.* II. §61 That Committee of the Council which used to be consulted in secret affairs. 1649 SELDEN *Laws Eng.* I. (1739) 201 The sense of State once contracted into a Privy Council, is soon recontracted into a Cabinet-Council, and last of all into a Favourite or two. 1668 HOWE *Bless. Righteous* Wks. (1834) 250/2 To know his [i.e. God's] Secrets; to be as it were of the Cabinet-Council. 1727 SWIFT *To very yng. Lady*, Never take a favourite waiting-maid into your cabinet-council. *a* 1734 NORTH *Lives* II. 51 Thus the cabinet council which at first was but in the nature of a private conversation, came to be a formal council, and had the direction of most transactions of the Government. 1846 MCCULLOCH *Acc. Brit. Empire* (1854) II. 143 Cabinet Council.—This body, though without any recognised legal existence, constitutes, in effect, the government of the country. It consists of a certain number of privy councillors, comprising the principal ministers of the Crown for the time being, who are summoned to attend at each meeting.

b. *now*, A meeting or consultation of the 'cabinet'.

1679 J. GOODMAN *Penitent Pardon.* I. iii. (1713) 54 God Almighty..never..leaves them to guess at the transactions in his Cabinet-Council. 1688 EVELYN *Mem.* (1857) II. 295 Carried to Newgate, after examination at the Cabinet

Council. **1726** BERKELEY in Fraser *Life* iv. (1871) 138 The point was carried..in the cabinet council.

9. Cabinet Counsellor, a private counsellor; a member of the Cabinet.

1611 SPEED *Hist. Gt. Brit.* IX. vi. 3 For a Cabanet-Counsellour at all times, he had his owne Mother, Matildis the Empresse. **1633** MASSINGER *Guardian* II. iii, You are still my cabinet counsellors. **1640** BASTWICK *Lord Bps.* i. A iv, It seems he is one of Christs Cabinet Counsellors, that he is so intimately privie to his thoughts.

III. *Attrib.* and in *Comb.*

10. Of the cabinet, as a private place; private, secret.

1607–23 *Cabinet Counsel* [see 8]. **1611–40** *Cabinet Counsellor* [see 9]. **1638** *Penit. Conf.* vi. (1657) 96 That laid open their Cabinet sins. **1654** WARREN *Unbelievers* 119 There are some Cabinet, secret thoughts, and purposes in God. **1655** FULLER *Ch. Hist.* I. 37 As if others had not received such private Instructions as themselves, being Cabinet-Historians. *a* **1674** CLARENDON *Hist. Reb.* (1704) III. XI. 197 He was likewise very strict in observing the hours of his private Cabinet Devotions.

11. Of such value, beauty, or size, as to be fitted for a private chamber, or kept in a cabinet. Sometimes more or less technical, as in ***cabinet edition***, one smaller and less costly than a library edition, but tastefully rather than cheaply got up; ***cabinet organ***, 'a superior class and size of reed organ'; ***cabinet photograph*** (see *cabinet-sized* in 14); ***cabinet piano***, etc.

1696 PHILLIPS, *Cabinet Organ*, a Portative Organ. **1708** KERSEY, *Cabinet-organ*, a little Organ, that may be easily carry'd, or remov'd from one Place to another. **1711** SHAFTESB. *Charac.* (1737) II. 430 One admires musick and paintings, cabinet-curiositys, and in-door ornaments. **1750** BEAWES *Lex Mercat.* (1752) 859 Cabinet Wares. **1817** L. HUNT *Let.* in *Gentl. Mag.* May (1876) 601 A cabinet piano. **1824** MISS MITFORD *Village* Ser. I. (1863) 147 It is quite a cabinet picture. **1859** GULLICK & TIMBS *Paint.* 18 Cabinet pictures are so named because they are so small in size as to be readily contained in a cabinet. *Mod.* The Cabinet edition of Macaulay.

12. Fit for cabinet making.

1849 FREESE *Comm. Class-bk.* 17 Cabinet woods, are the qualities used for making all kinds of household furniture, as mahogany, rose-wood, cedar, satin-wood.

13. Of or pertaining to the political cabinet, as ***cabinet minister***, etc.

1632, etc. [see sense 8]. **1806** *Deb. Congress* 5 Mar. (1852) 561 My answer was (and from a Cabinet Minister too) 'There is no longer any cabinet.' *Ibid.* 13 Mar. 765 The gentleman's [*sc.* Mirabeau's] fondness for Cabinet rank and Utopian glory. **1817** *Parl. Deb.* 1356 Did any body suppose that three years spent in a cabinet office were sufficient to entitle the individual to a cabinet pension? **1825** *Ann. Reg. 1812* (Chron.) 233 List of His Majesty's Ministers. January, 1812. Cabinet Ministers. Earl Camden..Lord President of the Council. **1867** W. BAGEHOT *Eng. Constitution* i. 22 This critical opposition is the consequence of cabinet government. **1938** *Ann. Reg. 1937* 31 The second reading of the Ministers of the Crown Bill..was moved on April 12 by Sir John J. Simon, who pointed out that it was for the first time placing on the Statute-book the terms 'Cabinet' and 'Cabinet Minister'.

14. *Comb.* **cabinet-box** = CABINET 5: **cabinet-founder; cabinet pudding**, a pudding made of bread or cake, dried fruit, eggs and milk, usually served hot with a sauce; **cabinet-sized** *a.*, of fit size for placing in a cabinet; (a photograph) of the size larger than a carte-de-visite.

1655 MRQ. WORC. *Cent. Inv.* Index 7 A total locking of Cabinet-boxes. **1800** *New Ann. Directory* 227 Underhill, J., Cabinet-founder and Ironmonger. **1821** KITCHINER *Cook's Oracle* (ed. 3) 430 Newcastle or Cabinet Pudding. Butter a half melon mould, or quart basin, and stick all round with dried cherries, or fine raisins, and fill up with bread and butter. **1822** UDE *French Cook* (ed. 7) 348 Cabinet Pudding or Chancellor's Pudding. **1883** LLOYD *Ebb & Flow* II. 186 A nice cabinet-sized photograph of her. **1958** B. HAMILTON *Too much of Water* i. 18 Picking with extreme caution at the last vestiges of a sort of cabinet pudding.

'cabinet, *v.* Pa. t. and pple. **-eted.** [f. prec.] *trans.* To enclose in or as in a cabinet.

c **1642** *Observator Defended* 11 That government, which our Laws are lockt and cabenetted in. *a* **1658** HEWYTT *Serm.* 87 (R.) To adore the casket, and contemn the jewel that is cabinetted in it. **1660** *Charac. Italy* 80 The Priest, who as yet was cabinetted up in the Merchants house. **1854** J. WARTER *Last of Old Sq.* v. 44 That a heart of hearts was cabinetted in a person the most attractive.

cabinetable ('kæbɪnɪtəb(ə)l), *a. colloq.* [f. CABINET *sb.* + -ABLE.] That is fit to be a member of a political cabinet.

1896 *Daily News* 28 Nov. 4/7 The Prime Minister is.. chosen..practically by public opinion, and a small knot of what we may call 'Cabinetable' men. **1905** *Westm. Gaz.* 5 Dec. 4/3 There is rather an unusually strong reserve of 'Cabinet-able' men.

'cabineted, *ppl. a. rare.* Enclosed as in a cabinet; shut up.

1680 CHARNOCK *Wks.* (1864) I. 53 Good men have providence cabineted in a promise. **18..** BLACKIE *Poems*, The cabineted skeleton Of fallen majesty!

cabine'teer. *nonce-wd.* One who has official connexion with a cabinet.

1837 *Fraser's Mag.* XVI. 531 Hume is the sole historian of whom the Cabineteer ever heard.

'cabinet-,maker.

1. One whose business it is to make cabinets (sense 5), and the finer kind of joiner's work.

1681 *Trial S. Colledge* 59 *Mr. Att. Gen.* What Trade are you? *Mr. Hickman.* A Cabinet-maker. **1689** LUTTRELL *Brief Rel.* (1857) I. 614 One Johnson, a popish cabinet maker. **1727** SWIFT *Gulliver* II. iii. The queen commanded her own cabinet-maker to contrive a box. **1872** YEATS *Techn. Hist. Comm.* 43 Joiners' and cabinet-makers' work.

2. *casual.* One who constructs a political cabinet.

1884 *Boston* (Mass.) *Jrnl.* 22 Nov. 2/4 The Cabinet-makers, office-seekers, and schemers who abound in Washington.

Hence **'cabinet ,making**, the cabinet-maker's occupation; the construction of a political cabinet.

1813 in *Examiner* 1 Feb. 71/2 They'll fit you..whatever your trade is; (Except it be Cabinet-making). **1882** BESANT *All Sorts* 116 The gentle craft of cabinet-making. **1885** *Pall Mall G.* 16 June 1/2 Hitches are inevitable whenever Cabinet-making is undertaken.

'cabinless, *a.* [f. CABIN *sb.* 5 + -LESS.] Not furnished with a cabin.

1850 S. ALLEN in D. J. Browne *Amer. Poultry Yd.* 310 Small dirty, cabinless shallops, of a few tons burthen. **1890** *Harper's Mag.* Mar. 558/1 The *topi*..are deckless and cabinless.

cabir, obs. form of CABER.

cabish, obs. form of CABBAGE.

cable ('keɪb(ə)l), *sb.* Forms: 3–4 **kable**, 5–7 **cabul(le, cabyl, -il, -ille, -el, -ell, -elle**, (5–6 **gable, gabyll**), 3– **cable**. [ME. *cable, cabel, kable*, identical with Du. *kabel*, MDu. *cābel*, MLG. *kabel*, MHG. and Ger. *kabel*, all app. from Romanic: cf. F. *câble*, Sp. *cable*, Pg. *cabre*, all meaning 'cable', It. *cappio* sliding knot, noose, gin:—late L. *capulum, caplum* a halter for catching or fastening cattle, according to Isidore f. *capĕre* to take 'quod eo indomita jumenta comprehendantur': cf. *capulum, -us*, 'handle, haft', *capulā-re* to take, catch, etc.

(There are difficulties as to F. *câble*, older forms of which were *caable, chaable, chéable, châble*, which point, through **cadable*, to a L. **catabola* a kind of BALLISTA for hurling stones, etc., in which sense *chaable* also occurs: see *Cabulus* in Du Cange. Littré supposes an early confusion between this and **cable* from Isidore's *capulum*; others think that as the *catabola* was put in motion with ropes, it may be the real source. But this does not account for the Sp. and It. words.]

1. a. A strong thick rope, originally of hemp or other fibre, now also of strands of iron wire.

Originally a stout rope of any thickness, but now, in nautical use, a cable (of hemp, jute, etc.) is 10 inches in circumference and upwards; ropes of less thickness being called *cablets* or *hawsers*. In other than nautical use (see 2), *rope* is commonly used when the material is hemp or fibre (as in the 'rope' by which a train is drawn up an incline), and *cable* when the material is wire.

c **1205** LAY. 1338 He hihte hondlien kablen [*c* **1275** cables]. *c* **1320** *Sir Guy* 4613 Sche come..Doun of þe castel in sel-coupe wise Bi on cable alle sleyeliche. *c* **1340** *Cursor M.* 24848 (Fairf.) þe mast hit shoke, þe cablis [*earlier MSS.* cordis] brast. *c* **1392** CHAUCER *Compl. Venus* 33 þaughe Ialousye wer hanged by a Kable Sheo wolde al knowe. *c* **1420** *Chron. Vilod.* 862 Alle þe gables of þe shippe þey broston a to. **1535** COVERDALE *Eccles.* iv. 12 A threfolde cable is not lightly broken. **1598** BARRET *Theor. Warres* v. iii. 135 Smal cables for the artillery. **1626** G. SANDYS *Ovid's Met.* VIII. 170 He..ouerthrowes With cabels, and innumerable blowes, The sturdy Oke. **1708** J. C. *Compl. Collier* (1845) 34 A Cable of three inches round and of good Stuff, will do better for Coal-work. **1842** *Penny Cycl.* XXIII. 336/2 The platform [of a suspension-bridge at the Isle of Bourbon] is suspended from four cables..and each cable consists of fifteen bundles of eighty wires each.

b. *fig.*

1600 HOOKER *Eccl. Pol.* VII. xviii. §10 The whole body politic should be..a threefold cable. **1604** SHAKS. *Oth.* I. ii. 17 He will..put vpon you what restraint or greeuance The Law..will giue him Cable. **1609** HOLLAND *Amm. Marcell.* XXIX. i. 351 He unfolded..a huge long cable of villanies. **1616** R. C. *Times' Whis.* VI. 2343 Linckt together with sinnes ougly cable.

c. ***it is easier for a cable to go through the eye of a needle***, a variant rendering of Matt. xix. 24, Mark x. 25, Luke xviii. 25, adopted by Sir J. Cheke, and cited by many writers.

[This represents a variant interpretation of Gr. κάμηλον in this passage, mentioned already by Cyril of Alexandria in the 5th c. Subsequently a variant reading κάμιλον (found in several late cursive MSS.) was associated with this rendering, and Suidas (? 11th c.) makes distinct words of κάμιλος 'cable', κάμηλος camel. Some Mod.Gr. dictionaries have also κάμιλος cable.]

c **1530** MORE *De Quatuor Nouiss.* Wks. (1557) 92 It were as harde for the riche manne to come into heauen, as a great cable or a Camel to go through a nedles eye. *c* **1550** CHEKE *Matt.* xix. 24 It is easier for a cable to passe thorough a nedels eie, yen for a rich man to enter in to yᵉ kingdoom of heaven. [*Marg. note.* Although yᵗ Suidas seem to sai κάμιλος to be for a cable roop, and κάμηλος for yᵉ beest, iet theophylactus..and Celius..taak κάμηλος to be booỳ yᵉ beest and yᵉ cable, as moost season agreeabli serveth heer.] **1581** MARBECK *Bk. of Notes* 540 It is impossible for a Camell (or Cable, that is a great rope of a ship)..to go through a needles eye. **1657** COLVIL *Whig's Supplic.* (1695) 49 An honest Clergyman will be When Cable passeth Needles eye. **1840** MARRYAT *Olla Podr.*, *S.W. & by W.* ¾ *W.*, If he were as incompetent as a camel (or, as they say at sea, a cable) to pass through the eye of a needle.

d. Short for *cable-stitch* (see 7).

1943 *Mary Thomas's Bk. Knitting Patt.* 74 The effect is a vertical Waved Rib, not a Cable.

2. a. *spec.* (*Naut.*) The strong thick rope to which a ship's anchor is fastened; and by transference, anything used for the same purpose, as a chain of iron links (***chain cable***).

'*Stream-cable*, a hawser or rope something smaller than the bower, used to move or hold the ship temporarily during a calm in a river or haven, sheltered from the wind and sea, etc.' (Smyth *Sailor's Word-bk.*)

c **1325** *E.E. Allit. P.* B. 418 With-outen mast, oþer myke, oþer myry bawe-lyne, Kable, oþer capstan to clyppe to her ankrez. *c* **1400** *Destr. Troy* 2848 þai caste ancres full kene with cables to grounde. **1490** CAXTON *Eneydos* xxvii. 96 Eneas..cutte asondre the cables that with helde the shippe within the hauen. **1593** SHAKS. *3 Hen. VI*, v. iv. 4 The Cable broke, the holding-Anchor lost. **1627** CAPT. SMITH *Seaman's Gram.* vii. 30 The Cables also carry a proportion to the Anchors, but if it be not three strond, it is accounted but a Hawser. **1769** FALCONER *Dict. Marine* (1789) s.v. *Admiral*, They may be ready to cut or slip the cables when they shall be too much hurried to weigh their anchors. **1836** W. IRVING *Astoria* I. 185 Slip the cable and endeavour to get to sea. **1885** ANNANDALE *Imp. Dict.* s.v., Chain-cables have now almost superseded rope-cables.

b. *fig.* Also in phr. ***to cut (the) cable(s)***: to depart; to make a break.

1635 QUARLES *Embl.* III. xi. (1718) 169 Pray'r is the Cable, at whose end appears The anchor hope. **1677** YARRANTON *Engl. Improv.* 22 The grand Banks..shall be the Anchor and Cable of all smaller Banks. **1851** MAYHEW *Lond. Labour* I. 360 Her cable had run out, and she died. **1859** GEO. ELIOT *Let.* 8 June (1954) III. 79, I want to get rid of this house —cut cables and drift about. **1895** G. B. SHAW *Let.* 30 Jan. (1965) 480 By cutting the cable before the supplies are exhausted you will prove that you are not merely making the best of a bad job. **1917** —— *Matter with Ireland* (1962) 156 Any nation less sheepish than the English would have cut the cable long ago and insisted on having a Parliament of its own for its own affairs.

c. ***a cable*** or ***cable's length***, as a unit of measurement, 'about 100 fathoms; in marine charts 607·56 feet, or one-tenth of a sea mile' (Adml. Smyth).

1555 EDEN *Decades W. Ind.* (Arb.) 381 Redde cliffes with white strakes like wayes a cable length a piece. **1665** *Duke of York's Fight. Instr.* xiv, To keep about the distance of half a cable from one another. **1702** *Lond. Gaz.* No. 3844/4 The Two Buoys..being distant near the Length of Two Cables. **1769** FALCONER *Dict. Marine* (1789) *Cable*..a measure of 120 fathoms, called by the English seamen a cable's length. **1778** CAPT. MILLER in Nicolas *Disp. Nelson* (1846) VII. Introd. 159 We got within a cable and a half of her. **1813** SOUTHEY *Nelson* (1854) 167 He veered half a cable, and instantly opened a tremendous fire. **1840** R. DANA *Bef. Mast* xi. 26 Within two cable lengths of the shore.

3. *Telegraphy.* **a.** A rope-like line used for submarine telegraphs, containing the wires along which the electric current passes, embedded in gutta percha or other insulating substance, and encased in an external sheathing of strong wire strands, resembling the wire cable of sense 1. Also **b.** a bundle of insulated wires, passing through a pipe laid underground in streets, etc.

1854 *Specif. Brett's Patent* No. 10939. 21 This said cable or rope I denominate my Oceanic Line. **1852** *Leisure Hour* Sept. 591 Complimentary messages were transmitted by means of the cable through the waters to Dover. **1855** WHEATSTONE *Roy. Soc. Proc.* VII. 328 Experiments made with the submarine cable of the Mediterranean Electric Telegraph. **1858** *Times Ann. Summary* 89 The unfortunate fracture of the oceanic cable. **1864** W. CROOKES *Q. Jrnl. Science* I. 44 The Atlantic Cable and its Teachings. **1865** RUSSELL *Atlantic Telegr.* 2 Mr. Wheatstone..as early as 1840 brought before the House of Commons the project of a cable to be laid between Dover and Calais. **1880** *Times* 17 Dec. 5/6 [She] is reported by cable to have put into St. Thomas. **1887** *Telegr. Jrnl.* 4 Mar. 203/2 In our system, the cables can be easily drawn out of the iron pipes if occasion demands it.

c. A cable message, a CABLEGRAM.

1883 *Bread-Winners* 175 It riled me to have to pay for two cables. **1884** *Pall Mall G.* 6 Aug. 11/1, I was desired by my chief in New York to..give them a long 'cable'. **1886** *Daily News* 4 June 6/4 The General..had received cables of greeting from the 'comrades' in Australasia and America.

d. Short for *cable television* (see 7).

1970 *Globe & Mail* (Toronto) 25 Sept. 14/8 Channel 12.. announced..that it would fight any attempt to drop it from cable. **1971** T. LEDBETTER in *Cable Television in Cities* 7/1 Cable was first introduced in remote mountainous areas where broadcast TV reception was poor. **1977** *Rep. Comm. Future of Broadcasting* 21 in *Parl. Papers 1976* (Cmnd. 6753) VI. 1 Cable is bound to give the viewer an increase in the choice of programmes at any given time. **1982** L. BLOCK *Eight Million Ways to Die* iv. 49 I'm watching a movie on cable. **1983** *Listener* 12 May 6/3 Cable..is an extremely expensive medium unless one can think of something remunerative which people want and which only cable can do. **1985** *Village Voice* (N.Y.) 8 Jan. 18/2 Cable's roots, after all, lie in the appropriation of over-the-air television signals ..and the reselling of those signals for a profit.

4. *Arch.*, *Goldsmith's work*, etc. Also ***cable-moulding***. A convex moulding or ornament made in the form of a rope.

1859 TURNER *Dom. Archit.* III. i. 9 Norman ornaments.. particularly the billet and the cable. *Ibid.* ii. vii. 359 The cornice is the cable-moulding on a large scale. **1862** *Athenæum* 30 Aug. 277 A figure of Science, on a coral base, with a cable border. **1877** W. JONES *Finger-ring* L. 140 The outer edge..is also decorated with a heavy cable-moulding.

5. (See quot.)

1877 PEACOCK *N.W. Lincoln. Gloss.* (E.D.S.) *Cable*, a long narrow strip of ground.

6. *Attrib.* and *Comb.*a. (senses 1, 2) ***cable-chain, -coil, -maker, -roots, -traction***; (sense 3) ***cable-advice, -despatch, -layer, -laying, -man, -message, -tank***; (sense 4) ***cable-border, moulding, pattern***, etc.

1882 *Mod. Trade Circular*, Further *cable advices from the Colonies. **1886** *Pall Mall G.* 27 Aug. 11/2 The *cable-chain makers..factory men, who make the marine or cable chains. **1667** DENHAM *Direct. Painter* II. ix. 24 See that thou ..spoil All their Sea-market, and their *Cable-coyl. **1908** *Daily Chron.* 25 Aug. 3/3 There is only room in the hearts.. of men for..one *cable-layer. **1901** *Westm. Gaz.* 17 Aug. 3/2 The primary object of *cable-laying is to facilitate communications. **1483** CAXTON *G. de la Tour* F j, A roper or *cable maker. **1865** *Daily Tel.* 19 Aug. 4/4 Mr. Canning showed the cable and the stab to the *cablemen. **1877** *Daily News* 3 Nov. 6/5 The following *cable message has been received..from New York. **1611** BEAUM. & FL. *Philaster* v. iii, Pines, whose *cable roots Held out a thousand storms. **1865** *Sat. Rev.* 12 Aug. 192 The first defect was occasioned —[by] the dropping of a fragment of wire into the *cable-tank. **1887** *Cable traction [see *cable-grip* below].

b. (sense 3 d) ***cable channel, company, movie, operator, service, show, subscriber, system***, etc.; ***cable-carried*** adj.

1962 *Television Soc. Jrnl.* X. 88/2 The system to be described, that is the coaxial cable v.h.f. system, was conceived on a rather different basis. **1971** T. LEDBETTER in C. Tate *Cable Television in Cities* 7/2 Cable subscribers in an isolated Pennsylvania town..actually got better reception.. than people living in Philadelphia. **1976** *National Observer* (U.S.) 18 Dec. 9/3 The FCC public-access doctrine.. requires cable operators regularly to turn over time free or at reduced rate, so local individuals..and community groups can produce their shows. **1981** B. PAULU *Television & Radio in U.K.* vi. 99 Cable services undoubtedly will continue... Currently the cable companies are losing customers as UHF broadcast coverage improves. **1982** *Daily Tel.* 11 Oct. 14/3 Its arguments are that a free cable system will lower standards, will be unfair to rural communities, and will favour the rich against the poor. **1983** *Wall St. Jrnl.* 5 Jan. 1/4, I got a room with droopy drapes..and free cable movies. **1983** *Listener* 3 Feb. 38/2 It is here, on the many cable-carried public stations, that *Sesame Street* can be seen. **1983** *Fortune* 2 May 125/1 Nickelodeon,..a children's cable channel.., has no ads... Some cable shows for kids carry ads.

7. Special comb.: **cable-bends, cable-buoy**, (see quot.); **cable-car**, a carriage moved by a chain or cable, e.g. on an overhead cable-way; **cable-carrier**, a system of tubs or buckets slung from an overhead cable for the purpose of carrying heavy materials across a space; **cable-grip** (see GRIP *sb.*[1] 5 b); so ***cable-gripper, -gripping***; **cable-hanger** (see quots.); **cable-hatband**, a twisted cord of gold, silver, or silk, worn round the hat (Halliw.); **cable-laid** *a.* (see quot.); **cable pattern** (see quot.); **cable-railroad, -railway, -road**, one along which carriages are drawn by an endless cable; **cable-range**, a given length of cable; a range of coils or rolls of cable; **cable-rope** = sense 1; also, cable-laid rope; **cable-ship**, a ship used to lay a submarine cable; **cable-station**, a station from which a cable message may be sent; **cable-stitch**, any of various twisted rope-like stitches in knitting and embroidery; **cable-stock**, the capstan; **cable system**, a system of traction by cable, or of telegraphy by submarine cables; **cable television, TV**, a system of television rediffusion whereby signals from a distant station are picked up by an antenna and transmitted by cable to subscribers' sets; see TELEVISION 1 a; **cable-tier**, the place in a hold, or between decks, where the cables are coiled away; **cable-tools** (see quot.); **cable tramway** (see quot. 1887); **cablevision** = *cable television* above (also a proprietary term in the U.S.); **cable-way**, (*a*) = *cable-railroad*; (*b*) an overhead cable and apparatus for the transport of materials or passengers.

1867 SMYTH *Sailor's Word-bk.*, **Cable-bends*, two small ropes for lashing the end of a hempen cable to its own part, in order to secure the clinch by which it is fastened to the anchor-ring. **1769** FALCONER *Dict. Marine* (1789) **Cable-Buoys*, common casks employed to buoy up the cables. **1887** J. B. SMITH *Cable Traction* 42 The excellent control of the *cable cars is..admirably demonstrated upon this line. **1888** S. HALE *Lett.* (1919) 200 Two rival processions which encumbered the streets..almost prevented our getting there in the cable-car. **1897** 'MARK TWAIN' *Following Equator* xvi. 161 It has an elaborate system of cable car service. **1902** E. BANKS *Newspaper Girl* 254, I..took a cable car for Capitol Hill. *a* **1884** KNIGHT *Dict. Mech.* Suppl., **Cable Carrier*, a means of transporting rough materials; stone, sand, lime, coal, earth, by a suspended bucket traveling on a wire cable. **1904** *Westm. Gaz.* 21 Nov. 8/2 Mr. Wall has discontinued the use of the overhead cable-carrier. **1887** J. B. SMITH *Cable Traction* 17 Elevated cable traction systems, for which he devised an ingenious *cable grip or catch. **1947** *Life* 24 Feb. 16 Cable grip fits into the slot between the tracks. With it the gripman inside the car can grasp or release the cable, which moves at a constant 9·5 mph. *a* **1877** KNIGHT *Dict. Mech.* I. 419/1 **Cable-gripper*, a lever compressor over the cable-well, and by which the cable is stopped from running out. **1887** J. B. SMITH *Cable Traction* 30 The intermediate slot through which the cable gripper passed into the interior of the tube. *Ibid.* 16 A able-gripping apparatus fitted with vertically moving clamping jaws. **1732** DE FOE *Tour Gt. Brit.* (1769) I. 149 Persons who dredge or fish for Oysters [on the Medway], not being free of the Fishery, are called *Cable-hangers. **1599** B. JONSON *Ev. Man out Hum.* Induct., Wearing a pyed feather The *cable hatband, or the three-piled ruff. **1602** MARSTON *Ant. & Mell.* II. i. (N.) More cable, till he had as much as my cable-hatband to fence him. **1723** *Lond. Gaz.* No. 6129/3 Stolen from the Fifth Moorings, Eleven Fathom of Eleven Inch *Cable laid Pendant. **1769** FALCONER *Dict. Marine* (1789) s.v. *Ropes*, Ropes are either cable-laid or hawser-laid: the former are composed of nine strands, viz. three great strands, each of which is composed of three smaller strands. **1882** CAULFEILD & SAWARD *Dict. Needlework* 287/1 *Cable Pattern.—This is also known as Chain Stitch. **1887** J. B. SMITH *Cable Traction* 33 The Claystreet *cable railroad was opened for public traffic in August, 1873. *Ibid.* 15 The success that attended the working performances of early *cable railways. **1883** W. C. RUSSELL *Sea Queen* II. ii. 34 The men were set to work to get the *cable-range along, ready for bringing up. **1882** *Ideographic* (San Francisco) 25 July 2/3 The *cable- or 'grip' road, as they term it in Cincinnati. **1523** SKELTON *Garl. Laurel* 833 From the anker he kutteth the *gabyll rope. **1556** *Chron. Gr. Friars* (1852) 53 At the west ende of Powlles stepull was tayed a cabelle roppe. **1711** *Lond. Gaz.* No. 4882/3 About sixty Fathom of Cable Rope, about nine Inches Circumference. **1885** *Electrician* XIV. 184/1 An additional cable..has been laid to Jersey by the Post Office's new telegraph *cable ship 'Monarch'. **1907** *Daily Chron.* 18 Jan. 7/4 The cableship Henry Holmes left here for Jamaica yesterday... She goes ..to repair the Colon cable. **1901** *Daily Colonist* (Victoria, B.C.) 8 Oct. 3/1 A staff of forty men will be kept at the *cable station, mostly operators. **1920** *Blackw. Mag.* Aug. 181/2 Chahbar was not a cable-station. *c* **1890** tr. *T. de Dillmont's Encycl. Needlework* 180 *Cable or chain stitch..used for strengthening..the edges. **1899** W. G. P. TOWNSEND *Embroidery* 95 Cable-stitch... The first stitch of all is to make a small link. **1950** J. CANNAN *Murder Included* ii. 29 His cable-stitch stockings. **1549** *Compl. Scot.* vi. 40 The maister..bald the marynalis lay the cabil to the *cabilstok. **1887** J. B. SMITH *Cable Traction* Introd. 3 From the capabilities of the '*cable system', it is now quite feasible to effect tramway communication in the most hilly districts. **1902** *Encycl. Brit.* XXXIII. 223/2 This spread of the cable system has naturally followed trade routes. **1965** *Variety* 9 June 34/1 The state of Indiana has been asked to exercise its regulatory charges for the use of telephone facilities in the transmission of *cable television. **1972** *Times* 21 Jan. 2 Cable television was originally introduced in the area in 1962 to provide better reception because Shooters Hill to the south consistently interfered with television pictures. **1982** *New Scientist* 9 Sept. 674 Reports that the government will soon approve plans to bring cable television to Britain have appeared in almost every newspaper. **1778** in *Essex Inst. Hist. Coll.* XXVI. 105 They drove us on board the frigate, and down in the *cable tier we must go. **1833** MARRYAT *P. Simple* (1863) 62 Knocking the man down into the cable tier. **1860** H. STUART *Seaman's Catech.* 62 The hemp cables are coiled in the cable tiers. **1881** RAYMOND *Mining Gloss.*, **Cable-tools*, the apparatus used in drilling deep holes, such as artesian wells, with a rope, instead of rods, to connect the drill with the machine on the surface. **1887** J. B. SMITH *Cable Traction* 2 A '*cable tramway', or in other words a tramway on which the cars are drawn or hauled by means of a cable or rope receiving its motion from a stationary and distant source of power. **1966** *Sat. Rev.* (U.S.) 11 June 90/1 (*heading*) The coming *cable TV war. *Ibid.* 17 Sept. 63/1 A more dramatic way of achieving full set efficiency is Community Antenna Television (CATV), also known as 'cable'..TV. **1970** *Globe & Mail* (Toronto) 26 Sept. 27/3 A number of Metro area residents wish to form a co-operative to own and operate their own cable T.V. **1983** *Listener* 21 Apr. 38/1 The Government White Paper on cable TV for Britain is now expected at the end of April or the beginning of May. **1965** *Variety* 14 July 31/3 A company to provide cable television service has been organized.., known as the Valley *Cablevision Corporation. **1971** *Official Gaz.* (U.S. Patent Office) 15 June 186/2 Cablevision Corporation of America... For Community Antenna Television Services. First use Aug. 4, 1969. **1972** *Daily Tel.* 10 Aug. 17/5 The idea of cablevision is to combine a service of strictly local television programmes, aimed at a restricted audience.., with a relay service which will improve the reception of conventional BBC and ITV programmes. **1981** *Economist* 28 Feb. 83 A joint offer to purchase the United Artists/Columbia cablevision interests. **1899** *Daily News* 11 Mar. 5/2 A *cableway right across the river. **1904** *Alpine Jrnl.* Nov. 336 The road which connects the Wetterhorn Hotel with the starting-point of the cable-way is finished. **1904** GOODCHILD & TWENEY *Technol. & Sci. Dict.* 78/2 *Cable ways*, overhead cables, suitable for haulage of materials. **1962** *Times* 3 Jan. 18/5 Erecting a pylon..for the 45 mile cableway.

cable ('keɪb(ə)l), *v.* [f. the sb.]

1. a. *trans.* To furnish with a cable or cables; to fasten with or as with a cable, to tie *up*.

c **1500** DUNBAR *Tua Mariit Wem.* 354 Se how I cabeld ȝone cout with a kene brydill! **1530** PALSGR. 473/1, I cable, I store a shyppe of cables. **1598** FLORIO, *Gomenare*..to cable an anker. **1605** T. RYVES *Vicar's Plea* (1620) 31 They are.. fortefied and cabled vp with the graunts and priuiledges of Gregory the 14. **1634** SHIRLEY *Example* I. i, Here I am cabled up above their shot. **1640** —— *Imposture* I. ii, I hope she's not turned nun..I do not like The women should be cabled up. **1800** *Naval Chron.* IV. 218 His Majesty's ships are insufficiently cabled. **1863** LD. LYTTON *Ring Amasis* II. II. III. xi. 273 The motive power of his being was cabled to Superstition.

b. To equip with cable for the reception of cable television. Also (*rare*) with *up*.

1979 *Washington Post* 7 Jan. K5/5 So far, only the east central part of the county is cabled. **1982** *Nature* 11 Mar. 102/1 If most British dwellings can be 'cabled up'—linked to some broadband distribution system capable of handling more like forty than four distinct video signals, as at present. **1982** *Daily Tel.* 1 Sept. 2/2 Country areas will not be cabled. **1982** *Times* 18 Oct. 13/1 British Linen Bank..is assessing the feasibility of cabling parts of central Scotland for multi-channel TV and 'telebanking'.

2. *Arch.* To furnish (a column) with vertical convex circular mouldings, which should properly occupy the lower part of the flutings, so as to represent a rope or staff placed in the flute (Gwilt).

1766 ENTICK *London* IV. 91 Cabled with small pillars bound round it, with a kind of arched work and subdivisions between. **1848** RICKMAN *Archit.* 13 These channels are sometimes partly filled by a lesser round moulding; this is called cabling the flutes. **1875** GWILT *Archit.* Gloss. s.v. *Cabling*. In modern times an occasional abuse has been practised of cabling without fluting, as in the church della Sapienza at Rome.

3. *trans.* and *intr.* To transmit (a message, news, etc.), or communicate, by submarine telegraph. (Const. as in *to telegraph*.)

1871 SCHELE DE VERE *Americanisms* (1872) 559 A late telegram by Atlantic Cable from the British Premier..said: 'Cable how match-tax works'. **1880** *Times* 28 Oct., The exciting news cabled from Ireland. **1881** *Ionia Standard* 24 Mar., He [i.e. Secretary Blaine] has been cabling constantly with Lord Granville. **1882** *Times* 14 Apr. 5/3 The Secretary of State..cabled the substance of them to Minister Lowell. **1884** *Kendal Merc.* 1 Nov. 5 Mr. Henry Irving cabled me from Boston..that, etc.

cable, obs. f. of CABALL, horse.

cabled ('keɪb(ə)ld), *ppl. a.* [f. CABLE *sb.* and *v.* + -ED.] **a.** Furnished or fastened with a cable or cables. **b.** *Arch.* **c.** *Her.* (See quots.)

1530 PALSGR. 473/1 My shyppe is as wel cabled as any in all the fleete. **1664** EVELYN tr. *Freart's Archit.* 130 Sometimes we find the Striges to be fill'd up with a swelling ..and these we may call Stav'd or Cabl'd Columns. **1751** CHAMBERS *Cycl.*, *Cabled flutes*, in architecture..filled up with raised or swelling pieces in form of Cables. *Ibid.* *Cabled*, in *Heraldry*, is applied to a cross formed of the two ends of a ship's cable. **1757** DYER *Fleece* II, In Myrina's port [they] Cast out the cabled stone upon the strand.

cablegram ('keɪb(ə)lgræm). [f. CABLE *sb.* + -GRAM, by superficial analogy with TELEGRAM *sb.* (in which both elements are Greek). (The substitution of CALOGRAM has been vainly urged by various writers.)] A message sent by submarine telegraph cable.

1868 *Daily News* 26 Sept., The new word *cablegram* is used by a New York contemporary to characterise a telegraphic despatch. **1873** in *Times* (D.) This libel appears in your journal as a cablegram, New York, 20th. **1879** *Let.* in *Daily News* 14 Oct. 6/2 If there is any necessity for a word to distinguish a telegram sent by cable..I would suggest that the word 'Calogram' be used in the place of 'Cablegram'. **1880** *Athenæum* No. 2764. 503/2 A cablegram has been received..from America, announcing the discovery of a 'large comet' by Mr. Lewis Swift. **1883** *High Commiss. of Canada* in *Times* 13 Aug., It may interest your association to be made acquainted with the following cablegram.

cablegraph ('keɪb(ə)lgrɑːf, -æ-), *v.* [f. prec. after *telegraph*.]

1887 *Standard* 14 Oct. 2/6 [He] cablegraphed from Loon.

cabler ('keɪb(ə)lə(r)). [f. CABLE *v.* + -ER.[1]] One who sends a cable message.

1890 *Daily News* 12 Dec. 6/3 The next I heard was that one of the cablers was among those who forced the offices. **1920** *Discovery* June 173/2 Those who held the view that the majority of cablers require speed without regard to cost were entirely mistaken.

cablese (keɪb(ə)l'iːz). [Contracted form of *cable-ese* (also used), f. CABLE *sb.* 3 c + -ESE.] The contracted or cryptic jargon used in cablegrams, esp. by journalists.

[**1895** A. ROBERTS *Adventures* viii. 104 The cold language of cablegramese fails to do justice to my prowess.] **1952** KOESTLER *Arrow in Blue* xxv. 205 And, thus transformed into French cablese, paste them on to telegram forms. **1955** H. KURNITZ *Invasion of Privacy* (1956) ii. 14 Messages were now framed in cablese..combining and contracting words until the output..bordered on gibberish. **1958** E. A. ROBERTSON *Justice of Heart* iv. 45 One of his correspondents ..was said to have wired back a long dispatch in plain English, and been told to use cable-ese, to save telegraph bills.

cabless ('kæblɪs), *a.* [f. CAB *sb.*[3] + -LESS.]

Of a place: unprovided with a cab or cabs. Also of a railway engine: without a cab.

1834 *Fraser's Mag.* X. 365 The cabless condition of St. James's Street. **1857** *Chamb. Jrnl.* VIII. 82 Ill-paved, unlighted, cabless regions. **1887** C. B. GEORGE *40 Yrs. on Rail* vii. 129 The cabless engines gave no shelter for engineer or fireman.

cablet ('keɪblɪt). [f. CABLE *sb.* + -ET[1].] A small cable or cable-laid rope less than 10 inches in circumference.

1575–6 in *4th Report Commiss. Hist. MSS.* (1874) 114/1 An Act for the true making of great cables and cabletts. **1613** *Voy. Guiana* in *Harl. Misc.* (Malh.) III. 176 By the..fury of the wind and sea, the cablet broke. **1794** *Rigging & Seamanship* I. 54 *Cablets*, cable-laid ropes, under nine inches in circumference. **1800** *Naval Chron.* III. 65 Made fast to the principal cablet, or hawser. **1803** *Rep. Commiss.* in *Naval Chron.* X. 48 Cablets—Inches, $9\frac{1}{4}$, 9, 8, $7\frac{1}{2}$..3. **1860** H.

STUART *Seaman's Catech.* 52 When three cablets are laid up together, it is called 'hawser-laid rope'.

cabling ('keɪblɪŋ), *vbl. sb.*[1] [f. CABLE *v.* + -ING[1].]

1. The filling up of the lower part of the flutes of a column with cylindrical mouldings.

1753 CHAMBERS *Cycl. Supp.* s.v., There are also cablings in relievo without fluting, especially on certain pilasters, as in the church of Sapienza at Rome.

2. The transmitting of a message by electric cable.

1903 *Westm. Gaz.* 9 Mar. 10/2 Cable Chess: Great Britain v. America... The cabling will be done in the room.

3. *collect.* Lengths of cable.

1927 *Daily Tel.* 1 Nov. 10/7 The mechanical apparatus consists of a generator, an air-screw.., cabling, [etc.].

4. Furnishing with cable for the reception of cable television.

1979 *Washington Post* 7 Jan. K1 The cabling of Arlington County will not be complete before 1980. **1982** *New Scientist* 9 Sept. 674 Why all the fuss about the 'cabling of Britain'? **1983** *Listener* 6 Jan. 34/1 Beyond all this talk of cable's boundless promise only two solid reasons for cabling ..emerge. **1986** *Daily Express* 21 Aug. 38 (Advt.), Previous site experience is essential as well as..knowledge of cabling installation practices.

cabling, erroneous or dial. form of CAVELLING.

1885 *Times* (Weekly ed.) 4 Sept. 6/1 This process known as cabling..the only fair method of allotting the work.

†'**cablish.** *Obs.* [prob. a. Anglo-Fr. *cablis = F. *chablis*, OF. *chaablis*, med.L. *cablicium*, pl. *cablicia*, in the Forest Laws, in same sense; of doubtful derivation: see Littré; but app. related to OF. *chaable*, and thus with L. **catabola*, see CABLE, and cf. Littré *chablis* and Du Cange *cabulus*.] Strictly, trees blown down, or branches blown off by the wind, but explained by the legal antiquaries of the 16th c. as = brushwood.

1594 R. CROMPTON *Jurisdict.* 196 Cablicia is properly brushwood. T. claimed the drie woods & cablish in his owne woods. **1664** SPELMAN, *Cablicia*, Cablish... Angl. Brushwood. Rectiùs..Windfalls. **1688** R. HOLME *Armoury* III. 75/2 Cablish is all sorts of Brushwood. **1852** SMITH *Eng. & Fr. Dict.*, Cablish..*bois chablis, broussailles*.

cabman ('kæbmən). [f. CAB *sb.*[3]] A man whose occupation is to drive a public cab.

1834 C. MATHEWS *Let.* 22 May in Mrs. Mathews *Mem. C.M.* (1839) IV. xiii. 284 This city of horrors—this collection of ruffianly Cab-men, and Buss-es. **1837** [see FIVE *sb.* 3 b]. **1850** MRS. BROWNING *Poems* II. 191 The cabman's cry to get out of the way. **1860** *Vacat. Tour.* 59 Half a dozen cabmen shouting in my ears. *Ibid.* 137 They know them as well as a London cabman does the streets.

cabob (kə'bɒb). Also **kabob**. [Arab. *kabāb* (also in Pers. and Urdu), in same sense.]

1. An oriental dish (see the quotations); also used in India for roast meat in general. (Now always in *plur.*)

1698 FRYER *Acc. E. Ind. & P.* 404 (Y.) Cabob is Rostmeat on Skewers, cut in little round pieces no bigger than a Sixpence, and Ginger and Garlick put between each. **1743** R. POCOCKE *Egypt* in Pinkerton *Voy.* XIV. 211 Cabobs, or meat rosted in small pieces, that may be eat without dividing. **1814** FORBES *Orient. Mem.* II. 480 (Y.), I often partook with my Arabs of a dish common in Arabia called Kabob or Kab-ab. **1854** THACKERAY *Newcomes* II. 242 Eats cabobs with city nabobs.

2. 'A leg of mutton stuffed with white herrings and sweet herbs' (Halliwell).

1690 B. E. *Dict. Cant. Crew, Cabob*, a Loin of Mutton Roasted with an Onyon betwixt each joint; a Turkish and Persian Dish..now used in England.

Hence **ca'bob** *v.*, to cook in the manner described. (Webster cites Sir T. Herbert.)

‖**caboceer** (kæbəʊ'sɪə(r)). [ad. Pg. *cabociero*, f. *cabo*, *cabeça* head.] The headman (of a West African village or tribe).

1836 MARRYAT *Midsh. Easy* xvi, My father appointed me a Caboceer. **1864** R. BURTON *Dahome* II. 38 The type of a Dahoman Caboceer. **1866** ENGEL *Nat. Music* i. 4 The melodies produced by a Caboceer, or chief of Dahomey, upon his sanko, deserve our attention.

†**caboche**, *sb. Obs.* [see next and CABOT.] A fish; the Bull-head, or Miller's Thumb.

c **1425** *Voc.* in Wr.-Wülcker 641 *Hic caput*, caboche. *c* **1440** *Promp. Parv.* 57 Caboche, *currulia*.

†**ca'boche**, *v.* ? *Obs.* Also 6 **cabage**. [f. F. *cabocher* (in same sense) implied in pple. adj. *caboché* CABOCHED, and used (as *cabacher*) by Palsgr., f. *caboche* = It. *capocchia* augm. and pejorative of *capo* head. The form *cabage* is identified with CABBAGE *v.*[1], which is ultimately the same word.] *trans.* To cut off the head of (a deer) close behind the horns.

a **1425** *Bk. Hunting* MS. Bodl. 546 fol. 93 þer nedeth no more but to caboche his heed. **1530** PALSGR. 596, I kabage a deere, *je cabaiche*. I wyll cabage my dere..*je cabacheray ma beste*. **1575** TURBERV. *Bk. Venerie* xliii. 134 It is cut off near to the head. And then the heade is cabaged [i.e.] cut close by the hornes through the braine pan, untill you come vnderneath the eyes, and ther it is cut off.

caboched, caboshed, cabossed (kə'bɒʃt, kə'bɒst), *ppl. a. Her.* Also **cabazed, cabaged**. [f. prec.; or ad. F. *caboché* in same sense.] Borne (as the head of a stag, bull, or other beast) full-faced, and cut off close behind the ears so as to show no part of the neck; trunked.

1572 BOSSEWELL *Armorie* II. 59 An hartes heade cabazed d'Or. **1610** GUILLIM *Heraldry* III. xiv. (1660) 162 These horned beasts..have also their heads borne Trunked: Which of some Armorists is blazoned Cabossed. **1751** CHAMBERS *Cycl.*, Caboched, caboshed or cabossed. **1761** *Brit. Mag.* II. 76 Three harts heads, caboshed, argent. **1797** *Churchw. Acc. St. Mary Hill, Lond.* (Nicholls) 95 *note*, A bull's head cabost. **1866** PEACOCK *Eng. Ch. Furniture* 36 A chevron between three bucks' heads cabossed argent.

ca'boching, ca'bossing, *vbl. sb. Her.* [f. as prec. + -ING[1].] (See quot.)

1727 BRADLEY *Fam. Dict.* I. s.v. *Cabosed*, A Term in Heraldry, for the Head of any Beast, being just cut off behind the Ears, by a Section parallel to the Face, or by a perpendicular Section; whereas Couping is usually express'd by a Horizontal one, and is never so close to the Ears as Cabosing.

‖**cabochon** (kabɔʃɔ̃). Also 6 *Sc.* **caboschoun, coboischoun, coboschoun.** [Fr.: augmentative of *caboche*; see above.] A precious stone when merely polished, without being cut into facets or receiving any regular figure but that which belongs to the stone itself, the rough parts only being removed. This fashion is chiefly applied to the garnet (carbuncle), ruby, sapphire and amethyst. Chiefly *attrib.*, as in ***cabochon shape, crystal, emerald***, etc.

1578 *Inventories* 265 (JAM.) Tua tabled diamantis, and tua rubyis coboischoun. *Ibid.* 266 Foure rubyis coboschoun. **1872** ELLACOMBE *Bells of Ch.* vii. 174 Under the foot of the cross is a large uncut crystal..at one side of this cabochon is a mitred figure. **1877** W. JONES *Finger-ring L.* 220 A pale cabochon sapphire. **1883** *Times* 14 July 7 The centre stone ..is encircled by ruby, emerald, sapphire, and five other stones, cut cabochon shape.

Caboclo (ka'bəʊkləʊ). [Brazilian Pg., derived by some from Tupi *caboculo* depilated.] A civilized Amerindian descended from aboriginals of Brazil. Also applied to others of mixed Indian and Negro or Indian and white parentage.

1816 KOSTER *Trav. Brazil* 387 Indians in a domesticated state, who are called generally Caboclos. **1825** CALDCLEUGH *Trav. S. Amer.* I. 80 Caboclos. *Note*, Mixture of the Indian races. **1874** R. F. BURTON in *Captivity of H. Stade* 45 Mamalucco, meaning the offspring of a white man by an 'Indian' woman, is obsolete in S. Paulo, where Caboclo.. has taken its place. **1918** *Times Lit. Suppl.* 28 Mar. 146/4 The Portuguese-speaking natives [in Brazil]..Caboclos in the south or Mulattos further north. **1956** R. REDFIELD *Peasant Soc.* 32 The more remote frontiersmen call for attention. Such are the *caboclo* of the Brazilian Amazon and coastal selva.

†**cabod**, *v. Obs. rare*[−1]. *trans.* ? To edge or border.

1753 *Songs Costume* (1849) 231 With fringes of knotting your Dickey cabod.

cabok, obs. f. of KEBBUCK, *Sc.*, cheese.

cabon, -et, early forms of CABIN, -ET.

caboodle (kə'bu:d(ə)l). *slang* (orig. *U.S.*). [Supposed to be a corruption of the phrase *kit and boodle* (see KIT *sb.*[1]).] ***the whole caboodle***: the whole lot (of persons or things).

a **1848** *Ohio State Jrnl.* (Bartlett, Add.), The whole caboodle will act upon the recommendation of the Ohio Sun. **1873** B. HARTE *Fiddletown* 3 She had more soul than the whole caboodle of them put together. **1901** B. PAIN *De Omnibus* 79, I was forced ter give 'im eleven coppers, which 'e took and then dropped the 'ole caboodle. **1904** *Daily Chron.* 6 May 8/4 'Give them a week's notice and start them.' 'What, the whole caboodle?' **1919** J. B. MORTON *Barber of Putney* xvi. 259 If we know they're comin', you can bet your sweet life them as runs the 'ole caboodle [*sc.* war] knows it too. **1923** *Strand Mag.* Oct. 351 Actually, the whole caboodle, sold, not pawned, produced seventy, not fifty—hundred and twenty in all.

cabook (kə'bu:k). Also **kabook**. ['Perhaps the Port. *cabouco* or *cavouco* a quarry. It is not in Singh. Dictionaries' (Yule).] The name given in Ceylon to a reddish gneissoid building-stone, soft when quarried but hardening by exposure to the air; laterite.

1834 S. C. CHITTY *Ceylon Gazetteer* 75 The houses are built of cabook, and neatly whitewashed with chunam. **1836** *Penny Cycl.* VI. 452/2 A reddish loam resulting from the decomposition of clay iron-stone called *cabook*. **1858** SIMMONDS *Dict. Trade*, Kabook. **1941** *Archit. Rev.* XC. 75/1 In more expensive types of building solid walls—of cabook, or stone and mud, or occasionally brick—replace the bamboo framework.

caboose (kə'bu:s). Also **cam-, can-, coboose.** [Identical with Du. *kabuis, kombuis*, earlier Du. *combûse, cabûse*, MLG. *kabhûse* (whence mod.G. *kabuse*), also F. *cambuse* 'app. introduced into the navy about the middle of the 18th c.' (Littré). The original lang. was perh. LG.; but the history and etymology are altogether obscure.]

1. a. 'The cook-room or kitchen of merchantmen on deck; a diminutive substitute for the galley of a man-of-war. It is generally furnished with cast-iron apparatus for cooking' (Smyth *Sailor's Word-bk.*).

1769 FALCONER *Dict. Marine* (1789), *Coboose*, a sort of box or house to cover the chimney of some merchant-ships. It somewhat resembles a centry-box, and generally stands against the barricade on the fore part of the quarter-deck. **1805** *N. York Chron.* in *Naval Chron.* XIII. 122 William Cameron drifted aboard on the canboose. **1805** DUNCAN *Marin. Chron.* IV. 70 A sea broke..and swept away the caboose and all its utensils from the deck. **1833** M. SCOTT *Tom Cringle* (1862) 6 Fishing boats at anchor, all with their tiny cabooses. **1844** *Regul. & Ord. Army* 341 A sentry is constantly to be placed at the cooking-place or caboose. **1879** FARRAR *St. Paul* II. 375 The caboose and utensils must long ago have been washed overboard.

b. A cooking-oven or fireplace erected on land.

1859 *Autobiog. Beggar-boy* 93 The man..requested me to put his pannikin on the caboose fire. **1882** *Harper's Mag.* Feb. 331 Outside are 'cambooses' for preparing fish in the open air. **1883** *Century Mag.* XXVI. 550 The lawn is studded with cabooses.

2. *U.S.* A van or car on a freight train used by workmen or the men in charge. Also *attrib.*

1861 H. DAWSON *Remin. Life Locomotive Engineer* 90 Another midnight ride in the 'Caboose' of a freight train. **1862** *Ashcroft's Railway Directory* 76 No. of Caboose Cars [on the Central Railroad of New Jersey], 6. **1881** *Chicago Times* 18 June, The caboose of the construction train, containing workmen and several boys. **1884** *Dakota paper* Jan., Four cars and a caboose running down the track. **1903** *New York Even. Post* 25 Aug., The rest of the crew..saw from the caboose windows the bodies..lying along the tracks.

3. a. A hut or poor dwelling. Chiefly *N. Amer.*

1839 *Congress. Globe* 15 Feb. App. 343/1 We have a postmaster in our village..and in his little caboose of a post office I found electioneering interferences. **1874** V. PYKE *Adv. G. W. Pratt* (1890) I. iii. 13 It's a darned wrong thing to allow in your caboose, mister. **1916** G. PARKER *World for Sale* xxiv. 308 'He's been lying drunk at Gautry's caboose ever since yesterday morning..' 'Gautry's tavern—that joint.'

b. A mobile hut or bunk-house, moved on wheels or runners. *Canad.*

1912 E. FERGUSON *Open Trails* 106 In the later winter one sees..a caboose on a sled, heading for the Peace River district or for some point up north. This is a comfortable way of travelling, and on arriving at his claim the homesteader shifts the caboose to the ground and uses it for a house. **1954** A. M. BEZANSON *Sodbusters invade Peace* xiv. 90 Our honeymoon trip was to be made in a caboose—a part-lumber part-canvas house built on a farm sleigh.

c. = CALABOOSE. *slang* (orig. *U.S.*).

1865 *Republican Banner* (Nashville, Tenn.) 12 Oct. 3/2 The 'caboose' is neatly packed with 'pickled' offenders of municipal law. **1929** F. BOWEN *Sea Slang* 21 *Caboose*... On shore it meant prison. **1939** *These are our Lives* (U.S.) 346 If they put me in the caboose for cruelty to roaches and water bugs.

cabos: see CABOT.

cabosh, -ed, cabossed, var. ff. CABOCHE, -D.

‖**cabot** (kabo, 'kæbət). [Earlier and N.Fr. *cabot*, mod.F. *chabot*, f. Romanic *cabo*, *capo* head + -OT.]

†**1.** A fish: the Bull-head or Miller's Thumb.

1611 COTGR., *Poisson royal*, the white Cabot.

2. A measure of dry goods in the Channel Islands; cf. the Sc. CAP.

1835 H. D. INGLIS *Channel Isl.* 124 In Jersey..sixteen cabots per perch, has been known to be obtained. **1862** ANSTED *Channel Isl.* IV. App. A (ed. 2) 566 In Jersey, the measure of dry goods is the cabot, or half-bushel.. containing 43 lbs. 7 ozs. of distilled water.

cabotage ('kæbətɪdʒ). *Naut.* [a. F. *cabotage* (also Sp., in It. *cabotaggio*) in same sense; f. F. *caboter* to coast; whence F. has also *caboteur, cabotier, cabotin, cabotinage, cabotiner*. Derivation uncertain.

Originally a shipping term of the north of France: M. Paul Meyer rejects Littré's guess from Sp. *cabo* cape, headland, as if 'to sail from cape to cape', as untenable phonetically and historically, and thinks the verb must be from the name of a kind of boat. The gloss '*cabo*, trabe, nave' occurs in (MS. Bibl. Nat. 1646 lf. 83 b) a 13th c. copy of an older glossary; and Littré has *cabot, chabot* as north French equivalents of *sabot*, which is still applied to a small vessel running two or three knots an hour. (Brachet guesses that *caboter* may be from the surname *Cabot*; which may have had the same origin, but cf. prec.)]

1. Coasting; coast-pilotage; the coast carrying trade by sea.

1831 SIR J. SINCLAIR *Corr.* II. 186 The Cabotage, as they call it, or carrying trade. **1876** R. BURTON *Gorilla L.* I. 6 Small vessels belonging to foreigners, and employed in cabotage. **1885** *Standard* 2 Jan. (Article) The Cabotage in China. [From Shanghai correspondent.]

2. *Aeronaut.* (The reservation to a country of) the air-traffic within its territory. Also *attrib.*

1933 *Aeroplane* 24 May 962/1 As far as the progress of international air transport is concerned cabotage is about the finest form of 'sabotage'. **1958** *Sunday Times* 15 June 3/5 India..though possessed of an enormous area protected by cabotage, has neither the resources to exploit this potential nor a population rich enough to indulge in mass air transport. *Ibid.* Members of the Commonwealth do not

form a cabotage unit. **1960** *Times* 11 Feb. 9/4 B.O.A.C.'s possession of end-to-end cabotage rights on these routes.

‖**cabotin** (kabɔtɛ̃). Fem. **cabotine** (-tin). [Fr., see next.] A low-class actor. Also *attrib.* Hence **cabotinism**, the state or quality of being a cabotin; = next.

1903 A. BENNETT *Truth about Author* xv. 196 He is terrible against *cabotins*, no matter where he finds them. **1909** H. JAMES *Tragic Muse* I. p. xvii, The mountebank, the mummer and the *cabotin*. **1926** R. FRY *Transformations* 120 The incalculable difference between Velasquez's distinction, detachment and scrupulous reserve as compared with Caravaggio's blustering Cabotinism. **1930** J. AGATE *Red Letter Nights* (1944) 129 There remain those impudences..which fell from Duse like sour benedictions, from Sarah with the cabotine's natural, slightly vulgar good nature. **1951** L. P. HARTLEY *My Fellow Devils* i. 8 He was a cabotin sort of character, always playing a lonely part. *Ibid.* xxi. 218 'Cabotin' character..seems to mean someone who enjoys playing..a rather second-rate part, who has no core of personality. **1966** *Punch* 30 Nov. 826/2 Sarah Bernhardt was a *cabotine*; she excelled in the art of self-advertisement.

‖**cabotinage** (kabɔtinaʒ). [Fr., f. *cabotin* strolling player, perh. ultimately f. *caboter* to coast, because of the resemblance between players who travel from town to town and coasting vessels.] The life or behaviour characteristic of low-class actors, with implication of 'playing to the gallery'.

1894 *Nation* (N.Y.) 22 Mar. 211 We can find the spirit of 'cabotinage'..even in the Church. **1895** *Daily News* 9 May 6/2 Dickens, yielding..to his native cabotinage, descended so low as to give readings from his own books! *Ibid.*, We cannot..blame the undeniable cabotinage of the great Napoleon. **1921** *Times Lit. Suppl.* 29 Sept. 626/2 In the narrow life of *cabotinage* there is little scope for originality.

†**cabow.** *Obs.* Also **cabbowe.**

1489 *Will of Rowley, Bristol* (Somerset Ho.) All my Cabowe or Stuf in Marchaundise. **1501** *Will of Barre* (Somerset Ho.) The Cabow that I haue in her [a ship]. **1501** *Bristol Wills* (Wadley) 173, xx marke of my Cabbowe in money or dettes..the Residue of my Cabbowe.

†'**cabre,** *v. Obs.* [a. F. *cabrer*, f. Sp. *cabra* goat: see CAPER.] *intr.* To caper (as a horse).

1600 HOLLAND *Livy* VIII. vii. 285 At the smart of which the horse reared and cabred with his forefeet.

‖**cabré** (kabre), *a.* [Fr.; f. *cabrer*: see prec.]

1. *Her.* Said of a horse: Capering, rearing on the hind legs.

†**2.** *Aeronaut.* = *tail-down* adj. (see TAIL *sb.*[1] 14). Also as *sb. Obs.*

1910 R. LORAINE in W. Loraine *R. Loraine* (1938) vi. 118, I was alarmed lest my biplane should suddenly do a cabré (fall backwards), if I kept her climbing. **1913** A. E. BERRIMAN *Aviation* iii. 22 So tilt the machine nose upwards into a position that is called *cabré.* **1914** H. M. BUIST *Aircraft in German War* i. 35 (*caption*) The craft flying cabré, or tail down, is also a biplane.

‖'**cabrie,** '**cabrit.** Also **cabree.** [cf. Sp. *cabrito* kid, dim. of *cabra* goat.] The Pronghorn Antelope, *Antilope Americana* (*furcifera*).

[**1624** T. SCOTT *2nd Pt. Vox Populi* 22 A peece of leane Kid, or Cabrito.] **1807** PIKE *Sources Mississ.* II. 136 Killed one cabrie, two deer, two turkies. **1834** *Penny Cycl.* II. 71/1 The Prongbuck..called cabree by the Canadian *voyageurs.*

cabriole ('kæbrɪəʊl). [In senses 1 and 4, a. F. *cabriole* (16th c.) a leap like that of a goat. Senses 2, 3, appear to be old errors for CABRIOLET.]

1. †**a.** A capriole, a caper (of a horse). *Obs.*

1814 SCOTT *Wav.* I. viii. 103 The occasional cabrioles which his charger exhibited.

b. = CAPRIOLE *sb.* 1; *spec.* in *Ballet*, a springing step in which one leg is extended and the second leg is brought up to the first.

1805 F. PEACOCK *Sk. Dancing* 110 The steps may be accompanied with bendings, risings, leaps, cabrioles. **1830** R. BARTON tr. *Blasis's Code of Terpsichore* II. vi. 78 An attitude upon one leg, as in..the *cabriole, brisés* and the *rond-de-jambe en l'air.* **1952** *Ballet Ann.* VI. 126/2 Eglevsky's special talent for hanging calmly in the air for an unbelievable moment during his *cabrioles.*

†**2.** *Obs.* A kind of small arm-chair (Littré). In full *cabriole chair*.

1781 *Eng. Chron.* 27–30 Jan. 1/2 The..original Manufactory for all sorts of Cabriole Chairs. **1785** MACKENZIE *Lounger* No. 36 ⁋8 Sofas and stuffed chairs in the drawing-room, which my Lady has made her change for cabrioles. **1848** H. R. FORSTER *Stowe Catal.* (Terminal Advt.) 15 Cabriole Drawing Room Chairs.

†**3.** *Obs.* = CABRIOLET.

1797 HOLCROFT *Stolberg's Trav.* (ed. 2) II. lxi. 403 The coaches are..less dangerous than the little one horse cabrioles. **1801** W. FELTON *Carriages* II. 180 The Cabriole is a two wheeled Carriage with the body like a Chariot, mostly used in France.

4. A form of curved leg, frequent in Queen Anne and Chippendale furniture, so called from its resemblance to a quadruped's foreleg making a leap or caper.

1888 J. MARSHALL in *Catal. Exhib. Decor. Handiwork, Edin.* 59 Settees and chairs with their cabriole legs and lion-claw feet. **1902** L. V. LOCKWOOD *Col. Furniture Amer.* 56 Walnut and Inlay Cabriole-legged Dressing-table. **1907** H. C. CANDEE *Decor. Styles* 202 The cabriole leg is the one great point of this decorative period with which collectors..must arm themselves. **1966** A. W. LEWIS *Gloss. Woodworking Terms* 11 *Cabriole leg*, furniture leg which curves outwards at the top and inwards at the bottom.

cabriolet (ˌkæbrɪəʊ'leɪ). [a. F. *cabriolet*, deriv. of *cabriole*, so called from its elastic bounding motion.] **1. a.** A light two-wheeled chaise drawn by one horse, having a large hood of wood or leather, and an ample apron to cover the lap and legs of the occupant. Contracted by 1830 to CAB, and in later times applied to any vehicle known by that name. Also, the top or open section of a carriage (see quot. 1815). Also *attrib.*

1766 SMOLLETT *Trav.* I. v. 73 He goes in a one-horse chaise, which is here called a *cabriolet.* **1770** H. WALPOLE *Let.* 7 July (1941) X. 313 We walked in the garden or drove about it in cabriolets, till it was time to dress. [**1789** *Let. fr. Paris* in *Public Advertiser* 3 Crushed to death by one of those machines called *Cabriolets*; on account of which infernal vehicles, the inhabitants..can no longer venture on foot at any hour. **1815** J. SCOTT *Visit to Paris* iii. 39 A conductor is attached to each Diligence, whose..chief business, according to his practice, is to sleep, closely shut up in the Cabriolet (which is a covered seat in front). **1816** *Ann. Reg.* 339 Lavalette was..conducted by Sir R. Wilson beyond the barriers in an English cabriolet.] **1820** J. S. MILL *Jrnl.* 27 May in *Boyhood Visit to France* (1960) 9, I..set off at 2 PM in the cabriolet of the diligence. We had chosen the cabriolet, thinking the interior would be too hot. **1823** *Gentl. Mag.* 463/2 April 23 Cabriolets were, in honour of his Majesty's birthday, introduced to the public this morning. **1840** BARHAM *Ingol. Leg.* 194 His lordship rang for his cabriolet [*rime* day]. *a* **1845** HOOD *Lost Heir*, I'm scared when I think of them Caboleys. **1846** DICKENS *Pictures from Italy* ii. 9 The Diligence..its cabriolet head on the roof, nodding and shaking, like an idiot's head. **1863** MISS BRADDON *J. Marchmont* I. ii. 41 Edward Arundel had driven over in a cabriolet. **1907** *Westm. Gaz.* 18 Jan. 3/1 Cabriolet-fares were one-third less than those for hackney coaches.

b. A motor car with fixed sides and a folding top.

1909 *Westm. Gaz.* 4 Feb. 4/3 The illustration given is that of a special type of cabriolet. *Ibid.* 17 Nov. 5/2 The exhibit [*sc.* a Lancia] is comprised of a 20-h.p. chassis fitted with a cabriolet body of admirable proportions.

2. A bonnet or hat shaped like a cabriolet.

1771 H. WALPOLE *Let.* 31 July (1904) 63, I have bespoken two cabriolets for her, instead of six, because I think them very dear. **1923** *Daily Mail* 22 June 11 Cabriolet hats are in fashion again... With a cabriolet you must have ribbon streamers falling over one shoulder.

cabul(le, -byl, obs. ff. of CABLE.

caburn ('kæbən). *Naut.* [? connected with CABLE.] (*pl.*) 'Spun rope-yarn lines, for worming a cable, seizing, winding tacks, and the like' (Smyth *Sailor's Word-bk.*).

1626 CAPT. SMITH *Accid. Yng. Seamen* 16 Cables serue.. for rope yarne, caburn, sinnit, an[d] okum. **1627** —— *Seaman's Gram.* v. 25 Caburne is a small line made of spun yarne to make a bend of two Cables, or to sease the Tackels, or the like. **1678** in PHILLIPS; also in mod. Dicts.

‖**caca'fuego.** Also 7 cacafugo, -fogo, cacofuego. [f. L. *cacā-re*, Sp. and Pg. *cagar* to discharge excrement + Sp. *fuego* (Pg. *fogo*) fire:—L. *focus* hearth.] A spitfire; a braggart.

(The name of the Spanish galleon taken by Drake in 1577.)

1625 FLETCHER *Fair Maid* III. i, She will be ravisht before our faces by rascalls and cacafugos, wife, cacafugoes! *c* **1661** *Argyle's Will* in *Harl. Misc.* (1746) VIII. 27/2 Presbytery will soon lose a prating, nonsensical Cacafuego. **1696** PHILLIPS, *Cacafuego*, a Spanish word signifying Shitefire; and it is used for a bragging vapouring fellow. **1721–90** in BAILEY. **1725** in *New Cant. Dict.* [**1775** ASH, *Cacafuego*, an insect in Spain said to dart fire from its tail.]

cacagogue, erroneous form of CACCAGOGUE.

ca'canny (ka'kænɪ). Also (after northern dialects) **-conny.** [See CALL *v.* 15, CANNY *a.* 10.] Moderation, caution; *spec.* the practice of 'going slow' at work; a deliberate policy of limiting output of work. Freq. *attrib.*

1896 *Westm. Gaz.* 25 Mar. 1/3 He was the first English Labour leader to reduce to a fine art the 'ca'conny' policy so well known in Western America. **1896** *Seamen's Chron.* 24 Oct. in *Times* 18 Nov. (1901) 10/1 What is ca'canny? It is a simple and handy phrase which is used to describe a new instrument or policy which may be used by the workers in place of a strike. **1902** *Westm. Gaz.* 25 Apr. 8/1 A 'ca-canny' policy said to have been deliberately adopted by certain trade union officials. **1958** *Economist* 29 Nov. 784/1 The teaching staff defends itself skilfully from battle to battle with cynicism and ca'canny.

Hence **ca''cannyism, ca''cannyness** (or **-iness**), ca'canny policy or behaviour; caution.

1917 *Glasgow Herald* 9 Aug. 3/7 The letter.. unintentionally detracts, by its extreme 'ca'cannyness', from the merits of the proposed scheme. **1921** *Glasgow Herald* 17 June 6 Mr. Ramsay Macdonald recommends 'a magnificently organised system of passive resistance', which, plainly interpreted by his followers, means Ca'-cannyism. **1926** W. S. BRUCE *Salt & Sense* 186 To-day we have a new word for a novel disease, which began first on the Clyde. It is called 'Ca'cannyism'. **1963** *Economist* 16 Mar. 976/2 The entrenched forces of ca'canniness.

cacao (kə'keɪəʊ, kə'kɑːəʊ). Also (6–7 caccao), 6–8 cacoa, 8 caco, cocao; and see COCOA *sb.* [Sp. *cacao*, ad. Mexican *caca-uatl* 'caca-tree'.]

1. The seed of a tropical American tree (*Theobroma Cacao*, N.O. *Byttneriaceæ*), from which cocoa and chocolate are prepared.

1555 EDEN *Decades W. Ind.* (Arb.) 342 In the steade [of money] the halfe shelles of almonds, whiche kynde of Barbarous money they [the Mexicans] caule cacao or cacanguate. **1594** BLUNDEVIL *Exerc.* v. (ed. 7) 568 Fruit, which the Inhabitants cal in their tongue Cacaco, it is like to an Almond..of it they make a certaine drinke which they love marvelous well. *a* **1687** PETTY *Pol. Arith.* iv. (1691) 83 The value of Sugar, Indico, Tobacco, Cotton, and Caccao, brought from the Southward parts of America. **1702** *Lond. Gaz.* No. 3842/3 A French Prize..laden with Sugar, Caco and Indigo from Martinico. **1748** ANSON *Voy.* II. v. (ed. 4) 248 Her load consisted of timber, cocao, coco-nuts, tobacco, hides. **1836** MACGILLIVRAY *Humboldt's Trav.* viii. 108 Cacao and sugar were also raised to a considerable extent. **1849** W. IRVING *Columbus* II. 315.

†**2.** The powder produced by grinding the seeds, often with other substances mixed; also the drink prepared from the seeds or powder; = COCOA *sb.*

1652 WADSWORTH *Chocolate* 2 Cacao..is cold and dry. **1662** H. STUBBE *Ind. Nectar* ii. 8 They had brought to them jarrs of Cacao.

3. The tree whose fruit yields this seed, more fully called **cacao-tree.**

1756 P. BROWNE *Jamaica* 11 They supply the most agreeable soils for the cacao. **1778** ROBERTSON *Hist. Amer.* II. VII. 296 The value..was estimated by the number of nuts of the cacao, which he might expect in exchange. **1832** *Veg. Subst. Food* 372 The seeds of the cacao were made use of as money in Mexico.

4. *attrib.*, as in *cacao-bush, -farm, -nut, -planter, -powder, -tree*, etc.; also **cacao-bean**, the seed of the cacao-tree; **cacao-butter**, a fatty matter obtained from the cacao-nut, used for making pomades, candles, etc.; **cacao-mother**, a tree used to protect the delicate cacao-tree; **cacao-walk**, a plantation of cacao-trees.

1652 WADSWORTH *Chocolate* 13 When they are growne up to a good hight, then they plant the Cacao-trees. **1661** HICKERINGILL *Jamaica* 30 Two of these little Cacoa Nuts (or Kernells) passe currant for one farthing. *Ibid.* 24 Cacoa-Walks..containing ten or twelve Acres of Ground. **1662** H. STUBBE *Ind. Nectar* ii. 9 They made a certain cooling-drink of the Cacao nuts. **1778** ROBERTSON *Hist. Amer.* II. VIII. 412 The cacao-tree grows spontaneously in several parts of the torrid zone. **1839** URE *Dict. Arts* 292 The cacao-beans lie in a fruit somewhat like a cucumber. **1871** KINGSLEY *At Last* vii, Lombardy poplar[s]..the beauty of these 'Madres de Cacao', Cacao-mothers as they call them here because their shade is supposed to shelter the Cacao-trees. *Ibid.* xiii, The cacao-bush which produces chocolate. *Ibid.* xvi, Can nothing be done to increase the yield of the cacao-farms? **1885** LADY BRASSEY *The Trades* 140 The ground is then prepared for the reception of the cacao pods, which are planted in rows called 'cacao-walks'. **1908** H. H. SMITH *Cacao Planting* 18 As long as cacao powder is so much in vogue. *Ibid.* 41 The Jamaica cacao planters. **1936** *Discovery* Feb. 41/2 In 1929 *Ephestia flutella*, formerly destructive to cacao beans and then to tobacco abroad, was found in London tobacco warehouses.

cacarootch, obs. form of COCKROACH.

†'**cacatory,** *a. Obs. rare*⁻¹. [ad. mod.L. *cacātōrius*, f. *cacāre* to evacuate the bowels; see -ORY.] Attended with looseness of the bowels.

1684 tr. *Bonet's Merc. Compit.* VI. 183 Cacatory, Dejectory, or Loose-fevers..ought wholly to be imputed to Choler. **1753** CHAMBERS *Cycl. Supp.*, *Cacatory-fever.*

caccagogue ('kækəgɒg). *Med.* [mod. f. Gr. κάκκη excrement + -αγωγος leading, leading away, f. ἄγ-ειν to lead, drive. Chambers *Cycl. Supp.* 1753 has mod.L. *cacagoga.*] An ointment made of alum and honey, and used to promote stool.

caccao, obs. f. of CACAO.

cacche(n, obs. f. CATCH *v.*

cace, obs. form of CASE.

†**ca'cemphaton.** *Obs. rare.* [Gr. κακέμφατον 'ill-sounding, equivocal'.] An ill-sounding expression.

[**1589** PUTTENHAM *Eng. Poesie* (Arb.) 260 This vice is called by the Greekes Cacemphaton, we call it the vnshamefast or figure of foule speech.] **1622** PEACHAM *Compl. Gentl.* (1661) 174 It had beene an harsh and unpleasing Cacemphaton, as your own eare will tell you. **1721–90** in BAILEY.

cachalot ('kæʃəlɒt, 'kæʃələʊ). Also 8–9 **-elot.** [a. F. *cachalot*, in the Bayonne dial. of 17th c. *cachalut*, app. meaning, 'toothed', from a Romanic word for 'tooth' or 'grinder', in Gascon *cachau*, Carcassone *caichal*, Cat. *caxal*, Pr. dials. *caissal, caysal.* The first notice of the word in Eng. writers is quoted from the French of Anderson's *Histoire Naturelle de Island*, etc. (Hamburg 1746). The word is now found in

most European langs., as Ger. *kachalot*, Da. *kaskelot*, Sw. *kaselot*, Du. *kazilot*, etc.

(In *Miscellanea Curiosa*, 1670 (Frankfort, and Leipzig 1681), observation cxxxvi. (p. 266) treats of this whale 'qui in Bayonna, Byaris, et in insula S. Johannis de Luca, et in locis ubi capitur *Cachalut*, latine *Orca* dicitur'.) A different derivation is proposed by Zobler, *Zeitsch. f. Rom. Philol.* IV. 176, whereby he would connect it with Sp. *cachuelo*, which derives from L. *catulus*.]

A genus of whales, belonging to the family *Catodontidæ*, distinguished by the presence of teeth in the lower jaw. The Common Cachalot, or Sperm Whale, which yields spermaceti, grows to the length of 70 feet, and has a head nearly one-half of the length of the body; it occurs in all seas, but its home is the Pacific Ocean.

1747 *Gentl. Mag.* XVII. 174 The figure which Mr. Anderson gives of the Cachelot..has the air of a monster. **1769** PENNANT *Zool.* III. 46 This genus..the French call Cachalot, a name we have adopted. **1832** LYELL *Princ. Geol.* II. 279 A herd of Cachalots, upwards of one hundred in number, were found stranded at Kairston, Orkney. **1833** SIR C. BELL *Hand* (1834) 298 The physeter or cachelot whale..has a very large head and is remarkable for having teeth. **1847** CARPENTER *Zool.* §213.

cache (kæʃ, formerly also kɑːʃ), *sb.* Also 6 casshe. [a. F. *cache*, f. *cacher* to hide.]

1. a. A hiding place, esp. of goods, treasure, etc.

1860 C. INNES *Scotl. in Mid. Ages* x. 310 The little cache on the Orkney sea-shore, produced 16 pound weight of silver. **1866** W. R. KING *Sportsm. & Nat. in Canada* iii. 57 Crouched in his cache of green boughs.

b. *esp.* A hole or mound made by American pioneers and Arctic explorers to hide stores of provisions, ammunition, etc.

1797 C. CHABOILLEZ *Jrnl.* in B. C. Payette *Northwest* (1964) 154 [He] had a large Cash of Provisions at..that river. **1805** LEWIS & CLARK *Jrnls.* (1904) II. 134 These holes in the ground or deposits are called by the engages caches (cachés). *Ibid.* VII. 99 We put in the carsh or hole..the bellowses. **1817** J. BRADBURY *Trav.* 118 The Aricaras could not spare any provisions, as the excessive rains had penetrated into their caches, and spoiled the whole of their reserved stock. **1837** W. IRVING *Capt. Bonneville* I. 267 Captain Bonneville..prevailed upon them to proceed..to the caches. **1856** KANE *Arct. Expl.* I. xii. 138 The power of the bear in breaking up a provision cache is extraordinary. **1878** MARKHAM *Gt. Frozen Sea* v. 62 Every cairn and cache was thoroughly examined.

2. The store of provisions so hidden.

183.. BACK *Jrnl. Arctic Voy.* (Bartlett), I took advantage of a detached heap of stones, to make a cache of a bag of pemmican. **1842** FREMONT *Report Exp. Rocky Mts.* (1845) 22 As this was to be a point in our homeward journey, I made a cache (a term used in all this country for what is hidden in the ground) of a barrel of pork. **1865** LUBBOCK *Preh. Times* xiv. (1869) 484 The Esquimaux..they all of them make 'caches' of meat under stone cairns.

3. *Computing.* A small high-speed memory in some computers into which are placed the most frequently accessed contents of the slower main memory or secondary storage. Also *cache memory*.

1968 *IBM Syst. Jrnl.* VII. 17 If the data is not present in the cache, additional cycles are required while the block is loaded into the cache from main storage. **1970** *Electronics World* Oct. 37/2 Cache or buffer storage, when used in a computer system, is interposed between the main memory and the CPU. **1979** *Sci. Amer.* May 1/2 An optional high-speed cache memory reduces main memory access time to accelerate program execution. **1983** *What's New in Computing* Jan. 6/2 The P/35 and P/60 utilize additional performance enhancements such as high speed cache memory. **1987** *Electronics & Wireless World* Jan. 105/1 If the information is held in the cache, which can be thought of as very fast on-chip local memory, then only two clock cycles are required.

cache (kæʃ, formerly also kɑːʃ), *v.* orig. *U.S.* [f. CACHE *sb.*: cf. F. *cacher*.] *trans.* To put in a cache; to store (provisions) under ground; said also of animals.

1805 LEWIS & CLARK *Jrnls.* (1904) VII. 139 We carried our baggage to where we concluded to carsh to the place of cashing. **1823** E. JAMES *Exped. Rocky Mts.* I. x. 193 They then proceed to *cache*, or conceal in the earth these acquisitions. **1856** KANE *Arct. Expl.* I. xxiii. 288 He accordingly cached enough provision to last them back. **1865** LD. MILTON & W. CHEADLE *N. West Pass.* v. 75 We now proceeded..to remove the cask from its hiding-place, and..to cache it safely at some distance. **1877** COUES *Fur Anim.* ii. 51 When they [wolverenes] can eat no more, they continue to steal the baits and câche them.

Hence **cached** (kæʃt), *ppl. a.*

1901 S. E. WHITE *Westerners* vii. 47 Lone Wolf's band took up quarters within striking distance of the cached schooners. *a* **1910** 'O. HENRY' *Trimmed Lamp* (1916) 230 The man from Nome, loyal to her who had resurrected his long cached heart..followed her.

cache, obs. form of CASH, Chinese money.

cache(n, obs. form of CATCH *v.*

cachectic (kəˈkɛktɪk), *a.* Also 7-8 -ick. [Ultimately ad. Gr. *καχεκτικ-ός* in a bad habit of body. Cf. CACHEXY. *Cachectique* occurs in F. in 16th c.; mod.L. *cachecticus* is prob. still earlier.] Of or pertaining to cachexy; affected with or characterized by cachexy or a bad state of body.

1634 T. JOHNSON tr. *Parey's Chirurg.* xx. vii. (1678) 461 A melancholick cachectick disposition of the whole body. **1744** BERKELEY *Siris* §94 The good effect of this medicine on cachectic and scorbutic persons. **1861** O. W. HOLMES *Elsie V.* 210 The flat-chested and cachectic pattern which is the classical type of certain excellent young females.

ca'chectical, *a.* [f. prec. + -AL[1].] = prec.

1625 HART *Anat. Ur.* iv. 43 She was of a whitish bleake colour, and of a cachecticall disposition. **1733** ARBUTHNOT *Air* (J.) Young and florid blood, rather than vapid and cachectical. **1755** in JOHNSON; also in CRAIG and mod. Dicts.

†**cachekow.** *Sc. Obs.* [f. CATCH *v.* + COW.] A cow-catcher or cattle-pounder; hence *gen.* a bailiff. Cf. CATCH-POLL.

1513 DOUGLAS *Æneis* VIII. Prol. 136 Sum wald be court man, sum clerk, and sum a cachekow, Sum knycht, sum capitane, sum Caiser, sum King.

‖**cache-peigne** (kaʃpɛɲ). [Fr., f. *cacher* to hide + *peigne* comb.] A bow or hat ornament, usually worn at the back of a woman's hat. Also *attrib.*

1873 *Young Englishwoman* Feb. 79/2 The cache peigne is quite gone out of fashion. **1896** *Westm. Gaz.* 7 May 3/1 A pretty Parisian toque..finished..with..a cache-peigne of peach-coloured roses. **1905** *Daily Chron.* 8 May 8/3 A very becoming..hat, which has a wreath of roses..finishing in the form of a cachepeigne at the back. **1936** *Burlington Mag.* June 261/1 The heavy cache-peigne cap helps to pull the reflection downwards.

‖**cache-pot** (kaʃpo, ˈkæʃpɒt). [Fr., f. *cacher* to hide + *pot* POT *sb.*[1]] An ornamental holder for a flower-pot.

1872 LADY C. SCHREIBER *Jrnl.* (1911) I. 162 Two fine Chantilly cachepots. **1898** *Daily News* 12 Mar. 6/6 The multi-coloured vases, jars, plaques, cache-pots, &c. **1968** *Times* 27 July 22/2 Staffordshire cache pot, decorated with pictures of H.M.S. Iron Duke and a Blériot monoplane about 1914.

†**'cachere.** *Obs. rare*[−1]. [a. ONF. *cachère*, *cacheor* (mod.F. *chasseur*), f. *cacher* to CHASE: cf. CATCHER.] A hunter.

c **1340** *Gaw. & Gr. Kt.* 1139 þenne þise cacheres þat couþe, cowpled hor houndez.

†**'cacherel.** *Obs.* Also 4 kacherel. [f. prec. + -EL. Cf. *scoundrel*, *wastrel*.] A catchpoll, beagle, 'bull-dog'.

a **1325** *Pol. Songs* (1839) 151 Aȝeyn this cachereles cometh thus y mot care. *a* **1340** *Ayenb.* 263 þe dyeuel a-ye huam and his kachereles..his hous mid greate strengþe wolde loky.

‖**cache-sexe** (kaʃ-, kæʃsɛks). [Fr., f. *cacher* to hide + *sexe* sex, genitals.] A covering for the genitals.

1926 *Spectator* 13 Feb. 270 Revues the feature of which was two *grandes ensembles* of women naked except for the minute *cache-sexe*. **1930** D. H. LAWRENCE *Nettles* 19 English artists might finally learn When they painted a nude, to put a *cache sexe* on. **1961** P. USTINOV *Loser* xi. 246 She oscillated listlessly in nothing but a spangled brassière and a sequin-covered *cache sexe* the shape of a heart.

†**cachespell, -pule.** *Sc. Obs.* Also 6 cache-puyll, -pill, -spale, caichpule, kaichspell, 7 catchpule. [app. corrupt form of MFlem. *caetse-speel*, f. *caetse* (= Fr. *chasse*, Eng. CHASE), Du. *kaats* place where the ball falls + *speel* play. The Flem. was evidently from a north. Fr. *cache*: cf. Picard *cacher* to chase.]

1. The game of tennis; also *attrib.*

1568 *Woman's Truth* in *Sc. Pasquils* (1868) 4 Ane handles man I saw but dreid, In caichpule faste playene. **1611** *Rates* (Jam.) Balles called Catchpule [**1670** Tennis] balls the thousand viijl. **1818** G. CHALMERS *Life Q. Mary* I. 255 Cachepole, or Tennis was much enjoyed by the prince.

2. A tennis-court.

1526 *Sc. Ld. Treasurer's Acc.* in Pitcairn *Crimin. Trials* I. 271 Item, for ballis in Crummise cache-puyll. **1538** *Aberdeen Registers* XVI. (Jam.) The bigging of the said Alex'ris cachespale wall. **1563** *Ibid.* XXV. (Jam.) The fluir of his cachepill laitly biggit. **1597** *Sc. Act Jas. VI* (1814) 155 (Jam.) Orcherdis, yardis, doucattis, kaichspell, cloistour.. cituat within the boundis..of the priorie..of Sanctandrois.

‖**cachet** (kaʃɛ). Also 6-7 catchet. [Fr.; f. *cacher* to conceal: in 18th c. treated as English.]

1. A seal. ***letter of cachet*** (F. *lettre de cachet*): a letter under the private seal of the French king, containing an order, often of exile or imprisonment.

a **1639** SPOTTISWOOD *Hist. Ch. Scotl.* IV. (1677) 193 She had appointed, in stead of his hand, a Cachet to be used in the signing of Letters. **1754** ERSKINE *Princ. Sc. Law* (1809) 177 On the accession of James VI. to the crown of England, a catchet or seal was made, having the King's name engraved on it, with which all signatures were to be afterwards sealed. **1753** *Scots Mag.* XV. 62/2 He obtained a letter of cachet.

2. *fig.* Stamp, distinguishing mark, 'sign manual'.

1840 THACKERAY *Paris Sk. Bk.* (1885) 69 All his works [pictures] have a grand cachet: he never did anything mean. **1882** PEBODY *Eng. Journalism* xxii. 176 The journal in which the cachet of fashionable life is to be distinguished.

3. *attrib.* Done under letter of cachet; privy, secret.

1837 *Fraser's Mag.* XVI. 293 Abominators of all close, cachet, muffled..proceedings.

4. A covering of paste, gelatine, or other digestible material, enclosing (nauseous) medicine; = CAPSULE 5.

1884 *Pharmac. Jrnl.* XV. 42/2 Cachets are..sheets of unleavened bread cut to a round or oval shape with a.. concave towards the centre,..intended to receive the powder to be taken. **1898** Q. HOGG in Ethel M. Hogg *Biography* (1904) 349 My experience and cachets were of use to him. **1901** *Contemp. Rev.* Mar. 405 One cachet..to be taken with the midday meal and one in the evening.

†**ca'chexicate, cacexicate**, *v. Obs. rare*[−1]. [f. next; see -ATE.] *trans.* To render cachectic.

1650 BULWER *Anthropomet.* ii. (1653) 71 Cacexicate their petty Corpusculums.

cachexy (see below). Also 7 **cacexy, -ie, cachexe, -ie, cakexy**; and in mod.Lat. form **ca'chexia**, (8 **cacexia**). [ad. mod.L. *cachexia* or F. *cachexie* (16th c. in Paré), ad. Gr. *καχεξία*, f. *κακ-ός* bad + *-εξια* = *ἕξις* habit or state, f. *ἔχ-ειν* to have, have oneself, be in condition. Walker accents (ˈkækɛksɪ) which is according to Eng. analogies; but mod. Dicts. have mostly (kəˈkɛksɪ).]

'A depraved condition of the body, in which nutrition is everywhere defective.' *Syd. Soc. Lex.*

1541 R. COPLAND *Galyen's Terap.* 2 Diij, The euyll habytude of the body (whiche the Grekes call Cachexie). **1555** EDEN *Decades W. Ind.* (Arb.) 58 The dysease which the phisicians caule Cachexia. **1651** WITTE tr. *Primrose's Pop. Err.* IV. xii. 262 Who can in a Cachexie draw all the vitious humours out of the body at once. **1775** SIR E. BARRY *Observ. Wines* 417 Liable to..cachexies..etc. **1843** BETHUNE *Sc. Fire-side Stor.* 65 Affected with fevers and cachexy.

b. A depraved habit of mind or feeling.

1652 L. S. *People's Lib.* xvi. 40 The Israelites desiring a King..out of a Cacexie and evill frame of spirit. **1657** REEVE *God's Plea* Ep. Ded. 5, I see..a cakexy of evill life amongst you. **1843** F. E. PAGET *Warden of Birkingholt* 161 He would think that a cachexy of chattering had become epidemic among the clergy of the nineteenth century. **1868** SYMONDS in *Fortn. Rev.* Dec. IV. 602 Both poets [Clough and De Musset] describe the *maladie du siècle*, the nondescript cachexy, in which aspiration mingles with disenchantment, satire and scepticism with a childlike desire for the tranquillity of reverence and belief.

c. Said of a body politic.

1654 L'ESTRANGE *Chas. I*, 187 Her high repletion brought her [the City] into a Cachexy. **1883** *Macm. Mag.* Nov. 33 Ireland..lies fretful and wrathful under a grim social cachexy of distressful centuries.

cachinnate (ˈkækɪneɪt), *v.* [f. L. *cachinnā-re*: see -ATE.] *intr.* To laugh loudly or immoderately.

1824 DE QUINCEY *Walladmor* in *London Mag.* X. 354 Not a publisher but cachinnates from Leipsic to Moscow. **1837** *Fraser's Mag.* XVI. 432 Groggan..only cachinnated the more vehemently.

cachinnation (kækɪˈneɪʃən). [ad. L. *cachinnātiōn-em*, n. of action f. *cachinnāre*: see prec.] Loud or immoderate laughter.

1623 COCKERAM, *Cachinnation*, a great laughter. **1635** PERSON *Varieties* II. 60 These Cachinnations or laughings.. which we heare, are rather Aerall spirits. **1815** SCOTT *Guy M.* iii, The hideous grimaces which attended this unusual cachinnation. **1868** BROWNING *Ring & Bk.* III. VIII. 767 He moved to mirth and cachinnation all.

'cachinnator. [agent-noun f. L. vb. in prec.] A loud or immoderate laugher.

18.. R. CHAMBERS *Wheesht*, They mark a cachinnator as a man to be avoided.

cachinnatory (ˈkækɪnəˌtərɪ), *a.* [f. prec.: see -ORY.] Of, pertaining to, or connected with loud or immoderate laughter.

1828 *Blackw. Mag.* XXIV. 188 Shall our cachinnatory muscles remain rigid? **1846** HAWTHORNE *Mosses* II. iii. (1864) 61 Which threatened instant death on the slightest cachinnatory indulgence.

cachique, obs. form of CACIQUE.

cacholong (ˈkætʃəlɒŋ). *Min.* [ˈ*Kaschtschilon* = "beautiful stone" of Kalmucks and Tartars' (Dana).] A variety of the opal, opaque, bluish-white, porcelain-white, pale yellowish or reddish.

1791 MACIE in *Phil. Trans.* LXXXI. 369 That variety of calcedony which is known to mineralogists by the name of Cacholong. **1868-80** DANA *Min.* 199 Cacholong..often adheres to the tongue, and contains a little alumina.

‖**cachou** (kaʃu). Also 8 cashou. [Fr.]

1. = CATECHU.

1708 MOTTEUX *Rabelais* v. viii, Store of Mirabolans, Cashou, Green Ginger preserv'd. **1750** BEAWES *Lex Mercat.* (1752) 787 Cardamome, Long Pepper, Cachou, etc.

2. A sweetmeat, generally in the form of a pill, made of cashew-nut, extract of liquorice, etc., used by tobacco-smokers to sweeten the breath.

1880 in WEBSTER Suppl. **1895** *Montgomery Ward Catal.* 261/2 Aromatic cachou lozenges for perfuming the breath. **1898** *Army & Navy Co-op. Soc. Price List*, Cachous, Atkinson's White Rose, Violet, Heliotrope, Citron..per box 0/8. **1909** *Daily Chron.* 23 Feb. 5/6 The tabloids might easily be taken for 'cachous'. **1922** *Glasgow Herald* 3 Apr. 4 He carried a little round, flat gilt box of Prince Albert cachous.

‖**cachrys** ('kækrɪs). *Bot.* [Gr. κάχρυς catkin.]

†**1.** 'The catkin of nut-trees, willows, etc.' *Obs.*

1708 in KERSEY. **1731** in BAILEY II.

2. A genus of umbelliferous plants.

‖**cachucha** (kə'tʃuːtʃə). Incorrectly **cachuca**. [Sp.] A lively Spanish dance.

1840 BARHAM *Ingol. Leg.* 480 A Court where it's thought in a lord or a duke a Disgrace to fall short in the Brawls (their Cachouca). **1841** THACKERAY *Profess.* in *Comic T. & Sk.* II. 154 In a very short time Miss Binse..could dance the cachuca. **1842** LONGF. *Sp. Stud.* I. iii, I see thee dance cachuchas. **1867** MISS BRADDON *Aur. Floyd* i. 8.

‖**cacique** (kə'siːk). Forms: 6 (L. *caccicus, caciquus,*) cacike, cazike, 7 cassique, casique, (casica), 8 cachique, 8– cazique, 6– cacique. [a. Sp. *cacique, cazique,* or F. *cacique,* native Haytian word for 'lord, chief' (Oviedo *Hist. de las Indias*).]

1. A native chief or 'prince' of the aborigines in the West Indies and adjacent parts of America.

1555 EDEN *Decades W. Ind.* I. II. (Arb.) 72 Makynge..a brotherly league with the *Caccicus* (that is to saye a kynge). **1577** EDEN & WILLES *Hist. Trav.* 219 b, These Indians gyue great honour and reuerence to theyr Cacique. **1578** T. N. tr. *Conq. W. Ind.* 33 A cruel and cursed Cacike, that is to say a Lord, in whose power we fell. *a* **1618** RALEIGH *Apol.* 46 The Mynes which the Cassique Carapana offered them. **1697** DAMPIER *Voy.* (1698) I. v. 124 They had a Casica too..but he could neither write nor speak Spanish. **1778** ROBERTSON *Hist. Amer.* I. II. 97 Here Columbus was visited by a prince or Cazique of the country. **1796** MORSE *Amer. Geog.* I. 757 The several nations are governed by their chiefs or cachiques. **1799** SHERIDAN *Pizarro* I. i, On yonder hill, among the palm-trees, we have surprised an old cacique. **1843** PRESCOTT *Mexico* II. i. (1864) 73 The cacique who ruled over this province.

2. In Spain or Latin America, a man who owes his ascendancy to his power or influence; a political 'boss'; also used *attrib.* of a political system in which the power is in the hands of such a man or men. Also *attrib.* Hence **ca'ciqu(e)ism**, the cacique system.

1872 SCHELE DE VERE *Americanisms* 71 The West India term *Cacique*..is often most absurdly applied..to mayors of New Mexican towns, and any somewhat pompous and self-sufficient man is apt to be nicknamed the Cacique of his town. **1903** *Times* 3 June 3/5 Caciquism, the Spanish equivalent for the methods of Tammany. **1923** *Glasgow Herald* 23 Oct. 7 This decree,..of great importance for the destruction of 'caciquism', will be applied to about 500 towns. **1923** *Contemp. Rev.* Nov. 613 The cacique whether an employer of labour or a moneylender has the majority of the constituency under his thumb. **1923** *Glasgow Herald* 13 Dec. 12 The whole cacique system is..an immense satire on local authority in Spain. **1964** *Economist* 4 July 37/2 The provincial *caciques* and city bosses.

Hence **ca'ciqueship**, †**caci'quesse**.

1760 tr. *Juan & Ulloa's Voy.* v. v. (1772) 266 The caciquesses, or Indian women, who are married to the alcades..and others. **1849** *Fraser's Mag.* XL. 411 The attainment of the caciqueship of that pseudo El Dorado by Gregor McGregor.

cack (kæk), *v. Obs.* or *dial.* [app. ad. L. *cacā-re* in same sense, whence also MDu. *cacken,* Du. *kakken,* early mod.Ger. *kacken,* Da. *kakke*; also Boh. *kakati,* Pol. *kakać.*]

1. *intr.* To void excrement.

1436 *Pol. Poems* (1859) II. 170 Wythoute Calise in ther buttere the cakked. *c* **1440** *Promp. Parv.* 58/1 Cakkyn, or fyystyn, *caco.* *c* **1500** DUNBAR *Fenȝeit Frier* 101 Ffor feir vncunnandly he cawkit. **1570** LEVINS *Manip.* 5 To cake, *cacare.* **1611** COTGR., *Chier,* to cacke. *a* **1710** POPE *Alley* i, Some cack against the wall. **1731** in BAILEY II.

2. *trans.* To void as excrement.

1485 CAXTON *Trevisa's Higden* IV. x. (1527) 158 One that hadde cacked golde. **1549** CRANMER in Strype *Life* (1694) App. 105 Because the Devil could not get out at his mouth, the man blew him, or cacked him out behind.

cack, *sb. Obs.* or *dial.* [f. same source as prec.: used already in OE. in the comb. *cac-hūs* 'latrina'.]

c **1600** *Timon* v. v. (1842) 89 Hee hath a face like one's that is at cack.

Hence **'cacky** *a. dial.* and *slang,* foul with excrement. (See also *Eng. Dial. Dict.*)

1937 PARTRIDGE *Dict. Slang* s.v. *cack.* **1977** C. MCCULLOUGH *Thorn Birds* xvii. 407 'Don't you want to get married?'..'Not bloody likely! Spend *my* life wiping snotty noses and cacky bums?'

†**cackerel** ('kækərəl). ? *Obs.* Also 7 **cackarel, cackrel.** [a. obs. F. *caquerel* (also *cagarel, cagaret*) Cotgr., ad. Pr. *cagarel, cagarello* (also, according to Duhamel, *gagarel,* whence Cuvier's specific name *gagarella*); app. f. Pr. *cagar*:—L. *cacāre* (see CACK *v.*), with which the name is popularly associated.

(Variously etymologized as 'a fish which voids excrements when pursued' or 'which when eaten relaxes the bowels'; M. Paul Meyer suggests that the name is merely one of contempt = 'méchant petit poisson', 'poisson chétif'. The allied *Mæna* is now in Pr. *picarel,* dim. of *picaro* 'rogue, rascal'.)]

1. A small fish of the Mediterranean: the name is applied by the fishermen of Marseilles and Toulon to *Smaris gagarella* (Cuv.), and perhaps to other similar species of the same genus of small sea-breams. Early writers used the word to english Pliny's *mæna* 'a kind of small sea-fish, eaten salted by the poor', now the name of a genus closely akin to *Smaris.*

1583 J. HIGINS tr. *Junius' Nomenclator, Mæna*.. a cackrell, so called, because it maketh the eaters laxative: some take it for a herring or sprat. **1601** HOLLAND *Pliny* I. 249 Cackarels change their colour: for these fishes being white all Winter, wax blacke when Summer comes. *Ibid.* II. 442 Salt Cackerels. **1632** SHERWOOD *Eng.-Fr. Dict.,* A cackerell (fish), *cagarel, caquerel, cagaret, juscle: bocque, mandole, mendole, mene.* **1634** SIR T. HERBERT *Trav.* 187 Fish, whose ordinary abode is in salt waters, namely porpoise,—cackrel, skate, soles, etc. **1721–90** in BAILEY. **1755** JOHNSON, *Cackerel,* a fish said to make those who eat it laxative.

2. [as if f. CACK.] Dysentery (F. *caquesangue*).

1659 HOWELL *Lex. Tetrag. It. Prov.* 19 May the Cackrel take him [transl. It *cacasangue*].

cack-handed (ˌkæk'hændɪd), *a. dial.* or *colloq.* Also **cag-, kack-, keck-handed.** [perh. f. CACK *sb.*] Left-handed; ham-handed, clumsy, awkward. Hence ˌ**cack-'handedness.**

1854 A. E. BAKER *Gloss. Northants.* I. 365 *Keck-handed,* awkward, left-handed. **1859** *N. & Q.* VIII. 483 If a man, at hay time or harvest, holds his fork with his left hand lowest, they say, 'Ah! he's no good! he's keck-handed!..' **1893** DARTNELL & GODDARD *Gloss. Wiltshire* 21 Cack-handed, cag-handed. **1955** M. ALLINGHAM *Beckoning Lady* vi. 91, I never met such a kack-handed jackass in all my born days. **1959** P. MCCUTCHAN *Storm South* iv. 52 He would..moan about the cack-handedness of Bacon (which was nonsense, for Bacon was a first-rate steward). **1961** *Spectator* 22 Sept. 384 An insanely slothful or cack-handed publican. **1964** S. JEPSON *Fear in Wind* i. 17 A series of kack-handed manœuvres..designed to keep one end of a stick on the ground. **1967** J. POTTER *Foul Play* x. 125 When he saw the ball going the wrong side of him, he lunged his [hockey] stick out behind him... 'Just thought I'd try a bit of your cack-handed stuff.'

cackle ('kæk(ə)l), *sb.* [f. the vb. stem: cf. Sw. *kackel* in same sense.]

1. A cackler. (Or ? *adj.* cackling.)

a **1225** *Ancr. R.* 66 Uolewe̊ð..nout þe kakele [*v.r.* chakele, kakelinde] Eue. *Mod. colloq.* or *dial.* What a cackle she is!

2. Cackling; as of a hen or goose.

1674 N. FAIRFAX *Bulk & Selv.* To Rdr., Dinn'd & grated with the Cackle. **1697** DRYDEN *Æneis* VIII. (R.) The silver goose..by her cackle, sav'd the state. **1833** TENNYSON *Goose* iii, The goose let fall a golden egg With cackle and with clatter.

3. a. *fig.* Stupid loquacity, silly chatter. Colloq. phr. ***cut the cackle*** (***and come to the horses***): stop talking (and get to the heart of the matter, the real business); hence ***cackle-cutting*** vbl. sb. and ppl. a.

1676 'A. RIVETUS, JUN.' *Mr. Smirke* 18 Bedawb'd with Addle Eggs of the Animadverters own Cackle. **1859** TENNYSON *Enid* 276 The rustic cackle of your bourg. **1862** THORNBURY *Turner* I. 262 The cackle about Claude. **1889** BARRÈRE & LELAND *Dict. Slang* I. 216/1 The great Ducrow ..was wont to apostrophise the performers in his equestrian drama after this fashion: 'Come, I say, you mummers, cut your cackle, and come to the 'osses!' **1899** *Westm. Gaz.* 27 June 2/1 Nine-tenths would be delighted if the famous phrase about 'cutting the cackle' were acted upon. **1919** G. B. SHAW in *Shaw on Theatre* (1958) 124 Out with the lot of them, then: let us cut the cackle and come to the 'osses. **1921** —— *Back to Methus.* v. 239 Cut the cackle; and come to the synthetic couple. **1930** WYNDHAM LEWIS *Apes of God* XII. vi. 469 Cut the cackle Arthur—I'm pressed for time! **1957** *Economist* 28 Dec. 1106/1 Nor..will delegates reassemble.. in September after parting only in March—a decidedly cackle-cutting feature of this last session. **1958** J. WAIN *Contenders* ix. 193 'You must be wondering what all this is about,' Ned put in, adopting his money-man's tone of directness and cackle-cutting.

b. A short spasmodic laugh, a chuckle.

1856 LEVER *Martins of Cro' M.* 410 'She hasn't got a nice day for pleasuring!' said the Jew, with a vulgar cackle.

4. cackle-berry *slang* (orig. *U.S.*), an egg.

1916 *Dial. Notes* IV. 272 Pass the *cackleberries.* **1925** G. P. KRAPP *Eng. Lang. in Amer.* I. v. 321 Sometimes slang is complicated in its suggestiveness, like *cackleberry,* meaning *egg.* **1962** *John o' London's* 14 June 571/1 A cackle berry is an egg [in naut. slang].

cackle ('kæk(ə)l), *v.*[1] Forms: 3 **kakelen, cakelen,** 4–5 **cackle(n,** 5 **cakele, -yn, kakyl,** 5–6 **cakle,** 6 **cakyll, cackyll, -el, cacle,** 7 **cakell,** 6– **cackle;** *Sc.* 6 **kekkyl, kekell,** 7 **kekcle:** see also KECKLE. [Early ME. *cakelen*: corresp. to Du. *kakelen,* LG. *kâkeln,* Sw. *kackla,* Da. *kagle*; cf. also Ger. *gackeln,* Du. *gaggelen,* and GAGGLE. The evidence does not make it certain to what extent the word has arisen separately in different langs. in imitation of the animal sounds, or has been adopted from one language into another. The word may have been WGer. or at least Saxon: but the Eng. may also have been from Scandinavian.]

1. *intr.* To make a noise as a hen, especially after laying an egg; also to make a noise as a goose (which is more specifically to GAGGLE).

a **1225** *Ancr. R.* 66 Þe hen, hwon heo haueð ileid, ne con buten kakelen. **1393** GOWER *Conf.* II. 264 Somtime cacleth as a hen. *c* **1440** *Promp. Parv.* 58 Cakelyn of hennys, *gracillo.* *c* **1470** *Hors, Shepe, & G.* (1822) 17 The ghoos may cakle. **1549** *Compl. Scot.* vi. 39 Quhilk gart the hennis kekkyl. **1552** HULOET, Cakle lyke a henne, *glocio.* **1596** SHAKS. *Merch. V.* v. i. 105 If she should sing by day When euery Goose is cackling. **1660** W. SECKER *Nonsuch Prof.* 43 Some persons are like hens that after laying must be cackling. *a* **1680** BUTLER *Rem.* (1759) II. 139 Like..a Wildgoose always cackling when he is upon the Wing. **1824** W. IRVING *T. Trav.* II. 253 A hen could not cackle but she was on the alert to secure the new-laid egg.

b. Said of the chattering of other birds, *esp.* crows, jackdaws, magpies, and starlings. *Obs.*

a **1225** *Ancr. R.* 88 Ane rikelot þet cakeleð hire al þet heo isihð. **1530** LYNDESAY *Test. Papyngo* 94 Bark lyk ane Dog, and kekell lyke ane Ka. **1553** T. WILSON *Rhet.* 117 b, Some cackels lyke a henne or a Jack dawe. **1613** MARKHAM *Eng. Husbandman* I. i. iii. (1635) 13 If Crowes flocke much together, and cakell and talke. **1675–7** HOBBES *Homer* 275 A cloud of starelings cackle when they fly.

2. *fig.* Said of persons: **a.** To be full of noisy and inconsequent talk; to talk glibly, be loquacious, prate, chatter. **b.** To talk loudly or fussily about a petty achievement, like a hen after laying an egg. **c.** To chuckle, 'to laugh, to giggle' (J.).

1530 PALSGR. 473/1 Howe these women cackyll nowe they have dyned. **1599** *Broughton's Lett.* ix. 34 Cease cackling of the vnlearnednes of thy betters. **1712** ARBUTHNOT *John Bull* (1727) 70 Then Nic. grinned, cackled, and laughed. **1847** DISRAELI *Tancred* II. v. (1871) 78 The peers cackle as if they had laid an egg. **1860** GEN. P. THOMPSON *Audi Alt.* III. cxix. 59 It is also the business of a sensible government, not to cackle on its discoveries. **1862** THACKERAY *Four Georges* iii. 162 The equerries and women in waiting..cackled over their tea.

3. *trans.* To utter with or express by cackling.

c **1225** *Ancr. R.* 66 ȝif hit nere icakeled. **1857** LIVINGSTONE *Trav.* vi. 114 Any man who..cackles forth a torrent of vocables. **1880** HOWELLS *Undisc. Country* i. 28 The ladies.. now rose..and joyously cackled satisfaction.

'cackle, *v.*[2] *Naut.* Also **kackle.** 'To cover a cable spirally with 3-inch old rope to protect it from chafe in the hawse hole' (Adm. Smyth).

1748 ANSON *Voy.* III. ii. (ed. 4) 427 They [cables] were besides cackled twenty fathom from the anchors. **1883** *Man. Seamanship for Boys' Training Ships R. Navy* (Admiralty) (1886) 128 The cable is then served, or, as is termed, kackled with $2\frac{1}{2}$-in. rounding, for the distance of 9 ft. from the eye.

cackler ('kæklə(r)). [f. CACKLE *v.*[1] + -ER[1].] One who cackles; *fig.* a tell-tale, tattler, blabber. *slang,* a fowl.

a **1400** *Cov. Myst.* 131 Kytt Cakelere and Colett Crane. **1598** FLORIO, *Gracchione*..a chatter, a cackler. **1673** R. HEAD *Canting Acad.* 192 A Prigger of the Cacklers. **1730–6** BAILEY, *Cackler,* a Prater, a Tell-tale, a noisy Person; also a humerous word for capons or fowl. **1878** BROWNING *Poets Croisic* 92 If they dared Count you a cackler.

cackling ('kæklɪŋ), *vbl. sb.* [see -ING[1].]

1. The crying of a hen on laying an egg; also that of a goose, or other fowl.

c **1374** CHAUCER *Parl. Foules* 562 Tho began The goose to speke, and in her cakelinge, She said. **1562** J. HEYWOOD *Prov. & Epigr.* (1867) 110 The cocke praide hir, hir cacklyng to seace. **1709** *Tatler* No. 133 ¶1 The cackling of cranes, when they invade an army of pigmies. **1821** CLARE *Vill. Minstr.* II. 70 Constant cacklings of new-laying hens.

2. Loud idle talk or chatter: sometimes with immediate reference to the cry of a hen on laying.

1530 PALSGR. 202/2 Cackelyng, bablyng, *cacquet.* **1601** DENT *Path-w. Heauen* 171 They spend the rest of the day.. in..cackling, prating and gossipping. **1860** GEN. P. THOMPSON *Audi Alt.* III. cxix. 61 This cackling about improved arms is not worthy of well-informed statesmen. **1866** GEO. ELIOT *F. Holt* (1868) 161 And when it takes to cackling, will have nothing to announce but that addled delusion.

'cackling, *ppl. a.* [see -ING[2].] That cackles.

a **1225** [see CACKLE *sb.* 1]. **1567** HARMAN *Caveat* 86 She hath a Cacling chete [i.e. a hen]. **1622** FLETCHER *Beggar's B.* v. i, Or surprising a boor's ken for grunting-cheats? Or cackling-cheats? **1674** FLATMAN *Belly God* 29 Pluck of[f] the cackling head. **1794** MRS. PIOZZI *Synon.* II. 174 *Ciarlatano* means a prating, cackling creature, and answers to our term *Quack.* **1841** CATLIN *N. Amer. Ind.* (1844) II. liv. 182 Some hundreds of cackling women and girls bathing.

caco- representing Gr. κακο- combining form of κακός bad, evil, forming many compounds in Greek, some of which, like *cacochymy, cacodæmon, cacoethes, cacophony,* have reached English through Latin (and French); others have been adapted directly from Greek in modern times (as *cacology, cacotrophy*); others have been formed on Greek analogies from their elements. Compounds of Greek and Latin, as *cacodorous* = malodorous, and the medical *cacosomnia* (sleeping badly) are exceptional. Occasionally *caco-* is used in looser or casual combination with words of Greek derivation, which may have been modelled on *cacodæmon,* as in *caco-magician, cacotype.* It is very freely used in medical terminology to form names of bad states of bodily organs, but most of these are not English in form, e.g. *cacoga'lactia* (a condition in which the milk is bad), *cacoglossia* (putrid state of the tongue), *cacomorphia* (malformation or deformity), *caconychia* (morbid state of the nails), *cacopharyngia* (a

putrid condition of the pharynx), *cacophthalmia* (malignant inflammation of the eyes), *cacoplasia* (formation of diseased structures from a depraved condition of the system), *cacopneumonia*, *cacorrhachitis* (disease of the vertebral column), *cacothymia* (disordered state of mind), *cacotrichia* (disease of the hair), etc.

cacoa, obs. form of CACAO, COCOA *sb.*

cacochylous (kækəʊ'kaɪləs), *a. Path.* [mod. f. Gr. κακοχυλ-ος with bad juice or flavour + -OUS.] Characterized by bad chyle; of difficult digestion, as ' cacochylous aliments'. *Syd. Soc. Lex.*

1859 in MAYNE *Exp. Lex.*

So **caco'chylia**, depraved chylification.

1706 PHILLIPS, *Cacochylia*, a bad chylification, when the chyle is not duly made. **1721-90** in BAILEY. **1839** G. RAYMOND in *New Monthly Mag.* LVI. 306 Persons.. using every diligence for a most unprofitable cacohylia.

† **'cacochyme**, *a. Obs. Path.* [a. F. *cacochyme* (16th c. in Paré), ad. Gr. κακόχυμος with unhealthy humours, f. κακο- bad + χυμός juice, humour.] Full of evil humours.

1614 W. BARCLAY *Nepenthes* in Arb. *App. Jas. I Counterbl.* 116 The body very cacochyme, or full of euil humours.

cacochymic (kækəʊ'kɪmɪk), *a.* and *sb. arch.* Also 6 cacochymyke, -chimick, -ike, 7 -chymick(e. [f. CACOCHYME (or its source) + -IC.]

A. *adj.* Having unhealthy or depraved humours; ill-humoured (in body).

1541 R. COPLAND *Guydon's Quest. Chirurg.*, In cacochymyke bodyes and replete. **1625** HART *Anat. Ur.* I. iii. 34 His bodie [was] plethoricke and cacochymicke. **1665** R. KEPHALE *Medela Pestil.* 71 If Cacochimick.. he must be well purged. **1863** T. THOMPSON *Ann. Influenza* 4 A pale caccochimic and depraved countenance.

B. *sb.* An 'ill-humoured' person.

1569 J. SANFORD *Agrippa's Van. Artes* 158 Made now of Alcumistes, Cacochimickes, of Phisitions, pewterers.

caco'chymical, *a. arch.* [f. as prec. + -AL[1].] Having the humours of the body depraved; 'ill-humoured' (in body, and jocularly, in disposition).

1606 HOLLAND *Sueton.* Annot. 18 In cacochymicall bodies, such as his was. **1656** RIDGLEY *Pract. Physic* 193 To cure a cacochymical person. **1707** FLOYER *Pulse-Watch* 97 The old Writers call'd these the different Species of cacochimical Choler. **1836** *Fraser's Mag.* XIII. 227 By what means did you.. arrive at a cacochymical old age? **1837** BEDDOES *Let.* Mar., Critical and cacochymical remarks on European literature.

† **caco'chymious**, *a. Obs.* [f. *cacochymia* (see below) + -OUS.] = CACOCHYMIC.

1676 SHADWELL *Virtuoso* II. Wks. 1720 I. 347 They were cacochymious, and had deprav'd viscera. **1702** E. BAYNARD *Cold Baths* II. (1709) 337 Cacocymious Juices.

† **caco'chymist**. *Obs.* [f. as prec. + -IST.] A person of depraved 'humours'.

1684 tr. *Agrippa's Van. Arts* xc. 313 In stead of Alchymists, Cacochymists; in stead of being Doctors, Beggers.

cacochymy ('kækəʊkaɪmɪ). *arch.* Also 6-8 -chymie, and in Latin form 6- **cacochymia**, (7 cacochym). [a. F. *cacochymie* (16th c. in Paré), and mod.L. *cacochymia*, a. Gr. κακοχυμία (Galen) badness of the humours, f. κακόχυμος: see above.]

In the medical system of the Humorists: Unhealthy state of the 'humours' or fluids of the body; 'ill-humoured' state (of the body).

1541 R. COPLAND *Galyen's Terap.* 2 Aij b, Yf eroysion habounde inwardely it is caused of cacochimie. **1665** G. HARVEY *Advice agst. Plague* 21 Cacochymies or fowl bodies of the Vulgar.. do require strong Purges. **1651** BIGGS *New Disp.* ¶ 184 The Anarchy of a cacochymia keeps not court in the veins. **1684** tr. *Bonet's Merc. Compit.* I. 20 The Melancholick Cacochymie. *Ibid.* XVI. 550 A great corruption of the Blood and Cacochym. **1744** MITCHELL in *Phil. Trans.* XLIII. 144 A peculiar kind of Cachexy, accompanied with an atrabilious Cacochymy. **1839** *New Monthly Mag.* LVI. 386 Are not their countenances disfigured by the cacochymy of their humours. **1852** HAMILTON *Discuss.* 248.

† **caco'demical**, *a. Obs. rare*[−1]. A humorous mixture of *cacodæmon* and *academical*.

1610 ROWLANDS *Mart. Mark-all* 6 Vp starts an old Cacodemicall Academicke with his frize bonnet.

cacodemon, -dæmon (kækəʊ'diːmən). [a. Gr. κακοδαίμων evil genius; also *adj.* possessed by an evil genius, ill-starred; whence sense 2.]

1. An evil spirit.

[**1398** TREVISA *Barth. De P.R.* II. xix. (1495) 45 Plato in Cuneo callith the deuyll Cachodemon, that is to vnderstonde knowynge euyll.] **1594** NASHE *Terrors of Nt.* Wks. 1883-4 III. 267 Anie terror, the least illusion in the earth, is a Cacodæmon vnto him. **1594** SHAKS. *Rich. III*, I. iii. 144 Leaue this World, Thou Cacodemon! **1664** BUTLER *Hud.* II. III. 644 Nor was the Dog a Cacodæman, But a true Dog. **1728** YOUNG *Love Fame* II. (1757) 95 Poor negroes, thus, to show their burning spite To cacodæmons, say, they're dev'lish white. **1870** LOWELL *Among my Bks.* Ser. I. (1873) 93 To make the pagan divinities hateful, they were stigmatized as cacodæmons.

† **b.** *Med.* A name for nightmare. *Syd. Soc. Lex.*

1811 in HOOPER *Med. Dict.*

c. *transf.* Applied to persons, etc.

1711 MRS. CENTLIVRE *Marplot* IV. Wks. (1760) 168 The old Cacademon is gone into that house. **1821** SCOT *Kenilw.* (1867) 109 My miller's thumb—my prince of cacodemons—my little mouse. **1854** BADHAM *Halieut.* 420 Untaught by their parents to know better, these little cacodemons, etc.

2. *Astrol.* The Twelfth House (or Scheme) in a figure of the Heavens, so called from its baleful signification.

a **1625** FLETCHER *Rollo* IV. ii. 442 The twelfth the Cacodemon. **1721-90** in BAILEY.

cacode'moniac. *rare.* [f. prec.: cf. DEMONIAC.] One possessed with an evil spirit.

1657 TOMLINSON *Renou's Disp.* 20 Unless some cacodemoniack, that refers them to his Philosophy.

† **cacode'monial**, *a. Obs. rare*[−1]. [f. as prec. + -AL[1].] Of or pertaining to an evil spirit.

1522 SKELTON *Why nat to Courte* 807 To his college conuentuall, As well calodemonyall As to cacodemonyall.

cacode'monic, *a.* [ad. Gr. κακοδαιμονικός 'bringing misfortune', in a sense taken from CACODEMON.] Of the nature of a cacodemon.

1886 *Pall Mall G.* 20 Aug. 4/2 One of these.. declines to have further dealings with cacodæmonic powers.

caco'demonize, *v. rare*[−1]. [see -IZE.] *trans.* To make into a demon.

1834-43 SOUTHEY *Doctor* (1849) 672 '*Beards*', The simple appendage of a tail will cacodemonise the Eudemon.

cacodorous (kæ'kəʊdərəs), *a. rare.* [A hybrid formation from Gr. κακο- bad + ODOROUS.] Ill-smelling, malodorous.

1863 *Press* 5 Sept., The August sun begins to make the Thames cacodorous. **1871** M. COLLINS *Mrq. & Merch.* III. 60 He.. made his way through a cacodorous crowd.

† **'cacodox**, *a. Obs.* [a Gr. κακόδοξος of the wrong opinion; cf. *orthodox*.] Holding wrong or evil opinions or doctrines.

1716 M. DAVIES *Athen. Brit.* III. 28 That Cacodox Alastor has.. abandon'd the true Principles of Reason and Religion.

cacodoxy ('kækəʊdɒksɪ). *rare.* [a. Gr. κακοδοξία wrong opinion, f. κακόδοξος (see prec.)] Wrong opinion or doctrine, heterodoxy.

a **1864** R. TURNBULL (Webster) Less anxious.. to favor or deny orthodoxy, heterodoxy or what Luther calls cacodoxy, than to establish the simple truth.

Hence **caco'doxian, caco'doxical** *a.*

1693 URQUHART *Rabelais* III. xxxviii. 318 Cacodoxical fool. **1716** M. DAVIES *Athen. Brit.* II. 431 These two Cacodoxian Alastors can Cant and Recant nothing but such quisquilian Nugaments. **1880** WEBSTER *Supp.*, *Cacodoxical.*

cacodyl ('kækəʊdɪl). *Chem.* Also **kakodyl**(e. [f. Gr. κακώδ-ης stinking, κακωδία stink (f. κακό-ς + ὀδ-, root of ὄζειν to emit smell) + -YL, matter.]

An organic compound of arsenic and methyl, $As(CH_3)_2$ = Kd, also called *arsendimethyl*, a colourless liquid, of most disgusting garlic odour and with extremely poisonous vapour, which takes fire on exposure to the air.

1850 C. DAUBENY *Atomic Theory* vii. 219 The body.. which Bunsen regards as the radical, and which from its offensive odour he denominates kakodyle. **1867** *Cornh. Mag.* Mar. 383 The well-known garlic-like odour characteristic of cacodyl. **1869** ROSCOE *Elem. Chem.* 341 Cacodyl is a colourless liquid, boiling at 170°. **1872** WATTS *Dict. Chem.* I. 405 Cacodyl takes fire in the air, at ordinary temperatures, even more readily than crude alkarsin.

caco'dylate. A salt of CACODYLIC acid.

1908 *Practitioner* Aug. 338 Arseniate of soda is more brutal, as it were, than cacodylate, the action of which is prolonged and deliberate.

cacodylic (kækəʊ'dɪlɪk), *a. Chem.* [f. CACODYL + -IC.] Of cacodyl, as in *cacodylic acid*, Kd O_2H, a crystalline solid.

1850 C. DAUBENY *Atomic Theory* vii. 219 Kd + O_3 forms kakodylic acid, or algargen. **1869** ROSCOE *Elem. Chem.* 341 One of the most important compounds is cacodylic acid; it is soluble in water, and is not poisonous.

cacœconomy (kækiː'kɒnəmɪ). *rare*[−1]. [f. Gr. κακ-οικονόμ-ος a bad steward: see ECONOMY.] Bad economy, bad management.

1819 SYD. SMITH in *Edin. Rev.* XXXII. 28 A mighty empire in spite of the cacœconomy of their government.

cacoëpy (kæ'kəʊɪpɪ). *rare.* [a. Gr. κακοέπεια faulty language.] Bad or erroneous pronunciation; opposed to *orthoepy*. Hence **cacoë'pistic** *a.*

1880 GRANT WHITE *Every-Day Eng.* 40 Phonology finds in orthoëpy only the materials upon which it works, which indeed it finds no less in cacoëpy. **1867** A. J. ELLIS *E.E. Pronunc.* I. iii. 224 Abnormal, cacoepistic, rare, vulgar and dialectic forms.

† **'cacoethe, -eth**, *a. Obs. rare.* [a. F. *cacoèthe*, ad. Gr. κακοήθης: see next. But in the examples, the word may represent L. *cacoēthē* pl. of the sb.] Of an ill habit; malignant (as a disease).

1541 R. COPLAND *Galyen's Terap.* 2 C iv b, It had ben better to haue called them [ulcers] Cacoethe, that is to say wycked, and nat inueterate. **1661** LOVELL *Hist. Anim. & Min.* 119 It helpes hardnesses, that are called cocoëth.

‖ **cacoethes** (kækəʊ'iːθɪs, -'iːθiːz). [L., a. Gr. κακόηθες ill habit, propensity, 'itch', subst. use of neuter of κακοήθης ill-disposed, f. κακο- bad + (ἦθος) ἠθε- disposition, character. (The Gr. (and L.) plural was *cacoēthē*.)] **a.** An evil habit. **b.** An obstinate or malignant disease. **c.** An 'itch' for doing something, as in the *insanabile scribendi cacoëthes* (incurable passion for writing) of Juvenal.

1563-87 FOXE *A. & M.* I. 657/1 Such is the malady and cacoethes of your pen, that it beginneth to bark, before it hath learned well to write. **1601** HOLLAND *Pliny* II. 142 Gangrenes and those morimall vlcers called Cacoethe. **1603** H. CROSSE *Vertues Commw.* (1878) 139 This cacoethes, or ill custome.. incroacheth so vpon the good maners of men. **1713** ADDISON *Spect.* No. 532 ¶ 1 Juvenal terms [this distemper] a Cacoethes, which is a hard word for a disease called in plain English, 'The itch of writing'. This Cacoethes is as epidemical as the small pox. **1726** MONRO *Anat.* (1741) 128 Unless the Patient labours under a general Cacoethes. **1836** *Fraser's Mag.* XIV. 578 One half of it was cacoëthes of building, the other half cacoëthes of painting.

† **cacoethic** (kækəʊ'ɛθɪk), *a. Med. Obs.* [f. prec.: after ETHIC.] Obstinate or malignant.

1684 tr. *Bonet's Merc. Compit.* VIII. 277 The Wound.. becomes cacoethick. *Ibid.* x. 347 Foul, cacoethick Ulcers.

cacogastric (kækəʊ'gæstrɪk), *a. nonce-wd.* [f. CACO- + GASTRIC f. Gr. γαστήρ belly.] Having a deranged stomach.

1833 CARLYLE *Diderot, Misc.* (1857) III. 221 (D). Indigestion succeeds indigestion.. The woes that chequer this imperfect cacogastric state of existence.

‖ **cacogenesis** (kækəʊ'dʒɛnɪsɪs). [mod.L. f. CACO- + Gr. γένεσις origin, birth.] Morbid or depraved formation; a monstrosity, a morbid pathological product. Also *transf.*

1880 in *Syd. Soc. Lex.* **1895** A. H. KEANE *Ethnology* ix. 200 From this 'kako-genesis' of speech taken in connection with the 'eugenesis' of races, there follow some important inferences.

cacogenic (kækəʊ'dʒɛnɪk), *a.* [f. CACO- after EUGENIC *a.*; cf. CACOGENESIS.] The reverse of *eugenic*; = DYSGENIC *a.* Hence **caco'genics** *sb. pl.*, the breeding of a weak race (opp. *eugenics*).

1917 W. R. INGE in *Edin. Rev.* Jan. 80 How will it escape the cacogenic effects of family restriction in the better classes combined with reckless multiplication among the refuse? **1920** —— in *Daily Tel.* 28 May 7/2 The new practice of subsidising the unsuccessful by taxes extorted from the industrious was cacogenics erected into a principle. **1929** R. R. GATES *Heredity in Man* 280 Out of 399 fertile marriages about 176 might be classed as eugenic matings and 223 as cacogenic.

cacography (kæ'kɒgrəfɪ). [perh. a. F. *cacographie* (16th c.), or ad. med. Gr. κακο-γραφία = bad writing. The analogous ὀρθογραφία orthography, καλλιγραφία calligraphy, and some of their derivatives, were used in classical Greek.]

1. Bad writing; bad handwriting. (Opposed to *calligraphy*).

1656 BLOUNT *Glossogr.*, *Cacography*, ill writing, or a writing of evil things. **1760** SWINTON in *Phil. Trans.* LI. 858 The cacography of the Etruscans, as their rude and uncouth manner of writing is termed. **1864** BURTON *Scot Abr.* II. 297 The crabbed cacography of the original manuscript. **1864** *Daily Tel.* 28 June, The compositors made very light of cacography.

2. Incorrect spelling; a bad system of spelling, such as that of current English. (Commonly opposed to *orthography*.)

1580 BARET *Alv.* Let. E. We may still wonder and find fault with our Orthographie (or rather Cacographie in deed). **1655** *Com. Hist. Francion* I. iii. 63 His clerk used a certain kinde of Cacographie, that admitted a multitude of superfluous letters. **1633** C. BUTLER *Eng. Gram.* in A. J. Ellis *E.E. Pronunc.* 155 The cause of this cacography which causeth such difficulty is a causeless affectation of the French dialect. **1806** SOUTHEY *Ann. Review* IV. 8 The orthography or rather kakography of many of the names is French. **1820** *Blackw. Mag.* VIII. 318 A celebrated critic who sometimes condescends to amend my cacography.

Hence **ca'cographer**, a bad writer or speller; **caco'graphic, -al** *a.*, of or pertaining to bad writing or incorrect spelling.

1838 *Athenæum* No. 3099 (1887) 383 A stupid series of cacographical errors. **1864** *Even. Standard* 29 Sept., The most remarkably ungrammatical and cacographical production. **1880** J. A. H. MURRAY *Addr. Philol. Soc.* 35 Before Norman cacographers spelt them with *o*.

cacokenny, perverted form of CACOCHYMY.

‖ **cacolet** (kakolɛ, -lɛt). [dial. F., applied in the Pyrenees to a contrivance fixed on the back of a mule or horse for carrying travellers over the mountains, a mule chair.] A military litter for the sick or wounded carried by mules; either in the form of arm-chairs suspended one on each

side of a mule, or of a bed laid along the beast's back. First employed by the French in the Crimean War, 1854–5.

1878 A. GRIFFITHS *Eng. Army* iv. 108 One hundred pack animals, seventy-six of which carry double litters, or 'cacolets', for patients. **1884** GEN. GRAHAM in *Times* 4 Apr. 11 Ambulances and mule cacolets were sent for. **1885** *Observer* 8 Feb. 5/4 The wounded who have been successfully removed from Gubat in cacolets.

† **'Cacolike, -leek.** *Obs.* A perversion of CATHOLIC, associating it with κακός bad, and used as a term of reproach.

1582 *Rhem. N.T.* Acts xi. Annot. 324 Some Heretikes of this time call them Cartholikes and cacolikes. **1600** O. E. *Repl. Libel* I. ii. 54 A Cacolike, or true member of the popes church. **1626** L. OWEN *Spec. Jesuit.* (1629) 20 The Iesuites should compell men by force, to be Romish Cacoleekes.

cacology (kæ'kɒlədʒɪ). [mod. ad. Gr. κακολογία evil speaking, vituperation, f. κακολόγος speaking evil, slanderous; = F. *cacologie*. The mod. use takes *bad* grammatically, not ethically.]

† **1.** Evil report. *Obs.*

1623 COCKERAM, *Cacologie*, ill report. **1656–81** BLOUNT *Glossogr.*, *Cacology*, evill speech or report, detraction.

2. Bad speaking, bad choice of words; vicious pronunciation.

1775 in ASH. **1826** PRAED *Poems* (1865) I. 263 Bishop Bembo mended her cacology. **1837** *Fraser's Mag.* XV. 571 Cacology amused the frequenters of the Haymarket Theatre. **1856** J. W. CROKER in *Croker Papers* (1884) I. i. 6 One Knowles, who..professed to remedy cacology and teach elocution.

caco-magician. [f. CACO- + MAGICIAN.] An evil magician or sorcerer; one versed in the black art.

1656 MORE *Antid. Ath.* III. ix. (1712) 167 That he is a Magician, not a Caco-Magician, and that he has nothing to do with the Devil. **1841** D'ISRAELI *Amen. Lit.* (1867) 647 The great adversary of Fludd..denounced the Rosacrucian to Europe as a caco-magician.

cacomistle ('kækəmɪs(ə)l). Also cacomixl, etc. [Amer. Sp. *cacomixtle* (also used), f. Nahuatl *tlacomiztli*.] A raccoon-like animal of the south-western United States and Mexico, *Bassariscus astutus*.

1869 W. H. FLOWER in *Proc. Zool. Soc.* 31 The interesting little American Carnivore the *Bassaris*... The animal was mentioned by Hernandez under the name of Tepe-Maxtlaton or Cacamitztli, meaning..the 'Rush-Cat'. **1889** *Cent. Dict.*, Cacomixl. **1931** *News Chron.* 12 Feb. 7/2 (*caption*) With the paws of a cat, the face of a fox and a ringed tail. A cacomixtle, the nocturnal prowler of the Mexican desert. **1958** RYHINER & MANNIX *Wildest Game* (1959) xvii. 302, I managed to pick up some cacomistles, or ring-tailed cats, in the Southwest.

caconym ('kækəʊnɪm). [f. CACO- + Gr. ὄνυμα name.] An example of bad nomenclature or terminology, esp. in biology and botany.

1889 in *Cent. Dict.* **1914** O. F. COOK in *Amer. Naturalist* XLVIII. 310 A name rejected for linguistic reasons [is] a caconym. **1956** *Nat. Cactus & Succulent Jrnl.* II. 3/1 A name may qualify as a caconym in different ways. First, from sheer length... Second, from the clash of consonants making it difficult (for a European at least) to articulate.

cacoon (kə'kuːn). [? A native African name.] The large flat polished bean of a climbing tropical shrub, *Entada scandens* (N.O. *Leguminosæ*), which has jointed pods six or eight feet long, containing in each joint one of these beans, about 2 inches across and half an inch thick. They are made into snuff-boxes, scent-bottles, spoons, etc., and are sometimes sold in the streets of London as West Indian Filberts.

1854 P. SIMMONDS *Comm. Product. Veg. Kingd.*, The horse-eyes and Cacoons of Jamaica..yield a considerable quantity of oil or fat. **1885** LADY BRASSEY *The Trades* 265 The pods..contain from ten to fifteen hard, brown, shining, flattened seeds, called cacoons.

† **ca'copathy.** *Obs. rare.* [mod. ad. Gr. κακοπάθεια distress, misery, f. κακοπαθής suffering ill.] An old term for a severe affliction or malady.

[**1708–21** KERSEY, *Cacopathia.*] **1721–90** BAILEY, *Cacopathy*, a suffering of evil, or lying under a painful disease. **1860** in MAYNE *Exp. Lex.*

† **ca'cophagy.** *Obs.* [f. Gr. κακο- evil + -φαγια eating.] 'A devouring'. Bailey 1730 (? for *catophagy*).

cacophonic (kækəʊ'fɒnɪk), *a.* [f. as CACOPHONOUS + -IC: after *euphonic*.] Ill-sounding.

1847 in CRAIG. **1862** *Temple Bar Mag.* IV. 187 Who rejoiced in the vulgarly cacophonic name of 'Hyrum'.

caco'phonical, *a.* = prec. (In Craig 1847.)

caco'phonically, *adv.* [f. prec. + -LY².] = CACOPHONOUSLY.

1864 DK. MANCH. *Court & Soc.* II. 387 'Hamlet', or 'Ambleto', as it is cacophonically rendered in Italian.

ca'cophonize, *v. rare.* [f. Gr. κακόφων-ος (see next) + -IZE.] *trans.* To make cacophonous.

1872 M. COLLINS *Pr. Clarice* I. v. 76 How should any one desire to mutilate and cacophonize so musical a name as Clarice?

cacophonous (kæ'kɒfənəs), *a.* [f. Gr. κακόφωνος ill-sounding + -OUS.] Ill-sounding, having a harsh or unpleasant sound.

1797 *Month. Rev.* XXIII. 579 The cacophonous repetition of rumpf displeases. **1807** SOUTHEY *Espriella's Lett.* (1814) I. 280 The names, like the language..are..sufficiently cacophonous to a southern ear. **1854** BADHAM *Halieut.* 318 The name of this illustrious but cacophonous benefactor of his kind was Wilhelm Deukelzoon. **1867** MACFARREN *Harmony* ii. 58 Thus divesting it of its cacophonous effect.

ca'cophonously, *adv.* [f. prec. + -LY².] With bad, harsh, or unpleasant sound.

1864 *Press* 21 May 481 Agricultural fiddlers and trumpeters playing cacophonously. **1880** *Gentl. Mag.* Dec. 726 The Opposition..cackled cacophonously.

cacophony (kæ'kɒfənɪ). [a. F. *cacophonie*, in 16th c. *cacofonie*, ad. (through mod.L.) Gr. κακοφωνία, f. κακόφωνος; see above. Formerly used in latinized form *cacophonia*.]

1. The quality of having an ill sound; the use of harsh-sounding words or phrases. (The opposite of *euphony*.)

1656 BLOUNT *Glossogr.*, *Cacophony*, an ill, harsh, or unpleasing sound, (in words) a vitious utterance or pronunciation. **1733** SWIFT *Let.* lxvi. Wks. 1761 VIII. 154 Alter rhymes, and grammar, and triplets, and cacophonies of all kinds. *a* **1745** —— *Wks.* (1841) II. 419 To allow for the usual accidents of corruption, or the avoiding a cacophonia. **1753** *Chesterf. Lett.* cclxvii, Avoid cacophony, and make your periods as harmonious as you can. **1847–8** DE QUINCEY *Protestantism* Wks. VIII. 140 My labours in the evasion of cacophony.

2. *Music.* A discordant combination of sounds, dissonance. Also *fig.* Moral discord.

a **1789** BURNEY *Hist Mus.* (ed. 2) I. viii. 133 What a cacophony would a complete chord occasion! **1831** MACAULAY *Let.* in Trevelyan *Life & Lett.* (1876) I. iv. 223 The oppressive privileges which had depressed industry would be a horrible cacophony. **1880** MADAME A. GODDARD in *Girl's Own Paper* 13 Mar. 166 The continual holding down of the loud pedal produces unutterable cacophony.

† **3.** *Med.* Old term for a harsh, grating, or discordant state of the voice (Mayne *Exp. Lex.*).

cacoplastic (kækəʊ'plɑːstɪk, -æ-), *a. Phys.* [mod. f. Gr. κακόπλαστος used in sense of 'ill-conceived' + -IC, after *plastic*.] Of morbid deposits: Imperfectly organized, of imperfect structure.

1839–47 TODD *Cycl. Anat. & Phys.* III. 748/2 The exudation verges towards a caco-plastic character. *Ibid.* 754/1 Between..the caco-plastic, and aplastic deposits, the gradations are almost insensible.

caco-rhythmic, cacorrhythmic (kækəʊ'rɪðmɪk), *a.* [f. Gr. κακόρρυθμος ill-modulated, irregular in measure + -IC, after *rhythmic*.] In bad rhythm; also formerly 'applied to an irregular or disorderly pulse' (*Syd. Soc. Lex.*).

a **1879** M. COLLINS *Pen Sketches* II. 191 Marvellous caco-rhythmic productions, which would remind some readers of Ossian, others of Tupper.

† **'caco,sphyxy.** *Path. Obs.* [ad. mod.L. *cacosphyxia*, f. Gr. κακο- bad + σφύξις pulse.] A bad or irregular state of the pulse.

1708 KERSEY, *Cacosphyxia.* **1775** ASH, *Cacosphyxy*, a bad pulse.

'caco,techny. *rare.* [mod. ad. Gr. κακοτεχνία bad art.] Bad art; a mischievous or hurtful art.

1775 ASH, *Cacotechny*, a hurtful invention. **1847** in CRAIG.

‖ **ca'cothesis.** *Path.* [f. CACO- + Gr. θέσις placing, position.] A bad or faulty position of any part of the body.

1880 in *Syd. Soc. Lex.*

Caco'topia. *nonce-wd.* (See quot., where *Utopia* 'nowhere' seems to be mistaken for *Eutopia* 'a place where all is well'.)

1818 BENTHAM *Parl. Ref. Catech.* 73 As a match for Utopia (or the imagined seat of the best government), suppose a Cacotopia (or the imagined seat of the worst government) discovered and described.

ca'cotrophy. [ad. med.L. *cacotrophia*, a. Gr. κακοτροφία bad nutrition.] Imperfect or disordered nutrition.

1708 KERSEY, *Cacotrophia.*
1721–90 BAILEY, *Cacotrophy*, an ill nutriment, proceeding from a fault in the blood. **1847** in CRAIG.

'cacotype. *rare.* [f. CACO- + TYPE: cf. CALOTYPE.] A faulty or imperfect description in print.

1853 READE *Peg Woff.* 58 How tame my cacotype of these words compared with what they were.

cacoxenite (kæ'kɒksɛnaɪt). *Min.* Also cacoxene. [f. Gr. κακο- bad + ξέν-ος guest + -ITE; so called because its presence in iron ore is injurious.] A native phosphate of iron, containing also water, peroxide of iron, and phosphoric acid, occurring in radiated tufts of yellow or brownish-yellow colour. (Dana.)

† **caco-'zeal.** *Obs.* [Formed after Gr. κακοζηλία unhappy imitation or rivalry, κακόζηλον bad affectation or imitation, f. κακόζηλος: see next.]

1. (Also in Gr. or L. form *cacozelon, cacozelia*): Perverse affectation or imitation, as a fault of style.

1579 E. K. *Spenser's Sheph. Cal.* Gloss., Rather a fault than a figure..called Cacozelon. **1589** PUTTENHAM *Eng. Poesie* (Arb.) 258 Cacozelia..we may call fonde affectation ..when we affect new words and phrases other then the good speakers and writers in any language, or then custome hath allowed. **1644** BULWER *Chiron.* 140 Take heed therefore, that Imitation degenerate into Caco-zeale, and of proving a Left-handed Cicero. **1721–90** BAILEY, *Cacozelia.*

2. Perverted or misdirected zeal.

1608 *2nd Pt. Def. Ministers Reasons Refus. Subscr.* 66 Who, from a hote fiery fierce cacozele, spare not, etc.

So **caco'zealot, caco'zealotry.**

1659 GAUDEN *Tears Ch.* 62 (D.) Some spitefull Cacozelots. *Ibid.* 623 The caco-zelotry of some men in our times.

† **caco'zealous,** *a. Obs.*⁻⁰ [f. Gr. κακόζηλ-ος + -OUS.] 'Ill-affected, or badly imitating'. Phillips 1676. (Ed. 1696 has 'or viciously devout'.)

1656 BLOUNT *Glossogr.*, *Cacozelous*, il-minded or affectioned, one that imitates badly. [Not in BAILEY.]

cacozyme ('kækəʊzaɪm). *Med.* [Gr. κακο- bad + ζύμη leaven.]

'A particle of matter...which is supposed to be the active agent in the production of infectious disease, either by its propagation or by acting as a ferment' (*Syd. Soc. Lex.*).

† **cacquet.** *Obs. rare.* [a. OF. *caquet* cackle of a hen, tattle.] Cackle, tattle, babble.

1567 FENTON *Trag. Disc.* 141 Open and publike cacquet in the streetes whiche brings their honour in question.

cactaceous (kæk'teɪʃəs), *a. Bot.* [f. CACTUS: see -ACEOUS.] Belonging to the old genus Cactus; or to the natural order *Cactaceæ*.

1854 BARTLETT *Mex. Boundary* I. viii. 196 Cactaceous plants abounded on the mountain sides.

cactal ('kæktəl), *a. Bot.* [f. CACT-US + -AL¹.] Allied to the cactuses, as in Lindley's 'Cactal alliance'.

cactoid ('kæktɔɪd), *a. Bot.* [f. CACT-US + -OID.] Resembling the cactus in form or structure.

1878 HOOKER & BALL *Marocco* 328 The curious cactoid Euphorbia, producing the Gum Euphorbium. **1885** J. BALL in *Jrnl. Linn. Soc.* XXII. 3 Cactoid plants..are seen on the rocky slopes.

cactus ('kæktəs). [a. L. *cactus*, a. Gr. κάκτος a prickly plant found in Sicily, the Cardoon or Spanish Artichoke (*Cynara Cardunculus*): taken by Linnæus as the generic name of the entirely different plants now so called.]

† **1.** In ancient Nat. Hist.: The Cardoon. *Obs.*

1607 TOPSELL *Four-f. Beasts* 102 There is a kinde of thorn called Cactus. **1753** CHAMBERS *Cycl. Supp.*, *Cactus*..the general acceptation of the word is, that it signifies the artichoak. **1803** REES *Cycl.*, *Cactus*, the name of a plant described first by Theophrastus.

2. The generic name of many succulent plants remarkable for their thick fleshy stems, generally without leaves, and armed with curious clusters of spines; they have usually few branches or none, and are often of grotesque shape, with flowers of great beauty and sweetness. The Linnæan genus *Cactus* is now subdivided into about 20 genera, as *Cereus*, *Echinocactus*, *Opuntia*, etc., constituting the natural order *Cactaceæ*, all of which however are popularly *cactuses*.

1767 J. ABERCROMBIE *Ev. Man own Gard.* (1803) Index, Cactus, or Melon and Torch-thistle. **1807** G. GREGORY *Dict. Arts & Sc.* I. 283/3 Cactus, melon thistle..in the natural method ranking under the 13th order Succulentæ. **1814** LUNAN *Hortus Jamaic.* I. 413 The slender parasitical currant cactus or Indian fig. **1836** MACGILLIVRAY *Humboldt's Trav.* iv. 63 Cactuses rose here and there, from a scanty soil. **1843** PRESCOTT *Mexico* (1850) I. 13 The device of the eagle and the cactus..the arms of the modern Mexican republic.

3. *attrib.*, as in ***cactus tribe, family***, etc.; ***cactus thorn***, etc.; **cactus dahlia**, a Mexican dahlia, so called from its cactus-like flame-coloured flower; **cactus wren** *U.S.*, a North American wren of the genus *Campylorhynchus*, frequenting cactus plants.

1865 TYLOR *Early Hist. Man.* vi. 119 To make rag-dolls, and stick cactus-thorns into them. **1869** *Amer. Naturalist* III. 183 The Rock Wren..and Cactus Wren (Campylorhynchus brunneicapillus) chirrup loudly. **1870** H. MACMILLAN *Bible Teach.* vii. 135 In the cactus tribe, the whole plant consists of jointed leaves. **1881** *Daily News* 14 Sept. 2/6 The latest importation from Mexico..the cactus dahlia, 'Juarezii'. **1881** *Amer. Naturalist* XV. 211 The cactus wren, so called from its habit of nesting in the cactus whenever available. **1882** *Garden* 19 Aug. 156/2 What a brilliant flower is that of the Cactus Dahlia.

cacuminal (kæ'kju:mɪnəl), *a. Phonetics.* [f. L. *cacūmināre* (see CACUMINATE *v.*) + -AL.] Of sounds: produced with the tip of the tongue 'inverted' or curled upwards towards the hard palate; retroflex. Hence as *sb.*

1862 *Jrnl. Amer. Oriental Soc.* VII. 354 Müller proposes 'cacuminal' as a name for the class [of consonants]. **1902** E. W. SCRIPTURE *Elem. Exper. Phonetics* xxi. 297 The term 'cacuminal' (or 'cerebral', or 'inverted') is applied to a frontal articulation, in which the point of the tongue is turned up and back. **1915** G. NOËL-ARMFIELD *Gen. Phonetics* xvii. 99 Indian grammarians class these consonants as *cerebrals*. The name for them in the terminology of phonetics is *retroflex* or *cacuminal*. *Ibid.* 100 To pronounce the cacuminals. **1931** [see CORONAL *a.* 5].

†**ca'cuminate**, *v. Obs. rare*$^{-0}$. [f. L. *cacūminā-re* to make pointed, f. *cacūmen*: see CACUMINOUS.] 'To make sharp or pyramidal' (J.).

1656 BLOUNT *Glossogr.*, *Cacuminate*, to make sharp or copped. **1678** PHILLIPS, *Cacuminate*, to form into a sharp top like a pyramid. **1721-90** BAILEY (as in BLOUNT).

†**cacumi'nation.** *Obs.*$^{-0}$ [f. as prec.] 'A making sharp at the top' (Phillips 1678).

cacuminous (kə'kju:mɪnəs), *a. rare.* [f. L. *cacūmen*, *-ūminis* a tree-top.] Of a tree: Having a pyramidal top.

1871 M. COLLINS *Inn Str. Meetings* 10 Hours Of youth.. and love 'neath trees cacuminous. *a* **1879** —— in *Pen Sketches* I. 248 Luminous books (not voluminous) To read under beech-trees cacuminous.

†**cad**[1]. *Obs.* [Deriv. uncertain: the dates are against its identification with next word, which the sense alone might permit.] A familiar spirit.

1657 BP. H. KING *Poems* III. (1843) 87 Rebellion wants no Cad nor Elfe But is a perfect witchcraft of it self. **1658** OSBORN *Adv. Son* (1673) 34 Love..cannot hold without Jealousie, nor break without Repentance, and must needs render their sleep unquiet, that have one of these Cadds or Familiars still knocking over their pillow.

cad[2] (kæd). [Apparently, an abbreviation of CADEE, CADDIE, CADET, the senses of which show the development of meaning, starting from sense 2 of CADET, and its popular form CADEE. The modern sense (5) appears to have arisen at the universities (or at least at Oxford), as an application of sense 4 to any one whose manners or conduct were like those of the class in question.]

†**1.** An unbooked passenger whom the driver of a coach took up for his own profit on the way.

1790 *Useful Hints* in *Globe* 12 May (1885) 1/5 To prevent his taking up short passengers, or (as they are termed) cads, to the robbery of his employer.

2. An assistant or confederate of a lower grade, as a bricklayer's labourer (*dial.*); a familiar, 'chum'.

1835 T. HOOK *G. Gurney* (1850) I. vii. 131, I will..appear to know no more of you, than one of the cads of the thimble-rig knows of the pea-holder. **1839** HOOD *Kilmansegg* 230 Not to forget that saucy lad (Ostentation's favourite cad) The page, who looked so splendidly clad.

†**3.** An omnibus conductor. *Obs.*

1833 HOOD *Sk. fr. Road*, Though I'm a cad now, I was once a coachman. **1837** DICKENS *Pickw.* xxxviii, Numerous cads and drivers of short stages. **1837** *Penny Mag.* 31 Mar. 117 He who hangs behind—who opens the door and receives the money..is conductor or in the vulgar tongue—cad. **1848** THACKERAY *Bk. Snobs* xlix, A sceptical audience of omnibus-cads and nursemaids.

4. = Sc. CADDIE, sense 2: '*Cads*, low fellows, who hang about the college to provide the Etonians with anything necessary to assist their sports'. Hone (note to quot.). So at Oxford, applied by collegians to town-lads of the same description, and contemptuously to townsmen generally.

1831 HONE *Year Bk.* 670 Preceded by one or two bands of music in two boats, rowed by 'cads'. **1838** *Leg. late Illumination* in *Oxf. Her.* 22 Feb., A gown-and-town row had got up, to testify their loyalty, By milling of all rads and cads, and other foes to royalty. **1844** PEGGE *Anecd. Eng. Lang.* (ed. 3) 34 *note*, The Oxford Townsman..in 1835 had been promoted to the title of *cad.* **1850** CLOUGH *Dipsychus* II. ii. 152 If I should chance to run over a cad, I can pay for the damage if ever so bad.

5. *colloq.* A fellow of low vulgar manners and behaviour. (An offensive and insulting appellation.)

1838 *Hints on Etiquette for Univ. Oxf.* 19 *note*, He was mentally considered a great 'cad' by the rest. **1850** KINGSLEY *Alt. Locke* xii, 'Box the cad's ears, Lord Lynedale,' said a dirty fellow with a long pole. **1862** A. BOYD in *Gd. Words* 694 People who talk of the great majority of their fellow-creatures as Cads. **1868** *Lessons Mid. Age* 142 You cannot make a vulgar offensive cad conduct himself as a gentleman.

6. *Comb.*, as **cad-catcher**: see quot.

1882 *Artist* 1 Feb. 63/1 'Cadcatchers' is an expressive, but not elegant, term now in use amongst artists for pictures painted to attract the undiscriminating.

Hence **'cadism**, the behaviour or action of a cad.

1876 *World* V. 8 It is the superlative 'cadism' of English residents in India which galls the natives.

†**cad**[3]. *Obs.* = CADE *sb.*[2], a cade-lamb.

cad[4]. Chiefly *dial.* [Another form of CADDIS[2] (dial. *caddy*); but there is nothing to show the actual relations to each other of *cad*, *caddy*, and *caddis*, nor which is the primitive form.] A caddis or caddis worm. Called more fully **cod-bait, cad-bait, cad-bit, cad-bote, cad-worm.**

1651-1653 [see CADDIS[2]]. **1653** LAUSON *Comm. Secr. Angling* in Arb. *Garner* I. 194 Cad bait is a worm bred under stones in a shallow river. **1677** N. COX *Gentl. Recreat.*, *Fishing* (1706) 41 Wasps, Gentles and Cad-bits are good baits for the Gudgeon. **1741** *Compl. Fam.-Piece* II. ii. 345 Tench delight chiefly in Worms..as the Lob-worm, Marsh-worm, Cad-worm, and Flag-worm. **1792** OSBALDISTONE *Brit. Sportsman* 85/1 Cadbate, a worm, good bait for trout. **1833** J. RENNIE *Alph. Angling* 34 The grubs which are known by the name of caddis-worms, case-worms, cad or cod bait and ruff coats. *a* **1888** *Northampton Dial.* We are going to the brook for some cads.

†**2. cad-worm**, applied in derision to a man. *Obs.*

1630 J. TAYLOR (Water P.) *Wks.* II. 155 This Cadworme, hauing onely got Rime, which is but the buttons and loopes to couple Verse together.

†**cad**[5]. *Obs.* = CADDOW[2].

1581 in *Bristol Wills* (1886) 233 The worne Irishe Cad [valued at] xxiiijs.

cadace, -as, obs. forms of CADDIS.

cadar, var. of CADER, a frame.

cadastral (kə'dɑ:strəl, -æ-), *a.* [a. mod.F. *cadastral* relating to the cadastre, as in *les registres cadastraux* (Littré).]

1. Of, pertaining to, or according to a cadastre; having reference to the extent, value, and ownership of landed property (strictly, as a basis of distributing taxation).

1858 GLADSTONE *Homer* I. 567 [Darius] divided the empire by a cadastral system under provincial governors. **1868** —— *Juv. Mundi* xiii, The catalogue of Homer is a great attempt to construct..a cadastral account of Greece. **1886** *Q. Rev.* Apr. 395 The following statement exhibits the cadastral distribution of properties.

2. *cadastral survey*: **a.** *strictly*, a survey of lands for the purposes of a cadastre; **b.** *loosely*, a survey on a scale sufficiently large to show accurately the extent and measurement of every field and other plot of land. Applied to the Ordnance Survey of Great Britain on the scale of $\frac{1}{2500}$ or 25·344 inches to a mile. So *cadastral map, plan*, etc.

1861 *Sel. Comm. Ho. Commons* 182 To inquire into the expediency of extending the Cadastral Survey to those portions of the United Kingdom which have been surveyed upon the scale of one inch to the mile only. **1861** A. S. AYRTON [in Parlt.] Thought that the question was very much mystified by calling the survey a cadastral survey, which meant all the details relating to the tenure of land, the condition of each property, and all such matters. **1862** TOULM. SMITH in *Parly. Remembrancer* Oct 182 The newfangled phrase 'cadastral survey' is as foolish as it is unquestionably mischievous. **1863** *Edin. Rev.* CXVIII. No. 242. 379 The French term 'cadastral'..is now used in England to denote a survey on a large scale. **1881** FITCH *Lect. Teaching* iii. 72 A special map of the province, and a cadastral plan (ordnance map) of the commune. **1885** SMITH in *Law Times* LXXIX. 400/2 The necessity of a complete cadastral survey of property in England and Wales. **1886** *Blackw. Mag.* Sept. 332 *note*, The Domesday Survey was in a sense a cadastral one: and the Ordnance Survey in its larger scale, as being the only comprehensive basis upon which a correct computation of areas and valuation of landed property for assessment of imposts is possible, may also be called 'Cadastral'.

‖**cadastre** (kadastr). [a. Fr. *cadastre*; = Sp., It. *catastro*:—late L. *capitastrum* 'register of the polltax', f. *caput* head, poll.]

a. (= L. *capitastrum.*) The register of *capita*, *juga*, or units of territorial taxation into which the Roman provinces were divided for the purposes of *capitatio terrena* or land tax. (Poste *Gaius.*) **b.** A register of property to serve as a basis of proportional taxation, a Domesday Book. **c.** (in mod.French use) A public register of the quantity, value, and ownership of the real property of a country.

1804 *Edin. Rev.* V. 17 To compile a general Cadastre, somewhat in the style of our old doomsday book. **1834** SOUTHEY *Doctor* ccxli. (1862) 660 Materials for a moral and physiological Cadastre, or Domesday Book. **1864** SIR F. PALGRAVE *Norm. & Eng.* IV. 62 The crown officers formed a new Cadastre according to the new principle which he laid down..the land was meted according to an invariable geometrical standard, without any reference to its productive worth. **1864** WEBSTER, *Cadastre*, an official estimate of the quantity and value of real property, made for the purpose of justly apportioning taxes: used in Louisiana. **1875** POSTE *Gaius* II. (ed. 2) 174 The list of capita was called a Cadastre (*capitastrum*).

cadaver (kə'deɪvə(r)). [a. L. *cadāver* dead body, perhaps f. *cad-ĕre* to fall. So F. *cadavre.*] A dead body, *esp.* of man; a corpse. (Now chiefly in technical lang.)

[**1398** TREVISA *Barth. De P.R.* VI. ii. (1495) 187 Careyne hath that name of cadauare of cadere . to falle.] *c* **1500** *Noble Life* I. xxxv, Zelio is a beste..it abydeth gladly in places wher as people be buryed, And it eteth the cadauers or wormes. **1524** *Will of J. Terry* (Somerset Ho.) I John Terry of Norwich..commende..my body to be Cadaver..to be buried. **1547** BOORDE *Brev. Health* lx. 18 Beware of..dead cadavers, or caryn. *a* **1626** DAVIES *Wit's Pilgrim.* ii, Whoever came From death to life? Who can cadavers raise? **1714** MANDEVILLE *Fab. Bees* (1725) I. 186 Time was when..the cadavers of the greatest emperors were burnt to ashes. **1874** ROOSA *Dis. Ear* (ed. 2) 19 Anatomical investigations on the human cadaver.

b. A skeleton.

1682 SIR T. BROWNE *Chr. Mor.* 91 Death's heads..and fleshless cadavers.

†**ca'daverable**, *a. Obs. rare.* [f. prec. + -ABLE.] Mortal.

1651 BIGGS *New Disp.* §287 By things cadaverable you may expect strange accidents.

†**ca'daverate**, *v. Obs.* [f. L. *cadāver* + -ATE.] To render lifeless; to reduce to dead matter.

1657 G. STARKEY *Helmont's Vind.*, [Excrementa]..which ..are by the heat of the body cadaverated, and cast forth.

cadaveric (kædə'vɛrɪk, kə'dævərɪk), *a.* [a. F. *cadavérique*, or f. L. *cadāver* (see above) + -IC (Gr. suffix: the L. forms are *cadāverīnus*, *cadāverōsus*).]

1. Of or pertaining to dead bodies; characteristic of a corpse. (More technical than *cadaverous.*)

1835-6 TODD *Cycl. Anat. & Phys.* I. 804/2 Chemical actions of a cadaveric description. **1865** *Reader* 2 Sept. 269/2 The earliest indications of cadaveric rigidity. **1880** B. DYER in *Daily News* 7 Oct. 6/7 Certain substances formed in decomposing animal tissues..[called] 'cadaveric alkaloids' ..owing to their formation subsequent to death. **1882** *Times* 8 Dec. 10 Evidence, previously given, with reference to the cadaveric lividities.

2. Caused by contact with a dead body.

1871 HOLMES *Syst. Surgery* (ed. 2) V. *Index*, Cadaveric boils. **1883** *Ibid.* (ed. 3) II. 940 Cadaveric warts have a somewhat special appearance.

†**ca'daverie.** *Obs. rare*$^{-1}$. = CADAVER.

1600 TOURNEUR *Transf. Met.* (1878) II. 187 Prol. 8 What ashie ghost, what dead Cadaverie..howles in my eares?

†**cadaveriety.** *Obs. rare*$^{-1}$. [f. L. *cadāver* (see prec.), ? after *variety*, *ebriety*, etc.] Deadness.

1651 BIGGS *New Disp.* §171 The cadaveriety, and dull lethargy of medicines, is contracted by the Opium.

ca'daverine. *Chem.* [f. as prec. + -INE.] One of the cadaveric alkaloids or Ptomaïnes.

1887 LAUDER BRUNTON *Pharmacol.* 98 Neurine, cadaverine, putrescine, and saprine have no marked physiological action.

ca'daverizable, *a.* [f. next + -ABLE.] Capable of being converted into lifeless matter.

1651 BIGGS *New Disp.* §287 Any putrefactible or cadaverizable thing.

cadaverize (kə'dævəraɪz), *v.* [f. CADAVER + -IZE: perh. in earlier use; see prec.] *trans.* To make into a corpse; to make cadaverous.

1841 *Fraser's Mag.* XXIII. 421 To effect a..suspension of the circulation, and cadaverise his countenance.

cadaverous (kə'dævərəs), *a.* [ad. F. *cadavéreux*, *-euse*, ad. L. *cadāverōs-us* corpse-like, f. *cadāver*: see above.] Of or belonging to a corpse; such as characterizes a corpse, corpse-like.

1627 FELTHAM *Resolves* II. xxxiv, A cadauerous man, composed of Diseases and Complaints. **1643** SIR T. BROWNE *Relig. Med.* I. (1656) §38 By continuall sight of Anatomies, Skeletons, or Cadaverous reliques. **1651** BIGGS *New Disp.* §26 Cadaverous dissection of bodies. **1713** DERHAM *Phys.-Theol.* IV. xi. 205 Some cadaverous smell those Ravens discover in the Air. **1776** WITHERING *Bot. Arrangem.* (1796) IV. 374 Cadaverous smell of the Phallus impudicus. **1855** BAIN *Senses & Int.* II. ii. §11 (1864) 172 The cadaverous odour is of the repulsive kind. **1848** DICKENS *Dombey* 36 The strange, unusual..smell, and the cadaverous light.

b. *esp.* Of corpse-like or deadly pallor.

1662 FULLER *Worthies* III. 67 His eye was excellent at the instant discovery of a cadaverous face..this made him at the first sight of sick Prince Henry, to get himself out of sight. *a* **1713** ELLWOOD *Life* 246 He found John Milton sitting in an Elbow Chair..pale, but not cadaverous. **1820** W. IRVING *Sk. Bk.* II. 145 He has a cadaverous countenance, full of cavities and projections. **1835** WILLIS *Pencillings* I. vi. 38.

ca'daverously, *adv.* [f. prec. + -LY[2].] In a cadaverous manner; like a dead body.

1847 in CRAIG.

ca'daverousness. [f. as prec. + -NESS.] Cadaverous quality; the condition of a dead body.

1669 W. SIMPSON *Hydrol. Chym.* 75 This depraved, circulated matter, hath reached so far..as to acquire a virulency or cadaverousness. **1839** POE *Fall Ho. Usher* Wks. 1846 I. 295 A cadaverousness of complexion.

cadaw, obs. form of CADDOW.

cad-bait, -bit, -bote: see CAD[4].

caddas, caddes, obs. ff. CADDIS.

†**caddee.** *Obs.* [The same word as CADEE, Sc. CADDIE. See also CAD[2].]

1803 *Ann. Reg.* (Chron.) 430/1 The York stage waggon was overturned from off the Bridge into the river at Casterton near Stamford..owing to the proper driver trusting to the guidance of a caddee, whilst he loitered behind.

caddee, var. of CADI.

caddel, obs. f. CAWDLE.

ˈcaddess. *nonce-wd.* [f. CAD² 5.] A female cad.

1870 *Illustr. Lond. News* 29 Oct. 443, I do not insult the people by including in the name the cads and caddesses. **1884** READE *Perilous Secr.* I. vii. 133 Caddess! What is that? .. I mean a cad of the feminine gender.

†**caddesse, cadesse.** ? *Obs.* = CADDOW, a jackdaw.

1565-73 COOPER *Thesaur.*, *Mōnedula*, a chough, a daw, a cadesse. **1567** MAPLET *Gr. Forest* 79 The Caddesse was first called *Monedula.* **1583** STANYHURST *Æneis* IV. (Arb.) 101 This that prat' pye cadesse labored too trumpet in eeche place. **1611** CHAPMAN *Iliad* XVI. 541 As a falcon frays A flock of stares or caddesses. **1655** MOUFET & BENN. *Health's Improv.* (1746) 187 The Cadesse or Jack-daw. **1688** R. HOLME *Armoury* II. 248/1 The Jack Daw, or Daw, is called a Caddesse or Choff.

caddet, obs. form of CADET.

caddi, variant of CADI.

caddice, variant of CADDIS.

caddie, cadie (ˈkædɪ). Also 7 caudie, 8 cawdie, cady, caddee, 8-9 caddy. [ad. F. *cadet*: see CADET and CADEE.]

†**1.** = CADEE, CADET 2, q.v. Also *attrib. Sc.*

1634-46 ROW *Hist. Kirk* (1842) 462 Ane young gentleman latelie come from France, pransing..with his short skarlet cloake and his long caudie rapier. **1724** RAMSAY *Tea-T. Misc.* (1733) I. 53 Commissions are dear Yet I'll buy him one this year; For he shall serve no longer a cadie. *a* **1776** *Ballad* in Herd *Coll.* II. 170 (Jam.) There was Wattie the muirland laddie..With sword by his side like a cadie.

2. a. A lad or man who waits about on the lookout for chance employment as a messenger, errand-boy, errand-porter, chair-man, odd-job-man, etc.; *spec.* a member of a corps of *commissionaires* in Edinburgh in the 18th c. (See also quot. 1883.) *Sc.*

c **1730** BURT *Lett. fr. N. of Scotl.* ii. (1754) I. 26 The Cawdys, a very useful Black-Guard, who attend..publick Places to go of Errands; and though they are Wretches, that in Rags lye upon the Stairs, and in the Streets at Night, yet are they often considerably trusted..This Corps has a kind of Captain..presiding over them, whom they call the Constable of the Cawdys. *a* **1774** FERGUSSON *Compl. Plainstanes*, A cadie wi his lantern. **1818** SCOTT *Hrt. Midl.* xxi, A tattered cadie, or errand-porter, whom David Deans had jostled. *c* **1817** HOGG *Tales & Sk.* V. 65 A caddy came with a large parcel to Mrs. Logan's house. *a* **1859** MACAULAY *Hist. Eng.* V. 209 Every Scotchman, from the peer to the cadie. **1883** *Wesleyan Mag.* 546 The Caddies—sturdy women with creels on their backs who acted as porters—struggled for the customer.

b. A golf-player's attendant who carries his clubs (generally a boy or lad). Also *attrib.*, as *caddie-car, -cart.*

1857 *Chambers' Inform. People* II. 696/2. **1864** *Bookseller* 31 Oct. 662 Twenty golfers, with their attendant caddies scattered over the link. **1883** *Standard* 16 Nov. 5/2 The 'caddy' who carries the clubs probably possesses theoretical knowledge. **1961** F. C. AVIS *Sportsman's Gloss.* 202/2 *Caddie-Car*, a light two-wheeled rack for holding golf-clubs, drawn by the golfer himself. **1962** *Punch* 21 Nov. 747/1 A moment's weakness, and you'll be hiring a caddy and a caddy-cart.

3. Young fellow, lad. (*ludicrous* or *familiar.*) *Sc.*

1786 BURNS *Earnest Cry* xx, Gie him't het, my hearty cocks, E'en cow the caddie [C. J. Fox]. **1788-1813** E. PICKEN *Misc. Poems* I. 186 (Jam.) A' ye canty cheerie caddies.

†**caddiˈnet.** *Obs.* [A dim. form; to be referred apparently to It. *cadino* 'basin, milk-pan, broad dish', var. of *catino*:—L. *catīnus, -um* bowl, dish.] A basin or vessel of some kind.

1662 J. OGILBY *King's Coronation* (1685) 15 The Officers of the Pantry..brought up the Salt of State and Caddinet.

caddis¹, caddice (ˈkædɪs). Forms: 5-9 cadas, 5 cadace, 6 cadys, -yas, -es, caddes, -iz, -esse, 6-7 caddys, 6-8 caddas, 6-9 caddis, caddice, 7 cadice, (8 cadduce), 8-9 cadis. [Here two words are apparently mixed up: 1 (sense 1), properly *cadas, cadace,* OF. *cadaz, cadas,* cf. Cotgr. *cadarce* 'the tow or coarsest part of silke, whereof sleaue is made'; cf. Irish *cadas* = *cadan* cotton; 2 F. *cadis* (15th c. in Littré) 'sorte de serge de laine, de bas pris'. Of both, the ulterior history is unknown.]

†**1.** Cotton wool, floss silk, or the like, used in padding: Scotch writers of the 18th c. applied the name to 'lint' used in surgery. *Obs.*

[HUE DE TABARIE *MS. Heber* No. 8336 in *Promp. Parv.* 57 Pur cadaz e cotoun de saunk fu le encusture.] *a* **1400** *Cov. Myst.* 241 Cadace wolle or flokkys..To stuffe withal thi dobbelet. **1440** *Promp. Parv.* 57/2 Cadas, *bombicinium.* **1458** *Will of Gist* (Somerset Ho.), Vnum Jakke stuffed cum Cadace. **1463** in *Rot. Parl.* in *Promp. Parv.* 57 No..bolstors, nor stuffe of woole, coton or cadas, nor other stuffer in his doublet. **1738** *Med. Ess, & Observ.* (ed. 2) IV. 334 Soft half-worn Linen, which the French call *Charpie*, the English, *Lint*, and we *Caddiss.* **1769** W. BUCHAN *Dom. Med.* (1790) 578 With soft lint, commonly called caddis.

†**2.** Worsted yarn, crewel. *Obs.*

1530 PALSGR. 202/1 Caddas or crule, *sayette.* **1548** W. PATTEN *Exped. Scotl.* in Arb. *Garner* III. 92 Hemmed round about..with pasmain lace of green caddis. **1721** C. KING *Brit. Merch.* I. 286 Tapestry with Caddas.

†**b.** Hence *attrib.* as a material. *Obs.*

1550-1600 *Customs Duties, Addit. MS. Brit. Mus.* No. 25097 Cruell or Caddas rybande. **1575** LANEHAM *Let.* (1871) 37 Seemly begyrt in a red caddiz gyrdl. **1596** SHAKS. *1 Hen. IV*, II. iv. 79 Wilt thou rob this Leatherne Ierkin..Puke stocking, Caddice garter. **1675** *Bk. of Rates* 293 Caddas or cruel ribbon.

†**c.** Short for *caddis ribbon*: A worsted tape or binding, used for garters, etc. *Obs.*

1580 LYLY *Euphues* (1868) 220 The country dame girdeth herselfe as straight in the waste with a course caddis, as the Madame of the court with a silke riband. **1584** B. R. *Herodotus* 79 Stitching to the inside of their vesture a tape or caddesse to gird their apparell. **1611** SHAKS. *Wint. T.* IV. iv. 208 Hee hath Ribbons..Points..Inckles, Caddysses. *a* **1664** QUARLES *Sheph. Orac.* VIII, Surely I was.. constrained to sell Cadice and inkle. **1691** *Lond. Gaz.* No. 2698/4 A..blue Saddle-Cloth bound with Green and White Caddis. **1739** DESAGULIERS in *Phil. Trans.* XLI. 190 Cadis, or a kind of Worsted Tape. **1751** S. WHATLEY *Eng. Gaz. Sturbridge (Camb.)*, All sorts of tapes, cadduces, and the like wares from Manchester. [**1822-76** NARES, *Caddis*, a kind of ferret or worsted lace.]

†**3.** A kind of stuff; perh. of worsted (or ? silk).

1536 *Inv. Kilburn Nunnery Middlesex* in *Monast. Anglicanum* III. 424/1 One Carpet of Cadys for the table xij *d.* **1552** *Berksh. Ch. Goods* 28 Ane other vestyment of grene caddes, a vestyment of Redd caddis. **1552** *Inv. Ch. Surrey* 54 Item a cope of blew cades. **1552-3** *Inv. Ch. Goods Staffs.* in *Ann. Diocese Lichfield* IV. 48 One vestement of cadyas, iiij albes. [**1876** ROCK *Text. Fabr.* iv. 31.]

b. A coarse cheap serge. [Mod.F. *cadis.*] (The first quot. is of doubtful meaning.) Cf. CADDOW².

1579 LYLY *Euphues* 79 In steede of silkes I will weare sackcloth: for Owches and Bracelettes, Leere and Caddys. **1714** *Fr. Bk. of Rates* 38 Cadis-Stuff per 100 Weight. **1755** JOHNSON *Caddis*..this word is used in Erse for the variegated cloaths of the Highlanders. **1862** WRAXALL *Hugo's Miserables* (1877) I. iv. 20 Who had acquired £80000 by manufacturing coarse clothes, serges, and caddis. **1887** J. H. NODAL in *Let.*, 'Caddies is still used in Bolton for a special make of sheets and quilts.' [Cf. CADDOW² *c* 1860.]

caddis², caddice (ˈkædɪs). Also 7 cadice, cados, 7-8 cadis. [Of uncertain origin: see the equivalent CAD⁴; parallel forms are dial. *cadew, caddy* (pl. *caddies*), perh. a false singular, from *caddi-s* (used as sing. and pl. by Walton); possibly a genuine dim. of *cad*: the relations of the forms have not been made out.]

1. The larva of the May-fly and other species of *Phryganea*, which lives in water, and forms for itself a curious cylindrical case of hollow stems, small stones, etc.; it is used as a bait by anglers.

1651 T. BARKER *Art of Angling* (1653) 9 Gentles, Paste or Cadice which we call Cod-bait. **1653** WALTON *Angler* 91 The May flie..is bred of the Cod-worm or Caddis. *Ibid.* 235, I have held you too long about these caddis. **1855** KINGSLEY *Glaucus* (1878) 207 Those caddises, which crawl on the bottom of the stiller waters, enclosed, all save the head and legs, in a tube of sand or pebbles. **1875** 'STONEHENGE' *Brit. Sports* I. v. iii. §12 Caddies, caterpillars and gentles.

2. *Comb.* **caddis-bait, caddis-worm** = prec.; **caddis-fly**, a Phryganea, as the May-fly.

1622 PEACHAM *Compl. Gentl.* xxi. (1634) 253 Other wormes as the Bobbe, Cadis-worme, Canker, or such like. **1658** ROWLAND *Mouffet's Theat. Ins.* 943 The great variety of those little Cados worms whereof they come. **1787** BEST *Angling* (ed. 2) 116 The Cadis-Fly..is a large four-winged fly, of a buff-colour. **1833** *Proc. Berw. Nat. Club* I. No. 1. 20 Caddis bait, which is the larva of different species of phryganea. **1847** CARPENTER *Zool.* §682 Caddice-flies..are very numerous in Britain; no fewer than 190 species having been described. **1863** KINGSLEY *Water-bab.* iii. 90 The caddis-baits in that pool. **1875** BRANDE & COX *Dict. Science, &c.* I. 341 Different species of the Caddice-worm protect themselves by means of different materials.

caddised (ˈkædɪst), *ppl. a.* [f. prec. + -ED².] Furnished or baited with a caddis.

1851 *Fraser's Mag.* XLIV. 63 Mute anglers drop their caddis'd hooks.

caddish (ˈkædɪʃ), *a. colloq.* [f. CAD² 5 + -ISH¹.] Of the nature of a cad; offensively ill-bred; the opposite of gentlemanly.

1868 *Imperial Rev.* 22 Feb. 180 We shall be understood when we say, that it is a still more *caddish* offence. **1881** *Blackw. Mag.* CXXIX. 186 A cad never seems more caddish than when he comes nearest to the most primeval simplicity of costume.

Hence ˈ**caddishly** *adv.*, ˈ**caddishness** *sb.*

1868 *Lond. Rev.* 15 Aug. 200/1 The cad takes his caddishness with him. **188.** MISS BRADDON *Just as I am* xlv. 307, Innate caddishness which must come out somewhere.

caddle, *sb. dial.*

1. Disorder, disarray, confusion, disturbance.

1825 BRITTON *Beauties Wiltsh.* Gloss. (E.D.S.), *Caddle*, a term signifying confusion or embarrassment. *To be in a caddle*, means to be overwhelmed with business. **1861** HUGHES *Tom Brown Oxf.* xxx. (D.) 'Ther wur no such caddle about sick folk when I wur a bwoy'. **1863** MRS. MARSH *Heathside Farm* I. 70 Mrs. Stone, a short, plump, Wiltshire matron..apologised for being found in such a caddle.

2. Trouble, bother.

1865 *Reader* 12 Aug. 182/2 The English won't take the trouble—won't, as they say with us in Somerset, *be at the caddle* to look after such things.

caddle, *v. dial.* [f. prec.] To trouble, disturb, worry.

1781 HUTTON *Tour Caves* Gloss., *Caddle*, to attend officiously. **1825** BRITTON *Beauties Wiltsh.* Gloss. (E.D.S.) s.v., *Don't caddle me*, don't teaze me. *A cadling fellow* means an impertinent or troublesome companion. **1862** T. HUGHES in *Macm. Mag.* V. 250 A caddled the mice in many a yield.

ˈ**caddow¹**. *Obs.* exc. *dial.* Also 5 cadaw, 5-7 cadowe, 6 cadow, caddawe, caddowe, 9 *dial.* caw-daw. [perh. f. *ca, ka* jackdaw (Sc. KAE) + DAW. (The Ir. *cudhóg*, Gael. *cathag*, Manx *caaig* jackdaw can hardly be connected.)]

A jackdaw.

1440 *Promp. Parv.* 57/2 Cadaw, or keo, or chowghe [*v.r.* ko; cadowe or koo], *monedula.* **1530** PALSGR. 202/1 Caddawe a byrde, *chucas.* **1552** HULOET, Caddowe, or choughe, byrde; some call them Jacke dawe. **1573** TUSSER *Husb.* (1878) 101 Kill crowe, pie, and cadow. **1579** *Marr. Wit. & Wisd.* (1849) 26 She can cackle like a cadowe. **1621** AINSWORTH *Annot. Pentat.* Lev. xi. 15 Crows, caddows, pies, and the like. **1792** OSBALDISTONE *Brit. Sportsm.* 85/1 Caddow, a bird, otherwise called a chough or jackdaw. **1842** *Few Words to Churchw.* (Camb. Camden Soc.) I. 14, Rubbish, brought together by the jackdaws or caddows. **1864** ATKINSON *Prov. Names of Birds*, Caddow, caw-daw.

ˈ**caddow²**. *Obs.* or *dial.* Also 6 caddo, 6-7 caddowe, 7 cadow(e, caddoe. [Cf. CADDIS¹ 3 b; also Gaelic *cudadh, cudath* tartan (not Irish—O'Reilly); but it is doubtful whether this is from Eng. or the converse. The Manx *cadee*, and the Ir. *cadas* cotton, can hardly be related.] A rough woollen covering: see quot. 1880.

1579 *Richmond Wills* (1853), ij fledg blankets *vs.* ij caddow blankets ij *s.* iiij *d.* **1588** *Middlesex County Records* I. 177 [Walter Hassellwrick stole]..vnum straggulum voc' an Irish Caddo [worth twenty shillings]. **1588** *Lanc. Wills* (1861) III. 135 A blankett and an Irish caddow checked. **1601** WEEVER *Mirr. Mart.* B iij, I stretcht my lims along the bed..Thrice ore the caddow I mine armes outspred. **1610** HOLLAND *Camden's Brit.* II. Ireland 63 They..make of their course wool Caddowes also or Coverlets. **1611** COTGR., *Couverture veluë*, an Irish Rug, Mantle, or Cadowe. **1681** CHETHAM *Angler's Vade-m.* xxxiv. §15 (1689) 190 Outlandish Cadows and Blanckets. *c* **1860** STATON *Rays fro' Loomenary* (Bolton) 40 Peggy wove caddows on a loom as they had ith back place. **1880** *Antrim & Down Gloss.* (E.D.S.) *Cadda, Caddaw*, a quilt or coverlet, a cloak or cover; a small cloth which lies on a horse's back.

cadduce: see CADDIS¹.

caddy (ˈkædɪ), *sb.*¹ [app. a corruption of CATTY *sb.*, Malay *kati*, a weight equal to $1\frac{1}{3}$ lb. avoirdupois.]

1. a. A small box for holding tea. Usually *tea-caddy.*

1792 *Madras Courier* 2 Dec. (Y.) A Quantity of Tea in Quarter Chests and Caddies, imported last season. **1793** COWPER *To Lady Hesketh* 19 Jan. (R.) When you went you took with you the key of the caddy. **1833** HT. MARTINEAU *Brooke F.* xii. 133 The best tea-tray and caddy. **1868** F. PAGET *Lucretia* 198 This house..instead of looking like a tea-caddy..might rather be said to resemble a litter of caddies.

b. *attrib.* and *Comb.*, as **caddy-spoon**, a short-handled spoon of a special shape used for measuring tea out of the caddy.

1927 *Daily Express* 31 Aug. 4 Old silver caddy-spoons that have survived from Georgian days.

2. a. orig. *U.S.* A can with a lid, for water, tobacco, biscuits, etc.

1883 *Harper's Mag.* Jan. 201/1 Near where his..saw and water caddy are lying. **1886** in *Alberta Hist. Rev.* (1971) Summer 16/1 A 28-pound caddy of tobacco. **1960** G. W. TARGET *Teachers* (1963) 18 The tin biscuit caddy on the mantelpiece.

b. *gen.* A storage container for objects (usu. small) in everyday use.

1976 *National Observer* (U.S.) 12 June 17/2 The 4-drawer caddy comes in your choice of red, yellow or orange. Sliding white drawers hold stamps, tacks, paper-clips, [etc.]. **1977** *Observer* 13 Feb. 13/7 (Advt.), Shoe Caddy holds 6 pairs of shoes in individual..compartments. **1982** *New Scientist* 21 Oct. 162/1 The discs are housed in caddies much like those used for the floppy discs in personal and mini computers.

ˈ**caddy**, *sb.*² [? f. CAD¹.] A ghost, bugbear.

1781 HUTTON *Tour Caves*, *Caddy*, a ghost, or bugbear.

caddy (ˈkædɪ), *v.* [f. *caddy*, var. CADDIE *sb.*] *intr.* To act as caddy *for* a golfer. Also *transf.*

1908 *Daily Chron.* 26 Aug. 4/7 You've caddied for me before. **1923** WODEHOUSE *Inimit. Jeeves* vii. 71 After lunch I should go off and caddy for Honoria on a shopping tour down Regent Street. **1928** *Daily Tel.* 29 May 9/4 The Prince had a local caddie named William Everett..who caddied for him once before.

caddy, var. of CADDIE.

cade (keɪd), *sb.*¹ [a. F. *cade* cask, barrel, ad. L. *cad-us* a large vessel usually of earthenware, a wine-jar, also a measure for liquids.]

1. A cask or barrel.

1387 in Rogers *Agric. & Prices* II. 428/4. *c* **1420** *Pallad. on Husb.* XI. 331 Kades thre Of wyne. **1706** J. PHILIPS *Cyder* II. 363 The Farmers Toil is done; his Cades mature, Now call for Vent. **1812** W. TENNANT *Anster Fair* II. vii, His lintseed stowed in bag or cade.

†**2.** *spec.* A barrel of herrings, holding six great hundreds of six score each; afterwards 500. *Obs.*

1337 in Rogers *Agric. & Prices* II. 555/3. *c* **1440** *Promp. Parv.* 57 Cade of herynge (or spirlinge) or oþyr lyke, *cada, lacista*, etc. **1466** *Mann. & Househ. Exp.* 207 Paid to Edwardes wyffe for j. cade of red herynge..vs. **1502** ARNOLDE *Chron.* (1811) 263, Xx. cadis rede hering is a last, v. C. in a cade, vi. score iiij. heringis for the C. **1593** SHAKS. *2 Hen. VI*, IV. ii. 36 Stealing a Cade of Herrings. **1599** NASHE *Lent. Stuffe* (1871) 106 The rebel Jack Cade was the first, that devised to put Red-Herrings in cades, and from him they have their name. **1704** WORLIDGE *Dict. Rust. et Urb.*, *Cade*..of Red-herrings 500, Sprats 1000; yet I find anciently 600 made the Cade of Herrings, Six score to the Hundred, which is called Magnum Centum. **1707** FLEETWOOD *Chron. Prec.* (1745) 82 A cade of red Herrings (720 the Cade). **1751** CHAMBERS *Cycl.*, *Cade*,..used in the book of rates for..500 herrings, and of sprats 1000. **1866** ROGERS *Agric. & Prices* I. xxiv. 610 Herrings..reckoned by the cade and the barrel.

3. *Comb.*, as **cade-bow** (see quot.).

1754 T. GARDNER *Hist. Dunwich* 20 The Cade, containing 600 Herrings, being a Frame called a Cade-Bow, made with Withs, having a Top and Bottom, with two Hinges folding, wherein Straw is laid inclosing the Fish.

cade (keɪd), *sb.*[2] (*a.*) Also 5 **kod**, 5–7 **cad**. [Origin and part of speech unknown. In *cade lamb*, 'cade' may be an adj. with some such sense as 'cast' or 'domestic, tame', or a sb. used *attrib.* as in *pet-lamb*: in the former case 'cade' as a sb. would be short for 'cade-lamb'; in the latter, 'cade-lamb' might be an expansion.

(As Cotgrave gives an alleged F. '*cadel* a castling, a starveling, one that hath need much of cockering and pampering', a sense not unlike Eng 'pet', it has been suggested that *cade-lamb* was perh. for an earlier **cadel-lamb*. But this is historically impossible. M. Paul Meyer says Cotgrave's word is not Fr., but app. the 16th c. Languedocien *cadel* 'little dog', and his explanation erroneous. The corresp. OF. word was *chael*, *cheel*, which has no likeness to the ME. *kod*, *cad*, even if the sense suited. Wedgwood compares Da. *kaad* wanton, petulant, sportive:—ON. *kát-r* merry, cheerful: but *cade* is not at all Sc., and apparently not properly northern, since Ray 1691 explains the 'North-Country words' *pet*, *pet-lamb* as 'a cade-lamb.')]

1. as *adj.* or in *comb.* Of the young of animals, *esp.* lambs and colts: Cast or left by the mother and brought up by hand, as a domestic pet.

c **1475** *Pict. Voc.* in Wr.-Wülcker 749 *Hic ricus*, a kodlomb. **1551** *Will of Jane Lovet* (Somerset Ho.) Three Cade lambes that go abowte the house. **1678** LITTLETON *Dict.* in *Cath. Angl.* 50 A cade lamb, *agnus domesticus, domi eductus*. **1681** WORLIDGE *Dict. Rust.* (E.D.S.) A *cosset* lamb or colt, or *cade* lamb or colt, that is a lamb or colt fallen and brought up by hand. **1698** F. B. *Modest Censure* 14 As mild and gentle as cade Lambs. **1792** in *Phil. Trans.* LXXXII. 366 We do not wean our cade-lambs till June. **1859** GEO. ELIOT *A. Bede* x. 95 It's ill bringing up a cade lamb. **1880** J. F. DAVIES in *Academy* 24 Dec. 456.

2. as *sb.* **a.** A pet lamb.

c **1450** *Nominale* in Wr.-Wülcker 698 *Hec agna*, a new lame; *hec cenaria*, a cad; *hec berbex*, a weder. **1483** *Cath. Angl.* 50 A Cade, *dome(s)tica vel domesticus, vt ouis vel auis domestica*. **1633** T. ADAMS *Exp. 2 Peter* iii. 18 He gave his poor godson a lamb for a cade. **1669** COKAINE *Ovid* 60 Pritty Spinella, you..Are tame enough, as Gentle as a Cad. **1830** HOWITT *Seasons, March* 58 Others [lambs]..are reared, generally by the assistance of a tea pot, with cow's milk and are called cades or pets.

b. The foal of a horse brought up by hand.

1617 MARKHAM *Caval.* II. 109 Such horses as we call Cades, which are those that neuer suck their dams, but vpon their first foaling are put vp into a house.

c. A spoiled or petted child. (*var. dial.*)

1877 PEACOCK *N.W. Linc. Gloss. Cade*, a child which is babyish in its manner. **1879** MISS JACKSON *Shropsh. Word-bk.* s.v., 'E's a reg'lar cade' said of a spoiled child.

3. Of fruit: Fallen, cast. *rare.*

1876 MISS BROUGHTON *Joan* III. 184 Austine is collecting the little cade cherries.

†**cade**, *sb.*[3] Variant of KED, a sheep-louse.

1570 LEVINS *Manip.* 8 A cade, sheepe louse, *pediculus ouis*.

cade (keɪd), *sb.*[4] [a. F. *cade*, in same sense.] A species of Juniper, *Juniperus oxycedrus*, called also Prickly Cedar, yielding *oil of cade*, or *cade oil*, used in veterinary surgery.

1575 TURBERV. *Bk. Venerie* lxvi. 187 If you rubbe a Terryer with Brymstone, or with the oyle of Cade, and then put the Terryer into an earth where Foxes be or Badgerdes, they will leaue that earth. **1800** tr. *Lagrange's Chem.* II. 251 The part most fluid is sold under the name of Cade-oil.

†**cade**, *sb.*[5] *Obs.*

c **1330** *Arth. & Merl.* 933 Telle schulen wiues twelue ȝif ani child may be made With-outen knoweing of mannes cade.

cade, *v.*[1] ? *Obs.* [f. CADE *sb.*[1]] *trans.* To put into a cade or keg.

1599 NASHE *Lent. Stuffe* (1871) 106 The rebel Jack Cade ..hauyng first found out the tricke to cade herring, they woulde so much honour him in his death as not onely to call it swinging but cading of herring also.

cade, *v.*[2] [f. CADE *sb.*[2]] 'To breed up in softness' (Johnson; with no quot. or reference).

1879 MISS JACKSON *Shropsh. Word-bk. Cade*, to pet; to bring up tenderly.

-cade, *suffix.* Taken by a false division of CAVAL)CADE *sb.* and used in various *Combs.*, as AQUACADE, MOTORCADE, etc., in the sense 'a procession, a show'. Chiefly *U.S.*

1936 MENCKEN *Amer. Lang.* (ed. 4) v. ii. 180 In the case of *motorcade*, *autocade*, *camelcade* and *aerocade*,..a new suffix, *-cade*, seems to have come in.

‖**cadeau** (kado). [Fr.] A present or gift.

1808 *Wynne Diaries* 10 Dec. (1940) III. 321 He has brought..a very handsome *joint Cadeau* to us of a Silver Tea Urn. **1826** M. KELLY *Reminisc.* (ed. 2) II. 320 Sheridan.. selected certainly not the worst for the *cadeau*. *a* **1845** BARHAM *Ingol. Leg.* **1882** *Cornh. Mag.* Jan. 13 A cadeau from his Highness. **1885** *Where Chineses Drive* 141 Some little present as a New Year's Cadeau.

†**cadee.** *Obs.* [Phonetic spelling of F. *cadet*.] The earlier form of CADET, CADDIE: A (gentleman) *cadet* in the army.

a **1689** MRS. BEHN *Widow Ranter* IV. ii, He listed us cadees for the next command that fell in his army. **1691** LUTTRELL *Brief Rel.* (1857) II. 234 The French convoy arrived at Limerick..two French lieutenant generalls, 106 subaltern officers, 150 cadees, 320 English and Scotch gentlemen. **1702** *Lond. Gaz.* No. 3856/3, 1 Captain, 1 Captain-Lieutenant, 1 Cadee, and 20 Soldiers killed. **1789** W. LAICK *Answ. to Presbyt. Eloq.* 33 (JAM.) A Cadee of Dunbarton's Regiment. *Ibid.* And from a Cadee become a curat.

cadee, obs. form of CADI.

cadelle (kə'dɛl). [Fr., ad. Pr. *cadello*.] The larva or adult of a beetle (*Trogosita mauritanica*) that is destructive to grain.

1861 *Chambers's Encycl.* II. 484/1 Cadelle (*Trogosita Mauritanica*..), an insect sometimes found in granaries in Britain.

cadence ('keɪdəns), *sb.* [a. F. *cadence*, ad. It. *cadenza* 'falling, cadence in music', on L. type *cadentia* sb., f. *cadent-* pr. pple. of *cad-ĕre* to fall. The literal sense is 'action or mode of falling, fall', and in this sense it was used by 17th c. writers; but at an early period the word was in Italian appropriated to the musical or rhythmical fall of the voice, and in this sense occurs as early as Chaucer. *Cadence* is in form a doublet of CHANCE, the direct phonetic descendant of *cadentia*.]

I. In verse and music.

1. 'The flow of verses or periods' (J.); rhythm, rhythmical construction, measure.

c **1384** CHAUCER *H. Fame* 627 To make bookes, songes, and dities In rime or else in cadence. *c* **1425** WYNTOUN *Cron.* V. xii. 315 Had he cald Lucyus Procurature..Ðat had mare grevyd þe Cadens, Ðan had relevyd þe sentens. **1513** DOUGLAS *Æneis* Prol. 46 Throu my corruptit cadens imperfyte. **1588** SHAKS. *L.L.L.* IV. ii. 126 The elegancy, facility, & golden cadence of poesie. **1642** MILTON *Apol. Smect.* (1851) 292 An eare that could measure a just cadence, and scan without articulating. **1763** J. BROWN *Poetry & Mus.* iv. 37 Measured Cadence, or Time, is an essential Part of Melody. **1824** DIBDIN *Libr. Comp.* 530 The periods flow with a sort of liquid cadence. **1873** SYMONDS *Grk. Poets* iv. 102 The Iambic is nearest in cadence to the language of common life.

b. The measure or beat of music, dancing, or any rhythmical movement; e.g. of marching.

1605 Z. JONES *De Loyer's Specters* 20 Now daunses..have neede of nothing..but only of Number, measure and true cadence. **1755** GRAY *Progr. Poesy* I. iii, To brisk notes in cadence beating Glance their many-twinkling feet. **1777** SIR W. JONES *Arcadia* Poems 109 Not a dancer could in cadence move. **1801** STRUTT *Sports & Past.* III. v. 195 Dancing round them to the cadence of the music. **1816** SCOTT *Old Mort.* vi, The occasional boom of the kettle-drum, to mark the cadence. **1862** F. GRIFFITHS *Artil. Man.* (ed. 9) 6 *Cadence*, in slow time 75 steps..are taken in a minute.

2. 'The fall of the voice' (J.).

1589 PUTTENHAM *Eng. Poesie* II. vii. (1811) 66 This cadence is the fal of a verse in euery last word with a certaine tunable sound which being matched with another of like sound, do make a [concord]. **1616** BULLOKAR, *Cadence*, the falling of the voice. **1768** STERNE *Sent. Journ.* (1778) II. 150 A low voice, with a..sweet cadence at the end of it. **1824** L. MURRAY *Eng. Gram.* I. 366 The closing pause must not be confounded with that fall of the voice, or cadence, with which many readers uniformly finish a sentence.

b. 'Sometimes, the general modulation of the voice' (J.).

1709 STEELE *Tatler* No. 9 ¶1 The Smallcoal-Man was heard with Cadence deep. **1710** *Ibid.* No. 168 ¶5 With all the..Cadence of Voice, and Force of Argument imaginable. **1760** STERNE *Tr. Shandy* 276 Amen, said my Mother..with such a sighing cadence of personal pity. **1844** A. WELBY *Poems* (1867) 87 The low cadence of her whispered prayer. **1855** BAIN *Senses & Int.* III. i. §22 (1864) 361 A third quality of vocal sounds is cadence or accent. **1862** TROLLOPE *Orley F.* xxxviii, 'No' said Peregrine, with a melancholy cadence in his voice. **1863** MISS BRADDON *J. Marchmont* 270.

c. Local or national modulation, 'accent'.

1727 SWIFT *Gulliver* III. i. 182, I returned an answer in that language, hoping..that the cadence might be more agreeable to his ears. **1771** SMOLLETT *Humph. Cl.* (1815) 241 The Scotchman who had not yet acquired the cadence of the English, would naturally use his own in speaking their language.

3. The rising and (*esp.*) falling of elemental sounds, as of a storm, the sea, etc.

1667 MILTON *P.L.* II. 287 Blustring winds, which all night long Had rous'd the Sea, now with hoarse cadence lull Seafaring men orewatcht. **1839** MRS. HEMANS *Release Tasso*, The low Cadence of the silvery sea. **1856** KANE *Arct. Expl.* I. xxix. 377 A murmur had reached my ear for some time in the cadences of the storm.

4. *Music.* The conclusion or 'close' of a musical movement or phrase. Also sometimes = CADENZA.

1597 MORLEY *Introd. Mus.* 73 A Cadence wee call that, when coming to a close, two notes are bound togither, and the following note descendeth. **1795** MASON *Ch. Mus.* I. 14 A perfect cadence then marks its termination. *c* **1860** GOSS *Harmony* xiii. 42 A Cadence or Close, signifies the last two chords of any passage; the principal cadences are those which conclude on the key-note. When the last chord is the triad on the key-note, preceded by the triad or chord of the 7th on the dominant, it is called the Perfect Cadence. **1867** MACFARREN *Harmony* I. 27 As performers insert a flourish at a close or cadence, we conventionally use the word cadence, to denote the flourish introduced at a close.

5. *Horsemanship.* 'An equal measure or proportion which a horse observes in all his motions when he is thoroughly managed' (*Farrier's Dict.* in Bailey). Cf. quot. 1833 under CADENCED.

6. *transf.* Harmonious combination of colours.

1868 SWINBURNE *Ess. & Stud.* (1875) 364 The cadence of colours is just and noble: witness the red-leaved book..on the white cloth, the clear green jug on the table, the dim green bronze of the pitcher.

II. In the Latin sense of falling.

†**7.** Falling, sinking down; mode of falling. *Obs.*

1613 R. C. *Table Alph.* (ed. 3) *Cadence*, falling, properly the ledging of corne by a tempest. *a* **1660** HAMMOND *Wks.* IV. 687 (R.) The cadence, or manner how Paul falls into those words, is worthy to be both observed and imitated. **1667** MILTON *P.L.* x. 92 Now was the Sun in Western cadence low.

†**8.** The falling out of an occurrence; chance.

1601 R. JOHNSON *Kingd. & Commw.* (1603) 8 This opportunitie is a meeting and concurring of divers cadences, which at one instant do make a matter very easie.

III. *Comb.* **cadence braking**, repeated rhythmic application of the brake pedal in order to slow a skidding vehicle (see quot. 1965).

1965 M. J. MCDERMOTT in *Autocar* 5 Nov. 990/1 The technique of '*cadence braking'..is to excite the vehicle into a vertical oscillatory motion by a series of suitably timed bursts of braking, until a considerable amplitude of the motion has developed. Hard braking as the vehicle descends then 'kills' the oscillation. **1971** *Daily Tel.* (Colour Suppl.) 22 Oct. 22/3 The urgent task [in a skid] is therefore to get them unlocked..and then to slow the car—if necessary by other means,..usually by cadence braking, which means gently but firmly applying and then releasing the brakes in sequence. **1982** *Advanced Motoring* (Inst. Advanced Motorists) (rev. ed.) vi. 26 Rally drivers..use what they call 'cadence' braking, in which the hard pushes on the brake pedal are timed to coincide with the spring frequency on the front suspension.

'**cadence**, *v. rare.* [f. prec.] **1.** *trans.* To put into cadence, to compose metrically.

a **1749** PHILIPS *To Ld. Carteret* (R.) These parting numbers, cadenc'd by my grief. **1873** SYMONDS *Grk. Poets* i. 18 Empedocles..cadenced his great work on Nature in the same sonorous verse.

2. *intr.* To flow in rhythm; to move in a cadence. So '**cadencing** *vbl. sb.* and *ppl. a.*

1907 P. L. FALZON *Love's Re-Awakening* 96 The cadencing majestic beat..Of poesy's most tender tone. **1918** QUILLER-COUCH *Studies in Lit.* 198 The verse cadences to the feeling. **1939** N. S. COLBY *Remembering* vii. 159 You could see her soft hands cadencing among the teacups. **1961** *Listener* 28 Dec. 1138/2 It [*sc.* a song]..moves..a little unexpectedly into E minor, and is on the point of cadencing in this key when the music skips nimbly back to the tonic key.

cadenced ('keɪdənst), *ppl. a.* [f. CADENCE *v.* and *sb.* + -ED.] Expressed or performed in cadence; characterized by cadence; rhythmical, measured.

a **1790** ADAM SMITH *Imit. Arts*, A certain measured, cadenced step, commonly called a dancing step. **1833** *Reg. Instr. Cavalry* I. 82 The horse has a firm, even, and cadenced pace. (Cadenced means that the time passed in making each step shall be exactly equal.) **1850** MRS. BROWNING *Lady Geraldine's C.* xlv, Her voice, so cadenced in the talking. **1851** —— *Casa Guidi Wind.* 3 Where the whole world might drop for Italy Those cadenced tears. **1870** LOWELL *Among my Bks.* Ser. II. (1873) 287 You hear the cadenced surges of an unseen ocean. **1958** P. GAMMOND *Decca Bk. Jazz* XV. 177 A harmonious and simple succession of thirds or single notes added in the form of a very flexible, cadenced conversation.

cadency ('keɪdənsɪ). [ad. L. **cadentia*: see -ENCY. In earlier use not distinguished from *cadence*; the sense of quality more proper to -ENCY comes out only in sense 3.]

†**1.** A falling out, happening, hap; = CADENCE 8.

1647 SPRIGG *Angl. Rediv.* I. xi. (1854) 10 How delightfully remarkable is it (as most apt cadency of Providence).

2. = CADENCE 1; cadent quality.

1627 FELTHAM *Resolves* I. lxx. Wks. (1677) 106 Poetry..is but a Play, which makes Words dance, in the evenness of a Cadency. **1642** HOWELL *For. Trav.* (Arb.) 48 The old Italian tunes and rithmes both in conceipt and cadency,

have much affinity with the Welsh. **1719** SWIFT *To Yng. Clergyman* Wks. 1755 II. II. 6 Rounded into periods and cadencies.

3. Descent of a younger branch from the main line of a family; the state of a cadet.

1753 CHAMBERS *Cycl. Supp.*, *Cadency*, in heraldry, the state, or quality of a cadet. **1858** R. CHAMBERS *Dom. Ann. Scotl.* I. 211 Not..a male descendant..in existence, of cadency later than the fifteenth century. **1866** —— *Ess. Fam. & Hum.* Ser. I. 18 He is recognised by a title of cadency from his wife, as Mrs. Thompson's husband. **1885** S. SALTER in *N. & Q.* VI. XII. 514/2 It might be thought that the label was for cadency of birth; but it was not so.

b. ***mark of cadency*** (Her.): a variation in the same coat of arms intended to show the descent of a younger branch from the main stock.

1702 A. NISBET (*title*) An Essay on additional Figures and Marks of Cadency. **1830** T. ROBSON *Hist. Heraldry* Lj/2 These marks of cadency..have crept into the general blazon of many coats of arms. **1882** W. A. WELLS in *N. & Q.* 25 Mar. 231 James..would *in vita patris* have borne as his mark of cadency the original crescent charged with a label.

cadene (kəˈdiːn). [a. F. *cadène* chain of iron, ad. Pr. *cadena*:—L. *catēna* 'chain'; in allusion to the chain-like character of the warp in weaving.]

A sort of inferior Turkey carpet imported from the Levant.

1847 in CRAIG; and later Dicts.

cadent (ˈkeɪdənt), *a.* [ad. L. *cadent-em*, pr. pple. of *cad-ĕre* to fall.]

1. Falling (literally). *Obs.* or *arch.*

1605 SHAKS. *Lear* I. iv. 307 With cadent Teares fret Channels in her cheekes. **1659** J. ARROWSMITH *Chain Princ.* 200 We ourselves have seen him Antichrist cadent. **1855** BAILEY *Mystic* 9 The moaning winds and cadent waters.

2. *Astrol.* Of a planet: Going down; in a sign opposite to that of its exaltation.

'Cadent Houses are the third, sixth, ninth and twelfth House of a Scheme or figure of the Heavens, being those that are next from the Angles' (Phillips 1696).

1586 LUPTON *Thous. Notable Th.* (1675) 201 If the part of Fortune be cadent from the Ascendent. **1671** BLAGRAVE *Astrol. Phys.* 164 Fixt Signs, and cadent Houses alwayes signifie the greatest distances.

3. Falling (rhythmically); having cadence.

1613 SIR E. HOBY *Counter-snarle* 13 Il current and worse cadent lines. **1857** EMERSON *Poems* 134 Far within those cadent pauses. **1859** F. K. HARFORD *Martyrs of Lyons* 24 Unfailing lips those cadent strains prolong.

4. *Geol.* Applied by Prof. H. Rogers to the tenth of his 15 divisions of the palæozoic strata of the Alleghanies, corresponding to the lower middle Devonian of British geologists.

†**ˈcadent**, *sb. Obs.* [f. prec.] One of the 'graces' in old English music.

1879 F. TAYLOR in Grove *Dict. Mus.* I. 43 'Shaked graces' are the Shaked Beat, Backfall, Elevation, and Cadent.

cadential (kəˈdɛnʃəl), *a.* [f. L. *cadentia CADENCE + -AL[1].] Of or belonging to a cadence. Also, of or pertaining to a cadenza.

1880 [see THIRTEENTH *sb.* 2]. **1882** *Athenæum* 8 Apr. 454/1 The examples..have in no one instance the slightest cadential character. **1954** L. R. PALMER *Latin Lang.* viii. 214 A return to concord in the cadential part of the line. **1955** E. DENT in H. van Thal *Fanfare for E. Newman* 103 Apart from a few cadential flourishes, the part of Leonor is entirely devoid of *coloratura*. **1958** *Times* 28 Mar. 3/7 Such a common feature of eighteenth-century recitative as a cadential appoggiatura. **1969** *Language* XLV. 253 Pāda-initial and pāda-final (cadential) occurrences account for 43 of 71 instances of *kāra-*.

cadenza (kəˈdɛnzə). *Music.* [It.; see CADENCE.] A flourish of indefinite form given to a solo voice or instrument at the close of a movement, or between two divisions of a movement. (Sometimes called *cadence*: the use of the Italian word is designed to differentiate the two.)

[**1753** CHAMBERS *Cycl. Supp.*, *Cadenza Sfuggita*, in the Italian music.] **1836** *Penny Cycl.* VI. 100/1 Formerly the *Cadenza* was, by Italian as well as English singers, considered indispensable..The French never admitted it. **1879** PARRY in Grove *Dict. Mus.* I. 294 The cadenza usually starts from a pause on a chord of 6-4 on the dominant, preparatory to the final close of the movement, and its object is to show off the skill of the performer..It was formerly customary to leave the cadenzas for improvisation.

†**ˈcader, cadar.** *Obs.* exc. *dial.* [Identical in form and meaning with, and prob. a. Welsh *cader* 'chair', in Mid. Welsh also 'cradle'; used also as in sense 2, and applied to a 'framework' of various kinds. (If sense 3 is not the same word, we may perh. compare F. *cadre* frame.)]

†**1.** A cradle. *Obs.*

a **1225** *Ancr. R.* 82 Heo makeð of hire tunge cradel [*MS. Cleop.* cader] to þes deofles bearn, and rockeð it. *Ibid.* 378 Hwon ȝe beoð ibunden wiðinnen uour large wowes, and he in a neruh kader [*MS. Titus D* cradel].

2. A light frame of wood put over a scythe to lay the corn more even in the swathe.

1679 PLOT *Staffordsh.* (1686) 353 Their barley they mow with the Sithe and Cadar in the South parts of the County.

3. 'A small frame of wood, on which a fisherman keeps his line' (*dial.*) Halliwell.

1880 MISS COURTNEY *West Cornwall Gloss.* (E.D.S.).

cadesse, var. CADDESSE, *Obs.*, jackdaw.

cadet (kəˈdɛt). [a. F. *cadet*, in 15th c. *capdet*, a. Pr. *capdet*:—Romanic type **capitetto*, dim. of L. *caput*, *capit-* head; hence, little chief, inferior head of a family. Cf. also CADEE, CADDIE, CAD.]

1. a. A younger son or brother.

1610 HOLLAND *Camden's Brit.* I. 463 From a younger brother or cadet of this house. **1671** CROWNE *Juliana* Ep. Ded. A iv, Leave that as a thread-bare portion to the Cadets. **1689** SWIFT *Ode to Temple* Wks. 1755 IV. I. 245 Poor we, cadets of heaven, Take up at best with lumber. *a* **1726** VANBRUGH *False Fr.* I. i, I am a cadet, and by consequence not rich. **1868** FREEMAN *Norm. Conq.* (1876) II. viii. 210 Spiritual preferments being turned into means of maintenance for cadets or bastards of the royal house.

b. A younger branch of a family; a member of a younger branch.

1690 LOCKE *Govt.* I. ix. §25 A Cadet, or Sister's Son, must have the Preference. **1726** WODROW *Corr.* (1843) III. 238, I suppose his family was a cadet of your Lordship's family.

c. The youngest son.

1646 SIR T. BROWNE *Pseud. Ep.* 348 Joseph was the youngest of twelve, and David the eleventh sonne, and but the caddet of Jesse. **1748** SMOLLETT *Rod. Rand.* (1812) I. 19 The cadet of a family.

2. a. A gentleman who entered the army without a commission, to learn the military profession and find a career for himself (as was regularly done by the younger sons of the French nobility before the Revolution). **b.** A junior in the East India Company's service. See also CADDEE, CADDIE.

1651 HOWELL *Venice* 7 This may be one reason why she connives at so many Courtisans for the use of the Cadett-gentlemen. [**1652** EVELYN *St. France* Misc. Writ. (1805) 84 The cadets and younger brothers minding for the most part no greater preferments than what they cut out with their sword.] **1690** B. E. *Dict. Cant. Crew*, *Cadet*, or *Cadee*, a Gentleman that Bears Arms in hopes of a Commission. **1691** *Lond. Gaz.* No. 2719/2 The Elector of Saxony..adds a Company of Cadets. **1704** *Hymn to Victory* lxx. 7 She serves Cadet and Voluntier. **1768** SIMES *Mil. Medley*, A cadet serves without pay. **1772** FOOTE *Nabob* I. 9 Go out Cadets and Writers in the Company's Service. **1816** 'QUIZ' *Grand Master* I. 10 His kit's pack'd up, and off he's set, To try his fortune—a cadet.

3. a. A student in a military or naval college.

1775 SWINBURNE *Trav. Spain* xliv. (L.) The royal apartments are now occupied by a college of young gentlemen cadets, educated at the king's expence. **1788** LD. AUCKLAND *Diary* in *Corr.* (1861) II. 91 An establishment of one hundred young cadets for the army. *a* **1845** HOOD *To J. Hume* iv, Watch Sandhurst too, its debts and its Cadets. **1860** DICKENS *Lett.* (1880) II. 122 Sydney has just passed his examination as a naval cadet.

b. A boy in an ordinary school who receives military training with or without a view to entering the army. Also *attrib.*, as **cadet corps**, a company of schoolboys who receive such training.

1873 *Programme of Review at Charterhouse School* 6 Aug., The young gentlemen (or Charterhouse Cadets) will be drawn up in Line at Open Order on the Cricket Ground. **1901** *Public School Mag.* Mar. 215 The Cadet Corps paraded in front of the school and stood 'at rest' while the band played 'The Land o' the Leal'. **1957** *Times* 3 Dec. 12/3 Cadet corps in Birmingham schools came under fire from many members of the city education committee to-day.

4. *N.Z.* A young man learning sheep-farming on a sheep-station. Hence **caˈdet(t)ing** *vbl. sb.*

1842 R. G. JAMESON *N.Z., S. Aust. & N.S.W.* xxiv. 337 We [are] in want of a college for colonial cadets. **1862** E. R. CHUDLEIGH *Diary* 21 Mar. (1950) i. 29 There were four Cadets learning sheepfarming. **1898** H. B. VOGEL *Maori Maid* xix. 147 A cadet is a young man, generally from England, who is paying a run-holder so much a year for the honour and privilege of working for him. *Ibid.* xix. 148 Otherwise cadetting..is a swindle. **1930** L. G. D. ACLAND *Early Canterbury Runs* ii. 23 Reginald Wade managed for the Chamberlains, and at one time had no fewer than ten cadets on the station.

Cadet[2] (kəˈdɛt). Also **Kadet.** [Russ. *Kadét*, f. the names (*Ka de*) of the initials of *Konstitutsiónnyĭ demokrát* Constitutional Democrat, with ending assimilated to that of CADET[1].] In Russian politics, a member of the Constitutional Democratic Party.

This party was formed in 1905 by a fusion of the group favouring autonomy for Poland and a federal constitution for the Russian empire with the (so-called) Independence Party formed by political exiles at Paris in 1903.

1906 *Daily Chron.* 22 May 7/5 The 'Cadets' (Constitutional Democrats)..have decided..to wait until the agrarian question comes on for discussion. **1908** *Westm. Gaz.* 19 Aug. 2/1 The more brilliant Zemstvo Liberals, who did so much to found the Cadet (or Liberal) Party. **1918** [see BOLSHEVIK *sb.*]. **1958** *Times Lit. Suppl.* 10 Jan. 14/3 The Kadets must properly be described as radicals. *Ibid.* 17 Jan. 31/4 The Cadets advanced the claim..to a sovereign and democratically elected legislature.

caˈdetcy. [see -CY.] = CADETSHIP 2.

caˈdetship. [f. CADET[1] + -SHIP.]

1. The status of a younger son.

1831 DISRAELI *Yng. Duke* III. iii. (L.) The ambitious prospects with which he had consoled himself for his cadetship.

2. The position or status of a military or naval cadet; the commission given to a cadet.

1845 STOCQUELER *Handbk. Brit. India* (1854) 55 For the artillery and engineers, it is a condition of the presentation of a cadetship that the candidate should have gone through a regular course of instruction at Addiscombe. **1854** *Blackw. Mag.* LXXVI. 667 The age of entering on their cadetship. **1884** *Harper's Mag.* May 866/1 Candidates for cadetship in the Royal Navy.

3. *N.Z.* The position or status of a young man learning sheep-farming on a sheep-station.

1842 R. G. JAMESON *N.Z., S. Aust. & N.S.W.* xxiv. 337 Colonial cadetships. **1853** J. ROCHFORT *Adv. Surveyor in N.Z.* ii. 20 They had just finished their 'cadetship', that is, they had been learning sheep-farming under a settler.

‖**cadette** (kəˈdɛt). [Fr.; fem. of *cadet.*] A younger daughter or sister.

1679 tr. *Marie Mancini's Apol.* 4 The order..seem'd to exclude my Sister as a Cadette.

cadew (ˈkædjuː). The same as CADDIS[2].

1668 WILKINS *Real Char.* II. v. §2. 125 Cadew, Strawworm. **1713** DERHAM *Phys.-Theol.* IV. xiii. 234 The several sorts of Phryganea or Cadews. **1774** WHITE in *Phil. Trans.* LXV. 268 They were taking..cadew-flies, may-flies, and dragon-flies. **1802** BINGLEY *Anim. Biog.* (1813) III. 239 The larvæ of the Great Cadew Flies, form a case with small bits of wood disposed longitudinally.

cadge (kædʒ), *sb.*[1] [App. a variant of CAGE perh. confused with CADGE *v.* to carry about; but it does not appear what is the source of the earliest quotation, which the later merely follow.]

1. *Falconry.* (See quots.)

1615 LATHAM *Falconry* (1633) *Wds. of Art expl.*, Cadge, is taken for that on which Faulconers carrie many Hawks together when they bring them to sell. **1721** BAILEY, *Cadge*, a round Frame of Wood, on which Hawks are carried to be sold. **1865** *Cornh. Mag.* May 623 We shall not trouble ourselves to take out the cadge to-day, for our party is quite strong enough to carry the hawks on the fist.

2. A pannier.

cadge, *sb.*[2] *vulgar.* [f. CADGE *v.*] The action of cadging or begging.

1812 J. H. VAUX *Flash Dict.*, *The Cadge* is the game or profession of begging. **1832–53** *Whistle-Binkie* (Sc. Songs) Ser. II. 68 He could 'lay on the cadge' better than ony walleteer that e'er coost a pock o'er his shouther.

cadge (kædʒ), *v.* Forms: 4 cagge(n, ? cache(n, (*pa. pple.* caget), (6 *Palsgr.* kadge), 6– cadge. [Derivation and original meaning uncertain: in some early passages it varies with *cache*, *cacche* CATCH, of which in branch I it may be a variant: cf. the pairs *botch*, *bodge*; *grutch*, *grudge*; *smutch*, *smudge*. Branch II may also be connected with *catch* or ONF. *cacher* in other senses; but it may be a distinct word: the whole subject is only one of more or less probable conjecture. Connexion of ME. *caggen* with CAGE *sb.* is phonetically impossible.]

I. Early senses.

†**1.** *trans.* ? To fasten, tie: cf. CADGEL *v.* (The early passages are obscure, and for one or other the senses *drive*, *toss*, *shake*, *draw*, have been proposed.) *Obs.*

c **1325** *E.E. Allit. P.* A. 511 For a pene on a day & forth þay [labourers in the vineyard] gotz..Keruen & caggen & man [= maken] hit clos. *Ibid.* B. 1254 þay wer cagged and kaȝt on capeles al bare. *a* **1400** *Alexander* 1521 And þen he caggis [*v.r.* cachez] vp on cordis as curteyns it were. *c* **1400** *Destr. Troy* 3703 Hit sundrit þere sailes & þere sad ropis; Cut of þere cables were caget to gedur. **1627** DRAYTON *Agincourt* 180 Whilst they are cadg'd contending whether can Conquer, the Asse some cry, some cry the man. **1875** *Lanc. Gloss.* (E.D.S.) *Cadge*, to tie or bind a thing.

†**2.** To 'bind' the edge of a garment. Cf. CADGING *vbl. sb.* I. *Obs.*

1530 PALSGR. 473/1, I cadge a garment, I set lystes in the lynyng to kepe the plyghtes in order. *Ibid.* 596/1, I kadge the plyghtes of a garment. *Je dresse des plies dune lisiere.* This kote is yll kadged: *ce sayon a ses plies mal dressés dune lisiere.*

†**3.** (See quots.) ? To tie or knot. Still *dial.*

1703 THORESBY *Let. to Ray* (E.D.S.) To *cadge*, a term in making bone-lace.

II. To carry about, beg, etc.

†**4.** *trans.* To carry about, as a pedlar does his pack, or a CADGER his stock-in-trade. *Obs.* exc. *dial.*

1607 WALKINGTON *Opt. Glass* 154 Another Atlas that will cadge a whole world of iniuries without fainting. **1691** RAY *N.C. Wds.* (E.D.S.) *Cadge*, to carry. **1718** RAMSAY *Contn. Christ's Kirk* III. xii, They gart him cadge this pack. **1788** MARSHALL *E. Yorksh.* Gloss. (E.D.S.) *Cadge*, to carry. **1858** M. PORTEOUS *Souter Johnny* 11 Weary naigs, that on the road Frae Carrick shore cadged monie a load. **1875** F. K. ROBINSON *Whitby Gloss.* (E.D.S.) *Cadge*, to carry; or rather, as a public carrier collects the orders he has to take home for his customers.

†**5.** To load or stuff the belly. *dial.*

1695 KENNETT *Par. Antiq.* Gloss. s.v. *Cade*, Hence..cadge-belly, or kedge-belly, is a full fat belly. *c* **1746** COLLIER (T. Bobbin) *View Lanc. Dial.* Wks. (1862) 68 While I'r busy cadging mey Wem. **1854** BAMPTON *Lanc. Gloss.*, *Cadge*, to stuff the belly.

6. *intr.* To go about as a cadger or pedlar, or on pretence of being one; to go about begging. *dial.* and *slang.*

1812 J. H. VAUX *Flash Dict.*, *Cadge*, to beg. **1846** LYTTON *Lucretia* II. xii, 'I be's good for nothin' now, but to cadge about the streets, and steal, and filch'. **1855** *Whitby Gloss.*, To Cadge about, to go and seek from place to place, as a

dinner-hunter. **1859** H. KINGSLEY *G. Hamlyn* xv. (D.) 'I've got my living by casting fortins, and begging, and cadging, and such like'. **1875** *Lanc. Gloss.* (E.D.S.) *Cadge*, to beg; to skulk about a neighbourhood. **1879** *Print. Trades Jrnl.* xxix. 32 Cadging for invitations to the Mansion House.

b. *trans.* To get by begging.

1848 E. FARMER *Scrap Book* (ed. 6) 115 Let each 'cadge' a trifle. **1878** BLACK *Green Past.* xi. 86 Where they can cadge a bit of food.

cadge, *a.* and *adv.* *Sc.* = CADGY.

1807–10 TANNAHILL *Poems* (1846) 12 My heart did never wallop cadger.

† **'cadgel.** *Sc. Obs.* 'A wanton fellow' (Jam.).

1603 *Philotus* xcvi, To tak a ȝoung man for his wyfe, ȝon cadgell wald be glaid.

† **'cadgel**, *v.* *Obs.* exc. *dial.* Also **cagel.**

† **1.** *trans.* To entangle. Hence **'cadgelled.**

1648 HEXHAM *Dutch Dict.* (1660) *In het garen vallen*, to be catch, cadgeld, or entangled in a net.. *Verwerret garen*, Cadgeld Yarne.

2. To harrow. *dial.*

1679 PLOT *Staffordsh.* (1686) 342 They cagel it with harrows to break the turf. **1847–78** HALLIWELL, *Cagel*, to harrow ground. *North.*

cadger ('kædʒə(r)). Also 5–6 *Sc.* cadgear. [f. CADGE *v.* + -ER[1].]

1. A carrier: *esp.* a species of itinerant dealer who travels with a horse and cart (or formerly with a pack-horse), collecting butter, eggs, poultry, etc., from remote country farms, for disposal in the town, and at the same time supplying the rural districts with small wares from the shops.

c **1450** HENRYSON *Mor. Fab.* 66 A Cadgear, with capill and with creils. *c* **1513** DOUGLAS *Æneis* VIII. Prol. 42 The cadgear callis furth his capill wyth crakis waill cant. **1641** BEST *Farm. Bks.* (1856) 103 The cadgers..call in the morninge, and if wee have anythinge for them, they goe on to Garton, and call for it againe as they come backe. **1695** KENNETT *Par. Antiq.* Gloss. s.v. *Cade*, *Cadger*, a butcher, miller, or carrier of any other load. **1816** SCOTT *Bl. Dwarf* iii, A buck hanging on each side o' his horse, like a cadger carrying calves. **1826** —— *Diary* in *Lockhart* (1839) VIII. 268 An instance of the King's errand lying in the cadger's gate. **1855** *Whitby Gloss.*, *Cadger*, a carrier to a country mill, or collector of the corn to grind. **1861** SMILES *Engineers* II. 99 Single horse traffickers, called cadgers, plied between country towns and villages, supplying the inhabitants with salt, fish, earthenware, and articles of clothing, carried in sacks or creels hung across the horse's back.

b. **1827** HONE *Every-day Bk.* II. 1654 A rosinante, borrowed..from some whiskey smuggler or cadger. **1843** *Proc. Berw. Nat. Club* II. xi. 66 Many..involved in smuggling..under the name of cadgers, carried on..their contraband commerce.

2. An itinerant dealer, a hawker, a street-seller.

1840 HOOD *Kilmansegg* cclvi, He fear'd..To be cut by Lord and by cadger. **1878** BLACK *Green Past.* x. 84 A cadger's basket stood on the table.

b. One who goes about begging or getting his living by questionable means.

1851 MAYHEW *Lond. Labour* I. 339 A street-seller now-a-days is looked upon as a 'cadger', and treated as one. **1861** *Sat. Rev.* 27 Nov. 537 Home Missions..to the interesting cadgers and thieves of her rookeries. **1877** *Holderness Gloss.* (E.D.S.) *Cadger*, a loose character who goes from door to door soliciting assistance.

3. *Falconry.* A man who carries hawks. (Cf. F. *cagier* 'celui qui porte les faucons à vendre' Littré; also CADGE *sb.*[1]) App. only modern in Eng.

1834 MAR. EDGEWORTH *Helen* xvii. (Rtldg.) 163 The German cadgers and trainers who had been engaged.

4. *Comb.*, as **cadger-like** adj.

1836–7 DICKENS *Sk. Boz* (1850) 289/2 A love of all that is roving and cadgerlike in nature.

cadgily ('kædʒɪlɪ), *adv.* *Sc.* [f. CADGY + -LY[2].] Cheerfully, merrily; wantonly.

a **1724** *Gaberlunzie Man* i, He..cadgily ranted and sang. *a* **1774** FERGUSSON *Poems* (1789) II. 28 Whare cadgily they kiss the cap. **1814** *Saxon & Gael.* I. 108 'Hoot gude-man' she wad say, sae cadgily 'set a stout heart to a stay brae'.

'cadginess. *Sc.* [f. as prec. + -NESS.] Wantonness, lasciviousness: sportiveness, cheerfulness.

cadging ('kædʒɪŋ), *vbl. sb.* [f. CADGE *v.*]

† **1.** The binding or edging of a garment. *Obs.*

1674 *Depos. York Castle* (1861) 209 After I toucht the cadgings of her skirts, she stept not many steps after.

2. The practice of a cadger in various senses. (See CADGER 2.) Also *attrib.*

1859 SALA *Tw. round Clock* 387 Defunct saturnalia of patrician 'cadging'. **1859** *Autobiog. Beggar-boy* 99 To join two genteel young men in the regular cadging trade. **1879** DIXON *Windsor* II. xxv. 254 No pride of place prevented him from cadging.

'cadgy, *a.* *Sc.* and *north. dial.* Also **cadgie, caidgie.** [Of uncertain origin. Cf. Suffolk *kedge* in same sense; also Da. *kaad* wanton, lascivious.]

1. Wanton, lustful: amorous.

a **1724** [cf. CADGILY]. **1733** *Cock-laird* in Chambers *Songs Scotl.* (1829) A cock-laird, fou cadgie, Wi' Jennie did meet. **1823** LOCKHART *Reg. Dalton* VII. v. (1842) 435 He may weel be cadgy in the chaise wi' her.

2. Cheerful, merry; glad.

1725 RAMSAY *Gentle Sheph.* IV. ii. 1 Wow! but I'm cadgie, and my heart lowps light. **1811** WILLAN *W. Riding Yorksh. Gloss.* in *Archæol.* XVII. (E.D.S.) *Cadgy*, cheerful, merry.

‖ **cadi** ('kɑːdɪ, 'keɪdɪ). Also 6–8 **cady**, 7 **kadi, caddi, -ee**, 7–8 **cadee**, 9 **kady**, (7 **cadis, cade**, 8 **cadjee**). [a. Arab. *qāḍī* judge, f. *qaḍa(y* to judge. (Whence, with *al-*, Sp. *alcalde*.)]

A civil judge among the Turks, Arabs, Persians, etc.; usually the judge of a town or village.

1590 WEBBE *Trav.* (1868) 33 In Turkie..the graunde Cady, that is their chiefest Iudg. **1613** PURCHAS *Pilgr.* I. VI. viii. 498 The house of the Cadi. **1653** GREAVES *Seraglio* 155 In the presence of the Cadee (who is the Justice). **1682** WHELER *Journ. Greece* VI. 419 The Veivode and Caddi.. came to make their Inspection. **1688** *Lond. Gaz.* No. 2328/1 The Kadis or Judges. **1703** MAUNDRELL *Journ.* (1721) 95 The Cadi at last gave sentence. **1852** WILLIS *Cruise in Medit.* xxxix. 236 The black-banded turban of a cadi.

Hence **'cadiship**, the office of a cadi.

1881 *Harper's Mag.* LXIII. 353 The judge or cadi—I am not positive as to the cadiship.

cadie, variant of CADDIE.

‖ **cadilesker** (kɑːdɪ'lɛskə(r)). Also **cadilisker, -escher, -esher, cadelesher, kadilesker.** [f. prec. + Turk. *leskar*, ad. Pers. *lashkar* army: his jurisdiction originally extended to soldiers.]

A chief judge in the Turkish empire.

1686 *Lond. Gaz.* No. 2196/1 Hussain Effendi Cadilisker of Romelia is made Great Mufti. **1688** *Ibid.* No. 2328/1 The Kadileskers, or chief Judges. **1703** *Ibid.* No. 3911/1 The Grand Signior had declared the Mufti's Son *Cadilescher*, or Judge Advocate. **1721–90** BAILEY, *Cadelesher*, *Cadilesher*, a chief Magistrate in Turkey, of which there are but two. [In mod. Dicts.]

cadis: see CADDIS.

'cadish, *a.* *dial.* [f. CADE *sb.*[2]] Tame, gentle.

1788 MARSHALL *Yorksh.* (ed. 2) II. 210 [Pigs].. remarkably cadish and quiet. **1879** MISS JACKSON *Shropsh. Word-bk.* (E.D.S.) *Cadish*, spoiled by over-indulgence.

‖ **cadjan** ('kɑːdʒən). *Anglo-Indian.* Also 7–8 **cajan.** [ad. Malay and Javan. *kājāng* palm-leaves, 'introduced by foreigners into Southern India' (Yule).]

1. 'Coco-palm leaves matted, the common substitute for thatch in Southern India' (Col. Yule).

1698 FRYER *Acc. E. India & P.* 17 (Y.) Flags..(by them called Cajans, being Co-coe-tree branches)..supplying.. Coverings to their Cottages. **1727** A. HAMILTON *New Acc. E. Ind.* I. xxiv. 294 His Palace..was..covered with Cadjans or Cocoa-nut Tree Leaves woven together. **1860** TENNENT *Ceylon* II. 126 (Y.) Houses are..roofed with its plaited fronds, which, under the name of cadjans, are likewise employed for constructing partitions and fences.

2. 'A strip of fan-palm leaf, i.e. either of the talipot, or of the palmyra, prepared for writing on; and so a document written on such a strip' (Col. Yule). Also *attrib.*, as in ***cadjan leaf, letter.***

1707 in J. T. Wheeler *Madras in Olden T.* II. 78 (Y.) The officer at the Bridge Gate bringing in..a Cajan letter that he found hung upon a post. **1716** *Ibid.* II. 231 (Y.) The President..has intercepted a villainous letter or Cajan. **1840** A. CAMPBELL *Code Madras Regul.* 323 Vellum parchment or any other material instead of paper or cadjan leaf. **1853** J. W. DYKES *Salem* 355.

cadjee, cadle, obs. ff. of CADI, CAUDLE.

'cadlock. Another form of CHARLOCK, a plant, including Wild Rape and Field Mustard.

1655 MOUFET & BENN. *Health's Improv.* (1746) 172 Tame Pidgeons..fed never at home but in Cadlock-time and the dead of Winter. **1790** MARSHALL *Midl.* Gloss. (E.D.S.) *Cadlock, Rough, sinapis arvensis*, wild mustard. *Cadlock, Smooth, brasica napus*, wild rape.

Cadmean (kæd'miːən), *a.* Also **Cadmian, -mæan.** [ad. L. *Cadmēus*, a. Gr. *Καδμεῖος*, f. *Κάδμος* Cadmus.] Pertaining to Cadmus, the legendary founder of Thebes in Bœotia, and introducer of the alphabet into Greece. ***Cadmean victory*** (Gr. *Καδμεία νίκη*), 'a victory involving one's own ruin' (Liddell and Scott); usually associated with Thebes or the Thebans.

1603 HOLLAND *Plutarch's Mor.* 12 A Cadmian victorie, that is to say, which turneth to the detriment and losse of the winner. **1678** CUDWORTH *Intell. Syst.* 146 Made them like the Cadmean Offspring, to do immediate Execution upon themselves. **1762** *Gentl. Mag.* 430 Our conquests would prove Cadmean victories. **1821** SHELLEY *Prometh. Unb.* IV, The cup Which Agave lifted up In the weird Cadmæan forest. **1868** TENNYSON *Lucr.* 50 Dragon warriors from Cadmean teeth.

† **'cadmia.** *Chem. Obs.* [a. L. *cadmĭa*, a. Gr. *καδμεία* or *καδμία γῆ* 'Cadmean earth'.] 'The ancient name of calamine' (Ure *Dict. Arts* I. 569); also applied to a sublimate consisting of oxide of zinc (tutty), and to an ore of cobalt.

1657 *Phys. Dict.*, *Cadmia officinarum*, tutty. **1674** A. A. BARBA *Art of Mettals* I. xxxiv. 146 Cadmia is also that which sticks to the walls of the Furnaces, principally wherein Copper is melted. **1753** CHAMBERS *Cycl. Supp.*, *Cadmia*, sometimes signifies a fossil substance, as the *Lapis calaminaris.* **1837** DANA *Min.* (1868) 409 The *cadmia* of Pliny and of other ancient authors included both the native silicate and carbonate, and the oxyd from the chimneys of furnaces (*cadmia fornacum*).

cadmic ('kædmɪk), *a.* [f. CADM-IUM + -IC.]

1. *Chem.* Of cadmium: as in cadmic oxide, etc.

1873 WILLIAMSON *Chem.* 173 Cadmic sulphide is a beautiful yellow compound.

2. Of cadmia, cadmean.

1873 A. W. WARD tr. *Curtius' Greece* I. I. iii. 91 The earth used for the refinement of copper was called Cadmic earth.

cadmiferous (kæd'mɪfərəs), *a.* *Chem.* [f. CADMI-UM + -FEROUS bearing.] Yielding cadmium.

1822 E. D. CLARKE *Cadmium* 5 The Cumberland Cave.. contains both silicate and carbonate of zinc, and both are cadmiferous.

cadmium ('kædmɪəm). *Chem.* [f. CADMIA calamine, the common ore of zinc, with which this metal is generally associated. The ending is that of other names of metals, as *sodium*, etc.]

a. A bluish-white metal, in its physical qualities resembling tin, found in small quantities chiefly in zinc ores. Symbol Cd.

1822 IMISON *Sc. & Art* II. 122 Cadmium..was discovered by M. Stromeyer in 1817, in ores of Zinc. **1863** WATTS *Dict. Chem.* (1879) I. 702 The only pure native compound of cadmium is the sulphide, called Greenockite. **1869** *Latest News* 10 Oct. 15 Cadmium is obtained for commercial purposes, from zinc ores and furnace deposits.

b. *attrib.* = CADMIC, as in ***cadmium oxide, sulphide***, etc., ***cadmium compounds***; **cadmium (mercury) cell**, a type of voltaic cell used as a standard of electromotive force; **cadmium green, orange, red**, pigments obtained from cadmium compounds; **cadmium yellow**, an intense yellow pigment, consisting of cadmium sulphide, artificially prepared.

1893 *Electrician* 13 Oct. 645/2 Notes on the E.M.F. and Temperature Coefficient of the Cadmium Mercury Cell. **1908** *Phil. Trans.* A. CCVII. 393 When the solution is saturated at all temperatures, i.e. when solid cadmium sulphate is always present in the cell, the name 'Cadmium Cell' has been frequently assigned to it in order to distinguish it from the original form. **1969** W. GARNER *Us or Them War* xxviii. 215 Jagger switched on the small cadmium cell torch, the light beam thrusting through the dark like a sword blade. **1873** FOWNES *Chem.* 395 Cadmium oxide is infusible. **1934** H. HILER *Technique of Painting* ii. 113 *Cadmium greens*..are mixtures of cadmium yellows and viridian or *vert emeraude.* **1936** A. HUXLEY *Olive Tree* 297 His grey trees have shadows of cadmium green. **1895** *Montgomery Ward Catal.* 253/1 Water colors..Pale cadmium yellow—cadmium orange—French blue. **1934** H. HILER *Technique of Painting* ii. 112 *Cadmium orange*, of the same chemical nature and composition as the yellow cadmiums,..and the most permanent of all the cadmium colours. **1886** H. C. STANDAGE *Artists' Man. Pigments* v. 47 *Cadmium red*..is a simple original pigment containing no base but cadmium. **1962** *Listener* 18 Jan. 126/2, I love cadmium red orange. **1879** ROOD *Chromatics* xi. 180 Bright yellow pigments, such as..chrome-yellow, cadmium-yellow.

† **'cadmy.** *Obs. rare*[−1]. [a. F. *cadmie* cadmia.] = CADMIA.

1756 C. LUCAS *Ess. Waters* I. 11 Lapis calaminaris, or cadmia; in our language..calamy, or cadmy.

ca'dogan (kə'dʌgən). [Said to be from the name of the 1st Earl Cadogan (died 1726). See Littré, and *N. & Q.* 7th Ser. IV. 467, 492.] A mode of knotting the hair behind the head.

c **1780** B'NESS D'OBERKIRCH *Mem.* (1852) II. ix, The duchess of Bourbon had introduced at the court of Montbéliard..[the fashion] of cadogans, hitherto worn only by gentlemen.

cados, obs. form of CADDIS.

† **ca'douk.** *Sc. Obs.* Also 7 **caddouk**, 9 **caduac.** [app. a. F. *caduc*, either with the notion of 'perishable' or of 'falling' to one.] 'A casualty, a windfall' (Jamieson).

1637 R. MONRO *Exped.* II. 123 His Majestie was liberall and bountifull..in bestowing on them cadouks and casualties. *Ibid.* 171 All other goods or caddouks in generall. **1819** SCOTT *Leg. Montrose* ii, The caduacs and casualties were all cut off.

cadow, obs. form of CADDOW.

‖ **cadre** (kadr). [F. *cadre* frame (e.g. of a picture), also used in sense 'l'ensemble des officiers et sous-officiers d'une compagnie' (Littré), ad. It. *quadro*:—L. *quadrum* four-sided thing, square.]

1. A frame, framework; scheme.

1830 SCOTT *Introd. Lay Last Minstr.*, This species of *cadre*, or frame, afterwards afforded the poem its name. **1868** M. PATTISON *Academ. Org.* sec. 5 §2. 174 It would seem..that no branch of human knowledge should be excluded..The corrective to the seeming infinity of this cadre is supplied by the old classification of faculties.

2. *Mil.* **a.** The permanent establishment forming the framework or skeleton of a regiment, which is filled up by enlistment when required. Also of an R.A.F. squadron. Also *attrib.*

1851 GALLENGA *Mariotti's Italy* 243 The number of officers..becomes inadequate to the sudden filling up of

their cadres, upon a transition from the peace to the war-footing. **1869** E. CARDWELL in *Daily News* 11 June, A larger number of battalions, with full cadres, ready to be expanded ..in a moment of emergency. **1884** *Sat. Rev.* 279 The principle of large permanent cadres in lieu of large standing armies. **1908** *Daily Chron.* 26 Nov. 6/4 The German Army ..is a 'cadre' army, which can only be set on a war footing by drawing on the reserves. **1929** *Air Ann. Brit. Empire* 54 The Service..is made up of three parts—the Regular Air Force, the Cadre Squadrons and the Auxiliary Air Force. **1931** *Flight* 1 May 374/2 The explanation is that the lower set of numbers indicates a Cadre squadron in which there is a proportion of Special Reserve *personnel*.

b. The complement of officers of a regiment; the list or scheme of such officers.

(After the Indian Mutiny, the cadres of Native Regiments which had been disbanded were kept in the Indian Army List for regulating promotions. In the parliamentary discussions about the amalgamation of the Indian with the British Army, the word was in constant use in this sense.)

1864 *Daily Tel.* 22 Aug., All staff corps lieutenant-colonels are to be removed from their cadre on promotion. **1870** *Pall Mall G.* 12 Oct. 7 The regimental cadres, that is, the officers of each regiment.

3. a. In Communist countries, a group of workers, etc., acting to promote the interests of the Communist Party; also, a member of such a group; = CELL *sb.*[1] 12 b.

1930 *Economist* 1 Nov. (Russian Suppl.) 10/2 The number, quality and devotion of these *cadres*, as the industrial army is called in Russia, will..decide the fate of the Industrial Revolution. **1931** *Times Lit. Suppl.* 9 July 536/4 The six 'cadres'..chosen as typical—Communist, Young Communist, shock worker, cultural worker, collectivized peasant and Red Army man—represent the sum total of the Soviet Government's supporters. **1937** E. SNOW *Red Star over China* ii. 61 Military training was secretly given to 2,000 cadres. **1950** D. HYDE *I Believed* ix. 92 In communist jargon to be a *cadre* meant to be someone trained and ready to do anything, anywhere, for communism. **1963** *Ann. Reg. 1962* 215 The specialized technical cadres needed for a further economic development [in Poland]. **1967** G. STEINER *Lang. Silence* 341 Around the hard core of French Stalinism, a harsh and disciplined *cadre* ..there has always flourished a large and animated world of intellectual Marxism.

b. In the People's Republic of China, an office-holder in a Party, governmental, or military organization; also more widely, one who holds a position, esp. in a local organization, school, etc. Also *attrib.*, esp. as *cadre school*.

1966 D. WILSON *Quarter of Mankind* i. 8 The cadres determined the class status of each villager. **1970** JENNER & YANG tr. *Mod. Chinese Stories* 181 What gave the local cadres some misgivings was that this cadre wanted to stay with an ordinary family, and said that he wanted to see the backward as well as the advanced aspects of the village. **1974** *Ann. Rev. 1973* 316 The role of cadre schools as places of re-education, where officials could participate in physical labour and political study, remained important. **1977** *Hongkong Standard* 12 Apr. 16/5 Wen, described as a plump, grey-haired cadre, is still being cross-examined, and has been branded a counter-revolutionary at mass criticism rallies. **1983** R. RENDELL *Speaker of Mandarin* i. 16 His father..was a party cadre, his mother a doctor, his sister and own wife doctors.

caduac, perversion of CADOUK.

caduc, variant of CADUKE *a. Obs.*

†**ca'ducal**, *a. Obs.* [f. L. *cadūcus* CADUCOUS + -AL[1].] Perishable, corruptible; = CADUKE 2.

1533 COVERDALE *Lord's Supper* Wks. 1844 I. 435 The caducal and corruptible meats wherewith the belly is fed. **1642** H. MORE *Song Soul* II. i. iii. xxiv, Nought..but vain sensibles we see caducall.

caducary (kə'djuːkərɪ), *a. Old Law.* [ad. L. *cadūcārius* relating to *bona cadūca* lapsed possessions. See CADUCOUS and -ARY.] Subject to, relating to, or by way of escheat or lapse.

1768 BLACKSTONE *Comm.* II. 265 The lord by escheat..is more frequently considered as being *ultimus haeres*, and therefore taking by descent in a kind of caducary succession. **1818** CRUISE *Digest* III. 452 Whether the escheat were considered as a reversion, as it once was, or as a caducary succession *ab intestato*, as it then substantially was.

†'**caduce.** *Obs.* = CADUCEUS.

1604 DANIEL *Fun. Poem on Earl of Devon*, Who equal bear the caduce and the shield. **1651** EVELYN *Diary* 7 Sept. (D.) Heralds in blew velvet semée with fleur de lys, caduces in their hand. **1681** COTTON *Wond. Peake* (ed. 4) 59 Ev'ry Wand a Caduce did appear. **1721–1800** in BAILEY.

†**ca'duce**, *a. Obs.* [ad. F. *caduc* or L. *cadūcus*.] = CADUKE, CADUCOUS.

1513 BRADSHAW *St. Werburgh* (1848) 118 This lyfe caduce and transytory. **1651** BIGGS *New Disp.* 2 That caduce, specious and seductive chameleon, Reason. **1657** TOMLINSON *Renou's Disp.* 279 Inclined to fall..imbecil and caduce.

ca'ducean, *a.* [f. CADUCE-US + -AN.] Of or pertaining to a caduceus.

1656 BLOUNT *Glossogr.*, *Caducean*, among the Romans was the name of a wand or rod. **1721–1800** in BAILEY. **1847** in CRAIG. **1879** J. TODHUNTER *Alcestis* 6 Of that caducean rod he [Apollo] drove our flocks To pasture with.

†**caduce'ator.** *Obs.* [L. *cādūceātor* one who bears a *caduceus*, a herald.] A herald, a messenger.

1684 tr. *Agrippa's Van. Arts* lxxxi. 279 Fecial Messengers and Caduceators. **1754** tr. *Josephus' Philo's Emb.* Wks. 797 Wars are determined by caduciators.

‖**caduceus** (kə'djuːsiːəs). Pl. **caducei** (-siːaɪ). [L. *cādūceus* (also *cādūceum*), ad. Dor. Gr. καρύκειον, καρύκιον (Att. κηρύκειον), a herald's wand, f. κῆρυξ herald.]

The wand carried by an ancient Greek or Roman herald. *spec.* The fabled wand carried by Hermes or Mercury as the messenger of the gods; usually represented with two serpents twined round it. (This is the earliest and proper sense in English.)

1591 SPENSER *M. Hubberd* 1292 He tooke Caduceus his snakie wand, With which the damned ghosts he gouerneth. **1606** SHAKS. *Tr. & Cr.* II. iii. 14 Mercury, loose all the Serpentine craft of thy Caduceus. **1668** *Lond. Gaz.* No. 243/2 The Heralds in their Coats of Armes, and Caducei in their hands. **1753** CHAMBERS *Cycl. Supp.*, *Caduceus*, is also a name given to a kind of staff covered with velvet, and decorated with *flower de luces*, which the French heralds of arms bear in their hands on solemn occasions. **1873** SYMONDS *Grk. Poets* xii. 410 Hermes..caduceus in hand. *fig.* **1860** R. VAUGHAN *Mystics* II. IX. iii. 137 The long process of vigil..which, with the caduceus of asceticism.. lulls to slumber the Argus-eyed monster of the flesh.

caduciary (kə'djuːʃ(ɪ)ərɪ), *a. Old Law.* [A non-etymological variant of CADUCARY, app. assimilated to *fiduciary*.] Subject to, relating to, or by way of escheat or lapse.

1757 SIR J. DALRYMPLE *Feudal Prop.* (1758) 67 To prevent his inheritance from being caduciary. **1880** MUIRHEAD *Gaius* II. §150 *note*, The L. Iulia et Papia Poppæa, whose caduciary provisions, etc.

Hence **ca'duciarily** *adv.*

1880 MUIRHEAD *Gaius* 504 Failure to take under a testament..The inheritance went to the heir-at-law caduciarily.

caducibranchiate (kəˌdjuːsɪ'bræŋkɪeɪt), *a. Zool.* [f. L. *cadūcus* falling + *branchiæ* gills, whence in mod.L. *Caducibranchia*, Latreille's name for the Batrachians.] Of Amphibians: Losing their gills before reaching maturity (like the frog). Also as *sb.*

[**1835** KIRBY *Hab. & Inst. Anim.* II. xxii. 412 Caducibranchia, or the proper Batrachians.] **1835–6** TODD *Cycl. Anat. & Phys.* I. 99/2 The early condition of the lungs in the caducibranchiate genera..is that of a mere rudimentary sac. **1839–47** *Ibid.* III. 448/2 The urodelous kinds of Caducibranchiates. **1870** ROLLESTON *Anim. Life* Introd. 67.

†**cadu'ciferous**, *a. Obs.*—[0]. [f. L. *cādūcifer* (f. *cādūc-eus* (see above) + *-fer* bearing) + -OUS.] Bearing a caduceus.

1656 BLOUNT *Glossogr.*, *Caduciferous*, that carries a white Rod in sign of peace. **1721–1800** BAILEY *Caduciferous*, bearing the Caduce. [Not in Johnson.]

caducity (kə'djuːsɪtɪ). [ad. F. *caducité*, as if:—L. **cadūcitātem*, f. *cadūcus*: see next.]

1. Tendency to fall; quality of being perishable or fleeting; transitoriness, frailty.

1793 W. ROBERTS *Looker-on* No. 49 (1794) II. 231 One of those evenings of autumn when the chilling damps of the air, and the caducity of nature, deepen the gloom of a melancholy mind. **1841** L. HUNT *Seer* II. (1864) 60 The stages of human existence, the caducity of which the writer applies to the world at large. **1879** M. PATTISON *Milton* 199 The ordinary caducity of language, in virtue of which every effusion of the human spirit is lodged in a body of death.

2. *esp.* The infirmity of old age, senility.

1769 CHESTERF. *Lett.* 426 IV. 272 This melancholick proof of my caducity. **1776–88** GIBBON *Decl. & F.* lxi. (R.) Count Henry assumed the regency of the empire, at once in a state of childhood and caducity. **1815** W. TAYLOR in Robberds *Mem.* II. 460 My father was attacked with symptoms of caducity. **1841** D'ISRAELI *Amen. Lit.* (1867) 345 The youth, the middle-age, and the caducity of the eminent personage.

3. *Roman Law.* Lapse of a testamentary gift.

1875 POSTE *Gaius* II. (ed. 2) 264 The leges caducariæ, which fixed the conditions of caducity. **1880** MUIRHEAD *Gaius* 464 If the party failing to take was sole heir, the caducity caused intestacy.

4. *Zool.* and *Bot.* Quality of being caducous.

1881 J. S. GARDNER in *Nature* XXIV. 75 The spores become detached before germination..this caducity always characterises the microspore.

caducous (kə'djuːkəs), *a.* [f. L. *cadūcus* falling, fleeting, etc. (f. *cadĕre* to fall) + -OUS.]

1. *Zool.* and *Bot.* Applied to organs or parts that fall off naturally when they have served their purpose; fugacious, deciduous.

1808 ROXBURGH *E. Ind. Butter Tree* in *Asiat. Researches* VIII. 500 Stipules..minute and caducous. **1835** LINDLEY *Introd. Bot.* (1848) II. 206 Fugacious, or caducous [leaves]. **1859** TODD *Cycl. Anat. & Phys.* V. 659/1 The placenta and other structures..become caducous.

2. Fleeting, transitory; = CADUKE 2.

1863 J. C. MORISON *St. Bernard* II. iii. 229 Monasticism.. was temporary, caducous, and charged with germs of evil.

3. *Roman Law.* Applied to testamentary gifts which for some reason lapsed from the donee.

1880 MUIRHEAD *Gaius* II. §206 The lapsed share becomes caducous, and falls to those persons named in the testament who happen to have children. **1880** —— *Ulpian* xvii. §1 A testamentary gift which..he to whom it was left has failed to take, although so left that according to the rules of the *ius ciuile* he might have taken it, is called caducous.

†**4.** Subject to the 'falling sickness', epileptic.

1684 tr. *Bonet's Merc. Compit.* v. 144 Treat the caducous but roughly, and disturb the manner of the Paroxysm.

†**ca'duke**, *a. Obs.* Also 5–6 caduc, 5–7 caduque. [a. F. *caduc* (fem. *caduque*):—L. *cadūcus*.]

1. Falling, liable to fall.

c **1420** *Pallad. on Husb.* XII. 134 The fruite caduke.

2. Fleeting, transitory, perishable, corruptible.

1484 CAXTON *Curial* 4 Our lyf..ne hath glorye mondayne ne pompe caduque wythoute aduersyte. **1509** FISHER *Wks.* I. (E.E.T.) 196 Euery thynge in this worlde is caduke. **1549** *Compl. Scotl.* 170 To fle thir varldly caduc honouris. **1651** STANLEY *Poems* 242 Caduque corruptible bodies. **1688** G. MIEGE *Gt. Fr. Dict.*, Caduke or crazy.

3. Of persons: Infirm, feeble.

1510–20 *Compl. to late maryed* (1862) 10, I am all caduc, and wery for age. **1541** R. COPLAND *Guydon's Quest. Chirurg.*, Yonge, vertuous and stronge, so that he be nat caduke nor shakynge of his handes.

4. Epileptic; = CADUCOUS 4.

1398 TREVISA *Barth De P.R.* XVIII. i. (1495) 746 Caduc men that haue the fallyng euyll.

cad-worm = caddis-worm: see CAD[4].

cady ('keɪdɪ). *local.* Also cadey, -i(e). [Origin unknown.] A hat or cap.

1846 *Spirit of Times* 6 June 170/2, I may be able to discover my lost 'Cady'. **1869** *N. & Q.* III. 406 In Lancashire..a straw hat [is vulgarly called] a cady or straw cady. **1887** *Walford's Antiquarian Mag.* XI. 251 Cadey found its way into a music-hall song some years ago. The chorus was something like this:—..Sixpence I gave for my cadey, A penny I gave for my stick. **1887** *Jamieson's Scot. Dict.* Suppl., *Cadie*..2. A boy's cap; generally applied to a glengary. **1898** J. D. BRAYSHAW *Slum Silhouettes* 220 Wot with 'is white cadi cocked a-outside, ter show orf 'is fringe. **1909** *Daily Chron.* 8 Dec. 6/7 The British navvy is never prouder than when he has, stuck in the ribbon of his best 'cady', a spray of the fateful [peacocks'] feathers. **1959** *Times* 28 Sept. 11/4 Isn't it time we relieved our modern rozzer of his incongruous cady?

cady, var. of CADI, CADDIE.

cadyas, obs. form of CADDIS[1].

†'**cadye**, *a. Sc. Obs.* [cf. Da. *kaad* lascivious, wanton; and see CADGY: the formal relation of the two words is obscure.] Wanton, lascivious.

1552 LYNDESAY *Monarche* 2657 Kyttoke thare, als cadye as ane Con. [**1877** PEACOCK *N.W. Lincoln. Gloss.* (E.D.S.) *Caddy*, hale, hearty.]

cæ-: see also CE-.

cæcal ('siːkəl), *a. Phys.* [f. CÆC-UM + -AL[1].] Pertaining to, or of the nature of, the cæcum; having a blind end.

1826 KIRBY & SP. *Entomol.* IV. xl. 121 Their cæcal appendages are numerous. **1858** LEWES *Sea-side Studies* Index, Cæcal prolongations of the intestines are.. ramifications without openings at the farther ends. **1881** *Jrnl. Microsc. Sc.* Jan. 99 It terminates behind in a cæcal extremity.

cæcally ('siːkəlɪ), *adv. Phys.* [f. prec. + -LY[2].] In the manner of a cæcum, with a blind end.

1872 NICHOLSON *Palæont.* 202 The intestine ends cæcally. **1877** HUXLEY *Anat. Inv. An.* viii. 463.

‖'**Cæcias.** ? *Obs.* Also 7 Cecias. [Lat.; a. Gr. καικίας.] The north-east wind personified.

1653 URQUHART *Rabelais* I. xl, Just as the winde called Cecias attracts the clouds. **1667** MILTON *P.L.* x. 701 Boreas, and Cæcias, and Argestes loud. **1824** T. FORSTER *Perenn. Calendar* in Hone *Everyday Bk.* II. 119 And Caecias blows his bitter blaste of woe.

cæciform ('siːsɪfɔːm), *a. Phys.* [f. CÆC-UM + FORM.] Having the form of a cæcum.

1871 R. JONES *Anim. Kingd.* 205 Cæciform appendages.. around the æsophagus and stomach.

cæcilian (siː'sɪlɪən). *Zool.* [f. L. *cæcilia* a kind of lizard (in Pliny *cæcus serpens* blind worm).] A member of the *Cæciliadæ*, a curious family of Amphibia, having the form of serpents, but the naked skin and complete metamorphosis of Batrachians; their eyes are very small and nearly hidden by the skin.

cæcitis (siː'saɪtɪs). *Med.* [f. CÆC-UM + -ITIS.] Inflammation of the cæcum, typhlitis.

1866 A. FLINT *Princ. Med.* (1880) 427 The inflammation limited to this portion of the large intestine..called typhlitis ..or cæcitis.

cæcity, var. of CECITY, blindness.

‖**cæcum** ('siːkəm). *Phys.* Also occas. **cecum**; *Pl.* **cæca**. [L.; for *intestinum cæcum*; neut. of *cæcus* blind.]

1. The blind-gut; the first part of the large intestine, so called because it is prolonged behind the opening of the ilium into a cul-de-sac. It is present in man, most mammals and birds, and in many reptiles.

1721 in BAILEY. **1727–51** CHAMBERS *Cycl.* s.v. *Intestine*, The cæcum..has a lateral insertion into the upper end of the colon; and hangs to it like the finger of a glove. **1872** HUXLEY *Phys.* vi. 150 The large intestine forms a blind dilatation beyond the ilio-cæcal valve..called the cæcum.

2. With pl. *cæca*: Any blind tube, or tube with one end closed. The ***intestinal cæca*** are two long blind tubes connected with the upper part of the large intestine in birds; ***pyloric cæca***, a series of blind tubes, from one to fifty in number, placed immediately behind the pyloric valve in the stomach of most fishes; also the prolongations of the stomach into the rays of star-fishes.

1753 CHAMBERS *Cycl. Supp.* s.v. *Intestinum*, The fish kind have in general a great number of these cæca; they are called by the ichthyologists Intestinula cæca. **1848** CARPENTER *Anim. Phys.* 172 Furnished with one or more little appendages, termed cæca. **1857** WOOD *Com. Obj. Sea-shore* 129 The stomach is assisted by certain supplementary stomachs which run through each ray..cæca as they are called. **1868** DUNCAN *Insect World* Introd. 10 The second are cæca, and larger and less numerous.

cæl-: see CEL-.

cænaculum: see CENACLE.

cæno- occas. var. CENO-, CŒNO-.

cænogenesis (siːnəʊˈdʒɛnɪsɪs). More regular form of KENOGENESIS (1879). So **cænogeˈnetic** *a.*

1909 *Cent. Dict.* Suppl., Cænogenesis. **1930** G. R. DE BEER *Embryol. & Evol.* i. 6 Haeckel concluded..that a new or caenogenetic stage had been intercalated in the ontogeny. *Ibid.* xv. 102 The appearance of characters in the early stages of development is caenogenesis. **1937** *Jrnl. R. Anthrop. Inst.* 192 It is clearly a caenogenetic character.

cænozoic (siːnəʊˈzəʊɪk), *a. Geol.* Another form of CAINOZOIC.

1863 *Q. Rev.* CXIV. 396 A general conspectus of the later cænozoic periods. **1869** PHILLIPS *Vesuvius* viii. 235 The extinct volcanoes manifested themselves very largely in early cænozoic periods. **1879** tr. *Haeckel's Evol. Man* II. xv. 15 The Tertiary, Cænozoic, or Cænolithic Epoch.

Caen-stone. A lightish-yellow building-stone found near Caen in Normandy; it is at first very soft, but hardens on exposure. Also *attrib.*

1421 in *Lett. Q. Margaret of Anjou* (1863) 20, I have purveyed xiij. tons tight [weight?] of Cane stone. **1598** STOW *Surv.* 361 Part of the ruines of the old Temple were seene to remaine builded of Cane stone. **1898** C. M. YONGE *J. Keble's Parishes* ix. 102 The material chiefly used in the cathedral was Caen stone. **1906** *Westm. Gaz.* 26 Apr. 12/1 The beautiful Caen-stone structure. **1924** F. M. FORD *Some do Not* I. iv. 99 They've got just a facing of Caen stone that the tide floated here.

Caerphilly (kɛəˈfɪlɪ). [The name of a town in S. Wales.] ***Caerphilly cheese***: a mild cheese (originally) made in Caerphilly; also *ellipt.*

1901 *Jrnl. R. Agric. Soc.* LXII. 153 The local variety of *Caerphilly* cheese was divided into two classes, according to size. *Ibid.*, Both the classes of Caerphilly cheese contained exhibits with good chances of a prize. **1951** *Good Housek. Home Encycl.* 376/1 *Caerphilly.* Originally a Welsh cheese, this is now also made in Somerset, Wiltshire, Devon and Dorset. **1958** M. DICKENS *Man Overboard* xv. 243 His face remained the colour of Caerphilly cheese.

cærule, -ean, etc.; see CER-.

Cæsar (ˈsiːzə(r)). Also 4–8 **Cesar.** [L. *Cæsar*, a proper name. This is generally held to be the earliest Latin word adopted in Teutonic, where it gave Gothic *kaisar* (cf. Gr. καῖσαρ), OS. *kêsar, -er*, OFris. *kaiser, keiser*, OHG. *keisar, -er*, OE. *câsere*, ON. *keisari*. But the OE. form of the word (which would have given in mod.Eng. *coser*—cf. *pope*) was lost in the ME. period. It was replaced in ME. by *keiser, cayser, kaiser*, from Norse and continental Teutonic, which has in its turn become obsolete, except as an alien term for the German emperor, and been replaced by the Latin or French form. See KASER, KAISER. Another form of the word is the Russian *Tsar* or CZAR.]

1. a. The cognomen of the Roman dictator Caius Julius Cæsar, transferred as a title to the emperors from Augustus down to Hadrian (B.C. 30 to A.D. 138), and subsequently used as a title of the heir-presumptive of the emperor. In modern use often applied to all the emperors down to the fall of Constantinople.

1382 WYCLIF *John* xix. 15 We han no kyng no but Cesar. [**1388** We han no king but the emperour.] **1586** FERNE *Blaz. Gentrie* 150 Amongst the Romaines vntill the time of their Cæsars, it was a common vse. **1776–88** GIBBON *Decl. & F.* xiii. (1875) 144 After the adoption of the two Cæsars, the emperors devolved on their adopted sons the defence of the Danube and of the Rhine. *Ibid.* lxviii. 1238 Mahomed the second performed the *namaz* of prayer and thanksgiving on the great altar, where the christian mysteries had so lately been celebrated before the last of the Cæsars. **1795** SOUTHEY *Joan of Arc* II. 337 Cæsars and Soldans, Emperors and Kings. **1869** FREEMAN *Norm. Conq.* (1876) III. xii. 91 Before whom Cæsars as well as Pontiffs were to quail.

b. ***Cæsar's wife***: In various uses with allusion to Plutarch *Cæsar* x. 6 ('I thought my wife ought not even to be under suspicion').

1579 LYLY *Euphues* (1868) 329 Al women shal be as *Cæsar* would have his wife, not onelye free from sinne, but from suspition. **1748** RICHARDSON *Clarissa* III. xvii. 108 The wife of Caesar must not be suspected. **1866** J. C. & A. W. HARE *Guesses at Truth* 187 Caesar's wife ought to be above suspicion. **1878** TROLLOPE *Is he Popenjoy?* II. xi. 161 But Cæsar said that Cæsar's wife should be above suspicion, and in that matter every man is a Cæsar to himself. *Ibid.* xiii. 182 Then there was that feeling of Cæsar's wife strong within his bosom. **1930** D. L. SAYERS *Strong Poison* xxi. 270 You've got a family and traditions, you know. Cæsar's wife and that sort of thing.

c. The emperor of the 'Holy Roman Empire'; the German KAISER.

1674 HICKMAN *Hist. Quinquart.* (ed. 2) 57 The very year before that Confession was presented to Cæsar, there was a Colloquy betwixt the Lutherans and Zuinglians. **1704** *Addr. Taworth* in *Lond. Gaz.* No. 4066/5 This..has rescued Germany from a Rebellious Incendiary; kept its Cæsar safe.

†**d.** A baby delivered by Cæsarean section. *Obs. rare.*

1540 R. JONAS tr. *Roesslin's Byrth of Mankynde* I. ix. fol. liii, They that are borne after this fashion be called cesares, for because they be cut out of theyr mothers belly, whervpon also the noble Romane cesar the .j. of that name in Rome toke his name.

e. (A case of) Cæsarean section. *Med. slang.*

1952 'R. GORDON' *Doctor in House* ix. 97 'How many babies have you had?'.. 'Forty-nine. That includes a couple of Cæsars.' **1956** 'J. BELL' *Death in Retirement* iii. 33 'I had to do a Caesar,' answered Dr. Clayton. **1963** *Economist* 20 Apr. 239/1 That 'caesar' in the maternity ward. **1964** *Guardian* 8 Feb. 8/5 One Roman Catholic doctor..will awaken this convenient custodian of his conscience with the words: 'I'm doing a fourth Caesar.'

2. a. *fig.* or *transf.* An absolute monarch, an autocrat, emperor.

1593 SHAKS. *3 Hen. VI*, III. i. 18 No bending knee shall call thee Cæsar now. **1594** —— *Rich. III*, IV. iv. 336 She shalbe sole Victoresse, Cæsars Cæsar. **1682** SIR T. BROWNE *Chr. Mor.* 3 Lead thine own captivity captive, and be Cæsar within thy self. **1697** DRYDEN *Virg. Georg.* IV. 314 The servile Rout their careful Cæsar praise. **1859** SALA *Tw. round Clock* (1861) 34 An Emperor will always be called Cæsar, and a dog 'poor old fellow'.

b. *contextually*, The temporal monarch as the object of his subjects' obedience (sometimes contrasted with the obedience due to God); the civil power. In allusion to *Matt.* xxii. 21.

[*c* **1000** *Ags. Gosp.* Matt. xxii. 21 Aȝyfað þam Casere þa þing þe þæs Casyres synt. *c* **1160** *Hatton G.* ibid., Caysere—Cayseres. **1382** WYCLIF *ibid.*, ȝelde ȝee to Cesar the thingis that ben Cesaris, and to God the thingis that ben of God. **1388** *ibid.*, ȝelde ȝe to the emperoure the thingis that ben the emperouris.] **1601** BP. BARLOW *Serm. Paules Crosse* 27 The things due from subjects to their Cæsar. **1679** PENN *Addr. Prot.* II. vi. (1692) 126 Caesar, by which Word I understand the Civil Government, engrosseth All. **1714** J. FORTESCUE-ALAND *Ded. Fortescue's Abs. & Lim. Mon.* 8 Impartially decides the rights of Caesar and his subject.

c. ***to appeal (un)to Cæsar*** (with allusion to *Acts* xxv. 11): to appeal to the highest authority.

1855 *Wesleyan Methodist Mag.* Apr. 305 The conduct of unreasonable..men made it right, as in St. Paul's case, for him sometimes to appeal unto Cæsar. **1894** T. B. REED *Dog with Bad Name* xv. 156 'Can't she come, Father?' said Percy, adroitly appealing to Cæsar. **1899** KIPLING *Stalky & Co.* 27 'I appeal to the Head, sir.'.. 'Thou hast appealed unto Caesar: unto Caesar shalt thou go.' **1903** J. CHAMBERLAIN in *Westm. Gaz.* 22 Oct. 5/1 If this policy..were not accepted as the policy of the Government..I should feel it my duty to appeal to Cæsar. **1926** P. GUEDALLA *Palmerston* II. ii. 70 In a formal reference to the Prince Regent the indignant soldier appealed to Caesar.

3. *attrib.* or in *comb.*, e.g. ***Cæsar-like, -worship***; **Cæsar baby**, a baby delivered by Cæsarean section.

1599 HAKLUYT *Voy.* II. I. 295 The most mightie Cesarlike maiestie of the Grand Signor. **1663** GERBIER *Counsel* C viij b, Matchless Buckingham most Cæsar-like glorious. **1861** J. SHEPPARD *Fall Rome* xii. 624 Between Christianity and Cæsar-worship there could be no compromise. **1975** H. JOLLY *Bk. Child Care* iii. 53 The Caesar Baby. The decision that delivery must be by Caesarean section is taken by the obstetrician. **1980** F. WELDON *Puffball* 246 'Lovely little baby', said the nurse. 'Of course Caesar babies usually are. They don't get so squashed.'

ˈCæsar, *v. nonce-wd.* [f. prec.] *trans.* To make into or like Cæsar, to call or style Cæsar.

a **1655** T. ADAMS *Wks.* (1861) I. 491 (D.) Crowned he villifies his own kingdom for narrow bounds, whiles he hath greater neighbours; he must be Cæsared to a universal monarch. **1726** AMHERST *Terræ Fil.* xliv. 233 After having Cæsar'd and Scipio'd him secundum artem.

ˈCæsardom. [see -DOM.] The dominion or dignity of the Cæsars.

1861 A. B. HOPE *Eng. Cathedr. 19th C.* 144 Charles the Frank..transporting the name and the pomp of the Cæsardom to the forests of Rhineland.

Cæsarean, Cæsarian (siːˈzɛərɪən), *a.* and *sb.* [ad. L. *Cæsariān-us* pertaining to Cæsar; also f. L. *Cæsare-us*, in same sense + -AN.]

A. *adj.*

1. Of or pertaining to Cæsar or the Cæsars.

1659 HOWELL *Lex. Tetragl.* To Philol., The Italian may be also calld..the Imperiall Cæsarean language. **1682** SIR T. BROWNE *Chr. Mor.* 95 A short Cæsarian conquest overcoming without a blow. **1776** GIBBON *Decl. & F.* I. 402 The Cæsarean ornaments. **1876** EMERSON *Ess.* Ser. II. iv. 105 Men of the right Cæsarian pattern.

2. (Also with lower-case initial): *spec.* (in *Obstet. Surg.*) **Cæsarean birth, operation, section**, the delivery of a child by cutting through the walls of the abdomen when delivery cannot take place in the natural way, as was done in the case of Julius Cæsar. Also *fig.*

1615 CROOKE *Body of Man* 344 Concerning this Cæsarian section. **1661** HICKERINGILL *Jamaica* 40 Neither heat nor cold can baracade the..womb of the earth from the Cæsarean Section..of the greedy Miners. **1751** CHAMBERS *Cycl.* s.v., Sometimes also denominated the Cæsarian birth ..as were [born] C. Julius Cæsar, Scipio Africanus, Manlius, and our Edward VI. **1818** CRUISE *Digest* I. 163 If the wife dies in childbed, and the issue is taken out of the womb by the Cæsarean operation, the husband will not be entitled to curtesy. **1865** CARLYLE *Fredk. Gt.* IV. II. v. 71 The Principality of Orange..clearly Prussia's; but it lies embedded deep in the belly of France: that will be a Cæsarean operation for you!

B. *sb.*

1. An adherent of Cæsar, of the Emperor (against the Pope), or of an imperial system.

1528 *Let.* in Brewer's *Reign Hen. VIII*, II. 323 The Archbishop of Capua and others of the Cæsarians. *c* **1555** HARPSFIELD *Divorce Hen. VIII* (1878) 182 If any such thing should by the Cæsarients..be attempted. **1618** BOLTON *Florus* (1636) 282 The eagernesse of the Cæsarians. **1869** SEELEY *Ess. & Lect.* i. 2 Then the Cæsarians become.. enlightened Liberals.

2. (Also with lower-case initial.) A Cæsarean section. *colloq.*

1923 S. P. WARREN in *Amer. Jrnl. Obstetr. & Gynecol.* VI. 338 (*heading*) What I have learned from my one hundred and six cesareans. **1948** *Parent's Mag.* Apr. 93/1 Hospitals generally let mothers recovering from a Caesarean remain longer than the ordinary five-day limit. **1971** H. & M. BRANT *Dict. Pregnancy, Childbirth, & Contraception* 46 It usually takes two to three months before you feel really well after a caesarean. **1985** *Washington Post* 13 Jan. K2/4 The AMA reports that a Caesarean commands an additional £250 over a vaginal delivery.

†**Cæˈsareate.** *Obs.* [f. L. *Cæsareus* of or pertaining to CÆSAR + -ATE.] The office of the Roman Cæsar; the imperial dignity.

a **1638** MEDE *Summ. View of the Apoc.* viii. 10 Wks. (1672) 920 The Western Cæsareate being extinct in Augustulus. **1685** H. MORE *Illustr.* 248 The sad final fate of the Western Cæsareate.

†**Cæˈsarical**, *a. Obs.* Of Cæsar, imperial.

a **1618** RALEIGH in Gutch *Coll. Cur.* I. 71 Particular custom, or Cæsarical law.

Cæsarism (ˈsiːzərɪz(ə)m). [f. CÆSAR + -ISM.]

1. The system of absolute government founded by Cæsar; imperialism.

1857 O. BROWNSON *Convert* Wks. V. 192 Monarchical absolutism, or what I choose to call modern Cæsarism. **1858** *Westm. Rev.* Oct. 313 Clumsy eulogies of Cæsarism as incarnate in the dynasty of Bonaparte. **1869** *Pall Mall G.* 1 Sept. 1 In Napoleon's Cæsarism there has been no flaw. **1870** JEVONS *Elem. Logic* vi. 47 The abstract word Cæsarism has been formed to express a kind of Imperial system as established by Cæsar. **1876** BANCROFT *Hist. U.S.* VI. xxxi. 97 Charlemagne..renewing Roman Cæsarism.

b. = ERASTIANISM.

1876 M. DAVIES *Unorth. Lond.* 460 Cæsarism, or the supremacy of the civil power in spiritual things.

So **ˈCæsarist**, an imperialist; **ˈCæsarize**, *v. intr.* to play the Cæsar; *trans.* to make like Cæsar, or like Cæsar's.

1603 DAVIES *Microcos.* 25 (D.) This pow'r..Cæsarizeth ore each appetite. **1652** BENLOWES *Theoph.* XI. lxxxiii. 203 Should trophies Cæsarize your power, Should beauty Helenize your flower. **1875** H. KINGSLEY *No. Seventeen* xl. 309 She is not a Cæsarist, because she says that the lady of Chiselhurst had never any taste in ribands. **1883** SWINBURNE *Victor Hugo* in *Fortn. Rev.*, German and Anglo-German Cæsarists.

Cæsaro-papism (ˌsiːzərəʊˈpeɪpɪz(ə)m). [f. CÆSAR + -O + PAPISM.] The supremacy of the civil power in the control of ecclesiastical affairs. So **ˌCæsaro-ˈpapal** *a.*, **-ˈpapalism, -ˈpapist** *a.*

1890 *Edin. Rev.* Apr. 349 Such a *régime* as the Cæsaro-papism of Justinian. **1903** *Cambr. Mod. Hist.* II. xvi. 567 A bill which went the full Henrican length in its Cæsaro-papalism and its severity. **1924** FOAKES-JACKSON *Studies in Life Early Ch.* 240 Another effect of the triumphant way in which Christianity won the respect and recognition of the Roman government was what is called Cæsaro-papalism. **1939** A. J. TOYNBEE *Study Hist.* IV. 592 The abortive resistance of the Church to the revival of 'Caesaro-Papism' in orthodox Christendom. *Ibid.*, The 'Caesaro-papal' authority. **1941** 'R. WEST' *Black Lamb* (1942) II. 249 A Cesaropapist empire whose emperor was the Vicar of Christ.

Cæsarship (ˈsiːzəʃɪp). The office of a Cæsar; imperial dignity.

1641 J. JACKSON *True Evang. T.* I. 22 During the Cæsarship of Nerva. **1864** BURTON *Scot Abr.* I. iv. 172 Germany, though nominally in possession of the Cæsarship.

cæsious (ˈsiːzɪəs), *a.* [f. L. *cæsi-us* bluish grey + -OUS.] Bluish or greyish green. (Chiefly in *Bot.*)

1835 LINDLEY *Introd. Bot.* (1848) II. 366 Cæsious; like glaucous, but greener. [**1880** GRAY *Bot. Text-bk.* 400 *Cæsius*, lavender colour; pale green with whitish or gray.]

cæsium (ˈsiːzɪəm). *Chem.* Also (*U.S.*) **cesium.** [f. L. *cæsium*, neuter of *cæsius* bluish grey.] One of the elementary bodies; a rare alkali-metal discovered by spectrum-analysis in 1860–61 by Bunsen and Kirchhoff; so called from two distinctive lines in the spectrum given by its compounds. Symbol Cs. Used *attrib.*, as in

cæsium compounds; **cæsium cell** (see quot. 1940).

1861 *Lond. & Edinb. Philos. Mag.* Ser. IV. No. 21. 86 A faint blue line not due to strontium or potassium or to the lately discovered cæsium. **1862** TIMBS *Year-bk. of Facts* 188 Cæsium and Rubidium. The new alkaline metals.. described..in the Philosophical Magazine. **1864** LYELL *Inaug. Addr.* in *Reader* 17 Sept. 358 It was necessary to evaporate fifty tons of water to obtain 200 grains of what proved to be two new metals..He (Professor Bunsen) named the first cæsium, from the bluish-grey lines which it presented in the spectrum. **1873** FOWNES *Chem.* 350 Caesium carbonate is soluble in absolute alcohol. **1931** *Engineering* 16 Jan. 87/1 The new Osram monatomic caesium cell being the most suitable for white light. **1940** *Chambers's Techn. Dict.* 125/2 *Caesium cell*, a photo-electric cell having a cathode consisting of a thin layer of caesium deposited on minute globules of silver; it is particularly sensitive to infra-red radiation. **1955** *Sci. News Let.* 27 Aug. 131/1 Cesium is a heavier and more active relative of sodium and potassium. **1958** C. C. ADAMS et al. *Space Flight* xiv. 346 Both rubidium and cesium have been considered as the propellant for the ion drive. **1958** *Times Rev. Industry* July 25/2 Machines now in service are stated to be equivalent in power to Cobalt 60 sources of well over 100,000 curies, and, in the isotope Caesium 137, of about 500,000 curies. **1960** *Gloss. Atomic Terms* (*H.M.S.O.*) 9 *Caesium* (*137*),..a long-lived (30 yr. half life) gamma-emitting radioactive isotope (caesium 137) is found in fission products, the 'ash' of nuclear reactors, and is used for cancer therapy in some hospitals..and for industrial radiography.

cæspitose, cespitose (ˌsɛspɪˈtəʊs), *a. Bot. & Zool.* [ad. mod.L. *cæspitōs-us*, f. *cæspit-em* turf: see -OSE.] Growing in thick tufts or clumps, turfy.

1830 LINDLEY *Nat. Syst. Bot.* 50 Little elegant herbaceous plants, with white flowers, cæspitose leaves. **1872** NICHOLSON *Palæont.* 95 The corallum is cæspitose, or tufted.

cæstus: see CESTUS.

cæsura (siːˈzjʊərə, siːˈsjʊərə). Forms: 6 **cesure**, 7 **ceasure**, 8–9 **cæsure**, 6– **cæsura**. [a. L. *cæsūra* 'cutting, metrical pause', f. *cæs-* ppl. stem of *cædĕre* to cut. The earlier form was immediately from French *césure*. (Some writers appear to have erroneously associated it with *cease*.)]

1. In Greek and Latin prosody: The division of a metrical foot between two words, especially in certain recognized places near the middle of the line.

In Dactylic Hexameter and Iambic Trimeter this usually occurs in the third foot (*penthemimeral cæsura*), but there may be subsidiary cæsuras as well; in the line *Tityre* | *tu patu* | *-læ recu* | *-bans sub* | *tegmine* | *fagi*, the main (penthemimeral) cæsura is after *-læ*, and there are subsidiary ones after *tu* and *-ans*.

[**1573** COOPER *Thesaur.*, *Cæsura*..a peece of a sentence or verse.] **1727–51** CHAMBERS *Cycl.*, *Cæsura* more properly denotes a certain and agreeable division of the words, between the feet of a verse; whereby the last syllable of a word becomes the first of a foot. **1871** ROBY *Lat. Gram.* I. 96 Occasionally..a short final closed syllable is lengthened by the arsis..this is chiefly in the cæsura. **1876** KENNEDY *Public Sch. Lat. Gram.* §260 This verse of Lucretius, *Auges* | *-cunt ali* | *-æ gen* | *-tes ali* | *-æ minu* | *-untur*, in which are four strong cæsuras, is faulty. **1884** MONRO *Homer's Iliad* Introd. §50 The third foot must not end with a word..such a break in the middle of the line is prevented by a Cæsura.

b. Used for the lengthening of the last syllable of a word by arsis which sometimes occurs in the cæsura.

1678 PHILLIPS, *Cæsura*, an accident belonging to the scanning of a Latin Verse, as when after a compleat foot a short syllable ends the Verse, that syllable is made long, as in this Verse of Virgil: *Ille latus niveum molli fultus hyacintho.* **1755** JOHNSON, *Cæsura*, a figure in poetry, by which a short syllable after a complete foot is made long.

2. In English prosody: A pause or breathing-place about the middle of a metrical line, generally indicated by a pause in the sense.

1556 ABP. PARKER *Psalter* A ij, Obserue the trayne: the ceasure marke To rest with note in close. **1581** SIDNEY *Def. Poesie* (1622) 529 The Cæsura, or breathing place in the midst of the verse. **1589** PUTTENHAM *Eng. Poesie* (Arb.) 88 Such Cesure must neuer be made in the middest of any word, if it be well appointed. **1603** DRAYTON *Odes* II. 40 That ev'ry lively Ceasure Shall tread a perfect Measure. **1751** CHAMBERS *Cycl.*, *Caesure*, in the modern poetry denotes a rest or pause towards the middle of a long Alexandrine verse. **1841** D'ISRAELI *Amen. Lit.* (1867) 170 In the most ancient manuscripts of Chaucer's works the cæsura in every line is carefully noted.

3. *transf.* **a.** A formal break or stop. **b.** A break, interruption, interval.

1596 SPENSER *F.Q.* II. x. 68 There abruptly it [a chronicle] did end, Without full point, or other Cesure right. **1846** D. W. PUGHE *Harlech Castle* 23 Ridge..extends with a few cæsures for nearly 22 miles.

†**cæ'sura**, *v. nonce-wd.* [f. prec. sb.] *trans.* To utter with a cæsura (*ludicrously*, in sing-song style).

a **1666** A. BROME *Sat. on Rebel.* (R.) No accents are so pleasant now as those That are cæsuraed through the pastor's nose.

cæ'sural, *a.* [f. CÆSURA *sb.* + -AL[1].] Of or pertaining to a cæsura.

1783 H. BLAIR *Rhet.* (1812) III. xxxviii. 98 A cæsural pause. **1861** CRAIK *Hist. Eng. Lit.* I. 262 Is this cæsural mark ..of any importance?

cæ'suric, *a.* [f. as prec. + -IC.] = prec.

1884 *Athenæum* No. 2981. 765 There are laws of cæsuric effect in blank verse.

†**caf.** *Obs. rare*[−1]. [cf. OE. *cofa*, mod. COVE: but the phonology does not fit.] ? A cask or box.

c **1375** ? BARBOUR *St. Tecla* 73 Of wod dry as teyndire þa mad a caf & put þar-in Bath pyk and tere, to ger it bryne.

caf, caff(e, obs. north. forms of CHAFF.

caf, var. of COFE *adv. Obs.*, quickly.

‖**cafard.** Also **cafart, caffard.** [F. *cafard*, *caphard*, of doubtful origin: some have proposed to identify it with Cat. *cafre* infidel, Sp., Pg. *cafre* cruel, which are app. ad. Arab. *kāfir*: see CAFFRE.] †**1.** A hypocrite, an impostor. *Obs.*

1539 *St. Papers Hen. VIII*, I. 593 We commoned of the cafart, Cornibus, that slaunderose frere. **1653** URQUHART *Rabelais* I. xlv, So did a certain Cafard or dissembling religionaire preach at Sinay, that, etc. *Ibid.* I. liv, Slipshod caffards, beggars pretending wants.

2. Melancholia; depression; 'the blues'.

1924 P. C. WREN *Beau Geste* I. i. 14, I see my handful of *cafard*-stricken men in my mud fort. **1926** GOULD *Med. Dict.* (ed. 8) 261/2 *Cafard*, a subacute melancholia, characterized by attacks of the 'blues'..; observed in soldiers. **1949** *Times Lit. Suppl.* 23 Sept., Don Juan was stricken with the superb *cafard* of the Romantics. **1951** W. SANSOM *Face of Innoc.* ix. 131 The itch of over-eating and the cafard that too much pernod leaves behind.

café (ˈkæfeɪ, formerly ‖kafe). Also vulgarly or jocularly pronounced (keɪf) or (kæf), and written in the form *cafe*; cf. CAFF. [Fr. *café* coffee, coffee-house.]

1. A coffee-house, a restaurant; strictly a French term, but in the late 19th c. introduced into the English-speaking countries for the name of a class of restaurant.

[**1789** A. YOUNG *Travels* 5 Sept. (1929) I. 229, I breakfasted at the *Café D'Acajou*.] **1802** C. WILMOT *Let.* 19 June in *Irish Peer* (1920) 73 All the Cafés are out of doors. **1816** J. SCOTT *Vis. Paris* (ed. 5) Pref. 43 A rushing whisper over Paris, encreasing to a buzz in the Cafés. **1851** GALLENGA *Mariotti's Italy* 389 Cafés and clubs roared incessantly. **1870** D. J. KIRWAN *Palace & Hovel* (1963) xvi. 151 In the corners of the saloon, up and down the stairs, were cafés and refreshment bars. **1871** MORLEY *Voltaire* (1886) 160 He wrote it as well as he knew how, and then went in disguise to the café of the critics. **1884** J. COLBORNE *Hicks Pasha* 85 The cafés are crowded with backgammon players. **1906** A. BENNETT *Whom God hath Joined* i. 5 Workshops, theatres, concerts, cafés, pawnshops. **1929** *S.P.E. Tract* XXXII. 374 If popular tea-shops paint their title of *cafe* over their doors the word will be pronounced like *chafe* and *safe*. **1938** [see TRANSPORT *sb.* 6]. **1965** I. FLEMING *Man with Golden Gun* v. 71 'There's the cafe' (she pronounced it caif).

2. *attrib.* and *Comb.* **a.** as *café-bar, -habit, -haunter, -restaurant, -window*; *café-haunting* adj.

1938 *Times Lit. Suppl.* 8 Oct. 641/3 In the other wing is a café-bar. **1910** *Daily Chron.* 5 Mar. 4/4 Any slight modification in the national temperament which the café habit might..bring. **1951** *Mind* LX. 331 It is the café-haunters, the preachers, the metaphysicians and the calendar-makers who talk of beauty. **1866** M. ARNOLD *Friendship's Garland* (1871) 167, I do not wish them [*sc.* my countrymen] to be the café-haunting, dominoes-playing Frenchmen. **1926** 'C. BARRY' *Detective's Holiday* iv. 40 The café-restaurant which the forester had called the canteen. **1907** W. O. LILLIBRIDGE *Where Trail Divides* 56 A complexion prairie wind had made like a lobster display in a café window.

b. café chantant (ʃɑ̃tɑ̃) [lit. 'singing café'], a café in which the customers are entertained by singers or other music; **café concert**, a musical or variety concert given in a café; also = *café chantant*; **café society** (orig. *U.S.*), a group of people who frequent fashionable restaurants, night-clubs, and resorts: also *attrib.*

1854 BAYLE ST. JOHN *Purple Tints Paris* II. iii. 67 Go out to the Luxembourg, to a *café chantant*,..or to the country. **1859** SALA *Twice round Clock* 164 Leicester Square..with.. the monster *cafés chantants*. **1908** *Westm. Gaz.* 18 June 1/3 The humbler rôle of café-chantant artist. **1968** *Times* 13 Nov. 10/4 Downstairs in the same new establishment there is a café-chantant. **1891** *Harper's Mag.* Dec. 49/2 A café concert over in the Bowery. **1934** C. LAMBERT *Music Ho!* III. 197 Chabrier's..tunes, though evocative of the café-concert are in no way pastiches of café-concert tunes. **1937** *Fortune* Dec. 123 A blending of old socialites and new celebrities called Café Society. **1952** *Time* 8 Sept. 4/2 All the other café society playboys and playgirls. **1958** *Times Lit. Suppl.* 9 May 250/5 His Jewish birth militated against his admission to what would now be called café society.

‖**3.** In French phrases, with the sense 'coffee', as **café au lait**, coffee taken with milk; white coffee; also, the colour of café au lait, a brownish cream colour; **café complet** (see quot. 1966); **café crème**, coffee with cream; **café-filtre**, (a cup of) coffee made by filtering boiling water through coffee; cf. FILTRE; **café noir**, black coffee, i.e. coffee without milk.

1763 H. WALPOLE *Let.* 18 Oct. (1904) V. 382 Pray send me some *café au lait*: the Duc de Picquigny..takes it for snuff. **1823** J. GRISCOM *Year in Europe* II. 32 We..refreshed ourselves..with an excellent cup of caffè [*sic*] au lait. **1839** URE *Dict. Arts* 420 Red with yellow, produces orange... To this shade may be referred flame colour,..*café au lait*,.. marigold. **1840** THACKERAY *Paris Sk.* -*Bk.* I. 19 Milk-women..selling the chief material of the Parisian *café-au-lait*. **1907** *Westm. Gaz.* 13 Nov. 12/3 Café-au-lait brocade. **1933** BLUNDEN & NORMAN *We'll shift our Ground* 120 These trays of frippery called *cafés complets*, with their couple of doughy *croissants* embracing in a teacup. **1937** M. V. HUGHES *London Home in Nineties* viii. 137 Our breakfast consisted of *café complet*. I made it as 'complet' as I could, but was ravenous by midday. **1966** P. V. PRICE *France* 31 *Café complet*, or, more accurately, *café au lait complet* means coffee with milk and lumps of sugar accompanied by bread or rolls and butter; sometimes jam is included. **1936** C. CONNOLLY *Rock Pool* viii. 203 A hundred café crèmes steamed on the marble tables. **1966** C. BUSH *Case of Good Employer* x. 99, I asked for a large *café crême*. **1922** W. H. UKERS *All about Coffee* xxxv. 675/1 Gatti's, where *café filtré*, or coffee produced by the filtration method, is a specialty; the cosmopolitan Savoy. **1958** M. STEWART *Nine Coaches Waiting* xvii. 252 A *café-filtre*, if you please. **1965** P. O'DONNELL *Modesty Blaise* vii. 79 He set out two large cups and the perforated metal containers for making café filtre. **1845** E. ACTON *Mod. Cookery* xxvii. 648 For the *café noir* served after dinner in all French families put less water. **1898** *Cornhill Mag.* Aug. 255 The widow brought our *café noir* to us after dinner. **1914** *Daily Express* 29 Sept. 2/7 Men the colour of ebony, café noir, café au lait.

cafeteria (kæfəˈtɪərɪə). orig. *U.S.* [a. Amer.-Sp. *cafetería* coffee-shop.] A coffee-house; a restaurant, esp. now a self-service restaurant.

1839 J. L. STEPHENS *Trav. Russian & Turkish Emp.* I. 157 Every third shop, almost, being a cafteria [*sic*] where a parcel of huge turbanded fellows were at their daily labours of smoking pipes and drinking coffee. **1894** *Lakeside Directory Chicago* 2188 Cafetiria Catering Co. 45 Lake. **1895** *Ibid.* 2231 'Cafetiria', 46 Lake, 80 Adams, 108 Quincy and 93 Vanburen. **1896** *Chicago Tribune* 28 June 4/1 Gerbach used to be a waiter in a West Side restaurant subsequent to his employment by the cafeteria company. **1912** *Jrnl. Home Economics* IV. 245 Exactly the same menu was served in a large college dining room and at the cafeteria. **1916** H. NEWMARK *Sixty Years in S. Calif.* x. 133 Then came the *cafeteria*... It was rather a place for drinking than for eating, and in this respect the name had little of the meaning current in parts of Mexico to-day, where a *cafeteria* is a small restaurant serving ordinary alcoholic drinks and plain meals. **1923** *Mod. Lang. Notes* Mar. 188 Every one knows by this time that a cafeteria is a 'help yourself' restaurant. **1925** *Glasgow Herald* 30 July, Cafeterias, although a commonplace in America, are just beginning to have a hold in Paris. **1958** *Oxf. Mag.* 8 May 410/2 Breakfast and lunch are served cafeteria style in Hall... How many colleges eat cafeteria-wise?

‖**cafetière** (kaftjɛːr). Also erron. **cafétiere, cafetiere, cafétière.** [Fr.] A coffee-pot; a coffee percolator.

1846 A. SOYER *Gastronomic Regenerator* 711 Pour either into the silver cafetière or the cups. **1888** *Queen* 17 Nov. in L. de Vries *Victorian Advertisements* (1968) 108/2 Royle's patent self-pouring cafetières and kettles. **1906** MRS. BEETON *Househ. Managem.* xlix. 1475 Place the coffee in the coffee chamber of a cafétiere, and pour the boiling water through the distributor on to the coffee. **1907** *Yesterday's Shopping* (1969) 169/1 Cafetiere, tin—2 cup... Simplex Circulating Cafetiere. **1927** FRANCIS BRETT YOUNG *Portrait of Clare* v. iv. 459 She..let her emotion flow into a laughing, triumphant recitation of her lavish purchases; the lordly Uffdown presents, Steven's bicycle, Aunt Cathie's cafétière.

caff (kæf). Vulgar or jocular slang for CAFÉ. Also *attrib.*

1931 D. MORSE-BOYCOTT *We do see Life!* i. 15, I was sitting in a caff in Compton Street. **1950** P. TEMPEST *Lag's Lexicon* 28 *Caff boys*, the youths and men, the 'spivs' and 'wide boys', who hang around certain cafés. **1959** G. FREEMAN *Jack would be a Gentleman* ix. 191 We'll find a caff somewhere an' 'ave our food out. **1959** *Daily Mail* 5 Mar. 7/1 The news reached Chrimes, 30-year-old boss of the low-life 'caff society' with his headquarters in a juke-box cafe in Uxbridge.

caff, obs. var. of CHAFE *v.* to warm.

†**caffa.** *Obs.* Also 6 **capha.**

1. A rich silk cloth, apparently similar to damask, much used in the 16th c.

1531 *Wardrobe Acc. Hen. VIII*, 18 May, White caffa for the Kinges grace. **1539** *Will of J. Hewes* (Somerset Ho.) A doblet of Satten wᵗ slevys of Caffa. **1552** in Strype *Eccl. Mem.* II. II. xiv. 359 The said bed-maker received.. twenty-two yards and three quarters of crimson capha for a damask to the same bed. **1587** FLEMING *Contn. Holinshed* III. 1290/1 Ouer the first loome was written, the weauing of worsted..ouer the sixt the weauing of caffa. **1641** CAVENDISH *Negot. Wolsey* in Beck *Draper's Dict.* 41 Rich stuffs of silk in whole pieces of all colours, as velvet, satin, damask, caffa..and others not in my remembrance.

2. A kind of painted cotton cloth made in India, and occurring in commerce in the 18th c.

1750 BEAWES *Lex Mercat.* (1752) 780 And some others [i.e. places] dependant on Caffa, which serves them for an Almagazen. **1810** *Encyl. Brit.* V. 49 *Caffa*..painted cotton cloths, manufactured in the East Indies, and sold at Bengal.

caffeic (kæˈfiːɪk), *a. Chem.* [ad. F. *caféique*, f. *café* coffee; partially assimilated to mod.L. *coffea*, which would properly give *coffeic*, *coffein*.]

Of or pertaining to coffee; esp. in **caffeic acid** ($C_9H_8O_4$), a substance found in brilliant yellowish prisms or plates. So **'caffeidine**, an uncrystallizable base ($C_7H_{12}N_4O$), produced by the action of alkalies on caffeine. **caffeone** (ˈkæfiːəʊn), the aromatic principle of coffee, a brown aromatic volatile oil, produced in the roasting of coffee berries. **caffe'tannate**, a salt of

caffe'tannic acid, an astringent acid found in coffee berries, Paraguay tea, and other plants.

1853 *Pharmac. Jrnl.* XIII. 383 Caffeic acid is precipitated. **1863** WATTS *Dict. Chem.* I. 709 Caffetannic acid colours ferric salts green. *Ibid.* 710 The caffetannates are but little known. **1876** HARLEY *Mat. Med.* 547 Caffeic acid is an astringent acid. **1880** *Cope's Tobacco Plant* Oct. 539 First Subdivision.—Caffeic Aliments: Coffee, Tea, Maté, Guarana, and the rest.

caffeine ('kæfiːn, formerly 'kæfiːaɪn). *Chem.* [ad. F. *caféine*, f. *café* coffee + -INE; see prec.] A vegetable alkaloid crystallizing in white silky needles, found in the leaves and seeds of the coffee and tea plants, the leaves of guarana, maté, etc.

1830 LINDLEY *Nat. Syst. Bot.* 206 Coffee is.. supposed to owe its characters to a peculiar chemical principle called Caffein. **1863** WATTS *Dict. Chem.* I. 707 Caffeine was discovered in coffee by Runge in the year 1820. Oudry, in 1827, found in tea a crystalline substance which he called *theine*, supposing it to be a distinct compound; but Jobat showed that it was identical with caffeine. **1869** *Daily News* 22 July, A piece of kaffeine, of the size of a breakfast plate, produced from 120 pounds of coffee.

So **'caffeinism** = CAFFEISM.

1889 in *Cent. Dict.*

caffeism ('kæfiːɪz(ə)m). [f. CAFFE(INE + -ISM.] A morbid condition arising from the prolonged or excessive use of beverages containing caffeine.

1886 *American* XII. 269 That class of diseases in which morphinism, caffeism and vanillism are found. **1906** *Westm. Gaz.* 27 Sept. 4/2 The beverage—I even hate its name: Guess it who can!—That makes the direful caffeism rage.

caffetan, var. of CAFTAN.

caffi'aceous, properly **coffeaceous**, *a. rare.* Allied to the botanical genus *Coffea*, of which *Coffea arabica* is the coffee shrub.

1865 LIVINGSTONE *Zambesi* xxvii. 563 Several caffiaceous bushes.. grew near, but no use was ever made of them.

caffle ('kæf(ə)l), *v. dial.* [Cf. CAVIL *v.*] *intr.* To cavil, argue; to prevaricate. Hence **'caffler**, **'caffling**. Cf. CAFFLING *ppl. a.*

1851 T. STERNBERG *Dial. Northants.* 16 *Caffle*,.. to quarrel. Probably a corruption of *cavil.* **1877** E. PEACOCK *Gloss. Manley* 45/1 Noo none o' your cafflin', tell us all about it straight out. **1883** A. EASTHER *Gloss. Almondbury* 21 *Caffler*,.. a shuffler, excuse-maker, &c. **1913** D. H. LAWRENCE *Love Poems* 50 To think I should ha'e to haffle an' caffle Wi' a woman an' pay 'er a price. **1932** S. O'FAOLÁIN *Midsummer Night Madness* 66 Are you going to be stopped by a city caffler?

† **'caffling**, *ppl. a.* ? var. of CAVILLING.

1591 HARINGTON *Orl. Fur.* xlv. 97 (N.) If I now put in some caffling clause I shall be called unconstant.

† **caffoy, cafoy.** *Obs.*

1. Some kind of fabric, imported in the 18th c.

1750 BEAWES *Lex Mercat.* (1752) 686 Products of Abbeville, as Plush, Caffoy, Ticking, etc.

2. *caffoy paper*: a kind of (?) flock paper used for covering walls in the middle of the 18th c.

1750 MRS. DELANY *Life & Corr.* II. 562 The [wall] paper is pearl coloured caffoy paper; the pattern like damask. **1755** —— III. 385 My dining room.. is hung with mohair cafoy paper.

Caffrarian (kæ'frɛərɪən), *a.* Also **Kaffrarian**. [See -AN.] Of, pertaining to, or characteristic of Caffraria (see CAFFRE 2).

a **1828** J. BERNARD *Retrosp. Amer.* (1887) 80 A certain German duchess had visited Paris, whose Caffrarian distinction fully equalled the magnificence of her other displays. **1874** GEO. ELIOT *Legend of Jubal* 193 No lions then shall lap Caffrarian pools. **1882** C. F. G. CUMMING *Fire Fountains* I. 258 From Crimean winters to Kaffrarian summers.

caffre ('kɑːfə(r), -æ-). Forms: 6 cafar, 6–7 caffare, 7 cafre, coffery, 8 coffrie, -ree, -re, 9 caffree, 8–9 cafer, caffer, caffre: see also KAFFIR. [ad. Arab. *kāfir* infidel, impious wretch, one who does not recognize the blessings of God, f. *kafara* to cover up, conceal, deny.]

‖ **1.** A word meaning 'infidel', applied by the Arabs to all non-Mohammedans, and hence to particular tribes or nations. More accurately *kafir*.

1680 *Taverner's Relat. of Tunquin* 86 The Cafer seeing his Child white, would have immediately fallen upon his Wife and strangled her. **1698** FRYER *Acc. E. India & Pers.* 91 (Y.) Why he suffers.. this Coffery (Unbeliever) to vaunt it thus. **1799** SIR T. MUNRO *Lett.* in *Life* I. 221 (Y.) He [Tippoo].. was to drive the English Caffers out of India. **1804** DUNCAN *Mariner's Chron.* I. 297 He.. put me in imminent danger of my life, by telling the natives that I was a Caffer, and not a Mussulman. **1812** A. PLUMTRE *Lichtenstein's S. Africa* I. 241 Being Mahommedans, they gave the general name of Cafer (Liar, Infidel) to all the inhabitants of the coasts of Southern Africa. **1817** KEATINGE *Trav.* I. 250 A Moor will .. point his musquet at, the women abuse, and the children pursue the caffre (infidel), the generic term for Christian here.

2. *spec.* In ordinary Eng. use: A member of a South African race of blacks belonging to the great Bantu family, and living in the north-east of the Republic of South Africa, in an area formerly known as *Caffraria* or *Caffre-land*. Also the name of their language, and used attributively.

Cust (*Modern Languages of Africa* II. 298) makes *Kafir* the general name of his Eastern subdivision of the Southern division of the Bantu family, and includes under it Xhosa, Zulu, and Gwamba; in popular use the term has been generally restricted to the Xhosa, or to these and the Zulu.

1599 HAKLUYT *Voy.* II. I. 242 The Captaine of this castle [Mozambique] hath certaine voyages to this Cafraria.. to trade with the Cafars. **1731** MEDLEY *Kolben's Cape G. Hope* I. 81 The Caffres.. are so far from bearing any affinity or resemblance with the Hottentots, that they are a quite different sort of people. **1833** *Athenæum* 2 Nov. 729 A mission among the Ammakosa, or Kaffers, as they have been erroneously denominated. **1834** PRINGLE *Afr. Sk.* xiv. 413 The Caffers are a tall, athletic, and handsome race.

3. A native of Kafiristan in Asia; see KAFFIR.

4. *attrib.* and in *comb.* as *Caffre-boy*, *-slave*; **Caffre-bread**, a South African cycadaceous tree with edible pith; **Caffre-corn**, one of the names of Indian millet, *Sorghum vulgare*, cultivated as a cereal in tropical Africa.

1781 *India Gaz.* No. 19 (Y.) To be sold by Private Sale two Coffree Boys. **1786** tr. *Sparrman's Voy. Cape G. Hope* II. 10 The colonists call it Caffer-corn. **1800** SYMES *Embassy Ava* 10 (Y.) The Caffre slaves, who had been introduced for the purpose of cultivating the lands. **1803** R. PERCIVAL in *Naval Chron.* X. 27 Which was the case with a Caffree boy. **1866** *Treas. Bot.* 450 *Encephalartos*.. the interior of the trunk, and the centre of the ripe female cones, contains a spongy farinaceous pith, made use of by the Caffers as food, and hence the trees are called.. Caffer-bread.

‖ **cafila** ('kɑːfɪlə). Also 6 caffylen, 7 caffalo, caphille, 8 caffilla, -la, 9 kafila. [Arab. *qāfilah* caravan, marching company.] A company of travellers, a caravan, in Arabia, Persia, or India.

1594 tr. *Linschoten's Voy.* in Arb. *Garner* III. 188 From thence, twice every year, there travelleth two caffylen. **1630** LORD *Banians* 81 (Y.) Some of the Raiahs.. making Outroades prey on the Caffaloes passing by the Way. **1671** CHARENTE *Let. Customs Tafiletta* 14 They sent yearly.. Caphilles or Caravans to Tombotum. **1786** tr. *Beckford's Vathek* (1868) 52 From the bells of a Cafila passing over the rocks. **1811** H. MARTYN in *Mem.* III. (1825) 339 At ten o'clock on the 30th our cafila began to move. **1867** *Q. Rev.* Jan. 102 (Y.) A carriage.. followed by a large convoy of armed and mounted travellers, a kind of Kafila.

cafoufle, cafuffle, varr. CURFUFFLE *sb.*

‖ **caftan** (kaf'tɑːn, 'kæftæn). Also 7–8 caffetan, cafetan, coftan, 9- kaftan. [Turkish *qaftān*, also used in Pers. In early use apparently taken immediately from the Fr. *cafetan*.]

1. A garment worn in Turkey and other eastern countries, consisting of a kind of long under-tunic or vest tied at the waist with the girdle.

1591 G. FLETCHER *Russe Commw.* (1657) 273 Yet he will have his Caftan or under-coat sometimes of cloth of gold. **1662** J. DAVIES tr. *Olearius' Voy. Ambass.* III. (1669) 56 Upon the *Kaftan* they wear a close Coat.. called *Feres.* **1671** CHARENTE *Let. Customs Mauritania* 41 The Jews wear a Shirt, Drawers, a black Close-coat, or Caffetan. **1695** MOTTEUX *St. Olon's Morocco* 90 They all wear a Cafetan or Cloth-Vest without Sleeves. **1700** RYCAUT *Hist. Turks* III. 533 A rich Coftan or Vest. **1716–8** LADY M. W. MONTAGUE *Lett.* I. xxxii. 111 My Caftan.. is a robe exactly fitted to my shape, and reaching to my feet, with very long strait falling sleeves. **1782** P. H. BRUCE *Mem.* II. 60 They [Turkish ladies] wear a Cafetan of gold brocade. **1813** MOORE *Twop. Post Bag* VI. 10 Through London streets with turban fair, And caftan floating to the air. **1835** WILLIS *Pencillings* II. xliii. 43 Wily Jews with their high caps and caftans. **1866** *Reader* 27 Oct. 887 The.. caphtan was during the first years of Peter's reign discontinued among the higher and middle classes of Russian society. **1889** HALL CAINE *Scapegoat* i, His Kaftan was of white cloth, with an embroidered leathern girdle.

2. A wide-sleeved, loose-fitting shirt or dress worn in Western countries, resembling the original garment worn in the East.

1965 *Vogue* July 43 Kaftan, 39 gns. **1966** *Daily Tel.* 17 Oct. 10/6 Caftans, the season's fashion talking point, won murmurs of delight in lightweight silk, hand-painted, in versions both short and long from artist Noel Dyrenforth. **1967** *Daily Mail* 10 Aug. 4/7 I'd like to see men in this country wearing kaftans—those long cotton robes—to relax at home. **1968** *Guardian* 6 June 5/5 [He] wore an astrakhan cap and a blue caftan shirt. **1969** *Daily Nation* (Nairobi) 31 Oct. 19/2 It comprises a Kaftan, slit on either side to the knees to reveal pencil slim hipster pants. **1972** J. WILSON *Hide & Seek* ii. 37 Her wedding dress.. had been an all enveloping Kaftan because she'd been hugely pregnant.

caftaned ('kæftænd), *ppl. a.* Clad in a caftan.

1863 SALA *Ischvostchik* 96 A bearded, caftaned man. **1879** R. S. EDWARDS *Russians at H.* I. 202 Caftaned merchants. **1898** *Blackw. Mag.* Oct. 537/2 Wild Kaftaned drivers.

† **cag** (kæg), *sb.*[1] ? *Obs.* Forms: 6 cagge, 7–8 cagg, 5, 7 kag, 7- cag. [Identical with ON. *kaggi*, Sw. *kagge* 'keg, cask'. From the fact that ships, or boats, and casks, or tubs, often go by the same name, some propose to identify these words with Du. *kaag* fishing-boat (see sense 2), early mod.Du. *kaghe*, LG. *kag*, with which Franck compares Rhenish *kac* (? from *kag*), found already in the 14th c. Cf. also F. *cague* fishing-boat (from Du.), and *caque* a herring-barrel. But of the origin and history of the word-group or groups, nothing certain is known. Now corrupted to KEG: cf. the Cockney *keb*, *ketch* for *cab*, *catch*.]

1. A small cask, a KEG. ? *Obs.*

1452 *Inv.* in *Test. Ebor.* III. 136, j saltkag lignei *xd.* **1596** *Wills & Inv. N.C.* (1860) II. 263 Iij cagges of strudg-shon .. ij cagges of eaylles. **1611** COTGR., *Encaquer*, to put into a little barrell, or cag. *Encacqué*.. incagged; put into a cag. **1690** MRS. BEHN *Wid. Ranter* III. i, To drink a cagg of Syder. **1704** WORLIDGE *Dict. Rust. et Urb.*, *Cagg* or *Keg*; this in respect of Sturgeon is 4 to 5 gallon. **1785** WOLCOTT (P. Pindar) *Lousiad* II. Wks. I. 246 A brandy cag. **1797** PRISC. WAKEFIELD *Mental Improv.* (1801) I. 50 Vast quantities are salted or pickled, and put up in cags.

† **2.** A small fishing-vessel. (Du. *kaag.*) *Obs.*

1666 *Lond. Gaz.* No. 113/3 Several Caggs from Holland, were.. suffered.. to pass. **1667** *Ibid.* 179/2 Privateers.. have .. taken 8 Kags or small ships near Wangerold.

† **cag**, *sb.*[2] *Obs.* exc. *dial.* A stiff point.

1604 EDMONDS *Observ. Cæsar's Comm.* 113 Great firme boughs.. spreading themselues at the top into sharpe cags. [**1847–78** HALLIW. *Cag*, a stump. *West.*]

cag (kæg), *sb.*[3] *Naut. slang.* Also **kagg**. [Cf. CAG *v.* 2.] An argument.

1916 M. T. HAINSSELIN *In Northern Mists* xviii. 69 We had a right-down regular genuine old-fashioned Ward-room Cag about it. **1918** 'BARTIMEUS' *Navy Eternal* 330 This.. is developing into a 'Branch-kagg'. **1932** C. MORGAN *Fountain* 150 He was one with.. a passion for argument on remote unprofessional subjects. He would sit down to what he called a 'cag' as eagerly and patiently as a dog before a rabbit bone.

So as *vb.*, to argue, to nag.

1919 'ETIENNE' *Strange Tales fr. Fleet* 23, I've never met such a crowd for 'kagging'. **1932** 'N. SHUTE' *Lonely Road* xi. 233 I'm not going to worry you, or cag about this any more.

cag, *v. dial.* [cf. CAGGY 2.] *trans.* To offend, insult. (Quot. 1504 is doubtful.)

1504 in *Plumpton Corr.* 186 The other tenaunts cannot pays ther housses, but they shalbe cagid. **1801** SOUTHEY *Lett.* (1856) I. 149 Pray, pray do not cag Horne Took for the sake of the debates. **1886** LONG *Isle of Wight Dial.* 9, *Cag*, to insult, offend. 'I've ben and cagged en now, I louz'—I have offended him now, I think. [*Cagged, Kegged* = offended, affronted, in various dialects.]

† **ca'gastric, ca'gastrical**, *a. Obs.* Used, after Paracelsus, to describe some supposed class of diseases; explained by some as = under a malignant star, 'ill-starred' [as if *cacastrical*, f. Gr. κακός evil + ἀστήρ star.]

1662 J. CHANDLER *Van Helmont's Oriat.* 322 He.. calls the Body of man Cagastrical or badly Planet-struck. **1753** CHAMBERS *Cycl. Supp.*, The pleurisy, plague, fever, &c., are ranked by that author in the number of cagastric diseases.

cage (keɪdʒ), *sb.* Also 5 kage, 6 kaig, cadge. [a. F. *cage* (= It. *gaggia*):—late L. **cavja*:—L. *cavea* hollow, cavity, dungeon, cell, cage, f. *cav-us* hollow. The phonetic development was as in *rage*, *sage*:—L. *rabies*, **sapius*.]

I. Generally and non-technically.

1. A box or place of confinement for birds and other animals (or, in barbarous times, for human beings), made wholly or partly of wire, or with bars of metal or wood, so as to admit air and light, while preventing the creature's escape.

a **1225** *Ancr. R.* 102 Ase untowe brid ine cage. *c* **1386** CHAUCER *Squieres T.* 611 Briddes.. that men in cages fede. *a* **1528** SKELTON *P. Sparowe* 324 Was neuer byrde in cage More gentle of corage. **1547** BOORDE *Introd. Knowl.* xxxii. 204 They do kepe in a kaig in the churche a white cocke and a hen. **1581** J. BELL *Haddon's Answ. Osor.* 500 Lyke a common skold in a Cage. **1649** LOVELACE *To Althea* 156 Stone walls do not a prison make Nor iron bars a cage. **1673** R. HEAD *Canting Acad.* 74 As nimble as a Squirrel in a Bell-Cage. **1727** SWIFT *Gulliver* II. viii. 162 Kept in cages like tame Canary birds. **1727** TINDAL tr. *Rapin's Hist. Eng.* (1757) III. 319 The Countess of Buquhan.. was put into a wooden cage, and placed as a ridiculous sight to the people on the walls of Berwick castle. **1875** BUCKLAND *Log-Bk.* 198 So we make water cages for our fish.

2. † **a.** 'A prison for petty malefactors' (J.); a lock-up. *Obs.*

c **1500** *Lancelot* 2767 As cowart thus schamfully to ly Excludit in to cage frome chewalry. **1593** SHAKS. *2 Hen. VI*, IV. ii. 56 His Father had neuer a house but the Cage. *c* **1600** *Distr. Emperor* V. iii. in *O. Pl.* (1884) III. 248 May constables to cadges styll comend theym. **1703** MAUNDRELL *Journ. Jerus.* (1732) 129 A small Timber Structure resembling the Cage of a County Burrough. **1836–7** DICKENS *Sk. Boz* (1850) 248/1 It has.. a market-place—a cage—an assembly-room. *a* **1850** THACKERAY *Fatal Boots* x, I found myself in a cage in Cursitor Street.

b. A (barbed-wire) camp enclosure for prisoners of war. *colloq.*

1919 DOWNING *Digger Dial.* 15 *Cage*, a prisoner of war compound. **1939** *War Illustr.* 7 Oct. 102 Polish prisoners are seen in a 'cage' to which they have been marched immediately after capture. **1956** A. CRAWLEY *Escape from Germany* xxvii. 280 Having seen that capture was inevitable .. he had.. packed three large suitcases.. to take.. to whatever 'cage' he was sent.

3. *fig.* That which confines or imprisons.

c **1300** *K. Alis.* 5011 Than she gooth to dethes cage. *c* **1450** CAPGRAVE *S. Katherine* 351 Thus was thy lyf, lady, kepte in cage. **1649** G. DANIEL *Trinarch., Hen. V*, ccxxxi, Soules enfranchis'd, from the torne-vp Cage Of flesh. **1730** BEVERIDGE *Priv. Th.* I. 77 The Cage of Flesh, Wherein the

Soul is penned. **1854** BREWSTER *More Worlds* 72 An immortal soul.. imprisoned in a cage of cartilage and of skin.

4. a. Anything resembling a cage in structure or purpose. †**b.** A scaffold, elevated stage or seat.

a **1400** *Cov. Myst.* (1841) 162, I am kynge knowyn in kage. *Ibid.* 166 Heyl, be thou kynge in kage full hye. *c* **1440** *Promp. Parv.* 57/2 Cage, *catasta*. **1553** EDEN *Treat. New Ind.* (Arb.) 15 Upon the packsaddels [of an elephant], they haue on euery side a little house, or towre, or cage (if you list so to call it) made of wood. **1592** SHAKS. *Rom. & Jul.* II. iii. 7, I must vpfill this Osier Cage of ours, With balefull weedes, and precious Iuiced flowers. **1884** *Western Daily Press* 28 Nov. 7/4 By the term crinolette, we by no means allude to the preposterously ugly and attached 'cage' which was formerly tied round the waist. **1887** *Pall Mall Budg.* 31 Mar. 2 The ludicrous and offensive object known as the 'cage' in the Ladies' Gallery of the House of Commons.

c. = CAGE-WORK 2.

1555 EDEN *Decades W. Ind.* III. v. (Arb.) 158 Defended by the cages or pauisses of the shyppes and their targettes.

II. In various technical uses.

5. *Mining.* **a.** 'A frame with one or more platforms for cars, used in hoisting in a vertical shaft'.

1851 J. HEDLEY *Coal-mines* 124 Tubs full or empty in the cage. **1855** *Leisure Hour* 474 We must step into this 'cage', which, you perceive, is a kind of vertical railway carriage. **1879** JEFFERIES *Wild Life in S.C.* 249 The rabbit has.. no cage with which to haul up the sand he has moved. **1883** *Chamb. Jrnl.* 733 The Cage, an iron structure open at two sides, fitted into two wooden guides fixed to the sides of the shaft.

b. The barrel of a whim on which the rope is wound; a drum.

1854 WHITNEY *Metal. Wealth U.S.* 73 The cage, or drum on which the rope is wound. **1856** W. BAINBRIDGE *Law Mines* 654 *Cage*.. also, the barrel for a whim-pipe.

6. A confining framework of various kinds.

a. *Carpentry* (see quot.).

1753 CHAMBERS *Cycl. Supp.*, *Cage*, in carpentry, signifies an outer work of timber, enclosing another within it. In this sense we say, the cage of a windmill. The cage of a stair-case denotes the wooden sides or walls which enclose it. **1876** GWILT *Archit.* Gloss.

b. The framework in which a peal of bells is hung.

c **1630** RISDON *Surv. Devon* §107 (1810) 108 A cage of four small broken bells. **1872** ELLACOMBE *Bells of Ch.* ix. 309 At East Bergholt, Suffolk, there is a ring of five heavy bells.. in a cage in the churchyard.

c. A framework confining a ball-valve within a certain range of motion.

d. A wire guard over the mouth of a pipe, etc., to allow the passage of liquids and prevent that of solids.

e. A cup with a glass bottom and cover, to hold a drop of water containing organisms for microscopic examination.

1839 *Penny Cycl.* XV. 181/1 s.v. *Microscope*, Capillary cages for containing animalculæ in water.

7. A vessel formed of iron hoops or bars, to contain burning combustibles (see quot. 1867).

1837 M. DONOVAN *Dom. Econ.* II. 171 Those who fish for them [anchovies] go out in boats with a cage of burning charcoal fastened to each boat. **1867** SMYTH *Sailor's Word-bk.*, *Cage*, an iron cage formed of hoops on the top of a pole, and filled with combustibles to blaze for two hours. It is lighted one hour before high-water, and marks an intricate channel navigable for the period it burns. **1875** BEDFORD *Sailor's Pock. Bk.* v. (ed. 2) 136 The entrances of channels .. shall be marked by special buoys with or without staff and globe, or triangle, cage, etc.

8. *Falconry.* A frame to carry hawks upon. See CADGE *sb.*[1]

1828 SEBRIGHT *Observ. Hawking* 64 The hawks are tied upon the cage as upon a perch. **1875** 'STONEHENGE' *Brit. Sports* I. IV. i. §3. 291 The oblong cage is four feet six inches by two feet.

9. (See quot.)

1883 WOOD in *Sunday Mag.* Oct. 628/2 The nest of the squirrel is known in some parts of England by the name of 'cage'.

III. 10. *attrib.* and in *comb.*, as *cage-bar*, *-bird*, *-ful*, *-maker*, *-mate*, *-seller*; *cageless* adj.; **cage aerial** (see quot. 1926); also CAGE-WORK.

1926 S. O. PEARSON *Dict. Wireless Techn. Terms*, *Cage *Aerial*, an aerial in which a number of component wires are held in position round small star-shaped spreaders or round small hoops in such a manner as to form a 'cage'. This is done to reduce the high-frequency resistance of the aerial. **1883** LLOYD *Ebb & Flow* II. 81 Beating their wings in vain against the mocking *cage-bars of necessity. **1626** BACON *Sylva* §834 Pigeons and Horses thrive best, if their Houses, and Stables be kept Sweet: And so of *Cage-Birds. **1881** *Athenæum* 5 Mar. 329/3 A *cageful of common finches. *a* **1849** MANGAN *Poems* (1859) 185 The *Cageless Wild-bird. **1693** *Lond. Gaz.* No. 2837/4 A Germain New Fashion *Cage-maker. **1904** *Westm. Gaz.* 26 Sept. 10/1 Till he becomes acquainted through the bars with the animals that are in future to be his *cage-mates. **1925** 'J. DOYLE' *Marmosite's Misc.* 10 Little David Garnett, a cage-mate of mine. *c* **1500** *Cocke Lorelles B.* (1843) 10 Pouche makers, belowfarmes, and *cage sellers.

cage (keɪdʒ), *v.* [f. prec. sb.] *trans.* To confine in, or as in, a cage; to imprison.

1577 HARRISON *England* II. xiv. (1877) 265 To be caged vp as in a coope. **1625** HART *Anat. Ur.* I. v. 46 The women are caged vp like linnets. **1805** SOUTHEY *Madoc in W.* vi, They lie.. Conquer'd and caged and fetter'd. **1813** BYRON *Br. Abydos* II. xx, When cities cage us in a social home. **1863** GEO. ELIOT *Romola* I. i. 16, I don't stay caged in my shop all day.

b. To fit as a cage in the shaft of a mine.

1860 *All Y. Round* No. 55. 103 Baskets that would rarely be dangerous if they were caged and supplied with proper guide-rods.

†**'cageat.** *Sc. Obs. rare.* [Perh. dim. of CAGE; Jamieson says 'App. corr. from F. *cassette*'. Cf. also F. *cachette* little place of concealment.] 'A small casket or box' (Jamieson).

1488 *Inv. Roy. Wardrobe & Jewell-ho.* (1815) 5 (JAM.) In a cageat, beand within the said blak kist, a braid chenye.. Item in the said cageat, a litill coffre of siluer oure gilt.

caged (keɪdʒd), *ppl. a.* [f. CAGE *v.* + -ED[1].]

1. Confined in, or as in, a cage. Also with *in*.

1596 SHAKS. *Tam. Shr.* Induct. ii. 38 Twentie caged Nightingales do sing. **1650** *Pref. verses Gregory's Posthuma* (T.) The cag'd votary did wider dwell Than thou. **1720** GAY *Poems* (1745) II. 170 The cag'd linnet. **1899** K. GRAHAME *Dream Days* 15 'What's that got to do with it?' retorted his sister, resuming her caged-lion promenade. **1937** W. DE LA MARE *This Year, Next Year*, A bookworm.. Timid, half-blind, caged-in, afraid.

†**2.** Closed like a cage. *nonce-use.*

1609 SHAKS. *Lover's Compl.* 249 She would the caged cloister flie.

cageling ('keɪdʒlɪŋ). [f. CAGE *sb.* + -LING.] A bird kept in a cage.

1859 TENNYSON *Vivien* 900 As the cageling newly flown returns. **1869** BLACKMORE *Lorna D.* xx. (D.) As a child.. chasing a flown cageling.

cager ('keɪdʒɛ(r)). [f. CAGE *v.* or *sb.* + -ER[1].]

1. One who encloses in a cage. *rare.*

1889 BROWNING *Asolando* 5 Boy-Cupid's exemplary catcher and cager.

2. An operative who attends to a cage (in various trades).

1908 *Daily Chron.* 24 Apr. 7/5 The cager was.. engaged in another part of the mine. **1921** *Dict. Occup. Terms* (1927) §§043, 056, 339, 399.

'cage-work. [f. CAGE *sb.* + WORK *sb.*]

1. Open work like the bars of a cage; also *fig.*

1625 GILL *Sacr. Philos.* II. 173 If this foundation of the mixture of the two natures in Christ bee taken away, all the Cage-worke of the Theodosians, that the Mediatour is mortall, and of the Armenians, that hee could not suffer, must needes bee rotten and unable to stand. **1756** C. LUCAS *Ess. Waters* II. 135 Malmeudy.. consists of about a thousand houses, mostly of cage-work.

†**2.** *Naut.* (see quots.) *Obs.*

a **1618** RALEIGH *Roy. Navy* 15 But men of better sort.. would be glad to find more steadinesse and lesse tottering Cadge worke. **1708** KERSEY, *Cage-work*, the uppermost carved Works of a Ship's Hull. **1721-1800** in BAILEY. **1855** KINGSLEY *Westw. Ho* xx. (D.) The English fashion was to heighten the ship.. also by stockades ('close-fights and cage-work') on the poop and fore-castle, thus giving to the men a shelter. **1867** SMYTH *Sailor's Word-bk.*, *Cage-wrock*, an old term for a ship's upper works.

cagey ('keɪdʒɪ), *a. colloq.* (orig. *U.S.*). Also **cagy**. [Etym. unknown.] Not forthcoming, reticent, wary, non-committal. Hence **'cagily** *adv.* Also **'cageyness**, **'caginess**, the state or quality of being cagey.

1909 *Sat. Even. Post* 1 May 5/3 See? He's cagey about going to 'em, but when a good medium gets him in front of her he swallows it all, lock, stock and barrel. **1922** *Short Stories* Feb. 158/2 The Battler was cagey and covered up for the greater part of the round. **1926** *New Yorker* 11 Sept. 36 The opinions of even the producing gentlemen's chauffeurs are being cagily sought. **1927** 'J. BARBICAN' *Confessions of Rum-Runner* xxiii. 259 We hoped they would come out and pick us off, but they were too cagey for that. **1948** *Time* 25 Oct. 23/1 The Yankee management had timed things cagily. **1950** A. LUNN *Revolt against Reason* x. 112 The caginess of a Darwinist when cross-examined on his claim. **1953** G. HEYER *Detection Unlimited* iii. 31 Aunt Miriam's always a bit cagy about it. What happened? **1955** *Archit. Rev.* CXVII. 278/3 This is not the first London retailer to eschew the conventions of 'cageyness'—of answering questions in the form that they are put but never volunteering information. **1966** *Listener* 10 Nov. 681/2 My son is a cagey mathematician where rent, food, and expenses are concerned.

cagg(e, var. of CAG *sb.*[1] *Obs.*

caggy ('kægɪ), *a. dial.* or *vulgar.*

1. Decaying, unfit for food. [f. CAGMAG.]

a **1848** MARRYAT *R. Reefer* xv, Mouldy bread, caggy mutton.

2. *dial.* 'Ill-natured, stomachful' (*Whitby Gloss.* 1855). [cf. CAG *v.*]

Cagian, var. CAJAN.

cagmag ('kægmæg), *sb.* and *a. dial.* or *vulgar.* [app. a word of dialectal origin, widely used in Lincolnshire, Yorkshire, and adjacent counties: of uncertain derivation.]

1. a. A tough old goose. **b.** Unwholesome, decayed, or loathsome meat; offal; hence anything worthless or rubbishy.

1771 PENNANT *Tour Scotl.* (1790) 11 The superannuated geese and ganders (called here cagmags) which by a long course of plucking prove uncommonly tough and dry. **1811** *Lex. Balatronicum*, *Cag Magg*, bits and scraps of provisions. Bad meat. **1847-78** HALLIWELL s.v., There is a small inferior breed of sheep called cagmags. **1864** SALA in *Daily Tel.* 27 Sept., Barrels full of kag-mag sweltering in the sun. **1875** TWEDDELL *Cleveland Dial.* 37 An awd cagmag of a silk gown. **1876** *Mid-Yorksh. Gloss.* (E.D.S.) *Cagmag*, sb. and adj., refuse; any worthless material. Used, also, of persons, contemptuously. **1877** PEACOCK *N.W. Linc. Gloss.* (E.D.S.) *Cagmags*, (1) old geese, (2) unwholesome meat. **1877** *Holderness Gloss.* (E.D.S.) *Cag-mag*, refuse, chiefly used in reference to meat, (2) a loose character. **1942** P. H. JOHNSON *Family Pattern* 80 Maudie is the best beloved woman in London, with the grandest manner. She makes Royalty look like cag-mag.

2. *attrib.* or *adj.* Unwholesome, decaying, refuse.

1859 SALA *Tw. round Clock* (1861) 295 The fumes of the vilest tobacco.. of ancient fish, of cagmag meat. **1864** —— *Streets of World* in *Temple Bar* Jan. 185 No kagmag wares are sold.

cagmag, *v. dial.* [f. the sb.] **a.** *intr.* To quarrel. **b.** *trans.* To nag.

1882 MRS. CHAMBERLAIN *Gloss W. Worcs. Words* 6 It's only them two aowd craters upstairs a cagmaggin' like thay allays be. **1932** H. J. MASSINGHAM *Wold without End* 296 Cotswold possesses a number of these dramatic words... The farm labourer.. will 'grizb',.. his wife 'cagmags', not henpecks, him.

†**'cagment.** *Obs.* [? f. CAG *v.*] ? Insult, affront.

1504 in *Plumpton Corr.* 187 It is sayd, that they have cagments for them that hath bought the wood, that they dare not deale therwith.

‖**cagnotte** (kaɲɔt). [F.] Money reserved from the stakes for the bank at certain gambling games (see quots.). Also *attrib.*

1928 *Daily Express* 29 Aug. 1/5 The club has adopted the equivalent of the Cagnotte system. A member winning a sum such as twenty-five pounds at a session is assessed approximately ten shillings. If he wins fifty pounds or over he pays the club one pound. **1959** *Times* 24 Feb. 11/7 The bank's cut, or *cagnotte*, may be some hundreds of pounds. **1961** I. FLEMING *Thunderball* xv. 156 One table of chemin de fer, whose cagnotte yields a modest five per cent.

‖**cagot** (kago). [Fr.; orig. proper name, perh. containing *-goth* (cf. *bigot*) of uncertain origin: see Littré.] Name of an outcast race or caste in southern France; sometimes, like 'pariah' etc., applied to other outcasts.

1844 L. COSTELLO *Béarn & Pyrenees* II. 262 At one period the Cagots were objects of hatred, from the belief that they were afflicted with the leprosy. **1871** TYLOR *Prim. Cult.* I. 104 Many a white man.. ascribes power of sorcery to despised outcast '*races maudites*', Gypsies and Cagots. **1883** T. WATTS *New Hero* in *Eng. Illust. Mag.* English cagots, pariahs, wretches convicted of the original sin of poverty.

‖**Cagoulard** (kagular). [F., lit. 'wearer of a monk's cowl', f. *cagoule* a sleeveless hooded garment + -ARD.] A member of a secret right-wing organization in France in the 1930s.

1937 *Times* 17 Sept. 11/7 A secret para-military organization of the extreme Right known as the *Cagoulards* (hooded ones). **1958** *Listener* 21 Aug. 277/2 When Raoul Dautry took over the Ministry of Armaments in September 1939, he was staggered to discover the chief Cagoulard in an important post. **1966** M. R. D. FOOT *SOE in France* vi. 137 We have his own word for it that he was not a *cagoulard*—that is, did not belong to the rough French equivalent of the Ku Klux Klan.

cagoule (kæ'gu:l). [a. Fr., lit. 'cowl'; cf. CAGOULARD.] A lightweight, waterproof (or windproof) hooded garment resembling an anorak, worn orig. by mountaineers and now generally.

1952 MORIN & SMITH tr. *Herzog's Annapurna* xiv. 201 We had both put on our cagoules, for it was very cold. **1962** *Times* 25 July 8/7 Fur-edged cagoule hoods. **1967** [see *international orange* s.v. INTERNATIONAL *a.* 2]. **1974** H. MACINNES *Climb to Lost World* iv. 56 'Are we here?' asked Joe, pulling his cagoule hood drawcord tight. **1983** *Times* 7 Apr. 24/3 The Haggs Safari, for children aged 8 and over (take wellies and cagoules if wet).

‖**cagui** ('kɑ:gɪ). [Native name.] A name of two Brazilian monkeys of the genus *Hapale*.

[**1693** RAY *Synop. Anim. Quadr.* 154.] **1753** CHAMBERS *Cycl. Supp.* s.v., The lesser cagui is a small and tender animal. **1774** GOLDSM. *Nat. Hist.* (1862) I. VII. i. 508 The Saki, or Cagui.. often termed the Fox Tailed Monkey.

cagy, var. CAGEY *a.*

cahch, -ar, -ynge, -polle, etc.: see CATCH-.

‖**cahier** (kaje). [F., in OF. *quaier*: see QUIRE.]

1. 'A book of loose sheets tacked together; whence, reports of proceedings contained in such a book'. More usually, an exercise-book, pamphlet, or fascicle.

c **1845** C. BRONTË *Professor* (1857) I. xvi. 271 Her eyes were fastened on the cahier open before her. **1849** in SMART (*Supp.*); whence in Worcester, Webster, etc. **1909** E. NESBIT *Daphne* iii. 37 You can divide my school books and *cahiers* among you. **1958** *N. & Q.* Nov. 488/1 A *cahier* is being prepared in commemoration of the centenary of Eleanora Duse's birth. **1964** E. BOWEN *Little Girls* I. ii. 24 He returned his *cahier* to it ostentatiously.

2. *Hist.* The instructions prepared by each of the three representative bodies as a guide for their policy at the National Assembly of 1789 in France.

1789 A. YOUNG *Travels* 27 June (1929) I. 162 These cahiers being instructions given to their deputies, I have

now gone through them all. **1805** *Edin. Rev.* VI. 152 Busily employed in preparing the *cahiers* or instructions for the direction of their deputies. **1879** *Encycl. Brit.* IX. 597/1 Early in 1789 all France was busy with the elections to the States-General, and in drawing up the *cahiers*, or papers of grievances. **1887** LECKY *Eng. in 18th Cent.* V. xx. 430 The cahiers of the clergy showed a frank willingness to surrender all privileges.

cahoot (kəˈhuːt). orig. *U.S.* [prob. a. F. *cahute* (see CAHUTE): cf. the uses of *cabin, cabinet.* But American dictionaries refer it to F. *cohorte.*] 'Used in the South and West to denote a company, or partnership' (Bartlett). Freq. in pl., esp. in phr. ***in cahoot(s)*** (***with***): in league or partnership (with).

18.. *Chron. Pineville* (Bartlett), I wouldn't swar he wasn't in cahoot with the devil. **1829** S. KIRKHAM *Eng. Gram.* 207 Hese in cohoot with me. **1834** S. S. PRENTISS in J. D. Shields *Life* (1884) 239, I will splice the member from North Carolina to you, and for a short time will consider you in cahoot. **1862** G. K. WILDER *MS. Diary* 14 May (D.A.E.), Mc wished me to go in cahoots in a store. **1889** K. MUNROE *Golden Days* 26 Are you willing to work in cahoots with yours truly? **1892** *Congress. Rec.* 16 Mar. 2133/1 Let's go into cahoots and go a coon hunting. **1899** G. ADE *Doc' Horne* xxv. 280, I have good reasons for thinking they were in cahoots. **1953** A. UPFIELD *Murder must Wait* xii. 108 She was in cahoots with a doctor.

Hence **cahoot** *v.* to act in partnership.

1857 *N.Y. Herald* 20 May (Bartlett), They all agree to cahoot with their claims against Nicaragua and Costa Rica.

cahoun, frequent variant of COHUNE.

cahow, var. COHOW.

†**caˈhute.** *Sc. Obs.* [a. F. *cahute* cabin, poor hut.] = CABIN *sb.*, senses 1-5.

c **1505** DUNBAR *Flyting* 449 Into the [ship] Katryne thou maid a foull cahute. **1513** DOUGLAS *Æneis* III. Prol. 15 Nyce laborynth..had neuir sa feill cahutis and wais.

cai, -age, obs. form of QUAY, -AGE.

Caiaphat. *nonce-wd.* [f. *Caiaphas*, after *pontificate, caliphate.*] A high-priesthood like that of Caiaphas (see *John* xi. 40, xviii. 14, 24).

1676 MARVELL *Gen. Councils* Wks. 1875 IV. 152 What new power had the bishops acquired, whereby they turned every *pontificate* into a *Caiaphat?*

caic, caïk(e, -jee: see CAÏQUE, -JEE.

caice, -able, obs. Sc. form of CASE, -ABLE.

caich, obs. Sc. form of CATCH.

caichpule, variant of CACHESPELL *Sc. Obs.*

‖**caid**, var. KAÏD.

caidgie, -ly, -ness, mod.Sc. ff. CADGY, etc.

†**caige**, *v. Sc. Obs.* [see CADGY.] *intr.* ? To wax wanton.

1603 *Philotus* v, Now wallie as the Carle he caiges, Gudeman quha hes maid ȝour mustages?

caigy, obs. form of CADGY.

caik, obs. Sc. f. CAKE; var. of CAÏQUE.

caikjee: see CAÏQUEJEE.

cail, obs. Sc. form of KALE, COLE.

cailcedra (kaɪlˈsɛdrə). [Origin unknown.] A lofty tree of West Africa, *Khaya senegalensis*, of which the wood is specially adapted for joinery and the bark furnishes a bitter tonic.

1866 LINDLEY & MOORE *Treas. Bot.*, *Cailcedra-wood*, the timber of *Flindersia australis.* **1886** *Encycl. Brit.* XXI. 662/1 The wood of the cailcedra..is used in joiner's work and inlaying. **1887** MOLONEY *Forestry W. Afr.* 297 Cailcédra or Mahogany Tree of the Gambia.

cailes, obs. form of KAYLES, nine-pins.

†**caille**, *v. Obs.* [ad. F. *caille-r* (= It. *cagliare, quagliare*:—L. *coagulāre.*] To curdle, to QUAIL. Hence **ˈcailling** *vbl. sb.*

1601 HOLLAND *Pliny* II. 397 In case this accident commeth by cailling of the milk.

‖**cailleach** (ˈkal(j)əx). In Scott **cailliach.** [Gaelic *cailleach* old woman, orig. 'nun', f. *caille* pallium, veil.] An old (Highland) woman, a crone.

1814 SCOTT *Wav.* I. xviii. 280 Some cailliachs (that is, old women) that were about Donald's hand. **1828** —— *F.M. Perth* III. 121 Think you the Clan Quhele have no cailliachs, as active as old Dorothy.

caimacam, var. of KAIMAKAM.

caiman, var. of CAYMAN, alligator.

cain, kain (keɪn). *Sc.* & *Ir.* Also 3-4 **can**, 3- **cane**, 6- **kane**, 8- **kain.** [a. Celtic *cáin*, in OIr. 'statute law', mod.Ir. 'rent, tribute, fine' (O'Reilly), Gaelic 'fine, tribute, payment in kind'. According to Skene (*Celtic Scotl.* III. 231) the primary meaning was 'law', whence it was applied to 'any fixed payment exigible by law'.]

1. A portion of the produce of the soil payable to the landlord as rent; a rent paid in kind. In later times used only of the smaller articles, as poultry.

c **1190** *Chartulary of St. Andrews* 45 (Skene) Ab can et cuneveth et exercitu et auxilio. **1251** [Skene cites] Cain, Coneveth, Feacht, Sluaged, & Ich. *a* **1758** RAMSAY *Poems* (1800) II. 525 (JAM.) The laird got a' to pay his kain. **1786** BURNS *Twa Dogs*, Our Laird gets in his racked rents, His coals, his kain, and a' his stents. **1818** SCOTT *Hrt. Midl.* viii. **1854** H. MILLER *Sch. & Schm.* (1858) 259 Under a tree on that inner island..the queen sits and gathers kain for the Evil One. **1876** GRANT *Burgh Sch. Scotl.* I. i. 7 The Cane of the lands..amounting to 40 Stones of cheese, 70 Measures of Barley, and a Sheep.

b. *attrib.*

1597 SKENE *Exp. Terms* s.v. *Canum*, This word, cane, signifies..tribute or dewtie, as cane fowles, cane cheis, cane aites, quhilk is paid be the tennant..as ane duty of the land. **1810** CROMEK *Nithsdale Song* 280 (Jam.) It is hinted..that Kain Bairns were paid to Satan, and fealty done for reigning through his division of Nithsdale and Galloway. **1828** SCOTT *F.M. Perth* III. ii. 45 Cooped up in a convent, like a kain-hen in a cavey. **1872** COSMO INNES *Sc. Legal Antiq.*, The cain fowls of a barony are quite well understood. Cain fowls are sometimes called reek hens—one payable from every house that reeked—every fire house.

c. ***to pay the cain***: (fig.) to 'pay' the penalty.

a **1774** FERGUSSON *Leith Races*, Though they should dearly pay the kain, And get their tails weel sautit. **1787** BURNS *Tam Samson's El.* ii, To Death she's dearly paid the kane, Tam Samson's dead! **1794** in Ritson *Sc. Songs* II. 78 (Jam.) For Campbell rade, but Myrie staid, And sair he paid the kain, man.

2. (Ireland) A fine or penalty for an offence.

1518 *Rental Bk. Earl Kildare* in *Trans. Kilkenny Archæol. Soc.* Ser. II. IV. 123 Item half kanys & penalties wtin the said Gleancappel.

Cain² (keɪn). Also 5-6 **Caym, Kaym.**

1. a. The proper name of the first fratricide and murderer (*Gen.* iv.), used descriptively.

c **1380** WYCLIF *Tract* xxiii. Sel. Wks. III. 348 þei bilden Caymes Castelis to harme of cuntreis. *c* **1400** *Ywaine & Gaw.* 559 The karl of Kaymes kyn. *c* **1505** DUNBAR *Flyting* 513 Cankrit Caym, tryit trowane, Tutiuillus. **1513** DOUGLAS *Æneis* VIII. Prol. 77 This cuntre is full of Caynis kyne.

b. ***to raise Cain***: see RAISE *v.*¹ 21 b. *colloq.* (orig. *U.S.*).

1840 *Daily Pennant* (St. Louis) 2 May (Th.), Why have we every reason to believe that Adam and Eve were both rowdies? Because..they both raised Cain. **1841** 'Dow, JR.' *Short Patent Sermons* xxix. 73 They will feel that they have been raising Cain and breaking things. **1852** [see RAISE *v.*¹ 21 b]. **1882** R. L. STEVENSON *Treasure Island* (1883) iii. 20 If I get the horrors, I'm a man that has lived rough, and I'll raise Cain. **1930** J. B. PRIESTLEY *Angel Pavement* vii. 345 If we stand here talking another minute the mistress'll be raising Cain the way she'll say she's destroyed with the draught.

†**2.** *Comb.*, as ***Cain-like***; **Cain-coloured**, of the reputed colour of the hair of Cain, to whom, as to Judas Iscariot, a 'red' or reddish-yellow beard was attributed.

1598 SHAKS. *Merry W.* I. iv. 23 He hath but a little wee-face; with a little yellow Beard: a Caine-colourd Beard. **1656** *Eirenicon* 21 Lay by this Cain-like disposition.

Hence also **ˈCainian** = *Cainite.* **ˈCainish** *a.*, of the temper of Cain. **Cainism**, the heresy of the Cainites. **ˈCainite**, (*a*) one of a sect of heretics in the second century who professed reverence for Cain and other wicked Scriptural characters; (*b*) a descendant of Cain; also *fig.* **Caiˈnitic** *a.*, pertaining to Cain or the Cainites.

1540 COVERDALE *Confut. Standish* Pref. Wks. 1844 II. 328 Some spice of Cainish stomach. **1620** BP. HALL *Hon. Mar. Clergy* I. §18 Censuring the opinion of Ambrose as sauouring too strongly of Cainisme and superstition. **1647** PAGITT *Heresiogr.* (ed. 4) 59 Possessed with a spirit of scoffing, terming..us..Cainites. **1659** GELL *Ess. Amendm. Last Transl. Bible* 105 The Lord hath given superiority.. unto the true Shem and all the Shemites..yea, unto Cain himself and the Cainites if they do well. **1653** A. ROSS *Πανσεβεια* (1658) 193 *Cainites*..worshipped Cain as the author of much goodnesse to mankind. **1657** COLVIL *Whig's Supplic.* (1695) But straight turned Anabaptists, Quakers.. And Mr. Gilbert Burnetans..Helvidians, Cainians. **1685** H. MORE *Illustr.* 377 Kainish persecutours. **1764** MACLAINE *Mosheim's Eccl. Hist.* (1844) I. 64/2 The more obscure and less considerable of the Gnostic sects..[as] the Cainites, who treated as saints..Cain, Cora, Dathan, the inhabitants of Sodom, and even the traitor Judas. **1877** DAWSON *Orig. World* xii. 255 Intermixture of Sethite and Cainite races. **1882-3** SCHAFF in *Relig. Encycl.* I. 358 Different turns in the Cainitic history.

cainell bone, var. of CANNEL-BONE.

ca'ing-whale (ˈkɑːɪŋhweɪl). *Sc.* Also **caa'ing whale.** [*Ca'ing* (*calling*: see CALL) = driving like a herd or flock.] The round-headed porpoise, which frequents the shores of Orkney, the Faroe Isles, and Iceland.

c **1865** LETHEBY in *Circ. Sc.* I. 103/1 The round-headed porpoise, or ca'ing whale (*Phocæna melas*). **1879** *Daily News* 23 Aug. 6/2 Upwards of a hundred whales—the *ca'ing whale* (*delphinus deductor*)—were driven ashore in Shetland. **1924** *Nature* CXIII. 532/1 Among the true dolphins (Delphinidae) the caa'ing whale (Globicephala melaena) and Risso's dolphin (Grampus griseus)..are known to subsist, partly at least, on cuttlefish. **1959** A. HARDY *Fish & Fisheries* xv. 287 Yet another northern species..is the pilot whale, blackfish or caa'ing whale.

cainosite, var. CENOSITE.

Cainozoic (kaɪnəʊˈzəʊɪk, keɪnəʊ-), *a. Geol.* Also **kainozoic, cænozoic.** [f. Gr. *καινό-ς* recent + *ζῷον* animal + -IC. The analogical form would be *Cænozoic*, as sometimes actually used; but *Caino-* is favoured by most authors as more evidently suggesting the derivation.]

Of or pertaining to the third of the great geological periods (also called TERTIARY), or to the remains or formations characteristic of it.

1854 PAGE *Introd. Text-bk. Geol.* 39 Cainozoic Period (Recent Life). **1865** LYELL *Elem. Geol.* 92 Some geologists ..have introduced the term Cainozoic, for tertiary. **1878** HUXLEY *Physiogr.* xvii. 290 One great group known as the Tertiary or Cainozoic series.

cainozoology (ˌkaɪnəʊzəʊˈɒlədʒɪ). [f. Gr. *καινό-ς* recent + ZOOLOGY.] (See quot.)

1861 R. E. GRANT *Divis. Anim. Kingd.* 8 The history of existing animals belongs to Cainozoology, and that of extinct forms to Palæozoology. —— (*title*) Cainozoology, the Natural History of Existing Animals.

caip, *sb.*, Sc. form of COPE in various senses.

caiper-caillie: see CAPER-.

caïque (kɑːˈiːk). Also 7 **caik, caic, caicche**, 8 **caick**, 7, 9 **kaik.** [a. Fr. *caïque*, ad. Turkish *kaik.*]

1. A light boat or skiff propelled by one or more rowers, much used on the Bosporus.

1625 PURCHAS *Pilgrims* II. 1623 Hee keepeth the Caiks and, always steereth when the Great Turke goeth vpon the water whose Caikes are most rich and beautifull to behold. **1653** J. GREAVES *Seraglio* 63 He..steers the Kings Kaik [*marg.* Barge]. **1702** W. J. *Bruyn's Voy. Levant* xi. 49 Caicks, Gondalos, and other smaller Wherries. **1812** BYRON *Ch. Har.* II. lxxxi, Glanced many a light caique along the foam. **1864** *Lond. Rev.* 28 May, There he found a solitary boatman, whom he hailed, and was soon seated in his kaik. **1884** J. COLBORNE *Hicks Pasha* 10 The Sultan going to mosque in a state caïque at Constantinople.

2. A Levantine sailing-vessel.

1666 *Lond. Gaz.* No. 95/2 Some Corsar Flutes belonging to Dulcigno..took a Caicche. **1852** CONYBEARE & H. *St. Paul* (1862) II. xxiii. 357 The Levantine caiques..preserve ..the traditionary build and rig of ancient merchantmen. **1861** GEIKIE *E. Forbes* x. 306 A crazy Turkish caique, with an old Turk, a stout Arab, and two little boys, by way of crew.

Hence **caïquejee, caïkjee** (kɑːˈiːkdʒiː) [Turkish], rower of a caïque.

1835 WILLIS *Pencillings* II. xlv. 53 The poorest caikjee might row his little bark under its threshold. **1864** *Daily Tel.* 24 Aug., His caïquejees can go close up to the ground with their flats and barges.

†**cair**, *v. Obs.* Forms: 4 **cayr(e, kayre, caire, kair(e**, (? **karre**), 5- **cair.** [ME. *kayre*, a. ON. *keyra* to drive, ride, thrust, toss about.]

1. *intr.* A poetic word for 'to go, proceed, make one's way': perh. orig. to drive, convey (oneself).

c **1300** in Wright *Lyric P.* x. 37 Ant ben y-cayred from alle that y kneowe. *c* **1325** *E.E. Allit. P.* B. 901 Cayre tid of þis kythe. *c* **1340** *Alex. & Dind.* 48 þe king..wiþ his peple Kairus cofli til hem. *c* **1350** *Will. Palerne* 5324 þei caired ouer cuntre & come neiȝ rome. *c* **1400** *Destr. Troy* 836, I counsell þe in kyrt, kaire to þi londe. *c* **1470** HENRY *Wallace* IX. 1240 Throu out the land to the Lennox thai cair.

2. *trans.* To bring.

c **1325** *E.E. Allit. P.* B. 1478 þe candelstik bi a cost watz cayred þider sone. [But perhaps = *caryed.*]

3. a. *trans.* To push backwards and forwards, to stir about. **b.** *intr.* To rake, stir about. (*mod.Sc.*). 'If ye dinna cair, ye'll get nae thick' (Jam.).

cair, Sc. form of CARE.

cair, -handit, var. of CAR *a. Sc.* left.

caird (kɛəd). *Sc.* Also 8 **kaird.** [Lowland Sc. a. Gaelic *ceard* 'artificer in metal, tinker, blackguard' = Irish *ceard* m. artist, artificer, metal-worker, tinker:—OIr. *cerd* (*cert*) smith, artificer, artist, composer, poet. The same word as Ir. *ceard* f. art, trade, business, function:—OIr. *cerd* art, craft, handicraft, Manx *keird* craft, trade, Welsh *cerdd* art, craft, now esp. musical art, minstrelsy.

(The Sc. thus shows a degraded use of an important Celtic word; cogn. with L. *cerdo* handicraftsman, cobbler; also Gr. *κέρδεα* 'cunning arts', *κερδώ* wily one, cunning fox.]

A travelling tinker; a gipsy, tramp, vagrant.

1663 SPALDING *Troub. Chas. I.* (1792) I. 243 Forbes.. nick-named Kaird, because when he was a boy he served a kaird. **1787** BURNS *To J. Smith* Yill an' whisky gie to cairds. **1818** SCOTT *Hrt. Midl.* xlix, This fellow had been originally a tinkler or caird, many of whom stroll about these districts.

Hence **ˈcairdman** *sb.*

? *a* **1800** *Knt. & Sheph. Dau.* ix. in Child *Ballads* IV. 474/2 A cairdman's daughter Should never be a true-love o mine.

caird, northern form of CARD.

Cairene (kaɪəˈriːn), *sb.* and *a.* Also **Caireen.** [f. *Cairo* + *-ene*, after *Nazarene*, etc.] **A.** *sb.* A

native or inhabitant of Cairo, the capital of Egypt. **B.** *adj.* Of or pertaining to Cairo.

1844 SOPHIA POOLE *Englishwoman in Egypt* I. xi. 156 If we were conducted by a Caireen, no Turkish ladies were likely to address us. **1851** *Illustr. London News* 8 Feb. 102/1 An interesting specimen of Caireen house-building. **1854** B. TAYLOR *Life fr. Egypt* xv. 205 A harem of Cairene ladies. **1855** R. F. BURTON *El-Medinah* I. 270 The people of Suez are a finer and a fairer race than the Cairenes. **1893** [see NILOT]. **1902** S. LANE-POOLE *Story of Cairo* i. 14 The Cairene tucks his legs up under him on the divan. **1936** E. M. FORSTER *Abinger Harvest* IV. 254 The joint authors..are Egyptian—one of them a Cairene Jew. **1945** R. HARGREAVES *Enemy at Gate* 107 A Cairene rebellion which was only suppressed at the cost of considerable bloodshed.

cairn (kɛən), *sb.* Also 6–8 **carne**, 8 **cairne**, **kairn**, 8–9 **carn**. [mod.Sc. form (cf. *bairn*, *wairn*, *airm*, etc.) of earlier *carn*, a. Gaelic *carn* masc. 'heap of stones'. Found in Lowland Sc. early in 16th c., and thence recently in Eng., as a term of prehistoric archæology, and more widely and popularly in connexion with the piles of stones used or raised by Ordnance Surveyors. The direct Eng. representative of the Celtic would be *carn*, which is common on the Ordnance maps of Wales, and in local use with tourists in Wales.

The word is found in all the Celtic langs.; OIrish *carn*, *carnn*, *carnd* occurs as neuter; Welsh, beside *carn* fem. 'heap', has *carn* masc. 'hoof' and 'haft of knife', etc., indicating an earlier sense 'horn'. If these are to be identified, the word must be = the recorded Gaulish *karn-on* neut. 'horn'; in which case the primary sense would apparently be 'cairn on a mountain top' i.e. the 'horn' on its 'head'; which is quite possible, though not certain. The word enters into the names of various mountains in Scotland and Wales. Welsh has also the collective derivative *carnedd*, as in *Carnedd Llewelyn*, etc.]

1. A pyramid of rough stones, raised for a memorial or mark of some kind: **a.** as a memorial of some event, or a sepulchral monument over the grave of some person of distinction (cf. *Gen.* xxxi. 45, *2 Sam.* xviii. 17, etc.). Hence, ***to add a stone to any one's cairn.***

1535 STEWART *Cron. Scot.* (1858) I. 87 Towardis the middis of that carne on hicht Ane greit lang stone gart set on end vprycht. *a* **1600** MONTGOMERIE *Flyting* 401 A cairne beside a croce. **1772** PENNANT *Voy. Hebrides* 209 (JAM.) As long as the memory of the deceased endured, not a passenger went by without adding a stone to the heap..To this moment there is a proverbial expression among the highlanders allusive to the old practice; a suppliant will tell his patron, *Curri mi cloch er do charne*, I will add a stone to your cairn; meaning, when you are no more I will do all possible honor to your memory. **1796** PEGGE *Anonym.* (1809) 424 Kairns, or piles collected for memorials of the dead. **1805** SCOTT *Last. Minstr.* III. xxix, On many a cairn's gray pyramid Where urns of mighty chiefs lie hid. **1807** G. CHALMERS *Caledonia* I. I. ii. 72 A large Carn of stones.. about twenty-five feet high. **1878** H. STANLEY *Dark Cont.* I. vi. 137 We..raised a cairn of stones over his grave.

b. as a boundary-mark, a landmark on a mountain top or some prominent point, or an indication to arctic voyagers or travellers of the site of a cache or depôt of provisions.

The local name of a summit-cairn in the south-east of Scotland and north of England previously to the period of the Ordnance Survey was *man*, as in *Coniston Old Man*, the *High Man* and *Low Man* on Helvellyn, etc.

1770 WESLEY *Wks.* (1872) III. 398 The Highlands are bounded..by Carns, or heaps of stones laid in a row, south-west and north-east, from sea to sea. **1790** BURNS *Elegy Henderson* iii, Ye hills, near neebors o' the starns That proudly cock your cresting cairns! **1805** J. GRAHAM *Sabbath* 167 On the distant cairns the watcher's ear Caught doubtfully at times the breeze-borne note. **1835** SIR J. ROSS *N.-W. Pass.* xli. 546, I..erected a cairn and a flagstaff. **1862** STANLEY *Jew. Ch.* (1877) I. iii. 53 The confines..are marked by the rude cairn or pile of stones erected at the boundary of their territories. **1871** *6-in. Ordn. Map Eng.* Sheet 78 Bangor, *has many instances of* 'carn'. **1872** JENKINSON *Guide Eng. Lakes* (1879) 301 The cairn on the summit of Scawfell Pike will now be a distinct object, and easily gained. **1878** MARKHAM *Gt. Frozen Sea* iv. 56 The depôt was placed on the north-easternmost island, and a large cairn was erected on the highest and most prominent point.

c. A mere pile of stones.

1699 *Phil. Trans.* XXI. 231 Three great Heaps of Stones in this Lake..we call Cairns in the Irish. **1786** BURNS *Brigs Ayr* 112 I'll be a Brig, when ye're a shapeless cairn.

2. ***Cairn terrier*** [said to be so named from being used to hunt among cairns], the smallest breed of terrier in Great Britain, somewhat long in the body and deep in the ribs, with short straight legs and a shaggy coat; also *ellipt.*

1910 *Kennel* Christmas No. 464/1 Cairn terriers promise to rank high in the near future, and already they are being bred to a fairly uniform standard. **1922** R. LEIGHTON *Complete Bk. Dog* xvii. 271 It is now rare to find a Cairn with a bad mouth. **1924** *Westm. Gaz.* 31 Oct., The handy little Sealyhams and Cairns.

cairn, *v.* [f. the sb., or back-formation f. CAIRNED *a.*] *trans.* To mark with a cairn. So **'cairning** *vbl. sb.*

1937 *Geogr. Jrnl.* XC. 309 Points were fixed with the latter, and where possible cairned. **1960** *Guardian* 12 Nov. 6/6 If any route marking is done in mountain districts, I hope it will be done by cairning.

cairned (kɛənd), *a.* [f. CAIRN *sb.* + -ED[2].] Furnished with, or surmounted by, a cairn.

1859 TENNYSON *Vivien* 488 The lake whiten'd and the pinewood roar'd, And the cairn'd mountain was a shadow.

cairngorm, -gorum ('kɛən'gɔəm, -'gɔərəm). [f. the mountain of that name (Gaelic *Carngorm*, i.e. blue cairn) between the shires of Aberdeen, Banff, and Inverness, where it is found.]

(More fully ***cairngorm stone***:) A precious stone of a yellow or wine-colour, consisting of rock-crystal coloured by oxide of iron or, according to Dana, by titanic acid; in common use for brooches and seals, and for ornamenting the handles of dirks, and other articles of Highland costume. Also *attrib.* and *Comb.*

1794 *Agric. Surv. Banffs.* 58 (Jam.) Scotch topazes, or what are commonly called Cairngorum stones. **1823** BYRON *Juan* IX. xliii, And brilliant breeches, bright as a Cairn Gorme. **1859** *All Y. Round* No. 29. 61 Scotch mulls, adorned with cairngorms set in silver thistles. **1861** C. KING *Ant. Gems* 1866 94 The Cairngorum..is only crystal coloured a dark orange or deep brown by some metallic oxide. **1870** MEREDITH *H. Richmond* (1871) I. viii. 136 In satisfying Janet's wishes for riding-whips, knives, pencil-cases, Cairngorm buttons, and dogs. **1881** *Instr. Census Clerks* (1885) 91 Lapidary. Cairngorm, Cameo..Cutter, Worker. **1883** H. DRUMMOND *Nat. Law in Spir. W.* (ed. 2) 372 The hidden amethyst and cairngorm in the rock beneath. **1921** *Dict. Occup. Terms* (1927) §638 Cairngorm grinder.

cairny ('kɛənɪ), *a. rare*$^{-1}$. [f. CAIRN *sb.* + -Y[1].] Abounding in cairns or heaps of stones.

1807 TANNAHILL *Poems* 150 The Rose blooms gay on cairny brae As weel's in birken shaw.

cairo: see COIR.

cairt, Sc. var. of CART; also in sense card.

†**'cairtar.** *Sc. Obs.* [f. *cairt*, Sc. f. CART *sb.*[2] + -AR[3], -ER.] A card-player.

1584 KNOX *Hist. Ref.* (1732) 132 Tables, quhairof sum befoir usit to serv for Drunkardis, Dycearis, and Cairtaris.

caiser(e, obs. form of KAISER, emperor.

caislip, dial. form of KEESLIP, CHEESELIP.

caisson ('keɪsən, keɪ'suːn). Also 8 **caissoon**. [a. F. *caisson* large chest, f. *caisse* chest. The first pronunciation is given by most orthoepists, the second (which agrees with the usual treatment of F. *-on* in the 18th c.) is given only by Perry, Worcester, and Cull.]

1. *Mil.* **a.** A chest containing bombs or other explosives, to be buried and fired as a mine.

1704 in J. HARRIS *Lex. Techn.* **1721** BAILEY, *Caisson* [in Fortification], a Chest of Wood holding four or 6 Bombs, or sometimes filled only with Powder, and buried under Ground, by the Besieged, to blow up a Work the Besiegers are like to be Masters of. **1755** JOHNSON, *Caisson*, a chest of bombs or powder, laid in the enemy's way to be fired at their approach. **1772** SIMES *Mil. Guide* s.v.

b. A chest containing ammunition; a wagon for conveying ammunition. Also *fig.*

1704 in J. HARRIS *Lex. Techn.* **1708** KERSEY, *Caisson*, a covered Waggon, or Carriage for Provisions, or Ammunition for an Army. **1730–6** in BAILEY. **1812** *Examiner* 24 Aug. 532/1, 20 caissons of ammunition. **1865** BUSHNELL *Vicar. Sacr.* III. iii. 233 The retributive causes of nature roll out their heavy caisson with us. **1870** *Echo* 14 Nov., Several artillery caissons captured at Orleans were found to be filled with wearing apparel.

2. *Hydraulics.*

a. A large water-tight case or chest used in laying foundations of bridges, etc., in deep water.

1753 CHAMBERS *Cycl. Supp.*, *Caisson* is also used for a kind of chest used in laying the foundations of the piers of bridges. **1765** *Ann. Reg.* 12/2 The greatest part of the first course [of the sixth pier of Blackfriars bridge] carried by the Caisson. **1823** P. NICHOLSON *Pract. Build.* 305 M. Labelye erected the piers [of Westminster Bridge] in caissons, or water-tight boxes. **1875** B. RICHARDSON *Dis. Mod. Life* 70 The effect of atmospheric pressure on men who are employed to work in caissons.

b. In *Canal-making.* Formerly, a large water-tight cistern or reservoir made at any point where the canal had to be extended over lower ground, in order to enable the boats to come forward with material for the embankment.

1769 *De Foe's Tour Gt. Brit.* III. 272 At Stretford, three Miles off, is the Caisson 40 Yards long by 32. **1838** SOUTHEY *Lett.* (1856) IV. 546. **1861** SMILES *Lives Eng.* I. 382 Brindley ..had the stuff required to make up the embankment brought in boats..conducted from the canal along which they had come into caissons or cisterns placed at the point over which the earth and clay had to be deposited.

c. A vessel in the form of a boat used as a floodgate in docks.

1854 FAIRBAIRN in *Proc. Inst. C. Engin.* 9 May, The employment of caissons for closing the entrance to wet or dry docks. **1867** SMYTH *Sailor's Word-bk.*, *Caisson*, a vessel fitted with valves, to act instead of gates for a dry dock.

d. 'A sort of float sunk to a required depth by letting water into it, when it is hauled under the ship's bottom,..and on pumping out the water floats her' (Smyth *Sailor's Word-bk.*); = CAMEL *sb.*

1811 *Naval Chron.* XXV. 219 This caisson or floating dock is made of wrought iron.

3. *Arch.* 'A sunken panel in ceilings, vaults, and cupolas'. Gwilt *Encycl. Archit.*

4. *attrib.* and in *comb.*, as **caisson disease** (see quots.); **caisson-gate** = sense 2c. **caisson sickness** = *caisson disease.*

1866 *Cornh. Mag.* Mar. 381, 23 feet depth of water when the caisson-gates are opened. **1883** *Harper's Mag.* July 945/1 The 'caisson disease' is the result of living under atmospheric pressure greatly above that to which the human system is normally adapted. **1887** *Health* 11 Mar. 394 What is known as the 'caisson disease' is not produced by the mere increase of atmospheric pressure, but by the sudden diminution of it on leaving the caisson, which produces ruptures of small blood-vessels. **1911** *Engineer* 10 Mar. 243 Caisson Sickness and Compressed Air.

Hence **caissonier** (keɪsə'nɪə(r)), one who works in a caisson; so **'caissoning.**

1903 *Strand Mag.* Jan. 98/2 The lives of 'the men in the box', *i.e.* the caissoniers, are in the greatest danger. *Ibid.* 101/2 After all these terrors it is perhaps astonishing to be told..that caissoning would be sought by any considerable number of men.

caitche, caiche, obs. *Sc.* variants of CATCH, a game played with a ball; tennis.

†**'caitifdom.** *Obs.* [f. next + -DOM.]

a. Captivity. **b.** Wretchedness, misery.

1382 WYCLIF *Ezek.* xxv. 3 The hous of Juda..is led into caitifdoom. *c* **1460** *Towneley Myst.* 156 With his blood he shall us boroo Both from catyfdam and from soroo.

caitiff ('keɪtɪf), *sb.* and *a.* Forms: α. 4 **caitef, -teff, -tyf, -tyue, kaitif, kaytefe**, 4–5 **caytef, -tif, -tyf, -tyue, kaytiff**, (4–6 *pl.* **kaytyves**), 4–7 **caitife, -tive, caytife, -tive**, 4–8 **caitif**, 5 **kaytif(f)e, catyffe, (caistiff)**, *Sc.* **catif**, (*pl.* **keyteyues, caytyveys, catyves**), 5–6 **kaytyf**, 5–7 **caytiffe**, 6 **caytyfe, -ttiue, -tief(e, catif**, *Sc.* **catife, -tive, tyue**, (*pl. Sc.* **catevis**), 6–7 **caitiffe, catiffe**, (*pl.* **catives**), 7 **catife**, 7– **caitiff**. β. 4 **chaytif, cheitefe, chaitif**, 5 **chaytyf.** [a. ONF. *caitif, caitive*, captive, weak, miserable (= Pr. *caitiu, captiu, -iva*, OCat. *captiu, -iva*, Sp. *cautivo*, OSp. *captivo*, Pg. *cativo* captive, It. *cattivo* captive, lewd, bad):—L. *captiv-um* CAPTIVE. The central OF. form *chaitif* (whence mod.F. *chétif, -ive*, of little value, wretched, sorry, miserable) gave the Eng. variant *chaitif*, frequent in 14–15th c., but did not displace the earlier Norman form. The transition of meaning has taken place more or less in most of the Romanic langs.]

A. *sb.*

†**1.** Originally: A captive, a prisoner. *Obs.*

1330 R. BRUNNE *Chron.* 172 Galwes do ȝe reise, and hyng þis cheitefe. *a* **1340** HAMPOLE *Psalter* cxxxvi. 3 The deuyl & his aungels led vs caitifs in synne. **1382** WYCLIF *Rom.* xvi. 7 Andronyk and Iuliane..myn euene caytifs, or prisoneris. **1449** PECOCK *Repr.* 479 Thei..that..leden Wommen Caitifis. **1502** ARNOLDE *Chron.* 161 In whoos power he is kepte as a kaytyf in myserable seruitude. **1533** BELLENDEN *Livy* II. (1822) 164 Thay have led you this day as vincust catives in triumphe. **1603** H. CROSSE *Vertues Commw.* (1878) 14 As catiues and slaues bend the will to such inhumane crueltie.

†**2.** Expressing commiseration: A wretched miserable person, a poor wretch, one in a piteous case. *Obs.*

c **1325** *Metr. Hom.* 31 Hou sal it far of us kaytefes, That in sin and foli lyes. *c* **1386** CHAUCER *Knts. T.* 859 Tuo woful wrecches been we, and kaytyves. **1480** CAXTON *Chron. Eng.* v. (1520) 56/1 Alas sayd he, to us wretches and catyves is sorowe for our greate synnes. *a* **1547** SURREY *Æneid* II. 977 From me catif alas bereued was Creusa then. **1604** SHAKS. *Oth.* IV. i. 109 Alas poore Caitiffe. **1631** WEEVER *Anc. Fun. Mon.* 46 The carcase of the poore caitiffe. **1678** BUTLER *Hud.* III. I. 344, I pity'd the sad Punishment The wretched Caitiff underwent.

3. Expressing contempt, and often involving strong moral disapprobation: A base, mean, despicable 'wretch', a villain. In early use often not separable from sense 2 (esp. when applied by any one to himself): 'it often implies a mixture of wickedness and misery' J.: cf. *wretch.*

a **1300** *Cursor M.* 11815 Þat caitif [Herod] vn-meth and vn-meke Nu bigines he to seke. *c* **1330** *Amis & Amil.* 1564 His wiif..With wordes hard and kene..seyd to him 'Thou wreche chaitif'. *c* **1400** *Destr. Troy* 10352 As a caiteff, a coward, no knighthode at all. **1481** CAXTON *Reynard* (Arb.) 96 He is a foule vylaynous kaytyt. **1509** BARCLAY *Ship of Fooles* (1570) 173 Another caytife or mischieuous vilayne. **1603** SHAKS. *Meas. for M.* v. i. 53 The wickedst caitiffe on the ground. **1632** G. FLETCHER *Christs Vict.* I. xvii, That wretch, beast, caytive, monster Man. **1713** SWIFT *Frenzy of J. Dennis* Wks. 1755 III. I. 144 Caitiffs, stand off, unhand me, miscreants! **1867** FREEMAN *Norm. Conq.* (1876) I. v. 274 Two caitiffs whose names are handed down to infamy.

¶ † Rarely as an error for *caitifte*: see CAITIFTY.

a **1340** HAMPOLE *Psalter* xiii. 11 Lord has turned away þe caitife of his folke. *c* **1340** *Cursor M.* 7353 (Trin.) Wiþ caitif [*Cott.* caitiuete] and care.

B. *adj.*

†**1.** Captive. *Obs.*

1382 WYCLIF *Isa.* v. 13 Therfor lad caitif is my puple. —— *Ephes.* iv. 8 He..ledde caitifte caytif, or prysonynge prisoned.

†**2.** Wretched, miserable. *Obs.*

a **1300** *Cursor M.* 9086 Yee helpe me in þis caitiue cas. **1393** LANGL. *P. Pl.* C. xv. 90 Noþer in cote noþer in caytyf hous was crist y-bore. *Ibid.* XXIII. 236 Þei chosen chile and chaytif pouerte. *c* **1400** *Rom. Rose* 211 Ful sade and caytif was she eek. *c* **1440** *Promp. Parv.* 58 Catyffe, *calamitosus, dolorosus.* **1583** STANYHURST *Æneis* I. (Arb.) 35 Wee caytiefe Troians, with storms ventositye mangled.

3. Vile, base, mean, basely wicked; worthless, 'wretched', 'miserable'.

a **1300** *Cursor M.* 16517 Ded es caitiue iudas nu. *c* **1325** *E.E. Allit. P.* B. 1426 A caytif counsayl he caȝt bi hym seluen. **1483** CAXTON *G. de la Tour* A vij, When the chaytyf body hath synned by his fals delytes. **1597** BP. HALL *Sat.* IV. ii. 120 When Lolioes caytive name is quite defast. **1626** T. H. *Caussin's Holy Crt.* 130 An age so caytiffe, where braue, and courageous magistrates are wanting. **1814** SCOTT *Ld. Isles* VI. xxxi, [He] cursed their caitiff fears. **1859** TENNYSON *Enid* 35 Bandit earls, and caitiff knights. **1871** BROWNING *Balaust.* 1804 This or the other caitiff quality.

† **'caitifhede, -ivehede.** *Obs.* [f. prec. + *-hede*, -HEAD.] **a.** Wretchedness, misery. **b.** Vileness, baseness, wickedness.

c **1340** *Cursor M.* 7353 (Fairf.) Wiþ caitef hede [*Cott.* caitiuete] and care out of þis werld he sal fare. *Ibid.* 22382 (Fairf.) Quen þat ilk warlagh brid [antecrist] his caitiuehede [*Cott.* caitiute] has ij. ȝere kid.

† **'caitifly, -ively,** *adv. Obs.* [f. CAITIFF *a.* + -LY-.] Like a caitiff: **a.** Wretchedly, miserably. **b.** Vilely, basely, despicably, badly.

1393 LANGL. *P. Pl.* C. IV. 242 Caytiflyche þow, conscience consailedist þe kyng. *c* **1425** WYNTOUN *Cron.* II. viii. 106 Lyve as Lowndreris caytevely. **1513** DOUGLAS *Æneis* IX. xiii. 22 Thynke ȝe na lak and schame..thus catyfly to fle?

† **'caitifness, -iveness.** *Obs.* [f. as prec. + -NESS.] **a.** Wretchedness, misery. **b.** Baseness.

1393 LANGL. *P. Pl.* C. x. 255 The cause of al þys caitifte [*v.r.* caiteefnes] comeþ of meny bisshopes. *c* **1400** *Judicium* (1822) 13 The day is comen of catyfnes. **1481** CAXTON *Myrr.* III. xxiii. 187 [In heuen] shal neuer be ony doubtaunce..of caytifnes ne of ony trybulacion. **1649** JER. TAYLOR *Gt. Exemp.* I. vi. 103 A strange caitivenesse and basenesse of disposition.

† **'caitifty, -ivetie.** *Obs.* For forms cf. CAITIFF. [a. OF. *caitivetet* (mod.F. *chétiveté*):—L. *captīvitāt-em* captivity, f. *captīvus* captive.]

1. Captivity.

a **1300** *Cursor M.* 23626 Þe gode..sal liue in fredom fre, þe wicked..euer in caitiuete. **1382** WYCLIF *Ephes.* iv. 8 He styȝinge into hiȝ, ledde caitifte caytif. —— *Isa.* Prol., The ten lynages led in to caitiftie.

2. Wretchedness, misery.

a **1300** *Cursor M.* 7353 Wit caitiuete and care He sal vte o þis werld fare. **1340** HAMPOLE *Pr. Consc.* 455 My moder has consayved me In syn and in caytefte. **1393** LANGL. *P. Pl.* C. x. 255 The cause of al þys caitifte · comeþ of meny bisshopes.

3. Vileness, wicked baseness.

a **1300** *Cursor M.* 22382 Quen þat ilk warlau bridd [antecrist] his caitiute has tua yeir kidd.

[**caitisned,** *pa. pple.* A misprint for *caytifued* = *caitived* (see next), copied in some Dicts.]

1678 PHILLIPS, *Caitisned*, chained, a word used by Chaucer. [So **1721–1800** BAILEY.]

† **caitive,** *v. Obs.* In 4–5 caityve, chatyue, caytifue. [f. CAITIFF *sb.*] *trans.* To make captive. Hence **caitived** *ppl. a.*

1382 WYCLIF *Bible* Pref Ep. iii, Chatyuynge al vndirstondyng for to obeishe to Crist. —— *Jer.* 2nd Prol., Sathan, caityuende the soules of them that ben forsaken of God. *c* **1400** *'Chaucer's' Test. Love* I. Wks. (1532) In this derke prisone caytifued [331/1, (1560) 272/2 *printed* caytisned] fro frendshippe and acquayntaunce, and forsaken of al. *c* **1440** *Relig. Pieces fr. Thorn. MS.* 36 Whyls we ere in þis caytifede worlde.

‖ **Cajan** (keɪdʒən, 'kɑːdʒan). [a. Malay *kāchang* applied to various leguminous plants (*Cajanus Lablab, Dolichos, Phaseolus, Soja,* etc.).]

A genus of plants, *Cajanus* (N.O. *Leguminosæ*), and esp. the species *C. Indicus*, a shrub native to the East Indies, but now naturalized in Africa, tropical America, and Polynesia, for the sake of the seeds or pulse, an esteemed article of food, called in India *Dhal, Dhol,* and *Urhur*, and in Jamaica *Pigeon-peas*, of which the *No-eye pea* and *Congo pea* are varieties.

1693 *Phil. Trans.* XVII. 688 The Thora Paerou or Cajan-Tree, an arborescent *Phaseolus* or Laburnum, much cultivated at the Cape. **1885** YULE *Hobson-Jobson* 109 The Cajan was introduced to America by the slave-traders from Africa.

Cajan, Cajen, Cajian, Cajun, etc., colloq. corruptions of ACADIAN *a.* and *sb. N. Amer.*

1868 *Putnam's Mag.* II. 54 Among them were..Cagians, the descendants of the old Acadians. **1878** *Hallberger's Illustr. Mag.* 577 (Farmer), The Native Louisianian..and the Acadian, more universally known..as the Cajen. **1880** *Scribner's Monthly* Jan. 383 Acadian—or rather its corruption 'Cajun', as they pronounce it—is regarded as implying contempt. **1885** *Outing* (U.S.) Feb. 337/1 The Cajan fisherman will gladly teach you his art of catching trout. **1942** T. H. RADDALL *His Majesty's Yankees* 26 We'd pluck the French off their farms—off the fat red 'Cajun lands around Fundy Bay. **1959** P. CAPON *Amongst those Missing* 43 My father's a Cajun from New Orleans.

cajaput, cajeput, variants of CAJUPUT.

cajole (kə'dʒəʊl), *v.* Also 7 caiole, cageole, cajoul, 7–8 cajol. [a. F. *cajoler*, in same sense, of uncertain origin and history.

Paré *c* 1550 has '*cageoller* comme un gay' to chatter like a jay. Littré has 16th c. examples of *cajoler, cajoller, cageoller*, in the senses 'to chatter like a jay or magpie', and 'to sing', also, in the modern sense 'to cajole'. Cotgr. 1611 has *cajoler, cageoler* 'to prattle or jangle like a jay (in a cage), to bable or prate much to little purpose'. Most etymologists taking *cageoler* as the original form, have inferred its derivation from *cage* cage, through an assumed dim. **cageole.* This is doubtful both in regard to sense and form; the early meaning 'to chatter like a jay' does not very obviously arise from *cage*, and does not clearly give rise to the modern sense. The Fr. dim. of *cage* is not **cageole* but *geôle* 'gaol', whence F. *enjôler* (OF. *engaioler, engauler*, Sp. *enjaular*) 'to put in gaol, imprison', also 'to inveigle, entice, allure, enthrall by fair words, cajole'. In Namur, *cajoler* has the sense *enjoliver*, to make *joli*, whence Grandgagnage would refer it to the stem *jol-* of *joli*, with 'prefix *ca-* frequent in Walloon with an iterative force'. It is possible that two or even three words are here confused; in the modern sense, F. *cajoler* is synonymous with *enjôler* above, and if not cognate with that word, its sense has probably at least been taken over from it by form-association of *cageoler* or *cajoler* with *enjôler*. But the working out of the history must be left to French etymologists.]

1. *trans.* To prevail upon or get one's way with (a person) by delusive flattery, specious promises, or any false means of persuasion. ('A low word' J.)

1645 *King's Cabinet Open.* Pref. 2 How the Court has been Caiolde (thats the new authentick word now amongst our Cabalisticall adversaries) by the Papists. *Ibid.* 46 He..gives avisoes to Caiole the Scots and Independents. **1649** MILTON *Eikon.* xxi, That the people might no longer be abused and cajoled, as they call it, by falsities and court-impudence. **1678** BUTLER *Hud.* III. i. 1526 'Tis no mean part of civil State-Prudence, to cajoul the Devil. **1723** SHEFFIELD (Dk. Buckhm.) *Wks.* (1753) II. 137 Cajoling a proud Nation to change their Master. **1735** POPE *Donne Sat.* iv. 90 You Courtiers so cajol us. **1823** LINGARD *Hist. Eng.* VI. 196 They sometimes cajoled, sometimes threatened the pontiff. **1863** W. PHILLIPS *Speeches* iii. 36 Leading statesmen have endeavored to cajole the people.

b. Const. *into, from* an action or state.

1663 PEPYS *Diary* 17 Mar., Sir R. Ford..cajoled him into a consent to it. *a* **1853** ROBERTSON *Lect.* ii. 55 Nor to cajole or flatter you into the reception of my views. **1862** TRENCH *Mirac.* xxviii. 310 He could neither be cajoled nor terrified from his..avowal of the truth.

c. Const. *out of*: (*a*) to do (a person) *out of* (a thing) by flattery, etc.; (*b*) to get (a thing) out of a person by flattery, etc.

1749 FIELDING *Tom Jones* XI. ix. (1840) 165/1 Everybody would not have cajoled this out of her. **1833** MARRYAT *P. Simple* (1863) 33 The stockings which she cajoled him out of. **1839** W. IRVING *Wolfert's R.* (1855) 247 The populace..are not to be cajoled out of a ghost story by any of these plausible explanations.

2. *intr.* or *absol.* To use cajolery. † *to cajole with*:—sense 1 (cf. *persuade with*).

1665 PEPYS *Diary* 12 Oct., He hath cajolled with Seymour, who will be our friend. **1789** BELSHAM *Ess.* I. iii. 40 [Elizabeth] knew how to cajole, how to coax, and to flatter. **1870** L'ESTRANGE *Miss Mitford* I. vi. 210 The well-fee'd lawyers have ceased to browbeat or to cajole.

† **ca'jole,** *sb. Obs. rare.* [f. prec. vb.] A delusive flattery.

1716 *Glossogr. Nova, Blandishment*, a Complement, a Cajole, a thing pleasantly done or spoken.

cajolement (kə'dʒəʊlmənt). [f. CAJOLE *v.* + -MENT.] The action of cajoling.

1816 KEATINGE *Trav.* II. 85 Neither official pomposity, threat, or cajolement, could blind him. **1825** COLERIDGE in *Rem.* (1836) II. 356. **1852** THACKERAY *Esmond* I. xii. (1867) 123 Plied them with tears, kisses, cajolements.

cajoler (kə'dʒəʊlə(r)). [f. as prec. + -ER[1].] One who cajoles or overcomes by flattery.

1677 HOBBES *Homer* 38 Cajoler, that confidest in thy face. **1814** *Monthly Rev.* LXXIV. 477 Cajolers of the people. **1841** CATLIN *N. Amer. Ind.* (1844) II. lviii. 238 The superior tact and cunning of their merciless cajolers.

cajolery (kə'dʒəʊlərɪ). Also 7 cajollery, 8 cajolry. [a. F. *cajolerie*, 16th c., in same sense, f. *cajoler* to CAJOLE.] The action or practice of cajoling; persuasion by false arts.

1649 EVELYN *Liberty & Serv.* iv. (R.) Those infamous cajolleries. **1698** SIDNEY *Disc. Govt.* iii. §45 (1704) 415 Others prefer'd the cajolerys of the Court before the honor of performing their duty to the Country. **1835** LYTTON *Rienzi* II. iii. 111 Is he familiar with the people?—it is cajolery! Is he distant?—it is pride! **1868** E. EDWARDS *Ralegh* I. xxv. 650 He had mingled the usual cajoleries with more than the usual slightly-veiled threats.

cajoling (kə'dʒəʊlɪŋ), *vbl. sb.* [f. CAJOLE *v.* + -ING[1].] The action of the verb CAJOLE.

a **1745** SWIFT *Wks.* (1841) II. 29 Fawning and cajoling will have but little effect. **1864** BURTON *Scot. Abr.* I. iii. 149 He tried cajoling, threats, and appeals to chivalrous feeling.

ca'joling, *ppl. a.* [f. as prec. + -ING[2].] That cajoles; deceitfully persuasive.

1715 BURNET *Own Time* (1766) I. 518 The king writ him a cajoling letter. *c* **1746** HERVEY *Medit. & Contempl.* (1818) 214 Vain images, and cajoling temptations. **1820** FOSTER in *Life & Corr.* (1846) II. 6 To assume a cajoling tone.

ca'jolingly, *adv.* [f. prec. + -LY[2].] In a cajoling manner.

1853 *Fraser's Mag.* XLVII. 672 'What man', asks another, cajolingly, 'can ever doubt the sincerity of our protestations?'

‖ **cajuput** ('kædʒəpət). Also cajeput, cajaput. [Ultimately a. Malay *kayu-putih* i.e. *kayu* wood + *puteh* white (whence also the spec. name *leucodendron*). The Eng. spelling, and F. *cajeput*, are due to the Dutch transliteration of the Malay, *kajoepoetih*, and mod.L. *cajuputi* (with *j* = *y*). The Malay name has passed into the vernaculars of Southern India as *kaya-puteh, kaya-poote*, etc.]

1. *cajuput tree*: one or more species of *Melaleuca* (N.O. *Myrtaceæ*), esp. *M. minor* (*Cajuputi*), and *M. leucodendron*, natives of the Eastern Archipelago and New Holland, and introduced in India.

1876 HARLEY *Mat. Med.* 610 The Cajuput Tree has been distributed over the whole of India.

2. *cajuput oil*: the aromatic oil obtained from these trees, used in medicine as a stimulant, antispasmodic, and sudorific.

1832 BABBAGE *Econ. Manuf.* xv. (ed. 3) 145 [In 1831] cajeput oil was sold..at 7*d.* per ounce. *a* **1845** HOOD *To Mr. Malthus* vii, Doors all shut, On hinges oil'd with cajeput. **1866** *Treas. Bot.* 728 The leaves..are distilled for the purpose of yielding the oil known as Cajuput or Cajeput oil, which is green, and has a powerful aromatic odour.

3. Also applied to a Californian tree, *Oreodaphne californica* (N.O. *Lauraceæ*).

Hence **cajuputene, cajputene,** *Chem.*, '$C_{10}H_{16}$ the hydrocarbon of which oil of cajuput is the hydrate' (*Syd. Soc. Lex.*).

1863–72 WATTS *Dict. Chem.* I. 711 Cajputene is obtained, together with two isomeric hydrocarbons, isocajputene and paracajputene. **1876** HARLEY *Mat. Med.* 611 Oil of Cajuput consists chiefly of hydrate of cajuputene.

ca'kate, *v.* humorous nonce-formation, intended to mean 'To serve with CAKE'.

1622 MIDDLETON & ROWLEY *Old Laws* v. i, *Enter Gustho and others, one bearing a bride-cake. Gus.* Will it please you to taste of the wedlock-courtesy?.. If your grace please to be cakated, say so.

cake (keɪk), *sb.* Also 4 **kaak**, 4–6 **kake**, 6 *Sc.* **caik.** [ME. *kake, cake*, 13th c., identical with, and prob. a. ON. *kaka* fem. (mod.Icel. and Sw. *kaka*, Da. *kage*) in same sense, pointing to an OTeut. **kakâ-*. An ablaut-derivative from the same root *kak-* is OHG. *chuohho* (MHG. *kuoche*, Ger. *kuche*), MLG. *kôke*, MDu. *coeke* (Du. *koek*), all masc., pointing to a WGer. **kôkon-*. The ulterior history is unknown, but the stem (Aryan type **gag-*) can in no way be related to L. *coquĕre* to cook, as formerly supposed.]

1. As name of an object, with plural: A baked mass of bread or substance of similar kind, distinguished from a loaf or other ordinary bread, either by its form or by its composition:

a. *orig.* A comparatively small flattened sort of bread, round, oval, or otherwise regularly shaped, and usually baked hard on both sides by being turned during the process.

c **1230** *Hali Meid.* 37 Hire cake bearneð o þe stan. *c* **1325** *E.E. Allit. P.* B. 635 Þrwe þryftyly þer-on þo þre þerue kakez. **1382** WYCLIF *1 Sam.* ii. 36 That..he offre a silueren peny, and a round kaak of breed. **1398** TREVISA *Barth. De P.R.* XVII. lxvii. (1495) 643 Some brede is bake and tornyd and wende at fyre and is callyd..a cake. **1483** *Cath. Angl.* 51 A Cake, *torta, tortula.* **1530** PALSGR. 202/2 Cake of fyne floure made in a print of yron, *gavfre.* **1542** BOORDE *Introd. Knowl.* xxvii. 194 A peny worth of whyte bread..ix. kakys for a peny; and a kake serued me a daye. **1611** BIBLE *Ex.* xii. 39 They baked vnleauened cakes. —— *Hosea* vii. 8 Ephraim is a cake not turned. **1685** BAXTER *Paraphr. N.T.* Mark viii. 4 Their Loaves then were but like our Cakes, by the custom of breaking them. **1719** DE FOE *Crusoe* (1840) I. v. 97, I..reduced myself to one biscuit-cake a day. **1879** FROUDE *Cæsar* xxii. 381 They made cakes out of roots, ground into paste and mixed with milk. *Mod.* King Alfred and the cakes.

b. In Scotland (parts of Wales, and north of England), *spec.* a thin hard-baked brittle species of oaten-bread. Hence the name *Land of Cakes* (i.e. of oaten bread), applied (originally in banter) to Scotland, or the Scottish Lowlands.

a **1572** KNOX *Hist. Ref.* (1732) 42 (Jam.) That winter following sa nurturit the Frenche men, that they leirnit to eit, yea, to beg caikis, quhilk at their entry they scornit. **1620** VENNER *Via Recta* i. 17 Of Oates in Wales, and some of the Northerne shires of England, they make bread, especially in manner of Cakes. **1669** SIR R. MORAY in *Lauderdale Papers* (1885) II. cxiv. 171 If you do not come out of the land of cakes before New Year's day. **1715** *Pennecuick's Tweeddale* Note 89 (Jam.) The oat-cake, known by the sole appellative of cake, is the bread of the cottagers. *c* **1730** BURT *Lett. N. Scotl.* (1818) II. 164 The Lowlanders call their part of the country the land of cakes. **1789** BURNS *Capt. Grose* i, Hear, Land o' Cakes, and brither Scots. **1864** A. MCKAY *Hist. Kilmarnock* 113 With abundance of cakes. *Mod.* Country children in Scotland still 'seek their cakes' on Hogmanay or 'Cake-day'. Among the rimes used, one hears 'My feet's cauld, my shoon's thin, Gie's my cakes, and let's rin.'

c. In England, cakes (in sense a) have long been treated as fancy bread, and sweetened or flavoured; hence, the current sense:

A composition having a basis of bread, but containing additional ingredients, as butter, sugar, spices, currants, raisins, etc. At first, this was a cake also in form, but it is no longer necessarily so, being now made of any serviceable, ornamental, or fanciful shape; e.g. a *tea-*, *plum-*, *wedding-cake*, etc.

c **1420** *Liber Cocorum* (1862) 50 Geder hit [the eggs, tansy and butter, for a tansy cake] on a cake.. With platere of tre, and frye hit browne. **1577** NORTHBROOKE *Dicing* (1843) 100 His mother left bringing of wine and cakes to the church. **1683** TRYON *Way to Health* 233 Observe the composition of Cakes, which are frequently eaten.. In them there are commonly Flour, Butter, Eggs, Milk, Fruit, Spice, Sugar, Sack, Rose-Water and Sweet-Meats, as Citron, or the like. **1710** ADDISON *Tatler* No. 220 ¶8 Banbury..was a Place famous for Cakes and Zeal. **1816** SOUTHEY *Poet's Pilgr.* I. 44 Assche for water and for cakes renown'd. **1841** LANE *Arab. Nts.* I. 71 Sweet cakes, or biscuits, of an annular form. *Mod.* At the conclusion of the ceremony each child was regaled with a cake. To buy a cake for the christening.

2. As a substance, without plural: Fancy bread of the kind mentioned in 1 c. (In Scotland, plain oatmeal bread of the kind mentioned in 1 b.)

1579 FULKE *Confut. Sanders* 591 The last answere is as good as cake and pudding. **1633** B. JONSON *T. Tub* II. i. (N.) If he ha' cake And drink enough, he need not vear [fear] his stake. *Mod.* Little boys are fond of cake. To buy a pound of cake at the confectioner's. To send wedding-cake to friends at a distance. No cards; no cake.

3. Applied to other preparations of food, not of the nature of bread, made in the form of a rounded flattened mass; e.g. a *fish-cake, potato-cake, pan-cake.* (The last named has the characteristics of a cake in the original sense, except that it is cooked soft, eaten hot, and is reckoned not as bread, but as a kind of pudding).

4. a. A mass or concretion of any solidified or compressed substance in a flattened form, as a cake of soap, wax, paint, dry clay, coagulated blood, tobacco, etc. See also AGUE-CAKE, ELF-CAKE.

1528 *Test. Ebor.* (Surtees) V. 267, ij cakes of wax. **1597** LANGHAM *Gard. Health* (1633) 2 Vse it..in thy potage to heale the elfe cake. **1587** FLEMING *Contn. Holinshed* III. 1368/1 Their cakes of waxe which they call Agnus Dei. **1626** BACON *Sylva* §552 A Cake that groweth upon the side of a dead tree..large and of a Chesnut colour, and hard and pithy. **1665** *Phil. Trans.* I. 36 It [earth] soon melted and became a Cake in the bottom. **1799** G. SMITH *Laborat.* I. 122 Take it [the enamel] off the fire, make it into cakes, and preserve it for use. **1833** MARRYAT *P. Simple* iv, Four cakes of Windsor, and two bars of yellow for washing. **1884** *Manch. Exam.* 29 Feb. 5/3 A parcel of cakes of dynamite.

b. *fig.*

1872 BAGEHOT *Physics & Pol.* (1876) 27 To create what may be called a cake of custom. **1879** H. GEORGE *Progr. & Pov.* x. i. (1881) 433 A body or 'cake' of laws and customs grows up.

c. A substance (such as cotton-seed, linseed, etc.) compressed in a flat form and used for feeding cattle, etc. Freq. with defining word, as COTTON-*cake*, LINSEED *cake*. Also *attrib.* and *Comb.*

1757 [see OILCAKE]. **1833** *Niles' Reg.* XLIV. 222/1 The cake is the very best food for stock. *a* **1884** KNIGHT *Dict. Mech.* Suppl. 152 *Cake grinder*, a machine for breaking linseed oil cake for food for stock. **1886** R. E. G. COLE *Gloss. S.W. Lincs.* 24 *Cake*, usual term for the Linseed Cake, used for fattening cattle. Some men run up a great *cäek* bill their last year. **1894** *Country Gentleman's Catal.* 14/2 A few acres of autumn cabbage will maintain and fatten, with the aid of corn or cake, of course, a large flock of sheep. **1907** *Yesterday's Shopping* (1969) 57 Patent Meat Fibrine Vegetable Dog Cakes... Patent Cod Liver Oil Dog Cakes. **1916** E. BLUNDEN *Barn* 20 The smell of apples..And homely cattle-cake. **1960** *Farmer & Stockbreeder* 26 Jan. 92/3 Those ewes whose body weights were maintained..by cake-feeding. *Ibid.*, The cake-fed ewes.

d. In the manufacture of artificial silk: (see quots.).

1927 T. WOODHOUSE *Artificial Silk* 42 An annular package of yarn is gradually built up by the succeeding layers of yarn. This annular package is called a 'cake'. **1963** A. J. HALL *Textile Sci.* ii. 46 Fibres..are collected into the form of a thread F to be drawn over rotating Godet wheel B and fall down into the rotating centrifugal Topham pot T to be built up inside as a ball or 'cake'.

5. *Heraldry.* A bearing resembling the bezant; a roundel.

1486 *Bk. St. Albans, Her.* C iij b, Besantys and lytill cakys differ not bot in colore, for besanttis be euer of golden coloure.

6. *dial.* and *slang.* A foolish or stupid fellow.

1785 GROSE *Dict. Vulgar Tongue, Cake* or *Cakey*, a foolish fellow. **1847–78** in Halliwell. **1877** PEACOCK *N. Linc. Gloss.* (E.D.S.) *Cake*, a silly person, especially one fat and sluggish. **1881** EVANS *Leicester. Was., Cake*, a noodle.

7. a. *Cake* is often used figuratively in obvious allusion to its estimation (esp. by children) as a 'good thing', the dainty, delicacy, or 'sweets' of a repast. So ***cakes and ale, cake and cheese*** (Scotl.). ***to take the cake***, (†U.S. ***cakes***): to carry off the honours, rank first; often used ironically or as an expression of surprise. Cf. BISCUIT 1 d.

1579 [see 2]. **1601** SHAKS. *Twel. N.* II. iii. 124 Dost thou thinke because thou art vertuous, there shall be no more Cakes and Ale? **1606** DAY *Ile of Gulls* III. i. (1881) 68 That's Cake and Cheese to the Countrie. **1847** W. T. PORTER *Quarter Race Kentucky* 120 They got up a horse and fifty dollars in money a side,..each one to start and ride his own horse,..the winning horse take the cakes. **1854** *Blackw. Mag.* LXXVI. 702 Malcolm is, *par excellence*, the 'cake' of the *corps dramatique*. **1884** *Lisbon* (Dakota) *Star* 25 July, Sherriff Moore takes the cake for the first wheat-harvesting in Ransom county. **1886** *Garden* 5 June 519/1 The gardener's life, as a rule, is not all 'cakes and ale'. **1886** *Pall Mall G.* 2 Sept. 5/1 As a purveyor of light literature..Mr. Norris takes the cake. **1900** T. DREISER *Sister Carrie* xxiii. 249 Pack up and pull out, eh? You take the cake. **1904** A. BENNETT *Great Man* xxv. 275 My bold buccaneer, you take the cake... There is something about you that is colossal, immense, and magnificent. **1938** G. HEYER *Blunt Instr.* ix. 158 I've met some kill-joys in my time, but you fairly take the cake.

b. In phrases, as ***the national cake***, or, allusively, ***(the) cake***, the assets or proceeds of a national, etc., economy, regarded collectively as something to be shared out.

1750 EARL HOLDERNESS in Ellis *Orig. Lett.* II. 466 IV. 390 If I stay in [office], I must now have my share of the Cake. **1949** *New Statesman* 22 Oct. 443/2 A general free fight between capital and labour for their respective shares of the national cake. **1957** *Listener* 8 Aug. 188/1 German labour may be about to demand a larger slice of the recovery cake. **1958** *Engineering* 28 Mar. 391/1 They [*sc.* trade unions] have for long thought that their job of getting more of the cake out of employers included advising on how to increase the cake.

c. Colloq. phr. ***a piece of cake***: something easy or pleasant.

1936 O. NASH *Primrose Path* 172 Her picture's in the papers now, And life's a piece of cake. **1942** T. RATTIGAN *Flare Path* I, Special. Very hush-hush. Not exactly a piece of cake, I believe. **1943** P. BRENNAN et al. *Spitfires over Malta* i. 31 The mass raids promised to be a piece of cake, and we anticipated taking heavy toll of the raiders. **1960** T. MCLEAN *Kings of Rugby* 205 They took the field against Canterbury as if the match were 'a piece of cake'.

8. Proverbs. ***you can't eat your cake and have it*** (see quots.). ***one's cake is dough***: one's project has failed of success. ***every cake has its make, mate***, or ***fellow*** (*northern dial.* and *Sc.*).

1562 J. HEYWOOD *Prov. & Epigr.* (1867) 79 What man, I trow ye raue, Wolde ye bothe eate your cake, and haue your cake? **1563** BECON *Displ. Popish Mass* in *Wks.* III. f. xlviii, Or ells your Cake is dough & al your fatte lye in the fyre. **1596** SHAKS. *Tam. Shr.* I. i. 110 Our cake's dough on both sides. Farewell. **1641** D. FERGUSON *Scot. Prov.* in Ray *Prov.* (1670) 293 There was never a cake, but it had a make. **1678** RAY *Prov.* 68 Every cake hath its make, but a scrape-cake hath two. **1687** SETTLE *Reflect. Dryden* 4 She is sorry his cake is dough, and that he came not soon enough to speed. **1708** MOTTEUX *Rabelais* IV. vi, You shall have rare Sport anon, if my Cake ben't Dough, and my Plot do but take. **1711** SHAFTESB. *Charac.* (1737) I. 130 As ridiculous as the way of children, who eat their cake, and afterwards cry for it.. They shou'd be told, as children, that they can't eat their cake, and have it. **1815** WELLINGTON *Let.* in Gurw. *Disp.* XII. 589 Our own government also..having got their cake, want both to eat it and keep it. **1860** [see DOUGH *sb.* 1 b]. **1934** J. FARNOL *Winds of Fortune* v. 31 Thy cake's dough, eh, Japhet; art cheated o' thy dear vengeance, lad!

9. *Comb.* **a.** (senses 1, 2), as ***cake-basket, -bowl, -cutter, -maker, -making, -man, -mould, -plate, -stall, -stand***; **b.** (sense 4), as ***cake-colour, -copper, -ink, -lac, -soap***; **c.** adjs., as ***cake-bearing, -like***; **d. cake-eater** *U.S. slang*, a self-indulgent or effeminate man; a playboy; † **cake-fiddler, cake-fumbler**, a parasite; **cake-hole** *slang*, a person's mouth; **cake-meal**, 'linseed meal obtained by grinding the cake after the expression of the oil' (*Syd. Soc. Lex.*); **cake-mix**, the prepared ingredients of a cake sold ready for cooking; **cake-mixer** (see quot. *a* 1877); **cake-tin**, (*a*) a tin in which cakes are baked; (*b*) a tin in which cakes are stored; **cake-urchin**, a popular name for Echinoderms of a discoid shape. See also CAKE-BREAD, -HOUSE.

1805 in Mrs. E. S. Bowne *Life* (1888) 205, I plated *Cake Basket silver rims. **1956** G. TAYLOR *Silver* vii. 145 The many elaborately pierced cake-baskets. **1667** *Phil. Trans.* II. 510 As in all *Cake-bearing (called..*Placentifera*), and in all Kernel-bearing (called *Glandulifera*) or Ruminating Animals. **1874** MRS. WHITNEY *We Girls* ii. 43 A *cake-bowl in one hand, and an egg-beater in the other. **1806–7** J. BERESFORD *Miseries Hum. Life* (1826) III. xxxvi, Rubbing ..*cake colours in a very smooth saucer. **1859** GULLICK & TIMBS *Paint.* 294 The pigments are prepared..as dry cake colours, as moist colours in earthenware pans..and in metal collapsible tubes. **1803** HATCHETT *Phil. Trans.* XCIII. 90 *note*, The fine granulated copper is made in this country from the Swedish *cake-copper. **1881** RAYMOND *Mining Gloss., Cake-copper, Tough cake*, refined or commercial copper. **1845** E. ACTON *Mod. Cookery* xi. 261 *Croutons*.. stamped out..with a round or fluted paste or *cake cutter. **1922** *Daily Ardmoreite* (Ardmore, Okla.) 6 Jan. 10/4 He calls us 'lounge lizards, tea drinkers, *cake eaters and all that'. **1513** DOUGLAS *Æneis, Transl. to Rdr.* 75, I am na *cayk fydlar [**1553** *caik fumler], full weil ye knawe. **1943** HUNT & PRINGLE *Service Slang* 20 **Cake hole*, the airman's name for his or anyone else's mouth. **1959** I. & P. OPIE *Lore & Lang. Schoolchildren* x. 194 Shut your cake-hole. **1704** *Lond. Gaz.* No. 4022/4 The Universal *Cake-Ink. **1883** *Cassell's Fam. Mag.* Oct. 686/1 The sediment..is formed into small, square cakes..known as lac-dye, or *cake-lac. **1835** TODD *Cycl. Anat. & Phys.* I. 764/2 The *cake-like organ..which covers the ear. **1591** PERCIVALL *Sp. Dict., Turronero*, a *cakemaker, *pistor placentarius*. **1824** MISS MITFORD *Village* Ser. I. (1863) 221 The preservings, the picklings, the *cake-makings. **1832** *Ibid.* Ser. v. (1863) 410 We turned off our old stupid deaf *cakeman. [**1938** FIENE & BLUMENTHAL *Handbook Food Manuf.* 332 Sponge *cake mix.] **1950** *Canad. Home Jrnl.* Jan. 24 The cake-mix... The package which would yield the principal makings for a good cake. **1957** *Which?* I. 1. 15/1 Packaged cake-mixes are undoubtedly time-and-labour-saving. *a* **1877** KNIGHT *Dict. Mech.* I. 422/2 **Cake-mixer*, a device for incorporating together the ingredients of cake, etc. **1906** *Daily Colonist* (Victoria, B.C.) 1 Jan. 5/5 Come down to 80 Douglas street and get..a Cake Mixer (it whips cream, beats eggs and mixes cake). *c* **1865** *Circ. Sc.* I. 343/1 Inspissated juice.. poured into..*cake-moulds. **1867** A. D. T. WHITNEY *L. Goldthwaite* x, *Cake-plates were garnished with wreathed oak-leaves. **1607** TOPSELL *Four-f. Beasts* 305 Dissolve therein one ounce of *Cake-sope. **1877** A. B. EDWARDS *Up Nile* i. 5 The old Turk who sets up his *cake-stall in the sculptured recess of a Moorish doorway. **1851** J. J. HOOPER *Widow Rugby's Husb.* 106 Here he went..clearing an old woman and her *cake-stand at a jump. **1895** *Montgomery Ward Catal.* 533/3 China Fruit or Cake Stand..measure[s] 12 inches across and $5\frac{1}{2}$ inches high. **1903** A. BENNETT *Leonora* iii. 80 A cakestand in three storeys. **1953** G. GREENE *Living Room* I. i, A cake-stand with bread-and-butter on one level and a plum cake on another. **1963** *Times* 25 May 6/1 He described the 'cake stand' of ministerial hierarchy—chocolate biscuits on top, cream buns underneath, and buttered scones at the bottom. **1846** 'A LADY' *Jewish Manual Cookery* vii. 139 Put the apples into an oval *cake tin. **1906** E. NESBIT *Railway Children* ii. 24 In the pantry there was only a rusty cake-tin and a broken plate. **1965** 'T. HINDE' *Games of Chance* II. i. 155 I'd..been relieved to find in the cake-tin that yesterday's Swiss roll had only been reduced by three inches.

cake (keɪk), *v.* [f. prec. sb.]

1. *trans.* To form or harden into a cake or flattish compact mass: also *fig.* (Chiefly *passive*.)

1607 SHAKS. *Timon* II. ii. 225 Their blood is cak'd: 'tis cold, it sildome flowes. **1708** J. C. *Compl. Collier* (1845) 17 Turn it over after it is Caked, it will again burn brisk. **1719** DE FOE *Crusoe* I. (1840) 98 It [a Barrel of Gun-powder] had taken Water, and the Powder was cak'd as hard as a Stone. **1848–77** M. ARNOLD *Sohrab & R.* Poems (1877) I. 115 The big warm tears roll'd down, and caked the sand.

b. To encrust or cover thickly *with*. Usu. *pass.*

1922 W. CATHER *One of Ours* III. viii. 233 Claude came downstairs early and began to clean his boots, which were caked with dry mud. **1957** 'R. WEST' *Fountain Overflows* xv. 328 She held up to us some lengths of string, some of them joined by knots caked with red sealing-wax. **1966** D. BAGLEY *Wyatt's Hurricane* ix. 248 Wyatt looked at the others—they were caked with sticky mud from head to foot and he looked down at himself to find the same. **1977** P. L. FERMOR *Time of Gifts* iii. 56 With freezing cheeks and hair caked with snow, I clumped into an entrancing haven of oak beams and carving and alcoves and changing floor levels.

2. *intr.* (for *refl.*) To form (itself) into a cake or flattened mass. Const. *together*.

1615 H. CROOKE *Body of Man* 88 Lead as soone as it is taken off the fire..caketh together. **1622** MALYNES *Anc. Law-Merch.* 49 Coale..such as will not cake or knit in the burning. **1719** DE FOE *Crusoe* (1840) I. xii. 212 The powder ..caking and growing hard. **1814** SIR H. DAVY *Agric. Chem.* 183 The stiff clays..in dry weather..cake, and present only a small surface to the air.

3. *trans.* To feed (cattle, etc.) on cake (see CAKE *sb.* 4 c). Also *absol.*

1851 *Jrnl. R. Agric. Soc.* XII. II. 334 Many farmers cake their hogs on the turnips. **1889** E. PEACOCK *Gloss. Manley* (ed. 2) I. 626 *Cake*, to feed cattle with linseed or cotton cake. I alus *caake* my yohs e' winter as well as th' hogs. **1904** KIPLING *They* (1905) 71 You've sixty-seven [bullocks] and you don't cake.

'cake-bread. [f. CAKE *sb.* + BREAD.] Bread made in flattened cakes; or of the finer and more dainty quality of cake.

1377 LANGL. *P. Pl.* B. XVI. 229 þei eten Calues flesshe and cakebrede. **1479** *Office Mayor Bristol* in *E.E. Gilds* 418 To take cakebrede & wyne. **1544** in *Latimer's Wks.* (1844) II. 484 Then cake-bread and loaf-bread are all one with you. **1547** BOORDE *Brev. Health* ccvii. I refuse Cake bread, Saffron bread..Cracknelles, Symnelles, and all maner of crustes. **1562** J. HEYWOOD *Prov. & Epigr.* (1867) 166 Beyng shod with cakebred that spurner marth all. *a* **1613** OVERBURY *A Wife* (1638) 204 In friendly breaking Cake-bread with the Fish-wives at funerals. **1882** O'DONOVAN *Merv.* II. xlv. 262 Some brown cake-bread of the coarsest description had been broken.

b. *attrib.* Like cake, brittle.

1579 J. STUBBES *Gaping Gulf* E vij, The Spanish genet wil soone champ thys cakebread snaffle a sunder.

caked (keɪkt), *ppl. a.* [f. CAKE *v.* + -ED[1].] Formed into a cake, concreted; cake-shaped.

a **1691** BOYLE *Wks.* V. 72 (R.) A very shallow and wide-mouthed vessel, called in the shops a clear caked glass. *a* **1821** KEATS *Fancy* 246 The caked snow..From the plough-boy's heavy shoon. **1866** LIVINGSTONE *Jrnl.* xii. (1873) I. 325 When we had dug down to the caked sand.

'cake-house. [f. CAKE *sb.* + HOUSE *sb.*]

† **1.** A house where cakes are sold. *Obs.* or *dial.*

1666 PEPYS *Diary* (1879) III. 421 Thence took them to the cakehouse, and there called in the coach for cakes and drank. **1782** V. KNOX *Ess.* (1819) III. clxx. 243 The cake-house at Hoxton. **1815** SCOTT *Guy M.* xvi, On the other side of the lake..is a..cake-house.

2. A building where cakes of anything, e.g. indigo, are stored.

1878 J. INGLIS *Sport & W. Nepaul* iv. 34 The cake-house boys run to and fro between the cutting-table and the cake-house with batches of cakes [of indigo].

cakelet ('keɪklɪt). [f. CAKE *sb.* + -LET.] A small cake.

1839 URE *Dict. Arts* 458 These cakelets must be dried upon laths. **1908** M. & J. H. FINDLATER *Crossriggs* xix. 134

Bits of cake and stale cakelets. **1928** *Daily Express* 13 June 3/6 These elusive cakelets [*sc.* cookies] are evolved by mixing [etc.].

cake-walk (ˈkeɪkwɔːk), *sb.* orig. *U.S.* [f. CAKE *sb.* + WALK *sb.*]

1. a. 'A walking competition among negroes, in which the couple who put on most style "take the cake"' (Thornton). **b.** A dance modelled on this.

It originated among the Negroes of the southern United States.

1879 *Harper's Mag.* Oct. 799/1 Reader, didst ever attend a cake walk given by the colored folks? **1888** FARMER *Americanisms* s.v. *Cake*, In certain sections of the country, cake-walks are in vogue among the colored people. It is a walking contest, not in the matter of speed, but in style and elegance. **1897** *Blackw. Mag.* Mar. 341/2'Cake-walks' and frolics and preachings filled the cabins with sound and merriment. **1902** HARBEN *Abner Daniel* 53, I was doing the cake-walk with that fat Howard girl from Rome. **1947** *Penguin Music Mag.* May 25 Ragtime was most certainly responsible for Debussy's 'Golliwog's Cake Walk'.

attrib. **1898** F. H. SMITH *C. West* 314 A certain—to him —cake-walk cut to the coat and white duck trousers. **1901** *Westm. Gaz.* 3 June 3/1 Although there is a painful amount of cake-walk music. **1903** *Daily Chron.* 21 Apr. 7/3 The closing number in the bill will be a grand cake-walk promenade.

c. *transf.* and *fig.* In quots. 1916, 1966 = 'something easy'.

1863 H. EDGAR *Jrnl.* in *Montana Hist. Soc. Contrib.* (1900) III. 133 Around and around that bush we went... We had a good laugh over our cake walk. **1894** 'M. TWAIN' in *Critic* 7 July 8/1 This Shelley biography.. is a literary cake-walk. **1916** J. B. COOPER *Coo-oo-ee* xi. 153 Whether they would give him victory in a fight that would not be a cake-walk, he did not know. **1966** J. M. BRETT *Cargo of Spent Evil* x. 87 This should be a cakewalk for you.

2. A form of entertainment consisting of a promenade moved by machinery on which people walk to the accompaniment of music.

1909 *Oxford Times* 11 Sept. 9/5 In dealing with the fair itself there were really no new features.. except that of the Brooklyn cake-walk, an ingenious rocking platform which gave those who patronised it the sensation of a cake-walk dance... The novelty was in operation at the White City last year. **1914** *Ibid.* 12 Sept. 10/3 The absence of the popular joy-wheel, the cake-walk [etc.]. **1968** D. BRAITHWAITE *Fairground Archit.* p. ix, The boneshaking old Cake-walk changes its name to suit the fashion of the day, becoming at one time the Jolly Jersey Bounce and more recently the Rock an' Roll.

Hence **ˈcake-walk** *v. intr.*, to walk or dance in the manner of a cake-walk (sense 1); also *transf.* and *fig.* So **ˈcake-walker**; **ˈcake-walking** *vbl. sb.* and *ppl. a.*

1898 WILLIAMS & WALKER *Let.* 16 Jan. in J. W. Johnson *Black Manhattan* (1930) x. 105 We, the undersigned world-renowned cake-walkers.. hereby challenge you to compete with us in a cake-walking match. **1898** *Daily Tel.* 14 Mar., Cake-walking is, in fact, a graceful motion, conducted upon the toes and ball of the foot. **1898** *Westm. Gaz.* 3 Dec. 7/7 The cake walkers at Covent Garden. **1904** *Daily Chron.* 22 Mar. 4/7 The genuinely tip-top men Were those who never cake-walked. **1904** 'SAKI' *Reginald* 90 A mouse used to cake-walk about my room. **1905** *Westm. Gaz.* 17 Aug. 8/1 French singers, cake-walking coons, and fifth-rate English dancers. **1927** *Melody Maker* Sept. 931/2 The syndicate.. cake-walks to prosperity. **1958** BLESH & JANIS *They all played Ragtime* 3 Soon the French were cakewalking in the streets of Paris to *le temps du chiffon*. *Ibid.* v. 99 Cakewalking developed into a real art. **1967** V. NABOKOV *Speak, Memory* (ed. 2) xv. 309 Pale-blue and pink underwear cakewalking on a clothesline.

caking (ˈkeɪkɪŋ), *vbl. sb.* [f. CAKE *v.* + -ING[1].] The forming of a cake; chiefly gerundial.

1816 CLEVELAND *Min.* 403 It burns without caking.

ˈcaking, *ppl. a.* That cakes.

1810 HENRY *Elem. Chem.* (1840) II. 319 *Caking coal*.. because its fragments melt at a certain temperature, and unite into one mass. *c* **1865** LETHEBY in *Circ. Sc.* I. 117/1.

caky (ˈkeɪkɪ), *a.* [f. CAKE *sb.* + -Y[1].]

1. In the form, or of the nature, of a cake.

a **1556** CRANMER *Wks.* (1846) II. 66 An horse, refusing to eat wafers so long as their caky god was among them. **1604** HIERON *Wks.* I. 568 A priest.. ore his head the wafer shakes ..Meane while the vulgar in a maze Vpon the caky idoll gaze. **1813** J. THOMSON *Lect. Inflam.* 483 Hard caky substances. **1860** O. W. HOLMES *Elsie Venner* (1887) 90 Charlottes, caky externally, pulpy within. **1869** *London Soc.* Christm. No. 49/1 Warm smells of a cakey description.

2. *dial.* Weak of intellect, silly.

1879 *Shropsh. Word-bk.*

cal (kæl). Also callen, kal, (?) gal. The name given by Cornish miners to the native tungstate of iron and manganese.

1875 URE *Dict. Arts* III. 1039 The most common ore of this metal [Tungsten] is *wolfram*, known also to the Cornish miner as 'cal' or 'callen'. *Ibid.* There remains a quantity of this mineral substance (gal). **1880** MISS COURTNEY *W. Cornwall Gloss.*, Cal.

cal, obs. form of CALL and CAUL.

‖**calaba** (ˈkæləbə). [A South American name.] A tropical evergreen tree (*Calophyllum Calaba*) growing in Brazil and the West Indies, from the seeds of which a lamp-oil is obtained; it also yields **calaba-balsam**, or **-resin**.

1753 in CHAMBERS *Cycl. Suppl.* s.v. **1866** *Treas. Bot.* 201/1 This tree is called Calaba in the West Indies.

calabar, var. of CALABER; obs. f. CALIBRE.

Calabar-bean (kæləˈbɑː ˈbiːn). [From *Calabar*, on the Gulf of Guinea, in Africa.] The seed of *Physostigma venenosum*, a climbing leguminous plant, called also the Ordeal-bean, administered by the natives to persons suspected of witchcraft.

1876 HARLEY *Mat. Med.* 654.

Hence **calabarine**, 'an alkaloid found in the Calabar bean' (*Syd. Soc. Lex.*).

1875 H. WOOD *Therap.* (1879) 310.

calabash (ˈkæləbæʃ). Forms: 6 calabaza, 7 callebass, 7–8 calabass(e, cali-, callabash, (?) 7–9 calobosh, 8 calobash, callebasse, 8– calabash. [a. F. *calebasse, calabace*, Cotgr.) ad. Sp. *calabaça, calabaza* gourd, pumpkin = Cat. *carabassa*, mod.Pr. *carabasso, calebasso, carbasso*, Sicil. *caravazza*. The ultimate source was perh. the Persian *kharbuz*, or *kharbuza*, also *kharpuza*, and *kharbūza*, 'melon', generally 'marsh-melon', occasionally 'water-melon', whence Arabic *khirbiz* 'melon', and *kirbiz* 'pumpkin, gourd'; also Turk. *qārpūz*, Albanian and mod.Gr. *καρποῦζι, καρβοῦζι*; also through Tartar *kharpuz, karpus*, in Slavonic langs., Serb. *karpuza*, Pol. †*harbuz*, †*garbuz*, †*karbuz, arbuz*, Little Russ. *harbuz*, Russ. *arbuz* (Miklosich). The Pers. word is explained as f. *khar* large, coarse, and *buza, puza*, odoriferous fruit. The Sicilian form may be from Arabic; but actual evidence is wanting.]

1. A name given to various gourds or pumpkins, the shell of which is used for holding liquids, etc.

[**1596** RALEIGH *Disc. Guiana* (1887) 32 He also called for his calabaza or gourds of the gold beads. (Though explained as a 'gourd', this was probably the tree calabash, sense 2.)] **1658** EVELYN *Fr. Gard.* (1675) 44 Their fruit resembling a gourd or callebass. *a* **1813** A. WILSON *Foresters*, Clustering grapes were seen, With ponderous calabashes hung between. **1866** LIVINGSTONE *Jrnl.* vii. (1873) I. 181 The manured space is planted with pumpkins and calabashes.

2. The fruit of the calabash tree (see 7) of America, the shell of which is used for household utensils, water-bottles, kettles, musical instruments, etc.; it is round or oval, and so hard externally as even to be used in boiling liquids over a fire. Also short for *calabash-tree*.

1596 [see 1]. **1657** R. LIGON *Barbadoes* 14 High and loftie trees, as the.. Fistula, Calibash, Cherry. **1699** L. WAFER *Voy.* (1729) 321 The Calabash grows up and down among the boughs, as our apples do. **1750** G. HUGHES *Barbados* 116 The fruit called calabashes are of two sorts. **1828** W. IRVING *Columbus* I. 159 The calabashes of the Indians.. were produced on stately trees of the size of elms.

3. The hollow shell of either of the preceding, used as a vessel.

1657 R. LIGON *Barbadoes* 15 With either of them a naturall Pitcher, a Calibash upon their arme. **1681** R. KNOX *Hist. Ceylon* 162 Two Calabasses to fetch Water. **1699** DAMPIER *Voy.* II. II. 115 Their Furniture is but mean, viz. Earthern Pots to boil their Maiz in, and abundance of Callabashes. **1746** *Lond. Mag.* 323 Water presented.. in a copious Calabash. **1836** MACGILLIVRAY *Humboldt's Trav.* vi. 84 Baling out the water with a calabash. **1866** ENGEL *Nat. Mus.* viii. 285 A stringed instrument of the guitar kind, the body of which was a calabash.

b. This vessel full *of* anything.

1679 *A Paradox* (Harl. Misc. 1753) I. 258 They will not give you a Calabash of Milk for it. **1843** CARLYLE *Past & Pr.* (1858) 234 One small calabash of rice. **1875** LUBBOCK *Orig. Civiliz.* vi. 280 Calabashes of wine.

4. A similar vessel or utensil of other material.

1772–84 COOK *Voy.* (1790) IV. 1377 Calibashes made of reeds, so closely wrought as to be water-tight. **1851** H. MELVILLE *Whale* xix. 104 Nothing about the silver calabash he spat into.

5. sweet calabash, the edible fruit of *Passiflora maliformis*.

1840 *Penny Cycl.* XVII. 304/1 *P. maliformis* bears what is called the sweet calabash. **1866** *Treas. Bot.* 851.

6. 'A humorous name for the head' Bartlett *Dict. Amer.* [Cf. Pg. *cabaça* = *calabaça* with *cabeça* head.]

7. *attrib.* and *Comb.*, as *calabashful*; **calabash fruit** = sense 2; **calabash gourd**, the bottle-gourd (*Lagenaria vulgaris*) = sense 1; **calabash-nutmeg**, *Monodora Myristica*; **calabash-tree**, a tree (*Crescentia Cujete*) native to tropical America and the West Indies, bearing the large oval or globular fruit called calabash (sense 2); also a name of the baobab tree.

1707 SLOANE *Jamaica* I. p. xvi, Horses feed on *Calabash fruit in dry times. **1824** BURCHELL *Trav.* II. 587 The *calabash gourd is much cultivated for the sake of its shell. **1866** *Treas. Bot.* II. 752/1 Called.. *Calabash Nutmegs from the entire fruit resembling a small calabash. **1737** MILLER *Gard. Dict.* (ed. 3) The *Calabash-Tree.. grows to a considerable Height in the warmer Parts of America, where it produces a very large Fruit. **1796** STEDMAN *Surinam* II. xx. 115 The gourd or callebasse tree procures them cups. **1816** KEITH *Phys. Bot.* I. 50.

†**calabass.** *Obs.* A small kind of gun.

1578 BOURNE *Invent.* 87 Certaine smal Ordinance.. as Markets.. and some Calabasses that doo shoote small stones.

calabaza (kæləˈbɑːzə, -ˈbɑːsə). Chiefly *West Indies.* [a. Sp.: see CALABASH.] A pumpkin, *spec.* = CALABASH 2; its fruit or shell.

1596 [see CALABASH 1]. **1970** *Tropical Agric.* XLVII. 303 Demands by new Spanish ethnic communities for indigenous foods.. have emphasized the need for quality in Puerto-Rican grown produce such as.. calabaza. **1975** E. L. ORTIZ *Caribbean Cooking* 300 *Calabaza*. Known as West Indian or green pumpkin.. not to be confused with pie pumpkin... The yellow flesh has a delicate flavour and is used mainly in soups and as a vegetable. **1983** *Washington Post* 21 Dec. E15/1 In Haiti... They also prepare a soup called *giraumon* or *giromon* made from *calabaza*, a type of pumpkin. Giraumon is fed to early morning visitors in a salute to the New Year.

calaber, calabar (ˈkæləbə(r)). Forms: 4–6 calabre, 5 calabere, 6 calubur, calober, callabre, calabrye, calliber, calloper, 6–7 callaber, 7 caliber, 9 calabar, 6– calaber. [app. a. F. *Calabre*, Calabria, a province of Italy; but why so called is unknown.]

1. A kind of fur, apparently obtained from some foreign species of the squirrel; now, commercially, applied especially to the fur of the grey or Siberian Squirrel: also *attrib.* ***calaber pencil***: an artist's colour-brush made of the hairs of this fur.

1362 LANGL. *P. Pl.* A. VII. 257 His cloke of Calabre with knoppes of Gold. **1483** CAXTON *G. de la Tour* E ij, Gownes of moche fyn cloth and furred of calabre, letuce, and ermyn. **1532–3** *Act 24 Hen. VIII*, xiii, Any maner of furres, other then black cony, budge, grey cony, shankes, calaber, gray, fiche. **1556** *Chron. Gr. Friars* (1852) 59 The ij. day of June [1549].. alle the gray ammesse with the calober in Powlles ware put downe. **1555** EDEN *Decades W. Ind.* (Arb.) 291 The people of Moscouia.. haue ryche furres as Sabels, Marteines, Foynes, Calaber. **1583** PLAT *Diuerse Exper.* (1594) 14 With a fine calaber pensill first dipped in y[e] coppres water. **1588** *Gifts to Queen* in Nichols *Progr. Q. Eliz.*, Furred thorough with mynnyover and calloper. *a* **1603** FLEETWOOD *ibid.* I. 355 We sitting in all our calabrye clokes of murrey, did geve the newe shereffs.. theire othes. **1720** *Stow's Surv.* (ed. Strype 1754) II. v. viii. 255/1 Those Aldermen that have not been Mayors are to have their Cloaks furred with Calabre. **1832–52** M[c]CULLOCH *Dict. Comm.*, *Calabar Skin*, the Siberian squirrel skin. **1875** URE *Dict. Arts* II. 516 Furs, Skins, and Pelts imported.. 1870.. Squirrel or Calabar 150, 668.

†**2.** The animal itself. *Obs.*

1607 COWELL *Interpr.* s.v. *Furre*, Calaber is a little beast, in bigness about the quantitie of a squirell, of colour gray. *a* **1626** MIDDLETON *Love & Antiq.* Wks. V. 289 Beasts bearing fur.. Lamb.. wolverin, caliber. **1721** in BAILEY.

calaber, obs. f. CALIBRE.

calaboose (kæləˈbuːz). *U.S.* [Negro French (of Louisiana) *calabouse*, ad. Sp. *calabozo* dungeon.] The name, in New Orleans and adjacent parts of the U.S., for a common prison.

1837–40 HALIBURTON *S. Slick, Hum. Nature* (Bartlett) A large calaboose chock full of prisoners. **1850** MRS. STOWE *Uncle Tom's C.* xv. 148 Send them to the calaboose, or some of the other places, to be flogged. **1883** *Century Mag.* Mar. 649/2 The terrors of the calaboza, with its chains and whips and branding irons, were condensed into the French tri-syllabic Calaboose.

Calabrese (kæləˈbreɪseɪ, -iːz). [It., = Calabrian.] A variety of sprouting broccoli.

1930 L. H. & F. Z. BAILEY *Hortus* 130 The Asparagus or Sprouting broccoli, *Calabrese*, is a different plant. **1939** *Times* 11 Jan. 15/4 Calabrese.. is one of the most quickly grown and delicately flavoured of all greens. **1957** E. HYAMS *Speaking Garden* 58 *Calabrese*, perhaps the most delicious of all cabbages.

Calabrian (kəˈleɪbrɪən), *a.* and *sb.* [f. *Calabria* (see below) + -AN.] **A.** *adj.* Of or pertaining to Calabria, a region of Italy (anciently the south-eastern, now the south-western, projection of the Italian peninsula). **B.** *sb.* A native or inhabitant of Calabria (see also quot. 1905).

1594 KYD *Cornelia* v. 239 As in the faire Calabrian fields. **1607** TOPSELL *Four-f. Beasts* 599 The Calabrian, Milesian, and Arentinean sheepe. **1615** SANDYS *Travels* IV. 250 There are not that professe Christ, a more vnciuill people then the vulgar Calabrians. *Ibid.*, A certaine Calabrian hearing that I was an Englishman, came to me. **1783** H. MORE *Let.* (1925) 88 The miseries which have visited the devoted Calabrians. *a* **1821** KEATS *Otho* (1848) v. v, What wine? The strong Iberian juice, or mellow Greek? Or pale Calabrian? **1833** [see *en règle*, s.v. EN *prep.*]. **1905** A. HOPWOOD *Old Eng. Sheep Dog* i. 1 The mighty Calabrian, or sheep dog of the Pyrenees,.. stands over thirty inches high. **1924** tr. *Pastor's Hist. Popes* XIII. viii. 223 A Calabrian, 33 years of age, was sent.. to the Jesuits. **1963** *Times* 22 Feb. 6/4 These people are Calabrian peasants.

Calaburne, variant of CALIBURN.

‖**ˈCalabur tree.** Name given in the West Indies to *Muntingia Calabura* (N.O. *Tiliaceæ*), the Silk-wood tree.

‖**calade** (kaˈlad, kəˈleɪd). [a. F. *calade* in same sense, ad. It. *calata* descent, f. *calare*:—L. *chalāre*, ad. Gr. *χαλᾶ-ν* to let down, let fall.] The

slope of a manège ground, down which a horse is ridden at speed, to teach him to ply his haunches.

1731 in BAILEY vol. II. **1792** OSBALDISTONE *Brit. Sportsm.* 87/1. [In mod. Dicts.]

‖**caladium** (kəˈleɪdɪəm). *Bot.* Also 9 calladium. [mod.L. adaptation, by Rumph, 1750, in *Herb. Amboinense* V. 318, of the Malay name *kélādy* (Forbes Watson) of *Caladium* (now *Colocasia*) *esculentum*. The genus in its present botanical acceptation was established by Ventenat in 1800, when, by a carelessness too frequent in botanical nomenclature, the actual species to which the name *kélādy* belonged, was excluded from the *Caladiums* and made a *Colocasia*.]

A genus of plants belonging to the Arum family, grown in this country as hot-house plants, but cultivated in their native regions for their underground corms, which contain much starch.

1845 *Penny Cycl. Suppl.* I. 264/1 *Caladium arborescens*.. yields a great quantity of starch. **1858** HOGG *Veg. Kingd.* 797. **1881** MRS. PRAED *Policy & Passion* I. 270 The verandah was adorned with stands of choice ferns and calladiums. **1882** *Garden* 4 Mar. 145/3 Caladiums.. will now be starting rapidly into growth. **1885** LADY BRASSEY in *Trades* 70 Caladiums and ferns growing in the wildest profusion.

†**caladrie.** *Obs. rare.* Wyclif's adaptation of the *Charadrius* of the Vulgate, Χαραδριός of the Septuagint. The latter was, 'according to Sundevall, the stone-curlew or thick-kneed bustard, *Charadrius Œdicnemus*' (Liddell and Scott). *Caladrius* occurs also in later writers (quoting from Aristotle) as some reputed white bird.

1388 WYCLIF *Deut.* xiv. 18 Ete ȝe not vncleene briddis.. a cormeraunt, and a caladrie [**1382** jay; **1611** the Storke and the Heron]. **1567** MAPLET *Gr. Forest* 76 The Caladrius, sayth Aristotle, is of milkie colour, without any black spot. **1601** CHESTER *Love's Mart.* clviii. (1878) 117 The snow-like colour'd bird, Caladrius.

‖**calaˈlu.** Also calaloo, -loe, caleloe, callalloo, -aloo, -alou, cullaloo. A West Indian name for various plants cultivated as culinary vegetables; also, a soup or stew made with them.

1756 P. BROWNE *Jamaica* 174 The branched Caleloe [*Solanum nodiflorum*].. The negroes make use of it every day almost in the year. *Ibid.* 232 Spanish Calaloe [*Phytolacca octandra*]. *Ibid.* 340 The prickly Calaloo [*Amarantus spinosus*].. used as a green, when the more valuable sorts are scarce. **1810** F. CUMING *Tour Western Country* 297 Mr. Green made me observe.. the cullaloo or Indian Kail [near Natchez, Mississippi]. **1884** MILLER *Plant-n.*, *Calalu.* **1892** J. C. HARRIS *On Plantation* 122 There was Callalou—a mixture of collards, poke salad, and turnip greens boiled for dinner and fried over for supper. **1929** W. J. LOCKE *Ancestor Jorico* viii. 107 We were given.. callaloo, which is an apotheosis of the American Okra soup. **1953** G. LAMMING *In Castle of my Skin* xiv. 273 A vegetable muddle called callalloo cooked with crab. **1969** *Daily Tel.* 11 Jan. 14/1 Calalu (sometimes spelt 'callaloo'), a green vegetable like spinach, makes wonderful soup—to bring tears to ex-patriate Jamaican eyes just mention calalu.

calamanco (kæləˈmæŋkəʊ). Forms: 6 calamance, 6–9 cali-, 7 calla-, 7–9 callimanco, (9 calamanca), 7– calamanco. [Found also in Du. *kalamink*, *kalmink*, Ger. *kalmank*, *kalmang*, F. *calmande*, Genev. *calamandre*: of unknown origin.

The form has naturally suggested connexion with med.L. *camelaucus*, a kind of cap, and a cloth of camel's hair; but evidence of connexion is wanting. See Du Cange.]

1. A woollen stuff of Flanders, glossy on the surface, and woven with a satin twill and chequered in the warp, so that the checks are seen on one side only; much used in the 18th c.

1592 LYLY *Midas* [see 2]. **1598** FLORIO, *Tesserino*.. a kinde of fine stuffe like.. calimanco. **1693** *Lond. Gaz.* No. 2832/3 His Wastcoat of a Striped Calamanco. **1760** STERNE *Tr. Shandy* (1802) VII. xvii. 32 A tawny yellow jerkin, turned up with red calamanco! **1848** THACKERAY *Bk. Snobs* iv, The body.. trimmed with calimanco.

b. *attrib.*

1605 *Lond. Prodigal* I. i. 223 What breeches wore I o' Saturday? Let me see: o' Tuesday my calamanco.. o' Thursday, my velure; o' Friday my calamanco again. **1639** FORD *Lady's Tr.* II. i, Diamond-button'd callamanco hose. **1710** STEELE *Tatler* No. 96 ⁋5 A Red Coat, flung open to show a gay Calamanco Wastcoat. **1812** H. & J. SMITH *Rej. Addr.* (1852) 41 A pair of black calamanco breeches. **1840** WHEELER *Westmoreland Dial.* Gloss, A calliminky petticoat.

c. *ellipt.* Garments of this material.

1859 THACKERAY *Virgin.* xxxii, The girls went off straightway to get their best calamancoes, paduasoys.. capes, etc. *a***1888** *U.S. Newspr.* The seat of his striped calimancoes.

2. *fig.* Applied to: **a.** language; **b.** a person.

1592 LYLY *Midas* IV. iii, Doest thou not understand their [huntsmen's] language? *Min.* Not I! *Pet.* Tis the best calamance in the world, as easily deciphered as the characters in a nutmeg. **1607** DEKKER & WEBSTER *Sir T. Wyat* 45 A Spaniard is a Camocho, a Calimanco.

3. Applied to wood and plaster buildings.

1792 *Misc. Ess.* in *Ann. Reg.* 150/2 The mansion.. was of plaister striped with timber, not unaptly called callimanco work. **1822** W. IRVING *Braceb. Hall* (1855) 267 *Calimanco* houses as they are called by antiquaries.

calamander (kæləˈmændə(r)). Also calaminder, (? calaminda). [Of uncertain origin: see quot. 1859. Clough *Singhalese Dict.* gives *kalumadīriya* as the Singhalese name; which Forbes Watson cites also as *calumidiriya*, *kalumederiye*, etc., but these may be adaptations of the Dutch.]

A beautiful and extremely hard cabinet wood of Ceylon and India, the product of *Diospyros quæsita* (N.O. *Ebenaceæ*), specifically akin to ebony.

1804 R. PERCIVAL *Ceylon* in *Ann. Rev.* II. 47/2 The banyan, the cotton-tree, the tickwood, and the beautiful calamander.. are indigenous here. **1828** HEBER *Journ. Upper India* (1844) II. 161 (Y.) The Calamander tree.. is become scarce from the improvident use formerly made of it. **1833** HT. MARTINEAU *Cinnamon & P.* v. 79 The finely-veined calaminda. **1859** TENNENT *Ceylon* I. I. iii. 118, I apprehend that the name Calamander, which was used by the Dutch, is but a corruption of Coromandel.

calamary (ˈkæləmərɪ). Also 6–7 calamarie, 9 calamer, calamury. [f. L. *calamāri-us* pertaining to a calamus or pen; in Sp. *calamar*, F. *calmar*. From the pen-like internal shell (and perhaps also having reference to the 'ink' or black fluid, which these animals squirt out).]

The general name for Cephalopods or Cuttle-fish of the family *Teuthidæ*, more especially of the genus *Loligo*, cuttle-fishes having a long narrow body flanked by two triangular fins, and with the internal shell 'a horny flexible pen': e.g. the Common Calamary, Squid, or Pen-fish.

1567 MAPLET *Gr. Forest* 75 Calamarie.. is like the Cuttle, but that she is a little longer. **1635** SWAN *Spec. M.* (1670) 342 The Calamary is sometimes called the Sea-clerke, having as it were a knife and a pen. Some call him the Ink-horn-fish. **1758** *Phil. Trans.* L. 778 The body of the.. Calamary is a sort of cartilaginous case.. of a roundish oblong shape. **1848** CARPENTER *Anim. Phys.* 101 The body.. furnished with a fin-like expansion behind, as in the calamary. **1854** WOODWARD *Mollusca* iii. 11 The calamary can even strike the surface of the sea with its tail.

‖**calambac** (ˈkæləmbæk). Also 7 callamback, calembuc, 7–8 calamba, 8 -bo, 8–9 -beg, 9 -bao. [*Kalambak* is given by Crawfurd and Forbes-Watson as Malay and Javanese: Col. Yule thinks 'it perh. came with the article from Champa' in Anam. The other forms are corruptions or adaptations in Portuguese and other European langs.: French has *calambac*, *-bart*, *-bouc*, *-bou*, *bour*.]

An eastern name of Aloes-wood or Eagle-wood, produced by *Aquilaria Agallocha*, Roxb. (See AGALLOCH.)

(So all recent authorities on Indian Botany. *Aloexylum*, regarded as the source by earlier authors, is now given up.)

[**1552** *Barros' Decades d'Asia* I. ix. 1 (transl. Yule) Campa, in the mountains of which grows the genuine aloes-wood, which the Moors of those parts call Calambuc.] **1594** *Merry Knack* in Hazl. *Dodsley* VI. 571 Then will I have.. Calambac and Cassia. **1667** H. OLDENBURG in *Phil. Trans.* II. 417 Where the best Calamba-wood, or Palo d'Aquila, grows. **1690** *Songs Costume* (1849) 189 Calembuc combs in pulvil case. **1751** CHAMBERS *Cycl.* s.v. *Aloes*, The calambo.. is brought in small bits of a very fragrant scent. **1871** E. BALFOUR *Cycl. India*, *Calambac*, *Calambao*, *Calambeg*, also called Aloes wood is the Agallochum of the ancients and the Agilla or Eaglewood of the moderns. It is produced in Siam and Silhet by *Aquilaria Agallocha*. **1885** G. WATT *Dict. Econ. Prod. India* s.v., In the interior of old trees we found irregular masses of harder and darker coloured wood, which constitutes the famous Eagle-wood.. called.. also Calambac, Agallochum, Aloe or Aloes Wood.

‖**calamˈbour.** In 7 callembour. One of the Fr. forms of prec. [See Littré.]

Said in modern English Dictionaries to be 'A species of Agallochum or aloes-wood, less fragrant than calambac, used by cabinet-makers': but this appears to be merely an error copied from dictionary to dictionary.

1685 *Lond. Gaz.* No. 2011/8 A little Callembour Box. **1847** CRAIG, *Calambac*, Aloes-wood. *Calambour*, the name given to a species of aloes-wood. [In WEBSTER, OGILVIE, CASSELL.]

calamel, obs. form of CALOMEL.

calament, obs. form of CALAMINT.

calamer, variant of CALAMARY.

calamiferous (kæləˈmɪfərəs), *a. Bot.* [f. CALAM-US + -FEROUS.] †**a.** Producing culms, culmiferous (*obs.*). **b.** Bearing reeds, reedy.

1753 CHAMBERS *Cycl. Suppl.*, *Calamiferous*, a denomination given by some to those otherwise called culmiferous plants. **1847** in CRAIG; and later Dicts.

ˈcalamiform, *a.* [f. as prec. + -FORM; cf. F. *calamiforme*.] Of the shape of a calamus, reed, or feather.

1881 in *Syd. Soc. Lex.*

‖**calamiˈnaris**, *a.* and *sb.* [L.: in full *lapis calamināris* 'calamine stone', f. med.L. *calamīna*: see CALAMINE.] Earlier name of CALAMINE.

1577 HARRISON *England* III. xii. (1878) 79 Those other which we call calaminares and speculares. **1585** LLOYD *Treas. Health* S vij, Take.. of the stones called Lazulus and Calaminaris. **1750** tr. *Leonardus' Mirr. Stones* 93 *Calaminaris*, is a Stone, yellow, tender, not lucid, nor transparent. **1750** BEAWES *Lex. Mercat.* (1752) 582 Somersetshire Produce.. Copper, Lapis Calaminaris, Crystal.

†**caˈlaminary, -ar**, *a. Obs.* Adapted forms of preceding.

1662 FULLER *Worthies* III. 17 The Calaminary-stone being of it self not worth above six pence in the pound. **1799** G. SMITH *Laborat.* II. 446 Prepare and calcine.. some small bits of calaminary stone. **1860** MAYNE *Exp. Lex.*, *Calaminaris*.. of or belonging to calamine.. calaminar.

calaminary, mistaken form of CALAMARY.

1620 VENNER *Via Recta* iv. 76 The Calaminary, the Cuttle-fish.. are euen of one and the same nature.

calaminda, -der, obs. ff. CALAMANDER.

calamine (ˈkæləmaɪn). [a. F. *calamine*, ad. med.L. *calamīna*, app. (like the Ger. *galmei*, formerly *kalmei*:—*calmia*) corrupted by the alchemists from L. *cadmīa*, Gr. καδμεία, καδμία, 'calamine'.

Agricola supposed the name to be from *calamus* reed, in allusion to the slender stalactitic forms common in the *cadmia fornacum* (oxide of zinc from furnace chimneys).]

An ore of zinc: originally applied, like med.L. *lapis calaminaris*, and the *cadmia* of Pliny, to both the carbonate $ZnCO_3$, and the hydrous silicate Zn_2SiO_4, H_2O but chiefly, in France and England, to the former, which is an abundant and important English ore of zinc. The silicate, found in Carinthia, Hungary, Belgium, New Jersey, etc., is distinguished as ***siliceous*** or ***electric calamine***.

The chemical difference between the two ores was established by Smithson in 1802; in 1807 Brongniart unfortunately chose *calamine* as the mineralogical name of the silicate, leaving the other ore as *zinc carbonatée*, which Beudant in 1832 named SMITHSONITE. This nomenclature is followed by Dana. But common English and French use (see Littré) continued to apply the name *calamine* to the carbonate; and in conformity with this Brooke and Miller in 1852 reversed Beudant's use of *calamine* and *smithsonite*. With British mineralogists, chemists, miners, and manufacturers, *calamine* therefore means the carbonate.

1601 HOLLAND *Pliny* II. 520 Some think it better to wipe.. the dust from the Calamine with wings. **1683** PETTUS *Fleta Min.* II. 18 Having here [in England] both the best Copper and Calamine of any part of Europe. **1794** SULLIVAN *View Nat.* I. 470 Zinc in the state of calamine. **1799** G. SMITH *Laborat.* I. 243 Calamine is dug in mines about Mendip, etc. in the West of England. **1802** SMITHSON in *Phil. Trans.* XCIII. 16 This calamine hence consists of—Carbonic acid, 0.352; Calx of zinc, 0.648. **1812** SIR H. DAVY *Chem. Philos.* 373 Calamine, which is a combination of zinc with oxygene and carbonic acid. **1839** URE *Dict. Arts* s.v. *Zinc*, The principal ores of zinc are the sulphuret called blende, the silicate called calamine, and the sparry calamine, or the carbonate. **1869** ROSCOE *Elem. Chem.* 231 Zinc Carbonate, an insoluble substance, occurring native as calamine. **1875** URE *Dict. Arts* III. 1187 Calamine is a mineral occurring usually in concretionary forms and compact masses, yellowish-white when pure.. it is a normal carbonate of zinc.. Calamine is worked in a rich mine of galena at Holywell.. The second locality of calamine is in the magnesian limestone formation. **1877** WATTS *Dict. Chem.* V. 1067 Zinc occurs as carbonate, forming the ore called calamine; as silicate or siliceous calamine; as sulphide or blende.

b. *attrib.*, as in **calamine stone** = *lapis calaminaris* (see CALAMINARIS).

1601 HOLLAND *Pliny* II. 486 Brasse.. Made.. of the Chalamine stone, named otherwise Cadmia. **1761** HUME *Hist. Eng.* II. xliv. 501 Oil, calaminestone, glasses.. had been appropriated to monopolists. **1802** SMITHSON in *Phil. Trans.* XCIII. 17 The smallness of these calamine crystals.

calamint (ˈkæləmɪnt). Forms: 4–7 calament, 5–6 calamynt(e, 6 -menthe, 7 calaminth, 8 calemint, 6– calamint. [ME. *calament*, a. F. *calament* (14th c. in Littré), med.L. *calamentum*, ad. L. *calaminthe*, a. Gr. καλαμίνθη, κάλάμινθος, applied to the same or some similar plant. The Gr. is explained from καλός beautiful + μίνθη, μίνθος mint: but this is perh. only popular etymology. The Eng. word was subsequently assimilated to the L. form, and to *mint*.]

A genus of aromatic herbs, *Calamintha* (N.O. *Labiatæ*), including the Common Calamint (*C. officinalis*), formerly in repute for its medicinal virtues, Lesser Calamint (*C. Nepeta*), Wood Calamint (*C. sylvatica*), and several other species.

[*c* **1265** *Gloss.* in Wr.-Wülcker 557 *Calamentum*, (Anglo-Fr.) calemente.] **1322** *Wardrobe Acc. 16 Edw. II*, 23 Calament 4*d* per lb. **1398** TREVISA *Barth. De P.R.* XVII. xxxiv. (1495) 623 Calament is an herbe like Mynte. *c* **1440** *Promp. Parv.* 58 Calamynt, herbe, *calamenta*, *balsamita*. **1551** TURNER *Herbal* I. (1568) 81 Calamynt.. is good for them that ar byten of serpentes. **1579** LANGHAM *Gard. Health* (1633) 112 Calament drunke three dayes, helpeth the Jaundies. **1596** SPENSER *F.Q.* III. ii. 49 But th' aged nourse.. Had gathered rew.. and calamint. **1625** B. JONSON *Pan's Anniv.* 25 Blue hare-bells, pagles, pansies, calaminth. **1688** R. HOLME *Armoury* II. 108/1 Calamint is purplish, and of a blush colour. **1835** HOOKER *Brit. Flora* 248.

†'**calamist**. *Obs.*⁻⁰ [f. L. *calam-us* reed + -IST.]

1. 'One who plays upon a reed, a piper.'
1656 in BLOUNT *Glossogr.* 1678 in PHILLIPS.

2. 'One hauing his haire turning vpwards.' (Cf. next.)
1623 in COCKERAM.

†**cala'mistrate**, *v. Obs. rare.* [f. L. *calamistrāt-us* crisped, curled, f. *calamistrum* curling-iron; cf. F. *calamistrer.*] *trans.* To curl, crisp, frizzle (the hair). Hence ˌ**calami'stration**.
1621 BURTON *Anat. Mel.* III. ii. II. ii. 469 Which belike makes.. great women to calamistrate and curl it up. *Ibid.* III. ii. II. iii, When those.. calamistrations, ointments, etc. shall be added, they will make the veriest dowdy otherwise, a goddess.

calamistrum (kælə'mɪstrəm). Pl. **-a**. [L., curling-iron.] A comb-like structure on the metatarsi of the fourth pair of legs of certain spiders, used to card and curl the silk as it issues from the spinnerets.
1866 E. F. STAVELEY *Brit. Spiders* 14 These [spines] are called calamistra, and are used in the construction of the web. 1875 *Encycl. Brit.* II. 292 The function of the calamistrum has been proved.. to be the carding, or teasing and curling, of a peculiar kind of silk, secreted and emitted from the fourth pair of spinners. 1958 W. S. BRISTOWE *World of Spiders* viii. 79 Three families of British spiders have a cribellum and a calamistrum.

calamite ('kæləmaɪt). [ad. mod.L. generic name *calamītes*, f. L. *calamus* reed; see -ITE.]

1. *Palæont.* A fossil plant, of a genus or order abundant in the Coal Measures, of which the stems are found in jointed fragments, ribbed and furrowed. They are generally considered to have been allied to the existing *Equisetaceæ* or Mare's-tails, but their stem was furnished with wood and bark.
1837 *Penny Cycl.* VII. 293/2 Calamites have been found with a diameter of fourteen inches. 1842 H. MILLER *O.R. Sandst.* vii. (ed. 2) 175 Some plant resembling a calamite of the Coal Measures. 1873 DAWSON *Earth & Man* v. 104 Calamites, gigantic and overgrown mares'-tails.

2. *Min.* A variety of tremolite (white hornblende) occurring in crystals sometimes reed-like.
1882 WATTS *Dict. Chem.* III. 169 *Calamite* is an asparagus-green variety of tremolite, found.. in Sweden.

†3. 'A name given by some to the osteocolla.. others have called some of the fossile coralloides by this name.' *Obs.*
1753 CHAMBERS *Cycl. Supp.*

calamitean (kælə'maɪtiːən), *a.* [f. CALAMITE 1 + -AN.] Belonging or relating to calamites.
1895 *Naturalist* Aug. 237 The histology of calamitean leaves. 1904 *Amer. Nat.* Apr. 250 Thus such transitions are well known, though of a relatively simplified form in the structure of the calamitean stem.

calamitous (kə'læmɪtəs), *a.* [ad. F. *calamiteux, -eus* (16th c. in Littré) ad. L. *calamitōsus*, contr. of *calamitāt-ōsus* adj., from *calamitāt-em* CALAMITY. (The contracted termination has supplied an analogy for several similar formations in French and Eng.: see -ITOUS, -OUS.)]

1. Fraught with or causing calamity; disastrous, distressful; full of distress, affliction, or misery.
1545 JOYE *Exp. Dan.* vii. (R.) Here is to be noted another heuey thretening which precheth the calamitous afflictions of yᵉ chirche. 1646 SIR T. BROWNE *Pseud. Ep.* 13 That calamitous error of the Jewes, misapprehending the Prophesies of their Messias. 1727 DE FOE *Eng. Tradesm.* vii. (1841) I. 45 In former times, it was a dismal and calamitous thing for a tradesman to break. 1772-84 COOK *Voy.* (1790) VI. 1949 The late calamitous accident. 1839 THIRLWALL *Greece* III. 189 Contests, in which victory would be unprofitable, defeat calamitous.

†2. Of persons: Involved in calamity, distress, or affliction; distressed, unfortunate, miserable. *Obs.*
1668 *Act Prevent. & Suppress. Fires in Lond.* 2 Fire.. rendring very many of the Inhabitants calamitous. 1726 AYLIFFE *Parerg.* 313 The Tears and Prayers of calamitous Persons. 1752 JOHNSON *Rambl.* No. 190 ¶6 Thou hast seen me happy and calamitous.

calamitously (kə'læmɪtəslɪ), *adv.* [f. prec. + -LY².] In a calamitous manner; disastrously.
1794 LD. AUCKLAND *Corr.* (1862) III. 232 Every subject in which he has borne a part.. has ended calamitously. 1896 *Home Missionary* (N.Y.) July 145 Churches.. brought suddenly and calamitously into missionary conditions.

ca'lamitousness. *rare.* [f. as prec. + -NESS.] Calamitous condition or quality.
1667 H. MORE *Div. Dial.* II. ix. (1713) 114 The Calamitousness of this Scene of things. 1852 SMITH *Eng. & Fr. Dict.* Calamitousness.. *affreuse misère.*

calamity (kə'læmɪtɪ). Also 5-6 **calamyte**, 6-7 **calamitie**. [a. F. *calamité*, f. L. *calamitāt-em* (nom. *calamitas*), damage, disaster, adversity; by Latin writers associated with *calamus* straw, corn-stalk, etc., in the sense of damage to crops from hail, mildew, etc. But there is difficulty in reconciling this with the force of the suffix, which etymologically could give only some such sense as 'the quality of being a *calamus*, reed, or straw' (cf. *cīvitas, auctoritas, bonitas*); hence some would refer it to a lost **calamis* 'injured, damaged', whence *incolumis* 'uninjured, sound'.
Bacon (*Sylva* §669) thus fancifully etymologized the word 'Another ill accident is drouth, at the spindling of the corn, which with us is rare, but in hotter countries common; insomuch as the word *calamitas* was first derived from *calamus*, when the corn could not get out of the stalke.']

1. The state or condition of grievous affliction or adversity; deep distress, trouble, or misery, arising from some adverse circumstance or event.
1490 CAXTON *Eneydos* xxii. 80 He was restored.. from anguisshe and calamyte in to right grete prosperite. c1529 WOLSEY in Ellis *Orig. Lett.* I. 103 II. 6, I shalbe releuyd and in this my calamyte holpyn. 1555 EDEN *Decades W. Ind.* II. I. (Arb.) 109 They fell from one calamitie into an other. 1592 SHAKS. *Rom. & Jul.* III. iii. 3 Thou art wedded to calamitie. 1623 COCKERAM, *Calamity*, misery. 1752 JOHNSON *Rambl.* No. 203 ¶3 So full is the world of calamity, that every source of pleasure is polluted. 1754 RICHARDSON *Grandison* III. xxx. 352, I am in calamity, my dear. I would love you if you were in calamity. 1841-44 EMERSON *Ess.*, *Compensation* Wks. (Bohn) I. 54 Yet the compensations of calamity are made apparent to the understanding also, after long intervals of time.

2. A grievous disaster, an event or circumstance causing loss or misery; a distressing misfortune.
1552 ABP. HAMILTON *Catech.* (1884) 32 Thair is na calamitie.. that may chance to man or woman. 1586 COGAN *Haven Health* lxxv. (1636) 81 A griefe of the head, proceeding of a rheume, which is a common calamity of Students. 1671 MILTON *Samson* 655 The bearing well of all calamities. 1683 BURNET tr. *More's Utopia* 143 Because of any great Calamity that may have fallen on their Person. 1748 JOHNSON *L.P.* Wks. 1816 X. 325 It was not his custom to look out for distant calamities. 1871 MORLEY *Voltaire* (1886) 60 Voltaire saw his [Newton's] death mourned as a public calamity.

3. *attrib.* and *Comb.*, as ***calamity-howler, -howling, -prophet, -shouting*** (U.S. colloq.); **Calamity Jane**, the nickname of Martha Jane Burke (*née* Canary) (? 1852-1903), a famous American horse-rider and markswoman, applied to a prophet of disaster.
1892 *Congress. Rec.* 2 Mar. 1654/1 We had some 'calamity howlers' here in Washington. 1905 D. G. PHILLIPS *Plum Tree* 264, I.. sent Woodruff East to direct a campaign of calamity-howling in the eastern press. 1876 *Cheyenne* (Wyoming) *Daily Leader* 23 Nov. in N. Mumey *Calamity Jane* (1950) 55 Calamity Jane.. now slingeth hash as a waiter in a Custer City Hotel. 1882 *Street & Smith's New York Weekly* 16 Jan. 1 Calamity Jane, the Queen of the Plains. A Tale of Daring Deeds by a Brave Woman's Hands. 1885 E. L. WHEELER (*title*) Deadwood Dick on deck; or, Calamity Jane the heroine of Whoop-up. 1930 *N. & Q.* 27 Sept. 232/1 A crepe-hanger is the ultimate in depressing persons; 'wet-blankets', 'gloomy Gus's', 'calamity Janes', are all a degree milder. 1960 *TV Times* 8 Jan. 11/1 I'm a real Calamity Jane. 1894 *Republican Campaign Text-bk. for 1894* 229 This is going to be a bad, sad year for the calamity prophets of both parties. 1911 J. C. LINCOLN *Cap'n Warren's Wards* i. 3 The pair of calamity prophets broke off their lament. 1892 *Congress. Rec.* 17 Mar. 2160/2 Calamity-shouters whose occupation is gone unless they can prove that calamity stalks abroad.

†'**calamize**, *v. Obs.*⁻⁰ [ad. Gr. καλαμίζειν to pipe on a reed, f. κάλαμος reed: see CALAMUS.] *intr.* To pipe or sing.
1656 in BLOUNT *Glossogr.*

‖ˌ**calamo'dendron**. *Palæont.* [f. Gr. κάλαμος reed + δένδρον tree.] A supposed genus of fossil trees; the fruits are found along with calamites, and are supposed by many to belong to them.
1873 DAWSON *Earth & Man* vi. 131 The.. Calamodendron or Reed-tree.. had stems with thick woody walls.

calamury, variant of CALAMARY.

‖**calamus** ('kæləməs). Also 6 **kalmus, calmus**. [a. L. *calamus*, Gr. κάλαμος reed.]

†1. A reed, a cane: vaguely used by early writers, after Latin or Greek authors. *Obs.*
1398 TREVISA *Barth. De P.R.* XVII. xxix. (1495) 622 Calamus is holowe wythin as a cane. *Ibid.* xxx. 622 Strawe is called *Calamus vsualis.* 1597 GERARD *Herbal* I. xlv. 63 Bastard or false Calamus grows naturally at the foot of a hill. 1601 HOLLAND *Pliny* I. 375 The shorter and thicker that the reed is, the better is the Calamus. 1712 tr. *Pomet's Hist. Drugs* I. 53 The true or bitter Calamus is a Kind of Reed.

2. **sweet calamus**, *C. aromaticus*: **a.** some eastern aromatic plant or plants (supposed by some to be *Andropogon Schœnanthus*, the Sweet-scented Lemon Grass of Malabar); **b.** applied by some English herbalists to the native Sweet Flag or Sweet Rush (*Acorus Calamus*).
1388 WYCLIF *Ezek.* xxvii. 19 Dan, and Greece, and Mosel, settiden forth in thi fairis.. calamus. 1398 TREVISA *Barth. De P.R.* XV. lxxiii. (1495) 515 Calamum smellyth full swete of yuory. 1535 COVERDALE *Jer.* vi. 20 Wherfore bringe ye me.. swete smellinge Calamus from farre countrees? 1611 BIBLE *Ex.* xxx. 23 Take thou.. of sweet calamus [*Coverdale* Kalmus] two hundred and fiftie shekels. 1650 RAWLEY tr. *Bacon's Life & Death* 45 Broath.. with.. a little Angellica Seed, and Calamus. 1741 *Compl. Fam.-Piece* I. iv. 243 Calamus Aromaticus 3 Ounces, leaves of Wall-Rue 4 Ounces. 1794 MARTYN *Rousseau's Bot.* xviii. 251 Of plants not ciliaceous.. Calamus Aromaticus or Sweet Rush. 1851 LONGF. *Gold. Leg., Nativity* vi, Another goblet!.. Stir.. drops of myrrh And calamus therein!

3. A genus of palms comprising many species, the stems of which grow to an extraordinary length, and form canes or rattans.
1836 *Penny Cycl.* VI. 135/2 Calamus.. the species.. grow in the forests, climbing over trees and bushes to a greater extent than any other known plants. 1885 H. STANLEY *Congo*, The luxuriant and endless lengths of calamus are useful for flooring and verandah mats.

4. 'A fistular stem without an articulation' (*Treas. Bot.*).

†'**calamy**¹. *Obs. rare.* Also **chaalamy**. Early form of CALAMUS, in sense 2.
1382 WYCLIF *Ex.* xxx. 24 Tak to thee swete smellynge thingis.. of chaalamy [1388 calamy]. ——*Jer.* vi. 20 Wherto to me.. ȝee bringen.. calamy swote smellende?

†'**calamy**². *Obs. rare.* [Cf. Ger. *kalmei.*]
1756 C. LUCAS *Ess. Waters* I. 11 Lapis calaminaris, or cadmia; in our language calamine, calamy, or cadmy.

calander, -re, obs. varr. CALANDRA.

calander, obs. form of CALENDER.

‖**calando** (ka'lando, -æ-, -æ-). [It. *calando* slackening, descending: cf. CALADE.] A musical direction indicating that the tone is to be gradually diminished, and the rate slackened.

calandra (kə'lændrə). Also 6 **calander**, 9 **calandre**. [a. F. *calandre*, It. *calandra* (= Sp. *calandria*), ad. med.L. *calandra*, Gr. κάλανδρος, all applied to the same bird.]
A species of lark (*Alauda Calandra*) with a body thicker than that of the sky-lark, found in the countries bordering on the Mediterranean Sea.
1599 NASHE *Lent. Stuffe* 65 He was a Triton of his time, and a sweete singing calander to the state. 1616 SURFL. & MARKH. *Countr. Farm* 726 Concerning the nature of the Calander.. she is hard to tame, if she be not taken in the nest. 1803 REES *Cycl.*, *Calandra*, the calandre lark. 1906 *Westm. Gaz.* 19 Apr. 12/1 In Milan, and also in Florence,.. he saw enormous masses of small birds.. field and calandra larks, and robin-redbreasts. 1953 BANNERMAN *Birds Brit. Isles* II. 8 The calandra is a Mediterranean species. *Ibid.*, The calandra lark is found almost exclusively in cultivated areas.

calandria (kə'lændrɪə). [Sp., lit. 'lark (bird); calander'.] A closed cylindrical vessel with a number of tubes passing through it, used as a heat exchanger in an evaporator and, in some nuclear reactors, to separate a liquid moderator from the fuel rods and coolant.
1929 B. HEASTIE in E. Hausbrand *Evap. App.* (ed. 4) xxvii. 445 The Kestner Salting Type Evaporator consists essentially of.. the separator and the calandria. The separator is a large cylindrical vessel around which the calandrias are grouped. *Ibid.* 446 Steam is admitted to the calandria, and the liquor then passes.. down into the bottom box of the calandria, up the calandria tubes, and back into the separator. 1955 *Bull. Atomic Sci.* Feb. 72/2 Working chiefly by remote control, the intensely 'hot' calandria, the heart of the reactor, was removed for safe burial. 1963 *New Scientist* 7 Nov. 305 In a tank (or 'calandria') which contains the heavy-water moderator there are fixed vertical tubes to contain the nuclear fuel.

†**calandring**. *Obs.* [cf. CALENDER *v.* and *sb.*²] A kind of stuff.
1697 EVELYN *Numism.* viii. 280 Several sorts of Stuffs, Calandring and Chambletings.

calangall, var. of GALINGALE, a plant.

‖**ca'langay**. A kind of white parrot, a native of the Philippine islands.
1753 CHAMBERS *Cycl. Supp.*, *Calangay*.. has a crest of white feathers. 1775 in ASH; and in subseq. Dicts.

calange, obs. form of CHALLENGE.

calapash, calapee, var. CALIPASH, CALIPEE.

'**calapite**, '**calappite**. [In Fr. *calapite*: f. Malay *calapa, kalappa*, the coco-nut.] A stony concretion sometimes found in the coco-nut, and used as an amulet; a vegetable bezoar.

calapyne, var. of CALEPIN.

calash (kə'læʃ), *sb.* Also 7 **gallesh, calleche, calesh, galeche**, 7-8 **caleche**, 9 **calèche**. [a. F. *calèche*, from Slavonic: Boh. *kolésa*, Pol. *kołaska*, dim. of *kołasa* 'wheel-carriage', f. *koło* wheel: cf. Russ. *kolaska* calash, *kolesó* wheel. In Eng., after many eccentricities, the word settled down as *calash*; but the Fr. form *calèche* is frequent in modern writers in reference to the Continent or Canada.]

1. A kind of light carriage with low wheels, having a removable folding hood or top. In Canada, a two-wheeled, one-seated vehicle,

usually without a cover, with a seat for the driver on the splashboard.

α. Form *calèche*, etc.

1666 *Lond. Gaz.* No. 104/1 The Pope..taking the air in a rich Caleche. **1673** DRYDEN *Marr. à la Mode* (1691) 16, I have been at your Lodgings in my new Galeche. **1676** ETHEREDGE *Man of Mode* III. ii. (1864) 36 Truly there is a bell air in Galleshes as well as men. **1678** BUTLER *Hud.* III. II. 871 Ladies hurried in Calleches, With Cornets at their Footmens Breeches. **1681** DINELEY *Jrnl. Tour Irel.* in *Trans. Kilkenny Archæol. Soc.* Ser. II. (1864) IV. 46 The Modell of a Calesh or Relune to be drawn with one Horse. **1702** *Lond. Gaz.* No. 3801/7 A Cannon Shot..carried away part of his Caleche. **1845** GRESLEY *Frank's First Trip to Continent* 24 A calèche was called. **1866** THOREAU *Yankee in Can.* i. 10 The Canadians..were riding about in caleches.

β. Form *calash*.

1679 R. MANSELL *Narr. Popish Plot* 43 Proposing first to go in his Calash, and pass for a French-man. **1711** F. FULLER *Med. Gymn.* 43 The Motion [of a]..light Calash..at first may seem a little troublesome, and the Shocks too rude. **1849** SIR R. WILSON *Life* (1862) I. iii. 129 Sleeping in the Calash.

2. The folding hood of such a carriage; also, the hood of a bathing machine, perambulator, etc.

1856 A. SMITH *Mr. Ledbury* I. xv. 117 The calash of a..bathing-machine.

3. A woman's hood made of silk, supported with whalebone or cane hoops, and projecting beyond the face. Formerly in common use.

1774 *Westm. Mag.* II. 352 Chip hats or calashes. **1791** WESLEY in *Wks.* (1872) VIII. 307 Give no ticket to any that wear calashes. **1848** THACKERAY *Van. Fair* xxxix, That lady in her clogs and calash. **1852** HAWTHORNE *Blithed. Rom.* II. xii. 212 Priscilla wore..a calash, which she had flung back from her head, leaving it suspended by the strings. **1867** MRS. GASKELL *Cranford* (1873) 52 Three or four ladies in calashes met at Miss Barker's door. A calash..is a covering worn over caps not unlike the heads fastened on old-fashioned gigs.

4. *attrib.*, as in ***calash-driver, -head, -top***.

1822 *Edin. Rev.* XXXVII. 255/4 His sketch of the calash-driver. **1824** SCOTT *St. Ronan's* (1832) 233 [The vehicle] had a calash head.

caˈlash, *v.* Also 9 callash. [f. prec. sb.] *trans.* To furnish with a calash.

1807 W. IRVING *Salmagundi* (1824) 32 Well callash'd without and well bolster'd within.

calash, obs. form of GALOSH.

calastic, *a.* so in Burton for *chalastick*, ad. Gr. χαλαστικός laxative.

1621 BURTON *Anat. Mel.* II. v. III. i. (1651) 401 Octavius Horatianus..prescribes calastick Cataplasms, or dry purging medicines. **1656** BLOUNT *Glossogr.*, *Calasticks*, purging medecines, or oyntments. **1678** PHILLIPS, *Calasticks*.

calat(e, var. of CALLET, *Obs.*, drab, strumpet.

calathian (kəˈleɪθɪən), *a.* [ad. L. *calathiāna*, otherwise, perh. correctly, *calatina (viola)*.] In *Calathian Violet*, a name transferred from Pliny, identified with a gentian (*Gentiana pneumonanthe*).

1578 LYTE *Dodoens* II. xxi, Of Autumne Belfloures, or Calathian Violets..Cordus calleth them *Pneumonanthe*: and truly it seemeth to be a certayne kinde of Gentian. **1601** HOLLAND *Pliny* II. 85 Some smell not at all, to wit, the Calathian Violet with the small leafe. *c* **1806** R. SURTEES *Poem* in Taylor *Life* (1852) 301 Our autumn fields are with pale gentian set, And the calathian glowing violet.

‖**calaˈthidium.** *Bot.* [mod.L.; dim. f. L. *calathus* (see below).] 'A name for the head of flowers (or better for the involucre only) of Compositæ' (Gray *Bot. Text-bk.*).

calathiform (ˈkæləθɪfɔːm), *a. Bot.* [mod. f. L. type **calathiformis* basket-shaped, f. *calathus* basket (see below) + *-formis* -FORM: cf. F. *calathiforme*.] (See quot.)

1880 GRAY *Bot. Text-bk.* 400 *Calathiform*, cup-shaped; of somewhat hemispherical outline.

‖**calathus** (ˈkæləθəs). Pl. -i. [L.: a. Gr. κάλαθος vase-shaped basket, as seen on the head of Demeter in ancient Greek statues.]

1. An ancient basket (in sculpture, etc.).

1753 CHAMBERS *Cycl. Supp.*, The *calathus* or work-basket of Minerva, is no less celebrated among the poets, than her distaff. **1846** ELLIS *Elgin Marb.* I. 20 On the head is a *calathus*, or basket. **1857** BIRCH *Anc. Pottery* I. (1858) 43.

2. *Bot.* = CALATHIDIUM; 'The head of flowers borne by composites' (*Treas. Bot.* 1866).

calavance (ˈkæləvæns). ? *Obs.* Forms: 7 garvance, caravance, 8 calla-, callevance, callvanse, kalavansa, 8 callivancy, 8– calli-, calavance. [Orig. *garvance, caravance*, a. Sp. *garbanzo* chick-pea, according to Larramendi ad. Basque *garbantzu*, f. *garau* seed, corn + *antzu* dry. (Diez says the question of derivation from Gr. ἐρέβινθος chick-pea is not worth consideration; though the Pg. form *ervanço* suggests connexion with the Gr.) *Calavance* appears to have come into Eng. through some foreign lang. which changed *r* into *l*.]

A name for certain varieties of pulse, as *Dolichos barbadensis, D. sinensis*, etc.

1620 *Cocks's Diary* II. 311 (Y.) They make their provition in abboundance..garvances, or small peaze or beanes. **1767** *Chron.* in *Ann. Reg.* 126/2 Orders of his Majesty in council ..Importation into this Kingdom of oats..peas, beans, tares, callivancies. **1772–84** COOK *Voy.* (1790) I. 246 Rice, callevances, and water-melons. *Ibid.* 255 To bring away the maize and callavances. **1779** FORREST *New Guinea* 104 Abounding with kalavansas (beans), but having no rice. **1829** MARRYAT *F. Mildmay* vi, Salt fish and calavances, for such was our cargo. *c* **1880** SIR J. HOOKER in Yule *Gloss.* s.v., When I was in the Navy, haricot beans were in constant use as a substitute for potatoes, and, in Brazil and elsewhere were called Calavances.

calaverite (kəˈlævəraɪt). *Min.* [f. *Calaveras* in California (where first found) + -ITE.] A tellurid of gold, or of gold and silver, bronze-yellow, massive, and without crystalline structure.

1868 DANA *Min.* 795 (Supp.) Calaverite is frequently associated with petzite. **1874** *Proc. Amer. Phil. Soc.* XIV. 229 Calaverite..is associated with sylvanite and quartz.

calaw, variant of CALLOO.

calawey, var. of CALEWEY, *Obs.*, a kind of pear.

calc- (kælk). *Min.* and *Geol.* [a. Ger. *kalk* lime, MHG. *kalc*, OHG. *chalch* (= OE. *cealc* CHALK), WGer. a. L. *calc-em* (*calx*) lime. In adopting the German term, English mineralogists have spelt it like Latin, and extended its use.]

Lime: used *attrib.* or in *comb.* = 'lime-, calcareous', as in CALC-SINTER, -SPAR, -TUFF; also **calcaphanite**, a calcareous variety of aphanite; **calc-schist**, calcareous schist, limestone shale.

1875 DAWSON *Dawn of Life* iii. 53 Dark grey micaceous limestone or calc-schist. **1879** RUTLEY *Stud. Rocks* xiii. 247 The calc-aphanite schist has a schistose structure.

‖**calcaire** (kalˈkɛːr). [Fr. (ad. L. *calcārius*); 'calcareous', sb. in Geology 'calcareous stone, limestone'.] In ***calcaire grossier*** and ***calcaire silicieux*** (lit. coarse and siliceous limestone) the French names of two Middle Eocene strata of the Paris basin, used by geologists generally.

1833 LYELL *Princ. Geol.* III. 64 The yellowish white building-stone of Paris, well known by the name of Calcaire grossier. **1838** —— *Elem. Geol.* (1865) 300 The calcaire siliceux and the calcaire grossier occupy distinct parts of the Paris basin. **1873** DAWSON *Earth & Man* x. 247. **1874** DAWKINS *Cave Hunt.* ii. 26 The same may also be said of the calcaire grossier of the basin of Paris.

†**calcane.** *Obs.* [see -ANE 2 a.] Davy's name for chloride of calcium; cf. *bismuthane*.

1812 SIR H. DAVY *Chem. Philos.* 348 Calcane consists of 31 chlorine and 19 of calcium.

calcaneal, calcanean (kælˈkeɪnɪːəl, -ən), *a. Phys.* [f. L. *calcāne-um* + -AL[1], -AN.] Of or belonging to the heel-bone.

1847–9 TODD *Cycl. Anat. & Phys.* IV. 770/1 A superior and inferior calcaneal branch are generally observed. **1855** OWEN *Skel. & Teeth* 65 There are three calcaneal processes.

Hence **calcaneo-** (-ˈeɪnɪəʊ), combining form, as in ***calcaneo-cuboid, -scaphoid, -tibial*** adjs.

1836–39 TODD *Cycl. Anat. & Phys.* II. 340 The strong calcaneo-cuboid ligament. **1842** E. WILSON *Anat. Vade M.* 131 The inferior calcaneo-scaphoid ligament is a broad and fibro-cartilaginous band of ligament. **1839–47** TODD *Cycl. Anat. & Phys.* III. 452/1 The calcaneo-tibial articulation.

‖**calcaneum** (kælˈkeɪnɪːəm). *Phys.* [L. (*os*) *calcāneum*. f. *calc-em* heel.] The bone of the heel.

1751 CHAMBERS *Cycl.* **1798** C. H. WILKINSON *Ess. Phys. & Philos.* 39 The Calcaneum or hock. **1866** HUXLEY *Preh. Rem. Caithn.* 94 The whole length of the limb from the..head of the femur to the under surface of the calcaneum.

†**calcanth.** *Obs.* Name of a plant.

1607 TOPSELL *Four-f. Beasts* 398 The fume of wall-wort, calcanth, parsely..do also kill mice.

calcanth, -thum, vitriol; see CHALCANTHUM.

calcanthus, improper f. CHALC-, CALYCANTHUS.

calcar[1] (ˈkælkɑː(r)). [ad. It. *calcara* 'a lime-kill' (Florio), 'a kind of oven or furnace to calcine vitreous matter in' (Baretti); cf. L. *calcāria* lime-kiln, fem. sing. of *calcārius*, f. *calx, -cis* lime.]

1. In *Glass-making*: 'A small furnace, in which the first calcination is made of sand and potash, for the formation of a frit' (Ure *s.v.*).

1662 C. MERRET tr. *Neri's Art Glass* 19 Mix & spread them well in the Calcar, with a rake, that they may be well calcined, & continue this till they begin to grow into lumps. **1712** tr. *Pomet's Hist. Drugs* I. 104 The English call the whole Quantity, bak'd at a time in the Calcar, a Batch. **1832** PORTER *Porcelain & Gl.* in *Lardner's Cab. Cycl.* 155 The Calcar is in the form of an oven about ten feet long, seven feet wide, and two feet high. **1875** URE *Dict. Arts* II. 654 A reverberatory furnace or calcar.

2. *Metall.* An annealing arch or oven.

‖**calcar**[2] (ˈkælkɑː(r)). *Bot.* [L. *calcar, calcāri-* spur, f. *calc-* heel + *-āri-* belonging to: see -AR.]

1. A hollow 'spur' from the base of a petal.

1832 J. LINDLEY *Introd. Bot.* I. 120 Sometimes a petal is lengthened at the base into a hollow tube, as in Orchis, &c.: this is called the spur or calcar, and by some nectarotheca. **1836** *Penny Cycl.* VI. 138/2 Calcar, or spur in flowers, is a hollow projection from the base of a petal, and has usually a conical figure. **1880** GRAY *Bot. Text-bk.* 400 *Calcar*, a spur; mostly used for the nectariferous one of a calyx or corolla.

2. *Anat.* Any of various spur-like bones of vertebrates, or the tibial spur of some insects.

1895 *Camb. Nat. Hist.* V. iii. 104 The spines at the top of the tibia [of insects], projecting beyond it, are called spurs, or calcares. **1898** PARKER & HASWELL *Textbk. Zool.* II. 254 On the tibial side of the first [digit] is a spur-like structure or calcar..: such a rudimentary digit is called a præhallux. **1951** C. K. WEICHERT *Anat. Chordates* x. 484 A small additional bone, the prehallux, or calcar, occurs on the tibial side of the tarsus in most salientians.

calcar, var. of CALKER[1], *Obs.*, a diviner.

calcarate (ˈkælkəreɪt), *a. Bot.* [f. CALCAR[2] + -ATE.] Furnished with a calcar or spur; spurred.

1830 LINDLEY *Nat. Syst. Bot.* 143 Sepals 4–5, combined at the base..the upper one calcarate. **1870** BENTLEY *Bot.* 221.

calcareo- (kælˈkɛərɪəʊ). Combining form of CALCAREOUS, used **a.** with adjectives, as ***calcareo-argillaceous*** (composed of clay with a mixture of lime), ***calcareo-magnesian, -sulphureous***, etc.; also ***calcareo-coralligenous***, producing a calcareous coral; **b.** with sbs. as ***calcareo-barite*** (see quot.)

1799 KIRWAN *Geol. Ess.* 127 Springs strongly impregnated with calcareous or calcareo-sulphureous matters. **1830** LYELL *Princ. Geol.* I. 204 Calcareo-magnesian limestone. **1837** DANA *Min.* (1868) 617 Calcareobarite is a white barite from Strontian containing..6·6°/ of lime. **1845** DARWIN *Voy. Nat.* iv. (1873) 75 The grand calcareo-argillaceous deposit. **1846** DANA *Zooph.* vii. (1848) 113 *Astræidæ*, calcareo-coralligenous.

calcareous, -ious (kælˈkɛərɪəs), *a.* [f. L. *calcārius* of lime (f. *calc-em* + *-ārius*) + -OUS. The spelling in *-eous*, which appeared about 1790, is erroneous, influenced by words in *-eous*, from L. *-eus*. The etymological sense of *calcar-eous* would be 'of the nature of a spur'.]

Of the nature of (carbonate of) lime; composed of or containing lime or lime-stone.

1677 PLOT *Oxfordsh.* 52 If..the stones be of the warm calcarious kind. **1774** GOLDSM. *Nat. Hist.* IV. 10 An animal or calcarious earth, which ferments with vinegar. **1792** A. YOUNG *Trav. France* 284 Rich loams on a calcareous bottom. **1802** BINGLEY *Anim. Biog.* (1813) I. 34 Eggs covered with a hard, calcareous shell. **1854** WOODWARD *Mollusca* 81 The calcarious grit of Berkshire. **1878** HUXLEY *Physiogr.* viii. 120 If a water be described simply as calcareous, it is generally assumed that the particular salt of lime which it holds in solution is the carbonate.

b. ***calcareous earth*** = lime, chalk; ***calcareous spar*** = CALC-SPAR; ***calcareous tufa*** = CALC-TUFF.

1756 WATSON in *Phil. Trans.* XLIX. 896 Ten grains of calcarious earth. **1799** MITCHILL *Med. Geog.* in *Med. Jrnl.* I. 255 Chalk, or calcareous earth. **1816** SIR H. DAVY in Faraday *Exp. Res.* 4 Calcareous tufas..found in every part of Italy. **1817** R. JAMESON *Charac. Min.* 107 Calcareous spar, heavy spar afford examples of the hexahedral prism.

Hence **calcareously** *adv.*, **calˈcareousness**.

1816 KEATINGE *Trav. France*, etc. II. 167 This bank appears to be calcareously stratified. **1864** WEBSTER *Calcareousness*.

calcariferous (kælkəˈrɪfərəs), *a.* [properly f. L. *calcar* spur + -(I)FEROUS; cf. F. *calcarifère*; the misuse (as if f. *calc-*) in 2 was app. due to thoughtless analysis of *calc-arious* as *calcar-eous*.]

1. 'Bearing spurs' (*Syd. Soc. Lex.*).

2. *catachr.* for CALCIFEROUS.

1853 TH. ROSS *Humboldt's Trav.* III. xxxii. 387 M. Boussingault..calls the rock of the Morros a 'problematic calcariferous gneiss'. **1881** *Syd. Soc. Lex.*, *Calcariferous*, containing, or mingled with, lime.

calcariform (kælˈkærɪfɔːm), *a.* [mod. f. L. *calcāri-* spur + -FORM, or a. F. *calcariforme*; with the same confusion of *calcar* with *calc-* as in prec.]

a. 'Shaped like a calcar or spur' (*Treas. Bot.*). **b.** *catachr.* 'Having a calcareous, rhomboidal appearance' (*Syd. Soc. Lex.* 1881).

calcarine (ˈkælkəraɪn), *a.* [f. L. *calcar* spur + -INE.] Spur-like.

1871 HUXLEY in Darwin *Desc. Man* vii. (1883) 205 The deep calcarine fissure.

calcarious, etymol. form of CALCAREOUS.

†**ˈcalcary**, *a. Obs. rare*[−1]. [ad. L. *calcārius*; see -ARY[1].] = CALCAREOUS.

1766 *Phil. Trans.* LVI. 232 The rocks below are mixed, calcary and noncalcary.

†'**calcate**, *v. Obs. rare.* [f. L. *calcāt-* ppl. stem of *calcāre* to trample under foot, f. *calx* the heel.] *trans.* To trample or stamp under the heel.
1623 COCKERAM, *Calcate*, to stampe. **1657** TOMLINSON *Renou's Disp.* 552 It should be calcated with ones feet.

cal'cation. *rare.* [f. prec.: see -ATION.] Trampling under the heel; kicking.
1656 BLOUNT *Glossogr.*, *Calcation*, a treading or stamping. **1721–90** in BAILEY. **1822** *Blackw. Mag.* XII. 342 Even a few supernumerary calcations would have been overlooked.

†'**calcatory.** *Obs. rare*$^{-1}$. [ad. L. *calcātōrium*, f. *calcāre* (see CALCATE).] A winepress, where the grapes are trodden.
c **1420** *Pallad. on Husb.* I. 461 Above it [thi wyne celar] well the calcatory make, A wyne pitte the oon half either to take.

‖**Calca'vella, Calca'vellos.** [so called from Carcavelhos (karka'veʎos) in Portugal.] A sweet white wine brought from Lisbon.
1816 ACCUM *Chem. Tests* (1818) 190 Various wines and spirituous liquors.. Calcavella.

calce, calce-vive: see CALX.

†'**calceate**, *a. Obs.* [ad. L. *calceātus*, pa. pple. of *calceāre* to shoe, f. *calceus* shoe; see -ATE[2].] Furnished with shoes, shod. ***Fathers Calceate***: the 'mitigated' or 'moderate' Carmelites, who do not go barefoot. Also as *sb.*
1669 WOODHEAD *St. Teresa* II. xvii. 117 He lived among the Fathers Calceate of the Rule relaxed. *Ibid.* II. xxi. 137 A Calceate Carmelite. *Ibid.* II. xxvii. 170 To live.. apart from the Calceates.

'**calceate**, *v. Obs.* [f. L. *calceāre*: see prec. and -ATE[3].] 'To shooe or put on shooes or socks' (BLOUNT *Glossogr.* 1656).
Hence '**calceated** *ppl. a.* = CALCEATE *a.*
1730–6 BAILEY, *Calceated*, shod, or fitted with Shoos. Hence in JOHNSON and mod. Dicts.

calced (kælst), *a. rare.* [f. L. *calc-eus* shoe + -ED[2].] Shod; = CALCEATE. (Cf. DISCALCED.)
1884 ADDIS & ARNOLD *Cath. Dict.* s.v. *Carmelite*, In Ireland there appear to be seven or eight Carmelite Friaries, calced and discalced.

calcedon, calcedony, etc.: see CHAL-.

calceiform ('kælsiːɪfɔːm), *a. Bot.* [mod. f. L. *calceus* shoe- + (I)FORM; cf. F. *calcéiforme.*] Shaped like a shoe or slipper; calceolate.
1860 WORCESTER cites GRAY.

calceolaria (ˌkælsiːəʊ'lɛərɪə, kælsɪə-). *Bot.* [f. L. *calceolus* 'small shoe, slipper', dim. of *calceus* + botanical suffix *-aria.*] 'Slipper-flower' or 'slipper-wort'; a genus of *Scrophulariaceæ*, the flower of which has some resemblance to a broad-toed slipper. Native to S. America, but cultivated in our gardens for the beauty of the flower.
1846 J. BAXTER *Libr. Pract. Agric.* I. 324 Cuttings of Calceolarias, Fuchsias, Linums, and Pelargoniums, should now be planted in a shady border. **1873** MISS BROUGHTON *Nancy* II. 35 The scentless flame of the geraniums and calceolarias.

calceolate ('kælsɪəleɪt), *a. Bot.* [f. as prec. + -ATE[2].] Shaped like a slipper.
1864 in WEBSTER. **1870** BENTLEY *Bot.* 221 A slight modification of the personate.. sometimes termed calceolate. **1872** OLIVER *Elem. Bot.* II. 216.
Hence '**calceolately** *adv.*
1881 DICKSON in *Jrnl. Bot.* X. 131 The far side of the funnel becomes calceolately pouched to an enormous extent.

calces, pl. of CALX.

†**cal'cescence.** *Obs.* [f. L. *calc-* lime, after *fluorescence*; so called because typically exhibited in the lime-light.] Earlier term for CALORESCENCE.
1881 *Nature* XXIV. 66 Akin gave the name of calcescence to the phenomenon of the change of non-luminous heat-rays into luminous ones as in lime-light, but the term has been superseded by Tyndall's term calorescence.

calcey, obs. form of CAUSEWAY.

†'**calcia.** *Chem. Obs.* [f. L. *calc(i)-* lime; cf. *magnesia*, *soda*, etc.] Oxide of calcium, lime.
1812 SIR H. DAVY *Chem. Philos.* 346 The important substance lime or calcia.

calcic ('kælsɪk), *a. Chem.* [f. CALC-IUM + -IC.] Of or containing calcium; = CALCIUM *attrib.*
1871 NICHOLS *Fireside Sc.* 275 Calcic carbonates. **1883** *Nature* 1 Feb. 325 Precipitated calcic and magnesic phosphates. **1884** *Harper's Mag.* Aug. 442/2 [It] contains so large a per cent. of lime that it may well be called a calcic-sulphur water.

calcicole ('kælsɪkəl), *a. Bot.* [f. L. *calc(i)*-lime, CALX + *colĕre* to inhabit.] That grows best in calcareous soil. Hence as *sb.*, a calcicole plant. So **cal'cicolous** *a.*
1882 *Encycl. Brit.* XIV. 562/1 As to saxicole lichens.. they may be divided into two sections, viz. *calcicole* and *calcifugous*. To the former belong such as are found on calcareous and cretaceous rocks. **1886** J. E. BAGNALL *Handbk. Mosses* 33 Another very characteristic calcicolous moss is Eucladium verticillatum. **1932** FULLER & CONARD tr. *Braun-Blanquet's Plant Sociol.* vi. 183 Mere traces of lime .. enable calcicoles to survive. *Ibid.* 184 The occurrence of calcicolous (lime-constant) communities. **1952** P. W. RICHARDS *Tropical Rain Forest* ix. 223 Calcicole and calcifuge species. *Ibid.*, True calcicoles.. dependent on the chemical rather than the physical properties of the limestone.

calcicrete ('kælsɪkriːt), see CALCRETE.

calcidoine, obs. form of CHALCEDONY.

calciferol (kæl'sɪfərəl). *Chem.* [f. CALCIFEROUS *a.* + -OL, as in ERGOSTEROL.] Vitamin D_2.
1931 T. C. ANGUS et al. in *Proc. R. Soc.* B. CVIII. 340 We think the provisional adoption of a name is justified.. and suggest 'Calciferol' in view of the high antirachitic activity of the substance. **1942** *Endeavour* I. 31/1 The first few almost microscopic crystals of calciferol were inspected by enthusiastic chemists. **1964** S. DUKE-ELDER *Parsons' Dis. Eye* (ed. 14) xv. 174 Cases of lupus frequently respond to calciferol.

calciferous (kæl'sɪfərəs), *a.* [f. L. *calc(i)-* lime + -FEROUS. Cf. F. *calcifère.*] Yielding or containing (carbonate of) lime. (Chiefly *Geol.*)
1799 KIRWAN *Geol. Ess.* 436 An effervescent calciferous clay. **1836–9** TODD *Cycl. Anat. & Phys.* II. 380/2 This calciferous fluid forms a layer of shell. **1876** PAGE *Adv. Text-bk. Geol.* xvii. 314 Some beds of calciferous sandstone.

calcific (kæl'sɪfɪk), *a.* [f. as prec. + -FIC.] Forming lime; belonging to calcification.
1861 BUMSTEAD *Ven. Dis.* (1879) 594 Gummatous tumors occasionally undergo calcific degeneration. **1866** A. FLINT *Princ. Med.* (1880) 59 We find calcific deposits in cheesy masses. **1869** HUXLEY *Phys.* xii. 324 A deposit of calcific matter takes place.

calcification (ˌkælsɪfɪ'keɪʃən). [n. of action f. CALCIFY (L. **calcific-āre*); see prec. and -ATION; cf. F. *calcification.*] Conversion into lime; replacement of other matter by lime; the hardening of a structure, tissue, etc. by the deposit of salts of lime, as in the formation of teeth, and many forms of 'petrifaction'.
1849–52 TODD *Cycl. Anat. & Phys.* IV. 876/1 As calcification of the tooth progresses towards its base. **1854** WOODWARD *Mollusca* II. 229 The shells.. differ from Rhynconella chiefly in the calcification of the oral supports.
b. *concr.* (the result of calcifying.)
1869 NICHOLSON *Zool.* xxx. (1880) 289 A calcareous shell formed by calcifications within the walls of the first three cephalic segments. **1872** —— *Palæont.* 88 The sclerodermic coral.. is an actual calcification of part of the tissues of the polype.

calciform ('kælsɪfɔːm), *a.* [f. L. *calc(i)-* lime a pebble + -FORM; but see also 3.]
†**1.** Of metals: In the state of CALX; oxidized.
1782 WITHERING in *Phil. Trans.* LXX. 333 Iron in a calciform state. **1784** KIRWAN *ibid.* LXXIV. 160 Many calciform iron ores become magnetic by calcination. **1812** SIR H. DAVY *Chem. Philos.* 47 Thus, as the metals have been distinguished by the termination 'um' as 'aurum', so their calciform or oxidated state might have been denoted by the termination 'a' as 'aura'.
2. 'Pebble-shaped' (*Syd. Soc. Lex.* 1881).
3. [f. L. *calx* heel.] 'Having a projection like a heel' (*Syd. Soc. Lex.* 1881).

calcifuge ('kælsɪf(j)uːdʒ), *a. Bot.* [f. *calci-* (see CALCICOLE *a.*) + -FUGE.] Not suited by calcareous soil; that grows best in acid soil. Hence as *sb.*, a calcifuge plant. So **cal'ci fugous** *a.*
1882 [see CALCICOLE *a.*]. **1909** *Cent. Dict.* Suppl., Calcifuge *a.* **1926** TANSLEY & CHIPP *Study of Veget.* vii. 122 When the acidity is well marked the soil bears special plant communities (often called *calcifuge*) excluding many species of plants altogether. **1946** *Nature* 17 Aug. 240/1 Several other blue-fruiting calcifuges. **1957** P. GREIG-SMITH *Quant. Plant Ecology* v. 109 Compare, for example, the occurrence of *Calluna vulgaris*, normally calcifuge, on calcareous soils under extreme climatic conditions.

calcify ('kælsɪfaɪ), *v. Phys.* [f. L. *calc(i)-* lime + -FY; on the type of a L. **calci-ficāre*, F. *calcifier.*]
1. *trans.* To convert into lime; to replace other matter by lime; to harden by the deposit of lime.
1854 WOODWARD *Mollusca* (1856) 42 Each layer was successively calcified.. and thrown off by the mantle to unite with those previously formed. **1861** HULME tr. *Moquin-Tandon* II. III. iii. 97 The stones are gradually dissolved, and serve to calcify and harden the new skin.
2. *intr.* To become calcified; see prec. sense.
1859 J. TOMES *Dent. Surg.* (1873) 3 The edges of the front teeth first assume their full dimensions in the form of pulp, and then calcify. **1876** tr. *Wagner's Pathol.* 259 The fibrin calcifies, becoming a fixed, continuous stone-like mass.
Hence '**calcified** *ppl. a.*; '**calcifying** *vbl. sb.* and *ppl. a.*
1836 TODD *Cycl. Anat. & Phys.* I. 116/1 The chorion of the ova is generally thin or coriaceous, seldom calcified or hard. *Ibid.* II. 381/2 The calcifying fluid from which the shell is formed. **1875** BLAKE *Zool.* 233 The calcifying processes continue to deposit shelly material. **1880** GUNTHER *Fishes* 315 Covered with calcified papillæ.

cal'cigenous, *a. Chem.* ? *Obs.* [f. L. *calc(i)-* in sense of CALX + *-gen-us* born, bearing + -OUS; cf. ALKALIGENOUS.] Producing a calx; said of those metals which with oxygen form a 'calx'.
1854 SCOFFERN in *Orr's Circ. Sc.* Chem. 434 Metals, the oxides of which were termed by ancient chemists *calces*, and which are, therefore, known as the calcigenous metals. *c* **1865** J. WYLDE in *Circ. Sc.* I. 311/1 Three classes; namely, Alkaligeneous, Calcigeneous, and Metals proper.

calcigerous (kæl'sɪdʒərəs), *a.* [f. L. *calc(i)-* + *-ger* bearing + -OUS.] Holding or containing lime.
1839–47 TODD *Cycl. Anat. & Phys.* III. 847/2 Calcigerous cells. **1842** E. WILSON *Anat. Vade M.* 53 True bone, characterised by the existence of numerous calcigerous cells.

calcimangite (kælsɪ'mæŋgaɪt). *Min.* [f. L. *calc(i)-* lime + MANG-ANESE + -ITE.] A synonym of Spartaite or manganiferous calcite.
1868 DANA *Min.* 678.

calcimine ('kælsɪmɪn, -maɪn). [Later modification of KALSOMINE, after L. *calci-*, *calx* lime + inorganic *-m-* + -INE[4].] A trade name given to a kind of white or coloured wash for walls.
1864 WEBSTER cites HART. **1885** *Spons' Mech. Own Bk.* 612 The wash or calcimine can be used for ordinary purposes. **1897** *Sears, Roebuck Catal.* 299/2 Should the ceilings and walls be calcimined or whitewashed, wash off old calcimine or whitewash. **1903** *Westm. Gaz.* 23 Jan. 4/3 The old-gold calcimine.. that covers the wall of the drawing-room. **1911** H. S. HARRISON *Queed* xi. 134 Sharlee tapped the calcimine with her pointed finger-nails. **1930** T. S. ELIOT tr. *St.-J. Perse's Anabasis* 27 My heart twittered with joy under the glare of the calcimine. **1953** A. UPFIELD *Murder must Wait* iii. 19 The faint smear on the cream calsomine.
Hence '**calcimine** *v.*, to whitewash; '**calci,miner**, a whitewasher, or wall-colourer.
1885 *Advance* (Chicago) 4 June 361 Yesterday the calciminers invaded our dwelling. **1919** *Chambers's Jrnl.* May 327/1 The quarters were.. somewhat garishly calcimined within. **1930** J. DOS PASSOS *42nd Parallel* 300 He was in a small room calsomined bright yellow.

calcimurite (kælsɪ'mjʊəraɪt). *Min.* [f. L. *calc(i)-* lime + *muri-ate* (= *chlor-ate*) + -ITE.] 'A chloritic calcareous earth' (Craig); a blue or olive-green earth of the consistency of clay.

calcinable (kæl'saɪnəb(ə)l), *a.* [f. CALCINE *v.* + -ABLE] Capable of being calcined.
1652 FRENCH *Yorksh. Spa* ii. 22. **1756** WRIGHT in *Phil. Trans.* XLIX. 675 Marble, sea-shells, chalk, and other calcinable matter. **1789** J. KEIR *Dict. Chem.* 93/1 By fire it [molybdena] is calcinable.

†'**calcinate**, *a.* and *sb. Obs.* [ad. med.L. *calcinātum* (that which is) calcined.]
A. *adj.* Calcined. **B.** *sb.* A calcined form or product, as *calcinate of magnesia*.
1610 MARKHAM *Masterp.* II. xli. 284 Eate it out either with verdigrease.. or else with Mercury calcinate. [**1685** BOYLE *Effects of Motion* iv. 37 Nitre itself may without Tartar be speedily reduced to a Calcinatum.]

†'**calcinate**, *v. Obs.* [f. med.L. *calcinat-* ppl. stem of *calcināre.*] = CALCINE.
1559 MORWYNG *Evonym.* 319 Sum put Tartarum to be calcinated in a newe pot in a potters oven. **1598** FLORIO, *Calcinare*, to calcinate. **1610** MARKHAM *Masterp.* II. lxxix. 355 Other Farriers vse to calcinate Tartar, and dissolue it in water. **1626** BACON *Sylva* §87 The Heat that these degrees; First, it indurateth and then maketh Fragile; And lastly it doth Incinerate, and Calcinate.
Hence '**calcinated**, '**calcinating** *ppl. adjs.*
1611 COTGR., *Calcinatoire*, calcinatorie, calcinating. **1615** DANIEL *Queen's Arcad.* (1717) 185 He sucks Out of a little hollow instrument Of calcinated Clay, the Smoak thereof. **1656** BLOUNT *Glossogr.*, *Cinnaber*, made of calcinated Sulphur and Quick-silver.

calcination (kælsɪ'neɪʃən). [n. of action f. med.L. *calcināre*: see CALCINE and -ATION.]
1. The action or process of calcining; reduction by fire to a 'calx', powder, or friable substance; the subjecting of any infusible substance to a roasting heat.
c **1386** CHAUCER *Chan. Yem. Prol. & T.* 251 Oure fourneys eek of Calcinacion [*v.r.* Calcynacion]. **1393** GOWER *Conf.* II. 86 The point of sublimation And forth with calcination. **1583** PLAT *Divers new Exper.* (1594) 22 Wheresoeuer there bee any stones that be subject to calcination. **1610** B. JONSON *Alch.* II. v. (1616) 632 Name the vexations, and the martyrizations Of metalls in the worke.. Putrefaction, Solution, Ablution, Sublimation, Cohobation, Calcination, Ceration, and Fixation. **1678** R. R[USSELL] tr. *Geber* II. I. IV. xiv. 120 Calcination is the Pulverization of a Thing by Fire. **1831** R. KNOX *Cloquet's Anat.* 167 Bones.. may be freed of the animal matter by calcination. **1875** URE *Dict. Arts* I. 573 The process of burning lime, to expel the carbonic acid, is one of calcination.
†**b.** Extended to other processes producing similar results; or used as synonymous with oxidation in general. *Obs.*
1612 WOODALL *Surg. Mate* Wks. (1653) 268 Calcination is solution of bodies into Calx or Alcool, by desiccation of the native humidity, by reverberate ignition, by Amalgamation,

by Aqua fortis, the Spirit of salt Vitriol, Sulphur, or the like. **1641** FRENCH *Distill.* i. (1651) 9 *Calcination*..may be done two waies—by firing, by Corosion. **1751** CHAMBERS *Cycl.* s.v. **1791** HAMILTON *Berthollet's Dyeing* I. I. I. i. 10 According to its degree of oxydation (calcination). **1822** IMISON *Sc. & Art* II. 20 The process of combining a metal with oxygen was called calcination, now oxigenation.

2. *gen.* A burning to ashes, complete combustion.

1616 BULLOKAR, *Calcination*, a burning, a turning into ashes. **1722** WOLLASTON *Relig. Nat.* v. 92 The earth reformed out of its ashes and ruins after such a calcination. **1822** *Blackw. Mag.* XII. 280 Those burnings of barns..and the general calcination which has gone through the country.

3. A calcined condition.

1830 LYELL *Princ. Geol.* I. 28 Steno had compared the fossil shells..and traced the various gradations from the state of mere calcination, when their natural gluten only was lost, to the perfect substitution of stony matter.

b. *concr.* That which has been calcined, a calcined product or 'calcinate'.

1712 tr. *Pomet's Hist. Drugs* I. 104 Fritt is..a Calcination of those Materials which make Glass. **1725** BRADLEY *Fam. Dict.* II. s.v., A quarter of an Ounce of this Calcination.

† **'calcinator.** *Obs.* [Agent-noun f. med.L. *calcināre.*] One who practises calcination.

1635 PERSON *Varieties* I. 42 What is your opinion concerning the potableness of Gold, after which, our Chymists..and Calcinators..make such search and labour?

calcinatory (kæl'sɪnətərɪ, 'kælsɪ-), *a.* and *sb.* [f. med.L. *calcināt-* ppl. stem of *calcināre* + -ORY.]

A. *adj.* Serving for calcination.

1611 COTGR., *Calcinatoire*, calcinatorie, calcinating. **1678** R. R[USSELL] tr. *Geber* v. i. 273 Let the Calcinatory Furnace be made square in length four foot.

B. *sb.* A vessel used for calcination [= *calcinātōrium* (*vas*) in Du Cange].

1730–6 in BAILEY; hence in JOHNSON and mod. Dicts.

† **'calcine,** *a.* *Obs.* *rare*⁻¹. [? ad. med.L. *calcineus*, or ? **calcinus*, f. *calx* lime.] Of lime.

1576 BAKER *Gesner's Jewel of Health* 206 a, An oyle will then issue, which shall be named the calcine oyle.

calcine (kæl'saɪn, 'kæl-), *v.* Also 4 **calcene**, 4–5 **calcyne**. [ad. med.L. *calcināre*, a term of the alchemists, 'to burn like lime, to reduce to CALX'.

Prob. the med.L. word arose in Italy, where *calcina* 'lime, quick-lime', deriv. of It. *calce*, L. *calcem*, is cited by Du Cange in a Latin document of 1215; Florio has also *calcinare* to burn lime, 'to burn minerals to correct the malignitie of them'. The accentuation '*calcening* occurs in Chaucer; *cal'cine* is the pronunciation in Ben Jonson, and all the poets since; though some recent Dictionaries give '*calcine* either as an alternative or sole pronunciation.]

1. To reduce to quick-lime, or to an analogous substance, by roasting or burning; 'to burn in the fire to a calx or friable substance' J.

By the alchemists and early chemists this was supposed to be to reduce a mineral or metal to its purest or most refined residuum by driving off or consuming all the more volatile and perishable constituents; in reality it yielded in most cases a metallic oxide, though sometimes only a finely comminuted or sublimed form of a metal, or a desiccated form of other substance.

c **1386** [see CALCINING *vbl. sb.*]. *c* **1460–70** *Bk. Quintessence* 9 The science to brynge gold into calx..in þe corusible ȝe schal fynde þe gold calcyned and reducid into erþe. **1580** R. DAY (*title*) The Key of Philosophie..howe to prepare, Calcine, Sublime, and dissolue all manner of Mineralls. **1601** HOLLAND *Pliny* II. 599 Fire burneth and calcineth stone, whereof is made that mortar which bindeth all worke in masonry. **1610** B. JONSON *Alch.* II. iii. (1616) 624, I sent you of his feces there, calcin'd. Out of that calx, I ha' wonne the salt of Mercvry. **1612** WOODALL *Surg. Mate* Wks. (1653) 199 Swines hoofs burnt or Calcined till they be white. **1643** SIR T. BROWNE *Relig. Med.* I. §50, I would gladly know how Moses with an actuall fire calcin'd, or burnt the Golden Calfe into powder. **1799** G. SMITH *Laborat.* I. 77 A little nitre thrown into the crucible, which effectually calcines the remaining regulus of antimony. **1822** IMISON *Sc. & Art* II. 318 Take some oysters-shells, calcine them, by keeping them in a good fire for about an hour. **1832** HT. MARTINEAU *Hill & Vall.* iv. 57 Mr. Wallace explained how the ironstone, or *mine* as it is called, is calcined in the kilns. **1874** KNIGHT *Dict. Mech.* s.v. *Calcination*, Copper and other ores are calcined, to drive off the sulphur, the sulphurets being oxidized and sulphuric acid being disengaged and volatilized.

b. To subject to a heat sufficient to desiccate thoroughly, destroy contained organisms, etc.

1880 MACCORMAC *Antisept. Surg.* 105 Schröder and Dusch established that it was not necessary to calcine air.

c. *fig.* To purify or refine by consuming the grosser part.

1634 HABINGTON *Castara* (1870) 130 Yet you by a chaste Chimicke Art, Calcine fraile love to pietie. **1648** EARL WESTMORLD. *Otia Sacra* (1879) 88 The Crimson streaks belace the Damaskt West, Calcin'd by night, rise pure Gold from the East. *a* **1711** KEN *Prepar.* Wks. 1721 IV. 159 Your Clay by the last Fire calcin'd, Shall to spiritual be refin'd.

2. *gen.* To burn to ashes, consume.

1641 M. FRANK *Serm.* (1672) 225 Though the general conflagration shall at last calcine these glorious structures into ashes. **1646** J. HALL *Poems* I Harmlesse reams.. Tobacco can Calcine them soon to dust. **1855** COSTELLO *Stor. Screen* 77 His body was found on the stone floor of his dormitory calcined to a cinder. **1882** FARRAR *Early Chr.* I. 214 Calcining the cities of Sodom and Gomorrah.

b. *fig.*

1633 G. HERBERT *Temple, Easter* i, As his death calcined thee to dust. *c* **1650** DENHAM *Progr. Learning* I. 157 Fiery disputes that union have calcined. **1879** FARRAR *St. Paul* I. 19 There are souls in which the burning heat of some transfusing purpose calcines every other thought.

3. *intr.* To suffer calcination.

1704 NEWTON *Opticks* (J.) This crystal is a pellucid fissile stone..enduring a red heat without losing its transparency, and, in a very strong heat, calcining without fusion. **1771** HAMILTON in *Phil. Trans.* LXI. 49 Its cone in many parts has been calcined, and is still calcining, by the hot vapours. **1861** A. B. HOPE *Eng. Cathedr.* vi. 226 The drawback of these stones [clunch and chalk] is..that under fire they calcine.

calcined (kæl'saɪnd). [f. CALCINE *v.* + -ED¹.] Reduced to dry powder or ash by burning; subjected to the thorough action of fire; purged by fire.

1583 PLAT *Divers new Exper.* (1594) 37 Weigh out of this calcined coppresse one part. **1605** TIMME *Quersit.* II. i. 105 Salts may be extracted out of all calcined metalls. **1732** ARBUTHNOT *Rules of Diet* 264 Calcin'd Hartshorn, which has something of this Quality. **1810** HENRY *Elem. Chem.* (1826) I. 619 Pure magnesia..is..prepared by the calcination of the carbonate, and hence its name of calcined magnesia. **1870** TYNDALL *Fragm. Sc.* (ed. 3) xi. 301 When a decoction of meat is effectually screened from ordinary air, and supplied solely with calcined air, putrefaction never sets in. **1876** ROUTLEDGE *Discov.* 28 The calcined ore is then ready for the blast furnace.

† **cal'cineous,** *a.* *Obs.* *rare*⁻¹. [a. med.L. *calcine-us* (f. *calx* lime) + -OUS.] Of the nature of quick-lime; caustic.

1660 tr. *Paracelsus Archidoxis* I. VI. 86 How acute or Calcineous soever it be..tis by that acuity alone that it Operates.

calciner (kæl'saɪnə(r)). [f. CALCINE *v.* + -ER¹.]

1. One who calcines.

1708 MOTTEUX *Rabelais* IV. xxix, A Calciner of Ashes.

2. An apparatus for calcining; *spec.* a kiln or furnace for roasting ore.

1837 *Penny Cycl.* VII. 502/1 The charge of ore usually put into the calciner weighs about three..tons. **1870** *Eng. Mech.* 21 Jan. 447/3 There are two calciners in use [in roasting copper ore], one of them known as an 'open', and the other as a 'blind' calciner. **1879** *Encycl. Brit.* IX. 842.

calcining (kæl'saɪnɪŋ), *vbl. sb.* [f. CALCINE *v.* + -ING¹.] The process of reducing to a calx, burning to ashes, or subjecting to a roasting heat.

c **1386** CHAUCER *Chan. Yem. Prol. & T.* 218 The care and wo That we hadden in oure matires sublymyng And in almalgamyng and calceniyng Of quyk siluer. **1601** HOLLAND *Pliny, Expl. Wds. of Art, Calcining*, the burning of a minerall, or any thing, for to correct the malignitie of it, or reduce it into pouder. **1641** FRENCH *Distill.* i. (1651) 9 Corrosion is the Calcining of bodies by corrosive things. **1861** W. FAIRBAIRN *Addr. Brit. Assoc.*, The different processes, from the calcining of the ore to the production of the bar.

attrib. **1662** MERRETT *Neri's Art of Glass* ii, The Calcar is a kind of calcining furnace. **1875** URE *Dict. Arts* I. 914 The Calcining Furnace rests upon a vault. **1876** ROUTLEDGE *Discov.* 28 Large calcining kilns.

calcining (kæl'saɪnɪŋ), *ppl. a.* [f. as prec. + -ING².] That calcines.

1644–58 CLEVELAND *Gen. Poems* (1677) 15 No more of your calcining Flame. **1757** DYER *Fleece* (1807) 97 Dissolving water's, and calcining sun's and thieving air's attacks.

calcinitre, synonym of NITROCALCITE.

† **'calcinize,** *v.* *Obs.* [see -IZE.] = CALCINE *v.*

1607 SYLVESTER *Du Bartas* II. iv. i. (1623) 437 Gods dread wrath, which quick doth calcinize The marble Mountains. **1656** BLOUNT *Glossogr.*, *Calcinize*, to burn to ashes, to reduce metals to powder by the fire, to refine.

calcio- ('kælsɪəʊ-), a combining form of CALCIUM, used in names of minerals: as **calcio-ce'lestite**, a variety of CELESTITE containing much lime; **calcio-'ferrite**, a hydrous phosphate of calcium and iron, occurring as a sulphur-yellow mineral (Dana).

calciphilous (kæl'sɪfɪləs), *a.* *Bot.* [f. *calci-* (see CALCICOLE *a.*) + Gr. φίλος (see -PHIL).] Of a plant: well suited to calcareous soil. So **'calciphile** *a.* (see also quot. 1952).

1909 *Cent. Dict.* Suppl., Calciphilous. **1934** WEBSTER, Calciphile. **1938** [see CALCIPHOBOUS *a.*]. **1952** J. CLEGG *Freshwater Life* xvi. 255 It is possible to group the freshwater Molluscs into those that need and are found only in 'hard' waters—the so-called *Calciphile* species..—and those that can thrive in quite soft waters.

calciphobous (kæl'sɪfəbəs), *a.* *Bot.* [f. *calci-* (see CALCICOLE *a.*) + Gr. -φόβος (see -PHOBE).] = CALCIFUGE *a.*

1907 W. R. FISHER *Schlich's Man. Forestry* (ed. 2) IV. 408 Holly makes excellent hedges, but requires plenty of humus. It is calciphobous like sweet-chestnut. **1938** WEAVER & CLEMENTS *Plant Ecology* (ed. 2) viii. 233 Certain species of plants have been grouped into lime-loving (*calciphilous*) and lime-fearing (*calciphobous*) species according to whether they grow on limestone or siliceous soils.

calcite ('kælsaɪt). *Min.* [mod. (Haidinger 1845 *calcit*) f. L. *calc-em* lime + -ITE, q.v.] The native crystallized rhombohedral anhydrous carbonate of lime (calcium carbonate), which exists in an immense variety of forms: calc-spar, calcareous spar. Taken by Dana as the type of the *Calcite Group* of anhydrous carbonates. Also *attrib.*

1849 MURCHISON *Siluria* App. 547 A change into crystalline calcite. **1874** DAWKINS *Cave Hunt.* ii. 64 Lined with glittering crystals of calcite. **1878** BATES *Centr. Amer.* vi. 81 Brown and black blende in quartz and calcite seams.

'calcitrant, *a.* *rare.* (*pedantic.*) [ad. L. *calcitrānt-em*, kicking: see next.] Kicking; that 'kicks' at any restriction. Cf. RECALCITRANT.

1866 *Lond. Rev.* 8 Dec. 621 A calcitrant son of Cambridge.

calcitrate ('kælsɪtreɪt), *v.* [f. L. *calcitrāt-* ppl. stem of *calcitrā-re* to strike with the heels, kick, f. *calc-em* heel; cf. obs. F. *calcitrer* (Cotgr.).] *trans.* and *intr.* To kick.

1623 COCKERAM, *Calcitrate*, to kicke, or wince. **1668** WILKINS *Real Char.* 179 Calcitrate, kick. **1708** MOTTEUX *Rabelais* IV. xiii. (1737) 54 The Filly..began to spurn it, to calcitrate it. **1832** *Fraser's Mag.* V. 242 They erect an idol.. which the succeeding generations, each for itself, calcitrates and heels over.

calcitration (kælsɪ'treɪʃən). [n. of action f. prec.: see -ATION.] Kicking. *lit.* and *fig.*

1652 A. ROSS *Arcana Microc.* 52 The birth of a child is caused partly by its calcitration. **1702** C. MATHER *Magn. Chr.* III. III. iii. (1852) 537. **1866** G. MACDONALD *Ann. Q. Neigh.* x. (1878) 181 There were signs of calcitration in the churchwarden, when he perceived whither I was leading him.

calcium ('kælsɪəm). *Chem.* [f. (by Sir H. Davy) L. *calx*, *calc(i)-* lime, on the type of other names of metals in -UM, -IUM.]

1. A chemical element, one of the 'metals of the alkaline earths', being the basis of lime; though one of the most widely diffused of elements, it is found in nature only in composition, and was first separated by Davy in 1808, as a light yellow metal, ductile and malleable, about as hard as gold, which rapidly oxidizes in air containing moisture, and forms 'quick-lime'. Symbol Ca.

1808 SIR H. DAVY in *Phil. Trans.* XCVIII. 346, I shall venture to denominate the metals from the alkaline earths barium, strontium, calcium, and magnium. **1815** W. PHILLIPS *Outl. Min. & Geol.* (ed. 3) 25 Lime has been proved by Sir H. Davy..to be a metallic oxide, consisting of 28 per cent. of oxygen and 72 of calcium. **1878** HUXLEY *Physiogr.* 81 A solid carbonate of calcium..more commonly termed carbonate of lime. **1881** LOCKYER in *Nature* No. 614. 321/2 Those short common lines of calcium which for years past we had watched coming out of the salts of calcium when decomposition was taking place.

2. *attrib.* = CALCIC; as in *calcium compounds*, *salts*, etc.; esp. **calcium carbonate**, $CaCO_3$, carbonate of lime, or limestone, and arragonite; **calcium chloride**, $CaCl_2$, chloride of lime, bleaching powder; **calcium fluoride**, $CaFl_2$, fluor spar; **calcium light**, the lime-light; **calcium oxide**, CaO, quick-lime; **calcium phosphate** $Ca_3(PO_4)_2$, phosphate of lime, the chief constituent of bone-ash; **calcium silicate**, $CaSiO_3$, found crystallized in tabular spar, etc.; **calcium sulphate**, $CaSO_4$, found crystallized as Gypsum.

1864 *Daily Tel.* 4 Oct., A blinding ray from a calcium light apparatus. **1869** ROSCOE *Elem. Chem.* 154 When bones are burnt, a white solid mass is left behind; this is called Calcium Phosphate. **1872** *Daily News* 7 Nov., Calcium lights shone on smiling multitudes. **1873** FOWNES *Chem.* 364 Calcium Carbonate is always precipitated.

calco- ('kælkəʊ), combining form of L. *calc-em* lime [not formed on L. analogies, which give *calci-*, but after Gr. words] in various technical terms.

1876 TOMES *Dental Anat.* 139 The 'calcospherites,' by which name he designated the globular forms seen and described by Rainie. *Ibid.* 140 For this modified albumen he proposes the name of 'calcoglobulin'. **1882** DANA *Min.* App. III. 20 *Calcozincite*..a mixture of zincite and calcite.

calcography, improper spelling of CHALC-.

† **'calcops.** *Obs.* A kind of fish.

1727 A. HAMILTON *New Acc. E. Ind.* II. xxxiii. 11 Fish-ponds to serve his Kitchin with Carp, Calcops and Mullet.

calcour, var. of CALKER, *Obs.*, a diviner.

calcrete ('kælkriːt). Also **calcicrete**. [f. L. *calc(i)-* lime, CALX + CON)CRETE *sb.*] A breccia or conglomerate formed by the cementation of rock debris, etc., by calcareous material.

1902 *Irish Naturalist* Oct. 231 Over the Boulder-clay and the calcrete is a bed of limestone sand and gravel. **1903** *Geol. Mag.* Mar. 139 No one would be likely to quarrel with 'calcicrete' and 'silicicrete', of which one would be two, the other three, letters longer [than 'calcrete', 'silcrete']. **1903** *Nature* 22 Oct. 614/1 In the Gulf of Manaar, calcareous masses ('calcretes') of great extent are formed *in situ* on the sea-bottom by the cementing of sand and other loose material by calcareous incrusting Polyzoa. **1959** J. D. CLARK *Prehist. S. Afr.* ii. 45 The tools of those times are found in calcretes and ferricretes.

calc-sinter ('kælk'sɪntə(r)). *Min.* [ad. Ger. *kalk-sinter*, f. *kalk* lime (a. L. *calc-em*; see CALC-) + *sinter* slag.] A hard crystalline deposit from

springs which hold carbonate of lime in solution.

1823 W. BUCKLAND *Relig. Diluv.* 115 Firmly cemented together by stalagmitic infiltrations of calc-sinter. **1830** LYELL *Princ. Geol.* I. 200 One of these springs .. has formed, by its incrustations, an elevated mound of solid travertin, or calc-sinter. **1850** LEITCH *Muller's Anc. Art* §268. 300 In Greece .. tufa and calc-sinter .. were also employed.

calc-spar ('kælk'spɑː(r)). *Min.* [see CALC-.] Calcareous spar or rhombohedral crystallized carbonate of lime.

1822 MRS. LOWRY *Convers. Min.* II. 28 Most of the fine calcspar of Derbyshire is of a deep topaz yellow colour. **1850** DAUBENY *Atom. The.* viii. (ed. 2) 267 Why .. do the particles of carbonate of lime, assume sometimes the form of calc-spar, sometimes of arragonite?

calc-tuff ('kælk'tʌf). *Min.* [see CALC-.] A porous deposit of carbonate of lime, formed by the waters of calcareous springs; calcareous tufa.

1822 MRS. LOWRY *Convers. Min.* II. 265 Acidiferous Earthy Minerals .. Calc-tuff. **1857** PAGE *Adv. Text-bk. Geol.* xx. (1876) 420 Calc-tuff .. is an open, porous, and somewhat earthy deposition of carbonate of lime from calcareous springs. **1863** WATTS *Dict. Chem.* I. 722 *Calctuff*, an alluvial form of carbonate of calcium.

calculability (ˌkælkjʊlə'bɪlɪtɪ). [f. next: see -ITY.] The quality of being calculable.

1873 B. STEWART *Conserv. Force* vi. 158 The characteristic of all such [machines] is their calculability.

calculable ('kælkjʊləb(ə)l), *a.* [f. L. *calculā-re* or F. *calcul-er* to calculate: see -ABLE, -BLE. So mod.F. *calculable.*] Capable of being calculated; that may be reckoned, measured, or computed.

a **1734** NORTH *Lives* II. 182 Eclipses .. being regular and calculable. **1809–10** COLERIDGE *Friend* (1865) 103 Incapable of producing any regular, continuous, and calculable effect. **1829** I. TAYLOR *Enthus.* vi. (1867) 113 The connexion of physical causes and effects is known and calculable. **1865** *Sat. Rev.* 25 Mar. 332/2 There is always a calculable risk of a vacancy.

b. Of a person: Such that his action in given circumstances can be reckoned upon and estimated.

1865 *Pall Mall G.* 1 May 2 He is the least consistent, reliable, and calculable of public men. **1876** GEO. ELIOT *Dan. Der.* 222 He was exactly the man to feel the utmost piquancy in a girl whom he had not found quite calculable.

calcular ('kælkjʊlə(r)), *a. Math.* [? f. CALCULUS + -AR[1].] Of or pertaining to a calculus.

1831 BREWSTER *Newton* (1855) II. xiv. 9 The rules are .. extricated from algebraical process, and presented in calcular form.

†**'calculary**, *sb.* ? *Obs.* [same deriv. as next.] Grew's name for a 'congeries of little stony knots' in a pear.

1674 GREW *Anat. Plants* vi. §3 The Calculary (most observable in rough-tasted, or Choak-Pears) is a Congeries of little stony Knots. **1677** —— *Anat. Fruits* ii. §6 Tartareous Grains .. in some Pears .. almost as hard as a Plum-stone; which I have thereupon named the Calculary. **1753** CHAMBERS *Cycl. Supp.* s.v., The calculary is no vital, or essential part of the fruit. **1852** SMITH *Eng. & Fr. Dict.*, Calculary, *pierre.*

calculary ('kælkjʊlərɪ), *a. Med.* [ad. L. *calculārius*, f. *calculus* stone: see -ARY.] Of or pertaining to a calculus; gravelly.

1660 GAUDEN *Bp. Brownrigg* 218 Motion was tedious .. to him, by reason of his calculary infirmity and corpulency.

†**'calculate**, *sb. Obs.* [f. L. *calculāre* to reckon: see next. Cf. *estimate* sb., and see -ATE[1], [2].]

A calculation, reckoning, estimate.

1695 E. BERNARD *Voy. fr. Aleppo* in *Misc. Cur.* (1708) III. 99 By a moderate Calculate there could not have been less at first than 560. **1700** RYCAUT *Hist. Turks* III. 432 An Exact and Secret Calculate was made of the true Number. *a* **1734** NORTH *Exam.* III. viii. ¶26. 602 Nor were these Brothers mistaken in their Calculate.

calculate ('kælkjʊleɪt), *v.*[1] [f. L. *calculāt-* ppl. stem of *calculā-re* to count, reckon, f. *calculus* a stone (see CALCULUS). Cf. It. *calcolare*, Sp., Pg. *calcular*, F. *calculer.* An early form of the pa. pple. was *calculat*, *-ate*, ad. L. *calculāt-us.*]

1. *trans.* To estimate or determine by arithmetical or mathematical reckoning; to compute, reckon.

1570 DEE *Math. Pref.* 42 Hable to Calculate the Planetes places for all tymes. **1656** tr. *Hobbes' Elem. Philos.* (1839) 92 When we calculate the magnitude and motions of heaven or earth. **1671** *True Non-Conf.* 152 About 165 years, before the Councel .. is the highest period from whence they can be calculat. **1833** HT. MARTINEAU *Manch. Strike* iii. 35 The men looked at the ground, and calculated how much digging and other work there would be. **1860** TYNDALL *Glac.* II. §1. 223 Bradley was able to calculate the velocity of light.

b. *absol.* To perform calculations, to form an estimate.

1601 SHAKS. *Jul. C.* I. iii. 65 Why Old men, Fooles, and Children calculate. **1613** R. C. *Table Alph.* (ed. 3) *Calculate*, cast a count, reckon. **1789** T. JEFFERSON *Writ.* (1859) III. 35 As yet, no vote has been given which will enable us to calculate, on certain ground.

2. *ellipt.* To ascertain beforehand the time or circumstances of (an event, e.g. an eclipse, a nativity) by astrology or mathematics.

1593 SHAKS. *2 Hen. VI*, IV. i. 34 A cunning man did calculate my birth And told me that by Water I should dye. **1667** MILTON *P.L.* VIII. 80 When they come to model Heav'n And calculate the Starrs. **1857** DE QUINCEY *China* 10 To calculate a lunar eclipse.

†**3.** To reckon in, count, include. *Obs.*

1643 *Sober Sadness* 32 [He] must have been calculated in the Black-bill, if he had not taken himselfe off.

4. To plan or devise with forethought; to think out; to frame. *arch.*

1654 G. GODDARD in *Introd. to Burton's Diary* (1828) I. 30 For the indenture, that was calculated at Court. **1672** GREW *Idea Hist. Plants* §3 That .. is but a Thought not well Calculated. **1708** SWIFT *Sentiments Ch. Eng. Man* Wks. 1755 II. I. 68 He doth not think the church of England so narrowly calculated, that it cannot fall in with any regular species of government. **1820** *Hoyle's Games Impr.* 171 Each [player] calculates his game without inspecting the tricks. **1856** EMERSON *Eng. Traits, Character* Wks. (Bohn) II. 61 The English did not calculate the conquest of the Indies. It fell to their character.

5. To arrange, design, prepare, adjust, adapt, or fit *for* a purpose. Const. *for*, or *inf.* with *to*; now only in *passive*.

1639 FULLER *Holy War* II. iii. (1840) 51 This vision, though calculated for this one bishop, did generally serve for all the nonresidents. **1691** T. H[ALE] *Acc. New Invent.* 16 Voyages all calculated for the proving her against the Worm. **1727** SWIFT *Modest Prop.* Wks. 1755 II. II. 66, I calculate my remedy for this .. kingdom of Ireland, and for no other. **1732** BERKELEY *Sermon to S.P.G.* Wks. III. 250 The Christian religion was calculated for the bulk of mankind. **1816** SCOTT *Antiq.* i, The coach was calculated to carry six regular passengers. **1848** THIRLWALL *Rem.* (1877) I. 137 The college is calculated for the reception of sixty students.

b. In the *pa. pple.* the notion of design gradually disappears, leaving merely the sense 'suited': see CALCULATED below. (Cf. the similar history of *apt*, *fit*, *adapted*, *fitted.*)

6. *intr.* To reckon or count *upon* or *on.*

1807 SOUTHEY *Life* (1850) III. 109 All those may almost be calculated upon. **1829** I. TAYLOR *Enthus.* vi. (1867) 114 Security in calculating upon the future. **1873** TRISTRAM *Moab* viii. 150 We had calculated on a quiet Sunday.

7. *U.S. colloq.* To think, opine, suppose, 'reckon'; to intend, purpose.

1830 GALT *Lawrie T.* II. v. (1849) 56, I calculate, that ain't no thing to make nobody afeard. **1833** MARRYAT *Peter S.* xliv. [*American speaking*] 'Well, captain,' said he, 'so you met with a squall?' 'I calculate not.' **1837** HALIBURTON *Clockm.* I. 291, I calculate you couldn't fault it in no particular. **1839** *Knickerbocker Mag.* XVII. (Bartlett), Mr. Crane requested those persons who calculated to join the singin' school to come forward.

†**'calculate**, *v.*[2] *Obs.* [f. L. *calculus* stone, pebble; cf. *coagulate*, etc.] *intr.* To form stone in the bladder. Hence **'calculating** *ppl. a.*

1607 TOPSELL *Four-f. Beasts* 197 The same .. with Parsley drunk in Wine .. dissolveth the stone in the bladder, and preventeth all such calculating gravel in time to come.

calculated ('kælkjʊleɪtɪd), *pa. pple.* and *ppl. a.* [f. CALCULATE *v.*[1] + -ED.[1]]

1. Reckoned, estimated, devised with forethought.

1863 GEO. ELIOT *Romola* III. xxvi. (1880) II. 266 When he did speak it was with a calculated caution. **1930** *Economist* 12 July 59/1 This important statement had been communicated to the Press as a result either of a misunderstanding or of a 'calculated indiscretion'. **1956** R. HEINLEIN *Double Star* (1958) i. 18 'You haven't any right to jeopardise everybody else by telling him. You don't know a thing about him.' 'It's a calculated risk.' **1959** *Listener* 22 Oct. 672/2 Obviously, the Soviet Union is taking a calculated risk.

2. Fitted, suited, fit, apt; of a nature or character proper or likely *to*.

1722 DE FOE *Col. Jack* (1840) 286 The state of life that I was now in was .. perfectly calculated to make a man completely happy. **1793** W. ROBERTS *Looker-on* (1794) No. 52 II. 273 These interlopers .. acted in a manner that was calculated to bring scandal upon the profession. **1795** SOUTHEY *Life* (1849) I. 256 Never had man so many relations so little calculated to inspire confidence. **1864** MANSEL *Lett., etc.* (1873) 298 These transparent disguises were not calculated, and, probably, were not intended, to deceive. **1868** GLADSTONE *Juv. Mundi* i. (1870) 3 A circumstance calculated to excite strong suspicion. **1879** in *Cassell's Techn. Educ.* IV. 76/2 Ireland is .. well calculated for the successful prosecution of ostreoculture.

Hence **'calculatedly** adv.

1899 *Westm. Gaz.* 8 Apr. 5/1 The *Freeman's Journal* says. .. 'The gentle wooing of the new unionism was so calculatedly seductive that a temporary aberration of the people would not have been unnatural.' **1931** BELLOC *Hist. Eng.* IV. 333 Cecil's danger was great. The power of Philip which had hitherto .. supported him he had calculatedly flouted. **1966** P. GREEN tr. *Escarpit's Novel Computer* vii. 97 My calculatedly excessive demand left these petty chiselers absolutely dumbfounded. **1984** *Observer* 26 Feb. 33/2 She has calculatedly reflected changing US tastes in looks and clothes.

calculating ('kælkjʊˌleɪtɪŋ), *vbl. sb.* [f. as CALCULATED *pa. pple.* and *ppl. a.* + -ING[1].] The action of the vb. CALCULATE; calculation: chiefly *attrib.*, as in ***calculating-engine***, ***-machine***, ***-machinery***, etc. **calculating machine**, any machine designed to carry out calculations, esp. one that performs arithmetical operations mechanically.

1710 *Brit. Apollo* III. 66 His Trigonometry for the Calculating of Sines, Tangents, etc. **1832** D. BREWSTER *Lett. Natural Magic* XI. 292 The calculating-machine now constructing under the superintendence of the inventor [*sc.* Babbage]. **1833** BREWSTER *Nat. Magic* xi. 292 The greater part of the calculating-machinery. **1855** *Proc. R. Soc.* VII. 499 Report of a Committee appointed by the Council to examine the Calculating Machine of M. Scheutz. **1878** TAIT & STEWART *Unseen Univ.* ii. §80. 90 Charles Babbage, the designer of the well-known calculating engine. **1890** CONAN DOYLE *Sign of Four* ii, You really are an automaton—a calculating machine. **1901** *Nature* 11 July 268/2 The advantages of the calculating machines .. are so great, and they are in so many ways preferable to logarithms where they can be used. **1955** KOESTLER *Trail of Dinosaur* 184 The calculating machines called electronic brains.

calculating ('kælkjʊˌleɪtɪŋ), *ppl. a.*[1] [f. as prec. + -ING[2].] That calculates; *esp.* that shrewdly or selfishly reckons the chances of gain or advantage. **calculating boy**, a child prodigy in arithmetic.

1809–12 MAR. EDGEWORTH *Absentee* ix, He was calculating and mercenary. **1828** SCOTT *F.M. Perth* xxxii, It had been resolved, with the most calculating cruelty. **1841** MIALL in *Nonconf.* I. 145 Men of a hardier, more sincere, less calculating religion. **1866** *North Brit. Rev.* XLV. 39 Colburn, the American 'calculating boy', who was then being exhibited as a curiosity in Dublin. **1937** H. G. WELLS *Star Begotten* vi. 91 The proportion of children of the calculating-boy and musical-prodigy type seemed to be increasing quite markedly.

Hence **'calcuˌlatingly** *adv.*

1855 MRS. WHITNEY *Gayworthys* i. (1879) 7 Huldah Brown looked calculatingly upon the gathered material.

†**calculating**, *ppl. a.*[2] *Obs.* See CALCULATE *v.*[2]

calculation (ˌkælkjʊ'leɪʃən). Also 4 calculacioun. [a. F. *calculation*, ad. L. *calculātiōn-em*, f. *calculāre* to reckon, CALCULATE. See -ATION.]

1. The action or process of reckoning; computation.

1393 GOWER *Conf.* II. 230 A great magicien Shulde of his calculation, Seche of constellation, How they the citee mighten gette. *Ibid.* III. 46 He maketh his calculations, He maketh his demonstrations. *c* **1400** MAUNDEV. 236 The Philosophres comen, and seyn here avys aftre her calculacions. **1614** RALEIGH *Hist. World* III. xxv. (R.) One Bartholomew Scullet .. hath by calculation found the very day. **1757** JOHNSON *Rambl.* No. 154 ¶5 No estimate is more in danger of erroneous calculations. **1875** JOWETT *Plato* (ed. 2) III. 412 All arithmetic and calculation have to do with number.

2. *concr.* The form in which reckoning is made; its product or result.

1646 SIR T. BROWNE *Pseud. Ep.* 134 If we suppose our present calculation, the Phaenix now in nature will be the sixt from the Creation. **1812** JANE AUSTEN *Mansf. Park* (1851) 81 If the first calculation is wrong, we make a second better. **1871** C. DAVIES *Metr. Syst.* III. 125 This calculation could not long suit the revenue.

3. Estimate of probability, forecast.

1847 EMERSON *Repres. Men* vi. *Napoleon* Wks. (Bohn) I. 372 His very attack was never the inspiration of courage, but the result of calculation. **1848** LYTTON *Harold* v. 142 Hitherto, he had advanced on his career without calculation. **1864** TENNYSON *En. Ard.* 470 The lazy gossips of the port, Abhorrent of a calculation crost.

calcu'lational, *a. rare.* [f. prec. + -AL[1].] Of or pertaining to calculation.

1874 PIAZZI SMYTH *Our Inherit.* ii. 14 Knowing well the numerical and calculational value of π.

†**'calculative**, *a.*[1] *Med.* ? *Obs.* [f. CALCUL-US + -ATIVE.] Liable to calculary disease.

1657 TOMLINSON *Renou's Disp.* 189 Foments applyed to pleuritical .. persons, as also to the calculative.

calculative ('kælkjʊlətɪv), *a.*[2] [f. CALCULATE *v.*[1]: see -ATIVE.] Of or pertaining to calculation; given to calculating.

c **1766** BURKE *Popery Laws* Wks. IX. 389 Habits of calculative dealings. **1840** *Fraser's Mag.* XXI. 307 Extraordinary calculative powers. **1865** CARLYLE *Fredk. Gt.* VIII. XIX. v. 170 Daun .. sits expectant; elaborately calculative.

calculator('kælkjʊˌleɪtə(r)). [a. L. *calculātor*, n. of agent f. *calculā-re*, corresp. to F. *calculateur*: see CALCULATE and -OR.]

1. One who calculates; a reckoner.

c **1380** WYCLIF *Sel. Wks.* II. 408 Siche ben many calkelatours. **1611** COTGR. *Calculateur*, a reckoner, calculator. **1722** DE FOE *Plague* (1884) 227 Calculators of Nativities. **1841** THACKERAY *Sec. Fun. Nap.* ii. (Pock. ed. 1887) 321 Economists and calculators. **1841–4** EMERSON *Ess. Experience* Nature hates calculators; her methods are saltatory and impulsive.

2. a. A set of tables to facilitate calculations.

b. A mechanical contrivance for performing certain calculations; a calculating machine.

1784 THOMSON (*title*) The Universal Calculator. **1824** W. WALTON (*title*) The Complete Calculator .. and Universal Ready Reckoner. **1876** *S. Kensington Museum Catal.* No. 831 This screw bears a calculator which serves to read angular displacements of less than 20 seconds.

c. An electronic device for performing calculations, now *esp.* one that is preprogrammed; *spec.* (more fully ***pocket calculator***) a flat hand-held calculator with a keyboard and visual display.

Formerly used where *computer* is now usual.

1946 [see *sequence-controlled* ppl. adj. s.v. SEQUENCE *sb.* 8]. **1946** *Sci. Amer.* June 248/3 (*heading*) Electronic calculator uses 18,000 tubes to solve complex problems. **1958** [see *electronic brain* s.v. ELECTRONIC *a.* 3]. **1965** *Product Engin.* 10 May 48 (*caption*) Electronic desk-top calculator. **1970** *Computer Design* June 34/1 (*heading*) LSI, electronic printout bases of 'pocket' electronic calculator. **1973** [see MICRO- 8 a]. **1976** *Globe & Mail* (Toronto) 23 Feb. 4/2 The digital watch is a natural followup to the electronic calculator and many watch distributors.. sell the calculators as well. **1978** [see POCKET *sb.* 12 a]. **1978** *John Moores Catal.* Spring–Summer 813 You can, of course, work out percentages on any calculator, but it is easier and quicker if you have a separate % key. **1983** *Austral. Microcomputer Mag.* Nov. 105/3 Casio is gearing up to make about 1 million thin credit-card calculators a month.

'calculatory, *a.* ? *Obs.* [f. CALCULATE *v.* + -ORY; corresp. to L. *calculātōrius*, F. *calculatoire.*] Of or pertaining to calculation or estimate.

1611 COTGR., *Calculatoire*, calculatorie, calculating. **1627** JACKSON *Creed* VI. Wks. V. 260 The argument is but calculatory, and this kind of argument is deceitful. **1649** BP. HALL *Cases Consc.* III. ii. (1654) 179 Calculatory or figure-casting Astrology. **1677** PLOT *Oxfordsh.* 286 The first Contriver of the Art Calculatory in disputation.

† **'calcule,** *sb. Obs.* Also 7 calcull, 8 calcul. [a. F. *calcul* in same sense, ad. L. *calculus*: see below.] = CALCULATION.

1601 HOLLAND *Pliny* XVIII. xxix, According to the calcull of others, the true reason and cause is this. **1682** WHELER *Journ. Greece* I. 20 He is much mistaken in the Calcule, both of its Longitude and Latitude. **1718** WODROW *Corr.* (1843) II. 407, I design.. to.. bring the matter to a close calcule with the printers. **1754** ERSKINE *Princ. Sc. Law* (1809) 480 Decrees.. founded on an error in calcul.

† **'calcule,** *v. Obs.* Forms: 4 calculen, calclen, 5 calkule, -el, -ylle, 5–6 -il(l, 4–6 calcule. [? a. F. *calcule-r* in same sense, ad. L. *calculā-re*: see CALCULATE.] To reckon; = CALCULATE *v.*

1377 LANGL. *P. Pl.* B. xv. 364 Of þat was calculed of þe element þe contrarie þei fynde. *c* **1380** WYCLIF *Serm.* xxix. Sel. Wks. I. 75 þei traveilen in veyn þat calculen þat, etc. **1387** TREVISA *Higden* (Rolls Ser.) II. 237 He calcleþ and accounteþ þe ages of þe world by þowsendes. **1496** *Dives & Paup.* (W. de W.) I. xxv. 62/1 They that calculen & casten yeres, dayes & monethes. **1549** *Compl. Scot.* 167 Quha can calkil the degreis of kyn & blude. **1559** H. BALNAVIS *Let.* in Keith *Hist. Aff. Sc.* App. 44 You may calkill what twa thousand futemen.. will tak monethlie.

† **'calculer.** *Obs.* [f. prec.] = CALCULATOR.

c **1391** CHAUCER *Astrol.* 14 Thin almury is cleped the denticle of capricorne or elles the kalkuler. **1470** HARDING *Chron.* clxxxviii. ix, The xx. daye of Maye.. as calculers it knowe.

calculiform ('kælkjʊlɪfɔːm), *a.* [f. L. *calculus* pebble + -(I)FORM.] Pebble-shaped.

1900 *Spectator* 24 Mar. 417/2 The people are still known as the Mayas, and the writing is called calculiform. **1930** *Antiquity* IV. 289 The calculiform signs.. have proved no Rosetta stone for the decipherment of.. surviving New Empire codices.

calculifrage ('kælkjʊlɪfreɪdʒ). *Med.* [a. F. *calculifrage* a. 'that breaks calculi', L. type **calculifrag-us*, f. *-frag-us* breaking, *frangĕre* to break.] An instrument introduced into the bladder for breaking down calculi (*Syd. Soc. Lex.*). Hence **calcu'lifragous** *a.*, (medicines) fitted for breaking or reducing calculi.

† **'calculing,** *vbl. sb. Obs.* [f. CALCULE *v.* + -ING[1].] Calculating, reckoning.

c **1374** CHAUCER *Troylus* I. 71 Whan þis Calcas knew by calkelyng. **1387** TREVISA *Higden* (Rolls Ser.) I. 39 þe calculynge of Denys.. haþ lasse by xxii ȝere þan þe calculynge of Jerom. **1582** BATMAN *Barth. De P.R.* VIII. xxvi. 131 Able to science and use of calkling and of accompts.

'calculist. [f. CALCUL-US + -IST.] One skilled in a mathematical calculus; a mathematician.

1829 CARLYLE *For. Rev. & Cont. Misc.* IV. 138 Mathesis, of which, it has been said, many a Great Calculist has not even a notion.

† **calcu'lose,** *a.* [ad. L. *calculōs-us* stony.]

1. Stony, pebbly.

c **1420** *Pallad. on Husb.* II. 274 The feldes calculose.

2. *Med.* = CALCULOUS 1.

1686 Sir T. Browne's *Pseud. Ep.* II. iv. 61 Calculose [ed. **1646** calculous] concretions in the kidney.

Hence **calculosity.** *rare*$^{-0}$.

1656 BLOUNT *Glossogr.*, *Calculosity*, fulness of stones or Counters.

calculous ('kælkjʊləs), *a.* [ad. L. *calculōs-us*, f. *calculus* stone, pebble; corresp. to F. *calculeux.*]

1. *Med.* Of or pertaining to a calculus or the stone; diseased with the stone; calculary.

1605 TIMME *Quersit.* III. 156 A remedy.. to mittigate and to dissolue such calculous & stony matter. **1683** ROBINSON in *Ray's Corr.* (1848) 137 A good medicine in some scorbutic and calculous cases. *a* **1801** W. HEBERDEN *Comment.* xvi. (1806) 84 In opening the bodies of calculous persons. **1803** *Med. Jrnl.* IX. 355 To ascertain the precise nature of calculous urine. *a* **1827** ABERNETHY *Surg. Wks.* (1827) II. 207 No calculous concretion was found after death. **1858** *Lond. Rev.* Oct. 230 A victim of confirmed calculous disease.

† **2.** Stony (as the 'calculary' of a pear). *Obs.*

1671 GREW *Anat. Plants* vi. §3 A simple Body, having neither any of the Lignous branches in it, nor any Calculous Knots.

calculus ('kælkjʊləs). *Pl.* -i, -uses. [L.; = 'small stone', dim. of *calx* stone, pebble; also, a stone or counter used in playing draughts, a stone used in reckoning on the abacus or counting board, whence, reckoning, calculation, account; and a stone used in voting, whence, vote, sentence.]

‖ **1.** *Med.* 'A stone. A generic term for concretions occurring accidentally in the animal body' (*Syd. Soc. Lex.*). Calculi are of many kinds, and receive names from the various parts of the body in which they occur, as *renal* (in the kidneys), *vesical* (in the bladder), *prostatic* (in the prostate), *intestinal* (in the intestines, chiefly of animals), etc., or from the nature of their composition, as *lithic acid*, *uric acid calculus*, etc.

[**1619** SCLATER *Exp. Thess.* (1627) I. To Rdr. 5 That flagellum studiosorum, Calculus Renum.] **1732** ARBUTHNOT *Rules of Diet* 420 A Human Calculus, or Stone. **1760** tr. *Keysler's Trav.* IV. 339 Bezoar is.. a stone or calculus taken from a species of the East and West Indian goats. **1807** M. BAILLIE *Morb. Anat.* 308 Calculi when divided.. exhibit most commonly a laminated structure. **1849** TODD *Cycl. Anat. & Phys.* IV 85/1 The oriental bezoard, a resinous intestinal calculus. **1880** *Med. Temp. Jrnl.* Oct. 6 Biliary calculi are not infrequently due to this influence.

† **2.** Computation, calculation. *Obs.*

1684 T. BURNET *The. Earth* I. 166 Suppose the abyss was but half as deep as the deep ocean, to make this calculus answer, all the dry land ought to be cover'd with mountains. **1693** E. HALLEY in *Phil. Trans.* XVII. 654 Were this Calculus founded on the Experience of a very great number of Years. **1817** COLERIDGE *Biog. Lit.* 140 For the purposes of mathematical calculus it is indifferent which force we term negative, and which positive.

3. *Math.* A system or method of calculation, 'a certain way of performing mathematical investigations and resolutions' (Hutton); a branch of mathematics involving or leading to calculations, as the DIFFERENTIAL, INTEGRAL calculus, etc. The differential calculus is often spoken of as 'the calculus'.

1672 *Phil. Trans.* VII. 4017, I cannot yet reduce my Observations to a calculus. **1750** *Ibid.* XLVII. xi. 62 Mr. Clairant.. kept his calculus a profound secret. **1804** *Ibid.* XCIV. 219 If the introduction of the new calculi, as they have been called, has extended the bounds of science. **1796** HUTTON *Math. Dict.* I. 234 We say the Arithmetical or Numeral Calculus, the Algebraical Calculus, the Differential Calculus, the Exponential Calculus, the Fluxional Calculus, the Integral Calculus, the Literal or Symbolical Calculus, etc... *Algebraical*, *Literal* or *Symbolical* Calculus is.. the same with algebra. **1837** CARLYLE *Fr. Rev.* (1872) III. II. i. 60 Science which cannot with all its calculuses, differential, integral, and of variations, calculate the Problem of Three gravitating Bodies. **1846** MILL *Logic* III. xxiv. §6 The general problem of the algebraical calculus. **1854** BOOLE *Invest. Laws Th.* i. (L.) The exhibition of logic in the form of a calculus. **1878** GEO. ELIOT *Coll. Breakf. P.* 279 Fount of spirit force Beyond the calculus.

cald, obs. f. COLD; obs. pa. t. of CALL.

‖ **caldarium** (kæl'dɛərɪəm). [L., f. *calid-us* hot.] A (Roman) hot bath or bath-room.

1753 in CHAMBERS *Cycl. Supp.* **1832** GELL *Pompeiana* I. vi. 106 The stove of the caldarium. **1856** R. VAUGHAN *Mystics* (1860) I. v. i. 110 It.. grinds their corn, fills their caldarium. **1881** DARWIN *Earth-worms* 227 The tops of the broken down walls of a caldarium or bath were likewise covered up with 2 feet of earth.

Caldee, obs. form of CHALDEE.

‖ **caldera** (kal'dera). *Geol.* [a. Sp. *caldera* = Pg. *caldeira*, F. *chaudière* cauldron, kettle, boiler:—L. *caldāria*, pl. of prec.] A deep cauldron-like cavity on the summit of an extinct volcano.

1865 LYELL *Elem. Geol.* (ed. 6) 632 Enlarged afterwards into a caldera. **1875** WATTS *Dict. Chem.* VII. 553 [In] the valley of Furnas.. the soil is now perforated by a number of geysers. The three largest and most active of these are called 'caldeiras'.

'calderite. *Min.* A variety of garnet.

1837 DANA *Min.* (1868) 269 *Calderite*, a mineral from Nepaul, is said to be nothing but massive garnet.

caldese, var. of CHALDESE *v.*, to cheat.

† **caldewelle.** *Obs.*

1463 *Mann. & Househ. Exp.* 192 Item payd ffor viij. pypys of caldewelle, ix.*s.*

† **caldmawe:** see CALMEWE.

caldrife, var. of CAULDRIFE *a. Sc.*, cold.

caldron, another spelling of CAULDRON *sb.*

† **cale,** *sb.*[1] *Obs.* [a. F. *cale* in same sense.] A kind of head-dress worn by women; a CAUL.

1588 DELONEY in *Roxburgh Ballads* (1887) VI. 391 Her Ladies.. in costly cales of gold.

† **cale,** *sb.*[2] *Obs.*

1708 *Lond. Gaz.* No. 4453/4 One black Gelding.. with a very large Star tending to a Cale, a charge lately laid on his Left Eye.

cale, *sb.*[3], early northern f. KALE, COLE, cabbage, and cabbage broth or soup.

cale: see also CALES.

† **cale,** *v. Obs.* [a. F. *cale-r* in same sense (= Pr., Sp. *calar*, It. *cálare*):—L. *chalā-re*, ad. Gr. χαλᾶ-ν to slacken, loosen, let down, lower.] *trans.* To lower (sails, yards, etc.).

1652 URQUHART *Jewel* Wks. (1834) 211 By the malignancie or over-mastering power of a cross winde, they should be forced to cale the hypocritical bunt.

‖ **calean, callean, calleoon.** [Pers. *qaliyān.*] 'A water-pipe for smoking; the Persian form of the hubble-bubble' (Yule).

1739 ELTON in Hanway *Trav.* (1762) I. I. v. 16 Several persians of distinction, who, smoaking their callean, observed a profound silence. **1811** H. MARTYN *Let.* in *Mem.* III. (1825) 412 Reclining in garden and smoking caleans. **1828** *Kuzzilbash* i. 59 (Y.) The elder of the men met to smoke their calleoons under the shade.

caleatour: see CALIATOUR.

calecannon, var. of COLCANNON.

caleche, calèche: see CALASH.

Caledonian (kælɪ'dəʊnɪən), *a.* and *sb.* [f. *Calēdonia*, Roman name of part of northern Britain, in modern times applied poetically or rhetorically to Scotland, or the Scottish Highlands, 'Caledonia, stern and wild' (Scott).]

A. *adj.* **1.** Of ancient Caledonia; of Scotland.

1656 BLOUNT *Glossogr.*, *Caledonian*, belonging to Scotland, formerly called Caledonia. **1785** WARTON *Milton's Silv. Lib.* (T.) Tinged with Caledonian or Pictish woad. *Mod.* Used in titles, as 'the Gentlemen of the Caledonian Hunt', 'the Caledonian Railway'.

2. *Geol.* Designating or pertaining to the great mountain-building episode of late Silurian and early Devonian times in Britain and Scandinavia; also applied to contemporary mountain-building elsewhere. Hence **'Caledonoid** *a.*, of or pertaining to the direction assumed by the Caledonian mountain-folds, generally from north-east to south-west.

1903 GEIKIE *Text-Bk. Geol.* (ed. 4) I. III. I. iii. 394 In north-western Europe, the prevalent line along which terrestrial plications took place during the earlier half of Palæozoic time was from S.W. or S.S.W. to N.E. or N.N.E. —the Caledonian chain of Professor Suess. **1906** SOLLAS tr. *Suess's Face of Earth* II. III. ii. 82 These pre-Devonian mountains, which proceed from Norway and form the whole of Scotland.. we call the *Caledonian mountains.* **1913** C. LAPWORTH in G. A. Auden *Handbk. for Birmingham* 598 The trend.. N.E., S.W... which suggests that trend characteristic.. of the 'Caledonian Movement' becomes.. naturally referred to as the *Caledonoid Trend.* **1929** L. J. WILLS *Physiogr. Evol. Brit.* II. vi. 76 'Caledonian' implies a fold produced during the post-Silurian orogeny, but 'Caledonoid' refers to a south-west to north-east fold of any age.

B. *sb.* A native of ancient Caledonia; *humorously* = Scotchman.

1768 J. MACPHERSON (*title*) Critical Dissertations on the Origin of the Ancient Caledonians. **1781** (*title*) The Unfortunate Caledonian in England. **1813** J. GRANT (*title*) Account of the Picts, Caledonians, and Scots. **1883** *Daily News* 4 Sept. 5/6 Those who go 'through' with the volatile Caledonian [Flying Scotchman].

caledonite ('kælɪdəʊ,naɪt). *Min.* [f. L. *Caledonia* Scotland + -ITE.] A mineral (see quot.) found at Leadhills in Lanarkshire and elsewhere.

1863 WATTS *Dict. Chem.* (1879) I. 722 *Caledonite*, cupreous sulpho-carbonate of lead, from Leadhills in Scotland.

caleduct, var. of CALIDUCT.

caleevere, obs. form of CALIVER.

calefacient (kælɪfeɪʃ(ɪ)ənt), *a.* and *sb.* [ad. L. *calefacient-em*, pr. pple. of *calefacĕre* to make warm, f. *calē-re* to be warm + *facĕre* to make.]

A. *adj.* Producing warmth.

B. *sb. Med.* A medical agent which produces warmth or a sense of heat.

1661 LOVELL *Hist. Anim. & Min.* 418 It's cured.. by.. calefacients. **1881** in *Syd. Soc. Lex.* **1885** LD. BRAMWELL in *19th Cent.* June 1027 Galen.. says: 'Old age is cold and dry, and is to be corrected by calefacients.'

† **cale'facted,** *ppl. a.* [f. L. *calefact-us* heated + -ED.] Heated, warm.

1599 A. M. *Gabelhouer's Bk. Physick* 85/1 Liquefye it in some calefactede locatione.

calefaction (kælɪ'fækʃən). Also 6 cali-, 7 calfaction, callifaction. Now *rare.* [ad. L. *calefactiōn-em*, n. of action f. *calefacĕre.*]

1. Making warm (*lit.* and *fig.*); warming, heating.

1547 BOORDE *Brev. Health* lxxiii. 22 It doth signifye califaction of the lyver. **1574** NEWTON *Health Mag.* 4 Exercise by motion and calefaction. **1658** R. FRANCK *North. Mem.* (1821) 35 Ardent are other some because influenced by callifaction. *c* **1750** FRANKLIN *Lett.* Wks. 1840 VI. 98 The blood is returned again to the heart for a fresh calefaction. **1852** J. H. NEWMAN *Scope Univ. Educ.* 10 The science of calefaction and ventilation is reserved for the north.

2. Heated condition.
1634 R. H. *Salerne Regim.* 196 The Calefaction or boyling ceaseth not by Blood-letting. **1844** *Blackw. Mag.* 509 [He] paused after his labours in a state of extreme calefaction.
† **3.** *Med.* (See quot.) *Obs.*
1612 WOODALL *Surg. Mate* Wks. (1653) 268 Calfaction is a..preparing simple and compound medicaments, not by boyling or burning, but by the moderate heat of the Sun, fire, *fimus equinus, vel ejus vicarius.*

calefactive (kælɪˈfæktɪv), *a.* Now *rare.* [f. L. *calefact-*, ppl. stem of *calefacĕre* to warm: see -IVE.] Having the tendency to warm; warming.
1576 NEWTON tr. *Lemnie's Complex.* (1633) 101 The warme and calefactive spirit, which..was infused into the whole world. **1678** HOBBES *Decameron* Wks. 1845 VII. 120 The air..had gotten a calefactive power. **1874** B. BERNARD *S. Lover* I. 158 Calefactive depths of Celticism.

calefactor (kælɪˈfæktə(r)). [Agent-noun of Latin type from *calefacĕre* to warm.]
† **1.** He who, or that which warms; a warmer.
1605 TIMME *Quersit.* II. vii. 133 It standeth in neede of a calefactor and restorer of heate.
2. Name of a small kind of stove.
1831 *Fraser's Mag.* III. 140 On the one hand..smokes (in patent calefactors) a Dinner of innumerable courses.

caleˈfactory (kælɪˈfæktərɪ), *a.* and *sb.* [ad. L. *calefactōrius* having heating power, f. *calefacĕre* to warm; in B, ad. med.L. *calefactōrium* a place or appliance for warming.]
A. *adj.* Adapted for or tending to warming.
1711 J. PUCKLE *Club* (1817) 53 Love, like sunbeams.. contracted to one object is fervent and calefactory. **1848** *Bachelor of Albany* 78 Calefactory arrangements and thermal comforts.
B. *sb.* **1.** The room in a monastery where the inmates warmed themselves.
1681 BLOUNT *Glossogr.*, *Califactory*, is a room in a Monastery, with one or more fires in it, where the Religious persons warm themselves, after they come from Matins. **1774** T. WEST *Antiq. Furness* (1805) 73 The locutorium, calefactory, and conversation room. **1844** S. R. MAITLAND *Dark Ages* 406 Warmed by hot air from the stove in the calefactory.
2. A warming-pan; the ball of precious metal containing hot water, on which the priest warmed his hands when administering the eucharist in cold weather; otherwise called the *pome.*
1536 *Inv. Lincoln Cathedral* in *Monasticon Anglic.* VIII. 1281 A calefactory, silver and gilt, with leaves graven, weighing nine ounces and half. **1536** *Regist. Riches* in *Antiq. Sarisb.* (1771) 198 A Fat of Silver for holy water..a calefactory, silver and gilt with divers Scriptures.
† **3.** = CALEFACIENT *sb.*
1657 TOMLINSON *Renou's Disp.* 203 Many calefactories.. as Pepper, Bartram, Bitumen.

† ˈ**calefy**, *v. Obs.* Also **califly**. [ad. med.L. *calefĭcāre*, f. *calēre* to be hot; see -FY.]
1. *trans.* To make warm or hot; to warm, heat. Also *absol.* Hence ˈ**calefied** *ppl. a.*
1526 *Pilgr. Perf.* (1531) 31 This spirituall sterre of grace.. calefyeth [*marg.* warmeth] & illumyneth our soules. **1599** A. M. *Gabelhouer's Bk. Physick* 13/1 Take the kernelles of wallnuttes, lay them in calefyede water. **1657** TOMLINSON *Renou's Disp.* 38 Which taken alone do greatly calefy.
2. *intr.* To become warm.
1646 SIR T. BROWNE *Pseud. Ep.* 51 Crystall will calefy unto electricity, that is a power to attract strawes or light bodies. **1658** R. FRANCK *North. Mem.* (1821) 350 Soils, which calify and indurate by the Sun's reflection.

calegarth, var. of CALGARTH *Obs.*, cabbage garden.

‖ **calembour** (kalɑ̃bur, ˈkæləmbʊər, -æ-). Also **calembourg**. [Fr. (According to Chasles, quoted by Littré, from the name of 'the Abbé de Calemberg, a witty personage in German tales', i.e. Pfarrer Wigand von Theben, known as the 'Pfaff von Kahlenberg' or Priest of Kahlenberg in Lower Austria.)] A pun.
1830 *Fraser's Mag.* II. 237 All British-born..people.. father their calembourgs on Rogers. **1876** A. S. PALMER *Word-hunter's Note-bk.* 167 A mere calembour on the resemblance between the word ebrius and Ebraeus.

calembuc(o, obs. form of CALAMBAC.

calemint, obs. form of CALAMINT.

calend, occas. obs. sing. of CALENDS.

calendal (kəˈlɛndəl), *a.* [f. L. *calend-æ* CALENDS + -AL[1].] Of or pertaining to the Calends.
1839 *Fraser's Mag.* XX. 204 In the most ancient calendal system. *Ibid.* 328 Each of the thirty calendal forms had its one or more animal representatives.

calendar (ˈkæləndə(r)), *sb.* Forms: 3-8 **kalender**, 4 **kalunder, calundere, kalendeere, -dre, -dare**, 4-5 **kalendere**, 4-8 **calender**, 5 **calendere, kalander**, 7 **callander**, 6- **kalendar**, 7- **calendar**. [a. AF. *calender*, = OF. *calendier* list, register:—L. *calendārium* account-book, f. *calendæ, kalendæ* calends, the day on which accounts were due; see CALENDS.]
1. The system according to which the beginning and length of successive civil years, and the subdivision of the year into its parts, is fixed; as the Babylonian, Jewish, Roman, or Arabic calendar.
Julian Calendar, that introduced by Julius Caesar B.C. 46, in which the ordinary year has 365 days, and every fourth year is a leap year of 366 days, the months having the names, order, and length still retained.
Gregorian Calendar, the modification of the preceding adapted to bring it into closer conformity with astronomical data and the natural course of the seasons, and to rectify the error already contracted by its use, introduced by Pope Gregory XIII in A.D. 1582, and adopted in Great Britain in 1752. See STYLE.
c **1205** LAY. 7219 He [Julius Caesar] makede þane kalender. *a* **1300** *Cursor M.* 24916 þat moneth þat man clepes..Decembre in þe kalunder. **1387** TREVISA *Higden* (1865) I. 247 Som monþe in þe kalendere haþ but foure Nonas, and som haþ sixe. **1413** LYDG. *Pylgr. Sowle* v. i. 73 The competister in the Craft of the Kalendar he cleped seculum the tyme of an honderd yeere. **1611** BIBLE *Pref.* 2 When he [Cæsar] corrected the Calender, and ordered the yeere according to the course of the Sunne. **1831** BREWSTER *Newton* (1855) II. xxiii. 311 When the public attention was called to the reformation of the Kalendar. **1854** TOMLINSON *Arago's Astron.* 188 The Arabic calendar, which is that of the Mahometans, is exclusively based on the course of the moon. **1856** EMERSON *Eng. Traits* x. *Wealth* Wks. (Bohn) II. 70 Roger Bacon explained precession of the equinoxes, [and] the consequent necessity of the reform of the calendar. **1886** R. THOMSON *Relig. Humanity* 20 The founder of the Church [Aug. Comte] drew up its calendar..Each of the thirteen lunar months of the year is sacred to the memory of a great leader of humanity.
2. A table showing the division of a given year into its months and days, and referring the days of each month to the days of the week; often also including important astronomical data, and indicating ecclesiastical or other festivals, and other events belonging to individual days. Sometimes containing only facts and dates belonging to a particular profession or pursuit, as *Gardener's Calendar, Racing Calendar*, etc. Also a series of tables, giving these facts more fully; an almanac.
c **1340** *Alisaunder* 623 If any wight..wilnes þem [þe twelue signes] knowe, Kairus to þe Kalender · & kenne yee may. *c* **1391** CHAUCER *Astrol.* I. §11 The names of the halidayes in the kalender. **1481** CAXTON *Myrr.* II. xxxi. 126 This is xii tymes so moche & more ouer as the calender enseigneth. **1549** *Bk. Com. Prayer*, The Table and Kalendar expressing the order of the Psalms and Lessons. **1595** SHAKS. *John* III. i. 86 What hath this day deseru'd?.. That it in golden letters should be set Among the high Tides in the Kalender? **1635** AUSTIN *Medit.* 207 Our Church keeps no Solemnitie for his [John the Baptist's] Death (though the Remembrance of it be in her Calender). **1759** MILLER *Gard. Dict.* Pref., The Gardeners Kalendar which was inserted in the former editions of this book. **1824** W. IRVING *T. Trav.* II. 38 Greatness..of a kind not to be settled by reference to the court calendar. **1846** J. BAXTER *Libr. Pract. Agric.* II. 423 Appendix, *Agricultural Calendar.* **1879** *Print. Trades Jrnl.* XXVIII. 11 Almanacks and calendars in great variety.
b. A contrivance for reckoning days, months, etc.
1719 DE FOE *Crusoe* I. 74 Every seventh Notch was as long again as the rest, and every first Day of the Month as long again as that long one, and thus I kept my Kalender. **1768** STERNE *Sent. Journ.*, *Captive* (1778) II. 31 A little calendar of small sticks..notch'd all over with the dismal days and nights he [a captive] had passed there. **1863** T. WRIGHT in *Macm. Mag.* Jan. 173 The Roman calendar of marble.. presented the more prominent attributes of the modern almanac.
† **3.** *fig.* A guide, directory: an example, model.
c **1385** CHAUCER *L.G.W.* 542 Thou..woste well that kalender ys she To any woman that wull louer be. *c* **1400** *Epiph.* (Turnb. 1843) 115 Lete hem afore be to yow a Kalendere. **1413** *St. Trials Hen. V* (R.) Images..introduced ..by the permission of the church, to be as a calendar to the laity and the ignorant. **1426** AUDELAY *Poems* 27. **1602** SHAKS. *Ham.* v. ii. 114 He is the card or calendar of gentry.
4. A list or register of any kind. (In the general sense, now only *fig.*)
? *a* **1400** *Morte Arth.* 2641 Kydd in his kalander a knyghte of his chambyre. **1479** *Office Mayor Bristol* in *Eng. Gilds* 429 To be called and named the Maire of Bristowe is Register, or ellis the Maire is Kalender. **1589** PUTTENHAM *Eng. Poesie* (Arb.) 141 He shoulde haue alwaies a little calender of them apart to vse readily. **1633** G. HERBERT *Temple, Ch. Militant* 243 When Italie..shall..all her calender of sinnes fulfill. **1664** H. MORE *Myst. Iniq.* 207 The last time in Daniel's Kalendar of his Four Kingdoms. **1689** *Myst. Iniq.* 16 Registred in the Kalender with those that stood precluded the King's Favour. **1857** H. REED *Lect. Brit. Poets* iii. 81 The calendar which opens so nobly with the name of Chaucer, closes worthily in our day with that of Wordsworth.
b. *esp.* A list of canonized saints, or the like. (Now usually treated as a form of sense 2, the days dedicated to the memory of the saints being usually registered in the 'calendar' or almanac.)
1601 HOLLAND *Pliny* II. 346 When they receiued Æsculapius as a canonized god into their Kalender. **1631** GOUGE *God's Arrows* III. §45. 266 Such as the Holy Ghost registreth in the Kalender of true Saints. **1781** GIBBON *Decl. & F.* II. xxxiii. 254 The calendar of martyrs received..a considerable augmentation. **1832** W. IRVING *Alhambra* II. 256 Peace offerings to every saint in the Kalendar.
c. A list of prisoners for trial at the assizes.
[**1591** *Declar. Gt. Troubles* in *Harl. Misc.* (1809) II. 214 To call those inquisitions, with their answeres to be put into writing..to keepe in a maner of a register or kalender]. **1764** R. SANDERS (*title*) The Newgate Calendar. **1768** BLACKSTONE *Comm.* IV. 376 The usage is, for the judge to sign the calendar, or list of all the prisoners' names. **1823** LAMB *Last Ess.*, *To Shade of Elliston*, Rhadamanthus..tries the lighter causes..leaving to his two brothers the heavy calendars. **1856** EMERSON *Eng. Traits* iv. *Race* Wks. (Bohn) II. 28 The crimes recorded in their calendars.
d. *spec.* A list or register of documents arranged chronologically with a short summary of the contents of each, so as to serve as an index to the documents of a given period.
[**1467** *Ordin. Worcester* in *Eng. Gilds* 370 The Kalender of the articles and acts afore specified.] **1830** (Rolls Series) (*title*) Calendars of the Proceedings in Chancery in the reign of Queen Elizabeth. **1856** (*title*) Calendar of State Papers, Domestic Series of the Reign of Edward VI.
† **5.** *fig.* A record. *Obs.*
1601 SHAKS. *All's Well* I. iii. 4 The Kalender of my past endeuours. **1649** SELDEN *Laws Eng.* I. lvii. (1739) 105 His meritorious Holy War could never wipe it out of the Calendar of story. *a* **1718** PENN *Tracts* Wks. 1726 I. 589 Once they were as Calendars, for weak People to read some Mystical Glory by.
† **b.** An outward sign, index. *Obs.*
1590 LODGE *Euphues Gold. Leg.* (1887) 13 Nor are the dimples in the face the calendars of truth.
† **6.** One who has charge of records or historical documents. Occurring in the name of an ancient guild in Bristol. *Obs.*
1479 *Office Mayor Bristol* in *Eng. Gilds* 417 The..prestis of the hous of the Kalenders of Bristowe. ? *c* **1600** *MS.*, *ibid.* 287 The rites and liberties of the Kalenders, of the fraternitie of the church of All Saincts in Bristow, who were a brotherhood consisting of clergy and laymen, and kept the ancient recordes and mynaments, not onely of the towne, but also of other societes in other remote places.
7. *attrib.* and *Comb.*, as ***calendar-day, -holiday, -saint***; **calendar-clock**, a clock which indicates the days of the week or month; **calendar-court**, a court of justice held on a day appointed in the calendar; **calendar month**, one of the twelve months into which the year is divided according to the calendar; also the space of time from any day of any such month to the corresponding day of the next, as opposed to a lunar month of four weeks.
1884 F. BRITTEN *Watch & Clockm.* 38 [A] *Calendar Clock [or a] Calendar Watch..[are] a clock or watch that denotes the progress of the calendar. **1865** *Morning Star* 26 May, The court was not a *calendar court. **1875** POSTE *Gaius* I. (ed. 2) 101 A *calendar day consisted of 24 hours measured from midnight to midnight. **1847** EMERSON *Repres. Men* iv. *Montaigne* Wks. (Bohn) I. 346, I mean to..celebrate the calendar-day of our Saint Michael de Montaigne. **1713** 'PHILOPATRIUS' *Refl. Sacheverell's Thanksgiv.-Day* 8, I.. consulted my Almanack, and found it was no *Calendar Holiday. **1788** J. POWELL *Devises* (1827) II. 255 Within six *calendar months after his decease. **1868** FREEMAN *Norm. Conq.* (1876) II. x. 507 This whole revolution..took less than one kalendar month. **1679** *Establ. Test.* 40 The Catalogue of their *Calender Saints.

† ˈ**calendar**, *a. Obs. rare*[−1]. [ad. L. *calendārius* belonging to the calends.] Of the calends: applied to the *Curia calabra* at the Capitol at Rome, where the calends were proclaimed.
1513 DOUGLAS *Æneis* VIII. xi. 29 Neyr the chymmys calendare.

calendar (ˈkæləndə(r)), *v.* [f. the sb.]
1. *trans.* To register in a calendar or list; to register, record.
1487 *Act 3 Hen. VII*, iii, The names of every such prisoner ..to be kalendred by fore the justices for the delyveraunce of the same gaole. **1547** *Act 1 Edw. VI*, v. §5 The said Wardens shall cause the Number of the said Horses..to be kalendered in a Book. **1624** HEYWOOD *Gunaik.* III. 150 Let that day never be callendred to memorise them. **1697** *View Penal Laws* 97 He shall shew his Licence to one of the Wardens of the Marches (that their number may be Kalendred). **1870** EMERSON *Soc. & Sol.*, *Work & Days* Wks. (Bohn) III. 69 Life was then calendared by moments.
2. *spec.* **a.** To register in the calendar of saints or saints' days.
1594 HOOKER *Eccl. Pol.* v. (1632) 388 Wee are generally more apt to Kalender Saints then Sinners dayes. *a* **1641** BP. MOUNTAGU *Acts & Mon.* 55 The Divines of Colen calendred Aristotle for a Saint. **1654** R. WHITLOCK *Manners Eng.* 21 (R.) Oft martyred names, as well as men, are calendared. **1842** TENNYSON *St. Sim. Stylites* 130 Holy men, whose names Are register'd and calendar'd for saints.
b. To arrange, analyse, and index (documents): see the *sb.* 4 d.
1859 RILEY *Liber Albus* Pref. 21 These books..that are thus calendared. **1878** *N. Amer. Rev.* CXXVI. 540 Treasures of the Record-Office..lately calendered and indexed. **1881** *Sat. Rev.* 24 Sept. 395/1 The task of analysing and calendaring [state-]papers.
Hence ˈ**calendaring** *vbl. sb.*
1671 F. PHILIPPS *Reg. Necess.* Ep. Ded., Allowances of Money..for the Calendring and well ordering of them.

calendar: see CALENDER *sb.*[1], [2].

calendarer (ˈkæləndərə(r)). [f. CALENDAR *v.* + -ER[1].] One who calendars (*esp.* documents).
1864 *Q. Rev.* CXVI. 354 The rules and regulations which he [the Master of the Rolls] has framed for the guidance of the Calendarers. **1881** S. R. GARDINER in *Academy* 29 Jan. 74 To a calendarer the work of writing a preface must be something like a holiday.

calendarial (kælən'dɛərɪəl), *a. rare.* [f. L. *calendāri-us* (or Eng. CALENDAR) + -AL[1].] = next.

1867 M. ARNOLD *Celtic Lit.* 59 Arthur and his Twelve (?) Knights..signifying solely the year with its twelve months; ..Stonehenge and the Gododin put to purely calendarial purposes. **1880** *Contemp. Rev.* Apr. 585 The calendarial system of Genesis.

calendarian (kælən'dɛərɪən), *a.* and *sb. rare.* [f. as prec. + -AN.]

A. *adj.* Of or pertaining to a calendar.

1839 *Blackw. Mag.* XLV. 372 The conventional calendarian principles of the poem. *Ibid.* 380 Calendarian festivals.

B. *sb.* A maker of a calendar.

1826 HONE *E.D. Bk.* I. 1378 A contemporary kalendarian.

†**calendari'ographer.** *Obs. rare*[−1]. [f. CALENDAR *sb.* or L. *calendārium*; cf. *biographer.*] A calendar- or almanac-maker.

1683 J. GADBURY *Wharton's Wks.* Pref., A Speculation.. little understood, even by our common Calendariographers.

'calendarist. *rare.* [see -IST.] One who calendars (events, days, etc.), one who assigns dates and periods.

1685 H. MORE *Paralip. Proph.* 411, I will allow more to the ingenious Calendarist than he requires. *Ibid.* Thus invalid is the Calendarist's ground. **1875** O'HANLON *Irish Saints* I. 379 All our calendarists agree in assigning St. Fechin's feast to the 20th of January.

†**'calendary,** *sb.*[1] and *a. Obs.* [ad. L. *calendārium* sb., *calendārius* adj.; see CALENDAR.]

A. *sb.* = CALENDAR *sb.*

c **1450** tr. *Higden* (1865) I. 247 Somme monethe in the calendary [1387 kalendere] hathe iiij nones oonly. **1694** FALLE *Jersey* i. 7 Recorded in the Kalendary or Martyrology of Coutance.

B. *adj.* Of, pertaining to, or according to, the calendar; = CALENDARIAN.

1633 CRESSY *Fun. Disc.* 115 To performe my Calendary and prescribed task. **1646** SIR T. BROWNE *Pseud. Ep.* 212 The usuall or Calendary month. **1783** W. F. MARTYN *Geog. Mag.* II. 191 The four seasons, the moveable feasts and other calendary information.

†**calendary,** *sb.*[2] *Obs.* [f. CALENDAR *sb.* or *v.*: cf. *registry.*] The act of calendaring.

1680 MARVEL *Gen. Councils* 12 A question..upon what day they ought to keep Easter; which though it were no point of Faith that it should be kept at all, yet the very calendary [ed. **1676** calending] of it was controverted.

calender ('kæləndə(r)), *sb.*[1] Also 6 calander, calendre, 8 calendar, 9 callender. [a. F. *calandre*:—med.L. *calendra, celendra,* L. *cylindrus,* a. Gr. κύλινδρος roller, cylinder. In sense 1 app. a corrupt form of *calenderer, calendrer.*]

†**1.** One who calenders cloth; a calenderer. *Obs.*

1513 *Act 5 Hen. VIII,* iv. §1 The said Strangers, called Dry Calanders..use the said dry calandring of Worsted. **1574** *Life Abp. Canterb.* B vij b *marg. note,* A scourer or Calender off worsteddes of Norwich. **1705** HEARNE *Collect.* 6 Aug. (O.H.S.) I. 26 A fire hapen'd..in a Calender's House. **1782** COWPER *Gilpin* 24 My good friend the calender Will lend his horse to go.

2. A machine in which cloth, paper, etc., is pressed under rollers for the purpose of smoothing or glazing; also for watering or giving a wavy appearance, etc.

1688 MIEGE *Gt. Fr. Dict.,* Calender, *calendre.* **1708** in KERSEY. **1751** CHAMBERS *Cycl., Calender* is also used for watering, or giving the waves to tabbies and mohairs. *Ibid. Supp.* s.v., At Paris they have an extraordinary machine of this kind, called the royal calender. **1791** HAMILTON *Berthollet's Dyeing* I. I. III. x. 295 The impressions of the calender, under which stuffs are passed to water them. **1802** *Hull Advertiser* 25 Dec. 2/3 A valuable Callender, complete. **1875** *Encycl. Brit.* III. 818/1 When it is desired to finish cloth with a stiff or with a glazed finish..it is finished in the calender.

3. *attrib.* & *Comb.,* as *calender-house, -mill, -roll.*

1727 SWIFT *Furth. Acc. E. Curll* Wks. 1755 III. I. 157 The calendar-mill-room at Exeter-change. **1875** URE *Dict. Arts* I. 576 The arrangements..are generally conducted at the calender houses where goods are finished. **1882** W. C. SMITH *Hilda* III. 125 'Twas a school of the calender kind, Meant to put a fine gloss on the mind. **1884** *Pall Mall G.* 25 Nov. 6/1 It [paper] is passed between calender rolls of chilled steel, which, by tremendous pressure, give it an even and polished surface.

'calender, *sb.*[2] Also kalender. [ad. Pers. *qalandar,* of unknown origin.] One of a mendicant order of dervishes in Turkey and Persia.

[**1614** SELDEN *Titles Hon.* 378 The Turkish Calendarlar (a kind of Monkish Order) wear in their Caps long Horse-haires hanging.] **1634** SIR T. HERBERT *Trav.* (1677) 70 Thirty Nobles in the habit of Pilgrim Kalenders. **1724** *Arab. Nights* (1812) I. 35 There are three calenders at the gate..they are all blind of the right eye. **1837** *Penny Cycl.* VIII. 430/1 Frequently the Calenders go about half naked, with their skin painted red or black.

†**'calender,** *sb.*[3] *Obs. rare*[−1]. [a. F. *calandre* weevil:—med.L. *calandrus* 'gryllus, cicada, curculio' (Du Cange).] A corn-weevil.

1708 in KERSEY. **1725** BRADLEY *Fam. Dict.* II. s.v. *Preserving Corn,* Mites, Weevils and Calenders.

'calender, *v.* Forms: 6 calandre, calendre, 7 calander, callendre, 7– calender. [a. F. *calandre-r,* f. *calandre*; see CALENDER *sb.*[1]]

trans. To pass through a calender; to press (cloth, paper, etc.) between rollers, for the purpose of smoothing, glazing, etc.

1513 *Act 5 Hen. VIII,* iv, Worsteds which been..shorn, dyed, and calandred. **1523** *Act 14 & 15 Hen. VIII,* iii. §10 The sayd craftes men..shall not..calendre any worstedes. **1696** J. F. *Merchant's Wareho.* 17 Frize..is not Callendred, or thickned as other Cloths. **1880** *Print. Times* 15 Feb. 31/2 The paper..must be heavily calendered before being used.

Hence **'calendered** *ppl. a.,* **'calendering** *vbl. sb.* (also *attrib.*).

1513 *Act 5 Hen. VIII,* iv. §1 The said dry Calandring is scorned and abhorred. **1832** BABBAGE *Econ. Manuf.* viii. (ed. 3) 54 Establishments for calendering and embossing. **1850** SMILES *Self Help* ii. 35 A woman who kept a calendering machine. **1878** *Cornell Rev.* Feb. 188 Beautifully printed on fine calendered paper.

calender(e, obs. form of CALENDAR.

calenderer ('kæləndərə(r)). Also 5 -derar, 8–9 -drer, 9 callenderer. [f. CALENDER *v.* + -ER[1].] One whose business it is to calender cloth, etc.

1495 *Act 11 Hen. VII,* x. §2 Calenderars of the same Worstedis. **1755** JOHNSON, *Calendrer,* the person who calenders. **1819** *Post Office Lond. Direct.* 365 Welsh, James, Calendrer and Embosser. **1832** MARRYAT *N. Forster* xxxi, Dyers, Callenderers, and Scourers.

†**calen'dographer.** *Obs. rare*[−1]. [f. CALENDS sense 5.] The constructor of a calendar.

a **1691** BOYLE *Wks.* VI. 154 (R.) That eclipse..that.. almost all calendographers had skipped over.

calendric, -ical (kə'lɛndrɪk, -ɪkəl), *a.* [f. CALENDAR *sb.* + -IC, -ICAL.] Of the nature of a calendar (in various senses); also, occurring on a special day or days indicated in a calendar.

1863 PINKERTON in *N. & Q.* Ser. III. III. 181 The labour of..precising in a calendrical form such a vast chaos of documents. **1878** T. HARDY *Return of Native* II. viii, Thomasin's hair..was braided according to a calendric system: the more important the day the more numerous the braids. **1949** G. BATESON in M. Fortes *Social Structure* 44 You made a beautiful structure of flowers and fruit for the calendric feast in his temple. **1959** I. & P. OPIE *Lore & Lang. Schoolchildren* xiii. 293 The calendrical framework in which folklorists commonly arrange their collectings. **1961** Y. OLSSON *Syntax Eng. Verb* vii. 202 A calendrical back-reference.

calendry. [f. CALENDER: see -RY.] A place where calendering is done.

1878 MORLEY *Diderot* I. 188 The gunpowder mill, the silk calendry.

calends, kalends ('kæləndz), *sb. pl.* Forms: [1 sing. calend, kalendus], 4–5 calendis, kalendis, -es, (sing. kalende, 5 calende), (4 kalendez, -us, 5 kalandes, 5–6 kalendas), 5–7 calendes, (6 kalendies, callends, 7 calands), 6– calends, kalends. [ad. L. *kalendæ, -as* sb. pl., first day of the month, on which the order of days was proclaimed; f. root *kal-, cal-,* which appears in L. *calāre,* Gr. καλεῖν to call, proclaim. (Or a. F. *kalendes,* 13th c. in Littré.) The singular *calend* is rare and obs.; it occurs in OE. in the sense 'month'. No sing. was used in Latin.]

1. The first day of any month in the Roman calendar: the term was more or less retained in actual use down to the 17th c.

(The Romans reckoned the days forward to the Kalends, Nones, or Ides next following. Thus, 'on the 27th of May' was 'ante diem sextum Kalendas Junias'. This was loosely rendered into English as 'the sixth of the Kalends of June', or 'the sixth Kalends of June'. Cf. NONES, IDES.)

1398 TREVISA *Barth. De P.R.* IX. xxi. (1495) 359 The fyrste daye of a monthe hath the name of Kalendis. ? *a* **1400** *Morte Arth.* 345 By the kalendez of Juny we schalle encountre ones. *c* **1400** *Apol. Loll.* 93 A waytiþ not þeis Egipcian daies, þat we call dysmal, ne kalendis of Janiuer. *c* **1420** *Pallad. on Husb.* III. 30 In Marche Kalendes in the soile ydight. **1496** *Dives & Paup.* (W. de W.) I. xlvii. 87/2 The fyrste daye of the yere, that is the fyrste Kalendas of Januarye. **1577** HOLINSHED *Chron.* III. 1239/1 In the yeare of our redemption, one thousand, one hundred, thirtie and three, the fift calends of June, being the three and thirtith yeare of the reigne of Henrie the first. **1598** HAKLUYT *Voy.* I. 94 Wee tooke our iourney..about the kalends of June. **1626** MASSINGER *Rom. Actor* V. i, Thou Shalt die to-morrow, being the fourteenth of The Kalends of October. **1665** MANLEY *Grotius' Low-C. Warrs* 337 Those that belonged to the City, marched out safe the Seventh of the Calends of August. *a* **1764** LLOYD *Two Odes* Wks. 1774 I. 121 On thy blest Calends, April. **1844** LINGARD *Anglo-Sax. Ch.* (1858) I. iii. 96 The calends of May and November.

b. With reference to debts and interest being then due: Settling day.

1643 MILTON *Divorce* (1851) Introd. 10 How they will compound, and in what Calends.

†**2. a.** In OE. A month; *also,* appointed time, season.

a **1000** *Menol.* 7 (Gr.) Se kalendus kymeð..us to tune; hine folc mycel Januarius heton. *Ibid.* 31 Kalend..Martius reðe. *a* **1000** *Sol. & Sat.* 479 (Gr.) Ær se dæȝ cyme, þæt sy his calend cwide (?) arunnen.

†**b.** In Scripture versions: Applied to the Jewish festival of the new moon. *Obs.*

1382 WYCLIF *Isa.* i. 14 ȝoure kalendis and ȝoure solempnetees hatede my soule [**1388** my soule hatith ȝoure calendis]. —— *1 Sam.* xx. 5 David seide to Jonathan, Loo! Kalendis ben to morwe. **1565** JEWELL *Def. Apol.* (1611) 60 God commanded the people to keepe the Calends and new Moones. **1609** BIBLE (Douay) *Numb.* xxviii. 11 In the Calendes you shal offer an holocaust to the Lord [**1382** WYCLIF, In the calendis forsothe, that is, in the bigynnyngis of monthes].

3. Phrases. †**a.** *calends of exchange*: ? a money changer's calendar, reckoning, or account; *hence,* business or practical reckoning.

c **1374** CHAUCER *Troylus* V. 1647 This Troylus this lettre thought al straunge..Hym thought it like a Kalendes of chaunge. **1470** HARDING *Chron.* xiii. i, Brutus..called this Isle Briteyn..So was the name of this ilke Albyon All sette on side in Kalandes of achaunge. *Ibid.* lxxii. ii, Her goodlyhede..chaunged all his corage and manhede, In Kalandes of eschaunge he was [so] impressed.

b. *on* (*at*) *the Greek Calends* (L. *ad Græcas kalendas*): humorous for Never; since the Greeks used no calends in their reckoning of time.

a **1649** DRUMM. OF HAWTH. *Consid. Parlt.* Wks. (1711) 185 That gold, plate, and all silver, given to the mint-house in these late troubles, shall be paid at the Greek Kalends. **1656** BLOUNT *Glossogr.* s.v., At the Greek Calends, never; for the Greks have no Calends. **1872** O. W. HOLMES *Poet Breakf. T.* i. 18 His friends looked for it only on the Greek Calends, say on the 31st of April, when that should come round, if you would modernize the phrase. **1882** *Macm. Mag.* 253 So we go on..and the works are sent to the Greek Calends.

†**4.** *fig.* First days, beginning, first taste, prelude. (Also in *sing.*) *Obs.*

c **1374** CHAUCER *Troylus* II. Prol. 7 Now of hope the kalendis bygynne. *c* **1380** WYCLIF *Serm.* xiv. Sel. Wks. II. 261 Kalendis of þis siȝt hadde Poul whan he was ravyshed. **1423** JAS. I *King's Q.* VI. v, Gave me in hert kalendis of confort. *a* **1618** RALEIGH *Rem.* (1644) 114 What is age, but the Calends of death?

5. A calendar, record. (Also in *sing. rare.*)

1470 HARDING *Chron.* ccxl. xxix, I make you a kalende Of all the waie to Edenbourgth. **1590** GREENE *Mourn. Garm.* (1616) 45 Their looks are like Calends, that can determine no certaintie. **1601** WEEVER *Mirr. Mart., Sir J. Oldcastle* F iij b, Him for a Saint within your Kalends hold. **1866** E. H. BICKERSTETH *Yesterd., to-day, &c.* XII. 317 Festivals that stand On the sidereal calends marked in light.

‖**ca'lendula.** *Bot.* [mod.L. dim. of *calendæ,* intended to express 'little calendar, little clock, or perh. little weather-glass'.]

1. The generic name of the Common Marigold, and its congeners.

1871 in M. Collins *Mrq. & Merch.* I. x. 309 The golden haze of the Calendula.

2. *Pharm.* A tincture of the flowers applied as a hæmostatic to wounds, etc. *attrib.* in *calendula ointment, plaster,* etc.

calendulin (kə'lɛndjʊlɪn). *Chem.* [f. prec. + -IN.] 'A mucilaginous substance extracted from the leaves and flowers of the common marigold' (Watts *Dict. Chem.* I. 722).

calenge, obs. form of CHALLENGE.

†**'calent,** *a. Obs. rare.* [ad. L. *calēns, calēnt-em* pr. pple. of *calēre* to be hot.] Warm, hot.

1607 TOPSELL *Four-f. Beasts* 377 Styled with the same epithets that the lion and the sun are; as heat-bearing, æstive, ardent, arent, calent, hot. **1656** in BLOUNT *Glossogr.* **1775** in ASH.

calenture ('kæləntjʊə(r)). Also 6 calentura, 6–7 callenture. [a. F. *calenture,* ad. Sp. *calentura* fever, f. *calentar* to be hot, f. L. *calēnt-em* hot, burning.]

1. A disease incident to sailors within the tropics, characterized by delirium in which the patient, it is said, fancies the sea to be green fields, and desires to leap into it.

The word was also used in the Spanish general sense of 'fever', and sometimes in that of 'sunstroke'.

1593 NASHE *Christ's T.* (1613) 92 Then (as the possessed with the Calentura,) thou shalt offer to leape. **1605** *Lond. Prodigal* V. i. 277 Such men die mad as of a calenture. *a* **1618** RALEIGH *Rem.* (1644) 223, I have suffered the most violent Calenture for fifteen dayes. *a* **1622** R. HAWKINS *Voy. S. Sea* (1847) 43 To avoyd the calmes, which..breed calenturas, which wee call burning fevers. **1719** DE FOE *Crusoe* I. 14 In this Voyage..I was continually sick, being thrown into a violent Calenture by the excessive Heat. **1721** SWIFT *S. Sea Proj.* vii, So, by a calenture misled, The mariner with rapture sees, On the smooth ocean's azure bed, Enamell'd fields and verdant trees. **1840** GEN. P. THOMPSON *Exerc.* (1842) V. 455 Demanding to jump overboard like the seaman in a calenture.

2. *fig.* and *transf.* Fever; burning passion, ardour, zeal, heat, glow.

1596 NASHE *Saffron Walden* 44 Ere hee bee come to the.. raging Calentura of his wretchednes. *a* **1631** DONNE *Poems* (1650) 158 Knowledge kindles Calentures in some. **1642** JER. TAYLOR *Episc.* (1647) 362 They were in the Calenture of primitive devotion. *a* **1711** KEN *Preparat.* Poet. Wks. 1721 IV. 27 Pure Chastity excells in Gust The Calentures of baneful Lust. **1841** HOR. SMITH *Moneyed Man* III. ix. 238

The mirage of a moral calenture, which conjures up unexisting objects.

Hence **calentural** *a.* (Carlyle), **calen'turist**.

1823 Lamb *Elia, All Fools D.* (1836) 96 You were founder, I take it, of the disinterested sect of the Calenturists.

† **'calenture**, *v. Obs. rare.* [f. prec. sb.] **a.** *trans.* To infect with the calenture; hence *fig.* to fever, fire. **b.** *intr.* To become hot or inflamed.

a **1678** Marvell *Poems* Wks. 1776 III. 336 Thirst of empire calentur'd his breast. **1649** G. Daniel *Trinarch., Rich. II*, ccix, A busie Age, where euery breath Calentur's into faction.

† **'calepin.** *Obs.* [a. F. *calepin*, ad. It. *calepino* dictionary, polyglot, from the cognomen of the Augustine friar, Ambrosio Calepino, of Calepio in Italy, the author of a famous Latin Dictionary, first published in 1502, which in its many editions was *the* Latin Dictionary of the 16th century, and the foundation of the later work of Forcellini. There was an octoglot edition by Passerat in 1609.]

A dictionary (sometimes 'a polyglot'); *fig.* one's book of authority or reference; one's notebook or memorandum-book.

Hence the French phrases 'je consulterai là-dessus mon calepin', 'cela n'est pas dans son calepin', 'mettez cela sur votre calepin' (make a note of that to serve as a lesson), and the English (*obs.*) 'to bring any one to his Calepin', i.e. to the utmost limits of his information.

1568 *Lanc. Wills* (1860) II. 226, I wyll that Henry Marrecrofte shall have my calapyne and my parafrasies. **1579** Fulke *Heskins' Parl.* 56 Let him turne ouer all his vocabularies, Calepines, and dictionaries. **1603** Florio *Montaigne* III. xiii. (1632) 602 A stone is a body: but he that should insist and urge: And what is a body?..and so goe-on: Should at last bring the respondent to his Calepine or wit's end. *a* **1649** Drumm. of Hawth. *Magic Mirr.* Wks. (1711) 174 Taxations, monopolies, tolls..and such impositions as would trouble many Calepines to give names unto. **1662** Evelyn *Chalcogr.* (1769) 22 We have weeded the calepines and lexicons. [**1772** Nugent *Friar Gerund* II. 53 Calepino is not..the title of a work, but a patronymic of the country of the author..a native of Calepio in Italy.]

† **cales.** *Obs. rare*$^{-1}$. The name of a fabulous creature: see quot.

c **1300** *K. Alis.* 7094 Ther he fond addren..And a feolle worm, Cales.

calescence (kə'lɛsəns). [f. calescent *a.* on L. type **calēscentia*: see -ence.] Increasing warmth or heat.

1846 Worcester cites Boase.

calescent (kə'lɛsənt), *a. rare.* [ad. L. *calēscent-em*, pr. pple. of *calēscĕre* to grow warm, inchoative from *calēre* to be warm.] Growing warm, glowing with heat.

1804 Huddesford *Weccam. Chaplet* 162 The calescent sanguine flood By vile vulgarity called Blood.

calesh, obs. form of calash.

calet(te, var. of callet, *Obs.*

calewe, obs. form of callow.

† **'calewey.** *Obs. rare.* Also caylewey, **kaylewey**, calawey, calwey. [a. OF. *caillouet*, *cailloel*, in Cotgr. *Caillouet*, f. *Cailloux* in Burgundy: see Skeat *Notes to P. Pl.* 376.] A kind of pear.

1377 Langl. *P. Pl.* B. xvi. 69 Contenence is nerre þe croppe as cal[e]wey bastarde. *c* **1400** *Rom. Rose* 7045 With deynte flawnes, brode and flat, With caleweis, or with pullayle [Fr. *la poire du caillouel*].

calf[1] (kɑːf). Forms: 1 cealf, celf, cælf, 2 *Kentish* chalf, 3 kelf, 3–5 kalf, 3– calf, (5 calffe), 6 caulf, *Kentish* chawlfe, 8 calve; (*Sc.* 6–9 cawf, 9 cauf). Pl. calves: 1 cealfru, calfru, calfur, cealfas, 4 calveren, calvys, 4–5 calfis, 7 calfes, 4– calves. (The genit. sing., esp. in comb., was frequently *calves*.) [Common Teut.: OWS. *cealf* (pl. *cealfru*), OMercian *cælf* (pl. *calferu*, *calfur*), ONorthumbrian *cælf*, *cęlf*, correspond to OS. and MDu. *calf* (Du. *kalf*), OHG. *chalb* (MHG. *kalp*, *kalb-*, mod.G. *kalb*):—OTeut. **kalboz*, *-iz* neut. In later WS. the word was often masc. (pl. *cealfas*) = ON. *kálfr*; in Goth. only the fem. *kalbô* (δάμαλις) = OHG. *chalba*, mod.G. *kalbe* female calf, is recorded.]

1. The young of any bovine animal, *esp.* of the domestic cow. 'Calf is applied to all young cattle until they attain one year old, when they are *year-olds* or *yearlings*' (Stephens *Bk. Farm* I. 179).

in calf, with calf (said of the cow): pregnant. ***golden calf***: the idol set up by Aaron, and the similar images set up by Jeroboam; sometimes proverbially with reference to the 'worship' of wealth. '***the calves of our lips***' (a doubtful transl. of a difficult Heb. passage, in *Hos.* xiv. 2 where the LXX and Peschito have 'fruit') is occas. quoted in the sense of 'an offering of praise'.

a **800** *Corpus Gl.* 2144 (O.E.T.) *Vitulus*, cælf; *vitula*, cucælf. *c* **1000** Ælfric *Exod.* xxxii. 4 þa nam he þæt gold and ʒet an cealf and hiȝ cwædon Israhel þis ys þin God. *c* **1000** *Ags. Gosp.* Luke xv. 27 þin fæder of-sloh an fæt celf [*c* **1160** *Hatton G.* chalf]. *a* **1225** *Ancr. R.* 138 Hit regibbeð anon, ase uet kelf and idel. *c* **1230** *Hali Meid.* 37 Hire calf sukeð. *c* **1250** *Gen. & Ex.* 1013 Kalues fleis, and flures bred. *a* **1300** *Cursor M.* 6503 þair goldin calf in tresur gadrid þai samen A goldin calf þar-of þai blu. *a* **1340** Hampole *Psalter* xxi[i]. 11 Many calfis has vmgifen me; fat bulles me has vmseged. *c* **1371** Wyclif *Begg. Friers* (1608) 12 Priests..wenten to calveren of gold. **1382** —— *Hosea* xiv. 2 We shuln ȝeelde the calues of our lippis [= Vulg. *vitulos*, LXX *καρπόν*]. *c* **1400** Maundev. ix. 105 Calveren of gold. **1483** *Cath. Angl.* 51 With Calfe, *fetosus*. **1534** *MS. Acc. St. John's Hosp. Canterb.*, Off yͤ cat' of cristchurch for a chawlfe, iijs. iiijd. **1539** Taverner *Erasm. Prov.* (1552) 10 He that hath borne a calfe, shall also beare a bull. **1562** J. Heywood *Prov. & Epigr.* (1867) 48 As wise as Waltam's calfe. **1607** Topsell *Four-f. Beasts* 89 A tail almost as long as a calves. **1629** J. Cole *Of Death* 105 Before we can offer unto God with a good conscience, the calves of our lips. **1671** Milton *P.R.* III. 416 They..fell off From God to worship Calves. **1727** Swift *Modest Prop.* Wks. 1755 II. II. 66 Their mears in foal, their cows in calf. **1861** Th. Martin *Horace's Odes* II. v. 80 Your heifer bounding in play With the young calves.

b. ***to slip (cast) the calf***: to suffer abortion; said of the cow, also (*humorously*) of women (*obs.*)

1664 Pepys *Diary* 19 Sept., Fraizer is so great with..all the ladies at court, in helping to slip their calfes when there is occasion. **1842–71** Stephens *Bk. of Farm* I. 178 A cow that suffers abortion slips her calf.

c. *transf.* Applied to human beings: A stupid fellow, a dolt; sometimes a meek inoffensive person. Also as a term of endearment. ***Essex calf***: a nickname for a native of that county.

a **1553** Udall *Royster D.* II. iv. in Hazl. *Dodsley* III. 94 You great calf, ye should have more wit, so ye should. **1611** Shaks. *Wint. T.* I. ii. 126 How now (you wanton Calfe) Art thou my Calfe? **1627** Drayton *Nymphid.* (1631) 171 Some silly doting brainless calfe. **1711** Steele *Spect.* No. 113 ¶3, I cried, like a Captivated Calf as I was. **1719** D'Urfey *Pills* IV. 43 It prov'd an Essex Calf. **1865** *Punch* 20 Apr., An Essex calf of the first magnitude.

2. *ellipt.* Leather made from the hide or skin of a calf. (More fully ***calf-leather***; see 7.)

1727 Swift *Furth. Acc. E. Curll* Wks. 1755 III. I. 156 As to the report of my poor husband's stealing o'calf, it is really groundless, for he always binds in sheep. **1879** *Print. Trades Jrnl.* XXVIII. 9 The material used is Calf. **1879** in *Cassell's Techn. Educ.* IV. 88 Calf is..prepared by the process called by tanners 'tawing'.

3. The young of other animals; as of deer, the elephant, the whale.

1398 Trevisa *Barth. De P.R.* XVIII. xxx. (1495) 793 The hynde etyth of the herbe Dragancia to be delyuerde of her calffe the more eesely. **1486** *Bk. St. Albans* E j b, Ye shall hym [a hart] a Calfe . call at the fyrst yere. **1597** *Return fr. Parnass.* II. II. v. 887 Your Hart is the first yeare a Calfe, the second yeare a Brochet. **1725** Dudley in *Phil. Trans.* XXXIII. 260 The Calf, or young Whale, has been found perfectly form'd in the Cow, when not above seventeen Inches long. **1860** Tennent *Ceylon* II. 397 An elephant, which had been captured by Mr. Cripps, dropped a female calf. **1875** 'Stonehenge' *Brit. Sports* I. XI. xi. §2. 155 The hounds also by their tongues indicate..the presence, if any, of a calf with the hind. **1884** Jefferies *Red Deer* iv. 63 The young of the..tall red deer are called calves.

4. sea-calf, a popular name of the seal, esp. *Calocephalus vitulinus* (or *Phoca vitulina*).

c **1613** Chapman *Odyss.* IV. (R.) In sholes the sea calues came. *a* **1711** Ken *Hymnar.* Poet. Wks. 1721 III. 182 The Calves Marine, who on firm Ground Are wont to take a Sleep profound. **1841** *Penny Cycl.* XXI. 161/2 The vulgar name is sea-calf, and on that account the male is called the bull, and the female the cow. **1853** Kane *Grinnell Exp.* xxvii. 221 Some overgrown Greenland calves..Very strange are these seal.

5. *transf.* **a.** A small island lying close to a larger one. [ON. *kálfr*; known in Eng. only in 'The Calf of Man'.]

1833 J. Gorton *Topogr. Dict.* I. 347 Calf of Man..An island, situated off the south-west extremity of the Isle of Man. **1860** H. Marryat *Jutland* I. vii. 91 The early Northmen often named these small islands calves. **18..** Backwell *Isle Man Guide* 60 Beyond..lies the Calf of Man..The Calf ..contains about 600 superficial acres of land.

6. An iceberg detached from a coast glacier; a fragment of ice detached from an iceberg or floe.

1818 *Edin. Rev.* XXX. 18 The fragments of ice, which the seamen term calves. **1853** Kane *Grinnell Exp.* xlii. (1856) 395 The interposition of floating fragments or calves. *Ibid.* xliii. 401 Calves..fragments of tables..which have been forced down by pressure, and afterward..have been liberated again from the floe and find their way upward wherever an opening permits.

7. *Comb.* **a.** Obvious and general, as ***calf-brains***, ***-flesh***, ***-guts***, ***-head***, ***-house***, ***-leather***, ***-pen***, ***-whale***, ***-worship***; ***calf-like*** adj. and adv. (For parts of the animal the genit. *calf's*, *calves'*, is now usual.)

? *c* **1600** *Distracted Emp.* I. i. in *O. Pl.* (1884) III. 181 You love the cubboarde Wherein your *calves brayns are lockt up for breakfast. *a* **1300** *Cursor M.* 2714 He..þam fedd wit *calf flesse [*Trin. MS.* calues flesshe]. *c* **1425** *Voc.* in Wr.-Wülcker 661 *Caro uitulina*, calfflesche. **1611** Shaks. *Cymb.* II. iii. 34 It is a voyce in her eares which..*Calues-guts, nor the voyce of vnpaued Eunuch to boot, can neuer amend. **1769** Mrs. Raffald *Eng. Housekpr.* (1778) 87 To dress a *Calf's Head Surprise. **1813** Moore *Post Bag* iii. 34 The dish..Was, what old Mother Glasse calls, 'a calf's-head surprised'! **1823** —— *Fab., Holy Alliance* II. 91 A Duke, of birth sublime..(Some calf-head, ugly from all time). **1807** Vancouver *Agric. Devon* (1813) 472 *Calves-house, 22 feet by 16, with their pens. **1879** in *Cassell's Techn. Educ.* IV. 416/2 The calf-house..should be a roomy, well-ventilated building. **1726** Amherst *Terræ Fil.* xxxviii. 200 Dress'd in a suit of *calve's-leather cloaths. **1610** Shaks. *Temp.* IV. i. 179 *Calfe-like, they my lowing follow'd. **1856** *Farmer's Mag.* Jan. 86 Have the *calf-pens opening into the cowshed for convenience of suckling. **1829** Marryat *F. Mildmay* xiii, I was going to swim to the *calf whale. **1650** Fuller *Pisgah* v. v. 152 *Calfe-worship..continued in the kingdome of Israel. **1860** Pusey *Min. Proph.* 82 He [Jeroboam] would have calf-worship to be the only worship of God.

b. Special combinations: **calf-bed**, a cow's matrix (*dial.*); also (*humorous*) parturition (of a cow), cf. *child-bed*; **calf-bound** *a.* (*Bookbinding*), bound in calf (cf. 2); **calf-country**, **calf-ground** (*Sc.*), the place of one's birth or early life; † **calf-haulm** (see quot.); **calf-kill**, a heath plant (*Kalmia latifolia*) injurious to cattle eating it; cf. 'lambkill' = *K. angustifolia*; **calf knee**, popular name for the malformation called *genu valgum*, or knock-knee; **calf-land** = *calf-country*; **calf-lea** (*Sc.*), 'infield ground, one year under natural grass' (Jamieson); **calf-lick** (*dial.*), a tuft of hair on the forehead which will not lie smoothly and evenly; a cowlick, a 'feather'; † **calf-lolly** (? *nonce-wd.*), a stupid calf; **calf-love**, romantic attachment or affection between a boy and a girl; **calf-lymph**, vaccine lymph obtained direct from the animal; **calf's-teeth** *sb. pl*, milk teeth; **calf-time**, the period of youth; **calf-trundle** (*dial.*), 'the entrails of a calf; *fig.* applied to the ruffle of a shirt, or flounces of a gown' (Halliwell); **calf-ward** (*Sc.*), a small field or enclosure for calves. Also calf's-foot, calf-skin, calves'-snout.

1822 Southey *Lett.* (1856) III. 305 Your uncle Tom has lost a cow, in *calf-bed. **1831** *Blackw. Mag.* Sept. 561 That, I believe, is his *calf-country. **1884** *Illust. Lond. News* 21 June 606/2 We'll go and take a look at my *calf-ground. **1741** *Compl. Fam.-Piece* III. 486 A Cow that strains in Calving, when their *Calf-haulm, Udder, or Bag, will come down and swell as much as a blown Bladder. **1765** Dickson *Agric.* xiii. 109 When it is only two or three years old, it is called, in some parts of the country, calf-lea. **1708** Motteux *Rabelais* IV. lxvii, I was..a *Calf-lolly, a Doddipole. **1823** Galt *Entail* I. xxxii. 284, I made a *calf-love marriage. **1863** Mrs. Gaskell *Sylvia's L.* II. 104 It's a girl's fancy—Just a kind o' calf-love—let it go by. **1884** *Christian World* 5 June 417/4 Any doctor can procure *calf-lymph for his patients. **1688** R. Holme *Armoury* II. 173/2 A *Calf Ride [is] a place made of Boughs..in which the Calf is kept whilst he is sucking. **1599** Porter *Angry Wom. Abingd.* (1841) 88 Ere your *calues teeth were out, you thought it long. **1822** Scott *Nigel* ix, Where have you been spending your *calf-time? **1785** Burns *Dr. Hornbook* xxiii, His braw *calf-ward whare gowans grew.

calf[2] (kɑːf). Also 4 caalf, 5–7 calfe, 7 calue. [app. a. ON. *kálfi* of unknown origin; adoption from Ir., Gael. *calpa* leg, calf of the leg, has been conjectured.]

1. The fleshy hinder part of the shank of the leg, formed by the bellies of muscles which move the foot.

c **1325** *Gloss. W. de Biblesw.* in Wright *Voc.* 148 *La jambe*, the caalf. *c* **1386** Chaucer *C.T.* Prol. 592, Ful longe were his legges and ful lene ylyk a staf ther was no calf ysene. *c* **1440** *Promp. Parv.* 58 Calfe of a legge, *sura*. *c* **1450** *Voc.* in Wr.-Wülcker 678 *Hic musculus*, the calfe of the lege. **1541** R. Copland *Guydon's Quest. Chirurg.*, The calfe ouer the leg mouyng the fote and ancle. **1588** Shaks. *L.L.L.* v. ii. 645 His legge is too big for Hector. More Calfe certaine. **1794–6** E. Darwin *Zoon.* (1801) I. 58 The contraction of the calf of the leg in the cramp. **1848** Thackeray *Van. Fair* xxxvii, A handsome person and calves.

b. *transf.* The corresponding part of a stocking.

a **1659** Cleveland *Pet. Poem* 55 My Stocking-calves.. Are paradiz'd as naked as my Nock. **1777** Sheridan *Trip Scarb.* I. ii, The calves of these stockings are thickened a little too much.

2. Applied to the corresponding part of the arm containing the belly of the triceps muscle.

1860 O. W. Holmes *Elsie V.* (1887) 33 The *triceps*.. furnishes the *calf* of the upper arm.

3. calf-length *a.* (of a garment, boots, etc.) reaching down to, or up to, the calf of the leg.

1965 G. McInnes *Road to Gundagai* ix. 143 Turning up.. in a calf-length white motoring coat. **1967** *Harper's Bazaar* Sept. 60/1 New calf-length skirt for the country. **1968** *Ottawa Jrnl.* 24 June 17/5 Sue Ellen..started down the aisle in white calf-length boots. **1969** J. Gardner *Founder Member* vii. 115 A pair of heavy calf-length stockings.

calf(e, obs. form of calve *v.*

† **calfam**, *sb. Obs. rare*$^{-1}$. ? = caliph.

1550 Bale *Apol.* 119 In thys poynte here hath he shewed hymselfe a very wyse calfam.

calfate, calfet: see calfret *v.*

calfhood ('kɑːfhʊd). Calf state or stage.

1880 G. Allen *Evolut., In Summer Fields*, Cows hate dogs instinctively, from their earliest calfhood upward.

† **'calfin**, *sb. Obs. Sc.* Also calfing, colfin. [Jamieson suggested connexion with F. *calfater* calfret.] The wadding or other stopping of a gun.

1676 W. Row *Contn. Blair's Autobiog.* xii. App. (1848) 587 Such other calfine as was at hand. **1722** in Wodrow

Sufferings Ch. Scot. II. App. 8 The burning Calfing was left on his Gown. **1736** *Trial Capt. Porteous* 21 (JAM.) He was so near as to see..the colfin flee out of the pannel's gun.

†'**calfin**, *v. Obs. Sc.* [f. prec. sb.] *trans.* To wad (a fire-arm).

1793 *Piper o' Peebles* 19 (JAM.) It's no been fir'd, I find it fu', Weel calfin'd wi' a clout o' green.

calfish ('kɑːfɪʃ), *a.* [f. CALF[1] + -ISH[1].] Akin to or resembling a calf; *fig.* raw, untrained.

1765 LAW *Behmen's Myst. Magnum* xxv. (1772) 115 Calfish understandings.

calfless ('kɑːflɪs), *a.*[1] Having no calf (*sb.*[1]).

1388 WYCLIF *Job* xxi. 10 The cow caluyde, and is not priued of hir calf [*v.r.* maad calflees]. *a* **1528** [see next].

'**calfless**, *a.*[2] Also calve-. [f. CALF[2] + -LESS.] Of the leg: Destitute of calf; thin, lean.

a **1528** SKELTON *Poem agst. Garnesche* 30 Your longe lothy legges..as a kowe calfles. **1822** W. IRVING *Braceb. Hall* (1845) 269 Long, lean, calfless legs. **1860** SMILES *Self-Help* x. 256 Calveless legs and limp bodies.

calfling ('kɑːflɪŋ). In 6 calueling. [f. CALF[1] + -LING.] A little calf.

1598 YONG *Montemayor's Diana* 79 Licking their yong and tender cauelings.

†'**calfret**, *v. Obs.* Also calfate, calfet, calfuter. [ad. F. *calfrete-r* (Cotgr.), *calfater*, *calfeutrer* to caulk (a ship). The word occurs also as It. *calafatare*, Sp. *calafatear*, *-fetear*; usually believed to be f. Arab. *qalafa*, in 2nd conjugation *qallafa* to caulk a ship with palm-tree fibre, etc.; cf. med.Gr. καλαφάτης caulker. The Fr. form *calfeutrer* is conjectured to have been influenced by *feutre* felt.] *trans.* To stop up (with oakum) the seams of (a ship); to caulk.

a **1600** HUME in Sibbald *Chron. Scot. Poetry* (1802) III. 381 (Jam.) Weill calfuterd [*printed* calsutered] bots. **1601** HOLLAND *Pliny* I. 482 They..therewith [viz. with reeds] calfret or calke the ioints of their ships. **1648** HEXHAM *Dutch Dict.* (1660) *Kleuteren*..to give Knocks or Blowes, or to Calfate. **1653** URQUHART *Rabelais* II. xiii, The Plaintiff truly had just cause to calfet..the gallion.

calf's-foot, calves-foot. Also 5 calvysfote, 6 calfes foote.

1. *lit.* The foot of a calf; hence, *calves-foot jelly*.

1620 VENNER *Via Recta* iii. 70 The vse of them (especially of Calues feete) is very profitable in consumptions. **1775** NOURSE in *Phil. Trans.* LXVI. 438, I now allowed him chicken broth..calves-feet jelly. **1785** W. SCOTT in *Med. Commun.* II. 85, I procured some calf's foot jelly. **1879** SALA in *Daily Tel.* 28 June, What purported to be mock-turtle soup..with pieces of calves-foot or cow-heel in it.

2. *Herb.* The Cuckoo-pint or Wake-robin (*Arum maculatum*): see ARUM. [So Fr. *pied-de-veau.*]

c **1450** *Voc.* in Wr.-Wülcker 588 *Jarus*, Cokkupyntel *et* Calvysfote. **1578** LYTE *Dodoens* III. vii. 322 Calfes foote or Cockowpynt. **1607** TOPSELL *Four-f. Beasts* 30 The hearb Arum, called in English Wake-Robbin or Calves-foot.

calf-skin. Also calf's-, calves-, calve-. The skin or hide of a calf; a superior kind of leather made from this, and used in bookbinding, shoemaking, etc. More rarely = *vellum.*

1590 SHAKS. *Com. Err.* IV. iii. 18 Hee that goes in the calues-skin, that was kil'd for the Prodigall. **1595** —— *John* III. i. 129 Hang a Calues skin on those recreant limbes! **1604** in *Shaks. C. Praise* 60 Master Bursebell the calves-skin scrivener. **1704** SWIFT *T. Tub* v. 75 Copies, well-bound in calf-skin. **1796** MORSE *Amer. Geog.* II. 74, 990 calve-skins [exported in 1 yr. from Petersburg]. **1870** EMERSON *Soc. & Solit., Courage* 207 Cowardice shuts the eyes till the sky is not larger than a calf-skin.

†**b.** A purse, etc., made of calf-skin. *Obs.*

1618 DEKKER *Owles Alman.*, This puts..coyne into the Painters calueskinne.

†**c.** *attrib.*

1606 *Wily Beguiled* Prol. (N.) His calfs-skin jests from hence are clear exil'd. **1785** GROSE *Class. Dict. Vulg. Tongue* Calf-skin fiddle, a drum.

calf's snout: see CALVES'-SNOUT.

calfuter: see CALFRET.

†'**calgarth, cale-garth.** [f. *cal(e*, KALE + GARTH.] A cabbage garden, a kale yard.

14.. *Harl. MS.* 1587 in *Promp. Parv.* 58 *Cauletum*, cawlegarthe. **1483** *Cath. Angl.* 51 A Cale garth, *ortus, etc.*; *vbi*, a gardynge. **1575** *Richmond Wills* (1853) 255, j old cal-garth spade and j haye spayde.

cali-, a non-etymological spelling of *calli-* in words formed from Gr. κάλλ-ος beauty; confused with *calo-* from Gr. καλό-ς beautiful. See CALLI-.

cali-: see also CALE-.

†**caliatour, caleatour.** In *Caliatour('s) wood*, a dye-wood from the Coromandel coast, identified by some with red sandal-wood.

1687 *Lond. Gaz.* No. 2269/2 Of Caleatours Wood.

caliawndyre, var. of COLIANDER, *Obs.*

Caliban ('kælɪbæn). [App. a variant of CANNIBAL[1], or perh. actually a form of *Carib.* It does not appear, however, where Shakspere found the form.] The name of a character in Shakspere's *Tempest*, 'a saluage and deformed slaue' (*Dram. Personæ*); thence applied to a man of degraded bestial nature. Also *attrib.* and *Comb.*, as ***Caliban-like*** adj. Hence '**Calibanish** *a.*; '**Caliba,nism**.

[**1610** SHAKS. *Temp.* I. ii. 308 Wee'll visit *Caliban*, my slaue, who neuer Yeelds vs kinde answere.] **1678** BUTLER *Hud.* III. I. 282, I found th' Infernal Cunning-man, and th' Vnder-witch, his Caliban, With Scourges..arm'd. **1839** KEMBLE *Jrnl. Georgian Plantation* (1863) 222 The Calibanish wonderment of all my visitors..is very droll. **1859** SALA *Tw. round Clock* (1861) 69 Where is the Dutch pug? Where is that Narcissus of canine Calibanism? **1872** DU CHAILLU *Country of Dwarfs* 62 The fiendish countenances of the living calibanish trio. **1876** GEO. ELIOT *Dan. Der.* IV. xxix, Grandcourt held that the Jamaican negro was a beastly sort of baptist Caliban. **1909** *Lady's Realm* Feb. 465/2 He was a Caliban-like creature, primitively ugly. **1921** *Chambers's Jrnl.* 22/2 A lunatic..indulges in Caliban-like gambols, unheeded. **1965** F. SARGESON *Memoirs of Peon* iv. 90 Mr. Gower-Johnson with his Caliban fish-eye.

calibash, obs. form of CALABASH, CALIPASH.

caliber, obs. form of CALABER.

calibogus (kælɪ'bəʊgəs). *U.S.* Also calli-. [Schele de Vere suggests that the *-bogus* is from BAGASSE: cf. BOGUS[2].] A mixture of rum and spruce-beer.

1785 GROSE *Dict. Vulg. Tongue, Calibogus*, rum and spruce beer, American beverage. **1861** L. DE BOILIEU *Recoll. Labrador Life* 162 Callibogus, a mixture of Rum and Spruce-beer, more of the former and less of the latter.

calibrate ('kælɪbreɪt), *v.* [f. CALIBRE + -ATE[3]: cf. F. *calibrer.*] **a.** *trans.* To determine the calibre of; *spec.* to try the bore of a thermometer tube or similar instrument, so as to allow in graduating it for any irregularities: to graduate a gauge of any kind with allowance for its irregularities. **b.** To determine the correct position, value, capacity, etc., of; to set an instrument so that readings taken from it are absolute rather than relative; *spec.* to mark (a radio) with indications of the position of various wavelengths or stations. Also *transf.* Hence '**calibrated** *ppl. a.*, '**calibrating** *vbl. sb.* (usu. *attrib.*).

1864 in WEBSTER. **1869** ROSCOE *Elem. Chem.* 27 The [thermometer] tube must be calibrated, i.e. the irregularities in the bore must be determined and allowed for. **1870** TYNDALL *Heat* x. App. 330, I give here the method of calibrating the galvanometer. **1881** TAIT in *Nature* XXV. 128 The external gauge was accurately calibrated. **1897** *Westm. Gaz.* 14 Jan. 6/3 The tube was handed on to a calibrating machine, which accurately 'shaped' it. **1909** *Installation News* III. 95/1 A very accurately calibrated check meter. *Ibid.* 160 A complete Testing and Calibrating Plant. **1930** *Daily Mail* 4 Jan. 7/1 To get the [wireless] set to do its best it must be calibrated. **1959** HALAS & MANVELL *Film Animation* xix. 228 All scene movements which he has to calibrate in terms of camera and rostrum movements. **1960** M. SHARP *Something Light* viii. 74 Calibrating a cup of char with Rossy as one extreme, and tea at Gladstone Mansions as the other, tea with the Meares..came about halfway.

calibration (kælɪ'breɪʃən). [f. prec. + -ATION.] The action or process of calibrating. Also, a set of graduations or markings; a classification. Also *attrib.*

1871 B. STEWART *Heat* §20 The relative diameter of the bore..having now been determined by Calibration. **1922** F. W. ASTON *Isotopes* v. 55 This is our first *calibration curve*—of necessity inaccurate owing to the gaps between the points. **1930** *Daily Mail* 4 Jan. 7/1 With calibration you can tune in at will to any foreign programme that is within the receptive powers of the set. **1959** HALAS & MANVELL *Film Animation* xix. 228 He may also have to readjust the camera-lens..for other effects of movement in the scene according to the calibrations he has previously worked out. *Ibid.* 337 *Calibrations*, markings to indicate the movement of a background in panning shots, the movement of the camera in tracking shots, or as a guide to the position of in-between drawings. **1965** *Language* XLI. 173 As an example of special calibration, consider 400 indirect object prefixes.

calibrator ('kælɪ,breɪtə(r)). [f. CALIBRATE *v.* + -OR.] One who, or that which, calibrates; *spec.* in *Med.*, an instrument for measuring the calibre of a passage, etc.

1900 DORLAND *Med. Dict.* 127/2 *Calibrator*, an instrument for dilating the urethra or for measuring the caliber of a passage. **1932** *News Chron.* 23 Sept. 7/4 A novel wireless calibrator, called the Easy Station Finder..enables owners of non-calibrated tuning arrangements to tune-in to any desired station with accuracy. **1958** *Spectator* 8 Aug. 201/2 The aisles and transepts are piled high with sheaves of crankshafts and bunches of calibrators.

calibre, caliber ('kælɪbə(r): occas. 'kəliːbr), *sb.* Also 6–8 caliver, 8 calabar, calliber, -bre, caliper, calabre. [a. F. *calibre* (*qualibre* in Cotgr. 1611) = It. *calibro*, Sp. *calibre* (OSp. also *calibo*, Diez) of uncertain origin; the Arab. *qālib* 'mould for casting metal', or some cognate derivative of *qalaba* to turn, has been suggested as the source. See CALLIPER.

(Mahn conjectured as source L. *quâ librâ* of what weight?) *Calibre* and *Calliper(s* are apparently originally the same word. Several 16th c. writers assign the same origin to CALIVER, the name of a species of harquebus, as if this were derived from *arquebuse de calibre*, or some similar name. Littré has 'douze canons de calibre d'empereur (12 cannons of *emperor's calibre*) pour la batterie' of 16th c. The frequent use of *caliver* in the sense of *calibre*, in the 16th and 17th c., appears to favour this.]

1. †**a.** The diameter of a bullet, cannon-ball, or other projectile. *Obs.* **b.** *Hence*, The internal diameter or 'bore' of a gun.

(As the 'calibre' of a piece of ordnance determines the weight of the projectile it can throw, phrases like 'guns of heavy calibre' often occur in popular use.)

1588 E. YORK *Ord. Marshall. City London* in *Stow's Surv.* (1754) II. v. xxxi. 570/1 We had our particular Calibre of Harquebuze..The Prynces..caused seven thousand Harquebuzes to be made, all of one Calibre. **1591** SIR J. SMYTHE *Instruct. Militarie* 189, I would that all their bullettes should be of one Caliver. *a* **1595** —— *Animadv. Capt. Berwick* in Grose *Mil. Antiq.* (1801) 297 A harquebuze and a currier, both..of one caliver heighthe of bullet. **1678** PHILLIPS, *Caliber*, in Gunnery the heighth of the bore in any peice of Ordnance. **1708** KERSEY, *Caliver* or *Caliper*, the Bigness, or rather the Diameter of a piece of Ordnance, or any other Fire-arms at the Bore or Mouth. **1746** *Rep. Cond. Sir J. Cope* 99 All the Cannon was of the same Caliber, being 1½ Pounders. **1727–51** CHAMBERS *Cycl.* s.v., The caliber is the rule by which all the parts of a cannon, or mortar, as well as of its carriage, are proportioned. **1778** *Phil. Trans.* LXVIII. 65 The bore..was nearly 20½ calibers long. **1803** WELLINGTON *Let.* in Gurw. *Disp.* II. 327 We..have taken about 60 pieces of cannon..of the largest calibres.

c. *transf.* The diameter of any body of circular section; *esp.* the internal diameter of a tube or hollow cylinder; in *Phys.* chiefly of an artery.

1727–51 CHAMBERS *Cycl., Caliber* or *Caliper*, in a general sense, notes the extent of any round thing in thickness, or diameter. In which sense we say, a column is of the same caliber as another, when they are both of the same diameter. **1764** REID *Inquiry* vi. §19 The caliber of these empty tubes. **1836** TODD *Cycl. Anat.* I. 77/2 If we brace the arteries..we shall find their calibres everywhere diminished.

2. *fig.* †**a.** Degree of social standing or importance, quality, rank. [The earliest cited sense; prob. from Fr.] *Obs.* **b.** Degree of personal capacity or ability; 'weight' of character; (often with conscious reference to 1). In wider sense: Quality, 'stamp', degree of merit or importance.

1567 FENTON *Trag. Disc.* 164 The forfeiture of the honor of a ladye of equall calibre [*elsewhere spelt* calabre] and callinge to mee. *a* **1649** DRUMM. OF HAWTH. *Skiamachia* Wks. (1711) 199 Sir Henry Vane, or others of such calibre? **1791** BURKE *App. Whigs* Wks. VI. 108 Declamations of this kind coming from men of their *Calibre*..were highly mischievous. **1808** SCOTT in *Lockhart* i. (1842) 9/1 The calibre of this young man's understanding. **1826** J. GILCHRIST *Lecture* 55 We know the Doctor's caliber well enough. **1857** HUGHES *Tom Brown* Pref., Playing against an eleven of their own calibre. **1860** MILL *Repr. Govt.* (1865) 57/2 Majorities would be compelled to look out for members of a much higher calibre. **1870** DISRAELI *Lothair* xxviii. 125 The host, with the Duke of Brecon on his right and Lothair on his left, and 'swells' of calibre in their vicinity.

3. pl. *calibers.* = CALLIPERS.

4. *attrib.* and in *comb.*, as in **calibre-rule, -scale** (see quots.); **calibre-compasses, -square**: see CALLIPER.

1729 SHELVOCKE *Artillery* I. 1 The Calibre Scale..an Instrument or Ruler..to determine the Weights of all Iron Bullets by their Diameters. **1753** CHAMBERS *Cycl. Supp.* s.v., Caliber-rule is an instrument, wherein a right line is so divided, as that the first part being equal to the diameter of an iron or leaden ball of one pound weight, the other parts are to the first, as the diameters of balls of two, three, four, etc., pounds, are to the diameter of a ball of one pound. The caliber is used by engineers, from the weight of the ball given, to determine its diameter, or caliber; or vice versa.

†**calibre, -ber** ('kælɪbə(r)), *v. Obs.* [f. prec. Cf. F. *calibrer.*] *trans.* To determine the calibre of; to measure with callipers. Hence '**calibered, -bred** *ppl. a.*

1731 in BAILEY, vol. II. **1775** in ASH.

'**calibred**, *a.* [f. CALIBRE *sb.* + -ED.] Of or having calibre: chiefly in *comp.*

1887 *Standard* 7 Nov. 5/7 The smaller calibred weapon.

Caliburn, -burno ('kælɪbɜːn, kælɪ'bɜːnəʊ). Also Calab-, caleb-. The name of King Arthur's sword. See EXCALIBUR.

1297 R. GLOUC. 174 Mid is suerd he was igurd..Calibourne it was icluped. *Ibid.* 208 Calebourne is gode suerd. ?*a* **1400** *Morte Arth.* (1847) 353 The kyng with Calaburne knyghtly hym strykes. **1799** S. TURNER *Anglo-Sax.* (1830) I. III. iii. 175 A sword, fancied to have been his caliburno. **1813** SCOTT *Trierm.* I. xv, On Caliburn's resistless brand.

calic(e, early form of CHALICE.

calicate, incorrect spelling of CALYCATE.

caliche (kə'liːtʃeɪ). *Min.* [Amer. Sp., f. Sp. *caliche* pebble in a brick, flake of lime.] In arid areas of North and South America, any of various mineral deposits (esp. native Chile saltpetre) containing sodium nitrate, calcium carbonate, or other salts.

1858 SIMMONDS *Dict. Trade, Caliche*, a name for nitrate of soda found in Peru. **1883** R. HALDANE *Workshop Rec.* 349/2

Iodine occurs in caliche or raw nitrate deposit, as iodate of sodium. **1892** E. S. DANA *J. D. Dana's Syst. Min.* (ed. 6) 871 In the district of Tarapaca, northern Chili,.. the dry pampa ..is covered with beds of this salt (caliche) several feet in thickness. **1939** W. H. TWENHOFEL *Princ. Sedimentation* ix. 342 Caliche..is a deposit of calcium carbonate and other salts made in semiarid regions.

caliciform ('kælɪsɪfɔːm), *a.* Also (*erron.*) calyciform. [ad. mod.L. *caliciformis*, f. L. *calicem* (*calix*) cup + -(I)FORM: cf. F. *caliciforme*.] **a.** In the form of a cup; cup-shaped.

1849–52 TODD *Cycl. Anat.* IV. 1122/1 A caliciform papilla.

b. *Archæol.* Resembling a calyx.

1902 [see *bell-beaker* (BELL *sb.*¹ 11 c)]. **1933** W. F. ALBRIGHT in *Ann. Amer. Sch. Oriental Res. 1931–32* XIII. 66 The caliciform vessels have a rudimentary stem. **1949** — *Archaeol. Palestine* v. 80 This ceramic culture came down from Syria, where is it known as 'caliciform' because of the tendency of potters to prefer the calyx form of vases to any other.

calicinated (kə'lɪsɪneɪtɪd), *ppl. a.* [app. irregularly f. L. *calix* cup.] Made cup-shaped.

1851 D. WILSON *Preh. Ann.* (1863) I. II. vi. 460 The beautiful calicinated fibula.

calicle ('kælɪk(ə)l). *Biol.* Also (*erron.*) calycle. [ad. L. *caliculus*, dim. of *calix* cup.] (See quot.)

1848 DANA *Zooph.* ii. 16 *note*, *Calicle*..is used for the prominences which contain the cells in many corals. *Ibid.* iii. 20 Every calicle is the site of a polyp-flower. **1874** A. WILSON in *Gd. Words.* 703 A row of little cup-like bodies.. known as 'hydrothecae' or 'calycles'.

calico ('kælɪkəʊ). Forms: α. 6 (Calȝecot), callicutt, 6–7 calecut, 6–8 calli-, calicut, 7 calicute, 7–8 callicot. β. 6 kalyko, calyco, calocowe, (callaga, -ca), 6–8 callico(e, 7–8 calicoe, 7– calico. [In 16–17th c. also *calicut*, from the name of the Indian city (sense 1), called in Malayâlam *Kōḻikōḍu*, in Arabic *Qaliqūt*, med.L. (Conti) *Collicuthia*, Pg. *Qualecut* (V. de Gama), *Calecut* (Camoens). It is not clear how the form *calico*, occurring in 1540 as *kalyko*, arose; it may have been merely an English corruption; the F. *calicot* has been suggested as the intermediate form, but the age of this is uncertain.]

1. The name of a city on the coast of Malabar; in the 16th c. the chief port, next to Goa, of intercourse between India and Europe; used *attrib.* in ***Calicut-cloth***, ***Calico-cloth***: see next.

α. [*c* **1505** DUNBAR *Warldis Instabilitie* 62 It micht have cuming in schortar quhyll Fra Calȝecot and the new-fund Yle.] **1541** (July) *Lett. Credence of T. Bellenden fr. Jas. V to Hen. VIII*, IX peces of Callicutt claith pertenyng to ane William Blaky in Leith. **1589** HAKLUYT *Voy.* (1886) I. 3 Of silke and linnen wouen together, resembling something Callicut cloth. — *Voy.* (1599) II. I. *Ep. Ded.*, Lapped vp almost an hundred fold in fine calicut-cloth.

β. **1540** *Lanc. Wills* (1860) II. 151 A surplyse and an elne kalyko cloth. [**1547** BOORDE *Introd. Knowl.* 142 The newe founde land named Calyco.] **1549** *Will. L. ap Rhes* (Somerset Ho.) Calocowe clothe. **1605** E. SCOT in *Middleton's Voy.* (Hakl. Soc.) App. iii. 165 (Y.) They [the Javanese] weare a kinde of Callico-cloth.

2. Hence: **a.** *orig.* A general name for cotton cloth of all kinds imported from the East (see quot. 1753); 'an Indian stuff made of cotton, sometimes stained with gay and beautiful colours' (J.); subsequently, also, various cotton fabrics of European manufacture (sometimes also with linen warp). **b.** Now, in England, applied chiefly to plain white unprinted cotton cloth, bleached or unbleached (called in Scotland and U.S. *cotton*). **c.** in *U.S.* to printed cotton cloth, coarser than muslin.

a. 1622–62 HEYLIN *Cosmogr.* III. (1682) 205 A Smock of Calicute, a kind of linnen cloth here made, and from hence so called. **1678** *Tavernier's Voy. Kingd. Tonquin* xiii. 43 Blue Calicuts. *Ibid.*, *Relat. Japon* 58 Chites or painted Calicuts which they call calmendar. **1688** R. HOLME *Armoury* III. 349/1 Dowlas, Scotch Cloth, Callicot. **1758** ELLIS in *Phil. Trans.* L. 453 Callicuts are painted with the juice of this shrub. **1789** COXE *Trav. Switz.* I. 30 Their manufactures are coarse callicots and muslins.

b. 1578 *Invent.* in *Drapers' Dict.* 42, iiij yards of Callaga, 6*s.* 4*d.* xij yards of Callaca, 12*s.* **1590** WEBBE *Trav.* (Arb.) 31 Fine Lawne or Callico thrust down my throate. **1616** *Trav. Eng. Pilgr.* in *Harl. Misc.* (Malh.) III. 326 A camel, laden with callicoes. **1665** G. HAVERS *P. della Valle's Trav. E. Ind.* 31 A very great Trade of fine Cotton Cloth or Callico. **1666** PEPYS *Diary* 24 Sept., Flags, which I had bought for the Navy, of Calico. **1714** *Fr. Bk. Rates* 230 The Arrest.. forbidding the Sale or Consumption of painted Callicoes from the East-Indies, or such as are printed or painted at Home. **1719** J. ROBERTS *Spinster* 347 A tawdry, pie-spotted, flabby, ragged, low-priced thing, called Callicoe..made.. by a parcel of Heathens and Pagans, that worship the Devil, and work for a half penny a day. **1740** JOHNSON *Drake* Wks. IV. 452 Dressed in white cotton or calicoe. **1753** CHAMBERS *Cycl. Supp.* s.v., Callicoes are of divers kinds, plain, printed, painted, stain'd, dyed, chints, muslins, and the like. **1774** *Act 14 Geo. III*, iii, Instead of the Word Callico, which stands for foreign Callicoes, each piece may be marked with the words British Manufacture. **1860** WARTER *Sea Board & Down* II. 22 The wind sounded like the tearing of calico. **1875** URE *Dict. Arts* I. 579 It was easy for needy adventurers to buy printed calicoes. — II. 565 Hung with black lustreless calico.

c. 1841–44 EMERSON *Ess. Prudence* Wks. (Bohn) I. 99 Calicoes [cannot] go out of fashion..in the few swift moments..the Yankee suffers..them to remain in his possession. **1863** *Life in South* II. 293 Cotton-prints..called 'calicoes' in America, for dresses. **1872** BRET HARTE *Prose & P.* I. 40 The furniture was extemporized from packing cases ..and covered with gay calico.

3. *simple attrib.* (or *adj.*) **a.** Of calico (cf. sense 1). ***calico ball***, a ball where the ladies wear only cotton dresses.

1612 *Rates* (Scotl.) 294 (Y.) Calico copboord claiths, the piece..xls. **1641** EVELYN *Mem.* (1857) I. 24 The men, wearing a large calico mantle yellow coloured. **1796** *Campaigns*, 1793–4 I. II. ii. 101 Callicoe sheets keep us decently warm. **1855** MACAULAY *Hist. Eng.* IV. xviii. 141 Flaunting in a calico shirt and a pair of silk stockings from Moorshedabad.

b. Coloured in a way suggestive of printed calico; variegated, piebald. Chiefly of horses. Also as *sb.*, a calico horse. *U.S.*

1807 W. IRVING *Salmag.* 24 Nov. 372 Bantering nature fairly out of countenance—representing her tricked out in all the tawdry finery of copper skies, purple rivers, calico rocks, red grass, [etc.]. **1812** — *Hist. N.Y.* (ed. 2) II. VII. iii. 182 Behold..Van Corlear, mounted on a..calico mare. *a* **1861** T. WINTHROP *Canoe & Saddle* (1883) x. 144 A hundred horses, roans, calicos..blacks and whites. **1878** B. F. TAYLOR *Between Gates* 207 There would be scant room for the calico horses to canter. **1954** J. POTTS *Go, Lovely Rose* (1955) ix. 60 Havelka's calico cat..was taking a fastidious stroll.

4. *Comb.*, as ***calico-glazer***, ***-making***, ***-smoother***, ***-trade***, ***-weaving***; **calico-bush**, the American mountain laurel (*Kalmia latifolia*); **calico-diaper** (see quot.); †**calico-lawn**, ? a fine quality of calico, lawn of calico or cotton; **calico-printer**, one whose trade is calico-printing; **calico-printing**, the art or trade of producing a pattern on calico by printing in colours, in mordants which produce colours on being dyed, or by other process.

1814 PURSH *Flora Amer. Sept.* I. 297 *Kalmia latifolia*.. called Laurel or in the mountains *Callico-bush. **1829** LOUDON *Encycl. Plants* 356 *Kalmia latifolia*, Calico-bush. **1914** L. H. BAILEY *Standard Cycl. Hort.* II. 627/2 Calico bush: *Kalmia.* **1969** HAY & SYNGE *Dict. Garden Plants* 314/1 *Kalmia* (*Ericaceae*) *latifolia.* Mountain Laurel, Calico Bush. **1696** J. F. *Merchant's Wareho.* 12 *Callico-Diaper..called so by reason it is made of Cotton, as the Callicoes are, and is wrought into little figures. **1723** *Lond. Gaz.* No. 6196/7 Mathew Bacon..*Callico-Glazer. **1809** A. STEWART in Lockhart *Scott* (1839) III. 180 Breaking into the workshop of Peter More, calico-glazer, Edinburgh. ?**1592** *Descr. Carrack Madre de Dios* (Y.) The calicos were book-calicos, *calico launes, broad white calicos, fine starched calicos, coarse white calicos, browne coarse calicos. **1683** *Lond. Gaz.* No. 1791/4 Two striped Muslins or Callico Lawnes. **1859** SMILES *Self-Help* 36 Robert Peel..began the domestic trade of *calico-making. **1706** *Lond. Gaz.* No. 4264/4 William Shirwin..*Callico-Printer. **1854** MRS. GASKELL *North & S.* xix, One of the half-dozen calico-printers of the time. **1753** HANWAY *Trav.* (1762) II. I. iii. 15 Sugar-baking and *callicoe-printing are the great articles. **1867** *N. & Q.* Ser. III. XI. 186/1 In 1676 Calico printing..was invented and practised in London. **1762** *Gentl. Mag.* 6 We have obstructed them in the *callico trade.

†**calicrat.** *Obs.* [app. f. *Callicrates*, name of a Greek artist celebrated for his minute ivory carvings of ants and other small animals (Pliny *N.H.* VII. xxi. §21, 'Callicrates ex ebore formicas et alia tam parva fecit animalia ut partes eorum a ceteris cerni non possent').] An ant.

1596 J. BUREL *Passage of Pilgremer*, The Calicrat, that lytle thing, Bot, and the hony Bie.

calicular (kə'lɪkjʊlə(r)), *a.* [f. L. *calicul-us*, dim. of *calix* a cup + -AR.] See also CALYCULAR.

†**1.** ? Resembling a little cup (? or perh. = CALYCULAR). *Obs.*

1658 SIR T. BROWNE *Gard. Cyrus* iii. 124 Contemplating the calicular shafts [of the teasel] and uncous disposure of their extremities.

2. *Biol.* Of or pertaining to a calicle.

1849 MURCHISON *Siluria* x. 221 They..produce their young clusters through this marginal calicular development. **1872** NICHOLSON *Palæont.* 94 Three chief forms of gemmation..amongst the compound Zoantharia—viz. basal, parietal, and calicular.

Hence **ca'licularly** *adv.*

1846 DANA *Zooph.* iv. §60 The coralla..may be described as calicularly branched.

caliculate (kə'lɪkjʊlət), *a.* [f. L. *calicul-us* (see prec.) + -ATE².] Having calicles.

1846 DANA *Zooph.* (1848) 437 Corallum below, short caliculate, calicles pariform.

caliculated, = prec; also obs. f. CALYCULATED.

ca'liculato-, combining form of CALICULATE, as in **caliculato-ramose**: see quot.

1846 DANA *Zooph.* iv. §82 The coralla of these species are ..styled caliculato-ramose (i.e. Each calicle forming a separate branch to the corallum: arising from segregate budding).

calid ('kælɪd), *a. arch.* [ad. L. *calidus* warm.] Warm, tepid; hot. (in *Med.*; cf. CALIDITY).

1599 A. M. *Gabelhouer's Bk. Physic* 41/2 Applye the same on the Foreheade..the salve beinge reasonable calide. **1657** TOMLINSON *Renou's Disp.* 141 A thin, calid, and chollerick humour. **1681** CHETHAM *Angler's Vade-m.* xxii. §1 Enlivened by the Suns calid Influence. **1854** SYD. DOBELL *Balder* xxiii. 98 Summer..Crowned with oak and ash, Her hot feet slippered in the calid seas.

†**ca'lidity.** *Obs.* [ad. mod.L. *caliditas*, f. L. *calid-us* (see prec.); = F. *calidité*: see -ITY.] Warmth, heat. (Chiefly *techn.* in *Med.*)

1528 PAYNELL *Salerne's Regim.* Q ij b, This walnut..is harde of digestion..by reason of hit calidite. **1599** A. M. *Gabelhouer's Bk. Physic* 47/2 For caliditye, and itchinge of the Eyes. **1620** VENNER *Via Recta* (1650) 5. **1646** SIR T. BROWNE *Pseud. Ep.* 51 The potentiall calidity of many waters.

calidity, var. of CALLIDITY, shrewdness.

caliduct ('kælɪdʌkt). [f. (app. by Wotton) L. *cali-dus* hot, or *cal-or* heat + *ductus*, after AQUEDUCT. Cf. F. *caliduc* (in the Academy's Dict. 1801).] A duct or pipe for the conveyance of heat by means of steam, hot water, or air.

1651 *Reliq. Wotton.* 254 Pipes..transporting heate to sundry parts of the House from one common Furnace..I am ready to baptize them Caliducts as well as they are termed Venti-ducts and Aquæ-ducts that convey winde and water. **1664** EVELYN *Kal. Hort.* (1729) 228 Since the Subterranean Caliducts have been introduced..the most tender..Plants..did outlive..those rigorous Seasons. **1753** CHAMBERS *Cycl. Supp.* s.v., The ancient caliducts. **1863** DRAPER *Int. Devel. Europe* xvi. (1865) 348 Earthen pipes, or caleducts, imbedded in the walls.

calif, variant of CALIPH.

California (kælɪ'fɔːnɪə). [The name of the state on the Pacific Coast of North America.]

†**1.** Money. *Obs. slang.*

1851 *London at Table* I. 5 Some 'California', as the fast young men of the day term 'money', is necessary for these houses. **1852** C. M. YONGE *2 Guardians* xi. 183 You had plenty of money... I know you keep California in your pocket.

2. Used *attrib.*, esp. in the names of various species of animals and plants; = CALIFORNIAN *a.*

1831 F. W. BEECHEY *Voyage to Pacific* II. 81 The California quail (*tetrao virginianus*). **1840** R. H. DANA *Bef. Mast* xiv, A few hides were brought down, which we carried off in the California style. *Ibid.*, Telling us that it was 'California fashion' to carry two on the head at a time. **1846** in *Calif. Hist. Soc. Q.* V. 380, I begin to conclude that californea Horses are not a hardy race of animals. **1874** COUES *Birds of Northwest* 363 Ferrugineous Buzzard, or California Squirrel Hawk. **1881** *Appleton's Ann. Cycl.* XII. 312/2 *Ceanothus thyrsiflorus* is a small tree producing an abundance of light blue flowers, and known as the California lilac. **1891** F. F. VICTOR *Atlantis Arisen* 225 The California poppy, *Eschscholtzia*, is found in Southern Oregon. **1911** *Daily Colonist* (Victoria, B.C.) 15 Apr. 6/3 A California grey whale, the first to be captured off the Island coast, has been brought in to the Sechart whaling station. **1926** *Ibid.* 16 July 4/4 My attention has been drawn recently to some California poppies, growing on the roadside along the Malahat [Road]. **1927** C. M. RUSSELL *Trails plowed Under* 3 A high-forked, full-stamped California saddle. **1967** 'E. QUEEN' *Face to Face* xxi. 96 A bottle of undistinguished California burgundy.

Californian (kælɪ'fɔːnɪən), *a.* and *sb.* [f. prec.]

A. *adj.* Of or belonging to, native or peculiar to, California; esp. in the names of species of birds, beasts, and plants.

1785 CUTLER in *Mem. Amer. Acad. Arts & Sci.* I. 400 The Spaniards are said to have procured from the Californian Indians, the art of dyeing the best black. **1801** LATHAM *Gen. Synop. Birds* Suppl. II. 281 Californian Quail. **1839** A. FORBES *California* 192 Many of the [Indian] baskets are ornamented with..the black crest feathers of the Californian partridge. *Ibid.* 251 The wheels of the Californian ox-cart..are of a most singular construction. **1845** J. C. FRÉMONT *Exped.* 245 Some of the banks being absolutely golden with the Californian poppy, (*eschscholtzia crocea*). **1884** R. L. STEVENSON *Silverado Squatters* iii. 34, I was interested in Californian wine.., still in the experimental stage. *c* **1900** in A. Davis *Package & Print* (1967) pl. 185 (*label*) Extract Eonia Californian Poppy. J. & E. Atkinson London. **1907** *Yesterday's Shopping* (1969) 34/1 Soaps..Californian Poppy—box of 3 tablets 3/3. **1926** A. HUXLEY *Jesting Pilate* IV. 260 Californian figs and oranges. **1938** G. GREENE *Brighton Rock* I. iii. 46 A handkerchief scented with Californian Poppy. **1956** *N.Z. Timber Jrnl.* July 54/2 Californian redwood, *Sequoia sempervirens.*

B. *sb.* A native or inhabitant of California.

1789 MORSE *Amer. Geogr.* 479 The characteristics of the Californian, are stupidity and insensibility. **1840** R. H. DANA *Bef. Mast* xiv, We saw three men..dressed partly like sailors and partly like Californians. **1893** K. A. SANBORN *Truthful Woman in S. Calif.* ii. 18 Some one says that Californians 'irrigate, cultivate, and exaggerate'. **1969** I. KEMP *Brit. G.I. in Vietnam* iii. 48 A soft-spoken Californian of medium build with hair already going a little grey.

californite (kælɪ'fɔːnaɪt). *Min.* [f. CALIFORNIA + -ITE¹ 2 b.] A compact form of green vesuvianite found in California.

1903 G. F. KUNZ in *Amer. Jrnl. Sci.* XVI. 397 (heading) *Californite* (*Vesuvianite*),—a new ornamental stone,.. recently [discovered] in California. *Ibid.* 398 This interesting mineral..is a form of vesuvianite distinctive enough to warrant giving it a special variety name,..I therefore propose the name 'Californite' for this massive, translucent mineral. **1955** BROWN & DEY *India's Min. Wealth* (ed. 3) 633 A compact green variety [*sc.* of idocrase] known as californite resembles jade.

californium (kælɪ'fɔːnɪəm). [f. the University of *California*, where it was discovered, + -IUM.]

A transuranic radioactive element; symbol Cf; atomic number 98.

1950 in *Amer. Speech* (1951) XXVI. 291/2 Scientists have created a new element—Californium—carrying the heaviest atom ever known, it was announced Friday. **1954** *Sci. News* XXXII. 109 Through the absorption of 13 successive neutrons and 4 emissions of electrons (beta decay), it [*sc.* plutonium-239] was converted into californium-252, which was separated chemically. **1969** *Times* 22 Apr. 6/6 Element 104 has successfully been synthesized by bombarding the artificial element californium.

calify, var. CALEFY *v. Obs.*

† **'caligate**, *a. Obs.* [ad. L. *caligātus* 'booted', f. *caliga* half-boot, esp. that worn by the Roman soldiers: see -ATE².] Wearing *caligæ* or military boots; *esp.* in ***knight caligate***.

c **1562** *Entertainm. Temple* in Nichols *Progr. Q. Eliz.* I. 134 After followed his messenger and Caligate Knight. **1562** LEIGH *Armorie* (1597) 40 b, These are Knightes in their offices, but not nobles, and are called knights Caligate of Armes, because they were startuppes to the middle legge. **1586** FERNE *Blaz. Gentrie* 106 A caligate knight, that is a souldior on foote. **1656** BLOUNT *Glossogr.*, *Caligate*, that wears stockings, buskings, or harness for the Legs.

† **cali'gation**. *Med. Obs.* Also 7 call-. [ad. L. *cālīgātiōn-em* dimness of the eyes, f. *cālīgāre* to be dim or misty.] Dimness or mistiness of sight.

1615 CROOKE *Body of Man* 252 The calligation or dimnesse of their sight, the hissing of their eares. **1646** SIR T. BROWNE *Pseud. Ep.* III. xviii. 153. **1657** TOMLINSON *Renou's Disp.* 195 Such medicaments as cure caligation.

caligi'nosity. *arch.* [f. as if ad. L. **cālīginōsitas*, f. *cālīginōsus*: see CALIGINOUS and -ITY; cf. F. *caliginosité*.] Dimness of sight.

1657 TOMLINSON *Renou's Disp.* 334 [Eyebright] takes away caliginosity and cures all pituitous diseases. **1876** GEO. ELIOT *Dan. Der.* v. xxxvii. 348, I prefer a cheerful caliginosity, as Sir Thomas Browne might say.

caliginous (kə'lɪdʒɪnəs). Also 6 calaginous. [ad. L. *cālīginōs-us* 'misty', f. *cālīgin-em* mistiness, obscurity: cf. F. *caligineux*.] Misty, dim, murky; obscure, dark; also *fig.* (Now *arch.*)

1548 *Compl. Scot.* 38 Al corrupit humiditeis, ande caliginus fumis. **1578** BANISTER *Hist. Man* viii. 98 The liuer maketh the thicker bloud and that which is calaginous. **1650** tr. *Caussin's Angel of Peace* 53 Those men..precipitate themselves into..caliginous observations. **1790** COWPER *Odyss.* XIII. 443 The goddess enter'd deep the cave Caliginous. **1794** MRS. PIOZZI *Synon.* II. 310 That caliginous atmosphere which fills London towards the 10th of November. **1849** LYTTON *Caxtons* II. XII. lxi, Her lone little room, full of caliginous corners and nooks. **1849** *Tait's Mag.* XVI. 218.

† **ca'liginousness**. *Obs.* [f. prec. + -NESS.] Caliginous quality; obscurity; dimness of sight.

1620 VENNER *Via Recta* viii. 166 Caliginousnes of the eyes. **1731** BAILEY, vol. II, *Caliginousness*, darkness, fullness of obscurity.

‖ **caligo** (kə'laɪgəʊ). [L.] Dimness of sight.

1801 *Med. Jrnl.* V. 139, I..examined her eye, but could discover no..appearance of caligo. **1881** in *Syd. Soc. Lex.*

caligrapher, -meter, etc.: see CALLI-.

Ca'ligulism. *nonce-wd.* [f. *Caligula*, cognomen of the third Roman Emperor + -ISM.] A mad extravagance such as Caligula committed.

1745 WALPOLE *Lett. to Mann* (ed. 2) II. 103 (D.) Alas! it would be endless to tell you all his Caligulisms.

‖ **Caligus** ('kælɪgəs). *Zool.* [mod.L., f. *caliga* 'shoe'.] A genus of pœcilopodous crustacean parasites, family *Caligidæ*. Hence **'caligoid**.

1836 *Penny Cycl.* VI. 161/1 Caligus..commonly known among the fishermen as fish-lice. **1852** DANA *Crust.* II. 1525 Few Caligoids have been reported from the Torrid zone.

calimanco, obs. form of CALAMANCO.

‖ **calin**. [Fr.: a. Pg. *calaim*, a. Arab. *qalaʻī*; the ultimate derivation is disputed. See *Calay* in Yule.] 'The tin of Siam and Malacca, of which the Chinese make tea-caddies, etc.', by some said to be an alloy of lead and tin.

1752 BEAWES *Lex Mercat. Red.* 817 A mixed metal called Calin. **1753** CHAMBERS *Cycl. Supp.*, *Calin*, the name of a sort of mixt metal, seeming composed of lead and tin. It is prepared by the Chinese, and they make several utensils of it, as tea-canisters, coffee-pots, and the like. **1847** in CRAIG; and in mod. Dicts.

calina (kə'liːnə). [Sp.] (See quot. 1887.)

1887 *Encycl. Brit.* XXII. 296/2 In July and August the plains of New Castile..are sunburnt wastes;..the atmosphere is filled with a fine dust, producing a haze known as *calina*. **1927** KENDREW *Climates of Continents* (ed. 2) 244.

calinda (kə'lɪndə). [American Sp.] An American Negro dance, found in Latin America and the southern United States.

1763 tr. *Le Page du Pratz's Hist. Louisiana* I. IV. iv. 271 Under pretence of *Calinda* or the dance, they [*sc.* the Negroes] sometimes get together to the number of three or four hundred. **1880** G. W. CABLE *Grandissimes* 121 There our lately met *marchande*..led the ancient Calinda dance. **1958** P. OLIVER in P. Gammond *Decca Bk. Jazz* i. 22 Dances such as the bamboula and the calinda, which are still to be found in the West Indies.

† **calino**. *Obs. rare*⁻¹. [Perh. suggested by 'calino custure me', the corrupt form of a popular Irish melody, frequently mentioned c. 1600. (Cf. Shaks. *Hen. V.* IV. iv. 4, and editors.) But cf. also F. *calin* 'a beggarly rogue or lazie vagabond that counterfeits disease' (Cotgr.).]

1599 NASHE *Lenten Stuffe* 24 Amongst our English harmonious calinos, one is vp with the excellence of the browne bill..another playes his prizes in print.

caliology (kælɪ'ɒlədʒɪ). [f. Gr. καλιά wooden dwelling, hut, nest + -OLOGY.] That department of ornithology which is concerned with birds' nests. Hence **calio'logical** *a.*

1875 *Encycl. Brit.* III. 772 There are not many works on nidification, for 'Caliology' or the study of nests has hardly been deemed a distinct branch of the science. **1884** COUES *N. Amer. Birds* (ed. 2) 227 One of the most delightful departments of ornithology, called caliology. **1902** C. DIXON *Birds' Nests* Introd. 4 The late J. G. Woods' popular treatment of birds' nests..practically exhausts the special literature of caliology.

† **'calion**. *Obs.* Also 5 calioun, 5–6 calyon. [Of uncertain etymology. Cf. obs. F. *caillon* 'a dot, clutter, clot, or congealed lumpe of flegme, bloud, etc.'(Cotgr.), app. f. *cailler* to coagulate, curdle, clot (:—L. *coagulāre*).] A flint nodule; a boulder or pebble; often *collective*.

c **1459** *Merlin* xx. 329 His horse..ran so swyfte that [?through] the felde that was full of smale caliouns that the fire sparkeled thikke. **1463** in *Bury Wills* 37 If..brykke be not sufficient to endure, lete it be maad with calyoun and moorter. **1499** *Promp. Parv.* 58/2 Calyon..rounde stone, *rudus.* **1555** *Fardle Facions* I. vi. 101 Criekes..whose entringes thenhabitauntes vse to stoppe vp with great heapes of calion and stones.

calipash ('kælɪpæʃ). Forms: 7 calapatch, 8 calibash, callepash, 8– calipash, callipash, (9 calapash). [Perh. *calipash* and CALIPEE may be adoptions of some West Indian words; the former suggests Sp. *carapacho* (see CARAPACE).]

† **a.** The upper shell or carapace of the turtle (*obs.*) **b.** That part of the turtle next to the upper shell, containing a dull green gelatinous substance.

1689 H. PITMAN *Relation* in Arb. *Garner* VII. 358 We left some peces of the flesh on the calapatch and calapee, that is, the back and breast shells. **1749** FIELDING *Tom Jones* I. I The tortoise..besides the delicious calibash and calipee contains many different kinds of food. **1768** STERNE *Sent. Journ.* (1775) 217 An alderman who swallows three pounds of callipash and callipee. *a* **1845** HOOD *Turtles*, Having.. Forestall'd the civic Banquet yet to be, Its callipash and callipee. **1883** *Pall Mall G.* 21 Nov. 11/2 The callipee is the white portion of the flesh which comes from the belly; the calipash is black in colour, and is taken from the back.

calipee ('kælɪpiː). Forms: 7 calla-, challapee, 7–9 calapee, 8 callepy, 8– calli-, calipee. [See prec.; not found in any other European lang.]

1. † **a.** The lower shell or plastron of the turtle. (*obs.*) **b.** That part next the lower shell, containing a light yellowish gelatinous substance.

1657 R. LIGON *Barbadoes* (1673) 36 Lifting up his [a Turtle's] belly, which we call his Calipee, we lay open all his bowells. **1679** TRAPHAM *Jamaica* in Sir T. Blount *Nat. Hist.* (1693) 354 The Callapee, viz. the Belly-part so called, baked, is an excellent dish. **1689** [see CALIPASH]. **1699** DAMPIER *Voy.* I. 102 The Challapee, or Belly [of a tortoise]. **1769** MRS. RAFFALD *Eng. Housekpr.* (1778) 15 Cut off the bottom shell, then cut off the meat that grows to it, (which is the callepy or fowl). **1829** MARRYAT *F. Mildmay* xviii, Turtle lying on their backs, and displaying their rich calapee. [see prec.]

† **2.** A kind of turtle. ? *Obs.*

1794 STEDMAN *Surinam* (1813) I. i. 16 The turtles are divided into two species, and are generally distinguished in Surinam by the names of calapee or green turtle, and carett.

caliper, -compasses: see CALLIPER.

cali'peva, calli-. Also calipeever, (-piver), callipiver. A fish: a mullet of the West Indies, *Mugil liza*, much esteemed as a delicacy.

1833 M. SCOTT *Tom Cringle* (1862) 239 Cold calipiver—our Jamaica Salmon. *Ibid.* (1859) 395 That calipeever so crisp in the boiling. **1866** *Morn. Star* 17 Mar., Such delicacies as the callipiver and turtle steaks. **1883** *Fisheries Exhib. Catal.* (ed. 4) 170 The Calipeva or Jamaica Salmon.

caliph, calif ('kælɪf, 'keɪlɪf). Forms: 5 calyphee, -iffe, -yffe(e, 5–7 caliphe, 6 calipha, 7 chalif, -iph, 7– calif, 8– khalif, caliph. [ME. *califfe, caliphe*, etc., a. F. *caliphe, calife*, ad. med.L. *calīpha*, ad. Arab. *khalīfah*, successor (f. *khalafa* to succeed, be behind), assumed by Abu-bekr after the death of Mohammed. Later forms attach themselves more directly to the Arabic: orientalists now favour *Khalīf*. The pronunciation with long *ā* (eɪ) is not justifiable.]

The title given in Mohammedan countries to the chief civil and religious ruler, as successor of Mohammed.

1393 GOWER *Conf.* I. 245 Ayein the caliphe of Egipte. *c* **1400** MAUNDEV. v. 36 Sahaladyn that toke the Califfe of Egypte and slough him. *Ibid.* xxi. 230 The Calyphee of Baldah. **1586** T. B. *La Primaud. Fr. Acad.* (1594) 597 The Caliphaes of the Sarasins were kings & chiefe bishops. *Ibid.* 754 Called by the calipha and inhabitants of Caire. **1613** PURCHAS *Pilgr.* I. I. xiii. 63 The story of this Bagded or Baldach and her Chalifs [also written *chalipha*]. **1614** RALEIGH *Hist. World* II. 199 The state of the Caliphe. **1615** BEDWELL *Arab. Trudg.*, One of the Chalifs. **1734** SALE *Koran* Prelim. Disc. 181 The third *Khalif* of the race of al Abbâs. **1758** JOHNSON *Idler* No. 101 ¶1 The favour of three successive califs. **1784** HENLEY in *Beckford's Vathek* (1868) 123 *note*, Caliph..comprehends the concrete character of prophet, priest, and king. **1837** WHEWELL *Hist. Induct. Sc.* (1857) III. 228 The califs of Bagdad. **1849** W. IRVING *Mahomed's Success.* ii, He contented himself..with the modest title of Caliph, that is to say, successor, by which the Arab sovereigns have ever since been designated.

caliphal ('kælɪfəl), *a.* [f. prec. + -AL¹.] Of or pertaining to a caliph.

1881 *Pall Mall G.* XXXIV. 1417 His Caliphal pretensions will not be seriously disputed.

caliphate ('kælɪfeɪt). Also -at. [f. as prec. + -ATE: in F. *caliphat*, med.L. *calīphātus*.]

1. The rank, dignity, or office of caliph.

1753 CHAMBERS *Cycl. Supp.* s.v., The Caliphate comprehended the power both of the royalty, and priesthood. **1817** KEATINGE *Trav.* I. 314 The grand signior is considered as the head of that religion since the extinction of the caliphat. **1841** ELPHINSTONE *Hist. Ind.* I. 519 The califate.

b. The reign or term of office of a caliph.

1734 SALE *Koran* Prelim. Disc. 56 Moseilama..had a great party, and was not reduced till the Khalîfat of Abu Becr. **1859** MACAULAY *Pitt* Misc. (1860) II. 359 His short and unreal caliphate. **1869** J. BALDWIN *Preh. Nations* vi. 232 In the year 637, during the califate of Omar.

2. The dominion of a caliph.

1614 SELDEN *Titles Honor* 93 Whil'st the Chaliphat remained vndeuided. **1871** FREEMAN *Hist. Ess.* I. vi. 140 The Empire even in the East was not a Caliphate.

† **ca'liphe**. *Obs.*⁻¹ A kind of sailing vessel.

1393 GOWER *Conf.* II. 258 With caliphe and with galey The same cours, the same wey, Which Jason toke.

'caliphship. *rare.* [f. CALIPH + -SHIP.] The office of caliph.

1677 SIR T. HERBERT *Trav.* 266 (T.) Ally, son-in-law to Mahomet..pretending to the caliphship.

Calippic: see CALLIPPIC.

calis, obs. form of CHALICE; var. of CALLIS.

‖ **calisaya** (kælɪ'seɪə). [? A native S. American name, adopted as the botanical specific name.] In *calisaya bark*: the most valuable sort of Peruvian Bark, obtained from *Cinchona calisaya*.

1837 *Penny Cycl.* VII. 173/2 The Carthagena yellow barks both contain quinia, but in less quantity than the Calisaya bark. **1875** H. WOOD *Therap.* (1879) 60 Calisaya or Royal Yellow Bark.

Hence **cali'sayine**, an alkaline substance from calisaya bark, used in making a kind of bitters.

calisthenic, -ics, variants of CALLISTHENIC *a.*, CALLISTHENICS *sb. pl.*

caliver ('kælɪvə(r), kə'liːvə(r)). *Obs.* exc. *Hist.* Forms: 6 qualivre, calliour, kalli-, qualli-, kaly-, calea-, 6–7 caly-, cally-, calee-, calever, 7 caliever, calivre, 6–9 calliver, 6– caliver. [App. the same word as CALIBRE; see the quotation from Littré there, and the following:

1588 E. YORK *Ord. Marshall* in *Stow's Surv.* (1754) II. v. xxxi. 570/1 When I was first brought up in Piemount..we had our particular Calibre of Harquebuze to our Regiment, that one Bullet should serve all the Harquebuzes of our Regiment..Of which Worde of Calibre, came first this unapt Term which we use to call a Harquebuze a Calliver, which is the Height of the Bullet and not the Piece. Before the Battell of Mounganter [= Moncontour, 1569], the Prynces caused seven thousand Harquebuzes to be made, all of one Calibre; which were called Harquebuze du Calibre de Monsieur le Prince. So as I think some men not understanding Frenche, brought hither the name of the Height of the Bullet for the Piece. **1594** BARWICK *Disc. conc. Weapons* 8 It is supposed by many that the weapon called commonly a Caliver is another thinge than a Harquebuze, whereas in truth it is not, but only a Harquebuze, sauing that it is of a greater circuite or Bullet then the other is of: wherfore the Frenchman doth call it a peece de Calibre, which is as much as to say, a peece of bigger circute. **1611** FLORIO, *Colibro*, as *Calibro*, an instrument that gunners vse to measure the height of any piece or bullet. Also the height or bore of any piece, from whence our word Caliuer is derived; being at first a piece different from others.]

1. A light kind of musket or harquebus, originally, it appears, of a certain calibre, introduced during the 16th c.; it seems to have been the lightest portable fire-arm, excepting the pistol, and to have been fired without a 'rest'.

1568 in *Archæologia* (1829) XXII. 78 [In an inventory of the goods at Grafton and Salwarpe 28th November 1568, occurs] 'Kalyvers'. **1569** [see 3]. **1574** *Lanc. Lieutenancy* (1859) I. 32 Ffitt men to serve wᵗʰ qualliuers. **1577** *Churchw. Acc. St. Margaret's, Westm.* (Nichols 1797) 19 Paid for newe stocking of five calyvers 12*s.* **1578** SIR R. CONSTABLE *Order of Campe* (*Harl. MS.* 847 lf. 53 b) The ordonnance.. halberts, harquebusses, qualivres, launces. **1587** HOLINSHED *Sc. Chron.* (1806) II. 303 A..hot skirmish.. between the Englishmen and Frenchmen with hagbuts, caleevers, and pistolets. **1588** LUCAR *Tartaglia's Colloq.* 61

His Caliver..must be in length at the least three foote and two ynches, and the bore must be in Diameter ⅝ of an ynch. His Musket..the bore in Diameter $\frac{20}{30}$ of an ynch. **1588** T. Deloney in *Roxb. Ball.* (1887) VI. 390 With Muskets, Pikes, and good Caleeuers, for her Graces safegarde then. **1598** Barret *Theor. Warres* I. i. 3 A good Calliuer charged with good powder and bullet. **1602** Fulbecke *1st Pt. Parall.* 53 He that shooteth in a Caleeuer at birdes. **1613** Hayward *Norm. Kings* 77 Of late yeeres..the harquebuze and calliuer are brought into vse. **1642** in Rushw. *Hist. Coll.* III. (1692) I. 670, 100 Colliers..whom he armed with Pikes, Musquets, and Calievers. **1678** Phillips, *Caliver*, or *Calliver*, a small Gun used at Sea. **1761** Hume *Hist. Eng.* II. xxvii. 129 The caliver..was so inconvenient that it had not entirely discredited the bow. **1821** Scott *Kenilw.* i, Then you are from the Low Countries, the land of pike and caliver? **1834** Planché *Brit. Costume* 278 During this reign [James I's] the caliver, a matchlock that could be fired without a rest, came greatly into use.

†**b.** A soldier armed with a caliver. *Obs.*

1581 Styward *Mart. Discip.* I. 44 The Caleuers or Coriers. Such must haue either of them a good and sufficient peece, flaske, touch bore, pouder, shot, &c. **1591** Garrard *Art Warre* 83 Calivers or Horgabuzieres or Musketieres.

†**2.**

1589 *Pappe w. Hatchet* (1844) 37 One of them lately at Yorke, pulling out his napkin to wipe his mouth after a lie, let drop a surgeans caliuer at his foote where he stood.

3. *attrib.* and *Comb.*, as ***caliver-man***, ***-shot***, etc.

1569 in Heath *Grocer's Comp.* (1869) 10 Furnyshed with calyuer matches with flasks. **1613** Purchas *Pilgr.* I. v. xv. 447 A calliver-shot could scarce reach from the one side to the other. **1622** R. Hawkins *Voy. S. Sea* (1847) 170 In a muskett, two calever shott, or many smaller. *a* **1642** Sir W. Monson *Naval Tracts* i. (1704) 174/2 The Fleet was to pass within Calliver Shot of this Fort. **1829** Scott *Hrt. Midl.* xxxii, Ye musquet and calliver-men.

'caliver, *v. nonce-wd.* [f. prec. sb.] *trans.* To shoot with a caliver.

1863 Sala *Capt. Dang.* I. iii. 43 He was averse to all high-handed measures of musketooning, and calivering.

caliver, obs. form of calibre.

†**caliverer.** *Obs. rare*⁻¹. [f. caliver *sb.* + -er¹.] A soldier armed with a caliver.

1590 Sir J. Smythe *Disc. Weapons* 5 Harquebuziers may skirmish with more dexteritie and certeintie than the Caliverers with their Calivers.

‖**calix** ('kælɪks). Pl. 'calices. [L. *calix* cup (see chalice). On account of the running together of this and the Græco-Latin *calyx* 'outer covering of a fruit or flower-bud' (cf. It. *calice*, Sp. *caliz*, F. *calice*), modern scientific writers rarely distinguish the two, but commonly write both as calyx. The diminutives calicle and calycle are more generally distinguished.]

A cup; a cup-like cavity or organ; e.g. the truncated termination of the branches of the ureter in the kidney; the wall of the Graafian follicle, from which an ovum has escaped; the cup-like body of a crinoid or coral which is placed on the top of the stem; the body of a Vorticella; a cup-shaped depression in the upper part of the theca of a coralligenous zoophyte, which contains the stomach-sac (sometimes in French form *calice*). Also, *Gr. Antiq.* = cylix.

1708 Motteux *Rabelais* v. xlii (1737) 180 A Carbuncle jetted out of its Calix or Cup. **1801** *Med. Jrnl.* V. 284 Remaining in one of the calices or infundibula in the kidneys. **1849** A. Rich *Illustr. Comp. Lat. Dict.* **1869** Nicholson *Zool.* xii. (1880) 160 A shallower or deeper cup-shaped depression, which contains the stomach-sac of the polype, and is known as the 'calice'. **1881** Mivart *Cat* 233 The part surrounding this prominence is called the calix. **1912** H. B. Walters in *Catal. Gr. Vases Brit. Mus.* I. II. 228.

Calixtin, -ine (ka'lɪkstɪn). *Eccl. Hist.*

1. [in F. *Calixtin*, in med.L. pl. *Calixtini*, *calix* cup, in sense 1 referred to L.] A member of a section of the Hussites, who maintained, as their chief article, that the cup as well as the bread should be administered to the laity; a Utraquist.

1710 tr. *Dupin's Eccl. Hist. 16th C.* I. II. xxxi. 185 Those called Calixtines, who administered the Sacrament in both kinds. **1753** Chambers *Cycl. Supp.* s.v., The Calixtins..in the main..still adhered to the Doctrine of Rome. **1838** *Penny Cycl.* XII. 361/1 The Hussites now divided into several branches, some..more moderate and rational, such as the Callixtines.

2. An adherent of the opinions of George Calixtus (1586–1656), a Lutheran divine and professor at the University of Helmstedt, Brunswick, noted for his moderate and conciliatory views and writings on controversial points; a syncretist.

1727–51 Chambers *Cycl.* s.v., The Calixtins are esteem'd a kind of Semi-Pelagians. **1826** C. Butler *Grotius* xii. 201 Denominated Syncretists or Calixtines from George Calixtus.

caliz, obs. form of chalice.

calk (kɔːk), *sb.*¹ Also 6 calke, cauke, 9 caulk. [app. ultimately f. L. *calc-em* (*calx*) heel, *calcāneum* heel, or *calcar* spur: but the history is wanting.]

1. A pointed piece of iron on a horse-shoe to prevent slipping; = calkin.

1587 Turberv. *Epitaphs & Sonn.* (1837) 387 He sets a slender calke, And so he rides his way. **1591** Percivall *Sp. Dict.*, *Rampones*, caukes in a horse shooe. **1881** *Daily Tel.* 17 Jan., Where would the poor horse be without the 'calks' on the hind feet?

2. A piece of iron projecting from the heel of a boot, shoe, or clog, which digs into the ice or frozen ground, and prevents slipping. *U.S.*

1805 *Naval Chron.* XIII. 113, In Canada it is customary during the winter season..to wear on the feet a sort of patten, called *caulks*. **1874** Knight *Dict. Mech.* s.v., The calk..attached to a boot consists of a plate with spurs, which project a little below the heel.

†**calk**, *sb.*² *Obs. rare.* Perh. calculation: cf. calk *v.*¹; perh. = chalk.

1535 Stewart *Cron. Scot.* I. 88 With astrologe and vther instrument, With compas, calk, and als with quadrent.

calk, obs. and northern form of chalk.

†**calk**, *v.*¹ *Obs.* Also calke, kalk. [app. shortened from calcule, *calkil*, *calkle*.]

1. *trans.* To calculate, reckon; *esp.* astrologically.

1401 *Pol. Poems* (1859) II. 61 If y cowde calkyn Al manere kyndes. *c* **1440** *Promp. Parv.* 58 Calkyn, *calculo*. **1509** Hawes *Past. Pleas.* xviii. i, On his boke he began to calke How the sonne entred was in Gemyne. **1559** *Mirr. Mag.*, *Dk. Clarence* xxvi. 3 Whose fortunes kalked made the father sad. **1646** J. Geree *Astrologom.* 19 Woolsey calked the Kings Nativity.

2. *intr.* or *absol.*

1398 [see calking 1]. **1455** in *Paston Lett.* I. 350 Oon Doktor Grene, a preest, hath kalked and reporteth, that, etc. **1483** Caxton *Gold. Leg.* 55/1 They kalked on his natyvyte. **1556** J. Heywood *Spider & F.* xliv. 26 If one diuell with an other for lies should calke.

3. ? To appropriate, lay claim to. [Perhaps a different word = to chalk out.]

1606 Birnie *Kirk-Burial* 30 By kirk-buriall the pavement [is] so partiallie parted to paticulare men, that if they cleaue to that they haue calked, the people that rests must byde at the doore.

calk (kɔːk), *v.*² [f. calk *sb.*¹] *trans.* To provide (a shoe) with a calk or calkin; to rough-shoe.

1624 Scott *2nd Pt. Vox Populi* 46 As many..as would suffice for sixe or eight thousand horse all calked sharpe and frost-nayled of purpose for trauaile ouer the Ice.

Hence **'calking** *vbl. sb.*; also *attrib.*, as in **calking-anvil**, an anvil for forming horse-shoe calks; **calking-tongs**, for sharpening these.

1695 Kennett *Par. Antiq.* Gloss. s.v. *Calciatura*, The calking or cauking of horseshoes, i.e. to turn up the two corners, that a horse may stand the faster upon ice. **1886** *Pall Mall G.* 5 Feb. 4/1 Colonel Myles's system was the exact opposite of the much-practised 'calking'.

calk (kɔːk, kælk), *v.*³ Also calque. [a. F. *calque-r*, in same sense, ad. It. *calcare* to press under:—L. *calcāre* to tread. (Cf. cauk.) Often supposed to be identical, etymologically, with chalk, with which it has nothing to do.]

trans. To copy (a design) by rubbing the back with colouring matter, and drawing a blunt point along the outlines so as to trace them in the colour on a surface placed beneath. Hence **'calking** *vbl. sb.*

1662 Evelyn *Chalcogr.* (1769) 52 Two plates exactly counter-calked. **1859** Gullick & Timbs *Paint.* 147 Transferred by tracing, or, as it is also called, calking.

calk, var. of caulk; obs. f. cauk *v.* to tread.

calkel, var. of calcule *v. Obs.* to calculate.

calken, local name of the Weaver Fish.

1674 Ray *Local Wds.*, *Sea Fishes, Collect.* 104.

†**'calker**¹. *Obs.* Also 6 calcar, 7 calcour. [f. calk *v.*¹ + -er¹.] A calculator of nativities, etc.; an astrologer; a magician, conjurer.

1535 Coverdale *Isa.* ii. 6 Calkers of mens byrthes, whereof ye haue to many. **1584** R. Scott *Discov. Witchcraft* VII. xv. 122 Imps, calcars, conjurors. **1662** Fuller *Worthies* I. 209 Forewarned (by what Calker I wot not).

calker² ('kɔːkə(r)). *Sc.* Also caulker. [f. calk *v.*² + -er¹.] = calkin. Also *fig.*

1794 Burns *To John Taylor* ii, Poor slip-shod giddy Pegasus Was but a sorry walker; To Vulcan then Apollo goes, To get a frosty calker. **1815** Scott *Guy M.* xxxix, They turn down the very caulkers of their animosities and prejudice, as smiths do with horses' shoes in a white frost. **1833** M. Scott *Tom Cringle* xvi. (1859) 434 The Bight of Leogane is a horseshoe, Cape St. Nicholas is the caulker on the northern heel.

calker³, var. of caulker.

calkes, illiterate spelling of calx.

calketrap(pe, -treppe, obs. ff. caltrop.

calkil, var. of calcule *v. Obs.* to calculate.

calkin ('kɔːkɪn, 'kælkɪn). Forms: (5 kakun), 6 calkyn, 7 cawkin, 7– calkin, calking. [Possibly going back to a ME. **calkain*, a. OF. *calcain* heel:—L. *calcāneum* heel; but the earliest form *kakun* agrees with the Du. *kalkoen*, MDu. *calcoen* 'ungula,' f. L. *calx*. Some orthoepists treat ('kɔːkɪn) as only a vulgar or colloquial pronunciation, but others know no other.]

1. The turned-down ends of a horse-shoe which raise the horse's heels from the ground; also a turned edge under the front of the shoe; applied esp. to these parts when sharpened in a frost.

1445 Bokenham *Female Saints* (1683) 223 Tweyn hors.. Of wych the toon hym greuously boot, And wyth hys kakun the tother hym smoot. **1587** Holinshed *Scot. Chron.* U iij b, Causyng a smyth to shoe three horses for him contrarily, with the calkyns forward. **1607** Topsell *Four-f. Beasts* 322 Little gravel stones getting betwixt the hoof, or calking, or spunge of the [horse's] shoee. **1610** Markham *Masterp.* II. xcvii. 387 Let your [horse-]shooes behinde haue a cawkin on the out-side. **1727** Bradley *Fam. Dict.* I. s.v. *Bleymes*, Calkings spoil the Feet of a Horse. **1868** *Regul. & Ord. Army* ¶1214 The calkins of the hind shoes are to be removed, as these are not needed on board.

2. The irons nailed on the heels and soles of strong shoes or clogs to make them wear longer.

1832 Southey *Lett.* (1856) IV. 314 The price of men's clogs is five shillings..This price includes calking, i.e. the iron-work.

†**'calking**, *vbl. sb.*¹ *Obs.* [f. calk *v.*¹ + -ing¹.]

1. Calculation, computation.

1398 Trevisa *Barth de P.R.* (Tollemache MS.) VIII. xxvii, þe science and use of calkynge [**1535** calclynge; Lat. *calculi*] and acountes.

2. *spec.* Astrological prognostication.

c **1400** *Epiph.* (Turnb. 1843) 103 Ych yere wer certeyn dayes three By calkyng cast and computacion Sowght and chosen. **1562** Phaër *Æneid* IX. Bb ij, To king Turnus deere he calkinges kest. But not with calking craft could he his plague beswitch that day.

calking *vbl. sb.*², var. of caulking.

calkling, var. of calculing *vbl. sb. Obs.*

calkule, -ylle, var. calcule *v. Obs.*

call (kɔːl), *v.* Forms: (1 ceallian), 3 callen, 3–6 calle, (4 cale, kal, kel), 4–5 kall, 4–7 cal, 5 callyn, 6 caal, (caul(e), 4– call. Also (*Sc.*) 7–9 caw, 8–9 ca'. [OE. shows a single instance of *ceallian*: but ME. *callen*, *kallen*, was originally northern, and evidently a. ON. *kalla* to call, cry, shout, to summon in a loud voice, to name, call by a name, also to assert, claim (Sw. *kalla*, Da. *kalde*). A common Teut. vb.: in MDu. *callen*, Du. *kallen* to talk, chatter, prattle, MLG. *kallen*, OHG. *challôn*, MHG. *kallin* to talk much and loud, to chatter:—OTeut. **kallôjan*, cogn. with *gol-* in Slav. *gólos* voice, sound, and perhaps with Aryan root *gar-* to chatter.

The connexion of meaning in Branch III seems far-fetched, but there appears to be no doubt of its identity.]

I. To shout, utter loudly, cry out, summon.

* *intr.*

1. To utter one's voice loudly, forcibly, and distinctly, so as to be heard at a distance; to shout, cry: often emphasized by *out*, to cry out. Const. *to*, *after* (a person whose attention it is desired to engage). One may also call *across* a river, *up* a shaft, *down* stairs, *into* a passage, etc. See also senses 21–23. (Not in Johnson.)

a **1000** *Byrhtnoth* (Gr.) 91 Ongan ceallian ofer cald wæter Byrhthelmes bearn. *a* **1225** *St. Marher.* 3 Ha bigon to cleopien ant callen þus to criste. *a* **1300** *Cursor M.* 5720 Sua lang þai cald, drightin þam herd. *Ibid.* 7341 þan bigan þai cal and cri þat godd o þam suld ha merci. **1393** Gower *Conf.* I. 148 Upon her knees she gan down falle..and to him calle. **1513** Bradshaw *St. Werburgh* (1848) 105 Callynge to her, in the name of Jhesu. **1596** Shaks. *Tam. Shr.* Induct. ii. 91 Sometimes you would call out for Cicely Hacket. **1604** —— *Oth.* I. i. 74 Heere is her Fathers house, Ile call aloud. **1667** Dryden *Mart. Mar-all* II. i, Do you hear, my aunt calls. **1711** Addison *Spect.* No. 44 ¶6 The Mother is heard calling out to her Son for Mercy. **1714** Ellwood *Autobiog.* (1765) 93 He calling earnestly after me. **1788** Dibdin *Mus. Tour* xxxvi. 143 *note*, He called to one of the sailors to tell him what it was. **1848** S. Bamford *Early Days* vi. (1859) 63, I thereupon called as loudly as I could. **1864** Tennyson *En. Ard.* 837 He call'd aloud for Miriam Lane.

b. Said of animals, chiefly birds, making certain cries or notes; of bees before swarming.

1486 *Bk. St. Albans* A ij, In the tyme of their loue they call and not kauke. **1552** Huloet, Call lyke a partryche. **1609** C. Butler *Fem. Mon.* v. (1623) L iij, After the second swarme, I have heard a young Ladie-Bee call. **1674** N. Cox *Gentl. Recr.* I. (1706) 73 Being almost spent, it is painful for them [the hounds] to call. **1704** Worlidge *Dict. Rust. et Urb.* s.v. *Bees*, In the Morning before they Swarm, they approach near the Stool, where they call somewhat longer. **1825** Cobbett *Rur. Rides* 289 The poor partridges..were calling all around us. **1847** Longf. *Ev.* I. v. 2 Cheerily called the cock to the sleeping maids of the farmhouse. **1851** Tennyson *To Queen* 14 While..thro' wild March the throstle calls.

c. Said of sounding a summons with a trumpet.

1606 Shaks. *Tr. & Cr.* I. iii. 277 Hector..will to morrow with his Trumpet call, To rowze a Grecian.

d. *fig.* Said of inanimate things.

1611 Bible *Ps.* xlii. 7 Deepe calleth vnto deepe at the noyse. **1842** Tennyson *Sea-fairies* 9 Day and night to the billow the fountain calls.

e. *Cards.* To make a demand (for a card, for one's opponents to show their hands, etc.): as (*a*) in *Long Whist*, at a certain point in the game, to call upon one's partner to produce an honour if he has one, in which case the game is won; *to call* (*for trumps*): see 22 d. (*b*) in *Poker*, to call upon one's opponents to show their hands. (*c*) in *Quadrille*, to 'call a king', i.e. demand and take into one's own hand a king from one's partner's hand. (*d*) in *Bridge* (*trans.* and *intr.*), to bid.

1680 COTTON *Compl. Gamester*, in Singer *Hist. Cards* 338 If he forgets to call after playing a trick, he loseth the advantage of can-ye for that deal. **1709** *Brit. Apollo* II. 36. 2/1 If either A. or B. have Honours they are at Liberty to Call. **1820** *Hoyle's Games Impr.* 44 (*heading*) Of calling honours. *Ibid.* 80 If both sides are eight, and no one calls, each player must possess an honour. *Ibid.* 93 (*Quadrille*) Call to your strongest suit except you have a queen guarded. **1883** *Longm. Mag.* Sept. 499 (*Poker*) When the bet goes round to the last player.. and he does not wish to go better, he may simply 'see it' and 'call'. **1906** A. SUTRO *Walls of Jericho* I I, *Duchess.* I call no trumps. *Tiny.* Shall I play to no trumps, partner? **1923** *Harmsworth's Househ. Encycl.* I. 532/1 The best that you can do is to call one of the suit you want led in case B goes no trumps. **1928** A. WAUGH *Nor many Waters* ii. 74, I called, 'Three No Trumps.' And the man on my left doubled. **1958** *Listener* 11 Dec. 1012/1 West was the dealer and the opponents did not call.

f. To make a telephone call. (Cf. sense 4 n.)

1882 J. E. K. *The Telephone* 19 The means by which the Exchange operator knows which subscriber is calling is very ingenious and very simple. *Ibid.* 38 An anxious mother.. called through the Exchange for the doctor. **1928** HECHT & MACARTHUR *Front Page* II. 72 *Endicott* (*into phone*): Endicott calling. Gimme a rewrite man.

2. *to call at a door*: orig. to call aloud there so as to make known one's presence and business to those within; hence, to knock or ring, and speak or make a communication to one who answers the door; whence, *to call at a house*, to go to the door, or enter, for the purpose of some communication—the extended notion of *entering* was at first expressed by *to call in*, still in familiar use = 'look in' in passing, or incidentally; *to call on* (*a person*): to pay him a short business, ceremonial, or complimentary visit; and absol. *to call* = make or 'pay' a call.

[*a* **1300** *Cursor M.* 10096 Mi saul es cummen, leuedi, þe to And calles at þi yatt 'vndo'! **1598** SHAKS. *Merry W.* IV. v. 9 Go, knock and call.] **1593** —— *Rich. II*, II. ii. 94 To day I came by, and call'd there. **1599** —— *Much Ado* III iii. 44 You are to call at all the Alehouses. **1603** —— *Meas. for M.* IV. v. 6 Goe call at Flauia's house, And tell him where I stay. **1711** BUDGELL *Spect.* No. 150 ¶9, I happened the other Day to call in at a celebrated Coffee-house near the Temple. **1787** COWPER *Lett.* 18 Jan., A young gentleman called here yesterday who came six miles out of his way to see me. **1831** GEN. P. THOMPSON *Exerc.* (1842) I. 366 If she is obliged to call again. **1834** MACREADY *Remin.* I. 420 Called at the Literary Fund office, and saw.. the secretary. **1881** MRS. RIDDELL *A. Spenceley* II. iii. 65 She thought of calling in Banner Square. *Mod.* Call in some time during the day. Have many visitors called to-day?

b. *to call at* (*a place*): to stop for a short time in passing, in order to speak or communicate in some way with people there: said e.g. of a carrier who 'calls' at a house or place to deliver or receive a parcel, and has his regular 'houses of call'; also of a vehicle, railway train, ship, steamer, which 'calls' or 'touches' at places on its way.

Merely 'to make a short stop or stay at a place' is not *to call*: purpose of speaking, dealing, visiting, or other communication.. is of the essence of the notion.

1670 COTTON *Espernon* II. VIII. 378 His Majesty continuing his way through Guienne, took occasion to call at Blaye. **1727** SWIFT *Gulliver* II. viii. 174 The captain called in at one or two ports. **1752** BEAWES *Lex Mercat.* 267 Where the vessel was to have liberty to call, in her way down, for a pilot. **1799** NELSON in Nicolas *Disp.* (1845) III. 147 Captain Blackwood.. calls at Minorca in his way down. *Ibid.* 352 Direct the Ships to call off here, but not to anchor. *a* **1888** *Railw. Time Table*, Trains call at this station when required.

** *trans.*

3. To utter (anything) in a loud voice; to read over (a list of names) in a loud voice; to proclaim, announce, give out, make proclamation of. Often with *out*. Also *absol.*

c **1325** *E.E. Allit. P.* C. 411 He callez A prayer to þe hyȝe prynce, for pyne, on þys wyse. *c* **1720** GAY (J.) Nor parish clerk, who calls the psalm so clear. **1768** TUCKER *Lt. Nat.* II. 530 How.. should it come into his head that calling a psalm was more holy employment than sawing a board? **1855** THACKERAY *Newcomes* II. xlii. 445 'Adsum'!.. the word we used at school when names were called. **1855** MACAULAY *Hist. Eng.* IV. 489 His duties were to call the odds when the Court played at hazard. **1886** *Manch. Exam.* 14 Jan. 4/7 Sir Erskine May called out the names of members in the order in which they were to.. take the oath.

b. To announce or proclaim authoritatively; to decree.

1647 in *Sc. Pasquils* (1868) 152 Might make the Pope a jubilee call. **1859** SALA *Tw. round Clock* 367 The newly made barristers 'call' carouse in Lincoln's Inn Hall. **1876** TREVELYAN *Macaulay* I. iii. 124 He could be angry as an opponent, but.. knew when to call a halt. *Mod.* Here the captain called a halt. We had better call a halt for a minute.

4. a. To summon with a shout, or by a call; *hence* to summon, cite; to command or request the attendance of, bid (any one) come; formerly also, to ask, invite, 'bid' formally or authoritatively. Also *absol.*; and with adverbial extension, as *away*, *back*, *home*, *in*, *out*, *into* a place, *to* a duty.

a **1300** *Cursor M.* 3712 Sithen his sun he cald him till. *Ibid.* 19793 þai þat war oute, in did he calle. **1377** LANGL. *P. Pl.* B. III. 3 The kyng called a clerke.. To take mede þe mayde. *c* **1500** *Blowbol's Test.* in Halliwell *Nugæ P.* 3 Whylis ye have your right memorie Calle unto you your owne secretory. **1535** COVERDALE *Mark* xv. 16 The soudyers.. called the whole multitude together. **1549** LATIMER *Serm. bef. Edw. VI*, ii. (Arb.) 57 They were not called to the feast. **1591** SHAKS. *Two Gent.* II. iii. 61 Come away man, I was sent to call thee. **1712** STEELE *Spect.* No. 264 ¶1 The Bell which calls to Prayers twice a Day. **1712** TICKELL *Ibid.* No. 410 ¶1 Sir Roger's Servant was gone to call a Coach. **1831** MACAULAY in *Life & Lett.* I. (1880) 209, I called a cabriolet. **1847** TENNYSON *Princess* II. 447 The chapel bells Call'd us. **1882** J. H. BLUNT *Ref. Ch. Eng.* II. 11 Southampton was called before the Council. *a* **1888** *Mod.* At the end of the play the chief actors were called before the house.

b. *fig.* Also *spec.*, to summon to another world.

a **1340** *Cursor M.* 19594 To call men vnto amendment. **1526** *Pilgr. Perf.* (W. de W. 1531) 13 b, Somtyme the Bell which calleth chyldren.. & calleth them to his glory. **1667** MILTON *P.L.* II. 92 The torturing houre Calls us to Penance. **1678** R. L'ESTRANGE *Seneca's Mor.* (1702) 41 Whensoever my Duty calls me. **1819** CRABBE *T. of Hall* II. Wks. 1834 VI. 43 While Richard's mind, that for awhile had stray'd, Call'd home its powers. **1830** TENNYSON *'All things will die'* 20 We are called—we must go. **1866** B. TAYLOR *My Mission, Poems* 256 Where the fairest blossoms call. **1886** *F. Leslie's Pop. Monthly* XXI. 611/2 All the doctors in Christendom.. can't save him. He's called.

c. To rouse from sleep, summon to get up.

1611 SHAKS. *Cymb.* II. ii. 7 If thou canst awake by foure o' th' clock, I prythee call me. **1711** STEELE *Spect.* No. 132 ¶1 The next Morning at Day-break we were all called. **1832** TENNYSON *May Queen* I You must wake and call me early, call me early, mother dear. **1858** *Merc. Mar. Mag.* V. 306 The Captain.. was called at 12.

†**d.** To invoke, appeal to. Cf. also *call to witness*, 20 c. *Obs.*

c **1250** *Gen. & Ex.* 3237 Qvað god, 'quor-at calles ðu me?' *c* **1500** *Melusine* (1888) 1 In the begynnyng of all werkes, men oughten first of alle to calle the name of the Creatour.

†**e.** Sometimes with the force of the modern 'call on', 23 g. *Obs.*

1601 SHAKS. *Twel. N.* III. ii. 56 Wee'l call thee at the Cubiculo. **1603** —— *Meas. for M.* IV. iv. 18 Ile call you at your house.

f. With the force of 'call for'; now *techn.*, as *to call a case* in court, *call the trial*.

c **1250** *Bestiary* 651 He remeð and helpe calleð. **1699** BENTLEY *Phal.* xi. 236 The Trial must be Call'd over again. **1697** DRYDEN *Virg. Georg.* IV. 480 One that once had call'd Lucina's Aid. **1731** SWIFT *Death Swift*, I wish I knew what King to call. **1746** HOYLE *Whist* (ed. 6) 10 A new Deal is to be call'd. *Mod.* The judge ordered the next case to be called.

g. To attract animals by a particular 'call', e.g. as in *moose-calling*.

h. With a thing as *obj.*: Chiefly with adverbs (senses 24–35); or in phrases, as *to call attention* (17 a), *call to mind* (20 b), etc.

1761 FRANCES SHERIDAN *Sidney Bidulph* (ed. 2) III. 160 But let us call another subject.—When did you hear from Mr. Faulkland?

i. *to call a bond*: to give notice that the amount of a bond will be paid.

j. *Sc.* = Call upon, call at, visit, go through.

1837 R. NICOLL *Poems* (1843) 72 The puir auld beggar bodie, ca'd The toun where I was born. *Mod.Sc.* 'I'll caw the haill town for't, or I want it.'

k. In various phrases: see 17–20.

l. *Cricket.* Of an umpire: to declare (a bowler) to have bowled a 'no ball'; to declare (a delivery) illegal.

1850 *Nottingham Rev.*, 11 Oct. 6/5 Regarding height in delivery as to warrant the umpire in calling them. **1862** *Baily's Mag.* Oct. 201 He was getting high, and if he did not keep it down he should have to 'call' him. **1902** A. SHAW *Reminisc.* xvi. 168 Will Oscroft.. bowled a wicket from outside the return crease, and as the umpire did not 'call' him he went down that path again.. every wicket taken being illegal. **1959** *Oxford Mail* 2 Feb. 8/6 His drag of the back foot was most noticeable but umpire McInnes, though watching him closely, did not 'call' him.

m. To communicate with (a person) by radio or telephone. (Cf. 1 f above.)

1889 'MARK TWAIN' *Connecticut Yankee* 477 In the telegraphic line.. I said.. 'Lively, now, call Camelot'. **1921** [see *call-sign* s.v. CALL *sb.* 15]. **1932** E. WALLACE *When Gangs came to London* xxii. 190 The operator.. said she would 'call her back'. **1936** N. COWARD *Hands across Sea* 23 *Clare* (at telephone):.. All right, darling—call me in the morning. **1968** *Globe & Mail* (Toronto) 17 Feb. 45 (Advt.), For more information, call Jud Newell 485-9191.

n. To summon (an actor, etc.) to be ready to appear on the stage; to inform an actor, etc., of (the part of a performance that is about to commence). Cf. CALL *sb.* 6 h.

1938 N. COWARD *Operette* II. vii. 127 *Duggie.* Overture beginners, please... *Dora.* He's calling the overture. **1962** *Listener* 25 Jan. 162/1 He was called for the last act.

5. To convoke, convene, summon (a meeting or assembly). See *call together*, 34.

c **1350** *Will. Palerne* 1460 þemperour calde his cunseil for to knowe here wille. *c* **1385** CHAUCER *L.G.W.* 1860 And Brutus.. let the peple calle, And openly the tale he tolde hem alle. **1503-4** *Act 19 Hen. VII*, xxviii. Preamb., His Highnes is not mynded.. to calle & somone a newe parliament. **1611** BIBLE *Joel* i. 14 Call a solemne assembly. **1618** BOLTON *Florus* (1636) 259 Cicero the Consull, calling a Senate made an Oration. **1848** MACAULAY *Hist. Eng.* II. 252 It might be necessary to call a Parliament. **1885** *Act 48 Vict.* xvi. §12 The notice calling the meeting.

6. To nominate by a personal 'call' or summons (to special service or office); *esp.* by Divine authority: 'to inspire with ardours of piety; or to summon into the church' (J.).

c **1300** *Harrow. Hell* 184 Loverd Christ, icham That thou calledest Habraham. **1535** COVERDALE *1 Cor.* i. 1 Paul, called to be an Apostle of Jesus Christ. —— *Rom.* viii. 30 Whom he hath called, them hath he also made righteous. **1591** SHAKS. *1 Hen. VI*, V. i. 29 What, is my Lord of Winchester .. call'd vnto a Cardinalls degree? **1606** —— *Ant. & Cl.* II. vii. 16 To be call'd into a huge Sphere. **1611** BIBLE *Acts* xiii. 7 Separate me Barnabas and Saul for the work where-unto I have called them. **1680** *Mem. J. Fraser* ix. in *Sel. Biogr.* (1847) II. 302, I was indeed called by the Lord to the exercise of the Ministry.

b. To invite in due form to the pastorate of a church (Presbyterian or Nonconformist).

1560 *1st Bk. Discipline* iv, In a church reformed.. none ought to presume either to preach, either yet to minister the sacraments, till that orderly they be called to the same. **1703** KIRKTON *Hist. J. Welsh* in *Sel. Biogr.* (1845) I. 33 [He] was speedily called to the ministry first in one village then in another. **1841** McCRIE *Sk. Ch. Hist.* I. 137 The Church to which he was afterwards called. **1862** MACFARLANE *Life Dr. Lawson* 53 In due time he was unanimously called to be Mr. Moir's successor.

c. *ellipt.* for *call to the bar*, 20 a.

1836-7 DICKENS *Sk. Boz* (1850) 218/1 A barrister?—he said he was not called. **1865** —— *Mut. Fr.* iii, 'I', said Euguene, 'have been "called" seven years'.

7. To ask with authority, bid, command, enjoin, call upon (a person) *to do* (something). Now esp. said of the call of God, or of duty.

[*a* **1300** *Cursor M.* p. 962. 23 (Cott. MS.) þai.. calden a blynd knight To wirk after þer lore.] **1580** BARET *Alv.* C 21 They began to cal Hortensius to pleade in good matters. **1678** WANLEY *Wonders* VI. xxix. §5. 616/1 Some were therefore called to open the Basilick vein. **1756** WESLEY *Wks.* (1872) XIII. 200, I am called to preach the Gospel both by God and man. **1769** ROBERTSON *Chas. V*, V. 536 *note*, The subject.. does not call me to write a history of the progress of society. **1853** MAURICE *Proph. & Kings* v. 80 The king believes that he is called to build a temple. **1882** R. W. DALE in *Gd. Words* Apr. 263 One may be specially 'called' to shelter the homeless.

b. *Amer. Land Law.* To require (objects, courses, distances, etc.) to answer to a description in a survey or grant of land (Webster).

†**8.** To challenge; to impeach, accuse *of*. *Obs.*

1470-85 MALORY *Arthur* (1816) II. 456 Now ye be called upon treason, it is time for you to stir. *c* **1489** CAXTON *Sonnes of Aymon* 566 Telle me, constans, false traytour, why dyde ye calle me of treyson.

9. *Hawking.* (See quot.)

1483 *Cath. Angl.* 52 To calle a hawke, *stupare.* **1500-32** *Ortus Voc.* ibid. 52 *Stupo*: to call a hawke with meat.

10. a. *Cards. to call honours*, *call a king*, *call for trumps*: see 1 e, 22 d.

b. To call ('heads' or 'tails'), in attempting to predict the result of tossing a coin.

1801 [see HEAD *sb.* 3 b]. **1931** P. A. TAYLOR *Cape Cod Mystery* viii. 120, I lost every bet I ever made in my life. If I called heads, it came tails. **1942** BERREY & VAN DEN BARK *Amer. Thes. Slang* §754/10 *Call the coin*, to call heads or tails at the toss of a coin. **1958** L. LITTLE *Dear Boys* I. x. 172 'Tails!' Flash Harry called. It was heads. **1987** *Washington Post* 8 Sept. c8, I flipped it. He called 'heads'.

II. To name, give a name or designation to.

11. *trans.* To give as name or title to; to name. With *complemental object*; also *to call by the name of*; *to call one's name so-and-so* (*arch.* and *dial.*).

c **1250** *Gen. & Ex.* 3686 Ðat stede beð cald ðor-for cabroth. *a* **1300** *Cursor M.* 11930 A haliday, þai þai calld sabat in þar lay. **1330** R. BRUNNE *Chron.* 42 Ane erle in þe North, Uctred men kalde. *c* **1400** MAUNDEV. Prol. 1 The Holy Lond, that men callen the Lond of Promyssioun. *c* **1400** *Destr. Troy* 5204 The same yle.. Cicill is calt. **1535** COVERDALE *Matt.* i. 25 He.. called his name Iesus. —— *Isa.* xlviii. 1 O thou house of Iacob: ye y^t are called by the name of Israel. **1562** LATIMER *Serm. in Lincoln* i. 66 A certaine secte which were cauled Flagellarii. **1611** BIBLE *Gen.* i. 5 God called the light, Day, and the darknesse he called Night. **1733** BERKELEY *Th. Vision* §16 Wks. 1871 I. 379 To call things by their right names. **1842** PRICHARD *Nat. Hist. Man* 206 The people whom the Russians call *Tschudes.*

b. To style, designate, term, address as, speak of as; to reckon, consider.

c **1340** *Cursor M.* 25143 (Cott. G.) þar calles him fader ful fele þat er noght to him suns lele. *Ibid.* 2426 (Trin.) Why mades þou vs in were to calle þi wif þi sister dere. *Ibid.* 27541 (Fairf.) Synnis.. þat clerkis callin veniale. **1481** CAXTON *Tulle of Old Age*, The poet Ennius callyd hym his swete hony. **1551** RECORDE *Pathw. Knowl.* I. xxvii, That quadrate is called properly to be drawen in a circle, when all his fower angles doeth touche the edge of the circle. **1581** *Confer.* II. (1584) I, The Papistes call iustice for treason, persecution for religion. **1611** BIBLE *Malachi* iii. 15 Now we call the proud happy. *a* **1631** DONNE *Paradoxes* (1652) 2 You can cal it pleasure to be beguil'd in troubles. **1720** DE FOE *Capt. Singleton* i. (1840) 1 The woman, whom I was taught to call mother. **1736** BUTLER *Anal.* I. i. Wks. 1874 I. 19 That living agent each man calls himself. **1795** SOUTHEY *Joan of Arc* I. 29 Her parents mock at her and call her crazed. **1875** JOWETT *Plato* (ed. 2) II. 426 Would you not call a man able who could do that?

12. To apply abusive names to; to abuse, vilify. Now *dial.* Cf. *to call* (*one*) *names*, 17 c.

1633 FORD *'Tis Pity* III. vi, I fear this friar's falsehood; I will call him. **1701** SWIFT *Mrs. Harris' Petit.* Wks. 1755 III.

II. 61 As though I had call'd her all to naught. **1825** BROCKETT *N. Country Gloss.* 37 *Call*, to abuse. They called one another! **1860** *Dial. Batley* s.v., In the unsophisticated Yorkshire dialect..*to call* is to put forth torrents of abuse. **1874** *Crowle Adv.* 19 Dec., No child in the Band of the Cross must use bad language or call any one.

III. To drive. *Sc.*

13. *trans.* To urge forward, drive (an animal or a vehicle). Perh. originally 'to drive with shouts'; but no trace of this is known since the 14th c., and the sense is not in ON.

1375 BARBOUR *Bruce* x. 223 Than Burmok..callit his wayn toward the peill. *c* **1470** HENRY *Wallace* IX. 718 Thir cartaris..callyt furth the cartis weill. *a* **1600** MONTGOMERIE *Flyting* 73 Many ȝeald ȝow hast thou cald ouer a know. **1785** BURNS *Cotter's Sat. Nt.* iv, Some ca' the pleugh. **1794** —— (*title*) Ca' the yowes to the knowes. **1832–53** *Whistle-binkie* (Sc. Songs) Ser. III. 29 My father wad lead wi' a bairn, But wadna be ca'd for the deil'.

b. To drive in the chase, to hunt.

1768 ROSS *Helenore* 122 (Jam.) We never thought it wrang to ca a prey.

c. To make to go; to turn, drive.

1724 RAMSAY *Tea-t. Misc.* (1733) II. 167 If that her tippony chance to be sma' We'll tak a good scour o't and ca't awa. *a* **1776** in Herd *Sc. Songs* II. 19 We ca'd the bicker aft about. **1818** SCOTT *Rob Roy* xxvi, Even if he were a puir ca'-the-shuttle-body [i.e. weaver]. **1863** J. NICHOLSON *The Burnie*, Ca' aboot the mill wheel. [So *to ca' ower*, to knock over.]

d. *fig.* as in *call clashes*: 'to spread malicious or injurious reports' (Jam.). *call the crack*: to keep the conversation going. *call one's way*: to pursue one's way, move on.

1768 ROSS *Helenore* 76 (Jam.) Ca' your wa', The door's wide open. **1785** BURNS *Ep. Lapraik* ii, On fasten-een we had a rockin, To ca' the crack and weave our stockin. **1858** M. PORTEOUS *Real Souter Johnny* 13 While Souter Johnnie ca'd the crack.

14. To drive (a nail); also, to fix, fasten, or join by hammering; to forge, weld. Also *ca' on.*

1513 DOUGLAS *Æneis* VIII. vii. 174 In every place sevin ply thai well and call. **1676** W. ROW *Contn. Blair's Autobiog.* xii. (1848) 504 Cawed in the boots by the hangman. **1768** ROSS *Helenore* 84 (Jam.) But to the head the nail ye mauna ca. **1789** BURNS *Kirk's Alarm*, He has cooper'd and cawt a wrong pin in't.

15. *absol.* To drive (a horse, cart, etc.). *to ca' canny*, to drive gently and carefully, also *fig.* Also to drive (a weapon) *at*, let fly *at*.

a **1500** *Sir Egeir* 45 (Jam.) His spear before him could he fang..And called right fast at Sir Gray Steel..And Gray Steel called at Sir Grahame. **1823** GALT *Entail* I. xxvii. 239 But..ca' canny. *Mod.* Will you come and ca'? [i.e. drive a skipping-rope].

16. *intr.* (for *refl.*) To drive, be driven.

1717 WODROW *Corr.* (1843) II. 246, I regret your want of health, and fear you may be calling off from an ill time to the joy of your Lord. **1768** ROSS *Helenore* 70 (Jam.), I mounts, and with them aff what we could ca'. **1794** BURNS *Young Jockey* 12 When Jockey's owsen hameward ca'. *a* **1803** in Scott *Minstr. Sc. Bord.* I. 199 (Jam.) There will never a nail ca' right for me.

IV. Phrases and Combinations.

* *Phrases.*

17. a. *to call attention to*: to direct or invite (a person's) notice to; to point out, show. (Cf. 4 g.)

1827 P. CUNNINGHAM *Two Yrs. in N.S. Wales* I. 204 To call their attention to the procuring of this valuable medicine. **1835** MARRYAT *Jac. Faithf.* xxvii, To which I shall soon have to call the attention of the House. **1885** SIR E. FRY in *Law Rep.* XXIX. *Chanc.* 484 It is not necessary to call attention to the evidence. *Mod.* Attention was called to the state of the Thames.

b. *to call cousins*: to address each other as 'Cousin'; to claim cousinship or kinship *with*. So formerly *to call brothers* or *sisters*. (Cf. 11.)

c **1603** MARSTON *Insat. Countesse* Wks. 1856 III. 112 We two, that any time these fourteene yeeres have called sisters. *c* **1623** MIDDLETON *Anyth. for quiet Life* Wks. (Dyce) IV. 443 So near I am to him, we must call cousins. **1751** H. WALPOLE *Corr.* (1837) I. 156 Pray do you call cousins. **1808** SCOTT *Autobiog.* in *Lockhart* (1839) 6 My father used to call cousin, as they say, with the Campbells of Blythswood.

c. *to call names*: to apply opprobrious names or epithets to (a person). (Cf. 12.)

[**1594** SHAKS. *Rich. III*, I. iii. 236 That thou hadst call'd me all these bitter names.] **1697** DAMPIER *Voy.* (1698) 117 They..content themselves with standing aloof, threatning and calling names. **1712** STEELE *Spect.* No. 274 ¶1 Calling Names does no Good. **1854** H. MILLER *Sch. & Schm.* xxii. (1860) 233/2 He replied to my jokes by calling names. **1884** *Times* (weekly ed.) 5 Sept. 3/1 They were not in the habit of calling one another names.

d. *to call (a thing) one's own*: to claim or regard as one's own. (Cf. 11 b.)

1613 SHAKS. *Hen. VIII*, III. ii. 454 My robe, And my integrity to Heaven, is all I dare now call my own. **1762** GIBBON *Jrnl.* in C. Morison *Life* 37, I had hardly a moment I could call my own. **1840** DICKENS *Old C. Shop* iii, She daren't call her soul her own. **1857** HUGHES *Tom Brown* I. v, The first place that he could call his own.

e. *to call out of one's name*, to address by a name other than the true one.

1848 DICKENS *Dombey* ii. 12 Perhaps if she was to be called out of her name, it would be considered in the wages. **1885** C. M. YONGE *Two Sides of Shield* I. iii. 38 She had rather not be called out of her name.

f. *to call it a day*: see DAY *sb.* 20 b; so *to call it a night.*

1934 'J. SPENSER' *Limey breaks In* xi. 180 There were at least sixty pounds there, and I quickly collared the lot and called it a night. **1968** K. WEATHERLY *Roo Shooter* 55 At length, when he had about half a ton of meat on the Rover, he decided to call it a night.

g. *to call one's* (or *the*) *bluff*: see BLUFF *sb.*[2] 3.

18. *to call in question*: to summon for trial or examination; to impeach; to challenge, impugn, dispute, cast doubt upon; formerly, also, to examine, make inquisition into; so †*to call in doubt.* (Cf. 4.)

1579 LYLY *Euphues* (Arb.) 119 That..I should call in question the demeanour of all. **1587** HARRISON *England* I. II. v. (1877) 130 This is alas too open and manifest..and yet not called into question. **1600** SHAKS. *A. Y. L.* v. ii. 6 Neither call the giddinesse of it in question. **1601** —— *Jul. C.* IV. iii. 165 Now sit we close about this Taper heere, And call in question our necessities. **1671** MILTON *Samson* 43 Let me not rashly call in doubt Divine prediction. **1831** BREWSTER *Newton* (1855) I. xiii. 371 This opinion..has only recently been called in question. **1844** THACKERAY *B. Lyndon* xix, For calling the honour of his mother in question.

19. *to call into being, existence*: to give life to, make, create. *call into play*: to bring into action.

1754 SHERLOCK *Disc.* (1759) I. ii. 76 To call Men from the Grave into being. **1868** FREEMAN *Norm. Conq.* (1876) II. x. 508 It was no small work to call into being that mighty abbey. **1873** MAX MÜLLER *Sc. Relig.* 29 By which a canon of sacred books is called into existence. **1874** BLACKIE *Self-Cult.* 45 An art which calls into play all the powers that belong to a prompt and vigorous manhood.

20. a. *to call to account*: to summon (one) to render an account, or to answer for conduct; *hence*, to reprove, rebuke: cf. ACCOUNT *sb.* 7, 8. *call to arms*: to summon to prepare for battle or war. *call to the bar*: to admit as a barrister; see BAR *sb.*[1] 24. *call to (one's) feet, legs*: to bid one stand up; *spec.* to bid one in a company rise and speak, propose a toast, sing, etc. (Cf. 4, 6.)

a **1618** RALEIGH *Rem.* (1664) D j a, Call your observation to accompt and you shall find it as I say. **1659** PEARSON *Creed* (1839) 13 They who heard St. Peter call a lame man unto his legs. **1711** ADDISON *Spect.* No. 89 ¶1 He was called to the Bar. **1833** HT. MARTINEAU *Manch. Strike* v. 61 This 'mob' declared their intention of calling Wentworth to account. **1848** MACAULAY *Hist. Eng.* I. 192 Calling the old soldiers of the Commonwealth to arms. **1875** JOWETT *Plato* (ed. 2) I. 139 He who transgresses them is to be corrected, or, in other words, called to account.

b. *to call to memory, mind, remembrance*: to recollect, recall, cause to be remembered; also with *back*: cf. 26 d. (Cf. 4.)

1472 *Paston Lett.* 700 III. 51 Preying yow to call to your mynd. **1583** STUBBES *Anat. Abus.* II. 1, I cannot call your name to remembrance. **1611** BIBLE *Mark* xiv. 72 Peter called to minde the word that Iesus said vnto him. **1701** EARL CLARENDON in *Pepys' Diary* VI. 207 Whose name I cannot call to mind. **1835** MARRYAT *Jac. Faithf.* xxiv, Calling to mind what had occurred. **1871** R. H. HUTTON *Ess.* (1877) I. 3 It is necessary to call to mind..a strangely-forgotten truth.

c. *to call to witness, record, surety*: to summon or appeal to (one) to bear witness, etc. (Cf. 4 d.)

1535 COVERDALE *Deut.* iv. 26, I call heauen and earth to recorde [**1611** to witnesse] ouer you this daie. **1601** SHAKS. *All's Well* v. iii. 108 She call'd the Saints to suretie, That she would neuer put it from her finger. **1848** MACAULAY *Hist. Eng.* I. 504 They were all ready to call God to witness that they renounced all spiritual connection with foreign prelates. **1859** TENNYSON *Elaine* 1291 To this I call my friends in testimony.

** *With prepositions.*

Formed on the intrans. senses 1 and 2; the combination, however, has often the force of a transitive verb, and takes an indirect passive, as 'a light was called for', 'we are not called upon to act'.

21. call after. See 1. †Also, to ask for, demand, summon (*obs.*).

c **1340** *Cursor M.* 17842 Anoon þei calde aftir parchemyne. **1377** LANGL. *P. Pl.* B. III. 100 The kynge called after Mede.

22. call for. a. To ask loudly or authoritatively for; to order; *fig.* to claim, require, demand.

1535 COVERDALE *Ezek.* xxxvi. 29, I wil call for the corne, and wil increase it. **1596** SHAKS. *Tam. Shr.* III. ii. 172 Hee calls for wine. **1601** —— *All's Well* I. i. 202 My Lord cals for you. **1737** BERKELEY *App. Querist* §104 Wks. 1871 III. 534 Whether our circumstances do not call aloud for some present remedy? **1801** I. MILNER *Life* xiii. (1842) 246 He said some things which, I thought, called for a fresh lashing. **1843** RUSKIN *Mod. Paint.* (1857) I. Pref. 9 The crying evil which called for instant remedy. **1875** SCRIVENER *Lect. Grk. Test.* 18 Few employments call for so much patience.

b. To call for (a speaker, actor, etc.) to appear in order to receive the applause of the audience.

1822 *New Month. Mag.* IV. 315 If the public call for an actor whom they have not seen a long time. **1831** MACREADY in *Remin.* I. 413 The audience called for me, and seemed pleased in applauding me. **1851** *Illust. Lond. News* 46 The author and the performers were called for.

c. To go to or stop at a place and ask *for.*

1641 BEST *Farm. Bks.* (1856) 103 The cadgers..call for it againe as they come backe. **1833** HT. MARTINEAU *Three Ages* III. 89 To be left at the Blue Lion till called for.

d. *Card-playing. to call for trumps*: to indicate by special play to one's partner that he is to play out trumps. Also *absol.*

1746 HOYLE *Whist* (ed. 6) 79 If your Partner calls..you are to trump to him.

23. to call on or **upon. a.** To call to a person with a request or entreaty; to address in a loud voice; to apostrophize the absent or dead.

c **1400** *Destr. Troy* 388 The Kyng was full curtais, calt on a maiden. **1475** CAXTON *Jason* 70 And whan he had so don he began to calle upon the two knightes. **1601** SHAKS. *Jul. C.* I. ii. 15 Who is it in the presse, that calles on me? **1718** J. CHAMBERLAYNE *Relig. Philos.* (1730) Ded., The Texts..in which he does so often call upon Atheists and Infidels.

b. To invoke, or make supplication to (God, etc.).

a **1300** *Hymn to Virg.* 1 in *Trin. Coll. Hom.* App. 257 Moder milde flur of alle..On þe hit is best to calle. *a* **1300** *Cursor M.* 5718 On drightin can þai cri and call. *Ibid.* 19670 All þat calles on þi nam. **1490** CAXTON *Eneydos* iv. 19 The goddis by hym adoured and callid on. **1611** BIBLE *Gen.* iv. 26 Then began men to call vpon the Name of the Lord. **1867** LYTTON *Lost T. Miletus* 67 One night on death he called And passed with death away.

c. (*a*) To appeal to, make direct application to (a person) *for* (something) or *to do* (something); to require, to make a demand upon. In the passive, said also of the call or requirements of duty.

1472 MARG. PASTON *Lett.* No. 695 III. 45 Yt is seyde here that my Lord Archebysschoppe is ded; and yf yt be so, calle up on hys suertes for the mony. *c* **1600** SHAKS. *Sonn.* lxxix. 1 Whilst I alone did call upon your aid. **1750** JOHNSON *Rambl.* No. 120 ¶2 He called for help upon the sages of physick. **1814** *Lett. fr. England* II. liii. 368 He called upon his congregation for horses.

1530 PALSGR. 473/2 Call upon them to remember my mater. **1603** SHAKS. *Meas. for M.* v. i. 287 Speake not you to him till we call vpon you. **1817** JAS. MILL *Brit. India* II. v. iv. 427 They would be called upon by parliament to produce their records. **1848** MACAULAY *Hist. Eng.* I. 530 Lord Berkeley called on all his friends to help him. **1883** SIR W. BRETT in *Law Rep. 11 Queen's B. Div.* 599 Without calling upon the defendant's counsel we are prepared now to give judgment. *a* **1888** *Mod.* A man is not called upon to make such sacrifices every day.

(*b*) To require or urge (a horse) to exert itself further. Cf. ASK *v.* 2 b.

1850 'H. HIEOVER' *Pract. Horsemanship* viii. 163 In the last few strides [of a race], where sudden and increased exertion is called for, and the horse is, in technical phrase, 'called upon'. **1886** LD. SUFFOLK & W. G. CRAVEN *Racing* v. 86 Romanus is seen to..lose his pace. Wood calls on him without mending matters. **1894** CUSTANCE *Riding Recoll.* xi. 162 When I called on the gallant animal for the final effort, he got up and won.

†**d.** To appeal to as an authority or precedent.

1647 CLARENDON *Hist. Reb.* I. (1843) 22/2 His [Earl of Manchester's] authority..was still called upon. **1655** FULLER *Ch. Hist.* VI. 312 Commonly Princes call on such Statutes when themselves are called on by their necessities.

†**e.** To make a claim for, demand (money due).

1472 MARG. PASTON *Lett.* 695 III. 44, I pray ȝow send me a kopy of the dyssecharge..bothe for my dyscharge and ȝowyrs wat sum ever that be callyd upon of eyther of us here after. **1607** SHAKS. *Timon* II. ii. 22 My Master is awak'd by great occasion To call vpon his owne.

†**f.** To impeach, challenge. *Obs.*

1606 SHAKS. *Ant. & Cl.* I. iv. 28 Full surfets, and the drinesse of his bones, Call on him for't. **1740** CHESTERF. *Lett.* I. clx. 295 You call upon me for the partiality of an author to his own works. **1791** SMEATON *Edystone L.* §73 Supposing his character called upon, not only as a professional man, but as a man of veracity.

g. To pay a short visit to, to make a call on.

1602 SHAKS. *Ham.* III. iii. 34 Ile call vpon you ere you go to bed. **1822** *New Month. Mag.* IV. 403 He had called on me in Wales, and stayed with me nearly three days. **1840** *Fraser's Mag.* XXI. 404, I can..occupy myself..in calling upon some friends.

*** *With adverbs.*

(See also the prec. senses, and the adverbs themselves for less specialized combinations.)

24. call again. a. See senses 1–3, and AGAIN.

†**b.** [sense 4.] To call back, recall, restore; to revoke, retract. *Obs.*

c **1340** *Cursor M.* 26459 If eft misdos wel es right þe laured call again his plight. *c* **1330** R. BRUNNE *Chron.* 215 (Mätz.) Calle ageyn thin oth. **1483** *Cath. Angl.* 52 To calle agane, *reuocare.* **1509** HAWES *Past. Pleas.* XXI. xvi, Dede done can not be called agayne. *a* **1528** SKELTON *Ph. Sparowe* 22 Nothynge it auayled To call Phylyp agayne Whom Gyb our cat hath slayne. **1562** TURNER *Herbal* II. 84 a, The juice..calleth them agayn that ar brought in to an extreme depe slepe. **1587** GOLDING *De Mornay* xiv. 211 Time can-not be called againe.

25. call away. [sense 4.] To summon or cause to come from one's actual place or occupation; *fig.* to divert, call off (the mind, thoughts, etc.).

a **1748** WATTS (J.) The passions call away the thoughts. **1741** H. WALPOLE *Lett. H. Mann* III. ix. 27, I..am called away and scarce know what I say. **1833** LAMB *Last Ess. Elia* (Chandos) 478 When..necessity calleth him away. **1875** JOWETT *Plato* (ed. 2) I. 41 Menexenus, who is called away to take part in a sacrifice.

26. call back. a. See senses 1, 3, and BACK.

b. [sense 4] *trans.* To summon (a person) to return; to recall; to bring back (a thing).

1594 CAREW *Huarte's Exam. Wits* viii. (1596) 117 The much cold..calleth backe the naturall heate inward by counterposition. **1611** BIBLE *1 Esdr.* i. 50 God.. sent by his messenger to call them backe. **1697** DRYDEN *Virg. Georg.* III. 409 The raging Tempest call'd him back in vain. **1875** JOWETT *Plato* (ed. 2) V. 68 Wine may call back the vital powers in disease.

c. To revoke, retract.

1553 BALE *Vocac.* in *Harl. Misc.* (Malh.) I. 356 He called a great pece of his tale backe againe. **1605** BROUGHTON *Corrupt. Handling of Relig.* 6 He calleth backe himselfe in particulars. **1611** BIBLE *Isa.* xxxi. 2 Yet he..wil not call backe his words. **1848** S. BAMFORD *Early Days* vii. (1859) 68 Rap out a round regimental oath, and as instantly call it back with a 'Lord help us'.

d. To recall to memory, remember.

1851 Trench *Poems* 38 Then calling back this day we will be strong.

e. *intr.* To revert to type; = *throw back*, throw *v.* 38 d.

1853 *Jrnl. R. Agric. Soc.* XIV. i. 112 Isolated individuals appear, which, in the phraseology of breeders, 'call back' to their more remote progenitors. **1855** *Ibid.* XVI. i. 22 The offspring are said..to call back to their grand parents.

27. call down. a. *intr.* See senses I, and down *adv.*

b. *trans.* See sense 4, and down; also *fig.* to invoke from above, bring down, cause to descend.

1810 Scott *Lady of L.* iii. x, On his name Shall call down wretchedness and shame. **1864** Tennyson *En. Ard.* 324 Calling down a blessing on his head. **1869** Freeman *Norm. Conq.* (1876) III. xii. 197 Irregularities which called down the censures of Pope Leo.

†**c.** [from 3.] To lower by proclamation; to denounce, decry. *Obs.*

1551 Robinson tr. *More's Utop.* (Arb.) 59 To calle downe the value of coyne to lesse then it is worthe. **1605** Bacon *Adv. Learn.* ii. §3 If an untruth..bee once on foot..it is never called downe. **1633** T. Stafford *Pac. Hib.* iv. (1821) 267 All other moneyes..shall bee decryed, annulled, and called downe. **1668** Child *Disc. Trade* (1698) 246 If the rate of Usury should be called down.

†**d.** [from 1.] To call to one to come or sit down, to stop (a speaker). *Obs.*

1656 in Burton *Diary* (1828) I. 295 He went on a little way in it, but was called down, in respect it was late.

e. To rate or reprove; to challenge sharply. *colloq.*

1896 Ade *Artie* iii. 27, I didn't want to call her down. **1897** Kipling *Capt. Courageous* ix. 196 An unsatisfied dough-faced youth who took delight in 'calling down the old man' and reducing his mother to tears. **1904** F. Lynde *Grafters* v. 58 He..so far lost his temper as to get himself called down by the judge. *a* **1910** 'O. Henry' *Trimmed Lamp* (1916) 209 When Fernando wanted to give me several thousand dollars for my trousseau he called him down something awful. **1940** H. G. Wells *Babes in Darkling Wood* i. i. 35 It's all very well for you to call it down, young lady, and criticise it.

28. call forth. a. *lit.* To summon or cause to come forward; to call out.

a **1300** *Cursor M.* 11083 Sir Zachari þai did call forth. **1526** Tindale *Acts* xxiv. 2 When Paul was called forth, Tartullus began to accuse him. **1590** Shaks. *Mids. N.* i. ii. 15 Call forth your Actors by this scrowle. **1667** Milton *P.L.* x. 649 Calling forth by name His mightie Angels.

b. *fig.* To summon *fig.*, to cause to appear; to draw forth, elicit; to summon up (courage).

1697 Dryden *Virg. Georg.* iii. 501 The Western Winds.. Call forth the tender Grass. **1709** Pope *Ess. Crit.* 666 And call new beauties forth from ev'ry line. **1713** —— *Prol. Addison's Cato* 16 He..calls forth Roman drops from British eyes. **1853** *Arab. Nts.* (Rtldg.) 731 He then called forth his courage, and went up.

29. call in. a. *intr.* See senses 1, 2, and in.

b. *trans.* See 4; *spec.* To withdraw from the outside, from an advanced position, from free action, from circulation or publicity.

1597 Shaks. *2 Hen. IV*, iv. iii. 28 Call in the Powers, good cousin Westmerland. **1633** Massinger *New Way* iv. ii, Call-in his license. **1644** Milton *Areop.* (Arb.) 32 If one of your publisht Orders..were call'd in. **1668** Child *Disc. Trade* (1698) 246 That money will be suddenly called in. **1676** R. Dixon *Two Test.* 70 If a Book be called in, I will therefore buy it. **1875** Jevons *Money* (1878) 114 The last proclamation of June, 1842, calling in light gold. **1885** *Law Rep. 29 Chanc. Div.* 461 The whole balance of the mortgage ..might be at once called in. **1885** *Manch. Exam.* 5 May 4/7 The Russians are willing to call in their outposts.

c. To summon for assistance or consultation.

1678 N. Wanley *Wonders* v. i. §103. 468/2 The Swedes, who were called in for the support of the German liberty. **1875** Jevons *Money* (1878) 36 To call in the aid of the microscope. **1885** Sir J. Hannen in *Law Rep. 10 Probate Div.* 90 Sir William Gull was called in.

d. To require the payment or repayment of (money outstanding): cf. call *sb.* 11.

1701 *Lond. Gaz.* No. 3749/8 Part of the 10 per Cent...to be called in. **1713** *Ibid.* No. 5114/3, 20s. per Share was.. called in.

30. call off. a. See senses 1, 3, and off.

b. [See 4.] To summon away, or from what one is doing; *fig.* to divert, call away (the attention).

1633 Bp. Hall *Hard Texts* 545 The Lord..will call off those evils wch they groane under. **1711** Steele *Spect.* No. 104 ¶2 My Eyes were suddenly called off from these.. Objects by a little Party of Horsemen. **1766** Goldsm. *Vic. W.* xxxi, But the appearance of..the jailer's two servants now called off our attention. **1810** Scott *Lady of L.* iii. iv, And in mid chase called off his hound.

c. *trans.* To cancel (an engagement, etc.), draw back from (an undertaking). Also *intr.*

1888 Mrs. Oliphant *Second Son* v, Why, in the name of all that's idiotic, do you call off now, and disappoint her.. and defy me? **1900** Ade *More Fables* 158 He was about to Call Off the Vestry Meeting, the Dinner, and all other Engagements for a Week to come. **1902** *Daily Chron.* 17 Oct. 5/3 The delegates of the Miners' Convention must first pass a vote upon the question of calling off the strike. **1927** *Observer* 14 Aug. 6 That he would have been profoundly relieved if the whole expedition had been called off. **1952** V. Gollancz *My Dear Timothy* 388 But I am almost certain that, war, or no war, I should have called it off.

31. call on. a. See senses 1, 3, and on *adv.* (*a.*, *sb.*[1])

†**b.** *trans.* To invite to come on, allure, incite; *fig.* to encourage the growth of, bring on. *Obs.*

1603 Florio *Montaigne* ii. xii. (1632) 296 It is a wonder, whither the perverse wickednesse of mans heart will proceed, if it be but called-on by any little successe. **1626** Bacon *Sylva* §546 How to multiply and call on mosses.

c. *intr.* Of hounds: To 'challenge'.

1704 Worlidge *Dict. Rust. et Urb.* s.v. *Fox-hunting*, And for such as are first cast off, let them be old stanch-hounds, which are sure; and if you hear such an one call on merrily, you must cast off some other to him. **1847–78** Halliwell s.v., When hounds are first cast off, and find game, they are said to call on.

32. call out. a. See senses 1, 3, and out *adv.*

b. To call or summon forth; *fig.* to evoke. *spec.* to summon to active or permanent service in a campaign or in a state of emergency.

c **1450** *Voc.* in Wr.-Wülcker 605 *Provoco*..to calle out. **1779** *Digest of Militia Laws* 112 Every such person, having served in the Militia when called out into actual service. **1840** *Fraser's Mag.* XXII. 697 The usual trick of being called out a dozen times, under pretence of a patient wanting me. **1849** Macaulay *Hist. Eng.* I. iii. 291 When the trainbands were called out against an enemy. **1853** Bunn *Old Eng.* II. 53 Shot by the military, who had been called out for the occasion. **1876** Green *Short Hist.* iv. §3 (1882) 176 [His] fiercest burst of vengeance was called out by an insult to his mother. *a* **1888** *Mod.* The military were called out. **1890** *Chambers's Jrnl.* 5 July 423/1 The fog-signalmen..are often called out for a night's 'fogging' just as they have finished a hard day's work. **1921** *Act 11 & 12 Geo. V* c. 15 §9 Where..a man of the Naval Reserves.. is called into actual service or called out for permanent service..on an occasion of great emergency.

c. To challenge to fight (*esp.* a duel).

1823 *New Month. Mag.* VIII. 111 Damme if I don't call them out. **1840** *Fraser's Mag.* XXI. 594 In modern.. parlance, 'I call you out'. **1882** Pebody *Eng. Journalism* xi. (1883) 78 [He] contrived..to be called out for a criticism which was too free and frank even for those times.

†**d.** To call for repayment of (money in a bank, or the like). *Obs.*

1682 Luttrell *Brief Rel.* (1857) I. 211 Severall persons who had money in the chamber of London..thought fitt to call it out, but were told there were no orders to pay any.

e. To summon (workers) to strike. orig. *U.S.*

1895 H. P. Robinson *Men born Equal* 284 Ugly threats, moreover, were being made by the strikers that the members of other labor organizations would be 'called out'. **1947** *Times* 1 May 5/2 The chairman..talked of launching a national strike and of calling out the seamen, the road transport workers, and the engineers. **1957** *Screen Printer & Display Producer* July 1/1 It was never the intention of the Union to call all its members out.

33. call over. a. See senses 1, 3, and over.

b. To read aloud (a roll or list of names), to which the persons called are to answer, in order to prove their presence. Also *absol.*

1687 Bp. Cartwright in *Magd. Coll. & Jas. II* (Oxf. Hist. Soc.) 117 We called over the College Roll. **1837** Dickens *Pickw.* xxxiv, A gentleman in black..proceeded to call over the names of the jury. **1864** H. Cox *Instit.* i. ix. 137 It has been the practice of the House of Commons, on several occasions of sufficient importance, to order that the House be called over at a future day.

†**c.** To read aloud, recite (an announcement), proclaim; to recite, rehearse (a story). *Obs.* or *dial.*

1681 *Select. fr. Harl. Misc.* (1793) 466 Here let me call over a story. **1865** Harland *Lanc. Lyrics* 137 Iv o' Sunday to't chourch theaw wilt gang, Ther axins tha'll yer um coed o'er.

d. *call over the coals*: see coal.

34. call together (see 5). To summon to assemble, to convoke.

1526 Tindale *Luke* xxiii. 13 And Pilate called [Wyclif clepid] to geder the hye prestes. **1611** Bible *Jer.* l. 29 Call together the archers against Babylon. *Mod.* Call the workmen together at once.

35. call up. a. See senses 1, 3, and up *adv.*

b. To summon, from some lower region or place (e.g. from Hades), to bring into the mind by an effort of memory or imagination.

1632 Milton *Penser.* 109 That thy power Might..call up him who left untold The story of Cambuscan bold. **1667** —— *P.L.* iii. 603 Philosophers..call up unbound..old Proteus from the Sea. **1847** L. Hunt *Men, Wom. & B.* II. viii. 146 A tinselled nymph..calling up commonplaces with a wand. **1871** Freeman *Norm. Conq.* (1876) IV. xvii. 32 Able to call up a personal image of several men of the days of Eadward.

c. To summon before an authority, tribunal, or examiner.

1753 *World* No. 35, I was unfortunately called up to give evidence against him. **1846** McCulloch *Acc. Brit. Empire* (1854) II. 323 In school..the master 'calls up' a certain number..with each of whom he construes a part.

d. To call to mind, recall.

1713 Addison *Cato* i. iv, Why do'st thou call my sorrows up afresh? **1848** Macaulay *Hist. Eng.* II. 155 The occasion ..could not but call up some recollections.

e. To call on or incite to rise and speak.

1848 Macaulay *Hist. Eng.* II. 524 These words called up Rochester. He defended the petition.

f. To call to battle; *spec.* to summon to military service. Cf. call-up.

[? **1684** in *Roxburghe Ballads* (1897) VIII. 453 Come fill up my cup, come fill up my Can; come saddle my horse and call up my man.] **1827** Scott *Bonnie Dundee* in *Lit. Gaz.* 8 Dec. 786 Come saddle my horses and call up my men. **1857** *Blackw. Mag.* LXXXII. 281/2 The landwehr of the first band are liable..in the event of war, to be called up. **1899** Atteridge *Wars of Nineties* 550/2 Thus Japan had an army of nearly 70,000 men on a peace footing, which by calling up the reserves could be expanded into a war force of more than a quarter of a million. **1914** *Eng. Rev.* Sept. 258 We saw young Belgians crowded in trains *en route* for the front, men who were 'called up' against the enemy.

g. To summon up (summon *v.* 7).

1889 *Illustrations, a Pict. Rev.* 143 Calling up whatever remnants of valour were left to me,..I advanced.

h. To summon (a person) on the telephone.

1898 [implied in *caller-up*]. **1900** [see phone *sb.*[2] and *v.*] *a* **1910** 'O. Henry' *Strictly Business* (1917) ii. 29 Kelley went to the nearest telephone booth and called up McCrary's café. **1921** G. B. Shaw *Back to Methuselah* iii. 137 Engaged! Who is she calling up now?

call (kɔːl), *sb.* Also 4–6 cal, calle, (8–9 *Sc.* ca, 9 *Sc.* and *dial.* caw, *dial.* cawal). [f. prec. vb.]

1. a. A loud vocal utterance or speech, a shout, a cry; a loud vocal address or supplication.

a **1300** *Cursor M.* 6790, I, for-soth sall here þair call. *Ibid.* 1377 An o þaim..Be-for ihesus þar made his call. **1678** Bunyan *Pilgr.* i. 207 They gave but a call, and in came their Master. **1704** Pope *Past., Summer* 83 But would you sing.. The moving mountains hear the pow'rful call. **1822** *New Month. Mag.* V. 150 You are amused with the perpetual opening and shutting of box doors, and the aubible calls of 'Mrs. So and so's places'.

b. *spec.* The reading aloud of a roll or list of names; a roll-call: see call *v.* 33 b.

1723 Bp. Nicolson in Ellis *Orig. Lett.* ii. 446 The Commons were very warm yesterday: and their Debates ended in a Call of their Members. **1780** Burke *Corr.* (1844) II. 318, I think to make my motion as soon as possible after the call of the House. *a* **1832** Mackintosh *Revol. 1688* Wks. 1846 II. 51 The attendance was partly caused by a call of the House..On the call..it appeared that forty were either minors, abroad, or confined by sickness.

c. A word or name called; a thing thus mentioned or indicated.

1801 Strutt *Sports & Past.* iv. ii. 296 The other calls at pleasure head or tail; if his call lies uppermost..he wins.

d. A summons or communication by telephone; a telephone conversation. (See also attrib. uses.)

1878 *Design & Work* IV. 306/3 Apparatus..to enable the sound of the voice while singing to be heard all over a room, and which I use as a 'call', instead of an electric bell. **1879** G. B. Prescott *Speaking Telephone* i. 23 It being necessary to keep the vibratory bells at each station in circuits, in order that the calls may be heard. **1882** J. E. K. *The Telephone* 19 The number of calls made upon the Exchange clerks. **1884** *Routledge's Every Boy's Ann.* 199/1 Before we follow the series of operations forming a complete call, let us examine the system of telephones used in the Broadway Office. This ..allows these batteries to be used for the calls to the subscribers by means of ordinary electric bells. **1899** *Post Office Guide* July 533 This deposit is refunded if the call is not extended. **1944** 'N. Shute' *Pastoral* ii. 22 Give me twopence for the call, and I'll give him a tinkle in the morning. **1953** R. Lehmann *Echoing Grove* 290 There was a call for you about a quarter of an hour ago. From London.

2. The cry of an animal, *esp.* of a bird.

1684 Bunyan *Pilgr.* ii. 62 The Hen by her common call, gives no meat to her Chickens. **1773** Barrington in *Phil. Trans.* LXIII. 250 The call of a bird, is that sound which it is able to make, when about a month old. **1833** *Chamb. Jrnl.* II. 148 They can hear the call of their calves. **1842** Tennyson *Locksley H.* 171 They shall..Whistle back the parrot's call. **1879** Jefferies *Wild Life in S.C.* 301 Neither redwing nor fieldfare sings during the winter; they of course have their 'call' and cry of alarm.

3. a. A particular cry or sound used to attract or decoy birds, etc.

1530 Palsgr. 202/2 Call for quaylles, *croquaillet*. **1590** Lodge *Euphues' Gold. Leg.* (1887) 98 Aliena smiled to see how Ganymede flew to the fist without any call. **1596** Raleigh *Disc. Guiana* (1887) 76 The deer came..as if they had been used to a Keepers call. **1851** *Illust. Lond. News* 15 Feb. 127 The birds after answering to the call..at last darted off again.

b. A small instrument or whistle to attract birds, etc., by imitating their note.

1654 Bate *Myst. Nature & Art* 73 They are known among some Shopkeepers by the name of Cals; and there are long white boxes of them, which are transported hither from France. **1704** Worlidge *Dict. Rust. et Urb.* s.v. *Calls*, As for the Artificial Calls..they are best made of Box and Walnut Tree, or such hard Woods. **1708** Kersey s.v., Among Fowlers, Calls are artificial Pipes, made to catch Quails, etc. **1753** Chambers *Cycl. Supp.* s.v., Different birds require different calls; but most of them are composed of a pipe or reed, with a little leathern bag, somewhat in the form of a bellows.

†**c.** A decoy-bird. *lit.* and *fig.* *Obs.*

1595 Shaks. *John* III. iv. 174 They would be as a Call To traine ten thousand English to their side. **1624** Massinger *Parl. Love* iv. iii, This fellow has a pimp's face, And looks as if he were her call, her fetch. **1725** Bradley *Fam. Dict.* s.v. *Lark*, Those live Birds tyed to the Packthreads are nam'd Calls.

4. *Hunting.* A strain or 'lesson' blown upon the horn to cheer and encourage the hounds.

1674 N. Cox *Gentl. Recreat.* i. (1706) 18 The Call, a Lesson blowed on the Horn to comfort the Hounds. **1721** in Bailey.

5. a. The act of calling at a door or place on the way: hence, house *of call*. **b.** A short and usually formal visit: *to make, pay, receive, a call*.

1783 Cowper *Task* i. 244 Dependant on the baker's punctual call. **1816** *Parody* in *Times* 25 Jan., Enumerate the principal houses of call in..London. **1862** Trollope *Orley F.* xiv, She had..made a morning call on Martha Biggs. **1875** B. Taylor *Faust* I. v. 90 We passed without a call to day. **1884** *Harper's Mag.* Sept. 493/2 The chief interest of Queenstown is as a port of call.

6. a. Summons, invitation, bidding. Also *fig.*

a **1300** *Cursor M.* 3022 Mete and drinc he gaue þam all þat wald cum al til his call. **1592** SHAKS. *Ven. & Ad.* 849 Tapsters answering every call. **1667** MILTON *P.L.* I. 378 Who first, who last..At thir great Emperors call..Came singly where he stood. **1752** JOHNSON *Rambl.* No. 204 ¶5 His call was readily obeyed. **1833** HT. MARTINEAU *Briery Cr.* iv. 92 A call to devotion. **1836** DICKENS *Sk. Boz* (C.D. ed.) 71 The bell rings and the orchestra in acknowledgment of the call play three distinct chords. **1875** EMERSON *Lett. & Soc. Aims, Eloquence* Wks. (Bohn) III. 193 Men who lose their talents, their wit..at any sudden call.

†**b.** A summons to answer to a charge; accusation, impeachment. *Obs.*

c **1340** *Cursor M.* 19138 (Fairf.) þai gedder bad bring forþ þe apostles alle for til ansquare to þaire calle.

c. A summons by applause for a speaker, actor, etc., to appear before an audience. Cf. CALL *v.* 22 b.

1825 *News* 4 Sept. 286/1 Mr. Kean came forward, and addressed the audience... 'It is impossible to withstand so gratifying a call.' **1887** *Punch* 12 Mar. 125/1 The enthusiastic..call that greeted him on the conclusion of his excellent work. **1921** 'IAN HAY' *Willing Horse* viii. 129 Seven *legitimate* calls after the first act.

d. A summons or signal sounded upon a bugle, trumpet, etc.; also *fig.*

1581 STYWARD *Mart. Discip.* I. 18 In sounding a march, a cal, yᵉ charge..yᵉ retrait. **1677** MILTON *P.L.* VII. 295 Armies at the call Of Trumpet..Troop to thir Standard. **1713** *Lond. Gaz.* No. 5135/3 The Drums beating a Call. **1875** B. TAYLOR *Faust* II. IV. iii. 269 The first clear call of bells is swept across the land.

e. *concr.* A whistle, or other instrument, on which such a call is sounded.

1769 FALCONER *Dict. Marine* (1789) The call can be sounded to various strains, each..appropriated to some particular exercise. **1818** SCOTT *Br. Lamm.* iv, She whistled on a small silver call which hung around her neck.

f. ***call to the bar***: admission to the status of barrister; see BAR *sb.*[1] 24, BARRISTER. Also †***call of serjeants*** (obs.).

a **1626** BACON (J.) Upon the sixteenth was held the serjeants feast at Ely place, there being nine serjeants of that call. **1698** CONGREVE *Way of W.* III. xv, In the country where great lubberly brothers slabber and kiss one another when they meet like a call of serjeants. **1868** M. PATTISON *Academ. Org.* v. 184 There shall be examinations and degrees required for the call to the Bar. **1878** R. H. HUTTON *Scott* ii. 27 The day of his call to the bar.

g. *spec.* An invitation to undertake the office and duties of pastor of a church.

1666 *Life J. Livingstone* in *Sel. Biogr.* (1845) I. 136, I got ane joynt call of the parish and presbytery and the old minister and my Lord Tarphichen patron of the church..to be minister there. *a* **1704** T. BROWN *2 Oxf. Scholars* (1730) I. 2, I shall receive a call to be a Pastor or Holder-forth in some Congregation or other. **1755** WESLEY *Wks.* (1872) XIII. 208 Both an inward and an outward call are requisite. **1818** SCOTT *Hrt. Midl.* xxxix, [The] presbyterians who had united in a harmonious call to Reuben Butler to be their spiritual guide. **1859** J. CUNNINGHAM *Ch. Hist. Scotl.* II. x. 422.

h. A notification, either verbal or written, summoning theatrical, etc., performers to attend (at a rehearsal or during a performance). Cf. CALL *v.* 4 n.

1780 G. COLMAN *Manager in Distress* 22 They were all drest, sitting ready for the call in the Green Room. **1876** *Jennie of 'The Princess'* 219 You are cast for Player Queen. Call is for eleven this morning. **1885** G. R. SIMS *Mustard & Cr.* in *Referee* 16 Feb., A 'call' is frequently made out for 'supers and ladies and gentlemen' when the principals are not required. **1933** P. GODFREY *Back-Stage* i. 16 The call-boy leaves the stage to cry: 'Overture beginners.'..As the call reaches them they take one last approving glance at their reflections. *Ibid.* 17 Each 'call' is plainly marked in the prompt book sufficiently ahead of the actual entrance to allow the actor concerned to receive an individual visit from the call-boy. **1955** *Times* 19 Aug. 4/1 The schedule for to-morrow's work arrived with all its facts and figures about the crew call, the set, [etc.].

i. *Whist.* A 'call for honours' (see CALL *v.* 1 e); also, a sign given to a partner by a special kind of play that he is to lead trumps (cf. CALL *v.* 22 d). In poker (orig. *U.S.*), 'a demand for a show-down; the show-down itself' (*Cent. Dict.*, 1889); in Bridge, a bid (*sb.* 2), pass, double, or redouble.

1850 'M. TENSAS' *Louisiana Swamp Doctor* 123 A gambler who has staked his whole pile, and found at the call that he has been bluffing up against a greenhorn with 'three white aces'. **1853** J. G. BALDWIN *Flush Times Alabama* 8 A negro *ante* and twenty on the call, was moderate playing. **1885** *Encycl. Brit.* XIX. 283/1 When all the stakes are thus equal, it becomes a *call*. **1887** *Temple-bar Mag.* Apr. 551 My partner..will lead trumps on the first opportunity in obedience to my 'call'. **1923** *Harmsworth's Househ. Encycl.* I. 531/1 Doubling..reopens the bidding and gives each player the chance of a fresh call. **1928** A. WAUGH *Nor many Waters* ii. 74 The man on my right suddenly cut into the bidding. 'Well, it's my call,' he said. 'Three spades.'

j. *Amer. Land Law.* 'An object, course, distance, or other matter of description in a survey or grant, requiring or calling for a corresponding object, etc., on the land' (Webster 1864).

k. *Cricket.* A shouted direction by a batsman to his partner either to run or to remain in his crease.

1854 J. PYCROFT *Cricket Field* (ed. 2) x. 212 Let men run by some call; mere beckoning..leads to fatal errors... 'Yes', 'no', or 'run', 'stop' are the words. **1898** G. GIFFEN *With Bat & Ball* viii. 103 Murdoch..was run out through a bad call of Tom Garrett's. **1955** *Times* 15 July 3/3 Fellows Smith failed to scramble home after being sent back for a ridiculous call.

l. A signification of impending death; *spec.* in phr. ***to get one's*** (or ***the***) ***call***, to die, be about to die. *dial.*

1884 D. GRANT *Lays & Legends* 172 His wife, wi' his grainin' sae weary, Was fain to have seen him awa'... Hersel' was the first gat the ca'. **1889** TENNYSON *Crossing the Bar* in *Compl. Wks.* (1896) 894/1 Sunset and evening star, And one clear call for me! **1892** C. M. YONGE *Old Woman's Outlook* ii. 39 There came a little robin about the door. We knowed it was a call, and we thought it must be for granfer; so we put 'im to bed. **1915** J. BUCHAN *Salute to Adv.* xxiii. 328 His breath laboured, and there was pain in his eyes. 'I've got my call,' he said faintly.

7. a. Demand, requisition, claim.

a **1300** *Cursor M.* 8705 þe barne atte dede is nauþer of thayme wille haue þer-til cal ne clayme. **1711** STEELE *Spect.* No. 206 ¶1 There is a perpetual call upon mankind to value and esteem those who set a moderate price on their own merit. **1751** JOHNSON *Rambl.* No. 141 ¶8 The call for novelty is never satisfied. **1832** A. FONBLANQUE *Engl. under 7 Administ.* II. 268 The Duke of Newcastle's call upon the anti-reformers to take up arms against the people. **1832** *Athenæum* No. 219. 19 The call of these times for cheap reprints. **1870** BRYANT *Iliad* I. IX. 269 The calls of thirst And hunger having ceased.

b. A need to defecate or urinate; freq. in phr. ***call of nature***. Colloq. phr. ***to pay a call***, to go to the lavatory.

1761 STERNE *Tr. Shandy* IV. 43 A city..who neither eat, or drank,..or hearkned to the calls either of religion or nature for seven and twenty days. **1852** in *Tailor & Cutter* (1966) 14 Oct. 111/1 The calls of Nature are permitted and Clerical Staff may use the garden below the second gate. **1858** G. RAWLINSON tr. *Herodotus's Hist.* I. cxxxiii. 274 To vomit or obey natural calls in the presence of another, is forbidden among them. **1926** GALSWORTHY *Escape* I. i, *Warder*... Where's your mate? *Fellow Convict.* 'Ad a call, sir... Went over to that wall. **1926** A. HUXLEY *Two or Three Graces* 249 He would suggest dropping in at the Monico, pretext a call of nature. **1939** F. THOMPSON *Lark Rise* 56 A type of complaint that could always be countered by pleading, 'Call o' Nature, please, sir.' **1959** 'O. MILLS' *Stairway to Murder* xv. 155 He'd had quite a bit of beer, and I'd an idea he might have to get up and pay a call. **1961** J. MCCABE *Laurel & Hardy* (1962) i. 33 On the way there we became aware of Nature's urgent call.

8. a. A requirement of duty; a duty, need, occasion, right.

a **1674** CLARENDON *Hist. Reb.* (1704) III. XIV. 377 He assured them..'that they had a very lawful Call to take upon them the supreme Authority of the Nation'. **1719** DE FOE *Crusoe* (1858) 243 What call, what occasion, much less what necessity I was in, to go. **1779** J. MOORE *View Soc. Fr.* (1789) I. xvi. 124 There was no Call for his interfering in the business. **1858** THACKERAY *Virginians* xxii, I don't know what call she had to blush so when she made her curtsey.

†**b.** Occasion or need to go; an errand. *Obs.*

1791 SMEATON *Edystone L.* §324 Having a call to St. Ives in Cornwall. *Ibid.* §325 Having a second call into Cornwall.

9. A divine, spiritual, or sacred appointment, or prompting, to a special service or office. See CALL *v.* 6.

1650 *Ministers New Eng.* in Ellis *Orig. Lett.* II. ccc, We came by a call of God to serve him here. **1755** *Mem. Capt. P. Drake* I. xi. 79 Proposals..to quit the World, and embrace that Course of Life, to which I told him I had no Call. **1790** MRS. FLETCHER in H. Moore *Life* (1817) II. VI. 121, I feel a call from the Lord to give my last testimony to his faithfulness. **1862** STANLEY *Jew. Ch.* (1877) I. xix. 368 It was a 'call'..or inward movement of the Divine Spirit through the conscience. *a* **1876** J. H. NEWMAN *Hist. Sk.* I. IV. i. 344.

†**10.** Calling, occupation, vocation. *Obs.*

1548 GESTE *Pr. Masse* 72 We must al be busely occupied ..eche man in his call accordingly. **1622** FLETCHER *Begg. Bush* II. i, Which lives Uprightest in his call. **1780** MRS. FLETCHER in H. Moore *Life* (1817) I. III. 161 Spending your time thus, for the bodies of the people. If that is your call, it is a mean call!

11. *Comm.* **a.** A demand for the payment of money; *esp.* a notice to a subscriber to pay up a portion of capital subscribed. Also *attrib.*

1709 *Lond. Gaz.* No. 4554/4 That..Two per Cent. on the Adventurers Stock be received in part of the said two Calls. **1776** ADAM SMITH *W.N.* I. II. ii. 319 A call of fifteen per cent. **1847** C. G. ADDISON *Contracts* I. i. §2 The directors must provide funds by making calls on the shareholders.

b. On the Stock Exchange.

a **1860** C. FENN *Eng. & For. Funds* (1883) 127 A 'Call' is an option of claiming stock at a certain time, the price and date being fixed at the time the option-money is given.

12. *dial.* Scolding, abuse. Cf. CALL *v.* 12.

13. *Sc.* (now in form *ca'*, *caw.*) Driving. In various applications: as, hard and forced respiration; a place where cattle are driven, a cow-gang; a pass or defile between hills.

1765 *Ogilvy & Nairns Trial* 83 (Jam.) There was a severe heaving at his breast, and a strong caw, and he cried to keep open the windows to give him breath. **1768** ROSS *Helenore* 22 (JAM.) In the ca, nor cow nor ewe did spare. **1795** *Statist. Acc. Scotl.* XVI. 168 (JAM.) By..the heights of Lead-na-bea-kach, until you arrive at the Ca (i.e. the slap or pass) of that hill. **1876** ROBINSON *Mid-Yorksh. Gloss.* (E.D.S.) s.v. *Caw.*

14. *Phrases.* **a.** with preps., as ***at call***: at command, ready to answer a call or summons; immediately available; ***within call***: within hearing or reach of a summons; hence, ***within call of*** (***a place***): near to (it); ***within call of*** (***a person***): *fig.* subject to (his) authority.

1594 HOOKER *Eccl. Pol.* Pref. (J.) Always at the call..of a number of mean persons. **1632** MASSINGER & FIELD *Fatal Dow.* III. i, A true friend at a call. **1668** CHILD *Disc. Trade* (1698) 227 It is our interest..not only to have many seamen, but to have them..within call in time of Danger. **1697** DAMPIER *Voy.* (1698) I. xx. 542 Those that subscribed to be at all calls. **1709** STEELE *Tatler* No. 182 ¶6 All the great Beauties we have left in Town, or within Call of it, will be present. **1830** TENNYSON *Dream Fair W.* 85, I saw a lady within call. **1885** *Manch. Exam.* 20 July 5/5 An unconscious desire to possess gold at call.

b. ***to have the call***: to be in chief or greatest demand; to be the favourite: in *Long Whist*, to be entitled to 'call honours'.

1840 *Fraser's Mag.* XXII. 674 Youth has the call. **1863** PARDON *Hoyle's Games* 18 The partners having eight points are said to have the call. **1867** F. FRANCIS *Angling* i. (1880) 31 Baited wheat has the call. *a* **1888** *Newspaper.* Heifers had the call of the market at £17 to £20 each.

15. *Comb.*, as **call-bell**, a bell for summoning attendance; a small stationary hand-bell for that purpose; *spec.* an electric bell giving the alarm at a fire-station, etc.; †**call-belt**, a belt for supporting a bugle or similar instrument; **call-bird**, (*a*) a decoy bird for attracting others by its note; (*b*) *transf.* , a lure used by tradesmen to promote sales; **call-board** *Theatr.*, a notice board; †**call-book**, a muster-roll; **call-box**, a telephone-booth; **call-boy**, a youth employed (*a*) (in a theatre) to attend upon the prompter, and call the actors when required on the stage; (*b*) (on a steamer) to transmit the captain's orders to the engineer; (*c*) (in a hotel) to answer the bells; (*d*) a messenger boy, *spec.* = *call-man*; (*e*) a device for transmitting messages and orders; (*f*) [after *call-girl*] a young male prostitute, *spec.* one who makes appointments by telephone; **call-button**, a push-button or other device for ringing a call-bell or alarm; **call-change** , a method of bell-ringing in which the ringers follow oral or written instructions; **call-day**, in the Inns of Court, the day appointed in each term for the ceremony of calling students to the bar; see also quot. 1720; **call-disc**, a disc indicating the provenance of a telephone call-signal; **call-down** *U.S.*, a scathing rebuke, an abusive tirade (cf. CALL *v.* 27 e); **call-duck**, a decoy duck; **call-girl** (orig. *U.S.*), a prostitute who makes appointments by telephone; also *attrib.*; **call-house** *U.S.*, a brothel; *spec.* a house occupied or used by call-girls; ; **call-letter**, a letter forming part of a call-sign; **call-loan**, a loan to be repaid at call; **call-man**, a man who calls up the members of a fire-brigade for duty; **call-money**, money at call; **call-night**, the night on which students of law are called to the bar; **call-note**, the note used by a bird or other animal in calling to its mate; **call number** (orig. *U.S.*), the press-mark or shelf-mark of a book; **call-off**, a cause of diversion or distraction; **call-office**, (*a*) a telephone office or central station where the call signals are received and where the connections necessary to intercommunication are made; (*b*) = *call-box*; **call-on** (see quot. 1958); also *attrib.*; **call-out**, the act of calling out (forces, etc.) (see CALL *v.* 32 b); **call-over** = CALL *sb.* 1 b; (also) in betting parlance, a calling over or reading aloud of a list of prices; **call-rocket**, a signal rocket; **call-room**, (*a*) = *call-box*; (*b*) *U.S.*, the room in a Stock Exchange where calls are announced; **call-sheet** *Theatr.* and *Cinemat.* (see quot. 1959); **call-sign**, a conventional sign used to indicate the identity of the sender of a wireless message, a transmitting station, etc.; **call signal**, (*a*) a signal for calling up on the telephone; (*b*) = *call-sign*; **call slip** *U.S.*, the slip on which a reader or borrower in a library enters details of the book or books required.

1872 ELLACOMBE *Bells of Ch.* iv. 53 A *call-bell to the Divine services. **1879** G. PRESCOTT *Sp. Telephone* 375 The introduction of call bells or alarms followed..with the early introduction of the electric telegraph. **1883** *Cassell's Fam. Mag.* Dec. 59/2 The alarms enable the [fire-]brigade to leave the station within a minute after the call-bell rings. **1686** *Lond. Gaz.* No. 2182/4 He had..an embroidered Buff *Call Belt, and an Agat-handled Sword. **1773** BARRINGTON in *Phil. Trans.* LXIV. 263 The fascinating power of their *call-birds. **1901** *Farm, Field & Fireside* 13 Dec. 358/1 Frequently a man buys two or three couples of English spring chickens, and then has a case of *eighty* 'Russians' sent in. He uses the English as 'call birds' on his shop front and those few Surreys are the means of disposing of his whole case of Russians. **1958** *Observer* 5 Jan. 7/4 Certain shops are studying..women's response to the 'call-bird'. That is the name they give to extraordinary bargains placed in the windows as lures for the sales-minded. **1886** J. B. HOWE *Cosmopolitan Actor* 134, I saw the cast of 'Colleen Bawn' still on the *call-board. **1901** C. MORRIS *Life on Stage* xxxiii. 277 On the wall..there hung that shallow, glass-covered frame or cabinet called, variously, 'the call-board', the 'call-case', or even the 'call-box'. **1663** PEPYS *Diary* 15 Jan., To examine the proof of our new way of the *call-bookes. **1803** *Naval Chron.* XV. 57 Are copies of the muster or call book

sent to the Navy Board? **1885** *Electrician* 13 Nov. 10/2 At intervals along the streets..we shall have '*call-boxes', by means of which conversation, by telephone, may be carried on with *any* desired person. **1893** *Cassell's Fam. Mag.* Apr. 338/2 Thus it was that I first became introduced to the call-box system. **1951** 'N. SHUTE' *Round Bend* 26 Her dad went down the road to the call-box and telephoned the police. **1794** MALONE *Shaks.* I. 88 *note*, His first office in the theatre was that of *Call-boy. **1848** THACKERAY *Van. Fair* li. 453 The gigantic footmen..were billeted off in the neighbouring public-houses, whence, when they were wanted, call-boys summoned them. **1863** SALA *Qualk the Circumn.* 65 A Woolwich steamboat..passengers and crew—down to the very call-boy. **1868** *Cassell's Mag.* 15 Aug. 256/1 Some of our great iron-clads have been furnished with electrical call-boys. **1887** *16th Ann. Rep. Oxf. Volunteer Fire Brigade* 9 The improved method of calling by electric bells, instead of by call boys. **1972** B. RODGERS *Queens' Vernacular* 111 Hustlers fall into two categories: the street variety and models (call boys). **1981** *Tuscaloosa* (Alabama) *News* 26 Nov. 9/5 The report quoted the unidentified 'call boy' as saying, 'Information is being collected, being systematically collected, being systematically filtered to other places, not just the Soviets either.' **1878** *Telegr. Jrnl.* VI. 113/2 When the attention of either station has been called on its bells by pressing the *call-button. **1966** J. CHAMIER *Cannonball* vi. 52, I..pressed the call button for the lift. **1872** ELLACOMBE *Bells of Ch.* iii. 35 The ringing 'rounds', and '*call-changes' was a good deal cultivated, a very long time before the birth of half-pull change-ringing. **1872** J. T. FOWLER *Bells, Sacristy* II. 137 When some variation..is rung again and again, then another variation, and so on, it is ringing 'call-changes', or 'set-changes'. **1880** GROVE *Dict. Mus.* I. 297/2 Ringers are said to be ringing call changes when the conductor calls to each man to tell him after which bell he is to ring. **1720** *Stow's Surv.* (ed. Strype 1754) II. v. xxvii. 469/2 The Lord Mayor and Court of Aldermen do meet at Guildhall, and sit in the orphan's Court once in every year to hear the names of all securities called over; wherefore that day is called *Call-day. **1886** *Whitaker's Almanack* 9 Inns of Court Law (Dining) Terms—Hilary begins 11 January, ends 1 February; Call Day, 26 January. **1884** *Routledge's Every Boy's Ann.* 124/2 The circles in the figure are the little windows at which the *call-disc makes its appearance. **1901** 'H. McHUGH' *John Henry* i. 11 The four-flush *call-down makes you back-pedal. **1917** WODEHOUSE *Man with Two Left Feet* 121 The feller that tries to get gay with me is going to get a call-down that'll make him holler for his winter overcoat. **1656** EARL MONM. *Advt. fr. Parnass.* 186 The true de quois, or *call-ducks. **1940** in *Amer. Speech* (1942) XVII. 204/1 *Call Girls Die Young. **1951** E. KEFAUVER *Crime in America* (1952) xvii. 193 The hotel..has shown up in some of the call-girl operations. **1957** *Economist* 7 Sept. 736/2 If the streets are cleared, however, there is certain to be an extension of prostitution off them—a growth of the 'call-girl' system. **1929** W. R. BURNETT *Little Caesar* VII. v. 270 Sometimes at night he would go to one of the *call-houses on a nearby street and spend a couple of hours with one of the women. **1936** J. DOS PASSOS *Big Money* 340 It wasn't a hotel or a callhouse. *a* **1940** F. SCOTT FITZGERALD *Last Tycoon* (1949) v. 106 She went to what you call call-houses. **1913** *Year-bk. Wireless Telegr.* 286 Combinations of '*call-letters' which are in turn allotted to ship and land stations. **1852** *N.Y. Wkly. Tribune* 10 Apr. 8/4 The rates are 4 @ 4½ on Government Stocks, 5 @ 6 on general *call loans. **1882** *Pall Mall G.* 7 June 5/2 Recourse had more and more to 'call' loans. **1905** *Westm. Gaz.* 19 Apr. 8/1 When instructions were sent to *call-man Hills to order out all the fogmen. **1885** *Daily News* 12 Feb. 7/2 Most of the banks affecting to consider *call money as the same thing [with cash on hand]. **1883** *St. James's Gaz.* 17 Nov., In the sister Inns of Lincoln and Gray, '*Call Night', like Grand Night, has its own peculiar and appropriate ceremonial. **1833** *Proc. Berw. Nat. Club* I. No. 1. 22 The mellow *call-note of the grey linnet was..heard. **1883** *Century Mag.* Aug. 484/1 The European partridge and Bob White differ in their call-notes. **1876** *Public Libraries U.S.* (Bureau of Educ.) I. 626 Determining the character of any book simply from its *call number. **1964** N. R. KER *Medieval Libraries* (ed. 2) 225 No entry follows the call number of the book if the inscription is in the common *ex dono* or *dedit* form. **1883** J. PARKER *Apost. Life* II. 186 No..*call-off from prolonged and arduous enquiry into profound and useful subjects. **1885** *Electrician* XIV. 102/1 Giving increased facilities to the public in the shape of '*call' offices. **1895** *Daily News* 13 Sept. 5/3 The charge for conversations..within a distance of 25 kilometres from the call-office..has so far been 5d. **1899** *Post Office Guide* July 533 The following additional charges..also apply to conversations between call offices. **1955** *Times* 28 June 8/3 There was a steady trickle of men arriving for the *call-on [at the docks]. *Ibid.* 4 July 8/2 It was decided to hold another meeting..before the normal docks call-on time to-day. **1958** *Ibid.* 7 Mar. 7/1 Dockers..having to attend a 'call-on' twice a day... They present themselves for work at 7.45 a.m. and again at 12.45 p.m. **1887** *Times* (Weekly ed.) 7 Oct. 17/1 The *call-out of the Russian reserves. **1887** *Charity Organ. Rev.* June 245 A Saturday *call-over at school. **1927** *Daily Tel.* 8 Mar. 15/1 That all such bets transacted at the club's 'calls-over' would be free of tax to the backer. **1882** J. E. K. *The Telephone* 33 *Call-rooms have been established in different parts of London, in which are placed telephones connected with the Exchanges. **1886** *Harper's Mag.* July 213/1 The Call Room daily presents an impressive spectacle of the traffic in grain. **1955** *Times* 25 Aug. 12/4 The rehearsal *call-sheet lists animals side by side with ladies and gentlemen of the chorus. **1959** W. S. SHARPS *Dict. Cinemat.* 82/2 *Call sheet*, the itemised schedule of calls for performers and production personnel. **1919** *Times* (weekly ed.) 17 Jan., She signalled the letters of her '*call-sign' and our wireless picked up her message. **1921** *Glasgow Herald* 4 Feb. 9 Shortly after two o'clock she was called, but did not answer her call-sign. **1884** *Routledge's Every Boy's Ann.* 120/2 This system can make a Bell telephone..speak loud enough to be heard throughout a room; and it comprises besides a *call-signal within itself. **1912** in *Year-bk. Wireless Telegr.* (1913) 52 The call signals must be differentiated from one another, and each one must consist of a group of three letters. **1881** *Amer. Library Assoc. Papers* 4/1 All books are to be asked for on *call-slips made out from the catalog.

call, obs. form of CAUL.

calla ('kælə). *Bot.* [mod.L. *calla* (C. Linnæus *Hortus Cliffortianus* (1737) 435).]

1. A monotypic genus of aquatic plants, native to northern Europe and eastern North America, and belonging to the family Araceæ.

1816 *Curtis's Bot. Mag.* 1831 Marsh Calla... Linnæus applied that [*sc.* the name] of Calla, a name borrowed from Pliny. **1845** A. WOOD *Class-bk. Bot.* 364 *C. Palustris.* Northern Calla. **1866** in *Treas. Bot.* 194. **1885** *Outing* (U.S.) Nov. 178/2 An interesting plant is the wild Calla, growing in cold, wet places. **1968** R. HAY *Gardening Year* 174/2 Calla (bog arum)..bears white lily flowers in spring.

2. A popular name for some plants of the genera *Zantedeschia* (esp. *Z. æthiopica*) and *Arum*, both members of the family Araceæ.

1805 *Curtis's Bot. Mag.* 832 Ethiopian Calla. **1870** H. MACMILLAN *Bible Teachings* vii. 143 The beautiful calla or Ethiopian lily. **1883** *Harper's Mag.* Mar. 606/2 Lilies, callas, and other water-plants. **1884** E. P. ROE *ibid.* Feb. 444/1 The plants are semi-aquatic, like this calla lily. **1949** L. H. BAILEY *Man. Cult. Plants* (rev. ed.) 187 Arum, L. A dozen species now recognized..a few occasionally grown for curiosity, often under the name Calla. **1951** *Dict. Gardening* (R. Hort. Soc.) IV. 2302/2 Zantedeschia... In gardens these plants are often known as Callas or Richardias. Calla is a different genus, typified by *Calla palustris*.

calla-: see CALA-.

callable ('kɔːləb(ə)l), *a.* [f. CALL *v.* + -ABLE.] That may be called (or called in, called upon, etc.).

1826 *Examiner* 673/2 Judges called, or callable, rural. **1889** *Sat. Rev.* 16 Mar. 313/2 Without a cash reserve, or without callable loans with bill-brokers. **1892** *Ibid.* 11 June 678/2 As there is no callable capital, the shareholders cannot suffer more than the loss of the capital paid up. **1959** *Economist* 18 Apr. 237/2 With $450 million of the amount for hard loans remaining callable as backing for ordinary bond issues.

callæs'thetic, -ics. [f. Gr. *κάλλος beauty* + *αἰσθητικός*; see ÆSTHETIC.] Name proposed by Whewell for æsthetics (see ÆSTHETIC B 2). Hence **callæs'thetical** *a.*

1847 WHEWELL *Philos. Induct. Sci.* II. 569 Since ..æsthetics would naturally denote the doctrine of perception in general..and since the essential point in the philosophy now spoken of [the theory of the Fine Arts] is that it attends to beauty..I should propose the term Callæsthetics, or rather Callæsthetic. *Ibid.* I. Pref. (ed. 2) 7 The progress of political, and moral and *callesthetical* truth.

ca'llainite. *Min.* [f. L. *callaïna* (Pliny) = *callais* (see next) + -ITE.] A hydrous aluminium phosphate, a massive translucent mineral of apple-green or emerald-green colour, with whitish and bluish lines or spots. (Dana *Min.*)

‖**callais** ('kæleɪs). [L. a. Gr. *καλλαΐς*.] A sea-green precious stone; probably turquoise.

1878 LUBBOCK *Preh. Times* iv. 83 Beads of Callais, a mineral. **1883** N. JOLY *Man before Metals* II. i. iv. 209 Amber, jet, callais, flint, slate..were adopted to make pendants.

callalloo, callaloo, callalou, varr. CALALU.

callamanco, callambac, etc.: see CALA-.

callant ('kalənt). *Sc.* and *north. dial.* Also **calland, callan,** (**calen**). [Identical with Flemish (and Du.) *kalant* customer, chap, blade, a. north. F. *caland* = F. *chaland* customer (literally): see Littré. A modern word in Scotch, taken from Flemish or Dutch by the fisher-folk of the east coast, with whom 'cannie callant' is a favourite form of address. The sense 'customer' has died out in Sc.; cf. *chap* = chapman, blade, lad, fellow.]

A lad, youth, stripling; a boy of any age.

1716 RAMSAY *On Wit* 21 The calland gap'd and glowr'd about. **1719** HAMILTON *Ep. Ramsay* i, O famed and celebrated Allan! Renowned Ramsay! canty callan! *a* **1774** FERGUSSON *Poet. Wks.* (1879) 31 An' ilka canty callant sing like me. **1790** A. WILSON *Miser*, I'm hunted hame wi' dogs and callans. **1814** SCOTT *Waverley* III. 249 'Ye're a daft callant, sir', said the Baron. **1816** J. GILCHRIST *Phil. Etym.* 205 College calens might become so free and bold, etc. **1819** J. HOGG *Hawick Commonriding Song*, Scotia's boast was Hawick callants. **1823** SCOTT *Quentin D.* xv, It will ruin the callant with the King. **1840** in *Westmorland Gloss.*, Callan.

callash, callavance, etc.: see CAL-.

callat, calle, obs. forms of CALLET, CAUL.

called (kɔːld). Pa. pple. of CALL *v.*, rarely used as adjective.

1477 EARL RIVERS (Caxton) *Dictes* 1 A worshipful gentylman callid Lowys de Bretaylles. **1611** BIBLE *Rom.* viii. 28 To them who are the called according to his purpose. **1614** J. ROBINSON *Relig. Commun.* 17 In respect both of the ..will of the Caller, and obedience of the Called. **1870** HARDY & WARE *Mod. Hoyle* 3 Called cards can only be called in compliance with the general laws. **1882** *Standard* 14 Dec. 5/7 Two millions of 'called' bonds.

callee (kɔː'liː). [f. CALL *v.* + -EE.] One who is called or called upon.

1872 BUTLER *Erewhon* xxi. 197 The callee would have been deaf to the caller. **1883** *Cambridge Staircase* v. 73 Our callee suggested that there were more comfortable seats. **1959** M. CHAMBERLIN *Dear Friends* (1960) iv. 29 It is the common practice of the caller to demand the number of the callee immediately.

callembour, obs. f. CALAMBOUR.

callen, same as CAL, wolfram.

†**'callent**, *a. Obs.* [ad. L. *callent-em* knowing.] 'Crafty, witty, cunning or wise by experience' (Blount *Glossogr.* 1656).

callepash, callepy, obs. ff. CALIPASH, -PEE.

caller ('kɔːlə(r)), *sb.* [f. CALL *v.* + -ER[1].] One who calls, in various senses of the vb.; *esp.*

1. a. One who cries aloud, or proclaims. **b.** One who invokes, summons, or exhorts in a loud voice. †**c.** A petitioner, an appellant, one who challenges. **d.** The convener *of* a meeting.

c **1502** J. YOUNGE in Leland *Collect.* (1774) IV. 288 The King called them before hym, and demaunded the Cause of ther Difference. The Caller sayd, Syre, he hath taken from me my Lady Paramour. **1532** MORE *Confut. Tindale* Wks. 823/1 Callers vppon the name of God. **1548** UDALL, etc. *Erasm. Par. Matt.* xx. 98 We be bounde to the caller for this also. **1577–87** HOLINSHED *Chron.* III. 907/1 The caller of the court was one Cooke of Winchester. **1635** *Vestry Bks.* (Surtees) 98 Item to the caller in the court, 4*d.* **1841** GEN. P. THOMPSON *Exerc.* (1842) VI. 246 Letting the callers of the meeting have their way. **1866** W. R. KING *Sportsman in Canada* iii. 52 [Moose-hunting] The caller..retires, with a reserve gun, to the rear of the sportsman.

e. One who announces the changes of steps during a dance. Also ***caller-out***. orig. and chiefly *U.S.*

1882 *Century Mag.* Oct. 878/2 The 'caller-out'..not only calls out the figures, but explains them at length to the ignorant, sometimes accompanying them through the performance. **1931** *Amer. Speech* VII. 50 To the 'fiddlin'' for the square dances the 'caller' sing-songs: All to your places, straighten up your faces, Join eight hands and circle left. **1938** *Times* 10 Jan. 10/4 The 'caller'..is a figure still prominent in American 'play-parties'. **1966** *Melody Maker* 7 May 18/1 (Advt.), Beckenham Ballrooms are interested in commencing a Country Style evening every Tuesday. They need a caller and musicians.

f. One who makes a call on a telephone. Also ***caller-up***.

1898 *Daily News* 6 June 6/2 The caller-up knowing whether he is through or not by the ringing or not ringing of his bell. **1899** *Post Office Guide* July 533 If a deposit has been made by the caller in the first instance to cover the fee for the second period of three minutes. **1954** K. AMIS *Lucky Jim* 95 Your second three minutes are up, caller. **1959** [see CALLEE].

g. A man or boy employed to knock up men for duty, esp. the members of a railway staff. Also ***caller-up***.

1898 H. E. HAMBLEN *Gen. Manager's Story* 72 The caller made his rounds with orders to call the first man he found off duty. **1899** R. WHITEING *No. 5 John St.* vi. 47 The caller-up begins his rounds with the dawn. **1935** A. J. CRONIN *Stars look Down* I. viii. 65 Next morning the caller woke him, at two o'clock he was in the pit working the early fore shift.

2. One who pays a short or complimentary visit. (The chief current sense.)

1786 MAD. D'ARBLAY *Diary* (1854) III. 30 Making him keep off all callers, by telling them I am dressing for the Queen. **1812** CHALMERS *Lett.* in *Life* (1851) I. 296 We have had a flow of forenoon callers. **1865** *Lond. Rev.* 23 Dec. 662/1 The most successful caller, i.e. the caller who finds no one at home.

3. *Sc.* A driver.

c **1450** HENRYSON *Mor. Fab.* 73 The caller cryed: How, haike vpon hight. **1805** BARRY *Orkney Isl.* 447 (Jam.) The caller goes before the beasts backward with a whip.

4. Of other than persons: **a.** *fig.* A thing which calls. **b.** A call-bird, a decoy-bird.

1607 HIERON *Wks.* I. 308 The sight of it is rather a common caller vpon him to bee faithfull to him. **1725** BRADLEY *Fam. Dict.* II. s.v. *Lark*, The Way of taking Larks is with Nets..the Callers are set upon the Ground.

5. With advbs., as ***caller away, off, on***, etc.

1555 EDEN *Decades W. Ind.* II. VII. (Arb.) 127 My importunate caulers on. **1628** EARLE *Microcosm.* lxvi. 142 His..caller away is his study. **1721** *St. German's Doctor & Stud.* 295 Callers on to have that point reformed. **1878** F. WILLIAMS *Midl. Railw.* 642 The 'caller-off' shouts out..the name.

caller ('kɑːlər), *a. Sc.* and *north. dial.* Forms: 4 caloure, 5–6 callour, 8 calour, ? callar, 8– caller, cauler, (9 cawler, cauller, calor). [prob. Sc. form of CALVER, q.v. Cf. *siller* from *silver*, etc.

It has generally been assumed to be derived in some way from stem of OTeut. *kal-an* to be cold. But this does not account for the form; nor does it yield the required sense, which in earlier times was not connected with *cold*: 'callour prey', *recens præda*, might be still warm.]

1. 'Fresh; as opposed to what is beginning to corrupt' (Jam.); without taint of decomposition; said of the flesh of animals used for food, *esp.* fish (which were specially liable to decay); 'as fresh as when taken out of the water'.

c **1375** ? BARBOUR *St. Cosmas & Damian* 360 In þe kirk-ȝard ȝestrevene wes lad Ane Ethiope, & ȝet his flesche Is caloure Inucht & als fres. *c* **1450** HENRYSON *Mor. Fab.* 2126 in *Anglia* IX, Ane side of salmond, as it wair, And callour. **1513** DOUGLAS *Æneis* VII. xiii. 110 The recent spreith and fresche and callour pray. [Cf. **1536** BELLENDEN *Descr. Alb.* xi. (1821) I. p. xliii. Quhen the salmondis faillis thair loup, thay fall callour in the said [boiling] caldrounis, and ar than maist delitious to the mouth.] **1768** ROSS *Helenore* 6 She.. was..As clear and calour as a water trout. **1862** *Macm. Mag.*

Oct. 501 The Newhaven fish-wife..shouting 'Caller herrings!' or 'Wha'll buy my caller cod?'

2. Of air, water, etc.: Fresh and cool; well-aired.

1513 DOUGLAS *Æneis* VII. Prol. 87 The callour air, penetrative and puire. *a* **1600** HUME in Sibbald *Sc. Poetry* III. 387 (Jam.) The rivers fresh, the callar streams. **1768** Ross *Helenore* 77 Behind the door a calour heather bed. **1816** SCOTT *Antiq.* xxi, 'Queer tirlie-wirlie holes that..keep the stair as caller as a kail-blade.' **1884** *Good Wds.* May 326/1 You ha'e the caller air, the caller earth; an' they're aye healthy.

calles, obs. form of CHALICE.

callesthetical: see CALLÆSTHETIC.

† **'callet**, *sb. Obs.* exc. *dial.* Forms: 6 **calat(e, calet, kallat, 6–7 callette, callot, 7 callat, calette, callott, 6–8 calot, callet.**

[Many have suggested its identity with F. *caillette* 'foole, ninnie, noddie, naturall' (Cotgr.), dim. of *caille* quail (esteemed a silly bird); but this does not quite answer phonetically, does not quite suit the sense, and was in French applied to men as readily as to women. Others have thought of F. *calotte* a kind of small bonnet or cap covering only the top of the head, but no evidence appears connecting this especially with a 'callet'. The Gael. and Ir. *caille* girl has also been suggested. It is not certain which is the earlier sense: perh. 'scold', as in the vb. and CALLETY.]

1. A lewd woman, trull, strumpet, drab.

c **1500** *Cocke Lorelles B.* (1843) 1 Yf he call her calat, she calleth hym knave agayne. *c* **1530** REDFORDE *Play Wit & Sc.* (1848) 17 Wyll I mar him, drabb? Thow, calat, thow! **1532** MORE *Confut. Tindale* Wks. 423/2 Frere Luther and Cate calate his nunne, lye luskyng together in lechery. **1569** J. SA[NFORD] tr. *Agrippa's Van. Artes* 94 Other Queenes which were queanes, and courtly callets. **1600** HOLLAND *Livy* I. lviii. 41 Any unhonest woman or wanton callot [*impudica*]. **1604** SHAKS. *Oth.* IV. ii. 121 A Begger in his drinke Could not haue laid such termes vpon his Callet. **1616** BULLOKAR, *Callette*, a Lewd Woman. **1731** BAILEY vol. II, *Calot*, a Drab. **1785** BURNS *Jolly Beggars* Air i, I'm as happy with my wallet, my bottle and my callet.

2. As a term of abuse; sometimes perhaps = 'scold' as in the vb. Also *attrib.* Still *dial.*

a **1528** SKELTON *El. Rummyng* 347 Than Elynour sayde, ye callettes, I shall breake your pallettes. **1530** PALSGR. 678, I rampe, I play the callet, *je ramponne* [I gibe, flout]. **1575** J. STILL *Gamm. Gurton* II. iii, Faith, would chad her by the face, chould crack her callet Crown. **1577** STANYHURST *Descr. Irel.* in *Holinshed* VI. 52 Let us..leave lieing for varlets..scolding for callets. **1611** SHAKS. *Wint. T.* II. iii. 90 A Callat Of boundless tongue, who late hath beat her Husband, And now bayts me.

Hence **callety** *a. dial.*, scolding, 'ill-tongued'.

1863 in ATKINSON *Provinc. Danby*.

'callet, *v. Obs.* exc. *dial.* [f. prec. sb.] *intr.* To scold, rail. Hence **'calleting** *ppl. a.*

a **1673** BRATHWAIT *Care's Cure*, To hear her in her spleen Callet like a butter queen. **1691** RAY *N.C. Wds.*, *Callet*, to cample, or scold; as, a calleting housewife. **1764** T. BRYDGES *Homer Travest.* (1797) I. 62 Mother, you know not what you're doing; To Callot thus will be your ruin. **1864** ATKINSON *Whitby Gloss.* (E.D.S.) *Callit*, to wrangle, to chide. 'They snap an' callit like a couple o' cur-dogs.'

calletrappe, -vance, obs. forms of CALTROP, CALAVANCE.

calliard ('kælɪəd). *local.* [Of doubtful origin; perh. connected with F. *caillou* pebble, and so ultimately with L. *calculus*. But cf. the later GALLIARD *sb.*[2]] A hard, smooth, flinty gritstone.

1781 J. HUTTON *Tour to Caves* (ed. 2) Gloss. (1873), *Callierd*, an hard stone. *a* **1835** J. PHILLIPS *Geol.* in *Encycl. Metrop.* (1845) VI. 587/2 Some less regular sandstone beds, called 'Cankstone', approach very nearly to the nature of the ganister or calliard rocks of the coal strata. **1865** PAGE *Handbk. Geol. Terms*, *Calliard*.., a local name for any hard siliceous stone; often applied by English miners and quarrymen to beds of cherty or siliceous limestone. **1876** WOODWARD *Geol. Eng. & Wales* 81 Some of the beds contain gritstone or greywacke, provincially called 'calliard'.

calliber, etc.: see CALI-.

† **calli'blephary.** *Obs. rare*$^{-1}$. [After Gr. καλλιβλέφαρον, neut. of καλλιβλέφαρος, f. καλλι- combining form of κάλλος beauty + βλέφαρον eyelid: see -ARY[1].] A dye for the eye-lids.

1661 LOVELL *Hist. Anim. & Min.* 34 The marrow of the right fore legge with sout..serveth for a calliblephary.

† **'callid**, *a. Obs. rare*$^{-0}$. [ad. L. *callidus*.] Crafty, cunning.

1656 in BLOUNT *Glossogr.* **1721–1800** in BAILEY; and in mod. Dicts.

callidity (kə'lɪdɪtɪ). Now *rare*. Also 7 (*erron.*) calidity. [ad. L. *calliditātem* cunning, craft (in good or bad sense), f. *callidus* skilful, cunning, crafty: see -ITY.] Craftiness, cunning.

1524 *St. Papers Hen. VIII*, VI. 280 His Holines, unto whom the callidities and crafty circumvencions of France be not unknowen. **1677** GALE *Crt. Gentiles* II. III. 99 Πανουργια signifies al manner of Calliditie or dexteritie to cheat & deceive. **1752** SMART *Hop Garden*, Her eagle-ey'd callidity, deceit And fairy faction. **1833** *Fraser's Mag.* VIII. 203 Suspect their own intimate friends of callidity.

callify, obs. form of CALEFY.

calligraph ('kælɪgrɑːf, -æ-), *sb.*[1] *arch.* Also cali-. [a. F. *calligraphe*, ad. med.L. *calligraph-us* fair writer, good penman, ad. Gr. καλλιγράφος, f. καλλι- comb. stem of κάλλος beauty + -γραφος 'writing, writer' (sometimes also 'written'). In this and the following cognate words the non-etymological spelling CALI- is frequently found.]

One who writes beautifully; *spec.* a professional transcriber of manuscripts.

1853 *Fraser's Mag.* XLVII. 83 The numerous scattered works of former zealous caligraphs. **1875** M. PATTISON *Casaubon* 38 The calligraphs, a race who long survived the invention of printing.

calligraph ('kælɪgrɑːf, -æ-), *sb.*[2] [f. same elements as prec., on analogy of *autograph*, *holograph*, which have Greek prototypes in -γράφον.] A beautiful specimen of writing.

1878 BROWNING *Poets Croisic* xxxvii, Over the neat crow-quill calligraph His pen goes blotting.

'calligraph, *v.* [f. prec., or F. *calligraph-er* (perhaps with some thought of Gr. γράφ-ειν to write); cf. to *photograph*, *telegraph*, etc.] *trans.* To write beautifully or ornamentally.

1884 *Athenæum* 3 May 570/1 The roll of Shiuten Doji, a famous Japanese outlaw of the tenth century..finely calligraphed and illuminated.

calligrapher (kə'lɪgrəfə(r)). [f. same elements as CALLIGRAPH + -ER: cf. *philosoph-er*.]

1. One who writes beautifully: sometimes (with qualification) merely = penman.

1815 SCOTT *Guy M.* xv, He should have been a calligrapher. **1824** D'ISRAELI *Cur. Lit.*, *Autographs*, Queen Elizabeth..was indeed a most elegant caligrapher.

2. *spec.* One who professes the art of elegant penmanship; a professional transcriber of manuscripts.

1753 CHAMBERS *Cycl. Supp.* s.v. *Calligraphy*, Calligraphy is also used to denote the calligrapher's work, in transcribing fair and at large. **1838–9** HALLAM *Hist. Lit.* I. I. ii. 140 *note*, Against Thomas à Kempis it is urged that he was a professed calligrapher. **1864** R. CHAMBERS *Bk. of Days* II. 309 A caligrapher, a writer and engraver of 'letters, knots and flourishes'.

calligraphic (kælɪ'græfɪk), *a.* [ad. Gr. καλλιγραφικός, in same sense, f. καλλιγράφος: see -IC.] **a.** Of or pertaining to calligraphers or calligraphy.

1774 T. WARTON *Hist. Poetry* Diss. II. (1840) I. 101 Excellence in the calligraphic art. **1809** *Monthly Mag.* XXVIII. 187 Two specimens of her calligraphic skill are carefully preserved in the Bodleian library. **1882–3** SCHAFF *Relig. Encycl.* III. 2556/1 The calligraphic principle, or effort to write beautifully and ornamentally, came in.

b. Of or pertaining to calligraphy (sense 4); having beauty of line.

1928 *Observer* 1 July 14/1 Swift calligraphic strokes which invest the picture with..vitality. **1930** *Times Lit. Suppl.* 9 Jan. 25/3 Leonardo displays his extraordinary gift of enclosing a volume by a flowing and calligraphic line. *Ibid.*, The calligraphic beauty of line. **1962** *Listener* 29 Nov. 909/2 These brilliantly coloured, calligraphic paintings.

† **calli'graphical**, *a. Obs.* [f. as prec. + -AL[1].] = prec.; also, Of a beautiful literary style. Hence **calli'graphically** *adv.*

1630 J. TAYLOR (Water Poet) *Wks.* III. 76 Dedicated..To the..Historiographicall Calligraphicall Relater and Writer ..Sir Thomas Coriat, Knight of Troy. **1882–3** SCHAFF *Relig. Encycl.* III. 2556/2 The Jews..may have perfected it calligraphically into the square character.

calligraphist (kæ'lɪgrəfɪst). [f. Gr. καλλιγράφ-ος or Eng. CALLIGRAPHY + -IST: cf. *zoologist*, etc.] = CALLIGRAPHER, esp. in sense 1.

1816 SINGER *Hist. Cards* 134 The same calligraphist furnished the prototype of both. **1849** MISS MULOCK *Ogilvies* 24 All the care of her governess and masters had never succeeded in making her a calligraphist. **1850** TEALE *Educ. in Eng.* 5 S. Dunstan was..a calligraphist.

calligraphy (kæ'lɪgrəfɪ). [Ultimately ad. Gr. καλλιγραφία, sb. of quality f. καλλιγράφ-ος: see CALLIGRAPH *sb.*[1]: perhaps immediately from L. *calligraphia* or F. *calligraphie*.]

1. Beautiful or fair writing as a product; also, elegant penmanship as an art or profession.

1613 R. C. *Table Alph.* (ed. 3) *Calligraphie*, faire writing. **1632** B. JONSON *Magn. Lady* III. iv, I have to commend me ..my kalligraphy, a fair hand, Fit for a secretary. **1753** CHAMBERS *Cycl. Supp.* s.v., Calligraphy made an article in the manual labour of the antient monks. **1816** SINGER *Hist. Cards* 93 Calligraphy was also another art which received considerable attention. **1866** FELTON *Anc. & Mod. Gr.* I. xii. 498 The age of calligraphy is gone.

2. Handwriting, penmanship generally; style of handwriting or written characters; a person's characteristic handwriting or 'hand'.

1645 MILTON *Colast.* Wks. (1847) 221/2 A divine of note had..stuck it here and there with a clove of his own calligraphy, to keep it from tainting. **1856** *Househ. Wds.* XIII. 240 His calligraphy suggests..the skating of an intoxicated sweep over a sheet of ice. **1859** GULLICK & TIMBS *Painting* 100 The study of the calligraphy, or penmanship, of ancient MSS. **1880** EARLE *Philol. E.T.* §99 In the eleventh century the fashion of our calligraphy was changed.

† **3.** Belles-lettres. *Obs.*

1860 WORCESTER cites R. PARK.

4. The brush-work (of a painting); beauty of line (of a painting, drawing, etc.).

1928 *Observer* 1 July 14/1 Gainsborough adopted the elegant calligraphy, the loose, flickering touch. **1962** *Listener* 2 Aug. 178/3 The three studies of 'Woman in Rocking Chair' show Kline's characteristic bold calligraphy in the process of being formed.

callimanco, obs. form of CALAMANCO.

ca'llimeter. *nonce-wd.* [f. Gr. καλλι- comb. stem of κάλλος beauty + μέτρον measure: see -METER.] A measure of beauty.

1862 J. BROWN *Horæ Subs.* 353 A flower..of a certain fixed and well-known value in Davie's standard calimeter.

calling ('kɔːlɪŋ), *vbl. sb.* [f. CALL *v.* + -ING[1].]

I. The action of the vb. CALL.

1. The action of emitting a loud voice; crying, shouting, proclamation. Applied also to particular cries of animals. ***calling on*** or ***upon***: invocation of.

c **1325** *E.E. Allit. P.* B. 1362 Þurȝ þe cuntre of Caldee his callyng con spryng. *c* **1340** *Cursor M.* 19095 (Trin.) þe callyng on [*v.r.* on-call] his holy name. **1490** CAXTON *Eneydos* xxi. 77 What complayntes, callynges, and lamentacyons. **1526** *Pilgr. Perf.* (W. de W. 1531) 38 By the inuocacyon and callyng on the name of Jesu. **1535** COVERDALE *Ps.* v. 1 Heare my wordes (o Lorde), considre my callynge. **1693** URQUHART *Rabelais* III. xiii, Bawling of mastiffs..calling of Partridges. **1864** TENNYSON *En. Ard.* 909 There came so loud a calling of the sea, That all the houses in the haven rang.

† **2.** An addressing; greeting, invitation. *Obs.*

a **1300** *Cursor M.* 11536 And thanked ioseph..O þair calling and herbergeri. **1535** STEWART *Cron. Scot.* II. 46 [He received] thame..With fair calling and hamelie cheresing.

3. a. The summoning *of* a person, a meeting.

c **1440** *Promp. Parv.* 58 Callynge or clepynge to mete, *invitacio*. *Ibid.* Callynge or clepynge to-gedyr, *convocacio*. **1580** BARET *Alv.* C 38 A calling or assembling to-gither, *conuocatio*. **1611** BIBLE *Numb.* x. 2 The calling of the assembly. **1712** PRIDEAUX *Direct. Ch.-Wardens* (ed. 4) 35 The calling of the said Meeting. **1848** MACAULAY *Hist. Eng.* I. 276 To prevent the calling of a parliament.

b. The summoning or inviting to a spiritual office or to the pastorate of a church.

1578 *2nd Bk. Discipline* iii, Vocation or calling..is a lawful way, by the which qualified persons are promoted to any spiritual office within the Kirk. **1864** J. M. DUNCAN *Paroch. Eccl. Law Scotl.* ii. 72 The presbytery by whose decision and authority the calling and entry of a particular ministry were effected.

† **4.** Naming, denomination; an appellation or name. *Obs.*

c **1460** J. RUSSELL *Bk. Nurture* 772 in *Babees Bk.* (1868) 169 'Colericus' by callynge. **1530** PALSGR. 202/2 Callyng, namyng, *apellance*. **1547** *Homilies* I. *Misery of Man.* I. (1859) 17 This, our right name, calling, and title, earth. **1563** T. GALE *Antidot.* Pref. 2 The diuersitie that is vsed in callinge of simples. **1576** LAMBARDE *Peramb. Kent* (1826) 291 Persons also, had their callings..of some note of the body, as Swanshalse, for the whitenesse of her necke. **1600** SHAKS. *A.Y.L.* I. ii. 245, I am..proud to be Sir Rolands sonne.. and would not change that calling.

5. Loud vituperation, scolding (*dial.*). ***calling (of) names***: the applying of reviling names or epithets.

1687 T. BROWN *Saints in Upr.* Wks. 1730 I. 72 There's such calling of names and giving the lie. **1844** DICKENS *Mar. Chuz.* iv, Such a bandying of words and calling of names. **1863** MRS. TOOGOOD *Yorksh. Dial.*, He behaved badly, so I gave him a good calling. **1864** ATKINSON *Whitby Gloss.*, *Calling*, a scolding. **1885** *Nonconf. & Independent* 22 Oct. 1019 Caling names was not argument.

6. The attracting of animals by a particular 'call' or cry.

1775 R. CHANDLER *Trav. Greece* (1825) II. 161 Calling is practised in still weather..The caller applies two of his fingers to his lips, and sucking them..produces a squeaking sound. **1880** LD. DUNRAVEN in *19th Cent.* 641 Moose-calling ..consists..in imitating the cry of the animal with a hollow cone made of birch bark, endeavouring by this means to call up a moose near enough to get a shot at him.

7. Driving. *Sc.*

c **1550** SIR J. BALFOUR *Practicks* 356 In..calling of his cattel throuch landis pertenand to the defendar. *Mod. Sc.* Cannie ca'ing.

8. With various advbs.: see CALL *v.* ***calling-down*** (orig. *U.S.*), a rebuke, upbraiding; ***calling-up*** (see CALL *v.* 35).

c **1440** *Promp. Parv.* 58 Callynge or clepynge a-ȝene, *revocacio*. *Ibid.* Callynge or clepynge yn to a place, *invocacio*. **1580** HOLLYBAND *Treas. Fr. Tong*, *Rappel*, a calling agaixne. **1626** BACON *Sylva* §316 The calling forth of the Spirits of the Body outward. **1813** HUSKISSON in *Examiner* 15 Mar. 166/2 The calling out the Local Militia. **1857** HUGHES *Tom Brown* v, The master..came down in cap and gown to calling-over. **1875** WHITNEY *Life Lang.* xiv. 285 A calling-out of many of the higher powers. **1877** *Design & Work* III. 713/3 For calling-up purposes I have a bell in the bedroom of a very drowsy domestic. **1890** *Peel City Guardian* 12 July 6/1 The calling up of constables on probation. **1901** G. ADE *40 Mod. Fables* 55 He would give the National Administration a sharp Calling Down every few Days. **1902** *Electr. & Magn.* xviii. 226 (Govt. Milit. Bk.) Calling-up may be done by means of an ordinary bell and battery. **1918** *Act 8 Geo. V* c. 5 §4 (2) With a view to preventing..the calling up of himself..for any form of military service. **1930** PERTWEE *Pursuit* I. xiii. 63 N.C.O.'s and other ranks were within hearing of the calling-down Frost was receiving. **1936** M. PLOWMAN *Faith called Pacifism* 94 When the calling-up paper comes along again, under the Conscription Act.

II. Summons, call, vocation.

9. a. The summons, invitation, or impulse of God to salvation or to his service; the inward feeling or conviction of a divine call; the strong impulse to any course of action as the right thing to do.

[**1382** WYCLIF *1 Cor.* i. 26 Se ȝe ȝoure clepinge, Britheren.] **1534** TINDALE, *ibid.* Brethren, loke on youre callinge. **1535** COVERDALE *Rom.* i. 7 Sayntes by callynge. *a* **1586** *Answ. Cartwright* 50 Our dumbe ministers haue as good a calling as the scribes.. had. **1641** MILTON *Ch. Govt.* Wks. 1738 I. 41 The conscious warrant of some high Calling. **1648** *Westm. Assembly's Shorter Catech.*, Effectual calling is the work of God's Spirit. **1811** SYD. SMITH *Wks.* (1859) I. 202/2 The doctrine of calling, or inward feeling, is quite orthodox in the English church. **1861** FLOR. NIGHTINGALE *Nursing* 84 What is it to feel a calling for any thing?

†**b.** The state of grace and obedience into which the Christian is called; duty. (Here the notion was affected by the next.) *Obs.*

1604 HIERON *Wks.* I. 482 The state and calling of a true Christian is a louely calling. **1644** *Direct. Publ. Worship* 10 Callings towards God and men.

c. In reference to the Christian ministry there is often a mixture of the notions of the divine 'call', the *vocatio* or call of the bishop, presbytery, or church, and the professional 'calling' as in 11.

1583 STUBBES *Anat. Abus.* II. 83 A good pastor, and diligent in his calling. **1575–85** ABP. SANDYS *Serm.* (1841) 80 Assisted from heaven with all helps necessary for their calling. **1732** LAW *Serious C.* xxiv. (ed. 2) 489 In the exalted virtues of his Apostolical calling. **1855** PRESCOTT *Philip II*, II. ix. (1857) 312 The dangerous calling of the missionary. **1883** FROUDE *Short Stud.* IV. I. iii. 28 The duties of his sacred calling.

d. Requirement of duty; occasion, right; = CALL *sb.*[8]

1857 *Lit. Churchman* III. 409 A sprightly American air which has no sort of calling to be a hymn-tune.

†**10.** Position, estate, or station in life; rank. [Founded on *1 Cor.* vii. 20, Gr. κλήσει, L. *vocatione*, where it stands for the condition or position in which one was when called to salvation; but afterwards often mixed up with sense 9, as if it meant the estate in life to which God has called a man.]

[**1382** WYCLIF *1 Cor.* vii. 20 Eche man in what clepynge he is cleped, in that dwelle he; **1534** TINDALE, in the same state wherein he was called; **1539** CRANMER and **1611**, in the same callinge, wherin he was called; **1557** *Geneva*, in the same state wherin he was called; **1582** *Rhem.*, in the vocation that he vvas called.] *a* **1555** LATIMER *Serm. & Rem.* (1845) 151 We are commanded.. to apply ourselves to goodness, every one in his calling. **1575–6** *Lansdowne MS.* 21 in *Thynne's Animadv.* (1865) Introd. 52 Righte honorable.. presuminge uppon the honor of your callinge. **1590** GREENE *Mourn. Garm.* (1616) 15 Seeing hee was a Gentleman of some calling, by his traine. **1603** KNOLLES *Hist. Turks* (1638) 304 As wel vnto them of the poorer sort, as others of greater calling. **1621** BURTON *Anat. Mel.* I. ii. IV. vi. (1651) 154 As it [Poverty] is esteemed in the worlds censure, it is a most odious calling. **1633** *Treas. Hid. Secrets* Pref., A Lady of Great calling. **1691** SHADWELL *Scowrers* IV. 376 Men of Calling, knaves of business.

11. a. Hence, Ordinary occupation, means by which livelihood is earned, business, trade. [Often etymologized in the same way as prec.]

1551 RECORDE *Pathw. Knowl.* To Rdr., As carefull familie shall cease hir cruell callinge, and suffre anie laiser. **1588** *Marprel. Epist.* (Arb.) 46 They continue in vnlawful callings. **1642** FULLER *Holy & Prof. St.* v. xiv. 413 They who count a calling a prison, shall at last make a prison their calling. **1687** T. BROWN *Saints in Upr.* Wks. 1730 I. 76, I was a ferry-man by my calling. **1768–78** TUCKER *Lt. Nat.* II. 488 The appellation given to all common trades and professions, which are termed lawful callings, that is, employments whereto each particular man is called by the courses of nature and fortune, those two ministers of Providence. **1841–4** EMERSON *Ess.* iv. *Spir. Laws* Wks. (Bohn) I. 68 Our choice of a calling. **1848** MACAULAY *Hist. Eng.* I. 284 A large class of mosstroopers, whose calling was to plunder dwellings and drive away whole herds of cattle. **1872** YEATS *Growth Comm.* 203 Navigation, with its many attendant callings.

b. *concr.* A body of persons following a particular profession or trade.

a **1660** HAMMOND (J.) A caution.. not to impose celibacy on whole callings, and great multitudes of men or women.

III. *attrib.* and *comb.* Freq. in the sense 'visiting'.

1814 T. CREEVEY *Let.* 14 June (1963) 109, I called on her this morning, and saw some very different names in her calling book from what I had ever seen before. **1848** BAMFORD *Early Days* xii. (1859) 118 Another calling house was Schofield's. **1853** MRS. GASKELL *Cranford* 4 From 12 to 3 are our Calling-hours. **1860** *Sat. Rev.* IX. 599/1 The calling-house of wits, the gathering-place of poets and connoisseurs. **1877** E. S. PHELPS *Story of Avis* 397 Lest society strike him from her calling-list. **1888** KIPLING *Plain Tales from Hills* 150 [He] put on his calling-clothes and called on the ladies of the Station. **1893** *Westm. Gaz.* 19 Apr. 6/2 There will be four calling stations. **1896** *Daily News* 24 Oct. 5/6 A note from him, written by himself on his calling card, placed the matter beyond all doubt. **1908** *Westm. Gaz.* 27 Apr. 10/2 To ensure regularity in arriving at the various calling ports.

'calling, *ppl. a.* [f. CALL *v.* + -ING[2].] That calls, cries, summons, etc.: in various senses of the verb.

1634 MILTON *Comus* 207 Calling shapes, and beckoning shadows dire. **1878** DICKENS *Dombey* x, Joey B., Sir, is not in general a calling man.

b. *spec.* in names of some animals: **calling crab**, a tropical genus of Land-crabs (*Gelasimus*) having one very large claw, which the animal extends, as if beckoning, but really in menace; **calling hare**, a rodent genus (*Lagomys*) nearly allied to the Hare, found in Siberia and other countries, and noted for their peculiar loud sonorous call or note.

1802 BINGLEY *Anim. Biog.* (1813) I. 411 The calling hare. These are solitary animals, and rarely to be seen. **1847** CARPENTER *Zool.* §786 Some of the Land-Crabs are remarkable for the inequality in the size of their claws; the larger is sometimes held up in a beckoning attitude, whence .. the name of Calling-Crabs. **1849** *Mammalia* IV. 162 The dwarf pika or calling-hare.

callino. ? = CALINO.

1602 DEKKER *Satiromastix* Lv, *Hor.* O, oh! *Tuc.* Nay, your o, oh's! nor your Callin-oes cannot serve your turn.

calliope (kə'laɪəpiː). *U.S.* [Gr. Καλλιόπη (beautiful-voiced), the ninth of the Muses, presiding over eloquence and heroic poetry.]

1. An instrument consisting of a series of steam-whistles toned to produce musical notes, played by a keyboard like that of an organ.

1858 J. COOK *Let.* 19 Sept. (1946) 45 On board the *Armenia*.. is a Calliope, or an instrument resembling an organ & played in connection with the engine. **1863** RUSSELL *Diary India* I. 269 The whistle sounds, and the calliope shrieks out 'Dixie' incessantly. **1908** E. C. BOOTH *Cliff End* v. 35 The calliope at the Crystal Palace would just about begin to realise our musical aspirations—with steam drum attachment. **1923** V. LINDSAY *Coll. Poems* 118 Proud men.. Call me the 'Calliope'... I am the Gutter Dream, Tune-maker, born of steam... I am the Kallyope. **1955** R. BLESH *Shining Trumpets* (ed. 3) v. 100 A calliope outside the circus tent.

2. *attrib.* **calliope hummingbird**, a hummingbird, *Stellula calliope*, of the Western United States and Mexico. *U.S.*

1878 *U.S. Nat. Museum Proc.* I. 426 *Stellula calliope.*—Calliope Humming-bird. **1962** *Amer. Speech* XXXVII. 28 There was a December–May marriage, conducted with all the calm and sobriety of a calliope concert.

Hence **ca'lliopeist**, one who plays the calliope.

1932 HEMINGWAY *Death in Afternoon* xiii. 150 An organist .. or a calliopeist.

callipash, callipee, see CALIPASH, -PEE.

calliper, caliper ('kælɪpə(r)). Forms: 6 calleper, 7 callaper, -par, calloper, 7–8 callipper, 8 caliber, (canniper), 7– calliper, caliper. [App. the same word as CALIBRE; *calliper compasses* being compasses for measuring the calibre of a bullet, etc. The earliest known English instances of *calliper compasses* occur in a book translated from Italian, with an Appendix 'to shew the Properties, Office, and Dutie of a Gunner'. Cf. also Florio (1611) '*Colibro*, as *Calibro*, an instrument that Gunners vse to measure the height of any piece or bullet; also, the height or bore of any piece'. It is however remarkable that from the beginning the words were spelt differently; only in modern times do we find occasional conscious identification with *caliber*, *calibre*.]

1. a. Originally used attrib., ***calliper compasses*** or ***compasses calliper***, compasses used to measure the calibre of shot; afterwards usually in pl. ***callipers*** or ***pair of callipers***: A kind of compasses with bowed legs for measuring the diameter of convex bodies; often with a scale attached for reading off the measurements; also a similar instrument with straight legs and points turned outwards for measuring the bore or internal diameter of tubes, etc.

1588 LUCAR *Colloq. Arte Shooting* App. 35 Measure first with a paire of calleper compasses the whole thickness of the peece. Measure likewise with a paire of other compasses, I mean straight compasses, the Diameter of the concauitie in the Peece. **1627** CAPT. SMITH *Seaman's Gram.* xiv. 68 Compasse Callipers belongs to the Gunner, and is like two half Circles that hath a handle and ioint like a paire of Compasses. **1644** NYE *Gunnery* I. (1647) 49 To take the said height or Diam. of the shot with a pair of Callaper compasses. *Ibid.* (1670) 50 Also by such a pair of Callapers you may find the Diameter of the Base-Ring, and of the Mussel-Ring of any Piece of Ordnance. **1677** MOXON *Mech. Exerc.* (1703) 196 Callippers measure.. any round Cilindrick Conical Body. **1692** in *Capt. Smith's Seaman's Gram.* II. viii. 97 To find the Diameter of any round Shot.. by a pair of Calloper Compasses, which are Compasses bowed at the Points. **1753** HOGARTH *Anal. Beauty* Introd. 47 These points may be marked upon a marble figure with calibers properly used. **1795** HOME in *Phil. Trans.* LXXXVI. 6 Measured by a pair of calliper compasses. **1821** CRAIG *Lect. Drawing* vii. 372 An anvil, a hammer, and a pair of calipers. **1859** SMILES *Self-Help* 267 Moral philosophy which proposes to measure our heads with callipers. **1876** *Catal. Sci. Appar. S. Kens.* No. 284 Universal Calliper, with slide and reverse action. No. 271 Calliper with Dial.. divided into eighths of an inch.

b. Applied to measuring rules of varying shape for taking the dimensions of other than round bodies. **calliper-square**, a rule or square carrying movable cross-heads, adapted for the measurement of internal and external diameters or sizes.

1708 KERSEY, *Callipers*, an instrument made like a Sliding-Rule, to embrace the two Heads of a Cask, or Barrel, in order to find the length of it. **1876** *Catal. Sci. Appar. S. Kens.* No. 293 Collection of Timber Callipers for the use of foresters. *Mod. techn.* Calliper (in Liverpool timber yards), a rule for measuring timber, something like that which shoemakers use to measure feet.

2. *transf.* The clip for holding the load in a crane.

1769 *De Foe's Tour Gt. Brit.* III. 272 Portable Cranes.. to draw Stone out of the Quarry with Callipers.

3. *Watch-making.* 'The disposition of the parts of a watch or clock; the arrangement of the train' (Britten). App. akin to CALIBRE.

1884 F. BRITTEN *Watch & Clockm.* 151 As a matter of convenience in arranging the caliper of the watch.

4. A metal support for a broken or diseased leg. Also ***calliper splint***.

1886 H. O. THOMAS *Contrib. Surg. & Med.* VI. 85 We decided to fix the whole extremity in a Calliper splint, which enabled him to resume his personal attention to business. **1890** *Ibid.* VII. 50 A most efficient mechanical means of assistance.. I found to be the 'calliper-knee-splint'... Its defects are, that it (the 'calliper') has to be altered in shape [etc.]. **1959** *B.S.I. News* Mar. 32 Thigh corsets and cuff tops for orthopaedic calipers.

'calliper, *v.* [f. prec. sb.] To measure with or use callipers. Hence **'callipering** *vbl. sb.*

1876 *Catal. Sci. Appar. S. Kens.* No. 477 Callipering Engine (British Horological Institute). **1881** HASLUCK *Lathe Work* 34 The diameter of the cylinder is tested by callipering.

Callippic (kə'lɪpɪk), *a.* [f. Gr. Κάλλιππος + -IC.] Of or pertaining to Callippus, a Greek astronomer who lived *c* 350 B.C. ***Callippic cycle*** or ***period***: a cycle proposed by him as an improvement on the Metonic cycle, consisting of 4 of the latter or 76 years, at the end of which, by omitting one day (i.e. making one month to have 29 days instead of 30) Callippus thought that the full and new moon would be brought round to the same day and hour.

1696 in PHILLIPS. **1708** KERSEY, *Callippick Period.* **1721–1800** in BAILEY. **1751** CHAMBERS *Cycl.* s.v., The Calippic period itself is not accurate.. it does not bring the new and full moons precisely to their places; but brings them too late, by a whole day, in 553 years. **1876** G. CHAMBERS *Astron.* 468 This cycle of 76 years (19 × 4) is known as the Cal[l]ippic period.

callipygian (kælɪ'pɪdʒɪən), *a.* [f. Gr. καλλίπῡγος, adj. f. καλλι- comb. stem of κάλλος beauty + πῡγή buttocks: the name of a famous statue of Venus'.] Of, pertaining to, or having well-shaped or finely developed buttocks.

[**1646** SIR T. BROWNE *Pseud. Ep.* IV. vi. 195 Callipygæ and women largely composed behinde.] *a* **1800** The Callipygian Venus. **1885** *Athenæum* 17 Oct. 497 The Callipygian luxuriance he so deplores.

callipygous (kælɪ'pɪdʒəs, -'paɪgəs), *a.* = CALLIPYGIAN *a.*

1923 A. HUXLEY *Antic Hay* iv. 64 One reality.. and that is callipygous. **1928** —— *Point Counter Point* vii. 122 One does not fall.. in love with a loud speaker.. however attractively callipygous. **1949** WODEHOUSE *Uncle Dynamite* vi. 95 He was unwilling to relinquish his memories of a callipygous Plank. **1967** J. RATHBONE *Diamonds Bid* ii. 22 The callipygous matrons with their shopping.

Hence **calli'pygously** *adv.*

1939 A. HUXLEY *After Many a Summer* ii. 14 Young ladies stretching, writhing, callipygously stooping to tie their sandals.

callis, obs. form of CULLIS.

c **1612** BEAUM. & FL. *Thierry* II. 455 Decoctions, Leaches, and callisies. **1641** in *Harl. Misc.* (Malh.) IV. 556 A spoonful or two of callis made of chickin.

Callis-sand. *Obs.* or *dial.* Also **Calis-, Calice-,** etc. [f. *Callis*, *Calleis*, *Callice*, *Calice*, etc. 16th c. forms of the name *Calais*, noted for its sand-dunes; the sands of Calais are frequently referred to in the 17th c. as a place for duels: see quots. in Nares.] A fine white sand, originally imported from Calais, used for blotting ink, scouring, etc.

1594 PLAT, *Jewell-ho.* II. 32 Take of right callis sand, and wash the same. **1659** HOOLE *Comenius Vis. World* (1777) 116 We dry a writing with blotting-paper, or calis-sand out of a sand-box. **1704** WORLIDGE *Dict. Rust. et Urb.* s.v. *Sand*, Calice-sand, burns reddish, but falls not in Water. **1877** E. PEACOCK *N.W. Lincoln Gloss.* (E.D.S.) *Callis-sand*, white scouring sand.

callisthenic (kælɪs'θɛnɪk), *a.* Also **cali-**. [f. Gr. καλλι- comb. stem of κάλλος beauty + σθένος strength (cf. the proper name Καλλισθένης 'beautifully or elegantly strong') + -IC.] Of or pertaining to the development of physical vigour in association with beauty; pertaining to callisthenics.

1847 CRAIG, *Calisthenic*, relating to calisthenics. **1859** SALA *Tw. round Clock* (1861) 193 The tyranny of the 'calisthenic exercises' and the French mark. **1863** S. W. MASON *Gymnastic Manual* Introd. 4 To hasten the

introduction of gymnastic, or calisthenic training into our schools.

callis'thenical, *a. rare*⁻¹. [f. as prec. + -AL¹.] Addicted to callisthenics.

1837 *Chamb. Jrnl.* 8 July 192 'Twere also as well she should be calisthenical.

callis'thenics, *sb. pl.* Also calisthenics. [f. CALLISTHENIC *a.*; cf. *gymnastic-s*. Mod.F. has *callisthenie*, repr. a regularly formed Gr. *καλλισθένεια 'beautiful strength'.] 'Gymnastic exercises suitable in the physical education of girls' (Littré); 'training calculated to develop the beauty of the human figure, and to promote elegant and graceful movement' (Craig). (Chiefly a term of young ladies' boarding-schools.) Also, *transf.* and *fig.* Occas. in *sing.*

1839 F. A. KEMBLE *Jrnl. Residence Georgian Pl.* (1863) 234 To follow me through half a day with any species of lively participation in my feelings would be a severe breathless moral calisthenic to most of my friends. **1847** in CRAIG. **1871** NAPHEYS *Prev. & Cure Dis.* I. vi. 168 Some theory of calisthenics is taught. **1871** *Daily News* 5 Jan., The exercises, perhaps, should be called 'callisthenics', rather than gymnastics, as they..consist simply in rhythmical movements with wooden rings and light wands, to the sound of piano music. **1872** F. THOMAS *Dis. Women* 57 An instructress or professor of calisthenics. **1946** MEZZROW & WOLFE *Really the Blues* viii. 117 We'd all raise our arms high, like a calisthenics class. **1956** M. STEARNS *Story of Jazz* (1957) xxiv. 301 *The Jazz Dance*..captures unerringly the stereotype notion..of frantic, abandoned calisthenics.

callis'thenium. [f. as prec., after *gymnasium*.] A place for the practice of callisthenics.

1883 *N.Y. Tribune* No. 13554/2 The calisthenium was thrown open and the girls danced until supper-time.

‖**callithrix, callitrix** ('kælɪθrɪks). Also 7 calitrich. [L. *callithrix*, pl. *callitriches* a kind of ape or monkey in Ethiopia (Pliny VIII. liv. 80 §216).] A genus of small Brazilian monkeys.

1607 TOPSELL *Four-f. Beasts* 7 The Calitrich..may be termed in English a bearded Ape. **1688** R. HOLME *Armoury* II. viii. §19 He beareth Gules, the Head of a Calitrich Ape. **1708** KERSEY *Callithrix*, a kind of Ape in Ethiopia, with a long beard, and a spread Tail. **1774** GOLDSM. *Nat. Hist.* (1862) I. VII. i. 507 The Callitrix, or Green Monkey of St. Iago.

callithump ('kælɪθʌmp), *sb.* and *v. U.S. colloq.* [App. back-formation from next.] **A.** *sb.* A callithumpian band; = CHARIVARI. **B.** *v. intr.* (See quot. 1888.)

1856 HALL *College Words* (ed. 2) 342 The band corresponds to the *Calliathump* of Yale. **1872** SCHELE DE VERE *Americanisms* 589 Callithump seems..to be of American origin. It represents the French *charivari*, the German *Katzenmusik*. **1888** FARMER *Americanisms*, *To callithump*, to caterwaul; to produce discordant 'musical' sounds by means of instruments, either incongruous in themselves or in conjunction—such as tin kettles, bells, rattles, etc.

callithumpian (ˌkælɪ'θʌmpɪən), *a.* and *sb. U.S. colloq.* [? fanciful formation; but cf. E.D.D. *Gallithumpians*. 1. A society of social reformers. 2. Disturbers of order at Parliamentary elections.] **A.** *adj.* Designating, pertaining to, or resembling, a band of discordant instruments. **B.** *sb.* A member of a callithumpian band.

1836 HILL *Yankee Stories* 9 (Weingarten), He said it was the *callathumpians*..that always went round New Year to kick up a sort of jollification. *c* **1845** G. FURMAN in *N.-Y. Hist. Soc. Q. Bull.* (1939) XXIII. 16 A celebrated detachment of these Rioters has long assumed the name of the 'Callithumpian Band', and has been distinguished for being more noisy and uproarious than the others. *Ibid.* 17 It was impossible for the Callithumpians to effect any meeting. **1848** BARTLETT *Dict. Amer.* s.v., This party is called the *Callithumpians* or the *Callithumpian Band*. **1886** *Harper's Mag.* July 213/2 The call [on the exchange] lasts ten or fifteen minutes, and occasionally has the accompaniment of callithumpian discord. **1946** R. BLESH *Shining Trumpets* (1949) vii. 155 Then the swift notes poured out, a black, calithumpian music.

‖**callitriche** (kə'lɪtrɪki:). *Bot.* [mod.Latin (Ruppius & Dillen.) f. Gr. καλλίτριχ-ος beautiful-haired.] A genus of small water-weeds inhabiting ponds and ditches; also called Water Star-wort.

1836 *Penny Cycl.* VI. 166/1 A few obscure floating species, all of which belong to the genus Callitriche. **1855** KINGSLEY *Glaucus* (1878) 206. **1882** *Cornh. Mag.* Jan. 34 Degraded blossoms like glasswort, callitriche and pondweed.

callivance, obs. form of CALAVANCE.

callixe, obs. form of CALX.

calloo (kə'lu:). Also calaw, callow. A species of Arctic duck, *Anas* (*Fuligula*, *Harelda*) *glacialis*, called also Long-tailed or Long-keeled Duck, a winter visitor to Orkney and Shetland.

1792 *Statist. Acc. Scotl.* V. 189 Lyres, calloos, wildgeese. *Ibid.* VII. 546 The calaw. **1806** NEILL *Tour Orkney & Shetl.* 79 (Jam.) The calloo—named from its evening call, which resembles the sound calloo, calloo, arrives from the arctic regions in autumn, and spends the winter here.

callop ('kæləp). [Aboriginal name.] An Australian freshwater fish, *Plectroplites ambiguus*.

1921 *Rec. S. Austral. Mus.* II, No. 1 (Index), *Plectroplites ambiguus* Richardson (Callop, Tarki). **1935** *R. Comm. Fishing Industry S. Austral., 2nd Progress Rep.* 23 Larger quantities of Callop are marketed than of any other river fish. **1949** VESEY-FITZGERALD & LAMONTE *Game Fish of World* 306 The callop is preferred to the cod by many people. **1966** *S. Austral. Yearbk.* 369 Approximately 210 part-time commercial fishermen using drum nets and set lines are engaged in fishing on the River Murray for Murray cod and callop.

calloper, obs. form of CALABER, CALLIPER.

callosal (kə'ləʊsəl), *a. Anat.* [f. L. *callōs-us* + -AL.] Of or belonging to the corpus callosum.

1868 R. OWEN *Anat. Vertebrates* III. xxviii. 101 Its [*sc.* that of the corpus callosum] hind part is embraced by the 'callosal convolution'. **1890** W. TURNER in *Jrnl. Anat.* XXV. I. 116 Marginal, callosal and hippocampal gyri are all differentiated. **1966** W. H. MCMENEMEY in Wright & Symmers *Systemic Pathol.* II. xii. 1275/1 The symptoms that might result from a callosal defect..are obscured by the mild dementia and loss of coordination that characterize the drunkard.

callose (kæ'ləʊs), *a. Bot.* [ad. L. *callōsus*: see CALLOUS.] Having callosities.

1864 in WEBSTER. **1880** GRAY *Bot. Text-bk.* 400.

ca'llosify, *v. rare*⁻¹. [see -FY; cf. *ossify*.] *trans.* To make callous.

1800 W. TAYLOR in Robberds *Mem.* I. 344 Smoking tobacco..may act by callosifying lungs too sieve-like.

callosity (kə'lɒsɪtɪ). [a. F. *callosité*:—L. *callōsitāt-em*, f. *callōs-us*; see CALLOUS.]

1. The condition of being callous; abnormal hardness and thickness of the skin or other tissues.

1578 BANISTER *Hist. Man* I. 4 b, The callositie of the Gowmes serueth some men in stead of teeth. **1671** SALMON *Syn. Med.* I. l. 119 If the Flesh about the Ulcer be dry, and sensless, it becomes a callous: and that Hardness is called Callosity. **1744** MITCHELL in *Phil. Trans.* XLIII. 108 The Thickness or Callosity of their Skins. **1831** BREWSTER *Nat. Magic* xii. (1833) 303 This callosity of the skin may be effected by frequently moistening it with dilute sulphuric acid.

2. *concr.* A callous formation, a callus; a thickened and hardened part of the skin, such as the hard lumps that arise from constant pressure or friction, or on the cicatrized surfaces of ulcers. Also applied to natural thickenings, such as those on the legs of the horse, the breast of the camel, etc.

1601 HOLLAND *Pliny* XVI. vii. 460 Certain hard callosities like Pumish stones. **1725** BRADLEY *Fam. Dict.* s.v. *Strangury*, If the Ischaria is caused by some Flesh Kernel or Callocity. **1818** *Art. Preserv. Feet* 42 A simple Callosity is nothing more than a thickening of the epidermis. **1878** TAIT & STEWART *Unseen Univ.* v. §165. 169 Asses..have callosities only on the inner side of the fore legs.

3. *fig.* A hardened state of mind or conscience; insensibility; = CALLOUSNESS 2.

1658 SIR T. BROWNE *Hydriot.* v. 28 To weep into stones are fables. Afflictions induce calosities. **1748** HARTLEY *Observ. Man* II. iii. §7. 311 When Men cease to regard God in due measure..they are very apt to relapse into Negligence and Callosity. **1874** FARRAR *Life Christ* 82 A callosity of heart, a petrifying of the moral sense.

calloso-marginal (kæˌləʊsəʊ'mɑ:dʒɪnəl), *a.* [cf. CALLOSAL *a.*, MARGINAL *a.*] *Anat.* Pertaining to the callosal and marginal gyri of the brain.

1876 *Quain's Elem. Anat.* (ed. 8) II. 531 The calloso-marginal fissure (cmf) commences beneath the anterior extremity of the corpus callosum. **1890** W. JAMES *Princ. Psychol.* I. 31 The calloso-marginal convolution. **1961** *Lancet* 30 Sept. 746/1 An inter-hemispheric clot may be recognised..by separation of the callosomarginal from the pericallosal artery.

callot, variant of CALLET.

callot(e, -ott(e, obs. ff. CALOTTE, skull-cap.

callo'technics, *sb. pl. rare.* [Improperly spelt for *callitechnics* or *calotechnics* (Gr. καλλιτεχνία, καλοτεχνία).] A proposed name for 'The fine or ornamental arts'.

1860 WORCESTER cites R. PARK.

†**callough.** *Obs. rare.* ? Some shell-fish.

1610 FOLKINGHAM *Art of Survey* IV. iii. 83 Winkles, Purples, Cutle, Callough, Cockles, Muskles, Shrimps.

callous ('kæləs), *a.* [ad. L. *callōsus* (cf. F. *calleux*) hard-skinned, callous, f. *callum* (*callus*) hardened skin: see -OUS.]

1. (Chiefly *Phys.* & *Zool.*) Hardened, indurated: as parts of the skin exposed to constant pressure or friction, or the cicatrized surfaces of ulcers. Also applied to parts which are naturally hard.

1578 BANISTER *Hist. Man* I. 4 b, With gowmes, which flesh is made so callous, and indurated. **1605** TIMME *Quersit.* III. 180 Callous and hollow ulcers. **1649** JER. TAYLOR *Gt. Exemp.* vi. §7 The flesh of beasts grows callous by stripes and the pressure of the yoke. **1695** CONGREVE *Love for L.* IV. xv, With labouring callous hands. **1797** BEWICK *Brit. Birds* (1847) I. 337 A callous conical protuberance. **1875** JOWETT *Plato* (ed. 2) I. 134 Hard and callous skins under their feet.

b. *Bot.*

1794 MARTYN *Rousseau's Bot.* xvi. 180 The tips of the leaves being callous. **1884** BOWER & SCOTT *Phaner. & Ferns* 174 The condition termed by Hanstein callous..consists in the thickening of the bands of membrane in all directions.

2. *fig.* Of the mind, feelings, conscience, etc., and of persons: Hardened, unfeeling, insensible.

1679 GOODMAN *Penitent Pardoned* I. iv. (1713) 109 The frequent injuries done to it [conscience] render it callous and insensible. **1729** BUTLER *Serm.* Wks. 1874 II. 85 Totally hard and callous to impressions of religion. **1776** HUME *My own Life* 18 Apr. in *Hist. Eng.* (1825) Introd. 4 Callous against the impressions of public folly. **1833** ARNOLD *Let.* in *Life & Corr.* (1844) I. vii. 343 It is an immense blessing to be perfectly callous to ridicule. **1844** DISRAELI *Coningsby* I. ix. 35 The callous bustle of fashionable saloons.

callous *sb.*, erroneous spelling of CALLUS *sb.*

'callous, *v.* [f. prec. adj.]

trans. To make callous, to harden. *lit.* and *fig.* Only in pple. (and ppl. adj.) **'calloused**, hardened.

1834 *Fraser's Mag.* X. 658 The whole English mind calloused against its efforts to make an impression. **1850** MRS. STOWE *Uncle Tom's C.* xx. 204 On the back and shoulders of the child, great welts and calloused spots. **1880** E. H. ARR *New Engl. Bygones* 108 Hands calloused by toil.

callousing ('kæləsɪŋ), *ppl. a.* [f. CALLOUS *a.* or *v.* + -ING².] That makes callous.

1921 *Sunday at Home* Jan. 214/1 My fellow-citizens are engaged on labour which is hard and callousing. **1928** *Sunday Express* 8 Jan. 9/1 The hardships and callousing brutalities of a mercenary force.

callously ('kæləslɪ), *adv.* [f. CALLOUS *a.* + -LY².] In a callous manner, unfeelingly.

1870 *Daily Tel.* 7 Oct., When they died she callously got rid of their bodies as best she could. **1883** *American* 184 No house..more callously indifferent to those it employed.

callousness ('kæləsnɪs). [f. as prec. + -NESS.]

†**1. a.** Callous quality or condition, induration; **b.** A callous formation; = CALLOSITY 1, 2.

c **1660** JER. TAYLOR *On Repent.* VII. viii, A callousness of his feet or a wart upon his fingers. *c* **1715** CHEYNE (J.) The skin becomes the thicker, and so a callousness grows upon it. **1765** *Phil. Trans.* LV. 82 There are often found in them [the lungs] tumours, callousnesses, etc.

2. *fig.* A hardened state of mind, conscience, etc.; want of feeling, insensibility.

1692 BENTLEY *Boyle Lect.* 12 Abandon'd to a callousness and numness of soul. **1726** BUTLER *15 Serm.* v. 91. **1781** JOHNSON *Lett.* 258 (1788) II. 194 As I have not the decrepitude I have not the callousness of old age. **1844** STANLEY *Arnold* (1858) I. vi. 236 The richer classes will again relapse into their old callousness. **1867** PEARSON *Hist. Eng.* II. 35 John's..utter callousness to honour.

Callovian (kæ'ləʊvɪən), *a. Geol.* Also KELLOVIAN. [ad. F. *callovien* (A. d'Orbigny *Paléont. française. Terrains jurassiques* (1842) I. 608), f. mod.L. *Callovien-sis*, f. *Kellaways* (given by d'Orbigny as *Kelloway*), a village in Wiltshire.] Epithet of a stage of the Jurassic between the Oxfordian in the Upper Jurassic and the Bathonian in the Middle Jurassic. Also *absol.*

1881 *Q. Jrnl. Geol. Soc.* XXXVII. 560 Near Bazinghen there is nothing but a few feet of clay between the Callovian grit with *Terebratula humeralis* (true) and *Rhynchonella varians* and the Nerinæan or so-called Astartian Oolite. **1885** A. GEIKIE *Text-bk. Geol.* (ed. 2) 801 Oxfordian, divisible into (*a*) Callovian, with zones of *Amm. macrocephalus*, and *A. anceps*, and (*b*) Oxfordian, with zones *A. Lamberti*, *A. Mariæ*, *A. cordatus*. **1946** W. J. ARKELL in *Bull. Geol. Soc. Amer.* LVII. 8 Formerly, (1933) the present author maintained that the Callovian should comprise only the Kellaways beds of Kellaways, Wiltshire, and that the whole of the Oxford Clay of Oxford should be included in the Oxfordian; however, he has come to the conclusion that this would be wrong... The line of division should..be drawn between the *Lamberti* and the *Mariae* zones. **1955** G. G. WOODFORD tr. *Gignoux's Stratigr. Geol.* vii. 338 The Callovian is a more or less calcareous or clayey sandstone.

callow ('kæləʊ), *a.* and *sb.* Forms: 1 calu, caluw, calo, 3 caluȝ, 4 calu, calouh, calewe, calouwe, 6 kallowe, 6– callow. [OE. *calu* (def. *calw-e*):—WGer. *kalwo-*, whence also MLG. *kale*, MDu. *cāle* (*calu*, gen. *caluwes*), OHG. *chalo* (def. *chalwe*, *chalawe*), MHG. *kal* (*kalwe*), Ger. *kahl*, by Kluge thought to be cognate with Lith. *gŏlŭ* naked, blank; but not improbably an adoption of L. *calv-us* bald. Cf. Ir. and Gael. *calbh* bald.]

A. *adj.* †**1.** Bald, without hair. *Obs.*

a **1000** *Prov.* (Kemble) 42 (Bosw.) Moniȝ man weorþ færlice caluw. *a* **1000** *Riddles* xli. 99 (Gr.) Ic eom wide calu. *c* **1375** *Cato Major* II. xxix, Þat forehed is lodly þat is calouh & bare. **1388** WYCLIF *Lev.* xiii. 40 A man of whos heed heeris fleten awei, is calu [**1382** ballid].

2. Of birds: Unfledged, without feathers.

1603 HOLLAND *Plutarch's Mor.* 63 Yoong callow birds which are not yet fethered and fledg'd. **1728** THOMSON *Spring* 667 The callow young..Their brittle bondage break. **1801** SOUTHEY *Thalaba* V. iii. Poems IV. 180 Her young in

the refreshing bath, Dipt down their callow heads. **1822** HAZLITT *Table-t.* II. xiv. 329 The callow brood are fledged.

b. Applied to the down of unfledged birds; and so, to the down on a youth's cheek and chin.

1604 DRAYTON *Owle* 245 His soft and callow downe. **1697** DRYDEN *Virg. Past.* VIII. 57 The callow Down began to cloath my Chin. **1735** SOMERVILLE *Chase* II. 457 Prove.. their Valour's Growth Mature, e'er yet the callow Down has spread Its curling Shade.

3. *fig.* Inexperienced, raw, 'unfledged'.

1580 HARVEY in *Spenser's Wks.* (Grosart) I. 40 Some, that weene themselves as fledged as the reste, being.. as kallowe. **1651** CLEVELAND *Poems* 31 Blasphemy unfledg'd, a callow curse. *a* **1797** H. WALPOLE *Mem. Geo. II* (1847) I. xii. 410 Teaching young and callow orators to soar. **1823** LAMB *Elia* Ser. II. xvii. (1865) 343 The first callow flights in authorship. **1849** C. BRONTË *Shirley* xxxiii. 474 In all the voluptuous ease of a yet callow pacha.

4. Of land: **a.** Bare; **b.** (*Ireland.*) Low-lying and liable to be submerged.

1677 PLOT *Oxfordsh.* 243 When these Lands are not swardy enough to bear clean tillage, nor callow or light enough to lie to get sward. **1878** LEVER *J. Hinton* xx. 138 Broad tracts of bog or callow meadow-land. **1882** *Science Gossip* Mar. 51 If a callow meadow is flooded all the winter.

5. *Comb.* †**callow-mouse**, a bat.

1340 *Ayenb.* 27 þe envious ne may ysy þet guod of oþren nanmore þanne þe oule oþer þe calouwe mous þe briȝtnesse of þe zonne.

B. *sb.*

†**1.** One who is bald; a bald-pate. *Obs.*

c **1305** *Life St. Dunstan* 89 in *E.E.P.* (1862) 37 Out, what haþ þe calewe [St. Dunstan] ido: what haþ þe calewe ido.

†**2.** A callow nestling; *fig.* a raw youth. *Obs.*

a **1667** JER. TAYLOR *Serm.* (1678) 310 Such a person.. deplumes himself to feather all the naked Callows that he sees. **1670** MRS. BEHN *Widow Rant.* IV. iii, She.. that can prefer such a callow as thou before a man.

3. The stratum of vegetable soil lying above the subsoil; the top or rubble bed of a quarry, which has to be removed to reach the rock. *dial.*

1863 MORTON *Cycl. Agric.* II. Gloss. (E.D.S.) *Callow* (Norf., Suff.), the soil covering the subsoil. **1875** URE *Dict. Arts* I. 673 *Callow*, the top or rubble bed of a quarry. This is obliged to be removed before the useful material is raised.

4. A low-lying damp meadow by the banks of an Irish river.

1862 H. COULTER *West of Ireland* 8 The extensive Callows lying along the banks of the Suck. **1865** *Gard. Chron. & Agric. Gaz.* 15 July 663/2 The callows consist of low flat land near a river, and liable to be overflowed, as well as being always in a damp state in the driest seasons. **1883** *Dundee Advert.* 25 Aug. 6/1 All the callows on the banks [of the Shannon] to Lusmagh.. are submerged.

Hence **'callowness**, **'callowy** *a.*

1855 DE QUINCEY in Page *Life* (1877) II. xviii. 90 Such advantage.. as belongs to callowness or freshness. **1823** *Monthly Mag.* LV. 240 Like to a bird, who bestows on her callowy nestlings the morsel.

callow, var. of CALLOO, wild duck.

'callowly, *adv.* [f. CALLOW *a.* + -LY².] In a callow manner; immaturely, naïvely.

1976 in *Conc. Oxf. Dict.* (ed. 6) 141/1. **1981** *N.Y. Times* 29 May C5/4 Callowly charismatic, the producer is a throwback to Mr. Dreyfuss' 'Duddy Kravitz', a man who can combine greed with guilelessness.

calltrop, obs. form of CALTROP.

‖**'callum.** *Obs.* [L. *callum.*] = CALLUS *sb.*

c **1420** *Pallad. on Husb.* IV. 599 Callum that in Elmes leves borne is. *a* **1640** JACKSON *Creed* x. xlii. Wks. IX. 499 Frequent calcitration against the edge of this fiery sword breeds a callum or complete hardness. **1646** FULLER *Wounded Consc.* (1841) 281 That callum, schirrus, or incrustation, drawn over it [the conscience] by nature, and hardened by custom in sin.

Calluna (kæ'lu:nə). *Bot.* [mod.L. (R. A. Salisbury 1802, in *Trans. Linn. Soc.* VI. 317), f. Gr. καλλύν-ειν to beautify, sweep clean, f. κάλλος beauty.] A monotypic genus of plants of the family Ericaceæ, the only known species being *C. vulgaris*, the common heather; also (with lower-case initial), a plant of this species. Also *attrib.*

1824 J. E. SMITH *Eng. Flora* II. 224 *Calluna.* Ling... Mr. Salisbury.. has judiciously called our common Ling, *Calluna*, from καλλυνω; which is doubly suitable, whether.. we take it to express a *cleansing* property, brooms being made of Ling; or whether we adopt the more common sense of the word, to *ornament* or *adorn*, which is very applicable to the flowers. **1920** G. JEKYLL *Wall & Water Gardens* (ed. 6) xxiv. 195 The Callunas should begin at the back.. and then come forward to the path. **1946** ZEUNER *Dating Past* iii. 56 Peats growing above the water level:.. *Calluna* peat (heather peat). **1962** *Amat. Gardening* 17 Feb. 2 The ericas and callunas have very much the same symmetrical habit of growth.

call-up. [CALL *v.* 35 f.] = CONSCRIPTION 4. Also *attrib.*

1940 *Economist* 10 Aug. 175/2 A continuous system of call-up and training for the Industrial Army. **1941** D. REED *Prophet at Home* 264 The rate of the call-up was too slow. **1945** *News Chron.* 1 June 4/2 We still propose to go on calling up young men under 30 as they reach the call-up age. **1958** *Spectator* 14 Feb. 191/2 The call-up cannot now be abandoned unless the bait for volunteers is made much tastier.

callus ('kæləs), *sb.* Also (*erron.*) callous. Pl. calluses. [a. L. *callus* hardened skin.]

1. *Phys.* and *Pathol.* A callous formation; a hardened and thickened part of the skin, or of some other tissue naturally soft; also applied to natural thickenings of the skin, etc.; = CALLOSITY 2.

1563 T. GALE *Antidot.* II. 56 It doth dry fistulas which haue not callus indurated. **1656** RIDGLEY *Pract. Physic* 157 The Callous must be first removed. **1722** DE FOE *Plague* (1884) 249 Spots.. as.. hard as a piece of Callous or Horn. **1769** PENNANT *Zool.* III. 280 Between the eyes and the mouth is a hard callus. **1858** O. W. HOLMES *Aut. Breakf. T.* 65 When I have established a pair of well-pronounced feathering calluses on my thumbs. **1873** TRISTRAM *Moab* xv. 292 Even in the young [ibex] kid there is a hard callous.. on the front of the knee.

2. *Pathol.* 'The bony material thrown out around and between the two ends of a fractured bone during the process of healing' (*Syd. Soc. Lex.*).

1678 JONES *Heart & Right Sov.* 396 Nature supplyes the .. breaches, in our bones, by a callus, or hardness of the like kind. **1713** CHESELDEN *Anat.* I. i. (1726) 8 The Callus from the broken ends of a bone that is not set. **1845** TODD & BOWMAN *Phys. Anat.* I. 125 The permanent callus has all the characters of true bone. **1855** HOLDEN *Hum. Osteol.* (1878) 37 This ferule termed the provisional callus is not removed until the fracture has been thoroughly repaired.

3. *Bot.* A hard formation in or on plants.

1870 HOOKER *Stud. Flora* 109 *Rubus fruticosus*.. rooting from a callus at the tip. **1882** VINES *Sachs' Bot.* 173 The callus formed between the bark and the wood, when the stem is cut off above the root.

4. *fig.* A callous state of feeling, etc.

1692 BURNET *Past. Care* vii. 73 A Callus that he Contracts, by his insensible way of handling Divine Matters. **1858** O. W. HOLMES *Aut. Breakf. T.* xii. 116 Editors have.. to develop enormous calluses at every point of contact with authorship.

callus ('kæləs), *v.* [f. the sb.] *intr.* To form a callus.

1864 J. S. HIBBERD *Rose-bk.* 284 In all cases keep cuttings and eyes alive and fresh by sprinkling their tops frequently rather than making the soil they are in very wet, they will in fact callus quicker if the soil is nearly dry. **1958** *Times* 22 Nov. 9/4 They allow the natural healing processes to carry on underneath so that in time the wound will callus over.

callvanse, obs. form of CALAVANCE.

†**cally'moocher.** *Obs. rare*⁻¹. [Cf. *moucher* loafer.] ? A raw cadger, a greenhorn.

1661 MIDDLETON *Mayor of Quinb.* in *Dodsley* XI. 132 (N.) Thou upstart callymoocher.

†**callyoan.** *Obs.* ? Some kind of fur.

c **1524** *Churchw. Acc. St. Mary Hill, London* (Nichols 1797) 125 Furred with callyoan and mynks.

calm (kɑ:m), *sb.*¹ Forms: 4–7 calme, 6 cawme, 7– calm. [ME. *calme*, a. F. *calme* (16th c. in Littré, in 15th c. *carme*) in same sense, ad. It. or Sp. (also Pg.) *calma.*

Since *calma* in OSp. and Pg. means also 'heat of the day', Diez, comparing mod.Pr. *chaume* 'resting-time of the cattle', and Rumansch *calma, cauma* 'a shady resting-place for cattle', thought *calma* possibly derived from late L. *cauma* (occurring in *Vulg.*, Job xxx. 30), a. Gr. καῦμα 'burning heat, fever heat, heat of the sun, heat of the day', used also in med.L. of the burning heat of the sun. Taken in connexion with the senses of the Rumansch and Provençal words this gives the possible development of meaning 'burning heat, heat of the day, rest during the heat of the day, quiet, stillness'; but it is notable that It. *calma* has no sense of 'heat', only 'a calme, or quiet faire weather' (Florio). As to the phonetic change of *au* to *al*, Diez suggested popular assoc. with *calēre* to be hot, *calor* heat, which Schuchardt also (*Romania* IV. 255) thinks probable; the latter has given other instances of the phonetic change in *Vokalismus des Vulgärlateins* I. 494–6 and III. 316.]

1. Stillness, quiet, tranquillity, serenity; freedom from agitation or disturbance.

a. *lit.* of the weather, air, or sea: opposed to *storm*; = CALMNESS.

1393 GOWER *Conf.* III. 230 As the.. rage Of windes maketh the see salvage And that was calme bringth into wawe. *c* **1400** *Destr. Troy* 13157 All the calme ouercast into kene stormes. *c* **1450** *Chaucer's Dreme* 1384 All was one, calme, or tempest. **1526** *Pilgr. Perf.* (W. de W. 1531) 252 The colde, the hete, the cawme, the frost, yᵉ snowe. **1530** PALSGR. 202/2 Calme, styll whether, *carme.* **1611** BIBLE *Matt.* viii. 26 There was a great calme. **1613** SHAKS. *Hen. VIII*, III. i. 166 A Soule as euen as a Calme. **1822** HAZLITT *Table-t.* Ser. II. iv. (1869) 85 Before and after earthquakes there is a calm in the air. **1850** TENNYSON *In Mem.* xi, Calm on the seas, and silver sleep. **1868** J. E. H. SKINNER *Roughing it* 253 By the rock of Pontiko there was a sheet of breathless calm.

b. Absolute want of wind: often in pl. *calms.* *region of calms*, a belt of the ocean near the equator, lying between the regions of the north-east and south-east trade winds.

1517 TORKINGTON *Pilgr.* (1884) 57 We.. fonde the wynde agens vs or ellys.. calmys. **1627** CAPT. SMITH *Seaman's Gram.* x. 46 When there is not a breath of wind stirring, it is a calme or a starke calme. **1709** *Lond. Gaz.* No. 4547/2 By reason of Calms he could not come up with them 'till the 6th. **1799** *Med. Jrnl.* I. 96 A calm prevailed, and the heat was extreme. **1812** J. WILSON *Isle of Palms* III. 923 Chain'd in tropic calms. **1857** H. REED *Lect. Brit. Poets* II. xii. 113 The misery of a dead calm beneath a torrid sky.

c. *fig.* (to **a.** and **b.**) of social or political conditions and circumstances.

1547 J. HARRISON *Exhort. Scottes* 210 The stormes of this tempestious worlde, shall shortely come to a calme. **1606** SHAKS. *Tr. & Cr.* I. iii. 100 The vnity and married calme of States. **1781** COWPER *Friendsh.* xxiii, Religion should.. make a calm of human life. *a* **1850** CALHOUN *Wks.* (1874) IV. 24 Till our free and popular institutions are succeeded by the calm of despotism.

d. *fig.* of the mind, feelings, or demeanour; = CALMNESS.

1606 SHAKS. *Tr. & Cr.* IV. i. 15 Our bloods are now in calme. **1719** DE FOE *Crusoe* (1840) I. xiv. 236 All my calm of mind.. seemed to be suspended. **1807** WORDSW. *Sonn. Lib., To Clarkson*, A good man's calm, A great man's happiness. **1879** FARRAR *St. Paul* II. 376 In that desperate crisis one man retained his calm and courage.

2. *attrib.* and in *comb.*

1865 *Intell. Observ.* No. 46. 253 The 'calm belt' of the equator. **1886** *Pall Mall G.* 20 July, Now the birds are storm-makers, and in another moment they are calm-bringers.

calm, *sb.*² Forms: 6 calme, cawm, 7 caulm, 8 calm, cam. Cf. also CAME.

†**1.** *Sc.* **a.** A mould in which metal objects are cast.

1535 *Sc. Acts Jas. V* (1814) 346 Twa hagbutis.. with powder and cawmys for furnessing of the samin. **1540** *Ibid.* (1597) §94 Ane Hagbutte of Founde, called Hagbute of Crochert, with their Calmes, Bullettes and pellockes of leed or irone. **1599** in Pitcairn *Crimin. Trials* II. 75 Prenting in calmis, maid of trie, fillit vp with calk, of fals adulterat money. *c* **1725** OREM *Hist. Aberdeen* in *Bibl. Top. Brit.* (1782) V. 152 Three hagbuts, with calms of stone. **1768** *Mauchline Less. Rec.* in *Old Ch. Life Scotl.* (1885) 139 A set of Cams or moulds.

b. *in the calms* (fig.): in course of construction, in the state of preparation.

a **1662** BAILLIE *Lett.* (1775) II. 197 (JAM.) The matter of peace is now in the caulms.

2. An enclosing frame, as of a pane of glass.

1577 HARRISON *England* II. xii. (1877) 236 Some.. did make panels of horne in steed of glasse, and fix them in wooden calmes. **1885** P. J. DAVIES *Standard Pract. Plumbing* 31 Put the sharpened end of the calme in between the cutters and turn the handle. **1885** *Spons' Mech. Own Bk.* 630 The use of lead 'calmes' for fixing window panes is of venerable antiquity. **1955** *Antiquity* XXIX. 217 No evidence was found of calms with horn panels. **1970** H. BRAUN *Parish Churches* viii. 111 A network of delicate grooved strips.. known as 'calms'—pronounced 'cames'.

3. The heddles of a loom. See CAAM.

calm (kɑ:m), *a.* Forms: 4–7 calme, 6 cawme, caulme, (? came), 7– calm. [a. F. *calme*, in same sense (15th c. in Littré), f. *calme* sb. The other langs. have not the adjective.]

1. Free from agitation or disturbance; quiet, still, tranquil, serene; without wind, not stormy.

a. *lit.* of the weather, air, or sea.

c **1400** *Destr. Troy* 2011 Stormes were stille.. All calme it become. *c* **1440** *Promp. Parv.* 58 Calme-wedyr, *malacia, calmacia.* **1550** JOYE *Exp. Dan.* Ded. A ij, The same sea.. wyl be so cawme and styll. **1573** TUSSER *Husb.* (1878) 125 Get home thy hawme, whilst weather is cawme. **1611** BIBLE *Jonah* i. 12 So shall the sea be calme. **1794** SULLIVAN *View Nat.* I. 63 The sea is much calmer.. at the bottom, than in any part nearer its surface. **1856** RUSKIN *Mod. Paint.* IV. v. xx. §6 The sea.. is never calm, in the sense that a mountain lake can be calm. **1878** HUXLEY *Physiogr.* 53 A calm atmosphere promotes the formation of dew.

b. *spec.* Absolutely without wind.

c **1440** *Promp. Parv.* 58 Calme or softe, wythe-owte wynde, *calmus, tranquillus.* **1547** BOORDE *Introd. Knowl.* i. (1870) 126 Although a man stande in neuer so came a place. **1711** *Lond. Gaz.* No. 4906/2 It fell stark Calm.

c. *transf.* and *fig.* of sound, utterance, etc.; of the mind, feelings, demeanour, or actions.

1570 ASCHAM *Scholem.* II. (Arb.) 100 A.. caulme kinde of speaking and writing. **1641** J. JACKSON *True Evang. T.* I. 6 Sweet and calm and sociable manners and conversation. **1729** BUTLER *Serm.* Wks. 1874 II. 87 He could have no calm satisfaction. **1798** COLERIDGE *Anc. Mar.* v. xiii, Be calm, thou Wedding-Guest! **1859** THACKERAY *Virgin.* xix. 147 He tried to keep his voice calm and without tremor. **1870** E. PEACOCK *R. Skirlaugh* III. 146 The placid river whose calm murmur was distinctly audible.

d. *fig.* of conditions or circumstances.

1667 MILTON *P.L.* VI. 461 Live content, which is the calmest life. **1751** JOHNSON *Rambl.* No. 185 ¶4 The calmest moments of solitary meditation. **1837** HT. MARTINEAU *Soc. Amer.* II. 352 In the calmer times which are to come. **1863** HAWTHORNE *Old Home, Lond. Suburb* (1879) 244 A calm variety of incident.

2. *Comb.*, as *calm-minded, -mindedness.*

1599 SANDYS *Europæ Spec.* (1632) 83 A calme-minded hearer. **1820** KEATS *Lamia* II. 158 With calm-planted steps. —— *Hyper.* III. 38 The thrush Began calm-throated. **1882** *Pall Mall G.* 26 Oct. 1 Public opinion has been cursed.. with an odious malady called calm-mindedness.

calm (kɑ:m), *v.* Forms: 4–6 calme, 7– calm. [f. CALM *a.*, or perh. a. F. *calme-r*, which however is only trans. Perh. the trans. sense was really the earlier in English, though evidence fails; the intrans. is not in Johnson.]

1. *intr.* Of the sea or wind: To become calm. *Obs.* exc. with *down.* Also *fig.*

1399 LANGL. *Rich. Redeless* III. 366 þan gan it to calme and clere all aboute. *c* **1400** *Destr. Troy* 4587 The course of the colde see calmyt. **1569** W. GIBSON in Farr's *S.P.* (1845) II. 244 If God command the seas to calme. **1598** W. PHILLIPS *Linschoten's Trav.* in Arb. *Garner* III. 22 It.. raineth, thundereth, and calmeth. **1599** SHAKS. *Pass. Pilgr.* 312 What though her frowning brows be bent, Her cloudy looks will calm ere night. **1684** *Lond. Gaz.* No. 1982/2 The wind

calming, they were forced to give over the pursuit. **1877** Mrs. Oliphant *Makers Flor.* xi. (1877) 265 The excited mass calmed down under this wonderful appeal.

2. *trans.* To make calm; to quiet, still, tranquillize, appease, pacify. *lit.* and *fig.*

1559 *Mirr. Mag., Dk. of York* xxiv. 7 Right shall raigne, and quiet calme ech crime. **1593** Shaks. *3 Hen. VI*, iii. iii. 38 Renowned Queene, With patience calme the Storme. **1667** Milton *P.L.* xii. 594 Go, waken Eve; Her also I with gentle Dreams have calm'd. **1709** Lady M. W. Montague *Lett.* lxv. 107 [She] can also..calm my passions. **1783** Pott *Chirurg. Wks.* II. 436 When..that inflammation is calmed. **1795** Southey *Joan of Arc* i. 122 She calm'd herself. **1841–44** Emerson *Ess., Heroism* Wks. (Bohn) I. 110 It may calm the apprehension of calamity.

†**3.** To delay (a ship) by a calm; to becalm.

1593 Shaks. *2 Hen. VI*, iv. ix. 33 A ship that, having 'scaped a tempest, Is straightway calm'd [**1623** calme]. **1604** —— *Oth.* i. i. 30, I..must be be-leed, and calm'd. **1753** Chambers *Cycl. Supp.* s.v., It is not uncommon for the vessels to be calmed, or becalmed, as the sailors express it.

calmant ('kælmənt, 'kɑːmənt), *sb. Med.* [a. F. *calmant*, pr. pple. of *calmer*; used as adj. and sb. in medical lang. and transferred.] = calmative *sb.*

1811 Melusina Trench *Leadbeater Papers* II. 210 What females call work..is a sort of composer, a calmant peculiarly useful..to the delicate and irritable spirits of women. **1862** *Med. Times* II. 390 Tobacco has always had the reputation of being a calmant rather than a stimulant. **1881** Mrs. Praed *Policy & P.* iii, Prussic acid..acted as a speedy calmant.

calmative ('kælmətɪv, 'kɑːm-), *a.* and *sb.* Chiefly *Med.* [f. calm *v.* + -ative. (The Latinic suffix is here defensible on the ground of the It. and Sp. *calmar*, F. *calmer*: but cf. -ative.)]

A. *adj.* Having a calming effect; sedative.

1871 Napheys *Prev. & Cure Dis.* ii. v. 569 Cool sponging of the body is grateful and calmative in delirium. **1875** H. Wood *Therap.* 59 A calmative action on the nervous system.

B. *sb.* A medical agent which quiets inordinate action of an organ; *transf.* and *fig.* anything which has a calming effect.

1870 *Pall Mall G.* 5 Nov. 4 The venerable Professor of Materia Medica tried to prescribe a calmative. **1875** H. Walton *Dis. Eye* 103 The combination of iron with calmatives and sedatives. **1883** *Brit. Q. Rev.* July 19 There is no more effectual calmative to the irritable nervous system than the healthy fatigue of sustained labour.

calmed (kɑːmd, *poet.* 'kɑːmɪd), *ppl. a.* [f. calm *v.* + -ed.] Made calm, reduced to calmness.

1590 Greene *Arcad.* (1616) 3 The Dolphines..fetcht their carreers on the calmed waues. **1795** Southey *Joan of Arc* viii. 669 The calm'd ocean. **1877** Mrs. Oliphant *Makers Flor.* iii. (1877) 86 A softened, calmed religious twilight.

†**b.** Detained by a calm, becalmed. *Obs.*

1634 in Ld. Campbell *Chancellors* (1857) III. lxiii. 251 For a more speedy passage of calmed ships.

calmer ('kɑːmə(r)). [f. calm *v.* + -er[1].] One who or that which calms.

1653 Walton *Angler* 33 Angling was..a calmer of unquiet thoughts. **1785** Keatinge *Trav.* (1817) I. 265 The duplication of the sum operated as a calmer to his mind. **1876** M. Arnold *Lit. & Dogma* 148 The calmer and pacifier.

†'**calmewe.** *Obs.* Also 5 caldmaw. [Deriv. uncertain; possibly f. *cald*, cold + mew (Sc. *maw*) a gull. Cf. colmow.] Some sea-fowl; perhaps the Winter Mew, or Gull in its immature plumage.

*c***1430** Lydg. *Min. Poems* (1840) 202 The semewe..Nor the caldmawe, nouthir fat nor lene. **14..** *Piers of Fullh.* 356 in Hazl. *E.P.P.* II. 15 The lampwynkes and thise calmewes That sweme on wawes whan it flowes, And som tyme on the sondis gone.

†'**calmey.** *Obs.* [a. Ger. *kalmei.*] = calamine.

1756 Nugent *Gr. Tour* (Netherl.) I. 273 Near this place there are several mines of lead, coal, vitriol, and calmey, or lapis calaminaris.

calming ('kɑːmɪŋ), *vbl. sb.* [f. calm *v.* + -ing[1].] Stilling, tranquillizing.

1711 Shaftesb. *Charac.* (1737) II. 61 To tend..towards the calming of the mind. **1883** *Daily News* 10 July 4/7 Time works wonders in the calming of national passions.

'**calming,** *ppl. a.* [f. as prec. + -ing[2].] That calms.

*a***1853** Robertson *Lect.* ii. (1858) 62 A question not altogether calming in these days. **1858** Froude *Hist. Eng.* III. xv. 328 A calming circular to the justices of the peace.

calmingly ('kɑːmɪŋlɪ), *adv.* [f. calming *ppl. a.* + -ly[2].] In a calming manner.

1908 A. Bennett *Buried Alive* viii, 'Of course you haven't,' she said calmingly. **1965** M. Frayn *Tin Men* xiii. 68 A paper whose language was..calmingly incomprehensible.

calmly ('kɑːmlɪ), *adv.* [f. calm *a.* + -ly[2].] In a calm manner; tranquilly, without agitation.

1597 Hooker *Eccl. Pol.* v. lxxix. §14 By quiet speech did thus calmly disclose itself. **1624** Capt. Smith *Virginia* v. 178 This threatning gust passed ouer more calmlier then was expected. **1671** Milton *P.R.* iii. 43 To whom our Saviour calmly thus replied. **1712** Addison *Spect.* No. 295 ¶1 When her Passion would let her argue calmly. **1856** Froude *Hist. Eng.* (1858) I. v. 424 They..settled themselves calmly down to transact..the ordinary business.

calmness ('kɑːmnɪs). [f. calm *a.* + -ness.] The state or quality of being calm; stillness, tranquillity, quietness.

a. *orig.* Absence of wind: now calm.

1516 Pynson *Life St. Birgette* 58 There arose anon suche a great calmenes that in a lytell smalle Bote they came..to londe. **1548** Udall, etc. *Erasm. Par.* Luke viii. 24 (R.) Immediately shall the tempeste be tourned into calmenesse.

b. Stillness of the sea or other surface of water, of the atmosphere, or general aspect of nature.

1580 Baret *Alv.* C 40 Calmenesse or quietnesse of the sea. **1719** De Foe *Crusoe* (1840) I. i. 9 The sea was returned to its ..settled calmness. **1860** Tyndall *Glac.* i. §16. 106 The calmness was perfect.

c. *transf.* and *fig.* Of the mind, feelings, or demeanour; of conditions and circumstances, etc.

1561 T. Norton *Calvin's Inst.* iv. ii. (1634) 513 The Church in calmenesse of time appeareth quiet and free. **1597** Hooker *Eccl. Pol.* v. lxii. §18 Calmness of speech. **1699** Luttrell *Brief Rel.* IV. 538 The dyet goes on with calmnesse. **1823** Lamb *Elia* (1860) 153 The Quakers go about their business..with more calmness than we. **1883** Lloyd *Ebb & Flow* II. 283 The almost rigid calmness of his features.

calm-stone, var. of cam-stone.

Calmuc(k, var. Kalmuck.

calmus, obs. form of calamus.

calmy ('kɑːmɪ), *a. poet. arch.* [f. calm *sb.* (or *a.*) + -y[1].]

1. Characterized by calm; tranquil, peaceful.

a. of the air, sea, etc.; of times and places.

1587 Churchyard *Worth. Wales* (1876) 107 When Calmie Skyes sayth bitter stormes are past. **1596** Spenser *F.Q.* ii. xii. 30 A still And calmy bay. **1598** Tofte *Alba* (1880) 130 A gentle calmie Winde. **1663** Cowley *Verses & Ess.* (1669) 17 That Sea, where she can hardly say, Sh' has known these twenty years one Calmy day. **1725** Pope *Odyss.* xv. 511 Six calmy days and six smooth nights. **1855** Singleton *Virgil* I. 335 All lies settled in the calmy sky.

b. *fig.* of thoughts, feelings, etc. (*rare.*)

1580 Sidney *Arcadia* (1622) 256 My calmie thoughts I fed On Natures sweete repast. *a***1649** Drummond Wks. (1711) 12 Sleep..Had..left me in a still and calmy mood.

2. Of or pertaining to the equatorial calms.

1818 Colebrooke *Import Colon. Corn* 156 Enabling them to hasten out of a calmy region.

†**calmy.** [cf. calmey.] ? Calamine.

1658 A. Fox *Wurtz' Surg.* ii. xxiii, Gray Calmy Stone.

‖'**calo.** *Obs. rare*[−1]. [L.] A camp-servant.

1617 S. Collins *Defence Bp. Ely* B iv b, A calo of that campe, but the meanest of many.

calo-, Gr. καλο- combining form of καλός beautiful: in some words interchanging with calli-.

calobash, calober, obs. ff. calabash, -ber.

†**calode'monial,** *a. Obs. nonce-wd.* Of or pertaining to beautiful or good spirits.

1522 Skelton *Why nat to Courte* 806 To his college conuenticall As well calo demonyall, As to caco demonyall.

'**calogram.** [f. Gr. κάλω-ς cable + -gram.] A suggested substitute for cablegram.

1868 *Let.* in *Daily News* 29 Sept., 'Cablegram'..is a mongrel and unsatisfactory term; instead of which, allow me to suggest one regularly and analogically formed—'Calogram', from the Greek word κάλως, a cable. **1879** *Ibid.* 14 Oct. 6/2, I would suggest that the word 'Calogram' be used in place of 'Cablegram'.

ca'lography. *rare*[−1]. In quot. kalo-. [f. calo- + -γραφία writing (not according to Greek precedents.] = calligraphy.

1804 Southey *Lett.* (1856) I. 296 An amateur of Gothic kalography. **1847** in Craig; and in mod. Dicts.

calomel ('kæləməl). Chiefly *Med.* Also 8 calamel. [In F. *calomel, calomélas*; according to Littré f. Gr. καλό-ς fair, beautiful + μέλας black.

Littré says 'so called, *it is said*, because the chemist who discovered it, saw a beautiful black powder change into a white powder in the preparation.' Chambers (*Cycl.* 1727–51) s.v. says 'The denomination *Calomel* rather seems to have first belonged to the Æthiops mineral; from καλος, *pulcher*, fair; and μελας, *niger*, black: for that white or pale bodies, rubbed herewith, become black. Some will have it first given to Mercurius dulcis, by a whimsical chymist, who employed a black in his laboratory; whose complexion, as well as that of the mercury, he alluded to in the term: the medicine being fair, the operator black.' Nothing appears as to when, where, or by whom the name was given: Littré calls it 'ancien nom'.]

Mercurous chloride, or 'protochloride' of mercury ($Hg_2 Cl_2$); a preparation much used in medicine in the form of a white powder with a yellow tinge, becoming grey on exposure to light; also found native as *horn-quicksilver* in crystals.

1676 Wiseman *Surg.* (J.) Lenient purgatives with calomel. **1727–51** Chambers *Cycl.*, *Calomel*, in pharmacy, a name given to Mercurius dulcis, further sublimated to a fourth time, or upwards. **1800** *Med. Jrnl.* IV. 410, I have been dissatisfied with the general and indiscriminate use of Calomel in the diseases of children. **1863** Kingsley *Water Bab.* v. (1878) 229 She dosed them with calomel and jalap. **1873** Watts *Fownes' Chem.* 402 Pure calomel is a heavy, white, insoluble, tasteless powder.

attrib. **1799** *Med. Jrnl.* I. 466 The calomel pill was given morning and evening.

calompniouse, obs. form of calumnious.

†**calo'phantic,** *a.* ? *nonce-wd.* [f. Gr. καλό-ς fair, excellent + -φαντης shower (f. φαίνειν to show) + -ic.] Pretending or making a show of excellence.

1602 Warner *Alb. Eng.* ix. liii. (1612) 238 In *Calophantick* Puritaines.

†**calor**[1], **-our.** *Obs.* [L. *calor.*] Heat, warmth.

1599 A. M. *Gabelhouer's Bk. Physic* 31/2 With a gentle & easye calor distille it. **1612** Woodall *Surg. Mate* Wks. (1653) 91 Of a moderate or temperate calour. *a***1618** Sylvester *Tobacco Battered* 517 (D.) The other drowns the Calor Naturall. **1656** Blount *Glossogr.*, *Calour.*

Calor[2] ('kælə(r)). [a. L. *calor* heat.] The proprietary name of liquefied gas (largely butane) supplied under pressure in containers for domestic use, etc.; usu. ***Calor gas.*** Also *attrib.*

1936 *Nature* 23 May 862/2 The manufacture of butane and isobutane in Great Britain has been undertaken by Imperial Chemical Industries, Ltd.,..and the gas is being marketed as 'Calor' gas. **1938** *Trade Marks Jrnl.* 8 June 699/1 *Calor*..Liquefied fuel gas. Calor-Gas (Distributing) Co. Ltd. **1938** 'G. Orwell' *Let.* 5 July (1968) I. 339 There is a Calor Gas Stove,..but there is also a little oil oven. **1948** *Times* 9 Jan. 2/3 Many people have to rely on calor gas for cooking and other essential purposes, particularly in rural areas. **1959** C. Fremlin *Uncle Paul* ii. 16 The Calor gas stove.

calorescence (kælə'rɛsəns). *Physics.* [f. L. *calor* heat; suggested by *calcescence*, *fluorescence.* (Etymologically, incorrect in form, and not expressing the fact to which it is applied.)] A name applied (Jan. 1865) by Prof. Tyndall to the change of non-luminous heat-rays into rays of higher refrangibility so as to become luminous. See also calcescence.

1865 Tyndall *Heat* xiii. (1870) §617 To express this transmutation of heat rays into others of higher refrangibility, I propose the term calorescence. **1869** —— *Notes Lect. Light* §248 In calorescence the atoms of the refractory body are caused to vibrate more rapidly than the waves which fall upon them; the periods of the waves are quickened by their impact on the atoms. The refrangibility of the rays is, in fact, exalted. **1881** *Nature* XXIV. 66 Akin gave the name of calcescence..but the term has been superseded by Tyndall's term calorescence, which is etymologically unfortunate, seeing that the Latin verb is *calesco*, not *caloresco.*

caloric (kə'lɒrɪk), *sb. Physics.* Also 8–9 -ique. [a. F. *calorique* (invented by Lavoisier), f. L. *calōrem* heat + *-ique* = -ic.]

1. The name given to a supposed elastic fluid, to which the phenomena of heat were formerly attributed. (Now generally abandoned, with the theory to which it belonged.)

[**1791** E. Darwin *Bot. Gard.* i. 8 *note*, This elastic matter of heat, termed Calorique in the new nomenclature of the French Academicians.] **1792** *Phil. Trans.* LXXXII. 88 The universally diffused caloric or matter of heat. **1801** *Month. Mag.* XII. 581 The laws of this *calorique* (or whatever it is to be called). **1826** J. Wilson *Noct. Ambr.* Wks. 1855 I. 84 Poor Vulcan has recently got A lingo that's almost historic And can tell you that iron is hot Because it is filled with caloric. **1834** Mrs. Somerville *Connex. Phys. Sc.* xxv. (1849) 238 The rays of caloric which produce the sensation of heat. **1864** Max Müller *Sc. Lang.* Ser. ii. xii. 579 Till very lately, Caloric was a term in constant use, and it was supposed to express some real matter.

2. Used simply for 'heat'; also *fig.*

1794 Pearson in *Phil. Trans.* LXXXIV. 386 Such a degree of caloric as was just sufficient to melt them. **1799** Southey *Nondescr.* iii. Wks. III. 63 A wretch..Who swells with calorique. **1870** Emerson *Soc. & Solit.*, *Eloquence* Wks. (Bohn) III. 24 The additional caloric of a multitude.

3. *Comb.* **caloric-engine**, the name given by Ericsson to his improved hot-air-engine.

1853 in *Proc. Amer. Phil. Soc.* V. 305 The experimental trial of the caloric-engine vessel. **1883** *Daily News* 10 Sept. 2/1 Two small caloric engines.

caloric (kə'lɒrɪk), *a.* [f. L. *calor* heat + -ic.] Of or pertaining to heat.

[**1853** (see caloric *sb.* 3)]. **1865** J. R. Mayer in W. R. Grove *Correl. Physical Forces* 275 The velocity of an asteroid when it strikes the sun measures from 445,750 to 630,400 metres; the caloric effect of the percussion is consequently equal to from 27½ to 55 millions of degrees of heat. **1896** F. W. Hume *Myst. Hansom Cab* (ed. 2) xxi. 198 To look at them merely was to increase one's caloric condition. **1925** T. Dreiser *Amer. Tragedy* i. viii. 69 Having acclimated himself to this caloric atmosphere. **1969** *Sci. Jrnl.* May 28/2 The animals were then dried to constant weight and combusted in a calorimeter to give caloric values.

ca'lorically, *adv. rare*[−1]. [f. an assumed adj. *calorical (f. caloric *sb.*) + -ly[2].] In the manner of heat, as heat.

1869 Baring-Gould *Orig. Relig. Belief* 176 In the sun it [Divine power] is gathered up and centred to act luminously, calorically, and attractively.

caloricity (kælə'rɪsɪtɪ). *Biol.* [f. caloric *sb.* + -ity: cf. F. *caloricité.*] The faculty in living

beings of developing heat so as to maintain nearly the same temperature at all times.
1836–9 TODD *Cycl. Anat.* II. 651/1 Caloricity or the power of evolving caloric.

caloriduct (kəˈlɒrɪdʌkt). [f. L. *calōr-em* heat + *dūct-us* conveyance, after *aqueduct*.] A tube or channel for conducting heat.
1864 in WEBSTER.

calorie (ˈkælərɪ). *Physics.* Also calory. [a. mod.F. *calorie*, arbitrarily f. L. *calor* heat.] A unit of heat or energy based on the specific heat of water; *esp.* **a.** The amount of heat required to raise the temperature of 1 kilogramme of water 1 degree centigrade; also used as a measure of the heat- or energy-producing value of food or for a quantity of food having this value; more fully ***great, kilogramme, large*** or ***major calorie***; also called *kilocalorie.* **b.** The amount of heat required to raise the temperature of 1 gramme of water 1 degree centigrade (see quot. 1963); more fully: ***gramme, lesser*** or ***small calorie.*** Also *attrib.*
The example in quot. 1821 corresponds in both sense and chronology to *caloric*, and is prob. due to a misreading or a misprint; the word has not been found in French before 1833 and was not in general English use before *c*1880.
[**1821** M. WILMOT *Let.* 21 June (1935) 116, I am writing to you, wrapped up in my rug cloak, with fur lined shoes to keep in an *atom* of *calorie*.] **1863** E. ATKINSON tr. *Ganot's Elem. Treat. Physics* IV. viii. 279 The unit chosen for comparison, and called the thermal unit, is not everywhere the same. In France it is the quantity of heat necessary to raise the temperature of one kilogramme of water through one degree centigrade: this is called a caloric [*corrected to* calorie *in ed. 2 (1866)*]. **1870** T. L. PHIPSON tr. *Guillemin's Sun* 37 The quantity of heat which is called a calorie is.. the amount required to raise 1 kilogramme of water 1° centigrade.. In England the.. calorie is sometimes stated to be the quantity required to raise 1 lb. of water from 60° to 61° Fahr., the equivalent of which in work is 722 foot-pounds. **1880** *Nature* XXI. 437 The amount of heat received from the sun is about twelve calories, per square metre, per minute. **1889** M. FOSTER *Text-bk. Physiol.* (ed. 5) II. 802 The following results expressed in calories, that is in gramme-degree units of heat. **1892** *Pall Mall Gaz.* 22 June 6/1 A pound of beefsteak contains.. 870 calories of energy. **1926** *Public Opinion* 13 Aug. 156/3 When the customary measure of calory value is applied to cake and bread, it is found that there is very little difference between these two staple foods. **1951** WODEHOUSE *Old Reliable* i. 9 A large, stout, elderly gentleman.. who looked like a Roman Emperor who had been doing himself too well on starchy foods and forgetting to watch his calories. **1957** J. I. M. STEWART *Use of Riches* 114 He had to admire an energy that didn't seem very substantially based on an intake of calories. **1963** JERRARD & MCNEILL *Dict. Scientific Units* 29 The energy represented by a calorie varies according to the temperature of the water, thus there was the International steam calorie (4·1868 joules), the 15° C calorie (4·1855 joules), the 4° C calorie (4·2045 joules), and the mean 0–100° C calorie (4·1897 joules). These differences were overcome when the calorie was replaced by the joule as the primary unit of heat in the metric system in 1950.

calorifacient (kəˌlɒrɪˈfeɪʃ(ɪ)ənt), *a.* *Phys.* [Formed as if from a L. *calōrifacient-em, pr. pple. of *calōrifacĕre (f. calōr-em + facĕre to make); but the true L. type was *calōrificāre: whence *calorify*, *calorifiant*, q.v.] Heat-producing.
1854 TODD & BOWMAN *Phys. Anat.* 263 in *Circ. Sc.* (1865) II. 21/2 Furnishing food to the calorifacient process. **1867** *Pall Mall G.* 19 July 16 The purely starchy or calorifacient group [of foods].

calorifiant (kəˈlɒrɪˌfaɪənt), *a.* [a. mod.F. *calorifiant*, pr. pple. of **calorifier*, repr. L. type **calōrificāre*, f. *calor* heat: see -FY.] = prec.
1860 WORCESTER cites THOMPSON; in mod. Dicts.

calorific (kæləˈrɪfɪk), *a.* *Physics.* [a. F. *calorifique*:—L. *calōrific-us* heat-making: see -FIC.]
1. Producing heat. Esp. in ***calorific value*** (see quot. 1904).
1682 GREW *Anat. Plants* (J.) A calorifick principle is either excited within the heated body, or transferred to it. **1686** GOAD *Celest. Bodies* II. ii. 161 Luminous and Calorifique Bodies. **1861** H. MACMILLAN *Footn. Page Nat.* 197 The sunbeam.. divided into actinic, luminous and calorific rays. **1869** TYNDALL *Notes Lect. Light* §246 The non-luminous calorific rays may be thus transformed into luminous ones. **1904** GOODCHILD & TWENEY *Technol. & Sci. Dict.* 81/2 *Calorific value*, the measure of the amount of heat obtainable from a given weight of fuel. **1950** *Ann. Reg. 1949* 465 Adjustments were made to coal prices in pursuance of the policy of making prices reflect relative calorific values.
2. *loosely.* Of or pertaining to heat; thermal.
1812 SIR H. DAVY *Chem. Philos.* 67 Active powers, such as gravitation, cohesion, calorific repulsion or heat. **1860** TYNDALL *Glac.* I. §22. 151 To make good the calorific waste.

†**caloˈrifical**, *a.* *Obs.* [f. as prec. + -AL[1].] = prec.
1620 VENNER *Via Recta* iv. 80 By reason of their moist and calorificall nature. **1635** SWAN *Spec. M.* v. §2 (1643) 149 Dew.. is of a calorificall nature.

caloˈrifically, *adv.* [f. prec. + -LY[2].] By way of heating, by means of heat.
1880 *Contemp. Rev.* Mar. 380 If the land be acted upon calorifically.

calorification (kəˌlɒrɪfɪˈkeɪʃən). *Phys.* [a. F. *calorification*, n. of action f. L. type **calōrificāre*: see CALORIFIANT.] The production of heat, *esp.* in living animal bodies.
1836 TODD *Cycl. Anat.* I. 804/2 Calorification is not the only function that may survive.. death. **1859** *Ibid.* V. 471/2 All the phenomena of excess of.. calorification.

caloriˈficient, *a.* [An utterly erroneous form.] = CALORIFACIENT.
In mod. Dicts.

calorifier (kəˈlɒrɪfaɪə(r)). [f. CALORIFY + -ER[1].] A name of an apparatus for heating air.
1881 *Daily News* 20 Oct. 2/3 In winter these fans will drive a current of air over 'calorifiers' into the courts.

calorify (kəˈlɒrɪfaɪ), *v.* [f. L. *calōr-em* heat + -FY, repr. L. type **calōrificāre*: cf. CALORIFIANT.] *trans.* To make hot. (In quot. only *humorous.*)
1841 *Fraser's Mag.* XXIII. 219 Feeling myself then somewhat calorified, I took off my wig.

calorimeter (kæləˈrɪmɪtə(r)). [f. L. *calōr-em* heat + -METER, Gr. μέτρον measure.] An instrument for measuring actual quantities of heat, or the specific heat of bodies.
1794 G. ADAMS *Nat. & Exp. Philos.* I. viii. 321 Calorimeter, or apparatus for measuring the relative quantities of fire in bodies. **1810** HENRY *Elem. Chem.* (1826) I. 109 Lavoisier ascertained that equal weights of different combustible bodies melt, by burning, very different weights of ice. The apparatus which he employed.. he has called the calorimeter. **1881** HILL in *Metal World* No. 22. 342 Two distinct forms of calorimeter have been used, one the continuous calorimeter.. the other the intermittent calorimeter.

calorimetric (kəˌlɒrɪˈmɛtrɪk), *a.* [f. prec. + -IC.] Of or pertaining to calorimetry; also loosely used for: pertaining to the measurement of temperature, thermometric. So **caˌloriˈmetrical** *a.*
1864 in WEBSTER. **1876** tr. *Wagner's Gen. Pathol.* 655 Exact calorimetric investigations. **1880** *Nature* XXI. 273 To obtain the temperature.. by a well-known calorimetric method. **1875** H. WOOD *Therap.* (1879) 121 Various calorimetrical experiments.

calorimetry (kæləˈrɪmɪtrɪ). [f. L. *calōr-em* heat + Gr. -μετρία measurement.] The measurement of heat.
1858 LARDNER *Nat. Phil.* iv. (*title*) Calorimetry. **1871** MAXWELL *Th. Heat* (1877) 9 The method of measuring heat may be called Calorimetry. **1882** WATTS *Dict. Chem.* III. 18 The measurement of temperature, or thermometry, is.. a preliminary to the measurement of heat, or calorimetry.

calorimotor (kəˌlɒrɪˈməʊtə(r)). [f. L. *calōr-em* heat + *mōtor* mover.] 'A voltaic arrangement consisting of one pair or a few pairs of very large plates, used chiefly for producing considerable heat effects' (Watts *Dict. Chem.* I. 723).
1832 *Nat. Philos.* II. *Galvan.* ii. §8 (U.K.S.) The first battery of this kind.. constructed by Dr. Hare, professor of chemistry in Philadelphia, and called by him a Calorimotor, from its remarkable power of producing heat.

calorist (ˈkælərɪst). *rare.* [f. CALOR-IC + -IST.] One who held that heat or caloric was a material substance. Hence **caloˈristic** *a.*
1864 *N. Brit. Rev.* Feb. 43 Any able Calorist.. maintaining the materiality of heat. *Ibid.* 6 The Caloristic idea [of radiant heat] seems to have been exactly analogous to the Corpuscular Theory of Light.

calorizing (ˈkælərаɪzɪŋ), *vbl. sb.* [f. L. *calor* heat: see -IZE.] The coating (of a metal) with aluminium by a process involving heat.
1930 *Engineering* 27 June 819/2 In cases where surface treatment is applied, e.g. calorising, whereby concentric zones of modified metal are produced. **1940** *Chambers's Techn. Dict.* 128/2 *Calorising*, a process of rendering the surface of steel or iron resistant to oxidation by spraying the surface with aluminium and heating to a temperature of 800° to 1000° C.

†**caˈlorous**, *a.* *Obs. rare.* [f. L. *calōr-em* heat + -OUS; cf. F. *chaleureux*.] Warm.
1737 OZELL *Rabelais* V. 232 Our outward Man wants something that's calorous.

calot, var. of CALLET. *Obs.*

calotte (kəˈlɒt). Forms: 7 **calot, callott(e, callote,** 7–8 **callot,** 9 **calotte.** [a. F. *calotte*, according to Littré, dim. of *cale* caul.]
1. A plain skull-cap; now *esp.* that worn by Roman Catholic ecclesiastics, etc.; formerly also the coif of a serjeant-at-law.
16.. *Songs Costume* (1849) 135 Then calot leather-cap strongly pleads. **1632** B. JONSON *Magn. Lady* I. vii. 68 The wearing the Callott; the politique hood. **1656** J. HARRINGTON *Oceana* (1700) 214 They wore black velvet Calots. **1670** LASSELS *Voy. Italy* II. 388 An ordinary callotte (or cap which we wear under our hats). **1776** PENNANT *Tours Scotl.* II. 243 A head of Cardinal Beaton, black hair, smooth face, a red callot. **1875** *Ceremonial Cath. Ch. U.S.* 137 Should any wear the calotte, it is taken off also when a genuflection is made; when the deacon sings the Gospel.
2. A cap-like set of feathers on a bird's head.
1874 COUES *Birds N.-W.* 616 Occiput subcrested.. forming a calotte of brownish-black.
‖**3.** Any thing having the form of a small cap; the cap of a sword-hilt; the cap of a pistol, etc. (Chiefly Fr. uses, but occas. used in Eng.)
1886 *Times* 3 Mar. 9/5 If.. the spherical *calotte* of the German system were put out of shape during the firing, it is doubtful whether the firing could be continued with the same precision. **1945** *Electronic Engin.* XVII. 326/2 The sensitiveness of this arrangement at low pressures may be materially improved by attaching a quartz calotte of a few μ thicknesses to the two quartz fibres where they are fused together.
‖**4.** *Arch.* (See quot.)
1727–51 in CHAMBERS *Cycl.* **1876** GWILT *Archit.* Gloss., *Calotte*, a concavity in the form of a cup or niche, lathed and plastered, serving to diminish the height of a chapel, alcove, or cabinet, which otherwise would appear too high for the breadth.
‖**5.** Any segment of a sphere, especially the smaller of two unequal segments. (A French sense; but given in some Eng. Dicts.)
6. An ice- or snow-cap.
1894 J. W. GREGORY in *Q. Jrnl. Geol. Soc.* L. 515 A 'calotte' or snow-cap, similar to those on Kibo.. and Chimborazo. **1957** COLLOMB *Dict. Mountaineering* 38 *Calotte*, a crest, tip or pyramid of snow which caps the summit of a mountain. The *calotte* of Mont Blanc is best known.

calotype (ˈkælətaɪp), *sb.* *Photography.* [f. Gr. καλός beautiful + τύπος type.] The name given by Fox Talbot to the process of producing photographs, invented by him in 1841, sometimes also called *Talbotype.* The picture was produced by the action of light upon silver iodide, the latent image being subsequently developed and fixed by hyposulphite of soda. Also *attrib.*, as in ***calotype process, picture,*** etc.
1841 FOX TALBOT *Specif. Patent* No. 8842. 3 The paper thus prepared, and which I term 'calotype paper', is placed in a camera. **1845** *Athenæum* 22 Feb. 202 The sharpness of the outline of the Calotype pictures is.. inferior to that of the Daguerreotypes. **1881** *Times* 4 Jan. 3/5 Calotype, or the waxed paper process, with its development by means of silver, superseded the daguerreotype, in which the image was developed by mercury vapour; and, again, calotype.. was ousted.. by Archer's collodion process, in which the paper picture gave way to.. glass and a substratum of collodion.
Hence **caloˈtypic** *a.*, **ˈcaloˌtypist.**
1854 SCOFFERN in *Orr's Circ. Sc.* Chem. 88 Paper suitable for taking Calotypic impressions. **1855** BROWNING *Mesmerism* ix, I imprint her fast On the void at last As the sun does whom he will By the calotypist's skill.

ˈcalotype, *v.* [f. prec. sb.; cf. *to photograph.*] *trans.* To represent or imprint by the calotype process; to photograph.
1853 *Blackw. Mag.* LXXIV. 754 Presenting the mind to it in a state of repose.. a blank sheet of paper, upon which the object may reflect or calotype itself. *a* **1879** M. COLLINS in *Pen Sk.* I. cxciv, Who could calotype Amy's laugh?

calouh, calouwe, obs. forms of CALLOW.

‖**caloyer** (kaloje). Also 7 **coloiero, caloiro, caloieri, caloier, caloire,** 9 **kaloyeri.** [a. F. *caloyer*, ad. It. *caloiero* (pl. *-ieri*), ad. late Gr. καλόγηρος, f. καλός beautiful + γηρο-, -γηρος in comb. old, aged, i.e. 'good in old age, venerable'. The It. *caloiero*, whence Fr. and Eng. immediately come, has *i* for palatal γ (= *y* cons.). The accentuation is shown in Byron quots.]
A Greek monk, *esp.* of the order of St. Basil.
1615 G. SANDYS *Trav.* 82 This mountaine is only inhabited by Grecian Monks whom they call Coloieros, vninterrmixed with the Laity. **1635** PAGITT *Christianogr.* I. ii. (1636) 47 Dedicated in honor of St. Basil, to the Greeke Caloiers. **1676** F. VERNON in *Phil. Trans.* XI. 582 Now there is a Convent of Caloieri's there. **1682** WHELER *Journ. Greece* II. 194 His usual Habit differeth not from the ordinary Caloyers, or Monks of the Order of St. Basil. *Ibid.* VI. 450 They consist of above a hundred Caloiroes. *Ibid.* 479 Here is also a Convent of Caloires, or Greekish Monks. **1812** BYRON *Ch. Har.* II. xlix, The convent's white walls glisten fair on high. Here dwells the caloyer, nor rude is he, Nor niggard of his cheer. **1813** —— *Giaour* 786 How name ye yon lone Caloyer? **1884** W. CARR *Montenegro* 29 The Vladika, the black caloyer of the Czernagora.

calp (kælp). *Min.* [See quot. 1862; mod.F. has also *calp.*] Local name of a species of dark-grey limestone occurring in Central Ireland.
1784 KIRWAN *Min.* (ed. 2) I. 233 Calp, or black quarry stone of Dublin. Colour, bluish black, or dark greyish blue, variously intersected with veins of white calcareous spar, and often invested with the same. **1803** *Ann. Rev.* I. 872/2 The calp quarries are situated in the neighbourhood of Lucan. **1862** JUKES *Stud. Man. Geol.* 512 This.. has been called Calp from a local term signifying black shale.

‖**calpac, calpack** (ˈkælpæk). Also **kalpack.** [Turkī *qalpāq* or *qālpāq*.] A felt cap of triangular form, worn by Turkīs, Tartars, etc.; also an oriental cap generally.
1813 BYRON *Giaour* 716 'Tis Hassan's cloven crest! His calpac rent. *Note,* The calpac is the solid cap or centre part of the head-dress; the shawl is would round it, and forms the

turban. **1835** WILLIS *Pencillings* II. xlvii. 71 The old trader, setting his huge calpack firmly on his shaven head. **1871** *Daily News* 10 Feb., The.. Persian Ambassador.. wearing his fur kalpack.

Hence 'calpacked *ppl. a.*, Wearing a calpack.
1852 WILLIS *Summer Cruise Medit.* xxxvii. 223 Calpacked and rosy Armenians.

calque (kælk). *Philol.* [Fr., lit. 'copy', f. *calquer* to trace (a design, etc.), ad. It. *calcare*, ad. L. *calcāre* to tread.] A loan-translation (see LOAN *sb.*[1]). Also as vb.
1937 *Amer. Speech* XII. 44 The speaker begins saying things in one form only, instead of using two forms which are almost exact *calques* of each other. **1941** C. T. ONIONS in *Medium Ævum* X. 160 The possibility of a direct 'calque' on a Norse **wrabba ok wrægja* should perhaps not be ruled out. **1957** G. V. SMITHERS *Kyng Alisaunder* II. 81 *Fecche mood*.. is evidently a calque on OF. *porter ire*, as in *Chanson de Roland*. **1958** A. S. C. ROSS *Etym.* 34 MnE *that goes without saying* is a translation-loan of (better, is calqued on) MnFrench *cela va sans dire*.

calque, variant of CALK *v.*

calsay, calsey, calsway: see CAUSEWAY.

calsomine, var. CALCIMINE, KALSOMINE.

calsoun, var. of CALZOON.

calstock, obs. f. KALE-STOCK, and CASTOCK (*casto'*), cabbage-stock.

calsydoyne, obs. f. CHALCEDONY.

||**caltha** ('kælθə). *Bot.* [L.] The Marsh Marigold; also the genus to which it belongs.
1599 CUTWODE *Caltha Poet.* lxii, To buz of Caltha now the Bee was bold.. For now no more he cals her Marygold, But newes from Lady Caltha he is bringing. **1718** PRIOR *Poems* 400 Wanting the Sun, why does the Caltha fade? **1882** *Garden* 10 June 404/3 The richly coloured double yellow Caltha.

calthrate (Cockeram), erroneous f. CLATHRATE.

caltrop ('kæltrɒp), **caltrap.** Forms: 1 (?) **coltetræppe, calcatrippe,** 3 **calketrap,** 3–5 **calketrappe,** 4 **calketreppe, kalketrappe;** 5 **calletrappe,** 5–6 **caltrappe,** 6 **caltrope, -troppe, -throppe, calltrop, calteroope,** 7 **calthrap,** (6 **galtrope, -troppe,** 7 **galtrap, -trop, -throp(e, gall-trappe, -throp,** 7–8 **gall-trap);** 7–9 **calthrop,** (5, 9 **calthorp),** 5– **caltrap,** 6– **caltrop.** [ME. *calke-, kalketrappe*, occurring in senses 1 and 3; OE. *coltetræppe* (? *colcetreppe*), *calcatrippe*, sense 3; corresp. to OF. *kauketrape*, *cauchetrepe* (*caudetrepe*) Godefroy, in sense 3, later *chauche-trape*, *chauces-trappes*, *chausse-trape* Littré (senses 1, 2, 3), which point back to an orig. *caulke-*, *caulce-trape*, cf. obs. It. *calcatrippa*, sense 3; these forms indicate a L. type **calcatrap(p)a* or **calcitrap(p)a* (the latter is in mod. botanical L.), app. f. *calc-em* heel + *trappa* trap, gin, snare (a. OHG. *trapo* trap, gin, noose); but perhaps in *calcatrappa* there was an association with *calcāre* to trample, tread. All the earliest examples are in sense 3; but it seems much more likely that the name should have been first used literally, and then transferred to plants. The mod.Eng. and Fr. sense 'star-thistle' is clearly transferred from 2. As a plant-name the word appeared (from med.L.) already in late OE.; sense 2 was probably adopted from French. *Galltrap*, frequent in 16–17th c., is an evident popular etymology referring to the *galling* of horses' feet.]

†**1.** A trap, gin, or snare, to catch the feet of beasts, of horses or men in war, and the like. *Obs.* (Still in Fr. in sense 'wolf-trap'.)
(Quots. *c* 1300 and 1393 lead on to sense 2.)
a **1300** *Gloss. Neckam's Treat.* in Wright *Voc.* 111 *Pedicam sive desciplulam, qua lupi capiantur, gloss.* calketrap. *c* **1300** *K. Alis.* 6070 They haden.. calketrappen maden ynowe, In weyes undur wode and bowe, Alisaundris men to aqwelle. **1340** *Ayenb.* 131 þise wordle þet ne is bote.. a forest uol of þyeues an of calketreppen and of grines. **1393** LANGL. *P. Pl.* C. XXI. 296 With crokes and with Kalketrappes a-cloye we hem echone. *c* **1440** *Promp. Parv.* 59 Caltrap of yryn, fote hurtynge, *hamus*. **1850** LEITCH *Müller's Anc. Art* §391, *note* 9 Psyche maltreated by Eros, singed as a butterfly.. caught in a caltrop.

2. a. *Mil.* An iron ball armed with four sharp prongs or spikes, placed like the angles of a tetrahedron, so that when thrown on the ground it has always one spike projecting upwards: Used to obstruct the advance of cavalry, etc.
1519 HORMAN *Vulg.* 266 b, They hydde pretely vnder the grounde caltroppys of yron to steke in horse or mennys fete. **1577** HOLINSHED *Chron.* II. 57/1 The Irishmen had strawed all alongest the shore a great number of caltrops of iron, with sharpe pricks standing vp, to wound the Danes in the feet. **1581** MARBECK *Bk. of Notes* 164 They did cast from them their Caltropes, which pricked their horses in the feete so sore, that down came the Chariots, horsemen and all. **1611** SPEED *Hist. Gt. Brit.* IX. xiv. (1632) 777 The murtherers to preuent pursuit, strewed galthrops behinde them. **1622** F. MARKHAM *Bk. War* III. ix. 114 Foards are soon choakt up by Calthropes. *a* **1626** FLETCHER *Love's Pilgr.* I. i, I think they ha' strewed the High-wayes with caltraps, No horse dare's pass 'em. **1659** HAMMOND *Paraphr. Matt.* xi. 6 Sharp stakes or other instruments to wound or gall the passengers, which are known by the name of Gall-trappes. **1816** SCOTT *Antiq.* iii, Ancient calthrops.. dispersed by Bruce to lacerate the feet of the English chargers. **1858** O. W. HOLMES *Aut. Breakf. T.* (1883) 255 One of those small *calthrops* our grandfathers used to sow round in the grass when there were Indians about,—iron stars.

b. *fig.*
a **1555** RIDLEY *Wks.* 368 The devil's galtropes that he casteth in our ways by some of his busyheaded younkers. **1607** DEKKER *Wh. Babylon* Wks. 1873 II. 224 If euer I come backe Ile be a Calthrop To pricke my countries feet, that tread on me. **1876** J. WEISS *Wit, Hum. & Shaks.* ii. 57 So he is a caltrop in men's path, with a spike always uppermost to impale the over-hasty feet.

†**c.** *attrib.*, as in *caltrop-thistle, -grass.*
1597 GERARD *Herbal* I. xiv. 18 Wee may call it in English, Round headed Caltrope Grasse. **1603** HOLLAND *Plutarch's Mor.* 59 With Calthrap-thistles rough and keen.

d. *Her.* A representation of a military caltrop in a coat of arms. (Now always spelt *caltrap*.)
1680 G. MACKENZIE *Sci. Herauldry* 95 The Earl of *Pearth*.. hath for his Compartment, a Galtrap used in Warr. **1716** S. KENT *Gram. Heraldry* s.v. *Trap of Gloucestershire*, The Field is Argent, three Cheval-Traps (or Caltrops) Sable. **1847** *Gloss. Heraldry* 76 Cheval-trap, sometimes called *Caltrap*, or *Galtrap*, and (chiefly by French heralds) *Chausse-trap*: an instrument thrown upon the ground to injure the feet of horses, and consisting of four iron spikes, one of which is ever uppermost. **1969** FRANKLYN & TANNER *Encycl. Dict. Heraldry* 340/1 Or, three caltraps gules. *Bellwood*.

3. *Herb.* **a.** Now usually *Caltrops*: A name given to various plants that catch or entangle the feet, or suggest the instrument described in 2. Applied in OE. to brambles or buckthorn, and apparently to Eryngo or Sea-holly; by 16th c. herbalists to Star-thistle (*Centaurea Calcitrapa*) from its round head garnished with long radiant spines; also by translators to the spiny-seeded *Tribulus terrestris* (**land caltrops**) of Southern Europe. **b. water caltrops**, a name for *Potamogeton densus* and *P. crispus*, which tend to entangle swimmers; also from its resemblance to the instrument (sense 2) for the seed of *Trapa natans* of Southern Europe.
c **1000** *Ags. Voc.* in Wr.-Wülcker 269 *Ramnus*, coltetræppe, þefanðorn. *a* **1100** *Ibid.* 298 *Heraclea*, calca-trippe. *c* **1265** *Ibid.* 557 *Tribulus marinus*, calketrappe, seaþistel. *a* **1387** *Sinon. Barthol.* in *Anecd. Oxon.* 37 *Saliunca*, wilde popi (*marg.* calketrappe). *c* **1440** *Promp. Parv.* 58 Caltrap, herbe, *saliunca*. **1578** LYTE *Dodoens* IV. lix. 521 This herbe is now called in.. English, Starre Thistel, or Caltrop. **1597** GERARD *Herbal* II. ccxcviii. 825 Most do call the fruit of this caltrops *castaneæ aquatiles* [= F. *châtaigne d'eau*, fruit of *Trapa natans*]. **1611** COTGR., s.v. *Achantique*.. Calthrop, or Star-thistle. **1671** SALMON *Syn. Med.* III. xxii. 437 Tribulus Τρίβολος Caltrop, abates inflamations. **1727** BRADLEY *Fam. Dict.* s.v., Land Caltrop.. the Seeds are inclosed in a Fruit that is furnish'd with several Prickles, and resembles the Cross of Malta. **1855** SINGLETON *Virgil* I. 80 Succeeds a prickly wood And burrs and caltrops. **1866** *Treas. Bot.* s.v. *Trapa*, The very singular four-horned fruits of the European species of *Trapa* (*T. natans*).. have been compared to the spiked iron instruments called caltrops.. growing in water, it is commonly called the Water Caltrops.

4. In the nomenclature of the spicular elements of sponges, a tetraxial spicule with four equal arms radiating from a central point, so called from its resemblance to a caltrop (sense 2).
1887 SOLLAS in *Encycl. Brit.* XXII. 416/2 Tetraxon Quadriradiate Type (Calthrops). **1940** L. H. HYMAN *Invertebrates* I. vi. 337 The typical spicule of the simpler tetractinellids is the calthrops, or tetraxon with four approximately equal rays.

†**'caltrop,** *v.* *Obs.*[—0] In 5 **caltrappyn.** [f. the sb.] *trans.* To catch or trap with a caltrop.
c **1440** *Promp. Parv.* 59 Caltrappyn, *hamo*.

calubur, obs. form of CALABER.

calumba (kə'lʌmbə). *Med.* Formerly also **calomba, calumbo, -ombo, columba, -umbo, -ombo.** [f. *Colombo*, in Ceylon. 'So called from a false impression that it was supplied from thence' (M. T. Masters in *Treas. Bot.* 636).]
The root of *Jateorhiza palmata* (or *Coccolus palmatus*) N.O. *Menospermaceæ*, a plant indigenous to the forests of Mozambique, used in medicine as a mild tonic and stomachic.
1811 HOOPER *Med. Dict.*, *Columbo*.. the root formerly so called is now termed Calumba in the London pharmacopœia.. As an antiseptic, Calumba root is inferior to the bark. **1876** HARLEY *Mat. Med.* 724 Calumba is indigenous to the forests of Eastern Africa, where it climbs to the tops of the loftiest trees. **1883** *Cassell's Fam. Mag.* Aug. 555/2 Take some of the milder bitter tonics—infusion of calumba, for instance.

Hence **ca'lumbin** [see -IN], **ca'lumbic acid** [see -IC], bitter substances found in calumba root.
1837 *Penny Cycl.* VII. 306/2 The active principle Calumbine.. may be obtained either by alcohol or æther. **1876** HARLEY *Mat. Med.* 725 Calumbin is the principal constituent. *Ibid.* Calumbic acid is a yellow amorphous substance.

calumet ('kæljʊmɪt). [a. F. *calumet* (Norman form of *chalumet*), given by the French in Canada to plants of which the stems serve as pipe-tubes, and to the Indian pipe. A parallel form to *chalumeau*, in OF. *chalemel* = Pr. *calamel*:—L. *calamellus*, dim. of *calamus* reed. The *u* in *chalumeau* began in the 16th c., and *chalumet, calumet*, was evidently modelled on it in the 17th c.
Charlevoix (1721) says 'Le calumet est un mot Normand, qui veut dire *chalumeau*, et est proprement le tuyau d'une pipe.']

A tobacco-pipe with a bowl of clay or stone, and a long reed stem carved and ornamented with feathers. It is used among the American Indians as a symbol of peace or friendship. To accept the calumet is to welcome terms of peace offered, to refuse it is to reject them.
[**1638** *Jesuit Relations* 35 Jamais ils ne tirent aucune conclusion que le calumet a la bouche. **1673** MARQUETTE *Voy. Mississippi* (*Recit. des Voy. en* 1673, ed. Lenox 54) Il y a un calumet pour la paix, et un pour la guerre.] **1717** *Atlas Geogr.* V. 780 They send 5, 10, or 20 Warriors to the Enemy, with the great Calumet of Peace... This Calumet is only a Tobacco-Pipe described by La Hontan, etc. **1754** *World* II. No. 102. 264 The French desired to smoak the calumet of peace. **1778** ROBERTSON *Amer.* I. IV. 393 The ambassadors present the calumet or emblem of peace. **1841** CATLIN *N. Amer. Ind.* (1844) I. xxix. 235 The calumet or pipe of peace.. is a sacred pipe and never allowed to be used on any other occasion than that of peace-making. **1849** THACKERAY in *Scribner's Mag.* (1887) I. 552/2, I wanted to have gone to smoke a last calumet at.. Portman Street. **1855** LONGF. *Hiaw.* I, Smoke the calumet together, And as brothers live henceforward!

†**calumner.** *Obs.* [irreg. f. CALUMNY *sb.* (cf. *astronom-er*). See CALUMNIER.] A calumniator.
1614 LODGE *Seneca, Life* vi, Senecas calumners, saith he, accuse him of diuers crimes. **1675** J. SMITH *Chr. Relig. Appeal* II. 38 (L.) The calumners of Lysimachus.

calumniate (kə'lʌmnɪeɪt), *v.* [f. L. *calumniāt-* ppl. stem of *calumniāri*; see -ATE[3]. Cf. 16th c. Fr. *calomnier*.]
1. *trans.* To asperse with calumny, utter calumny regarding; to accuse or charge falsely and maliciously with something criminal or disreputable; to slander.
1554 BP. HOOPER in Strype *Eccl. Mem.* III. App. xxiv. 67 So that hatred unto the trewth dyd alwayse falsly reporte and calumniate all godly mens doinges. **1611** BIBLE *Pref.* 2 *marg.*, The highest personages have been calumniated. **1620** N. BRENT tr. *Sarpi's Hist. Council Trent* (1676) 480 Mantua was.. calumniated to be ill affected. **1718** *Free-thinker* No. 2. 12 He was never heard to Calumniate his Adversary for want of Argument. **1837** WHEWELL *Hist. Induct. Sc.* (1857) I. 309 We must not calumniate even the Inquisition.
b. *intr.* (*absol.*) To utter calumnies.
1606 SHAKS. *Tr. & Cr.* V. ii. 124 Deceptious functions Created onely to calumniate. **1699** BENTLEY *Phal.* Pref. 27 The Editor and his Witnesses may calumniate as they please.
†**2.** To charge (a thing) calumniously *against* a person. *Obs. rare.*
1648 *Eikon Bas.* xii. 95, I thought, that.. the gaining of that respite could not be so much to the Rebels advantages (which some haue highly calumniated against me).

calumniated (kə'lʌmnɪeɪtɪd), *ppl. a.* [f. prec. + -ED.] Aspersed with calumny, slandered.
1793 W. ROBERTS *Looker-on* No. 67 The calumniated, like a city taken by night, are slain in their sleep. **1828** D'ISRAELI *Chas. I*, I. xii. 331 It requires.. more zeal to defend the calumniated than care to raise the calumny. **1848** MACAULAY *Hist. Eng.* II. 216 The calumniated Latitudinarians.

calumniating (kə'lʌmnɪeɪtɪŋ), *vbl. sb.* [f. as prec. + -ING.[1]] The action of slandering or defaming. (Now gerundial.)
1659 *Gentl. Call.* (1696) 7 A wronging, a calumniating even of the very Devil. **1855** MACAULAY *Hist.* III. 24 Calumniating and ridiculing the Church which he had deserted.

ca'lumniating, *ppl. a.* [f. as prec. + -ING.[2]] That calumniates, slandering.
1606 SHAKS. *Tr. & Cr.* III. iii. 174 Loue, friendship, charity, are subjects all To enuious and calumniating time. **1711** *Brit. Apollo* III. No. 154. 3/1 Calumniating Tongues.

calumniation (kəˌlʌmnɪ'eɪʃən). [n. of action f. CALUMNIATE. Cf. F. *calomniation* (14th c.)]
1. The action of calumniating; slandering; malicious detraction.
1548 HOOPER *Decl. 10 Commandm.* Pref., Clear and free from misconstruing and calumniation of such sycophants, etc. **1603** KNOLLES *Hist. Turks* (1621) 1051 By the calumniation of the envious. **1726** AYLIFFE *Parerg.* 25 Calumniation.. a Malicious and False Representation of an Enemys Words or Actions for an Offensive Purpose.
2. A libellous report, a slander, a calumny.
1588 *Let.* in *Harl. Misc.* (1809) II. 67 With many more such matters (which I nevertheless count to be very vain calumniations). **1601** HOLLAND *Pliny* II. 483 A notable calumniation framed against him. **1755** CARTE *Hist. Eng.* IV. 184 By their calumniations against his majesty.

calumniator (kə'lʌmnɪeɪtə(r)). In 7 also **-er, -our.** [a. L. *calumniātor*, n. of agent f. *calumniāri*; see CALUMNIATE and -OR. Cf. 16th c. F.

calomniateur.] One who calumniates; a slanderer.

1549 *Compl. Scot.* iv. 31 The peruerst opinions of inuyful calumniaturis ande of secret detrackers. *a* **1563** BECON *New Catech.* IV. (1844) 185 Satan..is called 'the tempter', 'the calumniator or quarrel-picker', and 'the accuser of the brethren'. **1663** COWLEY *Verses & Ess.* (1669) 85 The Calumniators of Epicurus his Philosophy. **1848** MACAULAY *Hist. Eng.* II. 148 To appoint, as his successor, his rival and calumniator, Tyrconnel.

calumniatory (kə'lʌmnɪəˌtərɪ), *a.* [f. L. type **calumniātōri-us*, f. *calumniātor*: see -ORY.] Slanderous, calumnious.

1625 BP. MOUNTAGU *App. Cæsar* 17 Your selves have related it in your calumniatory Information. **1836** *Random Recoll. Ho. of Lords* xv. 366 Never did personality, or anything calumniatory of an opponent escape his lips.

†**ca'lumnier.** *Obs. rare*⁻¹. = CALUMNIATOR.

1586 WHETSTONE *Eng. Mirr.* 165 Yea these calumniers and lybellers..slaunder their owne knowledge.

†**'calumning,** *vbl. sb. Obs. rare*⁻¹. [irreg. var. *calumnying*: cf. *calumner*.] Calumniating.

1541 WYATT *Let. Privy Council* 248 Touching the Bishop of London and Haynes' calumning in this matter.

calumnious (kə'lʌmnɪəs), *a.* Also 5 calomp-, 6 calumpniouse. [ad. L. *calumniōsus*, f. *calumnia*: see CALUMNY *sb.* and -OUS. But perh. Caxton took it immediately from a 15th c. F. *calompnieux*, *-euse* (though Littré has it only from 16th c.).] Characterized by calumny; of the nature of calumny or of a calumniator; slanderous, defamatory.

1490 CAXTON *Eneydos* xxvii. 98 Dydo seeng the first openyng of the daye sore besi to chasse the tenebres calompniouse away. **1508** FISHER *Sev. Penit. Ps.* Wks. 266 This calumnyous vyce of enuy. **1601** SHAKS. *All's Well* I. iii. 61 A foule mouth'd and calumnious knaue. **1667** MILTON *P.L.* v. 770 With calumnious Art Of counterfeted truth. **1711** STEELE *Spect.* No. 151 ¶7 He has been..unmercifully calumnious at such a Time. **1855** MACAULAY *Hist. Eng.* IV. 225 It might be true that a calumnious fable had done much to bring about the Revolution. **1871** MORLEY *Voltaire* (1886) 99 A calumnious journalist.

Hence **ca'lumniously** *adv.*, **ca'lumniousness**.

1625 BP. MOUNTAGU *App. Cæsar* 26 Dealing..so insincerely and calumniously. **1652** GAULE *Magastrom.* 350 [She] most calumniously charged the vertuous Queen with her own sorcerous act. **1633** BP. MORTON *Discharge Imputat.* 159 (R.) The bitterness of my stile was plainness, not calumniousness.

†**'calumnize,** *v. Obs.* [ad. med.L. *calum(p)nizā-re* or 15–16th c. F. *calompnise-r*; f. L. *calumnia*: see -IZE.] *trans.* To calumniate.

1606 WARNER *Alb. Eng.* XV. xcviii. 388 Saints, vnsanctified, that also sturre the State, Calumnize Church, our Liturgie, and Rites in criticke rate. **1636** HEYWOOD *Challenge* IV. i. Wks. 1874 V. 54, I have callumnis'd Your fame. *a* **1723** D'URFEY *Athen. Jilt* (D.) Rather than calumnize the king.

calumny ('kæləmnɪ), *sb.* [ad. L. *calumnia* and F. *calomnie* (15th c. in Littré).]

1. False and malicious misrepresentation of the words or actions of others, calculated to injure their reputation; libellous detraction, slander.

1564 Q. ELIZ. in Froude *Hist. Eng.* (1863) VIII. 103 Calumny will not fasten on me for ever. **1602** SHAKS. *Ham.* III. i. 141 Be thou as chast as Ice, as pure as Snow, thou shalt not escape Calumny. **1611** —— *Wint. T.* II. i. 72 The Shrug, the Hum, or Ha (these Petty-brands That Calumnie doth vse). **1751** JOHNSON *Rambl.* No. 144 ¶6 Calumny is diffused by all arts and methods of propagation. **1838** THIRLWALL *Greece* V. xl. 118 His conduct..had given a handle for calumny.

2. A false charge or imputation, intended to damage another's reputation; a slanderous report.

c **1611** CHAPMAN *Iliad* xx. (R.) What then need we vie calumnies, like women that will weare Their tongues out. **1675** BAXTER *Cath. Theol.* II. I. 108 The Synod of Dort rejecteth your accusation as a Calumny. **1751** JOHNSON *Rambl.* No. 183 ¶7 To spread suspicion, to invent calumnies, to propagate scandal, requires neither labour nor courage. **1836** GILBERT *Chr. Atonem.* vi. (1852) 168 A calumny against the revealed character of God.

ca'lumny, *v.* [a. F. *calomnier* (16th c. in Littré), ad. late L. *calumniāre* for classical *calumpniāri* to CALUMNIATE. Cf. *calumnier*, etc.] To calumniate. Hence **ca'lumnying** *vbl. sb.*

1563 FOXE in *Latimer's Serm. & Rem.* (1845) Introd. 10 Changing his old manner of calumnying into a diligent kind of conferring, etc. **1895** *Pall Mall Gaz.* 19 Jan. 7/1 The President has not been in office twelve hours..and is already calumnied. **1963** *Times* 10 May 13/5 We therefore consider it especially shameful that..the work of Pope Pius XII should be wrongly portrayed and his thoughts calumnied.

calutron ('kæljʊtrɒn). *Physics.* orig. *U.S.* [f. *Cal*ifornia *U*niversity cyclo*tron*.] (See quots.)

1945 H. DE W. SMYTH *Atomic Energy* xi. 187 The 'calutron' mass separator. *Ibid.* 189 The 37-inch cyclotron was dismantled..and its magnet was used to produce the magnetic field required in what came to be called a 'calutron'. **1946** *Ann. Reg. 1945* 355 An electromagnetic method [of separating 2 isotopes] using a magnetic separator, called a calutron, first constructed from the California University cyclotron. **1956** *Nature* 28 Jan. 157/1 The calutrons which are now used for enrichment of the isotopes of all the elements.

calvados ('kælvədɒs). Also **Calvados.** [f. *Calvados*, a department of Normandy, France.] A spirit distilled from cider, named after the region in which it is traditionally made; apple-jack.

1906 C. SCUDAMORE *Normandy* viii. 39 Calvados produces much cider and perry as well as a kind of brandy termed 'Calvados'. **1930** R. F. WILSON *How to wine & dine in Paris* v. 102 Cider, good ordinary wine, and fine old apple brandy (Calvados). **1942** E. WAUGH *Put out more Flags* 139 The principal ingredients were vodka and calvados.

†**calvair.** *Obs. rare*⁻¹. [a. F. *calvaire* 'the (bare) skull or skalpe of the head' (Cotgr.), ad. L. *calvāria* skull (see below).] A skull.

c **1420** *Pallad. on Husb.* I. 984 The calvair of an horsed asse or mare, Sette that uppe.

calvar, app. erroneous f. CARAVEL, q.v.

1590 GREENE *Orl. Fur.* (1599) 4 Stately Argosies, Caluars, and Magars, hulkes of burden great.

‖**cal'varia, cal'varium.** *Anat.* [L. *calvāria* skull, f. *calv-us* bald-headed, bare, *calva* the scalp. The form in *-um* is modern and not of Latin authority.] 'That portion of the skull which is above the orbits, temples, ears, and occipital protuberance' (*Syd. Soc. Lex.*).

1398 TREVISA *Barth. De P.R.* v. iv. (1495) 108 Caluaria the formest partye of the skulle hath that name of balde bones. **1866** HUXLEY *Preh. Rem. Caithn.* 88 The calvaria is remarkable for the projection of the supraciliary ridges. **1882** OWEN in *Longm. Mag.* I. 64 What is posed as the 'Neanderthal skull' is the roof of the brain-case, or 'calvarium' of the anatomist.

calvarial (kæl'vɛərɪəl), *a. Anat.* [f. L. *calvāria* + -AL¹.] Of or belonging to the calvaria.

1866 HUXLEY *Preh. Rem. Caithn.* 125 The calvarial sutures.

Calvary ('kælvərɪ). [a. L. *calvāria* skull, used to translate Aram. *gogulpō* or *gogolpā* 'the skull' (Heb. *gulgōleþ* skull, poll), in Gr. transliteration γολγοθά, the name of the mount of the Crucifixion, near Jerusalem.]

1. The proper name of the place where Christ was crucified. (Rendered in OE. *Headpanstow.*) Also used generically.

c **1000** *Ags. Gosp.* Luke xxiii. 33 Hiȝ comon on þa stowe þe is ȝenemned caluarie þæt is heafod-pannan stow. —— *Matt.* xxvii. 31 Golgotha, þæt ys, heafod-pannan stow. **1382** WYCLIF *Luke* xxiii. 33 And aftir that thei camen in to a place, which is clepid of Caluarie [**1388** Caluerie]. —— *Matt.* xxvii. 33 Clepid Golgatha, that is, the place of Caluarie. **1878** GEO. ELIOT *Coll. Breakf. P.* 293 A Calvary where Reason mocks at Love. **1878** *N. Amer. Rev.* 342 A new Calvary and a new Pentecost in reserve for these coheritors of the doom.

2. [F. *calvaire*] in *R.C. Ch.* **a.** A life-size representation of the Crucifixion, on a raised ground in the open air; **b.** A series of representations, in a church or chapel, of the scenes of the Passion.

1727–51 CHAMBERS *Cycl.*, *Calvary*, a term used in catholic countries for a kind of chapel of devotion, raised on a hillock near a city..Such is the Calvary of St. Valerian, near Paris; which is accompanied with several little chapels, in each whereof is represented in sculpture one of the mysteries of the passion. **1815** M. A. SCHIMMELPENNINCK *Demol. Port Royal* III. 206 She also took her for three weeks to the calvary of the Luxembourg. **1846** R. HART *Eccl. Records* (ed. 2) 223 Of the Golgotha, or Calvary, which represented on a large scale the circumstances of the Passion, with images of S. Mary and S. John, our Saviour on the Cross, and sometimes the two thieves, grouped in the open air, we have no English example. **1884** *Harper's Mag.* Nov. 852/1 By the side of the high-road..is one of those calvaries so associated with the landscape of Catholic countries.

3. **Calvary clover**, a name for *Medicago echinus*; **Calvary Cross, Cross Calvary**, in *Her.*, a cross mounted on a pyramid of three grises or steps.

1882 *Garden* 2 Sept. 220/2 Calvary Clover..makes a very pretty basket plant. **1678** in PHILLIPS *App.*, A Cross Calveri. **1730–6** BAILEY, *Calvary* (in Heraldry) as a cross calvary, is set on steps to represent the Cross on which our Saviour suffered. **1826** KIRBY & SP. *Entomol.* (1828) III. xxxiv. 483 The front is nearly the shape of a Calvary cross. **1863** D. WILSON *Preh. Ann. Scot.* II. 458 Engraved with floriated or Calvary Cross.

calve, obs. form of CALF.

calve (kɑːv), *v.*¹ Also 5 calfe, 5–6 calue, 7 calf, (9 *dial.* cauve). [OE. *cealfian*, f. *cealf* CALF *sb.*¹; cf. the corresp. MHG. *kalben*, Du. *kalven*, Sw. *kalfva*, Da. *kalve*. See sense 3.]

1. a. *intr.* To give birth to a calf. Said of kine, deer, etc.; cf. CALF *sb.*¹ 1, 3.

c **1000** ÆLFRIC *Hom.* II. 300 Ða wolde heo [seo cu] cealfian on ȝesihðe þæs folces. **1388** WYCLIF *Job* xxi. 10 The cow caluyed [**1382** bar] and is not priued of hir calf. **1398** TREVISA *Barth. De P.R.* XVII. xlix. (1495) 632 A Hynde..etith this herbe [diptannus] that she may calue eselier and soner. **1523** FITZHERB. *Husb.* §70 If a cowe be fatte, whan she shall calve, than..the calfe shall be the lesse. **1674** tr. *Scheffer's Lapland* xxviii. 131 The does..calve about May. **1828** SCOTT *F.M. Perth* II. 293 'What's the matter?' said Dwining, 'whose cow has calved?' **1860** *Merc. Mar. Mag.* VII. 213 They [whales] differ..in their habit of resorting to very shallow bays to calve.

b. *transf.*

1667 MILTON *P.L.* VII. 463 The grassie Clods now Calv'd, now half appeer'd The Tawnie Lion, pawing to get free His hinder parts.

2. a. *trans.* To bring forth (a calf, or young).

1388 WYCLIF *Job* xxi. 10 The cow..caluede [**1382** bar] not a deed calf. **1532–3** *Act 24 Hen. VIII*, vii, Any maner yonge suckynge calfe..which shall happen to fall or to be calued. **1607** SHAKS. *Cor.* III. i. 240, I would they were Barbarians, as they are, Though in Rome litter'd: not Romans, as they are not, Though calued i' th' Porch o' th' Capitoll. **1846** J. BAXTER *Libr. Pract. Agric.* II. 87 Of the origin of [the short horns]..little can be learned, prior to 1777, in which year the famous bull, Hubback, was calved.

b. *to calve down*: to breed from (a cow). Also *intr.* = *pass.*

1858 *Jrnl. R. Agric. Soc.* XIX. I. 27 These stock are generally calved down when little more than two years old, or else sold. *Ibid.* 28, I have myself known stock costing 6*l.* per head worth at the end of the same year 13 *l.* or 14 *l.*, and the increase is just as great when they calve down.

3. Of a glacier or iceberg: To detach and throw off a mass of ice. Cf. CALF *sb.*¹ 6, and CALVE *v.*²

1837 MACDOUGALL tr. *Graah's E. Coast Greenl.* 104 The Greenlanders believe that..the reverberation caused by the utterance of a loud sound, is sufficient to make an iceberg calve. *Ibid.* 132 One of the numerous large ice-blinks..calved a very considerable berg. **1873** A. L. ADAMS *Field & Forest Rambles* xi. 280 A vast field of ice at one time poured down the slope into the long fiord below, where it calved its bergs. **1882** H. LANSDELL *Through Siberia* I. 199 The icebergs 'calved' as they went along, with much commotion and splashing.

calve, *v.*² *dial.* [Of uncertain standing and derivation. It is possible that (kɑːv) is merely an earlier pronunciation of *cave* retained locally; but it is notable that *calve in* coincides in form and sense with W.Flemish *in-kalven* (cf. *de gracht kalft in* 'the ditch caves in' De Bo), in which the root part is the same as in Du. *afkalven*, to fall or break away, *uit-kalven* to fall or shoot out, said of the sides of a cutting or the like. De Vries refers this *-kalven* to *kalve*, *kaluwe*, surface of the ground, surface layer or soil (see CALLOW). *In-kalven* would thus signify the shooting in of the surface or earth above. Some, however, think that the word is, in its origin, identical with the preceding. The evidence is not decisive.

Calve (kɑːv, kɔːv) *in*, is the vernacular form in Lincolnshire, Notts, Hunts, Norfolk, and adjacent parts of Suffolk, Cambridge, Leicester, Derby, and Yorkshire. Wesley, who is quoted for it, was a native of Epworth, in the district covered by Mr. E. Peacock's *Gloss. of Manley and Corringham*, North Lincolnshire. Assuming the word to be from Dutch, it has been suggested that it was 'introduced by the Dutch navvies who came over for the large drainage works in the Lincolnshire fens' (Wedgwood).]

To fall in as an undermined bank or side of a cutting; to CAVE in.

1755 WESLEY *Wks.* (1872) II. 323 The rock calved in upon him, with a concave surface, which just made room for his body. **1788** *Ibid.* VI. 521 Instantly part of the pit calved in, and crushed him to death. **1873** E. PEACOCK in *N. & Q.* Ser. iv. XII. 274 In this part of the world we all say *calved in*, never *caved in*. **1877** —— *Manley & Corringham Gloss.* (E.D.S.) *Cauve*, to slip down as earth does in a cutting or in a bank undermined by water.

calved (kɑːvd), *ppl. a.* Also 6 caulfed. [f. *calve(s* (see CALF²) + -ED.] Having calves.

1593 *Pass. Morrice* 82 They that trode right, were either clouterly caulfed..spindle shankte, or bakerly kneed. **1870** HAWTHORNE *Eng. Note-bks.* (1879) II. 244 A Highlander..with..bare shanks, most enormously calved.

calveless, var. spelling of CALFLESS.

calven ('kɑːv(ə)n), *ppl. a.* [f. CALVE *v.* after strong pa. pples. like *shaken*.] That has calved.

1880 *Maidstone Newspr.*, For Sale, Fresh Calven Dairy Cows. **1863** ATKINSON *Danby Provinc.*, *Calven-cow*, a cow which has not long since had a calf.

calver ('kɑːvə(r)), *sb.*¹ [f. CALVE *v.* + -ER¹.] A cow that calves, or bears young.

1785 WORFAT *Bran New Wark* 322 (E.D.S.) He that sell'd me tother day a barren cow and a calf, for a calver. **1808** T. C. CURWEN *Hints on Feeding Stock* 177 The milk of the sixth, a winter calver, was reserved for the family. **1884** *York Herald* 26 Aug. 7/1 Calvers made up to £23 each, and half-breds and calving heifers up to £16 each.

†**calver,** *sb.*² *Obs. rare*⁻¹. [See CALVER *a.*] Only in Palsgrave, and it is difficult to determine what he intended by 'salmon scum'. Perh. the treatment as a sb. was some error.

1530 PALSGR. 202/2 Calver of saulmon, *escume de saulmon.*

[The following OE. passages possibly belong to these words. Unfortunately the OE. and Latin are alike uncertain in meaning:

a **700** *Epinal Gloss.* 471 *galmaria*, caluuær (*Erf.* caluuer). —— 476 *galbalacrum*, caluær (*Erf.* caluuer). *a* **800** *Corpus Gl.* 952 *galmaria*, caluuer. —— 956 *gabalacrum*, calwer. —— 954 *galmilla*, liimcaluuer. —— 427 *calvarium*, caluuerclim. *a* **1000** *OE. Gloss.* in Wr.-Wülcker 280 (*Incipit de mensa*) *calmaria*, cealfre. —— 281 *Caluiale*, calwerbriw. *a* **1100** *Alphabet. Gloss.* ibid. 369 *calmaria*, cealre, *Caluiale*, cealerbriw. *Ibid.* 413 *Galmaria*, calwere, *Gabalacrum*, calwer. Cf. also *Ags. Leechd.* 98 I. xxxviii. 2 Nim sur molcen, wyrc to cealre, and beþ mid þy cealre.]

† **calver**, *a. Obs.* In 4 calwar, 5 calvur. [Of this and its connected words, the origin and original sense are unknown: cf. prec. It may be the earlier form of Sc. CALLER (cf. *silver, siller*).]

An epithet applied to salmon or other fish. E. Müller thinks 'fresh'; Way (*Promp. Parv.*) 'fish freshly taken, when its substance appears interspersed with white flakes like curd'. See also CALVERED.

A good deal of evidence points to the condition of a fish, the dressing or cooking of which has begun while it is yet alive, instead of after it is dead. (Cf. also **1536** BELLENDEN *Descr. Alb.* (1821) I. xliii, Quhen the fish faillis thair loup, thay fall callour in the said [boiling] caldrounis, and ar than maist delitius to the mouth.)

a **1403** *Forme of Cury* in Warner *Antiq. Culin.* 19 Take calwar samon, and seeth it in lewe water. *c* **1440** *Promp. Parv.* 59 Calvur, as samoon or oþyr fysshe. **1526** *Ord. Hen. VIII*, ibid. 175 Calver Salmon 1 mess..2*s.* 6*d.* **1719** D'URFEY *Pills* V. 145 Your Pheasant, Pout, and Culver Salmon. **1865** WAY *Promp. Parv.* (note s.v.) In Lancashire, the fish dressed as soon as caught are called calver salmon.

† '**calver**, *v.* ? *Obs.* Also 7 calvor. [app. f. CALVER *a.*: cf. CALVERED, which is in form the pa. pple. of this vb., though earlier in our quots.]

1. *trans.* To treat or cook as a 'calver' fish. (The mode apparently differed at different times.) Nares says 'To prepare salmon, or other fish, in a peculiar way, which can only be done when they are fresh and firm'. Some identify it with to CRIMP. Some explain it To cut salmon into thin slices while 'fresh' (or 'alive') and then pickle these.

1651 BARKER *Art of Angling* (1653) 13 Trouts calvored hot with antchovaes sauce. *Ibid.* (1820) 33 A dish of close boyled Trouts buttered with eggs..Every scullion dresseth that dish against his will, because he cannot calvor them. **1660** R. MAY *Accompl. Cook* 354 To calver salmon to eat hot or cold. **1663** KILLIGREW *Parson's Wed.* in *Dodsley* (1780) XI. 445 The chines fry'd, and the salmon calver'd.

2. *intr.* Of fish: To behave when cooked as a 'calver' fish. Some recent writers conjecture 'To shrink by cutting and not fall to pieces' (Craig), some 'to bear being sliced and pickled'.

1651 BARKER *Art of Angling* (1653) 13 So the fierce boyling will make the fish to calvor. *Ibid.* (1820) 21 You shall see whether he calvors or no. **1676** COTTON *Angler* II. 310 A Grayling is a winter fish..his flesh even in his worst season is so firm and will so easily calver that..he is very good meat at all times. **1681** CHETHAM *Angler's Vade-m.* xii. §1 His flesh..is firm, white, will easily calver.

Hence '**calvering** *vbl. sb.*

1651–7 BARKER *Art of Angling* (1820) 12 When it [vinegar] boyles take it off the fire and pour it upon your fish, you shall see your fish rise presently, if they be new, and there is no doubt of calvoring.

calver, obs. form of *claver*, CLOVER *sb.*

1577 B. GOOGE *Heresbach's Husb.* (1586) 18b, Great calver, sperie, chick, and the other pulses.

'**calvered**, *ppl. a.* ? *Obs.* (exc. *Hist.*) Also 7 calvert, calvored. [f. CALVER *v.*] Used from end of 16th c. app. in room of the earlier CALVER *a.*: see CALVER *v.* Cf. quots. 1822 and 1860.

1610 B. JONSON *Alch.* II. ii. (1616) 622 My foot-boy shall eate phesants, caluerd salmons. *a* **1640** MASSINGER *Guardian* IV. i, Great lords sometimes For change leave calvert-salmon and eat sprats. **1651** BARKER *Art of Angling* (1820) 11 We must have two dishes of calvored Trouts. **1691** SHADWELL *Scowrers* II. Wks. 1720 IV. 330 Think on the Turbott and the Calvert Salmon at Locket's. **1822** NARES, Calver'd salmon..now means, in the fish trade, only crimped salmon. **1855** MACAULAY *Hist. Eng.* III. 560 Prince George, who cared as much for the dignity of his birth as he was capable of caring for any thing but claret and calvered salmon. **1860** KITCHENER *Cook's Orac.* 178 *note*, Calvered Salmon is the Salmon caught in the Thames, and cut into slices alive.

calveren, obs. = calves, irreg. pl. of CALF[1].

calves'-snout, calf's- ('kɑːvzsnaʊt, 'kɑːfs-). [f. CALF[1], *calves* + SNOUT.]

An old name of ANTIRRHINUM or Snapdragon; *esp.* of *A. Orontium* or Small Snap-dragon.

1548 TURNER *Names of Herbes* s.v. *Antirrhinon*, Plinies antirrhinon..maye be called in englishe calfe snoute. **1551** —— *Herbal* I. D ij b, Yellow Calfys snowte. **1629** PARKINSON *Paradisi in Sole* xlv. 270 In English Calues snout from the form of the seede vessels, and Snap-dragon, or Lyons mouth from the forme of the flowers. **1845** *Penny Cycl.* Supp. I. 125/2 *A. Orontium*..or Calves'-snout, occurs in dry sandy and gravelly soils.

‖ **calville.** ? *Obs.* Also 7 calvile, 8 calvil. [Fr.: of unknown origin (Littré).] A kind of apple.

1664 EVELYN *Kal. Hort.* (1729) 232 Apples..Pome Apis, Cour-pendue, Calvile of all sorts. **1727** BRADLEY *Fam. Dict.* s.v. *Apple*, The White Calville, is white both within and without; its Taste is more delicious than that of the red, for which reason 'tis more valued. **1755** in JOHNSON (from BAILEY); and in mod. Dicts.

calving ('kɑːvɪŋ), *vbl. sb.* [f. CALVE + -ING[1].] Of kine, etc.: The bringing forth of calves or young.

1398 TREVISA *Barth. De P.R.* XVIII. xxx. (1495) 792 After the caluynge the hynde etyth two manere herbes. *c* **1420** *Pallad. on Husb.* VIII. 66 Mete in mesure her calvyng wol advannce. **1587** HARRISON *England* III. i. (1878) II. 2 A cow ..which in six yeeres had sixteene calfes; that is, foure at once in three caluings, and twise twins. *a* **1854** E. FORBES *Lit. Papers* 152 (L.) Bay-whaling, a practice destructive to the cow whales about the time of calving.

b. *transf.* of a glacier or ice-berg.

1837 MACDOUGALL tr. *Graah's E. Coast Greenl.* 48 An occasional report, caused by the calving of the ice-blink.

c. *Comb.*, as ***calving-season, -time.***

1528 PAYNELL *Salerne's Regim.* E ij b, Hare fleshe and hartis fleshe..best before caluing tyme. **1881** DU CHAILLU *Land Midn. Sun* II. 197 The reindeers' calving season.

'**calving**, *ppl. a.* [-ING[2].] Bearing calves.

1886 *York Herald* 10 Aug. 7/4 Calving cows made up to £19..calving heifers £12 10*s.* each.

Calvinian (kæl'vɪnɪən), *a.* and *sb.* Also 6 Caluen-. [f. pr. n. Calvin, in Lat. *Calvinus* + -IAN.]

A. *adj.* Of, belonging to, or following the doctrine of, Calvin. (See CALVINISM.)

1566 T. STAPLETON *Ret. Untr. Jewell* Pref., The Lutheran and Caluinian Religion. **1688** BP. OF OXFORD *Reasons Abrog. Test* 54 Patron of the Calvinian Faction. **1862** *Lit. Churchman* 446 The Calvinian development of St. Augustin's idea of predestination was logically true.

† **B.** *sb.* = CALVINIST. *Obs.*

1582 MUNDAY *Eng. Rom. Life* in *Harl. Misc.* (1809) II. 206 He curseth all Caluenians, Lutherians, Zwinglians. **1691** WOOD *Ath. Oxon.* I. /193 Laurence Humphrey [was].. much of the Calvinian both in doctrine and discipline.

† '**Calvinish**, *a. Obs. rare.* = CALVINISTIC.

1637 *Declar. Pfaltzgrave's Faith* 30 A Calvinish heresie.

Calvinism ('kælvɪnɪz(ə)m). [f. as prec. + -ISM. Cf. F. *calvinisme*, mod.L. *calvinismus*.] The doctrines of John *Calvin* the Protestant Reformer (1509–1564), particularly his theological doctrines on grace, in which Calvinism is opposed to ARMINIANISM.

b. Adherence to these doctrines.

(The particular doctrines of theological Calvinism are contained in the so-called 'five points', viz. (1) Particular election. (2) Particular redemption. (3) Moral inability in a fallen state. (4) Irresistible grace. (5) Final perseverance.)

1570 LEVINS *Manip.* 146 Caluynisme, *caluinismus.* **1650** R. STAPYLTON *Strada's Low-C. Warres* III. 65 She was jealous lest Calvinisme, which then infected France, might be caught by their neighbours of Haynolt. **1655** L'ESTRANGE *Chas. I*, 127 The Doctrine of St. Augustine; which they who understand it not, call Calvinisme. **1863** FROUDE *Hist. Eng.* VII. 367 Thus spoke Calvinism, the creed of republics, in its first hard form.

fig. **1863** *Denise* I. 126 The destruction, the waste in Nature; the plants that bud and never bring forth fruit..the Calvinism of Nature, things predestined to destruction!

Calvinist ('kælvɪnɪst). [f. as prec. + -IST. Cf. F. *calviniste*.] An adherent of Calvinism.

1579 FULKE *Heskins' Parl.* 577 The seconde and thirde, he sayeth are denyed by the Caluenistes. **1673** MILTON *True Relig.* 7 The Calvinist is taxt with Predestination, and to make God the Author of sin. **1768** TUCKER *Lt. Nat.* I. 545 No Arminian will doubt a man being debarred of his liberty by shutting him up in a gaol; nor will the most rigid Calvinist deny, that upon being let loose he is at liberty to go which way he pleases. **1850** R. WILBERFORCE *Holy Bapt.* 253 Those who compiled the Service-Books of the Church of England were not Calvinists.

attrib. **1876** BANCROFT *Hist. U.S.* VI. Index 510 Union of Calvinist colonies proposed.

Calvi'nistic, *a.* [f. prec. + -IC.] Of or belonging to Calvinism, following the doctrines of Calvin. ***Calvinistic Methodists***: a section of the Methodists who follow the Calvinistic opinions of Whitfield, as distinguished from the Arminian opinions of Wesley; their chief seat is in Wales.

1820 SCOTT *Abbot* xiv, The cloak and band of the Calvinistic divine. **1850** R. WILBERFORCE *Holy Bapt.* 145 The Calvinistic doctrines of Election, Predestination, and Perseverance are incompatible with..Baptismal Regeneration.

Calvi'nistical, *a.* [f. prec. + -AL[1].] = CALVINISTIC; of the nature of, or pertaining to, Calvinism. Hence **Calvi'nistically** *adv.*

1606 W. CRASHAW *Rom. Forgeries* 78 Is not such a Caluinisticall sentence worthy to be razed out for euer? **1779** JOHNSON *Milton, L.P.* (1816) 128 His theological opinions are said to have been first Calvinistical. **1814** SCOTT *Wav.* xxv, This calvinistical Colonel. **1853** LYTTON *My Novel* I. 365 (Hoppe) Mrs. Avenel, in an awfully stiff, clean, and calvinistical cap.

1674 HICKMAN *Hist. Quinquart.* (ed. 2) 58 The Doctrine of Free-will is laid down as Calvinistically as one could wish. **1832** *Fraser's Mag.* XLVI. 588 Do not be so Calvinistically severe on their little amusements.

Calvi'nisticate, *v.* To make Calvinistic.

1834–43 SOUTHEY *Doctor* xlvi, If the old English worthy.. had been Calvinisticated till the milk of human kindness with which his heart was always ready to overflow had turned sour.

'**Calvinize**, *v.* [see -IZE.] **a.** *intr.* To follow Calvin, to teach Calvinism. **b.** *trans.* To imbue with Calvinism. Hence **Calvinized, 'Calvinizing** *ppl. a.*

1659 HEYLIN *Cert. Epist.* 175 He did not Arminianize in all things, I am sure he Calvinized in none. **1824** MᶜCULLOCH *Scotl.* II. 75 This Calvinised Country. **1861** *Q. Rev.* CX. 549 One brother Churchman was Romanising, or another Calvinising. **1862** *Ibid.* Apr. 325 The Calvinist has Calvinized..the services of his Church by his hymns. **1829** SOUTHEY *Sir T. More* (1831) II. 40 The Calvinizing Clergy.

'**Calvino-**, in *comb.* Calvinistic.

[**1584** FENNER *Def. Ministers* (1587) 39 Calling some *Anglo-puritani*, some *Caluino-papistæ*.] **1667** H. MORE *Div. Dial.* IV. xviii. (1713) 325 The Turks indeed are held great Fatalists, whence some in reproach call this Point of Calvin, Calvino-Turcism.

calvish ('kɑːvɪʃ), *a.* [f. CALF[1] + -ISH.]

1. Resembling a calf; calf-like, doltish, stupid.

b. Of or addicted to calf-worship.

1570 *Piththy Note Papists* (Collier) 4 The Bul bewitcht his caluish braine. **1660** GAUDEN *Brounrig* 48 He was transported with just indignation against the calvish Idolaters. **1834** BECKFORD *Italy* II. 71 Her Majesty's absolute commands having swept females off the stage, their parts are acted by calvish young fellows.

2. *nonce-use.* [f. CALF[2].] Pertaining to the calf of the leg (with pun on prec. sense).

1826 LAMB *Let.* in *Final Mem.* viii. (1850) 210 The cramp ..clawing me in the calvish part of my nature, makes me ever and anon roar bullishly.

calvity ('kælvɪtɪ). *rare.* [ad. L. *calvitiēs* baldness, f. *calv-us* bald: cf. F. *calvitie*.] Baldness.

1623 COCKERAM, *Caluity*, baldnesse. **1656** BLOUNT *Glossogr.*, *Calvity*, baldness, deceit. **1886** *Cornh. Mag.* 384 Middle-aged..and inclining to calvity and obeseness.

calvor, -ur, variants of CALVER *v.*

calvysfote, obs. form of CALF'S-FOOT.

calwey, var. form of CALEWEY, *Obs.*, a pear.

calx (kælks). Forms: 5 cals, 5–7 calce, 7 callixe, calxe, 8 calix, 7– calx. *Pl.* calces (formerly also calxes). [L. *calx, calc-em* lime; applied in an extended sense to substances produced in the same way as quick-lime.]

1. A term of the alchemists and early chemists for a powder or friable substance produced by thoroughly burning or roasting ('calcining') a mineral or metal, so as to consume or drive off all its volatile parts, as lime is burned in a kiln.

The *calx* was formerly taken as the essential substance or 'alcohol' of the crude mineral after all the grosser parts had been dispelled. The 'calx' of a metal was supposed to be the result of the expulsion of 'phlogiston'; in reality it was usually the metallic oxide, but in some cases the metal itself in a state of sublimation.

c **1460** *Bk. Quintessence* 7 Caste..cals of..gold..in wiyn ..and ȝe schule haue ȝoure licour..bettir gilt. **1605** TIMME *Quersit.* I. xiii. 56 The black feces..being reduced..into a calxe. *Ibid.* II. v. 123 Put fire thereunto..untill the earth.. is well calcined..Divide this thy callixe. **1610** B. JONSON *Alch.* II. v, *Sub.* How do you sublime him? *Fac.* With the calce of Egg-shells. **1612** WOODALL *Surg. Mate* Wks. (1653) 268 Calcination is solution of bodies into Calx or Alcool. **1670** *Phil. Trans.* V. 2042 Nor reduced into a calx but by a strong fire, by which it will turn into a substance like unslaked lime. *a* **1691** BOYLE *Wks.* I. 719 All brought into calces or powders that are white. **1756** C. LUCAS *Ess. Waters* I. 3 Lead by calcination..becomes a red calx or mineral earth. *Ibid.* Metals deprived of..phlogiston..are reduced to calces. **1781** J. T. DILLON *Trav. Spain* 233 Metallic calxes. **1791** HAMILTON *Berthollet's Dyeing* I. I. i. 7 Oxygen may be separated from some oxyds or metallic calces. **1812** SIR H. DAVY *Chem. Philos.* 23 Having ascertained the increase of weight of lead during its conversion into calx. **1822** IMISON *Sc. & Art* II. 20 The calx of tin, now the oxide of tin.

fig. **1799** SOUTHEY *Nondescr.* iii. Wks. III. 63 Some mass for the poor souls that bleach, And burn away the calx of their offences In that great Purgatory crucible.

† **2.** Sometimes in Latin sense 'lime': esp. in ***calx vive, calcevive*** (L. ***calx viva***, F. ***chaux vive***) quick-lime. *Obs.*

1581 STYWARD *Mart. Discip.* I. 12 They ought to haue.. Calx viue, Lint seede Oile, etc. **1641** FRENCH *Distill.* V. (1651) 129 Make a strong Lixivium of Calx vive. **1652** ASHMOLE *Theat. Chem. Brit.* 116 Our true Calcevive..our Ferment of our Bread. **1834** *Brit. Husb.* I. 439 Calx is lime combined with acids.

3. *Eton School slang.* [Another L. sense of *calx*, 'the goal, anciently marked with lime or chalk'.] The goal-line (at foot-ball).

1864 *Daily Tel.* 1 Dec., The Collegers were over-weighted ..and the Oppidans managed to get the ball down into their calx several times.

Calybite. [f. Gr. καλύβη little hut.] One of a class of early saints who passed their lives in huts.

'**calycanth.** *Bot.* [ad. L. CALYCANTHUS.] A book-name of the Natural Order *Calycanthaceæ*.

1866 *Treas. Bot.*, *Calycanthaceæ* (Calycanths).

caly'canthemy. *Bot.* [f. Gr. καλυκ- CALYX + ἄνθεμ-ον flower + -Y.] The conversion, partial or complete, of sepals into the appearance of petals, as in the variety of primrose called *Jack-in-the-box*. Hence **caly'canthemous** *a.*

1880 GRAY *Bot. Text-bk.* 400 *Calycanthemy*, name of the monstrosity in which the calyx imitates an exterior corolla.

‖ **Calycanthus** (kælɪ'kænθəs). *Bot.* [mod.L., f. Gr. κάλυκ- CALYX + ἄνθος flower.] A North

American genus of shrubs; esp. *Calycanthus floridus* or Carolina Allspice.

1864 MISS YONGE *Trial* I. 190 Come and reach me down some calycanthus out of the greenhouse. **1884** STEVENSON *Silver. Squatt.* 267 Cal[y]canthus crept, like a hardy weed, all over our rough parlor.

calycate ('kælɪkeɪt), *a. Bot.* Also **calicate**. [ad. mod.L. *calycātus*, f. L. CALYX: see -ATE[2].] Provided with a calyx.

1866 LINDLEY & MOORE *Treas. Bot.*, *Calicate*, furnished with a calyx.

calycifloral (ˌkælɪsɪ'flɔərəl, kəˌlɪsɪ-), *a. Bot.* [f. L. *calyc-em* (*calyx*) a. Gr. κάλυκ- + *flōr-em* flower + -AL[1].] Having the stamens and petals inserted in the calyx. So **calyci'florate, calyci'florous**, in same sense.

1872 OLIVER *Elem. Bot.* I. v. 58 Polypetalous flowers have their stamens inserted on the receptacle..or inserted upon the calyx, and are hence called Calycifloral, as Pea, Bramble, Apple. **1880** GRAY *Bot. Text-bk.* 400 *Calycriflorous*, petals (distinct or coalescent) and stamens adnate to the calyx.

calyciform ('kælɪsɪfɔːm, kə'lɪsɪ-), *a. Bot.* [f. as prec. + -FORM; cf. mod.F. *caliciforme*.]

Having the form of a calyx, calyx-shaped. Also erroneous spelling of CALICIFORM cup-shaped.

1831 J. DAVIES *Manual Mat. Med.* 453 Male flowers in elongate aments, caliciform scale diversely shaped. **1870** HOOKER *Stud. Flora* 463 *Woodsia*..involucre inferior, membranous, at first calyciform.

calycinal (kæ'lɪsɪnəl), *a. Bot.* [f. CALYCINE + -AL[1].] = CALYCINE I.

1831 J. DAVIES *Manual Mat. Med.* 453 *Salicineæ*..male flowers, calicinal scale supporting an unilocular ovary. **1835** LINDLEY *Introd. Bot.* (1848) I. 386 While the calycinal protuberance is making its appearance.

ca'lycinar, *a. Bot.* [f. as prec. + -AR.] **1.** = prec. **2.** (see quot.)

1866 *Treas. Bot.*, *Calicinar*, when a flower becomes double by an increase in the number of lobes of the calyx or sepals.

calycine ('kælɪsaɪn, -ɪn), *a.* [f. L. *calyc-em* (*calyx*) + -INE.] Of or belonging to the calyx; resembling a calyx.

1. *Bot.*

1816 COLEBROOKE *Asiat. Res.* XII. 539 Embraced at the base by the calycine hemispherical cup. **1830** LINDLEY *Nat. Syst. Bot.* 218 The symmetry of the stamens, corolline and calycine segments. **1861** S. THOMSON *Wild Fl.* III. (ed. 4) 239 Calycine sepals.

2. *Biol.* and *Phys.* (See CALYX 2.)

1872 NICHOLSON *Palæont.* 133 Sphæronites has each calycine plate perforated by two pores. **1877** HUXLEY *Anat. Inv. An.* ii. 96 A calycine investment for the whole animal.

calycle ('kælɪk(ə)l). *Bot.* [ad. L. *calycul-us* (which is now often used instead), dim. of *calyx*.]

1. A little calyx: **a.** A row of bracts or leaves surrounding the base of the calyx, and resembling a smaller outer calyx. **b.** The outer proper covering or crown of the seed, adhering to it to facilitate its dispersion. †**c.** Formerly, the outer envelope of a bud.

1731 BAILEY vol. II, *Calycle*, with Botanists, a small bud of a plant. **1803** REES *Cycl.*, *Calycle*, a term invented by Vaillant to express a series of leaves surrounding the base of the calyx. **1880** GRAY *Bot. Text-bk.* 400 *Calyculus*, an involucre or involucel imitating an additional calyx.

2. Erroneous form of CALICLE.

Hence '**calycled** *a.*, having a calycle, calyculate.

1794 MARTYN *Rousseau's Bot.* xxvi. 378 *note*, The calyx is ..calycled, or furnished with a second set of leaflets at the base. **1810** *Encycl. Lond.* I. 683/1 Calycled andromeda.

'**calycoid, -'oideous**, *a. Bot.* [f. Gr. κάλυκ- CALYX + -OID, + -EOUS; the Gr. was καλυκώδης.]

1866 *Treas. Bot.*, *Calycoideous*, resembling a calyx.

calycular (kə'lɪkjʊlə(r)), *a. Bot.* [f. L. *calycul-us* CALYCLE + -AR. Cf. mod.F. *caliculaire*.] Relating to or composing a calycle (in its various senses).

1658 SIR T. BROWNE *Gard. Cyrus* iii, Even the Autumnal buds, which await the return of the Sun, do after the winter solstice multiply their calicular leaves. **1707** SLOANE *Jamaica* I. 259 The calycular leaves are purple. **1866** *Treas. Bot.*, *Calicular*, a term of æstivation, when the outer bracts of an involucre are much shorter than the inner.

calyculate (kə'lɪkjʊleɪt). *a. Bot.* [f. L. *calycul-us* CALYCLE + -ATE[2] 2. Cf. F. *caliculé*.] Having a calycle. So formerly **ca'lyculated**, (having fruit) enclosed in a calyx or involucre.

1690 SLOANE in *Phil. Trans.* XVII. 466 Calyculated Berries of the bigness of a large Pea. **1693** *Ibid.* 928 Such.. have the Calyx of their Flower non deciduous, in which the Fruit standeth as in a Cup, and these he calls Calyculated Fruits. **1725** SLOANE *Jamaica* II. 95 Of Trees which bear berries, and are umbilicated or caliculated. **1880** GRAY *Bot. Text-bk.* 400 *Calyculate*, bearing bracts next to the calyx which imitate an external or accessory calyx.

'**calycule.** Another form of CALYCLE; see -CULE and cf. F. *calicule*.

calyon, variant of CALION, *Obs.*

calypso (kə'lɪpsəʊ). Pl. -os. [Origin unknown.] A West Indian ballad or song in African rhythm, usually improvised to comment on a topic of current interest. Also *attrib.* Hence **calypsonian** (kælɪp'səʊnɪən), an entertainer who composes and sings calypsos.

1934 A. HUXLEY *Beyond Mexique Bay* 18 A Calypso Tent ..is..a tin roof on posts—in which..the local talent assembles to rehearse certain songs composed against the coming of Carnival. *Ibid.* 19 The tunes to which these songs are sung is always some variant of an old Spanish air called Calypso; the words are home-made and topical. *Ibid.*, The singers..call themselves 'Calypsonians'. **1938** *Times* 26 May 17/6 'Calypso' songs (as they are curiously called), to judge from examples perhaps too discreetly chosen, are mere doggerel, and the music, if it does more than beat out the rhythm, is the most commonplace jazz. **1955** *Times* 28 Jan. 9/6 Calypso is a form of doggerel lampoon composed and sung to a guitar, often extempore... A Calypsonian both composes and accompanies his songs. **1957** *Observer* 24 Nov. 10/6 The calypso is a commentary. It seeks to tell of an event which has made an impression on the singer.

calypto'blastic, *a. Zool.* [f. Gr. καλυπτό-ς covered + βλαστός sprout, shoot.] (Hydroids) having the generative buds provided with an external protective receptacle.

1869 NICHOLSON *Zool.* viii. (1880) 122 The name of 'Calyptoblastic Hydroids' has been proposed by Professor Allman for the Sertularians and Campanularians.

calyptolite (kə'lɪptəlaɪt). *Min.* [f. Gr. καλυπτό-ς covered + -LITE.] A variety of Zircon.

1839 SHEPARD *Min.* (1858) 288 *Calyptolite*, very minute dark brown crystals, having the form of zircon.

‖**calyptra** (kə'lɪptrə). *Bot.* In 8 **calyptre**. [mod.L. a. Gr. καλύπτρα covering, veil, f. καλύπτειν to cover. Cf. F. *calyptre*.] A hood or cover; *spec.* **a.** the hood of the sporecase in mosses; **b.** 'the interior membranaceous and often hairy covering of the ovarium' (De Candolle and Sprengel *Philos. Plants* 61).

1753 CHAMBERS *Cycl. Supp.*, *Calyptra*. **1777** ROBSON *Brit. Flora* 26 A calyptra is the calyx of a Moss, covering the fructification like a hood. **1794** MARTYN *Rousseau's Bot.* xxxii. 493 A lidded capsule, covered with a smooth calyptre. **1807** J. E. SMITH *Phys. Bot.* 402 Mosses, which have..a hood-like corolla, or calyptra, bearing the style, and concealing the capsule. **1830** LINDLEY *Nat. Syst. Bot.* 60 [Of the Mangrove Tribe] Calyx superior..with the lobes varying in number..occasionally all cohering in a calyptra. **1858** CARPENTER *Veg. Phys.* §736.

calyptrate (kə'lɪptreɪt), *a. Bot.* [f. prec. + -ATE[2] 2. Cf. F. *calyptré*.] Having a calyptra, hood, or covering; hooded, operculate.

1830 LINDLEY *Nat. Syst. Bot.* 273 Each fibre of the roots has a calyptrate covering at the extremity. **1835** —— *Introd. Bot.* (1848) I. 327 The calyx is..calyptrate, if at the period of falling it bursts on one side, as in Eschscholtzia.

calyptriform (kə'lɪptrɪfɔːm), *a. Bot.* [f. as prec. + -FORM.] Calyptra-shaped.

1830 LINDLEY *Nat. Syst. Bot.* 46 The corolla is calyptriform in Antholoma. **1880** GRAY *Bot. Text-bk.* 400 *Calyptriform*, calyptra-shaped; as the calyx of *Eschscholtzia*.

So **calyptri'morphous** *a.* [Gr. μορφή form.] 'Applied in Botany to ascidia which have a distinct lid.' *Syd. Soc. Lex.* 1881.

calyptrogen (kə'lɪptrədʒɛn). *Bot.* [f. Gr. καλύπτρα covering + -GEN taken in sense of 'producer'.] The outer zone or layer of the meristem or primary tissue of the youngest part of plants.

1881 *Nature* XXIII. 288 Four zones of meristem:—calyptrogen, dermatogen, periblem and plerome. **1884** BOWER & SCOTT *De Bary's Phaner. & Ferns* 9 Since this accession originates in certain cases from a special layer of meristem, the latter is to be distinguished as the calyptrogen.

‖**calystegia** (kælɪ'stiːdʒɪə). *Bot.* [f. Gr. κάλυκ- CALYX + στέγη covering, in reference to the generic distinction.] A genus of plants separated by modern botanists from *Convolvulus*, because of the two large bracts which enclose the calyx; it contains the large White Convolvulus or Bindweed of the English hedges.

1880 *New Virginians* I. 85 A tangle, or wilderness of dewberries, white calystegias.

calyver, obs. form of CALIVER.

calyx ('kælɪks, 'keɪlɪks). Formerly also **calix**. Pl. **calyces** ('kælɪsiz), rarely **calyxes**. [L. *calyx*, a. Gr. κάλυξ outer covering of a fruit, flower, or bud; shell, husk, pod, pericarp (from root of καλύπτειν to cover). In med.L. and in the Romanic langs., this word has run together in form with the much commoner Latin word *calix* 'cup, goblet, drinking vessel'; and the two are to a great extent treated as one by modern scientific writers, so that the *calyx* of a flower is commonly (though quite erroneously) explained as the 'flower-cup', and the form *calyx* and its derivatives are applied to many cup-like organs, which have nothing to do with the *calyx* of a flower, but are really meant to be compared to a *calix* or cup. See sense 2 and cf. CALIX.]

1. a. *Bot.* The whorl of leaves (sepals), either separate or grown together, and usually green, forming the outer envelope in which the flower is enclosed while yet in the bud. Called by Grew, 1682, *Empalement*.

[**1671** MALPIGHI *Anat. Plant.*, *Calyx*..floris basis est. **1686** RAY *Hist. Plant.* I. A2 Calyx, folliculus sive, involucrum floris..the cup enclosing or containing the flower.] **1693** [see CALYCULATE]. **1704** in J. HARRIS *Lex. Techn.* **1718** R. BRADLEY *New Improv. Planting* II. (ed. 2) 83 The other [race] whose petals cannot contain themselves within the Bounds of the Chalyx, are call'd round podded Flowers. **1737–59** MILLER *Gard. Dict.* Explan. Terms, The empalement, *Calix*, is generally understood to mean, those less tender leaves, which cover the other parts of the flower. **1791** E. DARWIN *Bot. Gard.* I. 195 *note*, The effect of light.. occasions the actions of the vegetable muscles..which open their calyxes and chorols. **1802** MAR. EDGEWORTH *Moral T.* (1816) I. xvii. 144 The brown calyces of the geranium flowers. **1866** RUSKIN *Eth. Dust* 212 The calyx is nothing but the swaddling clothes of the flower; the child-blossom is bound up in it, hand and foot.

b. Applied to similar parts of other organisms.

1851 RICHARDSON *Geol.* viii. 224 In the sea-lily it [the stomach] reposes in the calyx surrounded by the arms. **1872** NICHOLSON *Palæont.* 119 At the summit of the stem is placed the body, which is termed the 'calyx'.

2. *Phys.* and *Biol.* Variant spelling of CALIX.

1831 R. KNOX *Cloquet's Anat.* 798 The Calyces (Infundibula) are small membraneous ducts which embrace ..the circumference of the mammillæ. **1836** TODD *Cycl. Anat.* I. 357/1 The part of the ovary in which the ovum is lodged is termed the calyx.

3. *Comb.*, as *calyx-base*, *-leaf*, *-limb*, *-lobe*, *-segment*, *-tooth*, *-tube*; *calyx-like* adj. **calyx-bursting**, bursting of the calyx, a defect in carnations; **calyx(-form) crater** or **krater** *Gr. Antiq.*, a crater (sense 1) of the shape of a calyx.

1870 HOOKER *Stud. Flora* 315 *Beta*..Fruit adnate to the disk and *calyx-base. **1900** *Westm. Gaz.* 7 May 4/2 *Calyx-bursting is a fatal objection to many varieties otherwise superb. **1896** C. H. SMITH in *Catal. Gr. Vases Brit. Mus.* III. 280 *Calyx-form Craters. **1912** J. D. BEAZLEY in *Ann. Brit. Sch. Athens* XVIII. 225 The pattern No. 15 does not occur on any other rf. kalyx-krater. **1915** *Oxf. Univ. Gaz.* 3 Feb. 378/2 The other vases include two *hydriæ*,..two amphoræ,..and a calyx-crater. **1872** OLIVER *Elem. Bot.* I. i. 7 *Calyx-leaves or Sepals. **1849–52** TODD *Cycl. Anat.* IV. 1137/2 A..*calyx-like arrangement. **1870** HOOKER *Stud. Flora* 176 *Calyx-limb deciduous. **1859** DARWIN *Orig. Spec.* vii. (1872) 173 The uppermost flower generally has two *calyx-lobes. **1870** HOOKER *Stud. Flora* 66 Stamens inserted on the *calyx-mouth. *Ibid.* 115 Bracts longer than the ovate *calyx-segments. *Ibid.* 265 *Calyx-teeth short. *Ibid.* 183 *Calyx-tube and corolla white.

†**cal'zoons**, *sb. pl. Obs.* Also **calsoun, -sound, -sune**. [From one or other of the Romanic langs.: F. *calçons*, *caleçons*, Sp. *calzones*, Pg. *calções*, It. *calzoni* breeches, drawers:—late L. *calciones*; augmentative forms of L. **calcea*, Sp. *calza*, Pg. *calça*, It. *calza*, F. *chausse* hose, f. L. *calceus* shoe, half-boot.] Drawers, hose, trousers: used of those of oriental nations.

1615 G. SANDYS *Trav.* 63 The next that they weare is a smock of callico with ample sleeves..vnder this a paire of calsouns of the same, which reach to their ancles. **1656** BLOUNT *Glossogr.*, *Calsounds* or *Calsunes*, a kind of drawers or such like garment of Linnen, which the Turks wear next their skin. **1677** HERBERT *Trav.* 115 The better sort of that sex here wear linen Drawers or Calzoons.

cam (kæm), *sb.*[1] Also **camb, camm**. [cf. Du. *kam* (MDu. *cam*), Ger. *kamm*, Da. and Sw. *kam*, the same word as Eng. COMB, but also applied to a 'toothed rim or part of a wheel, teeth of a wheel', as in Du. *kamrad*, Ger. *kammrad*, Da. and Sw. *kamhjul* 'toothed wheel, cog-wheel'; thence also mod.F. *came* 'cog, tooth, catch of a wheel, sort of tooth applied to the axle of a machine, or cut in the axle, to serve to raise a pestle or forge-hammer'. Taken into English prob. either from Du. or Fr.

The primary meaning of Teut. *kambo-* was 'toothed instrument'; cf. its cognates Gr. γόμφο- tooth, peg, Skr. *jambha-* tusk, OSlav. *zǫbŭ* tooth: see COMB.]

a. A projecting part of a wheel or other revolving piece of machinery, adapted to impart an alternating or variable motion of any kind to another piece pressing against it, by sliding or rolling contact. Much used in machines in which a uniform revolving motion is employed to actuate any kind of non-uniform, alternating, elliptical, or rectilineal movement. The original method was by cogs or teeth fixed or cut at certain points in the circumference or disc of a wheel, but the name has been extended to any kind of eccentric, heart-shaped, or spiral disc, or other appliance that serves a similar purpose.

1777 *Specif. W. Vicker's Patent* No. 1168 The wheel F turning a cylinder with a cam and two cranks. **1805** *Specif. J. Hartop's Patent* No. 2888 Upon any axis A..apply a pin, cam, crank or curve or curves C. **1831** G. PORTER *Silk Manuf.* 269 Camms, or wheels of eccentric form. **1832** BABBAGE *Econ. Manuf.* vi. (ed. 3) 44 If one or more

projecting pieces, called cams, are fixed on the axis opposite to the end of each lever. **1858** GREENER *Gunnery* 418. **1867** *Athenæum* No. 2084. 440/3 An iron camb for power-looms. **1879** *Cassell's Techn. Educ.* I. 407/2 Cams are variously-formed plates, or grooves, by means of which a circular may be converted into a reciprocating motion.

b. *Comb.*, as ***cam-ball valve, cam-groove, cam-gear wheel, cam-shaft, cam-wheel.*** **cam-box**, a frame surrounding a cam and designed to compel the rod which the cam drives to follow the return motion of the projecting lobe; also, a casing enclosing the cam and its rollers in order that copious lubrication may be secured by having the cams revolve in a bath of oil (*Cent. Dict.* Suppl. 1909); **cam-cutter**, a machine-tool specially adapted for cutting and finishing cams; **cam-pump**, a pump in which the valve motion is given by a cam; **cam-shaft**, a shaft bearing a cam or cams; also *attrib.*; **cam-yoke**, a frame attached to a valve-stem or other reciprocating piece to which it gives intermittent straight-line motion from a cam on the face of a rotating disc; used in steam-engine valve-gears (*Funk's Standard Dict.* 1893).

a **1884** KNIGHT *Dict. Mech.* Suppl. 156 Cam Cutter. **1922** JACOBS *Cam Design* 74 The hand-made master cam is now placed in position on the cam cutter head spindle. **1879** *Cassell's Techn. Educ.* IV. 393/1 A cam-groove cut in the reverse side of the crank-plate. *a* **1884** KNIGHT *Dict. Mech.* Suppl. 157 Drayton Cam Pump. *a* **1877** —— *Dict. Mech.* I. 435/2 *Cam-shaft*, a shaft having cams or wipers, for raising the pestles of stamping-mills. **1908** *Westm. Gaz.* 9 Jan. 4/1 Depressing the cam-shaft pedal. **1955** *Times* 20 Aug. 4/3 The new B.R.M. has a 2½-litre short stroke 4-cylinder engine with overhead cam-shafts. **1874** KNIGHT *Dict. Mech.* 435/2 The duty of the cam-wheel is to give an intermittent reciprocating motion to the bar.

cam, *sb.*[2] *north. dial.* [= Sc. *kame, kaim*, a. ON. *kamb-r* (Da. and Sw. *kam*) COMB, crest, serrated ridge, crest or ridge of a hill, etc. The same word originally as COMB, and CAM *sb.*[1], but the three come through distinct channels, and there is no consciousness of their identity.]

A ridge; a long narrow earthen mound; the bank on which a hedge is planted or the like.

1788 MARSHALL *E. Yorksh. Gloss.* (E.D.S.), *Cam*, any long mound of made earth. **1855** *Whitby Gloss.*, *Cam*, a mound of earth, a bank boundary to a field. **1861** RAMSAY *Remin.* Ser. II. Introd. 26 (*Yorksh. dial.*) Cum doun t' cam' soid. **1876** *Mid. Yorksh. Gloss.*, *Cam*, a rise of hedge-ground; generally *cam-side*.

cam, *sb.*[3] *dial.* [f. CAM *a.* or *v.*] Contradiction, crossing in purpose.

1875 *Lanc. Gloss.* (E.D.S.), When he meets wi cam, there's no good to be done.

CAM, *sb.*[4] (kæm). Also **C.A.M. ship, 'cam-ship.** [f. the initials of *C*atapult *A*ircraft *M*erchant-*ship*.] A merchant-ship equipped with a fighter plane launched by catapult.

1943 *Cosmopolitan* Aug. 14/1 Every eye was turned instinctively to the C.A.M., the convoy's Catapult Aircraft Merchantship, the defiant reply of the Royal Air Force to Nazi air assault on British merchant shipping. **1944** A. M. TAYLOR *Lang. World War II* 18 CAM: Catapult Aircraft Merchantship. Adopted by the RAF, to accompany and afford protection to convoys. **1945** L. R. GRIBBLE *Battle Stories RAF* vii. 18 Volunteered to fly with convoys as a catafighter on a Cam-ship. **1954** P. K. KEMP *Fleet Air Arm* 152 These catapult ships were known as Camships. **1956** 'TAFFRAIL' *Arctic Convoy* xix. 201 A 'C.A.M.' ship..an ordinary cargo-carrier fitted with a catapult forward with a single Hurricane fighter.

†**cam**, *a.* and *adv. Obs.* exc. *dial.* Also **kam**, (7 **kamme**). [Adopted from Celtic: in Welsh *cam* crooked, bent, bowed, awry, wrong, false; Gael. *cam* crooked, bent, blind of one eye; Manx *cam* (as in Gaelic); Ir. *cam*:—OIr. *camm* crooked, repr. an OCeltic **cambo-s*, as in the proper name *Cambodunum* 'crooked town'. In English probably from Welsh, and no doubt in oral use long before the 16th c. when first found in literature; the derived form *cammed* is in the Promptorium.]

A. *adj.* Crooked, twisted, bent from the straight. Hence *mod. dial.* Perverse, obstinate, 'cross'.

a **1600** HOOKER *Serm.* iii. Wks. II. 698 His mind is perverse, kam [ed. **1676** cam], and crooked. **1642** *Sc. Pasquils* (1868) 117 Cam is thy name, Cam are thyne eyies and wayes..Cam are thy lookes, thyne eyies thy ways bewrayes. **1853** AKERMAN *Wiltsh. Tales* 138 As cam and as obstinate as a mule. **1862** HUGHES in *Macm. Mag.* V. 236/2 As cam as a peg.

B. *adv.* Away from the straight line, awry, askew (also *fig.*). ***clean cam (kam)***, 'crooked, athwart, awry, cross from the purpose' (J.); cf. KIM KAM.

1579 TOMSON *Calvin's Serm. Tim.* 909/1 We speake in good earnest, and meane not..to say, walk on, behaue your selues manfully: and go cleane kam our selues like Creuises. **1607** SHAKS. *Cor.* III. i. 304, *Sicin.* This is cleane kamme. *Brut.* Meerely awry. **1611** COTGR. s.v. *Contrefoil*, The wrong way, cleane contrarie, quite kamme. **1708** MOTTEUX *Rabelais* v. xxvii, Here they go quite kam, and act clean contrary to others. **1755** JOHNSON, *Kam*, crooked.

cam (kæm), *v. dial.*; *trans.* and *intr.* [f. CAM *a.*] (see quots.)

c **1746** J. COLLIER (Tim Bobbin) *Tummus & M.* Wks. (1862) 53 So ot teh [so that they] camm'd little or none; boh agreed t' pey aw meeon [to pay all between them]. **1847–78** HALLIWELL s.v., A person who treads down the shoe heel is said to cam. *North.* **1875** *Lanc. Gloss.* (E.D.S.) *Colloq. use.* He cams his shoon at th' heel. *Ibid.*, *Cam*, to cross or contradict; to oppose vexatiously; to quarrel. I'll cam him, an' get up his temper.

cam, obs. and Sc. form of *came*, pa. t. of COME.

cam, obs. f. CHAM, KHAN, and var. CALM *sb.*[2]

†**'camaca.** *Obs.* Also **camaka, cammaka, -aca, camoca, cammoca, -oka.** [a. OF. *camocas* (*kamoukas* in Froissart) 'silk stuff approaching satin' (Godef.), or med.L. *camoca, camucum*, med.Gr. *καμουχᾶ*; also in Sp. *camocan, camucan*, acc. to Dozy, ad. Arab. *kamkhā* or *kimkhā*, which Devic thinks originally a Chinese word, and ultimately identical with OF. *canque.*] A kind of fine fabric, probably of silk.

1375 *Will of Edw. Ld. Despencer* (*trans.* Rock) My great bed of blue camaka, with griffins, also another bed of camaka striped with white and black. **1393** LANGL. *P. Pl.* C. XVII. 299 A cote of cammoka oþer of clene scarlett. *a* **1400** *Cov. Myst.* 163 In kyrtyl of cammaka kynge am I cladde. *c* **1475** *Sqr. lowe Degre* 835 Your curtaines of camaca, all in folde. *c* **1485** *E.E. Misc.* (1855) 4 The dosers alle of camaca.

[**1717** BLOUNT *Law Dict.*, *Camoca*, a Garment made of Silk, or something better. **1876** ROCK *Text. Fabr.* iv. 30.]

camack, Sc. form of CAMMOCK[2].

‖**camaieu** (kamajø). Also **camayeu.** [F. *camaïeu*, formerly *camahieu, camaheu*: see CAMEO.]

1. = CAMEO.

1596 DANETT tr. *Comines* (1614) 264 Goodly Camayeux excellently well cut. **1727–51** CHAMBERS *Cycl.*, *Camaieu* or *Camayeu*..a peculiar sort of onyx: also..a stone, whereon are found various figures, and representations of landskips, &c., formed..so as to exhibit pictures without painting. **1731** BAILEY vol. II. *Camaieu.* **1766** [ANSTEY] *Bath Guide* x. 65 And sure no Camayeu was ever yet seen Like that which I purchas'd at Wicksted's Machine.

2. A method of painting in monochrome.

1727–51 CHAMBERS *Cycl.*, *Camaieu* is also used for a painting, wherein there is only one colour; and where the lights and shadows are of gold, wrought on a golden, or azure ground. **1755** in JOHNSON. **1875** FORTNUM *Maiolica* xi. 96 A small plate, the painting of which in blue camaïeu is, etc.

†**camail.** *Obs.* exc. *Hist.* [a. F. *camail* = Pr. *capmalh*, It. *camaglio*; acc. to Diez f. *cap* head + *mail* MAIL, and thus orig. 'head-armour'.]

1. A piece of chain-mail armour attached to the basinet or head-piece, and protecting the neck and shoulders. In *comb.*, as ***camail-lace***.

1826 MRS. BRAY *De Foix* xi. (1884) 127 The dagger therefore slipped out, and sliding athwart the camail of his opponent fell to the ground. **1874** BOUTELL *Arms & Arm.* viii. 127 In England the basinet was constantly worn with the camail, but without any ventaile. *Ibid.* x. 197 The camail-lace or other mode of attachment was covered by a plate, generally enriched, which formed a part of the basinet.

2. (See quot.)

1670 LASSELS *Voy. Italy* (1698) I. 147 The Canons in the Quire wear a rochet and camail. **1681** BLOUNT *Glossogr.*, *Camail* (Fr.) a Hood to cover the head in foul weather: also a blew or purple ornament, worn by Bishops above their Rochets, and reaching as low as the bent of the arm. **1823** CRABB *Techn. Dict.*, *Camail* (*Eccl.*), a purple ornament worn by a bishop over his rochet.

3. 'A capuchin or short cloak, sometimes of fur'.

1858 in SIMMONDS *Dict. Trade.*

Hence **camailed** *a.*, having a camail.

1874 BOUTELL *Arms & Arm.* viii. 128 In England the camailed basinet ceased to be worn when the 15th century was only two or three years old.

camaile, obs. form of CAMEL *sb.*

Camaldolese (kəˈmældəliːz). Also **Camaldulese.** Pl. **-ese.** = CAMALDOLITE. Also *attrib.* or as *adj.*

1828 in B. Ward *Eve Cath. Emanc.* (1912) III. xlv. 198 Two have embraced the Order of Camaldolese Hermits. **1850** in *Ushaw Mag.* (1907) Mar. 62 In Rome the *Candela dell' Elevazione* is used by the Camaldolese only. **1873** NEWMAN *Mission Bened. Order* (1908) 75 Monte Cassino excelled in illumination and in mosaic, the Camaldolese in painting, and the Olivetans in wood-inlaying. **1880** H. COLLINS *Heaven Opened* II. xix. 247 The Carthusians and Camaldulese have but one fixed recreation in the week. **1929** D. GWYNN *Cdl. Wiseman* i. 16 Clothed in his white robes as a Camaldolese monk. **1952** S. RIGBY tr. *Bessières' Wife Mother & Mystic* III. ii. 164 The saintly Camaldolese used a capacious snuff-box.

Ca'maldolite. Also **Camaldulite, -dulian, -dule, -dolensian.** A member of the religious order founded by S. Romuald at Camaldoli in the Apennines, at the beginning of the 11th c.

1727–51 CHAMBERS *Cycl.*, *Camaldulians* or *Camaldunians.* **1764** MACLAINE tr. *Mosheim's Eccl. Hist.* (1844) I. 256/1 In the year 1023, Romuald, an Italian fanatic..founded the order or congregation of the Camaldolites. **1882–3** SCHAFF *Relig. Encycl.* I. 373 s.v. *Camaldules*..[Rudolf] also established Camaldule nunneries (1086). *Ibid.* II. 912/2 [Gregory XVI] since 1823 general of his order, the Cameldolensians.

camall, var. of CUMBLY, coarse (Indian) woollen.

‖**camalote** (ˈkæmələʊteɪ). Also **cameloté, -a.** [Amer. Sp.] An aquatic plant of the genus *Pontederia*, native to North and South America; also, floating islands of vegetation including this plant.

1881 E. W. WHITE *Cameos fr. Silver-Land* I. 243 When the river is high, it is no very uncommon circumstance to see the whole surface of this archipelago covered with the debris (*camelotas*) of these mud-formed islands, buoyed up by matted roots. **1882** *Ibid.* II. 3 Blue-flowered camalotes, consisting chiefly of *Pontederia*, which spread their broad leaves as sails. **1905** R. B. CUNNINGHAME GRAHAM *Progress* 63 Camelotes brought down by the flood were wreathed about them like gigantic eels. *Note*, The camelote is a very thick-growing water-lily, which sometimes chokes small streams. **1918** W. H. HUDSON *Far Away & Long Ago* xx. 261 The fourth lakelet..was..covered with a luxuriant growth of the floating *camaloté*, a plant which at a distance resembles the wild musk. **1950** J. G. KERR *Naturalist in Gran Chaco* i. 3 We passed on up the wide estuary with its muddy fresh water dotted with green floating islands of camelote (*Pontederia*). **1956** G. DURRELL *Drunken Forest* vii. 146 Then, round the bend of the river, appeared the vanguard of the camelotes..islands of lilies, convolvulus, and grass.

camalyon, obs. form of CAMELION.

camamel(le, -ille, -ylle, obs. ff. CAMOMILE.

caman (ˈkæmən). Also **camman.** [Gaelic.] The stick or club used in shinty.

1891 *Daily News* 12 Oct. 5/6 The *camman* is the club.. with which the Gaelic athletes play their favourite game. **1900** *19th Cent.* Aug. 307 Each man has a *caman* or hurley —a stick, about three feet long, with a bend or curve at the end. **1905** P. A. SHEEHAN *Glenanaar* i, The crack of the camans as they crossed in the air above or on the grass beneath.

camanchaca (kæmənˈtʃɑːkə). [Amer. Sp.] A heavy mist on the Peruvian coast.

1907 C. R. ENOCK *Andes & Amazon* i. 5 The heavy mist upon the coast, known as *Camanchaca.* **1922** *Daily Mail* 17 Nov. 8 In the Northern rainless zone, the camanchacas, or heavy, overhanging mists, became much denser.

camara[1] (ˈkæmərə). *Bot.* [a. Gr. *καμάρα* (see CAMERA); cf. F. *camare* (in sense a).]

a. A membranous fruit composed of two united valves and enclosing one or many seeds attached to the internal angle (Littré, and *Syd. Soc. Lex.*). **b.** One of the cells of a fruit. **c.** A carpel (*Treas. Bot.* 1866).

1880 GRAY *Bot. Text-bk.* 400 Camara and its diminutive Camerula (chamber) are sometimes used for the cells of a fruit.

‖**camara**[2] (ˈkæmərə). [Native name in Guiana.] 'A hard durable timber obtained from *Dipteryx odorata*' (N.O. *Leguminosæ*). *Treas. Bot.* 1866.

‖**cama'rada.** *Obs.* [Sp. *camarada*, lit. 'roomful': see COMRADE.]

1. A company of soldiers messing or lodging together. **2.** One of such a company in his relation to the others; a comrade.

1598 BARRET *Theor. Warres* I. ii. 9 With his Camaradas, hee is to demeane himself, sober, quiet, and friendly. *Ibid.* 10 Pescennius Niger did condemne vnto death, a whole Camarada of Soldiers. *Ibid.* Gloss. 249 *Camarada*, a Spanish word, is a small number of 11 or 12 soldiers, and is the one halfe of a squadra, being vnited together in their lodging.

camarade, obs. form of COMRADE.

‖**camaraderie** (kamaradri, kæməˈrɑːdərɪ). [Fr., f. *camarade* COMRADE.] 'The familiarity which exists between *camarades*' (Littré), comradeship; loyalty to, or partiality for, one's comrades; *esprit de corps*.

1840 *Fraser's Mag.* XXI. 721 A spirit of camaraderie and partisanship prevails in matters of art. **1863** RUSSELL *Diary North & S.* II. 107 The only camaraderie I have witnessed in America exists among the West Point men.

camarike, obs. form of CAMBRIC.

‖**camarilla** (kæməˈrɪlə, Sp. kamaˈriʎa). [Sp., dim. of *camara* room, CHAMBER.]

1. A small chamber.

1860 EMERSON *Cond. Life* Wks. II. 312 Now and then, one has a new cell or camarilla opened in his brain.

2. A private cabinet of counsellors; a cabal, clique, junto; a body of secret intriguers.

1839 R. M. BEVERLEY *Heresy Hum. Priesth.* 111 Conference is a camarilla of priests, who, with closed doors, make all the laws by which the society is regulated. **1858** *Sat. Rev.* V. 445/1 It is only a camarilla which demands Lord Palmerston's return to office. **1867** WARD in *Ess. Reunion* 117 No camarilla of worldly-minded politicians lay or sacerdotal.

‖**'Camarine.** *Obs.* Also **camerine.** [f. *Camarīna* (*Καμάρῖνα*), the name of a Sicilian town, beside

which was a pestilential marsh.] A fetid marsh or swamp. Also *fig.*

1576 NEWTON tr. *Lemnie's Complex.* To Rdr., This Author..doth not onely..wade into the very Gulph and Camarine of Mans apparant wilfulnesse. **1617** S. COLLINS *Def. Bp. Elie* 454 And doe wee meruaile now, if King Henry voyded such a Camarine? **1681** P. RYCAUT *Critick* 163 The danger of poisonous sents, and Camerines of Customs, which use to envenome and infect the soul.

camaron (kæmə'rəʊn, 'kæmərən). Also cammaron. [ad. Sp. *camarón* shrimp, f. L. *cam(m)arus* sea-crab.] A freshwater shrimp or prawn resembling the crayfish.

1880 T. H. HUXLEY *Crayfish* 329 These fluviatile prawns (known in many places by the name of '*Cammarons*') are not unfrequently confounded with true crayfishes. **1920** *Glasgow Herald* 31 Dec. 12 Camarons are excellent when boiled. **1947** M. LOWRY *Under Volcano* vii. 229 The boy brought them camarones, red shrimps in a saucer. **1967** *Oceanogr. & Marine Biol.* V. 371 Nephrops norvegicus... is known by the following common names:..Norway lobster, Dublin Bay prawn, North Shields prawn, Beardog (Britain)..Langostino, Camaron, Cigala, Maganto, Escamarlanch (Spain).

‖**camas, camash, cammas,** variant forms of QUAMASH (*Camassia esculenta*), a liliaceous plant, whose bulbs are eaten by North American Indians.

1837 W. IRVING *Capt. Bonneville* II. 221 The Indians.. come to it in the summer time to dig the camash root. **1884** JOAQUIN MILLER *Mem. & Rime* 83 The camas blossom..all Oregon in the early spring.

Hence **camas rat** (see quot.).

1868 WOOD *Homes without H.* i. 35 The Camas Rat (*Pseudostoma borealis*)..The name is derived from its food, which consists chiefly of quamash root.

camata (kə'mɑːtə, -'eɪtə). [It.] The commercial name for the half-grown acorns of *Quercus ægilops*, dried and used for tanning. Cf. next.

1858 SIMMONDS *Dict. Trade.* **1866** LINDLEY & MOORE *Treas. Bot.* 950/1.

camatina (kæmə'tiːnə, -'aɪnə). [dim. of prec.] The commercial name for the incipient acorns of *Quercus ægilops*.

1858 SIMMONDS *Dict. Trade.* **1866** LINDLEY & MOORE *Treas. Bot.* 950/1. **1884** *Encycl. Brit.* XVII. 694/2 The valonia of commerce, one of the richest of tanning materials, is the acorn of *Q[uercus] Ægilops*... Immature acorns are sometimes exported under the name of camatina.

camayeu: see CAMAIEU.

camayle, camaylle, obs. forms of CAMEL *sb.*

camb, obs. form of COMB.

cambace, ? obs. form of CANVASS (or CAMACA).

1460 CAPGRAVE *Chron.* 177 Thanne schuld thei clothe him, and gird him with a girdill of cambace.

cambake, obs. form of CAMMOCK.

†**cambal.** *Obs.* ? = CUMBLY (or next).

1599 HAKLUYT *Voy.* II. I. 257 Marchants which come out of China..come to buy muske, cambals, agats, silke.

cam'baye. [f. *Cambay* a sea-port of India.] A kind of cotton cloth made in India.

1727 A. HAMILTON *New Acc. E. Ind.* I. i. 9 Coarse chequer'd Cloth, called Cambaya Lungies, made of Cotton-yarn. **1874** KNIGHT *Dict. Mech.* 432 *Cambayes.*

Camber *a.*: see CAMBRIAN.

camber ('kæmbə(r)), *sb.* Also GAMBER. [a. F. *cambre*, f. *cambrer*: see next. Cf. CAMBREL.]

1. a. The condition of being slightly arched or convex above. Also *concr.* a flattened arch.

1618 [see *camber-keeled* in 4]. **1823** P. NICHOLSON *Pract. Build.* 220 Camber..the convexity of a beam upon the upper edge, in order to prevent its becoming straight or concave by its own weight, or by the burden it may have to sustain, in course of time. *Ibid.* 582 Camber; an arch on the top of an aperture, or on the top of a beam; whence Camber-windows, &c. **1876** GWILT *Archit.* 437 If the required rise or camber [in a riveted girder] equals *e* in the middle in inches. **1881** *Times* 11 Apr. 10/5 Boatbuilders insist on giving 'camber'.

b. The transverse arch of the surface of a road.

1905 *Westm. Gaz.* 13 Oct. 2/7 Another suggestion is that the 'camber' (i.e., the upward curve) of roadways should be lessened. **1907** *Ibid.* 30 July 8/1 The heavy camber of the sides..is the cause of very many mishaps. **1925** *Public Opinion* 11 Dec. 588/2 Hodge has always allowed his horse to take the top of the camber.

c. The curvature of the wings of an aeroplane. Also *attrib.*

1910 R. FERRIS *How it Flies* xx. 456 *Camber*, the distance from the chord of the curve of a surface to the highest point of that curve, measured at right angles to the chord. **1918** H. BARBER *Aeroplane Speaks* (ed. 6) 5, I must have a certain chord to make it possible for my Camber (that's curvature) to be just right for the Angle of Incidence. **1935** K. D. WOOD *Techn. Aerodynamics* ii. 52 The shape of the median camber line of the variable-density-tunnel series is nearly the same as for other good airfoils. *Ibid.* 53 The maximum median camber must next be located relative to the line through the leading and trailing edges.

d. *Automobile Engin.* (See quot. 1959[2].)

1936 *Motor Man.* (ed. 29) vii. 121 How a steering head is set to give castor action and camber. *Ibid.*, The point..is thrust forward by the slope or castor angle of the king pin and slightly to one side according to the camber chosen for the wheel and pin. **1959** *Ibid.* (ed. 36) v. 102 Each steering swivel..is also given..a camber angle so that its axis, when viewed from the front, meets the road at a point..close to the centre line of the wheel. **1959** *Motor* 2 Sept. 92/1 Camber (the sideways inclination of the wheel).

2. A piece of timber so bent; a camber-beam.

1677 MOXON *Mech. Exerc.* (1703) 158 Camber, a piece of Timber cut Arching. *c* **1850** *Rudim. Navig.* (Weale) 102.

3. 'The part of a dockyard where cambering is performed, and timber kept. Also, a small dock in the royal yards, for the convenience of loading and discharging timber' (Smyth *Sailor's Word-bk.*).

1885 LADY BRASSEY *The Trades* 403 Just outside the camber, [he] met us in the dockyard steam-launch.

4. *Comb.*, as **camber-beam, -slip** (see quots.); † *camber-bored, camber-keeled* (also *-keel*), adjs. **camber-nose,** 'an aquiline nose' (Halliwell, who cites 'Junius').

1721 BAILEY, **Camber-beam*..is a Beam cut hollow or arching in the middle. **1823** P. NICHOLSON *Pract. Build.* 129. **1626** CAPT. SMITH *Accid. Yng. Seamen* 32 To know whether she be equally bored, *camber, taper, or belbored. *a* **1618** RALEIGH *Royal Navy* 34 It is a great weakening to a ship to have so much weight..at both the ends, and nothing in the Mid-Ship, which causeth them to warpe, and (in the Sea-phrase, and with Marriners) is tearmed *Camberkeeld. *a* **1642** SIR W. MONSON *Naval Tracts* iii. (1704) 350/1 It will make the Ship Camberkeel. **1867** SMYTH *Sailor's Word-bk.*, *Camber-keeled*, keel slightly arched upwards in the middle of the length, but not actually hogged. **1823** P. NICHOLSON *Pract. Build.* 388 The *Camber-slip is a piece of board of any length or breadth, made convex on one or both edges, and generally something less than an inch in thickness; it is made use of as a rule..When the brick-layer has drawn his arch, he gives the camber-slip to the carpenter.

camber ('kæmbə(r)), *v.* [app. a. F. *cambre-r* 'to arch slightly' (16th c. in Littré), a semi-popular repr. of L. *camerāre* to vault (the natural repr. being *chambrer*), f. *camera* vault.]

1. *intr.* To be or become slightly arched or curved so that the centre is higher than the ends.

1627 CAPT. SMITH *Seaman's Gram.* ii. 6 The Decke doth camber or lie compassing. **1757** ROBERTSON in *Phil. Trans.* L. 288 Now it so happened, thro' the great weight of the head and stern, that the ship cambered very much.

2. *trans.* To bend (a beam, etc.) upwards in the middle; to arch slightly.

1852 P. NICHOLSON *Encycl. Archit.* I. 74 In all these instances the difficulty may be obviated by cambering the timber upwards. **1876** GWILT *Archit.* 437 It is usual to camber a riveted girder, so that on receiving the permanent load it may become nearly horizontal. **1882** *Nature* XXV. 247 At the centre of the span, where the bottom member has been cambered upwards to a height of 150 feet for navigation purposes.

Hence **'cambered** *ppl. a.*, **'cambering** *vbl. sb.* and *ppl. a.*

1627 CAPT. SMITH *Seaman's Gram.* ii. 6 A cambered Decke. **1757** ROBERTSON in *Phil. Trans.* L. 292 The resistance of the parts bent by the cambering. **1769** FALCONER *Dict. Marine* (1789) *Cambered Deck*, the deck..of a ship is said to be cambered, or to lie cambering, when it is higher in the middle of the ship's length, and droops toward the stem and stern. **1878** BARTLEY tr. *Topinard's Anthrop.* II. vi. 340 With head erect and cambered loins. **1909** *Flight* 20 Feb. 104/1 *Cambered*, this term denotes that the plane or wing has a curved transverse section. **1919** *Autocar Handbk.* (ed. 9) 223 When driving a car on a much-cambered or arched road. **1932** G. M. BOUMPHREY *Story of Wheel* 57 His roads were cambered (raised slightly in the middle to throw off water). **1951** W. F. HILTON *High-Speed Aerodynamics* II. x. 241 The 8% cambered wing would be outside the limits of accuracy at M = 10. **1967** *Gloss. Mining Terms (B.S.I.)* XI. 6 *Cambered girder*, a roof bar projecting forward to support the roof beyond the propped area.

'Camberwell 'Beauty. [from *Camberwell*, a parish of Surrey, now within the London area.] A collector's name for a species of butterfly (*Vanessa Antiopa*), occasionally seen in England.

1847 *Proc. Berw. Nat. Club* II. v. 198 Mr. Broderick remarked that he had seen the 'Camberwell Beauty' on Twizel-moor. **1847** CARPENTER *Zool.* §706.

cambial ('kæmbɪəl), *a.* [ad. late L. *cambiāl-is*, f. *cambium*: see CAMBIUM and -AL[1].]

1. Relating to exchange in commerce. [F. *cambial.*]

1864 in WEBSTER.

2. *Bot.* Pertaining to cambium.

1881 *Gard. Chron.* No. 414 XVI. 726 The adventitious roots in the cambial region of the vascular bundles. **1882** VINES *Sach's Bot.* 130 A middle layer of the cambial cells always remains capable of division.

cambiform ('kæmbɪfɔːm), *a. Bot.* [f. CAMBIUM + -FORM.] Of the form of, or like cambium.

1882 VINES *Sachs' Bot.* 114 Cambiform tissue. **1884** BOWER & SCOTT *De Bary's Phaner. & Ferns* 523 The narrow cambiform cells.

‖**'cambio.** *Obs.* [It. *cambio* change, exchange:—L. *cambium.*] **a.** A bill of exchange. **b.** A place of exchange, an exchange; = CAMBIUM 1.

1645 HOWELL *Dodonas Gr.* 20 (D.) Punctuality in payment of cambios. **1656** BLOUNT *Glossogr.*, *Cambio*, a Burse or Exchange as the Royal Exchange in London.

cambiogenetic (ˌkæmbɪəʊdʒɪ'nɛtɪk), *a. Bot.* [f. L. *cambium* + Gr. *γενετικός, f. γένεσις production.] Pertaining to the formation of cambium.

1884 BOWER & SCOTT *De Bary's Phaner. & Ferns* 473 The cambio-genetic production of tissue. *Ibid.* 585 An indication of cambiogenetic growth in thickness.

'cambism, *rare.* [see next and -ISM.] The theory and practice of exchanges.

1837 WHITTOCK *Bk. Trades* (1842) 334 The authors who have written..on cambism and the operations in exchanges.

cambist ('kæmbɪst). [a. F. *cambiste*, f. L. *cambium*, It. *cambio* exchange. (So Sp. *cambista*.)]

1. One who is skilled in the science or practice of exchanges; one who deals in bills of exchange.

1809 R. LANGFORD *Introd. Trade* 130 Cambist, one well versed in the knowledge of exchanges, a trafficker in bills. **1861** GOSCHEN *For. Exch.* 99 These speculators in exchange, or cambists, as they are technically called.

2. *transf.* As title of a manual of foreign exchanges.

1811 P. KELLY (*title*) The Universal Cambist, and Commercial Instructor. **1882** *Nature* XXVI. 55 The book is so far a cambist or dictionary of weights and measures.

'cambistry. [f. prec.: see -RY.] The science or operations of the cambist.

In mod. Dicts.

cambium ('kæmbɪəm). [a. late L. *cambium* exchange (found in the Laws of the Lombards); the physiological sense, 2, occurs in 14th c. in Arnold de Villa Nova ('cambium humiditas manifeste alterata membri continentis complexione').]

†**1. a.** Exchange, barter. **b.** A place of exchange, an exchange. *Obs.*

1708 KERSEY, *Cambium*, the exchanging or bartering of Commodities; also an Exchange, or Place where Merchants meet. **1721–1800** in BAILEY; and in mod. Dicts.

†**2.** One of the 'alimentary humours' formerly supposed to nourish the bodily organs. *Obs.*

1643 T. JOHNSON tr. *Parey's Wks.* I. vi. (1678) 9 The Arabians have mentioned four other humors, which they term Alimentary..The third [humor] they call by a barbarous name, Cambium, which, already put to the part to be nourished, is there fastned. **1708** KERSEY, *Cambium*, one of the three Humours sometime thought to nourish the Body, the other two being call'd Gluten and Ros. **1721–1800** in BAILEY; and in mod. Dicts.

3. *Bot.* A viscid substance, consisting of cellular tissue, lying immediately under the bark of exogens, in which the annual growth of the wood and bark takes place. 'The cells are inactive during winter, but very succulent in spring. This name was formerly given to the fluid contents only of the cells.' *Syd. Soc. Lex.*

(Quot. 1671 illustrates the origin of this sense from 2.)

1671 GREW *Anat. Plants* I. ii. §23 The said sap..becomes (as they speak of that of an Animal) the Vegetative Ros or Cambium: the noblest part whereof is at last..assimilated to the like substance with the said Lignous Body. **1813** SIR H. DAVY *Agric. Chem.* iii. 147 The Cambium which is the mucilaginous fluid found in trees between the wood and the bark. **1877** W. DALL *Tribes N.W.* 86 A species of red.. derived from pine bark or the cambium of the ground-willow.

b. *attrib.*, as in *cambium-layer, -ring.*

1842 GRAY *Struct. Bot.* iii. §3 (1880) 78 There is always a zone of delicate young cells interposed between the wood and the bark. This is called the Cambium, or better, the Cambium-layer. **1882** VINES *Sachs' Bot.* 654 The primary bundles..are united by a cambium-ring.

camblet, variant of CAMLET.

cambmok, camboc, -ok, obs. ff. CAMMOCK.

Cambodian (kæm'bəʊdɪən), *a.* and *sb.* [f. *Cambodia*, a country in S.E. Asia + -IAN.] **A.** *adj.* Of or pertaining to Cambodia or its inhabitants. **B.** *sb.* An inhabitant of Cambodia; also, the language of its people.

1770 W. GUTHRIE *New Geogr., Hist., & Comm. Gram.* 481 The betel..is the highest luxury of the Cambodians, from the King to the peasant. **1853** *Jrnl. Indian Archipelago & E. Asia* VII. 292 The most approved forms of Cambodian correspondence. *Ibid.*, The Cambodians always use Indian ink. *Ibid.*, The letter was then inserted into an envelope addressed in Cambodian. **1862** *Proc. R. Geogr. Soc.* VI. 82 The Cambodians had invented a written phonetic character, which they used at the present time; therefore there could be no difficulty in understanding a Cambodian manuscript. **1877** [see ANNAMITE *a.* and *sb.*] **1937** R. H. LOWIE *Hist. Ethnol. Theory* x. 162 Their first pyramids were erected five or six centuries later as copies of Cambodian..models. **1966** H. L. SHORTO in C. E. Bazell *In Memory of J. R. Firth* 398 In Cambodian, for example, words may be distinguished by a complex of features which includes both elements ascribed to 'register' and differences in vowel quality. **1966** *Guardian* 31 Aug. 11/3 Armed Cambodian terrorists..said to belong to the 'Free Cambodians'.

camboge, obs. form of GAMBOGE.

camboline, var. of CAMELINE *sb.*[1] *Obs.*

camboose, var. of CABOOSE.

‖**cambré** (kɑ̃bre), *a.* [Fr., pa. pple. of *cambrer* to arch, to bend: see CAMBER *v.*] Curved, arched; spec. in *Dancing* (see quots.). Also as *sb.*

1913 C. D'ALBERT *Dict. Dancing* 33 *Pas cambré*.. Open the heels and pivot on the toes; the points are inward, the feet in the form of an arch, toes nearly touching in front, heels open in the rear. Raise the shoulders.. then pivot on the heels, opening the toes.. and assemblé, letting the hands fall. **1929** D. H. LAWRENCE *Lovely Lady* (1932) 97 Her figure, though not stout, was full, strong, and *cambré*. **1952** KERSLEY & SINCLAIR *Dict. Ballet Terms* 22 *Cambré*, a bend of the body from the waist in any direction.

cambrel (ˈkæmbrəl). ? *Obs.* exc. *dial.* Forms: 5–8 **cambrel**, 6 **camborell**, 7 **cambrell**, **cambril**, **cammeril**, 9 *dial.* **camrel**, **cammeril**, **cambril**, **cameral**. See also CHAMBREL, GAMBREL. [It is uncertain whether this is a mere variant or alteration of CAMBREN (given as a synonym by Blount and Bailey, and really a Welsh word), or whether it is to be referred to the verb CAMBER, F. *cambrer*; cf. CAMBER *sb.* 2. The lateness of these words is against their being the source of *cambrel*; on the other hand, the variant forms *chambrel* (in sense 2) and *gambrel* (in both senses) make the Welsh derivation difficult. Perhaps there has been contact of distinct words, and action of popular etymology.]

1. A bent piece of wood or iron used by butchers to hang carcases of animals on.

c **1450** *Voc.* in Wr.-Wülcker 612 *Spatula*, a Cambrel, and a sclyse. **1641** J. JACKSON *True Evang. T.* II. 116 He.. was crucified.. with his head downward, just like a sheep upon the Cambrell. **1731–1800** BAILEY, *Cambren, Cambrel.* **1808** JAMIESON, *Camrel, Cammeril*, a crooked piece of wood, passing through the ancles of a sheep, or other carcase, by means of which it is suspended. **1863** *Glasgow Daily Her.* 14 Nov., He said a cameral was a beef-tree or piece of wood used for hanging up carcases. **1863** MORTON *Cycl. Agric.* II. Gloss., *Cambril* or *Gambril*, a butcher's stretch to hang carcases from or by. **1881** in *Leicestersh. Gloss.* (E.D.S.).

2. The bend or joint of the upper part of a horse's hind leg; the hock. Now chiefly *dial.*

1610 MARKHAM *Masterp.* II. i. 212 The length of his hinder hough would be twelue inches, and his cambrell fiue inches. *Ibid.* 295 The hinder legges will be all swolne.. from the cambrels or houghs vpward. *a* **1631** DRAYTON *Nymphal* x. Wks. 1519 (N.) A perfect goat below, His crooked cambrils arm'd with hoof and hair. **1725** BRADLEY *Fam. Dict.* II. 52/2 View his Cambrels, have an eye to the Joint behind. **1880** *O.C. & Farm. Wds.* (E.D.S.) 137 In the north the hocks of animals are called cambrils or gambrils.

3. *attrib.*

1523 FITZHERB. *Husb.* §107 A courbe is an yll sorance.. vnder the camborell place. **1611** COTGR., *Chapelet du iarret*.. the cambrell hogh of a horse. **1686** *Lond. Gaz.* No. 2121/4 Two hinder feet white towards the Cammeril Joint. **1877** E. PEACOCK *N.-W. Lincoln. Gloss.* (E.D.S.) *Cameril stick*, by which the carcase is suspended.

†ˈ**cambren.** *Obs. rare.* [a. Welsh *cambren*, a combination of *cam* crooked + *pren* wood, stick, applied in Wales both to the butcher's cambrel, and to the swingle-tree used when one horse is yoked in front of another. (The latter in Anglesea is called *bombren.*)] = CAMBREL 1.

1656 in BLOUNT *Glossogr.* **1721** BAILEY, *Cambren*, a crooked Stick with Notches on it, on which Butchers hang their meat. **1731–1800** [see prec. 1].

‖**cambresine** (kæmbrəˈziːn). Also 8 **cambrasine.** [F.] 'A species of fine linen made in Cambray' (Littré); also a similar eastern fabric.

1750 BEAWES *Lex Mercat.* 731 The Persians however drive a very considerable trade here in silk stuffs, Cambresines, Indianas, Carpets, Lizats, &c.

Cambrian (ˈkæmbrɪən), *a.* (*sb.*) [f. *Cambria*, var. of *Cumbria*, latinized derivative of *Cymry* (:—OCeltic *Combroges* 'compatriots') Welshmen, or of *Cymru* Wales. *Cumbria* and *Cambria* were originally the same, but were subsequently differentiated: *Cambria* was regularly applied to Wales by Geoffrey of Monmouth. (Some think that *Cymru*, a late word, is only a variant of *Cymry* the name of the people, parallel to the later Eng. use of *Wales* = OE. *Wealas* 'Welshmen', as the name of their country.)]

1. Pertaining to Wales, Welsh; *sb.* a Welshman.

[**1586** J. HOOKER *Girald. Irel.* in *Holinshed* II. 24/2 There came vnto him a Welsh or a Camber woman. **1626** W. SCLATER *Expos. 2 Thess.* (1629) 299 Wee, Brittans of t'other race, are growne all Cumber, Camber; quite changed from the temper of our peaceable forefathers. Cf. *kim kam*, CAM *a.*] **1656** BLOUNT *Glossogr.*, *Cambrian*, Welch, Brittish. **1780** VON TROIL *Iceland* 211 Among the ancient Cambrians. **1860** *All Y. Round* No. 68. 420 Change is too strong even for Cambrian nationality.

2. *Geol.* A name given by Sedgwick in 1836 to a group or 'system' of Palæozoic rocks lying below the Silurian, in Wales and Cumberland.

As originally defined, the Silurian of Murchison and Cambrian of Sedgwick, being established in different districts, were found on further investigation to overlap each other; the Cambrian is now generally held to include the Tremadoc slates, Lingula flags, Menevian beds, and Longmynd group, containing the Harlech grits and Llanberis slates; but the Geological Surveyors limit the term to the Longmynd group, while others extend it to include all the Lower Silurian of Murchison (Bala and Llandeilo groups).

1842 H. MILLER *O.R. Sandst.* xii. (ed. 2) 257 The geologist has learnt from Murchison to distinguish the rocks of these two periods,—the lower as those of the Cambrian, the upper as those of the Silurian. **1873** GEIKIE *Gt. Ice Age* xvi. 207 In Lewis we get boulders of Cambrian sandstone. **1876** PAGE *Adv. Text-bk. Geol.* xi. 193 The Cambrian may vary in composition in different regions.

cambric (ˈkeɪmbrɪk). Forms: 6 **camerick(e**, **-yk(e**, **-ike**, **camarick**, **-ike**, (*Sc.* **cammeraige**, **camorage**, **camroche**), 6–7 **cambricke**, **camerige**, 7 **cameric**, 6–8 **cambrick**, 8– **cambric**. [f. *Kameryk* or *Kamerijk*, Flemish name of *Cambray*:—L. *Camaracum*, in French Flanders.]

1. a. A kind of fine white linen, originally made at Cambray in Flanders. (Also applied to an imitation made of hard-spun cotton yarn.)

1530 *Privy Purse Exp. Hen. VIII*, 29 Oct. in Beck *Draper's Dict.*, xxiij elles of cameryk for vj shirtes for the King. *c* **1570** THYNNE *Pride & Lowl.* (1841) 19 His shirt had bands and ruffe of pure cambrick. **1578** *Royal Inv.* 232 (Jam.) Ane quaiff of camorage with twa cornettis. **1581** *Sc. Acts Jas. VI* (1597) §113 The wearing of coastelie Cleithing of Silkes.. Cammeraige. *a* **1586** *Maitland Poems* (1786) 326 (Jam.) Of fynest camroche thair fuk saillis. **1597** LOWE *Chirurg.* (1634) 367 Cover it with a linnen cloth, or for persons of higher dignitie take layre or camerige. **1607** SHAKS. *Cor.* I. iii. 95, I would your Cambrick were sensible as your finger. **1610** HOLLAND *Camden's Brit.* I. 478 Cameric, Calecut, &c. had.. their denomination from the places where they were first invented. **1712** STEELE *Spect.* No. 552 ¶1 The most delicate cambricks, muslins, and linens. **1735** BERKELEY *Querist* §552 Wks. 1871 III. 399 Diapers are made in one town.. in another cambrics. **1875** URE *Dict. Arts* I. 675 Linen cambric.. manufactured.. from power-spun flax.. frequently called cambric muslin.

b. As the material of handkerchiefs.

1886 *Sat. Rev.* 6 Mar. 328 It is not our habit.. to flourish cambric over the woes of any one.

c. *attrib.* Also **cambric tea** *U.S.*, a drink composed mainly of hot milk and water, given to children in place of tea.

1575 G. HARVEY *Letter-bk.* (1884) 98 Frenche camarike ruffes. **1714** GAY *Trivia* III. 82 Cambrick Handkerchiefs reward the Song. **1793** J. BERESFORD in *Looker-on* No. 79 A cambrick trophy of former achievements. **1888** *Union Signal* (Chicago) 21 Jan. 3 [She] gave me a vast easy chair to sit in.. and offered me tea, cambric tea to be sure, but in a beautiful cup. **1944** *Greeley* (Colo.) *Daily Tribune* 28 Sept. 6/4 Many children dearly love cambric tea, which is made by pouring about two tablespoons of weak tea into a cup of hot milk and adding a dash of sugar.

Cambridge (ˈkeɪmbrɪdʒ), the name of a university town in England, used *attrib.*, as **Cambridge blue**, a light blue; **Cambridge calf** (see quot. 1895); **Cambridge chimes**, the composition of Joseph Jowett and William Crotch, first employed in 1793 at the Church of St. Mary the Great, Cambridge; **Cambridge coprolite**, **greensand** *Geol.* (see quots. 1881, 1882); **Cambridge roller** *Agric.* (see quot. 1954); **Cambridge sausage**, a variety of sausage.

1580 in *Cath. Rec. Soc. Publ.* (1961) LIII. 194 Robert Kent prest, a cambridge man borne. **1830** M. R. MITFORD *Our Village* IV. 108 Your thoroughbred Londoner.. grumbling over.. his thin milk and his Cambridge butter. **1840** DICKENS *Let.* 1 Feb. (1969) 17 The Cambridge sassages of right down English Manafacter. **1850** DENISON *Clock & Watch-m.* 226 A clock made for a nobleman a few years ago, which intended to have the Cambridge chimes. **1877** E. S. DALLAS *Kettner's Book of Table* 94 It is notorious that what has been called Cambridge butter is a mixture of foreign butters. **1881** *Spon's Encycl. Industr. Arts* IV. 1260 The most valuable beds of the mineral in this country are in the Upper Greensand formation, lying chiefly in Cambridgeshire, and merging into Buckinghamshire. These are known as 'Cambridge' coprolites. **1882** GEIKIE *Text-bk. Geol.* 809 The so-called 'Cambridge Greensand'—a bed about 1 foot thick lying at the base of the Chalk of Cambridge, and largely worked for phosphate of lime derived from coprolites and bones. **1883** *Cassell's Fam. Mag.* Mar. 206/2 A huge wooden spoon, ornamented with bows of Cambridge blue. **1891** R. WALLACE *Rural Econ. Austral. & N.Z.* xviii. 262 About one pound of seed is sown per acre.. distributed from a sowing-box placed behind a Cambridge roller. **1895** *Windsor Mag.* I. 403/2 Knickerbockers of dark blue velveteen trimmed with Cambridge blue. **1895** ZAEHNSDORF *Short Hist. Bookbinding* 20 Cambridge Calf.—Fine and dark sprinkled calf of two tints, a square panel being left in centre of sides. **1898** *Westm. Gaz.* 3 Mar. 9/2 The bulky little volume.. in its Cambridge-blue cover. **1909** *Daily Chron.* 16 Feb. 4/6 As the 'Cambridge Chimes' at St. Stephen's strike 2 p.m. the King will arrive to open Parliament. **1947** G. GREENE *19 Stories* 227 A tin of Cambridge sausages. **1954** *Gloss. Terms Agric. Mach.* (*B.S.I.*) 12 *Cambridge roller*, a roller consisting of loosely mounted ring segments each usually about 3 in. wide and tapering at the periphery to a narrow rim. **1970** *Sunday Times* (Colour Suppl.) 1 Feb. 40/1 The finest breakfast I have ever had.. finnan haddock, Cambridge sausages, York ham.

Cambridgeshire (ˈkeɪmbrɪdʒʃə(r)). The name of an eastern county of England used attrib. in ***the Cambridgeshire handicap*** (***stakes***) as the name of a horse-race originated in 1839 and run annually at Newmarket (situated east of Cambridge): usually ellipt. *The Cambridgeshire.*

1840 J. C. WHYTE *Hist. Brit. Turf* II. 482 The Cambridgeshire stakes. **1856** 'STONEHENGE' *Brit. Sports* 373/1 Cambridgeshire Course.. 1 mile 240 yards. **1891** G. CHETWYND *Racing Remin.* I. 10 The next day Vestminster won the Cambridgeshire. **1930** WODEHOUSE *Very Good, Jeeves!* iv. 99 She married old Tom Travers the year Bluebottle won the Cambridgeshire.

cambril, cambuc, var. CAMBREL, CAMMOCK.

Cambro- (ˈkæmbrəʊ), mod.L. *Cambro-*, as in *Cambro-Britannicus* (1592), used as combining form in the sense 'pertaining to Cambria, Welsh'. Also in sense 'Cambrian' (Geol.)

1612 DRAYTON *Poly-Olb.* Pref., To my friends, the Cambro-Britans. **1748** SMOLLETT *Rod. Rand.* I. xxv. 233 A prescription.. which.. the Welchman.. got up to prepare... This Cambro Briton.. ordered the tar to run to his mess-mate. **1853** W. J. REES (*title*) Lives of the Cambro British Saints. **1871** LOWELL *Study Windows* 164 Tennyson in the Cambro-Breton cyclus of Arthur. **1925** J. JOLY *Surface-Hist. Earth* iii. 57 Almost complete submergence of North America in Cambro-Ordovician times. **1967** *Oceanogr. & Marine Biol.* V. 317 Permanent ocean basins which have not changed significantly in their area or position since Cambro-Ordovician times, some 500 million years ago.

cambugium: see GAMBOGE.

camcorder (ˈkæmkɔːdə(r)). [f. CAM(ERA + RE)CORDER[1].] A portable video camera incorporating a built-in video recorder.

1982 *Economist* 13 Mar. 73/2 Manufacturers of video tape recorders.. have agreed that these 'camcorders' will all use the same standard 8mm. video tape. **1983** *New Scientist* 21 Apr. 153/1 Discussions began in Tokyo in March 1982, after Sony, Matsushita, Sanyo and Hitachi had all separately demonstrated prototype 'camcorders' (video cameras with built-in recorders). **1984** *What Video?* Aug. 14/2 Kodak plans to launch an 8mm video camcorder, and until now everyone has thought of Kodak only as a film company. **1985** *Which?* Apr. 186/2 Panasonic have plans to introduce a camcorder which uses a standard VHS cassette.

came (keɪm). Also 7 **caum.** [app. the same as CALM[2] q.v.] A small grooved bar of lead used for framing the glass in lattice windows: chiefly in *pl.*

1688 R. HOLME III. ix. 384/2 Leads [Glasier's].. termed Caums. **1731** BAILEY vol. II, *Cames*, the small slender rods of cast lead of which they make their milled lead for joining the panes or quarrels of glass. **1734** *Builder's Dict.* s.v. *Cames*, Their Lead being cast into slender Rods, of twelve or fourteen Inches in Length, are called *Cames*; and sometimes they call each of those Rods a *Came.* **1875** URE *Dict. Arts* I 677 Cames.. were formerly called 'lattices', and hence leaded windows were termed lattice windows. **1875** GWILT *Archit.* §2228 The glazier's vice is for preparing the leaden slips called *cames* with grooves, etc.

came (keɪm), pa. t. of COME *v.*; Sc. f. COMB.

cameist (ˈkæmiːɪst). *rare.* [f. CAME-O + -IST.] A maker or connoisseur of cameos.

1866 *Reader* 10 Feb. 148/3 M. Saulini (the celebrated cameist).

camel (ˈkæməl), *sb.* Forms: 1 **camel**, **-ell**, 3 **kamel**, 4–5 **camele**, **kamell(e**, 4–7 **camell**, 5 **camelle**, **-ylle**, 6 **cammell**, 6–7 **cammel**, 3– **camel**. Also *β.* 3 **camayl(e**, 4–5 **camail(e**, 5 **cameile**, **cameylle**, **camayll(e**, (**camely**); *γ.* 4–5 **chamel**, 4–7 **chamell(e**; *δ.* 4–5 **chameyl(e**, 5 **chamayle**, **chamoil.** [Late OE. *camel*, *camell*, ad. L. *camēl-us* (*-ellus*), a. Gr. *κάμηλ-ος*, adopted from Semitic: Heb. and Phœn. *gāmāl*; if of native Semitic origin, perh. f. vb. **gāmal*, Arab. *jamala* to bear (Gesenius). In ME. affected by the OF. forms (see below).

The early Teutonic name for the camel was app. in some way identical (or rather, perhaps ultimately derived from a common source) with the Gr. *ἐλέφας*, *ἐλέφαντα*, L. *elephant-us*, elephant: viz. Gothic *ulbandus* (= *ulv-*), OHG. *olbenta*, MHG. *olbent*, OE. *olfend*, *oluend*, found in the Ags. Gospels, and coming down as late as Ormin in form OLFEND, q.v. But the Lindisfarne Gloss already in the 10th c. adopted the L. of the Vulgate as *camel*, *camell-*, which after the 12th c., helped by the influence of OF., became the only name. So in the other modern Teut. langs.: Ger. *kameel*, *kamel*, Du. *kameel*. The Romanic langs. follow two Latin types: (1) L. *camēlus*, whence ONF. *cameil*, OF. *chameil*, later *chamoil* (like *vēla*, *veile*, *voile*); (2) L. *camellus*, whence It. *cammello*, Sp. *camello*, ONF. *camel*, OF. *chamel*, mod.F. *chameau* (like *bellus*, *bello*, *bel*, *beau*). All the OF. forms appear in ME. (where *cameil* regularly became *camayl*); but the *camel* of OE. and ONF., being also most like the Latin, is the survivor.]

1. a. A large hornless ruminant quadruped, distinguished by its humped back, long neck, and cushioned feet; it is nowhere found wild, but is domesticated in Western Asia and Northern Africa, in the arid regions of which it is the chief beast of burden.

There are two distinct species, the Arabian or one-humped, and the Bactrian or two-humped; a lighter and fleeter variety of the former is known as the Dromedary.

c **950** *Lindisf. Gosp.* Matt. iii. 4 Gewede of hrum ðæra camella [*c* **975** *Rushw.* hrægl olbendena herum; *c* **1000** *Ags.* reaf of olfenda hærum; *c* **1160** *Hatton*, of oluende hære]. —— Mark i. 6 Mið herum camelles [*Rushw.* cameles, *Ags.* oluendes, *Hatton*, olfendes]. —— Matt. xix. 24 Eaður is camel [*Rushw.* olbende, *Ags.* olfende] ðerh ðyril nedles oferfæra. *c* **1250** *Gen. & Ex.* 1398 And fond good grið and good hostel, Him, and hise men, and hise kamel. *c* **1280** *E.E.P.* (1862) 3 As eþe forto bring a camel in to þe neld-is ei. *a* **1300** *Cursor M.* 3304 And þine camels [*Gött.* chameyles, *Trin.* camailes] sal drinc þair fill. *c* **1300** *K. Alis.* 6333 They no haveth camayle, no olifaunt. *c* **1382** WYCLIF *Judg.* viii. 21 The neckis of kyngis chamels [**1388** camels]. —— *1 Chron.* xii. 40 Assis, and chamoilis [**1388** camelis], and mulis. *c* **1386**

CHAUCER *Clerkes T.* 1140 Syn ye be strong as is a greet Camaille [*v.r.* camaile, camayle, *Harl. MS.* chamayle (*rime* bataille, -aile, aylle)]. *c* **1400** MAUNDEV. xxiii. 250 Mylk of mares or of camaylles or of asses. *c* **1400** *Apol. Loll.* 45 Blind foolis, clensing forþ þe knatt, but swelowyng þe camely. *c* **1440** *Promp. Parv.*, Camelle, or chamelle, *camelus.* *c* **1450** *Voc.* in Wr.-Wülcker 699 *Hic camelus*, a camylle. **1483** CAXTON *Gold. Leg.* 164/4 His knees were as harde as the horne of a camel. **1593** SHAKS. *Rich. II*, v. v. 16 It is as hard to come, as for a Camell To thred the posterne of a Needles eye. **1607** TOPSELL *Four-f. Beasts* 75 The wantonness thereof appeareth by the proverb of a dancing Camel. **1699** *Dampier's Voy.* (1729) III. I. 384 His Neck small, and resembling a Cammels. **1847** CARPENTER *Zool.* §278 Well, therefore, has the Camel..been termed 'the Ship of the Desert'. **1861** FLOR. NIGHTINGALE *Nursing* 71 It is the last straw that breaks the camel's back.

b. *fig.* A great awkward hulking fellow.

1606 SHAKS. *Tr. & Cr.* I. ii. 271 A Dray-man, a Porter, a very Camell. —— II. i. 58 Do rudenes, do Camell do, do.

c. *fig.* in allusion to *Matthew* xxiii. 24: Anything large and difficult to 'swallow' or do away with.

[*c* **1380** WYCLIF *Wks.* (1880) 172 Swolwynge þe grete camaile alhool.] **1637** GILLESPIE *Eng. Pop. Cerem.* II. v. 23 Christians..mocked & nicknamed *Puritans*, except they can swallow the Camell of Conformity. **1641** MILTON *Ch. Govt.* vi. (1851) 125 Can we believe that your government strains in good earnest at the petty gnats of schisme, when it makes nothing to swallow the Camel heresie of Rome? **1860** L. HARCOURT *Diaries G. Rose* I. 143 If the former was more than 'a gnat', the latter was not less than 'a camel' of immorality.

d. The characteristic colour of a camel, a shade of fawn.

1881 C. C. HARRISON *Woman's Handiwork* I. 50 Camel color is the most recent variety of écru shades, coming to us from England. **1922** *Daily Mail* 11 Dec. 14 Brushed Wool Scarf-wrap..Can be supplied..in plain colours—White,.. Camel, Beige, Grey. **1923** *Ibid.* 26 Feb. 1 In good shades of Grey, Camel, Fawn. **1924** *Tourist* Winter Sports No. 20 Sports hats..of camel check Tweed with scarves to match.

2. *techn.* A machine for imparting additional buoyancy to vessels, and thus enabling them to cross bars, shoals, etc., otherwise impassable; also for raising sunken ships, removing rocks, etc.

It consists generally of two or more huge water-tight chests provided with plugs and pumps. Water is admitted in order to sink the chests into position, and they are then fitted and braced to the sides of the vessel, which they are sometimes shaped to fit. On pumping out the water the camels rise, bearing up the vessel along with them.

1716 PERRY *State of Russ.* 168 His Majesty..sent a Person with me to shew me all the Camels (which are flat Vessels made to be fix'd to the bottom of Ships, and to come up like a Chest on each side). **1799** in *Naval Chron.* II. 283 Men of war..lifted over the bar by means of camels. **1805** *Ibid.* XIV. 227. **1847** A. KEY *Recov. H.M.S. Gorgon* 76 The construction of camels to be secured to the ship's bilge.

†**3.** (See quot.) *Obs.*

1753 CHAMBERS *Cycl. Supp.* s.v., Camel is also a denomination given to a kind of pit-coal, otherwise called canel.

4. *attrib.* and *Comb.*, as ***camel-back***, ***-battery***, ***-cart***, ***-corps***, ***-driver***, ***-dung*** (also ***camel's dung***), ***-guide***, ***-gulper*** (see 1 c), ***-hide***, ***-keeper***, ***-load***, ***-man***, ***-path***, ***-skin***, ***-trunk***; also ***camel-backed***, ***-faced***, ***-haired***, ***-like***, ***-shaped*** adjs.

1860 R. NOEL *Vacat. Tour* 464 For ladies to ride ten, twelve, and twenty-four hours on *camel back at a stretch. **1631** WEEVER *Anc. Fun. Mon.* 477 Crooked, crump-shouldred, or *Camell-backed. **1639** FULLER *Holy War* IV. xxvi. (1840) 227 Not that he was crookshouldered, or camel-backed. **1884** J. MACDONALD in *19th Cent.* June 987 The blue-jackets of the..*camel-battery poured a well-directed fire at..the redoubt. **1884** GILMOUR *Mongols* 112 The *camel caravan usually does a good part of its travelling at night. **1900** *Daily News* 25 Sept. 3/4 Our caravan..included ..six *camel carts for the ladies and children. **1907** *Westm. Gaz.* 25 Nov. 2/1 The most striking..conveyance is a camel-cart. **1884** *Times* 22 Nov., The *Camel Corps which marched from Assouan. **1818** KEATS *Endym.* III. 473 To slake My greedy thirst with nectarous *camel-draughts. **1753** HANWAY *Trav.* (1762) I. III. xxix. 125 The trifling conduct of the carriers and *camel-drivers. **1903** W. C. RUSSELL *Overdue* vi, Recollection reeks of the flavour of the *camel-dung cigarettes of Alexandria. **1886** R. F. BURTON *Arab. Nts.* X. 193 'Take care of the glass-phials!' cried the Prophet to a *camel-guide. **1829** SOUTHEY *Sir T. More* II. 27 Father Cressy, the *Camel-gulper. **1807** *Med. Jrnl.* XVII. 179 *Camel-faced boys and girls, and *camel-haired children. *a* **1300** *Cursor M.* 2250 þai þam hide Bath wit hors and *camel-hide. **1591** PERCIVALL *Sp. Dict.*, *Camelero*, a *Camel keeper. *a* **1603** T. CARTWRIGHT *Confut. Rhem. N.T.* (1618) 500 Knees..*Camell-like in the curtesie which you giue unto his name. **1761** *Chron.* in *Ann. Reg.* 59/2 A large camel-like protuberance of fat on the top of their shoulders. **1753** HANWAY *Trav.* (1762) I. III. xxx. 129 *Camel-loads of cloth. **1613** PURCHAS *Pilgr.* (1864) 68 Indian Merchants, with their..ten Camels, and fiue *Camel-men. **1883** E. ARNOLD *Pearls of Faith* XXII. 79 Amru the camel-man lay dead. **1884** *Daily News* 27 Sept. 5/3 Two *camel messengers ..came in to-day to ask for food and arms. **1824** *Edin. Rev.* XLI. 45 Beaten *camel-paths. **1827** *Every Night Book* 87 We strongly recommend you..to illumine the butt-end of your cigar with *camel's dung. **1879** W. J. LOFTIE *Ride in Egypt* xii. 261 There is an all-pervading smell..caused..by the use of camel's dung for fuel. *a* **1425** in *M.E.D.*, *Camel skyn. *c* **1450** CAPGRAVE *Life St. Aug.* 38 3e haue girdilis lich knytys; and þei with þongis of chamel skynnys, as Hely and Ion, go girt in her lendes. **1497** BP. ALCOCK *Mons Perfeccionis* E i b/1 Clothed in a camell skynne. **1903** *Month* Aug. 165 St. John in his camel-skin robe. **1660-3** J. SPENCER *Prodigies* (1665) 394, I think it hard to find a Faith that can swallow any such *Camel-stories. **1854** THACKERAY *Newcomes* II. 294 A *camel trunk or two which have accompanied him on many an Indian march.

5. Special comb.: **camel-back** orig. *U.S.*, an inferior or synthetic rubber used to retread tyres; **camel-bird**, name applied to the Ostrich; **camel-brown**, an artificial fly used in angling; **camel-engine**, = sense 2; **camel-gun**, a gun, as a machine gun, made light and short so as to be transportable by camels; **camel-gut**, the dried gut or intestines of a camel used to furnish strings for musical instruments; **camel's-hay**, a sweet-scented grass or rush growing in the East (*Andropogon Schœnanthus*); **camel-insect**, a name given to members of the genus *Mantis*, from their elongated thorax; **camel-kneed** *a.*, having hard or callous knees like those of a camel, caused by much kneeling; **camel-locust** = *camel-insect*; **camel's-meat** = *camel's-hay*; **camel's-straw**, an old name for the Common Rush (*Juncus conglomeratus* and *effusus*); **camel('s)-thorn**, (*a*) a leguminous plant (*Alhagi camelorum*); (*b*) *S. Afr.*, the tree *Acacia giraffæ* or *A. hirtella*; camel-tree; **camel-swallower**, **-swallowing** (see sense 1 c); **camel-tree**, *Acacia giraffæ*; **camel-trot**, **camel-walk**, a ball-room dance resembling the walk of a camel. Also CAMEL('S)-HAIR.

1942 in *Amer. Speech* (1943) XVIII. 302/2 The term '*camelback', broadly used, refers to the uncured rubber applied to the worn tire to make the new tread. **1959** *Times* 27 Apr. (Suppl. Rubber Ind.) p. vii/6 A general-purpose cold rubber for tyre stocks, camelbacks. **1771** T. SCOTT *Job*, *note*, The Ostrich is called by the Persians the *Camel-Bird. **1787** BEST *Angling* 107 September..2 *Camel brown..2 Dubbed with the hair pulled out of the lime of an old wall. **186.** *Athenæum* No. 1999. 240/3 A huge powerful *camel-engine. **1880** L. WALLACE *Ben-Hur* 7 Languishing acacias and tufts of *camel-grass. **1891** KIPLING *Light that Failed* ii. 29 Aren't the *camel-guns ever going to begin? **1879** STAINER *Music of Bible* 12 The Kinnor had, according to Fetis, nine strings of *camel-gut. **1597** GERARD *Herbal* I. xxix. §1. 40 *Camels haie hath leaues very like vnto Cyperus. **1718** QUINCY *Compl. Disp.* 81 Camels-Hay is also frequently call'd the sweet Rush. **1801** SOUTHEY *Thalaba* V. xxxvi, Some *camel-kneed prayer-monger. **1598** FLORIO, *Squinance*, squinanth, *cammels meate, or sweet rush, which is very medicinable. **1578** LYTE *Dodoens* IV. lii. 511 The first kinde [of Rushes] is called in English, the Rush candle, or Candle rushe: *Camels strawe. **1802** C. WILMOT *Let.* 15 Nov. in T. U. Sadleir *Irish Peer* (1920) 114 The Friar ..was a delightful sketch of a wholesale *camel swallower. He believed in the most extravagent miracles. **1840** C. H. TOWNSHEND *Facts in Mesmerism* 332 The gnat-strainers and *camel-swallowers may be content to accept this story. **1858** DICKENS *Lett.* (1879) II. 82 All manner of *camel-swallowing and of gnat-straining. **1607** TOPSELL *Four-f. Beasts* 74 There is a certain herb, which hath a seed like a myrtle-seed..and this seed is food for Camels..It is therefore called *Camel-thorn. **1824** W. J. BURCHELL *Trav. S. Afr.* II. 292 Some scattered trees of Camel-thorn, or *Mokaala.* **1850** LAYARD *Nineveh* xii. 306 Without a blade of vegetation, except a scanty tuft of camel-thorn. **1896** H. A. BRYDEN *Tales S. Afr.* 75 The camel-thorn trees [*f.n.* giraffe acacias] grew pretty thickly all around. **1947** L. HASTINGS *Dragons are Extra* i. 14 Among the scrub and camelthorn trees. **1961** L. VAN DER POST *Heart of Hunter* i. 21 Camel-thorn trees in leaf..growing in a part of the desert which was not typical camel-thorn country at all. **1923** *Weekly Dispatch* 8 Apr. 8 They call the modern dances *camel-trots. **1921** *Frontier* May 16 The morbid minded may read them as openly as they danced the shimmy and the *camel-walk a year ago. **1969** *New York* 15 Feb. 29/3 Rubbery-legged dances, like the Camel Walk.

'camel, *v. nonce-wd.* [f. prec. sb.] *to camel it*: to ride or perform a journey on camel-back.

1865 E. C. CLAYTON *Cruel Fort.* II. 144 He had.. camelled it through the deserts. **1885** *L'pool Daily Post* 9 Jan. 6/2 To day I have heard 'fueled' for taking in wood, and 'cameled' for using that ungainly beast in travelling.

'camelcade. *nonce-wd.* [after *cavalcade.*] A train of people on camels; a caravan with camels.

1886 *Contemp. Rev.* 860 The train..overtakes the crawling camelcade.

'cameldom. *nonce-wd.* [see -DOM.] The region of camels.

1885 *Daily News* 10 Jan. 4/6 Evolutions [of a camel].. which neither the most far-travelled Arab nor the oldest inhabitant of cameldom had ever seen or heard of.

cameleer (kæmə'lɪə(r)). Also camelier. [An analogical repr. of L. *camēlārius*: see -EER¹.] A camel-driver; a cuirassier mounted on a camel.

1808 A. PARSONS *Trav. Afr.* iv. 76 The cameliers (men who attend, feed, load, and unload the camels). **1837** DE QUINCEY *Revolt of Tartars* (1862) IV. 148 A body of trained cameleers, that is cuirassiers mounted on camels. **1883** COL. WARREN in W. Besant *Life Palmer* xi. 309 Six of these cameleers were of the Aligât tribe.

cameleon, obs. form of CHAMELEON.

camel-hair: see CAMEL'S-HAIR.

cameline ('kæməlɪn, 'kæmlɪn), *sb.*¹ Also 5 **kamelyne**, 5-6 **camelyn(e**, 6 **camboline**, 8 **camlin**, 9 **camaline**. [a. OF. *camelin*, ad. med.L. *camēlīnum*, f. *camēlus*: see CAMELINE *a.*]

a. *orig.* A kind of stuff made (or supposed to be made) of camel's hair: cf. CAMLET. Also the trade name of a modern fabric.

c **1400** *Rom. Rose* 7367 And dame Abstinence..Toke of a robe of kamelyne, And gan hir gracche [? graithe] as a bygynne. *a* **1450** *Acts of Christ, MS. Addit.* 11307, f. 97 (Halliw.) The cloth was ryche and ry3t fyn, The chaumpe it was of red camelyn. *c* **1450** *Voc.* in Wr.-Wülcker 569 *Camelinus*, camelyn. **1886** *Ripon Chron.* 4 Sept. 2/6 (*Advt.*) We can suit every taste in Cameline Prints.

b. A garment made of this material.

1599 HAKLUYT *Voy.* II. 261 The Tallipoies go very strangely apparelled with one camboline or thinne cloth next to their body of a browne colour. **1727** A. HAMILTON *New Acc. E. Ind.* I. i. 15 A Gown..called a Camlin; it is made of Camels Hair, or of their Sheeps Wooll. **1837** LARDNER *Steam Commun. w. India* 114 Their dress consists of a camaline, bound round the waist by a leathern girdle.

cameline ('kæməlaɪn), *sb.*² [a. F. *cameline* (in mod.L. *camelina*). Littré says 'the sauce is doubtless named from the plant'. (It has been conjectured to be a corrupt form of *chamælīnum*, corresp. to Gr. *χαμαίλινον 'dwarf flax'.)]

1. A genus of cruciferous plants; *spec.* the 'Gold of pleasure' (*Camelina sativa*). Also *attrib.*

1578 LYTE *Dodoens* IV. xxxv. 494 The oyle of the seede of Cameline or Myagrum..doth cleare and polish the skinne from all roughnesse. **1598** FLORIO, *Miagro*, the herbe Cameline. *c* **1865** in *Circ. Sc.* I. 105/2 Cameline or Dodder oil is extracted from the seeds of the *Camelina sativa.*

2. 'A certaine daintie Italian sauce' (Cotgr.).

c **1420** *Liber Cocorum* (1862) 30 þis sawce fyne, þat men calles camelyne.

cameline ('kæməlaɪn), *a.* [ad. L. *camēlīnus* f. *camēlus* CAMEL *sb.*: see -INE¹.] Belonging to a camel, or to the camel tribe.

1865 W. G. PALSGRAVE *Arabia* I. i. 39 The loss of his old master and cameline companions gives him no regret.

†**camelion.** *Obs.* Also 5 **camalyon.** [As a word app. the same as CHAMELEON, but in the 14th c. taken as made up of *camel* + *lion*, and identified with *camelo-pard.*] A camelopard or giraffe.

[Wyclif appears to have had before him a Latin text reading *cameleopardalum*; this he mistook for two words, rendering *cameleo* 'camelion' (with a description identifying it with the giraffe), and *pardalum* 'pardalun, that is a litil pard'. But some MSS. correct this by omitting the latter, thus taking 'camelion' as the translation of the whole *camelopardalum*: this was followed by Coverdale.]

1382 WYCLIF *Deut.* xiv. 5 Phigarg, origen, camelion [**1388** camelioun], that is a beest lijk a camele in the heed, in the bodi to a paard, and in the nek to an horse, in the feet to a bugle; and pardelun, that is, a litil pard. [*Vulg.* tragelaphum, pygargum, orygem, camelopardalum; *Douay* the pygargue, the wild beefe, the cameloparde; **1611** the pygarg, and the wild ox, and the chamois.] **1387** TREVISA *Higden* (1865) I. 159 Camelion is a flekked best in colour liche to a lupard. *c* **1400** *Sowdone* 1008 Wilde beestes bloode, Of Tigre, Antilope, and of Camalyon. **1535** COVERDALE *Deut.* xiv. 5 Vnicorne, Origen and Camelion.

camelion, obs. form of CHAMELEON.

camelious (kə'miːlɪəs), *a.* [f. CAMEL *sb.* + -IOUS.] Jocular word invented by Kipling (in form *cameelious*) to describe the hump given to the lazy camel in *Just So Stories.* Hence *allusively* (with ref. to HUMP *sb.* 3).

1902 KIPLING *Just So Stories* 27 Kiddies and grown-ups too-oo-oo, If we haven't enough to do-oo-oo, We get the hump—Cameelious hump—The hump that is black and blue! **1909** 'IAN HAY' *Man's Man* xvi, The men have both got camelious hump.

'camelish, *a.* [f. CAMEL *sb.* + -ISH¹.] Of the nature of the camel; obstinate as a camel.

Hence **'camelishness**.

1883 P. ROBINSON *Harml. Beasts*, Camelishness is a term of abuse for one who is obstinate past all reasoning.

'camelist. *nonce-word.* [f. CAMEL *sb.* + -IST.] A partisan of the camel.

1863 MISS POWER *Arab. Days & N.* 117 They, the camels, are patience itself, say the camelists.

†**'cameller.** *Obs. rare*⁻¹. [f. CAMEL *sb.* + -ER¹, probably after F. *camelier.*] A cameleer.

1615 G. SANDYS *Trav.* 137 Our Companions had their cradles struck down through the negligence of the Camellers.

camellia (kə'mɛlɪə). [Named (by Linnæus) after Kamel (latinized *Camellus*), a Moravian Jesuit who described the botany of the island of Luzon. (Often mispronounced as *ca'mēlia.*)] A genus of evergreen shrubs belonging to the tea family (*Ternströmiaceæ*), remarkable for the beauty of their flowers, and chiefly natives of China and Japan. Also *attrib.*, as in ***camellia-house***, ***-tree***; **camellia-red**, a bright red, the colour of red camellias.

1753 in CHAMBERS *Cycl. Supp.* **1832** *Veg. Subst. Food* 202 We are indebted to China for..species of the Camellia, Pœonia, and Rose. **1872** OLIVER *Elem. Bot.* 147 The favourite Camellias of our plant-houses, evergreen shrubs introduced from Japan. **1885** LADY BRASSEY *The Trades* 41 Camellia-trees of..gigantic proportions. **1890** *Daily News* 21 Oct. 2/1 Camellia red felt.

cameloid ('kæməlɔɪd), *a.* and *sb. Zool.* [ad. mod.L. *Cameloidea*: see CAMEL *sb.* and -OID.] **A.** *adj.* Of or pertaining to the Camelidæ or camel

family of ruminants. **B.** *sb.* An animal of this family.

1885 tr. *Schmidt's Mammalia* 156 The cameloid type of Ruminant. **1888** *Longman's Mag.* July 298 That the existing cameloids should be so strangely distributed. **1924** *Glasgow Herald* 8 Nov. 4 Herds of camels..trekked across..to Europe, leaving North America..with a glorious graveyard of cameloid progenitors.

camelopard (ˈkæmɪləʊˌpɑːd, kəˈmɛləpɑːd). Also 7 **-e**; and (*erron.*) 6 **cameleoparde**, 7–9 **cameleopard**; also (in Latin form) **camelopardus, -pardalis,** and **camelopardal.** [ad. L. *camēlopardus, -pardalis*, Gr. καμηλοπάρδαλις, f. κάμηλος CAMEL *sb.* + πάρδαλις PARD: so Fr. *camélopard*. Confusion with *leopard* led to the erroneous early spelling *cameleopard* in medL., Fr., and Eng., and to the vulgar pronunciation as '*camel-'leopard*. See also CAMELION.]

1. An African ruminant quadruped with long legs, very long neck, and skin spotted like that of the panther; now more commonly called GIRAFFE.

1398 TREVISA *Barth. De P.R.* XVIII. xx. (1495) 780 Cameleopardus hyghte cameleopardalis also, and hathe the heed of a camell..and speckes of the Perde. **1572** BOSSEWELL *Armorie* II. 53, P. beareth Or, a Cameleoparde, Sable, Maculé d'Argent. **1601** CHESTER *Love's Mart.* cxviii, The Horse, Cameleopard, and strong pawd Beare, The Ape, the Asse, and the most fearefull Deare. **1609** BIBLE (Douay) *Deut.* xiv. 5 The pygargue, the wild beefe, the cameloparde. **1613** PURCHAS *Pilgr.* I. VI. i. 464 The Giraffa or Camelopardalis, a beaste not often seene. **1653** H. COGAN *Diod. Sic.* 104 Those beasts called Cameleopards are procreated of them whose name they bear. **1708** MOTTEUX *Rabelais* V. xxx. (1737) 141 Hyæna's, Camelopardals. **1769** CARTERET in *Phil. Trans.* LX. 27 Inclosed I have sent you the drawing of a Camelopardalis. **1776** GIBBON *Decl. & F.* I. 350 Camelopards, the loftiest and most harmless creatures that wander over the plains of..Æthiopia. **1840** MACAULAY *Ranke, Ess.* (1851) II. 128 When camelopards and tigers bounded in the Flavian amphitheatre.

2. *Astr.* A northern circumpolar constellation, situated between Ursa Major and Cassiopeia.

1836 *Penny Cycl.* VI. 191/2 Camelopardalus, the camelopard or giraffe, a constellation formed by Hevelius.

camelo'pardel. *Her.* [f. prec.] A heraldic animal, figured as a camelopard with the horns of an ibex.

1830 in ROBSON *Hist. Heraldry.*

camelot, obs. form of CAMLET.

camelote, var. CAMALOTE.

camelry (ˈkæməlrɪ). [f. CAMEL *sb.* + -RY (in sense 1 after *cavalry*).]

1. Troops mounted on camels.

1854 LIDDELL & SCOTT *Greek Lex.* s.v. κάμηλος, ἡ κάμηλος, like ἡ ἵππος, the camels in an army, as one might say the camelry. **1883** G. A. SIMCOX *Latin Lit.* II. VI. iv. 176 It was Crœsus who frightened his enemy's cavalry by his camelry. **1885** *Times* 2 July 5 General Buller and the second half of the 'Light Camelry'..left Assouan to-day. *Ibid.* 16 July 12/3 The Camelry is a new force in the British Army. It is neither, properly speaking, cavalry nor infantry..A special flag had, therefore, been invented representing a black camel rampant upon a white ground.

2. 'A place where camels are laden and unladen.'

1882 in ANNANDALE *Imperial Dict.*

camel's hair. Also camel-hair.

1. a. The hair of the camel. (But cf. CAMEL-YARN.)

c **1325** *Metr. Hom.* 10 Wit camel hare was he cledde. *Ibid.* 41 Al men wist that knew sain Jon, That he hauid camel har him upon. *c* **1380** WYCLIF *Serm.* Sel. Wks. II. 3 Joon was cloþid wiþ camele heer. **1611** BIBLE *Matt.* iii. 4 The same Iohn had his raiment of camels haire. **1858** SIMMONDS *Dict. Trade* s.v., Camel's-hair is much longer than sheep's wool, and often as fine as silk.

b. Used *attrib.* of a cloth or garment, etc., made from the hair of the camel. Also *ellipt.*

1678 *New Castle Court Rec.* 361 A Camell haire Rugg. **1854** M. CUMMINS *Lamplighter* 178 That boy..has sent you home a camel's hair scarf. **1860** O. W. HOLMES *Elsie V.* (1887) 67 A camel's-hair scarf. **1865** *Atlantic Monthly* XV. 10 Cotton-bales, bound in striped camel's-hair cloth. **1918** W. OWEN *Let.* 10 Sept. (1967) 575 I'm sitting in my Camel Hair Coat at my bed-table. **1964** *McCall's Sewing* iv. 56/1 *Camel hair*, a coating fabric made from the natural-coloured hair of the camel, frequently mixed with wool. **1968** 'E. TREVOR' *Place for Wicked* v. 70 Well I'll bring my camel-hair. It's got pockets like rucksacks.

2. The long hairs from the tail of a squirrel, used to make artists' paint-brushes. Also *attrib.*, as in ***camel('s) hair brush, pencil.***

1771 SMEATON in *Phil. Trans.* LXI. 206 Take a middling camel's hair pencil. **1825** HONE *Every-day Bk.* I. 347 He could not procure camels' hair pencils. **1858** SIMMONDS *Dict. Trade, Camel-hair Pencil*, a small brush used by painters in water-colours, made of badgers' hair, camel's hair, or other suitable material. **1859** GULLICK & TIMBS *Paint.* 295 Brushes made of red sable, and also the squirrel—or 'camel hair' as it is called.

camel-yarn. [In Da. *kameelgarn*, Du. *kemelshaar*, Ger. *kämelhaar*: app. from a mistaken notion: cf. CAMLET and MOHAIR.] Yarn made from the wool of the Angora-goat, mohair yarn.

1670 *Bk. of Rates*, Yarne Camel, or Mohair Yarne.

Camembert (ˈkæmɑ̃bɛə(r)). [Name of a village near Argentan, France.] In full ***Camembert cheese***: a rich soft cheese made in the vicinity of Camembert; also, any cheese of the same type, wherever made.

1878 *Cassell's Fam. Mag.* Aug. 535/1 Gruyère, Camembert, and Gorgonzola are all delicious cheeses. **1910** [see GORGONZOLA]. **1951** *Good Housek. Home Encycl.* 381/1 The best Camembert cheeses are obtained during the summer-months.

camemille, obs. form of CAMOMILE.

camenes. *Logic.* A mnemonic word, representing the second mood of the fourth figure of syllogisms, in which the major premiss is a universal affirmative, the minor premiss and the conclusion universal negatives.

1851 WHATELEY *Logic* (ed. 2) 42 Camenes, viz. (*cam*) every A is B; (*en*) no B is C; therefore (*es*) no C is A.

cameo (ˈkæmiːəʊ). [a. It. *caméo, camméo*, corresp. to med.L. *cammæus* (Du Cange): of unknown derivation. Rarely accented as in It. on *e*.

The mod.F. *camée* (masc.) is ad. It. *cameo* (also *cammeo*, both in Florio 1611). Older F. forms were *camehu, cameu, camaheu, camahieu, gamahieu* (whence MHG. *gâmaheu*), *camahier, camayeu*, and *camaïeu* still in use, whence occasional Eng. CAMAIEU in 18th c. Sp. has *camafeo* (in Minsheu 1623) Pg. *camafeo* (also acc. to Diez *camafeio, camafeu*); med.L. had *camahutus* (in England) 1295, *camahotus, camahelus, camaheu*, 14th c.; Du Cange has also *camasil, camaynus, camayx*; *camæus* (Lives of Abbots of St. Albans). Some of these, possibly all, are formed from the modern langs., though the relations between the earliest known forms, med.L. *camahūtus*, and OF. *camehu, cameu*, all found in England in 13th c. documents, are uncertain. Of the derivation nothing is yet known: guesses may be seen in Mahn, Diez, and Littré.]

1. a. A precious stone having two layers of different colours, in the upper of which a figure is carved in relief, while the lower serves as a ground. For this purpose the ancients used the onyx, agate, etc., and especially the sardonyx, 'a variety of chalcedony, consisting of alternate parallel layers of white and red chalcedony', which was carved so as to leave a white figure in relief on a red ground. Thence extended to all lapidary's work of the same kind; and in modern times ('by abuse' Littré says) to similar carving in shells of molluscs, of which the inner stratum is differently coloured from the outer.

[**1222** *Ornamenta Eccl. Sarum* in *Register S. Osmund* (1884) II. 129 Item capa una..brodata cum morsu argent. in quo continetur lapis unus cameu..Item capa una..cum morsu argent. in quo continetur magnus camehu. **1295** *Visitat. Thesaur. S. Pauli* (*Monast. Angl.* III.) Septem annulos auri, novem cum saphyris..unum cum camahuto. **1530** PALSGR. 202/2 Camuse, precious stone, *chamahievx.* **1554** in *Bristol Wills* 193 My Ryng wth A white camfeo. **1596** DANETT tr. *Comines* (1614) 157 A ring set with a camée] **1561** HOBY tr. *Castiglione's Covrtyer* (1577) Gj a, Olde coynes, cameses[?-oes], grauings. **1670** LASSELS *Voy. Italy* I. 127 Rich jewels, strange stones, cameos, pictures. **1747** DINGLEY in *Phil. Trans.* XLIV. 506 The Merit both of Intaglio's and Cameo's. **1757** KEYSLER *Trav.* (1760) II. 27 Two exquisite cammei. **1762–71** H. WALPOLE *Vertue's Anecd. Paint.* (1786) I. 137 The ring which Henry sent..to Cardinal Wolsey, was a Cameo on a ruby of the king himself. **1791** E. DARWIN *Bot. Gard.*, The bold cameo speaks, the soft intaglio thinks. **1813** MAR. EDGEWORTH *Patron.* I. xvi. 269 A woman's accomplishment..ought to be..as Dr. South expresses it, more in intaglio than in cameo. **1865** *Athenæum* 28 June 127/3 Cameos and intaglios, ancient and modern. **1874** WESTROPP *Precious Stones* 45 Sardonyx..the Occidental variety..for camei.

attrib. **1860** *Print. Trades Jrnl.* No. 32. 30 The Cameo colour stamping-press. **1863** KINGSLEY *Water Bab.* v. (1878) 219 Her car of cameo shell. **1883** *Glasgow Weekly Her.* 5 May 8/6 Cameo checks in beautiful colourings at 8½d.

b. Special Combs.: **cameo-embossing** (see quot.); **cameo glass**, a decorative glass consisting of layers of different colours, the outermost being cut away so as to leave the design or designs in relief, an example being the Portland vase; **cameo-incrustation**, the art of producing bas-relief casts within a coating of flint-glass; **cameo-type**, in photography, a name formerly given to a small daguerreotype which could be mounted in a jewelled setting; **cameo ware**, pottery with figures in relief on a background of a different colour, as in Wedgwood ware.

1878 *Encycl. Brit.* VIII. 160/2 In the second variety [of colour embossing]—called cameo embossing—the colour is applied to the flat parts of the design by means of a small printing roller, and the letters or design in relief is left uncoloured. **1879** *Ibid.* X. 649/2 The first place among those processes in which one colour was superimposed on another may be given to that by which the cameo glass was produced. **1961** E. M. ELVILLE *Collector's Dict. Glass* (1967) 32 Cameo glass first made its appearance shortly after the Great Exhibition of 1851. **1849** A. PELLATT *Curiosities of Glass Making* 119 Cameo Incrustation was unknown to the ancients, and was first introduced by the Bohemians, probably about a century since. *a* **1877** KNIGHT *Dict. Mech.* I. 433/2 *Cameo-type*, a fanciful name given to a small vignette daguerreotype for mounting in a jeweled frame like a cameo.

2. *transf.* and *fig.* Esp. a short literary sketch or portrait; a small character part that stands out from the other minor parts. Freq. *attrib.*

1851 *Monthly Packet* I. 5 Cameos from English history. **1871** MISS YONGE (*title*) Cameos from English History. **1881** E. W. WHITE (*title*) Cameos from the Silver-Land. **1901** *Daily News* 19 Jan. 6/1 This volume is mainly composed of biographical sketches... Altogether there are here about ninety of these cameo-biographies. **1917** A. WAUGH *Loom of Youth* IV. vii. 314 He could give a clean-cut cameo impression of that monarch in two lines..: 'A dreamer who unfortunately allowed his dreams to encroach on his waking moments.' **1928** *Daily Mail* 6 Aug. 10/7 A daring act on motor-cycles..was followed by a cameo of the war. **1950** 'E. CRISPIN' *Frequent Hearses* i. 34 A cameo part ..the film equivalent of a bit part on the stage. **1967** D. PINNER *Ritual* x. 108, I was an actor. Beloved for my cameos in the Classics.

camera (ˈkæmərə). [a. L. *camera* (*camara*) vault, arched chamber, = Gr. καμάρα anything with an arched cover. In late L. in sense 'chamber', as also It., Pg. *camera*, Pg., Sp. *camara*, Pr. *cambra*, F. *cambre, chambre*: see CHAMBER. Used in Eng. only as a Latin or alien word, until popularized in connexion with photography.]

‖**1. a.** In Latin sense: An arched or vaulted roof or chamber. Given in mod. Dicts., but probably not in Eng. use, exc. in such cases as 'the Camera' of the Radcliffe Library at Oxford.

1708 KERSEY, *Camera*, (L.) a vaulted or arched Building, an Upper-Chamber or Gallery. **1730–6** BAILEY, *Camera*, a vault, roof, or upper gallery; (in the title of Mus. Books) signifies chamber-musick, or musick for private consorts, in distinction to musick used in chapels and publick consorts. **1863** *Oxf. Univ. Cal.* 63 The building known till lately as 'the Radcliffe Library' is now used as a Reading Room in connection with the Bodleian Library under the name of 'Camera Bodleiana'. [In the Latin Statute of 1856 the Radcliffe building was described as a *camera*.]

b. 'Used in the Latin law proceedings for the judge's chamber' (Tomlins); hence the phrase ***in camerâ***, i.e. in the judge's private chamber, instead of 'in open court'.

‖**2.** In reference to Italy and Spain: A chamber; a council or legislative chamber; one of the departments of the papal curia.

1712 *Lond. Gaz.* 5068/1 A Declaration read..by the Secretary of the Camera. **1832** DOWNES *Lett.* I. 343 The Camera, or Chamber, adjoining the body of the church, contains ten large frescoes by Raphael. **1841** SPALDING *Italy & It. Isl.* III. 114 The Camera or Treasury, whose president, the Camerlengo, is assisted by the Auditor, the Treasurer-general, and Assessors.

3. a. *Optics.* Short for *camera obscura* (see 4 a).

1727–51 CHAMBERS *Cycl.* s.v. *Camera Obscura*, Another portable *camera* may be thus made. **1760** STERNE *Tr. Shandy* (1793) I. 133 Others..will make a drawing of you in the Camera. **1770** *Court Misc.* Apr., In the plate we have represented the different sorts of cameras. Fig. I is of the first kind..or *camera obscura*. **1845** *Athenæum* 22 Feb. 202. **1878** FOSTER *Phys.* III. ii. 397 The eye is a camera.

b. *esp.* that form used in photography.

1840 E. RIDDLE *Sci. & Nat. Philos.* (1844) 359 Producing pictures with the aid of the Camera, by the..process of M. Daguerre. **1853** R. HUNT *Man. Photogr.* 36 The photographic picture, which is invisible when the plate is taken from the Camera. **1859** SALA *Tw. round Clock* 111 He throws the curtain of the camera over his head.

c. *Television.* That part of the equipment which forms the image and converts it into electrical impulses. See also OFF CAMERA, OFF-CAMERA *phr.* and *adv.*; ON-CAMERA *adv.* (*phr.*) and *a.*

1928 *Television* July 26 (*caption*) What the television 'camera' of the future may look like. **1936** *Nature* 19 Sept. 514/1 The system employs..scanning cameras..by means of which the scenes to be transmitted are directly and continuously transformed into electrical impulses without the intermediary of a film device. **1957** *Encycl. Brit.* IV. 218/1 The function of the television camera is analogous to that of the microphone in sound broadcasting.

d. *attrib.* and *Comb.*, as ***camera-angle, -crew, -work***; **camera booth** (see quot.); **camera-eye**, an eye that records detailed impressions, a camera-like eye; also, a person capable of unusually detailed or detached observation or memory; so ***camera-eyed*** adj.; **camera gun** *Aeronaut.* (see quots.); **camera-man**, a man who uses or operates a camera professionally; **camera-ready** *a. Printing*, of copy for printing by photographic means: supplied to the printer already typeset, typed, or pasted-up and in a form suitable for photographing; freq. as ***camera-ready copy***; **camera rehearsal**, a dress rehearsal for a film or for a television programme; **camera shake**, unintentional movement of the camera during photography or filming; **camera-shy** *a.*, fearful or nervous of cameras; not liking to be photographed or filmed.

1928 Camera angle [see ANGLE *sb.*^{2} 1 e]. **1930** J. B. PRIESTLEY *Angel Pavement* IV. ii. 168 He knew nothing about camera angles and 'cutting' and all the intricacies of crowd work. **1968** A. DIMENT *Gt. Spy Race* viii. 151 You could see

what was happening from two camera angles. **1929** *Photoplay* Apr., *Camera booth*, the movable sound-proof box with a glass front, in which cameras are enclosed in a talking picture studio in order that the sound of the camera may not intrude in the picture. **1940** *Chambers's Techn. Dict.* 129/2 Camera crew. **1950** 'E. CRISPIN' *Frequent Hearses* i. 8 Camera crews; continuity girls; youngish directors. **1968** *Listener* 8 Feb. 164/2 A BBC camera crew went round Washington collecting vox pops. **1930** J. P. BURKE in *Amer. Mercury* Dec. 455/1 *Camera eye*, a retentive memory for faces. 'Put him on the door. He's camera eye.' **1946** J. B. PRIESTLEY *Bright Day* v. 143 Staring at her with a cold camera eye. **1960** *Guardian* 17 Nov. 8/2 The 'I' will be speaking, not an uninvolved camera eye, but a very much involved eye. **1935** S. LEWIS *It can't happen Here* xxxv. 377 You were supposed to be the camera-eyed gink that kept up on everything that goes on. **1918** F. H. COLVIN *Aircraft Mechanics Handbk.* xxii. 316 For machine-gun practice at enemy airplanes, the camera gun is .. used. **1939** *War Illustr.* 2 Dec. 371 The first training of the gunners of fighting 'planes is given with a camera gun which registers on a photographic film the hits made by the gun. **1908** *Westm. Gaz.* 21 Apr. 7/1 After both had posed to the inevitable camera-men. **1920** *Q. Rev.* July 183 The camera-man will film you anything. **1957** *Times* 9 Oct. 18 (*caption*) Wild camels of central Asia .. dash to the safety of the foothills .. as cameramen made what is believed to be the first photographic record of these animals. **1967** KARCH & BUBER *Offset Processes* iii. 52 Reproduction proofs are sold to offset printers in 'kits' providing copy of form headings, bodies and body notes. Over 5,000 combinations make camera-ready copy available. **1979** *Jrnl. R. Soc. Arts* July 486/1 By the second deadline .. they were to have .. completed the lay-out and paste-up so that their camera-ready flats were ready for printing. **1959** W. S. SHARPS *Dict. Cinemat.* 83/1 *Camera rehearsal.* Otherwise *run through.* **1963** E. HUMPHREYS *Gift* II. v. 239 During camera rehearsals .. I always bought her a packet of glucose tablets. **1940** *Wall's Dict. Photogr.* (ed. 15) 364 *Camera shake.* Movement of the camera during the exposure is a very common cause of poor definition. **1962** L. DEIGHTON *Ipcress File* xxiv. 154 A slow motion movie would be less subject to camera shake. **1922** E. J. KIMBLE *Kimble's Vocational Vocab.* 189 Camera-shy. **1937** H. G. WELLS *Brynhild* i. 9 He had always been a little aloof and camera-shy in his publicity. **1958** *Manchester Guardian* 30 June 6/4 It is not difficult to sympathise with the camera-shy M.P. who fears that his daily life is to become too public with the arrival of television in the House. **1908** *Daily Chron.* 14 Mar. 3/3 They are most excellent examples of camera-work.

4. 'camera ob'scura [L.; lit. 'dark chamber']. **a.** *Optics.* An instrument consisting of a darkened chamber or box, into which light is admitted through a double convex lens, forming an image of external objects on a surface of paper, glass, etc., placed at the focus of the lens.

[**1668** *Phil. Trans.* III. 741.] **1727–51** CHAMBERS *Cycl.* s.v., Construction of a portable camera obscura. **1796** HUTTON *Math. Dict.* I. 237 Various sorts of camera obscuras. **1822** IMISON *Sc. & Art* I. 255 The eye is .. no more than a camera obscura. **1841** EMERSON *Misc.* (1853) 215 The Daguerreotypist, with camera-obscura and silver plate. **1874** KNIGHT *Dict. Mech.*, *Camera obscura* .. was described by Leonardo da Vinci, in 1500 .. Baptista Porta, in 1589, mentions it in his book on 'Natural Magic'.

b. *lit.* Dark chamber or room.

1725 POPE *Let. to E. Blount* 2 June, When you shut the doors of this grotto, it becomes on the instant, from a luminous room, a *Camera obscura.* **1753** RICHARDSON *Grandison* (1781) III. xvii. 144 Shall I .. make a Lover's *Camera Obscura* for you?

5. 'camera 'lucida [L.; lit. 'light chamber', after *camera obscura*]. *Optics.* †**a.** (see quot. 1753) *Obs.* **b.** An instrument by which the rays of light from an object are reflected by a peculiarly-shaped prism, and produce an image on paper placed beneath the instrument, whilst the eye at the same time can see directly the pencil with which the image is being traced.

[**1668** HOOK in *Phil. Trans.* III. 741.] **1753** CHAMBERS *Cycl. Supp.*, *Camera Lucida*, a contrivance of Dr. Hook, for making the image of anything appear on a wall in a light room, either by day or night. **1831** BREWSTER *Optics* xl. § 195 Camera Lucida .. invented by Dr. Wollaston .. has come into very general use for .. copying and reducing drawings. **1832** GELL *Pompeiana* I. v. 79 The original drawing as obtained by the camera lucida.

camerade, -ado, obs. forms of COMRADE.

'cameral, *a.* [a. Ger. *kameral*, ad. med.L. *camerāl-is*, f. *camera* in its late sense of 'chamber, bureau'.] Of or pertaining to the *camera* or 'chamber'; relating to the management of the state property (in Germany). Hence **,camera'listic** *a.*, **,camera'listics** *sb. pl.* (in Latin form *cameralia*).

1762 tr. *Busching's Syst. Geog.* IV. 103 The imperial royal representation and chamber, with which the cameral exchequer is connected. *Ibid.* IV. 522 The Amptskeller .. looks to .. œconomical and cameral matters. **1830** W. TAYLOR *Germ. Poetry* III. 242 Göthe .. was ennobled in 1782 with the appointment of Cameral President.

cameral, variant of CAMBREL.

cameralism ('kæmərəlɪz(ə)m). *Pol. Econ.* (now *Hist.*). [f. CAMERAL *a.* + -ISM, after G. *Kameralismus.*] An economic theory (prevalent in eighteenth-century Germany), which advocated a strong public administration managing a centralized industrial economy.

1909 A. W. SMALL *Cameralists* xxii. 591 Cameralism .. was a theory of managing natural resources and human capacities so that they would be most lucrative for the prince in whose interest the management was conducted. **1949** SLOAN & ZURCHER *Dict. Econ.* 37 Cameralism was concerned not only with the best ways in which a state might acquire wealth but also with the best uses to which that wealth, once acquired, might be put. **1983** M. RAEFF *Well-Ordered Police State* II. iv. 92 It is usually and quite correctly asserted that mercantilism, by whatever definition, inspired the economic theory and practice of cameralism.

So **'cameralist**, an advocate of such a theory.

1909 A. W. SMALL *Cameralists* i. 6 We may characterize these cameralists of the books as the group of writers .. constructing a 'science' or group of 'sciences' around the central consideration of the fiscal needs of the prince. **1962** MILLER & SPIELMAN (*title*) Rojas y Spinola. Cameralist and Irenicist. **1974** *Encycl. Brit. Macropædia* VI. 227/2 The German cameralists, whose ideas powerfully influenced the ambitious economic programs of Frederick II the Great of Prussia.

came'ranious, *a. nonce-word.* [f. L. *camera.*] Chamber-.

1791 T. TWINING *Country Clergym.* (1882) 147 Private cameranious fiddlings and singings.

camerata (kæmə'rɑːtə). [mod.L., f. *camera* CHAMBER.] Each of the groups into which students of English theological colleges at Rome are divided.

1846 J. H. NEWMAN *Let.* in W. Ward *Life* (1912) I. iv. 132 The whole body of students is divided into eight classes or portions (cameratas?)—who are never allowed to speak to each other. If you and Christie and Penny went, they would of course put you into three separate cameratas. **1912** B. WARD *Eve Cath. Emanc.* III. xxxiv. 13 The students .. likewise felt aggrieved at having to walk out in 'Camerata'.

camerate ('kæmərət), *a. Zool.* [ad. L. *camerāt-us*, taken as = 'chambered' (see next).] Divided into chambers; chambered; = CAMERATED 2.

1543 TRAHERON *Vigo's Chirurg.* II. xxi. 33 Some [exitures, i.e. abscesses] are called camerate, bycause they have many concavites and chambers. **1881** CLELAND *Evolution* iii. 83 Camerate eyes found in the invertebrata.

†**'camerate**, *v. Obs.* [f. L. *camerāt-* ppl. stem of *camerāre* to vault, f. *camera*: see -ATE[3].] *trans.* To vault, to arch.

1623 COCKERAM, *Camerate*, to siele, or vault. **1656** BLOUNT, *Camerate*, to vault, seil, or make an Arch or Roof.

camerated ('kæməreɪtɛd), *ppl. a.* [f. prec.]

1. *Arch.* Arched, vaulted. ? *Obs.*

1678 PHILLIPS, *Camerated*, vaulted, or arched, a term used in Architecture. **1708** E. HATTON *New View Lond.* II. 362/1 The roof within is camerated and covered with Lead. **1817** D. HUGHSON *Walks thro' London* 187 The roof of the interior is camerated.

2. *Zool.* Divided into chambers (as some shells).

1836 TODD *Cycl. Anat.* I. 547/1 The camerated portion of the shell. **1854** WOODWARD *Mollusca* (1856) 77 Shell external, camerated and siphuncled.

cameration (kæmə'reɪʃən). [ad. L. *camerātiōn-em* vaulting, f. *camerāre*; or f. CAMERATE *v.*]

1. *Arch.* Vaulting, arching. ? *Obs.*

1664 EVELYN tr. *Freart's Archit.* (R.) Where two arches intersect, which is the strongest manner of cameration. **1721** BAILEY, *Cameration*, Vaulting or Arching. **1755** JOHNSON.

†**b.** *Surg.* An old term (= Galen's καμάρωμα) for a fracture of the skull where the bones appear arched.

1730–6 in BAILEY. **1881** *Syd. Soc. Lex.*, *Cameration*; synonymous with *Camarosis.*

2. *Zool.* Division (of a shell, etc.) into chambers.

1877 HUXLEY *Anat. Inv. An.* xii. 658 The cameration of the skeleton.

†**camerelle.** *Obs. rare*$^{-1}$. [It. and med.L. dim. of *camera.*] A little chamber.

1483 *Cath. Angl.* 52 A camerelle, *camerella.*

camerie, var. of CAMERY.

camerige, camerike, obs. ff. CAMBRIC.

camerine: see CAMARINE.

'camerist[1]. *nonce-wd.* [app. a. F. *cameriste* chamber-woman, ad. It. *camerista*, f. *camera* chamber.] Chamber-woman, lady's maid.

1838 *New Month. Mag.* LII. 515 The fraternal camirist attacked the hair of her sister with combs, brushes, perfume, and all the tact of a genuine artiste.

camerist[2] ('kæmərɪst). Chiefly *U.S.* [f. CAMERA 3 b + -IST.] One who uses a camera, a photographer.

1890 *Anthony's Photogr. Bull.* III. 19 Theoretically, all camerists believe in a good negative. **1891** *Ibid.* IV. 85 A steady head is often needed to keep an enthusiastic camerist from being unduly depressed or exalted. **1906** *Westm. Gaz.* 15 May 12/3 Many of the pictures .. are excellent examples of artistic photography... They have been taken by camerists .. whose names are thoroughly well known. **1921** *Chambers's Jrnl.* Aug. 547/1 The camerist determines on some other makeshift foreground. **1936** *Discovery* June 191/2 The trick manœuvres of the 'camerist' in contracting or expanding the dimensions of time and space.

camerlingo (kæmə'lɪŋgəʊ). Also **camarlingo, camerlengo.** [It. *camerlingo*: see CHAMBERLAIN.] A chamberlain or treasurer. **a.** In a secular state. **b.** The Pope's chamberlain and financial secretary; the highest officer in the papal household. **c.** The cardinals' chamberlain, the treasurer of the sacred college. Hence **camer'lingate**, the office of camerlingo.

1625 PURCHAS *Pilgrims* II. x. 1834 The Inhabitants are governed by a *Camarlingo*, in the behalfe of Venice. **1753** CHAMBERS *Cycl. Suppl.* s.v., The *camerlingo* is the most conspicuous officer in the court of Rome... The cardinals have also their *camerlingo*, or treasurer of their college. **1759** A. BUTLER *Lives Saints* IV. I. 524 St. Charles .. absolutely refused the Camerlingate, the second and most lucrative dignity in the Roman court. **1923** *Glasgow Herald* 10 May 9 He was all confused when taken to the presence of Her Majesty by a camerlengo.

Cameronian (kæmə'rəʊnɪən), *a.* and *sb.* [f. the name *Cameron* + -IAN.] **A.** *adj.* Pertaining to Richard Cameron, his tenets, or his followers. **B.** *sb.* A follower of Richard Cameron, a noted Scottish Covenanter and field preacher, who rejected the indulgence granted to nonconforming ministers and formally renounced allegiance to Charles II. His followers afterwards constituted the body called the 'Reformed Presbyterian Church of Scotland'.

1690 B. E. *Dict. Cant. Crew*, *Cameronians*, Field-Conventiclers (in Scotland). **1691** LUTTRELL *Brief Rel.* (1857) II. 229 The Cameronians pretend neither to acknowledge king William or king James, but king Jesus, and declare for the old covenant. **1693** *Apol. Clergy Scot.* 15 Cameronian Zealots in the Western Shires. **1816** SCOTT *Old Mort.* Introd., The religious sect called Hill-men, or Cameronians, was at that time much noted for austerity and devotion. **1886** W. G. BLAIKIE in *Dict. Nat. Biog.* s.v. *R. Cameron*, It ought to be added that the 'reformed presbyterians' decline the term 'Cameronian', although to this day it is applied to them in popular use.

2. ***Cameronian Regiment***: the title of the old 26th Regiment of Foot in the British Army (now the 1st Battalion of the Scottish Rifles), formed originally of the Cameronians and other Presbyterians who rallied to the cause of William III, and fought at the Battle of Killiecrankie.

1848 MACAULAY *Hist. Eng.* xiii.

camerostome ('kæmərəʊstəʊm). *Zool.* [ad. mod.L. *camerostoma*, irreg. f. L. *camera* vault + Gr. στόμα mouth.] The anterior part of the body of arachnids which forms an arch over the mouth.

1888 ROLLESTON & JACKSON *Anim. Life* 523 A well-developed chitinoid piece—the camerostome .. overhangs the mouth anteriorly. **1949** *Trans. Connecticut Acad. Arts & Sci.* XXXVII. 260 The camarostome is formed by the upper lip and the pedipalpal coxae.

†**camery.** ? *Obs.* A disease of horses, in which pimples appear on the palate; the *frounce.*

1572 MASCALL *Govt. Cattle* (1627) 16 a, Camerie, is in his mouth venomed. **1610** MARKHAM *Masterp.* II. xxvii. 261 The Camery or Frounce in horses, are small pimples or warts in the midst of the palate. **1727** BRADLEY *Fam. Dict.*, *Camery* or Frounce, a distemper in horses, being small warts or pimples in the palate of a horse's mouth.

cames(e, var. of CAMMES, *Obs.*; see also CAMISE.

came-stone, another form of CAM-STONE.

1615 SIR R. BOYLE in *Lismore Papers* (1886) I. 90, I gave him a came stone for his arms.

camestres. *Logic.* A mnemonic word, representing the second mood of the second figure of syllogisms, in which the major premiss is a universal affirmative, the minor premiss and the conclusion universal negatives.

1551 T. WILSON *Logique* Hj a, *Ca.* The christian righteousnesse is the purenesse of the mynde. *mest.* To weare a tipete, a coule, a shauen croune is not the purenes of the minde. *tres.* Therfore the outwarde attyre is not the christian righteousnesse. **1870** BOWEN *Logic* vii. 200.

camesyd, var. of CAMOISED, *Obs.*

cameylle, camfeo, obs. ff. CAMEL *sb.*, CAMEO.

camfer, -fire, -fory, etc., obs. ff. CAMPHOR *sb.*

†**'camfering**, *ppl. a. Obs.*

1582 STANYHURST *Æneis* Ded. (Arb.) 4 Theyre Verses in camfering wise run harshe and rough. [Cf. *Shropsh. Word-bk.* (E.D.S.) *Campering*, mettlesome, high-spirited.]

Camford ('kæmfəd). [f. CAM(BRIDGE + OX)FORD.] = OXBRIDGE.

1850 THACKERAY *Pendennis* II. xiv. 135 He was a Camford man and very nearly got the English Prize Poem. **1924** [see OXBRIDGE]. **1939** H. G. WELLS *Holy Terror* I. ii. 37 Camford .. had never made the slightest attempt to give any coherent picture of the universe to the new generation that came to it for instruction. **1961** *Observer* 26 Mar. 29/4 The Camford-style Sermon on the Mount.

camforye, camfrey, obs. ff. COMFREY.

cami- ('kæmɪ), abbreviated form of CAMISOLE 2 b, used in *Comb.*, as **cami-bocker** [f. (*knicker*)*bocker*], **cami-knickers** or **-knicks**, an

undergarment which combines camisole and knickers; so **cami-petticoat**, etc.

1908 in C. W. Cunnington *English Women's Clothes* (1952) ii. 84 The cami-skirt, worn over the corsets, has its skirt usually divided into two. 1915 *Home Chat* 30 Oct. 229 My new cami-knickers. 1923 *Daily Mail* 2 May 1 Cami-petticoats made of..heavy Artificial Silk Stockinette. 1926 *Good Housekeeping* July 58 Cami-bocker in cotton crêpon. 1930 T. S. ELIOT tr. *St.-J. Perse's Anabasis* 37 The girls' camiknickers hanging at the windows. 1937 PARTRIDGE *Dict. Slang* 122/2 Cami-knicks. 1952 B. HAMILTON *So Sad, so Fresh* iv. 35 How are the cami-knicks coming along, Miss Demarest? 1966 *Punch* 5 Jan. 20/3 Her dress falls off to reveal eau-de-nil camiknickers.

‖**camion.** [F. *camion* a cart on low wheels, also in OF. *chamion*: see Littré.] A truck or wagon formerly used for transporting cannon (*obs.*). Also, a large dray; a lorry; a bus.

1885 WARREN & CLEVERLY *Wand. Beetle* 102 The ponderous camion thundered over the uneven pitching of the streets. 1922 *Blackw. Mag.* Jan. 23/2 The French..had in their turn a splash of khaki on each of their *camions*. 1942 'N. SHUTE' *Pied Piper* 46 There's lots and lots of camions and motors at the station. 1967 *Punch* 15 Feb. 234/1 Following the kerb does enable one to see past the camion along straight roads.

†'**camis, camus.** *Obs.* [Spenser's word was prob. meant to represent Sp. and Pr. *camisa*, = Pg. *camiza*, It. *camicia*, *camiscia* 'shirt, smock, priest's surplice', F. *chemise* (ONF. *kemise*):—late L. *camisia*, *camisa* linen tunic, alb, shirt (see CHEMISE); or else the cognate It. *cámice* surplice. It is hardly likely that he knew the Oriental *qamīç* or CAMISE (see below).] A light loose dress of silk or linen; a chemise, shirt, tunic.

1596 SPENSER *F.Q.* II. iii. 26 And [she] was yclad, for heat of scorching aire, All in a silken Camus lilly whight. *Ibid.* V. v. 2 [The Amazon] All in a Camis light of purple silke Woven uppon with silver, subtly wrought.

¶ Various foreign forms of the word *camisia*: **camesa, camisa, camiscia**, occur casually.

1690 B. E. *Dict. Cant. Crew*, *Camesa*, a Shirt or Shift. 1796 STEDMAN *Surinam* II. xx. 89 The rest of his [a rebel negro's] dress is a camisa, tied around his loins like a handkerchief. 1825 SCOTT *Talisman* xv, His..person was wrapped in the folds of his camiscia, or ample gown of linen.

cami'sade. *Mil. Obs.* or *arch.* [a. F. *camisade.*] = CAMISADO.

1560 DAUS tr. *Sleidane's Comm.* 268a, The Emperour attempteth the matter by a Camisade in the night, and chouseth out of the whole nombre the fotemen of Almaignes and Spanyardes, & comaundeth them to put on whyte shirtes ouer their harnesse. 1690 W. WALKER *Idiom. Anglo-Lat.* 80 Others were to set upon to give a camisade to the camp. 1819 SCOTT *Leg. Montrose* xiii, 'It was a pretty camisade, I doubt not..a very sufficient onslaught.' 1831 CARLYLE *Sart. Res.* II. i. 56. 1864 *Reader* 28 May 678 The word 'Camisade'..had its origin in the surprise of a French post near Rebéc by the Marquis de Pescaire; the Marquis's men on that occasion having worn white shirts over their clothes to distinguish them.

ˌ**cami'sado.** *Mil. Obs.* or *arch.* Also 6 **cammassado, camnesado, camisada**, 7 **camizado**, 8 **camiscado**. [ad. Sp. *camiçada*, *camisada*, f. *camisa* shirt: lit. 'an attack in one's shirt': see CAMIS, CHEMISE, and -ADO; also CANVASADO.]

1. A night attack; originally one in which the attacking party wore shirts over their armour as a means of mutual recognition. (A very common word in 16–17th c.)

1548 W. PATTEN *Exped. Scotl.* in Arb. *Garner* III. 89 Of whom, in a camisado..his Lordship killed above eight hundred. 1566 GASCOIGNE *Jocasta* Wks. 91 By night I wil the cammassado give. 1575 CHURCHYARD *Chippes* (1817) 110 The French came forth, at midnight..As though they would a camisado make. 1579 FENTON *Guicciard.* XII. (1599) 554 Ranse de Cere..gaue them a Camnesado in their lodging. 1598 BARRET *Theor. Warres* Gloss. 249 *Camisada*, a Spanish word, and doth signifie the inuesting or putting on of a shirt ouer the souldiers apparell or armour; the which is vsed in the night time, when any suddaine exploit..is to be put in practise vpon the enemy. 1663 *Flagellum* or *O. Cromwell* (1672) 83 Not dreaming of such a Camisado. 1721 DE FOE *Mem. Cavalier* (1840) 106 The garrison..gave us several camisadoes. 1865 CARLYLE *Fredk. Gt.* V. XIII. xiii. 125 Prince Karl..has been on march all night, intending a night-attack or camisado.

b. *fig.*

1565 JEWEL *Repl. Harding* (1611) 5 Howbeit (gentle Reader) be of good cheere. All this is but a camisado: These be but visards: they bee no faces. 1678 BUTLER *Hud.* III. ii. 296 Some for engaging to suppress The Camisado of Surplices..More proper for the cloudy Night Of Popery, than Gospel-Light. 1837 CARLYLE *Fr. Rev.* II. IV. vii. 216 A camisado, or shirt-tumult, every where.

2. (*erroneously*) The shirt worn over the armour in a night attack.

1618 SIR R. WILLIAMS *Actions Lowe Countr.* 82 (T.) Some two thousand of our best men, all in camisadoes with scaling ladders. *Ibid.* 83 Their armours and camisadoes: I mean the shirts that covered their armours.

†**camisard, camisar.** [a. F. *camisard*, f. Pr. *camisa* shirt- + ARD: cf. CAMISADE.] 'Name given to the Calvinist insurgents of the Cevennes, during the persecution which followed the revocation of the edict of Nantes' (Littré). Also *attrib.*

1703 *Lond. Gaz.* No. 3908/3 Accounts..of the Successes of the Camisars against the French King's Forces. *Ibid.* No. 3973/2 These Roman Catholicks call themselves the White Camisars, or the Florentines. 1710 STEELE & ADDISON *Tatler* No. 257 ¶12 Brownists, Independents, Masonites, Camisars, and the like. 1816 KEATINGE *Trav.* I. 30 They could effect little in a midnight warfare against Camisards. 1882–3 SCHAFF *Relig. Encycl.* I. 376 Without leaders the Camisard army gradually melted away.

'**camisated** *ppl. a. rare*$^{-0}$. See quots.

1731 BAILEY vol. II, *Camisated*, cloathed with a linen garment, surplice or shirt. 1755 JOHNSON, *Camisated*, dressed with the shirt outward. Hence in mod. Dicts.

camiscia: see CAMIS, CHEMISE.

‖**camise, camiss** (kə'miːs). Also (in Byron) camese. [Arab. *qamīç* under-tunic, shirt; occurring in the Koran, but generally thought to be ad. L. *camisia*, *camisa*: see CAMIS, CHEMISE; Mahn suggests Skr. *kshauma* linen stuff.] The shirt worn by Arabs and other Mohammedans.

1812 BYRON *Ch. Har.* II. *Tambourgi* ii, Oh! who is more brave than a dark Suliote, In his snowy camese and his shaggy capote? *c*1850 *Nat. Encycl.* I. 237 The national costume of the lower orders [in Afghanistan] is..a large shirt, 'camiss', worn over the trowsers, reaching down to the knees. 1859 SALA *Tw. round Clock* (1861) 143 The Suliote of the fruitship, in his camise and capote. 1865 S. EVANS *Bro. Fabian's MS.* 105 Snow-white the camise.

camisole ('kæmɪsəʊl). [a. F. *camisole*, ad. Sp. *camisola*, dim. of *camisa* shirt: see CHEMISE.]

‖**1.** A kind of sleeved jacket or jersey.

1816 *Gentl. Mag.* LXXXVI. I. 213 They wore short camisoles, huzar-sabres. 1828 G. W. BRIDGES *Ann. Jamaica* II. XIII. 121 Columbus found..a multitude..naked, or clothed only in a species of camisole.

2. a. A loose jacket worn by women when dressed in *negligée*.

1848 THACKERAY *Van. Fair* II. v. 56 Mrs. O'Dowd the good house-wife, arrayed in curl-papers and a camisole. 1857 C. BRONTË *Professor* I. viii. 134 She seldom wore a gown—only a shabby cotton camisole.

b. An underbodice, often embroidered and trimmed with lace. Also *attrib.*

1866 Advt. in A. Adburgham *Shops & Shopping* (1964) xii. 133, 2 Long-cloth petticoats..3 camisoles. 1895 *Army & Navy Co-op. Soc. Price List* 1062 Tucked Camisoles. 1903 *Daily Chron.* 14 Mar. 8/4 There are many camisole patterns. 1906 *Ibid.* 7 May 11/6 Camisole machinists. 1916 *Sphere* 19 Aug. p. vi/1 Cambric and nainsook combinations are..becoming obsolete, the camisole-knicker or camisole-chemise taking their place.

3. A strait-jacket, formerly put upon lunatics.

1881 in *Syd. Soc. Lex.*

'**camister.** *Thieves' cant.* [f. CAMIS in sense 'surplice' (? termination suggested by *minister*).] A clergyman, a minister.

1851 MAYHEW *Lond. Labour* I. 231 (Hoppe).

camizado, var. of CAMISADO.

camle. *Obs.* cf. CHAMELEON and CAMELION.

*c*1400 MAUNDEV. 289 There ben also in that contree manye Camles that is a lytille best as a goot, that is wylde, & he lyvethe be the Eyr, and etethe nought ne drynkethe nought.

camlee, camly, var. CUMBLY, Indian blanket.

camlet ('kæmlɪt), *sb.* Forms: 5 **chamlyt, chamelet(t**, 5–6 **chamlett**, 5–7 **cham(e)lot**, 6 **chambelot**, 6–7 **chamblet(t**, 6–8 **chamlet**, 6–9 **camblet**, 7 **chamolet, camelott, camlott**, 7–8 **camelot**, 7– **camlet**. [app. immediately from French: Littré cites *chamelot* 13th c., *camelot* 16th c.; Cotgr. translates F. *camelot*, 'chamlet'; Du Cange has med.L. *camelotum*; Anglo-French statutes of Edward IV have *chamelett*, and the spelling with *cham-* was the prevalent one in English till after the Restoration. The ultimate origin is obscure; at the earliest known date the word was associated (by Europeans) with *camel*, as if stuff made of camel's hair; but there is reason to think it was originally the Arabic *khamlat*, from *khaml*; Marco Polo (ed. Yule) I. 248 (Skeat). *Khaml*, *khamlat*, is explained by Lane as 'the nap or pile or villous substance on the surface of cloth'; *khamlat*, by Johnson, as 'camelot, silk and camel's hair, also, all silk or velvet, especially pily and plushy'. According to Littré, the *Journal officiel* of 1874, p. 3220/1, says *camelot* is so called from the Arabic *seil el kemel*, the Angora goat; cf. CAMEL-YARN.]

A name originally applied to some beautiful and costly eastern fabric, afterwards to imitations and substitutes the nature of which has changed many times over. 'A kind of stuff originally made by a mixture of silk and camel's hair; it is now made with wool and silk' (J.). 'A light stuff, formerly much used for female apparel, made of long wool, hard spun, sometimes mixed in the loom with cotton or linen yarn' (Ure). It is uncertain whether it was ever made of camel's hair; but in the 16th and 17th c. it was made of the hair of the Angora goat.

According to Beck, *Draper's Dict.*, 'In [the] production [of camlets], the changes have been rung with all materials in nearly every possible combination; sometimes of wool, sometimes of silk, sometimes of hair, sometimes of hair with wool or silk, at others of silk and wool warp and hair woof.. Those of our day have had cotton and linen introduced into their composition. They have been made plain and twilled, of single warp and weft, of double warp, and sometimes with double weft also'.

*c*1400 *Epiph.* (Turnb. 1843) 114 Wer ther of gold any clothes fownde..Or was ther any chamlyt or satyn. *a*1413 *Inv. Wardrobe Hen. IV* (Draper's Dict.), Seven yards of red chamlett at 13s. 4d. the remnant. 1423 JAS. I. *Kingis Q.* clvii, There sawe I..For chamelot, the camel full of hare. 1472 *Act 12 Edw. IV*, iii, Satens, Sarcenetz & Tarterons Chamelettis & autres Draps de soie, & dore & soie. 1532–3 *Act 24 Hen. VIII*, xiii, Silke, chamblet, or taffata. 1578 FLORIO *1st Fruites* 10, I wil buy..Velvet, Grograyne, Satten, Makadowe, Chambelot. 1615 G. SANDYS *Trav.* 15 Natolia affoording great store of Chamolets and Grogerams. 1634 SIR T. HERBERT *Trav.* 146 Some of rich gold or silver Chamlets, and other of cloth of gold. 1635 SWAN *Spec. M.* (1670) 398 Camblet..of Camels hair as some do affirm. 1644 EVELYN *Diary* (1871) 64, I went to see their manufactures in silke, their pressing and watering the grograms and chamblets. 1680 MORDEN *Geog. Rect.* (1685) 327 Famous..for good Chamlets. 1714 GAY *Trivia* I. 46 Show'rs soon drench the Camlet's cockled Grain. 1727 DE FOE *Eng. Tradesm.* xxvi. (1841) I. 266 Camlets from Norwich. 1756 NUGENT *Gr. Tour* I. 98 Here [Leyden] they make..camblets, tho' inferior to those of Great Britain. 1774 GOLDSM. *Nat. Hist.* II. 35 Stuffs made from the hair of [the Angora goat] are well known among us by the name of *camlet*. 1812 J. SMYTH *Pract. Customs* 256 Mohair..is commonly imported ready spun, and is woven into camblets. 1815 ELPHINSTONE *Acc. Caubul* (1842) II. 87 The tents..are of a kind of black blanket, or rather of coarse camlet.

b. *watered* (*water*) *camlet*: camlet with a wavy or watered surface; cf. Fr. *camelot à ondes* (Cotgr.).

1596 SPENSER *F.Q.* IV. xi. 45 Wav'd upon, like water chamelot. 1601 HOLLAND *Pliny* I. 228 The waued water Chamelot, was from the beginning esteemed the richest and brauest wearing. 1624 BACON *New Atl.* (1650) 3 A Gowne.. of a kinde of Water Chamolet, of an excellent Azure Colour. 1658 ROWLAND *Mouffet's Theat. Ins.* 961 Wings as if it were watered Chamblet. 1719 D'URFEY *Pills* (1872) VI. 95 A watered Camlet Gown she had.

c. A garment made of camlet. Also *fig.*

1613 SHAKS. *Hen. VIII*, V. iv. 93 You i' th' Chamblet, get vp o' th' raile. 1648 HERRICK *Hesper.* I. 64 Cloath'd in her chamlets of delight. 1847 L. HUNT *Men, Women, & B.* II. xi. 272 To see and be seen in his new camlet.

d. *attrib.*

1526 *Lanc. Wills* (1854) I. 13 My chamlett kyrtell. *a*1625 FLETCHER *Wom. Prize* V. i, His camblet breeches. 1662 PEPYS *Diary* 6 Mar., This night my new camelott riding coate..came home. 1696 BP. PATRICK *Comm. Exod.* xxvi. (ed. 2) 507 These Camlet Curtains (as I may call them [of Goats' hair]). 1789 MRS. PIOZZI *Journ. France* I. 5 The women..in long white camblet clokes. 1847 L. HUNT *Men, Women, & B.* 271 His black camletcloak with silver buttons.

e. *Comb.*, as *camlet-maker*; *camlet-mingled* adj.; also **camlet-fly**, a fly with mottled wings.

1658 ROWLAND *Mouffet's Theat. Ins.* 969 Nature bred this with a chamblet mingled coloured coat. 1676 COTTON *Angler* II. 335 In the middle of May [comes in] the Camlet-fly. 1750 BEAWES *Lex Mercat.* (1752) 686 Of the aforesaid wool the Camblet-makers alone take 80000 lb.

'**camlet**, *v.* For forms see CAMLET *sb.* [f. prec. sb.] *trans.* To mark or variegate as (watered) camlet; to mark with wavy veins. Hence '**camleted** *ppl. a.*; '**camleting** *vbl. sb.*

1618 BOLTON *Florus* I. v. 14 Embroydered Gownes, Cassockes chambleted with figures of palmes. 1626 BACON *Sylva* §658 Some have the Veines more varied and Chamloted: as Oake, whereof Wainscot is made. *Ibid.* §741 The Turks have a pretty Art of Chamoletting of Paper. 1652 EVELYN *Mem.* (1827) II. 53, I also inspected the manner of chambletting silk & grograms..in Morefields. 1652 BENLOWES *Theoph.* I. liii, In sackcloth chambleted with tears. 1727 BRADLEY *Fam. Dict.* I. s.v. *Alder*, They afford the Inlayer Pieces curiously chambletted and very hard.

camleteen, -ine (kæmlɪ'tiːn), *a.* Also 8 **camlettee, camletine**, 9 **cambleteen**. [f. CAMLET; cf. F. *camelotine*.] An imitation camlet; a 'camlet' of inferior kind.

1730–6 BAILEY, *Camlettee*, *Camleteen*, a Sort of fine worsted camlets or camelots. 1753 CHAMBERS *Cycl. Supp.*, *Camletine*, in commerce, denotes a slight, narrow kind of camblet, little valued..also..stuff made of hair mixed with wool, in imitation of a camblet. 1861 S. JUDD *Margaret* II. xi. (1871) 309 Dress of cambleteen.

camleting ('kæmlɪtɪŋ). In 7 **chambleting**. [f. CAMLET: cf. *coating*, *shirting*.] Stuff of camlet.

1697 EVELYN *Numism.* viii. 280 Several sorts of Stuffs, Calandring and Chambletings.

camlin, camlott, obs. f. CAMELINE *sb.*, CAMLET.

cammaka, -oka, var. CAMACA, a fine cloth.

cammamyll, -myld, obs. ff. CAMOMILE.

camman, var. CAMAN.

cammas, var. QUAMASH: see CAMAS.

cammassado, -esado, var. of CAMISADO.

cammauyne, obs. form of CAMOVYNE.

cammed (kæmd), *a. Obs.* exc. *dial.* [app. extended from CAM *a.*; cf. *wicked.*]

†**1.** = CAMOIS; having a cam or camois nose. *Obs.*

?*c* **1350** *Sat. Blacksmiths* in *Rel. Ant.* I. 240 The cammede kongons cryen after col! col! *c* **1386** CHAUCER *Reeve's T.* 14 Rounde was hese face and kammede was hese nose. *c* **1440** *Promp. Parv.* 59 Cammyd, or schort nosyd, *simus.*

2. Crooked, perverse. *dial.*

c **1746** J. COLLIER (Tim Bobbin) *Tummus & M.* Wks. (1862) 61 Its not to tell heaw camm'd things con happ'n! **1875** E. WAUGH *Old Cronies* vi. 60 (in *Lanc. Gloss.*) Thou'rt gettin' camm'd as a crushed whisket.

Hence **'cammedness.**

c **1440** *Promp. Parv.* 59 Chammydnesse [**1499** cammednesse], *simitas.*

cammel, cammeril, obs. ff. CAMEL *sb.*, CAMBREL.

†**cammes.** *Obs.* Also **cames, camwysse.** Apparently a corrupt form of CANVAS; 'a kind of gauze for samplers' (Jamieson).

1540 *Sc. Ld. Treas. Acc.* in Pitcairn *Crim. Trials* I. 301 For cammes to stuff the orpheis of þe samin. **1541** *Ibid.* 309 For xij boltis of cammes, to be salis. **1555** *Ch. Acc. Leverton, Linc.* in *Archæol.* XLI. 360 For iiij yardes of camwysse for the hye awlter. **1578** *Inventories* 215 (Jam.) A lang pece of cammes, sewit with the armes of Scotland.

cammock[1] ('kæmək). Forms: 1 cammocc, -uc, 1, 4 cammoc, 4–7 cammok, 5 cambmok, chambmok, camok, -oke, -ocke, 6–8 cammock, 7 camock, 9 *dial.* cammick. [OE. *cammoc*, generally assumed to be from Celtic, and to be the same word as the next, with a reference to 'crooked stems or roots'; but the plant is not so named in any Celtic language, and the root is not specially crooked, so that the actual origin remains doubtful.]

The plant *Ononis spinosa* (N.O. *Leguminosæ*) also called *Rest-harrow*, and according to Cockayne, *Cammock Whin.* Some earlier writers identified it with *Peucedanum*, and 'Petty Whin'; but it is not clear what plant or plants they meant.

c **1000** *Sax. Leechd.* I. 209 Ðas wyrte man peucedanum, & oðrum naman cammoc [*v.r.* cammuc] nemneþ. *c* **1000** *O.E. Voc.* in Wr.-Wülcker 300 *Nomina Herbarum, Peucedanum*, cammocc. *c* **1050** *Glosses* (Cott. Cleop.) ibid. 416 *Gotuna*, cammuc. **1377** LANGL. *P. Pl.* B. XIX. 319 For comunelich in contrees kammokes [*text C.* canmokes]..& wedes Fouleth þe fruite in þe felde. *a* **1387** *Sinon. Barthol.* (*Anecd. Oxon.*) 33 *Peucedona* i. cammoc secundum quosdam. *Ibid.* 36 *Resta bovis*, herba est retinens boves in aratro, an. Cammoc. **1398** TREVISA *Barth. De P.R.* XVII. cxxxviii. (1495) 695 The Cambmok is a pryckynge shrub. *Ibid.* Of the rotes and of the stalkes of Cambmok is made a medycyn that Physicyens call Licium. *Ibid.* Chambmok gendreth fyre of itselfe. *c* **1450** *Alphita* (*Anecd. Oxon.*) 156 *Resta bouis*..anglice hyseneherde uel cammok. **1578** LYTE *Dodoens* VI. ix. 668 The roote of Restharrow or Cammock. **1579** LANGHAM *Gard. Health* (1633) 527 Restharrow, Cammok, or Petywin. **1775** LIGHTFOOT *Flora Scot.* (1777) I. 386 Prickly Restharrow or Cammock. **1787** WINTER *Syst. Husb.* 123 The above field contained many cammocks.

2. Vaguely applied dialectally to other plants, as St. John's Wort, Ragweed, Fleabane, Yarrow, etc.

1878 BRITTEN & HOLL. *Plant-n.* s.v., In Hampshire almost any yellow flower is called Cammock.

3. *Comb.* **cammock whin** = sense 1.

cammock[2], **cambock** ('kæmək). *Obs.* exc. *Sc.* Forms: 5 cambok, -oke, -ake, 6 camok, -oke, -ock, -ocke, (7 cambuc(k), 6, 9 *Sc.* cammock, 9 *Sc.* camack. [ME. *kambok*, app. immediately ad. *cambuca*, a late L. word (Du Cange cites Papias *cambuta*, sustentamen vel baculus, flexus, pedum, crocia, and *Gloss. Corbeiense*, *cambuta*, baculus episcopōrum), app. of Gaulish origin, derived from *cambo-*, crooked, CAM; represented in mod. Welsh by *camawg*, *camog* fem. 'piece of bent wood, the felloe of a wheel'. Cf. also Gaelic *camag* 'curl, ringlet, crook,' and Manx *camag* 'crutch, crooked bat or shinty to play hurles, also the game itself'.

But some of the senses of the Manx word may be from Eng.; for the Irish and Gaelic for a bent stick for hurling, shinty, hockey, a golf-club, is *camán, caman.*]

1. A crooked staff, a crook; *esp.* a stick or club with a crooked head, used in games to drive a ball, or the like; a hockey-stick; hence, the game played with such a stick.

c **1425** *Voc.* in Wr.-Wülcker 666 (*Nomina Ludorum*) *Hoc pedum*, cambok. **1483** *Cath. Angl.* 52 A Cambake [*v.r.* Camboke], *cambuca.* **1547** SALESBURY *Welsh Dict.*, *Kamoc*, a camocke. **1720** *Stow's Surv.* (ed. Strype 1754) I. I. xxix. 302/2 People please themselves..some in Hand-ball, Foot-ball, Bandy-ball, and in Cambuck. **1821** *Edin. Even. Courant* 22 Jan., On Christmas and New Years day, matches were played..at the camack and football. **1885** *Inverness 30 Yrs. ago* ii. 80 A numerous party played a game of Cammack.

2. A crooked stick or piece of wood, a knee of timber; a cambrel.

c **1450** *Nominale* in Wr.-Wülcker 724 (*Nomina domo pertinentia*) *Hec cambuca*, a cambok. *c* **1510** BARCLAY *Mirr. Good Mann.* (1570) B vj, Soone crooketh the same tree that good camoke wilbe, As a common prouerbe in youth I heard this sayde. **1580** LYLY *Euphues* (Arb.) 237 Crooked trees proue good Cammocks. *Ibid.* 408 If my fortune bee so yll that searching for a wande, I gather a camocke. **1593** DRAYTON *Eclog.* VII 62 And earely crook'd that will a Camocke bee. **1615** CROOKE *Body of Man* 815 This tendon ..maketh an empty cauity, through which the Butchers peirce their Cammockes to hang the beast vpon in the shambles.

'cammocky, *a.* [f. CAMMOCK[1] + -Y[1].] Of or abounding in Cammock or Rest-harrow.

In mod. Dicts.

cammus, var. of CAMOIS, *Obs.*

camnesado, obs. form of CAMISADO.

cam-nosed, a variant reading of *cammosed*, CAMOISED: prob. only an error.

camoca, var. of CAMACA, *Obs.*, a fabric.

‖**ca'mocho.** *rare*[−1]. [Cf. It. *camoscio* 'a kinde of stuffe worne in Italie' (Florio).] A fabric. (In quot. applied contemptuously to a Spaniard.)

1607 DEKKER *T. Wyat* Wks. 1873 III. 115 A Spaniard is a Camocho, a Callimanco, nay which is worse a Dondego.

camock(e, obs. form of CAMMOCK.

†**'camois, camus**, *a.* (and *sb.*) *Obs.* Also 4 **cammus**, 5–8 **camoise, -oys, -oyse**, 6 ? **-ous**, 8 **chamois.** [a. F. *camus, -use*, 'having a short and flat nose'. Thurneysen refers it to a Celtic source, comparing the Ir. sb. *camus* hollow, retreating angle, bay, Gael. *camas* bought, bay, creek, space between the thighs: cf. *Cambus-* in place-names in Scotland. For another suggestion see Diez, and Littré.]

1. Of the nose: low and concave. Of persons: pug-nosed.

c **1380** *Sir Ferumb.* 4437 Ys browes were boþe rowe and grete, & ys nose cammus. *c* **1386** CHAUCER *Reeves T.* 14 Round was his face and camuse [*so* 3 *MSS.*; *v.r.* kamuse, camoyse, kammede, *Harl.* camois] was his nose. **1580** BARET *Alv.* C 44 A Camoise nose, that is to say, crooked vpwarde as the Morians. **1646** SIR T. BROWNE *Pseud. Ep.* VI. x. 328 Many Spaniards..of the race of Barbary Moores..have not worne out the Camoys nose unto this day. **1650** BULWER *Anthropomet.* vii. (1653) 123 The Inhabitants have all Camoyse or saddle Noses. **1745** tr. *Columella's Husb.* B vj, Such oxen..[as have] black eyes and lips, wide nostrils, a camoys nose. **1751** CHAMBERS *Cycl.* s.v., The Tartars are great admirers of camus beauties. **1877** R. H. HORNE in *Mrs. Browning's Lett.* II. 277 A gentleman..with a large camus nose.

b. *fig.* Low and curved like a camois nose.

1664 EVELYN tr. *Freart's Archit.* xxi. 52 The Cornice is camuse and blunt.

c. Hence *camois-nosed.*

1601 HOLLAND *Pliny* I. 336 The former haue flat noses, the other are hooked and camoise nosed vpward. **1656** BLOUNT *Glossogr.*, *Camoise-nosed*, hooked nosed.

2. *absol.* or quasi-*sb.* A person or animal with a camois nose.

1485 CAXTON *Chas. Gt.* (1881) 94 The camuse..is geffroy langeuyn. **1515** BARCLAY *Egloges* IV. (1570) C vj, She with Bacchus her camous did promote. **1618** SIR R. WILLIAMS *Actions Low Countr.* 49 White little hounds, with crooked noses, called camuses. **1751** CHAMBERS *Cycl.*, *Camus*, a person with a low, flat nose, hollowed or sunk in the middle.

†**'camoised**, *a. Obs.* Also 4–5 **camused**, 6 **camesyd, camoused, cammoised, cammosed**, 7 **camus'd, -oysed.** [f. CAMOIS + -ED.] Made camois; having a camois nose.

1393 GOWER *Conf.* II. 210 Some one, for she is noble of kinne..Some one, for that she is camused. *a* **1533** LD. BERNERS *Huon* xxxiii. 103 Grete eeres and a camesyd nose. **1583** STANYHURST *Poems* (Arb.) 141 This slut with a cammoysed haucks nose. *c* **1600** MONTGOMERIE *Flyting* 472 That cammosed [*ed.* **1688** camnosed] cocatrice they quite with them carie. **1625** LISLE *Du Bartas, Noe* 11 Camoysed dolphins. **1637** B. JONSON *Sad Sheph.* II. i. 49 Though my nase be camus'd, my lipps thick, And my chin bristled! **1650** BULWER *Anthropomet.* vii. 82 All children are a little camoised about the Nose, before the bridge riseth.

†**'camoisly, 'camously**, *adv. Obs.* [f. CAMOIS + -LY[2].] Like a camois nose; concavely.

a **1528** SKELTON *El. Rummyng* 28 Nose som dele hoked, And camously croked.

camok(e, obs. form of CAMMOCK.

camomile, cham- ('kæməmaɪl). Forms: 3–4 came-, camamille, 5 camamylle, -melle, -myle, camomelle, 5–6 camomylle, 6 cammamyll, -myld, cam(m)omyle, camamile, -mil, -mel, camimile, chamomyle, -myle, chamœmell, 6–7 cammomill, 6–8 camomil(l, 7 chamamil, chamæmell, cammomel, chamœ-, chamemile, chamomel, (8 camomoil), 8–9 chamomile, 6– camomile. [a. F. *camomille* (also formerly *camamille*), ad. L. *chamomilla* (Pliny, etc.), an altered form of *chamæmēlon* (Pliny, Palladius, etc.), a. Gr. χαμαίμηλον earth apple (f. χαμαί on the ground + μῆλον apple); so called from the apple-like scent of the blossoms. Cf. It. and Pr. *camomilla*, Sp. *camomila*, Fr. dial. *camomile, camamile.* The spelling *cha-* is chiefly in pharmacy, after Latin; that with *ca-* is literary and popular.]

1. a. The name of a Composite plant, *Anthemis nobilis*, an aromatic creeping herb, found on dry sandy commons in England, with downy leaves, and flowers white in the ray and yellow in the disk, but in cultivation often all white like a double daisy. The flowers are employed in medicine for their bitter and tonic properties. Also distinguished as Noble or Roman Camomile, White C., and in its single wild form as Scotch C.

c **1265** *Voc.* in Wr.-Wülcker 557 *Camomilla*, camemille, maiwe. **1313** in *Wardrobe Acc. Edw. II*, 20 Camamille, 12*d.* *c* **1440** *Promp. Parv.* 59 Camamyle, herbe, *camamilla.* *a* **1450** *E.E.P.* (1862) 141 Vn-to a benche of camomylle My wofulle hede I dyd inclyne. **1483** *Cath. Angl.* 52 Camomelle, *camomillum.* **1513** DOUGLAS *Æneis* XII. Prol. 116 The clavyr, catcluke, and the cammamyld. **1530** PALSGR. 202/2 Cammamyll herbe, *camamille.* **1540** ELYOT *Image Gov.* (1556) 63 b, The grounde was thicke covered with Camamile. **1548** TURNER *Names of Herbes* (E.E.T.S.) 13 Anthenus [Anthemis]..is called in englishe Cammomyle. **1573** TUSSER *Husb.* (1878) 95 Herbes of all sortes.. Camamel. **1586** COGAN *Haven Health* (1636) 77 Chamæmell is hot and dry in the first degree. **1605** TIMME *Quersit.* I. vii. 33 The flowers of chamamil. **1660** BOND *Scut. Reg.* 41 The Camomile the more it is trodden on, the better it groweth. **1748** THOMSON *Cast. Indol.* I. lviii, He bask'd him on the ground, Where the wild thyme and camomoil are found. **1794** MARTYN *Rousseau's Bot.* xxvi. 397 Common or true Camomile..sometimes covers a considerable extent of ground on dry sandy commons. **1878** T. BRYANT *Pract. Surg.* I. 51 Warm fomentations..medicated with.. chamomile.

b. Also used as an English book-name for the genus *Anthemis*, and popularly applied to several allied plants, esp. *Matricaria Chamomilla* (Wild Camomile, Dog's C., German C., or Camomile Goldins); *Anthemis Cotula* (Stinking Camomile, Dog's C., Mayweed); **blue** or **purple c.**, the Sea Starwort, *Aster Tripolium*; **red** or **purple c.**, *Adonis autumnalis* (from its foliage).

1578 LYTE *Dodoens* II. xxx. 184 Stinking Camomill or Cotula fœtida. *Ibid.* 185 Vnsauery Camomilla [*M. inodora*] or Cotula non fœtida. **1597** GERARD *Herbal*, Women that dwell by the seaside call it..blew camomill. **1783** AINSWORTH *Lat. Dict.* (Morell) VI, *Cauta*, Dogs camomile. **1790–1820** SOWERBY *Eng. Bot.* (ed. 3) VI. 52 Corn Chamomile, *Anthemis arvensis.* **1859** GEO. ELIOT *A. Bede* 214 The wild camomile that starred the road side.

2. *Comb.*, as *camomile-flower*; also **camomile-alley**, an alley planted with camomile (see quot.); **camomile-tea**, an infusion of camomile flowers.

1626 BACON *Sylva* §96 A Physitian prescribeth, for the cure of the Rheume that a Man should walk continually upon a *Camomill-alley; Meaning that he should put Camomill within his Socks. **1652** CULPEPPER *Eng. Physic* 18 Boiled with..*Chamomel flowers. **1753** *World* 37, I..am forced to attend with her *camomile tea. **1965** *New Statesman* 30 Apr. 674/3 At my daughter's kindergarten, the children drink camomile tea, not milk, at break. **1968** G. BUTLER *Coffin Following* ix. 200 She sipped her camomile tea delicately.

camooyne: see CAMOVYNE.

†**camoroche.** *Obs. rare.* The Wild Tansy or Silver-weed (*Potentilla anserina*).

c **1440** *Promp. Parv.* 204 Gosys gres, or camoroche, or wylde tanzy, *camaroca, vel tanasetum agreste.*

‖**camorra** (kə'mɒrə). [It. *camorra* (ka'morra), 'Irish rugge or mantle, a Mariners frocke' (Florio).]

1. A kind of smock-frock or blouse.

1869 W. GILBERT *L. Borgia* I. 211 She was dressed..in a camora of gold shot brocade.

2. A secret society of lawless malcontents in Naples and Neapolitan cities. Sometimes *transf.*

1865 *Sat. Rev.* 21 Jan. 87/1 The Camorra is a system of organized extortion, which has survived the Bourbon rule.. its name is conjectured to be that of a species of short coat worn by members of the society. **1880** *Fortn. Rev.* Feb. 174 The profits which..this official camorra divide between them are enormous.

Hence **Ca'morrism**, the principles or practice of this society; lawlessness, anarchy. **Ca'morrist**, a member of a camorra.

1863 *Sat. Rev.* 7 Nov. 625/2 The notes..treat..of the Neapolitan Camorrists. **1883** *Chamb. Jrnl.* 78 The Camorrist remains the personification of power and heroism to the Neapolitan.

†**camose.** *Obs.* [cf. CALMEWE.] A sea-gull.

1538–46 ELYOT, *Candosoccus*, a sea gull, or a camose.

camote (kə'məʊteɪ). [Mexican Sp., ad. Nahuatl *camotli.*] A name in Mexico and other Spanish-speaking countries for any one of several tuber-bearing plants, e.g. the sweet potato and yam.

1842 'A. T. MYRTHE' *Ambrosio de Letinez* I. 143 This is not a good country for praties, no how—save for the swate

ones, that the Mexican people call *camotes*. **1885** *Encycl. Brit.* XVIII. 751/1 Sweet potatoes (camote)..are pretty generally known [in the Philippines]. **1909** *Teachers' Assembly Herald* II. 44/2 [To] relieve the Igorot girls from their laborious toil in the camote patch.

camoudie (kəˈmuːdɪ). Also -di, camoodie, -oedi, -udi. [Native name.] A boa constrictor of tropical America.

1825 WATERTON *Wand. S. Amer.* i. 11 The Camoudi snake..from thirty to forty feet long. **1851** W. H. BRETT *Ind. Missions in Guiana* 35 The reptile, a large camudi, sprang upon him. **1866** R. DUFF *Brit. Guiana* 42 The camoedi was killed with a cutlass. **1887** *Timehri* Dec. 202 A very fine skin of a large Land-camoodie. **1898** H. KIRKE *25 Yrs. Brit. Guiana* 90 A camoudie shot over him and wrapped itself round his body. **1904** W. H. HUDSON *Green Mansions* ii. 31 If dangerous creatures had existed there—tigers, or camoodis, or solitary murderous savages.

camouflage (ˈkæməflɑːʒ), *sb.* [Fr., f. *camoufler* CAMOUFLET.] The disguising of any objects used in war, such as camps, guns, ships, by means of paint, smoke-screens, shrubbery, etc., in such a way as to conceal it from the enemy; also, the disguise used in this way; freq. *attrib.*

1917 *Daily Mail* 25 May 4/4 The act of hiding anything from your enemy is termed 'camouflage'. **1917** *Ibid.* 16 July 5/3 The King paid a visit to what is called a camouflage factory. **1922** C. E. MONTAGUE *Disenchantment* viii. 108 A French aerodrome across which the French camouflage painters had simply painted a great white high-road. **1948** *Sci. News* VII. 84 Features..which in a normal colour photograph might escape detection could often be clearly differentiated in this 'camouflage detection' film. **1957** *Granta* 9 Mar., We took home a few pieces of camouflage-painted aluminium.

b. *transf.* and *fig.*

1918 G. B. SHAW *Pen Portraits & Reviews* (1932) 35 The first necessity of such souls when truth is about, as it always is, is camouflage, or, better still, complete cover. **1920** R. MACAULAY *Potterism* I. iii, It's a very laudable object, and needs no camouflage. **1963** V. NABOKOV *Gift* iv. 251 Striped and spotted with words, dressed in verbal camouflage, the important idea he wished to convey would slip through.

camouflage (ˈkæməflɑːʒ), *v.* [f. the sb.] To conceal by or as by camouflage. So **ˈcamouflaged** *ppl. a.*, **ˈcamouflaging** *vbl. sb.*

1917 *Daily Mail* 16 July 5/3 The King saw all the latest Protean tricks for concealing or, as we all say now, for 'camouflaging' guns, snipers, observers. **1918** W. OWEN *Let.* Apr. (1967) 545 Your portrait is certainly slightly camouflaged. **1919** DOWNING *Digger Dialects* 15 *Camouflaged Aussy*, an Englishman serving with the A.I.F. **1920** *Blackw. Mag.* Mar. 332/1 Number One, ensconced in the little camouflaged control. **1921** *Spectator* 23 Apr. 518/2 The house telephone.., its extremely ugly box 'camouflaged' with the pattern of the paper. **1922** W. J. LOCKE *Tale of Triona* ii. 21 These are real eggs, although they're camouflaged in a Chinese scramble. **1924** GALSWORTHY *White Monkey* II. xi, Queer how Nature camouflaged her schemes. **1970** *Daily Mail* 24 Mar. 4/9 Television needs a lot more money to improve quality and variety. Colour merely camouflages the same old material.

‖**camouflet** (kamufle). *Mil.* [Fr.: see Littré.]

1. A mine containing a small charge of powder, placed in a wall of earth between the galleries of besieged and besieger, so as, in exploding, to bury, suffocate, or cut off the retreat of the miner on the opposite side; a 'stifler'.

1836 in *Penny Cycl.* VI. 197/1 *Camouflet* or *Stifler.* **1847** in CRAIG.

2. A subterranean cavity formed by a bomb exploding beneath the surface of the earth.

1941 *Nature* 17 May 596/2 If the bomb is too deep, the breaking of the surface does not occur; it is simply heaved up and drops back more or less into place. This is called a 'camouflet'.

camous, -ed: see CAMOIS, CAMOISED.

camovyne, -wyne. *Sc.* Also 6 cammauyne, 9 camooyne. = CAMOMILE.

1549 *Compl. Scot.* 67, I sau cammauyne, quhilk is gude for ane scabbit moutht. **1768** ROSS *Helenore* 112 (Jam.) On the camowyne to lean you down. **1884** MILLER *Plant-n.*, Camooyne, or Camowyne, *Anthemis nobilis*.

camow-nosed, *a.* = Camois-nosed. CAMOIS.

a **1600** HUME in Sibbald *Chron. Sc. Poetry* iii. 386 (Jam.) His little camow-nosed sheepe, And rowtting kie to feede.

camoys(e, var. of CAMOIS, *Obs.*

†**camp**, *sb.*[1] *Obs.* exc. *dial.* Also 1–3 comp, 3 komp, 4 kamp. [OE. *camp*, *cǫmp*, corresp. to OFris. *camp*, *cǫmp*, (MDu. *camp*, Du. *kamp*), MLG. *kamp*, OHG. *champf* (MHG. and Ger. *kampf*), combat, all masc., ON. *kapp* (*pp* from *mp*) neuter, (Da. and Sw. *kamp*) contest, keenness, vehemence. WGer. or OTeut. **kampo-z* was presumably an early Germanic adoption of L. *camp-us* in its transferred sense 'field of contest or combat', also 'duel, fight, battle, war'; see CAMP *sb.*[2] The word was thoroughly at home in WGer., and gave origin to numerous derivatives, particularly the vb. *kampjon*; see KEMP *v.* and cf. KEMP *sb.*:—OE. *cęmpa*, WGer. *kampjo-n* = late L. *campion-em* CHAMPION. In ME. the word survived longest in the north, esp. as an archaism of alliterative verse.

(Kluge and others, however, claim the word as native Teutonic, mainly on the ground of the improbability that the Germans who had so many native words to designate war, should adopt a foreign designation; but they offer no satisfactory account of its etymology.)]

†**1.** Martial contest, combat, fight, battle, war.

Beowulf 5003 In campe ʒecrong cumbles hyrde. *c* **1000** *Riddles* vii. 2 (Gr.) Mec ʒesette · Crist to compe. *c* **1205** LAY. 4215 þer heo weren on kompen [**1275** fihte]. *Ibid.* 4347 þu eært muchele betere cniht to halden comp [**1275** werre] and ifiht. *Ibid.* 14024 þer wes feht swiðe strong comp swiðe sturne. ? *a* **1400** *Morte Arth.* 3702 Alle þe kene mene of kampe, knyghtes and oþer.

2. Hence **camp-ball**: An ancient form of football in which large numbers engaged on both sides. See CAMP *v.*[1] 3, and CAMPING *vbl. sb.*[1]

c **1600** DAY *Begg. Bedn. Gr.* in Strutt *Sports & Past.* II. iii, I am Tom Stroud of Hurling, I'll play a gole at camp-ball. **1840** [see CAMPING *vbl. sb.*[1]] Fighting camps. **1847–78** HALLIWELL, *Camp*, an ancient athletic game of ball formerly in vogue in the Eastern Counties. **1887** *Illust. Lond. News* 26 Feb. /1 The game in very ancient times was not so properly called football as camp-ball. **1887** JESSOPP *Arcady* 236 Camp-ball..used to be a very favourite game in my parish some fifty years ago, and it was, by all accounts, a very rough one—something like football.

camp (kæmp), *sb.*[2] Also 6–7 campe. [a. F. *camp* (16th c. in Littré) in same sense: cf. It., Sp., Pg. *campo* 'camp', orig. 'field', and F. *champ*, Pr. *camp*, field, field of tournament, field of battle:—L. *camp-us* level field, *spec.* the Campus Martius at Rome, the place for games, athletic practice, military drills, etc., whence 'field of contest or combat', 'field of battle'. Although *camp* was the Norman form of *champ*, no trace of it appears in ME., which had only CHAMP from central OF., in the senses of 'field of duel or tournament' and heraldic 'field'. *Camp* was introduced early in the 16th c., from contemporary Fr. and with the sense *castra*, but was also at first used to render L. *campus* in other senses, as well as occasionally in the sense of the earlier *champ* 'field of combat'.

Littré supposed that the 16th century French use of *camp* was merely the literary adoption of the Picard form in a special sense; but evidently it was an adaptation of It. (or ? Sp.) *campo*, in a sense not used with F. *champ*.]

I. In the military sense.

1. The place where an army or body of troops is lodged in tents or other temporary means of shelter, with or without intrenchments. In common modern use the collection of tents, huts, and other equipments is the chief notion, the site being the 'camping-ground'; but as used of ancient works, Roman, British, Danish, etc., it usually means the intrenched and fortified site, within which an army lodged or defended itself; a modern *intrenched camp* includes both notions. The name is also given to a permanent station for the reception of troops, in order that they may be trained in manœuvring in large bodies, and in campaigning duties generally, as the camps at Aldershot, Shorncliffe camp, camp of Chalons.

1528 SIR GR. DE CASSALIS, etc. (*The King's Ambassadors with the Pope*) in Strype *Eccl. Mem.* I. II. xxiii. 61 It is very certain, that the Spanyards have refused batel, and conveyed themself out of ther camp neerer unto Naples in the night. **1560** BIBLE (*Genev.*) *2 Kings* vii. 7 They left their tentes and their horses and their asses, euen the campe as it was, and fledde for their liues. **1593** SHAKS. *Lucr.* Argt. 13 Sextus Tarquinius..departed with the rest back to the camp. **1683** BURNET tr. *More's Utopia* 170 They fortify their Camps well, with a deep and large Trench. **1697** DRYDEN *Virg. Georg.* III. 540 The Youth of Rome..pitch their sudden Camp before the Foe. **1727–51** CHAMBERS *Cycl.* s.v., Rhoe, describing the great Mogul's camp, says, it is twenty English miles round. **1856** EMERSON *Eng. Traits* v. *Ability* Wks. (Bohn) II. 33 He disembarked his legions, erected his camps and towers. **1870** F. WILSON *Ch. Lindisf.* 70 A fine ancient British camp, upon a neighbouring hill-top.

2. a. A body of troops encamping and moving together; an army on a campaign. (In earlier Eng. *the host.*)

a **1584** VICARY *Englishm. Treas.* 59 In anno 1551, when the said citie was taken and destroyed by the campe of Charles the first. *c* **1590** MARLOWE *Massacr. Paris* II. vi, Dismiss thy camp. **1598** GRENEWEY *Tacitus' Ann.* IV. vi. 97 This fleeting enemy was not to bee pursued with a maine campe. **1611** BIBLE *1 Sam.* iv. 7 God is come into the campe [COVERD. hoost, *Genev.* hoste]. **1706** FARQUHAR *Recruit. Off.* II. i, I hope you have more honour than to quit the service, and she more prudence than to follow the Camp. **1751** JOHNSON *Rambl.* No. 144 ¶4 Multitudes follow the camp only for want of employment. **1839** THIRLWALL *Greece* III. 451 The army was formed in a hollow square, inclosing the baggage and the followers of the camp.

b. *flying camp*, *camp-volant*: 'a little army of horse and foot, that keeps the field, and is continually in motion' (Phillips 1696–1706). See also quot. 1699. ? *Obs.*

1577 HOLINSHED *Chron.* III. 1040/2 Who..with a campe volant did what he could to stop the Englishmen within Hadington from vittels. **1726** DE FOE *Hist. Devil* (1822) 299 Some of his camp-volent are always present. **1611** COTGR., *Camp volant*, a flying campe, a campe of light-horsemen for ordinarie roades. **1699** B. E. *Dict. Cant. Crew*, *Flying-Camps*, Beggers plying in Bodies at Funerals. **1727–51** CHAMBERS *Cycl.* s.v. *Camp*, Flying Camp is a strong body of horse or dragoons.

c. *camp-royal*: the main or chief body of an army with the commander-in-chief; a great body of troops; hence *fig.* a great number, a host.

1593 NASHE *Christ's T.* 31 b, False witnesses they had in pay a Campe royal. **1601** DENT *Pathw. Heauen* 216 A Campe-royall, euen forty thousand strong. **1641** BROME *Jov. Crew* II. Wks. 1873 III. 377 This Doublet..might serve to furnish a Camp Royal of us.

3. Used for: The scene of military service; military service, the military life in general.

1725 RAMSAY *Gentle Sheph.* III. iv, I must..my Patrick soon remove To Courts and camps that may his soul improve. **1799** LAMB *Corr.* lxxi. (1870) 194 The world, the camp and the university have spoilt him among them. **1805** SCOTT *Last Minstr.* III. xv, Love rules the court, the camp, the grove. **1827** KEBLE *Chr. Y.* 1 Advent x, Through court and camp he holds his heavenward course serene. **1855** MACAULAY *Hist. Eng.* III. 204 His knowledge of courts and camps was such as few of his countrymen possessed.

II. *transf.* from the military sense.

4. a. The temporary quarters, formed by tents, vehicles, or other portable or improvised means of shelter, occupied by a body of nomads or men on the march, by travellers, gipsies, companies of sportsmen, lumbermen, field-preachers and their audiences, or parties 'camping out'; an encampment.

Connected with sense 1 by intimate gradations, *e.g.* the camp of the Israelites, or of North American Indians.

1560 BIBLE (*Genev.*) *Ex.* xvi. 13 At euen the quailes came and couered the campe [*Vulg.* castra, COVERD. tentes]. **1823** F. COOPER *Pioneer* xx, The sugar-boiler, who was busy in his 'camp'. **1864** W. CAMPBELL *My Indian Jrnl.* Contents.. Sport at Dharwar..A Civilian's Camp..Bison-Shooting, etc. **1886** F. H. GUILLEMARD *Cruise of Marchesa* I. 95 It is the hunter's rule to see that the fire is extinguished..before breaking camp.

b. *loosely.* 'Quarters.'

1747 H. WALPOLE *Corr.* (1837) I. 108, I am got into a new camp and have left my tub at Windsor.

c. *Austral.* and *N.Z.* A resting or assembly place (of sheep or cattle). Also *attrib.*

1891 D. FERGUSON *Bush Life* xxiv. 170 A long string of lambs and ewes..all making off as fast as they could for their camp. **1946** F. DAVISON *Dusty* x. 107 [The dog]..startled a few sheep huddled in camp. **1950** *N.Z. Jrnl. Agric.* Aug. 141 Variegated thistle established on a stock camp site under a tree.

d. Quarters for the accommodation of detained or interned persons, as *concentration camp*.

1917 *Sphere* 10 Feb. 128 Several copies have reached England of *The Ruhleben Camp Magazine* issued by the prisoners. *Ibid.*, The Lancashire and Cheshire civilians—who number over 500—in the camp [in Germany]. *Ibid.*, A parody of *The Mikado*..which jovial play seems to have been performed in the internment camp.

e. *S. Afr.* [ad. Afrikaans *kamp*.] A fenced-in portion of a farm.

1877 *Queenstown Free Press* 25 Sept. (Pettman), He purchased three birds to establish a camp at Somerset East in 1853. **1883** O. SCHREINER *Story Afr. Farm* I. i. 5 The.. Englishman, whose grave lay away beyond the ostrich-camps. **1896** R. WALLACE *Farm. Ind. Cape Col.* xi. 223 Ostriches require to be enclosed in camps. **1947** H. C. BOSMAN *Mafeking Road* 60 The wire he had borrowed from me for his new sheep-camp.

5. An encamping; a 'camping out'.

In Australia the regular term for an expedition or excursion for fishing, shooting, etc., in which the party camps out.

1865 *Intell. Observ.* No. 37. 15 A previous night's camp near the spot. **1880** INGLIS *Austral. Cousins* 233 We're going to have a regular camp; we..intend going to Port Hocking to have some shooting, fishing, and general diversion. **1886** *Pall Mall G.* 3 Aug. 13/2 Cadet corps (now out for a week's camp).

6. a. The whole company or body of persons encamped together, as surveyors, lumbermen, sportsmen, etc.; a company of nomads.

1750 BEAWES *Lex Mercat.* 797 The Chan of the Western Moungales Camp, tributary to China. **1864** in WEBSTER.

b. A local division or lodge of a society or league. *U.S.*

1880 TOURGÉE *Fool's Err.* II. v. 415 Sometimes several 'camps' or 'dens' [of the Ku-Klux] would, independently of each other, direct a warning to be sent to the same individual. **1904** HARBEN *Georgians* 132 The general is invited to address nearly all the veteran camps over the State when the badges of honor are presented once a year.

III. *fig.* from the military sense.

7. A 'host' or 'army' of arguments, facts, etc.

1566 PAINTER *Pal. Pleas.* Ded., Titus Liuius in whom is contayned a large campe of noble facts and exploites atchieued by valiaunt personages. **1871** E. BURR *Ad Fidem* xiv. 282 The main camp of allegations.

8. a. A body of adherents of a militant doctrine, or theory. So ***to have a foot in both camps***, to belong to or sympathize with two opposite groups, factions, etc. **b.** The position in which ideas or beliefs are intrenched and strongly defended.

1871 MORLEY *Voltaire* (1886) 23 No one who has marched ever so short a way out of the great camp of old ideas. **1885** CLODD *Myths & Dr.* II. vii. 182 Matters still dividing philosophers into opposite camps. **1933** J. G. COZZENS *Cure of Flesh* II. iii. 157 You never know when they may pull a fast one on you. I think you're in the wrong camp, George. **1935**

W. Empson *Versions of Pastoral* vi. 217 The divine Polly has a foot in both camps. **1958** *Listener* 6 Nov. 715/1 The world is in fact divided into two camps, Communist and anti-Communist, with a number of uncommitted nations standing on the sidelines.

IV. In sense of ME. champ.

†9. The field of combat, the lists. *Obs. rare*$^{-1}$.

1525 Ld. Berners *Froiss.* II. clxi. [clvii.] 446 Howe he durste..do armes with hym in campe or iustes mortall.

V. In various senses of L. *campus*.

†10. ***Campe of Mars, Camp Mart***: = Campus Martius. *Obs.*

1534 Ld. Berners *Gold. Bk. M. Aurel.* (1546) F viij, The emperour goynge to the campe of Mars. **1647** R. Stapylton *Juvenal* 109 Exercising and training like the tyrones or young souldiers in Camp Mart.

†11. Plain, level surface, field. ***watery camp*** (*cæruleus campus, campus latus aquarum*): the surface of the sea. *Obs.*

1598 Sylvester *Du Bartas* i. iii. (1641) 29/1 Whereby w'are stor'd with Truchman, Guide & Lamp, To search all corners of the watery Camp.

†12. Field of inquiry; field of discussion or debate, subject of debate. *Obs.*

1538 Leland *Itin.* I. p. xxi, I have more exspatiatid yn this Campe then they did. *c* **1538** Starkey *England* iv. 128 Wherfor I wyl not entur into that Camp.

‖**VI. 13.** = Spanish *campo*: see quot.

1877 *Athenæum* 1 Dec. 703/2 The Falkland Island word for expanses of bog land, 'camp,' is not derived from the French *champ*..but from the Spanish *campo*.

†14. (A sense of F. *camp*: see quot.) *Obs. rare*$^{-0}$.

1753 Chambers *Cycl. Supp.*, *Camp*, is also used among the Siamese and East-Indians, for a quarter of a town assigned to foreigners, wherein to carry on their commerce. In these camps, each nation forms itself a kind of city apart, in which their store houses and shops are, and the factors and their families reside. [So in *London Encycl.* 1829.]

VII. *attrib.* and *Comb.* **a.** Simple, as ***camp-boy, -craft, -diseases, -equipage, -equipment, -fare, -fashion, -frock, -guide, -hut, -keeper, -kettle, -kit, -language, -life, -mill, -money, -plot, -squire, -stove***, etc.

1813 Wellington in Gurw. *Disp.* XI. 27 Stores commonly called *camp equipments. **1820** T. Mitchell *Aristoph.* I. 121 The sack that holds our coarse *camp-fare. **1886** *Pall Mall G.* 28 July 2/1 Seated *camp-fashion on boxes. *a* **1849** J. C. Mangan *Poems* (1859) 338 In an uniform of blue and white And a grey *camp-frock he is dressed. **1828–40** Tytler *Hist. Scot.* (1864) I. 153 The servants who remained in the *camp-huts. **1805** *Naval Chron.* XIV. 35 Bailing it out with a *camp-kettle. **1850** Alison *Hist. Europe* XI. lxxvi. §39. 447 The ponderous iron camp-kettles hitherto used by the soldiers had been exchanged for lighter ones. **1861** Max Müller *Sc. Lang.* 303 Urdu-zeban, *camp-language, is the proper name of Hindustani. **1828** Macaulay *Hallam, Ess.* (1854) I. 72 The Judges would have given as strong a decision in favour of *camp-money as they gave in favour of ship-money. **1610** Holland *Camden's Brit.* i. 83 Maximus, a base *Campe-Squire.

b. Special comb., as **camp-bed, -bedstead**, a bed or bedstead for use in field-service; hence *spec.* a bedstead made to fold up within a narrow space; a trestle bedstead; **camp-chair**, a form of folding chair; †**camp-chaplain**, an army chaplain; **camp-colour**, a flag or colour used in marking out and arranging the camping-ground for a body of troops; hence ***camp colour-man*** (see quot.); **camp-disease, -duty** (see quots.); **camp-fever**, a name given to fevers of an epidemical character occurring in camps, chiefly typhus; **camp-fire**, a fire lit in a camp or encampment; hence a military social gathering in a garrison, etc.; *spec.* in *U.S.* a re-union of members of one or more clubs, 'posts', of the 'Grand Army of the Republic', a society of ex-volunteers; **camp-flux, -furniture** (see quots.); **camp-ground** *U.S.*, (*a*) the site of a camp-meeting; (*b*) a camping-ground; **camp-marshal** = F. *maréchal de camp*, see camp-master; **camp-muster** *Austral.* (see quot.); **camp-oven** *Austral.* and *N.Z.* (see quot. 1933); **camp-paper**, a kind of copying paper, like carbon paper; **camp-party**, a party forming a camp, a camping-out party; **camp-seat, -stool**, a light portable folding stool; **camp-vinegar**, a preparation made by mixing vinegar with Cayenne pepper, soy, walnut-ketchup, anchovies, and garlic, and afterwards straining it. Also camp-follower, -master, -meeting.

1690 *Lond. Gaz.* No. 2529/4 One large Tent fit for a Colonel, with Chairs and *Camp-Beds. **1825** Hone *Every-day Bk.* I. 940 A *camp-bedstead, of planks resting on bars of iron. **1885** *Harper's Mag.* Mar. 631/1 Winthrop found a *camp chair. **1679–88** *Secr. Serv. Money Chas. & Jas.* (1851) 196 One of the *camp chaplains..on his allowance of 8s. per diem. **1785** Ray in *Phil. Trans.* LXXV. 422 By arranging *camp colours in the intervals. **1753** Chambers *Cycl. Supp.* s.v., The *camp colour-men, are drawn a man out of a company. **1853** Stocqueler *Mil. Encycl.*, *Camp Colour men*, soldiers whose business it is to assist in marking out the lines of an encampment, etc.; to carry the camp colours to the field, on days of exercise, and fix them, for the purpose of enabling the troops to take up correct points in marching, etc. **1753** Chambers *Cycl. Supp.* s.v., The *camp disease, *morbus castrensis*, absolutely so called, is a malignant fever. Dudley Digges died of the camp disease which raged in the garrison at Oxford, in 1643. *Ibid.*, **Camp Duty*, in its utmost extent, includes every part of the service performed by the troops during the campaign. But in a more particular sense, denotes the guards ordinary and extraordinary kept in camps. *Ibid.* s.v. *Camp*, The *camp fever is the same with what is otherwise called the Hungarian fever, and bears a near affinity to the petechial fever. **1837** Thirlwall *Greece* IV. xxx. 121 Their *campfires first announced their presence. **1884** *Boston* (Mass.) *Jrnl.* 6 Sept., Edwin-Humphrey Post, No. 104, G.A.R., of this town celebrated its fifteenth anniversary by a camp-fire Friday evening. **1871** Forbes *War France & G.* 283 (Hoppe) During peace time, there is a camp-fire—or gathering equivalent to it—once a week in every Prussian Regiment. **1753** Chambers *Cycl. Supp.*, **Camp Flux*, a name frequently given to the dysentery. **1857** Simmonds *Dict. Trade*, **Camp-furniture*, articles of cabinet work made compact, light, and portable, so as to be easily folded and transported; such as camp-stools, camp-bedsteads, tables, etc. **1806** L. Dow *Travels* II. 94, I viewed the *Camp-ground, and preparations making for the meeting. **1816** U. Brown *Jrnl.* in *Maryland Hist. Mag.* XI. 360 Their Pilot..never could find their camp ground. **1895** *Outing* (U.S.) Dec. 254/2 The soil of the camp-ground is light and sandy. **1968** *North Carolina Travelbk.* 1968–69 20/2 Easily accessible public camp grounds, picnic areas, small lakes, fishing streams. **1670** Cotton *Espernon* i. iv. 152 The Count de Suze, Beszaudun, *Camp-Mareschal. **1707** *Lond. Gaz.* No. 4392/2 The Count Louvignies, a Camp-Marshal to the Spanish Forces. **1933** *Bulletin* (Sydney) 9 Aug. 21/3 The *camp muster was an annual event in the old days before general fencing, when every station had a general muster on the main cattle camps, and men from all the stations came along to identify and cut out their own cattle. **1846** H. Weekes *Jrnl.* 25 Feb. in Rutherford & Skinner *New Plymouth Settlement* (1940) i. vii. 118 Our cooking was now an open-air affair..with a *camp-oven and gypsy kettles. **1900** H. Lawson *On Track* (1945) 62 There was a camp-oven with a leg of mutton and potatoes sizzling in it on the hearth. **1933** L. G. D. Acland in *Press* (Christchurch, N.Z.) 23 Sept. 13/7 *Camp oven*, an iron pot with three short legs and a flat top, so that it can be used to boil, bake, or fry in. **1968** K. Weatherly *Roo Shooter* 21 There's a roast leg in the camp oven. *c* **1790** Imison *Sch. Art* II. 31 To make *Camp Paper, with which a Person may write or draw without Pen, Ink, or Pencil. **1794** R. Wellford *Diary* 29 Sept. in *William & Mary College Q.* (1903) XI. 5 To have three Canvass *Camp stools made directly, which will serve for seats in the day, & a bedstead at Night. **1817** Jane Austen *Sanditon* (1954) iv. 383 Two Females..with their books & camp stools. **1831** Peacock *Crotchet Cast.* 296 Sitting on a campstool with a portfolio on his knee. **1873** Black *Pr. Thule* vi. 87 He folded up and shouldered his camp-stool.

camp, *sb.*^{3} *dial.* [Of uncertain origin and history.] A conical or ridge-shaped heap of potatoes or turnips, in the open air, covered with straw and earth, for winter storage; called also a *bury, pie*, or *pit*. Cf. also clamp.

1790 Marshall *Midl. Counties* (E.D.S.) Camp, a hoard of potatoes, turneps, etc. **1881** *Leicester Gloss.* (E.D.S.) *Camp*, 'bury', a pit lined with straw in which potatoes are placed, and then earthed over so as to form a mound.

Hence **camp-cellar**, a temporary cellar made of clay heaped up.

1713 *Lond. & Countr. Brew.* ii. (1743) 110 This Salt, which is of a hot moist Nature, is that with which they make their Camp-cellars, by mixing it with Clay, to keep their Wine and other Liquors in.

†**camp**, *sb.*^{4} *Obs. rare*$^{-1}$. [a. ON. *kamp-r* beard, moustache.] *pl.* Whiskers (of a cat); stout bristly hairs: cf. kemp *sb.*

c **1450** Henryson *Mor. Fab.* 47 Hee [the Cat] lay so still, the Myce were not affeird..Some tirled at the Campes of his beird.

†**camp**, *v.*^{1} *Obs.* exc. *dial.* [OE. *campian, cǫmpian*, f. *camp* fight: a parallel formation to Du. *kampen*:—WGer. type **kampôjan*. The other langs. have forms from WGer. **kampjan*, viz. MDu. *kempen*, OHG. *chamfen, chemfan*, MHG. *kemphen, kempfen*, Ger. *kämpfen*; also Icel. *kęppa* (:—**kampja*), Sw. *kämpa*, Da. *kæmpe*, whence north. Eng. kemp.]

1. *intr.* To fight; to contend in battle. Cf. kemp.

(The rare 16th c. instance, may belong to camp *v.*^{2})

c **1000** *Guthlac* 316 (Gr.) Sceal oretta a..gode compian. [? *a* **1400** *Morte Arth.* 2634 There es no kynge undire Criste may kempe with hym one!] **1562** Leigh *Armorie* (1597) 61 Aristotle affirmeth that Rauens will gather together on sides, and campe and fight for victorie.

2. a. To contend in athletic contests; also *trans.*, as in ***to camp the bar***. *Obs.* or *dial.*

1774–6 J. Bryant *Mythol.* (T.) In our island, the exhibition of those manly sports in vogue among country people is called camping; and the enclosures for that purpose, where they wrestle and contend, are called camping closes. **1856** R. Vaughan *Mystics* (1860) I. vi. viii. 262 Those three tall fellows..fonder of sword-play, wrestling, and camping the bar, than of churchmen or church-going.

b. To strive with others in doing anything, e.g. drinking. Cf. kemp *v.*

1587 J. Melvill *Diary* (1842) 256 A banquet of wat and dry confectiones, with all sortes of wyne wharat his Majestie camped verie mirrelie a guid whyll.

c. *trans.* To excel or surpass in a contest. *Austral.*

a **1882** H. C. Kendall *Poems* (1886) 207 At punching oxen, you may guess There's nothing out can 'camp' him.

3. *esp.* To contend at camp-ball, to play a football match. Cf. camping *vbl. sb.*^{1}

c **1440** *Promp. Parv.* 60 Campyn, *pedipilo*. **1573** Tusser *Husb.* (1878) 60 Get campers a ball to campe therewithall *Ibid.* 64 In medow or pasture (to growe the more fine) let campers be camping in any of thine. *a* **1684** Sir T. Browne *Tract* viii. Wks. 1836 IV. 205 Words..of common use in Norfolk..as..kamp. **1691** Ray *S. & E.C. Wds.* (E.D.S.) *Camp*, to play at Football. This word..extends over Essex, as well as Norfolk and Suffolk. **1880** *Standard* 29 Dec. 6/2 Another field, called Camping Close, on which the inhabitants of Haverill, in Essex, used to Camp.

4. *intr.* To wrangle, scold. Cf. cample.

1606 *Wily Beguiled* in Hazl. *Dodsley* IX. 251 She'll camp, I warrant you. Oh she has a tongue! **1642** [see camping *ppl. a.*^{1}].

5. *trans.* To kick (a person) like a foot-ball.

1567 Drant *Horace' Epist.* ii. ii. H vij, Lest euen younge folke, seinge you drinke..Do make of you mere mockinge stockes and campe you with theire feete.

camp (kæmp), *v.*^{2} [a. F. *campe-r*, f. *camp* camp *sb.*^{2}]

1. a. *intr.* To live or remain in a camp; to form or pitch one's camp; to encamp.

1543 *Foray Fr. Country* in *Chron. Calais* (Camd.) 211 The hole oste departed owte of Callyes..and campid the same night without the walles of the towne in the feldes. **1556** J. Heywood *Spider & F.* lxvi. ad fin., At retret of trompet, they retyred a meyne, Where they before had campt. **1580** North *Plutarch* 152 (R.) Fabius camped always in the strong and high places of the mountains. **1611** Bible *Ex.* xix. 2 There Israel camped before the mount. **1808** J. Barlow *Columb.* iii. 533 To meet the expected war, Camps on the confines of an eastern plain. **1850** Blackie *Æschylus* I. 51 He Was camping far at Ilium.

b. With *down. lit.* and *fig. U.S.*

1781 T. Johnson *Jrnl.* 8 Mar. in G. Powers *Hist. Sketches Coos* (1841) 197 Camped down on the River Lamoille this night. **1850** W. Colton *3 Years Calif.* 310, I have seen this *savan* camp down and snore soundly through the night. **1869** L. M. Alcott *Lit. Women* (1870) II. vii. 100 I'll be hanged if I don't make them camp down before her table afterward. *a* **1888** *Spirit of Times* (Farmer), They..camped down a smart piece off the trail.

2. a. To sojourn or remain in a tent, pitch one's tent; also *famil.* to take up one's quarters, lodge.

1611 Bible *Nahum* iii. 17 The great grashoppers which campe in the hedges in the cold day. **1651** C. Cartwright *Cert. Relig.* i. 125 Bring it to the place, where they camped. **1857** Kingsley *Two Y. Ago* I. 106 Don't..ask me to come up and camp with you. **1859** Thackeray *Virgin.* vi. 48 The messenger from Virginia..camping at night in the snow by the forest fires. **1883** Gilmour *Mongols* xxvi. 307 A great, tall, blustering Mongol..advised me to camp beside him.

b. ***to camp out***: to lodge in the open in a camp. Also *transf.* and *fig.*

1748 Washington *Jrnl.* 18 Mar. in *Writ.* (1889) I. 3 We camped out in ye field this night. **1835** A. B. Longstreet *Georgia Scenes* 9 The old gentleman and his lady had consented to *camp out* for a day. **1837** H. Martineau *Soc. in Amer.* (1839) I. 294 Others besides emigrants camp out in the woods. **1853** Mrs. C. Clacy *Lady's Visit to Gold Diggings* iii. 33 We..determined to 'camp out' as much as possible. **1867** Smiles *Huguenots Eng.* xi. (1880) 181 They had to camp out at night in the public squares. **1884** T. E. Dawson *Handbk. Canada* 301 Canadians who camp-out upon these islands. **1901** 'L. Malet' *Hist. Sir R. Calmady* ii. ii. 96 He..took to camping-out on one of the broad window-seats of the Long Gallery.

3. *trans.* To establish or place in camp; to lodge; †also to place, put (*obs.*).

1549 *Compl. Scot.* 83 The tua gryt battellis of onnumerabil men of veyr var campit neir to giddir. **1598** Barret *Theor. Warres* ii. i. 20 In Garrisons it [Ensign]..is most often camped upon the wall. **1616** Shaks. *Ant. & Cl.* iv. viii. 33 Had our great Pallace the Capacity To campe this hoast. *a* **1888** *Mod.* The troops would be camped along the river side. **1920** J. M. Hunter *Trail Drivers of Texas* 63, I told the cook..to take the wagon and camp it up the river. **1930** L. G. D. Acland *Early Canterbury Runs* v. 98 An old circular manuka yard which had been put up to camp the sheep in at night.

4. *intr.* Of birds: to flock together, gyrate in the air (*dial.*). Of sheep or cattle: to flock together, usu. for rest or at night (*Austral.* and *N.Z.*).

1847 A. Harris *Settlers & Convicts* xii. 234 A flock of sheep 'camping', as the shepherds call it, under the shade of a tree from the noon-tide heat. **1879** *Norfolk Archæol.* VIII. 168 'The rooks are camping' is an expression often heard in the autumn when those birds assemble together and gyrate in the air. **1933** L. G. D. Acland in *Press* (Christchurch, N.Z.) 16 Sept. 15/7 Sheep which camp together are also said to 'break camp' when they move off to feed at dawn. **1938** F. S. Anthony in D. M. Davin *N.Z. Short Stories* (1953) 220 The first thing we saw was our twenty cows, camping alongside the fence, chewing their cuds.

5. ***to camp on*** (trans.): to reserve (a telephone call) *to* another, engaged, telephone using a camp-on facility. Also *absol.* Cf. camp-on.

1977 *Daily Tel.* 10 Mar. 2 (Advt.), An incoming call for an extension that is already engaged (busy) and the caller is willing to wait, can be 'camped' on to the engaged extension so that immediately the extension is free the call is automatically connected. **1985** *Telephone Syst. Man.* (Oxf. Univ. Press) 20 If you attempt to camp on to a phone after someone else you will hear the number unobtainable tone.

camp (kæmp), *v.*^{3} *slang.* [Etym. obscure.] **a.** *trans.* To make (something) 'camp' (see camp *a.*); esp. in phr. ***to camp it up***, to use exaggerated movements, gestures, etc., to over-act. **b.** *intr.* To be 'camp'; to be or behave like a homosexual.

1931 *New Broadway Brevities* (N.Y.) ii. 10/1 Boys and men with painted faces and dyed hair flaunt themselves camping and whoopsing for hours each night. *Ibid.* 10/2 His greatest triumph had been the management of a drag of his own at Bryant Hall, overlooking Bryant Park, so that most of the customers merely crossed the street to camp in a hall instead of a park. **1959** *Spectator* 13 Nov. 667/3 Most of the

time he camps it up for sniggers with manly gestures fading into womanly wriggles. **1960** *Encounter* Feb. 23/2 He..had taken to an open, defiant 'camping'. **1962** R. Cook *Crust on its Uppers* Foreword, You all love to shiver and say 'Ooh!' and camp about at the mention of the word 'crime'. **1965** G. Melly *Owning-Up* xv. 188 We were all very impressed by the thought of being used [in a film] as the basis for characters and camped it up like mad.

camp (kæmp), *a.* (and *sb.*[5]) *slang.* [Etym. obscure.] Ostentatious, exaggerated, affected, theatrical; effeminate or homosexual; pertaining to or characteristic of homosexuals. So as *sb.*, 'camp' behaviour, mannerisms, etc. (see quot. 1909); a man exhibiting such behaviour.

1909 Ware *Passing Eng.* 61/2 *Camp* (*Street*), actions and gestures of exaggerated emphasis. Probably from the French. Used chiefly by persons of exceptional want of character. 'How very camp he is.' **1931** *New Broadway Brevities* (N.Y.) II. 7/1 (*heading*) Drags, camps, flaunting hip-twisters and reefer peddlers run afoul of cops on the lam. **1933** M. Lincoln *Oh! Definitely* vi. 62 Dennis, slightly more 'camp' than usual, opened the front door. **1941** S. J. Baker *Dict. Austral. Slang* 16 *Camp* (adj.), homosexual. **1952** A. Wilson *Hemlock & After* I. v. 101 The..gossip of the golden spiv group...the 'camp' end of the room. *Ibid.* II. i. 112 The incoherence of his speech, the..absence of the customary 'camp'. *Ibid.* III. i. 191 Whether Terence was really 'queer'..how much happier he was when he was not being 'camp'. **1954** C. Beaton *Glass of Fashion* viii. 153 Hearty naval commanders or jolly colonels acquired the 'camp' manners of calling everything from Joan of Arc to Merlin 'lots of fun', and the adjective 'terrible' peppered every sentence. **1954** C. Isherwood *World in Evening* II. iii. 125 High Camp is the whole emotional basis of the Ballet.. and of course of Baroque art. **1956** L. McIntosh *Oxford Folly* vii. 103 'He was—you know—one of *those*'..'What, a pansy?' 'That's right,' said Julian, 'he was camp.' **1959** *Observer* 1 Feb. 17/1 The cute little dirty chuckle and the well-timed 'camp' gesture have made stage and audience indistinguishable from any would-be-smart cocktail-party. **1964** S. Sontag in *Partisan Rev.* XXXI. 515 (*title*) Notes on 'Camp'.

‖**campagna, campagnia** (kam'paɲɲa). *Obs.* [It. *campagna* open field, champaign, the country, a campaign:—L. *campania*: cf. campania, campaign *sb.*, champaign.]

†**1.** In 17th and 18th c. occasionally used for: champaign, level, open country, plain (esp. in reference to countries where Italian is spoken, but also in ordinary Eng.). *Obs.*

1641 M. Frank *Serm.* (1672) 413 This is a hill of Glory, hard to climb..no plain campagnia to it. **1703** Maundrell *Journ. Jerus.* (1732) 18 We pitch'd in the Campagnia. **1717** Berkeley *Tour Italy* Wks. 1871 IV. 568, 6 miles through the like flat campagna.

†**2.** In 17th c. occas.: a (military) campaign *sb.*

1652 Evelyn *State France* Misc. Writ. (1805) 84 He who hath not made two or three campagnas (as they use to term it) by the time that he is 18 years of age. **1663** Pepys *Diary* 11 Dec., He appoints such a day, and summonses all the country-people as to a campagnia, and, by several companies, gives every one their circuit.

3. Now only as proper name 'the Campagna (di Roma)' in Italy; see campania.

campagne, obs. form of campaign *sb.*

‖**campagnol** (kɑ̃mpaɲɔl). [Fr.; f. *campagne* country.] The Short-tailed Field-mouse.

[**1768** Pennant *Zool.* I. 104 The short-tailed Field Mouse. Names..Fr. *Le petit Rat de champs, Le campagnol*, Ital. *campagnoli*.] **1835** Kirby *Hab. & Inst. Anim.* I. ii. 92 The Campagnol, or short tailed rat of Pennant. **1868** Wood *Homes without H.* xxxi. 598 The Short-tailed Field Mouse otherwise termed Campagnol or Field Vole (*Arvicola arvensis*).

campaign (kæm'peɪn), *sb.* Also 7–8 **campagne,** 7 **-agn, -aine, -aigne.** [a. F. *campagne* country, open country, champaign, 'the field', campaign, which in the course of the 16th c. took the place of the earlier *champagne* in all its senses (except as the proper name of a French province). It was introduced into Eng. in the 17th c., and at first occasionally used in all the senses of the earlier champaign, but was at length differentiated, and restricted to the military sense, for which it is now the proper term. The forms *campagna*, *-agnia*, *-ania* were also in 17th c. use (see above).

Littré treats 16th c. Fr. *campagne* as a substitution of the northern or Picard dialect form for the Parisian *champagne*; but there can be no doubt that it was actually an adaptation of It. *campagna* (common in the military sense in 16th c., e.g. Caro *Virgil's Æn.* xii. 563 'Turno la campagna aprendo', Turnus opening the campaign), and may have been taken into F. first in military phraseology, and gradually extended to other senses, the advantage of a form which could not be confounded with the name of the province *Champagne* perhaps conducing to the result. For ultimate etymology see champaign, campania.]

†**1.** A tract of open country; a plain; = champaign. *Obs.*

1628 Hobbes *Thucyd.* (1822) 130 The River Achelous.. running through...most part of the campagne of Acarnania. **1647** Clarendon *Hist. Reb.* II. vi. 34 There was between the Hill and the Town a fair Campaigne. *a* **1718** Garth (J.) Where Tiber..fattens, as he runs, the fair campaign. **1765** Sterne *Tr. Shandy* (1802) VII. v. 12 The outworks stretch a great way into the campaign.

†**2.** Open country as opposed to hills, woods, etc.; country as opposed to town; = champaign.

a **1667** Cowley *Dang. in Much Company* Wks. 1710 II. 762 To be sure not to venture his Person any longer in the open Campaign, to retreat and entrench himself. **1684** *Scanderbeg Rediv.* ii. 9 For that the Countrey is there Composed of vast Campagn and level woods. **1699** Maundrell in *Journ. Jerus.* (1721) Tij b, We hunt in the most delightful Campaign. **1706** Collier *Refl. Ridic.* 194 They that see you in the Campaign in the Summer.

3. *Mil.* The continuance and operations of an army 'in the field' for a season or other definite portion of time, or while engaged in one continuous series of military operations constituting the whole, or a distinct part, of a war. (In Ger. *Feldzug.*)

The name arose in the earlier conditions of warfare, according to which an army remained in quarters (in towns, garrisons, fortresses, or camps) during the winter, and on the approach of summer issued forth into the open country (*nella campagna, dans la campagne*) or 'took the field', until the close of the season again suspended active operations. Hence the name properly signifying the 'being in the field', was also applied, now to the season or time during which the army kept the field, and now to the series of operations performed during this time. In the changed conditions of modern warfare, the season of the year is of much less importance, and a campaign has now no direct reference to time or season, but to an expedition or continuous series of operations bearing upon a distinct object, the accomplishment or abandonment of which marks its end, whether in the course of a week or two, or after one or more years. The history of the sense is seen in early Dictionaries; e.g.

1656 Blount *Glossogr.* s.v., A word much used among Souldiers, by whom the next Campaine is usually taken for the next Summers Expedition of an Army, or its taking the field. **1721** Bailey, *Campain*, [in Military Affairs] the space of time every Year, an Army continues in the Field, during a War. **1730–6** —— A summer's war. **1755** Johnson, *Campaign*, the time for which any army keeps the field, without entering into quarters.

1647 Clarendon *Hist. Reb.* I. i. 49 After he had made two or three Campaigns..he came in the leisure of the Winter to visit his Friends in England. **1667** Pepys *Diary* 28 June, Several commanders that had not money to set them out to the present campagne. **1693** *Mem. Ct. Teckely* i. 37 And prepared themselves to open the Campagn in good time. **1708** Swift *Predict. for 1708* Wks. 1755 II. i. 153 It will be a glorious campaign for the allies. **1790** Beatson *Nav. & Mil. Mem.* II. 218 The want of success in the last campaign. **1847** Emerson *Repres. Men, Napoleon* Wks. (Bohn) I. 375 In the Russian campaign he..said 'I have two hundred millions in my coffers, and I would give them all for Ney'.

4. *transf.* †**a.** A naval expedition; a voyage or cruise. *Obs.* (So F. *campagne*, It. *campagna.*)

1708 J. Bion *Suffer. Prot.* in Arb. *Garner* VI. 404 Being several Campaigns, Chaplain aboard one of the Galleys.

b. An expedition or excursion into the country; a summer's trip or sojourn.

1748 H. Walpole *Corr.* I. 123 A campaign at Twickenham furnishes as little matter for a letter as an abortive one in Flanders. **1749** Mrs. E. Montagu *Lett.* (1813) III. 82 The waters are good..the place agreeable, and you cannot make a better summer's campaign. **1789** Wolcott (P. Pindar) *Subj. for Painters* 59 A man in rather an exalted station..Made frequent curiosity campaigns; Sometimes caught grass-hoppers.

c. *Ironworks.* The period during which a furnace is in continuous operation.

1871 *Trans. Amer. Inst. Mining Eng.* I. 98 By their corrosive action on the lining..they shorten a campaign or run to a few days. **1881** in Raymond *Mining Gloss.*

5. a. *fig.* Applied to any course of action analogous to a military campaign, either in having a distinct period of activity, or in being of the nature of a struggle, or of an organized attempt aiming at a definite result.

1770 *Junius Lett.* xxxix. 201 They..rest from the.. labours of the campaign. **1773** Macklin *Man of World* (1793) 36 Their amorous equipage for the nuptial campaign. **1868** Dickens *Lett.* (1880) II. 388, I am now preparing for a final reading campaign. **1887** *Pall Mall Budg.* 31 Mar. 3 A campaign is being carried on in Paris..against the interlopers who sell tickets at the doors of the theatres.

b. esp. in *Politics*, An organized course of action designed to arouse public opinion throughout the country for or against some political object, or to influence the voting at an election of members of the legislature. Also *attrib.* orig. *U.S.* **c.** The ***Plan of Campaign*** in Ireland, entered upon in the winter of 1886–7, a method of conducting operations against landlords who refused to lower rents, according to which the tenants in a body were to pay what they considered the fair rent into the hands of a political leader, charged to retain it until the landlord should accept the sum offered, less any amount subsequently expended in maintaining the struggle.

1809 J. Steele *Papers* (1924) II. 601 The electioneering campaign having become much warmer than I had anticipated. **1844** *Talladega* (Ala.) *Dem. Watchtower* 12 June 2/6 We issue our Campaign Paper to meet the wants of numerous Associations. **1857** S. Bowles *Let.* 16 Feb. in G. S. Merriam *Life & Times S. Bowles* (1885) I. xxv. 291 We should get those amendments out of the way before we strike out for the summer campaign. **1880** Webster *Supp.*, *Campaign*, (U.S. Politics) the season of excitement and effort preceding an election; canvass. **1880** *Daily Union* (San Diego) 1 Sept. 1/1 He will take care of the Indiana campaign expenses, with the understanding that he be not called on to contribute to the campaign fund for other states. **1882** *Nation* 21 Dec. 522/3 Garfield seems to have reposed great confidence in Dorsey as a campaign manager. **1884** *Boston* (Mass.) *Jrnl.* 20 Sept., The attempt of the Republicans to introduce the tariff as one of the issues of the campaign. **1886** *United Ireland* 20 Nov. 272/2 The 'Plan of Campaign' as laid down in United Ireland of October 23rd. **1886** *Pall Mall G.* 24 Nov. 2/1 The plan of campaign is..the proposal that whenever a landlord refuses to settle at the abatement proposed by his tenants..the reduced rent of all the tenantry is to be banked with an unknown individual, who is to act as paymaster and dole out weekly allowances to such of the tenants as are evicted by the landlord for non-payment of rent. *a* **1888** *Mod.* The electoral campaign has now begun in earnest. **1907** *Daily Mail* 14 Jan. 7/3 A born campaign-manager. **1968** W. Safire *New Lang. Politics* 62/2 Just as there is an unwritten law that takes for granted campaign exaggerations, there is also an unwritten law that a candidate may not afterward disown his campaign statements.

†**6.** Short for *campaign-coat, -lace*: see 7 b. *Obs.*

1690 *Mundus Muliebris*, *Campaine*, a narrow kind of lace. **1692** Tryon *Good Housew.* i. 7 A Flannel Shirt, and a Wastcoat, Doublet, Coat, and Campaign, a Gown over all lin'd.

7. *attrib.* and in *Comb.*: **a.** Of the nature of open country; belonging to the open country.

1628 Hobbes *Thucyd.* (1822) 129 The campagne country beyond Strymon. **1634** Holland *Pliny* II. 84 The Campaign Rose bloweth early and is very forward. **1768** G. White *Selborne* xv. 43 The stone curlew..abounds in all the campaign parts of Hampshire and Sussex. **1882** Elwes tr. *Capello & Ivens* II. iv. 77 We plunged into the vast campaign country to the north.

b. Of, belonging to, or used on a military campaign: as ***campaign-coat***, ***-lace***, ***-oven***, ***-shoes***, ***-wig***. (Some of these were perhaps merely catch names referring to the famous campaigns of Marlborough.)

1677 *Lond. Gaz.* No. 1180/4 Wearing a brown serge Sute, and a brownish *Campaine Coat. **1690** B. E. *Dict. Cant. Crew*, *Campaign-coat*, originally only such as Soldiers wore, but afterwards a Mode in Cities. **1725** *New Cant. Dict.*, *Campaign-coat*, in a *Canting* Sense, the ragged, tatter'd.. Coat, worn by Beggars and Gypsies, in order to move Compassion. **1682** *Lond. Gaz.* No. 1769/4 A green Mohair Silk Petticoat, with a *Campain Gold and Silver Lace. **1708** Kersey, **Campaign-Oven*, a portable Oven..us'd by Confectioners. **1730–6** Bailey, *Campaign oven*, a portable oven made of copper, of a convenient length, and about three or four inches high, being raised on feet, so that fire may be kindled underneath, and on the cover or lid of it are ledges to hold fire also. **1693** *Lond. Gaz.* No. 2840/4 A Highway Robber..with a *Campagne Perriwig. **1691** *Satyr agst. French* 7 Our stockings must be Mill'd, our Shooes *Campaign. **1688** R. Holme *Armoury* ii. xviii. §118 A *Campaign Wig, hath Knots or Bobs (or a Dildo on each side) with a Curled Forehead, a Travelling Wig. **1846–60** Fairholt *Costume, Gloss.*, A wig called a 'campaign-wig' was introduced from France about 1712. It was plain, and close-fitting.

campaign (kæm'peɪn), *v.* [f. prec. sb.]

1. *intr.* To serve in, or go on, a campaign. Also *fig.* and *transf.*

1701 [see campaigning]. **1766** G. Canning *Anti-Lucretius* v. 401 Without an host what General could campaign? **1801** Sir R. Musgrave *Hist. Irish Reb.* p. vi. (T.) The officers, who campaigned in the late rebellion. **1875** Jowett *Plato* (ed. 2) III. 280 He..feeds his heroes, when they are campaigning, on soldiers' fare. **1885** *Pall Mall G.* 20 Feb. 2/2 You will campaign in the Soudan.

2. *trans.* (*nonce-use.*)

1768 Sterne *Sent. Journ.* (1778) I. 114 An old soldier.. campaign'd and worn out to death in the service.

campaigned (kæm'peɪnd), *ppl. a.* [f. campaign *v.* + -ed[1].] Of estates in Ireland which came under the Plan of Campaign (see campaign *sb.* 5 c).

1889 *Daily News* 24 July 3/3 Much light has been thrown on the grievous state of affairs..on the 'campaigned' estate of Mr. Leader in county Cork. **1892** *Sat. Rev.* 1 Oct. 381/2 Neither Mr. Dillon..nor Mr. Redmond..has as yet made it his business to stump the 'Campaigned' districts.

campaigner (kæm'peɪnə(r)). [f. campaign *v.* (or *sb.*) + -er.] One who serves in a campaign; *esp.* one who has served in many campaigns, a veteran; also *fig.*

1771 Smollett *Humph. Cl.*, Both horse and rider were old campaigners, and stood without moving a muscle. **1815** Scott *Guy M.* xi, I am an old campaigner, and perfectly used to it. **1858** Longf. *Emperor's Bird's-n.* vi, Forth the great campaigner came Slowly from his canvas palace.

cam'paigning, *vbl. sb.* The action of the verb campaign. Also *attrib.*

1701 Collier tr. *M. Anton., Med.* 186 This Campaining, Tempestuous Life you are engaged in. **1789** Wolcott (P. Pindar) *Expost. Odes* viii. 23 When Judges a campaigning go. **1859** G. Wilson *E. Forbes* iv. 118 Old soldiers who were past campaigning. **1856** Kane *Arct. Expl.* I. v. 45 Preparing sledges for our campaignings on the ice. **1872** Black *Adv. Phaeton* xxii. 314 His foraging adventures in campaigning time.

cam'paignlet. A diminutive campaign.

1885 *Sat. Rev.* 18 July 67/1 The campaign or campaignlet of 1885 cannot be considered a triumph.

campain(e, obs. f. campaign *sb.*, campane.

†'**campal,** *a. Obs.* [a. Sp. *campal* (cf. Minsheu 1599 '*Campál*, belonging to a champaine countrey, as *Batálla campál*, a champaine warre') = F. *campal*, It. *campale* in med.L.

campāl-is, f. *camp-us* CAMP *sb.*[2] V.; see -AL[1].] Pertaining to the open country or 'the field'.

1598 BARRET *Theor. Warres* III. ii. 82 If it shold come to campall fight. *Ibid.* IV. i. 116 Slaine..in a campall battell. *Ibid.* v. iii. 152 Sufficient with a campall fortification. **1611** COTGR., *Campal*, campall; of..a campe or field.

campan ('kæmpæn, ‖kɑ̃pɑ̃). [Name of a town in the French Pyrenees.] A marble of which there are several varieties.

1795 KIRWAN *Elem. Min.* (ed. 2) I. 115 The sp. gr. of green campan is 2,741. **1839** *Civil Eng. & Arch. Jrnl.* II. 452/2 Campan marble proper unites all these three varieties by very large stripes.

campan: see CAMPANY.

‖**campana** (kam'pana). [late L., It., and Sp. *campāna* a bell.

Isidore says, XVI. xxv. 6, Campana a regione Italiæ nomen accepit, ubi primum ejus usus repertus est. This refers to the ancient statement that *bells* were either invented or first used in churches at Nola in Campania.]

1. A church bell.

1706 in PHILLIPS; and in mod. Dicts.

2. Used by Drayton as the name of some bell-shaped flower; according to various Dictionaries, The pasque flower (*Anemone pulsatilla*).

1613 DRAYTON *Poly-olb.* XIII, For the laboring wretch that's troubled with a cough, Or stopping of the breath.. Campana heere he crops, approoued wondrous good.

3. *Arch.* (See quots.)

1823 P. NICHOLSON *Pract. Build.* 582 *Campana*, the body of the Corinthian capital. *Campanæ*, or *Campanula*, or *Guttæ*, the drops..of the Doric architrave.

4. A bell-shaped vase (see quot. 1957).

1802 *Christie's Catal. Etruscan Vases J. Clark Collection* 4 Two Vases, of the form called *Campana*. *Ibid.*, A campana Vase. *Ibid.* 5 A Vase of the campana form. **1957** MANKOWITZ & HAGGAR *Encycl. Eng. Pott. & Porc.* 41/2 *Campana vase*, a vase made in the neo-classic style, during the first decade of the nineteenth century.

campanal ('kæmpənəl), *a. rare*⁻¹. [f. late L. *campāna* bell + -AL[1].]

†**1.** Bell-shaped. *Obs.*

1571 DIGGES *Pantom.* (1591) 177 Conicall or Campanall.

2. *Campanal Alliance*: in *Bot.* Lindley's name for his alliance of natural orders, of which the *Campanulaceæ* or Bell-flowers were the type.

campanalian: see CAMPANILIAN.

campa'narian, *a. rare*⁻¹. [f. late L. *campānāri-us* bell-founder, bell-maker + -AN.] Of or pertaining to bell-founding or to bells.

1869 J. RAVEN *Ch. Bells Cambr.* (1881) 61 Campanarian luxuries in obiits were but sparingly indulged in at Cambridge.

campane (kæm'peɪn). In 7 campain. [a. F. *campane*:—L. *campāna* bell.]

1. *Her.* A bell. (Cf. CAMPANY.) Hence **campaned** *ppl. a.*, furnished or adorned with bells.

1688 in R. HOLME *Armory* III. 461/2 He beareth Argent, a Bell, or a Campain..by the name of *Campane*.

†**2.** A bell-shaped vessel forming the head or upper part of an alembic. *Obs.*

[**1641** FRENCH *Distill.* ii. (1651) 52 Put to the Water as much of the Spirit of Sulphur *Per Campanam*, as will give it a pleasant acidity.] **1662** J. CHANDLER *Van Helmont's Oriat.* 109 By a Campane or glassen Bell. **1670** W. SIMPSON *Hydrol. Ess.* 100 Sulphur burning under a Glass Campane (for the making its Oyl).

†**'campanel.** *Obs. rare.* [ad. F. *campanelle* or It. *campanella*, dim. of *campana* bell.]

1. A small bell.

1653 URQUHART *Rabelais* I. xvii, Tingling Tantans and ringing Campanels, to hang about his mares neck.

2. A sort of bit.

1611 COTGR., *Campanel*, campanell, or Bell-fashioned rowle in the mouth of a bitt. **1617** MARKHAM *Caval.* II. 58 If he..wryth his nether chappe, you shall then take that bytt which we call the Campanell. **1688** R. HOLME *Armoury* III. vii. §44 There are several sorts of Bits, as..The Bastonet Bit, The Campanell or Bell Bit. **1704** WORLIDGE *Dict. Rust. et Urb.* s.v., The Campanell, or the Curb and Hook, being the Chain and Hook under the Horse Chops.

‖**campanero** (kampa'nero). [a. Sp. *campanero* bell-man, f. *campana* bell.] The Bell-bird of South America.

1825 WATERTON *Wanderings* II. (1887) 157 No sound.. from any of the winged inhabitants of the forest..causes such astonishment as the toll of the campanero. **1860** GOSSE *Rom. Nat. Hist.* 21 The campanero or bell-bird of the Amazon..much like a snow-white pigeon, with a sort of soft fleshy horn on its forehead, three inches high.

†**cam'pania.** *Obs.* [In form, a. L. *campania* 'plain level country', *spec.* as the name of the rich and level province of Italy, lying south-east of the Tiber (afterwards particularly distinguished as *Campagna di Roma*); in later Lat. applied to many similar tracts, and as a common appellative; f. *campus* field. Hence (through Fr.), CHAMPAIGN, CAMPAIGN *sb.* But perh., in Eng. use, really the Italian word (also adopted as CAMPAGNA, *campagnia*), spelt as Latin, or phonetically.]

1. 'A large open level tract of ground without hills' (J.); plain; = CHAMPAIGN.

1647 CLARENDON *Hist. Reb.* I. v. 556 A clear view, upon an open Campania. **1663** CHARLETON *Chorea Gigant.* 42 In fields and spacious campanias. *a* **1698** TEMPLE (J.) In vast campanias, there are few cities.

2. *in campania*: in the flat open country where the operations of regular warfare are conducted; in open battle, 'in the field', 'in campaign' (in its original sense). Cf. CAMPAIGN *sb.* and CHAMPAIGN.

1601 R. JOHNSON *Kingd. & Commw.* (1603) 93 The Hungarians presuming..upon their valour in campania, have ever neglected to fortifie their frontiers. *Ibid.* 179 As they [cavalry] are of great consequence in campania, so amongst hils and rockes they are of small service.

3. Operations of an army in the field during a season; = CAMPAIGN *sb.* 3.

1679 EVERARD *Prot. Princes Europe* 8 Since the last Campania, the three..have entred into the entanglement of a War. *a* **1698** TEMPLE (J. s.v. *Attribute*), I have observed a Campania determine contrary to appearances, by the caution and conduct of a general.

campaniform (kæm'pænɪfɔːm), *a. Bot.* [f. late L. *campāna*: see -FORM.] Bell-shaped.

1757 PULTNEY in *Phil. Trans.* L. 65 Campaniform or bell-shaped flowers. **1759** MILLER *Gard. Dict.* (ed. 7). **1823** in CRABB *Techn. Dict.*

‖**campanile.** [It.; f. *campana* bell. The plural is in It. in *-i*, in Eng. usually in *-es*. Most frequently pronounced as Italian (kampa'nile), often as French (kɑ̃panil), but also anglicized as ('kæmpənɪl, -aɪl).]

A bell-tower; *esp.* applied to the lofty detached bell-towers of Italy; a steeple generally.

1640 SOMNER *Antiq. Canterb.* 160 Neere unto their Campanile or Steeple. **1691** WOOD *Ath. Oxon.* I./303 The Campanile or Tower at Darleston. **1762–71** H. WALPOLE *Vertue's Anecd. Paint.* (1786) III. 167 The great Campanile at Christ-church Oxford. **1855** TENNYSON *Daisy* 13 Slender campanili grew By bays the peacock's neck in hue. **1868** FREEMAN *Norm. Conq.* (1876) II. ix. 400 The rude art of English masons strove to reproduce the campaniles of Northern Italy.

attrib. **1842** S. LEWIS *Topogr. Dict. Eng.* I. 582 On the north side of the north aisle..is a detached campanile tower. **1865** *Morning Star* 4 Apr., The shaft is a splendid structure of the campanile order.

†**campa'nilian**, *a. Obs. rare*⁻¹. [f. prec. + -IAN.] Pertaining to a bell-tower, or peal of bells.

1693 URQUHART *Rabelais* III. xxviii, This Campanilian Oracle fretteth me to the Guts.

campa'niliform, *a.* [f. CAMPANILE + -FORM.] Shaped like a bell-tower or steeple. (In various Dicts. explained as 'shaped like a small bell'.)

1846 WORCESTER cites HARRIS.

campaniloger, incorrect f. CAMPANOLOGER.

campanist ('kæmpənɪst). [ad. med.L. *campanista* bellman, f. *campāna*.] One versed in the subject of bells.

1872 J. T. FOWLER in *N. & Q.* Ser. IV. IX. 531 Campanists all, Looke, Brothers, Looke! Loe! here's a passing goodlie Booke! **1881** J. P. BRISCOE *Old Nottinghamsh.* 110 It has been figured by most campanists.

Hence **campa'nistic** *a.*

1883 *Trans. Cumbld. Antiq. Soc.* VIII. 153 Our campanistic major, Jeremy Tolhurst.

campanology (kæmpə'nɒlədʒɪ). [ad. mod.L. *campanologia*, f. late L. *campāna* bell: see -LOGY.] The subject of bells; detailed examination of the principles of bell-founding, bell-ringing, etc.

[**1677** F. S[TEDMAN] (*title*) Campanologia. **1753** CHAMBERS *Cycl. Supp.*, *Campanologia*, the art or science of ringing bells.] **1847** CRAIG, *Campanology*, the art of ringing bells. **1857** LUKIS *Acc. Ch. Bells* I In investigating the subject of campanology, the belfry first presents itself. **1872** ELLACOMBE *Bells of Ch.* ii. 30 Writing a treatise on Campanology.

Hence **campa'nologer; campano'logical** *a.*, **-ly** *adv.*; **campa'nologist.**

1800 *Chron.* in *Ann. Reg.* 11/1 In the records of the Campaniloger's art. **1857** LUKIS *Acc. Ch. Bells* p. vi, Campanologist, campanological. **1882** *Athenæum* No. 2859. 205 Musical and campanological performances. **1884** *Ibid.* 18 Oct. 501/2 The..county of Surrey turned out..to be one of the poorest, campanologically speaking, which has come under review. **1822** J. TATE in *Parr's Wks.* (1828) VII. 250 A learned Grecian..a campanologist. **1868** *Guardian* 455/1 The Revd. H. T. Ellacombe, a well known campanologist.

campanula (kæm'pænjʊlə). *Bot.* [mod.L. *campānula*, dim. of *campāna* bell.] A bell-flower; a large genus of herbaceous plants, giving its name to the N.O. *Campanulaceæ*. The flowers are bell-shaped, and usually blue or white. The best-known species are *C. rotundifolia* (Bluebell of Scotland), and *C. Medium* (Canterbury Bells).

1664 EVELYN *Kal. Hort.* (1729) 205 Antirrhinum, Asphodel, Campanula. **1738–9** MRS. DELANY *Life & Corr.* (1861) II. 40 My lady Sutherland will be very glad of your campanula and vetch seed. **1806** BOWLES *Banwell Hill* I. 184 Along this solitary ridge, Where smiles, but rare, the blue campanula. **1846** RUSKIN *Mod. Paint.* I. II. I. vii. §22 The interwoven bells of campanula and heather. **1849** KINGSLEY *N. Devon Misc.* II. 262 The little ivy-leaved campanula.

campanu'laceous, *a. Bot.* [f. prec. + -ACEOUS.] Belonging to the N.O. *Campanulaceæ*.

1830 LINDLEY *Nat. Syst. Bot.* 187 More properly a Campanulaceous than a Lobeliaceous plant.

campanular (kæm'pænjʊlə(r)), *a.* [f. as prec. + -AR.] Bell-shaped; having a bell-shaped pedicle.

1813 BINGLEY *Anim. Biog.* III. 270 The campanular wasp. **1868** WOOD *Homes without H.* xiv. 259 Another species of..Tree Wasp is the Campanular Wasp (*Vespa sylvestris*).

‖**campanularia** (kæm,pænjuː'lɛərɪə). *Zool.* [mod.L.; f. CAMPANULA: see -ARIA.] A genus of hydroid Zoophytes having the polype-cells bell-shaped and supported on long footstalks.

1855 KINGSLEY *Glaucus* (1878) App. 234. **1883** *Harper's Mag.* Dec. 107/1 Graceful stalked vases of the campanularia appear as if by magic.

campanularian (,kæmpænjuː'lɛərɪən), *a.* and *sb. Zool.* [f. CAMPANULARIA + -AN.] Pertaining to, a hydroid of, the genus *Campanularia* or to calyptoblast hydroids generally. So **campanu'laridan.**

1868 T. HINCKS *Brit. Hydroid Zoophytes* p. iv, Some very skilfully mounted specimens of Campanularian and other zoophytes. **1883** *Science* I. 197/1 The Leptomedusæ..from the campanularian hydroids. **1888** ROLLESTON & JACKSON *Anim. Life* 247 In addition to the possession of hydrothecae, a Campanularian differs from a Tubularian in three important respects. *Ibid.* 766 The destruction of Campanularidan colonies by parasitic Protophytes. **1898** *Naturalist* 218 The empty campanularian cups. **1940** L. H. HYMAN *Invertebrates* I. vii. 370 Calyptoblastea or Leptomedusae or Thecophora, the campanularian hydroids.

campanulate (kæm'pænjʊlət), *a.* [ad. mod.L. *campānulātus*, f. *campānula*; see -ATE[2] 2.] Bell-shaped. (Used chiefly in *Botany & Zoology*.)

1668 WILKINS *Real Char.* 96 A flower of one intire leaf, whether Campanulate; such whose flowers have some resemblance to the figure of a Bell. **1794** MARTYN *Rousseau's Bot.* xvi. 185 Rather a funnel-shaped than a campanulate corolla. **1828** KIRBY & SP. *Entomol.* III. xxxv. 710 The pedicle is campanulate in many Vespidæ. **1842** DANA *Zooph.* 686 Calicles tubular or campanulate.

cam'panulated, *a.* [f. prec. + -ED.] = prec.

1757 PULTNEY in *Phil. Trans.* L. 69 The flowers..are large, of a campanulated figure. **1856–8** W. CLARK *Van der Hoeven's Zool.* I. 76 Cells campanulated, pedunculate.

cam'panulous, *a.* [f. mod.L. *campānula* + -OUS.] Bell-shaped, campanulate.

1727–51 in CHAMBERS *Cycl.* **1799** *Med. Jrnl.* I. 39 The calyx is undivided, campanulous.

†**'campany.** *Obs. rare*⁻¹. (See quot.)

1688 R. HOLME *Armoury* III. 461/2 A Bell..is termed a Campan, or Campany from the French word, Campaine.

Campari (kæm'pɑːrɪ). The name of an Italian firm, used to designate an aperitif. Also *attrib.*

1923 A. HUXLEY *Antic Hay* vi. 95 Cinzano, Bonomelli, Campari—illustrious names. **1930** H. CRADDOCK *Savoy Cocktail Book* I. 115 '*Old Pal*' *Cocktail.* ⅓ Canadian Club Whisky. ⅓ French Vermouth. ⅓ Campari. **1959** 'M. AINSWORTH' *Murder is Catching* xv. 171 He poured himself a half-glass of Campari and put an olive in it. **1959** P. MOYES *Dead Men don't Ski* iii. 28 A dark, smiling girl served them with Campari-sodas. **1960** *Spectator* 23 Dec. 1022 An account of their campari-drinking and conversations.

†**camparnole.** *Obs. rare*⁻¹. Also compur-, campre-, camper-. [app. a corrupt form of a dim. of *campāna*, such as **campanola*, *-uola*.] (See quot.)

1387 TREVISA *Higden* Rolls Ser. IV. 65 A compurnole [*v.r.* campurnole, camprenol, campernole; *anon. transl.* a gyrdelle of golde; L. *bullam auream*] of golde for his sone. **1398** —— *Barth. De P.R.* XIX. cxliv. (1495) 946 Tintinabuluz is a belle other a Camparnole.

camp-ball: see CAMP *sb.*[1] 2.

Campbellite ('kæmbəlaɪt). **1.** A follower of Alexander *Campbell*, a religious teacher of Virginia. Also *attrib.*

1830 *Massachusetts Spy* 22 Dec. (Th.), Elder Rigdon, one of the early Mormons, is described as having been 'a Campbelite leader of some notoriety'. **1834** J. M. PECK *Gaz. Illinois* I. 91 The Cambellites, or 'Reformers'..have several traveling, and a number of stationary preachers. **1847** J. PALMER *Jrnl. Trav. Rocky Mountains* 23 A Campbellite preacher, named Foster, was reading a hymn. **1881** *N.Y. Nation* XXXII. 401 We are quite sure these are the doctrines of the Campbellites. **1881** W. M. THAYER *Log-Cab. to White Ho.* ii, Abram Garfield..united with a comparatively new sect, called Disciples, though Campbellites was a name by which they were sometimes known, in honour of the founder of the sect, Alexander Campbell.

2. *transf.* A sunfish of the Mississippi region.

1872 *Harper's Mag.* July 315/2 'What do you call those fish?' 'Campbellites,' promptly responded the boy. **1884**

GOODE *Nat. Hist. Aquatic Anim.* 407 The Crappie—*Pomoxys annularis*... Other names are..'New Light' and 'Campbellite' in Kentucky and Indiana.

camp ceiling. *Arch.* [? from its shape resembling the roof of a camp tent.] 'A ceiling formed by an inclination of the wall on each side towards the plane surface in the middle, so as to form something like a coved ceiling. Most frequently used in garrets' (Crabb *Techn. Dict.* 1823).

Campeachy wood. Also 7 Campecha, Compeche, 7–9 Campeche, 8 Campechy, -chie, -chio. [From *Campeachy* on the west coast of Yucatan, in Central America, whence it was originally exported.] The red dye-wood yielded by *Hæmatoxylon Campechianum*, better known as LOGWOOD. So ***Campeachy tree.***

1652 WADSWORTH *Chocolate* 15 Three Cods of the Log-wood or Campeche tree. **1686** *Lond. Gaz.* No. 2186/1 Four Thousand Quintals of Compeche Wood. **1725** SLOANE *Jamaica* II. 184 Campeche wood good to dye withal. **1836** MACGILLIVRAY tr. *Humboldt's Trav.* xxiv. 370 Campeachy wood abounds in several districts. **1866** *Treas. Bot.*

‖**cam'pear**, *v. Obs.* [Sp. *campear* to pitch a field; *campear un vandero* 'to flourish an ensign' (Minsheu), f. *campo* field.] (See quot.)

1598 BARRET *Theor. Warres* II. i. 21 To aduance the Ensigne, and not to campear it, or pitch it on the ground.

†**Campechena, -pechiana, -puchina,** obs. by-forms of CAMPEACHY WOOD.

1703 *Lond. Gaz.* No. 3895/3 Goods out of the Mary, Man of War from Vigo, consisting of Sugars.. Campuchina. *Ibid.* No. 3912/3 Tobacco, Campechena. **1720** *Stow's Surv.* (ed. Strype 1754) II. v. xvii. 362/2 Cocheneal, Campechiana, etc.

‖**campement** (kɑ̃ːpəmɑ̃). [Fr.; f. *camper* to CAMP.] A detachment whose duty is to mark out the ground for a camp in advance of the army.

1821 V. BLACKER *Mahratta War* I. ix. 145 The *campement* was always attended by a *russalah* [division of native cavalry] of Mysore horse on the line of march. *Ibid.* 146 The *campement* was ordered to attach itself to the brigadier-general, instead of proceeding in advance.

†'**camper**[1]. *Obs.* or *dial.* [f. CAMP *v.*[1] + -ER[1].]

1. A player at camp-ball; a foot-ball player.

c **1440** *Promp. Parv.* 60 Campar or pleyar at foott balle. **1573** TUSSER *Husb.* (1878) 60 Get campers a ball, to campe therewithall. *Ibid.* 64 In medow or pasture (to growe the more fine) let campers be camping in any of thine.

2. ? A contentious person; a wrangler. Cf. CAMP *v.*[1] 4.

1730 OLDMIXON *Hist. Ho. Stuart* 281 Women of quality are wont to be campers.

camper[2] ('kæmpə(r)). [f. CAMP *sb.*[2], *v.*[2] + -ER.]

†**1.** One who belongs to a camp, or to the camp (cf. CAMP *sb.*[2] 3); a soldier, military man; a camp-follower. *Obs.*

1631 R. H. *Arraignm. Whole Creat.* xi. §1. 99 They promise.. more than Saul to his Courtiers and Campers. **1691** *New Disc. Old Intreague* xvi. 8 The running Campers.

2. One who goes into camp, or encamps; one who lives or lodges in a camp or tent. ***camper out***: one who lodges in a camp or tent in the open.

1856 KANE *Arct. Expl.* II. ix. 92 As ingeniously.. crowded together as the campers-out in a buffalo-bag. **1869** *Daily Tel.* 5 July, The new campers this year are the 7th Surrey, the 19th Surrey, and the London Irish. **1883** *American* VII. 169 A true and circumstantial delineation of the camper's life in the Maine forests.

3. One who takes part in a camp-meeting. *U.S.*

1806 L. DOW *Trav.* II. 61 We held Quarterly-meeting on Clarke's creek; some supposed I would get no campers... This prepared the way for the Camp-meeting. **1883** *Chicago Advance* 16 Aug., At the Sabbath services none but the regular campers were in attendance.

4. Chiefly *N. Amer.* A motor vehicle designed with a rear unit furnished with beds and other equipment for camping; = CARAVANETTE; also, a trailer furnished in this manner. ***pick-up camper***: see PICK-UP *a.* c. Also *attrib.*, esp. as ***camper shell***, and ***camper-van*** (cf. CARAVAN 4).

1960 *Better Homes & Gardens* (U.S.) May 155/1 These campers travel so well, even at road speeds, that you hardly know you're towing one. **1967** R. BRAUTIGAN *Trout Fishing in Amer.* 61 There were too many trailers and campers parked. **1970** N. ARMSTRONG et al. *First on Moon* ii. 39 He and a friend.. loaded their sons into a camper, drove to Cocoa Beach, camped out, fished and surfed. **1979** *Time* 2 July 23 A state policeman helps the campers and pickups thread in among the giant semis barreling along Route 25.

attrib., etc. **1961** *Sunset* Feb. 39/1 The length of the camper unit a truck can take depends on the truck bed. **1973** S. TRUEMAN *Fascinating New Brunswick* iv. 27 Most vehicles were family camper-vans. **1976** *Washington Post* 19 Apr. C10/2 (Advt.), 1972 GMC pickup,.. color blue,.. air cond, camper shell. **1977** *Caravan World* (Austral.) Jan. 45/1 Many more campervan owners than caravanners tend to travel off bitumen roads.

†'**campernoyle.** *Obs.* [A corrupt form of the word appearing in med.L. as *campinolius*, It. *campignuolo*, OF. *campigneul* (cf. mod.F. *campagnoule*); a deriv. of *campus* field: see CHAMPIGNON.] A champignon, mushroom, or toadstool.

1527 ANDREW *Brunswyke's Distyll. Waters* Cjb, Campernoyles that some men callyth tode stoles.

‖**campesino** (kampe'sino). [Sp.] A peasant farmer.

1937 *New Statesman* 20 Nov. 834/1 He stopped in the next village and.. took on board.. an aged *campesino* bearing two live cockerels. **1961** *Times* 10 Oct. 10/5 Fried banana, which is the staple of the Colombian *campesino*. **1965** C. D. EBY *Siege of Alcázar* (1966) iii. 70 A ragged *campesino* had smashed an image of the Virgin in San Vicente's Church. **1969** J. MANDER *Static Soc.* vii. 214 The Church has.. by distributing transistor radios to the *campesinos* of the backlands,.. ensured herself a captive audience.

campeson, var. of GAMBISON, *Obs.*, a stuffed doublet worn beneath the armour.

c **1325** *Coer de L.* 376 For plate, ne for acketton, For hauberk, ne for campeson.

campestral (kæm'pɛstrəl), *a. rare.* [f. L. *campester*, *campestris* pertaining to a level field (f. *campus* plain, field) + -AL[1]. (Cf. for the form L. *campestr-ātus*.)] Pertaining to fields or open country; growing or living in the fields.

a **1750** MORTIMER (J.) The campestral or wild beech, is blacker and more durable. **1880** HOWELLS *Undisc. Country* xiii. 188 The sylvan and campestral flowers.

†**cam'pestrial,** *a. Obs.* [See prec. and cf. *terrestri-al*, *equestri-an*. Both forms have analogies in Latin.] = CAMPESTRAL.

1606 BIRNIE *Kirk-Buriall* Ded., In all campestrial prowes and pas-tyming exploits. **1607** TOPSELL *Four-f. Beasts* 170 A wilde Campestrial Weasil. **1678** EVELYN *Sylva* (1776) 137 The Campestrial or wild [Beech].

†**camp-fight.** *Obs.* [A 17th c. rendering of AFr. *chaump bataile* (see CHAMP *sb.* 1), or of med.L. *pugna campi* (in a charter of 1122, in Du Cange), in which *campus* has the ordinary mediæval sense of the place enclosed for two champions to fight in single combat ('in campo decertare'), or of the duel or combat itself, 'singulare certamen quod rustice dicimus *campum*', 'pugna duorum, quod nostri *campum* vocant', 'pugna campi, id est, duelli' (Du Cange, s.v.). Cf. ACRE-FIGHT.] 'In law writers [from 17th c.] the trial of a cause by duel, or a legal combat of two champions in the field, for decision of some controversy'. Chambers *Cycl. Supp.*

1605 VERSTEGAN *Dec. Intell.* iii, If it were a crime deserving death then was the *Camp fight* for lyf and death. **1627** HAKEWILL *Apologie* (1630) 318 For their tryall by Camp-fight, the Accuser was with the perill of his owne body, to prove the accused guilty. **1644** COKE *Instit.* III. 221. *a* **1698** TEMPLE *Hist. Eng.* 572 The Trials Ordeal, and of Camp-fight.

ˌ**camp-'follower.** A man or woman who follows or hangs on to a camp or army, without being in military service.

1810 WELLINGTON *Let.* in Gurw. *Disp.* V. 464 The proceedings of the General Court Martial, on the trial of Edward Poole, camp follower. **1850** W. IRVING *Mahomet* II. 265 Here he and several thousand of his soldiers and camp-followers were cut to pieces. **1876** *Daily News* 3 Nov. 5/4 Those unfortunates who are known under the euphemistic appellation of 'camp followers'.

camph-, abbreviation of CAMPHOR, taken as a stem on which to form names of related chemical substances, as '**camphane** [-ANE], an inert, saturated bicyclic terpene, $C_{10}H_{18}$; now usu. called *bornane*; '**camphene**, a terpene contained in camphor oil from *Laurus camphora*; a crystalline colourless mass; generic name for the hydrocarbons isomeric or polymeric with oil of turpentine ($C_{10}H_{16}$); = TEREBENE; '**campherene**, a camphene of the second order (see quot.); '**camphilene**, 'Deville's name for the camphene obtained by treating hydrochlorate of turpentine oil with lime; also any camphene of the third order' (Watts); '**Camphine** (-aɪn), the commercial name of an illuminating oil procured by distillation from common turpentine; also *attrib.*; '**camphogen**, according to Watts = CYMENE, $C_{10}H_{14}$; but apparently also loosely used for *camphene* and *camphine*; '**camphoid** [-OID], a preparation of pyroxylin and camphor in alcohol; '**camphol**, †applied by Gerhardt to common camphor; but by Berthelot to $C_{10}H_{18}O$, regarded as the alcohol of a series of which Borneol is one variety, and common camphor the aldehyde; **cam'pholic acid**, $C_{10}H_{18}O_2$; '**campholide** (also †*-id*) [*-olid* (see quot. 1896)], either of two isomers of the lactone $C_{10}H_{16}O_2$, a crystalline substance resembling camphor; '**camphyl**, the radical of camphol, $C_{10}H_{17}$; whence **cam'phylic** *a.*

1895 *Jrnl. Chem. Soc.* LXVIII. I. 426 (*heading*) Action of Nitrous acid on Oximes of the Camphor (*Camphane) Series. **1932** J. L. SIMONSEN *Terpenes* II. v. 221 The saturated dicyclic hydrocarbon, camphane, $C_{10}H_{16}$, is of outstanding importance, since it is the parent hydrocarbon of the camphor group. **1952** *Chem. & Engin. News* 3 Mar. 930/3 The parent of borneol and camphor.. is called bornane rather than camphane because of conflicting names beginning with camph-. **1839–47** TODD *Cycl. Anat.* III. 152/6 Camphor.. is now found to be an oxide of *camphene. **1873** WATTS *Fownes' Chem.* 779 A crystallised hydrocarbon, called camphene. **1863–79** WATTS *Dict. Chem.* I. 724 A camphene often yields several isomeric modifications by treatment with different acids, or by repeated treatment with the same acid. The new camphenes thus produced are called *camphenes of the second order*, or sometimes **campherenes*. Another class, called *camphenes of the third order*, or sometimes **camphilenes*, are obtained by the action of lime or baryta at high temperatures on the hydrochlorates of other camphenes. **1842** *Mech. Mag.* XXXVII. 380 Lamp for burning oil and *Camphine. **1849** MISS MULOCK *Ogilvies* xxxvi. (1875) 275 This camphine is always too dull or too bright. **1850** KINGSLEY *Alt. Locke* iii. (1876) 37 Ye comfortable folks who.. grow wise in an easy chair with.. a camphine lamp. *c* **1865** LETHEBY in *Circ. Sc.* I. 106/1 Oil of turpentine, or camphine. **1863–79** WATTS *Dict. Chem.* I. 726 **Camphogen*, Dumas' name for the hydrocarbon $C^{10}H^{14}$, obtained from camphor by the action of phosphoric anhydride; it is identical with cymene. **1897** F. P. FOSTER *Reference-bk. Pract. Therapeutics* I. 203/2 **Camphoid*, a solution of 1 part of soluble gun-cotton and 20 parts of camphor in 20 parts of absolute alcohol, is used like collodion. **1929** WOOLLEY & FORRESTER *Pharmaceutical Formulas* (ed. 10) I. 54/2 Camphoid. Collodion Substitute. .. Used as a vehicle for iodoform, salicylic acid,.. and ichthyol. **1863–79** WATTS *Dict. Chem.* I. 726 The several bodies to which the name *camphol has been applied, are isomeric but not identical, being especially distinguished by their different rotatory power. **1876** HARLEY *Mat. Med.* 703 A solid crystalline camphor, called borneol or camphol. **1896** M. O. FORSTER in *Jrnl. Chem. Soc.* LXIX. I. 39 The isomeric lactone will be called **campholid*, the termination *olid* indicating, according to systematic nomenclature, a compound of lactonic character. **1938** *Thorpe's Dict. Appl. Chem.* (ed. 4) II. 247/2 Reduction of camphoric anhydride with sodium amalgam.. or catalytically.. gives α-campholide, whilst reduction of β-methyl hydrogen camphorate gives β-campholide, m.p. 218°–220°. **1876** HARLEY *Mat. Med.* 703 *Camphylic alcohol, of which common or laurel camphor is the aldehyd. **1876** tr. *Schutzenberger's Ferment.* 30 The presence of *camphyl alcohol.

campheer, obs. form of CAMPHOR *sb.*

camphor ('kæmfə(r), -ɔː(r)), *sb.* Forms: (4 caumfre), 5–9 camphire, (6 campher, camfory, -ie, camfery, camphora, camfora, canfora), 6–7 camphyre, (champhire, 7 camphory, campheer, -phir, -fer, -fire, canfir, 8 champhor), 7– camphor. [a. F. *camfre*, *camphre* = med.L., Pr., and Pg. *camphora*, It. *canfora*, Sp. and Pg. *alcanfor*, med.Gr. καφουρά ('Camphora, quam Aetius *caphura* nominavit' Herm. Barbaro, 15th c. commentator on Dioscorides, Devic), a. Arab. *kāfūr*, in Old Pers. *kāpūr*, Prakrit *kappūram*, Skr. *karpūram*; in Hindī *kappūr*, *kapūr*, *kāpūr*, Malay *kāpūr*. The European forms are immediately from Arabic, with *an* for long *ā*. Various forms of the word occur in 16th c. Eng., but the typical form down to *c* 1800 was *camphire*; the mod. *camphor* is conformed to the Latin.]

1. A whitish translucent crystalline volatile substance, belonging chemically to the vegetable oils, and having a bitter aromatic taste and a strong characteristic smell: it is used in pharmacy, and was formerly in repute as an antaphrodisiac.

common camphor ($C_{10}H_{16}O$) is prepared by distillation and sublimation from *Camphora officinarum* (*Laurus Camphora*), a tree indigenous to Java, Sumatra, Japan, etc., and from other lauraceous trees. Many essential oils, as those of feverfew, lavender, etc., deposit varieties of camphor differing only in their action on polarized light. ***Borneo camphor*** or *Borneol* ($C_{10}H_{18}O$) is yielded by *Dryobalanops Camphora*, N.O. *Dipteraceæ*, a tree growing in Sumatra and Borneo; it is less volatile than common camphor, and has a mingled camphoraceous and peppery smell. ***Ngai camphor***, of the same chemical composition as Borneol, is produced in China and Burmah by the distillation of *Blumea balsamifera*.

1313 in *Wardrobe Acc. 7 Edw. II*, 20 Caumfre 18*d.* **1530** PALSGR. 202/2 Camforie or gumme, *camfre*. **1553** EDEN *Treat. New Ind.* (Arb.) 22 Great plentie of *Camphora* called camphyre, whiche they affirme to be the gumme of a certayn tree. **1585** LLOYD *Treas. Health* I. ii, Gume of Arabicke, Dragance, Camfery. **1598** GILPIN *Skial.* (1878) 35 Tearmes of quick Camphire, & Salt-peeter phrases. **1599** HAKLUYT *Voy.* II. I. 242 Canfora being compound commeth all from China, and all that which growth in canes commeth from Borneo. **1605** TIMME *Quersit.* III. 177 Camphor. **1626** BACON *Sylva* §30 Brimstone, Pitch, Champhire, Wildfire.. make no such fiery wind, as Gunpowder doth. **1629** CAPT. SMITH *Trav. & Adv.* v. 8 Campheer, and powder of Brimstone. **1649** JER. TAYLOR *Gt. Exemp.* III. xiv. 15 Intemperance.. makes a fair estate evaporate like Camphire, turning it into nothing. **1657** W. COLES *Adam in Eden* cclxxxiv, In English camphire, camfire, camphor, and camfer. **1661** BOYLE *Spring of Air* II. i. (1682) 21 Camphire of which a little will fill a room with its odour. **1680** MORDEN *Geog. Rect.* (1685) 323 The Canfir of Borneo. **1681** DRYDEN *Sp. Fryar* i. Wks. 1725 V. 149 Prescribe her an Ounce of Camphire every Morning.. to abate Incontinency. **1764** CHURCHILL *Candidate* Poems (1769) II. 35 Her loins by the chaste matron Camphire bound. **1781–7** BP. WATSON *Chem. Ess.* (1789) V. 273 Camphor. **1814** SIR H. DAVY *Agric. Chem.* 146 Camphor is used to preserve the collections of

Naturalists. **1875** DARWIN *Insectiv. Pl.* ix. 209 Camphor is the only known stimulant for plants.

†**2.** A tree or plant which yields camphor: esp. *Camphora officinarum* and *Dryobalanops Camphora*; see prec. sense. *Obs.*

The shrub called 'camphire' in the 1611 version of the Bible is now identified with the *Lawsonia inermis* or henna-plant, N.O. *Lythraceæ*.

1570 LEVINS *Manip.* 72 Campher, herb, *camphora.* **1596** SPENSER *F.Q.* III. ii. 49 Rew, and Savine, and the flowre Of Camphora. **1611** BIBLE *Song of Sol.* i. 14 My beloued is vnto me, as a cluster of Camphire [**1885** *R.V.* henna-flowers]. **1633** H. COGAN *Pinto's Trav.* xxxix. (1663) 156 A Tent pitched upon 12 Ballisters of the wood of Camphire. **1684** BUNYAN *Pilgr.* II. 194 Here also grew Camphire, with Spicknard, and Saffron.

3. *attrib.* and in *Comb.*, as ***camphor ball, julep, oil, pill, posset, tree*** (see 2). **camphor-chest, -trunk** *U.S.*, a clothes-chest containing camphor as a protection against moths; **camphor ice** *U.S.*, a solid preparation of camphor; **camphor laurel** *Austral.* (see quots.); **camphor-wood**, the popular name for several trees (including prec.) of the families Dipterocarpaceæ and Lauraceæ, or the wood from these trees, which is fragrant.

1592 GREENE *Upst. Courtier* (1871) 38 Being curiously washed with no worse than a *Camphor ball. **1861** MRS. STOWE *Pearl of Orr's Isl.* I. viii. 59 That ar shawl your mother keeps in her *camfire chist. **1889** R. T. COOKE *Steadfast* v. 59 Mrs. Dennis was packing away blankets in the camphor chest upstairs. **1611** BEAUM. & FL. *Philast.* II. 26 Such *Camphire constitutions as this. **1880** A. A. HAYES *New Colorado* xv. 197 In the alkali regions, glycerine, or what is called '*camphor ice', should be used on face and hands. **1788** F. BURNEY *Diary* 5 Nov. (1891) III. 61, I gave her some *camphor julep. **1835** DICKENS *Let.* (1965) I. 73, I hope you are well and have taken some Camphor Julep. **1894** *Proc. R. Soc. Queensland* XI. 23 The identity of the camphor of *Cinnamomum oliveri* with that of *Camphor Laurel was proved by me. **1897** R. T. BAKER in *Proc. Linn. Soc. N.S.W.* XXII. 282 *Cinnamomum virens*, sp. nov. 'Wild Camphor Laurel'. **1932** R. H. ANDERSON *Trees N.S.W.* 50 Camphor Laurel (*Cinnamomum camphora*). A handsome, dense-topped tree. *Ibid.* 127 *Cinnamomum virens* is sometimes known as the Native Camphor Laurel. **1836** *Penny Cycl.* VI. 204 In that part of the stem [of *Dryobalanops Camphora*] which should be occupied by the pith it [Borneo camphor] is found along with *camphor-oil. **1671** MRS. BEHN *Amorous Pr.* IV. iv, To do penance In *Champhire Posset, this month. **1607** TOPSELL *Four-f. Beasts* 448 The leopard..delighteth in the *camphory tree. **1876** HARLEY *Mat. Med.* 451 The Camphor Tree is a large and handsome tree with evergreen shining leaves. **1869** MRS. STOWE *Oldtown Folks* 34 Mrs. Major had a real *Ingy* shawl up in her '*camphire' trunk. **1895** *Century Mag.* July 323/2 Cedar-chest and camphor-trunk and flowered bandbox have been called upon to disgorge their treasures. **1923** DALLIMORE & JACKSON *Handbk. Coniferæ* II. 173 *Callitris verrucosa*, R. Brown. Turpentine Pine..*Camphor Wood; Rock Pine. **1950** C. W. BOND *Colonial Timbers* 55 In spite of its hardness Borneo camphorwood is pleasant to work. *Ibid.* 63 East African camphorwood is interesting. **1955** *World Timbers* (Timber Development Assoc.) II. 9 Borneo Camphorwood [Dryobalanops aromatica] should not be confused with East African Camphorwood (*Ocotea usambarensis*)..nor with true camphorwood (Cinnamomum camphora). **1965** *Austral. Encycl.* II. 247/2 Camphorwood is the name standardized in the timber trade for the indigenous C[*innamomum*] *oliveri*.

'camphor, *v. rare.* [f. prec. sb.] *trans.* To impregnate or wash with camphor; to camphorate. Hence **'camphored** *ppl. a.*

1562 WHITEHORNE tr. *Macchiavelli's Arte warre* (1573) 26 b, Some moiste it..with camphored aqua vitae. **1607** TOURNEUR *Rev. Trag.* III. v, Does every proud and self-affecting Dame Camphire her face for this? **1696** TRYON *Misc.* 2 Camfired Spirit. **1709** STEELE *Tatler* No. 101 ¶5 Wash-Balls Perfumed, Camphired, and Plain, shall restore Complexions.

camphoraceous (kæmfə'reɪʃəs), *a.* [f. CAMPHOR *sb.* + -ACEOUS.] Of the nature of camphor.

1845 GARROD *Mat. Med. & Therap.* (1855) 225 The leaves..possess a powerful odour and camphoraceous taste.

camphorate ('kæmfərət), *sb. Chem.* In 8 **-at.** [see next, and -ATE[4].] A salt of camphoric acid.

1794 G. ADAMS *Nat. & Exp. Philos.* I. App. 547 Camphorats..white and transparent, bitterish..crystals irregular. **1800** tr. *Lagrange's Chem.* II. 244 The camphoric acid unites readily with earths and alkalies. Combinations of this kind are called Camphorates. **1874** SCHORLEMMER *Carbon Comp.* 306 Calcium Camphorate..is readily soluble in water.

camphorate ('kæmfərət), *a.* ? *Obs.* [ad. med.L. *camphorāt-us*: see -ATE[2].] Camphorated.

a **1691** BOYLE *Wks.* I. 433 (R.) Shaking the saline and camphorate liquors together. **1710** T. FULLER *Pharm. Extemp.* 94 A Camphorate Draught.

camphorate ('kæmfəreɪt), *v.* [f. as prec. + -ATE[3].] To impregnate or treat with camphor.

1641 FRENCH *Distill.* ii. (1651) 54 Crollius his Treakle water Camphorated. **1712** tr. *Pomet's Hist. Drugs* I. 182 Spirit of Wine camphorated. **1812** *Month. Rev.* LXXIX. 181 Who would..camphorate an ephemeron for immortality?

Hence **'camphorated** *ppl. a.*

1743-4 MRS. DELANY *Life & Corr.* (1861) II. 256 One ounce of Castille soap dissolved in half a pint of camphorated spirits of wine. **1786** tr. *Beckford's Vathek* (1834) 88 Two large torches..the camphorated vapour of which ascended and gathered itself into a cloud. **1811** A. T. THOMSON *Lond. Disp.* (1818) 324 Camphoretted oil of turpentine. **1830** LINDLEY *Nat. Syst. Bot.* 173 A fragrant camphorated smell.

camphored *ppl. a.*: see CAMPHOR *v.*

camphoretted. *Obs.*: see CAMPHORATED.

camphoric (kæm'fɒrɪk), *a. Chem.* [f. CAMPHOR *sb.* + -IC.] Of or pertaining to camphor; containing camphor in chemical combination, as in ***camphoric acid*** ($C_{10}H_{16}O_4$).

1794 G. ADAMS *Nat. & Exp. Philos.* I. 542 The camphoric acids. **1819** CHILDREN *Chem. Anal.* 280 Camphoric acid..forms snow white plumose crystals. **1884** *Health Exhib. Catal.* 63/1 Camphoric Antiseptics.

'camphorize, *v.* Also 8 **-irize.** [f. as prec. + -IZE.] = CAMPHORATE *v.* Hence **'camphorized.**

1736 BAILEY *Househ. Dict.* 155 To Camphorise Spirit of Wine. **1741** *Compl Fam.-Piece* I. i. 17 Nothing so effectually cures Kibe Heels, as doing them with camphiriz'd Spirits.

camphorous ('kæmfərəs), *a.* [f. as prec. + -OUS.] Of the nature of camphor, camphoraceous.

1881 *Syd. Soc. Lex.* s.v. *Borneol*, It..is..of a mingled camphorous and peppery smell.

camphory ('kæmfərɪ), *a.* = prec.

1826 H. H. WILSON tr. *Malati* 89 The camphory balm, and flowery perfume. *Mod.* It has a camphory smell.

camphyl: see CAMPH-.

camphyre, obs. form of CAMPHOR *sb.*

Campignian (kæm'pɪnjən), *sb.* and *a. Archæol.* [ad. F. *campignien* (P. Salmon in *Dict. Sci. Anthrop.* (1886)), f. Le *Campigny* (Seine-Maritime, France), the type site.] **A.** *sb.* A Stone Age culture of Europe. **B.** *adj.* Of or pertaining to this culture.

1921 M. C. BURKITT *Prehistory* xii. 156 The early Neolithic people (Campignians) owe nothing to their predecessors. *Ibid.* xiii. 164 The early Campignian industries also occur in Ireland. **1927** PEAKE & FLEURE *Hunters & Artists* 114 Campignian picks have been found in most parts of Europe except the extreme south. **1942** H. L. MOVIUS *Irish Stone Age* iv. 239 Although the main roots of the Campignian are Mesolithic, the real development began in Neolithic times.

campimeter (kæm'pɪmɪtə(r)). [f. L. *campus* field + -METER.] An apparatus designed to measure the field of vision, or the sensitivity of the retina to colour and space in indirect vision. Hence **cam'pimetry**, the use of the campimeter, the measuring of retinal areas; **campi'metrical** *a.*

1889 *Buck's Handbk. Med. Sci.* VII. 660/1 The campimeter of De Wecker. **1901** TITCHENER *Exper. Psychol.* I. 9 The Distribution of Colour Sensitivity over the Retina: Campimetry. *Ibid.* 10 The campimeter must be set so high above the mixer that no shadow is cast by it upon the spot of colour seen through the circular opening. *Ibid.* 12 The experiment may be repeated with as many combinations of the colour discs as the time allotted to campimetrical work permits. **1964** S. DUKE-ELDER *Parsons' Dis. Eye* (ed. 14) xiii. 138 For more accurate investigation of details campimetry must be employed.

Campine (kæm'piːn). [The name of a district of Belgium.] A breed of domestic fowl, resembling the Hamburgs.

1892 SIMMONDS *Dict. Trade* Suppl., *Campine*, a Belgian breed of fowls. **1902** *Encycl. Brit.* XXXI. 876/1 The hardy Campine or Braekel, resembling the pencilled Hamburgh in plumage, but larger and with a single comb, and laying a large egg in great numbers. **1924** *Glasgow Herald* 26 Apr. 5 Few birds make a prettier show than the still uncommon Silver Campine, a gallant little Belgian.

†**'camping,** *vbl. sb.*[1] *Obs.* [f. CAMP *v.*[1]]

1. Fighting in CAMP-FIGHT or single combat.

[Perh. taken by Caxton from Flemish *kampen.*]

1481 CAXTON *Reynard* (Arb.) 102 Reynard the foxe thought how come I on this Campyng, we ben not bothe lyke.

2. Contending, fighting.

1549 *Prayer-bk. Troubles* (1884) 148 Leave off..good countrymen, your camping at your own doors, and bestow that your stoutness of courage..against your enemies. **1563-87** FOXE *A. & M.* (1596) 410/2 A yong and a stout prelat, more fitter for the camping cure, then for the peaceable church of Christ.

3. Contending in a camp-ball match; foot-ball playing. Also *attrib.*, as in ***camping-ball.***

c **1430** LYDG. *Min. Poems* (1840) 200 Bolsteryd out of lenghth and breed, Lyche a large campyng balle. *c* **1440** *Promp. Parv.* 60 Campynge, *pedipiludium.* **1466** *Deed* in Sir J. Cullum *Hist. Hawsted* (1813) 124 The camping pightel joined to the East side of the churchyard. **1567** DRANT *Horace's A.P.* B iv, The stoole ball, top, or camping ball if suche one should assaye As hath no mannour skill therin..They all would..laughe at hym aloude. **1840** SPURDENS *Supp. Forby's Voc. East. A.* s.v., I have heard old persons speak of a celebrated camping, Norfolk against Suffolk, on Diss Common, with 300 on each side..The Suffolk men, after 14 hours, were the victors. Nine deaths were the result of the contest, within a fortnight. These were called fighting camps: for much boxing was practised in them.

camping ('kæmpɪŋ), *vbl. sb.*[2] [f. CAMP *v.*[2]]

1. Going into a camp, encamping; a lodging in tents, etc. ***camping out***, cf. CAMP *v.*[2] 2 b.

1572 N. ROSCARROCKE *Bossewell's Armorie* Prel. Verses, Campings, mornings, musterings. **1721** DE FOE *Mem. Cavalier* (1840) 53 The..order of their marchings, camping, and exercise was excellent. **1850** LYELL *2nd Visit U.S.* II. 234 The camping out of the people in the night when the first shocks occurred.

2. *attrib.*, as in ***camping-place, -ground.***

1606 BRYSKETT *Civ. Life* 94 (T.), I had rather be at a camping dinner than at your's. **1616** PURCHAS *Pilgr., Descr. Ind.* Many memorials and monuments of Alexanders Expedition to these Parts..Altars, Camping-places, and great Pits. **1835** W. IRVING *Tour Prairies* 187 In quest of a camping-place. **1867** LADY HERBERT *Cradle L.* viii. 207 A beautiful camping-ground.

†**'camping,** *ppl. a.*[1] *Obs.* [f. CAMP *v.*[1] 4.] Wrangling, contentious, scolding: cf. CAMPLE.

1642 MILTON *Apol. Smect.* Wks. (1849) 80/1 A troop of camping Huswives in Viraginia.

'camping, *ppl. a.*[2] [f. CAMP *v.*[2] + -ING[2].] That camps or lodges in a tent, etc.

1601 SHAKS. *All's Well* III. iv. 14, I..sent him forth, From Courtly friends, with Camping foes to liue. **1872** TAUNT *Map of Thames* 22/2 A camping man should not require more than three good meals per diem.

campinion, obs. f. CHAMPIGNON, mushroom.

†**'campion**[1]. *Obs.* Forms: 3 **caumpiun**, 4-7 **campion, -pioun**, 5 **campyon.** [A doublet of CHAMPION, in later times chiefly Scotch. ME. *campiun*, a. ONF. *campiun, -on* = central OF. *champiun, -on* (= Pr. *campio, -on*, It. *campione*):—late L. *campio, -ōnem* a combatant in the campus or arena, a professed fighter, f. *camp-us* field of athletic or pugilistic contest, place of fighting in single combat, lists: see CAMP *sb.*[1] and *sb.*[2]. *Campio* was formed on *campus*, like *tabellio* 'scrivener' on *tabella* 'written deed'. Practically also a doublet of KEMP *sb.*]

1. One who fights in single combat as a trial of strength or bravery, or to decide a judicial question; a gladiator, pugilist, or professional fighter; a combatant.

c **1320** *Cast. Love* 970, I am as campion [*v.r.* campioun] ouer-come. **1375** BARBOUR *Bruce* xv. 60 As ilk man war a campioun. *c* **1440** *Promp. Parv.* 60 Campyon or champyon, *athleta, pugil.* **1536** BELLENDEN *Cron. Scot.* xvi. (Jam.) Thay refusit na maner of besines nor laubour that mycht pertene to forsy campionis.

2. One who fights on behalf of another, or on behalf of any cause; a champion. *techn.* one who 'does battle' for another in wager of battle.

c **1270** *Saints' Lives* (Laud. MS.) (1887) 281 Ich habbe ane guode Caumpiun to þine bi-hofþe i-founde. **1552** LYNDESAY *Monarche* 5660 Mony one nobyll Campioun..The Law of God thay did defende. **1588** A. KING *Canisius' Catech.* 180 b, S. Paul that maist invincible campion of Christ. **1599** SANDYS *Europæ Spec.* (1632) 215 Their cheife Campions discouraged. **1609** SKENE *Reg. Maj.* 57 Anent the exchange of campions..gif..ane other campion is produced in the kings court then he quha waged the battell in the inferiour court. *a* **1651** CALDERWOOD *Hist. Kirk* (1843) II. 79 Our Head, and soverane Campioun, Jesus Christ.

campion[2] ('kæmpɪən). *Herb.* Also 7 **campian,** 7-8 **champion.** [This name appears first in Lobel (1576) and Lyte (1578) applied to the 'Rose Campion' or 'Garden Campions' (*Lychnis*, now *Agrostemma, coronaria*), and the 'Wild Campions'—Red and White—(*L. diurna*, and *vespertina*). As the first was identical with the plant called by Dioscorides λυχνὶς στεφανωματική, in Lat. *lychnis corōnāria*, where the second word in both means 'of or fit for a crown, chaplet, or wreath', and the λυχνίς is said by Theophrastus to have been used for garlands, the Eng. name has been conjectured to be identical with CAMPION[1] and = 'champion'.

But if so, we should have looked for some such name as 'Campions' flower' 'Campions' lychnis', and also that the name should have gone back to the 14th c. when the form 'campion' for 'champion' was in Eng. use. But of neither do we find any trace, and the conjecture must for the present be taken for what it is worth. The *Dict. des Sciences du Nat.* (1818) tome X, has '*Compagnon Blanc*, nom vulgaire *Lychnis dioica.*' HÉRICHER, *Philol. de la Flore de Normandie et d'Angleterre* 18, has Red and White Campion, *le rouge et le blanc Compagnon*, but the age of these names and their relation to *campion* is very doubtful. Others have conjectured formation from *campus* field.]

The name of certain plants, species of the genus *Lychnis*: under the name Lyte included the cultivated Rose Campion, *L.* (*Agrostemma* Linn.) *coronaria*, and the wild Red and White Campions, *L. diurna* and *L. vespertina.* It is doubtful whether it was a popular name even of these. Later writers have extended it, with qualifications, to a number of allied species, as **campion of Constantinople**, the Scarlet Lychnis (*L. chalcedonica*); **meadow campion**, the Ragged Robin, *L. Flos Cuculi*; **bladder campion**, *Silene inflata*; **corn c.**, the Corn Cockle, *Agrostemma Githago*; **moss campion**, *Silene acaulis*: these are only book-names.

1576 LOBEL *Stirpium Adversaria nova* (Antwerp) 142 *Lychnis Coronaria*, (Anglice) Rose Campion. **1578** LYTE

Dodoens II. x. 158 The wilde white Campion hath a rough white stemme. **1630** DRAYTON *Muses Elys., Nymphal* v, Sweet-williams, campions, sops-in-wine, One by another neatly. **1688** RAY *Hist. Plant.* II. 992 *Lychnis Coronaria*, Garden Campions or Rose Campion. **1688** R. HOLME *Armoury* II. 68/1 The double Champions are both red and white. **1859** CAPERN *Ball. & Songs* 128 The campion with its star of fire. **1863** BARING-GOULD *Iceland* 102 Here and there bloomed a little moss campion. **1881** G. ALLEN *Vignettes fr. Nat., Red Campion & White*, Known to.. village children as red and white campion.

campish (ˈkæmpɪʃ), *a.* [f. CAMP *sb.*[2] + -ISH.] Savouring of the camp, in manners, etc.

1581 MULCASTER *Positions* xiv. (1887) 67 Not for the soldiars saying..bycause his authoritie is to campishe. **1868** B. CRACROFT *Ess.* II. 290 He..was of military tastes, not a little campish in his licence.

cample (ˈkæmp(ə)l), *v. Obs.* exc. *dial.* [app. f. CAMP *v.*[1] + -LE, frequentative suffix.] *intr.* To enter on a wordy conflict; to answer in anger; to wrangle, scold, or quarrel.

1621 BURTON *Anat. Mel.* III. iii. IV. ii. 381 If they be incensed, angry, chid a little, their wives must not cample again, but take it in good part. **1640** G. ABBOTT *Job Paraphr.* 224 Not to cample, but humbly to yeeld obedience. **1691** RAY *N.C. Wds., Callet*, to cample or scold. **1709** HEARNE *Collect.* (1886) II. 280 In the North of England when a man complains they say he camples. **1811** WILLAN *W. Riding Yorksh. Gloss.* (E.D.S.) *Cample*, to answer pertly and frowardly when rebuked by superiors.

Hence ˈ**cample** *sb.*, ˈ**campling** *vbl. sb.* & *ppl. a.*

1660 H. MORE *Myst. Godl.* IV. xi. 126 His campling and cavilling with the Gymnosophists. **1867** E. WAUGH *Tattlin Matty* ii. 23 in *Lanc. Gloss.* (E.D.S.) Yo know aw've no neighbours to have a bit ov a cample to. **1881** *Leicestersh. Gloss.* (E.D.S.) s.v., Shay wur a very camplin' woman.

ˈ**campless**, *a.* [f. CAMP *sb.*[2] + -LESS.] Without a camp or camp-accommodation.

1863 *Life in South* II, Footsore soldiers, campless and blanketless.

†**camplete.** *Obs.* ? Some kind of wine.

c **1500** *Blowbol's Test.* in Halliw. *Nugæ P.* 10 Malmasyes, Rumneys, With Caperikis, Camppletes, and Osneys.

ˈ**camp-master.** *Obs.* exc. *Hist.* [f. CAMP *sb.*[2]] The term used in 16–17th c. to render Sp. *maestre de campo*, It. *maestro di campo*, and F. *maistre de camp*, a staff-officer of the army in these countries: also put for the L. *præfectus castrorum*. **camp-master-general**, a field-marshal.

In France, the staff-officers of infantry regiments at their institution in 1558 consisted of a colonel-general, a mestre de camp, and a sergeant-major; the mestre de camp subsequently became colonel of the regiment; in the cavalry the title of *maître de camp* was retained by the commander of the regiment. Sir D. Scott *Brit. Army* (1868) II. 382.

a **1569** KINGESMYLL *Confl. Satan* (1578) 21 So wicked that you might be a Campmaster, a General amongst them. **1581** SAVILE *Tacitus' Hist.* II. xxvi. (1591) 68 Iulius Gratus the Camp-master [*præfectus castrorum*] was put in prison. **1598** BARRET *Theor. Warres* Gloss. 249 *Campe-maister*, in Spanish Maestro del Campo, is a Colonell: being the chiefe Commander or officer ouer one Regiment. *Ibid., Camp maister Generall*, in Spanish, Maestre del Campo Generall, is a great Commander, and is with vs the high Marshall of the field. **1670** COTTON *Espernon* I. I. 2 He was made Camp-Master to the Light Horse of France. **1693** *Paris Rel. Batt. Landen* 4 The Regiment of the Camp-Master-General.

ˈ**camp-ˌmeeting.** [f. CAMP *sb.*[2] + MEETING.] A religious meeting held in the open air or in a tent (chiefly among Methodists in America), and usually lasting for some days, during which those who attend encamp on the spot.

1809 *Q. Rev.* II. 336 Our fanatics..have not yet ventured to hold camp-meetings. **1842** DICKENS *Amer. Notes* (1850) 174/1 Religious scenes..which can hardly be surpassed by an American camp-meeting.

campment. *rare.* Short for ENCAMPMENT.

1821 *Blackw. Mag.* VIII. 39 Nursoo's youth had Scindia's campments seen.

†ˈ**campo**[1]. *Obs. School-slang.* [? ad. L. *campus* field, perh. in some such phrase as *in campo* 'in the play-ground'; or ? a. It. *campo* field.] Play-field, play-ground.

1612 BRINSLEY *Lud. Lit.* 299 Without running out to the Campo (as they tearme it) at schoole times. *Ibid.* There is no day but they will all looke for so much time to the Campo.

‖**campo**[2] (ˈkampo). [American Sp., f. Pg. or Sp. *campo* field, open country (see CAMP *sb.*[2]).] In Brazil, a grass plain with occasional stunted trees, a savannah. Also *attrib.*

1863 BATES *Nat. Amazons* II. i, The country around Santarem..is a *campo* region; a slightly elevated and undulating tract of land, wooded only in patches, or with single scattered trees. **1931** L. D. STAMP in W. Rose *Outl. Mod. Knowledge* 831 The campos of Brazil. **1944** S. PUTNAM tr. *E. da Cunha's Rebellion in Backlands* ii. 79 Leaving the Alpine-like regions,..he will cross the great campos, a huge arena made to the measure of..the vaqueiros.

campodean (kæmˈpəʊdɪən), *a.* and *sb. Ent.* [f. mod.L. *Campodea*, f. Gr. κάμπη caterpillar + -ODE: see -AN.] (An elongated wingless insect) of the genus *Campodea*.

1895 *Naturalist* 62 The rediscovery of the blind campodean *Lipura stillicidii*.

campodeiform (kæmˈpəʊdɪɪfɔːm), *a. Ent.* [f. *Campodea* (see prec.) + -FORM.] Resembling insects of the genus *Campodea*, used esp. of larvæ.

1888 ROLLESTON & JACKSON *Anim. Life* 150 There are two types of larval (or young) Insecta: one known as Campodeiform, from a more or less close resemblance to the genus *Campodea* among *Thysanura*; the other as eruciform, of which a caterpillar may be taken as a good example. **1895** *Nature* 19 Dec. 155 Lubbock's far bolder attempt to derive his Campodeiform larva from a Rotifer-like ancestor. **1959** E. F. LINSSEN *Beetles* I. 28 The campodeiform type has the head, thorax, and abdomen well defined, and possesses three pairs of well-developed legs.

campoi (kæmˈpɔɪ). [Cantonese pronunc. of Chinese *kien* picked, selected + *pei* fire.] A fired variety of Congou tea.

1842 *Penny Cycl.* XXIV. 291/1 An Account of the Quantity and Prices of several sorts of Tea sold in England ..: Bohea..Congou..Campoi..Souchong..Pekoe. **1860** URE *Dict. Arts* (ed. 5) III. 855 To the black tea belongs [*sic*] the varieties known as Bohea, Congou, Campoi, Souchong, Caper, and Pekoe. **1875** [see CONGOU].

camp-on (ˈkæmpɒn). *Teleph.* [f. CAMP *v.*[2] + ON *prep.*] A facility of some telephone systems by which the caller of an engaged number can arrange for the system to ring it automatically as soon as it becomes free (in some cases ringing the caller also if he has replaced his receiver). Also ***camp-on busy***.

1975 *Telecommunications* Jan. 54/2 Standard Features include: attendant programmable class of service..add-on conference..camp-on busy, trunk busy display, [etc.]. **1982** *New Scientist* 21 Jan. 158/2 These [features] included 'camp-on' — whereby incoming [telephone] calls can automatically follow their targets around an office block. **1984** *UCL Bull.* July 18/2 Push-button telephones will enable an extensive range of facilities to be made available to the user, such as..camp-on (where a number dialled is busy, the system automatically sets up the call again when it becomes free), etc.

campoo (kæmˈpuː). *Anglo-Ind.* Rarely **campo.** [app. ad. Pg. *campo* camp.] 'Used for "a camp", but formerly specifically applied to the partially disciplined brigades under European commanders in the Mahratta service' (Yule).

1803 WELLINGTON in Grant *Hist. India* I. lxx. 368/1 Their infantry, of which there were three campoos, fought well. —— *Let.* in Gurw. *Disp.* II. 390 Two battalions of the Begum's Campoo escaped. **1883** *Q. Rev.* Apr. 294 (Y.) Campos and pultuns (battalions) under European adventurers.

campshed (ˈkæmpʃɪd), *sb.*, ˈ**campshot** (ˈkæmpʃɒt). Also 5 **camshide** 6 **cambshide**, 6–7 **camshed(d**, 7, 9 **campshead.** [Etymology unknown.

campshot has been conjectured to be Du. or Flem. with second element = *schot* 'boarding', as in *wain-scot*; **kant-schot* would be 'side-boarding'; but no trace of this or any similar compound is found in these langs. The thing is well known there, and called *schoeiing* i.e. 'shoeing'. The second element of the apparently earlier form *campshed* is probably, however, SHIDE *sb.*]

A facing of piles and boarding along the bank of a river, or at the side of an embankment, to protect the bank from the action of the current, or to resist the out-thrust of the embankment.

1471 in P. E. Jones *Calendar Of Plea & Memoranda Rolls 1458–82* (1961) 70 A tenement..at ende of vj fote of Assise from the Camshide and north-west Corner of the said wharf. **1531** in *Lett. & Pap. Hen. VIII* (1880) V. 183, 2 sawiers strangers, sawing with the sawers of the ordinary waigis, as nedylles, bynders, anckers, camp shedes, grete postes, planckes, and other necesares for the new frame of the est juttye. **1570** in *Crt. Min. Surrey & Kent Sewers Comm.* (1909) 85 To fill and to planke iiij roddes of the Cambshide againste the Thames. **1622** *Admir. Crt. Misc.* 1420, lf. 16 (MS.), The end of three piles at the topp of yt [*sc.* the wharf] are out of the campshead. **1632** in E. B. Jupp *Carpenters' Co.* (1887) 301 The making of Wharfes Camsheds Cranes and bridges of timber. **1691** T. H[ALE] *New Invent.* p. lxxi, Surveyors assured me that under St. Magnus Church they after the Fire met with an old Campshot and Wharfing, gain'd from the Thames, and.. that there were found Campshots much further from the Thames in digging of Cellars. **1841** *Civil Eng. & Arch. Jrnl.* IV. 106/1 These piles are placed from 3 to 4 feet apart from centre to centre, and have a capping or campshead 7 inches square. **1867** F. FRANCIS *Angling* i. (1880) 61 *note*, 'The campshot', as it is termed on the Thames, is the wooden boarding and piling that keeps up the bank of the river. **1888** *Times* 26 Mar. 4 The starting boats were moored in mid-stream at Putney opposite the end of the campshed on the Fulham side.

ˈ**campshed**, *v.* [see CAMPSHED *sb.*] *trans.* To face (the bank of a river or the side of an embankment) with piles and planks.

1882 *Daily News* 2 Oct. 6/2 The Richmond Vestry.. camp-shedded and otherwise improved it [the eyot below Richmond Bridge]. **1882** *Globe* 2 Oct. 7/2.

campshedding, -sheeting. [Prob. f. CAMPSHED *sb.*, app. the oldest form of the sb.

If the 17th c. *camp-shot* were the original form, it would be necessary to conjecture that *camp-shotting* had been variously corrupted to *-shutting, -sheeting, -sheathing, -shedding*.]

Collective form of CAMPSHED *sb.*

1819 REES *Cycl., Camp sheeting, camp shot*, or *campstead*, in inland navigation denotes a facing of piles and planks in the front of banks or wharfs, to prevent the banks being worn away. **1858** KINGSLEY *Chalk-stream Stud.*, Misc. I. 182 There is a campshutting (a boarding in English) upon which you can put your elbows. **1862** H. KINGSLEY *Ravenshoe* III. 201 The old gentleman..moved slowly down along the camp-shuting..Then the lad..slipped over the camp-shooting (will anybody tell me how to spell that word? Camps-heading won't do, my dear sir, all things considered). **1865** BAZALGETTE *Metropol. Drainage* 25 A channel is cut in the bed of the river..the sides protected by campsheathing. **1872** TAUNT *Map Thames* 13 The old weir, with its broken campsheding.

campsho, var. of CAMSHOCH *a. Sc.* crooked.

campshot. variant of CAMP-SHED *sb.*

campsin, camsim, obs. ff. KHAMSIN, simoom.

camptonite (ˈkæmptənaɪt). *Petrogr.* [a. G. *camptonit* (H. Rosenbusch *Mikrosk. Physiogr. d. Min. und Gesteine* (ed. 2, 1887) II. 333), f. *Campton*, a town in New Hampshire, U.S.A.: see -ITE[1].] Any of a group of dark-coloured, usu. porphyritic dike-rocks resembling basalt and typically consisting of phenocrysts of hornblende or barkevikite in a matrix of plagioclase.

1895 DANA *Man. Geol.* (ed. 4) 87 Camptonyte.—Rock resembling diabase and doleryte. Consisting of hornblende (as an original mineral of the rock) and probably anorthite. **1901** *Nature* 19 Sept. 513/1 The sills of camptonite and felsite intrusive in the Cambrian rocks. **1961** F. H. HATCH et al. *Petrol. Igneous Rocks* (ed. 12) IV. ii. 475 Localized intrusions of basic lamprophyric rocks including camptonites and monchiquites occur in or near the Ayrshire vents.

campus (ˈkæmpəs). orig. *U.S.* [a. L. *campus* field: see CAMP *sb.*[2] First used at Princeton, New Jersey.] The grounds of a college or university; the open space between or around the buildings; a separate part of a university. Hence allusively, university or college life or people. Also *attrib.*

1774 in J. F. Hageman *Hist. Princeton* (1879) I. 102 Having made a fire in the Campus, we there burnt near a dozen pounds [of tea]. **1826** R. MILLS *Statistics S. Carolina* 701 The whole disposed so as to form a hollow square containing about ten acres which is called the Campus. **1833** J. FINCH *Trav. U.S. & Canada* 282 In front of the College is a fine campus ornamented with trees. **1879** H. J. VANDYKE Jr. in *Princeton Bk.* 382 The central point of the Campus, the hub of the college world, is undoubtedly the big cannon. **1904** H. N. SNYDER in *Sewanee Rev.* Jan. 87, I am almost willing to shut my eyes to the excesses of the noisy strenuosity of the athletic mood if it bring into the campus life a warm, vital sense of college unity. **1939** *Nature* 26 Aug. 392/1 Frome Avenue, on the opposite side of which is the [Adelaide] University campus. **1958** *Times* 10 Mar. 12/7 Not only in the cloistered courts of Cambridge but also on college campuses in America. **1958** *Sunday Times* 27 Apr. 20/7 The first walls are rising of Sir Hugh Casson's new arts faculty campus. **1959** *Listener* 19 Feb. 326/2 As in this country, some of the best of this kind of history is written off campus. **1968** *Brit. Univ. Ann.* 30 To my eye, the Birmingham campus has now developed into one of the most attractive in the country.

Hence as *v. trans.*, to confine to the campus (see also quot. 1928). *U.S. colloq.*

1928 *Amer. Speech* III. 218 When a Freshman is campussed..he is not actually confined to the campus but merely deprived of some privilege or other. **1949** 'N. R. NASH' *Young & Fair* 79 You've campused Dru Eldridge?

ˈ**campward**, ˈ**campwards**, *adv.* [f. CAMP *sb.*[2] + -WARD.] Toward a camp.

[**1600** FAIRFAX *Tasso* XI. xlvi, Against that part which to his campe ward lay.] **1830** W. PHILLIPS *Mt. Sinai* I. 331 Hied then the Levite campward. **1881** *Philada. Times* No. 2228. 1 But proceeded campwards in modest civilian's state.

campy (ˈkæmpɪ), *a. slang.* = CAMP *a.*

1959 *Spectator* 2 Jan. 11/2 Kenneth Williams and Ted Durante as the campy sisters [in *Cinderella*] manage to seem five times the size of the two stars. **1961** *Harper's Bazaar* Apr. 138/2 Noël Coward (with his campy diaeresis above the 'e'). **1965** *New Statesman* 20 Aug. 263/1 The movie has been called 'campy', and yet I have never seen comedy direction of such conviction.

ˈ**campylite.** *Min.* [f. Gr. καμπύλ-ος bent + -ITE.] An arsenio-phosphate of lead, a variety of Mimetite.

1868 DANA *Min.* 537 Campylite, from Drygill in Cumberland, is in barrel-shaped crystals (whence the name, from καμπύλος, curved).

campylospermous (ˌkæmpɪləʊˈspɜːməs), *a. Bot.* [f. mod.L. *campylosperm-us* (f. Gr. καμπύλος bent + σπέρμα seed) + -OUS.] (See quot.)

1880 GRAY *Bot. Text-bk.* 400 *Campylospermous*, curved-seeded. Said of seed-like fruits or carpels, as those of some Umbelliferæ, in which the contained seed is incurved by the lateral edges, so as to produce a longitudinal furrow on the ventral face.

campyˈlotropal, *a. Bot.* = next.

1835 LINDLEY *Introd. Bot.* (1848) I. 397 Mirbel, who first distinguished these ovules, calls them campylotropal.

campylotropous (kæmpɪˈlɒtrəpəs), *a. Bot.* [f. mod.L. *campylotrop-us*, f. Gr. καμπύλος bent + -τροπος, f. τρέπειν to turn + -OUS.] Said of the ovule of phanerogamous plants when its

nucleus, with its integuments, is curved upon itself.

1835 HENSLOW *Phys. Bot.* 270 The ovule is then termed campulitropous. **1870** BENTLEY *Bot.* 324 The progressive development of the campylotropous ovule..in the Mallow.

campyon, var. of CAMPION[1], champion.

camrade, -ado, obs. forms of COMRADE.

camrel, dial. form of CAMBREL.

camroche, obs. form of CAMBRIC.

camrocke. Cf. CAMMOCK and CAMBREL.

?*a* **1400** *Chester Pl.* (Shaks. Soc.) 186 And with this crocket camrocke your backes I shall cloe.

camshachle (kam'ʃax(ə)l), *v.* *Sc.* Also camshauchel. [f. CAM *a.* crooked, awry + SHACHLE *v.* to distort.] *trans.* To crook, distort, twist all awry. Hence **camshachled** *ppl. a.*

1805 J. NICOL *Poems* I. 33 (JAM.) Nae auld camshaucheld warlock loun. **1819** *St. Patrick* II. 191 (JAM.) An ye think tae camshachle me wi' your bluidthristy fingers.

'camshell. In Orkney and Shetland: Cuttle-fish bone.

1693 WALLACE *Descr. Orkney* 18 On the shore is to be found..Camshells or *Os-Sepiæ*, that the Gold-Smith makes so great Use of. **1753** CHAMBERS *Cycl. Supp.* s.v. *Camshall*, a word used in Zetland to denote the *os sepiæ*.

camshoch ('kamʃəx, 'kamʃə), *a.* *Sc.* Also 6 camschow, -scho, 7 -schoche, 8 campsho, 8–9 camsheugh, 9 -shach. [The first part is evidently CAM *a.* 'crooked, perverse'; the second perh. represents OE. *sceoh* 'askew, perverse', of which *schoch* would be the normal Scotch form: Jamieson has also the Sc. verbs *sheuch*, *shach* to distort, and *shachle*, *shochle* to distort, wriggle.]

1. Crooked, distorted, awry; deformed.

1513 DOUGLAS *Æneis* III. x. 43 Thai elriche brethir..with mony camscho beik, And hedis semand to the hevin areik. *Ibid.* VII. Prol. 107 Laithlie of forme, wyth crukit camschow beik. *a* **1600** MONTGOMERIE *Flyting* 295 That cruiked, camschoche croyll, vncristned, they curse. **1730** RAMSAY *Twa Cats & Ch.* 13 A monkey with a campsho face. **1807–10** TANNAHILL *Poems* (1846) 21 Auld, swirlon, slaethorn, camsheugh, crooked Wight.

2. *fig.* Perverse (in disposition or fortune).

1606 BIRNIE *Kirk-Burial* (1833) 36 The camshoch commons now at last coms in a rere warde to debate the cause. **1787** W. TAYLOR *Scots Poems* 170 (JAM.) Bot camshach wife or girnin gett. **1790** A. WILSON *To E. Picken*, The queer carles sae camsheugh spak'. *a* **1809** *Christmas Ba'ing* in Skinner *Misc. Poet.* 129 (Jam.) Pate had caught a camshach cair At this uncanny wark.

camstairy (kam'steri), *a.* *Sc.* Also -stairie, -starie, -stary, -steary, -steirie. [Derivation uncertain: first element app. CAM crooked, awry.] Obstinately perverse, unruly, or wilful; fractious.

1776 HERD *Coll. Sc. Songs*, When she is fou she is unco camstarie. **1844** *Proc. Berw. Nat. Club* II. No. 12. 100 He had a wild, camstary pony. **1863** MISS TYTLER in *Gd. Words* Oct. 709/1 No wonder he is camsteary. **1868** G. MACDONALD *R. Falconer* I. 195 'What are ye sae camstairie for?'

camstone ('kæmstəʊn). *Sc.* In 8 calm-.

a. 'Common compact limestone probably of a white colour' (Jam.). **b.** A white or bluish-white clay used to whiten hearths, door-steps, etc.

1791 *Statist. Acc. Scotl.* I. 209 There is calmstone and plenty of ruddle. **1795** *Ibid.* XV. 327 (Jam.) At the base of the hill..you meet with several layers of camstone. **1815** SCOTT *Guy M.* xxxvi, A pail of whiting or camstane, as it is called, mixed with water—a circumstance which indicates Saturday night in Edinburgh. **1806** FORSYTH *Beauties Scotl.* III. 359 The third kind of limestone is..camstone or glenstone..It contains a considerable proportion of clay.

camus, var. of CAMIS and CAMOIS.

cam-wheel: see CAM.

cam-wood ('kæmwʊd). [According to some, ad. native African name *kambi*.] The hard red wood of *Baphia nitida* (N.O. *Leguminosæ*), imported from West Africa, and used for dyeing, and in turning and cabinet-making; called also BARWOOD.

1698 DAMPIER *Voy.* (1705) II. II. 58 At Cherburg near Sierra-Leone..there is Camwood, which is much like Blood-wood, if not the same. **1701** *Lond. Gaz.* No. 3758/8 Cam Wood and Elephant's Teeth, lately cast away upon the Goodwin Sands. **1788** CLARKSON *Impol. Slave Tr.* 7 The first African woods, that were known to be objects of commercial importance, were Camwood and Barwood. **1876** R. BURTON *Gorilla L.* I. 257 Corisco had long been celebrated for cam-wood..yielding a better red than Brazil.

camwysse, var. of CAMMES, *Obs.*, linen cloth.

†**'camy**, *a.* *Obs. rare.* [app. f. *came* = KAIM comb, crest.] Having a sharp or serrated ridge.

1513 DOUGLAS *Æneis* VII. xiv. 42 Thai that with scharp culter teill..the hylly knowis hie, Or camy eige.

can (kæn), *sb.*[1] Forms: 1 canne, (4 cane), 4–7 canne, kan, 5–6 kanne, 6–9 cann, 6– can. [app. Com. Teut.: OE. *canne*:—WGer. *kanna* weak fem. (whence MDu. *kanne*, Du. *kan*, OHG. *channa*, MHG. and Ger. *kanne*); also ON. *kanna* (Sw. *kanna*, Da. *kande*):—OTeut. type **kannôn-*. The word occurs also in med.L. *canna*, app. from Teutonic. The Germanic origin of the word is questioned; but the form is not derivable from L. *cantharus* pot, and L. *canna* 'reed, pipe', does not suit the sense. (In OE., only in a glossary, where it might be from L.)]

1. a. A vessel for holding liquids; formerly used of vessels of various materials, shapes, and sizes, including drinking-vessels; now generally restricted to vessels of tin or other metal, mostly larger than a drinking-vessel, and usually cylindrical in form, with a handle over the top.

a **1000** ÆLFRIC *Voc.* in Wr.-Wülcker 122 *Crater*, uel *canna*, canne. *c* **1375** ? BARBOUR *St. Laurentius* 361 He brocht a vatir-cane & Laurens hyme baptist þane. **1388** WYCLIF *John* ii. 6 There weren set sixe stonun cannes [**1382** pottis]. *a* **1400** *Cov. Myst.* 259 (Mätz.) Beryng a kan with watyr. **1485** *Inv.* in *Ripon Ch. Acts* 370 Duo kannes de ligno. **1535** COVERDALE *Hosea* iii. 1 They..loue the wyne kannes. **1562** J. HEYWOOD *Prov. & Epigr.* (1867) 49 Mery we were as cup and can could holde. **1598** B. JONSON *Ev. Man in Hum.* II. v. (1616) 27 Two cannes of beere. **1649** BLITHE *Eng. Improv. Impr.* (1653) 131 The Buckets or Kans to take up thy Water. **1719** D'URFEY *Pills* (1872) III. 247 Now what do you say to the Cans of wood? **1731** BAILEY *Cann*, a wooden Pot to drink out of. **1755** JOHNSON, *Can*, a cup; generally a cup made of metal, or some other matter than earth. **1800** WORDSW. *Pet Lamb* xi, I have brought thee in this can Fresh water from the brook. **1803** SCOTT *Bonnie Dundee*, Come fill up my cup, come fill up my can. **1838** DICKENS *O. Twist* xlv, The milk-can was standing by itself outside a public-house. **1842** TENNYSON *Will Waterpr.* xxii, The truth, that flies the flowing can, Will haunt the vacant cup.

b. (from its shape) A chimney-pot.

1833 *Act 3 & 4 Will. IV*, xlvi. §103 Chimney cans or pots. **1866** *Glasgow Police Act 29 & 30 Vic.* cclxxiii. §384 To repair any Chimney Head or Can.

c. A revolving cylinder open at the top to receive the sliver from a carding-machine. Also *attrib.* and *Comb.*

1825 J. NICHOLSON *Oper. Mech.* 382 The roving-frame.. used..where mule-spinning is carried on..is termed the *can roving-frame*. **1844** G. DODD *Textile Manuf.* i. 30 In the 'can-roving frame',..the cardings coming from two cans, and passing between the pairs of rollers, become elongated and fall into the can. **1853** URE *Dict. Arts* (ed. 4) II. 697 The missing band or sliver was supplied out of a can, being the produce of a single carding-engine working into cans. **1861** [see SLIVER *sb.*[1] 2 *attrib.*]. **1882** *Spon's Encycl. Industr. Arts* V. 2091 The several drawings are passed into a coiling-can, by which they are loosely twisted into one. **1912** BARKER & PRIESTLEY *Wool Carding* 201 A 'can' delivery apparatus. *Ibid.*, If the box is a 'can' box the sliver passes through a funnel and press rollers into a cylindrical can. *Ibid.* 228 The slivers are fed into the comb just as if they were fed out of the can-coiler from the carder.

d. A large, usu. cylindrical, metal container or bin, as in *ash-can*, *garbage can*. Chiefly *U.S.*

e. A lavatory, water-closet. *U.S. slang.*

1900 *Dialect Notes* II. 26 *Can*, water-closet. **1933** A. WOOLLCOTT *Let.* 22 Feb. (1946) 97 He was always organizing quartets and being fired for practicing in the can during working hours. **1951** J. D. SALINGER *Catcher in Rye* x. 90 She kept saying..corny..things, like calling the can the 'little girls' room'.

f. *to carry* (or *take*) *the can* (*back*) [origin of use unkn.; said to be the 'beer-can' which one (soldier) carries for all his companions]: to bear the responsibility, take the blame (also see quots.). *slang* (orig. *Services*').

1929 BOWEN *Sea Slang* 22 *A Can*, a reprimand. *Ibid.* 23 *To Carry the Can*, to be reprimanded (Navy). *Ibid.* 137 *To Take the Can Back*, to be reprimanded. **1936** *Daily Herald* 11 Aug. 8/5 Railwaymen and road transport workers use the phrase, 'Taking the can back' for (respectively) being held responsible for a mishap and being imposed upon. **1938** F. D. SHARPE *S. of Flying Squad* 333 '*Taking the Can Back*', being left to do the dirty work. **1943** HUNT & PRINGLE *Service Slang* 20 *Carrying the can back*, accepting the blame for your own or another's error. **1957** *Times* 23 Feb. 7/4 Senior officers who were forced to 'carry the can' because of the misdeeds of others. **1959** D. BARTON *Loving Cup* i. 11 Officially you have to take the can. **1959** J. BRAINE *Vodi* x. 148 It's always my fault, everything's my fault. I always carry the bloody can back. **1959** *Even. Standard* 6 July 5/2 He has enough political nous not to wish to carry the can for people like Aneurin Bevan. **1967** *Spectator* 30 June 763/3 No Department wanted to carry the can for cable-vetting —quite irrespective of security considerations.

g. The buttocks. *slang* (orig. and chiefly *U.S.*).

1930 L. HUGHES *Not without Laughter* xx. 229 If you offer a nigger a dime, he'll dance his can off. **1937** C. PRIOR *So I wrote It* xxv. 285 At last, the landlady threw me out and kept the few rags of luggage that I still owned. I was flat on my can. **1956** *Mademoiselle* Sept. 175/1 'What have you been doing?' 'Sitting on my can.' 'A writer I used to know once got sacroiliac trouble from sitting so long. Could that be coming on you?' **1965** J. MCCORMICK *Bravo* 1. 42 See this room... A primitive bed.., a toilet bowl in the corner with a scratched metal lid that freezes your can when you sit on it, [etc.].

†**2.** *Sc.* A measure of capacity. *Obs.*

1809 EDMONSTONE *Zetland Isles* I. 163 (JAM.) About three fourths of a can or gallon of oil.

3. a. A vessel of tinned iron, in which flesh of animals, fish, fruit, etc. are 'tinned', or sealed up air-tight for preservation (chiefly in U.S.).

1867 A. D. RICHARDSON *Beyond Miss.* 147 Mitchell..was fined two cans of oysters for contempt. **1874** *Harper's Weekly Jrnl.* 26 Sept. (Hoppe) Salmon..pickled, Smoked, and put up in cans. **1941** *Manch. Guardian Weekly* 26 Sept. 206/1 Cans of food are kept in the factory for a period before distribution. *Ibid.*, The can of carrots also contained gases at high pressure. **1968** *Gloss. Terms Mechanized & Hand Sheet Metal Work* (*B.S.I.*) 26 *Can*, lightweight container (usually for processed foods) fabricated from separate components, i.e. bottom, body and lid (or cover). (Usually known as an open-top can.)

b. A prison. *slang* (orig. *U.S.*).

1912 D. LOWRIE *My Life in Prison* xi. 125, I was in th' can ag'in, up against it f'r robbery. **1926** J. BLACK *You can't Win* xv. 216 Those two..never allowed any of 'their people' to languish in the 'can' overnight. **1961** *20th Cent.* Mar. 236 I'll stand by my man Though he's in the can.

c. *in the can*: of a cinema film or sequence, completed. *colloq.* Cf. CAN *v.*[3] b.

1930 C. BEATON *Diary* in *Wand. Years* (1961) 193 The scene was 'in the can' after twenty-five retakes. **1934** *Tit-Bits* 31 Mar. 12/2 When a film is completed it is 'in the can'. **1946** 'BRAHMS' & SIMON *Trottie True* I. vi. 158 John Bunny..was stirring a bucket of whitewash... When this shot was in the can Trottie..was due to come along..and push him into it. **1968** *Observer* (Colour Suppl.) 17 Nov. 48/4 Godard got the film into the can on schedule.

d. A protective jacket covering the fuel element in a nuclear reactor (see quot. 1962).

1945 H. D. SMYTH *Devel. Methods of using Atomic Energy for Mil. Purposes* 106 Mechanical jackets or cans of thin aluminum were feasible from the nuclear point of view. **1962** *Gloss. Terms Nuclear Sci.* (*B.S.I.*) 19 *Can*, a container used for a fuel element in a reactor to prevent the escape of fission products and possibly corrosion of the fuel, and sometimes to increase the mechanical strength of the fuel rod.

4. *Comb.*, as ***can-carrier***, ***-maker***; ***can-quaffing*** adj.; **can-opener** orig. *U.S.* = *tin-opener*. See also CAN-BUOY, CANDOCK, CAN-HOOK.

1597 *Return fr. Pernass.* II. I. ii. 170 Can-quaffing hucksters. *a* **1611** BEAUM. & FL. *Philaster* v. iii, My kind can-carriers. **1623** *Reg. St. Mary Bredman, Canterb.*, Thomas Colle Cannemaker. *a* **1877** KNIGHT *Dict. Mech.* I. 452/1 *Can-opener*, a domestic implement for opening cans containing fruit, oysters, and what not. **1936** *Economist* 4 Apr. 4/2 It is now possible to obtain complete meals in tinned form. The can-opener must surely be regarded as a sign of the times.

can, *sb.*[2] *Sc.* [f. CAN *v.*[1] Cf. *canny*.]

a. Skill, knowledge. **b.** Power, ability.

1768 ROSS *Helenore* 15 (Jam.) Thae auld warld foulks had wondrous cann Of herbs that were baith good for beast and man. *Ibid.* 134 I'll all Maggie's can and her cantraps defy.

can (kæn), *v.*[1] *irreg.* (Forms: see below.) [A defective verb, belonging to the small but interesting group of Teutonic *preterite-present* verbs (now chiefly used as auxiliaries of tense, mood, or predication), in form characterized by having as their present tense an original preterite, which retains the preterite form but has come to have a present signification, and from which a new weak past tense has subsequently been developed. Cf. *dare*, etc. OE. *cunnan*, pres. Ind. *can* (*cǫn*), pa. *cúðe* (:—*cunðe*), is identical with OFris. *kunna*, *kan*, *kunda* (*konda*), OS. *cunnan*, *can*, *consta*, *const*, (Du. *kunnen*, *kan*, *konde*), OHG. *kunnan*, *kan*, *kunda* (*konda*), or *kunsta* (*konsta*), (Ger. *können*, *kann*, *konnte*), ON. *kunna*, *kann*, *kunna* (:—*kunða*), Goth. (and OTeut.) *kunnan*, *kann*, *kunþa*. The OTeut. sense was 'to know, know how, be mentally or intellectually able', whence 'to be able generally, be physically able, have the power, L. *posse*'. Since the present was formally a preterite, its meaning 'I know' must have been derived from that of 'I have learned, I have attained to knowledge'; the original present stem being **kin-n-* or **ken-n-*, pre-Teut. **gen-n-*: cf. Lith. *zinaú* I know, Zend *ā-zaiñ-ti* knowledge, OIr. pret. *adgéin* he knew. Beside this Teutonic has *knǣ-* (ablaut form *knô-*), WGer. *knā-*, whence OE. *cnáwan* to KNOW, OHG. *ir-chnâ-an*, *bi-chnâ-an*, to recognize, *ûr-chnâ-t* recognition (answering to a Goth. *-*knêþs* fem.). This stem is widely diffused in the Aryan langs.; cf. L., Gr. *gnô-* in L. *gnô-sco*, Gr. *γι-γνώ-σκω* (*ἔ-γνω-ν*); OSlav. *zna-ti* to know; OIr. *gnáth* known. In Skr. the pres. has stem *jan-*, the preterite *jñā*, *jānā'mi*, *jajña'u*.

It has been further thought that the root was originally related to the Aryan *gen-* (with by-forms *gnā-*, *gnō-*), to bring forth, produce, Skr. *ja'nāmi*, pret. *jajā'na*, L., Gr. *gen-*, *gi-gn-* (see KIN, KING); but if so, they were already differentiated in Old Aryan, and the nature of the connexion of sense has not been determined.]

Here, as in BE, it will be convenient to illustrate the inflexions separately from the senses.

A. Inflexions.

1. *Pres. Indic.*

a. *1st* and *3rd sing.* can (kæn, kən, k(ə)n).

Forms: 1–4 cann, con, conn, 1– can, (4–5 conne, canne; also kan, etc.).

a 1000 *Cædmon Poems, Sat.* 250 Ic can eow læran. *Ibid.* 629 Ic eow ne con. c 1175 *Lamb. Hom.* 35 Nis nan sunne þet he ne con. a 1225 *Ancr. R.* 206 More vuel þen heo con. c 1250 *Gen. & Ex.* 309 Ic wene I can a red. c 1300 *Cursor M.* 20358 O me self can [*later MSS.* con, canne] I na rede. c 1320 *Cast. Loue* 555 Hose þis forbysene con. c 1420 *Avow. Arth.* xxxiii, I conne notte say. 1467 *Eng. Gilds* (1870) 407 The craft that he canne. 1556 J. Heywood *Spider & F.* G iij, Sure I can no false knackes. *Mod.* What can it be?

b. *2nd sing.* canst (kænst).

Forms: 1–4 const, 1– canst, (4–5 konst, kanst, 6 canest, 6–7 cannest), *northern* 3– can, kan.

a 1000 *Andreas* 68 (Gr.) þu ana canst ealra ȝehygdo. a 1225 *Juliana* 66 Greiðe hwet so þu const grimliche biþenchen. a 1240 *Lofsong* in *Cott. Hom.* 217 To þe þet const and wult wel don. a 1300 *Cursor M.* 12121, I can þe ken þat þou ne can. a 1400 *Ibid.* 824 (*Add. MS.*) Ynow þou canst fynde. c 1500 in Hazl. *E.P.P.* 36 Canst thou thy bylevе? 1526 Tindale *Mark* i. 40 Yf thou wilt, thou cannest [1557 *Genev., etc.,* canst] make me clene. 1600 [see B 6]. 1610 Shaks. *Temp.* iii. ii. 67 Canst thou bring me to the party?

c. *plural* can.

Forms: 1–2 cunnon (cunne-), 2–5 cunnen, (4–5 kunnen), 3–5 cunne, 4–5 connen, conne, 4–5 *south.* kunneþ, conneþ, 3– *north.* con, can, (kan), 5– can.

Beowulf 162 Men ne cunnon. a 1000 *Cædmon's Daniel* 141 3e ne kunnon. c 1175 *Lamb. Hom.* 75 Alle ȝe kunnen..ower credo. c 1205 Lay. 7301 Tweien wise men · þe wel cunnen a speche [c 1275 conne of speche]. *Ibid.* 23059 Ne cunne we demen [c 1275 ne con we telle]. a 1300 *Cursor M.* 9065 Quat rede can [*v.r.* con] we. 1340 *Ayenb.* 249 Þo þet conneþ.. onderstonde. a 1340 Hampole *Psalter* ix. 11 Oþer þat kan þaim noght. c 1350 *Will. Palerne* 4184 As wel as we kunne. c 1386 Chaucer *Sqrs. Prol.* 3 For certes ye konnen [*v.r.* konne, can]. 1387 Trevisa *Higden* (1865) II. 169 þese men ..kunneþ wel inow telle. c 1449 Pecock *Repr.* i. xvi. 89 Manye kunnen suche textis bi herte. 1550 Latimer *Serm. Stamford* ii. 104 All that can it not may learne. 1835 Browning *Paracels.* iv. Wks. I. 149 You can see the root of the matter.

d. *Negative* cannot ('kænɒt); *famil.* can't (kɑːnt). (*Sc.* canna). (The earlier mode was to prefix *ne.*)

? a 1400 *Cursor M.* (add. to Cott.) p. 959. 105 And þou þat he deed fore cannot sorus be. 1451 *Paston Lett.* 140 I. 186 Other tydyngs as yett can I non tell you. *Ibid.* 172 I. 229 Whethir it be thus or non I can not say. 15.. *Plumpton Corr.* 72, I canot get my money. 1706 *Col. Records Penn.* II. 256 The House cant agree to this. 1741 Richardson *Pamela* I. 56 If he..as you say can't help it. 1742 Young *Nt. Th.* i. 89 An angel's arm can't snatch me from the grave; Legions of angels can't confine me there. 1827 Keble *Chr. Y.* 4 Without Thee I cannot live. *Mod.* Can't you go?

2. *Past Indic.* **a.** *1st* and *3rd sing.* could (kʊd).

Forms: α. 1 cúðe, 2–3 cuþe, kuthe, 3–5 cowþe, cowthe, (4 coth), 4–5 couþe, 4–6 couthe, (5 couȝthe), 4 *north.* cuþ, cuth, 4–6 couth, (also in 4–5 with k-); β. 4–6 coude, k-, 5–6 coud, 7–8 *often* cou'd; γ. 6 coulde, 6– could, (6 coold, 6–7 cold, 6– *Sc.* culd).

The current spelling is erroneous: *l* began to be inserted about 1525, app. in mechanical imitation of *should* and *would*, where an etymological *l* had become silent, so that these words now rimed with *coud*, and might better have been written *shoud*, *woud*; cf. northern *wad*. In the sense *know*, the earlier form *couth* was retained longer.

α. c 893 K. Ælfred *Oros.* i. ii. §1 Ninus..se cuðe manna ærest dry-cræftas. c 1250 *Gen. & Ex.*, 289 Ne kuðe he noȝt blinne. a 1274 *Prisoner's Prayer* 1 in *Philol. Trans.* (1868) 104 Ar ne kuthe ich sorghe non. c 1297 R. Glouc. 29 He was y flowe an hey, & ne cowþe not a-liȝte. a 1300 *Cursor M.* 21420 (Cott.) Ful wel he cuth [*later MS.* cutht, couþe]. *Ibid.* 23945 (Edin.) I wald spek if I cuþe [*C.G.* cuth, *F.* couþe]. c 1325 *E.E. Allit. P.* B. 813 As þe wyf couþe. 1340 Hampole *Pr. Consc.* 7444 Wha couth þan telle. a 1450 *Knt. de la Tour* (1868) 75 He took fro them all that he couthe. 1519 *Mem. Ripon* (1882) I. 315 In as convenient hast as I couthe. 1530 Lyndesay *Test. Papyngo* 875 In Inglande couthe scho get none ordinance. 1579 Spenser *Sheph. Cal.* Jan. 10 Well couth he tune his pipe. 1607 Walkington *Opt. Glass* 18 Ne any couth his wit so hiely straine. 1652 C. Stapylton *Herodian* v. 37 So well his leere he Couth [*rime* South].

β. c 1350 *Will. Palerne* 4378 As he coude. c 1386 Chaucer *Sqrs. T.* 31 A Rethor excellent That koude [*v.r.* coude, couþe, kouþe, couþe] hise colours. a 1400 *Octouian* 111 (W.) The emperour, couthde no man kythe His ioye. c 1420 *Chron. Vilod.* 554 As he wel couȝthe and ouȝte to do. 1478 John Paston *Lett.* 812 III. 219 He koud get the good wyll. c 1500 in Hazl. *E.P.P.* 211 Yet could he neyther pates noster nor ave. c 1532 Ld. Berners *Huon* clxvi. 654 Al preuely as he coude. 1697 Dryden *Virg. Georg.* iii. 738 Th'..Entrails cou'd no Fates foretel. 1762 *Gentl. Mag.* 137 [Will] cou'd his fears impart.

γ. c 1530 Ld. Berners *Arth. Lyt. Bryt.* (1814) 129 There was none that coude..yet Gouernar dyd as moche as he coulde. 1530 *Myrr. Our Ladye* (1873) 20 The same Alphonse..coulde nothynge of her language. 1575 Laneham *Let.* (1871) 61, I coold my rulez, coold conster, and pars. 1584 Powel *Lloyd's Cambria* 315 [He] cold doo no good. 1588 A. King *Canisius' Catech.* 114 He culd nocht be præiudiciable to ye kirk. 1590 Spenser *F.Q.* i. ii 6 He could not rest. c 1620 A. Hume *Brit. Tong.* (1865) 20 Of this I cold reckon armies. 1848 Macaulay *Hist. Eng.* II. 265 He could not consent. 1882 Leslie Keith *Alasnam's Lady* III. 201 He really couldn't say where.

b. *2nd sing.* couldest, couldst (kʊdst).

Forms: 1 cúðest, 4 couthest, coudest, 6– couldest, couldst.

c 1000 *Ags. Gosp.* John i. 48 Hwanon cuðest ðu me [*Lindisf.* wistes ðu *vel* cuðes ðu]. 1377 Langl. *P. Pl.* B. v. 540 Koudestow auȝte wissen vs þe weye. *Ibid.* viii. 76 Þow couthest me wisse. 1526 Tindale *Mark* xiv. 37 Couldest not thou watche [so all exc. *Rhem.* couldst, Wyclif myȝtist not]. 1667 Milton *P.L.* iv. 950 And couldst thou faithful add?.. Faithful to whom?

c. *plural* could (kʊd).

Forms: 1 cúðon, 2–3 cuþen, 3–5 couthen, couthe, (4 coþen, 5 coothe), 4–6 couth, 4–5 koude, cowde, 5–6 coude, 6 kowd, colde, 6– could.

a 1000 *Cædmon's Daniel* 258 [Hi] dydon swa hie cuðon. c 1175 *Cott. Hom.* 223 Hi cuðon ȝeiðer god and yfel. a 1300 *Cursor M.* 12344 Wele þai couthe þaire lorde knaw. c 1340 *Ibid.* 14716 Þai cowd a-gayn him finde resoun nane. 1350 *Will. Palerne* 1033 Alle þe surgyens of salerne..ne couþen have ȝour langoures a-legget. c 1400 *Rom. Rose* 789 Welle koude they the gise. 1413 Lydg. *Pylgr. Sowle* iii. iii. (1483) 51 Ye that more good coothe. c 1449 Pecock *Repr.* i. vi. 28 As othere men miȝten and couthen do. c 1450 *Merlin* x. 146 Thei cowde heir tydynges. 1475 *Bk. Noblesse* (1860) 13 They..couthe have no socoure. 1510 Love *Bonavent. Mirr.* (Pynson) viii. D j, They coude the langage of Ebrewe. a 1533 Ld. Berners *Huon* vii. 16 The ii. brethern kowd not. 1580 Sidney *Arcadia* 397 Well my pipe they couth. 1646 E. F[isher] *Mod. Divinity* 237 They could skill to say. *Mod.* Could you or couldn't you?

3. *Pres. Subj.*: **a.** *sing.* can (kæn). Since 16th c. levelled with the Indic.

Forms: 1–4 cunne, (3–4 kunne), 4–5 conne, (4 cone, konne).

a 1000 *Satan* 702 Ðæt ðu cunne. a 1225 *Ancr. R.* 280 Hwat turn his fere ne cunne nout. c 1250 *Hymn Virg.* i. 45 Nis non maiden..þat swo derne louiȝe kunne. 1377 Langl. *P. Pl.* B. xix. 26 Thow knowest wel..And þow conne resoun. 1393 Gower *Conf.* I. 50 Though I ne conne but a lite. c 1450 *Merlin* ii. 40 With that thou conne me no magre. 1528 Roy *Sat.*, All though he canne many a wyle. 1596 Shaks. *1 Hen. IV*, ii. ii. 34 List if thou can heare the tread [*Qq.* canst]. *Mod.* He will come if he can.

b. *plural* can.

Forms: 1–3 cunnen, 2–3 cunne, 4–6 conne.

a 1000 *Elene* 374 Þæt [hi] andsware secȝan cunnen. 1735 Berkeley *Wks.* 1871 III. 320 Confute them if you can.

4. a. *Past Subj. sing.* could, *2nd sing.* could(e)st. (Like the Indicative.)

Forms: 1 cúðe, 3–5 couthe, (4 coþe, kouȝde), 4–6 couth, 4–6 coud, coude, 5 cowde, 6– could.

a 1300 *Cursor M.* 438 If he cuth [*v.r.* coude, couth, couþe]. *Ibid.* 4555 Coud þu [*v.r.* cuth, cowde; *Trin.* coudestou] tell me quat it ware. *Ibid.* 20024 Þof..i cothe. c 1380 Wyclif *Wks.* (1880) 382 No leyser to telle all ȝif I kouȝde. c 1440 *Gesta Rom.* (1878) 361 If thou couthiste peynte. 1508 Fisher *Wks.* (1876) 172 So yf he coude fynde x good and ryghtwyse personnes. c 1532 Ld. Berners *Huon* clxvi. 654 To seke yf he coude fynde the damoysell. 1586 Ferne *Lacyes Nobil.* 11, I had rather..my daughter Alice couth karoll a lay so lustilie. 1656 Bp. Hall *Occas. Medit.* (1851) Oh that thou couldest! 1697 Dryden *Virg. Georg.* iv. 705 Were Lovers Judges, or cou'd Hell forgive. *Mod.* I wish I could help you.

b. *plural* could.

Forms: 1 cúðen, 3–4 couthen, coude, 6– could.

a 1225 *Leg. Kath.* 1330 Þah we cuðen. a 1300 *Havelok* 369 Til þat he kouþen speken. 1394 *P. Pl. Crede* 623 If þei couþen her crede. 1611 Bible *2 Cor.* xi. 1 Would to God ye could bear with me.

5. *Infinitive* can (kæn). *Obs.* exc. *Sc.* or *dial.*

Forms: 1 cunnan, 2–4 cunnen, 3–5 cunne, 4 connen, 4–5 conne, 6– can (in 9 *dial.*; regular in *Sc.*) See also con *v.*

c 1175 *Lamb. Hom.* 73 Þet heo sculen..heore bileue cunnen. a 1240 *Moral Ode* 332 He sceal him cunne sculde wel. a 1300 *Finding Cross* 216 in *Leg. Rood* (1871) 93 þe laws wele better mai he cun. c 1320 *Cast. Love* 1071 He scholde konnen al þat God con. c 1340 *Cursor M.* 2570 Na mare saltow ham con rede þen sternes of heyuen. c 1374 Chaucer *Troylus* v. 1404 Cryseyde shal not conne knowe me. c 1380 Wyclif *Serm.* Sel. Wks. II. 245 To cunne no more þan is nede to cunne but to cunne to subrenesse. 1393 Gower *Conf.* II. 158 To conne arede. c 1460 *Towneley Myst.* 55 Wold I ken, And kun him thank. 1484 Caxton *Curial* 5 He shal neuer conne trotte. 1555 Eden *Decades W. Ind.* (Arb.) 52 To wyl to doo hurte & can not. 1607–12 Bacon *Gt. Place, Ess.* (Arb.) 282 In evill, the best condicion is not to will, the second not to can. 1816 Scott *Antiq.* xxvi, 'He'll no can haud down his head to sneeze, for fear o' seeing his shoon.' 1847 Frances Kemble (Mrs. Butler) *Rec. Later Life* (1882) III. 165 Lady Macbeth, which I never could, and cannot, and never shall can act. 1886 Stevenson *Kidnapped* 298 'Ye'll can name your business.'

†**6.** *Pres. pple.* cunning (in OE. cunnand), now only as adj., q.v. *Obs.*

†**7.** *Pa. pple.* could: in OE. cúþ, ME. couth, chiefly as adj.: see couth. As pple. *conne* (= *cun*, on model of str. vbs.) occurs anomalously, and in mod. dialects *could* is commonly so used. ***used to could***, a common phrase in certain dialects of England and in the United States for: used to be able to.

1413 Lydg. *Pylgr. Sowle* i. ii. (1859) 3 Yf thou haddest ony good conne. a 1888 *Mod. Sc.* He has not could come. If I had could find it. 1823–1940 dialectal examples in Wentworth's *Amer. Dial. Dict.* (1944).

1827 J. F. Cooper *Prairie* II. xvi. 257 A small and trifling matter is it, to what I used-to-could offer in the way of bargains. 1848 Bartlett *Dict. Amer.* 372 *Used to could*, a vulgarism used in the Southern States for could formerly. 1848 A. B. Evans *Leicestersh. Words.* 1872 Schele de Vere *Americanisms* 646. 1892 in *Eng. Dial. Dict.* s.v. *Can*, Ah can't walk five mile i' t' hahr nah, but ah used to could! 1899– in *Ibid.* Suppl. s.v. *Use.* 1940 *Sat. Even. Post* 6 Jan. 15/2 She used to could smell that old goat of yours from here to yonder.

8. *vbl. sb.* cunning, q.v. As a gerund **canning** has been used for the nonce, and is in mod.Sc.

1563–87 Foxe *A. & M.* (1684) II. 419 In canning the text of the whole New Testament..without book.

B. Signification.

I. As an independent verb.

†**1.** *trans.* To know. **a.** To know or be acquainted with (a person). **b.** To know or have learned (a thing); to have practical knowledge of (a language, art, etc.). ***to can by heart***: to know by heart. ***to can one's good***: to know what is good for one. *Obs.*

c 1000 *Ags. Gosp.* Matt. xxv. 12 Ne can ic eow. c 1200 *Trin. Coll. Hom.* 29 Cune sume meðe þenne þu almesse makest. c 1297 R. Glouc. 443 Of Engelond ne con ych non rede. a 1300 *Cursor M.* 13142 Sco sa well her mister cuth. a 1340 Hampole *Psalter* Comm. 22 Þe lord þat all þing can. c 1386 Chaucer *Miller's T.* 18, I can a noble tale for the noones. 1387 Trevisa *Higden* Rolls Ser. III. 281, I can nouȝt but þat I can nouȝt. c 1400 *Destr. Troy* 1251 For sleght þat he couth. 1480 Caxton *Descr. Brit.* 35 Now they lerne no frenssh ne can none. 1526 Skelton *Magnyf.* 561 Can you a remedy for the tysyke? 1538 Coverdale *N.T.* Ded., To..instruct such as can but English. 1541 Paynel *Catiline* l. 74 He coulde it by hart. 1548 Hall *Chron.* (1809) 363 An honest manne and one that could his good. 1563–87 Foxe *A. & M.* (1684) II. 325 Unlearned men that can no letters. 1591 Harington *Orl. Fur.* lxxxv. xxiii, It had bin well that he it never coud. 1600 Fairfax *Tasso* x. iv. 180 The way right well he could. 1602 Carew *Cornwall* 56 a, Most of the Inhabitants can no word of Cornish. 1632 B. Jonson *Magn. Lady* i. i, She could the Bible in the holy tongue. 1649 Lovelace *Poems* (1659) 120 Yet can I Musick too; but such As is beyond all Voice or Touch.

c. In phrase ***to can*** (***some, no, small, good,*** etc.) ***skill of*** or ***in***: to have skill in, be skilled in.

c 1518 Pace in Ellis *Orig. Lett.* iii. I. 186 They couth goodde skele in byldyngs. 1532 Hervet *Xenophon's Househ.* (1768) 52 A carpenter..that can good skylle therof. 1538 Leland *Itin.* II. 56 One Thomas Long..could skille of the Law. 1578 T. Proctor *Gorg. Gallery*, Talke thou of that, wherin some skill thou can. 1613 Chapman *B. D'Ambois' Rev.* Plays 1873 II. 180 Since I could skill of man. 1644 Bulwer *Chiron.* 19 One that could well skill in Manuall Rhetorique. 1710 Philips *Pastorals* iv. 23 No Skill of Musick can I, simple Swain.

2. *intr.* To have knowledge, to know *of*; also to know *much* or *little* of. *arch.*

a 1250 *Owl & Night.* 560 Bute thu canst of chateringe. a 1300 *Cursor M.* 740 Þat mast kan bath on crok and craft. *Ibid.* 7408 (Gött.) He coude of harpe mekil bi rote. c 1400 *Destr. Troy* 2529 A mad priste, That neuer colde of no knighthode, but in a kirke chyde. c 1420 *Avow. Arth.* xvii, The king couthe of venery. 1602 Rowlands *Greene's Ghost* (1860) 70, I neuer was there (that I can of). 1825 Scott *Talism.* (1854) 407 Thou canst well of wood-craft. a 1875 Kingsley *Poems, Little Baltung* 82 That cunning Kaiser was a scholar wise, And could of gramarye.

II. With infinitive, as auxiliary of predication.

(Many manuals of English Grammar have ineptly treated *can* so construed, as an auxiliary of the Subjunctive or 'Potential' mood!)

3. To know how (*to do* anything); to have learned, to be intellectually able.

a 1154 *O.E. Chron.* (Laud MS.) an. 1137 Suilc & mare þanne we cunnen sæin. a 1300 *Cursor M.* 14692 Your aun bok yee can noght spell. c 1400 *Rom. Rose* 176 Wel coude he peynte, I undirtake, That such ymage coude make. 1485 Caxton *Paris & V.* (1868) 64 On al the maners that ye shal conne demaunde. 1490 —— *How to Die* 2 To conne deye is to haue in all tymes his herte redy. a 1520 *Myrr. Our Ladye* 148 Dyscrecion to canne kepe peace . on all partyes. 1579 Spenser *Sheph. Cal.* Jan. 10 Well couth hee tune his pipe. 1726 Gay *Fables* ii. vi. 48 We country-folks Cou'd ope our gracious monarch's eyes.

This passes imperceptibly into the current sense:

4. a. To be able; to have the power, ability or capacity. (Said of physical as well as mental, and of natural as well as acquired ability; = L. *posse*, F. *pouvoir*.)

a 1300 *Havelok* 111 So yung þat sho ne couþe Gon on fote. 1375 Barbour *Bruce* iii. 431 Sum off thaim couth swome full weill. 1475 *Bk. Noblesse* 76 To can renne withe speer. 1526 Tindale *Mark* xiv. 37 Coudest not thou watche with me one hour? 1561 T. Norton *Calvin's Inst.* i. 6 Thou canst not with one view peruse the wide compasse of it. 1611 Bible *Ex.* vii. 21 The Egyptians could not drink of the water. 1650 T. B. *Worcester's Apoph.* 22, I..could not come to the speech of any of them. 1667 Milton *P.L.* i. 117 This Empyreal substance cannot fail. 1697 Dryden *Virg. Georg.* iv. 642 What Madness cou'd provoke A Mortal Man t' invade a sleeping God? 1709 Steele *Tatler* No. 11 ¶3 The whole Company..take Hands; then, at a certain sharp Note, they move round, and kick as kick can. 1875 Jevons *Money* (1878) 2 [She] could not consume any considerable portion of the receipts herself. *Mod.* What weight can you carry? Who can run farthest? The house can hold no more. Such language can do no good to the cause.

b. In this and the prec. sense it occurs, used for the nonce, as a main verb, with infinitive.

[Cf. 1555–1607 in A 5.]

1566 Drant *Horace's Sat.* i. iii. B vij, The wyse can rule; to can is full as muche As though he did. 1633 P. Fletcher *Pisc. Ecl.* vi. xxvi, If from this love thy will thou canst unbind, To will is here to can. [1837 Carlyle *Fr. Rev.* (1872) III. iii. iv. 118 What a Man kens he cans.]

5. Expressing a possible contingency; = May possibly.

c 1250 *Gen. & Ex.* 2872 Ic am sonder man, Egipte folc me knowen can [= may possibly know me]. 1609 Bible (Douay) *Numb.* xxxii. 17 Whatsoever we can have, shal be in walled cities. 1816 J. Wilson *City of Plague* i. i. 138 Dost think My mother can be living?

6. a. Expressing possibility: To be permitted or enabled by the conditions of the case; ***can you..?*** = is it possible for you to..?

1542 Udall *Erasm. Apoph.* 299 a, Thou cannest not haue of Phocion a frende & a flaterer bothe to gether. 1583 Stubbes *Anat. Abus.* ii. 38 And can you blame them? 1600 Heywood *Edw. IV*, i. ii. iii, Thou cannest bear me witness.

1611 BIBLE *1 Cor.* x. 21 Ye cannot drink the cup of the Lord, and the cup of devils. **1664** EVELYN *Kal. Hort.* (1729) 195 You can hardly over-water your Strawberry-Beds. **1667** MILTON *P.L.* III. 735 Thy way thou canst not miss. **1709** STEELE *Tatler* No. 45 ¶9 The best Sort of Companion that can be. *a* **1856** LONGF. *Vill. Blacksm.* iii, You can hear him swing his heavy sledge, With measured beat and slow. **1848** MACAULAY *Hist. Eng.* II. 221 Even if it could be believed that the court was sincere.

b. To be allowed to, to be given permission to; = MAY *v.*[1] 4 a. *colloq.*

1879 TENNYSON *Falcon* 12 Can I speak with the Count? **1894** T. B. REED *Dog with Bad Name* xv. 156 Father says you can come. **1905** *Ch. Times* 3 Feb. 136/3 No one can play the organ during service time without the consent of the Vicar.

7. In *past subjunctive*, expressing an inclination in a conditional form. (= Ger. *könnte.*)

1658–9 COL. WHITE in Burton *Diary* (1828) IV. 39, I could like well that they should be in that House. **1711** ADDISON *Spect.* No. 121 ¶8, I could wish our Royal Society would compile a Body of Natural History. **1786** MRS. INCHBALD *Such things are* in *Brit. Theat.* (1808) 14, I cou'd not think of leaving you so soon.

8. *ellipt.*, with verb to be supplied from the context, or with *do, make, come, get,* etc., understood. *can* or *cannot away with*: see AWAY 16. *cannot but*: see BUT 7 c.

c **1440** HYLTON *Scala Perf.* (W. de W. 1494) I. lxxii, I can wyth plente and I can wyth pouerte, I maye all in hym that strengthith me. *c* **1440** *Gesta Rom.* (1879) 38, I am a seruaunt of yourys in all þat I can and may. *c* **1500** *Mayd Emlyn* in *Anc. Poet. Tracts* (1842) 27 He coude well awaye, With her lusty playe. *a* **1536** TINDALE *Pathw. Holy Script.* Wks. I. 27 The more tangled art thou therein, and canst nowhere through. **1611** HEYWOOD *Gold. Age* II. i. Wks. 1874 III. 19 What cannot womens wits? they wonders can When they intend to blinde the eyes of man. *a* **1700** DRYDEN (J.) Mecænas and Agrippa, who can most With Cæsar. **1715** DE FOE *Fam. Instruct.* I. iii. (1841) I. 63, I will do all I can with them. **1718** POPE *Iliad* XIII. 987 What with this arm I can, prepare to know. **1719** YOUNG *Busiris* III. i. (1757) 53 What could your malice more? **1807** SIR R. WILSON in *Life* (1862) II. viii. 374, I could no more. I was really exhausted. **1869** J. MARTINEAU *Ess.* II. 394.

b. *Cards. can-ye, can-you*: see CAN-YOU?.

c. Colloq. phr. *can do*: it is possible, it is within the power of (the speaker). So *no can do.*

1903 KIPLING in *Collier's Weekly* 3 Oct. 16/3 'Four hundred and twenty knots'... 'Can do,' said Moorshed. **1923** H. C. WITWER *Fighting Blood* v. 141 I've tried everything *I* know to get this gil to fight us and no can do! **1951** 'E. CRISPIN' *Long Divorce* iii. 29 'Can do, sir,' said Mogridge with watery affability. **1958** L. A. G. STRONG *Treason in Egg* i. 11 'No. Sorry, old boy... No can do.'

III. Senses now written CON.

†**9.** To get to know; to learn, study. *Obs.* In this sense it was also treated as a weak vb. with pa. pple. *cand*: the variant *con* was at length established as a separate form, with weak inflexions (*cons, conned*): see CON *v.*

1394 *P. Pl. Crede* 107 A man þat my3te me wissen For to conne my crede. **1528** MORE *Dial. Heresyes* I. Wks. 111/1 He laboured..to can many textes thereof by harte. **1530** PALSGR. 93 If the lernar can perfitly these two exemples. **1563** *Mirr. Mag., Blacksm.* vii. 7 So fare they all that have not vertue cand. **1587** FLEMING *Contn. Holinshed* III. 1982/1 They had cand their lesson.

†**10.** *to can* or *con thank(s*: to express or offer thanks, to thank: app. originally 'to acknowledge' or 'recognize' one's gratitude. [ME. *thank cunne(n*, OE. *þonc cunnan*, = *þonc witan*, in OS. *thank witan*, OHG. *thank wizan.* Cf. also Gr. *χάριν εἰδέναι*, (L. *gratias meminisse*), It. *saper grado*, Pr. *saver grat*, F. *savoir gré*, whence also in ME. *to cunne gree, maulgre*, to express one's satisfaction or displeasure. These phrases were distinctly identified with *can, could* as late as 1525. But on the other hand, already in ME., the verb was often imagined to be different, and inflected as a weak vb. *can* or *cunn* (whence *cannes, canned; cunnest, cunnes, cunneth, cunned*) and in later times generally *con* (*connest, cons, conned*), rarely *ken.* See CON: the examples which follow illustrate its original form as belonging to *can.*]

c **1175** *Lamb. Hom.* 31 Ne con crist him nenne þonc. *a* **1300** *Cursor M.* 14065, I can hir mikel thank. *c* **1400** *Rom. Rose* 4400, I drede thou canst me gret maugre. **1483** CAXTON *G. de la Tour* xviii. 26 Yef he canne ani good, thanne he wille cunne her moche thanke. **1483** —— *Gold. Leg.* 364/4 The ladyes..couthe her moche thanke. **1483** *Vulgaria abs Terentio* 9 b, My maister cowde me grete thanke. **1523** LD. BERNERS *Froiss.* I. ccxxiv. 294 The good lady..coude hym great thanke. **1533** MORE *Apology* xii. Wks. 871/2 No man hath any cause to can him ani thank. **1545** ASCHAM *Toxoph.* (Arb.) 31 Not onelye I..but many other mo..wyll can you very moche thanke. **1584** R. SCOT *Discov. Witchcr.* XII. xiv. 201 The smiths will canne them small thankes for this praier. [**1672** —— : see CON.]

¶ The following examples show the tendency to make a separate vb. of it with regular inflexions. Some writers made it into *gan*, the converse of the change in CAN *v.*[2]

1534 MORE *Comf. agst. Trib.* II. Wks. 1210/1 Els would Christe haue canned her much more thanke. **1542** UDALL *Erasm. Apoph.* 110 b, I allowe hym and gan hym thanke. *Ibid.* 248 a, Augustus..after gannyng hym thanke, commaunded, etc. **1566** DRANT *Horace's Sat.* I. i. E vij b, And cannes me litle thankes.

IV. ¶*Can, cannot, can be, can do*, may for the nonce be used substantively in obvious senses. Also *can-doing*; *can't-doing*; *can't-eat, can't-work*: one who cannot eat, work, etc.

1626 FENNER *Hidden Manna* (1652) 62 Hee hath still, in every action, more Can-does than Wil-does. **1644** HUNTON *Vindic. Treat. Monarchy* vi. 51 Sure, by *cannot*, he understands fallaciously, as he useth to doe, a *morall cannot.* **1839** CARLYLE *Chartism* iii. 124 Let a man honour his craftsman, his can-do. *Ibid.* v. (1858) 25 How can do, if we will well interpret it, unites itself with shall-do among mortals; how strength acts ever as the right-arm of justice. **1842** J. AITON *Cler. Econ.* iv. 204 Let me have a first-rate goer, a good 'can do',—not that I mean in general to ride fast. **1900** *Westm. Gaz.* 15 Dec. 1/3 Achievement..is open to fewer persons than can't-doing. *Ibid.* 2/1 That the art of can't-doing has sprung from (1) the difficulty; (2) the barrenness of can-doing. *Ibid.*, Can't-eat, when applied, say, to lobster, is one thing; can't-eat, when relating to bread, is quite another. **1904** *Daily Chron.* 24 Feb. 6/5 We have then the 'Can't Works'.

¶ See also CAN-YOU?.

† **can**, *v.*[2] (*pa. tense.*) *Obs.* Also 4 cun, cunne, 4–5 **kan, con, conne.** [In ME. and early mod.Eng. used for GAN, pa. t. of *ginnan* to begin: see GIN *v.* In the early MSS. of Cursor Mundi *gan* and *can* constantly interchange, but the evidence shows that *can* was fully established in northern use early in the 14th c., and its beginnings were evidently in the period before 1300, from which no northern documents survive. It was in its origin a variant of *gan*, apparently merely phonetic; in later times, when used as a simple auxiliary of tense, its identity with *gan* tended to be forgotten; it was, from its form and construction, curiously associated with the preceding verb CAN, and this occasionally led to a forgetfulness of its being a past tense, and to the substitution of *couth, coud, could*, the pa. t. of that verb. *Can* prevailed in northern and north midland poets till the 16th c., and in the end of that century it was greatly affected by Spenser and his fellow-archaists and followers. Its main function is now filled by *did*, though the original *gan* is still a favourite note of ballad poetry.]

1. A verb in the past tense meaning *gan*, i.e. began, fell, set, proceeded *to.* Followed by an infinitive with *to*, it was much less usual than *gan.*

a **1300** *Cursor M.* 13557 Fast þai can [*G.* gan, *F.* con *T.*, gon] on him to stare. **1423** JAS. I *Kingis Q.* iv, And than how he..In philosophy can him to confort. *c* **1470** HENRY *Wallace* IV. 98 And so on ane hys eyne he can [*ed.* **1648** began] to cast.

2. It was usually followed by an infinitive without *to*, and then approached or passed into a simple auxiliary of the past tense = the modern *did.*

a **1300** *Cursor M.* 758 Þe nedder ner-hand hir gun [*G.* gan, *F.* con, *T.* gon] draw. *Ibid.* 2009 A neu liuelade cun [*G.* gan, *F.* con, *T.* dud] þai bigin. *Ibid.* 6390 Moyses on þe roche kan stand. *Ibid.* 6462 Moses..fourti dais can [*G.* gan, *F.* con, *T.* gon] þer-on duell. *Ibid.* 12129 Ho! all þan cun [*F.* con, *G. T.* gan] þai cri. **1375** BARBOUR *Bruce* I. 330 Sone to paryss can he ga. *c* **1400** *Destr. Troy* 11258 Antenor titly con ryse, fferkyt on fote, & to þe fre sayde. *c* **1420** *Chron. Vilod.* 128 Þis pore mon toke þis bred and..on his way con passe. *c* **1420** *Sir Amadace* liii, The king toke Sir Amadace..And to him conne he say. **1513** DOUGLAS *Æneis* I. viii. 116 Thus said Ilioneus, and sa can he seis. *c* **1570** THYNNE *Pride & Lowl.* (1841) 7 And straightly with his armes he can me fold. **1590** SPENSER *F.Q.* I. i. 50 Tho can she weepe [*ed.* **1679** gan]. *Ibid.* I. vi. 23 Till to ryper yeares he gan aspire. **1602** DAVISON *Rhapsody* (1611) 37 Then gan his Teares so swiftly for to flow..Then blustring sighes to boistrously can blow.

†**b.** 16th c. Scotch *can do* = 'did' auxiliary.

1513 DOUGLAS *Æneis* VII. vi. 11 As scho fure Doun from the skyis, on fer can do [*ed.* **1553** gan do] espy. *Ibid.* VIII. vi. 57 He can do [*ed.* **1553** gan do] schaw the altaire.

¶**3.** Erroneous forms *couth, coud, could*: = 'did'. (See above.)

1375 BARBOUR *Bruce* III. 460 The croune, that Ihesu couth ber. *a* **1550** *Christis Kirke Gr.* xvi, The carlis with clubbis coud udir quell. *Ibid.* xxi, Ane bent a bow, sic sturt coud steir him. *c* **1450** HENRYSON *Mor. Fab.* 27 (Bannat. MS. 1568 On euery side full warely could hee wate.

can, *v.*[3] [f. CAN *sb.*[1]] **1. a.** To put in a can or cans; to preserve by sealing up air-tight in a can; 'to tin'. See CANNED, CANNING.

1861 *Trans. Ill. Agric. Soc.* IV. 511 Good fruit..is always marketable in large cities..and much will be dried, or canned, for export. **1871** *San Francisco Weekly Bulletin* 17 Nov. (Hoppe) Full directions for canning fruit. **1884** *Harper's Mag.* July 297/2 The..facilities for canning beef.

b. *transf.* and *fig.* Esp., to record or preserve on film or as a recording. Cf. CAN *sb.*[1] 3 c.

1865 *Atlantic Monthly* XV. 395/1 The copper vessel wherein Solomon had so cunningly 'canned' the rebellious Afrit. **1914** *Wireless World* July 246/1 In their efforts to 'can' colloquial expressions the students have issued a manifesto. **1935** *Punch* 23 Oct. 456/2 *Anna Karenina*..has been rapidly canned for Greta Garbo. **1936** [see AD-LIB *v.*]. **1940** H. G. WELLS *Babes in Darkling Wood* IV. i. 307 Ten or twelve [discourses] on fundamental ideas which have to be embalmed or canned or potted or whatever you like to call it, upon steel gramophone records. **1958** *Times* 28 July 9/6 The progress towards 'canning' television programmes.

c. *spec.* To cover (the fuel element in a nuclear reactor) with a protective jacket. (Cf. CAN *sb.*[1] 3 d).

1945 H. D. SMYTH *Devel. Methods of using Atomic Energy for Mil. Purposes* 87 No one..is likely to forget the 'canning' problem, i.e., the problem of sealing the uranium slugs in protective metal jackets. **1955** *Times* 18 Aug. 6/2 Zirconium is used in atomic plants for canning nuclear fuel elements. **1957** *Listener* 9 May 738/1 There is the metal used to enclose the uranium rods, to 'can' them as they say. At Windscale the canning was done with aluminium.

2. a. To discharge or suspend from a situation; to expel from school or college. *U.S. slang.*

1905 *Dialect Notes* III. 73 Jim..got canned for two weeks. **1911** H. QUICK *Yellowstone N.* ii. 37 Did you get canned for letting me in? **1914** G. ATHERTON *Perch of Devil* ii. 269 They would merely be..canned—I beg pardon, fired. **1937** J. STEINBECK *Of Mice & Men* 41 Won't ever get canned 'cause his old man's the boss.

b. To stop, leave off (something); to 'cut out'. *slang* (orig. *U.S.*).

1906 H. GREEN *At Actors' Boarding House* 187 'Now, see here; can that line o' comedy!' shouted Miss Gray. **1912** A. H. LEWIS *Apaches N.Y.* 20 'Can that black-jack guff,' he retorted. **1920** WODEHOUSE *Coming of Bill* I. ix. 99 Can the rough stuff, Colonel. **1934** G. B. SHAW *Too True to be Good* III. 79 Can all that stuff, Sergeant. **1953** 'E. FERRARS' *Murder in Time* ix. 78 Carver winced at the noise. 'Can that bloody row, can't you?' he grunted.

can, obs. form of KHAN[1].

cañ-: see CAN-. (In Spanish ñ is a distinct letter (called *enye*), with its own alphabetical place, between N and O.)

caña ('kænjə). [Sp., = cane.] A spirit resembling rum made from sugar cane.

1881 E. W. WHITE *Cameos fr. Silver-Land* I. 40 Caña (White Rum). **1904** GALLICHAN *Fishing Spain* 211 A poor substitute for whisky is the spirit called caña. **1918** *Blackw. Mag.* Apr. 446/1 Supper and the tot of caña sacred to such occasions. **1967** A. LICHINE *Encycl. Wines* 536/1 The Uruguayans distil quantities of brandy... Caña—a type of rum—is popular.

Canaan ('keɪnən). [ad. Heb. *k'naʕan*]. The ancient proper name of Western Palestine, promised to the Children of Israel; hence *fig.* (esp. in hymns and devotional use) land of promise, land of heavenly rest across the Jordan of death, heaven.

1637 T. MORTON (*title*) New English Canaan. **1772** W. WILLIAMS *Hymn*, '*Guide me O thou great Jehovah*', Land me safe on Canaan's side. **1807** SOUTHEY *Espriella's Lett.* (1814) III. 328 It [Spain] is also the Canaan of Physicians.

Canaanite ('keɪnənaɪt), *sb.*[1] [f. prec. + -ITE.]

1. A native of Canaan. *fig.* 'No true Israelite.'

1382 WYCLIF *Judg.* i. 32 He dwellid in the mydil of Chananei [**1388** in the myddis of Cananey]. **1535** COVERDALE *ibid.* But dwelt amonge the Cananites. **1605** *Tryall Chev.* II. i. in Bullen *O. Pl.* (1884) III. 285 What foolish Canaanits were they to run in debt to their eyes for an houres sleepe. **1727** DE FOE *Syst. Magic* I. i. (1840) 35.

2. (more properly **Cananæan**): One of a Jewish sect desperate and fanatical in its opposition to the Romans: *hence*, a zealot, a fanatic.

1611 BIBLE *Matt.* x. 4 The names of the twelue Apostles are these..Simon the Canaanite [**1881** *Revised*, Cananæan.]

Hence '**Canaanitess**, a woman of Canaan; **Canaa'nitic, Canaa'nitish** *adjs.*, belonging to Canaan; of or like a Canaanite. Also *fig.*

1621 AINSWORTH *Annot. Pentat.* Numb. xxvi. 13 [Saul] the sonne of a Canaanitesse. **1882–3** SCHAFF *Relig. Encycl.* II. 1151 The Jebusites were a Canaanitic tribe. **1535** COVERDALE *Gen.* xlvi. 10 The Cananitish woman. **1872** SPURGEON *Treas. Dav.* Ps. lx. 6 Let not Canaanitish doubts and legalisms keep thee out of the inheritance of grace.

'**canaanite**, *sb.*[2] *Min.* A variety of pyroxene consisting of a greyish- or bluish-white rock, found near Canaan, Ct., U.S.

1844 W. PHILLIPS *Min.* 89 Canaanite occurs very extensively at Canaan, Ct. **1868** DANA *Min.* (1880) 803 Canaanite is a whitish pyroxene rock..and constitutes ridges.

canaby(e, obs. North. form of CANOPY.

†**Canace** ('kænəsiː). *Obs. rare.* [L. *Canace* = Gr. *Κανακη*.] The daughter of Æolus, who committed incest; formerly taken typically.

1623 COCKERAM, *Canaces*, incestuous women. **1678** PHILLIPS s.v., They use to call an Incestuous Woman, *Canace.*

†'**canacin, 'canakin.** *Obs.*

1673 *Cant. Academy*, *Canakin*, the Plague. **1721–1800** BAILEY, *Canacin*, the Plague. *C*[*ountry word*].

†'**canacle, 'conacle.** *Obs. rare.* [Of unknown derivation and meaning.] ? A cup.

c **1325** *E.E. Allit. P.* B 1461 Þe coperounes of þe canacles þat on þe cuppe reres, Wer fetysely formed out in fylyoles longe. *Ibid.* 1515 Þer watz..Clatering of conacles þat kesten þo burdes.

Canada[1] ('kænədə). The name of a country in N. America.

1. Used *attrib.* in the names of various commercial products, animals, and plants, as *Canada agaric, goose, stag*, etc.; esp. **C. balsam**, a pale balsam or resin derived from *Abies balsamea*, and *A. canadensis*, used in medicine, and as a transparent gum for

mounting microscopic objects; **C. rice**, an aquatic grass (*Hydropyrum esculentum*), whose seeds feed great flocks of water-fowl, and are also used as food by the natives; **C. tea**, the leaves of *Gaultheria procumbens*, used to flavour tea, or as a substitute for it; Mountain Tea; **C. turpentine** = *Canada balsam*.

[**1624** CAPT. SMITH *Virginia* VI. 205, I had..called it New England, yet so long he [Thomas Hunt] and his Consorts drowned that name with the Eccho of Cannaday.]

1840 GOSSE *Canadian Nat.*, The bark of the fir or balsam is covered with bladders full of a fluid resin..this is the *Canada-balsam of the apothecaries. **1861** MISS PRATT *Flower. Pl.* III. 284 *Canada Flea-bane..a dull-looking plant, with small heads of dingy flowers. **1772** FORSTER *Hudson's Bay Birds* in *Phil. Trans.* LXII. 414 The *Canada geese are very plentiful at Hudson's Bay. **1838** *Penny Cycl.* XI. 308/1 The Canada Goose generally builds its nest on the ground. **1842** *Ibid.* XXIII. 120/1 This [*Surnia funerea*] is the..*Canada Owl of Latham. **1869** T. BURROUGHS in *Galaxy Mag.* Aug., The tree or *Canada-sparrow. **1837** *Penny Cycl.* VIII. 359/1 The French in America call this beast [*Cervus Wapiti*] the *Canada Stag.

2. *ellipt.* for *Canada goose.* Chiefly *N. Amer.*

1871 W. N. LEWIS *Poultry Bk.* 90 The America Wild Goose is identical with the Canada. **1922** H. BIGELOW *Scatter-gun Sk.* 109 The old Canada came down in a heap. **1955** W. G. HARDY *Alberta Golden Jubilee Anthol.* 378 Then it was mostly drakes you saw, or Canadas that had lost their mates. **1965** *Water Prey & Game Birds N. Amer.* (Nat. Geogr. Soc.) 138 Our local geese are Canadas — large honkers, brown with black necks and white cheeks. **1980** *Outdoor Life* (Northeast ed.) Oct. 84/2 Our huge population of Canadas is due to several factors.

‖**cañada**² (ka'ɲada). [a. Sp. *cañada* 'a dale between two mountains', f. *caño* tube, gutter, *caña* reed.] In the Western States of N. America: A narrow valley or glen; a ravine or small cañon.

1850 B. TAYLOR *Eldorado* xiii. (1862) 131 Descending a long cañada in the mountains. **1879** BEERBOHM *Patagonia* iv. 51 The cañada..was about a mile and a half broad. **1881** RAYMOND *Mining Gloss.*, *Cañada*, a ravine, or small cañon.

Canader (kə'neɪdə(r)). *University slang.* [f. CANAD(IAN + -ER⁶.] A Canadian canoe.

1893 H. W. GREENE in *Oxford Mag.* 18 May, Beneath the Magdalen shadows, We'll drift in a 'Canader' When afternoons are warm. **1899** A. D. GODLEY *Lyra Frivola* 24 O it's Youth in a Canader with the willow boughs to shade her. **1919** R. B. DAWSON *Light & Shade in Sarawak* iv. 33 'Get in carefully, old man,' said he; 'it's like climbing into a *Canader* at Oxford.'

Canadian (kə'neɪdɪən), *a.* and *sb.* [f. CANADA¹ + -IAN, after F. *canadien*] **A.** *adj.* Of or belonging to Canada or its people.

1568 HACKET tr. *Thevet's New found World* lxxvi. 123 *marg.*, The amiable maners of these Canadiens. *Ibid.* 124 *marg.*, How these Canadiens doe chase the dere & other wilde beastes. **1697** C. MATHER *Pietas* 103 How beneficial an Undertaking it would have been for them to have pursued the Canadien Business, for which the New-Englanders were now grown too Feeble. **1746** SHIRLEY *Let.* 21 Nov. in E. Richard *Acadia* (1895) I. xii. 221 Some allowance may likewise be made for their bad situation between Canadians, Indians and English. **1757** in *General Orders of 1757 issued by the Earl of Loudoun & P. Lyman* (1899) 121 Two Canadian Prisoners..confined in yᵉ Fort at Albany. **1774** J. LANGHORNE *Country Justice* I. 18 Cold on Canadian Hills, or Minden's Plain, Perhaps that Parent mourn'd her Soldier slain. *c* **1789** *Encycl. Brit.* (1797) IV. 76/2 The commodities required by the Canadians from Europe are, wine, or rather rum;..linen; and wrought iron. *Ibid.* 77/2 The many specimens of profit to be made by the Canadian trade, at last induced the public to think favourably of it. **1836** *Penny Cycl.* VI. 215/1 The Canadians further urge that the province contains no aristocracy. **1862** *Brit. Canad. Rev.* Dec. 3 Shall we become a united people, truly Canadian in principle? **1887** *Trans. Hist. & Sci. Soc. Manitoba* XXVIII. 14/2 Thirty years ago, we, who speak French, were called by every one purely and simply 'Canadians'; others were known as English, Scotch or Irish. Lately the fashion has grown up of calling others Canadians and distinguishing us as French. **1907** *Yesterday's Shopping* (1969) 15/1 Cheese.. Canadian Cheddar, first quality, white or coloured—lb 0/8½. **1925** J. JOLY *Surface-Hist. Earth* viii. 131 The mountains themselves have long ago been base-levelled by denudation to the existing peneplanes of the Canadian Shield, where they extend over an area of at least a million square miles. **1964** *English Studies* XLV. (Suppl.). 11 He has grouped languages of Canadian Indians together. **1969** *Nature* 6 Sept. 994/2 The Canadian mayflower (*Maianthemum canadense*)..is usually only found in cold, high altitudes.

B. *sb.* A native or inhabitant of Canada.

1805 L. in *Naval Chron.* XIV. 30 Canadian balsam..had been shipped. **1825** SCOTT *Let.* in *Lockhart* (1839) VII. 362, I can get the Canadian geese..from Mr. Murray. **1868** MRS. OLIPHANT *Brownlows* I. 127 The Canadian had crept into his good graces. **1876** BANCROFT *Hist. U.S.* IV. xiv. 415 The French Canadians of that day.

Canadiana (kəneɪdɪ'ɑːnə). [f. *Canada* + -IANA *suff.*] Things relating to or characteristic of Canada.

1837 W. B. WELLS (*title*) Canadiana. **1921** *Daily Colonist* (Victoria, B.C.) 27 Mar. 24/3 Many have kept all the series for future reference, indexing them in a scrap book and thus making a unique piece of Canadiana. **1966** *Times* (Canada Suppl.) 28 Feb. p. ix/3 Until a few years ago it was mostly Canadiana—paintings, artifacts..from the Old West. **1968** *Globe & Mail* (Toronto) 3 Feb. 28/4 The now famous Apple Rose which is pure Canadiana with apple.

Canadianism (kə'neɪdɪənɪz(ə)m). [f. CANADIAN *a.* and *sb.* + -ISM.] The condition of being Canadianized; the spirit of the Canadians; a Canadian idiom or word.

1875 *Canadian Monthly* Nov. 429/2 In other words, the feeling of Canadianism is not yet sufficiently strong to override all conflicting local feelings and interests. **1899** *Daily News* 17 Nov. 6/6 He declares that Afrikanderdom is the very opposite to Canadianism. **1906** *Westm. Gaz.* 20 May 12/1 What is called Canadianism may grow more pronounced with the growth of population. **1926** *Brit. Weekly* 20 May 130/5 A flat in Charing Cross-road, London, from which he cultivated his virile Canadianism. **1928** *Daily Express* 4 Dec. 10/3 Perhaps one of the most descriptive Canadianisms is the word 'kick' instead of thrill. **1958** *Times* 24 Nov. p. iii/2 The feeling of unity and national identity and..other less tangible aspects of Canadianism.

Canadianize (kə'neɪdɪənaɪz), *v.* [f. CANADIAN + -IZE.] *trans.* To render Canadian in character. Also *intr.* Hence **Ca,nadiani'zation**.

1829 J. MACTAGGART *Three Years in Canada* I. 37 Some of the unthinking Scotch ape the manners of the latter [English], and are termed *Canadianized Scotchmen.* **1902** *Monthly Rev.* Oct. 55 When he calls himself 'French-Canadian', he simply wants to differentiate his racial origin from that of his English, Scotch, or Irish fellow citizens, who, in his mind, are but partially *Canadianised.* **1925** *Contemp. Rev.* Nov. 605 They are in process of rapid 'Canadianisation'. **1964** *Economist* 21 Mar. 1134/3 Corporations..will..have their own incentive to 'Canadianise'. *Ibid.*, Firms that do meet the requirements of Canadianisation.

‖**Canadien** (kanadjɛ̃), *sb.* and *a.* fem. **Canadienne** (-jɛn). [Fr., = Canadian.] **A.** *sb.* A French Canadian. (Cf. quot. 1568 s.v. CANADIAN *a.* and *sb.*) **B.** *adj.* French-Canadian.

1832 *Vindicator* (Montreal) 9 Mar. 2/5 [He] justly remarks that the Canadiens have good grounds for complaining. *Ibid.*, No man who feels as a Briton ought to feel would have thus prostituted a Canadien press. **1863** E. H. WALSHE *Cedar Creek* 82 The aged Canadienne arose, with the politeness so natural to her Gallic descent, and bade them welcome. **1906** *Daily Colonist* (Victoria, B.C.) 20 Jan. 8/1 (Advt.), This pretty Canadienne saved from terrible kidney disease by 'Fruit-a-tives'. **1952** D. HOFFMAN *Paul Bunyan* iv. 97 The idea persists that the origin of Paul Bunyan must be in *Canadien* folk tradition. **1958** *Times Lit. Suppl.* 31 Jan. 55/3 Some of the most important married into important 'Canadien' families. **1960** *Guardian* 5 Nov. 7/2 The 'Canadiens', the most self-centred, tenacious, clannish of minorities. **1963** *Western Weekly Suppl.* 13 Mar. 6/1 Louis loved his horses..almost as much as he did his petite Canadienne wife.

†**ca'nadoe.** *Obs. rare.* (? Drink from a CAN.)

1610 *Histrio-m.* ii. 104 And now, my maisters, in this bravadoe, I can read no more without Canadoe. *Omnes.* What ho! some Canadoe quickly!

'canage¹ ('keɪnɪdʒ). *Sc.* [f. *cane*, CAIN + -AGE.] The payment of cain; amount of cain paid.

1597 SKENE *Exp. Terms*, Canage of woll or hides is taken for the custome theirof.

'canage². *nonce-wd.* [f. CANE *sb.*¹; a humorous nonce-word formed after *vintage.*] A 'harvest of canes', i.e. a copious caning.

1881 HALES in *Antiquary* Nov. 190/1 Plautus's Virgidemia (a canage) a comical analogue of Vindemia (a vintage).

‖**ca'naglia.** *Obs. rare.* Also **canalia.** [a. It. *canaglia*; see CANAILLE.] = CANAILLE.

1605 B. JONSON *Volpone* II. ii. 73 Clamours of the Canaglia. **1681** RYCAUT *Critick* 231 Not trusting to these vile Canalia. *a* **1734** NORTH *Exam.* II. iv. ¶141. 306 Low Plebeian Invention, proper only for a Canaglia of Poltroons.

canaigre (kə'neɪgə(r)). [Mexican Sp.] A species of dock, *Rumex hymenosepalus*, which is grown on sandy soils from Texas to Lower California, and whose roots are rich in tannin; also, the tannin obtained from this plant.

1878 *Rep. Comm. Agric.* (U.S.) 119 In many respects cañaigre root resembled rhubarb. **1884** *Encycl. Brit.* XVII. 401/2 The cañaigre has long been known to possess powerful tanning properties. **1901** *Westm. Gaz.* 21 Oct. 5/1 A plant indigenous to New Mexico, Arizona, and Lower California, known as Rumex hymenosepalus, or 'canaigre'. **1902** *Encycl. Brit.* XXV. 629/1 Considerable promise attends..the experiments upon canaigre as a source of tannin. **1959** P. A. MUNZ *California Flora* 358 *R[umex] hymenosepalus*... Canaigre. Wild-Rhubarb... The dry roots contain as much as 35% tannin.

‖**canaille** (ka'nɑj, -'eɪl). Also 7 **canaile, cannale,** 8 **kennel,** 9 *Sc.* **cannailyie, canalyie.** [a. F. *canaille*, ad. It. *canaglia* (Sp. *canalla*, Pg. *canalha*), f. *cane*, L. *can-is* dog, with collective suffix, *lit.* 'pack of dogs'. In 17th and 18th c. app. naturalized; now again consciously used as French. The It. form was in earlier use: see CANAGLIA.] A contemptuous name given to the populace; the 'vile herd', vile populace; the rabble, the mob.

1676 ETHEREDGE *Man of Mode* V. i. (1684) 66 Let the Canaile wait as they should do. **1679** PENN *Addr. Prot.* I. 26 This Shameful Impiety..has not only prevailed with the Populace, the Cannale, the Vulgar. **1748** RICHARDSON *Clarissa* (1811) II. 73 Faulty morals deservedly..bring down rank and birth to the canaille. **1792** *Gentl. Mag.* LXII. I. 6 Like true Canaille..literally, a parcel of Dogs. **1805** J. NICOL *Poems* I. 37 (Jam.) The hale cannailyie, risin, tried In vain to end their gabblin. **1845** DISRAELI *Sybil* 103 Railroads ..and manufactories..are enterprises for the canaille, and I hate them in my heart.

b. A pack.

168. *Fears & Jeal. Ceas'd* 4 A most Powerful Party.. enrag'd against the whole Canaille of these Miscreants.

canakin, var. of CANIKIN.

canal (kə'næl), *sb.* Forms: 6 canall, 6–7 canale, 7 canalle, (cannal), 5, 7– canal. [a. F. *canal* (16th c. in Littré), a refashioning, after L. *canāl-em* or It. *canale*, of the earlier F. *chenal* (*chanel*, *chenel*): see CANNEL, CHANNEL. (The 15th c. instance may be from L.) The words *canel*, CANNEL, and *chanel*, CHANNEL, from the same Latin source, but immediately from old French, were in much earlier use in Eng.: when *canal* was introduced it was to some extent used as a synonym of these, but the forms were at length differentiated.

(There was an OF. (Picard) *canal*, a variant of *canel*, in the 12th c., but this had nothing to do with the 16th c. *canal* of literary French.)]

†**1.** A pipe used for conveying water or liquid; also a tube, or tubular cavity. *Obs.*

c **1449** PECOCK *Repr.* V. iii. 497 As thoruȝ a pipe or a canal. **1578** T. N. tr. *Conq. W. India* 193 The water is brought.. in two pipes or Canalls. **1601** HOLLAND *Pliny* II. 467 These canales (as I may so say of gold ore) follow the veins of such marble and stone in the quarry. **1626** BACON *Sylva* §138 If the sound which would scatter in open Air be made to go all into a Canale, it must needs give greater force to the Sound. **1670** E. KING in *Phil. Trans.*, [They, a sort of Wild Bee] first bore a Canale in the Stock. **1698** KEILL *Exam. The. Earth* (1734) 95 We take the Diameters and Axis..as small Canals or Tubes.

2. *Phys.* A tubular cavity in the body of an animal or in the tissues of a plant; a duct; as the ***alimentary canal***, the ***Haversian canals*** of the bones, the ***semicircular canals*** of the ear, etc. Rarely applied to small tubular passages in inorganic substances. (The second sense in current use.)

1626 BACON *Sylva* §30 A small Quantity of Spirits, in the Cels of the Braine, and Cannals of the Sinewes, are able to move the whole Body. *a* **1711** KEN *Hymnar.* Poet. Wks. 1721 II. 25 Through ev'ry soft Canal, Make vital Spirits sail. **1748** HARTLEY *Observ. Man* I. i. §1 ¶5. 27 The Cavities of the Vestibulum, semicircular Canals, and Cochlea [of the ear]. **1764** REID *Inquiry* iii. Wks. I. 115/2 The entrance of the alimentary canal..the entrance of the canal for respiration. **1801** *Med. Jrnl.* V. 172 The duplicature of membrane within the cranium and spinal canal. **1866** HUXLEY *Phys.* xii. (1869) 318 All bones, except the smallest, are traversed by small canals..These are called Haversian canals. **1869** PHILLIPS *Vesuv.* xi. 308 We found it [Vesuvian lava] pipy or full of canals.

†**3.** A water-course, a CHANNEL generally. *Obs.* (exc. as influenced by sense 6).

1538 LELAND *Itin.* II. 72 The..canales of eche partes of Sowey river kept from abundance of wedes. **1674** PETTY *Disc. bef. R. Soc.* 37 The different Velocity of Bodies.. experimented in large Canales, or Troughs of water, fitted with a convenient Apparatus for that purpose. **1756** WATSON in *Phil. Trans.* XLIX. 900 One of the canals, which carries off the waste water from the baths. **1771** CAVENDISH *ibid.* LXI. 607 The fluid shall be able to pass readily from one body to the other by that canal. **1860** TYNDALL *Glac.* II. §25. 366 We could see the water escape from it [moulin] through a lateral canal at its bottom.

†**4.** *Geog.* A (comparatively) narrow piece of water connecting two larger pieces; a strait. *Obs.*; now CHANNEL.

1686 *Lond. Gaz.* No. 2119/2 The Canal of the Black Sea near to Scutaret. **1704** *Collect. Voy. & Trav.* III. 32/1 In the Canal of Bahama. **1716** *Lond. Gaz.* No. 5473/1 The Turkish Fleet having entred the Canal of Corfu. **1750** BEAWES *Lex Mercat.* (1752) 8 In the bottom of the Adriatick Sea there were a quantity of small marshy isles, separated only by narrow canals. **1829** *Sun* 17 Sept. 1/5 The canal of Constantinople, or of the Bosphorus, gives vent to the waters of the Black Sea, which flow..by the canal of the Dardanelles or of the Hellespont.

†**5.** A long and narrow piece of water for the ornamentation of a garden or park. [App. directly from 17th c. French; see Littré.] *Obs.*

1663–4 PEPYS *Diary* 14 Mar., My Lord Southampton's canalle. **1666** *Ibid.* 15 July, Walked to the Park; and there (it being mighty hot, and I weary,) lay down by the Canalle. **1725** H. DE SAUMAREZ in *Phil. Trans.* XXXIII. 412 Having a Boat on the Canal in St. James's Park. **1725** *Lond. Gaz.* No. 6388/3 A Canal or Fish-Pond well stocked. **1751** JOHNSON *Rambl.* No. 142 ¶4 The wall which inclosed the gardens..and the canals. **1827** HONE *Every-day Bk.* II. 102 Skating..on the Canal in St. James's..park.

6. a. An artificial watercourse constructed to unite rivers, lakes, or seas, and serve the purposes of inland navigation. (The chief modern sense, which tends to influence all the others.)

1673 TEMPLE *United Prov.* iii. (R.) The great rivers, and the strange number of canals that are found in this province. **1703** L. HUDDLESTON (*title*) Method of conveying Boats or Barges from a higher to a lower level on Canals. **1797** J. RENNIE (*title*) Report concerning a Canal proposed between Edinburgh and Glasgow. **1836** *Penny Cycl.* V. 426/1 Shortly after this (1756) Brindley was consulted by he Duke of Bridgewater on the practicability of constructing a canal from Worsley to Manchester. **1857** BUCKLE *Civilis.* I. iii. 142 If we have no rivers, we make Canals.

transf. **1868** G. DUFF *Pol. Surv.* 176 From the basin of the Orinoco, the wonderful natural canal of the Cassiquiare leads us straight into the Rio Negro.

b. Any of the faint seasonal markings of doubtful nature observed on the planet Mars.

A misleading rendering of It. *canali* (Schiaparelli) = channels.

1888 *Edin. Rev.* Jan. 26 Indications derived as to the nature of the mysterious Martian canals. **1891** E. DUNKIN *Midnight Sky* 253 Networks of dark lines, to which Schiaparelli has given the name of 'canals', were noticed by him, in 1877 and 1882, to overspread the continents .. of the planet. **1926** H. MACPHERSON *Mod. Astr.* iv. 56 These lines he [*sc.* Schiaparelli] designated by the Italian word 'canali', which actually means 'channels', but was translated into English as 'canals'. **1969** *Times* 19 Feb. 13/4 The close-ups will pick out detail down to 900 ft. across and may resolve the question of the curious linear markings nicknamed canals.

†**7.** *fig.* A medium of communication, means, agency. *Obs.*; now CHANNEL.

1722 WODROW *Corr.* (1843) II. 658 You will not fail to send .. a full account of your Synod, and I shall be a canal to your friends at Edinburgh. **1751** SMOLLETT *Per. Pic.* III. lxxxiv, Ignorant of the canal through which he obtained that promotion. **1779** SIR W. HAMILTON in *Phil. Trans.* LXX. 43 The Royal Society .. through the respectable canal of its worthy president.

8. *Arch.* Applied to various semi-tubular grooves: see quot. More commonly CHANNEL. [These uses already in Latin, in Vitruvius.]

1727–51 CHAMBERS *Cycl.* s.v. **1876** GWILT *Archit.* Gloss., *Canal*, .. the flutings of a column or pilaster. The *canal of the volute* is the spiral channel, or sinking on its face, commencing at the eye, and following in the revolutions of the volute. The *canal of the larmier* is the channel or groove sunk on its soffite to throw off the rain.

9. *Zool.* The groove in the shells of certain univalve molluscs, for the protrusion of the siphon or breathing tube. (The third current sense.)

1835 [see CANALIFEROUS]. **1854** WOODWARD *Mollusca* 34 Protected by the canal of the shell.

10. *Comb.*, as *canal-barge*, *-boat*, *-bridge*, *-carrier*, *-lock*, *-man*, *-watered* adj.; **canal-built** *a.*, of a build adapted to canal navigation; **canal-cell** (*Bot.*), a cell in the archegonium of Vascular Cryptogams, which ultimately forms the canal through which fertilization takes place; **canal incline**, **canal-lift**, an incline or elevator used instead of a lock for transferring canal-boats from one level to another; **canal rays** [tr. G. *kanalstrahlen* (Goldstein 1886, in *Berl. Ber.* XXXIX. 691)]: from the openings in the cathode through which the ions pass, = *positive rays*; **canal-ways** *adv.*

1842 DICKENS *Amer. Notes* (1850) 104/2 The passengers being .. taken on afterwards by another *canal-boat. **1843** LEVER *J. Hinton* xix. (1878) 131, I started from Portobello in the canal-boat. **1819** *Post Off. Lond. Direct.* 319 *Canal-carriers to Manchester, Liverpool, and Staffordshire Potteries. **1875** BENNET & DYER *Sachs' Bot.* II. iv. 336 The *canal-cell penetrates between the rows of cells of the neck and becomes converted into mucilage. **1882** L. F. VERNON-HARCOURT *Rivers & Canals* I. 102 *Canal inclines are similar to inclines so common in mines. **1902** *Encycl. Brit.* XXVI. 555/1 Canal inclines were early adopted on canals where loss of water in lockage was of importance. **1858** SIMMONDS *Dict. Trade*, *Canal-lift. **1876** *Min. Proc. Instit. Civ. Eng.* XLV. 107 Hydraulic Canal Lift at Anderton, on the River Weaver. **1828** *Fall Brunswick Theatre* I Rivermen, *canalmen, and their families. **1904** RUTHERFORD in *Technics* July 12/2 The rays from radium are very similar to those produced when a strong electric discharge is sent through a vacuum tube... The *a* rays are very analogous to the '*canal' rays discovered by Goldstein. **1957** *Encycl. Brit.* XVIII. 882C/1 Goldstein first observed .. streams of luminous gas back of a perforated cathode .. as if .. ionizing particles were coming through the holes .. and ionizing the gas... These radiations .. were first called *kanalstrahlen*, or canal rays. **1869** *Notes N.-W. Prov. India* 86 Assessing *canal-watered estates to the land revenue. **1831** GEN. P. THOMPSON *Exerc.* (1842) I. 350 If the Chinese .. have conveyed their moral government *canal-ways to the other side of the Great Wall.

ca'nal, *v. rare* [f. prec. sb.] *trans.* To make a canal through; to furnish with canals. Also, to make (a river, etc.) navigable by furnishing it with locks like a canal.

1819 E. DANA *Geogr. Sketches* 20 The operation of canalling and locking the falls. **1870** EMERSON *Soc. & Solit.* vii. 131 Canalling the American Isthmus. **1876** C. WARNER *Winter on Nile* i. 18 All canaled and railwayed. **1905** *Daily Chron.* 29 July 9/2 The river .. has now been canalled, and is controlled by fourteen locks.

ca'nalage. *rare*⁻¹. [f. CANAL *sb.* + -AGE.] The construction of canals; canal-work.

1854 *Chamb. Jrnl.* 211 This extensive system of canalage.

canal-bone, -coal, var. CANNEL-BONE, -COAL.

canalia: see CANAGLIA.

canalicular (kænə'lɪkjʊlə(r)), *a. Nat. Hist.* [ad. mod.L. *canāliculāris*, f. *canālicul-us*; see below. Cf. F. *canaliculaire.*] Of, pertaining to, or resembling a canaliculus; minutely tubular.

1878 BELL *Gegenbauer's Comp. Anat.* 144 The special metamorphoses of the fibres into canalicular, or flattened cylindrical forms.

cana'liculate, *a. Nat. Hist.* [ad. mod.L. *canāliculāt-us*, f. *canāliculus*. In mod.F. *canaliculé.*] Having a longitudinal groove or hollow; minutely channelled.

1828 KIRBY & SP. *Entomol.* III. xxix. 183 They are all canaliculate. **1852** DANA *Crust.* I. 446 Tarsus of third pair of legs long, canaliculate. *Ibid.* 541 The beak .. is canaliculate or longitudinally concave. **1880** GRAY *Bot. Text-bk.* 401 *Canaliculate*, channelled, or with a longitudinal groove.

cana'liculated, *ppl. a.* = prec.; also, striated with minute grooves or flutings; also, pierced with a minute canal.

1761 DA COSTA in *Phil. Trans.* LII. 446 A kind of crystals canaliculated, or striated lengthwise. **1828** STARK *Elem. Nat. Hist.* II. 37 Shell .. canaliculated at the base. **1849** RUSKIN *Sev. Lamps* iv. §2. 95 The fluting of the column .. feebly resembled many canaliculated organic structures. **1882** C. C. HOPLEY *Snakes* xix. 372 Redi .. observed the canal .. in the fang .. and that these canaliculated teeth .. were for the conveyance of the venom.

,canalicu'lation. *Nat. Hist.* [see prec. and -ATION.] A canaliculate formation; a minute channelling or grooving.

1880 R. B. WATSON in *Jrnl. Linn. Soc.* XV. No. 82. 98 The slight canaliculation in which the mouth terminates. *Ibid.* XV. No. 87. 406 A very slight canaliculation on the suture.

ca'nalicule. [so in Fr.] = CANALICULUS 2.

1839 TODD *Cycl. Anat.* III. 91/2 The lacrymal canalicules.

‖**canaliculus** (kænə'lɪkjʊləs). Pl. canaliculi. [a. L. *canāliculus*, dim. of *canālis* pipe, groove, channel. The 16th c. plurals in *-icoli*, *-icolos* in Shute appear due to an It. *canalicolo.*]

†**1.** *Arch.* A groove, fluting, channel. (See CANAL and CHANNEL.) *Obs.*

1563 SHUTE *Arch.* C iij a, If your pillor shall haue *Canaliculos*. *Ibid.* C iij b, The *Canalicoli*, standing vpright within the Triglyphi. *Ibid.* D iij b, If this piller be garnished and filled with *Canaliculi*.

2. *Phys.* A small canal or duct; applied esp. to the minute tubes connecting the lacunæ in the bones, and to the lachrymal canals connecting each lachrymal sac with the eye-lids.

[**1727–51** CHAMBERS *Cycl.*, Canalis or *Canaliculus arteriosus*.] **1854** J. HOGG *Microsc.* I. ii. (1867) 67 The lacunæ and canaliculi of bone-structure. **1875** H. WALTON *Dis. Eye* 471 The division of a canaliculus.

canaliferous (kænə'lɪfərəs), *a. Nat. Hist.* [f. mod.L. *canālifer* (f. *canālis* channel + *-fer* producing) + -OUS. Cf. F. *canalifère.*] Having or bearing a canal: said of shells of molluscs.

1835 KIRBY *Hab. & Inst. Anim.* I. ix. 296 Lamarck's canaliferous Zoophagans, called so from the long straight canal which terminates the mouth of their shells. **1856–8** W. CLARK *Van der Hoeven's Zool.* I. 796 Shell spiral, with aperture entire, not canaliferous.

canaliform (kə'nælɪfɔːm), *a.* [f. L. *canalis* CANAL *sb.* + -FORM.] Having the form of, or resembling, a canal.

1826 KIRBY & SPENCE *Entomol.* IV. xlvi. 349 *Canaliform* .., when it [*sc.* the postscutellum] is a deepish elongate channel running from the postdorsolum to the abdomen. **1830** R. KNOX tr. *Béclard's Anat.* 132 The villosities do not appear conical, or cylindrical, or canaliform. **1926** H. MACPHERSON *Mod. Astr.* v. 75 Canaliform appearances.

canalization (,kænəlaɪ'zeɪʃən, kə,nælɪ'zeɪʃən). [f. CANALIZE + -ATION; or a. mod.F. *canalisation.*]

1. A furnishing with canals; the cutting of a canal through (an isthmus, etc.), the making (a river, etc.) into a canal; the construction of canals.

1844 *Blackw. Mag.* LVI. 193 A plan of canalization for the Hellenic kingdom. **1858** *Times* 26 Nov. 7/3 The canalization of the Isthmus [of Suez] .. may well cause hesitation. **1880** *Law Reports, 13 Chanc. Div.* 4 The canalisation of the rapids.

2. *Phys.* and *Pathol.* The formation of a canal or canals in the living organism: see also quot. 1881.

1876 tr. *Wagner's Gen. Pathol.* 203 Canalisation of the embolus .. leading to the permeability of the obstructed part. **1881** *Syd. Soc. Lex.*, *Canalisation*, the conversion of a vessel, especially a vein, into a rigid tube. Also, the boring through a structure, as of the prostate gland.

3. *transf.* A furnishing with (underground) ducts or channels for the conveyance of cables, etc.

1889 *Daily News* 7 Oct. 3/1 This is what Mr. Crompton, borrowing a French expression, calls his system of under-surface 'canalization'.

4. *fig.*

1929 *Atlantic Monthly* Sept. 387/1 He [*sc.* William James] went on to say that the 'canalization of pity was an engineering feat'. **1950** *Brit. Birds* XLIII. 344 On the West Coast a 'canalisation' of Gannets from various stations.

canalize ('kænəlaɪz), *v.* [f. CANAL *sb.* + -IZE: mod.F. *canaliser* was perh. the immediate source.]

1. *trans.* **a.** To cut a canal through; to furnish with canals. **b.** To make like a canal; to convert (a river) into a canal.

1860 PUSEY *Min. Proph.* 142 This system of canalising Egypt. **1865** *Times* 23 Mar. 10/6 The St. Lawrence .. has been canalized for such parts of its course as were naturally unfit for navigation. **1870** *Athenæum* 26 Feb. 299 We do not desire so to 'canalize' the Thames, as our neighbours have 'canalized' the Seine.

2. *Phys.* and *Pathol.*

1876 tr. *Wagner's Gen. Pathol.* 199 The symptoms .. of thrombosis disappear .. if the thrombus is reabsorbed or is sufficiently canalized.

3. *transf.* To furnish with (underground) ducts or channels for the conveyance of cables, etc.; to convey through cables so furnished.

1886 *Jrnl. Soc. Telegr. Engineers* XV. 547 Electricity, to use a French phrase, is so easily 'canalised', or conveyed through insulated conductors. **1889** *Daily News* 7 Oct. 3/1 He has 'canalized' nearly the whole length of the principal streets in the South Kensington-Knightsbridge region.

4. *fig.* **a.** To lead in a desired direction, so as to control or regulate.

1922 J. M. MUIR *Short Hist. Brit. Commonw.* II. IX. v. 359 The development of means for 'canalising' the nation's unspent wealth. **1943** H. READ *Politics of Unpolitical* II. 23 Organizations designed to canalize the national spirit. **1945** R. KNOX *God & Atom* x. 133 The urge to which it gave rise in the patient's nature may be canalized in a new direction. **1965** W. LAMB *Posture & Gesture* viii. 107 It is a pity that the new thinking on physical behaviour has become canalised to such an extent into the teaching of physical education as a subject.

b. *intr.* To take a certain direction, to form a channel.

1927 *Observer* 13 Nov. 8/5 A latent crisis in civilisation, a crisis which should have canalised into a religious revolution.

Hence **'canalized** *ppl. a.*

1855 *Househ. Wds.* XII. 54 The canalised river. **1885** *Athenæum* 605/2 Slowly descending the canalized Seine.

canaller (kə'nælə(r)). *colloq.* [f. CANAL + -ER¹.]

a. A person who works or lives in a canal-boat. **b.** A canal-boat. (Chiefly *U.S.*)

1864 T. S. NICHOLS *40 Yrs. Amer. Life* II, Steamboat men, sailors, canallers. **1884** *San Francisco Chron.* Aug., The 'canaler's' family is seen on deck. **1887** *Century Mag.* Aug. 487 Near the bow of each canaler was a lantern.

†**ca'nalliary.** *Obs. rare*⁻¹. [f. *canaglia* or *canaille* (q.v.) + -RY.] = CANAILLE (collectively).

1600 O. E. *Repl. Libel* I. viii. 210 Moriscoes and Negroes, and horseboies, and such Canalliary.

canalling (kə'nælɪŋ), *vbl. sb.* [f. CANAL *sb.* and *v.* + -ING¹.] **a.** The construction of a canal; canal-making; canal-work. **b.** Travelling or doing business by canal; canal traffic.

1834 *Chamb. Jrnl.* I. 40 The longest piece of canalling required to open the whole line. **1885** *Harper's Mag.* May 858/2 The journey .. is made up of twenty miles of .. canalling. **1885** *Graceville* (Minnesota) *Transcript* 3 Jan. 2/1 They say the days of canaling are over .. The railroads .. have taken all that business.

canalure, obs. form of CANNELURE.

canalyie, Sc. form of CANAILLE.

†**'canamell.** *Obs.* Also 5 **galamelle**. [ad. med.L. *cannamella* sugar-cane, f. *canna* cane + *mel* honey. Cf. CARAMEL.] The sugar-cane.

c **1400** MAUNDEV. xii. 141 Made of Galamelle; and that is that men maken Sugar of. **1506** GUYLFORDE *Pilgr.* (1851) 47 Infynyte plente of vynes, olyffe, fygges, and canamells.

canape, -pie, -py, obs. ff. CANOPY.

canapé ('kænəpɪ). [Fr. (both senses).]

1. A piece of bread or toast, etc., on which small savouries are served.

1890 *Mrs. Beeton's Cookery Bk.* 759/1 Anchovy Canapés. **1908** *Daily Chron.* 10 Apr. 7/5 As an appetiser nothing is better than a canape of chicken. **1955** J. CANNAN *Long Shadows* i. 11 She had sipped, smoked, examined pictures, nibbled canapés, moved here and there.

2. A sofa.

1892 F. LITCHFIELD *Illustr. Hist. Furn.* vi. 167 (*caption*) Carved and Gilt Canapé or sofa. **1955** R. FASTNEDGE *Eng. Furn. Styles* vi. 144 Settees .. were produced in emulation of Louis XV *canapés*.

‖**canard** (kanar, kə'nɑːd), *sb.* [Fr.; lit. 'duck'; also used in sense 1: see note there.]

1. An extravagant or absurd story circulated to impose on people's credulity; a hoax, a false report.

Littré says *Canard* for a silly story comes from the old expression 'vendre un canard à moitié' (to half-sell a duck), in which *à moitié* was subsequently suppressed. It is clear that to half-sell a duck is not to sell it at all; hence the sense 'to take in, make a fool of'. In proof of this he cites *bailleur de canards*, deliverer of ducks, utterer of *canards*, of date 1612: Cotgr., 1611, has the fuller *vendeur de canards a moitié* 'a cousener, guller, cogger; foister, lyer'. Others have referred the word to an absurd fabricated story purporting to illustrate the voracity of ducks, said to have gone the round of the newspapers, and to have been credited by many. As this account has been widely circulated, it is possible that it has contributed to render the word more familiar, and thus more used, in English.

[I saw the word in print before 1850 (J.A.H.M.).]

1864 in WEBSTER. **1866** *Even. Standard* 13 July 6 A silly canard circulated by the *Owl*, about England having joined France and Russia in 'offering' their mediation to the belligerents. **1880** W. DAY *Racehorse in Train.* xix. 185 The canards so industriously circulated as to the real cause of the deadly opposition he had met with.

2. A smaller surface on an aeroplane or hydrofoil providing stability or a means of control and placed forward of the main lifting

surface; also (and orig.) an aeroplane with its wings so placed. Also *attrib.*

1916 H. BARBER *Aeroplane Speaks* 137 *Canard*, literally 'duck', the name which was given to a type of aeroplane of which the longitudinal stabilizing surface (*empennage*) was mounted in front of the main lifting surface. **1928** C. F. S. GAMBLE *North Sea Air Station* Introd. 11 These monoplanes were of the 'Canard' (or 'tail first') type. **1931** *Flight* 2 Jan. 4/1 His brother experimented with canard models. **1961** *New Scientist* 16 Nov. 416/3 Most tentative designs for a Mach 3 liner provide for a canard form with the main wing at the rear. **1964** *Sci. Amer.* June 27/3 SCAT 17 is a delta-wing design with a canard, or balancing surface, at the nose. **1967** *Jane's Surface Skimmer Systems 1967–68* 95/2 The foils have been arranged..in a canard configuration, with one foil forward and two foils aft.

3. A bright, deep blue, like the colour which is found on a duck's wing.

[**1902** *Daily Chron.* 13 Dec. 8/4 The peculiar bright, yet deep, blue known in Paris as 'canard'.] **1908** *Westm. Gaz.* 22 Feb. 13/2 *Canard*—a new shade of blue inspired by the lovely patch of iridescent greeny blue that occurs on a duck's wing. **1923** *Daily Mail* 21 June 1 Over 40 shades including Ivory,..Apricot, Canard.

canard (kəˈnɑːd), *v.* [f. prec. sb.; in sense 2, a. F. *canarde-r.*]

1. *intr.* To fly abroad as a false report.

1862 RUSSELL in *Times* 27 Mar., Stories of all sorts last week respecting his resignation..which may be heard canarding about in the halls of the hotels.

2. To make a harsh sound like the cry of a duck, on a wind-instrument.

1841 *Fraser's Mag.* XXIII. 399 A ragged starveling, canarding on a clarionet.

Canarese, var. KANARESE.

Canarian (kəˈnɛəriən), *a.* and *sb.* [f. CANARY *sb.* + -IAN.] **A.** *adj.* Of or pertaining to the Canary Islands. **B.** *sb.* A Canary Islander.

1793 *Sporting Mag.* II. 23/2 His name, Ardagoma, signifies, in the Canarian language, shoulders of rock. *Ibid.* 24/1 These Canarians have given such remarkable proofs of their athletic powers. **1871** F. LOCOCK tr. *Pégot-Ogier's Fortunate Isles* I. vii. 97 The Canarians burning and plundering the ships. *Ibid.* xix. 304 Canarian ladies are not fond of walking. **1922** D. A. BANNERMAN *Canary Islands* i. 13 Carrying with him a number of the Canarians as captives. *Ibid.* iii. 57 The commoner forms of Canarian bird-life.

canariensis (kənɛərɪˈɛnsɪs). [app. popular alteration of the specific name *canariense* in *Tropæolum canariense*, a former systematic name of *T. aduncum*. (*Canariensis* occurs as the specific name of canary seed, *Phalaris canariensis*, and canary wood, *Persea canariensis*.)] Canary-creeper, *Tropæolum aduncum*.

1897 *Hearth & Home* 3 June 174/2, I have them [*sc.* tubs] filled with multi-coloured dwarf Nasturtiums, round which at the edges trailed Canariensis. **1908** *Daily News* 21 Sept. 4/2 They frequently attack both the nasturtium..and the canariensis. **1929** W. DEEPING *Roper's Row* xxiv. 260 She bought canariensis and climbing nasturtiums.

canary (kəˈnɛərɪ), *sb.* Forms: (6 canara), 6–7 canarie, (7 canari, cannaries, 8 kanary, canario), 7- canary. [a. F. *Canarie*, ad. Sp. *Canaria*, in L. *Canāria insula* 'Isle of Dogs' one of the Fortunate Isles, so called from its large dogs (*canāri-us* of or pertaining to dogs, f. *can-is* dog, Pliny), whence *Canāriæ insulæ* as the name of the group in Arnobius *c.* 300.]

The name of an island (*Gran Canaria*) on the west coast of Africa, and of the group Canary Isles or Canaries, to which it belongs. Hence in various uses, originally *attrib.*, but subseq. taken as sbs.

1. A lively Spanish dance, the idea of which is said to have been derived from the aborigines of the Canary Islands. In early use generally plural.

1592 NASHE *P. Penilesse* (ed. 2) 18 b, As gingerly as if she were dancing the Canaries. **1601** SHAKS. *All's Well* II. i. 77 A medicine That's able to breath life into a stone..and make you dance Canari. **1606** DEKKER *Sev. Sins* III. (Arb.) 27 They would make all the Hogges-heads that vse to come to the house, to daunce the Cannaries till they reeld againe. **1655** *Francion* VII. 5, I played the Canaries, which almost all the company danced. **1772–84** COOK *Voy.* (1790) II. 413 The canario, first used by the Canarians. **1789** BURNEY *Hist. Mus.* III. vii. 488 Country-dance and canaries. **1862** *Athenæum* 25 Jan. 111/3 Pécour it was who invented the 'Canary', a very lively dance, something like our Sir Roger de Coverley. **1880** GROVE *Dict. Mus.* I. 302 *Canarie*, a now antiquated dance.

attrib. **1609** *Ev. Wom. in Hum.* I. i. in Bullen *O. Pl.* IV, Another as she goes treads a Canarie pace. **1789** BURNEY *Hist. Mus.* (ed. 2) IV. ii. 89 Sometimes the canary and sometimes the courant step.

†2. = *Canary wine*, a light sweet wine from the Canary Islands. Formerly also in *pl. Obs.*

1597 SHAKS. *2 Hen. IV*, II. iv. 29 I' faith, you have drunk too much canaries. **1601** —— *Twel. N.* I. iii. 85 Thou lack'st a cup of Canarie. **1641** BROME *Jov. Crew* IV. i. Wks. 1873 III. 418 Good old Canary, I assure you. **1667** *Lond. Gaz.* No. 126/1 The St. Francis of Bilboa, laden with Canaries, and in her way was robbed..of one Hogshead of Wine. *a* **1711** KEN *Lett.* Wks. (1838) 80 Three bottles of canary for our sick friend. **1848** MACAULAY *Hist. Eng.* I. 320 To intoxicate large assemblies daily with claret or canary.

3. = CANARY-BIRD. Occasionally *fig.* = songster.

1655 MOUFET & BENN. *Health's Improv.* (1746) 189 So also doth the Canary, Finch or Fiskin. **1661** LOVELL *Hist. Anim. & Min.* Introd., Birds, which are..the..canarie, sparrow, finch. **1836** *Penny Cycl.* VI. 229 The hen canary will generally lay three or four times in the year. **1862** CALVERLEY *Verses & Trans.* 34 No darkringleted canaries Sing to me of 'hungry foam'.

4. Short for CANARY-BIRD (sense 2) in various slang and other uses (cf. Halliwell); also for *canary-grass* or *-seed.*

5. a. *Angling.* A 'fly' of a canary colour.

1867 F. FRANCIS *Angling* x. (1880) 372 The Canary..is more often called the 'Goldfinch'.

b. A gold coin, so called from its colour. Also *transf. slang.*

[**1785** [see CANARY-BIRD 2].] **1860** HOTTEN *Dict. Slang* 110 *Canary*, a sovereign. **1890** *Pall Mall Gaz.* 8 May 6/2 'Canaries', or promissory notes, were returned for considerably over £2,000. **1928** 'BRENT OF BIN BIN' *Up Country* xiii. 203 The 'Sweep Stakes', for which every entrant had to pay a 'canary' and the winner scoop the pool.

c. A convict. *Australian slang.*

1827 P. CUNNINGHAM *N.S. Wales* II. 117 Convicts of but recent migration are facetiously known by the name of *canaries*, by reason of the yellow plumage in which they are fledged at the period of landing. **1890** 'R. BOLDREWOOD' *Col. Reformer* vi. 49 Can't you get your canaries off the track here for about a quarter of an hour and let my mob of cattle pass?

¶ 6. A humorous blunder for *quandary* (put into the mouth of Mrs. Quickly).

1598 SHAKS. *Merry W.* II. ii. 61 You haue brought her into such a Canaries, as 'tis wonderfull: the best Courtier of them all could neuer haue brought her to such a Canarie.

7. *attrib.* and *Comb.*, as ***canary-coloured***, ***-sucking*** (sense 2), ***-yellow*** adjs.; **canary banana**, the dwarf banana, *Musa nana*; **canary-creeper**, 'a garden name for *Tropæolum aduncum*, (wrongly called *T. canariense*); **canary-finch** = CANARY-BIRD; **canary-grass**, the grass (*Phalaris canariensis*) which yields canary-seed; ***reed canary-grass*** = *canary-reed*; **canary pudding**, a lemon-flavoured sponge pudding; **canary-reed**, a British grass, *Phalaris* (*Digraphis*) *arundinacea*; †**canary-sack** = CANARY 2; **canary-seed**, the seed of *Phalaris canariensis*, used as food for canaries; also the plant itself; **canary-stone**, a 'beautiful yellow species of carnelian' (Simmonds *Dict. Trade*); †**canary-wine** = CANARY 2; **canary-wood**, the light orange-coloured wood of *Persea indica* and *P. canariensis*, obtained from Brazil.

1951 *New Biol.* XI. 67 The dwarf or *Canary banana (formerly *M. Cavendishii*) which flourishes in Mediterranean lands is also widespread in the Far East, and hence the synonym *M. Chinensis*. **1813** BINGLEY *Anim. Biog.* II. 174 The *Canary-finch. **1836** *Penny Cycl.* VI. 228 Canary bird, or Canary finch. **1668** WILKINS *Real Char.* II. iv. §3. 73 *Canary Grass. **1711** I. PETIVER in *Phil. Trans.* XXVII. 380 It's call'd Canary grass, because brought from thence, and is the common Food of those Birds. **1884** JEFFERIES in *Chamb. Jrnl.* 1 Mar. 130/2 The reeds and reed canary-grass come up. **1861** MRS. BEETON *Bk. Househ. Managem.* 636 **Canary pudding*..The weight of 3 eggs in sugar and butter, the weight of 2 eggs in flour, the rind of 1 small lemon, 3 eggs. **1951** *Good Housek. Home Encycl.* 382/2 Many different sponge puddings can be made, using the canary pudding mixture as a basis. **1884** MILLER *Plant-n.* 229 *Canary Reed. **1632** MASSINGER *City Mad.* IV. i, All the conduits Spouting *canary-sack. **1597** GERARD *Herbal* I. lxiv. 86 *Canarie Seed groweth naturally in Spain. **1794** MARTYN *Rousseau's Bot.* xiii. 133 Canary seed..is found in the Canary Islands..and is cultivated in Europe for the food of Canary and other small birds. **1836** *Penny Cycl.* VI. 230 Canary seed is chiefly cultivated in the Isle of Thanet in Kent, and about Sandwich. **1641** MILTON *Ch. Discip.* I. (1851) 18 His *canary-sucking, and swan-eating palat. **1620** VENNER *Via Recta* ii. 27 *Canarie-wine..is of some termed a Sacke, with this adiunct sweete; but yet very improperly..for it is not so white in colour as sack, nor so thin in substance. **1670** R. COKE *Disc. Trade* 6 The Canary Wines imported. **1875** URE *Dict. Arts* I. 679 *Canary wood.

ca'nary, *a.* [attrib. use of CANARY *sb.* 3.] Canary-coloured, bright yellow.

1854 THACKERAY *Newcomes* II. 128 The tall canary ones with white polls. *c* **1865** *Circle of Sc.* I. 228/2 The..liquid is ..of a canary-yellow colour. **1882** *Garden* 14 Oct. 347/2 Overlapping florets..of a clear canary yellow.

†**ca'nary**, *v. Obs.* [f. CANARY *sb.* 1.] *intr.* To dance the canary; to dance in a lively way.

1588 SHAKS. *L.L.L.* III. i. 12 To ligge off a tune at the tongues end, canarie to it with the feete. **1812** W. TENNANT *Anster F.* III. ii, The saffron-elbow'd Morning up the slope Of heaven canaries in her jewell'd shoes. *Ibid.* IV. lxxxi, Hoar-hair'd men..Canary in unconscionable rage.

canary-bird. [See CANARY *sb.*]

1. An insessorial singing bird, a kind of finch (*Fringilla* or *Carduelis canaria*, family *Fringillidæ*), originally brought from the Canary Islands, now a very common domestic songster. The wild bird, still found in Madeira, is green, but the domesticated breed is mostly of a characteristic yellow colour. (Also *canary-finch* and simply *canary*.)

1576 GASCOIGNE *Compl. Philomene* 33 Canara byrds come in to beare the bell, And Goldfinches do hope to get the gole. **1591** PERCIVALL *Sp. Dict.*, *Verdon*, a canarie bird, *Auis viridis ex insula Canaria*. **1685** *Lond. Gaz.* No. 2077/4 These are to give notice that there is lately come over from Canary, 700 Canary Birds. **1706** PHILLIPS, *Canary-bird*, an admirable Singing-bird of a green Colour, formerly bred in the Canaries, and no where else. **1802** BINGLEY *Anim. Biog.* (1813) II. 174 The Canary-bird must be considered as the musician of the chamber. **1850** MRS. STOWE *Uncle Tom's C.* xiv. 124 She [Eva] would perch like a canary-bird on some box or package near Tom.

2. *Thieves' slang.* (See quots.)

1673 R. HEAD *Cant. Acad.* 157 *Newgate* is a Cage of Canary-birds. **1725** *New Cant. Dict.*, *Canary-Bird*, a little arch or knavish Boy; a Rogue or Whore taken, and clapp'd into the Cage or Round-house. **1785** GROSE *Dict. Vulg. Tongue*, *Canary bird*, a jail bird, or person used to be kept in a cage, also in the canting sense, guineas. **1842** *Ainsworth's Mag.* II. 74 Leaving fifty good canary birds with their landlord when they go away.

†**ca'narye.** *Obs.* Also canayr. Used by Ld. Berners to render Froissart's *nacaire*, a sort of kettle-drum, otherwise called NAKER, q.v.

1523 LD. BERNERS *Froiss.* I. xii. 12 With trumpes and Canaryes. *Ibid.* lxxx. 102 Noyse of trumpettes and canarys.

canasta (kəˈnæstə). [Sp., lit. 'basket', ult. f. L. *canistrum* CANISTER.] A card game of Uruguayan origin, in which two packs are used with four jokers, combining features of rummy and pinochle; *canasta* is also the name of a meld of seven cards.

1948 *Harper's Bazaar* July 47 The Uruguayan rummy game, *canasta*,..is rapidly winning over even the most fervent Oklahoma devotees. *Ibid.*, Here the Baroness counts up the canastas at the end of a hand. **1949** *Bookseller* 12 Nov. 1171 (Advt.), A new card game—*Canasta*—is said to be sweeping the world. **1958** 'J. WELCOME' *Run for Cover* iv. 82, I resolved to go for my canastas as soon as possible.

canaster (kəˈnæstə(r)). [a. Sp. *canastra*, *canasta* (Fr. *canastre*, It. *canestra*):—L. **canastrum*, *canistrum*, a. Gr. κάναστρον basket. Cf. CANISTER.]

1. A rush basket used to pack tobacco in.

2. A kind of tobacco made of the dried leaves coarsely broken, so called from the rush basket in which it was formerly imported.

1827 HONE *Every-day Bk.* II. 196 The best tobacco.. the Dutch Canaster. **1850** THACKERAY *Imit. Horace*, Meanwhile I will smoke my canaster, And tipple my ale. **1853** *Blackw. Mag.* LXXIV. 132 The dried leaves, coarsely broken, are sold as canaster or knaster.

‖**canaut** (kəˈnɔːt). *Anglo-Indian.* Also 7 **canat**, **kanate**, 9 **kanaut**, **connaut**. [Urdū from Arab. *qanāt* (Yule).] 'The side-wall of a tent; a canvas enclosure' (Yule).

1625 PURCHAS *Pilgrimes* II. 1481 The Kings Tent.. incircled with Canats (made of red Calico stiffened with Canes at euery breadth, standing vpright about nine foot high). **1793** DIROM *Camp. India* 230 (Y.) The canaut of canvas..was painted of a beautiful sea-green colour. **1817** JAS. MILL *Brit. India* II. 201 (Y.) Silk of which they make tents and kanauts. **1834** T. MEDWIN *Angler Wales* I. ix. 163, I have known tents, though the 'canauts' (walls) and 'fly' (roof) consisted of four or five cloths, completely honeycombed in a very few weeks [by white ants].

canaveg, var. CANDAVAIG.

canayr: see CANARYE.

'can-buoy. *Naut.* [f. CAN *sb.*¹ + BUOY *sb.*] A large cone-shaped buoy, floated over sands, shallows, etc., and usually painted of a definite colour for purposes of recognition. (Formerly called *can-bodies*, Smyth, *Sailor's Word-bk.*)

1626 CAPT. SMITH *Accid. Yng. Seamen* 13 A boy, a can boy. **1769** FALCONER *Dict. Marine* (1789) *Can-Buoys*..are in the form of a cone, and of this construction are all the buoys which are floated over dangerous banks and shallows. **1858** *Merc. Mar. Mag.* V. 317 The Black Can Buoy on the Black Tail Spit. **1875** BEDFORD *Sailor's Pocket-bk.* v. (ed. 2) 136 Single-coloured can buoys..will mark the starboard side.

†**cancabs.** *Obs.* See quot.

1775 BRUCE in *Phil. Trans.* LXV. 417 The worst sort of Troglodyte Myrrh, called cancabs.

‖**cancan** (kɑ̃ːkɑ̃, ˈkænkæn). [F. (16th c. in Littré), noise, disturbance, 'rumpus' , also the dance. Of uncertain etymology, the popular fancy being that it is the L. *quanquam*, about the proper pronunciation of which a noisy wrangle is said to have occurred in the French schools. But Littré also points to an OF. *caquehan* tumultuous assembly; Scheler thinks it the vbl. sb. from *cancaner*, which he thinks was 'to quack as a duck'.]

A kind of dance made popular at the public balls in Paris, with extravagant and indecent gestures. *Comb.*, as ***cancan-dancing*** ppl. a.

1848 H. GREVILLE *Leaves fr. Diary* 269 Wearing a beard, smoking a short pipe, dancing the cancan. **1882** A. E. SWEET *Sk. from 'Texas Siftings'* 36 He usually compromises by dancing the Can-can. **1894** G. DU MAURIER *Trilby* II. VI. 201 This long-legged, cancan-dancing, Quartier Latin grisette.

Hence **'cancaning** *ppl. a.* [Cf. F. *cancaner* to dance the cancan.]

1865 *Daily Tel.* 5 Dec. 3/5 The shouting, dancing, cancaning crowd.

cancar, -d, -ous, obs. ff. CANKER, -ED, etc.

cancel ('kænsəl), *sb.* [(1) ad. L. *cancelli* (see CANCELLI); (2, etc.) f. following verb.]

†**I. 1.** *pl.* Prison bars, limits, bounds, confines. Chiefly *fig. Obs.*

1596 FITZ-GEFFREY *Sir F. Drake* (1881) 66 Bounded Within the cancels, that the world doe bound. *c* **1645** SIR E. DERING in Rushw. *Hist. Coll.* III. (1692) I. 295 As Mr. Speaker is bounded in and limited, by the Rules and Cancels of this House. **1649** JER. TAYLOR *Gt. Exemp.* III. xiv. 14 A person whose spirit is confined..and desires no enlargement beyond the cancels of the body. *a* **1667** —— *Serm.* (1678) 28 To put holy things into cancels, and immure them with acts and laws and cautions of separation.

II. 2. The act of striking out, erasing, annulling, rescinding, etc.

1884 *Manch. Exam.* 12 May 4/4 If an order is fairly executed it is a rare thing to receive a cancel.

3. *Print.* The suppression and reprinting of a page or leaf. Hence *concr.* **a.** a page so cancelled or struck out; **b.** (in full, ***cancel-leaf***) the new page substituted for that cancelled. Also ***cancel-page, -sheet.*** (Now the prevailing use.)

1806 SOUTHEY *Lett.* (1856) I. 394 Send me down a whole set of the sheets, that I may look them over; and see what cancels are necessary. **1824** D'ISRAELI *Cur. Lit.* (Rtldg.) 459/2 It was his pride to read these cancels [suppressed by the censor] to his friends. *Ibid.*, These cancel sheets or castrations. **1861** D. G. ROSSETTI *Let.* May (1965) II. 401 There are five *cancel* leaves already in the book. **1862** *National Rev.* Jan. 38 This title-page is a manifest cancel. **1872** J. A. H. MURRAY *Compl. Scotl.* Introd. 33 The leaf is a cancel replacing the original 31. **1908** F. MADAN in *Trans. Bibliogr. Soc.* IX. 62 Cancels are newly-printed leaves intended to take the place of cancelled leaves. **1908** POLLARD & GREG *Ibid.* 44 When we speak of a cancel nobody else ever knows whether we mean the leaf cut out and destroyed or the leaf inserted as a substitute. If we are careful we distinguish between a cancelled leaf and a cancel-leaf, but the person to whom we are speaking probably does not catch the subtle distinction. A change of terminology might be desirable. **1914** R. B. MCKERROW *Ibid.* XII. 299 In one case the leaf has been simply cut out, but in all the others it is replaced by a cancel-leaf. **1924** R. W. CHAPMAN in *Library* V. 249 Notes on Cancel Leaves. **1927** [see CANCELLANDUM]. **1964** F. BOWERS *Bibliogr. & Text. Crit.* V. iv. 152 Two versions of a cancel leaf.

4. ***pair of cancels***: an instrument for defacing or punching tickets (on the railway, etc.).

1887 *Daily Tel.* 11 Apr. 2/6 Charged with stealing a pair of Cancels, the property of the District Railway Company. **1887** *Standard* 18 Apr. 3/5 A pair of ticket cancels.

5. *Mus.* A natural sign, used to cancel the effect of a preceding sharp or flat. Cf. CANCEL *v.* 4 d. Chiefly *U.S.*

1912 *Nat. Educ. Assoc. U.S. Jrnl. Proc. & Addresses* 1022 The committee [on musical terminology] suggests to those who use 'cancel' as a noun, the use of 'primary' as an adjective. **1938** *Oxf. Compan. Mus.* 26/2 The American substitution of *Cancel* for *Natural* (after a sharp or flat) is defended on grounds that are decidedly logical. **1980** C. HEADINGTON *Illustr. Dict. Mus. Terms* 27/2 *Cancel*, same as 'natural' — as opposed to sharp, flat, etc.

cancel ('kænsəl), *v.* Also 5-6 cansel, 5-7 cancell, 6 *Sc.* cancil. [a. F. *cancelle-r* (15th c. in Littré):—L. *cancellāre* to make lattice-wise, to cross out a writing, f. *cancellus, cancelli* cross-bars, lattice. Cf. Pr. *cancellar*, Sp. *cancelar*, It. *cancellare*. F. *canceller* is a learned word: the native F. repr. of the L. is *chanceler*: see CHANCEL, etc.]

1. a. *trans.* To deface or obliterate (writing), properly by drawing lines across it lattice-wise; to cross out, strike out. Of legal documents, deeds, etc.: To annul, render void or invalid by so marking.

c **1440** [see CANCELLING *vbl. sb.* 1]. **1466** *Mann. & Househ. Exp.* 332 This day my mastyr reseyvid and canselled the said obligacyon. **1539** ELYOT in Ellis *Orig. Lett.* I. 142 II. 117 There was a former patente founde of the sayde Office, and myn was callid in and cancelled. **1592** GREENE *Art Conny catch* II. 2 Marry saies the prentise..then Bull shall cancell my indentures at Tiburne. *a* **1716** SOUTH *Serm.* II. x. (R.) The hand-writing against him may be cancelled in the court of heaven. **1767** BLACKSTONE *Comm.* II. xx. 309 A deed may be avoided, by delivering it up to be cancelled; that is to have lines drawn over it, in the form of lattice work or *cancelli*; though the phrase is now used figuratively for any manner of obliteration or defacing it. **1836** ARNOLD *Let.* in *Life & Corr.* (1844) II. viii. 34 In my Catholic Pamphlet..there is one paragraph which I should now cancel.

†**b.** To deface or destroy by cutting or tearing up.

1580 BARET *Alv.* C 50, I tore or rent in peces the verses that I made: I cancelled them. **1613** R. C. *Table Alph.* (ed. 3) *Cancell*, to vndoe, deface, crosse out, or teare. **1650** FULLER *Pisgah* III. iv. 385 That innocent Volume, first cancelled with a pen-knife to pieces, then burnt to ashes. **1659** PEARSON *Creed* (1839) 296 One ancient custom of cancelling bonds was, by striking a nail through the writing.

2. *fig.* **a.** To annul, repeal, render void (obligations, promises, vows, or other things binding). Also with *out*.

1494 FABYAN VII. 352 All such bandes and promysses that the Kynge or any other had made..shuld be adnulled & cancelled. **1594** DRAYTON *Idea* 845 Shake hands for ever, Cancell all our Vowes. **1692** BENTLEY *Boyle Lect.* ix. 335 Who can say that this [the Moral Law] is abrogated and cancelled by Jesus? **1772** PRIESTLEY *Nat. & Rev. Relig.* (1782) II. 34 That promise must have been cancelled. **1844** THIRLWALL *Greece* VIII. 138 All debts were to be cancelled. **1924** HICHENS *After Verdict* II. xix, Her will, so it seemed to her, had been cancelled out by little Clive's death.

†**b.** *intr.* To become void or null. *rare.*

a **1667** COWLEY, A rash oath that cancell'd in the making.

3. *gen.* **a.** To obliterate, blot out, delete from sight or memory.

1530 LYNDESAY *Test. Papyngo* 252 Quho bene Iniuste degraditar of glorie, And cancillat out of thy memorie. **1667** MILTON *P.L.* VI. 379 Canceld from Heav'n and sacred memorie, Nameless in dark oblivion let them dwell. **1827** MONTGOMERY *Pelican Isl.* II. 292 Great Babylon was like a wreath of sand, Left by one tide, and cancell'd by the next.

b. To frustrate, reduce to nought, put an end to, abolish.

1593 SHAKS. *Lucr.* 934 Why hath thy servant, Opportunity..Cancell'd my fortunes? **1608** *Yorksh. Trag.* I. ii. 203 Much good has been expected in your life; Cancel not all men's hopes. **1813** BYRON *Let. to Moore* 2 Oct., Your letter has cancelled all my anxieties. **1850** TENNYSON *In Mem.* xcv. 44 At length my trance Was cancell'd, stricken thro' with doubt. **1868** HELPS *Realmah* v. (1876) 87, I would cancel those offices which are becoming obsolete.

c. with *off.* (Cf. *cut off.*)

1608 SHAKS. *Per.* I. i. 113 We might proceed to cancel off your days.

4. a. *Arithm.* To strike out (a figure) by drawing a line through it; *esp.* in removing a common factor, e.g. from the numerator and denominator of a fraction; also *absol.* Hence **b.** To remove equivalent quantities of opposite signs, or on opposite sides of an equation, account, etc.; to balance a quantity of opposite sign, so that the sum is zero.

1542 RECORDE *Gr. Artes* 1575) 151, I must write that 1 ouer 3, and deface or cancell the 3. **1594** BLUNDEVIL *Exerc.* I. iv. (ed. 7) 12 Cancell the 2, and draw another line under the 2 severall Products. **1798** HUTTON *Course Math.* (1827) I. 161 Here the 2 to carry cancels the − 2, and there remains the − 1 to set down.

c. *fig.* To render (a thing) null by means of something of opposite nature; to neutralize, counterbalance, countervail; to make up for, compensate.

1633 G. HERBERT *Temple, The Bag* iv, Many a brunt He did endure to cancell sinne: And having giv'n the rest before, Here he gave up his life to pay our score. **1681** DRYDEN *Abs. & Achit.* 181 With publick Zeal to cancel private Crimes. *a* **1777** GOLDSM. *Prologue* 16 Here then at once I welcome every shame, And cancel at three score a life of fame. **1855** MAURY *Phys. Geog. Sea* xix. (1860) §792 One motion exactly cancels the other. **1881** JOWETT *Thucyd.* I. 29 The later kindness..may cancel a greater previous wrong.

d. *Mus.* To remove the effect of (a preceding sharp or flat), including an element of the key signature: marked by inserting a natural sign in the score.

[**1809** J. W. CALLCOTT *Mus. Gram.* I. v. 50 The Germans, consider this character as an alteration of the letter B, and call it a Cross (Kreuz), or *latticed* B (Gegittertes Be, B cancellatum).] **1836** L. MASON *Man. Boston Acad. Mus.* (ed. 2) 151 If a sharpened note is again to be restored, or the sharp is to be removed or canceled, it is done by a character called a natural, which is made thus ♮. **1880** [see NATURAL *sb.* 7 b]. **1983** *New Oxf. Compan. Music* I. 3/2 *Accidental.* Signs used in musical notation to indicate chromatic alterations from the key-signature or to cancel them.

e. *intr.* Const. *out.* To be rendered null or neutral by counterbalance.

1925 *Wireless Weekly* July 449/1 There will be a position where the effects of the two field coils cancel out. **1965** *Listener* 16 Sept. 421/1 The personal preferences of your contributors are..likely to cancel out.

5. *Printing.* To suppress (a page, sheet, etc.) after it has been set up in type or printed off.

1738 BIRCH *Milton's Wks.* I. 46 The Sheet otherwise the same, not cancell'd, but the Alteration made as it was printing. **1775** MASON *Mem.* in *Gray's Poems* (1775) 401, I once had an intention to cancel the pages, and correct the passages objected to. **1852** H. COTTON *Edit. of Bible* 276 Mr. Lea Wilson was of opinion that fol. xxxi. in the New Testament has been cancelled and reprinted.

†**6.**

1473 in Arnolde *Chron.* (1811) 78 That noo wullen cloth from thensforth be shorne excepte cancellyng but yf it be fully wet. **1483** *Act 1 Rich. III*, viii. §4 That no Sherman nor other persone..shere nor cancell any Cloth within this Roialme but if the same be afore fullye wette.

†**7.** To inclose with lattice-work or rails. *Obs.* [the literal sense of L. *cancellāre.*]

1644 EVELYN *Diary* (1827) I. 177 In a little obscure place cancelled in with yron worke. **1650** FULLER *Pisgah* IV. iii. 50 Cancelling, and railing it with posts.

cance'leer, *sb. Hawking.* Forms: 7 cancelleer, -ere, canceleer, cancileer, -ier, cancilleere, chancelleer, 7-8 cancellier, 8 cancelier, [a. the infinitive (taken subst.) of ONF. *canceler*, in mod.F. *chanceler* to swerve, shake to and fro, waver, totter, stagger, app. the same as OF. *canceler, chanceler* to place in the position of crossing bars or lattice-work, to cross; but since OF. had also *es-canceler, es-chanceler*, Littré takes the latter as the proper form in this sense, and explains it as:—L. **ex-cancellāre* to escape out of *cancelli*, 'sortir des barreaux, d'où *chanceler*', and thinks that the use of the simple verb in the sense of the derivative was due to confusion. But the simple *canceler* is quite as old in this sense (11th c.).] See quot. 1704.

1599 WEEVER *Epigr.* IV. v. (N.) Nor with the Falcon fetch a cancelleer. **1612** DRAYTON *Poly-olb.* xx, The fierce and eager hawks..Make sundry canceleers e'er they the fowl can reach. **1665** COTTON *Scarron.* IV. (1741) 141 Full swift she flew till coming near Carthage, she made a Chancelleer, And then a Stoop. **1704** WORLIDGE *Dict. Rust. et Urb.*, *Cancellier* ..when a light flown Hawk, in her stooping, turns two or three times upon the Wing, to recover herself before she seizes. **1823** in CRABB *Techn. Dict.*

b. *fig.*

1649 G. DANIEL *Trinarch., Hen. V*, cclvi, Enough if fame ..Scorne to Stoope, in well-wing'd Verse, To Single Names, in fainting Canciliers. **1655** L'ESTRANGE *Chas. I*, 20 His cancellier, his fall being only from the first loft.

cance'leer, cance'lier, *v. Hawking.* [f. prec.] Of a hawk: To turn (once or twice) upon the wing, in order to recover herself before striking.

1633 MASSINGER *Guardian* I. i, The partridge sprung, He makes his stoop, but, wanting breath, is forced To cancelier. **1834** MAR. EDGEWORTH *Helen* (Rtldg.) 166 Now right over the heron, and now she will canceleer.

b. *fig.* To turn aside, to swerve or digress.

a **1697** AUBREY *Nat. Hist. Surrey* (1719) V. 407, I will take the Boldness to cancelleer, and give a general Description of these Parts of England.

cancellable, cancelable ('kænsələb(ə)l), *a.* [f. CANCEL *v.* + -ABLE.] That may be cancelled.

1675 PENN *Eng. Pres. Int. Disc.* 22 The free People are the Original, not cancellable by a Transcript.

cancellandum (kænsə'lændəm). *Printing* and *Bibliography.* Also anglicized **'cancelland.** [neut. gerundive (sc. *folium* leaf) of L. CANCELLĀRE CANCEL *v.*] In full, ***cancellandum leaf***: a leaf, or portion thereof, for which another is substituted. So **'cancellans** [pres. pple.], the substituted leaf, etc.

1923 R. W. CHAPMAN in *Library* IV. 173 The function of a signature on a cancel is not to distinguish the *cancellans* from the *cancellandum*, but to tell the binder where the cancel is to be placed. **1927** MCKERROW *Introd. Bibliogr.* 223 It is convenient to have a means of distinguishing clearly between the original sheet or portion of a sheet which is intended to be cancelled and what is intended to replace it. We may call the former the *cancellandum* or 'cancelland', the latter the *cancellans* or simply 'cancel'. **1938** *Times Lit. Suppl.* 6 Aug. 524/2 There is also a presentation copy of Boswell's 'Life of Johnson', a first edition in boards, and Sheridan's copy with a rare cancelland. **1964** F. BOWERS *Bibliogr. & Text. Crit.* IV. v. 131 We know very little about the process of mutilating a cancellandum leaf. *Ibid.*, If the cancellans leaf had been machined before the printer collated the copies.

cancellarian (kænsə'lɛərɪən), *a. rare.* [f. L. *cancellāri-us* CHANCELLOR + -AN.] Of, or of the nature of, a chancellor.

1846 *Edin. Rev.* Apr. 288 (*Lord Chancellors*), Holding the Great Seals..for eighteen years together (a length of cancellarian days of which there is no other instance). **1887** *Pall Mall G.* 19 Sept. 4/2 It was only last year that he went out of the Vice-Cancellarian office.

cancellariate (kænsə'lɛərɪət). *rare.* [f. L. *cancellāri-us* + -ATE.] Chancellorship.

1846 WORCESTER has '*cancellareate*, belonging to a chancellor', app. an attrib. use.

†**'cancellate,** *v. Obs. rare.* [f. L. *cancellāt-* ppl. stem of *cancellā-re* to CANCEL: see -ATE³.] *trans.* **a.** To inclose, rail in; **b.** to strike out, cancel. Hence **'cancellating** *vbl. sb.*

1647 JER. TAYLOR *Dissuas. Popery* i. (1686) 16 He was forced to cancellate or blot out many sayings of St. Ambrose. **1649** —— *Gt. Exemp.* xix. §12 (1703) 375 This act was like to cancellating and a circumvallation of the holy mysteries.

cancellate ('kænsələt), *a.* [ad. L. *cancellātus* pa. pple. of *cancellāre* to CANCEL.] Marked with cross lines like lattice-work; reticulated.

1661 LOVELL *Hist. Anim. & Min.* Introd., The belly, in solipedes is rough and hard..in some mordaceous cancellate. **1835** LINDLEY *Introd. Bot.* (1848) II. 362 Cancellate, when the parenchyma is wholly absent, and the veins alone remain, anastomosing and forming a kind of network. **1880** GRAY *Bot. Text-bk.* 401 *Cancellate*, latticed.

cancellated ('kænsəleɪtɪd), *ppl. a.* [f. prec.]

1. Marked with crossing lines, like lattice-work; separated into spaces or divisions as by cancelli.

1681 GREW *Museum* (J.) The tail of the castor is almost bald..and cancellated, with some resemblance to the scales of fishes. **1800** YOUNG in *Phil. Trans.* XCI. 55 To this I adapted a cancellated micrometer. **1841** *Proc. Berw. Nat. Club* I. 272 Shell conical..cancellated with transverse striæ.

2. *spec.* Having a cellular structure formed by fine interlacing fibres and plates running in all directions, and separated by minute labyrinthine cavities, as in the less compact tissue of bones.

1836 TODD *Cycl. Anat.* I. 443 The cancellated structure in which the marrow is lodged. **1857** BIRCH *Anc. Pottery* (1858) II. 326 In quality from a coarse gritty and cancellated structure to a fine compact homogeneous paste. **1881** *Jrnl. Microsc. Sc.* 42 Labyrinthic or cancellated shelly growths.

cancellation (kænsə'leɪʃən). [ad. L. *cancellātiōn-em*, n. of action f. *cancellāre*: see

CANCEL *v.* and -ATION. So mod.F. *cancellation.* (In L. the sb. had only the sense of fixing a boundary.)]

1. a. The action of the vb. CANCEL: the crossing out or obliteration of writing, the suppression of a leaf or sheet of a book as originally printed, the annulling of a legal document; a making void or rescinding of an obligation; the neutralizing of opposing equal numbers or amounts.

1535 *Act 27 Hen. VIII*, xxvii, The said Chauncellour shall haue power..to make cancellacion of suche leases and letters patentes. **1628** COKE *On Litt.* 308 b, By cancellation of the Deed. **1855** MACAULAY *Hist. Eng.* III. 90 In spite of cancellations and interlineations, the original words can easily be distinguished. **1872** J. A. H. MURRAY *Compl. Scotl.* Introd. 20 They entailed the cancellation of no fewer than 33 of the original leaves, and the substitution of 37 others. **1875** POSTE *Gaius* II. (ed. 2) 247 The mere cancellation or obliteration of a will was an informal Revocation and left the will valid at civil law. **1878** F. A. WALKER *Money* I. iii. 68 In this cancellation of indebtedness.

b. The action or fact of cancelling a seat, room, place, etc., that has been reserved; a seat or room cancelled thus.

1953 E. S. GARDNER *Case Green-Eyed Sister* (1959) viii. 105 Luckily I managed to pick up a cancellation and came right through.

2. *etymologically.* The action of marking with cross lines lattice-wise. (*nonce-use.*)

1843 *Blackw. Mag.* LIV. 60 The cancellation of his back by stripes and scars.

cancelled ('kænsəld), *ppl. a.* [f. CANCEL *v.* + -ED.] Crossed or struck out, annulled, made void.

1539 TUNSTALL *Serm. Palm Sund.* (1823) 15 In cancellyng the bonde of our synne..and fastenynge it cancellyd to his crosse. **1557** RECORDE *Whetst.* K iv, I leave out..cancelled figures. **1631** *Star Chamb. Cases* (1886) 81 The said cancelled deed. **1820** SHELLEY *Prometh. Unb.* IV. i. 11 Many a cancelled year.

'canceller. [see -ER.] One who cancels.

1611 COTGR., *Quasseur*, a squasher, casser, canceller.

‖**cancelli** (kæn'sɛlaɪ), *sb. pl.* [L. *cancelli* crossing bars, gratings, lattice, railings, pl. of *cancellus*, dim. of *cancer*, pl. *cancri* crossing bars, grating.]

1. Bars of lattice-work; *spec.* the latticed screen between the choir and body of the church; hence the CHANCEL (mod.F. *cancel*) so railed off. (Hardly in Eng. use.)

1642 JER. TAYLOR *Episc.* (1647) 247 S. Ambrose his sending his Deacon to the Emperour, to desire him to goe forth of the Cancelli. **1703** MAUNDRELL *Journ. Jerus.* (1732) 27 The Altar is inclos'd with Cancelli.

2. *Phys.* 'The lattice-work of the spongy portion of bones, consisting of thin plates and bars interlacing with each other, and forming arches and buttresses in the direction of greatest pressure'. *Syd. Soc. Lex.*

1802 *Med. Jrnl.* VIII. 371 The bone of the cavity of the tympanum in the cetacea..shewing no vestige of fibres, cancelli, or vessels. **1871** *Proc. Amer. Phil. Soc.* XII. 25 The cancelli..always run parallel with the axis of the bone.

¶ **b.** Improperly applied to the interstices between these bars and plates of bones. (Probably first extended to the whole cancellous or cancellated tissue, including the interstices, and then carelessly misapplied to the latter.)

1845 TODD & BOWMAN *Phys. Anat.* I. 80 In the cancelli of bones there is a large deposit of fat. **1854** OWEN in *Circ. Sc.* (*c.* 1865) II. 47/2 Mere cancelli, or small medullary cavities. **1881** MIVART *Cat* 20 Some bones have their entire substance replete with cavities or cancelli, and such are called cancellated or spongy.

cancellier, variant of CANCELEER.

cancelling ('kænsəlɪŋ), *vbl. sb.* [f. CANCEL *v.*]

1. The action of crossing or blotting out, annulling, rescinding, etc. (see the verb); cancellation.

c **1440** *Promp. Parv.* 60/1 Cancellynge or strekynge owte a false word, *obelus*. **1552** HULOET, *Cancellynge*, or defacynge of wrytynge. **1631** *Star Chamb. Cases* (1886) 81 The supposed cancelling of the deed. **1870** GLADSTONE *Glean.* IV. xxv. 216 The King became a party to the cancelling of the whole arrangement. **1887** *Athenæum* 13 Aug. 211/2 Shelley cut it up freely with cancellings and alterations.

2. *Comb.*, as ***cancelling-press***, ***-stamp*** (contrivances for defacing printed stamps, to prevent their re-use).

cancellous ('kænsələs), *a. Phys.* [f. CANCELL-I + -OUS: cf. L. *cancellōsus.*] Having an open porous structure as of network, made up of fine interlacing fibres and plates, as in ***cancellous tissue***.

1836–9 TODD *Cycl. Anat.* II. 789/1 Deep in the cancellous structure of the bones. **1881** MIVART *Cat* 36 Cancellous bony tissue invested by compact bone.

cancelment ('kænsəlmənt). [f. as prec. + -MENT.] = CANCELLATION.

1621 ELSING *Debates Ho. Lords* (1870) 134 A breefe of the cancellments. **1881** MISS BRADDON *Asph.* III. 269 The cancelment of Madoline's engagement.

cancer ('kænsə(r)), *sb.* Also (4 cancre), 5 canser, (6 canker). [L. *cancer* (*cancrum*) crab, also the malignant tumour so called. (So in Greek, καρκίνος, καρκίνωμα 'crab' and 'cancer'; the tumour, according to Galen, was so called from the swollen veins surrounding the part affected bearing a resemblance to a crab's limbs.) The word was adopted in OE. as *cancer*, *cancor* for the disease, reinforced after 1100 by the Norman Fr. *cancre*, which gave the ME. and modern CANKER. The original Latin form was re-introduced in ME. in the astronomical sense, and about 1600 in the medical, as a more technical and definite term than *canker*, which had come to be applied to corroding ulcerations generally. (Cf. also CHANCRE, in 17th and 18th c. *shanker*.)]

1. a. A crab. (Now only as a term of Zoology.)

1562 BULLEYN *Bk. Simples* (1579) 76 [This castor..loueth to feede vpon Crabs and Cankers of the Sea.] **1607** TOPSELL *Serpents* 686 The like things are reported of the Asps, Cancers, and Tortoyses of Egypt. **1650** FULLER *Pisgah* IV. iii. 47 The slowest snail makes more speed forth-right, than the swiftest retrograde Cancer. **1791** E. DARWIN *Bot. Gard.* I. 121 The anchor'd Pinna, and his Cancer-friend.

b. *Med.* 'A term for an eight-tailed bandage; those resembling, it was thought, a crab's legs' (*Syd. Soc. Lex.*). Also called ***cancer-bandage***.

1753 in CHAMBERS *Cycl. Supp.*

2. *Astron.* (With capital initial.) **a.** The Zodiacal constellation of the Crab, lying between Gemini and Leo. **b.** The fourth of the twelve signs or divisions of the Zodiac (♋), beginning at the most northerly point of the ecliptic or summer solstitial point, which the sun enters on the 21st of June. The sign originally coincided with the constellation, but on account of the precession of the equinoxes, the first point of Cancer is now in the constellation Gemini. ***Tropic of Cancer***: the northern Tropic, forming a tangent to the ecliptic at the first point of Cancer, about 23° 28′ from the equator.

c **1391** CHAUCER *Astrol.* (1872) 9 In this heued of cancer is the grettest declinacioun northward of the sonne..this signe of cancre is cleped the tropik of Somer. *c* **1400** *Destr. Troy* 2344 In the season of somer, er the sun rose, As it come into canser. **1594** BLUNDEVIL *Exerc.* VI. xiv. (ed. 7) 624 The Sunne being in the fourth degree of Cancer. **1606** SHAKS. *Tr. & Cr.* II. iii. 206 And adde more Coles to Cancer, when he burnes With entertaining great Hiperion. **1727** THOMSON *Summer* 44 When..Cancer reddens with the solar blaze. **1833** MACAULAY *War Success. Sp.*, *Ess.* (1854) I. 239/1 The American dependencies of the Castilian crown still extended far to the North of Cancer and far to the South of Capricorn. **1859** *Pictures of Heavens* 32 Cancer..perhaps the Zodiacal sign was so called because the sun begins to return back..when it enters this sign, and its retrograde motion may be represented by that of a crab.

c. *Astrol.* A person born under the sign of Cancer. Also *attrib.* or as *adj.*

1894 E. KIRK *Influence of Zodiac upon Human Life* xvii. 145 The Cancer men are far more constant than the Cancer women. **1924** [see PISCES 1 b]. *a* **1963** L. MACNEICE *Astrol.* (1964) iii. 77 Many astrologers would advise a Pisces type to marry a Cancer but not a Virgo. **1970** L. GOODMAN *Sun Signs* 145 Cancer's heart is too soft not to be touched by someone's need. **1985** *London Portrait Mag.* Apr. 196/2 It would seem to tie in with Charles's chart that from August Cancer feels more secure, more nurtured and loved.

3. a. *Pathol.* A malignant growth or tumour in different parts of the body, that tends to spread indefinitely and to reproduce itself, as also to return after removal; it eats away or corrodes the part in which it is situated, and generally ends in death.

The earlier name was CANKER, q.v.

1601 HOLLAND *Pliny* II. Gloss., *Cancer* is a swelling or sore comming of melancholy bloud, about which the veins appeare of a blacke or swert colour, spread in manner of a Creifish clees. **1671** SALMON *Syn. Med.* I. xlviii. 114 Καρκινος, Cancer is a hard round Tumour blew or blackish having pain and beating. **1747** HERVEY *Medit. & Contempl.* (1818) 254 On some a relentless cancer has fastened its envenomed teeth. **1768** G. WHITE *Selborne* xviii. (1853) 80 The wonderful method of curing cancers by means of toads. **1877** ROBERTS *Handbk. Med.* I. (ed. 3) 274 Cancer is decidedly a hereditary disease.

b. *fig.* An evil figured as an eating sore.

1651 BAXTER *Inf. Bapt.* 274 This Cancer is a fretting and growing evil. *a* **1711** KEN *Edmund* Poet. Wks. 1721 II. 194 Sloth is a Cancer, eating up that Time Princes should cultivate for Things sublime. **1875** JOWETT *Plato* (ed. 2) II. 355 The incurable cancer of the soul.

†**4.** A plant: possibly *cancer-wort* (see 5).

1546 LANGLEY tr. *Pol. Verg. De Invent.* I. xvii. 31 b, Yf he be stynged with a spider, he healeth himself with eatinge Pylles or a certain herbe named Cancer. **1609** HEYWOOD *Brit. Troye*, Who taught the poore beast having poison tasted, To seek th' hearbe cancer, and by that to cure him?

5. *Comb.* (in sense 3), as ***cancer-cell***, ***-element***, ***-serum***; **cancer bush** *S. Afr.* [ad. Afrikaans *kankerbos*] (see quot. 1895); **cancer-root** (see quots); **cancer stick** *jocular* or *colloq.*, a cigarette; **cancer wort** (see quots.).

1895 A. SMITH *S. Afr. Materia Medica* (ed. 3) xxi. 138 *Sutherlandia frutescens*, R. Br.—Dutch, *Cancer bush. This shrub has been brought forward recently as a remedy for cancer. **1949** *Cape Argus* 9 July (Mag. Section) 1/3 This is where the..cancer bushes and chincherinchees for his rockeries are raised. **1966** E. PALMER *Plains of Camdeboo* xvii. 277 The early settlers..used..the pretty little *Sutherlandia humilis*—the cancer bush—not only for cancer but for flu. **1876** tr. *Wagner's Gen. Pathol.* 479 Cancer-juice consists of *cancer-cells and a usually scanty, fluid substance, the intercellular substance or cancer-serum. **1768** G. WHITE *Selborne* xviii. (1789) 53 This woman.. having set up for a *cancer-doctress. **1714** *Phil. Trans.* XXIX. 64 To this they add a Root call'd the *Cancer Root. **1884** MILLER *Plant-n.*, Cancer Root, *Conopholis* (*Orobanche*) *americana* and *Epiphegus virginiana*. —— one-flowered, *Aphyllon uniflorum*. **1959** J. BRAINE *Vodi* xxii. 242 There was a packet of cigarettes on the locker. She took one out and lit it. 'First *cancer stick today,' she said. **1967** *New Statesman* 20 Jan. 77/2 To be able to..tempt fate by a debonair pull on a cancer stick is a way of asserting the individual's right to choose his own end. **1597** GERARD *Herbal* Index (Britten & Holland) *Cancerwoort, that is Fluellen, 504. **1884** MILLER *Plant-n.*, Cancer-wort, *Linaria spuria* and *L. Elatine*; also an old name for the genus *Veronica*.

cancer ('kænsə(r)), *v.* [f. prec. sb.] *trans.* To eat into as a cancer; to eat (its way) slowly and incessantly like a cancer.

1840 DE QUINCEY *Casuistry Rom. Meals* Wks. III. 280 Other things advance *per saltum*—they do not silently cancer their way onwards. **1858** —— *Autobiog. Sk.*, Wks. (1863) XIV. 93 The strulbrug of Swift.. was a wreck, a shell, that had been burned hollow and cancered by the fierce furnace of life.

Hence **'cancered** *ppl. a.*, affected with cancer.

a **1774** GOLDSMITH *Nat. Hist.* (1776) VII. 102 The application of toads to a cancered breast.

cancerate ('kænsəreɪt), *v.* [f. L. *cancerāt-us* cancerous.] *intr.* To become cancerous, to grow into a cancer. Hence **'cancerated** *ppl. a.*

1688 R. HOLME *Armoury* III. 426/1 Breasts..Cancerated. **1694** R. L'ESTRANGE *Fables* 95 But striking his fist upon the point of a nail in the wall, his hand cancerated. **1736** BURTON *Cancers* II. in *Phil. Trans.* XLII. 110 The Right Lobe of the Lungs was full of scirrhous cancerated Tubercles. **1814** J. GILCHRIST *Reason Arbiter Lang.* 64, I would thank any man to put a cover on a cancerated nose.

canceratic (kænsə'rætɪk), *a. Pathol.* [ad. L. *cancerātic-us*: see -ATIC.] Of the nature of, or related to, cancer.

1881 in *Syd. Soc. Lex.*

canceration (kænsə'reɪʃən). [noun of action from CANCERATE *v.*] A growing cancerous or into a cancer.

1731 BAILEY vol. II, *Canceration*, a spreading abroad cancerously. **1755** in JOHNSON; and in mod. Dicts.

cancerd, cancered, obs. ff. CANKERED.

Cancerian (kæn'sɪərɪən), *sb.* (and *a.*) *Astrol.* [f. CANCER *sb.* + -IAN.] = CANCER *sb.* 2 c. Also *attrib.* or as *adj.*

1911 I. M. PAGAN *From Pioneer to Poet* iv. 50 The highly evolved Cancerian is the master of many moods. **1959** *Times* 21 Sept. 11/4 Cancerians were apparently expected to adopt the motto of Charlie Pendragon 'and put the family first'. *a* **1963** L. MACNEICE *Astrol.* (1964) viii. 256 The Sun is in Cancer, which gives Cancerian qualities to the 'deeper self'. **1972** D. LEES *Zodiac* 28 A typical Cancerian subject... She was born on July sixth... Physically she's a prototype Cancerian, even to that slight moustache. **1985** *Woman's Jrnl.* Mar. 16/4 The Good Samaritan was probably a Capricorn rather than a Cancerian.

cancerideous (kænsə'rɪdiːəs), *a. Pathol.* [f. L. *cancer*, on some mistaken analogy.] = CANCROID.

1881 in *Syd. Soc. Lex.*

cancerin ('kænsərɪn). An artificial guano from Newfoundland.

cancerism (kænsərɪz(ə)m). *Pathol.* [f. CANCER + -ISM.] 'The cancerous diathesis' (*Syd. Soc. Lex.*).

'cancerite, 'cancrite. *Palæont.* [see -ITE.] A fossil crab.

1848 WEBSTER *Cancrite*. **1860** WORCESTER *Cancerite*.

cancerous ('kænsərəs), *a.* In 6 canserous. [f. CANCER *sb.* + -OUS.] Of the nature of cancer; affected with cancer.

1563 T. GALE *Antidot.* II. 20 Canserous vlcerations. **1681** GLANVILL *Sadducismus* 91 Cancerous Knots in the breast. **1797** M. BAILLIE *Morb. Anat.* (1807) 198 When a portion of the intestinal canal becomes cancerous. **1872** COHEN *Dis. Throat* 125 Cancerous tumors..occur in the tonsils.

fig. **1655** H. VAUGHAN *Silex Scint.* 200 Frustrate those cancerous close arts. **1720** WELTON *Suffer. Son of God* II. xxi. 591 Cancerous and Calumniating Hearts. **1868** GEO. ELIOT *Sp. Gipsy* 317 Remorse was born within him, cancerous, Forcing each pulse to feed its anguish.

'cancerously, *adv.* In a cancerous manner.

1731 [see CANCERATION]. **1847** in CRAIG; and in mod. Dicts.

'cancerousness. Cancerous condition.
1731 in BAILEY vol. II. **1755** in JOHNSON. **1886** *Brit. Med. Jrnl.* 159/2.

cancheler, obs. form of CHANCELLOR.

cancil(l)eer, -ier, variants of CANCELEER.

cancker, -cred, etc., obs. ff. CANKER, -ED, etc.

†**'cancrenated**, *a. Obs. rare*$^{-1}$. [f. It. *cancrenare* to gangrene (f. *cancrena* gangrene) + -ATE + -ED.] Affected with gangrene.
1582 HESTER *Phiorav. Secr.* II. xix. 97 Woundes..beyng impostumated or cancrenated, thei chaunge their names.

cancriform ('kæŋkrɪfɔːm), *a.* [f. L. *cancr-* (*cancer*) crab + -FORM.]
1. Crab-shaped.
1826 KIRBY & SP. *Entomol.* (1828) III. xxxv. 714 The cancriform spiders. *Ibid.* IV. 394.
2. *Pathol.* 'Having the appearance of cancer' (*Syd. Soc. Lex.*).

cancrine ('kæŋkraɪn), *a.* [Formed on the normal L. type **cancrīnus*, f. *cancer*: see -INE.] Having the qualities of a crab; crab-like. ***cancrine*** (or palindromic) ***verse***: '(Latin) verses which are the same, read either forwards or backwards, as *Roma tibi subito motibus ibit amor*' (Bailey).
1755 in JOHNSON. **1846** R. HART *Eccl. Records* 245 At Hingham Church in Norfolk there is a curious cancrine inscription over the font.

cancrinite ('kæŋkrɪnaɪt). *Min.* [Named after *Cancrin*, a Russian statesman: see -ITE.] A massive mineral found at Minsk in the Urals, a silico-carbonate of aluminium and sodium.
1844 in DANA *Min.* **1850** DAUBENY *Atom. The.* xii. (ed. 2) 413 Silicates..with Carbonates. Example: Cancrinite. **1879** RUTLEY *Stud. Rocks* x. 108 Cancrinite is probably an altered condition of nepheline.

cancrizans ('kæŋkrɪzænz), *a. Mus.* [med.L., pres. pple. of *cancrizāre* to walk backwards, f. *cancr-*, *cancer* crab (CANCER *sb.*): see -IZE.] Applied to a canon in which the theme or subject is repeated backward in the second part. Hence as *sb.*, such a canon.
1782 C. BURNEY *Hist. Mus.* II. 494 The same part sings *in retro*, or, as it is called in the musical technica of the times, cancrizans. **1876** STAINER & BARRETT *Dict. Mus. Terms* 72/1 The following is a canon cancrizans with a bass part *per recte et retro*. **1879** GROVE *Dict. Mus.* I. 302/2 Sometimes a canon is both cancrizans and by contrary motion. **1926** A. B. SMITH *Studies & Caprices* 53 Inversions, diminutions, cancrizans exist only on paper. **1938** SCHOLES *Oxf. Compan. Music* 134/2 A highly artificial form in which the imitating voice gives out the melody backwards... This has been called the *Canon Cancrizans*..but crabs move *sideways*. **1942** *Scrutiny* XI. 10 This composer's elaborate *cancrizans*. **1969** *Listener* 24 Apr. 585/2, I strongly suspect that the obvious musical reversals were subtilised by the technical device of *cancrizans*.

‖**'cancro.** *Obs.* [It.: lit. 'the cancer (take you!)'] An imprecation. (Cf. *plague! pest!*)
c **1600** N. BRETON *Philiston's Lett.* (Gros.) 63 (Hoppe) Now and then [he would] rise off his bed in a rage, knitting his brows with cancro. **1612** CHAPMAN *Widowes T.* in *Dodsley* (1780) VI. 211 Cancro! what, thy husband's body?

cancroid ('kæŋkrɔɪd, -əʊɪd), *a.* and *sb.* In sense 2 also **-ide.** [f. L. *cancer*, *cancr-* crab + -OID. In sense 2 after F. *cancroïde.*]
A. *adj.* **1.** Like the crab in structure.
1826 KIRBY & SP. *Entomol.* (1828) III. xxxv. 705 In the cancroid spiders. **1852** DANA *Crust.* I. 65 These are Cancroid in the..branchial peculiarities.
2. *Pathol.* Resembling cancer.
1859 TODD *Cycl. Anat.* V. 591/1 Of a cancerous or cancroid nature. **1878** T. BRYANT *Pract. Surg.* I. 513 Cancer of the lips is generally applied to epithelioma or cancroid disease, true cancer or carcinoma being very rare.
B. *sb.* **1.** A crustacean of the crab family.
1852 DANA *Crust.* I. 48 The outer antennæ are small, as in the Cancroids.
2. A disease resembling cancer; also a synonym of epithelial cancer.
1851 in MAYNE *Exp. Lex.* **1859** TODD *Cycl. Anat.* V 593/2 Scirrhous or Hard Cancer and Cancroid are by no means so common. **1872** F. THOMAS *Dis. Women* 519 Malignant disease..in two forms, cancer and cancroid.

cancrous, obs. form of CANKEROUS.

cand (kænd). 'A name in some mining districts for Fluor spar' (Ure *Dict. Arts* I. 679).
1880 *W. Cornwall Gloss.* (E.D.S.) *Cam, cand*, fluor spar.

candareen (kændə'riːn). Also 7 **condrin.** ['In Malay, to which language the word apparently belongs, *kandūri*' (Yule).] A Chinese weight and money of account, equal to 10 cash or $\frac{1}{100}$ of a tael. As a weight of gold or silver estimated at about 6 grains Troy.
[**1554** A. NUNES 39 (Y.) In Malacca the weight used for gold, musk, &c., the cate, contains 20 taels, each tael 16 mazes, each maz 20 cumduryns.] **1615** R. COCKS *Diary* i. (1883) 1 (Y.) We bought 5 greate square postes of the Kinges master carpenter; cost 2 mas 6 condrins per peece. **1745** P. THOMAS *Jrnl. Voy. S. Seas* 260 A Moidore by those Weights weighs just thirty Candarines. **1796** MORSE *Amer. Geog.* II. 531 Candareen. **1802** *Naval Chron.* VIII. 382 Which will be settled at seven mace two candereen per head. **1854** in R. Tomes *Amer. in Japan* 410 The Japanese have a decimal system of weight, like the Chinese, of catty, tael, mace, candareen, and cash.

candavaig ('kændəveɪg). *Sc. dial.* Also **canaveg.** [According to Jamieson, f. Gael. *ceann* head + *dubhach* blacking; melancholy, sorry.] A salmon that lies in the fresh water till summer without going down to the sea, and is consequently reckoned as foul; a *black-fish*. Also a later-spawning variety of salmon.
1793 *Statist. Acc. Scotl.* IX. 109 (Jam.) We have—a species of salmon, called by the country people candavaigs, that frequently do not spawn before the month of April. **1847** STODDART *Angler's Comp.* 366 A variety of the salar, termed canavegs.

canded, obs. form of CANDIED.

†**'candefy, candify**, *v. Obs.*$^{-0}$. [Cf. L. *candefacĕre*: see -FY.] To make or become white.
1656 in BLOUNT *Glossogr.*; hence in BAILEY, and mod. Dicts.

candela (kæn'diːlə). [L., see CANDLE *sb.*] A unit of luminous intensity (see quot. 1968).
1950 *Commission Internat. de l'Éclairage, 1948* 14 It is recommended that the new unit for luminous intensity (which is such that the luminance or photometric brightness of a black body at the temperature of freezing platinum equals 60 units of intensity per square centimetre) shall be called in all countries by the Latin name 'candela', with the symbol '*cd*'. **1957** R. W. G. HUNT *Reprod. Colour* viii. 89 A purely physical or photometric quantity, measured, for instance,..in candelas or lumens per square foot if light units are used. **1960** *Aerodrome Lighting* (*B.S.I.*) 13 It may be said that in clear conditions the intensity of the runway lights should not exceed about 50 candelas. **1968** *Nature* 16 Nov. 651/2 The candela is the luminous intensity, in the perpendicular direction, of a surface of 1/600 000 square metre of a black body at the temperature of freezing platinum under a pressure of 101 325 newtons per square metre.

cande'labraed, *a.* [f. *candelabra* (see CANDELABRUM) + -ED.] Furnished with or as with a candelabrum. Also used as pa. pple. of a hypothetical verb **candelabra*.
1923 *Daily Mail* 19 Feb. 8 Throngs gather round the cheap lottery booths established under the candelabra'd lamp-posts. **1929** HEMINGWAY *Farewell to Arms* viii. 47 We passed stone farmhouses with pear trees candelabraed against their south walls.

‖**candelabrum** (kændɪ'leɪbrəm, -'lɑːbrəm). Pl. **-bra.** (Also in modern use, **candelabra**, *pl.* **-as.**) [L. *candēlābrum* candlestick, f. *candēla* CANDLE.]
1. *Greek* and *Roman Antiq.* **a.** A candlestick, usually an ornamental one. **b.** A stand on which lamps were supported.
1834 LYTTON *Pompeii* IV. vii, One of those tall and graceful candelabra, common to that day, supporting a single lamp. **1876** HUMPHREYS *Coin Coll. Man.* xxvi. 397 Bronze candelabra of Etrurian workmanship.
2. An ornamental branched candlestick holding a number of candles; a chandelier.
1815 *Edin. Rev.* XXV. 106 Some of these [cacti]..divided into several branches in the form of candelabras. **1820** SCOTT *Ivanhoe* vi, Four silver candelabras, holding great waxen torches. **1841-4** EMERSON *Ess. Art* Wks. (Bohn) I. 149 Galleries of statues, vases..and candelabra.
3. Simple *attrib.* Also prefixed (in form *candelabrum* or *candelabra*) to the names of trees with foliage shaped like a candelabrum, esp. a tropical African tree of the genus *Euphorbia*.
1834 [see EUPHORBIA]. **1878** R. J. HINTON *Handbk. Ariz.* 343 To what age the candelabra cactus attains is a matter of mere conjecture, their growth being exceedingly slow. **1892** J. G. BOURKE *On Border* 53 The majestic 'pitahaya', or candelabrum cactus, whose ruby fruit had long since been raided upon. **1909** WEBSTER, Candelabrum tree. **1927** D. H. LAWRENCE *Mornings in Mexico* 80 Even the organ cactus,.. and the candelabrum cactus, seem to be slowly wheeling and pivoting upon a centre. **1946** J. P. R. WALLIS *North. Goldfields Diaries T. Baines* I. 170 *Euphorbia ingenus* or candelabra tree. **1957** *Timber Technol.* LXV. 467 *Botanical name*: *Euphorbia* spp... *Trade name*: Candelabra tree... All species resemble each other in their giant cactus or candelabra formation. **1960** *Guardian* 7 Nov. 1/3 They had chased the Masai beyond the candelabra tree.

candelere, obs. form of CHANDELIER.

candelere, -deller, obs. ff. CHANDLER.

candelilla wax (kændə'liljə). [Amer. Sp. *candelilla*, f. Sp., little candle.] A vegetable product obtained from various American shrubs, esp. of the genus *Euphorbia*, prepared for some special purpose in the arts, dentistry, etc.
1909 *Jrnl. R. Soc. Arts* 25 June 664/2 Moulded into phonograph records, the candelilla wax will register the sounds perfectly. **1910** *Jrnl. Ind. & Engin. Chem.* II. 203/2 Candelilla wax..is found coating the entire surface of a plant that grows wild in the semi-arid regions of northern Mexico and southern Texas. **1951** R. MAYER *Artist's Handbk.* ix. 285 *Candelilla Wax*..obtained from a weed native to Texas and Mexico..is next in hardness to carnauba, and finds a use in industry as a cheaper substitute for it. **1961** J. N. ANDERSON *Appl. Dent. Mat.* (ed. 2) xv. 134 Candelilla wax is..light brown in colour.

†**'candency.** *Obs. rare*$^{-1}$. [ad. L. *candentia* whiteness, glow, sb. of quality f. *candent-em*: see next and -ENCY.] Warmth, fervency.
1723 M. WARD *Earnest Contend. Faith* 18 (Jam.) Your paper bewraying so much candency for the one, and coolness in the other.

candent ('kændənt), *a. Obs.* or *arch.* [ad. L. *candēnt-em*, pr. pple. of *candēre* to be white, glow.]
1. At a white heat; glowing with heat.
1577 DEE *Relat. Spir.* I. (1659) 356 The Colour of the fire of the 4 Arches is very red; The rest are very pure, Aerial, candent. **1646** SIR T. BROWNE *Pseud. Ep.* II. ii. 60 Wires totally candent. **1660** BOYLE *New Exp. Phys.-Mech.* xxxvi. 283 The heat of a candent Æolipile. **1790** COWPER *Iliad* XIX. 141 Lord of the candent lightenings. **1800** SIR W. HERSCHELL in *Phil. Trans.* XC. 296 Rays emanating from candent substances. **1832** FERGUSSON in *Blackw. Mag.* XXXI. 282 The candent hearth, the ruddy lurid row Of smiths.
2. *fig.* Fervent, impassioned. *rare.*
1723 McWARD *Earnest Contend. Faith* 170 (Jam.) Some men..are keen and candent against any who will do this.

†**canderros.** *Obs.*
1753 CHAMBERS *Cycl. Supp.*, *Canderros*, in the materia medica, a name of an East Indian gum..It has much of the appearance of common amber, only that it wants its yellow colour, being white and pellucid; we sometimes see it turned into toys of various kinds, which are very light.

can'descence. [f. next: see -ENCE.] Candescent state; dazzling whiteness or brightness.
1880 MISS BROUGHTON *Sec. Th.* I. I. vi. 83 The clear candescence of country snow.

candescent (kæn'dɛsənt), *a. rare.* [ad. L. *candēscent-em*, pr. pple. of *candēscĕre* to become white, begin to glow, inchoative from *candēre*: see CANDENT.] Glowing with, or as with, heat.
1824 BEDDOES *Let.* in *Poems* Introd. 34 The moment he [the sun] touched [the Alps], it appeared that all the snows took fire, and burned with a candescent brilliancy. **1863** *Q. Rev.* CXIV. 540 The spark..cast forth from the candescent metal. **1884** L. WALLACE *Ben-hur* I. xiv. 68 The star..less candescent than before.
Hence **can'descently** *adv.*, glowingly, dazzlingly.
1883 MISS BROUGHTON *Belinda* II. ii, Candescently white.

†**'candicant**, *a. Obs. rare*$^{-1}$. [ad. L. *candicānt-em*, pr. pple. of *candicāre* to be whitish or white.] Growing white, inclining to white, whitish.
1657 TOMLINSON *Renou's Disp.* 317 Small cups with candicant flowers. **1731** BAILEY vol. II, *Candicant*, waxing white. Hence in JOHNSON, and mod. Dicts.
Hence **'candicancy**, 'a whitening or making fair, etc.' (Bailey vol. II. 1731).

†**'candicate**, *v. Obs.*$^{-0}$ [f. L. *candicāt-* ppl. stem of *candicāre* (see prec.) + -ATE.]
1623 COCKERAM, Candicate, to waxe white.

candid ('kændɪd), *a.* [ad. L. *candid-us* white, glistening (also used in many fig. senses as below), f. stem of *candēre* to be white, to glisten. Perh. immediately from F. *candide*, 16th c. in Littré. (Not in Shaksp., Bible, Cotgrave, or Cockeram 1623.)]
†**1.** White. (Usually with reference to other meanings, or in translation from Latin.) *Obs.* or *arch.*
1630 JACKSON *Creed* VIII. xxvi. Wks. VIII. 105 Sending Him back to Pilate in a white or candid robe. *a* **1700** DRYDEN *Fabl., Pythagor. Philos.* 60 The stones came candid forth, the hue of innocence. **1738** WARBURTON *Div. Legat.* I. 54 That candid Appearance, which..does result from the Mixture of all Kinds of Colours. **1805** J. M. GOOD *Lucretius* I. 298 The candid milk.
2. *fig.* †**a.** Spendid, illustrious; fortunate.
1648 HERRICK *Hesper., To T. Shapcott* 179 Brave men.. whose candid actions are Writ in the poets endlesse kalendar. **1715** BENTLEY *Serm.* x. 371 This candid and joyful Day.
b. Pure, clear; stainless, innocent. *arch.*
1647 CLARENDON *Hist. Reb.* I. I. 72 Nor cared to make his designs..appear as candid as they were. *a* **1667** COWLEY *To Royal Soc.* ix, His candid stile like a clean stream does slide. **1868** BROWNING *Ring & Bk.* IX. 475 Where does the figment touch her candid fame?
3. Free from bias; fair, impartial, just.
1635 SWAN *Spec. M.* (1643) Pref. 1 Men of candid sinceritie will be readie..to give it a friendly welcome. **1754** CHATHAM *Lett. Nephew* vi. 46 Keep your mind in a candid state of suspense. **1828** ARNOLD *Let.* in *Life & Corr.* (1844) I. v. 243, I know that your mind is entirely candid: and that no man will conduct an inquiry with more perfect fairness. **1883** FROUDE *Short Stud.* IV. II. iii. 197 He was too candid to attribute such doubts..to wickedness of heart.
†**4.** 'Free from malice; not desirous to find faults' (J.); 'gentle, courteous' (Cotgr.); favourably disposed, favourable, kindly. *Obs.*
1633 MARMION *Fine Compan.* Ded., Candid dispositions who (in spite of malice and ignorance) dare countenance Poetry. **1660** STANLEY *Hist. Philos.* (1701) 79/2 To shun the censorious, and to apply our selves to such as are candid. **1718** *Free-thinker* No. 61. 37 Your Lectures meet with a very Candid Reception. **1732** POPE *Ess. Man* i. 15 Laugh where we must, be candid where we can. **1800** *Med. Jrnl.* IV. 502

The candid manner in which my Communication has been treated, lays me under strong obligations.

5. a. Frank, open, ingenuous, straightforward, sincere in what one says.

1675 OGILBY *Brit.* Advt., We shall gratefully accept Candid Informations. **1774** GOLDSM. *Retal.* 113 Let us be candid and speak out our mind. **1856** FROUDE *Hist. Eng.* (1838) I. ii. 121 A..very candid account of Henry's feelings is furnished by himself.

b. *ironically*, in phrase *candid friend*: one who claims to be a friend, and, in the name of candour, speaks unpleasant things.

1798 CANNING *New Moral.* in *Anti-Jacobin* 9 July (1852) 208 Save, save, oh! save me from the Candid Friend! **1867** *Habits & Cust. Working Classes* 26 Troops of friends..candid and sugar-candied. **1884** *Daily News* 5 Dec. 3/1 Mr. Raikes congratulated [Mr. Goschen] on being able to pose as the candid friend of the Conservative party.

c. Of a photograph or photography: unposed, informal. So ***candid camera***, a small camera for taking informal photographs of persons, freq. without their knowledge; also *attrib.* Also as *sb.*, an unposed photograph.

1929 *Graphic* 11 May 265 At the foreground table, unaware of the proximity of the candid camera, will be seen Dean Inge enjoying his cigar. **1935** *N.Y. Times* 8 Dec. Sect. xi. 14/3 Small enough to be manipulated without attracting attention, the miniature camera as used by 'candid camera' hobbyists is..becoming a highly revealing adjunct of the contemporary scene. **1937** *Miniat. Camera World* Dec. 5/2 'Candid' photography was at one time synonymous with 'miniature' photography. **1939** A. HUXLEY *After many a Summer* I. iii. 31 Candid Camera portrait of the President of Consol Oil. **1946** T. GODSEY *Free Lance Photogr.* iii. 36 He liked these 'candids' so well that a contract to do his new publication entirely with the miniature was the result. **1957** P. MANSFIELD *Final Exposure* i. 11 Those delightfully candid shots. *Ibid.* ii. 33 Candid photographs. *Ibid.* iv. 51 Can't you..take real candids—without people knowing?

candid, obs. form of CANDIED.

Candida ('kændɪdə). Also **candida**. [mod.L., coined in Du. (C. M. Berkhout *De Schimmelgeslachten Monilia, Oidium, Oospora en Torula* (1923) 41), fem. of L. *candidus* white: see CANDID *a.*] A yeast-like mycelium-forming parasitic fungus of the genus *Candida*, which includes species causing disease in man and animals; spec. *C. albicans*, common as a commensal in the alimentary tract and the vagina, and the cause of thrush.

1939 R. L. SUTTON *Dis. Skin* (ed. 10) II. xix. 1116 (*heading*) Candida infections. **1940** *Jrnl. Bacteriol.* XXXIX. 627 It is not surprising..that attempts to classify the '*Candidas*' should cause differences of opinion since these fungi can present variations in many features. **1947** *Bact. Rev.* XI. 239 A yeast, probably a Candida, has been used in the Soviet Union..for producing cattle feed. **1951** C. M. CHRISTENSEN *Molds & Man* ix. 181 Some species of Candida are common..on the outside of seeds such as corn and barley, some occur in soil, others on fruits. **1961** R. D. BAKER *Essent. Path.* ix. 210 Only rarely does Candida act as a deep fungus infection but cases of meningitis and endocarditis have been reported. **1970** PASSMORE & ROBSON *Compan. Med. Stud.* II. xviii. 19/2 The opportunist nature of candida infections is evident as the host is rarely attacked unless there is some predisposing factor. **1976** *Lancet* 11 Dec. 1271/2, 4 months after transplantation, she developed 7 mm of induration and erythema in response to the intradermal injection of candida. **1977** E. J. TRIMMER et al. *Visual Dict. Sex* (1978) xv. 154 Candida is mostly found in the vagina where it may cause no trouble.

Hence **candidiasis** (-'daɪəsɪs) = MONILIASIS.

1954 G. C. ANDREWS *Dis. Skin* (ed. 4) xvi. Candidiasis of the Mouth in Adults. Thrush infections similar to those observed in infants are sometimes seen on the buccal mucosa of adults. **1961** R. D. BAKER *Essent. Path.* ix. 210 The use of antibiotics and steroids may predispose to gastrointestinal candidiasis. **1963** C. W. EMMONS et al. *Med. Mycol.* xiv. 131 Candidiasis is an acute or chronic, superficial or disseminated mycosis caused by species of Candida. Its clinical varieties are so diverse that a more specific general definition can not be given. **1964, 1974** [see MONILIASIS]. **1980** *Brit. Med. Jrnl.* 29 Mar. 943/1 Napkin area eruptions can both be caused or complicated by candidiasis.

candidacy ('kændɪdəsɪ). [f. CANDIDATE: see -ACY 3; cf. *magistracy*.] The position or status of a candidate; CANDIDATESHIP, CANDIDATURE.

[**1852** D. G. MITCHELL *Batte Summer* 129 He..avows his own candidatecy.] **1864** FREMONT in *Daily Tel.* 21 June, In accepting the candidacy you propose to me. **1870** *Daily News* 22 Oct., The candidacy of the Duke d'Aosta for the throne of Spain.

candidate ('kændɪˌdeɪt), *sb.* [ad. L. *candidāt-us* adj., clothed in white, sb. a candidate (because candidates for office wore a white toga), f. *candidus* white: see CANDID. Cf. mod.F. *candidat* (16th c. in Littré).]

1. One who seeks or aspires to be elected or appointed to an office, privilege, or position of honour, or who is put forward or selected by others as an aspirant; *e.g.* one who seeks a seat in the House of Commons, or other representative body. Const. *for*; formerly sometimes *of*.

1613 R. C. *Table Alph.* (ed. 3) *Candidate*, a suiter for, or one elect for a place. **1685** *Lett.* in *Academy* (1876) 21 Oct. 408/2 Yesterday the newes came of the Lord Chamberlain's death..There are severall candidates for the place. **1704** NELSON *Fest. & Fasts* xiii. (1739) 158 Candidates for Holy Orders. **1741** MIDDLETON *Cicero* I. II. 150 A white Gown, the proper habit of all Candidates. **1818** in *Parl. Deb.* 1068 A court of law decided, that a man was not a candidate, who had not offered his services to the electors. **1844** STANLEY *Arnold's Life & Corr.* I. ii. 54 The head-mastership of Rugby became vacant..[Dr. Arnold] finally resolved to offer himself as a candidate. **1866** GEO. ELIOT *F. Holt* (1868) 14 Offering himself as candidate for North Loamshire.

in apposition. **1713** SWIFT *On Himself* Wks. 1755 IV. I. 12 Caress'd by candidate divines. **1845** STOCQUELER *Handbk. Brit. India* (1854) 153 A numerous supplementary class of candidate pupils.

b. Formerly the word had a *spec.* use in the Universities (cf. *licentiate*), but this is now merged in the general sense.

1691 WOOD *Ath. Oxon.* (R.) He published certain books against B. Jewell, being then a candidate of the Fac. of Theology. **1706** PHILLIPS, [after explaining the Ancient Roman sense, adds] the Word is still in use in the Universities. **1804** *Med. Jrnl.* XII. 287 His name as a Candidate for a Degree shall be entered in the minutes of Senate, and a day fixed when the Candidate shall read his Commentaries on the Aphorism and Case. **1846** MCCULLOCH *Acc. Brit. Empire* (1854) II. 339 The candidate for honours may seek to attain them in classical literature..or in mathematics.

2. *fig.* and *transf.* **a.** Sometimes simply = Aspirant, seeker for; sometimes with tacit allusion to the white dress of the Roman *candidati*, or the position of a Christian catechumen.

1647 CRASHAW *Poems* 149 Ye holy doves!..bright Candidates of blissful light, The heirs elect of love. **1673** CAVE *Prim. Chr.* III. ii. 275 They laid up the body as a candidate and expectant of a joyful and happy resurrection. *a* **1700** DRYDEN (J.) While yet a young probationer, And candidate of heav'n. **1750** JOHNSON *Rambl.* No. 21 ¶6 A candidate for literary fame. *a* **1847** R. HAMILTON *Rew. & Punishm.* iii. (1853) 145 The Christian is a candidate for the approval of his Judge. **1873** F. HALL *Mod English* 105 Thousands of words and uses of words, on their first appearance, or revival, as candidates for vernacularization.

b. One who is thought likely or worthy to gain a post, a position of honour, etc.

1766 GOLDSM. *Vic. W.* xxxi, If ever there was a candidate for Tyburn, this is one. **1781** GIBBON *Decl. & Fall* III. 260 Strength and majesty..marked him, in the popular opinion, as a candidate worthy of the throne.

†**3.** *Hist.* One of the *cohors candidatorum* (so called from their white dress) who served as the body-guard of the Roman Emperors after the time of the Gordians, A.D. 237.

1656 BLOUNT *Glossogr.*, *Candidats*..also gallent yong Gentlemen or Knights about the Emperors person. **1727–51** CHAMBERS *Cycl.* s.v., It was the younger Gordian who instituted the *Candidati*.

†'**candidate**, *a. Obs. rare.* [ad. L. *candidātus*: see prec.] Clothed in white. (*poetic.*)

1616 HOLYDAY *Persius* 329 He..Whom candidate chaulky ambition Draws gaping to her lure? **1648** HERRICK *Hesper.*, *Cloud*, Seest thou that cloud that rides in state, Part ruby-like, part candidate?

†'**candidate**, *v.*[1] *Obs. rare.* [f. L. *candidāt-* ppl. stem of *candidā-re* to make white, f. *candidus* white: see CANDID and -ATE[3].] *trans.* To make white, or as a candidate; to whitewash (*fig.*).

1628 FELTHAM *Resolves* II. 57 (T.) To purify and cleanse us, that we may be the better candidated for the court of Heaven. **1677** GILPIN *Dæmonol.* (1867) 437 This is his usual note to candidate iniquity.

'**candidate**, *v.*[2] *U.S. colloq.* [f. the sb.] To stand as a candidate. '**candidating** *vbl. sb.* and *ppl. a.*

1884 *Century Mag.* June 308/1 Let him put the question to some [choir-singers] who every spring have to candidate for a situation. **1885** *Chicago Advance* Aug. 538 To look upon the parish instead of himself as the candidating party. *Ibid.* 554 He holds candidating..to be absurd, delusive and sacrilegious. **1887** N. L. WALKER *Rel. Life Scot.* 264 The 'candidating' which..has given greater liveliness to preaching. **1909** *Springfield Weekly Republ.* 2 Sept. 14 Mr. Seccombe candidated in the Goschen church last spring.

candidatecy: see CANDIDACY.

candidateship ('kændɪdət-ʃɪp). [f. CANDIDATE *sb.* + -SHIP.] The position of a candidate.

1775 in PERRY. **1829** *Blackw. Mag.* XXV. 200 The candidateship for that uneasy and cheerless seat. **1861** J. SHEPPARD *Fall Rome* vii. 385 Genseric..supported..the candidateship of Olybrius.

candidature ('kændɪdətjʊə(r)). [a. F. *candidature*: see CANDIDATE *sb.* and -URE.] Standing as a candidate, candidateship.

1851 DIXON *W. Penn* xx. (1872) 171 The Court prepared to oppose his candidature. **1882–3** CALDERWOOD in Schaff *Relig. Encycl.* II. 936/2 [Hamilton] was supported in his candidature by Dugald Stewart.

candidly ('kændɪdlɪ), *adv.* [f. CANDID + -LY[2].]

1. Fairly, without prejudice or bias, with open mind.

1646 SIR T. BROWNE *Pseud. Ep.* 153 That proverbe must be candidly interpreted. **1647** SALTMARSH *Sparkl. Glory* (1847) 207. *c* **1650** TOMBES in Baxter *Inf. Bapt.* 211 He would have sought for truth candidly. **1745** *Season. Adv. Protest.* 28 So that the Children..may listen candidly to wholesome Instruction. **1817** MAR. EDGEWORTH *Harrington* (1832) 49 To think candidly of persons of his persuasion.

†**2.** Without malice; favourably, kindly, courteously. *Obs.*

1650 H. MORE in *Enthus. Tri.* (1656) 72, I will candidly passe over what may receive any tolerably good interpretation. **1768** STERNE *Sent. Journ.* (1778) I. 132 Candidly disposed to make the best of the worst. **1782** HELLINS in *Phil. Trans.* LXXII. 425, I hope this little piece will be candidly received. **1845** MAURICE *Mor. & Met. Philos.* in *Encycl. Metrop.* II. 581/1 He must not candidly and generously concede the truth and wisdom of those [propositions] which seemed to him plausible or reasonable.

3. Frankly, openly, straightforwardly, without reserve.

1762 GOLDSM. *Nash* 3 Montaigne or Colley Cibber, who candidly tells us what they thought of the world. **1783** LD. HAILES *Anc. Chr. Ch.* iv 98 Few judges have so candidly avowed their incapacity to discharge the duties of office. **1884** G. DENMAN *Law Times Rep.* LI. 666/2 The manager himself candidly answered that they took the risk. *Mod.* I candidly confess that I am ashamed of my party.

candidness ('kændɪdnɪs). [f. CANDID + -NESS.] State or quality of being candid.

†**1.** Purity, innocence. *Obs.*

1654 COKAINE *Dianea* I. 67 The candidness of my thoughts. **1655** FULLER *Ch. Hist.* x. 69 Whose plain Tombs, made of white Marble, shew..candidnesse of their natures. **1692** SOUTH *Serm.* II. xii. 459 (R.) The candidness of a man's very principles, the sincerity of his intentions.

2. Fairness, impartiality.

1628 FELTHAM *Resolves* II. lxii. (L.) The candidness of an upright judge.

†**3.** Favourable disposition, favour, courtesy.

1643 PRYNNE *Power Parl.* I. Perf. A ij b, Entertaine it therefore, with that candidnesse. **1688** I. CLAYTON in *Phil. Trans.* XVII. 790, I..have no reason to suspect their Favour, whose Candidness I so signally proved.

4. Frankness, straightforwardness, sincerity in speech.

candied ('kændɪd), *ppl. a.* Also 7 **canded**, 7–8 **candid**. [f. CANDY *v.* + -ED[1].]

1. Preserved or incrusted with sugar.

1616 R. C. *Times' Whis.* VI. 2771 Marmalade, Candid eringoes, & rich marchpaine stuff. **1620** VENNER *Via Recta* vi. 106 Candied ginger. **1712** tr. *Pomet's Hist. Drugs* I. 151 Candied Orange Peel. **1859** SALA *Tw. round Clock* 56 Candied horehound.

b. *transf.* and *fig.* Covered with anything crystalline or glistening, as hoar-frost.

1600 FAIRFAX *Tasso* VI. ciii. 114 The siluer moone..Spred frostie pearle on the canded ground. *c* **1750** SHENSTONE *Odes* Wks. 1764 I. 305 The winter's candy'd thorn. **1822** HAZLITT *Table-t.* Ser. II. vii. (1869) 144 My sensations are all glossy..they wear a candied coat.

2. Crystallized, congealed.

1641 BEST *Farm. Bks.* (1856) 68 Putte up before it [honey] wax cold and canded. **1648** EARL WESTMORLD. *Otia Sacra* (1879) 88 When the clumsie Winter doth incline His candid Icicles. **1746** G. ADAMS *Microgr.* 238 The inside Cavity of it [a Flint] appear'd to be crusted all over with a pretty candid substance. **1810** HENRY *Elem. Chem.* (1840) II. 198 Transparent crystals of sugar..called candied sugar.

3. *fig.* 'Sugared', 'honied', flattering, glozing.

1602 SHAKS. *Ham.* III. ii. 65 The Candied tongue. **1649** DRUMM. OF HAWTH. *Poems* Wks. (1711) 55 The candid poyson'd baits Of Jesuites.

candier ('kændɪə(r)). *rare.* One who candies.

1598 FLORIO, *Zuccheraio*, a sugar-maker, a comfet-maker, a preseruer, a candier.

†'**candify**, *v.* ? *Obs.* [In Bailey a variant of CANDEFY; but in mod. dicts. referred to CANDY.]

1721 BAILEY, *Candify*, to whiten. **1847** CRAIG, *Candefy*, to whiten, to make white. **1864** WEBSTER, *Candify*, to make or become white, or candied. **1885** ANNANDALE *Imp. Dict.*, *Candify*, to make or become candied, to candy.

†**candify**, *sb. Obs. Herb.* [cf. prec.] Name of a plant: app. = Fuller's Herb or Soapwort, *Saponaria officinalis*.

1727 R. BRADLEY *Fam. Dict.* s.v. *Fly*, Put some Candify or Fuller's Herb, and some Opium or Poppy Tears, amongst the Lime with which you whiten the House.

candiru (kændɪ'ruː). [a. Pg. *candirú*, a. Tupi *candirú*, *candérú*.] A tiny, bloodsucking catfish, *Vandellia cirrhosa*, of the family Pygidiidæ, found in the Amazon river, where it attacks other animals, including man.

1841 R. H. SCHOMBURGK in *Ann. Mag. Nat. Hist.* VI. 395, I was frequently warned by the inhabitants to be cautious while bathing of a small fish called *Cancliru* [sic]. **1897** J. BACH in *Proc. Zool. Soc.* 901 The 'Candyrú', as the fish is called, is much dreaded by the natives of the Jurua. **1930** E. W. GUDGER *Candirú* p. vii, 'Candirú' is the collective name given to certain small catfishes of the Amazon River and its tributaries to which are attributed the evil habit of entering the urethra of men and the vulva of women bathers. **1962** K. F. LAGLER et al. *Ichthyol.* xiv. 438 One fish that can perhaps be regarded as a true parasite is the small candiru, a South American catfish.

candi'sation. *Obs.*$^{-0}$ [a. F. *candisation*, f. *candir* to CANDY.] 'The Crystallizing or Candying of Sugar, after it has been dissolv'd in Water, and purify'd' (Phillips 1706).

Hence in KERSEY and BAILEY.

candite ('kændaɪt), *sb. Min.* [f. *Candy* in Ceylon.] A variety of Spinel, dark green or brown to black, found in Ceylon, also called Ceylonite or Iron-Magnesia Spinel. (Dana.)

1844 PHILLIPS *Min.* 138 It was called Candite by Bournon.

† **can'dite**, *v. Obs. rare*⁻¹. [After It. *candito* candied, pa. pple. of *candire* to candy; also *canditare* 'to candy with hard sugar'.] = CANDY *v.*

1693 SIR T. BLOUNT *Nat. Hist.* 61 [Ginger].. Transported Candited into Forreign Parts. [? error for *candied.*]

† **candi'teers.** *Obs.* 'In Fortification, Frames to lay faggots and brushwood on to cover the workmen' (Phillips 1696); whence in subsequent Dicts. to the present day.

candle ('kænd(ə)l), *sb.* Forms: 1-4 **condel, -ell,** 1-6 **candel, -ell,** 3 *Orm.* **kanndell,** 3-4 **kandel,** 4-5 **condle, -il, kandil,** 5 **candelle, -ylle, -yle, -ulle, -ul,** 5-6 **-yl,** 4- **candle,** (*dial.* **cannel, -le, kennel.**) [OE. *candel, cǫndel* fem., ad. L. *candēla* (or *candella*) 'candle', f. *candē-re* to shine. One of the Latin words introduced at the English Conversion, and long associated chiefly with religious observances: even in the 15th c. three of the glossaries in Wright-Wülcker include 'candle' among the 'names of things pertaining to the church' (*nomina pertinencia ecclesiæ*). This sacred character of the word bears on the OE. poetic compounds *Godes candel, heofoncandel,* etc. in 2. The southern ME. pl. was *condlen.*

L. *candēla* came down in Romance as It., Pr., Sp. *can'dela,* Pg. *can'dea.* OF. *chandeile, -doile,* ONF. *candeile, -doile.* The actual F. *chandelle* (OF. *chandele*) represents a late L. variant *candella* (usual in med.L.), assimilated to diminutives in *-ella.* (Cf. *querēla, querella.*) The occasional late ME. spelling *candelle* may have been after French.]

I. 1. a. A source of artificial light, consisting of a usually cylindrical body of wax, tallow, spermaceti, or other solid fat, formed round a wick of cotton or flax, formerly also, of the pith of a rush.

Candles are distinguished according to the method of manufacture, as ***dipped*** or ***mould candles***, by the material employed, or by some other peculiarity, as ***Paris candle, royal candle,*** etc. The word is also used without plural as a name of material, as in ***a piece of candle, an inch of candle.***

a **700** *Erfurt Gloss.* 382 (O.E.T.) *Emunctoria,* candeltuist. *a* **800** *Corpus Gloss.* 745 *Emunctoria,* candeltwist. *c* **1000** *Voc.* in Wr.-Wülcker 154 *Lampas,* candeles leoma. *a* **1154** *O.E. Chron.* an. 1140 Me lihtede candles to æten bi. **1297** R. GLOUC. 290 Þat chyld heo bete so stronge myd þe condlen long & towe. **1386** CHAUCER *Wif's Prol.* 334 A nigard that wol werne A man to light a candel at his lanterne. **1398** TREVISA *Barth. De P.R.* VIII. xvi. (1495) 322 A glasse sette byfore a candle receuyth lighte of a candil. **1477** EARL RIVERS (Caxton) *Dictes* 69 Is like to hym that lighteth a candelle to another. **1579** in Turner *Rec. Oxford* 402 A pound of the best cotton candells. **1613** SHAKS. *Hen. VIII,* III. ii. 96 This Candle burnes not cleere, 'tis I must snuffe it, Then out it goes. **1662** EARL ORRERY *State Lett.* (1743) I. 117 To provide fire and candle. **1708** *Brit. Apollo* No. 89. 2/1 Why should a Rush Candle burn longer than a Cotten one? **1771** SMOLLETT *Humph. Cl.* I. 15 May, Ten mould-candles, that had scarce ever been lit. **1851** W. P. SNOW *Jrnl. Arct. Seas.* iv. 46 Very little candle was required below at night. **1856** EMERSON *Eng. Traits* xii. *Universities* Wks. (Bohn) II. 91 No candle or fire is ever lighted in the Bodleian.

b. In religious or superstitious use.

a **1300** *Cursor M.* 20701 Gas þan wit fair processiun.. Wit cirges and wit candel bright. *c* **1400** *Apol. Loll.* 48 Wil þu offir a candil þat þu geyt merit & grace? **1554** WOODDE *Dial.* D j in Brand *Pop. Antiq.* (1870) I. 27 Wherefore serveth holye Candels? To light up in thunder, and to bless men when they lye a dying. **1561** PILKINGTON *Burn. St. Pauls* I iv b, *ibid.* We shuld bear our Candel at her [the Virgin's] Churching at Candlemas. **1611** COTGR. s.v. *Chandelle..* There was for euery Saint his candle. **1824** W. IRVING *T. Trav.* II. 101 A votive candle placed before the image of a saint. **1865** TROLLOPE *Belton Est.* I. 13 (Hoppe) Captain Aylmer was member for Perivale in the Low Church interest..He would say a sharp word or two..about vestments; he was strong against candles [*i.e.* the use of candles on the altar or communion-table in Anglican churches].

† **c.** as used at a sale by auction: see 5 d.

1662 PEPYS *Diary* 3 Sept., After dinner we met and sold the hulkes, where pleasant to see how backward men are at first to bid; and yet when the candle is going out how they bawl. **1690** *Records E. Ind. Comp.,* Mr. Thorowgood to manage the Company's Candle at the Sale.

d. A standard spermaceti candle formerly used as a unit of illuminating power: hence ***candle power***; freq. called ***international candle.*** Also, with prefixed numeral, = *candle power* (see 7). Replaced as a unit of luminous intensity by the ***new candle*** (see quot. 1937) = CANDELA.

[**1860** *Act 23 & 24 Vict.* c. 125 §25 The Quality of the Common Gas..shall be..such as to produce..a Light equal in Intensity to the Light produced by not less than Twelve Sperm Candles.] **1869** ROSCOE *Elem. Chem.* 98 Cannel gas is said to be equal to 34.4 candles. **1875** URE *Dict. Arts* II. 553, 10,500 cubic feet of 25-candle gas to the ton. **1880** J. W. URQUHART *Electr. Lt.* 279 A 2,000-candle light. *Ibid.* 282 A hundred-candle Sugg gas-burner. **1883** *Harper's Mag.* Feb. 482/1 One hour's light of two-thousand candle-power. **1917** *Trans. Illum. Engin. Soc.* XII. 440 *Candle,* the unit of luminous intensity maintained by the national laboratories of France, Great Britain and the United States... This unit, which is used also by many other countries, has..been referred to as the international candle. [**1937** *Com. Internat. Poids & Mesures* XVIII. 216 L'adoption d'une nouvelle définition de l'unité d'intensité lumineuse... Le Comité se rallie á la proposition d'appeler 'bougie nouvelle' l'unité qui vient d'être définie.] **1938** *Light & Lighting* XXXI. 186/1 The initiation of the new international candle, based upon..a primary standard of light (one-sixtieth of the luminous intensity of one square centimetre of a black body maintained at the temperature of solidification of platinum)... Laboratories are preparing groups of lamps to be measured in terms of the new candle, which is to come into operation in 1940.

† **2.** *fig.* A source of light; applied poetically (with attributes) to the natural luminaries. In OE. poetry *dæȝ candel, heofon-candel, rodor candel, woruld-candel, Godes candel,* were poetical terms for the sun. *Obs.*

Beowulf 3148 Hadre scineþ rodores candel. **937** *O.E. Chron.,* Glad ofer grundas Godes condel beorht. *c* **1374** CHAUCER *Compl. Mars* 7 Loo yonde the sunne the candel of Ialosye. **1592** SHAKS. *Rom. & Jul.* III. v. 9 Nights candles are burnt out. **1596** R. L[INCHE] *Diella* (1877) 37 He that can count the candles of the skie. **1634** BP. HALL *Occas. Medit.* xlix. Wks. (1808) 148 On a glow-worm. What a cold candle is lighted up, in the body of this sorry worm.

† **3.** *fig.* **a.** That which illuminates the mind.

1532 FRITH *Mirr. to know Thyself* (1829) 267 Yet will I set you up a candle which shall..clearly dispel his mist and vain poetry. **1555** LATIMER in Foxe *A. & M.* (1631) III. XI. 503/2 Wee shall this day light such a Candle by Gods grace in England, as I trust shall neuer bee put out. *a* **1619** DANIEL *Coll. Hist. Eng.* (1634) 2 Since the candle of letters gave us some little light therof.

b. The 'light' of life.

1535 COVERDALE *Job.* xxi. 17 How oft shal the candle of yᵉ wicked be put out. **1593** SHAKS. *3 Hen. VI,* II. vi. 1 Heere burnes my candle out; I, heere it dies. **1605** —— *Macb.* v. v. 23 Out, out, breefe Candle, Life's but a walking Shadow. **1642** FULLER *Holy & Prof. St.* I. ii. 6 Her candle was put out, as soon as the day did dawn in S. Augustine. **1768** BLACKSTONE *Comm.* II. 175.

4. *transf.* **a.** A preparation containing resinous or aromatic substances for diffusion during burning; a pastil. ***medicated candle***: (see quots.)

1621 BURTON *Anat. Mel.* I. iii. III. (1651) 210 Perfumes, suffumigations, mixt candles, perspective glasses, and such natural causes. **1753** CHAMBERS *Cycl. Supp.* s.v., Medicinal Candles, *candelæ fumales,* are compositions of odoriferous, aromatic, and inflammable matters, as benzoin, storax.. formed into masses in shape of candles. The effluvia and odours whereof when burnt, are supposed to be salutary to the breast. **1880** *Syd. Soc. Lex., Medicated candle,* a candle containing some drug for diffusion during burning.. Mercurial candle.

† **b.** A bougie; a suppository. *Obs.*

1684 tr. *Bonet's Merc. Compit.* XIX. 839 Suppositories are made round like Candles..whence they call them Candles from the similitude. **1753** CHAMBERS *Cycl. Supp.* s.v., Candles for caruncles of the urinary passage. [**1881** *Syd. Soc. Lex., Candela,* bougie.]

c. Mucus pendulous at the nose.

1858 GEO. ELIOT *Amos Bart.* ii. (D.) The inveterate culprit was a boy of seven, vainly contending against candles at his nose by feeble sniffing.

d. CHRISTMAS CANDLE, ROMAN CANDLE, q.v.

e. The inflorescence or panicle of a horse-chestnut tree. ***in candle***: of a chestnut tree, in flower.

1920 E. SITWELL *Wooden Pegasus* 48 The chestnut-candles flicker. **1938** T. H. G. STEVENS *Trees & Shrubs in my Garden* vii. 118 The Common Horse Chestnut from Albania is one of the finest flowering trees with its great candles of white flowers in May. **1954** 'C. DANE' *Flower Girls* I. 448 'Horse-chestnuts... The leaf prints off like a horse-shoe,' said Ernest, adding that the tree 'in candle' was the most beautiful sight. **1968** C. P. SNOW *Sleep of Reason* (1969) xxxviii. 357 In a public garden the candles stood bright on the flowering chestnuts. **1983** P. MORTIMER *Handyman* vi. 55 A huge horse-chestnut bearing a thousand candles hung over Slattery's wall.

II. 5. *Phrases.* **a.** ***candle, book, and bell***: see BELL *sb.*¹ 8.

a **1300** *Cursor M.* 17110 Curced in kirc þan sal þai be wid candil, boke, and bell. **1842** BARHAM *Ingol. Leg., Jackdaw of Rheims,* The cardinal rose with a dignified look, He called for his candle, his bell and his book.

† **b.** ***to set, light, proffer a candle before*** or ***to the devil***: to propitiate or humour him, as saints are supposed to be propitiated by a votive candle; later, ***to hold a candle to the devil*** (by confusion with c): to serve or assist an evil person, to be active in evil courses. *Obs.*

c **1461** *Paston Lett.* No. 428 II. 73 A man must sumtyme set a candel befor the devyle. **1562** J. HEYWOOD *Prov. & Epigr.* (1867) 20, I fearyng She would spit her venym, thought it not euyll To sette vp a candle before the deuyll. **1577** TUSSER *Husb.* (1878) 148 Thou maist find ease so proffering vp a candell to the deuill. **1599** MARSTON *Pigmal.* II. 145 A damn'd Macheuelian Holds candle to the deuill for a while, That he the better may the world beguile. **1649** HOWELL *Pre-em. Parl.* 20 According to the Italian Proverb, That one must sometimes light a candle to the Devil. *c* **1670** LADY ABERGAVENNY in R. Mansell *Narr. Popish Plot* 12 She could not endure to hear it, but yet was forced to hold a Candle to the Devil. **1828** SCOTT *F.M. Perth* II. 213 (D.) Here have I been holding a candle to the devil, to show him the way to mischief.

c. ***to hold a candle to another***: *lit.* to assist him by holding the candle while he works; hence, to help in a subordinate position. ***not to be able or fit to hold a candle to***: not fit to hold even a subordinate position to, nothing to be compared to.

1550 CROWLEY *Way to Wealth* 131 Dise playars..that haue nothynge to playe for..Holde the candle to them that haue wherewyth, and wyll sette lustily to it. **1590** GREENE *Never too late* (1600) 19 Driuen..when I am worst alle, forst to hold the candle. **1596** SHAKS. *Merch. V.* II. vi. 41 *Lorenzo.* Descend, for you must be my torch-bearer. *Jessica.* What, must I hold a Candle to my shames? **1614** T. ADAMS *Devil's Banq.* 225 Let Plato then, hold the candle to Moses. **1640** SIR E. DERING *Carmelite* (1641) 43 Though I be not worthy to hold the candle to Aristotle. **1773** BYROM *Poems,* Others aver that he to Handel Is scarcely fit to hold a candle. **1883** W. E. NORRIS *No New Thing* I. vii. 175 Edith is pretty, very pretty; but she can't hold a candle to Nellie.

d. ***to sell*** or ***let by the candle, by inch of candle,*** etc.: to dispose of by auction in which bids are received so long as a small piece of candle burns, the last bid before the candle goes out securing the article; hence in many *fig.* and *transf.* uses. Cf. AUCTION 3.

This appears to have been a custom adopted from the French; cf. Littré, also COTGR., s.v. *Chandelle.*

1652 MILTON *Lett. State* Wks. 1738 II. 169 The Council thinks it meet to propose the way of selling by inch of Candle, as being the most probable means to procure the true Value of the goods. **1672** SIR T. BROWNE *Lett. to Friend* xx. (1881) 141 Mere pecuniary matches, or marriages made by the candle. **1680** in Sir J. Picton *L'pool Munic. Rec.* (1883) I. 287 The new marked ground..was lett by inch of candle in the towne hall. **1697** COLLIER *Ess. Mor. Subj.* II. (1709) 53 To give Interest a share in Friendship, is in effect to sell it by Inch of Candle. **1700** *Act 11 & 12 Will. III,* in *Lond. Gaz.* No. 6129/1 All such Goods..shall be sold at publick Sale by the Candle. **1797** BURKE *Regic. Peace* iv. Wks. IX. 84 Where British faith and honour are to be sold by inch of candle. **1825** HONE *Every-day Bk.* I. 837 Four acres..are let by inch of Candle. **1851** *N. & Q.* 15 Nov. 383 Forty or fifty years ago goods were advertised for public sale by the candle.

1727-51 CHAMBERS *Cycl.* s.v., There is also a kind of Excommunication by Inch of Candle; wherein, the time a lighted Candle continues burning, is allowed the sinner to come to repentance; but after which, he remains excommunicated to all intents and purposes.

† **e.** ***to smell of the candle***: i.e. of work by night, of close and prolonged study. *Obs.*

1604 HIERON *Wks.* I. 504 If that bee commendation..for a mans labours to smell of the candle. (Cf. LAMP.)

f. ***the game, play,*** etc. ***is not worth the candle***: i.e. not worth the mere cost of supplying the necessary light (cf. 1550 in 5 c); not worth the labour expended.

(Of French origin: cf. COTGR. s.v. *Chandelle 'Le jeu ne vaut pas la chandelle,* it will not quit cost'.)

a **1690** TEMPLE *Ess. Health* Wks. 1731 I. 274 Perhaps the Play is not worth the Candle. *c* **1700** *Gentl. Instruct.* (1732) 556 (D.) After all, these discoveries are not worth the candle. **1874** P. BAYNE in *Contemp. Rev.* Oct. 706 The game would not be worth the candle.

g. ***to light*** or ***burn the candle at both ends***: to consume or waste in two directions at once.

(Cf. COTGR. '*Brusler la chandelle par lex deux bouts*'.)

1730-6 BAILEY, s.v., The Candle burns at both Ends. Said when Husband and Wife are both Spendthrifts. **1753** HANWAY *Trav.* (1762) II. I. iii. 19 Apt to light their candle at both ends; that is to say, they are apt to consume too much, and work too little. **1848** KINGSLEY *Saint's Trag.* III. i. 140 To double all your griefs, and burn life's candle, As village gossips say, at either end.

h. Various phrases obvious in meaning.

1551-6 ROBINSON tr. *More's Utop.* (1869 Arb.) 27 Setfurth the brightnes of the sonne with a candell as the Prouerbe saieth. **1579** GOSSON *Sch. Abuse* (Arb.) 41, I burnt one candle to seek another, and lost bothe my time and my trauell, when I had doone. **1581** LAMBARDE *Eiren.* III. iv. 361, I shal but set a Candle in the Sunshine. **1607** TOPSELL *Four-f. Beasts* Pref., Another Physitian, lighting his Candle by the former lights, succeeded them in this great undertaking. **1676** M. CLIFFORD *Hum. Reason* in *Phenix* (1708) II. 532 Men grope in the dark that light not their Candle at ours. **1728** YOUNG *Love Fame* vii. 97 How commentators each dark passage shun, And hold their farthing candle to the sun. *a* **1873** LYTTON *K. Chillingly* VIII. vii (Hoppe) Slothfully determined to hide his candle under a bushel [cf. *Matt.* v. 15].

III. *attrib.* and *Comb.*

6. General relations: **a.** attributive, as ***candle-dish, -flame, -grease, -rack, -screen, -shade, -shine, -smoke, -time, -wright,*** etc.; ***candle-lit*** adj. **b.** objective, as ***candle-bearer, -bearing, -maker, -making, -seller,*** etc.

1555 *Fardle Facions* II. xii. 267 The Acholite..occupieth the roume of *Candle-bearer. **1899** *Pall Mall Mag.* Jan. 77 Two silver *candledishes. **1887** *Spectator* 2 Apr. 463/1 Draughts which no *candle-flame was sensitive enough to indicate. **1774** GOLDSM. *Nat. Hist.* VII. iii. (Jod.) Drops of *candlegrease. **1868** WHITTIER *Meeting* in *Compl. Wks.* (1898) 486/1 No altar *candle-lit by day. **1890** *Pall Mall Gaz.* 22 Oct. 2/3 This candlelit old hall. **1916** H. G. WELLS *Mr. Britling* ii. §9 Equally unexpected was the supper on a long candlelit table without a cloth. **1611** COTGR., *Chandelier..*a Chaundler, or *Candle-maker, or Candle-seller. **1611** TOURNEUR *Ath. Trag.* v. ii. (1878) 142 Back to your *candle-making! *c* **1865** LETHEBY in *Circ. Sc.* I. 98/1 We do not employ much wax..for candle-making. **1863** BARING-GOULD *Iceland* 209 A curious *candlerack of wrought iron foliage. **1819** *Post Off. Lond. Direct.* 324 *Candle-screen Manufacturers. **1780** *Hickey's Bengal Gaz.* 8 Apr. (Y.), Borrowed last Month by a Person or Persons unknown..a very elegant Pair of *Candle Shades. *a* **1916** H. JAMES *Middle Years* (1917) 76 Milford Cottage, with its innumerable red candles and candle-shades. **1967** J. RATHBONE *Diamonds Bid* xvii. 147 The glass candle shade on my own table. **1853** *Charles Auchester* III. 230 By *candleshine, or the setting sun. **1647** R. STAPYLTON *Juvenal* 85 Foul'd with *candlesmoak. **1658** *Songs Costume* (1849) 168 But you keep off till *candle-time. **1766** ENTICK *London* IV. 3 A street occupied..by *candle-wrights, or candle-makers.

7. Special comb.: **candle-ball, -bomb,** a small glass bubble filled with water, which when held in the flame of a candle, bursts with a loud

explosion; **candle-bark** (*dial.*), a candle-box (cf. BARK *sb.*[1] 8); **candle-box**, a box for keeping candles in; †**candle-branch**, a chandelier (cf. BRANCH *sb.* 2 d); **candle-bush**, a South African plant, *Sarcocaulon patersoni*, so called from the readiness with which it burns; **candle-canting** (see quot. and cf. 5 d); †**candle-case**, a case or box to keep candles in; **candle-dipper**, a machine for making candles by dipping; **candle-dipping**, the process of manufacturing candles by dipping as distinguished from moulding; also *attrib.*, as in ***candle-dipping machine***; **candle-fir** (*Sc.*), 'fir that has been buried in a morass, moss-fallen fir, split and used instead of candles' (Jamieson); **candle-fish**, a sea-fish of the salmon family, frequenting the rivers of north-western America, which on account of its extreme oiliness is used when dried as a candle; †**candle-fly**, 'a flie that houering about a candle burnes itself' (Florio s.v. *Farfalla*), a moth; **candle-foot** = *foot-candle*; **candle-hour**, ? time when candles are burnt, night-time; †**candle-inch** (see 5 d); **candle-lamp**, a kind of lamp in which candles are used; **candle-match**, a match or fusee made of the wick of a candle, or of a piece of greased paper; **candle-metre**, the illumination of a standard candle at a distance of one metre; †**candle-mine** (*fig.*), a mine of fat or candle material; **candle-mould**, a mould or mould-frame for making candles in, now usually made of pewter or tin; **candle-nut**, the commercial name for the fruit of the candleberry tree, or *candle-nut tree*; **candle-paper**, a spill for lighting candles; **candle power**, (*a*) see sense 1 d above; (*b*) the illuminating power of an electric lamp, etc., reckoned in terms of the light of a standard candle; †**candle-quencher**, an extinguisher; †**candle-rush**, the common rush, formerly used for making rush lights; †**candle-shears**, snuffers; **candle-shrift**, penance done with candles; †**candle-silver**, a money-payment for the supply of candles; **candle-slate** (see quot.); †**candle-sniting**, the snuff of a candle; †**candle-stuff**, (*a*) study or work done by candle-light; (*b*) material for candles; **candle-teening** (*dial.*), **-tending**, **-tining**, the time for lighting or seeing to the candles, evening, nightfall. Also CANDLEBERRY, -END, -LIGHT, -STICK, etc.

1794 G. ADAMS *Nat. & Exp. Philos.* I. ix. 325 This effect of vapour is..exemplified by the small machines called *candle-balls. **1823** in CRABB *Technol. Dict.*, **Candle-bomb.* **1875** *Lanc. Gloss.* (E.D.S.) **Candle-bark, cannel-bark*, a candle-box. **1566** J. HARYNGTON in *Leisure Ho.* (1884) 630/1 That no mans bed be vnmade, nor fire or *candle box vncleane, after eight o'clock in the morning. **1837** CARLYLE *Fr. Rev.* II. IV. vii. 223 Amid candle-boxes and treacle-barrels. **1599** MINSHEU *Span. Dict.*, *Candeléro de tinieblas*, a *candle-branch that hath many candlestickes in it. **1890** A. MARTIN *Home Life Ostrich Farm* 60 The *kerzbosch*, or *candle-bush, a stunted, thorny plant, if lighted at one end when in the green state, will burn steadily just like a wax candle. **1966** E. PALMER *Plains of Camdeboo* xvi. 258 The men cut long forked sticks, spiked on the fork a Candlebush which burns like paraffin, and..moved quickly from clump to clump, burning off the noors spines. **1875** ROBINSON *Whitby Gloss.* s.v. *Canting* (E.D.S.) 'A *cannle-canting' when articles were appraised until a candle burned down to a certain mark, and the highest bidder got the bargain. **1596** SHAKS. *Tam. Shr.* III. ii. 45 A paire of bootes that haue beene *candle-cases. **1604** B. JONSON *Case is Altered*, Neither knive-cases, Pinne-cases, nor Candle-cases. **1882** *Standard* 7 Oct. 5/2 The wonderful *candle-fish, or 'oolachan', which ascends the North-Western rivers in March. **1886** *Montreal Gaz.* 14 Aug. 2/4 Advt., British Columbia 'Candle Fish'. This delicious fish, the 'oolachan' packed in small tubs—for family trade. **1626** COCKERAM II, *Farfalla*, a *Candle-Fly. **1733** BAILEY *Erasm. Colloq.* (1877) 392 (D.) Why should an owl be an enemy to small birds..a turtle-dove to a candle-fly? **1892** A. P. TROTTER in *Min. Proc. Inst. Civil Engineers* CX. 71 As the heights of lamp-posts and the width of streets are measured in feet, the *candle-foot, that is, the illumination produced by one standard candle at a distance of 1 foot, will be taken in the present Paper as the unit of illumination. **1902** *Encycl. Brit.* XXVIII. 83/2 In order that street surfaces may be well lighted, the minimum illumination should not fall below 0·1 candle-foot. **1928** *Sunday Dispatch* 30 Dec. 7/5 (L.C.C. Regulation) The lighting maintained in no part of the auditorium shall be less than ·025 candle-foot. **1650** G. DANIEL *Trinarch.*, *Crastini Anim.* 12 Till when, our Numbers (destin'd to more) Creeps to a corner, at a *Candle-Hower. **1719** D'URFEY *Pills* I. 355 Meaning by *Candle-Inch to buy my Lot. **1882** E. O'DONOVAN *Merv Oasis* I. xxvi. 448 On the table burned half a dozen *Candle-lamps. **1908** *Westm. Gaz.* 23 Mar. 4/2 The values are expressed in '*candle-mètres'. **1597** SHAKS. *2 Hen. IV*, II. iv. 326 You whorson *Candle-myne you. **1566** in Rogers *Agric. & Prices* III. 577/2 *Candle-mould. **1655** MRQ. WORCESTER *Cent. Inv.* Index 8 A Candle-mold. **1835–6** TODD *Cycl Anat.* I. 58/1 The fruits of the *Aleurites triloba*..the *candle-nuts of the inhabitants of these remote regions. **1884** *Leisure Ho.* Feb. 86/2 Candle-nuts, which are exceedingly hard, but yield good oil. **1854** SIMMONDS *Comm. Products Veget. Kingd.* (L.) The *candlenut tree grows in the Polynesian Islands. **1829** PRAED *Poems* (1865) I. 363 Twisting up his song Into the sweetest *candle-papers. **1877** *Engineering* XXIV. 333 In measuring the *candle power of the light produced by each machine. **1880** J. W. URQUHART *Electr. Lt.* 278 Six electric lights of 480-candle power each. **1883** Candle power [see CANDLE *sb.* 1 d]. **1894** SALOMONS *Electr. Lt. Install.* (ed. 7) II. 248 The amount of energy required to incandesce the lamp determines its candle-power efficiency. **1934** *Discovery* June 155/2 The official physical standards of the country, e.g., length, mass, temperature, candle-power. **1382** WYCLIF *Ex.* xxv. 38 *Candelquenchers, and forsothe where the snoffes ben quenchid, be thei maad of moost puyr gold. *c* **1440** *Promp. Parv.* 60 *Candylrysche [*v.r.* candel-rushe], *papirus.* **1578** LYTE *Dodoens* IV. lii. 511 The first [kind]..serueth for Matches to burne in lampes..is called..in English, the Rush candle, or candle rushe: Camels strawe. **1679** PLOT *Staffordsh.* (1686) 379 Both which it seems are Candle-rushes. **1483** *Cath. Angl.* 52 A *Candyl schers, *emunctorium.* **1611** *Rates* (JAM.) Candlesheares, the dozen pair xxx*s*. **1871** ROSSETTI *Dante at Ver.* lvii, This Dante writ in answer thus ..Hither to *candleshrift and mulct. **1420** *Will of T. Exton*, *Candelsilvyr qui in eadem ecclesia ut in aliis ecclesiis civitatis predicte tempore paschali colligi solent & levari. **1854** *Pharmac. Jrnl.* XIII. 623 *Candle-slates, and other bituminous shales. **1483** *Cath. Angl.* 53 A *Candylsnytynge, *licinus, licinum.* **1589** NASHE in Greene *Menaphon* (Arb.) 10 For recreation after their *Candle-stuffe. **1626** BACON *Sylva* §774 By the help of Oyl and Wax, and other Candle-stuff; the flame may continue and the wick not burn. **1519** HORMAN *Vulg.* 261 About *candell tendynge the fyghtynge broke of. **1613** T. GODWIN *Rom. Antiq.* (1625) 132 *Prima fax*, Candle-tining. **1746** *Exmoor Scolding* (E.D.S.) 314 Vrom candle-dowting to candle-teening.

'candle, *v. nonce-wd.* [f. prec.]

†**1.** ***to candle over***: to cover with the material of candles. *Obs.*

1676 MARVELL *Mr. Smirke* 16 Is it the Taeda, in which they candled a Man over in Wax, and he, instead of the wick, burnt out to his lives end like a Taper, to give light to the Company?

2. To test by allowing the light of a candle to shine through.

1879 *Daily News* 28 Aug. 3/7 Letters..'candled', like suspicious eggs, to detect whether more than one sheet was covered by the enclosure. **1883** *Ibid.* 1 Aug. 5/1 An old-fashioned post-office, with clerks 'candling' the letters.

†**candle-beam.** *Obs.* exc. *Hist.*

1. A beam between the chancel and the nave of a church, on which the rood stood, with candles placed on each side of it; a rood-beam.

1463 *Bury Wills* (1850) 15 And my body to be beryed by the awter of Seynt Martyn..under the percloos of the retourne of the candilbeem. **1499** in T. Gardner *Hist. Dunwich* (1754) 156 Paid Tho. Cuttyng for makyng of the Vyse unto the Candelbem. **1849** ROCK *Ch. of Fathers* III. x. 471.

2. ? A suspended beam of wood to support a number of candles; cf. quot. 1552.

c **1440** *Promp. Parv.* 60 Candelbem [**1499** candell beme], *lucernarium.* **1492** in *Bury Wills* (1850) 238 My candylbeme that hangyth in my hall w[t] vj bellys of laton standyng thereon. **1552** HULOET, *Candle beame*, suche as hangeth in gentlemens halles, with sockettes to set candels vpon.

candleberry ('kænd(ə)lbɛrɪ). [f. CANDLE *sb.* + BERRY *sb.*[1]] A name applied to the fruit of two plants and to the plants themselves.

a. properly **candleberry-myrtle**: (*a*) A shrub (*Myrica cerifera*) common in North America, whose berries yield myrtle-wax or bayberry tallow, a greenish-white wax, of which tolerable candles are made; called also *bayberry* and *wax-myrtle*, and in *U.S.* commonly ***candleberry tree***. (*b*) The name is sometimes extended to the other species of galeworts, esp. to the Sweet Gale (*Myrica Gale*).

1753 CHAMBERS *Cycl. Supp.*, *Candle berry tree*..an aromatic evergreen..also called the Virginia myrtle. **1761** WATSON in *Phil. Trans.* LII. 93 The candleberry myrtle of North America. **1858** CARPENTER *Veg. Phys.* §347 Wax.. exists in such abundance in the fruit of a Virginian myrtle, that this has received the name of Candleberry.

b. properly **candleberry tree**: A species of spurgewort, *Aleurites triloba*, a tree of the Moluccas and the S. Pacific Isles, which produces the candle-nut of commerce, the kernels of which are used by the natives as candles.

1866 *Treas. Bot.* 36/1 The Candleberry tree..attaining the height of thirty to forty feet..is commonly cultivated in tropical countries for the sake of its nuts.

candle-coal. A variant of CANNEL-COAL, frequent in the 18th c. See CANNEL[2] d.

candle-end ('kænd(ə)l ˌɛnd). Also 6–8 **candle's**.

1. The end piece of a burnt-down candle, which remains in the socket of the candlestick.

1547 BOORDE *Introd. Knowl.* vi. (1870) 141 Whan I ete candels ends, I am at a feest. **1668** R. L'ESTRANGE *Vis. Quev.* (1708) 65 The Brands and Candle-Ends, which they would still be filching, and laying out of the way. **1732** POPE *Ep. Bathurst* 292 When Hopkins dies, a thousand lights attend The wretch, who living sav'd a candle's end. **1871** MORLEY *Voltaire* (1886) 195 How Voltaire put his host's candle-ends into his pocket.

†**b.** ***to drink off*** (or ***eat***) ***candle-ends***: a romantic extravagance in drinking a lady's health by which gallants gave token of their devotion. *Obs.*

1597 SHAKS. *2 Hen. IV*, II. iv. 267 *Dol.* Why doth the Prince loue him so then? *Fal.* Because.. hee..eates Conger and Fennell, and drinkes off Candles ends for Flap-dragons. *a* **1626** FLETCHER *M. Thomas* II. ii. (N.) Carouse her health in cans and candle-ends. *a* **1637** B. JONSON *Masque Moon* in *Dodsley* VI. 62 (N.) But none that will hang themselves for love, or eat candle's-ends, as the sublunary lovers do.

†**c.** ***to rate by candle-end***: see CANDLE 5 d.

1687 J. M. *Elegy to Cleveland* 51 Wks. 283 The Cause by Candles-end he did not rate, When others Pens did Truth assassinate.

2. *fig.* A thing of short duration or of little value; a trifle, fragment, scrap. Usually *pl.*

a **1626** FLETCHER *Hum. Lieut.* III. v. (R.) We are but spans, and candles-ends. **1841** ORDERSON *Creoleana* ii. 16 A saving of cheese parings and candle ends. **1860** SALA *Lady Chesterf.* v. 81 This nip-cheese, candle-end saving..principle.

'candle-ˌholder. *rare*$^{-1}$. [See CANDLE 5 c.] One who holds a candle; an attendant or assistant who lights those who are engaged in any work or ceremony by night; a candle-bearer.

1592 SHAKS. *Rom. & Jul.* I. iv. 38 Giue me a Torch, I am not for this ambling. Being but heauy I will beare the light ..A Torch for me..Ile be a Candle-holder and looke on.

candleless ('kænd(ə)llɪs), *a.* [f. CANDLE *sb.* + -LESS.] Without a candle or candles.

1906 *Westm. Gaz.* 20 Jan. 5/1, I am left soapless, candleless, and forlorn. **1920** SANTAYANA *Char. & Opin. U.S.* i. 6 Like those candlesticks, probably candleless, sometimes displayed as a seemly ornament in a room blazing with electric light.

candlelight ('kænd(ə)llaɪt). Forms: 4 **candeliȝt**; see also CANDLE and LIGHT. [OE. *candel leoht*, f. *candel* CANDLE *sb.* + *leoht* LIGHT.]

1. The light given by a candle or by candles. Often, artificial light in general.

a **1000** *C.R. Benet* 53 (Bosw.) Candel-leoht. **1205** LAY. 23752 þer wes al longe niht songes and candel-liht. *c* **1380** *Sir Ferumb.* 2544 þay schyne þer in tal þat house so doþ þe candeliȝt. *c* **1430** *Hymns Virg.* (1867) 123 As cler as candyllyȝth. **1678** *Trial Coleman* 30, I cannot see a great way by Candle-light. **1710** ADDISON *Tatler* No. 240 ¶5 One who had studied Thirty Years by Candle-light. **1716–8** LADY M. W. MONTAGUE *Lett.* I. xix. 59 A very fine effect by candle-light. **1875** HELPS *Soc. Press.* ix. 133 Well, don't you think that most men fall in love by candle-light?

b. 'The necessary candles for use' (J.).

1523 FITZHERB. *Husb.* §149 Whether the warkes that thou ..& thy seruauntes shall do be more auauntage to the than the fyre & candell-lyghte, meat & drynk y[t] they shall spende. *a* **1704** MOLINEUX *Let. to Locke* (J.), I shall find him coals and candlelight.

c. A picture representing a scene by candlelight.

1762–71 H. WALPOLE *Vertue's Anecd. Paint.* (1786) III. 24 He frequently painted candle-lights.

†**d.** *fig.* 'Light' of life. Cf. CANDLE 3 b. *Obs.*

1596 SPENSER *F.Q.* VI. III. iii, A man of full ripe yeares.. weake age had dimd his candlelight.

2. The time during, or at, which candles are lighted; dusk, nightfall.

1663 PEPYS *Diary* 29 Aug., She and I, it being candlelight, bought meat for to-morrow. **1699** LUTTRELL *Brief Rel.* (1857) IV. 481 Yesterday the lords satt till after candlelight debating his majesties speech. **1699** BENTLEY *Phal.* Pref. 26 The Whole might be done..twice over before Candle-light. **1876** BANCROFT *Hist. U.S.* V. lix. 195 Soon after candle-light on the fourth..the firing was renewed.

3. *attrib.* Of or pertaining to candlelight.

1634–46 ROW *Hist. Kirk* (1842) 328 Unlawfull conventicles, candle-light congregations. **1645** QUARLES *Sol. Recant.* VIII. 80 Candle-light devotion. **1813** *Examiner* 22 Feb. 124/1 The candle-light glow of Titian. **1797–1803** FOSTER in *Life & Corr.* (1846) I. 178 Pages of vulgar truisms and candle-light sense. **1832** MARRYAT *N. Forster* xliv, A very pretty candle-light colour.

'candle-'lighter. [f. CANDLE + LIGHTER.]

1. One who lights candles; *spec.* an acolyte.

1753 CHAMBERS *Cycl. Supp.*, *Candle-lighter*, an officer in the antient church, called also accensor and acolythus. **1853** RUSKIN *Stones Ven.* II. iii. §35. 51 Watching the candle-lighter at his work, knocking his ladder about the heads of the capitals as if they had given him personal offence.

2. A thing for lighting a candle, etc.; a spill.

1855 MRS. GASKELL *North & S.* 240 (Hoppe) She knew that her mother slept, from the candle-lighter thrust through the keyhole of her bedroom door. **1859** W. COLLINS *After Dark* 67 (Hoppe) A piece of paper, rolled up tight like those candle-lighters that the ladies make.

So **candle-lighting** *vbl. sb.*

1605 L. HUTTEN *An Answer* 80 They washed at table and at candle-lighting. **1784** *Maryland Jrnl.* 17 Sept. Advt. (Th.), Said School to begin at Candle-lighting, and continue till Nine o'Clock, P.M. **1869** H. B. STOWE *Oldtown Folks* xxxiv. 449 Designing to bring up at the red school-house.. at 'early candle-lighting'. **1896** *Dialect Notes* I. 385 Evenin' meetin' took up at early candle-lightin'.

Candlemas ('kænd(ə)lmæs). Forms: 1–2 **candel mæsse**, 3–5 **-masse**, **-messe**, 5 **-mas**, 4 **candil-masse**, 5 **-messe**, **-mas**, **condulmas**, 5 **candylmesse**, 6 **-mas**, 6–8 **candlemass**, 6– **candlemas**. [OE. *candelmæsse*, f. *candel* CANDLE *sb.* + *mæsse* MASS. In Icel. *kyndilmessa*: cf. med.L. *candelaria*, F. *chandeleur*, Ger. *lichtmesse*.]

1. The feast of the purification of the Virgin Mary (or presentation of Christ in the Temple) celebrated with a great display of candles.

1014 *O.E. Chron.*, Her on þissum ʒeare Sweʒen ʒeendode his daʒas to candel mæssan iii nonas Febr. *a* **1225** [see 3]. *c* **1325** *Metr. Hom.* 155 The first nam es Candelmesse, The

tother Maryes clensing esse, The thred Cristes meting es cald. *c* **1410** LOVE *Bonavent. Mirr.* ix. (Gibbs MS.) þis feste of þe puryficacioun þat is cleped candelmasse. **1500** *Ortus Voc.* in *Cath. Angl.* 52 The feest of candelmas, or meetynge of candelles. **1590** GREENWOOD *Collect. Art.* F iiij b, Your solempne & double feasts of your hollomass, Christmass, Candlemass. **1879** SIMMONS *Lay Folks Mass Bk.* 242 *note*, Candles were offered at Candlemas and certain other festivals.

2. The date of this feast, February 2nd. It is one of the quarter-days in Scotland.

a **1123** *O.E. Chron.* an. 1101 Ðises ȝeares eac se b' Rannulf to þan[m] Candel mæssan ut of þan[m] ture on Lunden nihtes oðbærst. *c* **1200** ORMIN 7706 þatt daȝȝ..mang Ennglisshe menn Iss Kanndellmesse nemmnedd. *c* **1450** *Bk. Curtasye* in *Babees Bk.* (1868) 327 Frow alhalawghe day To candelmesse. **1631** BRATHWAIT *Whimzies, Zealous Bro.* 117 Hee holds all bonds bearing date at Lammasse, Michaelmasse, Candlemasse or any masse whatsoever to be frustrate and of no effect; but by changing masse into tide they become of full force and vertue. **1818** SCOTT *Rob Roy* vi, 'I wad sae for certain, that I am gaun to quit at Cannlemas.' **1876** GRANT *Burgh Sch. Scotl.* II. xiii. 469 The old quarterly terms for paying the school fees were, Lammas, Hallowmas, Candlemas and Beltane.

3. *attrib.* and *Comb.*, as ***candlemas-day, -eve, -even, -night, -season***, etc., and in Sc. ***candlemas-ball, blaze, crown, king, offering*** (see quots.).

a **1225** *Ancr. R.* 412 Condelmesse dei. **1389** in *Eng. Gilds* (1870) 54 After candilmesse day. *c* **1450** *Bk. Curtasye* in *Babees Bk.* (1868) 311 Bryng in fyre on alhalawgh day, To condulmas euen, I dar welle say. **1521** in Arnolde *Chron.* (1811) p. xliii, Candylmas day next after, the Kynge and the sayd Duke of Burgoyn bare theyr Candyls. **1655** L'ESTRANGE *Chas. I*, 129 February the 2[d]. (you may if you please call it Candlemas night) had been time out of minde celebrated at Court with somewhat more then ordinary solemnity. **1843** CARLYLE *Past & Pr.* (1858) 129 In that Candlemas season. **1857** CHAMBERS *Inform. People* II. 466 Candlemasday is a holiday at the public offices.

1794 *Statist. Acc. Scotl.* XIII. 211 (JAM.) The scholars.. pay..a Candlemas gratuity, according to their rank and fortune, from 5*s.* even as far as 5 guineas, when there is a keen competition for the Candlemas crown. The king, i.e. he who pays most, reigns for six weeks. **1825** JAMIESON, *Candlemas bleeze*, the gift made by pupils to school-master at Candlemas; elsewhere Candlemas offering. **1863** CHAMBERS *Bk. of Days* 2 Feb., The latter part of the day was usually devoted to what was called the Candlemass bleeze, or blaze, namely, the conflagration of any piece of furze which might exist in their neighbourhood..Another old popular custom in Scotland on Candlemas day was to hold a foot-ball match..the Candlemass Ba' as it was called.

'candler. [f. CANDLE *v.* 2.] One who tests eggs by the light of a candle or an electric bulb.

1906 *N.Y. Even. Post* 5 June 9 The candlers say ten hours' work on a stretch is harmful to their eyesight. **1921** *Dict. Occup. Terms* (1927) §449 Egg candler.

†**'candle-rent.** *Obs.* Rent or revenue derived from house-property (which is continually undergoing deterioration or waste).

1611 CHAPMAN *Mayday* ii, Candlerents: if the wars hold, or a plague come to the town, they'll be worth nothing. *a* **1613** OVERBURY *Charac., Ordinarie Widow*, She dare not venture upon..a souldier, though he have candle-rents in the citie, for his estate may be subject to fire. **1633** MARMION *Fine Compan.* I. iii, Candle rents that are subject to fire and ruin. **1655** FULLER *Ch. Hist.* VI. vi. §16 (1845) III. 447 The dean and chapter of Paul's..pretended themselves yearly losers by some of these chantries; for generally they were founded on candle-rents, (houses are London's land,) which were subject to casuality, reparation, and vacations. *Ibid.* XI. ii. §6 VI. 68 Bying them generally (as candle-rents) at or under twelve years' valuation.

'candle-snuff. The snuff or burnt wick of a candle.

1552 HULOET, Snuffer of a candle or candlesnuffe. **1683** CHALKHILL *Thealma & Cl.* 102 Her eyes like Candle-snuffs by age sink quite Into their Sockets. **1880** *Syd. Soc. Lex.*, *Candle snuff*..has been recommended for the cure of ague.

'candle-ˌsnuffer.

1. An instrument for snuffing candles.

1552 HULOET, Candle snuffer, or instrumente to snuffe candelles. **1766** SMOLLETT *Trav.* xxiii. I. 353 (JOD.) Hardware..such as knives, scissars, and candle-snuffers.

†**2.** An attendant whose duty it is to snuff and attend to candles; *spec.* in *Theatres*, the man in charge of the lights, when these were candles.

1711 ADDISON *Spect.* No. 42 ¶3 Two or three shifters of Scenes, with the two Candle-snuffers. **1821** CARLYLE in *Macm. Mag.* XLV. 236 Then shall I no longer play a candlesnuffer's part in the great drama. **1881** FITZGERALD *World behind Sc.* 17 'Not fit to be a candle-snuffer'. When oil lamps took the place of candles, the wicks required constant trimming, and the services of this official continued in requisition.

†**'candle-staff.** *Obs.* [OE. *candelstæf*, f. CANDLE + STAFF.] A candlestick; the main stem or shaft of a branched candlestick.

c **1000** *Ags. Gosp.* Matt. v. 15 Ne hi ne ælað hyra loeht-fæt [Vulg. *lucernam*] and hit under cyfe settað, ac ofer candelstæf [Vulg. *candelabrum*]. *a* **1100** *Voc.* in Wr.-Wülcker 326 *Candelabrum*, candelstæf. **1382** WYCLIF *Ex.* xxv. 33 Six ȝerdes, that ben to be brouȝt forth out of the candelstaf.

candlestick ('kænd(ə)lstɪk). Forms: see CANDLE and STICK. [OE. *candelsticca*, f. *candel* CANDLE + *sticca* STICK. Cf. prec.: there is no ground for the inference that it was originally 'a piece of pointed wood'; app. the earliest recorded meaning was the metallic 'stalk' or shaft of a candelabrum.]

1. A support for a candle; formerly a general name, including chandeliers, simple or branched, upright or pendent, branches, lustres, etc.; now chiefly a moveable stand for holding a candle.

c **970** *Chart. Bp. Æðelwold* in *Cod. Dipl.* VI. 101, .II. sylure candelsticcan and .II. ouergylde etc. *a* **1121** *O.E. Chron.* an. 1102 þet wæron roden..and candel sticcan. **1303** R. BRUNNE *Handl. Synne* 9374 A kandelstyke stode þe kyng before, þat oute of Ierusalem was bore. **1387** TREVISA *Higden* Rolls Ser. V. 207 He hadde a candle stikke [*candelabrum*] i-made by craft of honde so þat þe oyle schulde renne. **1552** in *Ch. Goods of Berks* 8 Fyve brasenne candlestickes for thaulter. **1552** HULOET, Candlestycke with thre braunches or lightes. **1599** MINSHEU *Sp. Dict.*, *Candeléro de tinieblas*, a candle-branch that hath many candlestickes in it. **1605** BACON *Adv. Learn.* I. iv. §6 (1873) 32 Set up one great light, or branching candlestick of lights. **1687** *Lond. Gaz.* No. 2217/4 Two pair of small silver Chamber Candlesticks. **1753** CHAMBERS *Cycl. Supp.* s.v., Larger, and more stately candlesticks contrived for holding a great number of candles, are called *branches* and *girondoles*; and when made of glass, *lustres*. **1862** C. WORDSWORTH *New Test.* Gen. Epist. 170 The word Candlestick has taken root in the English language as an emblem of a Church..but it does not rightly represent those λυχνίαι; which were similar to the Seven-branched λυχνίαι or Lampstands.

2. *fig.* (chiefly with reference to *Rev.* i. 20, in which the lighted candle is included.)

1483 CAXTON *Gold. Leg.* 259/1 Thou spouse of god..thou candelstyk of lyȝt withoute derkenes. **1709** *Refl. Sacheverell's Serm.* 9 The golden Candlesticks, as the seven petitioning Bishops were then call'd. **1882** FARRAR *Early Chr.* II. 359 The final removal of the candlestick of Judaism.

3. *Comb.*, as ***candlestick-caster, -maker, turner***, etc.

c **1510** *Cocke Lorelles B.* (1843) 10 Broche makers, glas blowers, candelstycke casts. **1599** NASHE *Lent. Stuffe* (1871) 94 Candlestick-turners and tinkers. **1845** DISRAELI *Sybil* (1863) 25 Some monster of the middle class, some tinker or tailor, or candlestick-maker, with his long purse, preaching reform and practising corruption. **1867** F. FRANCIS *Angling* x. (1880) 346 The Candlestick Maker. This is a fly to light the salmon to bed with. **1852** DICKENS *Bleak Ho.* II. 236 (Hoppe), With a look candlestickwards.

Hence **'candlesticked** *ppl. a.*, set on a candlestick.

1884 A. A. PUTNAM *Ten Yrs. Police Judge* xxviii. 226 A dozen such candles not hid under a bushel, but candlesticked and lighted on the bench.

'candle-tree.

1. = Candleberry Myrtle. Hence ***candle-tree oil.***

1691 RAY *Creation* II. (R.) The candletrees of the West Indies, out of whose fruit, boiled to a thick fat consistence, are made very good candles. **1753** CHAMBERS *Cycl. Supp.*

2. An American tree, *Parmentiera cerifera* (N.O. *Crescentiaceæ*): from the appearance of its fruit.

1866 *Treas. Bot.* 648/1 In the Isthmus of Panama.. termed the Candle-tree..because its fruits, often four feet long, have quite the appearance of yellow wax-candles. **1855** LADY BRASSEY *The Trades* 108 In the nursery and extension grounds are..candle-trees.

'candle-ˌwaster. He who or that which wastes candles by late study at night. So also **candle-wasting.**

1599 B. JONSON *Cynthia's Rev.* III. ii, A whoreson bookworm, a candle-waster. **1599** SHAKS. *Much Ado* V. i. 18 Patch griefe with prouerbs, make misfortune drunke With candle-wasters. **1600** E. BLOUNT *Hosp. Incur. Fooles* Ded. (N.) A thousand of these candlewasting book wormes.

2. A small bit of burning wick that falls upon the substance of the candle and causes it to run.

candle-wick ('kænd(ə)lˌwɪk). [OE. *candel-weoca*: see WICK.] **1. a.** The wick of a candle. Also *attrib.*

c **1000** ÆLFRIC *Voc.* in Wr.-Wülcker 154 *Funalia*, uel *funes*, candelweoca. **1483** *Cath. Angl.* 53 A Candylweke, *lichinus, lichinum.* **1576** NEWTON tr. *Lemnie's Complex.* (1633) 125 As Oyle doth nourish the flame in the Candlewike. **1611** COTGR., *Emmecher*, to furnish with a match or candle-weeke. **1777** HOWARD *Prisons Eng.* (1780) 397 The Keeper..employs the prisoners in spinning candle-wick. **1880** BROWNING *Clive* 129 Pray me trim your candle-wick!

†**b. candlewick mullein**, a name of the Great Mullein or Hag-taper, *Verbascum Thapsus*, the leaves and stalks having been used for wicks. *Obs.*

1597 GERARD *Herbal* cclvii. §3. 631 Candle weeke Mullein hath large, broade, and woollie leaues. **1611** COTGR., *Mescheniere*, candle-weeke Mullein.

2. As one word. A soft material, usually cotton yarn, used to produce a tufted surface, also called *candlewicking*; material embroidered with tufts of this yarn. Also *attrib.*

1930 *Sears Catal.* Fall 357 Candlewick Embroidery is a popular vogue in needlework. A candlewick tufted bedspread. **1934** *Archit. Rev.* LXXVI. 183 Candlewick work..is the apotheosis of the spot [design], consisting of blobs of fluffy wool stuck on to a material. **1939** M. B. PICKEN *Lang. of Fashion* 18/2 *Candlewicking*, tuftings of threads to give a napped surface to fabric. **1951** *Good Housek. Home Encycl.* 152/2 Tweeds, folk weave, and candlewick..provide a wide range of surface-texture. **1958** P. MORTIMER *Daddy's gone A-Hunting* xx. 119 Her candlewick dressing-gown.

'candle-wood.

1. Resinous wood, splinters of which are burned to give light.

1753 CHAMBERS *Cycl. Supp.*, *Candlewood*, slips of pine about the thickness of the finger, used in New England.... to burn instead of candles. **1857** HOLLAND *Bay Path* xv. 168 The Candle-wood blazed cheerfully upon the hearth.

2. A popular name of several trees which yield such wood: Californian C., *Fouquiera splendens*; Jamaica C., *Gomphia guianensis*; S. American C., *Sciadophyllum capitatum*; White and Black C. (of the West Indies), *Amyris balsamifera.*

1712 tr. *Pomet's Hist. Drugs* I. 62 Besides the Candle-Wood, we have..a certain red Wood which they call Coral-Wood. **1756** P. BROWNE *Jamaica* 208 White Candlewood, or Rose-wood..The younger trees are frequently cut for firewood..they are full of resin, burn very freely and with a most agreeable smell. **1884** MILLER *Plant-n.*

can-dock ('kændɒk). [f. CAN *sb.*[1] + DOCK *sb.*[1]] The Yellow Water-lily. Also applied to the White Water-lily; see quots.

1661 WALTON *Angler* (ed. 3) xx. 242 To kill the water weeds, as Water-lillies, Candocks..and Bull-rushes that breede there. [**1787** WITHERING *Bot. Arrangem.* (ed. 2) II. 555 (Britten & Holl.), *Nymphæa alba* [called Watercan] at Tamworth, from the half unfolded leaves floating on the water, being supposed to resemble cans.] **1820** SALTER *Troller's Guide* 88 Candock Weeds (by some called the Water Lily). **1821** S. F. GRAY *Brit. Plants* II. 707 *Nymphæa alba*, White Water-Lily..White water-can, Candock. **1879** PRIOR *Plant-n.*, *Can-dock*, from its broad leaves, and the shape of its seed vessel, like that of a silver can or flagon. Dan. *aa-kande*, the yellow water-lily.

candore, obs. form of CONDOR.

candour ('kændə(r)). Also 7-9 **candor.** [17th c. *candor*, a. L. *candor* (*-ōrem*) dazzling whiteness, brilliancy, innocency, purity, sincerity, f. root *cand-* of *candēre* to be white and shining, *accendĕre* to set alight, kindle: cf. *candid, candle.* F. *candeur* (16th c. in Littré) may have aided; the 14th c. example is properly Latin.]

†**1.** Brilliant whiteness; brilliancy. *Obs.*

[**1398** TREVISA *Barth. De P.R.* XIX. xi. (1495) 871 Candor is passynge whytnesse.] **1634** SIR T. HERBERT *Trav.* 91 This nights travaile was bettered by Cynthias candor. **1692** TRYON *Good House-w.* ii. 25 Milk..the Emblem of Innocence, deriving that aimable and pleasant Candor from a Gleam of the divine Light.

†**2.** Stainlessness of character; purity, integrity, innocence. *Obs.*

1610 B. JONSON *Alch.* V. v. (1616) 676 Helpe his fortune, though with some small straine Of his owne candor. **1675** TRAHERNE *Chr. Ethics* xxv. 388 If afterwards he comes to see the candor of his abused friend. **1703** ROWE *Fair Penit.* I. i. 376 Pure native Truth And Candour of the Mind. *a* **1704** T. BROWN *Eng. Sat.* Wks. 1730 I. 29 My lord Dorsets morals and integrity, his candor and his honour.

3. Freedom from mental bias, openness of mind; fairness, impartiality, justice.

a **1637** B. JONSON *Epigr.* cxxiii. (R.) Writing thyselfe, or judging others writ, I know not which th' hast most, candor or wit. **1653** *Hales' Dissert. Peace* in *Phenix* (1708) II. 388 If thou hast but a grain of Candor in thy heart, and wilt pass Sentence according to the Prescript of Truth. **1702** *Clarendon's Hist. Reb.* I. Pref. 2 The candor, and impartiality of what he relates. **1794** PALEY *Evid.* III. ii. (1817) 282 A species of candour which is shown towards every other book, is sometimes refused to the Scriptures. **1836** WHATELY *Chr. Evid.* v, To exercise candour in judging fairly of the evidences. **1857** H. REED *Lect. Brit. Poets* xv. 202 In criticism candour with its comprehensive sympathies, is as rare, as bigotry is frequent.

†**4.** Freedom from malice, favourable disposition, kindliness; 'sweetness of temper, kindness' (J.). *Obs.*

1653 WALTON *Angler* To Rdr., If he [the Reader] bring not candor to the reading of this Discourse, he shall..injure me..by too many Criticisms. **1666** DRYDEN *Ann. Mirab.* Ded. (Globe ed.) 42 Your candour in pardoning my errors. **1751** JOHNSON *Cheynel* Wks. IV. 508 He shews himself sincere, but without candour. **1765** —— *Pref. Shaks.* Wks. IX. 252 That bigotry which sets candour higher than truth. **1802** *Med. Jrnl.* VIII. 226 A gentleman of unbounded candor, and a most benevolent disposition.

5. Freedom from reserve in one's statements; openness, frankness, ingenuousness, outspokenness.

1769 *Lett. Junius* ii. 11 This writer, with all his boasted candour, has not told us the real cause of the evils. **1836** HOR. SMITH *Tin Trump.* (1876) 72 Candour in some people may be compared to barley sugar drops, in which the acid preponderates over the sweetness. **1876** J. H. NEWMAN *Hist. Sk.* I. II. iv. 257 Openness and candour are rare qualities in a statesman.

candred, var. of CANTRED.

candy ('kændɪ), *sb.*[1] [a. F. *candi* in *sucre candi*; cf. It. *zucchero candi* (found, according to Littré, in an It. author of 1310), Sp. *azucar cande*, Pg. *assúcar candi*, med.L. *saccharum candi*; a. Arab., orig. Pers. *qand* sugar, the crystallized juice of the sugar-cane (whence Arab. *qandah* candy, *qandī* candied); of Indian origin, cf. Skr. *khanda* 'piece', also 'sugar in crystalline pieces', f. *khand* to break. As in the other langs., the full SUGAR

CANDY (q.v.) appears much earlier than the simple *candy*.]

1. Crystallized sugar, made by repeated boiling and slow evaporation, more fully called SUGAR CANDY; also any confection made of, or incrusted with this. (In U.S. used more widely than in Great Britain, including toffee, and the like.)

[*c* **1420** *Liber Cocorum* 7 With sugur candy thou may hit dowce. **1543** TRAHERON tr. *Vigo's Chirurg.* Interpr. Straunge Wds., A syrupe they calle sugre candie.] **1769** MRS. RAFFALD *Eng. Housekpr.* (1778) 241 To a pound of double refined sugar put two spoonfuls of water, skim it well, and boil it almost to a candy, when it is cold, drain your plums out of the first syrup, and put them in the thick syrup. **1808–17** FOSTER in *Life & Corr.* (1846) I. lxxv. 410 Handing round candies and cowslip wine. **1844** EMERSON *Young Amer.* Wks. (Bohn) II. 302 One man buys..a land title.. and makes his posterity princes; and the other buys barley candy. **1850** MRS. STOWE *Uncle Tom's C.* xiv. 124 With her hands full of candy, nuts, and oranges. **1865** MRS. WHITNEY *Gayworthys* II. 44 The parson..approved only of white unflavoured candies for his children.

2. *Comb.*, as ***candy-girl***, ***-merchant***, ***pink***, ***-shop***, ***-stall***, ***-store***, ***-woman***; ***candy-coloured***, ***-pale*** adjs.; **candy-braid** (*U.S.*), a twist of candy or toffee; **candy-broad sugar** (*Sc.*), 'loaf or lump sugar' (Jam.); **candy butcher** (see BUTCHER *sb.* 3 b); **candy-floss** [FLOSS²], a sweet confection, usually pink, of fluffy spun sugar; also in *transf.* and *attrib.* use as a type of meretriciousness; **candy-high** *a.* or *adv.*, to the point of candying or crystallizing; so **candy-height**; **candy-man**, an itinerant seller of candy; in the north of England, a bum-bailiff or process-server; so called because in the great strike of coal-miners in 1844, when a large number of extempore bailiffs were employed to eject the miners wholesale from the cottages, there were recognized among them some well-known sellers of 'dandy candy' from the Newcastle streets, whose appellation was transferred to persons employed in the unpopular office; †**candy-plate**, an obsolete confection (see PLATE); **candy-pull** (*U.S.*), a turn at pulling or twisting toffee to make it tough and light-coloured, a party of young people at which toffee is made (in Scotland a *taffy-join*); **candy-stripe(d)**, pattern(ed) in alternate stripes of white and colour, as in a popular kind of candy; **candy-sugar** = SUGAR-CANDY.

1870 EMERSON *Soc & Solit.* Wks. vii. (Bohn) III. 64 Steam..can twist beams of iron like *candy-braids. **1732** R. MAXWELL *Trans. Soc. Improv. Agric.* 290 (JAM.) Three ounces of *candy-broad sugar. **1888** G. M. HOPKINS *Poems* (1918) 89 A *candycoloured..river. **1951** *Springfield Sunday Republican* 6 May 29A (Advt.), Salt water taffy.. pop corn—*candy floss. **1952** *Times* 2 Oct. 6/2 They could not solve problems of foreign policy on a diet of rhetorical candy floss. **1957** J. FRAME *Owls do Cry* II. xxii. 100 You won't get any ice creams or..candy-floss. **1957** R. HOGGART *Uses of Literacy* vii. 171 (*heading*) Invitations to a candy-floss world: the newer mass art. **1855** M. M. THOMPSON *Doesticks* xxxiii. 299 With what an affectionate air couldst thou..box the ears of the little *candy-girl. **1741** *Compl. Fam. Piece* I. i. 91 Boil it to a *Candy-height. **1769** MRS. RAFFALD *Eng. Housekpr.* (1778) 247 When it begins to candy round the edge of your pan it is candy height. **1750** E. SMITH *Compl. Housew.* 200 Sugar made into a syrup, and boiled *candy-high. **1863** *Newcastle Chron.* 31 Oct., The colliery carts and waggons stood at the doors and the furniture was handed out..It was evident that the '*candymen' had warmed to their work. **1880** PATTERSON *Antrim & Down Gloss.* (E.D.S.) *Candy-man*, a rag-man. These men generally give a kind of toffee, called 'candy', in exchange for rags, etc. **1886** *Leeds Merc.* 13 Jan., A large body of police and thirty 'candymen' arrived at Medoursley Collieries, Consett, near Durham, yesterday, for the purpose of evicting sixty unionists. **1870** 'FANNY FERN' *Ginger-Snaps* 61 To the delight of these youngsters and the *candy-merchants. **1920** E. SITWELL *Wooden Pegasus* 48 As they Shelter the children, *candy-pale. **1937** L. BROMFIELD *Rains Came* I. i. 15 He wore an enormous Rajput turban in shades of poison green and violet and *candy pink. **1649** G. DANIEL *Trinarch., Hen. V*, ccclxvi, Soe saue the Ipocras, and *Candy Plate. **1887** *Boston* (Mass.) *Jrnl.* 20 Aug. 5/3 The candies suggest pleasant winter evenings, and '*candy pulls' at the beach in summer. **1845** *Knickerbocker* XXV. 424 *Candy-shop keepers. **1886** *Harper's Mag.* June 93/2 A considerable portion of the refined sugars find their way to the candy shops. **1879** SALA in *Daily Tel.* 26 Dec., A very grand '*candy' stall, overbrimming with those lollipops so irrepressibly dear to the American palate. **1884** *New York Her.* 27 Oct. 7/6 Girl to learn to attend bakery, lunch room or *candy store. **1894** 'MARK TWAIN' *Pudd'nhead Wilson* 234 The *candy-striped pole..indicated..the barber shop. **1939** M. B. PICKEN *Lang. of Fashion* 18/2 *Candy stripe*, stripe like those in stick candy. **1941** 'R. WEST' *Black Lamb* (1942) I. 497 His candy-striped pyjamas. **1959** *Housewife* June 100/1 Candy-striped sheets and pillowcases. **1864** *Louie's last Term* 168 The *candy-woman..did not make any thing of the Dough-balls any how.

¶ *Candy* in mod. edd. of Shaks. *1 Hen. IV*, I. iii. 251: see CAUDIE.

†'**candy**, *sb.*² Obs. form of *Candia*, name of an island (now Crete): used in some obs. names of plants and products: also in CANDY-TUFT.

1597 GERARD *Herbal* I. xxiv. 31 It grows in Creet, now called Candy. **1601** HOLLAND *Pliny* II. 229 Touching the Candy Carot, it resembleth fennel. **1635** J. TAYLOR (Water P.) *Parr* in *Harl. Misc.* (Malh.) IV. 212 More sweet than candy oil. **1668** WILKINS *Real Char.* II. iv. 89 Candy Alexander. **1750** BEAWES *Lex Mercat.* (1752) 382 Oils, in Candy Barrels.

‖'**candy**, *sb.*³ [Mahr. *khandi*, Tamul and Mayal. *kandi*; in Pg. *candil* (Yule).] A weight used in southern and western India, varying greatly in different parts, but averaging 500 pounds av.

1618 PURCHAS *Pilgr.* I. 657 (Y.) The candee at this place [Batecola] containeth neere 500 pounds. **1862** BRIGHT *America, Sp.* (1876) 101 Every Candy of cotton—a candy is 7 cwt. or lbs. 784—costing 80 rupees. **1875** BEDFORD *Sailor's Pocket-bk.* ix. (ed. 2) 323 The Maund 25 lbs., and the Candy 500 lbs. English av.

candy ('kændɪ), *v.* [f. CANDY *sb.*¹, after F. *candir*, It. *candire* to candy. The formation of the French vb. was prob. assisted by taking *candi* in *sucre candi* as a pa. pple. = candied: cf. It. *zucchero candito*.]

1. *trans.* To preserve (fruits, etc.) by boiling with sugar, which crystallizes and forms a crust; to coat or incrust with sugar. Also *absol.*

1533 ELYOT *Cast. Helth* (1541) 72a, Gynger..candyd with Sugar. *a* **1634** RANDOLPH *To Feltham* 114 Neatly to candy o're the wholesome pill. **1741** RICHARDSON *Pamela* (1824) I. 126 To pot and candy, and preserve for the uses of the family. *c* **1760** GLASSE (*title*) Compleat Confectioner.. Method of..Candying Fruit. **1866** GEO. ELIOT *F. Holt* (1868) 24 If I've only got some orange flowers to candy.

2. *fig.* To sweeten, render pleasant or palatable; to give a pleasant appearance to; to sugar *over*.

1592 *Conspir. Pretend. Ref.* Pref. 2 To candie and sweeten them ouer with the louely shewe of peace. **1604** T. WRIGHT *Passions* v. iv. 203 That which was canded with semblable pleasure. **1642** FULLER *Holy & Prof. St.* IV. xix. 337 His Teachers..candy over his sourest studies with pleasure. *a* **1658** CLEVELAND *Gen. Poems* (1677) 15 For shame you pretty Female Elves, Cease thus to candy up your selves. *a* **1734** NORTH *Examen* 305 (D.) Thereby to candy them up to posterity.

3. To form into crystals, congeal in a crystalline form: **a.** sugar, honey, etc.; **b.** (*transf.*) other things resembling sugar, as salt, ice, etc.

1598 SYLVESTER *Du Bartas* I. ii. (1641) 14/1 Th' excessive cold of the mid-aire (anon) Candies-it [a dropping show'r] all in bals of Ycy-stone. **1601** HOLLAND *Pliny* I. 362 As for sugar..the best comes out of India. A kind of hony it is, gathered and candied in certaine Canes. **1713** *Lond. & Country Brew.* II. (1742) 110 The Sea-salt water candied or coagulated by the Sun. **1880** *Print. Trades Jrnl.* xxx. 37 Too much boiling candies the molasses.

4. *transf.* To cover or incrust with crystalline substance, as hoar-frost, etc. Also ***to candy over***.

1607 SHAKS. *Timon* IV. iii. 226 The cold Brooke Candied with ice. **1613** W. BROWNE *Brit. Past.* I. iv. (1772) I. 119 Hoary frosts had candy'd all the plaines. **1639** G. DANIEL *Ecclus.* xliii. 44 Frost, sent as salt..and Plants are Candid ore. **1703** BURCHETT *Naval Trans.* III. xix. (1720) 393 The Provisions sent to them were..candied with Salt.

5. *intr.* To crystallize or congeal, to become incrusted with sugar.

1657 S. PURCHAS *Theat. Pol. Flying-Ins.* 209 The hony.. ..of the new world, candies not, but is alwayes liquid like oyl. **1718** QUINCEY *Compl. Disp.* 34 After the Syrup comes to stand some time, it will candy. *Mod.* Preserves candy by long keeping.

candying ('kændɪɪŋ). *vbl. sb.* [f. CANDY *v.* + -ING¹.] The action of the verb CANDY, q.v.

1653 W. J. GENT (*title*) A Choice Manual..also most exquisite ways of Preserving, Conserving, Candying, etc. **1662** FULLER *Worthies, Essex* 318 The candying of them [Eringo roots] being become a staple commodity at Colchester. **1871** NICHOLS *Fireside Sc.* 99 The 'candying' results from boiling the molasses.

candytuft ('kændɪtʌft). Also erron. -turf. [f. CANDY *sb.*² = *Candia*, name of the island (now Crete) + TUFT.] A plant, *Iberis umbellata*, originally brought from Candia; and, by extension, the genus *Iberis* (N.O. *Cruciferæ*), consisting of herbaceous plants or small undershrubs with white, pink, or purple flowers in flat corymbs or 'tufts'.

[**1578** LYTE *Dodoens* v. lxiii 629 Candie Thlaspi is in complexion lyke to the other Thlaspies.] **1664** EVELYN *Kal. Hort.* (1729) 200 Sow divers Annuals..Candy Tufts. **1727** BRADLEY *Fam. Dict., Candy Tuft*, serves for an Ornament to great Parterres. **1741** *Compl. Fam.-Piece* II. iii. 362 Hardy annual Flowers, as..dwarf Lychnis, Candy Turf. **1858** GLENNY *Gard. Everyday Bk.* 146/1 The smaller kinds [of hardy annuals]..such as Larkspur, Candy Tuft.

cane (keɪn), *sb.*¹ Also 5 **canne**, **can**. [ME. *canne*, *cane*, a. OF. *cane*, later *canne* (= Pr. *cana*, Sp. *caña*, It. *canna*):—L. *canna*, a. Gr. κάννα, κάννη, reed, perh. from Semitic: cf. Heb. *qāneh*, Arab. *qanāh* reed, cane. In Latin the sense was extended from '(hollow) reed or cane' to 'tube or pipe', a sense retained in Romanic, and prominent in the derivatives *canneau*, *cannella*, etc.]

1. a. The hollow jointed ligneous stem of various giant reeds or grasses, as Bamboo and Sugar cane, and the solid stem of some of the more slender palms, esp. the genus *Calamus* (the Rattan); also the stem of the Raspberry and its congeners.

1398 TREVISA *Barth. De P.R.* XII. ix. (1495) 419 A noyse as it were wyth a canne other a grete reyd. *c* **1425** *Voc.* in Wr.-Wülcker 645 *Hec canna*, cane. *c* **1475** *Ibid.* 763 *Hic calamus*, a cane. **1481** CAXTON *Myrr.* II. x. 89 Ther growe in many places [of ynde] canes..ful of sugre. **1620** VENNER *Via Recta* vi. 101 The Sugar is nothing else but the iuyce of certaine Canes or Reedes. **1727** A. HAMILTON *New Acc. E. Ind.* II. xlvi. 152 The best Canes in the World grow hereabout. **1783** COWPER *Task* I. 39 Now came the cane from India, smooth and bright With Nature's varnish. **1861** DELAMER *Kitch. Gard.* 163 As soon as the last dish of fruit [raspberries] has been gathered, cut down..every cane on which it has grown. **1880** HOWELLS *Undisc. Country* xiii. 189 The canes of the blackberries and raspberries in the garden were tufted with dark green.

b. *contextually* = Sugar-cane.

1781 COWPER *Charity* 190 Has God then given its sweetness to the cane..in vain? **1837** HT. MARTINEAU *Soc. Amer.* II. 52 Some of the southern newspapers have recommended the substitution of beet for canes.

c. As name of a substance, without plural: usually the stem of the rattan or other palm.

Mod. A piece of cane. Ribs of whalebone or split cane.

d. *U.S.* (*a*) Canes collectively; (*b*) a field of cane; (*c*) = *cane-brake* (a).

1784 J. FILSON *Discovery Kentucke* 18 This great tract is.. covered with cane, wild rye, and clover. **1796** B. HAWKINS *Let.* in *Georgia Hist. Soc. Coll.* IX. 14 There is plenty of young cane and provisions. **1836** J. HALL *Statistics of West* ii. 27 The inhabitants drive their cattle to the cane in the autumn. **1847** in D. Drake *Life Kentucky* (1870) i. 14 Their practice was..to..lodge separately among the cane, which flourished in great luxuriance. **1925** Z. A. TILGHMAN *Dugout* 91 George secured men to..put in a crop of kafir and cane.

2. Hence, with various defining words, ***bamboo cane***, ***dragon cane***, ***rattan cane***, ***reed cane***, ***sugar cane***; see BAMBOO, etc. **Malacca cane**, a species (*Calamus Scipionum*) much thicker than the rattan, used for walking-sticks; **Tobago cane**, a slender West Indian palm, used for the same purpose. Also in the names of plants which are not canes: as **dumb cane**, an araceous plant, *Dieffenbachia seguina*; **Indian cane**, *Canna indica* (N.O. *Marantaceæ*); **sweet cane**, the Sweet Flag, *Acorus Calamus*.

1611 BIBLE *Isa.* xliii. 24 Thou hast bought mee no sweete cane with money. **1611** COTGR., *Acore*, Calamus aromaticus, the sweet Cane. **1842** *Penny Cycl.* XXIII. 227/2 The canes which grow immediately from the planted slips are called plant-canes..the canes which sprout up from the old roots, or stoles, being called rattoons. **1866** *Treas. Bot.* 116/1 Its [*Bactris minor*] stems..are said to be sometimes imported into this country under the name of Tobago canes. *Ibid.* 406 *Dieffenbachia*, It has acquired the name of Dumb Cane in the West Indies, in consequence of its fleshy cane-like stems rendering speechless any person who may happen to bite them, the juice of the plant being so excessively acrid as to..prevent articulation for several days. **1874** KNIGHT *Dict. Mech.* I. 443/2 Malacca canes have frequently to be colored in parts.

†**3. a.** A dart or lance made of a reed or cane; also *fig.* *Obs.* [cf. Lat. uses of *calamus*, *harundo*.]

1581 J. BELL *Haddon's Answ. Osor.* 77 You shall see how quickly he will take up your glove, and..crush your Sophisticall canes in peeces. **1677** SEDLEY *Ant. & Cl.* Wks. 1722 I. 162 Slain..by some flying Parthian's darted Cane. *a* **1700** DRYDEN (J.) The flying skirmish of the darted cane.

†**b.** ***play of (the) cane(s***: a translation of Sp. *juego de cañas* 'skirmish with throwing canes on horsebacke one at another' (Minsheu 1623). *Obs.*

1556 *Chron. Gr. Friars* (1852) 92 The play of the Spanyardes that was callyd the cane. **1574** HELLOWES *Gueuara's Fam. Ep.* (1577) 209 All the knights of the bande should..practise the play at the canes. **1627** R. ASHLEY *Almansor* 5 The Prince went downe, with all the Alcaydes.. to play at the Canes.

4. A suitable length of a cane stem, especially of one of the slender palms, prepared and used for a walking-stick, or as a rod for beating. Hence, by extension, a slender walking-stick of any sort.

1590 WEBBE *Trav.* (1868) 17 In Turkie they are beaten for debt vpon the soles of their feet with a Cane. **1662** PEPYS *Diary* 18 Apr., Sending the boy down into the cellar..I followed him with a cane, and did there beat him. **1686** *Lond. Gaz.* No. 2186/4 A Silver Sword, and a Cane of gilded Silver. **1722** DE FOE *Relig. Courtsh.* I. iii. (1840) 104 There are more ways of correction than the rod and the cane. **1799** SOUTHEY *Shufflebottom's Amat. Poems* iv, That portly Gentleman With gold-laced hat and golden-headed cane. **1853** *Arabian Nts.* (Rtldg.) 100 One of the slaves..gave me so many blows with a small pliant cane.

†**5. a.** A pipe or tube; in later use, esp. a slender glass tube, the tubular neck of a retort, or the like. [So L. and It. *canna*, F. *canne*.] *Obs.*

1430 LYDG. *Chron. Troy* I. vi, They take a quil..or a large can And in the ende this stone they set than. **1547** BOORDE *Brev. Health* lii. 23 b, The canes of the lunges [cf. L. *canna gutturis*]. **1605** SYLVESTER *Du Bartas* I. vi. I. 209 Least our eyes should bee As theirs that Heau'n through hollow Canes do see. **1684** R. WALLER *Nat. Exper.* 28 Take a Glass Cane AB..seal it at A, and..fill it with Mercury. **1693** E. HALLEY in *Phil. Trans.* XVII. 652, I took a smaller Bolt-head with a proportional Cane or Neck. **1720** *Ibid.* XXXI. 118 Let there be provided two small Glass Canes.

†**b.** ***cane of fire***: old term for a gun or fire-arm. [16th c. F. and It.; cf. F. *canne á vent* air-gun.]

1550 EDW. VI, *Jrnl.* in *Lit. Rem.* (1858) 279 With..canes of fire and bombardes assaulted the castel. **1591** HARINGTON

Orl. Fur. IX. lxvii. (R.) And brings with him his iron cane and fire, Wherewith he doth beate down and burne All those whom he to mischiefe doth desire. [1670 Lassels *Voy. Italy* I. Ev, They bring home nothing but firecanes, parots, and Monkies.]

6. Applied to a slender cylindrical stick or rod of various substances: **a.** of sealing-wax or sulphur; **b.** of glass (solid); †**c.** of tobacco.

a 1618 Sylvester *Tobacco battered* Wks. (1621) 1145 Impose so deep a Taxe On All these Ball, Leafe, Cane, and Pudding Packs. *a* 1612 Harington *Epigr.* IV. 34 (N.) Then of tobacco he a pype doth lack, Of Trinidade in cane, in leaf, or ball. 1645 Evelyn *Diary* (Chandos) 129 Sulphure made ..casting it into canes. 1746 *Phil. Trans.* XLIV. 27 Concerning the effects of a cane of black sealing wax, and a cane of brimstone, in electrical experiments. 1849 Pellatt *Curios. Glass-making* 108 'Cane' invariably means a solid stick of glass; and 'tube' hollow. 1884 *Public Opinion* 11 July 47/1 Glass blowers, with globes, cylinders, and canes.

7. Put for F. *canne*, It. *canna*, as a measure of length. Cf. CANNA²; also L. *calamus*, and REED.

At Naples = 7 ft. 3½ in., at Toulouse 5 ft. 8⅔ in.; in Provence 6 ft. 5½ in.

1653 Urquhart *Rabelais* I. xxxvii, A combe which was nine hundred foot long of the Jewish Canne-measure. 1750 Beawes *Lex Mercat.* (1752) 891. 1769 Hamilton in *Phil. Trans.* LX. 9 A Neapolitan cane is two yards and half a quarter, English measure.

8. = CANNEL.

1621 H. Ainsworth *Annot. Pentat.* Lev. i. 6 (1639) 6 The Cane (or channell bone) of the shoulder.

9. *Comb.*: **a.** attributive, as ***cane-arrow, -bill, -bottom*** (hence ***cane-bottoming***), ***-chair, -cut, -field, -grass, -piece, -seat, -slip -sugar, -wine***; **b.** objective, as ***cane-scraper, -seller, -splitter, -stripper; cane-carrying***; **c.** with pa. pple., as ***cane-bottomed, -seated*** adjs.; also **cane-like** adj., **cane-wise** adv.

1874 Boutell *Arms & Arm.* iii. 52 Long *cane arrows.. tipped..with sharp pieces of stone. 1831 J. Holland *Manuf. Metals* I. 142 The *cane bill. 1877 A. B. Edwards *Up Nile* ii. 40 A row of *cane-bottomed chairs. 1852 Mundy *Antipodes* I. iv. 137 They laughed at the *cane-carrying soldiers. 1924 *Glasgow Herald* 16 Apr. 10, I had not imagined..that cane-carrying was peculiar to some nations and not others. 1696 *Lond. Gaz.* No. 3213/4 *Cane-Chairs ..Tables, Stands. 1710 *Ibid.* No. 4646/4 Richard Lewis, born in Shropshire, a Cane-chair-maker. 1850 Marg. Fuller *Wom. in 19th C.* (1862) 263 Light cane-chairs. 1887 *Pall Mall G.* 5 Aug. 3/1 Three *cane-cuts over the palm of the hand. 1841 Orderson *Creol.* xvii. 202 A *cane field bordering the road. 1882 P. Robinson *Under Sun* III. v. 198 The tiger..crouches among the *cane-grass. 1866 *Treas. Bot.* I. 406/1 The stem has a *cane-like appearance. 1774 J. Schaw *Let.* 12 Dec. in *Jrnl. of Lady of Quality* (1921) ii. 84 We walked thro' many *cane pieces, as they term the fields of Sugar-canes. 1861 Trollope *Tales of all Countries* 134 He took Mr. Leslie through his mills and over his cane-pieces. 1875 Ure *Dict. Arts* III. 937 The cane-pieces were strewed..in the path of the wheel, and the juice expressed flowed away through a channel or gutter. 1881 *Mechanic* §40. 19 Beechen frames for *cane-seated chairs. 1875 Ure *Dict. Arts* III. 936 The proper season for planting the *cane-slips. 1887 *Daily News* 20 May 6/8 Sugar..*Cane sorts continue inactive. 1855 J. F. Johnston *Chem. Com. Life* I. 255 The *cane sugars are popularly distinguished from the grape sugars by greater sweetness. *Ibid.* 329 To this *cane-wine the negroes give the name of Guarapo. *c* 1654 Flecknoe *Trav.* 71 The body [of the Pinto tree] growing *cane-wise.

10. Special combs.: **cane-apple**, the Strawberry-tree, *Arbutus Unedo* (Chambers *Cycl. Supp.* 1753); **cane-brake**, (*a*) a brake or thicket of canes; (*b*) a genus of grasses, *Arundinaria*, allied to the bamboo; **cane-brimstone**, sulphur in rolls or sticks; **cane colour**, the colour of cane as applied to pottery ware; pottery of this colour; also as *adj.*; so **cane-coloured** *a.* (also *transf.*); **cane-fly**, a West Indian insect; **cane-fruit**, a commercial name for such fruit as raspberries and blackberries which grow on canes (*Cent. Dict. Suppl.* 1909); **cane grass**, (*a*) *U.S.*, the plant *Arundinaria macrosperma* forming the cane-brakes of the southern United States; (*b*) *Austral.*, *Glyceria ramigera*; **cane-gun**, a gun constructed in the form of a cane or walking-stick; **cane-harvester**, a machine for cutting standing (sugar) canes; **cane-hole** (in *Sugar-planting*), the hole or trench in which the slips of sugar-cane are planted; **cane-juice**, the juice of the sugar-cane; **cane-killer**, a plant (*Alectra brasiliensis*); **cane knife** *U.S.*, a large knife used in cutting cane; **cane-liquor** = *cane-juice*; **cane-mill**, a mill for crushing (sugar) canes; **cane-press**, a machine for pressing sugar-canes; **cane-rat**, any of several large African rodents, as *Thryonomys swinderianus* and *Aulacodus s.*; **cane-stripper**, a knife for stripping and topping the stalks of the sugar-cane; †**cane-tobacco**, tobacco in the form of cane (see sense 6); **cane-top** *U.S.* (see quot. 1833); **cane trash**, (*a*) the refuse of sugar-canes after the expression of the juice; (*b*) (see quot.); **cane-work**, strips of cane interwoven and used to form the backs of chairs and other articles of furniture; also *attrib.*; **cane-worker**, one who makes articles of cane.

1770 *South-Carolina Gaz.* 18 Oct., There is a large Neck, or Island, of Swamp or *Cane-Brake Land. 1839-40 W. Irving *Wolfert's R.* (1855) 201 They were generally pitched ..close by a canebrake, to screen us from the wind. 1876 Bancroft *Hist. U.S.* I. ii. 49 The impassable canebrakes, and the dense woods. *a* 1930 D. H. Lawrence *Last Poems* (1932) 14 So in the cane-brake he clasped his hands in delight. 1787 Jos. Wedgwood *Catalogue* (ed. 6) 2 Bamboo, or *cane-coloured bisqué porcelain. 1865 L. Jewitt *Wedgwoods* 311 The 'bamboo, or cane-coloured' ware. 1866 Meteyard *Jos. Wedgwood* II. p. xxiv, Cane-colour Inkstand. 1875 —— *Wedgwood Handbk.* Gloss. 393 *Cane-colour*, ware the colour of cane... Cane-colour was applied both to ornamental and to useful purposes. 1910 W. de la Mare *3 Mulla-Mulgars* xiv. 196 Short, fleecy, and cane-coloured whiskers. 1750 G. Hughes *Barbados*, The *Cane-fly..is a small whitish fly..It is chiefly to be seen among thick-planted ripe canes. 1827 *Western Monthly Rev.* (Cincinnati, U.S.) I. 209 The *cane grass of the vast swamps and savannahs on the Gulf of Mexico. 1898 Morris *Austral Eng.* 78/2 Cane-grass. 1953 A. Upfield *Murder must Wait* xxii. 195 A clump of low cane-grass. 1750 Beawes *Lex Mercat.* (1752) 751, I might add Sugar..if these People had the Art to cultivate and boil the *Canes Juice. 1764 Grainger *Sugar Cane* I. *note* (R.) A nation who made use of the cane-juice as a drink. 1798 A. Ellicott in *Life & Lett.* (1908) 159 [The country] could only be explored by using the *cane knife and hatchet. 1887 *Harper's Mag.* July 272/1 The children..squabbling for the possession of one cane-knife to split kindlers. 1875 Ure *Dict. Arts* III. 941 Recent *cane-liquor contains no appreciable portion of acid to be saturated. 1833 B. Silliman *Man. Sugar Cane* 30 The *cane mill consists of three cast iron cylinders. 1876 H. Brooks *Natal* 116 The cane-rat or ground-rat, that feeds upon the sugar-canes, is properly more of a porcupine than a rat. 1934 *Nature* 7 Apr. 524/2 Another addition to the Zoo worthy of note is three young cane-rats (*Aulacodus swinderianus*) from West Africa. 1954 G. Durrell *Bafut Beagles* ii. 39, I could see we had caught a very large Cane Rat... It measured about two and a half feet in length, and was covered with a coarse brownish fur. It had a chubby, rather beaver-like face, small ears set close to the head, a thick naked tail and large naked feet. 1600 Rowlands *Lett. Humours Blood* vi. 77 Out upon *Cane and leafe Tobacco smell. 1605 Chapman *All Fools* in *Dodsley* (1780) IV. 187 My boy once lighted A pipe of cane tobacco with a piece Of a vile ballad. 1608 *Merry Dev. Edmont.* in Hazl. *Dodsley* X. 215 Stuff'd With smoke, more chargeable than cane-tobacco. 1826 J. Bradford *Hist. Notes Kentucky* (1932) 11 *Cane tops. 1833 B. Silliman *Man. Sugar Cane* 12 But a part of the planting is done with cane tops, or that portion of the Cane which is rejected in cutting it for the mill. 1790 Castles in *Phil. Trans.* LXXX. 349 Burning the *cane trash (or straw of the cane). 1842 *Penny Cycl.* XXIII. 228/2 The canes..are reduced to the form of dry splinters, which are called cane-trash, and are used as fuel in heating the vessels for evaporating the juice. 1858 T. Vielé *Following the Drum* 53 Divans of *cane-work. 1887 A. Forbes *Insulinde* 25 The backs of the open canework chairs. 1934 *Burlington Mag.* Nov. 201/2 A back formed of a single panel of cane-work is something new. 1858 Simmonds *Dict. Trade*, **Cane-worker*, a maker of articles in rattans, Spanish and other canes; a basket-maker. 1901 *Daily Chron.* 24 Aug. 5/6 W.Y...cane-worker, pleaded guilty. 1921 *Dict. Occup. Terms* (1927) §472 *Caner, cane worker*,..fills in framework of baskets, wicker furniture, and other basket ware by interweaving cane.

†**cane**, *sb.*² Obs. form of KHAN². [Pers. *khān*.] An eastern inn or caravanserai.

1612 *Trav. four Englishm.* 77 The Canes that stand in high waies..for the protection of Trauellers. 1650 Fuller *Pisgah* IV. i. 18 Amongst these canes or turkish innes. 1743 R. Pocock *Egypt* in Pinkerton *Trav.* XIV. 194 Several canes at Buloc, in..which strangers are accommodated.

cane, *sb.*³ *local.* A weasel.

1789 G. White *Selborne* xv. (1853) 61 A little reddish beast..which they call a cane.

cane, *sb.*⁴ var. of CAIN, payment in kind.

cane, *sb.*⁵, obs. f. KHAN¹, an eastern prince or lord.

cane (keɪn), *v.*¹ [f. CANE *sb.*¹]

1. *trans.* To beat with a cane as a punishment.

a 1667 Jer. Taylor *Serm.* iii. 147 (L.) That it be esteemed ..more shame to fornicate than to be caned. 1715 De Foe *Fam. Instruct.* I. iv. (1841) Wks. I. 73 I'll cane the rascal if he don't. 1812 D'Israeli *Calam. Auth.* (1867) 142 To execute martial law, by caning the critic. 1825 Macaulay *Ess.* (1851) I. 25 Dressed up in uniforms, caned into skill.

2. To drive (a lesson) *into* (a person) with the cane.

1866 *Newspaper* I had a little Greek caned into me.

3. To fit or set (a chair, etc.) with cane.

1885 *Leisure Ho.* Jan. 47/1 Women and children..caning or rushing the 'bottoms'.

†**cane**, *v.*² *Obs.* exc. *dial.* To form a scum or 'head', as liquor in a state of fermentation, ale turning sour or becoming 'mothery'. Hence **caned** *ppl. a.*, **caning** *vbl. sb.*

1483 *Cath. Angl.* 53 Caned, *acidus*. *Ibid.* 53 Canynge of ale, *acor*. 1500 *Ortus Voc. ibid.* 53 *Acor*, canynge of ale. 1847-78 Halliw., *Caned*, mothery. *Yorksh.* 1876 Robinson *Mid-Yorksh. Gloss.* (E.D.S.) *Kêan*, to scum, or throw off as recrement. *Kêan*, a particle of this nature. *Kêaned*, scummed in this wise.

caned (keɪnd), *ppl. a.* [f. CANE *sb.*¹ and *v.*]

1. Beaten or chastised with a cane.

2. Furnished with cane, or with a cane.

1696 *Lond. Gaz.* No. 3206/4 Cain'd Chairs. 1848 Thackeray *Bk. of Snobs* ii, The long-caned ones [footmen] walked up and down the garden.

†'**canel**, *sb.* **canell(e.** *Obs.* Forms: 3–6 canel, 3–4, 7 canele, 4–7 canell, canelle, 5 canylle, cannell, 7–8 cannel. [ME. *canele*, a. OF. *canele*, *canelle* (mod.F. *cannelle*) cinnamon:—med.L. *canella*, dim. of *canna* cane.] Cinnamon; perhaps including the similar but inferior Cassia bark.

c 1205 Lay 17744 Muche canele & gingiuere & licoriz. 1382 Wyclif *Prov.* vii. 17 Myrre, and aloes, and canell. *c* 1460 J. Russell *Bk. Nurture* in *Babees Bk.* (1868) 125 Gynger, Canelle, longe pepur. 1575 Turberv. *Bk. Falconrie* 342 The powder of fine Canell whiche is nothing else but Cinnamon. 1608 Sylvester *Du Bartas* 268 Moluques Isles, that bear Cloves and Canele. 1651 *Rec. Pittenweem* in *Statist. Acc. Scotl.* IV. 376 (Jam.) Some great bunns.. baken with sugar, cannel, and other spices. 1721 Ramsay *Wks.* (1848) III. 70 Strains that warm our hearts like cannel gill.

†**canel, -ell.** Early form of KENNEL for dogs.

1509 Barclay *Ship of Fooles* (1570) 85 They make of the Church for their hawkes a mewe And Canell for their dogges. 1570 Levins *Manip.* 55 A canel of dogs, *canile*.

canel, -ell, var. CANNEL. *Obs.*, channel, neck, cannel-coal.

‖**canella** (kəˈnɛlə). [med.L. *canella* see CANEL.]

†**1.** Cinnamon, or Cassia bark; = CANEL. *Obs.*

1693 Sir T. P. Blount *Nat. Hist.* 40 Doubtless, the Shop-Cinnamon or *Canella*, is the true Cassia of the Ancients. 1876 Harley *Mat. Med.* 719 Canella was at one time applied to cinnamon.

2. a. *Bot.* A genus of plants (N.O. *Canellaceæ*), the most important of which is the West Indian tree, *C. alba*, or Wild Cinnamon. **b.** The inner bark of this tree, also called *white cinnamon*; used in medicine, and in the West Indies as a condiment. Also **canella bark**.

1756 P. Browne *Jamaica* 17 Large quantities of..canella or winter's bark. 1881 *Syd. Soc. Lex.*, *Canella*..the Pharmacopœial name, U.S.A., of the bark of the *C. alba*. 1865 *Treas. Bot.*, *Canella*, furnishes a pale orange-coloured bark, with an aromatic odour, which is used as a tonic.

ca'nellin. *Chem.* [f. prec. + -IN.] (See quots.)

1876 Harley *Mat. Med.* 720 A little Mannite, which was described by Petroz and Robinet as canellin. 1863-79 Watts *Dict. Chem.* I. 734 *Canella alba*..contains manna (formerly mistaken for a peculiar kind of sugar called canellin).

cane'ology. *humorous.* [f. CANE *sb.*¹; see -LOGY.] The doctrine of the use of the cane in corporal punishment.

1837 *Fraser's Mag.* XV. 572 When caneology was practised..in all well-disciplined schools. 1876 Clouston *Wine & Walnuts* I. 242 Deeply skilled in caneology.

ca'nephorus. Also 'canephor, ca'nephora. [a. L. *canēphora*, Gr. κανηφόρος adj. (f. κάνεον basket + -φορος carrying), also as sb. in senses given. In mod.F. *canéphore*, whence Eng. *canephor*.]

a. In ancient Greece, one of the 'maidens who carried on their heads baskets containing the sacred things used at the feasts of Demeter, Bacchus, and Athena' (Liddell and Scott); hence, **b.** *Arch.* applied to 'figures of young persons, of either sex, bearing on their heads baskets containing materials for sacrifice' (Gwilt *Encycl. Archit.* Gloss.).

1849 *Fraser's Mag.* XXXIX. 713 To be chosen canephor was as if 'Beautiful' were stamped on the lintel of a woman's door. 1880 Warren *Book-plates* iii. 23 The head of a canephorus.

caner. (ˈkeɪnə(r)) One who canes.

1868 *Daily News* 6 Oct., Described as a chair-caner.

canescence (kəˈnɛsəns). *rare*⁻¹. [f. as next; see -ENCE.] Hoariness, dull whiteness.

1855 R. Burton *El Medinah* (1861) I. 306 All colour melts away with the canescence from above. The sky is of a dead milk-white.

canescent (kəˈnɛsənt), *a.* [ad. L. *cānēscentem*, pr. pple. of *cānēscĕre* to grow hoary, f. *cān-us* hoary.] Rather hoary; greyish or dull white, like the down or hairs on the leaves of plants.

1847 in Craig.

‖**canette** (kəˈnɛt). [F. dim. of *cane*, *canne* CAN, jug.] A little (earthenware) can or pot.

1881 *Harper's Mag.* Feb. 366 These quaint canettes are pretty, with their gilded edges, colored bodies and footlines in black.

caneva, -as. 1. Obs. form of CANVAS.

2. Also, modern fancy name of a woollen fabric.

1885 *Yng. Ladies Jrnl.* 1 July 3/2 Caneva..made of the finest wool..closely woven together to resemble canvas.

caney, var. CANY *a.*

canezou (ˈkanzu). *Hist.* [Fr., of unknown origin.] A woman's blouse-like garment of muslin or cambric. Also *attrib.*

1827 *Lady's Mag.* Sept. 510/2 A canezou spencer of embroidered muslin. *Ibid.* 511/1 Muslin canezous over high dresses. 1893 G. Hill *Hist. Engl. Dress* II. 241 A cambric canezou..with sleeves full to the elbow. 1898 *Daily News* 26 Sept. 6/4 When the Restoration came in 1815,..Fleur-de-

lys appeared on everything... The canezou replaced the hideous spencer.

Canfield ('kænfiːld). *U.S.* [The name of R. A. *Canfield* (1855–1914), an American gambler.] A form of the game of patience similar to Klondyke.

1912 *Sat. Even. Post* 6 July 3/1 Playing double Canfield with my husband. **1932** N. MITFORD *Christmas Pudding* xx. 299 She would..play canfield on the schoolroom table. **1957** *Encycl. Brit.* XVII. 379/2 The most popular solitaire game of the U.S. is generally called Canfield..but..the game..should be called by its original name, Klondike... Canfield is a different though similar game.

canfieldite ('kænfiːldaɪt). *Min.* [f. the name of F. A. *Canfield* (1849–1926), Amer. mining engineer: see -ITE[1].] A rare sulphide of silver and tin.

1893 S. L. PENFIELD in *Amer. Jrnl. Sci.* XLVI. 113 There can be no doubt that canfieldite and argyrodite have the same chemical composition. **1894** —— in *Ibid.* XLVII. 454 As the Freiberg argyrodite has been shown to be isometric, and the name canfieldite cannot therefore be applied to the germanium compound, it is proposed now to transfer the name to the new isomorphous tin compound. **1957** *Encycl. Brit.* II. 340/1 Isomorphous with argyrodite is the corresponding tin compound Ag_8SnS_6, also found in Bolivia as cubic crystals, and known by the name canfieldite.

canfir, canfora, obs. forms of CAMPHOR *sb.*

'canful. As much as a can will hold.

1701 in *Fleet St. Mag.* (1887) I. 11 Having brought in a canfull of salt water. **1824** SCOTT *Redgaunt.* ch. xiii, A cup, or rather a canful, of tea.

† **cang,** *a.* and *sb. Obs.* Also **kang, chang, chank, cank.** [Of unknown derivation: the exchange of *ca-*, *cha-* suggests French origin; Godefroy has a quotation for *changon*, as a term of personal insult, which might be a deriv. of *chang.*]

A. *adj.* Foolish, silly. (In first quot. from *Ancr. Riwle* ? wanton.)

a **1225** *Leg. Kath.* 260 Ne kecched he creftiluker cang men. *a* **1225** *Ancr. R.* 56 To kesten kang [*v.r.* canh] eien upon ȝunge wummen. *Ibid.* 62 And nis heo to muche cang [*v.r.* chang, cangun]. *Ibid.* 358 Nis he a kang knit þet secheð reste iðe uihte.

B. *sb.* A fool.

a **1225** *Ancr. R.* 214 þis is al þes canges blisse. *Ibid.* 270 He is so old cang [*v.r.* ald fol; ald ganh] þat kumeð. *Ibid.* 362 Oðer we beoð kanges [*v.r.* changes].

Hence **canged** *a.*, foolish, besotted. **'cangliche** *adv.*, foolishly. **'kangschipe,** folly. **'cangun** = *canged.*

a **1225** *Ancr. R.* 362 (MS. T.) Oðer we arn cangede, þet weneð mid lihte scheapes buggen eche blisse. [See CANG *sb.*] *Ibid.* 56 þet te wummen lokede cangliche o weopmen. *Ibid.* 338 Nan more kangschipe [*v.r.* madschipe, kanhschipe] nis þen setten God terme. *Ibid.* 62 [see CANG]. *c* **1230** *Hali Meid.* 33 þu most to him halden, beohe cangun oðer crupel.

cang: see CANGUE.

† **'cangeant,** *a. Obs. rare*[−1]. [a. northF. *cangeant* = *changeant*: see CHANGE.] Changing.

a **1618** SYLVESTER *Du Bartas* II. iv. IV. (1641) 228/1 The cangeant colour of a Mallards neck.

cangenet. [Perversion or error.] = CANZONET.

1588 SHAKS. *L.L.L.* IV. ii. 124 Let me superuise the cangenet.

‖ **cangia** ('kandʒa). [cf. It. *cangia*, F. *cange.*] A light boat used on the Nile.

1715 *Lond. Gaz.* No. 5306/2 Cangi a Bashes (which..are small Vessels fit for carrying and landing 40 Men). **1859** *All Y. Round* No. 14. 334 A couple of cangias with large flapping sails. **1877** A. B. EDWARDS *Nile* xi. 300 Such ricketty, barbaric-looking craft as these Nubian cangias.

'cangica-wood. A wood from South America, of a light yellow-brown colour, used for cabinet-work and turnery. (Weale.)

1875 URE *Dict. Arts, Cangica wood*..is imported from the Brazils in trimmed logs, from eight to ten inches diameter.

cangle ('kæŋg(ə)l), *v. Sc.* [perh. onomatopœic: cf. *jangle, wrangle.*] *intr.* To dispute acrimoniously, to wrangle.

1619 Z. BOYD *Last Battell* (1629) 530 (JAM.) Only jangling and cangling, and at last returning to that where once wee beganne. **1839** *Chamb. Jrnl.* 19 Oct 310 To have..personal and domestic affairs harrowed up and cangled over.

'cangler, a wrangler, a quarrelsome disputant.

1730 RAMSAY *Cameleon*, 'Fy!' said a cangler, 'what d'ye mean?'

‖ **cangue, cang** (kæŋ). Also 8 **congo,** 20 **kang.** [In F. *cangue*, ad. Pg. *cango*, connected with *canga* 'yoke for oxen, porter's yoke'.

Prof. Legge thinks that the notion that the Portuguese name represents or was suggested by a Chinese word is baseless. The Chinese name is *kiá*, in modern Pekinese *chiá*, in Canton dial. *ka*, explained as 'one stick added to another, as a flail, a cangue or wooden collar.' The *kang-giai*, mod. Mandarin *k'ing-hiai*, *ch'ing-hiai* 'neck-fetter', cited from the *Kwang-yun* (a Dict. of 1009) is not the name, but merely one of the explanations of the character *kiá.*]

A broad heavy wooden frame or board worn round the neck like a kind of portable pillory as a punishment in China.

1727 A. HAMILTON *New Acc. E. Ind.* II. 175 (Y.) With his neck in the congoes. **1797** STAUNTON *Embassy* II. 492 (Y.) The punishment of the *cha*, usually called by Europeans the cangue, is generally inflicted for petty crimes. **1836** *Penny Cycl.* s.v., The cang most commonly in use weighs 50 or 60 pounds..As the cang prevents his making any use of his hands, he must be fed by others. **1883** *Q. Rev.* Jan. *Corea* 188 A sort of cangue was fastened round the neck. **1928** H. LAMB *Genghis Khan* 27 Targoutai..commanded that a *kang* be put upon him—a wooden yoke resting on the shoulders and holding the wrists of a captive prisoned at both ends.

Hence **cangue** *v.*

[**1696** BOWYER *Jrnl. Cochin China* in Dalrymple *Orient. Rep.* I. 81 (Y.) He was imprisoned, congoed, tormented.] **1883** *Daily Tel.* 2 Oct., Several men were brought up and cangued, the square boards being opened, their heads thrust through, the boards nailed up.

can-hook. [? f. CAN *sb.*[1] + HOOK *sb.*[1]] A contrivance for slinging a cask by the ends of its staves, consisting of a short rope or chain (little longer than the cask), with a flat hook at each end, the tackle being hooked to the middle of the rope or chain.

1626 CAPT. SMITH *Accid. Yng. Seamen* 13 The canhookes, slings, parbunkels. **1627** —— *Seaman's Gram.* v. 21 The Can-hookes..the Brewers vse to sling or carry their barrels on. **1769** FALCONER *Dict. Mar.* **1867** SMYTH *Sailor's Word-bk.*

canibal(e, obs. form of CANNIBAL[1].

'canicide. [f. on L. type **canicīda*, f. *canis* dog + *-cīda* killing: see -CIDE.] A dog-killer.

1852 WILLIS *Sum. Cruise Medit.* xli. 248 The dead dog is hung by his heels..and the canicide is compelled to heap wheat about him.

canicular (kə'nɪkjʊlə(r)), *a.* (*sb.*) Also 5 **cani-, canyculere,** 6 **canycular, canikeler, caniculare,** *Sc.* **-lair,** 6–7 **caniculer.** [ad. L. *canīculār-is* pertaining to the dog-star, f. *canīcula* little dog, dog-star, dim. of *canis* dog. Cf. F. *caniculaire.*]

A. *adj.*

1. ***canicular days***: the days immediately preceding and following the heliacal (in modern times, according to some, the cosmical) rising of the dog-star (either Sirius or Procyon), which is about the 11th of August; the DOG-DAYS, q.v.

1398 TREVISA *Barth. De P.R.* IX. xv. 356 In the mydle of the monthe Iulius the Canicular dayes begyn. **1502** ARNOLDE *Chron.* (1811) 172 The Canycular daies begynne y[e] xv. kalendas of August and endure to the iiij. nonas of Septembre. **1527** ANDREW *Brunswyke's Distyll. Waters* B vj b, In the canikeler dayes whan the leves begynne to fall. **1601** HOLLAND *Pliny* I. 19 All the time of the canicular daies they [dogs] are most ready to run mad. **1646** SIR T. BROWNE *Pseud. Ep.* 225 Some latitudes have no canicular dayes..as ..Nova Zembla..for unto that habitation the Dogge-starre is invisible. **1657** S. PURCHAS *Pol. Flying-Ins.* 132 The extraordinary heat of the Sun..in the Canicular dayes. **1753** CHAMBERS *Cycl. Supp.* s.v., Canicular days are computed by Harris to extend from the 24th of July to the 28th of August. **1756** C. LUCAS *Ess. Waters* III. 158 In the canicular days or other hot weather.

2. Of or pertaining to the dog-days.

1577 B. GOOGE *Heresbach's Husb.* (1586) 95 In Julie, before the Caniculer windes. **1594** GREENE *Look. Glasse* (1861) 144 The sun..Afflicts me with canicular aspect. **1710** T. FULLER *Pharm. Extemp.* 243 The Canicular Habit of the Body. **1847** DISRAELI *Tancred* III. iii, The canicular heat of Jerusalem.

3. ***canicular cycle*** or ***period***: the ancient Egyptian cycle of 1461 years of 365 days each, or 1460 Julian years, also called the *Sothic* or *Sothiac period*; in which time (as was supposed) any given day of the year of 365 days would have passed successively through all the seasons of the natural year (taken as = $365\frac{1}{4}$ days). ***canicular year***: the ancient Egyptian year, computed from one heliacal rising of Sirius to the next.

1660 STANLEY *Hist. Chald. Philos.* (1701) 2/1 A canicular Cycle, which consists of 1461 years (and are 1460 natural years). **1662** STILLINGFL. *Orig. Sacr.* I. vi. §1. **1837** WHEWELL *Hist. Induct. Sc.* (1857) I. 98 This period of 1461 years is called the Sothic Period, from Sothis, the name of the Dog-star, by which their fixed year was determined, and for the same reason it is called the Canicular Period.

4. *humorously.* Pertaining to a dog.

1592 G. HARVEY *Four Lett.* 7 If mother Hubbard.. Happen to tell one canicular tale; father Elderton..will counterfeit an hundred dogged Fables. **1833** LAMB *Elia* (1860) 425 Content with these canicular probations.

B. *sb.*

† **1.** The dog-star; (*pl.*) the dog-days. *Obs.*

c **1420** *Pallad. on Husb.* VIII. 13 Er the Caniculere the hounde ascende. **1430** LYDG. *Chron. Troy* v. xxxvi, At goyng out of the Canyculeres. **1727** M[c]URE *Hist. Glasgow* 119 Scorching heats of the Canicular.

2. *humorously.* (*pl.*) Doggrel verses.

1872 DE MORGAN *Paradoxes* 207 Some caniculars or doggrel verses.

canicule ('kænɪkjuːl). *rare.* [a. F. *canicule* dog-star, dog-days, ad.L. *canīcula.*] The dog-days.

a **1719** ADDISON *Let.* in *Student* II. 89 More afflicting to me than the canicule. **1819** H. BUSK *Vestriad* IV. 1000 Resembling more the baneful Canicule. **1834** *Fraser's Mag.* IX. 541 During the canicule of 1825.

'caniculture. *humorous.* [f. L. *canis* dog + *cultura.*] The rearing of dogs.

a **1888** *Newspaper.* The most philosophic of the protests against caniculture.

canid ('kænɪd). *Zool.* [f. mod.L. *Canidæ* (see def.), f. L. *canis* dog + -ID[3].] A member of the Canidæ, a family of digitigrade carnivorous mammals including dogs, wolves, and related animals.

1889 in *Cent. Dict.* **1945** G. G. SIMPSON *Princ. Classif. Mammals* III. 222/2 Fossil canids are very abundant. *Ibid.* 224/1 Borophaginae are large, later Tertiary canids with heavy jaws. **1950** *Proc. Prehist. Soc.* XVI. 128 An incomplete tibia of a canid.

canikin, variant of CANNIKIN.

† **ca'ninal,** *a. Obs.* [f. L. *canīn-us* CANINE + -AL[1].] = CANINE, dog-like.

1599 A. M. *Gabelhouer's bk. Physic* 20/1 People which are troubled with a Caninall hunger. **1660** FULLER *Mixt Contemp.* (1841) 186 Our English pulpits..have had in them too much caninal anger.

canine ('keɪnaɪn, 'kæn-, kə'naɪn), *a.* (*sb.*) [ad. L. *canīnus*, f. *canis* dog; cf. F. *canin*, 16th c.]

A. *adj.*

1. a. Of, belonging to, or characteristic of, a dog; having the nature or qualities of a dog.

1623 COCKERAM, *Canine*, doggish. **1664** H. MORE *Myst. Iniq.* Apol. 551 That Canine eloquence must needs sound harsh to their ears. **1735** SOMERVILLE *Chase* IV. 335 As the Dog..Raving he foams, and howls, and barks, and bites.. His Nature, and his Actions all Canine. **1870** L'ESTRANGE *Miss Mitford* I. iv. 101 Greyhounds, the most graceful and the most attached of all the canine race.

b. of appetite, hunger, etc.: Voracious, greedy, as that of a dog. ***canine appetite, hunger***: the disease BULIMY. ***canine madness***: hydrophobia.

1613 R. C. *Table Alph.* (ed. 3) *Canine*, dogge-hungry. **1648** *Hunting of Fox* 21 The Sectaries have canine Appetites. **1750** JOHNSON *Rambl.* No. 6 ¶6 The dreadful symptom of canine madness. **1804** *Med. Jrnl.* XII. 391 Characteristic marks of canine madness. **1818** T. JEFFERSON *Writ.* (1830) IV. 308 A canine appetite for reading.

c. ***canine letter*** = DOG'S LETTER.

1886 PHELPS & FORBES-ROBERTSON *Life S. Phelps* 15 He attached considerable importance to the canine letter, and often said that the rolling of the *r* [etc.]. **1890** HOWELLS *Shadow of Dream* 24 'Hermia' said Faulkner, sounding the canine letter in her name with a Western strength.

2. ***canine tooth***: one of the four strong pointed teeth, situated one on each side of the upper and lower jaw, between the incisors and the molars; a cuspidate tooth. (In some animals the canine teeth are immensely developed and become *tusks.*)

[**1398** TREVISA *Barth. De P.R.* V. xx. (1495) 124 Houndes wyth the sayd teeth that hyghte Canini gnawe bones.] **1607** TOPSELL *Four-f. Beasts* 113 They whose teeth hang over their canine teeth, are also adjudged railers. **1626** BACON *Sylva* §752 The Teeth are in Men of three kinds, Sharp, as the Fore-teeth; Broad, as the..Molar-teeth, or Grinders; and Pointed-teeth, or Canine, which are between both. **1836** TODD *Cycl. Anat.* I. 478/1 The canine teeth [of the Carnivora] are..preeminently strong, long and sharp.

3. *Anat.* and *Phys.* ***canine fossa***: a depression in the upper jaw-bone behind the canine prominence. ***canine laugh***: the expression of the face in sneering (so called because similar to that of a dog's face in snarling), *risus sardonicus*. ***canine muscle***: the *levator anguli oris*, which in the dog raises the corner of the mouth in snarling. ***canine prominence*** or ***ridge***: a ridge on the upper jaw-bone caused by the fang of the canine tooth.

1836–39 TODD *Cycl. Anat.* I. 223/1 From the inner part of the canine fossa. *Ibid.* 207/2 The canine ridge, which corresponds to the socket of the canine tooth.

B. *sb.* **a.** = Canine tooth (see 2). Also in *comb.*, as ***canine-shaped*** adj.

1835 SWAINSON *Nat. Hist. Quadrupeds* §71 (L.) The more perfect quadrupeds have three sorts of teeth, termed incisors, canines, and molars. **1870** ROLLESTON *Anim. Life* 7 The absence of canines is characteristic of the order.

b. A dog (sometimes *joc.*).

1869 E. FARMER *Scrap Book* (ed. 6) 61 As though 'Hullah' had tutored each canine to sing. **1886** *Pall Mall G.* 3 Apr. 13/2 A better-favoured canine was sacrificed. **1947** J. STEVENSON-HAMILTON *Wild Life S. Afr.* xii. 83 The little dogs rush in barking, as only such small canines can. **1969** *Nature* 18 Oct. 244/1 Rabies is believed to have originated as a disease of wild canines.

caning ('keɪnɪŋ), *vbl. sb.* [f. CANE *v.* + -ING.[1]] The action of CANE *v.*; a beating with a cane.

1715 DE FOE *Fam. Instruct.* I. viii. (1841) I. 150, I owe him a caning for all this. **1871** MORLEY *Voltaire* (1886) 53 Having a caning inflicted.

caniniform (kə'naɪnɪfɔːm), *a.* [f. L. *canīn-us* CANINE + -FORM.] Shaped like a canine tooth.

1876 TOMES *Dent. Anat.* 390 The outermost [incisor] being somewhat caniniform.

caninity (kə'nɪnɪtɪ). [f. L. *canīnus*, after *humanity.*]

1. Canine quality or trait; dog nature or race.

1794 MATHIAS *Purs. Lit.* (1798) 92, I surely may be excused for this caninity. **1879** G. MACDONALD *Sir Gibbie* I.

ix. 131 A lover of humanity can hardly fail to be a lover of caninity. **1884** A. Putnam *10 Yrs. Police Judge* xii. 86 These dog-masters have imbibed the worst qualities of caninity.

2. Sympathy with dogs, kindness to dogs.

1864 *N. & Q.* Ser. III. VI. 447 Our Duke's caninity had the more benevolent purpose, etc. **1886** *Sat. Rev.* 27 Feb. 289/1 The humanity of the wire muzzle, or rather its enlightened caninity.

† **'canion, 'cannion, canon.** *Obs.* Forms: 6 cannyon, 6–7 **canion, canyon,** 7–8 **cannion;** also 6–7 **canon,** 7 **cannon.** [In form *canion*, a. Sp. *cañon* tube, pipe, gun-barrel, 'the cannions of breeches' (= F. *canon*, It. *cannone*), augmentative of *caña*, It. *canna* tube: see CANNON. The F. form *canon* was also used in the same sense.]

pl. Ornamental rolls, sometimes indented, sometimes plain or straight, laid like sausages round the ends of the legs of breeches.

1583 Stubbes *Anat. Abus.* (1877) 56 Hose..with Canions annexed reaching down beneath their knees. **1598** Henslowe *Diary* Apr. (Fairholt) A payer of paned hose.. drawne out with cloth of silver and canyons to the same. *Ibid.* Hose..laid with silver lace and canons of cloth of silver. **1611** Cotgr., *Chausses à queue de merlus*, round breeches with strait cannions. **1660** Pepys *Diary* 24 May, Made myself as fine as I could, with the linning stockings on and wide canons. **1677** *Songs Costume* (1849) 182 By thy dangling pantaloons, And thy ruffling port cannons. **1706** Phillips, *Cannions*, old-fashioned ornament for the Legs. **1834** Planché *Brit. Costume* 266 Closer-fitting hose..with the canions, or canons attached. **1860** Fairholt *Costume* 412 Canions..are constantly seen in portraits of Henry III of France and his court.

Hence **canioned** *a.*, having canions.

1607 Dekker & Webster *Northw. Hoe* II. i. Wks. 1873 III. 20 The bragging velure-caniond hobbi-horses.

canister ('kænɪstə(r)). Also 8–9 **cannister.** [ad. L. *canistr-um* bread basket, basket for fruit or flowers, ad. Gr. κάναστρον wicker basket (app. f. κάννα reed).]

1. A small case or box, usually of metal, for holding tea, coffee, shot, etc.

1711 *Lond. Gaz.* No. 4915/4 A silver Canister for Tea. **1769** Falconer *Dict. Marine* (1789) Cccb, A case..or cannister, filled with case-shot. **1778** Johnson in *Boswell* (1887) III. 320 An author hunted with a cannister at his tail. **1828** J. W. Croker in *Cr. Papers* (1884) I. xiii. 404 A dog with a canister tied to his tail.

b. *R.C. Ch.* A metal vessel used to hold the wafers before consecration.

†**2.** An instrument used in racking off wine. *Obs.*

1678 Phillips, *Cannister*, a certain Instrument which Coopers use in the racking of [**1696** off] the Wine. Hence in Bailey, etc.

†**3.** A quantity of tea from 75 to 100 lbs. weight.

1704 Worlidge *Dict. Rust. et Urb.* s.v., Canister; of Tea, 75 to 1 c. weight. **1715** in Kersey. **1721** in Bailey.

4. A basket for bread, flowers, etc. [transl. or imitation of the Lat. or Gr.]

1697 Potter *Antiq. Greece* IV. viii. (1715) 233 Full Canisters of fragrant Lillies. **1697** Dryden *Virg. Æneid* I. (1886) 30. **1718** Pope *Odyss.* I. 184 They heap the glittering canisters with bread. **1847** Emerson *Poems, Monadnoc* Wks. (Bohn) I. 435 Weave wood to canisters and mats.

5. Short for *canister-shot* (see 6).

1801 *Naval Chron.* VI. 237 A brisk discharge of cannister and grape. **1833** Marryat *P. Simple* (1863) 331 'Put another dose of canister in.' We did so, and then discharged the gun. **1863** Kinglake *Crimea* (1877) III. i. 121 The storm of.. grape and canister came in blasts.

6. *Comb*, as ***canisterful***; **canister-shot**, a kind of case-shot consisting of 'a number of small iron balls..packed in a cylindrical tin case fitting the bore of the gun from which it is to be fired' (Smyth *Sailor's Word-bk.* s.v. *Case-shot*).

1809 *Naval Chron.* XXI. 25 Repeated broadsides of grape and cannister shot. **1810** Wellington in Gurw. *Disp.* VI. 376, 1000 rounds of canister shot. **1865** Dickens *Mut. Fr.* vi. 309 A canister-full of treasure.

'canister, *v.* [f. prec. sb.] *trans.* **a.** To put in a canister. **b.** To fasten a canister to the tail of (a dog). Hence **'canistered** *ppl. a.*

1815 *Hist. J. Decastro* ii. 58 No dog canistered but I held his tail. **1843** A. Fonblanque in *Life & Labours* ii. (1874) 144 The canistered genii..in the 'Arabian Nights'. **1862** Mark Napier *Life Dundee* II. 124 In the same spirit with which a cruel boy canisters a dog.

canities (kə'nɪʃiːz). *Path.* [L.] Whiteness or greyness of the hair.

1807 Morris & Kendrick *Edin. Med. Dict.* **1890** *Science* 3 Oct. 186/1 The sudden change in canities, when due to violent emotions. **1968** A. Rook et al. *Textbk. Dermatol.* II. xlvi. 1413/1 Canities is a physiological manifestation of the ageing process.

† **'canitude.** *Obs.*⁻⁰ [ad. L. *cānitūdo*, f. *cānus* grey.] (See quot.)

1656 Blount *Glossogr.*, *Canitude*, hoariness, whiteness, gravity. Hence in **1678–96** Phillips, and **1721–42** Bailey.

ca'nivorous, *a. nonce-wd.* [f. L. *canis* dog, after *carnivorous*.] Dog-devouring.

1835 *New Monthly Mag.* XLV. 287 They are fond of puppies..They do this not from a canivorous propensity.

† **cank,** *a. dial.* or *slang. Obs.* Dumb.

1673 R. Head *Canting Acad.* 36 *Cank*, dumb. **1688** R. Holmes *Armoury* II. iii. §68 *Canke*, a Dumb Man. **1731–1800** Bailey, *Cank*, dumb. C[*ountry Word*].

cank (kæŋk), *v. dial.* [Imitative of the sound.] *intr.* To cackle as geese; to talk rapidly, to chatter. Hence **cank** *sb.*², **'canking** *vbl. sb.*

1741 Shenstone *Let.* 23 Sept. Wks. 1777 III. 36 The canking of a goose. **1773** Graves *Spir. Quix.* IV. iii. (D.) The canking of some Spanish geese..threw poor Jerry into the utmost consternation. **1869** B. Brierley *Red Wind. Hall* xiv. in *Lanc. Gloss.* s.v., Aw'll just have a bit of a cank wi' thee. **1879** Miss Jackson *Shropsh. Word-bk.*, *Cank*, to cackle as geese; to talk rapidly, to gabble.

cank (kæŋk), *sb.*¹ *local.* The name in the Midland coalfields for a hard ferruginous sandstone. Also ***cankstone***.

a **1835** J. Phillips *Geol.* in *Encycl. Metrop.* (1845) VI. 587/2 Some less regular sandstone beds, called 'Cankstone', approach very nearly to the nature of the ganister or calliard rocks of the coal strata. **1860** *Engl. & For. Mining Gloss.* (ed. 2) 34 *Cank*, whinstone. **1877** [see galliard *sb.*²]. **1964** *Gloss. Mining Terms* (*B.S.I.*) v. 6 *Cank*, a hard, dark-grey massive rock consisting largely of ankerite.

cankar, -ard, -art, obs. ff. canker, -ed.

cankedort: see kankedort.

canker ('kæŋkə(r)), *sb.* Forms: 1 **cancer, -or,** 3 **cauncre,** 3–4 **cancre,** 4 **kankir,** 4, 6 **cankre,** 5 **cankyr, kankere,** 6 **cancar, cankar, kanker,** 6–7 **cancker,** 4– **canker.** [a. ONF. *cancre*, in Central OF. and mod.F. *chancre* (whence also in Eng. *shanker*, chancre, q.v.):—L. *cancr-um* (nom. *cancer*) crab, also gangrene. The word had been used in OE. directly from L.]

1. An eating, spreading sore or ulcer; a gangrene. †**a.** Formerly, often the same as cancer. **b.** Now *spec.* A gangrenous affection of the mouth, characterized by small fetid sloughing ulcers; gangrenous stomatitis, stomacace. Also called ***canker of the mouth*** or ***water-canker***. **c.** *Farriery.* A disease of the horse's foot, characterized by a fetid discharge from the frog.

For the specific sense a. the Latin *cancer* was introduced about 1600; but *canker* was used alongside of it till *c* 1700.

c **1000** *Sax. Leechd.* II. 110 Gemeng wiþ þam dustum, clæm on ðone cancer. *Ibid.* I. 370 Wið cancer-wund. *a* **1225** *Ancr. R.* 98 Ase holi writ seið, 'hore speche spret ase cauncre.' **1382** Wyclif *2 Tim.* ii. 17 The word of hem crepith as a kankir [**1388** canker, Vulg. *ut cancer*]. **1528** Paynell *Salerne's Regim.* Xij, A canker is a melancolye impostume, eatynge partes of the bodye. **1559** *Mirr. Mag.*, *Dk. Clarence* xi. 3 No cankar fretteth flesh so sore. **1563** T. Gale *Antidot.* II. 79 Cankers in the mouthes of the children. **1595** Shaks. *John* v. ii. 14 Heale the inueterate Canker of one wound, By making many. **1599** A. M. *Gabelhouer's Bk. Physic* 248/2 When as a woman getteth an obdurated Breste, & feareth leaste it be the Canncker. **1607** Topsell *Four-f. Beasts* 282 The Canker in the mouth..is a rawness of the mouth and tongue, which is full of blisters. **1630** Wadsworth *Sp. Pilgr.* viii. 88 Who had halfe his nose eaten away with a Canker. **1662** R. Mathew *Unl. Alch.* §99. 163 Women that have Cankers in their breasts. **1701** *Lond. Gaz.* No. 3723/4 Her [a mare's] Tongue almost eaten off with a Canker. *c* **1720** W. Gibson *Farrier's Guide* II. lxiii. (1738) 219 A mishapen or rusty Bit..will create those sort of Ulcers the Farriers call Cankers. **1752** Berkeley *Thoughts Tar-Water* Wks. III. 497 The foul disease, which with them passeth for a canker as they call it. **1831** Youatt *Horse* xix. (1847) 401 Canker is a separation of the horn from the sensible part of the foot.

†**2.** Rust. *Obs.* exc. *dial.*

1533 Elyot *Cast. Helthe* I. 9 Choler, grene lyke to grene cankar of mettalls. **1557** Bible (Genev.) *Matt.* vi. 19 Wher the mothe and kanker corrupt. **1570** Levins *Manip.* 71 The canker on iron, *ferrugo*. **1855** *Whitby Gloss.*, *Canker*, rust; oxidization on any metal, but especially iron.

3. A disease of plants, *esp.* fruit-trees, characterized by slow decay of the bark and tissues.

1555 Eden *Decades W. Ind.* (Arb.) 239 The disease of trees that the Latines caule *Caries*, which we may caule the worme or canker, being but a certeyne putrifaction. **1657** Austen *Fruit Trees* I. 54 Crab trees..are usually free from the Canker. **1813** Sir H. Davy *Agric. Chem.* v. (1814) 264 The canker or erosion of the bark and wood is a disease produced often..by a poverty of soil. **1846** J. Baxter *Libr. Pract. Agric.* I. 62 Such trees are..not liable to canker.

b. (See quot.)

1713 *Lond. & Country Brew.* II. (1743) 92 Suffering others with their Shoes to tread on many of the Corns of the Malt while they lie working on the Floor, which is often attended with ill Consequences; for, by bruising the Kernels, there immediately commences the Growth of a Canker, that will show itself in a Bunch, turn green, etc.

4. A caterpillar, or any insect larva, which destroys the buds and leaves of plants; a canker-worm.

c **1440** *Promp. Parv.* 60/2 Cankyr, worme of a tre, *teredo*. **1578** Banister *Hist. Man.* I. 6 The eyes of..Betles, Cankers, & such other. **1590** Shaks. *Mids. N.* II. ii. 3 Some to kill Cankers in the muske rose buds. **1637** Milton *Lycidas* 45 As killing as the canker to the rose. **1651** *Raleigh's Ghost* 111 The garden worm commonly called a Canker. **1782** Marshall in *Phil. Trans.* LXXIII. 217 Among the numerous enemies to which turnips are liable, none have proved more fatal here than the Black Canker (a species of Caterpillar). **1858** J. Martineau *Stud. Chr.* 103 The prophet [Jonah] was offended..that the canker was sent to destroy his favorite plant.

†**5.** An inferior kind of rose; the dog-rose (*Rosa canina*). *Obs.* exc. locally.

1582 Hester *Phiorav. Secr.* I. xi. 11 The buddes of Cankers or wilde Eglantine. **1596** Shaks. *1 Hen. IV*, I. iii. 176 To put downe Richard, that sweet louely Rose, And plant this thorne, this Canker Bullingbrooke. **1623** Fletcher *Maid of Mill* 20 A white rose or a canker. **1846** Sowerby *Eng. Bot.* (1864) III. 230 The Wild Rose is sometimes called the Canker in various parts of the Country.

b. A local name for (*a*) the common Wild Poppy (*Papaver Rhæas*); (*b*) the Dandelion (*Leontodon Taraxacum*); (*c*) a toadstool or other fungus. (Britten & Holl.)

6. *fig.* (from senses 1–4) Anything that frets, corrodes, corrupts, or consumes slowly and secretly.

1564 Palfreyman in *Bauldwin's Mor. Philos.* To Rdr., That pestilent and most infectious canker, idlenesse. **1583** Stubbes *Anat. Abus.* (1877) 105 Three cankers, which..wil eat vp the whole common welth. **1597–8** Bacon *Honour & Rep.*, *Ess.* (Arb.) 68 Enuie which is the canker of Honour. **1750** Beawes *Lex Mercat.* (1752) 36 An extravagant Interest ..is a sure Canker to their Fortunes. **1863** Kinglake *Crimea* (1876) I. i. 17 The canker of Byzantian vice.

7. (See quot.: cf. cankered 4.)

1607 Topsell *Four-f. Beasts* 455 The brains of a Leopard being mingled with a little quantity of the water which is called a Canker, and with a little Jasmine, and so mixed together, doth mitigate the pain or ach of the belly.

8. *Comb.*, as ***canker-bit(ten, -eaten, -hearted, -like, -mouthed, -poisonous, -stomached, -toothed*** adjs.; **canker-berry**, the fruit of the Dog-rose; also the West Indian plant *Solanum bahamense*; **canker-bloom**, the blossom of the Dog-rose; **canker-blossom**, a worm that cankers a blossom, a canker (sense 4); also *fig.*; **canker-eat** *v.*, to eat away like a canker; †**canker-fly**, app. some kind of caterpillar; **canker-rash**, a variety of scarlet fever in which the throat is ulcerated; **canker-rose**, (*a*) the Dog-rose (= sense 5); (*b*) the wild poppy (= sense 5 b), 'from its colour, and from its injuring corn-land' (*Syd. Soc. Lex.*); cf. Turner's name 'red corn rose'; **cankerweed**, a dial. name of Ragweed; †**cankerwort**, (*a*) the Dandelion (= sense 5 b); (*b*) ? = *cancerwort* (see cancer). See also cankerfret, cankerworm.

1756 P. Browne *Jamaica* 174 The *Canker Berry. The berries are bitterish and thought to be very serviceable in sore throats. **1605** Shaks. *Lear* v. iii. 122 My name is lost By Treasons tooth: bare-gnawne and *Canker-bit. **1753** Smollett *Ct. Fathom* (1784) 187/1 His reputation canker-bitten by the venomous tooth of slander. *c* **1600** Shaks. *Sonn.* liv. 5 The *Canker-bloomes have full as deepe a die As the perfumed tincture of the Roses. **1590** —— *Mids. N.* III. ii. 282 You iugler, you *canker blossome You theefe of loue. *a* **1619** Daniel *Hist.* 222 Those corruptions which Time hath brought forth to fret and *canker-eate [the state]. **1593** Drayton *Eclog.* x. 81 A leaveless *Canker-eaten Bow. **1711** *Lond. Gaz.* No. 4847/4 Her [a mare's] Tongue Canker-eaten. **1653** Walton *Angler* 98 There be of Flies, Caterpillars, and *Canker flies, and Bear flies. **1583** Golding *Calvin on Deut.* clxvii. 1034 *Cankerhearted against God. **1559** *Mirr. Mag.* 704 (R.) [Dissimulation] *canker-like devours it to the root. **1820** *Hoyle's Games Impr.* 434 They [cocks] may..become seam-eyed or *canker-mouthed. **1871** Palgrave *Lyr. Poems* 47 The *canker-poisonous chains. **1712** tr. *Pomet's Hist. Drugs* I. 112 The Wild, or *Canker-Rose, called Cinosbaton. **1861** Miss Pratt *Flower. Pl.* II. 233 *Rosa canina* (Common Dog-rose)..another of its names, the Canker-Rose. **1607** *Lingua* III. ii. in Hazl. *Dodsley* IX. 388 Those *canker-stomached, spiteful creatures. **1788** Burns *Let. Mrs. Dunlop* 27 Sept. (Globe) 428 A *canker-toothed, caterpillar critic.

canker ('kæŋkə(r)), *v.* [f. prec. sb.]

1. *trans.* To infect or consume with canker.

1398–1664 [see cankered 1, 3]. **1750** Johnson *Rambl.* No. 95 ⁋1 To canker the root.

†**b.** To corrode, rust, tarnish. *Obs.* exc. *dial.*

c **1420** [see 2]. **1570–1799** [see cankered 2].

2. *fig.* To infect, corrupt; to consume slowly and secretly like a canker.

a **1420** Occleve *De Reg. Princ.* 4003 God graunte knyghtes rubbe awey the ruste Of covetise, yf it her hertes cankir. **1641** Milton *Ch. Discip.* II. (1851) 33 There is no art that hath bin more canker'd in her principles..then the art of policie. **1750** Johnson *Rambl.* No. 85 ⁋11 Cankered by the rust of their own thoughts. **1850** Tennyson *In Mem.* xxvi, No lapse of moons can canker Love. **1875** E. White *Life in Christ* II. xi. (1878) 119 A world smitten with a curse which cankers half its blessings.

3. *intr.* To become cankered; †to rust, to grow rusty or tarnished; to fester (*dial.*). Also *fig.*

1519 Horman *Vulg.*, This latton basen cankeryth, for faulte of occupyeng. **1610** Shaks. *Temp.* IV. i. 192 As with age, his body ouglier growes, So his minde cankers. *a* **1626** Bacon *Physiol. & Med. Rem.* (L.) Silvering will sully and canker more than gilding. **1879** G. Macdonald *P. Faber* I. vii. 75 It cankers and breeds worms.

cankered ('kæŋkəd), *ppl. a.* Forms: 5 **cankerd,** 5–7 **-cred,** 6 **-karde, -card, -cerd, -ckerde, -ckered, -ckred, -crid,** (*Sc.* **-karit, -kerit, -kerrit, -kcart, -kart, kankyrryt**), 6–7 **cankard,** 6–8 **-kred,** 7 **-cered,** 6– **cankered.** [f. canker *v.* + -ed.]

1. Ulcerated, gangrened.

1398 TREVISA *Barth. De P.R.* XVIII. xxiv. (1495) 783 Rotyd woundes..cancred other festred. **1720** WELTON *Suffer. Son of God* II. xxiv. 654 Old cankered sores.

†**2.** Rusted, corroded; tarnished. *Obs.* exc. *dial.*

1570 LEVINS *Manip.* 49 Cankred, *ferruginosus.* **1597** SHAKS. *2 Hen. IV*, IV. iv. 72 The canker'd heapes of strange-atchieued Gold. **1611** BIBLE *Jas.* v. 3 Your gold and siluer is cankered. **1799** G. SMITH *Laborat.* I. 227 The iron..will become cankered.

3. Of plants: **a.** Infected with canker. **b.** Eaten by a cankerworm.

c **1530** MORE *De quat. Noviss.* Wks. 88/2 The cancred rote of pride. **1664** EVELYN *Kal. Hort.* (1729) 205 If you find any [Tulips] to be Canker'd. **1803** *Ann. Rev.* I. 767/1 A new and effectual method of..curing cankered trees. **1837** HAWTHORNE *Twice-told T.* (1851) I. vi. 115 To pine and droop like a cankered rosebud.

†**4.** Infected, polluted; infectious, venomous.

1633 MILTON *Arcades* 53 What the..hurtful worm with cankered venom bites. **1679** PLOT *Staffordsh.* (1686) 106 The Colepit waters, especially those they call Canker'd waters, that kill all the fish wherever they fall into the Rivers.

5. *fig.* Infected with evil; corrupt, depraved.

c **1440** *York Myst.* vii. 97 Here is a cankerd company. **1513** DOUGLAS *Æneis* v. iv. 72 Defend ȝow fra that cankyrit [*v.r.* kankeyryt] cast. **1535** COVERDALE *Susanna* 52 O thou olde canckerde carle, that hast vsed thy wickednesse so longe. **1555** HARPSFIELD *Divorce Hen. VIII* (1878) 296 Dangerous, pestilent, cankered heresy. **1695** KENNETT *Par. Antiq.* App. 693 The cancred greediness of worldly minded men. **1797** GODWIN *Enquirer* I. ii. 9 The..most cankered villain. **1857** H. REED *Lect. Brit. Poets* VIII. 290 A cankered profligate, case-hardened in sensuality.

6. *fig.* Malignant, envious; ill-natured, spiteful; ill-tempered, crabbed. (This and preceding sense were exceedingly frequent in 16th c.)

1513 DOUGLAS *Æneis* v. xi. 12 Rolling in mynd full mony cankarit bloik. **1535** STEWART *Cron. Scot.* I. 60 Cruell and crabit, and cankerit of kynd. **1555** *Fardle Facions* Pref. 20 Any cankered reprehendour of other mens doynges. **1595** SHAKS. *John* II. i. 194 A wicked will..A cankred Grandams will! **1618** STUKELEY *Petit.* in *Harl. Misc.* (Malh.) III. 394 A cancered enemy to God and his Sovereign. **1816** SCOTT *Antiq.* xxv, 'What ails ye to be cankered, man, wi' your friends?' **1859** C. BRONTË *Shirley* x 146 The vinegar discourse of a cankered old maid.

cankeredly ('kæŋkədlı), *adv.* [f. prec. + -LY[2].] Spitefully, malignantly; peevishly.

1535 STEWART *Cron. Scot.* III. 447 Rycht cankartlie he ansuerit him. **1559** *Mirr. Mag.* 401 So cankardly he had our kin in hate.

'cankeredness. [f. as prec. + -NESS.] Malice, spite; ill-humour; crabbed temper.

1538 SIR T. WRIOTHESLY in Ellis *Orig. Lett.* II. II. 109 Thinking..with his clemencye to conquerre their cancerdnes. **1548** UDALL, etc. *Erasm. Par., Pref. to Luke* 3 a, With malicious cancardnesse. **1660** HACKET *Serm. Whitehall* 22 Mar. 8 The cankardness of two men cost them fourty years bondage more.

'cankerfret, *sb. Obs.* or *dial.* [See next, and the verb.]

†**1.** Corrosion by rust. *Obs.*

1618 BOLTON *Florus* II. iii. 86 That the Armes of the Romans might not take dust, or canker-fret. [Or is this *vb.*?]

2. 'Copperas' (? Verdigris).

3. 'A sore or blister in the mouth. *East.*' Halliwell.

†**'cankerfret,** *a. Obs.* [f. CANKER *sb.* + FRET *pa. pple.* 'eaten away, gnawed'.] **a.** Eaten away with 'canker' or gangrene. **b.** Corroded with rust.

1297 R. GLOUC. 299 Somme by come cancrefrete, & somme blynde oþer wode. **1603** H. CROSSE *Vertues Commw.* (1878) 56 Blades..canker-fret and rustie within.

†**'cankerfret,** *v. Obs.* [f. CANKER *sb.* + FRET *v.*] **a.** *trans.* To eat with 'canker'. **b.** *intr.* To become cankered; to rust.

1642 ROGERS *Naaman* 36 Which else through ease and selfe-love would rust and cankerfret. *Ibid.* 103 Ere [this sin] have cankerfretted the soul.

cankering ('kæŋkərıŋ), *ppl. a.* [f. CANKER *v.* + -ING[2].] That cankers: see CANKER *v.*

1388 WYCLIF *Pref. Ep. Jerome* vii. 69 Thoroȝ cancrynge rust [**1382** rust wastynge]. **1513** MORE *Rich. III* (1641) 439 Neither fretting time, nor cancaring oblivion. **1673** T. MONCK (*title*) Cure for the Cankering Errors of the New Eutychians. **1775** ADAIR *Amer. Ind.* 196 The rust it had contracted, through the fault of cankering time. **1814** SOUTHEY *Inscript.* xxxvii. Wks. III. 158 A slow and cankering malady. **1832** LANDER *Exped. Niger* I. i. 32 Cutlasses..half devoured with cankering rust.

†**'cankerly,** *a.* and *adv. Obs.* [f. CANKER *sb.* + -LY.] = CANKERED, CANKEREDLY.

1580 H. GIFFORD *Gilloflowers* (1875) 6 That crabbed and canckerly naturde curre.

cankerous ('kæŋkərəs), *a.* Forms: 6–8 cancrous, 7 cankrous, -ckerous, -carous, 7– cankerous. [f. CANKER *sb.* + -OUS, after It. *cancheroso*, F. *chancreux.*]

1. Of the nature of a CANKER, or eating sore; cancerous, gangrenous.

1543 TRAHERON *Vigo's Chirurg.* II. iii. 18 The begynnynge of cancrous corruption. **1616** SURFL. & MARKH. *Countr. Farm* 390 Cankrous vlcers of the mouth. **1725** BRADLEY *Fam. Dict.* s.v. *Malanders*, Being a sharp Salve, it will kill the canckerous Humour.

†**b.** Rusty, like rust. *Obs.*

1651 BIGGS *New Disp.* ¶ 160 A canckerous and æruginous quality.

c. Of the nature of canker or blight in plants.

a **1866** B. TAYLOR *Vineyard Saint* Poems (1866) 206 The vines were brown with cankerous rust. **1866** FELTON *Anc. & Mod. Gr.* I. xi. 196 Cankerous blight, fruit-withering.

†**2.** Affected with canker; in a state of decay.

1609 W. M. *Man in Moone* in Halliw. *Charac. Bks.* (1857) 99 Your flesh, rotten; your bones, cankerous.

3. Having the qualities of a canker; eating into the flesh; corroding; infectious.

1691 T. H[ALE] *Acc. New Invent.* 17 A Cancarous and Corroding substance. **1833** MRS. BROWNING *Prometh. Bound* Poems 1850 I. 186 These cankerous fetters.

4. *fig.*

1620 DEKKER *Dreame* (1860) 18 Cank'rous enuy. *a* **1734** NORTH *Exam.* III. vi. ¶ 36. 450 His Words are cancrous, and fall as Excrements. **1735** THOMSON *Liberty* IV. 50 Tyrannick rule..whose cancrous shackles seiz'd The envenom'd soul. **1881** MRS. PRAED *Policy & P.* I. 100 A cankerous regret.

cankerworm ('kæŋkəwɜːm). [CANKER *sb.* 4.]

1. A caterpillar that destroys buds and leaves, a CANKER (sense 4). **b.** *spec.* (in U.S.) The larva of the *Geometra brumata* or winter moth.

1530 PALSGR. 202/2 Cancker worme, *uer de chancre.* **1611** BIBLE *Joel* i. 4 That which the locust hath left, hath the canker-worme eaten. **1634** CANNE *Necess. Separ.* (1849) 36 Viperous generation, caterpillars, moths, canker-worms. **1820** SCOTT *Monast.* v, Pestilential heresy..as a canker-worm in the rose-garland of the Spouse. **1841** EMERSON *Lect. Times* Wks. (Bohn) II. 260 The canker-worms have crawled to the topmost bough of the wild elm. **1863** LONGF. *Birds Killingw.* 196 From the trees spun down the canker-worms upon the passers-by.

2. *fig.*

1580 in Farr's *S.P.* (1845) II. 307 Unto the minde a canker-worme of care. **1641** MILTON *Ch. Govt.* vi. (1851) 121 Must tradition..be the perpetuall canker-worme to eat out Gods commandments? **1858** FROUDE *Hist. Eng.* III. xiii. 148 Lies..are cankerworms, and spoil all causes, good or bad.

cankery ('kænkərı), *a.* Also 4– cankry. [f. CANKER *sb.* + -Y[1].]

†**1.** Of the nature of a canker; gangrenous. *Obs.*

1398 TREVISA *Barth. De P.R.* VII. lix. (1495) 274 Noli me tangere is a cankry postume in the face.

2. a. Affected with CANKER.

1674 R. GODFREY *Inj. & Ab. Physic* 79 Others [seem'd to be] Cankery or Black-Chollery.

†**b.** Rusty; affected as if with rust. *Obs.*

1744 WOGAN in J. Burton *Genuineness Clarendon's Hist.* 140 The ink being turned brown and cankry.

c. Of trees.

1669 WORLIDGE *Syst. Agric.* (1681) 136 Cut off as much as you can of the Cankry Boughs. **1802** W. FORSYTH *Fruit Trees* vii. (1824) 188 Finding the pear-trees in Kensington gardens in a very cankery, and unfruitful state.

3. *fig.* Cankerous; ill-humoured, crabbed. *Sc.*

1786 BURNS *Ep. Major Logan* iv, Cankrie care. **1791** A. WILSON *Eppie & Deil* Poet. Wks. (1846) 85 Right cankry to hersel' she cracket. —— *Poems* (1816) 40 (Jam.) The cankriest then was kittled up to daffing. **1864** TROLLOPE *Can you forgive Her?* I. xxxviii. 296 One of them cankery chiels as never have a kindly word for man nor beast.

canking, *vbl. sb.*: see CANK *v.*

canmesse. *Obs.* A variant of CANVASS.

1570 LEVINS *Manip.* 85 Canmesse, *canabis.*

cann, *v. Naut.* See CON.

1751 SMOLLETT *Per. Pic.* (1779) I. ii. 14, I must confess you did not steer; but howsomever, you canned all the way. **1826** SCOTT in *Lockhart* xxiv. (Chandos) 571 Though I shall not desire to steer, I am the only person that can cann, as Lieut. Hatchway says, to any good purpose.

cann, obs. form of CAN.

‖**canna** ('kænə), *sb.*[1] [L. *canna* reed, CANE, taken in *Bot.* as the name of an entirely different genus.] A genus of endogenous plants (N.O. *Marantaceæ*), with brightly coloured flowers, yellow, red, or orange, and ornamental foliage, natives of warm climates, but cultivated in Britain.

1664 EVELYN *Kal. Hort.* (1729) 197 Sow on the Hot-bed ..Canna Indica..and the like rare and exotic Plants. **1767** J. ABERCROMBIE *Ev. Man own Gard.* 742/2 *Canna*, Indian shot, or canacorus. **1883** *Pall Mall G.* 17 Sept. 4/1 Mark also the crescent-shaped bed of Cannas—the Indian shot, as it is sometimes called, from the seed being so hard that the Indians used it as a missile.

‖**canna,** *sb.*[2] See CANE *sb.*[1] 7.

1600 PORY *Leo's Africa* II. 61 A Canna (a measure proper to this region containing two elles) of course cloth is solde for halfe a peece of gold.

canna (in 16th c. *cannocht*), Sc. form of *cannot*: see CAN *v.*

1721 RAMSAY *Poems* (1877) II. 267 He disna live that canna link The glass about. **1826** J. WILSON *Noct. Ambr.* Wks. 1855 I. 230, I canna read Greek—except in a Latin translation done into English.

canna, var. of CANNACH.

cannabal, obs. form of CANNIBAL[1].

cannabic (kə'næbık), *a.* [f. Gr. κάνναβις (L. *cannabis*) hemp + -IC.] Of the nature of hemp. ***cannabic composition***, a substance composed of a basis of hemp amalgamated with resin, and made into thick sheets, available for the same purposes as *papier mâché.* **'cannabene** (*Chem.*), a volatile, colourless, strong-smelling liquid obtained from Indian hemp. **'cannabin** (*Chem.*), the poisonous resin of the extract of Indian hemp. **'cannabine** *a.*, of or pertaining to hemp.

1731 BAILEY vol. II, *Cannabine*, of hemp or hempen. **1871** WATTS *Dict. Chem.* VI. 391 Cannabene exerts a powerful intoxicating action, though in this respect it is less energetic than cannabin, the resin of Indian hemp.

cannabidiol (ˌkænəbı'daıɒl). *Chem.* [f. CANNABI(S + DI-[2] + -OL I.] (See quot. 1949.)

1940 R. ADAMS et al. in *Jrnl. Amer. Chem. Soc.* LXII. 196/2 The isolation of a pure compound was accomplished. It proved to have one of the two empirical formulas suggested above [*viz.* $C_{21}H_{30}O_2$] and has been given the name cannabidiol. **1949** *Blackiston's New Gould Med. Dict.* 175/1 *Cannabidiol*, a constituent of cannabis which, on isomerization to a tetrahydrocannabinol, exhibits to a great degree the activity of cannabis. **1967** *New Scientist* 31 Aug. 436/1 The classical analysis of hashish..yielded three types of related compounds as the characteristic components of the drug. These were cannabidiol, cannabinol and tetrahydrocannabinol.

cannabie, obs. Sc. form of CANOPY.

cannabinol ('kænəbınɒl, kæ'næb-). *Chem.* [f. as CANNABIDIOL + -OL.] A crystalline phenol, $C_{21}H_{26}O_2$, obtained from cannabis resin.

1896 T. B. WOOD et al. in *Jrnl. Chem. Soc.* LXIX. 546 The name, 'cannabindon', which Leib Lapin proposes for his substance..does not recommend itself to the authors who propose the name *cannabinol* as the compound is undoubtedly a hydroxyl derivative. **1940** *Jrnl. Amer. Chem. Soc.* LXII. 196/1 Cannabinol is very toxic but has no marihuana activity. **1963** *Tetrahedron* XIX. 2073 Up till now the structure of only one compound of the cannabis group, namely the physiologically inactive cannabinol (I), has been fully elucidated. **1967** [see prec.].

cannabis ('kænəbıs). [mod.L. (Linnæus *Species Plantarum* (1753) II. 1027), f. earlier L. *cannabis*, Gr. κάνναβις hemp.] **1.** Common hemp, *Cannabis sativa*, a tall erect herb of the family Moraceæ having long dentate leaves on long petioles and common in central Asia and other warm regions; different regional varieties, occas. distinguished as *Cannabis americana*, *Cannabis indica* (Indian hemp), etc., are cultivated for their fibre, their intoxicating properties, or the oil obtained from their seeds.

[**1548** W. TURNER *Names of Herbes* s.v. Canabis. Canabis is called in Englishe Hemp. **1728** CHAMBERS *Cycl.* I, *Hemp*, by Naturalists call'd *Cannabis*, bears a near Analogy to Flax, *Linum.*] **1783** W. MARSDEN *Hist. Sumatra* 76 The *cannabis* or hemp..is cultivated in quantities, not for the purpose of making rope,..but for smoking. **1798** W. ROXBURGH *Plants Coast of Coromandel* II. 50/1 They have no idea of the superior quality of the bark of the common hemp-plant (Cannabis), which is indigenous in all parts of India. **1851** *Monthly Jrnl. Med. Sci.* XIII. 27 Two species of Cannabis have been described by many botanists—viz., *C. Sativa*, and *C. Indica*; but repeated comparison has not detected any material difference. **1871** WATTS *Dict. Chem.* I. 735 Cannabis indica..used in the East as an intoxicating agent. **1904** *Sci. Mem. Officers Med. & San. Depts. Govt. India* XII. 1 (*heading*) On the Morphology, Teratology and Diclinism of the Flowers of Cannabis. **1937** A. F. HILL *Econ. Bot.* xii. 293 Cannabis has been of little importance in the United States, but recently the use of marijuana cigarettes, illicitly made from hemp, seems to be increasing, in spite of all attempts to stamp out the habit. **1962** *Times* 7 May 11/7 Indian hemp, or cannabis as it is now generally termed, grows freely over great stretches of the earth.

2. (Orig. *ellipt.* for *Cannabis sativa* or (esp.) *indica.*) Any of various preparations of different parts of the hemp-plant which are smoked, chewed, or drunk for their intoxicating or hallucinogenic properties and were formerly used medicinally; bhang (marijuana), ganja, and charas (hashish) are different forms of these preparations and there are many other names.

1848 HEMPEL & QUIN tr. *Jahr's New Manual* I. 386 According to Noack and Trinks, Cannabis may be employed in the following affections: Hysterical conditions [etc.]. **1860** A. STILLÉ *Therapeutics & Mat. Med.* II. VI. 82 The mental effects of cannabis when fully developed are exceedingly curious. **1888** *Practitioner* Feb. 97 Even in more advanced cases of tropical diarrhœa cannabis will sometimes prove very useful. **1935** *Lancet* 6 Apr. 811/2 Frequent indulgence in cannabis..results in loss of judgment and restraint. **1939** *Times Lit. Suppl.* 9 Sept. 531/3 Marihuana, otherwise cannabis, hemp, hashish, nepenthe, bhang, ganja, dagga, and about a hundred other names, has not yet become in this country a popular way of escape from the worries of normal life. **1952** *Martindale's Extra Pharmacopœia* (ed. 23) I. 321 Cannabis was formerly employed in mania and nervous disorders as a cerebral sedative or narcotic, but owing to the uncertainty of its action it is now seldom employed in this manner. **1962** *Times* 7 May 11/7 The taking of cannabis does not at the moment present the Home Office with anything like a serious problem. **1967** *Guardian* 31 July 2 The general

effects of cannabis seem to be the liberation of certain inhibitions, accompanied by mild hallucinations. **1970** *Times* 12 Mar. 1/2 The Bill also halves the maximum prison sentence for possessing cannabis.

3. *attrib.* and *Comb.*, as ***cannabis plant, -smoker***; **cannabis resin**, the sticky resin produced by the hemp-plant, esp. the flowering tops of the female, and containing the active principles.

1896 K. L. DEY *Indigenous Drugs India* (ed. 2) 60 The *Charas* or cannabis Resin exudes naturally on the leaves, stem and fruits..on plants growing on the mountain tracts at an altitude of 6,000 to 8,000 feet. **1957** *Bull. Narcotics* IX. 4/1 In Europe, the cannabis plant produces a valuable fibre while showing little or no tendency to produce the narcotic principle. **1962** *Times* 7 May 11/7 Cannabis abuse is very likely to be the forerunner of addiction to more dangerous addicting drugs. **1967** *Listener* 3 Aug. 131/3 Only a tiny percentage of cannabis-smokers escalate to heroin. **1970** *Times* 10 Mar. 2/6 Three boys have been expelled..for smoking cannabis resin. **1970** *Oxford Mail* 8 Apr. 1/8 Flying Squad officers..charged them early today with possessing about 60 lb. of pure cannabis resin, worth about £30,000 on the black market.

cannach (ˈkanəx). *Sc.* Also **canna**. [a. Gaelic *cánach*.] The Cotton-grass (*Eriophorum*).

1803 MRS. GRANT *Poems* 42 (Jam.) The downy cannach of the wat'ry moors. **1804** GRAHAME *Sabbath* 244 Where the leafless cannachs wave their tufts Of silky white. **1810** SCOTT *Lady of L.* II. xv, Still as the canna's hoary beard. **1852** D. MOIR *Desert. Churchyard*, The hoary cannach.

cannailyie, cannale, obs. ff. CANAILLE.

cannakin, obs. form of CANNIKIN.

cannal, obs. f. CANNEL, CANAL, KENNEL.

cannapie, obs. form of CANOPY.

cannas, canness, obs. Sc. ff. CANVAS *sb.*

canne, obs. form of CAN *sb.*[1], KHAN[1].

canned (kænd), *ppl. a.* [f. CAN *v.*[3]] **a.** Put up or preserved in a can; tinned.

1859 R. B. MARCY *Prairie Traveler* 31 Canned vegetables are very good for campaigning. **1865** *Morn. Star* 13 Apr., Canned milk. **1879** BODDAM-WHETHAM *Roraima* 140 *note*, A small quantity of canned provisions. **1881** *Newspr.*, Canned beef and mutton. **1888** E. H. D'AVIGDOR *Antipodean Notes* xxiv. 173 Diggers all use immense quantities of jam and 'canned' fruits. **1937** *Daily Express* 24 Feb. 16/5 Canned beer has..flopped in Great Britain. **1954** *Sun* (Baltimore) 11 Dec. B. 15/2 The park area...where gather 'boys who like canned heat'.

b. *fig.* Mechanically or artificially reproduced, esp. of music.

1904 'O. HENRY' *Cabbages & Kings* vi. 93 'The Latin races..are peculiarly adapted to be victims of the phonograph.' 'Then,' says I, 'we'll export canned music to the Latins.' **1908** *Westm. Gaz.* 5 Aug. 2/2 The latest invention is the 'canned speech' delivered by a gramophone. **1930** *Punch* 2 July 21/1 'Canned music', by which is meant music transmitted by mechanism along with the film instead of being played by the theatre band. **1934** *B.B.C. Year-Book* 117 Broadcasting has been derided as 'canned' entertainment. **1959** *Camb. Rev.* 7 Feb. 321/1 The film as *pictures* (not merely as canned drama).

c. Intoxicated, 'tight'. *slang.*

1914 C. MACKENZIE *Sinister Street* II. IV. ii. 882 She was a bit canned that night, and I suppose I'd had one or two myself. **1926** 'J. J. CONNINGTON' *Death at Swaythling Court* iv. 70 Being rather canned, he sticks the candle on the table, and forgets all about it.

cannefas, obs. form of CANVAS *sb.*

†**cannel, canel** (ˈkænəl), *sb.*[1] *Obs.* Forms: 4–6 **canel**, 5 **canell**, 5–6 **kanel**, 6 **canelle**, **cannel(l**, 7–8 **cannal(l**. See also CANAL. [ME. *canel*, *kanel*, a. ONF. *canel* channel of a river, conduit, etc.; the central OF. form was *chanel*, whence the parallel ME. *chanel*, later *channel*. F. *canel*, *chanel*, correspond to Pr., Sp. *canal*, It. *canale*:—L. *canāl-em* pipe, groove, channel, etc. After CANAL was introduced in 16th c., *'cannel* gradually became obsolete, though sense 2 still exists in the form KENNEL, and CANNEL-BONE, from sense 5, is in 18th c. dictionaries. In both of these senses *channel* also occurs as a parallel form; and all the other senses have been taken up either by CHANNEL or by CANAL.]

†**1.** (form *canel*) The natural bed of a stream of water; a water-course. *Obs.* Now CHANNEL.

a **1300** *Cursor M.* 1866 He did þe waters ga til þair canels þat þai com fra. *Ibid.* 22577 (Gött.) In-til hir canel [*v.r.* chanel] sal scho [þe se] turn, And als til þairis ilk a burn.

†**2.** (forms *canel*, *cannel*) The gutter or surface water-course in a street, or by a road. This sense still survives as KENNEL *sb.*[2], q.v. (The 18th c. spelling *cannal* was app. influenced by *canal*.)

c **1380** WYCLIF *Serm.* Sel. Wks. II. 335 þei grutchiden aȝens þis water, and drunken podel water of þe canel. *c* **1450** LONELICH *Grail* xxxix. 244 Is likned to a flood..that trowbled as a kanel schal be. *c* **1440** *Promp. Parv.* 60/2 Canel, or chanelle [H. in the weye, P. in the strete], *canalis* [P. *aquagium*]. **1533** MORE *Apol.* xxxii. Wks. 896/1 They wyll..knele downe in the kanel and make their praiers in the open stretes. **1563** *Homilies* II. *Gluttony, etc.* (1859) 303 They lie stinking in our bodies, as in a lothsome sink or canell. **1666** PEPYS *Diary* 6 Sept., It was pretty to see how hard the women did work in the cannells, sweeping of water. **1756** C. LUCAS *Ess. Waters* I. 83 The common cannals in the streets.

fig. **1540** ELYOT *Image Gov.* (1556) 59 All the stynkynge canelles of vice. **1657** REEVE *God's Plea* 92 Unravell your lives, sweep the hid corners, rake the cannels.

†**3.** (form *canel*) A pipe or tube; a tap for a cask. *Obs.*

c **1420** *Pallad. on Husb.* I. 464 Canels or pipes wynes forth to lede Into the vat. *c* **1460** J. RUSSELL *Bk. Nurture* in *Babees Bk.* 121 Looke þow haue tarrers [and] wyne canels. **1629** *Church-w. Acc. Houghton-le-Spring* Giuen for a spidick and a Cannell—*jd.*

†**4.** Channel, passage. *Obs.*

1561 HOBY tr. *Castiglione's Courtyer* (1577) X ij a, When the canelles of the body be so feeble, that the soule can not through them worke hyr feates.

†**5.** The neck. *Obs.* = CHANNEL *sb.*[1] 10, KENNEL *sb.*[3] [An ancient sense, the origin of which is not quite clear. Cotgr. has F. *canneau du col* 'the nape of the neck', Littré 'le conduit qui traverse le cou', evidently the medullary canal of the cervical vertebræ (see F. *nuque* in Devic). Mätzner compares also L. *canālis animæ* windpipe. Hence CANNEL-BONE, CHANNEL-BONE.]

c **1340** *Gaw. & Gr. Knt.* 2298 Kepe þy kanel at þis kest.

†**6.** (See quot.) *Obs.*

c **1440** *Promp. Parv.* 60 (MS. K.) Canel of a belle, *canellus*.

7. *Comb.* (sense 2), ***canel-dung, -raker*** (cf. KENNEL); (sense 5) **canel-piece**, a piece of armour for the neck; see also CANNEL-BONE.

1593 H. SMITH *Serm.* (1866) II. 33 When we knocked at the *cannel-door, then the good door was shut. **1480** CAXTON *Chron.* ccxlviii. 316 The women..came out with stones & *canel dunge [FABYAN 599 'ordure of the strete']. **1430** LYDG. *Chron. Troy* III. xxii, Some wolde haue of plate a bauer That on the brest fastned be a forne The *Canell pece more easy to be borne. *c* **1500** *Cocke Lorell's B.* 10 Bewardes, brycke borners, and *canel rakers. **1541** BARNES *Wks.* (1573) 244/1 Carter or Cardinall, butcher or Byshop, tancardbearer or cannelraker. **1580** BARET *Alv.* C 58 A cannel raker, *purgator platearum*.

cannel (ˈkænəl), *sb.*[2] Forms: 6 **canel**, (7–8 **canole**, 7 **cannol**), 7 **cannell**, **cannal**, 8 **canal**, **cannil**, **kennel**, (7–8 **channel**, 8–9 **candle**), 7– **cannel**. [Of northern, prob. Lancashire origin. *Can'le*, *cannle* is the Sc. and northern form of *candle*, and the opinion has been expressed, at least since early in the 18th c., that *cannel-coal* is really = 'candle-coal'. It does not appear in evidence that the pronunciation of *candle* as *can'le* goes back in Lancashire to the 16th c., though such may be the case. A greater difficulty is that it is doubtful whether the original name was not simply *canel*, rather than *cannel coal*: see the first mention in Leland 1538. But no other etymological conjecture yet offered will bear examination. The following quotations refer to the derivation:

a **1734** NORTH *Lives* I. 294 Famous for yielding the Canal (or Candle) coal. It is so termed, as I guess, because the manufacturers in that country use no candle, but work by the light of their coal fire. **1796** KIRWAN *Min.* II. 52 Cannel Coal. This is found chiefly in Lancashire, its proper name is Candle Coal, as it burns like a Candle, but Candles in that shire are called Cannels. **1811** PINKERTON *Petral.* I. 572 Cannel coal, so called from the enunciation of the word candle, in Scotland and the north of England, because its flame is clear and pure, like that of a candle. **1836** SIR G. HEAD *Home Tour* 14 It seems to be the general opinion that having been used to light the men at their work, and serving as candle, it became by corruption 'Cannel' coal. **1875** ROBINSON *Whitby Gloss.* (E.D.S.) *Cannle*, a candle. *Cannle-coal* or *kennel-coal*, so called because it burns without smoke like a candle.]

A bituminous coal (in Scotland called *parrot-coal*), which burns with a very bright flame, and, from its richness in volatile matter, is much used in the manufacture of coal oils and gas: its texture is sufficiently compact and hard to allow of its being cut and polished like jet.

1538 LELAND *Itin.* VII. 47 Mr. Bradeshau hath a place caullid Hawe a myle from Wigan. He hath founde moche Canel like Se Coole in his Grounde very profitable to hym. **1673** R. BLOME *Brittania* in *N. & Q.* Ser. III. VII. 485/1 Wigan is famous for..the choicest Coal in England called cannell. **1690** B. E. *Dict. Cant. Crew*, *Cannal*, choice Coals ..that Blaze and Burn pleasantly. **1700** LEIGH *Lanc. & Chesh.* in *N. & Q.* Ser. III. VII. 485/2 The Kennel near Haigh, from which by distillation in a retort, will come over a very severe vitriolic water. **1836** SIR G. HEAD *Home Tour* 14 In Liverpool and elsewhere it is advertised by boards and placards 'Coal and Cannel sold here'. **1860** TYNDALL *Glac.* II. App. 437 Boghead Cannel..was once a mass of mud. **1864** *Daily Tel.* 16 July Advt., The 'Curly' Cannel of a small district in Flintshire yields a larger percentage of crude mineral oil..than any cannel.

attrib. **1869** ROSCOE *Elem. Chem.* 98 Cannel gas is said to be equal to 34.4 candles.

b. Also called *cannel coal*.

1610 HOLLAND *Camden's Brit.* I. 735 Commonly called Canole cole. **1679** PLOT *Staffordsh.* (1686) 125 The Cannel-coal being the hardest..will take a passable polish. *a* **1728** WOODWARD (J.) Our canal-coal nearly equals the foreign jet. **1773** *Gentl. Mag.* May, A head of his present majesty, cut in cannil coal. **1878** GREEN *Coal* i. 30 Cannel coal does not soil the fingers.

c. Occasionally, also *channel coal*, by assoc. with CANNEL *sb.*[1] and its variant CHANNEL.

1669 LISTER in *Ray's Philos. Lett.* (1718) 55, I do think them not Channel because they burn with much Difficulty. **1751** S. WHATLEY *Eng. Gazeteer, Wigan* (Lanc.) Channel-coal, which..may be taken up in a handkerchief without soiling it... They make snuff-boxes and other toys of it.

d. Often (since 1700) written *candle-coal*.

1734 [see above]. **1769** *De Foe's Tour Gt. Brit.* III. 281 Between Wigan and Bolton, is found great Plenty of what they call Canel or Candle Coal. **1793** *Statist. Acc. Scotl.* VII. 424 (Jam.) At Blair, beds of an inflammable substance, having some resemblance of jet, here called candle-coal, or light coal. **1805** FORSYTH *Beauties Scotl.* II. 467 That light, hard, grey-coloured species called here candle coal.

†**ˈcannel**, *v. Obs. Sc.* [a. F. *canne-ler*.] 'To channel, to chamfer' (Jamieson).

cannel, -ell, var. CANEL, *Obs.*, Sc. f. CANDLE.

†**ˈcannel-bone.** *Obs.* Forms; 4–7 **canel-**, 5 **canelle-**, 5–7 **cannell-**, 6 **cainell-**, 6–7 **canell-**, 7 **canal-**, **kannell-**, **cannel-**. [f. *canel*, *kanel*, *kenel* 'neck'; see CANNEL *sb.*[1] 5, and CHANNEL *sb.*, whence also the form CHANNEL-BONE.]

1. The 'neck-bone': perh. properly the cervical vertebræ, which form the medullary canal. (But it is not easy to know in what sense early writers used it. Quotations *c* 1420, 1593, may belong to sense 2; and the Dict. explanations of 17–18th c. are of uncertain authority.)

c **1369** CHAUCER *Dethe Blaunche* 943 Hyt [her neck] was white smothe streght, and pure flatte Wythouten hole or canel-boon. *c* **1420** *Anturs Arth.* xl. 12 The squrd squappes in toe His canel-bone allsoe, And cleuet his schild clene. **1557** *K. Arthur* (Copland) IV. xxviii, His swerd kerued him unto his canell boone. **1593** GOLDING *Ovid's Met.* 284 [He] thrust him through the place in which the necke and shoulders joine, He groand, and from his cannell-bone could scarcely pull the stake. **1656** BLOUNT *Glossogr.*, *Cannel bone*, the Neck or Throat-bone. **1664** EVELYN tr. *Freart's Archit.* 149 The cannel bone of the Throat. **1678–96** PHILLIPS, *Cannel-bone*, the neck-bone or wind-pipe. **1721** BAILEY, *Canel-bone*, the Neck or Throat Bone, so named, because of its resembling a Canal.

2. The collar-bone or clavicle.

c **1420** [see prec.]. **1470** HENRY *Wallace* v. 823 Baith cannell bayne [1st ed. **1570** collar-bane] and schuldir blaid in twa, Throuch the mid cost, the gud suerd gart he ga. **1548** PATTEN *Exp. Scot.* 47 (Jam.) The Lorde Hume..had a fall from his horse, and burst so the canell-bone of his neck, that he was fayne to be caryed straight to Edenborowe. **1603** HOLLAND *Plutarch's Mor.* 409 His cannell bone was broken which knitteth the two shoulders together in the forepart. **1611** COTGR., *Clavicules*, the kannell bones, channell bones, necke-bones, craw-bones; extending (on each side one) from the bottome of the throat vnto the top of the shoulder. **1656** DUGARD *Gate Lat. Unl.* §219. 61 The two Shoulder-blades (which the Cannel-bones, called in birds, furculæ, that is little forks, couple to the Chest).

3. ? The haunch-bone or ilium of an animal.

c **1460** J. RUSSELL *Bk. Nurture* in *Babees Bk.* (1868) 145 Betwene þe hyndur leggis [of þe cony] breke þe canelle boone. **1610** MARKHAM *Masterp.* II. clvii. 463 The vpper thigh bone goeth into the pot of the Cannel-bone.

cannel coal: see CANNEL *sb.*[2]

cannella, var. CANELLA.

1836 J. M. GULLY tr. *Magendie's Formul.* 91 Cannella powder. **1887** A. M. BROWN *Anim. Alkaloids* 53 A precipitate of a cannella colour.

†**ˈcannellate, -elate,** *a. Arch. Obs.* [After It. *cannellato* 'wrought hollow or chamfered as a reed' (Florio), and F. *cannelé*, pa. pple. of *canneler* to channel or flute, as *canneler une colonne*; cf. *canneau* fluting, and med.L. *canellus* channel. (The number of *n*'s and *l*'s is thus quite unfixed.) The Fr. and It. words are taken as immediately connected with *cannella*, *cannelle*, dim. of *canna*, *canne* reed, cane, but F. *canneau* can hardly be separated from OF. *canel*, one of the forms of *canal*: see CANAL, CHANNEL.] Channelled, fluted.

1673 RAY *Trav.* (1738) II. 359 They are cannellate, and there are now standing seventeen of them. **1676** F. VERNON in *Phil. Trans.* II. 579 These Pillars..are canellate.

cannelloni (kænɛˈləʊnɪ), *sb. pl.* Also formerly **cannelons.** (Both occas. used in *sing.*) [It. *cannellone*, pl. *cannelloni*, f. *cannello* stalk.]

1. (Only in form *cannelons.*) Rolls of pastry stuffed with a savoury filling or cream and eaten as a desert. **2.** Rolls of pasta filled with seasoned meat.

1845 E. ACTON *Mod. Cookery* xvi. 337 Cannelons. **1892** *Encycl. Pract. Cookery* I. 281/1 Cannelons..are composed chiefly of nouille paste in the shape of small pipes about 3 in. long and ½ in. in diameter. They are generally made by rolling the paste out very thin, cutting into strips 3 in. by 2 in., and rolling up round small pieces of wood, which are removed after baking. **1906** MRS. BEETON *Househ. Managem.* xvi. 511 (*heading*) Cannelon of beef. *Ibid.* xxiii. 669 (*heading*) Cannelons of chicken. **1937** C'TESS MORPHY *Good Food from Italy* 55 Toss the *cannelloni* in the *sugo*. **1952** P. BONNER *SPQR* (1953) vi. 52 A large slice of *cannellone*. **1960** *Guardian* 29 Aug. 5/6, I ate scampi and cannelloni with fresh Parmesan.

†**cannel-nail.** *Obs.*

1610 MARKHAM *Masterp.* II. xcviii. 389 Some canell naile, or other naile piercing the soale. **1639** T. DE GREY *Compl.*

Horsem. 199 If your horse have gotten a sore foot by meanes of any cannell-nayle.

cannelure (ˈkænəljʊə(r)). Also 8 canalure. [a. F. *cannelure* groove, f. *canneler* to CHANNEL.] A groove, fluting; also called CHANNELURE.

Hence **ˈcannelured** *a.*, grooved, fluted.

1755 *Gentl. Mag.* XXV. 128 The colour of this shell is the purest white; its canalures or ribs, which serpentize, are crossed by circular lines. **1866** *Cornh. Mag.* Sept. 350 The hinder cannelure of the bullet. **1881** GREENER *Gun* 153 Swiss long-range cannelured bullets.

‖**cannequin** (ˈkænɪkɪn). [a. F. *cannequin* = Pg. *canequim*, Sp. *caniqui*.] A kind of white cotton cloth from the East Indies.

1847 in CRAIG; and in mod. Dicts.

canner (ˈkænə(r)). [f. CAN *v.*[3] + -ER[1]; cf. CANNED.] **a.** One who cans meat, fish, fruit, etc.

1878 N. H. BISHOP *Voy. Paper Canoe* 120 The canners take a large portion of the best peaches. **1878** *Robinson's Epitome of Lit.* Sept. 136/2 A canner of tomatoes. *Mod. Newspaper*, Fifteen million lobsters are annually used by the Maine canners.

b. A beast fit only for canning. Chiefly *U.S.*

1890 *Stock Grower* (Las Vegas, New Mexico) 11 Jan. 5/2 Fit only for canners and feeders. **1892** *Pall Mall Gaz.* 8 Dec. 2/1 'Canners', which is the designation of all animals collected at the Chicago and other markets, that are refused by the butchers as unfit for their trade. **1906** *Daily Chron.* 13 June 7/3 A 'canner'..is an animal with little, if any, fat on it, in fact often nothing more than skin and bone. **1964** *Weekly News* (Auckland) 22 Jan. 40/3 The canner muttons and ewes were not so much in demand.

c. A machine for canning food.

1928 *Daily Express* 6 July 5/5 Until now canning has been beyond me for want of a canner.

cannery (ˈkænərɪ). [f. as prec. + -ERY.] A factory where meat, fruit, etc. are canned.

1879 *Echo* 18 Oct. 1/5 The salmon canneries in Oregon. **1880** *Libr. Univ. Knowl.* XI. 47 (*Oregon*) The first [salmon] cannery was established in 1868 by Mr. Hume, of Maine.

cannes, -ess, obs. Sc. forms of CANVAS.

cannet (ˈkænɪt). *Her.* [a. F. *canette*, dim. of *cane* duck.] A duck, borne as a charge, without feet or bill.

cannibal[1] (ˈkænɪbəl). Forms: 6-8 canibal, 6-7 caniball(e, canniball, 7 cannabal, 7- cannibal. [In 16th c. pl. *Canibales*, a. Sp. *Canibales*, originally one of the forms of the ethnic name *Carib* or *Caribes*, a fierce nation of the West Indies, who are recorded to have been *anthropophagi*, and from whom the name was subsequently extended as a descriptive term.

Professor J. H. Trumbull, of Hartford, has pointed out that *l, n, r* interchange dialectally in American languages, whence the variant forms *Caniba, Caribe, Galibi*: and that Columbus's first representation of the name as he heard it from the Cubans was *Canibales*, explained as 'los de Caniba or Canima'; when he landed on Hayti, he heard the name of the people as *Caribes* and their country *Carib*; the latter was afterwards identified with Puerto Rico, named by the Spaniards 'Isla de Carib', 'which in some islands', Columbus says, 'they call *Caniba*, but in Hayti *Carib*'. Apparently, however, it was only foreigners who made a place-name out of that of the people: according to Oviedo (*Hist. Gen.* II. viii.) *caribe* signifies 'brave and daring', with which Prof. Trumbull compares the Tupi *caryba* 'superior man, hero, *vir*'. CALIB-AN is app. another variant = *carib-an*; cf. *Galibi* above-mentioned.

Columbus's notion on hearing of *Caniba* was to associate the name with the *Grand Khan*, whose dominions he believed to be not far distant; he held 'que Caniba no es otra cosa sino la gente del Gran Can'. To connect the name with Sp. *can*, It. *cane*, L. *canis* dog, was a later delusion, entertained by Geraldini, Bp. of San Domingo, 1521-5; it naturally tickled the etymological fancy of the 16th c., and may have helped to perpetuate the particular form *canibal* in association with the sense *anthropophagi*. See Prof. Trumbull's article, in *N. & Q.* Ser. v. IV. 171.]

1. A man (*esp.* a savage) that eats human flesh; a man-eater, an anthropophagite. Originally proper name of the man-eating Caribs of the Antilles.

1553 EDEN *Treat. New Ind.* (tr. Sebastian Munster *Cosmog.* 15) Arb. 30 Columbus..sayled toward yᵉ South, and at yᵉ length came to the Ilandes of the Canibals. And because he came thether on the Sundaye called the Dominical day, he called the Iland..Dominica..Insula Crucis..was also an Ilande of the Canibales. **1555** —— *Decades New World* (tr. Peter Martyr 1511) I. (Arb.) 66 The wylde and myscheuous people called Canibales or Caribes, which were accustomed to eate mannes flesshe (and called of the olde writers Anthropophagi)..Vexed with the incursions of these manhuntyng Canibales. **1584** R. SCOT *Discov. Witchcr.* II. ix, Kin to the Anthropophagi and Canibals. **1594** J. DAVIS *Seaman's Secr.* II. (1607) 12 The Canibals of America flye the presence of men. **1604** SHAKS. *Oth.* I. iii. 143 The Canibals that each others eate. **1661** HICKERINGILL *Jamaica* 76 Thence they are call'd Caribs, or Cannibals. **1679** *Establ. Test* 18 The fierce Cannibals of the West Indies. **1748** ANSON *Voy.* III. vii. (ed. 4) 480 The necessity of turning cannibal. **1772** PRIESTLEY *Nat. & Rev. Relig.* (1782) III. 50 M. Voltaire..represents the Jews as canibals. **1852** TH. ROSS tr. *Humboldt's Trav.* III. 214 Geraldini, who sought to Latinize all barbarous denominations, recognized in the Cannibals the manners of dogs (*canes*). **1865** LIVINGSTONE *Zambesi* iii. 67 Nearly all blacks believe the whites to be cannibals.

b. *fig.* (sometimes formerly as a strong term of abuse for 'bloodthirsty savage').

1563-87 FOXE *A. & M.* (1684) III. 739 (On Boner's portrait) This Cannibal in three years space Two hundred Martyrs slew. **1593** SHAKS. *3 Hen. VI*, v. v. 61 Butchers and Villaines, bloudy Caniballes, How sweet a Plant haue you vntimely cropt. **1604** HIERON *Wks.* I. 559 Such are his carnall cardinals, Or rather bloudy canibals. **1845** STODDART in *Encycl. Metrop.* (1847) I. 159/1 The late Mr. Windham, an accomplished scholar..whom Mr. Tooke calls..a 'cannibal', and 'a cowardly assassin'. **1860** EMERSON *Cond. Life* vii. Wks. (Bohn) II. 420 Sickness is a cannibal which eats up all the life and youth it can lay hold of.

2. An animal that preys on its own species.

1796 MORSE *Amer. Geog.* I. 696 The shark and great black stingray, are insatiable cannibals. **1881** DARWIN *Earth Worms* i. 37 They [worms] are cannibals.

3. *attrib.* Pertaining to a cannibal, cannibal-like; bloodthirsty.

1596 NASHE *Saffron Walden* 120 He is such a vaine Basilisco..& swarmeth in vile Canniball words. **1607** CHAPMAN *Bussy D'Amb.* Plays 1873 II. 58 To feede The rauenous wolfe of thy most Canibal valour. *a* **1694** TILLOTSON *Serm.* xcix. (1742) VI. 1591 They have the face to complain of the cannibal laws, and bloody persecutions of the church of England. **1790** BURKE *Fr. Rev.* 210 To stimulate their cannibal appetites. **1855** MACAULAY *Hist. Eng.* III. xiv. 400 The street poets portioned out all his joints with cannibal ferocity. **1873** *Spectator* 22 Feb. 240/1 He [the shrike] is a cannibal bird.

ˈcannibal[2]. [? Corruption of *Camdeboo*: see Pettman *Africanderisms*.] Used *attrib.* in *cannibal stink-wood*, a South African name for *Celtis kraussiana*.

1859 R. J. MANN *Natal* 156 (Pettman), There is a variety of this wood known under the name of the Cannibal stink-wood. **1877** LADY BARKER *Yr.'s Housekpg. S. Afr.* 325 What rhyme or reason, what sense or satire can there be in such a name as 'Cannibal Stink-wood'?—applied..to a graceful, handsome tree whose bark gives out an aromatic..perfume.

cannibaˈlean, *a. rare.* In 7 canniˈballian. [f. CANNIBAL[1] + -EAN, -IAN.] = CANNIBALIC.

1602 CAREW *Cornwall* 34 a, His Canniballian fellowes. **1845** *Blackw. Mag.* LVII. 52 His cannibalean majesty.

cannibalic (kænɪˈbælɪk), *a.* [f. as prec. + -IC.] Of, pertaining to, or characteristic of a cannibal.

1837 DICKENS *Pickw.* (1842) I. 413 The fat youth gave a semi-cannibalic leer at Mr. Weller. **1844** —— *Mart. Chuz.* xxxvii, Preparers of cannibalic pastry. **1886** BLACKIE *What does Hist. Teach?* 111 In this worse than cannibalic style.

cannibalish (ˈkænɪbəlɪʃ), *a.* [f. as prec. + -ISH.] Savouring of cannibalism.

1837 *New Month. Mag.* XLIX. 522 It is rather a cannibalish proceeding. **1863** *Possibil. of Creation* 291 The poor fellow would be horrified at the cannibalish suggestion.

cannibalism (ˈkænɪbəlɪz(ə)m). [f. as prec. + -ISM.] The practice of eating the flesh of one's fellow-creatures. *fig.* Bloodthirsty barbarity.

1796 BURKE *Regic. Peace* I. Wks. VIII. 177-8 By cannibalism, I mean their devouring, as a nutriment of their ferocity, some part of the bodies of those they have murdered. **1824** D'ISRAELI *Cur. Lit.*, Dk. Buckhm. (1866) 312 The political cannibalism of the mob. **1879** WALLACE *Austral.* v. 93 Cannibalism is..practised in most of the tribes.

cannibalistic (ˌkænɪbəˈlɪstɪk), *a.* [f. as prec. + -IST + -IC.] Addicted to or pertaining to cannibalism. Hence **ˌcannibaˈlistically** *adv.*

1851 *Fraser's Mag.* XLIII. 476 They see Englishmen.. pugnacious, intemperate, and cannibalistic. **1884** *Pall Mall Budget* 22 Aug. 27/1 Badgers are equally cannibalistic. **1851** H. MELVILLE *Whale* x. 55 Queequey was General Washington cannibalistically developed.

canniˈbality. *rare.* [see -ITY.] = CANNIBALISM.

1796 *Monthly Mag.* I. 294 Cannibality, or man-eating, has always existed as a condition and practice of mankind.

cannibalize (ˈkænɪbəlaɪz), *v.* [f. CANNIBAL[1] + -IZE.] *trans.* To take parts from one unit for incorporation in, and completion of, another (of a similar kind). Hence **ˌcannibaliˈzation**, the removal of a part (of something) for incorporation in something else; **ˈcannibalized** *ppl. a.*

1943 REDDING & LEYSHON *Skyways to Berlin* (1944) xi. 173 One by one the other aeroplanes have gone, some destroyed by enemy action, others cannibalized for parts and still others retired because of age. **1947** *Hansard Commons* CCCCXLV. 973 It would be necessary to dismantle or, as they say, cannibalise half a dozen to provide one good Nissen hut. **1947** *Jrnl. R. Aeronaut. Soc.* LI. 981/2 The necessity for removing serviceable parts from one aircraft to service another. Cannibalisation, often of a new aircraft, was frequently the only method of maintaining reasonable serviceability. **1957** *Times Lit. Suppl.* 20 Dec. 771/1 The *Abwehr's* so-called Brandenburg Division was cannibalized, and five further Commando Battalions were formed. **1960** *How TV Works* 11/1 The whole process of cannibalising a travelling eye..began again in London. **1964** 'M. UNDERWOOD' *Crime of C. Wise* ii. 24 Wise had subsequently made him one [radio] out of cannibalised parts.

cannibally (ˈkænɪbəlɪ), *adv.* [f. CANNIBAL[1] + -LY[2].] After the manner of a cannibal. Also *fig.*

1607 SHAKS. *Cor.* IV. v. 200 And hee had bin Cannibally giuen, hee might haue boyld and eaten him too. **1702** C. MATHER *Magn. Chr.* II. App. (1852) 194 To have cannibally devoured one another.

†**ˈcannibe**, *a. Obs.* [Conjectured by some to be for F. *canif* or its OF. dim. *canivet*.]

c **1420** *Pallad. on Husb.* I. 1157 Showe forth also the cannibe knyves lite In planntes yonge a branch awaie to take.

cannie: see CANNY.

cannikin, canikin (ˈkænɪkɪn). Forms: 6-9 canni-, cani-, 7 canna-, 9 canakin. [dim. f. CAN *sb.*[1]: cf. Du. *kanneken*, Eng. *mannikin, pannikin*, and see -KIN.] **a.** A small can or drinking vessel.

1570 *Leg. Bp. St. Andrew* in *Sc. Poems 16th C.* 18. 313 (Jam.) Carruse, and hald the cannikin klynclene. **1604** SHAKS. *Oth.* II. iii. 71 And let me the Cannakin clinke, clinke. [**1658** HEXHAM *Du. Dict.*, *Kanneken*, a small Canne, Pot, or Cruse.] **1764** *Gentl. Mag.* XXXIV. 89 And clink the cannikin here below. **1845** BROWNING *Flight Duchess* xvi. 1 When the liquor's out why clink the cannikin? **1849** *Blackw. Mag.* LXVI. 570 With a canikin of rum.

b. *slang.* (See quots.)

1688 R. HOLME *Armoury* III. iii. §68 *Cannikin*, the Plague. **1690** in B. E. *Dict. Cant. Crew*.

cannily (ˈkænɪlɪ), *adv. Sc.* (and *north. dial.*) [f. CANNY *a.* + -LY[2].] Sagaciously, skilfully, prudently; cautiously, slily; gently, softly; comfortably, etc. (see various senses of CANNY).

1636 RUTHERFORD *Lett.* lxix. (1862) I. 178 Those who can take that crabbed tree handsomely upon their back and fasten it on cannily, shall find it such a burden as wings to a bird. *a* **1662** BAILLIE *Lett.* (1775) I. 147 (Jam.) He has.. carried himself far more cannily than any of that side. *a* **1758** RAMSAY *Poems* (1800) II. 386 Steering cannily thro' life. **1816** SCOTT *Antiq.* xxvii, Step lightly and cannily. —— *Bl. Dwarf* vii. **1839** *Cumbrld. & Westm. Dialog.* 18 Sae we dud varra connoly. **1866** KINGSLEY *Herew.* xv. 199, I told my story as cannily as I could.

canniness (ˈkænɪnɪs). *Sc.* [f. as prec. + -NESS.] Sagacity, skilfulness, prudence, cautiousness; gentleness, quietness.

a **1662** BAILLIE *Lett.* (1775) II. 92 (Jam.) When the canniness of Rothes had brought in Montrose to our party. **1878** P. BAYNE *Purit. Rev.* iii. 81 Native Scotch prudence and canniness.

†**canning**, *vbl. sb.*[1] *Obs.* [f. CAN *v.*[1] + -ING[1].] Being able, ability.

a **1555** BRADFORD *Wks.* (Parker Soc.) II. 28 (D.) Why would I not but because I could not? I mean because my canning is taken away by sin. **1615** T. ADAMS *White Dev.* 38 Cunning served his turn when canning did no good.

canning (ˈkænɪŋ), *vbl. sb.*[2] [f. CAN *v.*[3] + -ING[1].] The preserving of meat, fish, fruit, etc., by sealing up in cans or tins; tinning.

1872 in *Sacramento Weekly Union* 24 Feb. 6 (Hoppe). **1879** *Echo* 18 Oct. 1/5 In canning, every precaution is used to secure the native freshness and flavour of the article preserved. **1882** *Standard* 10 Feb. 5/3 The 'canning' of the vast shoals of salmon.

attrib. **1883** *Fisheries Exhib. Catal.* (ed. 4) 159 Thistle Haddie Canning and Curing Company. **1884** *Harper's Mag.* July 297/2 The canning house.

cannion, variant of CANION, *Obs.*

†**ˈcannipers.** *Obs.* Corrupted f. CALLIPERS.

1707 J. MORTIMER *Husb.* (J.) The square is taken by a pair of cannipers, or two rulers clapped to the side of a tree, measuring the distance between them. **1725** BRADLEY *Fam. Dict.* s.v. *Felling*, A pair of cannipers.

cannister, obs. form of CANISTER.

Cannizzaro (kænɪˈzɑːrəʊ). The name of Stanislao Cannizzaro (1826-1910), Italian chemist, used *attrib.* or in the possessive of a reaction of aldehydes with caustic alkali (see quot. 1964).

1912 *Chem. Abstr.* 1431 The conversion of aromatic aldehydes by alcoholates into acids and alcs. (Cannizaro's reaction) is found to be untenable. **1964** N. G. CLARK *Mod. Organic Chem.* x. 187 Cannizzaro reaction. When aldehydes containing no hydrogen atoms on the α-carbon atom (adjacent to the functional group) are treated in the cold with concentrated aqueous or alcoholic sodium hydroxide, a dismutation involving two molecules takes place. One molecule is reduced to the alcohol, while the other is oxidized to a salt of the corresponding carboxylic acid.

cannoa, cannoe, obs. ff. CANOE.

cannon (ˈkænən), *sb.*[1] Also 6 (chanon), 6-8 canon. [In 16th c. also *canon*, Sc. *cannoun*, a. F. *canon* (14th c. in Littré) = Pr. *canon*, Cat. *canó*, Sp. *cañon*, It. *cannone*, lit. 'great tube, barrel', augm. f. *canna*, *canne* CANE, reed, pipe, tube. The spellings *canon* and *cannon* occur side by side down nearly to 1800, though the latter is the more frequent after *c* 1660.]

†**1.** A tube, a cylindrical bore. *Obs.*

1588 LUCAR *Tartaglia's Arte Shooting* 30 How long the canon or concauitie of every Peece of Artillerie ought to bee. **1604** E. G. *D'Acosta's Hist. Indies* v. ix. 353 A small canon of cristall, in length half a foote. **1611** COTGR., *Trajectoire*, the cannon, or taile of a perfuming funnell. **1616** SURFL. & MARKH. *Countr. Farm* 358 You must make fast the foresaid Canon of the said barke of the new branch.

2. a. A piece of ordnance; a gun or fire-arm of a size which requires it to be mounted for firing. (The leading current sense.)

The following varieties are mentioned in the 16th-17th c.: *Canon Royall*, height 8½ in.; shot 66 lbs. *Canon*, height 8 in.;

shot 60 lbs. *Canon Sarpentine*, height 7½ in.; shot 53⅓ lbs. *Bastard Canon*, height 7 in.; shot 41¼ lbs. *Demy Canon*, height 6½ in.; shot 30¼ lbs. *Canon Petro*, height 6 in.; shot 24¼ lbs.

For the various ancient forms of cannon or great guns, see ASPIC, BASILISK, BASTARD, CARTHOUN, CULVERIN, DRAGON, FALCON, FALCONET, SAKER, SERPENTINE, SIREN, etc.

1525 T. MAGNUS in *State Papers* (1836) IV. 325, 5 gret gonnes of brasse called cannons, besides sondery other fawcons. **1545** EARL SHREWSBURY *ibid.* V. 441 To sende unto Tynmowthe..a cannon, a saker, etc. **1570** LEVINS *Manip.* 163 A chanon, gunne, *tormenti genus*. **1573** *Diurn. Occurrents* (1833) 330 Thrie houlkis of Ingland, ladunit with ane cannone ryell, four singill cannounis..with ane Scottis peice les nor ane cannoun. **1600** SHAKS. *A.Y.L.* II. vii. 153 Then, a Soldier..Seeking the bubble Reputation Euen in the Canons mouth. **1604** E. GRIMSTON *Siege of Ostend* 189 Canons of wood, a fadom long, with great bandes of Yron. **1633** T. STAFFORD *Pac. Hib.* xvi. (1821) 387 An other Cannon was brought up, and planted by the Demy-cannon. **1705** STANHOPE *Paraphr.* I. 18 They march directly up to the mouth of the loaded Canon. **1750** BEAWES *Lex Mercat.* (1752) 832 Iron Bars, Cannons, and Bullets. **1858** GREENER *Gunnery* 97 Mr. Nasmyth, whose monster cannon..was to astonish the whole world. **1864** H. JONES *Holiday Papers* 219 The Irishman's recipe for a cannon 'Take a long hole, and pour some brass round it'.

b. Also *collect.* (= 'artillery, ordnance') and *pl.*

1596 SHAKS. *1 Hen. IV*, II. iii. 56 Thou hast talk'd..Of Basiliskes, of Canon, Culuerin. **1666** PEPYS *Diary* (1879) III. 495 In the trial every one of the great guns, the whole cannon of seven..broke in pieces. **1760** *Keysler's Trav.* I. 184 The largest cannon here are about fifty pounders. **1855** TENNYSON *Charge Lt. Brigade* iii, Cannon to right of them, Cannon to left of them, Cannon in front of them Volley'd and thunder'd.

c. *Phrase.*

a **1639** SPOTTISWOOD *Hist. Ch. Scotl.* v. (1655) 239 He was apprehended, and by sentence of the Council of War condemned to ride the Cannon.

d. A pistol, a revolver. *U.S. slang.*

1901 'J. FLYNT' *World of Graft* 137 The thief had him covered with his 'cannon'. **1915** [see sense 10 below]. **1926** J. BLACK *You can't Win* xiii. 185 One of them.. started to lug out his 'cannon'.

e. A shell-firing gun in an aircraft.

1919 *Radio Pamphlet No. 30* (*Signal Corps, U.S. Army*) 3 These are..biplanes, mounting two to six or more machine guns and often a cannon. **1921** *Flight* XIII. 294/1 The machine carries one pilot and two gunners, operating in all eight machine-guns and one cannon. **1949** F. MACLEAN *Eastern Approaches* III. viii. 394 He showed me how the rear cannon fired, and how the intercom. worked.

3. *Mech.* **a.** A barrel or hollow cylindrical piece capable of revolving independently on a shaft, with a greater or less velocity than that of the shaft. **b.** The perforated barrel of a watch-key.

4. A smooth round bit. Also ***cannon-bit***.

1596 SPENSER *F.Q.* I. vii. 37 Could manage fair His stubborne steed with curbed canon bitt. **1614** MARKHAM *Cheap Husb.* I. ii. (1668) 24 A sweet smooth Cannon bit, with a plain watering chain. **1617** —— *Caval.* II. 50 The first byt a horse should weare, should be a smooth Cannon. **1617** J. LANE *Squire's T.* 273 The bitt, a canon bytt.

5. The part of a bell by which it is suspended; also called the *ear*. See also CANON *sb.*[2] 14.

1872 ELLACOMBE *Bells of Ch.* i. 4 The ear or cannon on its top or crown, by which it is hung..in the tower.

6. An empty zinc retort; see quot.

1871 *Trans. Amer. Inst. Mining Eng.* I. 74 Beneath the retorts is placed a row of six so-called cannons to break the heat.

7. a. *Billiards.* A stroke in which the player's ball is made to hit one of the other balls in such a way as to glance from it and strike the second.

(Also called *carambole* and *carrom*, of which *cannon* appears to be a perversion; probably influenced by the notion of a 'heavy shot'.)

1839 KENTFIELD *Billiards* 16 Canons..constitute by far the most interesting part of Billiards. **1844** MARDON *Billiards* 4 Scoring canons and hazards. **1850** THACKERAY *Pendennis* xxiii, 'I wish to the doose your wife was dead.' 'So do I. That's a cannon by Jove.' **1863** MISS BRADDON *J. Marchmont* II. i. 3, I am afraid she'll never make a cannon. **1872** BLACK *Adv. Phaeton* xi. 157 Even when he got a good chance of a cannon, the smallness of the balls caused him to fail entirely.

b. *transf.* An act of cannoning (see CANNON *v.* 3 b); a collision between persons or animals (as in racing).

1806-7 J. BERESFORD *Miseries Hum. Life* (1826) VII. ii, Briskly stooping to pick up a lady's fan when two other gentlemen are doing the same, and so making a cannon with your head against both of theirs. **1876** *Coursing Cal.* 35 Bellini came best out of a cannon, and never let Hawkseye have a look in, except to kill.

8. *attrib.*

1599 MARSTON *Sco. Villanie* II. vii. 203 His new stampt complement, his Cannon oathes. *a* **1668** DAVENANT *Siege Rhodes* Poems (1673) 40 With smoke of Cannon-Clouds. **1885** R. BUCHANAN *Master of Mine* I. xii. 175 Gusts, fitful though terrible—very cannon blasts of air.

9. *Comb.*, as ***cannon-bore***, ***-breech***, ***-bullet***, ***-casting***, ***-fever***, ***-flash***, ***-mouth***, ***-reek***, ***-smoke***; ***cannon-hot***, ***-moulded***, ***-mouthed***, ***-smoked*** adjs.; †***cannon-roared*** pa. pple.; **cannon-clock**, a cannon with a burning-glass so fixed over the vent as to fire the priming on the sun's reaching the meridian; **cannon-fly** (see quot.); **cannon-fodder** [tr. G. *kanonenfutter*; cf. Shakespeare's *food for powder* (1 Hen. IV, IV. ii. 72)]: men regarded merely as material to be consumed in war; **cannon-lock**, a contrivance for exploding the charge of a cannon; **cannon-metal**, a variety of bronze used for cannon; **cannon-mouth**, the mouth of a cannon-bit; **cannon pinion**, the perforated pinion which carries the minute hand of a watch, and drives the minute wheel; **cannon-royal** (see sense 1); **cannon-stove**, a stove for heating, shaped somewhat like a mortar. See also CANNON-BALL, -BASKET, etc.

1655 MRQ. WORCESTER *Cent. Inv.* §64 So clear from danger, that..a Pound of Butter did not melt being laid upon the *Cannon-britch. **1605** *1st Pt. Jeronimo* in Hazl. *Dodsley* IV. 382 Spleens big as a *cannon-bullet. **1724** WATTS *Logic* I. ii. §4 It is slow when compared with a cannon-bullet. **1833** *Edin. Rev.* LVII. 381 That..exciting sensation known to military men by the name of the *cannon-fever. **1860** HAWTHORNE *Marb. Faun* xxix. 229 The last *cannon-flash of a retreating army. **1787** T. BEST *Art of Angling* (ed. 2) 114 The Oak Ask, Woodcock, *Canon or Down hill fly. **1799** G. SMITH *Laborat.* II. 297 The oak-fly. Some call this..the cannon-fly. **1891** *Cannon-fodder [in N.E.D.]. **1898** G. B. SHAW *Our Theatres in Nineties* (1932) III. 287 Peter [the Great], regarding children as future cannon-fodder, was as terribly severe on infanticide as he was infinitely indulgent to illegitimacy. **1950** PARTRIDGE *Here, There & Everywhere* 65 *Cannon-fodder* was never very popular with British troops. **1567** in Tytler *Hist. Scotl.* (1864) III. 264 Knox thundered out..*cannon-hot against her. **1651** DAVENANT *Gondibert* II. xxxv, Deep *Cannon Mouth'd experienc'd Hounds. **1884** F. BRITTEN *Watch & Clockm.* 178 A long boss or pipe called the *cannon pinion. The cannon pinion drives the minute wheel. **1598** BARRET *Theor. Warres* v. iii. 134, 5000 Quintals or Centenaires of *Cannon powder. **1627** CAPT. SMITH *Seaman's Gram.* xiv. 71 Serpentine powder in old time was in meale, but now corned and made stronger, and called Canon corne powder. **1599** NASHE *Lent. Stuffe* (1871) 91 When the fame of the king of fishes was *canon-roared in her ears. **1813** SIR R. WILSON *Diary* II. 147 My new order ribbon: it is not in itself beautiful, but it becomes so when *cannon-smoked.

10. A thief, *spec.* a clever pickpocket. *U.S. slang.*

1915 JACKSON & HELLYER *Vocab. Criminal Slang* 22 *Cannon.* General currency. A revolver. In pickpocket parlance it signifies a pickpocket of indefinite order. **1936** *Evening News* 9 Dec. 8/5 The art of the 'dip' or 'cannon', as these light-fingered gentry are known in the underworld, probably reached its climax in the person of 'Diamond Dick'. **1955** D. W. MAURER in *Amer. Dial. Soc.* XXIV. 89 *Cannon*, an intensification..of *gun* was, and still is, used with some sense of indicating a better-than-ordinary pick-pocket.

ˈcannon, *sb.*[2] [Cf. CANION (also spelt *cannon*), and CANNON *sb.*[1]] A cylindrical or sausage-like curl, properly horizontal, like the canions of breeches. Hence ***cannon curls***.

c **1800** *Mem. Mary Somerville* iii. (1873) 41 He wore a powdered wig, with cannons at the ears, and a pigtail. **1857** GEO. ELIOT *Sc. Cleric. Life, Janet's Repent.* v. 218 With.. sandy hair, which was this morning arranged in taller cannon curls than usual. *Ibid.* II. 190 Old lawyer Pittman's daughters with cannon curls surmounted with large hats.

ˈcannon, *v.* [f. the sb.: cf. It. *cannonare*.]

1. *intr.* To discharge a cannon. *trans.* To cannonade.

1691 LUTTRELL *Brief Rel.* (1857) II. 170 To learn and use the art of canooning and bombarding. **1693** *Mem. Ct. Teckely* I. 43 At break of day they began to Cannon the Imperialists. **1865** *Spectator* 7 Jan. 5 He must..cannon them into material civilization.

2. *Billiards.* To play one's ball so as to make a CANNON (see sense 7). Also (of the ball), to strike and rebound.

1844 MARDON *Billiards* 11 Any bungler can canon full upon a ball. **1859** J. LANG *Wand. India* 114 He cannoned all over the table, went in off the red and white. **1864** *Spectator* 531 The art of cannoning as it were, against the miserable, the ball ultimately meant to strike the great and powerful. **1873** BENNETT & CAV. *Billiards* 225 If the spot-white is cannoned on full, the balls will be left together.

3. *trans.* To strike with rebounding collision (prop. laterally or obliquely), to come into violent collision with.

1864 VAMBÉRY *Trav. C. Asia* 197 Our heads were continually cannoning each other like balls on a billiard table.

b. *intr.* (with various preps.)

1872 *Daily News* 25 Mar., Franc Huron and Acton cannoned, and both fell. **1879** F. POLLOK *Sport Brit. Burmah* I. 111 He [a blind bear] used to get loose and run up the first tree against which he cannoned. **1880** MISS BRADDON *Just as I am* xvii. 106 Scampering over hedges and ditches, and cannoning at gates.

cannon, obs. form of CANON.

cannonade (kænəˈneɪd), *sb.* [f. CANNON *sb.* + -ADE: cf. It. *cannonata*, Sp. *cañonada* (Minsheu).] A continued discharge of cannon; an attack with cannon.

1655 FLECKNO *Trav.* 12 Your young gallants of the time.. talk of nothing but rampards and parapats, musquetads.. and canonads. **1769** ROBERTSON *Chas. V*, III. VIII. 96 A furious cannonade. **1776** W. HEATH in Sparks *Corr. Amer. Rev.* (1853) I. 333 We could not reduce the fort by cannonade. **1837** CARLYLE *Fr. Rev.* III. v. vi. 299 Twelve hours of raging cannonade. **1841** ELPHINSTONE *Hist. Ind.* II. 113 A cannonade was kept up on both sides.

fig. **1878** HUXLEY *Physiogr.* 167 A cannonade, more or less sharp, is constantly kept up against the coast.

b. *humorously*: at billiards.

1844 DISRAELI *Coningsby* xii, Where the echoing balls denoted the sweeping hazard or the effective cannonade.

cannonade (kænəˈneɪd), *v.* [f. prec.]

1. *trans.* To batter or attack with cannon; to discharge cannon against.

a **1670** SIR J. TURNER *Mem.* (1829) 68 Da. Leslie.. cannonading the royall troops, when they came in view of him. **1790** BEATSON *Nav. & Mil. Mem.* 221 Throwing shells and cannonading the ships. **1795** *Monthly Rev.* XVII. 569 Let fresh cities be cannonaded into rubbish. **1937** W. S. CHURCHILL *Great Contemp.* 104 The possibility of the German fleet..cannonading Calais.

2. *intr.* To discharge cannon continuously.

1702 *Lond. Gaz.* No. 3829/3 The Enemy cannonaded all day. **1841** ELPHINSTONE *Hist. Ind.* II. 443 After cannonading for three days..he ordered a general assault.

fig. **1886** PHELPS *Burglars in Par.* I. 9 The omnibus bobbed and cannonaded through..the streets.

cannoˈnading, *vbl. sb.* The action of the prec. vb.; the sustained discharge of cannon.

1704 E. WHITAKER in *Camden Soc. Misc.* (1881) 46 Admirall Byng, who commanded the cannonading. **1777** WATSON *Philip II* (1839) 245 He began a brisk cannonading.

fig. **1878** MORLEY *Crit. Misc.*, *Byron* 230 No..polemical cannonading can drive away the impalpable darkness of error.

ˈcannonarchy. [cf. *anarchy*, etc.] Government by cannon; usurpation supported by cannon.

1841 MRS. GORE *Cecil* (1860) 79 (Hoppe) The greatest despotism of modern times—the cannonarchy of Napoleon. **1864** *Atlantic Monthly* May 633 Our constitutional polity would give way to a cannonarchy.

ˈcannon-ˌball. [See BALL *sb.*[1] 5.]

1. a. A ball, usually of iron, to be thrown from a cannon. (Also *collect.* and as *pl.*)

1663 BUTLER *Hud.* I. II. 872 Heavy brunt of cannon-ball. **1704** *Lond. Gaz.* No. 4077/2 Colonel Fox was killed with a Cannon-Ball. **1704** *Collect. Voy. & Trav.* III. 764/2, 800 Cannon-ball. **1848** W. K. KELLY tr. *L. Blanc's Hist. Ten Y.* II. 265 Being battered down with cannon balls.

b. *Hist.* A nickname for the hard-headed remnant of the protectionist party in England.

1858 *Sat. Rev.* 30 Oct. 413/2 The amendment..which sealed for ever the fate of Protection, was carried [in 1852] with only fifty dissentient voices—the celebrated 'cannon-balls'.

2. cannon-ball fruit, the globular woody fruit of a South American tree, *Couroupita guianensis* (N.O. *Lecythidaceæ*) or **cannon-ball tree**. Also simple *attrib.*

1839 *Penny Cycl.* XIII. 381/1 Cannon-ball tree. **1866** *Treas. Bot.* 342 The Cannon-ball fruit: its shell is used as a drinking vessel, and its pulp when fresh is of an agreeable flavour. **1885** LADY BRASSEY *The Trades* 112 Perhaps the most remarkable of the order of Lecythidaceæ..was the so-called 'Cannon-ball tree'. **1920** TILDEN *Lawn Tennis* xiv. 146 A fast cannon-ball smash.

†**ˈcannon-ˌbasket.** *Obs.* A gabion.

1647 CLARENDON *Hist. Reb.* (1703) II. VIII. 419 The Governour..brought away their Cannon Baskets, and many Armes. **1656** DUGARD *Gate Lat. Unl.* §905 With Ordnance, placed behinde Canon-baskets (filled with earth). **1687** J. RICHARDS *Journ. Siege of Buda* 10 Cannon-Baskets and Faggots were brought to the Tower, in order to the raising a Battery.

cannon-bit: see CANNON *sb.* 4.

ˈcannon-ˌbone. [f. CANNON *sb.*[1] as being tube or reed-shaped; in F. *canon*.] The single bones between the knee or hough and fetlock of the fore and hind leg (of a horse or other quadruped), the metacarpal and metatarsal bones respectively.

1834 SIR C. BELL *Hand* 92 When we look in front, instead of the four metacarpal bones, we see one strong bone, the cannon bone. **1854** OWEN in *Circ. Sc.* (1865) II. 83/1 The single bone [of ox], called 'cannon-bone', which articulates with both these carpal bones, does not answer to the single 'cannon-bone' in the horse, but to the metatarsals of both the third and the fourth digits. **1872** NICHOLSON *Palæont.* 400 These are anchylosed together in the adult, and form a single mass which is known as the 'canon-bone'.

cannoned (ˈkænənd), *a.* [f. CANNON *sb.* + -ED[2].] Furnished with cannon.

1869 M. ARNOLD *South. Night* vi, There, where Gibraltar's cannon'd steep O'erfrowns the wave.

cannoneer (kænəˈnɪə(r)). Also 6- **cannonier.** [a. F. *canonnier* = It. *cannoniere*, Sp. *cañonero*, Pg. *canhoeiro*: see CANNON and -EER[1].]

An artilleryman who manages the laying and firing of a cannon; a gunner.

1562 *Act 5 Eliz.* v. §12 Gunners, commonly called Canoneers. **1590** MARLOWE *2nd pt. Tamburl.* III. iii. ad fin., To save our cannoneers from musket-shot. **1591** GARRARD *Art Warre* 303 The Cannoniers ought to be readie. **1674** WALLIS in Rigaud *Corr. Sci. Men* (1841) II. 588 Practical cannoneers..find the random of a bullet very different from the parabola. **1795** in Nicolas *Disp. Nelson* (1846) VII. Introd. 77 Ordnance stores for the siege, and cannoniers. **1855** MACAULAY *Hist. Eng.* III. 244 The Irish cannoneers stood gallantly to their pieces.

Hence **cannoˈneering** *vbl. sb.*, management of cannon; cannonading.

1756 BURKE *Vind. Nat. Soc.* Wks. I. 31 The present perfection of gunnery, cannoneering, bombarding, mining, and all these species of artificial..cruelty.

†**'cannonery.** *Obs.* Also 7 canonrie. [cf. F. *cannonière* = Sp. *cañonera.*] See quot.; also a loop-hole to shoot out at.

[**1598** BARRET *Theor. Warres* Gloss. 249 *Cannonera*, a Spanish word, and is the place or roome where the Cannon is placed in a bulwarke.] *Ibid.* v. ii. 130 Make the Cannoneries that they may shoot from aboue. **1611** FLORIO *Casamatta*, a casamat, a canonrie.

'cannoning, *vbl. sb.* [f. CANNON *v.* + -ING[1].]

1. The discharge of cannon; the noise of this discharge; any similar action or its noise.

1607 BREWER *Lingua* I. i. (R.) The loud cannoning of thunder-bolts. **1691** [see CANNON *v.* 1].

2. The making a cannon at billiards; a coming into violent collision.

1864 [see CANNON *v.* 2]. **1881** *Times* 14 Feb. 4/2 In riding for gates.. there was crowding and cannoning.

'cannon-proof, *sb.* and *a.* [see PROOF.]

A. *sb.* Impenetrability to cannon-shot; safety from cannon; cannon-proof armament.

1601 CORNWALLYES *Ess.* II. xxix (1631) 42 Put him in a Castle by Cannon proofe well guarded. **1611** BEAUM. & FL. *King & No K.* III. ii, If I might stand still in cannon-proof, and have fame fall upon me, I would refuse it.

B. *adj.* Impenetrable to cannon-shot; proof against cannon.

1632 G. HUGHES *Saints Losse* 37 It's canon-proofe, and a wall impregnable? **1667** EARL ORRERY *State Lett.* (1743) II. 222, I endeavour to make my batteries at Kingsale cannon proof. **1695** *Lond. Gaz.* No. 3100/4 The Lodgment on the Right was made Cannon proof.

cannonry ('kænənrı). [f. CANNON *sb.* + -RY: cf. *musketry, gunnery.*]

1. Discharge of cannon, cannonading.

1839-40 W. IRVING *Wolfert's R.* (1855) 157 Their columns were ripped up by cannonry. **1873** BROWNING *Red Cott. Nt. Cap* 114 Had not the dreadful cannonry drowned all.

2. Artillery, cannon collectively.

1851 MRS. BROWNING *Casa Guidi W.* 11, Long live the Duke!—how roared the cannonry!

3. *nonce-use.* Cannoneers as a force.

1866 RUSKIN *Crown Wild Olive* 210 You may have to call yourselves 'Cannonry' instead of chivalry.

'cannon-shot. [see SHOT *sb.*]

1. The shooting or discharge of a cannon.

1606 HIERON *Wks.* I. 46 If Hee had done it by cannon shot. **1876** BANCROFT *Hist. U.S.* III. xiii. 199 Triple line was formed, out of reach of cannon-shot.

2. Ammunition shot from a cannon; balls or other 'shot' for a cannon.

1591 SHAKS. *1 Hen. VI*, III. iii. 79 These haughtie wordes of hers Haue battred me like roaring Cannon-shot. **1653** URQUHART *Rabelais* I. xxxvii, These are cannon-shot. **1687** *Lond. Gaz.* No. 2282/6 Ply'd with Bombs and Cannon-shot. **1871** JOAQUIN MILLER *Songs Italy* (1878) 119 The hail like cannon-shot struck the sea.

3. The distance a cannon will throw a ball; the range of a cannon.

1580 SIR R. BINGHAM in *Spenser's Wks.* (Grosart) I. 463, I entered the harbour.. within canon shotte of the fortress. **1702** *Lond. Gaz.* No. 3844/4 Out of Cannon-shot of that Town. **1790** BEATSON *Nav. & Mil. Mem.* (1804) 327 To approach within cannon-shot.

cannopy, cannow(e, obs. ff. CANOPY, CANOE.

cannos, variant of CANOUS *a. Obs.*

cannot ('kænət), the ordinary modern way of writing *can not*: see CAN *v.*

‖**cannula** ('kænjʊlə). *Surg.* Also (*incorrectly*) canula. [a. L. *cannula* 'small reed or pipe', dim. of *canna* (q.v.) reed, pipe.] A tubular instrument introduced into a cavity or tumour in order to allow the escape of fluid.

1684 tr. *Bonet's Merc. Compit.* XIV. 484 Let a Cannula be made of a Linnen Rag besmear'd with White Wax. **1754-64** SMELLIE *Midwif.* I. 229 Blowing into the mouth with a silver canula so as to expand the lungs. **1866** FLINT *Princ. & Pract. Med.* (1880) 148 A canula or hollow needle introduced into the chest. **1876** FOSTER *Phys.* II. iv. (1879) 378 When a ureter is divided.. and a cannula inserted.

'cannular, *a.* [f. prec. + -AR.] Of the form of a cannula, tubular.

1823 H. H. WILSON *Wks.* (1864) III. 386 A sort of canular trochar. **1847** in CRAIG.

'cannulate, -ated, *a.* Also canu-. [f. as prec. + -ATE + -ED.] **a.** Made of a tubular shape, tubular. **b.** Channelled or grooved.

1684 tr. *Bonet's Merc. Compit.* VIII. 288 Putting a cannulated Catheter into the Wound. **1707** SLOANE *Jamaica* I. 171 Furrowed or cannulated calyces. **1775** ELLIS in *Phil. Trans.* LXVI. 4 A regular cannulated appearance on the surface. **1805** *Med. Jrnl.* XIV. 490 The canulated catheter. **1881** *Syd. Soc. Lex.*, *Cannulate*, tubular.

'cannulate, *v.* [f. the adj.] *trans.* To introduce a cannula into (a cavity). So **cannu'lation,** the action of the verb.

1926 *Jrnl. Amer. Med. Assoc.* 28 Aug. 641/2 The duct of Santorini was then cannulated, no attempt being made to cannulate or ligate the duct of Wirsung. **1944** *Science* 9 June 476/1 The 10 to 15 minutes used for the cannulation. **1956** *Nature* 18 Feb. 339/2 The blood-flow.. has been measured by cannulating the sagittal sinus. **1961** *Lancet* 19 Aug. 410/1 Repeated hæmodialysis by means of conventional cannulation techniques.

†**'cannule.** ? *Obs.* In 8 canule. [ad. L. *cannula*: see CANNULATE, -ATED *a.*] A minute canal or channel.

1718 BLAIR in *Phil. Trans.* XXX. 894, I find one Canulo entring the Bone from the sides of the Orifice for the Caretide Artery.

canny ('kænı), *a. Sc.* Also in north Eng. dial. conny. [A comparatively modern word: not found before 17th c. App. f. CAN *v.* in sense 'to know how, be able', or the derived Sc. sb. CAN, 'knowledge, skill' + -Y: cf. Sw. *kunnig. Canny, conny*, thus originally was nearly = *cunnand, cunning* in its primary sense. But it has developed an extensive series of meanings, two or three of which are in common use in Eng. literature to denote qualities considered characteristically Scotch. It is also current in the North of England as far south as Lancashire and the Humber, but in senses more or less distinct from the Scotch.]

1. Knowing, sagacious, judicious, prudent; wary, cautious. *Sc. arch.*

1637 RUTHERFORD *Lett.* lxxxiii. (1862) I. 212 Men's canny wisdom, who, in this storm, take the nearest shore and go to the lee and calm side of the Gospel. *a* **1661** *Ibid.* I. xi. (Jam.) I trust in God, to use the world, as a canny or cunning master doth a knave-servant;—he giveth him no handling or credit. *a* **1662** BAILLIE *Lett.* (1775) II. 138 (Jam.) The Parliament is wise to make, in a canny and a safe way, a wholesome purgation. *a* **1758** RAMSAY *Poems* (1800) II. 256 Ye gales that.. please the canny boatman.

b. *esp.* Cautious in worldly matters, worldly-wise, shrewd, having a constant eye to the main chance. (A somewhat sneering application of the Scotch word by English writers to 'a low prudence or roguish sagacity, which southern people are pleased to attribute to their northern kinsfolk' (*Chambers' Jrnl.*). Perh. from Scott's use.

1816 SCOTT *Antiq.* xxxviii, 'If ye'll let me hear the question,' said Edie, with the caution of a canny Scotchman, 'I'll tell you whether I'll answer it or no.' **1852** MISS YONGE *Cameos* (1877) II. vii. 90 Starving out the English, as the canny Scotch had so often done. **1870** LOWELL *Study Wind.* 145 It [the Hohenzollern] was an able and a *canny* house, a Scotch version of the word *able*, which implies thrift and an eye to the main chance. **1878** HOLBROOK *Hyg. Brain* 53 As they say in canny Scotland.

†**2.** Cunning, artful, wily. *Sc. Obs.* or *arch.*

a **1662** BAILLIE *Lett.* (1775) II. 67 (Jam.) Mr. Marshall.. by canny conveyance, got a sub-committee nominate according to his mind.—Vines, Herle, &c... seeing us excluded by Marshal's cunning, would not join. **1794** RITSON *Sc. Songs* I. 269 (Jam.) Well does the canny kimmer ken, They gar the scuds gae glibber down.

3. Skilful, clever, 'cunning' (in the old sense). ***canny wife***: 'wise woman', midwife (Fr. *femme sage*); hence ***canny moment***: moment of childbirth. *Sc. arch.*

1768 ROSS *Helenore* (1789) 15 (Jam.) [They] did with care the canny knack impart Unto their bairns. **1790** SHIRREFS *Poems* 266 (Jam.) A skilly wife, our parish howdy; Wha did her jobs sae freely canny. **1810** CROMEK *Rem. Nithsdale Song* App. 335 (Jam.) When the pangs of the mother seized his beloved wife, a servant was ordered to fetch the cannie wife who lived across the Nith. **1815** SCOTT *Guy M.* i, 'Ye'll be come in the cannie moment I'm thinking.'

†**4.** Supernaturally wise, endowed with occult or magical power. *Sc. Obs.*

1768 ROSS *Rock & wee pickle Tow* (Jam.) She was ne'er ca'd chancy, but canny and slim. **1816** SCOTT *Bl. Dwarf* iv, His popular epithet soon came to be Canny Elshie, or the Wise Wight of Mucklestane Moor.

†**5.** Lucky, fortunate, prosperous. *Sc. Obs.*

1715 PENNECUIK *Poems* 62 (Jam.) Farewel, old Calins, kannie all thy life. **1721** RAMSAY *Poet's Wish* ii, Whaever by his canny fate, Is master of a good estate.

b. Lucky or safe to meddle with; *esp.* with negative. Cf. UNCANNY. *Sc.*

1718 RAMSAY *Christ's Kirk* III. v, Word gae'd she was na kanny. **1829** SCOTT *Demonol.* v. 161 Which are not supposed to be themselves altogether canny.

6. Careful, frugal, thrifty. (An archaic Sc. sense, which has been taken up in English to characterize a quality considered specially Scotch.)

1725 RAMSAY *Gentle Sheph.* I. ii, Whate'er he wins, I'll guide with canny care. *c* **1800** *Maxim*, 'Be canny with the sugar!' **1866** HOWELLS *Venet. Life* 267 The number.. and cost of the dishes were carefully regulated by the canny Republic's laws. **1872** *Spectator* 7 Sept. 1129 A businesslike, thrifty, canny, constitutional government.

7. Careful or cautious in motion or action; *hence*, quiet, gentle, 'soft' of speech; free from commotion, disturbance, or noise. Said of persons or animals, in their action, speech, or disposition; and also applied to things, as running water, the sea, wind, etc. (The usual sense in modern Scotch.)

1785 BURNS *Cotter's Sat. Nt.* iv, Some tentie rin A cannie errand to a neebor town. **1786** —— *Salut. Auld Mare* v, Hamely, tawie, quiet and cannie. **1814** SCOTT *Wav.* lx, 'The plaids [Highlanders] were gay canny, and did not do so much mischief.' **1822** —— *Pirate* v, 'Speak her fair and canny.' **1820** *Glenfergus* II. 341 (Jam.) The canniest hand about a sick bed. **1861** RAMSAY *Remin.* v. (ed. 18) 125 Mounted upon a Highland pony as being the canniest baste. *Mod. Sc.* A cannie laddie. *Cannie Nannie*, a species of wild bee not given to stinging.

b. Of humour: Quiet, sly, 'pawky'. (*Sc.*, and used by Eng. writers as characteristic of Scotch humour.)

1876 GREEN *Short Hist.* viii. §2. 464 His canny humour lights up the political and theological controversies of the time.

8. Quiet, easy, snug, comfortable, pleasant, cosy. *Sc.*

a **1758** RAMSAY *Poems* (1800) I. 44 (Jam.) Edge me into some canny post. *Ibid.* II. 227 (Jam.) A canny soft and flowery den. **1787** BURNS *Ep. James Smith* xviii, Cannie, in some cozie place, They close the day. *Mod.* She [a servant] has a gey cannie place.

9. Agreeable to the eyes or perception, tidy, seemly, comely; good, worthy, 'nice', very satisfactory. In the north of England (in some parts pronounced *conny*) a general epithet of approbation or satisfaction, as in 'Canny Newcastle', 'the Canny Town'. In N. Lancashire, 'of good size or amount'. (Cf. the vulgar 'a tidy bit of money', and the like.) Not a Scotch sense.

1802 R. ANDERSON *Cumbrld. Ball.* 40 Tom Linton was bworn till a brave canny fortune. **1821** MRS. WHEELER *Westmrld. Dial.* 99 Saa yee awt else et wur conny while yee stayd? **1863** in Robson *Bards of Tyne* 237 We wish to be cleanly and canny. **1870** *Lancash. Gloss.* (E.D.S.) s.v., 'Jim had supp't a conny lot.' **1875** *Whitby Gloss.*, *Conny*, seemly: 'she's conny beeath to feeace an te follow.' **1877** *Holderness Gl.*, 'A conny lahtle bayn' [= bairn].

10. Also used *advb.*; esp. in phr. ***to ca' canny***: to go cautiously, quietly, gently, carefully, warily.

a **1796** BURNS *My Nannie O* vi, I maun guide it cannie, o. **1804** TARRAS *Poems* 82 (Jam.) The troddling burnie i' the glen Glides cannie o'er its peebles sma'. **1814** *Saxon & Gael* III. 73 (Jam.) 'Chaps like them sud ca' canny.' **1816** SCOTT *Antiq.* vii, 'Canny now, lad—canny now—tak tent, and tak time.' **1822** GALT *Entail* I. 239 (Jam.) 'But, Charlie and Bell, ca' canny.'

canoe (kə'nu:), *sb.* Forms: α. 6-8 canoa, 7 cannoa; β. 6-8 canow(e, 7 cannow(e, canou(e, 7-8 canoo; γ. 7- caano, cano, 7-8 cannoe, 8- canoe. [In 16th c. *canoa*, a. Sp. *canoa*, a. Haytian *canoa*, the native name found in use by Columbus. *Canoa* continued in Eng. use into the 18th c., but before 1600 there appeared a parallel form *canow*, used with varieties of spelling into the 18th c., which was apparently an Eng. modification of *canoa*; in the course of the 17th c. appeared the forms *caano, cano, canno, canoo, cannoe*, and *canoe*, of which *cano* is also the Du., and *canoe* an earlier Fr. form (in Cauxois' transl. of Acosta 1600).

(The mod.F. *canot* is considered by Diez and Scheler a dim. of OF. *cane* ship, boat (prob. of Teut. origin: cf. LG. *kane*, Du. *kaan*, Ger. *kahn*, also L. *canna* small vessel, gondola); but it is perh. the word *canoe* spelt according to a mistaken etymology. It is not however the equivalent of *canoe* in English, but means simply 'little boat'.)]

1. A kind of simple, keelless boat: **a.** Originally applied to those of the West Indian aborigines, which were hollowed out of a single tree-trunk, and thence to those of other primitive societies, or of prehistoric cultures, of this construction. **b.** Extended to those of other societies and other construction, and used generally for any roughly-made craft used by American Indians, Malayo-Polynesians, etc.; most of these use paddles instead of oars, whence 'canoe' is sometimes understood to be any vessel propelled by paddles (cf. sense 2).

α. **1555** EDEN *Decades W. Ind.* (Arb.) 45 The Indian language. *Canoa*, a boate or barke. *Ibid.* I. i. (Arb.) 66 Theyr lighters or small boates (whiche they call *Canoas*).. Theyr boates are made only of one tree, made holow with a certain sharpe stone.. And are very longe and narowe. Many affirme that they haue sene some of them with fortie ores. *a* **1618** RALEIGH *Invent. Shipping* 5 The Boate of one tree called the Canoa. **1622** R. HAWKINS *Voy. S. Sea* (1847) 90 With cannoas, which they have in this coast so great, that they carry seventie and eightie men in one of them. **1697** DAMPIER *Voy.* (1729) I. 29 Canoa's.. are nothing but the Tree it self made hollow Boatwise. **1727** A. HAMILTON *New Acc. E. Ind.* II. xxxviii. 71 The People come thronging on Board in their Canoaes.

β. **1590** GREENE *Fr. Bacon* (1630) 40 Persia [shall] downe her Volga by Canows, Send downe the secrets of her spicerie. **1613** W. BROWNE *Brit. Past.* I. ii, In a boate like the cannowes of Inde. **1661** HICKERINGILL *Jamaica* 48 In Boats and Canoues. **1756** NUGENT *Gr. Tour* I. 78 An Indian canow brought from the straights of Davis.

γ. **1622-62** HEYLIN *Cosmogr.* IV. (1682) 143 Making Caanos or Boats. **1637** HEYWOOD *Royal Ship* 9 Such the Indian Canooes. **1665** G. HAVERS *P. della Valle's Trav. E. Ind.* 343 Little Canoos (which are long narrow boats, but like troughs out of firm trees). **1685** *Phil. Trans.* XV. 980 Rowed up the River Mississippi, in a Canot. **1719** W. WOOD *Surv. Trade* 167 To work in any Cannoe or Wherry. **1760** T. HUTCHINSON *Hist. Col. Mass.* v. (1765) 467 They had two sorts of canoos. **1777** ROBERTSON *Hist. Amer.* (1783) I. 115 Canoes.. rudely formed out of the trunk of a single tree. **1825** *Bro. Jonathan* II. 29 Our birch canoe dipping, with every motion of the paddle. **1837** W. IRVING *Capt. Bonneville* I. 78 [He] descended the Platte from this fork, in

skin canoes. **1865** LUBBOCK *Preh. Times* xiii. (1869) 429 Each canoe being formed from a single trunk, probably hollowed by fire.

2. A small light sort of boat or skiff propelled by paddling, used chiefly for recreation in Europe, North America, etc.

The ordinary canoe is made of thin board, galvanized iron, caoutchouc, paper, etc., and like the *kayak* of the Eskimoes is covered in, except the small space occupied by the canoeist; it is propelled by a paddle having a blade at each end; but so-called 'Indian' or 'Canadian canoes', which are open, and hold several persons, are also in use as pleasure-boats, and are propelled by a single-bladed paddle.

1799 *Caldron or Follies of Cambridge* 9 Some mount the broad-built sloop, while others woo The well-oar'd funney or the slim canoo. **1807** SOUTHEY *Espriella's Lett.* II. 63 Many of the smaller boats [on the Isis] had only a single person in each; and in some of these he sat face-forward, leaning back as in a chair, and plying with both hands a double-bladed oar in alternate strokes.. One of these canoes is, I was assured, so exceedingly light that a man can carry it. **1818** *Visit to Oxford* 50 A young man who was drowned just below Folly Bridge by the over-setting of a dangerous kind of boat called a canoe, much used for pleasure till forbidden by the Governor of the university. **1865** J. MACGREGOR (*title*) A thousand miles in the Rob Roy Canoe.

b. See PADDLE *v.*[2] 2 b.

3. *attrib.* and *Comb.*, as ***canoe burial, load, travelling***; ***canoe-man***; ***canoe-like, -shaped*** (***shape***) adjs.; also **canoe birch**, a name for *Betula papyracea*; **canoe-shell**, a shell shaped like a canoe, spec. *Scaphander lignarius*; **canoe-song**, a song sung by a canoeist while afloat; **canoe wood**, the wood of the Tulip tree.

1835 *Penny Cycl.* IV. 349/2 *Betula papyracea*, the paper or *canoe birch. **1865** TYLOR *Early Hist. Man.* xii. 352 With this belief the *canoe-burial of the North West and of Patagonia hangs together. **1856** OLMSTED *Slave States* 359 A number of long, narrow, *canoe-like boats, of light draft. **1691** in J. Munsell *Annals of Albany* (1850) II. 115 Ye def't accused him of stealing 1/2 *canoe load of water millions. **1753** in Washington *Writ.* (1889) I. 15 They were sent from New-Orleans with..8 Canoe-Loads of Provisions. **1890** A. HENRY *Trav.* 63 Several canoe-loads of fish were exported. **1936** J. C. BEAGLEHOLE *New Zealand* i. 14 Canoe-loads of savages. **1698** L. HENNEPIN *New Discovery Amer.* xlv. 188 One of our *Canow-Men look'd after our Things. **1755** L. EVANS *Geogr. Essays* 17 The Canoe Men are often obliged to carry over Land. **1834** M. SCOTT *Cruise Midge* (1859) 360 Quoth Hanse to the black canoe man. **1885** F. POLLOCK in *Macm. Mag.* Feb. 261/2 An expert canoeman will almost turn it round with one twist of the paddle. **1711** PETIVER *Gazophyl.* VI. Tab. liii, Small Indian *Canoe-shell... It's of an odd Shape, and sticks to larger Shells. **1850** MISS PRATT *Common Things Sea-side* 216 The Tufted Canoe-shell. **1945** E. STEP *Shell Life* xvi. 272 The Canoe-shell (*Scaphander lignarius*) is a many-whorled spiral of reddish hue. **1882** W. BOYD *Aquatics in Canada*, One of the most popular French *canoe-songs. **1843** *Penny Cycl.* XXV. 341/2 *Tulip-tree*..in America, where it is native, it is also known by the names White wood, *Canoe wood, Saddle-tree, etc.

canoe (kə'nuː), *v.* Also 9 canoo. [f. prec. sb.]

intr. To paddle or propel a canoe; to move as in a canoe. ***to canoe it*** (colloq): to do the journey in a canoe.

1842 *Nabob at Home* in *Athenæum* 3 Dec., Stretching out the muslin, and canooing forward on his heels without getting up. **1883** *Harper's Mag.* Apr. 692/2 Many enterprising souls..would have..bicycled, or canoed. **1884** *Ibid.* Jan. 304/1 You go on your..vacation trip, canoeing it ..to Lake George.

canoeing (kə'nuːɪŋ), *vbl. sb.* [f. prec. + -ING[1].] The practice of paddling a canoe. Also *attrib.*

1870 *Daily News* 10 Oct., When it was not the fashion to regard..the Nile as a punting and canoeing stream. **1871** *Ibid.* 27 Sept., Recognised canoeing..dates..from the publication of the cruise of the Rob Roy in 1865. Since then a literature of canoeing has sprung up.

canoeist (kə'nuːɪst). Also canoist; spurious fem. -iste. [See -IST.] One who paddles a canoe.

1865 MACGREGOR *Rob Roy in Baltic* 2 The hard-won experience of a former voyage was a great advantage to the canoist. **1873** G. C. DAVIES *Mount. & Mere* xviii. 155 Panting canoeists stop for a refresher. **1872** M. COLLINS *Pr. Clarice* I. ii. 30 The pretty canoiste can move silently along the river with unfatiguing strokes of the paddle.

canon ('kænən), *sb.*[1] Forms: 4–5 canoun, (5 canown), 6–8 cannon, 1, 3– canon. [Found in OE. as *canon*, a. L. *canon* rule, a. Gr. κανών rule. Early ME. had *'canon*, prob. from OE., and *ca'nun, ca'noun*, a. OF. *canun, canon*, the Fr. descendant of the L. Senses 12–14 are of obscure origin; some or all may belong to CANNON, in F. spelt *canon.*]

1. a. A rule, law, or decree of the Church; esp. a rule laid down by an ecclesiastical Council. ***the canon*** (collectively) = *canon law*: see b.

The Canons, in Ch. of Engl. = 'The Constitutions and Canons Ecclesiastical' agreed upon by Convocation, and ratified by King James I under the Great Seal in 1603.

c **890** K. ÆLFRED *Bæda* IV. xxiv. (Bosw.) Canones boc. *a* **900** *Laws of Ælfred* xxi. in Thorpe II. 376 (Bosw.) Ða canonas openlice beodaþ. *a* **1300** *Cursor M.* 26290 Als þe hali canon [*v.r.* -oun] vs sais þat scrift on sere-kin sines lais. **1451** *Treaty w. Scotl.* in Rymer *Foedera* (1710) XI. 288 Maister Robert Dobbes, Doctor of Canon. **1489** CAXTON *Faytes of A.* IV. ix. 254 The canon deffendeth expresly al manere of bataille and violent hurt. **1597** HOOKER *Eccl. Pol.* v. lxi. §2 A sacred canon of the sixth reverend synod. **1601** SHAKS. *All's Well* I. i. 158 Selfe-loue, which is the most inhibited sinne in the Cannon. **1658** BRAMHALL *Consecr. Bps.* vii. 171 The Papall Canons were never admitted for binding Lawes in England. **1827** HALLAM *Const. Hist.* (1876) I. vi. 303 A code of new canons had recently been established in convocation with the King's assent. **1859** JEPHSON *Brittany* viii. 131 A priest is expressly forbidden by the canons..to enter a public inn.

b. ***canon law*** (formerly *law canon*: cf. F. *droit canon*): ecclesiastical law, as laid down in decrees of the pope and statutes of councils. (See Gratian, *Dist.* iii. §2.)

c **1340** *Cursor M.* 26290 (Fairf.) Squa sais lagh Canoun þat is wise, þat shrift on mani synnis lise. **1387** TREVISA *Higden* (1865) II. 117 (Mätz.) By dome of lawe canoun. *c* **1400** *Apol. Loll.* 73 Law canoun is callid law ordeynid of prelats of the kirk. **1494** FABYAN VII. 526 They sent ye estudyauntys of ye lawe, canon & cyuyle. **1511** in W. H. Turner *Select. Records Oxford* 7 John Prynne, bachiller of Canon. **1552** ABP. HAMILTON *Catech.* (1884) 1 Doctours of Theologie and Canon law. *a* **1586** *Answ. Cartwright* 3 The common Lawes are against the cannon Lawes in many hundreth poyntes. **1765** BLACKSTONE *Comm.* I. Introd. 82 The canon law is a body of Roman ecclesiastical law, relative to such matters as that church either has, or pretends to have, the proper jurisdiction over. This is compiled from the opinions of the antient Latin fathers, the decrees of general councils, the decretal epistles and bulles of the holy see. **1850** MRS. JAMESON *Leg. Monast. Ord.* (1863) 331 Where he made himself master of civil and canon law.

2. *gen.* **a.** A law, rule, edict (other than ecclesiastical). **b.** A general rule, fundamental principle, aphorism, or axiom governing the systematic or scientific treatment of a subject; *e.g.* canons of descent or inheritance; a logical, grammatical, or metrical canon; canons of criticism, taste, art, etc.

1588 FRAUNCE *Lawiers Log.* I. ii. 7b, Such rules, maximaes, canons, axioms..or howsoever you tearme them. **1602** SHAKS. *Ham.* I. ii. 132 Or that the Euerlasting had not fixt His Cannon 'gainst Selfe-slaughter. **1607** —— *Cor.* I. x. 26 Against the hospitable Canon. **1628** MILTON *Vacat. Exercise*, Substance with his Canons; which Ens..explains. **1788** REID *Aristotle's Log.* v. ii. 113 They have reduced the doctrine of the topics to certaine axioms or canons. **1806** *Med. Jrnl.* XV. 134 The canons of pathology. **1869** ROGERS *Pref. Adam Smith's W.N.* I. 17 The indirect taxation of France violated every canon of financial prudence and equity. **1874** SAYCE *Compar. Philol.* i. 58 The canons of taste and polite literature. **1879** FARRAR *St. Paul* I. 613 We may assume it as a canon of ordinary criticism that a writer intends to be understood.

c. A standard of judgement or authority; a test, criterion, means of discrimination.

1601 HOLLAND *Pliny* II. 497 Moreouer, he made that which workmen call Canon, that is to say, one absolute piece of worke, from whence artificers do fetch their draughts, simetries, and proportions. **1651** HOBBES *Govt. & Soc.* xvii. §16. 313 The sacred Scripture is..the Canon and Rule of all Evangelicall Doctrine. **1869** GOULBURN *Purs. Holiness* vii. 65 This Lord's Prayer, what a canon does it supply for testing and correcting our spiritual state. **1874** W. WALLACE *Hegel's Logic* §52. 93 [Reason] is a canon, not an organon of truth, and can furnish only a criticism of knowledge.

†**3.** *Math.* A general rule, formula, table; *esp.* a table of sines, tangents, etc. *Obs.*

c **1391** CHAUCER *Astrol.* II. §32 Lok how many howres thilke coniunccion is fro the Midday of the day precedent, as shewith by the canoun of thi kalender. **1594** BLUNDEVIL *Exerc.* II. (ed. 7) 130 If you shall not finde in the Canon, the Sine which by your calculation is found. **1656** tr. *Hobbes' Elem. Philos.* (1839) 292 The straight line BV..if computed by the canon of signs. **1706** PHILLIPS, In Mathematicks, Cannon is an infallible Rule to resolve all things of the same Nature with the present Inquiry. **1751** CHAMBERS *Cycl.* s.v. *Canon, Natural Canon* of Triangles is a table of sines, tangents, and secants together..*Artificial Canon* of Triangles is a table wherein the logarithms of sines and tangents are laid down. **1798** HUTTON *Course Math.* (1807) II. 3 A Trigonometrical Canon, is a table.

4. The collection or list of books of the Bible accepted by the Christian Church as genuine and inspired. Also *transf.*, any set of sacred books; also, those writings of a secular author accepted as authentic.

1832 WYCLIF *Apoc.* Prol., In the bigynnyng of canon, that is, of the bok of Genesis. **1591** T. NORTON *Calvin's Inst.* I. 13b, What reuerence is due to the Scripture, and what bookes are to be reckened in the canon therof. **1641** J. JACKSON *True Evang. T.* II. 116 S. Andrew the Apostle.. added nothing to the Canon of Scripture. **1870** MAX MÜLLER *Sc. Relig.* (1873) 29 The process by which a canon of sacred books is called into existence. **1882** FARRAR *Early Chr.* I. 98 The Epistle to the Hebrews is not a work of St. Paul, but it is pre-eminently worthy of its honoured place in the Canon. **1885** *Encycl. Brit.* XIX. 211/1 The dialogues forming part of the 'Platonic canon'. **1953** C. J. SISSON *Shakespeare: Compl. Works* p. xviii (*heading*) The canon and the text.

†**5.** A canonical epistle. See CANONICAL 3.

1483 CAXTON *Gold. Leg.* 25/3 Saynt John that saith in his canone, We have, etc. **1502** *Ord. Crysten Men* II. i. (W. de W. 1506) 84 Wherfore sayth well saynt Iames in his canon.

6. The portion of the Mass included between the Preface and the *Pater*, and containing the words of consecration.

a **1300** *Cursor M.* 21190 þe first mess þat sent petre sang, Was þar þan na canon lang Bot pater-noster in þaa dais, Na langer canon was, it sais. **1395** PURVEY *Remonstr.* (1851) 42 After the sacringe, in the canoun of the masse. *a* **1450** *Knt. de la Tour* (1868) 40. **1532** MORE *Confut. Tindale* Wks. 490/2 Luter himself casting away the holy canon of ye masse. **1656** BP. HALL *Tracts* (1677) 43 It was the farther solemnizing and beautifying that holy action which brought the Canon in. **1781** GIBBON *Decl. & F.* II. xlv. 695 He officiated in the canon of the mass. **1868** HOOK *Lives Abps.* II. II. iii. 284 *note*, The canon or rule was the part of the service containing the actual consecration.

7. *Mus.* **a.** A species of musical composition in which the different parts take up the same subject one after another, either at the same or at a different pitch, in strict imitation.

A passage in Burney's *Hist. Music* (1781) 480 suggests as an earlier meaning: 'The rule by which a composition (in canon-form), which is only partially indicted in the score, can be read out by the performers in full.' Cf. quot. 1609.

1597 MORLEY *Introd. Mus.* 104 Of how manie parts the Canon is, so manie Cliefes do they set at the beginning of the verse. **1609** DOULAND *Ornith. Microl.* 48 A Canon..is an imaginarie rule, drawing that part of the Song which is not set downe out of that part which is set downe. Or it is a Rule, which doth wittily discouer the secret of a Song. **1795** MASON *Ch. Mus.* I. 54 Such Organists as were Masters of Canon, Fugue, and Counterpoint. **1869** OUSELEY *Counterp.* xxiii. §13 The closest stretto should be reserved for the end ..especially if it be introduced in canon.

b. A long hymn, used in the Eastern Church, consisting of eight odes, each of many stanzas.

1862 *Q. Rev.* Apr. 338 If we might venture..to name the characteristics of these canons, we should say richness and repose, and a continuous thread of Holy Scripture..woven into them.

8. a. 'In old Records, a Prestation, Pension, or Customary payment upon some religious Account' (Phillips 1706). From *Roman Law.*

1633 CAVE *Ecclesiastici* Introd. 51 He restor'd the Corn-Canon, (as they call'd it) the yearly Allowance of Corn, which Constantine had settled upon the Church. **1726** AYLIFFE *Parerg.* 139 Which Allowance was, by the ancient Lawyers, called a Canon, and not a Prebend, as now it is. **1847–79** HALLIWELL, *Canon*, a portion of a deceased man's goods exacted by the priest.

b. A quit-rent. [cf. Littré, *Canon* 10.]

1643 PRYNNE *Power Parl.* App. 164 Therefore to sustaine the burthens of Peace, the demesne was instituted, (which among the Lawyers is called Canon). **1774** BP. HALLIFAX *Anal. Rom. Law* (1795) 69 On condition that the Tenant shall improve the Lands, and pay a yearly Canon or Quit-Rent to the Proprietor.

9. a. A chief epoch or era, serving to date from (Gr. *κανὼν χρονικός*); a basis for chronology. Cf. *canon monument* in 15.

1833 CRUSE *Eusebius* VI. xxii. 242 A certain canon comprising a period of sixteen years. **1876** BIRCH *Rede Lect. Egypt* 14 The Turin papyrus, the canon of history, a list of all the kings.

b. ***paschal canon***: the rule for finding Easter, to which was often appended a table of the dates of Easter and the feasts varying with it for a series of years.

1727–51 CHAMBERS *Cycl.* s.v. *Canon, Paschal Canon*, a table of the moveable feasts, shewing the day of Easter, and the other feasts depending on it, for a cycle of nineteen years.

10. a. (See quot.)

1727–51 CHAMBERS *Cycl.*, *Canon*, in monastic orders, a book wherein the religious of every convent have a fair transcript of the rules of their order, frequently read among them as their local statutes.

b. 'The list of saints acknowledged and canonized by the Church' (Chambers *Cycl.* 1727–51).

11. *Printing.* A size of type-body equal to 4-line Pica; the largest size of type-body that has a specific name.

So called perhaps as being that used for printing the canon of the Mass; but Tory is said by Reed (*op. cit.* 36) to have used the term Canon for letter cut according to rule—*lettres de forme*—as distinguished from *lettres bastardes.*

1683 MOXON *Mech. Exerc.*, French Canon $17\frac{1}{2}$ [types] to a foot. **1688** R. HOLME *Armoury* III. iii. 119/2 *Canon*, the great Canon is the name of the largest Letter for Printing that is used in England. **1721** BAILEY, *Canon*, (with Printers) a large sort of Printing Letter. **1887** T. B. REED *O. Eng. Lett. Foundries*, 36 The Canon of the Mass was..printed in a large letter, and it is generally supposed that this size of letter being ordinarily employed in the large Missals, the type-body took its name accordingly; a supposition which is strengthened by its German name of Missal.

12. (See quot.)

1696 PHILLIPS, *Canon*..a Surgeon's Instrument, made use of for the sewing up of Wounds. **1721** in BAILEY; **1755** in JOHNSON; and in mod. Dicts. (Not in *Syd. Soc. Lex.*)

13. (See quot.)

1847–78 HALLIWELL, *Canons*, the first feathers of a hawk after she has mewed. [Perh. the same as CANNON: cf. Sp. *cañon* a quill.]

14. A metal loop or 'ear' at the top of a bell, by which it is hung. Also written CANNON (*sb.*[1] 5).

1688 R. HOLME *Armoury* III. 461/2 This is called a St. Bell, because it hath not Canons on the head to fasten it to the stock. **1878** GROVE *Dict. Mus.* I. 219 [Bells] are first carefully secured by iron bolts and braces through the ears or 'canons' to the stock. **1882** *School Guardian* No. 315. 12 The height of the bell from the lip to the top of the canons is 8 ft.

15. *attrib.* and *Comb.*, as ***canon law*** (see 1 b), ***-lawyer, -making, monument*** (cf. 9), ***rule, type*** (cf 11): ***canon-like, -wise*** adjs.

1601 BP. BARLOW *Defence* 99 We acknowledge it *Canon-like, but not Canonicall. **1659** BAXTER *Key Cath.* xxv. 147 This is a cheaper way of *Canon-making in a corner. **1631** R. BYFIELD *Doctr. Sabb.* 149 You finde nothing..in any ..*cannon monument, and register of Antiquitie. **1603** HOLLAND *Plutarch's Mor.* 33 The very *Canon rule, and paterne of all vertue. **1641** MILTON *Reform.* Wks. 1738 I. 7 An insulting and only *Canon-wise Prelate.

canon ('kænən), *sb.*[2] Forms: (1 canonic), 3 canon, 3–4 canun, canoun, 3–4 chanun, 3–5 chanoun, 4–7 chanon, 5 chanowne, (cannon), 6–7 channon, 6– canon. [Found in OE. in the form

canonic, ad. L. *canonic-us*, a late L. sb. use of the adj. *canonicus* CANONIC, f. *canōn*, rule, etc.: see prec. L. *canonic-us* gave It. *canonico*, Sp. *canonigo*, Pr. *canorgue*. Cat. and Pr. *canonge*, ONF. *ca'nonie*, later *ca'noine*, central F. *chanoine*, derive from a late L. form **canonius*: cf. *canonia* in Du Cange. The 12th c. Eng. form was *ca'nun*, later ME. *ca'noun*: apparently an adaptation of the ONF. *canonie* (pron. ka'nonjə), with the ending imperfectly represented (perh. by confusing with CANON *sb.*[1]). When this was subsequently influenced by French of Paris, the central Fr. *chanoine* was represented in Eng. by *chanun, chanoun*, so common in 14–15th c. But *canon* reappeared in the 16th c. and is the surviving form, running together with the preceding CANON *sb.*[1], so that many dictionaries treat the two as one word.]

1. *Eccl. Hist.* A clergyman (including clerks in minor orders) living with others in a clergy-house (*claustrum*), or (in later times) in one of the houses within the precinct or close of a cathedral or collegiate church, and ordering his life according to the canons or rules of the church. This practice of the *canonica vita* or canonical life began to prevail in the 8th c.; in the 11th c. it was, in some churches, reformed by the adoption of a rule (based upon a practice mentioned by St. Augustine) that clergymen so living together should renounce private property: those who embraced this rule were known as *Augustinian* (*Austin*) or *regular*, the others were *secular* canons.

From the 'regular' canons, came in the 12th c. those who followed the still stricter rule of Norbert of Premontré, thence called *Premonstratensian* Canons. These two groups of 'canons regular' were popularly distinguished by the colour of their habits as ***Black Canons*** and ***White Canons***. As these vied, in strictness of living, with the monastic orders, the difference between a *canon regular* and a *monk*, became in the later Middle Ages (as now in the R.C. Ch.) so slight that the one is frequently confounded with the other. Thus Littré explains 'Augustinian Canons' as '*moines*, dits aussi hermites de Saint-Augustin'.

c **1205** LAY. 21861 Canones þer comen. *Ibid.* 24289 Canunes [**1275** many canoun] þer weoren. *a* **1300** *Cursor M.* 22002 Clerk, or munk, or canun [*v.r.* canoun, chanoun]. *c* **1386** CHAUCER *Chan. Yem. Prol. & T.* 20, I demed hym som Chanon for to be. **1393** LANGL. *P. Pl.* C. VI. 157 Boþe monkes and chanouns. *c* **1440** *Promp. Parv.* 69 Chanone, *chanonicus.* **1480** CAXTON *Chron. Eng.* cxcii. 168 Preestes and frerys and chanons and seculeres. **1518** WRIOTHESLEY *Chron.* (1875) I. 12 All the orders of friers, channons, moncks of Stratforde and Tower Hill. **1616** SURFL. & MARKH. *Countr. Farm* 580 Students, monks, chanons and other fine and daintie persons. **1682** N. O. *Boileau's Lutrin* II. 21 But Oh! these Chanters, Chanons make a Pother. **1861** PEARSON *Early & Mid. Ages Eng.* 275 An attempt of the anti-reformers to substitute canons for monks in Winchester was put down.

1387 TREVISA *Higden* (1865) I. 373 Patrik rered þere a chirche, and dede þere chanouns reguler. *c* **1400** MAUNDEV. vii. 79 In the Chirche of Seynt Sepulchre was wont to ben Chanouns of the ordre of Seynt Augustyn. *c* **1425** WYNTOUN *Cron.* I. Prol. 86 Of Sanct Androwys a chanowne Regulare. **1609** SKENE *Reg. Maj.* 54 Abbats and Priours of regular Channons. **1844** LINGARD *Anglo-Sax. Ch.* (1858) II. xii. 235 Regular canons, whether in holy orders or not, are always reckoned among those who are bound to a life of chastity.

1297 R. GLOUC. 282 Canons þer were Seculers. **1513** BRADSHAW *St. Werburg* (1848) 137 From secular chanons to monkes religious. **1531** *Dial. Laws of Eng.* II. xl. (1638) 132 Goods gotten by a Canon seculer by reason of his Church . . shall not goe to his successor. **1844** LINGARD *Anglo-Sax. Ch.* (1858) II. xii. 235 The conversion of the conventual and collegiate clergy into secular Canons. **1868** FREEMAN *Norm. Conq.* (1876) II. vii. 85 The chapter was formed of secular canons.

2. In the Church of England, since the Reformation, all the canons have been secular, and the system of canons has been retained mainly in connexion with cathedral churches, where the canons, with the dean at their head, constitute the body of resident ecclesiastical dignitaries, who manage the cathedral, and (formally) elect the bishop. (See CHAPTER.)

The name of ***minor*** or ***petty canons*** is now sometimes given to those clergymen of the cathedral establishment who assist in performing the daily service, but are not members of the chapter. ***honorary canons***, are titular members of the cathedral chapter, who are non-residentiary, and receive no emoluments. See also PREBENDARY.

[*c* **1305** in *E.E.P.* (1862) 82 Alle þe Canouns of þe queor. **1362** LANGL. *P. Pl.* A. XI. 33 Neuer kyng ne kniht ne Canoun of Seynt poules. **1483** CAXTON *Gold. Leg.* 223/2 Commaundyng hym . . that he shold assemble the chanones of Seint James for to burye thys pylgryme.] **1561** T. NORTON *Calvin's Inst.* IV. v. (1634) 535 There be commonly Canons with five, six or seven benefices. **1576** LAMBARDE *Peramb. Kent* (1826) 143 A college stored with two and twenty Chanons. *a* **1626** BACON (J.) Deans and canons, or prebends, of cathedral churches. **1628** EARLE *Microcosm.* iii. 8 He is a main pillar of our Church, though not yet Dean or Canon. **1709** STEELE *Tatler* No. 54 ¶3 One of our Petty-Canons. **1765** BLACKSTONE *Comm.* I. xi. 383 The chapter, consisting of canons or prebendaries. **1837** SYD. SMITH *Let. Singleton* Wks. 1859 II. 261/2 You are not a Dean nor a Canon-Residentiary. **1862** MRS. H. WOOD *Channings* i. 2 He was one of the senior minor canons.

b. prefixed as a title.

(This fashion has prevailed chiefly since the appointment of titular or *honorary* canons.)

1849 BIRKS *Horæ Apost.* Pref., The late Canon Tate.

cañon ('kænjən), *sb.*[3] Also **cannon, canon**, CANYON. [a. Sp. *cañon* tube, pipe, conduit, barrel, cannon, etc. (augm. of *caña*:—L. *canna* reed, pipe, quill, CANE; thus the same word as It. *cannone*, Pg. *canhão*, Pr. and F. *canon*, Eng. *cannon*, and *canion*), but spec. applied by the Spaniards of New Mexico in the sense in which it has been adopted from them by their English-speaking neighbours. In order to retain the pronunciation and prevent confusion with *canon*, which would result from the frequent want of the Spanish letter ñ, *ñ* (*enye*), in English typography, the word is frequently spelt CANYON, q.v.]

A deep gorge or ravine at the bottom of which a river or stream flows between high and often vertical sides; a physical feature characteristic of the Rocky Mountains, Sierra Nevada, and the western plateaus of North America.

1834 A. PIKE *Sketches* 20 Two cañons ran up into the bosom of the ridge (by which word *cañon* the Spaniards express a deep, narrow hollow among the mountains). **1846** R. B. SAGE *Scenes Rocky Mts.* 111 The Platte forces its way through a barrier of table lands, forming one of those striking peculiarities incident to mountain streams, called a 'cañon'. **1850** B. TAYLOR *Eldorado* xxvii. (1862) 287 The word cañon (meaning, in Spanish, a funnel) has a peculiar adaptation to these cleft channels through which the rivers are poured. **1863** *Let. fr. Vancouver's Isl.* in *Daily Tel.* 17 Nov. 7/2 Through what is called a *cannon* (pronounced *kanyon*), a vast gorge formed by perpendicular rocks. **1874** COUES *Birds N.-W.* 228 Deep, rocky cañons, where the dense foliage and precipitous walls shut out the sun, and a perpetual twilight prevails. **1882** GEIKIE *Geol.* III. II. ii. §3. 379 The Grand Cañon of the Colorado river is 300 miles long, and in some places more than 6000 feet in depth.

attrib. **1879** BEERBOHM *Patagonia* v. 65 The tracks suddenly turned and went up the cañon-side on to the plain.

canon, obs. form CANNON, CANION.

cañon ('kænjən), *v.*[1] [f. CAÑON *sb.*[3]]

1. *intr.* To form, or flow in, a cañon.

1851 MAYNE REID *Scalp-hunters* I. v. 58 The stream, after running parallel to the ridge, swept round and cañoned through it. **1911** J. S. CHASE *Yosemite Trails* 208 Above it 'cañons' to the long gorge that is known as the Grand Cañon.

2. *trans.* To pierce with cañons.

1889 J. S. DILLER in *8th Ann. Rep. U.S. Geol. Surv. 1886–87* I. 426 Deeply cañoned by numerous streams.

canon ('kænən), *v.*[2] [f. CANON *sb.*[1] 7.] *trans.* To treat (a musical theme) in canon fashion. Also *absol.* or *intr.*

1894 G. DU MAURIER *Trilby* I. I. 41 They . . fugued and canoned and counterpointed [that simple melody]. **1927** *Music & Lett.* July 347 The phrases [of bird singing] were more often alike and several times canoned one into the other in a most delightful way.

† **cano'neer.** *Obs.* Also **cannonier.** [humorously f. CANON *sb.*[1], after CANNONEER.] One who makes, cites, or interprets (ecclesiastical) canons; a canonist; a zealot or stickler for the canons.

1641 *Curates' Confer.* in *Harl. Misc.* (Malh.) IV. 376 They are the curates, who are set to be Cannoniers. **1659** BAXTER *Key Cath.* xvii. 71 We turn this Canon against the Canoneers. **1681** —— *Search Schism.* i. 1 The Diocesan-Militants, or Canoneers.

canoness ('kænənɪs). [f. CANON *sb.*[2] + -ESS; cf. F. *chanoinesse*, in 16th c. also *canoniesse*; in med.L. *canonica* and *canonissa*.]

1. *Eccl. Hist.* A member of a college or community of women living under a rule, but not under a perpetual vow; hence, a woman holding a prebend or canonry in a female chapter. (The *Augustinian Canonesses* are now practically an order of nuns.)

1682 *News fr. France* 36 The Nuns, or Regular Canonesses of the Blessed Virgin of the Nunnery of Charron. **1726** AYLIFFE *Parerg.* 140 There are also in Popish Countries, women which they call Secular Canonesses living after the Example of Secular Canons. **1772** PENNANT *Tours Scotl.* (1774) 246 The nunnery, filled with the canonesses of St. Augustine. **1844** MARG. FULLER *Wom. in 19th C.* (1862) 97 She may be one of the lay sisters of charity, a canoness bound by an inward vow. **1885** *Dict. Nat. Biog.* I. 216/2 Louisa was appointed at the age of seventeen a canoness of Mons, then the wealthiest . . chapter in the Austrian Netherlands.

2. *humorous.* The wife of a canon.

1873 E. BERDOC *Adv. Protestant* 213 The canons, canonesses, and minor canons.

† **ca'nonial**, *a. Obs.* [a. F. *canonial*, ad. late L. *canoniālis*: cf. *canonia* in Du C.] = CANONICAL.

a **1225** *Ancr. R.* 8 Sein James canoniel epistle. **1502** *Ord. Crysten Men* IV. xxvi. (W. de W. 1506) 314 The whiche ben bounde unto the houres canonyales. **1589** *Pasquill's Ret.* 13 Whatsoeuer he speakes, must be Canoniall.

Hence **ca'nonially** *adv.*, canonically.

1581 MARBECK *Bk. Notes* 115 To our Lord N., the Pope, and to his successours entring canonially.

canonic (kə'nɒnɪk), *a.* (and *sb.*) [ad. L. *canonic-us*, = Gr. κανονικός of or according to CANON[2]; or a. F. *canonique*. Already in OE. as sb. = modern CANON *sb.*[2]]

A. *adj.* **1.** Authorized by, or according to, ecclesiastical canons; = CANONICAL 1.

1483 CAXTON *Gold. Leg.* 219/1 Euery day atte vii houres canonyques. **1532** MORE *Confut. Tindale* Wks. 516/2 By an olde canonike and sure grounded custom of yᵉ churche. **1663** BUTLER *Hud.* I. I. 257. **1664** DRYDEN *Rival Ladies* I. ii, 'Tis Evening now, and the Canonick Hours For Marriage are past. **1812** COMBE (Dr. Syntax) *Picturesque* VIII, The Doctor, in canonic state, Now op'd at once the churchyard gate.

2. Of or pertaining to the canon of Scripture; = CANONICAL 2.

1634–46 ROW *Hist. Kirk* (1842) 53 Some portion of holie Canonick Scripture. **1645** RUTHERFORD *Tryal & Tri. Faith* (1845) 6 The Church's last prayer in canonic Scripture is for union. **1835** I. TAYLOR *Spir. Despot.* iv. 150 Not to be traced in the canonic writings.

3. *gen.* Having the authority of an accepted rule or type; classic; = CANONICAL 4.

1850 LEITCH tr. *Müller's Anc. Art* §138. 115 His numerous pictures of gods and heroes (as his Theseus) attained a canonic consideration in art.

4. *Mus.* Following the strict rules of canon-form. (Cf. CANONICAL 6.)

1854 tr. *Cherubini's Counterpoint* 45 Canonic imitation is that where the consequent responds to the antecedent, note for note, from beginning to end. **1879** GROVE *Dict. Mus.* I. 654 The voices move, in strict canonic imitation, on a groundbass.

5. Of or belonging to the order of canons; = CANONICAL 7.

1483 CAXTON *Gold. Leg.* 426/1 They toke not the canonyke breed, for the chanonnes that were at yᵗ tyme . . gouerned them self after the reule of Saynt Austyn.

B. *sb.* **1.** = CANON *sb.*[2]; one in canonical orders. (L. *canonicus*.)

a **1000** *Laws of Ethelbert* vi. 2 (Bosw.) Godes þeowas, biscopas and abbodas, munecas and mynecene, canonicas and nunnan. **1678** R. BARCLAY *Apol. Quakers* XII. §x. 443 Ten Canonicks, so called, were burnt for that Crime. *a* **1853** LANDOR *Wks.* I. 60/1 The bones had been verified . . in presence of the archbishop, the canonics, and the protonotary.

2. A scheme or system of logical rules or dialectic; = the Epicurean τὸ κανονικόν.

1655–60 STANLEY *Hist. Philos.* (1701) 548/2 Thus may this short Canonick or Treatise of Rules, serve instead of a laborious and prolix Dialectick. **1847** LEWES *Hist. Philos.* VIII. ii. (1871) I. 351 The Epicurean Logic called Canonic, which is a collection of rules respecting human reason and its application.

†**3. a.** The theory of music or harmony (ἡ κανονική). **b.** One who studies music theoretically (of the Pythagoreans, who were called οἱ κανονικοί).

1655–60 STANLEY *Hist. Philos.* (1701) 385/1 The Pythagoreans named that which we now call Harmonick, Canonick . . A Canonick in general is a Harmonick, who is conversant about that which consists of Harmony.

canonical (kə'nɒnɪkəl), *a.* (and *sb.*) [f. med.L. *canonicāl-is*, f. *canonic-us*: see prec. and -AL[1].]

1. Prescribed by, in conformity with, or having reference to ecclesiastical edict or canon law.

1570–6 LAMBARDE *Peramb. Kent.* (1826) 303 Rochester hath . . a lawful and canonicall Cathedral See. **1586** *Will* in *Spenser's Wks.* (Grosart) I. Introd. 17 For . . my wyfe for and in the name of her canonicall parte and porcion. **1768** BLACKSTONE *Comm.* I. (1793) 553 These canonical disabilities being entirely the province of the ecclesiastical courts. **1868** FREEMAN *Norm. Conq.* (1876) II. viii. 298 With the weapons of legal and canonical disputation.

b. ***canonical hours***: (*a*) stated times of the day appointed by the canons for prayer and devotion; (*b*) the hours (now from 8 a.m. to 3 p.m.) within which marriage can be legally performed in a parish church in England; (*c*) *transf.*

1483 CAXTON *Gold. Leg.* 218/2 And euery day at euery hour canonycal she was lift up in thayer of thangellis. **1526** *Pilgr. Perf.* (W. de W. 1531) 164 All suche meditacyons perteyneth to the houres canonicall. **1607** TOPSELL *Four-f. Beasts* Ded. 7 The canonical voice and watchfulness of a cock. *a* **1667** COWLEY *Friendship in Abs.*, Each Day think on me, and each Day I shall, For thee make Hours Canonical. **1859** HOOK *Ch. Dict.* 144/2 In the Church of Rome, the canonical hours begin with vespers.

1665 PEPYS *Diary* (1879) III. 207 We, fearing the canonicall hour would be past before we got thither, did with a great deal of unwillingness send away the license and wedding ring. **1719** D'URFEY *Pills* III. 270 Let us be wed, At Hours Canonical. **1847** BARHAM *Ingol. Leg.* (1877) 344 It's long past the canonical hour.

c. ***canonical dress***, etc.; the articles of dress worn by clergy according to canon.

1666 PEPYS *Diary* 27 Sept., I . . to speak for a cloak and cassock for my brother . . and I will have him in a canonical dress. **1685** LUTTRELL *Brief Rel.* (1857) I. 343 Titus Oates . . to be divested of his canonical habit for ever. **1862** SMILES *Engineers* III. 391 Two . . old men, whose canonical hats indicated their quality as village pastors.

d. ***canonical obedience***: the obedience to be rendered by inferior clergy to the bishop or other ecclesiastical superior, according to the canons.

1621 BURTON *Anat. Mel.* III. iv. I. ii. (1651) 650 A false perswasion..of canonical or blind obedience. **1769** BLACKSTONE *Comm.* IV. 87 His new engagements of canonical obedience to the pope. **1869** HOOK *Lives Abps.* II. ii. 150 At his consecration he made a profession of canonical obedience to the Archbishop.

2. Of or belonging to the canon of Scripture. (Also used of other sacred books.)

a **1568** COVERDALE *Carrying Christ's Cross* viii. Wks. II. 258 The canonical books of the old and New Testament. **1632** MASSINGER & FIELD *Fatal Dowry* III. i, If this new preacher..Could prove his doctrine for canonical. **1651** BAXTER *Inf. Bapt.* 167 Though it be not Canonicall, he was a wise man that said, etc. **1790** PALEY *Horæ Paul.* I. 6 Sentences from the canonical epistles. **1857** MAX MÜLLER *Chips* (1880) I. x. 267 The chief canonical books of the Buddhist faith. **1862** TRENCH *Miracles* Introd. 42.

3. ***canonical epistles***, more particularly, the seven catholic epistles of James, Peter, John, and Jude; also applied to certain epistles of St. Basil, etc. Also quasi-*sb.*, ***a canonical*** (obs.) = CANON *sb.*[2] 5.

(*Ἐπιστολὴ κανονικὴ* had various senses in ecclesiastical writers. In reference to the Catholic Epistles the meaning is disputed; in reference to those of St. Basil, it means 'having the authority of a canon'.)

[*a* **1225** see CANONIAL.] **1561** DAUS tr. *Bullinger on Apoc.* (1573) 292 He is greater, that is in vs (sayth S. John in his Canonicall) than is he that is in the world. **1755** CHAMBERS *Cycl. Supp.*, Canonical..or general epistles.

4. *gen.* Of the nature of a canon or rule; of admitted authority, excellence, or supremacy; authoritative; orthodox, accepted; standard.

1553 T. WILSON *Rhet.* 67 Suche as all the worlde hathe confirmed and agreed upon, that it is autentique and canonical. **1603** H. CROSSE *Vertues Commw.* (1878) 81 Wisedome vnder a ragged coate is seldome canonicall. **1651** HOBBES *Govt. & Soc.* xvii. §18. 315 There must bee some Canonicall Interpreter. **1796** *Monthly Rev.* XIX. 545 He..remained the canonical geographer of the antients. **1811** *Ibid.* LXV. 133 Before Polycletus had ascertained the canonical proportions of a beautiful human frame. **1868** *Sat. Rev.* 15 Aug. 229/1 Challenging all those who may be disinclined to accept his criticism as canonical.

5. *Math.* Furnishing, or according to, a general rule or formula (see CANON *sb.*[2] 3).

1738 LOGAN in Rigaud *Corr. Sci. Men* (1841) I. 331 A true canonical equation or power. **1851** J. J. SYLVESTER (*title*) On a remarkable discovery in the Theory of Canonical forms of Hyperdeterminants. **1876** SALMON *Higher Alg.* xv. Art. 164 The simplest form to which a quantic can without loss of generality be reduced is called the canonical form of the quantic.

6. *Mus.* According to the rules of canon, in canon form.

1609 DOULAND *Ornith. Microl.* 51 Virgular Syncopation is much vsed, Numerall seldome, Canonicall most seldome. **1869** OUSELEY *Counterp.* xxiii. §15 Some fragmentary imitation or canonical episode.

7. Of or belonging to an ecclesiastical chapter, or to one of its members (see CANON *sb.*[2]).

1579 HOOKER *Eccl. Pol.* v. lxxx. §11 No other benefices but only their canonical portions. **1600** *Ibid.* VIII. vii. §3 The very act of canonical election. **1634** *Abp. Laud's Visit. Exeter* in *4th Rep. Commiss. Hist. MSS.* 138/2 A canonicall house, due to a canon residentiary. **1662** J. BARGRAVE *Pope Alex. VII* (1867) 116 At my Canonical house, at the metropolitical church of Christ, Canterbury. **1881** FREEMAN *Subj. Lands Venice, Parenzo*, Among the canonical buildings on the south side of the church.

B. *sb. pl.* [cf. *academicals*.] Canonical robes.

1748 SMOLLETT *Rod. Rand.* ix, I did not at all wonder to find a cheat in canonicals. **1751** —— *Per. Pic.* (1779) IV. xcvi. 171 He was accosted by a person in canonicals. **1755** *Connoisseur* No. 65 Out of his canonicals, his constant dress is what they call parson's blue. **1848** MACAULAY *Hist. Eng.* I. 327 An ecclesiastic in full canonicals.

canonically (kəˈnɒnɪkəlɪ), *adv.* [f. prec. + -LY[2].] In a canonical manner (see the adj.).

1529 MORE *Supplic. Soules* Wks. 296 Stephen was well and canonically chosen archbishop of Caunterbury. **1609** BP. BARLOW *Answ. Nameless Cath.* 355 Then is he Sacrilegiously false, and Canonically irregular. **1759** H. WALPOLE *Corr.* (1837) I. 405 Marca was married yesterday ..the lawyers and milliners were all ready canonically. **1768** BLACKSTONE *Comm.* I. 387 The vicar..shall be canonically instituted and inducted. **1824** BYRON *Def. Transf.* I. i. 293 Would you..be a Titan? Or (To talk canonically) wax a son Of Anak? **1837** HAWTHORNE *Twice-told T.* (1857) I. v. 70 An English priest, canonically dressed. **1875** OUSELEY *Mus. Form* ix. 49 Treat the theme canonically, or with perpetual imitations.

canonicalness (kəˈnɒnɪkəlnɪs). [f. as prec. + -NESS.] The quality or fact of being canonical.

1638 CHILLINGW. *Relig. Prot.* I. iii. §28. 141 Their Authority and Canonicalnesse. **1715** BURNET *Own Time* an. 1711 (R.) Maintaining the canonicalness of the apostolical constitutions. **1747** CARTE *Hist. Eng.* I. 472 The canonicalness of whose election he had as abbot already acknowledged.

canonicate (kəˈnɒnɪkət). [a. med.L. *canonicāt-us*, f. *canonicus*; cf. F. *canonicat*.] The office or dignity of a canon; a canonry.

1652 WADSWORTH tr. *Sandoval's Civil Wars Spain* 237 The Bishopricks,..Canonicates, & other Ecclesiastical preferments. **1662** J. BARGRAVE *Pope Alex. VII* (1867) 41 The service..did scarce deserve a simple canonicate. *a* **1853** LANDOR *Wks.* II. 82 Within the walls of the canonicate. **1865** *Even. Standard* 3 June, His nomination to the canonicate of St. Peter is spoken of.

†**canoniˈcation.** *Obs. rare*[−1]. [n. of action f. med.L. *canonicāre* to make canonical, to canonize.] Canonization, consecration.

a **1641** SPELMAN *Wks.* 122 (R.) After his canonication, those that would consecrate the tenth part of their substance unto Hercules, should be very prosperous.

canonicity (kænəˈnɪsɪtɪ). [f. on type of a L. **canonicitas*, f. *canonic-us*, or ad. F. *canonicité*: see -ITY.] Canonicalness, canonical status, *esp.* the fact of being comprehended in the Canon of Scripture, or in any other sacred canon.

1797 *Monthly Rev.* XXIII. 485 To attribute canonicity to all those Scriptures of the Jews. **1841** MYERS *Cath. Th.* xix. 73 If none but a literal line and measure of Canonicity will be accepted. **1849** W. FITZGERALD tr. *Whitaker's Disput.* 46 Would Augustine, if he held all the books to have an equal right to canonicity..have preferred some to others?

caˈnonico-, combining form of CANONIC.

1689 *Apol. Fail. Walker's Acc.* 25 It being Canonico-Prelatically impossible, tho Schismatico-Presbyterially certain.

†**ˈcanonism.** *Obs.*[−1] [f. after next; see -ISM.] The principles of canon-law.

1621 W. SCLATER *Tythes Rev.* (1623) 161 Neede you, A man so skilled in Gratian, bee catechized in Canonisme?

canonist (ˈkænənɪst). [a. F. *canoniste* (15th c. in Littré), in med.L. *canonista*: see -IST.]

1. A professor of, or one skilled in, the canon law; a canon-lawyer.

1542 BRINKLOW *Complaynt* xxiv. (1874) 71 The greasy canonistes nosel the peple in idolatry. **1549** LATIMER *Serm. Ploughers* 38 A cannoniste, that is to saye, one that is broughte up in the studie of the Pope's lawes and decrees. **1643** MILTON *Divorce* (1851) Introd. 10 The shallow commenting of Scholasticks and Canonists. **1761** STERNE *Tr. Shandy* (1802) IV. xxiii. 99, I am a vile canonist, replied Yorick. **1868** FREEMAN *Norm. Conq.* (1876) II. App. 652 It offended against the strict laws of the Church as understood by continental canonists.

2. One who makes or upholds canons in science, criticism, etc.

1786–1805 H. TOOKE *Purley* I. vi. (1829) 93 If the etymological canonists..had not been so remarkably inattentive to the causes..of those literal changes of which they treat.

canonistic (kænəˈnɪstɪk), *a.* [f. prec. + -IC.] Of or belonging to a canonist; concerned with the exposition of canon-law.

1645 MILTON *Tetrach.* (1851) 223 The apt Schollers of this canonistic exposition. **1861** W. PERRY *Hist. Ch. Eng.* I. v. 218 Famous for his canonistic learning.

canoˈnistical, *a. rare.* [f. prec. + -AL[1].] Having relation to canonistic matters; also = prec.

1865 *Pall Mall G.* 27 July 10/2 Decisions, cases important for canonistical hermeneutics, and the like.

†**canoˈnistre.** *Obs.* [ad. F. *canoniste*: cf. *alkamistre*, *sophister*, etc., and see -ISTRE.] An earlier form of CANONIST.

1362 LANGL. *P. Pl.* A. VIII. 135 Bote Catoun construweþ hit nay And Canonistres boþe, And siggen bi hem-seluen *Sompnia ne cures.* **1393** *Ibid.* C. x. 303 Caton counteth hit at nouht and canonistres at lasse. *c* **1380** WYCLIF *Serm.* Sel. Wks. I. 32 Þis man of lawe..was neþir civilian ne canonistre. **1382** —— *Bible* Prol. xiii. 51 Sumtyme cyuylians and canonistris weren deuout.

canonizable (ˌkænəˈnaɪzəb(ə)l), *a.* [f. CANONIZE *v.* + -ABLE.] Worthy of canonization.

1913 *Nation* (N.Y.) 16 Jan. 58 A fictitious Crispi—..wise, righteous, canonizable. **1933** *Times Lit. Suppl.* 26 Oct. 736/1 Ampère, the scientist, whose laboratory was the home of 'a canonizable saint'.

canonizant (kəˈnɒnɪzænt), *a. Math.* [a. F. *canonisant*, pr. pple. of *canoniser* in sense 'regler'.] Attributive of an equation by the solution of which a quantic may be reduced to the 'canonical form'.

1879 SALMON *Higher Plane Curves* v. 186 A cubic identical with the Canonizant cubic of the last article.

†**caˈnonizate,** *pa. pple. Obs.* [ad. L. *canonizāt-us*, pa. pple. of *canonizā-re.*] = CANONIZED.

1538 BALE *Thre Lawes* 1223 To haue canonyzate Franciscus de pola. **1565** JEWEL *Repl. Harding* (1611) 271 Not Canonizate for a Saint as yet.

canonization (ˌkænənaɪˈzeɪʃən). [ad. L. *canonizātiōn-em*, n. of action f. *canonizāre* to canonize: cf. F. *canonisation.*] The action of canonizing; *esp.* formal admission into the calendar of saints.

c **1380** WYCLIF *Sel. Wks.* III. 433 To trow siche canonyzaciouns is lesse þan bileeue. *c* **1440** *Promp. Parv.* 60 Canonizacion, *canonizacio.* **1532** MORE *Confut. Tindale* Wks. 344/2 This new saint of Tindales canonisacion. **1538** BALE *Thre Lawes* 1635 He sent hym to heauen by hys canonyzacyon, And from thens to helle by an excommunycacyon. **1648** HERRICK *Hesper.* (1844) II. 158 To be number'd one Here, in my book's canonization. **1651** HOBBES *Govt. & Soc.* xviii. §14. 362 The canonization of Saints which the Heathen called Apotheosis. **1782** PRIESTLEY *Corrupt. Christ.* I. IV. 370 Before there were any regular canonizations.

b. *fig.*

1854 EMERSON *Lett. & Soc. Aims, Quot. & Orig.* Wks. (Bohn) III. 220 'Tis curious what new interest an old author acquires by official canonization in Tiraboschi or Dr. Johnson. **1877** MOZLEY *Univ. Serm.* IV. 87 The canonisation of men—the popular judgment which sets them up morally and spiritually upon the pinnacle of the temple.

canonize (ˈkænənaɪz), *v.* Also -ise. [ad. med.L. *canonizā-re* (also in 15th c. Fr. *canonizer*).]

1. *trans.* To place in the canon or calendar of the saints, according to the rules and with the ceremonies observed by the Church.

c **1380** WYCLIF *De Eccles.* Sel. Wks. III. 344 If þe pope canonise þis man þanne he must nedis be seint in hevene. **1460** CAPGRAVE *Chron.* (1858) 253 This same ȝere was Thomas of Lancastir canonized. **1516** PYNSON *Life St. Birgitte* in *Myrr. Our Ladye* (1873) Introd. 58 This blessyd woman seynt Birgette was canonyzed by pope bonyface. **1598** BARCKLEY *Felic. Man* (1631) 257 They assured him he should be canonized for a Saint. *a* **1680** BUTLER *Rem.* (1759) II. 195 A Fanatic..canonizes himself a Saint in his own Life-time. **1875** H. E. MANNING *Mission H. Ghost* vii. 191 A multitude who have not been canonised on earth, though they are saints in heaven.

†**2.** To install in any ecclesiastical dignity or office; to consecrate. *Obs.*

1393 GOWER *Conf.* I. 254 Thus was he pope canonised With great honour and intronised. *c* **1400** *Apol. Loll.* 57 Wan any auerous or couetous is canonizid in þe kirk, or maad cheef.

†**3.** To deify, apotheosize. *Obs.* or *arch.*

1553 EDEN *Treat. New Ind.* (Arb.) 20 Of them which amonge the gentiles were canonized into yᵉ numbre of the goddes. **1564** HAWARD *Eutropius* I. 2. **1601** HOLLAND *Pliny* II. 210 Circe our famous witch..was canonized a goddesse. **1669** GALE *Crt. Gentiles* I. II. viii. 106. **1794** SULLIVAN *View Nat.* II, Adventurers who were afterwards..canonized as a sign in the heavens..called Argonauts.

4. *fig.* To treat as a saint or glorified person.

1579 TOMSON *Calvin's Serm. Tim.* 683/1 But women are as it were canonized here: God putteth them into his register, and setteth them in an honourable degree. *c* **1590** MARLOWE *Faust.* I. 118 Faustus, these books, thy wit, and our experience, Shall make all nations to canonize us. **1825** *Bro. Jonathan* II. 282, I am not ready to canonize all women because I love one.

5. To make canonical; to admit into the Canon of Scripture, or (*transf.*) of authoritative writings.

1382 [see CANONIZED]. **1593** NASHE *Christ's T.* 38 b, Canonizing such a multifarious Genealogie of Comments. **1595** *Polimanteia* (1881) 36 To canonize your owne writers. **1645** USSHER *Body Div.* 5. **1657** COSIN *Canon Script.* ii. 14 They canonized the Books of the Maccabees. **1872** O. SHIPLEY *Gloss. Eccl. Terms* 86 Apocryphal books..were not canonized.

6. To sanction by the authority of the church; to give authoritative sanction or approval to.

1393 GOWER *Conf.* III. 280 Of the law canonized The pope hath bode to the men, that, etc. *c* **1400** *Apol. Loll.* 46 Þer wordis are canonized, & approuid of holi kirk. **1635** PAGITT *Christianogr.* I. iii. (1636) 89 These..doctrines are Canonized in their late meeting at Trent. **1670** G. H. *Hist. Cardinals* II. I. 132 The Popes are sure to have the Cardinals Canonize their errours. **1869** LECKY *Europ. Mor.* I. i 39 We should still be compelled to canonise a crowd of acts.

†**7.** (See quot.)

1578 COOPER *Thesaur.*, *Canonize*, to canonice: to examine by rule. **1656** BLOUNT *Glossogr*, *Canonize*, to examine by rule, to Register, to put in the rank and number.

ˈcanonized, *ppl. a.* [f. prec. + -ED.] Placed in the canon; sainted; consecrated, beatified, deified. †*canonized epistles*: cf. CANONICAL 3.

1382 WYCLIF *James* Prol., Not the same ordre is at Greekis ..of the seuen epistoelis that ben clepid canonysid. *c* **1440** *Promp. Parv.* 60 Canonyzyde, *canonizatus.* **1593** SHAKS. *2 Hen. VI*, I. iii. 63 Brazen Images of Canonized Saints. **1602** —— *Ham.* I. iv. 47 Thy Canoniz'd bones Hearsed in death. **1790** BURKE *Fr. Rev.* 49 Acting as if in presence of canonized forefathers. **1827** POLLOK *Course Time* IV, The lofty seat Of canonizèd bards. **1886** T. HARDY *Woodlanders* iv, No canonised antique.

canonizer (ˈkænənaɪzə(r)). [f. as prec. + -ER.] One who canonizes.

1588 A. KING tr. *Canisius' Catech.* K j, The canonizars of thir new sanctes. **1588** G. D. *Disc. Allen's Sedit. Drifts* 99 An open patrone of..trecherie, and a cannoniser of disloyall traytors. **1751** BP. LAVINGTON *Enthusiasm* (1754) III. 216 Such Canonizers and God-makers. **1821** *Blackw. Mag.* X. 697 The canonizer is worthy of the saint.

ˈcanonizing, *vbl. sb.* [f. as prec. + -ING[1].] The action of the vb. CANONIZE; canonization: **a.** Admission into the calendar of saints.

c **1380** WYCLIF *Serm.* xxix. Sel. Wks. III. 456 Þo canonysynge of þo seyntes. *a* **1638** MEDE *Apost. Latter Times* iv. Wks. (1672) 629 The Canonizing of the Souls of deceased Worthies..was an Idolatrous trick even from the days of the elder world. **1727** A. HAMILTON *New Acc. E. Ind.* II. li. 243 The Chinese are speedier in their canonizing than the Romans are.

b. Establishing as canonical.

1651 HOBBES *Leviath.* III. xlii. 282 The Canonizing, or making of the Scripture Law, belonged to the Civill Soveraigne.

ˈcanonizing, *ppl. a.* That canonizes.

1869 FREEMAN *Norm. Conq.* (1876) III. xi. 30 The canonizing voice of England.

†**ˈcanonly,** *adv. Obs. rare*[−1]. [f. CANON *sb.*[1] + -LY[2].] Canonically.

1502 *Ord. Crysten Men* IV. xxi. (W. de W. 1506) 234 If he hath not ben electe canonly.

canonry (ˈkænənrɪ). Also 4-5 chanonry(e. [f. CANON *sb.*² + -RY. (The L. was *canonia*, F. *chanoinie*.)] **1.** The benefice of a canon; the status, dignity, or office of a canon.

1482 CAXTON *Higden* (1527) 305 b, He..hadde geuen his letyll newe a chanonrye..in the chyrche of Lyncoln. **1687** *Lond. Gaz.* No. 2307/2 The Seizure of the Canonries and Prebendaries. **1691** WOOD *Ath. Oxon.* I. 81 This Tollard.. enjoyed his Canonry but few months. **1705** HEARNE *Collect.* (1886) I. 104 His Canonry of Xt Church. **1726** AYLIFFE *Parerg.* 139. **1862** MRS. H. WOOD *Channings* i. 2 A young man who had but just gained his minor canonry. **1886** *Law Times Rep.* LIII. 702/1 The profits of a canonry of Windsor were alienable by way of mortgage.

2. An establishment of canons or canonesses.

1877 SKENE *Celtic Scot.* II. 243 Boys and youths who are educated in the canonry. **1925** C. S. DURRANT *Flem. Mystics* I. ix. 130 John Busch himself travelled across Germany with three nuns of Bronope to reform an Austin Canonry.

ˈcanonship. [f. CANON *sb.*² + -SHIP.] = CANONRY I.

1534 HEN. VIII. *Liber Regis* p. viii, Every suche dignitie, prebend, vycarship, pety canonship. **1640** BP. HALL *Chr. Moder.* 31/2 The time was, when..none should be promoted..to canonships in cathedrals, but those which could read, sing, and competently construe. **1714** *Act. 13 Anne* vi. §8 in *Oxf. & Camb. Enactm.* 56 Canonship or Prebend in the Cathedral Church. **1762** tr. *Busching's Syst. Geog.* II. 602 Lautenbach..containing an important canonship.

†**ˈcanony, ˈchanonie.** *Obs.* [a. F. *chanoinie* or med.L. *canonia* in same sense.] = CANONRY I.

1641 MILTON *Ch. Discip.* II. (1851) 66 For their Bishopricks, Deaneries, Prebends, and Chanonies.

canoo, obs. form of CANOE.

canoodle (kəˈnuːd(ə)l), *v. slang* (orig. *U.S.*). Also 9 cannoodle, conoodle. [Origin obscure.] *intr.* To indulge in caresses and fondling endearments. Also formerly *trans.*, to persuade by endearments or deception. Hence **caˈnoodler, caˈnoodling** *vbl. sb.* and *ppl. a.*

1859 SALA *Tw. round Clock* 11 a.m., A sly kiss, and a squeeze, and a pressure of the foot or so, and a variety of harmless endearing blandishments, known to our American cousins..under the generic name of 'conoodling'. **1864** —— in *Temple Bar* Dec. 40 He is an adept in that branch of persuasive dialectics known as 'conoodling'. He will 'conoodle' the ladies..into the acquisition of whole packages of gimcrack merchandise. **1879** *Punch* 15 Mar. 117/2 Then he and the Matchless one struggle, snuggle, and generally conoodle together rapturously. **1894** *Mexborough & Swinton Times* 2 Feb. 2/7 The money which he had lent in return for the privilege of canoodling his daughter. **1894** *Idler* Sept. 207 She is not to be overcome by courting or *canoodling*. **1903** 'MARJORIBANKS' *Fluff-Hunters* 172 Two canoodlers tied up in knots and fastened with sealing-wax at the lips. **1919** J. M. BARRIE *Alice Sit-by-the-Fire* I. 31 She's not fond of a canoodlin' way. **1921** H. WALPOLE *Young Enchanted* III. iii, She's in there... I'm off on some business of my own for an hour or two, so you can canoodle as much as you damned well please.

canope, obs. form of CANOPY.

canophilist (kəˈnɒfɪlɪst). [irreg. f. L. *canis* dog + -PHIL + -IST.] A lover of dogs. So **canoˈphilia**, affection for dogs.

1879 W. L. LINDSAY *Mind in Lower Animals* I. I. iii. 24 A distinguished author, well known as a canophilist. **1889** *Macm. Mag.* Apr. 463/1 A great comfort to those who devote themselves to canine pets, and to canophilists generally (a pretty new word). **1935** AUDEN & ISHERWOOD *Dog beneath Skin* II. i, *2nd M.O.* Travelling with a dog. *1st M.O.* Hm. Canophilia. **1960** *Spectator* 7 Oct. 532 His canophilia..is chronic, sad and private.

Canopic (kəˈnəʊpɪk), *a.* [ad. L. *Canōpic-us*, f. *Canōp-us* a town of ancient Egypt.] Of or pertaining to Canopus. ***Canopic jar, vase***: a vase used in Egypt, chiefly for holding the entrails of embalmed bodies.

1878 WILKINSON *Anc. Egyptians* III. Index, Canopic vases. **1883** W. ARMSTRONG *Perrot's Art Anc. Egypt* I. 301 The canopic vases..were sometimes of stone, especially alabaster, sometimes of terra cotta, and now and then of wood, and were used to hold the viscera of the deceased. **1893** BUDGE *Mummy* 171 At each of the four corners or sides of the bier, is placed one of the so-called Canopic jars. **1957** *Encycl. Brit.* XV. 954/2 The internal organs were..placed in four vases known as the 'Canopic Jars'.

canopied (ˈkænəpɪd), *ppl. a.* [f. CANOPY *sb.* or *v.* + -ED.] Covered with, or as with, a canopy.

1593 SHAKS. *Lucr.* 398 Her eyes..canopied in darkness sweetly lay. **1611** CHAPMAN *Iliad* XIII. (R.) Mars..Sat canapied with golden clouds. **1796** MORSE *Amer. Geog.* II. 550 Palanquins..a kind of canopied couches. **1870** LOWELL *Among my Bks.* Ser. I. (1873) 196 These saints of literature descend from their canopied remoteness.

b. *Arch.* (Cf. CANOPY *sb.* 3.)

1849 FREEMAN *Archit.* 296 Rows of canopied niches. **1879** SIR G. SCOTT *Lect. Archit.* I. 182 A graceful canopied and crocketed panel to each intervening pier.

‖**Canopus** (kəˈnəʊpəs). [L., a Gr. Κάνωπος.]

1. The bright star α in the southern constellation Argo, situated in the rudder of the ship.

1555 EDEN *Decades W. Ind.* (Arb.) 278 When these are hydden, there is seene on the lefte syde a bryght Canopus of three starres of notable greatness..In the myddest of these is seene an other bryght Canopus. **1830** TENNYSON *Dream Fair Wom.* 146 We drank the Libyan Sun to sleep, and lit Lamps which out-burn'd Canopus.

2. = *Canopic vase.*

1836 *Penny Cycl.* VI. 244/2 *Canopus* is also the name of an Egyptian jar. **1857** BIRCH *Anc. Pottery* (1858) II. 204 The canopos or jar resembling those in which the Egyptians placed the entrails of their mummies. *Ibid.* (1873) 593.

canopy (ˈkænəpɪ), *sb.* Forms: 5-6 canape, -ope, 6 canapee, -opi, cannopy, canyppy, (? cannebe), *north.* canaby(e, 6-7 canapie, -apy, -opie, *Sc.* cannabie, 7 cannapie, canopey, 6- canopy. [In 15th c. *canape*, a. F. *canapé* (formerly also *conopée* masc. 'a canopie, tent, or pauilion', Cotgr.) = Sp., Pg. *canapé* 'couch, sofa', It. *canopè* (Diez), med.L. '*canopeum*, quod suspenditur super altare' (Du Cange), in cl. L. *cōnōpēum, -eum, -ium*, 'net of fine gauze about the bed, mosquito curtains' (Lewis & Short), 'pavilion, tent, or bed with a tester' (Scheller), a. Gr. κωνωπεῖον 'an Egyptian bed or couch with mosquito curtains' (L. & S.), f. κώνωψ gnat, mosquito. The Eng. forms may have been partly from med.L., and in Eng. the sense has adhered to 'curtain or tester', while in the mod. Romanic langs. that of 'couch' or 'sofa' has prevailed.]

1. a. A covering or hangings suspended over a throne, couch, bed, etc., or held over a person walking in procession.

1382 WYCLIF *Judith* xiii. 10 She toc awei his canope fro the pileris. **1454** *E.E. Wills* (1882) 133 My bed of grene sylke, wiþ the testour & Canape ther-to. *c* **1511** *1st Eng. Bk. Amer.* (Arb.) Introd. 29/2, Iiij of the noblest bereth the canapie ouer his hed. **1561** *Invent.* 138 (Jam.) Ane cannabie of grene taffetie..quhilke may serue for any dry stuill or a bed. **1576** LAMBARDE *Peramb. Kent* (1826) 113 They beare the foure staves of the Canapie over the Kings head at the time of his coronation. **1651** HOBBES *Leviath.* IV. xlv. 365 At this day the Popes are carried by Switzers under a Canopie. **1725** DE FOE *Voy. round World* (1840) 268 The mattress..had a large canopy over it, spread like the crown of a tent. **1843** PRESCOTT *Mexico* (1850) I. 28 Above the throne was a canopy of variegated plumage.

b. *spec.* A covering over a shrine, or over the Host when borne in procession.

1513 BRADSHAW *St. Werburgh* (1848) 146 Also ouer the shryne was prepared a canaby Of cloth of golde. *c* **1520** *Mem. Ripon* (Surtees) III. 201 Caruer framyng et carvyng j canape pro Corpore Xpi per iiij dies, 2*s.* **1556** *Chron. Gr. Friars* (1852) 94 The byshoppe bereynge the sacrament under a canapy. **1757** tr. *Keysler's Trav.* (1760) I. 70 The venerable host, which was carried under a splendid canopy.

2. a. *transf.* and *gen.* A covering, an overhanging shade or shelter. *spec.* the uppermost layer of branches in a forest.

1601 SHAKS. *Jul. C.* v. i. 88 Their shadowes seeme A Canopy most fatall, vnder which Our Army lies. **1641** MAISTERTON *Serm.* 23 Beautifull walks..shaded with the green canopy of every pleasant..tree. **1723** POPE *Let. to Digby* 10 Oct., The prospects begin to open..thro' the high canopies of trees to the higher arch of heaven. **1855** MAURY *Phys. Geog. Sea* v. (1860) §299 Under a canopy of perpetual clouds. **1874** HARTWIG *Aerial W.* i. 1 The atmosphere spreads its invisible canopy over sea and land. **1905** *Terms Forestry & Logging* 8 *Crown cover*, the canopy formed by the crowns of all the trees in a forest. **1952** P. W. RICHARDS *Tropical Rain Forest* ii. 23 A canopy means a more or less continuous layer of tree crowns of approximately even height.

b. *esp.* applied to the overhanging firmament.

1602 SHAKS. *Ham.* II. ii. 311 This most excellent Canopy the Ayre..this braue ore-hanging, this Maiesticall Roofe, fretted with golden fire. **1607** —— *Cor.* IV. v. 41 Where dwel'st thou? Vnder the Canopy. **1667** MILTON *P.L.* III. 556 Where he stood So high above the circling Canopie Of Nights extended shade. **1794** SULLIVAN *View Nat.* II. I. 453 At first, the celestial canopy was divided into three principal parts. **1869** FREEMAN *Norm. Conq.* (1876) III. xiii. 290 The people had met under the canopy of heaven.

c. *fig.* Covering, shelter.

1603 H. CROSSE *Vertues Commw.* (1878) 19 Shrowding thy selfe vnder the Cannapie of Vertue. **1650** HUBBERT *Pill Formality* 12 A form of Religion serves for a Canopie to cover all these abominations. **18..** SYD. SMITH, Withdrawing the canopy of his name from the bad passions of country gentlemen.

3. *Arch.* A roof-like ornamented projection, surmounting a niche, door, window, tomb, etc.

1682 N. O. *Boileau's Lutrin* IV. 31 The Pulpit now lifting its lofty Head With carved Canopy stands covered. **1874** PARKER *Illust. Goth. Archit.* I. v. 186 A niche was originally intended to contain an image, and the canopy over it was to protect the head of the image.

4. *Naut.* (See quots.)

1867 SMYTH *Sailor's Word-Bk.*, *Canopy*, a light awning over the stern-sheets of a boat. **1961** F. H. BURGESS *Dict. Sailing* 44 *Canopy*, a canvas covering on a metal frame or supported by stanchions, for protective coverings over hatchways, etc.

5. A hood over a carriage or motor car. Also *attrib.*

1895 *Montgomery Ward Catal.* 580/1 Canopy Top Surrey... A very nice carriage. **1906** W. W. BEAUMONT *Motor Vehicles* (ed. 2) II. 150 A..car with a closed tonneau body or limousine with canopy top and armed guard. **1930** *Motor Body Building* LI. 105/1 If the longitudinal framing is carried over the driver's seat the extension is called the canopy rail.

6. The 'umbrella' of a parachute, which fills with air when released from its packing.

1930 C. DIXON *Parachuting* vi. 53 The moment the silk canopy meets the full shock of the air currents—which spread it to its maximum extension—it pulls the airman off the wing and swings him into space. **1940** [see BROLLY 2]. **1959** *Times* 18 May 8/7, I heard the crack of the canopy opening above me.

7. The cover of the cockpit in an aircraft.

1939 *Jane's All World's Aircraft* 48c/1 Enclosed pilot's cockpit over wing. Sliding canopy with quick-release for emergency exit. **1944** *Aircraft of Fighting Powers* V. 29/2 The introduction of the 'tear-drop' cockpit canopy on the P-51D has resulted in a decrease in the keel area ahead of the tail assembly.

canopy (ˈkænəpɪ), *v.* [f. prec. sb.]

trans. To cover with, or as with, a canopy.

c **1600** SHAKS. *Sonn.* xii, Lofty trees..Which erst from heat did canopie the herd. **1698** CROWNE *Caligula* III. 28 That point of Heaven..Which canopys that holy happy land. **1791** E. DARWIN *Bot. Gard.* II. 65 Yon gay clouds, which canopy the skies. **1869** E. PEACOCK in *Athenæum* 22 May 710/3 A very graceful iron herse..canopies the alabaster effigies of a Marmion and his spouse.

‖**canor.** [L.] 'Melody or sweet singing' (Blount *Glossogr.* 1656).

canorous (kəˈnɔərəs), *a.* [f. L. *canōr-us* melodious (f. *canor* song, f. *canĕre* to sing) + -OUS.] Singing, melodious, musical; resonant, ringing.

1646 SIR T. BROWNE *Pseud. Ep.* VII. xiv. 368 Birds that are canorous..as Nightingales..Canary birds and Larkes. **1745** tr. *Columella's Husb.* VII. xii, The keeper of the manor house [*i.e.* a dog]..of a vast canorous bark. **1774** GOLDSM. *Nat. Hist.* III. 171 A beautiful & a canorous bird. **1822** DE QUINCEY *Confess.* Wks. V. 94 A long, loud, and canorous peal of laughter.

Hence **caˈnorously** *adv.*, **caˈnorousness**.

1680 H. MORE *Apocal. Apoc.* 293 The voice..as of a Trumpet talking loudly or canorously with him. **1870** LOWELL *Among my Bks.* Ser. II. 184 He chooses his language for its rich canorousness rather than for intensity of meaning.

‖**canot** (kano). The French word for 'canoe', used in certain French phrases relating to the Canadian fur trade: **canot du maître** (kano dy mɛːtr), the largest canoe of the fur trade, up to 40 feet long and carrying a cargo of 4 to 5 tons, formerly used esp. on the Great Lakes and St. Lawrence; **canot du nord** (kano dy nɔr), a canoe about 25 feet long and carrying over a ton of cargo, formerly used by the fur trade on the rivers of North-West Canada.

1828 A. MCDONALD *Peace River* (1872) 41 The largest kind of canoes used in the trade, viz., those which used to be dispatched from Lachine, on first open water, to Fort William, Lake Superior, and which were called '*Canots du Maître*'. *Ibid.*, The Canot du M. was of six fathoms, measured within, and the C. du Nord about four, more or less. **1961** H. MACLENNAN *Rivers of Canada* 23 The Nor'Westers used two types of canoe which they called the *canot du maître* and the *canot du nord*, the former for the run out of Montreal, the latter, which was lighter and carried less than a ton and a half of cargo, for the run west of Fort William where the streams were shallower. **1963** *Canad. Geogr. Jrnl.* Dec. 210/3 The bateaux were concealed, and the whole party of twenty-five embarked in a canot-du-maître for Fort Mackinac.

canou(e, canow(e, obs. ff. CANOE.

canoun, early form of CANON *sb.*²

†**ˈcanous**, *a. Obs. rare.* Also spelt -ois, -us, cannos. [f. L. *cānus* hoary.] Grey, hoary.

1513 DOUGLAS *Æneis* v. vii. 97 Or that wnfreindlie eild had thus besprent My heid and halfettis baith with canus [*ed.* **1553** canous] hair. *Ibid.* v. xii. 144 To Troiane ingill, and the cannos [*ed.* **1553** canois] Veste.

†**canque.** *Obs.* [So in F.] A Chinese cotton fabric: see quots.

1750 BEAWES *Lex Mercat.* (1752) 793 Cotton Linens, called Canques..of Nanquin. *Ibid.* 794 Coarse and fine Canques or Cotton Linen.

canroy (ˈkænrɔɪ). Also candroy. A machine, used in calico-printing establishments, through which cotton cloth is passed before printing. Hence **ˈcanroyer**, one in charge of a canroy.

1836 *Penny Cycl.* VI. 151/2 If they are not calendered, they are run through a machine called in Lancashire the *candroy*, which spreads them smoothly in the act of rolling them upon a cylinder. **1858** in SIMMONDS *Dict. Trade.* **1896** DUERR *Bleaching & Calico-printing* 26 After being sewn, each batch is taken to the shearing and winding-on machines, generally called a 'canroy'. Sometimes the shearing machine and canroy are two separate machines. **1921** *Dict. Occup. Terms* (1927) §384 *Canroyer*, a calenderer minding a canroy calender, having two iron rollers through which cloth is passed to break down stiffness after starching.

cansel, canserous: see CANCEL, etc.

cansonet, obs. form of CANZONET.

†**canstick.** *Obs.* Apparently a contracted form of CANDLESTICK. ***kit with the canstick***: Jack-o'-lantern, Will o' the wisp.

1562 J. HEYWOOD *Prov. & Epigr.* (1867) 20 Coll vnder canstyk, she can plaie on bothe handis, Dissimulacion well she vnderstandis. **1584** R. SCOT *Discov. Witchcr.* VII. xv. 122 They have so fraied us with bull beggars, spirits, witches.. kit with the cansticke, etc. **1596** SHAKS. *1 Hen. IV*, III. i. 131,

I had rather heare a Brazen Canstick [1623 candlestick] turn'd Or a dry Wheele grate on the Axle-tree. 1616 CHAPMAN *Batrachom.* 8 Their fencefull bucklers were The middle rounds of can'sticks. [COWPER has: The lamp contributed its central tin, A shield for each.] 1617 S. COLLINS *Def. Bp. Elie* A ij b, His . . wodden cansticke.

cant (kænt), *sb.*[1] Also 5–8 **kant**. [Found *c* 1400; rare before 1600. Words identical in form and corresponding in sense are found in many languages, Teutonic, Slavonic, Romanic, Celtic. Cf. Du. *kant*, MDu. *cant*, border, side, brink, edge, corner, MLG. *kant* (masc.) point, creek, border, also *kante* (fem.) side, edge, whence mod.G. *kante* edge, corner, border, brim, margin; also Du. and Ger. *kante* point-lace. (There is no trace of the word in the older stages of Teutonic.) Also OF. *cant* and mod.Norman *cant*, Walloon *can* side, Sp., Pg., It. *canto* edge, corner, side, med.L. *cantus* corner, side; with which some compare L. *canthus*, Gr. *κανθός* corner of the eye, and L. *canthus* tire (? felloe) of a wheel, according to Quintilian a 'barbarous' word. The Welsh *cant* edge of the circle, Breton *kañt* circle, circumference, which were thought by Diez to represent an original Celtic word, are held by Diefenbach and Thurneysen not to be native; so that at present we cannot go beyond the Romanic *canto*, and its possible identity with L. *canthus*. The Teutonic words were probably from Romanic. It is not clear whether the Eng. word was adopted from OF. or from LG., or, in different senses, from both.]

I. Original sb. senses.

†**1.** (probably) Edge, border, brink. *Obs.*

c 1375 ? BARBOUR *St. Lucas* 69, 70 Quhene he had drywyne wel oure þe kanttis of sewynty ȝeris & foure. *c* 1400 *Melayne* 1495 Under the cante of a hille Oure Britons beldis & bydis stille.

†**2.** A nook, corner in a building; a niche. *Obs.*

[1481–90 *Howard Househ. Bks.* (1841) 400 Item, for ij. panchons at the garden gate, with kant ther above viij*d.*] 1603 B. JONSON *Jas. I's Entert.* Wks. (1838) 530/1 Irene, or Peace; she was placed aloft in a cant, her attire white, semined with stars. 1604 DEKKER *King's Entert.* 297 Directly under her in a Cant by her selfe, Fame stood upright. 1605 VERSTEGAN *Dec. Intell.* v. 150 A nooke or corner being in our ancient language called a kant or cantell. 1624 WEBSTER *Mon. Honour.* Wks. (1857) 369 In several cants beneath sits, first Magistracy . . next Liberality.

†**3. a.** A corner or angle of a polygon. *Obs.*

1611 COTGR. s.v. *Pent*, *La figure hexagone à six pents*, hauing six Cants. 1688 R. HOLME *Armoury* III. xiii. §42 A Tower or Steeple of six Cants or six square . . Some term it an Hexagon or Octagon Tower, that is six or eight cornered; but Master Masons generally term it six or eight Cants or Corners. 1876 GWILT *Archit.* Gloss., *Cant*, an external angle or quoin of a building.

†**b.** ? A corner piece; a triangular piece. *Obs.*

1688 R. HOLME *Armoury* II. 118/2 Garden, part to be divided into Beds and them again to be cast into Ovals, Squares, Cants, Frets, Borders or Knots.

4. a. One of the side-pieces in the head of a cask; also *cant-piece*. (So in Welsh). Cf. *cantle-piece* (CANTLE *sb.* 8).

1611 COTGR., *Panneau de doile*, a cant pane or peece. 1848 J. A. CARLYLE tr. *Dante's Inferno* xxviii. 22 Even a cask, through loss of middle-piece or cant [*per mezzul perdere o lulla*] yawns not so wide as one I saw.

b. One segment of the rim of a wooden cog-wheel.

a 1877 in KNIGHT *Dict. Mech.*

5. The oblique line or surface which cants or cuts off the corner of a square or cube; an oblique face of a polygon, a crystal, etc.; an inclined or slanting face of a bank, or the like.

1840 FOSBROKE *Encycl. Antiq.* 148 *Cants* (parts which have inclined faces). 1850 *Gloss. Terms in Archit.* (ed. 5) 107 *Cant*, a term in common use among carpenters to express the cutting off the angle of a square. 1874 KNIGHT *Mech. Dict.*, *Cant*, an angle, a bevel, a chamfer, a slope, an arris, a hip, a ridge. 1875 BRANDE & COX *Dict. Science* I. 367 *Cant*, a term used in Architecture to express the sides of a polygon turned from the spectator. 1877 E. PEACOCK *N.-W. Linc. Gloss.*, *Cant*, part of a buttress wall or other building which is sloped off. 1880 *Standard* 20 May 13 Along the 'cant' of the ice the sealer coasts.

6. A squared log. *U.S.* Cf. CANTER *sb.*[1] 2.

1877 *Lumberman's Gaz.* 24 May, A cant or square-edged timber. 1879 *Ibid.* 5 Nov., The cheapest and most effective means yet devised for holding the cant in place.

7. *Naut.* A piece of wood laid upon the deck of a vessel to support the bulkheads, etc. Cf. CANT-PIECE, etc. in 12.

1794 *Rigging & Seamanship* II. 286 Fir cants nailed on the limber-strakes. 1865 *Reader* 12 Aug., Washing arrangements. Suitable places on board ship are to be set apart for the purpose, fitted with cants, to prevent the escape of water, and screens so arranged as to roll up when not in use.

II. from CANT *v.*

8. A toss, pitch, or throw, which overturns, casts down, etc.

1736 J. LEWIS *Hist. Thanet* Gloss., *Cant* . . likewise signifies a cast or throw; 'I gave him a cant'. 1755 *Mem. Capt. P. Drake* II. xiv. 244 To give me such a cant, as I never had before nor since, which was the whole Length of the Coffee-room; he pitched me on my Head and Shoulders, under a large Table, at the further End.

9. A sudden movement which tends to, or results in, tilting up or turning over.

1806 A. DUNCAN *Nelson* 308 The carronade . . took a cant from a roll of the ship. 1865 CARLYLE *Fredk. Gt.* XII. viii, Fortune's wheel made suddenly a great cant.

10. a. A slope, a slanting or tilted position; a deflection from the perpendicular or horizontal line.

1847 *Infantry Man.* (1854) 20 Giving the piece a cant with the forefingers. 1873 MRS. WHITNEY *Other Girls* xxxiv, The seat sloped with the sharp cant of the half-overturned vehicle. 1876 DAVIS *Polaris Exp.* x. 245 A large tongue of ice below the water was forced under the bows of the vessel, raising her . . and with the help of the wind giving her a cant.

b. An inclination.

1881 *Daily Tel.* 28 Jan., The helm had been lashed with a small cant to leeward.

11. *Whale-fishing.* (See quot.)

1867 SMYTH *Sailor's Word-bk.*, *Cant*, a cut made in a whale between the neck and the fins, to which the cant purchase is made fast, for turning the animal round in the operation of flensing.

III. Attributively and in combination.

12. Combs. with the sb. (or stem of the vb.) with the general sense of 'having canted corners or sides, on the slant, sloping, in a position diverging from the perpendicular or straight line', as in ***cant-buttress***, ***-floor***, ***-frame***, ***-piece***, ***-riband***; **cant-board**, a sloping board; in *Carriage building*, a board serving to show the plan of the side of a carriage; **cant-body**, *Naut.* (see quot.); †**cant-ceiling**, a ceiling which slants to meet the wall, as in attics, etc., apparently now corrupted into CAMP-CEILING; **cant-file**, a file with cutting faces at an obtuse angle to each other; **cant-line** (see quots.); **cant-moulding**, **-riband**, **-timber**, **-window** (see quots.); **cant-rail**, a timber or other stiffening member which supports the roof of a railway carriage either at an angle or longitudinally; also *transf.*

1759 SMEATON in *Phil. Trans.* LI. 103 A *kant-board, for throwing the water more directly down the opening . . into the lower cistern. 1879 *Carriage-building* in *Cassell's Techn. Educ.* IV. 131 The cant-board which shows the sidecant. *Ibid.* The diagram showing the cant-board. 1867 SMYTH *Sailor's Word-bk.*, **Cant-body*, an imaginary figure of that part of a ship's body which forms the shape forward and aft, and whose planes make obtuse angles with the midship line of the ship. 1879 W. H. WHITE *Ship-build.* in *Cassell's Techn. Educ.* IV. 190/1 In the cant-bodies the plan followed is almost identical with that sketched. 1663 in Cosin *Corr.* (Surtees) II. 367 Two *cant buttresses of hewen aishler neately jointed. 1688 R. HOLME *Armoury* III. xiii. §88 He beareth . . the like Tower with an Eve, or *Cant seileing Roofe. *a* 1877 KNIGHT *Dict. Mech.*, **Cant-file*, a file having the shape of an obtuse-angled triangle in its transverse section; used in filing the inner angles of spanners and wrenches for bolts with hexagonal and octagonal heads. *c* 1850 *Rudim. Navig.* (Weale) 119 One or two *cantfloors are added. 1833 RICHARDSON *Merc. Mar. Arch.* 21 The only guides in drawing the *cant frames. 1869 SIR E. REED *Ship Build.* viii. 151 The half-beams stand in the planes of the Cant frames and are consequently nearly at right angles to the side. 1867 SMYTH *Sailor's Word-bk.*, **Cant-line*, synonymous with *girt-line*, as to cant the top over the lowermast-head. 1909 *Cent. Dict.* Suppl., *Cantline*, the space between the sides or ends of barrels. 1961 F. H. BURGESS *Dict. Sailing* 44 The 'cant line' is the groove between strands of a rope, rows of casks or drums, etc. 1823 P. NICHOLSON *Pract. Build.* 582 **Cant-moulding*, a bevelled surface. 1876 GWILT *Archit.* Gloss., *Cant-moulding*, one with one or more bevelled, instead of curved, surfaces. 1794 *Rigging & Seamanship* I. 4 **Cant-pieces* are used in the angles of the fishes and side-trees. 1871 *Saddl. Harn. & Carriage Builder's Gaz.* 1 Dec. 12/2 Levers and links, aided by springs, to throw open the *'cant rails' and 'uprights' of carriage heads by inside pressure. 1930 *Motor Body Building* LI. 105/1 *Cant Rail*, the longitudinal framing of the Roof. 1951 *Engineering* 8 June 705/3 The roof cantrail is an interesting design. 1958 *Ibid.* 14 Mar. 344/1 Continuous longitudinal stiffening members such as cantrails. 1969 *Jane's Freight Containers 1968–69* 505/2 End frames: Fabricated hollow section corner pillars with 6·35 mm (¼ in) fixed end cantrail and hollow section. *c* 1850 *Rudim. Navig.* (Weale) 103 *Cant Ribands are those ribands that do not lie in a horizontal or level direction, or square from the middle line, but nearly square from the timbers, as the diagonal ribands. 1769 FALCONER *Dict. Marine* (1789) **Cant-timbers* . . those timbers which are situated at the two ends of a ship. They derive their name from being *canted*, or raised obliquely from the keel. *c* 1860 H. STUART *Seaman's Catech.* 67 Those timbers which form the bow and stern of a ship are called 'cant timbers'. 1663 GERBIER *Counsel* 13 Those Spectacle-like *cant Windows, which are of Glasse on all sides. 1877 E. PEACOCK *N. W. Linc. Gloss.* (E.D.S.) *Cant-window*, a bay-window whose angles are bevelled off. 1881 EVANS *Leicestersh. Gloss.* (E.D.S.) *Cant-window*, a projecting window with angles, as distinguished from a 'bow-window' which projects in a curve.

13. From other senses: as in *Whale-fishing* (see 11). **cant-blocks**, the large purchase blocks used by whalers to cant the whales round during the process of flensing. **cant-fall**, the tackle connected with the cant-blocks of a whaling ship. **cant-purchase** is formed by a block suspended from the mainmast-head, and another block made fast to the cant cut in the whale. So CANT-DOG, CANT-HOOK, CANT-SPAR.

1867 SMYTH *Sailor's Word-bk.*, *Spike-tackle and cantfalls*, the ropes and blocks used in whalers to sling their prey to the side of the ship.

cant (kænt), *sb.*[2] Now *dial.* and *Forestry*. [App. connected immed. with CANT *v.*[1] 'to share', and with CANTLE, though in some uses it closely approaches CANT *sb.*[1]; whether this is original or due to subsequent confusion is not clear.]

A portion; a share; a parcel; a division.

a 1541 WYATT in *Tottel's Misc.* (Arb.) 92 Lend in no wise, But if thou can be sure to win a cant Of half at least 1736 J. LEWIS *Hist. Thanet* Gloss, *Cant*, a corner of a field. 1812 J. H. VAUX *Flash Dict.*, *Cant of Dobbin*, a roll of riband. 1847–78 HALLIWELL s.v.. In Hampshire a small bundle of hay is termed a cant. 1863 MORTON *Cycl. Agric.* Gloss. (E.D.S.) *Cant-furrow*, a divisional furrow. 1875 PARISH *Sussex Dial.*, A haystack is said to be cut across in cants, and a field of wheat is divided into cants when it is portioned out in slips for the reapers, each of whom takes one or more cants as his share of work. 1928 *Forestry* II. 82 The season's *coupe* having been marked out previously into lots or 'cants'. 1953 H. L. EDLIN *Forester's Handbk.* xv. 255 The portion of the wood that is due for felling is marked out on the ground and, if it is large enough, divided into several parcels, called *cants* in Kent. 1965 *Punch* 15 Dec. 890/2 Our neighbour sold his at auction at the end of October in five cants—that is, slices, in this instance of roughly three acres apiece.

cant (kænt), *sb.*[3] [This and its accompanying vb. presumably represent L. *cant-us* singing, song, chant (Pr. and NFr. *cant*, Fr. *chant*), *cantā-re* NFr. *canter*) to sing, chant; but the details of the derivation and development of sense are unknown.

Cantare and its Romanic representatives were used contemptuously in reference to the church services as early as 1183, when according to Rigord (*c* 1200) *Gest Philip. August.* (1818) 11, the Cotarelli of the Bourges country 'sacerdotes et viros religiosos captos secum ducentes, et irrisoriè *cantores* ipsos vocantes, in ipsis tormentis subsannando dicebant: *Cantate nobis, cantores, cantate*; et confestim dabant eis alapas, vel cum grossis virgis turpiter cædebant'. So far as the evidence shows, the vb. appears in Eng. first applied to the tones and language of beggars, 'the canting crew': this, which according to Harman was introduced *c* 1540, may have come down from the religious mendicants; or the word may have been actually made from Lat. or Romanic in the rogues' jargon of the time. The subsequent development assumed in the arrangement of the verb is quite natural, though not actually established. Some have however conjectured that *cant* is the Irish and Gaelic *cainnt* (pronounced kaṇtj, or nearly kantʃ) 'language'. And as early as 1711 the word was asserted to be derived from the name of Andrew Cant or his son Alexander Cant, Presbyterian ministers of the 17th c. This perhaps means that the surname of the two Cants was occasionally associated derisively with canting. The arrangement of the sb. here is tentative, and founded mainly on that of the vb., which appears on the whole earlier.]

†I. (Sporadic uses, from L. *cantus* or its representatives; not directly related to II.)

†**1.** Singing, musical sound. *cant organ*: app. a technical term in music. *Obs.*

1501 DOUGLAS *Pal. Hon.* I. xlii, Fabourdoun, pricksang, discant, countering, Cant organe, figuratioun, and gemmell. 1704 SWIFT *T. Tub* Wks. 1760 I. 100 Cant and vision are to the ear and the eye the same that tickling is to the touch. 1708 *Brit. Apollo* No. 79. 2/2 That shrill Cant of the Grasshoppers.

†**2.** Accent, intonation, tone. *Obs.*

1663 *Aron-bimn.* 110 It depends not upon the cant and tone, or the wording of the Minister. 1763 *Ann. Reg.* 307/2 If these lines want that sober cant which is necessary to an epitaph.

II. The speech or phraseology of beggars, etc., and senses connected therewith.

3. 'A whining manner of speaking, esp. of beggars'; a whine.

1640 CLEVELAND in Wilkins *Polit. Ballads* I. 28 By lies and cants, [they] Would trick us to believe 'em saints. 1705 HICKERINGILL *Priest-cr.* IV. (1721) 227 With a Cant like a Gypsie, a Whine like a beaten Spaniel.

4. The peculiar language or jargon of a class: **a.** The secret language or jargon used by gipsies, thieves, professional beggars, etc.; *transf.* any jargon used for the purpose of secrecy.

1706 in PHILLIPS. 1707 J. STEVENS tr. *Quevedo's Com. Wks.* (1709) 226 They talk'd to one another in Cant. 1715 KERSEY, *Cant*, Gibberish, Pedler's French. 1734 NORTH *Exam.* II. v. ¶ 110. 383 To avoid being understood by the Servants, they framed a Cant, and called the Design of a general Rising the Lease and Release. 1865 DICKENS *Mut. Fr.* xvi. 127 The ring of the cant.

b. The special phraseology of a particular class of persons, or belonging to a particular subject; professional or technical jargon. (Always *depreciative* or *contemptuous.*)

1684 T. BURNET *Th. Earth* I. 214 There is heat and moisture in the body, & you may call the one 'radical' and the other 'innate' if you please; this is but a sort of cant. 1712 ADDISON *Spect.* No. 421 ¶ 3 In the Cant of particular Trades and Employments. 1750 JOHNSON *Rambl.* No. 128 ¶ 4 Every class of society has its cant of lamentation, which is understood by none but themselves. 1839 DICKENS *Nich. Nick* xxxiv, All love—bah! that I should use the cant of boys and girls—is fleeting enough. 1841–4 EMERSON *Ess.* xiii. *Poet* Wks. (Bohn) I. 156 Criticism is infested with a cant of materialism. 1861 HOLLAND *Less. Life* viii. 119 Repeating the cant of their sect and the cant of their schools.

†**c.** The peculiar phraseology of a religious sect or class. (Cf. 5 b.) *Obs.*

1681 DRYDEN *Abs. & Achit.* 521 Hot Levites . . Resum'd their cant, and with a zealous cry Pursued their old beloved theocracy. 1696 C. LESLIE *Snake in Gr.* (1698) Introd. 46 Really to understand the Quaker-Cant is learning a new

Language. **1709** Sacheverell *Serm.* 15 Aug. 15 Diabolical Inspiration, and Non-sensical Cant. **1711** *Spect.* No. 147 ¶3 Cant is by some people derived from one Andrew Cant who, they say, was a Presbyterian minister..who by exercise & use had obtained the Faculty, alias Gift, of talking in the Pulpit in such a dialect, that it's said he was understood by none but his own Congregation, and not by all of them.

d. Provincial dialect; vulgar slang.

1802 Mar. Edgeworth *Irish Bulls* (1832) 226 The cant of Suffolk, the vulgarisms of Shropshire. **1852** Gladstone *Glean.* IV. lxxxii. 122 The coarse reproduction of that unmitigated cant or slang.

e. *attrib.*

1727 Swift *Let. Eng. Tongue* Wks. 1755 II. I. 185 To introduce and multiply cant words is the most ruinous corruption in any language. **1824** W. Irving *T. Trav.* I. 273 Slang talk and cant jokes. **1841** Borrow *Zincali* (1843) II. 150 The first Vocabulary of the 'Cant Language'..appeared in the year 1680 appended to the life of 'The English Rogue'.

5. A form of words, a phrase:

†**a.** A set form of words repeated perfunctorily or mechanically. *Obs.*

1681 *Sejanus* in *Bagford Ballads* (1878) 758 *note*, A young Scribe is copying out a Cant, Next morn for to be spoke in Parliament. **1704** Steele *Lying Lover* I. i. 7 Sure..you talk by Memory, a Form or Cant which you mistake for something that's gallant. **1712** Addison *Spect.* No. 291 §6 With a certain cant of words.

b. A pet phrase, a trick of words; *esp.* a stock phrase that is much affected at the time, or is repeated as a matter of habit or form. (Formerly with *a* and *plural.*) *arch.*

1681 *Country-man's Compl. & Advice to King*, Gods! to be twice cajol'd by cants and looks. **1691** Wood *Ath. Oxon.* II./450 Enamour'd with his obstreperousness and undecent cants. **1692** Bentley *Boyle Lect.* 200 That ordinary cant of illiterate..atheists, the fortuitous or casual concourse of atoms. **1710** Hearne *Collect.* (1886) II. 365 The late happy Revolution, (so he calls it, according to the common Cant). **1769** *Junius Lett.* xxvi. 119 *note*, Measures, and not men, is the common cant of affected moderation. *c* **1815** Jane Austen *Northang. Ab.* (1833) I. v. 22 It is really very well for a novel..is the common cant.

c. *attrib.*

1712 Addison *Spect.* No. 530 ¶3 Enlivened with little cant-phrases. **1753** *Stewart's Trial* App. 130 It was a cant word through the country, That the tenants might sit, since the worst of it would be paying the violent profits. **1774** Gouvr. Morris in Sparks *Life & Writ.* (1832) I. 23 The belwethers..roared out liberty, and property, and a multitude of cant terms. **1790** Paley *Horæ Paul.* (1849) 396 There is such a thing as a peculiar word or phrase cleaving, as it were, to the memory of a writer or speaker and presenting itself to his utterance at every turn. When we observe this we call it a cant word or a cant phrase. **1855** Prescott *Philip II* (1857) I. v. 79 To borrow a cant phrase of the day, like 'a fixed fact'. **1868** Helps *Realmah* xvii. (1876) 465 He..can—to use the cant phrase—afford to support the dignity of the peerage.

6. As a kind of phraseology:

a. Phraseology taken up and used for fashion's sake, without being a genuine expression of sentiment; canting language.

1710 Berkeley *Princ. Hum. Knowl.* §87 All this sceptical cant follows from our supposing, etc. **1783** Johnson in *Boswell* 15 May, My dear friend, clear your mind of cant.. you may *talk* in this manner; it is a mode of talking in society; but don't *think* foolishly. **1809** Syd. Smith *Wks.* (1867) I. 174 The pernicious cant of indiscriminate loyalty. **1870** Lowell *Study Wind.* 157 Enthusiasm, once cold, can never be warmed over into anything better than cant. **1875** Smiles *Thrift* ii. 20 In fact there is no greater *cant* than *can't*. **1883** J. Parker *Tyne Ch.* 320 There is a cant of infidelity as certainly as there is a cant of belief.

b. *esp.* Affected or unreal use of religious or pietistic phraseology; language (or action) implying the pretended assumption of goodness or piety.

1709 Strype *Ann. Ref.* I. lv. 609, I set down this letter at large, that men may see the cant of these men. **1716** Addison *Freeholder* No. 37 (J.) That cant and hypocrisy, which had taken possession of the people's minds in the times of the great rebellion. **1789** Mrs. Piozzi *Journ. France* I. 256 Hypocritical manners, or what we so emphatically call cant. **1849** Robertson *Serm.* Ser. I. x. (1866) 182 Religious phraseology passes into cant. **1875** Hamerton *Intell. Life* vi. iii. 211 He had a horror of cant, which..gave him a repulsion for all outward show of religious observances. **1879** Froude *Cæsar* i. 6 The whole spiritual atmosphere was saturated with cant.

c. *attrib.*

1747 Carte *Hist. Eng.* I. 601 To make up what was wanting in the justice of their cause..by a cant and sophistical way of expression.

7. One who uses religious phrases unreally.

1725 *New Cant. Dict.*, *Cant*, an Hypocrite, a Dissembler, a double-tongu'd, whining Person. **1824** Mrs. Cameron *Pink Tippet* III. 16 Lest she should be called a cant. **1873** E. Berdoc *Adv. Protestant* 132 He was not a cant, but really felt what he said.

cant (kænt), *sb.*[4] [Goes with cant *v.*[4] The sb. (if not immediately from the vb.) may be an aphetic form of **encant*, or **acant*, a. OF. *encant*, mod.F. *encan* (Pr. *encant*, Sp. *encanto*, It. *incanto*), in same sense: of disputed origin. The loss of the initial syllable is found also in MHG. and mod.G. *gant* in same sense.

Diez takes the Romanic words as repr. L. *in quantum* 'to how much?' as the cry of the auctioneer; and with this agree the occas. med.L. form *inquantus*, Pr. *enquant*, and OF. *inquant*, and med.L. vb. *inquantare*. But no forms of the word appear to go back before the end of the 12th c.; the earliest and ordinary forms in med.L. were *incantus* (4th decl.), *incantum, incantare, accantare, incantator, accantator*; and OF. had *enchanteur, enchantement* (already in *Assizes of Jerusalem*). These show that the word was then identified with the Lat. *incantare, accantare*, derivs. of *cantare* to sing, in the sense of 'proclaim, cry'. Cf. Du Cange, under date 1351, 'quod incantator publicus dicti castri..debeat facere proclamationem', and the illustrative 'jussit ergo Moyses praeconis voce cantari'. M. Paul Meyer thinks the identification with *cantare* too old and general to be explained as an error; and that there is more ground for treating the connexion with *in quantum* as a later fancy. Cf. also the mod.Fr. *vendre a la criée* to sell by auction, and the Sc. and north. Eng. *roup*, cry, shout, auction, 'selling of goods by an outcry' (Phillips 1678).]

A disposal of property by public competition to the highest bidder; an auction. Chiefly *Irish.*

1705 *Lond. Gaz.* No. 4178/4 The Manor..is to be sold by publick Cant to the best Bidder. **1738** *Hist. Crt. Excheq.* vii. 134 The Goods are set up to Cant. **1832** Ht. Martineau *Ireland* ii. 27 Two or three lots of ground were to be let by auction, or, as the phrase goes, by cant. **1834** Southey *Doctor* cxxxix. (1862) 352 The whole of them were set up for sale by public cant in Dublin.

cant, *sb.*[5] *Sc.* [Of uncertain origin: possibly belongs to one of the prec. sbs. Cf. also *cantrip.*] ? 'Trick; slight, illusion' (Jamieson).

1790 Morison *Poems* 38 (Jam.) Williy's wisp wi' whirlin' cant Their blazes ca'. **1813** D. Anderson *Poems* 81 (Jam.) Superstition..Experiencing plans O' auld cants that night.

cant (kænt), *a. Sc.* and *north. dial.* Also 4–6 **kant**, 5 **kaunt**. [Common in early times (13–14th c.) in the allit. phrase 'kant and keen'. App. the same word as mod.Du. *kant* 'neat, clever', in phr. *kant en klaar* quite ready; also East Fris. *kant*; considered by Franck to have been developed out of the sb. *kant* edge, etc. (see cant *sb.*[1]); cf. the connexion of idea in 'keen' and 'edge'. The actual historical relation between the Low German and the northern English word does not appear. Hence canty, Flem. and LG. *kantig.*]

Bold, brisk, courageous, hearty, lusty, lively, hale. The Sc. sense leans to 'Lively, merry, brisk'; cf. Jamieson, who compares 'cant men' (armed followers) with 'merry men' of the ballads.

a **1300** *Cursor M.* 8943 Iuus þat war sa cant [*Gött. & Trin.* crabbed] and kene. **1330** R. Brunne *Chron.* 50 Knoute com with his kythe, þat kant was and kene. **1375** Barbour *Bruce* viii. 280 The kyng..Vith his men that war cant and keyn. ?*a* **1400** *Morte Arth.* 2195 The knyghte coue-ride on his knees with a kaunt herte. *c* **1440** *Gaw. & Gol.* ii. 2 (Jam.) Cant men and cruel. *c* **1450** Henryson *Mor. Fab.* 5 Ane Cocke..Right cant and crous. **1513** Douglas *Æneis* viii. Prol. 42 The cadgear callis furth his capill wyth crakis waill cant. **1535** Stewart *Cron. Scot.* II. 517 Alss blyth and als rejosit, And in him self that tyme als crous and kant. **1674** Ray *N.C. Wds.* 9 *Cant*, strong lusty; 'Very cant, God yield you', i.e. Very strong and lusty, God reward you. *Chesh.* **1849** C. Brontë *Shirley* I. 189 Th' wife's a raight cant body. **1868** E. Waugh *Sneck-Bant* iv. 76 As cant as a kitlin.

†**cant**, *v.*[1] *Obs.* [Of uncertain etym.: associated in sense with cant *sb.*[2], but of much earlier appearance, being the oldest vb. *cant* in the lang., and as a word preceded only by cant *a.* and cant *sb.*[1] Since the dim. of the latter word, *cantel, chanteau*, cantle, had the sense of 'piece, fragment', it is possible that this sense may have attached also to the primitive, and that a verb *to cant* 'to divide into pieces' may have been in LG. or ONF.: but it has not yet been found.]

1. *trans.* To part, divide, share, parcel out, apportion.

c **1440** *Promp. Parv.* 60 Cantyn or departyn, *partior, divido.* **1529** More *Comf. agst. Trib.* iii. Wks. 1245/2 Our very prison this earth is. And yet therof we cant vs out.. dyuers partes dyuerslye to our self. **1533** —— *Debell. Salem* Wks. 943/2 To diuide & cant it among good poore husband men, that should til the ground [with] theyr handes.

2. (See quot.) Cf. cant *sb.*[2] (quot. 1875).

1863 Morton *Cycl. Agric.* Gloss. (E.D.S.) *Cant*, (Kent), to let out land to mow, hoe, etc.

cant (kænt), *v.*[2] [f. cant *sb.*[1]; cf. Du. and Ger. *kanten* in several of the same senses.]

I. *trans.*

1. To give a cant edge to; to bevel; esp. to bevel *off* a corner.

1542–3 *Act 34 & 35 Hen. VIII*, vi, Pinnes..shal..haue.. the point well and rounde filled, canted, and sharped. **1791** Smeaton *Edystone L.* §274 The corners only were a little canted off. **1812** J. Hodgson in J. Raines *Mem.* (1857) I. 97 The several pillars which have their uppermost corner canted off. **1851–3** Turner *Dom. Archit.* II. ii. 30 The Abacus is square, with the angles canted.

2. To bring or put (a thing) into an oblique position, so that it is no longer vertical or horizontal; to slope, slant, tilt up.

1711 Duncan *Mariner's Chron.* (1805) III. 302 The sea broke in upon us, and the canoe being filled half full, canted her broadside to it. **1756** Winthrop in *Phil. Trans.* L. 11 Some [chimnies] were..canted horizontally an inch or two over, so as to stand very dangerously. **1792** *Munchausen's Trav.* ix. 30 The wind rose suddenly, and canted our barge on one side. **1826** Miss Mitford *Vill.* Ser. iii. (1863) 496 She sat..with her feet canted up on an ottoman. **1884** *Pall Mall G.* 12 Aug. 12/1 If the ship needs a 'list', she can be canted.

b. To turn *over* completely, turn upside down.

c **1850** *Rudim. Navig.* (Weale) 103 Canting, the act of turning anything completely over, so that the under surface shall lie upwards. **1855** Kingsley *Glaucus* (1878) 160 Without canting the net over, and pouring the contents roughly out.

†**c.** *fig.* (?) To incline, adapt with a bias. *Obs.*

1682 Southerne *Loyal Bro.* iv. Wks. 1721 I. 56 Gifted rogues, That cant their doctrine to their present wants.

3. To throw off, *e.g.* to empty out, the contents of a vessel by tilting it up. ***to cant off***: to decant.

1658 A. Fox *Wurtz' Surg.* iii. viii. 241 Let it stand in a warm place..then cant of the Aquavitæ cleanly. *a* **1845** Hood *Poems* (1864) 265 As vessels cant their ballast—rattling rubbish.

4. To pitch as by the sudden lurching of a ship; to toss, to throw with a sudden jerk.

1685 F. Spence *Ho. Medici* 120 Some couragious Priests had the leisure to joyn him, and cant him into a vestry, that was accidentally open. **1755** Smollett *Quix.* (1803) II. 130 This very innkeeper..held a corner of the blanket, and canted me into the air with great strength and nimbleness. **1791** Smeaton *Edystone L.* §254 *note*, The boat took a sudden yaw or sheer, which canted me overboard, headlong into the sea. **1805** *Naval Chron.* XIII. 387 The Ship gave a lurch, by which he was canted into the mizen shrouds! **1816** Scott *Antiq.* xvii, That spray of a bramble has..nearly canted my wig into the stream. **1861** G. Berkeley *Sportsm. W. Prairies* v. 82 'Does the cow-catcher', I asked, 'always cant the beef on one side'?

II. *intr.*

5. To tilt, take an inclined position, pitch on one side, turn over; often ***to cant over.***

1702 C. Mather *Magn. Chr.* vi. ii. (1852) 356 It fell on end and then canted along on the floor between two of the children. **1851** S. Judd *Margaret* iii. (1871) 15 It jolted over stones, canted on knolls, sidled into gutters. **1862** Smiles *Engineers* III. 410 *note*, A loose plank, which canted over. **1858** Carlyle *Fredk. Gt.* (1873) II. 88 The celestial sign of the Balance just about canting. *Ibid.* (1865) II. v. ii. 72 The History so-called of Europe went canting from side to side. **1884** *Manch. Exam.* 10 Sept. 5/1 The steamer, which had canted over, lay in a very dangerous position.

6. To have a slanting position, lie aslant, slope.

1794 *Rigging & Seamanship* II. 301 The upper fluke should cant down. **1882** Nares *Seamanship* (ed. 6) 135 The ..yard-arm should..cant abaft the yard rope.

7. *Naut.* To take, move into, or have an oblique position in reference to any defined course or direction; to swing round from a position.

1784 in Nicolas *Disp. Nelson* VII. Add. 7 At 7 weighed: in canting the ship got stern way. **1859** *Blackw. Mag.* LXXXVI. 655/2 The great length of the Nimrod and Cormorant caused them, when canting or swinging across the Channel, almost to block it up. **1887** Blackmore in *Harper's Mag.* Mar. 563 The boat canted round towards the entrance of the creek. *a* **1888** *Newspaper*, The stern of the Andalusian was seen to be canting to the southward.

†**8.** *fig.* ***to cant with***: ? to fall in with, take the direction of. (Cf. 2 c.) *Obs.*

1656 in Burton *Diary* (1828) I. 111 They were all cantings, such as could not cant with my thoughts.

†**9.** (See quot. 1877.) *Obs.* or *dial.*

1674 [see canting *vbl. sb.*[1]]. **1877** *Holderness Gloss.* (E.D.S.) *Cant*, to move about with a jaunty step. 'Why awd woman gans cantin aboot like a young lass.'

cant (kænt), *v.*[3] [See cant *sb.*[3] It is not certain whether the vb. or the sb. came first.]

I. 1. *intr.* To speak in the whining or singsong tone used by beggars; to beg.

1567 Harman *Caveat* (1869) 34 'It shall be lawefull for the to Cant'—that is, to aske or begge—'for thy living in al places.' **1612** Beaum. & Fl. *Cupid's Rev.* iv. 418 The cunning'st rankest rogue that ever Canted. **1687** Congreve *Old Bachel.* iii. vi, Thy master..lies canting at the gate. **1750** Johnson *Rambl.* No. 171 ¶10 [He] bad me cant and whine in some other place.

2. *intr.* To speak in the peculiar jargon or 'cant' of vagabonds, thieves, and the like.

1609 Dekker *Lanth. & Candle-L.* Wks. 1885 III. 194 He that in such assemblies can cant best, is counted the best Musitian. **1652** Gaule *Magastrom.* To Rdr., He cannot tell how to cant with him [a gypsie] in his own foysting gibborish. *c* **1652** H. More in R. Ward *Life* (1710) 307, I don't deny but that may sooner teach a Man to Cant and talk Gibberish. **1708** Kersey, *Cant*, to talk darkly, after the manner of Thieves, Beggars, &c. **1721–1800** in Bailey.

b. *slang* and *dial.* To speak, talk; in *Sc.* (see quot. 1788).

1567 Harman *Caveat* (1869) 84 The vpright Cofe canteth to the Roge. **1690** B. E. *Dict. Cant. Crew*, *Cant*, to speak. **1713** Ramsay *Elegy Maggy Johnstoun*, Of auld stories we did cant. **1726** Ayliffe *Parerg.* 309 Tho' it cants or speaks in another manner. **1788** Picken *Poems* Gloss., *Cant*, to tell merry old stories.

c. *trans.* To speak or utter in a cant way.

1592 Greene *Def. Coneycatch.* (1859) 5 To heare a pesant cant the wordes of art belonging to our trade. **1631** Brathwait *Whimzies, Wine-soaker* 102 Which sackes his capitall, makes his tongue cant broken English. **1633** Shirley *Gamesters* iii. iii, Canting broken Dutch for farthings.

†**3.** *intr.* To use the special phraseology or jargon of a particular class or subject. ? *Obs.*

1625 B. Jonson *Staple of N.* iv. iv, When my Muster-Master Talkes of his Tacticks, and his Rankes, and Files.. Doth not he cant? *Ibid.* Thou canst cant too. *Pic.* In all the Language in Westminster Hall, Pleas, Bench, or Chancery, *Fee-Farm, Fee-Tail, Tenant in Dower*, etc., etc. **1688** Miege *Gt. Fr. Dict.*, *Cant*, to speak a canting Language, to have an affected peculiar kind of Speech. **1698** Norris *Pract. Disc.* 262 The Quakers..only Cant in some loose general Expressions about the Light.

†4. To say or exclaim in the pet phraseology of the day, to use the phrases currently affected at the time. Also, *to cant it*: to phrase it in the cant of the period. *Obs.*

1648 JENKYN *Blind Guide* i. 6 No other import or tendency (as he *cants* it). **1660** S. FORD *Loyal Subject's Exult.* 13 The Sovereign Authority of the People (as our Times have learned to cant it). **1669** W. SIMPSON *Hydrol. Chym.* 24 Those..which they so much cant to be drying decoctions. **1710** SIR J. ST. LEGER *Managers Pro & Con*, in Somers *Tracts* Ser. IV. (1751) III. 242 To set right (as they cant) the ..Youth of the University. *a* **1716** SOUTH *12 Serm.* (1744) II. 64 There was thirty years more generation-work (as they canted it) cut out for him.

5. To affect the conventional phraseology of a school, party, or subject.

1728 YOUNG *Love Fame* VI. (1757) 155 Let them cant on, since they have got the knack, And dress their notions, like themselves, in black. **1784** JOHNSON in *Boswell* (1887) IV. 308 Don't cant in defence of savages. **1802** MAR. EDGEWORTH *Moral T.* (1816) I. xiv. 114 Who cants about the pre-eminence of mind. **1866** CARLYLE *Remin.* II. 215 A paltry print then much canted of. **1870** LOWELL *Among my Bks.* Ser. I. (1873) 340 Lessing..knew the classics, and did not merely cant about them.

6. *spec.* To affect religious or pietistic phraseology, *esp.* as a matter of fashion or profession; to talk unreally or hypocritically with an affectation of goodness or piety.

1678 BUTLER *Hud.* III. II. 765 Till they first began to Cant And sprinkle down the Covenant. **1778** JOHNSON in *Boswell* 12 Apr., He [Dr. Dodd] may have composed this prayer then. A man who has been canting all his life, may cant to the last. **1813** SCOTT *Rokeby* I. xviii, I could not cant of creed or prayer. **1851** KINGSLEY *Yeast* xi. (1853) 189 In Christian England Where they cant of a Saviour's name, And yet waste men's lives like vermin's. **1856** R. VAUGHAN *Mystics* (1860) II. VIII. ix. 102 Those dreamers who..cant about a general brotherhood which exempts them from particular charity.

7. *trans.* (in senses 5, 6.)

1641 M. FRANK *Serm. Transfig.* (1672) 514 To set up King Jesus; a phrase much canted. **1676** MARVELL *Mr. Smirke* I iij, Shall any sort of men presume to..force every man to Cant after them what it is not lawful for any man to utter? **1761** STERNE *Tr. Shandy* III. xii. 60 Of all the cants which are canted in this canting world..the cant of criticism is the most tormenting. **1825** *Edin. Rev.* XLII. 355 He may cant out his panegyricks. **1843** MACAULAY in *Life & Lett.* (1880) II. 146, I have heard the same cant canted about a much finer building.

8. *dial.* (See quots.)

1877 E. PEACOCK *N.-W. Linc. Gloss.* (E.D.S.) *Cant*, to deceive by pious pretences, to impose upon. **1881** EVANS *Leicestersh Gloss.* (E.D.S.) *Cant*, to wheedle; coax; humour. 'The pony'll be quiet enough when he's been canted a bit.'

II. †**9.** *trans.* To chant, sing; to repeat in a sing-song manner, intone. *Obs.*

1652 GAULE *Magastrom.* 24 Who is an Inchanter? A Sooth-singer, by canting numbers, or a Sooth-sayer by calculating numbers. **1705** HICKERINGILL *Priest-Cr.* II. iii. 35 Singing Men and singing Boys, that instead of rehearsing the Creed, cant it, like the tune called the *Mock-Nightingale*.

†**10.** *intr.* To chant, sing. *Sc.* or *dial.* ? *Obs.*

1768 ROSS *Helenore* 59 (Jam.) The birdies..Canting fu' cheerfu'.

cant (kænt), *v.*[4] [cf. CANT *sb.*[4], and the med.L. cognate verbs *incantāre*, *accantāre* to proclaim, cry, put up to auction, there mentioned.] To dispose of by auction. Chiefly *Irish*.

The first quotation may belong to CANT *v.*[1] to divide.

[**1570** *Wills & Inv. N.C.* (1835) 328, I will yt all my goods aftr my deathe shalbe canted & sold at my foredore & then to be distributed in money by euen portions to my executors.] **1720** SWIFT *Irish Manuf.* Wks. 1761 III. 4 Canting their own lands upon short leases, and sacrificing their oldest tenants for a penny an acre. **1723** —— *Power of Bps.* ibid. 262 [Irish] landlords..cant their lands to the highest bidder. **1828** C. CROKER *Fairy Leg. Irel.* II. 236 Tim the driver swears if we don't pay up our rent, he'll cant every ha'perth we have. **1839** W. CARLETON *Fardorougha* (ed. 2) 46 He..canted all we had at half price, and turned us to starve on the world. **1880** in *Antrim & Down Gloss.*

†**2.** To enhance by competitive bidding. *rare.*

a **1745** SWIFT *Hist. Eng., Will. II* (R.) When two monks were outvying each other in canting the price of an abbey.

†**cant,** *v.*[5] *Obs. dial.* [f. CANT *a.*] *intr.* To become 'cant' or well; to recover strength, to mend. Hence '**canting** *vbl. sb.*

1690 B. E. *Dict. Cant. Crew, Cant*..also (Cheshire) to grow Strong and Lusty. **1691** RAY *N.C. Wds.* s.v., 'A health to the good wives [wife's] canting' i.e. her recovering after lying-in.

cant, *v.*[6] = SCANT.

1580 TUSSER *Husb.* (1878) 184 Good huswiferie canteth [**1577** scanteth] the lenger to last.

can't (kɑːnt), a colloq. contraction of *cannot*; see CAN *v.*[1] A I.

Cantab ('kæntæb), *sb.* and *a.* **A.** *sb.* A colloquial abbreviation of CANTABRIGIAN.

1750 COVENTRY *Pompey Litt.* II. x. (1785) 68/1 The young Cantab..had come up to London. **1755** *Gentl. Mag.* XXV. 60 Upon gawdy, or exceeding days, as they are call'd by the Cantabs. **1807** BYRON *To Miss Pigot* 5 July, Sad dogs all the Cantabs.

B. *adj.* [Abbrev. of L. *Cantabrigiensis.*] Of the University of Cambridge. Usu. succeeding noun in titles, as ***M.A. Cantab.***

1870 (*title*) The French Genders in Rhyme. By A. M., Cantab. **1947** *Apostolic Succession* (Churchman's Mag.) p. ii The matter is of such moment that we are certain our readers will be glad to have the following article by 'M.A. (Cantab.)'. **1958** *Who was Who, 1941–1950* (rev. ed.) 254/2 Costello, Brig.-Gen. Edmund W.; V.C. 1897;..Hon. M.A. Cantab.

cantabank ('kæntəbæŋk). *rare.* [ad. It. *cantambanco*, f. *canta-re* to sing + *banco* bench.] A singer on a stage or platform; hence, *contemptuously*, a common ballad-singer.

[**1589** PUTTENHAM *Eng. Poesie* (Arb.) 96 Small and popular Musickes song by these *Cantabanqui* vpon benches and barrels heads.] **1834** SIR. H. TAYLOR *Artevelde* I. iii. i, He was no tavern cantabank.

‖**cantabile** (kan'tabile), *a.* and *sb. Music.* [It. = that can be sung, suited for singing.]

A. *adj.* In a smooth flowing style, such as would be suited for singing. Also as *adv.*

1724 *Short Explication Foreign Words in Musick Bks.* 17 *Cantabile*, is to play in a Kind of Singing or Chanting Manner. **1730–6** in BAILEY. **1792** J. W. CALLCOTT *Explan. Notes Mus.* 27/2 *Cantabile*, in a vocal stile. This word is sometimes used in the same sense as Cadenza, but very improperly. **1822** *Repository* No. 80. 103 The smooth, cantable, and expressive melody which pervades its structure. **1864** *Realm* 13 Apr. 8 Written in a simple cantabile style. **1893–7** J. S. SHEDLOCK tr. *H. Riemann's Dict. Mus.* 119/1 *Cantabile*, full of expression... In passages marked *c*, the principal melody is always made more prominent than the accompanying parts. **1931** D. F. TOVEY in Tovey & Craxton *Beethoven Piano Sonatas* III. 140/2 These bars are in double counterpoint to each other; therefore both hands must play *cantabile*.

B. *sb.* Cantabile style; a piece or passage of music of this style.

1744 J. GREEN *Psalmody* 140 *Cantabal*, Vocal Music. **1788** J. WILLIAMS (A. Pasquin) *Childr. Thespis* (1792) 137 Tho her sportive cantabilies win us. **1808** WOLCOTT (P. Pindar) Wks. 1812 V. 353 The tuneful Nymph..That in cantabile delights the soul. **1856** MRS. C. CLARKE tr. *Berlioz' Instr.* 81 It expresses them admirably in its cantabile.

Cantabrian (kæn'teɪbrɪən), *a.* and *sb.* [f. L. *Cantabria*: see -IAN.] **A.** *adj.* Pertaining to the Cantabri, an ancient warlike tribe of northern Spain, or to Cantabria, the region formerly occupied by them. **B.** *sb.* **a.** One of the ancient Cantabri. **b.** The language of the Cantabrians.

1642 J. HOWELL *For. Trav.* x. 124 The Cantabrian tongue in Biscaie. **1746** AKENSIDE *Hymn to Naiads* in Dodsley *Poems* (1758) VI. 8 The rough Cantabrian coast. **1747** [see SEPT *sb.*[2]]. **1797** *Encycl. Brit.* IV. 122/1 The Cantabrians had waged war with the Romans for upwards of 200 years. *Ibid.* 122/2 The Cantabrian does not appear to have any affinity with any other known language. **1813** *Q. Rev.* Oct. 256 Classes and Families of Languages... Indoeuropean... Cantabrian. Sclavic. **1861** *Chambers's Encycl.* II. 572/1 Their bravery was evinced in the Cantabrian war, a six years' contest with the Romans. *Ibid.*, *Cantabrian mountains*, the general name of the several ranges of coast and boundary mountains. **1904** T. R. GLOVER *Virgil* vii. 145 In the course of the Cantabrian war he wrote to the poet from Spain letters full of playful entreaties. **1957** P. KEMP *Mine were of Trouble* v. 97 These two victories forced the gateway through the Cantabrian Cordillera.

Cantabrigian (kæntə'brɪdʒɪən), *a.* and *sb.* [f. *Cantabrigia*, Latin form of the name *Cambridge* + -AN.] **1.** Of or belonging to Cambridge; a member of the University of Cambridge.

c **1540** [see OXONIAN *sb.* a]. **1616** J. CHAMBERLAIN *Let.* 27 Mar. (1939) I. 618 The King..had a play at Roiston acted by some of the younger sort of our Cantabrigians. *c* **1645** HOWELL *Lett.* (1650) I. 15 The Oxonians and Cantabrigians ..are the happiest Academians on earth. **1711** STEELE *Spect.* No. 78 ¶5 Some hardy Cantabrigian Author. **1856** EMERSON *Eng. Traits, 'Times'* Wks. (Bohn) II. 120 Every slip of an Oxonian or Cantabrigian who writes his first leader, assumes that we subdued the earth before we sat down to write this particular 'Times'.

2. Belonging to Cambridge, Mass., or to Harvard University.

1887 *Harper's Mag.* Mar. 589/1 Mrs. Sainsbury was Boston-born, as well as Mrs. Pasmer, and was Cantabrigian by marriage. **1893** W. K. POST *Harvard Stories* 26 The New Haven men struggled to the Cantabrigian twenty-yard line.

Hence, *nonce-wds.*, as **Cantabri'gicity**, '**Cantabrize** *v.*

1863 DE MORGAN in *N. & Q.* Ser. III. IV. 170 There is a general Cantabrigicity about it. **1655** FULLER *Ch. Hist.* IX. vii. §47 Know also that this university [Dublin] did so Cantabrize, that she imitated her in the successive choice of her Chancellours. **1885** *Academy* 10 Jan. 19/2 Readers.. might be excused for considering that Mr. Mullinger 'cantabrizes'.

†**can'taillie.** *Sc. Obs.* [A variant of CANTLE; cf. Du. *kanteel* battlement.] ? 'A corner-piece' (Jam.).

1561 *Royal Invent.* (1815) 165 (Jam.) Item, ane bed..with a litle cantaillie of gold furnisit with ruif head piece.

Cantal ('kæntəl). [Name of a district in south central France.] In full ***Cantal cheese.*** A hard cheese made chiefly in the Auvergne, France.

1890 J. MACDONALD *Stephen's Bk. Farm* (ed. 4) IV. 517/2 The Cantal cheese..is an extremely important one upon the Continent. **1918** [see BLEU]. **1961** *Listener* 20 Apr. 704/1 The delicious cheeses Cantal, Bleu d'Auvergne, and Saint-Nectaire. **1966** K. WHITE *Lett. from Gourgounel* xxii. 103 Last year in Auvergne..I was to be met on the hills with a bit of Cantal cheese.

'**cantalite.** *Min.* [a. F. *cantalite*, f. *Cantal* in France + -ITE.] A feldspathic rock from Cantal in France, formerly considered a variety of quartz.

†**canta'loon.** *Obs.* A woollen stuff manufactured in the 18th c. in the west of England.

1711 *Lond. Gaz.* No. 4806/4, 4 Trusses of Cantaloons or Serges. **1748** *De Foe's Tour Gt. Brit.* I. 94 (D.) Western Goods..Shalloons, Cantaloons, Devonshire Kersies, etc. *Ibid.* (1769) II. 25 In Bristol, and many Towns on that Side, Druggets, Cantaloons, and other Stuffs.

cantaloup, -loupe ('kæntəluːp). Also **cantalupe, -leup, canteleup, -lope, -loup, -lupe.** [a. F. *cantaloup*, ad. It. *Cantalupo*, the name of a former country seat of the Pope near Rome, where it is said, on its introduction from Armenia, to have been first cultivated.] A small, round, ribbed variety of musk-melon, of a very delicate flavour.

1739 MILLER *Gard. Dict.* II. s.v. *Melo*, The Cantaleupt [*sic*] Melon:..the Flesh..is of a rich vinous Flavour. **1763** MILLS *Pract. Husb.* IV. 169 The Cantaleupe..is held in the greatest esteem by all the curious in Europe. **1777** COWPER *Let.* 23 Oct. (1904) I. 143 The melon is a crimson Cantalupe. **1786, 1813** [see ROCK *sb.*[1] 9 e]. **1839** *Penny Cycl.* XV. 86/2 Varieties of melons..The Early Cantaloup. **1860** EMERSON *Cond. Life, Wealth* Wks. (Bohn) II. 354 The cantaloupes, crooknecks, and cucumbers will send for him. **1863** *Life in South* II. 343 A fine cantalupe melon, at five cents. **1883** F. M. CRAWFORD *Dr. Claudius* xiv, Behold also, his Grace eateth the cantelope. **1890** *Daily News* 18 Sept. 3/1 The very first item on the list is 'iced cantaloupes'. **1929** *Times* 2 Aug. 14/1 Melon or bailer shells..are almost exactly the same shape, size and colour as rock melons, or canteloups. **1970** *Natural History* Feb. 18/3 Cantaloupes..produce a crop only occasionally.

†**can'tanker.** *Obs. nonce-wd.* [A back formation from CANTANKER-OUS, like *canker*, *cankerous.*] = CANTANKEROUSNESS. So **cantankerate** *v.*, to provoke; **can'tankersome** *a.* = CANTANKEROUS (both *U.S. colloq.*).

1825 CANNING *Let.* in Stapleton *Canning & Times* (1859) App. iv, F. is cantankerous. He is also tricky. No man has a right to be both..Straightforwardness is the only excuse for cantanker. **1837–40** HALIBURTON *Clockm.* I. xxiv. (1862) 115 You may..cantankerate your opponents, and injure your own cause by it. *Ibid.* III. xii, A terrible cross-grained cantankersome critter.

cantankerous (kæn'tæŋkərəs), *a. colloq.* Also 8 **cantanckerous.** [Said by Grose, who spells it *contankerous*, to be a Wiltshire word. This spelling gives some support to the conjecture that the word was formed on ME. *contak*, *conteke*, contention, quarrelling, *contekour*, *conteckour* one who raises strife, whence **conteckerous*, **contakerous* would be a possible deriv. like *traitorous*, which might subseq. be corrupted under influence of words like *cankerous*, *rancorous*. Its oddly appropriate sound, and perh. some assoc. with these words, have given it general colloquial currency.]

Showing an ill-natured disposition; ill-conditioned and quarrelsome, perverse, cross-grained.

1772 GOLDSM. *Stoops to Conq.* II, There's not a more bitter cantanckerous road in all christendom. **1775** SHERIDAN *Rivals* V. iii, I hope, Mr. Faulkland..you won't be so cantanckerous. **1842** MISS MITFORD in L'Estrange *Life* (1870) III. ix. 142 As cantankerous and humorous as Cassius himself. **1865** LIVINGSTONE *Zambesi* ix. 195 A crusty old bachelor or..a cantankerous husband. **1873** *St. Paul's Mag.* I. 533 A cantankerous element in his nature.

Hence **can'tankerously** *adv.*, **can'tankerousness**.

1868 A. K. H. BOYD *Lessons Mid. Age* 217 One impracticable, stupid, wrongheaded, and cantankerously foolish person of the twelve. **1876** MRS. H. WOOD *Orville Coll.* 411 You have behaved cantankerously to him. **1881** A. R. HOPE in *Boy's Own Paper* 10 Sept. 794 The roller had crushed the cantankerousness right out of him. **1886** *Chr. Life* 2 Jan. 2/6 A member..expelled for general cantankerousness.

cantar ('kæntə(r)). Often in the native forms '**cantaro**, '**cantara.** [f. It., Sp. *cantaro*, *cantara*:—L. *canthar-us*, Gr. κάνθαρος tankard, drinking-pot.]

A measure of capacity and weight used in some of the countries bordering on the Mediterranean, varying greatly according to the locality, from $74\frac{3}{8}$ lbs. in Rome to $502\frac{3}{4}$ lbs. in Syria.

1730–6 BAILEY, *Cantar* [in Spain] wine measure, is about two gallons. *Cantar* [in Turky in Asia] 100 rotelloes, about 418 pounds averdupoise. *Cantar* [at Tunis] 114 pounds. **1773** BRYDONE *Sicily* xvii. (1809) 186 Mortars..to throw a hundred cantars of cannon-ball or stones. **1858** *Simmonds Dict. Trade, Cantara, cantaro*, a liquid measure of Spain ranging from $2\frac{1}{2}$ to 4 gallons. **1882** *Even. Standard* 16 Sept. 5/2 The cotton crop is estimated at 2,000,000 cantars. **1887** *Pall Mall G.* 24 June 12/1 Formerly twenty loaves [of sugar] went to the Moorish cantar, or hundredweight.

†'**cantarie.** *Obs.* [ad. L. *cantāria* CHANTRY, f. *cantāre* to sing: cf. CANTUARIE.] = CHANTRY.

c **1593** *Rites of Durham* (1842) 37 Within the said Gallelei in the Cantarie..stood Our Ladies alter.

cantarist ('kæntərɪst). *Hist.* [ad. med.L. *cantarista*, f. *cantaria* CHANTRY: see -IST.] A chantry priest.

1800 *Gentl. Mag.* Mar. 201 The almshouse..for one chaplain, or cantarist, and three almsmen. **1894** H. FISHWICK *Lancashire* ix. 213 Many of these cantarists, as they were called, were now pensioned off for life.

cantata (kæn'tɑːtə). *Music.* [It.; = 'a thing sung, a song, a composition to be set to music', f. *cantare* to sing; for the It. ending *-ata* see -ADE.]

1. Originally, a narrative in verse set to recitative, or alternate recitative and air, for a single voice, accompanied by one or more instruments; now applied to a choral work, either sacred and resembling an oratorio but shorter, or secular, as a lyric drama set to music but not intended to be acted. (See Grove *Dict. Mus.* I. 304.)

1724 H. CAREY (*title*) Cantatas for a voice, with Accompaniment. **1744** J. GREEN *Psalmody* 140 *Cantata*, a Song in an Opera Stile. **1751** SMOLLETT *Per. Pic.* (1779) I. ii. 22 Pipes perfomed the whole cantata. **1775** MRS. HARRIS in *Priv. Lett. 1st Ld. Malmesbury* I. 296 A very fine new cantata composed by Ranzini. **1861** WOODS *Pr. of Wales in Canada* 140 The Montreal Oratorio Society performed..a grand Cantata specially composed.

†**2.** A song, chant. (*nonce-use.*)

a **1754** FIELDING *True Patr.* Wks. 1775 IX. 311 The.. swan, whose last breath goes out in a cantata.

Hence **cantatize** *v. nonce-wd.* To perform cantatas.

1842 *Blackw. Mag.* LI. 24 The flexile trills of a cantatizing Signora.

cantate (kæn'teɪtiː, kæn'tɑːteɪ). [a. L. *cantate* 'sing ye', the first word of the psalm.] The ninety-eighth psalm (ninety-seventh in the Vulgate) used as a canticle (e.g. as an alternative to the Magnificat at Evening Prayer in the Church of England).

Cantate Sunday, the fourth Sunday after Easter, so called because the introit for that day is taken from this psalm.

c **1550** BALE *K. Johan* (Camden) 65 Now may we synge Cantate, And crowe Confitebor with a joyfull Jubilate. **1880** *Grove's Dict. Mus.* I. 305/2 The 17th canon of the council of Laodicea appointed lessons and psalms to be read alternately; and on this principle the 'Cantate' is to be considered as a 'responsory psalm' coming between the lessons. *Ibid.*, 'Cantate Services' are..rare. **1957** *Oxf. Dict. Chr. Church* 231/2 In the American Prayer Book of 1789, the 'Magnificat' was..replaced by the 'Cantate'.

can'tation. *rare.* [ad. L. *cantātiōn-em* singing, incantation, f. *cantāre* to sing: see -ATION.] †**a.** Singing (*obs.*). **b.** Incantation, magical charm.

1623 COCKERAM, *Cantation*, Singing. **1656** BLOUNT *Gloss.*, *Cantation*, singing or enchanting. **1846** FORD *Gath. fr. Spain* 237 As Ulysses stopped his bleeding by cantation.

‖**can'tator.** *rare.* [L.: agent-noun f. *cantāre* to sing; cf. CANTATRICE.] A (male) singer.

1866 ENGEL *Nation. Mus.* vii. 239 In describing a voyage, the cantator represents with his body the uneasy motion of the waves.

cantatory ('kæntətərɪ), *a. rare.* [f. on L. type **cantātōri-us*, f. *cantātōr-em*: see prec.] Of or pertaining to a singer or his singing.

1836 *Fraser's Mag.* XIII. 75 This specimen of his cantatory powers.

¶ Pertaining to cant; whining, sing-song.

In mod. Dicts.

‖**cantatrice** (It. kanta'tritʃe, Fr. kɑ̃tatris). [a. It. and F. *cantatrice*:—L. *cantātrix, cantātrīc-em*, fem. of *cantātor*.] A female professional singer.

1803 SCOTT *Let.* 6 Mar. (1932) I. 178 Immense parties where none dare tell his mind to his neighbour should it involve anything more important than an opinion on the merit of the newest *cantatrice* or *figurante*. **1866** *Daily Tel.* 16 Jan. 7/4 The rival cantatrice. **1871** SMILES *Charac.* xii. (1876) 350 A promising but passionless cantatrice.

cant-dog ('kæntdɒg). *north. dial.* [f. CANT *v.*² + DOG.] 'A hand-spike with a hook' (Halliwell); = CANT-HOOK 2.

1850 S. JUDD *R. Edney* 272 Leaning on a cant-dog, he could talk with Melicent and Barbara. **1868** *Harper's Mag.* XXXVI. 420 Six large logs were piled on to one large sled in a moment's time, two or three men assisting with their cant-dogs. **1885** *Boston* (Mass.) *Jrnl.*, Cant-dogs are coming into use for various purposes. **1942** *Amer. Speech* XVII. 220/2 *Cant dog*, a peavey; the riverman's tool. *a* **1951** B. CRONIN in *Austral. Short Stories* (1951) 167 The duty of a cant-dog man is to orient the logs.

canted ('kæntɪd), *ppl. a.* [f. CANT *sb.*¹ and *v.*² + -ED.] In various senses of CANT *v.*²: tilted up, caused to lean from the perpendicular; having a sloping or slanting surface; bevelled; placed at an oblique angle; having the corners bevelled off.

1649 in *Vetusta Mon.* (1748) II. Plates 23 & 24 One round Structure or Building of Free Stone, called the Canted Tower [of the Old Palace at Richmond, Surrey]. **1664** in Bp. Cosin *Corr.* (Surtees) II. 374 To make a canted stepp into the great roome. **1848** RICKMAN *Archit.* li, The general plan of the abacus is a square with the angles cut off, or what is called a canted square. **1872** O. SHIPLEY *Gloss. Eccl. Terms* 66 s.v. *Bevel*, A sloped or canted surface. **1874** KNIGHT *Dict. Mech.* s.v. *Cant*, A bolt with a hexagonal or octagonal head is said to be six or eight canted.

canteen (kæn'tiːn). orig. *Mil.* [a. F. *cantine*, ad. It. *cantina* cellar, cave, of doubtful deriv.: see Diez and Littré. The history and order of the senses is obscure. The quotations of date 1744 virtually carry senses 1 and 4 back to 1710–11, the date of the occurrences referred to. See also note under 4.]

1. a. A kind of sutler's shop in a camp, barracks, or garrison town, where provisions and liquors are sold to soldiers and non-commissioned officers. Now under regimental control. Also, in Indian and colonial use, applied to a victualling or refreshment house resembling this.

1744 M. BISHOP *Life & Adv.* 138, I took him to the Canteen, and gave him what he would drink. **1803** REES *Cycl.*, *Canteen* is the cabaret, tavern, or place in a garrison-town where the garrison have the privilege of purchasing spirits..and beer. **1832** *Life W. J. Neptune* 105 In the kitchen of the Canteen at the Citadel. **1837** F. OWEN *Diary* (1926) 7 The annoyance I had been put to, in one of the Hottentots being found on the floor at a canteen, at the time when he ought to have been at his place at the waggon. **1844** *Regul. & Ord. Army* 243 No civilians..are to be permitted to frequent, or in any way to make use of the Canteen, without the..sanction of the Commanding Officer. **1852** C. BARTER *Dorp & Veld* 9 (Pettman), But the inns sadly need reformation—they are in fact little better than canteens. **1886** The Canteen at the Indian and Colonial Exhibition. **1950** *Cape Times* 20 Sept. 16/2 Men in uniform have been encouraged by their officers to use their own canteens rather than public bars.

b. In extended use. Now usu. a refreshment-room at a factory, school, or the like.

1870 D. J. KIRWAN *Palace & Hovel* (1963) xv. 143 The Canteen of the Alhambra is..nothing more than a subterranean bar-room. **1908** *Parish Councils* (Fabian Tract No. 137) 13 At Limpsfield (Surrey) the school manager appointed by the parish council personally started a canteen, which fed 60 children who came from a distance. *a* **1930** D. H. LAWRENCE *Phoenix II* (1968) 18 Dinners are given in the canteen in one of the mean streets, where the children feed in a Church Mission room. **1937** *Discovery* Sept. 268/2 A works canteen, a matter on which employees are sensitive, especially if..the canteen is a virtual monopoly. **1955** *Times* 12 May 18/5 Every consideration will also be given to facilities for canteens and both indoor and outdoor recreation.

‖**2.** 'A small case divided into compartments for carrying flasks or bottles of wine and other liquors' (Littré); a French use, which however may have given rise to the next two English ones.

1737 OZELL *Rabelais* II. 235 Two Cantines (Bottle-Cases). The best Cantines are sold at Charing-Cross.

3. a. A box or chest with an outfit of cooking and table utensils, and other articles serviceable in a camp, or on an expedition, used by officers, etc.

1817 KEATINGE *Trav.* II. 6 Next follow the mules, with the tents and canteens. **1839** ANNE TYTLER *Leila* 13 Mr. Howard's canteen contained a small tea-service, etc. **1855** MACAULAY *Hist. Eng.* III. 627 The sumpter horses were unloaded: the canteens were opened.

b. A chest or case containing a set of table knives, forks, spoons, etc.

1895 *Army & Navy Co-op. Soc. Price List* 756 Canteens for wedding presents, yachting, college use, &c. **1963** *Times* 30 Jan. 4/3 Generous expenses and a canteen of cutlery!

4. A small tin or wooden vessel, of a capacity of from 3 to 4 pints, for water or liquor, carried by soldiers on the march, travellers, workmen, etc.

(This sense appears to be in vulgar Fr., since Littré says 'Il ne faut pas employer cantine pour cruche, ni dire: remplissez cette cantine'.)

1744 M. BISHOP *Life & Adv.* 8 The soldiers..ran into the Water..and after they had filled their Bellies, filled their Canteens. **1769** FALCONER *Dict. Marine* (1789) *Espoulette*, a tin canteen, or case, to carry fine powder. **1800** WEEMS *Washington* x. (1877) 129 Her soldiers often without a crust in their knapsacks or a dram in their canteens. **1811** *Monthly Mag.* 1 Dec. 464 *Canteen*, or *cantine*..a tin flat bottle, in which soldiers carry liquor on their shoulders. **1851** *Coal-tr. Terms Northumbld. & Durh.* 12 *Canteen*, a small wooden flat barrel, containing about half a gallon, in which a pitman carries water or coffee with him to his work. **1868** *Regul. & Ord. Army* §1128 The Men will..shift their pouches, havresacks and water canteens, round to the front of their bodies.

5. *attrib.* and *Comb.*, as (sense 1a) ***canteen-keeper, -sergeant, -steward***; (sense 1 b) ***canteen-manager, -work***; (sense 3) ***canteen-camel, -horse***; (sense 4) ***canteen-maker***.

1796 *Calvary Instruct.* (1803) 216 On a march, servants, led horses, and canteen horses remain with their squadrons. **1832** *Cape Gd. Hope Lit. Gaz.* 1 Feb. 243 (Pettman), We would call for certificates of character from every canteen-keeper. **1882–3** SCHAFF *Relig. Encycl.* I. 374 The canteen camel of Eastern tourists. **1886** *Pall Mall G.* 12 Sept. 2/2 The regimental and canteen supplies are left in the hands of canteen stewards and quartermasters. **1887** HAGGARD *Jess* 19 The canteen keeper sent for his boys to turn him out. **1918** A. BENNETT *Pretty Lady* xxvi. 171 Concepcion..had decided that she ought to take up canteen work. **1937** *Discovery* Sept. 268/2 A director who occasionally goes round dinners with his canteen manager.

‖**cante hondo, jondo** ('kante 'xondo). [Sp., lit. 'deep song'.] A popular type of Spanish song, often mournful.

1932 E. HEMINGWAY *Death in Afternoon* iv. 41 Do not look for beautiful women..in the brothels or the canta honda [*sic*] places. **1944** W. APEL *Harvard Dict. Mus.* 268/1 The gypsy style is supposed to have originated in the early 19th century from the *cante hondo* or *jondo*..of Andalusia, a highly emotional and tragic type of song probably influenced by the Sephardic Jews. **1961** *New Statesman* 22 Dec. 954/1 The agonised wail of *cante hondo* from beer-and-prawn cafés. **1969** D. CORY *Night Hawk* 48 Her voice had the real old cante jondo rasp.

cantel, var. of CANTLE; misreading of CAUTEL.

†'**cantel-cape, -cope.** *Obs.* [Cf. F. *chanteau* 'the quarter-piece of a garment, a cantle of cloth' (ONF. *cantel*).] A kind of cope or cape.

a **1121** *O.E. Chron.* an. 1070 Mæsse hakeles and cantel-capas and reafes. [transl. STEVENSON 1853, Mass-robes, and cantle-capes, and vestments.] *c* **1205** LAY. 29749 Godd clarc and wel idon, þa haueð his cantel-cape on. **1545** *Ludlow Churchw. Acc.* (Camden) 24 Payde for mendynge of iij. cantylcopes iijd. *Ibid.* 27 For mendynge of a cantilcop *vd.*

canter ('kæntə(r)), *sb.*¹ [f. CANT *v.*² + -ER¹. Cf. also CANT *sb.*¹ 6.]

1. a. One who cants, or tilts.

b. In a sawmill, a machine placed over the carriage and used to cant or roll over the log on the carriage in making the first cuts; a canting-machine (*Cent. Dict.* Suppl. 1909).

2. (See quot.)

1875 ROBINSON *Whitby Gloss* (E.D.S.) *Canter*, a timber-carrier; one who brings 'bauks' or tree-trunks from the woods to the ship-yards.

canter ('kæntə(r)), *sb.*² [f. CANT *v.*³ + -ER¹.]

1. One who uses the 'cant' of thieves, etc.; one of the 'canting crew'; a rogue, vagabond. *arch.*

1609 DEKKER *Lanth. & Candle-L.* Wks. 1885 III. 197 Stay and heare a Canter in his owne language, making Rithmes. **1610** S. R[OWLANDS] *Mart. Mark-all* E j b, Thus haue I runne ouer the Canter's Dictionary. **1630** J. TAYLOR (Water P.) *Wks.* II. 239/1 [They] gaue all their mony to the mendicanting Canters. **1652** GAULE *Magastrom.* 131 Astrologers, Soothsayers, Canters, Gypsies, Juglers. **1719** D'URFEY *Pills* III. 100 A Filcher my Brother, A Canter my Uncle. **1865** tr. *V. Hugo's Hunchback* II. vi. 76 Four or five canters..were quarrelling.

2. A talker of professional or religious cant; in 17th c. a nickname of the Puritans.

1652 EVELYN *Mem.* (1857) I. 292 On Whit-Sunday, I went to the church..and heard one of the canters. **1711** *Vind. Sacheverell* 42 The seditious Canter. **1821** *Blackw. Mag.* X. 731 The Schlegels are the great critical canters of modern Europe. **1848** MACAULAY *Hist. Eng.* I. 213 The days when he [Lauderdale] was a canter and a rebel.

canter ('kæntə(r)), *sb.*³ [cf. CANTER *v.*²] A Canterbury gallop; an easy gallop. 'The exertion is much less, the spring less distant, and the feet come to the ground in more regular succession,' than in the gallop proper (Youatt).

1755 *Connoisseur* No. 69 She never ventured beyond a canter or a hand-gallop. **1773** JOHNSON s.v. *Canterbury gallop*, The hand gallop of an ambling horse, commonly called a canter. **1831** YOUATT *Horse* (1843) 527 The canter is to the gallop very much what the walk is to the trot. **1851** LONGF. *Gold. Leg.* v, This canter over hill and glade.

b. *to win in a canter*: to distance all the other horses in a race so much that galloping is unnecessary at the end; *fig.* to come off victor with the greatest ease.

1853 LYTTON *My Novel* (Hoppe) He wins the game in a canter. **1874** *Sat. Rev.* Aug. 180 (ibid.) Hermitage won in a common canter.

2. *fig.* (cf. *run, scamper.*)

a **1864** SIR J. STEPHEN (Webster) A rapid canter in the Times over all the topics of the day. **1865** DICKENS *Mut. Fr.* xi. 86 Ma was talking then, at her usual canter. **1879** O. W. HOLMES *Motley* xvii. 118 He ever and anon relieves his prose jog trot by breaking into a canter of poetry.

†'**canter,** *sb.*⁴ *Obs. rare*⁻¹. [? ad. Sp. *cantera.*] A kind of Spanish fishing-boat.

a **1642** SIR W. MONSON *Naval Tracts* VI. (1704) 532/1 There are..employ'd out of Spain..Vessels call'd Canters, upon that Fishing. [**1867** SMYTH *Sailor's Word-bk.*, *Cantera*, a Spanish fishing-boat.]

canter, obs. var. of CANTOR.

†**canter,** *v.*¹ *Obs.* ? To chant, to intone.

1538 STARKEY *England* I. iv. (1871) 137 Thynke, yf Saynt Augustyn, Jerome, or Ambrose herd our curyouse dyscantyng and canteryng in churchys, what they wold say.

canter ('kæntə(r)), *v.*² [Shortened from CANTERBURY *v.*]

1. *intr.* Of a horse, etc.: To move in a moderate gallop, raising the two fore-feet nearly at the same time with a leap or spring.

1706 *Lond. Gaz.* No. 4247/4 Trots, Paces, and Canters very fine. **1804** G. ROSE *Diaries* (1860) II. 193 The horse, on

cantering down a..hill, came on his head. **1865** LIVINGSTONE *Zambesi* x. 212 The zebras..canter gracefully away.

2. Of the rider.

1768 STERNE *Sent. Journ.* (1778) I. 117 La Fleur..canter'd away..as..perpendicular as a prince. **1821** BYRON *Juan* IV. ciii, I canter by the spot each afternoon. **1870** E. PEACOCK *Ralf Skirl.* II. 164 He was cantering through the park.

3. *transf.* To run or move as in a canter; to move nimbly or briskly.

1761 STERNE *Tr. Shandy* (1793) IV. 157 'Tis..any thing which a man makes a shift to get astride on, to canter it away from the cares and solicitudes of life. *c* **1825** *Houlston Tracts* II. No. 38. 11 Away she canters, and tosses over and tries on before the looking-glass every article of dress.

4. *trans.* To make (a horse) go at a canter, to ride at a canter. Also *fig.*

1845 'TITMARSH' *Leg. of Rhine* xii, in *Cruikshank's Table-Bk.* 243 The knight gracefully cantering an elegant cream-coloured Arabian. **1856** R. VAUGHAN *Mystics* (1860) II. VIII. vii. 80 The islander catches..the first [pony] that comes to hand, puts on the halter, canters it his journey, and lets it go. **1930** V. WOOLF *Diary* 20 Feb. (1953) 156, I must canter my wits if I can.

5. *transf.* To impart a cantering motion to.

1821 *New Month. Mag.* II. 322 She would not be cantered in a swing set up in a kitchen-garden, because, as she whispered, the potatoes had eyes.

Canterburian (kæntə'bjʊərɪən), *a.* and *sb.* [f. CANTERBURY + -AN.] Of or pertaining to Canterbury, *esp.* to the archiepiscopal See; in the 17th c. taken as a representative of High Church Anglicanism. Hence **Canter'burianism.** So † **'Canterburiness,** mock designation of the Archbishop of Canterbury or his dignity.

1570 LEVINS *Manip.* 20 Canterburiane, *Cantuariensis.* **1660** T. FISHER *Rusticks Alarm* Wks. (1679) 216 Either Romish or Canterburian Catholicks. **1848** H. MILLER *First Impr.* xx. (1857) 351 The Canterburianism of the times of Charles the First did that hapless monarch much harm. **1588** *Marprel. Epist.* (Arb.) 15 The Pope..being far better than were John with his Canterburinesse. **1589** *Marprel. Epit.* (1843) 9, I hope his Canterburinesse will looke to this geare.

Canterbury ('kæntəbərɪ, -bərɪ), *sb.* [A city of England famous from ancient times as the see of the Archbishop and Primate of all England. The shrine of Thomas à Becket (St. Thomas of Canterbury) who was murdered in the cathedral 29 Dec., 1170, was in pre-Reformation times a favourite object of pilgrimage; and it was a company of pilgrims to this shrine that Chaucer made the narrators of his 'Canterbury Tales', to which some of the attributive uses refer.

c **1386** CHAUCER *Prol.* 16 Thanne longen folk to goon on pilgrimages. And specially from euery shires ende Of Engelond to Caunturbury they wende The hooly blisful martir for to seke That hem hath holpen whan þat they were seeke.]

A. *attrib.*

1. In phrases referring either (*a*) to the pilgrims, as ***Canterbury bells***; (*b*) to the tales told on the way (or Chaucer's work so called), as ***Canterbury tale*** or ***story***, in later times often taken as a long tedious story, a 'friar's tale', a fable, a cock-and-bull story; (*c*) or applied by the Puritans to the hierarchical position of Canterbury, as ***Canterbury trick.***

[*c* **1386** CHAUCER *Prol.* (*title*) Here bygynneth the Book of the tales of Caunterbury.] ? *a* **1550** in C. Wordsworth *Eccl. Biog.* (1818) I. 168 Pilgrimes..with the noise of their piping, and with the sound of their singing, and the jangling of their Canturburie bels. **1575** TURBERV. *Bk. Falconrie* 260 A verie olde womans fable or Cantorburie tale. **1579** FULKE *Heskins' Parl.* 422 A lewd lying counterfeter of more then Caunterburie tales. **1589** GREENE *Menaph.* Wks. 1881–3 VI. 86 Whosoeuer Samela descanted of that loue, tolde you a Canterbury tale. **1589** *Hay any Work* 1 There is a canterbury trick once to patch up an acusation with a lye or two. **1662** FULLER *Worthies* (1811) I. 527 (D.) Since that time Canterbury Tales are parallel to *Fabulæ Milesiæ*, which are characterized, *nec veræ, nec verisimiles.* **1709** STEELE *Tatler* No. 132 ¶ 10 One [Story] of a Quarter of an Hour long ..gathers Circumstances every Time he tells it, till it grows into a long Canterbury Tale of two Hours. **1737** in *N. & Q.* Ser. III. IX. 414/2 [He] would begin a long Canterbury Story of a duel he had fought. **1763** COLMAN *Deuce is in him* II. i. (D.) What, to come here with a Canterbury tale of a leg and an eye, and Heaven knows what!

2. ***Canterbury pace, rack, rate, trot, gallop,*** etc., supposed originally to designate the pace of the mounted pilgrims.

a **1636** W. SAMPSON *Vow-breaker* V. i, Have I practic'd..my smooth Ambles, and Canterbury Paces? **1675** *Charac. Fanatic* in *Harl. Misc.* VII. 637 (D.) A Canterbury rack, half pace, half gallop. **1717** E. WARD *Wks.* II. 6 With whip and spur he might beat-up Into a Canterbury tit-up. **1773** JOHNSON, *Canterbury gallop*, the hand gallop of an ambling horse, commonly called a canter; said to be derived from the monks riding to Canterbury on easy ambling horses. **1826** F. COOPER *Mohicans* ii, The most confirmed gait that he could establish, was a Canterbury gallop with the hind legs. **1830** GALT *Laurie T.* VI. vii. (1849) 280 On horseback, and off at a Canterbury trot.

3. ***Canterbury hoe*** (see quot. 1954).

a **1887** JEFFERIES *Field & Hedgerow* (1889) 79 A two-spean spud, or Canterbury hoe, with points instead of a broad blade. **1954** A. G. L. HELLYER *Encycl. Garden Work & Terms* 124/2 What is virtually a modification of the draw hoe, is a type known as the Canterbury hoe in which the blade consists of three fork-like prongs attached to the handle at right angles.

4. [Name of province in South Island, N.Z.] ***Canterbury lamb***, term used in Great Britain for lamb or mutton imported from New Zealand; in N.Z., for certain grades of such meat. Also *absol.*

1898 *N.Z. Farmer, Bee & Poultry Jrnl.* July 232/1 Does he mean to say that intrinsically as food..English mutton is worth about three times as much as prime Canterbury frozen? **1903** *Cyclopedia N.Z.* III. 80 We are basking in prosperity, now that we can turn off a large quantity of 'Prime Canterbury' from the plains. **1928** R. G. STAPLEDON *Tour Australia & N.Z.* viii. 58 A brief reference to the New Zealand 'Canterbury lamb'..may not be out of place. **1959** J. PASCOE *N.Z. Sheep-Station* 3 Every time we buy Canterbury lamb from the butcher we are reminded that the meat we are going to eat has come from a New Zealand sheep-farm. **1966** 'K. NICHOLSON' *Hook, Line & Sinker* ii. 25 We'll call at the butcher first; Len has saved a nice piece of Canterbury for us.

B. *sb.*

† 1. [From phrases in A 2.] An easy galloping pace; a hand-gallop; a CANTER. *Obs.*

1631 BRATHWAIT *Whimzies*, Hee rides altogether upon spurre..who is as familiarly acquainted with a Canterbury, as hee who makes Chaucer his author, is with his tale. **1710** SHAFTESB. *Charac.* I. iii. (1737) III. 25 The common Amble or Canterbury is not..more tiresom to a good Rider, than this See-Saw of Essay-Writers is to an able Reader. **1729** DENNIS *Pope's Dunc.* (N.) The Pegasus of Pope, like a Kentish post-horse, is always on the Canterbury.

2. A piece of furniture; a stand with light partitions to hold music-portfolios and the like.

1803 T. SHERATON *Cabinet Dict.* 127 *Canterbury*..has of late years been applied to some pieces of cabinet work, because, as the story goes, the bishop of that see first gave orders for these pieces. One piece is a small music stand... The other piece which receives this epithet, is a supper tray, made to stand by a table at supper. **1849** in SMART *Supp.* **1857** J. H. WALSH *Dom. Econ.* 202 Rosewood or mahogany plain Canterbury with drawer. **1880** *Argosy* XXX. 9 Look in the canterbury and find me that piece by Schubert. **1883** MISS BRADDON *Gold. Calf* i. 10 In an ancient canterbury under the ancient piano. **1904** A. BENNETT *Great Man* i. 2 The Canterbury with its spiral columns. **1962** *Times* 17 Nov. 11/7 In England the supper canterbury was essentially a specialized form of dumb waiter.

† **'canterbury,** *v. Obs. rare*$^{-1}$. [f. prec. sb.] *intr.* To canter.

1673 MARVELL *Reh. Transp.* II. 402 The Prelates trooping it up and down on the publick Post-horses and canterburing from Synod..to Synod.

Canterbury bell(s. [See BELL *sb.*^{1} 4; app. the full name was fancifully associated with the small bells worn on their horses by the pilgrims in pre-Reformation times, and often mentioned in the 16th c. (See Britten and Holland.)]

A flowering plant of the genus *Campanula*; originally applied to the native species *C. Trachelium*, the Nettle-leaved Bellflower or Throatwort; but in later times erroneously transferred to the cultivated exotic *C. Medium*, called in the 16th c. Coventry Bells or Marian's Violet. More loosely, the name has been applied to the Giant Bell-flower, *C. latifolia*, and perhaps to other species. (Until the present cent. always *bells.*)

1578 LYTE *Dodoens* II. xx. 170 Of Canterbury Belles or Haskewurte. *Ibid.* 172 In English they be called Belfloures, and of some Canterbury Belles. **1597** GERARD *Herbal* 163 (Britten & Holl 87) Of some about London Canterbury bels, but improperly, for that there is another kind of bell flower growing in Kent, about Canterbury, which may more fitly be called Canterburie bels, bicause they grow there more plentifully than in any other countrie. **1688** R. HOLME *Armoury* II. iv. §60 The Canterbury Bells have large rough leaves like Nettles. **1741** *Compl. Fam.-Piece* II. iii. 357 Towards the End of this Month, sow..Canterbury-bells. **1821** CLARE *Vill. Minstr.* II. 134 The wild stalking canterbury bell, By hedge-row side. **1861** MISS PRATT *Flower. Pl.* III. 339 Giant Bell-flower..often called Canterbury-bell. **1882** *Garden* 1 July 12/2 A collection of Canterbury Bells.

¶ Formerly Lady's Smock, *Cardamine pratensis.*

1597 GERARD *Herbal* 203 They are commonly called in Latine, Flos Cuculi; in English Cuckowe flowers; in Northfolke Caunterburie bels; at the Namptwich in Cheshire, where I had my beginning, Ladie Smocks.

canterer ('kæntərə(r)). A steed or rider that canters.

1820 *Blackw. Mag.* VII. 521 Her husband was..one of the gayest sparrers, swimmers..canterers, drinkers, revellers.

'cantering, *vbl. sb.* The action of the vb. CANTER.

1827 LYTTON *Pelham* xlii. (L.) For the rest, he loved trotting better than cantering.

attrib. **1867** LADY HERBERT *Cradle L.* vii. 167 A better track with occasional cantering ground.

'cantering, *ppl. a.* That canters.

1793 LD. AUCKLAND *Corr.* (1862) III. 81 A little cantering horse. **1846** PRESCOTT *Ferd. & Is.* I. i. 110 Cantering dactylic measure.

cantharic (kæn'θærɪk), *a.* [f. CANTHAR-IDES + -IC.] In ***cantharic acid***, a substance of the same composition as cantharidin (*Syd. Soc. Lex.*).

So **can'tharidal** *a. Med.*, pertaining to, made with, or caused by cantharides. **can'tharidate** *sb.*, a salt of cantharidic acid. **can'tharidate** *v.*, to impregnate or treat with cantharides. **cantha'ridian, -i'dean,** of the nature of, or composed of, cantharides. **cantha'ridic** *a.*, of the nature of cantharides, as in ***cantharidic acid***, a development of cantharidin by the absorption of one equivalent of water. **can'tharidin,** the vesicating principle of cantharides; also called ***canthari'dinic acid.*** **can'tharidism,** the poisonous action of cantharides. **can'tharidize** *v.*, to affect or treat with cantharides (esp. as an aphrodisiac); also *fig.*

1871 NAPHEYS *Prev. & Cure Dis.* II. iv. 534 Cantharidal collodion can be applied to the skin. **1875** H. WOOD *Therap.* (1879) 563 A constant symptom in cantharidal poisoning. **1881** *Syd. Soc. Lex.* s.v., Cantharidate of potash. **1786** BURNS *Holy Fair* xiii, O how they fire the heart devout, Like cantharidian plasters. **1873** MORLEY *Rousseau* II. 29 He writes..like a pedagogue infected by some cantharidean philter. **1833** CARLYLE *Misc.* (1857) III. 268 His love-philtres, his cantharidic wine of Egypt. **1877** WATTS *Fownes' Chem.* II. 608 Heated with alkalis it [cantharidin] dissolves, forming salts of cantharidic acid. **1819** CHILDREN *Chem. Anal.* 309 Cantharadin has the form of small crystalline plates with a shining micaceous appearance. **1861** HULME tr. *Moquin-Tandon* II. III. iii. 131 Cantharidin..taken internally, is a virulent poison. **1812** SOUTHEY *Omniana* II. 223 He may..very probably have cantharidized it [the language of a book] to the taste of the French court. **1832** MITFORD *Parnell's Poems* (Aldine ed.) *Life* 37 *note*, He has cantharadised the story.

‖ **cantharides** (kæn'θærɪdiːz), *sb. pl.* Also 6 **canterides,** 5–7 **cantarides,** 9 **cantharids.** Rarely in sing. 5 **cantharide.** [L.; pl. of *cantharis*, a. Gr. κανθαρίς blister-fly.]

1. (sing. *Cantharis* in *Entom.*) A genus of coleopterous insects of the family Trachelidæ; the officinal species (*C. vesicatoria* or Spanish Fly) has golden-green elytra. Early writers appear to have applied the name to Aphides.

1398 TREVISA *Barth. De P.R.* XVII. lxv. (1495) 642 Grene flyes brede in corne that ben callyd Ca[n]tarides. *c* **1420** *Pallad. on Husb.* I. 865 The cantharide in roses that we se. **1567** MAPLET *Gr. Forest* 112 One kind..is in colour greene: in humor or iuice verie poysonous, and is called Cantharis. **1593** NASHE *Christ's T.* 73 a, The greene venemous flies Cantharides. *a* **1625** COPE in Gutch *Coll. Cur.* I. 121 The Cantharides ever have, and will crop the fairest flowers. **1878** DOWDEN *Stud. Lit.* 418 The cantharides vibrating in the transparent air.

2. The pharmacopœial name of the dried beetle *Cantharis vesicatoria* or Spanish Fly. Used externally as a rubefacient and vesicant; internally as a diuretic and stimulant to the genito-urinary organs, etc. Formerly considered an aphrodisiac.

1541 R. COPLAND *Guydon's Quest. Chirurg.*, And make no scarres, but blysters as canterides. **1579** LANGHAM *Gard. Health* (1633) 531 Apply it on the bare skinne, to make blisters and holes, euen as Cantarides doth. **1611** BEAUM. & FL. *Philaster* IV. i, Before, she was common talk; now, none dare say, cantharides can stir her. **1831** YOUATT *Horse* xii. (1847) 252 Some stimulating liniment..consisting of turpentine or tincture of cantharides. **1847** EMERSON *Poems, Mithridates* Wks. (Bohn) I. 410 Give me agates for my meat; Give me cantharids to eat.

fig. **1598** E. GILPIN *Skial.* (1878) 32 They are Philosphicke true Cantharides To vanities dead flesh. **1601** B. JONSON *Poetast.* V. i, I, you whoreson cantharides! was it I? **1790** BURKE *Fr. Rev.* 93 Swallowing down repeated provocatives of cantharides to our love of liberty.

cantharus, kantharos ('kænθərəs). Pl. **canthari, kantharoi.** Also **cantharos.** [L. *cantharus*, Gr. κάνθαρος.]

1. *Antiq.* A large, two-handled drinking-cup.

1853 *Dict. Archit.*, *Cantharus*, the name of a peculiarly shaped drinking vessel particularly consecrated to the personifications of Bacchus. **1875** E. METEYARD *Wedgwood Handbk.* 393 Cantharos. **1885** *Encycl. Brit.* XIX. 180/1 Silver Cantharus from Rhodes, with gold mounts. **1909** *Daily Chron.* 18 Mar. 3/1 Twenty-six drinking cups, one kantharos. **1957** CHILDE *Dawn Europ. Civilization* (ed. 6) ii. 33 A two-handled tankard or cantharos with quatrefoil lip.

2. A fountain or laver placed in the courtyard of an ancient church for the use of worshippers.

1842 GWILT *Archit.* Gloss. 943. **1902** *Encycl. Brit.* XXXII. 626/2 A court enclosed the whole; near the porch was a laver (*cantharus*) for the ablutions of intending worshippers.

cantho-: see CANTHUS.

cant-hook ('kænthʊk). [f. CANT *v.*^{2} + HOOK.]

† 1. *pl. north. dial.* 'The fingers' (Halliwell).

2. *U.S.* A form of lever for canting over or turning timber, etc., consisting of a wooden bar with an iron catch or hooked arm near its lower end which passes over the log, grips it, and so affords a hold by which it may be pulled over; called also *cant-dog.*

a 1848 in BARTLETT *Dict. Amer.* 1883 *Harper's Mag.* Jan. 206/2 Chinese laborers easily roll them down upon the cars, aiding themselves with cant-hooks, jack-screws.

canthrip, dial. var. of CANTRIP.

‖**canthus** ('kænθəs). *Phys.* [L.; a. Gr. κανθός corner of the eye.] The outer or inner angle or corner of the eye, where the two lids meet. Hence, from combining form *canth(o-*, **can'thectomy** (*Surg.*), [Gr. ἐκτομή cutting out], 'excision or incision of either canthus' (*Syd. Soc. Lex.*). **can'thitis**, inflammation of the canthus. **cantho'plastic**, of or pertaining to **'canthoplasty** [Gr. -πλαστία moulding], the operation of enlarging the palpebral aperture when too small. **can'thorrhaphy** [Gr. -ῥαφία stitching], the operation of sewing up the canthus.

1646 SIR T. BROWNE *Pseud. Ep.* 174 They open at the inward canthus or greater angle of the eye. **1727–51** CHAMBERS *Cycl.* s.v., That corner next the nose, is called the great, inner, and domestic canthus. **1799** J. ROBERTSON *Agric. Perth* 316 By opening the vein below the canthus. **1874** COUES *Birds N.W.* 608 A conspicuous spot just at the anterior canthus of the eye. **1860** MAYNE *Exp. Lex.*, *Canthoplastic*, belonging to the operation of canthoplasty.

†**'cantic, -ick**, *sb. Obs.* [a. F. *cantique*, ad. L. *canticum*: see CANTICA] A song, a canticle.

1483 CAXTON *Gold. Leg.* 27 b/1 It is said in the Cantykes Canticorum ii Aryse thou my spouse, etc. **1613** R. C. *Table Alph.* (ed. 3), *Canticke*, a song. **1653** URQUHART *Rabelais* I. xxiii, Canticks, made in praise of the divine bounty. **1669** GALE *Crt. Gentiles* I. III. i. 2 We find not..in the Psalter, or Lamentations any Cantic bound up by Laws of Metre. [**1867** *Cornh. Mag.* 473 A cantique by the village-girls.]

cantic ('kæntɪk), *a.* [f. CANT *sb.*[1], or its Romanic cognates + -IC.] *cantic quoins* (coins): 'short three-edged pieces of wood to steady casks from labouring against each other' (Smyth *Sailor's Word-bk.*). Cf. also CANTLING 2.

1727–51 CHAMBERS *Cycl.* s.v. *Quoin*, Cantic Quoins are short, three legged [? edged] quoins, put between casks to keep them steady. **1753** —— *Supp.*, *Canting coins*, in ship building, the same as cantic coins.

‖**'Cantica.** *Obs.* [L.; pl. of *canticum* song; f. *canĕre*, *cant-* to sing.] The Song of Songs (in the Vulg. *Canticum Canticorum*). Cf. *Canticles*.

a **1300** *Cursor M.* 8472 Þe quilk man clepes cantica. **1563** 39 *Articles* vi, Cantica, or Songs of Solomon. **1577** tr. *Bullinger's Decades* (1592) 12 Ecclesiastes, and Cantica.

canticle ('kæntɪk(ə)l). Also 6 *Sc.* cantikil. [ad. L. *canticulum* dim. *canticum* song (CANTICA).]

1. A song, properly a little song; a hymn.

c **1250** *Gen. & Ex.* 4124 He [Moses]..wrot an canticle **1552** ABP. HAMILTON *Catech.* (1884) 33 In the Cantikil of Moyses. *c* **1705** POPE *Jan. & May* 524 Thus his morning canticle he sung, 'Awake, my love,' etc. **1870** LOWELL *Among my Bks.* Ser. I. (1873) 201 Religious canticles stimulant of zeal. **1881** J. C. SHAIRP in *Academy* 12 Feb. 112 The Queen's Wake contains several ballads which exhibit.. much more of his power than this tiny little canticle.

b. *spec.* One of the hymns (mostly taken from the Scriptures) used in the public services of the Church. (In the English Prayer-Book applied only to the *Benedicite*; but often used also of the *Benedictus*, *Jubilate*, *Magnificat*, *Cantate*, *Nunc Dimittis*, and *Deus misereatur*, and sometimes of the *Te Deum*.)

1625 BACON *Death, Ess.* (Arb.) 7 The sweetest Canticle is, Nunc dimittis. **1853** ROBERTSON *Serm.* Ser. III. iv. (1872) 55 The canticle which belongs to our morning service. **1874** H. REYNOLDS *John Baptist* ii. 72 The evangelic canticles contained in this chapter. **1880** T. HELMORE in Grove *Dict. Mus.* I. 336 The short melodies sung to the psalms and canticles in the English Church.

c. *transf.*

1851 LONGF. *Gold. Leg.* III. *Nativity* 5 Where robins chant their Litanies, And canticles of joy. **1863** KINGLAKE *Crimea* (1877) II. vii. 56 The time-honoured canticles of a doctrine already discarded.

2. *pl.* A name for the Song of Solomon.

1526 *Pilgr. Perf.* (W. de W. 1531) 284 b, Rede the canticles of Salomon. **1712** TICKELL *Spect.* No. 410 ¶5 A Translation of one of the Chapters in the Canticles into English Verse. **1845** J. H. NEWMAN *Ess. Developm.* v. (L.) The Canticles must be interpreted literally; and then it was..a necessary step, to exclude the book from the canon.

†**3.** A canto of a poem. *Obs.*

1596 SPENSER *F.Q.* IV. v. 46 The end whereof..Shall for another canticle be spared. **1647** H. MORE *Song of Soul* III. III. l, So large matter..for a fresh Canticle more fit.

b. A small canto. (*humorous.*)

1819 BYRON *Let. to Murray* 6 Apr., You shan't make *canticles* of my cantos.

‖**cantiga** (kæn'tiːgə). [Sp. and Pg.: cf. CANTICA.] A Spanish or Portuguese poem or folksong.

1915 A. F. G. BELL in *Mod. Lang. Rev.* X. 338 Written in the Galician—Portuguese language..there is not a page of the *Cantigas* which does not throw some curious light on the life of the thirteenth [century]... Some of these poems express beautiful and widely-extended legends. **1959** *Chambers's Encycl.* III. 56/2 *Cantiga* or *cantar* was the designation of all forms of poetry...*cantiga de amor*.. *cantiga de amigo*..*cantiga de escárneo* (satirical). The religious songs are represented by the *Cantigas de Santa Maria.* **1963** *Times* 18 May 11/3 The single-voiced *cantigas* of Alfonso the Wise (1221–1284), who turned the art of the *trobadors* to spiritual ends.

‖**canti'lena.** *Mus.* [It. or Lat.: see next.]

a. The plain-song or *canto-fermo* in old church music; the melody or 'air' in any composition, now usually the highest part. Also *attrib.* **b.** A ballad.

1740 GRASSINEAU *Mus. Dict.* 19 *Cantilenæ* are no more than songs, and signifies in general pieces of melody well composed. **1775** 'J. COLLIER' *Mus. Trav.* (ed. 3) 97 My *cantilena* was often rude. *a* **1789** BURNEY *Hist. Mus.* III. ii 165 The cantilena or principal melody was not given as it is by modern composers to the soprano or highest part. **1832** C. MACFARLANE *Lives Banditti* I. i. 38 They are sung in a sort of recitative, monotonous *cantilena* style. **1867** MACFARREN *Harmony* I. 20 The people may be said to make their cantilenas in the very act of singing them. **1964** *Listener* 8 Oct. 558/1 A singer's cantilena style.

‖**canti'lene.** *Obs.* (exc. as Fr.). [a. F. *cantilène*, ad. L. *cantilēna* a song, an old song, gossip, etc., f. *cantillāre*: see CANTILLATE.]

†**1.** An old song, silly prattle; idle tale, trick.

1535 LYNDESAY *Satyre* 4180, I knaw fals Schiphirds fyftie fidder,—War thair canteleinis kend. **1656** BLOUNT *Glossogr.*, *Cantilene*, a verse, a common speech or tale, a song.

2. A song, a melody.

1635 SWAN *Spec. M.* vii. §3 (1643) 348 They [birds] chaunt her [Aurora] out a mirthfull cantilene.

cantilever ('kæntɪliːvə(r)). Also 7 candi-, 7–9 canti-, 8–9 cantaliver, 8 cantaliever, 8–9 cantalever. [The spelling *candilever* found in the 17th c. (if of any authority) compared with the Sp. '*can debaxo de la viga*, mutilus super quem capita trabium imponuntur, a corbel in masonry' (Minsheu *Voc. Hisp.* 1617), naturally suggests some such Sp. phrase as *can de llevar*, 'modillion for carrying or bearing': but of this there is actually no trace. On the other hand the name 'flying lever bridge' used in *A treatise on Bridge-building* by T. Pope, New York, 1811, for what is now called a 'cantilever bridge', and the term 'framed lever' used for *cantilever* in Tredgold's *Carpentry* 1828, indicate that *lever* in its ordinary mechanical sense, is part of the word. For the first part we then think of CANT *sb.*[1], but as to the meaning in which that word might be here used, or the nature of the combination in *canti-lever* or *canta-lever*, no satisfactory suggestion can be offered. (Smyth *Sailor's Word-bk.*, has *canting-livre* = console-bracket.)]

1. *Arch.* A kind of bracket or support of stone, wood, or iron, whose length is many times its breadth and more than twice its depth, which projects from the wall of a building for the support of a balcony, the upper members of a cornice, eaves of a house, etc.; also *attrib.*, as in ***cantilever cornice, principle.***

1667 PRIMATT *City & C. Build.* 71 For Candilivers about eighteen inches deep and eight inches broad, handsomly carved with flowers. **1740** PINEDA *Span.-Eng. Dict.*, *Can*, a dog..In architecture, the end of timber or stone jutting out of a wall, on which in old buildings the beams used to rest, called Cantilevers. **1759** B. MARTIN *Nat. Hist. Eng.* I. 311 Wainscot Galleries round it, sustained by Cantilevers. **1869** *Latest News* 26 Sept. 14 A plan..for widening London Bridge by..forming footways upon cantilevers and brackets external to the road. **1880** *Contemp. Rev.* Mar. 421 Each architrave, each niche within the wall, Each cantilever, moulding, tooth or ball. **1884** *Pall Mall G.* 5 Dec. 11/2 The cantilever principle in its first development.

2. In *Bridge-building.* A projecting support or arm of great length, two of which, stretching out from adjacent piers, are used to support a girder which unites them and completes the span; also *attrib.*, as in ***cantilever arm, bridge***, etc.

[**1811** T. POPE *Treatise on Bridge-building* (N. York) *frontisp.* Flying lever bridge.] **1850** E. CLARK *Britannia & Conway Bridges* I. 276 The semi-beam or cantilever has to support half the weight of the beam suspended from its extremity [*At* p. 44 'bracket arch' *is used*]. **1867** B. BAKER in *Engineering* III. 338 (*Long Span-Bridges* The cantilever girder of uniform depth in appearance is identical with the independent girder. **1882** *American* IV. 70 A combination of two cantilevers with a central girder. **1887** *Hazell's Ann. Cycl.* 174/2 The main feature [of the Forth Bridge] will be the extraordinary spans, for a rigid structure, of a third of a mile in length, each of which is made by two cantilevers of 680 feet long, united by 350 feet of girder.

'cantilevered, *ppl. a.* [f. CANTILEVER + -ED[2].] Projecting like a cantilever; supported by a cantilever.

1910 H. BECHER *Reinforced Concrete* 229/1 Cantilevered beam. **1943** J. S. HUXLEY *TVA* xi. 85 The cantilevered overhead gantry crane. **1962** E. GODFREY *Retail Selling & Organ.* ii. 10 New stores..have made extensive use of pre-stressed concrete and cantilevered construction.

cantilie, var. of CANTILY *adv.*

cantillate ('kæntɪleɪt), *v.* [f. L. *cantillāt-* ppl. stem of *cantillā-re* 'to sing low, to hum' (Lewis and Short), f. *cantāre* to sing: see -ATE[3].]

To chant; to recite with musical tones: *spec.* applied to the intoning in Jewish synagogues.

1864 R. LEE *Reform Ch. Scotl.*, Singing can hardly be said to be used..in the Synagogues. Their cantillating much more resembles intoning. **1902** [See CANTILATIONARY *a.*].

cantillation (kæntɪ'leɪʃən). Also canti'lation. [f. prec: see -ATION.] Chanting, intoning, musical recitation; *spec.* that used in Jewish synagogues.

1864 ENGEL *Mus. Anc. Nat.* 328 The kind of singing which musicians call cantillation, and which may be heard in every synagogue. **1879** STAINER *Music of Bible* 158 The Arabs..recite the Koran to a sort of irregular chant or cantillation. **1901** W. B. YEATS *Let.* 16 Mar. (1954) IV. 348 Mr. Runciman said that I called a method of speaking verse ..'Cantilation'... You will perhaps permit me to say that Mr. Runciman invented the word. I never used it, and I don't mean to. **1919** E. POUND *Quia Pauper Amavi* 39 Up, up my soul, from your lowly cantilation.

Hence **canti'lationary** *a.*

1902 G. B. SHAW *Let.* 6 June in C. Bax *Farr, Shaw & Yeats* (1941) 19, I should do no good by entering into cantilationary polemics... Half the curates in the kingdom cantilate like mad all the time.

cantily ('kæntɪlɪ), *adv. Sc.* [f. CANTY + -LY[2].] In a canty manner, cheerfully, blithely, cheerily.

1721 RAMSAY *Addr. Town Council Edinb.*, And cantily Your supplicant shall sing. **1826** J. WILSON *Noct. Ambr.* Wks. 1855 I. 200 A' the bit bonny burdies are singing sae cantily.

‖**cantina** (kæn'tiːnə). [Sp. and It.] **a.** A (Spanish) canteen (sense 1, 1 b). **b.** A bar-room, a saloon (in Central and South America and south-west U.S.). **c.** An (Italian) wineshop.

1892 *Dialect Notes* I. v. 245 *Cantina*: bar-room; of frequent use [in Texas]. Often found on signs of Mexican bar-rooms. **1925** HEMINGWAY *In our Time* (1926) xi. 143 At the cantina near the bridge they trusted him for three more grappas. **1939** G. GREENE *Lawless Roads* i. 36 Life..went on behind the swing doors of the cantinas and billiard saloons. **1959** *Listener* 15 Jan. 125/3 When a station was reached the passengers swarmed down to the platform and round the tiny *cantina.* **1969** A. MARIN *Rise with Wind* xv. 190 Clay found a cantina on a side street. **1970** *Daily Tel.* Mag. 3 Apr. 43/1 Every hotel, every restaurant, every cantina paid him [*sc.* a Cuban chauffeur] his commission.

cantine, obs. form of CANTEEN.

cantiness ('kæntɪnɪs). *Sc.* [f. CANTY *a.* + -NESS] The quality of being canty; cheerfulness.

canting ('kæntɪŋ), *vbl. sb.*[1] [f. CANT *v.*[2] + -ING[1].] The action of the vb. CANT; tilting, sloping, turning over or about. **a.** *trans.* **b.** *intr.*

1769 FALCONER *Dict. Marine* (1789), *Canting*..the act of turning any thing about. *c* **1850** *Rudim. Navig.* (Weale) 105 *Canting*, the act of turning anything completely over, so that the under surface shall lie upwards. **1865** *Specif. Plimpton's Patent* No. 2190 These springs..control the turning, tilting, or canting of the stock or foot stand [of the roller skate]. **1865** CARLYLE *Fredk. Gt.* III. x. v. 262 Friedrich Wilhelm is amazed at these sudden cantings of Fortune's wheel.

†**c.** (See quot.) *Obs.*

1674 N. FAIRFAX *Bulk & Selv.* 102 It cannot well be call'd motion..But 'tis somewhat else that we have no right name for, (unless skipping or canting may in a low sort speak it).

'canting, *vbl. sb.*[2] [f. CANT *v.*[3] + -ING[1].]

1. The practice of using thieves' cant; the secret language or jargon used by thieves, professional beggars, etc.; see CANT *sb.*[3] 4 a.

1567 HARMAN *Caveat* (1869) 23 Their languag—which they term peddelars Frenche or Canting—began but within these xxx. yeeres. **1577** HARRISON *England* II. x. (1877) I. 218 They [beggers] haue devised a language among themselues, which they name 'canting'; but other 'pedlers Frenche', a speach compact thirtie yeares. **1641** BROME *Jov. Crew* II. Wks. 1873 III. 392, I understand their canting. **1670** COTTON *Espernon* II. VII. 327 Le Plessis in the Canting of that Cypher was call'd Floze. **1690** B. E. *Dict. Cant. Crew*, *Canting*, the Cypher or Mysterious Language, of Rogues, Gypsies, Beggers, Thieves, etc. **1725** in *New Cant. Dict.*

2. The use of the special phraseology of a particular class or subject (always *contemptuous*); jargon, gibberish; see CANT *sb.*[3] 4 b.

1625 B. JONSON *Staple of N.* IV. iv, *Pyc.* She bears, Argent, three Leeks vert, In Canton Or, and tassel'd of the first. *Pen. Can.* Is not this Canting? **1651** HOBBES *Leviath.* 21 Hypostatical, transubstantiate, consubstantiate..and the like canting of Schoolemen. **1693** *Phil. Trans.* XVII. 799 Nothing but Canting, and a Jargon of Scraps.

attrib. **1812** D'ISRAELI *Calam. Auth.* (1867) 146 The canting dictionary of criticism.

3. Unreal or affected use of language; *spec.* the formal use of religious or pietistic phrases; hypocritical talk; see CANT *sb.*[3], 5 b, 6. In 17th c. applied in ridicule to the preaching of Presbyterians and Puritans; hence ***canting coat***, the Geneva gown, or coat of the Puritan minister.

1659 *Character Engl.* in *Harl. Misc.* X. 191 [The Presbyterians]..make an insipid, tedious, and immethodical prayer, in phrases and a tone so affected and mysterious that they give it the name of canting: a term by which they do usually express the gibberish of beggars and vagabonds. **1687** DRYDEN *Hind & P.* III. 232 Quit the Cassock for the Canting-coat. **1698** NORRIS *Pract. Disc.* 190 Canting I call using Words without any real Sense or Notion under them. **1722** SEWEL *Hist. Quakers* (1795) II. VII. 23 *Judge.* Leave your canting. **1771** SMOLLETT *Humph. Cl.* (1815) 180 Here has been nothing but canting and praying since the fellow entered the place. **1809** SYD. SMITH *Wks.* (1867) I. 141 They hate canting and hypocrisy.

canting ('kæntɪŋ), *vbl. sb.*[3] *north. dial.* [f. CANT *v.*[4] + -ING[1].] Sale by auction.

1651 *Newsletter* 22 May in '*Milton' State Papers* (1743) 68 The Venetians made lately an edict that they should sell all the offices within the City, by way of cantinge, to rayse monies. **1691** RAY *N.C. Wds.*, Canting, *auctio.* **1825** BROCKETT *N. Country Gloss.* 37 *Canting*, a sale by auction, proclaimed publicly on the spot where it is to take place. **1875** ROBINSON *Whitby Gloss.* (E.D.S.) s.v., 'We will call a canting,' hold a sale. 'A cannle-canting' [= sale by inch of candle].

canting, *vbl. sb.*[4]: see CANT *v.*[5]

'canting, *ppl. a.*[1] [f. CANT *v.*[2] + -ING[2].]

1. That cants, tilts, or turns over; that stands or lies a-tilt; slanting, sloping.

1877 E. PEACOCK *N.-W. Linc. Gloss.*, *Canting*, sloping on a level. **1880** *Daily News* 18 Sept. 5/3 A Martin's self-canting anchor.

2. canting quoin, coin: see quot. and cf. CANTIC *quoin*. *canting-livre*: see CANTILEVER.

1626 CAPT. SMITH *Accid. Yng. Seamen* 13 Ballast, kintlage, canting coynes, standing coynes. **1730–6** BAILEY, *Canting-coins*, [in a Ship] are small, short pieces of wood cut with a sharp ridge to lie between the casks, and prevent them from rolling one against another.

'canting, *ppl. a.*[2] [f. CANT *v.*[3] + -ING[2].] That cants or uses cant.

1. Speaking in a sing-song tone; whining.

1625 B. JONSON *Staple of N.* I. v, An old Canting Beggar. **1748** DODSLEY *Preceptor* (1763) I. Introd. 37 Some have a singing or canting voice. **1841** BORROW *Zincali* I. iv. II. 278 The whining, canting tones peculiar to the gypsies.

2. Speaking the dialect of vagabonds, etc.; of the nature of, or belonging to, this dialect; see CANT *sb.*[3] 4 e. (Blending with *vbl. sb.* used *attrib.*)

1592 *Groundwork Coney-catch.* 99 The manner of their canting speech. **1620** MELTON *Astrolog.* 15 The Gypsies Canting Tongue. **1690** B. E. *Dict. Cant. Crew*, *Canting Crew*, Beggers, Gypsies. **1710** PALMER *Proverbs* 197 A canting catch that common rogues make use of.

3. Of, pertaining to, or using the phraseology or jargon of a special class or subject.

1629 MASSINGER *Picture* II. ii, This is no canting language Taught in your academy. *a* **1659** OSBORN *Observ. Turks* 341 The custom of Universitie requires..knowledge in the Arts so called, and a nimble mouthing of canting terms. *a* **1684** ROSCOMMON *Ghost Old Ho. Commons* (R.) While I..took for oracles that canting tribe [lawyers]. **1704** J. HARRIS *Lex. Techn.*, *Alkahest*, one of the Canting Terms of the Alchymists.

4. Given to using religious or pietistic language formally or affectedly; hypocritical; of, or belonging to, such phrases or pretensions.

1663 *Flagellum or O. Cromwell* 91 A letter..fraught with hypocritical canting expressions. **1703** DE FOE *Short Way w. Dissenters* Misc. 420 You..have set up your Canting Synagogues at our Church-Doors. **1781** COWPER *Truth* 233 On holy ground Sometimes a canting hypocrite is found. **1864** BURTON *Scot Abr.* I. v. 249 A clamorous quack or canting fanatic.

5. *Her.* **canting arms**: = *allusive arms* (see ALLUSIVE I b). So **canting heraldry, herald, coat.**

1727–51 CHAMBERS *Cycl.* s.v. *Arms*, Canting Arms are those wherein the figures bear an allusion to the name of the family. **1814** SCOTT *Wav.* xiv, Canting heraldry. **1830** —— *Monast.* xxxiv, A device of a punning or canting herald. **1852** MISS YONGE *Cameos* (1877) IV. iii. 38 Boleyn—or Bullen—had the canting arms of a black bull's head. **1864** SIR F. PALGRAVE *Norm. & Eng.* III. 30 His descendants gave a very clever canting coat, a bridge crossing a conventional similitude of water.

Hence **'cantingly** *adv.*, **'cantingness**.

1695 *Whether Preserv. Protest. Relig. Motive of Revol.* 4 Sycophant Divines..cantingly blow us into Triumphs of Thankfulness and Joy. **1740** *Trial Mr. Whitfield's Spirit* 40 (R.) In a suffering hour, as he [Whitfield] cantingly expresses it. **1840** HOOK in *New Monthly Mag.* LX. 429 To moralize, not tediously, boringly, or cantingly.

‖**cantinier.** [Fr.; f. *cantine* CANTEEN.] A canteen-keeper. (The feminine in F. is *cantinière*.)

1721 *Lond. Gaz.* No. 6001/3 The Cantinier acquainted him that neither Mr. Knight nor the Serjeant..were in his Lodgings.

cantino (kæn'tiːnəʊ). [It.] The treble string of a violin or similar instrument.

1876 in STAINER & BARRETT *Dict. Mus. Terms.* **1944** W. APEL *Harvard Dict. Mus.* 117/1 *Cantino*, the highest string of lutes, viols, etc.

†**'cantion.** *Obs.* [ad. L. *cantiōn-em* singing, incantation, f. *cant-* ppl. stem of *canĕre* to sing.]

1. A song.

1579 E. K. *Spenser's Sheph. Cal.*, *Oct.* Gloss., Singing a Cantion of Colins making. *c* **1660** WHARTON *Fasts & Fest.* Wks. (1683) 17 The Ecclesiastical Cantion thereon [Quinquagesima] used, taken from Psalm 30.

2. An incantation, charm.

1656 BLOUNT *Glossogr.*, *Cantion*, a song or enchantment, a sorcery or charm. **1678** CUDWORTH *Intell. Syst.* I. iv. 349 The Arcane Cantion..harps much upon this Point.

'cantish, *a. rare*[−1]. [f. CANT *sb.*[3] + -ISH[1].] Savouring of cant.

1880 GRANT WHITE *Every-Day Eng.* 461 The phrenological use of the word is..if not cant, at least cantish.

cantitate, *v. nonce-wd.* [f. L. *cantitāt-* ppl. stem of *cantitāre*, freq. of *cantāre* to sing.] *intr.* To sing as a bird. (Used contemptuously.)

1830 *Fraser's Mag.* I. 341 To play the cantitating gander to his wise group of admirers.

'cantity. *nonce-wd.* [f. CANT *sb.* [3] + -ITY.] Canting quality; cant.

1850 CARLYLE *Latter-day Pamph.* viii. 52 From the chair of verity this, whatever chairs be chairs of cantity.

cantle ('kænt(ə)l), *sb.* Forms: 4–9 **cantel**, 5–7 **cantell**, 6– **cantle**; also 4–5 **kantel, -tell**, 5 **cantelle, -tylle, chantel**, 6 **cantil**, 7 **kantle**. [a. ONF. *cantel* (in Central OF. *chantel*, now *chanteau*) = Pr. *cantel*, med.L. *cantell-us*, dim. of *cant*, *canto*, *cantus* corner. (Du. *kant* has, among other senses, that of 'piece' or 'cantle' of bread.)]

†**1.** A nook or corner; a corner-piece. *Obs.*

c **1350** *Magdalena* 383 in *Altengl. Leg.* (Horstmann) Opon þe heiȝe hurst in a grene cantel. ? *a* **1400** *Morte Arth.* 4232 The kyng with Calaburne knyghtly hym strykes The cantelle of þe clere schelde he kerfes in sondyre. *c* **1420** *Anturs of Arth.* xli, He keruet of the cantel, that couurt the knyȝte, Thro his shild and his shildur. **1575** in *Laneham's Let.* (1871) 42 A rich skarlet mantell, With a-leauen kings beards bordred aboout..and yet in a cantell lz leaft a place, the twelth to make oout. **1605** VERSTEGAN *Dec. Intell.* v. (1628) 150 A nooke or corner being in our ancient language called a kant, or cantell.

†**b.** A projecting corner or angle of land. *Obs.*

1583 STANYHURST *Æneis* III. (Arb.) 86 A cantel of Italye neereth. **1599** HAKLUYT *Voy.* II. 87 Constrained to leave the sayd plaine, save a cantell that was toward the sea. **1610** HOLLAND *Camden's Brit.* I. 601 It runneth far into the sea with a long cantle or Promontory. **1692** LUTTRELL *Brief Rel.* (1857) II. 613 A road to be made..crosse a cantell of land.

†**2.** A corner or other portion cut or sliced off; a shiver, a slice. *Obs.*

c **1400** *Melayne* 1032 Thay hewe theire scheldes to thaire handis In cantells hyngand by. *c* **1430** *Syr Gener.* 5934 Of his sheld floȝ of a grete cantel. **1470–85** MALORY *Arthur* I. xvi, But the stroke of kynge Ban felle doune and carfe a cantel of the sheld. **1530** PALSGR. 202/2 Cantell or shyver, *chanteau.* **1600** FAIRFAX *Tasso* VI. xlviii. 103 Their armours forged were of metalle fraile, On euery side, thereof huge cantels flies. **1627** DRAYTON *Agincourt* (1631) 58 The English..cut into Cantles all that them withstood.

3. A section, or segment, cut out of anything.

c **1440** *Promp. Parv.* 60 Cantel, of what euer hyt be, *quadra, minutal.* **1574** HELLOWES *Gueuara's Ep.* (1577) 12 The vniuersall earth, which..by the ambition of men hath bene diuided into cantels. **1596** SHAKS. *1 Hen. IV*, III. i, See, how this Riuer..cuts me from the best of all my Lands, A huge halfe Moone, a monstrous Cantle out. **1653** H. COGAN *Diod. Sic.* 119 Those great cantles of the Marble, which..they have hewed and cut off from the Quarry. **1823** LAMB *Last Ess. Elia, Superan. Man* 441 The huge cantle which it used to seem to cut out of the holiday. **1871** M. COLLINS *Mrq. & Merch.* I. i. 8 It has always cut an awkward cantle out of my property.

b. A thick slice or 'cut' of bread, cheese, meat, or the like.

c **1475** *Voc.* in Wr.-Wülcker 772 *Hec quadra*, a cantel of brede. *a* **1528** SKELTON *Elynour Rum.* 429 A cantell of Essex chese. **1552** HULOET, Cantel or shief of bread, *minutal.* **1627** FELTHAM *Low-Countr.* (1677) 46 A Cantle of green Cheese. **1737** OZELL *Rabelais* II. xxx, At the price of a cantle of bread. **1804** DUNCUMB *Herefords. Gloss.* (E.D.S.), *Cantle*, a piece of bread or cheese.

†**c.** A segment of a circle or sphere. *Obs.*

1551 RECORDE *Pathw. Knowl.* I. Def., If that part be separate from the rest of the circle..then ar both partes called cantelles. *Ibid.* Halfe globys and canteles of a globe. **1606** SHAKS. *Ant. & Cl.* III. x. 6 The greater Cantle of the world is lost With very ignorance.

4. A part, a portion (viewed as separate).

c **1315** SHOREHAM 33 Al i-hol Mot be thy schryfte, brother; Naȝt tharof a kantel to a prest And a kantel to another. *c* **1386** CHAUCER *Knts. T.* 2150 Nature hath nat take his bygynnyng Of no partye ne cantel of a thing, But of a thing that parfyt is and stable. **1552** *Let.* in *Edw. VI's Lit. Rem.* (1858) II. 418 That you might have soche a cantell of recreation. **1577** STANYHURST *Descr. Irel.* Ep. Ded., Perusing a cantell or parcel of the Irish historie that heere issueth. **1636** FEATLY *Clavis Myst.* xxxi. 401 Time is as it were a portion or cantle of eternity. **1860** GEN. P. THOMPSON *Audi Alt.* III. cxxxix. 116 A huge cantle of the folly.

5. The protuberant part at the back of a saddle; the hind-bow.

1592 GREENE *Art Conny catch.* II. 5 His sadle is made without any tree, yet hath it cantle and bolsters. **1652** SIR C. COTTERELL *Cassandra* II. II. (1676) 138 Nailed it to the cantle of his Saddle. **1859** *Art Taming Horses* viii. 120 Young men should learn to leap into the saddle by placing both hands on the cantle, as the horse moves.

b. cantle bar: a bar in the saddle of a camel, in place of the cantle.

1859 W. GREGORY *Egypt* I. 50 As the dromedary rises.. you..are..brought up by the cantle-bar just in your lower vertebræ.

†**6.** The crown of the head. *Sc.* [perh. from Du. *kanteel* a battlement, used fig. (Jam.).]

1822 SCOTT *Nigel* ii,'My cantle will stand a clour wad bring a stot down.' **1847–78** HALLIWELL, *Cantle*, the head. *Northumb. Mod.* To crack his cantle for him.

7. *dial.* (See quot.)

1811 WILLAN *W. Riding Yorksh.* Gloss, *Cantles*, the legs, chiefly in young animals. **1847–78** HALLIWELL, *Cantle*, the leg of an animal. *North.*

8. ? (Cf. SCANTLING.)

1536 *MS. Acc. St. John's Hosp., Canterb.*, To yᵉ sawers for sawyng ko[n]tyll bord. **1615** *Ibid.* Payd for saing of contellbordes and quarters. **1573** In *L'pool Munic. Rec.* (1883) I. 110 A cantel of a chest board. **1693** J. EDWARDS *Bks. O. & N. Test.* 428 Cantle [in Heraldry] quasi *Scantling*.

9. *Comb.* †**cantle-meal**, piecemeal; **cantle-piece**, a side piece of the head of a cask; cf. *cant-piece* (CANT *sb.*[1] 4), and F. *chanteau*; **cantle-wise** *adv.*, by cantles, in manner of a cantle (cf. CANTLE *v.*[1] 3). See also CANTEL-COPE.

c **1479** CAXTON *Bk. Curtasye* (1841) 409 (Mätz.) Men gete it now by *cantelmele. **1699** J. DICKENSON *Jrnl. Trav.* 46 The *Cantle-pieces of Sugar-Hogsheads. **1548** HALL *Chron., Hen. VIII*, an. 12 (R.) His garment was a chemew of clothe of siluer, culpond with clothe of golde, of damaske *cantell wise.

†**'cantle**, *v.*[1] *Obs.* Also 6 **cantel, kantel**. [f. prec. sb.]

1. *trans.* To cut into quarters or portions, divide.

1607 DEKKER *Wh. of Babylon* I. i. Wks. 1873 II. 193 This vast Globe Terrestriall should be cantled, And almost three parts ours. **1693** DRYDEN *Juvenal's Sat.*, For four times talking, if one piece thou take, That must be cantled, and the judge go snack.

2. *to cantle out*: to portion out, cut out.

1583 GOLDING *Calvin on Deut.* xcii. 570 Men are alwayes giuen to cantle out the poore folkes morsels as short as can be. **1674** N. FAIRFAX *Bulk & Selv.* 64 Their shape being nothing but their bulk so cantled out.

3. To piece together cantles of cloth.

1548 HALL *Chron.* (1809) 609 The garment was large & plited verie thicke & canteled of very good intaile. **1568** GRAFTON *Chron. Hen. VIII*, an. 6 Their apparell and bardes were cloth of golde, cloth of siluer, and crymsyn velvet kanteled together all in one sute.

†**'cantle**, *v.*[2] *Obs. rare.* = SCANTLE, to measure by a standard.

1603 HARSNET *Pop. Impost.* 80 Thyrœus..likely dooth Cantle all Exorcists by himselfe.

†**'cantler.** *Obs. rare.* App. = CANTER *sb.*[2].

1611 FLORIO, *Birrone*, a cheater, a conycatching cantler.

'cantless, *a. rare.* Void of cant.

1885 JEAFFRESON *Real Shelley* II. 10.

cantlet ('kæntlɪt). [f. CANTLE *sb.* + -ET[1].] A small cantle, a fragment.

a **1700** DRYDEN *Fab. Ovid's Met.* xii. 180 Huge cantlets of his buckler strew the ground. **1848** KINGSLEY *Saint's Trag.* I. i. 201 To spoil a waggon-load of ash-staves..And break a dozen fools' backs across their cantlets. **1849** C. BRONTË *Shirley* xxxiii, A cantlet of cold custard-pudding.

†**'cantling.** *Obs. rare.* [app. f. CANT, CANTLE; but cf. SCANTLING.]

1. A small part, corner, section, or division.

1674 N. FAIRFAX *Bulk & Selv.* 186 At Dooms-day a less cantling of it than England..will be enough to hold all the dwellers of it.

2. A support under a cask, to keep it steady when lying on the staves. Cf. *cantic-quoin* s.v. CANTIC *a.*

1616 SURFL. & MARKH. *Countr. Farm* 611 A vessell.. which hee shall cause to be set..vpon a cantling. *Ibid.* 617 Making two or three towres in the vessels, and afterward setting it againe vpon his cantling.

†**'cantly**, *adv.*[1] *Sc.* and *north.* [f. CANT *a.* + -LY[2].] Boldly, briskly, eagerly, energetically, cheerily.

1352 MINOT *Poems* v. 64 John of Aile of the Sluys..Was comen into Cagent cantly and kene. *c* **1400** *Destr. Troy* 6504 Then criet he full cantly þe knightes vpon.

'cantly, *adv.*[2] [CANT *sb.*[3] 4 e.] In canting phraseology; in slang.

1828 *Niles' Reg.* 27 Sept. XXXV. 66/2 This is cantly called 'talking to Bunkum'. **1890** *Field* 1 Nov. 655/2 They become open professionals, and 'go for the pieces', as it is cantly termed. **1906** CHESTERTON *Dickens* xii. 288 In attempting to decide whether an author will, as it is cantly expressed, live, it is necessary to have [etc.].

canto ('kæntəʊ). *Pl.* **-os**. [a. It. *canto* song, singing:—L. *cantus*, f. *canĕre* to sing.]

†**1.** A song, ballad. *Obs.*

1603 G. FLETCHER *Death of Eliza* iii, To heare a Canto of Elizae's death. **1633** P. FLETCHER *Purple Isl.* VI. lxxvi, Then should thy shepherd sing A thousand Canto's in thy heav'nly praise. **1656** BLOUNT *Glossogr.*, *Canto*, a Song or Sonnet. **1710** *Pict. Malice* 12 The Canto, or Poem in Dogrell Rhime.

2. One of the divisions of a long poem; such a part as the minstrel might sing at one 'fit'. (Used in Italian by Dante, and in Eng. by Spenser.)

1590 SPENSER *F.Q.* (*heading*) Canto I. **1596** *Ibid.* IV. ii. 54 The which, for length, I will not here pursew, But rather will reserve it for a canto new. **1603** DRAYTON *Bar. Wars* I. lxvii. 8 As the next Canto fearfully shall tell. **1759** DILWORTH *Pope* 20 This truly elegant piece in five cantos. **1883** LLOYD *Ebb & Flow* II. 195 In the twelfth canto of the Purgatorio.

‖**3.** *Mus.* [Ital.] See quot. 1879.

a **1789** BURNEY *Hist. Mus.* (ed. 2) II. iv. 325 Canto..the upper part or melody in a composition of many parts. **1879** HULLAH in Grove *Dict. Mus.* I. 306 Technically canto..is understood to represent that part of a concerted piece to which the melody is assigned. With the old masters this was, as a rule, the Tenor; with the modern it is almost always the Soprano.

‖**canto fermo** ('kanto 'fermo). *Mus.* [It.:—L. *cantus firmus* firm song, i.e. 'the melody which remains firm to its original shape while the parts

around it are varying with the counterpoint' (Grove *Dict. Mus.* I. 306).]

a. 'The simple unadorned melody of the ancient hymns and chants of the church' (Grove); plain-song. **b.** Hence applied to any simple subject of the same character to which counterpoint is added.

a **1789** BURNEY *Hist. Mus.* III. iii. 261 Making supplications to St. John in a fragment of simple melody, or Canto fermo. **1840** CARLYLE *Heroes* (1858) 253 His *Divine Comedy*..is, in all senses, genuinely a Song. In the very sound of it there is a *canto fermo*; it proceeds as by a chant. **1879** GROVE *Dict. Mus.* I. 306 [Palestrina's] motet 'Beatus Laurentius' is still more completely founded on the canto fermo, since the tune is sung throughout..in the first tenor, while the other four parts are moving in counterpoint above and below it.

canton ('kæntən, kæn'tɒn), *sb.*[1] [a. OF. *canton* corner, portion of a country, part of a shield, etc. = It. *cantone* corner, angle, augmentative of *canto* corner; see CANT *sb.*[1]]

†**1.** A corner, an angle; a retreating corner, angle, or nook. *Obs.*

1534 LD. BERNERS *Gold. Bk. M. Aurel.* xv, When I kept the Cantons, jetted in the streetes. **1598** YONG *Diana* 87 The house was quadrant, and at euery Canton was reared vp a high and artificiall tower. **1601** HOLLAND *Pliny* I. 73 In the inmost nouke of the creeke, the very canton and angle of Bœotia is washed by the sea. **1653** URQUHART *Rabelais* I. xlviii, He..with his Artillery began to thunder so terribly upon that canton of the wall.

2. *Her.* An ordinary of a shield or escutcheon, being a square division less than a quarter, occupying the upper (usually dexter) corner of the shield.

1572 BOSSEWELL *Armorie* II. 39 Whan ye shall see anye token abated, by the dignitie of the Canton. **1662** EVELYN *Mem.* (1857) I. 389 The King gave us [the Royal Society] the arms of England to be borne in a canton in our arms. **1808** *Regul. relat. to Service at Sea* IV. i. 79 Merchant Ships are to carry a Red Ensign with the Union Jack in a canton. **1864** BOUTELL *Heraldry Hist. & Pop.* (ed. 3) 208 Heirs of an heiress, who are not also heirs of their father, should bear on a Canton their father's arms. **1872** RUSKIN *Eagle's N.* §235.

b. 'Also used for the angular spaces between the branches of a cross or saltier' (Chambers *Cycl.*).

1830 E. CAMPBELL *Dict. Mil. Sc.* s.v. *Colours*, The Second Colour..is the St. George's Cross throughout, the Union in the upper Canton, the other three Cantons black.

†**3.** A quarter; a division of anything; a piece, or part. Cf. CANTLE 2–4. *Obs.*

1601 HOLLAND *Pliny* II. 434 A square piece or canton of the fish Tuny salted and condited. **1603** —— *Plutarch's Mor.* 462 If you regard number, all Greece..is not able to furnish us, for it would but answere one portion or canton of their [the Persians'] multitude. **1631** BRATHWAIT *Whimzies, Postmast.* 75 Hee quarters out his life into foure cantons, eating, drinking, sleeping, and riding. **1686** BURNET *Trav.* 255 (L.) Another piece of Holbein's..in which, in six several cantons, the several parts of our Saviour's Passion are represented. **1686** tr. *Chardin's Trav.* 405 How many Degrees are required to be a canton of thy knowledge?

4. A subdivision of a country; a small district.

1601 HOLLAND *Pliny* I. 56 The description by him made of all Italy, which be diuided into 11 Regions or Cantons. **1602** WARNER *Albion's Eng.* Epit. (1612) 360 The Saxon Heptarchia or their seuen Kingdomes, Cantons or Colonies here erected. **1702** *Eng. Theophrast.* 319 Men who have been the refuse of a little canton, and are now the honour of the world. **1760** T. HUTCHINSON *Hist. Coll. Mass. Bay* ii. (1765) 277 The Indians..divided into smaller cantons. **1796** T. JEFFERSON *Writ.* (1859) IV. 153 In the retired canton where I live, we know little of what is passing. **1839** THIRLWALL *Greece* I. 343 Cypselus, king of Arcadia, or of some Arcadian canton.

b. A parcel of ground; a portion of space.

1643 SIR T. BROWNE *Relig. Med.* I. §15 There are no Grotesques in nature: not any thing framed to fill up empty cantons and unnecessary spaces. **1690** LOCKE *Hum. Und.* IV. iii. §24 This little Canton, I mean this System of our Sun. **1693** EVELYN *De la Quint. Compl. Gard.* I. 180 All the Fruits of the same season, should be placed in the same Canton, or Parcel of Ground.

5. *spec.* **a.** One of the several sovereign states which form the Swiss confederation.

1611 COTGR., *Canton*..proper to Helvetia, or Switzerland; which, at this day consists of thirteene such Cantons). **1625** BACON *Nobility, Ess.* (Arb.) 191 The Switzers last well, notwithstanding their Diversitie of Religion, and of Cantons. **1720** *Lond. Gaz.* No. 5860/1 Berne, June 12..One of the Avoyers or Chief Magistrates of the Canton. **1868** G. DUFF *Pol. Surv.* 21 Pure democracy..has long existed in several of the small cantons.

b. In France, a division of an arrondissement containing several communes, answering somewhat to the hundred in England.

1611 COTGR., *Canton*..a Canton, or Hundred; a Precinct. **1838** *Penny Cycl.* X. 416/1 The smallest judicial divisions are cantons, each of which..in the rural districts comprehends several communes..The whole number of cantons in the kingdom is 2834. **1848** W. H. KELLY tr. *L. Blanc's Hist. Ten Y.* I. 50 An electoral college in each canton.

†'**canton**, *sb.*[2] *Obs.* [A variant form of CANTO; perh. from confusing the Italian words *canto* corner, *canto* song, *cantone* corner, *canzone* song.]

1. A song; = CANTO 1.

1594 *Zepheria* Canzon ii, How many Cantons then, sent I to thee? **1601** SHAKS. *Twel. N.* I. v. 289 Write loyall Cantons of contemned loue. **1609** HEYWOOD *Bryt. Troy* XII. xviii, They Oades and Cantons sing.

2. = CANTO 2.

1609 HEYWOOD (*title*) Troia Britanica, or Great Britaines Troy. A poem deuided into XVII. seuerall Cantons.

'**Canton**, *sb.*[3] The name of the city in southern China used *attrib.* to denote various manufactured articles, as ***Canton china, crape, enamel, flannel, matting.***

1860 *Texas Almanac* 244 Shirts, Carpets, Canton-Matting, shoes. **1865** M. EYRE *Lady's Walks* xvii. 195 A lady's worked Canton crape shawl. **1881** C. C. HARRISON *Woman's Handiwork* I. 47 *Canton flannel*,..a soft, downy fabric, the same on both sides. *Ibid.* III. 231 Blue Canton china of the willow pattern. **1889** *Anthony's Photogr. Bull.* II. 381 A good quality of canton flannel. **1910** S. W. BUSHELL *Chinese Art* (ed. 2) II. 82 Painted enamels on copper..often known as 'Canton enamels'. **1968** J. IRONSIDE *Fashion Alphabet* 222 *Canton crêpe.* Originally made of silk from Canton, this crêpe is widely used for dresses; it has a very pebbly surface and drapes and hangs beautifully.

canton ('kæntən, kæn'tɒn), *v.* Also 8 can'toon. [Partly f. CANTON *sb.*[1], partly repr. F. *cantonne-r* to quarter, It. *cantonare* to canton, to corner, f. F. *canton*, It. *cantone*: to which the 17th c. *cantoon* points.]

1. *trans.* To quarter, divide: **a.** To divide (land) into portions; to part, share. Also with *out*.

1598 FLORIO, *Cantonare*..Also to canton. **1602** W. WATSON *Decacordon 62 marg.*, The Iesuits are iolly fellowes to cap crownes, to canton Kingdoms. **1622–62** HEYLIN *Cosmogr.* III. (1673) 159/1 Cantoning his Estates amongst his children. **1701** DE FOE *True-born Eng.* I. 152 He Canton'd out the Country to his Men, And ev'ry Soldier was a Denizen. **1747** CARTE *Hist. Eng.* I. 287 The great lords, among whom the country was cantoned. **1875** H. ROGERS *Orig. Bible* ii. (ed. 3) 68 How contentedly they 'cantoned' out the world amongst them.

b. *spec.* To subdivide into cantons or districts.

1619 SIR D. CARLETON in *Relat. Eng. & Germ.* Ser. II. (1868) 7 Follow the example of..the Swisse, in cantoning themselves. **1697** POTTER *Antiq. Greece* III. i. (1715) 2 Being canton'd into a great number of States. **1713** DERHAM *Phys.-Theol.* IV. x. 172 They..begun to be Cantoned into distinct Nations. **1769** BLACKSTONE *Comm.* IV. 403 Where any kingdom is cantoned out into provincial establishments. **1851** THIRLWALL *Charge 16 note*, Hereupon they [the bishops] cantoned their great dioceses into Archdeaconries.

c. *transf.* To subdivide or cut out (generally).

1653 *Consid. Dissolv. Crt. Chancery* 36 The cantoning or cutting of the Courts at Westminster into so many County Courts, or parts. **1667** *Decay Chr. Piety* ix §10. 303 When they came to be..canton'd out into curious aerial notions. **1720** WELTON *Suffer. Son of God* I. x. 253 Who canton their Devotions in Quadrature with the World.

2. To divide (a part) *from*, or cut (it) *out* of a whole; to separate, sever by division. *arch.* or *Obs.*

1653 *Consid. Dissolv. Crt. Chancery* 63 To canton out a part of his Kingdom to be tryed by a Commission. **1681** *Whole Duty Nations* 14 A Nation or Kingdom is a part of Mankind canton'd from the whole world. *c* **1690** LOCKE *Conduct Und.* §3 They canton out to themselves a little Goshen in the intellectual world. **1741** WATTS *Improv. Mind* ix. Wks. (1813) 63 They canton out to themselves a little Province in the intellectual world.

†**3.** *intr.* (for *refl.*) To sever or separate oneself, secede, withdraw; *fig.* to digress. *Obs.*

1611 COTGR., *Se Cantonner*, to canton, or cantonnize, it; to seuer themselues from the rest of their fellowes, or from the bodie of a State, and fortifie, quarter, or erect a new State, apart. *c* **1630** DRUMM. OF HAWTH. *Poems* 56/1 Hold those subjects too too wanton, [That] Under an old king dare canton. *a* **1734** NORTH *Lives* II. 92, I have not cantoned much from the places intended express for particularities of this nature.

4. *trans.* To quarter (soldiers); to provide with quarters. (*Pronounced* kæn'tɒn *and* kæn'tuːn.)

1700 RYCAUT *Hist. Turks* III. 384 Leaving some of their Horse Cantoned near the City. **1751** *Phil. Trans.* XLVII. xxviii. 194 The Greys were cantoon'd in the village of Vucht near Boisleduc. **1755** *Mem. Capt. P. Drake* II. iii. 141 The small Corps, that were cantooned about that Neighbourhood. **1855** W. SARGENT *Braddock's Exped.* 142 An absurd plan for cantoning them in small divisions all over the country.

b. *fig.* To quarter, or locate in detachments.

1773 G. WHITE *Selborne* xxxviii. 96, I myself have found these birds in little parties in the autumn cantoned all along the Sussex downs. *Ibid.* (1853) II. xvii. 207 The variegated breed of his son-in-law, Jacob, were cantoned on the other. *a* **1779** H. WALPOLE *Mem. Geo. II* (1847) III. vi. 157 The whole body of Whigs were cantoned out in attachments to the Dukes of Newcastle and Bedford.

5. *intr.* (for *refl.*) To quarter (oneself), take up cantonments or quarters.

1697 POTTER *Antiq. Greece* (1715) I. iii. 10 His People..canton'd up and down the Country. **1707** *Lond. Gaz.* No. 4381/1 Our Army hath..received Orders to canton. **1841** ELPHINSTONE *Hist. Ind.* II. 279 He..cantoned for the rains near the present site of Calcutta.

6. *Her.* To furnish (a shield or cross) with a canton or cantons; to furnish the cantons with; to place in a canton. See also quot. 1688.

1688 R. HOLME *Armoury* I. viii. §45 This is of some Blasoned two Barrs Cantoned, thereby shewing that the higher hath a Canton joined to it. **1727–51** CHAMBERS *Cycl.* s.v., A cross argent, cantoned with four scallop-shells. **1864** BOUTELL *Heraldry Hist. & Pop.* xxi. §10 (ed. 3) 315 The cross of St. George cantoning in the 1st quarter a sword erect gules.

cantonal ('kæntənəl), *a.* [a. F. *cantonal*: see CANTON *sb.*[1] and -AL[1].] Of, pertaining to, or of the nature of a canton.

1842 *Penny Cycl.* XXIII. 426/1 In Switzerland several of the cantonal governments were parties to the bargain. **1847** GROTE *Greece* II. xxxi. IV. 176 It is well known..how unalterable are parochial or cantonal boundaries. **1861** M. ARNOLD *Pop. Educ. France* 41 The formation of cantonal committees, to watch over the..primary schools.

'**cantonalism**, a cantonal system or principle.

1873 *Echo* 13 Sept. 5/1. **1884** *Contemp. Rev.* June 887 The Vaudois Government..has..come back to Cantonalism.

cantoned (see the vb.), *ppl. a.* [f. CANTON *sb.*[1] and *v.* + -ED.]

1. Formed or divided into cantons.

1611 COTGR., *Cantonné*, cantonned, or cantonnized; seuered from the rest of their fellows, and fortified, or quartered apart. *a* **1649** DRUMM. OF HAWTH. *Skiamachia* Wks. (1711) 195 Conform to the government of a republick and cantoned towns. **1869** A. W. WARD tr. *Curtius' Hist. Greece* II. III. i. 259 The cantoned associations of Arcadia.

2. Quartered in cantonments.

1790 BEATSON *Naval & Mil. Mem.* I. 169 The army cantoned in the neighbourhood of Dunkirk. **1877** CLERY *Min. Tact.* ii. 20 Troops cantoned in and about the town.

3. *Arch.* (See quot.)

1727–51 CHAMBERS *Cycl.* **1876** GWILT *Arch.* Gloss., *Cantoned building*, one whose angles are decorated with columns, pilasters, rustic groins, or anything projecting beyond the naked of the wall.

4. *Her.* See CANTON *v.* 6.

cantoner. The inhabitant of a CANTON.

a **1670** HACKET *Abp. Williams* I. (1693) 67 These poor Cantoners [the Swiss] could not enjoy their own in quiet.

Cantonese (kæntə'niːz), *a.* and *sb.* [f. *Canton*, China + -ESE.] **A.** *adj.* Of or pertaining to Canton or its inhabitants. **B.** *sb.* **a.** An inhabitant of Canton. **b.** The dialect of Canton.

1857 *Bombardment of Canton* 29 Between you and ourselves, the Cantonese, there have been relations of friendship. **1857** 'AN ASIATIC' *China Question* 10 The Cantonese stir will be for the benefit of humanity. **1861** *Chambers's Encycl.* II. 575/2 The Cantonese are notorious for their turbulence and hatred of foreigners. **1877** EITEL (*title*) A Chinese dictionary in the Cantonese dialect. **1883** J. D. BALL (*title*) Cantonese made Easy. **1893** *Athenæum* 27 May 668/1 The book of English phrases compiled by a Cantonese for the use of those of his countrymen who aspire to become Hong Kong 'boys'. **1957** *Encycl. Brit.* IV. 772/2 The principal parts were played by Cantonese. *Ibid.*, The Cantonese delegates.

cantoning, *vbl. sb.* The action of the vb. CANTON; †*concr.* a portion, fragment (*obs.*).

1622–62 HEYLIN *Cosmogr.* I. (1682) 190 The dismembring and cantoning of this fair Estate. **1625** BP. MOUNTAGU *App. Cæsarem* 8 Popular cantonings of dismembred scripture. **1844** *Regul. & Ord. Army* 73 Quartering, Billeting, and Cantoning of Troops.

‖'**cantonist.** [ad. Russ. *kanto'nist*, from Fr.] The child of a (Russian) soldier in cantonment.

1854 *Fraser's Mag.* L. 481 The so-called military cantonists supply a yearly contingent of recruits, of which it is impossible to estimate the amount.

cantonite ('kæntənaɪt). *Min.* [Named from *Canton* in Georgia, U.S.; see -ITE.] A variety of Covellite, in cubes, with a cubical cleavage.

1858 SHEPARD *Min.* App. 3 Cantonite..a dimorphic form of covelline. **1868** DANA *Min.* 84.

cantoni'zation. [f. CANTONIZE *v.* + -ATION.] The process of making cantonal; a division into cantons.

1936 *Times Lit. Suppl.* 23 May 439/1 A cantonization after suppression of a serious revolt. **1949** KOESTLER *Promise & Fulf.* xii. 132 A scheme of Cantonization prepared by the Colonial Office.

†'**cantonize**, *v. Obs.* [f. CANTON *sb.*[1] + -IZE.]

1. *trans.* To divide into portions or parts; 'to parcel out into small divisions' (J.); to form into cantons.

1606 SYLVESTER *Du Bartas* II. iv. III. (1641) 217/1 To Cantonize the State. **1612** DAVIES *Why Ireland, etc.* (1787) 103 And thus was all Ireland cantonized among ten persons of the English nation. **1701** *Argument for War* 20 An unwarrantable reason for cantonizing the Spanish Territories. **1807** G. CHALMERS *Caledonia* I. I. ii. 57 Those kindred countries were each cantonized into many tribes.

b. *to cantonize out*: to separate.

a **1670** HACKET *Cent Serm.* (1675) 818 God cantonized out for himself but Twelve Families or Tribes out of all the Kingdoms of the Earth.

2. *intr.* To separate (oneself) into, or form, an independent community. Also *to cantonize it*. *Obs.*

1605 RALEIGH *Introd. Hist. Eng.* (1693) 6 Whether any parties did cantonize or were free Estates, or Commonwealths. **1611** [see CANTON *v.* 3]. **1711** SHAFTESB. *Charac.* II. §2 (1737) I. 113 To cantonize is natural; when the Society grows vast and bulky. **1809** *Edin. Rev.* XIII. 458.

3. *trans.* To canton (troops); to locate.

1626 T. H[AWKINS] tr. *Caussin's Holy Crt.* 127 The Diuells and Furyes were cantonnized. *c* **1674** *Scotland's Griev. under Lauderdale* 36 Neither is he content to have thus cantonized those [ministers] that were licensed.

Hence **cantonized** *ppl. a.*, **cantonizing** *vbl. sb.* and *ppl. a.*

1611 [see CANTONED 1]. **1651** DAVENANT *Gondibert* (1673) Pref. 4 Their cantonizing in Tribes. **1711** SHAFTESB. *Charac.* II. §2 (1737) I. 113 Sedition is a kind of cantonizing already begun within the State.

cantonment (kæn'tɒnmənt, -'tuːnmənt). Also 8–9 **cantoonment**. [a. F. *cantonnement*, f. *cantonner*: see CANTON *v.* and -MENT.]

1. The cantoning or quartering of troops.

1757 BURKE *Abridgm. Eng. Hist.* I. iii. (R.) No places of cantonment for soldiers.

2. The place of lodging assigned to a section of a force when cantoned out; also (often in *plural*) the place or places of encampment formed by troops for a more permanent stay in the course of a campaign, or while in winter quarters; 'in India the permanent military stations are so termed' (Stocqueler *Mil. Encycl.*).

1756 *Gentl. Mag.* XXVI. 554 They repaired to their respective cantonments. **1777** W. HEATH in Sparks *Corr. Amer. Rev.* (1853) I. 338 Every purpose..has been answered, by the troops in their present cantonment. **1813** WELLINGTON *Let.* in Gurw. *Disp.* XI. 311 The distress of the Spanish troops..induced me to order them into cantonments within the Spanish frontier. **1844** H. H. WILSON *Brit. India* I. 287 To withdraw from the cantonment to the Residency. **1844** *Regul. & Ord. Army* 270 No Officer is on any account to sleep out of Camp or Cantonments without leave.

3. *transf.* Quarters; places of occupation.

1837 W. IRVING *Capt. Bonneville* I. 166 All hands now set to work to prepare a winter cantonment. **1875** tr. *Schmidt's Desc. & Darw.* 227 The Mammalia, whose extraction may be inferred..from a comparison of their present cantonments..with the encampments of their former kindred.

†**can'toon.** *Obs.* A strong kind of fustian, showing a fine cording on one side and a smooth bright surface on the other.

1688 *Lond. Gaz.* No. 2328/4 A Cantoon grey cloth Bed. **1864** in WEBSTER; and in mod. Dicts.

cantoon, -ment, var. of CANTON *v.*, -MENT.

‖**cantor** ('kæntɔ(r)). Also 7 **canter**. [L. *cantor* singer, agent-noun f. *can-ĕre* to sing.]

†**1.** A singer. *Obs.*

1609 DOULAND *Ornith. Microl.* 4 A Cantor, who doth.. sing those things, which the Musitian..doth set downe. **1631** BRATHWAIT *Whimzies, Ballad-monger*, 18 Stanza's, which halt and hobble as lamely as that one-legg'd cantor that sings them. **1656** BLOUNT *Glossogr.*, *Cantor*, a singer.

2. He whose duty it is to lead the singing in a church; a precentor.

1538 LELAND *Itin.* V. 26 The Cantor of S. Davids. **1662** FULLER *Worthies* III. 155 Being Canter of that Church. *a* **1789** BURNEY *Hist. Mus.* (ed. 2) III. ii. 255 The Cantor or Chanter who directs the singing in Lutheran churches. **1867** LADY HERBERT *Cradle L.* vii. 176 The pillars where the Cantors stand during service. **1887** J. BADEN POWELL in *Ch. Union Gaz.* XVII. 145 A prose consists of a chorus, with intervening verses sung by cantors.

3. = CHAZZAN.

1893 I. ZANGWILL *Ghetto Tragedies* 3 The quaint monotonous sing-song of the Cantor reading the Law. **1945** A. KOBER *Parm Me* 120 Cards which she had received from the rabbis and cantors she had interviewed. **1958** *Times* 23 Sept. 2/7 A wandering synagogue-cantor.

Hence **'cantorship**.

1884 *Edin. Rev.* July 227 [Bach's] appointment to the Cantorship at Leipzig.

†**cantor-cope.** *Obs.* (Cf. CANTEL-COPE.)

1348 in *Eng. Gilds* (1870) 233 Two 'cantr copes' of 'blewe satyn'. **1450** *Voc.* in Wr.-Wülcker 721 *Hec dalmatica*, a canturcope.

†**can'tore.** *Obs.* [ad. Du. *kantoor* (in Ger. *kontor*), ad. F. *comptoir* (in 15–16th c. also *contouer*): see COUNTER.] Office, banking house.

1673 TEMPLE *Observ. United Prov.* Wks. 1731 I. 71 The common Revenue of particular Men lies much in the Cantores, either of the Generality, or the several Provinces, which are the Registries of these publick Debts. **1669** CHILD *Disc. Trade* (1694) 62 They have since reduced it by placart to 3 per cent. as to their cantors, and all publick receipts. *a* **1680** BUTLER *Rem.* I. 211 Like a Dutchman's Money i' th' Cantore..And whether he will ever get it out Into his own Possession is a Doubt.

cantorial (kæn'tɔərɪəl), **cantoral** ('kæntərəl), *a.* [f. on L. type **cantōri-us*, or f. CANTOR + -AL[1].] Pertaining to a cantor or precentor; applied to that side (the north side) of the choir of a cathedral or church on which the precentor sits.

1792 *Chron.* in *Ann. Reg.* 67/1 The pall bearers and executors in the seats on the decanal side, the other noble gentlemen and gentlemen on the cantorial side.

‖**cantoris** (kæn'tɔərɪs). [L., genitive of *cantor* CANTOR.] Of or belonging to the cantor or precentor; *cantoris side, stall*, the side occupied by the cantor, the north (exceptionally, the south) side. In *Music* used to indicate that side of the choir in antiphonal singing. (Correlative to DECANI.)

1641 J. BARNARD *First Book Sel. Ch. Mus.*, Tenor Cantoris..1 At Morning Prayer. First Service. **1760** BOYCE *Cath. Mus.* I. 67. **1880** *Grove's Dict. Mus.* I. 306/1. **1894** [see DECANI]. **1955** M. GILBERT *Sky High* i. 8 The Cantoris tenor ..bent across to say something to..the Cantoris alto.

'cantred. *Hist.* Forms: 4–5 **candrede**, 5 **candred**, 5–7 **cantrede**, 6–9 **cantred**. [app. an adaptation of CANTREF, assimilated to the Eng. *hundred*.] A hundred; a district containing a hundred townships.

1387 TREVISA *Higden* Rolls Ser. I. 343 A candrede is a contray þat conteyneþ an hondred townes. **1480** CAXTON *Descr. Brit.* 20 Hundred and candred is all one. **1495** *Act 11 Hen. VII*, xxxiv. Preamb., Cantredes, comotes, hundredes ..to the seid Castelles..belongyng. **1577** HOLINSHED *Chron.* II. 10/2 Meeth conteineth but sixteene cantreds. **1587** HARRISON *England* II. xix. (1877) I. 312 Essex hath in time past wholie beene forrest ground, except one cantred or hundred. **1610** FOLKINGHAM *Art of Survey* II. vii 60 Two Knights Fees make a Cantred. **1614** SPEED *Theat. Gt. Brit.* Pref., The Shires divisions into Lathes, Hundreds, Wapentakes, and Cantreds. **1747** CARTE *Hist. Eng.* I. 640 The city of Wexford and the two adjoining Cantreds. **1875** STUBBS *Const. Hist.* I. iv. 63 The cantred of Howel dha may answer to the hundred of Edgar.

†**b.** *transf. Obs.*

1674 N. FAIRFAX *Bulk & Selv.* 139 That this..is evenly dealt out amongst the sundry Clubs and Cantreds of bodies.

'cantref, -ev. Also *dial.* **canthrif**. [a. Welsh *cant* hundred + *tref* town, place.] = CANTRED.

1606 WARNER *Alb. Eng.* XV. xciii. (1612) 375 Wales, that had neere as many Kings as Cantrefes in times past. **1656** BLOUNT *Glossogr.*, *Cantred* or rather *Cantref* signifies an hundred villages. **1847** *Nat. Cycl.* I. 738 The county of Anglesey is divided into three cantrefs. **1875** ROBINSON *Whitby Gloss.* (E.D.S.). 'I'll whallop the whooal canthrif', i.e. fight the entire lot. **1887** *Edin. Rev.* Jan. 75, 12,800 erwr [= acres] formed the territorial division called a cymwd and about double that number a cantrev.

cantrip ('kæntrɪp) Also **-raip, -rap**. [A mod.Sc. word, of unknown origin: the orig. phrase appears to have been 'to cast cantrips', like to cast figures, horoscopes, nativities, lots, spells: perh. a perversion of some term of astrology. (Jamieson suggested *cant* to turn over + *raip* rope; Mahn Icel. *gan* frenzy, frantic gestures (which he renders 'witchcraft') + *trappa* a step.)]

A spell or charm of necromancy or witchcraft; a witch's trick or mischievous device. Also *jocosely*, any playfully mischievous trick; any whimsically mad, eccentric, or extravagant piece of conduct; in phr. ***to play one a cantrip***.

1719 RAMSAY *Ep. Hamilton* III. vi, Nor cantrapes cast to ken your fate. **1725** —— *Gent. Sheph.* II. ii, A witch, that for sma' price, Can cast her cantraips, and give me advice. **1790** BURNS *Tam O'Shanter*, By some devilish cantrip slight Each in its cauld hand held a light. **1816** SCOTT *Antiq.* xliv. 298, 'I think some Scottish deevil put it into my head to play him yon other cantrip.' **1872** *Daily News* 17 Aug. Our own young lady was permitted no such cantrips. **1884** TENNYSON *Becket* 171 Save from some hateful cantrips of thine own.

cant-spar. *Naut.* 'A hand-mast pole, fit for making small masts or yards, booms, etc.' (Smyth *Sailor's Word-bk.*).

1611 *Rates* (Jam.) Cant-spars or fire-poles, the hundreth, xx*l*. **1727** W. MATHER *Yng. Man's Comp.* 410 For which they import..Cantspares.

†**'cantuarie.** *Obs.* [ad. med.L. *cantuaria*, var. of *cantaria*, CHANTRY, q.v.] = CHANTRY 3.

1538 LELAND *Itin.* I. 4 And at the west end of the Chirche Yarde they made Lodgings for too Cantuarie Prestes. *Ibid.* I. 51 Ther is a Cantuarie.

cantus ('kæntəs). *Mus.* Pl. **cantus** (-tuːs). [L.] A song or melody, especially ecclesiastical melody; also, the principal voice. Also *attrib.*

[**1481** CAXTON *Reynard* (1895) xxvii. 63 What was it. prose or ryme. metre or verse..I trowe it was cantum. for I herde you synge.] **1590** WHYTHORNE (*title*) Cantus. (Bassus.) Of Duos, or Songs for two voices... Of the which, some be playne and easie to be sung, or played on Musicall Instruments. **1597** MORLEY *Introd. Mus.* 20 In this *Cantus* there is no difficultie if you sing your Semibreefes three Minyms a peece. **1662** T. DAVIDSON (*title*) Cantus, Songs and Fancies, To Three, Four, or Five Parts, both apt for Voices or Viols, With a brief Introduction to Musick. **1887** *Athenæum* 25 June 842/1 The work is written for cantus, altus, and tenor—a rather unusual combination of voices. **1965** *English Studies* XLVI. 269 The only extant cantus part in Hanover.

b. ***cantus firmus***: see CANTO FERMO.

1847 A. L. PHILLIPS *Little Gradual* p. xiv, The choir be directed by persons well skilled in the ecclesiastical chant (which is called *Cantus Planus* or *Firmus*). **1956** A. HUXLEY *Adonis & Alphabet* 234 Those composers who wrote their masses around a *cantus firmus*—a melody borrowed, almost invariably, from the closed, symmetrical music of popular songs. **1962** *Listener* 12 Apr. 652/2 The *cantus firmus* of Palestrina's early Mass, '*Ecce sacerdos magnus*'.

canty ('kæntɪ), *a. Sc.* and *north. dial.* [A deriv. of CANT *a.*, either native or of Low German origin: cf. Flem. and LG. *kantig*, similarly related to *kant*, there referred to.] Cheerful, lively, gladsome; esp. in *Sc.* manifesting gladness and cheerfulness; in north of England rather = lively, brisk, active: **a.** of persons.

a **1724** *Gaberlunzie Man* ii, He grew canty, and she grew fain. **1725** RAMSAY *Gent. Sheph.* I. i, I'll be mair canty wi't, and ne'er cry dool. *c* **1775** MRS. GRANT *Roy's Wife*, O, she was a cantie quean. **1789** BURNS *To Dr. Blacklock*, And are ye hale, and weel, and cantie? **1837** DICKENS *Pickw.* (1847) 406/2 Three or four..canty old Scotch fellows. **1845** EMILY BRONTË *Wuther. Heights* xxii. 193 My mother lived till eighty, a canty dame to the last. **1864** ATKINSON *Whitby Gloss.* s.v., 'She's a canty aud deeam for her years.' **1866** CARLYLE *Remin. E. Irving* 135 Canty, shrewd and witty fellows, when you set them talking.

b. of things.

1725 RAMSAY *Gent. Sheph.* I. ii, Little love or canty cheer can come Frae duddy doublets, and a pantry toom. **1786** *Harvest Rig* in Chambers *Pop. Hum. Sc. Poems* (1862) 34 Till they do lilt some canty song. **1789** BURNS *J. Anderson*, And mony a canty day, John, We've had wi' ane anither.

Canuck (kə'nʌk). *colloq.* Also **Kanuck**, etc. [App. f. the first syllable of *Canada*.] **A.** *sb.* **1.** A Canadian; *spec.* a French Canadian. **2.** A Canadian horse or pony. **3.** The French-Canadian patois. **B.** *adj.* Of or pertaining to Canada or its inhabitants.

In *U.S.* usage, *gen.* derogatory.

1835 H. C. TODD *Notes upon Canada* 92 Jonathan distinguishes a Dutch or French Canadian, by the term *Kanuk*. **1849** J. E. ALEXANDER *L'Acadie* I. xvi. 273 'Come boys and have some grog, I'm what you call a canuck:' a (Canadian). **1855** *Knickerbocker* XLV. 341 [We gave] our donkey into the keeping of a lively Canuck. **1860** HOLLAND *Miss Gilbert's Career* ii. 29, I'll hang on the tail of it and try legs with that little Kanuck of his. **1862** *Congress. Globe* 29 Apr. 1867/3 To Canada to buy the little Canuck ponies. **1884** *Harper's Mag.* June 125/1 A 'Kanuck' or French Canadian. **1895** *Century Mag.* Sept. 674/2 That would be convenient over the line among the Canucks. **1904** H. F. DAY *Kin o' Ktaadn* 145 'Roule, roulant, maboule roulant,' it's all Canuck but a good song. **1910** T. E. LAWRENCE *Let.* 17 Dec. (1954) 121 The three Canuck priests. **1964** *Calgary Herald* 19 Mar. 18/6 The Scottish skip missed a wide open takeout in the fifth leaving the Canucks another single. **1965** H. GOLD *Man who was not with It* xxvi. 249 *Bon jour, Grack, tu viens enfin?* That's Canuck for you ain't been a son to your ma.

canula, -lar, common var. of CANNULA, -LAR.

canun, early form of CANON *sb.*[2]

canvas, canvass ('kænvəs), *sb.* Forms: 4–5 **canevas**, 5 **kaneuas**, **canivas**, 5–6 **canwas**, 5–7 **canuas**, 6 **canvesse**, **canues**, (**cannefas**), 6–7 **canves**, 6–8 **canvase**, (7 **canuase**, **canvasse**, **canuasse**, 8 *dial.* **canvest**, **cannas**, **canness**), 5– **canvas**, 7– **canvass**. [ME. *canevas*, a. ONF. *canevas* (Central OF. *chanevas*) = Pr. *canabas*, Sp. *cañamazo*, It. *canavaccio*:—late L. type **cannabāceus* 'hempen', f. *cannabis* hemp. (From Lat. adjs. in *-āceus* were made, in Romanic, adjs. and sbs. of augm. and pejorative force, e.g. L. *populus*, *populāce-us*, It. *popolaccio*, Eng. *populace*.) The word has entered into most of the European langs.

The spelling *canvas*, with one *s*, plural *canvases* (cf. *atlases*) is, it will be seen, more etymological than *canvass*, and now predominates; this spelling is also better used in the verb with the literal sense of 'furnish or line with canvas', whence *canvased*, *canvasing*; but the old derivative verb with sense 'to toss in a sheet, discuss, debate, solicit votes', is now always spelt CANVASS, and this spelling is retained in the verbal sb. in turn derived from it, as 'the electoral *canvass*'.]

1. A strong or coarse unbleached cloth made of hemp or flax, used (in different forms) as the material for sails of ships, for tents, and by painters for oil-paintings, formerly also for clothing, etc.

1260 et seq. in Rogers *Agric. & Pr.* II. 511. *c* **1325** *Coer de L.* 2645 A melle he hadde..Four sayles wer theretoo..With canevas layd wel al bout. *c* **1450** *Voc.* in Wr.-Wülcker 570 *Canevasium*, Canevas. *c* **1460** FORTESCUE *Abs. & Lim. Mon.* (1714) 19 A pore Cote under their uttermost Garment, made of grete Canvas. **1537** *Bury Wills* (1850) 133 My best couerlett lyned wyth canwas. **1608** ROWLANDS *Humors Look. Glasse* 6 Sattin and silke was pawned long a goe, And now in canuase, no knight can him knowe. **1665** BOYLE *Occas. Refl.* (1675) Pref. 21 The fashion, that..allows our Gallants to wear fine Laces upon Canvass and Buckram. **1871** BRYANT *Odyss.* v. 312 Calypso..brought him store Of canvass, which he fitly shaped to sails.

b. ***under canvas***: in a tent or tents.

1864 *Soc. Science Rev.* 137 A life under canvas in the finer seasons of the year. **187.** F. GRIFFITHS *Eng. Army* i. 26 The residue lived all the year round under canvas.

2. A piece of canvas used for various purposes: as †**a.** A sheet, covering or screen; a filtering or bolting cloth; a blind for a carriage window, etc. *Obs.*

c **1386** CHAUCER *Chan. Yem. Prol. & T.* 387 And on the floor y-cast a canevas [*v.r.* kaneuas, canvas]. **1411** *E.E. Wills* (1882) 19 A reed bedde of worsteyd..with a canvase, a materas. **1483** CAXTON *Gold. Leg.* 397/2 There was a canuas that hynge ouer hys heed. **1561** HOLLYBUSH *Hom. Apoth.* 27 Wett a cannefas in Endiue water..and laye it vpon the lyuer. **1582** HESTER *Phiorav. Secr.* III. xlii. 61 Straine it harde through a Canues. **1667** SIR R. MORAY in *Phil. Trans.* II. 474 All the interposed Canvasses. **1754** RICHARDSON *Grandison* (1812) I. 210 On the contrary side of the chariot (his canvass being still up on that next me). **1785** MISS FIELDING *Ophelia* II. xviii, A chariot..having canvasses to let down.

b. A covering over the ends of a racing-boat to prevent water from being shipped; hence ***canvas-length*** (see 8).

1880 *Newspaper.* At the Farm he led by his forward canvas. **1887** *St. James's G.* 28 Mar. 13 Not a canvas-length (about 15 ft.) separated the boats.

c. *Boxing*, etc. A covering over the floor of a boxing or wrestling ring; hence by metonymy,

such a floor. Phr. *to hit* (or *kiss*) *the canvas*: to be floored in a contest.

1910 *Nevada State Jrnl.* 5 July 2/4 The fifteenth round lasted two minutes and 27 seconds. Out of this Jeffries was on the canvas 26 seconds. **1919** *Toledo* (Ohio) *News-Bee* 5 July 12/2 A salvo of heavy whacks from right and left again made Jess kiss the canvas. **1922** *Ring* June 21/1 He never got out o' the way of it and the first thing that hits the canvas is the back of his neck. **1942** BERREY & VAN DEN BARK *Amer. Thes. Slang* §699/1 Canvas, resin, rosin, rosin-covered canvas, the floor of the ring, hence a prize ring. **1967** C. POTOK *Chosen* I. ii. 45, I hit the canvas so hard I rattled my toenails. **1977** *Westindian World* 3–9 June 19/1 Frazier caught Ali with a vicious right hand which sent Ali crashing to the canvas for only the second time in his career.

3. *spec.* As material for sails; sail-cloth; *hence*, sails collectively. ***under canvas***: with sails spread.

1609 [see CANVAS-CLIMBER in 8]. **1645** QUARLES *Sol. Recant.* VII. 88 Pilots that are wise Proportion out their Canvase to the skies. **1697** DRYDEN *Virg. Georg.* I. 347 To spread the flying Canvass. **1794** *Rigging & Seamanship* I. 86 From No. 1 to 6 is termed double, and above No. 6 single, canvas. **1835** SIR J. ROSS *N.-W. Pass.* iii. 32 We were obliged to reduce our canvas. *c* **1860** H. STUART *Seaman's Catech.* 52 Canvas is made in lengths of 40 feet called bolts.. The stoutest is called No. 1, and so on in fineness to No. 8. **1873** BLACK *Pr. Thule* xv. 242 The small boat was put under canvas again.

4. *spec.* As material on which oil-paintings are executed; *hence*, a piece of canvas prepared to receive a painting.

1705 TATE *Warriour's Welc.* xxxiv, Then try your Skill: a well-prim'd Canvass stretch. **1756–7** tr. *Keysler's Trav.* (1760) II. 273 Damp, which is such a prejudice to the pictures on canvas or wood. **1769** *Junius Lett.* xxx. 135 Mark in what manner the canvass is filled up. **1805** N. NICHOLLS *Let.* in *Corr. w. Gray* (1843) 43 A power..of painting a scene, by judicious detail, as if it were on canvas.

b. An oil-painting; also, paintings collectively.

1764 GOLDSM. *Trav.* 137 The canvas glow'd beyond e'en Nature warm. **1835** LYTTON *Rienzi* II. i, Receptacles for the immortal canvas of Italian..Art. **1868** RUSKIN *Pol. Econ. Art* ii. 125 Cheques..freely offered, for such and such canvasses. **1882** *Athenæum* No. 2866. 439 The most important serial or cyclical group by Mr. E. Burne Jones.. consists of six canvasses in all.

c. *fig.*

1768–78 TUCKER *Lt. Nat.* (1852) II. 422 Striving to imprint..upon the imagination so much..as her coarse canvass can take off. **1822** HAZLITT *Table-t.* II. iii. 47 The canvas of the fancy is but of a certain extent. **1845** J. H. NEWMAN *Ess. Developm.* Introd. 7 History..does not bring out clearly upon the canvass the details.

‖**d.** [Fr.] (See quots. and cf. Littré.)

1727–51 CHAMBERS *Cycl.*, *Canvas*, is also used, among the French, for the model, or first words, whereon an air, or piece of music, is composed, and given to a poet to regulate and finish. The canvas of a song, is certain notes of the composer, which shew the poet the measure of the verses he is to make. Thus, Du Lot says, he has canvas for ten sonnets against the muses. **1730–6** in BAILEY. **1849** in SMART. **1864** in WEBSTER.

5. A clear unbleached cloth so woven as to present the appearance of close and regular lattice-work, used for working tapestry with the needle.

1611 COTGR., *Gaze*, Cushion Canuas; the thinne Canuas that serues women for a ground vnto their Cushions, or Purseworke, etc. **1753** CHAMBERS *Cycl. Supp.* s.v., Working canvas, for botts or cushions, narrow, broad, and broadest.

†**6.** *Hawking.* (An early use, of which the precise meaning is now obscure.) Cf. CANVAS *v.* 1.

1589 NASHE *Pasquill & Mar.* 10 Such canuaces made, such stales set, such traynes laide by the factious, to bring their Superiours into contempt.

7. *attrib.* (or *adj.*) **a.** Of canvas.

1563 T. GALE *Antidot.* II. 49 Straine it through a newe canues clothe. **1627** DRAYTON *Agincourt* (R.) Barks..with their canvass wings. **1720** GAY *Poems* (1745) I. 165 Thick rising tents a canvass city build. **1856** KANE *Arct. Expl.* II. xvi. 167 Canvas moccasins..for every one of the party.

†**b.** Having the colour or appearance of canvas; light grey. Cf. CANVAS-BACK 2. *Obs.*

1486 *Bk. St. Albans* A vij b, Hawkes haue white maill, Canuasmaill, or Rede maill..Canus maill is betwene white maill and Iron maill.

c. Pertaining to a canvas booth at a fair.

1860 MAYHEW *Lond. Labour* III. 131 A fair, or as we call it, a canvas clown. *Ibid.* 149 Strolling actors..as long as they are acting in a booth, are called canvas actors.

8. *Comb.*, as ***canvas-breadth***, ***-cutter***, ***-dauber***, ***-stretcher***; **canvas-bag**, a bag made of canvas; also *Mil.* (see quot. 1708); †**canvas-climber**, a sailor; **canvas-length** (see 2 b above).

1708 KERSEY, **Canvas-bags* or Earth-bags (in *Fortif.*) are Baggs fill'd with Earth, and us'd to raise [or repair] a Breast-work in haste. **1721–1800** in BAILEY. **1838** DICKENS *O. Twist* II. viii. 173 Guineas in a canvas bag. **1768** ROSS *Helenore* 27 (Jam.) The shade beneath a *Canuess-braid outthrow. **1608** SHAKS. *Per.* IV. i. 62 From the ladder tackle washes off a *Canuas-clymer. **1806** WOLCOTT (P. Pindar) *Tristia* Wks. 1812 V. 267 Behold the *Canvas-dauber!

canvas ('kænvəs), *v.* Also **canvass.** [f. prec. sb.: see also CANVASS *v.*, which has the same origin, but is unconnected in sense, and is now never spelt *canvas*. For spelling, see note to prec. sb.]

†**1.** *Hawking.* To entangle or catch in a net (see CANVAS *sb.* 6); also *transf.* and *fig. Obs.*

1559 *Mirr. Mag.* 230 (N.) As the canuist kite, doth feare the snare. **1576** PETTIE *Palace of Pleas.*, The hawke having bin once canvassed in the nettes, wil make it daungerous to strike againe at the stale. **1580** LYLY *Euphues* 402 Some thing I should [**1581** would] not utter which happylye the itchying eares of young gentlemen would so canuas, that when I would call it in, I cannot, and so be caughte with the Torteise, when I would not. **1653** E. CHISENHALE *Cath. Hist.* 95 Unless he..made a bait to fly at a Bishoprick, and being canvassed in Peters net, it stirred up some atra bilis.

†**2.** ? To stuff or pad *out* with canvas. *Obs.*

1606 CHAPMAN *Mons. D'Olive* Plays (1873) I. 200 Heers wit canuast out ans coate into's Jacket. **1630** J. TAYLOR (Water P.) *Wks.* II. 65/1 Linnen Drapers but for transportation Could hardly Canuase out their occupation.

3. To cover, line, or furnish with canvas.

1556 [see below]. **1865** DICKENS *Christmas Bks.*, *Dr. Marigold*, The door had been nailed up and canvassed over. **1881** MRS. PRAED *Policy & P.* I. 122 The walls were only canvased. **1885** *Manch. Guardian* 10 Jan. 6 More cotton was still to be baled and canvassed.

Hence **'canvased** *ppl. a.*

1556 ROBINSON tr. *More's Utop.* (Arb.) 80 *marg.*, Glazed or canuased windowes. **1559** [see 1 above]. **1875** *Daily News* 18 Mar., Canvassed verandahs.

†**canva'sado, -'zado.** *Obs.* Also canuassado, canuazado, canvissado, canuisado, -zado, canvisado, -zado. [Cf. CANVAS *v.*, and CANVASS *sb.* 2; but in sense 2, there was apparently confusion with CAMISADO, which might easily arise from the corrupt forms *cammassado*, *camnesado*, on one side, and *cammas*, *cammes*, *camwys*, *cannes*, on the other.]

1. A sudden attack.

1581 J. BELL *Haddon's Answ. Osor.* 381 That is wont to happen in a Canvizado or sodein skarmishe. **1593** *Bacchus Bounty* in *Harl. Misc.* (1809) II. 264 Which coppernosed crue..assaulted with a fresh canuazado the citie of Vinosa. **1599** NASHE *Lent. Stuffe* 51 Which had the worst end of the staffe in that sea iourney or canuazado.

2. A 'night attack', a CAMISADO.

a **1626** BRETON *Pilgr. Paradise* 19 (D.) And in the night their sodaine canuassados. **1605** Z. JONES tr. *De Loyer's Specters* 57 Which came thus by night to give them the [can]vazado. *a* **1618** RALEIGH *Mahomet* (1637) 79 The night following the Moores gave a Canvasado upon don Orpas. **1617** J. MOORE *Mappe Mans Mortal.* II. v. 131 To giue the enemie a canvisado.

3. ? A kind of stroke in fencing: a counter-check direct.

1601 DEACON & WALKER *Spirits & Dev.* 312 The one of them proferring the canuizado, or countercheck directly vnto the other. —— *Answ. Darel* To Rdr. 2 Giuing the Canuisado of late to her Maiesties high Commission. **1605** HEYWOOD *Troubles Q. Eliz.* Wks. 1874 I. 225 Holo, holo! thou hast giuen me the canvissado.

canvas-back. [f. CANVAS *sb.* + BACK *sb.*[1]]

1. A back of a garment made of canvas; hence *fig.* a reverse much inferior to the front.

1605 *Lond. Prodigal* III. i. 243 My father in a mocado coat a pair of red satin sleeves and a canvas back. **1668** CHILD *Disc. Trade* (ed. 4) 10 Many..would not go to the price of a whole satten doublet; the embroiderer made many hundreds of them..with canvas backs. *a* **1734** NORTH *Exam.* I. ii. ¶83, I thought it reasonable to bid Defiance to this bold Traducer, and turning him round, shew his Canvas Back.

2. A North American duck (*Fuligula valisneriana*), so called from the colour of the back feathers. Called also more fully ***canvas-back duck***, and ***canvas-backed duck***.

1785 JEFFERSON *Notes Virginia* vi. 130 Besides these [birds] we have..The Widgeon, Sheldrach, or Canvas back, Black head. **1809** W. IRVING *Hist. N.Y.* II. 282 The gastronomical merits of..canvas-back ducks. *a* **1813** A. WILSON *Foresters*, Four large ducks..The far-famed 'canvass-backs'. **1832** *Blackw. Mag.* May 846/2 The canvass-back stands alone. *Ibid.* The man who has feasted on canvass-back ducks, cannot philosophically be said to have lived in vain. **1859** HELPS *Friends in C.* Ser. II. I. i. 20 He had never tasted a canvas-back duck.

1842 DICKENS *Amer. Notes* (1850) 79/1 The water in both was blackened with flights of canvas-backed ducks.

canvass, canvas ('kænvəs), *v.* Forms: 6 **kanivas(se, kanvas,** 6–7 **canuas(e, canvase, canuasse, canvasse,** (6 **canvaze, canvisse, canuize,** 7 **canvise, canvize, canvace),** 6–8 **canvas,** 6– **canvass.** [f. CANVAS *sb.*, in its former spelling *canvass*, and some of its special senses. The development of senses 1–5 is plain enough, starting from the literal notion of 'toss in a sheet', whence 'shake up, toss to and fro (*agitare*), discuss, etc.; but that of the intrans. 6, which appears early, has not been explained. The two notions subsequently influenced each other, and produced connecting usages.

Johnson says 'from *canvass* as it signifies a sieve': cf. CANVAS *sb.* 2; but no clear example of the vb. in the literal sense 'sift or winnow' has occurred. Yet Cotgrave's explanation of F. *vanner* 'to vanne or winnow..also to course, chide, canuasse, bayt..rake up scoffingly the faults or imperfections of others', affords an analogy for such a development; not so the case of *berner* 'to vanne or winnow corne, also to canuasse or tosse in a siue (a punishment)', which points to the development in 1–4 below. With Johnson's derivation agrees his explanation 'to try votes previously to the decisive act', but this is not historically the original sense of 6, and is either a conjectural explanation, or at most a mixing up of the notions of soliciting and of discussing or investigating. The trans. sense in 'to canvass the constituency' is quite late.]

†**1.** *trans.* To toss in a canvas sheet, etc., as a sport or punishment; to blanket. *Obs.*

1508 *Dk. Buckhm's Acc.* in Brewer *Calendar* 497 To a child of the kitchen being kanivassed before my Lord. **1530** PALSGR. 596, I kanvas a dogge or a matter, *je trafficque.* **1591** SHAKS. *1 Hen. VI*, I. iii. 36 Ile canuas thee in thy broad Cardinalls Hat, If thou proceed in this thy insolence [cf. *2 Hen. IV*, II. iv. 243]. **1611** COTGR., *Berner* (see above).

†**2.** *transf.* To knock about, shake and shatter thoroughly; to buffet; to beat, batter, drub. *Obs.*

1573 RASTELL *12 Jests of Widow Edyth* XII. H iij b, I should canuas thee, and make thee lame. **1577** HOLINSHED *Chron.* IV. 242 How lustilie the English canons did canvass and batter his castell walles. **1612** WARNER *Alb. Eng.* II. vii. 27 Hercules did canuase so his carkas. **1643** *Subj. of Supremacie, etc.* 57 To play..at the cudgels, to canvase one another with crosse blowes.

†**b.** To subject to attack or assault. Cf. CANVASS *sb.* 2. *Obs.*

1599 HAYWARD *1st Pt. Hen. IV*, 53 The north parts were many times canvased, and..almost consumed by the Scots.

†**3.** *fig.* To buffet or 'thrash' (a person) in writing; to criticize destructively and unsparingly.

1590 GREENE *Never too late* (1600) 64 Some..haue for their satirical inuectiues been wel canuased. **1611** COTGR. s.v. *Berné*, He hath beene throughly canvassed; (a phrase most commonly applied to an ignorant or dull-headed fellow, that hath prouoked a learned penne, or tongue, to fall aboord him). **1618** *Barnevelt's Apol.* D ij, I leaue him to your learned penne: canuase him according to his merits.

†**b.** To pull to pieces, criticize or discuss destructively (a writing, etc.). *Obs.*

1577 tr. *Bullinger's Decades* (1592) 165 Therfore did the Gentiles bait and canuase it too and fro with wonderful preatie quippes. **1589** NASHE in Greene *Menaph.* (Arb.) Ded., Some desperate quipper will canvaze my proposed comparison. **1615** *Luther's Comm. 1 Pet.* v. 51 These words have been so canvassed and wrested by my Lord the Pope.

4. *fig.* To shake out or discuss (a subject or matter), so that its parts may be thoroughly investigated; to discuss, criticize, scrutinize fully.

1530 PALSGR. 596/2 This mater hath be canvassed in dede. **1573** G. HARVEY *Letter-bk.* (1884) 11 Sutch matters have bene thurrouly canvissid long ago. **1662** J. BARGRAVE *Pope Alex. VII* (1867) 15 Canvacing many titles, at length they pitched upon Eminency. **1753** RICHARDSON *Grandison* (1781) VI. xvii. 67 They canvassed the matter, with..much good-natured earnestness. **1798** DALLAS *Amer. Law Rep.* II. 343 An opportunity to canvass the character of the witnesses. **1845** DISRAELI *Sybil* (1863) 261 It was canvassed and criticised sentence by sentence. **1864** *Fraser's Mag.* Apr. 487 Clubs where the reputations of men are coolly canvassed.

†**b.** To investigate or examine physically. *Obs.*

1622–62 HEYLIN *Cosmogr.* IV. (1682) 105 Having thoroughly canvassed all the Eastern Shores, he turned his course.

†**c.** 'To discuss' (a dish). *Obs.*

1602 *Return fr. Parnass.* II. vi. (Arb.) 33, I inuited the hungry slaue..to the canuasing of a Turkey pie.

d. *intr.* To debate; to discuss.

1631 HEYLYN *St. George* 40 That he should neyther canvasse over idle Pamphlets, nor give beleefe to old wives Fables. *a* **1766** FRANCES SHERIDAN *Sidney Bidulph* (1767) V. 169 Having canvassed over the first part of Sir George's letter. **1794** GODWIN *Cal. Williams* 272, I canvassed for a moment whether I should make use of this. **1835** MARRYAT *Jac. Faith.* xxxii, We sat there canvassing over the affair.

e. *trans.* To scrutinize, so as to reject bad votes. Cf. CANVASSER d. *Obs.* exc. *U.S.*

1715 BURNET *Own Time* (1766) II. 182 The poll was closed when the Court thought they had the majority: but upon casting it up, it appeared they had lost it: so they fell to canvass it. **1778** *Laws State N.Y.* c. 16 §9 The said joint Committee..[shall] canvas and estimate the Votes. **1792** JAY *Corr.* (1891) III. 428 Tiogo will most probably not be canvassed, as the box was delivered by a person deputed by a deputy. **1888** BRYCE *Amer. Commw.* II. App. 682 The officers..whose duty it is..to receive and canvass the returns from the several precincts of their respective counties..must then and there proceed to canvass the returns. **1947** *Chicago Daily News* 17 Jan. 14/2 When the popular votes for governor are canvassed by the legislature only a candidate with a majority of all the votes shall be qualified.

†**5.** ? To bargain or deal with; to sound or try as to their expectations. *Obs.*

1688 EVELYN *Mem.* (1857) III. 289 The hero [William III] is now at St. James's..By what I collect, the ambitious and the covetous will be canvassed for places of honour, and rich employment.

6. *intr.* To solicit; *esp.* to solicit votes or support previously to an election; also, to solicit support, contributions, orders for goods, etc. (Johnson says 'To try votes previously to the decisive act'.)

a **1555** LATIMER *Serm. & Rem.* (1845) 296 This object is so seriously taken up, and canvassed for..in so eager or rather so ardent a spirit. *a* **1626** BACON (J.) Elizabeth being to resolve upon an officer, and being by some that canvassed for others, put in some doubt of that person she meant to advance. **1660** HAMMOND *Wks.* IV. 510 (R.) He that should give his voice unto Christ, because there was no body else to canvass for it. **1681** TEMPLE *Mem.* III. Wks. 1731 I. 342 Every one began to canvas for Elections in the ensuing Parliament. **1726** AYLIFFE *Parerg.* 119 This crime of canvassing or solliciting for Church-Preferment **1824** MISS FERRIER *Inher.* xv, She had begun to canvass with her brother and uncle, to bespeak their votes. **1831–55** BREWSTER *Newton* II. xix. 215 Unwilling to canvass personally for a seat in the new Parliament.

7. *trans.* †**a.** To sue for or solicit (a thing). *Obs.*

1768 H. WALPOLE *Hist. Doubts* Pref. 19 He..was not likely to canvass the favour of the father by prostituting his pen to the humour of the court. *a* **1774** GOLDSM. *Hist. Greece* I. 75 Even kings sometimes canvassed that title ['citizen of Athens'] for themselves and their children.

b. To sue or solicit (persons, a district) for votes, subscriptions, custom, orders, etc.; *esp.* to solicit the support of a constituency, by going through and interviewing the individual electors; to ascertain by this means the number of one's supporters.

1812 *Examiner* 5 Oct. 638/1 His inability to canvas the Livery in person. **1844** H. H. WILSON *Brit. India* I. 161 Mr. Paull, having canvassed unsuccessfully the borough of Westminster, ceased to be a member. **1855** MOTLEY *Dutch Rep.* (1861) II. 293 His most trustworthy agent..was now actively canvassing the governments and peoples of Germany. **1873** BURTON *Hist. Scot.* VI. lxxi. 236 Having canvassed the town and county of Aberdeen [for].. adherents to the Covenant.

canvass ('kænvəs), *sb.* Forms: 6 canvace, 7 -uasse, -uase, -vase, 7–8 canvas, 7– canvass. [f. prec. vb., the spelling of which it retains.]

†**1.** A shaking up; a tossing up and down. *Obs.*

1611 COTGR., *Demenée*.. a tumble tosse, canuasse.

†**2. a.** A shock; esp. that of a sudden attack or surprise. Cf. CANVASADO.

1611 COTGR., *Camisade*, a camisado, canuas, or cold Pie; a suddain assaulting, or surprisall of the enemie. **1627** F. E. *Hist. Edw. II* (1680) 69 Levies..sufficient to give a Canvas to the Royal Army.

†**b.** In *Fencing*. = CANVASADO 3. *Obs.*

a **1641** BP. MOUNTAGU *Acts & Mon.* 184 For it is the sorest canvase, that can be giuen an opposite, to beat him at his owne weapon.

†**3.** Repulse, rejection (e.g. at an election, in a suit). Phrase, ***to have or receive the canvass.*** Obs.

1621 BURTON *Anat. Mel.* I. ii. III. xi, If he chance to miss and have a canvass, he is in hell on the other side. *Ibid.* II. iii. VII. (1651) 352 But why shouldst thou take thy neglect, thy Canvas so to heart? It may be thou art not fit. **1626** SHIRLEY *Brothers* II. i, I have promised him As much as marriage comes to; and I lose My honour if my Don receive the canvas.

†**4.** Examination of the 'pros and cons'; full discussion. ? *Obs.*

1608–11 BP. HALL *Epist.* V. iv. (1627) 369 Learned canuases of the deepe points of diuinitie. *a* **1687** H. MORE *Pre-exist. Soul* Pref., I deem it worthy the canvass and discussion of sober and considerate men.

5. a. The action or process of personally soliciting votes before an election; including the notion of ascertaining the amount of support which a candidate may count upon. (Johnson makes it 'The act of sifting voices, or trying them previously to the decisive act of voting', but of this, apart from the actual solicitation of votes, there is no clear evidence. The first quot. is obscure, and may belong elsewhere, e.g. to CANVAS *sb.* 6.)

[**1612** BACON *Cunning, Ess.* (Arb.) 435 There are some that are good in Canuasses & factions, that are otherwise weake men.] **1691** WOOD *Ath. Oxon.* I./846 In the election..was the greatest canvas..in the memory of Man. **1788** LD. SHEFFIELD in *Ld. Auckland's Corr.* (1861) II. 222 In short their success on the canvass quite astonished them. **1791** MACKINTOSH *Parl. Suffrage* Wks. 1846 III. 229 Candidates and their..agents in every street during an active canvass. **1844** DISRAELI *Coningsby* v. iv. 201 The results of the two canvasses were such as had been anticipated.

attrib. **1881** *Daily News* 21 Jan. 5/4 It had never been their custom to preserve canvass books.

b. A scrutiny of votes in an election. *U.S.*

1778 *Laws State N.Y.* c. 16 §9 To determine upon such Canvas and Estimate. **1888** BRYCE *Amer. Commw.* II. App. 682 If all the returns have not been received, the canvass must be postponed... Upon the completion of said canvass and returns, the said Board shall immediately certify the same. **1903** *N.Y. Sun* 20 Nov. 5 The official canvass of the vote in the borough of Brooklyn was practically finished yesterday.

6. A solicitation of support, custom, etc.

1790 BURKE *Fr. Rev.* 219 The other mode of ecclesiastical canvas, subjects them [bishoprics and cures] infinitely more surely and more generally to all the evil arts of low ambition. **1817** COLERIDGE *Biog. Lit.* 78 One gentleman procured me nearly a hundred names for The Friend and..took frequent opportunity to remind me of his success in his canvass. **1846** PRESCOTT *Ferd. & Is.* I. vi. 290 Honours, which had before been..made the subject of a furious canvass.

canvassed ('kænvəst), *ppl. a.* [f. CANVASS *v.*] Subjected to canvassing; discussed.

Mod. A much canvassed appointment.

canvasser ('kænvəsə(r)). [f. CANVASS *v.* + -ER[1].]

1. a. One who canvasses: see CANVASS *v.* 1–5.

1599 MINSHEU *Sp. Dict., Manteador*, a canuasser or tosser in a blanket or sheet. **1628** LE GRYS tr. *Barclay's Argenis* 254 These busie Canuassers of causes. **1648** W. CLEMENT *Relat. & Observ.* 3 Old Canvasers of Factions. **1799** SHERIDAN *Pizarro* III. iii, Who seeks alone for living homage stands a mean canvasser in her temple's porch.

b. One who canvasses electors for votes.

a **1797** BURKE (R.) As real publick counsellors, not as the canvassers at a perpetual election. **1855** MACAULAY *Hist. Eng.* IV. 458 As a canvasser he was irresistible. **1869** *Daily News* 25 Jan., It has become practicable for an authorised canvasser to vitiate an election by excessive zeal.

c. One who solicits custom, or goes about soliciting orders, esp. in the book-trade.

1865 KNIGHT *Pass. Working Life* III. 18 Book-hawkers known as canvassers. **1879** *Print. Trades Jrnl.* XXVIII. 4 One of the greatest nuisances of the day is the canvasser.

d. *U.S.* 'One who examines the returns of votes for a public office' (Webster); a scrutineer.

1792 in Sparks *Life & Writ. G. Morris* (1832) III. 38 A majority of the canvassers rejected the votes of three counties. **1904** *Newark Even. News* 25 Nov. 5 Governor Murphy has appointed..as the State Board of Canvassers. .. The board will..officially determine the number of votes which were cast for the different candidates.

'canvassing, *vbl. sb.* The action of the vb. CANVASS, q.v.

1565 JEWEL *Repl. Harding* (1611) 86 This errour must needs hold by the canuasing of the Scriptures **1577** STANYHURST *Desc. Irel.* in *Holinshed* VI. 25 Through the canvasing of the towne merchants..that famous Mart was suppreст. **1589** COOPER *Admon.* 142 Such canuasing and working for Bishoprikes. **1606** HOLLAND *Sueton.* 34 a, That pastime with us in some places called the canvasing, and else where the vanning of dogs. **1613** R. C. *Table Alph.* (ed. 3) *Canuasing*, narrowly searching out of any thing. **1620** SHELTON *Quix.* IV. v. II. 55 She told likewise all the Story of his Canvasing. **1753** SMOLLETT *Ct. Fathom* (1784) 121/2 He ..after much canvassing agreed to discharge the defendant. **1838** DICKENS *Nich. Nick.* xvi. 121 At canvassing or election time.

†**b.** (*ellipt. const.* for 'a-canvassing'.)

1681 TEMPLE *Mem.* III. (R.) The elections were canvassing for a new parliament.

'canvassing, *ppl. a.* That canvasses.

1579 J. STUBBES *Gaping Gulf* F ij, Such a rablement of itching canuasing discoursing and subtile heads. **1865** KNIGHT *Pass. Working Life* III. 18 The persevering activity of the agents of the canvassing booksellers.

canvassy ('kænvəsɪ), *a.* Also **canvasy**. [f. CANVAS *sb.* + -Y[1].] Made of canvas, resembling canvas.

1892 *Dram. Opinions* 13 Jan. 1/1 The scenery..does not come up to the Lyceum standard, being more palpably *canvasy* than usual. **1903** *Westm. Gaz.* 12 Feb. 4/2 That nice crisp softness in the way they hang peculiar to things canvassy. **1923** *Blackw. Mag.* July 4/1 The material was quite loosely woven and canvassy.

cany ('keɪnɪ), *a.* [f. CANE *sb.* + -Y.]

1. Made or consisting of cane.

1667 MILTON *P.L.* III. 439 Where Chineses drive With Sails and Wind their canie Waggons light. **1738** GLOVER *Leonidas* IV. (R.) Scimitars..and cany bows. **1849** DE QUINCEY *Mail-coach* IV. 343 The little cany carriage.

2. 'Full of canes' (J.); cane-like.

1853 G. JOHNSTON *Nat. Hist. East. Borders* I. 75 They shoot up in freedom their cany boughs.

canyculere, canyon: see CANI-.

canyon ('kænjən), *sb.* Also **kanyon**. [A phonetic spelling of Sp. *cañon*, designed to represent the proper spoken word: cf. CANION.] = CAÑON *sb.*[3]

1837 O. RUSSELL *Jrnl.* (1955) 61 A deep narrow kanyon of rock. **1841** FARNHAM *Trav. Gt. Western Prairies* (1843) I. v. 267 About midway from the Great Gap and the Kenyon of the south Fork of the Platte. *Ibid.* 268 This Kenyon terminates thirty miles above the Gulf. **1861** R. BURTON *City of Saints* 117 *note*, The Spanish cañon—Americanised to kanyon—signifies a..ravine of peculiar form, common in this part of America. **1865** TYLOR *Early Hist. Man.* iii. 39 Traversed a kanyon or ravine. **1878** BLACK *Green Past.* xiii. 103 To explore the neighbouring canyons. **1946** *Nat. Geogr. Mag.* Jan. 33/2 High pine-studded canyons.

'canyon, *v.* [f. the sb.] **a.** *intr.* To flow in(to) a canyon. **b.** *trans.* To cut into canyons.

1869 S. BOWLES *Summer Vac. Colorado* 25 They 'canyon', as, by making a verb of the Spanish noun, the people of the country describe the streams as performing the feat of such rock passages. **1870** J. H. BEADLE *Utah* 441 Bear River.. forms a great U in Idaho, then turning southwest 'canyons' downward three miles. **1878** I. L. BIRD *Lady's Life in Rocky Mts.* (1879) xi. 195 Rocks, cleft and canyoned by the river. **1944** *Christian Sci. Monitor* 26 Dec., The great inland rivers of America, as wide as the Missouri and as canyoned as the Colorado.

can you? *Cards.* Also formerly **can-ye?** Now **can you one?** A 'call' at Long Whist; when one side has already scored eight ('ten' being the game), and a new hand is dealt, if a player on the winning side has two honours in his hand, he may thus ask his partner if he also has one, in which case, counting the majority of honours, they would score two and win.

1680 COTTON *Compl. Gamester* in Singer *Hist. Cards* 338 If either side are at eight groats he hath the benefit of calling *can-ye*, if he hath two honours in his hand, and if the other answers *one*, the game is up, which is nine in all, but if he hath more than two he shews them, and then it is one and the same thing; but if he forgets to call after playing a trick, he loseth the advantage of can-ye for that deal. **1709** *Brit. Apollo* II. No. 36. 2/1 The first are 8 Groats, which is generally call'd *Can-you*, the last are 6 Groats, which is generally call'd long *Can-you*.

'canzon. Now *arch.* [ad. It. *canzone* song: see next. In very common use in 17th c.] A song.

1590 LODGE *Euphues Gold. Leg.* in *Shaks. Wks.* (Halliw.) VI. 37 My canzon was written in no such humor. **1597** MIDDLETON *Wisdom of Sol.* Wks. V. 459 Deepest canzons of lament. **1633** P. FLETCHER *Purple Isl.* I. xiv, To frame Angelick strains, and canzons sing. **1687** WINSTANLEY *Lives Eng. Poets* 99 A writer of..canzons, and madrigals. **1952** E. POUND *Personae* 258 Safe may'st thou go my canzon whither thee pleaseth.

‖**canzona** (kan'tsona). [It.; deriv. form of *canzone*: see next.]

1. = CANZONE.

2. *Music.* **a.** The setting to music of the words of a canzone or canzona, for one or more voices. **b.** An instrumental piece written in the style of a madrigal. †**c.** Apparently an equivalent for sonata, as a piece of several movements. (Grove.)

1880 E. PROUT in Grove *Dict. Mus.* I. 306 A canzona by Sebastian Bach may be found in..his organ works.

‖**canzone** (kan'tsone). [It. *canzone* (= Sp. *cancion*, Pr. *canso*, *canson*. F. *chanson*):—L. *cantiōn-em* singing, song, f. *cant-* ppl. stem of *can-ĕre* to sing.] In *Ital.* or *Prov. Lit.*: A song, a ballad; a species of lyric, closely resembling the madrigal but less strict in style.

1590 GREENE *Never too late* (1600) 34 Francesco..to try the finesse of his wit, with a poeticall furie, began thus to make a Canzone. *a* **1789** BURNEY *Hist. Mus.* (ed. 2) II. iv. 325 When the song is written on a grave or tragic subject, says he it is called Canzone. **1877** MRS. OLIPHANT *Makers of Flor.* iv. 122 The Florentine public..sang the great poet's canzones about the streets.

canzonet (kænzəʊ'nɛt). [ad. It. *canzonetta* (= Pr. *cansoneta*, Fr. *chansonnette*), dim. of *canzone*.] A little or short song; a vocal solo in more than one movement; now usually, a short song of a light and airy character.

1593 T. MORLEY (*title*) Canzonets, or little short Songs to three Voyces. **1597** —— *Introd. Mus.* 180 Canzonets, that is little shorte songs..which is in composition of the musick a counterfet of the Madrigal. **1615** G. SANDYS *Trav.* 291 The lakes reechoing their continual canzonets and the like. **1763** J. BROWN *Poetry & Music* xii. 199 The common Song or Canzonette. **1792** S. ROGERS *Ital. Song* 118 The canzonet and roundelay Sung in the silent greenwood shade. **1847** TENNYSON *P'cess* IV. 117 A rogue of canzonets and serenades. **1880** W. H. CUMMINGS in Grove *Dict. Mus.* I. 306 Haydn has left us some admirable canzonets grave and gay; for example, 'She never told her love'.

‖**canzonetta** (kantso'netta). Pl. **canzonettas, canzonette.** [It., lit. 'little song'.] = CANZONET; CANZONE.

1724 *Short Explic. For. Words in Mus. Bks.* 19 *Canzonetta*, is a little Song, or Tune, Cantata, or Sonata. **1811** BYRON *Let.* 7 Sept. in *Wks.* (1832) II. 62 Spin canzonettas for Vauxhall. **1947** C. GRAY *Contingencies* ix. 149 Several of his madrigals and *canzonette*. **1958** *Listener* 14 Aug. 250/3 The canzonetta, villotta, carnival songs, and so on which are all offshoots of the madrigal.

Caodaism (kɑːəʊ'daɪɪz(ə)m). [Vietnamese *Cao Dai* (also used), lit. 'great palace' + -ISM.] A syncretistic religion founded in Cochin China in 1926. Hence **Caodaist** (-'daɪɪst), an adherent of Caodaism.

1937 V. THOMPSON *French Indo-China* vi. 474 The birth of a new politico-religious sect in Cochin-China called Caodaism in 1926. *Ibid.*, Nationalists and Caodaists use to good effect the plea for liberty of conscience. **1953** *Americana Annual* 332/2 The Caodaist sect fuses elements of all the great religions. **1953** *Newsweek* 4 May 48/3 Private armies of politico-religious sects such as the Caodaists (a hodgepodge of Buddhism, Confucianism, Spiritualism, and Christianity). *Ibid.* 21 Sept. 62/3 Among the most interesting religions..is Caodaism in Indo-China. **1955** *Times* 2 May 12/2 The Caodai 'pope', spiritual leader of the Caodai sect. **1958** A. J. TOYNBEE *East to West* xx. 62 A spiritual journey leading up to Caodai-ism as its goal. **1969** *New Yorker* 20 Sept. 110/3 The scattered religious elements in the South—the Buddhists, the Catholics, the Cao Dai sect.

‖**caoine** ('kiːnə). [Ir.] = KEEN *sb.*

1707 E. LHUYD *Archæologia Britannica* 309 *Caoine* is a sort of Verse used in Elegies or Funeral Poems; and sometimes also in Panegyricks and Satyrs. Each versicle of a *Caoine* consists of only four Feet, and each Foot most commonly of two Syllables. **1844** T. C. CROKER in *Percy Soc. Early Eng. Poetry* XIII. p. ix, *Keen*, which is here written according to its sound to the English ear, is, in its correct modern orthography, *Caòine*. **1916** STANFORD & FORSYTH *Hist. Music* x. 212 The principal styles [of Irish folk-music] are the songs, reels, jigs, caoines. **1954** *Grove's Dict. Mus.* (ed. 5) II. 50/1 The *caoine* is identical with the *qinah* of the Old Testament, where it is a lamentation for the death by professional wailing-women.

caoline, var. KAOLIN.

1895 BARING-GOULD *Noémi* x. 140 On the tops of the plateau..lies a film of caoline.

†**Caorsin.** *Obs.* (exc. *Hist.*) Also 4 **kauersin.** [a. Of. *caorsin*, *caoursin*, *coursin*, etc., in med.L. *caorcini*, *caourcini*, *caturcini*, in Matt. Paris *caursini*, an inhabitant of *Cahors*, L. *Cadurcum*, in Languedoc, a famous seat of Italian money-changers and financiers in the Middle Ages; hence, banker, usurer, money-lender. Commonly mentioned along with Lombards and Jews. See Godefroy and Du Cange.]

A banker or money-dealer from Cahors: usurer.

The Caorsins were expelled from England by Henry III in 1240, readmitted on the intervention of the Pope in 1250, and again proscribed and imprisoned 'on account of their unbounded and detestable usury' in 1251.

[*a* **1259** MATT. PARIS *Chron.* an. 1235 (Rolls Ser.) III. 328 Caursinorum pestis abominanda. *Ibid.* an. 1255 V. 519 Qui

[Judæi] si forte ab aliquibus Christianis plangerentur, ab æmulis eorum Cahursinis siccis lacrimis deplorabantur.] **1303** R. BRUNNE *Handl. Synne* 5555 Okerers, ande kauersyns, As wykkede þey are as sarasyns. **1340** *Ayenb.* 35 þe heȝe men..þet hyealdeþ and sosteneþ Iewes and þe Caorsins, þet leneþ and destruiþ þe contraye.

caoutchin ('kaʊtʃɪn). *Chem.* [f. CAOUTCH-OUC + -IN.] A hydrocarbon, $C_{10}H_{16}$, contained in the oils produced by distillation of caoutchouc and gutta percha: one of the elements of *caoutchoucin*.

1863-72 WATTS *Dict. Chem.* I. 736 Caoutchin is a transparent, colourless, mobile liquid, having an odour like that of oil of orange.

caoutchouc ('kaʊtʃʊk, 'ku:-). [a. F. *caoutchouc* (pron. kautʃu), ad. Carib *cahuchu* (Littré).]

1. India-rubber, or Gum Elastic; the milky resinous juice of certain trees in S. America, the E. Indies, and elsewhere, which coagulates on exposure to the air, and becomes highly elastic, and is waterproof; it is now a most important substance in arts and manufactures.

'Introduced to France early in the last century, but its origin was unknown till the visit of the French academicians to South America in 1735. They ascertained that it was the inspissated juice of a Brazilian tree, called by the natives *Hhvé*; and an account of the discovery was sent to the academy by M. de la Condamine in 1736' (*Penny Cycl.*). Chiefly obtained from the Brazilian *Siphonia elastica* (*Hevea caoutchouc*) N.O. *Euphorbiaceæ*, and E. Indian *Ficus elastica*. But many other tropical plants, *Euphorbiaceæ*, *Apocynaceæ*, *Artocarpads*, and others, yield it in considerable quantity. Chemically it is composed entirely of carbon and hydrogen, but is not a simple proximate principle, but a mixture of substances.

1775 *Phil. Trans.* LXVI. 258 An elastic gum bottle, otherwise called *boradchio* or *caout-chouc*. **1779** *Ibid.* LXIX. 384, I take the tube out of the phial, and thrust it..into a small caoutchouck, or elastic gum bottle. **1788-9** HOWARD *New Royal Encycl.* s.v., *Caoutchouc* in natural history..a very elastic resin..Very useful for erasing the strokes of black lead pencils, and is popularly called rubber, and lead-eater. **1827** FARADAY *Chem. Manip.* iv. 122 Cloth is rendered air-tight by caoutchouc. **1870** EMERSON *Soc. & Sol.*, *Work & Days* Wks. (Bohn) III. 65 What of this dapper caoutchouc and gutta-percha, which makes water-pipes.. and rain-proof coats for all climates? **1875** J. H. BENNET *Shores Medit.* I. i. 25 The secret of the luxuriant verdure [in the Euphorbia]..is the existence of a kind of caoutchu in their white acrid juices.

b. *attrib.* or in *comb.*

1833 BREWSTER *Nat. Magic* viii. 206 The country where the caoutchouc-tree was indigenous. **1859** JEPHSON *Brittany* iv. 38 Drinking..out of my caoutchouc cup. **1861** DU CHAILLU *Equat. Afr.* x. 121 The native caoutchouc collectors. *Ibid.* 122 The caoutchouc-vine grows equally well.

c. = 'Waterproof' (cloak).

1867 *Cornh. Mag.* Jan. 59 With the large hood of her caoutchouc heavy with snow.

2. ***artificial caoutchouc***: a substance formed by adding to a solution of glue tungstic acid or sodium tungstate, and then hydrochloric acid; it is elastic when warm. ***mineral c.***: = ELATERITE, a hydrocarbon found at Castleton in Derbyshire, and elsewhere. ***vulcanized c.***: caoutchouc kneaded with flowers of sulphur, with which it unites and becomes black and horny: see VULCANITE.

1863-72 WATTS *Dict. Chem.* I. 739 Sulphured or vulcanized caoutchouc is an excellent material for tubes for conveying water or gases.

caoutchoucin ('kaʊtʃu:sɪn). *Chem.* [f. CAOUTCHOUC + -IN.] A thin volatile oily liquid or empyreumatic oil, obtained from caoutchouc by dry distillation. It is composed of two polymeric hydrocarbons, *caoutchin* and *isoprene*.

1863-72 WATTS *Dict. Chem.* I. 739 Caoutchoucin..forms an excellent solvent for caoutchouc and other resins.

cap (kæp), *sb.*[1] Forms: 1 (cappa), cæppe, 3 keppe, 4-6 cappe, (5 cape), 5-7 capp, 6- cap. [OE. *cæppe*, a. late L. *cappa* 'cap' (It. *cappa*, Pr., Sp., Pg. *capa*, ONF. and Picard *cape*, F. *chape*, all meaning 'cloak, cape, or cope'). Isidore, *a.* 636, has (XIX. xxxi. 3, *De ornamentis capitis feminarum*) 'cappa..quia capitis ornamentum est'; Diez cites *cappa* from a document of 660, and an ancient gloss '*cappa* mitra'. Med.L. used indiscriminately *cappa* and *capa* (the latter, however, much more frequently), and commonly in the sense of 'cloak, cope'; *Chron. Treverti* anno 1146, has 'caracalla (i.e. a long cloak with a hood) quam nunc capam vocamus'. The presumption is that the name was transferred from a woman's cap, hood, or head-covering, as Isidore used it, to the 'hood' of a cloak, and then to a cloak or 'cape' having such a hood, and thus to a priest's 'cope'. The sense 'head-covering, cap, hat' was at an early period in Romanic appropriated by the dim. *cappellum*, *-ellus*, in It. *cappello*, Sp. *capelo*, Pr. *capel*, OF. *capel*, *chapel*, F. *chapeau*, 'hat'. (The sense 'little or short cloak' was retained by the fem. dim. *cappella*, *capella*, It. *cappella*, Pr., Pg. *capella*, Sp. *capilla*, ONF. *capelle*, F. *chapelle*, until this received the curiously transferred sense CHAPEL, q.v.)

An explanation of *capa*, from *capere* to take, 'quia quasi totum capiat hominem' (because it *takes* as it were the whole man) is erroneously cited by Du Cange, and many after him, from Isidore. It is really from Papias *c* 1053; and is manifestly a 'popular etymology' of a late age, after the application had passed from 'cap' to 'cloak with a hood'. (Mahn thinks that *cappa* may be of Iberian origin.) The evidence of OE. is important, since it points to two distinct L. types, viz. *cappa* (which gave *cæppe*, *cappe*, *cap*), and *cāpa* which gave *cāpe*, *cōpe*; the latter is also witnessed by Icel. *kápa* 'cowled cloak, cloak with a hood': see COPE.

It looks as if *cappa*, the living Romanic form, was first adopted in Eng. (say from Italy) in its 7th c. sense, and gave *cæppe*, and that at a later time *cāpa*, so common in med.L., was introduced specially for the ecclesiastical dress. The latter is not actually evidenced in OE., but it occurs in Layamon, and was in the language early enough to undergo the phonetic change of OE. *ā* into ME. *ǭ*. OHG. (late) had *chappa* 'cloak with a hood'; so MHG. *kappe*, MDu. *cappe* (both rarely in sense 'cap'); modG. *kappe*, Du. *kap* 'cap'.

Words to be distinguished are (1) *Cap*, OE. *cæppe*, L. *cappa*; (2) *Cap*, Sc. dial. form of *cop* (like *tap*, *stap*, for *top*, *stop*); (3) *Cape*, early ME. form of *cope*, retained in north. dial. and Sc. as *cape*, *caip* (cf. early ME. and north. *pape*, Sc. *paip* = *pope*); (4) *Cape*, mod.Eng., from F. *cape*, Sp. *capa* cloak, the same word in origin as 3, but re-introduced in a new connexion; (5) *Cape*, F. *cap*, It. *capo* headland; (6) *Cop*, OE. *cop*, *copp* top, summit, also cup; (7) *Cope*, early ME. *cāpe*, Icel. *kápa*, L. *cāpa*. In ME. *cape* also occasionally appears for *cappe*, *cap*.]

I. A covering for the head.

1. A hood, a covering for the head. (Precise sense not definable; in first quot. still in Latin form.)

c **1000** ÆLFRIC *Voc.* in Wr.-Wülcker 152 *Capitulum uel capitularium*, heafod-claþ uel cappa. *a* **1100** *Ags. Voc.* ibid. 328 *Cappa*, cæppe.

†**2.** A cloak with a hood; a cape or cope. (But prob. *cappa* here is really Latin, and not OE.)

a **1000** *Ags. Gloss.* in Wr.-Wülcker 200 *Caracalla*, cappa.

3. A head-dress for women, varying according to fashion and taste. In later times a light covering of muslin, or the like, for the head, ordinarily worn indoors, or under a bonnet. Cf. MOB-CAP.

a **1225** *Ancr. R.* 420 Ȝif ȝe muwen beon wimpel leas, beoð bi warme keppen. **1596** SHAKS. *Tam. Shr.* IV. iii. 70 Ile haue no bigger, this doth fit the time, And Gentlewomen weare such caps as these. **1598** B. JONSON *Ev. Man in Hum.*, Our great heads..never were in safety Since our wives wore these little caps. *c* **1830** MRS. SHERWOOD *Houlston Tracts* III. No. 67. 7 My lady's maid..with a fly cap, and a hat all puffed about with pea-green ribands. **1872** RUSKIN *Eagle's N.* §153 The quaint cap surrounds..the courtly and patient face. **1883** LLOYD *Ebb & Flow* II. 201 Count the nuns' caps and handkerchiefs. *Mod.* She insists on all the maids wearing caps.

4. a. A head-dress of men and boys: commonly applied to every kind of ordinary male head-dress which is not called a 'hat', from which it is distinguished by not having a brim, and by being usually of some soft material; also to a number of official, professional, and special head-dresses.

1382 WYCLIF *Ex.* xxiii. 14 [Men with] cappis died, *or steyned*, in the heedis of hem. *c* **1430** *Freemasonry* 697 When thou comest by-fore a lorde..Hod or cappe that thou of do. *c* **1450** *Nominale* in Wr.-Wülcker 735 *Hic pilius*, a cape. **1523** LD. BERNERS *Froiss.* I. cxix. 142 He toke of his cap and saluted the duke. **1553** EDEN *Treat. New Ind.* (Arb.) 22 Some [weare] high cappes lyke myters, of redde colour. **1594** SHAKS. *Rich. III*, III. vii. 35 Some followers of mine owne..hurld vp their Caps, And..cry'd, God saue King Richard. **1662** FULLER *Worthies* IV. 50 The best caps were formerly made at Monmouth, where the Cappers Chappel doth still remain. **1663** BUTLER *Hud.* I. III. 1151 Black Caps, underlaid with White, Give certain guess at inward Light. **1742** MIDDLETON *Cicero* III. ix. 6 *note*, A Cap was always given to Slaves, when they were made free, whence it became the emblem of liberty. **1772** *Hartford Mercury Suppl.* 18 Sept. 1/1 The Swedes were divided into two parties, distinguished by the names of Hats and Caps. *Mod.* Hats and caps of every shape.

b. Used contextually instead of *college cap* (esp. in phrase ***cap and gown***), *night-cap*, *skull-cap*, or other specific sense: see **e**.

1611 COTGR., *Calotte*..a little light cap, or night-cap, worne vnder a hat. *a* **1656** BP. HALL *Rem. Wks.* (1660) 242 We hold the head uncovered if the hat be off, though the cap be on. **1807** SOUTHEY *Espriella's Lett.* II. 63 The caps and tassels of the students. **1835** HOOD *Poetry, Prose, & Worse* xxix, Judge Park appears dreadfully prosy While dooming to death in his Cap. **1857** C. BEDE *Verdant Green* 341 While Mr. Green was paying for the cap and gown. *Mod.* Do we appear in cap and gown? Is it a cap-and-gown affair?

c. A helmet or headpiece: also ***cap of fence***.

1530 PALSGR. 202/2 Cappe of fence, *segrette de maille*. **1580** SIDNEY *Let.* in Arb. *Garner* I. 309 When you play at weapons, I would have you get thick caps and bracers. **1839** E. D. CLARKE *Trav.* 50/1 Their cap or helmet is the most beautiful part of the costume. **1874** BOUTELL *Arms & Arm.* ix. 161.

d. 'The ensign of the cardinalate' (J.); a cardinal's biretta.

1591 SHAKS. *1 Hen. VI*, V. i. 33 If once he come to be a Cardinall Hee'l make his cap coequal with the Crowne. **1666** *Lond. Gaz.* No. 26/2 The Pope expects more windfalls before he will give any Caps. **1670** G. H. *Hist. Cardinals* I. III. 74 He puts on the red Cap upon their heads..with these words, *Esto Cardinalis*. **1795** SOUTHEY *Vis. Maid of Orleans* II. 276 These..in scarlet, and in caps Like cardinals, I see. **1864** BURTON *Scot. Abr.* II. i. 69 It would have proved..as fatal..as another such like cap..had done to..Cardinal Betoun.

e. With some qualifying word, indicative of shape, origin, or character; as BLACK CAP, q.v.; ***college cap***, ***square cap***, that worn by academics, which in its present shape is also popularly styled ***trencher cap***, or ***mortar-board***, and in its earlier form is called in Scottish Universities the ***John Knox cap*** (see also CATER-CAP); ***forked cap***, a mitre; †***great cap*** (see quot.); †***Monmouth cap*** (see quot. 1662 in 4): ***Scotch cap***, the cloth cap worn with the Highland dress; also various recent modifications of that pattern; †***spiced cap***, ? a cap lined with a blister for the head; †***statute cap***, a cap of wool ordered by statute (see quot. 1571) to be worn by citizens on holydays for the benefit of the cappers' trade; hence, ***cap of wool***, taken as the mark of a tradesman or citizen. Also ***cricket-***, ***polo-***, ***football-cap***. And see CATER-CAP, NIGHTCAP, SKULL-CAP, etc.

1514 BARCLAY *Cyt. & Uplondysh.* (1847) Introd. 66 With forked cappes it folly is to mell. **1571** *Act 13 Eliz.* xix, Euery person..shall wear vpon the Sabbath and holy day..vpon their head a Cap of Wooll knit thicked and dressed in England. **1582** in W. H. Turner *Select. Rec. Oxford* 430 Scottyshe cappes partelie colored. **1588** SHAKS. *L.L.L.* V. ii. 281 Well, better wits have worne plain statute caps. **1599** —— *Hen. V*, IV. vii. 103 The Welchmen did good service.. wearing Leekes in their Monmouth caps. **1605** MARSTON *Dutch Courtezan* (N.) Though my husband be a citizen, and his cap's made of wool, yet I have wit. **1689** R. DAVIES *Jrnl.* (1857) 51 It was concluded..to put on a spiced cap by order of Dr. Willis for amaurosis. **1691** WOOD *Ath. Oxon.* I. 193 Sampson..was an enemy..to the square cap. **1732** BERKELEY *Alciphr.* I. §11 Philosophers in square caps and long gowns. **1751** CHAMBERS *Cycl.* s.v., Churchmen, and the members of universities..wear square caps. **1753** CHAMBERS *Cycl. Supp.*, *Cap* or *great Cap*, a denomination of a kind of compendious bandage, serving for almost all occasions of the head, being in figure not unlike a helmet. **1873** *Edin. Univ. Calendar* 174 Cap of black silk velvet after the John Knox fashion. **1885** *Cornh. Mag.* July, *Court Royal*, A silk cassock, red hood, and college cap.

f. *spec.* the cap, of a special form or colour, denoting selection as a member of a representative team, crew, etc.; hence, one who is awarded such a cap. Cf. CAP *v.*[1] 1 c.

1879 *Boy's Own Paper* 18 Jan. 1/3, I..was despairing of ever rising to win my 'first fifteen cap'. **1889** BARRÈRE & LELAND *Dict. Slang* I. 367/1 At Rugby when the school played football in white ducks, the probation 'caps' were allowed to wear *flannels*. **1895** *Cassell's Family Mag.* June 518/2 He may possibly be one of the crew, and the vision of the Light Blue cap flits before his enraptured eyes. **1902** *Football Who's Who 1901–2* 133 Cowan, James... Earned caps and medals galore. **1906** GIBSON & PICKFORD *Assoc. Football* IV. 28 He was eight seasons with the grand old club, and won his English cap. **1955** *Times* 10 Aug. 4/4 A brilliant first wood by Coulson, who gained his England cap this season.

g. ***cap of maintenance***: (*a*) see MAINTENANCE; (*b*) A cap borne as one of the insignia of office before the sovereign of England at the coronation, and before mayors of some cities; (*c*) in *Her.* A cap borne as a charge, or in place of a wreath, so ***cap of dignity***, ***estate***, ***honour***, ***state***. ***cap of liberty*** or *Phrygian bonnet*: the conical cap given in the Roman times to slaves on emancipation, and often used as a republican symbol. ***cap and bauble***, ***cap and bells***: the insignia of the fool or jester: cf. FOOL'S CAP. ***cap and feather days***: the days of childhood.

1489 WRIOTHESLEY *Chron.* (1875) I. 2 A capp of maynetenance brought from Rome to the Kinge. **1528** TINDALE *Obed. Chr. Man* Wks. I. 186 For their labour he [the pope] giveth to some a rose; to another a cap of maintenance. **1610** GUILLIM *Heraldry* VI. v. (1660) 400 This kind of Headtire is called a Cap of dignity. **1632** MASSINGER *City Mad.* IV. i, The cap of maintenance and city sword Borne up in state before him. **1663** BUTLER *Hud.* I. III. 1067 For who without a Cap and Bauble..Would put it to a second proof. **1709** ADDISON *Tatler* No. 161 ¶4 The Genius of a Common-wealth, with the Cap of Liberty on her Head. **1752** CARTE *Hist. Eng.* III. 191 The Earl of Surrey had re-assumed them, putting over them..a cap of maintenance purple with powdered furr. **1766** PORNY *Heraldry* (1787) Gloss., *Chapeau*..an antient Cap of Dignity, formerly worn by Nobility, being made of crimson Velvet in the outside, and lined with fur. **1821** in Cobbett *Rur. Rides* (1885) I. 50 Here I was got into the scenes of my cap-and-feather days! **1851** LAYARD *Nineveh* 97 The head dress of the Persian Monarchs appears to have resembled the Phrygian Bonnet or the French Cap of Liberty. **1874** BOUTELL *Arms & Arm.* x. 201 In this example [crested helm of King Richard II.] the lion-crest stands upon a 'cap of dignity'. **1884** *Punch* 1 Mar. 100 Where last he shook the cap and bells.

h. From the custom of uncovering the head (abridged to 'raising' or merely 'touching' the cap) in sign of reverence, respect, or courtesy, come many expressions, such as ***to come with cap in hand***, also ***cap-in-hand***, attrib. phr., †***with cap and knee***, bareheaded and bowing or kneeling, †***with cap and courtship***, or †***cap and curtsey***; and also the contextual use of *cap*, for the raising of the cap, respectful salute.

1565 GOLDING *Ovid's Met.* I. (1593) 3 No man would crouch..to Judge with cap in hand. **1573** G. HARVEY *Letter-bk.* (1884) 5 Neither aferding me a word, nor a cap. **1581** MARBECK *Bk. of Notes* 1189 They shall have cappe and knee,

and many gaye good morrowes in this lyfe. **1598** E. Gilpin *Skial.* (1878) 44 Cap and courtship complements. **1600** Holland *Livy* IX. xx. 328 They..importuned them..with cap and cursie. **1675** Brooks *Gold. Key* Wks. 1867 V. 486 Oh the caps, knees, and bows that Haman had. **1679** Penn *Addr. Prot.* I. 14 It [Apparel] opens Doors..carries away the Cap and the Knee from most other pretences. **1702** *Eng. Theophrast.* 109 A cap or a smile perhaps will serve to gain us the reputation of the opposite Virtues. **1887** *Pall Mall G.* 23 Feb. 3 Suppose that it went cap in hand to every Government in Europe. **1889** C. M. Yonge in *Monthly Packet* Xmas 33, I don't care for those cap-in-hand ways of your people here. **1960** *Farmer & Stockbreeder* 29 Mar. 109/1 A more militant approach is called for and an end to this cap-in-hand begging for fair play.

i. *fig.* (with some sense of top).

1607 Shaks. *Timon* IV. iii. 363 Thou art the Cap Of all the Fooles aliue.

5. In names of plants, as FRIAR'S CAP, SOLDIER'S CAP, TURK'S CAP, for which see these words.

6. *slang.* (From the expression 'to send round the cap (or hat) for an improvised collection') = *cap-money* (see 19).

1851 *Eureka*; *Sequel Ld. Russell's Post Bag* 21 What amount of Cap is realized out of an average field? **1902** *Westm. Gaz.* 9 Dec. 3/2 Masters of Hounds are naturally averse to that method of enriching their treasuries which consists in taking a 'cap' from strangers. **1928** *Daily Mail* 5 Nov. 12/3 If a visitor goes out with a pack like the Quorn he will have to pay a cap of £3 3s. per day. **1970** *Daily Tel.* 30 Jan. 19/6 The annual subscription to ride with the Exmoor Foxhounds is going up from £25 to £30 and the cap for visitors will be £3 instead of £2.

7. = Head; as in quot. 1659 in 9, and in such combs. as *fuddle-*, *huff-cap*.

8. Short for CAP-PAPER.

1630 J. Taylor (Water P.) *Wks.* (N.) Dunghill rags.. May be advanc'd aloft to sheets of cap. **1751** Chambers *Cycl.* s.v. *Paper*, Papers..may be divided..with regard to use..into cap, cartridge, copy, etc. **1874** Knight *Dict. Mech.* s.v., Flat cap is 14×17 inches; double cap is 17×28; foolscap and legal cap are of various sizes. **1875** Ure *Dict. Arts* III. 497 Under the characteristic names of coarse papers may be mentioned: Kent cap, 21 by 18; bag cap, $19\frac{1}{2}$ by 24; Havon cap, 21 by 26; imperial cap, $22\frac{1}{2}$ by 29.

9. Phrases. †***to cast one's cap at***: to show indifference to, give up for lost. †***to come, fall under, lie in one's cap***: to occur to, be in one's mind. ***to put on one's thinking*** or ***considering cap***: to take time for thinking over something. ***the cap fits***: the description or remark suits or is felt to suit (a particular person). ***to pull caps***: to quarrel, wrangle, struggle together (? in a noisy or undignified way). ***to set one's cap at***: (colloq.) said of a woman who sets herself to gain the affections of a man. †***to have one's cap set, to have*** (***enough***) ***under one's cap***: to be intoxicated. ***to throw up one's cap***: i.e. in token of joy. †***if your cap be of wool***: as sure as your cap is of wool. And other obvious proverbial phrases, such as ***my cap is better at ease than my head, ready as a borrower's cap***, etc.

1562 J. Heywood *Prov. & Epigr.* (1867) 136 My cap is better at ease then my hed. **1579** Tomson *Calvin's Serm. Tim.* 824/2 Hauing cast their caps into ye winde (as the prouerbe is) thinke no harme can touch them. **1582** *Long Meg of Westminster* (N.) Vicar..I'le make thee pay every farthing, if thy cap be of wooll. **1593** Shaks. *3 Hen. VI*, II. i. 196 He that throwes not vp his cap for ioy. **1597** —— *2 Hen. IV*, II. ii. 125 The answer is as ready as a borrowers cap. **1611** Cotgr. s.v. *Prendre, La pluye le prendra*, he will be well whitled, his cap will be set. **1624** Bp. Mountagu *Gagg.* 61 Goe cast your cap then at Peter's primacy from confirming his Brethren. *a* **1637** B. Jonson *T. Tub* II. ii. (N.) Slip, you will answer it, an if your cap be of wool. **1657** R. Ligon *Barbadoes* (1673) 42 They fall back, and put on their considering caps. *a* **1659** Osborn *Observ. Turks* (1673) Pref. 4 It lies not in my Cap to apprehend. **1719** D'Urfey *Pills* III. 52 He..casts his Cap, At the Court and her Cares. *a* **1734** North *Ld. Guilford* (1808) I. 84 (D.) It fell not under every one's cap to give so good advice. *Ibid.* II. 32 The reasons were special, and such as come not under every cap. **1749** Cleland *Mem. Woman of Pleasure* I. 99 Oh! he was such a beauty!..they would pull caps for him! **1754** Richardson *Let.* 12 Sept. (1804) V. 27 She scrupled not..to pull caps in good-humoured roguery. **1755** *Mem. Capt. P. Drake* II. v. 188 Mr. Miller, to show the Cap fitted him, made a Stroke with his Cane..at me. **1773** Goldsm. *Stoops to Conq.* I. i, Instead of breaking my heart at his indifference, I'll..set my cap to some newer fashion, and look out for some less difficult admirer. **1785** Wolcott (P. Pindar) *Ode to R. A.'s* x. Wks. 1812 I. 100 Our lofty Duchesses pull caps, And give each other's reputation raps. **1806** —— *Tristia* Wks. 1812 V. 341 Seven cities of the Grecian world Pull'd wigs, pull'd caps. **1816** 'Quiz' *Grand Master* III. 55 If the cap fits him, he may wear it. **1822** Byron *Juan* XI. lxxx, Some, who once set their caps at cautious dukes. **1830** Gen. P. Thompson *Exerc.* (1842) I. 195 Men are exhorted to struggle and pull caps. **1839** De Quincey *War* Wks. IV. 272 They could not have caused a war by pulling caps with each other. **1848** Thackeray *Van. Fair* I. iii, That girl is setting her cap at you. **1866** Geo. Eliot *F. Holt* (1868) 38 If anybody shows himself offended, he'll put the cap on for himself.

II. Things of similar shape, position, or use.

* *Of things natural.*

10. a. A cap-like covering of any kind; spec. the *pileus* or head of a mushroom, the *patella* or small bone protecting the knee-joint (KNEE-CAP); a cloud resting on a mountain top. **b.** A top stratum or layer, *esp.* when harder than that which it covers; a capping. **c.** A cap-like top.

1398 Trevisa *Barth. De P.R.* XVII. lxxxi. (1495) 653 Somme plantis beere sede in harde shales and in cappys wythout aboue the shalys: as nottes and other suche. **1664** Power *Exp. Philos.* II. 92 The little Cap of Air in the obtuse end of an Egge. **1671** Grew *Anat. Plants* I. vi. §8 In a Nut ..there are three general Parts, the Cap, Shell, and Pith. **1678** *Phil. Trans.* XII. 1052 The Mine..lies twenty yards under a surface or Cap of Earth. **1762** Hudson in *ibid.* LII. 496 Part of the base of one of the Fungi..rests on the pileus, or cap of the other. **1767** Sterne *Tr. Shandy* IX. xxxi, A wound upon the cap of a man's knee. **1791** Smeaton *Edystone L.* §108 The merchantable Beds are universally covered with a Stratum called the Cap, which is formed entirely of a congeries of petrified sea-shells. **1839** Murchison *Silur. Syst.* I. xxxvii. 516 The present form of the hills has alone been preserved by caps of semi-conglomerate cornstone. **1856** Longf. *Twilight*, Like the wings of sea-birds Flash the white caps of the sea. **1860** Tyndall *Glac.* I. §15. 101 On looking towards the Æggischorn we found a [cloud] cap upon its crest. **1865** Lubbock *Preh. Times* xii. (1878) 426 The ice cap at the Antarctic Pole.

d. *Ornith.* The pileum or top of a bird's head, especially when distinctively coloured. Cf. BLACK CAP 3.

1889 in *Cent. Dict.* **1890** Coues *Ornith.* 142 'Top of the head' is a collective term for all the upper surface, from base of bill to nape, and laterally to about the level of the upper border of the eyes; this is the *pileum* or 'cap'..; it is divided into three portions.

e. The calyptra of mosses.

1864 Oliver *Elem. Bot.* 281 The sporange is covered at first by a cap (*calyptra*). **1900** B. D. Jackson *Gloss. Bot. Terms.*

** *Of things artificial: general and technical.*

11. a. A cap-shaped part forming or covering the top of various things, e.g. of a thimble, furnace, etc.; the movable upper story of a windmill, the outer covering of a bee-hive, an extra box or case added on the top of a hive, the upper half of a journal-box (the lower half being the *pillow*).

1609 C. Butler *Fem. Mon.* (1634) 39 The Head [of the hive] is to be covered and bound fast with a Cap. **1674** Ray *Smelt. Silver* Coll. 114 The refining Furnace is covered with a thick cap of stone. **1693** Sir T. Blount *Nat. Hist.* 293 Full of little Pit-Holes, like the Cap of a Thimble. **1783** *Phil. Trans.* LXXIII. 452 The cap of the receiver. **1867** F. Francis *Angling* i. (1880) 10 Take off the cap of the float. **1881** *Mechanic* §970 The roof should be ornamented at its very apex by a cap.

b. The tire of lead and tin on the periphery of a glazing wheel.

c. (Also ***blue cap***.) In coal-mining, a circle of bluish flame appearing above and around the wick of a safety lamp when a dangerous quantity of fire-damp is present.

1877 *Encycl. Brit.* VI. 72/2 When a lighted candle is exposed in a non-explosive mixture of this gas [*sc.* fire-damp], the flame gradually elongates, forming a conical cap, floating above the wick. **1883** Gresley *Gloss. Coal-m.* s.v. *Blue Cap*, To carry on work in an atmosphere which shows a cap is unsafe. **1887** *Good Words* 99/1 The marsh gas is revealed..by the appearance of what is known as a 'cap' upon the flame. **1893** Lupton *Mining* 248 If there is 2 per cent. of fire-damp in the atmosphere, a small blue-cap may be observed.

12. A cap-like cover or similar part on the end of anything.

E.g. of a magnetic needle, a portable telescope, the lens of a camera; also the iron-banded piece on the end of a wooden pump-rod by which it is connected with a working-beam; the band of leather, etc. in a flail through which the middle-band passes = CAPLIN; the metal on the butt-end of fire-arms; a covering of tarred canvas on the end of a ship rope; an extra covering on the toe of a boot or shoe (= *toe-cap*); small pieces of leather used to confine temporary pins or bolts in carriages.

c **1440** *Promp. Parv.* 61 Cappe of a fleyle, *meditentum*. **1530** Palsgr. 203/1 Cappe of a flayle. **1680** *Lond. Gaz.* No. 1532/4 A Pair of French Pistols..the Stocks of Maple, Silver Side-plates, and Silver Caps. **1747** Knight in *Phil. Trans.* XLIV. 658 These [magnetic] needles..weighed.. with their caps 7 pennyweight. **1794** W. Felton *Carriages* (1801) Gloss., Pole pin caps, etc. **1870** *Eng. Mech.* 18 Mar. 661/3 Designs..suitable for the toe-caps of boots. **1876** Hiles *Catech. Organ* iv. (1878) 25 The cap [of a wood organ pipe] is a piece of hard wood at the lower end of the pipe, covering the block. **1879** *Cassell's Techn. Educ.* III. 99 When the camera has been placed in position..the cap of the lens should be removed. *a* **1884** Knight *Dict. Mech.* Suppl., *Cap*, a short terminal section of a pipe, with a removable stopper called a plug. **1885** *Law Rep.* XV. *Queen's B. Div.* 359 A metal cap was put over the shaft.. The cap kept the shaft in its place. **1886** *Cassell's Fam. Mag.* 638/1 An outer cap protecting the point [of a fountain pen]. **1895** Burns *Gloss. Techn. Terms* 18 *Cap and lining*, in gasfitters' work a joint used for connecting a composition pipe to an iron pipe. **1958** M. L. Hall *Newnes Compl. Amat. Photogr.* 110 Large flashbulbs are fitted with an ES(E27) cap and smaller types with an ASCC(B15s) cap.

13. a. A cap-like covering; a cover or case.

E.g. a *nipple* or *breast-cap*; the inner case, which encloses the movements in some forms of watches; in a cannon = APRON; the cover of a headband or the envelope of a book while binding.

1688 R. Holme *Armoury* III. xii. §18 A Brest Cap, or Nipple Cap..is made of silver in shape like an hat. **1704** J. Harris *Lex. Techn.* s.v., They call also that Piece of Lead which is put over the Touch-hole of a great Gun, to keep the Prime from being wasted or spilt, the Cap of the Gun. **1883** *Leisure Ho.* 244/2 Sewing the 'caps', or covers, on to the bales [of wool]. **1884** F. Britten *Watch & Clockm.* 4 The cap covers the escapement and balance. **1902** *Westm. Gaz.* 4 June 5/1 The effect of fitting shot or shell with a forged steel cap. **1921** *Dict. Occup. Terms* (1927) §254 *Cap maker* (electric lamps); a draw press hand making brass caps for electric lamps in a die press.

b. A small conical paper bag for holding groceries, etc., made by twisting up a sheet of paper; a 'cornet'.

c. *Mining.* ***in*** (***the***) ***cap***: see quots.

[**1871** R. W. Raymond *Mines of Pacific States* 313 The 'cap', a term usually employed to express the impoverished condition of the vein, may be due either to the pinching together of the walls of the fissure, or..to the filling of the vein with barren rock.] *a* **1884** Knight *Dict. Mech.* Suppl. s.v., A vein is 'in the cap' when it is much contracted. **1889** P. Milford *Dict. Mining Terms* (ed. 2) 14 A mine when the vein matter is barren or when the vein is pinched, or contracted, is said to be 'in cap'. *c* **1931** G. F. Willison *Here they dug Gold* vii. 122 Most of the hard-rock mines are in cap.

d. A contraceptive device, usu. made of rubber, covering the neck of the womb. Cf. *Dutch cap.*

1916 *Declining Birth-Rate* II. 247 A woman..will sometimes wear a cap over the neck of the womb, which takes the place, in the female, of the 'letters' that men wear. **1918** M. C. Stopes *Wise Parenthood* iii. 18 The great advantage of this cap is that once it is in and properly fitted it can be entirely forgotten. **1935** E. F. Griffith *Mod. Marriage* iv. 86 There are numberless caps on the market, most of which are made of rubber and vary considerably in thickness. **1970** *Sunday Times* 15 Mar. 50/4 Like the pill, the diaphragm, or cap..are used almost entirely by the more prosperous sections of the community.

14. a. = *gun cap*, *percussion cap*: A cap-shaped piece of copper lined with a fulminating composition, used to ignite the powder in fire-arms.

c **1826** Wellington in *Mem. R. Davenport-Hill* 231 'Croker, you may understand the battle of Waterloo, but I'll be d——d if you know anything of copper caps!' **1844** *Regul. & Ord. Army* 112 *note*, Copper caps [will be charged for] at the rate of ten shillings a thousand. **1868** *Sat. Rev.* No. 652. 561/2 Sometimes the caps would not explode; sometimes there were no caps at all. **1886** *Manch. Exam.* 6 Jan. 5/2 The cap missed fire.

b. The paper percussion cap of a toy pistol; = AMORCE.

1872 C. M. Yonge *P's & Q's* ii. 13 He was only just exploding a few caps to teach the child to stand fire. **1877** *Design & Work* III. 521/3 Those small caps..called French amorgies. **1883** [see AMORCE]. **1921** *Dict. Occup. Terms* (1927) §149 *Snap cap maker*, tends machine which makes snap caps, for toy pistols.

15. A part laid horizontally or flat along the top of various structures.

E.g. a horizontal beam joining the heads of a row of piles in a timber bridge, or the tops of a row of posts in a frame, a *plate*; the handrail of a balustrade, or of a stair railing; the lintel of a door or window frame; a piece of wood laid upon another in order to bring it up to a required height; the hood-sheaves of a shock of corn.

1677 Moxon *Mech. Exerc.* (1703) 151 If the Board be too thin, they underlay that Board upon every Joyst with a Cap. **1688** R. Holme *Armoury* III. xiii. §78 The first is a Wall with a Cap or Head over the Door. **1790** W. Marshall *Midl. Counties* (E.D.S.) *Caps*, hoodsheaves of cornshucks. *c* **1850** *Rudim. Navig.* (Weale) 103 *Caps*, square pieces of oak, laid upon the upper blocks on which the ship is built, to receive the keel.

16. *Arch.* The uppermost part of any assemblage of principal parts.

E.g. the capital of a column, the cornice of a room, the capping or uppermost member of the surbase of a room, etc.

1870 F. Wilson *Ch. Lindisf.* 50 The pillars are cylindrical; their caps primitively fluted. *Ibid.* 110 Its pillars..from floor to cap, are hexagonal.

17. *Naut.* A strong thick block of wood, having two large holes through it, used to hold two masts together, when one is erected at the head of the other in order to lengthen it (Smyth *Sailor's Word-bk.*). ***cap of a block***: see quot. 1794.

1626 Capt. Smith *Seaman's Accid.* 28 Strike your top masts to the cap. **1692** —— *Seaman's Gram.* XVI. 77 *To lower or strike the Flag*, is to pull it down upon the Cap. **1762–9** Falconer *Shipwr.* III. 583 The..stay Drags the main top-mast by the cap away. **1794** *Rigging & Seamanship* I. 150 *Cap*, a semi-circular projection from the sides and round the end of a block above the pin; through it two holes are bored ..through [which] the strap is passed, to prevent its being chafed. **1840** R. Dana *Bef. Mast* xxxv. 132 Rigging all let go ..topsail yards down upon the caps. *c* **1860** H. Stuart *Seaman's Catech.* 75 The lower caps are usually made of oak, with an iron band round them.

III. *attrib.* and in *comb.*

18. General relations: **a.** simple attrib., as ***cap-badge***, ***-border***, ***-box***, ***-peak***, ***-pocket***, ***-priming***, ***-riband***, ***-string***, ***-strip***, ***-worship***; **b.** appositive, 'formed or acting as a cap', as ***cap-glass***, ***-house***, ***-piece***, ***-roof***, ***-sill***; **c.** objective gen., as ***cap-knitter***, ***-maker***, ***-making***, ***-setting***; **d.** adjs., as ***capless***, ***cap-ended***, ***-roofed***.

1897 *Sears, Roebuck Catal.* 236/2 Nickel Plated *Cap Badges. *a* **1916** 'Saki' *Square Egg* (1924) 124 Men of divers variety of cap badges. **1969** D. Lambert *Angels in Snow* xii. 152 His Army cap badge, a couple of Service ribbons. **1878** Mrs. Stowe *Poganuc P.* xxii. 246 A thin old delicate face, with its aureole of white hair and its transparent *cap-border. **1798** W. Felton *Carriages* (1801) I. 219 A *Cap-Box is a case made convenient for carrying ladies' head-dresses safe. **1882** Vines *Sachs' Bot.* 145 Every such segment belonging to a root-cap is hence termed simply a *Cap-cell. **1843** *Jrnl. R. Agric. Soc.* IV. II. 365 *Cap-ended, that is, having no gables. **1660** Sharrock *Vegetables* 12 Those that use *Cap-Glasses..straw, litter, or the like. **1861**

C. INNES *Sk. Early Sc. Hist.* 443 A square keep surmounted by a *cap-house. **1465** in *Ripon Ch. Acts* 120 Marjoria Claton, *cappeknytter. **1600** HEYWOOD *Edw. IV*, I. II. ii, All kings or cap-knitters! **1840** GALT *Demon of Dest.* VIII. 53 His hoary hair streamed *capless. *c* **1440** *York Myst.* xxiv, The .*Cappemakers. **1488–9** *Act 4 Hen. VII*, ix, Hatmakers and Kapmakers doth sell their hattes and cappes at suche an outrageous price. **1713** *Lond. Gaz.* No. 5182/4 The Capmakers of Bewdley. **1796** MORSE *Amer. Geog.* I. 405 Each pier is composed of seven sticks of oak timber, united by a *cap-piece. **1844** *Regul. & Ord. Army* 92 With a view to the preservation of the *Cap Pockets, they are..to be carried inside the Pouch, over the Ammunition. **1879** G. MACDONALD *Sir Gibbie* xxi. 112 A turret with a conical *cap-roof. **1882** *Society* 30 Dec. 12/2 Caught by a *cap-setting woman. **1824** MISS MITFORD *Village* Ser. II. (1863) 263 Beautiful, in spite of age, and *cap-strip, and neckcloth, and spectacles. **1630** SANDERSON *Serm.* II. 262 The knee-worship, and the *cap-worship, and the lip-worship they may have that are in worshipful places.

19. Special combs.: **cap-bar** *Spinning*, an attachment to a drawing-frame supporting the bearings of draft rolls; †**cap-castle**, the chief village of a district; **cap-cell** *Bot.* (see quot. 1900); **cap-frame**, a type of spinning-frame in which the guide for the yarn takes the form of a cap; **cap-gun** = *cap-pistol*; **cap-head** (*Mining*), a top placed upon an air-box, used in sinking, etc.; **capland** (see quot.); **cap-man**, a cap-maker; a man who inspects the lamps attached to miners' caps; **cap-money** (see quot.); **cap-pistol**, a toy pistol which fires caps (sense 14 b); **cap-pudding**, a pudding containing plums or currants which form a black top or cap to it when it is served up; **cap-ribbon**, a band round a sailor's cap bearing the name of his ship; **cap rock** *Geol.*, an overlying rock or stratum; see also quot. 1956; **cap-screw** = *tap-bolt* (s.v. TAP *sb.*[1] 8); **cap-scuttle** (see quot.); **cap-sea** (see quot.); **cap-sheaf**, the top sheaf of a shock or stook, also *fig.*; **cap-shore** (see quot.); **cap-sick** *a.*, ? brain-sick, intoxicated; **cap-square**, † **-squire** (see quot.); **cap-tally** *Naut. slang*, = *cap-ribbon*; see also quot. 1946.

1897 W. S. TAGGART *Cotton Spinning* II. 91 It was formerly the practice to make the *cap bars of cast-iron. **1898** *Ibid.* III. 241 The cap bar, for keeping the top rollers in position, is pivoted..so that it can readily be moved over out of the way when the rollers require attention. **1664** SPELMAN s.v. *Metrocomiae*, Et nos in Gallia Narbonensi Metrocomias nunc *Capcastles appellamus. **1882** *Cap-cell [in N.E.D.]. **1900** B. D. JACKSON *Gloss. Bot. Terms*, *Cap Cells*, the upper sister-cells of the embryo-sac in the ovule which are compressed as the embryo-sac develops and for a time figure as a cap on its apex. **1884** W. S. B. McLAREN *Spinning* 160 For fine Botany yarns the *cap frame is always employed. **1921** *Dict. Occup. Terms* (1927) §365 *Spinner, cap; cap frame tenter*; minds a spinning frame in which guide over spindle is in form of a cap. **1931** *Kansas City Star* 22 July, They had bought two ice cream cones, a *cap gun, [etc.]. **1949** J. R. COLE *It was so Late* 71 Once he had brought him an old cap-gun. **1819** *Edin. Rev.* XXXII. 10 *Cap-land ..was held by the oaths of seven recognitors. **1647** in Rushw. *Hist. Col.* IV. II. 974 Two Thousand *Cap-Men from Bewdly. **1921** *Dict. Occup. Terms* (1927) §047 *Capman*; a lampman who attends to lamps attached to miners' caps; used only in a non-fiery mine. **1847–78** HALLIWELL, **Capmoney*, money gathered for the huntsman at the death of the fox. **1920** I. E. OSTRANDER *How many Cards?* 8, I found a gat on him that's like a toy *cap pistol compared to that gun lying there. **1962** A. LEJEUNE *Duel in Shadows* xii. 176 The shots sounded no louder than a child's cap-pistol. **1917** 'TAFFRAIL' *Little Ship* 20 At least ten thousand men must wear the H.M.S. *Victory* *cap-ribbon. **1960** *Times* 2 Apr. 8/7 The officer-of-the-watch moves down the line, his glance taking in every man, shoes to cap-ribbon. **1867** O. J. HOLLISTER *Mines of Colorado* 64 The quartz and *cap or wall-rock. **1874** R. W. RAYMOND *Statistics Mines, 6th Rep.* I. 317 The barren, or 'cap rock', now met with at the water-line in that mine. **1956** J. C. SWAYNE *Gloss. Geogr. Terms* 30 *Cap-rock*, (a) a stratum of resistant rock covering another of less resistant material; (b) the rock cover over the top of a salt-plug; (c) unproductive rock covering valuable ore. **1958** *New Scientist* 30 Jan. 8/3 If there exists suitable limestone or sandstone to form a reservoir rock, with an impervious 'cap-rock' layer above it, all the conditions for an oil field will be present. *a* **1884** KNIGHT *Dict. Mech.* Suppl., **Cap Screw*, a machine screw with a cubical head, used for screwing on the cylinder head. *c* **1850** *Rudim. Navig.* (Weale) 103 *A *cap scuttle*, a framing composed of coamings and head-ledges raised above the deck, with a flap or top which shuts closely over into a rabbet. **1880** ANDREWS *Daring Voy.* 135 Their course took them into the '*Cap Seas', or 'Rolling Forties' of Sailors, to the south and eastward of the Grand Banks. **1782** S. BALDWIN in S. E. Baldwin *Life & Lett.* (1919) 106 The whole was crown'd with a *cap-shief of Albany politeness. **1805** R. W. DICKSON *Pract. Agric.* II. 793 These [hattocks] ..are exposed to the action of the sun and air by taking off the hood, or cap-sheaves, in the day-time. **1851** H. MELVILLE *Whale* xlv. 296 The placing the cap-sheaf to all this blundering business was reserved for..Cuvier. **1873** M. E. HOLLEY *My Opinions & Betsey Bobbet's* 337 Of all the painted..critters I ever see, she was the cap sheaf. **1882** NARES *Seamanship* (ed. 6) 8 **Capshore*, a support under the forepart of a lower cap. **1619** H. HUTTON *Follies Anat.* (1842) 9, I could..tell a tale should..make them startle; fain themselves *cap-sick. **1611** COTGR., *Clavette*..also the *Capsquire, or Fore-locke of the carriage of a Canon. **1704** J. HARRIS *Lex. Techn.*, *Cap-Squares*, are broad Pieces of Iron, on each side of the Carriage of a great Gun, and lock'd over the Trunnions of the Piece with an Iron Pin: Their use is to keep the Piece from flying out of the Carriage when 'tis shot off with its Mouth lying very low. **1944** J. IRVING *Naval Life* 27 The '*cap-tally' with the ship's name on it is derived from the old-time sailor's habit of tying ribbons in his hat. **1946** —— *Royal Navalese* 47 *Cap-tally pint*, a tankard of beer in which deliberate short measure is concealed under a mound of froth. **1960** *Times* 2 Apr. 8/7 A grubby lanyard, over-bright collar, flamboyant bow on the cap-tally—these can mean you've missed the first boat.

†**cap**, *sb.*[2] *Obs.* Also 6 **cappe**. [Etymology uncertain: not easily connected with prec., and being exclusively Eng., it cannot be the Scotch CAP *sb.*[3]] A closed wooden vessel; a cask.

1519 HORMAN *Vulg.* 19 Valantynys be put and shocked in a close vessell as is a cappe. *a* **1672** WILKINS (J.) A barrel or cap, whose cavity will contain eight cubical feet of air, will not serve a diver above a quarter of an hour.

cap (kæp, kap), *sb.*[3] *Sc.* Also 5 **cop**, 8–9 **caup**. [app. a later Sc. form of *cop* (as in *tap*, *top*, etc.):—OE. *copp* cup, vessel, or ON. *kopp-r* cup, small vessel used in the dairy; but the form *caup*, unless merely phonetic, raises difficulties. A med.L. *caupus* is rendered by Ælfric 'cuppe'.]

1. A wooden bowl or dish, often with two ears or handles, formerly used as a drinking vessel.

1724 RAMSAY *Tea-t. Misc.* (1733) I. 91 There will be.. brandy in stoups and in caps. *c* **1730** BURT *Lett. N. Scotl.* (1818) I. 157 It is often drunk..out of a cap..a wooden dish with two ears or handles about the size of a tea-saucer and as shallow. **1785** BURNS *Holy Fair* xxiii, How drink gaed round, in cogs and caups. **1868** G. MACDONALD *R. Falconer* I. 272 A good slice of swack cheese with a cap of ale.

b. *to kiss caps with*: 'to drink out of the same vessel with' (Jam.); hence ***the kiss of a cap***. ***to drink cap-out***: to empty: see COP. Also proverb ***between cap and lip***.

1715 *Let.* in *Wodrow Corr.* (1843) II. 115 They..got not so much as the kiss of a caup. **1737** RAMSAY *Sc. Prov.* (1776) 53 (Jam.) Meikle may fa' between the cap and the lip. **1818** SCOTT *Rob Roy* xxix, 'Drink clean cap-out, like Sir Hildebrand.' **1879** JAMIESON *Sc. Dict.* s.v., 'I wadna kiss caps wi' sic a fallow.'

2. A measure of quantity: formerly COP, q.v.

1879 JAMIESON *Sc. Dict.*, *Cap*, *Capfou'*, *Capfu'*, the fourth part of a peck; as a capfu' o' meal, salt, etc.

3. *Comb.* **cap-ale**, 'a kind of beer between table-beer and ale' (Jam.); †**cap-ambry**, a cupboard: see COP-.

1864 A. MCKAY *Hist. Kilmarnock* 163 Sandy brewed within his own premises the cap-ale.

cap (kæp), *sb.*[4] Also **cap.**, **cap'**. Colloq. abbrev. of CAPTAIN.

1759 S. MERRIMAN *Diary* 21 June in G. Sheldon *Hist. Deerfield* (1895) I. 662 A covering party, consisting of wone cap, 3 subbs 4 sargents 100 rancks & file. **1840** *Porter's Spirit of Times* (N.Y.) 17 Oct. 391/3 The old cap. wanted to kill one of them varmints. **1902** KIPLING *Traffics & Discoveries* (1904) 29 'Well, Cap,' I says. **1909** WARE *Passing Eng.* 63/2 *Cap*, equivalent to 'Sir'—but really abbreviation of 'Captain'. Common in America—gaining ground in England. **1933** 'L. LUARD' *All Hands* 252 Where's the cap'?

cap (kæp), *sb.*[5] Colloq. abbrev. of CAPSULE. Chiefly *U.S.*

1942 BERREY & VAN DEN BARK *Amer. Thes. Slang* §509. 8 *Cap*, a capsule of narcotics. **1962** J. GLENN in *Into Orbit* 144 The Cap Sep or 'Capsule Separation' event. **1963** *New Society* 7 Nov. 11/2 If they were big dope pedlars, they gave you a cap [of heroin] for delivering something.

cap (kæp), *v.*[1] [f. CAP *sb.*[1]]

1. a. *trans.* To provide or cover with a cap; to put a cap on (a person, or his head); *esp.* as the sign of conferring a University degree (in Scotland). Also ***to cap about***.

1483 *Cath. Angl.* 54 To Cappe, *cappare*. *a* **1529** SKELTON *Elynour Rum.* in *Harl. Misc.* (Malh.) III. 479 With her clothes on her hed..like an Egyptian Capped about. **1620** VENNER *Via Recta* (1650) 302 Not by over much wrapping and capping the head. **1881** *Hist. Glasgow* lvi. 468 Their royal Highnesses were duly capped. **1883** W. C. SMITH *N. Country Folk* 44 When..he was capped, the town Gathered to see him.

b. To put a cap on (the nipple of a gun).

1856 KANE *Arct. Expl.* I. xxix. 387 While the men were loading and capping anew. **1872** BAKER *Nile Tribut.* xviii. 318, I had capped the nipples.

c. To award (a player) his cap (CAP *sb.*[1] 4 f); to select a representative player *for* a country, etc.

1902 *Football Who's Who 1901–2* 131 He was first capped as far back as 1893 against Ireland. **1963** *Times* 6 Feb. 4/2 Baker, capped five times for England in 1959–60.

2. a. To cover as with a cap or capping.

1602 CAREW *Cornwall* 115/2 When the top of Hengsten is capped with a cloud. **1691** T. H[ALE] *Acc. New Invent.* 82 To Capp the Bolt-heads with Lead. **1750** W. ELLIS *Mod. Husbandm.* V. i. 28 *Cap*, to cover a sheaf at the top. **1853** G. JOHNSTON *Nat. Hist. E. Bord.* I. 109 The turf has been pared off to cap stone-dikes.

b. To cover at the end; to protect the end of.

1794 *Rigging & Seamanship* I. 163 *To Cap a rope*, to cover the end with tarred canvas. **1823** P. NICHOLSON *Pract. Build.* 264 The extremities of beams, etc., have sometimes been capped with pitch. **1857** CHAMBERS *Inform. People* II. 703/1 Capping the end of the oar with the hand has a very awkward appearance.

3. a. To form, or serve as, a cap, covering, or top to; to crown; to overlie, lie on the top of.

1808 J. BARLOW *Columb.* III. 153 Columns of smoke, that cap the rumbling height. **1830** LYELL *Princ. Geol.* I. 58 The basalts..capping the hills. **1855** BROWNING *Fra Lippo Lippi*, Lodging with a friend..In the house that caps the corner. **1878** B. TAYLOR *Deukalion* IV. iv. 160 One block Shall cap the pediment.

b. To serve as a cover or wrapping for. ? *Obs.*

1735 POPE *Ep. Lady* 38 One common fate all imitators share, To save mince-pyes, and cap the grocer's ware.

4. a. To overtop, excel, outdo, surpass, beat. (At first *north. dial.*)

1821 MRS. WHEELER *Westmld. Dial.* Pref. 9 He wod giv a supper..if they cud cap him wie onny six words. **1848** C. BRONTË *J. Eyre* (1857) 386 'Well!..that caps the globe.' **1857** GEN. P. THOMPSON *Audi. Alt.* I. xix. 68 There is one story, which caps all the records religious war..can produce. **1876** GREEN *Short Hist.* ix. §4 (1882) 637 Oates capped the revelations of Bedloe by charging the Queen herself..with knowledge of the plot.

b. *dial.* To pass the comprehension of; to puzzle, bring to one's wit's end.

1736 BAILEY, *To Cap one*, to put him to a non-plus. **1857** HEAVYSEGE *Saul* (1869) 167 'Twould cap a monkey To say what I have gathered. **1863** MRS. TOOGOOD *Yorksh. Dial.*, It caps me how t' old man gets his work done.

c. Hence phrases, ***to cap the climax***, ***to cap all***.

1804 *Lancaster* (Pa.) *Intelligencer* 21 Feb. (Th.), Your correspondent caps the climax of Misrepresentation. **1836** W. IRVING *Astoria* III. 160 He capped the climax of this.. intelligence, by informing them that, etc. **1863** *Cornh. Mag.* VII. 323 As if to cap the climax of mismanagement. **1891** *Fur, Fin & Feather* Mar. 158 A section of country..that caps the climax for quail, especially along the little creeks.

5. ***to cap an anecdote, proverb, quotation***, etc.: to follow it up with another, a better, or one which serves as a set-off; to quote alternately in emulation or contest, so as to try who can have the last word. ***to cap verses***: to reply to one previously quoted with another, that begins with the final or initial letter of the first, or that rimes or otherwise corresponds with it.

1584 PEELE *Arraignm. Paris* IV. ii. (1829) 48 Sh' ath capt his answer in the cue. **1599** SHAKS. *Hen. V*, II. vii. 124 *Orleance*. Ill will neuer sayd well. *Const.* I will cap that Prouerbe with, There is flatterie in friendship. **1606** BP. W. BARLOW *Serm.* (1607) D 2 b, Had he bin to sit in the Consistory, only to cap voices, himself hauing no negatiue, etc. **1612** BRINSLEY *Lud. Lit.* 300 Or if time permit, sometime to cap verses. **1702** *Eng. Theophrast.* 59 He thinks the Roman Poets good for nothing but for Boys to cap verses. **1741** RICHARDSON *Pamela* (1824) I. 145 Don't think we are capping compliments as we used to do verses at school. **1856** R. VAUGHAN *Mystics* (1860) I. I. v. 32 Now you come to Shakspeare, I must cap your quotation with another.

6. To place or put on as or like a cap.

1612 T. JAMES *Jesuits' Downef.* 30 The Iesuits are iolly fellowes to cap crownes. **1823** *New Monthly Mag.* VII. 494 The hood will just cap itself over the horse's ears.

†**7.** To take away the cap from (a person). *Obs.*

1553 T. WILSON *Rhet.* 92 b, Boyes..will saye..Sir I wyll cappe you if you use me thus..meanynge that he will take his cappe from him. **1693** W. ROBERTSON *Phraseol. Gen.* 307 To cap one, or take away his hat.

8. a. *intr.* To take off the cap in token of respect; also, ***to cap it***. Const. *to* (a person), whence indirect passive ***to be capped to***.

1555 BRADFORD in Strype *Eccl. Mem.* III. App. xlv. 134 You must cappe to him in all places. *a* **1564** BECON *Humble Supplic.* in *Prayers* (1844) 238 They alone be capped, kneeled, and crouched to. **1687** in *Magd. Coll. & Jas. II* (1886) 216 They have denied any power over them in that College, and do refuse to cap. **1863** SALA *Capt. Danger.* III. iv. 115 Soon I was well known and Capped to.

b. *trans.* (by omission of *to*).

a **1593** H. SMITH *Serm.* (1871) I. 205 How would they cap me if I were in velvets. **1763–5** CHURCHILL *Author*, Poems II. 2 And cap the fool, whose merit is his Place. **1850** THACKERAY *Pendennis* I. xviii, He and the Proctor capped each other as they met.

9. Of a horse: ***to cap the hock***: to injure, and hence cause a swelling at, the point of the hock.

1886 *Sat. Rev.* 6 Mar. *Horse-idiocy* 327/2 Capable of exercising, sufficient discretion..to refrain from capping his own hocks.

10. *intr.* To take cap-money (see CAP *sb.*[1] 19).

1854 R. S. SURTEES *Handley Cross* IX. xxxiv. 269 Mr. Jorrocks allowed Pigg [his huntsman] to cap when they killed. **1896** MORDAUNT & VERNEY *Ann. Warwicks. Hunt* I. xiv. 288 They used to cap for us then.

†**cap**, *v.*[2] *Obs.* [app. a. OF. *cape-r* to seize, take, cf. *cape* 'bref de prise de corps' (Godef.): see CAPE *sb.*[4] But cf. also CAPIAS, the name of a writ; and CAPE *v.*[2], a. Du. *kapen* to take.]

1. *trans.* To arrest.

1589 R. HARVEY *Pl. Perc.* 11 Cap him sirra, if he pay it not. **1611** BEAUM. & FL. *Knt. Burning Pest.* III, Twelve shillings you must pay, or I must cap you.

2. 'To seize by violence, to lay hold of what is not one's own' (Jamieson). *Mod. Sc.*

cap, *v.*[3] *Obs.* Sc. form of CAPE *v.*

‖**capa** (ˈkɑːpə). [Sp.: see CAPE.] A Spanish cape or cloak.

1787 J. TOWNSEND *Journ. Spain* (1792) I. 335 The genteel young Spaniard in his capa. **1879** BEERBOHM *Patagonia* iv. 62, I drew my head under my capa and fell into a sound sleep again.

†**capaˈbilitate**, *v. Obs.* To make capable; to indicate the capabilities of (property).

1780 W. WOTY in Cussans *Hist. Herts* 104 Brown..whom Chambers may excel, But ne'er could capabilitate so well.

capability (ˌkeɪpəˈbɪlɪtɪ). [f. CAPABLE: see *-bility*, -ITY. Of mod. English formation; there is no

similar word in French.] The quality of being capable in various senses.

†1. The quality of having room for any thing; ability to receive or contain. Cf. CAPACITY. *Obs.*

1616 BULLOKAR, *Capability*, an aptnesse to containe or receiue. 1627 HAKEWILL *Apol.* 223 (R.) Discoursing of the arke and the capabilitie thereof. 1656 in BLOUNT *Glossogr.*

2. Power or ability in general, whether physical or mental; capacity.

1587 GOLDING *De Mornay* xv. 240 The abilitie or capabilitie that is in men to vnderstand things. 1602 SHAKS. *Ham.* IV. iv. 38 He..gaue vs not That capability and godlike reason To fust in us vnused. 1825 McCULLOCH *Pol. Econ.* II. ii. 125 Commodities, for the production of which they have no natural capability. 1856 SIR B. BRODIE *Psychol. Inq.* I. iii. 91 The capability of fixing the attention.

3. Legal or moral qualification or capacity.

1684 BUNYAN *Pilgr.* II. 58 The Righteousness of his Manhood giveth capability to his obedience to justifie. 1846 G. PHILLIPS in Spurgeon *Treas. Dav.* Ps. cv. 22 The capability of binding is to be regarded as an evidence of authority.

4. The quality of being susceptible of, or admitting of treatment, in any specified manner.

1794 G. ADAMS *Nat. & Exp. Philos.* II. xix. 331 If the ray ..have exactly the same capability or disposition to be refracted by the prism. 1816 KEATINGE *Trav.* (1817) I. 246 The charge has been very near capability of substantiation. 1875 JEVONS *Money* (1878) 40 The capability of a substance to receive such an impression. *Ibid.* The capability of a substance for being easily recognized. 1879 *Cassell's Techn. Educ.* I. 166 The capability of rapid movement.

5. (usually *pl.*) An undeveloped faculty or property; a condition, physical or otherwise, capable of being converted or turned to use. **capability-man**, one who makes it his business to discover the capabilities of estates.

1778 *Phil. Surv. S. Irel.* 169 Here are all the capabilities for a terrestrial paradise. 1831 DISRAELI *Yng. Duke* I. vi. (L.) Sir Carte..was immensely struck with Hauteville, particularly with its capabilities. 1841 EMERSON *Nature* viii. *Meth. Nat.* Wks. (Bohn) II. 221. 1882 A. W. WARD *Dickens* ii. 23 It was only as the author recognised the capabilities of the character. 1887 G. B. HILL *Boswell's Johns.* III. 400 *note* ['Capability Brown'] got his nickname from his habit of saying that grounds which he was asked to lay out had *capabilities*.

capable ('keɪpəb(ə)l), *a.* [a. F. *capable* (= Pr. *capable*), ad. late L. *capābil-em* (in early theological use: see Du Cange), irregularly f. L. *cap-ĕre* to take. The regular formation would have been *capibilis*; perh. *capābilis* was influenced by *capax*: Beda *Lib. de Orthogr.* has '*capax*, qui facile capit; *capabilis*, qui facile capitur' (Du Cange); so Augustine, but Cassiodorus *c.* 575 has it in the active sense = *capax*, as in the mod. langs.]

†1. Able to take in, receive, contain, or hold; having room or capacity for. Const. *of*, *for*, or *inf.* *Obs.*

1571 DIGGES *Pantom.* IV. xxv. Ggij, This transfygured, bodye is also capable of two internall spheres. 1601 T. WRIGHT *Passions* (1620) 330 They are almost capable of a bushel of wheate. *a* 1618 RALEIGH *Lett.* (1651) 87 The other five ships stand at Trinidado, having no other Port capable for them near Guiana. 1634 SIR T. HERBERT *Trav.* 25 Their Canoes..are..capable of three naked men. 1675 HOBBES *Odyssey* III. 450 The seat was large and capable of two. 1686 tr. *Chardin's Trav.* 246 Capable to lodge two hundred men. 1704 HEARNE *Duct. Hist.* (1714) I. 431 The Moselle..being not capable of Ships of Burden. 1775 JOHNSON *Western Isl.* Wks. X. 479 He has begun a road capable of a wheel-carriage.

†**b.** *fig.* Able to take in with the mind or senses; able to perceive or comprehend. *Obs.*

1561 T. NORTON *Calvin's Inst.* I. 26 Only those things be painted and grauen wherof our eies are capable. 1594 HOOKER *Eccl. Pol.* I. xi. (R.) Capable we are of God, both by vnderstanding and will. *a* 1662 HEYLIN *Laud* I. 222 The likeliest way to make them capable of the inconveniences they should run into. 1667 MILTON *P.L.* VIII. 51 Not capable her eare Of what was high.

†2. *absol.* Able to hold much; roomy, capacious.

1594 T. B. *La Primaud. Fr. Acad.* II. 343 The rounde forme is most capable. 1617 MORYSON *Itin.* III. II. iii. 86 The hugest and most capable vessels in his Cellar. 1650 FULLER *Pisgah* II. ii. 75 That capable vessell of brass.

†**b.** *fig.* Comprehensive. *Obs.*

1592 NASHE *P. Penilesse* (ed. 2) 33 b, You make this word Dæmon, a capable name of Gods, of men and of diuells. 1604 SHAKS. *Oth.* III. iii. 459 Till that a capeable, and wide Reuenge Swallow them vp.

3. Able or fit to receive and be affected by; open to, susceptible: †**a.** *of* anything material. *Obs.*

1611 TOURNEUR *Ath. Trag.* v. i. Wks. 1878 I. 136 If any roote of life remaines within 'em Capable of Phisicke, feare 'em not my Lord. 1612 DAVIES *Why Ireland, etc.* (1787) 3 The husbandman must first break the land before it be made capable of good seed. 1662 FULLER *Worthies* (1840) I. 263 Some have flesh, salt, and flesh capable thereof.

b. *of* things immaterial. *arch.*

1590 GREENE *Never too late* (1600) 95 Mirimidas eares are not capable of any amorous persuasions. 1597 SHAKS. *2 Hen. IV*, I. i. 172 You were aduis'd his flesh was capeable Of Wounds. 1667 MILTON *P.L.* IX. 283 His violence..being such As wee, not capable of death or paine..can repell. 1858 BUSHNELL *Nat. & Supernat.* x. (1864) 314 To be capable of his doctrine, only requires that the hearer be a human creature.

c. *absol.*

1602 SHAKS. *Ham.* III. iv. 127 His forme and cause conioyn'd, preaching to stones, Would make them capeable.

4. Able to be affected by; of a nature, or in a condition, to allow or admit of; admitting; susceptible. Const. *of*, also *absol.*

1597 HOOKER *Eccl. Pol.* v. lvii. §1 Infants which are not capable of instruction. 1652 NEEDHAM tr. *Selden's Mare Cl.* 11 The soil of a strange Citie is not capable of such a dedication. 1712 ADDISON *Spect.* No. 469 ¶5 He who is in any degree capable of Corruption. 1732 BERKELEY *Alciphr.* vii. §33 The being of a God is capable of clear proof. 1736 BUTLER *Anal.* I. v. Wks. 1874 I. 96 It is easy to see, that we are capable of moral improvement by discipline. 1794 SULLIVAN *View Nat.* I. 45 [A matter] capable of explanation. 1868 J. H. BLUNT *Ref. Ch. Eng.* I. 407 It was a system capable of very ready abuse. 1875 JOWETT *Plato* (ed. 2) V. 70 Men differ from the lower animals in that they are capable of musical discipline.

5. Having the needful capacity, power, or fitness for (some specified purpose or activity). Const. *of*; formerly also *inf.*

1597 HOOKER *Eccl. Pol.* v. lxxxi. §5 A quality which maketh capable of any function. 1634 BP. HALL *Occas. Medit.* Wks. (1808) 111 No other creature, besides man, is capable to apprehend this beauty. 1712 STEELE *Spect.* No. 264 ¶1 How few there are capable of a religious, learned, or philosophick Solitude. 1752 JOHNSON *Rambl.* No. 207 ¶8 Anything..capable of giving happiness. 1737–59 MILLER *Gard. Dict.*, The weaker trees being less capable to furnish a supply of nourishment. 1796 BP. WATSON *Apol. Bible* 338 You are capable of better things. 1863 E. NEALE *Anal. Th. & Nat.* 51 Animals must be capable of forming general thoughts. 1879 *Cassell's Techn. Educ.* IV. 91/3 A common compass-card, capable of free movement on a needle-point.

b. In a bad sense: Having the effrontery, depravity, wickedness for.

a 1680 S. CHARNOCK in Spurgeon *Treas. Dav.* Ps. x. 11 The criminal capable to practise them. 1777 BURKE *Corr.* (1844) II. 144 They who are capable of being forgers, are capable of being incendiaries. 1867 FREEMAN *Norm. Conq.* (1876) I. vi. 417 Eadric was capable of every wickedness.

6. *absol.* Having general capacity, intelligence, or ability; qualified, gifted, able, competent.

1606 SHAKS. *Tr. & Cr.* III. iii. 310 Let me carry another to his Horse; for that's the more capable creature. 1715 BURNET *Own Time* (1766) I. 31 The capablest man for business and the best speaker in that kingdom. 1728 MORGAN *Algiers* II. v. 294 Giving him, when capable, the whole management of all his domestic affairs. 1857 MRS. JAMESON *Leg. Madonna* 237 Joseph as the vigilant and capable guardian of the Mother and the Child. 1871 BLACKIE *Four Phases* i. 3 A more capable..witness could not be desired.

†7. Having some external, *esp.* a legal, capacity or qualification; qualified, entitled; in *Law*, qualified to hold or possess (property, etc.). Const. *of*, also *absol.* *Obs.*

1605 SHAKS. *Lear* II. i. 87 Of my land..Ile worke the meanes To make thee capable. 1610 GUILLIM *Heraldry* II. v. (1660) 65 Bastards are not capable of their Fathers patrimony. 1633 BP. HALL *Hard Texts* 134 To keepe themselves from all legall pollution, that they might be capable of eating the passover. 1760 T. HUTCHINSON *Hist. Coll. Mass.* ii. (1765) 327 Protestants..were capable of being made freemen. 1809 TOMLINS *Law Dict.* s.v. *Capacity*, An alien born..is capable of personal estate; but he is not capable of lands of inheritance. 1818 CRUISE *Digest* VI. 534 The devisee must be a person capable at the death of the devisor.

‖**capable de tout** (kapabl də tu), *adj. phr.* [Fr.] Capable of anything.

['Habacuc était capable de tout.' Attributed to Voltaire (*N. & Q.* (1941) CLXXXI. 46/2).]
1899 M. BEERBOHM *More* 166 He is *capable de tout*. 1953 'N. BLAKE' *Dreadful Hollow* vii. 93 You consider Celandine a vindictive character, *capable de tout*. 1962 N. MARSH *Hand in Glove* iv. 125 *He*..would certainly be capable of going too far—*capable de tout*.

'capableness. [f. CAPABLE + -NESS.] The quality or condition of being capable (in various senses); capability.

1587 GOLDING *De Mornay* xv. (1617) 261 So it [the mind] should euermore haue brought the ability and capablenesse of it into act. 1594 CAREW *Huarte's Exam. Wits* (1616) 27 Whereunto these ventricles serue, and their large or narrow capablenesse for the reasonable soule, all shall bee told by vs. 1607 HIERON *Wks.* I. 289 Where there is no capablenesse of faith, there ought to bee no baptisme. 1680 R. MANSEL *Narr. Popish Plot* 7 She there examined his capableness for business. 1731 BAILEY, *Appeasableness*, capableness of being pacified.

capably ('keɪpəblɪ), *adv.* [f. CAPABLE + -LY².] In a capable manner; in a way that shows capacity; with ability, ably.

1885 *Manch. Exam.* 18 Mar. 3/2 The details..are..freshly conceived and capably handled.

†**ca'pace.** *Obs.* [ad. L. *capāx*, *capāci-*, f. *capĕre* to take. (See -ACIOUS.) Ital. has *capace*, and there may have been a 16th c. F. *capace*, as the direct source.] Able to take in (with the mind) or comprehend; 'capacious' *of*.

1555 CDL. POLE in Strype *Cranmer* (1694) App. x. 216 The doctrine of the presence prevayling..above mans reason..may be capace of the same. 1658 LENNARD tr. *Charron's Wisd.* III. xiv. §36 (1670) 459 When they are great and capace of that whereunto they were instructed.

†**ca'pacify.** *Obs. rare.* [f. L. *capāci-* (see prec.) + -FY.] = CAPACITATE.

a 1677 BARROW *Serm.* I. i. (R.) Capacifying us to enjoy..all those good things. *Ibid.* (1823) II. xliv. 462 [To] enjoy the benefits he is capacified and designed for.

capacious (kə'peɪʃəs). [f. L. *capāci-* (see above) + -OUS: see -ACIOUS.]

†1. Of such size as to take in or hold; able to contain; having the capacity *of* or *to* (with infinitive).

1614 RALEIGH *Hist. World* I. vi. (R.) The ark..was sufficiently capacious to contain of all. 1624 MASSINGER *Parl. Love* III. ii, There cannot be room in one lover's heart Capacious enough to entertain Such multitudes of pleasures. 1634 BRERETON *Trav.* (1844) 154 A spacious harbour capacious of many thousand sail. 1656 COWLEY *Davideis* IV, What breast but thine capacious to receive The vast infusion? 1744 AKENSIDE *Pleas. Imag.* II. 244 Is thy short span Capacious of this universal frame? 1779 FORREST *Voy. N. Guinea* 232 A range of..china jars, each capacious of, at least, twenty gallons.

2. Able to hold much; roomy, spacious, wide.

1634 BRERETON *Trav.* (1844) 67 The Lutherans have..a mighty congregation, and a capacious church. 1656 tr. *Hobbes' Elem. Philos.* (1839) 488 Nature has bestowed upon them wide and capacious ears. 1690 NORRIS *Beatitudes* (1694) I. 14 The Importunity of such craving and capacious Appetites. 1700 MAIDWELL in *Collect.* (Oxf. Hist. Soc.) I. 311 He will erect a capacious *Auditorium*. 1818 HAZLITT *Eng. Poets* iv. (1870) 93 The capacious soul of Shakspeare. 1840 DICKENS *O.C. Shop* iii, A pair of capacious shoes. 1856 SIR B. BRODIE *Psychol. Inq.* I. ii. 64 There is no animal whose memory is equally capacious with that of man. 1872 YEATS *Growth Comm.* 202 Capacious quays.

3. Qualified, adapted or disposed for the reception *of*. *arch.* †Of capacity or qualified *to do* something (*obs.*).

1677 GALE *Crt. Gentiles* IV. II. 450 The more capacious he is to order al means and affaires in subservience to his end and designe. 1692 *Poems in Burlesque* 20 The girl began To grow capacious of a Man. 1709 *Brit. Apollo* II. No. 2. 3/1 Each Human Soul Capacious is to learn All Arts. 1725 POPE *Odyss.* v. 330 For the future sails Supplied the cloth, capacious of the gales. *Ibid.* XXIII. 201 Then posts, capacious of the frame, I raise. 1828–40 SIR W. F. NAPIER *Penins. War* VII. i. (Rtldg.) I. 328 A mind capacious of warlike affairs. 1850 MRS. BROWNING *Vis. Poets* ccxliii, Their eyes capacious of renown.

ca'paciously, *adv.* [f. prec. + -LY².] In a capacious manner.

1818 in TODD. 1846 in WORCESTER.

capaciousness (kə'peɪʃəsnɪs). [f. as prec. + -NESS.] The quality of being capacious; the power of holding or containing; largeness, roominess, wide extent. Cf. CAPACITY.

1642 T. GOODWIN *Heart of Christ* 129 There is..a greater capaciousnesse, vastnesse, and also quicknesse in his affections. 1658 ROWLAND *Moufet's Theat. Ins.* 1109 What thou speakest of the capaciousness of the place. 1685 H. MORE *Paralip. Prophet.* 169 By reason of the vast difference in their capaciousnesses. 1858 HAWTHORNE *Fr. & It. Jrnls.* I. 297 The vast capaciousness within St. Peter's is thrown away. 1874 PUSEY *Lent. Serm.* 98 We..gain..larger capaciousness for His endless Infinite love.

capacitance (kə'pæsɪtəns). *Electr.* [f. CAPACITY + -ANCE.] The ratio of the change in an electric charge to the corresponding change in potential; also, the ability to store a charge of electricity, capacity.

1893 *Trans. Amer. Inst. Electr. Engineers* X. 412 The term 'capacitance' is suggested as preferable to the already existing 'capacity'. 1916 *Standardiz. Rules Amer. Inst. Electr. Engineers* 18 It is..recommended that..the term 'Capacitance' be used when referring to the electro-static capacity of a device. *Ibid.* 53 Machinery of Low Capacitance. 1939 *Nature* 9 Sept. 458/2 The mica capacitor was compared by alternating current with an air capacitor, the capacitance of which can be evaluated in terms of resistance and time. 1940 *Chambers's Techn. Dict.* 132/1 *Capacitance grading*, grading of the properties of a dielectric so that the variation of stress from conductor to sheath is reduced. 1956 AMOS & BIRKINSHAW *Telev. Engin.* II. vii. 120 The input capacitance of a cathode follower is small only if the output load is high. 1962 A. NISBETT *Technique Sound Studio* iv. 79 In a building the size of a broadcasting studio centre there is a danger..of high frequency losses due to capacitance.

capacitate (kə'pæsɪteɪt), *v.* [f. CAPACITY + -ATE; see -ACITATE and -ATE³ 7.]

1. a. *trans.* To endow with capacity *for* or *to do* (something); to render capable; to qualify, fit.

1657 CROMWELL *Sp.* 8 Apr. (Carlyle) You can capacitate me to receive satisfaction in them. 1669 WORLIDGE *Syst. Agric.* ii. (1681) 10 It capacitates all sorts of Land..for some of the Improvements mentioned. 1704 SWIFT *T. Tub* Pref., He will please to capacitate and prepare himself by these directions. 1710 NORRIS *Chr. Prud.* iv. 175 This Temper that naturally qualifies and capacitates us for Happiness. 1853 ROBERTSON *Serm.* Ser. III. iii. (1872) 32 Long and careful study..capacitates him for his task.

absol. 1692 VILLIERS (Dk. Buckhm.), *Chances* (1714) 177 A Fund which might capacitate to make you Presents of my own.

b. *Physiol.* To cause (a spermatozoon) to undergo capacitation (see next).

1957 *Nature* 2 Feb. 258/2 'Capacitated' sperm were obtained from rabbits that had either been mated normally or inseminated with epididymal sperm. *Ibid.* 259/2 Epididymal sperm has to be capacitated. 1969 *Ibid.* 6 Sept. 1042/1 The Fallopian tube fluid is still effective in

capacitating sperm even when heavily diluted with a simple chemical medium.

2. To make legally capable; to qualify in law.

1657 CROMWELL *Sp.* 21 Apr. (Carlyle) It seems to capacitate all those who revolted from the parliament [to elect or be elected]. **1686** EVELYN *Mem.* (1857) II. 273, 2nd March Came out a proclamation..capacitating Papists to be chosen into all offices of trust. *c* **1792** WILKES *Corr.* (1805) V. 190 To admit all the other sectaries to be capacitated equally with the members of the church of England.

Hence **ca'pacitated** *ppl. a.*, **ca'pacitating** *vbl. sb.* and *ppl. a.*

a **1652** J. SMITH *Sel. Disc.* ix. 417 The capacitating of man for converse with God. **1669** W. SIMPSON *Hydrol. Chym.* 270 Being conveighed into a proper capacitated Matrix.

capacitation (kəpæsɪ'teɪʃən). [noun of action f. prec.: see -ATION.] **a.** A rendering capable.

a **1858** DE QUINCEY *Miracles* Wks. VIII. 234 The..supernatural birth..was essential as a capacitation for the work to be performed.

b. *Physiol.* The process or change that a spermatozoon undergoes in the female reproductive tract rendering it capable of penetrating the *zona pellucida* of an ovum and so fertilizing it.

1951 C. R. AUSTIN in *Austral. Jrnl. Sci. Res.* B. IV. 594 The principal conclusion..is that, at least in the rat and the rabbit, the sperm must undergo some form of preparation or capacitation before it can penetrate the zona. **1969** *Nature* 6 Sept. 1042/1 The acrosome, the cap-like structure on the head of the spermatozoon, is punctured in the course of capacitation and releases enzymes which dissolve materials such as compose the outer coverings of the egg.

capacitive (kə'pæsɪtɪv), *a.* *Electr.* Also **ca'pacitative.** [f. CAPACITY + -IVE.] Pertaining to electrostatic capacity.

1916 *Standardiz. Rules Amer. Inst. Electr. Engineers* 97 Capacitive Coupler. An apparatus which, by electric fields, joins portions of two radio frequency circuits. **1934** WEBSTER, Capacitative. **1943** *Gloss. Terms Telecomm.* (*B.S.I.*) 74 *Common-impedance coupling*, the coupling between two oscillating circuits by means of a current path which is common to both. (This coupling may be *inductive*, *capacitive* or *resistive*.) *Ibid.*, *Capacitive tuning*, a form of tuning in which the capacitance component is varied. **1946** *Electronic Engin.* XVIII. 71 There will be two forms of parasitic coupling present: capacitive and resistive. **1962** A. NISBETT *Technique Sound Studio* 256 An inductive impedance increases with frequency; a capacitative impedance decreases with frequency. **1964** R. F. FICCHI *Electrical Interference* 214 Capacitive coupling is the association of two or more circuits with one another by means of capacitance mutual to the circuits.

Hence **ca'pacitatively, ca'pacitively** *advs.*, by means of a capacitor or capacitors.

1950 *Physical Rev.* LXXIX. 696/1 A capacitatively loaded coaxial-line resonator. **1965** *Wireless World* Sept. 420/1 The r.f. stage is capacitatively coupled to the base of Tr_2. **1967** *Vacuum* XVII. 139 RF sputtering of metals can be achieved by capacitatively coupling the power supply to the metal electrode. **1984** *Sensors & Actuators* VI. 151 The device relies for its operation on the specific bulk absorption of an ionic species into a macroscopic phase deposited on a substrate, capacitatively coupled to a MOSFET. **1985** *Proc. 17th Internat. Conf. Physics of Semiconductors* 396 Capacitively coupled measurements of the magnetic resistance reveal new structure as the Fermi level moves between Landau levels.

capacitor (kə'pæsɪtə(r)). *Electr.* [f. CAPACITY + -OR.] A device which stores electricity during part of an operation; a condenser.

1926 *Gloss. Terms Electr. Engin.* (*B.S.I.*) 43 Condenser.. It is suggested that the new term capacitor shall be used for this device in order to avoid confusion with a steam 'Condenser'. **1939** [see CAPACITANCE]. **1946** *Electronic Engin.* XVIII. 13 A range of electrolytic capacitors of plain foil construction. **1962** A. NISBETT *Technique Sound Studio* 243 Capacitors are used in electronics for coupling, smoothing and tuning purposes.

capacity (kə'pæsɪtɪ). Also 5-6 -yte(e, 6-7 -itie, (6 -ite, -itye, -asitie). [15th c. *capacyte*, a. F. *capacité*, ad. L. *capācitāt-em*, noun of state f. *capāx*, *capāci-* able to take in: see -ACITY.]

†**1. a.** Ability to receive or contain; holding power. *Obs.* (in general sense).

1481 CAXTON *Myrr.* III. xx. 179 The capacyte and gretnes of heuene. **1555** EDEN *Decades W. Ind.* I. i. (Arb.) 66 Hauens of capacitie to harborowe greate nauies. *Ibid.* IV. (Arb.) 85 A potte of no bygger capacitie then to houlde them only. **1606** SHAKS. *Ant. & Cl.* IV. viii. 32. **1702** *Eng. Theophrast.* 228 There is a certain degree of capacity in the greatest vessel, and when tis full, if you pour in still, it must run out.

b. *fig.*

1578 *Chr. Prayers* in *Priv. Prayers* (1851) 513 That I may so drink of thee, according to my capacity, as I may live for ever. **1634** BP. HALL *Occas. Med.* Wks. (1808) 195 All favourable promises presuppose a capacity in the receiver. **1845** DE QUINCEY Wks. VI. 275 Men of genius have a larger capacity of happiness.

c. *capacity for heat, moisture*, etc.: the power of absorbing heat, etc. *capacity of a conductor* (Electr.): see quot.

1793 T. BEDDOES *Calculus, &c.* 233 The great capacity of the arterial blood for heat. **1863** R. S. CULLEY *Pract. Telegr.* (1871) 293 By the Capacity of a Condenser or Cable is meant its power to receive a charge. **1878** HUXLEY *Physiogr.* 68 The hotter the air the greater its capacity for moisture. **1885** WATSON & BURBURY *Math. The. Electr. & Magn.* I. 160 The capacity of a conductor in presence of any other conductors is the charge upon it required to raise it to unit potential, when all the other conductors have potential zero.

d. The power of an apparatus to store static electricity; also = CAPACITANCE. Also *attrib.*, denoting an apparatus which gives additional capacity, as *capacity cage, earth.*

1777 T. CAVALLO *Compl. Treat. Electr.* II. i. 103 The celebrated Father Beccaria supposes that the action of rubbing increaseth the capacity of the Electric, *i.e.* renders that part of the electric, which is actually under the rubber capable of containing a greater quantity of electric fluid. **1903** *Westm. Gaz.* 25 Feb. 5/1 The oscillatory circuit consists of a light wire cage, or 'capacity'. **1906** A. F. COLLINS *Man. Wireless Telegr.* 209 *Capacity cage*, a cylindrical cage made of wire and placed at the top of the aerial wire to give it additional capacity. **1923** *Daily Mail* 3 Mar. 5 If you are particularly bothered by the proximity of wires it is worth while to try the effect of substituting a 'capacity earth' for the ordinary earth connection. The capacity is a wire or wires stretched out below and parallel to the aerial above but insulated from the earth. **1932** C. J. SMITH *Intermediate Physics* xxxix. 507 The capacity of a sphere expressed in E.S.U. is numerically equal to its radius in centimetres. **1948** C. A. COULSON *Electr.* 43 If the potential difference between the plates is *V*, we define the capacity *C* by the formula $C = Q/V$. **1959** *Chambers's Encycl.* III. 826/1 The capacity of the charged conductor is ..increased, i.e. it can hold a bigger charge for a given potential.

e. Ability to provide accommodation (for the discharge, transport, etc.) of a certain amount or volume; also *spec.* in *Physical Geogr.*, ability to carry away detritus, measured by the quantity which passes a given point in a given time.

1885 *Eng. Illustr. Mag.* Sept. 813/2 The Nene does not discharge its waters so rapidly as it ought... Cut off the bends if you want a more efficient discharging capacity. **1892** *Jrnl. Soc. Arts* XLI. 96/2 The capacity of the present tunnel is sufficient to provide 100,000 horse-power applied to the turbines. **1900** *Ibid.* XLVIII. 835/1 The capacity of the larger canal would be over 20,000,000 tons a year.

f. The largest audience that a place of entertainment can hold; a situation in which a theatre, cinema, etc., is full; *spec.* in phr. *to capacity*: with all available room occupied; hence in general use, full; to the limit.

1908 L. MERRICK *Man who understood Women* 152 On the second Saturday night they played to 'the capacity of the house'. **1919** *Honey Pot* July 5 Why there is hardly a theatre in the West End playing to capacity, week in week out. **1929** J. B. PRIESTLEY *Good Compan.* II. iii. 328 We've got going in the town... Another week and it 'ud be capacity every night. *Ibid.* 329 Turning money away, my dear; capacity to the roof, ol' man. **1937** D. MARLOWE *Coming, Sir!* viii. 123 The other stows were filled to capacity. **1949** WODEHOUSE *Mating Season* xxii. 182, I..took my place among the standees at the back, noting dully that I should be playing to absolute capacity. **1958** *Spectator* 20 June 819/1 The bank-note paper mills worked to capacity throughout the year.

g. In industry: the ability to produce; equivalent to 'full capacity'.

1931 *Times Trade & Engin. Suppl.* 24 Jan. p. x/3 The production of bituminous coal [in U.S.] by 'mechanical mining' increased to 37·8 million tons in 1929, and this does not represent capacity, for short time and experimental work reduced the total below the maximum. **1940** *Economist* 8 June 999/1 The existing capacity must not only be worked to the limit, it must be expanded. **1959** *Listener* 12 Feb. 273/1 The British economy, so far from being inflationary, was suffering from a marked amount of excess capacity.

2. Hence, Content: †**a.** *superficial*, Area (*obs.*); **b.** *cubic*, Volume, solid content. ***measure of capacity***: the measure applied to the content of a vessel, and to liquids, grain, or the like, which take the shape of that which holds them.

1571 DIGGES *Pantom.* II. ix, You maye readely measure all equiangle figures, what capacitie..soeuer they bee of. *Ibid.* IV. xxiv, Rules for the inuention of his capacitie superficiall and Solide. **1658** SIR T. BROWNE *Hydriot.* II. (1736) 18 The present Urns were not of one Capacity, the Largest containing above a Gallon. **1697** DAMPIER *Voy.*, Of a Capacity usually of a Gallon or more. **1818** FARADAY *Exp. Res.* iv. 11 A glass globe of the..capacity..of about 140 cubic inches. **1866** HERSCHEL *Fam. Lect. Sc.* 192 Our ordinary measures of length, weight and capacity.

c. The total cylinder volume that is swept by the pistons in an internal-combustion engine.

1903 *Motor* 22 Apr. 237/2 Assuming that cylinder volume were taken as the standard..there would be no possibility of definitely ascertaining whether the two or four-stroke motor gave the better system, because the two-stroke would, on cylinder capacity, receive an enormous advantage. **1936** *Ibid.* 14 Oct. 514/1 The clever way in which eight cylinders, affording a total capacity of $4\frac{1}{2}$ litres, have been arranged in so compact a space. **1946** *Autocar Handbk.* (ed. 19) i. 33 On January 1, 1947..the H.P. tax will be superseded, for cars first registered after that date, by a tax on the cylinder capacity of the engine; that is, the volume swept by the pistons. **1966** S. BLACK *Man & Motor Cars* xi. 170 A six-cylinder engine..need be no more uneconomic in petrol consumption than a four-cylinder engine, if the cylinder capacity is suitably adjusted. **1977** 'E. CRISPIN' *Glimpses of Moon* xi. 213 There were Hondas and Suzukis and Yamahas and even a few Norton Commandos, ranging in capacity from 400 to 750 c.c. **1984** *Economist* 7 Apr. 85/2 The figures on..the fuel consumption of cars were calculated assuming that..lower transmission ratios or larger engine capacities would be used to compensate for performance losses as octane numbers..were reduced.

†**3. a.** A containing space, area, or volume. *Obs.*

1649 BLITHE *Eng. Improv. Impr.* (1653) 155 Into a long square..or an Ovall Capacity, or else into a Circular plot. **1756** BURKE *Subl. & B.* IV. ix, The whole capacity of the eye, vibrating in all its parts.

†**b.** *esp.* A space of three dimensions; a hollow space, a cavity. *Obs.*

1541 R. COPLAND *Galyen's Terap.* 2 G ij, In diuiding yᵉ tronke..betwene the necke & the legges, is two great capacytees. **1594** T. B. *La Primaud. Fr. Acad.* II. 216 There are two capacities or holow places in the heart. **1662** GLANVILL *Lux Orient.* xiv. 129 Not..a meer void capacity, for there are no such chasms in nature. **1704** J. HARRIS *Lex. Techn., Carcass*, is an Iron Case, or hollow Capacity, about the bigness of a Bomb.

†**c.** *fig.*

1587 GOLDING *De Mornay* xv. 248 Influence that floweth into the capasitie of our vnderstanding. **1752** JOHNSON *Rambl.* No. 204 ¶3, I will fill the whole capacity of my soul with enjoyment.

4. Mental or intellectual receiving power; ability to grasp or take in impressions, ideas, knowledge.

1485 CAXTON *Chas. Gt.* 1 After the capacyte of my lytel entendement..I haue ordeyned this book. **1580** BARET *Alv.* C 64 To apply himself to the capacitie of the scholer. **1671** MILTON *Samson* 1028 Capacity not raised to..value what is best. **1713** BERKELEY *Wks.* III. 145 He wants capacity to relish what true piety is. **1836-8** SIR W. HAMILTON *Metaph.* I. 253 Faculty is active power; capacity is passive power.

5. Active power or force of mind; mental ability, talent.

1485 CAXTON *Paris & V.* Prol., My capacity is not sufficient for the proper handling..of such subjects. **1597** HOOKER *Eccl. Pol.* v. lxvii. §12 Hath not perhaps the wit or capacity to tread out so endless mazes. **1673** MARVELL *Corr.* ccxi. Wks. 1872-5 II. 413 Ready to..serve them to the best of your capacityes. **1713** STEELE *Guardian* No. 17 ¶7 The fellow was a person of diligence and capacity. **1856** RUSKIN *Mod. Paint.* III. IV. x. §22 Everlasting difference is set between one man's capacity and another's.

6. *gen.* The power, ability, or faculty for anything in particular. Constr. *of*, *for*, or *inf.*

1647 JER. TAYLOR *Lib. Proph.* i. 10 Enable him with the capacities of our Saviour and Lord. **1736** BUTLER *Anal.* I. i. 19 We are endued with Capacities of action, of happiness and misery. **1749** FIELDING *Tom Jones* IX. vii, The capacity of removing themselves from one place to another. **1833** HT. MARTINEAU *Charmed Sea* i. 8 Sophia..seemed to have lost the capacity of loving. **1869** BUCKLE *Civilis.* II. i. 5 As society advanced there arose a capacity for self-protection. **1883** *Nature* 8 Mar. 435 The means of determining exact positions [in astronomy] and the capacity to reduce them.

7. The quality or condition of admitting or being open to action or treatment; capability, possibility.

1659 *Whole Duty Man* x. ii. 79 Several branches [of Justice] answerable to those capacities of injury. **1669** WORLIDGE *Syst. Agric.* iii. (1681) 17 Of Wet Meadows or Land under that capacity of being overflown. **1669** MARVELL *Corr.* cxiv. Wks. 1872-5 II. 274 You have yet..a capacity of straitning the project. **1719** DE FOE *Crusoe* II. v. 106 To deprive them of the capacity of ever returning. **1791** SMEATON *Edystone L.* §90 That there should be a level area ..or the capacity of making such a one. **1825** MᶜCULLOCH *Pol. Econ.* I. 23 Countries possessed of the greatest capacities of improvement. **1850** DAUBENY *Atom. The.* v. (ed. 2) 159 A capacity for infinite division.

†**8.** Hence *to be in, put into* or *out of a capacity*: i.e. a position which enables, or renders capable. *Obs.*

1649 JER. TAYLOR *Gt. Exemp.* II. vi. 17 He instantly, if he be in capacity, leaves the wife of his bosom. **1669** MARVELL *Corr.* cxxxi. Wks. 1872-5 II. 296 The House..not..in a capacity to finish that bill before their meeting in February. *a* **1672** WOOD *Life* (1848) 23 Being just..in capacity of spending the remainder of his dayes in ease and quietness, he died. **1697** DAMPIER *Voy.* I. xiii. 352 The capacity we were then in, of settling ourselves at Mindanas. **1725** DE FOE *Voy. round World* (1840) 282 Not willing to put ourselves out of a capacity of planting further. **1804** DUNCAN *Trident* I. 185 Our [galley] alone was in a capacity to begin the engagement.

9. a. Position, condition, character, relation.

a **1649** CHAS. I. *Wks.* 295 He should be in a capacity of Honor. **1655** FULLER *Ch. Hist.* III. 9 In what capacity these Jews came over, I finde not. **1710** POPE *Lett.* in *Wks.* V. 84, I am..dead in a natural capacity..dead in a poetical capacity..and dead in a civil capacity. **1747** HERVEY *Medit. & Contempl.* (1818) 266 The moon is..ready to act in the capacity of a guide. **1835** BUCHANAN *Ch. Establishm.* i. 7 Channels through which the mind of a people, in their collective capacity, can be expressed. **1848** MACAULAY *Hist. Eng.* I. 364 The King, in his individual capacity, had very little to give. **1871** SMILES *Charac.* iv. (1876) 111.

†**b.** Relation, tenor, sense (of words). *Obs.*

1720 WATERLAND *Vind. Christ's Divin.* 102 Irenæus understood those Texts..in that Capacity.

10. *Law.* Legal competency or qualification. *to be in capacity*: to be legally qualified.

1480 *Bury Wills* (1850) 66 Capacite in the lawe to purchase, take, and resceyue..possessiouns. *a* **1626** BACON *Use Com. Law* (1636) 42 Persons attainted of felony or treason, have no capacity in them to take, obtaine, or purchase. **1641** *Terms de la Ley* 44 Capacitie is when a man, or bodie politicke or corporate is able to give or take lands or other things, or to sue actions. **1768** BLACKSTONE *Comm.* II. 497 The ecclesiastical court is the judge of every testator's capacity. **1845** STEPHEN *Laws Eng.* II. 406 The capacity of an alien may be enlarged by his becoming a denizen.

11. a. *attrib.* and *Comb.*, as *capacity-catching*.

1904 *Westm. Gaz.* 17 Sept. 7/1 A certain groundwork of school knowledge, enough..to serve for what Professor Huxley called 'capacity catching'. **1905** *Daily Chron.* 31 Jan. 4/5 If you are out for what Mr. Sidney Webb would style 'capacity-catching'.

b. passing into *adj.* That reaches or fills the utmost capacity.

1920 *Times* (weekly ed.) 17 Sept., Profits are not unduly large in view of the fact that it is necessary to play almost to capacity business. **1925** *Times Lit. Suppl.* 27 Aug. 554/1 Both the play and film are now drawing capacity houses in London. **1928** *Morning Post* 20 Oct. 10/6 A 'capacity'

audience greeted the appearance of M. Ravel. **1929** *Ibid.* 28 Aug., Swimming baths, of course, attracted capacity crowds throughout the day. **1965** *Listener* 16 Sept. 416/3 *A Hard Day's Night* is running in six cinemas.. The Beatles do capacity business.

capacks, var. of CAPAX *a. Obs.*

†**capade** (kəˈpeɪd). [a. F. *capade*, f. *cap* head + -ADE.] In *Hat-making* = BAT *sb.*[2] 12.

1797 P. WAKEFIELD *Mental Improv.* (1801) I. 85 These pieces, or capades, as they are called, being formed in this manner. **1875** URE *Dict. Arts* II. 784 The bat or *capade.*

†'**capados.** *Obs. rare.* [? F. **cape à dos* 'cape to back' (but this does not appear in French Dicts.). Halliwell says *Captyhouse* occurs in same sense in MS. Arundel 249, lf. 88.] ? A hood; a piece to protect the back of the neck.

c **1340** *Gaw. & Gr. Knt.* 186 In þe wyse Of a kyngez capados, þat closes his swyre. *Ibid.* 572, & sythen a crafty capados, closed aloft.

cap-ambry: see COP.

cap-à-pie (kæpəˈpiː), *adv.* Also 6–9 cap(e-a-pe(e, (7 capp-a-pæ, cap a pea, capape(e, 7–9 cap a pied, etc.). [OF. *cap a pie* head to foot, mod.F. *de pied en cap.*] From head to foot: in reference to arming or accoutring.

1523 LD. BERNERS *Froiss.* I. ccccxvii. 730 Harnessed men cape a pe, lyke men of armes. **1556** J. HEYWOOD *Spider & F.* lii. 28 The rest all in bright harnesse capa pe. **1640** FULLER *Abel Rediv., Berengarius* (1867) I. 3 Confessors of the truth accoutred capp-a-pæ with undaunted courages. **1650** BULWER *Anthropomet.* Pref., Thus Capa peia is that Gallant great. **1682** BUNYAN *Holy War* 55 To arm you with cap-a-pe for your body. **1751** SMOLLETT *Per. Pic.* (1779) II. lxiii. 204 There was no possibility of furnishing them cap-a-pee at Antwerp. **1848** MRS. JAMESON *Sacr. & Leg. Art* (1850) 240 Mounted and armed cap-à-pie.

capar(s, obs. form of CAPER *sb.*[1]

caparison (kəˈpærɪsən). Also 7 caparisson, -izon, 8 -ason. [a. earlier F. *caparasson*, now *caparaçon*, a. Sp. *caparazon*, Pg. *caparação*, according to Littré, an augm. of med.L. *caparo* chaperon (a sort of cape worn by old women, etc.), deriv. of *capa* CAPE. See also COOPERISON.]

1. A cloth or covering spread over the saddle or harness of a horse, often gaily ornamented; housings, trappings; also of other beasts of burden.

1602 FULBECKE *Pandectes* 66 To esteeme.. a horse by his trappinges and caparison. **1627** *Lisander & Calista* x. 210 Seeing him without any caparison or other coverture but his saddle. **1751** JOHNSON *Rambl.* No. 120 ¶6 He covered his horses with golden caparisons. **1845** STOCQUELER *Handbk. Brit. India* (1854) 307 Elephants, with.. rich caparisons, and gorgeously painted trunks.

†**b.** A kind of defensive armour for a horse. *Obs.*

1598 HAKLUYT *Voy.* I. 62 Some of them haue.. caparisons for their horses made of leather, artificially doubled or trebled vpon their bodies. **1753** CHAMBERS *Cycl.* s.v., Antiently, the caparasons were a kind of iron armour, wherewith horses were covered in battle.

2. *transf.* The dress and ornaments of men and women: equipment, outfit. Also *fig.*

1598 *Pasquill's Ret.* 4 Spangled and trapt with a full caparison of the ornaments of this present age. **1611** SHAKS. *Wint. T.* IV. iii. 27. **1634** HEYWOOD *Lanc. Witches* IV. Wks. 1874 IV. 224 You have.. furnisht her with all the Caparisons that she hath worne. **1749** SMOLLETT *Regicide* III. iv. (R.) My heart groanes Beneath the gay caparison. **1868** MILMAN *St. Paul's* vi. 112 A.. rigidly restrictive caparison of the human mind.

caparison (kəˈpærɪsən), *v.* [a. F. *caparassone-r*, f. the sb.] *trans.* To put trappings on; to trap, deck, harness. Also *fig.*

1594 SHAKS. *Rich. III*, v. iii. 289 Come, bustle, bustle. Caparison my horse. *a* **1797** W. MASON *Ep. Sir W. Chambers,* O let the Muse attend thy march sublime And with thy prose caparison her rhyme. **1822** BYRON *Werner* IV. i, He shall be straight caparison'd.

Hence **caˈparisoned** *ppl. a.*, **caˈparisoning** *vbl. sb.* and *ppl. a.* **caˈparisonment**, *rare.*

1600 SHAKS. *A.Y.L.* III. ii. 205 Though I am caparison'd like a man. **1623** SIR F. COTTINGTON in Ellis *Orig. Lett.* I. 284 III. 142. **1841** ELPHINSTONE *Hist. Ind.* II. 343 Trains of caparisoned horses followed.

‖**capataz** (kæpəˈtæz, ˈkæ-). *rare.* Pl. capataces. [Sp., irreg. f. L. *caput* head: cf. CAPTAIN *sb.* 6 b, 9.] In Spanish-speaking countries: a headman of a ranch or farm; a foreman or overseer of a group of labourers.

1826 F. B. HEAD *Pampas* 43 The day before we started, the capataz came to me for some money to purchase hides, in order to prepare the carriages in the usual way. **1875** 'P. VERDAD' *From Vineyard to Decanter* 31 The sample having been tasted, the capataz is sent with his venencia into the cellar. **1904** CONRAD *Nostromo* I. ii. 15 The Company's lightermen, too, natives of the republic, behaved very well under their capataz.

†**caˈpax**, *a. Obs.* Also 6 capack(e)s. [a. OF. *capax*, a. L. *capāx*, f. *capĕre* to take: cf. CAPACE, CAPACIOUS.] Of capacity; able and ready to take or receive; capable.

1432–50 tr. *Higden* (Rolls) VI. 361 They scholde sende theire servauntes to the study, if thei were capax of conynge [TREVISA able to lerne]. **1483** CAXTON *Gold. Leg.* 271/2 Goo fight and be capax of perylles. **1491** —— *Vitas Patr.* (W. de W.) II. 282 a, Was capax and redy to receyue the euerlastyng blysse. *c* **1530** REDFORDE *Play Wit & Sc.* (1848) 2 Yoong, paynefull, tractable and capax. **1556** J. HEYWOOD *Spider & F.* xv. 49 Sure I can no false knacks, Alas, master spyder, ye be to capacks.

†**cap-bar, -barre.** *Sc. Obs.* = Capstan bar.

c **1550** *Aberd. Regist.* (Jam.) Serving of schippis with cap-barres.

†'**cap-case.** *Obs.* [? f. CAP *sb.*[1] or CAPE *sb.*[1]]

1. A travelling-case, bag, or wallet. (Representing the modern portmanteau or carpet-bag.)

1577 HARRISON *England* II. xvi. (1877) I. 283 Feeling whether their capcases or budgets be of anie weight or not, by taking them downe from their sadles. **1632** T. DELONEY *T. of Reading*, [He] turned backe and called for a capcase which lay in the Warehouse. **1641** HINDE *J. Bruen* 122 Thus many gamblers bring a Castle into a cap-case.

2. A receptacle of any kind; a box, chest, casket, case (L. *capsa*). Also *fig.*

1597 MORLEY *Introd. Mus.* 164 Your two last barres you haue robde out of the cap-case of some olde Organist. **1608** DEKKER *Belman Lond.* Wks. 1884–5 III. 109 These Bawdy baskets.. walke with baskets or capcases on their armes, wherein they haue laces, pinnes, needles. **1621** BURTON *Anat. Mel.* III. iv. I. ii. (1651) 645 S. Philanus arm.. shut up in a silver capcase. *a* **1625** BOYS *Wks.* (1630) 259 Wormes shall haue their carcase, and vnthrifty heires their cap-case. *a* **1627** MIDDLETON *Changeling* III. iv, 'Twill hardly buy a capcase for one's conscience though.

†'**cap-dates.** 'Perhaps Cape dates' (Nares).

15.. *Pathway of Health* (N.) Take.. halfe a quarter of cap dates.

†**cape** (keɪp), *sb.*[1] *Obs.* Also 4 **kape**, 6 *Sc.* **caip.** [Early form of COPE retained in north. dial. and Sc. Cf. ONF. *cape.*] A cloak with a hood; a cloak or mantle generally; an ecclesiastical cope.

c **1205** LAY. 7782 A cniht mid his capen [**1250** cope]. *Ibid.* 13097 He nom ane cape [**1250** cloke] of his ane cnihte. *c* **1320** *Seuyn Sag.* (W.) 3523 Thou sal be ful fayne For to hald my kapes sleue Whils I washe. **1423** JAS. I. *King's Q.* III. viii, There saw I stand, in capis wyde and lang, A full grete nowmer, but thair hudis all. *c* **1450** *Nominale* in Wr.-Wülcker 721 *Hec capa*, a cape. *c* **1520** *Treat. Galaunt* (W. de W.) xxvii, So many capes as now be, & so few good preestes. **1561** in *Inv. R. Wardr. Scotl.* (1815) 156 (Jam.) Nyne peces of caippis, chasubles, and tunicles.

cape (keɪp), *sb.*[2] [16th c. ad. F. *cape* (*cappe*), ad. Sp. *capa* or It. *cappa*, in same sense. Cotgr., 1611, has '*cape*, a shorte and sleeueless cloake or garment, that hath instead of a cape, a capuche behind it'.]

†**1.** A Spanish cloak (with a hood). *Obs.*

1565–78 COOPER *Thesaur.*, *Chlamys*, a cloke: a Spanish cape. **1580** BARET *Alv.* C 63 A spanishe cape: a cloke with an hoode.

2. The tippet of a cloak or similar garment, being an additional outer piece attached to it at the neck and hanging loose over the shoulders (e.g. in old riding-cloaks, infants' pelisses, etc.).

1596 SHAKS. *Tam. Shr.* IV. iii. 140, I said a gowne.. With a small compast cape. **1601** HOLLAND *Pliny* II. 199 Leaues ..resembling the cape of a cloke. **1818** BYRON *Juan* I. cxxxiv, The mountains.. clap a white cape on their mantles blue. **1828** SCOTT *F.M. Perth* III. 39 Having the cape of [his riding cloak] drawn up.

3. a. A separate article of attire, being a kind of short loose sleeveless cloak, fitting round the neck and falling over the shoulders as a protection against rain or cold. Waterproof capes of this kind are in common use.

[**1611** in Heath *Grocers' Comp.* (1869) 92 Or any other garments, safe only a cape of veluet.] **1758** JOHNSON *Idler* No. 49 ¶3 He.. buttoned up his cape, and went forwards. **1837** HAWTHORNE *Twice-told T.* (1851) II. xii. 190 To see the stream of ladies, gliding along the slippery sidewalks, with.. quilted hoods, boas, and sable capes. **1862** MISS YONGE *C'tess Kate* vii. (1880) 70 Adelaide had meantime picked out a nice black silk cape. **1885** *Law Rep.* 14 *Queen's B. Div.* 274 Such rain as they.. caught in their oilskin capes. *Mod.* A policeman in his waterproof cape. The fur capes at present worn by ladies.

b. *cape and sword* (also *cape and cloak*): phr. used to characterize romantic fiction or drama with a more or less historical background. Cf. CLOAK *sb.* 6.

Cf. F. *roman de cape et d'épée.*

1898 *Westm. Gaz.* 3 Nov. 2/3 Plays of poetry and passion, Cape and cloak, are all the fashion. **1898** *Daily News* 4 Nov. 3/5 The drama of the 'Cape and Sword'. **1910** *Westm. Gaz.* 2 Feb. 6/4 The cape-and-sword romanticism of Anthony Hope.

c. *transf.* The short feathers on a fowl's back falling below the hackle.

1899 A. H. EVANS *Birds* 548 *Xanthomelus aureus*.. has a.. black throat, tail, and part of wings and back, and a cape of hackled plumes falling over the last.

4. *Comb.*, as *cape-bonnet*, *-cloak*, *-coat*; **cape-work**, 'work' done by a bull-fighter in exciting and enraging the bull with his cape.

a **1613** OVERBURY *A Wife* (1638) 71 A picketooth in his Hat, a capecloak, and a long stocking. **1691** *Lond. Gaz.* No. 2631/4 A thin flaxen Hair'd Man, with a black Hat.. a brown Frize Cape-Coat. **1838** C. GILMAN *Recoll. Southern Matron* xix. 131 A young girl.. dressed in homespun, with a *cracker* or cape bonnet of the same material. **1870** LOWELL *Among my Bks.* Ser. I. (1873) 247 Decanting secrets out of the mouth of one cape-bonnet into that of another. **1926** HEMINGWAY *Fiesta* (1927) xv. 193 She liked Romero's cape-work. **1962** *Guardian* 29 Oct. 5/6 Instead of practising their capework during idle moments, Spanish boys nowadays play.. football.

cape (keɪp), *sb.*[3] [ad. F. *cap* head, cape, ad. Pr. *cap* or It. *capo*:—Romanic *capo*, for L. *caput* head. (The native Fr. repr. of Rom. *capo* is *chef.*)]

1. A piece of land jutting into the sea; a projecting headland or promontory.

1386 CHAUCER *Prol.* 408 ffrom Gootlond to the Cape of ffynystere. **1555** EDEN *Decades W. Ind.* I. III. (Arb.) 75 Inclosed on bothe sydes with capes or poyntes which receaue the water. **1598** HAKLUYT *Voy.* I. 311 A cape or headland called Sivetinoz. **1635** N. CARPENTER *Geog. Del.* II. xi. 189 A Promontorie.. whose extremity is called a cape. **1799** H. HUNTER tr. *St. Pierre's Stud. Nat.* III. 8 Between Cape Horn and the Cape of Good-Hope. **1812** BYRON *Ch. Har.* II. xl, Childe Harold hail'd Leucadia's cape afar.

transf. and *fig.* **1850** B. TAYLOR *Eldorado* xxxvii. (1862) 388 We approached a cape of the mountains. **1860** RUSKIN *Mod. Paint.* V. Pref. 6 Pieces of paper.. eaten away.. in capes and bays of fragile decay.

2. *the Cape*: some familiar headland; *esp.* the Cape of Good Hope in South Africa. Hence familiarly for *Cape Colony*, and ellipt. for ***Cape** (colony) wine, wool, funds*, etc. ***Cape** (or **cape**) hide*; also ellipt. for ***Cape** leather* or CAPESKIN, and *attrib.*

1667 MILTON *P.L.* ii. 642 Through the wide Ethiopian to the Cape. **1686** *Lond. Gaz.* No. 2180/4 The 25th of June they all sailed from the Cape. *c* **1800** SOUTHEY *Inscript.* xl, Vessels which must else have braved The formidable Cape, and have essayed The perils of the Hyperborean Sea. *a* **1845** HOOD *Public Din.* ii, Bucellas made handy, With Cape and bad Brandy. **1884** *York Her.* 23 Aug. 7/2 Wool Markets.. Capes are without improvement. **1884** *Pall Mall G.* 1 Oct. 5/2 Capes.. were practically unsaleable at the beginning of this week, investors fighting shy of the stock of a colony whose future, etc. *a* **1888** *Mod.* He has gone out to the Cape, to try sheep-farming. **1897** *Sears, Roebuck Catal.* 228/2 Men's Genuine Medium Weight Cape Goat Driving Gloves. **1915** K. J. ADCOCK *Leather* ii. 11 Large quantities of Cape hides are sent to England. **1921** B. E. ELLIS *Gloves & Glove Trade* iv. 58 Real Cape gloves are usually bark-tanned.. but many gloves sold as 'Capes' are tawed and dyed by the dipping process. **1929** [see BOULTON *a.*]. **1956** *Gloss. Leather Terms* (*B.S.I.*) 7 *Cape*, originally a soft, grain gloving or clothing leather made from South African hair sheep skin; now any similar leather made from hair sheep skin, but not finished leather made from E.I. native vegetable tanned hair sheep skin.

3. ***Cape** fly-away* (see quot.).

1769 FALCONER *Dict. Marine* (1789) *Terre de beurre*, cape fly-away, a cant-phrase applied to any illusive appearance of land in the horizontal clouds. **1867** SMYTH *Sailor's Word-bk.*, *Cape Fly-away*, a cloud-bank on the horizon, mistaken for land, which disappears as the ship advances.

4. *attrib.* **a.** chiefly in sense 2, as in ***Cape** boor, region, wine*, etc.; esp. in numerous names of animals, plants, etc. found at the Cape of Good Hope, as ***Cape** aloes, ant-eater, ash, badger, ebony, heath, marmot*, etc.; **Cape boy** (see BOY *sb.*[1] 3 e); **Cape cart**, a two-wheeled, horse-drawn hooded cart peculiar to South Africa; **Cape clouds** (see quot.); **Cape cobra**, a cobra (*Naja nivea*) of southern Africa, variable in colouring; **Cape Coloured** *a.*, of or designating the Coloured or brown population group of the Cape Province, especially of the Western Province of the Cape; *sb.*, a person (or the people) of this group; **Cape doctor**, a strong south-east wind in S. Africa (cf. DOCTOR *sb.* 6 b); **Cape Dutch**, (*a*) South Africans of Dutch extraction; (*b*) the Dutch spoken in South Africa, Afrikaans; also as *adj. phr.*; **Cape elk**, the Eland; **Cape gooseberry**, *Physalis peruviana*, a herb of the family Solanaceæ, native to South America, or its fruit; **Cape-hen**, a small kind of Albatross; **Cape jasmine**, *Gardenia florida*; **Cape jessamine**, any of various flowers of the genus *Gardenia*, esp. *G. jasminoides*; **Cape lobster**, the Cape crawfish (see CRAYFISH, CRAWFISH *sb.* 3 c); **Cape pigeon**, a pigeon-sized petrel, *Daption capensis*; **Cape robin**, a species of chat-like thrush, *Cossypha caffra*; **Cape salmon**, name given to various fishes having a resemblance to the European salmon, esp. the GEELBEK and the KABELJOU; **Cape smoke** *slang*, South African brandy; **Cape sparrow**, the S. African bird *Passer melanurus*; MOSSIE; **Cape wagon** (see quot. 1850); **Cape weed**, (*a*) *Roccella tinctoria* 'a dye lichen, obtained from the Cape de Verde Islands' (*Treas. Bot.* 1866); (*b*) a common yellow-flowered herb, *Cryptostemma calendulaceum*, now a troublesome weed in Australia and N.Z.; (*c*) (see quot. 1933). (See also Pettman *Africanderisms* for many other specific names.)

1822 BURROWES *Encycl.* V. 623/2 A *cape boor bestows no more labour on his farm than is absolutely necessary. **1892** J. R. COUPER *Mixed Humanity* ii. 20 Cape carts, driven by Malays and *Cape boys, rattled up and down the streets in numbers. **1896** F. C. SELOUS *Sunshine & Storm* 59 This force was, however, augmented by about 150 Cape boys, chiefly Amaxosa Kafirs and Zulus. **1877** LADY BARKER *Year's Housek. S. Afr.* i. 17 It was decided that I ought to take a drive in a *Cape cart. **1881** STATHAM *Blacks, Boers, & Brit.* 53 Do you know what a Cape cart is? It is a peculiar, but pleasant, institution—something like what was once in England called a 'Whitechapel'. **1910** J. BUCHAN *Prester John* vii, The half-caste who called him 'Sir' and drove his Cape-cart. **1880** AGNES GIBERNE *Sun, Moon & S.* 269 The famous Magellanic Clouds in the southern heavens. Sometimes they are called the *Cape Clouds. **1910** F. W. FITZSIMONS *Snakes S. Africa* vi. 74 The *Cape Cobra (*Naia flava*). Geel Slang, Bruin Slang, Spung Slang. The Cape Cobra is by far the commonest species of Cobra inhabiting South Africa. **1959** *Cape Argus* 31 Oct. 9/7 Cape cobras and puffadders provide most of the venom. **1897** *Milner Papers* (1931) iii. 89 The better treatment of *Cape Coloured people. **1927** W. M. MACMILLAN *Cape Colour Question* iii. 29 The great mixed mass, descended from Hottentots, slaves, and Europeans, but forming now one distinct class, whom we describe as 'Cape Coloured'. **1938** N. DEVITT *Spell of S. Afr.* xxi. 176 She jerks her body in a half-contemptuous shake, a common gesture among Cape coloureds of her class. **1943** *Cape Argus* 30 Jan. 7 Complaints and suggestions affecting the welfare of the Cape Coloured. **1960** *20th Cent.* Sept. 284 Kenneth Makeer..is a Cape Coloured, light enough in complexion to pass as white. **1861** LADY DUFF GORDON *Let.* 19 Oct. (1875) 213 It portends a 'south-easter'... This wind..is the *Cape doctor, and keeps away cholera, fevers [etc.]. **1890** A. MARTIN *Home Life on Ostrich F.* 15 That rough but benevolent south-east wind, which, owing to its kindly property of sweeping away the germs of disease, is called 'the Cape doctor'. **1966** *Listener* 18 Aug. 237/2 The Cape south-easter was blowing—the wind they call the Cape doctor because it blows the rubbish from the streets. **1826** *New Monthly Mag.* II. 488 The *Cape Dutch..possess many estimable qualities. **1850** APPLEYARD *Kafir Lang.* 11 A grammar, [with] 'Proeve van Kaapsch Taaleigen', where the peculiarities of Cape-Dutch usage are exposed. **1852** *Punch* 3 July 19/1 They've christened me Zekoe—that's Cape Dutch for Sea-Cow! **1944** *Archit. Rev.* XCVI. 97/1 The 'Cape Dutch' style in town and farm building. **1833** W. F. W. OWEN *Voyages* II. xix. 238 The physalis (*Cape gooseberry, or winter cherry) is here..a most delicious fruit. **1840** [see WINTER CHERRY 1]. **1870** *Cape Monthly Mag.* Oct. 218, I prefer the preserved *Cape* gooseberry to everything I have tasted. **1880** 'SILVER & CO.' *S. Africa* (ed. 3) 140 The Cape Gooseberry is a species of winter cherry. **1775** DALRYMPLE in *Phil. Trans.* LXVIII. 408 An uncommon birdlike *Cape hen. **1760** ELLIS *ibid.* LI. 932 The *Cape Jasmine..is the most rare and beautiful shrub, that has yet been introduced into the European gardens. *a* **1776** J. SCHAW *Jrnl. Lady of Quality* (1921) 246 While we were admiring a row of *cape jessamine, which even now is covered with flowers. **1804** J. BARROW *Trav. S. Afr. 1797–8* II. 82 The *Gardenia Thunbergia*, or the wild Cape Jessamine. **1858** T. VIELÉ *Following the Drum* 58 Cape jessamine hedges. **1793** tr. *Thunberg's Trav.* I. 240 The *Cape lobster (*Cancer arctos*)..has no large claws, and is craggy all over. **1902** H. J. DUCKITT *Hilda's Diary Cape Housekeeper* 47 'Crayfish', or 'Kreeft', is also plentiful all through the summer. We also call it 'Cape lobster'. **1913** W. W. THOMPSON *Sea Fisheries Cape Col.* ii. 51 The 'Cape lobster', as it [*sc.* the crawfish] is sometimes called. **1798** S. H. WILCOCKE tr. *Stavorinus' Voyages* II. 31 We saw..the birds called '*cape-pigeons'. **1858** *Merc. Mar. Mag.* V. 290 Albatrosses and Cape Pigeons about. **1867** E. L. LAYARD *Birds S. Afr.* 132 Bessonornis Phoenicurus..is the *Cape 'robin'. **1913** PETTMAN *Africanderisms* 114 *Cape robin.—Cossypha caffra*, a bird that resembles the English robin somewhat, but is without the red breast. **1846** H. H. METHUEN *Life in Wilderness* i. 17 The *cape salmon, a heavy fish, in size and in external aspect somewhat resembling its British namesake. **1865** *Hardwicke's Science-Gossip* 64/2 *Cape Salmon.*—Under this name the 'Geelbeck'..has been eulogized... Why call it Cape *Salmon*? **1906** [see KABELJOU]. **1846** H. H. METHUEN *Life in Wilderness* viii. 232 Revelling in the luxuries of *Cape smoke, or brandy, and sheep-tail fat. *a* **1871** J. GOLDSWAIN *Chron.* (1946) I. 36, I did not stop at this place Long for thear was to much Cape Smoke. **1954** 'D. DIVINE' *Golden Fool* v. 47 It was a better brandy than the Cape Smoke most of them drank. **1936** E. L. GILL *First Guide S. Afr. Bird* 21 *Cape Sparrow, Mossie, a very common bird about Cape Town and up the west coast region, and thence across the Karroo and High Veld. **1952** *Cape Times* 8 Nov. (Week-end Mag.) 6/5 What a handsome fellow the cock Cape sparrow is. **1798** LADY ANNE BARNARD *Let.* 6 June in *S. Africa a Century Ago* (1901) viii. 157 Of course, it was a *Cape waggon; any other sort..is impossible..for such an excursion. **1837** J. E. ALEXANDER *Narr. Voy. Observ.* xiv. 348 It is quite astonishing to a stranger what severe work Cape wagons undergo without injury. **1850** R. G. CUMMING *Hunter's Life S. Afr.* I. ii. 22 The Cape waggon is a large and powerful, yet loosely-constructed vehicle, running on four wheels. **1877** *Trans. N.Z. Inst.* X. 367 The *Cape weed, which is plentiful in Auckland. **1884** W. R. GUILFOYLE *Austral. Bot.* (ed. 2) 107 Cape Weed, *Cryptostemma calendulacea*. (Natural Order, *Compositæ*). This weed, which has proved such a pest in many parts of Victoria, was introduced from the Cape of Good Hope, as a fodder plant. **1933** L. G. D. ACLAND in *Press* (Christchurch, N.Z.) 23 Sept. 13/7 *Cape Weed*, Hypochaeris radicator. The English catsear is always so called in Canterbury. **1965** *Austral. Encycl.* II. 261/2 Capeweed is now so common on good pasture land..that the whole countryside may become a sea of yellow during late spring. **1797** HOLCROFT *Stolberg's Trav.* III. lxxxiv. (ed. 2) 351, I have seen it drunk..for red *Cape wine.

b. *attrib.* and in *comb.* in other senses; as ***cape-wise*** adv.

1849 THOREAU *Week Concord Riv.* 207 I jutted over the stream cape-wise.

†**cape**, *sb.*[4] *Old Law.* [a. OF. *cape* sb. fem., ad. L. *cape* imperat. of *capĕre* to take.] A judicial writ (now abolished) relative to a plea of lands or tenements; so named from its first word. Divided into ***cape magnum***, or the ***grand cape***, and ***cape parvum***, or ***petit cape***.

[**1292** BRITTON III. i. §4 A respouns par le graunt *Cape* et par le petit. *transl.* To answer by the great and little *Cape*.] **1588** FRAUNCE *Lawiers Log.* I. xii. 55 Replevyne of land upon a grand cape in olde time. **1641** *Termes de la Ley* s.v., Grand Cape lyeth before apparance, and petit Cape after..By the grand Cape the tenant is summoned to answer to the default, and over to the demandant: Petit Cape summoneth the tenant to answer to the default onely. **1706** in PHILLIPS.

†**cape**, *sb.*[5] *Obs.* exc. *dial.* [var. of CAP (see 10 b). Cf. also COPE, COPESTONE.] Top.

1650 HOWELL *Giraffi's Rev. Naples* 22 To negotiate with the cape leaders of the people. **1796** W. MARSHALL *Yorksh.* (ed. 2) I. 203 Setting the plants behind the 'cape-sod', or first-turned spit. **1812** H. E. STRICKLAND *Agric. E. Riding* 99 Turning the cape-sod, and planting the quickwood.

†**cape**, *v.*[1] *Naut. Obs.* Also 5–7 cap. [app. more or less directly, f. F. *cap* cape, also 'the forepart of a ship, in relation to the direction which it is following, as "porter le cap au nord"' (Littré).] *intr.* To head, keep a course, bear up; to drift. Said of sailors and of ship.

c **1500** DUNBAR in Maitland *Poems* 133 (Jam.) That ye man cap be wind and waw. **1513** DOUGLAS *Æneis* II. viii. 125 The port quham to we cappit was full large. **1535** STEWART *Cron. Scot.* I. 124 Sum with ane torss la capand on the wynd. **1627** CAPT. SMITH *Seaman's Gram.* ix. 41 Experience to try her drift, or how she capes. **1730–6** BAILEY, *Cap*..used of a ship, in the Trials of the running or setting of currents. **1867** SMYTH *Sailor's Word-bk.* s.v., How does she cape? How does she lie her course?

Hence, 'caping *vbl. sb.*

1594 DAVIS *Seaman's Secrets* (1607) 40 The ship..may make her way 2 or 3 points from her caping.

†**cape**, *v.*[2] *Obs.* [a. mod.Du. *kapen* to take, pilfer, plunder; *te kaap varen* to go a privateering: see CAPER *sb.*[3] Cf. also CAP *v.*[2]: but it is uncertain whether there is any original connexion.] To take or seize as a privateer; *also*, to go a privateering. Hence **caped** *ppl. a.*, 'caping *vbl. sb.*

1676 ROW *Supp. Blair's Autobiog.* xi. (1848) 489 Some of our grandees get much by their caping. **1721** WODROW *Hist. Ch. Scotl.* I. 220 (Jam.) Some private persons made themselves rich by caping or privateering upon the Dutch. **1759** FOUNTAINHALL *Decisions* I. 80 (Jam.) The buyers of caped goods in England are not liable in restitution.

cape, *v.*[3], var. of KEP to catch.

a **1802** *Lanckin* x. in Child *Ballads* IV. 332/2 A bason..To cape this ladie's blood.

cape, Sc. f. COPE; occas. var. CAP *sb.*

capeador (kæpiːə'dɔə(r)). [Sp. f. *capear*, to trick a bull with a cape, f. *capa* CAPE *sb.*[2]] One who aids a bull-fighter by distracting and tricking the bull with his cloak.

1909 in *Cent. Dict.* Suppl. **1924** KIPLING *Debits & Credits* (1926) 220 The capeadors—the men with the cloaks—were advancing to play Apis. **1932** R. CAMPBELL *Taurine Provence* iii. 73 Since Gordito's time..bandilleros have had most recourse to the aid of capeadors.

Cape Cod (keɪp kɒd). *N. Amer.* The name of a promontory in Massachusetts, U.S.A., used *attrib.* or *absol.* to designate a type of compact rectangular house, usually with a steep gable roof, reminiscent of dwellings on Cape Cod. Also *ellipt.*, as *Cape*.

1916 J. E. CHANDLER *Colonial House* ii. 60 The remembrance of a most charming Cape Cod cottage. **1926** *House Beautiful* Sept. 255/1 The Cape houses..were carefully constructed, with pitch roofs and walls hung on a solid frame of hewn oak. **1945** *Geogr. Rev.* XXXV. 445 Contemporary 'Cape Cod' invades the hills of the Los Angeles suburban zone to be neighbor to..'English half-timbered'. **1966** H. KEMELMAN *Saturday the Rabbi went Hungry* (1967) iii. 23 There was no confusing the Moderne with its flush door and three small diagonal panes of glass with the Cape Cod, which had a white panelled door flanked by two long narrow windows. **1967** *Boston Herald* 1 Apr. 8/1 (Advt.), A charming Cape with exquisite authentic detail. **1968** *Globe & Mail* (Toronto) 13 Feb. 30/1 (Advt.), Attractive Cape Cod, storey and a half, located on a well landscaped lot.

caped (keɪpt), *a.* [f. CAPE *sb.*[2] + -ED[2].] Having a cape; clad in a cape.

c **1550** *Pride & Abuse Wom.* 119 in Hazl. *E.P.P.* IV. 239 A caped cassoc, Moche lyke a players gowne. **1589** *Pappe w. Hatchet* D ij b, In a cap'de cloake. **1784** *New Spect.* I. 4/1 The treble-caped great coat and belt. **1859** SALA *Tw. round Clock* (1861) 362 A hackney coachman's many-caped coat. **1886** T. HARDY in *Athenæum* 16 Oct. 501/3 Quaintly attired in caped cloak, knee-breeches, and buckled shoes.

caped, *ppl. a.*: see CAPE *v.*[2]

capel[1] ('keɪp(ə)l). *Min.* Also **caple**. A composite stone of quartz, schorl, and hornblende, occurring in the walls of tin and copper lodes (Raymond *Mining Gloss.* 1881).

1801 HITCHINS in *Phil. Trans.* XCI. 162 The copper lode is filled with layers of ore and stony matter, the latter of which is here [in Cornwall] called Caple.

†**capel**[2], **cappell.** *Alch. Obs.* [ad. L. *capella*, app. so used in med.L. by alchemists; see Du Cange.] ? A kind of large crucible.

1527 ANDREW *Brunswyke's Distyll. Waters* A ij a, Ye must have cappellys of whyte claye..comonly halfe a yerde wyde and depe. *Ibid.* A ij b, As brode and longe as the cappell or fornays is. **1753** CHAMBERS *Cycl. Supp.* II. Plate 12 Cappels. [**1881** RAYMOND *Mining Gloss.*, *Capella*, Spanish, cupelling furnace.]

capel[3], variant of CAPLE, *Obs.*, a horse.

capelet[1] ('kæpəlɪt). Also **capellet.** [a. F. *capelet*, Picard for *chapelet*, from the resemblance to a wreath.] A wen-like swelling on the heel of a horse's hock, or on the point of the elbow.

1731–1800 BAILEY, *Capelé*. **1775** ASH, *Capelet*. **1792** OSBALDISTONE *Brit. Sportsm.* 93/2 *Capellet*, in horses, a particular swelling to which they are subject. **1847** in CRAIG. **1864** in WEBSTER.

capelet[2] ('keɪplɪt). [f. CAPE *sb.*[2] + -LET.] A small cape.

1912 *Home Chat* 1 June 444/2 The new Puritan capelet of white lawn. **1968** *Globe & Mail* (Toronto) 3 Feb. 11/5 The top is covered up by a broad-shouldered capelet that looks like a giant, beautiful bib.

capelet, obs. form of CHAPLET.

capelin, caplin ('kæpəlɪn, 'kæplɪn). Also 7 **capline, -ling**, 7–9 **capeling**, 8 **-elan, caplein**, 9 **capalan.** [= Fr. *capelan, caplan*, Sp. *capelan*.] A small fish very similar to a smelt, found on the coast of Newfoundland, and much used as a bait for cod.

1620 J. MASON *Newfoundland* 5, June hath Capline a fish much resembling Smeltes in forme and eating. **1623** WHITBOURNE *Newfoundland* 8 The Riuers..are stored with ..Launce, Capelin, Cod, and Trouts. *Ibid.* 89 Capeling. **1753** CHAMBERS *Cycl. Supp.*, *Capelan*. **1823** in W. Cobbett *Rur. Rides* (1885) I. 397 Innumerable small fry slip down unperceived, like caplins down the throats of the sharks. **1861** HULME tr. *Moquin-Tandon* II. III. i. 102 Other Gadoids ..the Haddock, the Capalan. **1861** L. NOBLE *Icebergs* 53 Four or five whales..were feeding upon the Capelin.

capeline ('kæpəlɪn). In 5 **capleyne**, 9 **capelline, cappeline.** [a. F. *capeline*, ad. It. (or med.L.) *cap(p)ellina* little hat, dim. of *cappella* (see CHAPEL), dim. of *cap(p)a* CAP, CAPE.]

1. 'A small skull-cap of iron worn by archers in the Middle Ages' (Fairholt). *Obs.* (exc. *Hist.*).

c **1470** HENRY *Wallace* III. 88 A steylle capleyne in his bonet but mar. **1834** PLANCHÉ *Brit. Costume* 204 The skull-caps of steel, called capellines [*temp.* Edw. IV.].

2. *Surg.* A bandage, which by its arrangement forms a kind of cap or bonnet.

1706 in PHILLIPS. **1751** *Phil. Trans.* XLVII. xl. 270, I bound the head with a strong capeline. *note.* A bandage peculiar to the head. **1753** CHAMBERS *Cycl. Supp.*, *Capeline*, a kind of bandage used by the French surgeons in cases of amputations; consisting of a roller with two equal heads.

3. A lady's hat; also, a woollen hood of loose texture, worn by ladies in going to or from an evening entertainment. [From mod.Fr.] Later, a hat for a girl or woman, having a wide brim often consisting of many folds of muslin, or the like.

[**1775** ASH, *Capeline* (from the French), a woman's hat adorned with feathers.] **1868** HOLME LEE *B. Godfrey* lxix. 412 She..drew the..capeline..over her head. **1899** *Westm. Gaz.* 13 July 3/2 A girl..in a black muslin *capeline* with a band round the crown and a big front bow of vivid cerise. **1901** *Daily News* 11 Feb. 3/2 The black tulle capeline made with a brim of perhaps twenty to thirty double folds of tulle. **1928** *Observer* 12 Feb. 23 Later on, brims will widen, and capelines of a particularly picturesque type will accompany the dainty dresses worn in the afternoon.

‖**Capella** (kə'pɛlə). [L. *capella* she-goat.] Proper name of a star of the first magnitude in Auriga.

1682 SIR T. BROWNE *Chr. Mor.* 121 The time might come when capella, a noble northern star, would have its motion in the æquator. **1868** LOCKYER *Elem. Astron.* lxii. 24 We read ..that Capella, which is now pale blue, was red.

capella: see CHAPEL.

†**ca'pellane.** *Obs.* [ad. late and med.L. *capellānus*. Cf. It. *cappellano*, F. *capelan*, *chapelain* chaplain.] **a.** A keeper of the sacred relics. **b.** One who officiates in a chapel; a chaplain.

a **1661** FULLER, The dignities and duties of the precentor, sacrist, subsacrist, capellane, ostiary. **1827** *Gentl. Mag.* XCVII. II. 541 At that time forty shillings a year was a common stipend for a capellane.

capelline, var. of CAPELINE.

cape'locracy. [f. Gr. κάπηλος shop-keeper + -κρατία rule.] The shopkeeping 'interest' or class.

1841 LYTTON *Nt. & Morn.* (1851) 236 A milliner's house (shop, to outward appearance, it was not), evincing..its degree above the Capelocracy, to use a certain classical neologism, by a brass plate. **1853** —— *My Novel* (Hoppe), The triumph of the capelocracy.

†'**cape-,merchant.** *Obs.* Also Cap-. [app. an adaptation of some foreign title in *cap* or *capo*,

meaning 'head merchant' or 'head of the traders'.] An old name for the supercargo in early voyages; also the head merchant in a factory. (Smyth.)

1613 PURCHAS *Pilgr.*, *Descr. India* (1864) 156 The Cape-Merchant Floris performed a worthy exploit. **1627** CAPT. SMITH *Seaman's Gram.* viii. 34 The Cape-merchant or Purser hath the charge of all the Carragasoune or merchandize. **1697** DAMPIER *Voy.* (1729) I. 272 Cape-Merchant, or Super-Cargo of Capt. Swan's Ship. **1708** KERSEY, *Cap-Merchant*. **1721–1800** in BAILEY.

b. *fig.*

1581 J. BELL *Haddon's Answ. Osor.* 138b, They..did admitte Grace to be cape marchaunt (as it were) with Free-will. **1639** FULLER *Holy War* 19 The French..were the cape-merchants in this adventure [Crusades]. **1649** SELDEN *Laws Eng.* II. vii. (1739) 39 The King shewed himself the Cape-Merchant of the world.

caper ('keɪpə(r)), *sb.*[1] Forms: α. with *-s* in *sing.* and *pl.* 4 **caperis**, 4–6 **cap(p)aris, -es**, 6–7 **caperes, -ers, -ars, cappers**; β. without *-s* in *sing.* 6–9 **caper**, 7 **capar**; γ. (from Fr.) 5–7 **capres**. [ME. *caperis*, *caperes*, a. L. *capparis*, a. Gr. κάππαρις; in OF. *caspres*, mod.Fr. *câpre*, It. *cappero*. The final *s* being treated as the plural sign, esp. in sense 2, was at length dropped in the singular. Cf. F. *câpres* in Littré.]

1. A shrub (*Capparis spinosa*) in habit of growth like the common bramble, abundant on walls and rocky places in the South of Europe.

1382 WYCLIF *Eccles.* xii. 5 The erbe caperis [**1388** capparis] shal be scatered. **1551** TURNER *Herbal* H iij b, Capers is a pricky bushe. **1578** LYTE *Dodoens* VI. xviii. 680 The Caper is a prickley plant or bush almost lyke the Bramble. **1597** GERARD *Herbal* II. cccxxxi. 896 It is generally called Cappers in most languages; in English Cappers, Caper, and Capers. **1688** R. HOLME *Armoury* II. 102/2 Capers hath a weak woody stalk. **1751** CHAMBERS *Cycl.*, Caper, Capparis. **1881** *Cornh. Mag.* Mar. 315 In sheltered nooks the caper hangs her beautiful purpureal snowy bloom.

2. (usually in *pl.*) The flower-buds of the same, gathered for pickling.

1481–90 *Howard Househ. Bks.* (1841) 311 He bout for my Lord..xxij. lb. capres. **1566** GASCOIGNE *Supposes*, Wks. (1587) 58, I will go into the towne and buy oranges, olives, and cappers. **1641** SUCKLING *Let.* 56 The Capers which will make my Lord of Dorset goe from the Table. **1732** ARBUTHNOT *Rules of Diet* I. 244 Capers, astringent and diuretic. **1882** *Garden* 9 Sept. 233/1 The Capers of commerce are the flower-buds gathered while in a young state.

3. *Capucine*, *Capuchin capers*, *English capers*: the seed-vessels of the nasturtium (*Tropæolum majus*: see CAPUCINE), or of the caper spurge (*Euphorbia Lathyris*), gathered for pickling; also the plants themselves.

1693 EVELYN *De la Quint. Compl. Gard.* II. 189 Capucine-Capers, or Nasturces, are annual Plants. **1721–1800** BAILEY, *Capuchin Capers*, a plant called Nasturces. **1750** JOHNSON *Rambl.* No. 51 ¶12 The art of making English Capers she has not yet persuaded herself to discover.

4. A sort of scented tea.

1864 W. WOOD *Wds. about Tea* 10 Scented Teas..a close twisted round shot-like leaf, termed Caper. **1883** *Daily News* 27 July 6/8 Tea..scented Caper 5d. to 1s. o½d.

5. *attrib.*, as in *caper-berry*, *-bush*, *-plant*, *-sauce*, *-shrub*, *-tree*; also **caper-bean** = *bean-caper* (see BEAN *sb.*); **caper-bush**, **caper-plant**, **caper-spurge**, different names of *Euphorbia Lathyris*; **caper-tree**, *Busbeckia arborea* of New South Wales.

1885 BIBLE (R.V.) *Eccles.* xii. 5 The *caper-berry shall fail. **1673** RAY *Trav.* (1738) II. 14, I found nothing by the way but a few *Caper-bushes. **1807** PINKERTON *Mod. Geog. Abr.* (1811) 209 The rocks on the [Spanish] coast..abound with samphire..vetch, caper bush. **1882** A. J. C. HARE in *Gd. Words* Mar. 185 The beautiful *caper plant, which is the hyssop of Scripture. **1791** WOLCOTT (P. Pindar) *Rights of Kings* Wks. 1812 II. 431 Dear as, to Legs of Mutton, *Caper-Sauce. **1609** BIBLE (Douay) *Eccles.* xii. 5 The *caper-tree shal be destroyed.

caper ('keɪpə(r)), *sb.*[2] [app. abbreviated from CAPRIOLE *sb.*: Florio has It. '*capriola* a capriole or caper in dancing'. Cf. the vb.; also *cab* from *cabriolet*.] **1. a.** A frolicsome leap, like that of a playful kid; a frisky movement, *esp.* in dancing; said also of horses; *fig.* a fantastic proceeding or freak.

1592 GREENE *Upst. Court.* in *Harl. Misc.* (Malh.) II. 248 You, Maister Usher of the dauncing schoole..stand upon your tricks and capers. **1600** SHAKS. *A.Y.L.* II. iv. 55 We that are true Louers, runne into strange capers. **1712** POPE *Spect.* No. 408 ¶5 An Hour in Secret, wherein he had his Frisks and Capers. **1856** OLMSTED *Slave States* 68 Jane [a horse] gave a little sympathizing caper.

b. *to cut a caper* or *capers*: to dance in a frolicsome way, to act fantastically. †*to cut a caper on nothing*: to be hanged.

1601 SHAKS. *Twel. N.* I. iii. 129 *And.* Faith, I can cut a caper. *To.* And I can cut the mutton too't. **1691** WOOD *Ath. Oxon.* II. /262 By his high dancing and cutting of Capers.. he did..sprain a vein. **1708** MOTTEUX *Rabelais* IV. xvi, Two of the honestest Gentlemen in Catchpole-land had been made to cut a Caper on nothing. **1711** STEELE *Spect.* No. 4 ¶8 He can Dance, though he does not cut Capers. **1826** DISRAELI *Viv. Grey* V. xv. 260 Executing splendid somersets, and cutting every species of caper.

c. *transf.* Any activity or pursuit, spec. a fashionable occupation. Also, a 'game', dodge, racket. (There are many shades of meaning in U.S., N.Z., and elsewhere.)

1839 *Spirit of Times* 9 Nov. 423/2 When they are short on't for cradles, a feedin trof is jest the caper. **1840** C. F. HOFFMAN *Greyslaer* I. 84 The bizness is a bad one, any how you can fix it, capting; but I think I understand the caper on't. **1851** MAYHEW *Lond. Labour* I. 416/1, I used to dress tidy and very clean for the 'respectable broken-down tradesman or reduced gentleman' caper. **1867** *London Herald* 23 Mar. 221 'He'll get five years penal for this little caper,' said the policeman. *a* **1889** *Boston Herald* (D.A.E.), Mind-reading is now the proper caper. **1897** CONRAD *Nigger Narcissus* iv. 81 'I know his caper,' he said, in a low voice. **1926** J. BLACK *You can't Win* x. 131 If anything had gone wrong with this caper and we had to take a pinch. **1944** J. A. LEE *Shining with Shiner* 75 It's getting worse for this caper every year. **1959** *N.Z. Listener* 12 June 5/2 Marxism was the caper. **1959** *Times* 26 May 12/7 Now let's see if the car stops at all after that little caper. **1964** J. BURKE *Hard Day's Night* v. 104, I know your caper. The kidney punch and the rabbit clout.

2. *Comb.* **caper-cut**, the cutting of a caper; **caper-cutting** *a.*, that cuts capers: **caper-witted** *a.*, of frivolous or unsteady mind.

a **1626** FLETCHER *Love's Pilgr.*, My poor child..Your caper-cutting son has run away with. *a* **1670** HACKET *Abp. Williams* I. 227 (D.) Whatsoever any caper-witted man may observe. **1875** BROWNING *Aristoph. Apol.* 361 Those flute-girls—trash who..fed eye with caper-cuts.

†**'caper**, *sb.*[3] *Obs.* exc. *Hist.* [a. mod.Du. *kaper* privateer, corsair, f. *kapen*, E.Fris. *kapen* to take away, steal, rob, plunder (see CAPE *v.*[2]).]

1. A privateer (also *caper-vessel*); the captain of a privateer; a corsair.

1657 COLVIL *Whig's Supplic.* (1695) 23 Capers bringing in their prizes, Commons cursing new excises. **1666** LAMONT *Diary* (1810) 243 Divers persons contributed to the reaking out of smaller Vessels to be capers. **1667** *Ibid.* 246 A caper vessel..did spleit on upon the Sands. **1668** *Treaty* in Magens *Insurances* (1755) II. 447 The Captains and Capers shall..give good and sufficient Security. **1821** SCOTT *Pirate* xxvi, Brenda..ran from her like a Spanish merchant-man from a Dutch caper.

fig. **1719** D'URFEY *Pills* V. 349 Wit Capers, play Sharpers, loud Bullies.

†**2.** A captor, seizer. *Sc. Obs.*

1759 FOUNTAINHALL *Decisions* I. 333 (Jam.) The oft debated cause of the Capers of the two prize Danish ships.. that they were free ships, but that the Capers had probable grounds to bring them up.

caper ('keɪpə(r)), *sb.*[4] *Sc.* Also **kaper**. [a. Gael. *ceapaire* piece of bread and butter.] 'A piece of oatcake and butter with a slice of cheese on it' (Jamieson).

1815 *Clan Albin* I. 211 (Jam.) Hugh..I gave you a kaper, and a crogan of milk. **1818** *Trial Sons of Rob Roy* 107 She gave the deponent..bread, butter, and cheese, which they call a caper.

caper ('keɪpə(r)), *sb.*[5] *slang.* (See quot.)

1851 MAYHEW *Lond. Labour* I. 287 And capers (chorister boys and ballet-girls).

caper ('kæpə(r)), *sb.*[6] Colloq. abbrev. of CAPERCAILYE, CAPERCAILZIE.

1902 *Westm. Gaz.* 30 Dec. 4/3 The great 'caper' can fly as noiselessly as an owl. **1920** J. RITCHIE *Animal Life Scotl.* vi. 355 Bishop Jhone Leslie..shows clearly that the range of the Caper was limited. **1937** R. A. KNOX *Double Cross Purposes* ix. 146 A caper rocketed up suddenly a few feet away from him. **1958** *Listener* 23 Oct. 660/3 Many other species..from the grand old Caper to diminutive shore waders.

caper ('keɪpə(r)), *v.*[1] [app. abbreviated from CAPRIOLE *v.*: Florio has It. '*capriolare* to caper or capriole'. Cf. the sb.] *intr.* To dance or leap in a frolicsome manner, to skip for merriment; to prance as a horse. Also with *about*, *away*.

1588 SHAKS. *L.L.L.* V. ii. 113 The third he caper'd, and cried All goes well. **1635** SWAN *Spec. M.* VI. ii. (1643) 221 As if it danced or capered up and down. **1691** BOYLE *Wks.* II. 282 (R.) Dancing and capering like a kid. **1768** TUCKER *Lt. Nat.* (1852) II. 445 The complete horseman..may let him sometimes prance and caper and curvet. **1802** MAR. EDGEWORTH *Moral T.* I. viii. 50 A number of people capering about. **1847** BARHAM *Ingol. Leg.* (1877) 168 Capering away in a Spanish bolero. **1859** TENNYSON *Elaine* 788. Making a roan horse caper and curvet For pleasure.

b. *transf.* and *fig.* of a singer or singing bird.

a **1593** H. SMITH *Serm.* I. 410 A nightingale..quavers and capers and trebles. **1609** DOULAND *Ornith. Microl.* 88 The Italians..caper with their voyces. **1850** BLACKIE *Æschylus* I. Pref. 6 The old Hellenic dialect can caper gracefully through movements, that..would twist our English tongue into.. dislocation.

†**caper**, *v.*[2] *Obs.* [f. CAPER *sb.*[3]] To privateer. See CAPERER[1] and CAPERING.

†**'caperate**, *v. Obs.* [f. L. *caperāt-* ppl. stem of *caperā-re* in same sense.] **a.** *trans.* To wrinkle. **b.** *intr.* To frown. Hence **'caperated** *ppl. a.*

1623 COCKERAM, *Caperate*, to frowne. **1657** TOMLINSON *Renou's Disp.* 372 Its pill more crasse, rugous, and caperated. **1731** BAILEY II. *Caperated*, wrinkled like a goat's horn. **1775** in ASH.

capercailye, capercailzie (kæpə'keɪljɪ, keɪ-, -'keɪlzɪ). *Sc.* Forms; 6–9 **capercailye, -llie, -ly, -le, capercalʒe, -calye, -calzeane (-callzie)**, 7 **-kelly**, 7–9 **-caley, -cally**, 8 **-coille, -colze, -colly, (cobberkely)**, 9 **capercailzie, -kayle, caipercaillie**. [Corruption of the Gael. name *capull coille* (kapəl 'kɒlje) great cock (*lit.* horse) of the wood (*coille* = genitive of *coll* wood). The *lz* for *lʒ* is a 16th c. Sc. way of representing *l mouillé*, as in Sc. *spulʒe*, Fr. *espouille* spoil, and is properly represented by *ly*.]

The Wood-grouse (*Tetrao urogallus*), the largest of European gallinaceous birds; the male is also called Mountain Cock or Cock of the Woods. Formerly indigenous in the Scottish Highlands, where, after having become extinct, it has again been introduced from Scandinavia.

1536 BELLENDEN *Cron. Scot.* (1821) I. Introd. 42 Caper-cailye, ane foul mair than ane ravin quhilk leiffis allanerlie of barkis of treis. **1596** J. DALRYMPLE tr. *Leslie's Hist. Scotl.* (1885) 39 The Capercalʒe..with the vulgar peple, the horse of the forest. **1630–56** SIR R. GORDON *Hist. Earl. Suthd.*, In these fforests..ther is great store of partriges, pluivers, capercaleys. *c* **1730** BURT *Lett. N. Scotl.* (1818) II. 71 The Cobberkely which is sometimes called a wild turkey. **1797** *Statist. Acc. Scotl.* XX. 307 (Inverness) The caper coille or wild turkey was seen in Glenmoriston about 40 years ago. **1799** R. JAMIESON *Ballad, Ld. Kenneth & Ellinour*, The Caiper-caillie and Tarmachin, Craw'd crouse on hill and muir. **1830** LYELL *Princ. Geol.* (1875) II. III. xlii. 460 The larger capercailzies..had been quite destroyed. **1884** Q. VICTORIA *More Leaves* 50 Saw a capercailzie, of which there are many here.

†**'caperclaw**, variant of CLAPPERCLAW.

1589 *Hay any Work* (1844) 60 His Bishopdome was reasonably caperclawed.

caper-cousin, corruption of CATER-COUSIN.

†**caper'dewsie, caper'dochy.** *Obs.* [app. corruptions of CAPPADOCHIO.] The stocks; prison.

1600 HEYWOOD *1 Edw. IV*, IV. iv. Wks. 1874 I. 72 My son's in Dybel here, in Caperdochy, iria gaol. *Ibid.* I. I. 86 He's in Capperdochy, Ned, in Stafford Jail, for a robbery. **1663** BUTLER *Hud.* I. II. 832, I here engage myself to loose ye And free your heels from caperdewsie.

†**caperer**, *sb.*[1] = CAPER *sb.*[3], privateer.

1676 W. ROW *Contn. Blair's Autobiog.* xii. (1848) 508 At this time our capereres set to sea.

caperer ('keɪpərə(r)), *sb.*[2] [f. CAPER *v.* + -ER[1].]

1. One who capers.

1693 DRYDEN *Juvenal*, The nimble caperer on the cord. **1812** BYRON *Waltz* x, Columbia's caperers to the warlike whoop.

2. A caddis-fly (*Phryganea*); from its flight.

1855 KINGSLEY *Glaucus* (1878) 208 Caperers and sandflies. **1863** —— *Water-bab.* 80 Fly away as a caperer, on four fawn-coloured wings, with long legs and horns.

†**'caperhay**, *v. Obs.* [? f. CAPER *v.* + HAY a kind of country-dance.]

1600 *Look About You* in Hazl. *Dodsley* VII. 421 Come, caperhay, set all at six and seven.

caperik, var. of CAPRIKE, *Obs.*

capering ('keɪpərɪŋ), *vbl. sb.*[1] [f. CAPER *v.* + -ING[1].] Frolicsome dancing or leaping.

1599 MARSTON *Sco. Villanie* 193 To shew his capring skill. **1793** W. ROBERTS *Looker-on* No. 84 The leaping and capering she [the hare] displays. **1868** HELPS *Realmah* xv. (1876) 410 Not to be indulged in caperings of their own.

†**'capering**, *vbl. sb.*[2] *Obs.* [f. CAPER *v.*[2] + -ING[1].] Privateering.

1676 W. ROW *Contn. Blair's Autobiog.* xii. (1848) 491 The Scots capering did not a little irritate the Dutch.

'capering, *ppl. a.* [f. CAPER *v.* + -ING[2].] That capers, dancing.

1595 MARKHAM *Sir R. Griniule* xxiv, A winde-taught capring Ship. **1597** *1st Pt. Ret. fr. Parnass.* v. i. 1418 A capringe page. **1698** ROWE *Amb. Stepm.* Prol. 21 Nor capering monsieur from Active France. **1828** SCOTT *F.M. Perth* ii, Those gallants, with their capering horses.

Hence **'caperingly** *adv.*

1641 BROME *Jov. Crew* I. Wks. 1873 III. 366 Most crowse most capringly.

caperis, -es, obs. ff. of CAPER *sb.*[1], the plant.

Capernaite (kə'pɜːneɪaɪt). Also 6 **caparnaite**. [f. *Capernaum* a town of Galilee + -ITE.] An inhabitant of Capernaum; *hence* (with reference to *John* vi. 52) A controversial designation for a believer in transubstantiation.

Hence †**Caper'naitan** *sb.*, **Ca,perna'itic** *a.*, **Ca,perna'itical** *a.*, **Ca,perna'itically** *adv.*, †**Caper'naitish** *a.*, †**Ca'pernize** *v.* (All frequent in the doctrinal polemics of the 16th & 17th c.)

1549 RIDLEY *Determ. Sacrament* Wks. (1841) 175 They which affirm transubstantiation are indeed right Sacramentaries and Capernaites. **1579** FULKE *Heskins' Parl.* 217 To be Caparnaites. **1642** ROGERS *Naaman* 230 Calling them Capernaits and Carnall. **1661** S. FISHER *Spir. Verities Rev.* Wks. (1679) 851 No High-climbing Capernaites..can ever soar high enough to enter. **1641** MILTON *Animadv.* (1851) 234 O race of Capernaitans..capable onely of loaves and belly-cheere! **1880** tr. *Hagenbach's Hist. Chr. Doctr.* II. 338 Cardinal Humbert was carried so far..as to interpret the phrase [This is my body] in the grossest Capernaitic manner. **1882–3** SCHAFF *Relig. Encycl.* III. 2368 The carnal Capernaitic misunderstanding. **1563–87** FOXE *A. & M.* (1684) II. 7/2 The absurd, gross, and Capernaitical opinion of the new Schoolmen. *a* **1656** BP. HALL *Rem. Wks.* (1660)

192 They will admit of [no] other then a grosse capernaiticall sence. **1640** SIR E. DERING *Prop. Sacr.* (1644) 41 Forbear this carnall barbarisme of eating our Saviours body thus Capernaitically. **1643** HERLE *Answ. to Ferne* 7 A Capernaitish following the King for loaves. **1624** A. DARCIE *Birth Heresies* xxi. 98 Did he determen we should hereby Capernize & Nicodemize, to..make doubt of Gods power?

capernoitie (kæpər'nɔɪtɪ), *sb. Sc.* [Etymology unknown.] Head, noddle. Hence perhaps **caper'noity** *a.*, **caper'noited** *a.*, 'crabbed, irritable, peevish' (Jam.); slightly affected in the head by drinking, muddle-headed, wrong-headed; also **caper'noitedness**.

1719 W. HAMILTON *Ep.* ii. in *Ramsay's Wks.*, I thought I shou'd turn capernoited. **1769** HERD *Sc. Songs* II. 23 She is ..Sae capornoytie, and sae bonny. **1819** *St. Patrick* III. 42 (Jam.) His capernoitie's no oure the bizzin' yet wi' the sight of the Loch fairies. **1824** SCOTT *Redgauntlet* ch. ii, Capernoited maggots and nonsense. **1832–53** *Whistle-Binkie* (Sc. Songs) Ser. II, Of the stark aquavitæ they baith lo'ed a drappie, And when capernutie then aye unco happy.

caperoile, -oilie. *Sc.* The Heath-pea (*Orobus tuberosus*), or CARMELE.

1795 *Statist. Acc. Scotl.* (*Lanark*) XV. 8 (Jam.) Carameile or Caperoiles—the root so much used in diet by the ancient Caledonians.

caperon, obs. var. of CHAPERON a hood.

capersome ('keɪpəsəm), *a.* [f. CAPER *v.* + -SOME.] Given or inclined to capering.

1852 AIRD *Life D. Moir* in *Moir's Wks.* I. 29 We are in a frivolous capersome humour. **1857** HEAVYSEGE *Saul* (1869) 206 I've never seen a cat..more capersome.

capes (keɪps), *sb. pl. north. dial.* and *Sc.* **a.** Grains of corn to which the husk continues to adhere after threshing; **b.** The grain which is not sufficiently ground; **c.** Flakes of meal which come from the mill when the grain has not been sufficiently dried. (Jamieson.)

1641 BEST *Farm. Bks.* (1856) 103 The chaffe, capes and heads gather togeather on the toppe and are taken off. **1790** MORRISON *Poems* 110 Wi' capes, the mill she gard them ring ..Then Goodie wi' her tentie paw, Did capes an' seeds the gether ca'. **1796** W. MARSHALL *Yorksh.* (ed. 2) I. 362 To separate the chaff, the capes, and the grain. **1847–78** HALLIWELL, *Capes*, ears of corn broken off in thrashing.

capeskin ('keɪpskɪn). [f. CAPE *sb.*³ 2 + SKIN *sb.*] A soft leather made from South African hair sheepskin.

[**1915** K. J. ADCOCK *Leather* ii. 13 Of the imported varieties, the..Cape sheep skins are the best.] **1934** in WEBSTER. **1938** *Times* 11 Mar. 19/3 The Gay Nineties type of flat crown... Of particular interest are those of patent leather or capeskin. **1959** *Observer* 5 Apr. 13/1 The supplest and lightest weight of capeskin leathers, silky to the touch, printed in delicate marbled designs.

capestan, obs. form of CAPSTAN.

capestone, north. form of COPESTONE.

capet, obs. form of CAPOT *v.*

Capetian (kə'piːʃ(ɪ)ən), *a.* [ad. F. *Capétien.*] Pertaining to the third dynasty of French kings, founded by Hugh Capet in A.D. 987. Also as *sb.*

1836 *Penny Cycl.* VI. 264/1 The third, or,..Capetian dynasty of French princes. **1839** K. H. DIGBY *Mores Cath.* IX. xi. 333 The Capetians, whose title dates from Robert-le-fort. **1929** BELLOC *Joan of Arc* ii. 39 From him all the Kings were descended, and that Crown Capetian which was the centre and prop of the world and the eye of Christendom.

capful ('kæpfʊl). [f. CAP *sb.* + -FUL.] As much as a cap will contain. ***a capful of wind*** (*Naut.*): 'a light flaw, which suddenly careens a vessel, and passes off' (Smyth *Sailor's Word-bk.*).

1719 DE FOE *Crusoe* 7 You were frightened, wa'n't you, last night, when it blew but a cap-full of wind? **1851** LONGF. *Gold. Leg.* v. *At Sea*, I was whistling to Saint Antonio for a capful of wind to fill our sail. **1873** C. ROBINSON *N.S. Wales* 44 When down the shaft one night he picked up a capful of quartz worth £20.

capha, -e, obs. forms of CAFFA, COFFEE *sb.*

†**ca'phar.** *Obs.* [In F. *caphar*, a. Arab. *khafārah* defence, premium for defence or protection, f. *khafara* to protect, patronize.] See quot.

1703 MAUNDRELL *Journ. Jerus.* (1732) 4 A place where we paid our first Caphar. *Ibid.* 119 The excessive demand made upon us by the Caphar-men. **1751** CHAMBERS *Cycl.*, *Caphar*, a toll, or duty imposed by the Turks on the Christian merchants, who carry or send merchandise from Aleppo to Jerusalem.

Capharnaism (kə'fɑːneɪ,ɪz(ə)m). [f. *Capharnaum*, Aramaic form of *Capernaum* + -ISM.] The doctrine of the Capernaites. Also †**Ca'pharnaite, -nite** = CAPERNAITE.

1656 BLOUNT *Glossogr.*, *Capharnaits.* **1706** tr. *Dupin's Eccl. Hist. 16th C.* II. v. 25 The impious Capharnites. **1828** SOUTHEY in *Q. Rev.* XXXVII. 217 Bishop Ricci..would have taxed him with Capharnaism.

caphtan, capiai, var. of CAPTAN, CABIAI.

†'**Capian**, *a. Obs. rare*⁻¹. Of or belonging to the Cape of Good Hope.

1731 MEDLEY *Kolben's Cape G. Hope* II. 80 Capian wine.

‖**capias** ('kæpɪæs). *Law.* [L. *capias* 'thou mayest take'.] A writ or process commanding the officer to take the body of the person named in it, that is, to arrest him; also called ***writ of capias.***

The term *Capias* includes writs of various kinds; ***capias ad respondendum***, to enforce attendance at court; ***capias ad satisfaciendum***, after judgement, to imprison the defendant, until the plaintiff's claim is satisfied; ***capias utlagatum***, to arrest an outlawed person; ***capias in Withernam***, to seize the cattle or goods of any one who has made an unlawful distraint (see WITHERNAM).

1467 in *Eng. Gilds* (1870) 390 That no seriaunt take..for servynge of a capias eny thynge but in maner folowynge. **1543** *Ludlow Churchw. Acc.* (Camden) 14 Payde for ij capias ..vjd. **1622** FLETCHER *Span. Cur.* v. ii, A capias from my surgeon and my silkman. **1648** PRYNNE *Plea for Lords* 52 Walter Clerke..was arrested..upon a *Capias Utlagatum.* **1682** LUTTRELL *Brief Rel.* (1857) I. 234 If his lordship had not appeared, a capias in Withernam would have gone out, whereon he must have been committed. **1689** HICKERINGILL *Modest Inq.* ii 17 Excommunications, Capias's, Fines, and Imprisonments. **1812** COMBE (Dr. Syntax) *Picturesque* xxv, Near Clifford's-Inn appear'd to stand Of Capiases an ugly band. **1865** *Dublin Univ. Mag.* I. 563 A distinguished general officer..who was just going out to India and who had been stopped by a capias.

capibara, var. of CAPYBARA.

capidan, obs. form of CAPITAN.

†'**capidoce, 'capydois.** *Sc. Obs.* [perhaps the same as CAPADOS.]

1548 *Aberd. Regist.* V. 20 (Jam.) Vij capidocis of velvet. *Mod.Sc.* Capie-dossie, a hairy cap.

capie-hole: see CAPPY-HOLE.

capil, -pill, -pyl, var. of CAPLE, *Obs.*, a horse.

capillaceous (kæpɪ'leɪʃəs). [f. L. *capillāce-us* hairy, hair-like, f. *capill-us* hair: see -ACEOUS.] Of the nature of, or resembling hair; hair-like, thread-like. Cf. CAPILLARY 5. Hence **capi'llaceously** *adv.*; **capi'llaceo-'multifid** *a.*, divided into many hair-like filaments.

1731–7 MILLER *Gard. Dict.* s.v. *Crocus*, Spring Crocus, with a capillaceous Leaf. **1858** GRAY *Bot. Text-bk.* 401 *Capillaceous*, so slender that it may be compared with the hairs of animals. **1877** F. E. HULME *Wild Fl.* Introd. 10 Water-Buttercup, —Submerged leaves capillaceo-multifid.

‖**capillaire** (kapilɛr). [F. *capillaire* maidenhair fern, ad. L. *capillāris* of hair, *capillaris herba* the maidenhair.] A syrup or infusion of maidenhair fern (*Adiantum capillus Veneris*). **b.** A syrup flavoured with orange-flower water. Also ***syrup of capillaire.***

1754 *Connoisseur* No. 38 Whatever orgeat or capillaire can inspire. **1791** BOSWELL *Johnson* (1831) I. 482 He used to pour capillaire into his port wine. **1794** MARTYN *Rousseau's Bot.* xxxii. 491 True Maiden-hair, which is used, or supposed to be so, in the syrup of capillaire. **1851** T. MOORE *Brit. Ferns* (1864) 17 Capillaire..is prepared by pouring boiling syrup over the fronds, and flavouring the infusion with orange flowers.

†**ca'pillament.** *Obs.* [ad. L. *capillāment-um* the hair collectively, f. *capillus* hair. Cf. F. *capillament.*] An organic structure, presenting a slender and hair-like appearance; a hair-like fibre, filament; one of the ultimate ramifications of the root of a plant, or of a nerve in animals.

1681 tr. *Willis' Rem. Med. Wks.* Gloss., *Capillaments*, small hairy threds of the Nerves. **1727** BRADLEY *Fam. Dict.* I. s.v. *Adder's Tongue*, The Root is small, and divided into a few Capillaments. **1748** HARTLEY *Observ. Man* I. i. I. ¶5. 17 The Nerves are rather solid Capillaments than small Tubuli. **1785** REID *Int. Powers* 83 Capillaments of the optic nerve.

†**b.** *Bot.* A filament; a stamen. *Obs.*

c **1720** QUINCY (J.), Those small threads or hairs which grow up in the middle of a flower, and adorned with little herbs at the top, are called capillaments. **1727** A. HAMILTON *New Acc. E. Ind.* II. xxxix. 81 Fruit..with a tough Skin, beset with Capillaments. **1751** CHAMBERS *Cycl.*, *Capillaments, more usually called stamina.*

†**ca'pillar**, *a. Obs.* Also 7 capillare. [ad. L. *capillār-is* of or pertaining to hair, f. *capillus* hair: cf. F. *capillaire*, 14th c. in Littré.] Of or pertaining to hairs, hair-like.

1. = CAPILLARY 5.

1601 HOLLAND *Pliny* II. 127 No root at all these Capillar hearbes haue. *Ibid.* 232 Polytricha & Callitrica (both capillare herbs).

2. = CAPILLARY 3.

1612 WOODALL *Surg. Mate* Wks. (1653) 22 The cutis.. hath many capillar veines in it. **1666** G. HARVEY *Morb. Angl.* x. 96 The chyle..sticks in the Capillar veins.

3. = CAPILLARY 2.

1638 A. READ *Chirurg.* xxii. 162 If the chink [in fractured skull] be only capillar, and hard to be seene..the Chirurgeon may be excused. **1693** EVELYN *De la Quint. Compl. Gard.* I. 7 All the Capillar Roots must be taken away.

capillarimeter (kə,pɪlə'rɪmɪtə(r)). [f. L. *capillāri-s* + -METER.] An instrument for determining the strength of wine or the quality of oil on the principle of capillary attraction.

1874 in KNIGHT *Dict. Mech.* **1881** in *Syd. Soc. Lex.*

capillariness, -arious, etc.: see after CAPILLARY.

capillarity (kæpɪ'lærɪtɪ). [ad. F. *capillarité*, f. L. *capillār-is* CAPILLARY + -ITY.] Capillary quality; *esp.* that of exerting capillary attraction or repulsion. Also, capillary attraction.

1830 HERSCHEL *Stud. Nat. Phil.* 234 Capillary attraction, or capillarity as it is sometimes called. **1850** DAUBENY *Atom. The.* (ed. 2) 315 The affinity of capillarity..which acts solely between the surfaces of the attracting body and of that which combines with it. **1882** GEIKIE *Text-bk. Geol.* III. I. iv. §2. 299 The power possessed by water of penetrating rocks, in virtue of the porosity and capillarity.

capillary ('kæpɪlərɪ, kə'pɪlərɪ), *a.* and *sb.* [f. L. *capillāris*: see CAPILLAR and -ARY².]

A. *adj.* **1.** Of, pertaining to, consisting of, or concerned with hair.

1656 BLOUNT *Glossogr.*, *Capillary*, of or like hair. **1853** KANE *Grinnell Exp.* xxxvi. (1856) 326 Another, remarkable for a dirty person, of well used-up capillary surface. **1863** *Possibilities of Creat.* 182 [A whisker] shooting its capillary herbage in a curving direction across the cheek. **1885** *Truth* 11 June 932/1 It is as good for the dentists as for the capillary artists.

2. Hair-like; resembling a hair in tenuity.

1664 POWER *Exp. Philos.* I. 37 All diaper'd or branched over with pure white capillary little veins. **1704** SWIFT *Mech. Operat. Spirit* Misc. (1711) 294 Certain capillary Nerves. **1742** H. BAKER *Microsc.* II. v. 86 This Dunghill-Water abounds..with a sort of capillary Eels, that are extreamly active. **1811** PINKERTON *Petral.* I. 261 Capillary virgin silver. **1872** OLIVER *Elem. Bot.* II. 182 Lesser Helosciad, submerged leaves, with capillary segments.

3. Having a very minute or hair-like internal diameter; as a ***capillary tube*** or ***vessel.***

1664 POWER *Exp. Philos.* II. 142 Take a small Capillary Glass-pipe, or Tube, open at both ends. **1669** W. SIMPSON *Hydrol. Chym.* 297 Rain-water..meeting with capillary veins (as I may call them) or small pores [in the rocks]. **1742** H. BAKER *Microsc.* II. x. 132 The Blood..in the minute Capillary Veins and Arteries. **1819** PLAYFAIR *Nat. Phil.* I. 191 The reason why the water between the two narrow plates of glass rises only to half the height it does in a capillary tube. **1871** B. STEWART *Heat* §16 A tube of glass.. which has a capillary bore.

4. a. Of, pertaining to, or taking place in, capillary vessels or capillaries. For ***capillary attraction, repulsion***, see those words.

1809 (*title*) An Examination of M. La Place's Theory of Capillary Action. **1831** BREWSTER *Optics* iv. 30 A drop of the fluid..will be retained by the force of capillary attraction. **1836** TODD *Cycl. Anat.* I. 77/2 The capillary system.. becomes infinitely less extended.

b. (See quot. 1962.)

1895 F. H. KING *Soil* v. 176 The slower rise of capillary water in a dry soil. **1929** WEAVER & CLEMENTS *Plant Ecol.* ix. 182 The water-retaining capacity..includes the hygroscopic water as well as the much larger quantity that the soil holds besides, commonly called capillary water. **1932** FULLER & CONARD tr. *Braun-Blanquet's Plant Sociol.* vii. 212 The capillary water of the soil forms a thin, coherent water film around each solid particle. **1962** HANSON *Dict. Ecol.* 66 *Capillary water*, the portion of soil water which is held by cohesion as a continuous film around particles and in spaces; most of it is available to plants.

†**5.** See quots. *Obs.* (Cf. B. 3.)

c **1720** QUINCY (J.), Capillary, or capillaceous plants, are such as have no main stalk or stem, but grow to the ground, as hairs on the head; and which bear their seeds in little tufts or protuberances on the backside of their leaves. **1753** CHAMBERS *Cycl. Supp.* s.v., Capillary plants amount to much the same with what are denominated acaulose plants.

B. *sb.*

†**1.** Anything resembling a hair or collection of hairs. *Obs.*

1697 EVELYN *Numism.* vi. 214 As it were Capillaries, hairy Lines and tender Rays.

2. A capillary vessel. Cf. A. 3. *esp.* One of a number of extremely minute blood-vessels, in which the arterial circulation ends, and the venous begins.

1667 *Phil. Trans.* II. 511 The capillary's of the Arteries, and Veins. **1744** BERKELEY *Siris* §56 Mercury..may justly be suspected of hurting the fine capillaries. **1794** G. ADAMS *Nat. & Exp. Phil.* II. xxi. 420 Secreted by the fine capillaries ..in the bodies of plants and animals. **1873** MIVART *Elem. Anat.* x. 406 Minute tubes, capillaries, which convey the blood to the tissues.

†**3.** *Bot.* **a.** A name given apparently at first to the Maidenhair Fern, *Adiantum capillus Veneris* (in ancient Lat. *Capillus Veneris* and *herba capillaris*), and thence to other ferns or allied plants.

[**1578** LYTE *Dodoens* III. lxviii. 409 Apuleius calleth it Capillus Veneris, Capillaris, and Crinita.] **1646** SIR T. BROWNE *Pseud. Ep.* 351 Some kinde of the capillaries, which are very small plants and only grow upon wals and stony places. **1692** RAY *Disc.* II. iv. (1732) 191 The leaves of Ferns and other Capillaries. **1751** CHAMBERS *Cycl.* s.v., The ancients thought that the capillaries were all without seed.

†**b.** Any stemless or acaulous plant. *Obs.*

1664 EVELYN *Kal. Hort.* (1729) 217 All Fibrous Plants.. Also the Capillaries; Matricaria, Violets, Primroses, etc. may now be transplanted. **1675** —— *Terra* (1729) 45 Violets, Auricula, Primroses, and other Capillaries planted in Beds, or Bordures.

Hence †**ca'pillariness** = CAPILLARITY; †**capi'llarious** *a.* = CAPILLARY; also **capi'llarian** *a. nonce-wd.*

1775 ASH, *Capillariness*, the state of being capillary. [Also in mod. Dicts.] **1750** G. HUGHES *Barbados* 252 Its..

capillarious, fringy branches are divided into .. smaller ones. **1825** LAMB in *Life & Lett.* xv. (Wks. 1865) 443, I call all good Christians the Church, Capillarians and all.

capillate (ˈkæpɪleɪt), *a.* [ad. L. *capillāt-us* hairy, f. *capill-us* hair: see -ATE².] Furnished with hair.
1881 in *Syd. Soc. Lex.*

† **capiˈllation.** *Obs. rare.* [ad. L. *capillātiōn-em*, f. *capillātus* hairy, f. *capillus* hair.] The state or condition of being hairy or hair-like; hence, *concr.* **a.** a hair-like blood-vessel, a capillary; **b.** a capillary fracture of the skull.
1646 SIR T. BROWNE *Pseud. Ep.* 110 Nor is the humour contained in smaller veines, or obscure capillations, but in a vesicle or little bladder. **1656** BLOUNT *Glossogr.*, *Capillation*, hairiness, a making a thing hairy, or a causing hair to grow. **1704** J. HARRIS *Lex. Techn.*, *Capillation* .. is a Fracture in the Skull, so small that it can scarce be found, which yet often proves mortal. **1751** in CHAMBERS.

† **caˈpillature.** *Obs. rare.* [ad. L. *capillātūra* in same sense.] (See quot.)
1656 BLOUNT *Glossogr.*, *Capillature*, a frizling of the hair, the bush of hair on the head. **1721–1800** in BAILEY; and in mod. Dicts.

capilliform (kəˈpɪlɪfɔːm). [f. L. *capill-us* + -FORM.] Having the form of a hair; hair-shaped.
1835 LINDLEY *Introd. Bot.* (1848) II. 104 Long capilliform pedicels.

‖ **capillitium** (kæpɪˈlɪʃɪəm). *Bot.* [a. L. *capillitium* the hair collectively, f. *capillus.*] Entangled filamentary matter in fungals, bearing sporidia. (*Treas. Bot.* 1866.)
1871 COOKE *Fungi* (1874) 34 The spinulose projections from the capillitium .. are the remains of pedicels. **1875** BENNETT & DYER tr. *Sachs' Bot.* 255 The mass of slender filaments remains as a delicate Capillitium.

capiˈllose, *a.* and *sb.* [ad. L. *capillōs-us* full of hair, f. *capillus.*] **A.** *adj.* Full of hair, hairy.
In mod. Dicts.
B. *sb. Min.* A synonym (in Chapman 1843) for Millerite or sulphide of nickel, also called *capillary pyrites.* (Dana *Min.* 57.)

† **ˈcapilmute, ˈcabalmute.** *Sc. Law. Obs.* [app. f. *capil*, CAPLE, CABLE horse + *mute*, MOOT, pleading, plea. The synonym *cattelmute* is f. CATTLE.] The form of legal action by which the owner of strayed or stolen cattle proved his ownership, and obtained restoration.
Quoniam Attachiamenta x. Note (Jam.) Forma controversiæ vulgo appellatur *capilmute*, *cabalmute*, vel *cattelmute*; nam *mote* vel *mute* significat placitum, querelam, etc.

capiloˈtade. Also 7–8 capirotade, -adoe. [a. F. *capilotade*, formerly *capirotade*, in Rabelais *cabirotade*, ad. Sp. *capirotata* (cf. It. *capperottato*), according to Littré f. *capirote* hood, as if 'a dish with a hood', but Scheler and others doubt this.] A kind of dish (see quot.); *fig.* a cooked-up story, hash, medley.
1611 COTGR., *Capirotade*, Capirotadoe, or stued meat, compounded of Veale, Capon, Chicken, or Partridge, minced, spiced, and layed upon several beds of Cheese. **1696** PHILLIPS, *Capilotade*, a stew'd meat, compounded of the heads, legs, carcasses of Capons, Partridges, etc. **1705** VANBRUGH *Confed.* III. ii, What a capilotade of a story's here! **1731–1800** BAILEY, *Capirotade* .. Minc'd Meat. **1889** *Mrs. Marshall's Cookery Bk.* 111 Capilotade of sweet-bread. **1892** T. F. GARRETT *Encycl. Pract. Cookery* I. 284/1 Capilotade .. is literally the French term for a hash or ragoût, consisting usually of giblets and pieces of cold meat or poultry. **1950** *Mrs. Beeton's Househ. Managem.* xxv. 594 Giblets, capilotade of.

caping, *vbl. sb.*, see CAPE *v.*¹, ², and COPING.

capisten, obs. form of CAPSTAN.

† **caˈpistrate,** *v. Obs. rare.* [ad. L. *capistrāt-* ppl. stem of *capistrāre* to halter, f. *capistrum* halter.] *trans.* 'To halter, muzzle, or tye' (Cockeram 1623).
Also **1656** in BLOUNT *Glossogr.* **1721–1800** in BAILEY.

capital (ˈkæpɪtəl), *sb.*¹ Forms: 3 **capitale,** 5 **capital,** 6–7 **capitell,** -el, (7 capitull, -ol), 7– **capital.** [Answers to L. *capitell-um* in same sense (dim. of *caput* head, or rather of its dim. *capitulum*), and its representatives, It. *capitello*, OF. *capitel*, *chapitel*, now *chapiteau*; but from the beginning tending to confusion with the adj. CAPITAL, to which it is now assimilated. Italian influence favoured *capitel(l)* in the 17th c.]
1. The head or top of a column or pillar.
c **1290** *Land Cokaygne* 69 in *E.E.P.* (1862) 158 Þe pilers .. Wiþ harlas, and capitale Of grene jaspe and rede corale. **1413** LYDG. *Pylgr. Sowle* IV. xxxvi. (1483) 83 The legges ben as it were pylers .. the knees ben the capitals and the feete the bases. **1563** SHUTE *Archit.* B j b, In the Capitel, was set Voluta .. for an ornature and garnishment of the Capitell. **1604** DRAYTON *Owle* 629 From the Base, up to the Capitell. **1660** BLOOME *Archit.* E a, Corinthian Capitall. **1670** LASSELS *Voy. Italy* II. 157 Four great Pillars .. adorned with Capitels .. of brasse guilt. **1747** *Scheme Equip. Men of War* 60 On the Capitol, Victory, Trade, Peace and Plenty might be expressed. **1851** RUSKIN *Stones Ven.* (1874) I. vii. 72 A capital is only the cornice of a column.
2. The head or cap of a chimney, crucible, etc.
1715 DESAGULIERS *Fires Impr.* 79 Such a Capital will wholly hinder the Wind from going into the Chimney. **1753** CHAMBERS *Cycl. Supp.* s.v., Capital of a lanthorn .. Capital of a mill. **1800** HENRY *Epit. Chem.* (1808) 148 An alembic, covered with its capital.
¶ **3.** A chapter of a book. (for CAPITLE.)
1819 SCOTT *Ivanhoe* xxxvii, Holy St. Bernard in the rule of our .. profession, hath said, in the fifty-ninth capital, etc.

capital, *sb.*²: see B. under the adj.

capital (ˈkæpɪtəl), *a.* and *sb.*² Forms: 3–4 **capitale,** 5–7 **capitall(e,** 5–6 **capytal(l,** 7 **capitoll,** 4– **capital.** [a. F. *capital* (12th c.), ad. L. *capitāl-is*, in legal and ecclesiastical use. The actual F. descendant of the L. word is *cheptel* (pronounced *chetel*).]
A. *adj.* **I.** Relating to the head.
† **1.** Of or pertaining to the head or top. *Obs.*
a **1225** *Ancr. R.* 258 Wiðuten eddren capitalen þet bledden on his hefde. **1486** *Bk. St. Albans, Her.* F j, Sparris .. put .. by the maner of an hede, and ij syche sparris ionyt togedyr make a capitall sygne. **1616** CHAPMAN *Homer's Batrachom.* 9 Their parts capitall They hid. **1667** MILTON *P.L.* XII. 383 His [the Serpent's] capital bruise. **1688** R. HOLME *Armoury* III. xiii. 34 A Pillar Composed in the Capital part.
2. a. Affecting, or involving loss of, the head or life.
1483 CAXTON *Gold. Leg.* 184/3 To haue capytal sentence & be beheded. **1581** LAMBARDE *Eiren.* I. xii. (1588) 67 Capitall (or deadly) punishment is done sundry wayes. **1770** LANGHORNE *Plutarch* (1879) I. 181/2 Cimon .. narrowly escaped a capital sentence. **1868** *Spectator* 19 Dec. 1487 We never remember a capital verdict upon such insufficient evidence.
b. Punishable by death. For the distinction (from 1957 to 1965) of ***capital murder***: see quot. 1957.
1526 FRITH *Purgat.* 201 Whosoever hath committed a capital crime. **1688** STRADLING *Serm.* (1692) 168 The Egyptians made it Capital to affirm that their God Apis was dead. *a* **1745** SWIFT *Wks.* (1841) II. 154 Guilty of a capital crime. **1827** HALLAM *Const. Hist.* (1876) III. xvii. 330 It was capital to preach even in houses. **1957** *Act 5 & 6 Eliz. II* c. 11 §5 The following murders shall be capital murders .. (*a*) any murder done in the course or furtherance of theft; (*b*) any murder done by shooting [etc.]. *Ibid.*, Where it is alleged that a person accused of murder is guilty of capital murder, the offence shall be charged as capital murder in the indictment.
† **c.** Of persons: Dealing with capital crimes; also, capitally condemned. *Obs.*
1583 STUBBES *Anat. Abus.* II. 106 They, as Capytall Iudges, geue definytiue sentence of lyfe and death. **1631** GOUGE *God's Arrows* III. §60. 295 Putting capitall malefactors to death. **1644** PRYNNE *Check to Britan.* 4 An impenitent, obdurate, Capitall Delinquent.
† **d.** Fatal. *Obs.*
a **1626** BACON (J.) War, which is capital to thousands. **1701** COLLIER *M. Antoninus* 11 In the Reign of Adrian an excellency of almost any kind was sometimes Capital to the Owner.
e. *Roman Law.* Involving loss of civil rights.
1838 ARNOLD *Hist. Rome* (1846) I. xiv. 289 The punishment of a libeller involved in it a *diminutio capitis*, and was thus in the Roman sense of the term capital.
† **3.** Said of an enemy or enmity: Deadly, mortal. *Obs.*
1375 BARBOUR *Bruce* III. 2 The lord off lorne .. That wes capitale ennymy To the king. **1502** ARNOLDE *Chron.* (1811) 283 A capital enmyte lyke to haue endured for euer. **1670** COTTON *Espernon* I. III. 109 The Bishop was his capital Enemy. **1762** HUME *Hist. Eng.* (1806) IV. liv. 162 The capital enemy of their country.
4. *fig.* Of defects, errors, and the like: Fatal, vitally injurious, most serious, radical. (Passing into sense 6 d.)
1538 STARKEY *England* 128 You have notyd such [faults] as be most capytal. **1581** MULCASTER *Positions* xxxiii. (1887) 121 Immoderate exercise .. a very capitall enemie to health. **1612** T. TAYLOR *Comm. Titus* ii. 10 (1619) 429 It is more capitall to smite the master then a stranger. **1734** tr. *Rollin's Anc. Hist.* (1827) II. II. 34 Hannibal's stay at Capua was a capital blemish in his conduct. **1855** PRESCOTT *Philip II*, II. v. (1857) 249 In the outset, he seems to have fallen into a capital error.
II. Standing at the head. *lit.* and *fig.*
5. a. Of words and letters: †Standing at the head of a page, or at the beginning of a line or paragraph, initial (*obs.*). ***capital letters***: letters of the form and relative size used in this position.
c **1391** CHAUCER *Astrol.* 8 This same bordure is devyded .. with 23 lettres capitals. **1432–50** tr. *Higden* (Rolls Ser.) IV. 299 The capitalle letters .. expresse this sentence. **1490** CAXTON *Eneydos* xxii. 84 The grete capitalle lettres of the bygynnynge .. of the psalmes and chapytres .. ben alle mayde fayre. **1584** POWEL *Lloyd's Cambria* 9 It is easy for the C. Capitall to creepe in. **1662** PEPYS *Diary* 11 June, To have the capitall words wrote with red ink. **1676** MOXON *Print. Lett.* 10 Use a Capital Letter .. in all Proper Names. **1811** J. BANNATINE in *Monthly Mag.* XXXIV. 429 One very modern improvement in writing and printing .. dropping the capital letters, except in the beginning of sentences, etc.
b. Introducing (a repetition of) the initial letter of a word, for emphasis, etc.
1863 DICKENS in *All Yr. Round* Christmas 3/2 'Capital D her!' bursts out Caroline. **1892** I. ZANGWILL *Childr. Ghetto* (1893) II. xv. 381 'Oh, Leon, Leon, you'll turn Catholic soon!' said Strelitski reprovingly. 'Not with a capital C,' said Raphael, laughing. **1902** H. JAMES *Wings of Dove* iv. 66 Kate had mentioned .. that her aunt was Passionate .. uttering it as with a capital P. *a* **1930** D. H. LAWRENCE *Phoenix* (1936) IV. 534 Life with a capital L is only man alive. **1956** A. J. TOYNBEE *Historian's Appr. Relig.* xi. 147 He assumed that this was the mature and perfect form of Civilized Society: Civilization with a capital 'C'. **1966** *Sunday Times* 13 Nov. 10/4 A subtle attack upon the stability of our very own Monarchy, with a capital M.
6. Chief; head-: **a.** of persons. *arch.* or *Obs.*
c **1425** WYNTOUN *Cron.* VI. xix. 37 Of þis Lawch are thre capytale. **1461–82** *Liber Niger Edw. IV* in *Househ. Ord.* 73 This sergeaunt, capitall Buttler. **1530** *Test. Ebor.* (Surtees) V. 293 Capital Sanctes under God of the aforsaid kirkes. **1614** T. ADAMS *Divel's Banq.* 213 Diseases, which be Deaths capitall Chirurgions. **1683** *Lond. Gaz.* No. 1866/4 The Mayor, Aldermen, Bayliff, Capital Burgesses, and Commonalty of .. Waymouth. **1753** CHAMBERS *Cycl. Supp.*, *Capital lord* .. the lord of the fee. **1810** in *Risdon's Surv. Devon* 426 A Mayor, assisted by 18 capital burgesses.
b. of mansions, estates, towns, and cities. ***capital manor***: one held *in capite*, or directly from the King. ***capital messuage***: that occupied by the owner of a property containing several messuages. ***capital town*** or ***city*** = CAPITAL *sb.* (see B. 2 below).
1539 *Act 31 Hen. VIII*, v, The saide manour of Hampton courte shall .. be the chiefe and capitall place and parte of the saide honour of Hampton courte. **1601** HOLLAND *Pliny* I. 125 From thence .. to the capitoll towne of the Arachosians, 515 miles. **1642** PERKINS *Prof. Bk.* v. §406. 175 The heire is not compellable to assigne unto his mother .. the capitall messuage which was his Fathers. **1667** MILTON *P.L.* II. 924 Battering Engines bent to rase Som Capital City. *Ibid.* XI. 343 This had been Perhaps thy Capital Seate, from whence had spred All generations. **1768** BLACKSTONE *Comm.* II. 214 The eldest son had the capital fee or principal feud of his father's possessions. **1774** T. WARTON *Hist. Eng. Poetry* (1840) I. 18 Chained in the cloister, or church, of some capital monastery. **1809** BAWDEN tr. *Domesday Bk.* 589 The Abbot of Westminster claims all this because the capital manor is given to St. Peter.
c. of ships: 'Of the line'; first-rate.
1652 in *Mariner's Mirror* (1926) XII. 399 They are between the I. of Wight and Portland with 45 sail, 12 of which are capital ships. **1688** *Lond. Gaz.* No. 2397/4 The Capital Ships are off of Torbay about 4 Leagues from the Shore. **1766** SMOLLETT *Hist. Eng.* (1804) V. 248 Of these capital ships (those of the line), 17 were stationed in the East Indies. **1793** LD. HOWE in Barrow *Life* (1838) 214 Under a repeated fire from three or four of their capital ships. **1805** D. MACPHERSON *Ann. Commerce* III. 250 They .. took from our English East-India company their most important fort .. ; they also took one of that company's capital ships. **1909** *Hansard Commons* I. 1110/2 Mr. Robert Harcourt asked the First Lord of the Admiralty if he was prepared to give an official definition of the term capital ship? Mr. M'Kenna: The Board of Admiralty have never sanctioned the official use of the term, and they do not deem it expedient to do so. **1919** *Daily Tel.* 11 Aug. 9/6 The battle-fleet force became a vast assemblage of capital vessels, cruisers, light cruisers, destroyers and submarines. **1928** *Britain's Industr. Future* v. xxx. 426 A capital-ship base at Singapore.
d. of other things.
a **1535** MORE *De quat. Noviss.* Wks. 85/2, Ii. capitall vyces, that is to wit enuye and couityce. **1597** J. PAYNE *Royal Exch.* 44 Love ys the capitall affection in men and women. **1671** MILTON *Samson* 394 To win from me My capital secret. **1749** CHESTERF. *Lett.* II. clxxxv. 189 The Last Supper, by Paul Veronese .. is reckoned his capital performance. **1872** R. W. DALE *Commandm.* 7 The old traditions .. made Obedience the capital virtue of childhood.
e. *less strictly.* Main, leading, weighty, important, first-class.
1724 A. COLLINS *Gr. Chr. Relig.* 20 Several capital places in the sacred Writers. **1767** GOOCH *Treat. Wounds* 182 These preparatory rules, generally necessary before any capital operation. **1788** PRIESTLEY *Lect. Hist.* I. i. 5 All history has a capital advantage over every work of fiction. **1793** W. ROBERTS *Looker-on* No. 47 He .. espoused the daughter of a capital grocer. **1818** HAZLITT *Eng. Poets* VI. (1870) 146 So capital and undeniable a proof of the author's talents.
7. In mod. use: Excellent, 'first-rate'. Often as an exclamation of approval.
1762 LD. RADNOR in *Priv. Lett. 1st Ld. Malmesbury* I. 85 The Hobbema is also a very capital picture. **1791** 'G. GAMBADO' *Ann. Horsem.* vi. (1809) 91 He clears every thing with his fore legs in a capital style. **1835** T. HOOK *G. Gurney* I. ii, Nobody said capital, or even good, or even tolerable. **1870** E. PEACOCK *Ralf Skirl.* III. 26 He was a capital companion. **1875** JOWETT *Plato* (ed. 2) I. 100 Capital, Socrates; by the gods, that is truly good.
8. Of or pertaining to the original funds of a trader, company, or corporation; principal; *hence*, serving as a basis for financial and other operations.
1709 *Lond. Gaz.* No. 4534/1 An Act for Enlarging the Capital Stock of the Bank of England. **1776** ADAM SMITH *W.N.* I. I. ix. 98 The capital stock of Great Britain was not diminished even by the enormous expense of the late war. **1825** SOUTHEY in *Q. Rev.* XXXII. 41 Compelled .. to encroach largely upon its capital fund. **1884** LD. SELBORNE in *Law Rep.* 25 Chanc. Div. 689 She may commute into a capital sum .. the benefit given to her .. by way of annuity.
III. † **9.** ***capital lye***: the first or strongest alkaline solution employed in the process of soap-making. *Obs.* [Cf. F. *capitel* in same sense, med.L. *capitellum* 'aqua saponis *vel* lixivium', It. *capitello* 'lie to wash and skoure with' (Florio). So that strictly this is a distinct word.]
1704 WORLIDGE *Dict. Rust. et Urb.* s.v. *Soap*, The Magistral or Capital Lye .. is so strong, that an Egg will swim therein. **1731** BAILEY, *Capital Lees*, are the strong Lees, made by Soap-boilers from Pot-ashes.
B. *sb.* [Several elliptical uses of the adjective.]

1. A capital letter. Hence *to speak in capitals*: i.e. with emphasis. (Cf. A. 5.)

1649 G. DANIEL *Trinarch., Rich. II*, cxvii, Noe Character so small, But through that Glass appeares a Capitall. **1676** MOXON *Print. Lett.* 5 A, B, C, etc. are Capitals. **1733** SWIFT *On Poetry* 99 When in Capitals exprest, The dullest reader smokes the jest. **1871** L. W. LOCKHART *Fair to See* I. 4 (Hoppe) 'AND I AM!' cried Fuskisson, a little white ensign, speaking in large capitals, with a voice like a Jew's harp. **1873** BURTON *Hist. Scot.* VI. lxviii. 147 The Service-book was amply decorated with pictorial capitals.

2. A capital town or city; the head town of a country, province or state.

1667 MILTON *P.L.* I. 756 Pandæmonium, the high Capital Of Satan and his Peers. **1750** JOHNSON *Rambl.* No. 49 ¶4 He that, like Cæsar, would rather be the first man of a village, than the second in the capital of the world. **1853** ROBERTSON *Serm.* Ser. III. ix. 115 §2 A constant round from the capital to the watering place, and from the watering place to the capital.

3. A capital stock or fund. **a.** *Commerce.* The stock of a company, corporation, or individual with which they enter into business and on which profits or dividends are calculated; in a joint-stock company, it consists of the total sum of the contributions of the shareholders. Also, the general body of capitalists or employers of labour, esp. with regard to its political interests and claims (cf. LABOUR *sb.* 2 b). **b.** *Pol. Econ.* The accumulated wealth of an individual, company, or community, used as a fund for carrying on fresh production; wealth in any form used to help in producing more wealth.

[**1611** COTGR., *Capital*, wealth, worth; a stocke, a man's principall, or chiefe, substance.] **1630-9** WOTTON *Lett. & Treat.* 459 (K.O.) **1647** CLARENDON *Hist. Reb.* VII. (1847) 441/1 Such anticipations upon all kinds of receipts for monies borrowed and already spent, that they had no capital for future security. **1727-51** CHAMBERS *Cycl.* s.v., Power given by Parliament to the South-Sea Company to increase their capital. **1790** BURKE *Fr. Rev.* 51 You began ill..You set up your trade without a capital. **1793** BENTHAM *Emancip. Col.* Wks. 1843 IV. 411 In proportion to the quantity of capital a country has at its disposal, will..be the quantity of its trade. **1796** MORSE *Amer. Geog.* I. 442 The gentlemen of fortune turn their capitals into this channel. **1825** McCULLOCH *Pol. Econ.* II. ii. 73 The accumulation..of the produce of previous labour, or, as it is more commonly termed, of capital or stock. *Ibid.* 114 Credit..enables those who have capitals..to lend them to those who are desirous to obtain them. **1863** FENN *Eng. & For. Funds* 26 Bank Stock..is the capital of the Corporation of the Bank of England. **1869** *Eng. Mechanic* 4 June 237/3 We might feel inclined to despair over the chances of Giant Capital and Dwarf Labour ever working harmoniously. **1874** HELPS *Soc. Press.* iii. 54 The immense difficulty that it is for any human being without capital to ensure himself a living. **1929** D. H. LAWRENCE in *Star Rev.* Nov. 626 The Soviet hates the real physical body far more deeply even than it hates Capital. **1940** W. TEMPLE *Thoughts in War-time* iv. 26 When we reach the stage of justice in the relations between capital and labour.

c. *fixed capital*: that which remains in the owner's possession, as working cattle, tools, machinery, etc. *circulating, floating capital*: that which is constantly changing hands or passing from one form into another, as goods, money, etc.

1776 ADAM SMITH *W.N.* (1869) I. II. i. 276 His capital is continually going from him in one shape, and returning to him in another. Such capitals..may..be called circulating capitals. **1825** McCULLOCH *Pol. Econ.* II. ii. 95 What could he do without the assistance of fixed capital or tools?

d. *fig.*; also phrase, *to make capital out of*: to turn to account.

1847 HELPS *Friends in C.* (1851) I. 28 To reject the accumulated mental capital of ages. **1855** MACAULAY *Hist. Eng.* xxv. (1869) IV. 314 He tried to make..political capital out of the desolation of his house. **1865** MRS. RIDDELL *G. Geith* II. ii. 26 The quietest, most conciliating manners that ever a man made capital out of. **1885** STEVENSON *Dr. Jekyll* i. 8 If you choose to make capital out of this accident.

4. *Fortif.* (See quot.)

1706 PHILLIPS, *Capital*, the line..drawn either from the angle of the Polygon to the point of the Bastion, or from the point of the Bastion to the middle of the Gorge. **1853** STOCQUELER *Mil. Encycl.*, *Capital*..is an imaginary line bisecting the salient angle of a work.

†**5.** (See quot.) *Obs.*

1799 G. SMITH *Laborat.* I. 188 One part of capital or cream of clay.

6. (attrib. use of 3) *capital account, stock*; *capital bonus*, a pro rata bonus distributed in shares; *capital expenditure* (see quot. 1959); *capital gain* (orig. *U.S.*), a profit from the sale of investments or property; freq. used *attrib.* in *capital gains tax*; *capital goods*, commodities forming capital; economic goods (e.g. railways, ships, machinery, buildings) destined for use in production, opp. to *consumers' goods*; *capital levy*, the confiscation by the state of a proportion of privately-owned wealth or property; *capital transfer tax*, a tax levied on transfer of capital by gift, bequest, etc. (replacing estate duty in 1975 and replaced by inheritance tax in 1986).

1895 *Min. Proc. Inst. Civil Engin.* CXXII. 224 When the North-Eastern Railway Company..includes the cost of between three and four hundred locomotives, which had presumably been charged to revenue, in the capital stock without any increase in capital account. *Ibid.* 234 The engine-miles run (excluding those by 'capital' engines) were 58,202,648. **1898** S. S. DAWSON *Accountant's Compendium* 47/2 *Capital expenditure*..In its more restricted sense the term implies the expenditure of the capital receipts of a company or other body upon the construction of a particular work, *e.g.*, a railway. **1899** J. B. CLARK *Distrib. Wealth* ix. 116 The differences that science must recognize between 'capital' and 'capital-goods'. **1919** *Hansard Commons* CXVI. 235, I do not see how you can have a capital levy under war conditions. **1921** *Washington Post* 16 Aug. 4/2 The bill redefines capital gain and capital loss, declaring the former to mean 'taxable gain from the sale or exchange of capital assets'. **1928** *Daily Chron.* 9 Aug. 8/4 The directors..have distributed a number of capital bonuses among their fortunate Ordinary shareholders. **1931** *Times Trade & Engin. Suppl.* 24 Jan. 430/4 The production of 'capital goods' which are not 'consumed' immediately the money is spent upon them, but contribute a quota to the national wealth over many future years. **1951** L. H. SELTZER *(title)* The nature and tax treatment of capital gains and losses. **1959** JOWITT *Dict. Eng. Law* I. 310/1 *Capital expenditure*, expenditure from which benefits may be expected over a relatively long period, as opposed to revenue expenditure;..expenditure on capital or fixed assets. **1962** *Times* 10 Apr. 13/2 The Chancellor of the Exchequer..proposed an uncommonly large number of tax changes... Several are controversial: the pledge on ending Schedule A; the capital gains tax, [etc.]. **1970** *Money Which?* Mar. 4/1 Capital Gains Tax. You may have to pay this tax on most capital gains—for instance, the gain you make when you sell shares at a higher price than you bought them for. **1974** *Hansard Commons* 12 Nov. 276 The new capital transfer tax will replace the estate duty on deaths after the Bill has received Royal Assent. **1978** *Listener* 8 June 718 Now comes the new squirearchy: bowler-hatted money managers from the City, eased into landed power with the help of capital transfer tax and the..demise of the wealthy owner-farmer. **1986** *Daily Tel.* 24 May 14/5 The president of the Historic Houses Association..plays down too much euphoria over the Chancellor's proposed substitution of inheritance tax for capital transfer tax.

capital ('kæpɪtəl), *v.* [f. the sb.] *trans.* To furnish or adorn with a capital.

1851 RUSKIN *Stones Ven.* I. ix. §29 They shod and capitaled the mouldings till they looked like a group of shafts.

capitaled ('kæpɪtəld), *ppl. a.* [f. CAPITAL *sb.* + -ED².] **a.** *Arch.* Furnished with a capital. **b.** Supplied with capital. (Chiefly in *comb.*)

1803 *Ann. Rev.* I. 383/1 The..sluggish proceedings of an under-capitaled community. **1851** RUSKIN *Stones Ven.* I. i. §17 All Romanesque, massy-capitaled buildings. **1853** C. BRONTË *Villette* xx. (D.) The white column capitalled with gilding.

capitalhood ('kæpɪtəlhʊd). [f. CAPITAL *sb.*² + -HOOD.] The condition of being a capital city.

1865 *Examiner* 25 Nov. 743 Her [Florence's] half forgotten dreams of capital-hood are more than realized.

capitalism ('kæpɪtə,lɪz(ə)m). [f. CAPITAL *sb.*² + -ISM.] The condition of possessing capital; the position of a capitalist; a system which favours the existence of capitalists.

1854 THACKERAY *Newcomes* II. 75 The sense of capitalism sobered and dignified Paul de Florac. **1877** A. DOUAI *Better Times* (1884) 10 This institution of private capitalism is of a comparatively recent origin. **1884** *Pall Mall G.* 11 Sept. 6/1 A loophole for capitalism to creep in upon the primitive Christian communism.

capitalist ('kæpɪtəlɪst). [f. CAPITAL *sb.*² + -IST.] One who has accumulated capital; one who has capital available for employment in financial or industrial enterprises. Also *attrib.* and *Comb.*, as ***capitalist-imperialist***.

1792 A. YOUNG *Trav. France* 529 A gross evil of these direct imposts is, that of moneyed men, or capitalists, escaping all taxation. **1823** COLERIDGE *Table-t.* 27 Apr., The poor-rates are the consideration paid by..capitalists for having labour at demand. **1845** DISRAELI *Sybil* (1863) 95 The capitalist flourishes, he amasses immense wealth; we sink, lower and lower; lower than the beasts of burthen. **1845** J. S. MILL in *Edin. Rev.* LXXXI. 525 This is true of capitalist farmers..but not of labourer-farmers. **1867** J. B. KINNEAR *Quest. for Refd. Parlt.* 213 The capitalist class. **1937** 'G. ORWELL' *Road to Wigan Pier* xii. 247 The capitalist-imperialist governments..will not fight with any conviction against Fascism.

capitaˈlistic, *a.* [f. CAPITALIST + -IC.] Of or pertaining to capitalists.

1873 in *Doc. Hist. Amer. Industr. Soc.* (1910) IX. 371 The growth of capitalistic association and monetary institution. **1877** A. DOUAI *Better Times* (1884) 7 The offshoot of capitalistic production. **1884** *Christian Union (N.Y.)* 24 Apr. 390 The substitution of some form of co-operation in production and exchange for the capitalistic method. **1935** *Discovery* Mar. 81/1 These two systems 'communistic' or 'capitalistic'.

capitalistically (,kæpɪtə'lɪstɪkəlɪ), *adv.* [f. CAPITALISTIC: see -ICALLY.] In a capitalistic manner.

1889 W. WILSON *State* (1893) xvi. 666 Churches are spiritually convenient; joint-stock companies are capitalistically convenient. **1921** *Glasgow Herald* 24 June 9 When the concern was capitalistically owned. **1931** *Time & Tide* 3 Oct. 1130 The *rentier* has been unfeeling enough to practise what is capitalistically called virtue.

capitalization (,kæpɪtəlaɪ'zeɪʃən). [f. CAPITALIZE + -ATION.]

1. a. The action of converting into capital, or of representing an annual income or payment by its capital value.

1860 *Sat. Rev.* IX. 3/2 Her creditors..agreed to the capitalization of their overdue dividends. **1885** SIR H. COTTON in *Law Rep.* 30 Chanc. Div. 243 The profits..were to be capitalized, and she was only to have the income arising from that capitalization.

b. The sum or figure resulting from the action of converting into capital.

1906 *Daily Chron.* 13 Feb. 5/1 The companies have a capitalisation of 80,000,000 dols. **1970** *Daily Tel.* 22 Apr. 21/3 IBM—whose market capitalisation is larger than that of any other United States company—is the post-war growth stock *par excellence*.

2. Conversion into a capital city.

1865 *Pall Mall G.* 9 Oct. 10 Florence is being summarily subjected to the advantages of capitalization.

3. The action of printing in capitals.

1864 in WEBSTER, etc. **1906** R. L. RAMSAY in *Skelton's Magnyf.* p. xx, The orthography is that of the original; punctuation and capitalization are modern. **1908** M. W. SAMPSON *Milton's Lyr. & Dram. Poems* p. v, The text follows the first editions as closely as modern spelling, capitalization and punctuation permit. **1964** F. BOWERS *Bibliogr. & Text. Crit.* VI. iii. 177 The details of spelling, capitalization, punctuation, and word-division.

capitalize ('kæpɪtəlaɪz), *v.* [f. CAPITAL *sb.*² + -IZE.]

1. a. *trans.* To convert into capital.

1868 ROGERS *Pol. Econ.* xxiii. (ed. 3) 307 Notes bearing interest, to be subsequently capitalised into a funded debt. **1885** SIR E. KAY in *Law Times Rep.* LII. 369/2 The company were authorised..to capitalise the reserved fund. *fig.* **1878** *N. Amer. Rev.* CXXVII. 241 They should teach us to capitalize our philosophy.

b. To invest with capital. *U.S.*

1870 J. K. MEDBERY *Men & Myst. Wall St.* 11 The variations of its [*sc.* Wall St.'s] share market affect the whole volume of capitalized indebtedness the country through. **1897** *Daily News* 13 Mar. 2/2 This Company is very moderately capitalised at £80,000 in Shares of £1 each. **1948** *Chicago Tribune* 18 Aug. III. 5/5 The Canadian unit..will be capitalized at 5,000 shares of $100 par value stock. **1970** *Sci. Amer.* Mar. 35/2 A conglomerate can..apply the debt capacity of safe, mature businesses to capitalize rapidly growing but unstable ventures.

c. To make capital out of, turn to account. Also *absol.* orig. *U.S.*

1869 in *Trans. Kansas Hist. Soc.* (1900) VI. 64 To capitalize this land in the hands of speculators. **1926** *Publishers' Weekly* 22 May 1701 The book-stores and the libraries can capitalize on that same interest. *Ibid.* 29 May 1795 The publishers..do not intend to capitalize the publicity. **1935** *Punch* 15 May 578/3, I can only 'capitalize'..something which already belongs to me... And therefore I condemn the advertisement..which asserts that the makers..have 'capitalised this mother-instinct'. **1953** *Encounter* Nov. 9/1 The *Tokyo Evening News*..capitalises on the time-difference between Japan, America, and Europe to be up-to-the-minute with the news. **1958** *Times* 18 Nov. 13/5 His material was indifferent..but..he was able to capitalize brilliantly on every disadvantage.

2. To convert (a periodical income or payment) into an equivalent capital sum; to compute or realize the present value of such a payment for a definite or indefinite length of time. Also *spec.* in *Accounting*, to reckon (a current outgoing) as though it were a capital asset on the basis of its expected earnings in the future, less any maintenance costs.

1856 *Times* 22 Jan., As to the project of capitalizing incomes, that is another affair. **1861** GEN. P. THOMPSON *Audi Alt.* III. cxlv. 131 The hundred millions..must be, as the term learnt in France I think is, *capitalized*. **1972** *Nature* 28 Jan. 183/1 It may be proper to capitalize the cost of research and development.., yet there should have been more anxious questions much sooner about the scale on which Rolls-Royce had been..turning paper losses into paper profits. **1982** *N.Y. Times* 17 Dec. D8/6 The companies will also be required to capitalize leases in the same manner as unregulated companies. **1985** *Metals Week* 30 Dec. 1 The company will decrease ore reserves..allowing for a 'significant writedown of certain assets and capitalized preproduction expenditures'.

3. To print in capitals. Also, to print an initial letter in capitals. Also in *vbl. sb.* = CAPITALLING *vbl. sb.*

1764 *Acc. Coll. New-Jersey* 25 All these compositions..are critically examined with respect to the..pointing, capitalizing, with the other minutiæ. **1809** W. CUNNINGHAM Jr. *Let.* 23 Sept. (1823) xlix. 165, I capitalized the prophetic parts of the letter..and italicized the Latin. **1850** WHIPPLE *Ess. & Rev.* II. 264 Capitalizing the names of abstract qualities. **1890** *Phonetic Jrnl.* 26 Some peculiarity in capitalising. **1944** [see AFRO-]. **1964** F. BOWERS *Bibliogr. & Text. Crit.* VI. iv. 186 The single Q capitalization is also capitalized in F.

Hence **'capitalized** *ppl. a.*, **capitalizer** ('kæpɪtə,laɪzə(r)) *sb.*, **'capitalizing** *vbl. sb.*

1863 GLADSTONE *Financ. Statem.* 33 The capitalized value of the income. **1880** *Atlantic Monthly* Dec. 849 The administrator of capital and labour is not a mere middleman; he is a capitalizer. **1882** W. B. WEEDEN *Soc. Law Labor* 28 Small farmers..are almost always capitalizers. **1880** *Atlantic Monthly* Dec. 848 Capitalizing; that is the converting of capital and labour into more capital.

capitalless ('kæpɪtəllɪs), *a.* [f. CAPITAL *sb.* + -LESS.] Without capital; having no capital.

1866 CRUMP *Banking* ii. 65 Dishonest speculation which thoroughly bad and capitalless houses have practised.

capitalling ('kæpɪtəlɪŋ), *vbl. sb.* [f. CAPITAL *sb.*[2] + -ING[1].] The furnishing of a word with a capital letter.

1683 MOXON *Mech. Exerc., Printing* 261 The Correcter.. examines the Proof, and considers the Pointing, Italicking, Capitalling, or any error. **1770** LUCKOMBE *Hist. Printing* 249 Some [authors] give themselves no concern about capitaling. **1904** *Athenæum* 13 Feb. 210/2 The first variation, apart from detail of pointing and capitalling, is in line 17.

capitally ('kæpɪtəlɪ), *adv.* [f. CAPITAL *a.* + -LY[2].] In a capital manner.

1. In a manner involving loss of life, as in *to punish* or *accuse capitally*.

1619 N. BRENT tr. *Sarpi's Hist. Counc. Trent* (1676) 410 Those that are infected with Heresie ought to be proceeded against capitally. **1695** BP. PATRICK *Comm. Gen.* xlii. 15 He was punished capitally. **1741** MIDDLETON *Cicero* I. v. 378 The people could not condemn, nor even try a man capitally. **1837** THIRLWALL *Greece* IV. xxxv. 396 He was capitally impeached.

2. Fatally, seriously.

1606 WARNER *Alb. Eng.* xv. c. 394 So capitally bad. **1741** RICHARDSON *Pamela* II. 77 None but the Presumptuous, the Conceited, and the Thoughtless, err capitally. **1835** I. TAYLOR *Spir. Despot.* ix. 376 Those who are capitally.. in fault.

3. Principally, mainly, eminently, in an important degree.

1786 T. JEFFERSON *Writ.* (1859) I. 586 The commerce.. so far as it depended on that article, which was very capitally too. **1836** FOSTER in *Life & Corr.* (1846) II. 304 Capitally fantastic, witty, and brilliant.

4. Excellently, admirably.

1750 WARBURTON *Julian* Wks. 1811 VIII. 90 The action too was capitally interesting. **1810** SCOTT *Lett.* in *Lockhart* (1842) 191 Miss Baillie's play went off capitally here. **1875** JOWETT *Plato* (ed. 2) I. 331 You understand me capitally, Socrates.

5. In capital letters: in large characters.

1755 YOUNG *Centaur* vi. Wks. IV. 259 In heaven's.. effort for our welfare, is capitally written the Dignity of Man.

'capitalness. [f. CAPITAL *a.* + -NESS.] The condition or fact of being capital.

1611 COTGR., *Capitalité*, capitalnesse; or a capitall fact.

‖**capitan** (kapɪ'tan, 'kæpɪtæn). Also 8 **capidan**, (7–8 **captain**). [Sp. *capitan* CAPTAIN.] Mostly *attrib.*, as in *Capitan* (or *Captain*) *Pacha*, the chief admiral of the Turkish fleet. Hence *capitan galley* = CAPITANA.

[**1688** *Lond. Gaz.* No. 2320/3 The Captain Bassa or Lord Admiral. **1707** *Ibid.* No. 4336/6 The Captain Pasha will go .. with the Gallies.. into the Archipelago.] **1755** SMOLLETT *Quix.* (1803) II. 150, I rowed in the capitan galley of the Three Lanthorns at Navarino. **1835** WILLIS *Pencillings* II. v. 96 He was formerly capitan pasha, or admiral-in-chief of the fleet. *a* **1849** J. C. MANGAN *Poems* (1859) 182 Many a Capitan, and bey.

capitan(e, obs. form of CAPTAIN.

‖**capitana** (kapɪ'tana). [It., Sp., and Pg. *capitana* in same sense, prop. adj., fem. of *capitan, -o*, qualifying *nave* 'ship' or other word.] The chief or admiral's ship.

1684 *Lond. Gaz.* No. 1988/1 The Capitana of the Gallies of Naples.. was in a great storm cast away. **1728** MORGAN *Algiers* II. v. 315 Algiers lost.. their Capitana or Admiral. **1843** PRESCOTT *Mexico* II. iv. (1864) 87 Orders were given.. to take the direction of the capitana or admiral's ship.

'capitanate. [ad. It. *capitanato.*] The office of a Capitano.

1818 J. C. HOBHOUSE *Hist. Illustr.* 523 Ye.. were.. injured first by what was called a Senate, then under the name of a Capitanate.

capitanery, -ry: see CAPTAINRY.

‖**capitano** (kapɪ'tano). [It.; = CAPTAIN.] A captain, headman, or chief.

1611 CORYAT *Crudities* 283 The Præfectus otherwise called the Capitano.. over all their [Venitian] forces. **1705** ADDISON *Italy* (1766) 87 The chief officers of the commonwealth are the two Capitaneos. **1779** FORREST *Voy. N. Guinea* 110, I made him a Capitano, by giving him a frock and drawers of chintz. **1847** DISRAELI *Tancred* v. viii.

‖**capitao** (kæpɪ'taʊ). Also capitow, capito. [Pg. *capitão*, = CAPTAIN.] A head-man, leader of a gang, etc., in Africa.

1899 *Daily News* 21 Mar. 7/7 Parties of villagers who elect to work on the lines are in charge of the 'Capitows', or gang-leaders. **1925** *Chambers's Jrnl.* Oct. 655/2 Accompanied by my 'capitao', I reached the river bank. **1926** *Blackw. Mag.* Apr. 550/1 Our Safari consisted of A. and myself, two capitos (headmen), a few personal boys and gun-bearers, and forty-six porters. **1957** V. W. TURNER *Schism in Afr. Soc.* iv. 95 A capitao in charge of road maintenance.

capitate ('kæpɪteɪt), *a. Nat. Hist.* [ad. L. *capitāt-us* headed, f. *caput, capit-* head: cf. next, and see -ATE[2] 2.]

1. Having a distinct head, knob-headed.

1661 LOVELL *Hist. Anim. & Min.* Introd., Gudgin, capitate and not capitate. **1807** J. E. SMITH *Phys. Bot.* 274 [The Pistil] capitate, forming a little round head. **1848** DANA *Zooph.* 135 Tentacles long and capitate.

2. *Bot.* Having the inflorescence in a close terminal cluster or head, as in composite flowers.

1686 *Phil. Trans.* XVI. 285 The capitate Herb, whose flowers are fistular. **1794** MARTYN *Rousseau's Bot.* x. 103 Capitate flowers like the thistles. **1861** MISS PRATT *Flower. Pl.* V. 298 Dense-headed Rush, or Capitate Rush.

Hence **'capitated** *ppl. a.*, with same meaning.

1676 GREW *Anat. Flowers* App. §15 Without Stalks, that is, Capitated, as in Scabious. **1763** EHRET in *Phil. Trans.* LIII. 132 Having a globular or capitated stigma.

capitate ('kæpɪteɪt), *v. Math.* [f. as prec.] (See quot.)

1884 CAYLEY *Mem. Seminvariants* in *Amer. Jrnl. Math.* VII. I. 10 We capitate a symbol by prefixing to it a number which is not less than the highest number contained in it: thus 552 may be capitated into 5552, 6552, etc.

capitation (kæpɪ'teɪʃən). [ad. L. *capitātiōn-em* (sense 2), f. *caput, capit-* head, having the form of noun of action from a vb.: see prec. and -ATION.]

1. The counting of heads or persons.

1614 RALEIGH *Hist. World* II. 418 This law of capitation. **1646** SIR T. BROWNE *Pseud. Ep.* 360 For not performing the commandement of God concerning capitation.

2. a. The levying of a tax or charge by the head, i.e. upon each person. **b.** A tax or fee paid for each head; a poll tax. **c.** A payment or fee of so much per head from pupils, etc.

1641 EWES (*title*), Speech, touching the Bill of a Capitation or Poll-money. **1696** LUTTRELL *Brief Rel.* (1857) IV. 156 To make the whole capitation about 5 millions. **1745** FIELDING *True Patr.* Wks. 1775 IX. 317 Demanding two millions, to be immediately raised by capitation. **1796** MORSE *Amer. Geog.* II. 281 According to the last capitation, there were 166,871 Jews in Poland.. who paid the tax. *Ibid.* 463 All other religions are.. included in this system of toleration, on paying a certain capitation. *Mod.* The Head Master's salary, paid partly by a capitation on each pupil.

3. *Attrib.* and *Comb.*, as *capitation-consumption, -tax*; also † **capitation-drugget, stuff**, etc. (see quots.); **capitation grant**, a grant of a certain sum for every person who fulfils certain conditions, as to a school for scholars who pass a test examination, to volunteers, etc.

1886 *Pall Mall G.* 19 Oct., We find.. the average *capitation consumption of tobacco about 8 lb. 3 oz. **1690** B. E. *Dict. Cant. Crew*, **Capitation-Drugget*, a Cheap, Slight Stuff, called so from the Tax of that Name. **1862** *Sat. Rev.* 15 Mar., It would be quite possible to merge several of the existing grants [for education] into a single *capitation grant. **1704** *Lond. Gaz.* No. 4031/4 Some Druggets, *Capitation Stuffs, and Shalloons. **1776** ADAM SMITH *W.N.* (1869) II. v. ii. 466 *Capitation taxes are levied at little expense. **1844** H. H. WILSON *Brit. India* I. 112 A capitation tax upon pilgrims to the temple of Jagannath. **1701** *Lond. Gaz.* No. 3740/4 An Olive *Capitation Wastcoat.

capitative, *a.* [f. L. *capitat-* (see prec.) + -IVE.] Reckoned by the head; 'per head'.

1879 GLADSTONE in *19th Cent.* Sept. 571 The capitative addition made by their population to our commerce.

† **'capitaynate.** *Sc. Obs.* [f. *capitayn*, obs. f. CAPTAIN + -ATE[1].] A captainship.

1593 DEE *Diary* (1842) 43 Jan. 7th I receyved letters from the Lord Lasky from his capitaynate in Livonia.

‖ **'capite** ('kæpɪtiː). L., ablat. of *caput* head, occurring in the phrase *tenēre in capite* to hold (of the king) in chief; whence ***tenant, tenure in capite***, and attrib. uses, as ***capite-lands***, and the treatment of *capite* in Law Dicts. as 'The name of a tenure (abolished by *Act 12 Chas. II*, xxiv.), by which land was held immediately of the King, or of the crown'.

1616 BULLOKAR s.v. *Capite*, a tenure, when a man holdeth lands, immediately of the king as of his crowne. *a* **1626** BACON *Use Com. Law* (1636) 39 If a man be seized of capite lands and soccage, he cannot devise but two parts of the whole. **1634** SANDERSON *Serm.* II. 291 A single rood of capite-land will bring the whole estate into wardship. **1641** *Termes de la Ley* 46 Capite is a Tenure that holdeth immediatly of the King, as of his Crowne. **1755** in JOHNSON.

† **capite-berne.** *Sc. Obs.* Also capy-. [app. f. *cappit*, CAPPED or CAPED + Fr. '*berne* a kind of Moorish garment, or such a mantle as Irish gentlewomen weare' (Cotgr.).] Perh. a cape or hood.

1473 in *Acc. Ld. Treas. Scotl.* I. 29, ij½ elne of blak for a clok and capiteberne for the Quene. **1474** *Ibid.* 22, j½ elne of satyne to lyne a cipiberne of the Kingis clok. *Ibid.* 24, v quarteris of vellus to lyne a capitbirne for a riding gowne to the King.

capitel(l, -ele, -il, obs. ff. CAPITAL, CAPITLE.

capitellate (kə'pɪtɛleɪt), *a.* [f. L. *capitellum* (see next) + -ATE[2] 2.] Furnished with a capitellum or small head; terminating in a small knob. Cf. CAPITATE.

1870 HOOKER *Stud. Flora* 240 Stigma capitellate.

‖ **capi'tellum.** [L. dim. of *caput* (or its dim. *capitulum*) head.] A little head. In *Phys.* The rounded eminence on the outer surface of the lower end of the humerus or upper arm.

1872 MIVART *Elem. Anat.* 148 A rounded prominence, called the capitellum, which joins the outer bone of the fore-arm or radius.

† **'capitle.** *Obs.* Also 4–5 itil, -ytle, -itele. [a. ONF. *capitle*:—L. *capitulum*, dim. of *caput* head. Another form of CHAPITLE, chapter.]

1. ? A chapter; or ? a capital city.

1340 *Ayenb.* 43 Þe zenne of ham þet.. purchaceþ þe stryfs and þe werres in cites oþer ine capiteles, oþer betuene þe heȝe men.

2. A chapter of a book (or the like).

1340 *Ayenb.* 1 Þise byeþ þe capiteles of þe boc uolȝinde. *c* **1380** WYCLIF *Serm.* Sel. Wks. I. 134 As tellip þe Gospel of Joon in þe same capitle. *c* **1430** LYDG. *Bochas* I. x. (1554) 20 b, In this Capitle (*ed.* **1558** chapitle) [Bochas] gan direct his stile To write the story. *c* **1440** *Promp. Parv.* 61 Capytle, or chapytle, or captur, *capitulum*.

3. A summary.

1382 WYCLIF *Hebr.* viii. 1 Forsothe a capitle vpon tho thingis that ben seid. **1388** *Ibid.* (Gloss) A capitil, that is a schort comprehending of many thingis.

Capitol ('kæpɪtəl). Forms: 4 capitole, (-hole, -olye), 4–5 capit-, capytoile, -olie, 7 capitoll, 7– capitol. [ME. *capitolie, capitoile*, a. ONF. *capitolie*, Parisian *capitoile* (= It. *capitolio*), ad. L. *capitōlium*, a derivative of *caput* head. The mod.F. *capitole* and Eng. *capitol* are new adaptations of the L.]

1. Literally, A citadel on the head or top of a hill. *esp.* The great national temple of Rome, dedicated to Jupiter Optimus Maximus, on the Saturnian or Tarpeian (afterwards called Capitoline) Hill; sometimes applied to the whole hill including the *arx* or citadel.

1375 BARBOUR *Bruce* I. 543 Syne in hys capitole wes he [Caesar] Throw thaim of his consaill priue, Slayne. *c* **1386** CHAUCER *Monkes T.* 713 This Iulius to the capitolie [*v.r.* capitolye, capithole, capitoile] went. ? *a* **1400** *Morte Arth.* 96 At Rome.. Appere.. In þe kydd capytoile before þe kyng selvyne. **1475** *Bk. Noblesse* 10 Brenus.. wanne and conquered Rome, except the capitoile of Rome. **1601** SHAKS. *Jul. C.* I. iii. 36 Comes Cæsar to the Capitoll to morrow? **1671** MILTON *P.R.* IV. 47 There the Capitol thou seest.. On the Tarpeian rock. **1838** ARNOLD *Rome* I. 315 The commons in that revolution occupied the Capitol.

b. *transf.* and *fig.*

c **1630** DRUMM. OF HAWTH. *Poems* Wks. (1711) 29 The spot-less sp'rits of light.. Greet their great victor in his capitol. **1682** SIR T. BROWNE *Chr. Mor.* 26 Triumphs not leading up into capitols, but up into the highest heavens. **1751** CHAMBERS *Cycl.* s.v., Antiently the name capitol was.. applied to all the principal temples, in most of the colonies.

2. *U.S.* 'The edifice occupied by the congress of the United States in their deliberations. Also, in some states, the state-house, or house in which the legislature holds its sessions' (Webster).

1699 *Acts Assembly Virginia* (1727) I. 205 An Act directing the Building the Capitol and the City of Williamsburgh, &c. **1706** *Cal. Virginia St. Papers* (1875) I. 109 The main street.. extending from the Capitol to ye utmost Limits of the City Westward. **1752** J. BLAIR in *Official Records of R. Dinwiddie* (1883) I. 146, I laid the last top Brick on the Capitol Wall. **1793** JEFFERSON *Let.* 1 Feb. in *Writ.* (1854) III. 508 Doctor Thornton's plan of a capitol. **1795** J. SCOTT *U.S. Gazetteer* s.v. *Washington* (D.C.), The capitol is now building and is situated upon a beautiful eminence. **1834** C. D. ARFWEDSON *United States* I. 318 The Capitol, as it is called, or Statehouse occupied by the legislature of the State. **1843** *Penny Cycl.* XXVII. 98 The president's house is situated at the opposite extremity of Pennsylvania avenue from the Capitol. **1888** *Harper's Mag.* June 50/1 The part of the Capitol which is completed (Senate Chamber, House of Representatives, Library, Historical Society, etc.). **1928** S. V. BENÉT *John Brown's Body* 155 Muddy Washington, with its still-unfinished Capitol. **1943** *Chicago Daily News* 12 June 6/6 To provide the State of Texas with a new capitol.

Hence **Capi'tolian, Ca'pitoline** *a*, of or pertaining to the Capitol; ***Capitoline games***: games in honour of Capitoline Jove.

1618 HOLYDAY *Juvenal* 142 He could not add the capitolian oaken garland to the Alban olive garland. *a* **1822** SHELLEY *Liberty* vii, Gold profaned thy capitolian throne. **1667** MILTON *P.L.* IX. 508 Ammonian Jove, or Capitoline, was seen. *a* **1789** BURNEY *Hist. Mus.* (ed. 2) II. i. 6 In the time of this Emperor [Constantine].. the Capitoline games were abolished.

capitol(l, obs. form of CAPITAL.

‖**capitonné** (kapitɔne), *a.* [Fr., pa. pple. of *capitonner* to upholster, quilt.] (See quots. 1882 and 1957.)

1873 *Young Englishwoman* Mar. 131/2 A dress of tulle over white tafettas, capitonné into bouillons with small clusters of Parmese violets. **1882** CAULFEILD & SAWARD *Dict. Needlework* 61/1 *Capitonné*. This is a French term, signifying drawn in at intervals, as a stuffed sofa, chair, or pincushion, which is buttoned down at each attachment of the double material, at the front and back. **1939** C. BEATON *My Royal Past* ii. 17 She graciously patted the *capitonné* sofa. **1957** M. B. PICKEN *Fashion Dict.* 53/1 *Capitonné embroidery*, decorative tufting similar to that used on furniture, but adapted and modernized for use on hats, yokes, panels of dresses, etc., giving quilted appearance. **1968** *Home & Garden* Nov. 86/2 Deep capitonné Chesterfield... In black hide it costs £237 10s.

capitose (ˌkæpɪ'təʊs), *a.* [f. L. *caput, capit-* head + -OSE.] **a.** Having a large head. **b.** Obstinate, headstrong.

1881 in *Syd. Soc. Lex.*

‖**capitoul** (kapıtul). [F. *capitoul*, a. Pr. *capitol*:—late L. *capitōlium*, for *capitulum* chapter, town-hall.] A name given to the municipal magistrates of Toulouse.

1753 CHAMBERS *Cycl. Supp.* s.v. **1756** NUGENT *Gr. Tour* IV. 243 Their eschevins were called capitouls. **1818** HALLAM *Mid. Ages* (1872) I. 347 The capitouls of Toulouse pretend to an extravagant antiquity.

†**capitoulate.** *Obs.* Also capitolat, -ulate. [ad. Fr. *capitoulat*, f. *capitoul*: see prec.] **a.** The dignity of a capitoul. **b.** A ward or quarter of a city presided over by a capitoul.

1586 T. B. *La Primaud. Fr. Acad.* (1589) 591 The Stats yeerely held in the Provinces, the Mairalties of townes, Shreevalties, Consulships, Capitolats, & Church-wardens, are as it were the forme of a Democraty. **1753** CHAMBERS *Cycl. Supp.* s.v., Tholouse is now divided into eight capitoulates or quarters.

capitulant (kəˈpıtjʊlənt). [a. F. *capitulant*, pr. pple. of *capituler* to CAPITULATE.] One who capitulates.

1839–57 ALISON *Hist. Europe* xxvii. §99 Gaining possession of the fortress which the capitulants held.

capitular (kəˈpıtjʊlə(r)), *a.* and *sb.* [ad. med.L. *capitulār-is* adj., *capitulāre* sb., f. *capitulum* in its various senses: see below.]

A. *adj.*

1. Of or pertaining to an ecclesiastical chapter; governed by a chapter.

1611 COTGR., *Capitulaire*, capitular; of, or belonging to, a chapter. **1651** *Life Father Sarpi* (1676) 36 That in a capitular action..should be sent forth two Apostolical Briefs. **1747** CARTE *Hist. Eng.* I. 787 Seizing the temporalities of bishops and capitular bodies. **1861** A. B. HOPE *Eng. Cathedr. 19th C.* 182 Some of the old cathedrals had been served by chapters of canons, others by monks—all were hereafter to be capitular.

2. *Phys.* Of or pertaining to a terminal protuberance of bone. Cf. CAPITULUM 2.

1872 MIVART *Elem. Anat.* 28 The first of these articular sources is termed 'capitular'. **1881** —— *Cat* 37 One kind, attached to the centrum, are called capitular.

3. *Bot.* Growing in small heads, as the Dandelion does.

1846 WORCESTER cites LOUDON; and in mod. Dicts.

B. *sb.* [various elliptical uses of the adj.]

1. A member of an ecclesiastical chapter.

1726 AYLIFFE *Parergon* 201 The Chapter may..make Decrees and Statutes which shall bind the Chapter itself and all its Members or Capitulars. **1761** STERNE *Tr. Shandy* (1802) IV. 20 The dean of Strasburg..the capitulars and domiciliars (capitularly assembled)..all wished, etc.

2. = CAPITULARY B. 2.

1660 JER. TAYLOR *Rule Conscience* IV. i. (R.) The capitular of Charles the Great joyns dicing and drunkenness together. **1751** CHAMBERS *Cycl.* s.v., In these capitulars did the whole French jurisprudence antiently consist. **1809–10** COLERIDGE *Friend* (1818) I. 142 Nothing gives us a better notion of the ..French monarchy, than the third capitular of the year 811.

3. ? A law or statute of a chapter, or of an ecclesiastical council; a canon; also *fig.*

a **1667** JER. TAYLOR *Serm.* (1678) 90 Our Blessed Saviour made those capitulars and canons of Religion. **1721–1800** BAILEY, *Capitulars*, ordinances or injunctions of kings or bishops, about Ecclesiastical Affairs. **1751** CHAMBERS *Cycl.*, *Capitular* or *capitulary*, denotes an act passed in a chapter, either of knights, canons, or religious.

4. ? A heading or title of a chapter.

1846–7 MASKELL *Mon. Rit.* I. p. liv, Here must be mentioned a Capitular which not unfrequently is to be met with in MSS. of the New Testament in English..'Here begynnythe a rule, that tellith in whiche chapitris of the bible..ye mown fynd the epistlis and the gospels'.

†**ca'pitularly,** *adv. Obs.* [f. CAPITULAR *a.* + -LY².] In the form of, or as, a chapter.

1702 *Acc. Transact. Present Convocation* 5 The Dean and Prebendarys..meeting Capitularly in the Jerusalem Chamber. **1711** SWIFT *Let. Mr. St. John* 11 May (R.) You could do nothing but when all three were capitularly met. **1761** [see CAPITULAR B. 1].

capitulary (kəˈpıtjʊlərı), *a.* and *sb.* [ad. med.L. *capitulārius*, *-ium* in same senses; F. *capitulaire*. Cf. CAPITULAR.]

A. *adj.* Of or pertaining to a chapter.

1774 T. WARTON *Hist. Eng. Poetry* III. §35 (R.) The register of the capitulary acts of York Cathedral. **1861** *Times* 23 May (*Milan*), The Capitulary Vicar has prohibited the clergy from taking part in the approaching national fête.

B. *sb.*

1. A member of an ecclesiastical chapter. ? *Obs.*

1694 LUTTRELL *Brief Rel.* (1857) III. 298 The grand dean ..adjourned the chapter..and retired with 22 capitularies.

2. A collection of ordinances (in mod.L. called *capitula*), especially those made on their own authority by the Frankish kings.

1650 ELDERFIELD *Tythes* 111 And the capitularies [say] that they were the vows of the faithful. **1747** CARTE *Hist. Eng.* I. 240 Enjoined by the capitularies of Charle-Magne. **1844** LD. BROUGHAM *Brit. Const.* iii. (1862) 54 We have also an ordinance of 829, the Capitulary of Worms. **1875** STUBBS *Const. Hist.* I. i. 10 Germany, except in the few Capitularies of the Frank sovereigns, has no central or common written law.

3. A heading, title, category.

1824–9 LANDOR *Imag. Conv.*, *Southey & Porson* I. All that portion of our metre..ranged under the capitulary of lyric.

†**ca'pitulate,** *ppl. a. Obs.* [ad. med.L. *capitulāt-us*, pa. pple. of *capitulāre* 'capitulis aliquid distinguere' (Du Cange), to draw up under distinct heads, f. *capitulum* head of a discourse, chapter, title, dim. of *caput* head.]

Reduced to heads; agreed or laid down in a number of distinct heads or items; stipulated.

1528 GARDINER in Pocock *Rec. Ref.* I. l. 99 It is capitulate between the king's highness and the French king to make actual war in Flaundres. **1574** HELLOWES *Gueuara's Ep.* (1577) 19 It was a law made and capitulate by the Lawyers. **1600** HOLLAND *Livy* XXIV. vi. 512 It was capitulate and covenanted, that..the river Himera, etc.

capitulate (kəˈpıtjʊleıt), *v.* [f. prec. or on analogy of vbs. so formed: see -ATE³.]

†**1.** *trans.* To draw up in chapters, or under heads or articles; to specify, enumerate. *Obs.*

1593 LODGE *Wm. Longbeard* E ij b, The lawes..which we capitulate at sea are not..used on lande. **1608** TOPSELL *Serpents* 600 The places of serpents abode being thus generally capitulated. *c* **1645** HOWELL *Lett.* (1678) 116. **1678** MARVELL *Def. Howe* Wks. 1875 IV. 182 The Discourse.. capitulates that Mr. Howe should by efficacious intend infallibility, etc.

†**b.** *intr.*

1596 NASHE *Saffron Walden* 81 For an assay..of his pen, he capitulated on the births of monsters.

†**2.** *intr.* To draw up articles of agreement; to arrange or propose terms; to treat, bargain, parley.

1596 SHAKS. *1 Hen. IV*, III. ii 120 Percy, Northumberland,..Mortimer, Capitulate against vs. **1618** SIR T. LAKE in *Fortescue Papers* 38 He did not intend to capitulate with his Majesty. **1669** BAXTER *Call Unconv.* 247 Think not to capitulate with Christ, and divide your heart betwixt him and the world. **1697** DAMPIER *Voy.* (1729) I. 220 The Spaniards..capitulated day after day to prolong time. **1748** RICHARDSON *Clarissa* (1811) VII. 344 It had the appearance of meanly capitulating with you. **1815** WELLINGTON in Gurw. *Disp.* XII. 355 We must not capitulate with mutiny in any shape. **1816** SOUTHEY *Ess.* (1832) I. 322 Those magistrates..who capitulated with the ..agricultural rioters, and..acceded to the demands of a mob.

†**b.** With various constructions: To make conditions, stipulate, agree. *Obs.*

1580 NORTH *Plutarch* (1676) 965 Plemminius..did capitulate with Lepidus to render up the Town. **1580** SIDNEY *Arcadia* IV. (1590) 432 To capitulate what tenements they should have. **1602** SEGAR *Hon. Mil. & Civil* III. xiii. 126 Two gentlemen capitulate to fight on horseback. **1715** DE FOE *Hon. & Just.* (1841) 16, I capitulate for so much justice as to explain myself. **1818** MRS. SHELLEY *Frankenst.* iv, The man who thus capitulated for his safety.

†**3.** *trans.* **a.** To make terms about, agree upon the terms of; to formulate, arrange for, conclude. **b.** To make the subject of negotiation. *Obs.*

1593 LODGE *Wm. Longbeard* F ij b, A peace lately capitulated betwixt Dagobert, kinge of France and Grimoald. *a* **1649** CHAS I. *Wks.* 230 He had no Commission ..to capitulate anything concerning Religion. **1661** WEBSTER *Thracian Wonder* II. i, How dare you, sir, capitulate the cause?

4. *intr.* To make terms of surrender; to surrender or yield on stipulated terms, in opposition to surrendering at discretion. The ordinary use; said of a general, force, garrison, fortress, town, etc.

1689 LUTTRELL *Brief Rel.* (1857) I. 547 The 12th, the duke of Gourdon beat a parly, and desired to capitulate. **1705** *Lond. Gaz.* 4160/3 The Castle of Mittau began to capitulate the 14th instant. **1769** ROBERTSON *Chas. V*, V. v. 439 Want of provisions quickly obliged Trevulci to capitulate. **1874** BANCROFT *Footpr. Time* iii. 160 Washington..after defending himself one day, capitulates.

fig. **1714** *Spect.* No. 566 ¶8, I still pursued, and, about two o'clock this afternoon, she thought fit to capitulate. **1841–4** EMERSON *Wks.* (Bohn) I. 21, I am ashamed to think how easily we capitulate to badges and names.

b. *trans.* To surrender upon terms.

1847 R. HAMILTON *Rew. & Punishm.* vi. (1853) 264 We cannot capitulate the premises. **1870** *Daily Tel.* 22 Sept., The new Minister..seems..disposed to the policy of capitulating France.

Hence **ca'pitulated** *ppl. a.* **ca'pitulating** *vbl. sb.* and *ppl. a.*

1586 FERNE *Blaz. Gentrie* 331 A Combate capitulated, that is to wit, a Combate, wherin are set downe..diuers Articles or conditions, as to the manner of the battaile. **1654** EARL ORRERY *Parthenissa* (1676) 281 This capitulating Traytor. **1753** SMOLLETT *Ct. Fathom* (1784) 154/1 He put on his capitulating face.

capitulation (kə,pıtjuːˈleıʃən). [a. F. *capitulation*, ad. med.L. *capitulātiōn-em*, n. of action f. *capitulāre* to draw up under heads.] The action of the verb CAPITULATE.

†**1.** The action of arranging in chapters or heads; a portion of a work so arranged. *Obs.*

1613 R. C. *Table Alph.* (ed. 3) *Capitulation*, distinguishing by parts, bringing to hands [? heads].

2. A statement of the heads of a subject; summation, summary, enumeration; cf. *recapitulation.*

1579 FENTON *Guicciard.* I. (1599) 15 This is the capitulation and summe of them [the conditions of a convention]. **1638** HEYWOOD *Port Piety* 264, I should but spend paper in a meere capitulation of their names. **1882** STEVENSON *Men & Bks.* 124 Capitulation is not description.

†**3.** The making of terms, or of a bargain or agreement; stipulation. *Obs.*

1589 PUTTENHAM *Eng. Poesie* (Arb.) 298 In conuersation simple, in capitulation subtill and mistrustfull. **1647** CLARENDON *Hist. Reb.* VI. (1843) 347/2 **1721** STRYPE *Eccl. Mem.* I. I. xii. 103 Appointing by capitulation what the pope should do.

†**b.** *pl.* Articles or terms of a treaty, stipulations, covenants, conditions. *Obs.*

1580 NORTH *Plutarch* (1676) 377 The capitulations which the Ephori sent unto him, were these. **1667** *Treaty* in Magens *Insurances* II. 530 The Kings of Great Britain and Spain shall..keep..all and singular the Capitulations in this present Treaty agreed. **1721** STRYPE *Eccl. Mem.* II. I. xxvii. 221 Soldiers..had been paid for their service.. according to their capitulations. **1728** MORGAN *Hist. Algiers* II. iv. 285 The Capitulations between his Imperial Majesty and his new Ally.

†**c.** An agreement on specified terms, a covenant, convention, treaty. *Obs.*

1535 GARDINER in Strype *Eccl. Mem.* I. II. lxv. 161 In case .. any of them should swerve from any piece of the capitulation by force of the emperor. **1642** BRIDGE *Wound. Consc. Cured* §4. 29 Then the Doctor comes to the matter of capitulation or covenant. **1691** LUTTRELL *Brief Rel.* (1857) II. 212 The French at Mons had already broke their capitulation with the burghers. **1798** DALLAS *Amer. Law Rep.* II. 459 The rights which descended to him in consequence of his father's original capitulation. **1843** PRESCOTT *Mexico* VII. iv. (1864) 444 The terms of his [Columbus] original 'capitulation' with the crown.

d. *spec.* (*a*) The agreement or conditions sworn to by the former German emperors at their election. (*b*) The agreements made by the Swiss cantons with foreign powers respecting the regiments of Swiss who took service under them. (*c*) The articles by which the Porte gave special immunities and privileges to French subjects; extended subsequently to those of other nations.

1622 *Prot. Princes* in Rushw. *Hist. Coll.* I. 74 As was agreed upon in the Capitulation Royal, and Fundamental Law of the Empire. **1756** NUGENT *Gr. Tour* II. 26 Every Emperor is tied down at his coronation to some new articles, which are called terms of capitulation. **1796** MORSE *Amer. Geog.* II. 472 European merchants live here in..splendour and safety..owing to particular capitulations with the Porte. **1863** KINGLAKE *Crimea* (1876) I. viii. 116. **1872** FREEMAN *Growth Eng. Const.* 209 The system of military capitulations..by the Cantons. **1884** TWISS *Law Nations* I. 463 It may be doubted whether the term 'Capitulations' came into use before the Treaty of 1535 between France and the Porte.

4. The making of terms for surrender; the action of surrendering to an enemy upon stipulated terms.

1650 CROMWELL *Let.* 18 Dec. (Carlyle) The gentlemen you desire..to treat and conclude of the capitulation. **1769** ROBERTSON *Chas. V*, V. IV. 407 Clement..was soon obliged to demand a capitulation. **1876** J. H. NEWMAN *Hist. Sk.* I. I. i. 17 In Greece to offer earth and water was the sign of capitulation. *Mod.* The capitulation of Metz.

b. The instrument containing the terms.

1793 LD. AUCKLAND *Corr.* III. 9, I..enclose the capitulations of Breda and Gertruydenberg. **1849–50** ALISON *Hist. Europe* VIII. lv. §34. 590 At daybreak the capitulation was signed.

capitulationism (kə,pıtjuːˈleıʃənız(ə)m). [f. CAPITULATION + -ISM.] The act or principle of capitulation; *spec.* in Communist usage (see quots.). Hence **ca,pitu'lationist** *sb.* and *a.*, one who advocates capitulationism; characterized by capitulationism.

1957 R. N. CAREW HUNT *Guide to Communist Jargon* xlv. 152 Wilhelm Zeisser and Rudolf Herrnstadt were..expelled ..on account of the attitude they were said to have adopted at the time of the Berlin rising of the previous June, the specific charges against them being that they had advocated 'capitulationism', and had exalted the spontaneous role of the masses at the expense of the Party. **1962** [see ADVENTURIST *sb.*]. **1963** *Economist* 5 Jan. 18/3 Peking's campaign against such 'capitulationists' as Mr. Khrushchev. **1963** *Times* 8 Jan. 7/1 Scarcely veiled accusations of Russian 'capitulationism' and 'Trotskyism', and the abandonment of peaceful coexistence by the Chinese, were exchanged between Peking and Moscow. **1963** *New Statesman* 1 Feb. 145/1 The reported Chinese memorandum..[refers to] Krushchev's 'capitulationist' attitudes towards the 'imperialists'.

ca'pitulator. [agent-noun in L. form, from CAPITULATE *v.*] One who capitulates.

1611 COTGR., *Capituleur*, a capitulator. **1632** in SHERWOOD; **1846** in WORCESTER; and in mod. Dicts.

capitulatory (kəˈpıtjʊlə,tərı), *a.* [f. as prec. + -ORY.] Of or pertaining to capitulation; cf. *recapitulatory*.

1833 LAMB *Elia* (1860) 243 In their tedious genealogies, or their capitulatory brass monuments?

capitule, -ull, obs. ff. CAPITLE, CAPITAL.

‖**capitulum** (kəˈpıtjʊləm). [L.; dim. of *caput* head.] A little head or knob.

1. *Eccl.* A short 'lesson' from Scripture.

1753 in CHAMBERS *Cycl. Supp.* **1885** MᶜCRIE *Sketches & Stud.* 29 The last page of the capitula of St. John's Gospel.

2. *Phys.* 'A protuberance of bone received into a hollow portion of another bone' (*Syd. Soc. Lex.*).

1755 in CHAMBERS *Cycl. Supp.* 1881 MIVART *Cat* 37 They articulate with the heads, or the capitula, of the ribs.

3. *Bot.* a. 'A close head of sessile flowers. Also a term vaguely applied among fungals to the receptacle, pileus, or peridium' (*Treas. Bot.*).

1721–1800 BAILEY, *Capitulum* [among Botanists] is the Head or Flowring Top of any Plant. 1830 LINDLEY *Nat. Syst. Bot.* 106 The neutral florets.. being quite open in very many capitula. 1861 S. THOMSON *Wild Flowers* I. (ed. 4) 91 The flower-head or capitulum of such a plant as the daisy.

b. In characeous plants, a head-cell borne by each manubrium.

1875 BENNETT & DYER tr. *Sachs's Bot.* 520. 1877 HUXLEY & MARTIN *Elem. Biol.* (ed. 4) 45 At the free end of the manubrium is a rounded body, the *capitulum*, which bears six smaller, *secondary capitula*. 1898 H. C. PORTER tr. *Strasburger's Bot.* 339 Each manubrium terminates in a knob-like cell or capitulum, from which a large number of short cells grow out into the cavity of the antheridium.

4. *Zool.* a. The body of a barnacle together with the case containing it; so called from its forming a head to the peduncle or foot-stalk.

1872 NICHOLSON *Palæont.* 152 At its free extremity the peduncle bears the 'capitulum'.

b. (See quots.)

1920 I. F. & W. D. HENDERSON *Dict. Sci. Terms* 42/1 *Capitulum*.. the exsert part of the head in ticks. 1964 M. HYNES *Med. Bacteriol.* (ed. 8) xxx. 460 Ticks are eight-legged arthropods with no division between head, thorax or abdomen. Their mouth-parts are carried on a separate movable *capitulum*.

capivara, var. of CAPYBARA.

capivi, var. of COPAIBA.

capkin ('kæpkɪn). *nonce-wd.* [f. CAP *sb.* + -KIN.] A little cap.

1844 *Blackw. Mag.* LVI. 215 The small mannikins had.. thrown down their broad brown capkins.

caplan, obs. form of CAPELIN.

'caple, capul. *Obs.* exc. *dial.* Forms: α. 4–5 capel, 4–6 capil, 5 capylle, 5–6 capill, 6 capyl, 4–7 caple. β. 4–9 capul, 5 capulle, 5–6 capull. In Drayton **cauple**. [ME. *capel, -il, -yl, -ul*, corresponds to Icel. *kapall* (for *kapal-r*) nag, hack, mare; also to Ir. *capall, capull* horse, mare, Gael. *capall* mare, the relations between which are uncertain; the ultimate source is prob. L. *caball-us* horse, hack. See also CABALL, and its variants.

Not in Old Irish (Windisch): Manx has *cabbyl*, Welsh *ceffyl* (Davies, not in Pughe), Cornish *cevil, kevil, keffyl* (also in place names as *Nankevil, Penkevil*), Breton *caval* (in Lagadeuc's Catholicon 1499, and in Rostrenen 1732, not in Legonidec). These forms point to no common Celtic source, but to separate adoption from L., Norman Fr., and perh. Eng. The Irish *capall* was evidently directly from L. *caballus*. The Icelandic word is chiefly in ecclesiastical documents after 13th c., and may be directly from L., or perh. immed. through Irish. The immediate source of the ME. word is not determined.]

A horse: in ME. chiefly *poetical*; now only *dial.*

c 1290 *Land Cokaygne* 32 in *E.E.P.* (1862) 157 Hors, no capil, kowe, no ox. *c* 1325 *E.E. Allit. P.* B. 1254 þay wer cagged and kaȝt on capeles al bare. 1362 LANGL. *P. Pl.* A. IV. 22 þenne Concience on his Capul Carieth forþ Faste. *c* 1386 CHAUCER *Frere's T.* 254 Bothe hey and Cart and eek hise caples thre. *c* 1440 *Promp. Parv.* 61/2 Capul, or caple, horse, *caballus*. *c* 1475 *Rauf Coilȝear* 114 The ane of ȝow my Capill ta, The vther his [the king's] Coursour alswa. 1547 SALESBURY *Welsh Dict.*, *Kephyll*, a capull. 1600 HOLLAND *Livy* III. vii. 1365 *note*, Grasse and food, for sheepe, caples, and goats. 1603 DRAYTON *Bar. Warres* VI. l, Phœbus tooke his lab'ring Teame.. To wash his Cauples in the Ocean Streame. 1670 RAY *Proverbs* 48 It is time to yoke when the cart comes to the caples, *Cheshire*. 1799 R. JAMIESON *Pop. Ballads* (1806) I. 233 (Jam.) And hark! what capul nicker'd proud? 1819 SCOTT *Ivanhoe* xxxviii, I will get me.. my neighbour Buthan's good capul.

2. A name for a hen. *rare*.

c 1460 *Towneley Myst.* 99 Sely Capyll, oure hen, both to and fro She kakyls.

caple, variant of CAPEL.

capless ('kæplɪs), *a.* [f. CAP *sb.*[1] + -LESS.] Without a cap; having no cap.

a 1839 GALT *Demon Destiny* (1840) viii. 53 His hoary hair streamed capless. 1891 *Daily News* 30 July 2/7 He could not have a capless maid to answer the door. 1904 H. G. WELLS *Food of Gods* I. ii. 22 A very little old woman, capless, with dirty white hair. 1958 M. L. HALL *Newnes Compl. Amat. Photogr.* 110 A range of capless fitting flashbulbs.

capleyne, obs. form of CAPELINE.

caplin, capling ('kæplɪn, -lɪŋ). [f. CAP.] The cap of leather on a flail, through which the thongs pass that connect the swingel and staff.

1688 R. HOLME *Armoury* III. 333/1 The Cap-lings.. of a Flail or Threshal.. are the strong double Leathers made fast to the top of the Hand-staff and the top of the Swiple. 1704 in WORLIDGE *Dict. Rust. et Urb.* s.v. *Flail*. 1727 in BRADLEY *Fam. Dict.* s.v. *Flail*.

caplin, -ling, var. of CAPELIN, a small fish.

capnite ('kæpnaɪt). *Min.* [in Ger. *Kapnit* (Breithaupt 1841), f. *Kapnik* (in Hungary) + -ITE.] A variety of Smithsonite, containing carbonate of iron.

1868 in DANA *Min.*

capnomancy ('kæpnəʊmænsɪ). [f. Gr. καπνός smoke + μαντεία divination. Cf. F. *capnomancie* (in 16th c. *capnomantie*).] Divination by smoke.

1610 HEALEY *St. Aug. City of God* 294 Divination.. was done.. by smoake, Capnomancy. 1663 J. SPENCER *Prodigies* (1665) Pref., Those thin and curious arts, capnomancy, augury, Sooth saying. 1883 STEWART *Neth. Lochaber* xxxiv. 206 In books on.. divination it is called Capnomancy.

capnomor ('kæpnəʊmɔː(r)). *Chem.* [f. Gr. καπνός smoke + (?) μόρα, Doric for μοῖρα part.] A colourless transparent oil of peculiar smell, one of the constituents of smoke, obtained from wood-tar.

1838 T. THOMSON *Chem. Org. Bodies* 736 Capnomore.. was discovered by Reichenbach,.. and was so named by him.. because it exists in the smoke of organic bodies. 1863–79 WATTS *Dict. Chem.* I. 741 Capnomor is contained, together with creosote and another oil, in the portion of wood-tar which is soluble in potash.

‖**capo**[1] ('kɑːpəʊ, 'kapo). [It., lit. 'head'.] The leader of a branch or 'family' of the Mafia. Also **capo mafioso** (cf. MAF(F)IOSO).

1952 E. REID *Mafia* xvi. 183 Di Martini took over as *Capo Mafioso* of New Orleans. 1959 G. MAXWELL *Ten Pains of Death* iv. 65 There used to be two great *capo* (chief) *mafia* families in Castellamare... The present holder of the title of *capo* is a nephew of the last, now an old man of eighty. 1969 M. GILBERT *Etruscan Net* III. iii. 242 Those men were of the Mafia. You hired their services... You were responsible to their *capo* for their safe return. 1972 [see MAFIA]. 1978 G. VIDAL *Kalki* vii. 165 Various Mafia capos all around the country have denied any knowledge of the murder of what many believed was a leading trafficker in drugs.

capo[2] ('kæpəʊ), ellipt. for CAPO TASTO.

1946 J. SAMPSON *Specialized Course Guitar Lessons* XIII. 6 A 'Capo' should only be used by those who find that pieces of music are written too *low* for them to comfortably sing while playing. 1968 *Melody Maker* 30 Nov. 22 (Advt.), Ask for Hamilton capos. 1987 *Folk Roots* Apr. 9/3 Cast off capos.. will be found littered around any guitar player's stomping ground.

‖**'capoc.** 'A fine short-stapled cotton wool, used in India for stuffing cushions and lining palanquins, etc.' (Simmonds 1858). See KAPOK.

1750 BEAWES *Lex Mercat.* (1752) 817 Capoc (a sort of very fine Cotton).

‖**ca'pocchia.** [It.; fem. of *capocchio* silly, simple (*capoccio, capocchio* 'shallow skonce, loggerhead' Florio); lit. 'blockhead', f. *capo* head.] Theobald's correction of the reading *chipochia*, in

1606 SHAKS. *Tr. & Cr.* IV. ii. 13 (Fol. 1) Alas poore wretch: a poore chipochia.

†**ca'poche**, *v. trans. Obs. rare*[−1]. Meaning uncertain: Johnson suggests 'perhaps to strip off the hood', f. CAPOUCH; it might also be a sportive use of CABOCHE *v.*

1664 BUTLER *Hud.* II. II. 529 We still have.. Capoched [*ed.* 1689 *has* o'er-reach'd] your Rabbins of the Synod And snapt their Canons with a Why-not.

Capo di Monte ('kɑːpəʊ diː 'mɒnteɪ). Also **Capodimonte.** The name of a palace near Naples applied *attrib.* to a type of porcelain first produced there in the mid-eighteenth century. Also used *absol.* and *ellipt.*

1850 MARRYAT *Hist. Pott. & Porc.* xi. 217 The Capo di Monte tea and coffee services are perhaps the most beautiful description of Porcelain which has ever been manufactured in Europe. 1869 LADY C. SCHREIBER *Jrnl.* (1911) I. 34 One small Mennecy figure (marked), and a white Capo ditto (unmarked). *Ibid.* 49 Saw Mr. Gladstone's collection... The Capo di Monte I do not understand. 1926 V. TREE *Castles in Air* iii. 123 Beardsley drawings or better, and Capo di Monte china. 1942 A. E. W. MASON *Musk & Amber* vi. 64 Candlesticks of the Capodimonte porcelain. 1969 *Times* 25 Mar. 12/4 The Antique Porcelain Company gave 9,500 gns. for a very rare Capodimonte Italian comedy group.

capon ('keɪpən), *sb.* Forms: 1, 3 capun, 4 capoun, (kapoun, chapon), 4–6 capone, 5 capun(e, (capvne), capoone, 4– capon. [OE. *capun*, ad. L. *capōn-em* in same sense, whence also ONF. *capun, capon* (F. *chapon*, Pr. and Sp. *capon*, It. *cappone*), which prob. reinforced the Eng. word.]

1. A castrated cock.

c 1000 ÆLFRIC *Voc.* in Wr.-Wülcker 132 *Capo*, capun. *Gallinaccus*, capun. *c* 1250 *Bestiary* 390 in *O.E. Misc.* 13 Ðe coc and te capun. *a* 1300 *Floriz & Bl.* 260 Bute he also capun beo idiȝt. 1377 LANGL. *P. Pl.* B. IV. 38 For a dozeine chickenes Or as many capones. 1398 TREVISA *Barth. De P.R.* XII. xviii. (1495) 425 The capon is a cocke made as it were female by keruynge away of his gendringe stones. 1481 CAXTON *Reynard* 26 He.. hadde to fore hym as fatte capone as a man myght fynde. 1598 BARCKLEY *Felic. Man* I. (1603) 11 Is made fat with daintie and delicate fare like a capon. 1600 SHAKS. *A.Y.L.* II. vii. 154 The Iustice In faire round belly, with good Capon lin'd. *a* 1704 T. BROWN *Wks.* (1760) III. 26 (D.) To truck.. justice for fat capons to be delivered before dinner. 1847 BARHAM *Ingol. Leg.* (1877) 161 On capons fine they daily dine. 1865 LIVINGSTONE *Zambesi* x. 216 Some fine fat capons.

b. Formerly used in payment of rent in kind.

1495 *Act 11 Hen. VII*, xl. Preamb., xl. acres of wood x*lti*. rent and the rent of L. capons. 1523 LD. BERNERS *Froiss.* I. ccccxlvii. 789 They gadered vp the rentes, as Capons, and other thynges in his townes.

c. As a type of dullness, and a term of reproach.

1542 UDALL *Erasm. Apoph.* 307 b, [He] came flyngiNg home to Roome again as wyse as a capon. 1551 T. WILSON *Logike* 11 Some [men] are capones by kinde, and so blunt by nature, that no arte at all can whet them. 1590 SHAKS. *Com. Err.* III. i. 32 Mome,.. Capon, Coxcombe, Idiot, Patch.

†2. *transf.* A eunuch.

1594 CAREW *Huarte's Exam. Wits* (1616) 279 Of a 1000 such capons who addict themselues to their booke, none attaineth to anie perfection, euen in musicke (which is their ordinarie profession). 1605 *Tryall Chev.* II. i. in Bullen *O. Pl.* (1884) III. 289. 1691 D'URFEY *All for Money* 65 If there be a Capon in Christendom, I'll make thee one.

3. Humorously applied to various fish; *esp.* a red-herring.

c 1640 J. SMYTH *Hundred of Berkeley* (1885) 319 The Sole wee call our Seuverne Capon. 1699 B. E. *Dict. Cant. Crew*, *Yarmouth-Capon*, a Red Herring. 1719 RAMSAY *Hamilton* ii. iii, A Glasgow capon and a fadge Ye thought a feast. 1812 W. TENNANT *Anster F.* iv, Each to his jaws A good Crail's capon holds [*note* 'a dried haddock']. 1847–78 HALLIWELL, *Capon*, a red-herring. *Kent*.

†4. A billet-doux. Cf. F. *poulet* 'a chicken; also, a loue-letter, or loue-message' (Cotgr.). *Obs.*

1588 SHAKS. *L.L.L.* IV. i. 56 O thy letter, thy letter.. Boyet, you can carue, Breake vp this Capon.

5. *Comb.*, as ***capon-broth, -flesh***; ***capon-crammed, -like, -lined*** adjs.; **capon-beer**, ? capon-broth made with beer; **capon-bell**, the passing-bell (Halliwell cites Dekker); †**capon-cote**, a house for keeping capons; **capon-justice**, a corrupt magistrate who is bribed by gifts of capons; **capon-money**, money in commutation of a payment of capons; †**capon's-feather**, the feather of a capon; also, Common Columbine (*Aquilegia vulgaris*); †**capon's-tail**, a plant, *Valeriana pyrenaica*; **capon's-tail grass**, *Festuca Myurus* (Britten and Holland).

1626 BACON *Sylva* §411 Drink incorporate with Flesh or roots (as in *Capon-beer &c.) will nourish more easily. 1691 T. H[ALE] *Acc. New Invent.* 78 If the Alderman thought that an impossibility, he was certainly far gone in *Capon-broth. 1393 LANGL. *P. Pl.* C. VII. 136 Hue hadde a childe in the *chapon-cote. 1597 *2nd Pt. Return fr. Parnass.* III. ii. 1214 His mawe must be *Capon crambd each day. *a* 1662 HEYLIN *Hist. Ref.* (1849) I. 212 (D.) Salcot of Salisbury [otherwise called Capon].. redeems his peace.. by making long leases of the best of his farms and manors; known afterwards most commonly by the name of *Capon's feathers. 1847–78 HALLIWELL, *Capon's-feather*, the herb columbine. *c* 1425 *Voc.* in Wr.-Wülcker 662 *Caro spadonia*, *capuneflesche. *Caro caponina*, caponflesche. *a* 1639 WARD *Serm.* (1862) 128 (D.) Judges that judge for reward, and say with shame, 'Bring you', such as the country calls *capon justices. 1856 R. VAUGHAN *Mystics* (1860) I. 150 A portly, *capon-lined burgomaster. 1714 *Lond. Gaz.* No. 5246/3 In Arrear to the Corporation of Portsmouth, for Town-Rents, Reliefs, *Capon-Money or other Dues. 1548 TURNER *Names of Herbes*, Phu is called in englishe setwal, of other some *Capons tayle. 1598 FLORIO, *Amantilla*, the herbe Valerian, Capons taile or Setwall. 1597 GERARD *Herbal* I. xxii. 29 My friend.. gave it the title.. *Capons-taile Gracce.

'capon, *v.* [f. prec.; = F. *chaponner*.] *trans.* To make a capon of; to castrate. Hence **'caponed** *ppl. a.*, **'caponing** *vbl. sb.*

1624 MASSINGER *Renegado* I. i, Had it been discovered, I had been caponed. 1668 R. L'ESTRANGE *Vis. Quev.* (1708) 184 Nothing but a Capon'd, a thing unman'd, could ever, etc. 1693 DRYDEN *Juvenal's Sat.* VI. 487. 1886 *N. Zealand Her.* 1 June 2/6 The caponing of male fowl birds.

†**'caponet.** *Obs.* [f. CAPON + -ET[1]: prob. OF; mod.F. has *chaponneau*.] A little or young capon.

1570 LEVINS *Manip.* 93 A caponet, of capon, *capunculus*. 1619 H. HUTTON *Follies Anat.* (1842) 21 To shelter the scorcht caponet or hen. 1708 MOTTEUX *Rabelais* IV. lix. (1737) 243 Caponets, Caviar and Toast.

caponier (kæpə'nɪə(r)). Also **caponiere, caponnière, kaponier.** [a. F. *caponnière*, ad. Sp. *caponera* in same sense; orig. a capon-cote or mews, f. *capon* CAPON. Many modern writers have used the French form.]

'A covered passage across the ditch of a fortified place, for the purpose either of sheltering communication with outworks or of affording a flanking fire to the ditch in which it stands' (Stocqueler *Mil. Dict.* 1853).

1683 *Lond. Gaz.* No. 1858/6 A Retrenchment.. which we still maintain, to cover the Caponiers we have in the Ditch. 1704 J. HARRIS *Lex. Techn.*, *Caponniere*. 1772 SIMES *Mil. Guide*, *Caponier*. 1830 E. CAMPBELL *Dict. Mil. Sc.*, *Caponière*. 1863 KINGLAKE *Crimea* (1877) III. v. 364 Of its eight angles, every other one was supplied with a little bastion or caponiere. 1879 *Cassell's Techn. Educ.* IV. 138/2 Kaponiers are large casemated masonry buildings for the defence of the ditches of permanent works on the polygonal system. 1882 *St. James's Gaz.* 6 Feb., Strong caponiers for flanking the ditches.

caponize (ˈkeɪpənaɪz), *v.* [f. CAPON *sb.* + -IZE.] *trans.* To make a capon of; to castrate.
1654 GAYTON *Fest. Notes* IV. ii. 180 [To] dishonour a Cock of his spurrs: that is to Caponize the gallant spirit of the Creature. **1736** BAILEY *Househ. Dict.* 140 These bustards may likewise be caponiz'd, as well as turkeys, to make them larger. **1859** R. BURTON *Centr. Afr.* in *Jrnl. R.G.S.* XXIX. 350 The habit of caponizing cattle and poultry prevailed.. before the arrival of the Arabs.

capoone, obs. form of CAPON.

‖**caporal** (kapoˈral). [a. Sp. and F. *caporal.*]
†**1.** A corporal. (*Sp.*)
1598 BARRET *Theor. Warres* II. i. 23 Of the best approued souldiers to chuse for Caporals. *Ibid.* Gloss. 249 Cabo de esquadra or Caporall, a Spanish word, is the head or chiefe vnder the Captaine of a small number of souldiers.
2. A kind of (superior) tobacco. (*Fr.*)
1850 THACKERAY *Pendennis* lxix. (1885) 680 Couldn't find a bit of tobacco fit to smoke till we came to Strasburg, where I got some Caporal.

caporcianite (kəˈpɔːʃənaɪt). *Min.* [f. Monte de Caporciano in Tuscany + -ITE.] A variety of Laumontite.
1868 DANA *Min.* 399 Caporcianite occurs in pearly monoclinic crystals of a flesh-red color.

capot (kəˈpɒt, formerly ˈkæpət), *sb.*[1] Also 7 capet. [a. F. *capot* (*t* always mute) 'said of the player who fails to make a trick', also 'the stroke by which a player is made *capot*' (Littré).]
In *Piquet.* The winning of all the tricks by one player (which scores 40).
1651 *Royall Game Picquet* 32 Which of them soever wins all the Cards,.. he shall reckon Fourty; and this is called a Capot. **1674** COTTON *Compl. Gamester* vi. (1676) 87 (*Picket*) A Capet. **1700** FARQUHAR *Const. Couple* II. ii. i, The Capot at Piquet. **1823** LAMB *Elia, Mrs. Battle* (1853) 55 She would ridicule the pedantry of the terms—such as pique—repique—the capot—they savoured (she thought) of affectation.

‖**capot** (kapo), *sb.*[2] [a. F. *capot*, dim. of *cape* CAPE.] = CAPOTE.
1775 R. CHANDLER *Trav. Asia M.* (1825) I. 195 Wrapped in their thick capots or loose coats. **1836** W. IRVING *Astoria* (1849) 47 They wear a capot or surcoat, made of a blanket.

capot (kəˈpɒt), *v.* [f. CAPOT *sb.*[1]: formerly accented on first syllable.] *trans.* In *Piquet.* To score a capot against, to win all the tricks from.
1651 *Royall Game Picquet* 41 And so by this meanes he come to be Capotted. **1659** *Shuffling, Cutting, & Deal.* 3, I have thrown out all my best Cards.. so I may very well be capetted. **1700** FARQUHAR *Const. Couple* II. I. i, I have capotted her my self two or three times in an evening. **1818** SCOTT *Rob Roy* x, He hazarded everything for the chance of piqueing, repiqueing, or capoting his adversary.
b. *transf.* To 'score off' (a person) heavily. Also as an imprecation *capot me!*
1649 DR. DENTON to *Sir R. Verney* 15 Oct., If it be to come in by a Privy Seal.. I doubt you will be capotted. **1760** FOOTE *Minor* I. i, Capot me, but those lads abroad are pretty fellows.

ˈ**capotaine**, *a.* [? Fr.] perh. = CAPOTE 2.
1821 SCOTT *Kenilw.* xxxiii, She laid aside her travelling cloak and capotaine hat.

capo tasto (ˈkapo ˈtasto). *Mus.* Also **capodastro.** [It., lit. 'head stop'.] A device consisting of a bar or movable nut attached to the fingerboard of a stringed instrument for the purpose of raising the pitch of all the strings at once.
1876 STAINER & BARRETT *Dict. Mus. Terms* 75 The capo tasto, or capodastro as it is sometimes called, is screwed over the strings on to the finger-board and forms a temporary nut. **1879** GROVE *Dict. Mus.* I. 306/2 The construction of a capo tasto varies according to the stringing and shape of the neck of the instrument it is to be applied to. **1897** *Army & Navy Co-op. Soc. Price List*, Capodastros. **1961** C. BUNTING in A. Baines *Mus. Instr.* VI. iii. 141 The use of the thumb as a movable 'nut' (like the guitarist's *capotasto*).

capote (kəˈpəʊt). [a. F. *capote*, a fem. form, answering to *capot* masc., dim. of *cape* CAPE.]
1. a. A long shaggy cloak or overcoat with a hood, worn by soldiers, sailors, travellers, etc. **b.** A long mantle reaching to the feet, worn by women.
1812 BYRON *Ch. Har.* II. lii, The little shepherd in his white capote. **1836** W. IRVING *Astoria* I. 76 Emerging.. like spectres from the hatchways, in capotes and blankets. **1854** THACKERAY *Newcomes* II. 299 The ladies came down, pretty capotes on. **1857** EMERSON *Poems* 97 Frocks and blouses, capes, capotes. **1877** KINGLAKE *Crimea* VI. vi. 94 His troops in their sombre capotes.
2. A close-fitting hat of cap-like form.
1882 *Society* 14 Oct. 24/1 Some of the *capôtes* have had their dimensions reduced to such a degree as to attain merely the form of a skull-cap. **1886** *St. James's Gaz.* 25 Sept. 11/1 New bonnet and capote shapes.

†**caˈpouch.** *Obs.* A variant of CAPUCHE, a hood or cowl.
1592 CHETTLE *Kinde-Harts Dr.* (1841) 47 Conueying a massy sault vnder his capouch. **1656** BLOUNT *Glossogr.*, *Capouche*, a coul, hood or cover for the head. **1742** JARVIS *Quix.* I. IV. xxix. (1885) 171 He.. put on him a grey capouch. **1783** AINSWORTH *Lat. Dict.* (Morell) II, *Capitium*, as some say, a hood, a capouch.

capoun, obs. form of CAPON.

cappa (ˈkæpə). *Eccl.* [It.: see CAPE *sb.*[2]] A cloak (cf. CAPA); a cloak forming part of a religious habit; a cope.
1859 J. MORRIS *S. Thomas Becket* vii. 64 [S. Thomas of Canterbury] put on a black cappa, which was closed all round and reached his feet... The black cappa with lambs-wool.. was not the monastic habit of his monks of Christ Church. It was that of the Black Canons Regular, to which order Merton belonged. **1867** R. PALMER *Philip Howard* 15 In tropical climates where the cappa is less worn. **1923** *Glasgow Herald* 10 May 9 Camerlengos and attendants with the spada and cappa.

cappadine (ˈkæpədɪn, -diːn). [perhaps from CAPADE.] 'A sort of silk flock or waste obtained from the cocoon after the silk has been reeled off' (Simmonds *Dict. Trade* 1858).
1678 PHILLIPS, *Cappadine*, is a kind of Silk whereof the shagg of some kind of Ruggs is made. **1721** in BAILEY.

†**cappaˈdochio.** *Obs.* Also CAPERDEWSIE, -DOCHY, q.v. [Nares suggested 'a corruption of Cappadocia', of which country 'the king, says Horace, was rich in slaves, but had little money'. But this reason seems far-fetched.] 'A cant name for prison' (Nares); perhaps rather, the stocks.
1607 W. S. *Puritan* in *Supp. Shaks.* II. 510 (N.) How, captain Idle? my old aunts son, my dear kinsman, in Cappadochio?

Cappadocian (kæpəˈdəʊʃ(ɪ)ən), *a.* and *sb.* Also †**Capadocian.** [f. *Cappadocia*: see -AN.] **A.** *adj.* Of or pertaining to Cappadocia or its inhabitants. **B.** *sb.* **a.** An inhabitant of Cappadocia, an ancient kingdom of Asia Minor, now part of Turkey. **b.** The language of the Cappadocians.
1607 TOPSELL *Four-f. Beasts* 285 The Capadocians do breed of the Parthian horsses. *Ibid.* 286 The Cappadocian horsses are swift and lusty in their old age. **1762** STERNE *Tr. Shandy* V. xxvii. 98 The Phoenicians,—the Arabians,—the Capadocians.. did it. **1836** *Penny Cycl.* VI. 272/1 The Cappadocians were very generally known during the Roman occupation of their country for their unprincipled and vicious character. **1845** *Encycl. Metrop.* XIV. 253/1 The Cappadocian horses have been the theme of much deserved panegyric from the pens of several historians. **1876** *Encycl. Brit.* V. 74/2 In the time of Herodotus, the Cappadocians occupied the whole region from the chain of Mount Taurus on the south to the shores of the Euxine. **1934** A. TOYNBEE *Study of Hist.* II. 80 The Cappadocian Fathers of the Church. **1954** PEI & GAYNOR *Dict. Linguistics* 35 *Cappadocian*, an extinct language.. of undetermined linguistic affinities.. classified as Asianic.

Cappagh (ˈkæpə). A place near Cork, in Ireland; whence ***Cappagh*** or ***Cappah brown***, a brown pigment, consisting of a bituminous earth coloured by oxide of manganese and iron; manganese brown.
1875 URE *Dict. Arts* I. 896 Vandyke, Cappah.. and Cologne Browns.

cap-paper (ˈkæp,peɪpə(r)). [See below.]
1. A kind of wrapping paper: the precise application has apparently varied from time to time.
1577 *Richmond. Wills* (1853) 269, Vj quare of capp paper, xijd., xij quaire of paper. **1583** J. HIGINS *Junius' Nomenclator* 6 (N.) Packe paper or cap-paper, such paper as mercers.. use to wrappe their ware in. **1634** *Althorp MS.* in Simpkinson *Washingtons* Introd. 65, 4 quire of cappe paper to pack up yᵉ plate, 00 01 04. **1693** ROBERTSON *Phraseol. Gen.* 973 Cap paper or brown paper, wherein grocers wrap their ware. **1745** STUKELEY *Corr.* I. 371 Send it to me by the carrier, tyed up in a bit of cap-paper. *a* **1847** MRS. SHERWOOD *Lady of Manor* IV. xxiv. 92 She was offering to Henry a small parcel contained in cap-paper. **1877** E. PEACOCK *N.W. Linc. Gloss.* (E.D.S.) *Cap-paper*, a whity-brown, thin paper, such as milliners fold their wares in.
†**2.** Used as filter-paper. *Obs.*
1634 BATE *Myst. Nature & Art* 30 Strain them through a cap paper. **1667** BOYLE *Orig. Formes & Qual.*, Glasse Funnel lin'd with Cap-paper. **1704** J. HARRIS *Lex. Techn.* s.v. *Caustick*, Then filtrate through Cap-paper. **1788** WITHERING in *Phil. Trans.* LXXVIII. 321 Saturated with vegetable alkali it converted cap paper into touch paper.
3. A size or kind of writing paper.
1854 LANDOR *Lett. American* 52 Meanwhile on what cap-paper were employed the unseasoned crow-quills of the Continent! **1875** URE *Dict. Arts* III. 494. **1874** KNIGHT *Mech. Dict.*, *Cap-paper*, 1. a kind of writing paper. Ruled with blue lines, and folding on the back, it is foolscap; with red lines to form a margin on the left hand, and made to fold on the top, it is legal cap. 2. A size of paper from $7\frac{1}{2}$ × 12 to $8\frac{1}{2}$ × 14.
[Probably, senses 1 and 3 are quite distinct in origin. Sense 1 has been conjectured to have originated in the use to which the paper was put, as a 'cap' to hold groceries, or as the material for the paper caps of workmen. Sense 3 may have been named from the watermark of a cap, employed to indicate a certain size. Cf. also FOOLSCAP.]

†ˈ**cappard**, *a. Obs.* [Cf. CAPERATE.]
1653 PLAT *Gard. Eden* 110 A Peare.. graffed upon a white thorn will be small, hard, cappard, and spotted.

capparid (ˈkæpərɪd). *Bot.* [f. L. *capparis* the caper: see -ID.] A plant akin to the caper; one of the *Capparidaceæ.* So **cappariˈdaceous**, *a.*, of the natural order Capparidaceæ, of which the caper is the type. [*Capparidaceæ* is erroneously formed for *Capparaceæ.*]
1866 LIVINGSTONE *Jrnl.* xii. (1873) I. 316 A species of Capparidaceous fruit.

capped, capt (kæpt), *ppl. a.* [f. CAP *sb.* and *v.* + -ED.]
1. a. Provided with or wearing a cap, either as an article of dress, or of defensive armour.
c **1370** WYCLIF *Agst. Begg. Friers* (1608) 30 Capped Friars, that beene called Maisters of Divinitie. **1401** *Pol. Poems* (1859) II. 107 Aske thi cappid maistres. **1587** FULWELL *Like will to L.* in Hazl. *Dodsley* III. 321 Where learn'd you to stand capp'd before a judge? **1667** J. CHAMBERLAYNE *St. Gt. Brit.* I. III. x. (1743) 243 Anciently it was not permitted to any Subject to be so much as capped in presence of the King of England. **1859** JEPHSON *Brittany* xvi. 269 Crowds of white-capped laundresses.
b. Having a natural cap or head-covering.
1704 WORLIDGE *Dict. Rust. et Urb.* s.v. *Fishing Flies*, The Steel-Fly.. capt about with the Feathers of a Peacocks-tail. **1783** AINSWORTH *Lat. Dict.* (Morell) I. s.v. *Lark*, The capped, or chit, lark.
c. *fig.*
1856 R. VAUGHAN *Mystics* (1860) I. VI. i. 150 The friar.. went capped with the name of Brother Brimstone ever after.
2. a. Covered on the top as with a cap; crowned.
1610 SHAKS. *Temp.* IV. 152 The Clowd-capt Towres. **1665** BOYLE *Exp. Hist. Cold* xix. (R.) Savoy, and the neighbouring countries.. have mountains almost perpetually capped with snow. **1816** BYRON *Ch. Har.* III. lxxxvi, Darken'd Jura, whose capt heights appear Precipitously steep. **1878** HUXLEY *Physiogr.* 25 London clay capped by Lower Bagshot sand.
b. *fig.*
c **1605** MONTGOMERIE *Flyting* 624 Great fraud.. Cappit with quyet conceit. **1847** EMERSON *Repr. Men* iv. *Montaigne* Wks. (Bohn) I. 338 You are bottomed and capped and wrapped in delusions.
c. Having the surface caked or hardened into a crust. *dial.*
1750 W. ELLIS *Mod. Husbandm.* III. i. 78 (E.D.S.) When heavy rains presently succeed.. the surface is apt to become what we call capped. **1807** A. YOUNG *Agric. Essex* (1813) II. 89 He found the surface slightly bound (called here capt).
3. Fitted with a cap, as a ship's mast with protective covering, a loadstone with a piece of steel or magnetic iron, a fire-arm with a percussion cap.
1575 LANEHAM *Let.* (1871) 38 A payr of capped Sheffeld kniuez. **1613** M. RIDLEY *Magn. Bodies* 3 Artificially capped and armed with steele, or iron. **1667** H. OLDENBURG in *Phil. Trans.* II. 423 The two pieces [of Load-stone].. uncapped as well as capped. **1685** BOYLE *Effects of Mot.* iv. 38 The Load-stone vigorous.. and well capped. **1803** *Naval Chron.* IX. 329 All the lower and upper masts up, capped, rigged over head. **1887** *Times* (weekly ed.) 23 Sept. 4/2 The muzzle-loading rifle was also loaded and capped.
4. Of a horse's hocks: Having a swollen appearance, as if covered with a cap. Cf. CAPELET.
1831 YOUATT *Horse* xvii. (1847) 366 Capped Hock.. is seldom accompanied by lameness. *Ibid.* (1872) 392 A horse.. with a capped hock is regarded with a suspicious eye.
5. *dial.* Puzzled, beaten. Also, astonished, surprised. Cf. CAP *v.*[1] 4 b.
1862 C. C. ROBINSON *Dial. Leeds* 262 *Capt*, surprised; astonished. 'I wur capt to see him thear'—surprised. 'Fair capt'—clean astonished; as at the tricks of a juggler. **1866** J. SCHOLES in J. Harland *Lancashire Lyrics* 133 Aw'm capt' 'at folk wantin' to wed. **1876** F. K. ROBINSON *Gloss. Whitby* 32/1, I was sair capp'd te tell. **1959** J. AUSTWICK *Murder in Borough Library* xvii. 135 Just saw them disappearing into the wall. I was fair capped for a moment because I didn't know there was a door. **1967** 'S. WOODS' *And shame Devil* ii. 41 'Why should she have been lying?'.. 'Beats me. I was fair capped when they called her.'
6. capped quartz, a variety of crystallized quartz, embedded in a matrix of compact quartz.

capped, cappit, Sc. var. of COPPED, crabbed.

caˈppelenite. *Min.* A silico-borate of yttrium and barium, from Norway.
1886 *Amer. Jrnl. Science* Mar. 230 Cappelenite occurs in hexagonal crystals of a brown color.

cappeline, var. of CAPELINE.

capper (ˈkæpə(r)), *sb.*[1] Also 6 cappar. [f. CAP *sb.* and *v.* + -ER[1].]
†**1.** A capmaker. *Obs.*
1389 *Eng. Gilds* (1870) 12 Philippo atte Vyne, Cappere, ciui Londonie. **1488–9** *Act 4 Hen. VII*, ix, No hatter nor capper.. [shall] put to sell any hatte.. above the price of xxd. **1574** *Ludlow Churchw. Acc.* (Camden) 158 Richarde Philipes, capper. **1581** W. STAFFORD *Exam. Compl.* i. (1876) 14 He.. bryngeth wyth him.. a Capper of the same towne. **1677** YARRANTON *Engl. Improv.* 162 The benefit that may come.. to the Cappers of Bewdley. **1805** LUCOCK *Nat. Wool* 67 In the reign of Elizabeth the cappers made a violent struggle to counteract the trade of their rivals.
2. One who caps; in various senses of the verb.
1587 GOLDING *De Mornay* xviii. (1617) 320 A thousand flatterers, and as many crouchers and cappers. **1850** L. HUNT *Autobiog.* 100 An excellent capper of verses. **1876** *Mid-Yorksh. Gloss.* (E.D.S.) *Capper*, an extinguisher.
3. *dial.* A person or thing who 'caps' or 'beats' all others; a thing which 'beats' one's comprehension.

1790 Mrs. Wheeler *Westmld. Dial.* (1840) 13 Nea yan knas what it means, it's a capper. **1802** R. Anderson *Cumbld. Ball.* 52 Then at dancin, O he was a capper! **1868** E. Waugh in *Lanc. Gloss.* That's a capper of a tale, as heaw! **1877** *Holderness Gloss.* It's a capper wheear mah knife's gone teeah.

4. One who or that which caps: in various technical senses.

a **1884** Knight *Dict. Mech.* Suppl., *Capper*, a tool used in placing the priming cap on its seat in the rear end of the metallic shell. **1890** *Pall Mall Gaz.* 28 June 4/3 Employed by the prosecuting firm [of perfumers] as 'cappers'. **1921** *Dict. Occup. Terms* (1927) §138 *Glass capper*, cuts off glass as it leaves tubes of glass blowing machine. *Ibid.* §459 *Capper, bottle*,.. fixes a small paper, tin, or lead foil cover over corks of bottles. **1955** J. G. Davis *Dict. Dairying* (ed. 2) 90 A combined unit which fills the bottle and applies its own aluminium cap... A 20-head filler and 8-head capper.

5. An accomplice, esp. a confederate in a gambling game; a dummy bidder at an auction. *slang* (chiefly *U.S.*).

1753 J. Poulter *Discoveries* (ed. 2) 27 There is generally four Persons concerned, that is, the Sailor, call'd a Legg Cull, to pinch the Nobb; the next is the Capper, who always keeps with the Sailor. **1853** *Alta California* (San Francisco) 25 Apr. 1/7 A glib-mouthed auctioneer and at least two cappers, puffers, or decoy-ducks. **1872** Schele de Vere *Americanisms* 319 Cappers they ['strikers'] are called, when the game is the famous Three-Card Monte. **1926** J. Black *You can't Win* xiii. 184 His 'cappers', 'boosters', and 'shills' ..always beat them to the pieces of soap containing the money.

capper, Sc. var. of copper.

capper-: See caper-.

cappie ('kæpɪ). *Sc.* [dim. of cap *sb.*[3]]

1. A small drinking vessel.

1824 Scott *St. Ronan's* xiv, I think ye hae been at the wee cappie this morning.

2. 'A kind of beer between table-beer and ale, formerly drunk by the middling classes' (Jamieson).

capping ('kæpɪŋ), *vbl. sb.* [f. cap *v.*[1] + -ing[1].]

1. a. The action of the vb. cap in various senses.

1592 Greene *Groatsw. Wit* (1617) 3 Schollers..receiued (after long capping and reuerence) a sixepenny reward. **1602** *Return fr. Parnass.* i. iv. (Arb.) 17 Letts leaue this capping of rimes. **1717** De Foe *Hist. Ch. Scot.* ii. 45 The Bishop.. would have proved that Capping, or pulling off the Hat, and kneeling, were synonimous. **1863** Geo. Eliot *Romola* i. xvi. (1880) I. 225 To be swamped in the capping of impromptu verses. **1883** *Athenæum* 3 Nov. 564/1 A capping of the Cervantic with the Rabelaisian spirit. **1885** M. Pattison *Mem.* 57 In the thought of how I ought to perform my first act of 'capping' I omitted the ceremony altogether.

b. *spec.* The putting of a gun-cap upon a gun, etc. Also *attrib.*

1847 *Infantry Man.* (1854) 34 Bring the firelock down to the capping position. **1866** *Cornh. Mag.* Sept. 345 A capping system..entails a loss of not less than fifty per cent. in rapidity. **1881** Greener *Gun* 105 The best capping breech-loader ever invented.

c. The ceremony of conferring a University degree in Scotland. Also *N.Z.*

1905 *Westm. Gaz.* 28 Aug. 2/3 Sir Robert Stout.. announced at the last capping at Wellington that..if the students persisted in their senseless conduct there would be no more capping ceremonies in public. **1966** *Weekly News* (N.Z.) 27 Apr. 10/4 Invading students from Massey University did not have permission from the Auckland City Council to sell their capping magazine in Queen St.

d. The practice of taking a definite sum of money for a day's hunting from a non-subscriber to the hunt. (See cap *sb.*[1] 6.)

1890 *Pall Mall Gaz.* 26 Feb. 3/1 The proceeds of the capping should go to a damage fund. **1897** *Daily News* 16 Jan. 7/6 It has just been decided by the Hunt Committee to introduce the 'capping' system into the Quorn country next season.

2. Cap-making; the capper's trade.

1662 Fuller *Worthies, Wales* 49 Capping anciently set fifteen distinct Callings on work.

3. That with which anything is capped, covered at the top, or overlaid. *spec.* of honey or cells in a honeycomb.

1713 *Lond. & Country Brew.* iii. (1743) 207 Under its Capping of fresh Malt. **1792** *Phil. Trans.* LXXII. 374 The upper plate of lead which served as a capping to the junction of the hip with the ridge of the roof. **1832** De la Beche *Geol. Man.* 409 It is here without that great capping of the oolitic group. **1850** Leitch tr. *Müller's Anc. Art* 316 A truncated pillar..with base and capping. **1878** Huxley *Physiogr.* 25 The capping of sand..of insignificant thickness. **1934** in Webster. **1950** *N.Z. Jrnl. Agric.* Jan. 27/2 When drained free of surplus honey, wax cappings [of cells] should not be thrown away.

4. *attrib.* and *Comb.*, as ***capping-sheaf, -stone***; **capping-leather**, leather from which the upper leather of a shoe is made; **capping-plane** (*Joinery*), a plane for working the upper surface of the balustrade on a staircase; **capping-woollen**, woollen stuff for cap-making.

1641 Best *Farm. Bks.* (1856) 142 *Cappinge leather is soe deare. **1877** E. Peacock *N.W. Linc. Gloss.* (E.D.S.) **Capping-sheaves*, the hood-sheaves of a 'stook' of corn. **Capping-stones*, the coping stones of a wall or other building. **1555** *Fardle Facions* ii. ix. 198 Rounde about these sparres thei straine *cappyng wollen.

capping ('kæpɪŋ), *ppl. a.* [f. cap *v.*[1] + -ing[2].] That caps, that makes an obeisance.

1602 Breton *Mother's Bless.* lxii. (D.) A smoothing tongue, a capping knee.

‖**cappuccino** (kapput'tʃino). [It., see Capuchin.] Coffee with milk; white coffee, esp. as served in espresso coffee-bars, topped with white foam. Also, a cup of such coffee.

1948 R. O'Brien *This is San Francisco* 84 You drink a *cappuccino*, gray, like the robe of a capuchin monk, and made of chocolate that is laced with brandy or rum, and heated by steam forced through coffee. **1955** *Archit. Rev.* Sept. 166 Do you think I dare say cappucino? **1959** C. MacInnes *Absolute Beginners* 17 She blew a little brown nest in the white froth of her *cappuccino.* **1960** *Guardian* 25 Mar. 16/6 The first meal in a café should be a cappuccino or two and a dry roll or bun.

cappuce, obs. form of capuche.

cappy ('kæpɪ), *a.* [f. cap *sb.* + -y[1].] Characterized by a cap; like a cap.

1865 *Sat. Rev.* 24 June 758/1 Hairless and cappy age. **1865** Mrs. Whitney *Gayworthys* i. 10 Cappy headdress.

†'**cappy-hole.** *Sc.* Also **capie-hole, coppihool, coppiehoall.** A school-boys' game, in which the object is to throw a marble into a hole.

1605 *Session Rec. Ayr* 24 Mar., To summon Thomas Smal for playing at yᵉ coppihool in the Kirk-door. *c* **1675** A. Peden *Lord's Trump.* (Jam.) Adam played it [his stock] at the Capie-hole one morning with the Devil at two or three throws at the game. **1722** *Life Sc. Rogue* 7 in Brand *Pop. Antiq.* (1870) II. 304, I was..readier at..Cappy Hole than at my Book.

caprate ('kæpreɪt). *Chem.* [f. capr-ic + -ate[4].] A salt of capric acid.

1836 *Penny Cycl.* VI. 273/1 In order to procure capric acid, caprate of barytes is first obtained. **1863–79** Watts *Dict. Chem.* I. 742 The caprates are mostly difficultly soluble in water.

capreall, capreol, obs. forms of capriole.

caprel, corruption of capriole.

†'**capreol(e.** *Obs.* [ad. L. *capreolus* (in same senses), dim. of *capreus* roe, f. *caper* goat.]

1. A kind of deer; a roebuck or variety of it.

1655 Moufet & Benn. *Health's Improv.* (1746) 155 Of all Venison, Roebuck and Capreol beareth away the Bell.

2. A tendril. [Cf. It. *capriolo.*]

1578 Lyte *Dodoens* v. xxx. 589 A kind of Cucumber..full of Capreoles or clasping tendrelles. **1725** Bradley *Fam. Dict.* II. s.v. *Sallet*, The Capreols, Tendrels and Claspers of Vines.

capreolate ('kæpriːəleɪt, kə'priːəleɪt), *a. Bot.* [ad. L. **capreolāt-us* (cf. *capreolātim*), f. *capreolus*: see capreol.] Furnished with tendrils.

1737–59 Miller *Gard. Dict.*, *Capreolate plants*..such plants as twist and climb upon others, by means of Tendrils. **1880** Gray *Bot. Text-bk.* 401 *Capréolate*, bearing a tendril.

capreoline (kə'priːəlaɪn), *a. Zool.* [f. L. *capreol-us* roebuck + -ine.] Of or belonging to the genus Capreolus of Cervidæ.

1835 Swainson *Quadrupeds* §299 The Capreoline group is formed to contain the roebucks.

capres, obs. form of caper *sb.*[1]

†**capret.** *Obs.* [Cf. It. *capretto*, *capretta* kid, fawn, dim. of *capro*, *capra* goat: in Fr. *chevret*, *chevrette*. (Perh. in med.L.)] A roe.

1382 Wyclif *Deut.* xii. 15 As capret and hert thow shalt eete. —— *2 Sam.* ii. 18 Ceertis Asahel was a moost swift renner, as oon of the caprettis that dwellen in wodis.

†**ca'prettie.** *obs. rare*[−1]. [Some corruption of F. *capriot* or It. *capriccio*, or irreg. formation from caper.] A fantastic motion of some kind.

1575 Laneham *Let.* (1871) 18 By an Italian, such feats of agilitiee..gambaud, soomersauts, caprettiez and flights.

Capri (kæ'priː). [Name of an island in the Bay of Naples.] **1.** Any of various wines produced originally in Capri. Cf. caprik(e.

1877 E. S. Dallas *Kettner's Bk. of Table* 482 Some of the Italian white wines—as White Capri, or White Lachryma Christi—would do as well. **1890** Kipling *Life's Handicap* (1891) 209 Raw, rasping Capri with all the strength of whisky. **1961** B. Malamud *New Life* (1962) 137 George, the fine waiter, served..manchiego cheese and some dry white capri, iced in buckets.

2. ***Capri pants***: women's close-fitting trousers with tapering legs, reaching to just above the ankle. Also *ellipt.* as *Capris*. orig. *U.S.*

1956 *Amer. Speech* XXXI. 307 *Capri pants*, pants tapered to just above the ankle. **1966** H. Nielsen *After Midnight* (1967) i. 12 The shrieking pink Capris and the wild silver blonde hair-do. **1967** P. McGerr *Murder is Absurd* ix. 113 He appraised the high-necked sweater and capri pants. **1969** R. Airth *Snatch!* iv. 31 She was wearing capris, green and tight.

capric ('kæprɪk), *a.* [f. L. *caper*, *capr-um* goat + -ic. Cf. F. *caprique*.]

1. Of or belonging to a goat (*nonce-use*).

1881 *Academy* No. 491. 252 Capric and porcine flesh.

2. *Chem.* **a.** ***capric acid*** ($C_{10}H_{20}O_2$), a fatty acid obtained from butter, cocoa-nut oil, fusel oil, etc.: a colourless crystalline body, having a slight odour of the goat. Otherwise known as *rutic acid*, the name preferred by various chemists, who would apply *capric* to what is otherwise called *caprylic*. (Formerly sometimes *caprinic acid*).

1836 *Penny Cycl.* VI. 273/1 Capric acid crystallizes in small needles. **1853** F. Hall in *Ledlie's Misc.* II. 183 The odour in question..may possibly be influenced by the formation of capric acid, a much more pungent substance than the caproic acid of the fair subject.

b. ***capric series***: the series of chemical compounds allied to capric acid, as *capric aldehyde*, etc.

From same source '**capramide**, the primary amide of capric acid (formerly called '**caprinˌmide**). '**caprone**, the ketone of the capric series. Also caprate, capryl, q.v.

‖**capriccio** (ka'prittʃo). Also 7 **caprichio, capritio**, 7–8 **capricio.** [a. It. *capriccio* sudden start, motion, or freak, app. f. *capro* goat, as if 'the skip or frisk of a goat' (in Sp. *capricho*):—L. type **capriceus*. (For the sense cf. capriole.)]

1. A sudden sportive or fantastic motion; a prank, trick, caper.

1665 Glanvill *Sceps. Sci.* Addr. 16 The shifts, windings, and unexpected Caprichios of distressed Nature. **1693** Bentley *Atheism, Boyle Lect.* v. 9 All the various Machins and Utensils would now and then play odd Pranks and Capricio's quite contrary to their proper Structures. **1761** Sterne *Tr. Shandy* (1802) I. xxiii. 117 To have..viewed the soul stark naked, watched her loose in her frisks, her gambols, her capricios. **1823** Lamb *Elia* Ser. ii. v. (1865) 267 Magnificent were thy capriccios on this globe of earth, Robert William Elliston!

†**2.** = caprice 1. *Obs.*

1601 Shaks. *All's Well* ii. iii. 310 Will this Caprichio hold in thee, art sure? *a* **1634** Chapman *To Pan*, In quite oppos'de capriccios. **1686** W. de Britaine *Hum. Prud.* §xx. 92 The Capricio's of Fortune. **1690** Locke *Hum. Und.* iv. xvi. §11 A thousand odd Reasons, or Caprichio's, Men's Minds are acted by. **1794** Mathias *Purs. Lit.* (1798) 379 Another little capriccio of..the late Adam Smith. **1824** Scott *Redgauntlet* Let. v, Folks who..partake of their fantastic capriccios.

3. A thing or work of fancy; = caprice 2.

1678 Cudworth *Intell. Syst.* i. iii, [They] look upon the plastick life of nature as a figment or phantastick Capritio. **1824** Heber *Jrnl.* (ed. 2) II. xxi. 353 It is a mere capriccio, with no merit except its carving. **1873** Symonds *Grk. Poets* xi. 390 These exquisite little capricci, engraved by Greek artists upon gems.

b. *Music.* A name variously applied (see Grove s.v.) but usually denoting a composition of lively character, and more or less free in form.

1696 Phillips, *Capriccio's* are pieces of Music, Poetry, and Painting, wherein the force of Imagination has better success than observation of the Rules of Art. **1789** Wolcott (P. Pindar) *Subj. Painters* 42 Still is that voice, of late so strong, That many a sweet Capriccio sung. **1845** E. Holmes *Mozart* 155 This is not a prelude..but a capriccio to try a piano. **1882** Statham in Grove *Dict. Mus.* I. 225/1 His next published work, the 'Capriccio in D minor'.

‖**capriccioso** (kaprit'tʃoso), *a. Music.* [It., f. *capriccio* + *-oso* = -ous.] A direction in music to denote a free fantastic style.

caprice (kə'priːs). [a. (after 1660) F. *caprice*, It. *capriccio*: see capriccio, and caprich, which both preceded this. About 1700 '*caprice* was a usual accentuation; Pope rimed the word with *vice*.]

1. A sudden change or turn of the mind without apparent or adequate motive; a desire or opinion arbitrarily or fantastically formed; a freak, whim, mere fancy.

1667 G. Digby *Elvira* v. in Hazl. *Dodsley* XV. 82 Dependent on the wild caprice of others. **1673** Dryden *Marr. à la Mode* iv. iv, *Rho.* Now I have the oddest thought ..*Melan.* This is the strangest caprice in you. **1727** Swift *Gulliver* iii. ii. 192 The caprices of woman-kind are not limited by climate or nation. **1732** Pope *Ess. Man* ii. 239 That counter-works each folly and caprice; That disappoints th' effect of ev'ry vice. **1776** Adam Smith *W.N.* I. ii. i. x. 146 He was liable to be removed..at the caprice of any church-warden. **1856** Froude *Hist. Eng.* (1858) I. ii. 120 The restraint which ordinary persons..are able to impose on their caprices.

b. The disposition of a mind subject to such humours; capriciousness.

1709 Pope *Ess. Crit.* 287 Critics of less judgment than caprice. **1712** Addison *Spect.* No. 435 §1 The Folly, Extravagance, and Caprice of the present Age. **1728** Young *Love Fame* vii. 161 Say, Britain! whence this caprice of thy sons? **1855** Macaulay *Hist. Eng.* IV. 433 There was something appalling in the union of such boundless power and such boundless caprice.

c. *transf.* of things.

1748 *Anson's Voy.* ii. ii. (ed. 2) 178 The vessel..left to the caprice of the winds and waves. **1793** T. Beddoes *Catarrh* 150 This caprice of our climate. **1867** Freeman *Norm. Conq.* (1876) I. iii. 136 By a caprice of language.

2. A work of irregular and sportive fancy.

1721 Bailey, *Caprichio, Caprice*..also a particular Piece of Musick, Painting and Poetry. **1838** Hallam *Hist. Lit.* I. i. iii. §82. 199 Extravagant combinations of fancy, caprices

rapid and sportive as the animal from which they take their name.

b. *Music.* = CAPRICCIO 3 b.

1880 E. PROUT in Grove *Dict. Mus.* s.v. *Capriccio*, In the present day the word Caprice is usually.. applied to a piece of music constructed either on original subjects, and frequently in a modified sonata- or rondo-form (as in Mendelssohn's 'Three Caprices,' op. 33, or Sterndale Bennett's Caprice in E), or to a brilliant transcription of one or more subjects by other composers.

3. A kind of scarf so called.

1838 *Workwoman's Guide*, A kind of scarf made of broad ribbon, and called a caprice.

† **'capricerve.** *Obs. rare*⁻¹. [ad. mod.L. *capricerva* the antelope, f. *capra* she-goat + *cerva* hind.] The antelope.

1661 LOVELL *Hist. Anim. & Min.* 28 Capricerve.. The flesh of the last is not very pleasant.

† **ca'prich.** *Obs.* [ad. It. *capriccio*: see above. This adapted form of the It. preceded the adoption of F. *caprice.*] = CAPRICCIO, CAPRICE.

1656 BLOUNT *Glossogr.*, *Caprichio, Caprich*, an humour, fancy, toy in ones head, a giddy thought. **1664** BUTLER *Hud.* II. i. 18 Till drawing blood o' th' Dames, like Witches Th' are forthwith cur'd of their Capriches. **1698** S. CLARK *Script.-Just.* Introd. B ij, If once we give way to the Caprich, Luxury and intemperance of a wanton Fancy herein.

caprichio, capricio, obs. ff. CAPRICCIO.

capricious (kəˈprɪʃəs), *a.* Also 7 **-ichious, -itious.** [ad. F. *capricieux*, ad. It. *capriccioso* (= Sp. *caprichoso*): see above. The by-form *caprichious* belongs to the corresp. forms of the sb.]

† **1.** Characterized by play of wit or fancy; humorous, fantastic, 'conceited'. *Obs.*

1594 CAREW *Huarte's Exam. Wits* 153 (L.) The inventive wits are termed in the Tuscan tongue capricious (capriciuso) for the resemblance they bear to a goat, who takes no pleasure in the open and easy plains, but loves to caper along the hill-tops. **1600** SHAKS. *A.Y.L.* III. iii. 8, I am heere with thee, and thy Goats, as the most capricious Poet honest Ouid was among the Gothes. **1710** SHAFTESB. *Charac.* (1737) III. 142 The capricious Point, and Play of Words.

2. Full of, subject to, or characterized by caprice; guided by whim or fancy rather than by judgement or settled purpose; whimsical, humoursome.

1605 CAMDEN *Rem.* 57 A friend of his that knew him to be Caprichious. **1644** *Eng. Tears* in *Harl. Misc.* (Malh.) V. 450 The monstrous exorbitant liberty, that almost every capricious mechanick takes to himself. **1753** JOHNSON *Adventurer* No. 111 ¶6 Our estimation of birth is arbitrary and capricious. **1833** J. RENNIE *Alph. Angling* 49 We have known the salmon.. so capricious as often to prefer a fancy fly. **1884** *Law Times Rep.* 10 May 325/1 The defendants' refusal was not capricious, but a bonâ fide exercise of their judgment.

3. *transf.* Of things: Subject to change or irregularity, so as to appear ungoverned by law.

1823 LAMB *Elia* Ser. II. vii. (1865) 283 The capricious hues of the sea, shifting like the colours of a dying mullet. **1830** LYELL *Princ. Geol.* (1875) II. II. xlix. 617 The capricious distribution of coral reefs. **1874** HELPS *Soc. Press.* vi. 75 The vicissitudes of a capricious climate. **1875** TAIT & STEWART *Unseen Univ.* iv. §118 To give to the atoms a perfectly arbitrary and capricious side movement.

capriciously (kəˈprɪʃəslɪ), *adv.* [f. prec. + -LY².] In a capricious manner, according to caprice: arbitrarily.

1746 HERVEY *Medit.* (1818) 23 One is tempted to exclaim against the King of Terrors, and call him capriciously cruel. **1771** *Junius Lett.* xlviii. 250 A power arbitrarily assumed, and capriciously applied. **1853** KANE *Grinnell Exp.* xxvi. (1856) 217 This ice-opening was instructive.. because it taught.. us.. how capriciously insecure was our position. **1869** FREEMAN *Norm. Conq.* (1876) II. App. 663 How capriciously Scottish and Northumbrian affairs are entered or not entered in our national annals.

capriciousness (kəˈprɪʃəsnɪs). Also 7 **caprichiousness(e, caprytchyousnes.** [f. as prec. + -NESS.] The quality of being capricious.

1617 MARKHAM *Caval.* II. 53 Inuented.. to showe caprytchyousnes of cunning mens braines. **1671** DRYDEN *Evening's Love* IV. i, You have a just Exception against the Caprichiousness of Destiny. **1752** FIELDING *Amelia* IV. v, From nothing better than a capriciousness in his friend's temper. **1828** D'ISRAELI *Chas. I*, I. xi. 301 The capriciousness of popular favour. **1863** GEO. ELIOT *Romola* vi, I.. marvel at the capriciousness of my daughter's memory.

Capricorn (ˈkæprɪkɔːn). [a. F. *capricorne* or ad. L. *capricornus* 'goat-horned' (the Zodiacal sign), f. *caper, capr-um* goat + *cornu* horn; cf. Gr. αἰγόκερως. The Latin form also is common in English books in sense 1.]

1. *Astron.* **a.** The Zodiacal constellation of the He-Goat, lying between Sagittarius and Aquarius. **b.** The tenth of the twelve signs of the Zodiac, beginning at the most southerly point of the ecliptic or winter solstitial point, which the sun enters about the 21st of December. ***Tropic of Capricorn***: the southern Tropic forming a tangent to the ecliptic at the first point of Capricorn.

c **1391** CHAUCER *Astrol.* I. §17 Wiche declinacioun.. is 23 degrees & 50 Minutes, as wel in cancer as in Capricorne. **1430** LYDG. *Chron. Troy* Prol., Whose lordshyp cheifest is in Capricorne. **1509** HAWES *Past. Pleas.* XXXIII. i. (1845) 161 Whan golden Phebus in the Capricorne Gan to ascend fast unto Aquary. **1595** J. DAVIS *Seamans Secr.* II. 5 What is the Tropick of Capricorn? **1667** MILTON *P.L.* x. 677 As deep as Capricorne. **1687** DRYDEN *Hind & P.* III. 598 That very morn The Sun was entered into Capricorn. **1833** [see CANCER 2]. **1867** DENISON *Astron. without Math.* 37 The tropic of Capricorn, which the sun reaches in our winter and the southern midsummer.

c. *Astrol.* A person born under the sign of Capricorn. Also *attrib.* or as *adj.*

1894 E. KIRK *Influence of Zodiac upon Human Life* xvi. 130 Capricorn people resent all interference, and never meddle with the affairs of others. **1936** 'J. TEY' *Shilling for Candles* xix. 206 Capricorn people are often melancholic. **1958** *20th Cent.* Aug. 153 A horoscope.. tells Emma that this week, if her man is an Aquarius.. 'Be patient and subtle'; if he is an Aries, '.. guide his enthusiasm..' and if a Capricorn, 'Use a little diplomacy.' **1970** D. GILMAN *Amazing Mrs Pollifax* (1971) iii. 27 Colin's Capricorn.. that's why he's so inherently precise. **1977** *Rolling Stone* 30 June 73/2 At her kitchen table, we talk about being Capricorns and being pigeonholed in all the astrology books as humorless.

† **2.** A 'goat-horned' animal; ? a chamois. *Obs.*

1646 EVELYN *Diary* (Chandos) 189 He shew'd two heads and hornes of the true capricorne, which animal he told us was frequently kill'd among the mountaines.

3. ***capricorn beetle***: a name given to beetles of the genus Cerambyx.

1700 KING *Transactioneer* 18 A Scarlet Butterfly, an Ash-coloured Capricorn. **1781** SMEATHMAN in *Phil. Trans.* LXXI. 168 *note*, The Caterpillar of a large Capricorn Beetle, or Goat Chafer. **1828** KIRBY & SP. *Entomol.* IV. xlix. 517 In the wood itself may be found the Anobidæ and the Capricorn beetles.

¶ ? Humorously used for *capriccio*, with a reference to *horn* (as in next verb).

1612 CHAPMAN *Widows T.* in *Dodsley* (1780) VI. 183 Have you no other Capricorns in your head, to entrap my sister in her frailty.

† **'capricorn,** *v. Obs. rare*⁻¹. [f. prec. sb.] *trans.* To fit with (goat's) horns; to horn.

1665 R. B. *Comment. 2 Tales* 85 A wily Wench there was .. Who us'd to Capricorn her Husband's head.

Capricornian (kæprɪˈkɔːnɪən). *Astrol.* [f. CAPRICORN + -IAN.] = CAPRICORN 1 c.

1901 M. MAYO *Our Fate & Zodiac* 129 The heirs of Virgo or Pisces.. will make but a few demands upon the affectional impulses of these cold dignified Capricorians [*sic*]. **1911** I. M. PAGAN *From Pioneer to Poet* x. 161 Capricornians are said to attain their best period between the ages of fifty-six and seventy. **1970** 'D. HALLIDAY' *Dolly & Cookie Bird* iv. 60 Lord Luck.. said that Capricornians would find that a discussion.. had restored all their confidence. **1984** *Observer* 11 Mar. 12/7 Capricornians (22 December–20 January) are given an encouraging forecast for 1984.

† **capri'cornify,** *v. Obs. rare*⁻¹. [f. CAPRICORN + -FY.] = CAPRICORN *v.*

1611 CORYAT *Crudities* (1776) 40 So consequently they should be capricornified.

capri'cornity. *nonce-wd.* [f. as prec. + -ITY.] Goat-horned or he-goat quality.

1837 *Fraser's Mag.* XV. 227 Billy [a goat], as if perceiving some indefinite symptoms of capricornity about him.

caprid (ˈkæprɪd), *a. Zool.* [f. mod.L. *caprid-æ*, f. *caper* goat: see -ID.] Of or belonging to the Capridæ or goat tribe.

1864 in WEBSTER.

ca'prificate, *v.* [f. L. *caprificāre*; see next and -ATE³.] *trans.* To ripen by caprification.

(In mod. Dicts.)

caprification (ˌkæprɪfɪˈkeɪʃən). [ad. L. *caprificātiōn-em*, n. of action f. *caprificāre* 'to ripen figs by the stinging of the gall-insect', f. *caprificus* the wild fig-tree (f. *caper, capr-um* goat + *ficus* fig-tree, fig).]

1. A process resorted to for ripening figs by means of the puncture of insects produced on the wild fig (*Caprificus*), or by puncturing them artificially.

'According to the investigations of modern science, it is proved to be not only unnecessary but positively injurious.' (R. Thompson in *Treas. Bot.*)

1601 HOLLAND *Pliny* I. 545 As touching the ripening of Figges by Caprification, true it is, that there be certain flies like gnats engender in greene figs, which are the occasion thereof. **1751** *Phil. Trans.* XLVII. 171 The effects of caprification in fig-trees. **1794–6** E. DARWIN *Zoon.* (1802) II. 411 Caprification, or the piercing of figs in the island of Malta, is said to ripen them sooner. **1835** LINDLEY *Introd. Bot.* (1848) II. 217 Causes so essentially different as fertilisation and caprification. **1870** A. L. ADAMS *Nile V. & Malta* 107 The Maltese practice caprification extensively, by attaching the fruit of the wild fig by strings to the branches of the domesticated trees.

¶ **2.** Erroneously used for: Artificial fertilization.

1836 *Penny Cycl.* VI. 273 This kind of caprification.. practised with the date palm, and which has been mentioned by Herodotus. **1859** R. BURTON *Centr. Afr.* in *Jrnl. R.G.S.* XXIX. 368 §2 Bees.. performing an important part.. by masculation or caprification, and the conveyance of pollen. **1879** *Cassell's Techn. Educ.* I. 243/2 An artificial means of ensuring fertilisation.. a small feather is inserted and turned round in the cavity. This operation is called caprification.

† **'caprifig.** *Obs. rare*⁻¹. [ad. L. *caprific-us*: cf. F. *caprifiguier*; see CAPRIFY.] The wild fig.

c **1420** *Pallad. on Husb.* IV. 589 Sum men sette amonge hem caprifige Tree that it nede not for remedie To honge on every tree that trees fige. **1866** *Treas. Bot.* 492 A wild sort called the Caprifig.

caprifoil (ˌkæprɪfɔɪl). Also 6 **caprifole, -foly.** [ad. med.L. *caprifolium* 'goat-leaf' or honeysuckle; cf. It. *caprifoglio*, F. *chèvrefeuille.*] **a.** Old name for the Honeysuckle or Woodbine; **b.** English name for plants of the N.O. *Caprifoliaceæ*, including the honeysuckle.

1578 LYTE *Dodoens* III. li. 391 Called.. in Englishe Honysuckle, or Woodbine, and of some Caprifoyle. **1596** SPENSER *F.Q.* III. vi. 44 Eglantine and Caprifole emong. **1597** GERARD *Herbal* II. cccxxviii. 891 Called in English Honisuckle and Caprifoly. **1678** PHILLIPS, *Caprifoile.* **1849** JOHNS *Forest Trees* II. 440 Caprifoils, *Caprifoliaceæ*.

caprifoliaceous (ˌkæprɪˌfəʊlɪˈeɪʃəs), *a. Bot.* [see -OUS; cf. F. *caprifoliacé.*] Belonging to the N.O. *Caprifoliaceæ* (see prec.).

1852 TH. ROSS *Humboldt's Trav.* I. vi. 212 The family of the honeysuckle, or caprifoliaceous plants.

capriform (ˈkæprɪfɔːm), *a.* [f. L. *caper, capr(i)*-goat + -FORM.] Goat-shaped.

1847 in CRAIG. **1847** CARPENTER *Zool.* §267 The Capriform Antelopes are more widely diffused.

† **'caprify,** *v. Obs. rare*⁻¹. [f. L. *caprificāre*: on the analogy of vbs. in *-ficāre* see -FY.] To ripen by caprification.

c **1420** *Pallad. on Husb.* IV. 592 In Juyn, as sonne is hiest, to caprifie The fig-tree is, that is to signifie The figges grene of caprifigtree rende With tree made like a sawe on hem suspende.

caprigenous (kəˈprɪdʒɪnəs), *a.* [f. L. *caprigen-us* (f. *capr(i)*- goat + *-genus* produced by, of the kind of) + -OUS.] Produced by a goat; of the goat kind.

1731 in BAILEY vol. II; and in mod. Dicts.

† **'caprik(e.** *Obs.* Also 6 **capryck, caperik.** A kind of wine.

c **1460** J. RUSSELL *Bk. Nurture* 120 in *Babees Bk.* (1868) 125 Greke, Malevesyn, Caprik, & Clarey. **1514** BARCLAY *Cyt. & Uplondyshm.* 36 Muscadell, Caprike, Romney, and Malvesy. **1587** HARRISON *England* II. vi. (1877) I. 149 Caprike, Clareie, and Malmesie.

† **'capril.** *Obs.* [cf. CAPREOLE.] ? A wild goat.

1514 *Exam. Cokeye More* 15 in *Chetham Misc.* II. Sum caprils of Redclyf yᵗ were wyld and wold not be dryven.

caprine (ˈkæpraɪn, -ɪn), *a.* [ad. L. *caprīn-us*, f. *caper* goat; cf. F. *caprin.*] Of or pertaining to a goat; goat-like.

1607 TOPSELL *Four-f. Beasts* (1673) 228 These eyes.. their colour varieth as it doth in Men, according to the caprine and glazie humour. **1660** GAUDEN *Brounrig* 236 That which in their Physiognomy is canine, vulpine, caprine. **1824** J. MᶜCULLOCH *Highl. Scotl.* II. 310 The Caprine population has undergone the same revolution. **1847** CARPENTER *Zool.* §267 Other Caprine Antelopes (often designated as Goats) are found in Asia.

capring, -ly, obs. ff. CAPERING, -LY.

ca'prinic, *a. Chem.* [f. L. *caprīn-us* of a goat, CAPRINE + -IC.] In ***caprinic acid***: an older name for CAPRIC acid.

c **1865** J. WYLDE in *Circ. Sc.* I. 333/2.

[**capriny,** ? mispr. for CAPRING.

a **1687** C. COTTON *Æneid* II. *Burlesqued* Pref., As frolicksome as a capriny Monsieur.]

capriole (ˈkæprɪəʊl), *sb.* Also 6 **capreall,** 7 **capreol, caprioll(e, (caprel),** 7–8 **capriol.** [a. F. *capriole* (now *cabriole*) 'a caper', or ad. It. *capriola* 'a fawn, a kid, a young hind; also, a capriole or caper in dancing, also a Capriole or Goat's leap that cunning riders teach their horses' (Florio), dim. of *capra* she-goat:—L. *capra*: cf. *caprea, capreolus*, applied to wild goats, etc.]

1. A leap or caper, as in dancing.

1594 DAVIES *Orchestra* in Arb. *Garner* V. 40 With lofty turns and caprioles in the air. **1630** B. JONSON *Chloridia* Wks. (1692) 657/2 Ixion.. does nothing but cut capreols, fetch friskals, and lead lavoltaes with the Lamiæ. **1760** FOOTE *Minor* I. (1781) 15 Italy [has] equip'd him with capriols and cantatas. **1832–4** DE QUINCEY *Caesars* (1862) IX. 107 All possible evolutions of caprioles and pirouettes. *fig.* **1599** MARSTON *Sco. Villanie* III. ii. 225 His heeles doe caper.. His very soule, his intellectual Is nothing but a mincing capreall. *a* **1670** HACKET *Cent. Serm.* (1675) 326 In the Capreols of our own fancy. **1852** HAWTHORNE *Blithedale Rom.* ix, Permitting no caprioles of fancy.

2. *Horsemanship.* A high leap made by a horse without advancing, the hind legs being jerked out together at the height of the leap.

c **1605** MONTGOMERIE *Flyting* 509 While ky kest caprels behind with their heeles. **1617** MARKHAM *Caval.* II. 239 That sault which.. Italians call Caprioll, and wee heere in England the Goates leape. *a* **1634** RANDOLPH *Poems*, Thy Pegasus, in his admir'd careere Curvets no capreols in nonsence here. **1814** SCOTT *Wav.* viii, The occasional caprioles which his charger exhibited. **1884** E. L. ANDERSON

Horsemanship II. xvii. 153 The Capriole, the most vigorous of all the school movements.

3. A kind of head-dress worn by ladies.

1756 *Connoisseur* No. 112 (1774) IV. 58 The milliner told me..that the name of this ornament..was a Capriole or Cabriole. **1864** in WEBSTER.

capriole ('kæprɪəʊl), *v.* [f. prec. sb., or directly from It. *capriolare* 'to caper, to capriole' (Florio).] *intr.* To leap, skip, caper. Also said of horses (and their riders); and *fig.*

1580 SIDNEY, etc. *Ps.* cxiv. (R.) Hillocks, why capreold ye, as wanton by their dammes We capreoll see the lusty lambs. **1690** CROWNE *Eng. Frier* III. 20 If you had been starv'd you wou'd not have caprioll'd with your witty conceits. **1788** DIBDIN *Mus. Tour* xc. 365 Leap, skip, and pound would poor Ap Hugh, And capriole, and caper too. **1837** CARLYLE *Fr. Rev.* (1857) I. I. VII. x. 220 Rascality, caprioling on horses from the Royal Stud.

Hence **capri'oling** *vbl. sb.* and *ppl. a.*

1628 LE GRYS tr. *Barclay's Argenis* 41 To have their stables full..of capreoling Horses. **1821** DE QUINCEY *Wks.* (1863) XIII. 121 The wild..dancing, waltzing, caprioling..of the chamois. **1824** SCOTT *Redgauntlet* let. xii, In the midst of her exuberant caprioling.

capriole, obs. var. of CAPREOLE.

†**'caprious**, *a. Obs. rare*$^{-1}$. (See quot.)

1623 COCKERAM, *Caprious*, a goatish desire, lustfull.

'capriped, *a.* (and *sb.*) [ad. L. *capripēs, -pedem*, f. *caper, capr(i)-* goat + *pēs* foot.] Goat-footed. Also as *sb.*

1730–6 BAILEY, *Capripede*; and in mod. Dicts. **1916** E. POUND *Lustra* 46 And what, pray, do you know about horticulture, you capriped? **1925** A. HUXLEY *Those Barren Leaves* I. iv. 46 I'm nothing but an old capripede.

capritio, -ious, obs. ff. CAPRICCIO, CAPRICIOUS.

'caprizant, *a. Med.* [ad. medical L. *caprizāns* (*pulsus*), f. *caper* goat.] Of the pulse: 'Bounding', uneven in motion.

1730–6 BAILEY; and in mod. Dicts.

'caprizate, *v. Med.* [cf. prec.] 'To leap like a goat; a term applied to the pulse' (Crabb *Techn. Dict.* 1823).

caproic (kə'prəʊɪk), *a. Chem.* [f. L. *caper, capr-* goat (from its smell) + *-oic*, -IC; in form purposely varied from CAPRIC, with which it is associated. *Capronic* was another form used by some.]

1. *caproic acid*: a peculiar acid found along with the capric and butyric acids in butter, etc; chemically also called ***normal caproic*** or *pentylformic acid*; this and ***iso-caproic*** or *isopentylformic acid* being forms of the hexoic acids ($C_6H_{12}O_2$), the monatomic monobasic or fatty acids of the hexyl series.

1839–47 TODD *Cycl. Anat.* III. 359/1 The butyric, caproic, and capric acids. **1873** WATTS *Fownes' Chem.* 686 Caproic Acid is produced by the action of alkalis on amyl cyanide.

2. *caproic series*: the series of chemical compounds allied to caproic acid, or containing the radical caproyl; as *caproic alcohol, caproic aldehyde, caproic ethers*, etc.

From same source **'caproate**, a salt of caproic acid. **'caproone**, the ketone of the caproic series. **'caproyl** or **'capronyl**, $C_6H_{11}O$, the radical of the caproic series; whence **'caproyla,mine**, etc.

1845 DAY tr. *Simon's Anim. Chem.* I. 76 Nearly the whole of the caproate salt is deposited. **1873** WATTS *Fownes' Chem.* 687 The metallic caproates are soluble and crystallisable.

caprolactam (kæprəʊ'læktəm). *Chem.* [f. CAPRO(IC *a.* + LACTAM.] A crystalline amide, $C_6H_{11}NO$, used esp. in the manufacture of a type of nylon.

1944 *Chem. Abstr.* XXXVIII. 122/2 Production of *N*-(ethylmercaptomethyl)caprolactam. **1946** L. H. SMITH *Synthetic Fiber Dev.* iii. 452 Perlon..Caprolactam was the main nylon-type raw material used during the war. **1960** *Times* 2 Nov. 19/5 An arrangement with Courtaulds to produce the chemical caprolactam in Britain. **1961** *Economist* 10 June 1144/3 Caprolactam, the raw material for the nylon 6 polymer.

†**'capron**[1]. *Obs.* Also **chappron**, (**capon**). [a. F. *capron*, NF. dial. form of *chaperon* hood.] A hood. *capron hardy* [F. = bold hood or cap; cf. *mad-cap, wild-cap*, etc.]: an appellation for an impudent fellow.

c **1460** *Bk. Curtesye* (Oriel MS.) lxvi. (1868) 46 To his souereyne Chappron [CAXTON capron] hardy no bonet lust avale. **1546** BALE *Eng. Votaries* II. (1550) 67 The monkes had their cowles, caprones, or whodes, and their botes. **1561** AWDELAY *Frat. Vacab.* 12 This knave with his cap on his head lyke Capon hardy, wyll syt downe by his Maister. [**1611** COTGR., *Vn Chaperon fait à l'en veux*, a notable whipster or twigger; a good one, I warrant her.]

‖**capron**[2]. *Obs.* [F. *capron, caperon*: see Littré.] A sort of strawberry.

1693 EVELYN *De la Quint. Compl. Gard.* Gloss., *Caprons*, Straw-berry Plants that have large Velvet Leaves, and bear large Whitish Straw-berries which have but a faint taste.

caprone. *Chem.* See under CAPRIC.

ca'pronic. *Chem.* An early variant of CAPROIC.

1859 TODD *Cycl. Anat.* V. 392/1 A variety of volatile fatty acids..known under the names of..caprylic, capronic, capric and vaccinic acids. *c* **1865** J. WYLDE in *Circ. Sc.* I. 333/2.

caproone, caproyl: see CAPROIC.

†**capruch.** *Obs.* ? = CAPRICH, caprice.

1634 SHIRLEY *Example* II. i, A mental tiphon, a windy Capruch.

†**ca'pruncle.** *Obs. rare*$^{-1}$. [ad. L. *caprunculum.*] An earthen vessel.

1657 TOMLINSON *Renou's Disp.* 489 The vessels in a Pharmacopoly..are Bottles, Capruncles, etc.

capryck, caprytchyous, etc.: see CAPRI-.

capryl ('kæprɪl). *Chem.* [f. CAPR-IC (acid) + -YL.] Applied by some to the radical ($C_{10}H_{19}O$) of capric or rutic acid; by others to the radical ($C_8H_{17}O$) of caprylic acid, which some distinguish as *caprylyl*. In the latter sense it appears in **'capryla,mide**, the amide of the caprylic series; **'caprylate**, a salt of caprylic acid; **caprylonitrile**, etc.

ca'prylic, *a. Chem.* [f. as prec. + -IC.]

caprylic acid ($C_8H_{16}O_2$): a fatty acid of a faint but unpleasant odour, found as a glyceride in butter, cocoa-nut oil, etc.; one of the octylic or 8-carbon fatty acids. So *caprylic series*, etc.

1845 DAY tr. *Simon's Anim. Chem.* I. 75 Two of these acids, the capryllic and vaccinic, were discovered only a few months ago. **1859** [see CAPRONIC]. **1873** WATTS *Fownes' Chem.* 688.

caps. A printers' abbreviation of *capitals*, capital letters.

1850 THACKERAY *Pendennis* xxxii, We'll have that in large Caps., Bungay, my boy. **1856** GEO. ELIOT in *Westm. Rev.* X. 450 That particular view of Christianity which..condenses itself into a sentence of small caps. **1960** K. HOPKINS *Dead agst. Principles* ii. 15 'Original designs TATTOOED'—large caps, Manciple.

capsa ('kæpsə). [L., see CASE *sb.*[2]] (See quot. 1959.)

1932 B. L. ULLMAN *Anc. Writing* xvii. 204 The grouping of the books of Livy in decades is due to the fact that ten books were kept in each *capsa*. **1954** C. H. ROBERTS in *Proc. Brit. Acad.* XL. 193 The hypogaeum of Trebius Justus where codices, roll, and capsa are all represented. **1959** L. M. HARROD *Librarians' Gloss.* (ed. 2) 58 *Capsa*, a cylindrical box used in Roman libraries to hold one or more rolls standing upright.

†**capse.** *Obs. rare.* [a. OF. *capse*, ad. L. *capsa* box.] A coffer, chest.

1447 BOKENHAM *Seyntys* 100 In a capse of sylvyer it for to close.

Capsian ('kæpsɪən), *a.* and *sb. Archæol.* [ad. F. *capsien* (J. de Morgan et al. 1910, in *Rev. de l'École d'Anthrop.* XX. 110), f. L. *Capsa*, substituted for Gafsa (see def.) + -IAN.]

A. *adj.* Belonging to the palæolithic period represented by remains found at Gafsa in central Tunisia. **B.** *sb.* **a.** The culture of Gafsa. **b.** A person of this period.

1915 W. J. SOLLAS *Anc. Hunters* (ed. 2) viii. 290 In the greater part of Spain, almost the whole of Italy, and across the Mediterranean, as in Tunisia..this industry..persists throughout the Solutrian and Magdalenian ages... It is known as the Capsian or Getulian. **1921** R. A. S. MACALISTER *Textbk. Europ. Archæol.* I. 537 The Capsian thus corresponds chronologically to the European Upper Palæolithic, and culturally to the Aurignacian stage. **1931** *Times Lit. Suppl.* 1 Jan. 6/2 The so-called Capsians of Eastern Spain. **1951** *Proc. Prehist. Soc.* XVII. 91 The large backed blades, so characteristic of the Capsian, suggest that comparison should be made with the north rather than Africa. **1958** A. R. RADCLIFFE-BROWN *Method in Soc. Anthropol.* I. iv. 107 The affinities of the Solutrean or Capsian culture.

‖**capsicum** ('kæpsɪkəm). *Bot.* [mod.L. (Tournefort) of uncertain composition. Linnæus explained it from Gr. κάπτειν 'to bite' (rather 'to gulp down'); but it is generally referred to L. *capsa* case, as if named from the pods. In either case the formation is etymologically irregular.]

1. A genus of tropical plants or shrubs (N.O. *Solanaceæ*), characterized by their hot pungent capsules and seeds.

The common annual capsicum or Guinea Pepper (*C. annuum*), and Spur Pepper (*C. frutescens*) produce the chillies of commerce, the chief source of Cayenne pepper. Other species are Bird Pepper (*C. baccatum*), Bell Pepper (*C. grossum*), Goat Pepper (*C. fruticosum*), etc.

[**1664** EVELYN *Kal. Hort.* (1729) 19 Sow on the Hot-bed.. *Capsicum Indicum*..and the like rare and exotic Plants.] **1796** C. MARSHALL *Garden.* xvi. (1813) 264 Capsicum is sometimes raised for its young pods to pickle. **1878** H. M. STANLEY *Dark Cont.* II. xii. 351 The capsicum with its red-hot berries rose in embowering masses.

2. The fruit of the capsicum; *esp.* the prepared fruit of *Capsicum fastigiatum*, an active stimulant, used chiefly as a condiment.

1725 BRADLEY *Fam. Dict.* II. s.v. *Sallet*, The Indian Capsicum superlatively hot and burning. **1787** J. COLLINS in *Med. Commun.* II. 372 The active ingredient..is the capsicum. **1801** *Med. Jrnl.* V. 425 The gangrenous disposition of the throat was only checked by capsicum. **1845** DARWIN *Voy. Nat.* xiii. (1852) 279 After tobacco, indigo came next in value; then capsicum.

Hence **'capsicine**, *Chem.*, the active principle extracted from the capsules of capsicum.

1831 J. DAVIES *Manual Mat. Med.* 161 Capsicine..when perfectly pure, is tasteless, inodorous, and crystallizes in acicular fragments. **1866** *Treas. Bot.* 219/1 A peculiar acrid fluid called capsicin, which is so pungent that half a grain of it volatilised in a large room, causes all who respire the contained air to cough and sneeze. **1863–79** WATTS *Dict. Chem.* I. 747 Capsicine. **1875** H. WOOD *Therap.* (1879) 85 The name of Capsicin has been applied by different observers to the oil, to the resin, and to their combination, but should..be dropped, as having no definite meaning.

capsid ('kæpsɪd), *a.* and *sb.*[1] [f. mod.L. *Caps-us* (see def.) + -ID[3].] **A.** *adj.* Belonging to the Capsidæ, a family of heteropterous insects including the genus *Capsus*. **B.** *sb.* An insect of this family.

1889 in *Cent. Dict.* **1932** *London Gaz.* 28 Oct. 6796 The Apple Capsid (Essex) Order of 1932... On being satisfied that the Apple Capsid exists on any such trees or bushes [etc.]. **1934** *Discovery* Sept. 252/2 In Kenya..it [*sc.* pyrethrum] is effective against capsid and antestia bugs, which are harmful to coffee plants. **1959** SOUTHWOOD & LESTON *Land & Water Bugs* viii. 201 Great care should be taken when collecting capsid bugs. **1960** *Times* 25 July 11/6 Scales, capsids, tsetses.

capsid ('kæpsɪd), *sb.*[2] [ad. F. *capside* (A. Lwoff et al. 1959, in *Ann. de l'Inst. Pasteur* XCVII. 286), f. L. *capsa* box (see CAPSA) + -ID[2].] (See quots.)

1964 *Inst. Biol. Jrnl.* XI. 93 *Capsid*, the quasi-crystalline shell, built up by the regular arrangement of capsomeres, to produce the structure that is the stable and transmissible form of some viruses. **1964** *New Scientist* 23 July 210 Some viruses consist of a single protein coat or 'capsid' enveloping the infective nucleic acid. **1964** G. H. HAGGIS *Introd. Molecular Biol.* iv. 83 A number of other small spherical viruses have been shown to contain nucleic acid within similar protein envelopes, now called *capsids*.

capsizal (kæp'saɪzəl). [f. CAPSIZE *v.* + -AL[1] II. 5.] The act of capsizing; an upset.

1881 W. C. RUSSELL *Sailor's Sweeth.* III. v. 218, I was none the worse for my capsizal. **1882** *Fraser's Mag.* XXV. 687 To protect..against all risks of further 'capsizals'.

capsize (kæp'saɪz), *sb.* [f. next.] = prec.

1807 E. S. BARRETT *All the Talents* 62 Shou'd he get a capcise How..could he rise? **1848** J. GRANT *Adv. Aide-de-C.* xxxviii, We escaped a capsize. **1882** NARES *Seamanship* (ed. 6) 152 In the event of a capsize they..will float.

capsize (kæp'saɪz), *v.* [Origin unknown; app. originally a sailor's expression: not in Bailey, Johnson, Ash, nor in Todd 1818. The first element may possibly be CAP *sb.*[1]

(Prof. Skeat suggests corruption of Sp. *cabezar* 'to nod, pitch as a ship', or of *capuzar* 'to sink a ship by the head', from *cabeza, cabo* head.)]

1. *trans.* To upset, overturn (*esp.* on the water).

1788 DIBDIN *Mus. Tour* xxxv. 142, I began to think, with the sailors below, that there was certainly a chance of 'our being capsized'. **1803** REES *Cycl.*, *Capsize*, in Naval Language to upset or turn over anything. **1823** BYRON *Juan* IX. xviii, What if carrying sail capsize the boat? **1847–78** HALLIWELL, *Capsize*, to move a hogshead or other vessel forward by turning it alternately on the heads. *Somerset.* **1870** E. PEACOCK *Ralf Skirl.* II. 286 He..capsized the stool on which he had been seated.

fig. **1833** MARRYAT *P. Simple* xvii, I was capsized..when I looked at the house.

2. *intr.* (for *refl.*) To be upset or overturned.

1805 A. DUNCAN *Mariner's Chron.* IV. 75 The captain.. expressed his surprise that the ship should remain so long on her beam-ends, in such a heavy sea, without capsizing. **1882** NARES *Seamanship* (ed. 6) 140 The sail..will capsize behind the top-gallant sail.

Hence **cap'sized** *ppl. a.*, **cap'sizing** *vbl. sb.*, etc.

1882 *Daily News* 1 June 3/6 She fell in with a capsized vessel, apparently a schooner.

capsomere ('kæpsəʊmɪə(r)). [ad. F. *capsomère* (A. Lwoff et al. 1959, in *Ann. de l'Inst. Pasteur* XCVII. 286), f. as CAPS(ID *sb.*[2] + -O + *-mere*, f. Gr. μέρος part.] (See quot. 1964[2].)

1962 *Lancet* 5 May 965/1 Preliminary evidence suggested that the antigens A and C were in fact the two kinds of capsomeres believed to form the outer shell of the virus particle. **1964** M. HYNES *Med. Bacteriol.* (ed. 8) xxiv. 349 A typical virus consists of a core of either DNA or RNA surrounded by numerous identical subunits of protein, termed capsomeres. **1964** *Inst. Biol. Jrnl.* XI. 93 *Capsomere*, one of the units from which the closed shell or tube of some viruses is built up.

capstan ('kæpstən). Forms: α. 4 **capstan**, 5–6 **capstayne**, 6 **capestan**, 6–7 **capstain(e, -sten**, 7–8 **-stane**, 7 **-stone, -stang**, 7– **capstan**; β. 7 **capsterne**, 7–9 **-stern**, (7 **capstorm**); γ. 7–8 **capstand**; δ. 7–8 **capstall**; see also CAPSTRING. [either a. F. *cabestan*, also in 16th c. *capestan* (Littré), or else

directly from the source of the Fr., viz. Pr. *cabestan*, earlier *cabestran* (Cat. *cabestrant*, Sp. *cabestrante*, *-estante*, *cabrestante*, Pg. *cabrestante*):—L. **capistrānt-* pr. pple. of *capistrāre* (Pr. *cabestrar*), to halter, bind fast, fasten, f. *capistr-um* (It. *capestro*, Sp. *cabestro*, Pg. *cabresto*, Pr. *cabestre*, F. *chevêtre*) halter, f. *cap-ĕre* to take hold of.

The Fr. *cabestan* is not known to us earlier than Palsgr. 1530; since the word occurs in Eng. in 14th c., it may have been learned from the shipmen of Marseilles or Barcelona at the time of the Crusades. In Pg., *capistrum* and its derivatives have the *r* transposed, *cabresto* 'halter', nautically 'ropes, cables belonging to the bowsprit', *cabresteiro* 'halter-maker', *cabrestante*; the last is also the approved form in mod. literary Sp.; this form gave rise to the untenable conjecture that the derivation was from *cabra* goat + *estante* 'standing', ingeniously supported by the known application of the name of the goat in various languages (*cabria, chèvre, bock*, etc.), to various mechanical devices. The attempt to find a meaning in the word, in English, produced many popular perversions of the second element, as *stain, stone, stand, stall, stern, storm, string*. Other names were *capstock*, and *cablestock*.]

1. a. A piece of mechanism, working on the principle of the wheel and axle, on a vertical axis, the power being applied by movable bars or levers inserted in horizontal sockets made round the top, and pushed by men walking round, whereby the apparatus is made to revolve and wind up a cable round its cylinder or barrel; it is used especially on board ship for weighing the anchor, also for hoisting heavy sails, etc., and for raising weights out of quarries, mines, coal-pits (see GIN), and the like.

double capstan, one that has two barrels on different decks, so as to be worked by two sets of men. Phrases, ***to heave at the capstan, to man the capstan, to bring the cable to the capstan; to rig the capstan***, to insert the bars, etc.; ***to pawl the capstan***, to drop the pawls or catches into their sockets so as to prevent recoil, when heaving is stopped; ***to come up the capstan***, to slacken the cable by lifting out the pawls and walking back; ***to surge the capstan***, to slacken the rope while heaving so as to prevent riding or fouling.

α. forms *capstan, -stain, -sten, -stone, -stang.*

c **1325** *E.E. Allit. P.* B. 418 þe arc..with-outen..kable oþer capstan to clyppe to her ankrez. *c* **1500** *Cocke Lorell's B.* (1843) 12 Some wounde at yᵉ capstayne..Some stode at yᵉ slynge. **1530** PALSGR. 607/2 Let go your capestan..*laschez vostre cabestan.* *a* **1608** SIR F. VERE *Comm.* 28 The Cap-stain being too strong for my men. **1615** *MS. Acc. St. John's Hosp. Canterb.*, A nyorne pynne for the capsten. **1618** RALEIGH *Invent. Shipping* 16 The weighing of Anchors by the Capstone is also new. **1622** R. HAWKINS *Voy. S. Sea* (1847) 132 With our capstens [we] stretched the two byghtes. **1633** T. JAMES *Voy.* 25 Bringing the Cable to Capstang, to heaue in our Cable. **1706** PHILLIPS, *Capstan, Capstand* or *Capstern*..Come up Capstan, or Launce out the Capstan, when the Sea-men would have the Cable that they heave by slacked. **1729** DESAGULIERS in *Phil. Trans.* XXXVI. 196 A Capstane, or upright Shaft, drawn round by Horses. **1832** BABBAGE *Econ. Manuf.* vii. (ed. 3) 48 In mines it is sometimes necessary to raise or lower great weights by capstans.

β. forms *capstern, -storm.*

1624 CAPT. SMITH *Virginia* I. 14 The men..were throwne from the Capstern, by the breaking of a barre. **1670** DRYDEN *Tempest* I. i, Hands down! Man your Main-Capstorm. **1759** WESLEY *Wks.* (1872) II. 521 The capstern of the ship. **1769** FALCONER *Dict. Marine* (1789) *To come up the Capstern*, is to let go the rope which they had been heaving. **1836** MARRYAT *Midsh. Easy* xiii. 45 Mind you leave all your pistols on capstern.

γ. form *capstand.*

1616 BULLOKAR, *Capstand*, an instrument to wind up things of great weight, some call it a Crane. **1791** SMEATON *Edystone L.* §154, I tried them by a strain from the Capstand.

δ. form *capstall.*

1610 HOLLAND *Camden's Brit.* I. 318 Enforced to worke their vessels to land by a Capstall or Crane. **1714** STEELE *The Lover* (1723) 190 Anchors, Cables, Rudders..Capstals.

b. (See quot. 1959.)

1948 *Sat. Rev.* 28 Feb. 56 Tape..is usually capstan driven at constant linear speed. **1949** FRAYNE & WOLFE *Sound Recording* xxix. 580 The recording material is pulled by a capstan against which it is held by a roller. The capstan may be driven directly by a motor or by means of a belt drive. **1959** W. S. SHARPS *Dict. Cinemat.* 84 *Capstan*, in magnetic tape recording, this is the motor-controlled spindle surmounted by a roller which grips the tape and draws it past the sound head at constant speed.

2. *attrib.* and *Comb.*, as ***capstan-bar, -barrel, -heaver, labourer, -man***; ***capstan-headed*** adj.; **capstan-house**, see quot.; **capstan-swifter**, 'a rope passed horizontally through notches in the outer ends of the bar..the intent is to steady the men, and to give room for a greater number to assist, by manning the swifters both within and without' (Smyth); **capstan table**, a round table on a column, often with a revolving top.

1627 SMITH *Seaman's Gram.* ii. 7 Holes thorow which you put your *Capstaine barres, for as many men as can stand at them to thrust it about, and is called manning the Capstaine. **1798** CAPT. MILLER in Nicolas *Disp. Nelson* (1846) VII. Introd. 157 They dropped under the capstan-bars, and were asleep in a moment. **1706** PHILLIPS s.v., **Capstan-barrel* is the main part of the whole piece. **1790** ROY in *Phil. Trans.* LXXX. 147 *Capstan-headed screws. **1791** BENTHAM *Panopt.* II. 115 The *capstern-heaver would be dead before the wheel-walker felt the sensation of fatigue. **1809** C. MILWARD in *Naval Chron.* XXII. 309 The mess-room door of the *capstan-house. **1863** BARRY *Dockyard Econ.* 101 Capstan-houses. These are the houses in which capstans, anchor stocks, pump boxes, etc., are manufactured, repaired, and stored. **1881** *Instr. Census Clerks* (1885) 94 *Capstan labourer. **1889** P. H. EMERSON *Eng. Idyls* 67 On deck, a countryman who had shipped as *capstan-man, was standing for'ard with the master. **1921** *Dict. Occup. Terms* (1927) §706 *Capstan man*.., moves trucks in goods depôt by depressing foot lever actuating automatic capstan. *Ibid.* §741 *Capstan man*, operates capstan,..allows capstan to revolve,..etc. **1921** *Glasgow Herald* 1 June 9 Cranemen, capstanmen, and others. **1927** *Daily Tel.* 31 May 4/1 An old English '*capstan' writing table.

†'capstock. *Obs.* [Cf. CAPSTAN and CABLESTOCK.] = CAPSTAN.

1551 RECORDE *Pathw. Knowl.* Pref., To sette forth the Capstocke, and eche other parte, wold make a greate showe of Geometries arte.

cap-stone ('kæpstəʊn). [f. CAP + STONE.]

1. A stone which caps or crowns: **a.** the top-stone. Also *fig.*

1685 *Gracian's Courtier's Orac.* 150 Here is the fair occasion..to put the cap-stone upon his other perfections. **1791** SMEATON *Edystone L.* §293 They had put on the cap-stone of the stair-head. **1863** MRS. C. CLARKE *Shaks. Char.* xvii. 447 The capstone to his revelry is when he accepts Falstaff's pledge to a bumper.

b. The overlying horizontal stone of a cromlech or dolmen.

1851 D. WILSON *Preh. Ann.* (1863) II. 9 Much greater mechanical skill.. was required to..upheave the capstone of the cromlech on to the upright trilith. **1879** LUBBOCK *Addr. Pol. & Educ.* ix. 157 A dolmen..of which only the capstone now remains.

c. Coping-stone, coping.

1665 *Lond. Gaz.* No. 6/1 The Sea here threw up several Capstones and Keys. **1828-41** TYTLER *Hist. Scot.* (1864) I. 137 So near the walls as to be able to fix their movable bridges on the capstone.

d. The uppermost bed of stone in a quarry.

1791 SMEATON *Edystone L.* §108 Were it not for these cavities, the cap-stone would not readily be worked.

2. *Geol.* A fossil Echinite of the genus Conulus, so called from its cap-like shape.

1677 PLOT *Oxfordsh.* 92 By the Country people called commonly Cap-stones, from their likeness to a Cap laced down the sides.

capstone, obs. form of CAPSTAN.

†'capstring. A perversion of CAPSTAN.

1609 HEYWOOD *Brit. Troy* (N.) Some to the cap-string call, some pray, some sweare. **1655** HEYWOOD & ROWLEY *Fort. Land & Sea* IV. iii, Part of their Capstring too I with a Piece abaft shot overboard.

capsular ('kæpsjʊlə(r)), *a.* [ad. mod.L. *capsulār-is*, f. *capsula*: see CAPSULE and -AR[1].] Of, pertaining to, or of the nature of a capsule.

[**1679** PLOT *Staffordsh.* (1686) 196 The bicapsular seed vessel of Digitalis ferruginea.] **1730-6** BAILEY, *Capsular*, pertaining to a coffer, chest or casket. **1748** HARTLEY *Observ. Man* I. ii. vii. ¶74. 245 The capsular Ligaments of the Joints. **1794** MARTYN *Rousseau's Bot.* xvi. 175 A berry covered with a capsular shell. **1831** R. KNOX *Cloquet's Anat.* 766 Capsular Lymphatics..come from the supra-renal capsules. **1822-44** GOOD *Study Med.* (ed. 4) III. 167 Capsular cataracts are those in which the front, or back, of the capsule of the lens is alone affected. **1845** LINDLEY *Sch. Bot.* iv. (1858) 37 Fruit berried or capsular.

†'capsulary, *a. Obs.* [ad. mod.L. *capsulāri-us* = *capsulāris* (see prec.).] = prec.

1615 CROOKE *Body of Man* 360 A small braunch from the Axillary veine which they call the Capsulary or purse-braunch. **1646** SIR T. BROWNE *Pseud. Ep.* 172 A capsulary reception of the breast bone. **1656** in BLOUNT *Glossogr.*

†capsulate ('kæpsjʊlət), *a. Bot. Obs.* [ad. mod.L. *capsulātus*, f. *capsula*: see -ATE[2].] Furnished with or enclosed in a capsule; formed into a capsule; capsuled.

1668 WILKINS *Real Char.* II. 102 Capsulate herbs. **1688** R. HOLME *Armoury* II. 115/1 Capsulate Pods [are] little short seed Vessels. **1803** REES *Cycl.* s.v., Capsulate plants..bear their seeds in short capsulæ.

†'capsulated, *a. Obs.* [f. prec. + -ED.] = prec.

1646 SIR T. BROWNE *Pseud. Ep.* 194 The seed of plants lockt up and capsulated in their husks. **1664** POWER *Exp. Philos.* I. 40. **1737-59** MILLER *Gard. Dict.*, Capsulated Plants.

capsu'lation. *Med.* [f. CAPSULE *v.* + -ATION.] 'The enclosure of a drug in a capsule to render it more convenient or more pleasant in administration' (*Syd. Soc. Lex.*).

capsule ('kæpsju:l), *sb.* (and *adj.*) Also 7 capsul; and in Latin form **capsula**, *pl.* -æ. [a. F. *capsule*, ad. L. *capsula* small box or case, dim. of *capsa* box, repository.]

A. *sb.*

†1. *gen.* A little case or receptacle. *Obs.*

1652 URQUHART *Jewel* Wks. (1834) 233 Brought their disorderly raised spirits into their former capsuls. **1713** DERHAM *Phys.-Theol.* x. *note* 1 (R.) The little cases or capsules which contain the seed in this species [the fern].

2. *Phys.* A membranous integument or envelope; a bag or sac. **capsule of Tenon**, Tenon's capsule (TENONIAN *a.*).

a **1693** URQUHART *Rabelais* III. xxxi. 262 The left Capsul of the Heart. **1738** *Med. Ess. & Observ.* (ed. 2) IV. 193 When this Capsule is opened the Crystalline escapes. **1804** ABERNETHY *Surg. Obs.* 13 The tumour will..acquire for itself a kind of capsule. **1855** OWEN *Skel. & Teeth* 7 The capsule of the eye-ball..is a fibrous membrane. **1866** HUXLEY *Phys.* v. The tubules [of the kidney]..terminate in dilatations..called *Malpighian capsules.* **1867** *Amer. Jrnl. Med. Sci.* July 241 The capsule of Tenon,..which incloses the whole eyeball, with the exception of the cornea, consists of two very different portions. **1884** [see CAPSULITIS]. **1964** S. DUKE-ELDER *Parsons' Dis. Eye* (ed. 14) x. 112 At the time of an operation after the capsule of Tenon has been opened.

3. *Bot.* **a.** A dry dehiscent seed-vessel, containing one or more cells, and opening when ripe by the separation of its valves. **b.** Applied to certain kinds of perithecia or receptacles in Fungi.

1693 LEEUWENHOEK in *Phil. Trans.* XVII. 706 So soon as the Capsula breaks upon the ripening of the Seed. **1776** WITHERING *Bot. Arrangem.* (1796) I. 96 A Capsule with two boat-shaped Valves, and one Cell; the Valves opening length-ways. **1830** LINDLEY *Nat. Syst. Bot.* 182 The dehiscence of their capsule. **1874** LUBBOCK *Wild Flowers* iii. 77 The seed capsules, when ripe, burst open if touched.

4. *Chem.* A shallow saucer, for roasting samples of ores, or for evaporating.

1727-51 CHAMBERS *Cycl.*, *Capsula*, in chymistry, is an earthen vessel, in form of a pan; wherein things are frequently placed, that are to undergo very violent operations of the fire. **1727** BRADLEY *Fam. Dict.* s.v. *Distilling*, Two Bars of Iron..to support the Retort or Capsula. **1853** GREGORY *Inorg. Chem.* 181 If we heat a capsule of platinum a little beyond 212°, and drop water into it. **1873** W. LEES *Acoustics* III. v. 111 A small capsule containing water.

5. *Med.* A small envelope of gelatine to enclose a dose of nauseous medicine.

1875 H. WOOD *Therap.* (1879) 503 When patients object to the taste, the drug may be given in gelatine capsules.

6. A metallic cap or cover for a bottle.

1858 in SIMMONDS *Dict. Trade.*

7. A percussion cap; the shell of a metallic cartridge. [Fr.]

In mod. Dicts.

8. (*a*) A pressurized compartment in an aircraft, also used for an emergency escape. (*b*) The detachable nose-cone of a rocket or space missile for carrying an astronaut, instruments for recording and transmitting scientific data, etc. orig. *U.S.*

1954 M. CAIDIN *Worlds in Space* v. 105 The ship could be controlled from within the sealed capsules. **1955** *Sci. News Let.* 11 June 377/3 An escape capsule for pilots flying supersonic aircraft..has been patented. **1958** *Wall St. Jrnl.* 9 Oct. 1/3 Later efforts would be made to send a man, again encased in a pressurized capsule, circling the earth for 24 hours. **1959** *Daily Tel.* 23 Feb. 11/6 For the space pilot.. there must be the ability, in emergency, to eject the whole capsule in which one sits. **1959** *Listener* 17 Sept. 440/1 The first American space capsule. **1964** *Ann. Reg. 1963* 185 Because of a fault in some of the automatic control equipment he had had to control the Mercury capsule manually during the critical period of re-entry into the earth's atmosphere. **1968** *Times* 10 Dec. 6/8 Solar telescopes which can be linked up in space to an Apollo capsule.

B. As *adj.* Brief, condensed, compressed; small and compact. orig. *U.S.*

1938 in J. Beatty *Saturday Rev. Gallery* (1959) 279 One of those capsule biographies of the author that sometimes appear on the jackets of detective stories. **1944** *Amer. N. & Q.* June 42/2 (*heading*) Capsule language for fighting men. **1953** R. STOUT *Golden Spiders* 55 An estimated million and a quarter New Yorkers got an impressive capsule demonstration of the might of American armed forces. **1955** KEEPNEWS & GRAUER *Pict. Hist. Jazz* xiv. 149 It's not so much a Kansas City 'style' as a capsule history of jazz in one town. **1958** *Vogue* May 199 Blue and white blazer..slim skirt, really a capsule wardrobe in itself.

'capsule, *v.* [f. prec.] *trans.* To furnish or close (a bottle, etc.) with a capsule or metallic cover. Hence **'capsuled** *ppl. a.*, **'capsuling** *vbl. sb.*, etc.

1859 *All Year Round* No. 30. 77 Any patent capsuled colour tubes. **1886** *Brit. Manuf. Export Jrnl.* 1 Oct., The necessity for wiring, sealing, or capsuling.

capsuli-, capsulo-, comb. forms of L. *capsula*, CAPSULE; as in **capsu'liferous** *a.*, bearing capsules. **'capsuliform** *a.*, having the form of a capsule. **capsu'ligenous** *a.*, giving origin to capsules. **,capsulo-len'ticular** *a.*, of the capsule of the lens of the eye.

1857 BERKELEY *Cryptog. Bot.* §474. 430 Variously formed capsulæform organs. **1870** HOOKER *Stud. Flora* 471 Lycopodium Selago..leaves erect..upper capsuliferous. **1870** ROLLESTON *Anim. Life* 125 The so-called capsulo-genous glands. **1875** WALTON *Dis. Eye* 741 Traumatic cataract is always capsulo-lenticular.

capsulitis (kæpsju:'laɪtɪs). *Path.* [f. CAPSULE + -ITIS.] Inflammation of a capsule (e.g. of the eyeball); tenonitis.

1830 W. MACKENZIE *Pract. Treat. Dis. Eye* x. 470 By the term aquo-capsulitis is meant inflammation of the cartilaginous membrane..which lines the internal surface of the cornea. **1884** H. R. SWANZY *Handbk. Dis. Eye* xxii. 414 Capsulitis, or Inflammation of the Capsule of Tenon, is an affection concerning the occurrence of which there is some doubt. **1951** W. S. C. COPEMAN in *Brit. Encycl. Med. Pract.* (ed. 2) V. 437 A number of these cases appear to progress to the formation of intra-capsular adhesions, resulting

ultimately in what the Americans term the 'frozen shoulder', or 'fibrosing capsulitis'.

capsulize ('kæpsju:laɪz), *v.* orig. *U.S.* [f. CAPSUL(E + -IZE.] *trans.* To compress or condense (information, news, etc.) into a brief and compact form. (Cf. CAPSULE B.) Hence **'capsulized** *ppl. a.*

1950 *Sat. Rev. Lit.* 11 Nov. 17/1 This is a brief, almost capsulized account of postwar USSR. **1958** *New Yorker* 11 Oct. 39/1, I wanted..a slogan that would capsulize the lip-smacking flavor of the soups. **1959** *Economist* 7 Feb. 497/2 The Readers' Digest supplements its capsulised journalism.

capsulotomy (kæpsju:'lɒtəmɪ). *Surg.* [f. CAPSULI-, CAPSULO- + -TOMY.] The incision of a capsule, *spec.* that of the lens of the eye in an operation for cataract.

1877 *Arch. Ophthalmol. & Otology* VI. 550 The peripheric capsulotomy may lessen the danger still attending Graefe's method of extraction. **1907** *Practitioner* Dec. 778 The operation of capsulotomy for some cases of acute nephritis with threatened suppression of urine. **1969** S. DUKE-ELDER *Syst. Ophthalmol.* XI. I. iii. 272 The subsequent capsulotomy which is required if the posterior capsule remains intact should be undertaken soon after the eye has become quiet.

capt, var. of CAPPED *ppl. a.*

†**'captable**, *a. Obs.* [ad. L. *captābilis*, f. *captāre* to catch at (see CAPTATE).] Liable or open to be caught or taken.

1649 J. ECLISTON tr. *Behmen's Epist.* xv. (1886) 12 Our precious life..lying captable to both [i.e. heaven and hell].

captain ('kæptɪn), *sb.* Forms: α. 4-5 **capitain**, **-tayn**, **-tane**, **-tein**, 5 **capytayn**, **-tein**, **capeteigne**, 5-6 **capi-**, **capytayne**, 5-7 **capitaine**, 6 **capitan**, 7 *Sc.* **capitane**; β. 4-5 **capteyn**, 5 **-tayn**, **-tan**, 5-7 **-tayne**, 6-7 **-taine**, 7 *Sc.* **-tane**, 5- **captain**. [ME. *capitain*, a. late OF. (14th c.) *capitaine*, *capitain*, ad. late L. *capitāne-us capitān-us* adj. 'chief, principal', sb. 'chief, headman', f. *caput*, *capit-* head.

Had L. *capitāneus* been an old word, which lived on in French, its OF. form would have been *catain*, *chatain* (:—*captāneum*); being of somewhat later (10-11th c. origin) the actual OF. form was *cata-niē*, *cataigne*, *chataigne*; a still later (12th c.) semipopular form, preserving the intertonic *i* of *capitāneus*, was *chevetaine* (whence Eng. CHIEFTAIN). *Capitaine* was again a much later adaptation of the L.]

I. A chief or headman.

1. a. One who stands at the head of others and leads them, or exercises authority over them; a headman, chief, or leader. Now only as *fig.* use of special senses.

c **1380** WYCLIF *De Eccles.* ix. Sel. Wks. III. 360 It were good to obeishe to Petre, and þat sich a captein were in þe Chirche. **1485** CAXTON *Chas. Gt.* 231 Thou hast ben capytayn ayenst the fayth. **1534** MORE *Picus* Wks. 21 Christ our lorde and soueraine captayne. **1611** BIBLE *Heb.* ii. 10 The Captaine of their saluation. **1683** tr. *Erasmus' Moriæ Enc.* 50 Homer, that Captain of all Poetry. **1875** JOWETT *Plato* (ed. 2) III. 489 He [Homer] is the great captain and teacher of the whole of that charming tragic company.

b. ***captain of industry***, an industrial magnate, a merchant prince.

1843 CARLYLE *Past & Pr.* IV. iv. 361 (*heading*) Captains of Industry. **1896** G. B. SHAW *Our Theatres in Nineties* (1932) II. 179 Attentive observers of great 'captains of industry' know that their success often comes to them in spite of themselves. **1931** *Economist* 10 Jan. 51/2 A representative conference of trade union leaders and captains of industry. **1933** J. M. KEYNES *Essays in Biogr.* I. iii. 42 Mr. Bonar Law has liked to think of himself as..handling wars and empires and revolutions with the coolness and limited purpose of a first-class captain of industry.

2. *esp.* A military leader; a commander of a body of troops, of a fortress, castle, etc.

1375 BARBOUR *Bruce* VIII. 52 Thai off the castell..tauld it to thair capitane. **1450** W. SOMNER in *Four C. Eng. Lett.* 4 Peris Brusy was cheffe capteyn. **1535** COVERDALE *Judg.* i. 1 Who shall..be oure Captayne of warre against yᵉ Cananites? **1603** SHAKS. *Meas. for M.* II. ii. 130 That in the Captaine's but a chollericke word, Which in the Souldier is flat blasphemie. **1618** BOLTON *Florus* II. xviii. 157 Such as the Captaine is, such is the Souldier. **1671** MILTON *Samson* 1651 Lords, ladies, captains, counsellors, or priests. **1752** JOHNSON *Rambl.* No. 190 ⁋2 The captains of thousands awaited his commands. **1855** MACAULAY *Hist. Eng.* III. 200 Of all the Irish captains the most dreaded and the most abhorred.

3. A military leader of skill and experience; an able general or commander; a strategist.

1590 A. COPE (*title*) The History of two most noble Captaynes of the World, Anniball and Scipio. **1689** EVELYN *Mem.* (1857) III. 297 Authors of sects, great captains and politicians. **1701** SWIFT *Contests in Athens & Rome* Wks. 1755 II. I. 18 Miltiades..is reckoned to have been the first great captain, not only of Athens, but of all Greece. **1838** MACAULAY *Sir W. Temple*, *Ess.* (L.) Condé and Turenne will always be considered as captains of a very different order from the invincible Lewis. **1868** FREEMAN *Norm. Conq.* (1876) II. x. 477 The world first fully learned how great a captain England had in her future King.

II. The head of a division.

4. *gen.* A subordinate officer holding command under a sovereign, a general, or the like.

c **1380** WYCLIF *Serm.* Sel. Wks. I. 323 Folk, þat weren þe fendis capteyns in killing of martiris. **1535** COVERDALE *1 Macc.* xv. 38 The kynge made Cendebeus captayne of the see coost. **1594** SHAKS. *Rich. III*, v. iii. 108 O thou, whose Captaine I account my selfe..Make vs thy ministers of Chasticement. **1609** BIBLE (Douay) *Lament.* I. *comm.*, His capitaine Nabuzardan spoyled al. **1611** BIBLE *Deut.* i. 15 Captaines ouer fifties, and captaines ouer tennes, and officers among your tribes. **1830** SPARKS *Biog. S. Cabot* ii. 109 On Cabot's arrival..he gave him the title of his Captain.

5. *spec.* **a.** In the army: The officer who commands a company of infantry or foot artillery, or a troop of cavalry or horse artillery, ranking between the major and the lieutenant. The grade is the third in order of promotion.

1567 *Confed. Popish Princes* in Strype *Ann. Ref.* I. II. l. 538 The principall lievetenaunts and capytaines. **1598** BARRET *Theor. Warres* II. i. 15 Regiment [divided] into companies, ouer every company a Captaine. **1641** *Sc. Acts.* (1870) V. App. 679/2 Petitione be the Lieutenant Colonellis and Majoris..desyring the pay of ane captaine. **1814** SCOTT *Wav.* v, Captain Waverley of the —— regiment of dragoons. **1845** S. AUSTIN *Ranke's Hist. Ref.* II. 347 Who had now risen to the rank of captain.

b. An officer in the Salvation Army.

1878 *Christian Mission Mag.* Dec. 320 These stray remarks added to the interest we felt in our contemplated visit to the command of Captain Louise Agar. **1884** W. BOOTH *General's Lett.* 6 Dec. (1890) 18 Go to the crowd of sinners, or spot them individually..because out of them you may make Lieutenants, and Captains, and Majors, and Generals. **1965** R. COLLIER *General next to God* iii. 75 Not all in those pioneer years could afford..a guinea for a captain's outfit.

c. *U.S.* A police officer ranking between chief officer and lieutenant; one who commands a precinct or division.

1909 L. F. FULD *Police Admin.* ii. 57 An officer called a captain is placed in charge of each precinct. **1926** J. BLACK *You can't Win* iv. 32 One of the detectives went into an office ..and came out at once with a man in uniform he called 'captain'. **1932** W. FAULKNER *Light in August* iv. 81 Captain McLendon said, 'I don't reckon about it at all.' **1978** J. WAMBAUGH *Black Marble* iv. 48 'Sometimes a fellow shouldn't work homicide that long,' Captain Hooker offered.

6. a. The officer who commands a man-of-war. In the British navy, the title of an officer who ranks between a rear-admiral or a commodore and a commander. The title is also often given by courtesy to a commander.

Captain of the Fleet: an officer, temporarily appointed by the admiralty, who acts as adjutant-general of a naval force, carries out all orders issued by the commander-in-chief, but whose special duty it is to keep up the discipline of the fleet; he wears the uniform of a rear-admiral. ***Captain of the Port***: an officer of the Board of Health who 'controls the entries and departures, the berthing at the anchorage, and general marine duties in a port, but possesses no naval authority. Hence, the port-captain is quite another officer' (Smyth *Sailor's Word-bk.*).

1554 EDEN *Decades W. Ind.* VII. (Arb.) 375 This capitayne Wyndam, puttyng furth of his shyp at Porchmouth. **1593** SHAKS. *2 Hen. VI*, IV. i. 107 This Villaine heere, Being Captaine of a Pinnace. **1626** CAPT. SMITH *Accid. Yng. Seamen* 1 The Captaines charge is to commaund all, and tell the Maister to what Port he will go. **1745** *Observ. Conc. Navy* 36 A Captain of a Man of War of the Line, is equal in Rank to a Colonel. **1804** G. ROSE *Diaries* (1860) II. 194 Captain Prescott, a commander in the navy. **1836** MARRYAT *Midsh. Easy* xxii, The captain of the frigate.

b. Applied to the chief sailor of a gang of men to whom the duties of a certain portion of the ship are assigned, as ***captain of the forecastle***, ***captain of the hold***, ***captain of the maintop***, etc.

1801 *Naval Chron.* VI. 103 He was captain of a gun at the Battle of the Nile. **1833** MARRYAT *P. Simple* II. vii, The captain of the main-top was there with two other sailors. **1859** F. GRIFFITHS *Artil. Man.* (1862) 208, No. 1, the Captain [of a gun] commands, attends the breech, primes, points, and fires. **1882** *Navy List* July 459 Captain of Quarter-deck Men, Captain of the Forecastle, Captain of the Foretop, Captain of the Hold, etc.

7. a. The master or commander of a merchant ship or of any kind of vessel.

1704 ADDISON *Italy* 6 Our Captain thought his Ship in so great Danger. **1822** J. FLINT *Lett. Amer.* 144 The persons who take the charge of keel-boats are also Captains. **1858** *Merc. Mar. Mag.* V. 39 Capt. Baker had every confidence in the ship. **1873** MORLEY *Rousseau* II. 55 A kidnapper of coolies or the captain of a slaver.

b. The pilot of a civil aircraft.

1929 *Proc. Internat. Civil Aeronaut. Conf.* 253 It will be indispensable..that a uniform juridical system govern..the aircraft, its owner..its captain and crew, as well as the passenger. **1955** *Times* 13 May 7/1 Having decided to retire from commercial flying after being an airline captain continuously since 1922 [etc.].

8. The superintendent or manager of a mine (in Cornwall, etc.).

1602 CAREW *Cornwall* 10/1 Their ouerseer, whome they terme their Captaine. **1757** BORLASE in *Phil. Trans.* L. 504 This very intelligent captain of the mine observes, etc. **1852** *Leisure Ho.* 632 *note.* **1864** MRS. LLOYD *Ladies Polc.* 16.

9. a. The foreman of a company of workmen or of a workshop in various trades. (Cf. also 6 b.)

1886 *Newspaper*, D. H., 'captain' of Messrs. Davies' [tailors'] shop, said that he never saw a coat worse made.

b. One in charge of a group of waiters or bell-boys in a hotel. Chiefly *U.S.*

1942 L. BEMELMANS *Hotel Splendide* iii. 43 These two have been nothing but waiter and captain for twenty years. *Ibid.* 44 Captains, ah! Maîtres d'hôtel they call themselves. **1952** M. STEEN *Phoenix Rising* iii. 59 He indicated his wants to the waiter... The captain went to his table..and nodded sharply to the waiter. **1968** *Globe & Mail* (Toronto) 3 Feb. 23/1 The Imperial Room opened when the hotel was built in 1929 (one captain and one waiter have been there from the beginning).

10. The head boy of a school, or of a form in it.

1706 *Spect.* No. 307 ⁋13 Every Boy is bound to have as good a Memory as the Captain of the Form. **1730** *Etoniana* x. 156 There was a speech made by the captain. **1825** SCOTT in *Lockhart* (1839) VIII. 149 A schoolboy who writes himself Captain of Giggleswick School. **1864** *Blackw. Mag.* XCVI. 226 (Hoppe) The late captain of Harrow..gives it as his opinion that the small houses have their necessary advantages.

11. In *Cricket*, *Football*, and other sports: The leader of a side or team, the chief of a club, etc.

1823 MISS MITFORD in *Lady's Mag.* July 387/1 Our captain applied to him instantly to play. **1857** HUGHES *Tom Brown* I. v, Old Brooke is talking to the captain of quarters [at foot-ball]. *Ibid.* II. viii, And then the Captain of the eleven..what a post is his in our School world. **1865** (*title*) The Rob Roy on the Jordan..By J. Macgregor, Captain of the Royal Canoe Club. **1884** *Harper's Mag.* Jan. 299/1 They [bowling club] have a captain, and a treasurer.

12. As a term of address (without implying any office or rank). *familiar* or *slang*. Cf. '*governor*'.

1607 SHAKS. *Timon* II. ii. 76 Why how now Captaine? what do you in this wise Company? **1611** —— *Wint. T.* I. ii. 122 Come Captaine, We must be neat; not neat, but cleanly, Captaine. **1862** RUSSELL *Diary, North & S.* I. xiii. 139 All the people who addressed me by name prefixed 'Major' or 'Colonel'. 'Captain' is very low..The conductor who took our tickets was called 'Captain'.

III. 13. A name for the Grey Gurnard.

[*c* **1520** ANDREWE *Noble Lyfe* in *Babees Bk.* (1868) 232 Capitaius is a lytel fisshe with a great hede, a wyde rounde mouthe.] **1810** P. NEILL *Fishes* 14 (Jam.) Grey Gurnard; Crowner.—It is known by a variety of other names, as Captain, Hardhead, etc.

IV. 14. *Comb.*, as ***captain-craft***, ***-commandant***, ***-hackum***, ***-sharp***; **captain's biscuit**, a hard variety of fancy biscuit; †**captain-pacha**: see CAPITAN.

1844 DICKENS *Mar. Chuz.* v. (C.D.) 53 He took a *Captain's biscuit. **1876** BANCROFT *Hist. U.S.* IV. xv. 419 Commissioned..as *captain-commandant for Pittsburg. **1639** FULLER *Holy War* III. xxiv. (1840) 162 There were some mysteries in the *captain-craft. **1877** MAJOR *Discov. Pr. Henry* x. 131 Prince Henry..gave Cabral the rank of *Captain Donatary. **1690** B. E. *Dict. Cant. Crew*, **Captain-hackum*, a Fighting, Blustering, Bully. *Ibid.* **Captain-sharp*, a great Cheat; also a Huffing, yet Sneaking, Cowardly Bully.

†**captain** ('kæptɪn), *a. Obs.* [In part perh. ad. med.L. *capitāneus* chief, principal; but in many cases not to be distinguished from an attrib. use of prec. sb.] Chief, principal, leading, head-.

1566 DRANT *Horace Sat.* ii. B, He lays it to the captaine heape Whereof it rose, and grew. **1566** T. STAPLETON *Ret. Untr. Jewell* iv. 50 A manifest and Captain Untruthe. **1581** MULCASTER *Positions* xxxiii. (1887) 121 Sound sleepe, the captaine cause of good digestion. *c* **1600** SHAKS. *Sonn.* lii, Like stones of worth..Or captain jewels in the carcanet. **1635** R. BOLTON *Comf. Affl. Consc.* iv. 182 Some Captaine and Commanding sinne.

captain ('kæptɪn), *v.* [f. the sb.] **a.** *trans.* To act as captain to, lead as captain, head.

1598 BARRET *Theor. Warres* II. i. 24 Captained as we are, our blind ignorance may chance breed our owne woe. **1700** SOUTHERNE *Fate of Capua* I. i, This head-long rout..Is captain'd, headed, and led on by some. **1815** SOUTHEY *Roderick* XIV. 103 Who called them to the field, who captained them. **1885** *Manch. Even. News* 29 May 2/4 Lord Harris captained the team. **1885** *Sat. Rev.* 4 July 1/2.

b. *intr.*

1671 DRYDEN *Even. Love* 19 As if I were gone a Captaining to Flanders.

Captain Cooker ('kæptɪn 'kʊkə(r)). *N.Z.* Also **Captain Cook**. [f. Captain James *Cook* (1728-79), navigator and explorer.] A wild boar, *Sus scrofa* (supposedly descended from the domesticated pigs introduced into New Zealand by Cook).

1879 *N.Z. Country Jrnl.* III. 55 The immense tusks.. attest..the size of the wild boars or 'Captain Cooks' as the patriarchs are generally termed. **1892** W. E. SWANTON *Notes on N.Z.* 116 The old boars among them are called 'Captain Cooks', after the esteemed founder of their order. **1902** W. S. WALKER *Zealandia's Guerdon* iv. 42 [The dog] got ..'bailed up' a regular 'Captain Cooker', long, lean and very muscular. **1957** D. GLOVER in J. Reid *Kiwi Laughs* (1961) 206 He has taken the liberty of bringing along a complete history of the district from the sighting of the first Captain Cooker by a white man.

captaincy ('kæptɪnsɪ). [f. CAPTAIN *sb.* + -CY (cf. *aldermancy*); after *infancy*, *lieutenancy*, etc., in which the suffix, really *-y*, is apparently *-cy*.]

1. The post or position of captain.

1818 SCOTT *Hrt. Midl.* xvi, The captaincy of the Tolbooth. **1840** CARLYLE *Heroes* (1858) 275 Enlisted, under Heaven's captaincy. **1884** *Cyclist* 13 Feb. 242/1 Mr. G... after seven years of captaincy duties, retires from the post.

2. a. The action or control of a captain; generalship.

1850 CARLYLE *Latter-d. Pamph.* i. 43 To bring these hordes of outcast captainless soldiers under due captaincy. **1864** WENDELL PHILLIPS in *Boston* (Mass.) *Commonw.* 27 May, We have had neither statesmanship in the White house nor captaincy in the head quarters of the army.

b. *spec.* in *Cricket*.

1853 *Bell's Life* 22 May 6/2 The England side was under the captaincy of Mr. Nicholson. **1873** *Baily's Mag.* Aug. 44 The good captaincy added quite a new attraction.

3. The district under the rule of a captain (e.g. in Brazil). [= Sp. *capitania*.]

1821 SOUTHEY *Lett.* (1856) III. 255 Disputes and divisions between the great captaincies will be the next step.

4. captaincy-general = CAPTAIN-GENERALCY.

1846 WORCESTER (citing Murray). **1876** *Gentl. Mag.* XVI. 433 We want.. changes of supreme importance:—Abolition of the Captaincies-General, [etc.].

captainess ('kæptɪnɛs). [f. CAPTAIN *sb.* + -ESS. Cf. F. *capitainesse* in sense 2.]

1. A female captain or commander. (Formerly frequent.)

1465 MARG. PASTON *Lett.* 502 II. 187, I had lever.. to be captensse here then at Caster. **1581** SIDNEY *Astr. & Stella* lxxxviii, From my dear Captainnesse to run away. **1658** USSHER *Ann.* VI. 354 A Company of woemen whose Captainesse was Archidamia. **1864** R. BURTON *Dahome* II. 75 *note*, The captainesses of the life-guards.

†**2.** The flagship of a fleet of galleys. *Obs.*

1600 HOLLAND *Livy* XXXV. xxvi. 903 The rest of the fleete having lost their captainesse [*prætoria nave amissa*].

Captain 'General, captain-general. [= F. *capitain général*, Sp. *capitan general*.] Chief commander of a force: commander-in-chief of an army (*obs.* in Eng. use). Also the governor of a Spanish province or colony.

1514 *Summ. Terouane* in *Rel. Ant.* I. 317 The Lord Pont Deremy, capeteyn generall. **1606** SHAKS. *Tr. & Cr.* II. iii. 279 Honour'd Captaine Generall of the Grecian Armie, Agamemnon. **1708** *Proclam.* 30 Dec. in *Lond. Gaz.* No. 4503/1 John Duke of Marlborough, Captain General of our Forces. **1777** WATSON *Philip II* (1839) 159 The marquis of Mondejar, captain-general of the province. **1809** WELLINGTON *Let.* in Gurw. *Disp.* V. 3 Appointing me one of the Captains General of the Spanish armies. **1845** DARWIN *Voy. Nat.* i. (1879) 3 It is here the governors and captain-generals of the islands have been buried.

captain-generalcy. The office or province of a captain-general. So **captain-generalship.**

1846 WORCESTER (citing *Sat. Mag.*), Captain-generalcy. **1896** *Cosmopolitan* XX. 412/1 The captain-generalcy of Venezuela had then been under the Spanish crown two hundred and forty years. **1898** *Daily News* 28 Nov. 7/4 Before the colonies had secured their independence four of them were rated as Viceroyalties, and five as Captain-Generalships. *Ibid.* 10 Dec. 6/1 Promotion to the Captain-Generalship of Cuba. **1900** *Ibid.* 9 May 9/3 A headquarter [cyclist] corps in London, of which Mr. A. J. Balfour had accepted the Captain Generalcy.

'captaining, *vbl. sb.* [f. CAPTAIN *v.* + -ING¹.] In Cricket, etc.: acting as the captain of a side.

1903 *Westm. Gaz.* 28 May 8/2 On fielding and on captaining. **1904** *Daily Chron.* 10 Aug. 7/3 Their captaining capacities.

'captainless, *a.* Without a captain.

1586 WARNER *Alb. Eng.* III. xix. (R.) But captainless Confusedly they deale. **1796** SOUTHEY *Joan of Arc* VIII. 587 (R.) All captainless, Ill marshalled. **1850** CARLYLE *Latter-d. Pamph.* i. 43 Captainless, uncommanded, these wretched outcast 'soldiers'.. must needs become banditti.

captain-lieu'tenant. A military officer who commanded a company or troop, with a captain's rank, and lieutenant's pay. (The rank no longer exists.)

a **1658** CROMWELL in Rushw. *Hist. Coll.* III. II. 278 My captain-lieutenant slew him. **1745** *Observ. Conc. Navy* 48 In the Army there are Captain-Lieutenants whose Commissions are superiour to all other Lieutenants and inferiour to Captains. **1770** DAVIES in *Phil. Trans.* LX. 187 Tho. Davies, Captain Lieutenant of Artillery. *c* **1880** GRANT *Hist. India* I. lvi. 289/2 Captain-Lieutenant Clark.. was struck on the breast by a spent ball.

†**'captainly,** *a. Obs.* Befitting a captain.

1597 J. PAYNE *Royal Exch.* 34 Endowed wth courrage and Captaynely knowlege.

captain-pasha: see CAPITAN.

†**'captainry.** *Obs.* Also 6 capitanry, -ery. [ad. F. *capitainerie*, in med.L. *capitaneria* (Matt. Paris): see CAPTAIN *sb.* and -RY.]

The office of captain, captaincy; a district under a captain.

1536 BELLENDEN *Cron. Scot.* I. 276 The king of Pichtis.. promittit.. to geif the capitanry of Camelon to him. *c* **1565** LINDESAY (Pitscottie) *Chron. Scot.* (1728) 51 Under the Captainry and Government of James Hamilton. **1577** HOLINSHED *Chron. Irel.* an. 1568 (R.) Fearing that their capteinries should be taken away. **1762** tr. *Busching's Syst. Geog.* III. 740 The capitanery of Luggarus. **1796** MORSE *Amer. Geog.* I. 749 The 16 captainries, into which this country is divided.

'captainship. [f. CAPTAIN *sb.* + -SHIP.]

1. The office, position, authority or rank of a captain; commandership; leadership.

c **1465** *Eng. Chron.* (Camd. Soc.) 79 To dyscharge hym [Capteyn of Caleys] of the capteynshyppe. **1495** *Act 11 Hen. VII*, xxxiii. §25 The Captainshippe of the Castell of Aberwstoyth. **1542** UDALL *Erasm. Apoph.* 234 a, He was putte from the capitaineship of a compaignie of horsemen. **1643** PRYNNE *Power Parl.* II. 63 The Earle of Warwick was elected to the Captainship of Calice. **1752** CARTE *Hist. Eng.* III. 223 The captainship of the Scotch Guards. **1841** W. SPALDING *Italy & It. Isl.* II. 150 A still more terrible host, called the Great Company.. then under the captainship of Lando, a German.

2. The dignity or personality of a captain. *humorous*; cf. *lordship*.

1611 BARREY *Ram Alley* in Hazl. *Dodsley* X. 324 Is this the fittest place Your captainship can find to puff in? **1612** CHAPMAN *Widowes T.* in *Dodsley* (1780) VI. 224 Your Captainship commands my service no farther. *c* **1817** HOGG *Tales & Sk.* VI. 154, I advise your lordship, your captainship, and your besiegership.

3. A district under the rule of a captain.

[transl. Sp. & Pg. *capitania*.]

1680 MORDEN *Geog. Rect.* (1685) 258 The Portugueses enjoy.. the Captainships of Para, etc. **1825** WATERTON *Wand. S. Amer.* II. ii. 173 He has been shot south of the line, in the captainship of Para.

4. Skill in performing the part of captain or leader, 'skill in the military trade' (J.).

1606 SHAKS. *Ant. & Cl.* III. xiii. 8 The itch of his Affection should not then Haue nickt his Captain-ship.

‖**'captal.** *Obs.* [Pr.:—L. *capitāl-is*.] An old title of rank in the south of France = chief, captain, as in the famed *Captal de Buch*, here referred to:

1592 WYRLEY *Armorie* 159 Truth and courage bold That Chandos, and the Captall true did hold.

captan ('kæptən). [Shortened from MERCAPTAN.] The name of a fungicide and pesticide produced from mercaptan.

1953 A. R. KITTLESON in *Jrnl. Agric. & Food Chem.* I. 677/1 SR-406 or captan, the common name.. is a member of a new class of highly active organic fungicides, which is currently undergoing commercial development as an agricultural pesticide. *Ibid.* 678/1 Captan is synthesized by the reaction of sodium.. with perchloromethyl mercaptan. **1955** *Rose Annual* 193 (Advt.), Orthocide Wettable 50% Captan for black spot on roses.

†**'captate,** *v. Obs.* [f. L. *captāt-* ppl. stem of *captāre* to catch at, freq. of *capĕre* to take, seize.] *trans.* To catch at, strive to obtain, seek after.

1628 HOBBES *Thucyd.* I. xxii. *note*, [They] recited their histories to captate glory. **1659** GAUDEN *Tears Church* 255 (D.) Condescending oft.. in order to captate the love and civil favour of people. **1671** *True Non-Conf.* Pref., I do not captate the empty praise of an affected modesty.

captation (kæp'teɪʃən). [a. L. *captātiōn-em*, n. of action f. *captā-re* (see prec.); cf. F. *captation*.] A catching at, an endeavour to get, *esp.* by address or art; the making of *ad captandum* appeals.

1523 SKELTON *Garl. Laurel* 815 With proper captacyouns of benevolence. **1613** R. C. *Table Alph.* (ed. 3), *Captation*, procuring, purchasing. **1628** BP. HALL *Quo Vadis* xv. 700 Neuer generation was so forward as the Jesuiticall for captation of wils [cf. L. *captatio testamenti*] amongst their owne, or of soules amongst strangers. **1648** *Eikon Bas.* 107 Popular captations which some men use in their speeches. **1656** BLOUNT *Glossogr.*, *Captation*, subtilty to get favour, a cunning endeavor to get a thing. **1873** *Daily News* 28 July 4/7 To induce candidates to rely.. less on the arts of political captation.

†**capte.** *Obs.* [ad. L. *capt-us* taking, comprehension, capacity, f. *capt-* ppl. stem of *cap-ĕre* to take.] Capacity, comprehension.

1542 UDALL *Erasm. Apoph.* Pref. 23 b, Helpe the weake and tendre capte of the vnlearned reader. *Ibid.* 321 b, A mery conceipte to those that are of capte to take it.

caption ('kæpʃən), *sb.* Also 4 capcioun. [ad. L. *captiōn-em* taking, f. *capt-* ppl. stem of *capĕre* to take. Cf. OF. *capcion*, *-tion*.]

1. a. Taking, catching, seizure, capture. *now rare.*

1382 WYCLIF *2 Peter* ii. 12 Beestes, kyndeli in to capcioun [Vulg. *in captionem*], or takinge. **1680** *Sess. Admir.* 18 Feb. in Beawes *Lex Mercat.* 238 A caption in order to an adjudication. **1689** *Treaty* in Magens *Insurances* (1755) II. 471 Ships present at the Caption. **1813** *Monthly Mag.* XXXVI. 14 To handle is to exercise the instrument of caption. **1886** *Pall Mall G.* 3 June 16/1 (*Advt.*) Mineral water.. an improved method of caption, by which dilution is avoided.

b. *Law.* Arrest or apprehension by judicial process. (*esp.* in Scotch law.)

1609 SKENE *Reg. Maj.* Table, 70 The forme of the breive of caption of ane debtour. **1635** PAGITT *Christianogr.* III. (1636) 35 Letters of Caption sent forth against the said Prebend. **1702** J. CHAMBERLAYNE *St. Gt. Brit.* II. III. x. (1743) 434 The last step.. is called a caption, which is a warrant to seize the debtor's person. **1739** *Col. Rec. Penn.* IV. 391 Yᵉ Day and Cause of his Caption and Detention. **182.** SCOTT *Rob Roy* Introd., Sentenced by letters of horning and caption. **1837** *New Month. Mag.* XLVII. 310 The caption of some of the most violent appeased the riot.

2. The action of cavilling or taking exception; an objection or cavil; fallacious or captious argument; a quibble, sophism. (L. *captio*.)

1605 BACON *Adv. Learning* II. xiv. §6. 55 The degenerate and corrupt vse is for Caption and contradiction. **1622–62** HEYLIN *Cosmogr.* Introd. (1674) 2/1 Not to spend more time in answering so vain a Caption. **1655** FULLER *Ch. Hist.* II. 84 How causelesse is the Caption of the Papists at the Consecration of Matthew Parker. *a* **1734** NORTH *Lives* I. 365 He.. showing them the proclamation, asked if they could find any caption to be made upon it. **1922** *Public Opinion* 14 July 36/1 Genius like hers stands above envy and caption.

3. *Law.* 'That part of a legal instrument, as a commission, indictment, etc., which shows where, when, and by what authority it is taken, found, or executed' (Tomlins *Law Dict.* 1809). This appears to be short for 'certificate or note of caption or taking'; and it is sometimes used for the 'making or execution' of this certificate.

1670 BLOUNT *Law Dict.* s.v. *Caption* (*Captio*), When a Commission is executed, and the Commissioners names subscribed to a Certificate, declaring when and where the Commission was executed, that is called the Caption. **1790** DALLAS *Amer. Law Rep.* I. 131 The time from which they are bound: whether from the caption or from the inrolment of the recognizance. **1818** CRUISE *Digest* V. 123 Unless the caption of such fine be before one of the justices or barons. **1885** J. WOODCOCK in *Law Times* LXXIX. 233/1 A customary tenant.. must attend before the steward to be sworn to the caption.

The foregoing is sometimes explained as 'the beginning or heading of a warrant, commission, or indictment', whence comes

4. The heading of a chapter, section, or newspaper article (chiefly used in U.S.). Also used (orig. *U.S.*) for the title below an illustration; in cinematography and television, a sub-title. Also *attrib.* and *Comb.*

1789 J. MADISON *Writ.* (1904) V. 355 You will see in the caption of the address that we have pruned the ordinary stile of the degrading appendages of Excellency, Esqrs. &c. **1821** *Massachusetts Spy* 24 Oct. (Th.), [The statute] is under the caption of 'Fees in the Secretary's office'. **1848** BARTLETT *Dict. Amer.*, *Caption*: This legal term is used in the newspapers where an Englishman would say *title*, *head*, or *heading*. **1854** *N. & Q.* Ser. I. IX. 245/1 [A review] having three works as the caption of the article. **1865** GROSART *Palmer's Mem.* Introd. 21 Prof. De Morgan.. delighting the readers of the Athenæum with the treasures of his.. reading, under the caption, 'A Budget of Paradoxes'. **1879** G. PRESCOTT *Sp. Telephone* 111 A short article.. in.. this journal under the caption 'Galvanic Music'. **1894** H. FREDERIC *Copperhead* 83 Spreading eagles in front, over the printed captions. **1919** H. L. WILSON *Ma Pettengill* ii. 43 The caption says of Vida Sommers: 'Her love has turned to hate.' **1920** *Glasgow Herald* 23 July 7 The Speaker said that this part of the bill—the caption, he believed was its proper title—was not submitted to the House. **1923** *Yorkshire Post* 17 Dec. 6/8 A continuous alternation of pictures and those pieces of text that are, one believes, known as captions. **1924** D. MCCARTHY *Drama* (1940) 360 It is true that the expression on a film actor's face may occasionally suggest that he, or she, is saying something worth hearing, but the audience cannot supply it from their imaginations; neither can 'the caption' writer. **1936** *Punch* 10 June 654/2 The film *The Emperor's Candlesticks*.. is in German, and.. those who do not know German.. have to collect the sense through captions in our own tongue. **1938** [see CUT *sb.*² 36]. **1964** T. RATTIGAN *Heart to Heart* in *Coll. Plays* III. 426 In on David. Super his caption. *Ibid.*, Take out caption. Cue David. **1968** *Listener* 20 June 814/2, I have seen one of these pictures used in a Chinese magazine over the caption 'US aggressor flees'.

caption, *v.* [f. the sb.] *trans.* To provide with a caption, heading, or title; to entitle. Hence **'captioning** *vbl. sb.*

1901 *Science* 22 Nov. 808 An effective poem.. captioned 'The Song of the Innuit'. **1912** J. LONDON *Son of Sun* VII. ii, It means the feathers of the sun. Thus does this base interloper caption himself. **1927** *Observer* 27 Nov. 14/5 [His] article captioned 'Cecil Sharp'. **1957** *Listener* 12 Dec. 1001/2 The captioning sometimes strays awkwardly on to the picture.

'captionless, *a.* Of a cartoon: without a caption.

1944 *Newsweek* 25 Sept. 102 This captionless effort.. is from a collection of cartoons. **1961** *Times* 23 Nov. 17/4 The captionless jokes in the *New Yorker*.

captious ('kæpʃəs), *a.* Forms: 4, 6 **capcious,** 5 **-cyows,** 6 **-tius,** 7 **-tiose,** 6– **captious.** [ad. F. *captieux* or L. *captiōs-us* fallacious, sophistical, f. *captiōn-em* (see CAPTION *sb.*).]

I. Apt to catch or take one in; fitted to ensnare or perplex in argument; designed to entrap or entangle by subtlety; fallacious, sophistical.

1447 BOKENHAM *Seyntys* 7 At Caimbrygge.. Where wyttys be manye ryht capcyows And subtyl. **1530** PALSGR. 307/1 Capcious, crafty in wordes to take one in a trap, *captieux*. **1548** UDALL, etc. *Erasm. Par. Mark* ii. 23 a, Wherfore they went vnto Iesus, & moued vnto hym this capcious question. **1677** GALE *Crt. Gentiles* II. III. 31 Verbal, Captiose, Sophistic Questions. **1784** COWPER *Tirocinium* 903 A captious question, sir, and yours is one, Deserves an answer similar, or none. **1871** BLACKIE *Four Phases* I. 113 By captious questions to worm answers out of other people.

†**b.** Crafty. *Obs.*

1590 SWINBURN *Testaments* 147 This former kinde of disposition which by reason of the cunning condition appeareth to be made in hope of gaine, and is therefore properlie tearmed captious. **1608** TOPSELL *Serpents* 779 Spiders.. have given themselves.. to captious taking at advantage, watching and espying their prey.

2. Apt to catch at faults or take exception to actions; disposed to find fault, cavil, or raise objections; fault-finding, cavilling, carping.

c **1380** WYCLIF *Serm.* Sel. Wks. II. 13 þes wordis ben soþeli seid aȝens alle capcious men. **1538** COVERDALE *N.T.* Prol., The world is captious, and many there be that had rather find twenty faults, than to amend one. **1561** EDEN tr. *Cortes' Arte de Navigar* Pref. ad fin., Enemies to vertue & captious of other mens doinges. **1655** FULLER *Ch. Hist.* Pref., To cut off all occasions of Cavill from captious persons. **1804** *Med. Jrnl.* XII. 359 The objections of the captious. **1865** TROLLOPE *Belton Est.* vi. 60 He was captious, making little difficulties, and answering him with petulance.

3. In various nonce-uses.

†**a.** Able to take in or contain, capacious. *Obs.*

1601 SHAKS. *All's Well* I. iii. 208 Yet in this captious, and intenible Siue, I still poure in the waters of my loue And lacke not to loose still.

†**b.** Alluring, taking, plausible. *Obs.*

1776 Sir P. Francis in *Mem.* (1867) II. 55 The proposition was captious, and if made at an earlier period, might have been listened to by some of us.

c. *humorous.* ?

1808 W. Irving *Knickerb.* (1861) 134 Little captious short pipes, two inches in length, which..could be stuck in one corner of the mouth.

captiously ('kæpʃəslɪ), *adv.* [f. prec. + -ly^2.] In a captious manner.

1539 Bible (Great) *Luke* xi. 53 The lawears and the Pharyses began..capciously to aske him many thynges. 1563-87 Foxe *A. & M.* (1684) III. 239 Captiously asking often of Bradford a direct answer concerning Oaths. 1657 J. Smith *Myst. Rhet.* 78 A fallacy in sophistry, that is, when a saying is captiously taken and turned to another sense. 1812 J. & H. Smith *Rej. Addr.* x. (1873) 96 Objections..captiously urged. 1866 G. Macdonald *Ann. Q. Neighb.* xxiii. (1878) 415 The father..had been behaving captiously and unjustly to his son.

captiousness ('kæpʃəsnɪs). [f. as prec. + -ness.] Captious quality or disposition.

1545 Udall, etc. *Erasm. Par. Luke* (1548) 71 a, The malicious capciousnesse of the Pharisees and of the Scribes. 1664 H. More *Myst. Iniq.* 101 Who put questions..for captiousness, contention and a conceited hope of puzzling him. 1750 Johnson *Rambl.* No. 74 ¶5 The captiousness of old age. 1861 *Sat. Rev.* 30 Nov. 562 [He] sometimes pushes his criticism to the length of captiousness.

†**captivable,** *a. Obs. rare*$^{-1}$. [f. captive *v.* + -able.] That can be taken captive.

1675 H. More in R. Ward *Life* (1710) 244 If we find our selves Captivable by them.

†**cap'tivance.** *Obs. rare.* Also -aunce. [f. F. *captiver* to captive + -ance.] = captivation, captivity.

1596 Spenser *F.Q.* iii. vii. 45 That wofull squyre Whom he had reskewed from captivaunce. *Ibid.* v. vi. 17 With that he gan at large to her dilate The whole discourse of his captivance sad.

captivate ('kæptɪveɪt), *v.* [f. late L. *captīvāt-* ppl. stem of *captīvāre* to take captive, f. *captīvus* captive; cf. F. *captiver* and captive *v.*]

†1. a. *trans.* To make captive, take prisoner, capture. *Obs.* or *arch.*

c1555 Harpsfield *Divorce Hen. VIII* (1878) 186 The Emperor would yet again captivate the Pope. 1641 J. Jackson *True Evang. T.* iii. 209 Crœsus..when he was captivated by Cyrus. 1768 C. Beatty *Two Months' Tour* 11 The Indians..killed and captivated all. 1796 Morse *Amer. Geog.* I. 428 They were mostly taken or destroyed by the enemy, and their seamen captivated. 1825 *Bro. Jonathan* III. 86 The British..captured or captivated four successive patroles. 1840 C. F. Hoffman *Greyslaer* I. x. 114 We can captivate those chaps complete,..if they only move a little further down stream. 1873 J. M. Bailey *Life in Danbury* 137 Captivating coons is not a very easy task.

†b. To capture, secure, hold captive (animals and things). *Obs.*

1595 *Locrine* iii. iv. 165 Thy bragging banners..Shall all be captivated with this hand. 1613 Purchas *Pilgr.* I. vi. i. 466 Another captivateth his legges with a Rope. 1696 Tryon *Misc.* i. 6 There this dark furious Spirit is hid or captivated.

†2. *fig.* To make or hold captive, put or keep in subjection, subjugate (the mind, mental attributes, etc.) Const. *to*. *Obs.* exc. as passing into 3.

c1526 Frith *Disput. Purgatory* (1829) 118 Let us ever captivate our reason unto that. 1603 Florio *Montaigne* (1634) 189, I captivate more easily my conceits under the auctoritie of ancient opinions. 1611 Bible *Pref.* 116 They that are wise, had rather haue their iudgements at libertie in differences of readings, then to be captiuated to one. 1698 Norris *Pract. Disc.* (1707) IV. 269 That requires us to captivate our Reason to the Obedience of Faith. 1838 J. Halley in *Life* (1842) 163 Lord, subdue me to thyself; captivate me to thyself.

3. *esp.* 'To overpower with excellence' (J.): to enthrall with charm or attractiveness; to enslave, fascinate, enamour, enchant, charm.

1535 Coverdale *Judith* xvi. 9 Hir bewtye captyuated his mynde. 1592 Shaks. *Ven. & Ad.* 281 This I do to captivate the eye Of the fair breeder that is standing by. 1665 Boyle *Occas. Refl.* vi. x. (R.) Princesses..who captivate by proxy. 1713 Addison *Guardian* No. 111 Wisdom..so captivates him with her appearance, that he gives himself up to her. 1768 Beattie *Minstr.* ii. xxxvi, Lured by the toys that captivate the throng. 1814 Scott *Wav.* xiv, The sort of beauty or merit, which captivates a romantic imagination in early youth. 1828 D'Israeli *Chas. I*, I. v. 92 A tale..to captivate the listeners, and humour the nation.

†'**captivate,** *ppl. a. Obs.* Also 6-7 -at. [ad. L. *captīvāt-us*: see prec.] = captivated. Hence †'**captivately** *adv.*, in captive condition or form.

1556 J. Heywood *Spider & F.* lxxiii. 12 Before nor since my suffrance captiuatlie. 1581 J. Bell *Haddon's Answ. Osor.* 137 b, It is bond, servile and altogether captivate. 1591 Shaks. *1 Hen. VI*, v. iii. 107 Tush, women haue bene captiuate ere now. 1610 Holland *Camden's Brit.* i. 247 That Arke In Balaims temple Captivate. 1671 *True Non-Conf.* 427 His Majestie..was so possessed and captivat by a design.

'**captivated,** *ppl. a.* [f. prec. vb. + -ed.] Made captive, enthralled.

1621 Molle *Camerar. Liv. Libr.* Ded., This captiuated and exhausted Kingdome. 1636 Featly *Clavis Myst.* xiii. 183 To release your long captivated attention. 1692 South *12 Serm.* (1697) I. 294 The Victorious Philistines were worsted by the Captivated Ark. 1750 Beawes *Lex Mercat.* (1752) 213 The Captor must exhibit all the..captivated mariners to be examined. *Mod.* A captivated admirer.

captivater, obs. f. captivator.

captivating ('kæptɪveɪtɪŋ), *vbl. sb.* The action of the verb captivate.

1623 Hart *Arraignm. Ur.* Ded., The captivating of the French King. 1659 Pearson *Creed* (1839) 354 By captivating he ascended.

'**captivating,** *ppl. a.* That captivates, takes captive, or enthralls. (See the vb.)

1675 H. More in R. Ward *Life* (1710) 244 The Captivating Desires of the Animal Life. 1690 Baxter *Kingd. Christ* i. (1691) 6 Their Persecuting, Captivating..Enemies. a1711 Ken *Hymnoth.* Poet. Wks. 1721 III. 213 When captivating Death he captive led. 1772 Wilkes *Corr.* (1805) IV. 109 Mrs. Garrick is..the most captivating of the whole circle. 1868 Freeman *Norm. Conq.* (1876) II. viii. 219 The tale is one of the most captivating in the whole range of monastic history.

Hence '**captivatingly** *adv.*

1861 *Temple Bar* III. 533 The child is captivatingly modelled. 1863 E. C. Clayton *Queens of Song* II. 326 Never did she sing or act more captivatingly.

captivation (kæptɪ'veɪʃən). [ad. L. *captīvātiōn-em*, n. of action f. *captīvāre* to captivate.]

1. The action of taking or holding captive; the fact or state of being taken or held captive; now only *fig.*, of the attention, mind, fancy, affections.

1610 Healey *St. Aug. City of God* 712 In the seaventith yeare after their captivation they [i.e. Jews] returned home. a1656 Bp. Hall *Rem. Wks.* (1660) 21 No small part of our servitude lyes in the captivation of our understanding. 1751 Johnson *Rambl.* No. 147 ¶5 By some occult method of captivation, he animated the torpid..and opened the reserved. 1868 Holme Lee *B. Godfrey* xxiv. 129 It was a case of mutual captivation. 1878 C. Stanford *Symb. Christ* 49 They are bound, not in captivity, but in captivation.

2. A captivating influence, a fascination.

1824 Scott *St. Ronan's* xviii, Lady Penelope threw out the captivations of her wit.

captivative ('kæptɪveɪtɪv), *a.* [f. L. *captīvāt-* (see above) + -ive.] Fitted or tending to captivate.

1772 J. Ross *Winterdine Rocks* 42 The warbling tenants of the Grove, Which captivative trill the voice of love.

captivator ('kæptɪveɪtə(r)). In 7 also -er. [f. captivate *v* + -or.] One who captivates.

1651 Baxter *Inf. Bapt.* 151 Captivaters of the best of their Brethren. 1690 —— *Kingd. Christ* ii. (1691) 41 Babylonish Conqueror and Captivater. 1862 F. Hall *Hindu Philos. Syst.* 62 Nature is both the captivator and the emancipator of the soul.

captive ('kæptɪv), *a.* and *sb.* Also 4-5 captif(e, -yfe, 6- yue. [a. F. *captif, -ive*, ad. L. *captīv-us* taken prisoner, a prisoner, f. *capt-us* taken: see -ive. Cf. caitiff.]

A. *adj.* (In early use, and in many phrases, the adj. and sb. are hardly separable.)

1. a. Taken prisoner in war, or by force; kept in confinement or bondage.

c1374 Chaucer *Troylus* iii. 333 Stocked in prison..Captive to cruell king Agamemnon. 1535 Coverdale *Ezra* x. 6 Put out from the congregacion of the captiue. 1611 Bible *2 Macc.* viii. 10 To make so much money of the captiue Iewes. a1700 Dryden *Pal. & Arc.* i. 511 Nor hopes the captive lord his liberty. 1855 H. Reed *Lect. Eng. Lit.* iv. (1878) 128 Kings were captive in England's capital.

b. *transf.* Said of animals caught and kept in confinement, e.g. *a captive lark*; also of things restrained from escaping, as *a captive balloon*.

1855 *Househ. Words* XI. 150/2 Pilâtre de Rosier..had already the honour of being the first man who ascended..in a captive balloon. 1897 *Aeronaut. Jrnl.* Jan. 5/2 My own apparatus..is simply a system of large kites only for captive use. *Ibid.*, My present object is to get an apparatus to serve instead of a captive balloon. 1939 G. Greene *Lawless Roads* x. 251 The twenty-four churches rose like captive balloons.

c. *to lead, take, hold captive*: perh. this was orig. the sb., as in *to take prisoner*, but it remains unchanged in the pl.

[1382 Wyclif *2 Chron.* xxx. 9 Their lordis that hem laddyn caityf.] 1535 Coverdale *Jer.* xxii. 11 In the place, where vnto he is led captyue. 1575 Laneham *Let.* (1871) 32 Many led captiue for triumph. 1611 Bible *Gen.* xiv. 14 His brother was taken captiue. 1806 A. Knox *Rem.* I. 33 Temptations by which..we were led captive. 1884 Gustafson *Found. Death* i. (ed. 3) 4 Setting free the waters they had held captive.

d. *captive audience*: an audience of captives; esp. in extended use, an audience that cannot escape a particular form of entertainment or instruction. orig. *U.S.*

1902 W. D. Howells *Lit. & Life* 57 It was on a Sunday that we crouched in an irregular semicircle..within the prison pale, and faced the captive audience in another semicircle. 1949 in *Amer. Speech* (1951) XXVI. 208/1 It [tram radio] gives a radio station what is referred to in less polite circles as a 'captive' audience. 1956 A. Huxley *Adonis & Alphabet* 119 If they [*sc.* publishers]..possess a large enough captive audience for their text-books to be able to implement their good intentions. 1956 *Kenyon Rev.* XVIII. 463 The captive audience of the class-room. 1959 Thurber *Years with Ross* v. 82 The captive audiences in Grand Central Station, where passengers had been forced to listen to broadcast commercials. 1966 *Listener* 2 June 785/2 We must be especially careful with a captive audience. No airline would inflict a stream of dirty stories..on the helpless passengers on a long-distance journey. 1970 B. Aldiss *Hand-reared Boy* 42, I cannot remember a word she said, being merely a captive audience and bored with the whole visit.

e. Applied to a mine that supplies its products only to commercial concerns under the same ownership, i.e. not to the open market. *U.S.*

1924 *Min. Resources U.S. 1922* II. 546 It was not possible, however, to distinguish..between the output of commercial mines and the output of the 'captive mines' owned or controlled by consumers. 1948 *Economist* 10 July 59/2 The steel companies which operate 'captive' coal mines.

2. *fig.* Captivated, enslaved in will and feeling.

1594 Shaks. *Rich. III*, iv. i. 80 My Womans heart, Grossely grew captiue to his honey words. 1601 —— *All's Well* v. iii. 17 Whose words all eares took captiue.

3. Of or belonging to a captive.

1590 Spenser *F.Q.* i. vii. 49 That he my captive languor should redeeme. 1671 Milton *Samson* 1603, I sorrowed at his captive state.

¶4. Used for caitiff *a.* or *sb.*

1634 *Malory's Arthur* (1816) II. 239, I am the most wretch and captive of the world.

B. *sb.*

1. a. A person taken prisoner, in war, or by brigands or savages; one taken and held in confinement.

?a1400 *Morte Arth.* 1580 To comone with his captifis fore covatys of silver. 1494 Fabyan iv. lxvii. 45 To be a Captyue or a prysoner to ye Romaynes. 1611 Bible *Dan.* ii. 25 A man of the captiues of Iudah. 1713 Young *Force Relig.* i. (1757) 53 But whither is the captive borne away, The beauteous captive, from the chearful day?

fig. c1600 Shaks. *Sonn.* lxvi, And captiue-good attending Captaine ill.

b. *transf.* Said of an animal or thing.

1820 *Hoyle's Games Impr.* 313 He [a piece at draughts] becomes king and is crowned by placing one of the captives upon him. 1885 *Pall Mall G.* 7 Feb. 3/2 The balloon committee at Chatham is only busy with 'captives'.

2. *fig.* One captivated or enslaved by beauty, personal influence, or the like.

1732 Lansdowne *Beauty & Law* (R.) The fairest of the sex complain Of captives lost, and loves invok'd in vain.

C. *Comb.* **captive-like** *a.* and *adv.*

1583 T. Watson *Poems* lxxiii. (Arb.) 109 The winged boy..led him captiuelyke from all delight.

captive ('kæptɪv), *v. arch.* [a. F. *captive-r* (15th c.):—L. *captīvāre*, f. *captīv-us* captive *a.*

In very common use in 16-18th c.; rare in 19th. Orig. pronounced *cap'tive*, as still in Milton; but *'captive*, used by Shaks., and frequent in 17th c., alone survives.]

To take captive, bring into captivity: a. *lit.*

c1430 Lydg. *Min. Poems* (1840) 38 Thei hym captived, whereby he was y-lore. 1596 H. Clapham *Briefe Bible* i. 91 Tiglath Pileeser had before tyme captived them [the Israelites]. 1599 Shaks. *Hen. V*, ii. iv. 55 When Cressy battell fatally was strucke, And all our princes captiu'd. 1702 C. Mather *Magn. Chr.* ii. (1852) App. 217 They butchered and captived many of the inhabitants. 1756 Burke *Vind. Nat. Soc.* Wks. 1842 I. 8 And their inhabitants slaughtered, and captived. 1828 W. Taylor *Surv. Germ. Poetry* I. 300 Thusnelda has been captived by the Romans.

b. *fig.* To captivate, enthrall (the understanding, reason, affections, will, etc.).

1528 More *Heresyes* i. Wks. 169/1 To captiue and subdewe oure vnderstandyng. 1581 J. Bell *Haddon's Answ. Osor.* 142 b, Freewill being captived hath no power to worke anything but sinne. a1595 Southwell *Peter's Compl.*, O women! woe to men; traps for their falls..Earth's necessary ills, captiving thralls. c1605 Rowley *Birth Merl.* ii. ii. 305 That face..Captiv'd my senses. 1640 Bastwick *Lord Bps.* ii. B ij b, Captiving them with manyfold ceremonies. c1720 Prior (J.) How she the vagrant might inthral, And captive him, who captives all. 1761 Churchill *Rosciad* (R.) If music..Captives the ear.

Hence '**captived** *ppl. a.*, '**captiving** *ppl. a.*, etc.

1591 Horsey *Trav.* (1857) 182 To by and redeme divers..of those captived people. 1596 Spenser *F.Q.* iii. i. 2 But the captiv'd Acrasia he sent..a nigher way. 1613 Purchas *Pilgr.* I. i. xvii. 79 The Philistins placed the Captived Arke in Dagon's Temple. 1671 Milton *Samson* 33. 1724 Ramsay *Tea-t. Misc.* (1733) II. 125 My captiv'd fancy. 1798 *Monthly Mag.* VI. 99 The captived king Zedekiah.

†'**captivement.** *Obs. rare*$^{-1}$. [f. captive *v.* + -ment, or a. obs. F. *captivement*, f. *captiver*.] A taking captive, captivity.

1714 'Nestor Ironside' *Orig. Canto Spenser* xxv, And eas'd the Pain of her sad Captivement.

†**captiver.** *Obs.* [f. captive *v.* + -er.] One who takes captive; a captor.

1613 Forbes *On Rev.* 200 The captiuers are captiued. 1640 Featly *Reinolds* in Fuller *Abel Rediv.* (1867) II. 222 Without captiver both are captive led.

captivity (kæp'tɪvɪtɪ). Also 4 (captyuide), 4-6 captyuyte, 6-7 captiuitie. [perh. a. F. *captivité*, ad. L. *captīvitas, -tātem*, f. *captīv-us* captive. The OF. was *chetiveté*: as Littré has *captivité* only from 15th c., the ME. may have been direct ad. Lat.]

1. The condition of a captive; the state of being held prisoner by an enemy or conqueror; sometimes *spec.* that of the Jews at Babylon.

c1325 *E.E. Allit. P.* B. 1612 þat caȝt watz in þe captyuide in cuntre of Iues. c1380 Wyclif *Wicket* (1828) 2 They shall fall..into captyvyte manye dayes. 1480 Caxton *Chron. Eng.* ccliv. 328 There were many cristen men..put in captyuyte. 1593 Shaks. *3 Hen. VI*, iv. v. 13 To set him free from his

Captiuitie. **1662** STILLINGFL. *Orig. Sacr.* I. vi. §8 How durst Ezra..after the Captivity, profane so sacred a thing? **1794** SULLIVAN *View Nat.* II. 238 Their several captivities, dispersions, and desolations. **1860** PUSEY *Min. Proph.* 135 A captivity implies a removal of the inhabitants.

b. of a captive animal.

1774 GOLDSM. *Nat. Hist.* V. 305 A malicious joy in these call-birds to bring the wild ones into the same state of captivity.

2. *fig.* The servitude or subjection of the reason, will, or affections.

1538 STARKEY *England* 31 Wyse conseyl may at the lest.. restore the wyl out of such captyvyte. **1552** ABP. HAMILTON *Catech.* (1884) 38 The miserable captivitie of the devil. **1605** BACON *Adv. Learn.* I. IV. §12 Disciples do owe unto masters ..not an absolute resignation or perpetual captivity. **1611** BIBLE *2 Cor.* x. 5 Bringing into captiuitie euery thought to the obedience of Christ. **1651** HOBBES *Leviath.* III. xxxii. 196 By the captivity of our understanding is..meant a Submission..of the Will to Obedience. **1714** ADDISON *Cato* III. i. (L.) The strong, the brave, the virtuous, the wise Sink in the soft captivity together.

†**3.** Those who are in captivity; captives collectively. (A Hebraism.) *Obs. to lead captivity captive*: a Scriptural phrase used in *Judges* v. 12, *Ps.* lxviii. 19 in the sense of 'lead off one's captives in triumph'; but often taken (after *Eph.* iv. 8) in the sense 'to lead away into captivity those who have held others in bondage'.

1526 TINDALE *Eph.* iv. 8 He is gone vp an hye, and hath ledde captivitie captive [WYCLIF, ledde caitifte caitif]. **1597** HOOKER *Eccl. Pol.* v. lxxviii §9 He led captivity captive. **1611** BIBLE *Judg.* v. 12 Leade thy captiutie captiue, thou sonne of Abinoam [**1382** WYCLIF, Tak thi chaytyues; **1388** thi prisoneris; **1535** COVERD. Catch hem y^t catched thee, thou son of Abinoam]. —— *Dan.* vi. 13 That Daniel which is of the captiuity of the children of Iudah. **1667** MILTON *P.L.* x. 188 And with ascention bright Captivity led captive through the Aire.

captor ('kæptə(r), -ɔː(r)). [a. L. *captor*, agent-n. f. *cap-ĕre* to take (see CAPTURE): cf. F. *capteur.*]

1. One who takes by force a prisoner or a prize; *spec.* (in 18th c.) one who makes a capture at sea.

1688 MIEGE *Gt. Fr. Dict.*, *Captor*, celui qui a fait la prise. **1712** *Act 10 Anne* xxvi. §113 Her Majesty's Declaration made in favour of the Captors of prizes. **1722** CAPT. OGLE in *Lond. Gaz.* No. 6091/3, I being Captor, was disqualified. **1755** MAGENS *Insurances* I. 487 Before the Ship or Goods, can be disposed of by the Captor. **1805** SOUTHEY *Madoc in Azt.* xviii, Ririd..Close on the captors, with avenging sword, Follow'd right on. **1871** BLACKIE *Four Phases* i. 56 Lysander the captor of Athens.

†**2.** A censor. (Cf. *caption.*) *Sc. Obs.*

1646 ROW *Hist. Kirk* (1842) 186 There were captors appointed to observe what speeches ministers uttered.

captress ('kæptrɪs). *rare.* [f. CAPTOR + -ESS.] A female captor.

1867 *Pall Mall G.* 21 Feb. 3 He has followed his captress with heavy heart and sickly smile.

capturable ('kæptjʊərəb(ə)l), *a.* [f. CAPTURE *v.* + -ABLE.] Capable of being captured.

1865 CARLYLE *Fredk. Gt.* IX. xx. iii. 36 Breslau capturable. **1876** *Tinsley's Mag.* XIX. 109 Less capturable than the sleeping weasel.

capture ('kæptjʊə(r)), *sb.* [a. F. *capture* (16th c. in Littré), ad. L. *captūra* taking, seizing, f. *capt-* ppl. stem of *cap-ĕre* to take: see -URE.]

1. a. The fact of seizing or taking forcibly, or by stratagem, or of being thus seized or taken; catching; seizure; arrest; *esp.* the seizing as a prize.

1541-2 in Pitcairn *Crim. Trials* 257* Remission to John Lausone..for his capture and apprehension. **1611** COTGR., *Capture*, a capture or taking. **1713** *Guardian* No. 159 Being concerned in several captures, he brought home with him an estate of about twelve thousand pounds. **1841** ELPHINSTONE *Hist. Ind.* II. 197 After Akber's capture of Ahmednagar. **1848** ARNOULD *Mar. Insur.* (1866) II. III. ii. 706 *Capture* is the forcible taking of a ship, etc. in time of war, with a view to appropriating it as prize. **1873** MORLEY *Rousseau* II. 124 The primitive usages of..marriages by capture, purchase, and the rest.

b. *Physical Geogr.* The process by which a stream by headwater erosion encroaches on the basin of a stream at a higher level, and diverts the upper waters of the latter into its own channel; also the point of such diversion; said also of a glacier.

1898 *Geogr. Jrnl.* XI. 441 M. Meunier explains the distribution of erratics in the neighbourhood of the Alps by the 'capture' of one glacier by another, the head of which has eaten back through the dividing wall, and thus tapped the ice-supply. **1908** J. LOMAS in *Nature Book* I. 165 Standing at the elbow of the capture of the Hodder, and looking seawards. **1965** A. HOLMES *Princ. Phys. Geol.* (ed. 2) xix. 560 Eventually C_2 is intercepted, its headwaters are diverted into S_1 and its lower course is beheaded. This process is called river capture. The rectangular bend *e* at the point of diversion is known as the elbow of capture.

c. *Astr.* The process whereby a star or planet brings an object within its gravitational field. Also *attrib.*

1910 T. J. J. SEE *Res. Evolution Stellar Systems* II. xxiv. 731 The Capture Theory is so overwhelmingly indicated by the most diverse phenomena of the Starry Heavens, that I cannot doubt that it represents an ultimate truth... Moons and planets..always drift towards the powerful centres of attraction, and are finally captured or absorbed. **1940** *Monthly Not. R. Astron. Soc.* C. 552 The decisive moment for capture is when the parent stars have only just separated after the collision. **1958** *Listener* 20 Nov. 821/2 A few years ago Hoyle also believed in the capture theory but in a different form.

d. *Physics.* The process in which an atomic particle is absorbed by another particle, an atom, or a nucleus. (Formerly believed to be a process by which one particle cohered to another.)

1923 RUTHERFORD in *Proc. Camb. Phil. Soc.* XXI. 510 The capture of electrons by flying α particles has thus opened up a new and interesting field of enquiry. **1929** J. CHADWICK in *Proc. Roy. Soc.* A. CXXIII. 383 The disintegration [of the nucleus] is supposed to occur when an α-particle penetrates into a nucleus and is captured by it, the result of the capture being the emission of a proton. **1938** R. W. LAWSON tr. *Hevesy & Paneth's Man. Radioactivity* (ed. 2) ii. 33 In the course of the flight of an α-particle this capture and loss of electrons is repeated several thousand times. **1955** FRIEDMAN & WEISSKOPF in W. Pauli *Niels Bohr* 136 The actual predominance of capture over scattering in low energy resonances is easily described.

e. = *data capture* s.v. DATUM 3.

1971 [see TELECOMMUNICATION]. **1984** *Glaxo Group News* Apr. 8/5 The systems installed are used for a wide variety of applications such as the capture of cancer research data. **1986** *Pract. Computing* Oct. 32/1 The simplest form of file transfer is using the capture or log to disc facility of your software.

2. The prize, prey, or booty so taken.

1706 in PHILLIPS. **1750** BEAWES *Lex Mercat.* (1752) 213 It is allowable to bring a dubious capture into port. **1775** JOHNSON *West. Isl.* Wks. X. 399 Produces a plentiful capture of herrings. *Mod.* He had been butterfly-hunting, and now exhibited his captures.

'capture, *v.* [f. prec. sb.: cf. F. *capture-r.* Not in Johnson 1755–73; replaces CAPTIVE *v.*]

1. a. *trans.* To make a capture of; to take prisoner; to catch by force, surprise, or stratagem; to seize as a prize in war.

1795 SOUTHEY *Joan of Arc* III. 121 His bravest Chiefs Or slain or captured. **1814** WELLINGTON *Let.* in Gurw. *Disp.* XII. 8 The value of the property so captured. **1850** PRESCOTT *Peru* II. 175 To disperse the enemy, and, if possible, to capture their leader. **1879** LUBBOCK *Sci. Lect.* i. 5 To capture small aquatic animals.

fig. **1873** BLACK *Pr. Thule* xviii. 281 As if women were to be captured by millinery! **1882** HINSDALE *Garfield & Educ.* I. 60 He took great pleasure in 'capturing boys', as he called it.

b. *Physical Geogr.* Of a river or glacier: to divert by capture (see prec. 1 b).

1900 *Geogr. Jrnl.* XVI. 36 It may then have happened that whole basins, like that of Lake Mascardi, drained formerly towards Nahuelhuapi, have been captured towards the Pacific slopes. **1908** J. LOMAS in *Nature Book* I. 166 Along the Vale of York, where the rocks are softer than those of the Pennines or East Yorkshire, the Don sent up a tributary and successively captured the rivers to form what is now the Ouse. **1965** A. HOLMES *Princ. Phys. Geol.* (ed. 2) xix. 562 The headwaters of the Aire..were captured by the Ribble.

c. *Astr.* Of a star or planet: to bring an object within its gravitational field (see prec. 1 c).

1910 [see CAPTURE *sb.* 1 c]. **1958** tr. *J. Verne's Round Moon* 11 It had however travelled so near to the moon that it had been 'captured' by the lunar gravitation. **1959** *Listener* 23 Apr. 708/1 Mercury has a captured rotation; that is to say, its sidereal period is equal to its axial rotation period, eighty-eight Earth days in each case. **1961** *Ibid.* 9 Nov. 766/1 According to one theory, minor satellites of this sort are really in the nature of captured asteroids. **1969** *Times* 13 June 7/7 It seems that the moon was either a wandering planet that was captured by the earth or else was formed from a cloud of matter.

d. *Physics.* To bring about the capture of (a particle) (see prec. 1 d).

1923 RUTHERFORD in *Proc. Camb. Philos. Soc.* XXI. 506 The α particle in passing through matter occasionally captures an electron. **1929** [see CAPTURE *sb.* 1 d]. **1956** A. H. COMPTON *Atomic Quest* 18 The uranium atom when it captured the neutron, became unstable and divided into roughly two equal parts.

e. To cause (data) to be entered into a computer.

1971 *Computers & Humanities* VI. 46 A terminal that cannot capture text without the help of the main computer cannot therefore be considered. **1977** *Building Societies Gaz.* July 697/2 Datapad requires no specialist training, captures data at source, eliminates punching and verifying errors, accepts most freehand writing styles and produces clean input data for any mainframe system. **1980** *Regional Lang. Stud.—Newfoundland* IX. 22 Twenty or thirty pages are being captured experimentally, with appropriate codes, on a diskette for printing out. **1980** *Nat. Westminster Bank Ltd. Ann. Rep. 1979* 26 Feb. 20/1 Equipment of this type..will enable customer accounting data to be captured for subsequent posting to accounts at the same time as the transaction at the counter is being completed. **1985** *DSNA Newslet.* Fall 7/1 No further data will be supported at Waterloo until the entire text of the Dictionary has been captured and proofed.

2. *Chess, Draughts*, etc. To take (an opposing piece). Cf. TAKE *v.* 2 d.

1820 [see CAPTURED *ppl. a.*]. **1876** *Encycl. Brit.* V. 593/1 The king, queen, rooks, and bishops may capture any foeman which stands anywhere within their respective ranges. **1960** R. C. BELL *Board & Table Games* I. ii. 60 If a checked king was unable to move out of check, or it was impossible to capture the checking man, or to interpose another man to protect him from the check, the game was lost. **1973** D. B. PRITCHARD *Go* 19 A stone once played is not moved again, but if captured, is removed from the board and retained until the end of the game by the player who makes the capture.

3. To represent, catch, or record (something elusive, as a quality) in speech, writing, etc. Esp. in literary and artistic contexts.

1901 G. B. SHAW *Three Plays for Puritans* p. xi. The authors had no problematic views: all they wanted was to capture some of the fascination of Ibsen. **1967** E. SHORT *Embroidery & Fabric Collage* iii. 57 They at the same time were able to convey the pose and to capture the muscular strength of the animal concerned. **1979** P. ROTH *Ghost Writer* II. 28 She wrote stories about the college which capture the place in a sentence.

Hence **'captured** *ppl. a.*; **'capturing** *ppl. a.*, etc.

1795 SOUTHEY *Joan of Arc* VI. 168 Of every captured town the keys Restore. **1820** *Hoyle's Games Impr.* 357 Should all the captured pieces not be taken off the board. **1855** MACAULAY *Hist. Eng.* IV. 240 The English..turned the captured guns against the shore. **1800** LD. SPENCER in Nicolas *Disp. Nelson* (1845) IV. 225 *note*, The capturing Squadron. **1864** *Morning Star* 2 Feb., The capturing of vessels when not carrying contraband of war was unlawful.

capturer ('kæptjʊərə(r)). One who captures.

1820 *Hoyle's Games Impr.* 357 The capturer in that case is forfeited or huffed. **1829** J. KNAPP *Jrnl. Nat.* 149 A very skilful capturer of these animals. **1884** O'DONOVAN *Story of Merv* i. 17 The capturer of Schamyl.

captyhowse, obs. var. of CAPADOS.

‖**capuccio** (kap'puttʃo). *Obs. rare.* [a. It. *cappuccio* (*capuccio* in Florio).] = CAPUCHE.

1596 SPENSER *F.Q.* III. xii. 10 In a discolour'd cote of straunge disguyse, That at his backe a brode capuccio had.

capuche (‖kapyʃ, kə'puːtʃ). Also 7 **capuch, -uce, cappuce.** See also CAPOUCH. [a. F. *capuche* (also *capuce*), ad. It. *cappuccio* (= Sp. *capucho*), augm. of *cappa*: see CAP, CAPE.] The hood of a cloak; *spec.* that of the Capuchin monks.

a **1600** *Aberdeen Register* (Jam.) Ane sie [i.e. say] capusche. **1611** COTGR., *Capuchon*, a Capuche; a Monks Cowle, or Hood..also, the hood of a cloake. **1658** CLEVELAND *Rustick Ramp.* Wks. (1687) 424 His Hood or Capuch (which was a part of the Cloak..and served to cover the Head). **1670** G. H. *Hist. Cardinals* I. II. 46 He put his Cappuce or Cowle upon his head. **1726** CAVALLIER *Mem.* I. 49 Nothing else was to be seen there but Cassocks and Capuches. **1843** JAMES *Forest Days* (1847) 105 A jolly friar, clothed in grey, with his capuche thrown back.

Hence **ca'puched** *a.*, hooded.

1646 SIR T. BROWNE *Pseud. Ep.* v. iii. 236 They are differently cucullated or capuched upon the head and backe. **1656** BLOUNT *Glossogr.*, *Capuched*, hooded.

Capuchin ('kæpjʊtʃɪn, kapyʃin), *sb.* (and *attrib.*) Also **-ine**. [a. 16th c. F. *capuchin* (now *capucin*), ad. It. *capuccino*, f. *capuccio*, *capuche* hood: see above.]

1. A friar of the order of St. Francis, of the new rule of 1528. So called from the sharp-pointed capuche, adopted first in 1525, and confirmed to them by Pope Clement VII. in 1528.

1599 MARSTON *Sco. Villanie* I. ii. 178 When impropriat gentles will turn Capuchine. **1603** BP. HALL *Serm.* v. 5 More strict and Capuchin-like. **1712** tr. *Pomet's Hist. Drugs* I. 163 The invention of Friar Auge the Capuchin. **1771** SMOLLETT *Humph. Cl.* (1785) I. 63/2 He..traversed..France, in the disguise of a Capuchin. **1876** BANCROFT *Hist. U.S.* II. xl. 494 The Capuchin missionary.

2. 'A female garment, consisting of a cloak and hood, made in imitation of the dress of capuchin friars; whence its name' (J.).

[**1706** tr. *C'tess D'Aunoy's Trav.* 5 Wrapping up their Heads in their Hooded-Gowns, they seemed to me to be Thieves disguised in Capuchins.] **1749** FIELDING *Tom Jones* Wks. 1775 III. 72 The young lady had on her hat and capuchin. **1752** —— *Covent Gard. Jrnl.* 9 May, Within my memory the ladies..covered their lovely necks with a Cloak; this was exchanged for the manteel, this again was succeeded by the pelorine, the pelorine by the neckatee, the neckatee by the capuchine, which hath now stood its ground a long time. **1858** THACKERAY *Virgin.* I. 377.

b. = CAPUCHE, hood.

1834 PLANCHÉ *Brit. Costume* 322 In..1752 we find a successor to the hood in the capuchin. **1887** *Cornh. Mag.* Mar. 266 Attached to the collar of the coat, and hanging midway down the back, is the uncouth capuchin.

3. A plant, *Impatiens.*

1756 P. BROWNE *Jamaica* 322 The Capuchine or Balsamine [Impatiens]..introduced to Jamaica many years ago.

4. Capuchin monkey, an American monkey (*Cebus capucinus*) with black hair at the back of the head, looking something like a cowl; **Capuchin pigeon**, a sub-variety of the Jacobin pigeon, with a range of inverted feathers on the back of the head, suggesting a cowl or hood.

1785 J. E. SMITH in *Leisure Ho.* (1883) June 353/2 The Capuchin monkey..whose horrid yellings are intolerable to the ears. **1855** H. SPENCER *Princ. Psychol.* (1872) I. I. i. 11 The movements of the little Capuchin monkey. **1855** OWEN *Skel. & Teeth* 300 Capucin-monkey (*Cebus*).

1735 J. MOORE *Columb.* in Tegetmeier *Pigeons* xvi. (1867) 146 Under the title of the Capuchine Moore alludes to a breed which is evidently nothing more than an inferior or cross-bred Jacobine.

5. Capuchin's beard, a variety of endive used for salad; **Capuchine capers**, see CAPER *sb.*[1] 3.

1861 DELAMER *Kitch. Gard.* 111 Barbe de Capucin, or Capuchin's Beard, is consumed in large quantities in Paris during winter and early spring. It is the same thing as the foregoing chicory.

‖**capuchon.** *Obs.* [Fr.; augm. of *capuche* hood.] A hood; a kind of head-dress.

1604 E. G. *D'Acosta's Hist. Indies* IV. xii. 245 An earthen vessell, like to..a capuchon or hoode. **1613** R. C. *Table Alph.* (ed. 3) *Capuchon*, a hoode or coule. **1834** PLANCHÉ *Brit. Costume* 120 The capuchon, instead of being worn as a cowl, was sometimes twisted into a fancilful form and placed upon the top of the head like a modern toque.

†**Ca'pucian, -'uccian.** *Obs.* = CAPUCHIN.

1597-8 BP. HALL *Sat.* VI. i. 198 And dieth like a starv'd Cappucien. **1645** QUARLES *Sol. Recant.* II. 2 T'abjure delight, and turn Capuccian.

‖**capucine** (kapysin). *Obs.* [Fr.; fem. of *capucin*: see CAPUCHIN.]

1. The French name of the Tropæolum (*majus* and *minus*) or Indian Cress, in England commonly known as Nasturtium. ***capucine capers***: the pickled seeds of this plant.

1693-1721 [see CAPER *sb.*[1] 3]. **1719** LONDON & WISE *Compl. Gard.* i. 289 Violet Capucins, or Nasturces Camamils.

2. The dark orange colour of these flowers.

1791 HAMILTON *Berthollet's Dyeing* II. II. 352 To make these colours incline to mor-doré and capucine.

capul(l, obs. form of CAPLE, horse.

capulet ('kæpjʊlɪt). = CAPELET.

1848 JOHNSON *Sportsm. Cycl.* 104 *Capulet*, or Capped Hock.

'capulin. 'The Mexican Cherry' (Webster).

capun, obs. form of CAPON.

capusche, obs. Sc. form of CAPUCHE.

‖**caput** ('kæpʌt). [L.; = head.]

1. Sometimes used in technical language instead of the vernacular 'head' or 'top'; esp. in *Anat.* In *Bot.* the peridium of certain fungi.

†**2.** Short for CAPUT MORTUUM, q.v.

†**3.** The former ruling body or council of the University of Cambridge.

1716 KENNET in Monk *Life Bentley* (1833) I. 423 The Caput, as they call them, complain much of a breach of their privilege, that it was not laid before them preparatory to its being laid before the Senate. **1797** *Cambridge Univ. Cal.* 144 The vice-chancellor, a doctor of divinity, a doctor of laws, a doctor of physic, a regent master of arts, and a non-regent master of arts, form the caput. They are to consider and determine what graces are proper to be brought before the university. **1823** LAMB *Elia* (1860) 16 Your caputs, and heads of colleges care less than any body else. **1830** BP. MONK *Life Bentley* (1833) I. 423 The..mistake of confounding the Caput Senatus with the Heads of Colleges.

4. Occas. used in certain L. phrases in *Astron.*, etc., as ***Caput Draconis***, i.e. Dragon's Head, a star in Draco; ***caput lupinum*** (lit., wolf's head), an outlaw: see WOLF'S-HEAD 2; ***Caput Medusæ***, the star Algol or Medusa's Head in Perseus; also a species of fossil Pentacrinite; ***caput radicis***, the crown of the root in a plant.

1649 G. DANIEL *Trinarch, Hen. V*, lxxxii, Irresolution, doth as Dreadfull rise As Caput Algot in Nativities. [**1797** *Encycl. Brit.* IV. 156/1 Anciently an outlawed felon was said to have *caput lupinum*.] **1837** MACAULAY *Crit. & Hist. Essays* (1843) II. 393 That a valetudinarian..should be treated as a *caput lupinum* because he could not read the Timæus without a headache, was a notion which the humane spirit of the English school of wisdom altogether rejected. **1888** *Guardian* 4 Apr. 488/2 The National League, if it did not formally decree the death of Fitzmaurice for disobedience to its orders, at least proclaimed him as a *Caput Lupinum*.

‖**'caput 'mortuum.** [L.; = dead head.]

†**1.** A death's head, a skull. *Obs.*

1658 R. FRANCK *North. Mem.* (1821) 153 Fancying..he lived now in his grave, and every object a *Caput Mortuum*.

2. *Alch.* and *Chem.* The residuum remaining after the distillation or sublimation of any substance, 'good for nothing but to be flung away, all vertue being extracted' (Willis 1681).

1641 FRENCH *Distill.* i. (1651) 4 Adde the *Caput Mortuum*, of Vitriall, or Aqua fortis. **1662** R. MATHEW *Unl. Alch.* §89. 153 Take out the Retort with the Capud. **1741** *Compl. Fam. Piece* I. i. 80 Take..the *Caput Mortuum* of the Scull of a Man 1 Dram. **1794** SULLIVAN *View Nat.* I. 135 Earth, or ..*caput mortuum*..is the last element of all bodies which can be no farther altered by any art whatsoever.

3. *fig.* Worthless residue.

a **1711** KEN *Edmund* Poet. Wks. 1721 II. 138 His youthful Heat and Strength for Sin engaged, God has the *Caput Mortuum* of his Age. **1812** *Examiner* 5 Oct. 633/1 The *caput mortuum* of the Addington administration. **1876** A. M. FAIRBAIRN in *Contemp. Rev.* June 124 The Pietists..hailed it as the *caput mortuum* of the speculative..school.

capy-: see CAPI-.

capybara (kæpɪ'bɑːrə). Also **capibara.** [A native name in Brazil.] The largest extant rodent quadruped (*Hydrochœrus Capybara*), nearly allied to the Guinea-pig; it lives about the rivers of tropical S. America. Cf. CABIAI.

1774 GOLDSM. *Nat. Hist.* (1862) I. III. iii. 350 The capibara resembles a hog of about two years old..Some naturalists have called it the water-hog. **1849** *Sk. Nat. Hist., Mammalia* IV. 155 The food of the capybara consists exclusively of grass and vegetables, as water-melons, gourds, etc. **1852** TH. ROSS tr. *Humboldt's Trav.* II. xviii. 168 A herd of capybaras which was crossing the river.

capyl, obs. form of CAPLE, horse.

†**'capyous,** *a.* *Obs.* [f. L. *cap-ĕre* to take.] = CAPABLE.

c **1430** LYDG. *Lyf our Ladye* xlv. ii. (Caxton) The wonderfullest and most meruaylous [things]..Wherof no wyght by kynde is capyous.

car (kɑː(r)), *sb.*[1] Forms: 4-7 carre, (5 *Sc.* caar), 7-8 carr, 6- car. [ME. *carre*, a. ONF. *carre*:—late L. *carra*, a parallel form to *carrus*, *carrum* (whence It., Sp. *carro*, Pr. *car*, *char*, ONF. *car*, F. *char*, ME. CHAR), a kind of 2-wheeled wagon for transporting burdens. The L. was a. OCelt. **karr-os*, **karr-om*, whence OIr. (also mod.Ir. and Gael.) *carr* masc. 'wagon, chariot,' OWelsh *carr*, Welsh *càr*, Manx *carr*, Bret. *karr*.

(Late L. *carra* also gave WGer. *carra* fem., in OHG. *charra*, Ger. *karre*, MDu. *carre*, Du. *kar* fem., Sw. *karra*, Da. *karre*.)]

1. A wheeled vehicle or conveyance:

a. *generally*—a carriage, chariot, cart, wagon, truck, etc. (Now little used in this wide sense.)

1382 WYCLIF *Isa.* lxvi. 16 His foure horsid carres [**1388** charis]. *c* **1400** MAUNDEV. xi. (1839) 130 Ne Hors ne Carre nouther. *c* **1440** *Promp. Parv.* 62 Carre, carte, *carrus, currus*. **1480** *Wardr. Acc. Edw. IV* (1830) 122 For cariage..of the Kinges carre..from Grenewiche. **1600** HOLLAND *Livy* XXV. xiii. 556 They sent little above forty carres [*vehicula*]. **1611** BIBLE *1 Esdras* v. 55 They gaue carres that they should bring Cedar trees from Libanus. **1750** BEAWES *Lex Mercat.* (1752) 399 Merchants, and others that use Carrs or Carts.

b. From 16th to 19th c. chiefly poetic, with associations of dignity, solemnity, or splendour; applied also to the fabled chariot of Phaëthon or the sun, and so to that in which the moon, stars, day, night, time, are figured to ride in their grand procession. Also in prose, a chariot of war, triumph, or pageantry.

1590 SPENSER *F.Q.* I. ii. 1 Phoebus fiery carre In hast was climbing up the Easterne hill. **1594** SHAKS. *Rich. III*, v. iii. 20 The weary Sun..by the bright Tract of his fiery carre. **1667** MILTON *P.L.* IX. 65 Four times [he] cross'd the Carr of Night. **1697** DRYDEN *Virg. Georg.* III. 795 To draw the Carr of Jove's Imperial Queen. **1738** GLOVER *Leonidas* III. 133 The king arose. 'No more; prepare my car.' **1758** JOHNSON *Idler* No. 51 ¶9 A slave was placed on the triumphal car. **1852** TENNYSON *Ode Wellington* 55 And a reverent people behold The towering car, the sable steeds. **1853** ROBERTSON *Serm.* Ser. III. vii. 93 Whose body opposing the progress of the car of Juggernaut is crushed beneath its monstrous wheels.

c. *spec.* Applied locally and at special periods to various vehicles in particular; also with defining words, as *Irish car*, etc.

1576 *Act 18 Eliz.* x. §4 Cars or Drags, furnished for..Repairing..Highways. **1704** WORLIDGE *Dict. Rust. et Urb.* s.v. *Beech*, Some approve it much for Cars. **1716** *Lond. Gaz.* No. 5446/2 Carts, Drays, Carrs and Waggons. **1824-7** HONE *Every-day Bk.* II. 240 The common Irish Car is used throughout the province of Leinster..The Irish 'jaunting car' [is a] wholly distinct and superior vehicle. **1838** *Murray's Handbk. N. Germany* 318 A Russian Mountain, down which visitors descend in cars. *Mod.* In some provincial towns (e.g. Birmingham) 'car' means a four-wheeled hackney carriage, 'cab' meaning a hansom.

d. *transf.* A miniature carriage or truck used in experiments, etc.

1831 BREWSTER *Nat. Magic* iv. (1833) 87 The living object AB, the mirror MN, and the lens LL, must all be placed in a moveable car for the purpose of producing the variations in the size of the phantasms.

e. = MOTOR CAR.

1896 L. SERRAILLIER tr. *Farman's Auto-Cars* 132 The latter drove with a daring which may have been dangerous to himself, but which never affected his car. *Ibid.* 135 The three cars which came in next after Mr. Levassor's were all Peugeot cars. **1900** W. W. BEAUMONT *Motor Vehicles* I. 615 Hill-climbing trials alone would not of course be sufficient as a test of the wearing power or durability of a car. **1902** HARMSWORTH *Motors & Motor Driving* 23 The first car built by the Daimler Company at Coventry. **1948** A. HUXLEY *Ape & Essence* (1949) i. 12 He threw the car into gear and we were off.

2. a. 'In the United States the term has become restricted almost entirely to vehicles designed for travelling on railways' (in Great Britain known as carriages, trucks, wagons, etc.), or to those used on tramways. Hence in U.S. ***passenger-car, sleeping-car, coal-car, freight-car, petroleum-car, provision-car, tool-car***, etc. (also used in Great Britain, usu. as the second element in combinations). In Great Britain formerly applied regularly to those of street tramways.

1826 *Laws Commonw. Mass.* 4 Mar. c. 183 §5, p. 331 The conveyance of stone and other property, in their cars and vehicles on said railways. **1837** HT. MARTINEAU *Soc. Amer.* II. 181 During my last trip on the Columbia and Philadelphia rail road, a lady in the car had a shawl burned to destruction on her shoulders. **1850** LYELL *2nd Visit U.S.* II. 110 Here we..entered the cars of a railway built on piles. **1854** THOREAU *Walden* iv. (1886) 113 For the last half-hour I have heard the rattle of railroad-cars. **1873** C. M. YONGE *Pillars of House* IV. xlv. 274 Even Pullman's cars shook him. **1875** [see PULLMAN]. **1879** HARLAN *Eyesight* viii. 109 Straining the accommodative apparatus of the eye by reading in a car or carriage. *Mod.* On account of the snow, the cars on the tramways in London ceased running at eight o'clock. **1899** [see BUFFET *sb.*[2] 3 b]. **1901** M. CARMICHAEL *In Tuscany* 284 The restaurant car has come in since. *a* **1930** D. H. LAWRENCE *Phoenix II* (1968) 252 One sits in the breakfast car in the train, coming to London... In America the Pullmans..don't shake like our cars. **1939** T. S. ELIOT *Old Possum's Practical Cats* 40 It is Skimble who's in charge Of the Sleeping Car Express. **1967** *Jane's World Railways 1967–68* p. iii, Computers..are being extended into every possible field of operation.., from sending messages to locating freight cars.

b. *ellipt.* A car-load. *U.S.*

1869 *Trans. Ill. Agric. Soc. 1867–9* VII. 446 A farmer had far better send..one car of good sheep in the twelve months, than six cars of..bad breed. **1902** G. H. LORIMER *Lett. Merchant* 133 The last car of lard was so strong that it came back of its own accord from every retailer they shipped it to. **1948** *Green Bay* (Wis.) *Press-Gaz.* 30 June 23/4 Receipts were: wheat 38 cars, corn 83, oats 34 and soy-beans 9.

†**3.** Formerly extended to a sleigh or hurdle without wheels. *Obs.* (So in Gaelic.)

c **1400** MAUNDEV. xi. 130 Thei let carye here vitaylle upon the yse, with carres that have no wheeles, that thei clepen scleyes. *c* **1470** HENRY *Wallace* II. 263 On a caar wnlikly thai him cast.

4. a. The part of a balloon in which aeronauts sit.

1794 G. ADAMS *Nat. & Exp. Philos.* III. xxxiii. 404 (Of Air Balloons) To this a sort of carr, or rather boat, was suspended by ropes. **1822** IMISON *Sc. & Art* I. 171 The car, or boat, is made of wicker-work covered with leather. **1825** in HONE *Every-day Bk.* I. 443 Mr. Graham..seated himself in the car of his vehicle.

b. The cage of a lift. Chiefly *U.S.*

1870 *Gold Hill* (Nevada) *News* 25 Aug., The cable fell..upon the car and cage. **1904** *N.Y. Even. Post* 2 Feb. 2 The elevator man seemed to lose control of the elevator at the fifth floor. The car made a sheer drop from the fourth story to the basement. **1943** D. BAKER *Trio* III. 171 When leaving car, close car gate and landing door, otherwise elevator becomes inoperative.

†**5.** The seven stars in the constellation of the Great Bear, called also the Plough or Wain. *Obs.*

1633 P. FLETCHER *Purple Isl.* I. li, None nam'd the stars, the North Carres constant race. **1697** DRYDEN *Virg. Georg.* I. 210 The Pleiads, Hyads, and the Northern Car.

6. *Comb.*, as ***car-borne***, ***-carrying*** adjs.; chiefly attrib., as ***car-body***, ***-boy***, ***-drive***, ***-driver***, ***-ferry***, ***-gear***, ***-hire***, ***-horse***, ***-key***, ***-load***, ***-nail***, ***-ride***, ***-ring***, ***-wheel***, etc., etc.; ***car-owner***; ***car-owning*** vbl. sb. and ppl. a.; see also CAR-LESS *a.*; and esp. in U.S. in sense 2 (where *carriage-*, *truck-*, *wagon-* are used in Britain), as ***car-axle***, ***-buffer***, ***-conductor***, ***-coupling***, ***-door***, ***-fare***, ***-heater***, ***-lamp***, ***-seat***, ***-spring***, ***-starter***, ***-wheel***, ***-window***, etc., etc.; **car bomb**, a bomb concealed by terrorists in a car, esp. in one that is parked; hence **car-bomber**, one who plants or employs a car bomb; also **car-bombing**; **car-boot sale**, an outdoor sale at which people gather to sell unwanted possessions, produce, etc., from the boots of their cars; **car-coat**, a short coat designed especially for the use of car-drivers; **car-ful**, as many or as much as a car will hold; **car-hop** *U.S. colloq.*, a waiter or waitress who serves customers in their parked cars; cf. *bell-hop*; hence as *v. intr.*, to act as a car-hop; **car-loading**, the amount of freight carried in goods trains within a given period; freq. in *pl.*; also *fig.*; **car-park**, a building, open space, etc., for the parking of motor vehicles; also *attrib.*; **car-phone**, a radio-telephone designed for use in a motor vehicle; **car-port** (orig. *U.S.*), a motor-car shelter, open at the side or front, adjoining or built into a house; **car-sick** *a.* [after *sea-sick*], sick from the motion of a motor car; so ***car-sickness***. Also CARMAN, etc.

1838 *Civil Eng. & Archit. Jrnl.* I. 390/1 The truck is guided by the *carbody with..mathematical precision. **1959** *New Statesman* 1 Aug. 141/1 A car-body firm. **1972** *Times* 18 May 1/1 The explosion of a *car bomb without warning in a loyalist street. **1986** *Daily Tel.* 16 June 1/1 The government blamed the outlawed African National Congress for a car bomb explosion in central Durban that killed three women and injured 68 other people. **1974** *Ann. Reg. 1973* 32 A terrorist campaign to secure the transfer to Northern Ireland of the London *car-bombers sentenced at Winchester. **1985** *Listener* 2 May 4/1 Car bombers are but the most dramatic manifestation. **1972** *Times* 12 May 2/1 With two *car-bombings and the death of a soldier here today, a period of comparative peace in Northern Ireland appears to be ending. **1985** *Globe & Mail* (Toronto) 9 Oct. A15/2 It is the fifth car bombing in a week. **1985** *Company* Dec. 160/1 We cram our own homes solid with junk and then cruise the local *car-boot sales in the hope of acquiring someone else's. **1986** *Daily Tel.* 30 Aug. 10/2, I have furnished the balcony with..a variety of terra-cotta pots bought in France and found in jumble and car-boot sales here. **1827** HEBER tr. *Pindar* v. 4 *Car-borne Psaumis. **1959** *Times* 10 June 9/7 The Boulogne–Lyons *car-carrying trains. **1963** *Punch* 10 Apr. p. xiv, Men's wear..includes foam-backed *car coats. **1965** *Guardian* 31 Mar. 16/3 The now ubiquitous car-coat..is usually made from a cotton suedette or brushed nylon shell fabric and lined with an acrylic pile liner. **1863** 'G. HAMILTON' *Gala-Days* 22 The heads of the two columns collide near the *car-door. **1924** GEIKIE *Long Life's Wk.* 220 We had long walks and still longer *car-drives. **1870** 'FANNY FERN' *Ginger-Snaps* 182 What troubles me most is, whether I am to pay six cents for *car-fare. **1900** *Dial. Notes* II. 16 A fish-scale..is the nickel

with which a [Yale] student pays his car-fare. **1958** S. Ellin *Eighth Circle* (1959) II. x. 104 She said she needed carfare to get back to school. **1884** H. Hall in *Rep. U.S. Census of 1880* VIII. 221 Side-wheel *car-ferry Transport..with three railroad tracks on deck. **1898** *Strand Mag.* Apr. 443/2 The..necessity for appeasing the ire of passengers, who were compelled in the old days to change from train to ferry-boat, and then to train again, is the real reason for the existence of the car ferry. **1955** 'Lory' *Brit. Railways' Sands across Sea* 264 A Car Ferry Terminal has been constructed at..Dover. **1832** G. Downes *Lett. Cont. Countries* I. 207 An occasional *car-full of priests. **1808** Anderson *Cumbld. Ball.* (1819) 43 The *car-gear at Durdar she wan. **1959** *Listener* 31 Dec. 1156/1 Even *car-hire services possess a long ancestry. **1937** *Amer. Speech* XII. 320/1 At roadside drive-ins..the waitresses are now being called *curbies* or **car-hops*. **1960** J. McManus in *Introduction* 188, I had another job..*car-hopping six days a week at a little beef-and-burger kerb-stand. **1800** M. Edgeworth *Parent's Assistant* V. 75 He had been used..to lead *car-horses. **1907** M. H. Norris *Veil* v. 38 A car-horse, sore-footed and generally weather-beaten..completed this part of his purchase. **1962** M. Kelly *Due to a Death* vii. 123, I dropped the *car key in the table drawer. **1854** Thoreau *Walden* 40, I do not see in my mind any retinue at their heels, any *car-load of fashionable furniture. **1958** R. Godden *Greengage Summer* vi. 72 The car-loads and char-à-bancs of visitors. **1959** N. Mailer *Advts. for Myself* (1961) 210 A *carloading of homogenized words. **1963** *Economist* 21 Dec. 1292/2 Railway shares have benefited especially from such things as consistent increases in carloadings. **1605** Sylvester *Du Bartas* I. iv. (1641) 32/2 *Car-nails fastned in a wheele. **1903** *Motoring Ann.* 91 *Car-owners always consider it a privilege to have Miss Wilson on their front seat. **1925** A. Huxley *Along Road* I. 16, I can talk for hours about motors with other car-owners. *Ibid.* 17 *Car-owning may have the worst effect on the character. **1959** *Daily Tel.* 15 Oct. 12 The traffic problems of a car-owning democracy. **1926** *Daily Mail* 1 Dec. 9/6 Glastonbury *Car Park. Indignation has been aroused..by a proposal..to purchase part of the land ..as an extra parking space for motor cars. **1935** *Archit. Rev.* LXXVIII. p. xlvi, The car-park problem. **1955** *Times* 9 May 18/2 A large construction programme [in Canada] of multi-deck car parks with direct access to the stores. *Ibid.* 25 Aug. 8/6 The car park attendant. [**1956** *Autocar* 25 May 615/2 Stockholm now has a regular subscription scheme for car telephone installations.] **1965** *Newsweek* 12 July 63/1 There is a pocket of mobile phone owners in New York.. but the fad hasn't yet caught on in other cities, where *car phones are generally for professional purposes. **1971** 'A. Burgess' *MF* xi. 131 Rod, he said to the constable, get on the carphone to..the manager at the circus. **1986** *Sunday Tel.* 15 June 8/1 It must have been caused by a police mobile transmitter or someone using a car phone nearby. **1939** *Life* 8 May 17/1 At the left is the '*carport' which opens on main entrance of building. **1947** *Archit. Rev.* CII. 117 Above the living-room-kitchen part is an open roof-deck, below the bedrooms a car-port. **1963** *Sunday Times* 21 Apr. 45/6 Terrace houses overlooking Torbay which incorporate tiled carports under the houses. **1902** Harben *Abner Daniel* 25 Now I have a long *car-ride before me, and it's growing late. **1801** Southey *Thalaba* XII. xiii, And clench'd the *car-rings endlong and athwart. **1881** *Chicago Times* 14 May, The employés of the Grand Trunk *car shops are on strike. **1908** *Lancet* 12 Sept. 828/1 Individuals who are *car-sick may be good sailors and *vice versâ*. *Ibid.*, By car-sickness is meant a series of unpleasant symptoms, as giddiness, staggering, nausea, and vomiting due to riding in a vehicle or even in a baby-carriage. **1941** J. P. Marquand *H. M. Pulham* xxxi. 343 You always get car-sick if you eat too much. **1947** C. P. Stewart *Sword Between* xv. 80 Maria suffered from car-sickness, and frequent stops had to be made. **1884** *Western Daily Press* 2 Apr. 5/7 A *car-washer in the employ of the Great Western Railway. **1854** M. J. Holmes *Tempest & Sunshine* xvii. 239 From the *car windows Fanny watched the long blue line of hills. **1903** Kipling *5 Nations* 115 Where the white car-windows shine.

car *sb.*²: see carr.

car, *a. Sc.* Also **kar, ker.** [a. Gael. *cearr* wrong, awkward, Ir. *cearr* left-handed, wrong, *cearr-lamhach* left-handed, Manx *kiare* in *lauechiare* left hand.]

a. Left, sinister: commonly in ***car-hand, car-handed***. **b.** Awkward; perverse; wrong; sinister.

c **1420** *Anturs Arth.* xlviii, With a cast of the carhonde, in a cantelle he strikes. *c* **1450** *Wisdom Solomon* in *Ratis Raving* 23 The visdome of the wysman is in his rycht hand, and the foly of the ful in his kere hand. **1548** *Compl. Scotl.* 115 He resauit the vryting in his kar hand. **1597** Skene *Exp. Wds.* s.v. *Hebdomas*, Vpon the ker and wrang side, was placed the thrid Idole, Frigga. **1808–79** Jamieson s.v., If you meet a car-handit person, or one who has flat soles. *Ibid. Sc. Prov.* You'll go a car gate yet.

car, *v.* [f. car *sb.*¹] *trans.* To place or carry in a car; ***to car it*** (colloq.): to go by car. Also *intr.*: to go by car.

1791 E. Darwin *Bot. Gard.* I. 119 Car'd on the foam your glimmering legion rides. **1861** E. Forbes in *Life* xiv. 501 The ladies and I prepared to car it to Killarney. **1907** *Daily Chron.* 23 Sept. 4/4 You just get out of your train, walk or 'car' to your hotel.

† **'carab.** *Obs. rare.* [ad. L. *carab-us* (see Du Cange) 'a small wicker-boat covered with raw hide': cf. Gr. κάραβος 'a kind of light ship'. English writers appear to have identified it with Ir. *corrach*, curragh.] (See quot.)

1387 Trevisa *Higden* (Rolls Ser.) VI. 389 Þe Scottyshe men..took a carabum, þat is a schippe i-made but of tweie hydes and an half. **1610** Holland *Camden's Brit.* II. 228 Devout men, that in a Carab (or Carogh) made of two tanned hides only and an halfe, sailed out of Ireland into Cornwall.

carabe, obs. form of carob.

'carabid, ca'rabidan, *sb. Ent.* [f. mod.L. pl. *cārabidæ*, f. L. *cārabus* a kind of crab, used in Zool. for a genus of beetles.] One of the *Carabidæ*, a family of large carnivorous beetles.

1835 Kirby *Hab. & Inst. Anim.* II. xx. 359 Evidently belonging to the Carabidans. **1880** D'Albertis *New Guinea* I. 369, A large number of insects, especially carabids.

carabid ('kærəbɪd), *a.* [f. the sb.] Of or pertaining to the Carabidæ.

1901 *Trans. Entomol. Soc.* 193 (*title*) The Carabid genus Pheropsophus. **1966** C. Sweeney *Scurrying Bush* iv. 52 Our search disclosed a number of tenebrionid and carabid beetles, the former feeding on the dung, the latter carnivorous.

carabideous (kærə'bɪdɪəs), *a. Ent.* [f. carabid + -eous.] = prec.

1835 J. Duncan *Nat. Hist. Beetles* 119 The majority of carabideous insects secrete an acrid and caustic fluid. **1835** [see square *a.* 1]. **1889** A. R. Wallace *Darwinism* 44 The curious little carabideous beetles of the genus Notiophilus.

† **carabin** ('kærəbɪn). *Obs.* Also 6–7 **carbine**, 6 **-yne**, 7 **carbeene, carabine, carrabin.** See also carbine, the weapon: the two words have been taken as one in English. [a. F. *carabin* (16th c. in Littré), of disputed origin: Roquefort alleges an earlier *calabrin*, according to Diez, f. *calabre* an ancient engine of war, the name *calabrin* being transferred from the man who worked that to those who carried these fire-arms; but Littré inclines to see in it a transl. of *Calabrinus* Calabrian.

Calabre, also Pr. and OSp., is regarded by Diez as repr. medL. *chadabula* an engine for throwing stones, earlier *catabola*, a. Gr. καταβολή overthrow, destruction.]

A mounted musketeer; a carabineer. (See 1611.)

(Not in Johnson 1755.)

1590 Webbe *Trav.* (Arb.) 19 Much like to Carbines or Horsemen readie to yᵉ warre. **1591** Sir J. Smythe *Instr. Milit.* 202 Musters of Carabins or Argolettiers. **1611** Cotgr., *Carabin*, a Carabine or Carbeene; an Arguebuzier armed with a morrian, and breast-plate, and seruing on horsebacke. **1625** Markham *Souldier's Accid.* 42 Hargo-busseirs, or Carbines. **1626** T. H. *Caussin's Holy Crt.* 266 To leaue it, like a Carbine, who hath shot of his pistoll. **1735** Carte *Ormonde* I. 97 A troop of horse which consisted..of sixty Carabins. [**1885** R. Burton *1001 Nights* I. 202 *note*, Men who formerly would have half starved as curates and ensigns, barristers and carabins.]

b. (See quot.; cf. *free lance*.)

1816 Singer *Hist. Cards* 234 Carabin a term used at the game of lansquenet, to designate an occasional player who takes the chance of a card or two..and then ceases to play.

carabineer (ˌkærəbɪ'nɪə(r)), **carbineer** (kɑːbɪ'nɪə(r)). Also **carabinier.** [a. F. *carabinier*, f. *carabine* carbine.] A soldier who carries a carbine. (The 6th Dragoon Guards are distinctively called ***the Carabineers***.)

1672 T. Venn *Milit. Observ.* vi. 15 That the Harquebuzier and Carabinier be often exercised to shoot bullets at a mark. **1721** Bailey *Carabineers*, horse-men who carry Carabines. **1819** Rees *Cycl.* s.v., Formerly, all regiments of light armed horse were called Carabineers. **1820** Byron *Let. to Moore* 13 July, I have heard no more of the carabiniers. **1873** *Daily News* 17 Sept. 5/4 Yesterday, five Carabineers..gave evidence in favour of the Claimant.

‖ **carabinero** (karabi'nero). [Sp.] A customs or revenue officer; a frontier guard.

1845 R. Ford *Handbk. Spain* I. III. 324 The expensive preventive service of *Resguardos, Carabineros*, etc. which is every where established to put down the smuggler. **1843** Ld. Saltoun *Scraps* I. ii. 216 The *carabineros*, or revenue officers, might be so disposed of as to leave the coast clear. **1955** J. Thomas *No Banners* viii. 67 They knew they could never hope to reach Barcelona with a pack of irate *carabineros* on their trail. **1957** P. Kemp *Mine were of Trouble* i. 13 *Carabineros*, or frontier guards, in light green and flat peaked caps.

‖ **carabiniere** (kærəbɪ'njɛərɪ). Pl. **-ieri.** [It.] A member of an Italian Army Corps which serves as a police force.

1847 J. H. Newman *Let.* 25 July (1962) XII. 104 Minardi ..the head of the Carabinieri, was found to be implicated. **1924** D. H. Lawrence in M. Magnus *Memoirs of Foreign Legion* 52 The carabinieri wanted to arrest him at the monastery, so he escaped here. **1946** G. Millar *Horned Pigeon* ix. 129 The four of us squeezed into the middle of a first-class compartment with the officer and the *carabinieri* occupying all the corners and another *carabiniere* in the corridor. **1969** P. Loraine *Mafia Kiss* I. i. 13 What if the carabinieri had taken the child, questioned him?

caraboid, *a. Ent.* [f. L. *cārabus* (see carabid *sb.*) + -oid.] Like or related to the genus *Carabus* of beetles.

caracal ('kærəkæl). [a. F. *caracal*, a. Turkish *qarah-qulaq*, f. *qarah* black + *qulak* ear.] A feline animal (*Felis caracal* Linn.) found in northern Africa and south-western Asia; it belongs to the sub-genus of the lynxes, and is generally supposed to be the 'lynx' of the ancients.

1760 *Phil. Trans.* (1809) XI. 474 *note*, The caracal is an animal of great strength and fierceness. **1774** Goldsm. *Nat. Hist.* (1862) I. IV. i. 381 The siagush, or, as Mr. Buffon names it, the caracal. **1834** Jardine *Felinæ* 251 The caracal has always been considered to be the lynx mentioned by the ancients as possessing such wonderful power of sight. **1839** *Penny Cycl.* XIV. 218/2 The Caracals hunt in packs like the wild dogs.

‖ **caracara** (kɑrə'kɑːrɑ). Also **carcara.** [See quot.] Name for the South American birds of the *Polyborinæ*, an aberrant sub-family of the *Falconidæ*, with affinities toward the Vultures.

1838 *Penny Cycl.* X. 168 Marcgrave was the first to introduce into Europe the name of Caracara, the vulgar appellation of the bird in Brazil, derived from its hoarse and peculiar cry.

caracature, obs. f. caricature.

carack, var. of carrack, a ship.

caracol ('kærəkɒl), **caracole** (-kəʊl), *sb.* Also 7 **caragolo, carrocol.** [a. F. *caracol, caracole*, ad. It. *caracollo* wheeling of a horse, ad. Sp. (and Pg.) *caracol* snail, periwinkle, spiral shell, also winding stair; in sense 1 Cat. has *caragol*, It. also *caragollo*. Ulterior derivation doubtful: see Diez and Skeat.]

† **1.** A spiral shell. *Obs.*

1622 R. Hawkins *Voy. S. Sea* (1847) 94 Certaine shels, like those of mother of pearles, which are brought out of the East Indies, to make standing cups, called caracoles.

2. *Arch.* 'A term sometimes applied to a staircase in the form of a helix or spiral' (Gwilt).

1721–1800 Bailey, *Caracol.* **1753** in Chambers *Cycl. Supp.* **1823** in Crabb *Techn. Dict.*; and in mod. Dicts.

3. A half-turn or wheel to the right or left executed by a horseman. Littré gives the sense in Fr. as 'a succession of such wheels to right and left alternately, movement in a zigzag course', which appears to have been the earlier sense in Eng. also. Many writers have used the word without any clear notion of its meaning: see next.

1614 Markham *Cheap Husb.* I. i. (1668) 21 In the Art of Horsemanship, there are divers and sundry turns..those we call Caragolo. **1643** Slingsby *Diary* (1836) 103 Now was Sʳ Wᵐ Constable crept out of Hull wᵗʰ their Horse making their Carrocols upon yᵉ woulds. *a* **1679** Earl Orrery *Guzman* iv, What a Caracole he made, when you fac'd about. **1792** Osbaldistone *Brit. Sportsm.* 94/1 They sometimes ride up in caracols, to perplex the enemy. **1810** *Encycl. Brit.* (ed. 4) V. 171 In the army, the horse always makes a caracol after each discharge, in order to pass the rear of the squadron. **1825** Scott *Talism.* xxviii, The Scottish knight.. made his courser carry him in a succession of caracoles to his station. **1863** Thornbury *True as Steel* I. 145 Chargers pacing with curvets and caracoles.

'caracol, caracole, *v.* [a. F. *caracole-r*, It. *caracollare* to caracol, wheel about: see prec.]

1. *intr.* Of a horseman or horse: To execute a caracol or caracols. Often used loosely for 'to caper about'. Also *transf.* of other animals.

1656 Blount *Glossogr.*, *Caracol*, to cast themselvs into a round ring, as souldiers do. **1785** *Sportsman's Dict.*, To caracol is to go in the form of half rounds. **1813** Scott *Trierm.* II. xix, Now caracoled the steeds in air. **1840** Thackeray *Catherine* ii, The Captain on his..steed caracolling majestically. **1861** G. Meredith *Evan Harr.* xli. 466 Once that sound used to set me caracoling before an abject multitude.

2. *trans.* To make (a horse) caracol.

1835 W. Irving *Tour Prairies* 44 He was fond of caracolling his horse. **1845** Saunders *Cab. Pict., Chaucer* 82 The youthful knight..caracolled his horse along the pavement.

Hence **'caracoling, -colling** *vbl. sb.* and *ppl. a.*

1837 Carlyle *Fr. Rev.* (1857) I. I. VII. vi. 205 Caracoling Bodyguards. **1843** Miall *Nonconf.* III. 209 We crave indulgence for a little caracolling.

'caracoler, -coller. [f. prec. + -er¹.] One who caracols.

1837 Carlyle *Fr. Rev.* (1857) I. I. VII. vi. 205 Himself and his Women are dispersed by caracolers. **1861** *Sat. Rev.* 27 Apr. 421/1 The trained caracoller of Batty's circus.

‖ **caracoli.** *Obs.* [? the Carib name.] A mixed metal or alloy formerly used by the natives of the Caribee Islands, and imitated by Europeans by mixing 6 parts of silver, 3 of copper, and 1 of gold. Chambers *Cycl. Supp.* 1753.

‖ **caracore.** [Also in F. *caracore*, Sp. *caracora*.] 'A sort of vessel used in the Philippine Isles' (Littré).

1794 *Rigging & Seamanship* I. 240 *Caracores* are light vessels used by the natives of Borneo..and by the Dutch as guarda costas in those latitudes.

† **caract, carect**, *sb. Obs.* Forms: 4–6 **caracte, carecte**, 4–7 **carect**, 5 **karect**, 6 **carracte, karecte, carrect**, 7 **caract, carract.** See also charact. [ME. *caracte, carect*, OF. *caracte, carecte* fem., *caract* masc., correspond to L. types **characta, -um*, app. a. Gr. χαρακτός, -ή, -όν 'graven, impressed as a mark', taken absol. as =

character. *Caracta* occurs in Pr. rendering *characterem* in the Vulg., *Rev.* xiii. 15: possibly the form arose only in Romanic from L. *charácter.*]

1. A mark, sign, or CHARACTER.

1377 LANGL. *P. Pl.* B. XII. 80 þorw carectus þat cryst wrot. **1382** WYCLIF *Rev.* xiv. 11 If ony man toke the carecte of his [the beast's] name. *c* **1449** PECOCK *Repr.* II. v. 166 Sum seable cros or mark or carect. **1570** BILLINGSLEY *Euclid* II. v. 68 The greatest and least karectes or numbers. **1587** GOLDING *De Mornay* iii. 37 The Egiptians..described him [God] in their holy Carects as a Pilot alone gouerning a ship. **1603** SHAKS. *Meas. for M.* v. i. 56 In all his dressings, caracts, titles, formes. **1655** TRAPP *Comm. 1 Cor.* x. 21 An altar.. which must have its prints and carects.

spec. **1530** PALSGR. 203/1 Carracte in pricke song, *minime.*

2. *spec.* A magical character or symbol; a charm.

1393 GOWER *Conf.* I. 57 Whan that a man..With his carecte him [a serpent] wolde enchaunte. *Ibid.* III. 138 Of sorcerie the caractes. **1522** SKELTON *Why nat to Court* 694 By nycromancy, By carectes and coniuracyon.

†**caract,** *v. Obs.* [f. prec. sb. Cf. med.L. *caranāre* in Du Cange.]

trans. To mark (with a sign or letter).

1662 FULLER *Worthies* I. 61 We have in the Margin caracted them with a Rem: for Remove.

caract(e, obs. form of CARRACK and CARAT.

caracter, -ere, earlier spelling of CHARACTER.

caracul(e), var. KARAKUL.

Caradoc (kæ'rædɒk). *Geol.* [f. Caer *Caradoc*, name of sandstone hills in Shropshire.] Applied *attrib.* to a stage or series or to the rocks of the Ordovician System in Britain. Hence **Cara'docian** *a.*

1835 R. I. MURCHISON in *Phil. Mag.* vii. 47 *Caradoc sandstones.* This name..has been derived from the..ridge of Caer Caradoc. **1855** J. PHILLIPS *Man. Geol.* 192 There is also a narrow tract of Caradoc sandstone running N.N.W. in the Lickey Hills. **1910** *Encycl. Brit.* V. 300/1 In the Lake district the Coniston limestone series represents the Upper Caradocian. **1960** L. D. STAMP *Britain's Struct.* (ed. 5) xii. 109 Caradocian and Ashgillian..being the lower and upper parts respectively of the old Bala Group.

carafe (kə'rɑːf, -æ-). Also caraff, -affe. [a. F. *carafe* = It. *caraffa* (Neapol. *carrafa* a measure of liquids), Sp. and Pg. *garrafa*, Sicil. *carrabba*. According to Littré identified by Mohl with Pers. *qarābah* 'a large flagon' (see CARBOY); but Dozy refers it to Arabic *gharafa* to draw or lift water: cf. the derivatives *ghuruf* little cup, *ghirāf* a great and full measure of dry things, *gharrāf* having much water, *ghirāfah* a draught, etc., no one of which however exactly answers to the Romanic forms.]

A glass water-bottle for the table, bedroom, etc. Also, one used at table, etc., for wine; *attrib.*, designating an ordinary wine served in a carafe.

The word has long been in common use in Scotl.; in England it is of later appearance, and often treated as still French. Also vulgarly corrupted to *craft, croft.*

1786 *Lounger* (1787) II. 178 Called for a..*caraff* of water. **1845** THACKERAY in *Fraser's Mag.* Nov., Caraffes, with the tumblers..placed over them. **1851** *Art Jrnl. Catal. Exhib.* 91 A Water-caraft and Tumbler. **1860** RAMSAY *Remin.* Ser. I. (ed. 7) 260 [With old-fashioned Scotch people] the crystal jug or decanter in which water is placed upon the table was a caraff (Fr. carafe). **1861** TRAFFORD *City & Sub.* I. 28 On the table stood a croft of water, surmounted by a tumbler. **1868** MISS BRADDON *Run to Earth* I. xi. 277 A claret jug, a large carafe of water, and an empty glass. **1939** E. AMBLER *Mask of Dimitrios* xiii. 274 The carafe burgundy which his host had recommended so warmly at dinner. **1950** J. CANNAN *Murder Included* iii. 58 A *carafe* of white wine, biscuits, butter and cheese. **1957** R. POSTGATE *Good Food Guide 1957–58* 263 A small carafe of white wine. **1959** *Ibid. 1959–60* 260 Carafe wines, white and red. **1962** *Punch* 26 Dec. p. x, The 'Tent'..serves simple English dishes and carafe wines for the hurried or the hard-up. **1966** *Guardian* 15 Dec. 6/6 An admirable carafe Sancerre.

carag(h(een, var. of CARRAGEEN.

carage, obs. form of CARRIAGE.

carain(e, -ing, obs. forms of CARRION.

carak(e, obs. form of CARRACK, a ship.

caral(le, caralde, obs. forms of CAROL.

caramba (kæ'ræmbə), *int.* Also carramba. [Sp.] An exclamation of surprise or dismay: gracious! strange! confound it! damn!

1835 J. H. INGRAHAM *South-West* I. 139 'Sacré diable!' 'Carramba!'—fell upon the ear. **1845** R. FORD *Handbk. Trav. Spain* I. i. 36 More becoming will it be to the English gentleman to swear not at all; a reasonable indulgence in *Caramba* is all that can be permitted. **1851** H. MELVILLE *Moby Dick* II. i. 2 Caramba! have done, shipmate, will ye? **1906** *Daily Chron.* 3 Jan. 3/4 An obvious villain had snapped 'caramba!' at her.

caramba. = CARAMBOLA.

1866 *Treas. Bot.*, *Averrhoa Carambola*, the Caramba.

‖**carambola.** [a. Pg. (and mod.Lat.) *carambola.* Several Portuguese writers of the 16th c. state that this was the native name in Malabar: Molesworth has Mahrattī *karanbal*; Forbes Watson has a Hindī name *karmal*, Singhalese and Hindī *kāma-ranga*, Skr. *karma-ranga.* (Marsden has Malay *karambil* coco-nut.) Linnæus took the Pg. name into botanical Latin.]

The acid fruit (golden-yellow, ellipsoid, obscurely 10-ribbed) of a small East Indian tree *Averrhoa Carambola*, (N.O. *Oxalidaceæ*); also the tree itself.

1598 tr. *Linschoten's Voy.* 96 *note*, The fruite which the Malabars and Portingales call Carambolas, is in Decan called *Camarix*, in Canar *Camarix* and *Carabeli.* **1887** *Standard* 16 Sept. 5/3 The carambola and the Otaheite apple.

carambole ('kærəmbəʊl), *sb. Billiards.* [a. F. *carambole*, ad. Sp. *carambola* the red ball at billiards, the stroke so called, a trick: derivation unknown. As the word is in Pg. identical in form with the prec., suggestions as to their identity have been made, but without any evidence.]

†**a.** In billiards, the red ball which is placed on the mark. (But it is doubtful whether this sense has ever been practically in English use.) †**b.** The game in which this ball is used. *Obs.* **c.** The stroke otherwise called a CANNON.

1775 C. JONES *Hoyle's Games Impr.* 205 Billiards ..*Carambole*, is played with three Balls, one being red which is neutral..The chief Object of the Game is to hit with your own Ball the two other Balls, which is called a Carambole. **1788** J. BEAUFORT *ibid.* iii. 195 *Carambole* is a game newly introduced from France. *Ibid.* 196 The *Russian carambole*.. has still more lately been introduced. **1820** *Hoyle's Games Impr.* 371 Each of the hazards and the carambole counts two. *Ibid.* 372 Which stroke, called a *carambole* or *carom.* **1850** Bohn's *Handbk. Games* 519 If with his own ball he strike two others successively, the stroke is called a canon (formerly *carom* or *carambole*).

d. *attrib.*, as in ***carambole game*** = b.

1807 in *N. & Q.* (1886) 27 Feb. 167. **1820** *Hoyle's Games Impr.* 371 The Red or winning and losing carambole game. **1850** Bohn's *Handbk. Games* 544 The Carambole Games.. are played with three balls.

carambole, *v.* [a. F. *carambole-r*, f. *carambole*; see prec.] *intr.* To make a carambole or cannon at billiards. Hence **'caramboling** *vbl. sb.*

1775 C. JONES *Hoyle's Games Impr.* 205 Seven may be gained in one Stroke, by caramboling and putting in both Balls. **1820** *Hoyle's Games Impr.* 380 If the striker caramboles and holes both the red and his adversary's ball, he gains seven points. **1870** *Daily News* 6 Oct., A good deal of..domino-playing, and caramboling at billiards.

carameile: see CARMELE.

caramel ('kærəmɛl), *sb.* [a. F. *caramel*, ad. Sp. (It., Pg.) *caramelo*, of uncertain origin.

Scheler suggests that the Sp. represents L. *calamellus* little tube, in reference to its tubular form; Mahn thinks it from med.L. *cannamella* sugar-cane: an Arabic source is conjectured by Littré.]

a. A black or brown porous substance obtained by heating sugar to about 210° C., by which it loses two equivalents of water; burnt sugar. It is used for colouring spirits, etc. **b.** A kind of 'candy' or sweet. **c.** *attrib.* as ***caramel-walnuts.***

1725 BRADLEY *Fam. Dict.* s.v. *Sugar*, When it is boiled to Caramel, it breaks and cracks. *c* **1865** J. WYLDE in *Circ. Sc.* I. 413/1 High-dried malt..contains a substance termed *caramel.* **1884** *Philadelphia Times* Sept., An article so generally a favorite with all classes as caramels. They are made of cream, sugar, vanilla, pistache, etc.

d. The colour of caramel brown. Also *attrib.*

1909 *Daily Mirror* 4 Oct. 10/3 Caramel is the name for various new shades of brown. **1927** *Daily Express* 12 Mar. 3/5 Caramel, a useful light brown, suitable for all kinds of walking costumes. **1970** C. DRUMMOND *Stab in Back* vi. 135 She was wearing the caramel suit she disappeared in.

Hence **'caramel** *v. trans.* and *intr.*, **'caramelize** *v.* [cf. F. *caraméliser*], *trans.* and *intr.*, to turn into caramel.

1727 BRADLEY *Fam. Dict.* s.v. *Apple*, Let it boil so long till the Sugar be red enough and caramel'd. **1842** *Penny Cycl.* XXIII. 230/1 By caramelizing the syrup. **1883** *Knowledge* 20 July 36/1 Partial carbonisation, or 'caramelising'. **1887** *Century Mag.* Nov. 114/1 He seeks to keep the temperature down to 130°. If it is too high some of the sucrose will 'invert' or 'caramel' into glucose. **1897** *Yearbk. U.S. Dept. Agric.* 515 The sugar in the milk caramels in baking and browns the crust.

,carameli'zation. [f. CARAMELIZE *v.* + -ATION.] The production of caramel; conversion into caramel or into the colour of caramel.

1889 in *Cent. Dict.* **1955** J. G. DAVIS *Dict. Dairying* (ed. 2) 163 *Caramelisation*, the browning of sugar solutions by heat. **1960** *Times Rev. Industry* July 19/3 Care must be taken to prevent browning caused by caramelization of the sugars.

‖**caramoussal, carmousal.** *Obs.* Also caramousal, -musall, -mosil; carmasal, carmizale, carmusol. [In It. '*caramusáli*, a kind of ship in Ormuz, *caramusalino*, a kind of pinnace or bark' (Florio), *caramussále*, a Turkish merchantman (Baretti), Sp. *caramuzal* 'transport vessel used by the Moors' (Velasquez), F. *carmoussal* 'a kind of Turkish ship' (Cotgr.), 16th c. L. *caramussallus*, Turkish *qarāmusāl* a kind of ship (Meninski 1680, Zenker 1866). (*Kara-mussal* is also the name of a place in the Gulf of Nicomedia near the Bosphorus.)] A Turkish and Moorish ship of burden, noted in the 17th c.

THOS. HYDE *Notes on Peritsol's Trav.* (1691) says (p. 81) 'navis cujus prora ac puppis sunt elevatiora quam media pars': cf. the description of the old Caravel.

[**1565** HIERON. COMES ALEXANDRINUS *Comment. de bello in insulam Melitam* (in Du Cange, and Jal) Tria navigia quæ vulgo appellant Caramussalos; minora sunt autem onerariis navibus, et figura prope ovali.] **1587** SAUNDERS *Voy. Tripoli* in Hakluyt *Voy.* II. 187, I and sixe more..were sent forth in a Galeot to take a Greekish Carmosell. **1603** KNOLLES *Hist. Turkes* (1621) 1329 There were two gallies, a caramoussal, and a Greeke brigandine. **1615** G. SANDYS *Trav.* (1670) 20 Turkish Carmasals and Gallies. **1628** DIGBY *Voy. Medit.* (1868) 33, I made her for a carmizale. **1651** HOWELL *Venice* 195 Som Gallies and Caramusalls that carried passengers upon a Pilgrimage to Mecha. **1656** BLOUNT *Glossogr.*, Carmasal, carmusol. **1668** WILKINS *Real Char.* II. xi. 280 Galeot, Caramosil, Carrack, Caravel. **1696** PHILLIPS, *Carmousal*, a Turkish ship with a very high poop. **1721–1800** BAILEY, *Caramousel*, and *Carmousal.*

‖**caraña, caranna** (ka'raɲa, kə'rænə). Also 7 -agna. [a. Sp. *caraña*, from the native name.] A resin obtained from a West Indian tree, *Bursera acuminata* (N.O. *Amyridaceæ*).

1616 BULLOKAR, *Caranna.* **1678–1706** PHILLIPS, *Caranna*, a Gum coming from the West-Indies, good for the Tooth-ach, if applyed to the Temples. **1712** tr. *Pomet's Hist. Drugs* I. 198 It is call'd Caranna Gummi, or Caragna.

carancha, carancho, varr. CARRANCHA.

carangid (kə'rændʒɪd), *a.* and *sb.* [f. mod.L. *Carangidæ.*] **A.** *adj.* Pertaining to or resembling the Carangidæ, a family of perciform fish. **B.** *sb.* A member of this family.

1889 *Cent. Dict.*, Carangid *n.* **1931** J. R. NORMAN *Hist. Fishes* v. 94 The Scad or Horse Mackerel (*Trachurus*), a member of a large group of fishes known as Pampanos or Carangids (Carangidae). **1931** J. R. NORMAN in W. P. Pycraft *Standard Nat. Hist.* xi. 461 (*caption*) A Carangid fish known to the ancients as Pompilus. **1962** K. F. LAGLER et al. *Ichthyology* xi. 337 Certain carangids such as *Trachurus* have prominent paired swellings designated the cristae cerebelli.

carangoid (kə'ræŋgɔɪd), *a.* and *sb.* [f. as prec. + -OID.] = prec.

1862 *Proc. Acad. Nat. Sci. Philadelphia* IX. 430 My attention having been..attracted especially to the Carangoids, it has been discovered that the nomenclature of several was quite erroneous. **1926** H. M. KYLE *Biol. Fishes* v. 113 Many normal fishes among the Carangoids show this stage.

carant, caranto: see CORANTO.

‖**caranx** ('kæræŋks). [mod.L.; in F. *carangue.*] A genus of fishes of the family *Scomberidæ.* ***C. trachurus*** is the Scad or Horse-mackerel.

1836 *Penny Cycl.* VI. 278/2. **1854** BADHAM *Halieut.* 227 At Rome..during Lent..this caranx is often seen, heard, and smelt, sputtering in rancid grease.

caranye, obs. form of CARRION.

'carap. [from the native name.] ***carap oil***: an oil obtained from the seeds of the *Carapa guianensis*, a large tree found in Guiana.

c **1865** LETHEBY in *Circ. Sc.* I. 95/1 A semi-solid oil, named Crab or Carapa oil. **1866** *Treas. Bot.* I. 220 s.v. *Carapa*, By pressure the seeds yield a liquid oil, called Carap oil or Crab oil, suitable for burning in lamps..In this country it hardens into a solid fat.

carapace ('kærəpeɪs). [a. mod.F. *carapace*, ad. Sp. *carapacho* upper shell of a tortoise: of doubtful origin; taken by Barcia as a by-form of **carapazon*, by metathesis for *caparazon* caparison, body-armour of a horse, augmentative of *capara, -o*, in med.L. a hood, a covering of the head and shoulders, f. L. *capa*, CAPE.]

The upper body-shell of tortoises, and of crustaceans. Extended to the hard case investing the body in some other animals, as certain Infusoria.

1836 TODD *Cycl. Anat.* I. 202/1 If the carapace is raised in a crab. **1854** H. MILLER *Sch. & Schm.* x. (1857) 201 The carapace of some tall tortoise. **1878** BELL *Gegenbauer's Comp. Anat.* 38 A continuous covering for the body, like the carapace of the Arthropoda.

fig. **1860** O. W. HOLMES *Prof. Breakf.-t.* ii, Nothing.. could have got me to leave the shelter of my carapace.

Hence **'carapaced** *a.*

1876 PAGE *Adv. Text-bk. Geol.* xix. 357 Carapaced turtles.

carapacial (kærə'peɪʃ(ɪ)əl), *a.* [f. CARAPACE + -IAL.] Of or pertaining to a carapace.

1880 T. H. HUXLEY *Crayfish* iv. 217 The lateral portions of the carapacial ridge.

So **carapacic** (kærə'peɪsɪk) *a.*

1903 *Ann. & Mag. Nat. Hist.* XI. 442 The carapacic portion of the dorsal scute.

carapato, var. CARRAPATO.

ˈ**carapax.** = CARAPACE.

1847–9 TODD *Cycl. Anat.* IV. 10/2 Amœbæ endowed with a power of constructing for themselves a carapax or shelly covering. **1862** DANA *Man. Geol.* 345 Turtles or Chelonians. Body having a carapax, or shell.

carat (ˈkærət). Forms: 6 **caracte, carette, carret,** (**carrotte**), **charect,** 6–7 **karect(e, carrect,** 6–9 **caract,** 7 **caratt, karat, charat, charact, charract,** (**corrat, carack, carrack**), 7–8 **carrat, carract,** 7– **carat.** [a. F. *carat*, ad. It. *carato*: cf. Sp. and Pg. *quilate*, earlier *quirate*, a. Arab. *qīrāṭ* (and *qirrāṭ*) 'weight of 4 grains', acc. to Freytag ad. Gr. κεράτιον 'little horn, fruit of carob or locust tree, a weight = $\frac{1}{3}$ of an obol'. Isidore (XVI. xxv. 10) has '*ceratum* oboli pars media est, habens siliquam unam et semis'; but originally the Gr. κεράτιον was identical with the L. *siliqua*, and was called the *siliqua Græca*. (Formerly confounded with *caract* mark, sign, character: see sense 4.)

As a measure of weight and fineness, the *carat* represents the Roman *siliqua*, as $\frac{1}{24}$ of the golden solidus of Constantine, which was $\frac{1}{6}$ of an ounce: hence the various values into which $\frac{1}{24}$ and $\frac{1}{144}$ enter or originally entered.]

†**1.** The seed or 'bean' of the carob-tree. *Obs.*

1601 HOLLAND *Pliny* I. 447 The fruit called Carobes or Caracts. [**1846** LINDLEY *Veg. Kingd.* (1853) 550.]

2. A measure of weight used for diamonds and other precious stones, originally $\frac{1}{144}$ of an ounce, or $3\frac{1}{3}$ grains, but now equal to about $\frac{1}{150}$ of an ounce troy, or $3\frac{1}{5}$ grains, though varying slightly with time and place. It is divided into 4 *carat-grains.* Also *attrib.*, as in *a one-carat diamond.*

1575 LANEHAM *Let.* (1871) 48 As for the valu, yoor iewellers by their Carrets let them cast, and they can. **1598** HAKLUYT *Voy.* II. I. 225 These pearles are prised according to the caracts which they weigh, euery caract is 4 graines. **1667** E. KING in *Phil. Trans.* II. 429 A Diamond of 10 Carats. **1679** *Lond. Gaz.* No. 1462/4 Lost..a parcel of Rough Diamonds..containing 38 Caracks $\frac{1}{2}$. **1743** S. MADDEN *Boulter's Mon.* (1745) 57 Augmenting Carracts vastly raise Th' advancing Value of the Diamond's Blaze. **1750** BEAWES *Lex Mercat.* (1752) 873 The Jewellers divide the Ounce into 152 Parts, or Carats, and these into Grains, whereof four make a Carat. **1868** SEYD *Bullion* 146 Six carats are equal to 19 grains Troy weight. **1875** JEVONS *Money* (1878) 36 A one carat diamond. **1887** *Whitaker's Alm.* 362 The jewellery ounce is divided into $151\frac{1}{2}$ carats and 600 pearl-grains.

3. A proportional measure of one twenty-fourth used in stating the fineness of gold; e.g. if the mass contain 22 parts of pure gold and 2 of alloy, it is said to be 22 carats fine, or gold of 22 carats. Also *attrib.* with numeral, as ***22-carat gold.***

1555 EDEN *Decades W. Ind.* (Arb.) 211 The golde is of .xxii. caractes or better in fynesse. **1575–6** *Act 18 Eliz.* xv, No..Golde lesse in fynesse than that of xxij Carrottes. **1627** DONNE *Serm.* clvii. Wks. 1839 VI. 266 All their clods of Earth are Gold..of innumerable Carats. **1676** B. W[ILLIS] *Man. Goldsm.* 57 In his report of a Gold assay he [the Assay-master] sets it down by Carracts and Carract-grains. **1722** *Lond. Gaz.* No. 6059/2 The Gold..will be of the Standard of 22 Carrats. **1806** HUTTON *Course Math.* (1806) I. 129 It is said to be 22 caracts fine. **1820** G. CAREY *Funds* 94 The whole weight of any piece of pure gold is supposed to be divided into twenty four parts, called carats.

fig. **1581** SIDNEY *Astr. & Stella* xvi, Beauties which were of many carrets fine.

†**b.** The tradition that the carat was originally a definite weight of gold, and = $\frac{1}{24}$ of some weight (see the etymology), survived in dictionaries, arithmetical works, etc., but these have erroneously taken it as $\frac{1}{24}$ of an ounce (= 1 scruple), and $\frac{1}{24}$ of a pound Troy (= $\frac{1}{2}$ oz.); also as $\frac{1}{3}$ of an ounce.

1552 HULOET, *Scruple*, a certayne measuer called a charect, whereof thre make a dramme. **1558** WARDE tr. *Alexis' Secr.* (1568) 49a, Take Damaskene Roses..an unce, Lignum Aloes, Galanga, Penyworth, of eche of them a carette. **1656** BLOUNT *Glossogr.*, *Carat*..is the third part of an ounce. **1667** E. CHAMBERLAYNE *St. Gt. Brit.* I. (1684) 12 The pound weight or 12 Ounces Troy of Gold, is divided into 24 parts which are called carrats so that each carrat is 10 penny weight troy, or half an ounce. **1686** W. HARRIS tr. *Lemery's Chym.* I. i. 75 A Carat of Gold is properly the weight of one Scruple. **1755** *Gentl. Mag.* XXV. 361 Weigh a small vial which holds about 4 ounces..fill it with water, and weigh that..1–128th of the whole..is called a caract. **1852** A. RYLAND *Assay Gold & S.* 28 The ounce containing 24 carats.

†**4.** *fig.* Worth, value; estimate. *Obs.*

(Here a confusion with CARACT character, is evident.)

1597 SHAKS. *2 Hen. IV*, IV. v. 162 Thou best of Gold, art worst of Gold. Other, lesse fine of Charract, is more precious. **1598** B. JONSON *Ev. Man in Hum.* III. iii. 22 No beautie, no; you are of too good caract, To be left so, without a guard. **1650** HOWELL *Giraffi's Rev. Naples* 125 Authority doth commonly discompose the mind of man, specially one of a base carat. *a***1680** BUTLER *Rem.* (1759) II. 14 Counterfeit Jewels of any Caract.

‖**caratch** (kaˈrɑːtʃ). [Arab. *kharāj* tribute.] The tribute or poll-tax levied by the Turks on their Christian subjects.

1682 WHELER *Journ. Greece* VI. 479 The Inhabitants were all run away, not being able to pay their Caratch. **1753** HANWAY *Trav.* (1762) II. v. iii. 138 The abolition of the carak, imposed on the sunnis. **1775** R. CHANDLER *Trav. Greece* (1825) II. 7 They pay..caratch or tribute money. **1796** H. HUNTER tr. *St. Pierre's Stud. Nat.* (1799) III. 481 The carach or tribute is paid only by the Greeks.

caraus: see CAROUSE.

Caravaggiesque (ˌkærəvæˈdʒɛsk, -dʒɪˈɛsk), *a.* Also **Caravaggioesque.** [f. the name *Caravaggio* (see below) + -ESQUE.] Of, resembling, or characteristic of the Italian painter Michelangelo Merisi Caravaggio (1573–1610), or his works.

1925 A. HUXLEY *Along Road* III. 184 The most spectacular Caravaggioesque light and shade. **1936** *Burlington Mag.* Mar. 132/1 A Caravaggiesque *Madonna.* **1938** *Ibid.* Jan. 4/1 The third great style of the century is the 'Caravaggesque'. **1958** *Spectator* 24 Jan. 106/2 As a painter of religious or genre subjects in artificial light he has obvious associations with the Caravaggesque.

caravan (ˈkærəvæn, kærəˈvæn), *sb.* Also 6 **carouan,** 7 **carrauan, caruan, karavan,** 8 **karrawan.** [In 16th c. *carouan*, a Pers. *kārwān*, in same sense. Found in med.L. *carvana* (Hoveden), *caravanna, caravenna* (Matt. Paris), and F. *carvane*, from Crusading times, but app. not in Eng. before 16th c. The form *caravan* was perhaps *caravane* from French.]

1. a. A company of merchants, pilgrims, or others, in the East or northern Africa, travelling together for the sake of security, esp. through the desert. Also *attrib.*, as in ***caravan route.***

1599 HAKLUYT *Voy.* II. I. 204 The maner and order which the Carouan obserueth in marching. **1601** W. PARRY *Sherley's Trav.* 23 A caravan is a great many of camels laden, and men in a company. **1602** WARNER *Alb. Eng.* XI. lxvi. (1612) 282 Their Marchants trauailing by Carauan, that is, Great Droues of laden Camels. **1615** G. SANDYS *Trav.* 122 Brought ouer-land by Caruan from Mecha. **1760** GOLDSM. *Cit. W.* xxii, He..hired himself as a camel-driver to a caravan that was crossing the desert. **1761** STERNE *Tr. Shandy* IV. (1770) 62 (D.) From thence by karrawans to Coptos. **1872** YEATS *Growth Comm.* 31 Various caravan routes. **1873** LONGF. *Kambalu* 3 At the head of his dusty caravan.

†**b.** *Thieves' cant.* An object of plunder. *Obs.*

1688 SHADWELL *Sqr. Alsatia* I. i, Thy cousin here is the wealthiest Caravan we have met with a long time. **1690** B. E. *Dict. Cant. Crew*, *Caravan*, a good round Sum of Money about a Man, and him that is Cheated of it.

2. a. A fleet of Turkish or Russian ships, *esp.* of merchant vessels, with their convoy.

1605–74 CAMDEN *Rem.* 493 The sinking of the great Galeasse of the Saracens, the taking of their Convoy, which ..is called a Caravana. **1654** FULLER *Comm. Ruth* (1868) 119 A caravan..sailing in the vast ocean. **1686** *Lond. Gaz.* No. 2177/2 News..of the rencounter between Signior Venier, Captain Extraordinary of the Ships of this State, and the Turkish Caravan. **1753** CHAMBERS *Cycl. Supp.* s.v., Sea Caravans..conveyed by ships of war.

b. (See quots.)

1727–51 CHAMBERS *Cycl.*, Caravan is also an appellation given to the voyages, or campaigns, which the knights of Malta are obliged to make at sea, against the Turks and Corsairs. **1858** W. PORTER *Hist. Knts. Malta* II. xx. 209 Every Knight, during his residence in Malta, was bound to complete four caravans, or cruises of six months each.

3. *transf.* **a.** A troop of people going in company [so in Fr.]; a company in motion. Also *fig.*

1667 MILTON *P.L.* VII. 428 [Birds] rang'd in figure wedge thir way..and set forth Their Aierie Caravan. **1681** COTTON *Poet. Wks.* (1765) 332 We a Caravan of dead Folks were. **1683** *Argum. for Union* 4 [Arians, Socinians, etc.] may associate in a Caravan, but cannot joyn in the Communion of a Church. **1711** SWIFT *Lett.* (1767) III. 223 We got out before eleven, a noble caravan of us. **1719** DE FOE *Crusoe* (Hotten) 177 Attacking a whole Caravan of them.

b. A company of travellers, traders, or emigrants, with their wagons, mules, or packhorses, esp. in the Western States; a train (of wagons, etc.). *U.S.*

1748 CATESBY *Carolina* App. p. iv, Indian Traders, whose Caravans travel these uninhabited Countries. **1791** W. BARTRAM *Trav. Carolina* (1792) 376 Our caravan consisting of about twenty men and sixty horses, we made a formidable appearance. **1817** S. R. BROWN *Western Gaz.* 77 General Harrison..was accompanied in his march through the wilderness by a caravan of waggons. **1897** J. L. ALLEN *Choir Invisible* ii. 14 A company of travellers with pack-horses—one of the caravans across the desert of the Western woods.

4. A covered carriage or cart: In 17–18th c. applied to a private or public covered vehicle carrying passengers or a company of people together (later shortened to *van*); hence early in 19th c. to a third class 'covered carriage' on a railway; now, usually, a house on wheels, e.g. the travelling house of gipsies, a showman, or (according to recent fashion) a party on a pleasure tour; one of the covered vehicles of a travelling menagerie, etc. Now freq. one able to be towed by a motor car and used as a stationary dwelling (esp. while on holiday). Also *attrib.*, as **caravan park, site,** a place where caravans are parked and used as dwellings.

1674 BLOUNT *Glossogr.*, *Caravan* or Karavan..also of late corruptly used with us for a kind of Waggon to carry passengers to and from London. **1689** *Lond. Gaz.* No. 2450/4 A Fair easie going Caravan, with a very handsome Roof Brass Work, good Seats, Glasses on the sides to draw up, that will carry 18 Persons. **1741** *Act 14 Geo. II*, xlii. §5 Nothing in this act shall..extend..to Caravans or the covered Carriages of Noblemen or Gentlemen for their private use. [So **1751** 24 Geo. II, xliii. §5.] **1754** *Connoisseur* No. 25 We should laugh at a nobleman who..should..be content to have his family dragged to his country seat, like servant maids in the caravan. **1797** BEWICK *Brit. Birds* (1847) I. 369 One of these birds which was kept in a caravan. **1823** *Mechanic's Mag.* No. 19. 290 The steam-engine employs its force to impel the caravans..and coaches. **1824** W. IRVING *T. Trav.* I. 272 Several caravans containing wild beasts, and other spectacles. **1872** BROWNING *Fifine* iv. 5 A slow caravan, A chimneyed house on wheels. **1886** W. G. STABLES *Cruise of Wanderer* 9 Nice curtains divide the caravan at pleasure into two compartments. *Ibid.* 3 He is unsuited for a caravan life. **1935** *Caravan Ann.* (*sub-title*), A list of over 1,200 caravan sites in Britain. **1937** 'G. ORWELL' *Road to Wigan Pier* iv. 61 The dreadful caravan-dwellings that exist in numbers in many of the northern towns. *Ibid.*, Parts of the population have overflowed into supposedly temporary quarters in fixed caravans. *Ibid.*, Some of the caravan-dwellers. **1959** M. STEEN *Tower* I. iii. 44 The back streets, the caravan sites and the pre-fabs. **1963** *Times* 18 Feb. 16/5 The difficult problem of finding enough caravan parks on which to put the end product.

Hence **caravaˈneer**, the leader or conductor of an (oriental) caravan; one who lives or travels in a caravan. ˌ**caraˈvaning** *vbl. sb.*, travelling by caravan or house on wheels. ˌ**caraˈvanist**, one who practises this mode of making a tour. **caraˈvannish** *a.*, resembling or smacking of a caravan.

1768 E. BUYS *Dict. Terms of Art*, *Caravanier*, a Person who leads the Camels, and other Beasts of Burden, commonly used in the Caravans in the East. **1856** RUSKIN *Mod. Paint.* IV. v. ii. §15 Great diligences going in a caravannish manner, with whole teams of horses. **1885** *Chr. Leader* 5 Nov. 680 Caravaning in Scotland. **1887** *Pall Mall G.* 19 Sept. 6/1 The caravanist reverses matters..every night finds him encamped in meadow, in wood, or on moorland. **1893** *Cornhill Mag.* Mar. 288 The joy of the caravaneer was ours.

caravan, *v.* [f. the sb.] **1.** *intr.* To travel or live in a caravan.

1885 [see CARAVANING *vbl. sb.*]. **1909** R. BROOKE *Let.* Sept. (1968) 184 Will you Caravan with me in the Spring, or Summer? **1930** W. DE LA MARE *Desert Islands* 39 In the 'second part' of his adventures Crusoe is transformed into a mere globe-trotter, caravanning from Nanking to Tobolsk. **1963** *Times* 12 Mar. p. iv/1 Having caravanned all over this continent, he admitted that there is an awful lot of it to love.

2. *trans.* To convey by caravan. *rare.*

1898 G. W. STEEVENS *With Kitchener to Khartum* 118 The Greek gets his stuff up everywhere:..he caravans it with a double-barrelled rifle on his shoulder.

caravance, obs. form of CALAVANCE.

caravanette (kærəvæˈnɛt). [f. CARAVAN + -ETTE.] A motor vehicle designed with a caravan-like rear compartment for eating, sleeping, etc., esp. while on holiday; a motorized caravan or camper.

1961 *Motor Caravanner* Oct. 21 Nomad Ltd... '*Nomad Caravanette*' on B.M.C. 16/18 cwt, £895. **1974** *Oxford Times* 22 Feb. 6 A sleeping man was flung to his death when an articulated lorry crashed into his parked caravanette. **1979** *Daily Tel.* 31 July 6/7 Mr Young..was a passenger in a caravanette which overturned on an S-bend. **1984** *Observer* 11 Mar. 3/5 Haynes was picked up at a caravanette in Liskeard, Cornwall.

caravanner (ˈkærəvænə(r)). Also **-aner.** [f. CARAVAN + -ER.[1]] **a.** One who lives in or travels in a caravan (esp. on a pleasure tour). **b.** The conductor of a caravan in the East (Cf. CARAVANEER).

1909 *Westm. Gaz.* 5 Apr. 4 The [Caravan] club decided to spell 'caravanner', 'caravanning', with two n's—not one. **1916** C'TESS VON ARNIM (*title*) The Caravaners. **1923** *Weekly Dispatch* 21 Jan. 5 Victor Maclaglen, who gives a magnificent performance as a gipsy king in the story, was urged to prolong his stay by the caravanners. **1929** *Daily Tel.* 22 Jan. 11/3 There is little doubt that information which caravanners gave me yesterday has now reached Kabul. **1958** *Economist* 25 Oct. 310 The shanty towns into which caravanners have been herded.

caravanning (ˈkærəvænɪŋ), *vbl. sb.* Also **caravaning.** [f. CARAVAN *v.* + -ING[1].] Travelling or living in a caravan. Also *attrib.*

1885 [see CARAVANING *vbl. sb.*]. **1892** *Pall Mall Gaz.* 5 May 3/1 The rage of this season is to be caravanning. **1914** *Lancet* 9 May 1369/1 Caravanning offers freedom, movement, variety, open-air life. **1957** *Listener* 24 Oct. 643/2 A caravanning holiday. **1958** *Times* 19 Mar. 6/6 Caravanning, he said, was 'not a question of poverty or squalor'. It was a 'new way of life'. **1962** *Listener* 5 July 14/2 Facilities are provided for camping and caravanning in special fields.

caravanserai, -era, -ary (kærəˈvænsəraɪ, -ərə, -ərɪ). Forms: (6 **cauarzara**), 7 **carauansara, car(r)avans-raw, karavan serai, quervanseray,** 8 **caravanserie,** 8–9 **caravansera, -sary,** 9 **caravansery,** (**caravensary**), 8– **caravanserai.** [ult. a Per. *kārwān-sarāī*, f. *kārwān* caravan + *sarāī*, or *sarā* palace, mansion, inn. In F. *caravansérai*, Pg. *caravançara*. The endings *-ary, -ery*, are due to popular analogy.]

A kind of inn in Eastern countries where caravans put up, being a large quadrangular building with a spacious court in the middle.

1599 HAKLUYT *Voy.* II. I. 196 We lay in one of the great Cauarzaras [? caruanzaras], that were built by Mahomet

Bassha with so many goodly commodities. **1615** tr. *De Monfart's Surv. E. Ind.* 8 The Sophie hath caused to bee erected certaine..huge lodgings..called *Carauan-sara* or Surroyes, for the benefit of Carauans. **1634** Sir T. Herbert *Trav.* 51 Where is a Carravans-raw. **1682** Wheler *Journ. Greece* II. 192 Publick Buildings they call *Karavan Serais*, or *Kans.* **1687** tr. *De Thevenot's Trav.* III. I. v. 8, I went to lodge in a Quervanseray. **1712** Addison *Spect.* No. 289 ¶9 A house that changes its inhabitants so often, and receives such a perpetual succession of guests, is not a Palace but a Caravansary. **1798** T. Maurice *Hindostan* IV. iii. (1820) II. 252 The birth of Christ [in]..the stable of the caravansera..in the lowly village of Bethlehem. **1801** Southey *Thalaba* V. viii, Not in sumptuous Caravansery. **1855** Milman *Lat. Chr.* (1864) IV. VII. vi. 170 In Jerusalem there were public caravansaries.

b. *transf.* and *fig.*

1760 Sterne *Serm. Yorick* III. 17 What provision the Author of our being has prepared..how many caravanseras of rest! **1805** Foster *Ess.* I. vii. 88 The man whose mind has been a kind of caravansera of opinions. **1864** Sala in *Daily Tel.* 13 Oct., The palatial caravanserais of New York.

Hence **caravan'serial** *a.*

1864 Sala in *Daily Tel.* 13 Oct., Hotels..at Saratoga Springs [and] their caravanserial congeners in other parts of the United States.

caravel ('kærəvɛl). *Naut.* Forms: 6 carauelle, 6–7 -vell, 7 -vall, 8–9 -val, 6– caravel: see also CARVEL. [a. F. *caravelle* (16th c. in Littré—in earlier F. *caruelle*), ad. It. *caravella* (Sp. *carabela*, Pg. *caravela*), prob. dim. of Sp. *caraba*; cf. late L. *carabus*, Gr. *κάραβος* a kind of light ship.

Isidore XIX. i. 26 explains *Carabus* as 'parva scapha ex vimine facta, quæ contecta crudo corio genus navigii præbet'.]

1. A kind of ship: variously applied at different times, and in relation to different countries.

a. The same as CARVEL, which was the earlier vernacular form; but since the term came to be only historical, usually written *caravel*, like b and c. In later times applied to **b.** The Portuguese *caravela*, a small ship with lateen sails; **c.** The Turkish war-frigate, called in Italian *caravella*.

1527 R. Thorne in Hakl. *Divers Voy.* (1582) B iv b, A flote of three shippes and a carauell that went from this citie. **1555** Eden *Decades W. Ind., Interpr.* (Arb.) 45 A *Carauel* or *Caruel. Ibid.* I. I. (Arb.) 65 Light marchaunte shyppes without deckes whiche the Spaniardes call *Carauelas*. **1600** Holland *Livy* XXVIII. viii. 673 Three Galleaces or Caravels. **1642** Fuller *Holy & Prof. St.* II. xxi. 138 The King of Spain..sent a Caravall of adviso to the West Indies. **1738** Earl Sandwich in *Naval Chron.* (1799) II. 324 The [Turkish] Caravels or frigates under forty guns. **1769** Falconer *Dict. Marine* (1789) *Caravelle*, a small square-sterned Portuguese vessel, navigated with lateen sails; and esteemed very expeditious. **1796** Morse *Amer. Geog.* II. 463 Caravellas [Turkish war-vessels]. **1843** Prescott *Mexico* (1850) I. 221 The vessel..in which Cortes himself went, was of a hundred tons' burden..the remainder were caravels and open brigantines. **1848** W. Irving *Columbus* I. 123 Two of them were light barks, called Caravels..They are delineated as open, and without deck in the centre, but built up high at the prow and stern, with forecastles and cabins.

2. The floating mollusc *Ianthina*.

1707 Sloane *Jamaica* I. 7 What seamen call a Caraval or Portuguese Man of War.

caravette (kærə'vɛt). [f. CARAV(AN + -ETTE.] = CARAVANETTE.

1958 *Motor* 8 Jan. 906/1 The Caravette provides holiday accommodation for two adults and one or two children. **1965** *Punch* 6 Oct. 498/2 You can now buy a 'caravette' or rent a 'centrally heated Dolomette' in the Dolomites. **1967** *Motor Caravanner* Feb. 96 The vehicle used was a 1962 VW Devon Caravette. **1970** *AA Camping & Caravanning Handbk.* 246 *Devon*, Torvette VW Kombi..Caravette VW Microbus. **1976** *Norwich Mercury* 19 Nov. 13/3 (Advt.), Contact Reliance Rentals for all your van, car and caravette requirements.

caraway ('kærəweɪ). Forms: (5–7 carway), 6 caruway(e, carowaye, -weie, 6–7 careway(e, carawey, 7 carrowaye, 7–9 carraway, 5– caraway. [From med.L. *carui*, or some allied Romanic form: cf. F., It., Sp. *carvi* (whence Sc. *carvy, kervie*), OSp. *alcaravea, alcarahueya*, Pg. *alcaravia, alcorovia*, a. Arab. *al-karawiyā* or *-karwiyā*: cf. Gr. *κάρον, κάρεον* (in L. *carum, careum* Pliny), forms however which could not immediately give the Arabic.]

1. An umbelliferous plant (*Carum Carui*): its small fruits, commonly called 'caraway-seeds', are aromatic and carminative; they are used in cakes, sweetmeats, etc., and yield a volatile oil.

c **1440** *Promp. Parv.* 62 Caraway herbe, carway, sic scribitur in campo florum. **1551** Turner *Herbal* H iv b, Caruwayes..the poticaries call it *carui*. **1579** Langham *Gard. Health* (1633) 125 Carway breaketh winde. **1794** Martyn *Rousseau's Bot.* xvii. 236 Carraway has no proper involucre. **1861** Delamer *Kitch. Gard.* 124 Caraway is the object of field culture in Essex, and on other stiff soils.

†**2.** The fruit or 'seed' of the caraway; also a sweetmeat or confection containing caraway-seeds. *Obs.* exc. as Sc. CARVY.

1557 Seager *Sch. Vertue* in *Babees Bk.* (1868) 343 Bisketes or Carowayes. **1586** Cogan *Haven Health* (1636) 101 To eat Carawayes or Biskets, or some other kinde of Comfits or seedes together with Apples. **1597** Shaks. *2 Hen. IV*, v. iii. 3 We will eate a last yeares Pippin of my owne graffing, with a dish of Carrawayes. **1620** Melton *Astrol.* 75 A piece of Cheese, Pippins, or Carrowayes. **1620** Venner *Via Recta* vii. 162 In meates, I prefer the Carewayes before..Fennel-seeds. **1712** tr. *Pomet's Hist. Drugs* I. 5 The Caraways that the people of Paris buy out of the Shops.

3. *Comb.*, as **caraway-comfit**, a sweetmeat containing caraway-seeds; **caraway-seed** (see 1); also *attrib.*, as in ***caraway-seed biscuit***.

1710 Steele *Tatler* No. 245 ¶2 One Silver gilt [box] of a large Size for Cashu and *Carraway Comfits. **1548** Turner *Names of Herbes* s.v., Ye may use *carawey seede or carot seede. **1626** Bacon *Sylva* §54 Adding a little Coriander-seed and Carraway seed. **1694** *Phil. Trans.* XVIII. 212 Oyl of Carui-Seeds. **1836–7** Dickens *Sk. Boz* (1850) 141/2 Some sweet carrawayseed biscuits.

†**carawimple.** *Obs.* (Cf. CARRIWITCHET.)

1672 Eachard *Lett.* 2 A meer fiction..a dream, device, and carawimple.

carayne, obs. form of CARRION.

carb, colloq. abbrev. of CARBURETTOR, -ETTER b.

1942 Berrey & Van den Bark *Amer. Thes. Slang* §82/4 *Carburetor*, carb, jug, juicer, juice pot. **1943** *R.A.F. Jrnl.* Aug. 22 He..did courses on Mags, Carbs, Turning, Forging, Sheet-bashing. **1963** *Times* 16 Oct. 7/7 (Advt.), Austin Mini Cooper 997 cc engine. Twin carbs. Disc brakes. **1977** *Hot Car* Oct. 21/2, I would like to fit an S.U. carb from a Mini or a Morris 1100 to the Escort.

carb-. *Chem.* Combining form of CARBON *sb.*, used (instead of CARBO-) before vowels, in names of carbon compounds, as **carba'llylic** (or **tricarballylic**) **acid** [ALLYL], a 3-basic acid obtained by the action of potash on allylic tricyanide; its salts are **car'ballylates.** **'carbanil** [ANIL], an amido-derivative of the benzene group, cyanate of phenyl, $CO{=}N{-}C_6H_5$, a mobile liquid with a pungent odour; hence **carbanilamide**, $NH_2{\cdot}CO{\cdot}NH{-}C_6H_5$, **carbanilic acid**, $HO{\cdot}CO{\cdot}NH{-}C_6H_5$, **carbanilide**, $CO{=}2(NH{\cdot}C_6H_5)$. **'carbazol** [AZO- + -OL], an amidophenyl, $2\ C_6H_4{=}NH$, occurring in coal-tar oil, and as a by-product in the manufacture of aniline. **carba'zotic acid** [AZOTIC], an earlier name of Picric acid; its salts are **car'bazotates.**

1873 *Fownes' Chem.* 730 Carballylic Acid is produced by the action of nascent hydrogen on aconitic acid. *Ibid.* The carballylates of the alkali-metals are easily soluble in water. **1877** *Ibid.* II. 56 Carbazol crystallizes in shining laminæ. **1881** *Athenæum* 14 May 658/3 'On some Carbazol Compounds'. **1836–9** Todd *Cycl. Anat.* II. 405 The properties..closely resemble the carbazotates. **1830** Lindley *Nat. Syst. Bot.* 93 A peculiar acid, called Carbazotic. **1883** *Chamb. Jrnl.* 226 A yellow, intensely bitter mass..known also as Carbazotic Acid.

carbage: see CABBAGE, GARBAGE.

carbamide ('kɑːbəmaɪd). *Chem.* [f. CARB- + AMIDE.] Analytical name of the organic compound UREA, $CO{\cdot}2(NH_2)$, as a primary diamide of Carbonyl. Hence ***sulpho-carbamide*** or sulphur urea, in which CS takes the place of CO.

Also **car'bamic** [see AMIC] *a.*, related to carbamide, as in ***carbamic acid***, $CO{\cdot}NH_2{\cdot}OH$, ***carbamic ethers***. **'carbamate**, a salt of carbamic acid, as ***ammonium carbamate***, $CO{\cdot}NH_2{\cdot}O{\cdot}NH_4$.

1865 Mansfield *Salts* 367 The compound 'Carbamide' is not yet known in the separate state. **1877** Watts *Fownes' Chem.* II. 391 Carbamide or Urea..was the first instance of the artificial formation of a product of the living organism. **1869** Roscoe *Elem. Chem.* xxxv. 382 Carbamic Acid.

carbanion (kɑː'bænaɪən). *Chem.* [f. CARB- + ANION.] An organic ion containing negatively charged carbon. Cf. CARBONIUM (*b*).

1933 Wallis & Adams in *Jrnl. Amer. Chem. Soc.* LV. 3838 For the sake of clearness in discussion all tricovalent carbon compounds may be divided into three classes: (1) 'carbanions'..(2) free radicals..(3) carbonium ions... The above word [carbanion] is here proposed for a negatively charged carbon ion in contrast to the term 'carbonium', which indicates a positively charged ion. **1956** J. E. Leffler *Reactive Interm. of Org. Chem.* ix. 187 Many of the reactions of the weak carbon acids are reactions of the carbanion, the rate being the rate of ionization.

†**'carberry**, *v. Sc. Obs.* [? f. *Carberry Hill* where Queen Mary was finally routed.] *trans.* ? To defeat, get the better of.

1692 *Babell* 551 We, for all the Councell's threats, On that day neither pray nor preach..By which we doe the state Carberrie.

carbide ('kɑːbaɪd). *Chem.* [f. CARB- + -IDE.] A compound of carbon with an element, as hydrogen or a metal, as ***iron carbide***; less usual than the older equivalent *carburet*. *spec.* Short for 'calcium carbide'.

c **1865** J. Wylde in *Circ. Sc.* I. 308/2 The combinations of sulphur with metals are termed sulphides..of carbon, carbides. **1879** *Athenæum* 6 Sept. 312/2 Native iron carbides of Greenland. **1879** G. Prescott *Sp. Telephone* 434 Carbides of hydrogen obtained as secondary products. **1898** W. E. Gibbs *Lighting by Acetylene* 70 Water from an elevated reservoir enters T until the carbide is reached. **1904** A. B. F. Young *Compl. Motorist* 257 Carbide lamps give a beautiful light when they are working properly. **1957** P. Kemp *Mine were of Trouble* iv. 59 A bare room..lit by a single smelly carbide lamp.

carbinado, obs. spelling of CARBONADO.

carbine ('kɑːbaɪn), **'carabine.** Also 7 car(r)abin, 8 carrabine. [In 17th c. *carabine*, a. F. *carabine*, in It., Sp., and Pg. *carabina*, the weapon of the CARABIN, q.v.]

A kind of fire-arm, shorter than the musket, used by the cavalry and other troops; 'a kind of medium between the pistol and the musket' (J.).

1605 Verstegan *Dec. Intell.* i. (1628) 23 The names of Lances, Carabines, pykes, muskets. **1640** T. Carew *On Death K. Sweden* (R.) The thunder of their carabins. *c* **1645** Howell *The Vote* ii, No pistolls or some rare-spring carrabins. **1660** H. More *Myst. Godl.* v. xvi. 189 Discharging their carbines. **1721** De Foe *Mem. Cavalier* (1840) 182, I discharged..my carabin twice. **1799** Earl Ancram in *Trans. Roy. Soc. Edin.* (1805) V. 246, I had a carabine made at Drogheda. **1815** Wellington in Gurw. *Disp.* XII. 345, I will apply for the Carbines for your Cavalry. **1858** Greener *Gunnery* 399 Double rifled carbines can be constructed of so light a weight that their exclusive use for cavalry is not far distant. **1859** Jephson *Brittany* x. 152 His double-barrelled carabine..slung over his shoulder.

b. *Comb.*, as ***carbine-ball, -lock, -proof, -shot.***

1643 *Cromwell's Lett. & Sp.* App. 29 July, Retreating in order, near carbine-shot of the enemy. **1655** Mrq. Worcester *Cent. Inv.* §44 A Brest-plate..of Carabine-proof. **1721** De Foe *Mem. Cavalier* (1840) 66 A salvo of carbine-shot. **1802** Wellington in Gurw. *Disp.* I. 380 Ordering..20,000 carbine balls to be cast. **1814** Byron *Corsair* I. vii. 24 Free from rust, My carbine lock.

carbinol ('kɑːbɪnɒl). *Chem.* [f. CARBON *sb.* + -OL (the ending of *alcohol*, used to indicate an analogous compound).] A generic name introduced by Kolbe *c* 1868 for the monatomic alcohols.

Simple *Carbinol* is methyl alcohol or wood spirit (taken as $COH.H_3$), a compound of 1 atom of carbon with 1 of hydroxyl OH, and 3 of replaceable hydrogen, any one or more of which may be replaced by the same number of alcohol radicals, the name or names of which are prefixed. When only one hydrogen atom is replaced, the carbinol is a 'primary alcohol', as ***methyl carbinol*** $COH.H_2.CH_3$ = ethyl or ordinary alcohol, C_2H_5OH; ***ethyl carbinol*** $COH.H_2.C_2H_5$ = propyl alcohol C_3H_7OH. When two atoms of hydrogen are replaced, the carbinol includes the 'secondary alcohols' as ***dimethyl carbinol*** $COH.H.(CH_3)_2$ = secondary propyl alcohol C_3H_8O; ***methyl-propyl-carbinol*** $COH.H.CH_3.C_3H_7$. When all three atoms of hydrogen are replaced, the carbinol includes the 'tertiary alcohols', as ***trimethyl carbinol*** $COH.(CH_3)_3$ = tertiary butyl alcohol $C_4H_{10}OH$, ***dimethyl-ethyl-carbinol*** $COH.(CH_3)_2.C_2H_5$. The nomenclature of the complicated members as *carbinols* is more simple and definite than as alcohols.

carbinyl ('kɑːbɪnɪl). *Chem.* [f. CARBON *sb.* + -YL, as in *ethyl*, etc.] A term for the alcohol radicals of the corresponding *carbinols*, as ***dimethyl carbinyl iodide*** $C(CH_3)_2{\cdot}H{\cdot}I$. (Watts.)

carbo-. *Chem.* Combining form of CARBON *sb.*, used before consonants, in names of carbon compounds. ***carbo-hydrogen***; ***-hydrous, -methylic*** adjs.; **carbo-cyclic** *a.*, containing a ring of carbon atoms only; **carbo-dynamite**, a patented explosive, in which fine charcoal is used as the absorbent.

1873 *Fownes' Chem.* 823 Carbo-cresylic and Cresotic Acids are formed simultaneously by the action of carbon dioxide and sodium on cresol. **1899** *Jrnl. Chem. Soc.* LXXVI. I. 59 Carbocyclic Compounds. **1904** *Nature* 11 Aug. 341/1 The stability of carbocyclic and heterocyclic chains. **1888** *Times* 2 Oct. 3/1 Some carbo-dynamite, which had lain for eight months in water. **1866** Odling *Anim. Chem.* 75 The carbo-hydrogen of vegetable tissue. **1881** *Ann. Rep. Smithsonian Inst.* 393 The carbohydrous material which is present in the plant. **1838** R. D. Thomson in *British Annual* 323 Carbo-methylic acid. **1810** Henry *Elem. Chem.* (1826) I. 468 The bi-sulphuret of carbon was found by Berzelius to be capable of..forming compounds which may be called Carbo-Sulphurets.

carbohydrate (ˌkɑːbəʊ'haɪdreɪt). *Chem.* Also **carbo-hydrate.** [f. CARBO- + HYDRATE, q.v.] An organic compound of carbon with oxygen and hydrogen in the proportion to form water. They are divided into *sugars proper* ($C_{12}H_{22}O_{11}$), *grape-sugars* or *glucoses* ($C_6H_{12}O_6$), and *amyloses*, comprising starch and woody fibre ($C_6H_{10}O_5$). Also *attrib.* and *Comb.*

1869 Roscoe *Elem. Chem.* 393. **1876** tr. *Wagner's Gen. Pathol.* 531 Carbo-hydrates and fats serve chiefly to the production of heat, and of vital force. **1882** Vines *Sachs' Bot.* 668 Cell-walls and starch-grains..consist mainly of carbo-hydrates insoluble in water. **1886** *Jrnl. Franklin Inst.* CXXII. 274 (*title*) Carbohydrate and fatty foods. *Ibid.* 285 The glycogen of the liver greatly diminishes in amount in the absence of carbohydrate food stuffs. **1888** *Jrnl. Chem. Soc.* LIV. 972 Acid in Healthy and Disordered Stomachs during a Carbo-hydrate Diet. **1900** *Westm. Gaz.* 21 Dec. 3/2 Concerning malt liquors, we are told that the large quantity of carbohydrate matter in them [etc.]. **1908** *Carnegie Trust Rep.* 22 The carbohydrate material and ferments of blood. **1910** *Practitioner* Jan. 129, I want to insist that pyorrhoea alveolaris is a local disease due to germ, or carbohydrate-germ. **1964** M. Hynes *Med. Bacteriol.* (ed. 8) i. 7 Carbohydrate-fermenting bacteria may produce enough acid in culture to kill themselves.

carbokull, obs. form of CARBUNCLE.

carbolate (ˈkɑːbəʊleɪt). *Chem.* [f. CARBOL-IC + -ATE.] A salt of carbolic acid; a phenate.
1875 H. WOOD *Therap.* (1879) 628 An alkaline carbolate. 1876 BARTHOLOW *Mat. Med.* (1879) 523 Carbolic acid exists in the blood, probably, as a carbolate.
So ˈ**carbolated** *ppl. a.*, made into a carbolate; impregnated with carbolic acid, carbolized.
1884 *Sat. Rev.* 7 June 760/2 Cotton-wool..moistened with carbolated oil. 1884 *Health Exhib. Catal.* 62/1 Concentrated Carbolated Creosote Disinfecting Fluid.

carbol-fuchsin, -ine (ˌkɑːbɒlˈfuːksɪn). [f. CARBOL(IC *a.* + FUCHSINE.] A mixture of fuchsine and carbolic acid, used as a staining-solution.
1897 PEARMAIN & MOOR *Appl. Bacteriol.* iii. 84 *(heading)* Ziehl's Carbol-Fuchsine. 1909 *Practitioner* Feb. 304 Leprosy bacilli..can be stained with carbol-fuchsin in the ordinary way. 1956 *Nature* 3 Mar. 430/2 Sections were..stained with..dilute carbol fuchsin.

carbolic (kɑːˈbɒlɪk), *a. Chem.* [f. CARB- + -OL, the ending of *alcohol, benzol* + -IC.] In **carbolic acid**, a substance more systematically called *phenol* or *phenyl alcohol*, $C_6H_5{\cdot}OH$, a secondary monatomic aromatic alcohol (consisting of benzol in which one atom of H is replaced by OH), found in the heavy coal oils, and elsewhere, forming, when pure, white deliquescent crystals, melting at 35° to an oily liquid, with penetrating odour and burning taste. It has powerful antiseptic qualities, and is much used as a disinfectant. Hence ***carbolic soap***, etc. Also *ellipt.* for *carbolic acid* or *soap*.
c 1865 LETHEBY in *Circ. Sc.* I. 118/2 The acid of creosote, or carbolic acid. 1865 LD. BURY in *Morn. Star.* 6 Nov. Cowsheds were carefully cleansed and washed with gas-tar, carbolic acid, and water. 1872 BLACK *Adv. Phaeton* (Hoppe) My lady doubted the efficacy of carbolic soap. 1881 LUBBOCK in *Nature* 405 Some substance capable of killing the germs, without being itself too potent a caustic..Dilute carbolic acid fulfilled these conditions. 1884 *Medical Uses Carbolic Acid* (F.C. Calvert & Co.) 35 The Carbolic will be readily given off in vapour sufficient to fill an ordinary room. *Ibid.* 47, I used 1 pint of Carbolic to each room. 1907 M. C. HARRIS *Tents of Wickedness* I. iv. 58 The stone floors are so cold, and there is such a smell of carbolic.

carbolize (ˈkɑːbəlaɪz), *v.* [f. prec. + -IZE.] *trans.* To impregnate with carbolic acid. Hence ˈ**carbolized** *ppl. a.*
1870 *Daily News* 24 Oct., Fine hemp or tow carbolised with crystallised carbolic acid. 1884 W. H. STONE in *Times* 30 Oct. 9/6 A small tent of carbolized gauze, to prevent the dispersion of poisonous membrane.

carbomycin (ˌkɑːbəʊˈmaɪsɪn). *Med.* [f. CARBO- + Gr. μύκης fungus (see MYCO-) + -IN¹.] An antibiotic obtained from the fungus *Streptomyces halstedii*.
1952 *Antibiotics & Chemotherapy* II. 441 Magnamycin is the trade-mark name of Chas. Pfizer & Co.'s antibiotic carbomycin. 1960 M. E. FLOREY *Clinical Appl. Antibiotics* IV. ii. 36 Like erythromycin, the antibiotic carbomycin.. was isolated in 1952 and has similar antibacterial properties.

carbon (ˈkɑːbən), *sb.* [ad. F. *carbone* (same sense), made by Lavoisier from L. *carbo, carbōnem* coal, charcoal.]
1. a. *Chem.* One of the non-metallic elements, very abundant in nature, occurring uncombined in three allotropic forms—two crystalline (diamond and graphite) and one amorphous (charcoal), and in combination in carbonic acid gas, the various carbonates, and nearly all organic compounds (thence often called 'the carbon compounds'). Carbon (symbol C) is a tetrad; atomic weight 12.
1789 PRIESTLEY in *Phil. Trans.* LXXIX. 279, Suppose that even the whole of this plumbago afforded only one of the elements of the fixed air, viz. that which the French chemists call *carbone*. 1794 G. ADAMS *Nat. & Exp. Philos.* I. xii. 496 Their *carbonne* is supposed to be the remaining part of charcoal after it has been divested of earth and fixed salts. 1810 HENRY *Elem. Chem.* (1826) I. 335 The diamond ..was first shown by Guyton to contain carbon. 1813 SIR H. DAVY *Agric. Chem.* ii. (1814) 46 Carbon is considered as the pure matter of charcoal. 1856 DOVE *Logic Chr. Faith* VI. iv. 352 Is man's body mere carbon? 1862 R. H. PATTERSON *Ess. Hist. & Art* 8 Carbon..in its amorphous state, is charcoal; when crystallised in prisms, it becomes black and opaque graphite; and when crystallised in octohedrons, it is etherealised into the limpid and transparent diamond.
b. A form of diamond, the black diamond or carbonado.
1869 *Eng. Mechanic* 20 Aug. 475/1 Diamond or carbon (the latter name is preferred) stands the severest tests for mechanical purposes without apparent wear. 1903 *Westm. Gaz.* 6 June 9/1 'Black diamonds'..technically known as 'carbons'.
c. Short for *carbon-paper* (*b*).
1895 COLLYNS *Typists' Man.* 55 Errors must not be erased while the carbons are in the machine. 1913 E. W. SARGENT *Technique of Photoplay* (ed. 2) 25 For carbon copies get the carbon second sheets. 1920 R. MACAULAY *Potterism* I. iv. 46 Jane extracted carbons from a drawer and fitted them to her paper.
d. Short for *carbon-copy*.
1937 in PARTRIDGE *Dict. Slang* 127/1. 1940 H. INNES *Trojan Horse* iii. 62, I signed the carbon and placed it in a foolscap envelope. 1964 R. PETRIE *Murder by Precedent* iii. 46 There has to be something in the file first. The carbon of the finished letter.
e. carbon 14: a long-lived radioactive isotope of carbon, of mass-number 14, the regular decay-rate of which makes possible the dating of organic materials from ancient deposits; also used as a tracer element in biochemistry. Symbol: C^{14} or ^{14}C. Cf. RADIO-CARBON.
1936 *Physical Rev.* XLIX. 778/1 McMillan has obtained evidence of a radio-active C^{14}. 1941 *Ibid.* LIX. 349 There are 5 known isotopes of carbon, stable C^{12}..C^{13}..C^{10}..C^{11} and C^{14} (half-life 10^3–10^5 years). *Ibid.* 351/2 Production of C^{14} is achieved as a by-product of cyclotron operation. 1946 *Lancet* 12 Oct. 535/2 A so-called unit of carbon 14 (C^{14}). 1950 *Amer. Speech* XXV. 25 Carbon 14..is being extensively used as a tracer. 1951 *Proc. Prehist. Soc.* XVII. 7 There can be age-determination..by the Carbon 14 method. 1958 *Listener* 6 Nov. 720/1 Carbon 14 dating has become vital to the study of archaeology. 1958 *Times* 12 Dec. 17/6 Carbon 14..breaks down only slowly—half of it in about 5,600 years. 1969 E. H. PINTO *Treen* 5 The scientific system of radio carbon dating, or carbon-14 dating, as it is also called, has come into being.
2. *Electr.* A pencil of fine charcoal (usually made of condensed lamp-black), used in one form of the electric light. Two of these are placed with their points close to each other, and a current of galvanic electricity transmitted through them renders the carbon points intensely luminous.
Also sometimes used for the delicate filament of charcoal in the incandescent form of the electric light.
c 1860 FARADAY *Forces Nat., Electric L.* 184 The light is essentially given by the carbons. 1879 G. PRESCOTT *Sp. Telephone* 403 The light..is soon extinguished by the burning or wasting away of the carbons.
3. *attrib.* **a.** In general sense, Of, like, or pertaining to charcoal or coal, or some form of carbon; **carbon-black** = LAMP-BLACK; also *attrib.*; **carbon-copy**, a copy made by using carbon-paper; also *fig.* and *attrib.*; **carbon cycle**, (*a*) *Biol.*, the cycle in which carbon dioxide is absorbed from the atmosphere by plants and replaced mainly by the respiration of plants and animals and the decay of organic matter; (*b*) a cycle of thermonuclear reactions in stellar regions, in which carbon acts as a catalyst in the conversion of hydrogen into helium, the consequent energy released being held to be the source of the energy radiated by the sun and stars; **carbon fibre**, a fibre of carbon; *spec.* a very thin, polycrystalline filament of carbon, freq. very strong, obtained by the pyrolysis of organic textile fibres and consisting of crystallites that are preferentially aligned parallel to the axis of the filament; used esp. to increase the strength-to-weight ratio of plastic or other material in which filaments are incorporated as in a matrix; also, such filaments collectively; **carbon-paper**, (*a*) *Photogr.*, paper used in carbon printing (*disused*); (*b*) thin paper coated on one side with a preparation of carbon-black or some other pigmented material, used between two papers to make a duplicate copy of what is written, typed, etc., on the upper sheet (earlier called *carbonic paper*); **carbon printing, process**, a photographic process introduced by Poitévin in 1855, producing permanent prints in black and white, the shades of which are produced by the carbon of lamp-black; **carbon steel**, a steel the properties of which are determined mainly by the percentage of carbon present.
1889 *Cent. Dict. s.v.*, Carbon-black..is almost pure carbon in a finely divided form. 1930 *Engineering* 9 May 605/3 The carbon-black industry in the United States. 1934 *Discovery* May 138/2 Indian ink contains carbon black. 1808 J. BARLOW *Columb.* v. 669 When at his word the carbon clouds shall rise. 1895 Carbon copy [see *carbon-paper*]. 1944 AUDEN *For Time Being* (1945) 58 Everything, the massacres, the whippings, the lies, the twaddle, and all their carbon copies are still present. 1959 *Observer* 15 Mar. 11/5 A group of indolent, shiftless, carbon-copy 'West Side' youths. 1961 *Daily Tel.* 3 Apr. 7/4 Victim of the week-old 'carbon copy' murder. 1912 E. J. RUSSELL *Soil Conditions* iv, The carbon and nitrogen cycles in the soil. 1940 H. A. BETHE in *Astrophysical Jrnl.* XCII. 118 The nuclear reactions involved in the carbon cycle. 1946 *Ann. Reg. 1945* 356 It is generally accepted that the Bethe carbon cycle..provides the main source of stellar energy. 1960 *Chem. Abstr.* LIV. 1966 *(heading)* The morphology of carbon fibers. 1966 *Engineer* 27 May 816/1 Work on the application of these new carbon fibres is directed toward the manufacture of carbon-fibre composites having resinous matrices. 1969 *Guardian* 10 June 4/1 The Lotus car company is examining ways in which carbon fibre can be used in car production. 1878 *Jrnl. Chem. Soc.* XXXIV. 919 *(heading)* Carbon-paper rendered sensitive without a chrome-bath. 1895 COLLYNS *Typists' Man.* 55 In correcting the carbon copies, a narrow strip of carbon paper should be placed upon the ribbon to prevent the corrections being conspicuous. 1879 *Cassell's Techn. Educ.* III. 326 The perfecting of a carbon process has been the work of considerable time. *a* 1888 *Mod. Newspaper*, The majority of the works shown are permanent carbon photographs. 1903 A. H. HIORNS *Steel & Iron* xix. 336 The mild blister steel is used for springs, and the higher carbon steel after fagoting and welding is termed 'shear' steel. 1925 *Jrnl. Iron & Steel Inst.* CXI. 305 Plain carbon steels high in carbon have a partially austenitic structure when sufficiently intensely quenched.
b. *Chem.*, as in ***carbon compounds***, etc., and specific names, as **carbon dioxide**, CO_2, systematic name of carbonic acid gas; **carbon-dioxide snow**, carbon dioxide solidified by cooling (cf. CARBONIC *a.* 1 a); **carbon disulphide**, see DISULPHIDE; **carbon monoxide**, CO, a highly poisonous gas, also known as carbonic oxide gas; etc; **carbon tetrachloride**, see TETRA- 2 a.
1869 ROSCOE *Elem. Chem.* xxvii. (1874) 289 Organic Chemistry is defined as the chemistry of the carbon compounds. 1873 *Fownes' Chem.* 161 Carbon Dioxide, or Carbonic Oxide, is always produced when charcoal burns in air or oxygen gas. *Ibid.* 163 Carbon Monoxide is a combustible gas. 1910 *Lancet* 14 May 1350/1 The beneficial effects of treatment by carbon dioxide snow in Xeroderma pigmentosum. 1934 *Discovery* Aug. 223/2 In its solid state it [*sc.* carbon dioxide] is used by hospitals for cauterisation, in the form of ' carbon dioxide snow'.
c. *Electr.*, as in ***carbon light, points, poles***, etc. **carbon-arc**, an arc between electrodes that consist wholly or mainly of carbon; also *attrib.*; **carbon microphone**, a microphone depending for its action on the varying electrical resistance of carbon granules when subjected to sound waves of varying pressure (see quot. 1962); **carbon transmitter**, = *carbon microphone*.
1908 *Jrnl. & Proc. R. Soc. N.S.W.* XLII. 201 An investigation of the phenomena associated with the relighting of the carbon arc. 1922 GLAZEBROOK *Dict. Appl. Physics* II. 145/2 The cored carbons which are used in ordinary open type or enclosed type lamps, for the so-called pure carbon arc, have the core canal filled with a mixture of carbon and potassium silicate. 1927 *Lancet* 1 Jan. 15 The therapeutical use of the carbon-arc light. 1871 tr. *Schellen's Spectr. Anal.* 74 Instead of the carbon-cylinder thick rods or wires of zink..may be employed. *Ibid.* 33 To reach the carbon holders. 1879 *Telegraphic Jrnl.* VII. 1/1 The carbon microphone..has already proved a practical instrument for sending articulate sounds. 1962 A. NISBETT *Technique Sound Studio* 244 *Carbon microphone*, microphone in which the audio signal is produced by varying the resistance of a button of granular carbon to which a polarizing voltage is applied (a diaphragm presses on the carbon button). 1875 HAMERTON *Intell. Life* VII. iii. 238 The light that plays between the wedded intelligences as the electric light burns between two carbon points. 1871 tr. *Schellen's Spectr. Anal.* 30 As soon as the current passes through the carbon poles the electric arc is formed. 1879 G. PRESCOTT *Sp. Telephone* 39 C is a carbon transmitter included with battery B in the primary circuit. 1889 *Telephone* I. 248/1 A carbon transmitter is used in connection with this receiver.

carbon, *v.* [f. the sb.] *intr.* or *pass.* Of the cylinders in the engine of a motor car: to become coated with carbon deposit. Const. *up*.
1922 *Daily Mail* 28 Nov. 6 [A motor engine] longer to carbon up and easier to decarbonise than its rivals. 1925 *Morris Owner's Man.* 70 Thanks to good carburation, the Morris engine carbons up very slowly. 1928 *Daily Express* 3 Aug. 9 Even if the engine is carboned up, you get wonderful pulling.

carbona (kɑːˈbəʊnə). *Cornish Mining.* [Origin unknown.] An irregular mass of ore, usually found in the vicinity of a lode.
1843 W. J. HENWOOD in *Trans. R. Geol. Soc. Cornwall* V. 21 The extraordinary deposit of tin ore which..has obtained the name of the *Carbona*. 1855 LEIFCHILD *Cornwall* 40 The formation of the tin ore in this mine is very singular, and is provincially termed *carbona*.

carbonaceous (kɑːbəˈneɪʃəs), *a.* [f. L. *carbōnem* charcoal, coal + -ACEOUS.]
1. Of the nature of coal, charcoal, or other common form of carbon; coaly.
1791 HAMILTON *Berthollet's Dyeing* I. 8 It destroys the carbonaceous or coaly matter. 1863 *Possibil. Creation* 53 Manchester would soon be enveloped in a great carbonaceous fog. 1872 YEATS *Techn. Hist. Comm.* 101 Bellows, chimneys, and carbonaceous fuel were certainly employed by the ancients.
2. *Chem.* Of or pertaining to the chemical element carbon; consisting of or containing carbon.
1794 SULLIVAN *View Nat.* I. 243 The acid is decomposed, the carbonaceous principle combines, and is fixed in the vegetable, while the oxigene is thrown off. 1794 G. ADAMS *Nat. & Exp. Philos.* I. xii. 497 Carbonaceous inflammable gas. 1807 ALLEN & PEPYS in *Phil. Trans.* LX. 268 To consume certain known quantities of diamond and other carbonaceous substances in oxygene gas. 1879 *Christian World* 19 Dec. 814/1 Food..is made up of two constituents, the nitrogenous or flesh-forming part, and the carbonaceous or heat-producing part.
3. *Geol.* Of the nature of coal, abounding in coal, coaly.
1833 LYELL *Princ. Geol.* III. 222 In one part of the series, carbonaceous shales occur. 1872 W. SYMONDS *Rec. Rocks* vi. 208 Carbonaceous markings of plants. 1878 GREEN *Coal* i. 27 The beds..more or less coaly or carbonaceous in character.

carboˈnade, *sb.* [a. F. *carbonade*, 'a rasher on the coales' (Cotgr.).] †**1.** *Obs.* = CARBONADO.
1631 MASSINGER *Beleeve as you l.* IV. iii, I was tolde that I had fleshe enough of mine owne, And, yf that I were hungrie, I might freelye Eate mine owne carbonades.
2. (Also in Fr. form *carbonnade.*) A beef stew (see quots.).

1877 E. S. DALLAS *Kettner's Bk. of Table* 101 The carbonade has degenerated in France into a stew, having meant originally a grill; and attempts are made to introduce the word into England as corrupted by the French cooks. **1935** MORPHY *Recipes of all Nations* 550 (*heading*) Les Carbonnades Flamandes (Flemish carbonades). This is one of the most well known of all Belgian dishes... The word 'carbonnades'..is now used for a method of slow stewing. *Ingredients*..boned neck of beef..onions..1 bottle of beer. **1959** R. POSTGATE *Good Food Guide 1959–60* 73 Occasionally a more unusual dish appears, such as carbonade of beef (braised with onions in beer). **1970** *Times* 7 Mar. (Suppl.) p. v/2 Carbonnade of beef is a rich stew, combining beef, onions and beer.

† **carbo'nade**, *v. Obs.* [f. the sb.] = CARBONADO *v.*

1629 MASSINGER *Picture* II. i, With his keen-edge spear He cut and carbonaded them. **1634** SIR T. HERBERT *Trav.* 150 Carbonaded or rosted in the fire. **1655** *Francion* I–III. 73 The Gyants, who carbonaded one another as small as minced meat. **1748** RICHARDSON *Clarissa* (1811) VI. xxv. 106 [I'll] carbonade and broil the traitress.

Hence † **carbo'nading** *vbl. sb.*

1599 NASHE *Lent. Stuffe* (1871) 87 To have the scorching and carbonading of it. **1673** RAY *Journ. Low-C.* (1738) I. 350 Their roasting differs not much from our broiling or carbonading. **1736** BAILEY *Househ. Dict.* 156, *Carbonading.*

† **carbo'nado**, *sb.*[1] *Obs.* Also 7 carbinado, charbonado. [ad. Sp. *carbonada* 'a Carbonado on the coles' (Minsheu) = It. *carbonata*, F. *carbonade* (Cotgrave); see -ADO.] A piece of fish, flesh, or fowl, scored across and grilled or broiled upon the coals. Often *transf.*

1586 MARLOWE *1st Pt. Tamburl.* IV. iv. 47, I will make thee slice the brawns of thy arms into carbonadoes and eat them. **1591** LYLY *Sapho* II. iii. 175 If I venture..to eate a rasher on the coales, a carbonado. **1607** SHAKS. *Cor.* IV. v. 199 He scotcht him, and notcht him like a carbinado. **1651** MARKHAM *Eng. Housw.* 70 Charbonadoes. **1656** HEYLIN *Surv. France* 72 A suit of Turkie grogram..cut with long slashes or carbonado's. **1656** H. MORE *Antid. Ath.* III. iii. They made goodly Carbonado's of Witches. **1687** B. RANDOLPH *Archipel.* 19 His Buttocks were like unto Carbonados.

carbonado (kɑːbɒ'neɪdəʊ), *sb.*[2] [Pg.] A dark, opaque variety of diamond, found near Bahia in Brazil, used in rock-drilling and stone-polishing.

1853 J. TENNANT *Gems & Prec. Stones* 94 A considerable quantity of a black substance was found, of specific gravity like the Diamond, but lamellar... It was termed 'Carbonado' by the discoverers from its charcoal like appearance. **1879** *Encycl. Brit.* IX. 345/1 The dressing and grooving of mill-stones is generally done by hand-picking, but sometimes black amorphous diamonds (carbonado) are used. **1951** J. R. PARTINGTON *Gen. & Inorg. Chem.* (ed. 2) xvii. 439 Black or dark-coloured..diamonds, carbonado and bort (or boart), of no value as gems, are used for rock-drills.

carbo'nado (kɑːbəʊ'neɪdəʊ), *v. arch.* [f. CARBONADO *sb.*[1]]

1. *trans.* To make a carbonado of; to score across and broil or grill.

1611 SHAKS. *Wint. T.* IV. iv. 268 How she long'd to eate Adders heads, and Toads carbonado'd. *c* **1630** JACKSON *Creed* IV. cvii. Wks. 1844 III. 105 Having..lastly his raw bulk broiled or carbonadoed quick. **1679** *Hist. Jetzer* 5 The colour of his face was as if it had been newly Carbanadoed, and laid upon a Gridiron. **1820** SCOTT *Monast.* xvi, On a level with Richard Cœur-de-Lion, when he ate up the head of a Moor carbonadoed. **1823** [see CARBONARI].

fig. **1647** WARD *Simp. Cobler* 62 Whose heart hath been long carbonado'd..in flames of affection towards you. **1672** R. WILD *Poet. Licent.* 27 Raw men you were, raw still you are, I Do scarce believe you'l carbonado'd die.

b. quasi-*intr.* (from elliptic use of gerund).

1675 J. SMITH *Chr. Relig. App.* II. 7 His Arm not to shrug, while it was carbonadoing, with that live Coal that fell into his Sleeve. **1863** THORNBURY *True as Steel* III. 2 While some venison stakes, dipped in wine and spiced, were carbonadoing at a fire.

2. *transf.* To cut, slash, hack.

1596 NASHE *Saffron Walden* 20, I am the man will deliuer him to thee to be scotcht and carbonadoed. **1605** SHAKS. *Lear* II. ii. 41 Draw, you Rogue, or Ile so carbonado your shanks. **1650** BULWER *Anthropomet.* 259 Barbarous Gallants ..slash and carbonado their Bodies. **1748** SMOLLETT *Rod. Rand.* (1812) I. 58, I would flea him, carbonado him. **1832** W. IRVING *Alhambra* II. 166 He..has been..so cut up and carbonadoed that he is a kind of walking monument of the troubles of Spain.

carbo'nadoed *ppl. a.*, **carbo'nadoing** *vbl. sb.*

1601 SHAKS. *All's Well* IV. v. 107 Your carbinado'd face. **1615** MARKHAM *Eng. Housew.* II. ii. (1668) 78 The manner of carbonadoing. **1635** QUARLES *Embl.* I. v. (1718) 21 To broil the carbonado'd hearts of men. **1655** GURNALL *Chr. in Arm.* II. 223 Satan's plundering him of his estate..carbonadoing (as I may say) his body with sores and boiles (which were as so many deep slashes in his flesh).

‖ **Carbonari** (karbo'nari), *sb. pl.* Rarely in sing. carbonaro. [It.; pl. of *carbonaro* collier, charcoal-burner, an appellation assumed by the society.] The members of a secret political association formed in the kingdom of Naples during the French occupation under Murat, with the design of introducing a republican government.

1823 BYRON *Age Bronze* xii, Have Carbonaro cooks not carbonadoed Each course enough? **1840** MARRYAT *Olla Podr.* (Rtldg.) 245 The *Carbonari* had become formidable in Italy. **1870** DISRAELI *Lothair* viii. 33 How they can be got together, I marvel: priests and philosophers, legitimists and carbonari! **1880** W. CORY *Mod. Eng. Hist.* I. 148 *note*, In 1799..when driven to the forest of the Abruzzi they [republicans] are believed to have disguised themselves as charcoal-burners. In the course of twenty years the name *Carbonari* was borne by a society, or confederate societies, ranging all over Italy.

Hence **carbo'narism**, the political principles of the Carbonari, or (*transf.*) of similar revolutionists.

1832 *Athenæum* No. 243. 399 A touch of carbonari-ism. **1857** *Sat. Rev.* III. 51/1. **1878** SEELEY *Stein* III. 487 His subjects..were almost all imbued with the principles of liberty, and indeed with some ideas of carbonarism.

carbonatation (ˌkɑːbəneɪ'teɪʃən). [f. CARBONATE *v.*[1] + -ATION.] = CARBONATION.

1887 *American* XIV. 24 The process of carbonatation, or removing the excess of lime used in defecating the juice by carbonic acid gas. **1888** *Harper's Mag.* June 47 The best method of 'carbonatation' of the saccharine juice.

carbonate ('kɑːbənət), *sb.* Also 8–9 carbonat. [a. F. *carbonate*, ad. mod.L. *carbonātum* 'a carbonated (product)', f. CARBON *sb.* or L. *carbōn-em* + -ATE 1 c. Cf. CARBONATED.]

1. *Chem.* A salt of carbonic acid, a chemical compound formed by the union of carbonic acid with a base or basic oxide. These constitute a very numerous class of bodies, some of which, e.g. Carbonate of lime, $CaCO_3$, exist in great quantities in nature.

Since *carbonic acid* (the hydrate), $CH_2O_3 = 2HO.CO$, contains two atoms of replaceable hydrogen, there exist two sets of carbonates, viz. ***normal carbonates*** in which both atoms of H are replaced by a metal, and ***hydrogen carbonates***, in which only one atom of H is so replaced. Thus ***normal sodium carbonate*** (carbonate of soda) 2NaO.CO, ***hydrogen sodium carbonate*** (bicarbonate of soda) HO.NaO.CO.

1794 PEARSON in *Phil. Trans.* LXXXIV. 394 Carbonate of lime (chalk) readily dissolved, with effervescence, in the liquid. **1794** G. ADAMS *Nat. & Exp. Philos.* I. App. 546 The alkaline carbonats are soluble in water. **1807** MARCET in *Phil. Trans.* XCVII. 308 Common carbonat of magnesia. **1876** PAGE *Adv. Text-bk. Geol.* iii. 70 The alkalis and alkaline carbonates attack many rocks with great facility. **1876** HARLEY *Mat. Med.* 245 Carbonate of lead has been known from the highest antiquity.

2. *ellipt.* 'The common term in the West for ores containing a considerable proportion of carbonate of lead. They are sometimes earthy or ochreous (soft carbonates), sometimes granular and comparatively free from iron (sand carbonates), and sometimes compact (hard carbonates)' (Raymond *Mining Gloss.*). In full ***carbonate ore***.

1890 W. J. GORDON *Foundry* 96 The hæmatite,..unlike the carbonate ores,..requires no roasting. **1892** *Daily News* 29 Oct. 6/4 The new bodies of carbonate ore.

3. = CARBON *sb.* 1 b.

1883 GRESLEY *Gloss. Coal-m.*, *Carbonates*, black imperfectly crystallised form of diamond used for rock boring; the abrasion of the diamond removes the rock in an annular form, producing cores.

carbonate ('kɑːbəneɪt), *v.*[1] [f. prec.: cf. F. *carbonater*.]

1. *trans.* To burn to carbon, char, CARBONIZE.

1831 *Fraser's Mag.* III. 744 Witches..were carbonated in the fire because they unreasonably resisted drowning in the millrace.

2. *Chem.* To form into a carbonate. **b.** To impregnate with carbonic acid gas, to aërate.

1805 W. SAUNDERS *Min. Waters* 237 Caustic alkali.. becoming itself carbonated by means of the water. **1853** W. GREGORY *Inorg. Chem.* 279 The slow action of air, moisture, and the vapour of acetic acid on thin sheets of lead, by which the metal is oxidised and carbonated.

† **carbonate**, *v.*[2] *Obs.* [var. of CARBONADE *v.*] = CARBONADO *v.* Hence **carbonated** *ppl. a.*

1629 GAULE *Holy Madn.* 255 To carbonate his Flesh. **1675** EVELYN *Terra* (1729) 22 How men carbonate and cut so many Rills, and narrow Trenches irregularly crossing one another, to drain their Meadows. **1659** GAUDEN *Tears Ch.* 580 (D.) Antiepiscopall Preachers..being loth to be Carbonated or Crucified Christians.

carbonated ('kɑːbəneɪtɪd), *a.* [f. mod.L. *carbonātus*, *-um*, or F. *carbonaté*, f. L. *carbōn-em*; see CARBON *sb.*]

† **1.** Reduced to carbon, carbonized; burnt black; covered with carbon. (Cf. CARBONATE *v.*[1] 1.)

1799 KIRWAN *Geol. Ess.* 249 Coal, and bituminous and carbonated wood. **1825** in Hone *Every-day Bk.* I. 883 Blacksmiths are super-carbonated.

† **2.** Chemically combined with carbon; CARBURETTED. *Obs.*

1797 HENRY in *Phil. Trans.* LXXXVII. 402 The heavy inflammable air..is termed, in the new nomenclature, carbonated hydrogenous gas. *Ibid.* 409 The carbonated hydrogen. **1805** BRANDE *ibid.* XCVI. 96 Mixed gases, consisting chiefly of carbonic acid and carbonated hydrogen.

3. Chemically combined with carbonic acid; made into a carbonate.

N.B. *Carbonate of lime, soda, ammonia*, etc. were originally called *carbonated lime, soda, ammonia*.

1803 SIR H. DAVY in *Phil. Trans.* XCIII. 269 The carbonated alkalis. **1805** W. SAUNDERS *Min. Waters* 43 The mild or carbonated ammonia, will decompose all the earthy salts by double affinity. *Ibid.* 50 Carbonated soda is readily procured. *Ibid.* 280 A wine pint of Pyrmont water contains —Of oxyd of iron ·56; carbonated lime 4·46; carbonated magnesia 10·03. **1808** HENRY *Epit. Chem.* (ed. 5) 135 This water..will effervesce with carbonated alkalis. **1887** *Pall Mall G.* 16 Dec. 11/1 To separate the carbonated lead from what remains of the metallic.

4. Impregnated with or containing carbonic acid gas.

1858 GEIKIE *Hist. Boulder* viii. 144 Formed by the percolation of carbonated water. **1875** URE *Dict. Arts* III. 1098 Acidulous or carbonated waters are characterised by an acid taste, and by the disengagement of gas. **1876** PAGE *Adv. Text-bk. Geol.* ii. 48 Highly carbonated atmosphere.

carbo'nation. [f. CARBONATE *v.* + -ION[1].] Formation of a carbonate; impregnation with carbonic acid.

1881 *Daily News* 6 June 3/2 Defecation of the beet juice with lime, carbonation with carbonic acid.

carbonator ('kɑːbəneɪtə(r)). [f. CARBONATE *v.*[1] + -OR.] One who or that which carbonates.

1896 *Voice* (N.Y.) 21 May 4/5 (*title*) American Bottler and Carbonator. **1921** *Dict. Occup. Terms* (1927) §459 *Carbonator*..runs a specified quantity of carbonic acid gas, in solution, into beer. **1935** *Discovery* Dec. 363/1 The juice with the milk of lime then passes into the first carbonators where it is treated with carbon dioxide gas.

† **carboned**, *ppl. a. Obs.*$^{-1}$ = CARBONADED (for which it may be a misprint).

1660–1 PEPYS *Diary* 1 Jan., Where we had a calf's head carboned, but it was raw, we could not eat it.

carbonic (kɑː'bɒnɪk), *a. Chem.* [f. CARBON *sb.*, or its L. source *carbōn-em* + -IC.]

1. a. Of or pertaining to carbon. *esp.* in certain chemical names, as **carbonic acid**, a name originally given to the gas now more systematically called **carbon(ic) dioxide** or **carbonic anhydride**, CO_2, formerly also known as *fixed air*, the gas which is formed in the ordinary combustion of carbon, disengaged from fermenting liquors, given out in the breathing of animals, and largely evolved from fissures in the earth, constituting the choke damp or foul air of mines and caves. This is still popularly called ***carbonic acid gas***, but the name ***carbonic acid*** is applied in chemistry to the hydrate or compound CH_2O_3 supposed to be formed when carbon dioxide comes in contact with water, of which the carbonates are the salts; **carbonic-acid snow** or **carbonic anhydrase** (see quot. 1949); **carbonic oxide** = *carbon monoxide*, CO; **carbonic snow**: carbon-dioxide snow.

1791 E. DARWIN *Bot. Gard.* I. 82 *note*, The various kinds of acids, as Carbonic acid (or fixed air). **1793** T. BEDDOES *Calculus* 234 It returns to the lungs surcharged with carbonic-hydrogene air. **1794** SULLIVAN *View Nat.* I. 232 This aerial, or carbonic acid. **1794** J. HUTTON *Philos Light, &c.* 161 The azotic and carbonic air. **1812** SIR H. DAVY *Chem. Philos.* 105 An inflammable gas, called carbonic oxide, which burns with a blue flame. **1841** [see SNOW *sb.*[1] 5 b]. **1863** A. RAMSAY *Phys. Geog.* i. (1878) 4 The carbonic acid in the air. **1873** J. COOKE *New Chem.* 143 This aeriform material is now called in chemistry carbonic dioxide. **1877** ROBERTS *Handbk. Med.* I. 383 The expired air may be cool, and is deficient in carbonic anhydride. **1932** MELDRUM & ROUGHTON in *Jrnl. Physiol.* LXXV. 4 P, Recently we have succeeded in separating the catalytic system from hæmoglobin... For this new enzyme system we suggest the name Carbonic Anhydrase. **1940** *Nature* 3 Aug. 164/1 (*heading*) Sulphanilamide as a specific inhibitor of carbonic anhydrase. **1949** S. & L. M. MIALL *New Dict. Chem.* (ed. 2) 109/2 Carbonic anhydrase is an enzyme which serves to accelerate the formation of carbon dioxide from bicarbonate in the blood vessels of the lung. **1964** S. DUKE-ELDER *Parsons' Dis. Eye* (ed. 14) xxi. 309 Further lowering of the tension may be obtained by the systemic administration of carbonic anhydrase inhibitors. **1905** GOULD *Dict. New Med. Terms* 197/2 A bag filled with carbonic snow at a temperature 176° F. below zero is applied daily for half an hour to the pit of the stomach.

b. Of or caused by carbonic acid gas.

1872 AITKIN *Sc. & Pract. Med.* II. 735 Carbonic narcosis may possibly, in some cases, retard the heart's action.

c. ***carbonic paper***, early name of *carbon-paper* (*b*).

1808 S. NAPIER *Let.* 14 Nov. in H. A. Bruce *Life Gen. Sir William Napier* (1864) I. iii. 66, I am enabled to write this with my own hand upon carbonic paper, invented by Wedgwood for taking copies. **1876** PREECE & SIVEWRIGHT *Telegraphy* 289 The rest of the message..is transcribed on the public copy by carbonic paper. **1881** *Instr. Census Clerks* (1885) 82 Carbonic Paper Maker. **1884** W. LYND *Pract. Telegraphist* 26 The carbonic paper must be changed sufficiently often to admit of a clear and distinct impression being made. **1895** *Army & Navy Co-op. Soc. Price List* 548 Carbonic Paper. For Tracing and Transfers, Black both sides.

2. Of coal or charcoal; of the Carbonari. (Also *sb.*)

1819 H. BUSK *Dessert* 421 Come share the heat of our carbonic fire. **1821** BYRON *To Moore* 19 Sept., The cause has been the exile of all my fellow Carbonics.

carboniferous (kɑːbɒˈnɪfərəs), *a.* [f. L. *carbōn-em* coal, CARBON *sb.* + *-fer* bearing + -OUS. Cf. mod.F. *carbonifère*.]

1. Producing coal. Applied in *Geol.* to the extensive and thick series of palæozoic strata, with which seams of coal are associated, the ***Carboniferous System*** or ***Formation***, lying next above the Devonian or Old Red Sandstone, and including the Coal Measures, Millstone Grit, and Mountain or Carboniferous Limestone; also to the rocks, fossils, etc., of this formation, and to the age of geological time, the ***Carboniferous Age, Era,*** or ***Period***, during which these strata were deposited, and the luxuriant vegetation existed that formed the coal-beds.

1799 KIRWAN *Geol. Ess.* 290 By carboniferous soils, I mean the various sorts of earth or stone among or under which coal is usually found. **1802** PLAYFAIR *Illustr. Hutton. The.* 152 The facts which Mr. Kirwan produces in treating of what he calls carboniferous soils. **1830** LYELL *Princ. Geol.* (1875) II. III. xlv. 529 The Scar Limestone, a member of the carboniferous series. **1842** H. MILLER *O.R. Sandst.* x. (ed. 2) 224 During the vastly-extended term of the carboniferous period. **1857** —— *First Impr.* i. 14 Deep in the carboniferous ocean. **1851** RICHARDSON *Geol.* i. 6 Lead is chiefly confined to the carboniferous limestone. **1881** A. RAMSAY in *Nature* 419 The Apalachian chain is chiefly of post-Carboniferous date.

2. *jocularly.* Coal-bearing, carrying coals.

1865 *Daily Tel.* 20 July, There was a set-to between some of the speakers and the coalporters.. One speaker suggested .. the expulsion of the carboniferous brawlers.

carˌbonifiˈcation. [Noun of action f. next.] Conversion into coal.

1883 *Standard* 31 Jan. 5/3 Lignite is vegetation further advanced in the process of carbonification.

carbonify (kɑːˈbɒnɪfaɪ), *v.* [f. L. *carbōn-em* coal + -FY: on L. type *carbōnificāre*.] *trans.* To convert into coal or charcoal, to CARBONIZE. Hence **carˈbonified** *ppl. a.*

1803 *Med. Jrnl.* IX. 371 The phenomenon of Scintillation produced by the concussion of carbonified wood.

carbonigenous (kɑːbɒˈnɪdʒɪnəs), *a.* [f. L. *carbōn-em* + *-genus* born, bearing + -OUS.] Producing or developing carbon.

1865 *Reader* 29 Apr. 477/3 A carbonigenous era composed of stemmy herbage and productive trees.

carbonite (ˈkɑːbənaɪt). [f. CARBON *sb.* + -ITE[1].] (See quots.)

1891 THORPE *Dict. Applied Chem.* II. 83/2 Carbonite is an explosive introduced by Hellhoff, of Berlin; stated to be composed of nitrobenzene, potassium nitrate, sulphur, and Kieselguhr. **1892** H. W. HUGHES *Coal-mining* 79 Carbonite is another explosive of late introduction. It is said to be composed of nitro-glycerine, sulphur, and nitro-benzol. **1898** A. W. & Z. W. DAW *Blasting of Rock* xix. 204 H.M. Inspectors of Mines strongly condemn the use of blasting powder in coal mining.. and they recommend that a high explosive practically free from flame, which property is claimed for carbonite, should be substituted. **1910** *Encycl. Brit.* VIII. 764/1 Carbonite contains 25% of nitroglycerin. **1922** *Ibid.* XXX. 86/2 Bombs of a type known as 'Carbonite'. **1931** PAYMAN & STATHAM *Firedamp Explosions* viii. 123 The latter regulation cuts out the old 'Carbonite' class of explosives, which.. appears to be the one class of explosive capable of causing the ignition of coal dust more rapidly than firedamp.

carbonium (kɑːˈbəʊnɪəm). *Chem.* [f. CARBO- + *-onium* as in AMMONIUM.] (*a*) Formerly, 'the univalent radical CH_3 in the capacity.. of a base former analogous to ammonium' (WEBSTER 1909); (*b*) used *attrib.* of an organic ion containing positively charged carbon. Cf. CARBANION.

1902 *Jrnl. Chem. Soc.* LXXXII. I. 600 Triphenylmethyl. .. Carbonium Salts. **1905** *Ibid.* LXXXVIII. I. 282 Distinction is drawn between an ionisable and a non-ionisable valency; the former is termed a 'carbonium valency'. *Ibid.* 282 Carboxonium salts.. are regarded as carbonium salts, corresponding with the salts of triphenylmethyl. **1933** [see CARBANION]. **1936** *Nature* 8 Aug. 224/1 Ionic reactions.. generally involve carbonium anions and cations. **1962** J. HINE *Physical Org. Chem.* (ed. 2) vii. 163 The carbonium ion is a very reactive intermediate that is rapidly transformed into the final product.

carbonizable (ˈkɑːbəˌnaɪzəb(ə)l), *a.* [f. CARBONIZE *v.* + -ABLE.] That can be carbonized.

1883 *Brit. Pat.* 5978, Carbonisable material in a plastic or semi-liquid state.

carbonization (ˌkɑːbɒnaɪˈzeɪʃən). [f. next. + -ATION.] **a.** Conversion into (mere) carbon, charcoal, or coke. **b.** Charging with carbon or carbonic acid. **c.** Combining chemically with carbon; CARBURIZATION.

1804 HATCHETT in *Phil. Trans.* XCIV. 390 Vegetable matter in an incipient state of carbonization. **1830** LYELL *Princ. Geol.* I. 351 The heat of the tuff.. was proved by the carbonization of the timber, corn, papyrus-rolls.. there discovered. **1875** H. WOOD *Therap.* (1879) 182 These changes of the blood.. its secondary excessive carbonization. **1875** URE *Dict. Arts* III. 899 (Steel) The *carbonization* or conversion is effected, as it were, in layers.

carbonize (ˈkɑːbɒnaɪz), *v.* [f. CARBON *sb.* + -IZE.]

1. *trans.* To convert into mere carbon; to reduce to charcoal or coke.

1806 HATCHETT in *Phil. Trans.* XCVI. 131 *note*, Caoutchouc and elastic bitumen were only superficially carbonized by the sulphuric acid. **1816** J. LAURENCE in *Monthly Mag.* XLII. 298 Diamond.. we can carbonize that precious gem, and prove it to be charcoal. **1870** F. POPE *Electr. Tel.* iv. (1872) 44 A flash of.. electricity frequently carbonizes the paper between the plates.

2. To carburet or carburize. *arch.*

1808 [see CARBONIZED]. **1875** URE *Dict. Arts* III. 899 (Steel) The combination of the carbon with the iron.. extends from one lamina to another until the whole is carbonized.

3. To cover with charcoal, lamp black, etc. See CARBONIZED.

4. To destroy vegetable impurities in (wool, etc.) by treatment with an acid and heat, which reduces the vegetable matter to carbon dust.

1892 *Sci. Amer.* 6 Feb. 84/3 Washing.. follows, by which the chloride is removed and the residue of carbonized matter washed away. **1920** *Glasgow Herald* 6 July 7 Australian wool... There will be a considerable surplus of low and medium cross-breds and carbonising wool. **1964** *Times Rev. Industry* Mar. 45/1 Carbonising has become the almost universally recognised method of burr removal.

Hence **ˈcarbonizing** *vbl. sb.* and *ppl. a.*

1867 *Morning Star* 7 Aug. 5 The men employed in the carbonising departments in the gas factories. **1898** *Westm. Gaz.* 17 Feb. 8/3 The company.. pays 3s. 6d. per ton of coal for carbonising wages. **1921** [see CARBONIZER]. **1955** *Times* 5 July 5/1 The carbonizing industries had been allocated 3,000,000 tons more than dispatches in the summer of last year. This should produce nearly 1,500,000 tons more coke.

ˈcarbonized, *ppl. a.* [f. prec. + -ED.] **1.** Converted into mere carbon or charcoal, charred.

1858 GEIKIE *Hist. Boulder* iv. 53 A.. mass of carbonized matter. **1863** *Q. Rev.* 380 In the Lake of Constance.. have been found.. carbonised wheat, grains of barley, etc.

2. = CARBURETTED, CARBURIZED. *arch.*

1808 HENRY in *Phil. Trans.* XCVIII. 285 Carbonized hydrogen, from Stagnant water. **1875** URE *Dict. Arts* III. 899 Steel so produced being more carbonized on the surface than at the centre of the bar.

3. Covered or prepared with carbon so as to yield a copy of anything written over it.

1883 *Daily News* 19 Sept. 7/1 To keep an account of the sales and receipts.. and, by means of carbonised papers, to make duplicate copies.

carbonizer (ˈkɑːbənaɪzə(r)). [f. CARBONIZE *v.* + -ER[1].] One who or that which carbonizes.

1908 *Daily Chron.* 24 Aug. 9/6 (Advt.), Foreman (Working) wanted for gas works; must be a good carboniser. **1912** G. MARTIN *Industr. & Manuf. Chem., Org.* 392 Continuous carbonisers, such as Woodall-Duckham and Glover-West, have also been tried. **1921** *Dict. Occup. Terms* (1927) §361 *Piece carboniser*; carbonises woollen fabrics in the piece. *Ibid.* §693 *Carboniser, carbonising man*.. general terms for men charging retorts or furnaces either by hand or machine.

ˈcarbonless, *a.* **1.** Void of carbon.

1850 *Fraser's Mag.* XLI. 295 The carbonless.. hydrogen.

2. Of paper: that enables writing or typing done on it to appear simultaneously on any paper underneath it, without the insertion of carbon paper.

1956 *TAPPI* June (Suppl.) 142A/1 The National Cash Register Co... announced development of the carbonless forms system approximately two years ago. *Ibid.* (*caption*) Carbonless duplicating paper in sheets makes it possible for any printer to manufacture business forms without using carbon inserts. **1961** *Stationery Trade Ref. Bk.* 72/2 (Advt.), Manufacturers of cash registers.., carbonless paper, carbon paper, bank proof machines. **1979** *Now!* 21 Sept. 77/1 It has concentrated on high-margin special products, particularly carbonless copying paper. **1982** *What's New in Computing* Nov. 90/2 It can.. trim sprocket margins from continuous forms (whether plain or carbonless, single or multipart).

carbonnade: see CARBONADE *sb.* 2.

carboˈnometer. [f. CARBON *sb.* + -(O)METER.] An instrument for testing the presence of an excess of carbonic acid.

1864 in WEBSTER.

†**carboˈnose,** *a. Obs. rare*[−1]. [f. L. *carbōn-em* + -OSE.] Of the character of coal.

1811 PINKERTON *Petral.* I. 249 Weight, from carbonose to granitose.

carbonous (ˈkɑːbənəs), *a.* [f. CARBON *sb.* + -OUS: perh. after F. *carboneux*.] Of the nature of or containing carbon.

1794 G. ADAMS *Nat. & Exp. Philos.* I. xi. 483 A carbonous substance, which is disengaged from the blood in the lungs. **1865** MANSFIELD *Salts* 501 We.. see the epibasic attachment for metal salts, which is so strongly marked in H_3N, considerably weakened in its carbonous congeners.

carbonyl (ˈkɑːbənɪl). *Chem.* [f. CARBON *sb.* + -YL(E) = Gr. ὕλη substance, base.] A name for the divalent compound radical CO (known in the free state as *carbon monoxide* or *carbonic oxide gas*) considered as a constituent of urea, alloxan, creatin, etc. Also *attrib.*, as in ***carbonyl series, compound, chloride***, etc., and in *comb.*, as ***sulpho-carbonyl***, CS, in which the combination is with sulphur instead of oxygen.

1869 ROSCOE *Elem. Chem.* xxxv. 381 Carbonyl chloride is formed when dry carbonyl and dry chlorine gases are brought together in sunlight. **1880** *Libr. Univ. Knowl.* VIII. 493 Carbonic oxide or carbonyle, CO.

Carborundum (kɑːbəˈrʌndəm). *orig. U.S.* Also **carborundum.** [Trade-name, f. CARBO(N *sb.* + CO)RUNDUM.] A compound of carbon and silicon, SiC, a very hard crystalline substance, used either as a powder or in blocks for polishing and scouring, for grinding tools and as a refractory lining in furnaces. Also *attrib.*

1892 *Official Gaz. U.S. Patents* LIX. 1914/1 [Trade-mark registered by] The Carborundum Company, Monongahela City, Pa. *Ibid.*, Trade-marks registered June 21, 1892 [include] Carborundum. **1893** *Amer. Jrnl. Sci.* XLVI. 472 While examining the hardness of 'carborundum', a carbide of silicon, made by Mr. Acheson of Pittsburg, it was found that it readily scratched red, blue, white, pink, and yellow corundum in the form of fine gems. **1895** *Bloxam's Chem.* (ed. 8) 127 Silicon carbide (carborundum).. is prepared by heating silicon or silica with carbon in the electric furnace. **1917** *Mod. Boot & Shoe Maker* III. 250 The rough scouring on the coarse sandpaper roll or the felt roller covered with carborundum. **1924** *Chambers's Jrnl.* 39/1 The cutting edge is bestowed by grinding on a carborundum wheel. **1963** J. OSBORNE *Dental Mechanics* (ed. 5) xv. 343 The sprues must next be removed with either a diamond disc or a carborundum-type 'cut-off' disc.

carboxy- (kɑːˈbɒksɪ), comb. form of CARBOXYL; as in **carboxy-hæmoglobin**, a combination of carbon monoxide and hæmoglobin formed in the blood when carbon monoxide is inhaled; **carboxy-(poly)peptidase**, an enzyme (e.g. in the pancreas) that hydrolyses peptides and polypeptides by removing the amino acids containing free carboxyl groups.

1891 *Jrnl. Chem. Soc.* LX. 1522 Conversion of carboxy-hæmoglobin into methæmoglobin, and detection of carbonic oxide in blood. **1908** *Practitioner* Dec. 842 Carbon-monoxide has a marked affinity for the colouring matter of the blood, and forms carboxy-haemoglobin, the chief characteristic of which is stability. **1962** *Lancet* 13 Jan. 68/1 Each animal was gassed until the blood-level of carboxyhaemoglobin was 70%. **1930** *Chem. Abstr.* 1129 Proteinase and carboxy-polypeptidase of the pancreas. **1935** *Science* LXXXI. 467/1 Carboxypolypeptidase splits the amide linkages of certain amino-acid compounds, such as chloracetyl tyrosine,.. with the liberation in each case of an amino-acid which in the intact compound has a free carboxyl group. **1940** *Chem. Abstr.* 2397 Ext[ract]s of pancreas contg. carboxypeptidase were subjected to adsorption. **1955** *Sci. Amer.* July 78/2 The enzyme carboxypeptidase.. removes amino acids from the ends of protein chains. **1956** *Nature* 17 Mar. 527/2 Treatment with carboxypeptidase.. revealed leucine as the C-terminal amino-acid.

carboxyl (kɑːˈbɒksɪl). *Chem.* [f. CARBON *sb.* + OX(YGEN) + -YL = substance.] A name given to the monad group −CO·OH, contained in all the fatty acids; thus *Formic acid* is H−CO·OH, *Acetic acid* CH_3−CO·OH, *Butyric acid* C_3H_7−CO·OH.

1869 ROSCOE *Elem. Chem.* 346 Carboxyl we thus regard as contained in all the fatty acids: it is formed by the oxidation of methyl. **1878** KINGZETT *Anim. Chem.* 33 Hydrogen is replaced by a monad carboxyl group.

carboxylase (kɑːˈbɒksɪleɪs, -eɪz). *Chem.* [G. (Neuberg and Karczag 1911, in *Biochem. Zeitschr.* XXXVI. 73), f. CARBOXYL + -ASE.] An enzyme that breaks down ketonic acids into the corresponding aldehydes and carbon dioxide.

1911 *Jrnl. Chem. Soc.* C. II. 1020 These decompositions are not brought about when yeast which has previously been heated is employed... It is therefore due to an enzyme to which the name *carboxylase* is given. **1953** *Biochem. Jrnl.* LIV. 378/1 Carboxylase is a thiol enzyme. *Ibid.* 389/2 Highly purified carboxylase is sensitive towards thiol reagents such as heavy metals, trivalent arsenicals, [etc.].

carboy (ˈkɑːbɔɪ). Also 8 **karboy.** [Evidently a corruption of Pers. *qarābah, qarrābah*, 'a large flagon' (for wine, rose-water, etc.): see the quots. Kaempfer (loc. cit.) 'gives an exact etching of a carboy' (Yule).]

A large globular bottle, of green or blue glass, covered with basket-work for protection, used chiefly for holding acids and other corrosive liquids.

[**1712** KAEMPFER *Amœn. Exot.* 379 (Y.) [Referring to the wine trade of Shiraz] Vasa vitrea, alia sunt majora, ampullacea et circumducto scirpo tunicata, quae vocant Karabà.. Venit Karaba una apud vitriarios duobus mamudi, raro carius.] **1753** HANWAY *Trav.* I. 154, I delivered a present.. of oranges and lemons.. and 6 Karboys of Ispahan wine. **1800** SYMES *Emb. to Ava* 488 (Y.) Six corabahs of rose-water. **1813** MILBOURNE *Orient. Comm.* II. 330 (Y.) Carboy of Rose-water. **1838** POE *A.G. Pym* Wks. 1864 IV. 106 A carboy containing nearly three gallons of excellent Cape Madeira wine. **1883** *Times* 7 Apr., Two carboys were.. found to contain nitro-glycerine.

Hence **ˈcarboyed** *ppl. a.*, put into a carboy.

1855 *Fraser's Mag.* LI. 536 Shrimps and anemones live in water carboyed many miles off shore.

carbuncle (ˈkɑːbʌŋk(ə)l). Forms: α. 3–4 **charbucle, -bokel,** 3–5 **-bocle,** (3 **-bugle**), 4 **-bokyll,**

-bukel(le, 5 -bokill, -bokell, 6 cherbukkill; β. 5 carbokyl, -bokull, (? 6 -bocle); γ. 5 charboncle, -bonkkel, -bouncle, 5–6 -buncle; δ. (4 carbunculum), 5 karboncle, carbunacle, 5–6 carboncle, 6 -bonkel, 6–7 -bunckle, 7 -bunkle, 4– carbuncle. [ME. *charbucle, -bocle*, a. central OF. *charbucle, -boucle*, var. of *charbuncle*, in ONF. *carbuncle, carboucle* (= Pr. *carbuncle*, Sp. *carbunclo*, (†*carbonco*, †*carboncol*), It. *carbonchio*):—L. *carbuncul-us* small coal, carbuncle stone, red tumour, dim. of *carbo* coal. At a later period the forms in *char-* were displaced by *carboucle, -buncle*, which came nearer to the Lat.; these alone occur in the medical sense.

The mod.F. *escarboucle* is a by-form with a prefix *es-* (L. *ex-*), which goes back also to the 11th c. Cotgr. has also *carboucle*; *charboucle* remains in rural use for 'smut of corn' (Littré). Prob. both the change of *-buncle* to *-boucle*, and the prefixed *es-* were owing to popular etymology.]

1. (Formerly often more fully **carbuncle-stone**): A name variously applied to precious stones of a red or fiery colour; the carbuncles of the ancients (of which Pliny describes twelve varieties) were probably sapphires, spinels or rubies, and garnets; in the Middle Ages and later, besides being a name for the ruby, the term was esp. applied to a mythical gem said to emit a light in the dark; in mod. lapidary work the term is applied to the garnet when cut *en cabochon*, or of a boss form, usually hollowed out to allow the colour of the stone to be seen.

α. *c* **1230** *Hali Meid.* 43 Alswa as a charbucle is betere þen a iacinet iþe euene of hare cunde. *a* **1300** *Floriz & Bl.* 234 On þe tur anouen-on Is a charbugle ston. *c* **1400** *Destr. Troy* 3170 Chaundelers full chefe, & charbokill stones. *c* **1489** CAXTON *Sonnes of Aymon* iii. 74 A charbokell..whiche stone full precyous was shinyng as a torche that brenneth.

β. *c* **14..** *Sir Beues* (MS. C.) In the hylte was a carbokull [*v.r.* charbokyll] stone. *c* **1475** *Pict. Voc.* in Wr.-Wülcker 769 *Hic carboculus*, a carbokylstone.

γ. *c* **1400** MAUNDEV. xxii. 239 A rubye and a charboncle of half a fote long. *c* **1430** LYDG. *Chorle & Byrde* xxxviii, The white Charbonkkel that rolleth in wave.

δ. *c* **1305** *Land Cokaygne* 90 in *E.E.P.* (1862) 158 þer is.. Carbuncle and astiune, Smaragde, lugre and prassiune. **1481** CAXTON *Myrr.* II. vii. 79 Carboncle, the whiche by nyght..shyneth as a cole brennyng. **1567** MAPLET *Gr. Forest* 5 The Carbuncle..giueth light, but especially in the night season. **1614** RALEIGH *Hist. World* I. 96 The Hebrewes ..suppose that the Arke was lightened by a Carbuncle. *a* **1691** BOYLE *Wks.* I. 790 (R.) There are very learned men, who (plausibly enough) deny that there are any carbuncles or shining stones at all. **1787** GLOVER *Athenaid* IV. (R.) Carbuncles, gems of native light, Emitting splendour. **1816** CLEAVELAND *Min.* 296 The carbuncle of the ancients was probably a garnet. **1866** KINGSLEY *Herew.* viii. 138 They were all lighted by a single carbuncle.

†**b.** *fig.* applied to a thing or person of resplendent quality. *Obs.*

c **1430** LYDG. *Bochas* III. ix. (1554) 81 b, Charboncle of armes! mirrour of policie! **1513** DOUGLAS *Æneis* Prol. 7 Thow peirles perle..Chosin cherbukle, cheif flour, and cedir tree. *c* **1630** DRUMM. OF HAWTH. *Poems* Wks. (1711) 1 The wand'ring carbuncles which shine from high.

c. Carbuncle as a substance; also *fig.* resplendent substance.

1413 LYDG. *Pylgr.* v. iii. (1483) 93 This other world whiche thou seest sowen with sterres of Charbouncle. **1667** MILTON *P.L.* IX. 500 His Head Crested aloft, and Carbuncle his Eyes. **1847** EMERSON *Repr. Men* iii. *Swedenborg* Wks. (Bohn) I. 313 If you will have pure carbon, carbuncle, or diamond, to make the brain transparent.

2. *Her.* A carbuncle borne in a shield, and hence, a charge or bearing representing a carbuncle with its rays; = ESCARBUNCLE.

c **1386** CHAUCER *Sir Thopas* 160 His sheeld..And therin was a bores hed, A charboucle [*v.r.* charbokele, charbokil, charbokel] beside. ? *a* **1400** *Morte Arth.* 2523 A charbocle in þe cheefe, chawngawnde of hewes. **1557** *K. Arthur* (Copland) v. ix, Griffons of golde in sable charbuncle yᵉ chefe of syluer. **1572** BOSSEWELL *Armorie* II. 55 b, The field is parted per Pale Nebule, Carboncle and Diamonde. **1727** in CHAMBERS *Cycl.* **1730–6** in BAILEY; and in mod.Dicts.

3. *Med.* An inflammatory, circumscribed, malignant tumour, caused by inflammation of the skin and cellular membrane. It differs from a boil in having no central core; an anthrax.

[**1398** TREVISA *Barth. De P.R.* VII. lix. (1495) 275 Antrax ..is callyd also Carbunculus.] **1530** PALSGR. 157 *Vne charboncle*, a carboncle, a sore pestylenciall. **1562** BULLEYN *Bk. Simples, &c.* 16 b, [It] healeth Antrax, called the Carbuncle. **1605** SHAKS. *Lear* II. iv. 227 A Byle, A plague sore, or imbossed Carbuncle In my corrupted blood. *a* **1691** BOYLE *Wks.* III. 676 (R.) Which turned to a pestilential carbuncle, that could scarce be cured in a fortnight after. **1859** *Times* 20 Apr. 8/2 The original complaint of the King of Naples was carbuncle (anthrax).

b. A red spot or pimple on the nose or face caused by habits of intemperance.

1682 N. O. *Boileau's Lutrin* I. 87 Her Nose, emboss'd with Carbuncles Divine, Before her steps did like a Flam-boy shine. **1709** ADDISON *Tatler* No. 131 ¶5 The Council for the Brewers had a Face..inflamed..with Carbuncles. **1830** JAMES *Darnley* (1846) 25 Sundry carbuncles illuminated his countenance, and gave an air of jollity to a face..not otherwise very amiable.

4. *transf.*

1805 *Naval Chron.* XIV. 368 The description of the carbuncles and the cotyledons [of a cuttle-fish].

†**5.** (See quots.) *Obs.*

1577 B. GOOGE *Heresbach's Husb.* (1586) 17 b, Carbuncle, that is ground over heated and parched with the sunne; which will burne the rootes of whatsoever commeth in it. [**1601** HOLLAND *Pliny* I. 503 The hot earth, called.. Carbunculus, which vseth to burn the corne sown therupon.]

6. *attrib.* and *Comb.*, as ***carbuncle-face, -nose, -tumour***; **carbuncle-stone**: see 1 above.

1658 ROWLAND *Moufet's Theat. Ins.* 928 Their sting.. causeth a carbuncle tumor. **1690** B. E. *Dict. Cant. Crew, Carbuncle-Face*, very Red and full of large Pimples. **1710** *Tatler* No. 260 ¶7 A Carbuncle Nose likewise bore an excessive Rate. **1864** *Daily Tel.* 17 Mar., A carbuncle ring on his finger.

carbuncled (ˈkɑːbʌŋk(ə)ld), *ppl. a.* [f. prec.]

1. Set or adorned with carbuncles.

1606 SHAKS. *Ant. & Cl.* IV. viii. 28 Carbunkled Like holy Phoebus Carre.

2. Affected with a carbuncle or carbuncles; spotted, pimpled; red or shining like a carbuncle.

1664 BROME *Good fellow* in *Songs & Poems* 155 A carbuncled face Saves a tedious race, For the Indies about us we carry. **1709** STEELE & SWIFT *Tatler* No. 66 ¶4 Our Friend is to drink till he is carbuncled and Tun-bellied. **1845** MIALL *Nonconf.* V. 181 Look at that carbuncled nose, and those trembling hands.

3. *transf.*

1805 *Naval Chron.* XIV. 368 The carbuncled appendages [in a cuttle-fish] might be tentacles.

†**4.** (Cf. CARBUNCLE 5.) *Obs.*

1577 GOOGE *Heresbach's Husb.* (1586) 24 Carbunckled [land], that is burnt with the sonne, rotten, and mossie.

carbuncly (ˈkɑːbʌŋklı), *a.* [f. CARBUNCLE + -Y[1].] Of or resembling a carbuncle; bearing carbuncles.

1873 LELAND *Egypt. Sketch-Bk.* 74 Their combs and wattles became of a deep carbuncly red. **1922** JOYCE *Ulysses* 348 His carbuncly nose with the pimples on it.

carbuncular (kɑːˈbʌŋkjʊlə(r)), *a.* [f. L. *carbuncul-us* CARBUNCLE + -AR[1].] Of, pertaining to, resembling, or characterized by carbuncles.

1737 OZELL *Rabelais* II. 78 Who ow'd the carbuncular Richness of their Phyz to..Drinking. **1754** WALPOLE *Lett. H. Mann* No. 252 (1834) III. 63 Such a carbuncular state of blood as carried off my brother. **1840** DICKENS *Old C. Shop* viii, Sticking his fork into a carbuncular potatoe. **1882** *Pop. Sci. Monthly* 422 Carbuncular germs in the soil.

carˈbunculate, *a.* [ad. mod.L. *carbunculāt-us*, f. *carbuncul-us*: see -ATE[2].] Having carbuncles, 'like to carbuncle, tuberculate' (*Syd. Soc. Lex.*). So **carˈbunculated** *a.*

1860 in MAYNE *Exp. Lex.* **1842** *Blackw. Mag.* LII. 97 Their carbunculated physiognomies.

†**carˈbunculate**, *v. Obs.* [f. as prec.: see -ATE[3].] 'To burne like a coale' (Cockeram 1623).

†**carˌbuncuˈlation.** *Obs.* [ad. L. *carbunculātiōn-em* a disease of plants, f. *carbunculā-re* to have *carbunculus* or blasting.] (See quots.)

a **1673** CARYL in Spurgeon *Treas. Dav.* Ps. cxlvii. 16 Unseasonable frosts..scorch the tender fruits, which..is usually expressed by carbunculation or blasting. **1704** J. HARRIS *Lex. Techn.*, *Carbunculation*, is the blasting of the new-sprouted Buds of Trees and Plants, either by excessive Heat..or else by excessive Cold. **1755** in JOHNSON, etc.

†**carˈbunculine**, *a. Obs. rare*[−1]. [f. L. *carbuncul-us* + -INE: cf. *carbunculosus* (*ager*) land containing red toph-stone.]

c **1420** *Pallad. on Husb.* XII. 272 Black erthe is apte, and londe carbunculyne, And ragstoon all to rapte is for hem digne.

carˈbunculous, *a.* [ad. L. *carbunculōs-us*, f. *carbuncul-us* CARBUNCLE: see -OUS.] Of, abounding in, or of the nature of carbuncles.

1612 WOODALL *Surg. Mate* Wks. (1653) 405 Pestilential or Carbunculous spots. **1882** MOZLEY *Remin.* I. ix. 69 An angry eye, and a carbunculous complexion.

carburant (ˈkɑːbjʊərənt). [f. CARBUR(ET *v.* + -ANT[1].] A liquid or vaporized hydrocarbon used to carburet air or gas for the production of light or mechanical energy. Also **ˈcarburetant**.

1893 *Funk's Standard Dict.*, Carburetant. **1909** *Cent. Dict.* Suppl., Carburant. **1928** *Daily Tel.* 4 Sept. 9/3 To find a carburant less inflammable than petrol.

carburation (kɑːbjʊəˈreıʃən). [f. CARBUR(ET + -ATION.] The process of charging air with hydrocarbon in a finely divided liquid form, the resulting gas being burnt for the production of energy.

1896 B. DONKIN *Gas, Oil, & Air Engines* (ed. 2) II. xxi. 303 The carburation of the air takes place in the middle division. **1902** HARMSWORTH *Motors & Motor-Driving* 166 There may be a slight flare up, but this will assist the carburation. **1920** *Westm. Gaz.* 1 Apr. 4/2 Few improvements have been made to the various carburation systems. **1959** *Motor* 1 Apr. 319/2 Carburation is by means of a pair of..carburetters.

†**carbure.** *Obs. Chem.* [a. F. *carbure*, f. CARBON *sb.*: see -URE.] = CARBURET.

1790 WEDGWOOD in *Phil. Trans.* LXXX. 319 Lavoisier.. mentions a carbure of zinc also, and says that both these carbures are called plumbago, or black-lead. **1799** G. SMITH *Laborat.* I. Pref. 6 Black lead is well known to be a compound of iron; called carbure of iron.

carburet (ˈkɑːbjʊərɛt), *sb. Chem.* [f. CARB-ON + -URET, q.v.] A compound formed by the chemical combination of carbon with another element; = CARBIDE.

1795 PEARSON in *Phil. Trans.* LXXXV. 335 A compound of iron and carbon..which in the new system is denominated a carburet of iron. **1820** FARADAY *Res.* xvi. 68 Pure steel..and good iron mixed with charcoal powder were heated intensely for a long time..they formed carburets. **1836** MACGILLIVRAY tr. *Humboldt's Trav.* ii. 33 Carburet of iron, which gives the green colour to the parenchyma of plants.

ˈcarburet, *v.* [f. prec.] *trans.* To combine (any element) chemically with carbon; to impregnate or charge with carbon. Hence **ˈcarbuˌretting, -eting**, *vbl. sb.* and *ppl. a.*

1869 *Eng. Mech.* 31 Dec. 379/1 A small gas-making machine, founded upon the principle of the carburetting of the atmospheric air. *Ibid.* It feeds the..vessel in which is placed the carburetting element.

carburetted, -eted (ˈkɑːbjʊəˌrɛtıd), *ppl. a. Chem.* [f. prec. + -ED.] Combined with carbon, as in ***carburetted air***, air which has been impregnated with fine particles of hydrocarbon, and which provides the power by which petrol engines are driven; ***carburetted hydrogen***, the 'fire-damp' of miners, and chief constituent of coal-gas. Also impregnated with, or holding carbon in solution; ***carburetted water-gas***, water-gas which has been enriched by mixing with a hydrocarbon gas.

1802 HENRY in *Phil. Trans.* XCIII. 37 Carburetted hydrogen gas. **1812** SIR H. DAVY *Chem. Philos.* 306 Carburetted hydrogene..is the gas evolved in stagnant waters. **1836** TODD *Cycl. Anat.* I. 60/2 Animal fat is chiefly a..highly carburetted hydrate of oxygen. **1861** SMILES *Engineers* II. 227 He suggested..the employment of carburetted hydrogen gas, then coming into extensive use for lighting purposes. **1879** *Encycl. Brit.* X. 101/2 The efforts to introduce carburetted water-gas have been numerous and persistent. **1881** P. SMYTH in *Nature* 430 The existence there of carburetted gas of some kind. **1896** B. DONKIN *Gas, Oil, & Air Engines* (ed. 2) II. xxi. 298 Inflammable petroleum essence..is perhaps best distinguished by the term usually applied to it abroad—'carburetted air'. **1899** *Motor-Car World* Oct. 9/1 A 'carburettor', the function of which is the production of a saturated mixture of spirit, vapour, and air, known as 'carburetted air'. **1958** *Times Rev. Industry* May 34/2 Publicizing the carburetted water gas process in Europe.

ˈcarburettor, -etter. [f. prec. *v.* + -OR, -ER.]

a. That which carburets; *spec.* an apparatus for charging hydrogen, coal-gas, or atmospheric air, with carbon, by passing it through or over a liquid hydrocarbon, so as to add illuminating power.

1866 *Morning Star* 21 Sept. 5/3 A dull, sluggish gas-flame is brightened to an extent almost marvellous when a carburettor is placed in the course of the pipe supplying it. **1882** *Echo* 20 Jan. 1/5 The hydrogen is passed through carburetters, and is stored in holders.

b. (Also formerly **carburator.**) In petrol engines, the apparatus for impregnating air with fine particles of fuel and thus preparing the explosive mixture for the cylinders.

1896 *Jrnl. Soc. Arts* 27 Nov. 22/1 Where a vaporiser is employed, or a carburettor. **1898** tr. *L. Lockert's Petroleum Motor-cars* 145 The carburator, in which the petroleum essence..is vaporized. **1900** *Motor-Car World* Aug. 254 Supplemental exhaust tube for heating carburettor tank. **1902** HARMSWORTH *Motors & Motor-Driving* 166 Too rich a mixture may be caused by the presence of too much petrol in the carburator. **1912** *Motor Man.* 12 To obtain an explosive mixture of paraffin and air a special form of carburetter is required. **1959** [see CARBURATION].

carburiˈzation. [noun of action f. next; see -ATION.] The process of combining an element or substance with carbon, as in the conversion of wrought iron into steel.

1864 *Reader* 9 Apr. 450 The degree of carburization is regulated by the addition of 'Spiegeleisen'—a material containing a known quantity of carbon. **1881** *Metal World* 133/1 The history of our knowledge concerning the carburisation of iron, from the work of Clonet at the end of last century to that of Margueritte in 1856.

carburize (ˈkɑːbjʊəraız). [f. F. *carbure* carburet + -IZE.] *trans.* To combine with carbon or a carbon compound; used esp. of the process of imparting carbon to wrought iron in making cement steel; also = CARBURET *v.*

carbyl (ˈkɑːbıl). *Chem.* Also **carbyle.** [f. CARB- + -YL.] **1.** [a. G. *carbyl*, in *carbylsulphat* (G. Magnus 1839, in *Ann. d. Physik und Chem.* XLVII. 512).] A name for the basic hydrocarbon radical derived from ethylene; little used except in **carbyl sulphate**, ethionic

anhydride, $(-CH_2\cdot SO_3-)_2$, a white, deliquescent, crystalline substance.

1844 Fownes *Chem.* 395 Carbon, hydrogen, and the elements of sulphuric acid... Sulphate of carbyle. **1890** *Bloxam's Chem.* (ed. 7) 479 The compound formed by SO_3 with ethylene..is termed carbyl sulphate or ethionic anhydride. **1950** N. V. Sidgwick *Chem. Elements* II. 903 With alcohol it [*sc.* sulphur trioxide] forms 'carbyl sulphate', which is..the anhydride of ethionic acid.

2. [a. F. *carbyl*, in *carbylamine* (A. É. J. Gautier 1867, in *Compt. Rend.* LXV. 902).] A divalent radical of carbon; little used except in **carbylamine** (kɑːbɪˈlæmiːn, kɑːˈbaɪləmiːn), the isocyanide radical, $-NC$; also, any of the compounds (also called carbamines, isocyanides, isonitriles) consisting of this radical attached to a hydrocarbon radical, which are foul-smelling poisonous liquids; *spec.*, phenyl isocyanide, $C_6H_5\cdot NC$; **carbylamine test**, a test for detecting primary amines by heating the substance with chloroform in a basic solution, the presence of an amine being indicated by the characteristic smell of an isocyanide.

1879 Watts *Dict. Chem.* (ed. 2) VI. 522 In the one class..the alcohol-radicle is in direct union with the carbon; in the other, discovered independently by Hofmann and by Gautier in 1867, and designated as isocyanides, carbylamines, or carbamines, it is combined directly with the nitrogen. **1886** E. F. Smith tr. *V. von Richter's Org. Chem.* 246 The carbylamine test of Hofmann for detection of primary amines. **1887** A. M. Brown *Contrib. Anim. Alkaloids* 36 Heated with potash and chloroform, cadaverine does not give carbylamine. **1946** *Nature* 31 Aug. 295/2 The presence of amines by carbylamine test could not be shown. **1963** W. E. Flood *Orig. Chem. Names* 59/1 A comparison of the structure of a carbylamine with that of a simple amine..shows that the carbylamine may be regarded as an amine in which the two hydrogen atoms of the amino-group are replaced by carbyl (i.e. a carbon 'radical').

carcage, Sc. form of carcass.

1477 *Charter Jas. III* in *Hist. Edinburgh* I. i. (1753) 8 The Nolt-Market of Carcages and Mutone. **1513** Douglas *Æneis* xi. v. 35 Full mony carcage of thir oxin greyt.

‖**carcajou** (ˈkarkaʒu, ˈkɑːkə(d)ʒuː). [Fr. of N. America, app. of Indian origin.]

1. A name given in N. America to the Glutton or Wolverene (*Gulo luscus*).

1703 tr. *La Hontan's Voy. N. Amer.* I. 62 The Holes or Dens of the *Carcaioux*. *Ibid.* 232 Carcaious, an Animal not unlike a Badger. **1744** A. Dobbs *Hudson's Bay* 40 The beavers have three enemies, man, otters, and the Carcajon [*sic*]. **1774** Goldsm. *Nat. Hist.* (1862) I. iv. iii. 425 The glutton..in the north of Europe and Siberia, as in the northern parts of America, where it has the name of the carcajou. **1796** Morse *Amer. Geog.* I. 196 The Wolverene, called in Canada the Carcajou, and by hunters the Beaver eater. **1865** Ld. Milton & Cheadle *N.W. Pass.* vii. 103 The fur-hunter's greatest enemy is the..wolverine or carcajou.

¶**2.** According to Littré, Webster, and the Dicts. generally, 'The American badger (*Meles Labradorica*) found in the sandy plains or prairies of N. America'. (Apparently some error.) Also erroneously applied by Charlevoix to the Canadian Lynx.

1839 *Penny Cycl.* XIV. 231/1 The mistake of Charlevoix in applying to it [the Canadian Lynx] the appellation of Carcajou..has produced some confusion of synonymes amongst subsequent writers. **1866** W. R. King *Sportsman & Nat. in Canada* i. 16 The name 'Carcajou' is erroneous as applied to this animal [the Canadian Lynx].

carcake (ˈkɑːkeɪk). *Sc.* Also in Jamieson **care-**, **ker-**. [First part as in Care Sunday, Ger. *Karfreitag*, etc.] A kind of small cake baked with eggs, and eaten on Fastern's Een (Shrove Tuesday) in some parts of Scotland. ***blood kercake***: a cake made of blood and oatmeal, formerly used in the south of Scotland. (Jamieson).

1816 Scott *Antiq.* xxvi, The dame was still busy broiling car-cakes on the girdle. **1818** —— *Hrt. Midl.* xxix, They arena that bad at girdles for carcakes neither. **1818** Hogg *Brownie of Bodsb.* I. 277 (Jam.) Ye'll crush the poor auld body as braid as a blood-kercake.

†**carcan.** *Obs.* Forms: 6 *Sc.* **carkanne**, (carcant), 6–7 **carquan**, 7 **carkan**, **carkeyne**, 6–8 **carcan**. [a. F. *carcan* (in OF. also *quercant*, *cherchant*, *charchant*, Pr. *carcan*, late L. *carcannum*, It. *carcame*), f. Teut.: cf. OHG. *quercka* (fem.), ON. *kverk*, in comb. *kverka*-throat.]

1. An iron collar used for punishment.

1534 Ld. Berners *Gold. Bk. M. Aurel.* iv. D iij b, Carcans for blasphemers, chaynes for sclaues. **1596** Danett tr. *Comines* 236 A fetter to put on their feete, very hard to be opened, like to a carquan. **1777** Brand *Pop. Antiq.* (1849) III. 109 An iron collar or carcan.

2. An ornamental collar or necklace; = next.

1539 *Ld. Treas. Acc.* in Pitcairn *Crim. Trials* I. 299 New-ȝeris Giftis, in chenȝeis, tabullatis, ringis, stanis, carkannis. **1601** Holland *Pliny* xxxiii. xii, Carquans and such ornaments for their shooes of silver. **1603** —— *Plutarch's Mor.* 215 The gorgeous trappings and caparisons, the brooches, collars and carkans of riches. **1694** Strype *Cranmer* App. iii. 7 One carkeyne of gold antique warke.

carcanet (ˈkɑːkənɛt). *arch.* Forms: 6 **karknett**, **garganet**, 7 **carckanet(t**, **-kenet**, **-quenet**, **-conet**, **-kaneth**, 7–8 **carknet**, 7–9 **carkanet**, 6– **carcanet**. [f. prec. + -et¹, dim. suffix.

(No Fr. *carcanet* appears to be recorded, but it is difficult to believe that the word was entirely of Eng. formation.)]

1. An ornamental collar or necklace, usually of gold or set with jewels. *arch.*

(App. *obs.* from *c* 1670 to 19th c.)

c **1530** in Gutch *Coll. Cur.* II. 313 A Karknett for my Lorde of Richemount. **1542** *P'cess Mary's Jewels* in Madden *Privy Purse Exp.* 180 A carckanet. *Ibid.* 198 Item a karkenet. **1572** *Gifts to Queen* in Nichols *Progr. Q. Eliz.* I. 323 One riche carkanet or collor of golde, haveing in it two emeraldes. **1583** Stanyhurst *Æneis* i. 25 Thee pearle and gould crownes..with garganet heauye. **1601** Holland *Pliny* I. 357 To weare costly pearles and rich stones in carkanets about our necke. **1616** W. Browne *Brit. Past.* ii. iv, He might but see the Carknet where it lay. **1649** Jer. Taylor *Gt. Exemp.* ii. vii. 36 A gold chaine, or a carkenet of pearle. **1670** G. H. *Hist. Cardinals* ii. iii. 204 A Carcanet of Gold. **1815** Moore *Lalla R.* (1850) 56 Around the white necks of the nymphs..Hung carcanets of orient gems.

[*erroneously* **1863** Sala *Capt. Danger.* I. i. 5 The Don wears jewelled rings and carcanets on all his fingers.]

†**b.** A similar ornament for the head. *Obs.*

1611 Cotgr., *Fermaillet*, a Carkanet, or border of gold, etc., such as Gentlewomen weare about their heads. **1630** Marston *Ant. & Mel.* ii. i. ii, Curled haires, hung full of sparkling carcanets. **1822** Scott *Nigel* v, His high-crowned grey hat..encircled by a carcanet of large balas rubies.

2. *transf.* and *fig.*

1593 Nashe *Christ's T.* (1613) 148 For thy Carcanets of pearle, shalt thou have Carcanets of Spiders. **1648** Herrick *Hesper.* (1869) I. 43 Making a carkanet Of maiden-flowers. **1830** Tennyson *Adeline* v, A carcanet of rays. **1876** Macfarren *Harmony* vi. (ed. 2) 191 This a carcanet of smiles, the other, a rosary of tears.

Hence ˈ**carcaˌneted** *a.*, furnished with a carcanet.

a **1652** Brome *City Wit* iv. i, Her lip painted, her neck carkanetted.

carcass, carcase (ˈkɑːkəs), *sb.* Forms: α. 4 **carcays**, **karkeis**, 4–6 **carcas**, 5 **carkoys**, 5–6 **carkes**, 5–7 **carkeis**, **-keys**, **-kas**. β. 6 **carkace**, **carckesse**, **karkaise**, 6–7 **karcasse**, **carcasse**, **-kasse**, **-kesse**, **-keise**, 7 **-caise**, **-kase**, **karcase**, 7–8 **carkass**, 8 **carkess**, 6– **carcase**, 7– **carcass**. [Of this we have two types: α. ME. *carkoys*, *-cays*, *-keis* (which survived to 16th c. and even to 1611 as *carkeis*, *-eys*), a. Anglo F. *carcois*, *carcas* (in Central OF. *charcos*, *charcois*, *charchois*, *charquois*, still dial. in W. of France) answering to med.L. *carcosium* (see Du Cange and quot. 1450 in sense 1); β. 16th c. *carcasse*, later *carcase*, *carcass*, a. 16th c. Fr. *carcasse*, ad. It. *carcassa* (Pg. *carcassa*, Sp. *carcasa*) 'carcass'. The 16–17th c. forms *carkaise*, *-keise*, *-kesse*, are app. a mixture of α and β. In mod. spelling *carcass* and *carcase* are almost equally common: the Dictionaries from Bailey and Johnson downward give *carcass* alone or by preference.

(The ulterior etymology presents many difficulties: see Diez, Littré, Scheler, Skeat. It is to be noted however that OF. *carcois*, med.L. *carcosium*, must app. be separated from OF. *tarquais* quiver (repr. med.Gr. ταρκάσιον, evidently ad. Pers. (Arab., Turk. *tarkash* quiver, arrow-case), although some confusion of the two words may be suspected in mod.F. *carquois* (since 15th c.), It. *carcasso* and *turcasso*, Pg. *carcaz* quiver. M. Paul Meyer thinks it must also be separated from the 17th c. F. *carquois* in sense 'mast-head', repr. L. *carchēsium*. But the actual derivation of *carcosium*, *carcassa*, and their mutual relation remains quite uncertain. Diez's suggestion of L. *caro* flesh, and It. *casso* chest, breast, or *cassa* case, trunk, is untenable for *carcosium*, and not very likely for *carcassa*.]

1. a. The dead body of man or beast; but no longer (since *c* 1750) used, in ordinary language, of the human corpse, exc. in contempt (see 3). With butchers, it means the whole trunk of a slaughtered animal, after removal of the head, limbs, and offal.

α. [**1299** *Lib. Custum.* I. 192 (Godef.) Le carcois de boef. **1321** *Ibid.* 304 Le carcas de porke. **1314** Sir R. Clifford in *Hist. Lett, &c.* (Rolls 1873) 228 Carcois de beef sale, xx. carcois de moton.]

1340 Hampole *Pr. Consc.* 874 Wormes..sal..gnaw on þat stynkand carcays. **1388** Wyclif *Ex.* xxi. 35 The karkeis [**1382** careyn] of the deed oxe. *c* **1400** *Ywaine & Gaw.* 470 A Karcas of Saynt Martyne. *c* **1440** *Promp. Parv.* 62 Carkeys, *corpus, cadaver*. *c* **1450** *Voc.* in Wr.-Wülcker 570 *Carcosium*, a carkoys. **1530** Palsgr. 203/1 Carkes of a foule, *granche*. *a* **1535** More *Wks.* 190 (R.) Setting hys carcas in a gay shrine, & then kissing his bare scalpe. **1555** Eden *Decades W. Ind.* (Arb.) 56 Lefte theyr carkeses in the wildernesse. **1575** *Brieff Disc. Troubl. Franckford* (1846) 195 No skermishe, where some..left not their karkaises in the felde. **1611** Bible *Judg.* xiv. 8 A swarme of Bees, and honie in the carkeis of the Lion. —— *2 Kings* ix. 37 The carkeise of Iezebel. **1630** Lord *Banians* 11 That he might strowe..the earth with dead carkeyses.

β. **1528** Roy *Satire* (1845) A dedde stynkynge carkace. **1583** Stanyhurst *Æneis* i. (Arb.) 19 His carcasse on rockish pinnacle hanged. **1590** Shaks. *Mids. N.* iii. ii. 64 I'de rather giue his carkasse to my hounds. **1650** Milton *Lett. State* Wks. 1738 II. 160 That the breathless Carcass may be deliver'd to his Friends. **1663** *Flagellum or O. Cromwell* (1672) 120 On the 17th December his Carcase was landed at Bristol. **1727** Swift *Gulliver* i. viii. 90 The carcasses of an hundred oxen. **1750** Johnson *Rambl.* No. 33 ⁋4 Famine who scattered the ground everywhere with carcasses. **1835** W. Irving *Tour Prairies* 124 To bring home the carcass of the doe. *a* **1849** H. Coleridge *Poems* (1850) II. 162 She wept O'er the new-ransom'd carcase of her..Hector. **1875** Jevons *Money* (1878) 6 A carcase of meat.

†**b.** Said of part of a dead body. *Obs. rare.*

1663 Gerbier *Counsel* B v a, The carcass of his head on a Pole.

c. *Cookery.* The bones of a cooked bird, esp. as used for making stock, etc.

1883 *Cassell's Dict. Cookery* p. xxvii, In all large establishments..there is much left of cooked meat, bones, carcases of fowls and game, &c., and which materially help to fill up the stock-pot. **1956** C. Spry *Cookery Bk.* 115 Ordinary household stock..may contain cooked meat bones, chicken carcasses, vegetables, [etc.]. **1963** Hume & Downes *Penguin Cordon Bleu Cookery* 35 Use good chicken stock..made from the liquor from a poached chicken and strengthened with the carcass bones after carving the bird.

†**2.** The living body considered in its material nature. *Obs.* exc. as in 3.

1406 Occleve *Misrule* 350 My carkeis repleet with hevynesse. **1571** Digges *Pantom.* Pref. A iij, This man notwithstanding he were imprisoned in a mortall carkasse..yet his diuine minde, etc. *a* **1618** Raleigh *Mahomet* 9 His Trances proceeded through the weaknesse of his earthly Carcase. *a* **1683** Oldham *Poems* (L.), Was ne'er so fair a creature For earthly carcass had a heavenly feature. **16..** R. L'Estrange (J.), He that finds himself in any distress, either of carcass or of fortune. **1701** Collier tr. *M. Aurel.* 57 The Declension of your Health, or the Accidents in your Carcass, need not affect you. **1717** J. Fox *Wanderer* No. 12 (1718) 77 The injur'd Animal only sought to secure his little Carcase from farther danger.

3. In later times, in application to the human body, dead or alive, it has gradually come to be a term of contempt, ridicule, or indignity.

[**1528** Roy *Sat.* (1845) Fye on his carkes bothe quycke and dead. **1563–87** Foxe *A. & M.* (1684) III. 115 Laden with a heavier lump of this vile carcase.] **1586** Warner *Alb. Eng.* ii. vii. 27 Hercules did canuase so his carkas. **1692** South *Serm.* IV. ii. (R.) He thinks that Providence fills his purse, and his barnes, only to pamper his own carcass. **1775** Adair *Amer. Ind.* 265 That they might shed blood, like wolves, without hazarding their own carcases. **1827** Pollok *Course T.* vii, The miser drew His carcass forth, and gnashed his teeth, and howled. **1870** Bryant *Homer* I. ii. 47 Cloak and tunic and whatever else Covers thy carcass.

4. *fig.* Anything from which the 'life', 'soul', or essence is gone; the lifeless shell or husk, the 'corpse', 'skeleton'.

1612–5 Bp. Hall *Contempl.* v. *Quails & Manna* (1628) 909 The carkasse of the sacrament cannot giue life; but the soule of it. *a* **1617** Hieron *Wks.* II. 484 Hee is but..almost a Christian. Hee is but the out-side and carkasse and sheath. **1641** J. Jackson *True Evang. T.* ii. 148 No better than a counterfeit or carcasse of true patience. *a* **1763** Shenstone *Ess.* 19 The mere carcase of nobility. **1883** Bright in *Edin. Daily Rev.* 15 June 3/1 The corrupt carcase of an old commercial body.

attrib. **1612** T. Taylor *Comm. Titus* ii. 8 The dead and carkase faith not of a few.

5. *transf.* The decaying skeleton of a vessel or edifice; a ruin.

1596 Shaks. *Merch. V.* iii. i. 6 The Goodwins..very dangerous flat, and fatall, where the carcasses of many a tall ship, lye buried. **1637** Heywood *Royal Ship* 3 In the very Apex and top thereof [Mᵗ Ararat], there is still to be discerned a blacke Shadow, resembling a Darke Cloud..by the Natives..held, to be the still remaining carkasse of the Arke of Noah. **1662** Fuller *Worthies* (1840) II. 505 The carcass of a castle. **1879** J. Hawthorne *Laugh. Mill* 43 The carcase of a dismantled and deserted house.

6. The naked framework or 'shell' of a building before it is plastered, etc., the 'skeleton' of a ship; see quots. The framework of a cabinet or other piece of furniture. Also *attrib.*

1663 Gerbier *Counsel* 67 Oaken Carcasse. **1677** Moxon *Mech. Exerc.* (1703) 159 Carcass is (as it were) the Skeleton of an House, before it is Lath'd and Plastered. **1704** Worlidge *Dict. Rust. et Urb.* s.v. *Wind-Mill*, The Body or Carcase, or outside of the Mill. **1805** *Edinb. Cabinet Makers' Bk. of Prices* (1821) 10 A Library Book Case. Six feet six inches long, seven feet nine inches high, in six carcases. **1823** P. Nicholson *Pract. Build.* 221 *Carcase of a Building*, the naked walls, and the rough timber-work..before the building is plastered or the floors laid. **1865** *Daily Tel.* 18 Oct. 7/3 They get the land on a ground-rent, and 'run up' carcases with money borrowed. **1867** Smyth *Sailor's Word-bk.*, *Carcass of a ship*, the ribs, with keel, stem, and stern-post, after the planks are stripped off. **1940** *Burlington Mag.* Sept. 93/2 The carcase-work and the doors are of soft pine. **1959** G. Savage *Antique Coll. Handbk.* 113 Veneers are thin sheets of wood..which are used to cover a 'carcase' of commoner and cheaper wood.

7. *Mil.* A spherical iron shell, filled with an inflammable composition, and having three holes through which the flame blazes; fired from a mortar or gun to set fire to buildings, wooden defences, etc. Formerly also of other shape and material; see quot. 1751.

(In this sense regularly spelt *carcass*.)

1684 *Lond. Gaz.* No. 1980/1 To attack that place with Bombs and Carcasses. **1731** J. Gray *Gunnery* 67 Bombs, granadoes, carcasses, and other shot. **1751** Chambers *Cycl.*, *Carcasse*, or *Carcuss*, a kind of bomb, usually oblong, or oval, rarely circular; consisting of a shell, or case, sometimes of iron, with holes; but more commonly of a coarse strong canvas, pitched over, and girt with iron hoops; filled with combustible matters. **1790** Beatson *Nav. & Mil. Mem.* I. 322 The carcasses, bombs, and red-hot balls..fired into the town, had little or no effect. **1810** Wellington *Let.* in Gurw. *Disp.* VI. 577 No opportunity of trying the 24 pound carcasses which you have been so kind as to offer him. **1859** F. Griffiths *Artil. Man.* (1862) 86 Carcasses..the flame from which is..nearly unextinguishable.

8. *Comb.*, as *carcass-carrier*; *-less*, *-like* adj.; **carcass-butcher**, a butcher who sells meat by

the carcass; also *fig.* (cf. BUTCHER 1 b); **carcass-flooring, -roofing** (*Arch.*), the framework of timber which supports the boarding of the floor or roof (see 6); **carcass meat**, raw meat as distinct from corned or tinned meat; **carcass-shell** = sense 7.

1773 *Gentl. Mag.* XLIII. 599 The trades of the fell-monger and *carcase-butcher are intolerable. **1835** GEN. P. THOMPSON *Exerc.* (1842) III. 446 An exercise of despotic power such as is not usual among the carcase-butchers of the continent. **1837** WHITTOCK *Bk. Trades* (1842) 81 When the bullock is killed, skinned, and dressed, the carcass butcher sells it to the retail butcher. **1609** DAVIES in Farr's *S.P.* (1848) 182 'Cast out your dead!' the *carcase-carrier cries. **1736** H. WALPOLE *Corr.* (1837) I. 7 Headless carcases and *carcaseless heads. **1548** UDALL, etc. *Erasm. Par. Mark* ii. 20 b, The *karkaslyke sicke man. **1948** E. SUMMERSKILL in *Hansard Commons* 12 July 821 The dock strike caused us to issue canned corned meat in lieu of..*carcase meat. **1952** *Meat Trades' Jrnl.* 20 Mar. 647/1 In February, 1948, an agreement was reached under which Argentina undertook to send us 400,000 tons of carcase meat and offal. **1823** P. NICHOLSON *Pract. Build.* 582 *Carcase roofing, that which supports the covering by a grated frame of timber-work.

'carcass, *v.* [f. prec. sb., sense 6.] **1.** *trans.* To put up the carcass of (a building). Hence **'carcassing** *vbl. sb.*

1881 *Mechanic* §163. 56 Battens, deals and planks for carcassing and rough purposes. **1886** *Standard* 18 May 3/5 Buildings which were to be carcassed by the 24th of January.

2. To make a carcass of.

1906 *Daily Chron.* 7 June 5/4 These animals realise only one-third as much as those fit for carcassing.

carcassed ('kɑːkəst), *ppl. a.* [f. CARCASS *sb.*]

†**1.** Turned into a carcass; dead, corrupt. *Obs.*

a **1603** T. CARTWRIGHT *Confut. Rhem. N.T.* (1618) Pref. 3 As vnto Vitellius, the dead citizen was alwayes of good sauour, so vnto you, the dead and carcased soules are of pleasant smell.

2. Having a carcass. (In parasynthetic comb.)

1724 *Lond. Gaz.* No. 6318/3 A grey Mare..strong carcassed.

carcat, var. of *carknet*, CARCANET.

15.. *Songs Costume* (1849) 92 Thair collars, carcats, and hals beidis!

carcedony: see CARCHEDONY.

†**carceir**, *v. Sc. Obs.* [a. OF. *carcere-r*, ad. L. *carcerāre*, f. *carcer* prison.] *trans.* To imprison.

1630–56 SIR R. GORDON *Hist. Earld. of Sutherl.* (1813) 406 This Felton had bein tuyse carceired by the Duke.

carcel ('kɑːsəl). [f. proper name of inventor, a Frenchman, early in 19th c.] **1.** *carcel-lamp*, a lamp in which the oil is pumped up to the wick by clockwork. Called also the *French* or *mechanical lamp*.

1845 *Mechanic's Mag.* XLIII. 402 One of the most deserving of notice is the improved carcel lamp. *c* **1865** LETHEBY in *Circ. Sc.* I. 105/1 Colza oil is generally consumed in the Carcel or French lamp. **1881** MISS BRADDON *Asph.* v. 60 In the bright white light of the carcel lamps.

2. A French unit of illumination, equal to the light emitted by a standard carcel lamp burning 42 grammes of colza-oil an hour and with a flame 40 millimetres in height. (*Disused.*)

a **1884** KNIGHT *Dict. Mech.* Suppl., *Carcel-bec*, the French unit of illumination. Given the preference over candle-power..at the Electrical Congress, in Paris, 1881. **1884** F. KROHN tr. *Glaser de Cew's Magn. & Dyn.-Electr. Mach.* 119 The expenditure of work per second per Carcel-burner (7·4 candle power)... An illuminating power of 1·40 Carcels (10·36 candles). **1902** *Encycl. Brit.* XXX. 260/2 The values are expressed in carcels (9·5 candles) per square centimetre of the mean horizontal focal plane of the luminous source.

†**'carcelage.** *Obs.*—0 [ad. med.L. *carcelagium* 'quod..carceris custodi præstatur ab incarcerato pro victu et potu qui ei subministrantur'(Du Cange s.v. *Carcerarium*). Cf. Sp. *cárcel* prison, *carcelage* prison fees, f. L. *carcer*.] 'Prison fees'(J.).

1678–96 PHILLIPS, *Carcellage*, the Fees of a Prison. **1721** BAILEY, *Carcellage*, Prison-Fees. **1755** JOHNSON, *Carcelage*. (So in mod. Dicts.)

'carceral, *a.* [ad. L. *carcerālis*, f. *carcer* prison.] Of or belonging to a prison.

1563–87 FOXE *A. & M.* (1596) I. 605/2 Released from his carceral indurance. **1656** in BLOUNT. **1678–96** in PHILLIPS. **1909** *Westm. Gaz.* 5 Jan. 2/1 Any punishment, carceral or otherwise. **1960** V. NABOKOV *Invit. to Beheading* xix. 191 The [prison] door opened, whining, rattling and groaning in keeping with all the rules of carceral counterpoint.

carcerate ('kɑːsəreɪt), *v.* [f. L. *carcerāt-* ppl. stem of *carcerāre* to imprison: see -ATE[3].] *trans.* To imprison, incarcerate, confine.

1839 F. BARHAM *Adamus Exul.* 19 Living souls.. carcerated in matter.

carce'ration. [n. of action f. prec.: see -ATION.] Imprisonment, incarceration.

1870 TROLLOPE *Vicar of Bullh.* 91 Talking of..the injustice of carceration without evidence of guilt.

'carcerist. *nonce-wd.* [f. L. *carcer* + -IST.] One who advocates or has to do with prisons.

1821 SYD. SMITH *Wks.* (1859) I. 338/1 How comes our loyal carcerist to forget all these sorts of tides?

'carcerule ('kɑːsər(j)uːl). *Bot.* [ad. mod.L. *carcerulus*, dim. of *carcer* prison, taken as = cell.] (See quot.)

1870 BENTLEY *Bot.* 309 The Carcerule is a superior, many-celled fruit, each cell being dry, indehiscent, and one or few-seeded. **1875** BENNETT & DYER tr. *Sachs' Bot.* II. v. 537.

†**carchedony, carcedony.** *Obs.* [ad. L. *carchēdōnius* (*carbunculus*) a brilliant precious stone from Carthage (Pliny), f. Gr. Καρχηδών Carthage. Some MSS. read καρχηδών instead of χαλκηδών CHALCEDONY in *Rev.* xxi. 19: the two words were evidently confused.]

1678 PHILLIPS, *Carcedony*, see *Calcedonie*. **1721–1800** BAILEY, *Carchedony*, a kind of Carbuncle, a precious Stone.

carchef, obs. form of KERCHIEF.

carcinogen (kɑːˈsɪnədʒən). *Path.* [f. CARCINO(MA + -GEN 1.] A substance or agent that produces cancer.

1853 J. PAGET *Lect. Surg. Path.* xv. 590 Is there one material for cancer, one carcinogen, which..may form different yet closely allied compounds? **1936** *Nature* 10 Oct. 651/2 This result affords some support for the suggestion that the 'substrates' upon which carcinogens act are protein in nature. **1937** *Ann. Reg. 1936* 55 Carcinogens can excite œstrus and œstrin can have carcinogenic effects. **1955** *Sci. News* XXXVI. 14 Continued treatment with a true carcinogen..speeds up tumour formation.

carcinogenesis (ˌkɑːsɪnəʊˈdʒɛnɪsɪs). *Path.* [f. CARCINO(MA + -GENESIS.] The production of cancer in living tissues. Also, (the study of) the changes that occur in tissues or cells during the origin of cancer.

1926 in *Gould's Med. Dict.* (ed. 8) 279/2. **1930** *Lancet* 21 June 1354/2 (*heading*) Experimental carcinogenesis. **1952** R. J. LUDFORD in G. H. Bourne *Cytology* (ed. 2) ix. 407 Such cases render it improbable that cellular differentiation can be an essential factor in carcinogenesis.

carcinogenic (ˌkɑːsɪnəʊˈdʒɛnɪk), *a.* [f. CARCINO(MA + -GENIC.] Cancer-producing.

1926 *Jrnl. Cancer Res.* X. 229 Separation of the crude coal tar into its various substances has disproved the presence of a specific carcinogenic agent. **1928** *Observer* 12 Feb. 22 The carcinogenic substance. **1954** *Sci. News* XXXI. 81 In respect of their cancer-producing properties these compounds resemble the older carcinogenic hydrocarbons. **1957** *Times* (Agric. Suppl.) 2 Dec. p. vi/4 Fear of the carcinogenic effects of oestrogenic hormones.

Hence **ˌcarcinoge'nicity**, carcinogenic ability.

1930 *Jrnl. Path. & Bacteriol.* XXXIII. 134 We had practically detoxicated the tar as far as its carcinogenicity is concerned. **1955** *Times* 13 July 4/2 Cigarette tobacco extracts from the butts of naturally smoked cigarettes have also proved inactive in tests for carcinogenicity. **1962** *Lancet* 13 Jan. 102/2 Benzidine, because of its carcinogenicity, must not be used as a routine reagent.

carcinoid ('kɑːsɪnɔɪd), *a.* and *sb. Path.* [f. CARCIN(OMA + -OID. In mod. use ad. G. *karzinoid* sb. and adj. (S. Oberndorfer 1907, in *Frankf. Zeitschr. f. Path.* I. 431).]

A. *adj.* †**1.** (See quot.) *Obs.*

1889 *Cent. Dict.*, *Carcinoid*, a...cancroid; carcinomorphic.

2. Of, pertaining to, or of the nature of a carcinoid (see B); *carcinoid syndrome*, a syndrome sometimes associated with the presence of carcinoids, marked by excessive production of serotonin and with symptoms that include severe flushing.

1925 *Bull. Johns Hopkins Hosp.* XXXVII. 134/2 The protoplasm of the carcinoid cells gives a striking chrome reaction. **1931** *Arch. Surg.* XXII. 568 Carcinoid tumors of the small intestine. **1955** *Circulation* July 1/2 Before the recent reports of the carcinoid-cardiac syndrome we had studied a patient who fell into this category. **1956** *Amer. Jrnl. Med.* XXI. 868/1 It appears somewhat unexpected to find lesions only of the right side of the heart occurring with the carcinoid syndrome. **1974** PASSMORE & ROBSON *Compan. Med. Stud.* III. xviii. 61/2 Rarely, a carcinoid adenoma produces the clinical picture known as the carcinoid syndrome, most commonly associated with carcinoid tumours in the abdomen. **1983** *Oxf. Textbk. Med.* I. XII. 56 Many carcinoid tumours are slow growing and followed a prolonged course of up to 20 or more years from the development of the first carcinoid symptoms.

B. *sb.* = ARGENTAFFINOMA.

1925 *Bull. Johns Hopkins Hosp.* XXXVII. 133/2 Burkhardt studied a group of carcinoids of the small intestine. **1948** R. A. WILLIS *Path. Tumours* xxii. 414 Many 'carcinoids', of the small intestine especially, are dangerously invasive and metastasizing growths. **1984** TIGHE & DAVIES *Pathology* (ed. 4) xvii. 173 Tumours of the endocrine portion of the pancreas are much less common... A true carcinoid, producing serotonin, may occur.

carcinology (kɑːsɪˈnɒlədʒɪ). *Zool.* [f. Gr. καρκίνος crab + -λογία: see -LOGY.] That part of zoology which treats of crabs and other crustaceans.

Hence **ˌcarcino'logical** *a.*, **carci'nologist**.

1852 DANA *Crust.* II. 1592 The Carcinological collections ..in the United States. **1864** WEBSTER, *Carcinology*. **1876** BENEDEN *Anim. Parasites* 7. **1886** *Athenæum* 3 July 20/1 The Challenger..could never afford to operate for the conchologist, or carcinologist, or ichthyologist..separately.

‖**carcinoma** (kɑːsɪˈnəʊmə). Pl. **carci'nomata**. [L., a. Gr. καρκίνωμα (-ματ-), the disease cancer, f. καρκίνος crab; cf. CANCER.]

1. *Med.* The disease CANCER. Now usually restricted to a malignant tumour of epithelial origin (the general term being CANCER).

'This word has been applied by authors in other ways. Indolent non-malignant tumours, [and] those forms only of cancer in which the structure resembles brain matter, have been thus called..By some..restricted to the early stages only of cancer' (*Syd. Soc. Lex.*).

1721 BAILEY, *Carcinoma*, the Cancer before it comes to an Ulcer. **1751** CHAMBERS *Cycl.*, *Carcinoma*, in medicine, a tumour more usually called a Cancer. **1805** *Med. Jrnl.* XIV. 83 Possessing a similar life with carcinoma, and multiplying in the same manner. **1878** T. BRYANT *Pract. Surg.* I. 99 Secondary carcinomata can only be produced by the direct propagation of the epithelial cells.

†**2.** *Med.* A disease of the cornea. *Obs.*

1731 BAILEY, *Carcinoma*..a Disease in the horny Coat of the Eye. **1753** CHAMBERS *Cycl. Supp.*, *Carcinoma* is..used to denote a disorder of the tunica cornea of the eye, wherein the little veins of the part appear turgid and livid.

3. *Bot.* 'A disease in trees when the bark separates, an acrid sap exuding and ulcerating the surrounding parts' (*Treas. Bot.*).

†**carciˌnoma'tose**, *a.* *Obs.* [f. as CARCINOMATOUS *a.* + -OSE.] = CARCINOMATOUS *a.*

1740 ZOLLMAN in *Phil. Trans.* XLI. 304 The Flesh was hard, and, as it were, carcinomatose.

carcinomatosis (ˌkɑːsɪnəʊməˈtəʊsɪs). *Path.* [mod.L., f. L. *carcinōmat-* (see CARCINOMATOUS *a.*) + -OSIS.] Widespread dissemination of carcinoma throughout the body; applied also to a more limited spread when it is substantial in amount but diffuse, without the usual separate nodules.

1905 GOULD *Med. Dict.* Suppl. 153/1. **1964** S. DUKE-ELDER *Parsons' Dis. Eye* (ed. 14) xxv. 372 The patient is generally in the stage of general carcinomatosis.

carcinomatous (kɑːsɪˈnəʊmətəs, -ˈɒmətəs), *a. Med.* [f. L. *Carcinōmat-* (see CARCINOMA) + -OUS.] Characterized by, or of the nature of, carcinoma.

1700 *Phil. Trans.* XXII. 478 The growth of carcinomatous Tumours. **1753** *Scots Mag.* XV. 51 With carcenomatous eye. **1847–9** TODD *Cycl. Anat.* IV. 430/2 Carcinomatous degeneration. **1878** A. HAMILTON *Nerv. Dis.* 191 The carcinomatous growth.

‖**carcinosis** (kɑːsɪˈnəʊsɪs). *Med.* [mod.L. f. Gr. καρκίνος crab, cancer; see -OSIS.] 'The production and development of cancer; also, a synonym of the disease cancer' (*Syd. Soc. Lex.*).

1866 A. FLINT *Princ. Med.* (1880) 282 In so-called general carcinosis, many small cancerous nodules may appear in the various organs and tissues of the body. **1876** tr. *Wagner's Gen. Pathol.* 131 Tuberculosis, carcinosis, etc., not arising from an exterior cause, are not ranked among the infectious diseases.

carck, var. of CARK *v.*

carckesse, obs. form of CARCASS.

‖**carcoon** (kɑːˈkuːn). *Anglo Ind.* Also **-koon**. [Mahrattī *kārkūn* clerk, a. Pers. *kār-kun* operator, manager, f. *kār* action, work, business.] A clerk.

1803 WELLINGTON *Let.* in Gurw. *Disp.* II. 161 A carkoon whom he sent to me this morning. **1816** ELPHINSTONE in *Q. Rev.* (1884) 374 The carcoon who brought it missed the detachment. **1858** BEVERIDGE *Hist. India* III. VIII. i. 267 'He laboured', says Duff, 'as assiduously as any carcoon under his government.'

card (kɑːd), *sb.*[1] [a. F. *carde* teasel-head, wool-card (15th c. in Littré); app. ad. Sp. or It. *carda* thistle, teasel, card, a deriv. fem. form from com. Romanic (It., Sp., Pg.,) *cardo* masc., thistle:—med.L. *cardus*:—L. *carduus* thistle. Adopted in WG. as **karda*, OHG. *charta* (wk. fem.), MHG. *charte*, MLG. *karde*, MDu. *caerde*, Du. *kaarde*, Ger. *karde* (from LG.). In Eng., the related verb (CARD[2]) occurs in the 14th c.

The Romanic sense, 'teasel', does not seem to occur in English, unless in the comb. *card-gatherer* = *card-thistle-gatherer*.]

1. † **a.** An implement for raising a nap on cloth, consisting of teasel-heads set in a frame (*obs.*). **b.** An iron instrument with teeth, or (later) a wire brush (see 2 a, b), used for the same purpose.

[**1401** See 3. Some of the early quots. in 2 may belong here.] **1511–12** *Act 3 Hen. VIII*, vi. § 1 The Walker and Fuller..shall not rowe nor werke any Clothe or Webbe with any Cardes. **1550** *Act 3–4 Edw. VI*, ii, No Person shall.. occupy any yron cards or pickards, in rowing of any set cloth. **1611** COTGR., *Applaneur de draps*, the Clothworker; who with his thistle cards doth smooth and stroake down clothes. **1819** REES *Cycl.* s.v. *Cloth*, The instruments used in this operation [dressing cloth] are the wire cards, and teazels.

2. a. An instrument with iron teeth, used in pairs to part, comb out, and set in order the fibres of wool, hemp, etc., one of the cards being held in the hand, and the other fastened to a 'stock' or support. **b.** In later use a sort of wire brush for the same purpose, consisting of a strip of leather, vulcanized rubber, or similar material, into which short steel wires are inserted. These strips are fixed on a flat surface or on the cylinder of a carding-machine, and the wool is passed between two sets of them working with each other.

Also with defining prefix as *hand-card*, *stock-card*, *tow-card*, *wool-card*, etc.

1401 [see 3]. **1418** *Bury Wills* (1850) 3 Assigno Sibill Chekyneye seruienti mee..j par de wollecombes, j. kembyngstok; j. rot j. par de cardes. *c* **1440** *Promp. Parv.* 62 Carde, wommanys instrument, *cardus*. **1483** *Act 1 Rich. III*, xii. §2 No Merchant Stranger..shall bring into this Realm ..Cards for Wooll. **1548** R. Crowley in Strype *Eccl. Mem.* II. i. 142 Honest matrons brought to the needy rock and cards. **1563-87** Foxe *A. & M.* (1684) III. 747 It is no Womans matter, at Cards and Tow. **1614** Markham *Cheap Hvsb.* (1623) 125 Take a Wool-Carde and..combe off all the scurfe and filth from the Swines backe. **1757** Dyer *Fleece* III. (R.) Behold the fleece beneath the spiky comb Drop its long locks, or from the mingling card, Spread in soft flakes. **1791** E. Darwin *Bot. Gard.* II. 58 With wiry teeth revolving cards release The tangled knots. **1851** *Art Jrnl. Illust. Catal.* p. iv**/1 From the lap machine, the cotton passes to the carding engines, or cards.

3. *attrib.* and *Comb.*, as **card-board**, **-room**, **-stock**, **-tack**, **-wire**; also **card-can**, the receptacle into which the carded cotton or wool falls; **card-cloth**, the leather or indiarubber backing of a card; hence *card-clothing*; **card-end**, the soft mass or rope or fibre delivered by the carding machine; **card-gatherer**, a gatherer of carding-thistles or teasels; **card-maker**, one who makes cards for combing wool, etc.; **card-tenter**, one who attends to a carding-machine; **card-thistle**, the teasel.

1688 R. Holme *Armory* III. ix. 383 The third is a *Card Board or Leaf..as yet without Leather or Teeth. **1796** Morse *Amer. Geog.* I. 403 In manufacturing card-boards, card-tacks, and finishing the cards. **1887** *Manch. Guard.* 26 Feb. 12 Frame pulleys, *card cans. **1851** *Art Jrnl. Illust. Catal.* p. v**/1 To make *card-cloth, hides of leather are cut up into strips. **1864** R. Arnold *Cotton Fam.* 29 The *'card end'..deposits itself in circular tin 'pots'. **1725** *Lond. Gaz.* No. 6400/6 James Hand, late of Lyneham in the County of Wilts, *Cardgatherer. **1401** *Pol. Poems* (1859) II. 109 Carpenters ne sowters, *card-makers ne powchers. **1483** *Act 1 Rich. III*, xii. §1 Founders, Cardmakers, Hurers, Wyremongers. **1596** Shaks. *Tam. Shr.* Induct. ii. 20 Christopher Slie..by byrth a Pedler, by education a Cardmaker. **1885** *Manch. Exam.* 24 July 5/1 An appeal has been issued by the *cardroom hands to the trade unionists of the country. **1562** *Richmond. Wills* (1853) 156 *Cardstocks, iij^s. Stockcards and hande cards, iij^s. **1851** *Art Jrnl. Illust. Catal.* p. v**/1 The carding depends more on the quality of the cards than upon any..skill in the..*card-tenters. **1578** Lyte *Dodoens* IV. lx. 521 The *Cardthistel or Teasel is of two sortes, the tame and the wild. **1597** *Act 39 Eliz.* xiii, Their trade..of Card-making and drawing of *Cardwyer.

card (kɑːd), *sb.*² Also 5-7 carde. See also cart *sb.*², chart *sb.*¹ [An altered representative of F. *carte* (14th c. in Littré in sense 'playing-card'), ad. It. *carta*, in same sense (cf. quot. 1816 in 1), a specific use of It. *carta* paper, leaf of paper, leaflet:—L. *charta* (*carta*) papyrus leaf, paper, ad. Gr. *χάρτης* leaf of papyrus, leaf, thin plate; perh. of Egyptian origin. (It does not appear how the Eng. form came to be *carde*, instead of *carte*, which was established in Sc.)

The native Fr. repr. of L. *carta* was *charte*; after the introduction of *carte* from Ital. it was gradually extended to other senses, belonging to *charte* (as in *charte blanche*), or to med.L., It., or Sp. *carta*, as those of map, chart, card. The Eng. word has had a parallel history; the shape and stiffness of a playing-card being generally present to mind in the later extensions of the word.]

I. 1. a. One of a 'pack' or set of small oblong pieces of pasteboard, used in playing games of chance, or chance and skill combined: now called more specifically *playing-cards*. Unless otherwise indicated by the context, always referring in this sense to the particular species of cards which are marked with 'pips' or conventional figures of four different kinds or 'suits', called severally *spades*, *clubs*, *hearts*, and *diamonds*. The 'pack' consists of 4 'suits', each of 13 cards, 10 of which bear respectively 1, 2, 3, etc. (up to 10) pips all of one form, and the remaining 3 have habited figures called 'King', 'Queen' and 'Knave', whence they are called court (i.e. *coat*) or *picture-cards*. (The earliest sense in Fr. and English.)

? *a* **1400** *Chester Pl.* II. (1847) 83 Usinge cardes, dice, and cupes smalle. **1463** *Act 4 Edw. IV*, iv. §1 That no Merchant ..shall bring, send nor conuey..Chessemen, playing Cardes. **1562** J. Heywood *Prov. & Epigr.* (1867) 29 Tell thy cardes, and then tell me what thou hast wonne. **1577** Northbrooke *Dicing* 111 The Kings and Coate cardes that we use nowe were in olde time the images of idols and false gods. **1589** *Hay any Work* A iij b, Cards..though they bee without hornes..are parlous beasts. **1650** Sir E. Nicholas in *N. Papers* (1886) I. 192 If a Presbiterian or Scotch court card were trumpe. **1732** Pope *Ep. Bathurst* 142 Mighty Dukes pack Cards for half-a-crown. **1816** Singer *Hist. Cards* 4 Cards are mentioned as being in common use among the Italians at the end of the thirteenth century. **1858** O. W. Holmes *Aut. Breakf. T.* (1883) 251 Turn up the faces of your picture-cards!

¶ One of the tablets in the game of 'dominoes'.

1820 *Hoyle's Games Impr.* 182 At the commencement of the game [of Domino], the cards (as they are called) are shuffled with their faces on the table.

b. *a house* (*castle*) *of cards*: built by children in their play; hence applied *fig.* to any insecure or unsubstantial scheme, system, etc.

1641 Milton *Reform.* Wks. 1738 I. 18 Painted Battlements..of Prelatry, which want but one puff of the King's to blow them down like a past-board House built of Court-Cards. **1645** Bp. Hall *Remed. Discontent.* 27 It is for Children to cry for the falling of their house of Cards. **1665-9** Boyle *Occas. Refl.* IV. xviii. (1675) 275 As children oftentimes do with their Cards, when having taken a great deal of pains to build fine Castles with them, they themselves afterwards ruine them with their Breath.

c. *pl.* A game or games played with cards; card-playing. Phrase, *to play cards* or *at cards* (Sc. *at the cards*); *a game at* or *of cards*; formerly, † *on the cards*.

1484 Marg. Paston *Lett.* 881 III. 314 Pleyng at the tabyllys, and schesse and cards. **1502** *Privy Purse Exp. Eliz. York* (1830) 84 Item to the Quenes grace..for hure disporte at cardes this Crismas. **1589** *Hay any Work* A iij b, Our brother Westchester had as liue playe twentie nobles in a night, at Priemeero on the cards. **1661-2** Pepys *Diary* 13 Jan., My aunt Wight and my wife to cards. **1699** B. E. *Dict. Cant. Crew*, *Knave-Noddy*, a Game on the Cards. **1715** De Foe *Fam. Instruct.* I. iii. (1841) I. 63 Spend no more precious time at Cards. **1775** *Annals of Gaming* 86 Every thing that can be done upon the cards by the most expert *joueurs*. **1787** T. Jefferson *Corr.* (1830) 95 After supper, cards; and after cards, bed. **1826** J. Wilson *Noct. Ambr.* xxv, While an occasional evening away..at an innocent and cheerful game at cards.

2. In many fig. phrases arising out of the game: **a.** (in *sing.*) from technical terms of play. † *card of ten*: one that has ten pips, a 'ten'; from its function in some game appears to come the phrase *to face* (*brag*) *it out with a card of ten*, i.e. to brag, put on a bold front. † *cooling card*: app. a term of some unknown game, applied *fig.* or punningly to anything that 'cools' a person's passion or enthusiasm. †*facing card*: ? = *card of ten*. *leading card*: a card which determines the 'suit' which must be played by those who follow the first player; *fig.* 'an example or precedent' (*Dict. Cant. Crew* 1690). *loose card* (see quot.).

1542 Brinklow *Compl.* xix. (1874) 45 He shal haue fauor for his masters sake, or els bragg it owt with a carde of x. **1579** Lyly *Euphues* (Arb.) 105 A certeine pamphlet which he termed a cooling carde for Philautus. **1580** *Ibid.* 320 All louers (he onelye excepted) are cooled with a carde of teene [tenne]. **1591** Shaks. *1 Hen. VI*, v. iii. 84 There all is marr'd: there lies a cooling card. **1600** Breton *Pasquill's Mad-cap* (1626) D ij b, Feede their humours with a Card of Tenne. **1606** *Sir G. Goosecappe* II. i. in Bullen *O. Pl.* (1884) III. 37 For temper sake they must needs have a cooling carde plaid upon them. **1621** Jas. I *Answ. Commons* in Rushw. *Hist. Coll.* (1659) I. 51 God sent us a Cooling-card this year for that heat. *a* **1624** Bp. M. Smith *Serm.* (1632) 33 If yee [goe away] for these facing-cardes of multitudes or chaire, vnhappy are yee. **1683** Tryon *Way to Health* 474 Drunkenness being the leading Card to all Evils. **1690** B. E. *Dict. Cant. Crew*, *Cooling Card*, cold comfort, no hope. **1706** Hearne *Collect.* (1885) I. 164 A great Duke (as a Leading Card) has subscrib'd 30,000*l.* **1820** *Hoyle's Games Impr.* 49 Loose card, is a card of no value, and consequently, the properest to throw away.

b. *sure card*: an expedient certain to attain its object; a person whose agency, or the use of whose name, will ensure success. Similarly with other adjs., as *good*, *safe*, *likely*, *doubtful*, etc., and in phrases, *to play one's best card*, *to have played one's last card*, etc.; *to have a card* (or *cards*) *up one's sleeve*: to have a plan, resources, etc., in reserve; *to play the Orange card*: to appeal to N. Irish Protestant sentiment for political advantage (see quot. 1886); hence in extended use (*to play the..card*), applied to other political gambits.

c **1560** *Enterlude Called Thersytes* (1848) 87 Nowe thys is a sure carde, nowe I maye well saye. **1579** Lyly *Euphues* (1636) A iv, A cleere conscience is a sure card. **1589** R. Harvey *Plain Perc.* 12 To get a sure card on their side, either calles for Iustice. **1605** *Tryall Chev.* v. ii. in Bullen *O. Pl.* (1884) III. 343 Here's Cavaliero Bowyer, Core and Nod.. sound cards. **1649** Selden *Laws Eng.* I. xv. (1739) 28 It cannot be denied that the Pope and Kings were good Cards in those days. *Ibid.* xlvii. 78 The Bishop..had formerly no other Cards to shew but that of the Canon. **1690** B. E. *Dict. Cant. Crew*, *A sure Card*, a trusty Tool, or Confiding Man. **1707** J. Stevens *Quevedo's Com. Wks.* (1709) 164 Is this the Service I am to expect from you, Paul! I must turn a new Card. **1711** *Brit. Apollo* II. No. 102. 3/2 Don Gimcrack his last Card has plaid. **1742** Fielding *J. Andrews* IV. iii, We have one sure card, which is to carry him before justice Frolick. **1755** Young *Centaur* I. Wks. 1757 IV. 123 All their objections to Christianity seem to be no more, nor less, than playing the best card they have. **1763** Fr. Brooke *Lady J. Mandeville* in Barbauld *Brit. Novelists* (1820) XXVII. 23 Poor fellow! I pity him; but marriage is his only card. **1811** Wellington *Let.* in Gurw. *Disp.* VIII. 454 The Prince d'Aremberg..is too great a Card to give up for the Marquis de Santa Cruz. **1812** J. Bellingham in *Examiner* 25 May 336/1, I have been called upon to play an anxious card in life. **1826** Scott *Woodst.* III. xiv. 358 No card seemed to turn up favourable to the royal cause. **1836** Dickens *Let.* ? 22 Aug. (1965) I. 167 Harley wrote, when he had read the whole of the opera, saying 'It's a sure card—nothing wrong *there*'. **1872** J. P. Kennedy *Quodlibet* (ed. 3) i. 40 Consider me a sure card in that line. **1898** *Tit-Bits* 23 July 3289/3, I took the precaution of having what, I believe, you sporting men call a card up my sleeve. **1907** E. Phillips Oppenheim *Secret* xxxvii. 231 If Guest has yet another card up his sleeve, he has kept it secret from me. **1933** 'G. Orwell' *Down & Out* v. 38, I have got a few cards up my sleeve. There are people who owe me money, for instance. **1953** R. Lehmann *Echoing Grove* 206 It was only years later, in rooms with Jocelyn, that she guessed or suspected the possibility of another motive—the card up her sleeve she had always shut her eyes to guessing that she held. **1886** R. Churchill *Let.* 16 Feb. in R. R. James *Ld. Randolph Churchill* (1959) viii. 233, I decided some time ago that if the G.O.M. went for Home Rule, the Orange card would be the one to play. **1955** *N.Y. Times* 2 May 12/5 The Russians have not played this captive-soldier card yet, but they can play it not only in their negotiations with the Germans but in the conversations that will be starting with the Japanese in London next month. **1973** *Times* 31 May 10 British policy toward Ireland has been paralysed by the fear that the Protestants of Ulster will play the Orange Card and fight to preserve their British tie. **1982** *Christian Science Monitor* 3 Nov. 1/2 Western newspapers have been full of speculation as to whether China was playing a 'Soviet card' against the United States.

c. *mod. slang.* [app. suggested by such expressions as *sure card*, etc.; see prec.], applied to a person, with adj. (as *knowing*, *old*, *queer*, etc.) indicating some eccentricity or peculiarity. Also without adjective: a 'character', an 'original'; a clever, audacious, etc., person.

1836 Dickens *Sk. Boz* 264 (Hoppe) Mr. Thomas Potter whose great aim it was to be considered as a 'knowing card'. **1852** —— *Bleak H.* xx. 199 But such an old card as this. **1853** *Ibid.* lxii. 596 You know what a card Krook was for buying all manner of old pieces of furniter. **1873** Black *Pr. Thule* x. 151 You are the most romantic card I know. **1905** A. Bennett *Tales of Five Towns* I. 9 It would be..a topic for years, the crown of his reputation as a card. **1911** —— (*title*) The Card—a Story of Adventure in the Five Towns. **1929** W. Deeping *Roper's Row* xxi, 'What the Midlanders call "a card".' 'What's that?' 'An original, a person.' **1942** 'W. B. Johnson' *Widening Stain* (1943) iii. 34 That old Witch-Hammer was really quite a card.

d. (in *pl.*) from the comparison of any enterprise to a game of cards, as *to play one's cards well, badly*, etc. Also *to throw* or *fling up one's cards*: to abandon a project. *to show one's cards*: to reveal one's plans, the extent of one's resources. † *to have* or *go in with good cards*: to have good grounds for expecting success. † *to cast* or *count one's cards*: to reckon up one's chances, take stock of one's position. † *cards and cards* (see quot. 1584). See also cut, deal, shuffle *vbs.*; trump. Also *to lay*, *put* (or *play with*) (*all*) *one's cards on the table*: 'to show one's cards', to reveal one's resources.

1577 Holinshed *Chron.* IV. 207 Choosing rather to die in battell (if hap had so cut their cards). **1581** Campion in *Confer.* II. (1584) U iv, I would I might be suffered to shewe my cardes. **1584** R. Scot *Discov. Witchcr.* XIV. viii. 311 Calculating and casting his cards in this maner. **1584** B. R. *Herodotus* I b, It was cardes and cardes betwene them, the one beyng full meete and quit with the other. *c* **1590** Marlowe *Massac. Paris* I. ii, Since thou hast all the cards within thy hands..deal thyself a King. **1597** *1st Pt. Ret. fr. Parnass.* IV. i. 1373 Let us caste our cardes before wee goe. **1621** Quarles *Argalus & P.* (1678) 119 Amphialus.. trusting to his Cards. **1622** Bacon *Hen. VII*, They went in upon farre better Cardes to ouerthrow King Henry, then King Henry had to ouerthrow King Richard. **1638** Chillingw. *Relig. Prot.* I. ii. §155. 114 There being nothing unwritten, which can goe in upon halfe so faire cards. **1645** Quarles *Sol. Recant.* III. 86 And let thy wisdome play Bad Cards with best advantage. **1664** *Floddan F.* IV. 32 Our Cards we had both need to count and cast. **1688** W. Darrel *Ignatius no Phanat.* 18 If I cannot oppose more weighty Reasons to the contrary, I'll fling up my Cards. **1710** *Subst. of Late Conf.* 3 The Cards run so much against him. **1753** [see play *v.* 22 b]. **1801** M. Edgeworth *Belinda* I. i. 24 A man of gallantry..who was known to play his cards well, and to have good luck whenever *hearts* were trumps. **1848** Mrs. Gaskell *M. Barton* I. xi. 198 Thou'st played thy cards badly... At one time he were desperate fond o' thee. **1868** Browning *Ring & Bk.* I. III. 176 Come, cards on table; was it true or false? **1871** W. S. Gilbert *Palace of Truth* II. p. 29 One who shows her cards so candidly. **1907** E. Phillips Oppenheim *Secret* viii. 55, I began to think that I had been rash to lay my cards upon the table. **1914** Shaw *Fanny's First Play* III, Tramps are often shameless; but theyre never sincere. Swells—if I may use that convenient name for the upper classes—play much more with their cards on the table. **1923** J. M. Murry *Pencillings* 195 He seems to put his cards on the table and to be saying in the friendliest way: 'That's my opinion. What's yours?' **1925** W. Deeping *Sorrell & Son* xvi. 155 There is no reason why we should put all our cards on the table. **1930** W. S. Maugham *Cakes & Ale* vii. 85 If you play your cards right you ought to marry well. **1956** A. Wilson *Anglo-Saxon Att.* I. iii. 96 Mrs. Middleton played her last card, '*I* know, children,' she said, 'the Vicar is hungry, that is what it is.'

e. *on the cards*, † *out of the cards*: within (*or* outside) the range of probability.

On the cards appears to mean with Dickens 'liable to turn up', as any thing in the game may when the cards are turned up. But it is very possible that the phrase originated with cartomancy, when the cards were consulted as to the issues of enterprises. Other sources have also been conjectured.

1813 Sir R. Wilson *Diary* II. 40 It is not out of the cards that we might do more. **1849** Dickens *Dav. Copp.* xi, 'If in

short, if anything turns up.' By way of going in for anything that might be on the cards, I call to mind that Mr. Micawber ..composed a petition to the House of Commons. **1852** —— *Bleak H.* iv, It don't come out altogether so plain as to please me, but it's on the cards. **1865** CARLYLE *Fredk. Gt.* (1873) V. 303 Lest a scalade of Prag should be on the cards. **1868** MILL *Engl. & Irel.*, It was on the cards whether Ireland should not belong to France. *Mod.* It was quite on the cards that he was to be raised to the Upper House.

†**II. 3. a.** A map or plan; = CHART *sb.*¹ *Obs.*

1527 R. THORNE in Hakluyt *Divers Voy.* (1582) B iv b, A little Mappe or Carde of the worlde. *Ibid.* C ij a, The first lande from the sayd beginning of the carde towarde the Orient is certaine Ilandes of the Canaries. **1555** EDEN *Decades W. Ind.* (Arb.) 45 Of the vniuersall carde & newe worlde. **1570** J. CAMPION in Arb. *Garner* I. 53 In our way to Scio, as you may plainly see by the Card. **1577** EDEN & WILLES *Hist. Trav.* 231 If Ortelius generall Carde of the world be true. **1591** BURGHLEY *Let.* in *Unton Corr.* 88 The best particular cardes of Normandie and Picardie. **1602** SHAKS. *Ham.* v. ii. 114. **1605** BACON *Adv. Learn.* II. xxiii. §46 (1873) 246 Not only that general map of the world.. but many other more particular cards. **1650** FULLER *Pisgah* v. xx. 183 Such an elbow appears not in the late cardes of this country.

†**b.** *card of the sea, mariner's card* or *sea card*; = CHART *sb.*¹ 1 b. *Obs.*

1534 LD. BERNERS *Gold. Bk. M. Aurel.* R vij, What profitte is it to the mariner to know the carde of the see. **1555** EDEN *Decades W. Ind.* II. x. (Arb.) 134 Manye of those mappes which are commonly cauled the shipmans cardes or cardes of the sea. **1594** BLUNDEVIL *Exerc.* VII. xxvii. (ed. 7) 690 The Mariners Card..is none other thing but a description..of the places that be in the Sea or in the land next adioyning to the Sea, as Points, Capes, Bayes. **1613** PURCHAS *Pilgr.* VIII. ii. 729 Pirats..robbing him..forced him to sustaine himselfe with making of Sea-Cardes. **1649** G. DANIEL *Trinarch., Rich. II*, cccx, Harry..by his Card knew how farr on His Voyage he might be. **1678** PHILLIPS, *Card*, a Sea-Map..Vulgarly so called for Chart. **1721–1800** in BAILEY. [Not in JOHNSON.]

4. a. The circular piece of stiff paper on which the 32 points are marked in the mariner's compass.

16th c. quotations are doubtful since they may belong rather to 3 b 'chart'. Possibly the compass-card was at first so called rather because it was regarded as a sort of 'chart' than on account of its material.

[**1555** EDEN *Decades W. Ind.* II. VII. (Arb.) 127 Knowleage of the sea carde & compasse.] **1605** SHAKS. *Macb.* I. iii. 17 All the Quarters that they know I' th' Ship-mans Card. **1656** J. HARRINGTON *Oceana* (1700) 140 What Seaman casts away his Card, beause it has four and twenty Points of the Compass? **1732** POPE *Ess. Man* II. 98 On Life's vast ocean diversely we sail, Reason the card, but Passion is the gale. **1751** CHAMBERS *Cycl.* s.v. *Compass*, The flower de lis, wherewith all nations still distinguish the north point of the card. **1770** *Phil. Trans.* LX. 133 At noon it [the Scilly light-house] bore directly north by true card. **1867** SMYTH *Sailor's Word-bk.*

b. *fig.*

1594 HOOKER *Eccl. Pol.* I. (1617) 5 That Law..is the Card to guide the World by. **1636** FEATLY *Clavis Myst.* xxix. 382 Let us..carefully steere by the Card of God's word. *a* **1703** BURKITT *On N.T.* 2 Peter ii. Pref., Our apostle.. recommended the holy scriptures to us..as our card and compass. **1786** BURNS *To Mount. Daisy* vii. 39 Unskilful he to note the card Of prudent lore.

c. *to speak by the card*: to express oneself with care and nicety; to be exact to a point.

1602 SHAKS. *Ham.* v. i. 149 Wee must speake by the Carde, or equiuocation will vndoe vs. **1875** JOWETT *Plato* (ed. 2) IV. 315, I speak by the card in order to avoid entanglement of words.

III. 5. a. *gen.* A flat piece of stiff paper or thin pasteboard, usually rectangular; used as a surface to write or draw upon, or for other purposes.

1610 G. FLETCHER *Christ's Vict.* I. xv, There hung the.. Card Where good and bad and life and death were painted. **1622** PEACHAM *Compl. Gentl.* xiii. (1634) 129 My booke.. will teach you the use of colours for Limning..the manner of preparing your card. **1724** SWIFT *Drapier's Lett.* iii. (1724) VI. 415 If we are driven to the expedient of a sealed card [i.e. as a substitute for coin]. **1828** SOUTHEY *Ep. A. Cunningham*, Thou..didst wilfully Publish upon a card, as Robert Southey's, A face..as like Tom Fool's. *Mod.* Cards bearing the names of the prize-winners are affixed to the successful exhibits.

b. *transf.* Anything having the form of a card. *U.S.*

1823 J. F. COOPER *Pioneers* ix, With 'cards of gingerbread'. **1853** J. G. BALDWIN *Flush Times Alabama* 103 He distributed..a plug of tobacco there, or a card of *town* gingerbread to the little snow-balls. **1884** PHIN *Dict. Apiculture* 20 *Card*, a frame filled with honeycomb. A sheet of honeycomb.

6. In many specific applications (in most of which small size, not greatly exceeding that of a playing card, is implied):

a. A small sheet on which a letter or message may be written; hence formerly a short letter, note, or message, whether literally on a *card* or otherwise. Around 1870 the use of actual cards for this purpose was revived, whence POST-CARD (in U.S. *postal card*). So *message-card*, *correspondence-card*.

1596 COLSE *Penelope* (1880) 173 With scoffing cardes she doth vs load. **1781** COWPER *Let. to Newton* 4 Oct., Send Dr. Johnson..my poems, accompanied with a handsome card. **1784** —— *Task* II. 384 Never at his books Or with his pen, save when he scrawls a card. **1797** *Encycl. Brit.* II. 432/2 These..are to be noted down..upon a large message-card. **1873** MORLEY *Rousseau* II. 289 Hume was the friend of Walpole, and had given Rousseau a card of introduction to him. *Mod.* Send me a card to let me know of your arrival. I'll drop you a card when I hear from him.

b. conveying an invitation to a party, a ball, etc.; or serving as a ticket of admission to an exhibition or entertainment, as evidence of membership in a society; or the like.

1771 SMOLLETT *Humph. Cl.* (1815) 80, I can't resist the curiosity I have to know if you received a card on this occasion? **1824** BYRON *Juan* XVI. lxix, All country gentlemen ..May drop in without cards. **1876** *World* V. No. 114. 17 Astonished by an invitation to dinner, which she declines, and then by cards for parties, which she refuses. *Mod. Advt.* House to be sold..Cards to view may be obtained of the auctioneer.

c. bearing a person's written or printed name, or name and address. More fully with prefixed sb. indicating the special purpose, as (*a*) *visiting card*: used chiefly for presentation on making a call, or to be left in token that a call has been made. Phrase, *to leave a card on* (a person). (*b*) *wedding cards*: bearing the names of the bride and bridegroom, and sent as a notification of the wedding. (*c*) *business card*: see BUSINESS 24.

1795 S. ROGERS *Words for Mrs. Siddons* 51 A thousand cards a day at doors to leave. **1848** THACKERAY *Bk. of Snobs* xxviii. (L.) Our first cards were to Carabas House. —— *Van. Fair* III. 178 (Hoppe) The Scape tradesmen..left their cards, and were eager to supply the new household. **1855** O. W. HOLMES *Poems* 160 Brattle Street and Temple Place Were interchanging cards! **1856** EMERSON *Eng. Traits* vi. *Manners* Wks. (Bohn) II. 47 If he [an Englishman] give you his private address on a card, it is like an avowal of friendship. *Mod.* He called, and sent up his card.

d. with defining sbs. prefixed, as *birthday*, *Christmas*, *Easter*, *New Year cards*, printed with ornamental designs, etc. to be sent (on the occasions indicated) as an expression of compliments or good wishes; *collecting cards*, on which small donations received by collection for charitable institutions are recorded; *menu cards*, etc.

a **1869** E. GARRETT *Occup. Retired Life* vii. 133 A Christmas card gives as much delight as a Christmas-box.

e. A programme, official or not, of the 'events' at races, regattas, and the like. *spec.* in *Cricket*, a score-card.

1849 *Punch* XVII. 12/1 Paid..2d. for a Card of the Innings. *a* **1888** *Mod.* Here's the c'rect card, sir! **1903** A. D. TAYLOR *Annals of Lord's* 111 The printing tent was introduced at Lord's, on June 26th, 1848,..and the public, for the first time, could secure a 'correct card' of the game.

f. A card held by a delegate at a trade union meeting or congress and representing a certain number of the members of his union. Cf. *card vote*.

1902 *35th Ann. Rep. Trades Union Congress* 69 A vote by card was then demanded, and resulted in the Committee being supported by 796,000 to 375,000. *Ibid.* 85 The method of voting shall be by card, to be issued to the delegates of trade societies according to their membership, and paid for..on the principle of one card for every 1,000 members or fractional part thereof represented.

g. *pl.* An employee's documents (e.g. national-insurance card, etc.) held by an employer and returned when employment ceases; hence in various phrases alluding to dismissal or resignation from employment. *colloq.*

1929 H. GREEN *Living* vii. 103 Arthur Bridges was sending for his cards after 54 years' work. **1958** M. DICKENS *Man Overboard* xi. 176 You're planning to ask for your cards this morning, I suppose. **1958** 'A. GILBERT' *Death against Clock* 51 Wouldn't surprise me to know he'd helped himself from the till, and that's why they gave him his cards.

h. A rectangular piece of stiffened plastic issued by banks and other institutions, with information embossed or otherwise represented, used chiefly in obtaining credit, guaranteeing cheques, or for use with cash-dispensing and other devices. Principally as the second element: *Access card*, *cash card*, *credit card*, etc., see under first word.

1967 *Times Rev. Industry* Mar. 66/3 The Midland..took the decision to honour the National Provincial and Lloyds cards at its own branches. **1982** *Daily Tel.* 28 Sept. 8/1 British Telecom is increasing the number of public call boxes using plastic cards instead of coins. **1984** S. BELLOW *Him with his Foot in his Mouth* 20 Walish, after computing interest and service charges to the fourth decimal, cut up Reg's cards.

7. *transf.* U.S. A published note, containing a short statement, request, explanation, or the like. (Webster.)

1769 *Boston News-Letter* 2 Feb. (Th.), A Card from the London and British Merchants to the American Merchants. **1788** *Gen. Even. Post* (London) 1–3 Jan. 2/3 A Card. Dr. Norris..desires to inform the public [etc.]. **1887** *Chr. Leader* 21 July 462 When news reached the saloon keepers that a prohibitory law had been passed, they published the following card: 'To all prohibitionists,' etc. **1931** G. T. CLARK *Leland Stanford* viii. 305 That there might be no misunderstanding as to where they stood they published the following card over the signature of James Anthony and Company. **1945** *Bristol* (New Hampshire) *Enterprise* 15 Feb. 4/1 (Advt.), Births, marriage and death notices inserted free. Card of thanks, $1.00.

8. A large rectangular piece of pasteboard containing an advertisement, or the like, for placing in a window, hanging on a wall, etc. So *window-card*, *show-card*, etc.

9. *Comm.* (more fully *pattern-card*, *sample-card*): Sometimes simply a sheet of pasteboard, sometimes an elaborate contrivance resembling a portfolio, on which samples of manufactured articles are fastened for exhibition to customers.

10. *Mech.* One of the perforated pasteboards or sheet metal plates in the Jacquard attachments to looms for weaving figured fabrics.

1831 G. PORTER *Silk Manuf.* 252 Figure weaving..These fixed cards thus become substitutes for the intermediate blank spaces on the revolving card slips. **1859** *Encycl. Brit.* XIII. 143 Since 1841..scarcely a machine has been worked without the ornaments being applied by means of cards.

11. *slang* or *colloq.* '*the card*': = 'the correct thing', the TICKET, q.v.

1851 MAYHEW *Lond. Lab.* II. 47 (Hoppe) I've got 10s. often for a great coat, and higher and lower..but 10s. is about the card for a good thing.

IV. *attrib.* and *Comb.*

12. *attrib.* with prefixed numeral in names of games (sense 1), as *three-card monte*, *trick*, *five-card*, *eight-card cribbage*: see the sbs.

13. General combs., as (sense 1 a) *card-dealer*, *-game*, *-play*, *-sense*; (sense 1 b) *card-castle*, *-house*; (sense 2) *card assembly*, *box*, *-cheat*, *-cheating*, *-maker*, *-making*, *-meeting*, *-party*, *-player*, *-playing*, *-room*, *-table*; *card-devoted* adj.; (sense 6 c) *card-basket*, *-exchanging* adj., *-leaving*, *-plate*, *-tray*.

1751 SMOLLETT *Per. Pic.* (1779) III. lxxxiii. 285 Our hero forthwith repaired to a *card-assembly. **1841** A. BACHE *Fire-Screen* viii, To this treasury does the tasteful disposer of drawing-room decorations consign her antiquated *card-baskets. **1872** C. M. YONGE *P's & Q's* vi. 58 She began to search in the card basket. **1829** CARLYLE *Misc.* (1857) II. 76 A mere intellectual *card-castle. **1859** SALA *Tw. round Clock* 153 Skittle sharps, *card-cheats, 'duffers' and ring droppers. **1608** DEKKER *Belman Lond.* Wks. 1884–5 III. 131 This *card-cheating..is called Batt fowling. **1902** O. WISTER *Virginian* iii. 31 Into my thoughts broke the voice of that *card-dealer. **1784** COWPER *Task* IV. 229 Sit pupils in the school Of *card-devoted time. **1899** *Westm. Gaz.* 26 May 10/1 The Hague, in the opening days of the Peace Conference, was simply a mass of *card-exchanging foreigners. **1864** *Once a Week* 19 Mar. 364/1 Other principal *card-games of the period were Iodam, noddy, bankerout.. and post-and-pair. **1824** MISS MITFORD *Village* Ser. I. (1863) 14 Knocking down the rest of the line like a nest of *card-houses. **1853** E. RUSKIN *Let.* 30 Nov. in M. Lutyens *Millais & Ruskins* (1967) 113 Continual letter-writing and note-sending and *card-leaving on every body in and around Edinburgh. **1900** *Manners & Rules of Good Society* iii. 16 The etiquette of card-leaving is a privilege which society places in the hands of ladies. **1564** J. RASTELL *Confut. Jewell's Serm.* 2 *Karde-makers, tapsters, gailers. **1694** LUTTRELL *Brief Rel.* (1857) III. 381 Mr. Whitfeild, the late kings cardmaker. **1732** BERKELEY *Alciphr.* II. §2 This idle amusement [gaming] employs the card-maker. **1751** CHAMBERS *Cycl.* s.v. *Cards*, The great letters, in our old manuscripts..are apparently done by the illuminers after this method of *card-making. **1824** MISS MITFORD *Village* Ser. I. (1863) 196 He belonged..to every *card-meeting of decent gentility. **1777** JOHNSON in *Boswell* II. 574, I advised Mrs. Thrale who has no *card-parties at her house, to give sweetmeats, and such good things, in an evening. **1840** MARRYAT *Poor Jack* li, She..was considered quite a catch at card-parties. **1852** MRS. E. TWISLETON *Let.* 1 July (1928) i. 9 Mr. Twisleton having gone out to order a *cardplate for me. **1919** A. E. M. FOSTER *Auction Bridge Table Talk* v. 37 Any form of gambling—*card play, racing, or whatever else it may be. **1931** *Essays & Studies* XVI. 182 The terms of card-play. **1589** *Hay any Work* A iij b, What, a bishop such a *cardplaier? **1816** SINGER *Hist. Cards* 38 Ferdinand V... promulgated more severe laws and penalties against Card-players. **1577** NORTHBROOKE *Dicing* (1843) 142 What say you to *carde playing? **1848** MACAULAY *Hist. Eng.* I. 255 Most of the time which he could save..was spent in racing, cardplaying, and cock-fighting. **1760** A. MURPHY *Way to keep Him* III. 67 I'll go this Moment into the *Card-Room, and watch whom she whispers with. **1876** GEO. ELIOT *Dan. Der.* I. 211 Who is that standing near the card-room door? **1930** W. S. MAUGHAM *Cakes & Ale* ix. 108, I did not play well, but Mrs. Driffield had a natural *card sense. **1713** ADDISON *Guardian* No. 120 (Jod.) There is nothing that wears out a fine face like the vigils of the *cardtable. **1785** COWPER *Let. to Newton* 19 Mar., The card-table..is covered with green baize.

14. Special combs.: **card-carrying** *a.*, having a membership card of a specified organization, esp. of the Communist Party; so *card-carrier*; **card-case**, a case for carrying visiting cards; **card-catalogue**, a catalogue (of a library, etc.) in which each item is entered on a separate card; †**card-conny-catching**, †**card-gospeller**, *nonce-wds.* (see quots.); **card-edge gilder**, a man who, or machine which, gilds the edges of cards; **card-holder**, one who holds the cards for a great personage while he is playing; also *fig.*; one who possesses a membership-card of a certain organization; a member; **card-index** (orig. *U.S.*), an index in which each item is entered on a separate card; a card-catalogue; also *transf.* and *fig.*; hence **card-index** *v. trans.* and *intr.*, to make a card-index (of); also *fig.*; so *card-indexed* ppl. adj., *card-indexing* vbl. sb.; †**card-man** (see 3), a maker of maps or charts; †**card-match**, a piece of card dipped in melted sulphur; also *fig.*; **card-money**, money allowed a person to enable him to play cards; **card-paper**

= CARDBOARD; **cardphone**, a public telephone operated by means of a prepaid plastic card holding details of outstanding credits, instead of by coins; **card-press**, a small press for printing cards; **card-rack**, a rack for holding business or visiting cards; **card-sharp** (orig. *U.S.*), a card-sharper; **card-sharper**, one who makes a trade of cheating at cards; **card-sharping**, the practices of a card-sharper; **card vote**, in trade union meetings, etc., a method of voting by which the vote of each delegate counts for the number of his constituents (cf. sense 6 f above); †**card-work**. Also CARDBOARD.

1966 'W. HAGGARD' *Power House* iii. 27 His wife was a communist... She wasn't a *card-carrier. **1948** B. ANDREWS *Washington Witch Hunt* ii. 96 The most dangerous Communists in the nation today are not the open, avowed, *card-carrying party members. **1953** *Wall St. Jrnl.* 18 Aug. 2/3 'Millions of workers who are just card-carrying members' and who take no interest in union affairs. **1835** MARRYAT *Olla Podr.* viii, Again drawing out his *card-case. **1870** MISS BRIDGMAN *R. Lynne* I. xiv. 235 Margaret took out her card-case. **1878** H. STEVENS (of Vermont) (*title*) Photo-Bibliography, or a word on printed *Card Catalogues of old rare beautiful and costly books.. Six sample Cards of the proposed Titles. **1592** GREENE *Def. Conny-catch.* Wks. 1881–3 XI. 76 Let mee vse it for an excuse of our *Card Conny-catching: for when wee meet a country Farmer with a full purse, a miserable miser.. we hold it a deuotion to make him a Conny, in that he is a Caterpillar to others. **1902** *Westm. Gaz.* 1 Jan. 1/7 Book *Card-edge Gilders. **1921** *Dict. Occup. Terms* (1927) §538 *Card edge gilder*;.. places cards in press after they are trimmed..; brushes them over with size, lays on gold leaf and allows it to dry; burnishes gold leaf by hand with agate or bloodstone burnishing tool. **1550** LATIMER *Serm. Stamford* I. 269 Among so great a number of gospellers, some are *card-gospellers, some are dice-gospellers, some pot-gospellers. *a* **1659** OSBORN *Essex's Death* Wks. (1673) 677 With what Circumspection Princes ought to play their Game, since Counsellors their *Card-holders, are not seldome Cheaters. **1934** WEBSTER, *Cardholder*, a person who has a card issued by a library entitling him to borrow books. **1955** *Times* 17 June 7/5 A fellow traveller is not a card-holder. **1970** *Daily Tel.* 25 Apr. 17/3 Individual card holders may find their credit ceiling upgraded and find Barclaycard less pressing in asking them to pay their bills in future. **1850** *Rep. Comm. Patents 1849* (U.S.) 344, I also claim the *card index formed with the shoulder *b*, to suspend the card in the slit of the plate or false bottom *a*. **1900** *Engineering Mag.* XIV. 767 Those who desire to clip the items for card-index purposes. **1908** *Modern Business* Dec. 544/2 Card indexing has become nowadays an essential requirement of modern business. **1911** H. S. HARRISON *Queed* vi. 67 She had touched the spring of the automatic card-index system, known as his memory. **1911** *Cosmopolitan* June 130/1 All the vast store of information that he had treasured up in that marvelous brain of his, ready to be called on almost as if his mind were card-indexed. **1917** TWYFORD *Purchasing & Storing* 16 Card indexing them [*sc.* specifications].. will make them available for rapid reference. **1920** ROSE MACAULAY *Potterism* I. iv, Jane, sitting in her father's outer office, card-indexing, opening and entering letters. **1924** KIPLING *Debits & Credits* (1926) 188 He pulled out a drawer of card-indexed photographs. **1927** *Daily Express* 31 Oct. 13 The film is an interesting example of the 'card-index' method of film construction. **1929** *Sunday Dispatch* 13 Jan. 5 The little books have made it possible to 'card-index' my mind and systematise my memory. **1625** LISLE *Du Bartas* 92 The poet followeth Mercator, Ortelius and the common opinion of the *Cardmen of our times. **1673** [R. LEIGH] *Transp. Reh.* 102 Crying Chimney Sweep, Ay, or *Card-Matches and Save-alls. **1730** FIELDING *Tom Thumb* II. vi, Where are those eyes, those card-matches of love. **1760** in HONE *Every-day Bk.* II. 1628 Two of the lady's servants.. agreed.. to dispose of the *card money. **1858** LD. ST. LEONARDS *Handy Bk. Prop. Law* xvii. 114 For.. ornaments of her person, pocket-money, card-money, charities, or any other objects. **1777** MUDGE in *Phil. Trans.* LXVII. 336 There must.. be two other circular pieces of *card-paper cut out. **1830** MISS MITFORD *Village* Ser. IV. (1863) 260 A house of card-paper would be the solider refuge. **1978** *Daily Tel.* 14 Aug. 11/3 A caller would insert the card into a slot and dial in the normal way. The '*cardphone' would deduct the cost of the call from the value of the card. **1981** *Times* 28 July 2/4 Public telephones.. which use prepaid plastic cards, are now in operation in London... The telephones, called Cardphones, take cards of the same shape and size as a credit card. **1984** *New Scientist* 26 Jan. 27 Cardphones are proving so popular.. that British Telecom.. is planning to introduce three thousand more this year. **1790** *Pennsylvania Packet* 11 Dec. 3/2 *Card racks or containers. **1803** *Lett. Miss Riversdale* III. 198 As to sending one's name to grace her card rack, I don't think there's much in that. **1826** MISS MITFORD *Village* Ser. II. (1863) 342 Painted shells and roses .. on card-racks and hand-screens. **1884** HARTE *On Frontier* 273 To make a *card sharp out of him. **1963** *Punch* 3 July 33/3 George Manolesco was a Rumanian thief and cardsharp. **1859** SALA *Tw. round Clock* 336 German swindlers and *card-sharpers. **1887** EDNA LYALL *Donovan* xvi. 183 Beware of pickpockets and cardsharpers dressed as gentlemen. **1870** *Daily News* 20 Apr., Two men.. were charged with.. *card-sharping in a railway carriage. **1902** *35th Ann. Rep. Trades Union Congress* 74 Should a *card vote be demanded, it would of course be taken. **1924** H. G. WELLS in *Westm. Gaz.* 8 Mar., Should its [*sc.* the League of Nations'] members have a card vote after the pattern of a British Trade Union Congress? **1966** *Listener* 22 Sept. 411/2 Representation, two different forms of voting procedure—a show of hands and the card vote—and accountability are all clearly laid down. **1653** H. COGAN *Pinto's Trav.* xxxix. (1663) 157, 12 Ballisters of the wood of Camphire.. wreathed about with silver in the fashion of *Card-work.

†**card**, *sb.*³ *Obs.* See also CHARD. [a. F. *carde*, in same sense; cf. Sp. *cardo*, lit. 'thistle', used as a name of the artichoke, from its thistle-like flower.] **a.** The tender central leaf-stalk of the Artichoke, *Cynara Scolymus*, blanched for table use. **b.** The prepared midrib of a variety of white beet.

1658 EVELYN *Fr. Gard.* (1675) 205 If you would have them abound in fair cards, you must keep them well hous'd. **1704** *Collect. Voy. & Trav.* III. 34/1 They pare it like a Lettice, or Artichoke Card. **1727** BRADLEY *Fam. Dict.*, *Cardes*: They are of two Sorts, viz. Cardes of Beet and Cardes of Artichoke; those of the Beet are.. the Stalks or Ribs.

†**card**, *sb.*⁴ *Obs.* [Cf. CHAR, also '*Cardui*, Sc., a kind of trout found in Lochleven, probably the char' (Jam.).] Some sort of fish.

c **1640** J. SMYTH *Hundr. Berkeley* (1885) 319 A Cod, a Card.

card (kɑːd), *v.*¹ Also 4 **karde**, 5 **cardyn**. [f. CARD *sb.*¹, or, perhaps rather a. F. *carder*; in our quots. the vb. appears earlier than the sb.]

1. *trans.* To prepare wool, tow, etc., for spinning, by combing out impurities and parting and straightening the fibres with a card. Also with *out*, and *absol.* Also, †To dress cloth with teasels or cards (*obs.*); see CARD *sb.*¹ 2. †To remove (impurities) from flax, etc. with cards (*obs.*).

1393 LANGL. *P. Pl.* C. x. 80 Boþe to karde and to kembe. *c* **1440** *Promp. Parv.* 62 Cardyn wolle, *carpo*. **1447** BOKENHAM *Seyntys* (1857) 294 To spynnyn and cardyn she hadde no shame. **1553** EDEN *Treat. New Ind.* (Arb.) 21 The men spinne and carde and make clothe. **1577** GOOGE *Heresbach's Husb.* I. (1586) 39 Some use agayne to carde of the knoppes [of flax] with an iron Combe. **1661** HICKERINGILL *Jamaica* 31 The Natives, card out this Rind into a kind of course Tow. *a* **1687** PETTY *Pol. Arith.* (1690) 19 Cloth must be cheaper made, when one Cards, another Spins, another Weaves. **1757** DYER *Fleece* III. (R.) These card the short, those comb the longer flake. **1804** EARL LAUDERD. *Publ. Wealth* (1819) App. 409 Machines which at once clean, card, and reduce the cotton into a state adapted for spinning.

fig. **1377** LANGL. *P. Pl.* B. x. 18 Wisdome and witte now is nouȝt worth a carse, But if it be carded with coueytise as clotheres kemben here wolle. **1786** BURNS *Wks.* II. 45, I inclose you two poems I have carded and spun since I past Glenbuck.

b. *transf.* Said of bees and spiders. Also, *to card up* (dial.): see quot.

1608 TOPSELL *Serpents* 786 As for separating, dividing, picking, carding, or suting their stuffe, they [a kind of spiders] are very bunglers to the first mentioned. **1829** *Family Libr.* I. 70 The bees.. carded it with their feet into a felted mass. **1876** *Mid. Yorksh. Gloss.* (E.D.S.) s.v., To 'card up' a hearthstone is.. merely to separate and remove the ashes and cinders. To 'card up' a room means, to put it generally to rights.

†**2.** To stir and mix with cards (see quot. 1607); to stir together, to mix. *Obs.*

1591 G. FLETCHER *Russe Commw.* (1857) 92 They drinke milke or warme blood, and for the most part carde them both together. **1592** GREENE *Upst. Courtier* in *Harl. Misc.* (Malh.) II. 241 You Tom Tapster.. carde your beere.. halfe smal & halfe strong. **1607** TOPSELL *Four-f. Beasts* 277 As for his diet, let it be warm mashes, sodden wheat and hay, thoroughly carded with a pair of Wool-cards. **1635** PAGITT *Christianogr.* I. iii. (1636) 133 Wine, carded together with a little warme water.

fig. **1597** SHAKS. *2 Hen. IV*, III. ii. 62 The skipping King .. carded his State, Mingled his Royaltie with Carping Fooles. **1627** FELTHAM *Resolves* II. xliii, Calm discussions do card affections into one another.

†**3.** To comb or cleanse (of impurities). *Obs.*

1612 SHELTON *Quix.* I. vi. I. 42 'Tis necessary that this Book be carded and purged of certain base things.

4. To scratch or tear the flesh with a wool-card or similar instrument, as a method of torture.

1556 *Chron. Gr. Friars* (1852) 74 For cardynge of hare mayde wyth a payer of carddes soche as doth carde wolle with-alle. **1603** FLORIO *Montaigne* (1634) 393 With Cardes and Teazels.. he made him to be carded.. untill he died of it. **1827** *Q. Rev.* XXXV. 87 On the overthrow of his party he was taken prisoner, and carded to death. **1881** W. E. FORSTER in *Standard* 25 Jan., 'Card' him—that is to say, an iron comb used for agricultural purposes is applied to the man's naked body.

5. *Sc.* 'To scold sharply' (Jamieson). [cf. Sp. *cardar* 'to reprimand severely', *carda* 'a severe reprimand'.]

card (kɑːd), *v.*² [f. CARD *sb.*²]

†**1. a.** *intr.* To play at cards; to play one's cards. Also, *to card it. to card a rest*: to set up a REST (in Primero); *fig.* to stand to one's point.

1548 LATIMER *Serm. Ploughers* (1868) 25 Thei hauke, thei hunt, thei card, thei dyce. **1613** SHERLEY *Trav.* 136 You shall hazard to Card ill, that play to please one by displeasing another. *a* **1617** BAYNE *On Eph.* I. (1658) 166 Many that live revelling, carding, dicing. **1637** HEYWOOD *Royal King* II. ii. Wks. 1874 VI. 32 Will you card A rest for this? **1728** FIELDING *Love in sev. Masks* Wks. 1775 I. 42 Lasses, that sleep all the morning, dress all the afternoon, and card it all night. **1766** ANSTEY *Bath Guide* xiv. 6 Brother Simkin's grown a Rakehell, Cards and dances ev'ry Day.

†**b.** *trans. to card away.*

a **1620** J. DYKE *Divers Sel. Serm.* (1640) 169 It may bee they card and dice it [their trouble] away.

2. *trans.* (*U.S.*) To send a message by post-card to a person. Cf. WIRE *v.*

1875 in *Newspaper*, Fulcitus carded almost daily his friend Ruisseaux. **1880** (*from a letter*) Will you card to me here an answer to my friend the professor's question?

3. a. To fix on a card. (Frequent colloq. in trades where pattern-cards are used: see CARD *sb.*² 9.)

1884 *Harper's Mag.* Oct. 522/2 They are carded, and boxed in cotton-wool.

b. To write (something) on a card, e.g. for use in a card-index. Also const. *up*.

1925 MAWER & STENTON *Place-Names Bucks.* p. v, Mrs. Stenton.. has given invaluable help.. in the work of carding up and identifying the place-names. **1934** J. E. MANSION *Harrap's Standard Fr. Dict.* I. p. vi, To supplement these we must collect and 'card' our own material. **1968** *Times Lit. Suppl.* 30 May 559/4 This isn't to say.. that other readers may not have found and carded them [*sc.* words] earlier.

cardakew, var. of CARDECU, *Obs.*

‖**cardamine** (kɑːˈdæmɪniː, ˈkɑːdəmaɪn). *Bot.* [mod.Lat. (Linnæus), a. Gr. καρδαμίνη some cresslike plant, f. κάρδαμον cress: cf. F. *cardamine.*] A genus of cruciferous plants, including the common Lady-smock or Cuckoo-flower (*C. pratensis*); Meadow-cress.

1753 in CHAMBERS *Cycl. Supp.* **1875** VEITCH *Tweed* 27 The slender cardamine, first lilac hued, Then growing white and pure. **1882** *Garden* 22 Apr. 284/1 A regular bed of lovely pink Cardamine.

cardamom (ˈkɑːdəməm). Forms: 6–8 **cardamome**, 7 **-dumome**, **-damony**, **-damon(e**, (9 **cardemon**), 7–9 **cardamum**, 7– **cardamom**. [ad. L. *cardamōmum*, a. Gr. καρδάμωμον, f. κάρδαμον cress + ἄμωμον AMOMUM: cf. F. *cardamome.*]

A spice consisting of the seed-capsules of various species of *Amomum* and *Elettaria* (N.O. *Zingiberaceæ*), natives of the East Indies and China; used in medicine as a stomachic, and also for flavouring sauces and curries. (Rarely applied to the plant from which the spice is obtained.) The only kind included in the British pharmacopœia is the Malabar cardamom, obtained from *E. Cardamomum*. **b.** Also occas. applied to the capsules of *A. Meleguetta* of Western Africa, usually called Grains of Paradise.

[**1398** TREVISA *Barth. De P.R.* XVII. xxxiii. (1493) 623 Cardomomum helpyth ayenst wamblyng and indygnacyon of the stomak.] **1553** EDEN *Treat. New Ind.* (Arb.) 15 There begin spyces to be found as ginger.. Cardamome, Cassia. **1579** LANGHAM *Gard. Health* (1633) 122 Cardamom, or Graines of Paradise, are good to be drunke against the falling sicknesse. **1712** tr. *Pomet's Hist. Drugs* I. 21 The lesser Cardamome is enclos'd in a Pod of the Length of a Child's Finger. **1799** SOUTHEY *Nondescr.* iii. Wks. III. 63 Give Boreas the wind-cholic, till he roar For cardamum. **1841** ELPHINSTONE *Hist. India* I. 11 Pepper and cardamums grow in abundance on the western coast. **1870** YEATS *Nat. Hist. Comm.* 151 Cardamoms are shipped to this country from Ceylon.

attrib. **1789** W. BUCHAN *Dom. Med.* (1790) 183 Powdered cardamum seeds. **1883** *Athenæum* 21 July 75/1 Cardamom gardens in Coorg.

cardan (ˈkɑːdən). The name of *Cardan* (Geronimo Cardano, 1501–1576, Italian mathematician), used attrib. in ***cardan joint***, a universal joint, a joint permitting free motion of the different parts of the mechanism; ***cardan shaft***, a shaft having a universal joint at one end or at both ends for transmitting motion from one shaft to another not in a direct line with it. Also *absol.*

1902 HARMSWORTH *Motors & Motor-Driving* 191 In order to permit of the free vertical movement of the wheels under the springs, two universal or 'Cardan' joints.. are fitted within the length of the shaft. **1906** *Daily Chron.* 14 July 6/4 The cardan shaft, which connects the gear-box with the differential gear that works the driving wheel. **1906** *Westm. Gaz.* 2 Oct. 7/1 While oiling his motor as it was running, M. Santos-Dumont caught the sleeve of his leather jacket in the cardan. **1907** *Ibid.* 13 Nov. 9/2 The 15-h.p. is the only model having a cardan drive. **1908** *Ibid.* 16 Apr. 4/2 A very short cardan-jointed shaft. **1951** *Engineering* 22 June 752/2 A twin-motor cardan-shaft drive.

carˈdanic, *a. Math.* Pertaining to *Cardan* (see prec.). ***cardanic equation***: a cubic equation (for which Cardan discovered a general method of solution). ***cardanic suspension***, a form of support in which an instrument is hung on gimbals, so as to allow free movement in all directions.

1684 *Phil. Trans.* XIV. 575 A cardanick Æquation. **1892** *Review of Reviews* July 718/2 A highly sensitive vibrator, with cardanic suspension.

ˈ**cardboard.** [f. CARD *sb.*² + BOARD.]

a. Pasteboard of the thickness of card, for cutting cards from, or for making boxes and the like. Also *attrib.* in ***cardboard box***, etc.

1848 A. BRONTË *Tenant Wildf. Hall* I. xviii. 325 The pencil.. leaves an impression upon card-board that no amount of rubbing can efface. **1858** in SIMMONDS. **1863** WYNTER *Subtle Brains* 309 The rooms in which the portraits are gummed on cardboard and packed up. **1879** *Print. Trades Jrnl.* XXVIII. 16 They are printed on stout, fine cardboard.

b. *fig.* (*attrib.* or as *adj.*). Unsubstantial, unreal, 'pasteboard'.

1893 *Jrnl. Soc. Arts* XLI. 476/1 When his cardboard empire of the East fell to pieces. **1927** J. DEVAL (*title*) Her Cardboard Lover. **1952** *Illustrated* 6 Dec. 8 The cardboard family that has become larger than life.

cardboardy ('kɑːdbɔːədɪ), *a.* [f. CARDBOARD + -Y[1].] Resembling cardboard; also *fig.*

1925 D. H. LAWRENCE *Refl. Death of Porcupine* 233 All you can do now is to twiddle-twaddle about golden boughs, because you are empty.., hollow, deficient, and cardboardy. **1966** N. FREELING *King of Rainy Country* 37 A huge piece of pastry..that had gone slightly cardboardy from being kept in the fridge. **1968** H. R. F. KEATING *Inspector Ghote hunts Peacock* i. 8 The big, light brown, rather cardboardy—no, very cardboardy—suitcase. **1969** *Listener* 6 Mar. 324/1 Mrs Spark probably intended Miss Brodie to be cardboardy in her passions.

†**carde.** *Obs.* Some fabric anciently used for canopies, curtains, and linings. The explanation in quot. 1882 does not suit quot. 1295, which indicates a linen material.

[**1295** DU CANGE s.v., Visitatio Thesaurariæ S. Pauli Lond...linea una Carda Indici coloris..similiter Carda Inda cum zona de filo..Unum velum Quadragesimale de Carde croceo et Indico. **1396** *Mem. Ripon* (Surtees) III. 124 In card emp. pro coopertorio Corporis Xpi. in die Corporis Xpi. 2s. **1401** *Will of Furneux* (Somerset Ho.) Gounam de nigro Burneto dupplicat cum Carde.] **1426** *E.E. Wills* (1882) 76 A blewe bedde of Tapecery..& a selour with curteyns of carde. [**1882** BECK *Draper's Dict.*, *Carda*, *Carduus*, an inferior silk, supposed to have been made of the coarse outer filaments of cocoons, probably used for linings. Fourpence an ell was paid in 1278 for 119 ells of carda, for thirty-four surcoats to be used in a tournament.]

carde, perhaps = CARDER. But cf. CAIRD, CARD *sb.*[2] 2 c.

1572 in W. H. TURNER *Select Rec. Oxf.* 341 No fuller.. may kepe..in their houses journeymen, otherwise called cardes.

†'**cardecu.** *Obs.* Also 7 cardicue, -akew, -ecue, -ekue, -eque, -ecew, -escue. [a. F. *quart d'écu* quarter of an *écu* (usually englished 'crown').] An old French silver coin, worth ¼ of the gold *écu*, or 15 sous tournois.

In 1580, when the silver *quart d'écu* was first struck, the value of the gold écu is said to have been about 8/6 (see Larousse s.v. *Ecu*), whence the *cardecu* would be worth about 2/1½ by a gold standard. English writers of 17th c. make it = about 1/6.

1605 *Tryall Chev.* III. i. in Bullen *O. Pl.* (1884) III. 305 There's a Cardicue to wash downe melancholy. **1606** CHAPMAN *Mons. D'Olive* Plays (1873) I. 202, I could neuer yet finger one Cardicue of her bountie. **1611** CORYAT *Crudities* 69, I compounded with them for a cardakew. **1662** FULLER *Worthies* I. 95 In the Court of France, the Kings Jester moved to have..a Cardescue of every one who carried a Watch about him, and cared not how he employed his Time. **1727** W. MATHER *Yng. Man's Comp.* 236 Silver.. Old Cardecus..value 1s. 6d. 1 farthing. **1819** SCOTT *Ivanhoe* xxxii, The bunch of them were not worth a cardecu.

carded ('kɑːdɪd), *ppl. a.* [f. CARD *v.* + -ED.]

1. Dressed with a card, or by a carding machine.

1547 BOORDE *Brev. Health* ccclxx. 119 Stuffe it with carded wolle or cotton. **1858** LONGF. *M. Standish* III. 44 The carded wool like a snow-drift Piled at her knee.

2. Supplied or furnished with a card.

1521 *Test. Ebor.* (Surtees) V. 140 My cardyd and my best compass.

†**3.** Mixed, or adulterated by mixing. Also *fig.*

1596 NASHE *Saffron Walden* 99 Being constrained to betake him to carded ale. *a* **1625** FLETCHER *Wom. Prize* IV. iv. (R.) Mine is..Such a strange carded cunningness. **1626** BACON *Sylva* §46 To be drunk either alone or Carded with some other Beer.

4. Entered on a programme card, score-card, filing-card, etc.

1900 *Daily News* 18 Aug. 7/3 The next race carded was for the Rear-Commodore's Cup. **1927** *Daily Express* 19 Oct. 3/4 Nine times out of ten the carded distance is wrong.

‖**cardel.** Also kardel. [ad. Du. *kardeel*, *quardeel*.] A hogshead containing in 17th c. 64 gallons, used in the Dutch whaling trade. See QUARDEEL.

1694 *Acc. Sev. Late Voy.* (1711) II. 178 The Train-oyl runs into the Warehouse into a Vatt, whereout they fill it into Cardels or Vessels..A Cardel or Hogshead holds 64 Gallons. *Ibid.* 11 Cutting the great pieces of fat into lesser pieces, to fill our Kardels with them. **1857** *Polar Seas & Regions* (ed. 20) 461 The Dutch..took 57,590 whales, yielding 3,105,596 quardeelen of oil..A quardeel of oil contains..from 77 to 90 imperial standard gallons.

cardenal, -ale, -all, obs. ff. CARDINAL.

carder[1] ('kɑːdə(r)). [f. CARD *v.*[1] + -ER[1].]

1. One who cards wool, etc.; one who attends to a carding machine.

c **1450** *Voc.* in Wr.-Wülcker 692 *Carpetrix*, a carder. **1514** *Act 6 Hen. VIII*, ix. § 1 The Carder and Spinner to deliver ..Yarn of the same Wooll. **1613** SHAKS. *Hen. VIII*, I. ii. 33 The Clothiers..haue put off The Spinsters, Carders, Fullers, Weauers. **1725** *Lond. Gaz.* No. 6380/13 Charles Banton..Spinner and Carder. **1862** *Athenæum* 30 Aug. 265 Potters, grinders, carders, hacklers.

b. A species of wild bee, *Bombus muscorum*; so called from its tearing moss into shreds for the construction of its nest. Cf. CARD *v.*[1] 1 b.

1854 H. MILLER *Sch. & Schm.* (1858) 68 There were the buff-coloured carders, that erected over their honey-jars domes of moss. **1868** WOOD *Homes without H.* xxiv. 463 Carder Bees..prepare the materials for their nest in a manner similar to that..employed in carding cotton-wool.

2. See quot. Cf. CARD *v.*[1] 4.

1812 *Gent. Mag.* Mar. 282/2 Persons who call themselves Carders, from the instrument they use (a wool card) to enforce compliance with their demands for the regulation of the price of land [in Ireland]. **1833** MAR. EDGEWORTH *Love & L.* II. iii. (D.) Carders and thrashers, and oak-boys, and white boys, and peep o'day boys.

†'**carder**[2]. *Obs.* Also 6 cardar. [f. CARD *v.*[2] + -ER.] A card-player.

c **1530** *Hickescorner* in Singer *Hist. Cards* 251 Walkers by nyght..and joly carders. **1580** LUPTON *Siquila* 94 There is not one dicer nor yet carder in all our countrey. **1712** STEELE *Spect.* No. 308 ¶6 The Carders..never begin to play till the French-Dances are finished.

‖'**cardia.** *Anat.* [Gr. καρδία heart, also 'cardiac orifice of the stomach' (Liddell and Scott); so in mod.F.] The upper or cardiac orifice of the stomach, where the œsophagus enters it.

1782 W. HEBERDEN *Comm.* xxv. (1806) 140 From the fauces to the cardia. **1880** HUXLEY *Cray-Fish* ii. 52 In a man's stomach the opening by which the gullet communicates with the stomach is called Cardia.

cardiac ('kɑːdɪæk), *a.* (and *sb.*) Forms: 5 cardiake, 7 -aque, -acke, 7–8 -ack, 8– cardiac. [a. F. *cardiaque* of the heart, ad. L. *cardiacus*, a. Gr. καρδιακός, f. καρδία heart.]

A. *adj.*

1. Of or pertaining to the heart, anatomically, physiologically, or pathologically. †*cardiac passion* [L. *cardiaca passio*]: 'an old name for cardialgia or heartburn' (*Syd. Soc. Lex.*); but app. *orig.* palpitation of the heart. *cardiac arrest*, sudden cessation of the heart's pumping action.

1601 HOLLAND *Pliny* II. 153 The Cardiacke passion, which is a feeblenesse and trembling of the heart. **1629** CHAPMAN *Juvenal* v. 65 His longing friend..blown in fume up with a cardiack fit. **1726** MONRO *Anat. Nerves* (1741) 74 The Cardiac Nerves. **1810** *Encycl. Brit.* (ed. 4) V. 177 Cardialgia..better known by the name of cardiac passion, or heartburn. **1835–6** TODD *Cycl. Anat.* I. 192/1 The cardiac arteries arise from the aorta close to its origin. **1883** *Nature* 15 Mar. 468 The cardiac action became stronger. **1950** *Ann. Surg.* CXXXII. 855 The sudden onset of ventricular fibrillation in 15 and cardiac arrest in two as observed in the continuous electrocardiographic image. **1961** *Lancet* 5 Aug. 293/2 The technique..has been used in all cases where the period of cardiac arrest was expected to exceed about 15 minutes. **1977** *Rolling Stone* 30 June 35/1 Jazz pianist Hampton Hawes died May 22nd in Los Angeles of a cardiac arrest following a cerebral hemorrhage. **1982** *Macmillan Guide Family Health* 388/1 If cardiac arrest happens when nobody else is present, it is fatal. **1983** *Oxf. Textbk. Med.* II. xiii. 90/1 Signs of cardiac arrest such as dilated pupils, apnoea, and absent heart sounds.

2. a. 'Applied to medicines supposed to invigorate the heart' (*Syd. Soc. Lex.*); cordial, strengthening.

1661 EVELYN *Fumifug.* Misc. III. (1805) 241 Strawberries, whose very leaves..emit a cardiaque & most refreshing halitus. **1718** QUINCY *Compl. Disp.* 77 Whatsoever raises the Spirits, and gives sudden Strength..is term'd Cardiack, or Cordial, as comforting the Heart. **1744** BERKELEY *Siris* §64 The stomachick, cardiack, and diuretick qualities of this fountain. **1807** in G. GREGORY *Dict. Arts.*

b. *cardiac glycoside*, any of a group of steroid glycosides (as digoxin, ouabain) that occur in certain plants and are heart stimulants; similarly *cardiac glucoside*, a glucoside of this group.

1927 *Jrnl. Biol. Chem.* LXXIV. 787 (*heading*) The relationship between the structure and the biological action of the cardiac glucosides. **1937** A. STOLL (*title*) The cardiac glycosides. **1951** A. GROLLMAN *Pharmacol. & Therapeutics* xviii. 332 The cardiac glycosides have been used from time immemorial principally because of their toxic effects. **1983** *Oxf. Textbk. Med.* II. XIII. 61/1 Many patients on maintenance cardiac glycosides do not require them, and in view of their potential danger the need for continued treatment should be reviewed frequently.

3. Pertaining to or affected with disease of the heart.

1748 tr. *Vegetius' Distemp. Horses* 50 Such [Horses] as have the Head-ach, or the Staggers, or are mad or are cardiac. **1856** KANE *Arct. Expl.* II. 30 We both suffered from cardiac symptoms.

4. *Anat.* Distinctive epithet of the upper orifice of the stomach; hence applied to the corresponding end or region of the stomach, or to some organ connected with it. Cf. CARDIA.

1843 J. WILKINSON tr. *Swedenborg's Anim. Kingd.* I. ii. 70 The cardiac orifice guards the stomach. **1866** HUXLEY *Phys.* vi. (1869) 166 Its [the stomach's] left end is produced into an enlargement which, because it is on the heart side of the body, is called the cardiac dilatation. The opening of the gullet into the stomach, termed the cardiac aperture.

5. Heart-shaped (in *cardiac wheel* = HEART-CAM).

1864 in WEBSTER.

B. *sb.*

†**1.** A disease or affection of the heart, or referred to the heart; ? = *cardiac passion* (see A. 1).

c **1450** *Destr. Jerus., Addit. MS.* 10036, f. 29 Suche joie Titus gan undretake, That him toke a cardiake. **1468** *Medulla* in *Cath. Angl.* 54 *Cardiaca*; *quidam morbus*, a cardyake. **1483** *Cath. Angl.* 54 A Cardiakylle or cardiake, *cardia, cardiaca.*

2. A medicine supposed to stimulate the heart, a cordial. Also *fig.*

1746 BERKELEY *2nd Let. Tar-water* §6 This medicine of tar-water worketh..as a..cardiac. **1803** *Man in Moon* (1804) 65 No. 9 How many cardiacs has the fertile invention of modern dramatists mixed up..to please an audience?

3. A person suffering from heart disease.

1934 in WEBSTER. **1957** *Amer. Heart Jrnl.* LIV. 352 These patients represent an important group of cardiacs who are often denied surgical relief. **1972** I. L. RUBIN et al. *Treatm. Heart Dis. Adult* (ed. 2) xviii. 445 All cardiacs should be watched carefully for fall in blood pressure.

‖**car'diaca.** *Obs.* [Lat.; short for *cardiaca passio.*] = *cardiac passion*; see CARDIAC A. 1.

c **1375** ? BARBOUR *St. Margarete* 10 Vertuyse..Agayne ane II, callyt cardiaca. **1561** HOLLYBUSH *Hom. Apoth.* 19 b, Cardiaca is a disease of trembling of the harte.

†**car'diacal,** *a.* ? *Obs.* Also 5 cardyacle, 7 cardiacall. [f. as CARDIAC + -AL[1].]

1. = CARDIAC A. 1.

1447 BOKENHAM *Seyntys* (1835) 9 The cardyacle passyoun. **1620** VENNER *Via Recta* vii. 113 The Cardiacall Passion proceeding of choler. **1656** in BLOUNT *Glossogr.*

2. = CARDIAC A. 2.

1620 VENNER *Via Recta* vi. 106 Cardiacall medicines. **1727** BRADLEY *Fam. Dict.* s.v. *Bezoar Stone*, The great cardiacal virtues with which the Bezoar is endowed.

3. = CARDIAC A. 3.

1748 tr. *Vegetius' Distemp. Horses* 135 They..turn mad, furious, phrensical, and cardiacal.

cardiace. 'A precious stone in the shape of a heart.'

1730–6 in BAILEY. **1775** in ASH. **1846** in WORCESTER.

†**cardiacle.** *Obs.* Also 4 cardiakill, 5 -kyll, cardyakyll(e. [ad. L. *cardiaca*, OF. *cardiaque*, perh. with excrescent *-le* as in *chronicle*, *treacle* (OF. *triacle* from L. *thēriaca*), assimilated to sbs. in *-acle.*] = CARDIACA, *cardiac passion.*

1377 LANGL. *P. Pl.* B. xx. 81 Coughes, and cardiacles, crampes, and tothaches. *c* **1386** CHAUCER *Pardoneres Prol. & T.* 27, I have almost y-caught a cardiacle. **1398** TREVISA *Barth. De P.R.* VII. xxxii. (1495) 246 There is dowble maner of Cardiacle. *c* **1485** *Digby Myst.* (1882) III. 1363 þe Ientyll Ielopher a-ȝens þe cardyakylles wrech.

cardiagraphy, erron. f. CARDIOGRAPHY.

cardial ('kɑːdɪəl), *a.*[1] *rare.* [f. Gr. καρδί-α heart + -AL[1]: etymologically irregular.] Pertaining to the heart; = CARDIAC A. 1.

1868 DUNCAN *Insect. World* Introd. 141 The cardial portion of the dorsal vessel. **1887** SALA in *Illust. Lond. News* 9 Apr. 402 Everyone whose cardial arrangements are not as hard as the nether millstone.

'**cardial,** *a.*[2] *Archaeol.* [f. mod.L. *cardium* cockle, so called from its heart-shaped shell, + -AL.] Of or pertaining to a variety of early Neolithic impressed ware of the western Mediterranean, decorated by patterns made with the edge of a cockle-shell, usu. *Cardium edule*; also, of or pertaining to the Neolithic peoples who used this method of pottery decoration.

1939 V. G. CHILDE *Dawn European Civilization* (ed. 3) 338 *Cardial*, decorated with lines executed with a shell-edge. *Ibid.* xiv. 242 Pottery..decorated with semi-circles executed in cardial and stab-and-drag technique. **1975** P. PHILLIPS *Early Farmers W. Mediterranean Europe* iii. 52 Early Neolithic Cardial site at Leucate. **1982** *Times* 13 Apr. 8/1 The earliest period is marked by the presence of the pottery known to archaeologists as 'Cardial ware', because it is decorated with zigzag impressions made by the edge of a shell of the cockle *Cardium edule.*

cardialgic (kɑːdɪ'ældʒɪk), *a.* [ad. Gr. καρδιαλγικός; cf. F. *cardialgique*: see CARDIAL *a.*[1]]

1. Pertaining to cardialgia.

1620 VENNER *Via Recta* vii. 124 They..helpe the Cardialgicke paines of the stomacke. *Ibid.* viii. 188.

2. *fig.* (*nonce-use.*) Producing 'heart-ache'.

1817 COLERIDGE *Own Times* (1850) III. 951 Twice as many cardialgic teeth, that have given ten-fold more heart-aches than, etc.

cardialgy ('kɑːdɪældʒɪ). *Med.* [ad. mod.L. *cardialgia* (also used), a. Gr. καρδιαλγία heartburn, f. καρδία heart + ἄλγος pain; cf. F. *cardialgie.*]

The disease or affection popularly known as 'heartburn' (because anciently referred to the heart), consisting of pain and a sensation of heat about the cardiac orifice of the stomach, often accompanying indigestion.

1655 *Phys. Dict.*, *Cardialgia*, Heart-burning. **1710** T. FULLER *Pharm. Extemp.* 414 Effectual against..Cardialgy. **1725** BRADLEY *Fam. Dict.* s.v. *Stomach*, The Cardialgia or gnawing at the Stomach. **1803** *Med. Jrnl.* IX. 144 Mr. H. P. M. had been frequently affected with cardialgies.

cardiform ('kɑːdɪfɔːm), *a.* [f. CARD *sb.*[1] (or F. *carde*) + -FORM.] Resembling a wool-card: applied to the teeth of certain fishes: see quot.

1875 BLAKE *Zool.* 191 When..with their points bent back, they are cardlike or cardiform.

cardigan ('kɑːdɪgən). [Named from the Earl of Cardigan, distinguished in the Crimean war

(1855).] A knitted woollen over-waistcoat with or without sleeves.

1868 ROWE in *Gd. Words* 699/1 Rubbing..the sleeve of his brown Cardigan. **1879** MISS BIRD *Rocky Mount.* I. 278, I bought a cardigan for myself..and some thick socks. **1883** *Daily News* 22 Oct. 7/1 Jersey frocks and Cardigans.

†**cardimelech.** *Obs.* [f. Gr. καρδί-α heart + Heb. *melek* king.] 'A supposed active principle in the heart, superintending what are now called the vital functions' (*Syd. Soc. Lex.*).

1684 *Phil. Trans.* XIV. 704 Vice-royes residing in the Principal Viscera as in Provinces..Cardimelech in the heart.

cardinal ('kɑːdɪnəl), *a.* Forms: 4 **cardinale,** 5 **-enale,** 5-6 **-ynall,** 6-7 **-inall,** 4 **-inal.** [a. F. *cardinal*, ad. L. *cardinăl-is* pertaining to a hinge, principal, chief, f. *cardo, cardin-em* hinge.

The specific applications in Eng. (found also in other mod. European langs.) follow those of the Latin word (classical or post-classical). The analogy of *cardinal winds* (L. *venti cardinales*), whence *cardinal points*, etc., led to a certain association of the adj. with the number *four*, as in *cardinal virtues, cardinal humours*.]

I. From fig. uses of the Latin adj.

1. a. *gen.* On which something else hinges or depends, fundamental; chief, principal, of special importance. (Almost always of abstract things.)

c **1440** *Promp. Parv.* 62 Cardenale, *cardinalis*. **1593** NASHE *Christ's T.* 36 b, For the cardinall iudgement against it. *a* **1639** W. WHATELEY *Prototypes* I. xi. (1640) 94 The cardinall grace, that on which all other graces move as the doore upon its hinges. **1650** R. GELL *Serm.* 8 Aug. 19 Ye read of..four cardinal Angels. **1796** MORSE *Amer. Geog.* II. 629 One of the above cardinal crimes [theft, adultery, murder]. **1821** SYD. SMITH *Wks.* (1867) I. 316 One cardinal fault which pervades the work. **1868** GLADSTONE *Juv. Mundi* i. (1870) 5 A cardinal argument for placing the date of the Poet near that of his subject. **1875** BRYCE *Holy Rom. Emp.* xv. (ed. 5) 245 To that position three cardinal duties were attached.

b. *cardinal vowel*: one of a series of vowel-sounds proposed as a standard for phonetics.

1922 D. JONES *Outl. Eng. Phonetics* (ed. 2) p. ii, By referring the vowels of all languages to a set of Cardinal Vowels, the relations between them are made clearer. **1932** *Ibid.* (ed. 3) vii. 28 There is only one way of making written descriptions of vowels intelligible to a large circle of foreign readers, and that is to describe the sounds with reference to a scale of 'Cardinal Vowels', i.e. a set of fixed vowel-sounds having known acoustic qualities and known tongue and lip positions. **1943** K. L. PIKE *Phonetics* vii. 137 Jones's 'cardinal vowel' scheme is perhaps the most convenient and objective classification.

2. a. *cardinal virtues* (Lat. *virtutes cardinales*): in scholastic philosophy, justice, prudence, temperance, and fortitude, accounted the four chief 'natural' virtues as distinguished from the 'theological' virtues of faith, hope, and charity. Some modern writers include these, and speak of 'seven' cardinal virtues; so the 'seven cardinal sins'.

a **1300** *Cursor M.* 10008 þas er four vertus principals, þe quilk man clepes cardinals..þat es rightwisnes, and meth, For-sight, and strenght. **1340** *Ayenb.* 123 Zeue oþre uirtues huer-of þe þri byeþ ycliped godliche and þe uour byeþ y-cleped cardinals. *c* **1470** *Hors, Shepe, & G.* (1822) 5 The foure vertues callyd cardynall. **1526** *Pilgr. Perf.* (W. de W. 1531) 11 The vertues cardynall, with the vertues morall. **1611** SHAKS. *Hen. VIII*, III. i. 103, I thought ye..two reuerend Cardinall Vertues, But Cardinall Sins, and hollow hearts I feare ye. **1649** ROBERTS *Clavis Bibl.* 363 The 4 chief cardinal vertues. **1852** MRS. JAMESON *Leg. Madonna* (1857) 94 The seven cardinal virtues. **1875** H. E. MANNING *Mission H. Ghost* x. 266 The four Cardinal virtues are prudence, justice, fortitude, and temperance.

b. *Cardinal virtues* also occurs in the general sense (1).

1640 WATTS *Bacon's Adv. Learn.* Pref. 33 A seperate history of their virtues: we mean, such as in nature may be accounted Cardinall. **1651** HOBBES *Leviath.* I. xiii. 63 Force, and Fraud, are in warre the two Cardinall vertues. **1749** FIELDING *Tom Jones* 103 That cardinal virtue, patience. **1855** BAIN *Senses & Int.* II. §11 (1864) 217 In every kind of expression clearness is a cardinal virtue.

3. *cardinal number* (Arith.): a number which answers the question 'how many?'; one of the primitive or 'natural' numbers (*one, two, three*, etc.), as distinguished from the ORDINAL numbers (*first, second, third*, etc.).

1591 PERCIVALL *Sp. Dict.* B iij b, The numerals are either Cardinall, that is, principall, vpon which the rest depend, etc. **1668** WILKINS *Real Char.* 328 Adverbs Cardinals; as semel, bis, ter, etc. **1711** J. GREENWOOD *Eng. Gram.* 277 There is a cardinal number. **1845** STODDART in *Encycl. Met.* (1847) I. 45/1 Numerals are commonly divided into cardinal and ordinal.

4. *cardinal points*; **a.** the four points of the horizon (or the heavens) which lie in the direction of the earth's two poles (*cardines*), and of sunrise and sunset respectively; the four intersections of the horizon with the meridian and the prime vertical; the north, south, east, and west points. *cardinal winds*: the four chief or main winds which blow from these points.

1549 *Compl. Scot.* vi. (1872) 61 Ther is iiij. callit vyndis cardinal. **1643** *Parables on Times* 15 All the winds in the compasse, both collaterall and cardinall. *c* **1645** HOWELL *Lett.* (1650) II. 26 They..subdivided the four cardinal winds to two and thirty. **1755** B. MARTIN *Mag. Arts & Sc.* III. ii. 179 Four of them are called the Cardinal Points..S, the South; W, the West; N, the North; E, the East..sometimes called the four Winds of Heaven. **1862** RAWLINSON *Anc. Mon.* I. v. 96 The angles of the building exactly face the four cardinal points.

†**b.** of the ecliptic: *Astrol.* and *Astron.* The two equinoctial and two solstitial points of the ecliptic; also applied to the corresponding signs of the zodiac, viz. Aries, Cancer, Libra, Capricornus, called also *cardinal signs*. Also, in a horoscope, 'the First, Fourth, Seventh, and Tenth Houses' (Bailey). *Obs.*

1594 BLUNDEVIL *Exerc.* III. I. xvi. (ed. 7) 311 The two Equinoxes, and the two Solstices, are commonly called the foure cardinall or principall points. **1646** SIR T. BROWNE *Pseud. Ep.* Wks. (1686) 235 The cardinal intersections of the zodiack. **1839** BAILEY *Festus* viii. (1848) 94 Diurnal, cardinal, nocturnal, equinoctial.

c. of the prime vertical: '*Astrol.* The rising and setting of the sun, the zenith and nadir' (Webster); = *cardines* (see CARDO).

5. *Phys.*

†*cardinal humours*: 'an old term for four principal humours, viz. blood, phlegm, yellow bile, and black bile.' (*obs.*)

cardinal veins: 'the venous trunks..which transmit the blood in the early embryo from the Wolffian bodies, the vertebral column and the parietes of the trunk to the sinus venosus by means of the ducts of Cuvier. Similar veins from the anterior part of the body join the duct of Cuvier. These are sometimes called anterior cardinal veins and the others posterior cardinal veins' (*Syd. Soc. Lex.*).

6. In R.C. Ch. *cardinal bishop, priest, deacon*: a rendering of Lat. *episcopus, presbyter, diaconus cardinalis*; see CARDINAL *sb.*, which arose from the absol. use of the adj. in this sense. Also (*Hist.*) *cardinal church*: rendering of *ecclesia cardinalis*, the name given in early times to the principal or 'parish' churches of Rome, to distinguish them from the 'oratories' subordinate to them.

1670 G. H. *Hist. Cardinals* I. III. 68 The Title of Cardinal was first given to the Places, that is, to the Cardinal Churches, but apply'd afterwards to the persons that Govern'd them. *Ibid.* 72 There are six Cardinal Bishops, fifty Cardinal Priests, and fourteen Cardinal Deacons.

II. 7. *Zool.* Pertaining to the hinge of a bivalve shell.

1836 TODD *Cycl. Anat.* I. 708/1 The part of the shell..upon which the hinge occurs, is called its cardinal edge. **1850** DANA *Geol.* App. i. 691 The cardinal area is nearly wanting. **1862** —— *Man. Geol.* 180 The insertions of the cardinal muscle.

III. [f. CARDINAL *sb.*] **8.** Of the colour of a cardinal's cassock; deep scarlet.

1879 *Daily News* 13 June 2/2 A black satin dress with 'cardinal' trimmings. **1882** *Garden* 7 Oct. 309/2 Single Dahlias..fine deep cardinal. **1887** *Sat. Rev.* 1 Jan. 19 The young lady in cardinal hose and a scarlet hood.

cardinal ('kɑːdɪnəl), *sb.* Forms: 4 **cardenal, -ynal(le, -inarl,** (*pl.* **-inaus**), 5 **-inalle,** 5-6 **-ynall,** 6 **-enall,** (**cartdenall**), 6-7 **-inall,** 2- **cardinal.** [absol. uses of prec., after those of *cardinālis* in later Latin.]

I. The ecclesiastical sense and its derivatives.

1. a. One of the seventy ecclesiastical princes (six cardinal bishops, fifty cardinal priests, and fourteen cardinal deacons) who constitute the pope's council, or the sacred college, and to whom the right of electing the pope has been restricted since the third Lateran council in 1173.

The cardinals hold the highest rank next to the pope, who is chosen from their number. [See CARDINAL *a.* 6.]

1125 *O.E. Chron.*, On þes ilces ʒæres sende se papa of Rome to ðise lande an cardinal Johan of Creme. **1297** R. GLOUC. 476 Tueie cardinals the pope him sende iwis. **1393** LANGL. *P. Pl.* C. XXII. 415 Ich knew neuere cardinal þat he ne cam fro þe pope. *c* **1538** STARKEY *England* iv. 124 Hys College of Cardynallys. **1613** SHAKS. *Hen. VIII*, I. i. 51 The right Reuerend Cardinall of Yorke. **1647** CLARENDON *Hist. Reb.* I. I. 23 Rochel..was then straitly besieged by the Cardinal Richelieu. **1782** PRIESTLEY *Corrupt Chr.* II. x. 251 Cardinals..have the rank of princes in the Church. **1845** S. AUSTIN tr. *Ranke's Hist. Ref.* I. 341 The Council..prescribed to Cardinal Raimund very strict conditions.

b. Preceding other titles, indicating dignities held by one who is also a cardinal.

1670 G. H. *Hist. Cardinals* I. III. 79 The Cardinal Nephew, whom they call *Padrone*. *Ibid.* 84 The Cardinal Vicar. **1709** *Lond. Gaz.* No. 4525/1 In the Cardinal-Legate's Coach. **1783** WATSON *Philip III* (1839) 225 The cardinal-archbishop went himself to Rome.

†**c.** *the cardinal's blessing*: a blessing merely without any further advantage. *Obs.*

1702 C. MATHER *Magn. Chr.* VII. 32 What will they merit but the Cardinal's Blessing who will take no warning? **1758** JORTIN *Erasm.* I. 53 A gift, which, in all probability, would never be worth more than a Cardinal's Blessing.

d. Either of two (Senior and Junior) of the minor canons of St. Paul's Cathedral (see quot. 1868).

1748 CHAMBERLAYNE *Pres. St. Gt. Brit.* (ed. 37) II. III. 231, 12 Minor Canons [of St. Paul's Cathedral]... The Rev. Mr. William Rayner, Subdean, sen. The Rev. Mr. Dechair sen. Cardinal, The Rev. Mr. Hilman jun. Cardinal, [etc.]. **1868** WALCOTT *Sacred Archæol.* 113 Cardinal. The word, when applied to an altar, means the high or principal altar, and from their attendance upon it two minor canons at St. Paul's are still called the senior and junior cardinals. **1877** J. D. CHAMBERS *Divine Worship* 90 At S. Paul's, London..there were four Vicars called Cardinals.

†**2.** Name of a variety of apple. *Obs.*

1664 EVELYN *Kal. Hort.* (1729) 223 Apples..Lording-Apple, Pear-Apple, Cardinal, Winter Chestnut.

3. A short cloak worn by ladies, originally of scarlet cloth with a hood.

1745 MRS. DELANY *Life & Corr.* (1861) II. 382 You are capering about in your fine cardinals. **1775** SHERIDAN *Duenna* I. iii. 193 My cardinal & veil are in her room. **1826** MISS MITFORD *Village* Ser. II. (1863) 451 The thickest and brightest red cardinal that ever came out of a woollen-draper's shop. **1858** THACKERAY *Virgin.* xxxii. (1878) 248.

4. = *cardinal-bird*; see 7.

1756 P. BROWNE *Jamaica* 467 The Cardinal. This bird is frequently imported from South Carolina. **1851** *Voy. Mauritius* iv. 160 The cardinal, though scarcely larger than a bullfinch, is conspicuous for his bright scarlet plumage.

5. *slang.* 'Mulled red wine'.

II. 6. In *plural* (for the adj. with a sb. pl.). = cardinal points, winds, virtues, numbers, muscles, etc.

1398 TREVISA *Barth. De P.R.* VIII. vi. (1495) 304 The endes of this lyne that hyghte Axis ben pyghte in the poles and hyghte Cardinales. **1735** P. GORDON *Geog. Anat.*, It is impossible to distinguish properly in it any one of the intermediate points of the compass; nay, or so much as two of the four cardinals themselves. **1768** TUCKER *Lt. Nat.* (1852) II. 402 Philosophy..classes the virtues under the four cardinals of prudence, fortitude, temperance, and justice. **1816** J. SMITH *Sc. & Art* II. 183 Each segment between the several cardinals and their compounds, is subdivided into four equal portions. **1841-71** T. R. JONES *Anim. Kingd.* 553 Three pairs [of muscles]..denominated respectively 'adductors', 'cardinals', and 'accessory cardinals'. **1871** ROBY *Lat. Gram.* I. 442 The genitive plural of the cardinals and distributives.

III. 7. *Comb.* (all in sense 1), as *cardinal-making* vbl. sb.; **cardinal-bird, grosbeak,** a North American singing-bird (*Cardinalis virginianus*) with scarlet plumage; **cardinal's** (†**cardinal) hat,** the red hat worn by a cardinal, taken typically for his dignity or office; **cardinal lace,** the name of a modern pattern of lace; **cardinal spider** (see quot.). Also CARDINAL-FLOWER.

1802 BINGLEY *Anim. Biog.* (1813) II. 161 The *Cardinal Grosbeak..is an inhabitant of several parts of North America. **1885** LADY BRASSEY *In Trades* 422 Cardinal grosbeaks (*Petylus Cardinalis*) are a kind of Virginian nightingale. **1538** BALE *Thre Lawes* 1225 And as moch besydes he had not longe afore For a *Cardynall hatte. **1832** G. DOWNES *Lett. Cont. Countries* I. 349 The devices of a cock and a Cardinal's hat. **1881** *Daily News* 12 Sept. 3/5 *Cardinal laces are still wanted. **1662** FULLER *Worthies* (1840) I. iv. 16 This custom of *cardinal-making. **1883** WOOD in *Gd. Words* Dec. 762/1 The common House-spider..sometimes grows to an enormous size, and it is then known by the name of the *Cardinal Spider.

cardinalate ('kɑːdɪnəleɪt), *sb.* [a. F. *cardinalat* (It. *cardinalato*), ad. med.L. *cardinālātus*; see -ATE[1].] The office or dignity of a cardinal; the rank of a cardinal church.

1645 EVELYN *Mem.* (1857) I. 170 Bearing also the title of a Cardinalate. **1716** POPE *Let. to Swift* 20 June, I have not the least hopes of the Cardinalat. **1839** JAMES *Louis XIV*, II. 105 The refusal..to nominate De Retz to the Cardinalate.

†'**cardinalate,** *v. Obs.* Also 6 **-ite.** [f. CARDINAL *sb.* + -ATE[3].]

trans. To raise to the rank of cardinal.

1577 HOLINSHED *Chron.* III. 1167/1 Polydor..affirmeth him to be cardinalited by Pope Nicholas 5. **1620** BP. HALL *Hon. Mar. Clergie* I. xxi. (1628) 763 Panormitan was cardinalated by an intruding Pope.

cardinalatial (ˌkɑːdɪnəˈleɪʃɪəl), *a.* = CARDINALITIAL *a.*

1888 *Scottish Leader* 1 June 3/7 Two names..are being considered by Leo XIII for elevation to the Cardinalatial dignity. **1961** *Times* 31 July 17/3 The Pope..gave them [*sc.* two cardinals] the cardinalatial privileges of preaching or hearing confessions anywhere in the world.

cardinal-flower. [From its scarlet colour, like that of a cardinal's robe or hat. (In F. *cardinale rouge*; also *cardinale bleue*.)] The Scarlet Lobelia (*L. cardinalis*), a native of North America, cultivated for the splendour of its blossoms. **b.** *blue cardinal-flower*: (rare) for *L. syphilitica*.

1698 PETIVER in *Phil. Trans.* XX. 405 American Scarlet Cardinal-Flower. **1767** J. ABERCROMBIE *Ev. Man his own Gard.* (1803) 233 Perennials and biennials of the fibrous rooted tribe..crimson cardinal flower. **1831** J. DAVIES *Manual Mat. Med.* 241 Blue Lobelia, or Blue Cardinal Flower. *Lobelia syphilitica*. **1868** LOSSING *Hudson* 9 The splendid Cardinal flower..glowing like a flame.

cardi'nalic, *a. rare.* [f. CARDINAL *sb.* + -IC.] Pertaining to a cardinal. So **cardi'nalical** *a.*

1650 A. B. *Mutat. Polemo* 32 The Cardinalical party, (I mean the Jesuitical). **1886** FORTNUM in *Archæol.* L. 120 Some bronze casts from other cardinalic seals.

'**cardinaˌlish,** *a. rare*[−1]. [see -ISH[1].] Savouring of a cardinal.

1624 T. SCOTT *Aphor. State* 13 It not onely sheweth the Cardinalish Prince, but that which lyeth next vnder.

'cardinaˌlism. [see -ISM: in F. *cardinalisme.*] The institution or system of cardinals.

1670 G. H. *Hist. Cardinals* I. II. 33 Cardinalism receiving its form and essence from the Power of the Pope. **1849** CLOUGH *Remains* (1869) I. 148 Papa Pfyffer (my landlord)..protests against cardinalism loudly.

'cardinaˌlist. *Hist.* [see -IST. In F. *cardinaliste*, a partisan of Cardinal Richelieu or Mazarin.] A partisan of cardinals or of a cardinal.

Applied esp. to the adherents of Cardinal Granvella during the Dutch revolt from the Spanish rule in the 16th c.

1650 R. STAPYLTON *Strada's Low-C. Warres* IV. 81 The faction of the Cardinalists. **1855** MOTLEY *Dutch Rep.* I. 390 They stigmatized all who refused to enter into their league as cardinalists.

cardinalitial (ˌkɑːdɪnə'lɪʃ(ɪ)əl), *a.* [f. L. type **cardinālīci-us* (cf. It. *cardinalizio*, F. *cardinalice*): see -ITIAL.] Pertaining to cardinals as a class.

1670 G. H. *Hist. Cardinals* II. i. 108 The Cardinalitial Authority is great. **1716** M. DAVIES *Athen. Brit.* III. 96 Renewing his attack against the Jesuits..with the aforesaid cardinalitial success. **1849** ROCK *Ch. of Fathers* II. 70 All the other cardinalitial robes.

cardinalitian (ˌkɑːdɪnə'lɪʃ(ɪ)ən), *a.* [f. as prec. + -AN.] = prec.

1716 M. DAVIES *Athen. Brit.* III. 95 Advanced to the Cardinalitian eminency. **1770** BARRETTI *Journ. Genoa* II. 68 Badajoz..is no very cardinalitian residence. **1866** *Daily Tel.* 30 Oct. The Cardinalitian discourse.

cardi'nality. [f. on L. type **cardinālitās*: see -ITY.] †**1.** Condition of a cardinal; cardinalate. *Obs.*

1525 LD. BERNERS *Froiss.* II. cxcvi. [cxcii.] 605 All his Cardynalles to be putte out of their Cardynalyties. **1616** BRENT tr. *Sarpi's Counc. Trent* (1676) 615 The Archbishop of Otranto, and others, who aimed at the Cardinality.

2. *Math.* The property of having a certain cardinal number.

1935 *Mind* XLIV. 343 We may imagine set out before us all the examples, of whatever cardinality, involving a single dyadic relation. **1959** K. R. POPPER *Logic Sci. Discovery* vi. 114 The concept of the cardinality (or power) of a class. **1966** *McGraw-Hill Encycl. Sci. & Technol.* XII. 205 An ordering is one way of setting up a 1-1 correspondence between two sets of the same cardinality.

'cardinaˌlize, *v.* [a. 16th c. F. *cardinaliser*: see -IZE.]

1. *trans.* To raise to the rank of a cardinal.

1616 R. SHELDON *Surv. Miracles Ch. Rome* 306 His carnall kinred, whereof, he hath..cardanalized diuers. **1921** S. LESLIE *Manning* xiii. 196 Meantime Cullen had been Cardinalised.

†**2.** *humorously.* To make scarlet. *Obs.*

1653 URQUHART *Rabelais* I. xxxix, Crayfishes, which are cardinalised with boyling.

cardinally ('kɑːdɪnəlɪ), *adv.* [f. CARDINAL *a.* + -LY².] Fundamentally, pre-eminently.

1866 P. G. MEDD in *Ch. & World* 348 That cardinally important subject. **1874** MORLEY *Compromise* (1886) 36 Our own [age] is characteristically and cardinally an epoch of transition.

¶ Humorous perversion of *carnally* (cf. *cardinal sins*).

1603 SHAKS. *Meas. for M.* II. i. 81 My wife, who, if she had bin a woman Cardinally giuen, might haue bin accus'd in fornication.

†**'cardinalˌric.** *Obs.* [see -RIC; cf. *bishopric.*] = CARDINALATE.

1688 R. HOLME *Armoury* II. 37 Lesser dignities, as, Cardinalricks, archbishoprics, etc.

cardinalship ('kɑːdɪnəlʃɪp). [f. CARDINAL *sb.* + -SHIP.] The state or office of a cardinal; tenure of office of a cardinal.

1537 ? TINDALE *Exp. St. John* 64 All his doctrine..of benefyces..cardinalships. **1651** *Reliq. Wotton.* 656 (R.) During the time of his cardinalship. **1783** W. F. MARTYN *Geog. Mag.* II. 332 In elevating foreign prelates to the cardinalships. **1872** *Athenæum* 8 June 713/1 Montalto's cardinalship was passed in worries.

†**'cardine,** *a. Obs.* [Badly f. Gr. καρδί-α + -INE.] = CARDIAC.

1769 WHYTT *Vital Motions* in *Phil. Trans.* LX. 34 The cardine nerves.

cardines, pl. of CARDO.

carding ('kɑːdɪŋ), *vbl. sb.*¹ Also 5 **gardyng.** [f. CARD *v.*¹ + -ING¹; with the form *gardyng* cf. OF. *guerder* = *carder* (Littré *Suppl.*).]

1. a. The dressing of wool, cotton, etc. with cards or in a carding-machine.

1468 in *Ripon Ch. Acts* (1882) 134 Spynnyng et cardyng in festo S. Mathi. *a* **1485** *Pol. Poems* (1859) II. 284 Thei putt owte of purse, As myche for gardyng, spynnyng, and wevyng. **1727** DE FOE *Eng. Tradesm.* xlvii. (1841) II. 189 The carding is generally done by hired servants. **1851** *Art Jrnl. Illust. Catal.* p. v**/1 The carding depends more on the quality of the cards than upon any attention or skill in the operatives.

b. *concr.* The carded product.

1837 WHITTOCK *Bk. Trades* (1842) 170 The fibres of the cotton..when sufficiently combed are called cardings.

2. Torturing with wool-combs. Cf. CARD *v.*¹ 4.

1828 HEBER *Journ. India* III. 348 The work of carding..murder and robbery, goes on as systematically.

3. *attrib.* (sense 1), as in ***carding-cylinder***, ***-mill***, ***-room***; **carding-engine, -machine,** a machine for combing or cleansing wool or cotton, in which a large cylinder set with cards works in connexion with smaller cylinders and a hollow shell similarly set with cards.

1860 SMILES *Self-help* ii. 35 One of the first..to adopt the *carding cylinder. **1795** *Edin. Advertiser* 6 Jan. 15/3 The whole Cotton Machinery..consisting of five common *carding engines, etc. **1835** URE *Philos. Manuf.* 111 Towards one end of this floor are distributed the carding-engines. **1788** *Salem Mercury* 25 Nov., A Providence paper informs, that the *Carding and Spinning Machines used in England in manufacturing cotton stuffs, are introducing into that town by some publick spirited gentlemen. **1831** J. KENNEDY in *Mem. Lit. & Phil. Soc. Manchester* V. 321 In 1784 or 5 he [*sc.* Samuel Crompton] made a carding machine, the working of which was a little different from those in common use. **1822** J. FLINT *Lett. Amer.* 72 A fulling-mill, a *carding-mill, and a mill for bruising flax-seed. **1854** MRS. GASKELL *North & S.* xiii, I began to work in a *carding room soon after, and the fluff got into my lungs, and poisoned me.

'carding, *vbl. sb.*² [f. CARD *v.*² + -ING¹.] Card-playing. Also *attrib.*

1495 *Act 11 Hen. VII*, ii. §5 Where disyng, cardyng, tenys pleiyng..shalbe used. **1594** BP. KING *Jonas* (1618) 125 To erect dicing and carding houses. **1654** TRAPP *Comm. Job* xxxi. 22 In Carding and Dicing he had often wished himself hanged if it were not so and so. **1885** *Pall Mall G.* 24 June 2 The sole..income was derived from the carding.

carding ('kɑːdɪŋ), *ppl. a.* [f. CARD *v.*¹ + -ING².] That cards; as in ***carding bee*** = *carder bee* (see CARDER¹ 1 b).

1802 BINGLEY *Anim. Biog.* (1813) III. 288 The Carding Bees nearly all perish in the winter.

cardio- ('kɑːdɪəʊ-; with dissyllabic endings ˌkɑːdɪ'ɒ-), combining form of Gr. καρδία heart, as in **'cardioblast,** in insect embryology, one of a row of mesodermal cells from which the heart develops; **ˌcardio-diaphrag'matic** *a.*, pertaining to the heart and the diaphragm; **'cardiogram,** the tracing made by a cardiograph or electrocardiograph; **'cardiograph** (-grɑːf, -æ-), [Gr. -γράφος writing, writer], an instrument which registers the motions of the heart by tracing a curve on paper, etc.; **cardi'ographer,** one who uses a cardiograph or electrocardiograph; esp. a technician who has received training in (electro)cardiography; **ˌcardio'graphic** *a.*, of or pertaining to a cardiograph; hence ***cardiographically*** adv.; **cardiography** (-'ɒgrəfɪ), [Gr. -γραφία writing], (*a*) in anatomy, 'a description of the heart' (Craig); (*b*) 'the application and use of the cardiograph' (*Syd. Soc. Lex.*); **ˌcardio-in'hibitory** *a.*, checking or arresting the heart's action; **ˌcardio'lipin,** a substance extracted from beef hearts, capable of acting as an artificial antigen in serum tests for syphilis; **ˌcardio'logical** *a.*, of or pertaining to cardiology; **cardi'ologist,** one who specializes in the study or treatment of the heart and its diseases; **cardiology** (-'ɒlədʒɪ), [Gr. -λογία discourse], knowledge of, or a treatise on, the heart; **cardi'olysis,** resection of portions of the cardiac area in order to free the heart from surrounding structures to which it has become adherent; **cardiometer** (-'ɒmɪtə(r)), [Gr. -μέτρον measure], an instrument for measuring the force of the heart's action; also *fig.*; hence **cardiometrical** (-əʊ'mɛtrɪkəl), *a.*; **cardiometry** (-'ɒmɪtrɪ), [Gr. -μετρία measurement], 'the measurement of the size of the heart by percussion and auscultation' (*Syd. Soc. Lex.*); **ˌcardio'motor** *a.*, pertaining to the action of the heart; **cardiopathy** (-'ɒpəθɪ), [Gr. -παθία suffering], disease of the heart; **ˌcardiop'tosis,** displacement of the heart downwards; **ˌcardio-'pulmonary** *a.*, pertaining to the heart and the lungs; **ˌcardio-'renal** *a.*, pertaining to the heart and the kidneys; **ˌcardio-re'spiratory** *a.*, relating to the action of both heart and lungs; **ˌcardio-scle'rosis,** induration of the tissues of the heart; **'cardioscope** (see quot. 1890); **'cardiospasm,** spasmodic contraction of the cardiac sphincter of the stomach; **ˌcardiota'chometer,** an instrument for measuring the rate at which the heart beats; **cardi'otomy,** dissection or incision of the heart; **ˌcardio'tonic** *a.*, serving to invigorate the heart; **ˌcardio-'vascular** *a.*, relating to both the heart and the blood-vessels.

1898 A. S. PACKARD *Text-Bk. Ent.* II. 572 A long string or row of cells (**cardioblasts*), which on each side border the mesodermal layer of the primitive band. **1907** *Practitioner* Apr. 528 A smaller movement of the right *cardio-diaphragmatic angle. **1876** *Nature* 13 Apr. 471/2 More than one physiologist has obtained far more satisfactory '*cardiograms' by applying the sphygmograph. **1888** *Buck's Handbk. Med. Sci.* VI. 95/2 The Cardiogram.—A graphic record of the impulse of the heart against the chest-wall can be obtained by means of sphygmographs constructed on the principle of Marey's; or by modifications of the same for their better application to the thorax, as Galabin's cardiograph. **1892** A. E. SANSOM *Dis. Heart* 493 Dr. Hercules Macdonald obtained cardiograms from the posterior aspect of the heart. **1870** S. GEE *Auscult. & Percuss.* iii. 48 The *Cardiograph is an instrument invented by Chauveau and Marcy whereby the movements of the cardiac impulse may be registered. **1964** *Whitley Councils for Health Services P.T.B. Circular* No. 174, 2 A *Cardiographer is an officer who has completed..appropriate..training..and is employed on electrocardiography. **1884** B. BRAMWELL *Dis. Heart* 751 *Cardiographic tracings are usually obtained from the pulsations of the left apex-beat. **1907** *Practitioner* Nov. 610 Both *cardiographically and clinically, its duration is well defined. **1884** B. BRAMWELL *Dis. Heart* 31 The *cardio-inhibitory centre in the medulla. **1907** *Practitioner* Nov. 693 The conservative influence of cardio-inhibitory action. **1942** M. C. PANGBORN in *Jrnl. Biol. Chem.* CXLIII. 247 It is proposed to designate this substance '*cardiolipin'. **1946** *Nature* 27 July 119/2 Almost as active preparations could be obtained with cardiolipin. **1922** *Encycl. Brit.* XXXI. 350/2 Another aspect of the *cardiological problem..is the so-called 'nervous or irritable heart'. **1927** *Daily Tel.* 21 June 15 The cardiological department contains an electrocardiograph. **1885** *Lancet* 26 Sept. 576/1 Being near the great *cardiologist, he thought he would hear what he had to say. **1965** *Math. in Biol. & Med.* (*Med. Res. Council*) I. 34 He claims that the computer can diagnose correctly as often as three experienced cardiologists using the same clinical data. **1847** CRAIG, **Cardiology*. **1903** *Lancet* 18 July 188/2 Dr. Brauer performed an operation which has been called *cardiolysis and which consists in resecting some costal cartilages and a part of the sternum so that the heart would have more freedom of movement. **1918** F. W. PRICE *Dis. Heart* 346 The advisability of performing the operation of 'cardiolysis' in some cases of severe adhesions between the pericardium and the chest wall. **1860** READE *Cloister & H.* II. 334, I called little Kate's hand a *Kardiometer, or heart-measurer, because it graduated emotion, and pinched by scale. **1875** H. WOOD *Therap.* (1879) 151 The..beat will influence the mercurial column of the cardiometer. **1878** *Rep. Smithsonian Inst.* 423 Careful *cardiometrical studies showing that the arterial pressure is not seriously affected. **1910** J. MACKENZIE *Dis. Heart* (ed. 2) 399/1 *Cardio-motor centres. **1924** R. W. G. HINGSTON in E. F. Norton *Fight for Everest: 1924* (1925) 250 The cardiomotor mechanism of the vigorous man at a height of 16,000 feet closely resembles that of the physically inefficient person at sea-level. **1885** *Lancet* 1 Aug. 219/2 The commonest age at which the *cardiopathy manifests itself..is from forty to forty-six. **1905** *Medical Annual* 185 Palpitations, attacks of vertigo, and occasionally inability to lie on the left side, are the principal symptoms... *Cardioptosis does not endanger life. **1918** F. W. PRICE *Dis. Heart* 24 The apex-beat..may be displaced downwards in cardioptosis, emphysema, and pneumothorax. **1908** *Practitioner* Mar. 324 Such murmurs are louder during inspiration, and are literally *cardio-pulmonary, the pulmonary artery being compressed by the flattened chest-wall through the medium of the lung. **1959** *Times* 14 Oct. 14/5 A cardio-pulmonary research centre. **1913** *Jrnl. Chem. Soc.* CIV. I. 1022 Respiration and Metabolism in *Cardio-renal Disease. **1892** OSLER *Princ. Med.* 227 The so-called *cardio-respiratory murmur. **1908** J. MACKENZIE *Dis. Heart* 26 A cardio-respiratory reflex. **1964** L. MARTIN *Clinical Endocrinol.* (ed. 4) II. 61 A cardio-respiratory syndrome. **1894** GOULD *Dict. Med.*, *Cardio-sclerosis. **1908** J. MACKENZIE *Dis. Heart* p. xviii, The term cardio-sclerosis, unless qualified, will always refer to the group with arterial degeneration. **1890** BILLINGS *Nat. Med. Dict.* I. 230/2 **Cardioscope*, instrument for examining the movements of the heart. **1900** DORLAND *Med. Dict.* 135/1 *Cardiospasm. **1914**, **1939** Cardiospasm [see ACHALASIA]. **1928** *Arch. Internal Med.* XLI. 403 The *cardiotachometer, an instrument to count the totality of heart beats over long periods of time. **1956** *Newsweek* 26 Nov. 104/2 The cardiotachometer..detects heart stoppage on the operating table seconds before it is recognizable to the surgeon. **1922** *Encycl. Brit.* XXXI. 348/1 Doyen attempted *cardiotomy on a patient believed to be suffering from mitral stenosis. **1936** *Nature* 19 Sept. 484/1 None of the recognized *cardiatonic [*sic*] drugs seems to have been used in China at the date, A.D. 1596, when this list was compiled. **1949** *Blakiston's New Gould Med. Dict.* 182/1 Cardiotonic. **1879** *St. George's Hosp. Rep.* IX. 798 *Cardio-vascular pulsation. **1909** *Practitioner* Nov. 617 The cardio-vascular hypertrophy. **1918** F. W. PRICE *Dis. Heart* 79 Those articles of food which especially stimulate the cardio-vascular system. **1962** *Lancet* 29 Dec. 1386/2 Deaths should be assigned to the cardiovascular or cerebrovascular class of disease.

†**'cardiogˌnost.** *Obs.* [ad. Gr. καρδιογνώστης, f. καρδία heart + -γνώστης knowing, knower.] One who knows the heart.

1652 URQUHART *Jewel* Wks. (1834) 276 As if they were his cardiognosts, and fully versed in his intentions.

So †**ˌcardiog'nostic,** *a.* and *sb.* (= prec.).

1640 SIR E. DERING *Carmelite* (1641) 39 You will make the Saints to be Gnosticks indeed, Cardiognosticks! **1643** *True Informer* 40 Greater Kardiognosticks than God Almightie. *c* **1645** HOWELL *Lett.* (1650) I. 436 The omniscient Creator, he is only kardiognostic. **1656** in BLOUNT *Glossogr.*

cardioid ('kɑːdɪɔɪd). *Math.* Also **-oide.** [ad. Gr. καρδιοειδής heart-shaped, f. καρδία + εἶδος form.] A curve somewhat resembling a heart in shape.

If through a fixed point in the circumference of a circle straight lines be drawn, intersecting the circle at different points, and such that the length of each line on each side of the point of intersection is equal to the diameter of the circle, the extremities of these lines will trace out a cardioid, having its cusp at the fixed point. The cardioid is also traced out by a point in the circumference of one circle rolling round the circumference of another equal to it.

1753 in CHAMBERS *Cycl. Supp.*, The Cardioide. **1852** SALMON *Higher Pl. Curve* (1879) II. 44 The curve is of the form of a heart and is called the cardioide. **1879** THOMSON

& TAIT *Nat. Phil.* I. I. §94 We have . . the case of a circle rolling externally on another of equal size. The curve in this case is called the Cardioid.

cardiphonia (kɑːdɪˈfəʊnɪə). [f. Gr. καρδία heart + -φωνία, f. φωνή voice.] The title given to a collection of letters by the Rev. John Newton (1781), intended to mean 'utterance of the heart', in which sense it has been occas. used by later writers.

1781 J. NEWTON (*title*) Cardiphonia, or Utterance of the Heart. **1881** *Contemp. Rev.* 330 The work [In Memoriam] . . became at once a text-book and a cardiphonia.

cardite (ˈkɑːdaɪt). *Zool.* A genus of molluscs (*Cardita*) of the family *Cyprinidæ*. [So in Fr.]

1852 TH. ROSS tr. *Humboldt's Trav.* I. vi. 204 The cardites, the turbinites, the ostracites, and shells of small dimension.

‖**carditis** (kɑːˈdaɪtɪs). *Med.* [mod.L. f. Gr. καρδία + -ITIS.] Inflammation of the muscular substance of the heart.

1783 CULLEN *Wks.* (1827) II. 69 Carditis and Pericarditis, or the inflammations of the heart and Pericardium. **1836–9** TODD *Cycl. Anat.* II. 637/1 True carditis seems to be generally admitted to be rare.

‖**cardo** (ˈkɑːrdəʊ). Pl. cardines (ˈkɑːdɪniːz). [L. *cardo* hinge; adopted in some special senses.]

†**1.** *Astrol.* in *pl.* = CARDINAL *points. Obs.*

1571 DIGGES *Pantom.* I. xxix. I iij, The foure cardines or quarters of the Horizon. *a* **1625** FLETCHER *Rollo* IV. ii, How are the cardines? **1660** H. MORE *Myst. Godl.* VII. xv. 341 Starres and Planets do most potently act in the Cardines of the Celestiall Theme, of which Imum Cœli is one.

†**2.** *fig.* A 'hinge', turning-point. *Obs.*

a **1638** MEDE *Wks.* I. xxvi. (1672) 109 The main Cardo and hinge of Repentance. **1657** COLVIL *Whig's Supplic.* (1695) 89 This is the Cardo of the Dispute.

3. *Conch.* The hinge of a bivalve shell.

1755 *Gentl. Mag.* XXV. 31. **1789** G. WHITE *Selborne* (1853) III. 19 The cardo passing for a head and mouth. **1877** HUXLEY *Anat. Inv. An.* vii. 429 The cardines.

cardol (ˈkɑːdɒl, -əʊl). *Chem.* Also 9 -ole. [a. G. *cardol* (G. Städeler 1847, in *Ann. d. Chem. und Pharm.* LXIII. 141), f. mod.L. *ana-card-ium*, generic name of the cashew tree + -OL 3.] A vesicatory oil, $C_{15}H_{27}{\cdot}C_6H_3(OH)_2$, obtained from the pericarp of the cashew-nut.

1848 G. STÄDELER in *Chem. Gaz.* 15 Jan. 30, I propose for this fatty acid the name of anacardic acid, and for the active constituent that of cardol. *Ibid.* 1 Feb. 61 The medicinal effects of pure cardol far exceed those of the mixture extracted from the pericarp by æther. **1884** H. G. GREENISH tr. *Dragendorff's Plant Analysis* 146 Cardol is a colourless oil accompanying anacardic acid in the cashew nut. **1954** *Current Science* Aug. 265/1 A sample of cardol, isolated from Indian cashew nut shell liquid.

carˈdooer. *Sc.* [f. vb. *cardoo, cardow, curdow*, expl. by Jamieson as 'To mend old clothes, patch, botch': of uncertain origin.]

1837 LOCKHART *Scott* (1839) VII. 217 A little hunchbacked tailor . . one of the race who creep from homestead to homestead . . the great gossips and newsmen of the parish,—in Scottish nomenclature cardooers.

cardoon (kɑːˈduːn). Forms: 5 **cardoun**, 7–8 **cardon**, 7– **cardoon**. Also β. 7–9 **chardon**, 8 **chardoon**. [a. 16th c. F. *cardon* cardoon, ad. It. *cardone* (or Sp. *cardon*) great thistle, teasel, cardoon, augm. of *cardo*:—L. *cardus, carduus* thistle, cardoon, or artichoke. In origin, the same word as F. *chardon* thistle, the northern form of which, *cardon*, had appeared in ME. as CARDOUN.]

A composite plant (*Cynara Cardunculus*), closely allied to the Artichoke (see quot. 1845); a native of the south of Europe and north of Africa, and cultivated in kitchen-gardens, esp. on the continent, for the fleshy stalks of the inner leaves, which are made tender by blanching. (By Cotgrave applied also to the similar CARD of the Artichoke.)

The cardoon was prob. first cultivated in Northern France in the 16th or ? end of 15th) c.; it is mentioned by Parkinson (*Paradisus* 1629) under the name of *Carduus esculentus* (Edible Thistle), and is said in *Treas. Bot.* to have been first cultivated in England in 1656.

1611 COTGR., *Means* . . spaces left for Cardoons betweene rowes of Onyons. *Ibid., Cardons*, Cardoones; the stalkes of Artichokes, or of the white thistle, buried in the ground, or otherwise vsed, to get them a whitenesse (excellent meat). **1640** PARKINSON *Theat. Bot.* 974 The Cretanes use their wilde Artichoke in the same manner that the Italians, Spaniards and French use their Cardui or Chardons. **1658** EVELYN *Fr. Gard.* (1675) 162 The Spanish chardons. **1796** C. MARSHALL *Garden* xx. (1813) 4 Blanch . . endive, beet, and chardons by tying. **1845** DARWIN *Voy. Nat.* vi. (1873) 119 Botanists are now generally agreed that the cardoon and the artichoke are varieties of one plant. **1882** MRS. REEVE *Cookery & Housek.* xxv. 325 *Cardoons*, this excellent vegetable is little known in England.

‖**carˈdophagus.** *nonce-wd.* Pl. -gi. [f. Gr. κάρδος (L. *carduus*) thistle + -φαγος -eater.] A thistle-eater, i.e. donkey.

1857 THACKERAY *Virgin.* xix. (D.) Kick and abuse him, you who have never brayed; but bear with him, all honest fellow-cardophagi.

†**carˈdoun.** *Obs.* [a. ONF. *cardon* = central F. *chardon* thistle = Pr. *cardó*, It. *cardone*, augm. of Romanic *cardo*:—L. *cardus, carduus* thistle: cf. CARDOON.] A thistle.

c **1425** *Voc.* in Wr.-Wülcker 645 *Cardo*, cardoun.

†**cardue.** *Obs.* [ad. L. *carduus*.] A thistle.

1388 WYCLIF *2 Kings* xiv. 9 The cardue, *that is a low eerbe and ful of thornes* [**1382** thistill], of the Liban sente to the cedre. —— *2 Chron.* xxv. 18 A cardue, *ether a tasil* [**1382** the thistil].

†ˈ**carduel.** *Obs.* [ad. L. *carduēlis*.] A goldfinch.

1572 BOSSEWELL *Armorie* III. 22 On a wreathe d'Or and Sable, a Carduell volante, beaked and legged Argente.

cardumome, obs. form of CARDAMOM.

†**cardus.** *Obs. rare*⁻¹.

1716 *Lond. Gaz.* No. 5481/4 The Pannel with red Cardus near the Crupper.

‖**carduus** (ˈkɑːdjuːəs). The Latin word for 'thistle', formerly sometimes used in Eng. as the name of the *Carduus benedictus* or Blessed Thistle; esp. *attrib.*, as in †*carduus posset*, †*water*.

1398 TREVISA *Barth. De P.R.* XVII. xxxvi. (1495) 625 Carduus ben thystels grete and smale. **1599** SHAKS. *Much Ado* III. iv. 73 Get you some of this distill'd carduus benedictus and lay it to your heart. *a* **1613** OVERBURY *A Wife* (1638) 204 He utters a most abominable deale of Carduus water. **1647** ASHMOLE *Diary* (1774) 305 Taking a carduus posset at night, and sweating upon it. **1789** W. BUCHAN *Dom. Med.* (1790) 677 *Infusion of Carduus.* Infuse an ounce of the dried leaves of carduus benedictus.

cardy (ˈkɑːdɪ). Also **cardi(e)**. Colloq. abbrev. of CARDIGAN.

1968 N. MARSH *Clutch of Constables* iv. 88 I'll just get my cardi. I won't be a tick. **1969** *Guardian* 3 Nov. 7/2 Grey gentlemen in shrunken cardies. **1970** *Sunday Times* 3 May 28/2 Midi dresses with brief tops . . matching midi cardis. **1981** *Daily Tel.* 29 Aug. 11/2 A flock of over-50s wearing pastel cardis and floppy hats. **1983** *Austral. Personal Computer* Nov. 6/4 The city is colder than you would believe. Even Santa Claus puts on an extra cardie when he visits. **1986** J. MILNE *Dead Birds* xix. 144 He wore his yellow cardy with the leather buttons.

cardyacle, cardynal: see CARDI-.

care (kɛə(r)), *sb.*¹ Forms: 1 caru, cearu, 2–4 kar(e, 4 car, 3– care. [Common Teut.: OE. *caru, cearu* = OS. *cara*, OHG. *chara*, MHG. *kar*, Goth. *kara*, trouble, grief, care, ON. *kör* (:—*karu*), gen. *karar*, bed of trouble or sickness :—OTeut. *karâ*-. (In no way related to L. *cura*.)]

†**1. a.** Mental suffering, sorrow, grief, trouble. *Obs.*

Beowulf 1303 (Gr.) Cearu wæs ȝeniwod ȝeworden in wicim. *c* **1250** *Hymn to God* 33 in *Trin. Coll. Hom.* 259 Bring us ut of wo and kare. *a* **1300** *Cursor M.* 3212 Sara . . deȝed . . and Abraham for hir hadde care. *Ibid.* 3612 þar i lig her now, in bedd o care [*Trin.* wo]. **1330** R. BRUNNE *Chron.* (Rolls) 3204 þys body ȝow bar wiþ wo & kare! *c* **1430** *Syr. Gener.* 7256 Comen he is to doo vs care. *c* **1440** *Promp. Parv.* 62 Care, *tristicia*. **15..** *Frere & Boye* 23 in Ritson *Anc. Pop. P.* 36 Euer she dyde the lytell boye care, As fer forth as she dorste. **1596** SPENSER *F.Q.* IV. viii. 5 Him to recomfort in his greatest care. **1648** HERRICK *Hesper., Sorrowes succeed*, When one is passed another care we have, Thus woe succeeds a woe. **1718** POPE *Iliad* XVII. 89 His words infix'd unutterable care Deep in great Hector's soul.

†**b.** Utterance of sorrow; lamentation, mourning. ***clothing of care***: mourning-dress. *Obs.*

a **1000** *Ags. Ps.* lxxviii. 11 Geonge for þe gnornendra care [*gemitus*]. *a* **1300** *Cursor M.* 10419 Sco tok on hir cleþing o care. *Ibid.* 10444, I se þe leuedi ma sli care.

2. Burdened state of mind arising from fear, doubt, or concern about anything; solicitude, anxiety, mental perturbation; also in *pl.* anxieties, solicitudes. †***withouten care***: without doubt. †***to be in care***: to be troubled, anxious, concerned.

c **1000** *Ags. Gosp.* Luke xxi. 34 On ofer-fylle and on druncennesse and þises lifes carum. *a* **1240** *Sawles Warde* in *Cott. Hom.* 255 Ich habbe þeruore sar care. *c* **1297** R. GLOUC. 457 Of þe erl of Chestre ȝe ne dorre abbe non care. *c* **1320** *Cast. Loue* 1509 O God hit is, wiþ-outen care, Of alle schaftes schuppare. **1362** LANGL. *P. Pl.* A. I. 170 þei beoþ cumbred in care · and cunnen not out-crepe. *c* **1420** *Sir Amadace* xxxi, Gode Sirs, haue ȝe no care. **1576** GASCOIGNE *Steel Gl.* (Arb.) 61 In my glasse . . I can perceive how kingdomes breed but care. **1593** SHAKS. *2 Hen. VI*, II. iv. 4 So Cares and Ioyes abound as Seasons fleet. **1682** N. O. *Boileau's Lutrin* IV. 332 Fretting Care, that kills a Cat! **1714** T. ELLWOOD *Autobiog.* (1765) 92, I was in care how to speak with some Friend about it. **1796–7** COLERIDGE *Poems* (1862) 2 The sorrow-clouded breast of Care. **1864** TENNYSON *En. Ard.* 222 Cast all your cares on God. **1884** *Illust. Lond. News* 27 Sept. 307/3 Black care who sits behind the horseman.

3. a. Serious or grave mental attention; the charging of the mind with anything; concern; heed, heedfulness, attention, regard; caution, pains.

c **1000** *Ags. Gosp.* Luke x. 40 Nis þe nan caru [**1160** care] þæt min swustur let me ænlipie þenian. **1548** UDALL, etc. *Erasm. Par. Matt.* xxvi. 116 Buryed with the busy care of a noble man. **1580** LYLY *Euphues* (Arb.) 320 Dost thou now commit Idolatrie with them with-out care? **1616** R. C. *Times' Whis.* v. 1673 Many . . only vse their care In dainty banquetes. **1697** DRYDEN *Virg. Georg.* IV. 791 His Mother's Precepts he performs with Care. **1742** POPE *Dunc.* IV. 431 Rose or carnation was below my care. **1828** SCOTT *F.M. Perth* (1860) Introd. 10 Mustaches which had lately been arranged with some care. **1847** TENNYSON *Princ.* Prol. 171 As a parrot turns . . And takes a lady's finger with all care.

b. Const. *of* (*arch.*), *for*, and *inf*. Here, and in c., the sense may pass, esp. in negative construction, to Regard arising from desire or estimation, liking, inclination *to* or *for*.

c **1400** *Destr. Troy* 427 Criste on the crosse for our care deghit. **1590** GREENE *Poems* (1861) 295 Care to live or sweet delight in life Draws me. **1623** LISLE *Ælfric on O. & N.T.* Judg., They worshipped the God of heaven with care of his commandements. **1651** HOBBES *Leviath.* I. xii. 52 Man, which looks too far before him, in the care of future time. **1705** I. NORRIS in *Pa. Hist. Soc. Mem.* X. 82 They stand in care of nobody's censure. **1850** TENNYSON *In Mem.* xxxviii, If any care for what is here Survive in spirits render'd free. **1863** GEO. ELIOT *Romola* I. (1880) Introd. 8 Public spirit . . its essence is care for a common good.

c. ***to have a care***, †***keep a care***, ***take care***.

1588 SHAKS. *L.L.L.* V. ii. 511 We will turne it finely off sir, we wil take some care. **1590** —— *Mids. N.* IV. i. 15 Good Mounsieur haue a care the hony bag breake not. **1596** —— *Tam. Shr.* I. i. 191 He tooke some care To get her cunning Schoolemasters to instruct her. **1610** —— *Temp.* II. i. 301 If of life you keep a care, Shake off slumber and beware. **1677** MOXON *Mech. Exerc.* (1703) 221 You must take great care, that the Solid Ball . . be . . exactly Spherical. **1697** DRYDEN *Virg. Georg.* IV. 160 Take a timely Care to bring the Truants back. **1819** BYRON *Juan* I. xiii, For native Spanish she had no great care. **1876** BLACK *Madcap V.* xviii. 161 'Have a care, Jack!' Peter called out.

4. a. Charge; oversight with a view to protection, preservation, or guidance. In the address of a letter or package '*care of* ——'. *in care of* (U.S.): = *care of*.

c **1400** *Destr. Troy* 6196 Noble knightes all, Vnder care of two kynges. **1560** BIBLE (Genev.) *2 Cor.* xi. 28, I . . have the care of all the Churches. **1647–8** COTTRELL *Davila's Hist. Fr.* (1678) 4 He left the Care of the whole Enterprize. **1710** PRIDEAUX *Orig. Tithes* ii. 67 Upon the Evangelical Priesthood . . is incumbent . . to take on them the Care of their Souls. **1841** LANE *Arab. Nts.* I. 99, I commend thee to the care of God. **1850** MRS. STOWE *Uncle Tom's C.* xxiii. 230 'I'll take her under my care.' **1852** DICKENS *Bleak Ho.*, Address to Nemo, care of Mr. Krook. **1875** JEVONS *Money* (1878) 207 The ship-master . . is obliged to retain the identical cases committed to his care. **1917** S. MERWIN *Temperamental Henry* 256 If you care to write a good-bye, address me in care of the ship. **1928** *N. & Q.* 4 Aug. 90 If owners of such letters will write to me in care of the Oxford University Press. **1967** *Boston Sunday Globe* 23 Apr. B. 63/7 Questions on home improvement and repair may be addressed to The House Doctor in care of this newspaper.

b. Hence ***to have the care of***, etc. ***to take care of***: to look after (see LOOK *v.* 12 f); to deal with, provide for, dispose of.

1579 TOMSON *Calvin's Serm. Tim.* 363/2 O Lorde . . I thanke thee, for that thou vouchsafest to haue care vppon so wretched a creature as I am. **1582** N. T. (Rhem.) *Luke* x. 32 [He] brought him into an Inne, and tooke care of him. **1611** BIBLE *Pref.* 2 It doth certainely belong vnto Kings to haue care of Religion. **1620** SHELTON *Quix.* III. xxxiii. 240, I desired this Waiting-woman to have a Care on him. **1711** ADDISON *Spect.* No. 37 ¶4 She has no Children to take care of. *a* **1724**, etc. [see PENNY 9 h]. **1747** LD. CHESTERFIELD *Let.* 6 Nov. (1932) III. 1051, I recommend to you to take care of minutes; for hours will take care of themselves. **1762** BOSWELL *London Jrnl.* 31 Dec. (1950) 113 She mentioned one consequence that in an affair of gallantry might be troublesome. . . 'Why, to be sure, if such a person should appear, he must be taken care of.' **1801** T. JEFFERSON *Let.* 18 Sept. in *Writings* (1897) VIII. 94 We are bound to take care of them. Could we not procure them as good berths as their former at least, in some of the custom-houses? **1816** JANE AUSTEN *Emma* II. xvi. 309 Young ladies should take care of themselves.—Young ladies are delicate plants. They should take care of their health and their complexion. **1847** TENNYSON *Princ.* iii. 69 She had the care of Lady Ida's youth. **1861** MILL *Repr. Govt.* ii. 22 Things left to take care of themselves inevitably decay. **1875** JOWETT *Plato* (ed. 2) I. 173 You take care of your money. **1925** *Ladies' Home Jrnl.* May 26/2 'Never mind, ma. I'll take care of them,' put in Edd. **1926** *Publishers' Weekly* 22 May 1709/2 Such an information desk should take care of all inquiries regarding books and reading. **1930** *Ibid.* 31 May 2728 The budget . . was not sufficient to take care of the increasing expenses. **1931** H. F. PRINGLE *Theodore Roosevelt* I. xiv. 198 He . . found himself besieged with petitions for jobs . . . It was impossible to take care of all of them. **1932** *Atlantic Monthly* Apr. 421/2 Money . . which would enable him to take care of all arrears on the property. **1959** *Listener* 9 Apr. 628/1 That little problem had been taken care of.

c. (***in need of***) ***care or*** (also ***and***) ***protection***, a legal formula (see quot. 1933) used of a destitute or dangerously circumstanced child who is judged fit for official guardianship; also *attrib.*, as ***care or (and) protection order***, one by which a magistrate effects such guardianship; also *ellipt.*, as ***care order***; ***in care***, under official guardianship.

1932 *Act 22 & 23 Geo. V* c. 46 §9 (*heading*) Juveniles in need of Care or Protection. **1933** *Act 23 Geo. V* c. 12 §61 For the purposes of this Act a child or young person in need of care or protection means a person who is (a) a child . . who, having no parent or guardian . ., is either falling into bad associations, or exposed to moral danger, or beyond control; or (b) a child . . in respect of whom any of the offences mentioned in . . this Act has been committed; [etc.]. **1944** A. E. IKIN *Education Act 1944* 102 Children and young persons in need of care and protection. **1948** *Act 11 & 12 Geo. VI* c. 43 §10 (*heading*) Duty of parents to maintain contact with local authorities having their children in care. **1969** *Listener* 15 May 666/1 The family . . ends with the father in lodgings and the mother and children in a hostel (and frequently some children in care). **1969** *Children & Young Persons Act*

17 & 18 Eliz. II c. 54 §20 (1) Any provision of this Act authorising the making of a care order in respect of any person shall be construed as authorising the making of an order committing him to the care of a local authority. **1985** *Daily Tel.* 30 Apr. 3/1 On August 17 an interim care order was made, and at a case conference three days later it was decided to place the children with foster parents.

5. a. An object or matter of care, concern, or solicitude.

1590 SPENSER *F.Q.* II. x. 37 Gathered the Princes..To taken counsell of their common cares. **1634** BP. HALL *Occas. Med.* §123 The main care of any creature is self-preservation. **1732** BERKELEY *Alciphr.* I. §1. **1750** GRAY *Elegy* vi, Or busy housewife ply her evening care. **1812** BYRON *Ch. Har.* I. ix, Pomp and power alone are woman's care. **1855** TENNYSON *To Maurice*, Come, when no graver cares employ. **1875** JOWETT *Plato* (ed. 2) I. 298 He could not himself spare the time from cares of state.

b. of persons and things. Cf. '*youthful charge*'.

1697 DRYDEN *Virg. Past.* II. 59 Come to my longing Arms, my lovely Care. **1704** POPE *Messiah* 49 The good shepherd tends his fleecy care. **1735** SOMERVILLE *Chase* II. 465 Each watchful Eye Fix'd on his youthful Care. **1863** AYTOUN in *Tales fr. Blackwood* IX. 39 Wintry frosts shall never see The rose that is my care!

6. *Comb.* **a.** attrib., as ***care-line***, ***-wrinkle***; **care-and-maintenance** *attrib.*, describing a building, area, etc., maintained in good condition though not in present use; **care-bed**, a bed of suffering or grief; **care-committee**, a committee which charges itself with the care of the poor; **care-labelling**, the securing of labels on clothes and fabrics, giving advice about cleaning and ironing processes; so ***care-label***; †**care-weed**, mourning attire. **b.** objective, (*a*) with pr. pples. forming adjs., as ***care-bewitching***, ***-bringing***, ***-charming***, ***-defying***, ***-drowning***, ***-eluding***; (*b*) with vbl. sbs. or agent-nouns forming sbs., as ***care-charmer***, ***-killing***, etc.; **c.** instrumental, as ***care-accloyed***, ***-crazed***, ***-crossed***, ***-encumbered***, ***-fraught***, ***-laden***, ***-lined***, ***-pined***, ***-scorched***, ***-tired***, ***-tuned***, ***-untroubled***, ***-wounded***, etc., and esp. **care-worn**. Also CARE-TAKER, -TAKING, etc.

1596 FITZ-GEFFREY *Sir F. Drake* (1881) 81 Poore *care-accloyed pilgrime traveler. **1930** *Economist* 13 Sept. 475/1 Once estates are put on to a '*care and maintenance' basis, it will take a considerable increase in price to bring them back into production. **1958** *Times Rev. Industry* Aug. 40/2 Two former..sites (one of which had been kept on a partial care-and-maintenance basis) were reopened. *a* **1400** *Sir Perc.* lxvii, The kyng to *Carebedd es gane. **1768** ROSS *Helenore* 56 (Jam.) In care-bed lair for three lang hours she lay. **1645** QUARLES *Sol. Recant.* vii. 5 *Care-bewitching sweets. **1597** DRAYTON *Mortimer.* 72 Prest with a *care-bringing Crowne. **1592** DANIEL *Delia* Wks. (1717) 415 *Care-Charmer Sleep, Son of the sable Night. **1908** *Times* 3 Feb. 11/5 He had been told to devote the whole of his time to assisting the *Care Committee. **1909** M. FRERE *Children's Care Committees* 35 In 1902 the name [*sc.* Charitable Funds Committee] was changed to Children's Relief Committee, and finally, in 1908, to Children's Care Committee. **1931** W. HOLTBY *Poor Caroline* v. 157 He schooled his..sense of humour to docility in the face of care committees and church workers. **1594** SHAKS. *Rich. III*, III. vii. 184 A *care-crazed mother of a many sonnes. **1876** M. ARNOLD *Lit. & Dogma* 249 *Care-crossed, toil-stained millions. **1802** LAMB *Corr.* cxliii. (1870) 376 *Care-drowning night. **1730** THOMSON *Autumn* 605 With every gentle *care-eluding art. **1841-6** LONGF. *Bridge* xii, Thousands of *care-encumbered men. **1835** WILLIS *Pencillings* II. lvii. 140 Their *care-fraught profession. **1962** *Rep. Comm. Consumer Protection* 39 in *Parl. Papers 1961-62* (Cmnd. 1781) XII. 317 The next topic we explored in relation to clothing and textiles was the very important subject of *care-labelling. **1967** *Spectator* 1 Dec. 682/1 The most recent spot check by *Which*? found that only two thirds of garments had care labels of any kind. **1880** BURTON *Q. Anne* III. xiv. 11 Whispers and *care-laden looks. **1603** DEKKER *Grissill* Wks. 1886 V. 115 Coy dames, who..Fly the *care-pined hearts that sue to them. **1610** *Histriom.* III. 68 Cast water on the *care-scorcht face. **1593** SHAKS. *Rich. II*, III. ii. 92 My *care-tun'd tongue. **1611** A. STAFFORD *Niobe* II. 241 (T.) [The nightingale] begins to carol out her care-tuned musick. **1794** BURNS *Wks.* IV. 279 *Care-Untroubl'd, joy-surrounded. *c* **1500** DUNBAR *Tua Mariit Wem.* 422, I go to the kirk, cled in *cair weid. **1828** CARLYLE *Misc.* (1857) I. 219 His *careworn heart. **1856** DICKENS *Lett.* (1880) I. 443 A face too careworn for her years. **1882** *Three in Norway* xix. 149 We met a very careworn-looking man. **1627** MAY *Lucan* v. (T.) Cornelia, his *care-wounded breast clasping.

†**care**, *sb.*[2] *Obs.* Some kind of stuff. (Perh. the same word as CARY.)

1429 *Test. Ebor.* (1836) I. 420 A russet cloke, lynd w^{t} care aboute ye schuldyrs. *a* **1440** *Sir Eglam.* lxxi, Thys lady was in care cladd.

care (kɛə(r)), *sb.*[3] The name for the Mountain Ash, in the south-west of England.

1849 KINGSLEY in *Life* I. 173 (D.) Of old Dartmoor was a forest..its hill-sides clothed with birch, oak, and 'care'. **1880** *W. Cornw. Gloss.* (E.D.S.) *Care*, the mountain ash.

care (kɛə(r)), *v.* Forms: 1 **carian, cearian**, 2-3 **carien**, 3-4 **car, kar**, 4- **care**. [Com. Teut.: OE. *carian* = OS. *carôn*, OHG. *charôn*, *-ên*, MHG. *caren*, *karn*, Goth. *karôn*:—OTeut. **karôjan* to mourn, sorrow, have trouble, trouble oneself, f. **karâ-* CARE *sb.*[1]]

†**1. a.** To sorrow or grieve. *Obs.*

a **1000** *Crist* 277 (Gr.) Hwæt bemurnest ðu cearizende. *a* **1175** *Cott. Hom.* 243 þa cearodon þa sunder halʒan. *c* **1230** *Hali Meid.* 27 Moni þing schal ham wraððen..ant makie to carien. **1350** *Will. Palerne* 3182 Whi carestow? sede þe quene. *c* **1400** *Pol. Poems* (1859) II. 4 The lond..for defalte of help hath longe cared. **1530** PALSGR. 475/1, I care for his losses, *Je me chagrine de ses pertes.*

†**b.** To mourn, lament. *Obs.*

a **1300** *Cursor M.* 3212 Sarra..deid..and abraham can for hir car. *c* **1386** CHAUCER *Clerkes T.* 1156 Lat hym care and wepe and wryng and waille.

2. †**a.** To be troubled, uneasy, or anxious (*obs.*).

b. To feel concern (great or little), be concerned, trouble oneself, feel interest. Also in colloq. phrases expressing or implying lack of interest or concern: ***for all I care***, ***see if I care***, ***who cares?***

Beowulf 1536 Na [man] ymb his lif cearað. *a* **1225** *Ancr. R.* 48 Sore mei anoðer of hire fluht carien. *c* **1300** *Beket* 1573 Ich wole sigge..whi ich carie so. *c* **1340** *Cursor M.* 11675 (Fairf.), I care mare for a-noþer þing. *c* **1460** *Towneley Myst.* 88 (Mätz) Ye nede not to care if ye folow my sawe. **1535** COVERDALE *1 Sam.* ix. 20 As for the Asses..care not thou for them for they are founde. **1593** SHAKS. *2 Hen. VI*, III. i. 173 Those that care to keepe your royall Person. **1611** BIBLE *2 Sam.* xviii. 3 Neither if halfe of vs die will they care for vs. **1844** 'J. SLICK' *High Life N.Y.* I. vi. 68, I didn't exactly like the feel of it, but 'Who cares', sez I to myself. **1856** FROUDE *Hist. Eng.* (1858) I. v. 421 He cared only..for his own interests. **1856** *Harper's Mag.* Sept. 561/2 Who cares? **1861** FABER *Hymn*, '*Sweet Saviour*,' Labour is sweet, for Thou hast toiled; And care is light, for Thou hast cared. **1931** *Maclean's Mag.* 15 Dec. 24/2 'I'll be killed,' the man gasped. 'Who cares?' was the brutal reply. **1934** J. HILTON *Goodbye Mr. Chips!* viii. 55 You can go to blazes for all I care. **1947** V. M. AXLINE *Play Therapy* 356 Fall on the floor, damn you! See if I care.

c. To be careful, to take care. Now only *dial.*

a **1593** H. SMITH *Serm.* (1637) 302 It is not enough to heare but you must care how you heare; it is not enough to pray, but you must care how you pray. *Ibid.* (1866) II. 47 Let them which are down care to rise. **1883** *Harper's Mag.* Jan. 200/2 Unless a man cares to fall her right, she'll break all up.

3. *to care for*: to take thought for, provide for, look after, take care of. Also with *indirect pass.*

c **1230** *Hali Meid.* 5 He wile carien for hire. **1377** LANGL. *P. Pl.* B. II. 161 þanne cared þei for caplus to kairen hem þider. **1535** COVERDALE *Ps.* xxxix. 17, I am poore & in mysery, but the Lorde careth for me. **1607** SHAKS. *Cor.* I. i. 79 Who care for you like Fathers? **1676** HALE *Contempl.* I. 183 He careth for us that knows what is fittest for us. **1858** GEO. ELIOT *Sc. Cleric. Life*, *Janet's Rep.* xxv. 318 Infinite Love was caring for her. **1887** *Manch. Guard.* 14 Apr. 7 The child had..been well cared for.

4. In negative and conditional construction: **a.** ***not to care*** passes from the notion of 'not to trouble oneself', to those of 'not to mind, not to regard or pay any deference or attention, to pay no respect, be indifferent'. Const. *for*, etc.

c **1489** CAXTON *Sonnes of Aymon* vi. 139, I departed fro my londe poure & exyled but I dyd not care for it. **1535** COVERDALE *Matt.* xxii. 16 Master we knowe that thou..carest for no man. **1596** SPENSER *F.Q.* II. ii. 18 Ne ought he car'd whom he endamaged By tortious wrong. **1610** SHAKS. *Temp.* I. i. 18 What cares these roarers for the name of King? **1633** P. FLETCHER *Pisc. Ecl.* v. 28 Full little caren they To make their milkie mothers bleating stay. **1711** STEELE *Spect.* No. 145 ¶4 The young Man is rich, and, as the Vulgar say, needs not care for any body. **1748** THOMSON *Cast. Indol.* II. iii, I care not, Fortune, what you me deny. *a* **1774** GOLDSM. *Hist. Greece* II. 61 This important pass, which Philip did not care attempting to force. **1816** J. WILSON *City of Plague* II. iv. 174 In thy embrace what do I care for death. **1871** MORLEY *Voltaire* (1878) 3 Men had almost ceased to care whether there be any moral order or not. **1875** JOWETT *Plato* (ed. 2) III. 13 Cephalus appears not to care about riches. **1883** LLOYD *Ebb & Fl.* I. 18, I don't care what people say.

(*a*) with some strengthening word, as ***a pin***, ***a button***, ***a straw***, ***a rush***, ***a fig***, ***a farthing***, ***a rap***, etc.

1590 SPENSER *F.Q.* I. ii. 12 He..cared not for God or man a point. **1633** MARMYON *Fine Compan.* II. i. 68, I do not care a pin for her. **1709** STEELE *Tatler* No. 50, I do not care a farthing for you. **1760** GOLDSM. *Cit. W.* xlvi, Not that I care three damns what figure I may cut. **1828** *Thaumaturgus* 23 If for the truth you care a button. **1856** R. VAUGHAN *Mystics* (1860) I. 4 A subject..for which not ten of your friends care a straw. **1876** GEO. ELIOT *Dan. Der.* 236, I don't care a toss where you are. *Ibid.* 211 You suppose I care a damn for that? **1880** SPURGEON *Treas. Dav.* II. 4 Pharisees care not a fig for the Lord's hearing them.

(*b*) Sc. ***to care na by***: not to care about (it).

1788 E. PICKEN *Poems* I. 189 (Jam.) Alake, she cared na by. *a* **1796** BURNS *My Nannie O.* viii, Come weal, come woe, I care na by.

(*c*) Colloq. phr. (*I*, etc.) ***couldn't care less***: (I am, etc.) completely uninterested, utterly indifferent; freq. as phr. used *attrib.* Hence ***couldn't-care-less-ness***.

1946 A. PHELPS (*title*) 'I couldn't care less.' **1947** B. MARSHALL *Red Danube* vi. 53 The couldn't-care-less boys, the chaps who imagined that now that the war was over there was no need for further effort. **1947** *People* 22 June 2/4 If I suggest that it should be good because the book was by a top-line author she simply couldn't care less. **1955** *Essays in Criticism* V. 76 Exhibiting a vulgar couldn't-carelessness. **1957** F. H. KING *Man on Rock* iv. 120 The phrase he most used was 'I couldn't care less': which seemed to sum up his character. **1965** *Times Lit Suppl.* 25 Nov. 1083/1 The couldn't-care-less attitude of people with little to lose.

(*d*) U.S. colloq. phr. (*I*, etc.) ***could care less*** = sense (*c*) above, with omission of negative.

1966 *Seattle Post-Intelligencer* 1 Nov. 21/2 My husband is a lethargic, indecisive guy who drifts along from day to day. If a bill doesn't get paid he could care less. **1973** *Washington Post* 5 Jan. B1/1 A few crusty-souled Republican senators who could care less about symbolic rewards. **1978** J. CARROLL *Mortal Friends* III. iii. 281 'I hate sneaking past your servants in the morning.' 'They know, anyway. They could care less. Thornton mistreats them horribly.'

b. Not to mind (something proposed); to have no disinclination or objection, be disposed *to*. Now only with *if*, *though*.

1526 *Pilgr. Perf.* (W. de W. 1531) 18 Some for a fewe tythes, with Cayn, careth not to lese the eternall rychesse of heuen. *c* **1590** MARLOWE *Dido* IV. v, So you'll love me, I care not if I do. **1597** SHAKS. *2 Hen. IV*, I. ii. 142, I care not if I be your Physitian. **1611** FLORIO, *Scrócca il fuso*..a light-heeled trull that cares not to horne hir husband. **1646** ROW *Hist. Kirk* (1842) 324 We care not to lett you see what we wrot up to the King. **1748** RICHARDSON *Clarissa* (1811) V. 265 Will you eat, or drink, friend?.. I dont care if I do. **1841** GRESLEY *C. Lever* 58, I don't care if I go with you for once.

5. To have a regard or liking for. Orig. only in neg. or interrog. constructions ('not to regard' as in 4 a); now also in affirmative, but usually as the alternative or negative of an implied negation.

a. To have a regard, liking, or inclination *for* (a thing); to be inclined or disposed *to*, to think it worth while *to do*.

1560 A. L. tr. *Calvin's Foure Serm.* iii. (R.) He cared for nothing more then that kynde of lyfe. **1631** GOUGE *God's Arrows* III. §4. 189 Malice..onely careth to satisfie its owne venomous humour. **1697** DAMPIER *Voy.* I. ix. 275 We..baked of these Roots..but none of us greatly cared for them. **1762** GOLDSM. *Nash* 12 He never cared to give money. **1868** J. H. BLUNT *Ref. Ch. Eng.* I. 98 Few cared for reformation; many cared for destruction. **1875** JOWETT *Plato* (ed. 2) III. 511 They become rulers in their own city if they care to be. **1883** H. WACE *Gospel & Witn.* ii. 36 The main positions for which a Christian writer cares to contend.

b. To have regard, fondness, or attachment *for* (a person).

c **1530** LD. BERNERS *Arth. Lyt. Bryt.* (1814) 244, I care not for hym that is ayenst my heart. **1590** LODGE *Euphues Gold. Leg.* (1887) 163 Creep not to her that cares not for thee. **1657** R. LIGON *Barbadoes* 47 He never car'd much for her afterward. **1750** LADY HERVEY in *Bk. of Days* II. 299, I dread to see people I care for quite easy and happy. **1878** MRS. WOOD *Pomeroy Ab.* I. vi. 93 She was sure she cared for the lord at heart.

6. *trans.* in various senses: †**a.** To cause care to, trouble (*obs.*). †**b.** To care for, regard (*obs.*). **c.** To take care of, guard, preserve with care (*dial.*).

[*c* **1230** *Hali Meid.* 29 Lutel þarf þe carien for þin anes liueneð.] *c* **1386** CHAUCER *Miller's T.* 112 Nay ther of care thee noght quod Nicholas. *c* **1420** *Iudicium* (1822) 13 The day is comen of Catyfnes all those to care that ar uncleyn. *c* **1565** LINDESAY Pitscottie *Chron.* 301 (Jam.) He cares you not in his just quarrell. **1612** JAS. I in Ellis *Orig. Lett.* I. 266 III. 106 Ye littill care youre olde freindis. **1628** FELTHAM *Resolves* I. 76 (L.) Care them [jewels] up, and wear them but on festivals. **1881** MRS. P. O'DONOGHUE *Ladies on Horseb.* vi. 84 If you care your things..it is surprising how long they may be made to serve.

care, var. of CHARE, *Obs.*

careage (see quot.). [? for CARUAGE.]

1704 WORLIDGE *Dict. Rust. et Urb.*, *Careage* is a term sometime used in Agriculture, and signifies the Ploughing of Ground, either ordinary; or extraordinary. **1727** so in BRADLEY *Fam. Dict.*

careatides: see CARYATID.

†**care-away**, *phr.* and *sb.* *Obs.*

a. An exclamation of merriment or recklessness; 'care begone! away with care!' Hence, a reckless fellow, roisterer. **b.** Something that drives away care (with a pun on *caraway*, quot. 1633).

1440 *Promp. Parv.* 61 Care-awey, sorowles, *tristicia procul.* **1471** RIPLEY *Comp. Alch.* v. xxxvi. in Ashm. (1652) 157 Hay hoe, careaway, lat the cup go rounde. **1575** NEWTON tr. *Lemnie's Complex.* 99 (D.) Wanton yonkers and wilfull Careawayes. **1588** FRAUNCE *Lawiers Log.* I. xix. 71 b, False forsworne knaves, desperate careawaies. *c* **1633** T. ADAMS *Wks.* (1862) II. 466 (D.) If worldly troubles come too fast upon a man, he hath a herb called care-away.

careck(e, carect, careke, obs. ff. CARRACK.

†'**care-cloth**. *Obs.* exc. *Hist.* Also 6 **carke-cloth**. [Etymology uncertain:

Palsgrave's 'carde, clothe (? read *carde-clothe*) for brides' seems to be the same word, and, if not merely a blunder, would seem to point to identity of the first element with CARDE. Some have conjectured F. *carre* sb. or *carré* adj., square; the word can hardly be CARE *sb.*[1], though that sense has been played on.]

A cloth formerly held over (or placed upon) the heads of the bride and bridegroom as they knelt during the marriage-service.

Cf. med.L. *jugalis*, for which Du Cange quotes an example of 4th c., showing that it denoted a cloth placed upon the head of the bride and the shoulders of the bridegroom.

1530 PALSGR. 203/1 Carde, clothe for brides: they [*i.e.* the French] use none. **1534** in PEACOCK *Eng. Ch. Furnit.* (1866) 204 A care cloth of silke dornex. **1550** in *Surrey Ch. Goods* (1869) 42 A care cloth of silk. **1552** *Ibid.* 12 Item a carke clothe. *Ibid.* 63 Item on lynyn care cloth. **1559** FABYAN VII. 716 Thei cam foorthe, and kneled before the altare all the masse tyme, and the care clothe was holden. **1624** W. WHATELEY (*title*) A Care-Cloth, or a Treatise of the Cumbers and Troubles of Matrimony. **1878** ROCK *Text. Fabr.* 72 The care cloth was a sort of canopy held over the bride and bridegroom as they knelt for the nuptial blessing.

cared (kɛəd), *ppl. a.* [f. CARE *v.* + -ED[1].] In comb. with prep., as *cared-for*, attended to, looked after; liked.

1901 *Westm. Gaz.* 7 May 2/1 Never may we have to see any cared-for play therein produced. **1911** *Rep. Labour & Social Condit. Germany* VI–VII. 190 The..cared for appearance of the children. **1924** R. MACAULAY *Orphan Island* xviii, He..had a cared-for looking white skin.

careen (kəˈriːn), *sb. Naut.* Also 6–7 carine, 7 carene, careene, 8 creen. [a. F. *carène* fem., keel, in phrases such as *en carène* = 'on the careen', helped by the use of the verb.]

1. The position of a ship laid or heeled over on one side. *on (upon) the careen*: turned over on one side for repairing, or by stress of weather, etc.

1591 *Hon. Actions E. Glemham*, Which compeld them to lie vpon the carine, to stop their leakes. **1627** CAPT. SMITH *Seaman's Gram.* ii. 13 Breaming her..either in a dry dock or vpon her Careene. *c***1645** HOWELL *Lett.* I. I. xxviii, Many Gallies, and Galeasses..either in Cours, at Anchor, in Dock, or upon the Carine. **1651** —— *Venice* 36 She hath bin so often trimmd, putt upon the Carine, and metamorphosed. **1678** *Lond. Gaz.* No. 1359/4 The Algierine..had so great a hole made in her, that [s]he was brought to her Carene. **1707** *Ibid.* No. 4380/2 We saw him on the Careen [from being struck between wind and water]. **1769** FALCONER *Dict. Marine* (1789) Liij b, When a ship is laid on a careen, every thing is taken out of her. **1798** *Naval Chron.* (1799) I. 171 A broadside, which laid him on a creen. **1836** MARRYAT *Pirate* iii, The [ship] righted from her careen.

2. The process of careening: see the vb.

1712 W. ROGERS *Voy.* (1718) 217 The Dutchess began to make ready for a careen.

3. A careening over. (See the vb. 4.)

1880 L. WALLACE *Ben-Hur* I. i. 6 The charm [of the camel] is not..in the movement, the noiseless stepping, or the broad careen.

careen (kəˈriːn), *v. Naut.* Forms: 6–7 carene, 7 carine, (careene, carreene, caren, carrine, 7–8 carreen, 8 creen), 7– careen. [corresponds to mod.F. *caréner*, earlier *cariner*, Sp. *carenar*, It. *carenare*, f. F. *carène*, Sp. or It. *carena* keel:—L. *carīna* keel.

(The precise source of the vb. does not appear; it may even have been f. the sb.: the Fr., Sp., It. verb is not in Cotgr., Minsheu, Florio.)]

1. a. *trans.* To turn (a ship) over on one side for cleaning, caulking, or repairing; to clean, caulk, etc. (a ship so turned over).

1600 HAKLUYT *Voy.* (1810) III, A fit place to carene the ship. **1628** DIGBY *Voy. Medit.* (1868) 56 To stay att Milo to carine and fitt her. **1682** WHELER *Journ. Greece* I. 28 A Fountain of Pitch..with which they caren Vessels. **1687** B. RANDOLPH *Archipel.* 11 To carine his ship. **1747** *Col. Records Penn.* V. 71 His Sloop cou'd not go to Sea without being Careen'd. **1849** W. IRVING *Columbus* III. 25 Finding a convenient harbor..he unloaded and careened his vessels. *fig.* **1763** H. WALPOLE *Corr.* (1837) II. 189 After an Irish voyage I do not wonder you want careening.

†**b.** *transf.* Humorously *to careen a wig.*

1675 *Character Town Gallant* 5 He..pulls out his Comb, Carreens his Wigg. **1702** *Eng. Theophrast.* 53 He [the beau] is two long hours careening his wig. **1702** *Poet Banter'd* 48 Swiming Line careend with Flies.

2. a. *absol.*

1697 DAMPIER *Voy.* I. xvi. 443 A fine small Cove..fit to Careen in. **1790** BEATSON *Nav. & Mil. Mem.* I. 227 The Commodore..informed the Captains, that his orders were ..to careen, and refit. **1821** BYRON *Juan* III. xx, He left his ship..With orders to the people to careen.
fig. **1737** M. GREEN *Spleen* (1807) 173 Once in seven years I'm seen At Bath or Tunbridge, to careen. **1874** *Sat. Rev.* 19 Jan. (Hoppe) We got him safe to Eskmount..There he is at present, careening, and the ladies take the best care possible of him.

b. *intr.* for *pass.* Said of the ship itself.

1667 *Lond. Gaz.* No. 145/3 Some that were driven to shore, were since forced to unlade and Carine. **1670** MARVELL *Let. Mayor Hull* Wks. I. 155 Liberty for our ships to careen and victual in any of his ports. **1720** *Lond Gaz.* No. 5827/1 The Barfleur..is now carreening.

3. *trans.* To cause (a ship) to heel over.

1833 M. SCOTT *Tom Cringle* xii. (1859) 281 Do you mean to careen the ship that you have all run to the starboard side? **1836** MARRYAT *Pirate* xi, The heavy blows of the seas upon the sides of the vessel careened and shook her.

4. a. *intr.* 'A ship is said to careen when she inclines to one side, or lies over when sailing on a wind' (Smyth *Sailor's Word-bk.*).

*a***1763** SHENSTONE *Love & Hon.* 99 The fleet careen'd, the wind propitious fill'd The swelling sails. **1762** FALCONER *Shipwr.* II. 32 Careening as if never more to right. **1863** DICEY *Federal St.* I. 4 The ship staggered, careened, and reeled, as wave after wave came thundering on her. **1883** G. C. DAVIES *Norfolk Broads* ix. 76 If the wind is strong then the yachts careen over to the very verge of safety.

b. *transf.* To lean over; to tilt.

1883 G. MEREDITH *Poems* 157 Now his huge bulk o'er Africa careened. **1895** CONRAD *Almayer's Folly* xii. 260 The big office desk, with one of its legs broken, careened over like the hull of a stranded ship. **1920** C. H. STAGG *High Speed* (ed. 2) ix. 152 A hundred times their throats choked as the car careened on a bank. *Ibid.* xiv. 251 The car should have careened until it almost turtled. *Ibid.* xv. 272 A sickening skid,..a careening lurch that brought a cry from Dan. **1938** *British Birds* XXXI. 333 The bird was careening from side to side as though there were waves.

5. [Influenced by CAREER *v.* 2.] To rush headlong, to hurtle, esp. with an unsteady motion. Chiefly *U.S.*

Quot. 1925 may belong to sense 4 b.

1923 [see CRUISER 2]. **1925** T. DREISER *Amer. Tragedy* (1926) II. xxiii. 312 There came a contact..which set his thoughts careening in an entirely different direction. **1928** F. HURST *President is Born* xiii. 146 With terrible, terrifying, careening strides, that zigzagged crazily. *Ibid.* xxxi. 315 The tears jetted and careened down to her lips. **1940** *Amer. Speech* XV. 72 *Careen* of recent years has come to mean 'to rush headlong', or 'hurtle', doubtless because of its resemblance to *career*. **1957** H. ROOSENBURG *Walls came tumbling Down* iv. 91 A lot of Russians careening along the road on liberated bicycles. **1965** H. GOLD *Man who was not with It* (1965) v. 46 A shrill cry careened down the street.

careenage (kəˈriːnɪdʒ). [f. CAREEN *v.* + -AGE; cf. F. *carénage.*] **a.** The careening of a ship; *ellipt.* the expense of this. **b.** A careening-place (cf. *anchorage*).

In sense b the Fr. *carénage* is much used, esp. in W. Indies, and parts of N. America.

1794 SIR J. JERVIS in *Naval. Chron.* X. 462 The Asia and Zebra were appointed..to enter the careenage. **1829** *Lond. Encycl.* V. 161 Careenage is the place where the operation is performed, and also the money given for careening. **1841** ORDERSON *Creoleana* v. 45 The whole line of the carenage being..one continuous sloping bank of slime.
attrib. **1877** KINGLAKE *Crimea* V. ii. 372 [He] crossed the Careenage Ravine.

caˈreening, *vbl. sb.* [f. as prec. + -ING[1].] The action of the verb CAREEN.

1668 in WILKINS *Real. Char.* 283. **1692** in *Capt. Smith's Seaman's Gram.* xvi. 76 *Careening*, is bringing a Ship to lye down on one side while they trim and caulk the other. **1833** BREWSTER *Nat. Magic.* vi. 141 They were greatly heeled-to on one side, or in the position called careening.
attrib. **1697** DAMPIER *Voy.* I. iii. 38 A good careening place. **1790** BEATSON *Nav. & Mil. Mem.* II. 52 The careening-wharfs, etc. are entirely decayed.

career (kəˈrɪə(r)), *sb.* Forms: 6–7 carriere, careere, (6 carire, -eire, carrire), 6–8 carier(e, carrier, -eer, 7 carrere, carere, (carrear, -eere, -eir, careir), 6– career. [a. F. *carrière* racecourse; also career, in various senses; = It., Pr. *carriera*, Sp. *carrera* road, carrer:—late L. *carrāria* (*via*) carriage-road, road, f. *carr-us* wagon.

The normal Central Fr. repr. of late L. *carraria* is OF. *charriere*, still usual in the dialects; it is not clear whether *carrière* is northern, or influenced by It. or Pr.]

†**1. a.** The ground on which a race is run, a racecourse; also, the space within the barrier at a tournament. **b.** *transf.* The course over which any person or thing passes; road, path way. *Obs.*

1580 SIDNEY *Arcadia* (1622) 286 It was fit for him to go to the other end of the Career. **1642** HOWELL *For. Trav.* (Arb.) 46 In the carrere to Her mines. *a***1649** DRUMM. OF HAWTH. *Poems* Wks. (1711) 6 Rowse Memmon's mother..That she thy [Phœbus'] career may with roses spread. **1651** HOWELL *Venice* 39 Since the Portuguais found out the carreer to the East Indies by the Cape of Good Hope. **1751** CHAMBERS *Cycl.*, *Career*, or *Carier*, in the manage, a place inclosed with a barrier, wherein they run the ring.

†**2. a.** Of a horse: A short gallop at full speed (often in phr. *to pass a career*). Also a charge, encounter (at a tournament or in battle). *Obs.*

1571 HANMER *Chron. Irel.* (1633) 139 Seven tall men.. made sundry Carreers and brave Turnaments. **1591** HARINGTON *Orl. Fur.* xxxviii. 35 (N.) To stop, to start, to pass carier. **1598** BARRET *Theor. Warres* v. ii. 142 The Lanciers..ought to know how to manage well a horse, run a good carrier, etc. **1617** MARKHAM *Caval.* II. 203 To passe a Cariere, is but to runne with strength and courage such a conuenient course as is meete for his ability. **1667** MILTON *P.L.* I. 766 Mortal combat or carreer with Lance. **1751** CHAMBERS *Cycl.*, *Career*..is also used for the race, or course of the horse itself, provided it do not exceed two hundred paces. **1764** HARMER *Observ.* XXVII. vi. 284 Horses..walking in state and running in full career.

†**b.** 'The short turning of a nimble horse, now this way, nowe that way' (Baret *Alvearie*); *transf.* a frisk, gambol. *Obs.*

1577 HOLINSHED *Chron.* III. 809/1 Manie a horsse raised on high with carrier, gallop, turne, and stop. **1594** *2nd Rep. Faustus* in Thoms *Pr. Rom.* (1858) III. 338 Careers and gambalds. **1599** SHAKS. *Hen. V*, II. i. 132 The king is a good king, but..he passes some humors, and carreeres.

3. a. By extension: A running, course (usually implying swift motion); formerly [like Fr. *carrière*] applied *spec.* to the course of the sun or a star through the heavens. Also *abstr.* Full speed, impetus: chiefly in phrases like ***in full career***, †***to take, give (oneself or some thing) career***, etc., which were originally terms of horsemanship (see 2).

*c***1534** tr. *Pol. Verg. Eng. Hist.* (1846) I. 55 Theie..tooke privilie there carier abowte, and violentlie assailed the tents of there adversaries. **1591** SPENSER *Ruins Time* xvi, As ye see fell Boreas..To stop his wearie cáriere suddenly. **1626** T. H. *Caussin's Holy Crt.* 31 Dolphins..leape and bound with full carrere in the tumultuous waues. **1667** MILTON *P.L.* IV. 353 The Sun..was hasting now with prone carreer To th' Ocean Iles. *a***1677** BARROW *Serm.* Wks. 1716 III. 35 Sooner may we..stop the Sun in his carriere. **1762** FALCONER *Shipwr.* II. 258 Vast torrents force a terrible career. **1810** SCOTT *Lady of L.* III. xiii, Stretch onward on thy fleet career! **1863** MARY HOWITT tr. *F. Bremer's Greece* II. xvi. 137 Away we went in full career with the waves and the wind.

b. *Hawking.* (See quot.)

1727–51 CHAMBERS *Cycl.*, *Career*, in falconry, is a flight or tour of the bird, about one hundred and twenty yards.

4. *fig.* (from 2 and 3) Rapid and continuous 'course of action, uninterrupted procedure' (J.); formerly also, The height, 'full swing' of a person's activity.

1599 SHAKS. *Much Ado* II. iii. 250 Shall quips and sentences..awe a man from the careere of his humour? **1611** —— *Wint. T.* I. ii. 286 Stopping the Cariere Of Laughter, with a sigh. **1603** FLORIO *Montaigne* I. ix. (1632) 15 He takes a hundred times more cariere and libertie unto himselfe, than hee did for others. **1643** W. BURTON *Beloved City* 57 Antichrist, in the full course and carrére of his happynesse. **1663** COWLEY *Verses & Ess.* (1669) 35 Swift as light Thoughts their empty Carriere run. **1675** TRAHERNE *Chr. Ethics* xxv. 389 Quickly stopt in his careir of vertue. **1722** WOLLASTON *Relig. Nat.* ix. 174 Not to permit the reins to our passions, or give them their full carreer. **1767** FORDYCE *Serm. Yng. Women* II. viii. 29 A..beauty..in the career of her conquests. **1848** MACAULAY *Hist. Eng.* II. 599 In the full career of success.

5. a. A person's course or progress through life (or a distinct portion of life), *esp.* when publicly conspicuous, or abounding in remarkable incidents: similarly with reference to a nation, a political party, etc. **b.** In mod. language (after Fr. *carrière*) freq. used for: A course of professional life or employment, which affords opportunity for progress or advancement in the world. Freq. *attrib.* (orig. *U.S.*), esp. (*a*) designating one who works permanently in the diplomatic service or other profession, opp. one who enters it at a high level from elsewhere; (*b*) ***career girl, woman***, etc., one who works permanently in a profession, opp. one who ceases full-time work on marrying. Also, **careers master, mistress**, a schoolteacher who advises and helps pupils in choosing careers.

1803 WELLINGTON in Gurw. *Disp.* II. 424 A more difficult negotiation than you have ever had in your diplomatic career. **1815** *Scribbleomania* 200 That great statesman's public career. **1860** MOTLEY *Netherl.* (1868) I. i. 7 A history ..which records the career of France, Prussia, etc. **1868** GEO. ELIOT *F. Holt* 20 Harold must go and make a career for himself. **1884** *Contemp. Rev.* XLVI. 99 An artist, even in the humblest rank, had a career before him. **1927** *Lit. Digest* 25 June 14/2 The foundation of any sound Foreign Service must consist of 'career men' who have become expert. **1931** F. J. STIMSON *My U.S.* xviii. 190 The career professors look somewhat askance at one who comes in from the outside world—just as career secretaries in diplomacy do upon a chief who has not gone through all the grades. **1936** *Yale Rev.* XXV. 288 Other steps essential to a well-rounded career service remain to be taken... The prospect of permanent undersecretaryships for career men needs to be realized. **1937** *Collier's Wkly.* 26 June 20 (*heading*) Career girl. **1937** *Sat. Rev. Lit.* 9 Oct. 16/3 Most career women are different. **1943** *Assistant Masters' Year Book* 24 The Committee enables members who are careers masters to exchange information. **1947** *Daily Mail* 25 Aug. 2/3 (*heading*) Should the career woman make dates? **1951** R. HOGGART *Auden* vi. 200 The career-girl Rosetta yearns for her lush English landscape. **1954** F. P. KEYES *Royal Box* viii. 101 He might well have expected the offer of an embassy... It's only occasionally that they go to career diplomats like me. **1959** *Times* 15 Apr. 13/4 As careers mistress in a grammar school it is certainly not my habit. **1970** *New Yorker* 17 Oct. 167/1 Philip Habib, a competent, if unusually brusque, career diplomat.

career (kəˈrɪə(r)), *v.* For forms see the sb.

†**1.** *intr.* To take a short gallop, to 'pass a career'; to charge (at a tournament); to turn this way and that in running (said of a horse); also *fig.* Also *trans.* with cognate object. *Obs.*

1594 WILLOBIE *Avisa* F ij, Shamelesse Callets..That.. can carire the whores rebound, To straine at first, and after yeeld. **1611** SPEED *Hist. Gt. Brit.* IX. xv. 52 His horse of a fierce courage carrierd as he went. **1672** VILLIERS (Dk. Buckhm.) *Rehearsal* (1714) 87 How we Tilt and Career.

2. *transf.* and *fig.* To gallop, run or move at full speed. (Also *to career it.*)

1647 WARD *Simp. Cobler* 87 If's tongue doth not career't above his wit. **1679** *Sc. Pasquils* (1868) 248 Episcopie must quit the cause, And let old Jack carrear boys. **1795** SOUTHEY *Joan of Arc* I. 368 When Desolation royally careers Over thy wretched country. **1823** SCOTT *Peveril* v, The little Julian was careering about the room for the amusement of his infant friend. **1851** *Househ. Narrative* 13 Two heavy seas.. careered towards one another. **1856** MRS. BROWNING *Aur. Leigh* III. 331 Sap..Careering through a tree.

3. *trans.* To make (a horse) career.

1829 W. IRVING *Conq. Granada* lxxxiii. (1856) 450 A Moor is born..to career the steed..and launch the javelin.

4. To move swiftly over. (Cf. '*run the streets*'.)

1830 W. PHILLIPS *Mt. Sinai* I. 47 In living clouds careering the expanse, These fleck the firmament.

Hence **caˈreerer**, **caˈreering** *vbl. sb.* and *ppl. a.*, **caˈreeringly** *adv.*

1844 *Blackw. Mag.* 691 Careerers of the skies! **1627** BP. HALL *Heav. upon Earth* vii. 80 All..fall to plunging and careering. **1817** COLERIDGE *Sibyl. Leaves* (1862) 66 The mad careering of the storm. **1599** NASHE *Lent. Stuffe* (1871) 48 The careeringest billow. **1667** MILTON *P.L.* VI. 756 Careering Fires. **1838** DE QUINCEY *Wks.* XIV. 295 Huge careering leaps. **1832** J. WILSON in *Blackw. Mag.* 272, I came down waveringly, careeringly, flourishingly.

careerism (kəˈrɪərɪzm). [f. CAREER *sb.* + -ISM.] The practice or policy of a careerist.

1933 RAHMAT ALI *Now or Never* (1934) 4 They [*sc.* Muslim leaders] have, time and again, sacrificed their own political principles and our national patrimony for the sake

of sheer opportunism and sordid careerism. **1946** E. BENTLEY *Playwright as Thinker* 58 The striving of modern careerism with all its vast implications.

careerist (kəˈrɪərɪst). [f. CAREER *sb.* + -IST.] A person (esp. a holder of a public or responsible position) who is mainly intent on the furtherance of his career, often in an unscrupulous manner. Also *attrib.* or as *adj.*

[**1910** H. G. WELLS *Mr. Polly* vii. 225 He called him the 'chequered Careerist'.] **1917** *Times* 5 June 7/2 Half the present unpopularity of the 'lawyer-politician'..is due to the fact that he is too often a 'carpet-bagger' and a 'careerist'. **1926** S. JAMESON *Three Kingdoms* v. 153 I'm one of those damned careerist women. **1929** G. B. SHAW in *Times* 6 Aug., There were already..members of it [*sc.* the Labour party] who were 'careerists'—men who wanted to have a political career and joined the party they thought would give them the best prospects. **1934** *Punch* 21 Mar. 336/2 He states plainly that he was a 'careerist', power and money were in his hands and it is no wonder that he was dazzled by them. **1940** G. BARKER *Lament & Triumph* 15 The careerist politician and the vague thinker. **1969** *Daily Tel.* 4 Jan. 23/2 Accused..of being a 'double-dealer' and 'political careerist'.

carefox, obs. form of CARFAX.

carefree, care-free (ˈkɛəfriː), *a.* [f. CARE *sb.*[1] + FREE *a.*] Free from care or anxiety. Hence **ˈcarefreedom, ˈcarefreeness**, the state or quality of being carefree.

1795 S. J. PRATT *Gleanings through Wales* III. lxiii. 121 As heart-whole, and care-free, as any man in the circle of Westphalia. **1854** B. TAYLOR *Life & Landscapes fr. Egypt* vii. 96 We..wander..as happy and care-free as two Adams in a Paradise without Eves. **1919** E. GRUBB *Relig. Exper.* xi. 133 This joyous, care-free, self-abandoning life. **1924** *Public Opinion* 21 Mar. 292/2 It makes for joyous indolence and carefreeness of heart. **1928** G. COOKE *Theory of Music* 75 The apparently carefree joyousness of individual performance. **1960** *House & Garden* May 79/1 A special kind of carefreedom in the furnishings.

careful (ˈkɛəfʊl), *a.* Forms: 1 carfull, cearful, 3, 5 karefull, 4–5 carful, 6 *Sc.* cairfull, 3– careful. [OE. *carful*, *cearful*, f. *caru* care + -FUL.]

†**1.** Full of grief; mournful, sorrowful; also (of cries, etc.), expressing sorrow. *Obs.*

a **1000** *Soul's Address* 15 Cleopaþ þonne swa cearful..se gæst to ðam duste. *c* **1205** LAY. 16761 Duden of claðes karefulle cnihtes. *c* **1394** *P. Pl. Crede* 441 þey crieden alle o cry a carefull note. **1470–85** MALORY *Arthur* (1816) I. 161 A careful widow wringing her hands and making great sorrow. *c* **1505** DUNBAR *Tua mariit Wem.* 418 My clokis thai ar caerfull in colour of sabill. **1592** DANIEL *Compl. Rosamond*, Her Tears upon her Cheeks (poor careful Girl!). **1599** *Parismus* II. (1661) 26 To..ease her careful heart.

2. Full of care, trouble, anxiety, or concern; anxious, troubled, solicitous, concerned. *arch.*

a **1000** *Guthlac* 549 (Gr.) Cwædon cearfulle Criste laðe to Guðlace. *a* **1300** *Cursor M.* 23116 þaa care-ful eth sal be to kene. *c* **1400** *Rowland & Ot.* 1066 He crakkede full many a carefull croun. **1535** COVERDALE *Tobias* v. 12 That I make the not carefull, I am Azarias. **1582** N. T. (Rhem.) *Matt.* vi. 34 Be not careful therefore for the morrovv. **1606** MARSTON *Fawne* III. Wks. (1856) 63 Necessarie as sleepe To carefull man. **1714** STEELE *Arriv. Ulysses*, The King arose, and beat his careful Breast. **1814** BYRON *Lara* I. xx, It is a sight the careful brow might smooth.

3. Full of care or concern *for*, attentive to the interests *of*, taking good care *of*.

a **1000** *Lambeth Ps.* xxxix. 18 (Bosw.) Drihten carful oððe ymhydiȝ is mines. **1535** COVERDALE *2 Macc.* xv. 19 They that were in the cite, were most carefull for those which were to fight. **1553** BALE *Vocacyon* in *Harl. Misc.* (Malh.) I. 357 A woman..which was to me a carefull creature. **1590** SHAKS. *Err.* I. i. 79 My wife more carefull for the latter-borne. **1594** —— *Rich. III*, II. ii. 96 Bethinke you like a carefull Mother Of the young Prince your sonne. **1732** POPE *Ep. Bathurst* 13 Then careful Heav'n supply'd two sorts of men. **1795** SOUTHEY *Joan of Arc* VIII. 47 She..stretch'd forth her careful hands To ease the burthen. **1850** MRS. STOWE *Uncle Tom's C.* vi. 38 Be careful of the horses, Sam ..don't ride them too fast.

4. Applying care, solicitous attention, or pains to what one has to do; heedful, painstaking, attentive to one's work; circumspect, watchful, cautious.

c **1050** *Gloss.* in Wr.-Wülcker 172 *Curiosus*, carful. **1583** GOLDING *Calvin on Deut.* xxii. 129 That they should be the earnester and carefuller in teaching their children. **1588** SHAKS. *Titus A.* IV. iii. 21 Goe get you gone, and pray be carefull all, And leaue you not a man of warre vnsearcht. **1640** BP. HALL *Episc.* I. vii. 29 The carefullest Ambassador may perhaps swerve from his message. **1845** GRAVES in *Encycl. Metrop.* (1847) II. 752/1 Dionysius of Halicarnassus, a careful and learned antiquary. **1860** TYNDALL *Glac.* I. §22. 155, I felt just sufficient fear to render me careful. **1878** MORLEY *Crit. Misc.* 192 None the less careful, minute, patient, systematic, in examining a policy.

b. Const. *to do* a thing, *that* a thing be done, or with relative clause.

1579 LYLY *Euphues* (Arb.) 144 The master would be more carefull what he did teach. **1622** SPARROW *Bk. Com. Prayer* (1661) 40 Careful to maintain the ancient usage. **1677** MOXON *Mech. Exerc.* (1703) 48 Be very careful that the Spindle stand exactly Perpendicular. **1771** *Junius Lett.* xlviii. 252 He was careful not to assume any of those powers. **1820** *Hoyle's Games Impr.* 431 Be careful that they are neither thrown about nor changed. **1836** MACGILLIVRAY tr. *Humboldt's Trav.* 290 Both males and females are careful to ornament their persons with paint.

†**5.** Applying care to avoid; on one's guard against, cautious, wary. *Obs.*

1580 LYLY *Euphues* (Arb.) 446 Not disdainefull to conferre, but careful to offende. **1666** SPURSTOWE *Spir. Chym.* (1668) 217 Be more careful of doing anything to lose your Peace. **1711** STEELE *Spect.* No. 118 ¶2 Orestilla is.. particularly careful of new Acquaintance. **1728** R. MORRIS *Anc. Archit.* 91 Ever careful of acting so indiscreetly.

†**6.** Causing trouble or fear, dreadful. *Obs.*

c **1340–70** *Alex. & Dind.* 158 Careful cocodrillus..þe king lette. *c* **1505** DUNBAR *Gold. Targe* 243 So carefull was the crak. **1552** LYNDESAY *Monarche* 5747 Herode..With mony vther cairfull Kyng. **1579** SPENSER *Sheph. Cal.* Dec. 133 The carefull cold hath nypt my rugged rynde.

7. a. Of things: Fraught or attended with sorrow, trouble, or anxiety. *Obs.* or *arch.*

c **1200** *Trin. Coll. Hom.* 171 On þe careful dai þan he cumeð al middeneard to demen. *a* **1300** *Cursor M.* 3632 Ar þat he deied in car-ful bedd. **1413** LYDG. *Pylgr. Sowle* II. xliv. (1859) 50 Alas! the careful tyme that euer we were conceyued. **1577** tr. *Bullinger's Decades* (1592) 633 He casteth him..into a careful and miserable exile. **1634** FORD *Perkin Warb.* III. ii, Paths which lead..to a careful throne. **1814** SOUTHEY *Roderick* xv, He upon his careful couch.

b. Showing care, done or performed with care.

1651 HOBBES *Leviath.* III. xxxii. 198 By wise.. interpretation, and carefull ratiocination. **1756–7** tr. *Keysler's Trav.* (1760) III. 245 After a careful survey of this place. **1797** BEWICK *Brit. Birds* (1847) I. 59 A careful examination of the specimin. **1848** MACAULAY *Hist. Eng.* I. 617 Careful watch was kept all night. **1883** LLOYD *Ebb & Fl.* I. 32 His drawing was careful.

carefully (ˈkɛəfʊlɪ), *adv.* [OE. *carful-líce*: see prec. and -LY[2].] In a careful manner; with care: in various senses of the adj.; now chiefly, Heedfully, attentively, circumspectly, cautiously.

a **1000** in Thorpe *Laws* II. 360 Se sacerd sceal don carfullice Godes þenunga. *a* **1300** *Cursor M.* p. 989. 333 Ful carfully me-think be þis way ȝe walk. **1393** LANGL. *P. Pl.* C. XXIII. 201 For drede gan ich quaken, And criede carfully. **1551** ROBINSON tr. *More's Utop.* (Arb.) 147 Whome they see depart from his life carefullie and agaynst his will. **1559** MORWYNG *Evonym.* 7, I began carefully to muse. **1588** SHAKS. *Tit. A.* II. ii. 8 Let it be your charge..To attend the Emperours person carefully. **1710–11** SWIFT *Lett.* (1766–8) III. 95, I walkt plaguy carefully, for fear of sliding. *a* **1726** COLLIER (J.) Envy, how carefully does it look? how meagre and ill-complexioned? **1856** FROUDE *Hist. Eng.* (1858) I. v. 429 The parliament, in asserting the freedom of England, carefully chose their language. **1875** JOWETT *Plato* (ed. 2) III. 160 We must examine carefully the character of his proposals.

carefulness (ˈkɛəfʊlnɪs). [OE. *carfulnys*: see CAREFUL and -NESS.] The quality or state of being careful.

a. Solicitude, anxiety, concern. *arch.* **b.** Heedfulness, vigilance, attentiveness, exactness, caution.

a **1000** in Thorpe *Hom.* II. 280 (Bosw.) Godes cwydas sind to smeaȝenne mid micelre carfulnysse. *c* **1000** *Sax. Leechd.* III. 210 Briwas niman ȝestreon mið carfulnysse ȝe[tacnað]. *c* **1175** *Lamb. Hom.* 115 Mið carfulnesse haldan þas bebo-dan. **1535** COVERDALE *Ps.* cxxvi[i]. 2 Eate the bred of carefulnesse. **1553** GRIMALDE *Cicero's Offices* I. (1558) 13 It is harde to haue a carefulnesse ouer other mens matters. **1605** BACON *Adv. Learn.* I. i. §3 (1873) 8 There groweth carefulness and trouble of mind. **1685** BAXTER *Paraphr. N.T.* 1 Cor. vii. 32 Carefulness about the World is so bad a thing. **1823** LAMB *Elia* (1860) 213 The face..full of thought and carefulness. **1863** FR. KEMBLE *Resid. Georgia* 16 You may rely upon the carefulness of my observation. **1865** MONSELL *Hymn*, '*O Worship the Lord*' ii, Low at His feet lay thy burden of carefulness.

carein(e, obs. form of CARRION.

Careing: see under CARE SUNDAY.

1785 *Newark Fair* in Brand *Pop. Antiq.* (1870) I. 67 Careing Fair will be held on Friday before Careing Sunday.

carek, obs. form of CARRACK.

carel, -eld, obs. form of CAROL, CARREL.

careless (ˈkɛəlɪs), *a.* [OE. *carléas*, repr. OTeut. type **karalaus*: see CARE *sb.* and -LESS.] The opposite of CAREFUL in its various senses.

†**1.** Free from care, anxiety, or apprehension. (Since *c* 1650 *arch.*, *poetic*, or *nonce-word.*)

a **1000** *Rule Ben.* 2 (Bosw.) He on ðam dome freoh and carleas biþ. *c* **1205** LAY. 12478 Nu we maȝen to ȝere careles wunien here. *a* **1225** *Ancr. R.* 246 þe kastel is wel kareleas aȝean his unwines. **1548** UDALL, etc. *Erasm. Par. Matt.* ix. 6 Depart in peace with a quyet and careles mynde. **1611** BIBLE *Judg.* xviii. 7 They dwelt carelesse, after the maner of the Zidonians, quiet and secure. [**1671** MILTON *P.R.* IV. 299 In corporal pleasure he, and careless ease.] **1705** POPE *Ep. Miss Blount* 11 Thus wisely careless, innocently gay. **1816** J. WILSON *City of Plague* I. i. 352 That book, With whose worn leaves the careless infant plays. **1857** HUGHES *Tom Brown*, The may-fly is the carelessest fly that dances..by English rivers.]

2. Unconcerned; not caring or troubling oneself; not solicitous, regardless; having no care *of*, *about*, or †*to*.

a **1000** *Cædmon's Exod.* 151 (Gr.) Wulfas sungon, carleasan deor. *c* **1205** LAY. 19658 þenne weoren heo care-læse of Costantines cunne. **1579** LYLY *Euphues* (Arb.) 144 Seeing the father carelesse what they learne, he is also secure what he teacheth. **1585** ABP. SANDYS *Serm.* (1841) 148 A governor like to Moses..not careless to be zealous in God's cause. **1596** SHAKS. *Tam. Shr.* IV. ii. 79 And come to Padua carelesse of your life. **1614** MARKHAM *Cheap Husb.* I. ii. (1668) 10 Gingle the..stirrops about his ears, to make him careless of the noise. **1697** DRYDEN *Virg. Georg.* IV. 504 'Tis Aristæus..Who to his careless Mother makes his Moan. **1727** DE FOE *Eng. Tradesm.* (1841) I. vii. 48 Careless of the event of things. **1770** GOLDSM. *Des. Vill.* 161 Careless their merits or their faults to scan. **1800** WORDSW. *Michael* 28, I was yet a Boy Careless of Books. **1807** CRABBE *Par. Reg.* III. 859 Careless what he said. **1847** tr. *J. De Vega's Jrnl. Tour* iii. 18 Quite resigned and careless about the loss. **1883** LLOYD *Ebb & Fl.* II. 202 'Not at all'..said Frank, in one of his most careless tones.

3. Not taking due care, not paying due attention to what one does, inattentive, negligent, thoughtless; inaccurate.

1579 LYLY *Euphues* (Arb.) 195 As farre be they carelesse from honour as they be from awe. **1579** THYNNE *Animadv.* (1865) 6 By oure carelesse..printers of Englande. **1732** BERKELEY *Alciphr.* v. §25 It is natural for careless writers to run into faults they never think of. **1805** WORDSW. *Prelude* XIII. (1851) 276 Souls that appear to have no depth at all To careless eyes. **1871** MORLEY *Voltaire* (1886) 29 Writers so acutely careless as Montaigne.

4. Of things:

†**a.** Uncared for, untended (*obs.*); **b.** Arranged or uttered without art; artless, unstudied, *négligé* (*arch.*); **c.** (*esp.* in mod. use) Done, caused, or said heedlessly, thoughtlessly, negligently. Esp. in phr. ***careless talk***, applied during the war of 1939–45 to talk which, if overheard, might assist the enemy.

1590 MARLOWE *Hero & L.* I, A country maid, Whose careless hair..Glistered with dew. **1596** SPENSER *F.Q.* IV. iv. 38 Their many wounds and carelesse harmes. **1605** SHAKS. *Macb.* I. iv. 11 To throw away the dearest thing he ow'd As 'twere a carelesse Trifle. **1660** STANLEY *Hist. Philos.* (1701) 32/2 Causing a careless rupture in the State. **1704** STEELE *Lying Lover* I. (1747) 12 My Sword..does it hang careless? **1706** POPE *Lett.* Wks. 1736 V. 52, I have seen.. women..look better in a careless night-gown..than Mademoiselle Spanheim drest for a ball. *a* **1763** SHENSTONE *Wks.* (1764) I. 128 My limbs with careless ease reclin'd. **1768** BEATTIE *Minstr.* II. vi, One evening, as he framed the careless rhyme. **1798** S. ROGERS *Ep. to Friend* 190 Careless my course, yet not without design. *Mod.* Nothing could show better the contrast between careful and careless work. **1940** *War Illustr.* 16 Feb. 98/3 A Finnish soldier is reading a Government poster warning the people that careless talk may help the enemy. **1942** T. RATTIGAN *Flare Path* I. 95 Talk about careless talk! *Ibid.* 100 There must be some news, or are you going all careless talk on me?

5. quasi-*adv.*

1812 J. WILSON *Isle of Palms* II. 447 The dripping sail is careless tied Around the painted mast. **1855** TENNYSON *To Maurice* 15, A careless-order'd garden.

carelessly (ˈkɛəlɪslɪ), *adv.* [f. prec. + -LY[2].] In a careless manner, without care; without apprehension (*obs.*); without attention, art, or study; (now *esp.*) heedlessly, thoughtlessly, negligently.

1561 T. NORTON *Calvin's Inst.* IV. xviii. (1634) 711 Evill men..more carelesly follow their owne lusts. **1592** GREENE *Groatsw. Wit* (1617) 39 The one carelesly skiping, the other carefully prying. **1611** BIBLE *Ezek.* xxxix. 6 Among them that dwell carelesly in the yles. —— *Zeph.* ii. 15 This is the reioycing citie that dwelt carelesly. **1667** OLDENBURG in *Phil. Trans.* II. 432 Course Hemp, carelesly twisted. **1726** ADDISON *Dial. Medals* ii. 46 Leaning carelessly on a pillar. **1747** BERKELEY *Let.* Wks. 1871 IV. 315 Things hastily and carelessly written. **1847** HELPS *Friends in C.* (1851) I. 7 Looking at everything so carelessly that they see nothing truly. **1876** GEO. ELIOT *Dan. Der.* III. xxxvii. 130 Many a carelessly-begotten son of man.

carelessness (ˈkɛəlɪsnɪs). [OE. *carléasnes*: see CARELESS and -NESS.] The quality or state of being void of care, or of taking no care; freedom from trouble or anxiety (*obs.*); heedlessness, inattention, thoughtlessness, negligence, indifference.

c **1000** ÆLFRIC *Voc.* in Wr.-Wülcker 172 *Securitas*, karleasnes. **1561** T. NORTON *Calvin's Inst.* III. 204 Consider how great is our carelesnesse, or drowsinesse, or sluggishnesse. **1597** HOOKER *Eccl. Pol.* v. lxviii. §9 Carelessness to whom we impart the mysteries of Christ. **1613** R. C. *Table Alph.* (ed. 3) Securitie, carelesnesse, feare of nothing. **1641** J. JACKSON *True Evang. T.* II. 148 The Stoicks..patience..was..onely a..wretched carelessnesse. **1729** BUTLER *Serm.* Wks. 1874 II. 97 Men do indeed resent what is occasioned through carelessness. **1823** LAMB *Elia* (1860) 211 With what ineffable carelessness would he twirl his gold chain! **1849** RUSKIN *Sev. Lamps* v. §ix. 144 Accidental carelessnesses of measurement or of execution.

ˈcareless,wise, *adv.* In a careless way.

1880 EMMA MARSHALL *Mem. Troubl. Times* 15 With a violet velvet cloak thrown carelesswise over his shoulder.

caren, obs. form of CARRION.

carenage: see CAREENAGE.

†**carenayre.** *Obs. rare*[−1]. [ad. L. *carēnāria* vessel for making *carēnum*: see CARENE[1].]

c **1420** *Pallad. on Husb.* VIII. 129 In carenayres naked children goo And glocke it oures v to and froo.

†**carency.** *Obs. rare*[−1]. [ad. med.L. *carēntia*, f. *carēre* to lack; cf. Fr. *carence*, It. *carenzia*.] The state of being without; wantingness, want.

1655 BP. RICHARDSON *Observ. O.T.* 185 (L.) This sense of dereliction and carency of Divine favour.

†**caˈrene**[1]. *Obs. rare*[−1]. [ad. L. *carœnum*, a. Gr. *κάροινον*.] A sweet wine boiled down.

c **1420** *Pallad. on Husb.* XI. 484 Defrut, carene, and sape, in oon manere of must is made.

†**carene**[2]. *Obs. rare*$^{-1}$. [ad. med.L. *carēna* a forty days' fast, also a remission of such fast; according to Du Cange formed from *quadragēna* or *quarantena*. Cf. QUADRAGESIMA, QUARANTINE.]

A forty days' fast; a remission or indulgence from forty days of fasting. ? = CARENTANE.

1647 JER. TAYLOR *Dissuas. Popery* I. iv. §4 (R.) Were you well advis'd? it may be your Quadragenes are not Carenes, that is, are not a quitting the severest penances of fasting so long on bread and water.

†**carene**[3]. *Obs. rare*$^{-1}$. [a. F. *carène* keel:—L. *carīna*.] (See quot.)

1755 *Gentl. Mag.* XXV. 31 Carene, the bottom or keel of a shell, when in its natural situation, as that part of the Nautilus, on which it swims.

carene, obs. form of CAREEN.

†**carentane**. *Obs.* [Cf. It. *quarantana, -ena, -ina*, Pr. *quarantena, carantena*, F. *quarantaine*, med.L. *quarantena* collection of 40, space of 40 days; f. Romanic *quaranta* (:—L. *quadraginta*) forty + *-ana*, F. *-aine* (see *dozen*).] A group of 40; a space of forty days; a forty days' indulgence.

1647 JER. TAYLOR *Dissuas. Popery* I. §3 (R.) In the church of Sancta Maria de Popolo there are for every day in the year 2800 years of pardon, besides 14,014 Carentanes, which in one year amount to more than 1,000,000.

carer ('kɛərə(r)). [f. CARE *v.*] **a.** One who cares.

1691 NORRIS *Pract. Disc.* 185 The immoderate Carers for the World. **1850** BROWNING *Christm. Eve* 166 A carer for none of it, a Gallio?

b. *spec.* A person whose occupation is the care of the sick, aged, disabled, etc.; one who looks after a disabled or elderly relative at home, esp. one who is therefore unable to work. Cf. CARING *ppl. a.*

1978 *Age & Ageing* VII. 107 A much lower proportion of patients with chief carers in social classes one and two were admitted than those in three, four and five. **1980** *Times Lit. Suppl.* 9 May 530/4 Some professional 'carers'..make therapeutic work a substitute for living and can no longer even tell whether they like or dislike a person in ordinary life. **1982** *Times* 7 May 2/6 More money should be spent on the carers—those people, mainly women and mainly unpaid, who look after old and handicapped relations. **1985** *New Age* Summer 7/3 Believers in Cosmic nursing..distribute information and supportive literature to carers in hospital and in homes, and to relatives of elderly people. **1985** *Brit. Med. Jrnl.* 17 Aug. 465/1 Carers, usually women, are the welfare state's solution to an expensive problem.

carerie, var. of CAREER: perh. erroneous.

1599 PORTER *Angry Wom. Abingd.* (1841) 123 Giue roome and let us have this hot carerie.

caresay, obs. f. KERSEY, a cloth.

†'**caresome**, *a. Obs.* In 6 *Sc.* **cairsum**. [f. CARE *sb.* + -SOME.] Troublesome, burdensome.

1535 STEWART *Cron. Scot.* II. 588 He fell in sic trubill war cairsum for to tell.

caress (kə'rɛs), *sb.* Also 7 carresse, caresse, (charesse). [a. F. *caresse*, 16th c. ad. It. *carezza*:—late L. **cāritia*, f. *cārus* dear.] An action of endearment, a fondling touch or action, a blandishment.

[**1611** COTGR., *Caresse*, a cheering, cherishing..hugging ..making much of.] **1651** JER. TAYLOR *Holy Living* x. xiv. (R.) All the caresses and sweetness of love. **1667** MILTON *P.L.* VIII. 56 Solve high dispute With conjugal Caresses. **1774** GOLDSM. *Nat. Hist.* (1776) III. 52 The goat..easily attaches itself to man, and seems sensible of his caresses. **1863** GEO. ELIOT *Romola* II. xxxii. (1880) I. 386 She felt his caress no more than if he had kissed a mask.

b. *fig.*

1647 CLARENDON *Hist. Reb.* I. II. 98 The Scots made all the Caresses to many of the English. **1649** G. DANIEL *Trinarch. Hen. V*, cclxxi, 'T wer in vaine To frame Carresses of Discourse. **1750** JOHNSON *Rambl.* No. 77 ¶2 When the gifts and caresses of mankind shall recompense the toils of study. **1761-2** HUME *Hist. Eng.* (1806) V. lxx. 233 The caresses of faction, and the allurements of popularity.

caress (kə'rɛs), *v.* [a. F. *caresse-r* to caress, fondle, ad. It. *carezzare*, f. *carezza*; see prec.]

1. *trans.* To treat affectionately or blandishingly, to touch, stroke, or pat endearingly; to fondle.

1697 DAMPIER *Voy.* (1729) I. 359 (*heading*) The natives caress them. **1716-8** LADY M. W. MONTAGUE *Lett.* I. xiii. 46 She caressed me as if I had been her daughter. **1851** LONGF. *Gold. Leg.* VI. *Cott. Odenwald*, My very hands seem to caress her. **1870** E. PEACOCK *Ralf Skirl.* III. 141 Isabell was caressing the fawn.

b. *transf.* and *fig.*

c **1746** HERVEY *Medit.* (1818) 161 Fondly caressing this little flower. **1853** C. BRONTË *Villette* xiv. (1855) 128 Acacia-boughs caressed its panes. **1870** LOWELL *Among my Bks.* Ser. II. (1873) 195 Its prolonged echoes caress the ear.

2. *fig.* To treat with kindness of favour, pet, make much of. *arch.*

1658 MILTON *Lett. State* Wks. 1738 II. 230 For the Sweetness of his Disposition caress'd by all Men. **1682** *Addr. fr. Chester* in *Lond. Gaz.* No. 1764/4 [We] do further resolve and promise not to Caress or Encourage any person who shall obstinately persist in courses disliked by Your Majesty. **1728** MORGAN *Algiers* II. iv. 287 Sultan Suliman highly caressed a Person, concerning whom he had heard so much. **1740** JOHNSON *Blake* Wks. IV. 359 Without being much countenanced or caressed by his superiors. **1771** R. HENRY *Hist. Gt. Brit.* II. 5 The poets of the north were.. greatly caressed by our Anglo-Saxon kings. **1804** A. DUNCAN *Mariner's Chron.* II. 227. **1876** FREEMAN *Norm. Conq.* IV. xviii. 128 William was thus busy in half caressing, half coercing, his English subjects.

†**b.** *fig.* To 'treat'. *Obs.*

1670 HOBBES *Behemoth* (1840) 409 Lambert..caressed his soldiers with an entertainment at his own house. **1699** T. COCKMAN *Tully's Offices* (1706) 199 Sums..daily thrown away to Caress the People.

3. *absol.*

1683 D. A. *Art of Converse* 96 To treat with your Friend as a Serpent caressing with the Tail. **1752** JOHNSON *Rambl.* No. 200 ¶15 Some..offend when they design to caress. **1875** B. TAYLOR *Faust* I. v. 214 She slept while we were caressing.

ca'ressable, *a.* [f. CARESS *v.* + -ABLE.] That may be caressed. Also **caressible**.

1663 SIR G. MACKENZIE *Relig. Stoic* i. (1685) 16 The most caressable of opinions. **1890** W. CORY *Let.* 21 Aug. (1897) 554 Anglican curates, invitable to garden-parties at Lambeth, caressible for ladies. **1900** M. CORELLI *Master-Christian* 343 A small, slight gossamer thing of beauty,.. soft and caressable as a dove. **1969** R. WOLLHEIM *Family Romance* 148 The lovely caressable girl.

caressant (kə'rɛsənt), *a. rare* and *poetic.* [a. F. *caressant*, pr. pple.] Caressing, fondling.

1861 TEMPLE & TREVOR *Tannhäuser* 12 The caressant airs of Heaven. **1871** R. ELLIS *Catullus* xxv. 10 Those tender hands caressant.

ca'resser. [see -ER[1].] One who caresses.

1822 BEDDOES *Brides' Trag.* III. v, Close to my heart, dear caresser, you creep.

ca'ressing, *vbl. sb.* and *ppl. a.* [f. CARESS *v.*]

A. *vbl. sb.* The action of the verb CARESS. **B.** *ppl. a.* That caresses; fondling, endearing.

1665 J. SPENCER *Prophecies* 69 In caressing of Christ by some pretty attributes. *a* **1774** GOLDSM. tr. *Scarron's Com. Rom.* (1775) I. 153 The same civility and caressing expressions. **1855** MACAULAY *Hist. Eng.* IV. 441 His caressing manners.

Hence **ca'ressingly** *adv.*, in a caressing manner.

1834 MRS. HEMANS in *Blackw. Mag.* XXXV. 634 A bright rill wound Caressingly about the holy ground. *a* **1845** HOOD *Cupid Greyb.*, Passing his hand caressingly over her curls.

ca'ressive, *a.* [f. CARESS *v.* + -IVE; formed after words like *express-ive*.] Habitually caressing; of the nature of a caress.

1801 *Monthly Mag.* XII. 98 Diminutives easily acquire a caressive character. **1880** *Harper's Mag.* 909 Much caressive handling.

caressively (kə'rɛsɪvlɪ), *adv.* [f. CARESSIVE *a.* + -LY[2].] Caressingly.

1913 D. H. LAWRENCE *Sons & Lovers* i. 10 'Now do come and have this one wi' me,' he said caressively. **1922** —— *England, my England* (1924) 113 Her gloomy black eyes softened caressively to me for a moment.

Care Sunday. *Sc.* Also cair-. [German has the corresp. *kar-freitag* (in MHG. *karvrîtac, kartac*) Good Friday, and *karwoche* (also in MHG.) Passion week; *kar-sonntag* appears not to be in use. OHG. *chara*, OE. *caru*, CARE in its earlier sense of 'sorrow, trouble, grief'.]

'According to Bellenden, Sunday immediately preceding Good Friday; but now generally used for the fifth in Lent' (Jamieson).

1536 BELLENDEN *Cron. Scot.* (1821) II. 497 Thus entrit Prince James in Scotland; and come, on Care Sonday, in Lentern, to Edinburgh [BOETH. *dominicae passionis obviam*.] **1538** *Aberd. Reg.* V. 16 (Jam.) Betuixt this & Cair Sonday. *a* **1575** *Diurn. Occurr.* (1833) 23 Lestit quhill caris sonday in Lentrone. **1825** HONE *Every-day Bk.* I. 415 Care, or Carle Sunday is the fifth Sunday in Lent.

†**caresweet**. *Obs.* An old name for Gentian.

a **1387** *Sinon. Barthol.* (*Anecd. Oxon.*) 22 *Gentiana*, baldemoyne, careswete, idem.

caresye, obs. f. KERSEY, a cloth.

caret ('kærɪt, 'kɛərɪt). [L. *caret* (there) is wanting, f. *carēre* to be in want of.]

A mark (^) placed in writing below the line, to indicate that something (written above or in the margin) has been omitted in that place.

1710 W. MATHER *Yng. Man's Comp.* (1727) 38 That which is called Caret (that is to say in English, it is wanting) markt with a Latine Circumflex, thus (^) which is to shew where a Word forgotten..and placed above the Line, is to come in. **1824** J. JOHNSON *Typogr.* II. viii. 218 Should a letter have been omitted, a caret is put at the place. **1870** LOWELL *Study Wind.* (1886) 301 Like the *carets* on a proof-sheet.

caret, obs. form of CARROT *sb.*

caretake ('kɛəteɪk), *v.* [Back-formation f. CARETAKER.] *trans.* To take charge of, watch over, and keep in order (a house, estate, business premises, etc.) in the absence of the owner or customary occupants. Also *absol.*

1893 *Cornhill Mag.* Nov. 507 Martha caretakes a decrepit City warehouse. **1904** *Daily Chron.* 14 Apr. 9/5 (Advt.), Housekeeper (Working): reliable; occasionally to caretake. **1921** *Glasgow Herald* 6 Aug. 6 They have to be electrical and mechanical engineers, and to 'care-take' the whole establishment, as well as to operate. **1960** H. PINTER *Caretaker* III. 81 I'll keep an eye on the place for you.., I'll caretake for you.

'**care-ˌtaker**. Also **caretaker**. [f. CARE *sb.* + TAKER, f. TAKE *v.*] **a.** One who takes care of a thing, place, or person; one put in charge of anything.

1858 M. PORTEOUS *Souter Johnny* 17 The souter's wife.. was servant to Gilbert Brown..and..acted as nurse and care-taker to Agnes his daughter. **1859** W. G. WILLS *Life's Foreshad.* II. xvii. 205 The caretaker of the house met them, hat in hand. **1869** *Daily News* 19 July, The votes of Parliament to the caretakers of the parks.

b. *esp.* in Ireland, a person put in charge of a farm from which the tenant has been evicted.

1868 *Times* 24 June 12 (Irish Correspt.) Three companions assaulted the caretaker. **1887** *Illust. Lond. News* 29 Jan. 113 The evicted tenants were readmitted as caretakers.

c. *attrib.*, esp. designating a government, administration, etc., in office temporarily; = STOP-GAP 5.

[**1885** J. CHAMBERLAIN in *Cobden Club Dinner, Special Rep.* 11 It is only upon those terms that what will be known in history as the 'Stop-gap' Government can invite the toleration of its opponents... I see no reason why they should not remain as caretakers on the premises—(great laughter and cheering)—until the new tenants are ready in November for a prolonged..occupation.] **1945** *Times* 26 May 5/2 This is evidently not 'a caretaker administration', but a carefully balanced team. **1945** *New Statesman* 2 June 346/3 There are already plenty of signs that the advent of the 'caretaker' Government means a serious setback to reconstruction. **1946** *News* (Birmingham, Ala.) 13 Nov. 20/4 A stopgap or caretaker operation will be established to carry on at the state's biggest college. **1963** *Ann. Reg. 1962* 370 Far from being a 'caretaker' Pope,..he was proving one of the most popular Popes.

'**care-ˌtaking**, *vbl. sb.* (Also written as one word.) [f. as prec. + -ING[1].] †**a.** Anxiety (*obs.*). **b.** Taking care *of*, esp. in the sense of taking charge of a house, etc.

1625 K. LONG tr. *Barclay's Argenis* IV. viii. 266 Shee was very ill, both by caretaking and sicknesse. **1765** STERNE *Tr. Shandy* VIII. xx, The want of caretaking of me. **1879** 'E. GARRETT' *House by Works* I. 174 There will be none to send to market but that caretaking woman. **1883** A. THOMAS *Mod. Housewife* 139 To rely solely upon..'trusty' servants, or care-taking models. **1895** *Atlantic Monthly* July 61 The feeding and care-taking inseparable from life in the nest.

So **care-taking** *ppl. a.*, that takes care, careful.

1825 in Cobbett *Rur. Rides* (1885) II. 12 Industrious and care-taking creatures reduced to beggary by bank-paper.

carete, -ette, obs. ff. CART *sb.*[2], CARTE, CARAT.

carew, var. of CARUE, *Obs.*, a measure of land.

careway, obs. form of CARAWAY.

†**care-worm**. *Obs.* [? error for EAREWORM.]

1598 W. PHILLIPS *Linschoten's Voy.* (1864) 222 They can hardly keepe any Paper or Bookes from wormes, which are like care wormes, but they doe often spoile and consume many Papers and euidences of great importance.

‖**carex** ('kɛərɪks). *Bot.* Pl. **carices** ('kɛərɪsiːz). [L. *cārex* sedge.] A large genus, N.O. *Cyperaceæ*, comprising various grassy-looking plants; a sedge.

1398 TREVISA *Barth. De P.R.* XVII. xxxv. (1495) 624 Carix, Sedge is an herbe moost harde and sharpe. **1833** J. HODGSON in J. Raine *Mem.* (1858) II. 305 Narrow haughs edged with carexes. **1834** MUDIE *Brit. Birds* (1841) II. 27 Carex, and stunted rushes. **1859** DARWIN *Orig. Spec.* iii. (1878) 56 Not counting grasses and carices.

careyn(e, obs. form of CARRION.

Carey Street ('kɛərɪstriːt). A street in London, formerly the location of the Bankruptcy Department of the Supreme Court, used allusively to indicate a state of bankruptcy.

1922 J. AGATE in *Sat. Rev.* 29 July 172/2 The melancholy gentleman in direful Carey Street. **1936** N. COLLINS *Trinity Town* v. 80 A man like Mr. Broster who might find himself in Carey Street at any moment.

†**carf**. *Obs.* exc. *dial.* In 1 **cyrf**, 4 **kyrf, kerfe**, 4–7 **carfe**, 5 **carffe**. [OE. had *cyrf* fem. repr. OTeut. *kurbjô-* from ablaut stem of CARVE *v.* Cf. MHG. *kerbe*, MLG. and MDu. *kerve*, Du. *kerf* fem. Thence ME. *kyrf, kerfe*; the later form may be modified after the vb., in OE. *ceorfan*; cf. LG. *karf*.]

1. Cutting, a cut, incision; a wound; a fissure.

a **1000** *Rule St. Benet* 28 (Bosw.) Cyrf *abscissio*. *c* **1340** *Gaw. & Gr. Knt.* 372 Kepe þe cosyn..þat þou on kyrf sette. **1393** GOWER *Conf.* II. 152 With sondry kerfe and portreture. ? *a* **1400** *Morte Arth.* 2714 And whene þe carffes ware clene, þat clede them aȝayne. **1559** MORWYNG *Evonym.* 64 A thin borde with a slitt or carfe in the midst cut out over-thwarth. **1565** GOLDING *Ovid's Met.* VIII. (1593) 205 The bloud came spinning from the carfe. **1639** *MS. Acc. St. John's Hosp. Canterb.*, For sawinge of a carfe in a peece of timber, ijd. **1847-78** HALLIWELL, *Carf*, the breadth of one cutting in a rick of hay. *Kent.* **1879** JAMIESON, *Carf*, a cut in timber, for admitting another piece. *Dumfr.*

2. ? The cut part at the end of a piece of wood.

1502 ARNOLDE *Chron.* 97 I iij fote of assise be syde the carf. **1542-3** *Act 34-5 Hen. VIII*, iii, Euerie shyde of tal-wood to

conteyne in length .iiii. foote of assise at least, besyde the carfe. **1799** S. FREEMAN *Town Off.* 151 All cord wood for sale shall be four feet long, including half of the carf.

carf, obs. pa. t. of CARVE *v.*

carfax, -fox ('kɑːfæks, -fɒks). Forms: 4 **carfuks, carfouk,** 5 **carfowgh, carfoukes,** 6–7 **carfox,** 7 **carfoix, carefox,** 8 **cairfax,** 5– **carfax.** [ME. *carfuks, -fouk*, repr. an earlier *carreforc(s, -furcs*, corresp. to Pr. *carreforc*, OF. *carrefor(s, -four* (mod.F. *carrefour*):—L. *quadrifurc-us* four-forked, f. *quadri-* = *quatuor* four + *furca* fork.
As the F. had lost the final *c* before the 12th c., it is not quite clear how this came into Eng.;—possibly from the Latin form—it could hardly be from the Provençal. The total absence of the *r* in Eng. is also notable, esp. as *fork* was a well-known word from OE. times. But notwithstanding these and other obscure points in the phonetic history, the derivation itself appears to be beyond doubt.]

1. A place where four roads or streets meet. (Sometimes extended to more than *four*.)
1357 *London City Rec., Lett. Bk.* G 72 Item qe nul Pulter nautre denzein de la Citee nestoise as Carfuks del ledenhalle ouesqz conyns volatil nautre Pulletrie pur vendre. *c* **1440** *Promp. Parv.* 62 Cartehowse [*v.r.* Carfax, or Carfaus], *quadrivium.* *c* **1450** *Merlin* xvii. 273 Thei enbusshed hem a-gein a carfowgh [? carfowrgh] of vj weyes. *c* **1500** *Partenay* 1819 No place ther had, neither carfoukes [Fr. *carrefours*] non. **1662** PHILLIPS, *Carefox, quasi, quatre-four*, or a place parted into four wayes, a market place in Oxford. [*ed.* **1678** Carfax.] **1886** C. W. BARDSLEY *Jim's Psalm* 17 He comes to a country carfax. Four roads meet.

2. Hence, the proper name of a place formed by the intersection of two principal streets in various towns, as at Oxford and Exeter.
1527 *Will of W. Secoll of Stanton Harcourt* (Somerset Ho.) My house in Eynesham before the Carfaxe. **1580** VOWELL *Exeter* (1765) 6 The Conduit at Quatrefois or Carfox. *c* **1630** RISDON *Surv. Devon* §107 (1810) 104 Four.. streets.. do all meet in the midst of the city, called corruptly Carfox. **1656** BLOUNT *Glossogr.*, *Carefox*, a market place in Oxford so called. **1673** *Will of H. Ellis of Horsham* (Somerset Ho.) Scarfolkes. **1693** J. EDWARDS *Bks. of O. & N.T.* I. 429 Carfax.. the place where Four Ways meet in Oxford. **1709** HEARNE *Collect.* 24 July, Ad quadrivium, vulgo Cairfax. **1751** S. WHATLEY *Eng. Gazeteer* Exeter (Devon), Here are 4 principal streets.. all centering in the middle of the City, which is therefore called Carfox. **1880** *Sussex Gloss.* (E.D.S.) The Carfax at Horsham. **1886** T. NORTHY *Hist. Exeter* xiii. 66 They were taken to Exeter and executed at the Carfoix.

†**3.** (In form *carfouk*): Used to render med.L. *quadrivium*, in the academic sense of the four 'arts', arithmetic, geometry, music, and astronomy (cf. ART 7). *Obs.*
1387 TREVISA *Higden* VI. xiv. Rolls Ser. VII. 69 þat carfouk ich leve [*illud quadrivium omitto*], but he [Gerebertus] drank þerof þat he passed al oþere.

†**carfe.** *Obs.* [? error for CARSE.]
1704 WORLIDGE *Dict. Rust. et Urb.*, *Carfe*, signifies Ground unbroken in Husbandry. **1721** in BAILEY. **1775** in ASH.

carfe, *sb.*: see CARF.

carferal ('kɑːfərəl). [f. the first syllables of *carbon*, *fer-rum* (iron), and *al-umina*, of which substances it is compounded.] (See quots.).
1881 *Nature* XXV. 62 The powers of carferal, well known as a filtering medium in the removal of ammonia from sewage. **1884** *Health Exhib. Catal.* 65/1 *Carferal*, a new.. filtering material compounded of alumina, iron and carbon.

†'**carfle,** *v. Obs. rare*$^{-1}$. A verb applied to one of the operations in preparing flax for spinning.
1398 TREVISA *Barth. De. P.R.* XVII. xcvii. (Tollemache MS.) It [flax] is knokked and bete, breyed and carfled [*ed.* **1495** carflyd], rodded and gnodded, ribbed and hecchelid.

carfoix, -ouk(es, -owgh, -ox: see CARFAX.

†'**carfour, carrefour.** *Obs.* In 5 quare-, quarfour, 6 quare-, quarrefoure, 6–8 carfour, 6– carrefour, carri-. [a. F. *carrefour*, in 13th c. *quarrefour*: see CARFAX.] A place where four ways meet, a 'carfax'. (Formerly quite naturalized, but now treated only as French.)
1477 CAXTON *Jason* 28 In alle the quarefours of the cyte. **1490** —— *Eneydos* xxvii. 100 By the grete quarfours and by wayes. **1502** *Ord. Crysten Men* (W. de W. 1506) v. ii. 362 In a quarefoure of a towne. **1600** HOLLAND *Livy* XXVII. iv. 628 Neere unto the carrefour or crosse waie [*compitum*] of Anagnia. *Ibid.* XXXVIII. xxxvi. 1005 In all quarrefours or crosse streets of the citie. **1601** —— *Pliny* I. 59 Rome.. containeth.. 265 crosse streets or carfours. **1652** EVELYN *State France* Misc. (1805) 93 You walk the Streets and public Carfours. *c* **1730** BURT *Lett. N. Scotl.* (1818) I. 22 It [Glasgow] has a spacious *carrifour*, where stands the cross. *a* **1734** NORTH *Exam.* III. vii. ¶86. 572 Their Seat was in a Sort of Carfour at Chancery-Lane End.

carfuffle, variant of CURFUFFLE, *Sc.*

‖'**carga**¹. In 8 cargo, cargau. [Sp. *carga* load, cogn. with F. *charge*, It. *carica*, f. *caricare*, in late L. *carricāre* to load: see CHARGE, CARGO.] A 'load' as a measure of weight (see quots.).
1622 MALYNES *Anc. Law-Merch.* 26 They account also by Cargaos of 400ˡᵇ smal weight. **1704** J. HARRIS *Lex. Techn.* s.v. *Weight*, At Antwerp.. The carga, or charge, 400 l., which is two Bales of 200 l. each, for an Horse to carry. **1712** W. ROGERS *Voy.* (1718) 199 Each Cargau 81 Pound weight. **1753** CHAMBERS *Cycl. Supp.*, *Cargo* also denotes a weight used in Spain and Turky, amounting to about 300 English pounds. **1850** PRESCOTT *Peru* II. 103 Two hundred cargas, or loads of gold.

‖'**carga**². *Obs.* [Sp. *carga* charge.] (See quot.).
1625 MARKHAM *Souldiers Accid.* 60 [Of] the Sounds and Commands of the Trumpet.. (which we generally call Poynts of Warre) there are sixe:.. The fift is Carga, Carga, or an alarum, Charge, Charge which sounded, every man (like Lightning) flyes vpon his enemie.

cargador (kɑːgə'dɔə(r)). Pl. **cargadores.** [Sp.] In Spanish America: a porter (see also quot. 1892).
1811 J. BLACK tr. *Humboldt's Polit. Essay* I. 39 The existence of these valleys prevents the inhabitants from travelling except on horseback, afoot, or carried on the shoulders of Indians, (called *cargadores*). **1844** G. W. KENDALL *Santa Fé Exped.* II. xix. 362 Cargadores, with their leather trousers rolled up. **1889** K. MUNROE *Golden Days* iv. 36 Nearly naked *cargadores*, or native porters [bent] beneath heavy burdens. **1892** *Dialect Notes* I. 245 *Cargador*, the man in charge of the packs, in a pack train. **1904** CONRAD *Nostromo* viii. 81 A cargador would fly out head first and hands abroad. **1926** D. H. LAWRENCE *Plumed Serp.* xvi. 245 The cargadores were busy at the charcoal boats, carrying out the rough sacks. **1958** *Alaska Sportsman* Dec. 34/3 The 'cargodore' is Chinese, two of the packers are Tahitan natives and the cook.. is Chinese.

†'**cargason, cargazon.** *Obs.* Forms: 6–7 (9) **cargason,** 7 **cargazon, cargosoon, car(r)agasoune, (cargaison).** [a. Sp. *cargazon* 'load of a ship, cargo', double augm. (*-azo, -on*) of *carga*, *cargo* load: cf. F. *cargaison*.]
1. The cargo or freight of a ship.
1583 J. NEWBERY *Let.* in Arb. *Garner* III. 172 There should come in euery ship the fourth part of her cargason in money. **1626** CAPT. SMITH *Accid. Yng. Seamen* 2 The Cape-merchant and Purser hath the charge of all the Caragasoune or Merchandize. *c* **1645** HOWELL *Lett.* III. vi, Her cargazon of broad cloth. **1657** R. LIGON *Barbadoes* (1673) 8 That part of the Cargosoon that was consign'd for that place. **1722** DE FOE *Col. Jack* (1840) 315 We will not fail to.. bring money enough for any cargaison. **1882** MYERS *Renew. Youth* 65 They lade thy bark for nought, they pile thereon With vain largess the golden cargason.
b. *fig.*
1625 DONNE *Serm.* Wks. 1839 VI. 67 Discretion is the ballast of our ship.. but zeal is the very freight, the cargason, the merchandise itself. **1642** HOWELL *For. Trav.* (Arb.) 67 A cargazon of Complements and Cringes. *c* **1645** —— *Lett.* I. xi, My body is but a Cargazon of corrupt humours.
2. An inventory of goods shipped, a bill of lading. [So F. *cargaison*.]
1599 HAKLUYT *Voy.* II. I. 217 These Marchants as soone as they are come on land, do give the cargason of all their goods to that Broker that they will haue to do their businesse for them, with the marks of all the fardles and packs.

carge, obs. Sc. form of CHARGE *sb.*
c **1470** HENRY *Wallace* VIII. 396 He had leuer haiff had him at his large.. than off fyne gold to carge [*ed.* **1570** charge] Mor than in Troy was fund.

carged, carging: see CARGUED.

cargo ('kɑːgəʊ), *sb.*¹ Also 8 cargoe. Pl. cargoes. [17th c. a. Sp. *cargo* loading, burthen, or perhaps *carga* load, freight, cargo, in It. *carico*, *carica*, med.L. *carricum*, *carrica* load, f. late L. *carricāre* to load, f. *carrus* CAR: see CHARGE.]
1. a. The freight or lading of a ship, a ship-load.
1657 R. LIGON *Barbadoes* 8 As we had Cause to suspect him for the Cask, so wee had for the Cargo. **1697** POLLEXFEN *Disc. Trade & Coyn* 116 The Ships Adventure and Bristol, whose Cargoes cost in England about 60000*l.* **1705** *Lond. Gaz.* No. 4151/4 The Catharine Maurice.. with her Cargo of Brown Sugar and Ginger. **1725** DE FOE *Voy. round World* (1840) 7 We had a very rich cargo on board. **1796** MORSE *Amer. Geog.* I. 321 The specie was leaving the country in cargoes. **1840** R. DANA *Bef. Mast* xxii. 67 Having discharged her cargo and taken in ballast.
†**b.** A bill of lading. *Obs.*$^{-0}$ (Cf. CARGASON 2.)
1678 LITTLETON *Lat. Dict.*, A cargo or Bill of lading or list of goods, *mercium catalogus.* **1721** BAILEY, *Cargo*.. Also a Bill of Lading, or List of the Goods of a Ship.
2. a. *transf.* (cf. *load*). †**b.** *slang.* (see quot. 1690.)
1690 B. E. *Dict. Cant. Crew*, *Cargo*, a good round Sum of Money about a Man. **1714** H. GROVE *Spect.* No. 558 ¶5 Advancing towards the Heap, with a larger Cargo than ordinary upon his Back. *a* **1762** LADY M. W. MONTAGUE *Lett.* xciv. 155, I am promised a cargo of lampoons from Bath. **1806–7** J. BERESFORD *Miseries Hum. Life* (1826) II. xxxi, A cargo of novels. **1845** DARWIN *Voy. Nat.* xv, Six were intended for riding, and four for carrying cargoes.
3. *Comb.*, chiefly *attrib.*, as **cargo-boat**, *-book*, *-fall*, *-hold*, **liner**, *-man*, *-port* (an opening in the side of a ship for delivering cargo), *-rice*, *-ship*, *-steamer*, *-winch*; **cargo-cult** (see quots.).
1859 *Merc. Mar. Mag.* (1860) VII. 8 *Cargo boats conveying goods to Canton from Ships. **1867** SMYTH *Sailor's Word-bk.*, **Cargo-book*, shows the mark, number, quality, and (if measurement goods) the dimensions of such packages of a ship's cargo. **1949** *Sydney Morning Herald* 18 June 2/4 The fantastic '*cargo cult' among New Guinea natives has become a serious problem for Australian administrators... Natives influenced by it believe that the spirits of their ancestors will arrive shortly in ships and aeroplanes carrying cargoes of food, tobacco, axes, and other goods. **1951** R. FIRTH *Elem. Soc. Organization* iii. 112 The extraordinary economic operations of some groups, particularly in what has been termed the Cargo cults of some of the New Guinea natives. **1966** 'E. LINDALL' *Time too Soon* (1967) iii. 26 The cargo cults, in which the cultists sat waiting for ships to come sailing from America laden with all the luxuries and gee-gaws of white civilisation. **1924** R. CLEMENTS *Gipsy of Horn* viii. 151 Making the harpoon-line fast to the *cargo-fall. **1920** *Blackw. Mag.* Mar. 316/2 The *cargo-holds were refurbished. **1922** *Glasgow Herald* 14 June, A homeward bound *cargoman. **1832** J. R. MCCULLOCH *Dict. Commerce* 908 There are an immense number of different sorts of rice. The rice exported from Bengal is chiefly of the species denominated **cargo* rice. **1884** *St. James's Gaz.* 10 Apr. 5/1 The owners of *cargoships and steamers. **1907** *Motor Boat* 19 Sept. 190/2 A good, simple, and cheap *cargo winch.
¶ See also CARGA.

†'**cargo,** *sb.*² *Obs.* [Both of the following uses seem explicable from the senses of the Sp. *cargo*, *carga* burden, load, weight, bundle, fardle, truss, etc.; but they appear earlier than the prec., and have no contact with it in Eng.
There is however no evidence that *cargo* was so used in Sp. The suggestion that the exclamation was meant for the Sp. *ca'rājo*, appears phonetically out of the question, as does that of its being for It. *coraggio* (ko'raddʒo).]
1. A contemptuous term applied to a person.
1602 B. JONSON *Poetast.* V. iii, A couple of condemn'd caitiue calumnious Cargo's.
2. As an exclamation or imprecation.
1607 G. WILKINS *Miseries Enf. Marr.* IV. in Hazl. *Dodsley* IX. 533 But cargo! my fiddlestick cannot play without rosin. **1615** *Albumaz.* in *Dodsley* (1780) VII. 251 Twenty pound a year For three good lives? Cargo! hai Trincalo!

cargo ('kɑːgəʊ), *v.* [f. CARGO¹.] *trans.* To load. Also, to carry as cargo; to package (goods) for distribution. Hence '**cargoed** *ppl. a.*
1889 *Guardian* 10 July 1050/3 In the race for literary immortality the heavy Spanish galleon may be cargoed with golden ingots. **1892** *Congress. Rec.* 18 Mar. 2188/1 Pelts and peltries, and anything else the teamster may be cargoed with. **1909** *Westm. Gaz.* 5 Nov. 2/3 Our ship with store of cargoed memories. **1924** R. MACAULAY *Orphan Island* i. 15 They were for leaving the island with the two boats, cargoed with fruit and cocoa-nuts. **1934** DYLAN THOMAS in *New Verse* June 8 And drown the cargoed apples in their tides. **1959** *Amer. Speech* XXXIV. 159 Cargo that pile of beds. **1984** *Times* 1 Mar. 1/8 They found new British Leyland cars waiting to be cargoed to Switzerland, the keys were in the ignitions.

'**cargoose.** [app. f. CARR *sb.*² + GOOSE: the bird breeds in meres and fens: cf. *carr swallow*.] A name for the Crested Grebe.
1677 CHARLETON *Exerc. de Nomin. Animal.* 107 Avis quædam anate paulo major.. agri Cestrensis incolis (ubi frequens est) a *Cargoos* dicta. **1789** MRS. PIOZZI *Journ. France* II. 232 Why there are no.. cargeese upon these lakes nobody informs me. **1879** JOHNS *Brit. Birds* 609/2.

†**cargued, carged,** *a. Naut. Obs.* [? cf. F. *carguer* to charge, lade (Cotgr.).] In *high-cargued* or *-carged*; which is found also in the form *high-charged*, and appears to be the same as *high-carved*. The original form and sense are unknown.
High-caged (*-cadged*) has been suggested: cf. CAGE 4c, CAGE-WORK 2.
1580 NORTH *Plutarch* (1676) 105 The Persian galleys, being high cargued, heavy, and not yare of stereage. **1591** RALEIGH *Last Fight Rev.* (Arb.) 19 So huge and high carged was the Spanish Ship.
So (**high**) **cargeing** *vbl. sb.*
1618 RALEIGH *Lett.* (1651) 131 The high Cargeing of Ships, is that that brings many ill qualities.

†**cariacare.** *Obs.* Put for the Vulgate *caricarum* 'of dried figs' (*1 Sam.* xxv. 18). [L. *cārica*.]
1483 CAXTON *Gold. Leg.* 67/1, ii C masses of cariacares.

cariama: see SERIEMA.

Carian ('kɛərɪən), *sb.* and *a.* [f. L. *Caria*, Gr. Καρία Caria + -AN.] **A.** *sb.* A native or inhabitant of Caria, an ancient province of Asia Minor; the language of Caria. **B.** *adj.* Of or belonging to Caria.
1607 TOPSELL *Four-f. Beasts* 142 Among the Carians.. they sacrificed a Dog in stead of a Goate. **1680** OLDHAM in *Rochester's Poems* 122 Thus the vain glorious Carian, I'll out do. **1818** KEATS *Endym.* II. 374 This Dew-dropping melody, in the Carian's ear. *Ibid.* IV. 52 Thou, Carian lord, hadst better have been tost Into a whirlpool. **1839** *Civil Engin. & Arch. Jrnl.* II. 435/1 Jassos.. was named also Carian marble. **1876** *Encycl. Brit.* V. 102/2 The Carians are spoken of by all ancient writers as a distinct nation from their neighbours. **1891** W. CORY *Ionica* 7 My dear old Carian guest. **1902** *Encycl. Brit.* XXXIII. 896/2 Symbols exactly like ϕ, χ, ψ.. are found in the Carian alphabet. **1933** BLOOMFIELD *Language* iv. 65 We have copious inscriptions in Lycian.. and less extensive ones in Carian, from the seventh century B.C. **1948** DIRINGER *Alphabet* 466 Names of Carian mercenaries scratched upon Egyptian monuments.

carian, obs. form of CARRION.

†'**cariate,** *v. Obs.* [f. CARI-ES + -ATE, prob. after F. *carier*: see -ATE.] *trans.* To affect with caries or decay.
Hence '**cariated** *ppl. a.*, decayed, carious.
1665 G. HARVEY *Advice agst. Plague* 24 Light cariated dusts of Vegetables. **1702** *Eng. Theophrast.* x. 139 And cariate the very bones. **1758** J. S. *Le Dran's Observ. Surg.* (1771) 20 The Hole of the Cariated Alveol.

cari'atic, *a.*: for CARYATIDIC.
1789 P. SMYTH tr. *Aldrich's Archit.* (1818) 107 Cariatic columns in any temple would have been ridiculous.

cariatid, -al, etc.: see CARYATID.

Carib ('kærɪb), *sb.* and *a.* In 6 pl. **caribeis, caribes, cariues.** [a. Sp. *caribe*: see CANNIBAL[1].]
A. *sb.* One of the native race which occupied the southern islands of the West Indies at their discovery: in earlier times often used with the connotation of *cannibal*.
1555 EDEN *Decades W. Ind.* I. I. (Arb.) 66 The wylde and myscheuous people called *Canibales* or *Caribes*, whiche were accustomed to eate mannes flesche. **1578** T. N. tr. *Conq. W. India* 4 Others..looking for death, and to be eaten of the Cariues. **1602** *Metamorph. Tabacco* (Collier) 10 Which at the Caribes banquet gouern'st all, And gently rul'st the sturdiest Caniball. **1876** BANCROFT *Hist. U.S.* VI. xlii. 259 The oppressed and enslaved Caribs.
B. *adj.* Of or pertaining to the Caribs of South and Central America and the West Indies, their culture or language. Cf. CARIBBEAN *a.*
1881 *Encycl. Brit.* XII. 828/2 In British Guiana the Carib tribes are the Ackawais and Caribisi of the coast and foreign regions, the Arecumas and Macusis of the savannah region. **1933** L. BLOOMFIELD *Language* iv. 73 In South America, we note..the *Arawak* and *Carib* families, which once prevailed in the West Indies. **1951** W. FAULKNER *Requiem for Nun* 37 It was said..that the man slept at night in a kind of pit at the site of the chateau he was planning, tied wrist to wrist with one of his captor's Carib slaves. **1970** S. SELVON *Plains of Caroni* i. 9 It [*sc.* the river] might have sung some primitive Carib tune. **1984** *Lang. & Communication* IV. II. 93 Their motivation for attending the dügü is different (curiosity, boredom, a desire to learn about Carib culture).
Hence **'Caribal** *a.* (after *cannibal*); **Cari'bbean** *a.* and *sb.*, applied to certain of the West Indian isles, and to the sea between them and the mainland; **Cari'bee** (= CARIB).
1849 CARLYLE *Disc. Nigger Question* 37 Under the incompetent Caribal (what we call 'Cannibal') possessors. **1719** DE FOE *Crusoe* (1858) 319 Their battles with the Caribbeans. *Ibid.* (1858) 320 How 300 Caribbees came and invaded them. **1777** ROBERTSON *Hist. Amer.* (1783) II. 449 A Caribbean canoe. *Ibid.* II. 450 The Caribbees still use two distinct languages.

caribe (kæ'riːbeɪ, 'kærɪbeɪ). Also **cariba.** [Sp.: see CARIB.] A characinoid fish of the genus *Serrasalmus*, in the rivers of tropical S. America, noted for its voracity and sharp bite; the piranha.
1868 R. PAEZ *Trav. S. & Cent. Amer.* v. 62 Several dangerous fish..such as..the *caribe*, whose ravenous and bloodthirsty propensities have caused it to be likened to the cannibal tribe of Indians. **1880** GÜNTHER *Fishes* 613 The fish hooked is immediately attacked by the 'Caribe' (as these fishes are called). **1904** BOULENGER in *Cambr. Nat. Hist.* VII. 578 The 'Piranha' or 'Cariba' (*Serrasalmo*)..whose bite has been compared to the cut of a razor. **1904** W. H. HUDSON *Green Mansions* xiii. 181 Some little caribe fishes had made their appearance. **1931** J. H. NORMAN *Hist. Fishes* vii. 130 Another fish which is renowned for its ferocity is the Caribe or Piraya (*Serrasalmus*).

caribou, cariboo ('kærɪbuː, -'buː). Also **carr-.** [Canadian F. *caribou*: prob. of native American origin.] **a.** The North American Reindeer.
c **1665** P. E. RADISSON *Voyages* (1885) 202 We killed severall..Carribboucks. **1672** JOSSELYN *New Eng. Rarities* 20 The Maccarib, Caribo, or Pohano, a kind of Deer. **1703** tr. *La Hontan's Voy. N.-Amer.* I. 59 Harts and Caribous are kill'd both in Summer and Winter. **1774** GOLDSM. *Nat. Hist.* (1862) I. II. v. 336 The North Americans also hunt the rein-deer under the name of the caribou. **1848** THOREAU *Maine W.* i. (1864) 11 Deer and caribou, or reindeer, are taken here in the winter. **1879** LD. DUNRAVEN in *19th C.* July 63 The American Cariboo is identical with the reindeer of Europe.
b. *attrib.* and *Comb.* **Caribou Eskimo**, one of a group of Eskimos living in the Barren Grounds of N. Canada and depending on caribou; **caribou moss**, reindeer moss.
1779 in *Essex Inst. Hist. Coll.* XLIX. 112 Sold..82 caribou skins, at £6 10. 0. **1860** H. Y. HIND *Narr. Canad. Red River Exped.* I. v. 110 The general surface was either bare..or else thickly covered with caribou moss and tripe de roche. **1887** *Harper's Mag.* Feb. 458/2 The hunter..covers his feet with..a pair of moose or caribou shanks, with the hair outside. **1903** S. E. WHITE *Conjuror's House* viii. 94 She felt..the hunger that yet could not stomach the..hairy, black caribou meat. **1904** —— *Silent Places* xiii. 137 The foundation he made of caribou moss. **1929** K. B. SMITH *Caribou Eskimos* I. 9 'Caribou Eskimo' is the name which the Fifth Thule Expedition has attached to a group of Eskimo tribes in the southern part of the extensive Barren Grounds west of Hudson Bay. **1936** *Discovery* July 200/2 According to his view the eastern or Caribou Eskimo are neither original nor degenerate, but represent a fusion of Eskimo and Indian cultures. **1963** *Times* 25 Feb. (Canada Suppl.) p. xvi/5 The Chipewyan Indians—the greatest of the caribou-eating tribes.

‖**cari'cado.** *Obs.* Also **carr-.** [prob. f. It. *caricare* to load, *caricata* a loading: see -ADO.] A movement in fencing.
1595 SAVIOLO *Practice* L ij a, You maie vse a caricado. **1599** MARSTON *Sat.* 227 The carricado, with th' enbrocata.

†**carica'tura.** *Obs.* Also 8 **carri-, carra-,** 8–9 **cara-.** [It.; lit. 'charge', 'loading', f. *caricare* to charge, load, exaggerate. Superseded in English by *caricature*.]
1. = CARICATURE 1.
a **1682** SIR T. BROWNE *Misc. Tracts* 207 Pieces and Draughts in Caricatura. **1690** *Sir T. Browne's Let. to Friend* §10 *note*, When men's faces are drawn with resemblance to some other animals, the Italians call it, to be drawn in Caricatura. **1773** GOLDSM. *Stoops to Conq.* iv, I shall be stuck up in caricatura in all the print shops. **1829** CUNNINGHAM *Brit. Paint.* I 187 Heidegger..had a face beyond the reach of caricatura.
2. = CARICATURE 2.
1712 HUGHES *Spect.* No. 537 ¶2 Those burlesque Pictures, which the Italians call *Caracatura's*; where the Art consists in preserving, amidst distorted Proportions and aggravated Features, some distinguishing Likeness of the Person. **1751** CHESTERF. *Lett.* 10 May, Rembrandt paints caricaturas. **1814** J. CAULFIELD *Calcograph.* Pref., The multiplicity of caracaturas of my person already appeared.
b. = CARICATURE 2 b.
1732 BERKELEY *Alciphr.* v. §20 Nothing is easier than to make a Caricatura (as the Painters call it) of any Profession upon Earth. **1756–82** J. WARTON *Ess. Pope* II. viii. 42 A caricatura of Cowley. **1783** W. F. MARTYN *Geog. Mag.* II. 172 Their plays being mere extravagant caricaturas.
3. = CARICATURE 3.
1752 (*title*) Lusus Naturæ, or Carracaturas of the present Age. **1789** MRS. PIOZZI *Journ. France* II. 313 Every thing appears to me a caricatura of London. **1809** *Q. Rev.* I. 347 Who can believe such a caricatura..ever existed?
4. *attrib.*
1680 SIR T. BROWNE *Let. to Friend* §10 What Caricatura Draughts Death makes upon pined Faces. **1682** —— *Chr. Mor.* iii. 14 Caricatura representations.

caricatural (ˌkærɪkətjʊərəl), *a.* [f. CARICATURE + -AL[1].] Of the nature of caricature, resembling a caricature.
1881 *Daily News* 4 May 5/4 This caricatural biography of Lord Beaconsfield. **1882** *Illustr. Lond News* 25 Mar. 278 To adorn the boulevards by their caricatural presence.

caricature ('kærɪkəˌtjʊə(r)), *sb.* [a. F. *caricature*, ad. It. *caricatura*, which it has superseded in English. The stress was, and is often still, on *u*, esp. in the verb and derivatives *caricaturing*, etc.]
1. In *Art.* Grotesque or ludicrous representation of persons or things by exaggeration of their most characteristic and striking features.
1827 MACAULAY *Machiav.*, *Ess.* (1851) I. 50 The best portraits are perhaps those in which there is a slight mixture of caricature. **1850** LEITCH tr. *Müller's Anc. Art* §13. 4 A thorough destruction of beauty and regularity by exaggerated characterizing is caricature. **1865** WRIGHT (*title*), History of Caricature and Grotesque in Literature and Art.
b. *transf.* of literary description, etc.
1871 FREEMAN *Hist. Ess.* Ser. I. i. 5 Stories..which.. illustrate, if only by caricature, some real feature in his character.
2. A portrait or other artistic representation, in which the characteristic features of the original are exaggerated with ludicrous effect.
1748 H. WALPOLE *Let. G. Montagu* 25 July, They look like caricatures done to expose them. **1788** STORER in *Ld. Auckland's Corr.* (1861) II. 207 A pleasant caricature of Lady Archer is lately come out. **1826** SYD. SMITH *Wks.* (1859) II. 88/1 You may draw caricatures of your intimate friends. **1883** LLOYD *Ebb & Flow* II. 128 His marked features stood out so strongly that it made his face seem almost like a caricature of himself.
b. *transf.* of literary or ideal representation.
1756 *Connoisseur* No. 114 Their ideal caricatures have perhaps often represented me lodged at least three stories from the ground. **1841–44** EMERSON *Ess. Nom. & Realism* Wks. (Bohn) I. 254 If you criticise a fine genius, the odds are that you are..censuring your own caricature of him. **1853** MARSDEN *Early Purit.* 245 An early Puritan comes down to us as a distorted caricature, known only as misrepresented in the next century by profligate wits and unscrupulous enemies.
3. An exaggerated or debased likeness, imitation, or copy, naturally or unintentionally ludicrous.
1767 SIR T. MEREDITH in *Burke's Corr.* (1844) I. 129 You are a caricature of St. Thomas, not to believe, till you saw, what I could do in an election. **1839** W. IRVING *Wolfert's R.* (1855) 166 Where they were served with a caricature of French cookery. **1860** SMILES *Self-Help* ix. 251 The monkey, that caricature of our species.
4. *attrib.*
1845 DARWIN *Voy. Nat.* vii. (1879) 139 A caricature-likeness of the Common Swallow. **1853** KANE *Grinnell Exp.* xl. 365 A rough caricature drawing by one of the men.

caricature (see prec.), *v.* [f. the sb. Cf. F. *caricaturer*.]
trans. To represent or portray in caricature; to make a grotesque likeness of.
1762–71 H. WALPOLE *Vertue's Anecd. Paint.* IV. iv. (R.) In revenge for this epistle, Hogarth caricatured Churchill under the form of a canonical bear. **1760** LYTTELTON *Dial. Dead* iv, He could draw an ill face, or caricature a good one, with a masterly hand. **1851** RUSKIN *Stones Ven.* (1874) I. App. 398 The appointed fate of the Renaissance architects, to caricature whatever they imitated.
b. *transf.* and *fig.* To burlesque.
1749 SMOLLETT *Gil Bl.* 431 It would be caricaturing the peerage to confer it on me. **1862** GOULBURN *Pers. Relig.* IV. vii. (1873) 307 The Faith once given to the saints is grievously caricatured.
Hence (from sb. and vb.) **carica'turable** *a.*; **caricatured** *ppl. a.*; †**caricaturely** *adv.*; †**caricaturer** (= CARICATURIST); **caricaturing** *vbl. sb.*; **caricaturish** *a.* (For pronunc. see the sb.)
1886 *Sat. Rev.* 31 July 170 A grotesque and caricaturable ugliness. **1813** *Examiner* 5 Apr. 223/1 Those caricatured rogues which give eclat to celebrated plays. **1865** *Public Opin.* 28 Jan. 104 It is the caricatured crinolines that have brought their originals into disfavour. **1759** MACKLIN *Love à la Mode* I. i. (1793) 10 His manner..has something so caricaturely risible in it. **1758** *Monthly Rev.* 319 The most eminent Caracaturers of these times. *Ibid.* All the humourous effects of the fashionable manner of Caracaturing. **1859** DICKENS *T. Two Cities* II. xiv, With beer-drinking, pipe-smoking, song-roaring, and infinite caricaturing of woe. **1819** *Blackw. Mag.* V 401 Either that.. they are rude or weak, caricaturish or insufficient.

ˌcarica'turist. [f. CARICATURE + -IST; or a. F. *caricaturiste*.] One who practises caricature.
1798 FERRIAR *Illustr. Sterne* i. 8 Exaggeration is also the art of caricaturists. **1865** WRIGHT *Hist. Caricature* xxviii. (1875) 480 Gillray was, beyond all others, the great political caricaturist of his age. **1866** FELTON *Anc. & Mod. Gr.* II. ix. 156 Aristophanes..was a brilliant caricaturist.

carices, plural of CAREX, sedge.

carick(e, carik(e, obs. forms of CARRACK.

cari'cography. [f. CAREX, *caric-* + -(O)GRAPHY, after pure Gr. compounds.] A description of the genus Carex and its species.
1846 in WORCESTER. **1864** WEBSTER cites DEWEY.

caricous ('kærɪkəs), *a.* [f. L. *cārica* a kind of dry fig + -OUS.] Resembling a fig.
1730–6 BAILEY, *Caricous Tumour* (with Surgeons) a swelling resembling the figure of a fig. **1751** in CHAMBERS *Cycl.* **1847** in CRAIG; and in mod. Dicts.

Caridea (kə'rɪdɪə), *sb. pl. Zool.* [mod.L. (neut. pl.), f. Gr. καρίς, καριδ- shrimp.] A group of macrurous decapod crustaceans, containing the shrimps and prawns. Hence **carid** ('kærɪd), a member of this tribe; also *attrib.*; **ca'ridean, 'caridid** *adjs.*, of or belonging to the Caridea; **'caridoid** *a.*, resembling the Caridea.
1852 DANA *Crustacea* I. 528 In arranging the Caridea into groups, much stress is usually laid upon external form and length of beak. **1877** THOMSON *Voy. Challenger* II. iii. 193 Scarlet caridid and peneid shrimps. **1904** *Ann & Mag. Nat. Hist.* XIII. 147 This combination of characters [in Malacostraca] goes to make up what might be called the caridoid 'facies'. **1907** *Ibid.* XIX. 460 The absence [in the Penæidea] of the Caridean bend in the abdomen. *Ibid.* 461 The gill-series in the lower Reptantia are fuller than in either Penæids or Carids. **1909** G. SMITH in *Cambr. Nat. Hist.* IV. 158 Two of the Caridea, viz. the Shrimp..and the Prawn. **1964** BODEN & KAMPA in *Oceanogr. & Marine Biol.* II. 354 The penaeid and carid decapod crustaceans.

†**carie.** *Obs.* perhaps = CARRY *sb.* load.
c **1300** *K. Alis.* 6695 With besauns, a thousand camailes; Y wol geve the gymmes, and byghes, Ten thousand caries.

carie(n, obs. form of CARRY *v.*, CARE *v.*

'caried, *ppl. a. rare*[−1]. [f. CARIES + -ED. Cf. F. *carié*.] Affected with caries, decayed.
1884 VERN. LEE *Euphor.* I. 181 Unfleshed, caried carcases.

carien, obs. form of CARRION.

caries ('kɛəriːz). [L. *cariēs*. Cf. F. *carie*.]
a. *Pathol.* Decay of the bones or teeth. Also *attrib.* and *Comb.* **b.** *Bot.* Decay of vegetable tissue.
1634 T. JOHNSON *Parey's Chirurg.* xix. 27 The excrementitious humours..to wit the matter of the *Caries*. **1655** CULPEPPER *Riverius* II. xv. 89 A Caries or foulness of the Bone. **1836** TODD *Cycl. Anat.* I. 746/1 Caries..attacks the cranium in common with the rest of the osseous system. **1859** J. TOMES *Dental Surg.* 305 The enamel and the dentine are the tissues..affected by caries. **1937** T. W. & E. V. B. WIDDOWSON *Dental Surgery* (ed. 3) ix. 228 Many teeth are caries-free until cementum is exposed late in life. **1944** MARZELL & BRONNER *Dental Surgeon's Handbk.* 10 Caries prophylaxis should begin in early infancy. **1963** J. OSBORNE *Dental Mech.* (ed. 5) x. 193 These may form a caries-prone area.
Hence †**'cariez'd** *ppl. a.*
1634 T. JOHNSON *Parey's Chirurg.* XXIX. (1678) 689 His leg all ulcered, and all the bones cariez'd and rotten.

carillon (‖karijɔ̃, 'kærɪljɒn, kə'rɪljən). [Fr.; f. 'med.L. *quadriliōn-em* a quaternary, because carillons were formerly rung on four bells' (Littré); cf. It. *quadriglio* 'a crue, troupe, companie' (Florio); but some think the *carillon* was orig. the melody.]
1. 'A set of bells so hung and arranged as to be capable of being played upon either by manual action or by machinery' (Grove).
1775 J. COLLIER *Mus. Trav.* (ed. 2) 39 Dr. Burney treats all *Carillons* with sovereign contempt, I confess I was much pleased with these. **1776** *Ibid.* (ed. 4) App. 15 An accurate history of the carillons and church-clock. **1836** *Fam. Tour S. Holland* 111 A fine set of carillons, which emit pleasing silvery tones. **1854** BADHAM *Halieut.* 377 Adjust to each a little carillon of bells. **1872** ELLACOMBE *Bells of Ch.* x. 349 There are in the tower of Notre Dame at Antwerp two Carillons..accords or harmonies of four and six notes can be played on them.
2. An air or melody played on the bells.
1803 REES *Cycl.*, *Carillons*, a species of chimes frequent in the Low Countries, played on a number of bells. **1873**

LONGF. *Elizabeth* Pref. 81 When ceased the little carillon To herald from its wooden tower The important transit of the hour. **1879** DOWDEN *Southey* iv. 85 Flanders..where the carillons ripple from old spires.

3. A musical instrument, or appendage to one, to imitate a peal of bells.

1819 REES *Cycl.* VI, *Carillon*, is likewise the name of a small keyed instrument to imitate a peal of hand bells. **1876** HILES *Catech. Organ* x. (1878) 98 The Carillon [in the organ] is a series of sonorous steel bars. **1881** C. A. EDWARDS *Organs* 68 In Mr. Holmes' organ the echo, the solo, and the carillon are all three commanded from the fourth clavier.

Hence ‖**carillo'nneur**. [Fr.]

1772 BURNEY *Pres. St. Mus.* 15 The Carillonneur was literally at work, and hard work indeed it must be. **1871** HAWEIS *Music & Mor.* III. iii. 472 The best living carillonneurs. **1879** GROVE *Dict. Mus.* I. 593 As carilloneur his duties were to play..to keep the chimes in tune and to set fresh tunes..on the drum of the carillon.

carilloner (kə'rɪljənə(r)), anglicization of CARILLONNEUR.

1930 *Aberdeen Press & Jrnl.* 20 Jan. 6/6 Again and again the carilloner had to give encore pieces.

‖**carina** (kə'raɪnə). *Zool.* and *Bot.* [L. *carīna* keel.] Applied to various structures of the form of a keel or ridge; esp. **a.** the two petals forming the base of a papilionaceous corolla; **b.** the median ridge on the mericarp of an umbelliferous fruit; **c.** the median ridge on the sternum of birds; **d.** the dorsal single plate of the shell of Cirripedes; **e.** the vertebral column of an embryo. (*Syd. Soc. Lex.*)

1704 J. HARRIS *Lex. Techn.*, *Carina*, is a Term used..by the Anatomists for the first Rudiments of the intire Vertebræ, as they appear in a Chicken's Embryo..because it is crooked in the form of the Keel of a Ship. **1774** GARDEN in *Phil. Trans.* LXV. 104 This carina, or keel, is very distinguishable..by its thinness, its apparent laxness. **1828** STARK *Elem. Nat. Hist.* II. 187 Dorsal carina prolonged and pointed. **1842** GRAY *Struct. Bot.* (1880) 185 In a Papilionaceous Corolla..the two anterior [petals]..partly cohering to form a prow-shaped body, the Carina or Keel. **1872** NICHOLSON *Palæont.* 151 The compartment at the end of the shell where the animal thrusts out its cirrated limbs, is called the 'carina'. **1872** OLIVER *Elem. Bot.* App. 304 Alæ roundish, converging, shorter than the compressed, curved carina.

carinal (kə'raɪnəl), *a. Zool.* and *Bot.* [f. prec. + -AL[1].] Pertaining to the carina; see prec.

1872 NICHOLSON *Palæont.* 151 The carinal Margin. **1872** OLIVER *Elem. Bot.* II. 181 The carinal ridges are opposite to the stamens. **1877** HUXLEY *Anat. Inv. An.* vi. 292 The carinal and the rostral compartments.

‖**carinaria** (kærɪ'nɛərɪə). *Zool.* [f. L. *carīna* keel.] A genus of Heteropodous Molluscs, having the heart and liver protected by a small and delicate shell of glassy translucency, known to collectors as Glass Nautilus and Venus's Slipper.

1847 CARPENTER *Zool.* §901. **1873** DAWSON *Earth and Man* iv. 76 Those singular molluscous swimmers by fin or float known to zoologists as..Carinarias.

carinate ('kærɪnət), *a. Zool.* and *Bot.* [ad. L. *carīnāt-us*, f. *carīnā-re*: see next, and -ATE[2].] Furnished with a CARINA or ridge; keeled.

1781 KERR in *Phil. Trans.* LXXI. 374 The back is carinate; the belly flat. **1876** HARLEY *Mat. Med.* 391 Leaves linear..smooth, channeled above, carinate below.

Hence **cari'nato-**, comb. f. L. *carīnātus*.

1846 DANA *Zooph.* (1848) 327 Lobes carinato-angular. *Ibid.* 166 Exterior often..finely carinato-striate.

carinate ('kærɪneɪt), *v. Zool.* and *Bot.* [f. L. *carīnāt-* ppl. stem of *carīnāre* to furnish with a keel (or shell), f. *carīna* keel: see -ATE[3].] *trans.* To furnish with a carina, keel, or central ridge.

Hence **'carinated** *ppl. a.*, keeled, ridged; also of pottery (cf. CARINATION); = CARINATE *a.*; **'carinating** *ppl. a.*, ? forming a carina; **cari'nation**, a keel-like formation, ridging resembling a keel.

1698 J. PETIVER in *Phil. Trans.* XX. 324 The Stalk is round and carinated. **1880** WATSON in *Jrnl. Linn. Soc.* XV. No. 84. 228 Two threads whose prominence slightly carinates each whorl. **1788** GRAY in *Phil. Trans.* LXXIX. 28 Carinated scales..a character of venomous Serpents. **1846** DANA *Zooph.* 384 The twelve large carinating lamellæ. **1880** WATSON in *Jrnl. Linn. Soc.* XV. No. 82. 117 Each whorl..projects in an angular carination. **1881** —— *ibid.* No. 87. 411 The line of the tubercles forms a rather acute carination. **1936** *Oxoniensia* I. 49 This contained pottery of the first century, including a carinated bowl with cordons. *Ibid.* 60 Bowl with heavy moulded rim and slight carination at base. **1937** *Proc. Prehist. Soc.* III. 338 The commonest grave-vessel is a plain carinated bowl with pronounced shoulder. **1963** H. N. SAVORY in Foster & Alcock *Culture & Environment* iii. 35 The fine, carinated bowls of Clegyr-boia.

†**carine.** *Obs.* [a. F. *carine*:—L. *carīna*.] Keel.

1656 BLOUNT *Glossogr.*, *Carine*, the keel or bottom of a ship. *Howel.* **1678** in PHILLIPS.

carine, obs. form of CAREEN.

caring ('kɛərɪŋ), *vbl. sb.* [f. CARE *v.* + -ING[1].] The action of the verb CARE.

1553 GRIMALDE *Cicero's Offices* II. (1558) 87 No painfulnesse, no diligence, no caring. **1607** HIERON *Wks.* I. 318 A caring and studying to prooue what is the good will of God. **1633** P. FLETCHER *Purple Isl.* VI. xxxv, Daintie joyes laugh at white-headed caring. *a* **1797** H. WALPOLE *Lett.* I. 39 (L.) If the god of indolence is a mightier deity with you than the god of caring for one.

'caring, *ppl. a.* [f. CARE *v.* + -ING[2]; cf. UNCARING *ppl. a.*] That cares; compassionate, concerned; *spec.* with reference to professional social work, care of the sick or elderly, etc. Freq. as *caring profession, society*.

1966 *Punch* 6 July 28/3 This was good, caring, committed television, of the kind I am always begging for in these columns. **1976** *Economist* 21 Aug. 93/3 The shift from relative scarcity to relative abundance in the supply of social service manpower has meant that it is now much more difficult to enter the 'caring professions'. **1976** *Glasgow Herald* 26 Nov. 28/2 But you can't have it both ways. Either the much-vaunted 'caring society' is a myth, or a complete change in the value judgements of the people who govern television is needed. **1980** M. DRABBLE *Middle Ground* 52 The welfare state itself, and all the caring professions, seemed to be plunging into a dark swamp of uncertainty. **1984** *Listener* 10 May 20/2 (Advt.), A friendly caring atmosphere in co-educational boarding houses. **1985** *Sunday Tel.* 29 Dec. 17/6 The word *caring* in the context of the Tory Party meant that Mrs Thatcher intended to lower her voice another octave.

carino-, comb. form of CARINA, keel.

1872 NICHOLSON *Palæont.* 151 The one nearest the carina, 'carino-lateral'.

carioca (kærɪə'ʊkə). [Pg.] **1.** A native of Rio de Janeiro. Also *attrib.*

1830 R. WALSH *Notices of Brazil* I. 499 A fountain in the largo or square of the Carioca. *Ibid.* 500 The term Carioca is applied to a citizen of Rio in the same sense as cockney to a citizen of London. **1925** L. E. ELLIOTT in *Countries of World* V. XXXIII. 3364/2 Every one born in the capital [Rio de Janeiro] is a 'carioca'; the true native is supposed to be born within sight of the historic Largo de Carioca (a fine square with a great fountain). *Ibid.* 3372/1 The freedom of the carioca pencil and the pungency of carioca wit. **1965** *New Statesman* 10 Dec. 922/2 The *Cariocas* have left the cool and attractive hillsides to the shanty-dwellers.

2. A type of dance related to the samba, originating in Brazil; also, the music for this dance.

1934 *Washington Post* 13 Mar. 3/5 The polka has gone out of fashion, but why don't they learn the carioca? **1935** WODEHOUSE *Luck of Bodkins* xviii. 216 A certain brand of cigarette—one puff of which..will make a week-old corpse spring from its bier and dance the Carioca. **1962** —— *Service with Smile* iii. 43 A pal of mine who had sprained an ankle while trying to teach choirboys the carioca.

carioch, obs. form of CAROCHE.

carion, obs. form of CARRION.

†**cari'ose**, *a. Obs. rare*[−1]. [ad. L. *cariōs-us*, f. *cariēs*.] = CARIOUS.

1762 WOLLASTON in *Phil. Trans.* LII. 585 The os calcis, and astragalus, are both of them cariose.

cariosity (kærɪ'ɒsɪtɪ). *Pathol.* [ad. mod.L. *cariōsitāt-em*, f. *cariōsus* rotten, carious.] Carious state or condition; a carious formation.

1638 A. READ *Chirurg.* xviii. 130 Moist medicaments are not to be applied to bones, because they cause cariositie. **1746** AMYAND in *Phil. Trans.* XLIV. 199 A..Cariosity in the Body of the Os Humeri.

carious ('kɛərɪəs), *a.* [ad. F. *carieux* (16th c. in Paré), or L. *cariōs-us*, f. *cariēs*: see -OUS.]

1. *Pathol.* Of bones, teeth, etc.: Affected with caries, decayed.

1676 WISEMAN *Chirurg. Treat.* IV. iv. 309 Finding the bone carious. **1789** W. BUCHAN *Dom. Med.* 357 A rotten or carious tooth. **1831** YOUATT *Horse* viii. (1847) 202 Carious or hollow teeth are occasionally..seen.

2. *transf.* Decayed; rotten with dry rot.

1530 *Test. Ebor.* (Surtees) 295 My cariouse bodye to be beride in the Trenyte qweir. **1832** *Veg. Subst. Food* 49 The ..carious grains are..often housed with the sound grain. **1842** *Blackw. Mag.* LI. 286 Fire racing along the old carious timbers. **1848** RUSKIN *Mod. Paint.* I. Pref. 37 The earth yields and crumbles beneath his foot..for its substance is white, hollow, and carious.

Hence **cariousness**.

1818 *Art Preserv. Feet* 116 A cariousness which has rendered the amputation of one or more toes..necessary.

‖**carissima** (kə'rɪsɪmə). [It., superl. of *cara* beloved, dear.] A term of affection addressed to a woman: darling, best-loved.

1857 W. C. YELVERTON *Let.* in D. Crow *Theresa* (1966) ix. 109 How are you getting on in health, carissima, and how do the dreams progress? **1909** KIPLING *Actions & Reactions* 87 Don't be provincial, *carissima*. **1969** M. GILBERT *Etruscan Net* II. iv. 121 The old woman put an arm round her waist and said, 'Nothing is wrong, carissima, and nothing shall be wrong.'

†**caritably,** *adv. Obs.* = CHARITABLY.

1533 MORE *Debell. Salem* Wks. 973/1 To do otherwise truly and caritably their duty. [Perh. only a misprint.]

caritas ('kærɪtɑːs). [a. L. *cāritās*: see CHARITY.] = CHARITY I. Also *attrib.*

1862 GEO. ELIOT *Let.* 29 Dec. (1956) IV. 72 What charity meant in the elder English and what the translators of the Bible meant in their rendering of the XIIIth chapter of I Corinthians—*Caritas*, the highest love or fellowship. **1911** (*title*) Caritas. The quarterly review of the Guild of the Love of God. **1932** A. G. HEBERT tr. *Nygren's Agape & Eros* I. I. i. §5. 36 Mediæval Caritas is a complex conception, containing elements both of Agape and of Eros. **1936** H. G. WELLS *Anat. Frustration* xix. (*b*). 241 A free wide, generous, unpossessive caritas for the individuals about us. **1939** P. S. WATSON tr. *Nygren's Agape & Eros* II. II. iv. 391 Mediæval Christianity as a whole is Caritas-religion and Caritas-ethics.

caritative ('kærɪteɪtɪv), *a.* [f. L. *cāritāt-em* charity + -IVE.] **1.** Of charitable or benevolent tendency. Cf. CHARITATIVE.

1884 M. KAUFMANN in *Gd. Words* 617 Thus by a 'caritative system'—a term first introduced into text books of political economists by Wagner—to secure social peace.

2. *Gram.* Endearing, hypocoristic.

1906 DRIVER *Jeremiah* 368 It seems more probable that it has a diminutive, caritative force.

caritive ('kærɪtɪv), *a. Gram.* [f. L. *carit-* ppl. stem of *carēre* to lack + -IVE.] Applied to the case used (in Caucasian languages, etc.) to express the lack of something. Also *absol.*

1860 [see ADESSIVE *a.*]. **1939** L. H. GRAY *Found. Lang.* vii. 201 The caritive denotes 'lack of'.

†**'carity.** *Obs.* [ad. L. *cāritās*, *-ātem*, f. *cārus* dear. Cf. CHARITY, CHERTY.] Dearness, dearth.

1530 *St. Papers Hen. VIII*, I. 367 A gret carystye in Italye of all maner of grayn. **1620** VENNER *Via Recta* iii. 56 Notwithstanding the raritie and caritie of it. **1656** BLOUNT *Glossogr.*, *Carity*, dearth, scarcity, dearness.

cariune, obs. form of CARRION.

cark (kɑːk), *sb. Obs.* or *arch.* Also 4–5 **carke, kark(e**. [a. Af. *karke*, *kark*, a northern F. form of *carche*, *charche*, bearing the same relation to *karkier*, *carchier*, *charchier* (see next), that *charge* does to *chargier*.

The pretended OE. '*cearc*, *carc*, care' and its derivatives in Bosworth are baseless figments. There is no word of this form in Teutonic.]

†**1.** (?) A load; a weight of 3 or 4 cwt. *Obs.*

[*a* **1300** RILEY *Lib. Alb.* (1859) 223 *De Scawinga*, Qe toutz les avers des queux serra prys custume par karke, doit le karke poysera iiii centaines..kark du grein iii centaines.] **1473** *Acta Audit.* 31 (Jam.), Ii tun of wad, a cark of alum, a pok of madyr. *a* **1502** ARNOLDE *Chron.* (1811) 99 A karke of peper. A kark of gynger. *Ibid.* 99 The kark therof shal wey iij. C. *c* **1550** SIR J. BALFOUR *Practicks* (1754) 87 (Jam.) For ane hundreth carkes of kelles at the entrie ij, at the furthcoming ii. [**1637** COWELL *Interpr.*, *Carke* seemeth to be a quantity of wooll whereof thirtie make a Sarpler, 27 H VI. cap. 2. [Some error—the word there is *sackes*.] Hence in *Termes de la Ley*, BLOUNT, PHILLIPS, BAILEY, etc.]

†**2.** Charge, burden of responsibility. *Obs.*

a **1300** *Cursor M.* 20790 (Cott.) He wil noght tak þe cark [*MS. F.* charge] on him. *c* **1330** *Arth. & Merl.* 3952 This ich seuen saunfail, The cark hadde of the batayl. *c* **1400** *Gamelyn* 760, I see that al the cark schal fallen on myn heed. **1580** BABINGTON *Exp. Lord's Prayer* (1596) 148 Them that haue any great cark vpon their hands.

3. That which burdens the spirit, trouble; *hence*, troubled state of mind, distress, anxiety; anxious solicitude, labour, or toil. (In later use generally coupled with *care*.) *arch.*

c **1325** *E.E. Allit. P.* B. 4 Fayre formez myȝt he fynde in for[þ]ering his speche & in þe contrare, kark & combraunce huge. *Ibid.* C. 265 He knew vche a cace [? care] and kark þat hym lymped. **1330** R. BRUNNE *Chron.* 135 He quath..fiue thousand to þe hospitale, for þei were in karke. *c* **1449** PECOCK *Repr.* III. xv. 377 This seid cark and caring & attendaunce is miche more in a man for that he hath wijf & children. **1542** BOORDE *Dyetary* v. (1870) 240 Euer in carcke & care, for his purse wyll euer be bare. **1567** DRANT *Horace Epist.* II. ii, Mongst so much toyle, and such a coyle, such soking carke, and spyte. **1590** SPENSER *F.Q.* I. i. 44 Downe did lay His heavie head, devoide of careful carke. **1626** MASSINGER *Rom. Actor* II. i, What then follows all your carke & caring? **1639** H. AINSWORTH *Annot. Ps.* x. 3 He woundeth himselfe with his greedy carke. **1841–6** LONGF. *Nuremberg* xxii, The swart mechanic comes to drown his cark and care.

†**4.** Care, heed, pains. *Obs.*

1482 *Monk of Evesham* (Arb.) 78 The gret carke that they had of her riches..and imoderate carke of her kynnefolke. **1549** COVERDALE *Erasm. Par. Phil.* iii. 1, I haue with muche carke and care oftentymes warned you. **1576** WOOLTON *Chr. Man.* 66 The cark & care which Gods Spirit..taketh that justice may overcome. **1603** FLORIO *Montaigne* I. xxiv. (1632) 61 The carke and care men tooke about good husbandry.

cark (kɑːk), *v. Obs.* or *arch.* [ME. *carke-n*, *karke-n*, is identical in form with ONF. *carkier*, *karkier*, *carquier*, *qarkier*, later (and mod. Pic.) *carker* (in other dials. *carcier*, *carchier*, *charchier*) to load, burden:—late L. *carcāre*, contr. f. *carricāre* to load (whence came the OF. duplicate form *chargier*, in ONF. *carguer*, *cargier*, to CHARGE).]

†**1.** *trans.* To load, burden; *also*, to charge or impose as a charge upon. *Obs.*

a **1300** *Cursor M.* 8253 (Gött.) It was sua karkid [*F.* karked, *C.* cherged, *T.* charged], ilka bow, wid lef, and flour, and fruit, enow. *Ibid.* 23002 þai sal haue na might vp to win, Sua heui carked of þair sin. **1330** R. BRUNNE *Chron.* 110 Anoþer oth..þe clergie did him karke. **1340** *Ayenb.* 138 þe ilke..þet naȝt ne heþ bote þane nhicke y-carked mid zenne dyadlich. *Ibid.* 142 þe milde herten y-carked mid þornes of ssarpnesse of penonce. **1393** LANGL. *P. Pl* C. IV. 472 Shal noþer kyng ne knyȝt..Ouer-cark þe comune.

2. To burden *with care*, burden as care does; to worry, harass, vex, trouble. (Mostly in pa. pple.) *Obs.* or *arch.*; but see CARKING *ppl. a.*

a 1300 *Cursor M.* 5654 þan þai ware carked [*v.r.* fillud] in þat land [Egypt] wit care. *Ibid.* 23994 (Gött.) Bot carked [*C.* charked, *F.* carkid] sua i was wid care. *Ibid.* 24233 þou cark þe noght sa fast wit car. *c* 1330 *Arth. & Merl.* 4464 The king Cradelman Was soure carked and alle his man. 1830 TENNYSON *Dirge* 8 Thee nor carketh care nor slander.

3. *intr.* To be anxious, be full of anxious thought, fret oneself; to labour anxiously, to toil and moil. *Obs.* or *arch.*

a 1400 in Wright *Lyric P.* xvi. 54 For hire love y carke ant care. 1530 PALSGR. 476, I carke, I care, I take thought, *Je chagrine.* 1556 ABP. PARKER *Psalter* xxxvi. Argt., How he careth and carkth for his lytheir gayne. 1580 TUSSER *Husb.* (1878) 209 To carke [*ed.* 1573 carp] and care, and euer bare .. What life it is. 1609 HOLLAND *Amm. Marcell.* XIX. x. 136 Constantius .. sat carking [L. *curantem*] and musing upon the matter. 1649 BLITHE *Eng. Improv. Impr.* (1652) 79 He need neither Moyle nor Carke as he did before. *a* 1677 BARROW *Serm.* Wks. 1716 I. 54 A covetous man .. carking about his bags. 1732 BERKELEY *Alciphr.* ii. §20 Old Bubalion in the city is carking, starving, and cheating, that his son may drink, game, and keep mistresses. 1848 KINGSLEY *Alt. Locke's Song* 9 Why for sluggards cark and moil?

†**4.** In weakened sense (cf. CARE *v.*): To take thought or care, busy oneself. *Obs.*

a 1375 *Joseph Arim.* 30 þei carke for here herbarwe. *c* 1420 *Pallad. on Husb.* IV. 701 For boles eke now tyme is forto kark. 1602 *2nd Pt. Return fr. Pernass.* III. v. (Arb.) 47 Our doting sires, Carked and cared to haue vs lettered. 1603 *Engl. Mourn. Garm.* in *Select. fr. Harl. Misc.* (1793) 207 To cark for sheep and lambs, that cannot tend themselves.

†**5.** ? (Morris explains 'to produce'.) *Obs. rare.*

1340 *Ayenb.* 230 A donghel þet ne carkeþ .. bote þornes and netlen.

cark- in various words: see CARC-.

carke-cloth: see CARE-CLOTH.

†'**carket.** *Obs.* Also 6–7 **carcat, -kat.** [Contracted f. CARCANET, *carknet.*] = CARCANET.

15.. *Songs Costume* (1849) 92 Thair collars, carcats, and hals beidis. 1580 HOLLYBAND *Treas. Fr. Tong, Collier & autre bague pendant au col,* a coller or carket. 1603 *Philotus* xxviii, For to decoir ane Carket craif That cumlie Collour bane. 1814 *Discipline* III. 26 (Jam.) There's a glen where we used to make carkets when we were herds.

†'**carkful,** *a. Obs.* [f. CARK *sb.* + -FUL.] Full of care or trouble; anxious.

c 1449 PECOCK *Repr.* III. xv. 377 Ouer thouȝtful and ouer carkful. 1482 *Monk of Evesham* (Arb.) 60 Ouer carkefulle of hys bodely helþe.

'**carking,** *vbl. sb. Obs.* or *arch.* [f. CARK *v.* + -ING[1].] The action of the verb CARK; grieving, being anxious; trouble, solicitude; anxious toil.

1583 GOLDING *Calvin on Deut.* cxxxvii. 844 They which are maried .. must needes be giuen ouer to many cares and carkings. *a* 1639 W. WHATELEY *Prototypes* I. vi. (1640) 73 Without any further carking and perplexity of mind. 1659 *Gentl. Call.* v. 414 Those carkings and solicitudes to which needier persons are exposed. 1691 E. TAYLOR *Behmen's Threef. Life* xvii. 312 Distrustful carking and toiling. 1861 P. YOUNG *Daily Read.* ccxvi. 75 With all our carking and caring, we cannot increase our stature.

carking ('kɑːkɪŋ), *ppl. a. Obs.* or *arch.* [f. as prec. + -ING[2].] That carks.

1. An attribute of *care*, or the like: Burdening, distressing, grieving, wearing, fretting.

c 1565 T. ROBINSON *Mary Magd.* lxviii, Solace in her brest no place can finde, For carking care doth all delights together binde. 1748 THOMSON *Cast. Indol.* II. i, Ate up with carking care & penurie. 1840 DICKENS *Old C. Shop* lxiv, Some carking care that would not be driven away.

2. Of persons: **a.** Fretting, anxious; **b.** Toiling, moiling; **c.** Miserly, niggardly.

1567 DRANT *Horace Epist.* ii. C iij, Duke Nestor, sillie carking segge. 1579 TWYNE *Physicke agst. Fort.* II. lxxxiii. 266 a, A labouryng and carkyng man, whose lyfe ought to be a patterne of all quietnesse. 1600 HEYWOOD *1 Edw. IV*, Wks. 1874 I. 21 Whose recreant limbs are notcht with gaping scars, Thicker than any carking craftsmans score. 1720 WELTON *Suffer. Son of God* II. xv. 402 Who are so extremely carking and caring about this Life. 1748 RICHARDSON *Clarissa* (1811) VIII. lxxi. 331 Immensely rich and immensely carking. 1750 BERKELEY *Patriotism* §22 Ibycus is a carking, griping, closefisted fellow. 1789 D. DAVIDSON *Seasons* 62 (Jam.) List'ning to the chirp O' wandring moose, or moudy's carkin hoke.

†'**carkingly,** *adv. Obs.* [f. prec. + -LY[2].] Anxiously, fretfully, solicitously.

1611 COTGR., *Chagrinement*, pensiuely, heauily, sadly, carkingly. 1633 BP. HALL *Hard Texts* 11 Be ye not anxiously, distrustfully, carkingly careful for the things of this life. 1656 DUGARD *Gate Lat. Unl.* xvi. 193 Neither immoderately desire riches, or carkingly heap them up. 1660 S. FISHER *Rusticks Alarm* Wks. (1679) 326 Your .. false Translations ye are so carkingly careful of.

carl, carle (kɑːl), *sb.*[1] Also 4–7 **karl(e, 5 karll, 6 carril, cairle, carll.** [a. ON. *karl* (Sw. Da. *karl*) man, male, freeman, man of the people; found in OE., from the time of the Danish kings, in *hús-carl*, later also in *butse-carl*, and *carlman*, but not as a separate word. ON. *karl* = OHG. *charal*, *karl*, MHG. *karl*:—OTeut. type **karlo-z*. OHG. had also *charlo*, MHG. *charle*, *karle*:—OTeut. type **karlon-*. Besides these the LG. dialects have an ablaut form repr. an OTeut. type **kerlo-z*, viz. OE. *ceorl* (from *cerl*), MDu. *kērel*, *kerle*, Du. *kerel*, MLG. *kerle* (whence mod.G. *kerl*), Fris. *tzerl*: see CHURL. The form *karl* appears as the proper name *Karl*, OE. *Carl*, L. *Carolus*, Fr. and Eng. *Charles*: cf. CHARLES'S WAIN.]

1. A man of the common people; more particularly a countryman, a husbandman. *arch.*

[1000 See HOUSE-CARL, BUS-CARL, CARMAN[2].]
1375 BARBOUR *Bruce* III. 226 Stalwart karlis .. and wycht. *Ibid.* x. 158 He wes a stout carle and a sture. *c* 1386 CHAUCER *Prol.* 545 The Mellere was a stout carl for the nones. *c* 1425 WYNTOUN *Cron.* VIII. xi. 90 Thai sparyt nowther carl na page. *c* 1440 *Promp. Parv.* 62 Carle or chorle, *rusticus.* *c* 1450 *Merlin* xi. 167 They saugh come a grete karl thourgh the medowes. 1509 BARCLAY *Ship of Fooles* (1570) 159 Fye rurall carles, awake I say and rise. *c* 1550 SIR J. BALFOUR *Practicks* 510 (Jam.) Cairles, and men of mean conditioun. 1552 HULOET, Churle or carle of the countrey, *rusticus.* 1757 DYER *Fleece* II. 435 They clothe the mountain carl or mariner. 1820 SCOTT *Monast.* xvii, It seems as if you had fallen asleep a carle, and awakened a gentleman. 1821 JOANNA BAILLIE *Malcom's Heir* xii. 2 By lord and by carle forgot. 1876 MORRIS *Sigurd* II. 87 And kings of the carles are these.

†**b.** *esp.* A bondman, a villain; cf. CHURL. *Obs.* (after 1500 blending with prec.)

a 1300 *Cursor M.* 29444 þe toþer .. es woman, carl o feild, and child þat es wit-in eild. *c* 1400 *Cato's Morals* 313 in *Cursor M.* p. 1673 If þou haue carlis boȝt to serue þe in þi þoȝt. *c* 1440 *Promp. Parv.* 62 Carle or chorle, bondeman or woman, *servus nativus, serva nativa.* *c* 1440 *York Myst.* xi. 191 We are harde halden here als carls vndir þe kyng. 1483 CAXTON *Gold. Leg.* 148/2 He tormented a uylayn or a carle for the couetyse of hys good. 1530 PALSGR. 203/1 Carle, chorle, *uilain.* 1549 *Compl. Scot.* xvii. 144 The discriptione of ane vilaine (quhilk ve cal ane carl in our scottis langage). [1844 LD. BROUGHAM *Brit. Const.* x. (1862) 140 The oath of a .. king's thane, being of equal avail with that of six carles or peasants.]

2. Hence, A fellow of low birth or rude manners; a base fellow; a churl. In later times, passing into a vague term of disparagement or contempt, and chiefly with appropriate epithets. *Sc.* (*kerl*) or *arch.*

a 1300 *Cursor M.* 13808 'þou carl, qui brekes þou vr lau.' *c* 1325 *E.E. Allit. P.* B. 876 An out-comlyng, a carle, we kytte of þyn heued. *c* 1400 *Ywaine & Gaw.* 559 The karl of Kaymes kyn. 1476 SIR J. PASTON *Lett.* 776 III. 163 They weer ffrowarde karlys. 1526 SKELTON *Magnyf.* 1844 A knave and a carl, and all of one kynd. 1549 *Compl. Scotl.* xvii. 146 Thai that var vicius & couuardis, var reput for vilainis ande carlis. 1597 *1st Pt. Return fr. Parnass.* v. i. 1479 Farewell, base carle clothed in a sattin sute. 1728 THOMSON *Hymn to May* (R.), I deem that carl, by beauty's pow'r unmov'd Hated of heav'n. 1818 SCOTT *Hrt. Midl.* xvii, 'Ye donnard carle'. 1829 —— *Demonol.* iv. 123 Wrinkled carles and odious hags. 1882 MISS FOTHERGILL *Kith & K.* xiii, A rough-hewn, cross-grained carle like him.

b. *spec.* One who is churlish or mean in money matters; a grabber; a niggard. Now only *Sc.*

1542 BRINKLOW *Compl.* ii. (1874) 9 Another rich covetos carl. 1564 BECON *Jewell of Joye* Wks. II. 15 Those riche carles and couetouse churles. 1593 T. NASHE *Christ's T.* 53 None is so much the thieues mark as the myser and the Carle. 1597–8 BP. HALL *Sat.* II. iv. 34 The liberal man should liue, and carle should die. 1642 ROGERS *Naaman* 354, I will not say, as a Carle lately did, of great wealth, I shall dye a beggar. 1730–6 BAILEY s.v., An old Carle, an old doting, covetous hunks, a surly niggard. 1753 RICHARDSON *Grandison* (1781) II. xxxvi. 341 Mercantile carle. 1837 R. NICOLL *Poems* (1843) 90 He was a carle in his day, And siccar bargains he could mak.

3. Without any specific reference to rank or manners, but usually including the notion of sturdiness or strength, and sometimes of roughness; = Fellow. *Sc.*

[Cf. 1375–86 in 1.]
a 1550 *Christis Kirke Gr.* xxi, The carlis with clubbis coud udir quell. 1668 CULPEPPER & COLE *Barthol. Anat.* I. xxxi. 74 If he be a lusty Carle. 1724 RAMSAY *Tea-t. Misc.* (1733) I. 84 The night was cauld, the carle was wat. 1794 BURNS *The Carles of Dysart*, Up wi' the carles o' Dysart, And the lads o' Buckhaven. 1798 WORDSW. *P. Bell* I. xvii, He was a carl as wild and rude As ever hue-and-cry pursued. 1828 SCOTT *F. M. Perth* vii, The town hold me a hot-headed carle. 1857 J. WILSON *Chr. North* I. 156 A rosy-cheeked carle, upwards of six feet high. 1858 M. PORTEOUS *Souter Johnny* 7 A blither cantier carl.

b. Sc. *to play carl again*: 'to return a stroke, to give as much as one receives' (Jamieson).

1862 in Hislop *Prov. Scotl.* 161 Play carle wi' me again.

4. = CARL HEMP, q.v.

5. *attrib.* and *Comb.*: **a.** *simple attrib.* or in apposition: That is or acts as a carl; knavish.

c 1450 *Erle of Tolous* 1081 Thou carle monke, wyth all thy gynne .. Hur sorowe schalt thou not cees. 1593 PEELE *Order Garter* Wks. 1829 II. 238 The carl Oblivion stol'n from Lethes lake.

b. In sense of 'male', as ***carl cat, carl crab***; ***carl doddie***, a flowering stalk of ribgrass, scabious, etc. (cf. *curl doddy*); also CARL HEMP, CARMAN[2].

(The asserted occurrence of *carl-catt*, *carl-fuȝol*, etc. in OE. appears to be an error: they have not been found by us even in ME.)

c 1605 MONTGOMERIE *Flyting* 670 Carle cats weepe vinegar with their eine. 1691 RAY *N. C. Wds.* (E.D.S.) Carl-cat, a boar or he-cat. 1803 SIR R. SIBBALD *Fife* 132 (Jam.) The common sea-crab .. the male they call the Carle crab. 1868 G. MACDONALD *R. Falconer* I. 65 'He kneipit their heids thegither, as gin they hed been twa carldoddies'.

carl, *sb.*[2] *dial.* [Cf. CARL *v.*[2]]

1. = CARLING[2].

1875 ROBINSON *Whitby Gloss.* (E.D.S.) Carlings or Carls, are gray peas steeped in water and fried the next day in butter or fat .. They are eaten on the second Sunday before Easter, formerly called 'Care Sunday'.

2. Carl Sunday = Carling or Care Sunday.

1688 R. HOLME *Armoury* III. 130/1 The 5 Sunday in Lent called Carle Sunday. 1788 MARSHALL *E. Yorksh.* (E.D.S.) s.v. *Carlings*, The Sunday next but one before Easter, which is called Carl-Sunday.

carl, *v.*[1] [? f. CARL *sb.*[1]]

†**1.** *intr.* (?) To act or behave like a carl; to talk with a gruff, snarling voice, to snarl. Still *dial.*

1602 *Return fr. Parnass* v. iv. (Arb.) 72 Nought can great Furor do, but barke and howle, And snarle and grin, and carle, and towze the world, Like a great swine. 1621 BURTON *Anat. Mel.* I. ii. I. v. (1651) 60 They Carle many times as they sit, and talk to themselves, they are angry, waspish. 1875 ROBINSON *Whitby Gloss. Carl*, to snarl.

2. *trans.* To provide or suit with a male. *Sc.*

1807 KNICKBIE *Wayside Cott.* 177 (Jam.) If she could get herself but carl'd .. She wi' her din ne'er deav'd the warld.

carl, *v.*[2] *dial.* [Of uncertain origin.

(Perh. a back-formation from CARLING[2] 'parched peas', taken as a participial form.)]

trans. To prepare as carlings; to parch (peas); to birsle or bristle. Hence **carled** *ppl. a.*

1611 COTGR. s.v. *Groule*, *Febves groulées*, parched or carled Beanes. 1862 *Leeds Dial.* 263 *Carled peas*, grey peas steeped all night in water and fried the following day with butter. 1863 MRS. TOOGOOD *Yorksh. Dial.*, The sun carls the hay and makes it crackly. *Ibid.*, T'ground is sumpy underneath, but carled on top.

carlage, obs. Sc. var. of CARLISH *a.*

car-less, carless ('kɑːlɪs), *a.* [-LESS.] Not possessing, or unprovided with, a (motor) car; without cars.

1927 *Blackw. Mag.* Nov. 696/1 The transport problem —for of course I was carless—was solved by the arrival of Bosworth, one of whose cars I instantly seized. 1955 T. H. PEAR *Eng. Social Diff.* 147 The car-less middle-class man. 1970 *Daily Tel.* 26 Nov. 16/6 Car-less shopping areas.

'**carlet.** [ad. F. *carrelet*, in same sense, dim. of *carrel*, *carreau* file:—Romanic **quadrello*, dim. of *quadro*:—L. *quadrum* square.] A file of triangular section, two sides being single-cut, and one smooth; used by comb-makers.

1688 R. HOLME *Armoury* III. 383/2 Combmakers Tools .. a Carlett .. three square, whereof the smooth side is up, and one of the Teeth side seen. 1874 in KNIGHT *Dict. Mech.*; and in mod. Dicts.

[**Carlet** in Richardson, etc., a mistake for *Carlel*, i.e. (the earl of) Carlisle, in the following:

1630 DRAYTON *Barons Warres* iv. 7 That craftie Carlel closely apprehended.]

Carley ('kɑːlɪ). The name of an American, Horace S. *Carley*, used *attrib.* (chiefly as *Carley float*) to designate a type of large raft carried on board ships for use in emergency (see quot. 1922). Also *ellipt.*

[1903 *U.S. Pat.* 734,118 Horace S. Carley of Hydepark, Massachusetts, Assignor to Carley Life Float Company, of Philadelphia... I, Horace S. Carley, .. have invented a new and useful Improvement in Life-Rafts.] 1915 *Illustr. War News* 26 May 23/2 Our illustration shows a valuable life-saving device in the form of the Calley [*sic*] Life-Buoys. 1922 *Encycl. Brit.* XXXII. 451/1 The Carley Life Raft .. is made in various sizes. A large copper pipe is bent into the form of an O, brazed up to be airtight, surrounded by cork and canvas, provided with a strong rope netting to form a floor within the O, and fitted with hand ropes, etc. 1925 FRASER & GIBBONS *Soldier & Sailor Words* 82 'Carley Floats', life-saving rafts of circular shape. 1942 *Ann. Reg. 1941* 131 A search .. produced no more evidence of the catastrophe than two empty life-boats and a Carley float. 1951 N. MONSARRAT *Cruel Sea* III. vi. 161 Alongside the boats were the Carley floats. *Ibid.*, There were two Carleys.

carl hemp. Also 6 **churle hempe, charle hemp.** [from CARL *sb.*[1] in sense 'male'; but the name was actually given in 16th c. to what is now known to be the *female* plant (being the robuster and coarser).

(So in med.L., and other langs.; the popular error was pointed out by RAY *Hist.* (1686) I. 159 'Mas robustior (*haec nobis foemina dicitur quia prolifica*)', also by LINNÆUS *Amœnitates* (1746) I. 329; and fully discussed by BLAIR, *Botan. Essays* (1730) 246.)]

1. The female or seed-bearing hemp plant, which is of stronger growth, and produces a coarser fibre.

1523 FITZHERB. *Husb.* §146 Thy female hempe must be pulled from the churle hempe, for that beareth no sede .. The churle hempe beareth sede .. the hemp therof is not soo good as the female hempe. 1573 TUSSER *Husb.* (1878) 32 Karle hempe, left greene, now pluck vp cleene. 1597 GERARDE *Herbal* ccxxvii. 572 The male is called Charle Hempe, and Winter Hempe. The female Barren Hempe, and Sommer Hempe. 1691 RAY *N.C. Wds.* (E.D.S.) s.v., Nostrates dicunt karl-cat pro fele masculo, et karl-hemp pro cannabo majori vel masculo. 1877 E. PEACOCK *N.-W. Linc. Gloss.* (E.D.S.) The carl or male hemp was used for ropes, sackcloth, and other coarse manufactures; the fimble, or female hemp, was applied to .. domestic purposes.

fig. 1721 KELLY *Sc. Prov.* 373 (Jam.) You have a stalk of carle hemp in you;—spoken to sturdy and stubborn boys. 1789 BURNS *To Blacklock*, Come Firm Resolve, take thou the van, Thou stalk o' carl-hemp in man.

2. Also called shortly **carl.**

1573 TUSSER *Husb.* (1878) 113 The fimble to spin and the karl for hir seede. **1577** B. GOOGE *Heresbach's Husb.* (1586) 39b, The female or firble Hempe is first pulled up, afterward the male or the carle, when his seede is ripe, is plucked up. (In mod. Trade and other Dicts.)

carlicue, U.S. var. CURLICUE.

'carlie. *Sc.* [f. CARL *sb.*[1] + -IE = -Y[4].] A little carl, a man short of stature.

1697 CLELAND *Poems* 68 (Jam.) Some peevish clownish carlie. **1822** GALT *Sir A. Wylie* I. 40 (Jam.) Andrew settled into a little gash carlie, remarkable chiefly for a straightforward simplicity.

†**'carlin.** *Obs.* Also **carline**. [a. F. *carlin*, ad. It. *carlino*, f. *Carlo* Charles, the name of several rulers, esp. Carlo I, 1266.] 'A small silver coin current in Naples and Sicily, equivalent to about four-pence English' (Chambers *Cycl. Supp.*), or, in later times, twopence.

1705 HICKERINGILL *Priest-Cr.* II. i. 7 The Pardon will cost ..a Dukat and 5 Gross or..5 Carlins. **1799** SIR T. TROUBRIDGE in Nicolas *Disp. Nelson* (1845) III. 329 Sailors ..all driven into the gun-boats without a carline. **1818** HOBHOUSE *Hist. Illust. Ch. Harold* 541, 26 pence of the ancient small money (now, worth a carline).

carline[1], **-ing** ('kɑːlɪn). Chiefly *Sc.* Forms: 4 kerling, -lyng, 6 carlyng, 6–9 carling, carlin, carline. [Northern ME. *kerling*, a. ON. *kerling* woman, esp. old woman, fem. of *Karl* (with umlaut and *-ing*, Norse form of *-in*, -EN). *Carlin* is assimilated to CARL, and in the ending follows the Sc. pronunciation of -ING as *-in*, as in *mornin'*, *flittin'*, etc. In Sc. commonly ('kɛrlɪn).]

A woman, esp. an old one; often implying contempt or disparagement, like CARL *sb.*[1] 2.

a **1300** *Cursor M.* 11056 Þe tan was leuedi maiden ying, þe toþer hir hand-womman kerling. *c* **1375** ? BARBOUR *St. Theodera* 21 Thru flatry Of kerlyngis, þat in mony wyse ȝung mene betresis oft-syse. **1501** DOUGLAS *Pal. Hon.* 1942 Vnto the nimphe I maid a busteous braid, Carling [*v.r.* Carline] (quod I) quhat was ȝone. **1630** B. JONSON *New Inn* v. i, Why..sold'st him then to me..for ten shillings, carlin? **1712** ARBUTHNOT *John Bull* II. iv, [*Peg* says] There's no living with that old carline his mother. **1787** BURNS *To J. Smith*, That auld, capricious carlin, Nature. **1810** TANNAHILL *When John and me were married*, My minnie, cankert carling, Would gi'e us nocht ava. **1827** SCOTT *Chron. Canong.* Introd. (1863) 242 It was but about a young cateran and an auld carline. **1870** MORRIS *Earthly Par.* III. IV. 56 Goodwife..Thou art a sturdy carline yet.

b. Applied particularly to a witch or one charged with being such.

1528 LYNDESAY *Dreme* 45 Off the reid Etin and the gyir carlyng. **1535** STEWART *Cron. Scot.* II. 514 How King Duffois was witchit be..ane Witche Carling that duelt in Forres. *a* **1700** in *Sc. Pasquils* (1868) 44 A witches son, shame fa' his face Sa carling lyke. **1790** BURNS *Tam O'Shanter*, The carlin caught her by the rump, And left poor Maggie scarce a stump. *a* **1835** HOGG *Witch of Fife* lix, The kerlyngs drank of the bishop's wyne Quhill they scentit the morning wynde.

carline[2] ('kɑːlɪn). [a. F. *carline*, Sp., It., and med.L. *carlina*, reputed to be for *Carolina*, from the emperor Karl or Carolus Magnus (Charlemagne)—'Herba quam Carolinam vocant, quod Magno quondam Carolo divinitus ostensa fuerit, adversus pestiferam luem salutaris' (Ruelle *c* 1525 in Du Cange).]

A genus of Composite plants, closely allied to the thistles, and hence generally called Carline Thistle. The common species (*Carlina vulgaris*) grows on dry soil, and is conspicuous for the straw-coloured, hygrometric involucre which surrounds the dull purple disk of the flower.

1578 LYTE *Dodoens* IV. lxvii. 529 Carline Thistel..White Carline Thistel. *Ibid.* 530 They call it Carlina, or Carolina, bycause of Charlemaigne Emperour of the Romaynes, vnto whom an Angel first shewed this Thistel, as they say when his armie was striken with the pestilence. *Ibid.*, The roote of Carline boyled in wyne, is very good..against the Sciatica. **1605** TIMME *Quersit.* III. 177 The rootes of angelica, of the Carline-thistle. **1861** MISS PRATT *Flower. Pl.* III. 182 Carline-thistle. **1879** LUBBOCK *Sci. Lect.* xi. 36 The heads of the common carline..present a sort of thicket, which must offer an almost impenetrable barrier to ants.

carline[3], *a.* and *sb.* Also **Caroline**. Applied to one of the balls in a particular game at billiards; also to the game in which this is used.

1820 *Hoyle's Games Impr.* 372 The Caroline or Carline game is played either on a round or square table with five balls, two white, one red, another blue, and the caroline ball yellow. **1863** PARDON *Hoyle's Games* 408 The carline holed in a centre pocket scores six.

carling[1], **carline** ('kɑːlɪŋ, -lɪn). [Of uncertain etymology: in mod.F. *carlingue* 'the step of a mast, the peece of timber whereinto the foot thereof enters' (Cotgr.), (according to Littré from English); Pg., Sp., It. *carlinga*. Icel. *kerling* (in the *þulur*), as if the same word as CARLINE[1].]

1. *Naut.* One of the pieces of timber about 5 inches square in section, lying fore and aft under the deck of a ship, with their ends let culvertail-wise into the beams. 'On and athwart these the ledges rest, whereon the planks of the deck and other portions of carpentry are made fast' (Smyth *Word-bk.*).

1611 COTGR. s.v. *Aileurs*, Our Ship-wrights name them Comings or Carlings. **1627** CAPT. SMITH *Seaman's Gram.* ii. 7 Carlings..lieth along the ship from beame to beame. **1775** FALCH *Day's Diving Vess.* 5 These stanchions were again supported with cross beams or carlings in the middle of the chamber. **1804** A. DUNCAN *Mariner's Chron.* II. 325 The first explosion..struck them against the carlings of the upper deck, so as to stun them. **1840** R. DANA *Bef. Mast* xxxi. 119 The water dropping from the beams and carlines. *c* **1850** *Rudim. Navig.* (Weale) 103 The carlings by the side of, and for the support of the mast..are much larger than the rest. **1863** *Times* 19 Mar. 14/2 Iron carlines.

2. *dial.* (see quot.).

1875 ROBINSON *Whitby Gloss.*, *Carlin*, or *Carelin*, the portable beam beneath a hatchway in the floor, for giving cross-support to the hatch-lid.

3. carling-knee, a piece of timber lying transversely from the ship's side to the hatchway, serving to sustain the deck between the two.

1626 CAPT. SMITH *Accid. Yng. Seamen* 30 Carling-knees, for the Dauid. **1627** —— *Seaman's Gram.* ii. 7 The Carling knees..comes thwart the ship from the sides of the Hatches way. **1704** in J. HARRIS *Lex Techn.* **1867** in SMYTH.

carling[2] ('kɑːlɪŋ). In 6 carline, 7 carlin. [Possibly f. *care* in CARE SUNDAY + -LING. Peas, parched, or otherwise prepared, appear to have been long associated with Lent: see Brand 'Mid-Lent Sunday', and PALSGRAVE 652, 'I parche pesyn, as folkes use in Lent, *je grasle des poys.*' This being so, CARL *v.*[2] would be from *carling.*]

1. (See quots.)

1562 TURNER *Herbal* II. 93a, The perched or burstled peasen which ar called in Northumberland Carlines. *a* **1724** in Ramsay *Tea-t. Misc.* (1733) I. 90 There lads and lasses.. Will feast..On sybows, and rifarts and carlings. *c* **1746** J. COLLIER (Tim Bobbin) *Lanc. Dial.* Gloss., *Carlings*, peas boiled on Care-Sunday. **1875** [see CARL *sb.*[2] 1].

2. Carling Sunday, the fifth Sunday in Lent, on which it was customary to eat parched peas.

c **1680** in Law *Mem.* 191 *note*, [Protest of the Gibbites] They solemnly renounce..'old wives fables and bye words, as Palm-Sunday, Carlin-Sunday..etc.' **1777** BRAND *Pop. Antiq.* (1849) I. 112. **1786** *Gentleman's Mag.*, In Northumberland the day is called Carling Sunday. The yeomanry..steep peas, and afterwards parch them, and eat them on the afternoon of that day, calling them carlings. **1825** HONE *Every-day Bk.* I. 378 Care Sunday is the fifth Sunday from Shrove Tuesday..It is also called *Carle* Sunday, and in some parts *Carling* Sunday.

carling[3], var. of CARLINE.

†**carlip.** *Obs. rare*$^{-1}$. ? A species of fire-arm.

1659 *Unhappy Marksman* in *Harl. Misc.* (1812) IV. 7 (D.) The carlip is but short, wanting some inches of a yard in the barrel.

carlish ('kɑːlɪʃ), *a.* Also 3 karl-. [f. CARL *sb.*[1] + -ISH[1].] Of or pertaining to a carl or carls; churlish, clownish, vulgar, coarse; rude, mean. Hence **'carlishness**.

a **1240** *Wohunge* in *Cott. Hom.* 273 Ne þole me neauer mi luue nohwer to sette o karlische þinges. *c* **1375** BARBOUR *Troy-bk.* I. 86 Hyme lykis erare to be Carlyche þane curtase. *c* **1440** *Promp. Parv.* 77 Chorlysche or carlysche, *rusticanus*. *a* **1500** *Colkelbie Sow* II. 513 (Jam.) This carlage man, this foirsaid Colkelbe. **1542** UDALL *Erasm. Apoph.* 179b, At suche a carlishe aunswer. **1552** HULOET, Carlishnes or churlyshnes, *rusticitas*. *a* **1624** BP. M. SMYTH *Serm.* 245 When a poore Dauid, as it were, would borrow a sheep of carlish Nabal. **1803** W. S. ROSE tr. *Amadis de G.* 78 Two carlish knights stood by.

Carlism ('kɑːlɪz(ə)m). [a. F. *carlisme*, Sp. *carlismo*, f. *Carlos* Charles + -ISM.] Attachment to Don Carlos, second son of Charles IV of Spain, and his heirs, as the legitimate successors of Ferdinand VII (died 1833), to the exclusion of the daughter of the latter, and her heirs; Spanish legitimism. So **Carlist** *sb.*, an adherent of Don Carlos; *adj.*, pertaining to Carlism.

1830 *Ann. Reg.* 287 The Carlists were in fact the party of the Church. **1834** *Gentl. Mag.* CIV. I. 97 Vittoria, the seat of Carlism. **1836** GEN. THOMPSON *Brit. Legion* v. 130 Lest the eloquence of the Carlist had been of a nature to induce the Christino to desert. **1873** *Spectator* 23 Aug. 1061/2 The delinquencies of some foolish partisans of Carlism.

†**carllein.** *Obs. rare*$^{-1}$. [? for *carling*, f. CARL *sb.*[1] + -LING, or ? -ING.] A little carl.

c **1460** *Towneley Myst.* 146 *Herod.* Shuld a carllein, a knafe, bot of oone yere age, Thus make me to rafe?

carloc, -lock, -lok(e, obs. ff. of CHARLOCK.

carlock ('kɑːlɒk). [a. Russ. *karlúk* isinglass; in F. also *carlock.*] Isinglass from the bladder of the sturgeon, imported from Russia.

1768 in E. BUYS *Dict. Terms of Art.* **1819** in *Pantologia*; and in mod. Dicts.

†**'carlot.** *Obs. rare*$^{-1}$. [f. CARL *sb.*[1] + -OT.] A churl, carl, peasant.

1600 SHAKS. *A.Y.L.* III. v. 108 He hath bought the Cottage and the bounds That the old Carlot once was Master of.

Carlovingian (kɑːləʊ'vɪndʒɪən), *a.* and *sb.* [ad. F. *carlovingien*, for *carlingian*, after *Merovingian* (f. *Mérovée* + *-ing*). Another form is CAROLINGIAN.] **A.** *adj.* **a.** Belonging to the second dynasty of French kings, founded by Carl or Karl the Great (Charlemagne).

1781 GIBBON *Decl. & F.* xlix, The Carlovingian Sceptre was transmitted..in a lineal descent of four generations. **1879** SIR G. SCOTT *Lect. Archit.* I. 45 The weakness of the Carlovingian monarchs.

b. = CAROLINE *a.* 1 a (*spec.* use).

1853 H. N. HUMPHREYS *Orig. & Progress Art of Writing* xi. 119 The more regular style of writing adopted about this time in France is termed, by paleographers, *Caroline*, or Carlovingian. **1906** E. JOHNSTON *Writing & Illuminating* (1977) I. i. 7 (*heading*) Caroline (or Carlovingian) writing. **1957** A. NESBITT *Hist. & Technique Lettering* I. iv. 27 Carlovingian writing was named after the dynasty of which Carl the Great is the chief representative. **1980** M. DROGIN *Med. Calligraphy* iv. 50 We know the script today as *Carolingian Minuscule, Carlovingian Minuscule, Caroline Half-Uncial*, [etc.].

B. *sb.* = CAROLINGIAN *sb.*

1845 J. S. MILL in *Edin. Rev.* LXXXII. 415 Five centuries..extended from Clovis to the last of the Carlovingians. **1882** C. T. LEWIS *Hist. Germany* II. v. 111 In the year 987, by the death of a fifth Louis ('le Fainéant', the lazy), the family of the Carlovingians ingloriously died out in France.

Carlowitz ('kɑːləvɪts, -wɪts). Also **Karlowitz(er)**. [a. G. *karlowitzer.*] A red wine of Carlowitz on the Danube (above Belgrade).

1858 *Murray's Handbk. Trav. S. Germany* 519 A good full-bodied red wine, known under the name of Karlowitzer. **1888** *Catal. Cellar Wines* (Christie, Manson & Woods) 24 July 7 One Bottle of Carlowitz. **1892** W. & A. GILBEY *Price List Wines* 9 Castle Hungarian Claret Karlowitz. **1920** G. SAINTSBURY *Notes Cellar-bk.* 93 The commoner vintages were not intolerable; you *could* drink Carlowitz if you tried, and the Austrian Vöslauer was not to be despised.

Carlsbad ('kɑːlzbæd). The German form of the name of Karlovy Vary, a town in Czechoslovakia, used *attrib.* in ***Carlsbad plum***, a blue-black dessert plum, usu. crystallized.

1885 *Army & Navy Co-op. Soc. Price List* Jan. 72 Carlsbad plums..per lb. 1/7. *a* **1916** 'SAKI' *Toys of Peace* (1919) 130 Trying to decide between the merits of Carlsbad plums and confected figs as a winter dessert. **1960** R. COLLIER *House called Memory* vi. 92 Sweet purple-black Carlsbad plums that would not [keep].

Carlsbad twins. 'Large felspar crystals which are porphyritically embodied in a regularly constituted rock, as in the granite of Carlsbad in Bohemia, and the granite of some parts of Cornwall' (Ure *Dict. Arts*).

Carlylism (kɑː'laɪlɪz(ə)m). [f. the name of Thomas *Carlyle* (1795–1881) + -ISM.] **a.** The characteristic literary manner or teachings of Carlyle. **b.** A mannerism of Carlyle (chiefly in language or style).

1841 *Fraser's Mag.* XXV. 722 It is Carlyleism in manner, but not in matter. **1881** *Athenæum* 9 Apr. 488/3 Fighting the good fight of liberty against tyranny, Christian kindness against Carlylism. **1881** *N.Y. Nation* XXXII. 231 The emptiness, or, to use a Carlylism, the 'putrescent cant' of most of the talk.

So also **Car'lylean, -'eian, -ian** *a.*, of, pertaining to, or like Carlyle; *sb.*, an admirer or imitator of Carlyle. **Carly'lese**, the literary style or dialect of Carlyle. **Carly'lesque** *a.*, **Carlyli'ana, Car'lylite**, etc.

1878 MORLEY *Carlyle* 188 Two conspicuous qualities of Carlylean doctrine. **1884** *Illust. Lond. News*, 23 Sept. 243/2 Thence the Carlyleian gigmanity. **1878** T. SINCLAIR *Mount* 104 Carlylians are good guides, if there are no better. **1858** *Sat. Rev.* V. 414/1 The Quarterly will..talk Kingsleyism, and the Edinburgh Carlylese. **1886** F. HARRISON *Choice Bks.* 181 The finest Carlylese is never equal to the finest English. **1866** *Cornh. Mag.* Oct. 414 His letters..took a curiously Carlylesque tone. **1865** *Sat. Rev.* 11 Nov. 607 The Carlylites retort that Mr. Disraeli is 'a Jew'.

‖**carmagnole** (karmaɲɔl). [Fr. *carmagnole* a kind of dress much worn in France during the Revolution of 1789; also in senses given below.]

1. Name of a lively song and dance, popular among the French revolutionists in 1793.

1827 SCOTT *Napoleon* Prose Wks. 1835 II. 99 *note.* **1837** CARLYLE *Fr. Rev.* (1857) II. II. v. xi. 82 Duke Brunswick is not dancing carmagnoles, but has his drill-sergeants ready. **1871** FARRAR *Witn. Hist.* v. 189 That liberty which has for her lullaby the carmagnole.

2. A nickname for a soldier in the French revolutionary army; applied by Burns to the devil, as the author of mischief or ruin.

1796 BURNS *Poem on Life*, That curst carmagnole, auld Satan. **1823** GALT *Entail* III. xii. 115 Switching away the heads of the thistles..as if they had been Parisian carmagnols.

3. The bombastic style adopted in reporting the successes of the French revolutionary army.

1860 *Times* 16 Apr. 10/2 A fair specimen of the style called the Carmagnole, so much cultivated by the newspaper and pamphlet writers of the first Revolution.

†**carmalle.** *Obs. rare*$^{-1}$. ? Carmelite.

c **1528** SKELTON *Image Hypocr.* II. 429 Be they not carnalles, And lordes infernalles? Yea gredy carmalles, As any carmarante.

carman[1] ('kɑːmən). [f. CAR *sb.* + MAN.] A man who drives a car; a carter, carrier. Also name of one of the London City Companies.

1580 BARET *Alv.* C 146 A carman or carter. **1598** B. JONSON *Ev. Man in Hum.* III. ii, Serue..in Thames-street, or at Custome-house key, in a ciuill warre against the car-men. **1663** GERBIER *Counsel* 26 That no Car-men turne or tumble down their Bricks. **1735** in *Swift's Lett.* (1768) IV. 141, I promise..to send the paper by the carman. **1880** *Times* 15 Nov. 6/2 The carman who drove me..to Ballinroe. **1887** *Whitaker's Alm.* 309 The fee for taking up freedom by purchase in the Carmen's Company is £9 15*s.*

† **'carman**[2]. *Obs.* Also 2 carlman, 4 carmanne, careman. [a. ON. *karmann*, var. of *karlmann* (in nom. *karmaðr*) male, man, f. *karl* man, male + *mann* man.] A man, an adult male.

1135 *O.E. Chron.*, þa namen hi þa men..carl men and wimen. *a* **1300** *Cursor M.* 27166 Quar he carman be, woman, or barn. *c* **1325** *Metr. Hom.* 156 Simeon hiht the carmanne And the womman was cald dam Anne. ? *a* **1400** *Morte Arth.* 957 Carefulle careman, thow carpez to lowde.

carmasal, var. CARAMOUSSAL, *Obs.*

† **Carme**, *sb.* and *a. Obs.* Also 4 **karme**. [a. F. *carme*:—*Carmel.*] = CARMELITE.

c **1380** WYCLIF *Sel. Wks.* III. 353 Carmes seien þat þei weren bifore þe tyme þat Crist was born. *c* **1394** *P. Pl. Crede* 340 Two frere karmes wiþ a full coppe. **1479** *Will of Stoughton* (Somerset Ho.) Freres mynors, freres carmes. **1535** *Compl. too late Maryed* (N.) A grey friar, Jacobin, or a Carm. **1631** WEEVER *Anc. Fun. Mon.* 139 This Order of Carmes, or Carmelites. **1797** *Archaeol.* XIII. 272 Discalced Carmes at Tongres.

'carmele. *Sc.* Also carameile. [a. Gael. *cairmeal, corra-meille*, Ir. *cara meala*, 'heath-pea, wild licorice'.] The Heath Pea (*Lathyrus macrorrhizus*), a leguminous British plant with an edible tuberous root.

1771 SHAW in Pennant *Tour Scotl.* (1769) App. 310 (Jam.) One root..which we call carmele..grows in heaths and birch woods to the bigness of a large nut..I have often seen it dried, and kept for journeys through hills where no provisions could be had. **1884** MILLER *Plant-n.*, Carameile.

† **'Carmelin**, *a.* and *sb. Obs. rare.* [a. OFr. *carmelin*, ad. L. *carmelīn-us*.] = CARMELITE. Hence also **'Carmeliness**. *rare.*

1631 WEEVER *Anc. Fun. Mon.* 139 There were likewise Carmelin or Carmelinesse Nunnes here in England. **1655** *Francion* VI. 14.

† **'Carmelitan**, *a.* and *sb. Obs.* = next.

1599 SANDYS *Europæ Spec.* (1632) 67 The Carmelitans and Augustines. **1736** J. SERCES *Popery Enemy Script.* 50 *note*, A Carmelitan Monk.

Carmelite ('kɑːməlaɪt), *sb.* and *a.* [a. F. *carmélite*:—L. *Carmēlītēs, -a* inhabitant of Carmel.]

1. a. A member of an order of mendicant friars (called also, from the white cloak which forms part of their dress, *White Friars*), who derive their origin from a colony founded on Mount Carmel by Berthold, a Calabrian, in the 12th century. Also *attrib.*, or as *adj.*

The order was introduced into Europe in the 13th c., and in the 16th divided into several branches, one of which, the *bare-footed Carmelites*, were distinguished by the severity of their rule.

c **1500** DUNBAR *Freiris of Berwik* 25 The Jacobene freiris of the quhyte hew, The Carmeleitis and the monkis eik. **1505** *Test. Ebor.* (1869) IV. 239 To the Freerres Carmelites a certayne of bookes. **1648** MILTON *Observ. Art Peace* (1851) 572 Most grave and reverend Carmelites. **1756–7** tr. *Keysler's Trav.* (1760) III. 81 The above-mentioned Carmelite church. **1766** ENTICK *London* IV. 281 The church of the White-friars, or Carmelites, stood on the south side of Fleet-street. **1823** LINGARD *Hist. Eng.* VI. 501 Pallavicino, a carmelite friar.

b. Belonging to, or a member of, an order of nuns organized on the model of the Carmelite or White Friars.

1611 T. CORYAT *Crudities* 14, I was at the Nunnery of the Carmelite Nunnes. **1670** CRASHAW *Steps to Temple* 61 The Admirable Sainte Teresa Foundresse of the Reformation of the Discalced Carmelites, both Men and Women. **1739** GRAY *Lett.* 1 Apr. (1900) I. 17 We saw the chapel of Minims and the Carmelite Nuns. **1888** H. J. COLERIDGE *St. Teresa* III. 9 St. Mary Magdalene of Pazzi was a 'Mitigated' Carmelite. **1909** *Dublin Rev.* Jan. 61 We have..Carmelites at Lanherne, Darlington, and Chichester.

†**2.** A variety of pear. *Obs.*

1704 WORLIDGE *Dict. Rust. et Urb.*, *Carmelite*, is a large flat Pear, one side gray, and on the other a little tinged with red..It is ripe in March. **1755** in JOHNSON.

3. A fine woollen stuff, generally of a grey or other obscure colour: perh. = Fr. *carmeline* 'wool of the *vicugna*' (a species of llama), Littré.

1828 J. T. SMITH *Nollekins* I. 19 Among her dresses was one of a fashionable Carmelite, a rich purple brown. **1859** *Lady's Tour Monte Rosa* 7 Every lady..should have a dress of some light woollen material such as carmelite or alpaca. **1873** MISS BRADDON *Str. & Pilgr.* I. vii. 77 [She] put on her Puritan hat, and sober gray carmelite gown.

'Carme,litess. A female Carmelite.

1669 WOODHEAD *St. Teresa* II. xxx. 183 The life of St. Ann, a Carmelitess.

† **'carminate**, *v. Obs.* [f. L. *cārmināt-* ppl. stem of *cārmin-āre* to card (wool), f. *cārmen* a card for wool + -ATE[3]. Cf. It. *carminare* 'to card or teazell wool, also to make grosse humors fine and thin' (Florio). Cf. CARMINATIVE.]

trans. Of medicines: To expel (wind) from the stomach or bowels.

1601 HOLLAND *Pliny* XXVI. viii, To carminate or dissolve ventosities. *Ibid.* (1634) Gloss., To Carminat, is to make more fine and thin the grosse humours..a terme..borrowed from those that card wooll. **1655** *Phys. Dict.* s.v., Carminating medicines, are such as do break wind.

¶ To card wool, etc. (Only in Dicts.)

1613 R. C. *Table Alph.* (ed. 3) *Carminate*, to card wool, or deuide. **1623** COCKERAM, *Carminate*, to spin. **1656** BLOUNT *Glossogr.*, *Carminate*, to card wool, or hatchel flax, to sever the good from the bad.

† **carmi'nation.** *Obs. rare*[−1]. [noun of action, f. *carmināre* to make verses, f. *carmen* verse, song.] Charming, incantation.

1620 MELTON *Astrolog.* 80 Seducing and blinding the ignorant..by Incantations, Carminations, Annual Observations.

carminative ('kɑːmɪneɪtɪv), *a.* and *sb.* [f. L. *cārmināt-* ppl. stem of *cārmināre* to card + -IVE.

'A medical term from the old theory of humours. The object of carminatives is to expel wind, but the theory was that they dilute and relax the gross humours from whence the wind arises, combing them out like the knots in wool.' Wedgwood.]

A. *adj.* Of medicines, etc.: Having the quality of expelling flatulence.

1655 in *Phys. Dict.* **1710** ADDISON *Tatler* No. 224 ¶8 The Carminitive Wind-expelling Pills. **1804** *Med. Jrnl.* XII. 555 Fennel..The seeds..supposed to be stomachic and carminative. **1875** H. WOOD *Therap.* (1879) 291 Chloroform ..exerts..a stimulant carminative action.

B. *sb.* A carminative medicine or agent.

1671 SALMON *Syn. Med.* III. xvi. 366 Carminatives are such as by a heating, rare and Anodyne quality expell winde. **1731** SWIFT *Strephon & C.*, Carminative and Diuretick, Will damp all Passion Sympathetick. **1807** *Med. Jrnl.* XVII. 560 Peppermint water is well known as a carminative.

carmine ('kɑːmɪn), *sb.* and *a.* [a. F. or Sp. *carmin*, in med.L. *carmīn-us*, contracted from *carmesīn-us*, f. Sp. *carmesí* CRIMSON, a. Arab *qirmazī* 'crimson', f. *qirmiz*, KERMES, ALKERMES, the scarlet grain insect.]

1. A beautiful red or crimson pigment obtained from cochineal. **b.** *Chem.* The colouring matter of cochineal; = CARMINIC *acid.*

[*c* **1450** *Alphita* (Anecd. Oxon) 93 Lacca..de qua et urina humana fit carminum.] **1712** tr. *Pomet's Hist. Drugs* It is of no other use that I know of..but to make Carmine. **1756** *Connoisseur* No. 110 Fixing a high duty upon rouge and carmine. **1791** HAMILTON *Berthollet's Dyeing* II. II. III. iii. 180 Carmine is the lake obtained from cochineal by means of alum. **1882** VINES *Sachs' Bot.* 39 Weak acetic solution of carmine [has] no power of colouring living protoplasm.

2. *transf.* As the name of a colour.

1799 H. HUNTER tr. *St. Pierre's Stud Nat.* I. 583 The azure insect deposited in a goblet of carmine. **1828** SOUTHEY *Ep. Cunningham*, To give his cheeks that deep carmine engrain'd. **1870** EMMA MARSHALL *C. Kingscote* 30 A sky where amber melted into the softest carmine.

3. a. *attrib.* or as *adj.* Of this colour; deep crimson. ***carmine spar*** = CARMINITE. **b.** in *comb.*, qualifying other adjs. of colour, as ***carmine-crimson, -purple***, etc.

1737–59 P. MILLER *Gard. Dict.*, Anchusa..2..Perennial wild Borage with a Carmine Flower. **1845** DARWIN *Voy. Nat.* i. (1873) 14 A most beautiful carmine-red fibrous matter. **1882** *Garden* 1 Apr. 210/1 The fine bright carmine flowers of this plant. *Ibid.* 21 Oct. 354/1 Bracts of a bright carmine-crimson colour. *Ibid.* 14 Oct. 347/2 Dahlias..rich carmine-purple.

carmined ('kɑːmɪnd), *a.* [f. CARMINE *sb.* + -ED[2], after *rouged.*] Reddened with carmine.

1893 *Scribner's Mag.* June 702/2 These coarse carmined Delilahs. **1902** G. MEREDITH in *Westm. Gaz.* 4 Mar. 8/2 Warfare with carmined savages. **1920** *Chambers's Jrnl.* 344/1 Two parted, carmined lips.

carminic (kɑː'mɪnɪk), *a. Chem.* [f. CARMINE *sb.* + -IC.] ***carminic acid***: the colouring matter of cochineal; = CARMINE 1 b.

1876 HARLEY *Mat. Med.* 791 The latter is called carmine, cochinellin, or carminic acid. **1880** *Academy* 20 Nov. 368/3 Carminic acid and Tyrian purple.

'carminite. *Min.* An arsenate of lead and iron of a colour varying from carmine to tile-red.

1854 in DANA *Min.* 410.

carminophilous (kɑːmɪ'nɒfɪləs), *a. Biol.* [f. CARMINE *sb.* + Gr. φίλος loving + -OUS.] Epithet of those cytoplasmic granules which are readily stained by carmine.

1901 G. N. CALKINS *Protozoa* 143 Carminophilous granules..are easily stained by carmine and many aniline colours. **1903** E. A. MINCHIN in E. R. Lankester *Zool.* I. II. 182 The so-called carminophilous granules,..composed apparently of an albuminoid substance which is stained red by picrocarmine and acetocarmine.

carmizale, carmousal, var. CARAMOUSSAL.

† **carmot.** *Alch.* Name for the substance of which the 'philosopher's stone' was supposed to consist.

1851 in MAYNE; and in recent Dicts.

carmuiche, -usche, obs. Sc. ff. SKIRMISH. [Fr. *éscarmouche.*]

1535 STEWART *Cron. Scot.* (1858) I. 243 With countering and with carmuiches also. *Ibid.* II. 610 With greit scrymmyng and carmusche euerie da.

carmusol, var. CARAMOUSSAL, *Obs.*

carn, carne, var. of CAIRN *sb.*

Carnaby Street ('kɑːnəbɪ ˌstriːt). The name of a street in central London, used allusively to refer to fashionable clothing designed for young people. Also *ellipt.* as ***Carnaby***.

[**1964** *New Statesman* 29 May 853/1 Window dressers and Carnaby street pants-peddlers.] **1965** *Observer* (Colour Suppl.) 29 Aug. 21/1 A mother's-boy spy, still living at home to save all his income for Carnaby Street. **1966** K. GILES *Provenance of Death* iii. 86 Leicestershire wore..his Carnaby Street gear. **1966** *Guardian* 25 Apr. 7/1 Discothèque-crazed tele personalities jerking in Carnaby plumage. **1969** C. BOOKER *Neophiliacs* iii. 80 Why was it going to be Britain that would produce the Beatles and Carnaby Street and television satire..?

‖**carnac** ('kɑːnæk). *rare.* [in F. *cornac*, Pg. *cornáca*, supposed to be of Indian origin, but not now found in any Indian vernacular. (Dr. Rost, quoted in Yule, suggests Singhalese *kūrawa* elephant-stud + *nāyaka* leader; others propose, for the first part, Skr. *karī* elephant.)] The driver of an elephant, a mahout.

1704 *Collect. Voy.* (Churchill) III. 825/2 Old Elephants..oftentimes kill their *Carnak* or Guides. **1727** A. HAMILTON *New Acc. E. Ind.* II. xli. 110 Going to the River to be washed, with his Carnack, or Rider on his Back. *a* **1832** in LYELL *Princ. Geol.* xxxv. II. 43 The elephant only allows himself to be led by the carnac whom he has adopted. **1884** C. BOCK *Temples & Eleph.* 22 The carnac or driver was quite unable to control the beast.

'carnadine. *Obs.* Also carnatine, carnardine. [ad. It. *carnadino* 'a carnation colour' (Florio); cf. *carnato* 'the hue or colour of one's skin and flesh' (Florio), 'complexion' (Baretti), f. *carne* flesh: *carne, carnat-o, carnat-in-o*, constitute a regular series. Cf. INCARNADINE.]

'Red, or carnation colour; or a stuff of that colour' (Nares).

1598 TOFTE *Alba* (1880) 74 How ill fits you this Ribbon Carnatine. *a* **1627** MIDDLETON *Any Thing for Q. Life* Com. (N.) Grograms, sattins, velvet fine, The rosy coloured carnadine. [**1847–78** HALLIWELL, *Carnadine*, the carnation.]

carnage ('kɑːnɪdʒ). [a. F. *carnage* (16th c. in Littré), ad. It. *carnaggio* 'carnage, slaughter, murther; also all manner of flesh meate' (Florio 1611):—late L. *carnāticum* flesh-meat, also, the flesh-meat supplied by tenants to their feudal lords.

OFr. had the corresp. word *charnage*, ONF. *carnage*, 'flesh of animals, meat, feast of flesh, season or day during which flesh is eaten'; it stills exists dialectically.]

†**1.** (See quots.) *Obs.* (only in Dicts.)

1656 BLOUNT *Glossogr.*, *Carnage*, flesh-time, or the season wherein 'tis lawful to eat flesh. Also a term in Venery, signifying that flesh which is given the dogs after hunting. **1662** so in PHILLIPS. **1721–1800** BAILEY, *Carnage*, Flesh that is given to Dogs after the Chace.

2. Carcases collectively: a heap of dead bodies, *esp.* of men slain in battle. ? *Obs.* (or confused with next.)

1667 MILTON *P.L.* x. 268 Such a sent I [Death] draw Of carnage, prey innumerable. **1714** GAY *Trivia* II. 471 As vultures o'er a camp..Snuff up the future carnage of the fight. **1774** GOLDSM. *Nat. Hist.* (1776) II. 124 The animals of the forest..mostly live upon accidental carnage. **1842** BARHAM *Ingold. Leg.*, *Black Mousquetaire*, Where those, who scorn'd to fly or yield In one promiscuous carnage lie.

3. The slaughter of a great number, esp. of men; butchery, massacre.

Frequent in HOLLAND, then rare till late in the 18th c.

1600 HOLLAND *Livy* II. 16 The carnage and execution was no lesse after the conflict than during the fight. **1601** —— *Pliny* VII. vii, Such as delight only in carnage and bloudshed. **1696** PHILLIPS, *Carnage*, a great slaughter. **1776** GIBBON *Decl. & F.* I. xiii. 281 A slight resistance was followed by a dreadful carnage. **1813** BYRON *Br. Abydos* II. xx, Mark! where his carnage and his conquests cease! He makes a solitude, and calls it—peace!

b. Slaughter personified.

1814 BYRON *Lara* II. x, Carnage smiled upon her daily dead. **1816** WORDSW. *Thanksgiv. Ode* viii, Yea, Carnage is Thy daughter.

4. *Comb.*, as ***carnage-field, -lover***; ***carnage-coloured, -covered, -loving*** adjs.

1721 CIBBER *Refusal* II, These Carnage Lovers have such a Meanness in their Souls. **1800** CAMPBELL *Pleas. Hope* 92 Carnage-cover'd fields. **1826** E. IRVING *Babylon* I. II. 90 The dragon, carnage-coloured, signifies Rome. *Ibid.* II. VI. 131 The carnage-loving character of the infidel Anti-christ. **1837** CARLYLE *Fr. Rev.* (1857) III. II. VI. viii. 121 One of those Carnage-fields, such as you read of by the name 'Glorious Victory'.

carnaged (ˈkɑːnɪdʒd), *a.* [f. prec. + -ED².] Strewn with carnage or slaughtered bodies.

1795 SOUTHEY *Joan of Arc* IX. (D.) Look yonder to that carnaged plain. **1852** D. MOIR *Castle of Time* xvi, Death's vultures crowd o'er carnaged Ascalon.

carnaill, obs. Sc. form of CARNAL *a.*

†**carnal**, *sb.*¹ *Obs.* [Presumably for F. *corneille* crow: but there may be some connexion or association with *carnal* adj.] ? A crow.

17.. '*Carnal & Crane*' i. in Child *Ballads* II. iv. (1885) 8/1 In argument I chanced to hear A Carnal and a Crane.

†**carnal**, *sb.*² *Obs.* A perversion of *cardinal*.

a **1528** SKELTON *Image Hypocr.* II. 429 Be they not carnalles, And lordes infernalles? **1543** BECON *Pol. Warre* Pref., One.. an Englishe man borne daunceth now like a Traytoure in a Carnalles wede at Rome. **1598** BARKCLEY *Felic. Man* (1631) 51 This Cardinall.. or rather Carnall and his Brother were both extremely in love with one woman.

carnal (ˈkɑːnəl), *a.* Forms: 5 *Sc.* carnaill, 5–6 carnell, 6 karnale, 5–7 carnall, 5– carnal. [ad. L. *carnāl-is* fleshly (in Tertullian and other Christian writers), and frequent in med.L. as an attribute of relationship, as *frater* or *soror carnalis*, brother or sister by blood, in which use it appears in Eng. in 15th c. The theological sense appears equally early, but app. not in Wyclif. The Fr. repr. is *charnel*: see CHARNEL.]

†**1.** Of or pertaining to the flesh or body; bodily, corporeal. *Obs.*

c **1470** HENRY *Wallace* XI. 1348 Bot Inglissmen him seruit of carnaill fud. **1555** in Strype *Eccl. Mem.* III. App. xliv. 125 Look not you for it with carnal eyes. **1579** FULKE *Refut. Rastel* 745 The Lutheranes admitte the carnall presence. **1658** SIR T. BROWNE *Hydriot.* i. 22 Carnal Interrment or burying. **1847** tr. *St. Aug. on Psalm* xlv. III. 240 The Church which coming from the Gentiles did not consent to carnal circumcision.

†**2.** Related 'in blood', 'according to the flesh'.

c **1450** *Merlin* vii. 117 Noble knyghtes.. many of hem carnell frendes. **1490** CAXTON *How to Die* 8 His wyf, his chyldren, & his frendes carnall. **1509** BARCLAY *Ship of Fooles* (1570) 181 Christ our Sauiour.. His carnall mother benignly did honour. **1598** HAKLUYT *Voy.* I. 66 Two carnall brothers.

3. Pertaining to the body as the seat of passions or appetites; fleshly, sensual.

a **1400** *Cov. Myst.* (1841) 84 Myghty soferauns of carnal temptacion. **1526** *Pilgr. Perf.* (W. de W. 1531) 148 b, Blynded with sensualite & carnall pleasure. **1670** WALTON *Hooker* 33 The visible carnal sins of gluttony and drunkenness, and the like. **1829** SOUTHEY *All for Love* iv, To carnal wishes would it [Heaven] turn The mortified intent?

b. Sexual.

c **1450** *Merlin* i. 17 That myght haue childe with-owte carnall knowynge of man. **1533** T. WILSON *Rhet.* 25 b, Without wedlocke and carnal copulation. **1667** MILTON *P.L.* IX. 1013 That false fruit.. Carnal desire inflaming. **1686** *Col. Rec. Penn.* I. 176 He was accused of having Carnall Knowledge of his Brother in Law's woman Servant.

4. Not spiritual, in a negative sense; material, temporal, secular. *arch.*

1483 [see CHARNEL]. *c* **1510** BARCLAY *Mirr. Good Mann.* (1570) D ij a, Suche one in carnell troubles can no displeasour finde. **1611** BIBLE *Rom.* xv. 27 Their duetie is also to minister vnto them in carnall things. **1781** GIBBON *Decl. & F.* xxviii. §5 III. 80 Judge whether Martin was supported by the aid of miraculous powers, or of carnal weapons. **1839** STONEHOUSE *Axholme* 207 [Wesley] began to doubt the utility, and even the lawfulness of carnal studies.

†**b.** as *sb.* in *pl.* 'Carnal things', temporal or worldly goods. [Rendering τὰ σαρκικά, or Vulg. *carnalia*, in *Rom.* xv. 27. 1 *Cor.* ix. 11.] *Obs.*

1607 S. COLLINS *Serm.* (1608) 89 They haue aduanced.. the spirtualls of other men, with the loss.. of their own carnalls. **1625** BURGES *Pers. Tithes* 10 Euery man.. that is made partaker of the Minister's Spirituals, must render Carnals. *Ibid.* 14 Spirituals doe well deserue carnals.

5. Not spiritual, in a privative sense; unregenerate, unsanctified, worldly.

c **1510** MORE *Picus* Ded., All faithfull people are rather spirituall then carnall. **1526** TINDALE *Rom.* vii. 14 The lawe is spirituall, but I am carnall [WYCLIF fleischli]. **1611** BIBLE *Rom.* viii. 7 The carnall minde is enmitie against God. **1667** MILTON *P.L.* XI. 212 Had not doubt And carnal fear that day dimm'd Adams eye. **1712** ADDISON *Spect.* No. 494 ¶1 To abstain from all Appearances of Mirth and Pleasantry, which were looked upon as the Marks of a Carnal Mind. **1865** MOZLEY *Mirac.* iii. 65 To a carnal imagination an invisible world is a contradiction in terms—another world besides the whole world.

†**6.** Carnivorous; *fig.* bloody, murderous. *Obs.*

1594 SHAKS. *Rich III*, IV. iv. 56 This carnall curre Preyes on the issue of his mothers body.

7. *Comb.*, as ***carnal-minded*** adj., ***-mindedness***; **carnal securitan** [f. carnal security; sense 5], etc.

1664 H. MORE *Antid. Idol.* x. 123 Abusing the credulous and *carnal-minded. **1607** HIERON *Wks.* I. 105 This must needes condemne our *carnall mindednesse. **1849** HARE *Par. Serm.* (1849) II. 30 Spiritual pride.. is apt to settle down into carnalmindedness. **1627** BERNARD *Isle of Man* 18 One Mr. Outside, in the inside a *carnall Securitan, a fellow that will come to his Church. **1655** FULLER *Ch. Hist.* IX. 112 A most *carnall-spirituall exposition. **1818** SCOTT *Hrt. Midl.* xii, This *carnal-witted scholar, as he had in his pride termed Butler.

†**ˈcarnal**, *v. Obs. rare.* [f. CARNAL *a.*] **a.** *trans.* To make carnal, fill with sensuality. **b.** *intr.* To have carnal intercourse *with*.

1643 SIR T. BROWNE *Relig. Med.* II. §7 This was the Temper of that Lecher that carnal'd with a Statua. *a* **1653** G. DANIEL *Idyll* iii. 90 The Lust of Tyrants.. carnalls the world at Will.

ˈcarnalism. *rare.* [f. CARNAL + -ISM.] The practice of what is carnal; sensualism.

1864 *Times* 17 Aug. 6 There is a degree.. of carnalism, so to speak, in all this. **1876** M. DAVIES *Unorth. Lond.* 119 To avoid the Charybdis of carnalism, there is no need to seek the Scylla of Quietism.

†**ˈcarnalist.** *Obs.* [f. as prec. + -IST; cf. *sensualist.*] A habitual follower of carnal things; a 'fleshly-minded' or unspiritual man.

1621 BURTON *Anat. Mel.* III. iv. II. i. (1651) 685 Meer carnalists, fleshly minded men. **1659** *Eng. Univ. Distract.* 21 Shallow headed, narrow-hearted Carnalists are pusled in it. **1829** *Lond. Encycl.* V. 172 A Carnalite is a worldly-minded man; a carnalist seems to be some shades darker in character.

†**ˈcarnalite.** *Obs.* [f. as prec. + -ITE.] = prec.

1573 ANDERSON *Exp. Benedictus* 7 b (L.), We feare not what the pope or any other carnalite can do against us.

carnality (kɑːˈnælɪtɪ). [ad. L. *carnālitās* (Augustine), f. *carnāl-is*. Cf. F. *charnalité*.]

1. The state of being flesh; fleshly condition, fleshliness; fleshiness.

a **1400** *Cov. Myst.* (1841) 114 Parfyte God and parfyte man, Havyng alle schape of chyldly carnalite. **1526** *Pilgr. Perf.* (W. de W. 1531) 82 b, This vertue toke from Hely the prophete all carnalite, and made hym apte.. to be lyfted up to god in the fyry chare. **1646** SIR T. BROWNE *Pseud. Ep.* v. v. 240 His carnallity and corporall existence. **1881** *Daily News* 31 Jan. 2/1 The carnality of Nana's beauty, which would have been to the taste of Rubens.

2. a. Sensuality, indulgence of the 'flesh' or body with its appetites. **b.** Carnal intercourse.

c **1440** *Gesta Rom.* I. xlvi. 158 Thow hast slepte to longe in the slepe of carnalite. **1483** CAXTON *Cato* D iij, In carnalitees and in many vyces delectable and swete to the persone. **1675** BAXTER *Cath. Theol.* II. ix. 200 He may give up himself to lewd carnality. **1720** GAY *Equivocation*, Marriage at best Is but carnality profest. **1866** J. MURPHY *Comm. Ex.* xxiii. 24 To bury all moral feeling in the grave of carnality.

3. a. The state of being unspiritual or unregenerate; unspirituality, worldliness. **b.** *concr.* A carnal thing, action, etc.

1483 CAXTON *Gold. Leg.* 129/1 Many doo almesses that abyde in theyr carnalytees. **1548** UDALL, etc. *Erasm. Par. Luke* xix, 154 b, The carnalitie of the lawe. **1660** INGELO *Bentivolio* I. (1682) 90 He exploded Reason as a meer Carnality. **1684** CHARNOCK *Attrib. God* (1834) I. 252 Spirituality is the genius of the Gospel, as carnality was of the law. **1748** HARTLEY *Observ. Man* II. iii. §2. 234 Mankind .. tending ever from Carnality to Spirituality. **1751** BP. LAVINGTON *Enthus. Method. & Papists Comp.* (1754) II. 155 The most infamous Carnalities. **1834** H. MILLER *Scenes & Leg.* x. (1857) 153 The deadness and carnality of the church at this.. time. **1879** CHR. ROSSETTI *Seek & F.* 254 Christ saw that great company approach whom he fed by a miracle .. and whom later he rebuked for carnality.

carnalize (ˈkɑːnəlaɪz), *v.* [f. CARNAL *a.* + -IZE.]

1. *trans.* To make carnal; to rob of spirituality; to sensualize. Hence **ˈcarnalized** *ppl. a.*

1685 J. SCOTT *Chr. Life* i. §2 A sensual and carnalized spirit. **1755** YOUNG *Centaur* vi. (1757) IV. 264 We are so carnalized by our lusts. **1850** MᶜCOSH *Div. Govt.* (1852) 21 A tendency to carnalize the Divine character by representing it in symbol. **1884** MISS COBBE in *Contemp. Rev.* Dec. 803 It will not merely belittle life, it will carnalize it, to take Religion out of it.

†**2.** *intr.* To act carnally, have carnal intercourse. *Obs.*

1706 T. BAKER *Tunbr. Walks* II. i, Tell him you are sorry you shou'd carnalize without his consent.

ˈcarnallite. *Min.* [Named (by H. Ross 1856) after *Von Carnall* of the Prussian mines (Dana).]

A hydrous chloride of potassium and magnesium, occurring as a milk-white mineral (but often reddish from admixture of oxide of iron and organic matter) in the salt mines in Prussia and Persia. It is now an important source of potash.

1876 PAGE *Adv. Text-bk. Geol.* xvi. 305 A series of saliferous strata.. carnallite, kieserite, etc. **1882** PLAYFAIR in *Macm. Mag.* XLV. 335 Potash.. now found in the minerals carnallit and kainit, in such inexhaustible quantity.

carnally (ˈkɑːnəlɪ), *adv.* [f. CARNAL *a.* + -LY².]

1. Corporeally, bodily; 'in the flesh'.

1539 TONSTALL *Serm. Palm Sund.* (1823) 43 That Christe .. shall reygne with all his syntes here in erthe carnally. **1561** T. NORTON *Calvins's Inst.* I. 25 Men do not beleue that God is among them, vnlesse he shew himself carnally present. **1607** DEKKER *Northw. Hoe* IV. i. Wks. 1873 III. 49 What saies the deuill.. for Ime sure thou art carnally possest with him. **1847** DE QUINCEY *Sp. Mil. Nun* Wks. III. 21 Gross men, carnally deaf from eating garlic and onions.

2. In the way of carnal intercourse.

1474 CAXTON *Chesse* 114 He knewe hys doughters carnelly. **1533–4** *Act 25 Hen. VIII*, xii, To the whiche prince Arthur, the said lady Catherine was lawfully maried, and by him carnallie knowen. *c* **1610** *Female Saints* (1886) 180 Some may thinke perhaps that.. he vsed her carnallie. **1611** BIBLE *Lev.* xviii. 20. **1686** *Col. Rec. Penn.* I. 176 Being Carnally Concerned with a Woman Servant.

3. In an unspiritual manner; as a 'carnal' or unregenerate person; 'according to the flesh'.

1527 TINDALE *Doct. Treat.* (1848) 43 Because either of us looked carnally for him. **1561** T. NORTON *Calvin's Inst.* I. xi. (1634) 38 They carnally worshipped God in stocks and stones. **1611** BIBLE *Rom.* viii. 6 To be carnally minded, is death. **1685** BAXTER *Paraphr. Mark* xii. 24 Carnal Men think carnally of things Heavenly. **1714** NELSON *Bp. Bull* xxxvi, Either spiritually or carnally.

ˈcarnalness. [f. CARNAL *a.* + -NESS.] Carnal quality or state; unspirituality; sensuality.

1549 COVERDALE *Erasm. Par. Rom.* viii. 10 Ye haue forsaken your carnalnes, and begunne now to be spirituall. **1646** P. BULKELEY *Gospel Cov.* I. 20 The carnalnesse and licentiousnesse of the lives of Christians.

carnaptious (kɑːˈnæpʃəs, kən-), *a. Sc.* and *Irish dial.* Also **carnapshus, curnaptious.** Bad-tempered; quarrelsome; cantankerous.

1858 *Ulster Jrnl. Archæol.* VI. 44 A nivver seen wan so carnaptious. **1879** W. G. LYTTLE *Readings by Robin* 48 (S.N.D.), He's a cross carnapshus wee brat, so he is! **1931** H. S. ROBERTSON *Curdies* 114 (S.N.D.), That belangt to ane they ca'd Rab Frew, a carnaptious auld deevil he was. **1963** *Times Lit. Suppl.* 21 June 459/3 The carnaptious old Irish hotel-keeper.

carnardine, erron. form of CARNADINE.

†**carnary** (ˈkɑːnərɪ). *Obs.* [ad. med.L. *carnārium* in same sense, in ancient L. a place for flesh, a larder, etc., neut. of *carnārius* belonging to flesh, f. *caro, carn-em* flesh. In F. *charnier*.]

A charnel or charnel-house; also *attrib.*

1538 LELAND *Itin.* III. 59 The Carnarie Chapelle in the Cimitery. *Ibid.* 100 A fair Chapelle on the North side of S. Mary Abbay Church.. under it is a Vault for a Carnarie.

carnassial (kɑːˈnæsɪəl), *a.* (*sb.*) *Comparative Anat.* [f. F. *carnassier* carnivorous = Pr. *carnacier*, med.L. *carnacerius* butcher, bourreau, f. L. type **carnāce-us* of or pertaining to flesh, f. *carn-em* flesh + -AL¹.]

A. *adj.* 'Relating to flesh eating' (*Syd. Soc. Lex.*); used of certain teeth of carnivorous animals, specially adapted for tearing flesh. **B.** as *sb.* A tooth adapted for eating flesh.

1849–52 TODD *Cycl. Anat.* IV. 907/1 The tooth.. has a.. carnassial modification of form. *Ibid.* 911/2 The fourth premolar is the carnassial tooth. **1854** OWEN in *Circ. Sc.* (*c* 1865) II. 109/2 The lower carnassials of the lion. **1875** BLAKE *Zool.* 78 The carnassial apparatus of these predaceous marsupials.

carnatine, var. CARNADINE, carnation-colour.

†**carˈnation**¹. *Obs.* [a. OF. *carnation, -acion* = *incarnation* (perh. aphetic form).] = Incarnation.

c **1410** LOVE *Bonavent. Mirr.* iii. (Gibbs MS.) þe secund Adame cryste god and man reformed his ymage in his carnacioun. **1570–87** HOLINSHED *Scot. Chron.* (1806) I. 395 He was slain the year of the carnation 1057. **1710** HOPKINS *Wks.* 716 (R.) The.. temporal carnation of the Son of God.

carnation² (kɑːˈneɪʃən), *sb.* and *a.* [ad. L. *carnātiōn-em* (in Cælius Aurelianus *c* 420 in sense 'fleshiness, corpulence'), f. *carn-em* flesh; cf. F. *carnation*, and It. *carnagione* 'the hew or colour of ones skin and flesh' (Florio).]

A. *sb.* **1.** †**a.** The colour of human 'flesh' or skin; flesh-colour (*obs.*); **b.** a light rosy pink, but sometimes used for a deeper crimson colour as in the carnation flower.

c **1535** DEWES *Introd. Fr.* in *Palsgr.* 921 Carnatyon, *carnation*. **1577** B. GOOGE *Heresbach's Husb.* II. (1586) 67 Some of them glitter.. with a deepe purple, and some with a passing beautifull Carnation. **1599** SHAKS. *Hen. V*, II. iii. 35 A could neuer abide Carnation, 'twas a Colour he neuer lik'd. **1622** PEACHAM *Compl. Gentl.* xiii. 129 Flesh-colours or Carnations for the face and complexion. **1662** PHILLIPS, *Carnation*, a kind of colour resembling raw flesh. **1827** LYTTON *Pelham* iii, Her complexion of the most delicate carnation. **1863** MISS BRADDON *Eleanor's Vict.* III. viii. 108 The pink-blossom tint of her cheeks was intensified into vivid carnation.

2. *pl.* 'Flesh tints' in a painting; those parts of a painting which represent the naked skin.

1704 J. HARRIS *Lex. Techn.*, *Carnation*, is a Term in Painting, signifying such Parts of an Human Body as are drawn naked.. or what express the bare Flesh; and when this is done Natural, Bold, and Strong, and is well coloured, they say of the Painter, that his Carnation is very good. **1760** GOLDSM. *Cit. W.* xxxiv, What attitudes, carnations, and draperies! **1812** *Examiner* 25 May 327/1 He has been.. less happy then usual in his carnations.

3. Name of a variety of cherry.

1664 EVELYN *Kal. Hort.* (1729) 210 Cherries: Carnations, Morella. **1767** J. ABERCROMBIE *Ev. Man own Gard.* (1803) 674/1 Cherries, early May, Carnation, Amber. **1846** J. BAXTER *Libr. Pract. Agric.* I. 163.

B. *adj.* [attrib. use of the *sb.* in sense 1.] †**a.** Flesh-coloured (*obs.*); **b.** rose pink. See A. 1.

1565–78 COOPER *Thesaur.*, *Carnosus candor*, a carnation whitenesse. **1578** LYTE *Dodoens* II. lvi. 217 [The flowers of the orchis are].. of a carnation or fleshly colour like the colour of mans body. **1588** SHAKS. *L.L.L.* III. i. 146 How much Carnation Ribbon may a man buy? **1607** TOPSELL *Four-f. Beasts* 13 A certain four-footed beast of a yellowish-carnation colour. *Ibid.* 232 [Of Horses] the chief colours are these; bay, white, carnation, golden, russet, mouse-colour,

flea-bitten, spotted, pale and black. **1653** H. COGAN *Pinto's Trav.* li. §1. 202 In a Carnation Satin Suit. **1820** SCOTT *Monast.* xvi, Hanging garters of carnation silk. **1824** BYRON *Juan* xvi. xciii, Juan grew carnation with vexation.
fig. **1647** WARD *Simp. Cobler* 86 To sugar your papers with Carnation phrases.

C. *Comb.*, as ***carnation-coloured, -painted*** adjs.
1596 NASHE *Saffron Walden* 64 When these Italionate carnation painted horses tayles were in fashion. **1786** tr. *Beckford's Vathek* 99 His superb carnation-coloured tent.

carnation³ (kɑːˈneɪʃən). Also 6 **incarnacyon, coron-, cornation.** [Some 16th c. authors give one form of the name as *coronation*, apparently from its 16th c. specific name, *Betonica coronaria*, in allusion to its use in chaplets (cf. CAMPION), or from 'the floures..dented or toothed aboue..like to a littell crownet' (Lyte). On the other hand, Turner calls the plant *an incarnacyon*, Lyte has *carnation* as well as *coronation*, and Gerarde expressly identifies it with the colour 'carnation'. Prior takes *coronation* as the original form, and Britten and Holland think his opinion 'probably correct'.

One or other name must have been due to popular mistake; *carnation* is alone found after 1600, and has apparently even modified the later application of 'carnation' as a colour-name: the flower, however, is not always of this colour: as Lyte says, 'some be of colour white, some carnation or of a liuely flesshe colour, some be of a cleare or bright redde, some of a darke or deepe redde, and some speckled'.]

The general name for the cultivated varieties of the clove-pink (*Dianthus caryophyllus*).
1538 TURNER *Libellus* Aiij, Betonica altilis siue coronaria, que a quibusdam uocatur cariophillatum, est herba quam uernacula lingua uocamus a Gelofer, aut a Clowgelofer aut an Incarnacyon. **1578** LYTE *Dodoens* II. vii. 156 In English garden Gillofers, Cloaue gillofers, and the greatest and brauest sorte of them are called Coronations or Cornations. *Ibid.* 154 Vetonica altilis, Carnations, and the double cloaue Gillofers. **1579** SPENSER *Sheph. Cal.* Apr. 138 Bring Coronations, and Sops in wine, Worne of Paramoures. **1597** GERARD *Herbal* II. clxxii. 473 The great Carnation Gilloflower..flowers of an excellent sweete smell, and pleasant Carnation colour, whereof it tooke his name. **1611** SHAKS. *Wint. T.* IV. iv. 82 Carnations, and streak'd Gilly-vors. **1779** SHERIDAN *Critic* II. ii, The striped Carnation, and the guarded rose. **1814** WORDSW. *Excurs.* I. 757 Carnations, once Prized for surpassing beauty. **1861** MISS PRATT *Flower. Pl.* I. 207 Clove-Pink, Carnation, or Clove-Gilly-flower.
attrib. **1631** MILTON *Epit. Mch'ness Winchester* 37 The pride of her carnation train. **1796** H. HUNTER tr. *St. Pierre's Stud. Nat.* (1799) III. 107 Basilicons, with a carnation smell, exhaled the sweetest of perfumes.

carnationed (kɑːˈneɪʃənd), *a.* [f. prec. + -ED².] †**a.** Flesh-coloured (*obs.*); **b.** reddened, made ruddy.
1649 LOVELACE *Lucasta* 12 (L.) Court gentle zephyr, court and fan Her softer breasts carnation'd wan. **1823** BYRON *Manfr.* II. ii. 18 Carnation'd like a sleeping infant's cheek. **1876** T. HARDY *Hand Ethelb.* II. xxxv. 76 Her hair getting frizzed and her cheeks carnationed by the wind.

carnauba (kɑːˈnɔːbə, -ˈnaʊ-, kɑːnəˈuːbə). [Pg.] The Brazilian wax-palm, *Copernicia cerifera*; so ***carnauba wax***, a wax exuded from the leaves of the carnauba and used in the manufacture of polishes, candles, etc.
1854 R. D. THOMSON *Dict. Chem.* 521/2 *Wax, Carnauba.* .. From the leaves of a palm in Brazil; soluble in hot alcohol and ether. **1866** LINDLEY & MOORE *Treas. Bot.* I. 225 *Carnäuba*, a Brazilian palm, *Corypha cerifera*, the leaves of which yield a wax, which is used for making candles. **1919** *Chambers's Jrnl.* Apr. 271/1 It is a question whether there is a more wonderful or more useful tree to man than the carnauba (or carnahuba) tree of Brazil. **1958** *Listener* 4 Dec. 967/1 The hard, most efficient polishing waxes (carnauba wax, for instance) had often to be mixed with less efficient, softer wax.

carnaval, obs. var. of CARNIVAL.

†**carˈneity.** *Obs rare*⁻¹. [f. L. *carne-us* of flesh + -ITY.] The state or quality of being flesh.
1691 G. KEITH *2nd Narr. Proc. Turner's Hall* 31 Flesh is a Substance, Carneity is but a Mode or Quality of it.

†**ˈcarnel.** *Obs.* Also 4 **karnel.** [a. ONF. *carnel* (Cotgr. *carneau*), var. of *kernel*, in OF. *crenel*: see KERNEL.] An early variant of the word KERNEL, CRENEL, battlement, embrasure.
c **1320** *Cast. Loue* 695 þe carnels so stondeþ vp-riht, Wel i-planed and feir i-diht. *c* **1325** *E.E. Allit. P.* B. 1382 With koynt carneles aboue, coruen ful clene. *c* **1330** R. BRUNNE *Chron. Wace* (Rolls) 1035 þey wyþynne stode in karneles, Wyþ arblastes schotten ageyn quarels. *c* **1340** *Cursor M.* (Trin. & Laud MSS.) þis castel..with carneles is hit set ful wele. **1362** LANGL. *P. Pl.* A. VI. 78 þe carnels beþ of Cristendom..brutaget with þe bileeue.

carnel, obs. f. KERNEL (of fruit).

[**carnel, carnel-work**, error for *caruel*, CARVEL, CARVEL-WORK, in Phillips, whence copied by Blount, Harris, Bailey, Chambers, Webster, etc.]

†**carneled**, *a. Obs.* [f. CARNEL + -ED². Cf. F. '*carnelé* imbattled, having battlements' (Cotgr.) and CARNILATE.] Embattled.
c **1330** R. BRUNNE *Chron. Wace* (Rolls) 14646 Castels aboute þe toun dide make, Bretaxed & carneled.

carnelian (kɑːˈniːlɪən). Forms: 7–8 **carnelion**, 9 **carnelian.** [A variant of CORNELIAN, altered under the influence of med.L. *carneolus* CARNEOL, or otherwise etymologized from L. *carn-em* flesh, with the notion of expressing 'flesh-coloured'.] CORNELIAN; a flesh-coloured, deep red, or reddish-white variety of chalcedony.
1695 WOODWARD *Nat. Hist. Earth* (T.) The common carnelion has its name from its flesh colour..which is, in some of these stones, paler, when it is called the female carnelion; in others deeper, called the male. **1789** MRS. PIOZZI *Journ. France* II. 335 Carnelions much amaze one in so northern a latitude. **1816** J. SMITH *Panorama Sc. & Art* II. 463 The carnelion is an agate nearly transparent, of different shades. **1861** C. KING *Ant. Gems* (1866) 5 The Carnelian is a semi-transparent quartz of a dull red colour, arranged often in different shades.

†**ˈcarnell.** *Sc. Obs.* [According to Jamieson, dim. of *carn* heap.] 'A heap' (Jamieson).
1536 BELLENDEN *Cron. Scot.* (1821) I. Introd. 40 Ane carnell of stanis, liand togidder in maner of ane croun.

†**ˈcarneol**¹. *Obs.* [ad. med.L. *carneol-us* cornelian; dim. of L. *carneus* fleshy, with the sense of 'slightly flesh-coloured'; but perh. an alteration of the forms in *corn-* under the influence of this supposed derivation.] = CORNELIAN.
1398 TREVISA *Barth. De P.R.* XVI. xxxiii. (1495) 563 Carneolus is a red stoon and dymme..yf it is hanged aboute a mannys necke..in stryfes it alayth wrathes. **1708** KERSEY, *Carneol*, a precious Stone. **1731** in BAILEY, vol. II.

†**ˈcarneol**². *Obs.* Some (? fleshy-leaved) plant.
1678 LITTLETON *Lat. Dict.*, *Carneol*, an herb, *acesi.* **1708** KERSEY, *Carneol*, a kind of Herb. [Hence in BAILEY, 1731.]

carneous (ˈkɑːnɪəs), *a.* [f. L. *carne-us* fleshy (f. *carn-em* flesh) + -OUS.]
1. Consisting of flesh, fleshy.
1578 BANISTER *Hist. Man* IV. 45 a, Of carneous and Musculous substance. **1662** FULLER *Worthies* III. 98 All their [carps'] mouths are Tongues, as filled with a Carneous substance. **1836** TODD *Cycl. Anat.* I. 575/1 The carneous parts of the fishes.
†**2.** Flesh-coloured, pale red. *Obs.*
1673 RAY *Journ. Low C.* 466 The one with a carneous, the other with a blew flower. **1880** GRAY *Bot. Text-bk.* 401.

carnet (ˈkɑːneɪ). [F., lit. 'note-book, booklet'.]
1. A note-book.
1897 *Daily News* 17 Sept. 6/2 Little scenes..that might have been taken bodily from the jottings of the artist's 'carnet' of subjects for illustration.
2. (*a*) A permit issued to an aviator (see quot. 1926²). (*b*) A permit allowing a motor-vehicle, etc., to be taken across a frontier. (*c*) A permit giving admission to some camping-sites.
1926 *Spectator* 20 Mar. 556/2 The A.A. issues Triptyques or Carnets to its members. **1926** *Flight* 2 Dec. 774/1 A 'carnet'..serves as a Customs pass on foreign aerodromes and relieves the holder of all troublesome formalities. **1955** *Times* 13 Aug. 7/7 One in eight of the motoring parties..took camping carnets which give them the run of camping sites recognized by the Alliance Internationale de Tourisme.

carney, *sb.*¹ ? *Obs.* [perh. connected in some way with L. *caro, carn-em* flesh: F. *acharné* would be in ONF. *acarné*, but evidence is wanting.] (See quot.)
1678 PHILLIPS, *Carney*, a disease in Horses, whereby their mouth becomes furred and clammy that they cannot eat. Hence in BAILEY, CHAMBERS *Cycl. Supp.*, and mod. Dicts.

carney, carny (ˈkɑːnɪ) *v. dial.* and *colloq.* [Widely diffused in midland and southern dialects, from Whitby to Cornwall, but origin unknown.
(There have been numerous conjectures, e.g. referring to *caro, carnem* flesh, or *cāra* dear, but no evidence. Cf. *blarney.*)]
a. *intr.* To act in a wheedling or coaxing manner. **b.** *trans.* To wheedle, coax, cajole. Hence **ˈcarneying** *ppl. a.*; also **carney** *sb.*² 'soft, hypocritical language' (*Slang Dict.* 1874); also, a smooth talker, a flatterer.
1811 WILLAN *West Riding Wds.* (E.D.S.) *Carny*, to flatter, to coax. **1818** *London Guide & Stranger's Safeguard* p. x, *Carney*, softening talk. *Ibid.* 205 The thoroughbred sycophant may be known by his *carney* or small talk. **1836–49** SMART, *Carny* v.n., to interlard discourse with hypocritical terms or tones of endearment. (*Colloq.*) **185.** *Household Wds.*, That carneying old woman..who is pulling Mr. S. by the arm. **1867** A. SKETCHLEY in *Cassell's Mag.* I. 479/2 Them 'umbugs that carneys over good ladies and gets reglar supported. **1869** *Good Words* 1 Oct. 561/1 He's a little bit too much of a carney. **1870** READE *Put yourself*, II. v. 91 'Well, sir,' said Cole, in a carneying voice. **1923** J. MANCHON *Le Slang* 79 *To come the carney*, flatter, flagorner.

carney, carny (ˈkɑːnɪ), *a. slang.* [f. CARNEY, CARNY *v.* (and *sb.*²).] Artful, sly.
1881 *N. & Q.* 6th Ser. III. 318 Eh, she *was* carny when she was a-sayin' that. **1925** in FRASER & GIBBONS *Soldier & Sailor Words* 47. **1955** E. BLISHEN *Roaring Boys* IV. 203 Macbeth was pretty carney in the way he handled Banquo.

carniferous (kɑːˈnɪfərəs), *a. rare*⁻¹. [f. L. *carn-em* flesh + -FEROUS.] Flesh-bearing.
1841 L. HUNT *Seer* (1864) 27 There is also a milk tree; but we nowhere find a carniferous, a flesh-bearing tree.

‖**carnifex** (ˈkɑːnɪfɛks). *Obs.* exc. *Hist.* [L. *carnifex, carnific-em*, f. *carn-em* flesh + *-fex, -ficem*, maker, f. *fac-* (in comb. *-fic-*) make, making; in ancient L. 'executioner', but in med.L. often 'butcher' (the trade), e.g.
1521 *Crt. Rolls of Northall, Middx.* [Presentment] quod Johannes Swycote est carnifex et vendit carnem corruptam. **1662** FULLER *Worthies* I. (1840) 497.]
An executioner.
1561 *Godly Q. Hester* (1873) 40 Auoide the murder of this carnifex Aman. **1617** MIDDLETON *Fair Quar.* IV. iv, Let the carnifexes scour their throats. **1823** SCOTT *Nigel* v, The carnifex, or executioner there. **1882** J. MARTINEAU *Spinoza* 21 The chief carnifex undertaking the high-born folks.

†**carˈnificate.** *Obs.* [f. L. *carnific-āre* to execute: see prec.] 'To hang' (Cockeram 1623).

carnification (ˌkɑːnɪfɪˈkeɪʃən). [sb. of action f. CARNIFY: see -FICATION.]
†**1.** The formation of flesh or sarcose tissue. *Obs.*
a **1734** NORTH *Lives* III. 224 If a wound was..come to carnification.
2. *Pathol.* Alteration of certain tissues so that they become like flesh; esp. fleshy condition of the lung, as in the fœtus.
1758 J. S. *Le Dran's Observ. Surg.* (1771) 351 The Carnification of the Bone. **1834** J. FORBES tr. *Laennec's Dis. Chest* 183 The lung has entirely lost its crepitous feel under the finger, and has acquired a consistence and weight altogether resembling those of liver..modern anatomists have named this condition of the organ hepatization or carnification. **1881** *Syd. Soc. Lex.*, *Carnification of the lung*, a term applied by Laennec to simple condensation of the lung, without inflammation, in which it becomes tough, leathery, inelastic, and having the appearance of muscle; it is the condition which is found in the fœtal lung, etc.
3. The conversion of bread into flesh by transubstantiation.
1826 SOUTHEY *Vind. Eccl. Angl.* 418 Giving their sanction to miracles of carnification. **1827** *Q. Rev.* XXXVI. 341 A famous wafer in which the miracle of carnification had been manifested.

†**ˈcarnifice.** *Obs. rare*⁻¹. [ad. L. **carnificium* execution, butchery, f. *carnifex, -ficem*: cf. *officium, office*, etc.] Butchery, murder, torture.
1657 TOMLINSON *Renou's Disp.* 470 It..were carnifice to adhibite sixty of them [Spanish Flies].

carnificial (kɑːnɪˈfɪʃəl), *a.* [f. as prec. + -AL¹.] Belonging to an executioner, or to a butcher; butcherly.
1632 LITHGOW *Totall Disc.* B ij a, I bequeath thee to a Carnificiall reward. **1822** SCOTT *Nigel* xxx, By the blow of my adversary's weapon..and not by any carnificial knife. **1863** *N. & Q.* Ser. III. IV. 482 The carnificial curiosity of Selwyn and Boswell. **1882** *Pall Mall G.* 1 Dec. 2 The carnificial view of the uses of the Cattle Show.

†**carnificine**, *sb.* and *a. Obs. rare*⁻¹. [ad. L. *carnificīna* the executioner's office, **carnificīnus* adj., f. *carnifex, -icem*: see above.]
A. *sb.*
1656 BLOUNT *Glossogr.*, *Carnificine*, the place of execution, the office of hangman. **1678** in PHILLIPS.
B. *adj.* Of the executioner; butcherly.
1681 BAXTER *Apol. Nonconf. Min.* 201 Set up this Carnificine trade.

carnify (ˈkɑːnɪfaɪ), *v.* [On type of F. **carnifie-r*, L. *carnificā-re* to execute: see CARNIFEX.] Hence **ˈcarnified, ˈcarnifying** *ppl. a.* and *vbl. sb.*
1. *trans.* To make or convert into flesh.
1643 SIR T. BROWNE *Relig. Med.* I. § 37. 89 All these creatures..are but the herbs of the field digested into flesh in them, or more remotely carnified in our selves. **1826** SOUTHEY *Vind. Eccl. Angl.* 415 The miraculous image, or carnified and bleeding host.
b. *Pathol.* To alter (bone or other tissue) so that it becomes of the structure of flesh: cf. CARNIFICATION 2. Chiefly *passive.* Also *intr.* To undergo this alteration.
1746 AMYAND in *Phil. Trans.* XLIV. 205 The Bone is carnified, that is, turned into Flesh. **1830** R. KNOX *Béclard's Anat.* 158 The nails soften, carnify, become imperfect horny tissue. **1862** H. FULLER *Dis. Lungs* 11 The lung is carnified and reduced to a small inelastic mass.
†**2.** *trans.* and *intr.* To generate flesh. *Obs.*
1639 T. DE GREY *Compl. Horseman* (1656) 341 That the carnifying flesh may heale the better. **1677** HALE *Prim. Orig. Man.* (J.) In inferiour faculties I walk, I see, I hear, I digest, I sanguify, I carnify. **1704** WORLIDGE *Dict. Rust. et Urb.* s.v. *Burnings*, Heal the Sore with your carnifying and healing Salves. **1829** *Lond. Encycl.* V. 174 To Carnify is to generate flesh.
†**3.** 'To quarter or cut in pieces.., to torment' Blount *Glossogr.* 1656. [Only a Latinism.]

†**ˈcarnilate**, *v. Obs. rare.* [f. med.L. *kernellāre, quernellāre* (KERNELLATE); cf. F. *carnelé* 'imbattled, having battlements' (Cotgr.): see

CARNEL, and CRENELLATE.] To KERNEL, CRENELLATE, or furnish with battlements.

1577 HARRISON *England* II. xix. (1878) I. 310 It is not lawfull for anie subject to carnilate, that is, build stone houses.

carnival (ˈkɑːnɪvəl). Forms: 6 **carnoval, carnevale**, 7 **carnevall, carnivall**, 7–8 **carnaval**, 7– **carnival**. [a. It. *carnevale, carnovale* (whence F. *carnaval*), evidently related to the med.L. (11–12th c.) names *carnelevārium, carnilevāria, carnilevāmen*, cited by Carpentier in additions to Du Cange. These appear to originate in a L. **carnem levāre*, or It. **carne levare* (with infinitive used subst. as in *il levar del sole* sunrise), meaning 'the putting away or removal of flesh (as food)', the name being originally proper to the eve of Ash Wednesday. The actual It. *carnevale* appears to have come through the intermediate *carnelevale*, cited by Carpentier from a document of 1130.

The history of the word is illustrated by the parallel med.L. name *carnem laxare* (cited by Carpentier from a charter of 1050), corresp. to It. **carne lasciare* 'leaving or forsaking flesh', whence, app. by contraction, the modern *carnasciale* = *carnevale*. *Carnem laxare, *carne lasciare, *carnelasciale, carnasciale*, form a series exactly parallel to **carnem levare, *carne levare, carnelevale, carnevale*. Other names having a similar reference are, for Shrove Tuesday, *carnicapium* 'flesh-taking', and *carnivora* [*dies*]; for Lent or its beginning, *carniprivium, carnisprivium, privicarnium*, f *privare* to deprive. In all these, 'flesh' means *meat*, and that it was understood to mean the same in *carnelevare* is shown by many early quotations in Du Cange; e.g. in a MS. of beg. of 13th c. 'De ludo Carnelevar. In Dominica dimissionis carnis,' etc. Also 'Dominica ad vel ante carnes tollendas'; with which compare the Spanish *carnes tolendas*, 'shrove-tide'. We must therefore entirely reject the suggestion founded on another sense of *levare*, 'to relieve, ease', that *carnelevarium* meant 'the solace of the flesh (i.e. body)' before the austerities of Lent. The explanations 'farewell flesh, farewell to flesh' (from L. *vale*) found already in Florio, and 'down with flesh!' (from F. *aval*), belong to the domain of popular etymology. (Cf. Dr. Chance in *N. & Q.* s. 7 IV. 82.)]

1. The season immediately preceding Lent, devoted in Italy and other Roman Catholic countries to revelry and riotous amusement, Shrove-tide; the festivity of this season. ***High Carnival***: the revelry of the Carnival at its height.

Originally (according to Tommaseo and Bellini) 'the day preceding the first of Lent'; commonly extended to the last three days or the whole week before Lent; in France it comprises *Jeudi gras, Dimanche gras, Lundi gras* and *Mardi gras*, i.e. Thursday before Quinquagesima, Quinquagesima Sunday, Monday, and Shrove Tuesday; in a still wider sense it includes 'the time of entertainments intervening between 'Twelfth-day' (or Boxing Day) and Ash Wednesday' (Littré).

Mid Lent Carnival (*Carnaval de la mi-carême*): a festivity held on the middle Thursday of Lent, to celebrate the fact that the first half of that season is at an end.

1549 THOMAS *Hist. Italie* 85 a, In theyr Carnoual time (whiche we call shroftide). **1565** JEWEL *Repl. Harding* Wks. (1609) 4 The Italians..contrary to the Portuise, call the first weeke in Lent the Carneuale. **1632** MASSINGER *City Mad.* IV. iv, After a carnival Lent ever follows. **1646** EVELYN *Diary* Jan., Shrovetide, when all the world repaire to Venice, to see the folly and madnesse of the Carnevall. **1739** GRAY *Let. to West* 16 Nov., This Carnival lasts only from Christmas to Lent; one half of the remaining part of the year is past in remembering the last, the other in expecting the future Carnival. **1756** NUGENT *Gr. Tour, Italy* III. 88 The carnival is the season devoted intirely to pleasure, and begins the second holiday after Christmas. **1763** J. BROWN *Poetry & Mus.* 202 The Carnaval is, in many Circumstances, almost a Transcript of the ancient Saturnalia of Rome. **1817** BYRON *Beppo* vi. **1873** MORLEY *Rousseau* I. 208 Like distracted masks in high carnival. **1886** *Pall Mall G.* 3 Apr. 10/2 A tragical finale to the gaieties of the Mid-Lenten Carnival.. The Carnival of the Mi-Carême..is the great festival of the Parisian blanchisseuses.

2. a. *fig.* Any season or course of feasting, riotous revelry, or indulgence. Now usu. = FESTIVAL *sb.* 1 a (see also quots. 1950).

1598 TOFTE *Alba* (1880) 102 The Carnouale of my sweet Loue is past, Now comes the Lent of my long Hate. **1649** JER. TAYLOR *Gt. Exemp.* II. xii. 93 To avoid..freer revellings, carnivals and balls. **1765** STERNE *Tr. Shandy* VII. xxvii, During that carnival of sporting. **1816** BYRON *Siege of Cor.* xvi, He saw the lean dogs..Hold o'er the dead their carnival. **1870** LOWELL *Study Wind.* (1886) 348 It was a carnival of intellect without faith. **1916** JOYCE *Portrait of Artist* v. 257 She passed now dancing lightly across his memory as she had been that night at the carnival ball, her white dress a little lifted, a white spray nodding in her hair. **1921** *Daily Colonist* (Victoria B.C.) 19 Mar. 11/5 The Arena was the scene of a brilliant assemblage of people last night when over eighteen hundred guests attended the ice carnival, and well over one thousand guests joined in the skating. **1950** *Oxf. Jun. Encycl.* IX. 114/2 We now use the word 'carnival' in a general sense to describe a particular kind of public celebration or entertainment which includes a fancy dress procession through the streets. *Ibid.* 115/1 During the summer holiday season,..seaside resorts sometimes arrange imitations of the continental carnival, the main feature being a beauty competition for the election of the Carnival Queen. **1966** *Oxf. Mail* 1 Oct. 1/5 It was not a serious demonstration. Grinning youngsters..baited the police and the crowd of 3,000 turned the occasion into a boisterous carnival. **1968** M. ALLINGHAM *Cargo of Eagles* xiv. 158 Travels for a small firm..who make carnival novelties, streamers, funny hats and so on.

b. A fun-fair; circus. *N. Amer.*

1931 J. LITTELL *Carnival Girl* (1933) ii. 41 An oblong of trucks surrounding a village of tents. A carnival company! *Ibid.* iii. 45 The man was offering her a job—with the carnival! **1939** [see CARNY *sb.*]. **1955** D. W. MAURER in *Amer. Dial. Soc.* XXIV. 31 A bank robber would be likely to distrust a carnival grifter on principle. **1968** *Globe & Mail* (Toronto) 17 Feb. 6/5 Nobody would be allowed to set up a permanent carnival ride on the grounds of any church in the City of Toronto.

3. *attrib.*

1605 B. JONSON *Volpone* IV. ii. (1616) 498 For your carniuale concupiscence [cf. COTGR. *Carnavalée*]. **1611** CORYAT *Crudities* 315 Carnival Shows in Italy like Shrove-Tuesday ones in England..Their Carniuall day..is obserued amongst them in the same manner as our Shroue-tuesday with vs in England. **1709** STEELE *Tatler* No. 94 ⁋2 Both of them were at a Play in a Carnival Evening. **1800** COLERIDGE *Wallenst.* IV. ii, This is a carnival night.

Hence ˌ**carnivaˈlesque** *a.*, characteristic, or of the style, of the carnival; ˈ**carnivaling**, ˈ**carnivalizing** *vbl. sbs.*; also ˈ**carnivalite**, ˈ**carnivaller**, one who takes part in a carnival.

1791 H. WALPOLE in *Jrnls. & Corr. Miss Berry* (1866) I. 289 Your [letter] whets no reply, being merely carnivalesque. **1833** *Blackw. Mag.* XXXIII. 374 This unique and carnivalesque drama. **1841** THACKERAY *Shrove Tuesday in Paris* in *Wks.* (1900) XIII. 570 When they grow old, perhaps, they leave off gallantry and carnivalising. **1866** *Reader* 1 Sept. 760 [The Lord Mayor] in grand carnivalesque pomp. **1881** *Pop. Sci. Monthly* XIX. 151 All shouting and cheering, merry as carnivallers. **1893** *Westm. Gaz.* 25 Feb. 5/3 Feasting on wonderful and uncanny—but very dainty—dishes is another important part of carnivaling. **1896** *Daily News* 19 Feb. 3/4 These fashionable Shrove-tide carnivalites.

‖**Carnivora** (kɑːˈnɪvərə), *sb. pl. Zool.* [L. *carnivora* (sc. *animalia*) flesh-eating (animals); see CARNIVOROUS.]

A large order of flesh-eating Mammalia, including among others the feline, canine, and ursine families. (For a singular, see CARNIVORE.) Also, sometimes applied to orders or groups of other animals, e.g. to a large family of pentamerous beetles.

1830 BENNETT *Gardens Zool. Soc.* 99 The most typical group of the Carnivora. **1847** CARPENTER *Zool.* §645 The aquatic Carnivora [Beetles]..live during their larva and perfect states in water. **1865** *Daily Tel.* 7/2 In a land like Hindostan..what a veritable power the great carnivora are.

ˌ**carnivoˈracity.** *nonce-wd.* [f. L. *carni-* flesh + VORACITY: cf. *carnivorous.*] Appetite for flesh.

1730 POPE *Let. Gay* 18 Aug., Wondring at the superior carni-voracity of our friend.

carnivore (ˈkɑːnɪvɔə(r)). [a. F. *carnivore*, ad. L. *carnivor-us* flesh-eating.] A carnivorous animal; one of the Carnivora. Also, a carnivorous plant.

1854 OWEN in *Circ. Sc.* (1865) II. 86/1 The..talons.. enable the carnivore to seize the prey. **1881** G. ALLEN *Vignettes* i. 5 Fighting with their teeth, like carnivores. **1884** *Pall Mall G.* 14 July 5 Great tropical carnivores like the beautiful Sarracenias, with their ingeniously devised traps for luring unhappy insects to their living tomb.

carnivorous (kɑːˈnɪvərəs), *a.* [f. L. *carnivor-us* (f. *carni-* flesh + *-vorus* devouring) + -OUS.]

1. Eating or feeding on flesh; applied to those animals which naturally prey on other animals, and *spec.* to the order CARNIVORA.

1646 SIR T. BROWNE *Pseud. Ep.* IV. x, Many there are.. which eate no salt at all, as all carnivorous animals. **1664** POWER *Exp. Philos.* I. 6 In all Flyes, more conspicuously in Carnivorous or Flesh-Flyes. **1797** BEWICK *Brit. Birds* (1847) I. Introd. 9 Birds may be distinguished, like quadrupeds, into granivorous and carnivorous. **1833** MRS. BROWNING *Prometh. Bd.*, Poems (1850) I. 187 Zeus's winged hound, The strong carnivorous eagle. **1845** DARWIN *Voy. Nat.* i. (1852) 34 The carnivorous beetles or Carabidæ. **1879** WALLACE *Australasia* iii. 56 Carnivorous marsupials preying upon the other groups.

2. *Bot.* Applied to those plants which absorb and digest animal substances as food.

1868 *Sci. Opinion* i. 16 The highly interesting carnivorous plants. **1878** MᶜNAB *Bot.* iv. (1883) 95 Some plants..obtain a part of [their nitrogenous food] in a peculiar manner. These are the so-called carnivorous plants.

3. *Med.* Applied to caustics as destructive of flesh.

1881 in *Syd. Soc. Lex.*

Hence **carˈnivorously** *adv.*, **carˈnivorousness.**

1837 MARRYAT *Dog-Fiend* xxxviii, The sow..was carnivorously inclined. **1858** HOGG *Life Shelley* II. 446 He dined carnivorously. **1856** *Chamb. Jrnl.* V. 133 Carnivorousness is an aberration of humanity, and a semi-return to the diet of beasts.

carnivory (kɑːˈnɪvərɪ). [f. CARNIVORE + -Y³.] The eating of flesh; the consumption of animal tissue; carnivorousness.

1901 *Morning Post* 10 May 4/7 Vivisection seems to us demonstrably a less evil than carnivory. **1967** D. MORRIS *Naked Ape* vi. 193 Perhaps this is one way in which we resisted the move towards full-blooded carnivory. **1976** *Endeavour* XXXV. 114 The study of the physiology of plant carnivory began with Darwin, whose classical work appeared just over a century ago.

†**carnoggin.** *Obs.* [a. Welsh *cyrniogyn* a piggin, dim. of *cyrniawg* horned (Owen Pughe); perh. in reference to the longer stave left projecting as a handle.] (See quot.)

1656 BLOUNT *Glossogr.*, *Carnogan* (Brit.), a little kind of a wooden dish with hoops, a Piggin. [Hence in PHILLIPS, KERSEY, & BAILEY.] **1682** *Wit & Drollery* 203 (N.) That country [Wales] yeilds flannel, carnoggins, Store of Metheglin in thy waggons.

carnose (kɑːˈnəʊs), *a.* [ad. L. *carnōs-us* abounding in flesh, fleshy, f. *caro, carn-em* flesh.] Consisting of or resembling flesh; fleshy.

1562 TURNER *Herbal* II. 59 a, Yᵉ Cypres tre and the Tamarisk haue carnose or flesshy leues. **1677** GALE *Crt. Gentiles* II. III. 122 The mortification of some carnose part. **1731** MASSEY in *Phil. Trans.* XXXVII. 217 Two short carnose Antennæ. **1854** BADHAM *Halieut.* 77 Cartilaginous fish..are carnose in fibre and difficult to digest.

carnosity (kɑːˈnɒsɪtɪ). [a. F. *carnosité* (14th c. in Littré, with parallel forms in Pr., Sp., It.), f. L. *carnōs-us* fleshy: see -ITY.]

†**1.** Fleshiness; pulpiness; flesh or pulp. *Obs.*

1533 ELYOT *Cast. Helthe* I. 2 Carnositie or fleshynes, etc. **1601** HOLLAND *Pliny* XV. iii. I. 431 They erre..that they suppose an Oliue the more growen it is in carnositie, to be the fuller of oile. **1657** TOMLINSON *Renou's Disp.* 670 Their [Golden Apples'] carnosity is very sapid and sweet.

2. A morbid fleshy growth, a caruncle.

1559 MORWYNG *Evonym.* 280 If an eye be diseased with blerednes..or any swelling carnosity bred upon it. **1618** FLETCHER *Chances* III. i, What's good for a Carnosity in the bladder? **1751** STACK in *Phil. Trans.* XLVII. 328 Strictures and carnosities of the urethra. **1810** *Encycl. Brit.* (ed. 4) V. 189 Carnosities are very difficult of cure.

†**b.** *fig. Obs.*

1613 SPELMAN *De non temer. Eccl.* (1668) 105 Overgrown with so hard a carnosity, as it requireth strong and potent corrosives to make an entrance. **1689** N. LEE *Princ. Cleve* IV. i, Your thoughts are swell'd with a Carnosity.

carnoso- (kɑːˈnəʊsəʊ), combining form of L. *carnōsus*, used in sense 'carnose and..', 'with carnous modification'; as in ***carnoso-fibrous, carnoso-tuberose***, etc.

1846 DANA *Zooph.* 644 Carnoso-tuberose. **1866** BERKELEY in *Intell. Observ.* No. 50. 96 The carnoso-fibrous stem.

Carnot (ˈkɑːnəʊ). *Physics.* The name of N. L. S. *Carnot* (1796–1832), French physicist, used *attrib.* and in the possessive to designate thermodynamic concepts devised by him or arising out of his work, as **Carnot('s) cycle**, the cycle of an ideal heat engine in which a substance is successively and reversibly expanded at constant temperature, expanded adiabatically, compressed at constant temperature, and compressed adiabatically to its initial temperature and volume; **Carnot('s) principle** or **theorem**, the principle that all heat engines operating reversibly between the same temperatures have the same efficiency, which is greater than the efficiency achievable by irreversible operation between the same temperatures.

1849 W. THOMSON in *Trans. R. Soc. Edin.* XVI. 541 (*heading*) An account of Carnot's theory of the motive power of heat. *Ibid.* 544 So generally is Carnot's principle tacitly admitted as an axiom, that its application in this case has never..been questioned. **1887** *Encycl. Brit.* XXII. 481/2 This is the fraction of the whole heat given to it which an engine following Carnot's cycle converts into work. **1930** *Engineering* 4 July 25/1 Later, the reheat cycle had been exploited, also combination cycles of various kinds, many of which approach the Carnot cycle in efficiency. **1937** [see KELVIN, KELVIN 3]. **1956** *Nature* 21 Jan. 111/2 Solar radiation may be converted to electricity by thermo-couples in which heat is an intermediate form of energy and which, therefore, are subject to the toll of the Carnot efficiency. **1977** I. M. CAMPBELL *Energy & Atmosphere* vi. 149 The maximum theoretical thermodynamic efficiency of a water/steam working cycle is achieved in the Carnot cycle. **1984** D. C. GIANCOLI *Gen. Physics* xxi. 411 Carnot's theorem can be shown to follow from..the second law of thermodynamics.

carnotite (ˈkɑːnətaɪt). *Min.* [ad. F. *carnotit* (Friedel & Cumenge 1899, in *Compt. Rend. Acad. Sci.* CXXVIII. 534), f. the name of Marie Adolphe *Carnot* (1839–1920), French inspector-general of mines: see -ITE¹.] A yellow earthy hydrated vanadate of potassium and uranium, found in south-western Colorado, and worked as a source of vanadium, uranium, and radium. Also *attrib.*

1899 *Jrnl. Chem. Soc.* LXXVI. II. 434 A new mineral containing uranium and vanadium, to which the authors give the name *carnotite*, is found in yellow, friable masses, mixed with very variable quantities of silica, together with malachite and chessylite, in pockets at the surface of a grit in Montrose Co., Colorado. **1920** *Discovery* May 143/1 The carnotite beds on the borders of Utah and Colorado. **1945** *Times* 8 Aug. 4/2 In 1938 the United States produced 4,290 short tons of carnotite ore.

carnous (ˈkɑːnəs), *a.* ? *Obs.* [ad. L. *carnōs-us* fleshy, f. *carn-* flesh: see -OUS.]

1. Consisting of or abounding in flesh; fleshy.

1577 VICARY *Englishm. Treas.* Kj, A carnous pannicle. *a* **1682** SIR T. BROWNE *Misc. Tracts* (1684) 17 A fair and carnous state of Body. **1694** J. TURNER in *Phil. Trans.* XVIII. 17 Much more like a Sceleton than a carnous

Substance. **1758** J. S. *Le Dran's Observ. Surg.* (1771) 24 All the Parts, both carnous and osseous. **1783** POTT *Chirurg.* II. 63.

2. Of fruits, roots, etc.: Pulpy, fleshy.

1601 HOLLAND *Pliny* XV. iii, [The] stones and carnous matter [of olives]. *Ibid.* II. 19 The roots of some be carnous and fleshie..namely of the Beet. **1679** PLOT *Staffordsh.* (1686) 199 Such [Herbs] as have a carnous substance, and will never become lignous.

†**car'nouse.** *Obs.* Also 7 **-nooze, -nose.** 'The base-ring about the breech of a gun' (Kersey).

1626 CAPT. SMITH *Accid. Yng. Seamen* 32 Her carnooze or base ring at her britch. **1627** —— *Seaman's Gram.* xiv. 65 Carnouse..is the greatest circle about her britch. **1678** PHILLIPS, *Carnose.* **1708** in KERSEY. **1731** in BAILEY.

carny ('kɑːnɪ), *sb. U.S. slang.* Also **carney, carni(e).** [f. CARNIVAL 2 b + -Y[6].] = CARNIVAL 2 b; also, a person who works at a carnival. Also *attrib.* or as *adj.*

1931 *Amer. Speech* VI. 330 *Carnifolks*, persons who engage in the carnival business. **1933** B. J. CHIPMAN *Hey Rube* 193/2 *Carny*, carnival. **1939** *New Yorker* 12 Aug. 22/2 Sixty thousand outdoor show people, the 'carnies', who travel from town to town with carnivals. **1948** F. BROWN *Dead Ringer* i. 5 All around the midway carneys were letting down banners and running rope. *Ibid.* 10 A town kid might possibly be around the sideshow top this late at night, but not without his clothes on. For a carney kid that wasn't too strange. *Ibid.* 11 One of the new girls with the posing show. She'd been with the carney only a week. **1955** R. BRADBURY *October Country* (1956) 10 Life fixed him so he's good for nothing but carny shows. **1956** H. GOLD *Man who was not with It* (1965) i. 4 Joy..stopped in her roaming through this carnie where she dwelled and listened. *Ibid.*, He was a sallow stooped carnie with vapors fuming in his eyes. **1961** *Times Lit. Suppl.* 27 Jan. 62/2 Ernie, the carni man, is violent, stupid, and wholly untouched by any kind of decency.

carny, *v.*: see CARNEY.

caroach, obs. form of CAROCHE.

carob ('kærəb). Forms: 6–7 **carobe, carrob,** 7 **carabe,** 9 **carubbe, caroub,** 6– **carob.** [a. F. *carobe, carrobe* (also *carroube, carrube*) Cotgr. (now *caroube*), corresp. to It. *carrubo*, Sp. *garrobo, algarrobo*, a. Arab. (*al*) *kharrūbah*, in Pers. *khirnūb*, 'bean-pods, carobs'.]

1. The fruit of an evergreen leguminous tree (*Ceratonia siliqua*), Carob-tree, a native of the Levant: a long flat horn-like pod containing numerous hard seeds embedded in pulp. Also called ***carob-bean, carob-pod.***

Generally identified with the 'husks' eaten by the prodigal in the parable, *Luke* xv. 16; and by some taken to be the 'locusts' eaten by John the Baptist, whence the names *locust-pods*, and *St. John's bread.*

1548 TURNER *Names of Herbes* s.v. *Siliqua*, It may be called in english a Carobe tree, and the fruite Carobes or Carobbeanes. **1591** PERCIVALL *Sp. Dict.*, *Algarrova*, Carobes, or S. Johns bread. **1601** HOLLAND *Pliny* II. 172 As for those Carobs or Cods of Syria. **1682** WHELER *Journ. Greece* VI. 424 Ægina hath..abundance of Almonds, and Keratia, or Carobs. **1880** V. L. CAMERON *Our Future Highw.* I. ii. 28 The carob harvest was going on as well as the olive gathering. **1886** A. H. CHURCH *Food Grains Ind.* 170 Carob pods are 6 inches to 1 foot in length, and about 1 inch broad.

2. The tree, more fully called ***carob-tree.***

1548 [see 1]. **1568** TURNER *Herbal* III. 20 The leafe is lyke unto Carobe, or saint Johannis breadis tre. **1685** BAXTER *Paraphr. Luke* xv. 15 They would not let him fill his Belly with the Cods of the Carabe Tree, which was the swines meat. **1842** L. S. COSTELLO *Pilgr. Auvergne* I. 45 Where the tall carob's branches spread. *c* **1854** STANLEY *Sinai & Pal.* ii. (1858) 146 The large dark-leaved, widespread tree called the 'Carob', common apparently in the forests of Galilee. **1886** A. H. CHURCH *Food Grains Ind.* 173 The carob tree was introduced into India about the year 1840.

caroce, obs. form of CAROSSE: cf. next.

ca'roche, *sb. arch.* Forms: 6–7 **carroch(e,** 7 **caroch(e, caroach, carioch,** 9 **caroche, carroch.** [a. 16th c. F. *carroche*, ad. It. *carroccio, -ia*, augmentatives of *carro* chariot:—L. *carrus*; see CAR. Cf. the parallel word CAROSSE.]

The 17th c. name of a coach or chariot of a stately or luxurious kind; the representative of the modern 'carriage' for town use. *Obs.* exc. *Hist.*

1591 PERCIVALL *Sp. Dict.*, *Carrucha*, a carroch, a coche. **1606** DEKKER *Sev. Sins* II. (Arb.) 20 They harnessed the Grand Signiors Caroach. **1610** HOLLAND *Camden's Brit.* I. 42 To ride in a Carroch, or hanging Coach. **1611** CORYAT *Crudities* 85 Seven or eight stately Carochs of great personages. **1614** COOK *Tu Quoque* in *Dodsley* VII. 28 The keeping of a coach For country, and a carroch for London. **1671** F. PHILLIPS *Reg. Necess.* 213 He did in..1666 prohibit the Duke of Newcastles Footmen the wearing of black Velvet Caps whilst they attend his Caroch. **1678** BUTLER *Hud.* III. III. 211 To mount two wheel'd Carroches. [**1822** SCOTT *Nigel* i, The court ladies..when visiting his shop in their caroches. **1848** THACKERAY *Bk. Snobs* ii, When the caroches of the nobles had set down their owners.]

b. Used to represent It. *carroccio*, the car of state which accompanied the army of an Italian republic and bore the standard.

1840 BROWNING *Sordello* I. 263 We shut..in..all noises but The carroch's booming.

c. *attrib.* (trade name of a kind of tricycle).

1885 *Bazaar* 30 Mar. 1274/3, 46 in. Caroche Gem, central gear, front steerer..44 in. Caroche tricycle, rear steerer.

†**ca'roche**, *v. Obs.* [f. the sb.; or ad. It. *carrocciare, carozzare*, F. *carrosser* 'to ride in a caroch'.] **a.** *intr.* To ride or travel in a caroche. **b.** *trans.* To convey in a caroche. Hence **ca'roched** *ppl. a.*, seated or driven in a caroche.

1618 WITHER *Motto* (1633) 560 If but he and's whore Carrocht a Furlong are, the Coach man may For sennight after let his Horses play. **1619** BP. WILLIAMS *Serm. Apparell* (1620) 11 To Caroach it abroad, to go out and see. **1636** HEYWOOD *Challenge* I. i. Wks. 1874 V. 12 Came hee on horse-backe or Caroach't? **1650** A. B. *Mutat. Polemo* 30, I speedily caroatcht thither.

caroigne, obs. form of CARRION.

carol ('kærəl), *sb.* Forms: 4–6 **karol(e, karolle, carole,** 4–7 **caroll(e,** 4–9 **carrol(l,** 5 **(careld), caroul,** 5–6 **caral(le, carowl,** 6 **carralle, caril, caryl, carrell, karrel,** 7 **karil, (carrold),** 4– **carol.** [a. OF. *carole*, also *kar-, char-, quar-, quer-, kerole, -olle*, in all the senses in which it occurs in Eng. (exc. 3); still in French dialects. (Marne *carole* dance, fête, joy; Swiss Rom. *coraula, coraulo*, round dance, dance-song, *coraul* ball, round dance (Godef.), Pr. and It. *carola*; Old Pr. also *corola*. The ulterior etymology of OF. *carole* and its accompanying vb. *caroler*, is uncertain; nor is it clear whether the vb. or the sb. takes priority etymologically. There are many indications that the first syllable had originally *co-* (see Diez, 1878, p. 539, and cf. the Swiss and Breton forms); hence Romanic etymologists generally agree with Diez, in seeking the etymology in the Gr.-L. *chorus*, and its derivatives *chorēa, choraules*, etc.: cf. esp. 'corolar *vel* coreiar, *coreas ducere*' quoted by Diez from Faidit *Gram. Prov.*, of 13th c. Wackernagel would take the vb. (coraulare '*conculcare*' to tread, dance, Ugutio) as a derivative of the sb. *coraula, choraula, choraules*, the fluteplayer who accompanied the chorus dance, and the sb. as a derivative of the vb. Another conjecture, assuming 'ring' to be the original sense of the sb., has proposed as its source L. *corolla* 'little crown, coronet, garland'. In any case, a Celtic origin is out of the question: Welsh *carol* (Christmas) carol, and vb. *caroli* to sing carols, are from English (Rhŷs), and Breton *koroll* dance, *korolli* to dance, *koroller* dancer, are from French. The arrangement of the senses here followed is tentative.]

I. A ring-dance, and derived senses.

†**1.** A ring-dance with accompaniment of song; ? a ring of men or women holding hands and moving round in dancing step. *arch.*

a **1300** *Cursor M.* 7601 O þair karol suilk was þe sang. *c* **1300** *K. Alis.* 1845 Faire is carole of maide gent, Bothe in halle and eke in tent. **1303** R. BRUNNE *Handl. Synne* 3460 Wymmen..þat borwe cloþes yn carol to go. *c* **1330** *Arth. & Merl.* 1722 Miri time it is in may..Damisels carols ledeth. **1387** TREVISA *Higden* (Rolls) VII. 123 He saw a mayden..daunsynge in a carrole among oþer maydouns. **1394** GOWER *Conf.* III. 365 With harpe and lute and with citole, The love daunce and the carole..A softe pas they daunce and trede. *c* **1420** *Chron. Vilod.* 1022 And daunceden with a caralle þe chirche abouȝt. **1483** *Cath. Angl.* 54 A Caralle, *corea, chorus, pecten.* **1612** DRAYTON *Poly-olb.* xi, In carrolds as they course. **1616** BULLOKAR, *Carol*, a song, sometimes a dance. **1865** TYLOR *Early Hist. Man.* vi. 115 The circles of upright stones..have suggested the idea of a ring-dance, and the story has shaped itself..that such a ring was a party of girls who were turned into stone for dancing carols on a Sunday. **1866** ENGEL *Nat. Mus.* viii. 273 We learn that the term Carole was applied by the Trouvères to a dance in which the performers moved slowly round in a circle, singing at the time. **1867** LONGF. *Dante's Parad.* XXIV. 16 Those carols dancing in different measure.

†**b.** Diversion or merry-making of which such dances formed a leading feature. *Obs.* [So in mod.F. dial. = 'fête, joie'.]

a **1300** *Cursor M.* 28146 Caroles, iolites, and plaies, ic haue be-haldyn and ledde in ways. **1340** *Ayenb.* 71 Oure blisse is ywent in-to wop, oure karoles into zorȝe. *c* **1340** *Gaw. & Gr. Knt.* 43 Iusted ful Iolile þise gentyle kniȝtes, Syþen kayred to þe court, caroles to make. **1483** CAXTON *G. de la Tour* C ij, To be att feestes, Joustes, and carolles.

†**c.** A company or band of singers, a choir. (? Or simply 'assembly, company' as in Godefroy 'assemblée, cercle, réunion'.) *Obs.*

1483 CAXTON *Gold. Leg.* 253/1 Thassembles of martirs, the Couentes of Confessours, the Carolles of Virgyns.

2. A song; originally, that to which they danced. Now usually, a song of a joyous strain; often *transf.* to the joyous warbling of birds.

1303 R. BRUNNE *Handl. Synne* 9043 Þys ys þe karolle þat þey sunge. **1393** GOWER *Conf.* I. 133 And eke he can carolles make, Roundel, balade and virelay. *c* **1440** *Promp. Parv.* 92 Caral, songe [*P.* caroll], *palinodium* [*K.* Psalmodium]... Caroolyn, or synge carowlys. **1595** SPENSER *Epithal.* 259 The whiles the maydens doe theyr carroll sing. **1600** SHAKS. *A.Y.L.* v. iii. 27 This Carroll they began that houre, With a hey and a ho, & a hey nonino. *c* **1750** SHENSTONE *Elegy* ix, To sing soft carrols to your lovely dames. **1800** WORDSW. *Hart-leap Well* II. xv, He heard the birds their morning carols sing. *a* **1824** CAMPBELL *Dead Eagle* 99 The fife-like carol of the lark.

3. a. A song or hymn of religious joy.

a **1547** SURREY *Æneid* II. 300 Children, and maides, that holly carolles sang. **1625** BACON *Ess.*, *Adversity* (Arb.) 505 Yet, euen in the old Testament, if you Listen to Dauids Harpe, you shall heare as many Herselike Ayres, as Carols. **1830** TENNYSON *Dream Fair Wom.* 245 'Glory to God' she sang, and past afar..Losing her carol I stood pensively.

b. *esp.* A song or hymn of joy sung at Christmas in celebration of the Nativity. Rarely applied to hymns on certain other festal occasions.

1502 *Priv. Purse Exp. Eliz. York* (1830) 83 Item to Cornishe for setting of a carralle upon Cristmas day. **1521** W. DE WORDE (*title*), Christmasse Carolles. **1530** PALSGR. 203/1 Carole a song, *chancon de noel.* **1573** TUSSER *Husb.* (1878) 70 A Christmas Caroll of the birth of Christ vpon the tune of King Salamon. **1590** SHAKS. *Mids. N.* II. i. 102 No night is now with hymne or caroll blest. **1641** J. JACKSON *True Evang. T.* III. 175 The Dity of that hymne, or Caroll, [was] Peace on earth. **1667** MILTON *P.L.* XII. 367. **1774** T. WARTON *Hist. Eng. Poetry* xxviii. (1840) II. 397 These coronation carols were customary. **1806–7** J. BERESFORD *Miseries Hum. Life* (1826) ii. 29 Screaming and bellowing Christmas carols under your window. **1845** S. AUSTIN tr. *Ranke's Hist. Ref.* I. 371 Singing hymns before the doors of houses, and new year's carols in the villages.

II. A ring, and related senses. (perh. ought to be I.)

†**4.** A ring or circle, *e.g.* of standing stones.

[All these instances refer to Stonehenge, also called the *Giants' Dance*; cf. quot. 1865 in sense 1; but Du Cange has instances of a very different kind, e.g. 'Unum annulum cum saphyro magno, et karola in circuitu 7 lapidum et 8 perlarum'.]

1330 R. BRUNNE *Chron. Wace* in Hearne Pref. R.B. 194 Þis Bretons renged about þe feld, Þe karole of the stones beheld, Many tyme ȝede þam about. *Ibid.* 195 Whan he had gon alle aboute Within þe karole & withoute. *c* **1470** HARDING *Chron.* lxx. x, Within [the] Giauntes Carole, that so ther hight, The [Stone hengles] that nowe so named been.

¶ A precinct, a space enclosed by rails, etc. See Du Cange.

†**5.** A small enclosure or 'study' in a cloister.

[See numerous OF. examples in Godefroy, and quot. from Premonstrat. Statutes in Du Cange 'in claustro carolæ vel hujusmodi scriptoria'.]

1593 *Descr. Monuments, &c. Ch. Durham* §41 (1842) 70 In every wyndowe three Pewes or Carrells, where every one of the old monks had his carrell, severall by himselfe, that when they had dyned they dyd resorte to that place of Cloister, and there studyed upon there books, every one in his carrell all the after nonne. **1721** BAILEY, *Carrel*, a Closet or Pen in a Monastery. **1810** *Acc. Gloucester Cath.*, The ten divisions for the windows in the south cloister are divided into twenty carrols; two carrols in each window;—their width four feet.

b. ***carol-window***: ? a bay-window.

c **1600** JUPP *Acc. Comp. Carpenters* 223 In 1572 the Carpenters Company of the City of London ordered a caroll-window to be made in the place wher the window now standethe in the gallerie.

†**6.** A chain. [So F. *quarole*, two examples in Godef.: see also Du Cange.]

c **1425** *Seven Sag.* (P.) 2885 Scho putte ilke resche in other, And made a karole in a stounde, The ton hende touched to grounde, And the othir scho helde on heygh.

7. *Comb.* and *attrib.*, as ***carol service, singer, singing*** (also as *pr. pple.*); ***carol-song, -wise***; ***carol-chanting*** ppl. adj.

c **1385** CHAUCER *L.G.W.* 201 (Camb. MS.) And songyn as it were in carolewyse. **1583** T. WATSON *Poems* (Arb.) 137 Let those lament who lust, Ile sing a carroll song for obsequy. **1601** CHESTER *Love's Mart.* (1878) 5 And carroll-chanting birds are sudden mute. **1876** STAINER & BARRETT *Dict. Mus. Terms* 77/2 Carol singing is of great antiquity among Christian communities. **1911** E. DUNCAN *Story of Carol* xiv. 180 On Christmas Eve country carol-singers spent half the night tramping the ice-bound ways. *Ibid.* 191 An amusing story, connected with carol-singing, is related in *Pasquil's Jests.* **1928** P. DEARMER et al. *Oxford Bk. Carols* p. xvi, William Hone..anticipated that carol-singing would entirely disappear in a few years. *Ibid.* p. xxii, 'Carol services' are indeed not infrequently held even to-day at which not a single genuine carol is sung. **1954** T. S. ELIOT *Confidential Clerk* I. 17 I've always sung in our voluntary choir And at the carol service. **1954** *Radio Call* (Austral.) 22 Dec. 10 As on previous Christmas eves, they'll be carol singing for appreciative audiences. **1978** *Washington Post* 19 Nov. F2/2 Its four holiday stamps..showing carol singers through the ages will go on sale Wednesday.

carol ('kærəl, -ɒl), *v.* For forms see prec. [a. OF. *caroler*, f. *carole*; see prec. The derivative forms in *-ed, -ing, -er*, are now most commonly spelt (in England) with *ll* (*carolled*, etc.) though for no good reason: cf. F. *caroler, carolant, caroleur.*]

†**1.** *intr.* To dance in a ring to the accompaniment of song; to dance and sing, make merry. *Obs.*

a **1300** *Cursor M.* 7600 [Þar] karold [*Gött.* dauncid] wimmen be þe wai. **1303** R. BRUNNE *Handl. Synne* 9041 Þese wommen ȝede and tollede here oute Wyþ hem to karolle þe cherche aboute. *Ibid.* 9138 Þese men þat ȝede so karol-lande Alle þat ȝere hande yn hande. *c* **1400** *Rom. Rose* 810, I wolde have karoled right fayn, As man that was to daunce right blithe. *c* **1530** LD. BERNERS *Arth. Lyt. Bryt.* (1814) 327 Ladyes and damoyselles did carowle and sing.

2. To sing, *orig.* in accompaniment to a dance. Now usually: To sing a lively or joyous strain. (Chiefly *poet.*)

c **1369** CHAUCER *Dethe Blaunche* 848, I sawe her daunce so comely, Carol and sing so swetely **1393** GOWER *Conf.* III. 30 If she carole upon a songe, Whan I it here, I am so fed. *c* **1440** *Promp. Parv.* 62 Caroolyn, or synge carowlys [*P.* carallyn], *psalmodio.* **1579** SPENSER *Sheph. Cal.* Feb., Tho

wouldest thou learne to caroll of love. **1633** P. Fletcher *Pisc. Ecl.* xi. i, And carol lowd of love, and loves delight. **1791** Cowper *Iliad* xviii. 712 Carolling to it with a slender voice. **1853** De Quincey *Sp. Mil. Nun* viii. 17 Juvenal's qualification for carolling gaily through a forest full of robbers.

b. *ironically.*

1440 J. Shirley *Dethe K. James* (1818) 18 Sirs the spows is foundon, wherfore we bene cumne, and all this nyght haf carold here.

c. *transf.* of the warbling of birds, etc.

1595 Spenser *Epithal.* 79 Hark, how the cheerfull birds do chaunt.. And carroll of Loves praise. **1768** Beattie *Minstr.* i. v, Where the grey linnets carol from the hill. **1830** Tennyson *Sea-Fairies*, Merrily merrily carol the gales.

3. *trans.* **a.** with cognate object.

1575 Laneham *Let.* (1871) 60 Then carroll I vp a song withall. **1589** Greene *Menaphon* (Arb.) 37 To carroll out this roundelay. **1718** Prior *2nd Hymn Callimachus* (R.) Hovering swans..carol sounds harmonious. **1797** *Philanthrope* No. 25 Many a feather'd warbler..Carrol'd the melodious lay. **1859** Tennyson *Elaine* 700 Carolling as he went A true-love ballad.

b. To sing of, celebrate in song.

1634 Milton *Comus* 849 The shepherds..Carol her goodness loud in rustic lays. **1683** Chalkhill *Thealma & Cl.* 40 Shepherds Swains still Carol out her Fame. **1774** *Westm. Mag.* II. 374 The Muse That carrol'd Sir John Hill!

ca'rolathine. *Min.* [f. *Karolath* in Silesia.] A variety of allophane, found in rounded balls of a honey-yellow colour at Zabize in Upper Silesia.

1858 in Dana *Min.* 500.

Carolean (kærəˈliːən), *a.* and *sb.* [f. L. *Carolus* Charles + *-ean* as in Jacobean *a.* (*sb.*).] **A.** *adj.* = Caroline *a.* 1 b. **B.** *sb.* One who lived in the reign of Charles I or II.

1911 *Chambers's Jrnl.* 15 July 513/1 The rapacity and meanness of the Ministers in the Carolean era. **1927** *Observer* 8 May 15/2 The spirit that animated the restored Caroleans in their exhumatory operations against the regicides. **1927** *Daily Tel.* 12 July 5/5 A Carolean Poet [*sc.* Marvell]. **1939** *Archit. Rev.* LXXXV. 58/1 This seeming late 18th century window is in strange company, surrounded as it is by what appear the familiar swags of essentially Carolean aspect.

caroler, -oller (ˈkærələ(r)). [f. carol *v.* + -er¹.] One who carols; a carol-singer; a singer, bard.

1806–7 J. Beresford *Miseries Hum. Life* ii. (1826) 29 'Sunt et mihi carmina'..says the caroller. **1852** Miss Yonge *Cameos* (1877) III. xxxiii. 345 Coming down with some alms for the carollers.

†ˈ**carolet.** *Obs. rare*⁻¹. [dim. of carol *sb.*; see -et¹.] A little carol or song.

1593 Drayton *Sheph. Garl.* vii, Repeat a carowlet in rime.

‖**carolin** (ˈkærəlɪn). [Ger. *Karolin.* f. L. *Carolus* Charles.] The name of a gold coin formerly current in Bavaria and in Würtemburg; the Bavarain carolin was worth 20*s.* 4·23*d.* sterling, that of Würtemburg 20*s.* 1·47*d.*

1821 in Kelly *Cambist.* **1847** in McCulloch *Dict. Comm.* 326.

Carolina (kærəˈlaɪnə). The name (after Charles II.) of a North American colony, now forming two states (North C. and South C.) of the American Union; hence applied to the Sweet Potato (see quot.), and used in the names of various plants and animals, as ***Carolina ash, osprey, whiting***; also **Carolina Allspice**, the flowering shrub *Calycanthus floridus*; **Carolina Pink**, *Spigelia Marilandica*, also called Indian Pink, of which the root is an active anthelmintic; **Carolina rice**, a variety of rice, the ripe husk of which is yellowish. See also Caroline *a.* 2.

1734 Mortimer *Nat. Hist. Carolina* in *Phil. Trans.* XXXVIII. 317 *Alburnus Americanus*, the Carolina-Whiting. **1787** Jefferson *Let.* 30 July in *Writings* (1853) II. 195 The Carolina rice..crumbles in certain forms of preparation. **1845** E. Acton *Mod. Cookery* i. 44 The Patna ..rice..is not so good as the Carolina for the general purposes of cookery. *Ibid.* 45 The Carolina rice even answers, well dressed, in this way. **1884** *Century Mag.* Jan. 442/1 The sweet potato was adopted from the aborigines in all the Southern colonies, and it is yet known in the market as the 'Carolina'. **1866** *Treas. Bot.* 203 Carolina Allspice or Sweet-scented shrub. **1962** *Guardian* 12 Jan. 8/5 Soak a breakfast-cupful of Carolina rice.

ˈ**caroline,** *sb.* [see carolin, carlin.] A name of coins of various countries and of different values; sometimes = carline, or carolin.

1555 Eden *Decades W. Ind.* (Arb.) 195 A rounde plate of syluer as brode as the coyne cauled a Corolyne. **1709** *Lond. Gaz.* No. 4571/2 (*Naples*) A Captain is to receive five Carolines a Day. **1717** Berkeley in Fraser *Life* (1871) 578 The clergy of Ischia get each a Caroline a mass. **1783** W. F. Martyn *Geog. Mag.* II. 78 (*Sweden*) A caroline, (about one shilling and two-pence value). **1865** *Athenæum* No. 1953. 448/2 The forty golden carolines with which the Grand-Duke..repaid the dedication.

Caroline (ˈkærəlaɪn), *a.* [f. *Carol-us* Charles.] **1.** Of or pertaining to Charles: *esp.* **a.** of Charles the Great (Charlemagne); *spec.* designating a style of minuscule handwriting developed in France at the time of Charlemagne; **b.** of Charles I. and II. of England, or their period.

1652 Needham tr. *Selden's Mare Cl.* 322 Under the Caroline kings. **1805** W. Saunders *Min. Waters* 314 The village of Carlsbad..as well as..the Caroline Waters [named after] the emperor Charles IV. in 1370. **1839** Hallam *Hist. Lit.* IV. iv. v. §22. 234 Waller has a more uniform elegance..than any [other] of the Caroline era. **1850** F. Madden tr. *J. B. Silvestre's Univ. Palæogr.* I. cxxix. 346 The text is in clear, well proportioned, Caroline minuscules, with the words not divided, the tails and tops of the letters of proper length, and the strokes of the *m* and *n* inclined towards the left; graphic characters which indicate the ninth century, and the kind of writing termed Caroline. **1874** F. Hall in *N. Amer. Rev.* CXIX. 310 Our Caroline divines. **1883** I. Taylor *Alphabet* II. viii. 181 Owing to its manifold excellencies..the rapidity with which it could be written, the ease with which it could be read, and economy of parchment, the Caroline minuscule, as it is usually called, grew rapidly in favour. **1884** Courthope *Addison* i. 20 The Caroline dramatists. **1897** [see Carolingian A]. **1957** N. R. Ker *Catal. MSS. containing Anglo-Saxon* p. xxii, It should be assumed that..writing dated s. xi or later is caroline minuscule. **1962** D'Ardenne in Davis & Wrenn *Eng. & Medieval Studies* 85 The manuscript is written in Latin on parchment in a smooth round English form of the caroline minuscule.

†**2.** Applied in end of 17th c. to a fashion of hat.

1687 *Lond. Gaz.* No. 2246/4, 25 black Hats, commonly called Caroline. **1695** *Ibid.* No. 3119/4 A Young Man, aged about 17..wears..a Carolina Hat.

caroling, -olling (ˈkærəlɪŋ), *vbl. sb.* [f. carol *v.* + -ing¹.] The action of the vb. carol.

c **1300** *K. Alis.* 1045 At theo feste was trumpyng.. Carolyng, and turneieyng. *c* **1386** Chaucer *Chan. Yem. Prol. & T.* 792 Was never..lady lustier in carolynge. **1523** Ld. Berners *Froiss.* I. ccxix. 279 On a Sonday after dyner.. ther was great daunsyng and karolynge. **1596** Spenser *Heav. Beauty* 265 Carolings Of Gods high praise. *a* **1834** Coleridge *Lit. Rem.* I. 82 (L.) The sweet carolings of *As you like it.* **1853** C. Brontë *Villette* xxiv. (1876) 256.

caroling, -olling, *ppl. a.* That carols.

1867 Miss Braddon *R. Godwin* I. i. 5 Carolling music of birds. **1880** *Atlantic Monthly* Sept. 329 The singer's caroling lips are dust.

Caroˈlingian, *a.* and *sb.* **A.** *adj.* = Carlovingian, q.v.; *spec.* = Caroline *a.* 1 a.

1881 *Athenæum* No. 2803. 86/2 The accessories preserve something that is Carolingian. **1882–3** Schaff *Relig. Encycl.* III. 1777 Ornaments of the Carolingian period. **1897** H. W. Johnston *Latin MSS.* ii. 72 Of the better forms the Caroline (Carolingian) may be regarded as the type, as it finally became the literary hand of all Western Europe. **1912** E. M. Thompson *Introd. Gr. & Latin Palaeogr.* xvi. 367 At Tours, where, under the rule of Alcuin of York, who was abbot of St. Martin's from 796 to 804, was specially developed the exact hand which has received the name of the Carolingian Minuscule. **1962** D. B. Updike *Printing Types* (ed. 3) I. iii. 50 This Carolingian minuscule..became the dominant handwriting of western Europe.

B. *sb.* A member of the Carlovingian dynasty.

1894 E. F. Henderson *Hist. Germany in Middle Ages* vii. 100 (*heading*) The later Carolingians. **1910** *Encycl. Brit.* V. 381/2 In Italy the Carolingians kept their position until the deposition of Charles the Fat in 887. **1942** H. & R. Norden tr. *Ludwig's Germans* i. 34 From the Carolingians to the Great Revolution, France experienced no real change of dynasty. **1959** *Chambers's Encycl.* III. 129/1 The Frankish monarchy under the Carolingians was fundamentally different from that of the Merovingians. **1974** *Encycl. Brit. Macropædia* XI. 931/2 Under the Carolingians, the slaves in Gaul formed only a residual class, although the slave trade was still active.

Caroˈlinian, *a.* [f. med.L. *Carolīnus* of Charles; and its derivative *Carolina.*] **a.** Belonging to Charles the Great. **b.** Belonging to one or both of the Carolinas in U.S. Also *sb.*

1705 Penn *Let.* 9 Dec. in *Penn-Logan Corr.* (1872) II. 105 The Carolinian Lords. **1707** J. Archdale *New Descr. Carolina* 15 By the Encouragements of several Carolinians than in England my Going was concluded on. **1818** *Mass. Agric. Repository & Jrnl.* V. 60 Populus Angulata—Carolinian Poplar, name given to it in Europe, because first brought from Carolina. **1847** *Secret Soc. Mid. Ages* 321 The Fehm-Gerichte..named..Carolinian Tribunals, as having been (as was believed) instituted by Charles the Great. **1775** Adair *Amer. Ind.* 226 Sharp and cold to a Carolinian. **1876** Bancroft *Hist. U.S.* IV. xlvii. 228 It became the pride of native Carolinians not to accept a seat in [the king's council].

c. = Caroline *a.* 1 b. Also as *sb.*, a poet of the time of Charles I or II.

1949 M. Bewley in *Scrutiny* Mar. 16 The tone of the colloquialism is Carolinian. *Ibid.* 19 The Carolinians exploit the fashion for the grace and elegance of conceit it allows them.

caroˈlitic, *a. Arch.* Erroneous f. corollitic.

1842–76 Gwilt *Archit.* Gloss., *Carolitic column*, one with a foliated shaft.

carolus (ˈkærələs). [f. *Carolus*, Latinized form of Karl, Charles.] A gold piece struck in the reign of Charles I.; originally valued at 20*s.*, but afterwards at 23*s.* The name has been given to various other coins bearing 'Carolus' as the name of the monarch; e.g. a *Carolus dollar.*

1687 *Lond. Gaz.* No. 2258/4 A Boy about 18 years old.. Run away with..5 Carolus pieces of Gold. **1753** Richardson *Grandison* (1781) II. xx. 216, 120 Carolus's were also in this purse. **1855** Macaulay *Hist. Eng.* IV. 490 Every trader had his own strong box..and..told down the crowns and Caroluses on his own counter.

carom, carrom (ˈkærəm). An abbreviation of carambole, applied to the stroke so called in Billiards; now corrupted to cannon *sb.*¹ 7.

A. *sb.*

1779 C. Jones *Hoyle's Games Impr.* 260 Which stroke is called a Carambole, or for shortness, a Carrom. **1826** *Hoyle Impr.* 396 A carombole or carom. **1850** Bohn *Handbk. Games* 519 A canon (formerly *carom* or *carombole*). **1872** Mark Twain *Innoc. Abr.* xii. 84 We accomplished very little in the way of caroms.

B. *v. intr.* (*transf.* in quots.) To strike or glance and rebound. Also *fig.* Chiefly *U.S.*

1860 O. W. Holmes *Prof. Breakf.-t.* 67 She glanced from every human contact, and 'caromed' from one relation to another. **1883** *Harper's Mag.* Mar. 494/2 A single stone was made to 'carom'. **1911** Mulford *Bar-20 Days* iv. 45 The table skidded through the door on one leg and caromed off the bar at a graceful angle. **1943** K. Tennant *Ride on Stranger* (1968) xvii. 219 It was here that Mrs. Brewster made the mistake..of caroming off a telegraph post into the ditch. **1946** H. Croome *Faithless Mirror* xviii. 192 The car lurched crazily..up the gully, caroming from side to side. **1952** B. Wolfe *Limbo '90* xix. 284 The phrase caromed through his mind. **1967** *Boston Globe* 18 May 36/8 Rockets carom to the moon.

caromel, variant of caramel.

ˈ**carony bark.** 'A synonym of true *Angustura bark*' (*Syd. Soc. Lex.*).

1853 Th. Ross tr. *Humboldt's Trav.* III. xxv. 2 *note*, The trade carried on..in the Carony bark, which is the beneficial bark of the Bonplandia trifoliata.

†**caˈroon¹, caˈrroon, caˈroome.** *Obs.* [Etymol. obscure. Derivation from car or F. *carre* has been conjectured; cf. also OF. *carron* paving tile: was the impost originally levied to defray paving?] 'A licence by the Lord Mayor of London to keep a cart' (Wharton *Law Lex.* 1860).

1720 *Stow's Surv.* (ed. Strype 1754) II. v. xviii. 389/1 If the yearly Rent of 17*s.* 4*d.* a piece be not paid to the said President and governors, the Caroon, that is, the License of such person so wanting or refusing shall be forthwith suspended. **1730–6** Bailey, *Carroon*, a Rent received for the Privilege of driving a car or cart in the city of London. **1800** Colquhoun *Comm. Thames* xi. 331 To regulate and control Carroons, or privileged Carts. **1832** E. V. Williams *Executors & Adm.* I. 531 A caroome, or a license by the Mayor of London to keep a cart.

caroon² (kəˈruːn). [Etymol. unknown. (Mahn compares Ir. *caor*, dim. *caoran*, the rowan-tree berry; but there is no connexion.)] A species of cherry.

1858 in Simmonds *Dict. Trade.*

caross, var. kaross, an African cloak of skins.

†**caˈrosse.** *Obs.* Also in 7 caroce. [a. F. *carosse* (now *carrosse*), ad. It. *carozza*, augmentative of *carro* chariot, etc.: cf. the parallel caroche.] A carriage, a caroche.

1598 Florio, *Carroccia*..a caroce, a coche, a chariot. **1608** Chapman *Byron's Trag.* Plays (1873) II. 297 The Carosse of the Marquis of Rhosny Conducted him along to th' Arcenall. **1657** Colvil *Whigs Supplic.* 89 And when ye travel in carosses, Ye will salute the high-way crosses.

‖**caroˈteel, -el.** [possibly ad. Arab. *qirṭāl*, collective of *qirṭālat*, *qartillat* ass's burden, basket, fruit-basket.] 'The commercial name for a tierce or cask, in which dried fruit and some other commodities are packed, which usually averages about 7 cwt.' (Simmonds *Dict. Trade*).

1704 Worlidge *Dict. Rust. et Urb.*, Caroteel of Cloves 4 to 5 C. Weight; Currants 5 to 9 C.; Malt about 3 C. **1721** Bailey, *Caroteel*, a quantity of some Commodities; as of Cloves, from 4 to 5 Hundred Weight.

carotene, carotin (ˈkærətiːn, -ɪn). [a. G. *carotin* (H. W. F. Wackenroder 1831, in *Mag. Pharmacie* XXXIII. 148), f. L. *carota* carrot + -ene, -in¹.] An orange or red hydrocarbon, $C_{40}H_{56}$, synthesized in several isomeric forms by carrots and many other plants, and an important source of vitamin A. Also *attrib.*

1861 Mrs. Beeton *Bk. Househ. Managem.* 563 A peculiar crystallizable ruby-red neuter principle, without odour or taste, called carotin. **1895** *Naturalist* 24 [Berries of mountain ash.] Their colouring matter is due to carotin. **1897** *Jrnl. Chem. Soc.* LXXII. ii. 225 The author does not attempt to decide whether the crystals formed in this reaction are all xanthophyll or all carotin crystals, or whether these are identical or whether they consist in part of colouring matters nearly related to carotene. **1951** *Science News* XXII. 75 Vitamin A..is one half of a carotene molecule and is formed from carotene in the intestinal wall of animals. **1960** [see cryptoxanthin].

Hence ˌ**caroteˈnæmia** (U.S. -nem-), ˌ**carotiˈnæmia**, the presence of carotene in the circulating blood.

1919 A. F. Hess & V. C. Myers in *Jrnl. Amer. Med. Assoc.* LXXIII. 1745/1 In cases of carotinemia the urine was colored yellow as well as the serum. **1959** *Listener* 11 June 1017/1 Occasional cases of a condition known as carotinaemia were encountered... It arose from an over-indulgence in carrots.

carotenoid, carotinoid ('kærətɪnɔɪd). *Biochem.* [ad. G. *Carotinoïde* (M. Tswett 1911, in *Ber. d. Deut. Bot. Ges.* XXIX. 630); see prec. + -OID.] Any one of a group of pigments including the carotenes, the xanthophylls, and fucoxanthin, found in many plants and animals. Also *attrib.* or as *adj.*

1913 *Chem. Abstr.* 2956 (*title*) The Occurrence of Carotinoids in Plants. **1917** HAAS & HILL *Introd. Chem. Plant Products* (ed. 2) v. 229 Carotin, Xanthophyll, and Fucoxanthin..are known collectively as the Carotinoids. **1922** L. S. PALMER (*title*) Carotenoids and related pigments. **1930** *Brit. Jrnl. Exper. Path.* Apr. 81 The relation between the carotenoid pigments and vitamin A. **1952** *New Biol.* XIII. 40 Doubling the number of chromosomes in pure yellow corn caused a 40% increase in the carotenoid pigment content, including the active provitamin A fraction of the carotenoids. **1968** *Times* 16 Nov. 9/7 Sporopollenin is a polymer formed of sub-units known as carotenoids.

carotic (kə'rɒtɪk), *a. Pathol.* and *Phys.* [ad. Gr. καρωτικός stupefying, soporific, f. καροῦν to stupefy. Cf. F. *carotique.*]

1. a. 'Having power to stupefy or produce stupefaction' (*Syd. Soc. Lex.*). **b.** Of the nature of or pertaining to stupor or carus; in a state of carus.

1684 tr. *Bonet's Merc. Compit.* xvi. 567 He was thought to be carotick, but he was not so; for at length he awaked. **1881** *Syd. Soc. Lex., Carotic sleep*, profound drowsiness.

2. = CAROTID. (*rare.*)

1656 RIDGLEY *Pract. Physic* 53 The temporal muscle, and the Carotick Arteries. **1843** J. WILKINSON *Swedenborg's Anim. Kingd.* I. ii. 85 The cranial or carotic blood.

carotid (kə'rɒtɪd), *a.* and *sb.* [ad. Gr. καρωτίδ-ες, f. καροῦν 'to plunge into deep sleep, to stupefy', because compression of these arteries is said to produce carus or stupor. (Galen.)]

A. *adj.* Epithet of the two great arteries, one on either side of the neck, which supply blood to the head.

Each of the two primitive carotid arteries afterwards divides into two branches, called the external and internal respectively. **1667** E. KING in *Phil. Trans.* II. 450 Which made me open the Carotid Artery. **1804** ABERNETHY *Surg. Obs.* 193 It had passed beneath, and torn the internal carotid artery. **1831** R. KNOX *Cloquet's Anat.* 649 They ascend..to the upper part of the larynx, where they divide into the external carotid and the internal carotid arteries.

b. Pertaining to or adjoining the carotid arteries; e.g. ***carotid canal***, the tunnel through the temporal bone which gives passage to the internal carotid, and its plexus of nerves (***carotid plexus***).

1842 E. WILSON *Anat. Vade M.* 26 Nearer to the apex of the bone is a large oval opening, the carotid foramen. **1877** BURNET *Ear* 88 The carotid canal is the simplest in structure ..of the canals in or about the tympanum.

B. *sb.* A carotid artery.

1741 MONRO *Anat.* (ed. 3) 90 The Arteries derived from the external Carotids. **1806** *Med. Jrnl.* XV. 477 After the incision into the carotid of a horse. **1862** CALVERLEY *Verses & Tr.* 46 With vest blood-spotted, and cut carotid.

†**ca'rotidal**, *a. Obs.* [f. prec. + -AL[1].] = prec.

1664 POWER *Exp. Philos.* I. 66 The carotidal Arteries. **1737** BRACKEN *Farriery* (1763) 83 The Blood which is brought to the Brain by the Carotidal and the Vertebral Arteries.

carotidean (kærəʊ'tɪdɪən), *a.* [f. as prec. + -EAN. Cf. F. *carotidien.*] = prec.

1836–39 TODD *Cycl. Anat.* II. 285/5 He would exclude the Vidian nerve, or at least its carotidean branch.

carouba (ka'ruːba). A variant of CAROB (tree), following the Arabic form of the word.

1856 J. H. NEWMAN *Callista* (1885) 330 A few olives and caroubas. **1867** LADY HERBERT *Cradle L.* ix. 233 The so-called 'Forest' of Carmel..with dwarf oak, bay, carouba. **1884** *Harper's Mag.* 209/1 Looking at the carouba-trees.

caroul, obs. form of CAROL.

carousal (kə'raʊzəl). [f. CAROUSE *v.* + -AL[1]; but the formation may have been aided by the misunderstanding of *carousel*, and its association with CAROUSE *v.*] A fit of carousing, a drinking-feast or carouse; revelry in drinking.

1765 STERNE *Tr. Shandy* VII. xliii. (R.) The swains were preparing for a carousal. **1801** SOUTHEY *Thalaba* VI. xxviii, Sounds of carousal came, and song. **1814** BYRON *Lara* I. vii, Join'd the carousals of the great and gay. **1872** YEATS *Techn. Hist. Comm.* 124 The Germans were celebrated for their hospitality..and their carousals.

¶Erroneously put for CAROUSEL q.v.

†**ca'rouse**, *adv. Obs.* Also garaus, carous. [a. Ger. *gar aus*, in *gar-aus trinken* to drink 'all out', to empty the bowl. Cf. ALL OUT, the English phrase in same sense. In 16th c. F., Rabelais has *boire carrous et alluz.*] In the phrase ***to drink, quaff (pledge one) carouse***: i.e. to the bottom, to drink a full bumper to his health.

1567 DRANT *Horace Ep.* i. 18 The tiplinge sottes at midnight which to quaffe carowse do vse. **1586** T. B. tr. *La Primaud. Fr. Acad.* (1589) 193 Rather than they wil refuse to drink carouse. **1600** ROWLANDS *Lett. Humours Blood* (1874) 43 His hostesse pledg'd him not carouse [*rime* house]. **1609** HOLLAND *Amm. Marcell.* XXVII. i, Some againe drinking garaus. **1667** E. CHAMBERLAYNE *St. Gt. Brit.* I. (1684) 40.

carouse (kə'raʊz), *sb.* Forms: (6 garouse), 6–7 carous, car(r)owse, -ouse, 7 car(r)ousse, carrouze, (caraus, garaus, -ausse, karausse), 7–9 carouze, 6– carouse. [The prec. adv. in phrase *to drink carouse*, taken for obj. of the vb.: cf. F. *une carrousse*, Sp. *carauz*, also from Ger. The word formerly rimed with *house*, *mouse*; the pronunciation (-aʊz) appeared first in the vb., *c* 1660 (cf. *grass*, *graze*, *advice*, *advise*, etc.), and subsequently spread to sense 3 of the sb., taken as a deriv. of the vb.]

†**1.** The action or fashion of 'drinking carouse'.

1559 *Mirr. Mag.* 610 (R.) Lyæus fruitful cup with full carowse Went round about. **1600** ROWLANDS *Lett. Humours Blood* vii. (1874) 13 Drinke some braue health vpon the Dutch carouse..Or visit Shorditch, for a bawdie house. **1611** RICH *Honest. Age* (1844) Introd. 19 Their best was, I drinke to you, and I pledge yee; some shallow-witted drunkard found out the Carowse.

†**2.** A cupful drunk 'all out', a full draught of liquor, a full bumper to one's health, a toast. *Obs.* bef. 1700 (but used by Scott).

1594 DRAYTON *Ideas* vii, Quaffing Carowses in this costly Wine. **1596** SHAKS. *Tam. Shr.* I. ii. 277 Quaffe carowses to our Mistresse health. **1611** ROWLAND *Four Knaves* (1843) 13, I..will drinke a healths carouse. **1611** COTGR., *Carous*, a carousse of drinke. **1617** MORYSON *Itin.* III. II. iii. 86 All which garausses he must drinke. **1674** MILTON *Moscov.* Wks. 1738 II. 145 The Emperor standing up, drank a deep Carouse to the Queen's Health. **1813** SCOTT *Rokeby* I. vii, Quaff the full carouze.

3. A drinking bout; a carousal; carousing.

1690 W. WALKER *Idiomat. Anglo-Lat.* 228 Bassus at the Thracian carowse. **1725** POPE *Odyss.* I. 480 The early feast and late carouse. **1833** HT. MARTINEAU *Manch. Strike* i. 8 To go to the Spread-eagle and have a carouse. **1851** LONGF. *Gold. Leg., Refectory* ad fin., What means this revel and carouse?

carouse (kə'raʊz), *v.* Forms: 6 karous, garouse, carous, 6–7 carrouse, car(r)owse, 7 garousse, carrowze, -ouze, 7–8 carowze, -ouze, 6– carouse. [f. CAROUSE *adv.*: cf. F. *carousser* 'to quaff, swill, carouse it' (Cotgr.).]

1. *intr.* To drink 'all out', drink freely and repeatedly. So ***to carouse it.***

1567 DRANT *Horace Ep.* xiv, I that in tune and out of time, karoust it without measure. **1596** RALEIGH *Discov. Guiana* (1848) 64 Some..garoused of his wine til they were reasonable pleasant. **1601** HOLLAND *Pliny* II. 349 To quaffe and carouse again vpon it more lustily. **1656** BLOUNT *Glossogr., Carouse*..to drink all out. **1727** A. HAMILTON *New Acc. E. Ind.* I. xv. 173 To procure Wine and carouze with him, which they did, and he got beastly drunk. **1779** JOHNSON *L.P., Thomson* Wks. IV. 167 Thomson.. carousing with lord Hertford and his friends. **1827** POLLOCK *Course T.* iv, Drinking from the well of life, And yet carousing in the cup of death. **1875** B. TAYLOR *Faust* I. vi. 102

b. To drink a bumper *to* (any one), to drink health or success *to.*

1583 STUBBES *Anat. Abus.* (1877) I. 107 Swilling, gulling and carowsing from one to another. **1594** LYLY *Moth. Bomb.* II. i. 92, I carouse to Prisius, and brinch you mas Sperantius. **1604** SHAKS. *Ham.* v. ii. 300 (2nd Qo.) The Queene Carowses [1st Qo. drinkes] to thy fortune Hamlet.

†**2.** *trans.* To drink off or up, to drain, to quaff, to swill; to drink (a health). *Obs.*

1580 LYLY *Euphues* (Arb.) 432 The Glasses wher-in you carouse your wine. **1604** SHAKS. *Oth.* II. iii. 55 Roderigo.. To Desdemona hath to night Carrows'd Potations, pottle-deepe. **1617** MORYSON *Itin.* III. 162 Some Gentlewomen were so free in this excesse, as they would..garousse health after health with men. **1683** TRYON *Way to Health* 168 To Carrouze strong Drink, Brandy, Wine. **1742** YOUNG *Nt. Th.* v. 545 Egypt's wanton queen, Carousing gems.

b. *fig.*

1589 R. HARVEY *Pl. Perc.* 23 Carrouse vp your owne quarrels in the cup. **1645** QUARLES *Sol. Recant.* I. 20 Why doe we thus..carouse full Bowles Of boyling anguish? **1660** W. SECKER *Nonsuch Prof.* 11 If the Cup be lawful we must not carouze it.

carousel (kæruː'zɛl). Also 9– carrousel. [a. F. *carrousel*, ad. It. *carosello*, *garosello* 'a kind of joust or feat on horseback'. Littré takes It. *carosello* or *garosello* as dim. of *garoso*, quarrelsome, contentious, f. *gara* quarrel, strife; but this is doubtful, and possibly the etymological form was *carrosello*, from *carro* chariot.)]

1. 'A tournament in which knights, divided into companies (quadrilles) distinguished by their liveries and dresses, engaged in various plays and exercises; to this were often added chariot races, and other shows and entertainments' (Littré).

1650 MARVELL *Death Ld. Hastings*, Before the Crystal Palace where he dwells The Armed Angels hold their Carousels. **1686** *Lond. Gaz.* No. 2117/4 A great carousel is preparing here [Paris] against Easter. **1697** DRYDEN *Virg. Æneid* v. (1806) III. 131 This Game, these Carousels Ascanius taught. **1753** HANWAY *Trav.* (1762) I. VII. xc. 414 The carousel, the expence of which amounted to seventy thousand crowns. **1839** JAMES *Louis XIV*, III. 27 Those carousels and mock-fights. **1865** CARLYLE *Fredk. Gt.* VI. XVI. vi. 187 Carrousel..is, in fact, a kind of superb betailored running at the ring.

¶Many writers employing the word historically, have erroneously identified it with *carousal.*

1709 STEELE *Tatler* No. 33 ¶ 10 A Carousal, wherein many of the Youth of the first Quality..ran for the Prize. **1762** HUME *Hist. Eng.* (1806) IV. l. 35 His fine taste in dress, festivals, and carousals. **1774** T. WARTON *Hist. Eng. Poetry* (1840) II. 28 A royal carousal given by Charles the Fifth of France to the Emperor. **1823** LINGARD *Hist. Eng.* VI. 23 The young king loitered for weeks at Calais, spending his time in carousals and entertainments. **1858** PLANCHÉ *D'Aulnoy's Fairy T.* 440 After which, there were ballets, carousals, and a thousand other things.

2. A merry-go-round, a roundabout. Also *attrib.* Chiefly *U.S.* (where freq. written *carrousel*).

1673 R. FOLYARTE *Let.* in D. Braithwaite *Fairground Archit.* (1968) iii. 34 A new and rare invencon knowne by the name of the royalle carousell or tournament being framed and contrived with such engines as will not only afford great pleasure to us and our nobility in the sight thereof, but sufficient instruction to all such ingenious young gentlemen as desire to learne the art of perfect horsemanshipp. **1899** *N.Y. Times Illustr. Mag.* in F. Fried *Pict. Hist. Carousel* (1964) iii. 82 A carousel costs from $300 to $10,000 according to the decoration and finish... A carousel that will seat 60 riders measures 40 feet in diameter and costs $2,200. **1909** *Sat. Even. Post* 13 Mar. 64/1 We make everything.. from a hand-power Merry-Go-Round to the highest grade Carousselles. **1951** J. D. SALINGER *Catcher in Rye* xxv. 250 She sat down on this big..horse. Then the carousel started, and I watched her go round and round. **1956** E. AMBLER *Night-Comers* iii. 58 There was even a small fair in progress. A carousel had been set up. **1958** S. ELLIN *Eighth Circle* (1959) II. xi. 122 A faraway sound of carrousel music. **1968** R. PETRIE *MacLurg goes West* x. 89 Bracketed on, so that they hung semi-rampant..were the two carousel horses.

3. (See quot. 1961.) Now esp. one at airports for the delivery of passengers' luggage.

1961 WEBSTER, *Carrousel*, a conveyor (as for assembly-line work) on which objects are placed and carried round a complete circuit on a horizontal plane. **1970** *Which?* Nov. 352/1 Older people..found it hard to tug their cases off the carousels.

carouser (kə'raʊzə(r)). One who carouses.

1596 RALEIGH *Discov. Guiana* (1848) 64 The greatest garousers and drunkards of the world. **1598** R. BARCKLEY *Felic. Man* I. (1603) 24 Carowsers that will match Nero. **1732** LD. LANSDOWNE *To Garth* (R.) The bold carouser and advent'rous dame. **1849** W. IRVING *Mahomed* viii. (1853) 27 The noise brought the carousers from their tents.

carousing (kə'raʊzɪŋ), *vbl. sb.* The action of the verb CAROUSE. Often *attrib.*

1583 STANYHURST *Æneis* III. (Arb.) 81 They kept a myrry carousing. **1592** NASHE *P. Penilesse* (ed. 2) 23 b, Downe to yᵉ bottome of his carrowsing cups. **1617** MORYSON *Itin.* III. II. 87 Which kind of karoussing they call the crowning of the Emperor. **1650** HUBBERT *Pill Formality* 137 Drowned in carowsing bowls. **1756** NUGENT *Gr. Tour, Germ.* II. 208 At Vienna, Their chief diversion is feasting and carousing. **1861** RAMSAY *Remin.* iii. 62.

ca'rousing, *ppl. a.* That carouses. Hence **ca'rousingly** *adv.*

1603 FLORIO *Montaigne* II. ii. (1634) 188 Our carowsing tospot German souldiers. **1704** ROWE *Ulysses* II. i. 955 These Carousing Lovers. **1848** CRAIG, *Carousingly.* **1875** MYERS *Poems* 58.

carowaye, -weie, obs. ff. CARAWAY.

carowl, carowse, obs. f. CAROL, CAROUSE.

caroygne, -oyne, obs. ff. CARRION.

carp (kɑːp), *sb.*[1] Also 5–7 carpe. Pl. carp, formerly carps. [a. OF. *carpe* (Sp. *carpa*):—late L. *carpa* (Brachet cites Cassiodorus *a* 575 'destinet carpam Danubius'). The same name (modified in termination, etc.) appears in Romanic, Celtic, Teutonic, and Slavonic: cf. esp. OHG. *charpho*, MLG. *karpe* masc. pointing to a possible WGer. **karpo*. But the original source is unknown.]

1. A freshwater fish, *Cyprinus carpio*, the type of the family *Cyprinidæ*; introduced into England as early as the 14th c., and commonly bred in ponds.

c **1440** *Promp. Parv.* 62 Carpe, fysche, *carpus.* **1462** *Mann. & Househ. Exp.* 561 My master putte into the said ponde, in gret carpes, xxj. **1584** R. SCOT *Disc. Witchcr.* XIII. x. 248 A bone taken out of a carps head, stancheth bloud. **1653** WALTON *Angler* I. ix, The Carp is the Queen of Rivers: a stately, a good, and a very subtle fish. **1718** LADY M. W. MONTAGUE *Lett.* liv. II. 80 In the fish ponds are kept tame Carp, said to be, some of them, eighty years of age. **1770** WHITE *Selborne* xl. 103 In this water are many carps. **1854** BADHAM *Halieut.* 257 That singular fleshy palate which is popularly but incorrectly known all over the world as carp's tongue. **1867** F. FRANCIS *Angling* iii. (1880) 84 In rivers carp bite more boldly than in ponds.

2. Applied to other species of the genus *Cyprinus*, or family *Cyprinidæ*, to which belong the Gold and Silver Fish, the Prussian or Crucian Carp (*C. gibelio*), the Norwegian Carp (*Scarpæna norvegica*), and others.

1786 WHITE *Selborne* xcviii, Gold and silver fishes.. Linnæus ranks..under the genus of *cyprinus* or carp. **1847** CARPENTER *Zool.* §567 The *Cyprinidæ* or Carp tribe. **1883** *Fisheries Exhib. Catal.* (ed. 4) 107 Collection of Stuffed.. Carp, Crucian Carp, Gold Carp.

3. *Comb.* **carp-louse**, a name for small crustaceans of the family Argulidæ, parasitic on fishes; cf. FISH-*louse*.

1678–1706 PHILLIPS, *Carp-stone*, a triangular stone found in the chop of a carp, white without and yellow within. **1889** in *Cent. Dict.* **1909** J. J. LISTER in A. Sedgwick *Textbk. Zool.* III. 410 Carp-lice. Copepods with large compound eyes. **1931** J. R. NORMAN *Hist. Fishes* xx. 417 Mention may also be made of the so-called Carp Louse (*Argulus*), another Crustacean parasite.

carp, *sb.*[2] [f. CARP *v.*[1]]

†**a.** Discourse. *Obs. rare.* †**b.** Power of speech. *Obs. rare.* **c.** Carping speech, cavil (with play on CARP *sb.*[1]).

c **1325** *E.E. Allit. P.* A. 882 In sounande notez a gentyl carpe. *Ibid.* B. 23 Kryst kydde hit hymself in a carp onez. *Ibid.* B. 1327 Þat he ful clanly bi-cuv-er his carp bi þe laste. **1618** MYNSHUL *Ess. Prison* 1st Ep. Ded. i, Carpes haue bin good cheap this Lent, for I haue had more than I desired for nothing. **1904** *Westm. Gaz.* 9 May 4/1 Criticism—what a lady I know calls 'the carpers carping with their carps'. **1922** F. SCOTT FITZGERALD *Let.* Jan. (1964) 331 But one more carp before I close. **1967** *Observer* 24 Oct. 25/2, I have one carp, however. His own performance..tends to become confusing.

¶ Associated with CARK.

1548 UDALL, etc. *Erasm. Par. Mark* viii. 57 a, Their vayne and superfluous carpe and care.

carp (kɑːp), *v.*[1] Also 4 **karp**, 5 **karpe**, 4–7 **carpe**. [Senses 1–3, chiefly in northern poetry (especially in alliterative verse), were probably a. ON. *karpa* to brag; but the later prose senses 4–6 appear to be derived from, or influenced by, L. *carpĕre* to pluck, *fig.* to slander, calumniate. The ulterior history of the ON. word is uncertain.]

†**1.** *intr.* To speak, talk. *Obs.*

a **1240** *Wohunge* in *Cott. Hom.* 287 Carpe toward ihesu and seie þise wordes. *a* **1300** *Cursor M.* App. *Resurrect.* 388 Als þai come narre þe castelle, to-geder carpand. *c* **1400** *Destr. Troy* 829 The Kyng þan full curtesly karpes agayne. **1420** *Siege Rouen* 1235 in *Archæol.* XXII. 381 Vnnethe thay myȝt brethe or carpe. **1470** HARDING *Chron.* Proem. x, Leonell..that wedded..The erles daughter of Vister, as man do Karpe. **1570** LEVINS *Manip.* 33/3 To carpe, talke, *colloqui, confabulari.* **1575** TURBERV. *Bk. Falconrie* Epil. Aa iij, To carpe it fine with those that haue no guile.

†**b.** To discourse *of*, in speech or writing. *Obs.*

1350 *Will. Palerne* 216 þe kowherdes bestes i carped of bi-fore. **1393** LANGL. *P. Pl.* C. XXII. 199 Thus conscience of crist and of þe croys carpede. *c* **1425** WYNTOUN *Cron.* III. Prol. 26 (Jam.) Of thame..Carpe we bot lityl. *a* **1605** MONTGOMERIE *Flyting* 575 Of his conditions to carp for a while.

†**2.** *trans.* To speak, utter, say, tell. *Obs.*

1350 *Will. Palerne* 503 To karp þe soþe. **1393** GOWER *Conf.* III. 325 To carpe Proverbes and demaundes sligh. *c* **1400** *Destr. Troy* 4610 When Calcas his counsell had carpit to the end. **1515** *Sc. Field* 73 in Furniv. *Percy Folio* I. 216 Our Knight full [of] courage carpeth these words.

†**3.** *intr.* To sing or recite (as a minstrel); to sing (as a bird). *Obs.*

c **1425** *Thomas of Erceld.* 313 'To harpe or carpe, whare-so þou gose, Thomas, þou sall hafe þe chose sothely': And he saide 'harpynge kepe I none, For tonge es chefe of mynstralsye'. **1515** BARCLAY *Egloges* iv. (1570) C iv/2 In goodly ditie or balade for to carpe. *a* **1528** SKELTON *Agst. comely Coyst.* 13 In his gamut carp he can. *c* **1570** THYNNE *Pride & Lowl.* (1841) 8 Many was the bird did sweetly carpe Among the thornes. **1802** *Lochmaben Harper* vii. in Scott *Minstr. Scott. Bord.* (1869) 94 Then aye he harped, and aye he carped Till a' the lordlings footed the floor.

†**4.** *Vituperatively*: To talk much, to prate, chatter. Cf. CARPER. *Obs.*

1377 LANGL. *P. Pl.* B. x. 69 Clerkes..carpen of god faste, and haue [him] moche in þe mouthe. *a* **1528** SKELTON *Col. Cloute* 549 Some..Clatter & carpe Of that heresy. **1530** PALSGR. 476/1, I carpe (Lydgate), *Je carquette*..This is a farre northen verbe. **1557** *Praise Maistr. Ryce* in *Tottel's Misc.* (Arb.) 202 Came Curiousness and carped out of frame.

5. *spec.* To talk querulously, censoriously, or captiously; to find fault, cavil. (The current sense.)

(*Certain* examples of this before the 16th c. are wanting: the early ones may have merely the sense of 1 with contextual colouring. Cf. CARPER.)

[**1377** LANGL. *P. Pl.* B. x. 286 Abasshed To blame yow or to greve, And carpen noght as they carpe now, Ne calle yow dumbe houndes. **1401** *Pol. Poems* (1859) II. 77 Thou carpist also of oure coveitise, and sparist the sothe. **1515** BARCLAY *Egloges* i. (1570) Aj, Some in Satyres against vices dare carpe.] **1548** *Soul John-Nobody* in Strype *Cranmer* (1694) App. 139 They will currishly carp. **1561** T. NORTON *Calvin's Inst.* I. xiii. (1634) 49 Servetto carpeth, that God did beare the person of an Angell. **1655** DIGGES *Compl. Ambass.* 377 The King..carpeth upon the marriage. *a* **1677** BARROW *Serm. Malice of Soc.*, In carping and harshly censuring..their neighbours. **1785** BURNS *2nd Ep. Lapraik*, Ne'er grudge an' carp, Tho' fortune use you hard an' sharp. **1863** MRS. C. CLARKE *Shaks. Char.* xv. 386 The bulk of society did not assemble to carp and to cavil.

b. Const. *at.*

1586 THYNNE *Contn. Holinshed* Pref., Curiouslie carping at my barrennes in writing. **1794** BURKE *Corr.* IV. 235 That faction and malice may not be able to carp at it. **1879** M. ARNOLD *Falkland* Mixed Ess. 207 We will not carp at this great writer.

†**6.** *trans.* To find fault with, reprehend, take exception to. *Obs.*

1550 CRANMER *Sacrament* 100 a, Whiche my saiyng diuers ignorant persones..did carpe and reprehende. **1582** N. T. (Rhem.) *Luke* vii. *marg.*, The Pharisees did alwaies carpe Christ. **1598** GRENEWEY *Tacitus Ann.* v. ii. (1622) 117 Courtly carping the Consull Fufius. **1605** CAMDEN *Rem.* (1637) 230 Carping whatsoever hath been done or said heretofore. **1678** R. BARCLAY *Apol. Quakers* iii. §vii. 87 Our Adversaries shall have nothing from thence to carp.

†**7.** *intr.* (?) To censure; to judge, discriminate.

1591 *Troub. Raigne K. John* (1611) 21 Any one that knoweth how to carpe, Will scarcely iudge us both one countrey borne.

†**8.** (?) To contend, fight. *Obs. rare.*

1535 STEWART *Cron. Scot.* I. 606 With brandis bricht that scherand wer and scharp So cruellie togidder did tha carp.

¶ Associated with CARK, q.v.

c **1465** *Chevy Chace* II. 135 Tivydale may carpe off care. **1522** *World & Child* in Hazl. *Dodsley* I. 267 Ever he is carping of care. **1670** G. H. *Hist. Cardinals* I. II. 49 Poor drudgeing..Priests that carp and moyl all day long. **1702** *Eng. Theophrast.* 312 Carping for the unprofitable goods of this world.

carp, *v.*[2] [? ad. L. *carpĕre* to pluck, card.] (See quot.) Hence **carper**, **carping** *vbl. sb.*

1835 URE *Philos. Manuf.* 202 The business to which children are first put in this business is carping; that is, preparing thistle-teasels for the workman, who fits them into the rods and handles for dressing the cloth. The little carpers sit at this easy work.

†**car'pacious**, *a. Obs. rare*[−1]. [f. Lat. *carpĕre*, taken in sense of Eng. CARP: after *loquacious*, *rapacious*, etc.: see -ACIOUS.] Given to carping.

1574 R. SCOT *Hop Gard.* (1578) 62 Corrupt and hastye Judges..carpacious Controllers, and..impudent Scoffers.

carpal ('kɑːpəl), *a. Anat.* [ad. mod.L. *carpālis*, f. *carpus* wrist.] Of or pertaining to the carpus or wrist.

1743 BEVAN in *Phil. Trans.* XLII. 489 Several Anchylosses's formed in the small Joints, viz. carpal and meta-carpal Bones. **1840** G. ELLIS *Anat.* 402 The posterior carpal artery is very small. **1800** *Med. Jrnl.* IV. 416 The articulation between the carpal and metacarpal bones. **1856** YARRELL *Hist. Birds* I. 390 From the carpal joint to the end of the wing.

b. *sb. pl.* = Carpal bones.

1855 OWEN *Skel. & Teeth* 15 The row of short bones joined with these are the 'carpals'.

Carpano (kɑː'pɑːnəʊ). [Name of Antonio *Carpano*, who made the first commercial preparation of vermouth in Italy in 1786.] The proprietary name of an Italian vermouth; a drink of this.

1921 *Chambers's Jrnl.* 6 Aug. 572/2 The little waiter had that moment emerged..with a wet tray and a cool glass of *carpano*. **1950** D. AMES *Corpse Diplomatique* xii. 89 Dagobert ordered a *Carpano* for me and a *Campari* for himself. **1961** *Guardian* 21 Nov. 13/2 Carpano is..a dark, bitter-sweet vermouth. **1968** HURD & OSMOND *Send him Victorious* 20 Raikes began to fumble in his pockets for money to pay for his Carpano.

carpar, -are, obs. f. CARPER.

Carpathian (kɑː'peɪθɪən), *a.*[1] [f. *Carpathos*: see -IAN.] Of or pertaining to Carpathos or Karpathos, an island in the Ægean Sea.

1634 MILTON *Comus* 872 By hoary Nereus wrincled look, And the Carpathian wisards hook. **1797** *Encycl. Brit.* IV. 179/1 The sea which, from this island, is called the Carpathian Sea. **1925** *Glasgow Herald* 30 July 6 In a spell of Carpathian silence.

Carpathian (kɑː'peɪθɪən), *a.*[2] and *sb.* [Prob. immediately ad. G. *Karpathen* (*Karpatisch* adj.) Carpathian mountains:—L. *Carpatus*, Gr. *Καρπάτης ὄρος* (Ptolemy), of uncertain ulterior etymology: see -IAN.] **A.** *adj.* Epithet of a range of mountains extending from northern Czechoslovakia to Romania; pertaining to the region of these mountains. **B.** *sb. pl.* The Carpathian mountains.

1673 E. BROWNE *Trav. Hungary, Servia* 3 The Carpathian Mountains which divide Poland and Hungary. **1694** *Phil. Trans. 1693* XVII. 470 Next, Let us suppose this Ocean interspersed with wide and spacious Tracts of Land; with high ridges of Mountains such as the Pyrenean, the Alps, the Apennine, the Carpathian in Europe. **1776** GIBBON *Decl. & F.* I. ix. 218 A ridge of hills, rising from the Danube, and called the Carpathian mountains, covered Germany on the side of Dacia or Hungary. **1835** J. B. ROBERTSON tr. *F. von Schlegel's Philos. of Hist.* ii. 84 The great Danubian countries, extending from the South of the Carpathian mountains, down to the other mountainous chain northward of Greece. **1845** *Encycl. Metrop.* XX. 390/1 The Carpathians, extending from West to East in a semicircular line of 200 leagues, are, according to Beudant, not so much a chain as a high terrace..terminated at both extremities by high mountain masses. **1862** MACKENZIE & IRBY *Across Carpathians* i. 1 The Carpathian or Krapack chain of mountains incloses the kingdom of Hungary on three sides, in the form of a bow... In the north..it fully merits the epithet from which etymologists have derived its name—Chrib, Chrebet, the high mountain, or still more literally, the high *back.* **1919** G. B. SHAW *Inca of Perusalem* 215 Before ten years have elapsed every civilized country from the Carpathians to the Rocky Mountains will be a Republic. **1932** J. S. HUXLEY *Probl. Relative Growth* vii. 206 The Red Deer is by nature a forest species; driven from the lowlands, ..it grows stunted. This, however, takes no account of the difference in relative size of antlers between Scotch and e.g. Carpathian strains. **1959** *Chambers's Encycl.* III. 131/2 The territory of the Carpathians is shared by Czechoslovakia, the U.S.S.R., Poland, Hungary and Rumania. **1974** *Encycl. Brit. Macropædia* III. 947/1 Today, each of the Carpathian countries has its own general geological maps.

‖**carpe diem** ('kɑːpɪ 'daɪɛm). [L., 'enjoy the day, pluck the day when it is ripe'.] An aphorism quoted from Horace (*Odes* I. xi) affirming the need to make the most of the present time. Also *attrib.*

1817 BYRON *Let.* 2 Jan. in Moore *Life* (1830) II. 68, I never anticipate,—*carpe diem*—the past at least is one's own, which is one reason for making sure of the present. **1853** 'C. BEDE' *Verdant Gr.* x. 89, I daresay old Horace gives very good advice when he says, 'carpe diem'. **1867** 'OUIDA' *Under Two Flags* II. ii. 41 The reckless life of Algeria..with..its gay, careless carpe diem camp-philosophy. **1901** *Daily News* 7 Mar. 6/1 The 'Carpe diem' philosophy is not the philosophy of happy people. **1914** T. A. BAGGS *Back from Front* xix. 91 'Carpe diem' is their motto, and indeed, they enjoy life while they may. **1957** N. FRYE *Anat. Criticism* 299 The *carpe diem* poem based on a moment of pleasure in experience.

carpel ('kɑːpəl). *Bot.* [mod. f. Gr. *καρπ-ός* fruit, on type of mod.L. dim. **carpellum*; see -EL, and cf. F. *carpelle*.] One of the divisions or cells of a compound pistil or fruit; or the single cell of which a simple pistil or fruit consists.

[**1817** DUNAL *Monogr. des Anonacées* 13 Il serait utile et commode d'avoir un mot particulier pour exprimer dans un fruit multiple, le fruit partiel résultant de chaque ovaire féconde et développé; je propose ici celui de *carpelle*, *carpellum*.] **1835** LINDLEY *Introd. Bot.* (1848) I. 372 Carpels are modified leaves. **1869** GRAY *Bot.* §547 It is convenient to have a name which shall designate a single pistil-leaf, whether occurring as a distinct simple pistil, or as an element of a compound pistil. For this purpose the name of Carpel has been devised. **1881** G. ALLEN in *Knowledge* No. 4. 65 A little central boss or cushion, supporting several carpels or unripe fruitlets.

†**carpell.** *Obs. rare*[−1].

1593 PEELE *Edw. I* (1829) 155 'God save her grace, & give our young prince [Edw. II] a carpell in their kind.'

carpellary ('kɑːpələrɪ), *a. Bot.* [f. CARPEL; see -ARY, and cf. F. *carpellaire*.] Pertaining to, or of the nature of, a carpel.

1830 LINDLEY *Nat. Syst. Bot.* 216 The two carpellary leaves of which the fruit is formed. **1835** —— *Introd. Bot.* (1848) I. 372 The carpellary theory of structure.

†**carpencloth, carpyncloth.** *Obs.* [Cf. *carpent* obs. f. CARPET.] Probably carpet-cloth; table-cloth or bed-covering of carpet.

1577 *Wills & Inv. N.C.* (1835) I. 414, Beddinge, iij carpenclothes of tappestarye iiij*l.* *xs.*—iij grene carpynclothes.

†**carpenel.** *Obs.* Some kind of fabric; ? = CARPMEAL.

1523 *Act 14 & 15 Hen. VIII*, xi, Clothes called carpenel whites, commonly made for lining of hosen.

carpent ('kɑːpənt), *v. rare.* [ad. med.L. *carpent-āre* to cut or make as a carpenter; cf. F. *charpenter*, in the senses here given.] *trans.* To make as a carpenter; *fig.* to put together, construct mechanically. Hence '**carpented** *ppl. a.*

1623 FAVINE *Theat. Hon.* II. xiii. 231 Extended upon the Crosse, made and carpented of Oake. **1878** T. SINCLAIR *Mount* 75 With carpented 'Columbiads', unfortunately he [Poe] condemned poetry not founded at all on the tour de force plan of little ambitious prosaic spirits.

carpent(e, obs. (erroneous) f. CARPET.

†'**carpentage.** *Obs.* [f. CARPENT + -AGE.] Carpenter's work, carpentry.

1660 HEXHAM *Dutch Dict.*, *Barckoener*, a certaine Beame of carpentage.

carpentarie, -ary, obs. f. CARPENTRY.

†**carpentaries.** *Obs.* perh. pl. of *carpentarie*, *-ary*, as a variant form of CARPENTER; perh. for *carpentaris*, pl. of form *carpentar*: see -AR[2].

1486 *Bk. St. Albans, Her.* f j b, Carpentaries and makeris of howses.

carpenter ('kɑːpəntə(r)), *sb.* Forms: 3 **carpenter**, (4 **carpunter**, 5 **-pentour**, **-pynter**, 6 **-pintor**, (*Sc.*) **charpenteir**). [a. AngloFr. *carpenter*, ONF. *carpentier* (F. *charpentier* = Pr. *carpentier*, Sp. *carpentero*, It. *carpentiero*):—late L. *carpentāri-us* originally 'carriage-maker', f. *carpent-um* two-wheeled chariot, wagon.

L. *carpent-um* was app. a. OCelt. **carpentom*, whence OIr. *carpat*, mod.Ir. & Gael. *carbad* carriage, chariot, litter, bier; prob. related to OCelt. **carr-om*: see CAR. Isidore XIX. xix. 1 says 'Lignarius generaliter ligni opifex appellatur. Carpentarius speciale nomen est. Carpentum enim solum facit.']

1. 'An artificer in wood' (J.); as distinguished from a joiner, cabinet-maker, etc., one who does the heavier and stronger work in wood, as the framework of houses, ships, etc.

c **1325** *Coer de L.* 5934 My fadyr n'as mason, ne carpentere. **1387** TREVISA *Higden* (Rolls) II. 367 Of Dedalus þe carpunter. *a* **1400** *Leg. Rood* (1871) 30 Þat holi tre was fairest þo..þe carpenters it let[e] adoun. *c* **1400** *Destr. Troy* 1597 Carpentours, cotelers, coucheours fyn. **1495** *Act 11 Hen. VII*, xxii. §1 A maister Ship Carpenter..havyng men

undre hym. **1548** *Compl. Scot.* 10 Ane merchant, ane cordinar, charpenteir. **1564** BULLEYN *Dialogue* (1886) 8 Suche Carpenter, suche chips. **1567** DRANT *Horace Ep.* xiv, The carpintor dothe grudge. **1611** BIBLE *Mark* vi. 3 Is not this the carpenter, the sonne of Mary? **1665–9** BOYLE *Occas. Refl.* (1675) 376 Like the Carpenters that toyl'd to build the Ark to save Noah from the Deluge, themselves perisht in. **1835** MISS MITFORD in L'Estrange *Life* III. iii. 31 Captain Gore is..a capital working carpenter. **1851** RUSKIN *Stones Ven.* (1874) I. App. 381 The trade which of all manual trades has been most honoured; be for once a carpenter.

2. *fig.* cf. '*builder, constructor.*'

1393 LANGL. *P. Pl.* B. x. 410 Carpenters vnder criste holy kirke to make. **1597** *2nd Pt. Return fr. Pernass.* IV. ii. 1722 The chiefe Carpenter of Sonets.

3. *Naut.* 'An officer appointed to examine and keep in order the hull of a wooden ship, and all her appurtenances' (Smyth *Sailor's Word-bk.*). Hence *carpenter's crew, mate, yeoman*, etc.

1627 CAPT. SMITH *Seaman's Gram.* viii. 35 The Carpenter and his Mate. **1708** *Royal Procl.* 20 May in *Lond. Gaz.* No. 4440/1 Trumpeters, Quarter-Gunners, Carpenters Crews. **1753** CHAMBERS *Cycl. Supp.* s.v., The carpenter has a mate under him, and a crew or gang to command on necessary occasions. **1833** MARRYAT *P. Simple* xvii, The captain..sent for Mr. Muddle, the Carpenter.

4. Short for *carpenter-ant, carpenter-bee*, etc.

1883 *Knowledge* 13 July 20/1 [One species of tree-ants] bore into the trunk of the tree itself, by reason of which.. they are designated Carpenters.

5. *attrib.* and *Comb.*, as ***carpenter-fashion, -shop, -theory***. In possessive case, frequently designating varieties of tools and instruments specially used by carpenters, as ***carpenter's axe, chisel, clamp, gauge, level, plane, square***, etc. **carpenter-ant** (see 4); **carpenter-bee**, a genus of solitary bees, *Xylocopa*, the females of which excavate cells in decaying wood in which to deposit their eggs; †**carpenter-grass**, common Yarrow, *Achillea millefolium*; **carpenter's herb**, common Self-heal, *Prunella vulgaris*; erroneously, bugle and yarrow; **carpenter's measure**, tonnage as measured by the cubic foot; **carpenter's** or **carpenter-scene** (*Theat.*), (*a*) a scene introduced on the front of the stage to give the stage-carpenters time to arrange complicated scenery behind for the next act; (*b*) the painted scene which forms the background of this, and shuts off the part of the stage behind, where the stage-carpenters are at work; **carpenter-work**, carpentry; also *fig.*

1844 *Penny Cycl.* XXIII. 635/1 The wings of the ..*carpenter-bees are most frequently black, with a fine purple or violet gloss. **1857** SEARS *Athan.* xii. (1858) 102 The idea of the universe as a building which..God put up *carpenter-fashion. **1526** *Gt. Herball* (Britten & H.) In some places is called *Carpenter-grasse, it is good to reioyne, and soudre woundes. **1578** LYTE *Dodoens* I. xc. 133 Brunella, in English Prunell, *Carpenters herbe, Selfe heale & Hooke heale. **1611** COTGR., *Herbe au charpentier*..Carpenters-hearbe, Sickle-worte, Hooke-heale, Selfe-heale. **1737** OZELL *Rabelais* (1807) II. 119 He should go search for some millefoil, commonly called the carpenter's herb. **1861** MISS PRATT *Flower. Pl.* IV. 176. **1768** *Phil. Trans.* LVIII. 312 Secured in a tube from the wind, in the manner of *carpenters levels. **1756** in Picton *L'pool Munic. Rec.* (1886) II. 147 A bounty of ten shillings a ton..of *Carpenter's measure. **1860** *Cornhill Mag.* Dec. 750 (Hoppe) The dialogue of a front-scene (known technically as a *carpenter's scene) when your play requires a complicated view to be arranged behind it. **1864** *Athenæum* No. 1928, 506/2 Carpenter-scenes. **1874** *Graphic* 31 Jan. 111/2 A Carpenter's Scene is generally a flat in the first grooves consisting of some murky picture or other. **1882** FREEMAN in *Longm. Mag.* I. 88 'Barber-shop', '*carpenter-shop'. **1688** R. HOLME *Armoury* III. ix. §13 A Joyners Rule..and a *Carpenters Square. **1862** H. SPENCER *First Princ.* I. v. §33 (1875) 120 He declines to accept the *carpenter theory of creation as the most worthy. **1553** UDALL *Respublica* (1952) v. vi, I woulde ere long of yowe [haue] made suche *carpenter weorke, That ye shoulde haue saide Policie had been a clerke. **1720** in *Jrnl. Derbysh. Archæol. Soc.* (1905) XXVII. 216 Carpenter work 1 6 0. **1844** H. STEPHENS *Bk. Farm* I. 168 They embrace the particulars of mason-work, carpenter-work, slater-work,..smith-work. **1909** *Daily Chron.* 2 June 5/2 The play is at best a piece of very crude carpenter-work.

ˈcarpenter, *v.* [f. prec.]

intr. To do carpenter's work. *trans.* To make by carpentry; to do carpenter's work; to put together mechanically. Also *fig.*

c **1815** JANE AUSTEN *Persuas.* (1833) I. xi. 301 He drew, he varnished, he carpentered. **1844** [see CARPENTERED *ppl. a.*]. **1861** *Sat. Rev.* 7 Dec. 582 The man who ploughs or carpenters sees a satisfactory fruit of his labours. **1885** A. BRERETON *Dram. Notes* 50 Mr. Paul Meritt and Mr. Henry Pettitt..know how to carpenter a play for the stage. **1908** *Daily Chron.* 23 Oct. 6/1 The acting may be bad, the play cribbed and carpentered, but if people are genuinely moved the essence is there. **1909** MRS. STRATTON-PORTER *Girl of Limberlost* xi. 212 When I think of how you are carpentered, I'm adoring the result.

Hence **ˈcarpentered** *ppl. a.*, **ˈcarpentering** *vbl. sb.* (also *attrib.*).

1837 CARLYLE *Fr. Rev.* I. IV. iii. (D.) The Salle des Menus is all new carpentered. **1838** DICKENS *O. Twist* liii, Here he took to gardening, planting, fishing, carpentering. **1840** THACKERAY *Catherine* vii, He succeeded to..the carpentering business. **1844** W. G. WILLS in *Pall Mall G.* 28 July 4/1 A playwright may take a month..and only produce a carpentered thing at last. **1884** BLACK *Jud. Shaks.* xxviii, She even tried her hand at carpentering.

carpentership. [See -SHIP.] The art or occupation of a carpenter; *fig.* workmanship.

1574 WITHALS 30 Carpentership, *architectura.* **1885** *Blackw. Mag.* July 98/2 One man gave up his carpentership.

carpentry (ˈkɑːpəntrɪ). Also 4 **carpentarie**. [a. ONF. *carpenterie* = F. *charpenterie* (= Pr. *carpentaria*, Sp. *carpinteria*):—L. *carpentāria* (sc. *fabrica*) carriage-maker's workshop: cf. -RY.]

1. The trade or art of a carpenter; the art of cutting, working, and joining timber into structures.

1377 LANGL. *P. Pl.* B. x. 178 Tooles of carpentrie. **1382** WYCLIF *Ex.* xxxv. 33 Werkis of carpentarye. **1523** LD. BERNERS *Froiss.* I. cxx. 144 Two connyng men maisters in carpentre. **1586** FERNE *Blaz. Gentrie* 72 Carpentarie.. dealeth with wood. **1677** MOXON *Mech. Exerc.* (1703) 117 It had been more proper for me in these Exercises to have introduced Carpentry before Joinery. **1836** EMERSON *Nature, Spirit.* Wks. (Bohn) II. 166 Idealism is a hypothesis to account for nature by other principles than those of carpentry and chemistry. **1873** ROORKEE *Civil Engineer.* I. iii. §241 Carpentry is the art of combining pieces of Timber for the support of any considerable weight or pressure.

2. Timber-work constructed by the carpenter; 'an assemblage of pieces of timber connected by framing, or letting them into each other, as are the pieces of a roof, floor, centre, etc.' (Gwilt).

1555 *Fardle Facions* I. iv. 46 The chiefe citie..stondeth not by building of masonrie, & carpentrie as ours. **1616** MARKHAM *Countr. Farm* 333 Borne vp with carpentrie or frames of timber. **1770** FRANKLIN *Lett.* Wks. 1840 VI. 335 The carpentry of the roof..is sheeted or covered with deals. **1865** CARLYLE *Fredk. Gt.* VII. iii, Solid well-painted carpentry.

3. *attrib.*

1750 BEAWES *Lex Mercat.* (1752) 832 Carpentry Wood.. brought here from Lower Saxony. **1796** MORSE *Amer. Geog.* I. 542 The inward carpentry-work.

carper[1] (ˈkɑːpə(r)). [f. CARP *v.* + -ER[1].] One who carps. †**a.** A talker, prattler. *Obs.* **b.** A fault-finder, a caviller, a captious critic.

c **1440** *Promp. Parv.* 62 Carpare, *fabulator, garulator.* **1547** RECORDE *Judic. Ur.* A ii b, The besye brabling of curyouse carpers. **1579** GOSSON *Sch. Abuse* (1841) 36 Every Duns will bee a carper. **1581** J. BELL *Haddon's Answ. Osor.* 501 A carper of other mens faultes. **1658** A. FOX *Wurtz' Surg.* Ep. Ded. 9 He will meet with very many Carpers and Cavilers. **1666** J. SMITH *Old Age* (1752) 51 That audacious carper at the works of God. **1868** BROWNING *Ring & Bk.* VIII. 1007 Carpers abound in this misjudging world.

carper[2]. One who prepares teasels: see CARP *v.*[2]

†**carpese.** *Obs. rare*[−1]. [a. 16th c. F. *carpase*, ad. L. *carpasum*, a. Gr. κάρπασον.] A plant with narcotic juice mentioned by ancient authors.

1598 SYLVESTER *Du Bartas* II. I. III. 161 The stifning Carpese, th' eyes—foe Hemlock stinking. [**1611** COTGR., *Carpase.*]

carpet (ˈkɑːpɪt), *sb.* Also 4 **karpete**, (6 **carpente**), 5–6 **carpette**, **-pyte**, 6 **carpett**, **-pete**, 6–7 **carpit**. [ME. *carpete*, varying with *carpette*, and in 16th c. *carpyte*: from F. or med.L., and this from It. OF. had *carpite* (13th c.), sort of coarse cloth (mod.F. *carpette* rug, small (Turkish) carpet is app. from Eng.). Med.L. had *carpita, carpeta*, explained by Carpentier in Du Cange as 'a kind of villose or thickish cloth, and a garment of that cloth'; also *carpetta*. Florio has It. *carpetta* 'a carpet for a table'; mod.Ital. dicts. *carpita* a coarse carpet; La Crusca says 'a coarse hanging for a table, made of rough woollen materials, and of patches, of motley colours'.

Carpīta is etymologically identical with F. *charpie* (Pic. *carpie*, Latinized *carpia* 13th c.) 'lint (for surgical purposes) procured by the unravelling of old linen,' the pa. pple. fem. of OF. *charpir* to card wool, to unravel cloth & reduce it to threads, to tear to shreds, corresp. to It. *carpire*, pa. pple. *carpito*, representing (with change of conjugation) L. *carpĕre* to card, pick, pluck, tear, pull in pieces. The name *carpita* may have been originally given to a fabric formed of unravelled cloth, or of shreds of cloth patched together. The variants *carpeta, carpetta* also occur in later med.L., doubtless from Italian *carpetta*, which assumes the form of a diminutive.]

I. As a simple sb.

¶ In med.Lat. use, 'A kind of villose or thickish cloth, and a garment of that cloth'. Carpentier cites, *inter alia*,

1291 *Carmelite Rule*, Habeat unusquisque frater unam Carpitam, quod est nostræ Religionis signum, non de petiis consutam sed contextam [a carpet which is the distinctive dress of our order, not sewed together of pieces (or patches) but woven together]. **1295** Unam carpitam de pann serico velluto [a carpet of silk velvet cloth].

†**1. a.** A thick fabric, commonly of wool, used to cover tables, beds, etc.; a table-cloth. *Obs.*

1345 *Sacrist's Roll Lichfield Cathed.* (*Derbysh. Archæol. Trans.*) 9 Item unus pannus qui vocatur Karpete. **1434** in Rogers *Agric. & Prices* IV. 577. **1513** *Bk. Keruynge* in *Babees Bk.* 283 Laye carpentes about the bedde. **1527** *Inv. Sir H. Guildford's Goods* (MS.), A carpett of grene cloth for a lytill foulding table. **1563** FOXE *A. & M.* an. 1555 Oct., The carpet or cloth, which lay upon the table whereat M. Ridley stood, was remoued. **1642** FULLER *Holy & Prof. St.* IV. x. 287 A Communion-table will not catch cold with wanting a rich carpet. **1702** *Lond. Gaz.* No. 3851/4 One green Cloth Carpet, with a small Fringe round it, for the Communion Table. **1727–51** CHAMBERS *Cycl.*, *Carpet*, a sort of covering..to be spread on a table, trunk, an estrade, or even a passage, or floor. **1728** NEWTON *Chronol. Amended*, To adorn their beds and tables with rich furniture and carpets.

b. *on the carpet* (i.e. of the council table): under consideration or discussion [cf. F. *sur le tapis.*] Also *colloq.* (orig. *U.S.*) (with admixture of sense 2 a): undergoing, or summoned to receive, a reprimand. Cf. sense 2 d and MAT *sb.*[1]

1726 WODROW *Corr.* (1843) III. 255 The great cry made for the people's powers in election..which is the case now upon the carpet. *a* **1734** NORTH *Lives* Pref. 21 These three brothers, whose lives are upon the carpet before me. **1773** R. GRAVES *Spirit. Quix.* x. xi. (D.) He..contrived to bring another subject upon the carpet. **1800** WEEMS *Washington* xii. (1877) 187 A question of importance being on the carpet. **1855** MOTLEY *Dutch Rep.* IV. iii. (1866) 604. **1900** G. ADE *Fables in Slang* 120 Next Morning she had him up on the Carpet and wanted to know How About It. **1902** LORIMER *Lett. Merchant* 134 The boss of the canning-room [will be] called up on the carpet and made to promise that it will never happen again. **1921** LD. DUNSANY *If* I. i. 9 You been on the carpet, Bill? **1936** *Sketch* 22 Jan. 148/1 His manager had just had him on the carpet, pointing out that his work had been getting steadily bad for the last few months. **1944** 'N. SHUTE' *Pastoral* v. 136 After the first shock of realising that she herself was on the carpet. **1961** *Times* 8 May 13/2 Such a solution is not on the carpet now.

2. a. A similar fabric, generally worked in a pattern of divers colours, used to spread on a floor or the ground, for standing, sitting, or kneeling on, or (now usually) to cover a floor, or stair. Also the material, as in 'a piece of carpet'.

1438–60 *Lib. de Antiq. Legib.* ccvi, Duas vestes vocatas Carpette sternendas coram fontem ecclesiæ. **14..** *MS. Addit.* 6113 f. 106 a in *Dom. Archit.* III. 107, Iij chambres of pleasaunce..all the floures covered with carpettes. **1513** MORE *Rich. III* (1641) 439 On a carpit in a Ladies chamber. **1548** HALL *Edw. IV*, 234 (R.) A prelate, more mete for a ladyes carpet, than for an ecclesiasticall pulpet. **1580** BARET *Alv.* C 144 A carpet of Turky, *Polymeta phrygia.* **1682** DRYDEN *Mac Fl.* 91 No Persian carpets spread th' imperial way. **1712** ADDISON *Spect.* No. 289 ⁋9 The Dervise..laid down his Wallet, and spread his Carpet after the Manner of the Eastern Nations. **1839** tr. *Lamartine's Trav. East* 155/1 [In] the mosques..I found a small number of Turks, seated cross-legged, or kneeling on the carpets. **1861** FLOR. NIGHTINGALE *Nursing* 61 A dirty carpet..infects the [sick] room.

b. Being, at first, chiefly a luxury of a lady's chamber, it became an attribute of luxury and effeminacy (see esp. 6); also of the chamber, drawing room, or court, as opposed to the camp or field.

1581 STYWARD *Mart. Discip.* To Rdr. 2 Whereby we maie not be reputed sleepers, or followers too much of the carpet. **1630** NAUNTON *Fragm. Reg.* (Arb.) 32 For the times began to be quick and active, and fitter for stronger motions, than those of the Carpet. *Ibid.* 40 They were of the Court and Carpet, not led by the genius of the Camp.

†**c.** ***knight of the carpet***: see quotations; also = CARPET-KNIGHT. *Obs.*

? **1547** in Strype *Eccl. Mem.* II. II. App. E, The Knights of the Carpet dubbed by the King on Shrove Tuesday. [These were evidently *Knights Bachelors*; the list follows that of the *Knights of the Bath* made at same time.] **1586** FERNE *Blaz. Gentrie* 105 A Knight..may be dubbed..in the time of peace vpon the Carpet..he is called a Knight of the carpet, bycause that the King sitteth in his regall chaire of estate and the Gentleman..kneeleth before his Soueraigne vpon the carpet or cloth vsually spred..for the Soueraignes footestoole. **1630** NAUNTON *Fragm. Reg.* (Arb.) 47 A worse Christian than he was, & a better knight of the carpet than he should be. **1688** R. HOLME *Armoury* III. 57/2 Knights of the Carpet, or Knights of the Green Cloth; to distinguish them from Knights that are Dubbed as Soldiers are in the Field.

d. ***to walk the carpet***: said of a servant summoned before the master or mistress for a reprimand. (Cf. CARPET *v.* 4.)

1823 GALT *Entail* III. xxix. 278 Making..her servants 'walk the carpet'.

e. ***to sweep*** (or ***push***) (something) ***under the carpet***: to conceal (something embarrassing or unpleasant), in the hope that it will go unnoticed or be forgotten.

1963 *Times* 24 Jan. 6/1 It would be self-deception to think that unemployment could be dealt with by emergency measures and pushed under the carpet. **1966** *Listener* 17 Mar. 390/2 You cannot sweep these problems under the carpet as the Labour Government is doing.

3. *fig.* **a.** Applied to a covering or expanse, as of grass or flowers, resembling a carpet in smoothness, softness, or varied colouring.

1593 SHAKS. *Rich. II*, III. iii. 50 Vpon the Grassie Carpet of this Plaine. **1670** EVELYN *Diary* 22 July, At either end of the towne, upon the very carpet where the sports are celebrated. **1757** DYER *Fleece* I. 26 They..The close-wov'n carpet graze. *c* **1854** STANLEY *Sinai & Pal.* ii. (1858) 122 The carpet of flowers..on the banks of the Chebar.

b. *spec.* in *Cricket*, the surface of the field, the ground. Also *attrib.*, as ***carpet drive***.

1882 *Cricket* 22 June 93/3 His hits..are never high; on the contrary they are mostly, to use the slang of the cricket field, 'on the carpet'. **1896** *Westm. Gaz.* 23 July 7/2 A grand carpet drive to the off-boundary. **1899** SNAITH *Willow the King* v. 74 It flew like a streak to mid-off all along the carpet. **1908** W. E. W. COLLINS *Country Cricketer's Diary* xiv. 233 Leaving us in a parlous bad condition by putting catch after catch..upon the carpet. **1927** M. A. NOBLE *Those 'Ashes'* 201 Bowley tried a carpet drive through the covers. **1950** W. HAMMOND *Cricketers' School* x. 98 The batsman's art..is to learn how to turn the ball..so that..it shall stay 'on the carpet'.

c. *Aeronaut. slang.* The ground; ***on the carpet***, at or near ground level.

1918 J. M. Grider *War Birds* (1926) 258, I was right on the carpet and over a little ruined village. **1934** V. M. Yeates *Winged Victory* xxi. 165 He could not go down on to the carpet again point blank into the mouths of the machine guns.

d. *Civil Engin.* (See quot. 1954.)

1920 H. E. Goldsmith *Mod. Road Constr. & Maintenance* App. I. 86 *Carpet*, a bituminous surface of appreciable thickness, generally formed on top of a roadway by the application of one or more coats of bituminous material with gravel, sand, or stone chippings added. **1930** *Engineering* 15 Aug. 210/1 It consisted of a 2 in. stone-filled asphalt carpet laid on a reinforced-concrete foundation. **1954** *Gloss. Highway Engin. Terms (B.S.I.)* 31 *Carpet*, a wearing course containing a road tar or bitumen binder and having a compacted thickness not greater than $1\frac{1}{2}$ inches.

e. A large number of bombs dropped to damage an area intensively, esp. to clear the way for advancing ground troops. Also *attrib.* and *Comb.*

1944 T. H. Wisdom *Triumph over Tunisia* xxiii. 181 Our massed bombers..set off to lay Tedder's bomb carpet; to blast a passage for the armies right through to Tunis. **1945** *Baltimore Sun* 23 Feb. 3/5 Several ministries were laid in ruins that Saturday as a result of the American carpet bombing. **1945** *Life* 4 June 25 A carpet raid is an effort to pulverize an area in front of ground troops to facilitate a breakthrough. **1946** *Aviation Ann.* 16 Carpet bombing.. consists simply of dropping such a heavy concentration of bombs in a small area that the defenders are stunned and demoralized for a short time. *Ibid.*, A carpet attack in a certain sector. **1968** L. van der Post *Portrait Japan* i. 29 Carpet bombing by the United States Air Forces flattened the capital.

4. Short for *carpet-moth*; see 5.

1856 R. Shield *Pract. Hints* 108 Those beautifully marked Geometræ called 'carpets' by collectors. **1859** Stainton *Butterf. & Moths* II. 73 In the month of May the 'Carpets' enter on the scene. **1866** E. Newman *Brit. Butterf. & Moths* 64 The Satin Carpet..the Ringed Carpet.

II. In combination or attributively.

5. *Comb.* **a.** attributive (pertaining to a carpet, or made of carpet), as ***carpet-cloth***, ***-shoe***, ***square***, ***-web***, ***-work***; **b.** objective, as ***carpet-beater***, ***-beating***, ***-dusting***, ***-maker***, ***-planner***; **c.** instrumental, as ***carpet-covered*** adj.; **d.** similative (resembling a carpet of smooth turf), as †***carpet-grass***, †***-ground***, †***-hill***, †***-walk***, †***-way***; also ***carpet-smooth***, ***-woven*** adjs. Spec. combs. as **carpet-bed** (*Gardening*), a bed in which dwarf foliage-plants of different colours are arranged so as to form a pattern like that of a carpet; so ***carpet-bedding***, ***-garden***; **carpet beetle**, any of various beetles or their larvæ, especially *Dermestidæ*, destructive to carpets and other fabrics; **carpet-broom**, **-brush**, one used for sweeping a carpet; **carpet-dance**, a dance on the carpet, an informal dance (the carpet being taken up for dancing on great occasions); **carpet-moth**, a name for several species of Geometer moths, from their variegated colouring; **carpet-rod**, a metal rod to keep a stair-carpet in its place, a stair-rod; **carpet shark**, a shark of the genus *Orectolobus* having spots on the back suggesting the pattern of a carpet; **carpet slipper**, a slipper the uppers of which were orig. made of carpet-like material; also used *attrib.* to express an informal or slip-shod method of work; **carpet-snake**, a large Australian snake (*Morelia variegata*) with a variegated skin; see also quot. from Whitworth; **carpet sweeper**, a household implement with a revolving brush or brushes for sweeping carpets; **carpet-weed**, the genus *Mollugo* (N.O. *Caryophyllaceæ*). See also carpet-bag, -knight.

1836–7 Dickens *Sk. Boz* (1850) 44/1 A jobbing-man—*carpet-beater and so forth. **1883** *Pall Mall G.* 7 Sept. 4/1 The *'carpet beds', where some intricate pattern is worked out in a variety of colours. Here no flower is allowed, the effect being due entirely to the colours of the leaves. **1889** *Cent. Dict.*, *Carpet-beetle*, a popular name of *Anthrenus scrophulariæ*, a beetle of the family *Dermestidæ*. **1961** *Which?* July 157/1 The varied carpet beetle, often known in its larval phase as the woolly bear (*Anthrenus verbasci*). **1615** *Churchw. Acc. Gt. Wigstone, Leicestersh.* (Nichols 1797) 149 New *Carpet-cloth for the communion table. **1835** T. Hook *G. Gurney* I. v. 84 Hard *carpet-covered benches. **1846** R. Ford *Gatherings from Spain* xxiii. 325 An extempore ball, which might be called a *carpet-dance, if there were any. **1861** T. Peacock *Gryll Gr.* xxiii. 198 On these occasions, it was of course a carpet-dance. **1865** Dickens *Mut. Fr.* (Hoppe), A well-conducted automaton to come and play quadrilles for a carpet-dance. **1756** Mrs. Calderwood *Jrnl.* (1884) 26 Fine *carpet-grass. **1677** N. Cox *Gentl. Recreat.* v. (1706) 30 He will tread as boldly on Stones as on *Carpet-ground. **1759** Dilworth *Pope* 144 An ambling muse running on a carpet-ground. **1732** Mrs. Pendarves in *Mrs. Delaney's Autobiog* (1861) I. 376 This house lies on the top of a *carpet hill. *c* **1500** *Cocke Lorell's B.* (1843) 9 Brouderers,..and *carpyte makers. **1863** Trafford *World in Ch.* I. 90 Another corridor..reduced upholsterers and *carpet planners to despair. **1848** Thackeray *Van. Fair* iii, She looked for one instant in his face, and then down at the *carpet rods. **1929** S. Elliott Napier in *Times* 2 Aug. 14/1 The 'Leopard' or '*Carpet' shark. **1956** *Coast to Coast 1955–56* 128 The two spearsmen came in with a five-foot carpet shark. **1851** Mayhew *Lond. Labour* I. 157/1 The large *carpet slippers that served her for shoes. **1902** *Chambers's Jrnl.* 10 May 353 Etymologists relieve the tedium of a hard day's work by a relapse into the carpet-slipper side of their science. *Ibid.*, The old monks were adepts at carpet-slipper derivation. **1905** H. A. Vachell *Hill* i. 17 He slimes about in carpet slippers—the beast! **1967** S. Beckett *Eh Joe* 15 Joe, late fifties, grey hair, old dressing-gown, carpet slippers, in his room. **1844** Mrs. Browning *Lost Bower* xviii, *Carpet-smooth with grass and moss. **1863** Wood *Nat. Hist.* III. 115 The Diamond Snake..[and] The *Carpet Snake..are variable in their colouring. **1864** *Glasgow Herald* 12 Apr., An enormous carpet snake which ..was found to measure 12 feet 6 inches in length. **1885** G. C. Whitworth *Anglo-Ind. Dict.*, *Carpet snake*..Loosely applied to any kind of snake found in a dwelling house, other than a cobra or a dhâman..most commonly the *lycodon aulicus*. **1901** F. H. Burnett *Making of Marchioness* i. 20 She..bought herself a Kensington *carpet-square, as red as Kensington art would permit it to be. **1973** 'H. Carmichael' *Too Late for Tears* vi. 80 The carpet square patterned in reds and browns and greens. **1859** *Rep. Comm. Patents 1858* (U.S.) II. 444 That description of *carpet or floor sweepers in which a revolving brush..is made to take up and deposit the sweepings in a case covering the brush. **1892** *Ladies' Home Jrnl.* Dec. 19/4 Bissell carpet sweeper. **1960** *Which?* Apr. 85/1 The ideal carpet sweeper is one which picks up a lot of dirt, but only a little carpet pile, and which is easy to use and empty. **1664** Evelyn *Kal. Hort.* (1729) 201 Mow *Carpet-walks. **1664** H. More *Myst. Iniq.* 549 To keep rank and file..not to break order though all be not *Carpet-way. *a* **1658** Cleveland *The Times* 31 We.. Must not expect a Carpet way. **1884** Browning *Ferishtah* 128 A *carpet-web I saw once leave the loom. **1611** W. Barksted *Hirem* (1876) 81 All the floore with *Carpet-worke was strawn. **1816** Jane Austen *Emma* i. x. 72 If I give up music, I shall take up carpet-work. **1768** Tucker *Lt. Nat.* (1852) II. 414 The *carpet-woven grass that beautifies our lawns.

6. a. *attrib.* and *Comb.* arising out of sense 2 b, as ***carpet-consideration***, ***courtship***, ***friend***, ***gentry***, ***toy***; †**carpet-man**, †**carpet-monger**, one who frequents ladies' boudoirs or carpeted chambers, one who deals in 'carpet-trade'; †**carpet-trade**, the occupations and amusements of the chamber or boudoir. Also carpet-knight (q.v.), and many appellations akin to it (in which *carpet* implies haunting the chamber or boudoir), as ***carpet captain***, ***champion*** (champion of the dames), ***coward***, ***peer***, ***shield***, ***squire*** (= squire of dames), or modelled on it (with the sense of dilettantism, shirking of practical work, difficulty, or danger), as ***carpet geologist***, ***poet***, ***soldier***, etc.

1548 Hall *Chron.* (1809) 153 Like a *Carpet capitaine he ..removed his Campe & fled to Crespy. **1623** Cockeram iii, *Paris*, a Carpet Captaine, rather than a Warriour. **1600** Fairfax *Tasso* xvi. xxxii. 286 A *Carpet champion for a wanton dame. **1601** Shaks. *Twel. N.* iii. iv. 258 He is knight dubb'd with vnhatch'd Rapier, and on *carpet consideration. **1636** Massinger *Bashf. Lov.* i. i, You are not to be won By carpet-courtship, but the sword. **1605** *Play Stucley* in *Sch. Shaks.* (1878) 201, I am a soldier And hate the name of *carpet-coward. *a* **1616** Beaum. & Fl. *Valent.* iv. ii, Have I lived Only to be a *carpet-friend, for pleasure? **1571** Fortescue *Forest of Hist.* 153 b, The daintie coward and *carpette man. **1599** Nashe *Lent. Stuffe* Ded., Any other *carpet-munger or primerose knight of Primero. **1592** —— *P. Penilesse* (N.) The..insinuating curtesie of a *carpet-peere. **1854** Emerson *Lett. & Soc. Aims, Poet. & Imag.* Wks. (Bohn) III. 167 Your *carpet poets, who are content to amuse. **1869** Rawlinson *Anc. Hist.* 470 No *carpet soldiers, but hardy troops. **1605** *Play Stucley* in *Sch. Shaks.* (1878) 188, I shall be thought..a coward, A sleepy dormouse, and a *carpet squire. **1660** Waterhouse *Arms & Arm.* 68 Adorned with rich Clothes, precious Jewels, and *Carpet toyes. **1581** Rich *Farew. Milit. Profess.* (N.) This noble duke had no maner of skill in carpet-trade.

b. Sometimes passing into an adjective.

a **1639** Ward *Serm.* 119 (D.) Our strait-buttoned, carpet, and effeminate gentry. **1884** *St. James's Gaz.* 20 Apr. 4 The carpet markmanship which is the special fruit of Wimbledon.

7. *Criminals' slang. Ellipt.* for carpet-bag 2.

[**1903** 'No. 77' *Mark of Broad Arrow* xi. 166 Your 'Autoleyne' cares little about a 'drag' (three months), a sixer (a 'carpet' it is generally called), or a 'stretch'.] **1917** E. Wallace *Just Men of Cordova* x. 133 'Carpets' (three months' hard labour) almost innumerable had fallen to his share. **1936** J. Curtis *Gilt Kid* 17 Long enough to've been in Wandsworth and done a carpet. **1963** T. & P. Morris *Pentonville* xi. 227 A *carpet* (3 months).

carpet (ˈkɑːpɪt), *v.* [f. prec. sb.]

1. *trans.* To cover or spread with a carpet. Hence ˈ**carpeted** *ppl. a.*

a **1626** Bacon *New Atl.*, A fair Chamber richly hanged and carpeted under Foot. **1811** *Lett. fr. Engl.* I. xiv. 161 The room is carpeted. **1849** C. Brontë *Shirley* x. 142 She noiselessly paced..the carpeted floor. **1860** Emerson *Cond. Life, Wealth* Wks. (Bohn) II. 348 A sumptuous ship has floored and carpeted for him the stormy Atlantic.

2. *transf.* To cover or strew as with a carpet.

1728 Ramsay *Ep. Somerville*, These delightful flowers, Which carpet the poetic fields. **1817** J. F. Pennie *Royal Minstr.* v. 339 The yellow leaves That carpet autumn's groves. **1865** Gosse *Land and Sea* (1874) 216 Clumps of pale primroses are carpeting the hollows.

3. To place on a carpet. *rare.* (Cf. *pillow*.)

1821 Byron *Juan* iii. lxvii, Haidee and Juan carpeted their feet On crimson satin.

4. *colloq.* To call (a servant) into the parlour, etc., to be reprimanded; to reprimand, 'call over the coals'. (Cf. carpet *sb.* 2 d.)

1840 H. Cockton *Val. Vox* xli, They had done nothing! Why were they carpeted? **1871** *Daily News* 23 Sept., When they [Colonel Burnaby and Captain Annesley] were 'carpeted' [by the Jockey Club] to account for the suspicious running of the mare Tarragona with Michel Grove.

ˌ**carpet-ˈbag**, *sb.* **1. a.** A travelling bag, properly one made of carpet.

1830 *Boston Directory* 28 (Advt.). **1836** Dickens *Early Coaches* in *Sk. Boz* II. 173 The new carpet-bag you bought. **1844** Disraeli *Coningsby* i. v. (R.) Coningsby..had lost the key of his carpet-bag. **1858** Hawthorne *Fr. & It. Jrnls.* (1872) I. 1 Our dozen trunks and half-dozen carpet-bags, being already packed and labelled.

b. *attrib.*, as in ***carpet-bag adventurer***, ***government***, ***rule*** (U.S. slang): see carpet-bagger.

1874 *Fraser's Mag.* Aug. 155 The double curse of negro and carpet-bag rule. **1878** *N. Amer. Rev.* CXXVI. 279 A ring composed of carpet-bag adventurers. **1886** Dicey *Engl. Case agst. Home Rule* 108 The so-called Carpet Bag Governments, that is..the rule of Northern adventurers who were kept in office throughout the South by the Negro Vote.

2. *Rhyming slang.* = drag *sb.* 8 b.

1938 Sharpe *S. of Flying Squad* 330 *Carpet* (or *Carpet Bag*, or *Drag*), three months' imprisonment.

3. *Comb.* **carpet-bag steak**, a steak stuffed with oysters.

1958 *Times* 28 Aug. 7/7 At the Gas Council stand she can see ground nut stew, carpet bag steaks, biryani..being prepared. **1969** *Times* 22 Dec. 9/8 Many 'foreign' dishes are really British. Like Australian 'carpetbag steak'—rare fillet stuffed with oysters.

ˈ**carpet-ˌbag**, *v. colloq.* (orig. and chiefly *U.S.*). [f. the sb.] *intr.* To travel with very little luggage (see also quot. 1889). Also *transf.*

1872 *Trans. Ill. Dept. Agric. 1871* IX. 266 Almost the entire force of our common schools tends to..send [our young men]..'carpet bagging', down South. **1889** *Century Dict.*, *Carpet-bag*, to act or live in the manner of a carpet-bagger. (U.S. slang.) **1890** *Congress. Rec.* 4 June 5598/2 It has been stated that Mr. McDuffie carpet bagged from somewhere down into Alabama... Now I will tell the House how Judge McDuffie happened to carpet-bag down into that district. **1968** A. Williams *Brotherhood* i. iv. 51, I don't have to carpet-bag to your kind of publicity, Owen. Now piss-off.

carpet-ˈbagger. *U.S. Political slang.* [f. carpet-bag *sb.* + -er.] A scornful appellation applied, after the American Civil War of 1861–5, to immigrants from the Northern into the Southern States, whose 'property qualification' consisted merely of the contents of the carpet-bag which they had brought with them. Hence, applied opprobriously to all Northerners who went south and tried, by the Negro vote or otherwise, to obtain political influence; and generally to any one interfering with the politics of a locality with which he is thought to have no permanent or genuine connexion.

Hence **carpet-ˈbaggery**, **carpet-ˈbaggism**.

1868 *Daily News* 18 Sept., All 'carpetbaggers' and 'scalawags' are whites. The carpet baggers are immigrants from the North who have thrown themselves into local politics, and through their influence with the negroes obtained office. **1872** *Spectator* 21 Sept. 1194 At the elections which took place in June, 1868, 'Carpet-baggers' and other adventurers who put themselves forward as the friends of the freedmen were everywhere successful. **1880** Gen. Grant in *New York Her.* 26 Oct., See the prosperity and the thrift that has been brought to these new States by these carpet baggers! **1881** *Philada. Record* No. 3459. 2 The 'solid south' is a protest against carpetbagism..in the form of Northern men going down in person to take charge of Southern politics. **1884** *Milnor* (Dakota) *Teller* 30 July, To abolish this infamous system of territorial carpet-baggery, and to require all appointees to territorial offices to have been two years residents of the territory. *Mod. Eng. Newsp.* The electors have preferred the local man to a carpet-bagger from London.

ˈ**carpet-ˌbagging.** orig. and chiefly *U.S.* Travelling with only a carpet-bag to contain one's effects; *spec.* the practice of a carpet-bagger. Also *attrib.*

1869 *Atlantic Monthly* June 747 After three weeks' delightful Carpet-Bagging. **1888** Bryce *Amer. Commw.* iii. lxxv. II. 621 Negro suffrage produced, during the few years of 'carpet-bagging' and military government which followed the war, incredible mischief. **1904** *N.Y. Even. Post.* 1 Feb., The infernal 'carpet-bagging' system at present in vogue should be done away with. **1955** *Times* 26 May 4/3 In this carpet-bagging age, a home-grown politician is as rare as a home-grown professional footballer.

carpeting (ˈkɑːpɪtɪŋ), *sb.* [f. carpet *sb.* or *v.* + -ing[1].]

1. The action of covering (as) with carpet.

2. Material for carpets.

1758 B. Franklin *Corr.* in *Wks.* (1840) VII. 165 Some carpeting for a best room floor. **1806–7** J. Beresford *Miseries Hum. Life* ii. ix, This [is] carpeting compared with what follows. **1813** L. Hunt in *Examiner* 22 Feb. 114/1 Matting and carpeting have done much for the stone floor. **1835** Ure *Philos. Manuf.* 139 In Wilton carpeting, there is both a linen warp and a worsted warp.

3. *transf.* A carpet-like covering.

1883 *Century Mag.* Dec. 174/1 Its rich carpeting of wild flowers. **1885** S. O. Jewett *March Island* xiv, The frayed whitish carpeting of their last year's leaves.

4. See carpet *v.* 4.

Mod. colloq. 'She received from her mistress a thorough good carpeting.'

'carpet-'knight. [f. CARPET *sb.* 2 b + KNIGHT.] Originally, perhaps = *knight of the carpet* (see CARPET 2 c); but, usually, a contemptuous term for a knight whose achievements belong to 'the carpet' (i.e. the lady's boudoir, or carpeted chamber) instead of to the field of battle; a stay-at-home soldier. In modern use with less reference to the lady's boudoir, and more to the drawing-room with its avoidance of practical work.

1576 WHETSTONE *Rock of Regard* 55 He consults with carpet knights about curious masks. **1580** H. GIFFORD *Gilloflowers* (1875) 85 Yee curious Carpet knights that spend the time in sport & play. **1580** BARET *Alv.* B956 Those which serue abhominable and filthy idlenesse, and as we vse to call them carpet knightes. **1611** COTGR. s.v. *Couchette, Mignon de couchette*, a Carpet-Knight, one that euer loues to be in womens chambers. **1621** BURTON *Anat. Mel.* I. ii. II. ii. (1651) 75 As much valor is to be found in feasting, as in fighting, and some of our City Captains and Carpet Knights will make this good. **1719** D'URFEY *Pills* (1872) IV. 276 Brave Carpet Knights in Cupid's fights. **1810** SCOTT *Lady of L.* v. xiv, I..hold your valour light As that of some vain carpet-knight. **1860** A. L. WINDSOR *Ethica* vi. 297 Their authors had been no carpet-knights, but had lived and acted the lives of their heroes.

'carpetless, *a.* Without a carpet.

1835 *Fraser's Mag.* XII. 631 In spite of carpetless floors. **1838** DICKENS *Nich. Nick.* xiv. (C.D. ed.) 100 The common stairs of this mansion were bare and carpetless.

carpholite ('kɑːfəlaɪt). *Min.* [Ger. *karpholith* (Werner 1819), f. Gr. κάρφος straw + λίθος stone.] A hydrous silicate of alumina and manganese, occurring in silky fibres of a straw-yellow colour, in the tin mines of Schlackenwald.

1844 PHILLIPS *Min.* 18. **1868** DANA *Min.* 419.

carphology (kɑː'fɒlədʒɪ). *Med.* Also in L. form **carphologia.** [ad. Gr. καρφολογία (Galen), f. κάρφος twig, straw, bit of wool + λέγειν to collect.]

The movements of delirious patients, as if searching for or grasping at imaginary objects, or picking the bed-clothes; floccilation.

1851 in MAYNE *Exp. Lex.* **1866** A. FLINT *Princ. Med.* (1880) 703 Subsultus, carphologia, and fumbling with the bed-clothes are frequent symptoms. **1880** *Med. Temp. Jrnl.* Jan., When carphology has given place to a mere trembling of the fingers.

carpho'siderite. *Min.* [f. Gr. κάρφος straw + σίδηρος iron + -ITE.] A hydrous sulphate of iron with sand and gypsum, occurring as a straw-coloured mineral, found in reniform masses and incrustations, in Labrador.

1850 DANA *Min.* 452.

carpid ('kɑːpɪd). *Bot.* [In mod.L. *carpidium*, dim. (on Gr. type) of καρπός fruit.] A synonym of CARPEL.

1880 GRAY *Bot. Text-bk.* 401.

carpincho (kɑː'pɪntʃəʊ). [Native name.] A local name in South America for the capybara.

1839 DARWIN *Jrnl.* iii. 57 These great Rodents are generally called 'carpinchos'. **1869** W. H. HUDSON *Let.* 14 Dec. in *Ornithol. Buenos Ayres* (1951) i. 2, I have known the *ciervo jaguar* aguará and carpincho with other large mammels. **1904** *Westm. Gaz.* 6 Sept. 10/1 When alarmed the carpincho utters a kind of grunting cry. **1949** *Oxf. Jun. Encycl.* (1955) II. 81 The Capybaras, or Carpinchos, are 4 feet long and weigh about 98 pounds.

carping ('kɑːpɪŋ), *vbl. sb.*[1] The action of the verb CARP: †**a.** Speaking or saying; speech, talk; faculty of speech. *Obs.*

c **1325** *E.E. Allit. P.* B. 1550 Sone so þe kynge for his care carping myȝt wynne. *a* **1400** *Relig. Pieces fr. Thornton MS.* (1867) 7 Ryghte sayeyng and carpyng of þe wordes. *a* **1400** *Cov. Myst.* (1841) 166 Suche a carpynge is unknowe.

b. Censorious speech: cavilling, fault-finding, captious criticism.

c **1400** *Ywaine & Gaw.* 127 This kene karping of Syr Kay. **1599** SHAKS. *Much Ado* III. i. 71 Such carping is not commendable. **1697–1712** LESLIE *Short Method w. Deists, &c.* iii, All those little carpings..that are made as to the passage through the Red Sea. **1868** NETTLESHIP *Browning* i. 49 The alloy of harsh criticism, of ungrateful carping.

carping, *vbl. sb.*[2] The preparing of teasels: see CARP *v.*[2]

'carping, *ppl. a.* That carps; fault-finding, censorious, captious.

1581 SIDNEY *Apol. Poetrie* (Arb.) 48 Their carping disprayse. *c* **1591** SHAKS. *I Hen. VI*, IV. i. 90 With enuious carping tongue. **1730** LD. LANSDOWNE *To Mem. Waller* 20 No carping critic interrupts his praise. **1865** TROLLOPE *Belton Est.* xi. 120 That carping spirit in which she had been wont to judge of his actions.

¶ Confused with CARKING *ppl. a.*

1580 T. MARSHALL in Farr's *S.P.* (1845) II. 312 With carpyng cares did call and crie. *a* **1703** BURKITT *On N.T.* Luke xii. 30 By our carping care.

Hence **'carpingly** *adv.*, in a carping way.

1579 J. ROGERS (*title*), An answer unto a wicked..Libel made by Christopher Vitell..carpingly answering to certain points. **1577–86** HOLINSHED *Chron. Irel.* (1808) VI. 13 Through his procurement carpinglie published. **1755** in JOHNSON.

carpit(e, obs. form of CARPET.

†**carples.** *Obs. rare*⁻¹. [? Cf. CARPELL.]

1537 *Will of W. Walwyn* (Somerset Ho.) A carplese of olde wole.

†**Carpmeal, Carptmeal.** *Obs.* [from *Cartmel* on Morecambe Bay.] (See quots.)

1610 *Act 7 Jas. I*, xvi. §2 All Cogware, Kendalles, course Cottons, and Carptmeales..made within the said Counties of Cumberland and Westmerland, or within the said Townes and Parishes of Carptmeale, Hawkeshead, and Broughton, in the said Countie of Lancaster. **1677–1692** COLES, *Carpe-meals.* **1704** WORLIDGE *Dict. Rust. et Urb.*, *Carpmeals*, a coarse kind of Cloth made in the North of England, and formerly mentioned. I know not whether the Name continues still. **1799** STRUTT *Dress & Habits* II. 195.

carpo-[1], combining form of Gr. καρπός, CARPUS, wrist, as in **car'pocerite** [Gr. κέρας horn]. **,carpometa'carpal** *a.*, 'relating to the carpus and metacarpus'. **carpo'pedal** *a.*, 'relating to the hand and the foot' (in *carpopedal spasm* 'a term applied to the local convulsions which affect the hands and feet of children'). **car'popodite**, 'the fifth basal joint of the hinder antennæ of certain Arthropods'. (*Syd. Soc. Lex.*)

1877 HUXLEY *Anat. Inv. An.* vi. 314 To its inner portion the ischiocerite is connected, bearing a merocerite and carpocerite, while the last segment, or procerite, consists of a long multi-articulate filament. **1836–9** TODD *Cycl. Anat.* II. 510 The carpo-metacarpal joint of the thumb enjoys motion forwards, backwards, inwards, and outwards. **1877** ROBERTS *Handbk. Med.* I. 362 Carpopedal contractions. **1870** ROLLESTON *Anim. Life* 94 The fifth segment is known as the Carpopodite.

carpo-[2], combining form of Gr. καρπός fruit, as in **'carpogone, carpo'gonium** *Bot.* [cf. *archegonium*], the female reproductive organ of Thallophytes which produces a sporocarp or spore-fruit; hence **carpo'gonial** *a.*, relating to the carpogonium. **car'pophagous** *a. Zool.* [Gr. -φαγος eating], fruit-eating. **'carpophore** *Bot.* [Gr. -φορος bearing, f. φέρειν to bear], a prolongation of the axis of a flower, raising the pistil above the stamens, as in *Geraniaceæ* and *Umbelliferæ*; also, in Thallophytes, the stalk of a sporocarp or spore-fruit. **'carpophyll** *Bot.* [Gr. φύλλον leaf], 'the modified leaf which by its folding produces a carpel' (*Syd. Soc. Lex.*). **'carpospore** *Bot.* [Gr. σπόρος sowing, seed], in Thallophytes, the spore formed in a sporocarp or spore-fruit; hence **carpo'sporous** *a.*, applied to Algæ which produce sporecarps or spore-fruits with carpospores.

1882 VINES *Sachs' Bot.* 236 The female organ [of Thallophytes]..may be designated by the general term Carpogonium. *Ibid.* 292 The true fertile carpogonial branches. **1839–47** TODD *Cycl. Anat.* III. 302/1 The Carpophagous Phalangers. **1870** BENTLEY *Bot.* 298 The axis is prolonged in the form of a columella or carpophore. **1871** M. COOKE *Fungi* (1874) 168 A germ-like tube, which, without originating a proper mycelium, develops at the expense of the nutritive material stored in the zygospore into a carpophore, or fruit-bearer. **1880** GRAY *Bot. Text-bk.* 401 *Carpophyll*, literally fruit-leaf; synonym of Carpel. **1882** VINES *Sachs' Bot.* 267 The carpospores are here precisely like the ordinary non-sexual conidia. **1887** *Nature* 21 Apr. 577/2 The carposporous forms of Algæ.

Carpo'cratian. A follower of Carpocrates of Alexandria (A.D. 120), who asserted the mortality of Christ's body and the creation of the world by angels. Also †**Car'pocratite.**

1585–7 T. ROGERS 39 *Art.* (1607) 65. **1677** GILPIN *Dæmonol.* (1867) 138 The filthy Carpocratians, who taught that men must sin and do the will of all the devils. **1882–3** SCHAFF *Relig. Encycl.* II. 880 The Antinomianism of the Carpocratians. **1579** FULKE *Confut. Sanders* 590 The Gnostikes and Carpocratites haue Images painted in collours.

carpolite ('kɑːpəlaɪt). Also **-lithe.** [f. Gr. καρπο- fruit + λίθος stone: see -LITE.] A fossil or petrified fruit.

1847 CRAIG, *Carpolite.* **1851** RICHARDSON *Geol.* 196 *Carpolithes.*

carpology (kɑː'pɒlədʒɪ). [f. Gr. καρπο- fruit + -λογια: see -LOGY.] The part of botany which is concerned with the study of fruits. Hence **carpo'logical** *a.*, **carpo'logically** *adv.*, **car'pologist.**

1806 *Edin. Rev.* VIII. 66 Those botanists..are..aware of the necessity of the study of carpology. *Ibid.* 67 A carpological tour in France, England and Holland. **1869** in *Eng. Mech.* 24 Dec. 370/2 Carpological specimens. **1819** COLEBROOKE in *Trans. Linn. Soc.* XIII. (1822) 46 That eminent carpologist.

'car pool. *N. Amer.* Also **car-pool, carpool.** [f. CAR *sb.*[1] + POOL *sb.*[3]] An arrangement whereby a group of people share their cars (to travel to work, take children to school, etc.); a car carrying members of a car pool; a group sharing cars in this way or the meeting-place of such a group. Cf. *van pool* s.v. VAN *sb.*[3] 3.

1942 *Reader's Digest* Dec. 138, I don't believe I care for anything, thank you. I'm just in their car pool. **1943** *McCall's Mag.* Apr. 15 On a master map of the city car pools are plotted. **1959** A. HARRINGTON *Life in 'Crystal Palace'* (1960) viii. 112, I look out of my picture-window to watch the late-arriving car-pools whirling up the long driveway. **1968** MRS. L. B. JOHNSON *White House Diary* 18 Dec. (1970) 759, I always wondered how she managed to make 8 A.M. car pools. **1974** *State* (Columbia, S. Carolina) 1 Apr. 2-A/3 Special driving lanes and other plans favoring carpools are developing. **1986** *Jrnl.* (Fairfax Co., Va.) 28 May A15/6 Disputes have sometimes arisen over the number of people that constitute a car pool.

Hence **'car-pool, 'carpool** *v. intr.*, to join a car pool; to drive or travel in a shared car, esp. to work; also *trans.*, to drive (passengers, esp. children) in a car pool; also **car-pooler, car-pooling.**

1962 *National Rev.* (U.S.) 22 May 361/2 You have to proceed to the consideration of the relative values of carpooling with large or small families. **1966** *N.Y. Times* 19 Apr. 46/1 There she was the other day, as unruffled as if her only thought were carpooling her two children to school. **1973** *Sunday Bull.* (Philadelphia) 7 Oct. (Parade Suppl.) 12 Car poolers tell us..that when they are not at the wheel.., they come to work relaxed. **1975** *Atlantic Monthly* Dec. 65 If we won't car-pool, and if we won't or can't use mass transportation, can we at least get more mileage from the gallon? **1976** *Billings* (Montana) *Gaz.* 1 July (Advt. Suppl.) 1/1 The number of cars on the road can also be reduced if more people could be encouraged to 'triple-up' and carpool to work. **1985** *U.S.A. Today* 18 Oct. A5/2 Gov. Lamm, Mayor Frederico Pena kicked off winter Better Air campaign stressing car-pooling, mass transit. **1983** *Mass Transit* Apr. 24/1 The company subsidizes each vanpool rider $25 a month while allowing sliding subsidies for carpoolers. **1986** *New Yorker* 17 Mar. 86/2 Ollar ships with a crew of eight, most of whom carpool to work together in the morning.

‖**carpus** (kɑːpəs). *Anat.* [mod.L. *carpus*, a. Gr. καρπός wrist.] The part of the skeleton which unites the hand to the fore-arm, consisting in the higher vertebrates of eight small bones, in birds of two. In man it forms the *wrist*; in the horse, the *knee.*

1679 PLOT *Staffordsh.* (1686) 295 From the Carpus to the end of the middle finger. **1726** MONRO *Anat.* (1741) 259 The Hand is..divided into the Carpus, Metacarpus and Fingers. **1833** SIR C. BELL *Hand* (1834) 91 The carpus, forming [in the horse] what by a sort of license is called the knee. **1840** G. ELLIS *Anat.* 417 Other small arteries are given off to the carpus and hand.

carquan, carquenet, obs. ff. CARCAN, -ET.

carr[1] (kɑː(r)). *dial.* [Old Northumbrian *carr* rock.] A rock: now especially applied to insulated rocks off the Northumbrian and Scottish coasts.

c **950** *Lindisf. Gosp.* Matt. vii 24 Se ðe ȝetimbres hus his ofer carr. *Ibid.* Mark xv. 46 Byrȝen þæt wæs ȝeheawen of carre. **1856** *Berwick Nat. Club* III. 223 *Farne Islands*—The *Utt Carres*, modernized into *Out Carres*, are not far from Monkshouse.

carr[2], **car** (kɑː(r)). *local.* Also 4 **kerr,** 5 **ker,** 6–7 **carre.** [From ON. Cf. Da. *kær, kjær* pool, pond (e.g. *gade-kær* village pond), Sw. *kærr* fen, morass, marsh, moor, Norw. *kjær, kjerr* pool, marsh, wet copse, Icel. *kjarr* copse-wood, brushwood, *kjarrmýrr* marsh grown with brushwood.]

1. A pond or pool; a bog or fen; now, usually, wet boggy ground; a meadow recovered by draining from the bog.

c **1330** R. BRUNNE *Chron. Wace* (Rolls) 14574 Sire Thadok, þe erchebischop of ȝork, He liuede in kerres, as doþ þe stork. **1538** LELAND *Itin.* V. 53 This Fenne..hath many Carres of Waters in it. *Ibid.* V. 122 There is a praty Car or Pole in Bishops Dale. **1556** *Scotter Crt. Roll* in E. Peacock *N.-W. Linc. Gloss.* (E.D.S.) s.v., Euery inhabytant of Scotter shall put ther geyse in the carre. **1614** MARKHAM *Cheap Husb.* (1623) 46 Which pastures may be either high woods, commons, carres, or such like spacious pieces of ground. **1691** RAY *N.C. Wds*, *Carre*, a hollow place where water stands. **1843** *Jrnl. Roy. Agric. Soc.* IV. II. 293 These redeemed meadows, or carrs [Lincolnshire]..consist of an unctuous peat. **1880** *Times* 17 Sept. 8/5 In the carrs and marishes both corn and turnips are under water. **1881** *Archæol.* XLVI. 378 There are lands called cars in most of the neighbouring parishes. **1887** *York Herald* 16 Apr. 2/1 Agistments in Everingham Carr. Horses and Cattle may be Pastured on the above Carr from 10th May to Old Michaelmas Day, 1887.

2. A fen or bog grown up with low bushes, willows, alders, etc.; a boggy or fenny copse.

c **1440** *Promp. Parv.* 272 Ker, where treys growyn be a watur or a fenn, *cardetum*; ker for aldyr, *alnetum.* **1681** WORLIDGE *Dict. Rust. et Urb.*, *Carre*, woody moist boggy ground. **1691** RAY *S. & E.C. Wds.*, *Carre*, a wood of alder, or other trees in a moist boggy place. **1865** W. WHITE *East. Eng.* II. 98 The larger islets are known as 'carrs', and 'alder carrs' to denote those on which the waterside tree grows thickly. **1874** *N. & Q.* Ser. v. I. 132 In Norfolk..osier or alder carrs. One is called the bird-carr from the fact of the black-headed gull breeding there. **1883** G. C. DAVIES *Norfolk Broads* xv. (1884) 111 In the upper marshes, low copses, locally called 'carrs,' are numerous.

3. *attrib.* and *Comb.*, as **carr fir, oak, wood,** timber and trees dug up in carrs; †**carr-grave,**

† **-graver**, an officer appointed to attend to the carrs; † **carr-sick** (see quot.): **carr swallow**, a local name of the Black Tern (*Sterna nigra*). Also CARGOOSE.

1691 RAY *N.C. Wds.*, *Car-sick*, the kennel, a word used in Sheffield. **1802** MONTAGUE *Ornith. Dict.* II, It is found in the fenny parts of Lincolnshire and Cambridgeshire, and is called at this last place Car-Swallow.

carr[3], **car** (kɑː(r)). *local.* [perh. identical with prec.] (See quot.)

1679 PLOT *Staffordsh.* (1686) 146 Whether they can find any coal water, i.e. an acid water having a Car, or yellow sediment. **1880** R. HOLLAND in *O.C. & F. Words* (E.D.S.) 77 The brown sediment (humate of iron) deposited in water from boggy ground is called carr in Cheshire.

Hence **carr-water**, **carry** *a.*

1875 *Lanc. Gloss.* 70 *Carr-water*, red peaty water. *Carry*, red, peaty. **1888** *N. & Q.* VII. V. 135.

carr, var. of CAR.

carrabin, **carrat**, etc.: see CARA-.

carracature, obs. form of CARICATURE.

† **carrack**, **carack** (ˈkærək). *Obs.* exc. *Hist.* Forms: 5-6 caryk(e, 5 carikke, careke, karik, carrik(ke, carryk(e, carrake, carryg, 5-7 carak, carack(e, carrike, carricke, 6 carake, caryck, (caracte, carect), carrek(e, 6-7 carike, carick(e, careck(e, carracke, carreck(e, carrick, carrak, 7 (carract), carraque, 7-8 (caract), 7-9 carack, carrack. [a. OF. *carraque*, *caraque* = med.L. *carraca*, *carrica*, *carica*, Sp., Pg. *carraca*, It. *caracca* (whence also MDu. *ka'râke*, now *kraak*), of uncertain origin; see Diez.]

A large ship of burden, also fitted for warfare, such as those formerly used by the Portuguese in trading with the East Indies; a galleon.

c **1386** CHAUCER *Sompn. T.* 24 Brodder than of a carryk [*MSS.*, carrik, carik, carike, caryke] is the sayl. *a* **1422** HEN. V. in Ellis *Orig. Lett.* Ser. III. 31 I. 72 Maistres for owr grete shippes, carrakes, barges, and balyngers. *a* **1422** TOMA *ibid.* I. 72 *note*, Ther be twey new Carrakas of makyng at Bartholem. **1480** CAXTON *Chron. Eng.* ccxliii, With 3 carrickes [*v.r.* carrikkes, FABYAN carykes] of Jene. **1483** *Act 1 Rich. III*, viii. Preamb., In Caraks, Galeis, and Shippes. **1495** *Act 11 Hen. VII*, v. Preamb., Carrykis..of other regions and Cuntreies. **1509–10** *Act 1 Hen. VIII*, xx. §1 Any Carrek or Galey. **1512** WRIOTHESLEY *Chron.* (1875) I. 7 A carike of France. **1523** LD. BERNERS *Froiss.* I. xxvii. 41 Shyppes, careckes, and galyes. **1529** RASTELL *Pastyme, Hist. Brit.* (1811) 250 Toke .iii. of the greattest of theyr Caryckes. **1534** LD. BERNERS *Gold. Bk. M. Aurel.* (1546) Uvb, In greate carrackes. **1579** NORTH *Plutarch* 338 (R.) One of the greatest carects or hulkes of the king. **1581** J. BELL *Haddon's Answ. Osor.* 459 A great Carrick would be skarce able to beare them all. **1590** SHAKS. *Com. Err.* III. ii. 140 Spaine, who sent whole Armadoes of Carrects. **1600** ABP. ABBOT *Exp. Jonah* 146 The hugest mightiest Carickes that ever came on the water. **1628** WITHER *Brit. Rememb.* VII. 1045 The Carraks, and the Argosies of Spaine. **1655** HEYWOOD *Fort. by Land* IV. i. Wks. 1874 VI. 414 With any Carract that do's trade for Spain. **1670** COTTON *Espernon* III. IX. 441 The wrack of the Carricks. **1703** DE FOE *Sp. Descent* Misc. 130 Here a vast Carrack flies, while none pursue. **1860** MOTLEY *Netherl.* (1868) II. xvi. 283 Drake..fell in with one of those famous Spanish East Indiamen, called carracks.

carract, obs. form of CARAT.

carrageen, **-gheen** (ˈkærəgiːn). Properly **Carragheen moss**. [From *Carragheen* near Waterford in Ireland, where it grows abundantly.]

A kind of seaweed (*Chondrus crispus*), also called *Irish moss*, common on the British coasts, of a cartilaginous texture and a purplish colour, becoming yellowish-white when dried. It yields on boiling a nutritive demulcent jelly, used for food and in medicine. Introduced into medical use by Mr. Todhunter of Dublin. (See Reece's *Monthly Gazette of Health*, Jan. 1831.)

1834 ESTHER COPLEY *Housekpr's Guide* 57 Carraghan moss..in the time of the dreadful destitution in Ireland, in 1831, was the means of preserving many families from starving. **1837** M. DONOVAN *Dom. Econ.* II. 323 *Carrageen*, commonly called Irish moss, introduced from Ireland as an article of food within the last ten years. **1841** *Penny Cycl.* XXI. 156 Carrageen moss..is frequently employed instead of isinglass for the manufacture of blanc-mange and jellies.

Hence **carra'geenin** (*Chem.*), the form of PECTIN found in Carragheen.

carraine, **carran**, **carren**, obs. ff. CARRION.

carralle, **-ell**, obs. forms of CAROL.

carrancha (kəˈræntʃə). Also **carancha**, **car(r)ancho**. [Native name.] A South American caracara or carrion-hawk, *Polyborus tharus*.

1839 DARWIN *Jrnl.* iii. 64 *Polyborus Braziliensis*..is most numerous on the grassy savannahs of La Plata (where it goes by the name of Carrancha). **1869** W. H. HUDSON *Let.* 22 Dec. in *Ornithol. Buenos Ayres* (1951) ii. 10 This *sayno* swamp is a great breeding place for the Carranchos, and for hawks. **1889** SCLATER & HUDSON *Argent. Ornithol.* II. 81 *Polyborus tharus*..Carancho Carrion-Hawk. **1911** *Encycl. Brit.* XX. 901/1 The carrancha or carrion-hawk..is one of the characteristic features of a Patagonian landscape. **1920** W. H. HUDSON *Birds of La Plata* II. 76 South of Paraguay the Spanish name is *Carancho*, possibly a corruption of *Keanché*, the Puelche name for the allied *Milvago chimango*, in imitation of its peevish cry. *Ibid.* 77 The Caranchos pair for life, and may therefore be called social birds.

carrapato (karəˈpɑːtəʊ). Also **carapato**; and in Sp. form **garrapata**. [Pg.] A tick of the genus *Ixodes*. Also *attrib.*, as ***carrapato disease*** (quot. 1903).

1886 [see *bush-tick*]. **1892** G. FLEMING *Neumann's Treat. Parasites* 103 These are popularly designated by such names as Ticks..and Carapatos. **1903** *Jrnl. Tropical Med.* 2 Nov. 341/1 The carapato disease of the Zambesi basin is certainly produced by the bite of a tick—*Argas moubata*. **1906** F. C. GLASS *Through Heart Brazil* 20 The carrapato is a kind of minute tick. **1930** *Discovery* July 229/2 Such parasites as the garrapato and pinalia abound.

Carrara (kəˈrɑːrə). The name of a town in N. Italy, used *attrib.* to designate a variety of marble quarried there; *spec.* in *Pottery* (see quot. 1957).

a **1728** [see MARBLE *sb.* 1 b]. **1795** R. KIRWAN *Elem. Min.* (ed. 2) I. VI. 85 Carrara marble is next in purity. **1883** *Encycl. Brit.* XV. 528/2 It is in Carrara marble that the finest works of Michelangelo and of Canova are executed. **1907** E. WHARTON *Fruit of Tree* I. iii. 32 The numerous gas-jets..shed their lights..on Carrara busts and bronze Indians. **1928** D. H. LAWRENCE *Lady Chatt.* vii. 87 She began to be afraid of the ghastly white tombstones, that peculiar loathsome whiteness of Carrara marble. **1957** MANKOWITZ & HAGGAR *Encycl. Eng. Pott.* 43/1 *Carrara*, name given to the parian paste by Josiah Wedgwood & Sons. **1967** J. RICHARDSON *Courtesans* i. 22 In Blanche d'Antigny's bathroom, the bath was made of the finest Carrara marble.

carrat, **carraway**: see CARAT, CARAWAY.

carrawitchet: see CARRI-.

carreck(e, **carrek(e**, obs. ff. CARRACK.

† **carre-crow**. *Obs.* = CARRION CROW.

1611 COTGR., *Corbin*, (carrion, or carre) crow.

carrect, **carret**, obs. forms of CARAT.

carreen(e, **carrell**, etc.: see CARE-.

carrefour: see CARFOUR.

† **ˈcarrel**[1]. *Obs.* Also **carele**. A fabric mentioned in the 16th and 17th c.

1570 *Bk. of Drapery* in Beck *Draper's Dict.* (1882) *Carrells, Currelles*, [mentioned with bays, fustians, and mockadoes, as] works mixed with silk, saietrie, or linen yarn. **1611** *Bk. of Rates* (Jam.) Carrels, the peece, conteining 15 elnes, viij *l.* **1720** *Stow's Surv.* (ed. Strype 1754) II. v. ix. 266/1 There were Carells, Fustians, Blankets.

carrel[2] (ˈkærəl). Also **carrell**. **a.** Var. of CAROL *sb.* 5 a. *Obs.* exc. *Hist.*

1593, **1721** [see CAROL *sb.* 5 a]. **1890** J. W. CLARK *Cambr.* 274 They..retired thither for study after dinner, each sitting in his 'carrell' as it was called. **1893** F. MADAN *Bks. in MS.* 34 These carrels were fully open on one side of the cloister walk. **1911** L. WEAVER *House & Equipment* 39 In monastic houses reading was generally done in carrells, which were little bays in one or more of the Cloister walks.

b. A private cubicle provided in a library for use by a reader.

1919 *Library Jrnl.* XLIV. 635 The provision of carrels for research workers. **1933** *Times* 11 Dec. 19/5 Experiments in library administration, including the use of carrels and research rooms adjoining appropriate sections of the stack. **1957** V. NABOKOV *Pnin* iii. 76 He then returned to his carrell for his own research. **1960** *Medium Ævum* XXIX. 109 The study cubicles in the college library at Ampleforth are still called 'carrels'. **1970** *Libr. Assoc. Rec.* Apr. 161/2 In the Reference Library there are ten carrels and six semi-carrels, as well as open study-desks.

‖ **carretera** (kareˈtera). [Sp.] A main road.

[**1845** R. FORD *Handbk. Spain* I. i. 12 The cross roads and minor roads of Spain are bad... They are divided into those which are practicable for wheel-carriages '*camino carretero*', '*de carruage*', '*carretera*', and those which are only bridle-roads.] **1900** *Engineering Mag.* XIX. 683 A *carretera*, or macadamized road is the 'best road' or route of the 'fast mail' in Porto Rico. **1923** *Blackw. Mag.* Aug. 178/1 The extreme provincialism of the Spanish *carratera*. **1924** *Ibid.* June 804/2 Very pretty they look sailing slowly along the dusty *carretara* to do the day's marketing. **1958** L. R. MUIRHEAD *Blue Guide to Northern Spain* (ed. 2) p. cxlii, Apart from the Carreteras Nacionales, however, many of the roads are stony and often under repair.

carriable, **carryable** (ˈkærɪəb(ə)l), *a.* [f. CARRY + -ABLE.] That may be carried.

1611 COTGR., *Portatisse*, portatiue, portable, carryable. **1887** *Pall Mall G.* 10 June 10/1 A simple motion, carryable by a simple majority.

carriage (ˈkærɪdʒ). Forms: 4-7 **cariage**, 5 **karyage**, 5-6 **caryage**, 5-7 **carryage**, (*Sc.* 5-7 **carage**, 6 **carraige**), 6- **carriage**. [a. ONF. *cariage*, in mod.F. *charriage*, Picard *carriage* action of conveying in a vehicle, f. *carier*, mod.F. *charrier* to carry (in a cart, etc.): see -AGE.]

I. The action of carrying.

1. **a.** Carrying or bearing from one place to another; conveyance.

1388 WYCLIF *Gen.* xlv. 19 That thei take waynes..to the cariage [**1382** kariying] of her little children. *c* **1440** *Promp. Parv.* 62 Caryage, *vectura, portagium*, etc. **1534** LD. BERNERS *Gold. Bk. M. Aurel.* (1546) Fb, The horse, that hathe..passed his course of caryage, shoulde reste hym. **1626** BACON *Sylva* §193 The carriage of the Sounds. **1693** URQUHART *Rabelais* III. lii. 422 Their Carriages by Wains and Carts of the Wines. **1725** DE FOE *Voy. round W.* (1840) 299 Mules or horses for carriage. **1825** MᶜCULLOCH *Pol. Econ.* III. v. 284 For the expences of carriage as for those of production.

b. with *obj. genitive*, or special reference to the object: = 'being carried'.

1611 SHAKS. *Cymb.* III. iv. 190 Least..I be suspected of Your carriage from the Court. **1719** DE FOE *Crusoe* (1840) I. xx. 359 Trees, which..lay there for carriage. **1826** SIR J. SEBRIGHT *Observ. Hawking* (1828) 35 By constant carriage, not only by day, but also..during a part of the night.

2. *esp.* Conveyance of merchandise; commercial transport; traffic of transport; carrying trade.

1523 FITZHERB. *Husb.* §128 The erthe swelleth & bolneth..with treadynge, and specyally with caryage. **1547** *Act 1 Edw. VI*, v. §5 The cariage or conveyaunce of anny horses..into Scotelande. **1684** BURNET tr. *More's Utopia* 73 The Streets are made very convenient for all Carriage. **1727** DE FOE *Eng. Tradesm.* xxvi. (1841) I. 260 Our river navigation is not to be named for carriage with the vast bulk of carriage by packhorses and by wagons. *a* **1797** BURKE *Late State Nation* (R.) The largest proportion of carriage had been engrossed by neutral nations. **1834** SOUTHEY *Doctor* xxiii. (1862) 52 The whole carriage of the northern counties..was performed by pack-horses.

† **3.** An impost on the transport of goods through a country or territory; a customs duty, toll, or carrier's licence. *Obs.*

[*c* **1200** in Dugdale *Monast.* I. 310 Soluta et quieta de omnibus Geldis..et lastagio et stallagio et carriagio.] **1771** *Antiq. Sarisb.* 80 Free from Toll, Pontage, Passage, Pasture, Lestage, Stallage, Carriage and every other Custom.

† **4.** An obsolete service of carrying, or a payment in lieu of the same, due by a tenant to his landlord or feudal superior, or imposed by authority. Cf. AVERAGE *sb.*[1] *Obs.*

c **1386** CHAUCER *Pers. T.* ¶677 Distreyned by taylages, custumes, and cariages. **1480** CAXTON *Chron. Eng.* ccxxii. 214 Touchyng vitails and also of caryages. **1549** *Compl. Scot.* xv. 125, I am maid ane slaue of my body to ryn and rashe in arrage & carraige. **1571** CAMPION *Hist. Irel.* II. viii. (1633) 102 The Irish imposition of Coyne, Livery, Cartings, carriages, loadings. **1611** BIBLE *Pref.* 2 He [Solomon] had..troubled them with some cariages. **1703** in Keble *Bp. T. Wilson* (1863) 194 To leave all such carriages, Boones and services on the same foot as already provided for by Law. **1755** in *United Presbyter. Mag.* Apr. (1884) 156 To answer all carriages and days' dargs exacted by the laird. **1754–1835** [see AVERAGE *sb.*[1]].

5. (*ellipt.* or *contextually*) The price, expense, or cost of carrying.

1753 CHAMBERS *Cycl. Supp.*, *Carriage*, also denotes the money or hire paid to a carrier, or other bearer of goods. The carriage of letters is called postage. **1866** ROGERS *Agric. & Prices* I. xx. 504 Sometimes the carriage is given as a separate item.

† **6.** (*contextually*) Power, ability, or capacity for carrying; (in quot. 1588 quibblingly). *Obs.*

1588 SHAKS. *L.L.L.* I. ii. 74 Sampson..was a man of good carriage, great carriage; for hee carried the Towne-gates on his backe like a porter. **1740** PINEDA *Eng. Span. Dict.* s.v., A Beast of Carriage, a Ship of Carriage.

7. *Arith.* See CARRY 7.

1847 DE MORGAN *Arithmet. Bks.* Introd. 22 Proceed with each figure, and carriage.

† **8.** 'Bearing', course, direction. *Obs.*

1668 CULPEPPER & COLE *Barthol. Anat.* I. vi. 10 The insertion of many Nerves, and the oblique carriage of many fibres. *Ibid.* 12 The carriage of Fibres.

9. The carrying of a fortress, etc.; also ***carriage away***: cf. CARRY 16, 46.

1603 KNOLLES *Hist. Turks* (1631) 610 Solyman..resolued forthwith to besiege Vienna, the chiefe citie of Austria, in good hope that by the carriage away of that, the other cities..would without any resistance be yeelded vnto him.

10. Action of conducting, carrying out; execution; conduct, management, administration.

1601 R. JOHNSON *Kingd. & Commw.* (1603) 82 The whole Government and carriage of affaires. **1611** SPEED *Hist. Gt. Brit.* x. i. (1632) 1241 A Proclamation against all griping Monopolies..and Protections..as also against other abuses in other inferiour carriages. **1650** B. *Discollim.* 21 The carriages or miscarriages of these affaires. **1652** NEEDHAM tr. *Selden's Mare Cl.* Ep. Ded. 18 The carriage and conduct of this noble Enterprise. **1876** *Belfast News* 22 Nov. 3/3 Messrs. —— solicitors, had the carriage of the sale. **1884** *Law Times Rep.* 26 Apr. 246/1 The carriage of the order [for winding up a company] is given to the first petitioner.

11. The carrying (of a motion).

1879 O'CONNOR *Beaconsfield* 397 The consequence of the carriage of the motion would be the expulsion of Lord John Russell from power.

II. Manner of carrying; conduct, behaviour.

12. Manner or way of carrying or bearing (e.g. anything in the hand, the body, or any part of it).

1621 BURTON *Anat. Mel.* III. ii. III. iii. (1651) 470 'Tis not the eye, but carriage of it. **1653** WALTON *Angler* I. v, The ill carriage of the line..makes you lose your labour. **1688** R. HOLME *Armoury* III. 150/1 A good Graver..[must] have a curious & exact carriage of the Hand. **1711** BUDGELL *Spect.* No. 67 ¶11 An handsome carriage of the body. **1821** DE QUINCEY in Page *Life* I. v. 97 A peculiar and graceful carriage of her head.

13. Manner of carrying one's body; bodily deportment, bearing, mien.

1596 SHAKS. *1 Hen. IV*, II. iv. 466 A goodly portly man..of a most noble Carriage. **1653** H. COGAN tr. *Pinto's Trav.* xxxviii. §3. 153 A stately carriage, far different from that he was wont to have. **1705** ADDISON *Italy* 45 A free and easie

Carriage. **1866** G. MACDONALD *Ann. Q. Neighb.* ix. (1878) 135 He had the carriage of a military man.

14. a. Manner of conducting oneself socially; demeanour; deportment, behaviour. (Referring to *manners.*) *arch.*

1590 SHAKS. *Com. Err.* III. ii. 14 Teach sinne the carriage of a holy Saint. **1642** FULLER *Holy & Prof. St.* III. xxi. 211 Others have so scornfull a carriage. **1697** DAMPIER *Voy.* xiii. (1698) 372 A pretty ingenious young man..of a very civil carriage and behaviour. **1741** MIDDLETON *Cicero* II. vii. 6 Her husbands peevishness and churlish carriage. **1818** BYRON *Juan* I. lxvi, Her very prudent carriage.

b. Manner of acting *to* or *towards* others; treatment of others. *arch.*

1598 BACON *Hypocrites, Ess.* (Arb.) 117 Their..honest carriage towardes men. **1612** —— *Faction* ibid. 83 The even carriage betweene two factions, proceedeth not alwaies of moderation. **1646** SIR T. BROWNE *Pseud. Ep.* I. x. (1686) 30 Who can but laugh at the carriage of Ammon unto Alexander? **1692** SOUTH *12 Serm.* (1697) I. 125 We have treated of men's carriage to Christ in this world. **1725** DE FOE *Voy. round W.* (1840) 158 The affectionate carriage of this poor woman to her infant. **1844** DISRAELI *Coningsby* IV. xii. 171 Lucretia's carriage towards her gave her little discomfort. **1856** EMERSON *Eng. Traits* vi. *Manners* Wks. (Bohn) II. 48 Nothing can be more delicate..than the courtship and mutual carriage of the sexes.

†**c.** (with *pl.*) An act of behaviour towards another. *Obs.*

1649 BP. HALL *Cases Consc.* I. ix, In all which mutuall carriages, we ought to be guided by those respects which we could wish tendered to ourselves in the like occasions. **1682** BUNYAN *Holy War* 338 After some mutual carriages of love. **1684** —— *Pilgr.* II. 6 All her unkind, unnatural, and ungodly carriages to her dear Friend.

15. a. Habitual conduct or behaviour. (Referring to *morals* or *character*.)

1588 THYNNE *Let.* in *Animadv.* (1865) Introd. 92 Makinge my actions the towchestone of the honest cariage of myself. **1648** HERRICK *Hesper., Epit. sober Matron*, With blamelesse carriage I liv'd here. **1712** STEELE *Spect.* No. 480 ¶2 Something of their own Carriage they would exempt from Examination. **1759** STERNE *Tr. Shandy* (1802) I. vii. 14 A person of decent carriage. **1844** DISRAELI *Coningsby* II. i. 50 That irregular and unsettled carriage of public men which so perplexed the nation.

b. Conduct or action *in* given circumstances.

1587 FLEMING *Contn. Holinshed* III. 1402/2 His fidelitie and good carriage in small things. **1634–46** ROW *Hist. Kirk* (1842) 217 His cariage in relation to Gowrie's Conspiracie. **1663** GERBIER *Counsel* C iv a, Negotiations..wherein your Lordships carriage hath justly deserved the respects of those. **1868** FREEMAN *Norm. Conq.* (1876) II. ix. 409 Harold's energetic carriage in the Welsh campaign.

†**c.** Short for 'good carriage'. (Also in sense 13.)

1618 FLETCHER *Island P'cess* II. i, One without carriage or common sense. **1621** ELSING *Debates Ho. Lords* (1870) 106 Protested his innocencye and carryage in that place. **1666** PEPYS *Diary* 27 Sept., She is poor in clothes, and not bred to any carriage.

†**16.** A piece of conduct; action; proceeding.

1609 TOURNEUR *Fun. Poems* 120 His former carriages. **1633** BP. HALL *Hard Texts* 244 All her actions & carriages are full of honor. **1696** STILLINGFL. *Serm.* iv. 159 Men, sober, just, humble and meek in all their carriages.

†**17.** Manner or way of conducting or managing (an affair). *Obs.*

1612 DAVIES *Why Ireland, &c.* (1747) 9 Touching the carriage of the Martiall affaires from the seventeenth year, etc. **1658** BP. REYNOLDS *Lord's Supp.* xvii, To leave every man in the external carriages of his worship unto the conduct of his private fancy. **1683** EVELYN *Diary* 13 July, Some dislike of the present carriage of matters at Court.

III. That which is carried.

†**18. a.** Something carried; a burden, a load. *Obs.*

1458 *MS. Christ's Hosp., Abingdon* in *Dom. Archit.* III. 41 For cartis with cariage may goo & come. **1523** LD. BERNERS *Froiss.* I. lv, Their horses with caryages entred in: and the two that came last [were] laden with coles. **1583** BABINGTON *Commandm.* (1590) 339 The pismire..whose many little cariages..make a great heape at last. **1598** BARRET *Theor. Warres* II. i. 27 The musket is a heauie cariage, and painfull to be handled. **1607** TOPSELL *Four-f. Beasts* Ded. 5 When our backs be broak, they must take up the carriage. **1704** WORLIDGE *Dict. Rust. et Urb.* s.v. *Saddle*, To keep the Portmanteau, or other Carriage off the Riders back.

b. A load, as a quantity definite or indefinite.

1596–7 S. FINCHE in *App. Hist. Croydon* (1783) 152 We get in carriages of stone and bricke. **1704** WORLIDGE *Dict. Rust. et Urb.* s.v., Carage of Lime is 64 Bushels. **1805** FORSYTH *Beauties Scotl.* I. 519 Bringing..carriages of lime.

c. *fig.* Burden, load.

a **1553** UDALL *Royster D.* III. ii, *Mery* Doth not love lade you? *Cust.* I feele no such cariage. **1610** SHAKS. *Temp.* V. i. 3 Time Goes vpright with his carriage.

†**19.** Baggage. (Originally *collect.*; later often in *pl.*) *Obs.* **a.** The portable equipment of an army, L. *impedimenta*; = BAGGAGE 2. Sometimes including the whole baggage-train.

1375 BARBOUR *Bruce* VIII. 275 The cariage..Behynd hym levyt he all still. ? *a* **1400** *Morte Arth.* 2282 They kaire to the karyage and take whate them likes. **1460** CAPGRAVE *Chron.* 313 In the tyme of the batail al her cariage was stole be the Frenschmen. **1586** J. HOOKER *Girald. Irel.* in *Holinshed* II. 84/1 The cariage was dragging after the armie, and slenderlie manned. **1598** GRENEWEY *Tacitus' Ann.* I. xi. (1622) 21 The carriages inclosed in the middest [*mediis impedimentis*]. **1611** SPEED *Hist. Gt. Brit.* IX. iv. 43 The King ..had sent his maine Army to conduct the Carriages. **1611** BIBLE *1 Sam.* xvii. 22 Dauid left his cariage in the hand of the keeper of the cariage. **1644** SLINGSBY *Diary* (1836) 130 His carriage could not pass. **1655** STANLEY *Hist. Philos.* (1701) 116 To burn their Carriages and Tents.

b. Movable or portable property; baggage or luggage carried with one on a journey, etc.

1398 TREVISA *Barth. De P.R.* XVIII. xix. (1495) 778 The camell is..gode..to bere charge and caryage of men. *c* **1425** *Three Kings Cologne* 40 Euery kyng..had with hym his cariage, þat is to seye beestys, as oxen and schepe and oþer beestis þat longeth to mannys lyuyng and sustynaunce. **1563** FOXE *A. & M.* (1583) 988 This Cardinall [Wolsey]..hauing in his cariage lxxx wagons. **1598** HAKLUYT *Voy.* I. 94 Constrained at euery baite to take downe my carriages and lift them up againe on sundry horses backs. **1611** BIBLE *Acts* xxi. 15 We tooke vp our cariages, & went vp to Hierusalem. **1655** *Francion* IX. 2 A little waggon..to be made here, to put my Carriages in it, which is too heavy for my Sumpter-horse. **1743** R. POOLE *Journ. France & Holl.* (1744) I. 200, I would greatly have lessen'd my Carriage, and my expence also thereby.

†**20.** Leaves and branches carried away by a stag with his antlers when passing through a thicket or wood. *Obs.*

1616 SURFL. & MARKH. *Countr. Farm* 684 If the Hart be tall and large, the cariages will also be somewhat large.

†**21.** Meaning carried by words; burden, import, purport, bearing. *Obs.*

1602 SHAKS. *Ham.* I. i. 94 By the same cov'nant And carriage of the article design'd. **1607** HIERON *Wks.* I. 367 This was the question, as appeareth by the whole carriage of the former chapter. **16..** *Time's Store-ho.* 112 (L.) The Hebrew text hath no other carriage.

IV. Means of carrying.

* *In general use.*

†**22.** *collect.* Means of conveyance. *Obs.*

c **1450** *Merlin* X. 144 On the tother side come all the cariage of the londe, and brought vitaile. **1612** BRINSLEY *Lud. Lit.* Introd. 16 Knowing languages to be the carryage of knowledge. **1710** *Act 9 Anne* xi.[x.] §6 Letters and Packets, passing or repassing by the Carriage called the Penny-Post. **1800** WELLINGTON *Let.* in Gurw. *Disp.* I. 104 To proceed with that quantity for which they have at present carriage.

†**23.** A vehicle or means of conveyance of any kind. *Obs.* exc. in ***wheel carriage***; = next.

15.. *Dk. Northumb. Household Bk.* xlix. (1827) 386 Ther shall be a Caryage apontide at every Remevall for the Cariage of my Lordes Childre Stuff. **1665** G. HAVERS *P. della Valle's Trav. E. India* 90 One of those Carriages which the Portugals call Rete..a net of cords ty'd at the head and feet, and hanging down from a great Indian Cane. **1740** JOHNSON *Drake* Wks. IV. 441 The most useful animals of this country..serving as carriages over rocks and mountains. **1771** SMOLLETT *Humph. Cl.* 23 Apr., The poor chair-men and their carriages. *Ibid.* 26 Apr., Coaches, chaises, chairs, and other carriages. **1776** ADAM SMITH *W.N.* (1869) II. v. i. 307 A high way, a bridge, a navigable canal, may..be..made and maintained by a small toll upon the carriages that make use of them. **1786** BURNS *Inventory*, Wheel carriages I hae but few, Three carts..ae auld wheelbarrow. **1837** CARLYLE *Fr. Rev.* (1872) III. 94 No wheel-carriage rolls this morning in these streets.

†**24.** A wheeled vehicle generally. *Obs.* or *arch.*

1560 WHITEHORNE *Arte Warre* (1588) 41 Euery ten men of armes, should haue fiue carriages. **1611** COTGR., *Charroy*, a cart, or other cariage. **1693** *Pittington Vestry Bk.* (Surtees) 210 For mending the church gate that carriages comes in at, 2*s*. 6*d*. **1711** *Lond. Gaz.* No. 4935/4 Wheels of all manner of Carriages. **1741** *Act 14 George II*, xlii. §5 Carts, waggons, or other carriages, employed only about Husbandry, or carrying of only Cheese, Butter, Hay, Straw, Corn. **1757** *Gentl. Mag.* 528 Laws..for..regulating the drivers of carriages within this city [London].

25. A wheeled vehicle for conveying persons, as distinct from one for the transport of goods. Often in comb., as ***hackney-carriage, railway-carriage, travelling-carriage***, etc. *spec.* ellipt. for *railway-carriage*.

1706 PHILLIPS, *Carriage*, also a kind of cover'd or close waggon. **1748** SMOLLETT *Rod. Rand.* xi, The master of the waggon..fearing the captain and his lady would take umbrage and leave his carriage, etc. **1751** —— *Per. Pic.* lii. (*heading*), The whole company set out for Ghent in the Diligence..Our Hero is captivated by a Lady in that Carriage. **1828** E. GROSVENOR *Jrnl.* Aug. (1965) vi. 127 There were 3 steam engines and carriages attached to each. **1837** CARLYLE *Fr. Rev.* II. IV. v, Monsieur in a commonplace travelling carriage is off Northwards. **1859** *Carriage Builders' & Harness Makers' Art Jrnl.* I. 66/1 A train started from Worcester at half-past three, p.m., and consisted of six carriages with an engine and tender. **1875** *Echo* 29 Oct., The Supervisor of Excise..said that the word 'carriage' as defined by the Act of Parliament, meant any vehicle not used for carrying merchandise or any kind of goods. **1884** MISS BRADDON *Ishmael* xxix, Lolling in the corner of a railway carriage. **1921** A. HUXLEY *Crome Yellow* i. 2 What right had he to sit in the sunshine, to occupy corner seats in third-class carriages, to be alive? **1958** J. BETJEMAN *Coll. Poems* 265 The train at Pershore station was waiting that Sunday night Gas light on the platform, in my carriage electric light.

26. *spec.* A wheeled vehicle kept for private use for driving in; especially an elegant four-wheeled vehicle having accommodation for four persons inside, and drawn by two or more horses. ***carriage and pair***: one drawn by a pair of horses.

This use began about the middle of the 18th c.; *coach* was the word in earlier use.

[**1741** *Act 14 Geo. II*, xlii. §5 The covered Carriages of noblemen and Gentlemen for their private use.] **1771** SMOLLETT *Humph. Cl.* 24 May, The postilion behind, endeavouring to stop the carriage. **1794** W. FELTON (*title*), A Treatise on Carriages, comprehending Coaches, Chariots, Phætons, Curricles, Gigs, Whiskies, etc. **1848** THACKERAY *Van. Fair* viii, A carriage and four splendid horses. **1879** *Times* 27 Aug., The party drove off in a carriage and pair. **1884** MISS BRADDON *Ishmael* xxix, I wonder that you can drive in an open carriage in such weather.

** *In technical use.*

27. The wheeled support on which a piece of ordnance is mounted; a *gun-carriage*.

1560 WHITEHORNE *Arte Warre* (1588) 97 To make the carriage of the artillery, with the spokes of ye wheele crooked. **1603** KNOLLES *Hist. Turks* (J.), He commanded the great ordnance to be laid upon carriages, which before lay bound in great unweildy timber. **1706** PHILLIPS, *Carriages* for Pieces of Ordinance, a kind of long, narrow Carts, each made to the proportion of the Gun it is to carry. **1776** W. HEATH in Sparks *Corr. Amer. Rev.* (1853) I. 278, I should be glad to have the carriages for the four pounders sent forward. **1874** KNIGHT *Dict. Mech.*, s.v. *Cannon*, The gun is mounted on a steel carriage weighing 15 tons.

28. *Carriage-building.* The wheeled framework which supports the body of a coach or similar vehicle (see quot. 1794).

1761 *Official Descr. Royal State Coach*, The whole of the carriage and body is richly ornamented. **1794** W. FELTON *Carriages* (1801) I. 39 Its [carriage's] meaning is frequently confined to the under part only, on which the body is placed. *Ibid.* 40 All four-wheeled carriages are divided into two parts—the upper and under carriage. The upper is the main one, on which the body is hung; the under carriage is the conductor, and turns by means of a lever..The hind wheels are placed on the upper part; the fore wheels on the under.

29. Applied to various mechanical contrivances which move and carry some part of a machine.

1688 R. HOLME *Armoury* III. iii. 114/1 (*Several Parts of a Press*) The Carriage, is the sliding Plank on which the Marble Stone is laid. **1833** J. HOLLAND *Manuf. Metals* II. 229 The type carriage is caused to move steadily along. **1879** *Cassell's Techn. Educ.* IV. 395/2 From seven hundred to nine hundred spindles..arranged upon the 'carriage', or movable part of the mule.

30. †**a.** The loop attached to the sword-belt, through which one passed his sword. *Obs.* (Perh. only an affectation.)

1602 SHAKS. *Ham.* V. ii. 161 *Ham.* What call you the Carriages? *Osr.* The Carriages, Sir, are the hangers. *Ham.* The phrase would bee more Germaine to the matter; If we could carry Cannon by our sides.

b. **1847–78** HALLIWELL, *Carriage*, a belt which carries a whetstone behind a mower. (*Var. dial.*) **1879** in MISS JACKSON *Shropsh. Word-bk.*

31. *Agric.* An artificial channel for conveying water for irrigation, drainage, etc. *Obs.* or *dial.* (Cf. CARRIER 5.)

1669 WORLIDGE *Syst. Agric.* iii. §2 (1681) 22 Let the main Carriage narrow by degrees, and so let it narrow till the end, that the Water may press into the lesser Carriages, that issue all along from the main. **1679** PLOT *Staffordsh.* (1686) 356 Smaller carriages or trenches 40 or 50 yards asunder. **1704** WORLIDGE *Dict. Rust. et Urb.* s.v. *Drains*, The lesser Drains must be made among the Carriages in the lowest places. **1885** *Hampsh. Gloss.* (E.D.S.) *Carriage*, a drain, water carriage.

32. a. = BEARING *sb.* 12. **b.** A rail-chair.

1788 SMEATON in *Phil. Trans.* LXXIX. 3 A piece of brass, or brass carriage, made to fit upon the vertical part of the meridian..This piece of brass carries the spindle. **1816** *Specif. Losh & Stephenson's Patent* No. 4067. 6 The half lap joinings of the rails *c, c* placed in their carriages.

c. *Arch.* 'The timber framework on which the steps of a wooden staircase are supported' (Gwilt).

1823 P. NICHOLSON *Pract. Build.* 188 This additional wood-work, which is necessary to the firmness and durability of the construction, is called the carriage of the stairs.

†**33.** = PORTAGE. *Obs.* Also *attrib.*

1690 H. KELSEY *Papers* (1929) 2 Through Rivers wch run strong with falls [there were] thirty three Carriages five lakes in all. **1744** A. DOBBS *Hudson's Bay* 34 The River..having about 30 Falls..where they must carry their Canoes. Two or three of them are Carriages of a League or two. **1753** CHAMBERS *Cycl. Supp.*, *Carriage* is also used to denote a space of ground, over which the inhabitants of New France, and other colonies of North America..are obliged to carry their boats and provisions. **1775** J. MELVIN *Jrnl.* (1857) 10 The carriage-place is about a mile in length.

V. *Attributively*, and in *Combination.*

34. General: †**a.** (used for carrying), as ***carriage-beast, -bier, -bullock, cattle***, etc.; †**b.** (concerned with the baggage), as ***carriage-man, -master***; **c.** (referring to vehicles, senses 23–26, esp. 26), as ***carriage-blind, -break, -builder, -building, -clock, -door, -exercise, -frame, -head, -ladder, -lamp, -road, -spring, -tax, -top, -wheel, -window***.

1548 THOMAS *Ital. Gram.*, *Giumente*, any *carriage beastes. **1623** BINGHAM *Xenophon* 28 Lay your baggage vpon the carriage-beasts. *a* **1825** *Gay Goshawk* xi. in Child *Ballads* IV. xcvi. (1886) 362/2 Rise up..And make her *carriage-bier. **1837** CARLYLE *Fr. Rev.* III. I. iv. 33 Pull up your *carriage-blinds. **1803** WELLINGTON *Let.* in Gurw. *Disp.* I. 399 Every *carriage Bullock..should have a saddle. **1884** F. BRITTEN *Watch & Clockm.* 113 Used for striking the hours on in ..*carriage clocks. **1860** W. G. CLARK *Vacat. Tour* 53 Like a *carriage-lamp. **1375** BARBOUR *Bruce* VIII. 275 The *cariage-men and the pouerale. **1598** BARRET *Theor. Warres* IV. iii. 110 The *carriage-maister is to furnish him with cartes and cariages. **1798** SOUTHEY *Eng. Eclog.* I, A *carriage road That sweeps conveniently from gate to gate. **1869** PHILLIPS *Vesuv.* viii. 208 Wide enough for a broad carriage-road. **1869** NICHOLSON *Zool.* xliii. (1880) 390 In many Brachiopods the arms are supported upon a more or less complicated internal calcareous framework or skeleton.. sometimes called the 'carriage-spring apparatus'. **1887** *Spectator* 5 Mar. 318/1 Carriage-builders and others interested in the *Carriage-tax. **1853** DOUGLAS *Milit.*

Bridges vii. 359 A very good substitute for a capstan may be formed of a carriage wheel. **1856** EMERSON *Eng. Traits, Wealth* Wks. (Bohn) II. 70 Two centuries ago.. the carriage wheels ran on wooden axles.

35. Special comb.: **carriage-bridge**, a military bridge running on wheels; **carriage-company**, people who keep private carriages; **carriage-coupling**, the coupling for uniting the fore and hind carriages of a four-wheeled vehicle, or for connecting the fore-carriage with the body; **carriage-cradle**, a luggage-rack; **carriage dog**, a coach-dog, a Dalmatian dog; **carriage-drive**, the roadway for carriages in private grounds, parks, etc.; **carriage-folk** = *carriage-company*; **carriage free** *a.*, free of charge for conveyance; used esp. as *advb. phr.*; **carriage-guard**, a guard to prevent the fore-wheels of a carriage from rubbing against the body in turning sharp round; †**carriage-gun**, a gun mounted on a carriage; **carriage-horse**, †(*a*) a horse used for carrying purposes; (*b*) one that runs in a carriage; **carriage-house**, a coach-house; **carriage-lady** (cf. *carriage-company*); **carriage-lock**, a brake for a carriage; **carriage-lubricator**, a self-acting contrivance for oiling a carriage wheel-box and axle; **carriage paid** *a.* (with hyphen) and *advb. phr.*, for which the cost of carrying has been paid; **carriage-piece**, one of the slanting pieces forming the support of the steps of a wooden stair-case, a string-piece (see 32 c); **carriage-step**, a step or set of folding steps fixed below the door of a carriage; **carriage trade**, (*a*) the trade of conveyance, carrying-trade; (*b*) trade or custom from those who use carriages, i.e. from the wealthy (Webster 1909); *transf.* (*colloq.*), wealthy people collectively; **carriage-way**, that part of roads, etc. open to, or intended for, vehicular traffic; cf. *dual carriageway*.

1853 DOUGLAS *Milit. Bridges* vi. 277 Neither bateaux, pontoons, nor *carriage-bridges can be conveyed. **1833** *Chamb. Jrnl.* No. 72. 155 Affluent merchants and tradesmen ..vulgarly denominated *carriage company. **1855** THACKERAY *Newcomes* ix. (D.) No phrase more elegant and to my taste than that in which people are described as 'seeing a great deal of carriage-company'. **1866** *Chambers's Jrnl.* 28 July 466, I saw [him] clutch at the *carriage-cradle above his head, as though it would have relieved his mind to climb. **1824** MISS MITFORD *Village* Ser. I. (1863) 221 The very *carriage-dog, Sancho, was individualized. **1863** MISS BRADDON *J. Marchmont* (Hoppe), A wretched equestrian making his way along the *carriage-drive. **1819** C. BROWN *Let.* 24 Jan. in *Lett. of Keats* (1931) II. 302 The whole of the family are *shuffling* to *carriage folks for acquaintances, *cutting* their old friends. **1952** W. DE LA MARE in *N.Y. Times* 7 Sept. VII. 30/2 They were carriage-folk, and thoroughly genteel. **1769** J. WEDGWOOD *Let.* 11 Nov. (1965) iii. 83 He delivers them safe, and *carriage free to London. **1873** *Young Englishwoman* IV. 131/2 The Little Yankee Sewing Machine..is delivered carriage free. **1742** WOODROOFE in Hanway *Trav.* (1762) I. II. xvii. 76 The ship..having six *carriage guns of three pounders. **1804** A. DUNCAN *Trident* I. 261 A French privateer..mounted 10 carriage guns and 9 swivels. **1596** DANETT tr. *Comines* 333 Their Estradiots tooke all our *carriage horses. **1647** LILLY *Chr. Astrol.* lvii. 381 The Carriage-Horse attending the Army seem serviceable. **1761** in F. H. Stewart *Notes on Old Gloucester County, N.J.* (1917) I. 316 Their fine *carriage house is finished and painted. **1883** ROE in *Harper's Mag.* Dec. 43/1 The drive passed to an old-fashioned carriage-house. **1837** CARLYLE *Fr. Rev.* I. VII. v. (D.) No *carriage-lady..but must dismount in the mud roads..and walk. **1771** SMOLLETT *Humph. Cl.* I. p. xv, I have sent an Almanack.. directed for him at Mr. Sutton's, bookseller, in Gloucester, *carriage paid. **1869** TROLLOPE *He knew*, etc. II. lviii. 68 A parcel..sent by the railway, carriage paid. **1894** *Daily News* 13 Nov. 5/4 Carriage-paid tickets, with which the carriage of letters for any place within the capital could be prepaid. **1970** *Observer* 29 Mar. 31/6 Tubular steel fruit cages... Immediate despatch. Carriage paid. **1848** DICKENS *Dombey* III. 211 (Hoppe), I put up the *carriage-steps. **1719** T. GORDON *Cordial Low Spir.* 274 These advantages..will give us all the *carriage trade of the Mediterranean. **1958** *Spectator* 25 July 136/3 For the carriage trade there is still polished mahogany. **1800** *Act 39 & 40 Geo. III* c. 47 §1 Where there is a regular Continuation of *Carriage Way Pavement from either of the said Cities. **1833** *Act 3–4 Will. IV*, xlvi. §116 Whenever the width of the carriageway in such street..will allow thereof. **1875** POSTE *Gaius* IV. §3 A right of horse-way or carriage-way through his land. **1957** *Times* 3 Dec. 7/7 Although the 16ft. carriageway is marked as two 8ft. lanes, in practice many of the larger lorries occupy more than one lane, so that the traffic at this point is often reduced to a single line.

Hence **'carriageful**, as much or as many as a carriage will hold. **'carriageless** *a.*, without carriage. **'carriagewards** *adv.*, towards a carriage.

1837 MARRYAT *Olla Podr.* xxxii, A carriagefull of children. **1872** BLACK *Adv. Phaeton* xviii. 244 A carriageful of luggage. **1861** TRAFFORD *City & Suburb.* I. 284 Accordingly, carriageless John Perman was..fain to hand his sister..into a Tottenham omnibus. **1871** *Daily News* 23 Feb., Some men hurrying carriagewards.

carriageable ('kærɪdʒəb(ə)l), *a.* [f. prec.: see -ABLE, and cf. *marriageable*.]

1. Capable of being carried; portable. *rare.*

1702 C. MATHER *Magn. Chr.* II. (1852) App. 196 What billets of wood were..carriageable for them. **1857** RUSKIN *Pol. Econ. Art* ii. (1868) 101 Works of carriageable art.

2. Practicable for wheeled carriages.

1813 WELLINGTON *Let.* in Gurw. *Disp.* XI. 44 There are only two carriageable roads across it. **1878** *Fraser's Mag.* XVIII. 699. **1884** J. COLBORNE *Hicks Pasha* 276 Carriageable roads might be made all over the country with little labour.

carriaged ('kærɪdʒd), *a.* [f. CARRIAGE + -ED.] †**a.** Having a carriage, deportment, bearing; behaved, mannered (*obs.*); **b.** furnished with carriages. Only with qualifying adv., as ***handsome-, ill-, many-, well-carriaged.***

1633 AMES *Agst. Cerem.* I. 131 A well cariaged man outwardly. **1650** W. FENNER *Christ's Alarm* 57 Any fine-carriaged man under heaven. **1664** PEPYS *Diary* 14 June (D.) A fine lady..and very well carriaged, and mighty discreet. **1710** *Lond. Gaz.* No. 4674/8 A brown bay Gelding ..handsome carriaged. **1883** *Daily News* 1 Mar. 5/3 A.. many-carriaged excursion train. **1887** *County Gentl.* 25 June, The Queen's guests were certainly well carriaged.

carrick, carrik, obs. forms of CARRACK.

'carrick 'bend. *Naut.* [See BEND *sb.*[1] 3. *Carrick* was a frequent variant of CARRACK ship of burden; and may have that sense here.]

A knot for splicing two ropes together, formed by looping the two ends to be joined, and interlacing them, each going at every intersection, now over, now under, the other.

1819 REES *Cycl.* s.v. *Bend*, For a carick bend, lay the end of a rope or hawser across its standing part, etc. *c* **1860** H. STUART *Seaman's Catech.* 2 Or a carrick bend, or a bowline knot.

'carrick 'bitts. *Naut.* [app. f. *carrick* = CARRACK ship of burden (cf. prec.) + BITT(S, q.v.]

1847 in CRAIG. *c* **1850** *Rudim. Navig.* (Weale) 103 *Carrick-bitts*, the upright pieces of timber near the ends of the windlass, in which are the gudgeons for the spindles to work on: they are also called 'windlass-bitts'.

ˌCarrickma'cross. The name of a town in Co. Monaghan, Ireland, used to designate certain forms of lace made there (see quots.).

1861 QUEEN VICTORIA *Let.* 23 Aug. in *Dearest Child* (1964) 346 A very pretty flounce... But it is not Carrick Mackross. **1864** *Morning Post* in B. Palliser *Hist. Lace* (1875) XXXV. 394 A lady's dress is described as having the train, and petticoat 'trimmed with Carrickmacross point lace'. **1888** A. S. COLE *Irish Art Lace-making* 6 Carrickmacross *Appliqué* Lace..stitched on to net (*appliqué*)..has an appearance somewhat similar to Brussels *appliqué* lace. **1919** R. FIRBANK *Valmouth* viii. 141 A rich muff of Carrickmacross lace. **1947** J. E. PETHEBRIDGE *Man. Lace* 11 Carrickmacross lace is the oldest lace made in Ireland. **1970** *Sunday Tel.* 22 Mar. 9/2 An industry that 10 years ago was..based on Irish tweeds, hand-knitted sweaters, and hand-made Carrickmacross lace.

carried ('kærɪd), *ppl. a.* [f. CARRY *v.* + -ED.] In various senses of CARRY *v.*; esp.

1. *Mil.* Of arms: Held in the position described in CARRY *v.* 36.

1833 *Regul. Instr. Cavalry* I. 28 Standing steady with carried arms. **1844** *Regul. & Ord. Army* 265 Remain with their arms carried.

2. *Sc.* 'Transported' or 'carried away' in mind; rapt, abstracted; not 'collected'.

1825–79 JAMIESON s.v., Jenny's gotten an heirscaip left her, and she's just carryit about it. **1825** E. IRVING *Let.* in Mrs. Oliphant *Life* 285 Sarah Evans..was somewhat carried in her mind if you remember. **1832** *Gloss. Waverley Novels, Carried*, in nubibus: having the mind fixed upon something different from the business in hand: having the wits gone 'a wool-gathering'.

carrien, carrine, -ing, obs. ff. CARRION.

carrier ('kærɪə(r)). Forms: 5 caryare, -our, 5–6 -er, 6 cariar, -ier, carryar, 6–7 -er, 6– carrier. [f. CARRY *v.* + -ER[1].]

1. a. One who or that which carries, in various senses of the verb; a bearer.

1398 TREVISA *Barth. De P.R.* v. lxi. (1495) 178 A veyne is berer and caryer of blode. *c* **1440** *Promp. Parv.* 62 Caryare, *vector, vectitor.* **1571** GOLDING *Calvin on Ps.* lxxiv. 16 The sonne as the cheef caryer thereof [*i.e.* of light]. **1580** BARET *Alv.* C 129 A carier of letters. **1592** *Let. Univ. Cambridge* in Payne Collier *Annals Stage* I. 292 The most ordinary carriers and dispensers of the infection of the plague. **1697** DRYDEN *Virg. Georg.* IV. 13 Winds..will drive The loaded Carriers from their Ev'ning Hive. **1844–57** G. BIRD *Urin. Deposits* 99 Blood-discs, the reputed carriers of oxygen. **1884** *Spectator* 12 July 913/1 To obtain carriers for the dead.

b. A bearer of a message, letter, etc.

1588 SHAKS. *Tit. A.* IV. iii. 86 What sayes Iupiter I aske thee? Why villaine art not thou the Carrier? **1598** —— *Merry W.* II. ii. 141 This Puncke is one of Cupid's Carriers. **1621** BURTON *Anat. Mel.* III. ii. 111, The very carrier that comes from him to her is a most welcome guest, if he bring a letter. **1774** GOLDSM. *Nat. Hist.* IV. viii, These birds are employed..as the most expeditious carriers. **18..** THACKERAY *Fatal Boots* xi, Being a letter-carrier.

c. *slang.* (See quot.)

1725 *New Cant. Dict., Carriers*, a Sett of Rogues.. employ'd to look out, and watch upon the Roads, at Inns, &c., in order to carry Information to their respective Gangs, of a booty in Prospect.

d. *Techn.* Applied to particular parts of instruments and machines which act as bearers and transmittors; in *Mech.* esp. a piece of iron in a lathe by which what is being turned is carried round in the machine.

1858 GREENER *Gunnery* 201 A carrier is then secured on a part of the plug that projects out of the breech-end of the barrel, and then put into the face-plate of the lathe, which carries it round. **1870** TYNDALL *Heat* iv. §114 As long as the rocker is able to communicate sufficient heat to the Carrier on which it rests. **1881** MAXWELL *Electr. & Magn.* I. 295 The moveable conductors are called Carriers.

e. A small low detached cloud, betokening rain. *local.*

1844 [see *water-wagon*, WATER *sb.* 29]. **1884** R. LAWSON *Upton-on-Severn Words* 23 *Messenger*, a small detached cloud (*cumulus*) floating low, and supposed to betoken rain. Sometimes called a Carrier.

f. A case in which letters, etc., are enclosed for dispatch by pneumatic tube. Also, a small light capsule for carrying messages, attached to a homing pigeon.

1872 *Min. Proc. Inst. C.E.* XXXIII. 7 The carriers for the reception of telegrams, letters, or light parcels, consist of small cylinders made of gutta percha [etc.]. **1876** *Ibid.* XLIII. 60. **1892** *Pall Mall Gaz.* 18 Aug. 1/3 The actual form on which the message was written is put into a little cloth box, called a carrier, and blown through a tube to the central telegraph office. **1908** H. R. KEMPE *Engineer's Year-Bk.* 253 The carriers in which the messages are placed consist of a cylindrical tube of gutta-percha covered with felt. **1920** *Blackw. Mag.* Dec. 762/1 He took a message form, wrote a few words on it, and taking a pigeon from the basket, fixed a carrier to its leg. **1969** C. R. HILL *Pet Library's Pigeon Guide* i. 16 In a small waterproof envelope were message carriers, message pad and pencil.

g. A vessel which conveys fish from the fishing-ground to a port or market.

1883 R. F. WALSH *Irish Fisheries* 16 Many plans of steam carriers have been devised and proposed... Amongst [them] is the vessel with false hold or bottom, which allows the water to pass through with a view to bringing the fish alive to market. **1896** *Daily News* 27 Feb. 8/7 The fish.. arrived in eight carriers. **1907** *Westm. Gaz.* 25 Feb. 6/3 The 'Speed-well', a steam carrier.

h. A device for filling the magazine of a gun or rifle with a group of cartridges; a charger.

1885 *Marine Engineer* 1 July 95/2 The carrier which draws the cartridges out of the belt, and deposits them in the feed wheel. **1901** *Westm. Gaz.* 21 Mar. 4/3 By means of the carrier the cartridges are dropped into the magazine receptacle and the empty carrier thrown away. **1903** C. B. MAYNE *Infantry Weapon* 139 This..can only be done by rapidly loading the rifle by means of groups of cartridges temporarily held together by 'clips' or by 'carriers', also called 'chargers'. [*Note*] The 'carrier', or 'charger', is a strip of tin that grips the cartridges by their projecting bases only; the 'clip' is a tin framework that, more or less, grips the whole cartridge-case.

i. A box, metal plate, or other contrivance attached to a bicycle or motor-cycle for carrying parcels, luggage, or a pillion-rider.

1885 *Naturalist's World* Jan. 6 A 'carrier' can be fixed on to the rod supporting the seat. **1887** BURY & HILLIER *Cycling* 201 Luggage..should be carefully affixed [to the machine] by means of one or other of the carriers described elsewhere. *Ibid.* 429 The Carrier Cycle. **1911** C. S. LAKE *Motor Cyclist's Handbk.* 253 Luggage Carrier and Stand. It is common practice to make the carrier of tubular material. **1915** B. E JONES *Motor Cycles* 137 A very light carrier can be fitted, as this machine is not strong..enough for passenger-carrier riding. **1967** N. FITZGERALD *Affairs of Death* ii. 20 The bicycle..was a new one;..to the carrier had been affixed a small bundle.

j. A substance used as a base or supporting medium.

(i) An insoluble substance (e.g. barytes, china clay, gypsum) used as a base to receive the colouring matter in the preparation of certain pigments.

1892 G. H. HURST *Painters' Colours* 268 The base or carrier exerts a most important influence on the value of the lake as a pigment. **1915** J. C. SMITH *Manuf. Paint* (ed. 2) 170 Many so-called lakes consist simply of a carrier..saturated with a soluble dye.

(ii) *Chem.* A supporting medium for a catalyst.

1923 E. E. REID tr. *Sabatier's Catalysis in Org. Chem.* §946 It is best to use the palladium precipitated on an inert carrier. **1943** H. GILMAN *Org. Chem.* (ed. 2) I. ix. 785 Asbestos has also been employed as a carrier for platinum black.

(iii) An inert gas used to convey volatile material, esp. in chromatographic analysis. Also ***carrier gas***.

1940 *Nature* 27 July 129/1 The vapour of the iodides at low pressure..and diluted with a carrier gas..was passed through a tube. **1955** L. B. LOEB *Basic Processes of Gaseous Electronics* ii. 185 Since carriers in gases are in constant contact with the ambient gas molecules, they partake of the random chaotic heat motions of the molecules. **1956** *Nature* 14 Jan. 84/2 Low-boiling materials prove difficult to remove from the carrier-gas stream. **1959** R. L. PECSOK *Gas Chromatogr.* i. 5 A carrier gas containing the vapor of a substance..is passed through the column.

(iv) A substance (usu. non-radioactive) that will carry a trace of a substance of similar chemical properties (but usu. radioactive) with it through a chemical or physical reaction.

1947 M. D. KAMEN *Radioactive Tracers* ii. 38 It is usual to add small quantities..of the element to be purified so that ordinary chemical manipulation is possible... Such material is called 'carrier'. **1950** *Thorpe's Dict. Appl. Chem.* X. 432/1 The carrier is simply a macroscopic concentration of an ion of similar properties to the tracer component. **1953** A. F. RUPP in J. R. Bradford *Radioisotopes* ix. 170 It is.. desirable to produce as many radioisotopes as possible by other processes in which they are obtained carrier-free, or

nearly so. *Ibid.* 183 Carrier-free separation of radioisotopes by adsorption of radiocolloids. **1959** C. E. FRANCIS et al. *Isotopic Tracers* (ed. 2) iii. 42 If this radioactive isotope is purified and separated from any 'carrier' or non-radioactive isotope of the same element, it is described as carrier-free.

(v) A substance that transports an ion across a cell membrane.

1957 H. H. USSING in Q. R. Murphy *Metab. Aspects of Transport across Cell Membranes* iii. 52 The principal property of the hypothetical membrane-carrier is to bind specifically the ion to be transported. **1964** G. H. HAGGIS *Introd. Molecular Biol.* vi. 181 The number of carrier molecules required to account for known membrane effects is so small that it may be impossible to detect their presence among membrane lipids by current chemical methods.

k. (i) *Chem., Biochem.* A substance that effects a transference of an element or property, etc. (See quots.)

1892 BEDSON & WILLIAMS tr. *Meyer's Theoret. Chem.* 214 Certain bodies act as carriers of chlorine in a similar way to the oxygen carriers. **1902** J. B. COHEN *Theoret. Org. Chem.* 368 If chlorine or bromine acts upon benzene in presence of a 'carrier', substitution occurs. **1921** D. LL. HAMMICK *Org. Chem.* 156 [The iron] probably acts as a halogen 'carrier', ferric bromide being first formed, and then 'handing on' bromine to the benzene molecules. **1929** *Biochem. Jrnl.* XXIII. 128 Will a hydrogen donator react with a hydrogen acceptor in the presence of their specific enzymes but in the absence of any intermediate hydrogen carrier? **1934** *Ibid.* XXVIII. 1819 These substances might catalyse carrier-linked reactions.

(ii) *Physics.* An electron, atom, or group carrying an electric charge.

1901 RUTHERFORD in *Phil. Mag.* II. 221 The velocity of the negative carrier produced by ultra-violet light is about the same as that of an ion produced by *x*-rays;..it behaves at low pressures as if it were identical with the cathode-ray carrier. **1902** —— & BROOKS in *Phil. Mag.* IV. 20 Excited radio-activity is due to the conveyance of radioactive matter of some kind on positively charged carriers, which travel through the air in an electric field.

(iii) *spec.* In a semi-conducting material: any of the mobile electrons or holes which carry charges.

1939 A. H. WILSON *Semi-conductors & Metals* iv. 47 Since the 'holes' behave in many ways like positive electrons, this question can be settled by measuring any quantity which depends on the first power of the charge of the carrier. **1945** *Jrnl. Appl. Physics* XVI. 564/2 Such 'holes' will give rise to a conductivity described by Eqs. (1)-(3) but the sign of the charge carriers will appear to be positive. **1946** *Chem. Abstr.* XL. 6907 (*title*) Measurement of mobilities of charge carriers in real semiconductors. **1964** K. W. CATTERMOLE *Transistor Circuits* (ed. 2) ii. 10 The main charge carriers, holes and electrons respectively, are called majority carriers.

l. (i) A person, animal, or plant that carries a pathogenic agent and acts as a potential source of infection without suffering from clinically obvious disease; sometimes restricted to organisms that are hosts of the pathogenic agent (cf. VECTOR).

[**1899** *Leisure Hour* 176/2 Two-winged flies..act as carriers of disease.] **1906** *Medical Annual* 182 Carriers [of diphtheria] without symptoms or demonstrable contact. **1908** [see TYPHOID B c]. **1910** R. ROSS et al. *Prevent. Malaria* 195 If the local carrier belongs to a species..which feeds almost entirely upon man. **1930** *Discovery* June 198/2 The human carrier of typhoid fever and other diseases... A person, himself immune, bears the germ of the disease and is capable of infecting other healthy but more susceptible persons. **1937** F. D. HEALD *Introd. Plant Path.* xvi. 319 A virus may exist in a plant without causing any external evidence of its presence, and such symptomless 'carriers' may yield the virus to insects feeding upon them. **1955** GAIGER & DAVIES *Vet. Path. & Bacteriol.* (ed. 4) vii. 152 Convalescent animals are often carriers... In some diseases ..the carrier state may remain for years and the animal becomes a danger to other susceptible animals.

(ii) *Genetics.* An organism that has a recessive gene for some genetic characteristic (as a hereditary disease) and so can pass the characteristic on to a descendant although not itself showing it.

1933 *Brit. Jrnl. Psychol.* July 7 An intermediate type of inheritance of mental defect in which the heterozygote or 'carrier' is recognizable as a dull person. **1944** DARLINGTON in *Nature* 5 Aug. 167/1 Viruses..[are] suppressed by some host genotypes and permitted by others... There are, therefore, 'susceptible' and 'carrier' genotypes... Infection of one susceptible species can take place from another through an immune carrier species. **1970** *Observer* 12 Apr. 25/4 It's estimated that every human being is a carrier for about half a dozen lethal and perhaps a dozen crippling recessive genes.

m. = *aircraft carrier.* Also *attrib.*

1917 W. L. WADE *Flying Book* 12 The big cruising sea-plane, operating either from port or from a seaplane carrier. **1919** L. R. FREEMAN *To Kiel* 114 Aeroplanes launched from the 'carrier' *Furious*. **1922** *Advis. Committee for Aeron., Techn. Rep. 1918–19* I. 29 A large amount of wind channel work has been done on models of different aeroplane carrier ships. **1958** *New Statesman* 28 June 822/2 Fighters and bombers operating from the fleet's three carriers.

n. *Telecomm.* An electromagnetic wave or an alternating current or voltage that is modulated by a wave, etc., of lower frequency representing the signal to be transmitted.

1921 *Jrnl. Inst. Electr. Engin.* Apr. 402/2 The most valuable feature of the high-frequency carrier-wave system is its adaptability to multiplex telephony. **1921** COLPITTS & BLACKWELL in *Ibid.* 412/2 Carrier-current Telephony and Telegraphy. **1922** *Encycl. Brit.* XXXII. 712/1 The high frequency current serves as a 'carrier' for the telephone current over the line. **1923** *Electr. Communication* I. IV. 16 In a carrier current system a number of telephone or telegraph messages are simultaneously superposed on a single pair of wires by means of high frequency currents of different frequencies on which individual messages are impressed. **1929** E. MALLETT *Telegr. & Teleph.* ix. 249 The frequency ω_1 is called the *carrier* frequency. **1931** *B.B.C. Year-Bk.* 437/2 *Carrier Wave*, the high frequency oscillations emitted by a wireless telephone transmitter. These are modulated during telephony. The analogy is that the telephony (music, speech, etc.) is 'carried' by the high-frequency oscillations from the transmitter to the receiver. **1933** *Ibid.* 443 The television signals are made to modulate the carrier-wave sent out by the broadcasting station. **1962** A. NISBETT *Technique Sound Studio* 254 Unless two carriers on the same wavelength have almost the same strength, the stronger 'captures' the area. *Ibid.* 267 Systems of carrier modulation in use are amplitude modulation and frequency modulation.

o. A carrier-bag.

1936 W. HOLTBY *South Riding* I. v. 58 Mothers with laden paper carriers. **1959** S. DELANEY *Taste of Honey* I. i. 7 Pass me that bottle—it's in the carrier.

2. a. One whose occupation it is to carry loads, a porter. Also in comb., as *water-carrier*, etc.

c **1511** *1st Eng. Bk. Amer.* (Arb.) Introd. 35/2 Cariers that go with the olyphantes, and cary our harneys and vitales. **1528** *MS. Acc. St. John's Hosp., Canterb.*, Paid for..the hay makers & cariars. **1688** R. HOLME *Armoury* III. 72/1 A Bearer or Carrier..attend Merchants Cellars and Grocers Shops, to carry their Goods..on their Backs or Shoulders. **1885** *Pall Mall G.* 25 Nov., His carriers, thirty Malays, are following.

b. (With capital initial.) [See quot. 1906.] A people of Athapascan Indians inhabiting British Columbia; a member of this people; also, the language of this people. Also *attrib.*

1793 A. MACKENZIE *Voy. fr. Montreal* 3 July (1801) II. vii. 284, I found no difference in their language from that of the Nagailas or Carriers. **1820** D. W. HARMON *Jrnl. Voy. & Trav.* 403 (*heading*) A specimen of the Tacully or Carrier tongue. **1845** C. WILKES *U.S. Exploring Exped.* IV. xiii. 480 This part..is inhabited by the two great nations of the north, the Takali, and Atnaks or Shouswaps: the former are also known by the name of the Carriers. **1846** [see ATHAPASCAN *sb.* 1]. **1890** FRAZER *Golden Bough* I. iii. 239 Amongst the Takilis or Carrier Indians of North-West America. **1906** A. G. MORICE *Hist. N. Int. Brit. Columbia* 6 Among the Carriers, the widow of a deceased warrior used to pick up from among the ashes of the funeral pyre the few charred bones..and *carry* them on her back in a leathern satchel—hence the name of the tribe—until the co-clansmen had amassed a sufficient quantity of eatables and dress skins to be publicly distributed..in the course of an ostentatious ceremony called 'potlatch'. **1921** E. SAPIR *Language* iv. 71 Athabaskan languages..including..Navaho..Carrier, Chipewyan. **1957** *Encycl. Canadiana* II. 253 The Carrier have not made a successful adjustment to European civilization.

3. a. *spec.* One who undertakes for hire the conveyance of goods and parcels (usually on certain routes, and at fixed times). The most familiar current sense.

In the legal sense the term *carrier* or *common carrier*, includes any person or association of persons undertaking, for payment, the transport of goods by land or water, as stage coach proprietors, railway companies, parcel delivery companies, owners and masters of ships, etc.

1471 *Will* in *Ripon Ch. Acts* 154 Rog. Brounfeld de Ebor', caryour. *c* **1500** *Cocke Lorell's B.* (1843) 10 Carryers, carters, and horskepers. **1533–4** *Act 25 Hen. VIII*, viii, The poore cariers..repairynge wekely and monthely to your citee of London. **1592** GREENE *Art Conny-catch.* III. 8, I haue..a Cheese from my Vncle..which I receiued of the Carrier. **1642** *Declar. Lords and Comm.* 31 Dec. 3 The robbing of the common Carriers and Trawnters. **1746** BERKELEY *Let.* Wks. 1871 IV. 308 My wife..sends you a present by the Cork carrier. **1774** JOHNSON *Let.* 29 Jan. in *Boswell*, If anything is too bulky for the post, let me have it by the carrier. *a* **1888** *Mod.* Inscription on Vans, etc.: 'The North Western Railway Company, carriers.' **1903** E. R. JOHNSON *Amer. Railway Transp.* 124 A copy of the bill must be sent to each of the railroads..and to any freight association of which the carrier may be a member.

fig. **1583** BABINGTON *Commandm.* (1590) 455 Our senses, the common carriers of conceits unto us.

b. Applied to a nation or community who conduct the commerce between distant parts of the world.

1673 TEMPLE *Observ. Unit. Prov.* Wks. 1731 I. 60 Their Sea-men being, as they have properly been call'd, the common Carriers of the World. **1776** ADAM SMITH *W.N.* IV. ii, The Dutch were..the great carriers of Europe. **1861** GOSCHEN *For. Exch.* 18 The country which becomes the carrier for others. **1875** MERIVALE *Gen. Hist. Rome* xvii. (1877) 98 The Carthaginians made themselves the common carriers of this vast population.

4. A CARRIER-PIGEON; also the breed of these, though not used for carrying purposes.

1641 WILKINS *Mercury* xvi. (1707) 68 A smaller sort of Pigeon, of a light Body, and swift Flight..called by the Name of Carriers. **1741** *Compl. Fam.-Piece* III. 512 The Carriers [are valuable] for their swift Return home, if carried to a Distance. **1859** DARWIN *Orig. Spec.* xi. (1873) 306 Varieties between the rock-pigeon and the carrier. **1862** HUXLEY *Lect. Wrkg. Men* 105 'Homing' birds..used as carriers are not 'carriers' in the fancy sense. **1867** TEGETMEIER *Pigeons* vii. 75.

5. A conduit or drain for water, etc. Cf. CARRIAGE 31.

1797 A. YOUNG *Agric. Suffolk* 157 A carrier or master drain, into which all the single drains empty themselves..I strongly recommend these carrier ditches to be open. **1872** *Daily News* 12 Oct., Liquid flows gently from the delivering carriers. **1883** *Pall Mall G.* 16 Oct. 4/2 This liquid..is lifted by a sludge pump into an underground carrier and deposited in earth tanks.

6. With advbs., as *carrier about, on*; cf. CARRY *v.*

1556 T. HOBY tr. *Castiglione's Courtyer* II. (1561) N iij b, No carier about of trifling newes. *c* **1661** *Argyle's Last Will, &c.* in *Harl. Misc.* (1746) VIII. 30/2 A most indefatigable Carrier on of his Designs. **1884** in *Law Times Rep.* 8 Mar. 45/2 The carriers on of the business.

7. *Comb.*, as ***carrier-block, -pin, -rocket***; **carrier-bag**, a strong (usu. paper) bag fitted with a handle; **carrier-based** or **-borne** *a.*, of aircraft: operating from or accommodated on an aircraft-carrier; **carrier-bird**, applied to the pelican, the carrier-pigeon; **carrier-shell, -trochus**, a genus of molluscs, remarkable for the habit of attaching pieces of stone, coral, etc., to their shells.

1907 *Yesterday's Shopping* (1969) 339/3 The 'Sensible' *carrier bag. With strings..is the only paper Bag with a firm bottom, and capable of carrying wet fruit, pastry &c., without..bursting the bag. **1956** *Times* 7 Aug. 6/7 Most of the new arrivals stepped out of the train with nothing more than one small suitcase or a paper carrier-bag. **1935** *Flight* 9 May 498 American *carrier-based aircraft. **1968** *New Scientist* 1 Feb. 230/1 United States bases in the Pacific were warned to expect a carrier-based air strike..some days before the attack upon Pearl Harbour. **1801** SOUTHEY *Thalaba* v. iv, And journeying onward, blest the *Carrier Bird. **1850** TENNYSON *In Mem.* xxv, But this it was that made me move As light as carrier-birds in air. **1881** GREENER *Gun* 162 To throw the cartridges upon a *carrier-block in the rear. **1939** K. EDWARDS *Navy of Today* iv. 81 The number of *carrier-borne aircraft accounted for by the ships already building. **1884** F. BRITTEN *Watch & Clockm.* 104 Holes..to receive the *carrier pin. **1946** H. HARPER *Dawn of Space Age* p. vii, The large '*carrier' rocket would have a flat nose, and to this would be attached the small rocket. **1959** *Listener* 18 June 1057/1 The carrier rocket of the Russian sputnik. **1854** WOODWARD *Mollusca* (1856) 15 The *carrier-trochus cements shells and corals to the margin of its habitation.

'carrier-'pigeon. [see prec. 4.] A breed of pigeons in which the instinct for finding the way home is very strongly developed, used for bearing communications or letters. Also *fig.*

1647 R. STAPYLTON *Juvenal* 66 Letters brought by carryer-pidgeons. **1650** —— *Strada's Low-C. Warres* VII. 79 The antient invention of Carrier-Pidgeons. **1840** BP. E. STANLEY *Birds* v, Carrier Pigeons. These are a particular breed, which can be so trained, that when carried to great distances from the place of their usual abode, and turned out, they will find their way back. **1871** TEGETMEIER (*title*) Homing, or Carrier Pigeon. *a* **1856** LONGF. *Childr. Lord's Supper* 157 Prayer..the carrier-pigeon of heaven.

carrine, obs. form of CAREEN.

carriole ('kærɪəʊl). Also cariole. [a. F. *carriole* small covered carriage, = Pr. *carriol, carriola*, Sp. *carriola*, It. *carriuola*, med.L. *carriola* vehicula feminarum (Papias, in Du Cange), dim. of med.L. *carra* CAR.]

1. a. A small open carriage with a seat for a single person. **b.** A covered light cart.

1834 BECKFORD *Italy* I. 65 These goddesses stepping into a car, vulgarly called a cariole. **1860** *All Y. Round* No. 64. 334 Obliged to burn his carriole, or covered cart. **1868** HAWTHORNE *Amer. Note-bks.* (1879) II. 41 Through the curtain of the cariole. **1878** BLACK *Green Past.* xxxii. 257 The people shot by us in the light little carrioles.

2. A kind of sledge used in Canada.

1808 PIKE *Sources Mississ.* I. 68, I rode in a cariole, for one person, constructed in the following manner. **1820** SILLIMAN *Tour Quebec* 337 The Carriole..gaily careers over the frost-bound river. **1833** *Chamb. Jrnl.* No. 67 118 When 'beautified' with a little paint and a few trifling ornaments the sledge assumes the name of cariole.

Hence **'carrioling** *vbl. sb.*, riding in a carriole.

1884 *Sat. Rev.* LVII. 636 All carioling is not of this agreeable character. The tourist may now and again have to drive for many hours together through pine-woods, gloomy, monotonous, and empty of sound.

carrion ('kærɪən), *sb.* (and *a.*) Forms: α. 3 caroine, caronye, (charoine), 4–5 caroigne, -oygne, -oyne, 5 karoyne, -oigne; β. 4 caraing, 4–5 careyn(e, kareyne, 4–6 carayne, 5 caranye, 5–6 careine, 6 caraine, carrayne, -eyne, karreine, 6–7 carraine; γ. 4 karyn, 4–6 caren, caryn(e, 6 carrine, 6–7 carren, carring, 7 carran; δ. 4 karyun, 4–6 cariune, caryon(e, 4–8 carion, 5 caryonne, 5–6 caryen, carien, carrien, carryon, cariong, 6–7 carian, 6– carrion. [ME. *caronye, caroine*, a. ONF. *ca'ronië*, later *caroine, caroigne*, in central OF. *charoigne* (mod. F. *charogne*, and in other sense *carogne*, Picard *carone, carongne*) = Pr. *caronha*, It. *carogna*, Sp. *carroña*, pointing to a Romanic type **carōnia*, supposed to be a deriv. of *caro* flesh, but not regularly formed on the stem *carn-*. The phonetic history of the English β. and δ. forms is obscure.]

A. *sb.*

†**1. a.** A dead body; a corpse or carcass. *Obs.*

a **1225** *Ancr. R.* 84 þe bacbitare..bekeð mid his blake bile o cwike charoines as þe þet is þes deofles corbin of helle. **1297** R. GLOUC. 265 [They] slowe..eyȝte hondred & fourty men, & her caronyes [*v.r.* caroines] to drowe. *a* **1300** *Cursor M.* 22906 Ded þar gun his [a lion's] caroigne [*v.r.* carion, caroyne, careyn] li. *c* **1308** *Pol. Songs* (1839) 203 A vilir caraing nis ther non. **1382** WYCLIF *Hebr.* iii. 17 Whos careyns ben cast down in desert. *c* **1386** CHAUCER *Knts. T.* 1157 The careyne [*v.r.* careyn, caroyne, karoigne, caroigne] in the busk with throte ycorue. *c* **1440** *Promp. Parv.* 61

Caranye or careyn, *cadaver*. **1494** FABYAN V. cxxiv. 102 Y^e cource of the riuer was let by the multitude of the caryens or dede bodyes. **1590** L. LLOYD *Diall Daies* Oct. 51 The raven ..returned not, but fed upon the carrens. *c* **1645** HOWELL *Lett.* I. I. xx, Dogs which..eat the Carrens. **1718** *Free-thinker* No. 47. 342 The Raven..stay'd to prey upon the Carrions of the Dead. **1763** C. JOHNSTON *Reverie* II. 235 They all flocked about him, croaking like so many ravens about a carrion.

†**b.** = Applied to a dead man or corpse that 'walks' or returns to earth. *Obs.*

c **1430** LYDG. *Min. Poems* (1840) 143 Blissid Austyn the careyn gan compelle, 'In Jhesu name..What that thu art trewly for to telle'. **1483** CAXTON *Gold. Leg.* 174/3 Thenne the caryon broughte hym thyder to the graue.

2. a. Dead putrefying flesh of man or beast; flesh unfit for food, from putrefaction or inherently.

1297 R. GLOUC. (Rolls) 6544 þo ne vond he atte laste Noȝt of hom bote caroyne. *a* **1340** HAMPOLE *Psalter* cxlvi. 10 þe deuyl..fedis þaim wiþ karyun. *c* **1400** *Destr. Troy* 1972 Caste vnto curres as caren to ete. **1430** LYDG. *Chron. Troy* I. vii, Whan a beast is tourned to careine. *c* **1510** MORE *Picus* Wks. 25 Vile carein and wretched wormes meate. **1557** NORTH *Gueuara's Diall Pr.* (1619) 698/2 The wormes in carring. **1791** WOLCOTT (P. Pindar) *Remonstr.* Wks. 1812 II. 457 Like flies in Carrion. **1837** M. DONOVAN *Dom. Econ.* II. 127 The vulture..feeds on putrid carrion.

†**b.** ? = Death. *Obs.*

1387 TREVISA *Higden* IV. xxxiii, þerof cometh tweie manere of careyns, for we beeþ i-slowe wiþ wepoun, oþer we beeþ adreent. [Hence **1494** in FABYAN.] **1481** CAXTON *Myrr.* I. v. 18 They come the sooner to their ende and to carayne.

3. *transf.* **a.** Used (contemptuously) of a living human body; cf. CARCASS (? *obs.*). †**b.** The fleshly nature of man, 'the flesh' in the Pauline sense (*obs.*).

1377 LANGL. *P. Pl.* B. XIV. 331 Ne noyther sherte ne shone ..To keure my caroigne. *a* **1450** *Knt. de la Tour* xxvii. (1868) 39 To aorne suche a carion as is youre body. **1491** CAXTON *Vitas Patr.* (W. de W.) I. xxxv. 31 a, To leue thy careyne and folowe Ihesu Cryste. **1549** *Compl. Scotl.* xvii. 154 Our carions ande corporal natur..is bayth vile ande infekkit. **1596** SHAKS. *Merch. V.* III. i. 38 *Shy.* My owne flesh and blood to rebell. *Sol.* Out vpon it old carrion, rebels it at these yeeres. **1832** HT. MARTINEAU *Demerara* ii. 27 Much good may your tender mercies do your carrion.

†**4.** Used (contemptuously) of a living person, as no better than carrion. *Obs.*

1547–64 BAULDWIN *Mor. Philos.* (Palfr.) x. §1 It were better for a woman to be barren Than to bring forth a vile wicked carren. **1601** SHAKS. *Jul. C.* II. i. 130 Priests and Cowards, and men Cautelous, Old feeble Carrions. **1661** PEPYS *Diary* 15 Sept., Pegg Kite..will be..a troublesome carrion to us executors.

†**5.** Used of animals: sometimes app. in sense 'noxious beast', 'vermin'; sometimes merely 'poor, wretched, or worthless beast'. *Obs.*

1477 EARL RIVERS (Caxton) *Dictes* 142 The euill creatures ben wors than serpentes, lyons or caraynes. **1562** J. HEYWOOD *Prov. & Epigr.* (1867) 119 Daws ar carren. **1573** TUSSER *Husb.* xvi. (1878) 35 Let carren & barren be shifted awaie, For best is the best, whatsoever you paie. **1634** W. WOOD *New Eng. Prosp.* I. vi, The beasts of offence be Squunckes, Ferrets, Foxes. *Ibid.* I. viii, Having shewed you the most offensive carrions that belong to our Wildernesse. *a* **1639** W. WHATELEY *Prototypes* I. xix. (1640) 227 They [dogs and monkeys] be paltry carrions.

6. *fig.* Anything vile or corrupt; †corrupt mass; 'garbage', 'filth'.

1524 S. FISH *Supplic. Begg.* 18 Declaring suche an horrible carayn of euyll ageinst the ministres of iniquite. **1597** *1st Pt. Return Parnass.* V. i. 1455, I woulde prove it upon that carrion of thy witt. **1845** CARLYLE *Cromwell* (1873) I. 21 Flunkyism, falsity and other carrion ought to be buried! **1870** EMERSON *Soc. & Sol., Courage* Wks. (Bohn) III. 113 Melancholy sceptics with a taste for carrion, who batten on the hideous facts in history. **1879** FROUDE *Cæsar* xxiii. 402 *note*, Roman fashionable society hated Cæsar, and any carrion was welcome to them which would taint his reputation.

B. *attrib.* passing into *adj.*

1. a. Consisting of, or pertaining to, corrupting flesh. (Usually with some notion of contempt.)

a **1535** MORE *De quat. Noviss.* Wks. 101 No man findeth fault, but carrieth his carien corse into ye quere, and.. burieth ye body boldly at the hie alter. **1583** STANYHURST *Æneis* III. (Arb.) 77 A stincking Foule carrayne sauoure. *c* **1613** ROWLANDS *More Knaves* 30 Some carion beast, Whereon the Rauens and the crowes doe feast. **1860** PUSEY *Min. Proph.* 454 The carrion-remains should be entombed only in the bowels of vultures and dogs.

†**b.** As an epithet of Death personified; also of Charon. *Obs.*

1566 ADLINGTON *Apuleius* 62 Deliver to carraine Charon one of the halfepens, which thou bearest, for thy passage. **1587** *Mirr. Mag. Q. Cordila* xlvii. 4 By hir elbowe carian death for me did watch. **1576** *Parad. Daynty Dev.* (N.) Seeing no man then can death escape..We ought not feare his carraine shape. **1596** SHAKS. *Merch. V.* II. vii. 63 A carrion death, Within whose emptie eye there is a written scroule.

2. Applied in contempt to the living human body, as no better than carrion (cf. 3).

1537 *Surr. Northampton Priory* in Prance *Addit. Narr. Pop. Plot* (1679) 36 In continual ingurgitations and farcyngs of our carayne Bodies. **1563** *Homilies* II. *Excess Appar.* (1859) 316 Why pamperest thou that carreyne flesh so hye? **1577** STANYHURST *Desc. Irel.* in *Holinshed* VI. 14 By the imbalming of their carian soules with the sweet and sacred flowers of holie writ. **1606** SHAKS. *Tr. & Cr.* IV. i. 71 For euery scruple Of her contaminated carrion weight.

3. †**a.** Carrion-lean, skeleton-like. *Obs.* **b.** Rotten; vile, loathsome; expressing disgust.

1565 HARDING *Confut. Apol.*, Ye will haue your spiritual Bankets so leane and Carrien. **1580** HOLLYBAND *Treas. Fr. Tong.*, *Eslance*, as *chevaux eslancez*, carren horses. **1645–6** EVELYN *Diary* 28 Jan., My base, unlucky, stiffnecked trotting carrion mule. **1653** H. COGAN *Pinto's Trav.* xxii. §3. 79 Mounted on horses, or to say better, on lean carrion Tits that were nothing but skin and bone. **1826** in Cobbett *Rur. Rides* (1885) II. 82 The foul, the stinking, the carrion baseness, of the fellows that call themselves 'country gentlemen'. **1867** *N. & Q.* Ser. III. XI. 32/2 Then she called me all sorts o' carrion names.

C. *Comb.* **a.** attributive with sense 'having to do with, feeding on carrion', as ***carrion-bird***, ***-chafer***, ***-fly***, ***-hawk***, ***-kite***, ***-raven***, ***-vulture***; **b.** objective and instrumental, as ***carrion-feeder***, ***-nosing*** ppl. adj., ***-strewn*** pa. pple.; **c.** similative, as ***carrion-like*** adj. or adv., ***-scented*** ppl. adj. Also **carrion-beetle**, any beetle of the family *Silphidæ*, which feed on carrion; **carrion-flower**, a name for the genus *Stapelia*, also for *Smilax herbacea*, from the scent of their blossoms; †**carrion-lean** *a.*, lean as a wasting corpse or skeleton; *fig.* meagre, very deficient; †**carrion-row**, a place where inferior meat or offal was sold. Also CARRION CROW.

1817 KIRBY & SPENCE *Entomol.* II. xxi. 242 Those unclean feeders, the *carrion beetles (*Silphæ*, L.)..are at the same time very fetid. **1959** E. F. LINSSEN *Beetles* I. 159 Burying beetles, carrion beetles, rove beetles, etc. **1839** THIRLWALL *Greece* III. 137 Neither dogs, nor *carrion-birds, would touch them..so long as the pestilence lasted. **1816** KIRBY & SP. *Entomol.* (1828) II. xxiv. 386 The *carrion-chafers, and others of the lamellicorn beetles. **1855** J. JOHNSTON *Chem. Com. Life* I. 332 The Stapelias are called *carrion-flowers because of the disagreeable putrid odours they exhale. **1852** THOREAU *Summer* (1884) I/23 The Smilax herbacea, carrion flower, a rank green vine..It smells exactly like a dead rat in the wall, and apparently attracts flies like carrion. **1787** BEST *Angling* (ed. 2) 114 The Oak, Ask, Woodcock, *Carion or Down hill fly comes on about the sixteenth of May. **1796** WOLCOTT (P. Pindar) *Sat.* Wks. 1812 III. 395 Court-sycophants, the Carrion-flies. **1861** HULME tr. *Moquin-Tandon* II. IV. i. 241 Larvæ of the carrion fly. **1581** T. HOWELL *Deuises* (1879) 234 Art thou so fond, with *carren kyte to haunt. **1542** UDALL *Erasm. Apophth.* 245 b, Because it was so *caren leane. **1554** J. PROCTER tr. *Vincentius* To Rdr., How owgle and carrion-lean ye are to se. **1581** J. BELL *Haddon's Answ. Osor.* 135 So carrion leane in the knowledge of Scriptures. **1602** FULBECKE *1st Pt. Parall.* 74 It is better to haue a declaration too copious then carion-leane. **1710** *Brit. Apollo* III. 18. 2/1 He is so Carrion-lean. **1620** VENNER *Via Recta* viii. 189 It maketh them *carran-like leane. **1878** TENNYSON *Q. Mary* IV. iii. 171 The *carrion-nosing mongrel. **1589** COOPER *Admon.* 140 As *carren Rauens flye ..to stinking carcasses. **1728** SWIFT *Answ. Memorial* Wks. 1755 V. II. 173 The district in the several markets, called *carrion-row. **1829** SCOTT *Anne of G.* ii, The huge *carrion vulture floated past him.

carrion crow. [see prec.] A species of Crow (*Corvus Corone*) smaller and more common than the Raven, and rather larger than the Rook, which feeds on carrion, small animals, poultry, etc. It is the 'Crow' of most parts of England, and the 'Corbie' of Scotland.

1528 MORE *Heresyes* III. Wks. 225/2 We fare as doo the rauens and the carein crowes y^t neuer medle with any quicke flesh. **1774** GOLDSM. *Nat. Hist.* III. 122 The Carrion Crow is less favored by mankind. *a* **1811** J. LEYDEN *Ld. Soulis* xliii, And they heard the cry, from the branches high, Of the hungry carrion crow.

b. Applied by Dampier, Sloane, etc., to a Vulture.

1699 DAMPIER *Voy.* II. II. 67 Carrion Crows are blackish Fowls, about the bigness of Ravens; they have bald Heads, and redish bald Necks like Turkeys; and..are often mistaken for such. *Ibid.* Some of the Carrion Crows are all over white..The Logwood-Cutters call the white ones King Carrion Crows. **1802** BINGLEY *Anim. Biog.* (1813) II. 28 The Carrion Vulture..Synonyms. Vultur Aura. Linn. .. Carrion Crow. Sloane.

†**carrio'nere.** *Obs.* ? *nonce-wd.* [cf. F. *salière* saltcellar, *poivrière* pepper-box, etc.] A holder or dispenser of carrion, or of that which stinks like it.

1648 HERRICK *Hesper.* (Grosart) II. 184 Fie, quoth my lady, what a stink is here? When 'twas her breath that was the carrionere.

†'**carrionize**, *v.* *Obs. rare*$^{-1}$. [f. CARRION + -IZE.] *trans.* To turn into carrion, to corrupt.

1593 NASHE *Christ's T.* (1613) 43 Her Heart, her Lungs.. al are carioniz'd and contaminated with surfets of selfewill. **1623** COCKERAM, *Carionized*, stinking.

†'**carrionly**, *a.* and *adv.* *Obs.* Also 6 **carrenly**. [f. CARRION + -LY.]

A. *adj.* Of the nature of carrion; corrupt, vile, loathsome. **B.** *adv.* Like carrion.

1547–64 BAULDWIN *Mor. Philos.* (Palfr.) viii. §6 Pampering his carrionly carkasse. *Ibid.* 7 The rumor of no vice stinketh more carrionly, then the name of lechery. **1573** TUSSER *Husb.* (1878) 52 Such pestilent smell of a carrenly thing. **1609** BP. BARLOW *Answ. Nameless Cath.* 68 A Carrionly Curre.

carritch, -es ('kɑːrɪtʃ, -æ-, -iːz). *Sc.* [*Carritches* is a corruption of CATECHIZE *sb.* F. *catéchèse*, which has been treated as a plural, with sing. *carritch.*] = CATECHISM.

1761 *Mem. Magopico* 5 (Jam.) A blind woman..taught him the A, B, C, and the Mother's Carritch. *a* **1774** FERGUSSON *Poems* (1789) II. 112 (Jam.). **1818** SCOTT *Hrt. Midl.* xvi, I can say the single carritch, and the double carritch, and justification, and effectual calling. *Mod. Sc.* He knows the carritches thoroughly.

b. *to give carritch*: to take to task.

1776 HERD *Sc. Songs* II. 219 (Jam.) The very first night the strife began, And she gae me my carriage.

Hence '**carritch** *v. trans.*, to catechize.

1837 R. NICOLL *Poems* (1842) 83 The Minister..duly carritchin' the bairns.

carri'witchet, car'witchet. Forms: 7 carwhichet, -whitchet, -wichet, corwhichet, 7–9 carwitchet, 8 carrawitchet, cary-whichit, carry witchet, 9 carwhichit, carriwitchet. [Derivation unknown. Dr. Fitzedward Hall in *Mod. Eng.* asks 'can it be a corruption of F. *colifichet*?']

A pun, quibble; a hoaxing question or conundrum.

1614 B. JONSON *Barth. Fair* V. i. (1631) 69 All the fowle i' the Fayre, I meane, all the dirt in Smithfield, (that's one of Master Littlewit's Carwhitchets now). **1630** J. TAYLOR (Water P.) *Wks.* (N.) Devices..of planting the Ile of Dogs with whiblins, corwhichets, mushromes and tobacco. **1662** DRYDEN *Wild Gall.* I. i, A bare Clinch will serve the turn; a Carwichet, a Quarterquibble, or a Punn. **1669** BUTLER *Rem.* II. 120 Carwitchets, Clenches and Quibbles. *a* **1743** SAVAGE *Author to be let* §4, I..deal in clinches, puns..and carry-which-its. *c* **1750** ARBUTHNOT *Dissert. Dumpling* (N.) Conundrums, and carrawitchets,—at which the king laughed till his sides crackt. **1822** SCOTT *Nigel* xiii, Mortally wounded with a quibble or a carwitchet at the Mermaid. **1874** *Slang D. Carriwitchet*, a hoaxing, puzzling question.. as 'How far is it from the first of July to London Bridge?'

‖**carro** ('kɑːrəʊ). [Pg.] In Madeira, a sledge usu. drawn by bullocks.

1882 E. M. TAYLOR *Madeira* 198 Those Mount sledges, or *carros*, in which people are impelled down the steep Mount road at a very rapid rate. **1900** A. J. D. BIDDLE *Madeira Isl.* I. 118 The *carros* (bullock-cars mounted on runners). **1928** J. E. HUTCHEON *Things seen in Madeira* iii. 64 Madeira is indebted to Englishmen for two of these unique modes of conveyance, the bullock-carro, and the running-carro of the mountains. *Ibid.* 66 There are ox-carros and mule-carros. **1953** E. NICHOLAS *Madeira & Canaries* viii. 59 In the old days horses, mules, and bullock carros were used as a means of transport.

carrob, carroch(e: see CAROB, CAROCHE.

carrogh, erroneous f. CURRAGH, coracle.

carrol(l, -old, obs. ff. CAROL.

Carrollese ('kærəliːz), **Carrollian** (kæ'rɒlɪən), **Carrolline** ('kærəlaɪn), *adjs.* [See -ESE, -IAN, -INE[1].] Resembling, or characteristic of, the style of 'Lewis Carroll' (C. L. Dodgson (1832–98), author of 'Alice's Adventures in Wonderland'). So **Carrolli'ana** [see -IANA].

[**1899** S. D. COLLINGWOOD *L. Carroll Picture Bk.* vii. 321 (*heading*) Miscellanea Carrolliana.] **1907** *Westm. Gaz.* 25 July 2/3 There is nothing Carrollese about the lines. **1924** S. H. WILLIAMS (*title*) Some rare Carrolliana. **1927** *Observer* 3 Apr. 8 The book has the Gilbertian or, rather, Carrolline, title of 'Ships and Sealing Wax'. **1932** *Times Lit. Suppl.* 28 Jan. 49/2 The Carrollian heroine. **1963** *Listener* 14 Mar. 474/3 The King Shag, which, with Carrollian panache, makes its nest from guano, scurvy-grass, and mesembryanthemum. **1969** J. BROWN *Rhapsody of Words* 70 The Carrolline adjective galumphing. **1970** *Guardian* 10 Apr. 10/4 Membership of the society..includes most of the important collectors of Carrolliana in this country and abroad.

carrollite ('kærəlaɪt). *Min.* [Named from Carroll Co. Maryland, where found.] A variety of cobalt pyrites containing copper.

1887 DANA *Man. Min.* 181.

carrom, var. of CAROM, CARAMBOLE.

carronade (kærə'neɪd). *Mil.* [f. *Carron*, near Falkirk in Scotland (where originally cast) + -ADE.] A short piece of ordnance, usually of large calibre, having a chamber for the powder like a mortar: chiefly used on shipboard.

(Said in *N. & Q.* 5th Ser. II. 247 (1855) to be the invention of Gen. Robt. Melville.)

1779 *Admiralty Minute* 16 July (*MS. Record Off.*), Experiments having lately been made..of the utility of small pieces of cannon called carronades, and the Comptroller of the Navy..having recommended the use of them. **1781** *Gentl. Mag.* LI. 485 Trials were made of an hundred pound carronade, mounted on a battery at Leith. **1809** WELLINGTON *Let.* in Gurw. *Disp.* IV. 439 You have omitted to require carriages for the carronades. **1833** MARRYAT *P. Simple* (1863) 131 Our large boats had carronades mounted in their bows. **1858** GREENER *Gunnery* 67 Carronades..short..ordnance without trunnions, but fastened by a loop under the reinforce. **1861** SMILES *Engineers* II. 61 The manufacture of carronades or 'smashers' at the Carron works.

attrib. **1833** MARRYAT *P. Simple* (1863) 52 To take a seat upon the carronade slides.

carron oil. [From *Carron* ironworks, where much used.] A liniment composed of equal parts of linseed oil and lime water (*Syd. Soc. Lex.*).

1884 *Chamb. Jrnl.* 4 Oct. 655/2 The best thing to apply to a burned or scalded part is Carron oil spread on lint.

carroon, var. of CAROON[1].

carrot (ˈkærət), *sb.* Forms: 6 caret, carete, carette, carot, carote, carotte, 6–7 carret, 7 carrat, carroote, 7– carrot. [a. F. *carotte*:—L. *carōta*; ad. Gr. καρωτόν ? f. κάρā head, top. (Cf. κεφαλωτόν, headed, said of plants, as garlic.)]

1. An umbelliferous plant (*Daucus Carota*) having a large, tapering root, which in cultivation is bright red, fleshy, sweet, and edible.

1538 TURNER *Libellus*, Daucus creticus..mihi uidetur anglis esse, *Wylde carot.* **1548** —— *Names of Herbes* 60 Carettes growe in al countreis in plentie. **1565–78** COOPER *Thesaur.*, *Carota*..the wilde caret. **1794** MARTYN *Rousseau's Bot.* xvii. 232 Carrot has a large winged involucre. **1832** *Veg. Subst. Food* 237 Unsuccessful attempts to change by culture the wild carrot into the esculent one.

2. a. Usually, the edible root itself. *fig.* (with allusion to the proverbial method of tempting a donkey to move by dangling a carrot before it) an enticement, a promised or expected reward; freq. contrasted with 'stick' (= punishment) as the alternative.

1533 ELYOT *Cast. Helthe* (1541) 28 Parsnepes and carettes..do nourishe with better iuyce than the other rootes. **1634** *Althorp MS.* in Simpkinson *Washingtons* Introd. 26 Parsenipps and carrootes. **1776** JOHNSON in *Boswell* (1887) II. 439 You would not value the finest head cut upon a carrot. **1783** COWPER *Epit. Hare*, Slic'd carrot pleas'd him well. **1832** *Veg. Subst. Food* 244 The quantity of nutritive matter..in the whole weight of carrot, being 98 parts in 1000. **1895** *Westm. Gaz.* 24 Aug. 2/2 Among other carrots dangled before the electors last month was Bimetallism. **1916** E. W. GREGORY *Furnit. Collector* 228 The spectacle of an otherwise intellectual individual engaged in trying to plumb the depths of duplicity to which dealers can descend in faking old furniture is like that of the donkey pressing eagerly forward after the dangling carrot. It would..be very pleasant to possess the carrot of complete knowledge, but the conditions render it impossible. **1948** *Economist* 11 Dec. 957/2 The material shrinkage of rewards and the lightening of penalties, the whittling away of stick and carrot. **1954** J. A. C. BROWN *Social Psychol. of Industry* i. 15 The tacit implication that..most men..are..solely motivated by fear or greed (a motive now described as 'the carrot or the stick'). **1963** *Listener* 21 Feb. 321/2 Once Gomulka had thrown away the stick of collectivization, he was compelled to rely on the carrot of a price system favourable to the peasant.

b. Something shaped like a carrot; a plug. Chiefly *U.S.*

1646 SIR J. TEMPLE *Irish Rebell.* 106 The Rebels..put a gag or carret in the said Master Bingham's mouth. **1808** PIKE *Sources Mississ.* I. 17, I..presented him with two carrots of tobacco. **1857** *Trans. Ill. Agric. Soc.* II. 360 The creoles manufactured the tobacco into carrots, as they were called. A carrot is a roll of tobacco twelve or fifteen inches long, and three or four inches in diameter at the middle of the roll, and tapered towards each end. **1890** *Congress. Rec.* 27 Aug. 9213/2, I have here some carots [*sic*] of Cuban tobacco.

3. *pl.* Applied humorously or derisively to 'red' or 'carroty' hair, or to one who has such hair. (In the latter case used like a proper name.)

c **1685** *Yng. Man's Counsellour*, *Roxb. Ball.* II. 559 The Carrots I'd like to forgot, which is the worst colour of all. **1685** S. WESLEY *Maggots* 57 The Ancients..Pure Carrots call'd pure threads of beaten gold. **1690** B. E. *Dict. Cant. Crew*, *Carrots*, Red hair'd People. **1775** SHERIDAN *Rivals* I. i, Jack Gauge, the exciseman, has ta'en to his carrots. **1876** MRS. MOLESWORTH (*title*) 'Carrots,' Just a little boy.

4. *attrib.* or as *adj.* = CARROTY. ? *Obs.*

1671 GLANVILL *Disc. M. Stubbe* 28 If I had said your head was Red, I had not been such a Liar neither; it was direct Carrot. *c* **1680** *Roxburgh Ball.* (1886) VI. 219 The Carrot pate be sure you hate, for she'l be true to no man. **1710** PALMER *Proverbs* 114 To picture Judas with..a squint eye..a carrot beard. **1877** BLACKIE *Wise Men* 95 The roving Scythian, with his carrot curls.

5. *Comb.*, as ***carrot-coloured***, ***-eating***, ***-headed***, ***-pated*** adjs., ***carrot-fly***, ***-poultice***, ***-root***, ***-seed***; **carrot (rust) fly**, a small fly (*Psila rosæ*) whose larva feeds mainly on carrots; **carrot-tree**, an umbelliferous shrub (*Monizia edulis*) with an edible root, found in Deserta Grande, an uninhabited island S.E. of Madeira.

a **1659** CLEVELAND *Smectymn.* 63 Robson and French..May tire their *Carret-Bunch. **1684** *Lond. Gaz.* No. 1935/4 A *Carrot coloured Beard and Hair. **1672** DAVENANT *News fr. Plymouth* (1673) 13 These *Carrot-eating Dutch. **1840** J. & M. LOUDON tr. *Kollar's Treat. Insects* II. 161 The larva of the *carrot-fly is cylindrical. **1882** *Garden* 1 Apr. 219/1 The Carrot fly (*Psila rosæ*) is one of the true flies. **1951** COLYER & HAMMOND *Flies Brit. Isles* xv. 197 The common Carrot Fly or Carrot-rust Fly, an agricultural pest of some significance. **1719** D'URFEY *Pills* II. 323 Confound the *Carrot Pated Jade. **1808** *Med. Jrnl.* XIX. 349 The *carrot poultice..would perhaps be useful. **1595** *Househ. Bk. Earl Cumbrld* in Whitaker *Hist. Craven* (1812) 320 Pd. for vi cabishes, and some *caret roots bought at Hull, 11*s*. **1831** J. DAVIES *Manual Mat. Med.* 187 Carrot Root..has been employed in decoction as a stimulant. **1832** *Veg. Subst. Food* 242 *Carrot-seed is raised..in Essex. **1866** *Treas. Bot.* II. 750 The *Carrot-tree, has a crooked woody stem one to four feet high..The orchil-gatherers and fishermen..eat the roots.

carrot (ˈkærət), *v.* [f. the sb., from the yellow colour imparted to the fur.] *trans.* To treat (fur) with nitrate of mercury (see quot. 1906). Cf. CARROTING *vbl. sb.* and SECRETAGE.

1862 *Chambers's Encycl.* IV. 560/1 Furs have their felting property sometimes increased by the process of *carroting*, in which the action of heat is combined with that of sulphuric acid. **1879** *Encycl. Brit.* IX. 837/1 Furs..of the hare and the rabbit,..dressed, carroted, and cut from the skin. **1906** WATSON SMITH *Chem. Hat Manuf.* 17 The *sécretage* or 'carrotting' process..consists in a treatment with a solution of mercuric nitrate in nitric acid, in order to improve the felting qualities of the fur.

ˈcarrotiness. [f. CARROTY + -NESS.] Carroty quality or colour, 'redness of hair' (J.).

1730–6 BAILEY, *Carotiness.* **1755** in JOHNSON.

ˈcarroting, *vbl. sb.* (See quot.)

1880 *Libr. Univ. Knowl.* VII. 357 Furs intended for felting..are treated with a solution of nitrate of mercury, an operation called carroting or secretage.

carroty (ˈkærətɪ), *a.* [f. CARROT *sb.* + -Y[1].]

a. Like a carrot in colour, red; said of hair. Also, of persons: red-haired.

1696 TUTCHIN *Pind. Ode* v. 18 Long was his Chin, and carotty his Beard. **1728** MORGAN *Algiers* I. iv. 106, I have never met with any North-Briton, Dane, or any other, more carotty and freckled. **1748** SMOLLETT *Rod. Rand.* xiv. (1804) 77, I had parted with those carroty locks. **1826** DISRAELI *Viv. Grey* VI. i. 276 Long, carroty hair. **1887** *Daily News* 9 Dec. 8/5 He was a tall, carroty man. **1912** C. N. & A. M. WILLIAMSON *Heather Moon* III. 297 The plainest, oldest, and carrotiest of the three red-headed maids. **1947** W. S. MAUGHAM *Creatures of Circumstance* 16 A shock of untidy carroty hair.

b. *Comb.* as *carroty-haired*, *-headed*, *-polled*.

1795 WOLCOTT (P. Pindar) *Hair Powder* Wks. 1812 III. 285 Poor Carroty-polled Phyllis. **1840** MARRYAT *Poor Jack* viii, A carroty-headed boy. **1856** THACKERAY *Christmas Bks.* 251 That carroty-haired Angelica.

carrouse, -ouze, -owse, obs. ff. CAROUSE.

carrousel, var. CAROUSEL.

†**ˈcarrow.** *Obs.* [Ir. *cerrbach* (mod. spelling *cearrbhach*) gambler. See O'Donovan's *Tribes and Customs of Hy Many*, 104, 122, where other Anglo-Irish spellings are given.] (See quots.)

1577–87 HOLINSHED *Chron.* I. 45/1 A brotherhood of karrowes, that proffer to plaie at cards all the yeare long. **1596** SPENSER *State Irel.* Wks. (1862) 527/1 There is another..much more lewd and dishonest, and that is, of their Carrows, which is a kinde of people that wander up and downe to Gentle-mens houses, living onely upon cardes and dice. **1829** SCOTT *Antiq.* Introd. 8 In the character of the Irish itinerant gambler, called in that country a carrow.

carry (ˈkærɪ), *v.* Forms: 4–5 carie, carye, cary, 5–6 carrie, 5– carry. [a. ONF. *carie-r*, mod. Pic. *carrie-r* = Central F. *charier*, *charrier*:—late L. *carricāre* to cart, convey in a car, f. *carr-us* CAR.

An earlier L. *carricare* in sense of 'load', became *carcare*, *cargare*, whence OF. *charchier*, *chargier*: see CHARGE. After this, was formed a new *carricāre* in sense of 'transport in a cart', which gave OF. *carier*, *charier*. Ultimately therefore *carry* has the same etymology as CARK, CHARGE, and CARGO.]

From the radical meaning which includes at once 'to remove or transport', and 'to support or bear up', arise two main divisions, in one of which (I.) 'removal' is the chief notion, and 'support' may be eliminated, as in 4, 5, and several of the fig. senses; while in the other II.) 'support' is the prominent notion, and 'motion' (though usually retained) may entirely disappear. Cf. 'Do not leave the carpet-bag here; carry it up stairs', with 'Do not drag it along the floor; carry it'. For the former *take* is now largely substituted.

I. To transport, convey while bearing up.

* *Of literal motion or transference in space.*

1. *trans.* To convey, originally by cart or wagon, hence in any vehicle, by ship, on horseback, etc.

[*c* **1320** in Dugdale *Monast.* (1661) II. 102 De libero transitu cum plaustris carectis & equis..cariandi decimas suas et alia bona sua.] **1330** R. BRUNNE *Chron.* (Rolls) 13987 He..dide þem carie to þer contres, & byried þem at here cites. **1489** CAXTON *Faytes of A.* I. xiv, Vpon cartis he shal doo carye wyth hym. **1538** STARKEY *England* 65 To the hole destructyon..of al other caryd in theyr schyp. **1611** BIBLE *Gen.* xlii. 19 Carry corne for the famine of your houses. —— *2 Kings* ix. 28 his seruants caried him in a charet to Ierusalem. **1719** DE FOE *Crusoe* (1840) I. ii. 18, I carried about 40*l*. in..toys.

spec. a. To bear a corpse to burial. b. To carry corn from the harvest field to the stackyard.

1466 *J. Paston's Funeral* in *Let.* II. 268 Geven to Martyn Savage..awaytyng upon my master at London be vii. dayes before that he was caryed, iis. *xd*. [**1526** *Pilgr. Perf.* (W. de W. 1531) 23 After that he..repeth it, byndeth it, shocketh it, and at the last caryeth it home to his barne.] **1801** BP. OF LINCOLN in G. Rose *Diaries* 1860 I. 427 Our wheat is all carried. **1851** H. MAYO *Pop. Superst.* (ed. 2) 170 It is a field of wheat, but it has been cut and carried.

c. *absol.* Said e.g. of a carrier.

c **1631** MILTON *On Univ. Carrier* ii. 18 If I mayn't carry, sure I'll ne'er be fetched. *Mod.* The common carrier who carries between London and Totteridge.

d. *intr.* (for *pass.*). Of soil: to stick to the feet, or to horses' hoofs.

1892 *Field* 30 Jan. 155/2 The frost..caused the fallows and seeds to 'carry' a good deal, and they could only hunt very slowly. *Ibid.* 156/3 An expanse of ploughed soil which 'carries' considerably.

2. a. To bear from one place to another by bodily effort; to go bearing up or supporting. So *to fetch and carry*. *to carry coals* (fig.): see COAL.

c **1340–70** *Alex. & Dind.* 725 ȝe..carien by costum corn to hure temple. *c* **1384** CHAUCER *H. Fame* 1280 Y saugh him carien a wyndmelle. *c* **1386** —— *Prol.* 130 Wel coude she carie a morsel. *c* **1449** PECOCK *Repr.* I. vi. 30 His apostlis..wolden aftirward carie fischis in paniers. **1511** *1st Eng. Bk. Amer.* (Arb.) Introd. 32/2 He [gryffon] wyll well cary in his neste an oxe. **1610** SHAKS. *Temp.* II. i. 90 Hee will carry this Island home in his pocket. *Ibid.* III. i. 25 Ile beare your Logges..Ile carry it to the pile. **1611** BIBLE *1 Kings* xxi. 10 Carie him out, and stone him. —— *Isa.* xl. 11 He shall gather the lambes with his arme, and carrie them in his bosome. **1711** STEELE *Spect.* No. 41 ¶6 Honeycomb..carried off his Handkerchief full of Brushes. **1791** 'G. GAMBADO' *Ann. Horsem.* iv. (1809) 83 A horse..which does not carry me at all in the same way he did the man I bought him of. **1816** SCOTT *Guy M.* xxiii, 'Dumple could carry six folk, if his back was lang eneugh.' **1884** MISS BRADDON *Ishmael* iv, The lad..carried the youngest on his shoulder across the sands.

b. *Falconry.* To bear a hawk upon the fist.

1826 SIR J. SEBRIGHT *Observ. Hawking* (1828) 35 The passage-hawk, when first taken, must be carried all day upon the fist, and fed at night by candle-light. **1881** E. B. MICHELL *Falconry in Min.* in *Macm. Mag.* Nov. 39 He [the young hawk] is 'carried' for some hours amongst men, children, dogs, and horses, so as to become accustomed to their presence.

c. *absol.* † *to carry double*: said of a horse with saddle and pillion. See also quot. 1677.

1577 HOLINSHED *Chron.* III. 813/1 They were put to carie and draw. **1591** SHAKS. *Two Gent.* III. i. 274 Shee can fetch and carry: why a horse can doe no more; nay a horse cannot fetch, but onely carry. **1677** N. COX *Gentl. Recreat.*, *Hunting* (1706) 17 When a Hare runs on rotten Ground, or in a Frost sometimes, and then it sticks to her Feet, we say, she *Carryeth*. **1678** BUTLER *Hud.* III. I. 569 A Beast..Which carries double. *c* **1720** PRIOR *Alma* III, To go and come, to fetch and carry. **1862** HUXLEY *Lect. Wrkg. Men* 105 The Carrier [pigeon], I learn..does not 'carry'.

3. Also said of a cart, wagon, railway train, ship, bicycle, or other vehicle; so running water carries bodies floating on it, or suspended in it, wind carries leaves, balloons, slates, etc.

1377 LANGL. *P. Pl.* B. XIX. 326 A carte hyȝte cristendome to carie Pieres sheues. **1590** SHAKS. *Com. Err.* I. i. 88 And floating straight, obedient to the streame, Was carried towards Corinth. **1652** EVELYN *Diary* 22 Mar., Flinging it into a rapid streame, it..carried away the sand, etc. **1803** *Med. Jrnl.* X. 363 Blood carries with it the basis of nutrition. *Mod.* This tricycle has carried me five thousand miles.

4. To bear or take (a letter, message, report, news, and the like). (Without reference to weight).

c **1340–70** *Alex. & Dind.* 184 And bad him in haste To þe king..carien his sonde. **1591** SHAKS. *Two Gent.* I. i. 112 Nay Sir, lesse then a pound shall serue me for carrying your Letter. **1641** SIR E. NICHOLAS in *N. Papers* (Camd.) I. 53 He being dessigned to carry that newes. **1670** MILTON *P.L.* v. 870 These tidings carrie to th' anointed King. **1820** *Hoyle's Games Impr.* 467 On such complaint being carried to any one of the stewards. **1848** MACAULAY *Hist. Eng.* I. v. 600 The news..had been carried to the Earl of Pembroke.

5. a. To conduct, escort, lead, 'take' (a person) with one, without reference to the mode of transit; to 'take' (a horse, a ship) *to* a place, a given distance, etc. Now *arch.* and *dial.*

1513 DOUGLAS *Æneis* XIII. i. 57 The Troianis..by power of hie Jove ar hiddir cary. **1584** POWEL *Lloyd's Cambria* 79 Carieng with them the Archbishop. **1611** BIBLE *2 Kings* ix. 2 Look out there Jehu..and carry him to an inner Chamber. **1659–60** PEPYS *Diary* 27 Feb., My landlord carried us through a very old hospital. **1725** DE FOE *Voy. round World* (1840) 2 He that can carry a ship to Lisbon may with the same ease carry it round the world. **1750** BEAWES *Lex Mercat.* (1752) 795 The Japonese Pilots..come aboard and carry the Vessel into Port. **1758** JOHNSON *Idler* No. 6 ¶9 The lady carried her horse a thousand miles in a thousand hours. **1771** FRANKLIN *Autobiog.* Wks. 1840 I. 7 My father carried his wife with three children to New England. **1818** *E. Burt's Lett. N. Scotl.* I. 66 *note*, The Scots..talk of..getting on the back of a cart-horse, and carrying him to grass. **1822** J. FLINT *Lett. Amer.* 264 (Americanisms) Carry the horse to water. **1861** RAMSAY *Remin.* Ser. II. iv. 51 'Carry any ladies that call up stairs.' **1886** BURTON *Arab. Nts.* (abridged ed.) I. 286 As soon as it was dusk, the slave-girl came to him and carried him to the house.

b. *esp.* To take by force, as a prisoner or captive.

1584 POWEL *Lloyd's Cambria* 93 Caried him towards the ships. **1588** *Pittington Vestry Bk.* (Surtees) 27 Nicolas Yonger was carried to Littleburne about the rogge monie. **1597** SHAKS. *2 Hen. IV*, v. v. 97 Go carry Sir Iohn Falstaffe to the Fleete. **1665** PEPYS *Diary* 10 Aug., My she-cosen Porter..to tell me that her husband was carried to the Tower. **1799** S. FREEMAN *Town Off.* 99 Apprehend and carry him before a justice.

c. in *Backgammon*.

1820 *Hoyle's Games Impr.* 294 Directions how to carry your men home. *Ibid.* 296 Six and five, a man to be carried from your adversary's ace-point, as far as he can go, for a gammon, or hit.

6. a. ***to carry all before one***: (i.e.) like a body moving with irresistible force and carrying away or propelling everything in its course.

1672 R. WILD *Poet. Licent.* 35 Some men there be that carry all before 'em. **1848** L. HUNT *Jar Honey* vii. 81 That, indeed, carries everything, even truth itself, before it. **1878** Bosw. SMITH *Carthage* viii. 169 The Irreconcilables carried everything their own way.

b. To shoot down, 'bring to the ground'.

1653 H. COGAN *Pinto's Trav.* xlix. §1. 190 Having discovered this game [wild boars], we got as near to them as we could, and discharging amongst them, we carried two of them to the ground.

7. a. To transfer (a number, cipher, or remainder) to the next column or unit's place before or after, in the elementary operations of arithmetic.

1798 HUTTON *Course Math.* (1806) I. 23 To carry as many to the next figure as were borrowed before. *Ibid.* (1827) I.

161 The 1 to carry from the decimals is set down. **1825** in COBBETT *Rur. Rides* (1885) II. 35 You are to put down the 4 and carry 2.

b. To transfer (entries) from one account book to another.

1745 *De Foe's Engl. Tradesm.* (1841) II. 41 This carrying things from the journal..to the ledger..is called posting.

8. A channel, drain, pipe, etc. is said to *carry* water or other liquid or fluid, sound, etc.

1601 HOLLAND *Pliny* VI. xxvii, When it begins once to carry a more forcible streame it is called Tigris. **1607** TOPSELL *Four-f. Beasts* 389 The voice of a man carryed in a trunk, reed or hollow thing. **1749** FIELDING *Tom Jones* I. iv, A constant cascade not carried down a regular flight of steps. **1750** BEAWES *Lex Mercat.* (1752) 733 The Canal..serves to carry the water..to this city. **1878** HOLBROOK *Hyg. Brain* 55 The nerve filaments carry the will. **1886** *Law Times* LXXXI. 59/2 A 9-inch sewer, which carried the drainage from the houses into the main brick sewer.

9. a. A bow, a gun, or the like is said to *carry* an arrow, a ball, or other missile to a specified distance or in a specified way. Usually *absol.*; and *transf.* or *fig.*

1636 HEALEY *Theophrast.* 19 Hee, that saluteth a man as farre off as his eye can carry levell. **1643** SIR T. BROWNE *Relig. Med.* ii. §3 Scholars are men of Peace, but..their pens carry farther, and give a lowder report than thunder. **1644** NYE *Gunnery* (1670) 4 After you have made one shot, and find the Peece carry just over the Mark. **1869** PHILLIPS *Vesuv.* viii. 226 About as high as a crossbow can carry. **1870** LOWELL *Study Wind.* 377 A fine, telling phrase that will carry true.

b. *Golf* and *Cricket.* Of the ball, or the player hitting it, or the club, etc.: to cover (a distance) or pass (a point) at a single stroke. Also *absol.* Cf. CARRY *sb.* 4 b.

1875 R. CLARK *Golf* 213 The balls carried considerably higher than the weather-cock. **1887** W. G. SIMPSON *Golf* 155 Many prefer it [*sc.* a dragging shot] to an ordinary loft at shortish distances, the latter being more difficult within, say, thirty yards than when the player has further to carry. *Ibid.* 184 His game is easily insulted by being made to go round, or play short of, a bunker, it ought to be allowed to try to carry. **1903** J. BRAID in Benson & Miles *Bk. Golf* 30 At a greater distance where the mashie will not carry I should very often use an iron. **1929** *Morning Post* 17 June 16/2 Off the next ball—a full-pitch—he only just failed to carry the ring. **1953** B. LOCKE *On Golf* II. xvi. 117 It is important at times to be able to hit very high iron shots to carry formidable obstacles, such as big bunkers or even trees.

c. *intr.* Of sound: to travel or be heard at a distance. Cf. CARRYING *ppl. a.* 1 b.

1896 M. CORELLI *Mighty Atom* iii. 54 Lionel's voice could not now 'carry' far enough to echo the farewell. **1932** E. V. LUCAS *Reading, Writing* ii. 45 He [*sc.* Andrew Lang] had a voice that did not carry—'roupy' he himself called it. **1934** *Discovery* Dec. 354/2 The sound..carries remarkably well.

10. The wind is said to *carry* a ship along, which it drives or impels over the sea.

1526 TINDALE *Acts* xxvii. 17 We let doune a vessell and soo were caryed. **1565–78** COOPER *Thesaur.* s.v. *Nauis*, The shippe fleeteth beyng caryed with winde and sale. **1590** SHAKS. *Com. Err.* I. i. 110 Her part..Was carried with more speed before the winde. **1722** WOLLASTON *Relig. Nat.* v. 99 The wind, which carries one into the port, drives another back to sea. **1737** POPE *Horace's Epist.* I. vi. 70 Where winds can carry, or where waves can roll.

11. To cause to go or come.

a. The impelling moral cause or motive is said to *carry* one to a place.

1876 GREEN *Short Hist.* v. §1 (1882) 213 A mission carried him [Chaucer] in early life to Italy.

b. A march, journey, a space traversed, is said to *carry* one to a point.

1871 FREEMAN *Norm. Conq.* (1876) IV. xviii. 240 The great march which carried Harold from London to Stamford bridge.

12. Provision, or money, which lasts out till one reaches a distant point of space or time, is said to *carry* one to that point.

1703 BURCHETT *Naval Trans.* IV. xxi. (1720) 553 They intended to take in Provisions, being so much streighten'd that they had not enough to carry them to the Havana. **1855** MACAULAY *Hist. Eng.* IV. 695 A scanty stock of silver, which ..was to carry the nation through the summer.

13. *fig.* To continue to have with or beside one, as one moves on; to 'take with' one.

1777 W. DALRYMPLE *Trav. Sp. & Port.* xxxv, A hollow way, which we carried with us to Aranjuez. *Ibid.* lxxxiii, We carried a mountainous country along with us, on the left hand. **1840** MARRYAT *Poor Jack* xlvii, We made sail, carrying with us three-fourths of the flood. **1857** *Merc. Mar. Mag.* (1858) V. 9, I carried a steady Trade [wind], all sail set.

14. a. To extend or continue (a line, a piece of work) in the same direction to a specified distance, or in a given direction.

1393 GOWER *Conf.* II. 112 Ne yet the mone, that she carie Her cours alonge upon the heven. **1704** WORLIDGE *Dict. Rust. et Urb.* s.v. *Lapis Calam.*, They should carry Air-shafts with them, as in Lead-Mines. **1715** DESAGULIERS *Fires Impr.* 32 Such a Pipe may be carried into a Bed and warm it. **1772** *Hist. Rochester* 28 [They] did not carry this tower to the height it now is. **1871** FREEMAN *Norm. Conq.* (1876) IV. xviii. 154 The defences were not carried down to the water. **1878** BOSW. SMITH *Carthage* 424 The man who.. could carry a wall from sea to sea.

b. *fig.* of things immaterial: as in *to carry to excess, too far*, etc.

1711 ADDISON *Spect.* No. 119 ¶5 This kind of Good-manners was perhaps carried to an Excess. **1728** T. SHERIDAN *Persius* v. (1739) 67 The highest, and most generous Notions of Friendship. How high does Cicero carry it in his first Book of Laws. **1878** MORLEY *Crit. Misc.* Ser. I. 194 He carries the process a step further.

*** With notion of taking away by force.*

15. a. To take as the result of effort, to win (as a prize), succeed in obtaining: also *to carry off.* (F. *emporter.*) Cf. 17.

1607 SHAKS. *Cor.* II. i. 254 He would misse it [the consulship], rather then carry it But by the suite of the Gentry to him. **1611** COTGR., *Enchere*..any Portsale, Outrope..wherein he that bids most for a thing is to carrie it. **1625** BACON *Friendsh., Ess.* (Arb.) 169 He had carried the Consulship, for a Frend of his. **1647** W. BROWNE *Polex.* I. 69 He alwaies fights alone, and alone carries the victory. *a* **1716** SOUTH *12 Serm.* (1717) VI. 379 Consider..what the Issue may be, if the Tempter should carry thy Choice. **1734** tr. *Rollin's Anc. Hist.* (1827) V. XIV. 312 He had carried the prize at the Olympic games. **1862** MERIVALE *Rom. Emp.* (1871) V. xlii. 169 He strove to carry with his own hand the victory.

b. Hence *to carry it*: to gain the advantage, win the contest, 'win the day', 'bear the palm'.

1580 NORTH *Plutarch* 621 Cæsar carried it by much. **1598** SHAKS. *Merry W.* III. ii. 70. **1601** —— *All's W.* IV. i. 30 It must be a very plausiue inuention that carries it. **1647** W. BROWNE *Polex.* II. 98 Love carried it from Jealousie. **1690** LOCKE *Hum. Und.* IV. xviii. §8 Revelation..must carry it against the probable Conjectures of Reason. **1779** FORREST *Voy. N. Guinea* 181 The name Selangan carries it generally over the other [name]. **1870** GOULBURN *Cathedral Syst.* i. 7 Where the two come into collision, the second must carry it over the first.

c. So *to carry the day.*

a **1685** N. LOCKYER in Spurgeon *Treas. Dav.* Ps. xciv. 15 He returns, and then his people carry the day. **1855** MACAULAY *Hist. Eng.* IV. 429 The French King had..said that the last piece of gold would carry the day. **1879** MCCARTHY *Own Times* II. xix. 59 The phrase had carried the day.

16. a. To take away or win from the enemy by military assault (a town, position, ship, etc.).

1601 SHAKS. *All's W.* III. vii. 19 The Count..Layes downe his wanton Siedge before her beautie, Resolue to carrie her. **1622** BACON *Hen. VII*, Wks. 1857–62 VI. 129 The town would have been carried in the end. **1677** *Govt. Venice* 101 Dying of pure indignation that he could not carry the Town. **1703** BURCHETT *Naval Trans.* III. xix. (1720) 384 Lawson..pressed so hard upon De Ruyter, that he had like to have carried him. **1797** SIR J. JERVIS in A. Duncan *Nelson* (1806) 46 Boarded and carried two of the enemy's gun-boats. **1876** BANCROFT *Hist. U.S.* V. x. 444 Horne directed eight regiments..to carry this position.

b. *fig.* and *transf.* (Often with mixture of senses.)

1622 SPARROW *Bk. Com. Prayer* Pref., To court the affections and..by their help, to carry the understanding. **1868** FREEMAN *Norm. Conq.* (1876) II. ix. 340 They were words which at once carried the whole assembly with them. **1884.** READE *Perilous Secr.* xiii, Always kept his temper and carried everybody, especially the chaplain.

c. To gain (a district, etc.) in an election. (Cf. 17.) *U.S.*

1848 LOWELL *Biglow P.* ix. 124, I thought our ticket would ha' caird the country with a resh. **1905** D. G. PHILLIPS *Plum Tree* 122 We, our party, carried the state, as usual. Our legislative majority was increased by eleven. **1965** T. C. SORENSEN *Kennedy* viii. 212, I told him [*sc.* J. F. Kennedy]—mistakenly as it turned out—that he had carried California.

17. a. To gain victory for, to be victorious or successful against opposition with (a matter or measure for which one contends). Hence such phrases as *to carry one's candidate*; *to carry* (= win) *an election*, etc.

a **1619** FOTHERBY *Atheom.* I. i. §5. 7 Arguments.. sufficient to carry the matter. **1715** BURNET *Own Time* II. 9 If the King would have acted with the spirit that he sometimes puts on, they might have carried their business. **1723** WODROW *Corr.* (1843) III. 9 Several of the elders.. have carried a call for Mr. John Hepburn. **1848** MACAULAY *Hist. Eng.* II. 125 The government had been unable to carry its measures. **1870** STANHOPE *Hist. Eng.* II. xiii. 178 They carried their candidates in the centres of popular election.

b. frequent in phrase *to carry one's point*; cf. 16.

1699 BENTLEY *Phal.* 429 If I can carry this Single Point. **1759** FRANKLIN *Ess.* Wks. 1840 III. 416 The surest way of carrying his point. **1885** MRS. MACQUOID *Louisa* III. ii. 21 She had carried her point with her husband.

18. *esp.* To carry *a motion* in a meeting, *a bill* in a legislative assembly, etc.: to get it passed or adopted by the whole or a majority of the votes.

1666 MARVELL *Corr.* lix. Wks. 1872–5 II. 198 Upon division of the House..'twas caryed for the provisos being committed. **1682** N. O. *Boileau's Lutrin* IV. 147 Let faithful tellers take the Poll, and note the Ay's and Noe's; And if we carry't, then Sir! Down goes the Innovation, once agen Sir! **1837** THIRLWALL *Greece* IV. xxx. 135 This motion was carried, probably by a very small majority. **1863** H. COX *Instit.* I. viii. 100 The second Reform Bill was carried by a large majority. *Mod.* The remaining clauses were carried unanimously.

**** Of figurative transference.*

19. a. In a variety of figurative uses taken from 1 or 2, the subject, or object, or both, being things immaterial, or the motion not in space, but from or into a sphere of thought or action = take, conduct, transport, transfer, cause to go.

1526 *Pilgr. Perf.* (W. de W. 1531) 29 b, But at his ende, caryenge it out of this worlde with hym, he shall neuer dye. **1713** BERKELEY *Wks.* III. 189 If we carry our thoughts from the corporeal to the moral world. **1754** ERSKINE *Princ. Sc. Law* (1809) 257 Heritable rights may be carried from the debtor to the creditor either by, etc. **1818** CRUISE *Digest* III. 45 It does not appear that this case was ever carried to the House of Lords. **1857** BUCKLE *Civiliz.* I. ix. 589 [Private judgment] carried into politics, over-turned the government. **1885** *Act. 48 & 49 Vict.* I. §25 All sums received..shall be carried to the consolidated loans fund.

1662 *Bk. Com. Prayer, Collect 4th Sund. after Epiph.*, Such strength and protection as shall..carry us through all temptations. *a* **1778** CHATHAM *Lett. Nephew* i. 3, I will recommend to Mr. Leech to carry you quite through Virgil's Æneid. **1781** BURKE *Corr.* (1844) II. 438 The grand principles of justice and policy are not dear enough to us to carry us through the difficulties which we should encounter. **1873** BLACK *Pr. Thule* xviii. 280 The perfect independence of that gentle young lady..might carry her too far.

b. *to carry the war into the enemy's camp*, etc.: to move the scene of fighting to the enemy's camp, to take up the attack; freq. *fig.*; *to carry the war into Africa* (*U.S. colloq.*): to act aggressively, to go over to the attack.

1828 *Reg. Deb. Congress* IV. I. 1315/1, I shall not..act in mere self-defence. I shall carry the war into Africa. **1835** R. J. MACKINTOSH in J. Mackintosh *Life* I. 81 Nor was this production altogether defensive; the war was now and then carried into the enemy's quarters. **1845** *Q. Rev.* II. 162 Having in so far attempted to vindicate Condorcet, we carry the war into the enemy's camp by asserting that Lord Brougham's biography is obnoxious to all the charges. **1855** J. B. JONES *Winkles* 202 But the way to be redressed..is to carry the war into Africa. **1927** L. P. HARTLEY in C. Asquith *Black Cap* 47 'I don't think Rollo is slow,' remarked Jimmy, hoping to carry the war into her country. **1938** H. MCCLOY *Dance of Death* xx. 237 Her smile annoyed Basil. He carried the war into Africa. 'Are you aware that M. Pasquale takes morphine?'

20. To impel or lead away as passion does, or by influencing the mind or feelings; to incline, move, urge, sway, influence. Now usually *carry away*; cf. 46 b.

1577 *St. Aug. Manuell* (Longmans) 62 The soule..is caried with desirousnes, drawen with longyng. **1596** SPENSER *F.Q.* IV. iv. 34 Caried with fervent zeale. **1601** F. GODWIN *Bps. of Eng.* 335 Subiect to flatterers, who carried him to their pleasure. **1608** GOLDING *Epit. Frossard's Chron.* III. 152 The king..was altogether carryed by this man, in such sorte as he both neglected and hated his vnckles in respect of him. **1621** BURTON *Anat. Mel.* II. ii. VI. i. (1651) 291 We should moderate our selves, but we are furiously carryed. **1715** BURNET *Own Time* I. 556 That idleness to which youth is naturally carried. *a* **1844** CAMPBELL '*How delicious is the winning*' iii, Just as fate or fancy carries.

21. *to be carried*: to be rapt, to be moved from sobermindedness, to have the head turned. *Obs.* exc. *Sc.*

1561 T. NORTON *Calvin's Inst.* I. ix. §1 They are not caried with such giddinesse [*tantâ vertigine raptari*]. **1827** SCOTT *Surg. Dau.* iii, If their heads were not carried with the notice which the foolish people..took of them.

***** To conduct (a business).*

22. a. To conduct, manage (a business or affair), *arch.* Now usually *to carry on.*

1590 SHAKS. *Mids. N.* III. ii. 240 This sport, well carried, shall be chronicled. **1599** —— *Much Ado* IV. i. 212 This wel carried, shall..Change slander to remorse. **1607–12** BACON *Ess., Seditions, &c.* (Arb.) 395 When Discordes, and quarrells..are carryed openly. **1612** —— *Vain-glory* ibid. 462 If they haue neuer so little Hand in it, they thinke it is they that carry it. **1715** BURNET *Own Time* II. 193 The elections were carried with great heat. **1845** BROWNING *Soul's Trag.* (1868) 23 So will you carry matters, that the rest of the world must at length unite and put down, etc.

†**b.** Hence *to carry it*: to conduct matters, behave, act. *Obs.*

1601 SHAKS. *Twel. N.* III. iv. 150 We may carry it thus for our pleasure. **1625–6** SHIRLEY *Maid's Rev.* III. i, She will carry it so, that Velasco shall be suspected. **1671** FLAVEL *Fount. Life* iv. 9 The Lord seemed to carry it as one at a distance from his Son. **1742** RICHARDSON *Pamela* III. 306 Sir Jacob carried it mighty stiff and formal.

c. with extension *to carry into effect, execution, practice*, etc. (Cf. next.)

1731–59 MILLER *Gard. Dict.* Pref., Carrying this into practice. **1769** GOLDSM. *Hist. Rome* (1786) I. 483 [They] were appointed to carry it into execution. **1828** SCOTT *F.M. Perth* iv, He would find it difficult to carry it into execution. **1871** FREEMAN *Norm. Conq.* (1876) IV. xviii. 123 He did not tarry long in carrying his purpose into effect.

****** intr. or absolute uses implying motion.*

†**23.** To drive, ride, move with energy or speed.

1362 LANGL. *P. Pl.* A. Prol. 28 Coueyte not in cuntre to carien [*some B. MSS. have* kairen] aboute. *Ibid.* IV. 22 Thanne Conscience on his capul carieth forth faste. **1399** —— *Rich. Redeless* III. 301 Whanne realles remeveth and ridith thoru tounes, And carieth ouer contre. *c* **1450** HENRYSON *Mor. Fabl.* 58, I tuke my club and homeward could I carie, So ferlying as I had seene ane Fary. **1513** DOUGLAS *Æneis* VIII. iv. 100 In haist Hercules com at hand Wyth furius mynd careing ouyr the land. *Ibid.* XII. xi. 136 Lat ws follow that way, and thiddir cary.

24. *Falconry.* To fly away with the game or quarry. [so Fr. *charrier.*]

1615 LATHAM *Falconry* (1633) 14 Affirming that Doves will make Haggards carry: which is not so, for this is idlenesse and want of skill in their keepers, that causes them to Carry. **1677** N. COX *Gentl. Recreat.* (1706) II. 49 Should she be guilty of Carrying, yet by this means she will be reclaimed, and forget that Error. **1826** SIR J. SEBRIGHT *Observ. Hawking* (1828) 8 Less disposed to carry, *i.e.* to fly away with the game; a fault to which all hawks are more or less inclined.

II. To support, sustain.

** With more reference to motion.*

25. To hold, hold up, sustain, while moving on or marching; to bear. *to carry weight* (in

Horseracing): i.e. such additional weight as equalises the competitors.
1563 FOXE *A. & M.* (1583) 73 The myracles of the foresayde Helenus..how he caried burning coales in his lap. **1782** COWPER *John Gilpin* 115 'He carries weight!' 'He rides a race!' **1818** SCOTT *Rob Roy* iii, 'You ride four stone lighter than I.' 'Very well; but I am content to carry weight.' **1852** TENNYSON *Ode Wellington* 6 Warriors carry the warrior's pall.

26. a. To bear, wear, hold up, or sustain, as one moves about; habitually to bear about with one (e.g. any ornament, ensign, personal adjunct; also a name or other distinction).
c **1380** WYCLIF *Sel. Wks.* III. 266 Carie a swerd in a scaberge. **1601** HOLLAND *Pliny* XXXVII. vii, Rubies of India ..which carry the name also of Carchedonij. **1631** WEEVER *Anc. Fun. Mon.* 149 Deacons, for a difference from the Priests, carried a round wreath of white cloth. **1631** GOUGE *God's Arrows* v. §11. 421 More fit..to carrie a bush-bill rather then a battell-axe. **1703** BURCHETT *Naval Trans.* III. xix. (1720) 389 The victorious Fleet..under the Command of the Earl of Sandwich, who carried the Standard. **1875** JOWETT *Plato* (ed. 2) III. 46 We do not know whether they are to carry arms. *Mod.* He carries a snuff-box.

b. To bear within one, contain.
1509 HAWES *Past. Pleas.* xvi. vii, My sadde body my hevy hert did cary. **1748** SMOLLETT *Rod. Rand.* lxvii, A sailor having drunk more new rum than he could carry. **1880** *Daily Tel.* 3 Dec., Valuable carbonates of lead, which carry silver.

c. To be pregnant with.
1776 JOHNSON in *Boswell* (1831) III. 458 Mrs. Thrale is big, and fancies that she carries a boy. **1788** J. POWELL *Devises* (1827) II. 361 The mother supposed to be now carrying a third child.

27. To bear about (mentally); to have or keep in the mind.
1583 BABINGTON *Commandm.* 315 O let us carrie some greater care to observe His will. **1602** CAREW *Cornwall* 107/1, I carried once a purpose, to build a little wooden banqueting house. **1709** BERKELEY *Ess. Vision* §91 We ought to carry that distinction in our thoughts. **1878** MORLEY *Crit. Misc.* Ser. I. 195 To carry ever with us the unmarked, yet living tradition.

28. To bear as a character, mark, attribute, or property; to exhibit, display: **a.** to the senses.
1581 *Act 23 Eliz.* ix. §2 Whiche Coulers, althoughe they carrye a Shew of a good, true and perfitte Couler. **1596** SPENSER *F.Q.* I. i. 46 That Lady trew, Whose semblance she did carrie under feigned hew. **1633** BP. HALL *Hard Texts* Isa. xi. 15 That baye..carries the forme of a tongue. **1671** MILTON *Samson* 1073 His habit carries peace, his brow defiance. **1704** WORLIDGE *Dict. Rust. et Urb.* s.v. *Foal*, The same Shape he carries at a Month, he will carry at six Years old. **1791** BURKE *App. Whigs* Wks. VI. 30 Any writer who has carried marks of a deranged understanding. **1873** HOLLAND *A. Bonnic.* xv. 236 Both carried grave faces.

b. to the mind.
1589 PUTTENHAM *Eng. Poesie* III. xxiii. (Arb.) 279 Rude and vnciuill speaches carry a marueilous great indecencie. **1597** MORLEY *Introd. Mus.* 76 Make your descant carrie some forme of relation to the plaine song. *Ibid.* 114 These waies of double descant carie some difficultie. **1677** HALE *Prim. Orig. Man.* I. ii. 45 Something that carries a kind of analogy to Sense. **1693** *Mem. Ct. Teckely* Ep. Ded. 6 At this Day they carry the highest Value. **1845** STEPHEN *Laws Eng.* II. 576 The liability..may at first sight carry the air of hardship.

†**c.** To bear (affection, respect, etc.) *to*, *towards*.
1598 BARRET *Theor. Warres* II. i. 19 He ought to carie great respect vnto the Sergeant Maior. **1605** VERSTEGAN *Dec. Intell.* v. (1628) 147 The naturall affection they carried vnto the Country-men. **1709** STEELE *Tatler* No. 112 ¶2 To carry an universal Benevolence towards every Thing that has Life. *a* **1718** PENN *Wks.* (1726) I. 538 The Over-fondness some carry to their Opinion.

d. So, ***to carry weight, authority***, and the like. In ***to carry conviction*** there is a mixture of notions.
1613 SHAKS. *Hen. VIII*, III. ii. 233 Words cannot carrie Authority so weighty. **1662** STILLINGFL. *Orig. Sacr.* II. vii. §2 Such as do not carry an immutable obligation along with them. **1691** T. H[ALE] *Acc. New Invent.* 13 The Navy Officers, with whom it carries so much weight. **1729** BUTLER *Serm.* iii. Wks. 1874 II. 33 Conscience..carries its own authority with it. **1870** E. PEACOCK *Ralf Skirl.* III. 192 The voice almost carried conviction.

29. To bear or convey (a meaning, sense, etc.).
1651 HOBBES *Leviath.* III. xxxiv. 207 The sense they [words] carry in the Scripture. **1881** TYLOR *Anthrop.* vi. 162 The root, which carries the sense..is followed by suffixes strung on to modify it.

30. To bear implicitly or as a consequence; to involve.
1662 STILLINGFL. *Orig. Sacr.* II. vi. §5 Those predictions which have seemed to carry the greatest improbabilities with them. **1717** *Col. Rec. Penn.* III. 39 Understood to Carry their assent along with it. **1835** I. TAYLOR *Spir. Despot.* iv. 168 The determination of [these questions] carries..the question of ecclesiastical polity. **1877** F. CONDER *Bas. Faith* ii. 66 A positive judgment carrying immense consequences.

31. A loan, etc. is said to ***carry interest***, a bill to ***carry grace***.
1693 W. ROBERTSON *Phraseol. Gen.* 313 Corn carries a price, *Annona cara est.* **1711** *Lond. Gaz.* No. 4870/4 Notes carrying 6 per Cent. Interest. **1767** BLACKSTONE *Comm.* II. xxx, A contract, which carries interest. **1767** A. YOUNG *Farmer's Lett. People*, These little farms carry twenty shillings..an acre. **1866** CRUMP *Banking* v. 104 Bills or notes on demand carry no grace.

** *With chief reference to manner.*

32. a. To hold (the body, head, etc.) up in a certain way.
1583 BABINGTON *Commandm.* (1590) 352 Till hee and his counsell have brought his maintainers to carie but a small port. **1619** R. WEST *Bk. Demean.* in *Babees Bk.* (1868) 295 To carry up the body faire, is decent. **1723** S. MORLAND *Spec. Lat. Dict.* 12 His coming to an Estate makes him carry his Head so high. **1724** *Lond. Gaz.* No. 6258/3 Stolen..a Mare..does not carry her Tail well.

b. said of a ship.
1796 in Nicolas *Disp. Nelson* (1846) VII. Introd. 223* The Captain gets on..and carries a good helm. **1836** MARRYAT *Pirate* iii, 'How does she carry her helm, Matthew?' inquired Oswald..'Spoke a-weather'.

c. *absol.*
1829 *Lond. Encycl.* V. 194 A horse is said to carry well, when his neck is arched, and he holds his head high.

33. *refl.* **a.** To comport, demean, behave oneself. Also of conduct.
1593 BILSON *Govt. Christ's Ch.* 253 To carrie himselfe for a Presbyter. **1653** H. COGAN *Pinto's Trav.* xv. §3. 49 Let us carry ourselves in such sort, as they may not perceive we fear them as Enemies. **1719** *Col. Rec. Penn.* III. 86 Carrying themselves very rudely. **1847** L. HUNT *Men, Women, & B.* I. iii. 43 The way in which sheep carry themselves on abrupt and saltatory occasions. **1876** G. ELIOT *Dan. Der.* v. xxxvi. 331 She carried herself with a wonderful air.

b. of conduct or behaviour *to* or *towards* others. *arch.* or *Obs.*
1594 T. B. *La Primaud. Fr. Acad.* II. *Seneca*, How to cary our selues towardes our neighbours. **1668** PEPYS *Diary* 4 Nov., The Duke of York do..carry himself wonderfull submissive to the King. **1714** ELLWOOD *Autobiog.* 74 My Sisters..carried themselves very kindly to me.

†**c.** *intr.* (for *refl.*) To behave. *Obs.*
1634–46 ROW *Hist. Kirk* (1842) 95 He craved the advise of the Assemblie how to carie in the mater. **1673** O. WALKER *Education* 285 It is an action of very great Prudence to carry even between adulation and sowreness. **1726** WODROW *Corr.* (1843) III. 269, I hope the youth will carry so as he may not be ashamed of the God of his fathers.

†**34.** ***to carry a hand*** (***over, upon, to***): to treat in a specified way; so ***to carry an eye on***: to watch, oversee. *Obs.*
1596 J. NORDEN *Progr. Pietie* (1847) 22 We must carry a very short hand over our affections. **1622** MASSINGER, etc. *Old Laws* II. ii, I'll carry an even hand to all the world. **1633** T. STAFFORD *Pac. Hib.* xxi. (1821) 215 To carrie a strict hand upon the Commissaries. **1646** SIR T. BROWNE *Pseud. Ep.* I. viii. 30 If any man..shall carry a wary eye on..many other. **1723** S. MORLAND *Spec. Lat. Dict.* 12 To Carry a severe Hand over any one.

†**35.** To wield; ***to carry a*** (***great***) ***stroke***, to wield or have great influence. *Obs.*
1598 BARRET *Theor. Warres* II. i. 22 The Lieutenant..in the absence of his Captaine, carieth his roome, charge and command. **1633** BP. HALL *Hard Texts* Dan. xi. 4 To carry that sway and greatnesse wch that great monarch bore before them. *c* **1645** HOWELL *Lett.* (1678) 205 My Lord Wentworth ..carries a mighty stroke at Court. **1646** SIR T. BROWNE *Pseud. Ep.* VI. x, Though Sulphur seem to carry the master stroak. **1651** CULPEPPER *Astrol. Judgem. Dis.* (1658) 6 The time of the year carries a great stroke in this businesse.

36. *Mil.* To hold a weapon in the position for saluting.
1796 *Instr. & Reg. Cavalry* (1813) 239 Carry swords! Eyes —right! **1833** *Ibid.* I. 60 The men remain at 'Carry Swords', till ordered to 'Slope'. **1844** *Regul. & Ord. Army* 265 Reliefs are to carry their Arms when passing Officers who are dressed in their Uniforms. **1859** F. GRIFFITHS *Artil. Man.* (1862) 152 The officers recover and carry swords.

*** *With chief reference to sustaining.*

37. ***to carry sail***: said of a ship, or of those who work it. [F. *charrier de la voile*.]
1631 MASSINGER *Emperor of E.* IV. iii, You carry too much sail for your small bark. **1703** BURCHETT *Naval Trans.* v. xiii. (1720) 641 The Adventure..stood away with all the Sail she could carry. **1836** MARRYAT *Midsh. Easy* xxvi. 103 'I fear, sir, we cannot carry the mainsail much longer.' **1840** R. DANA *Bef. Mast* xxxi. 119 No one could say that he was slow to carry sail.

38. a. To support, sustain the weight of, bear.
1626 BACON *Sylva* §530 Carry Camomile, or Wilde Thyme..upon sticks, as you do Hops upon Poles. **1831** BREWSTER *Optics* x. 93 An armed natural loadstone, which could carry $1\frac{1}{2}$ Roman pounds. **1851** RUSKIN *Stones Ven.* (1874) I. i. 30 Main arches..carried by..pillars. **1875** BUCKLAND *Log-Bk.* 59 The thick skin which carries the hair.

b. said of plants.
1626 BACON *Sylva* §425 They will put forth many, and so carry more Shoots vpon a Stemme. **1712** tr. *Pomet's Hist. Drugs* I. 2 This Plant..carries its Seed in little Bunches or Clusters on its Top. **1828** STEUART *Planter's G.* 368 The Trees of the present year..all carried a healthy leaf.

c. To hold or keep on hand (securities, merchandise, a stock, etc.). orig. *U.S.*
1848 W. ARMSTRONG *Stocks* 10 It is nominally considered that the stock is meanwhile 'carried' or possessed by the seller. **1869** J. H. BROWNE *Gt. Metrop.* iii. 48 (Funk), Operators can..carry such an amount of stocks as astounds the weaker ones of the street. **1870** MEDBERY *Men & Myst. Wall St.* 77 When a broker agrees to 'carry' stock, he says, Seven per cent, unless the market tightens. **1898** *Westm. Gaz.* 14 Jan. 8/3 The only remedy we see..is for the sufferers to carry smaller stocks. **1917** TWYFORD *Purchasing & Storing* 325 It is not economical to carry in stock several variations of articles of a similar nature. **1930** *Publishers' Weekly* 11 Jan. 214/1 Mr. Brady explained that he did not carry the book. **1963** J. MITFORD *Amer. Way Death* 233 *Casket and Sunnyside* is carried in only six eastern libraries.

d. To maintain or keep up with financial (or other) support. orig. *U.S.*
1879 *Bradstreet's* 8 Oct. 4/4 He is forced to pay on loans necessary to 'carry' the farmer. **1883** *Harper's Mag.* Nov. 877/2 The men of business..have for years carried the New York Academy of Music. **1917** ATWOOD *Exch. & Specul.* 51 In common parlance the customer trades on a 'margin'. Expressed in another way the broker 'carries' the customer for all except a small part of the cost. **1931** *Times Lit. Suppl.* 19 Feb. 124/3 When the production period of capital goods ends, therefore, there will be no savings to 'carry' them, and the boom must end. **1944** *Ann. Reg. 1943* 157 The Central Government could not continue indefinitely to 'carry' a province to which Nature had given so generous a crop. **1947** J. BERTRAM *Shadow of War* VII. i. 211 If one man 'swings the lead' in a coal gang of four, the other three must 'carry him' by working all the harder. **1959** G. SLATTER *Gun in Hand* ii. 23, I been carryin ya all mornin.

†**39.** To bear, endure, 'take' (anything grievous).
1583 BABINGTON *Commandm.* (1590) 431 He is a slave to the thing that he gapeth for, and to make up his mouth he will cary any thing. **1605** SHAKS. *Lear* III. ii. 48 Mans Nature cannot carry Thaffliction nor the feare. **1679–1715** BURNET *Hist. Ref.* 351 Queen Anne did not carry her death so decently.

40. a. To bear as a crop; to sustain, support (cattle). Also, to maintain (a population).
1799 J. ROBERTSON *Agric. Perth* 166 The foot of every brook..carries amazing crops of lint. **1846** GROTE *Greece* (1862) II. xvi. 395 The cold central plain did not carry the olive. **1884** *Times* (weekly ed.) 12 Sept. 7/4 A grazing farm ..which is said to carry 600 head of cattle. **1905** *19th Cent.* Nov. 816 Mackay, with back country carrying about 15,000 people.

b. Of a journal, newspaper, etc.: to print (an article) in its pages. Also *transf.*, to broadcast. orig. *U.S.*
1926 *Publishers' Weekly* 22 May 1676/1 There are many towns in which the newspapers do not carry book reviews. **1927** *Ibid.* 12 Feb. 609 *Publishers' Weekly* of January 8th carried a letter signed by a committee of the American Booksellers' Association..which commented adversely on the Literary Guild. **1929** E. WALLACE *Kennedy the Con Man* iv. in *Red Aces* 178 We carry big ads. in all the papers. **1946** D. L. SAYERS *Unpopular Opinions* 128 Any proposal to control the branded goods..will be violently opposed (on the loftiest hygienic grounds) by the papers that carry the branded advertising. **1957** *BBC Handbk.* 73 The Light Programme carries the People's Service in the morning and the 'Sunday Half-hour' of community hymn singing in the evening. *Ibid.* 170 The German Service carried programmes and discussions on this subject.

41. To support (an inference, analogous case, etc.); to give validity to.
1835 I. TAYLOR *Spir. Despot.* vii. 298 The end being of infinite moment carries all means and makes all lawful. **1885** G. DENMAN in *Law Times' Rep.* LIII. 785/1 It is impossible to say that any one case is so in point as to carry this case.

42. *Cards.* To retain the cards of one suit in one's hand, while those of another are thrown out.
1744 HOYLE *Piquet* ii. 9 Which of these suits are you to carry? **1820** *Hoyle's Games Impr.* 121 (*Piquet*), Suppose elder-hand, that you have the ace, queen, seven, eight and ten of clubs, also the ace, knave, seven, eight and ten of diamonds, etc., carry the ace, knave, etc.

†**43.** To have (specified dimensions). *Obs.* [So F. *porter*, 'avoir telle dimension'.]
1601 HOLLAND *Pliny* II. 574 Another Obeliske, which carried in length a hundred foot wanting one. **1631** WEEVER *Anc. Fun. Mon.* 382 The height of the West arched roofe.. carrieth an hundred and two foot. **1670** LASSELS *Voy. Italy* (1695) II. 60 The walls shew you what compass it carried.

III. Combined with adverbs.
See also the preceding senses and the adverbs for non-specialized combinations.

44. carry about.
a. See senses 1–3, and ABOUT.
Mod. It is too valuable to carry about with you.
b. *trans.* To move or drive hither and thither.
1539 BIBLE (Great) *Ephes.* iv. 14 Caryed aboute with euery wynde of doctrine. **1611** —— *Hebr.* xiii. 9 Be not caried about with diuers and strange doctrines.
†**c.** To cause to revolve, set in motion. *Obs.*
1677 MOXON *Mech. Exerc.* (1703) 180 Wheels turn'd with Wind, Water, or Horses, to carry the Work about.

45. carry along. See senses of CARRY and ALONG.
1833 *Chamb Jrnl.* No. 70. 141 A stone bridge carrying along the road from Peebles to Selkirk.

46. carry away.
a. *trans.* = *carry off*, a.
[*c* **1600** SHAKS. *Sonn.* lxxiv, When that fell arrest Without all bail shall carry me away.] **1603** FLORIO *Montaigne* (1632) 432 A popular sickenesse..carried away an infinite number of persons.

b. To move forcibly from the firm footing of reason and judgement.
1570 HULOET, This thing rauished or caried me awaye, whether I would or no. **1587** GOLDING *De Mornay* Pref. 1 Their reason is caried awaie and ouermaistered by the course of the world. **1709** STEELE *Tatler* No. 151 ¶2 Woman-kind..are carried away with every Thing that is showy. **1879** FROUDE *Cæsar* xvii. 275 Carried away by the general enthusiasm for liberty.

c. To break off and remove by force. Also, to lose by breakage; and *intr.* Chiefly *Naut.*
1537 WRIOTHESLEY *Chron.* (1875) I. 61 Carriinge a parte of the house awaye with him. **1703** BURCHETT *Naval Trans.* v. xxii. (1720) 723 The best Bouer Ancher carried away with a Shot. *c* **1750** *Narrative Byron's Voy.* 4 (L.) We carried away our mizen-mast. **1840** R. DANA *Bef. Mast* xv. 41 Her jib-boom ran between our..masts, carrying away some of our rigging. **1853** KANE *Grinnell Exp.* iii. (1856) 27 We ran into an iceberg..and carried away our jib-boom. **1867** SMYTH *Sailor's Word-bk.* s.v., That ship has carried away her fore top-mast. **1881** *Daily News* 9 June 5/4 Something may carry away on board the leading boat.

†**d.** To win, gain for oneself, or as one would have it. *Obs.*

1581 NOWELL & DAY in *Confer.* I. (1584) C iiij, His wordes ..were [not] of sufficient credite to carry away such a matter. **1633** BP. HALL *Hard Texts* Hebr. ii. 2 Every transgression..carryed away a terrible judgement from the just hand of God. **1677** EARL ORRERY *Art of War* 157 Whoever keeps in Reserve a Body of Men..rarely misses to carry away the victory.

†**e.** *to carry it away*: to have the advantage, carry the day. *Obs.*

1598 GRENEWEY *Tacitus' Ann.* XIII. vi. (1622) 187 This opinion carried it away. **1602** SHAKS. *Ham.* II. ii. 377 Do the Boyes carry it away? **1633** BP. HALL *Hard Texts* Matt. xxvi. 25 Doe not thinke that either thy secrecy or impudence can carry it away without notice.

47. carry back.

trans. To take back in time by process of thought or retrospective action.

1722 DE FOE *Plague* (1756) 221 None knows how far to carry that back, or where to stop. **1876** GREEN *Short Hist.* ii. §7 (1882) 95 The legend..carries us back to the times of our own Ælfred.

48. carry forth. See simple senses and FORTH.

49. carry forward.

trans. To transfer from one column, page, or book to its successor, or to the next account.

1839 *Reply Lockhart's Pamph.* 97 Carry forward £41.478 15*s.* 5*d.*

50. carry in. See senses 1–5, and IN *adv.*

51. carry off.

a. *trans.* To remove from this life, be the death of.

c **1680** TEMPLE *Health & Long L.* Wks. 1770 III. 275 Old Parr..might have..gone further, if the change of country diet and air for that of the town had not carried him off. **1710** ADDISON *Tatler* No. 221 ¶2 A Fever, which..at last carried him off. **1878** SEELEY *Stein* III. 559 A serious cold, which in seven days carried him off.

b. To win (the prize, honours, etc.: cf. 15); so *to carry it off.*

1828 SCOTT *F.M. Perth* vi, Some of those who think they carry it off through the height of their plumed bonnets. **1882** PEBODY *Eng. Journalism* vii. 57 The North Briton carried off the palm.

c. To cause to pass; to take away the adverse effect of; to render passable.

1715 BURNET *Own Time* II. 177 They promised..to carry off his impeachment with a mild censure. **1863** GEO. ELIOT *Romola* I. iii, A rapid intellect and ready eloquence may carry off a little impudence. **1879** MISS BRADDON *Vixen* III. 152, I have not enough diamonds to carry off black velvet.

d. To bear it out, face or brave it out.

a **1704** R. L'ESTRANGE (J.) If a man carries it off, there is so much money saved. **1886** STEVENSON *Dr. Jekyll* i. (ed. 2) 8 Frightened too..but carrying it off, sir, really like Satan.

e. To take away, abduct, steal.

1817 JANE AUSTEN *Sanditon* (1954) viii. 405 If she could not be won by affection, he must carry her off. **1829** PEACOCK *Misf. Elphin* xi. 141 The mountain sheep are sweeter, But the valley sheep are fatter; We therefore deemed it meeter To carry off the latter. **1855** MACAULAY *Hist. Eng.* IV. 423 A body of constables..carried off the actors to prison. **1969** G. PAYTON *Payton's Proper Names* 266/1 *Lochinvar*, the hero of a song in Scott's *Marmion* who carries off the fair Ellen at her wedding feast.

52. carry on.

a. *trans.* To continue or advance (a proceeding) from the stage already attained.

1649 MILTON *Eikon.* Wks. 1738 I. 377 To carry on the solemn jest. **1774** J. BRYANT *Mythol.* I. 374 Which.. assisted to carry on the mistake. **1858** TRENCH *Parables* i. (1877) 68 They did but carry on the work which he had.. begun. **1876** GREEN *Short Hist.* viii. §5 (1882) 511 Poetic Satire had become fashionable in Hall..and had been carried on vigorously by George Wither.

b. To maintain, keep up, prevent from stopping.

1606 SHAKS. *Tr. & Cr.* II. iii. 174 He..carries on the streame of his dispose, Without obseruance or respect of any. **1707** FLOYER *Pulse-Watch* 32 The Circulation will be carry'd on more rarely. **1790** PALEY *Horæ Paul.* I. viii, They carry on no connexion of argument. **1813** JANE AUSTEN *Pride & Prej.* xii. 232 The conversation was carried on. **1856** BREWSTER *Mart. Sc.* II. ii. (ed. 3) 125 We at the same time carried on a regular series of observations. **1877** BROCKETT *Cross & Cr.* 34 The conflict which has been carried on for nearly three hundred years.

c. To practise continously or habitually; to conduct, manage, work at, prosecute.

1644 SLINGSBY *Diary* (1836) 127 Carrying on his business with so much success. **1712** ADDISON *Spect.* No. 305 ¶5 The last War, which had been carried on so successfully. **1748** *Anson's Voy.* I. v. (ed. 2) 61 Besides the battery mentioned above, there are three other forts carrying on for the defence of the harbour. **1791** SMEATON *Edystone L.* §101 Plan for carrying on the works. **1802** MAR. EDGEWORTH *Moral T.* (1816) I. 217 His trial must be carried on in open day. **1884** LD. COLERIDGE in *Law Times Rep.* 8 Mar. 45/1 Brickmaking, which is undoubtedly a business, was being carried on.

d. *intr.* (orig. *Naut.*) To continue one's course, move on. Also, in military use, to continue as before, resume the former situation or occupation; to proceed to carry out instructions, to 'go ahead'. Hence *gen.*, to 'keep going', to persist; to make the best of things.

1832 *Blackw. Mag.* Apr. 643 Carry on, carry on; reef none, boy, none. **1840** R. DANA *Bef. Mast* xxxiii. 125 As we were going before it [the gale], we could carry on. **1853** DE QUINCEY *Sp. Mil. Nun* Wks. III. 35 She carried on, as sailors say, under easy sail. **1909** *Daily Chron.* 24 July 4/4 'Carry on!' is a word they have in the Navy. It is the 'great word' of the Service... To-morrow the workaday life of the Fleet begins again, and the word will be, 'Carry on!' **1915** 'BARTIMEUS' *Tall Ship* i. 14 The ship..began to heel slowly over. The Captain..raised the megaphone to his mouth. 'Carry on!' he shouted. 'Every man for himself.' **1915** A. D. GILLESPIE *Lett. from Flanders* (1916) 183 All except the officers were just carrying on as usual, which meant that, except for the sentries, you could see nothing except boots sticking out from the dug-outs. **1915** 'IAN HAY' *First Hundred Thou.* xiv. 190 'Do you understand my order?' thundered the Colonel... 'I do, sir,' replied Blaikie politely, 'but—' 'Then, for heaven's sake, carry on!' **1919** —— *Last Million* vii. 97 I'm not one to ask for sympathy when there's others needs it more... Carry on—that's my motto! **1927** C. E. MONTAGUE *Right off the Map* 156 'We'll let the men carry on resting,' said Willan. **1932** 'F. ILES' *Before Fact* xv. 261 Linda said..'I want to talk to you.' 'Carry on, sergeant,' said Mr. Thwaite amiably. **1940** *War Illustr.* 19 Jan. 623 But War caught these essential transport toilers at their job, and in the good British spirit they—not perhaps without an excusable grumble—felt they could but 'carry on'.

e. To continue a course of conduct or relations; *esp.* (colloq.) to behave or 'go on' in some conspicuous way which one does not more minutely characterize. Also *spec.* (*a*) To behave, esp. to speak, in a rowdy, excited, or bad-tempered way; (*b*) to engage in flirtation, esp. of a dishonourable nature, to have an affair (with).

1828 MRS. ROYALL *Black Bk.* II. 27 They romped and squalled, and to use a Yankee phrase, 'carried on' at such a rate that he and Mrs. C. were greatly annoyed. **1856** WHYTE-MELVILLE *Kate Cov.* iii, How Lady Carmine's eldest daughter is carrying on with young Thriftless. **1863** BATES *Nat. Amazon* vii. (1864) 195 More drinking is then necessary..and thus they carry on for many days in succession. **1876** BESANT & RICE *Golden Butterfly* xxxv, She and I carried on for a whole season. People talked. *a* **1876** E. LEIGH *Gloss. Cheshire* (1877) 37 *Carry on, v.* 'She carried on shameful', *i.e.* she used very unladylike language, or she shewed bad conduct. **1886** STEVENSON *Dr. Jekyll* iv. (ed. 2) 37 Stamping with his foot..and carrying on (as the maid described it) like a madman. **1892** R. L. STEVENSON *Uma* i, in *Illustr. London News* 2 July 11/1 What's she carrying on about? *Ibid.* ii, 9 July 42/1 There was Adams in the middle, gone luny again, and carrying on about copra like a born fool. **1930** W. S. MAUGHAM *Cakes & Ale* viii. 92 It was impossible that she could be 'carrying on' with Lord George. **1947** 'N. SHUTE' *Chequer Board* 4 She don't half carry on about the beer I drink.

53. carry out. (See senses 1–5, and OUT.)

†**a.** *trans.* To transport (the mind) in ecstasy or devotion. *Obs.*

1599 DAVIES *Immort. Soul* xxxv. (L.) These things transport and carry out the mind. **1639** HARVEY in Carlyle *Cromwell* (1872) V. x. 154 His requests, wherein his heart was so carried out for God and His People.

b. To conduct duly to completion or conclusion; to carry into practice or to logical consequences or inferences.

1605 SHAKS. *Lear* V. i. 61 Hardly shall I carry out my side, Her husband being aliue. **1840** *Fraser's Mag.* XXII. 317 His jackass brother..'carried out', as the phrase now is, the principle so far that it drove him from the throne. **1856** FROUDE *Hist. Eng.* (1858) I. ii. 117 Henry..proceeded to carry out his father's ultimate intentions. **1875** JOWETT *Plato's Crito* (ed. 2) I. 391 The law which requires a sentence to be carried out. **1885** SIR H. COTTON in *Law Rep.* 30 Chanc. 13, I do not think that the cases..carry out the proposition for which he has cited them.

c. *to carry out one's bat* (in Cricket): to leave the wickets (esp. at the close of the game) without being 'out'. Also freq. with omission of *out*. So *to carry one's bat through*: to go in first and remain undismissed at the end of the innings.

[**1833** J. MITFORD in *Gentl. Mag.* Sept. 236/1 Tom scored the amazing number of 95 runs in his first innings, and brought his bat out with him.] **1833** *New Sporting Mag.* Sept. 325 Take care..or through the game Your bat you will not carry. **1846** W. DENISON *Cricket: Sk. Players* 18 Brown carried his bat out with 112 runs marked against his name. **1859** *All Y. Round* No. 13. 306 We had made our 80 runs in less than two hours, and carried out our bats. **1867** G. H. SELKIRK *Guide Cr. Ground* ii. 23 If the player carrying his bat out was one of the two who first went in, he is said to have carried his bat through. **1882** *Cliftonian* June 228 The former carried his bat for a lucky 14. **1895** *Westm. Gaz.* 18 May 7/1 Grace has carried his bat twenty-two times when scoring centuries. **1933** D. L. SAYERS *Murder must Advertise* xviii. 311 The satisfaction of carrying out his bat for 14.

d. *trans.* To bear out (a corpse) for burial.

1526 TINDALE *Acts* v. 6 And the yonge men roose vp..and caryed him out, and buryed him [so **1611**]. **1832** TENNYSON *May Q., New Year's Eve* 42 When I have said goodnight for evermore, And you see me carried out from the threshold of the door.

54. carry over.

a. *trans.* To influence (any one) to pass over to the other side.

1855 MACAULAY *Hist. Eng.* xvii. IV. 64 To carry over a regiment or two would do more harm than good. *Ibid.* xxii, Marlborough had promised to carry over the army, Russell to carry over the fleet.

b. To carry to a new account; to keep over to the next settling day on the Stock Exchange; to allow an account to remain open over the day when its settlement is due; also said of the debtors.

1745 *De Foe's Engl. Tradesm.* (1841) II. 19 Carried over £10 14*s.* 2*d.* **1839** *Reply Lockhart's Phamph.* 13 Balance carried over..£2932 4*s.* 4*d.* **1880** *Standard* 15 Dec, The charge for 'carrying over' English Railways advanced in the later hours. **1887** *Daily News* 26 Feb. 6 The smaller brokers and dealers were 'carried over' on sufferance.

c. To transfer.

1889 E. CARPENTER *Civilis.* iv. 105 The ideal passion of that period..was that of comradeship, or male friendship carried over into the region of love.

55. carry through.

trans. To conduct or bring safely through difficulties, or a crisis; to prosecute to the natural end.

1605 SHAKS. *Lear* I. iv. 3 My good intent May carry through it selfe to that full issue For which I raiz'd my likenesse. **1832** *Blackw. Mag.* Jan. 67/2 It is by similar means that conservative meetings..may be carried through in every part of the country. **1863** tr. *V. Hugo's Miserables* viii. (ed. 7) 163 Impudence had carried him through before now. **1874** *Act 37 & 38 Vic.* xciv. §10 Such petition shall be presented, published and carried through.

56. carry up.

a. *trans.* To continue (building, etc.) to a given height.

1705 STANHOPE *Paraph.* I. 80 For carrying up his Spiritual House. **1747** *Col. Rec. Penn.* V. 61 So much of the Buildings as was carried up before such Notice. **1876** GWILT *Archit.* 566 Where walls..are to be carried up.

b. To bring up (one portion of a series or subject) so as to preserve its due relation to the rest.

1630 WADSWORTH *Sp. Pilg.* iii. 17 Wee march forth..by two and two, Father Thunder himselfe carrying vp the reare. **1817** JAS. MILL *Brit. India* II. v. iii. 392 Unable to carry up its payment to the level of the taxation.

c. To trace back in time.

1677 HALL *Prim. Orig. Man.* II. ii, He carries up the Egyptian Dynasties before the Flood. **1862** STANLEY *Jew. Ch.* (1877) I. iv. 64 The feud..is carried up by them to the feud between Joseph and his brethren.

†**d.** To bear, holding up; to hold up. *Obs.*

1563 FOXE *A. & M.* (1596) 66/2 She was caried up from drowning. **1613** SHAKS. *Hen. VIII*, IV. i. 51 She that carries vp the Traine. **1685** LUTTRELL *Brief Rel.* (1857) I. 340 These six persons following carried up the pall.

e. = *carry over* or *forward* to the top of a new column, in accounts.

carry ('kærɪ), *sb.* [f. prec. in various unconnected applications, of dialectal or technical origin.]

1. a. A means of transport; a vehicle. **b.** *spec.* 'A two-wheeled barrow' (Jamieson). *Sc.* and *north. dial.*

1605 STOWE *Ann.* 1272 On the last of March, Henry Barrow and John Grenewood were brought to Tyborne in a carry. **1820** *Caldeonian Merc.* 20 July, Alexander then asked the loan of her carrie. **1863** ATKINSON *Danby Provinc.*, *Carry*, a kind of waggon with solid floor but unplanked sides ..Used for carting stone, wood, etc., and in hay and harvest time. **1887** *Scott. Leader* 20 May 4 One of the..horses.. started, violently throwing Wilson on to the front of the 'carry'.

c. (See quot.)

1881 *Antrim & Down Gloss.* (E.D.S.) *Carry*, a weir or mill-lead.

†**2.** *Falconry.* Manner of carrying. *Obs.*

1618 LATHAM *2nd Bk. Falconry* (1633) 90 Shee is a buzzard; shee is of a bad carry, he can make her do nothing.

3. The position required by the command to 'carry arms'; cf. CARRY *v.* 36.

1833 *Regul. Instr. Cavalry* I. 170 The lance to be brought to the 'Carry'.

4. a. The range (of a gun); cf. CARRY *v.* 9.

1858 MAYNE REID *Oceola* lxxxiii, Our position was beyond the 'carry' of their guns.

b. *Golf.* The distance between the spot from which a ball is struck and that where it first lands; also, the trajectory of the ball. Cf. CARRY *v.* 9b.

1887 W. G. SIMPSON *Golf* 112 Getting both hands well under the club also produces a low carry. **1890** H. G. HUTCHINSON *Golf* xvii. 445 *Carry*, the distance from the place where the ball is struck to the place where it pitches. Hence a *long carry*, and a *short carry*. **1896** W. PARK *Golf* 104 A well hit drive should be almost all carry; the ball should not run any distance after it falls. *Ibid.* 262 A long carry or a short carry are used to signify the distance a ball must be lofted usually over a hazard. **1899** *Golf Illustrated* 29 Dec. 319/2 The carry alone is estimated to have been close on two hundred and fifty yards. **1953** B. LOCKE *On Golf* II. xvi. 118 You must not take a divot with this shot, otherwise you will not get the loft and the carry needed.

5. A portage between navigable rivers or channels *U.S.* and *Canada*. Cf. CARRIAGE.

1860 *All Y. Round* No. 75. 588 We crossed the carry at day-break. **1884** *Harper's Mag.* June 125/1 Boats came to St. Louis from Montreal with but few 'portages' or 'carries'.

6. a. The drift of the clouds as they are carried along by the wind. *Sc.*

1819 H. BUSK *Vestriad* v. 870 Still towering, till the faithless currents change, And adverse carries floating hopes derange. **1828** J. WILSON in *Blackw. Mag.* XXIV. 292 The clouds are driving fast aloft in a carry from the sea. **1857** R. WHITE *Madeira* 170 The direction of the wind..registered from the 'carry' of the lower strata of clouds.

b. The clouds collectively, firmament, sky.

1788 PICKEN *Poems* 60 (Jam.), I min'..sin' he used to speel Aboon the carry. **1807–10** TANNAHILL *Sleeping, Maggie*, Mirk and rainy is the night, No a starn in a' the carry.

7. a. *gen.* The action or an act of carrying; a posture or manner of carrying.

1880 G. FRASER *Lowland Lore* 134 She [*sc.* a hare] got a guid lang carry [in a sack]! **1925** E. F. NORTON *Fight for Everest: 1924* I. v. 117 We hoped that their [*sc.* porters] reluctance would be reduced..by the fact that the carry had now been once successfully accomplished. **1951** J. FRAME

Lagoon 66 I'm having first go, Minnie said. But I haven't even had a carry of it [*sc.* a kite], I protested. **1966** J. CHAMIER *Cannonball* i. 4 The barman, with the glass of vodka stopped dead in his carry. **1967** 'G. BAGBY' *Corpse Candle* (1968) xiii. 165 Schmitty hung him over his shoulder in a comfortable carry. **1979** *United States 1980/81* (Penguin Travel Guides) 624 Basque games and contests (50-pound carries, walking weight carries,..and a granite-ball lift).

b. *N. Amer. Football.* An act or instance of carrying the ball in order to gain ground. Cf. RUSH *sb.*[2] 3 a.

1949 *Pittsburgh Press* 6 Nov. 40/4 The 20-year-old junior from University City, Mo., averaged more than 10 yards a carry..at Harvard stadium. **1962** *Springfield* (Mass.) *Republican* 18 Nov. 131/2 Grisham, who outrushed the entire Missouri team by getting 116 yards on 23 carries, sparked the scoring drive with a 30 yard run. **1970** *Globe & Mail* (Toronto) 26 Sept. 36/5 Raimey..is leading the Eastern Football Conference in rushing. He has run for 571 yards, 6.9 a carry. **1984** *News* (Mexico City) 12 Mar. 30/1 Dupree's 11 carries made him the Breakers' most active rusher.

carry-all, carryall ('kærɪɔːl). *U.S.* [f. CARRY *v.* + ALL: app. altered by 'popular etymology' from CARRIOLE.] **a.** A light carriage for one horse, usually four-wheeled and capable of holding several persons. Now also, a closed motor vehicle with facing seats along the sides, a station wagon.

1714 J. STODDARD *Jrnl.* in *N.-E. Hist. & Gen. Reg.* V. 27 Mr. Longuille sent a carryall for us. **1837** HT. MARTINEAU *Soc. Amer.* (1839) I. 276 We mounted our carry-all, a carriage which holds four. **1851** HAWTHORNE *Twice-told T.* I. xvi. 249 A four wheeled carryall, peopled with a round half dozen of pretty girls. **1882** HOWELLS in *Longm. Mag.* I. 45 The neighbouring farmer-folks in buggies and carryalls. **1939** in WEBSTER Add. **1940** *Austral. Motorist* 1 Apr. 366/1 The first commercial models to issue from the Vauxhall-Bedford factories since the declaration of war.. are a 6 cwt. model, known as the 'Carryall', and a ½-ton model. **1977** D. J. NARUS *Great Amer. Woodies & Wagons* 42 Chevrolet took a giant leap forward in 1935 and introduced the Suburban Carryall. **1978** *Detroit Free Press* 5 Mar. C22/7 (Advt.), Stakes, carryalls, stepvans, [etc.]. **1983** *Washington Post* 15 Aug. A6/2 Their hard-sell advertising drew dune buggies and four-wheel drive carryalls down the beach by the hundreds.

b. In Canada applied to a sleigh (Bartlett). Cf. CARRIOLE 2.

c. *transf.* That which carries everything one has.

1884 J. HABBERTON *My Friend Moses* 216 A haversack; could he find one of these carry-alls.

'carry-away. [f. *carry away*, CARRY *v.* 46 c.] In *Yachting*, the breakage of a spar, rope, etc.

1901 *Westm. Gaz.* 23 May 5/1 The 'carry-away'..was the most serious that could have happened. First bowsprit snapped, and topmast bent to leeward. **1928** *Daily Tel.* 11 Sept. 15/6 Mrs. Percy Sabel's Widgeon had a carry-away, and was forced to give up when well placed.

†**'carry-castle.** *Obs.* A descriptive term for an elephant, which carries a castle.

1598 SYLVESTER *Du Bartas* I. vi. (1605) 193 The scalie Dragon, being else too low For th' Elephant, vp a thicke Tree doth goe..To watch the Carrie-Castell. **1599** T. M[OUFET] *Silkewormes & Flies* 34 To see a Norway whale, or Libian cat, A Carry-castle or a Crocodile.

'carry-cot. [COT *sb.*[4]] A portable cot for a baby.

The proprietary name *Karri-Kot* and variants also occur.

1943 H. CROOME *O Western Wind* xvi. 131 He slept all day long in his carry-cot. **1951** A. BARON *R. Hogarth* 140 Young couples..carrying two-handled carry-cots between them from which..babies bellow.

carry-forward. *Comm.* [f. *carry forward*, CARRY *v.* 49.] A balance of money carried forward, esp. after providing for a dividend, reserves, etc.

1898 *Westm. Gaz.* 17 May 8/1 The last carry-forward was £132. **1901** *Ibid.* 7 Aug. 7/1 This is one of the few companies which does not announce its carry forward with the dividend. **1959** *Economist* 28 Feb. 817/2 The ordinary dividend..is paid by drawing upon the carry-forward.

carryg, obs. var. of CARRACK.

carrying ('kærɪɪŋ), *vbl. sb.*

1. The action of the vb. CARRY in various senses.

c **1440** *Promp. Parv.* 62 Caryynge. **1521** in *Bury Wills* (1850) 123 Item for carieng of tymber. **1626** CAPT. SMITH *Accid. Yng. Seamen* 13 The sheathing, furring, carrying, washing, and breaming. *a* **1719** ADDISON (J.), In the carrying of our main point. **1769** in Picton *L'pool Munic. Rec.* (1886) II. 220 The slave carrying and limitation Bills. *c* **1865** *Circ. Sc.* 435/1 In subtraction the carrying can never amount to more than 1.

2. with advbs. **carrying-over** = CARRY-OVER a.

1597 HOOKER *Eccl. Pol.* v. lxxv. §3 The carrying him forth upon a bier. **1611** BIBLE *Matt.* i. 17 Vntill the carrying away into Babylon. **1642** HOWELL *For. Trav.* (Arb.) 43 There are many things..worth the carying away. **1711** ADDISON *Spect.* No. 73 ¶5 The carrying on of Traffick, the Administration of Justice. **1729** in Picton *L'pool Munic. Rec.* (1886) II. 87 The carrying on the building. **1907** POLEY & GOULD *Stock Exch.* 168 The General Contango Day (these days are also known as Continuation or Carrying-over Days). *Ibid.* 175 Where the broker is himself the taker-in rendering a carrying-over note, he is not entitled to charge both commission and contango. **1910** H. WITHERS *Stocks & Shares* 277 If no charge is made for carrying over, a full commission is usually paid when the bargain is finally closed.

3. An act of carrying; that which is carried. ***carryings-on*** (pl.): questionable or *outré* proceedings, flirtations, frolics; also *sing.*; cf. CARRY *v.* 52 e.

1663 BUTLER *Hud.* I. II. 556 Is this the end To which these Carryings-on did tend? **1821** BYRON *Foscari* II. i. 305 Your midnight carryings off and drownings. **18..** *Peter Cram* in *Knickerbocker Mag.* (Bartlett) Wherever there were singin' schools, there would be carryings-on. *c* **1865** *Circ. Sc.* I. 510/2 The carryings from the rejected decimals are to be taken account of. **1866** BRIERLEY *Fratchingtons* i. 5 Theau'd weary th' patience ov a jackass wi' thi carryins on. **1890** J. SERVICE *Notandums* xi. 80 What carryin's on have I no seen there! **1909** MASEFIELD *Trag. Nan* I. 13 You'll let 'er marry 'im, after 'is carrying on along o' Jenny?

4. *attrib.*, as in *carrying corporation, horse, power, vessel*; **carrying-capacity**, the number of people or animals (esp. sheep or cattle) that a given area of land will support; also *transf.*; **carrying-chair**, a chair in which a person is carried; **carrying-place**, a place where goods, etc. have to be carried overland in inland navigation (cf. CARRIAGE, CARRY *sb.*); **carrying trade**, the trade or business of carrying goods, *esp.* over sea between different countries.

1883 'MARK TWAIN' *Life on Mississippi* 570 Demands made upon their [boats'] *carrying capacity. **1930** L. ACLAND *Early Canterbury Runs* vii. 151 Hoare.., by ploughing, had raised the carrying capacity [of the station] to over 30,000 sheep in 1890. **1958** *Geogr. Rev.* XLVIII. 5 By relating actual to potential use the capability of the land to support population—that is, its 'carrying capacity'—can be measured. **1880** *Queen* 13 Mar. (Advt.), Invalid furniture ..*carrying chairs, £2. 16s. 6d. **1894** *Outing* (U.S.) XXIV. 129/2 The Chinese mandarin..when seated proudly in his fancy carrying-chair. **1905** *Westm. Gaz.* 25 Feb. 16/3 The carrying-chair used by Leo XIII. **1887** *Manch. Guard.* 2 Apr. 7 Business of a carrying corporation. **1689** in *Mass. Hist. Soc. Coll.* (1861) 4th Ser. V. 221 Then we marched down to..several of the *carrying-places. **1786** W. GRAYSON in Sparks *Corr. Amer. Rev.* (1853) IV. 133 The navigable waters and the carrying-places between them are made common highways. **1876** BANCROFT *Hist. U.S.* V. liii. 124 The shortest carrying-place from the Kennebec to the Dead River. **1878** HUXLEY *Physiogr.* 133 If a river has a steep bed it generally possesses great *carrying power. **1776** ADAM SMITH *W.N.* I. II. v. 377 The coal trade..employs more shipping than all the *carrying trade of England. **1878** F. WILLIAMS *Midl. Railw.* 157 A monopoly of the carrying trade of the district. *c* **1440** *Promp. Parv.* 62 *Caryynge vesselle, or instrument of caryynge.

¶ Examples of the passage of the vbl. sb. into a gerund, and its subsequent apparent use as a passive pple., through omission of preceding preposition *a*, as in 'the ark was a building'.

1684 *J. Peter's Siege of Vienna* 4 The Fortifications.. which were vigorously carrying on by Count Staremberg. **1736** BUTLER *Anal.* II. iv. 186 A mysterious Oeconomy, which has been carrying on from the Time the World came into, etc. **1742** JARVIS *Quix.* I. III. viii. (*heading*) Several unfortunate persons, who were carrying, much against their wills, to a place they did not like. **1777** SHERIDAN *Trip Scarb.* II. i, I met a wounded peer carrying off. **1816** JANE AUSTEN *Emma* II. xviii. 266 Tea was carrying round. **1849** GROTE *Greece* (1862) V. lxi. 338 The operations now carrying on in Chios.

'carrying, *ppl. a.* **1. a.** That carries: see CARRY *v.*

1627 FELTHAM *Resolves* I. liii, The carrying stream is greater, than the bringing one. **1887** *Scotsman* 19 Mar., Fourteen high-class weight-carrying hunters.

b. Of sound: far-reaching, penetrating. Cf. CARRY *v.* 9 c.

1893 YONGE & COLERIDGE *Strolling Players* ii. 9 A small, slight girl..sending her clear, sweet 'carrying' voice before her. **1932** *Punch* 6 Jan. 14/1 My offices are just above and you have a carrying voice. I am not known as Towser to the staff. **1940** WODEHOUSE *Eggs, Beans & Crumpets* 156 Beamish's voice is of a robust and carrying timbre.

2. Special combinations: **carrying comb** *Spinning* (see quots.); **carrying party** *Mil.*, a party detailed to carry or bring up supplies.

1866 *Brit. Pat. 1123* 5 In Figure 6 an arrangement is shown for obtaining motion to the parts from a column in the centre of the main circle of *carrying combs. **1884** W. S. B. MCLAREN *Spinning* (ed. 2) 94 The carrying-comb carries off the wool from between its two plates. **1889** BURNLEY *Wool & Woolcombing* 269 The carrying comb advances in as near as possible a perpendicular position close to the nipper mouth and takes off the tuft of fibres. **1884** *Instr. Mil. Engin.* (*H.M.S.O.*) (ed. 3) I. II. 109 A certain number..will be told off as *carrying party. They will be provided with bags of hay, shavings, wool, &c., boards, fascines. **1928** BLUNDEN *Undertones of War* ix. 95 A carrying-party from another battalion was to meet me in Hamel.

carryke, obs. variant of CARRACK.

†**carry-knave.** *Obs.* A common prostitute.

1630 J. TAYLOR (Water P.) *Wks.* (N.) Our hyreling hackney carry knaves, and hurry-whores.

carryon, obs. form of CARRION.

carry-on ('kærɪɒn). *dial.* and *slang.* [f. *carry on*, CARRY *v.* 52 e.] Fuss, to-do, excitement; carryings-on.

1890 J. SERVICE *Notandums* v. 29 Byla [bailie] Stech, who had been cheated out of his dinner by a' the carry on. **1927** *Scots Observer* 23 Apr. 2/3 Ladies of the Hannah More type lamented the 'voluptuous' carry-ons of miners. **1948** L. WALMSLEY *Master Mariner* I. vii. 123 There's a different carry on up here than what we've had at the other bazaar concerts. **1959** P. BULL *I know the Face* vi. 111 We were all engaged for a radio version of Hamlet... I had never realized the incredible carry-on connected with these productions. **1963** V. GIELGUD *Goggle-Box Affair* iii. 29 Hargest was completely sold on Eurovision and all that carry-on. **1964** *Guardian* 2 Mar. 7/6 They want madmen and blood and wild carry-ons and all that.

'carry-out, *a.* and *sb.* orig. and chiefly *U.S.* Also **carry out, carryout.** [f. vbl. phr. *to carry out*, CARRY *v.* 53: cf. TAKE-OUT *a.* and *sb.*] **A.** *adj.* Of or pertaining to (the trade in) prepared food and drink sold for consumption away from the premises of sale. Cf. TAKE-AWAY *a.* and TAKE-OUT *a.* 1 b, 2.

1935 *Soda Fountain* June 41/2 Soda fountain operators will find it profitable now to carry a good supply of ginger ale and bottled carbonated water..in the cold storage compartment for the carry-out trade. **1957** *Fast Food* Sept. 100/2 In comparing the merits of the counter and carry-out sales, owner Gault points out that size of the order is the big factor. Most carry-out customers purchase food for groups of two to seven. **1963** *Ibid.* Feb. 35 Carry-out catering. No delivering. No serving. **1977** *Washington Post* 17 Mar. (Maryland Weekly Suppl.) 8/4 Paradise Restaurant... Available for carryout food and banquets on premises. **1978** *Detroit Free Press* 5 Mar. C18/4 (Advt.), Service station, party store, lottery tickets, carry-out pizzas, living quarters plus a small cottage. **1985** *Money* Mar. 149 While still working for the restaurant in 1956, he began his franchising career, buying rights that allowed him to sell carryout Kentucky Fried Chicken from his employer's location.

B. *sb.* (The selling of) prepared food and drink for consumption away from the premises of sale; a shop selling take-away food.

1940 *Soda Fountain* July 20 (*heading*) Tapley chalks up a success with carry-outs. **1964** *Fast Food* Feb. 92/2 Carry-out frequently goes 'By the Bucket'. **1970** *Cornell Hotel & Restaurant Q.* May 86 (*caption*) Schueler's 7 kitchens in Cincinnati serve seven menu selections..for eating on the premises or carry out. **1972** S. CONN *Ear to Ground* 36 Outside The Silver Slipper the boys wait, Trousers flared, jacket-pockets Bulging with carry-outs. **1974** *Evening News* (Edinburgh) 12 Apr. 3/5 One of them had a 'carry-out', and when informed that it was illegal to take it off the premises at that time he left it with one of the bar staff. **1975** *Business Week* 27 Oct. 56/2 Kresco Inc...operates everything from quick-service carryouts to higher-priced restaurants. **1983** *N.Y. Times* 6 Apr. C7/1 These days there are almost as many carryouts as supermarkets on street corners.

carry-over. [f. *carry over*, CARRY *v.* 54 b.] On the Stock Exchange: postponement of payment of an account until the next settling-day; the amount so kept over. Also *attrib.* Cf. CONTANGO.

1894 *Daily News* 29 Jan. 2/5 Grand Trunk stocks are from 2 to 4 per cent. higher than at the last 'carry over'. **1895** *Ibid.* 19 Oct. 2 The carry-over price was fixed at 2⅞. **1922** *Daily Mail* 12 Dec. 3 It was Carry-over day in the Mining market, and 'new-time' dealing there was on a small scale. In view of to-day being the general Carry-over, there was a certain amount of realising.

b. *transf.* Something remaining or transferred from one period, process, etc., to the next; a balance carried forward; a transference.

1925 *London Teacher & Lond. School Rev.* 13 Nov. 393/2 The Board in 1921 announced suddenly that they would not pay grants on the full carry-over of the three Burnham scales. **1927** *Observer* 27 Nov. 21/2 A very heavy carry-over of work from the adjournment on December 21 is inevitable, as hundreds of cases are awaiting trial in the King's Bench Division. **1931** *Economist* 17 Jan. 104/1 To make room for the absorption of the present unprecedentedly huge carry-over by restricting further production or export during the coming five years. **1934** BALMER & WYLIE *After Worlds Collide* 43 'He was indubitably wrong about hundreds of other theories.' Tony grinned at this carry-over of this curious man's prejudices and attitudes. **1940** H. G. WELLS *All aboard for Ararat* iii. 85 Will they evaporate with the rest of their class? Will there be no carry-over from them for the Ark? **1952** *Scrutiny* XVIII. III. 197 *Women in Love* is wholly self-contained, and, for all the carry-over of names of characters, has no organic connexion with *The Rainbow*. **1955** J. G. DAVIS *Dict. Dairying* (ed. 2) 107 Carry-over in many [milk-bottle-washing] machines of the ordinary detergent solution is inevitable.

†**'carry-tale.** *Obs.* A tale-bearer, a tell-tale.

1577 HOLINSHED *Chron.* III. 1062/1 By reason of carietales and flatterers, the loue continued not long. **1588** SHAKS. *L.L.L.* v. ii. 463 Some carry-tale, some please-man. **1619** SCLATER *Expos. 1 Thess.* (1630) 131 We haue our carry-tales..to acquaint vs with their priuate actions & speeches. *a* **1652** BROME *Queen* II. vi. Wks. 1873 II. 35, I can be here no carry-Tale. **1824** *Lond. Encycl.* V. 192.

carsay, carsey, obs. ff. of KERSEY.

carse (kɑːs, Sc. kɛrs). *Sc.* Forms: 4 kerss, 6 cars, 7– carse. [Of uncertain derivation, but perhaps the same word as *carres, carrs, cars*, pl. of CARR *sb.*[2] fen, low wet land.

This suits the sense: the early quotations speak of the *kerss* as full of pools and mires: Trivet describes the Carse of Falkirk in the time of Edwd. I. as *loca palustria* (Jam.). The suppression of the vowel of the plural is phonetically regular, and the retention of the (s) sound instead of its change to (z) is seen also in *pence, dice, mice, truce* (the latter also, like *carse*, made into a singular). Cf. also the change of *Pieres, Peres* to *Piers, Pierce*. The difficulty is that no early examples of *kerris* or *carres* are found in Sc.: in Barbour the word is already *kerss*. The Welsh *cors* 'marsh' suits the sense, but presents a difficulty in the vowel, as well as in the geographical localization of the word.]

The stretch of low alluvial land along the banks of some Scottish rivers:

'Thus all the flat lands, on the north side of Tay, between Perth and Dundee, are called *the Carse of Gowrie*; those on the Forth, *the Carse of Stirling*, and *the Carse of Falkirk*' (Jam.). The name appears to have originally referred to their wet fenny character, but is now associated with their rich fertility.

1375 BARBOUR *Bruce* XII. 392 Thai herbryit thame that nycht Doune in the kerss..in the kerss pollis [= pools] ther war. **1535** STEWART *Cron. Scot.* II. 554 Into the cars of Gowrie quhair tha la. **1657** COLVIL *Whigs Supplic.* 100 When mires grew hard, like toasted bread, That men might through the Carses ride. **1787** BURNS *Let. G. Hamilton* 28 Aug., The windings of Forth through the rich carse of Stirling, and skirting the equally rich carse of Falkirk. **1822** SOUTHEY *After King's Visit Scotl.* i, Highland and lowland, glen and fertile carse. **1873** BURTON *Hist. Scot.* I. iii. 83 The haughs or carses on the borders of the rivers.

b. *attrib.*

1797 *Statist. Acc. Scotl.* XIX. 448 What lies next the river is carse clay. **1806** FORSYTH *Beauties Scotl.* III. 52 The soil ..formed by the slime deposited in floods, is of the nature of carse-ground. **1873** GEIKIE *Gt. Ice Age* xxii. 287 The great carse-lands of the estuaries. **1881** *Alloa Advertiser* No. 1617. 2/1 Carse farmers have..got their fallow wheat sown.

Carshuni, var. GARSHUNI.

carstone ('kɑːstəʊn). *Geol.* [app. = *carn-stone*, for *quarn stone*, local form of QUERN-STONE.] A species of the Lower Greensand.

1815 W. SMITH *Mem. Map Strata Eng. & Wales* 43 Iron Sand, or Carstone. **1822** CONYBEARE & PHILLIPS *Outl. Geol. Eng. & Wales* 136 Iron Sand... We are able to trace and identify the present series throughout the island. In different counties it has received the name of Carstone and Quern stone. **1840** SPURDENS *Suppl. Forby's Voc. E. Anglia* (1858), *Car-stone*, a peculiar stone, found principally near Swaffham. **1876** WOODWARD *Geol. Eng. & Wales* 230 The hard beds, locally termed Carstone (or Quern stone), are worked for building-purposes. **1940** *Nature* 8 June 902/1 A carstone rubble bed. **1961** M. W. BARLEY *Eng. Farmhouse & Cottage* II. iv. 103 Chalk, like carstone, was little used before the end of the eighteenth century.

cart (kɑːt), *sb.* Forms: 3–7 **carte**, (3 **karte**, 3–4 **kart**), 6 (**charte**), *Sc.* **cairt**, 3– **cart**. [OE., had *cræt* neut., pl. *cratu*, app. related to Du. *krat* neut. 'hind part of a cart' (which is, however, only mod.Du. and suspected to be of recent adoption). Some compare OHG. *cratto*, *crezzo*, masc., MHG. *kratte*, *kretze* (m. and f.) basket, hamper, panier, mod.G. dial. *krätze* fem., basket (cf. CRATE), and suppose that OE. *cræt* was prop. a cart of basketwork, but of this there is no actual evidence. ON. had *kart-r* masc. 'cart', generally considered to be cognate with the OE. word; and since the ME. was always *cart(e*, and never *crat*, its direct source appears to have been the ON., rather than the OE. word.

If ME. *cart(e* had merely arisen by metathesis of *r* from OE. *cræt*, we should expect some overlapping of forms as in the case of *brid*, *bird*; one may note, however, that OE. *cræt-wǽn* exists in mod. Welsh as *cartwen*. *Cart* has entered from Eng. into most of the Celtic langs.; but is there palpably a foreign word.]

†**1.** A carriage of any kind; a chariot, car. *Obs.*

[*a* **800** *Corpus Gloss.*, *Carruca* (MS. *carcura*), cræt. *c* **1000** ÆFLRIC *Gen.* l. 9 He hæfde..cratu and ridende men. *c* **1050** *Gloss.* in Wr.-Wülcker 426/6 *In carruca* on cræte.]

c **1200** ORMIN 48 Alls iff þeȝȝ karrte wærenn off wheless fowwre. *c* **1205** *Lay.* 11396 Mid carte he [Aldolf] for to Lundene. *a* **1300** *Cursor M.* 6220 He..cuppel did his cartes all. *a* **1340** HAMPOLE *Psalter* lxvii. 18 þe kart of god is ten thowsand manyfald. **1382** WYCLIF *Matt.* Prol., They ben as foure whelis in the foure horsid carte of the lord. *c* **1384** CHAUCER *H. Fame* 943 Pheton wolde lede Algate hys Fader Carte. *c* **1440** *Promp. Parv.* 62 Cart, *biga*, *reda*, *quadriga*. **1483** CAXTON *Gold. Leg.* 72/2 Salamon had xl M. Packes for the horses of his cartes, chases, and curres. **1596** SPENSER *F.Q.* v. viii. 34 On every side of his embatteld cart. **1602** SHAKS. *Ham.* III. ii. 165 Full thirtie Times hath Phoebus Cart gon round Neptunes salt Wash, and Tellus Orbed ground.

2. a. *spec.* A strong vehicle with two wheels, and without springs, used in farming operations, and for carrying heavy goods of various kinds. (Distinguished from a *wagon*, which has four wheels.)

1297 R. GLOUC. (1724) 189 So gret charge..Of mules, of cartes, and of hors mydde alle gode. *c* **1325** *E.E. Allit. P.* 1259 To cayre at þe kart & þe kuy mylke. *c* **1386** CHAUCER *Nonnes Pr. T.* 200 A carte ful of donge ther shalt thou see. *c* **1450** *Merlin* ii. 37 This erthe may be hadde a-wey..in cartes. **1523** FITZHERB. *Husb.* §19 Any wodde, cole, or tymbre to cary..with thy charte or wayne. **1621** BURTON *Anat. Mel.* II. iii. VII. (1651) 350 As good horses draw in carts as coaches. **1623** J. TAYLOR (Water P.) *World on Wheeles* (1630) 235 A Cart is the Embleme of a Man, and a Coach is the Figure of a Beast: for as man hath two legges, a cart hath two wheeles. **1847** EMERSON *Poems*, *Monadnoc*, Their talismans are ploughs and carts. **1877** PAGE *De Quincey* I. vii. 128 A common farmer's cart was brought.

b. With various sbs. indicating its use, as ***baggage-***, ***dung-***, ***dust-***, ***harvest-***, ***hay-***, ***luggage-cart***, etc., or the animal that draws it, as ***donkey-cart***.

1642 in Thornbury *Haunted London* (1865) 385 Paid to the same for the night-cart and cover..£7 9*s.* **1710** *Brit. Apollo* III. No. 26. 3/2, I..was Poyson'd with Night-Carts. **1791** 'G. GAMBADO' *Ann. Horsem.* v. (1809) 89 On a hay, pea, or dust cart. *Ibid.* xv. 126 Some Mackerel carts on the road. **1802** *Med. Jrnl.* VIII. 52 Conveyed here on the baggage cart. **1849** ROBERTSON *Serm.* Ser. I. ii. (1886) 23 Wheat, dropped by a harvest cart upon a road.

†**c.** Formerly used for conveying convicts to the gallows, and instead of a drop; also for the public exposure and chastisement of offenders, esp. lewd women. Cf. CART *v.* 2, CART'S-TAIL. *Obs.*

1624 HEYWOOD *Captives* v. iii. in Bullen *O. Pl.* IV, They will spitt at us and doom us Unto the post and cart. **1682** DRYDEN *Loyal Bro.* Prol. 34 Like thief and parson in a Tyburn-cart. **1708** in Picton *L'pool Munic. Rec.* (1886) II. 81 That Marg[t] Justice be whipt next day att a cart's arse, and ..Jane Justice be carryed in the cart at the same time from the Exchange to Jane Justice's house. **1800** COLERIDGE *Piccolom.* I. xii, Your windows and balconies all forestall'd To see him on the executioner's cart. **1861** THACKERAY *Lovel* 263 (Hoppe) She was always fitting the halter and traversing the cart..but she for ever declined to drop the handkerchief and have the business over.

3. A two-wheeled vehicle of lighter or more elegant make, with springs, drawn by one horse at a rapid pace. Often specified as ***spring-cart*** (which varies least from 2), ***mail cart***, ***village cart***; also DOG-CART, TAX(ED) CART, q.v.

1823 *Act 4 Geo. IV*, xcv. §19 Any..chaise, curricle, gig, chair, or taxed cart. **1835** SIR G. STEPHEN *Adv. in Search Horse* ii. 34 Tradesmen who require light carts for the conveyance of their goods. **1848** THACKERAY *Let.* 1 Nov., A party of us drove in an Oxford Cart to Blenheim. *Mod.* He met me at the station with his village cart.

†**4. a.** Some kind of transport vessel. (? error.)

1568 C. WATSON *Polyb.* i. 26 After the third Navy came the carts [τὰς ἱππηγους] and foists in which their horses were transported.

b. The carapace or upper shell of a crab. *colloq.* or *dial.*

1860 HOTTEN *Dict. Slang* (ed. 2) s.v. *Carts*, In Norfolk the carapace of a crab is called a *crab cart*. **1887** *Girl's Own Paper* 16 July 661/2 Pick the meat from the cart, the breastplate, and the claws.

5. *Proverbs* and *Phrases.* ***to set*** or ***put the cart before the horse***: to reverse the natural or proper order. †***to be left out of the cart's tail***: (see quot.). †***to keep cart on wheels***: ? 'to keep straight', or 'to keep things going'. Also ***in the cart***: in an awkward, false, or losing position; in serious difficulties (cf. sense 2 c) (*slang*).

[**1340** *Ayenb.* 243 Moche uolk of religion zetteþ þe zuolȝ be-uore þe oksen.] **1520** WHITTINTON *Vulg.* (1527) 2 That techer setteth the carte before the horse that preferreth imitacyon before preceptes. *a* **1541** WYATT *Defence* 265 It is a common proverb, 'I am left out of the carts tail,' and it is taken upon packing gear together for carriage, that it is evil taken heed to, or negligently, slips out of the cart, and is lost. **1587** *Mirr. Mag.*, *Q. Cordila* v. 5 Lest I set the horse behinde the cart. **1589** PUTTENHAM *Eng. Poesie* (Arb.) 181 We call it in English prouerbe, the cart before the horse, the Greeks call it Histeron proteron, we name it the Preposterous. **1605** SHAKS. *Lear* I. iv. 244 May not an Asse know, when the Cart drawes the Horse? **1611** COTGR. s.v. *Oye*, The cart leads the horse; the young instruct the old. **1662** NEWCOME *Diary* (1849) 56, I must walke closer with God or I cannot keep cart on wheeles. **1705** E. WARD *Hud. Rediv.* II. iii. p. 26 Excuse me, that the Muses force The Cart to stand before the Horse. **1863** KINGSLEY *Water-Babies* iv. 176 They.. having, as usual, set the cart before the horse, and taken the effect for the cause. **1889** *Evening Standard* 25 June 1/3 In two races..Sir George Chetwynd—to use a vulgarism—had been 'put in the cart' by his jockey. **1908** *Punch* 12 Feb. 110 We were simply all over 'em, and had 'em in the cart in no time. *Ibid.* 4 Nov. 334 Something..tells me I am fairly in the cart. **1909** A. BENNETT *Literary Taste* 27 The passionate few do not read 'the right things' because they are right. That is to put the cart before the horse. **1914** W. S. MAUGHAM *Smith* 13 Emily was left in the cart? **1924** J. B. HOBBS *Cricket Mem.* 158 We made 238, which was enough practically to put South Africa hopelessly in the cart. **1945** R. HARGREAVES *Enemy at Gate* 152 There is a glib saying.. that 'trade follows the flag'; an apophthegm that succeeds in putting the cart before the horse with greater aplomb than almost any other cant phrase in common use. **1966** G. W. TURNER *Eng. Lang. Austral. & N.Z.* vi. 137 Sargeson's French translator..had some slang shared with English to translate, and job (boulot), tight (noir), spree (nouba), in the cart (dans le pétrin)..are neatly managed.

6. *Comb.*, as ***cart-driver*** (formerly also = charioteer), ***-filler***, ***-gelding***, ***-grease***, ***-harness***, ***-horse***, ***-jade***, ***-maker***, ***-pitch***, ***-road***, ***-room***, ***-rope***, ***-shed***, ***-thill***, ***-track*** (*-tract*); **cart-aver** (*Sc.*) a cart-horse (see AVER *sb.* 3); †**cart-band**, ? the tire of a cart-wheel; **cart-body**, that part of a cart which holds the load (see BODY *sb.* 8 g); †**cart-bote**, **-boot** (*Feudal Syst.*), an allowance of wood to a tenant for making and repairing carts (see BOOT *sb.*[1] 5 b); †**cart-bread** (see quot.); †**cart-clout**, an iron plate to protect the axle-tree from wear; †**cart-gate** = CART-WAY; †**cart-gun** ? a cannon mounted on a carriage; **cart-head**, the front of a cart (cf. CART'S-TAIL); **cart-ladder** (**-leather**), a rack or framework at the front, back, or sides of a cart, to increase its carrying capacity; called also *lead-trees*; **cart-lodge** [LODGE *sb.* 1 c] *local*, a shed or out-house where carts are kept; **cart-man**, a man who drives a cart; †**cart-nave**, ? the nave of a cart-wheel; †**cart-piece**, ? = *cart-gun*; †**cart-ritt** = *cart-rut*; **cart-road** = CART-WAY; **cart-ruck**, **-rut**, the deep rut cut in soft ground by the wheels of a cart; hence **cart-rutted** *a.*; **cart-saddle**, the small saddle placed on the back of a cart- or carriage-horse to support the shafts; also †as *v. trans.*, to put a cart-saddle on, to yoke; †**cart-spur**, **-spirn**, a cart-track [OE. *spor* track; cf. SPOOR]; †**cart-staff**, the shaft of a cart; also applied to other parts of a cart; †**cart-taker**, the officer who impressed carts for the king's service; so †**cart-taking**; **cart-tire**, the tire of a cart-wheel; **cart-track**, a track along which a cart has gone; a cart-rut; **cart-warping** (see quot.). See also CART-FUL, -HORSE, -HOUSE, -LOAD, -TAIL, -WAY, -WHEEL, -WHIP, -WRIGHT.

1822 SCOTT *Pirate* iv, The carles and the *cart-avers.. make it all; and the carles and the cart-avers eat it all. **1483** *Cath. Angl.* 54 A *carte band, *crusta*. *c* **1325** *Gloss. W. de Bibbesw.* in Wright *Voc.* (1857) 167 *Le chartil*, the *carte body. **1407** in Kennett *Par. Antiq.* (1818) II. 213 Et pro sarratione et dolatione unius Cartbody..vi[d]. **1779** in *Narrag. Hist. Reg.* I. 93 Went to Tower hill for a cart body. **1834** W. G. SIMMS *Guy Rivers* 414 The conflagration.. destroyed his cart-body and calicoes. **1594** WEST *Symbol.* ii. *Chancerie* §88 Surrender..the said tenement and premisses ..with sufficient *cartbote, heybote, and hedgebote. **1726** AYLIFFE *Parerg.* 506 If a man cuts Trees for..Cartboot, Ploughboot and Fireboot. **1580** BARET *Alv.* C 149 Bread solde in markets in London; *cart bread. **1446** *Wills & Inv. N.C.* (1835) I. 95, J carecta cum rotis iiij hopis et viij *cartecloutez. **1622** F. MARKHAM *Bk. War* III. x. 119 Nailes for Tyers, and all other purposes..Spunges, Chaines, Cart-clouts, Weights. **1611** SPEED *Hist. Gt. Brit.* VI. viii, A Prince? nay an Incendiary..a Stage-plaier, a *Cart-driuer. *c* **1505** DUNBAR *Compl. to King* 25 Chaff-midden churls cuming off *cart-fillaris. **1594** *Manch. Crt. Leet Rec.* (1885) II. 89 There hath bene a *Cartgate..betwixte the landes. **1773** *Gentl. Mag.* XLIII. 644 *Cart-grease must be used. **1550** HALL *Chron. 18 Hen. VIII*, 156 The Cardinal..had there *cart gonnes ready charged. **1818** SCOTT *Ht. Midl.* xviii, Mending his *cart-harness. **1812** W. TENNANT *Anster F.* ix, On his *cart-head, sits the goodman. **1580** SIDNEY *Arcadia* (1622) 174 With al his clownes, hoist vpon such *cart-jades, so furnished, etc. **1523** FITZHERB. *Husb.* §5 And a *carte ladder behinde whan he shall carye eyther corne or kyddes or such other..Theyr waynes haue carte ladders bothe behynde and before. **1727** BRADLEY *Fam. Dict.* I. s.v. *Cart*, The Cart-Leathers. **1753** CHAMBERS *Cycl. Supp.* s.v. *Cart*, *Cart-ladders*, the crooked pieces set over the wheels to keep hay and straw loaden off them. **1888** *Cart lodge [see LODGE *sb.* 1 c]. **1915** KIPLING *Div. Creatures* (1917) 432 A little cart-lodge was sliding sideways amid a clatter of tiles. **1933** *Brit. Birds* XXVII. 25 A Blackbird..built a nest on the horizontal beam..above the open front of a cart-lodge in south-west Kent. **1580** NORTH *Plutarch* 138 *Cart-makers ..Sadlers, Coller-makers. **1719–54** W. SEWEL *Eng.-Dutch Dict.* s.v. *Sleeper*, The *Cart-men at London. **1807** W. IRVING *Salmag.* (1824) 212 A cartman driving full-tilt through Broadway. **1881** *Echo* 28 Jan. 4/3 Embezzlement by a Cartman. **1882** *Atlantic Monthly* XLIX. 678 Nearly all the cartmen and porters are negroes. *c* **1450** *Voc.* in Wr.-Wülcker 628 *Timpana* *cartenave. *a* **1670** SPALDING *Troub. Chas. I*, 14 May, Thair cam..tua uther iron *cart peices to the schoir. **1865** TYLOR *Early Hist. Man.* ix. 255 Well smeared with *cart-pitch and tar. **1649** G. DANIEL *Trinarch.*, *Rich. II*, clxxxv, Revenue run's faire..The other *Cart-Ritt holds but for a while. **1607** TOPSELL *Foure-Footed Beasts* 536 The Shrew, which falling by chaunce into a *Cart-roade or tracke doth die vpon the same. **1868** HOLME LEE *B. Godfrey* xxx. 157 A cart-road which plunged deep into a wood. **1832** MISS MITFORD *Village* Ser. v. (1863) 445 A miniature farm-yard, with stabling for two, *cart-room for one. **1535** COVERDALE *Isa.* v. 18 Wo vnto vayne personnes, that drawe..synne as it were with a *cart rope. **1623** MASSINGER *Bondman* I. iii, A cart-rope Shall not bind me at home. **1659** GAUDEN *Brownrig* (1660) 162 He drew all ..not by the cart-ropes of rigor and imperiousness. **1818** SCOTT *Rob Roy* xi, I will have his meaning from him..if I should drag it out with cart-ropes. **1823** LAMB *Elia*, *Oxford in Vac.* 319 The..quill, that has plodded..among the *cart-rucks of figures and ciphers. **1601** HOLLAND *Pliny* II. 351 The earth taken from a *cart-rut where a wheele hath gon. **1669** WOODHEAD *St. Teresa* II. xxxv. 233 To pull the coaches out of the cart-rotes. **1821** CLARE *Vill. Minstr.* I. 135 The cart-rut rippled down With the burden of the rain. **1881** POYNTER *Among Hills* I. 153 A steep, *cart-rutted lane. **1377** LANGL. *P. Pl.* B. II. 179 *Cartesadel the comissarie, Oure cart shal he lede. **1692** *Lond. Gaz.* No. 2777/4 A black punch Gelding..gall'd with the Cart-Saddle on the off side. **1483** *Cath. Angl.* 55 A *carte spurre, *orbita*. **1528** *St. Papers Hen. VIII*, IV. 496 It haith chaunced me..to take a fall of my horse, and to breke my left arme, overthuart a cartspirn. **1297** R. GLOUC. (Rolls) 2198 ȝe beþ men bet iteiȝt to ssofle & spade To *cartstaf & to ploustaf. **1753** CHAMBERS *Cycl. Supp.* s.v. *Cart*, *Cartstaves*, those that hold the cart and the raers together. **1455** in *Househ. Ord.* (1790) 24 *Carte Takers—Richard Rede, etc. **1653** A. WILSON *Jas. I*, 11 Purveyors, cart-takers, and such insolent officers. **1782** S. PEGGE *Cur. Misc.* (1818) 33 The King's Cart-takers, a post which is now in being though out of use. **1671** F. PHILIPPS *Reg. Necess.* 46 To be freed from Pourveyance and *Cart-taking. **1601** HOLLAND *Pliny* I. 493 The French white Ash ..will bend well for *cart-thills and fellies. *Ibid.* II. 365 Snailes (such..as are found betweene two *cart-tracts). **1827** MISS MITFORD *Village* Ser. I. (1863) 60 The roads through the coppice..have the appearance of mere cart-tracks. **1839** STONEHOUSE *Axholme* 43 Another method by which the sediment of the Trent water is made highly beneficial to the adjoining land..is termed *'cart warping', the alluvial soil being led on the land during a hard frost or in very dry weather.

cart (kɑːt), *v.* [f. prec. sb.]

1. a. *trans.* To carry or convey in a cart; also *fig.* ***to cart off*** or ***away***: to carry off or away in a cart; hence *gen.* to carry off, take away, remove.

c **1440** *Promp. Parv.* 62 Cartyn or lede wythe a carte, *carruco*. **1663** *Aron-bimn.* 7 When the Ark was to be Carted to the City of David. **1807** DE QUINCEY in Page *Life* I. vii. 129 We were all carted to the little town.

†**b.** To mount on a cart or carriage. *Obs.*

1550 HALL *Chron.* 5 *Hen. VIII*, 27 The pece of ordinaunce was raysed & carted, and furthe was it caried.

c. *Anglo-Indian.* (See quot.)

1837 T. BACON *First Impr. Hindostan* I. 137 Carting a girl, or riding out with her, is considered in India as a regular publication of the banns.

d. *Cricket. trans.* and *intr.* To hit (a ball) hard and high. So with the bowler as obj.

1903 WODEHOUSE *Tales St. Austin's* 35 Half-way through the over I carted a half-volley into the pav. **1903** —— *Prefect's Uncle* xiii. 188 'When have you seen him?' 'In a scratch game between his form and another. He was carting all over the shop. Made thirty something.' **1961** *Times* 30 May 4/1 He carted Halfyard to square leg for six.

e. *trans.* fig. To carry as in a cart, to convey (something heavy or cumbersome) over a long distance or with considerable effort; to carry or take unceremoniously. Freq. with advbs., as *about, away, off*, etc. *colloq.*

1864 J. H. NEWMAN *Apol.* 31, I hereby cart away as so much rubbish, the impertinences, with which the Pamphlet swarms. **1881** *Punch* 8 Oct. 166/2 Napier and Havelock might be carted off to join the poor Duke of Kent at the top of Portland Place. **1891** FARMER *Slang.* **1889** J. K. JEROME *Three Men in Boat* v. 71 Then Harris and I..carted out our luggage on to the doorstep, and waited for a cab. **1898** J. D. BRAYSHAW *Slum Silhouettes* 215 I've just seed Liz Dukeson ..her that Cocky uster cart abaht. **1909** R. A. WASON *Happy Hawkins* 241 We knew that Barbie carted around at all times what they call a spirit of combativity. **1936** A. RANSOME *Pigeon Post* xvi. 161 What about taking spades? We don't want to cart them up there for nothing. **1951** R. CAMPBELL *Light on Dark Horse* i. 22 This was by no means the only time cousin Ethelbert carted animals about in trains or lorries. **1959** F. ASTAIRE *Steps in Time* (1960) ii. 13 Married in her teens, she was in her early twenties when she took on the challenging job of carting her two brats to New York in search of a career. **1982** B. TRAPIDO *Brother of More Famous Jack* xi. 46, I tell him how..we carted home a great quantity of accumulated litter from our desks in a plaid blanket which we carried between us down the hill.

†**2.** *spec.* To carry in a cart through the streets, by way of punishment or public exposure (esp. as the punishment of a bawd). *Obs.*

1596 SHAKS. *Tam. Shr.* I. i. 55 Leaue shall you haue to court her at your pleasure. *Gre.* To cart her rather. She's to rough for mee. **1607** DEKKER, &c. *Northw. Hoe* I. iii. Wks. 1873 III. 13, I was neuer Carted (but in haruest) neuer whipt but at Schoole. **1664** BUTLER *Hud.* II. I. 81 Democritus ne'er laugh'd so loud, To see Bawds carted through the crowd. **1738** POPE *Epil. Sat.* I. 150 Vice..lifts her scarlet head, And sees pale Virtue carted in her stead. **1812** CRABBE *T. of Hall* I. (D.) Suspected, tried, condemned, and carted in a day.

3. *intr.* or *absol.* To work with a cart; to use a cart.

1393 LANGL. *P. Pl.* C. VI. 62 Hit by-comeþ for..knaues vncrouned to cart and to worche. **1463** MARG. PASTON *Lett.* 480 II. 143 Your grey hors..nowthyr ryght good to plowe nor to carte. **1707** J. MORTIMER *Husb.* (L.) Oxen are not so good..where you have occasion to cart much.

4. *trans.* To put (someone) 'in the cart' (see prec. 5); to cause to feel let down. *slang.*

1889 BARRÈRE & LELAND *Dict. Slang* I. 228/2 An owner is said to be 'in the *cart*', or *carted*, when his horse is prevented winning by some fraud on the part of those in his employment. **1923** T. E. LAWRENCE *Let.* 13 June (1938) 425 A temporary job at a high salary would only cart me worse than ever in the end. **1934** —— *Let.* 16 Nov. 825 Poets are always..savagely political: and the real politician..always carts them properly. Poets hope too much. **1948** *Hansard* CDXLVIII. 1054 Many had lived in camp according to the promised scale of pay, with the result that they lived beyond their means. To use an Army expression, 'They were properly carted'.

'cartable, *a.* [f. CART *sb.* or *v.* + -ABLE.] That can be carted; that can be traversed by carts.

1684 *Phil. Trans.* XVII. 744 Above Twenty Miles from Keswick, and none of the way Cartable.

cartaceous: see CHARTACEOUS *a.* papery.

†**cartafi'lago, -phi'lago.** *Obs.* Given by Turner as an English name of *Gnaphalium sylvaticum* or *Filago germanica.*

1551 TURNER *Herbal* I. (1568) Ijb, Centunculus [cudweed]..in englyshe in some places cartaphilago. **1562** *Ibid.* II. 11 b, Cottenweede..I thinke that the herbe which is called in Englande Cartafilago is a certain kynde of the same herbe. **1578** LYTE I. lxii. 90 Called of Turner.. Cartaphilago.

cartage ('kɑːtɪdʒ). [f. CART *sb.* or *v.* + -AGE.] The process of conveying by cart; the price paid for this.

1428 in Heath *Grocers' Comp.* (1869) 6 For chalke and stoon and cartage £18 11*s.* 5*d.* **1755** MAGENS *Insurances* I. 327 Cartage of the Sugars from the Keys to the Warehouse. **1878** F. WILLIAMS *Midl. Railw.* 297 The proposed line would free the streets..from an enormous amount of cartage.

cartage, obs. form of CARTRIDGE.

cartall, obs. form of CARTEL.

carte[1] (kɑːt, kart). Forms: 4- **carte**, 6 **cart,** (**carete**), *Sc.* **cairt.** [a. F. *carte* card:—L. *carta, charta* paper: adopted at two different times; first in ME. in branch I; secondly, after this had become obs. (exc. perhaps in Sc. *cartes* 'playing-cards'), from mod.Fr. in branch II.]

I. †**1.** ? A treatise, exposition of a science. (? *spec.* of astrology). *Obs.*

1393 GOWER *Conf.* III. 130 As it is written in the carte, Complexion he [*i.e.* Canis Minor] taketh of Marte. **1560** ed. of *Chaucer's Astrol.* 249/2 In any carts [*ed. Skeat* tretis] of the Astrolabie that I have yseene, there ben some conclusions, that, etc.

†**2.** A chart, map, plan, diagram. Also *fig. Obs.*

1502 ARNOLDE *Chron.* (1811) Introd. 15 The Copye of a Carete cumpasyng the Circuet of the Worlde. **1558** *Treas. Acc.* in Lauder *Tractate* (1864) Pref. 8 For paynting of the vii Planetis, of the kart, with the rest of the convoy xvi *li.* **1578** *Invent.* (1815) 237 (Jam.) Tua litle cairtis of the yle of Malt. **1669** MARVELL *Wks.* 1872–5 II. 273 A cart of the flats and sands that we meet with at Court. **1670** COTTON *Espernon* II. VII. 333 Very expert in the Geographical Cart. **1683** *Weekly Memorial* 85 Having referred his readers to the common Sea-carts..for the situation of the island.

†**3.** A charter; a legal 'paper' or document. *Obs.*

c **1449** PECOCK *Repr.* 402 Cartis or chartouris conteyning the formes of ȝeuyng the seid greet endewing. **1640** FULLER *Joseph's Coat* v. (1867) 155 Though these outlandish sins have of late been naturalized and made free denizens of England; yet our ancientest carte is for gluttony.

4. *Sc.* A playing-card; *pl.* the game of cards.

1497 *Sc. Treas. Acc.* in Pitcairn *Crim. Trials* I. 117 Augt. 7. Item, giffen to þe king to play at þe Cartis with þe Spanyartis, at Noreme, xx Vnicornis. *a* **1555** LYNDESAY *Tragedy* 81 Playng at cartis, and Dyse. **1785** BURNS *Epist. Davie* viii, Tent me, Davie, ace o' hearts! (To say aught less wad wrang the cartes). **1816** SCOTT *Antiq.* xv, 'Take a hand at the cartes till gudeman comes hame.'

‖**II. 5.** A bill of fare.

1818 MOORE *Fudge Fam. Paris* iii. 6 The Carte at old Véry's. **1850** THACKERAY *Pendennis* xlvi, The carte was examined on the wall, and Fanny was asked to choose her favourite dish. **1856** KANE *Arct. Expl.* I. xxix. 387 Our carte is comprised in three lines—bread, beef, pork.

6. Short for CARTE-DE-VISITE.

1861 DICKENS *Lett.* (ed. 2) II. 148, I think the 'cartes' are all liked. **1867** YATES *Black Sheep* II. 292 (Hoppe) Mr. Felton had some letters yesterday..and there was a carte of his son in 'em.

carte[2] (kɑːt). *Fencing.* [(Also written QUART(E): a. F. *quarte*, ad. It. *quarta* fourth.

First introduced in the form *quarte*; in 18th c. naturalized as *carte*; recent writers, using French authorities, show a tendency to revert to *quarte*.]

A position in fencing; one of the eight parries and two usual guards of the small-sword. See quot. 1861.

1707 SIR W. HOPE *Method of Fencing* 15 The only sure defence and preservative upon the ordinary Quart and Tierce Guards. **1709** STEELE *Tatler* No. 26 ¶11 Questions about the Words Cart and Terce, and other Terms of Fencers. **1809** ROLAND *Fencing* 37 In parrying either carte or tierce the same edge of your blade will parry both parades, provided you turn your wrist in its proper position for each parade. **1840** BARHAM *Ingol. Leg., Tragedy* iv, He thrust carte and tierce Uncommonly fierce. **1861** G. CHAPMAN *Foil Practice* 11 Quarte—The hand turning to the left, the point raised and inclined to the left, the finger-nails turned up (slightly). **1878** BROWNING *Poets Croisic* 137 No carte-and-tierce Observes the grinning fencer.

b. as *vb.* (nonce-word).

1765 *Universal Mag.* XXXVII. 41/1 I'll carte and terce you, you scoundrel.

‖**carte blanche** (kart blɑ̃ʃ). Also 8 **chart blanch, charte blanche.** [Fr. (formerly *charte blanche*): = blank paper.]

1. A blank paper given to any one on which to write his own conditions.

1707 LD. RABY in Hearne *Collect.* (1886) II. 43 Who sent Chart Blanch to make a Peace. **1712** ADDISON *Spect.* No. 299 ¶2, I threw her a *Charte Blanche*, as our News Papers call it, desiring her to write upon it her own Terms. **1864** KIRK *Chas. Bold* II. III. ii. 154 Louis..returned a carte blanche which was filled up with the government of Guienne and a long list of inferior posts and emoluments.

b. *lit.* Blank paper.

1790 BURKE *Fr. Rev.* Wks. V. 285, I cannot conceive how any man can..consider his country as nothing but carte blanche, upon which he may scribble whatever he pleases.

2. Hence *fig.* Full discretionary power granted.

1766 CHESTERF. *Lett.* cccc. (1792) IV. 235 Mr. Pitt, who had *carte blanche* given him, named every one of them. **1809** WINDHAM *Let.* in *Speeches Parl.* (1812) I. 114 Unless I can have *carte blanche* as to my military plans. **1861** A. B. HOPE *Eng. Cathedr. 19th C.* 185, I may venture to assume carte blanche in arguing the impossibility of basilican revival. **1879** *Lond. Soc.* Christm. No. 47/1 Our good easy vicar gave me carte blanche to use this organ.

3. *Piquet.* A hand containing no picture-cards. (The French is *avoir cartes blanches* to have blank cards; the earlier Eng. was *blank* or *blanche.*)

[**1651** *Royal Game Picquet* 6 If he..find that he hath never a Coat Card in his hand, he saies..I have a Blanche. **1659** *Shuffling, Cutting, & Deal.* 7, I am blanck. **1676** COTTON *Compl. Gamester* vi. 88 (*Picket*) He that hath a Blank..his Blank shall hinder the other Picy..and Repicy.] **1820** *Hoyle's Games Impr.* 112 *Carte Blanche*, means a hand without a court card in the twelve dealt, which counts for ten. **1850** Bohn's *Handbk. Games* 200. **1882** *Laws of Piquet* Law xviii, Carte blanche..scores first, and consequently saves a pique or a repique.

carted ('kɑːtɪd), *ppl. a.* [f. CART *v.* + -ED[1].] Carried in a cart; *spec.* as a punishment.

1683 SOAME & DRYDEN tr. *Boileau's Art Poetry* (L.) Thespis..with his carted actors. **1692** SOUTHERNE *Wives Excuse* II. i, Like a carted bawd justly punish'd for the sins of the people. *c* **1730** SWIFT *Clad in Brown* Wks. 1755 IV. I. 263 Old carted bawds such garments wear.

‖**carte-de-visite** ('kartdəvi'zit). Pl. **cartes-de-visite.** [Fr.; = visiting card.] A small photographic portrait mounted on a card, $3\frac{1}{2}$ by $2\frac{1}{4}$ inches: so called from the purpose for which they were first proposed.

1861 *N. & Q.* Ser. II. XII. 322/2 A carte de visite in old times. In these days of *cartes de visite*, etc. **1869** *Eng. Mech.* 17 Dec. 328/2 The former style of cartes-de-visite. **1875** tr. *Vogel's Chem. Light* iv. 36 The collodion process..acquired an immense impetus through the introduction of cartes de visite. *Ibid.* vi. 53 The Carte de visite was introduced at Paris by Disderi in 1858..and has been diffused over the whole earth.

‖**carte d'identité** (kart didɑ̃tite). [Fr.] An identity card; a document which gives personal particulars.

1923 *Michelin Guide to Gt. Brit.* (ed. 7) III. 861 Passports are indispensable... It is also advisable to obtain a 'Carte d'Identité' at the Passport Office. **1933** 'G. ORWELL' *Down & Out* vii. 56, I had not sufficient papers of identification; my *carte d'identité* was not enough. **1947** *Horizon* XVI. Oct. 100 As indispensable to the common man as a birth certificate, a passport, a *carte d'identité*. **1965** G. LYALL *Midnight plus One* xxiv. 183, I wanted him on the defensive in the hope he'd forget to ask for my *carte d'identité*.

‖**carte du pays** (kartdypei). [Fr., lit. 'map of the country'.] The lie of the land; also *fig.*

1744 H. WALPOLE *Let.* 22 July (1955) XVIII. 483 Not being quite perfect in the *carte du pays*, told my Lady, [&c.]. **1840** J. B. FRASER *Trav. Koordistan* II. xviii. 436 My companion, who knew the *carte-du-pays* well, had been prowling about to discover..the means of getting on. **1853** MRS. GASKELL *Ruth* II. ix. 228 [He] knew, from the *carte du pays* which the scouts of the parliamentary agent had given him, that Mr. Benson was a person to be conciliated. **1905** R. BROUGHTON *Waif's Progress* ii. 11, I want, before you go, to give you a tiny *carte du pays*.

cartel ('kɑːtəl; in senses 3 c, d kɑː'tɛl), *sb.* Forms: α. 6–7 **cartell,** 7 **-all,** 7– **-el.** β. 6 **chartale, -ell,** 6–7 **-el.** [a. F. *cartel*, ad. It. *cartello* (= Sp. *cartel*, med.L. *cartellus*), dim. of *carta* paper, letter, bill. (The fem. dim. *cartella* has a different sense.)]

1. A written challenge, a letter of defiance.

1560 SIR T. CHALONER *Let.* 15 Jan. in Froude *Hist. Eng.* VI. 313 Our professed enemies..instead of cartels of defiance, will send us solemn letters of congratulation. **1598** B. JONSON *Ev. Man in Hum.* I. v. 89, I should send him a chartel presently. **1650** JER. TAYLOR *Holy Dying* iii. §8 Xerxes..sent a chartel of Defiance against the Mount Athos. **1769** ROBERTSON *Chas. V* (1813) V. 431 He..sent back the herald with a *cartel* of defiance. **1841** D'ISRAELI *Amen. Lit.* (1867) 454 To the unknown libeller..Sir Philip Sidney..designed to send a cartel of defiance. **1880** S. COX *Comm. Job* 213 Job breaks out into this brief cartel of defiance.

†**2.** A slanderous writing, a libel. *Obs.*

1590 DAVIDSON *Reply Bancroft* in *Wodr. Soc. Misc.* 516 That calumnious chartale, fraughted with as many lies almost as it hath lines. **1600** O. E. *Reply Libel* Ep. Ded. 5 One of our friends doth only term it a chartell or libell.

3. a. A written agreement relating to the exchange or ransom of prisoners, etc.; such exchange itself.

1692 BENTLEY *Boyle Lect.* ix. 335 The agreements of the Cartel do expire of their own accord when the Peace is concluded. **1715** BURNET *Own Time* an. 1659 (R.) By a cartel that had been settled between the two armies, all prisoners were to be redeemed at a set price. **1774** *Westm. Mag.* II. 483 A cartel being soon after established for the exchange of prisoners. **1809** WELLINGTON *Let.* in Gurw. *Disp.* V. 69, I shall endeavor to establish a cartel of exchange as soon as possible. **1832** W. IRVING *Alhambra* II. 184.

b. = *cartel-ship*: see quot. 1769.

1769 FALCONER *Dict. Marine* (1789) *Cartel*, a ship commissioned in time of war to exchange the prisoners of any two hostile powers; also to carry any particular proposal from one to another. **1795** in Nicolas *Disp. Nelson* (1845) II. 38 Three Cartels are expected from Toulon with sick prisoners. **1813** *Examiner* 10 May 304/2 He was coming home in the cartel.

c. [After G. *kartell.*] (Orig. in Germany) an agreement or association between two or more business houses for regulating output, fixing prices, etc.; also, the businesses thus combined; a trust or syndicate. Also *attrib.* and *transf.*

1902 *Daily Chron.* 24 May 6/3 He laid stress on the injury which would be done to the Indian industry if the country were flooded with 'Cartel' sugar. **1902** *Pol. Sci. Q.* XVII. 381 The cartel, or producers' syndicate. **1902** *Westm. Gaz.* 24 Nov. 10/1 The new cartel includes practically every important iron and steel interest in the Dual Monarchy. **1934** *Punch* 4 Apr. 377/1 The cartel of American lyrists has drawn up regulations forbidding the use of any adjective other than 'swell', 'red-hot' or 'blue'. **1935** *Economist* 12 Jan. 68/2 The Vienna coal trade has arranged a cartel for house coal, and a 4 per cent. price rise has occurred. **1958** *Times Rev. Industry* Apr. 12/1 A powerful world cartel.., controlling about 95 per cent of world production, was formed to restore balance.

d. *Hist.* The coalition formed in 1887 between the Conservatives and the National Liberals in Germany to support each other's candidates, for the furtherance of Bismarck's military and imperial policy. Hence as a name for similar coalitions in other countries.

1889 *Ann. Reg. 1888* 270 On this occasion the German Unionists, or 'Cartell party', composed of the Conservatives and National Liberals, again spoke for the Government measure. **1918** C. G. ROBERTSON *Bismarck* 453 The Chancellor's political cartel was complete; it consisted of the

Conservatives, the old National Liberals, and the Centre; and the union gave him a decisive and obedient majority. **1919** A. W. Ward *Germany* III. 125 The entire *Cartel*, this time with the Centre, agreed to proceed with the loan. **1926** *Encycl. Brit.* II. 94/1 The Radicals, Radical-Socialists and Socialists formed a Cartel [France, 1924]. **1927** *Contemp. Rev.* Aug. 154 Hence an electoral cartel was inevitable, and to this the Transylvanians and Tsaranists consented. **1928** *Daily Tel.* 21 Aug. 8/3 The 'cartel' of Republican parties formed by him [*sc.* M. Veniselos]. **1959** B. & R. North tr. *Duverger's Political Parties* (ed. 2) II. i. 231 The Left-wing Cartel, the Popular Front, and so on. *Ibid.* ii. 326 The Cartel ..which won the 1887 elections and lost the 1890 one.

4. *gen.* A paper or card, bearing writing or printing; a tablet.

1693 Urquhart *Rabelais* III. viii. 68 Covering them with Husks..Films, Cartels, Shells..Rinds. **1762–71** H. Walpole *Vertue's Anecd. Paint.* (1786) I. 210 He ordered a cartel with some Greek verses..to be affixed to the frame [of a portrait]. **1850** Mrs. Browning *Poems* II. 324 Wipe such visionings From the Fancy's cartel. **1875** Stubbs *Const. Hist.* I. xiii. 584 To send in a cartel or report of the number of knights' fees.

5. *attrib.*, as in ***cartel ship***, a ship employed in exchanging prisoners; see 3, 3 b; **cartel clock** (see quots.).

1757 Wesley *Wks.* (1872) II. 425 Some hundred English, who had been prisoners in France, were landed at Penzance, by a cartel ship. **1826** Kent *Comm.* 69 The same interdiction of trade applies to ships of truce, or cartel ships. **1899** F. J. Britten *Old Clocks & Watches* 275 Hanging or 'Cartel' Clocks of Louis XV period were usually of metal thickly gilt and graceful in form. **1960** H. Hayward *Antique Coll.* 57/1 *Cartel clock*, a mural clock, usually of somewhat flamboyant design... English are usually of carved wood, whereas the French are usually of cast brass or bronze and gilt.

Hence †**cartel** *v. trans.*, to serve with a challenge; †**ˈcarteller**, †**ˈcartelist**, one who challenges; **ˈcartelling** *vbl. sb.*, making of cartels, exchanging of prisoners; **ˈcartel(l)ism**, the system of cartels, cartelization; **ˈcartel(l)ist**, a member or supporter of a cartel; **cartel(l)iˈzation**, the formation of or into cartels; **ˈcartel(l)ize** *v. trans.* and *intr.*, to form (into) a cartel; hence ***cartel(l)ized*** ppl. adj., ***cartel(l)izing*** vbl. sb.

1598 B. Jonson *Ev. Man in Hum.* I. iv, Come hither, you shall chartel him. **1611** Florio, *Cartellante*, a challenger, a carteller. *a* **1679** Earl Orrery *Guzman* III, The Mode of fighting Duels with single Rapier, which..has been call'd, by the Cartelists, *à la Bouteville.* **1865** Carlyle *Fredk. Gt.* V. xix. ix. 628 No more exchanging or cartelling. **1923** *Contemp. Rev.* June 716 Hitherto textiles were not regarded as favourable fields for cartelisation. **1925** *Glasgow Herald* 16 Apr. 9 Passionate Cartelist though he is. **1926** *Ibid.* 4 Jan. 7 The leading exponent of Cartellism. **1927** F. S. Browne tr. *R. Liefmann's Internat. Cartels* 98 Baron Tibbaut (Belgium) believed that cartellization spelled the death of 'protectionism'. *Ibid.* 101 In the face of a cartellized industry, strong organization of the consumers..was necessary. **1929** *Times* 5 June 15/3 In the late Council Anti-Cartellists and Cartellists were exactly balanced. **1935** *Economist* 6 Apr. 779/1 The Conservative advocates of the cartelising policy known euphemistically as 'Self-government for Industry'. **1955** *Times* 4 July 9/7 Whereas only lately, at the request of the Allies, decartelization in Germany was the order of the day, it is now again cartelization. **1961** *Economist* 25 Nov. 819/2 This [air travel], the most highly-cartelised industry in the world.

cartel, cartle, varr. KARTEL.

carter¹ (ˈkɑːtə(r)). Also 3–6 **cartare**, 4 **karter**, 5 **cartere**, 6–8 **cartar**. [f. CART *sb.* + -ER¹. (Littré and Cotgr. have F. *chartier* in this sense in 16–17th c.)]

†**1.** The driver of a chariot; a charioteer. *Obs.*

a **1300** *Cursor M.* 21287 Þe carter self is iesus crist. *c* **1374** Chaucer *Boeth.* v. iv. 163 As men seen þe karter worken in þe tournynge..of hys kartes or chariottes. **1513** Douglas *Æneis* XII. viii. 60 Metiscus the cartar, That Turnus chayr had for to rewle on hand. **1551** Recorde *Cast. Knowl.* (1556) 264 This constellation is also named Auriga the Cartar. **1580** Baret *Alv.* C 150 A chariot man, a carter.

2. a. One who drives a cart.

a **1250** *Owl & Night.* 1184 Drah to the cwaþ þe cartare. **1463** *Mann. & Househ. Exp.* 226 The carteris that browt hame the sayd yryn. **1549** Olde *Erasm. Par. Ephes.* Prol. C ij, As vnmete for this..as a carter of husbandry to be a caruer at a noble mans table. **1697** Dampier *Voy.* (1729) I. 432 A piece of Buffaloe-hide, shaped like our Carters Frocks. **1840** Hood *Up Rhine* 194 The carters drive along the streets smacking a tune with their whips.

b. As a type of low birth or breeding; a rude, uncultured man, a clown. (Common in 16th c.)

1509 Barclay *Ship of Fooles* Pref., Why are they [poets] dyspysed of many rude carters of nowe a dayes whiche vnderstonde nat them? **1581** J. Bell *Haddon's Answ. Osor.* 3 b, There is no Carter but knoweth it. **1589** Puttenham *Eng. Poesie* I. xx. (Arb.) 57 Continence in a king is of greater merit, then in a carter. **1848** Macaulay *Hist. Eng.* iii. (1849) I. 322 A man with the deportment, the vocabulary, and the accent of a carter.

†**3.** ? Some kind of missile. *Obs.*

1751 Smollett *Per. Pic.* (1779) I. ii. 8 Heaving..round and doubleheaded partridges, crows, and carters.

4. a. More fully **carter-fish**: a kind of flat-fish (*Pleuronectes megastoma*), otherwise called WHIFF.

1884 *St. James's Gaz.* 18 Jan. 6/1 The carter, etc...belong to that strange family of fish.

b. In full **carter spider**: an arachnid of the order Opiliones; = HARVESTMAN 2.

1665 Hooke *Microgr.* 198 The Carter, Shepherd Spider, or long-legg'd Spider. **1736** Hooke in E. Albin *Nat. Hist. of Spiders* 57 Microscopical observations on the Carter Spider and Jumping Spider. **1746** B. Martin *Ess. Electricity* 22 That Sort [of spider] we call a Carter, or Father Long-legs.

†**ˈcarter**². *Sc. Obs.* Also **cairtar**. [f. CARTE¹ 4 + -ER¹.] A card-player.

1566 Knox *Hist. Ref.* Wks. 1846 I. 345 Tables, whairof sum..used to serue for drunkardis, dysaris, and carteris.

carter, obs. form of CHARTER.

carter-cap (Nashe): = CATER-CAP, collegian.

†**ˈcarterlike,** *a.* and *adv. Obs.* [f. CARTER¹ + LIKE *a.*] Like a carter; rude(ly, clownish(ly.

1561 T. Hoby tr. *Castiglione's Courtyer* I. I iij, Rude and cartarlyke singing. **1580** Hollyband *Treas. Fr. Tong.*, *Roturièrement*, carters like. **1678** Flamsteed in Baily *Acc. Flamsteed* 117 That you should think me of that carter-like temper that I cannot move without a goad.

†**ˈcarterly,** *a.* and *adv. Obs.* [f. as prec. + -LY.]

A. *adj.* Like or befitting a carter; clownish, boorish, rude, ill-bred.

1519 Horman *Vulg.* 280 A carterly or a rebaud songe. **1579** Lyly *Euphues* (Arb.) 40 Diogenes a philosopher, yet who more carterly? **1611** Cotgr. s.v. *Charterie*, A carterlie, or churlish tricke. **1644** Sir E. Dering *Prop. Sacr.* E iiij b, This is carterly language.

B. *adv.* In a rude or boorish manner.

1553 Grimalde *Cicero's Offices* I. (1558) 57 We must.. take hede..that.. nothing blockishly or carterly wee do. **1593** Nashe *Lett. Confut.* 57 Not the most exquisite thing that is, but the Counsel Table Asse Richard Clarke, may so Carterly deride. **1598** Florio, *Villanamente*..clounishlie, carterly, basely, inciuilie.

Cartesian (kɑːˈtiːzɪən, -ʒ(ɪ)ən), *a.* (*sb.*) [ad. mod.L. *Cartesiānus*, f. *Cartesius*, latinized form of the name of *René Descartes*, the famous French philosopher and mathematician (1596–1650).]

A. *adj.* **a.** Pertaining to Descartes, or to his philosophy or mathematical methods.

1656 H. More *Antid. Ath.* Gen. Pref. 18 So perfectly agreeable to the Cartesian Philosophy. **1691–8** Norris *Pract. Disc.* (1711) III. 128 When I happen to fall into that Cartesian doubt and perplexity. **1837** Hallam *Hist. Lit.* III. iii. §86 *Cogito*; *Ergo sum*, this famous enthymem of the Cartesian philosophy. **1854** Scoffern in *Orr's Circ. Sc.* Chem. 73 Varying the form of lenses from sections of spheres to sections of certain ovals, which, from the name of Descartes, are termed the Cartesian ovals. **1882** Minchin *Unipl. Kinemat.* 20 The Cartesian equation of the curve.

b. ***Cartesian co-ordinates***: see CO-ORDINATE *sb.* 2; ***Cartesian devil, C. diver***: a philosophical toy, consisting of a hollow figure, partly filled with water and partly with air, and made to float in a vessel nearly filled with water, having an air-tight elastic covering. This covering being pressed down, the air inside the vessel is compressed, and more water forced through a small aperture into the figure, which consequently sinks, to rise again when the external pressure is removed.

1731 *Phil. Trans.* XXXVII. 79 The Glass for shewing the Experiment with the Cartesian Devils.

B. *sb.* A follower of Descartes; one who accepts the philosophy of Descartes.

1660 Boyle *New Exp. Phys-Mech.* Digress. 347 Divers of the new Philosophers, Cartesians, and others. **1692** Bentley *Boyle Lect.* 59 The Cartesians and some others.. have asserted that brutes are meer machins and automata. **1758** Johnson *Idler* No. 10 ¶4 The Cartesian who denies that his horse feels the spur. **1837** Hallam *Hist. Lit.* III. iii. §86 *note*, This word [Ego], introduced by the Germans, or originally perhaps by the old Cartesians.

Carˈtesianism, the philosophy of Descartes.

1656 H. More *Antid. Ath.* Gen. Pref. 17 Not only Platonism, but that which now deserves to be called Cartesianism, for Des-Cartes his so happily recovering it again into view. **1870** *Athenæum* 3 Dec. 716 Cartesianism, if logically followed into its conclusions, surely lands us in Spinozism.

cartful (ˈkɑːtfʊl). [see -FUL.] As much or as many as a cart will hold.

1399 Langl. *Rich. Redeles* II. 158 Cauȝte of the kytes a cartfull at ones. **1453** Marg. Paston *Lett.* I. 256 This day I have had inne ij. cartfull of hey. **1465** *Mann. & Househ. Exp.* 316 Payd for a cartfolle of charcolle vjs. **1651** *Reliq. Wotton.* 614 (R.) Wood..at twenty-five crowns the cart-full. **1863** J. Brown *Horæ Subs.* (ed. 3) 143 A cartful of irrepressible youngsters.

Carthaginian (kɑːθəˈdʒɪnɪən), *a.* and *sb.* Also 6–9 **Carthagenian**. [f. L. *Carthago*, *-inis* Carthage + -IAN.] **A.** *adj.* Of, pertaining to, or characteristic of Carthage, an ancient city of north Africa, or its people; ***Carthaginian faith***: see FAITH *sb.* 11 b; ***Carthaginian peace***, a peace settlement that is very severe to the defeated side. **B.** *sb.* A native or inhabitant of Carthage. Cf. PUNIC *a.* and *sb.*

1592 [see PERFIDY]. **1594** Kyd *Cornelia* II. 484 Fought, before the fearefull Carthagenian walls. **1596** Spenser *View Irel.* in *Wks.* (1893) 627/2 The Carthagenians in all the long Punicke Warres. **1601** [see PUNIC *a.* 1]. **1618** [see TRICK *sb.* 3]. **1652** [see CONTROVERSY *sb.* 1 a]. **1671** Milton *P.R.* III. 35 Young Scipio had brought down The Carthaginian pride. **1711** [see FAITH *sb.* 11 b]. **1846** R. Ford *Gatherings from Spain* ii. 11 The lower classes partake of the Greek and Carthaginian character, being false, cruel, and treacherous. **1869** 'Mark Twain' *Innoc. Abr.* viii. 79 The Phoenicians, the Carthagenians, the English, Moors, Romans, all have battled for Tangier. **1940** *Economist* 3 Feb. 191/2 Intending to annex slices of German territory, or to impose a Carthaginian peace. **1948** Kroeber *Anthropology* xvii. 729 The Etruscans and the Carthaginians..were slow in taking up coinage. **1967** *Guardian* 11 July 6/5 The idea that the Israelis are anxious to..dictate a Carthaginian peace is ludicrously wide of the mark.

‖**carthamus** (ˈkɑːθəməs). Also 7 **cartamus**, 8 **carthame**. [mod.L. *carthamus* (in F. *carthame*), ad. Arab. *qarṭum*, *qirṭim*, in same sense.]

A small genus of annual composite plants; esp. *C. tinctorius* (Safflower or Bastard Saffron), cultivated from southern Europe to China, the flowers of which yield red and yellow dyes. **b.** The florets used in the mass as a dye, and as a drug.

1548 Turner *Names of Herbes*, *Cnecus*..is called..in englishe Bastarde saffron or mocke-saffron..The Poticaries call thys herbe carthamus. **1662** Fuller *Worthies* I. 317 No precious drug is more adulterated [than Saffron] with Cartamus. **1750** Beawes *Lex Mercat.* 806 Commodities of the Country's [Java's] Growth..Carthame (or Bastard Saffron). **1814** Sir H. Davy *Agric. Chem.* 146 The Carthamus contains a red and a yellow colouring matter.. from the red, rouge is prepared.

Hence **carˈthamic** *a.*, as in ***carthamic acid***, the same as **ˈcarthamin**, the red colouring matter of safflower, $C_{14}H_{16}O_7$.

1838 T. Thomson *Chem. Org. Bodies* 405 Carthamin. This..Dobereiner considers as an acid, to which he has given the name of carthamic acid. **1863–72** Watts *Dict. Chem.* I. 808 The carthamin is precipitated in red flocks.

†**Cartholic.** *Obs.* A derisive perversion of CATHOLIC.

1582 N. T. (Rhem.) *Acts* xi. Annot. 324 Some Heretikes of this time call them Cartholikes and cacolikes.

ˈcart-ˌhorse. A horse used to draw a cart. (In first quot. transl. *bigalis* 'horse drawing two-wheeled chariot'. Now, a large thick-set horse used for heavy work.)

1398 Trevisa *Barth. De P.R.* XVIII. xli. (1495) 802 Charyotte horse were ordeyned and halowed to the sonne, and carte horse were halowyd to the mone. **1483** *Cath. Angl.* 55 A carte hors; *veredus, caballus.* **1535** Coverdale *1 Kings* iv. 26 Salomon had fortye thousande cart horses, and twolue thousande horsmen. **1623** J. Taylor (Water P.) *World on Wheeles* Wks. II. 235/2 Scarse any Coachhorse in the world doth know any letter in the Booke, when as euery Carthorse doth know the letter G very vnderstandingly. **1813** Macaulay in *Life & Lett.* (1880) I. 48, I will work like a cart-horse.

†**carthoun.** *Obs.* [= Ger. *kartaune*, *kartane*, ad. It. and med.L. *quartana*, which, as well as the former Ger. transl. *viertelsbüchse* 'quarter-gun', designated originally 'a 25-pounder cannon in relation to the largest siege-pieces of 100 lbs.' (Kluge). Also CARTOW, q.v.]

A kind of cannon, also called a quarter-cannon; recent writers identify it (app. through some error) with the *cannon-royal.* See also CARTOW, CURTALL.

1849 *Mem. Kirkaldy Gr.* xxviii. 335 These consisted of one cannon-royal or carthoun a 48 pounder, two sakers, etc. **1867** Smyth *Sailor's Word-bk.*, *Carthoun*, the ancient cannon royal, carrying a 66 lb. ball. **1874** Knight *Dict. Mech.* I. 446 Cannon royal or carthoun 48 pounds.

cart-house (ˈkɑːthaʊs).

1. A shed or outhouse in which carts are kept.

1483 *Cath. Angl.* 54 A Carte hows, *carectarea.* **1805** Forsyth *Beauties Scotl.* II. 230 The barn, cart-house, and granary [formed] the third side.

†**2.** A house on wheels. *Obs.*

1601 R. Johnson *Kingd. & Commw.* (1603) 161 Moving houses, built upon wheels like a shepperds cottage..they plant these cart-houses verie orderlie in a ranke.

carthouse, obs. corrupt f. CARTOUCHE.

Carthusian (kɑːˈθjuːzɪən, -ʒ(ɪ)ən), *a.* and *sb.* Earlier forms were **Charthous, Chartous, Cartusier.** [ad. L. *Cartusiān-us*, *Cartusiensis*, 'from the *Catursiani montes*, or from *Catorissium*, *Caturissium*, *Chatrousse*, a village in Dauphiné, near which their first monastery was founded' (Littré). In F. *chartreux*, OF. *charteus*, *-ous.*

Most English dictionaries erroneously explain their name from la Grande-Chartreuse, their chief convent, near Grenoble; but this is really named after the order: see CHARTER-HOUSE.]

1. a. *adj.* Of or belonging to an order of monks founded in Dauphiné, by St. Bruno, in the year 1086, remarkable for the severity of their rule. **b.** *sb.* A monk of this order.

c **1394** *P. Pl. Crede* 674 Monkes ne preistes, Chanons ne Charthous þat in chirche serueth. **1526** *Pilgr. Perf.* (W. de W. 1531) 26 b, The order of the cartusiensys. **1536** Bellenden *Cron. Scot.* (1821) II. 299 He..deit a chartour [? -ous] monk. **1563–87** Foxe *A. & M.* II. 375 The house of the Carthusian monks. **1605** Stow *Ann.* 559 The religion of the Cartusiers. **1633** Massinger *Guardian* III. i, Live, like a Carthusian, on poor-John. **1828** Scott *F.M. Perth* xxv, In the Carthusian convent. **1847** Sir J. Stephen *Eccl. Biog.* (1850) 113 The Carthusians with their self-immolations.

2. a. *adj.* Of the 'Charterhouse' School, founded on the site of a Carthusian monastery in London. **b.** *sb.* A scholar of the Charterhouse School.

1860 *All Y. Round* No. 66. 367 There is plenty of space for the Carthusians to play in. **1864** *Blackw. Mag.* XCVI. 449 (Hoppe) Carthusians regard their old school with loyalty and gratitude.

cartilage ('kɑːtɪlɪdʒ). [a. F. *cartilage* (16th c. in Littré), ad. L. *cartilāgo* gristle.]

1. A firm elastic flexible tissue, of a whitish translucent colour, in vertebrate animals; gristle.

temporary cartilage is that which occurs only in very early life, and subsequently ossifies or changes to bone; ***permanent cartilage*** is that which permanently retains its character, e.g. the ***articular cartilage*** which coats the ends of bones at the joints, and the ***membraniform cartilage*** which occurs in the walls of cavities.

1541 R. COPLAND *Guydon's Quest. Chirurg.*, What is cartylage?.. It is a substaunce as it were of the kynde of bones, but it is softer or sowpler than the bone is. **1633** P. FLETCHER *Purple Isl.* IV. 44 *note*, The winde-pipe..is framed partly of cartilage, or grisly matter. **1797** GODWIN *Enquirer* I. iii. 15 What at first was cartilage..gradually becomes bone. **1873** MIVART *Elem. Anat.* ii. 24 The adjacent surfaces of bones are coated with smooth cartilage.

b. A structure or formation consisting of cartilage, a gristly part; as the ***cartilages of the ribs***.

1541 R. COPLAND *Guydon's Quest. Chirurg.*, The bones, grystles, or cartilages, the synewes. **1827** F. COOPER *Prairie* II. i. 5 Ornaments..pendant from the cartilages of his ears.

†**2.** Applied to the coats of an onion. *Obs.*

1563 HYLL *Art Garden.* (1593) 131 The..number of cartilages, with the which the bodie [of an onion] is included.

3. *Comb.*, as ***cartilage-corpuscle***, ***-like*** adj.

1847 TODD *Cycl. Anat.* IV. 518/1 The cartilage-like tendon. **1876** tr. *Wagner's Gen. Pathol.* 154 Bone and cartilage-corpuscles.

cartila'ginean. *rare.* A cartilaginous fish.

1835 KIRBY *Hab. & Inst. Anim.* II. xxi. 388 Cartilagineans in which [the skeleton] is cartilaginous.

†**cartila'gineous,** *a. Obs.* Also 7 -ious. [f. L. *cartilāgine-us* (f. *cartilāgin-em* cartilage) + -OUS.] = CARTILAGINOUS.

1646 SIR T. BROWNE *Pseud. Ep.* III. xix, The Lamprey hath..for the spine or back-bone, a cartilagineous substance. **1693** *Phil. Trans.* XVII. 930 Cartilagineous Fishes.

cartilaginification (ˌkɑːtɪləˌdʒɪnɪfɪ'keɪʃən). [So. in mod.Fr.: f. L. *cartilāgini-* stem of *cartilāgo* cartilage; see -FICATION. Cf. *ossification*.] The formation of or conversion into cartilage.

1842 E. WILSON *Anat. Vade M.* 5 The semi-opaque jelly becomes dense, transparent, and homogeneous, the change ..constituting cartilaginification. **1847–9** TODD *Cycl. Anat.* IV. 131/1 Some alterations of texture..(the so-called cartilaginification and ossification).

cartilaginiform (ˌkɑːtɪlə'dʒɪnɪfɔːm), *a.* [f. as prec.; see -FORM.] Resembling cartilage.

1830 R. KNOX *Béclard's Anat.* 238 Cartilaginiform ligamentous organs. **1835–6** TODD *Cycl. Anat.* I. 249/1 This remarkable structure..called by the older anatomists.. cartilaginiform ligament.

cartilaginoid (kɑːtɪ'lædʒɪnɔɪd), *a.* [f. as prec.; see -OID.] Of the form or nature of cartilage.

1859 TODD *Cycl. Anat.* V. 517/1 A cartilaginoid thickening of the periosteum. **1881** E. R. LANKESTER in *Jrnl. Microsc. Sc.* Jan. 131 A homogeneous cartilaginoid substance.

cartilaginous (kɑːtɪ'lædʒɪnəs), *a.* [ad. F. *cartilagineux*, or L. *cartilāginōs-us*, f. *cartilāgin-em* cartilage: see -OUS.]

1. Of the nature of, or consisting of, cartilage.

1541 R. COPLAND *Guydon's Quest. Chirurg.*, The places about the lachrymall..and the palpebres neyghbours cartylagynouses. **1710** STEELE & ADDISON *Tatler* No. 260 ¶5 The Gristle or Cartilaginous Substance. **1851** RICHARDSON *Geol.* viii. 278 In the Sturgeon the skeleton is cartilaginous.

b. *Zool.* ***cartilaginous fishes***: an order of fishes having a cartilaginous skeleton.

1695 WOODWARD *Nat. Hist. Earth* VI. (1723) 271 Fish..of the cartilaginous and squammose..kinds. **1769** PENNANT *Zool.* III. 57 Many of the cartilaginous fish are viviparous. **1847** CARPENTER *Zool.* §579.

2. *Bot.* Of the texture of cartilage.

1677 GREW *Anat. Seeds* iv. §22 The Inner Cover [of the Seed] is also Cartilaginous or Horney. **1830** LINDLEY *Nat. Syst. Bot.* 137 Albumen..between horny and cartilaginous. **1870** HOOKER *Stud. Flora* 80 [Holly] leaves glossy..with waved spinous cartilaginous margins.

carting ('kɑːtɪŋ), *vbl. sb.*[1] [f. CART *v.* + -ING[1].] The action of conveying in a CART. In specific senses: **a.** exposure to public ignominy in a cart; **b.** the transport of coal underground to the shaft.

1554 MARTIN *Marriage of Priestes* LL ij b (L.) In carting, and ploughing. **1587** GOLDING *De Mornay* xii. (1617) 188 Haddest thou once shamed him by the pillory or by carting. **1642** T. TAYLOR *God's Judgem.* II. iv. 57 Scarce a monthely Sessions..without hanging and carting. **1645** *Mercurius Anti-Brit.* 11 Aug. 11 Have you ever, at a Carting, seen People throw rotten eggs?

†**'carting,** *vbl. sb.*[2] *Sc. Obs.* [f. CARTE[1] 4 + -ING[1].] Card-playing.

1535 STEWART *Cron. Scot.* III. 345 Sic carting, dysing, hurdome, and harlatrie. **1536** BELLENDEN *Cron. Scot.* II. 167 The young men..followit dising and carting.

'cart-load. The load which a cart can carry.

a **1300** *Havelok* 895 A carte lode Of segges, laxes, of playces brode, Of grete laumprees, and of eles. **1626** BERNARD *Isle of Man* (1627) 165 David..that gaue..3300 Cartload of Treasure for the building of the Temple. **1641** S. MARSHALL *Peace-Offering* 48 Above three and thirtie thousand cart-load of silver. **1757** tr. *Keysler's Trav.* (1760) II. 322 The many thousand cart-loads of earth or sand, taken out of the catacombs. **1870** EMERSON *Farming* Wks. (Bohn) III. 61 See what the farmer accomplishes by a cartload of tiles.

b. Often *fig.* for a large quantity, 'load,' 'heap'.

1577 HOLINSHED *Chron.* II. 123 Whole cart lodes of complaints and greevances. **1645** PAGITT *Heresiogr.* (1647) 158 The Anabaptists brought Cart-loads of lyes to maintaine their..opinions. **1789** J. WOLCOTT (P. Pindar) *Expost. Ode* vii. Wks. 1812 II. 230 Of fun you rob him of cart-loads.

cartogram ('kɑːtəʊgræm). [ad. Fr. *cartogramme*.] (See quot. 1965.)

1890 *Rep. Insane, Feeble-Minded, &c.* (11th Census U.S.) 9 Cartogram 1 indicates by depths of shading the ratios of the insane to each 100,000 of the population in the different states. **1909** WEBSTER, *Cartogram*, a map showing geographically, by shades or curves, statistics of various kinds; a statistical map. **1934** E. RAISZ in *Geogr. Rev.* XXIV. 292 The statistical cartogram is not a map. Although it has roughly the proportions of the country..the cartogram is purely a geometrical design to visualize certain statistical facts and to work out certain problems of distribution. **1937** *Geogr. Jrnl.* LXXXIX. 349 A cartogram is arithmetically accurate but topographically untrue. **1938** E. RAISZ *General Cartography* xxiii. 257 How 'diagrammatic' a map must be in order to be called a cartogram depends largely on individual judgment. **1965** F. J. MONKHOUSE *Dict. Geogr.* 55/2 *Cartogram*, a map on which statistical information is presented in diagrammatic form.

cartographer (kɑː'tɒgrəfə(r)). Also **charto-**. [f. F. *carte* card, chart, or L. *charta*, *carta* (a. Gr. χάρτη, χάρτης), leaf of paper + Gr. -γράφ-ος writer + -ER[1]; cf. *geographer*. The *ch-* spelling is in accordance with the ultimate etymology (the Gr. would be *χαρτογράφος); but the other is commoner, and perh. preferred, as not suggesting the pronunciation of *ch-* in *chart*.]

One who makes or compiles charts or maps.

1863 *Reader* 12 Dec. 705/3 Each cartographer only delineated one lake. **1880** HAUGHTON *Phys. Geog.* vi. 308 The speculations of chartographers. **1885** *Athenæum* 29 Aug. 274/2 No cartographer since the 15th century had ventured to indicate it.

cartographic (kɑːtə'græfɪk), *a.* Also **charto-**. [f. as prec. + -IC.] Of or pertaining to cartography. So **carto'graphical**, of, belonging to, or dealing with cartography.

1885 *Academy* 19 Sept., A good specimen of.. cartographic work. **1880** *Ibid.* 11 Dec. 428 The cartographical art being only in its infancy. **1881** *Nature* XXIV. No. 607. 150 Valuable chartographical matter.

cartography (kɑː'tɒgrəfɪ). Also **charto-**. [f. as prec. + Gr. -γραφία writing; as if ad. Gr. *χαρτογραφία.] The drawing of charts or maps.

1859 R. BURTON *Centr. Afr.* in *Jrnl. Geog. Soc.* XXIX. 28 The circles which in cartography denote cities or towns. **1859** J. R. JACKSON (*title*), A Manual of Geographical Science..Part I..Chartography. **1884** *Bookseller* 6 Nov. 1177/1 A clever piece of cartography.

cartomancy ('kɑːtəʊˌmænsɪ). [f. It. *carta* in sense 'playing-card' + Gr. μαντεία divination.] Divination by playing-cards.

1871 TYLOR *Prim. Cult.* I. 114 Cartomancy, the art of fortune-telling with packs of cards. **1886** *Newscastle Weekly Chron.* 29 May 3/1 It is said that the earliest work on cartomancy was written or compiled by Francesco Marcolini, and printed at Venice, in 1540..Cartomancy was very fashionable in England during the eighteenth century. Numbers of young ladies used to consult the cards to know whom, when, and where they would marry.

carton[1] ('kɑːtən). [app. a. F. *carton* papier-mâché, pasteboard, f. *carte*: see CARTOON.] In rifle practice: A white disc or circle within the bull's-eye of a target; also a shot which strikes this; *attrib.* as in ***carton-target***.

1864 *Daily Tel.* 15 July, Captain Heaton, out of 27 shots ..made 26 bull's-eyes, of which 13 were cartons..These Swiss carton targets, at which the Vernon prizes are shot for, were..crowded during the day.

carton[2] ('kɑːtən). [a. F. *carton*: see CARTON.]

a. Light pasteboard or cardboard used for making boxes, etc. Also *attrib.*

[**1786** T. BLAIKIE *Diary Scotch Gardener* (1931) 202 The Marquis de Cray..proposed to make buildings of Paper or as he called it Carton. *Ibid.* 203 The Marquis still persisted in his carton projects.] **1891** MAHAFFY *Flinders Petrie Papyri* 9 The coffins..were made of layers of papyrus,..stuck together so as to form a thick carton, painted within and without with designs and religious emblems. These carton-cases were made to fit the swathed body. **1908** J. H. JUDD (*title*) The 'A.L.' Carton Work. **1910** —— Carton Designing for Juniors. **1913** *Bk. School Handwork* I. 188 Domestic Handicraft for Girls in Paper, Carton, Cardboard, and Woodwork. *Ibid.* 195 Paper folding and carton work..in the making of toys.

b. A box or case made of light pasteboard, cardboard, or plastic, for holding goods. Hence **cartoned** ('kɑːtənd) *a.*, packed in a carton.

1906 *Daily Chron.* 24 Oct. 6/6 A pound carton [of soap]. **1921** C. C. MARTIN *Export Packing* 559 Sundry Cartoned Goods. **1924** *Public Opinion* 12 Sept. 258/3 Motorists' sandwich papers and cigarette cartons. **1926** *Spectator* 18 Sept. 412/1 The fish..are packed in specially designed cartons. **1957** *Encycl. Brit.* III. 989/1 Cartons form an important branch of paper box manufacture. **1971** *Garden News* 25 June 14/4 Transparent yoghurt cartons.

cartonnage ('kɑːtənɪdʒ). *Archæol.* Also **cartonage.** [Fr., f. *carton*: see prec. and -AGE.]

An Egyptian mummy-case made of layers of linen or papyrus tightly pressed and glued together and fitting closely to the embalmed body; also, the material thus used. Also *attrib.*

[**1834** T. J. PETTIGREW *Egypt. Mummies* 116 The case I am describing is called by the French the 'Cartonage', from the resemblance of its composition to pasteboard.] **1841** J. G. WILKINSON *Anc. Egyptians* II. 477 The innermost covering of the body..was the *cartonage*. This was a pasteboard case fitting exactly to its shape. **1881** RAWLINSON *Hist. Anc. Egypt.* I. 512 The swathed body was covered by a 'cartonnage', consisting of twenty or forty layers of linen tightly pressed and glued together, so as to form a sort of pasteboard envelope, which then received a thin coating of stucco, and was painted in bright colours with hieroglyphics and figures of deities. **1889** PETRIE *Hawara* 15 Mummies with gilt cartonnage heads. **1957** G. CLARK *Archaeol. & Society* (ed. 3) iii. 78 A number of papyri..were recovered from the cartonnage of a mummy excavated by Flinders Petrie.

‖**carton-pierre** (kartɔ̃ pjɛːr). [Fr., = 'cardboard (of) stone'.] A kind of papier mâché made to imitate stone or bronze.

1850 THACKERAY *Pendennis* I. xxxviii. 372 Old family portraits from Wardour Street..and battle-axes made of *carton-pierre*. **1851** *Illustr. Catal. Gt. Exhib.* III. 747/1 Bracket-table,..the figures supporting it of carton-pierre. **1858** SIMMONDS *Dict. Trade*, *Carton-pierre*..has been used for roofing, and is composed of the pulp of paper mixed with whiting and glue. **1961** *Connoisseur Guide to Antique Eng. Furn.* 115 A great deal of Early Victorian furniture made use of patent materials such as gutta-percha, stamped leather, carton-pierre, [etc.].

cartoon (kɑː'tuːn), *sb.* Also 8 **carton**, **cartone**. [a. F. *carton* or (its source) It. *cartone*, augm. of *carta* paper.]

1. A drawing on stout paper, made as a design for a painting of the same size to be executed in fresco or oil, or for a work in tapestry, mosaic, stained glass, or the like.

1671 EVELYN *Diary* 18 Jan., I perceived him [Gibbon], carving that large cartoon, or crucifix, of Tintoretto. **1683** *Ibid.* 9 May, To ask whether he [the Duke of Norfolk] would part with any of his cartoons and other drawings of Raphael. **1697** C. HATTON *Corr.* (1878) II. 229 But yᵉ sight best pleased me was yᵉ cartoons by Raphael, wᶜʰ are far beyond all yᵉ paintings I ever saw. **1711** STEELE *Spect.* No. 226 ¶1 The Cartons in Her Majesty's Gallery at Hampton-Court. *a* **1721** PRIOR *Alma* III. 440 When Rarus shows you his Cartone, He always tells you, with a groan, etc. **1762–71** H. WALPOLE *Vertue's Anecd. Paint.* (1786) I. 240. **1852** MRS. JAMESON *Leg. Madonna* (1857) 24 The set of cartoons for the tapestries of the Sistine Chapel. **1867** *Even. Standard* 14 Feb., Coloured cartoons for church windows in stained glass.

2. a. A full-page illustration in a paper or periodical; *esp.* applied to those in the comic papers relating to current events. Now, a humorous or topical drawing (of any size) in a newspaper, etc. Cf. *strip-cartoon*.

1843 *Punch* 24 June 258/2 *Punch* has the benevolence to announce, that in an early number of his ensuing Volume he will astonish the Parliamentary Committee by the publication of several exquisite designs, to be called Punch's Cartoons! *Ibid.* 15 July 22/2 Substance and Shadow. Cartoon No. I. **1863** MISS BRADDON *Eleanor's Vict.* xl, One of Mr. Leech's most genial cartoons. **1879** *Print. Trades Jrnl.* XXIX. 8 The cartoons bearing on colonial politics. **1900** M. BEERBOHM *Lett. to R. Turner* (1964) 298 His [*sc.* Pellegrini's] famous *Vanity Fair* cartoons. *Ibid.*, A pair of original cartoon-drawings. **1910** *Daily Chron.* 1 Mar. 6/6 The cartoon nowadays..is merely party-political. You find a scratchy sketch in the corner of a paper devoted to the week-end football matches or the spring handicaps, or Mr. Asquith's breakfast with the King. 'Cartoon!' **1959** *Chambers's Encycl.* III. 117/1 Daumier's example can still be traced in the modern newspaper cartoon. *Ibid.*, Caricatures..began to appear as political cartoons.

b. *Cinematography.* An animated cartoon (see ANIMATED *ppl. a.* 1 d). Also *attrib.*

1916 *Sci. Amer.* 14 Oct. 354/1 Knowledge of motion is a requisite in properly animating a drawing, in spite of the seeming simplicity of the cartoons when viewed on the screen. *Ibid.*, Here may be learned..the production of cartoon films, from the inception of the idea to the projection of the film on the screen. **1923** *Lit. Digest* 5 May 27/2 The moving cartoons now familiar at the picture shows are made with the aid of transparent sheets of pyralin. **1936** *Discovery* Apr. 122/2 The making of motion pictures, cartoons, and sound recording. **1956** *Ann. Reg.* 1955 385 The first feature-length cartoon film, *Animal Farm*. **1959** I. & P. OPIE *Lore & Lang. Schoolchildren* vii. 112 Popeye.. another cartoon character originating in America.

car'toon, *v.* [f. prec. sb.]

1. *trans.* To design, as a cartoon (sense 1); to make a preparatory sketch or tracing of.

1887 *Athenæum* 12 Mar. 348/3 Rossetti was greatly struck by this story, and immediately the subject for 'Michael Scott's Wooing' was 'mentally cartooned'.

2. To represent by a cartoon (sense 2); to caricature, or hold up to ridicule.

1884 A. A. PUTNAM *10 Yrs. Police Judge* xxii. 194 They make bold to cartoon..the goodly profession of the law.

cartoonery (kɑːˈtuːnərɪ). [f. CARTOON *sb.* + -ERY.] The making of cartoons; cartoons in general.

1902 *Strand Mag.* Oct., The cartoon which we reproduce ..appealed particularly to the intellectually-minded, who hold that cartoonery should be something else than buffoonery. **1914** *N.Y. Herald* 16 June 10/7 Typical of a vast amount of cartoonery.

car'tooning, *vbl. sb.* [f. CARTOON *v.* + -ING[1].] The drawing or execution of cartoons; representation in a cartoon.

1846 BROWNING *Lett.* 9 July (1899) II. 319 Then comes the rest from cartooning and exhibiting. **1887** *Athenæum* 12 Mar. 348/1 The mental cartooning that foreshadowed those masterpieces. **1927** *Sunday at Home* June 540/1 The cartooning of nature has been aided by some touching up from a tricksy human hand. **1967** *Punch* 27 Dec. 954 Within the limits of cartooning.

car'toonist. An artist who draws cartoons.

1880 *Daily News* 28 Dec. 3/1. **1883** *Glasgow Her.* 12 July, The cartoonist of the comic papers.

†**car'toose.** *Obs.* **1.** Var. of CARTOUSE.

2. Of doubtful meaning; cf. CARTOUSE and CARTOUSH.

1607 DEKKER, etc. *Northw. Hoe* III. i. Wks. 1873 III. 37 A close sleeue with a cartoose collar.

cartophily (kɑːˈtɒfɪlɪ). [f. F. *carte*, It. *carta* (see CARD *sb.*[2]) + -O + -PHIL + -Y[3].] The pursuit of collecting, arranging, and studying cigarette-cards and similar items. So **car'tophilist**, a person devoted to cartophily; **carto'philic** *a.*

1936 C. L. BAGNALL in *Cigarette Card News* Apr. 87, 30,000 people in the British Isles..collect cigarette cards... I have coined a new word for my clients and call them cartophilists. **1936** *Morning Post* 11 Aug. 12/6 There is a magazine entirely devoted to 'cartophily'... For every one serious 'cartophilist' in 1930 there are 25 now. **1937** *Cigarette Card News* Apr. 120 In a mansion..the new cartophilic headquarters is to be found.

cartouche (kɑːˈtuːʃ). Also (7 **catouche, carthouse,** 8 **catooch**), 7–9 **cartouch.** See also CARTOUSE, CARTRIDGE. [a. F. *cartouche* fem. 'the cornet of paper wherein..grocers put the parcels they retaile; also, a Cartouch, or full charge, for a pistoll put vp within a little paper to be the readier for vse, etc.' (Cotgr.). Also = '*Cartoche*, a cartridge, or roll (in Architecture)' (Cotgr.): the latter is in mod.Fr. *cartouche*, masc. a. It. *cartoccio* 'a coffin of paper' (Florio), a 'cornet' of paper, augmentative f. *carta*:—med.L. *carta*, L. *charta* paper; see CARTE[1], CHART.]

I. = Fr. *cartouche* fem.

1. *Mil.* **a.** A roll or case of paper, parchment, etc., containing the charge of powder and shot for a gun or pistol; a cartridge. ? *Obs.* Also, in *Pyrotechnics*, the case containing the inflammable materials in some fireworks.

1611 COTGR. [see above]. **1625** J. GLANVILL *Voy. Cadiz* 20 To fill Carthouses of powder. **1662** PHILLIPS, *Cartouch* (Fr.), a charge of powder and shot, made ready in a paper, called also a Carthrage [*ed.* 1678: also sometimes mistakenly used for Carthrage]. **1704** J. HARRIS *Lex. Techn.*, *Cartouche*, the same with Cartridge. **1718** J. CHAMBERLAYNE *Relig. Philos.* II. xxi. §24 A little Cartouch or Case, of that kind which they use in making Squibs in common Fire-Works. **1725** DE FOE *Voy. round W.* (1840) 257 A harquebuss..with cartouches, powder and ball. **1850** MAZZINI *Roy. & Repub. Italy* 37 Women were rivals in the enthusiasm..they prepared cartouches.

†**b.** A case of wood, pasteboard, etc., containing iron balls, to be fired from a cannon or howitzer.

1611 COTGR., *Cartouche*, also, a peece of pastboord or thick paper stuffed (in a round or pudding like forme) with bullets, etc., and to be shot out of a great peece. **1693** *Paris Rel. Batt. Landen* 19 Whose Cannon play'd upon them with Cartouches. **1768** SIMES *Mil. Medley*, *Cartouch*, a case of wood..holding about four hundred musquet-balls, besides six or eight balls of iron.

c. = *cartridge-box*.

1808 J. BARLOW *Columb.* VII. 595 No cramm'd cartouch their belted back attires.

¶ 'A ticket of leave or dismission given to a soldier.' (In mod. Dicts., but app. purely Fr.)

II. = Fr. *cartouche* masc.

2. *Arch.* **a.** A corbel, mutule, or modillion. The earlier form was CARTOUSE, q.v. ? *Obs.*

1726 R. NEVE *Builder's Dict.* (1736), *Cartooses, Cartouzes*, or as some call 'em *Cartouches* are the same as Modilions.. under the cornice at the Eaves of a House..ornaments representing scrolls of paper: But most commonly are flat Members with Wavings for a device. **1762–71** H. WALPOLE *Vertue's Anecd. Paint.* (1786) II. 50 Three cartouches to support the balcony. **1850** PARKER *Gloss. Archit.* [see 2 c].

b. Any ornament in the form of a scroll, as the volute of an Ionic capital.

1611 COTGR., *Volute*..the writhen circle, or curle tuft that ..sticks out of the chapter of a piller, etc., and is tearmed by our workmen, a Rowle, Cartridge, or Carthouse. **1662** PHILLIPS, *Cartouch* (F.)..a Roll, with which they adorn the Cornish of a Pillar. **1708** *New View Lond.* II. 489/2 A white marble monument adorn'd with Cartouches. **1789** P. SMYTH tr. *Aldrich's Archit.* (1818) 105 Twisted columns, which are called cartouches.

c. A tablet for an inscription or for ornament, representing a sheet of paper with the ends rolled up; a drawing or figure of the same, for the title of a map, or the like; a drawn framing of an engraving, etc. Often *attrib.*

a **1776** J. GRANGER *Lett.* (1805) 69 The roof of this church is painted in cartouches or compartments. **1824** J. JOHNSON *Typogr.* I. 540 The print itself has a large cartouche oval frame, with pinks and gillyflowers issuing from the four corners. **1850** PARKER *Gloss. Archit.*, *Cartouch, Cartouche*, F., a term adopted from the French for a tablet, either for ornament or to receive an inscription, formed in the resemblance of a sheet of paper with the edges rolled up. **1875** FORTNUM *Maiolica* xiii. 146 Panels edged with cartouche ornament.

3. *Her.* The oval escutcheon of the Pope and 'churchmen of noble descent'.

1828 BERRY *Dict. Heraldry* (1830) *Cartouche*, is an oval shield in which the Popes and churchmen of noble descent in Italy place their armorial bearings.

4. *Archæol.* Name given to the oval or oblong figures in Egyptian hieroglyphics, inclosing characters expressing royal or divine names or titles.

1830 *Q. Rev.* May 118 (*Egypt. Antiq.*) It was soon found that royal names were inclosed in a sort of oval ring, called by Champollion a cartouche. **1850** LAYARD *Nineveh* x. 246 Between the figures is a cartouche containing a name in hieroglyphics.

III. *Comb.* (from sense 1) as **cartouche-box** = *cartridge-box*.

1697 DAMPIER *Voy.* I. 231 Some..that had not waxt up their Cartrage or Catouche Boxes, wet all their Powder. **1711** *Lond. Gaz.* No. 4850/3, 3 Chests Catooch Boxes. **1753** HANWAY *Trav.* (1762) I. VII. xciii. 429. **1808** *Regul. Service at Sea* VII. ii. §28. 223 He..is to be very careful that there are not any cartridges left in the cartouch-boxes.

†**car'touse.** *Obs.* Also 7–8 **-oose, -ouze, -oese.** [A variant of CARTOUCHE, or ad. It. *cartoccio*; formerly appropriated to the architectural sense.]

1. A modillion or corbel; = CARTOUCHE 2 a.

1611 COTGR., *Modillon*, a cartridge or cartoose, a foulding bracket or corbell. **1624** WOTTON in *Reliq.* (1672) 25 In the Cornice both Dentelli and Modiglioni (our artizans call them Teeth and Cartouzes). **1660** BLOOME *Archit.* A a, *Mutils*, that which we commonly call in English a cartouse. **1663** GERBIER *Counsel* 43 Masons put stone Cartoeses in the top of the inside walls, which are bearers to the Summers. **1726** [see CARTOUCHE 2].

2. A volute; see CARTOUCHE 2 b.

car'toush. *dial. Sc.* [According to Jamieson f. F. *courte* short, and *housse* 'a short mantle of course cloth worne in all weather by countrey women about their head and shoulders' (Cotgr.). Du Cange has *houcia curta* of date 1360.]

A kind of 'bed-gown' worn by working women in parts of Scotland, e.g. Fife. (Jamieson.)

†**car'tow.** *Sc. Obs.* [app. ad. 16th c. Flem. *kartouwe* 'genus bombardæ maioris, vulgo *cartuna* et *quartana*, Ger. *cartaun*, It. *courtaun*' (Kilian); meaning 'quarter-cannon' (CARTHOUN).

The Flemish word and the form *curtall* 'a great gun' mentioned by Hall, suggest F. *quartaut*, in the 16th c. *quartault*, the measure of a fourth of a bushel, which Littré refers to med.L. *quartāle*: but no evidence of the application of the F. word to a gun has been found. *Cartow* was apparently sometimes associated in the 17th c. with *cart*, as if the same as *cart-piece*, i.e. carriage-gun.]

A kind of cannon, also called a quarter-cannon, which threw a ball of a quarter of a hundred-weight. See also CARTHOUN.

1650 Row *Hist. Kirk* (1842) 519 June 15..The Covenanters Lords..had..with them tuo great cartowes and some lesser field-peeces. *a* **1670** SPALDING *Troub. Chas. I* (1830) I. 109 Two cartowis or quarter canons, haveing the bullet to about 24 pound weight each. *Ibid.* II. 228 On Tuysday 14 of May, the tua Cartowis wes brocht about fra Montrois to Abirdene be sea: bot thair wheilles wes hakit and hewin by the Gordouns, as ye have hard. Thair cam also tua uther iron cart peices to the schoir.

cartre, obs. form of CHARTER.

cartridge (ˈkɑːtrɪdʒ). Forms: 6–7 **cartage,** 7 **cartrage, -redge, -rege, cartharidge, (cartalage), cartruce,** 7–8 **carthrage,** 8 **cartrouche,** 7– **cartridge.** [A corruption of CARTOUCHE, q.v. for other forms and examples.]

1. a. *Mil.* The case in which the exact charge of powder for fire-arms is made up; of paper, parchment, pasteboard, flannel, serge, metal, etc., according to its use. Generally, for small-arms, the cartridge contains the bullet as well as the powder (called distinctively a ***ball-cartridge***); if it contains no ball, it is a ***blank cartridge***.

1579 DIGGES *Stratiot.* 116 Cases of Haileshot in manner of Cartages. **1611** FLORIO, *Scarnuzzo*, a cartage so called of gunners. **1625** MARKHAM *Souldiers Accid.* 42 Cartalages.. for this or any other peece on horsebacke. **1626** CAPT. SMITH *Accid. Yng. Seamen* 2 The Maister Gunner hath the charge of the..Spunges, Cartrages, Armes. **1644** NYE *Gunnery* I. (1647) 38 Canvas or strong paper, to make Cartredges. **1656** BLOUNT *Glossogr.*, *Cartouche* (Fr.), a charge of powder and shot ready made up in a paper; we corruptly call it a *cartage*. **1665** *Phil. Trans.* I. 84 A Cartridge full of Gunpowder. **1677** EARL ORRERY *Art of War* 58 If the Powder in the Cartruce be wet. **1678** PHILLIPS, *Carthrage*..a bag of Canvas..of such a depth as to contain just so much Powder as the Charge of the Piece: Also a Charge of Powder and Shot made ready in a Paper for any smaller Gun. **1702** E. CHAMBERLAYNE *St. Gt. Brit.* (ed. 20) 369 Ordnance..with cartrouches and ball for service. **1868** *Regul. & Ord. Army* §630 a, 90 rounds of ball Cartridge and 60 rounds of blank Cartridge. **1887** *Murray's Mag.* Aug. 181 The famous buckshot-cartridges were ordered by the Government that preceded him [Mr. Forster].

b. *transf.* and *fig.*

1673 MARVELL *Reh. Transp.* II. 182 'Tis pity that you.. did not..fill the cartridges or distribute them to each magistrate according to his calibre. **1679** PLOT *Staffordsh.* (1686) 221 Pellets or Cartrages of the same forme..made not of the leaves of the same tree..but plainly of the Rose. **1826** SHERIDAN in *Sheridaniana*, Every line is a cartridge of wit in itself. **1872** LEVER *Ld. Kilgobbin* lxvii, What rare wisdom it is not to fire away one's last cartridge.

†**c.** = *cartridge-box*. *Obs.*

1627 CAPT. SMITH *Seaman's Gram.* xiv. 66 They haue also Cartrages or rather cases for Cartrages made of Lattin to keepe the Cartrages in. **1704** J. HARRIS *Lex. Techn.* s.v., There are also Tin Cartridges, in which the Paper or Parchment ones are both formed and carried.

d. (i) *Photogr.* A spool of film in a (cylindrical) light-proof container designed for daylight loading; *esp.* one that requires mere insertion into a suitable camera.

1918 *Photo-Miniature* Mar. 9 *Film Cartridge*, roll of sensitive film (for negatives) wound on a spool and enclosed within a longer band of black paper for daylight changing. **1940** A. L. M. SOWERBY *Wall's Dict. Photogr.* (ed. 15) 111 The term cartridge is sometimes applied to roll films in spools. **1969** *New Yorker* 11 Oct. 17/2 (Advt.), This is it... The most automatic automatic. Just drop in the film cartridge. **1970** *Amat. Photographer* 11 Mar. 32/3 The 126 cartridge consists of two film chambers joined by a double 'bridge' which forms a channel for the film to pass through.

(ii) A small container for chemicals.

1920 WEBSTER, *Cartridge*, a small case or capsule of chemicals. **1940** A. L. M. SOWERBY *Wall's Dict. Photogr.* (ed. 15) 111 Dry photographic chemicals are often put up in cartridge form for the use of tourists.

(iii) = CASSETTE 1 d.

1960 *Tape Recording & Hi-Fi Mag.* 20 Apr. 18/2 Sufficient tape is contained within the three-inch wide cartridge to provide 65 minutes' playing time without interruption. **1966** *Tape Recording Year Bk.* 7 For some years tape recorder manufacturers have been trying to come to terms with the tape cassette (alternatively called a cartridge, or sometimes a magazine). **1970** *Daily Tel.* 16 Mar. 24/2 The '8 track' cartridge..gives four stereo tracks of about 20 minutes each on a closed loop of tape.

e. Part of the pick-up arm of a gramophone or record-player (see quots. 1961, 1962).

1941 J. F. RIDER *Automatic Record Changers & Recorders* ii. 43/1 In the case of crystal pickups..it is inadvisable to make any attempt to repair the crystal, it being preferable to replace the defective crystal with a new cartridge. **1946** *Electronics* Sept. 164/2 A standard type of crystal pickup arm with the carbon button assembly mounted in place of the crystal cartridge. **1961** G. A. BRIGGS *A to Z in Audio* 28 *Cartridge*, the head of a pickup containing the voltage generating mechanisms and stylus assembly, which clips on or plugs in to the tone arm. **1962** A. NISBETT *Technique Sound Studio* 243 Cartridge can mean removable pick-up head or capsule. A tape capsule (or cartridge) is a double spool of tape in a single container (comprising both feed and take up) which does not need to be laced up before replay. **1963** *Which?* Jan. 8 The head contains the cartridge, and set into the cartridge is the stylus.

†**2.** *Arch.* **a.** A modillion or corbel; **b.** The volute of an Ionic capital; **c.** A tablet representing a sheet of paper with the ends rolled up; = CARTOUCHE 2 a, b, c. *Obs.*

1611 COTGR., *Cartoche* as *cartouche*; also a Cartridge or roll (in architecture). **1756** NUGENT *Gr. Tour, France* IV. 90 The cartridges in the cieling are also by [Le Brun].

3. (See quot.)

1747 HOOSON *Miner's Dict.* E 1 b, When the Miner haums a Pick, there is always some of the Haum comes through the Eye on the other Side..that part he calls the Cartridge.

4. *attrib.* and in *comb.*, as **cartridge-bag**, a flannel bag, etc., containing the charge of powder for a cannon; **cartridge-belt**, a belt having pockets for cartridges; **cartridge-box**, a box for storing or carrying cartridges; the case in which a soldier carries his supply of cartridges; also see quot. 1867; **cartridge-case**, (*a*) = *cartridge-box*; (*b*) the paper which contains the powder of a cartridge; **cartridge-filler**, (*a*) one who fills cartridges; (*b*) an appliance for charging cartridge-cases with the proper quantity of powder; **cartridge-paper**, a strong kind of paper, used for making cartridges, and also for rough drawings, etc.; **cartridge-shot**, shot contained in cartridges; **cartridge starter**, a device for starting an internal-combustion

engine, esp. in an aeroplane, by means of an explosive charge.

1699 DAMPIER *Voy.* II. I. iv. 70 The Soldiers have each a *Cartage Box, covered with leather. **1802** HOME *Hist. Reb.* iv, A musket, bayonet, and cartridge-box, were delivered to each volunteer. **1867** SMYTH *Sailor's Word-bk.*, *Cartridge-box*, a cylindrical wooden box..just containing one cartridge, and used for its safe conveyance from the magazine to the gun..The term is loosely applied to the ammunition-pouch. **1769** FALCONER *Dict. Marine* (1789) *Lanterne*..a *cartridge-case, to carry the cartridges from the ship's magazine to the artillery. **1858** J. B. NORTON *Topics* 7 The *cartridge-cry..did not originate with the sepoys. **1871** RUSKIN *Fors Clav.* vi. 8 Every collier and *cartridge-filler is as fit for Elysium as any heathen could be. **1712** *Act 10 Anne* in *Lond. Gaz.* No. 5018/3 Paper called..*Cartridge Paper. **1739** BEIGHTON in *Phil. Trans.* XLI. 750 Fine Paper pasted on Cartridge-paper, or Two Papers pasted together. **1690** *Lond. Gaz.* No. 2544/3 Major la Borde was kill'd with *Carthrage-shot from the last Cannon that was fired. **1753** HANWAY *Trav.* (1762) II. 396 *note*, These [swivel guns or harquebuses] carried cartridge-shot to a great distance. **1922** *Flight* XIV. 65/1 For use when no accumulators are carried there is the '*cartridge' starter, originated and, we believe, patented by Farmans. **1956** J. JOHNSON *Wing Leader* 68 Which provided extra power and incorporated the Coffman cartridge starter.

cart's-tail. Rarely cart-tail. The hinder part of a cart, to which offenders were tied to be whipped through the streets. Hence **cart's-tailing** *vbl. sb.*, **cart's-tailable** *a. nonce-wds.*

1563-87 FOXE *A. & M.* (1596) 1868/1 They..should be tyed to a Carts tayle, and be whipped three market dayes through the City. **1642** in Rushw. *Hist. Coll.* III. (1721) IV. 559 b, He shall be whipped from thence at a Cart's-Tayl. **1753** CHAMBERS *Cycl. Supp.* s.v. *Cart*, Bawds and other malefactors are whipped at the Cart's tail. **1856** FROUDE *Hist. Eng.* i. (L.) The rough remedy of the cart-tail.

1808 SOUTHEY *Let.* 22 Nov., Your phrase of 'eking out' is cart's-tailable without benefit of clergy. *Ibid.* I am not quite sure which deserves the severest cart's-tailing.

† **'cartuary, 'chartuary.** *Obs.* [ad. med.L. *cartuarium* = *cartularium*.] = next.

1523 FITZHERB. *Surv.* (1539) Pref., The other small bokes, as court-baron, court hundred, and chartuary. **1708** J. CHAMBERLAYNE *St. Gt. Brit.* II. I. ii. (1743) 311 The cartuary of Kelsoe. *a* **1754** CARTE in Gutch *Coll. Cur.* II. 77 Entered into Cartuaryes or Registers.

cartulary ('kɑːtjʊlərɪ). Also spelt CHARTULARY, q.v. [ad. med.L. *cart-*, *chartulārium*, f. L. *cartula*, *chartula*, dim. of *carta*, *charta*, a paper, writing, charter; see CHART and -ARY. Cf. F. *cartulaire* (14th c. in Littré).]

'A place where papers or records are kept' (J.); whence the whole collection of records (belonging to a monastery, etc.); or the book in which they are entered; a register.

1541 R. COPLAND *Guydon's Formul.* T ij, Taken at the cartulary of mayster Peter [of Bonaco]. **1631** WEEVER *Anc. Fun. Mon.* xiv. 99 Those cartularies, by which Saxon princes endowed their sacred structures. **1761** HUME *Hist. Eng.* x. I. 217 An action..in which..the King of France's cartulary and records..were taken. **1848** H. MILLER *First Impr.* iii. (1857) 37 The Cartulary of Moray—contains the Constitutiones Lyncolnienses. **1868** FREEMAN *Norm. Conq.* (1876) II. App. 528 The cartulary of Saint Michael's Mount contains two charters in which Eadward is called 'rex'.

† **'cartware.** *Obs.* [see WARE.] A team of horses; used by Harrison 1577 also in the sense of CARUCATE (L. *jugum*).

1562 J. HEYWOOD *Prov. & Epigr.* (1867) 142 There cumth, a carteweare, of good hors by. **1563** GOLDING *Ovid's Met.* II. (1593) 32 Which when the cart-ware did perceive, they left the beaten way. **1577** HARRISON in Holinshed *Descr. Brit.* I. x. *marg.*, For Hide they used the word Carucate or Cart-ware, or Teme. —— *England* II. xix. (1877) I. 309 So manie hundred acres..called in some places of the realme, carrucats or cartwares.

cart-way ('kɑːtweɪ).

A way along which a cart can be driven; sometimes = highway, as in the phrase 'common as the cart-way'; but now usually a rough road on a farm or in a wood, passable by a heavy cart, but not by a carriage or other spring-vehicle.

1362 LANGL. *P. Pl.* A. III. 127 Heo is..As Comuyn as þe Cart-wei to knaues and to alle. **1532-3** *Act 24 Hen. VIII*, v, Any common high way, cartway, horseway, or foteway. **1590** H. SWINBURN *Testaments* 162 Albeit the wife were as common as the Cart-waie. **1673** in Ansted *Channel Isl.* I. iv. (1862) 78 There is a cartway cut by art down to the sea. **1725** BRADLEY *Fam. Dict.* s.v. *Copse*, Where the Woods are large, it is best to have a Cart-way along the Middle of them. **1768** BLACKSTONE *Comm.* (1793) 442 Every cartway leading to any market-town must be made twenty feet wide at the least. **1824** MISS MITFORD *Village* Ser. I. (1863) 46 Cross-roads, mere cart-ways, leading to the little farms.

'cart-wheel, *sb.*

1. The wheel of a cart.

c **1386** CHAUCER *Sompn. T.* 549 Twelf spokes hath a cart whel comunly. **1585** PARSONS *Chr. Exerc.* II. i. 152 A drye cart wheel..cryeth and complayneth, vnder a small burden. **1858** J. MARTINEAU *Stud. Chr.* 342 Armed men, with a clouted shoe and a cart-wheel for their standards.

2. *humourously* said of a large coin, as a crown or dollar.

1867 A. SKETCHLEY in *Cassell's Mag.* 327/1 He..says 'This 'ere cart wheel's a duffer'. **1885** LADY BRASSEY *The Trades* 195 The old Spanish doubloons..by irreverent travellers from the United States termed 'cartwheels'.

3. *to turn cart-wheels*: to execute a succession of lateral summersaults, as if the feet and hands were spokes of a wheel; also *Catherine-wheels.* (Street-boys did this by the side of a moving omnibus, etc., for chance coppers thrown to them.) Also without 'to turn' and in *sing.* Also *transf.* and *attrib.*

1864 SALA in *Daily Tel.* 23 Dec., I saw a little..blackguard boy turning 'cartwheels' in front of the Clifton House. **1895** [see SPLIT *sb.*[1] 4 b]. **1917** 'CONTACT' *Airman's Outings* 246 A medley of swift darts, dives, and cart-wheel turns. **1933** P. GODFREY *Back-Stage* xv. 187 The girls in these troupes..must be expert in high kicks, cartwheels, and splits. **1955** *Simple Gymnastics* ('Know the Game' Series) 27/1 *Cartwheel.* Start from standing aside... Swing your legs up as high as you can and look over your shoulder with the head well back. **1960** B. KEATON *Wonderful World Slapstick* (1967) 149, I could do..a series of cartwheels in a circle, without touching hands to the floor.

4. A kind of fire-work. Cf. CATHERINE WHEEL 3.

1840 R. H. DANA *Bef. Mast* xiii. 72 We had..everything ..from Chinese fire-works to English cart-wheels.

5. A hat with a wide circular brim. Also *attrib.*

1884 L. TROUBRIDGE *Life amongst Troubridges* (1966) 169 Mr. and Mrs. Oscar Wilde to tea, she dressed for the part in ..a huge cartwheel Gainsborough hat. **1895** *Westm. Gaz.* 29 Jan. 3/1 Complaints in respect to the cart-wheel hat. *Ibid.*, The indignant playgoer who happens to be seated directly behind a superb cart-wheel of the latest Parisian make. **1946** KOESTLER *Thieves in Night* 99 Four boys in khaki shorts and cartwheel hats of straw. **1959** B. GOOLDEN *For Richer, for Poorer* iv. 61 They come in to buy a cart-wheel..and they happen to see a completely entrancing cloche.

cart-wheel, *v.* [f. the sb.] *intr.* To move like a rotating wheel; said esp. of an aeroplane which makes a crash landing on one wing-tip.

1920 *Blackw. Mag.* July 85/1 He cart-wheeled round right-handed to get behind her again. **1925** E. F. NORTON *Fight for Everest, 1924* 114 Somervell's axe slipped from his numb fingers and went cart-wheeling down the slopes below. **1928** *Daily Express* 24 Sept. 7/4 The machine continued to lose height, and suddenly cartwheeled vertically to the ground. **1962** *Daily Tel.* 29 Dec. 1/6 A Carvair aircraft..hit a snow-covered dyke and 'cartwheeled' four times as it came in to land.

'cart-whip. A whip used in driving a cart, a long heavy horse-whip.

1713 *Lond. Gaz.* No. 5144/10 Carters are to ride with long Cart Whips. **1823** CANNING in *Ann. Reg.* (1824) 129/1 Driving the slaves, by means of a cart-whip.

Hence **cart-whip** *v.*, to flog with a cart-whip.

1788 DIBDIN *Mus. Tour* liv. 222 They are cart-whipt and treated with much other cruelty. **1811** *Edin. Rev.* XIX. 141 After a cart-whipping..he was carried to a sick-house.

cartwright ('kɑːtraɪt). [f. CART *sb.* + WRIGHT.] A carpenter who makes carts.

14.. *York Myst.* Introd. 26. **1483** *Cath. Angl.* 55 A Cartewright, *caractareus.* **1589** *Pappe w. Hatchet* B iij b, Be a ship-wright, cart-wright, or tiburn-wright. *a* **1619** FOTHERBY *Atheom.* II. i. §8. 193 Some, Housewrights; some, Shipwrights; some, Cartwrights; and some, the Ioyners of smaller workes. **1829** CARLYLE *Misc.* (1857) I. 268 As essential..as the millwright or cartwright.

Hence **'cartwrighting,** doing cartwright's work.

1850 MARG. FULLER *Life without & within* (1860) 124 The blacksmithing, cartwrighting..and grain-grinding.

'carty, *a. fam.* [f. CART *sb.*[1] + -Y.] Of the breed and build of a cart horse.

1863 *Reader* 7 Nov. 529 The early illuminators' variations of a few podgy fat-calved knights, and the carty fetlocked horses they should have ridden. **1875** 'STONEHENGE' *Brit. Sports* II. III. i. 521 Well-bred but very strong and carty.

† **'caruage.** *Old Law.* (erron. spelt **carvage**). [a. ONF. *caruage*, in mod.F. *charruage*, on L. type **carrūcāticum*; but actually made in med.L. *carrucāgium*, and *car(r)uāgium.*]

1. Ploughing.

1610 FOLKINGHAM *Art of Survey* I. vii. 14 This Deluage is distinguishable into Caruage and Scaphage. Caruage comprehends all sorts of plowing of Grounds. *Ibid.* x. 24 Crust-clung and Soale-bound soyles craue Caruage. **1688** R. HOLME *Armoury* III. 333/2 Carvage is Plowing of Ground.

2. = CARUCAGE.

[**1664** SPELMAN *Gloss.* 126 *Carucagium*, alias *caruagium*, est tributi genus quod singulis aratris..imponitur.]

1610 FOLKINGHAM *Art of Survey* III. iv. 71 Infeoffing with Toll, implies Freedome from Custome, etc. With Caruage, from taxation by Carues. **1641** *Termes de la Ley* 47 A priviledge by which a man is freed from Carvage. **1670** BLOUNT *Law Dict.* s.v. *Carrucate.* **1700** TYRRELL *Hist. Eng.* II. 711 The late unreasonable Carvage or Tax in his Diocese. **1846** *Dugdale's Monast.* III. 103/1 He desired the convent to lend him their annual carucatage, carucagium, or carvage.

carucage, carrucage ('kærjuːkɪdʒ). *Feudal Syst.* (Also 6 **charugage.**) [ad. med.L. *car(r)ūcāgium* (= ONF. *caruage*, F. *charruage*), f. med.L. *carrūca* plough. (If of Latin age, the type would have been **carrūcāticum*; but the word was of later origin, after F. *-age*, med.L. *-āgium*, had become familiar formatives: see -AGE.)]

A tax levied on each plough or carucate of land.

1577 HOLINSHED *Chron., John* an. 1200 (R.) The dutie called charugage, that was, three shillings of euerie plough-land. **1592** STOW *Annals* 271 The same time King Henry [III] tooke Carucage, that is two Marks of Silver of every Knights Fee, towards the Marriage of His Sister Isabell to the Emperour. **1611** SPEED *Hist. Gt. Brit.* IX. ix. 68 After the taking of Bedford, he had Carrucage, that is, two shillings vpon euery Ploughland. **1700** TYRRELL *Hist. Eng.* II. 851 The King had granted him..a Carucage of Two Shillings on each Plough-Land. **1875** STUBBS *Const. Hist.* I. xi. 382 [Danegeld] was in very nearly the same form reproduced under the title of Carucage by the ministers of Richard I.

† **carucate, carrucate** ('kærjuːkeɪt). *Feudal Syst.* [ad. med.L. *car(r)ūcāta* plough-gate, plough-land, f. *car(r)ūca* plough (see CARUE). The ONF. regular repr. of *carrūcāta* was *car(r)uée*, central F. *char(r)uée*: see -ATE[1].

L. *carrūca* (f. *carr-us* CAR) was originally 'a sort of state coach or chariot'; this sense is still found anno 700 'carruca in qua sedere consuevi' (see Diez); but in Gaul it was early applied to the wheel-plough, in which sense *carruca*, *carruga*, *carrua* appear in the Salic and Allemannic Laws. Cf. the s.w. Eng. *plough* = 'wagon'.]

A measure of land, varying with the nature of the soil, etc., being as much as could be tilled with one plough (with its team of 8 oxen) in a year; a plough-land.

The acreage of the carucate varied according to the system of tillage. If the land lay in three arable common fields the carucate, according to *Fleta*, contained 180 acres; 60 for fallow, 60 for winter corn, and 60 for spring corn. If the land lay in 2 fields the carucate consisted of 160 acres, 80 for fallow, and 80 for tillage. Commonly only the land under plough in any one year was reckoned, the fallow being thrown into common pasturage. Hence in ancient deeds the normal carucate is either 120 acres or 80 acres by the Norman number (5 score to the hundred) and 144 acres or 96 acres by the English number (6 score to the hundred). —*Rev. I. Taylor.*

[**1086** *Domesday Bk. Hampsh.* (Du Cange) In dominio sunt 2 carucatæ. *c* **1190** *Chart. Rich. I* (Du Cange) Viginti carrucatas terræ scilicet unicuique carrucatæ sexaginta acras terræ.] **1432-50** tr. *Higden* I. xlix. (Rolls) II. 91 Which alle William Conquerour kynge of Englonde causede to be describede, and the hides and carucates of londe to be measurede [*et per hydas seu carucatas dimetiri*]. **1577** HARRISON *England* II. xix. (1877) I. 309 So manie hundred acres or families (or as they haue been alwaies called in some places of the realme, carrucats or cartwares). **1614** STOW *Annales Will. I*, an. 1080. 118 How many carucates of lande, how many plough-lands. *c* **1630** RISDON *Surv. Devon* §295 (1810) 305 Some hold a hide and a carucate to be all one, but not of any certain content, commonly said to be so much land as a plough can..plough in a year. **1788** KELHAM *Domesday Bk.* 168 (T.) Twelve carucates of land make one hide. **1841** TYTLER *Hist. Scot.* (1879) I. 284 A bovate.. contained eighteen acres; a carucate contained eight bovates; and eight carucates made a knight's fee. **1875** STUBBS *Const. Hist.* I. x. 302 The old English hide was cut down to the acreage of the Norman carucate.

'carucated, *a. Hist.* Measured and assessed by carucates.

1908 W. G. COLLINGWOOD *Scandin. Britain* 111 Leicestershire..was a carucated district.

† **'caruck.** *Obs. rare*[−1]. [ad. med.L. *car(r)ūca*, as occasionally used for *carucāta*, like mod.F. *charrue* in sense of *charruée*.] = CARUCATE.

1627 SPEED *England Abr.* xxviii. §3 These Parishes are measured by Hides, and Carucks, or Plough-lands.

† **carue.** *Old Law.* Also 6 **carewe,** (7- *erron.* **carve**). [a. ONF. *carue* (mod.F. *charrue* = Pr. *carruga*, It. *carruca*):—L. *carrūca* (med.L. *carrūca*, *carrūga*, *carrūa*), used already in the Salic Law in the sense 'plough'. See note to CARUCATE. Mod.F. *charrue* is both plough and plough-land (or carucate), whence the Eng. use.

The spelling *carve* is a blunder of transcription, after the differentiation of *u* and *v*, owing to the fact that *v* was right before *e* in most words, e.g. *carve*, *starve*, *serve*.]

A plough-land or CARUCATE.

[**1292** BRITTON III. xxi. §1 Une carue de terre ove les apurtenaunces (one carucate of lande with the appurtenances).] **1593** NORDEN *Spec. Brit. M'sex* I. 5 The vsuall account of lande at this day in Englande is by acres, yardes, carewes, hydes, knightes fees, cantreds, baronies and counties. **1610** FOLKINGHAM *Art of Survey* II. vii. 60 A Plow-land or Carue of land is said to containe 4 Yard-land at 30 acres to the Yard-land. **1628** COKE *On Litt.* 17 b, If a man bee seised in fee of a carue of Land by iust title. **1642** W. BIRD *Mag. Hon.* 155 A Carve of land, or Plow land. **1670** BLOUNT *Law Dict.*, *Carrucate* or *Carve of Land.*

caruncle (kəˈrʌŋk(ə)l, ˈkærʌŋk(ə)l). Also 9 caruncule, and 8-9 in Lat. form **caruncula.** [ad. 16th c. F. *caruncule* 'a little peece of flesh', Cotgr. (mod.F. *caroncule*), ad. L. *caruncula*, dim. of *caro*, *carnem* flesh.]

1. A small fleshy excrescence: applied in Anatomy to certain natural formations, as the lachrymal and urethral caruncles, the wattles of the turkey-cock, etc. In *Pathol.* formerly applied to a stricture.

1615 CROOKE *Body of Man* 143 Caruncles or teats, with very fine perforations..opening into the..pipes of the Vreters. **1661** LOVELL *Hist. Anim. & Min.* Introd., A

caruncle like a tongue. **1688** R. HOLME *Armoury* II. 306/1 The Caruncles [are] knotty pieces of flesh, hanging about the Bill..as in Turky-cocks. **1720** BECKET in *Phil. Trans.* XXXI. 51 A Caruncle in the Urethra. **1794** G. ADAMS *Nat. & Exp. Philos.* II. xvii. 255 At the inner corner of the eye.. stands a caruncle. **1871** DARWIN *Desc. Man* II. xii. 13 The fleshy caruncles on the heads of certain birds.

2. *Bot.* 'An excrescence at or about the hilum of certain seeds' (Gray).

1830 LINDLEY *Nat. Syst. Bot.* 144 Having a remarkable tumour, called a caruncula, at one end of the seeds. **1870** HOOKER *Stud. Flora* 328 Cuticle brown, caruncle large.

Hence **caruncled** *a.* = CARUNCULATE.

1870 HOOKER *Stud. Flora* 366 Seeds caruncled.

caruncular (kəˈrʌŋkjʊlə(r)), *a.* [on type of L. **carunculār-is*, F. *caronculaire*: see prec. and -AR.] Of the nature of or resembling a caruncle.

1847 in CRAIG.

caˈrunculate, *a.* [ad. mod.L. *carunculātus*, f. *caruncula* (see prec. and -ATE² 2): cf. F. *caronculé*.] Having a caruncle or caruncles.

1835 LINDLEY *Introd. Bot.* (1848) II. 31 The umbilicus.. is said to be..carunculate. **1870** HOOKER *Stud. Flora* 326 Euphorbiaceæ..seeds carunculate.

caˈrunculated, *a.* [f. as prec. + -ED.] = prec.

1804 BEWICK *Brit. Birds* (1847) II. 285 A naked, red, warty, or carunculated skin. **1868** DARWIN *Animals & Pl.* I. v. 139 The skin over the nostrils swollen and often carunculated or wattled.

caˈrunculous, *a.* [= F. *caronculeux*, on L. type **carunculōs-us*.] = prec.

1847 in CRAIG.

‖**carus** (ˈkɛərəs). *Med.* [med.L. *carus*, L. *caros*, a. Gr. κάρος heavy sleep, torpor.] A term applied to various forms of profound sleep or insensibility; *esp.* 'the fourth and extremest degree of insensibility, the others being sopor, coma, and lethargy' (*Syd. Soc. Lex.*).

1678 PHILLIPS, *Caros*, a disease in the Head which is caused by an over full stomach and want of concoction. **1696** —— *Caros*, or *Carus*, a Sleep wherein the person affected being pull'd, pinch'd and call'd, scarce shews any sign of hearing or feeling. **1782** HEBERDEN *Comm.* lxix. (1806) 340 Paralytic debility of the senses and intellect..as carus, coma, lethargy.

caruway, obs. form of CARAWAY.

carvacrol (ˈkɑːvəkrəl). Also 9 carvacrole. [a. G. *carvacrol* (E. Schweizer 1841, in *Jrnl. f. prakt. Chem.* XXIV. 263), f. mod.L. *carv-i* in *Carum carvi*, botanical name of CARAWAY, + L. *ācr-is* (see ACRID *a.*) + -OL 2.] A liquid phenol, $C_{10}H_{14}O$, obtainable from camphor, origanum, oil of caraway, savory, etc., and used in perfumery and as a fungicide, etc.

1854 R. D. THOMSON *Cycl. Chem.* 153/1 *Carvacrole*, a colourless oil, heavier than water. **1860** H. WATTS tr. *Gmelin's Chem.* XIV. 414 Carvol when *heated* appears to be transformed into carvacrol. **1911** *Brit. Pharm. Codex* 266 An iodide of carvacrol, in the form of a light yellow or brownish powder, has been used as a substitute for iodoform. **1963** D. L. WEDDERBURN in H. W. Hibbott *Handbk. Cosmetic Sci.* xxi. 452 The isomeric methyl isopropyl phenols, thymol and carvacrol, are about 28 times as effective as phenol against *Salmonella typhosa*.

carvage, bad spelling of CARUAGE, ploughing.

carval (ˈkɑːvəl). *Isle of Man.* Also carvel. [Manx *carval*.] A carol, a ballad on a sacred subject.

1873 W. HARRISON in *Mona Miscellany* 2nd Ser. p. x, A specimen of a Manx *carval* is given... It would have been easy to have given many of these *carvals*, which may be termed a literature entirely peculiar to the Manx people, consisting chiefly of ballads on sacred subjects which have been handed down in writing... Most of these carvals are from 50 to 150 years old, and amongst the favourites may be mentioned 'Joseph's History', 'Susannah's History', 'The Nativity', 'The Holy War', 'David and Goliath', 'Samson's History', 'Birth of Christ'. **1887** HALL CAINE *Deemster* III. xxxiii. 60 Sometimes he crooned a Manx carval. **1910** *Encycl. Brit.* V. 639/2 Most of the existing literature.. consists of ballads and carols, locally called carvels. **1956** *Archivum Linguisticum* VIII. I. 88 The carval manuscripts with their ryhmes and abundant non-literary spellings.

carve (kɑːv), *v.* Forms: 1 ceorfan, 2 keruen, 2–3 keoruen, 3 keorfen, (curuen), 4 cerue, 4–6 kerue, 5–7 kerve, 6–7 karve, 5- carve. *Pa. t.* α. 1 cearf, 3–5 carf, 3 kerf, (*subj.* kurue), 4 karf, karue, carue, corue, 4–5 carfe, 5 kerue, carff; *pl.* 1 curfon, 3–4 corue(n, 4 corwen. β. 4 keruet, 5 carft, 5- carved. *Pa. pple.* α. 1 corfen, 3–4 i-coruen, 3–6 coruen , 4 coruun, koruun, ykoruen, corn, caruen, kerue, 4–5 (y)corue, (y)coruyn, 5 coruene, 6 keruen, 6, 9 carven; β. 5 keruyd, 6 kerued, 6- carved. [Common Teut.: OE. str. vb. *ceorfan, cearf*, pl. *curfon, corven*, corresp. to OFris. *kerva*, MDu. and Du. *kerven*, MHG. and mod.G. *kerben*, to notch, carve, (pa. pple. *gekurben* occurs in MHG., in Niederrheinisch); not known in OHG. or Gothic: OTeut. type **kerfan, karf*, pl. *kurbum, korban*. Cf. also Icel. *kyrfa* to carve, Da. *karve* to notch, indent, Sw. *karfwa* to notch, carve. The Teut. word is generally held to be cognate with Gr. γράφ-ειν to write, orig. to scratch or engrave; pointing to an Aryan *gṛph-*. The original strong conjugation has become weak as in all the mod. langs, but the pa. pple. *carven* is still used as an archaic form.

The normal mod. repr. of *ceorf-* would be *cherve*: *c* was prob. retained here by influence of *curfon, corven*. The *ar* for earlier *er* is as in ARBOUR, *bark*, etc.]

I. †1. a. *trans.* To CUT: formerly the ordinary word for that action in all its varieties.

c **1000** *Ags. Gosp.* Mark v. 5 Hine sylfne mid stanum ceorfende. *c* **1200** *Trin. Coll. Hom.* 87 To keruen þat fel biforen on his strenende lime. *a* **1300** *Cursor M.* 7241 Quils sampson slepped..His hare sco kerf. *c* **1325** *E.E. Allit. P.* A. 40 Quen corne is coruen with crokez kene. *c* **1386** CHAUCER *Prioresses T.* 159 Ther he with throte ykoruen lay. *c* **1420** *Liber Cocorum* (1862) 40 Kerve appuls overtwert and cast þerin. *c* **1450** *Bk. Curtasye* 765 in *Babees Bk.*, With brede y-coruyn. **1480** CAXTON *Descr. Brit.* 45 They wolde..pricke and kerue her owne bodyes. **1560** ed. of *Chaucer's Boeth.* I. 198 b/2 They..corven and renten my clothes.

†b. With various extensions, as ***of kerven***, to cut off; ***to carve*** (a limb) ***from*** any one; ***to carve asunder, in two, in*** or ***to pieces***; ***to carve*** (a knight) ***out of*** his armour. *Obs.*

c **1000** ÆLFRIC *Lev.* viii. 20 Hiȝ curfon ðone ram eall to sticceon. *c* **1025** *O.E. Chron.* an. 1014 He cearf of heora handa and heora nosa. **1297** R. GLOUC. (1810) 560 Sir Willam Mautrauers Carf him of fet & honde. *c* **1325** *Chron. Eng.* 757 in Ritson *Metr. Rom.* II. 301 Hys legges hy corven of anon. **1330** R. BRUNNE *Chron.* (1810) 244 þe dede body þe[i] britten on four quarters corn. **1382** WYCLIF *Hosea* xiv. 1 Wymmen with chijld of it ben coruen out. *c* **1386** CHAUCER *Knts. T.* 1838 Tho was he corven out of his harneys. *c* **1400** *Destr. Troy* 9468 He karve hit of cleane. *Ibid.* 9832 He kylles our knightes, kerues hom in sonder. *c* **1430** *Syr Gener.* (Roxb.) 4223 Laces and stringes he kerue on twoo. **1485** CAXTON *Chas. Gt.* 222 He carf hym asondre in the myddes.

†c. *fig. Obs.* (with influence of other senses).

c **1230** *Hali Meid.* 17 þeo þat habbið fram ham icoruen flesches lustes. **138.** WYCLIF *Serm.* Sel. Wks. I. 231 A sworde sharpe..to kerve awey synne. *c* **1386** CHAUCER *Monkes T.* 467 His estate fortune fro him carf.

†d. *intr.* or *absol. Obs.*

a **1225** *Ancr. R.* 384 Gif eax ne kurue, ne þe spade ne dulue ..hwo kepte ham uorte holden? *c* **1314** *Guy Warw.* (A.) 4066 Thai corwen þurch liuer and þurch lunge. *c* **1400** *Destr. Troy* 6674 He..Corve euyn at the kyng with a kene sword. **1430** LYDG. *Chron. Troy* II. xi, Yᵉ lyue yᵗ carueth through the centre. **1513** DOUGLAS *Æneis* XII. v. 217 Onto hys chyn the edge did carvin doun.

e. *trans.* (*slang*). To slash (a person) with a knife or razor; esp. ***to carve*** (a person) ***up***. Hence **carved** *ppl. a.*, **carving** *vbl. sb.*

1929 D. HAMMETT *Dane Curse* xi. 113 The man had.. stood..waiting to carve me when I came out; and my fall had saved me, making him miss me with the blade. **1938** G. GREENE *Brighton Rock* II. i. 73 How do we make you safe, Spicer?... If carving'd do it... *Ibid.* III. i. 98 They just meant to carve him up, but a razor slipped. **1938** SHARPE *S. of Flying Squad* v. 65 He feared that they would 'carve him up'. *Ibid.* xiv. 157 Carve him with a razor. **1960** M. SPARK *Ballad of Peckham Rye* ix. 188 We got to carve up that boy one of these days.

†2. *trans.* To cleave (as by cutting). *Obs.*

c **1325** *E.E. Allit. P.* B. 1547 As a coltour in clay cerues þo forȝes. *c* **1374** CHAUCER *Former Age* 21 No ship yit karf the wawes grene. *c* **1430** LYDG. *Bochas* II. xvii. (1554) 56 a, A great hyl..carf on twain, Not farre asyde from the towne. **1604** T. WRIGHT *Passions* v. §2. 170 The filing of iron.. almost all men..abhorre to heare..for that the aire so carued, punisheth and fretteth the heart.

†3. a. To circumcise. **b.** To castrate (a cock).

c **1420** *Circumcision* (*Tundale's Vis.* 86) The chylde was corve therwith. **1586** BRIGHT *Melanch.* xxxix. 252 Generally of fowle the carued is better than the others..of beastes the gelded have preferment. **1601** HOLLAND *Pliny* I. 280 If they be once carued and made capons they crow no more. **1678** LITTLETON *Lat. Dict.*, To carve as cockrels are carved.

4. To cut (a way or passage). Also *fig.*

1490 CAXTON *Eneydos* xxvii. 97 The shippes..carfe waie in the water. **1813** BYRON *Giaour* xxxv, To such let others carve their way. **1856** KANE *Arct. Exp.* II. xxiii. 232 The axe was indispensable to carve our path through the hummocks. **1865** HOLLAND *Plain T.* iii. 115 It is by work that man carves his way to that measure of power.

II. To cut artistically or ornamentally.

5. *trans.* **a.** To hew, cut, or sculpture (any solid figure, an image, *out of* stone, *in* ivory, etc.); to make or shape artistically by cutting.

a **1000** *Rood* 66 (Gr.) Curfon hie ðæt moldern of beorhtan stane. *c* **1420** *Chron. Vilod.* 292 He..carff welle ymagus and peynted bothe. **1535** COVERDALE *Isa.* xl. 20 Morouer shal the ymage maker..carue therout an ymage. *a* **1700** DRYDEN (J.) And carv'd in iv'ry such a maid so fair. **1855** TENNYSON *Maud* I. viii, An angel watching an urn Wept over her, carved in stone. **1878** HUXLEY *Physiogr.* 207 Each column has been carved out of a single block of green marble.

b. To fashion (a material) *into* some shape by cutting, chiselling, or sculpturing.

1535 COVERDALE *Wisd.* xiii. 13 He carueth it [wood] diligently..and..fashioneth it after the similitude of a man. **17..** BENTLEY (J.) Had Democrates really carved mount Athos into a statue of Alexander the Great.

6. a. To cut or engrave figures, either in relief or intaglio, *on* (*in, into*) a surface.

c **1250** *Gen. & Ex.* 2700 He carf in two gummes of pris Two likenesses. *c* **1386** CHAUCER *Milleres T.* 132 With Powles wyndowes corven on his schoos. **1483** CAXTON *Gold. Leg.* 219/1 Thistory of her was..entayled & coruen in the sepulcre. **1542** UDALL tr. *Erasm. Apoph.* 332 b, An other [chaire of estate] with whippes kerued in it. **1600** SHAKS. *A.Y.L.* III. ii. 9 Carue on euery Tree, The faire, the chaste, and vnexpressiue shee. **1643** MILTON *Divorce* II. vi. (1851) 77 To carve into his flesh the mark of that strict and pure cov'nant. *c* **1800** SOUTHEY *Retrospect*, Some idle hind Carves his rude name within a sapling's rind. **1807** WOLFE *Bur. Sir J. Moore* viii, We carved not a line and we raised not a stone.

b. to cover or adorn (wood, stone, etc.) with figures so cut on or in the surface.

c **1384** CHAUCER *H. Fame* 1295 Which [gate] that so wel corven was. *c* **1394** *P. Pl. Crede* 161 þe pileres weren.. queynteli i-coruen wiþ curiouse knottes. **1570** LEVINS *Manip.* 34/21 To carve wood, *insculpere*. **1611** BIBLE *1 Kings* vi. 29 Hee carued all the walles of the house round about with carued figures of Cherubims. **1698** DRYDEN *Virg. Georg.* II. 632 Nor Box..smooth-grained..which curious Hands may kerve. **1703** MAUNDRELL *Journ. Jerus.* (1732) 77 Carv'd in such a manner, as to resemble a piece of wainscot. **1832** TENNYSON *Pal. Art* 138 A million wrinkles carved his skin. **1875** LONGF. *Masq. Pandora* v, Yon oaken chest, carven with figures. **1883** LLOYD *Ebb & Fl.* II. 84 Sarcophagi carved with old Christian emblems.

7. *intr.* or *absol.* To cut figures or designs; to practise the sculptor's or engraver's art.

1567 MAPLET *Gr. Forest* 12 b, Kaman the stone..is easie to be engrauen and carued in. **1591** HARINGTON *Orl. Fur.* II. xxxiii, He that carves and drawes with equall praise. **1841–4** EMERSON *Ess. Art* Wks. (Bohn) I. 147 We carve and paint, or we behold what is carved and painted. **1858** GLADSTONE *Homer* I. 14 Where other poets sketch, Homer draws; and where they draw he carves.

III. 8. a. *intr.* To cut up meat at table. †***to carve to***: to serve, 'help' (any one at a meal).

a **1300** *K. Horn* 233 Tech him..Biuore me to kerue, And of the cupe serue. *c* **1386** CHAUCER *Prol.* 100 He..carf biforn his fader at the table. **1484** CAXTON *Chyualry* 17 Euery man that wylle come to knyghthode hym behoueth to lerne in his yougthe to kerue at the table. *c* **1530** LD. BERNERS *Arth. Lyt. Bryt.* (1814) 283 There Gouernar carued to the lady ryght goodly with his knyfe. **1625** SANDERSON *Serm.* (1681) I. 133 Give them from your own, but do not carve them from another's trencher. **1665** BOYLE *Occas. Refl.* III. v. (1675) 152 Upon his being Carv'd to at a Feast. **1727** SWIFT *Gulliver* II. iii. 122 A bit of meat..out of which I carved for myself. **1751** CHESTERF. *Lett.* ccxi, A man who tells you gravely that he cannot carve. **1868** Q. VICTORIA *Life Highl.* 148 General Grey and Lady Churchill carved.

b. *trans.* e.g. ***to carve a fowl, a joint***, etc.

c **1529** FRITH *Antith.* (1829) 301 Men to carve his [Pope's] morsels. **1599** SHAKS. *Much Ado* v. i. 157 A calues head and a Capon, the which if I doe not carue most curiously, say my knife's naught. *c* **1611** CHAPMAN *Iliad* IX. (R.) Till I had.. carued thee tendrest meate. **1865** TROLLOPE *Belton Est.* xxiv. 286 Captain Aylmer..would have carved the roast fowl with much more skill.

9. *fig.* **a.** *intr.* To help or serve (oneself or others) at one's own discretion, to do at one's pleasure, indulge oneself.

1602 SHAKS. *Ham.* I. iii. 20 Hee may not, as vnuallued persons doe, Carue for himselfe. **1602** WARNER *Alb. Eng.* IX. li. (1612) 232 Which of the Patriarks, Prophets, or Gods people..vnto their owne Affections caru'd. **1633** BP. HALL *Hard Texts* 581 They shall carve themselves of your punishment, and their owne advancement at their pleasure. **1649** —— *Cases Consc.* II. x. (1654) 159 Thus to carve himselfe of Justice, is..to violate lawfull authority. **1691** LOCKE *Money* Wks. 1727 II. 35 When some common and great Distress..emboldens them to carve to their wants with armed Force.

†b. *trans.* To apportion at discretion, to assign as one's portion or lot, to take at one's pleasure.

1578 BANISTER *Hist. Man* IV. 51 Be sapient therfore Reader..not captious in caruing a fault. **1650** HOBBES *De Corp. Pol.* 35 Where every man carveth out his own right, it hath the same effect, as if there were no right at all. **1662** FULLER *Worthies* (1840) I. iv. 18 Carving a good portion of honour to themselves. **1742** MIDDLETON *Cicero* I. I. 33 Licence being indulged to an insolent army of carving for themselves what fortunes they pleased. **1755** YOUNG *Centaur* ii. (1757) IV. 159 God's promises are better than anything we can carve for ourselves.

10. a. To cut up or subdivide.

1711 SHAFTESB. *Charact.* (1737) III. 112 Our second head we shou'd again subdivide into firsts and seconds, but that this manner of carving is of late days grown much out of fashion. **1818** CRUISE *Digest.* VI. 379 The testator..has carved the whole fee in particular estates. **1870** BRYANT *Iliad* I. 25 All the rest was carved into small portions. **1875** STUBBS *Const. Hist.* I. v. 97 The Country was carved into equal districts.

b. ***to carve up***: to cheat, swindle. *slang.*

[**1909** WARE *Passing Eng.* 65 *Carve up* (Amer.), to annihilate completely. That dear grave holds a disappointed chap who cum out here from Reno to carve me up.] **1933** C. E. LEACH *On Top of Underworld* x. 138 *Carve up*, swindle accomplice out of share. **1936** J. CURTIS *Gilt Kid* ix. 96 I'm going to trust you to play square with me at the end. No carving-up or else. **1959** H. PINTER *Birthday Party* I. 10 Then after that, you know what they did? They carved me up. Carved me up. It was all arranged, it was all worked out.

11. The alliterative phrase ***cut and carve*** goes back to the 14th c. when the two words were equivalent, and *cut* was beginning to take the place of *carve*: it is still used, though mostly *fig.*, and prob. *carve* is now usually taken in the preceding or some of the extant senses.

1398 TREVISA *Barth. De P.R.* v. lxiv. (1495) 181 The skynne is callyd cutis in latyn, for it..is ofte kytte and coruen. *Ibid.* XVII. cii. 667 Bowes of mirra ben kerue and kytte and slytte. *c* **1400** *Rom. Rose* 1887 This arwe was kene grounde, As ony rasour that is founde, To kutte and kerve. **1633** G. HERBERT *Temple, Divinitie* ii, Which with the edge of wit they cut and carve. **1799** H. HUNTER tr. *St. Pierre's Stud. Nat.* (ed. 2) I. Introd. 8 Mr. L. T. Rede..proceeds to cut and carve me down into..a careful abridgement. **1812** COMBE (Dr. Syntax) *Picturesque* XIX. 72 To the last he'd cut and carve.

12. *to carve out*: **a.** (in *Legal lang.*) To cut a smaller or subordinate estate out of a larger one.

1625 Burges *Pers. Tithes* 21 To carue out his whole maintenance out of their estates. **1767** Blackstone *Comm.* II. 107 The fee-simple..is generally vested and resides in some person or other; though divers inferior estates may be carved out of it. **1876** Digby *Real Prop.* v. §2. 215 The estate of tenant in tail was, according to the metaphorical expression of the lawyers, 'carved out of', that is, less than an estate in fee simple and different from it. **1879** Castle *Law Rating* 66 The interests carved out or subordinate to his occupation. **1885** *Law Rep.* 29 Chanc. Div. 255 A lease.. carved out of a term created by a lease of the 27th of June, 1797.

b. *transf.* (Sometimes also in other senses, esp. 1 and 4.)

1605 Shaks. *Macb.* I. ii. 19 Braue Macbeth..with his brandisht Steele..caru'd out his passage. **1695** Blackmore *Pr. Arth.* VII. 579 The valiant..carve out to themselves propitious Fate. **1716–7** Bentley *Serm.* xi. 374 Carving out his own satisfaction in every object of Desire. **1867** Freeman *Norm. Conq.* (1876) I. vi. 465 Roger now sought to carve out a dominion for himself. **1874** Blackie *Self-Cult.* 77 Persistency will carve out a way to unexpected success. **1875** McLaren *Serm.* Ser. II. viii. 144 No matter what honour they have carved out for themselves with their swords.

†**13.** *fig.* (with reference to speech) Schmidt suggests 'To show great courtesy and affability'. *Obs.*

1588 Shaks. *L.L.L.* v. ii. 323 He can carue too, and lispe: Why this is he That kist away his hand in courtesie. **1598** —— *Merry W.* I. iii. 49 Shee discourses: shee carues: she giues the leere of inuitation.

carve, *sb.* [f. the vb.] An act or stroke of Carving. See also carf.

Mod. Give it a carve.

carve, erroneous spelling of carue ploughland.

carved (kɑːvd, -ɪd), *ppl. a.* [f. carve *v.* + -ed[1].] Cut, sculptured, engraved; see the vb.

1526 *Pilgr. Perf.* (W. de W. 1531) 192b, No kerued ne grauen ydoll. **1593** Shaks. *Rich. II*, III. iii. 152 A payre of carued Saints. **1611** Bible *Ps.* lxxiv. 6 They breake downe the carued worke thereof. **1662** Fuller *Worthies* (1840) III. 188 The carved chapel of Wainscot. **1822** Procter (B. Cornwall) *Flood of Thess.* II. 102 Phidias—whose carved thoughts Threw beauty o'er the years of Pericles. **1870** Bryant *Iliad* I. III. 100 At rest on his carved couch.

b. *Naut.* ***high-carved***: app. = *high-cargued*; see cargued, and carving.

a **1642** Sir W. Monson *Naval Tracts* III. (1704) 374/1 The difference in the Built of Ships, betwixt a flush Deck and high Carv'd. **1667** *Lond. Gaz.* No. 170/4 Two great Frenchmen of War, being high carved ships.

carvel (ˈkɑːvɪl). *Naut.* Forms: 5 kervel, -yle; 5 caruyll, 5–7 carvell, 6 caruile, karuell, 6–7 carvill, 7 carvile, -eile, karval, 6–7, 9 carvel; see also caravel. [a. OF. *caruelle*, *kirvelle* (16th c. in Littré): see caravel. *Carvel* was the vernacular Eng. form from 15th to 17th c., and still continues to be so, so far as the word is truly at home, as in the comb. *carvel-built*, etc.]

The ordinary name from the 15th to the 17th c., of a somewhat small, light, and fast ship, chiefly of Spain and Portugal, but also mentioned as French and English. (Rarely mentioned after 1650 exc. as a thing of history, and then usually written *caravel*, after mod.F. *caravelle*, Pg. *caravela*.)

1462 *Rep. Fr. Prisoners* in *Paston Lett.* II. 93 In to Scotland ward in a kervyle of Depe. **1494** Fabyan VII. 447 Of ye Englyshe men..ii. barkys, and a caruyll: the whiche thre small shyppys escaped by theyr delyuer Saylynge. **1513** Douglas *Æneis* VIII. ii. 61 The payntit carvellis fleting throu the flude. **1575** Laneham *Let.* (1871) 13 Hoounds harroing after [the deer], az they had bin a number of skiphs too the spoyle of a karuell. **1590** Greene *Fr. Bacon* ix. 262 Rich Alexandria drugs, Fetch'd by carvels from Ægypt's richest streights. **1613** Purchas *Pilgr.* VIII. ii. 729 Thus Columbus is set forth with three Caruels at the King's charges. **1622** Heylin *Cosmogr.* IV. (1682) 29 An infinite number of karvals and small Boats. **1627** Capt. Smith *Seaman's Gram.* ix. 40 A Caruell whose sailes stand like a paire of Tailers sheeres. **1631** Heywood *Fair Maid of W.* I. IV. i. Wks. 1874 II. 313 It did me good To see the Spanish Carveile vaile her top Vnto my Maiden Flag. **1686** *Lond. Gaz.* No. 2201/1 Besides ..they have 9 or 10 Carvels or small Frigats, from 18 to 6 Guns. **1830** James *Darnley* xxxv. 154 From the biggest man-of-war to the meanest carvel. **1854** H. Miller *Sch. & Schm.* iii. (1857) 42 All sorts of barques and carvels..correctly drawn on the slate.

†**2. a.** The Paper Nautilus or Argonaut. **b.** The floating mollusc *Ianthina*. **c.** A jelly-fish (*Medusa*). *Obs.*

1657 R. Ligon *Barbadoes* 6 This little Fish, the Carvill, riseth to the top of the sea..and there..raises up his Maine Mast, spreads his sayles, which he makes of his own sinews, and begins his voyage. **1688** J. Clayton *Virginia* in *Phil. Trans.* XVII. 783 In the Sea I saw many little things which the Seamen call Carvels..they Swim like a small Sheeps Bladder above the Water, downwards there are long Fibrous Strings, some whereof I have found near half a yard long. **1690** J. Banister *Virginia* ibid. 671 The Nautilus or Carvil (as the Sailors call it). [**1707** Sloane *Jamaica* I. 7 When we were in about 46 degrees of Northern Latitude, I first saw what seamen call a Caraval or Portuguese Man of War.]

3. *Comb.* **carvel-built**, (*Naut.*) applied to a vessel 'the planks of which are all flush and smooth, the edges laid close to each other..in contradistinction to clinker-built, where they overlap each other' (Smyth *Sailor's Word-bk.*). So **carvel-planked** *a.*, **carvel-work**.

1678 Phillips [erroneously] *Carnel-work*, the building of ships first with their Timbers, and after bring on their planks. **1798** Capt. Miller in Nicolas *Disp. Nelson* VII. clix, The pains I had taken to get carver-built boats. **1805** *Mariner's Dict.*, *Carvel Work*, in contradistinction to clincher work; is the common method of planking vessels by laying the edges close to each other, and caulking them to make them water tight. **1859** McClintock *Voy. Fox* (1881) 249 She had been originally 'carvel' built. **1886** R. C. Leslie *Sea-painter's Log* xi. 252 The heavy carvel-planked boats of the French, Spaniards, or Italians.

carven (ˈkɑːv(ə)n), *ppl. a.* [Strong pa. pple. of carve *v.*: in ME. *corven*; *carven* occurs in 16th c., but its present use is a 19th c. revival, orig. poetical, but now frequent in rhetorical prose.] = carved.

1330 R. Brunne *Chron.* (1810) 336 Of arte he had þe maistrie, he mad a coruen kyng. **1430** Lydg. *Chron. Troy* II. xi, The corue knottes. *c* **1449** Pecock *Repr.* I. xix. 114 Graued werk or coruun werk. **1528** More *Heresyes* I. Wks. 117/2 Hys ymage painted or caruen. **1820** Keats *St. Agnes* xxiv, Garlanded with carven imageries. **1856** Mrs. Browning *Aur. Leigh* IV. 1004 A screen of carven ivory. **1879** Dowden *Southey* 32 A miracle of carven tracery branches overhead.

carvene (ˈkɑːviːn). *Chem.* A hydro-carbon $C_{10}H_{16}$ found in oil of caraway.

1876 Harley *Mat. Med.* 578 Carvene boils at 343°.

carver[1] (ˈkɑːvə(r)). [f. carve *v.* + -er[1].]

1. *gen.* One who carves or cuts.

c **1380** Wyclif *Sel. Wks.* III. 320 Clipperis and purse-kerveris. **1398** Trevisa *Barth. De P.R.* v. xx. (1495) 125 Of the teeth some ben keruers. **1605** Bacon *Adv. Learning* (1873) 56 A carver or a divider of cummin seed.

2. *spec.* One who carves wood, ivory, stone, etc.; a sculptor: most frequently (when not otherwise qualified) applied to one who carves in wood.

c **1386** Chaucer *Knts. T.* 1041 Ne portreyour, ne kerver of ymages. **1495** *Act 11 Hen. VII*, xxii. §1 A Freemason.. Tyler, Plommer, Glasier, Kerver nor Joyner. **1589** Puttenham *Eng. Poesie* (Arb.) 311 The painter or keruers craft. **1605** *Tryall Chev.* IV. i. in Bullen *O. Pl.* III. 336 A cunning Carver had cut out thy shape..in white alabaster. **1754** Dodsley *Agric.* ii. (R.) Smooth linden best obeys The carver's chissel. **1768–74** Tucker *Lt. Nat.* (1852) II. 604 The carver, the gilder, and the paper-hanger. **1840** Hood *Kilmansegg, Death* xvii, Its foreman, a carver and gilder.

†**b.** *attrib.* (A tree) used for carving.

1590 Spenser *F.Q.* I. i. 9 The carver holme, the maple seldom inly sound.

3. One who carves at table.

1432–50 tr. *Higden* (Rolls) VI. 435 Whom the kynges kerver hurte soore. *a* **1450** in *Eng. Gilds* (1870) 446 To bere his swerd & be his keruere tofore him. **1509–10** *Act 1 Hen. VIII*, xiv, Hys Cuppe berers Carvours and Sewers. **1670** Lassels *Voy. Italy* I. 16 Several carvers cut up all the meat at a side table. **1710** *Lond. Gaz.* No. 4672/1 First Carver, and Brother to the Empress. *Mod.* An expert carver.

b. A carving knife. ***a pair of carvers***: a carving knife and fork.

1840 Thackeray *Catherine* ii, You had got the carver out of her hand.

c. [Distinguished from Carver[2].] An armchair among a set of dining-chairs, usu. set at the head of the table as for the one who carves.

1927 *Daily Tel.* 3 May 3/3 A set of Hepplewhite chairs and carver upholstered in pigskin. **1952** J. Gloag *Short Dict. Furniture* 172 *Carver chair*... Another use of the term is to distinguish the arm chair or elbow chair in a set of dining-room chairs, used at the head of the table by the carver. **1978** *Morecambe Guardian* 14 Mar. 9/8 Top selling lines.. are dining room suites with a choice of table style..together with dining chairs, matching carver chairs and sideboards.

†**4.** *fig.* One who assigns any one his 'portion'. †*to be one's own carver*: to take or choose for oneself at one's own discretion. *Obs.*

1579 Lyly *Euphues* (Arb.) 55 In this poynte I meane not to be mine owne caruer. **1598** —— *Moth. Bombie* (Halliw.) Neither father nor mother, kith nor kinne shall bee her carver in a husband. **1583** Babington *Commandm.* 343 That everie souldier should be his owne carver and take what he can get. **1614** Raleigh *Hist. World* v. v. §7. II. 595 Plainly told them, that the Romans would be their owne Carvers, and take what they thought good. **1645** Bp. Hall *Contentation* 39 Wee are ill carvers for our selves; hee that made us, knows vvhat is fit for us. *a* **1714** Abp. J. Sharp *Serm.* I. i. (R.) He himself, were he to be the carver of his fortunes..would chuse for himself. **1797** Holcroft *Stolberg's Trav.* li. (ed. 2) 250 Peter..has..been the carver of his own fortune.

Carver[2] (ˈkɑːvə(r)). *U.S.* The name of John *Carver* (1576–1621), the first governor of Plymouth Colony in America, used *attrib.* to designate a chair of a type owned by him, having a rush seat, arms, and a back usually consisting of three horizontal and three vertical spindles.

1902 L. V. Lockwood *Colonial Furnit. Amer.* v. 129 Figures 85 and 86 are Elder Brewster's and Governor Carver's chairs respectively, and were, according to tradition, brought over in the Mayflower... Chairs in the fashion of Figure 86 are commonly known as 'Carver chairs', and are more frequently met with than any other pattern of the turned chair. **1913** —— *Furnit. Collectors' Gloss.* 10 *Carver*, an Americanism for a turned chair of the early seventeenth century, the back of which has three horizontal turnings and three vertical spindles, between the two lower horizontal turnings. So called because of one owned by Gov. Carver. **1923** *Furnit. Jrnl.* 3 Feb. 69 (*caption*) No. 1461 Carver. **1924** Nutting *Furniture Pilgrim Cent.* 299 This great Carver chair has a back superior to any other that we have seen, in its massiveness, and the character of its turnings. **1937** Langdon *Everyday Things* 32 The Carver Chair and the Brewster Chair.

ˈcarvership. [see -ship.] The office of carver (to the king).

1830 Nicolas in *Priv. Purse Exp. Eliz. York* 192/1 He was ..protected in the enjoyment of the carvership.

ˈcarvery. [see -ery.] **a.** Meat to be carved. **b.** Carved or sculptured work. *nonce-wds.*

1839 *New Monthly Mag.* LV. 129 The tin was lifted from his share of the carvery. **1845** T. Cooper *Purgat. Suicides* (1877) 23 O'ercanopied with perforated carvery.

c. A buffet or restaurant where meat is carved from a joint as required.

1962 *Hotels & Restaurants in Gt. Brit. & Irel.* (ed. 33) 186/2 'The Carvery', carve for yourself from the joint of your choice. **1977** *Logophile* v. 7/1 The huge billboard outside the carvery in Leicester Square. **1978** *Washington Post* 21 May 68 The other adult, wanting roast beef from the carvery..waits in the carvery line, also holding a tray.

carve-up (ˈkɑːvʌp). *slang.* [f. carve *v.* 10 and 10 b.] (The situation resulting from) a sharing of spoils; a division, sharing-out, cutting-up (with derogatory contextual overtones).

In quot. 1935 the reference is to money bequeathed in a will.

1935 M. Harrison *Spring in Tartarus* I. 27 The de Launes hadn't a tosser between them. Oh my Lord, what a carve up! **1936** J. Curtis *Gilt Kid* ix. 92 There would probably be a carve-up at the end when it came to sharing out the dough. Scaley was certainly the sort of man to stick to more than his fair share. **1943** 'R. Llewellyn' *None but Lonely Heart* xxxiv. 251 'How much can we make a week?'..'Depends on the carve up,' Slush says. **1959** *News Chron.* 3 July 6/6 In practice it is a carve-up among the Big Four. **1961** *Guardian* 12 Jan. 8/2 Public monopoly is preferable to commercial carve-up. **1963** *Times* 24 Jan. 5/1 Is the selection of justices of the peace in Britain..a 'political carve-up', as alleged by some of the more vociferous of the system's opponents? *Ibid.* 29 Apr. 7/6 Apart from one farcical carve-up of a passage from *Coriolanus*, the exercises owed nothing to written drama.

carvey, -vie, var. of Sc. carvy.

carving (ˈkɑːvɪŋ), *vbl. sb.* [f. carve *v.*]

1. The action of the verb carve, in various senses.

In senses 5–7 of the vb., *carving* is now usually restricted to work in wood, ivory, etc., *sculpture* being used of work in stone, and *chasing* of work in metal.

a **1225** *Ancr. R.* 344 Of keorfunge, oðer of hurtunge. *a* **1240** *Lofsong* in *Cott. Hom.* 207 In umbe keoruunge. *c* **1380** Wyclif *Sel. Wks.* III. 264 Kervynge of mete. **1530** Elyot *Gov.* I. viii, He shulde be..enstructed in painting or keruinge. **1561** T. Norton *Calvin's Inst.* I. 26 Caruing and painting are the giftes of God. *a* **1613** Overbury *Charac.*, *Very woman*, Her wrie little finger bewraies carving. **1641** Milton *Ch. Govt.* (1851) 118 To say Episcopacy is partly of divine institution, and partly of mans own carving. **1768** *Priv. Lett. 1st Ld. Malmesbury* I. 168 Ladies here never interfere with carving, etc. **1841–4** Emerson *Ess.*, *Hist.* Wks. I. 5 The value which is given to wood by carving.

2. Carved work; a carved figure or design.

c **1384** Chaucer *H. Fame* 1302 More to tellen..Ne of compasses ne of kervynges. **1633** G. Herbert *Temple*, *Sion* i, Wood..embellished with flowers and carvings. **1826** Scott *Woodst.* i, The carving on the reading-desk. **1867** Lady Herbert *Impress. Spain* 20 The choir..is very rich in carving.

3. *Naut.* ***high-carving***: see carved b.

a **1642** Monson *Naval Tracts* (Churchill) III. 322/1 A ship that carries her ordnance low, and her hull high built, has a great advantage of a galley..if she [sc. the galley] be desperately forced to board the same ship, she will not be able to enter her, in respect of her heighth and high carving.

4. *attrib.* and in *comb.*, as ***carving-board***, ***-fork***, ***-knife***, ***-machine***, ***-machinery***, ***-table***, ***-tool***, etc.

c **1450** *Bk. Curtasye* 673 in *Babees Bk.*, Two keruyng knyfes. **1503** *Priv. Purse Exp. Eliz. York* (1830) 96 A payre of carving knyves. **1673–4** Grew *Anat. Trunks* vii. §3 Shoomakers..make use of it [sallow] for their Carving-boards. **1678** *Lond. Gaz.* No. 1332/4, 1 silver carving fork. **1680** *Ibid.* No. 1487/4 A great Carving Spoon. **1875** Ure *Dict. Arts* I. 739 The most perfect carving machine..made for strictly artistic works. *Ibid.* The carving machinery.. invented by Mr. Jordan and patented in 1845.

ˈcarving, *ppl. a.* [f. as prec. + -ing[2].] That carves or cuts; cutting, sharp.

a **1225** *Ancr. R.* 212 Scherpe & keoruinde wordes. *c* **1400** *Destr. Troy* 8640 Hit was keruond & kene. **1413** Lydg. *Pylgr. Sowle* III. i. (1483) 50 Sharp keruyng rasours.

†**carvist.** *Obs. Falconry.* A hawk in its first year, of proper age to be carried on the fist.

1677 N. Cox *Gent. Recreat.* II. (1706) 21 The fourth [Falcon] is termed Murzarolt (the latest term is Carvist, as much as to say, *Carry on the Fist*) they are so called January, February, March, April, and till the middle of May, during which time they must be kept on the Fist. **1704** Worlidge *Dict. Rust. et Urb.* s.v. **1720–1800** in Bailey.

carvy (ˈkɑːvɪ). Also 7 carvi, 7– carvie, 9 carvey. Sc. form of caraway, esp. (in *pl.*) in sense 2, small confections containing caraway seeds.

a **1648** Digby *Closet Open.* (1671) 149 If you shew a few carvi comfits on the top, it will not be amiss. **1689** A. Hay tr. *St. Germain's R. Physic* 58 (Jam.) Seeds of the four greater hot seeds, viz. Annise, Carvie, Cumin, Fennel. **1802** *Agric. Surv. Peebles* 397 (Jam.) A small handful of camomile flowers, two tea-spoonfuls of anise-seeds, and as much carvey-seeds. **1820** *Blackw. Mag.* Oct. 14 (Jam.) She had

preserved, since the great tea-drinking..the remainder of the two ounces of carvey, bought for that memorable occasion.

carway, obs. form of CARAWAY.

carwhichet, -witchet, var. CARRIWITCHET.

car'widgeon. ? = CARRIWITCHET.
a **1626** MIDDLETON *Mayor of Queenb.* v. i, *2nd Player.* The Whirligig, the Whibble, the Carwidgeon. *Simon.* Heyday! what names are these? *2nd. Pl.* New names of late.

†**cary.** *Obs.* Some textile fabric. Cf. CARE *sb.*[2]
c **1394** *P. Pl. Crede* 422 His cote was of a cloute þat cary y-called.

caryatid (kærɪ'ætɪd). *Arch.* Pl. usually in L. form **caryatides**; also **caryatids**, and (*erron.*) 8 **careatides**, 9 **caryatidæ**. [ad. L. *caryātid-es*, a. Gr. καρυᾶτιδες, pl. of *Caryātis*, Καρυᾶτις a priestess of Artemis at Caryae (Καρύαι a village in Laconia), also a female figure as below.]
A female figure used as a column to support an entablature. Also *attrib.*, as in ***caryatid figures***.
1563 SHUTE *Archit.* B iij a, Ymages, figured like women.. named Cariatides..for pillers. **1679** *Confinement, a Poem* 9 Alas, the Order solely is, That of the captiv'd Cariatides. **1776** R. CHANDLER *Trav. Greece* (1825) II. 86 The entablature is supported by women, called caryatides. The Greeks..destroyed Carya, a city which had favoured the common enemy, cut off the males, and carried into captivity the women, whom they compelled to retain their dress..in a state of servitude. **1804** *Ann. Rev.* II. 351 To place like caryatids our perfection in our supportance. **1844** DISRAELI *Coningsby* VII. viii. 275 Caryatides carved in dark oak. **1846** ELLIS *Elgin Marb.* II. 39 Caryatid figures. **1847** TENNYSON *Princ.* IV. 183 Two great statues, Art And Science, Caryatids, lifted up A weight of emblem.
Hence **cary'atidal, caryati'dean, carya'tidic** adjs., like, or of the nature of, a Caryatid.
1835 *Gentl. Mag.* III. 192/2 Cariatidal statues. **1865** E. C. CLAYTON *Cruel Fort.* I. 143 Caryatidean attitudes. **1881** O'DONOVAN *Merv Oasis* xxxvii. (1882) II. 126 Caryatidic appendages of the architecture of my residence.

carycke, caryk(e, obs. ff. CARRACK.

caryen, caryne, caryon, obs. ff. CARRION.

caryinite (kə'raɪnaɪt). *Min.* [f. Gr. καρύιν-ος nut-brown.] A lead-manganese-calcium arsenate.
1887 DANA *Man. Min.* 234.

caryo-: see KARYO-.

caryophyllaceous (ˌkærɪəʊfɪ'leɪʃ(ɪ)əs), *a. Bot.* [ad. mod.L. *Caryophyllāceæ*, f. *caryophyllus* (ad. Gr. καρυόφυλλον), the clove-pink.]
a. Belonging to the N.O. *Caryophyllaceæ*. **b.** Applied to a corolla having five petals with long claws, as in the clove-pink.
1835 LINDLEY *Introd. Bot.* (1848) I. 335 A caryophyllaceous [corolla] has long, narrow, distant claws.

†**cary'ophyllate**, *v. Obs.*[−1] [f. as prec. + -ATE.] To flavour with cloves. Hence **caryophyllated** *ppl. a.*
1641 FRENCH *Distill.* iv. (1651) 99 On this pour Spirit of Wine Caryophyllated.

ˌcaryo'phylleous, *a. Bot.* = CARYOPHYLLACEOUS, **a.**
1794 MARTYN *Rousseau's Bot.* xix. 272 Caryophylleous plants.

‖**caryopsis** (kærɪ'ɒpsɪs). *Bot.* Pl. **-ides** (-ɪdiːz). [mod.L., f. Gr. κάρυ-ον nut + ὄψις appearance.] A small one-seeded dry indehiscent fruit, whose pericarp adheres to the seed throughout so as to form one body with it, as in wheat and other kinds of corn.
1830 LINDLEY *Nat. Syst. Bot.* 6 Dry nuts or caryopsides. **1872** OLIVER *Elem. Bot.* II. 278 In Barley and Oats, the pale, or the pale and flowering glume, adhere to the caryopsis, after the time of flowering.

†**cas.** ? Overthrow, fallen mass. (But in the passage quoted the Ellesmere and two other MSS. have *tas* heap.)
c **1386** CHAUCER *Knts. T.* 147 (Harl., Corpus, Petw, Lansd.) To ransake in the caas of þe bodies dede [so ll. 151 162; *here Harl. has* chaas].

cas, obs. form of CASE *sb.*

ca. sa. (kɑː sɑː). *Law.* The usual abbreviation of *capias ad satisfaciendum* (see CAPIAS).
1796 J. ANSTEY *Pleader's G.* (1803) 70 [He] conceives that *Ca' Sa's* are vexatious, And shudders at a Fieri facias. **1864** *Daily Tel.* 30 Aug., The bankrupt had not only been arrested on a ca. sa. but on a capias, and the proper course would be to apply to a judge at chambers. **1865** *Dublin Univ. Mag.* I. 562 I've got a ca. sa. against you, Captain.

casakene, obs. form of CASSAKIN.

casal ('keɪsəl), *a.* [f. CASE + -AL[1].] Of or belonging to grammatical case.
1834 J. M. MCCULLOCH *Eng. Gram.* 57 *note*, The casal termination of the Saxon possessive.

‖**casal, casale.** [It. *casale*, f. *casa* house.] A hamlet (in Italy, Malta).
1506 GUYLFORDE *Pilgr.* (1851) 56 We landed..and wente to suche casales as we founde, and refresshed us. **1810** COLERIDGE *Friend* (1818) III. 321 A venerable old man, belonging to one of the distant casals. **1834** F. F. HEAD *Bubbles of Brunnen* 190 People who had come from the most remote casals [in Malta] to see the execution.

casamat(e, obs. form of CASEMATE.

casamunar, var. CASSUMUNAR a medical root.

Casanova (kæzə'nəʊvə, kæs-). Used as *sb.* allusively of a man whose amorous activities resemble those of the Italian adventurer, Giovanni Jacopo *Casanova* de Seingalt (1725–98), author of memoirs, in French, describing his escapades and amours in most countries of Europe. So **Casa'nova-ish, Casano'vesque, Casa'novian** *adjs.*; also **Casa'novism**.
[**1888** *Encycl. Brit.* XXIII. 215/1 There is also no doubt a touch of Casanova in Barry Lyndon's character.] **1903** G. B. SHAW *Man & Superman* p. xiv, Don Juanism is no longer misunderstood as mere Casanovism. **1925** A. HUXLEY *Those Barren Leaves* I. vii. 68 Boasting..of one's Casanovesque capacities. **1928** E. CANTOR *My Life is in your Hands* v. 52 My grandmother..came to box my ears and take the infant Casanova home. **1932** W. FAULKNER *Light in Aug.* (1933) i. 4 Young bachelors, or sawdust Casanovas. **1940** *Time* 4 Mar. 74/3 It concerns the adventures of a Casanovian Irishman, Gideon Ouseley, among the English. **1958** J. KEROUAC *On Road* 170 Decadent, Casanova-ish men. **1959** J. BRAINE *Vodi* vi. 94 A resplendent Casanova in a royal blue sports jacket.

‖**casaque** (kazak). [Fr. *casaque* CASSOCK.] A woman's blouse or jumper.
1872 *Young Englishwoman* Dec. 646/2 Walking costumes are still made with either polonaise or casaque tunic. **1894** *Daily News* 30 Oct. 6/6 The 'casaque', or Louis XVI jacket, in brocade or very handsome fancy cloth, is another revival of this season. **1923** *Daily Mail* 19 Feb. (Advt.), Knitted Wool Casaques.

‖**casaquin** (kazakɛ̃). [Fr.: see CASSAKIN.] A kind of bodice or jumper.
1879 J. R. PLANCHÉ *Cycl. Costume* II. 181 A *casaquin* (a loose jacket) of grey velvet laced with silver..and lined with cloth of silver. **1922** *Daily Mail* 4 Dec. 15 The casaquin bodice was joined to a full ankle-length skirt. **1923** *Ibid.* 18 Jan. 11 Another frock from Paris has a casaquin..over a plain skirt. *Ibid.* 12 Feb. 15 The casaquin jumper of this three-piece suit.

†**casard.** *Obs.* = CASINGS.
1499 PYNSON *Promp. Parv.*, Casard netes donge [**1516** W. de W. casan], *bozetum*.

casareep, casava: see CASS-.

†**casbald.** *Obs.* A term of reproach (addressed in places quoted to Mary Magdalene).
c **1440** *York Myst.* xxxiv. 194 Go home, casbalde with þi clowte. *c* **1450** *Towneley Myst.* 213 Go home, thou casbald, with that clowte.

cascabel ('kɑːskəbɛl, 'kæs-). Forms: 7 **caskable, casacabel(l**, 9 **cascable**, 7– **cascabel**. [a. Sp. *cascabel* little round bell, child's rattle, rattlesnake; which has been conjectured to be connected with L. *scabellum* a kind of castanet played with the foot: see Diez.]
1. *Gunnery.* Formerly the knob or pommel at the rear end of a cannon; now the whole rear part behind the base ring, including knob and base.
1639 R. WARD *Animadv. Warre* 129 The Center of the pummell or Caskable of the Peece. **1672** W. P. *Compl. Gunner* iv. 5 The Pumel or Button at her Coyl or Britchend is called the Casacabel. **1795** *Phil. Trans.* LXXXV. 439 A circular cavity..to receive the cascabel of the gun. **1797** RUMFORD *ibid.* LXXXVII. 240 A cannon of metal..placed vertically upon its cascabel. **1858** GREENER *Gunnery* 9 Furnished with trunnions, cascable, and touchhole. **1864** *Daily Tel.* 25 May, The knob of the cascable.
†**b.** called also ***cascabel deck***. *Obs.*
1669 S. STURMY *Mariner's Mag.* v. xi. 48 (*On engraving of a Gun*) Casacabell deck. **1706** PHILLIPS, *Cascabel*, the Pummel or hindermost round Knob at the Breach of a great Gun, by some called the Cascabel-deck.
‖**2.** A rattle-snake; also its rattle. [Sp.]
1760–72 tr. *Juan & Ulloa's Voy. S. Amer.* I. vii. 60 The cascabel or rattle-snake..at the end of its tail is the cascabel or rattle. **1852** TH. ROSS tr. *Humboldt's Trav.* I. iv. 152 The Cascabel, or rattle-snake, the Coral, and other vipers.

cascade (kæ'skeɪd), *sb.* Also 7 **cascata, cascate, caskade**. [a. F. *cascade*, ad. It. *cascata* fall, f. *cascare* to fall: see -ADE.]
1. A waterfall. **a.** Usually, a small waterfall; *esp.* one of a series of small falls, formed by water in its descent over rocks, or in the artificial works of the kind introduced in landscape gardening.
1641 EVELYN *Diary* 8 Oct., Divers springs of water, artificial Cascades. **1670** LASSELS *Voy. Italy* II. 315 The fountains, the *Cascatas*, the *Grottas*, the *Girandolas*, and the other rare water works. **1789** MRS. PIOZZI *Journ. France* I. 11 The underwork of an artificial cascade. **1808** PIKE *Sources Mississ.* I. App. 50 Springs which form small cascades as they tumble over the cliffs. **1873** G. C. DAVIES *Mount. and Mere* xiii. 101 For a quarter of a mile the water comes down in a series of small cascades.
†**b.** Formerly in a wider sense.
1671 *Phil. Trans.* VI. 2151 On this side of the Cascata's of the Nile. **1673** RAY *Journ. Low C.* 105 A great Cascate or Catarract of the river Rhene. **1684** T. BURNET *Th. Earth* I. 99 Great spouts or caskades of water. **1718** ROWE *Ode King's Birth-D.* vi, Volga tumbling in Cascades.
2. *transf.* and *fig.* **a.** In general uses.
1860 TYNDALL *Glac.* I. §2. 20 The ice cascade. **1869** PHILLIPS *Vesuv.* iii. 70 Forming a most beautiful and uncommon cascade [of red-hot ashes, etc.]. **1878** GEO. ELIOT *Coll. Breakf. P.* 389 Anti-social force that sweeps you down The world in one cascade of molecules.
b. A pyrotechnic device imitating a fall of water.
1749 in A. St. H. Brock *Pyrotechnics* (1922) iv. 30 A large vertical Sun moved by double Fires, Cascades, Pyramids. **1875** W. H. BROWNE *Art Pyrotechny* xii. 118 The chapter will contain instructions for the construction of..brilliant suns, cascades [etc.]. **1922** A. ST. H. BROCK *Pyrotechnics* v. 128 Cascade..a feature of the Crystal Palace displays.
c. A loose wavy fall or ruffle of lace, etc.
1882 *World* 21 June 18/1 [The jacket] had a sailor collar.. and cascade of lace down the front. **1885** *New York Weekly Sun* 13 May 6/5 Morning dresses..are made dressy with profuse use of ribbons in bows, flots, cascades.
d. *Electr.* ***charge by cascade***: a method of charging a series of insulated Leyden jars by connecting the outer coating of the first with the knob of the next, and so on; the last outer coating being connected with the ground. Also applied to other electrical devices connected in such a manner that each operates the next one in turn; freq. in phr. ***in cascade***.
1868 *Q. Jrnl. Sci.* V. 117 We have here a compact form of Leyden battery, arranged for 'cascade'. **1870** R. FERGUSON *Electr.* 89 Called the charge by cascade. **1915** *Proc. Inst. Radio Engin.* III. 230 Where a greater amplification than can be obtained with one audion is required, cascade working of the radio frequency systems may be resorted to by coupling two or more audion systems. *Ibid.* 286 The 'exponential' method of tuning, involving the use of radio frequency pliotron amplifiers in cascade, is shown to have given remarkable selectivity. **1930** *Engineering* 7 Mar. 312/3 The two 500,000-volt transformers are connected in cascade to give 1,000,000 volts. **1940** *Jrnl. R. Aeronaut. Soc.* XLIV. 373 The current control can be carried out..mechanically by means of a special cascade transformer. **1946** *Electronic Engin.* XVIII. 151 The required high voltage may be obtained..by the use of cascade transformers and rectifiers.
e. *spec.* Applied to a succession of stages or processes in some operation or event in Physics, Chemistry, etc. Freq. *attrib.*
1902 *Encycl. Brit.* XXVII. 187/1 The method by which we try to obtain successively lower temperatures by making use of successive gases is called the 'cascade method'. **1937** *Nature* 13 Nov. 837/2 In the cascade process, showers are built up from the successive conversion of electron energy into radiation, radiation into pair production and then further loss of electron energy to radiation. **1940** *Rep. Progr. Physics* VI. 65 Hertz has..arranged these in a cascade similar to the cascade used for the diffusion of isotopes through porous walls. Figure 3 shows cascades of three units. **1945** *Ann. Reg. 1944* 383 Cascade showers are largely initiated by electrons. **1958** *Chambers's Techn. Dict.* 963/2 *Cascade*, separation of isotopes by similar successive stages in a process, each stage increasing the concentration of each. **1960** *Economist* 15 Oct. 268/3 The production method..is to turn the uranium into a gas and filter it through porous membranes through which the lighter uranium 235 passes first. This process works on a 'cascade' principle. **1964** N. G. CLARK *Mod. Org. Chem.* v. 86 The necessary low temperatures are obtained by a 'cascade' process involving the pressure liquefaction and evaporation of propane.
f. The practice of relegating stock to successively less exacting uses. See sense 4 of the vb.
1984 *Railway Mag.* June 227/2 Refurbishing all the vehicles for the new services has cost just over £2m, which compares with £1m a time for a comparable new e.m.n. The advantages of the cascade principle are thus well demonstrated.
3. *Comb.*, as ***cascade-garden***.
a **1667** COWLEY *Greatness* (1684) 123 Nor vast Parks, nor Fountain, or Cascade-Gardens.

cascade (kæ'skeɪd), *v.* [f. the sb.]
1. a. *intr.* To fall or pour in a cascade.
1702 S. P[ARKER] tr. *Tully's De Finibus* 70 Wines.. Caskading from a mighty Goblet. **1732–48** DE FOE, &c. *Tour Gt. Brit.* II. 218 (D.) In the middle of a large octagon piece of water stands an obelisk of near seventy feet, for a *Jet-d'-Eau* to cascade from the top of it. **1791** SMEATON *Edystone L.* §100 The waves cascaded through this gap. **1830** LYELL *Princ. Geol.* (1875) II. II. xxvi. 34 A much more copious stream of melted matter, had cascaded down the same height and overflowed the plain below. **1880** MISS BIRD *Japan* I. 123 A vigorous mountain torrent cascading its way between rocky walls.
b. *transf.* (Cf. CASCADE *sb.* 2 c.)
1861 THACKERAY *Philip* xix. 258 Who wore a large high black-satin stock cascading over a figured silk waist-coat.
c. *vulgar.* To vomit. ? *Obs.*
[**1771** SMOLLETT *Humph. Cl.* III. 4 Oct. iii, She cascaded in his urn.] **1805** *Naval Chron.* XV. 35, I had cascaded two or three times. **1847–78** HALLIWELL, *Cascade*, to vomit. *Var. dial.* [Webster says: *colloq.* or *vulgar* in Amer.]
2. *trans.* To pour, like a cascade. *nonce-use.*
? **1796** COLERIDGE *Lett. to Estlin* (1884) 21 The Monthly has *cataracted* panegyric on my poems, the Critical has *cascaded* it.
3. *Electr. trans.* and *intr.* To link or connect (valves, etc.) in stages to form a cascade (cf. prec. 2 d).

1930 *Jrnl. Inst. Radio Engin.* XVIII. 1007 Consideration ..must be given to characteristics of any other selective devices of the amplifier system..if single or coupled circuits are cascaded with the coupled circuit under consideration. **1956** AMOS & BIRKINSHAW *Telev. Engin.* II. vii. 114 Decrease in stage gain to give constant passband when cascading. **1971** *Physics Bull.* Apr. 208/3 It is possible to cascade either germanium-silicon or lead telluride type modules thermally with bismuth telluride.

4. *trans.* To relegate (old but still serviceable stock, esp. buses, railway coaches, etc.) by stages to successively less exacting uses.

1980 [implied at CASCADING *vbl. sb.*]. **1983** *Forward Look* (Vicrail Freight Business Group, Victoria, Austral.), Relaying secondary freight lines. Relay selected routes with rail cascaded down from main interstate lines. **1984** *Railway Mag.* Dec. 496/2, I wonder how many Hastings line passengers have given thought to the forthcoming rolling stock? Present proposals are for '4-VEP'..multiple-units 'cascaded' from other services. **1985** *Buses Extra* Apr.-May 43/2 No fewer than 30 VRs would be cascaded in Western National's direction.

Hence **ca'scaded** *ppl. a.*, **ca'scading** *vbl. sb.*

1791 SMEATON *Edystone L.* §100 The cascading of the water through the gully before mentioned. **1919** *Wireless World* July 187/1 These types of alternator..may be classified as follows:—1. Machines in cascade. 2. Internally-cascaded machines. *Ibid.* 189/2 In effect the machine Figure 2 represents in a single machine the summation of the four cascaded machines of Figure 1. **1930** *Jrnl. Inst. Radio Engin.* XVIII. 994 Cascading must give the same type of transmission curve as coupled circuits with very weak coupling... Two staggered single-circuit curves of the same shape cascade into a coupled-circuit transmission curve... The amount of transmission is improved in the cascaded case. **1949** *Electronic Engin.* XXI. 61 Simple cascading (i.e. direct coupling between anode and grid) requires a relatively high potential source for the later stages. **1956** AMOS & BIRKINSHAW *Telev. Engin.* II. viii. 122 A conventional cascaded amplifier has an upper frequency limit beyond which it is impossible to amplify. **1980** *Internat. Railway Jrnl.* Mar. 18/2 In the 1980 rail laying programme, 235 track miles of worn welded rail not meeting Southern's rail wear limits for heavy tonnage lines will be released for cascading to lighter density track segments. **1984** *Buses* Oct. 440/1 The arrival of 'cascaded' VRs in the country allowed dual-door VRs to return to the city as FLF replacements. **1985** *Buses Extra* Apr.-May 45/2 Bristol Omnibus Company had already indulged in secondhand VR purchases before the cascading policy began.

ca'scading, *ppl. a.* [f. CASCADE *v.* + -ING[2].] Falling in or as in a cascade.

1889 C. EDWARDES *Sardinia* 199 The cascading stream. **1916** 'BOYD CABLE' *Action Front* 179 From overhead..there came..the clatter and rattle of cascading bricks and tiles. **1923** *Glasgow Herald* 9 May 11 Climbing and cascading plants. **1957** *Encycl. Brit.* XXIII. 412/2 Another cause for hanging tributaries and consequently a sheer or cascading plunge..is simply more rapid deepening of that valley.

‖**cascalho** (ka'skaljo). Also **-hao.** [Pg.] In Brazil, a deposit of pebbles, gravel, and ferruginous sand, containing diamonds or gold.

1812 J. MAWE *Trav. Brazil* v. 77 The gold lies..in a stratum of rounded pebbles and gravel, called *cascalhão*. **1823** —— *Diamonds* (ed. 2) 35 In one part of the Diamond District the *cascalho* forms a solid breccia. **1867** C. W. KING *Precious Stones* (ed. 2) 59 The gravel—*cascalhao*—filling their beds is dug out. **1910** *Encycl. Brit.* VIII. 160/1 The diamond is found..in the gravels of the present rivers, embedded in a ferruginous clay-cemented conglomerate known as *cascalho*. **1957** *Ibid.* IV. 838/2 Carbonado..is found almost exclusively in the state of Bahia in Brazil, where it occurs in the *cascalho* or diamond-bearing gravel.

†**cascan.** [a. obs. F. *cascane*.] (See quots.)

1696 PHILLIPS, *Cascans*, in Fortification, Wells digg'd to clear the Mines from Water. **1704** J. HARRIS *Lex Techn.*, *Cascan*..is a certain Hole or Hollow-place in form of a well, from whence a Gallery dug in like manner under Ground is convey'd, to give Air to the Enemies Mine. **1721-1800** in BAILEY.

‖**cascara** ('kaskara). [Sp. *cáscara* bark.]

1. A bark canoe (in Spanish America).

1882 *Athenæum* 4 Feb. 155/2 Birch-bark canoes, dug-outs, cedar canoes, balsas, woodskins, and cascaras. **1882** *Standard* 10 Feb. 5/3 The cascara of the Caripuna..or the coracle of the Mandans and the Welsh.

2. *Med.* (An extract of) the bark of a Californian buckthorn, *Rhamnus purshiana*, used as a laxative or cathartic; in full *cascara sagrada*, 'sacred bark' (see SACRED *a.* 7). Popularly pronounced (kæ'skɑːrə).

1879 A. O'NEILL in *New Preparations* (Detroit) III. 140. **1885** *Brit. Pharmacopœia* 151 Extract of Cascara Sagrada. *Ibid.* 152 Mix the cascara with two pints of the spirit. **1922** JOYCE *Ulysses* 68 One tabloid of cascara sagrada. **1951** A. GROLLMAN *Pharmacol. & Therapeutics* xix. 390 Cascara sagrada is a very popular remedy in habitual constipation. **1966** J. GARDNER *Amber Nine* ii. 35 If you are given any reason to think you've been detected, move like an overdose of cascara.

cascarilla (kæskə'rɪlə). [a. Sp. *cascarilla*, dim. of *cascara* rind, bark. In F. *cascarille*.] The bitter aromatic bark of the plant *Croton eleuteria*, used as a tonic. Also called *cascarilla bark*.

1686 *Lond. Gaz.* No. 2186/1, 200 thousand pounds of the Bark of Trees, called Cascarilla. **1759** B. STILLINGFL. tr. *Beyerstein's Physic* in *Misc. Tracts* (1762) 210 They use the cascarilla, which is certainly a very good medicine in shiverings. **1826** GOOD *Bk. Nat.* (1834) I. 191 The cascarilla bark and castor oil are obtained from plants poisonous in some part or other. **1870** YEATS *Nat. Hist. Comm.* 234.

Hence **casca'rillin,** a bitter substance ($C_{12}H_{18}O_4$) obtained from cascarilla bark.

1875 H. WOOD *Therap.* (1879) 83 Cascarillin, a neutral, bitter, crystallizable principle.

†**casceis.** *Sc. Obs.* Some article of attire.

1578 *Invent.* (1815) 231 (Jam.) Ane white casceis pasmentit with silvir.

†**caschielawis.** *Sc. pl. Obs.* Also **caschelawes.** [Cosmo Innes, *Sketches of Early Sc. Hist.* compares *glaslavis* = Gael. *glas-lamh* handcuff; this has suggested the possibility of formation from Gael. *caisg* (kaʃk) restrain + *lamh* (lav) hand, or that the derivation includes *cas* foot (genitive *coise*, 'koʃe) and *lamh*. But these are merely conjectures. The torture, however, appears to have been allied to that called 'the three smalls,' in Gaelic folk-lore.]

An instrument of torture, said to have been invented by the 'Master of Orkney' in 1596. Its action appears to have been forcibly to draw together the body and limbs of the victim, and hold him in this cramped position.

(An unlucky 'shot' at a derivation, hazarded by Dr. Jamieson ['It might be deduced from Teut. *kausse*, *kousse* (Fr. *chausse*) a stocking, and *lauw* tepidus q. the warm hose'], although absolutely pre-scientific and worthless, is the sole foundation for the imaginary description of this 'frightful machine', adopted by Mr. Lecky, *Hist. Rat.* (1865) I. 142. The assumption that it was in legal use is equally baseless; all the references are to legal proceedings *against* those who were charged with applying this cruel torture.)

1596 in Pitcairn *Crim. Trials* I. II. 375 The said Alesoun was, be vehement tortour of the caschielawis quhairin sche was kepit be the space of fourtie-aucht houris, compellit to mak the said pretendit Confessioune. *Ibid.* I. 376 He being kepit in the caschielawis ellewin dayis and ellewin nychtis; tuyise in the day, be the space of fourtene dayis, callit in the buites. [**1607** *Indictment of Master of Orkney* in *Sc. Acts* (1816) IV. 396/2 Novo et inusitato crudelitatis tormento a se invento vulgo lie caschelawes.] **1599** (11 Oct.) *Regr. of Privy Council of Scotl.* VI. 49 Without ony offens or fault committit be him [he] patt him to tortour in ane instrument nameit the caschielawis, and held him thairin the space of twa houris, drawing his body, nek, armes, and feit togidder within the boundis of ane span.

‖**caschrom** ('kasxrom). Also **cascrome, -croim, casschron.** [Gael. *cas* foot, *crom*, *chrom*, crooked.] An instrument of tillage formerly used in the Scottish Highlands, called also 'foot-plough'.

1806 *Gazetteer Scotl.* 513 The cascroim or crooked spade is almost the only utensil used by the common class of tenants in labouring the ground. **1808** J. WALKER *Hist. Hebrides & Highl. Scot.* I. 170 The cascrome, or crook spade. **1824** MᶜCULLOCH *Highl. & W. Isl. Scotl.* IV. 297 Dugald who drives at the Caschrom. **1861** SMILES *Engineers* II. 375 An instrument called the cas-chrom—literally the 'crooked-foot'..was almost the only tool employed in tillage.

‖**casco.** [Sp. *casco* hull, hulk.] **a.** The hull of a ship. **b.** A kind of boat used at Manila in lading and unlading ships.

1755 MAGENS *Insurances* II. 211 Upon the Casco as it is call'd or the Hull of the Ship.

cascode ('kæskəʊd). *Electr.* [f. CASC(ADE *sb.* 2 d + CATH)ODE.] (See quot. 1958.) Also *attrib.*

Quot. 1939 does not illustrate the current sense: see quot. 1948.

1939 HUNT & HICKMAN in *Rev. Scient. Instruments* X. 16/2 This tube connection we have called the 'cascode'... It is generally useful for d.c. amplifier work in which it is inconvenient to supply the additional bias voltages for a pentode. The dual triode, as connected, may be shown to be equivalent to a single triode. **1948** H. WALLMAN et al. in *Proc. Inst. Radio Engin.* XXXVI. 701/1 Search for a concise name for the grounded-cathode, grounded-grid combination led to the designation 'cascode', after a somewhat similar arrangement employed by Hunt and Hickman. *Ibid.*, The low-noise property that forms the feature of the present circuit is, however, entirely unconnected with the original use of the cascode as a d.c. amplifier in a voltage stabilizer. **1955** *Electronic Engin.* XXVII. 323 The features of the cascode type of amplifier. **1958** *Chambers's Techn. Dict.* 964/1 Cascode, thermionic valve circuit in which a grounded-cathode triode followed by a grounded-grid triode provides a low noise amplifier for very high radio frequencies. **1960** *Electronic Engin.* XXXII. 44 A transistor cascode amplifier does not require neutralization.

case (keɪs), *sb.*[1] Forms: 3-5 cas, (4 cais, caice, cass), 4-5 caas, caace, 4-6 cace, kace, 6 *Sc.* caice, 4- case. [ME. *cās*, *caas*, a. OF. *cas* in same sense:—L. *cāsu-s*, *cassu-s* fall, chance, occurrence, case, f. stem *cas-* of *cadĕre* to fall.]

I. † 1. a. A thing that befalls or happens to any one; an event, occurrence, hap, or chance.

a **1225** *Ancr. R.* 340 Swuch cas and swuch auenture biti-með to summe monne. **1297** R. GLOUC. (1810) 24 þar fore me clepude þat Water þo Homber..for þe cas þat Homber ..þer ynne a-dreynt was. *c* **1314** *Guy Warw.* (A.) 1698 In lasse while þan þat was Might falle mani wonder cas. **1375** BARBOUR *Bruce* III. 592 The Erle off the leuenax was, I can nocht tell ȝow throw quhat cass, Lewyt behynd. *c* **1384** CHAUCER *H. Fame*, 254 How Eneas tolde Dido every caas That hym was tyd upon the see. *c* **1460** FORTESCUE *Abs. & Lim. Mon.* (1714) 38 For doute of sodeyn Casys, which mowe fal to hym. **1596** SPENSER *F.Q.* I. ix. 26, I you recount a ruefull cace.

†**b.** A deed, a thing. *Obs.*

1297 R. GLOUC. (1810) 282 þys gode kyng and he dude þys gode cas. *c* **1340** *Cursor M.* 1497 (Fairf.) Quen cayn had done þat sari cas [*G. & T.* dede, *C.* plight]. *c* **1532** LD. BERNERS *Huon* clxiv. (1883) 646 Such a kyng traytoure that hathe done suche a case [*ed.* **1601** deede].

†**2. a.** Chance, hazard, hap. *Obs.*

1340-70 *Alisaunder* 24 Case fell, þat this Kyng Was with siknes of-sought. **1375** BARBOUR *Bruce* II. 24 He tauld hys brodyr halyly..how he chapyt wes throw cass. *c* **1440** *Gesta Rom.* lii. 230 (Harl. MS.) Fel cas, that ther was a knyȝt namid andronicus. **1483** CAXTON *Gold. Leg.* 237/3 And thus by caase of fortune..she toke the body of the prothomartir.

†**b.** Chiefly in phrases: *by* (*be, bi*) *case*, *of case*, *on*, *upon case* = 'perchance perhaps'; so PERCASE.

1297 R. GLOUC. (1810) 140 Gorlois, erl of Cornewail, þerforþ com bi cas. *c* **1340** *Ayenb.* 70 And be cas hit is þet Salomon zayþ. *c* **1375** ? BARBOUR *St. Andreas* 249 Syne eftir hapnyt of case. **1387** TREVISA *Higden* (Rolls) I. 13 On cas [*forsan*] despised of envious men and proude. *c* **1420** *Chron. Vilod.* 220 Upon a day hit fell by case. **1513** DOUGLAS *Æneis* I. vi. 99 The schippis that on caice war redy thair. **1560** ROLLAND *Crt. Venus* I. 692 In argument I and that gentill man Fell heir on case.

3. a. An instance or example of the occurrence or existence of a thing (fact, circumstance, etc.).

a **1300** *Cursor M.* 26679 In þat case man most nede sceu quam wit he did þat foli. *c* **1340** *Ayenb.* 42 þet hi ham loki uram þise zenne ine þri cas. *c* **1400** *Apol. Loll.* 79 In þis cas he schal not be cursid. *c* **1449** PECOCK *Repr.* 243 In manye Caasis. **1581** MARBECK *Bk. Notes* 297 The case shall bee this: My..neighbour..is so oppressed with povertie, that he is not able to paie. **1651** HOBBES *Leviath.* III. xli. 265 In a certain case that rarely happens. **1769** *Junius Lett.* xvi. 70 Some case or cases, strictly in point, must be produced. **1872** HELPS *Anim. & Mast.* i. (1875) 15 The most recent case within my knowledge.

b. An infatuation; a situation in which two people fall in love. So *to have a case on*: to be infatuated with or enamoured of. *slang* (orig. *U.S.*).

1852 *Harper's Mag.* V. 338/2 Young America..voted it 'a case'. The elderly ladies thought it a 'shocking flirtation'. **1860** HOTTEN *Slang Dict.* 112 Among young ladies at boarding-schools a *case* means a love affair. **1872** M. E. BRADDON *To Bitter End* III. xvii. 285 They have only been engaged three weeks; but from the day we first met Lord Stanmore..the business was settled. It was a 'case', as you fast young men say. **1893** 'S. GRAND' *Heavenly Twins* I. II. iv. 237 Edith..blushed. She could not reason about him... 'That's a case, I think,' said Mrs. Guthrie Brimston. **1928** F. N. HART *Bellamy Trial* iii. 73 Everybody knew they had a terrible case on each other. **1931** *Story-Teller* Aug. 598/2 By the end of the second year the girls were saying that Salesby *had* quite *a case on* Chips. **1951** M. KENNEDY *Lucy Carmichael* VII. iii. 372 'I think it's a case all right.'..'Yes,' said Melissa. 'She's lost to the world.'

4. a. *the case*: The actual state or position of matters; the fact. *it is not the case*: it is not the fact, it is not what actually is or happens.

c **1400** *Destr. Troy* 12025 Euen the couenand to kepe, as þe cas was, þat bertat hom þe toun. **1463** *Bury Wills* (1850) 29, I wil the seid iijs. iiijd. go therto, or part therof, as the case requireth. *a* **1626** BACON (J.) Here was the case; an army of English, wasted and tired with a long winter's siege, engaged an army of a greater number than themselves..fresh and in vigour. **1650** JER. TAYLOR *Holy Living* (J.) He hath no need to use them, as the case now stands. **1758** S. HAYWARD *Serm.* i. 4 This is the case not only with men of years, but with infants of a day old. **1830** MACAULAY *Let.* in Trevelyan *Life* II. vii. 8 The case with me is the reverse. **1888** SIR L. W. CAVE in *Law Times Rep.* LII. 627/2 A short consideration of the different sections will show that this is not the case.

b. A state of matters relating to a particular person or thing. *in the case of*: as regards (a specified thing or person); *in that case*: if that is true; if that should happen; that being so; similarly, *in the first case*, etc. Also *in any case*: whatever may happen, whatever the fact is (cf. 13); *in many cases*: in a number of instances; similarly, *in some cases*.

1393 GOWER *Conf.* III. 42 Delicacy in loves cas Withoute reson is and was. *a* **1586** SIDNEY (J.) Well do I find each man most wise in his own case. **1680** BURNET *Rochester* (1692) 30 What sense this noble Lord had of their Case when he came at last seriously to reflect upon his own. **1711** ADDISON *Spect.* No. 108 ¶7 Will Wimble's is the Case of many a younger Brother of a great Family. **1726** GAY *Fables, Hare & many Friends* 41 And when a lady's in the case, You know all other things give place. **1791** J. WALKER *Pron. Dict.* s.v. *Medicinal*, Poets..who have, and, perhaps, in some cases, ought to have, a language different from prose. **1848** MACAULAY *Hist. Eng.* II. 178 But..he regarded the case of the Church of Rome as an exception to all ordinary rules. **1848** *Sporting Life* 11 Mar. 23/1 'In that case,' replied the guard, 'I will go and fetch the steward myself.' **1872** THUDICHUM & DUPRE *Treatise on Wine* xiii. 435 When he comes to his vineyard he finds his crop either eaten by the flies, or rotten, or over-ripe, and in any case yields him a lesser quantity or quality of wine. **1881** *Spons' Encycl. Industr. Arts* IV. 1252 In many cases, flax-spinning establishments have weaving branches in connection with them. **1894** SWEET *Anglo-Saxon Reader* (ed. 7) 227 The parts of speech are not marked in the case of adjectives, pronouns and weak verbs. **1896** L. FLETCHER *Introd. Study Meteorites* 36 In some cases the chondrules consist wholly or in great part of glass. **1909** BEYNON *Drapery* 76 'And if I can show you cheaper lines than you are buying, you won't buy?' 'No, I will not buy even in that case.' **1912** C. N. & A. M. WILLIAMSON *Heather Moon* II. iii. 128 'It didn't seem to me there was anything romantic about Mr. Douglas, except his name.' 'In that case, you are a little flirt,' said he. **1916** E. W. GREGORY *Furnit. Collector* 227 But in any case worm-eaten furniture is not at all desirable. **1921** A. L. SIMON *Wine* 59 In the first case, the wines are sent over here, as a rule two

years after vintage. **1929** PINERO in *Eighteen-Seventies* 133 The difficulties of great men are intensified in the case of little ones.

†**c.** *all a case*: all one. *Obs.*

1660 JER. TAYLOR *Duct. Dubit.* 341 He that swears by Heaven, or by the Earth, by the Temple, or by the Gold, it is all a case. **1666** BUNYAN *Grace Ab.* ¶313 Believe or disbelieve me in this, all is as a case to me. *a* **1704** R. L'ESTRANGE (J.) Taken or not taken, tis all a case to me.

5. a. Condition, state (of circumstances external or internal), plight. *in good case*: well off.

c **1300** *K. Alis.* 4428 With sweord ryden he dud amere In this strong fyghtyng cas, He mette with Dalmadas. **1482** CAXTON *Chron. Eng.* ccxlix. 319 Our enbassatours came home ageyne in werse caas than they wente. **1529** MORE *Comf. agst. Trib.* I. Wks. 1140/1 He..neuer leaueth his seruantes in case of a coumfortlesse Orphanes. **1535** COVERDALE *Hosea* iv. 3 Therfore shal the londe be in a miserable case. **1560** BIBLE (Genev.) *Gen.* xl. 14 When thou art in good case show mercie unto me. **1611** —— *Ex.* v. 19 And the officers of the children of Israel did see that they were in euill case. **1614** RALEIGH *Hist. World* III. 80 Thereby leaving their old enemies in case of much contempt and disabilitie. **1693** W. ROBERTSON *Phraseol. Gen.* 315 In good case for estate, *beatus.* **1782** COWPER *Gilpin* xlviii, But stop and eat, for well you may Be in a hungry case. **1875** JOWETT *Plato* (ed. 2) I. 281 And now I know not what virtue is, and you seem to be in the same case.

b. *esp.* Physical condition, as *in good case* (arch.); also simply, *in case, out of case* (? obs.). Also, esp. in U.S., *spec.* of tobacco.

1640 in *Archives of Maryland* (1883) I. 98 Bad Tobacco shall be judged..[what is] sooty, wett, or in too high Case. **1640–1** *Kirkcudbr. War-Comm. Min. Bk.* (1855) 60 Ordaines..that William keip the horss in good caice. **1660** STANLEY *Hist. Philos.* (1701) 121/1 By this means their Horses are the better in Case, but the worse for Service. **1674** *Diary of W. Cunningham* (1887) 3 The houses are out of case. **1693** W. ROBERTSON *Phraseol. Gen.* 315 In good case for flesh, *pinguis.* **1704** SWIFT *Batt. Bks.* (1711) 231 Their Horses large, but extreamely out of Case. **1725** BRADLEY *Fam. Dict.*, *Jockey*..one that brings Horses into Case. **1755** JOHNSON s.v., In ludicrous language, *In case* is *lusty* or *fat.* **1800** W. TATHAM *Cult. & Com. Tobacco* 37 It must be stretched gently over the ends of the fingers and knuckles, and if it is in good case, *i.e.* plight, or condition, it will discover an elastic capacity. **1808** SCOTT *Marm.* I. xxi, Our Norham vicar..Is all too well in case to ride. **1845** DODD *Brit. Manuf.* 132 An exposure to the air for..about five weeks makes the leaves of tobacco elastic and tough, and slightly covered with a glossy kind of moisture. The tobacco is then said to be *in case.* **1852** MRS. STOWE *Uncle Tom's Cabin* xii. 72 What he would sell for, if he was kept fat and in good case. **1865** *Trans. Ill. Agric. Soc. 1863* V. 667 The fires should be suffered to go out, and the tobacco be suffered to come in case, or get soft again. **1944** *Dial. Notes* Nov. 65 *In case*: adj. phr., in proper condition—cured and having the correct amount of moisture to ensure handling without injury or loss.

c. *in case to* or *for*: in a condition or position *to* or *for*; prepared, ready. *arch.*

[**1461** *Paston Lett.* 430 II. 77 Sche is in the cas to have the lyf in stede of damages.] **1523** LD. BERNERS *Froiss.* I. cxxx. 157 We be nat in case to do any great dede of armes. **1610** SHAKS. *Temp.* III. ii. 29, I am in case to iustle a Constable. **1653** H. COGAN *Pinto's Trav.* viii. §2. 23 When thou art in better case to hear me I will tell thee. **1663** BUTLER *Hud.* I. III. 745 Quoth Ralph, I should not, if I were In Case for Action, now be here. **1824** MISS MITFORD *Village* Ser. I. (1863) 70 Even if they escaped hanging for that exploit, I should greatly doubt their being in case to attempt another. **1865** CARLYLE *Fredk. Gt.* VII. XVIII. ix. 261 Breslau; which is in no case to resist and be bombarded.

6. *Law.* 'The state of facts juridically considered' (J.). **a.** A cause or suit brought into court for decision. **b.** A statement of the facts of any matter *sub judice*, drawn up for the consideration of a higher court. **c.** A cause which has been decided: *leading case*, one that has settled some important point and is frequently cited as a precedent.

1523 LD. BERNERS *Froiss.* I. cccxxvi. 510 The pope gaue the duke full puyssance..reseruyng certayne cases papall, the which he myght nat gyue. **1552** HULOET s.v. *Preiudice*, As the ruled cases and matters of the lawe be called boke-cases. **1602** SHAKS. *Ham.* v. i. 108 Why might not that bee the Scull of a Lawyer? Where be his Quiddits now? his Quillets? his Cases? **1621–31** LAUD *Serm.* (1847) 204 This..is a great leading case for Kings. **1689** *Tryal Bps.* 26 This being a Case of the greatest Consequence, peradventure, that ever was in the Westminster Hall. **1710** PRIDEAUX *Orig. Tithes* ii. 42 Precedents and judged Cases have ever had the like authority. **1863** H. COX *Instit.* II. ix. 524 If the justices refuse to state a case, application may be made to the Queen's Bench for a rule commanding them to do so. **1877** (*title*) Leading Cases done into English. **1886** *Daily News* 17 July 2/1 There is a very strong Bar engaged in the case.

d. The case as presented or 'put' to the Court by one of the parties in a suit; hence, the sum of the grounds on which he rests his claim. Also *fig.* as in *to make out one's case, a case.*

[**1375** BARBOUR *Bruce* I. 52 And othir sum nyt all that cass And said that he thair king suld be That war in als ner degre.] **1596** DRAYTON *Legends* iv. 40 My doubtfull Case to plead. **1602** *2nd Pt. Returne fr. Pernass.* iv. ii. 1647 Till at length, *per varios casus*, by putting the case so often, they make their client so lanke, that, etc. **1660** JER. TAYLOR *Worthy Commun.* Introd. 7 This is a breviate of our case. **1863** MRS. C. CLARKE *Shaks. Char.* xvi. 391 Shakespeare has made out a strong case for Shylock. **1883** *Law Times* 20 Oct 407/2 A litigant without a case. **1885** *Law Rep. 29 Chanc. Div.* 452 If he abandoned the point it must be assumed that he had no case. *Mod.* This concluded the case for the prosecution. 'That is our case, my lord.'

e. A form of procedure in the Common Law: see quots. *Obs.* in England.

1590 SHAKS. *Com. Err.* IV. ii. 42. **1591** LAMBARDE *Arch.* (1635) 61 Suits at the Common Law, for remedie in Cases, where no proper helpe was formerly knowne..called the Action or Writ upon the Case. **1594** HOOKER *Eccl. Pol.* (1617) 656 We should shortly have no actions upon the case, nor of trespass, but all should be pleas of the crown. **1631** *Star Chamb. Cases* (1886) 77 The plaintiff had brought an action of the case against Rickby. **1768** BLACKSTONE III. 122 *Action upon the case*, This action of trespass, or trangression, on the case, is an universal remedy given for all personal wrongs and injuries without force..so called because the plaintiff's whole case or cause of complaint is set forth at length in the original writ. **1863** H. COX *Instit.* II. ix. 523 Action of trespass on the *Case*, so called from the words *in consimili casu*..in the Statute of Westminster the Second, which authorizes such actions..Injuries caused by negligence are usually remediable by action on the case.

f. An incident or set of circumstances requiring investigation by the police or other detective agency.

1838 C. ROWAN in *Parl. Papers 1837–8* XV. 359 The constable who..has been successful..in pursuing the case, is rewarded. **1878** A. K. GREEN (*title*) The Leavenworth case. **1926** G. DILNOT *Story of Scotland Yard* xxxiv. 284 Finger-prints are only of incidental use in the solution of a mystery... Nevertheless, it was on a case of murder that Scotland Yard scored its first spectacular triumph with the new system. **1930** D. L. SAYERS *Strong Poison* ii. 35 Consider the circumstances of the case as a whole, and say what conclusion you have come to. **1959** L. LEE *Cider with Rosie* 116 The police left at last with the case unsolved. **1978** in D. B. Hughes *Erle Stanley Gardner* xxix. 295 By February 14 [1969], Erle was writing Larry that *The Case of the Careless Corpse* was dictated and transcribed.

7. *case of conscience*: A practical question concerning which conscience may be in doubt; a question as to the application of recognized principles of faith and obedience to one's duty in a particular case or set of circumstances.

A transl. of L. *casus conscientiæ* (F. *cas de conscience*), according to Ames (1576–1633), 'called *casus*, because it is wont to happen or occur (*cadere*) in life; and *casus conscientiæ*, because when it happens, conscience ought to give a judgement with the greatest carefulness'. These cases or questions are divided into two classes, (1) those which concern a man's state before God, (2) those which concern his actions in that state. It is mainly to the second of these, or cases of conduct, that CASUISTRY is understood to refer.

[*a* **1400** ASTEXANUS *Summa de casibus Conscientiæ* (1469).] **1592** W. PERKINS (*title*), A Case of Conscience, the greatest that euer was; How a Man may knowe whether he be the Child of God or no: resolued by the Worde of God. **1605** BACON *Adv. Learn.* II. xxv. §21 In this part I commend much the deducing of the law of God to cases of conscience. [**1655** in Ellis *Orig. Lett.* II. 309 IV. 5 *note*, He [Cromwell] hoped..to have had some clearing of the Case as to his conscience: but instead of that they had made the matter more doubtful..than it was before.] **1660** JER. TAYLOR (*title*), Ductor Dubitantium; or the Rule of Conscience in all her general measures; serving as a great instrument for the determination of cases of conscience. **1851** ROBERTSON *Serm.* Ser. IV. xii. I. 81 This epistle [1st to Corinthians] is one of Christian Casuistry, or the application of Christian principles to the various circumstances and cases of conscience which arise continually in the daily life of a highly..artificial community.

8. *Med.* **a.** The condition of disease in a person.

1709 *Tatler* No. 121 ¶1 It is the general fault of physicians, they are so in haste, that they never hear out the case. **1732** BERKELEY *Alciphr.* VI. §9 A patient must have full liberty to explain his case, and tell all his symptoms. **1848** MACAULAY *Hist. Eng.* I. 441 The fourteen doctors who deliberated on the king's case.

b. An instance of disease, or other condition requiring medical treatment; 'a record of the progress of disease in an individual' (*Syd. Soc. Lex.*). Also (*colloq.*), a patient.

1732 ARBUTHNOT *Rules of Diet* 256 [They] are hurtful in Cases where the Blood is too much dissolv'd. **1758** GOOCH (*title*), Cases and Practical Remarks in Surgery. **1804** ABERNETHY *Surg. Observ.* (*title*), A classification of Tumours, with cases to illustrate the history of each species. **1851** DIXON *W. Penn* xxiii. (1872) 207 At Deal they shipped a case of small-pox. **1864** MISS YONGE *Trial* II. 325 Nothing else could teach him that patients are not cases but persons. **1881** *Brit. Med. Jrnl.* 18 June, About two hundred cases of ulcerated legs pass through my wards annually. **1940** N. MITFORD *Pigeon Pie* xiii. 197 Heatherley and Winthrop..would not be able to leave the Treatment Room for a moment, except to carry 'cases' upstairs to the Hospital.

c. *U.S. slang.* of persons: A 'specimen', 'cure'.

1848–60 BARTLETT *Dict. Amer.*, *Case*, a character, a queer one; as 'That Sol Haddock is a case'. 'What a hard case he is', meaning a reckless scapegrace, *mauvais sujet.* **1884** P. ROE in *Harper's Mag.* May 922/2 There was a little wheat in all that chaff of a man..But the wife is a case.

9. *Grammar.* [L. *cāsus* used to translate Gr. πτῶσις lit. 'falling, fall'.

By Aristotle πτῶσις was applied to any derived, inflected, or extended form of the simple ὄνομα or ῥῆμα (i.e. the nominative of nouns, the present indicative of verbs), such as the oblique cases of nouns, the variations of adjectives due to gender and comparison, also the derived adverb (e.g. δικαίως was a πτῶσις of δίκαιος), the other tenses and moods of the verb, including also its interrogative form. The grammarians, following the Stoics, restricted πτῶσις to nouns, and included the nominative under the designation.]

a. In inflected languages, one of the varied forms of a substantive, adjective, or pronoun, which express the varied relations in which it may stand to some other word in the sentence, *e.g.* as subject or object of a verb, attribute to another noun, object of a preposition, etc. **b.** But as many modern languages have nearly or quite lost these variations of form, *case* is sometimes loosely used for the *relation* itself, whether indicated by distinct form or not.

Thus, by a mixture of the two notions, in modern English, substantives are commonly said to have three cases, *nominative, objective*, and *possessive*; the two former being merely relations, and the latter entirely formal; in modern French to have two (or three) cases, *cas-sujet* and *cas-régime* (the latter subdivided into *direct* and *indirect*), which are in the noun merely relations, while of the pronouns some retain only one case-form, some have four (e.g. *ils, les, leur, eux*). Thus also, in quot. 1824, 'nominative' case is loosely used for *subject.*

1393 LANGL. *P. Pl.* C. IV. 339 [As] adiectif and substantyf vnite asken Acordaunce in kynde in cas and in numbre. *c* **1440** *Gesta Rom.* xci. 416 (Add. MS.) And so we han the nominatif case. **1530** PALSGR. Introd. 30 But thre cases, nominatyve, accusatyve and oblique as *je, me, moy.* **1581** SIDNEY *Def. Poesie* (Arb.) 70 Those cumbersome differences of Cases, Genders, Moodes, and Tenses. **1598** SHAKS. *Merry W.* IV. i. 46 Well: what is your Accusatiue-case? **1612** BRINSLEY *Pos. Parts* (1669) 5 What is a Case? Every severall ending of a Noun in the declining of it. **1751** HARRIS *Hermes* II. iii. (1786) 273 Whatever we may be told of Cases in modern Languages, there are in fact no such things. **1824** L. MURRAY *Gram.* I. 341 *To err*, is the infinitive mood, and the nominative case to the verb 'is'. **1868** BROWNING *Ring & Bk.* VIII. 965 A complete list Of the prepositions each with proper case.

II. *Phrases.*

†**10.** *in case*: **a.** in the event, in fact (cf. 3). (See also 5, 5 b, for a different sense.)

1340–70 *Alex. & Dind.* 228 For more may hit in cas ȝou menske þan greue. *c* **1384** WYCLIF *Sel. Wks.* III. 377 In veyn preyers of ypocrites, þat in caas ben dampned devels. *c* **1449** PECOCK *Repr.* II. xiv. 231 Thouȝ in caas it can not be founde speciali witnessid bi Holi Scripture. **1526** *Pilgr. Perf.* (W. de W. 1531) 2 Except in case whan you vnderstande not y[t] ye rede therin. **1629** W. SCLATER *Exp. 2 Thess.* 75.

b. as conjunction (with sentence): in the event or contingency that, if it should prove or happen that, if. *in case*, esp. in *just in case*, orig. with aposiopesis, *in case* ——, to indicate an unspecified apprehension of accident.

c **1400** MAUNDEV. xviii. 191 In cas that he had ony Werre aȝenst ony other Kyng aboute him. **1418** *E.E. Wills* 25 Yn case I deye. **1554** PHILPOT *Exam. & Writ.* (1842) 327 In case one sudden chance..had not interrupted me. **1596** SPENSER *State Irel.* 12, I would tell you in case you would not challenge me anon. **1646** FULLER *Wounded Consc.* (1841) 324 In case his leg be set, he flings, flounces..unjointing it again by his misemployed mettle. **1863** P. BARRY *Dockyard Econ.* 195 To be in readiness in case anything should happen to the present Board of Admiralty. **1864** D. MITCHELL *Sev. Stor.* 76 In case his papers were not all right. **1898** KIPLING *Fleet in Being* 28 One leg over the edge of the bunk—in case. **1929** WODEHOUSE *Mr. Mulliner Speaking* ix. 301 She rather thought she wouldn't be able to, but she said leave her ticket at the box-office in case. **1951** *Teazle's News-Let.* 24 Apr. [5] A picture..of a London policeman directing the traffic at a busy point in Paris, with a French traffic constable standing by, just in case.

c. lest, in provision against the case that.

1588 A. KING *Canisius' Catech.* 152 Thou sall pay him the price of his labour..incaice he cry to God agains the. *Mod.* Take your umbrella, in case it should rain.

d. *in case of*: in the event of.

1736 BUTLER *Anal.* I. iii. 70 Obnoxious to it [punishment] in case of a discovery. **1745** P. THOMAS *Jrnl. Anson's Voy.* 65 All the Ships had Orders..in case of not meeting there, to make the best of their way to Macao. **1832** W. IRVING *Alhambra* I. 90 More apt to trust to the length of his legs than the strength of his arms, in case of attack.

†**11.** *if case be that*: if it should prove or happen that, if perchance. So *if case. Obs.*

1535 COVERDALE *Job* xxxi. 38 But yf case be that my londe crie agaynst me. —— *Jer.* xxxviii. 17 Yf case be, that thou wilt go forth vnto the kynge off Babilons prynces. **1541** R. COPLAND *Guydon's Quest. Chirurg.*, It ought nat to be applyed, but yf case be that the pacyente were faynte herted. **1593** SHAKS. *3 Hen. VI*, v. iv. 34 If case some one of you would flye from vs. **1630** J. TAYLOR (Water P.) *Wks.* (N.) If case a begger be old, weake or ill.

12. *to put* or *set the case*, formerly *to put* or *set case* (*that*): to propound a hypothetical instance or illustration, to suppose.

c **1400** *Destr. Troy* 2932 With Sossyngs, & Sotelte, Settyng of cases. *a* **1420** OCCLEVE *De Reg. Princ.* 1058, I putte cas..Thow were yfalle in indigent povert. *c* **1440** *Gesta Rom.* iv. 10 (Harl MS.), I sette cas, þat a thefe make an hole in a hous. **1579** TOMSON *Calvin's Serm. Tim.* 142/2 Let vs put the case that nothing is sought for. **1654** JER. TAYLOR *Real Pres.* Ep. Ded., Put case the Turke should invade Italy. **1751** JORTIN *Serm.* (1771) III. 39 Either there is a future state, or there is not. Put the case that there is not. **1850** TENNYSON *In Mem.* xxxv, O me, what profits it to put An idle case?

13. *in any case*: by any means (*obs.*); at all events, anyhow. *in* (†*by*, †*for*) *no case*: by no means (? *obs.* in this sense).

a **1400–50** *Alexander* 1362 How he miȝt couir in any cas to come to þe cite. *Ibid.* 2350 Þat þai suld corde be na cas vnto þe kingis hestis. *c* **1440** *Ipomydon* 355 But she kowde wete for no case Whens he come ne what he was. **1577** B. GOOGE tr. *Heresbach's Husb.* I. (1586) 12 b, Varro wyll in any case have two courtes. **1596** SHAKS. *1 Hen. IV*, v. ii. 25 Let not Harry know In any case, the offer of the King. **1611** BIBLE *Matt.* v. 20 Yee shall in no case enter into the kingdome of heauen. *Mod.* In any case you had better hear what he has to say.

III. 14. *Comb.*, as (sense 9) **case-distinction, -ending, -form, -function, -system**; **case-book**, a book containing an account of legal or medical cases; also *transf.*, *fig.* and *attrib.*; **case**

conference, a meeting of professionals (such as doctors, teachers, social workers, etc.) to discuss the case of a particular individual or family in their care; † **case-divinity**, casuistry; **case-form** *Gram.*, a morphological variant (of a noun, adjective, pronoun, etc.) that indicates its case by its form; **case frame** *Linguistics*, in case grammar: the underlying set of semantic and syntactic relationships linking the verb with the nominal phrases of the sentence at the level of deep structure; **case grammar** *Linguistics*, a version of transformational grammar in which case relationships are used to describe the semantic deep structure of sentences; **case-history**, the record of a person's origins, personal history, etc., orig. *Med.*, compiled for diagnostic or other purposes and comprising all matters relevant to an episode of illness in a patient; in extended use, any brief conspectus of individual development, cf. *life-history*; **case-law**, the law settled by decided cases; **case-load**, the total number of cases that a doctor, social worker, probation officer, or other professional person or agency, is concerned with at any one time; **case-phrase** *Gram.*, a phrase expressing a relation by means of a preposition and a noun instead of the bare case-form of the noun; † **case-putter**, one who puts cases or the (legal) case; so † **case-putting**, stating of a legal case, the making of hypotheses; **case-sheet** *Med.*, a document giving a patient's clinical history; also *transf.*; **case-study**, the attempt to understand a particular person, institution, society, etc., by assembling information about his or its development; the record of such an attempt.

1762 CANNING in *Poet. Register* (1807) 459 Now adieu, my friend Jacob—I'll close up my *case-book. **1862** BURTON *Bk.-hunter* II. 129, I know not whether 'lay gents'.. can feel any pleasure in wandering over the case-books. **1934** WEBSTER, *Casebook*, a compilation of detailed information concerning actual cases, legal, medical, psychological, economic, etc., for reference and study. **1949** E. COXHEAD *Wind in West* iv. 102 They sat discussing the literature of the passions, but let somebody present them with.. a case-book page and.. they all thought fit to take offence. **1953** *Proc. Prehist. Soc.* XIX. 129 This paper is a small selection from our 'case-book' in the Department of Environmental Archaeology. **1958** *Times Lit. Suppl.* 15 Aug. 457/3 The first pages are casebook reportage; then there appears to be an attempt at a symbolist dimension. **1954** *Brit. Med. Jrnl.* 16 Jan. 116/2 Each course lasted for a term and consisted of weekly *case conferences of two hours each. **1977** *Economist* 24 Sept. 140/2 Staff.. allowed her to follow them as they went about their work.. and to be present at case conferences. **1986** *Professional Teacher* Summer 3/3 There is consultation time, involving attendance at staff meetings, department meetings, pastoral discussions, case conferences and parent consultations. **1894** JESPERSEN *Progress in Lang.* 31 The doing away with the old *case distinctions in English has facilitated many extremely convenient idioms. **1934** PRIEBSCH & COLLINSON *German Lang.* 153 The loss of case-distinctions.. becomes still more marked in M.H.G. **1628** BP. HALL *Righteous Mamm.* 721 That which law and *case-diuinity speakes of life. **1642** FULLER *Holy & Prof. St.* II. x. 90 In Case-divinity Protestants are defective. **1874** SAYCE *Compar. Philol.* vii. 286 The so called *case-ending in *-a*. **1875** WHITNEY *Life Lang.* iii. 41 A *case-form of a compounded adjective. **1922** JESPERSEN *Lang.* xviii. 345 English shows that a small number of case forms is not incompatible with perfect clearness and perspicuity. **1951** R. H. ROBINS *Anc. & Med. Gram. Theory* i. 34 The most systematic semantic analysis of case-forms in antiquity is by the Byzantine scholar, Maximus Planudes. **1968** C. J. FILLMORE in Bach & Harms *Universals in Linguistic Theory* 27 The insertion of verbs.. depends on the particular array of cases, the '*case frame', provided by the sentence. **1978** *Language* LIV. 87 His choice of the case-frame 'object' rather than the category 'noun' was necessary, because several nouns may be associated with a verb, but it is only the object noun which retains a consistent.. ordering with the verb. **1984** *Fremdsprachen* XXVIII. 84 One could suggest particular case-frames for particular types of verbs. **1894** JESPERSEN *Progress in Lang.* 161 The apostrophe was at that time used (without any regard to *case-function) where a syllable was added in pronunciation. **1968** C. J. FILLMORE in Bach & Harms *Universals in Linguistic Theory* 88 One criticism of *case grammar.. is that it is too strongly motivated by semantic considerations. **1977** *Language* LIII. 493/2 The long expositions of case grammar (146–70) and performative analysis (Ch. 9) seem completely out of place. Neither concept has been generally accepted by linguists, and their value in an introductory text is dubious. **1984** *Fremdsprachen* XXVIII. 19, I propose to show how a knowledge of some aspects of case grammar may be useful to the translator. **1912** *Lancet* 2 Mar. 589/2 (*title*) *Case Histories in Neurology. **1931** E. WILSON *Axel's Castle* v. 185 Is he telling us his own case-history with symbols? **1934** C. DAY LEWIS *Hope for Poetry* iv. 18 A very instructive entry in the case-history of poetic feeling. **1935** WOODWORTH *Psychol.* (ed. 10) ii. 23 Reconstructing the individual's history.. from his memory, the memories of his acquaintances... This case history method has obvious disadvantages. **1945** 'L. LEWIS' *Birthday Murder* (1951) iii. 40 A good many of our friends were case histories. They belonged in a textbook on mildly abnormal psychology. **1958** *Engineering* 14 Mar. 346/3 This practice of giving applications in the form of case histories is now common in the industrial engineering field. **1861** MAINE *Anc. Law* (1870) 13 English *case-law is sometimes spoken of as unwritten. **1871** MARKBY *Elem. Law* (1885) 58 English case law does for us what the Roman law does for the rest of Western Europe. **1885** *Law Times* LXXIX. 153/1 The unwieldy mass of case-law which now cumbers every practitioner's shelves. **1950** C. MORRIS *Social Case-work in Gt. Brit.* ii. 51 Pseudo-cases are soon dropped from the *caseload. **1961** R. KEE *Refugee World* 1 The.. human beings who are the refugees are lumped together into the 'case-load'. **1961** 'C. H. ROLPH' *Crime & Punishment* x. 158 It used to be thought that the maximum 'case-load' a good probation officer could carry was about fifty. **1911** *Rep. Joint Comm. Gram. Terminol.* 27 Recommendations... That in English and French the combination of a Preposition with a Noun or Pronoun may be called a **Case-phrase*. **1927** E. A. SONNENSCHEIN *Soul of Gram.* 44 In Indo-European the case-system was supplemented.. by.. the case-phrase system. **1681** OTWAY *Soldier's Fort.* II. i, He's a tatter'd worm-eaten *case-putter; some call him Lawyer. **1645** MILTON *Tetrach.* (1851) 159 Some heroick magistrat, whose mind.. dares lead him both to know and to do without their frivolous *case-putting. **1687** R. L'ESTRANGE *Answ. Diss.* 21 The Case-putting-Humour goes on still too; though the Author succeeds no Better in his Third Supposition. **1925** W. DEEPING *Sorrell & Son* xxviii. 273 A few words had been written in haste on the back of a *case-sheet. **1958** *Listener* 16 Oct. 621/2 What we saw was the case sheet of Sinforth. **1933** *Proc. Brit. Acad.* XVIII. 371 His [*sc.* Kenny's] ideas as to the value of *case-study fitted neatly into his general conception of English legal education. **1940** WOODWORTH *Psychol.* (ed. 12) v. 162 Those who are professionally concerned in judging personality.. depend largely on the interview and the inclusive procedure known as the case study. **1956** *Planning* XXII. 148 It is intended to illustrate the findings by brief case-studies of industries, firms, or products. **1959** *Listener* 29 Oct. 744/3 A shrewd and stimulating case-study of the Lancashire election of 1868. **1875** WHITNEY *Life & Growth of Lang.* vi. 107 The downfall of the *case-system was accompanied by the uprise of the class of prepositions. **1953** W. J. ENTWISTLE *Aspects of Lang.* xi. 349 The Caucasian languages develop the case system up to twenty-three places.

case (keɪs), *sb.*[2] Forms: 4– case; also 4 cas, caas, kase, 4–6 cass, 5 kace, 5–6 casse, 6 (*Sc.*) cais. [a. ONF. *casse*, in central OF. *chasce*, *chasse*, mod.F. *châsse* (= It. *cassa*):—L. *capsa* case, receptacle, f. *cap-ĕre* to take, hold.]

1. a. A thing fitted to contain or enclose something else; a receptacle or holder; a box, chest, bag, sheath, covering, etc.; *spec.* in very early use (as in OF.) a reliquary.

a **1300** *Cursor M.* 21617 And ilk paskes.. wit-vten case.. þis cros was men þan wont to se. **1375** BARBOUR *Bruce* xx. 304 Ane cass of siluir fyne. *c* **1386** CHAUCER *Knts. T.* 1500 The arwes in the caas. **1398** TREVISA *Barth. De. P.R.* XVII. cxxvi. (1495) 686 Of russhes ben made.. cuppys and casses and baskettes to kepe in lettres and other thynges. *c* **1440** *Promp. Parv.* 269/1 Kace, or casse for pynnys, *capcella*. **1597** SHAKS. *2 Hen. IV*, III. ii. 351 The Case of a Treble Hoeboy was a Mansion for him. *a* **1639** WOTTON (J.), A fair case for books. **1859** TENNYSON *Elaine* 973 Full meekly rose the maid, Stript off the case, and gave the naked shield. **1872** E. YATES *Castaway* I. 12 (Hoppe) Lighting a cigar and handing his case to his friend.

b. with various substantives or adjs. indicating special use or purpose; e.g. *book-case*, *card-case*, *cigar-case*, etc. (for which see their first element).

1382 WYCLIF *Isa.* xxii. 6 And Elam toc an arewe caas. **1552–3** *Inv. Ch. Goods Staffs.* 46 Ij corporas casys of sylke with ij corporases. **1596** SHAKS. *Tam. Shr.* III. ii. 45 A paire of bootes that haue beene candle-cases. *Mod.* A collector of plants with his botanical case.

c. A box or frame in which choice or delicate plants are grown, e.g. fern-case, Wardian case.

1664 EVELYN *Kal. Hort.* (1729) 205 The least size of Cases ought to be of sixteen Inches.. supported from the Ground with Knobs or Feet four Inches. **1704** WORLIDGE *Dict. Rust. et Urb.* s.v. *Fir*, Sow the Seeds in Beds or Cases.. during March. **1842** TENNYSON *Amphion* xi, Squares of tropic summer shut And warm'd in crystal cases.

d. *U.S.* In the game of faro, the fourth card of a denomination, when the other three have been taken from the dealing-box. So ***to keep cases***: to note the cards as they come from the dealing-box; also *transf.*, to keep a close watch (*on*). Also, ***to come*** (or ***get***) ***down to cases*** (chiefly *U.S.*): to come to the point.

1856 *Harper's Mag.* Dec. 69/1 He has no great faith in 'cases', but believes in betting on three cards at a time. [**1856** *San Francisco Bull.* 4 Dec. 2/2 He was sitting in front, keeping the 'cases'.] **1896** G. ADE *Artie* iii. 24 A Johnny-on-the-spot.. was tryin' to keep cases on her. *Ibid.* xi. 103 When it comes down to cases they're just as good as a lot of people that make a bigger front. **1902** O. V. LIMERICK *B. Burgundy's Opinions* 58 To get right down to cases, she was a human-four-card-flush. **1903** A. ADAMS *Log of Cowboy* xiii. 199 We found Quince Forrest and Wyatt Roundtree playing the faro bank, the former keeping cases. **1918** MULFORD *Man fr. Bar-20* ii. 21 Comin' down to cases, you ain't really a cow-puncher. **1920** —— *J. Nelson* xiv. 144 I'm keepin' cases on these cattle. **1937** RUNYON *More than Somewhat* i. 7 It takes him some time to get down to cases and tell me what is eating him.

2. a. The outer protective or covering part of anything, as the case of a watch, a fire-work, a sausage; a natural outer covering, sheath, or receptacle; *e.g.* a seed-vessel, the 'case' of a pupa or chrysalis, of a case-worm, etc.

1398 TREVISA *Barth. De P.R.* v. xl. (1495) 155 The blood sholde be brent but yf the superfluyte therof had place within the caas of the galle. **1605** SHAKS. *Lear* IV. vi. 147 *Lear.* Read. *Glou.* What, with the Case of eyes? **1611** —— *Wint. T.* v. ii. 14. **1605** TIMME *Quersit.* III. 178 All the kindes of poppey, with their cases which containe the seed. **1660** BOYLE *New Exp. Phys.-Mech.* xxvii. 206 We took a Watch, whose Case we open'd. **1665** *Phil. Trans.* I. 89 This Insect leaves two Coats.. in the Theca or Case. **1691** RAY *Creation* (J.), Other caterpillars produced maggots, that immediately made themselves up in cases. **1856** KANE *Arct. Expl.* II. vi. 70 This solid case of nine-foot ice. **1870** EMERSON *Soc. & Solit.* Wks. (Bohn) III. 41 The care which covers the seed of the tree under tough husks and stony cases.

b. So in comb., as *clock-case*, *pillow-case*, *watch-case*; *seed-case*, *pupa-case*: see CLOCK, etc.

1848 C. A. JOHNS *Wk. at Lizard* 298 The unusual hardness of the seed-case.

c. *spec.*

1869 *Eng. Mech.* 24 Dec. 354/1 Galls are of two kinds, called respectively *galls* and *cases*. *Galls* are more or less solid or ligneous, and contain *one* insect. *Cases* are hollow and horny, comprising a *colony* of insects.

d. ***book-binding*** (= BOOK CASE.) The boards and back, cloth-covered or otherwise, in which books are 'cased' or 'bound in cloth', and which are often prepared and issued to the public for the annual volumes of magazines, etc. Also a cover of a similar kind made to hold separate pamphlets, etc., without binding, so that they can be arranged among books in a library.

1868 E. ARBER (*Prospectus of Eng. Reprints*), Handsome cases, in best roan and cloth, Roxburghe style, to contain six of the 'Reprints'. One shilling each. *Mod.* Cloth cases, gilt-lettered, for binding the volume will be issued with the December number.

3. *fig.* **a.** The body (as enclosing the soul, etc.).

1547–64 BAULDWIN *Mor. Philos.* (Palfr.) ii. 6 The body.. the case & sepulchre of the soule. **1606** SHAKS. *Ant. & Cl.* IV. xv. 89 This case of that huge Spirit now is cold. **1883** J. GILMOUR *Mongols* xviii. 214 The body is merely the case or shell in which the soul lives.

†**b.** The exterior (of a man). *Obs.*

1655 FULLER *Ch. Hist.* VIII. i. §26 On the inside thereof walked the proper case of a man well habited.

†**4. a.** The skin or hide of an animal. *Obs.*

a **1569** KINGESMYLL *Man's Est.* vi. (1580) 31 Every mans skinne is the case of a sinner. **1575** TURBERV. *Venerie* lxxii. 198 His [Raynard's] case will serue to fur the cape of master huntsmans gowne. **1633** *Costlie Whore* II. ii. in Bullen *O. Pl.* IV, For Hares and Asses weare the lion's case. **1704** WORLIDGE *Dict. Rust. et Urb.* s.v. *Wild-Cat*, Tho her case be not so good as that of the Martern, yet it is very warm.

b. Applied to clothes or garments. *Obs.*

1593 NASHE *Christ's T.* 73 b, Our garments (which are cases and couers for our bodies). **1597** *1st Pt. Return fr. Parnass.* I. i. 370 Then he steps, and bringes out Signior Barbarisme in a case of nightcapps, in a case of headpeeces all-to-be-wrought. **1650** FULLER *Pisgah* II. xi. §21 [Samson] bestowed their corps on the earth, and their cases on their fellow countrymen. **1667** DRYDEN *Ind. Emperor* II. ii, A Man of bearded Face, His Limbs all cover'd with a shining Case.

5. The frame in which a door or window is set; cf. STAIR-CASE.

1663 GERBIER *Counsel* (1664) 44 That doore cases.. be made as high again as they are wide, and so must well proportioned window cases be. **1719** DE FOE *Crusoe* (1840) I. xiv. 248, I made a formal framed door-case, and a door to it of boards. **1827** HONE *Every-day Bk.* II. 25 Affixed to the outer door-case. **1876** GWILT *Archit.* Gloss., *Case of a Stair*, the wall surrounding a staircase.

6. a. 'The outer part of a house or building' (J.); the shell or carcass.

1677 HALE *Prim. Orig. Man.* I. iii. 75 That case or Sceleton of the World. *Ibid.* 76 The case or Fabrick of the House. **1704** WORLIDGE *Dict. Rust. et Urb.* s.v. *Oak*, The rough-grain'd body of a stubbed Oak, is fittest for the Case of a Cyder-Mill, and such Engines. **1704** ADDISON *Italy* 147 The Case of the Holy House is nobly design'd. **1876** GWILT *Archit.* Gloss., *Case*.. is also a term used to denote the carcass of a house.

b. *Masonry.* 'An outside facing of a building, of material superior to that of the backing' (Knight *Dict. Mech.* 1874).

c. In the following some have suggested influence of It. *casa* house. Also, a brothel.

1536 R. COPLAND *Hye Way to Spyttell Hous* Eiii, Toure the patryng coue in the darkman cace. *a* **1678** MARVELL *Wks.* (1875) III. 497 A net.. That Charles himself might chase To Caresbrook's narrow case. **1690** B. E. *Dict. Cant. Crew*, *Case*, a House, Shop, or Warehouse. **1699** B. E. *Dict. Cant. Crew*, *Case*,.. also a Bawdy-house. **1730–6** BAILEY, *Case*.. a house where thieves, pick-pockets, whores, house-breakers, highway-men, and all the loose, idle, furacious crew meet and drink.. and revel. **1821** P. EGAN *Life in London* II. ii. 177 In the motley group are several *Coves* of *Cases* and procuresses... The proprietors of houses of ill-fame. **1905** A. M. BINSTEAD *Mop Fair* viii. 135 They arranges to stop 'private' in Brighton, at a little case in Black Lion Street where Tom Reeder annually took his old woman every August. **1931** *Police Jrnl.* Oct. 501 Whilst he was sleeping (kipping), she told a detective (bogey) she knew that Jack was in the brothel (case). **1942** A. GARDNER *Lower Underworld* xx. 58 It's used as a case, you see, by some of the girls.

7. a. A box or chest with its proper contents; often of definite character (e.g. a case of surgical instruments, a dressing-case); or of determinate quantity, as a case of glass. † ***case of drawers***: chest of drawers (*obs.*).

1540 *Act 32 Hen. VIII*, xiv, For euery case of veluet conteinyng xiiii. pieces of veluet v.*s.* **1686** *Lond. Gaz.* No. 2118/4 Looking-Glasses, Screwtores, Cases of Drawers. **1704** WORLIDGE *Dict. Rust. et Urb.*, *Case*; this of Normandy-Glass is 120 Foot. **1745** P. THOMAS *Jrnl. Anson's Voy.* 58 Cases of Spanish Brandies and Wines. **1848** MACAULAY *Hist. Eng.* I. 556 Cases of arms from Holland. **1883** *Fisheries Exhib. Catal.* 217 Nail set cases, dressing cases.. work cases, writing cases.

b. Hence (or from 8), a set.

1599 SHAKS. *Hen. V*, III. ii. 5 The knocks are too hot: and for mine owne part, I haue not a Case of Liues. **1824** SCOTT

Redgauntlet ch. xvii, Cicely..displayed a case of teeth which might have rivalled ivory.

8. a. ***a case of pistols*** **(*dags*)**: a couple, brace. So †***a case of rapiers.*** Also *transf.* A brace, a pair.

1579 *Lanc. Wills* (1860) II. 126 One case of pystolles..a case [of] dagges. *c* **1590** MARLOWE *Faust* vi, I have run up and down the world with this case of rapiers. **1598** B. JONSON *Ev. Man in Hum.* Pref. 82 An inseparable case of coxcombs, city-borne; The Gemini or Twins of foppery. **1667** EARL ORRERY *State Lett.* (1743) II. 118 A hundred case of pistols. **1832** G. DOWNES *Lett. Cont. Countries* I. 304 [He] discharged in the act a case of pistols.

†**b.** ? One of a pair, the fellow to another.

1623 FLETCHER *Maid of Mill* II. ii, The other is the case of this.

9. *Printing.* The receptacle or frame in which the compositor has his types, divided into compartments for the various letters, figures, and spaces.

In ordinary printing the compositor has two such cases before him on a slanting stand, the upper case containing the capitals, etc., the lower the small letters, ordinary spaces, etc.

1588 *Marprel. Ep.* (Arb.) 22 His Letters melted, with cases and other tooles defaced. **1637** *Decree Star Chamb.* 11 July §23 That no Master-printer shall imploy either to worke at the Case, or the Presse [any but Freemen]. **1824** J. JOHNSON *Typogr.* II. i. 9 The compositor is materially retarded by moving from one case to another. **1880** *Printing Trades Jrnl.* No. 32. 25 Many eminent journalists began life at a compositor's case.

10. *Mil.* Short for *case-shot.*

1667 *Lond. Gaz.* No. 160/4 Being all laden below with double and barrs, and above with Case and Baggs. **1810** WELLINGTON *Let.* in Gurw. *Disp.* VI. 151 Let there be 20 rounds of Case for each gun. **1879** *Athenæum* 1 Nov. 556/3 The fire of case from the Russian batteries.

11. *Mining.* (see quot.)

1881 RAYMOND *Mining Gloss.*, *Case*, a small fissure, admitting water into the workings.

12. *Comb.*, as ***case-maker, -plant, -spring, -tree, -wing***; **case-bay**, in *Building* (see quot.); **case-house** *slang*, a brothel; **case-keeper**, (*a*) *U.S.*, one who 'keeps cases' in faro (see 1 d); the device used for this purpose; (*b*) a brothel-keeper; **case-man** (*Printing*), one who works at the case, a compositor; **case-oil**, oil or other petroleum products transported in containers packed in wooden cases; **case paper**, ? a corruption of CASSE-paper; †**case-pepper**, a species of Capsicum (prob. *C. baccatum*); **case-rack**, the wooden frame in which printers' cases are kept; **case-room**, the compositors' room; **case-work**, 'a book glued on the back and stuck into a "case" previously prepared' (Knight). Also CASE-BOTTLE, -WORM, etc.

1876 GWILT *Archit.* Gloss., **Case Bays*, the joists framed between a pair of girders in naked flooring..The extent of the case-bays should not exceed ten feet. **1912** C. MACKENZIE *Carnival* xxx. 322 You don't suppose I'd go on living in what's no better than a common *case-house. **1924** M. KENNEDY *Constant Nymph* viii. 118, I wonder at you for bringing the young lady here, for it's nothing better than a dirty case-house. **1867** *Terr. Enterprise* (Virginia, Nevada) 18 Aug. 3/1 A '*case keeper'..at a game kept on C Street. **1890** J. P. QUINN *Fools of Fortune* 201 A record of the game is kept by means of an instrument known as a 'case-keeper'. **1909** *Cent. Dict.* Suppl., *Case-keeper*, in *faro*, the player who marks the cards as they come from the dealing-box... Small buttons are pushed along wires for this purpose. **1914** C. MACKENZIE *Sinister St.* II. IV. ii. 879 You call me a case-keeper? What men have I ever let you bring back here? **1938** H. ASBURY *Sucker's Progr.* 14 Case-keeper, a device for keeping a record of the cards as they were drawn. Also, the man who operated this device. *c* **1450** *Voc.* in Wr.-Wülcker 688 *Hic cassarius*, a *casmaker. **1664** PEPYS *Diary* (1879) III. 36 Thence to my case-maker for my stone case. **1858** SIMMONDS *Dict. Trade*, *Case-maker*, a carpenter who makes wooden packing-cases for shipping goods. **1892** *Daily News* 13 May 5/8 A steamer's carrying her oil in small hermetically sealed tin cases..would not necessarily secure her..from fire... But..no instance is on record of a fire having occured on board a steamship laden with *case-oil while in transit through the Canal. **1930** MASEFIELD *Wand. Liverpool* 49 The ship discharged her chalk..and loaded case-oil. **1953** tr. *F. C. Gerretson's Hist. R. Dutch* I. v. 226 In order to sell the remaining supplies of Russian case oil, the cases had to be removed first. **1615** MARKHAM *Eng. Housew.* II. i. (1668) 26 Seven corns of *case pepper. **1675** EVELYN *Terra* (1729) 45 Exoticks and choicer *Case Plants. **1884** F. BRITTEN *Watch. & Clockm.* 47 [He] fixes the *case springs in a thin brass ring between the movement and the case. **1664** EVELYN *Sylva* (1776) 139 To shelter Orange and other tender *Case-trees from the parching Sun. **1770–4** A. HUNTER *Georg. Ess.* (1803) III. 100 The elytra, or *case wings are of a reddish brown colour.

case, *sb.*[3] Also **case-char.** A fish of the family *Salmonidæ.*

1751 S. WHATLEY *Engl. Gazetteer* (*Winander Meer*) There is a fish very much like it [the char] (but of another species, supposed to be the case) called *torgoch*, or *red-belly.* **1769** PENNANT *Zool.* III. 260 The jaws in the Case Charr are perfectly even.

case, *sb.*[4] (See quot. 1854.)

1851 MELVILLE *Moby Dick* II. xxxv. 238 The upper part, known as the Case. *Ibid.* III. viii. 64, I am ready to squeeze case eternally. **1854** *Chamb. Jrnl.* I. 53 The greater part of the head of the sperm-whale is composed of soft parts, called junk and case. The junk is oily fat; and the case is a delicate fluid, yielding spermaceti in large proportion.

†**case**, *v.*[1] *Obs.* [f. CASE *sb.*[1] 12.] **a.** *trans.* To put or bring forward as a supposition. **b.** *intr.* = *to put cases* (see CASE *sb.*[1] 12).

1647 WARD *Simp. Cobler* 52 Good Casuists would case it, and case it, part it, and part it; now it, and then it, punctually. **1687** R. L'ESTRANGE *Answ. Diss.* 21 For this way of Casing a Matter, has the Force of Asserting it. *a* **1704** —— (J.) They fell presently to reasoning and casing upon the matter with him, and laying distinctions before him.

case (keɪs), *v.*[2] [f. CASE *sb.*[2]]

1. a. *trans.* To enclose in a case; to put up in a case or box; to incase, surround *with.*

1575 TURBERV. *Falconrie* 161 When he hath armed or cased the hearons tronke with a cane or reed. **1608** SHAKS. *Pericles* V. i. 112 Her eyes as iewell-like, and cast as richly. **1664** POWER *Exp. Philos.* I. 30 Long wings, like those of Flyes, which lye folded up, and cased within the former. **1748** *Anson's Voy.* I. viii. 111 A great quantity of snow and sleet, which cased our rigging, and froze our sails. **1825** HONE *Every-day Bk.* I. 1524 The felloes are cased in brass. **1856** KANE *Arct. Expl.* I. xxiii. 309 Bones of seals, walrus, and whales—all now cased in ice. **1876** SMILES *Sc. Natur.* ix. (ed. 4) 161, I procured the whole of them myself, preserved them and cased them.

b. with *up, over.*

1593 SHAKS. *Rich. II*, I. iii. 163 Like a cunning Instrument cas'd vp. **1713** *Guardian* No. 95. **1741–3** WESLEY *Jrnl.* (1749) 95 The sleet..froze as it fell, and cased us over presently. **1815** SIR W. GRANT in G. Rose *Diaries* (1860) II. 522 He insisted on having them cased up, and sent back.

c. To cover or clothe with the hide of an animal, etc. (Chiefly said with reference to armour.)

1583 STANYHURST *Æneis* II. (Arb.) 66 With lion his yellow darck skyn my carcase I cased. **1596** SHAKS. *1 Hen. IV*, II. ii. 55 Case ye, case ye; on with your vizards. **1613** HEYWOOD *Silver Age* III. i. Wks. 1874 III. 129 Yet I ere night will case me in his skin. **1725** POPE *Odyss.* XXIV. 535 They case their limbs in brass; to arms they run. **1854** PATMORE *Angel in Ho.* I. iii. 5. **1863** W. PHILLIPS *Speeches* iii. 40 Men cased in iron from head to foot.

d. *fig.*

1606 SHAKS. *Tr. & Cr.* III. iii. 187 If thou would'st not entombe thy selfe aliue, And case thy reputation in thy Tent. **1871** BLACKIE *Four Phases* I. 127 A people..cased in the hard panoply of unreasoned tradition.

2. Technical uses.

a. *Building.* To cover the outside of a building with a facing of different material.

1702 W. J. *Bruyn's Voy. Levant* lxiii. 235 It is a Building Cased with great Free-Stone. **1734** *Builder's Dict.*, *Casing* of Timber-Work, is the Plaistering a House all over on the Outside with Mortar, and then striking it wet by a Ruler, with the Corner of a Trowel..to make it resemble the Joints of Freestone. *a* **1735** ARBUTHNOT (J.), Then they began to case their houses with marble. **1876** GWILT *Archit.* Gloss. s.v., A brick wall is said to be cased with stone, or with a brick superior in quality.

b. *Book-binding.* To glue (a book), after sewing, into its 'case' or cover.

c. To line (a shaft, tube, etc.).

1879 *Cassell's Techn. Educ.* IV. 337/1 The shaft is sunk as in ordinary mines, cased with timber.

d. *Glass-making.* (See quots.)

1849 PELLATT *Curios. Glass-making* 74 The modern practice of casing flint glass with one or more thin coatings of intensely coloured glass. *Ibid.* 114 The principle of casing a layer of colour upon flint crystal glass.

e. *dial.* (See quot.)

1813 A. YOUNG *Agric. Essex* I. 261 The whole was clover; part of it was what is called cased, in June, that is, made a bastard fallow; tempered as they call it in Norfolk; and the operations of this casing were, first to clean plough it shallow; then it was roved across; then stitched up, and ploughed once more.

3. To furnish or fit with cases (cf. *shelved*).

1884 *Athenæum* 5 Jan. 23/3 The narrow gallery beyond (not yet completely cased) will contain, when arranged, a good stratigraphical series.

4. To strip of the case or skin; to skin. *Obs.* exc. *U.S.*

1601 SHAKS. *All's Well* III. vi. 111 Weele make you some sport with the Foxe ere we case him. **1634** SIR T. HERBERT *Trav.* 212 The Bats, some case like Rabbets. **1796** MRS. GLASSE *Cookery* vi. 126 Take a full grown hare and let it hang four or five days before you case it. **1803** REES *Cycl.* s.v. *Casing*, They say, flay a deer, case a hare. **1821** J. FOWLER *Jrnl.* (1898) 44 The Hunters killed two deer, [and] Cased the Skins for Baggs. **1900** N. SMITHWICK *Evol. State* 178 The vessels for carrying water were made of deer skins cased—stripped off whole—the legs and necks tied tightly with sinews.

5. To examine, inspect, size up beforehand. Phr. *to case the joint* (*gaff, job*), to study the layout of premises before robbing them. *slang* (orig. *U.S.*).

1915 JACKSON & HELLYER *Vocab. Criminal Slang* 23 *Case*, ..to watch; to observe; to scrutinize. **1928** *Amer. Mercury* May 81/1 Has it [*sc.* a building] been *cased*? '*Casing* a mark without getting a rank' is the most difficult part of a robbery. **1929** *Sat. Even. Post* 13 Apr. 54/3 If he [a crook] intends to prowl a place, he first cases the joint. **1934** 'D. HUME' *Too Dangerous to Live* x. 108 We've cased a job, and it looks good. **1940** J. O'HARA *Pal Joey* (1952) 36, I..cased the mouse and got a look at her kisser. **1946** *Amer. Speech* XXI. 69/2 *To case*..to criminals..means simply to look at, to watch, or to look over. **1947** M. GILBERT *They never looked Inside* vii. 106 He was one of the curious specialists who flourish on the fringe of the kingdom of crime; he was infinitely patient at 'casing' a job and infinitely crafty at finding or making a way in. **1954** J. STEINBECK *Sweet Thursday* ii. 15 He was casing the field for a career. **1957** M. GAIR *Sapphires* iii. 42 What he was doing was casing the gaff; or, in police terms, 'loitering with intent to commit a felony'.

†**'caseable**, *a. Sc. Obs.* Also 6 caiceable, 7 casible. [f. CASE *sb.*[1] + -ABLE. Cf. *chanceable.*] Able or liable to happen, possible; natural in the case.

c **1565** LINDESAY (Pitscottie) *Chron. Scot.* (1728) 115 No man can say, it is bot caiceable to ane man to fall in ane offence. *a* **1662** R. BAILLIE *Lett.* (1775) I. 185 (Jam.) Of this symptom, very caseable, more din was made by our people than I could have wished. **1671** *True Non-Conf.* 97 As is very casible.

caseate ('keɪsiːeɪt), *sb. Chem.* [f. L. *case-us* cheese + -ATE[4].] A salt of caseic acid.

1840 HENRY *Elem. Chem.* II. 448 Caseate of ammonia has a sharpe saline bitter taste mixed with that of cheese.

caseate ('keɪsiːeɪt), *v. Path.* [f. L. *cāseus* cheese + -ATE[3].] *intr.* To undergo caseous degeneration. See CASEATION b.

1871 T. H. GREEN *Introd. Pathol.* 76 In..fatty degeneration..subsequent changes invariably take place; the part either softening, caseating, or becoming the seat of calcification itself. **1907** *Practitioner* Dec. 737 If the appendix is subsequently removed, you may find a caseating centre near it. **1910** *Ibid.* June 743 Caseated glands. **1964** S. DUKE-ELDER *Parson's Dis. Eye* (ed. 14) xvii. 226 *Tuberculosis of the Sclera*..may be primary, forming a localized nodule which caseates and ulcerates.

caseation (keɪsiː'eɪʃən). [f. L. *caseāt-us*, treated with cheese: see -ATION.] **a.** The coagulation of milk, conversion into cheese. **b.** *Pathol.* A type of necrosis characteristic of tuberculosis, in which the infected tissue becomes a firm, amorphous, yellowish-white material resembling cheese in appearance; also, caseated material.

1866 A. FLINT *Princ. Med.* (1880) 162 Caseation of the products of lobar pneumonitis. **1876** BRISTOWE *The. & Pract. Med.* (ed. 2) 64 A tendency to..that form of degeneration which is termed caseation. **1954** E. P. ABRAHAM in H. W. Florey *Lect. Gen. Path.* viii. 165 Caseation is a form of coagulation necrosis in which the dead tissue looks like cheese and contains a mixture of coagulated protein and fat. **1965** WALTER & ISRAEL *Gen. Path.* (ed. 2) xx. 348 There is now produced the tubercle follicle.., which consists of a central mass of caseation surrounded by epithelioid and giant cells.

case-bottle ('keɪs,bɒt(ə)l). [f. CASE *sb.*[2]]

a. A bottle, often square, made to fit into a case with others. **b.** A bottle protected by a case.

1719 DE FOE *Crusoe* (1840) I. vi. 108, I filled a large square case-bottle with water. **1815** SCOTT *Guy M.* xxiv, A case-bottle of brandy. **1851** THACKERAY *Eng. Hum.* v. (1858) 244 Under their arms, sword, hanger, and case-bottle.

cased (keɪst, *poet.* 'keːsɪd), *ppl. a.* [f. CASE *v.* + -ED.] **1.** Enclosed in or furnished with a case, put into a case, etc. (see the verb).

1595 SHAKS. *John* III. i. 259 Thou maist hold..A casèd Lion by the mortall paw. **1634** BRERETON *Trav.* (1844) 11 Adorned over mantle-tree with birds cased. **1694** *Acc. Sev. Late Voy.* I. (1711) 38 The Armadillo is cased over the Body with a shell. **1849** PELLATT *Curios. Glass-making* 115 Cased coloured glass for windows. **1876** GWILT *Archit.* Gloss., *Cased Sash Frames*, those which have their interior vertical sides hollow, to admit the weights.

2. Slang phr. *to be cased up*: (*a*) to cohabit (*with* someone); (*b*) to be in a brothel. Cf. CASE *sb.*[2] 6 c.

1936 J. CURTIS *Gilt Kid* ii. 23 She was cased up with a bloke... She's got a bloke, a regular customer, get me, who pays the rent of the flat. **1939** H. HODGE *Cab. Sir?* xv. 219 A 'Case', or 'Knocking shop', is what the police call a 'disorderly house'. To be 'cased up' is to be in one.

case-harden ('keɪs,hɑːd(ə)n), *v.* [f. CASE *sb.*[2] (in locative constr.) + HARDEN *v.*] *trans.*

1. To harden on the surface; *spec.* to convert iron superficially into steel by partial cementation.

1677 MOXON *Mech. Exerc.* (1703) 56 Rasps have formerly been made of Iron and Case-hardned, because it makes the outside of them hard. **1864** *Daily Tel.* 11 Aug., Till the ship-men find some way of case-hardening their plates. **1881** GREENER *Gun.* 253 Some work is case-hardened by plunging when at a red heat into a solution of prussiate of potass.

2. *fig.* To harden in constitution or spirit, so as to render insensible to external impressions.

1713 STEELE *Guardian* No. 95 §15 Adieu, old fellow..e'en get thyself case-harden'd. **1771** SMOLLETT *Humph. Cl.* III. 26 Oct., In order to case-harden the constitution. **1871** R. H. HUTTON *Ess.* (1877) I. 100 He can so easily case-harden his spirit against the supernatural pain.

'case-'hardened, *ppl. a.* Hardened on the surface. **a.** *lit.*

1691 *Lond. Gaz.* No. 2624/4 A small screwed Case-hardened Lock. **1831** J. HOLLAND *Manuf. Metals* I. 288 The method will succeed well with case-hardened goods.

b. *transf.* and *fig.*

1769 FALCONER *Dict. Marine* (1789) Aa2, A case-hardened or weather-beaten tar. **1836** MARRYAT *Midsh. Easy* v, Eventually, I cared nothing for a flogging. I had become case-hardened. **1863** MRS C. CLARKE *Shaks. Char.* xiii. 328 The callous and case-hardened of the old world.

'case-'hardening, *vbl. sb.* The process expressed by the verb CASE-HARDEN. **a.** *lit.*

1677 MOXON *Mech. Exerc.* 54 The manner of case-hardening is this. Take cow-horn or hoof, etc. **1816** J. SMITH *Panorama Sc. & Art* I. 8 The depth of the steel induced by case-hardening. **1866** LIVINGSTONE *Jrnl.* iv.

(1873) I. 89 They are unacquainted with the process of case-hardening.

b. *transf.* and *fig.*

1755 *Gentl. Mag.* XXV. 60 Absolutely necessary for the further case-hardening our hero. **1813** SCOTT *Let.* in *Lockhart* (1839) IV. 128 A few years of..oppression would bring us back to the same case-hardening in body and sentiment.

caseic (keɪˈsiːɪk), *a. Chem.* [f. L. *case-us* cheese + -IC.] In ***caseic acid***, a synonym of *lactic acid*; also (*obs.*) = *caproic acid.*

1840 HENRY *Elem. Chem.* II. 448 Caseic acid is of the colour and consistence of syrup..and has an acid bitter taste mixed with that of cheese. *c* **1865** J. WYLDE in *Circ. Sc.* I. 333/1 Caseic, sudoric, and capric acids.

caseiform (ˈkeɪsiːɪfɔːm), *a.* [f. L. *case-us* cheese; see -FORM.] Having the form of cheese.

1847-9 TODD *Cycl. Anat.* IV. 107/2 [Tuberculous matter] of two materials, the one soft, friable, and caseiform.

casein (ˈkeɪsiːɪn, ˈkeɪsiːn). *Chem.* (Incorrectly -ine.) [f. L. *case-us* cheese + -IN.] **1. a.** A substance belonging to the class of Proteids or Albuminoids, forming one of the chief constituents of milk; chemically identical with the Legumin (also called ***vegetable casein***), of the seeds of leguminous plants; also, the product precipitated as curd and applied to various commercial uses. Casein is coagulated by acids, and forms the basis of cheese.

On the applications of *casein* and *caseinogen* see next.

1841 *Lond. Edin. & Dub. Jrnl.* Dec. No. 126 Vegetable Caseine. **1845-6** G. DAY tr. *Simon's Anim. Chem.* II. 55 However much the nutriment of the mother may vary, no great influence is thereby exerted on the relative quantities of casein and sugar. **1863** WYNTER *Subt. Brains & Liss. Fing.* 157 Casein, or cheese, exists more abundantly in peas and beans than it does in milk itself. **1869** ROSCOE *Elem. Chem.* 434 Casein is the nitrogenous substance contained in milk and cheese. **1891** [see CASEINOGEN]. **1919** E. E. SLOSSON *Creative Chem.* 142 A mixture of casein and celluloid has something of the merits of both. **1939** *Nature* 29 Apr. 734/1 A wool-like fibre is made from casein by dissolving in alkali solution and forcing under pressure into a solution containing acid, formaldehyde and either salts or sugars. **1966** A. W. LEWIS *Gloss. Woodworking Terms* 37 *Casein* or *cold-water glue.* Curd obtained from skimmed milk is dried and ground to powder and then mixed with lime and sodium carbonate.

b. Jocularly for 'the cheese', 'the correct thing'.

1856 KINGSLEY *Let.* May (D.) Horn minnow looks like a gudgeon, which is the pure caseine.

2. *attrib.*, as **casein plastic**, a plastic material prepared by a reaction of casein with formaldehyde.

1889 *Cent. Dict.*, *Casein glue*, a glue made by dissolving casein in a strong solution of borax, used as a substitute for ordinary glue by bookbinders and joiners. **1934** *Thorpe's Dict. Appl. Chem.* Suppl. I. 255 (*heading*) Casein plastics. **1937** *Jrnl. R. Aeronaut. Soc.* XLI. 526 Unlike casein cements, they are proof against the attacks of mould and fungus. **1943** V. E. YARSLEY in R. S. Morrell *Synth. Resins* (ed. 2) ii. 59 Casein plastic works in all respects like horn and ivory, and it can be turned, drilled, polished, stamped, moulded, and engraved. **1951** R. MAYER *Artist's Handbk.* iv. 179 Emulsions of casein solutions with oils are easily made.

caseinogen (keɪsiːˈɪnədʒən). [f. CASEIN + -O + -GEN.] A protein of milk producing casein when acted upon by rennin; = CASEIN (see quots. 1938 and 1961).

1891 W. D. HALLIBURTON *Textbk. Chem. Physiol.* xxvi. 580 It will be more convenient..to reserve the term casein for the clotted proteid, and to use the word *caseinogen* for its precursor in the milk. **1906** *Jrnl. Chem. Soc.* XC. I. 56 A comparison of solutions of casein and paracasein (or, as they are usually called in English, caseinogen and casein respectively). **1914** *Chem. Abstr.* VIII. 3059 The conversion of caseinogen into casein by enzyme action is accompanied by the cleavage of N, P, and Ca. **1934** *Times Lit. Suppl.* 1 Nov. 758/3 Caseinogen hydrolysates completely freed from tyrosine are still able to support growth in young rats. **1938** *Thorpe's Dict. Appl. Chem.* II. 411/1 Many American and some English authors have preferred to use the term *casein* for the commercial product produced by precipitation from milk, and the word *caseinogen* for the protein..of milk in its natural condition... In view of the doubt whether the latter term refers to a single specific chemical compound, and of the fact that there are two quite distinct types of the commercial product, the term *casein* is used in both senses throughout this article. **1961** *Brit. Med. Dict.* 262/1 *Caseinogen*, a phosphoprotein present in milk and convertible by the enzyme chymosin (rennin) into casein. (In the U.S.A. caseinogen is called *casein* and casein *paracasein.*) It is the substance which is precipitated when milk goes sour by the formation of lactic acid, and the precursor of the casein formed by rennin in the coagulation of milk.

case-knife (ˈkeɪsnaɪf). [f. CASE *sb.*² + KNIFE.]

a. A knife carried in a case or sheath; a hunter's knife. **b.** 'A large kitchen or table knife' (Craig).

1704 ADDISON *Italy* Wks. 1721 II. 34 The King always acts with a great case-knife stuck in his girdle. **1712** ARBUTHNOT *John Bull* (1727) 106 He pulled out a case-knife ..and threatened to cut his own throat. **1833** J. HOLLAND *Manuf. Metals* II. 5 The description of knife..used for cutting food, or a case-knife, as it was long afterwards called, from being fitted with a sheath. **1841** LANE *Arab. Nts.* I. 126 A dagger or case-knife is..now more commonly worn.

ˈcaseless, *a.* Without a case.

1884 A. A. PUTNAM 10 *Yrs. Pol. Judge* xii. 70 A caseless day. What better condition of a court than to be without business?

casemate (ˈkeɪsˌmeɪt). Forms: 6-7 **casamat(t**, **casamate**, (6 **cassamate**, 7 **casemat**, **cazimate**), 6- **casemate**. [The actual form is a. F. *casemate* (in 16th c. also *chasmate*, *casmate*, *-matte*); the earlier forms were ad. Sp. *casamata*, It. *casamatta.* Of these the first element is app. Sp. and It. *casa* house, but the second is uncertain. Diez mentions It. *matta* in dial. sense 'pseudo-', also Sicilian *matta* dark. Wedgwood, comparing the Eng. equivalent 'slaughter-house', suggests Sp. *matar* 'to kill, slaughter', but it is difficult on this theory to account for the form of the word.]

1. a. *Fortif.* A vaulted chamber built in the thickness of the ramparts of a fortress, with embrasures for the defence of the place; 'a bomb-proof vault, generally under the ramparts of a fortress, used as a barrack, or a battery, or for both purposes' (Stocqueler 1853). †**b.** An embrasure (*obs.*).

The original sense is thus given by BARRET *Theor. Warres* (1598) Gloss.: '*Casamatta*, a Spanish word, doth signifie a slaughter-house, and is a place built low vnder the wall or bulwarke, not arriuing vnto the height of the ditch, seruing to scowre the ditch, annoying the enemy when he entreth into the ditch to skale the wall.' The Sp. and It. is explained in the same words by PERCIVALL and FLORIO; the latter adds as an English equivalent *canonrie*, i.e. CANNONERY, loop-hole, embrasure.

1575 GASCOIGNE in Turberv. *Venerie* Pref. A iv, Plotformes, Loopes and Casamats, deuised by warlike men. **1589** IVE *Fortif.* 26 Casemate..any..edifice that may be made in the ditch to defend the ditch by. **1591** GARRARD *Art Warre* 160 As curtaines or bulwarkes with their casamates do flancke a fortresse. **1600** DYMMOK *Ireland* (1843) 38 Their correspondency hindered by the cassamates in the ditch. **1620** DEKKER *Dreame* (1860) 12 Forts, gabions, palizadoes, cazimates. **1647-8** COTTERELL *Davila's Hist. Fr.* (1678) 527 Raising new Forts, and making new Casamats. **1656** BLOUNT *Glossogr.*, *Casemate.* **1790** BEATSON *Nav. & Mil. Mem.* App. 138 The fort has good casemates. **1859** F. GRIFFITHS *Artil. Man.* (1862) 248 Casemates, or vaulted batteries, are made bomb-proof. **1877** W. THOMSON *Cruise Challenger* i. 19 Galleries in the solid rock, forming a kind of casemate.

†**c.** *fig.* ? Batteries.

1635 HEYWOOD *Hierarch.* VII. 441 Of Thunder, Tempest, Meteors, Lightning, Snow, Chasemates, Trajections, of Haile, Raine.

d. *Naut.* An armoured enclosure for guns in a warship.

1888 *Engineering* 17 Feb. 159/2 Italian Ironclad 'Italia'... The barbettes are contained in an armoured casemate, which is supported by the unarmoured structure of the ship. **1899** *Daily News* 21 July 10/4 Twelve out of the sixteen 6-inch guns are in casemates, a term borrowed, I fancy, from the land gunner. It is a neat little apartment, containing one gun, with the hoist from the magazine into it, and all complete.

2. *Arch.* 'A hollow moulding, such as the *cavetto*' (Gwilt); = CASEMENT 1.

1611 COTGR., *Nasselle*..a hollow in a piller, etc., called, a Casemate.

Hence **ˈcasemated** *a.*, provided with casemates; *transf.* strongly fortified.

1751 SMOLLETT *Per. Pic.* xvii, Casemated as he was, the instrument cut sheer even to the bone [of his skull]. **1851** *Ord. & Regul. R. Eng.* iv. 18 Casemated Barracks, and Hospitals. **1870** *Daily News* 5 Oct., A perpendicular rock, like Gibraltar, 200 feet high, casemated, and nearly impregnable.

casement (ˈkeɪsmənt, ˈkeɪz-). Also 5 **casment**, 6 **casemund**, **cazement**, 7 **kesment**. [app. ad. med.L. *casamentum*, in It. *casamento* a building or house-frame; cf. OF. *enchacement* 'cadre'; or ? of Eng. formation, from CASE *sb.*² or *v.*² Sense 1 is perh. a distinct word.]

1. *Arch.* **a.** A hollow moulding, a cavetto, not exceeding a quarter-round; = CASEMATE 2.

1430 LYDG. *Chron. Troy* II. xi, The ryche coyning, the lusty tablementes, Uinettes ronning in casementes. *a* **1490** BOTONER in Gwilt *Archit.* 928 [Names of mouldings on sketch], A cors wythoute; a casement, a bowtelle..a casement wyth Levys..a casment wyth trayler of Levys. **1660** BLOOME *Archit.* A a, *Scotia*, a hollow casement. **1677** MOXON *Mech. Exerc.* (1703) 268 A Cavetto, or Casement. **1875** GWILT *Archit.* §2531 The cavetto..By workmen it is frequently called a casement.

b. The matrix cut in stone to receive a monumental brass.

1454 in Dugdale *Antiq. Warwicksh.* (1656) 354/1 Either of the said long plates for writing shall be in bredth to fill justly the casements provided therefore. **1890** J. T. FOWLER in *Proc. Soc. Antiq.* XIII. 34 It has been proposed to revive 'casement', an equally good word at one time in use. **1891** W. H. ST. JOHN HOPE *Ibid.* 213 Beneath the figure is the casement of the inscription. **1903** *Yorks. Archaeol. Jrnl.* 307 The top slab with the casement of the brass taken up and inserted in the north wall.

2. a. A frame or sash forming a window or part of a window, opening on hinges attached to the upright side of the frame in which it is fixed. (The usual sense.) From the early pronunciation popular etymology made a form *gase-*, *gazement.*

1556 J. HEYWOOD *Spider & Fl.* xcvii. 5 Ech copweb..she full defaces: No wem seene in casemunds, nor casemund cases. **1575** TURBERV. *Venerie* xxxv. 91 Where casements neede not opened be. **1590** SHAKS. *Mids. N.* III. i. 57 Why then may you leaue a casement of the great chamber window open. **1595** BARNFIELD *Cassandra* iii, Through her light cazements cleare, He [Phœbus] stole a kisse. **1620** VENNER *Via Recta* Introd. 5. **1662** J. BARGRAVE *Pope Alex. VII* (1867) 132 The kesment being taken away, or a pannel of glass broken. **1704** WORLIDGE *Dict. Rust et Urb.* s.v. *Green-Houses*, Some use Glass-doors, Casements, or Chases. **1722** DE FOE *Plague* (1884) 138, I seldom opened the Casements. **1822** W. IRVING *Braceb. Hall* i. 5 When I throw open my jingling casement. **1879** SIR G. SCOTT *Lect. Archit.* I. 229 If a window were beyond the width of a single casement, a small pillar was often interposed.

†**b.** App. used by Gerbier for *window-frame.*

1662 GERBIER *Princ.* 18 Windows to be fitted in woodden Casements. **1663** —— *Counsel* 95 Shutters..framed..to the witdth and height of the stone casement of the window.

c. *fig.* (cf. *window.*)

1642 R. CARPENTER *Experiences* VI. vii. 182 Hee that hath set the Casements of his curious eyes wide open to vanitie. **1691** RAY *Creation* II. (R.) By these casements enter in adulterous thoughts in the mind. **1696** J. EDWARDS *Existence & Provid. God* II. 29 The clear and pellucid casements of the body to let light in.

3. †**a.** ? = CASE *sb.*² I. *Obs.*

1668 *Lanc. Wills* (1884) 165, I give to my Grand-child.. one great Cupboard and a little one wᶜʰ wee call a casement.

b. Casing, covering.

1689 SWIFT *Ode to Temple*, Some ('tis said) for their defence Have worn a casement o'er their skin. **1862** LYTTON *Str. Story* 13 The mailed knight..in his casement of iron.

4. *Fortif.* ? Corruption of CASEMATE.

1772 SIMES *Mil. Guide*, *Casement*, is a bomb-proof work made under the rampart.

5. *attrib.* as ***casement pane***, ***window***; **casement cloth**, a fabric (*spec.* a cotton or mock-linen cloth) used primarily for casement curtains, but also as a dress material, etc.; so **casement fabric**, which is of wider application; **casement curtain**, a curtain made to fit a casement window; **casement flux**, the orig. name of casement cloth (in the *spec.* sense).

1903 *Popular Fallacy* (*Heal & Son*) (back cover), Pattern books of..printed cottons, printed linens and woollen casement cloths. **1908** *Home Chat* 6 June 572/2 Linen, or casement cloth, employed as concluding note to a skirt of the same. **1932** *Manchester Guardian* 28 Jan. 15/7 Furnishing and casement cloths have been in rather better demand. **1957** *Encycl. Brit.* VI. 572/1 *Casement cloth*, flat, lustrous, British curtain fabric. **1830** TENNYSON *Mariana* ii, She drew her casement-curtain by. **1910** *Daily Chron.* 5 Apr. 9/4 Our windows are furnished with casement curtains. **1912** *Queen* 27 July 180/2 Patterns of Sundour casement fabrics and washing materials. **1920** *Home Chat* 4 Dec. 428 Casement Fabrics made to measure. **1903** *Popular Fallacy* (*Heal & Son*) (back cover), Casement flux: 36 ins. wide. **1805** WORDSW. *Waggoner* I. 76 Those casement panes. **1789** MRS. PIOZZI *Journ. France* II. 120 We have got the little casement windows clean.

Hence **ˈcasemented** *a.*, furnished with casements.

1841 HOR. SMITH *Moneyed Man* I. iii. 51 Its panelled rooms, and casemented windows. **1885** T. MOZLEY *Remin. Towns, Vill. & Schools* 343 A large irregular room..with little casemented windows.

caseous (ˈkeɪsɪəs), *a.* [f. L. *case-us* cheese + -OUS.]

1. Of the nature of cheese, cheesy.

1661 LOVELL *Hist. Anim. & Min.* 3 The Asses [milk] having more serum and lesse of the caseous, or cheesy matter. **1781** KERR in *Phil. Trans.* LXXI. 380 [It] forms a coagulum with the caseous part of the milk. **1881** *Daily Tel.* 23 Feb., Not Parmesan, but some inexpensive and wholesome caseous product.

b. *humorously.* Abounding in cheese; fond of cheese.

1807-8 SYD. SMITH *Plymley's Lett.* Wks. 1859 II. 168/1 A universal state of disaffection among that caseous and wrathful people [the Welsh]. **1859** SALA *Tw. round Clock* (1861) 271 Parma, in which caseous Italian city, etc.

2. *Pathol.* Resembling cheese in appearance.

1753 CHAMBERS *Cycl. Supp.* s.v., Cataracts are by some divided into milky, and caseous, differing only in the degree of hardness or consistence. **1804** ABERNETHY *Surg. Observ.* I. 43 Cysts..containing a kind of caseous substance. **1878** T. BRYANT *Pract. Surg.* I. 5 The formation of caseous deposits..in the bones, joints, skin, or lungs.

†**caser**¹. *Obs.*

1585 *Wills & Inv. N.C.* (1860) 112, j caser, j chair and a launce, 12*d.*

caser² (ˈkeɪsə(r)). *slang.* [Yiddish; f. Heb. *kesef* silver.] A crown; five shillings; in the *U.S.*, a dollar.

1849 'A. HARRIS' *Emigrant Fam.* I. ix. 212 A caser (dollar) if you fine him a night of it; and four if he gets what'll make him quiet. **1860** HOTTEN *Slang Dict.* 111. *Caser* is the Hebrew word for a crown. **1879** J. W. HORSLEY in *Macm. Mag.* Oct. 501/2 One morning I found I did not have more than a caser (5s.). **1899** *Bulletin* (Sydney) 14 Jan., *Caser*, a five-shilling piece [cited as N.Z. slang]. **1900** H. LAWSON *Over Sliprails* (1945) 145, I borrowed half a caser off a murderer once. **1939** J. B. PRIESTLEY *Let People Sing* x. 256 Knocker brought some money and examined it... 'A nicker, half a bar, a caser an' a hole.' **1967** *Sunday Mirror* 19 Mar. 24/4, 5s.—Oxford scholar or coser.

casern, -e (kəˈzɜːn). *Mil.* Also cazern. [a. F. *caserne*, ad. Sp. (and Pg.) *caserna*, f. *casa* house: Littré compares *cava caverna.*] One of a series

of small (temporary) buildings between the ramparts and houses of a fortified town for the accommodation of troops; also a barrack.

1696 PHILLIPS *Cazerus.* **1703** *Lond. Gaz.* No. 3913/2 They set fire to their Caserns. **1716** *Prot. Mercury* 3 Aug. 3 To build Cazernes or Barracks in Hide Park. **1858** BEVERIDGE *Hist. India* I. III. xi. 638 All the tents and temporary caserns were blown to pieces. **1863** KINGLAKE *Crimea* (1877) IV. xiii. 314 The fronting walls of the cazern..were in some places destroyed. **1867** SMYTH *Sailor's Word-bk., Casernes* ..correctly small lodgments erected between the ramparts and houses of a fortified town, to ease the inhabitants by quartering soldiers there.

case-shot (ˈkeɪsʃɒt). *Mil.* [f. CASE *sb.*[2] + SHOT.] A collection of small projectiles put up in cases to fire from a cannon; canister shot. Its composition and fashion have changed from time to time. Also, a shrapnel-shell, or spherical iron case containing a number of bullets.

1625-8 *Camden's Hist. Eliz.* an. 1601 (R.) A continuall storm..of chain-shot and case-shot. **1627** CAPT. SMITH *Seaman's Gram.* xiv. 66 A Case is made of two peeces of hollow wood ioyned together like two halfe Cartrages fit to put into the bore of a Peece, and a case shot is any kinde of small Bullets, Nailes, old iron, or the like to put into the case to shoot out of the Ordnances. **1769** FALCONER *Dict. Marine* (1789) Mmb, Case-shot..is formed by putting a great quantity of musket-bullets into a cylindrical tin-box called a canister. **1877** CLERY *Min. Tact.* xi. 134 Case-shot is serviceable against troops under the same conditions.

casevac (ˈkæzɪvæk). *Mil. colloq.* [Abbrev. of *casualty evacuation*; cf. MEDEVAC.] The emergency removal of casualties from a war-zone to hospital by air. Hence as *v. trans.*

1959 *Times Rev. Industry* May 40/2 The last link with the Far East 'casevac' service was forged when..in 1950.. aircraft loaded with stretcher cases flew from Singapore to the U.K. **1965** *She* Nov. 46/1 It is recorded that the very first casualty evacuation flights (nicknamed 'Casevac' and so-called until recent years) brought patients to hospitals from battlefields in the last year of the 1914–18 war. **1982** R. FOX *Eyewitness Falklands* 253 Kim Sabido..moved with one of the rifle companies. A man next to him was hit and had to be casevaced. **1986** *Airextra* Aug. 11/3 In the casevac role, the 'Hip-C' can carry 12 stretchers.

caseway, var. of CAUSEWAY.

ˈcase-weed. Also 6 **casse-weede**, 7 **cass-weed.** [f. CASE *sb.*[2] + WEED.] An old name for Shepherd's Purse (*Capsella Bursa pastoris*).

1578 LYTE *Dodoens* I. lv. 81 In English Shepherds purse, Scrippe, or Pouche: and of some Casseweede. **1597** GERARD *Herbal* xxiii. §2. 215 Called..in the North part of England ..Caseweede. **1879** PRIOR *Plant-n., Case-weed*, or *casse-weed*, in allusion to its little purse-like capsules.

case-work (ˈkeɪswɜːk). [f. CASE *sb.*[1] 8 b + WORK *sb.* 2.] Social work carried out by the study of individual persons or groups. Hence ˌ**case-ˈworker**, one engaged in such study.

1896 *Westm. Gaz.* 23 Mar. 8/2 There are two kinds of criticism urged frequently against this body—one, from outside, that it is all organisation and no charity; the other, from among its own members, that the officials are buried in 'case' work and do no organising. **1935** C. F. WARE *Greenwich Vill. 1920–1930* xiii. 374 The presence of 'begging tendency' as a possible problem to be checked on a case worker's record. **1940** *Economist* 30 Mar. 573/2 The weakness of Miss Hill's book is her lack of interest in the 'case work' side of the problem. **1942** *Soc. Insurance* (App. G to Beveridge Rep.) 36 The Health Centre could be the focus for all social work among the incapacitated, and its social workers could act as case workers for the Ministry. **1959** *Times Lit. Suppl.* 24 Apr. 244/4 She is a magistrate herself, and a social worker, apparently gifted with a lawyer's appreciation of the one function and a caseworker's knowledge of the other. **1959** B. WOOTTON *Soc. Sci. & Path.* App. II. 360 The difference between caseworker and the intrained or untrained worker lies in the skill required in assessing the effect of environment.

ˈcase-worm. [f. CASE *sb.*[2] + WORM *sb.*] A caddis-worm; see CADDIS[2]. Hence, *case-worm fly* = *caddis-fly*, phryganea.

1606 S. GARDINER *Angling* 95 The case-worme, the dewe-worme, the gentile. **1681** CHETHAM *Angler's Vade-m.* iv. §11 (1689) 40 Cod-bait, Cadis-worm, Cad-bait or Case-worm, are all one and the same Bait. **1826** KIRBY & SP. *Entomol.* (1828) II. xxiii. 300 Those caseworm-flies that are remarkable for their long antennæ. **1836-39** TODD *Cycl.* II. 865/1.

cash (kæʃ), *sb.*[1] [ad. F. *casse* 'a box, case, chest, to carrie or kepe wares in, also a Marchants cash or counter' (Cotgr.), or its source It. *cassa* 'a chest,..also, a merchants cashe or counter' (Florio 1598):—L. *capsa* coffer, CASE. Mod.F. has *caisse*, Sp. *caxa*, Pg. *caixa*: the phonetic history of the Eng. word is not clear; the earliest known instances have *cash*; the sense 'money' also occurs notably early, seeing that it is not in the other langs.]

†**1. a.** A chest or box for money; a cash-box, till.

1598 FLORIO, and **1611** COTGR. [see above] A Marchants cash, or counter. *a* **1617** WINWOOD *Memorials* III. 281 (T.) 20,000*l.* are known to be in her cash. **1673** TEMPLE *United Prov.* ii. (R.) This bank is properly a general cash, where every man lodges his mony. *a* **1693** URQUHART *Rabelais* III. xli. 342 They had..emptied their own Cashes and Coffers of ..Coin. *a* **1734** NORTH *Lives* III. 387 He always carried a cash on purpose for them [the beggars].

†**b.** A sum of money. *Obs.*

1677 YARRANTON *Eng. Improv.* 20 As the Land and Personal Security is at this day, no living man..can take a great Cash into his hands, and pay six in the hundred for it. **1707** C. N. *Poem on Union* 19 A flowing Cash, an Universal Trade. **1715** BURNET *Own Time* (1766) I. 327 There was a considerable cash in his hands, partly for the pay of his men. **1752** HUME *Ess. & Treat.* (1777) I. 372 No merchant thinks it necessary to keep by him any considerable cash.

2. Money; in the form of coin, ready money. **a.** Formerly in literary and general use; but now only commercial (see b), or consciously used as a sort of commercial slang.

1596 NASHE *Saffron Walden* 106 He put his hand in his pocket but..not to pluck out anie cash. **1661** NEEDHAM *Hist. Eng. Rebellion* 48 For a twelve months cash. **1667** MILTON *P.L.* IV. 188. **1686** BURNET *Trav.* ii. (1750) 95 There was great store of Cash and many Jewels in the House. **1724** SWIFT *Drapier's Lett.* Wks. 1755 V. II. 55 Very near as much as the current cash of the kingdom in those days. **1727** A. HAMILTON *New Acc. E. Ind.* II. xlv. 149 Bees-wax is the current Cash in that Country. **1782** MISS BURNEY *Cecilia* II. iii. (1783) 187 Where's the cash? who's to pay the piper? **1788** PRIESTLEY *Lect. Hist.* III. xv. 124 The quantity of circulating cash in different nations. **1810** SIR A. BOSWELL *Edinburgh* 155 Those who have cash, come here to spend. **1858** GREENER *Gunnery* 231 Let but some individual, with the head and the cash, try the experiment.

b. As a term of banking and commerce, used to signify, in its strictest sense, specie; also, less strictly, bank-notes which can at once be converted into specie, and are therefore taken as 'cash', in opposition to bills or other securities. Also in the phrases ***hard cash***, ***ready cash***, ***cash in hand***. ***cash on delivery***: applied to the forwarding of goods to order, payment being made to the carrier or postman when the goods are delivered. Abbreviated C.O.D.

1599 SHAKS. *Hen. V*, II. i. 120 *Nym.* I shall haue my Noble? *Pist.* In cash, most iustly payd. **1641** *Jrnls. Ho. Commons* II. 235 Three hundred Pounds ready Cash. **1696** LUTTRELL *Brief Rel.* (1857) IV. 100 Only bills or notes, and not cash. **1753** *Scots Mag.* Oct. 512/1 He had then but little cash in hand. **1782** T. PICKERING in Sparks *Corr. Amer. Rev.* (1853) III. 512 These notes are not received there as cash, but only as pledges. **1817** *Parl. Debates* 1528 On and after the 1st October next, the Bank will be ready to pay cash for their notes of every description, dated prior to the 1st Jan. 1817. **1837** W. IRVING *Capt. Bonneville* (1849) 38 He required hard cash in return for some corn. **1851** *Illustr. London News* 11 Oct. 442/2 One Sydney merchant has sold one ton of flour..for £70, cash on delivery. **1852** McCULLOCH *Comm. Dict., Cash*, in commerce, means the ready money, bills, drafts, bonds, and all immediately negotiable paper in an individual's possession. **1885** *Manch. Exam.* 21 July 5/2 To pay down the price in ready cash. **1904** *Daily Chron.* 13 Apr. 6/3 The cash-on-delivery system of transmitting goods by parcel post.

fig. **1715** BURNET *Own Time* (1766) I. 266 He had the most learning in ready cash of any he ever knew.

†**c.** Minted coin, current coin. *Obs.*

1614 T. ADAMS *Devil's Banq.* 205 To buy leaden trash, with golden cash. **1691** LOCKE *Money* Wks. 1727 II. 92 The current Cash being..computed..to want half its Standard Weight. —— *Lower. Interest* 93 Clipping had left none but light running cash. **1708** MOTTEUX *Rabelais* V. xv. (1737) 60 A few cropt Pieces of White Cash.

d. It is also the regular term for 'money' in Book-keeping. See *cash account* in 3.

1651 in *Index Royalists* (Index Soc.) 18 The said treasurers or their clerk of the cash. **1875** POSTE *Gaius* III. §131 The entry of a person as debtor to cash does not constitute an obligation, but is evidence of an obligation.

e. Phrases. ***out of cash***, ***in cash***.

1593 PEELE *Edw. I* (1830) 57 Now the Friar is out of cash five nobles, God knows how he shall come into cash again. **1609** ROWLANDS *Doctor Merrie-m.* 23 If once I doe begin perceiue That out of cash they bee. **1752** W. STEWART in *Scots Mag.* (1753) Sept. 445/2 He was not in cash, and could not send the five pounds. **1771** SMOLLETT *Humph. Cl.* (1815) 157 With his credit when he is out of cash. **1848** THACKERAY *Snobs* xxxvi. He bets..freely when he is in cash.

f. ***cash down*** (DOWN *adv.* 12): ready money. orig. *U.S.*

[**1722** P. LLOYD *Let.* 28 July in *Maryland Hist. Soc. Publication* (1894) XXXIV. 31 A Reserve was made of Allmost all the Lands upon the Western shore, for the Value of £120 Cash pd downe.] **1800** *Green's Impartial Observer* I. 29 Nov. 4 (Advt.), I have for sale..a few Negroes, for Cotton or Cash down. **1817** CUMMINGS & HILLIARD *Let.* 22 July in *Proc. Amer. Antiq. Soc. 1938* (1939) XLVIII. 38 We now address you to ascertain on what terms you would sell us six terrestrial, & one celestial globe, that is—for what each, cash down. **1855** HALIBURTON *Nat. & Hum. Nat.* II. 111 What's the price..cash down on the nail? **1907** I. ZANGWILL *Ghetto Comedies* 238 You should have made it a rule—cash down.

g. ***cash and carry***, a system whereby the purchaser pays cash for goods and takes them away himself. Usu. *attrib.* Also *ellipt.*, a shop or supermarket operating on this system. *spec.* used with reference to purchases of arms from the U.S. in the period immediately before 1941. Also, ***cash and carry away***. orig. *U.S.*

1917 *Ladies' Home Jrnl.* July 27/3, I would recommend to every woman that you follow the 'cash and carry' plan of buying in preference to the 'credit and delivery' plan. **1921** *Dialect Notes* V. 112. **1922** S. LEWIS *Babbitt* iv. 54 One of those cash-and-carry chain stores. **1927** *Mag. of Business* July 35/1, I located my store in a veritable nest of 'cash and carries'. **1930** *Economist* 24 May 1178/2 Marks and Spencer, being a 'cash and carry' concern, is liquid in every respect. **1937** *Ann. Reg. 1936* 294 The President should be given some measure of discretion to permit, say, the victims of aggression to buy, pay for, and transport at their own risk such supplies, not actually munitions of war, which they might need. This policy was described by its proponents as the 'cash and carry' policy. **1940** *Ann. Reg. 1939* 308 It [*sc.* a Bill of U.S. Senate] permitted the country to sell arms to belligerents on a 'cash-and-carry' basis. **1962** H. E. BEECHENO *Introd. Bus. Stud.* xi. 101 These [discount] shops restrict themselves to selling goods on a cash-and-carry-away basis. **1970** *Times* 16 Mar. 15 The number of cash and carries has grown from 398 in 1967 to 610 at the end of the year.

3. a. *attrib.* and *Comb.*, as ***cash-box***, ***-chest***, ***-girl***, ***-remittance***; **cash-account** (see quot. 1852); **cash-book**, in *Book-keeping*, a book in which is entered a record of cash paid and received; **cash-boy**, in large shops, a boy who carries the money received by the salesman from a customer to the cashier, and brings back the change; **cashcard**, a card [CARD *sb.*[2] 6 h] issued by a bank, etc., to a depositor, which allows money to be drawn from a cash-dispensing machine; **cash carrier** *U.S.*, a device employed in shops by which money is carried in a receptacle running on a line between the cash-desk and the several counters; **cash-credit** (see quot. 1864); **cash-crop** (orig. *U.S.*), a crop cultivated primarily for its commercial value (opp. to one for subsistence, etc.); hence **cash-cropping** *vbl. sb.* and (as back-formation) **cash-crop** *v.*; **cash desk**: in a shop, restaurant, etc., a desk or counter at which the customer pays; **cash dispenser**, an automatic machine from which bank (building society, etc.) customers may withdraw cash, esp. from a current account; = *automated teller machine* s.v. AUTOMATED *ppl. a.*; **cash flow**, the flow of money, as receipts and payments into and out of a business, esp. considered as a measure of liquidity or profitability; *spec.* (N. Amer.) the net income of a company plus allowances for depreciation, etc.; †**cash-house**, a counting-house; **cash-keeper**, one who has charge of cash, a treasurer, a cashier; **cash-nexus**, a relationship constituted by, and usu. consisting solely in, monetary transactions; also *attrib.*; **cash-payment**, payment in ready money, *spec.* the payment of cash for government paper money or bank-notes; **cashpoint** = *cash dispenser* above; freq. *attrib.*; **cash-price**, the price at which an article is sold for ready money; **cash register** orig. *U.S.*, a till for recording and adding the amounts put into it; **cash-sale**, a sale for ready money; **cash-store** *U.S.*, a store in which credit is not given; **cash-value**, the value in cash; *spec.* in *Insurance* (in full ***cash surrender value***), the value of a policy, etc., cashed before it matures; *fig.* (Philos.), the empirical content of a concept, word, or proposition; †**cash-weight** (see quot.).

1768 J. WEDGWOOD *Let.* 13 June (1965) 65 Your *Cash Account is much wanted. **1786** BURNS *Poems* 88, I might, bythis, hae..strutted in a Bank and clarket My Cash-Account. **1852** McCULLOCH *Comm. Dict., Cash account*, in book-keeping, an account to which nothing but cash is carried on the one hand, and from which all the disbursements of the concern are drawn on the other... *Cash account*, in banking, is the name given to the account of the advances made by a banker in Scotland, to an individual who has given security for their repayment. **1954** T. S. ELIOT *Confid. Clerk* II. 59 Claude has just accepted me like a debit item Always in his cash account. **1622** MALYNES *Anc. Law-Merch.* 371 To keepe an orderly *Cash Booke of all the moneys receiued and payed out. **1875** POSTE *Gaius* III. 410 The Roman account-book, he supposes, was essentially a Cash-book. **1834** *Chambers's Edin. Jrnl.* III. 149/1 Tills, or *cash-boxes in counters, are now..banished from the higher class of the trading community in London. **1864** SKEAT *Uhland's Poems* 85 That on the cash-box watchful sits. **1967** *Bankers' Mag.* CCIV. 274/2 Following 'Barclaycash'..and the Westminster's 'cash dispenser service'..the National Provincial has started up its '*cash cards' dispenser—like the others good for £10 when inserted into a machine located outside a branch. **1969** *Times* 1 Apr. 6/2 (Advt.), Go to a branch with a cash dispenser in the wall. You pop in your cashcard. Tap out your number. And the money's yours. **1984** *Business Rev. Weekly* 14 Apr. 96/2 The building societies' card..gives access to about 250 cashcard ATMs throughout Australia. **1889** *Century Dict.*, *Cash-carrier. **1903** G. ADE *In Babel* 18 He had thought out an overhead cash-carrier of the kind used in retail stores. **1649** G. DANIEL *Trinarch., Hen. V*, ccxcviii, *Cash-catchers is a Trade to ravish Clownes. **1719** W. WOOD *Surv. Trade* 335 It [money] must lie dead in the *Cash-Chest. **1832** *Chambers's Edin. Jrnl.* I. 186/1 It is now a hundred and three years since the first *cash credit was instituted. **1866** CRUMP *Banking* iii. 76 Over-drawn accounts, or, as they are sometimes called, 'cash-credits'. **1869** *Rep. U.S. Dept. Agric. 1868* 18 Wheat is a *cash crop, and demands a small outlay of labor. **1934** F. R. IRVINE *Text-bk. W. Afr. Agric.* p. vii, (*heading*) Cash Crops. **1937** *Geogr. Jrnl.* XC. 75 This grafting of cash-crop production on subsistence agriculture in tribal communities. **1942** *Rep. Comm. Land Utilisation in Rural Areas* 5 Cash crops are crops sold directly off the farm, as opposed to those used on the farm. **1950** *N.Z. Jrnl. Agric.* Apr. 365/2 Peas and potatoes also play an important part in the cash-cropping programme. **1957** M. GLUCKMAN in V. W. Turner *Schism & Continuity* p. xiii, The development of

wage-earning and cash-cropping. **1960** *Farmer & Stockbreeder* 8 Mar. 91/1 Try to reduce the acreage per cow to $1\frac{1}{2}$ and cash-crop what you save. **1879** *Birmingh. Weekly Post* 8 Feb. 1/4 The same discount that most tradesmen will gladly allow to a *cash customer. **1904** A. Bennett *Jrnl.* 14 July (1932) I. 187 One *café*.. was open. The stout lady in the *cash-desk seemed just as usual. **1962** E. Godfrey *Retail Selling & Organization* ix. 86 In some shops customers are asked to take the money to the cash desk and return to the counter to collect the parcel. **1983** *Financial Times* 11 Apr. III. p. xi, They are linked throughout the operation—from goods received through to despatch or the trade buyer at the cash desk. **1967** *Banker* Apr. 351/1 (*caption*) Chubb's *cash dispenser. **1984** *Financial Times* 5 June IV. p. v, Nixdorf.. is the biggest supplier to the European banking market (of cash dispensers, automatic teller systems and the like). **1954** *Harvard Business Rev.* Jan.–Feb. 128/1 'Discounted *cash flow'.. computes rate of return as the maximum interest rate which could be paid on the capital tied up over the life of the investment without dipping into earnings produced elsewhere in the company. *Ibid.* 128/2 The mechanics of the cash-flow method consist essentially of finding the interest rate that discounts future earnings of a project down to a present value equal to the project cost. **1964** *Financial Times* 12 Mar. 10/4 Our gross cash flow from operations has increased considerably, to $3,293,600 or $2.48 per share, as against $2.22 the previous year. **1975** J. De Bres tr. *Mandel's Late Capitalism* vii. 230 Financial analysts now increasingly employ the concept of *cash-flow* to judge the solidity of a corporation—a notion which refers to the sum of profits and depreciation charges. **1985** A. Blond *Book Book* iii. 37 Faber's cash flow has been helped by what they have received from the musical *Cats*. **1880** *Harper's Mag.* June 37/1 The *cash-girls are paid a dollar and a half a week. *a* **1910** 'O. Henry' *Trimmed Lamp* (1916) 78, I was a cash-girl and a wrapper and then a shop girl. **1633** T. Adams *Exp. 2 Peter* i. 11 The oppressor doth more hurt sitting silently in his *cash house. **1626** *Raleigh's Ghost* in *Harl. Misc.* (Malh.) III. 539 Gondomar.. chief *cash-keeper for the order of Alcantara. **1705** Vanbrugh *Confed.* I. ii, Her Cash-Keeper's out of humour, he says he has no money. [**1839** Carlyle *Chartism* vi. 149 Cash Payment had not then grown to be the universal sole nexus of man to man.] **1855** Mrs. Gaskell *North & South* II. xxvi. 353 My only wish is to have the opportunity of cultivating some intercourse with the hands, beyond the mere '*cash nexus'. **1904** *Society in New Reign* iv. 93 London is a European suburb, united by a cash nexus to New York. **1936** C. Day Lewis *Friendly Tree* II. xiii. 193 I'm bound to them by a cash-nexus. They paid for my ticket down here. **1803** *Edin. Rev.* II. 102 The statute of 1797 for stopping the *cash-payments. **1852** McCulloch *Taxation* II. xi. 380/1 When the currency recovered its value, and cash payments were resumed. **1875** Jevons *Money* (1878) 35 Iron money could not be used in cash payments at the present day. **1973** *Times* 15 Jan. 16/4 A cash dispenser which can issue variable amounts of money has been introduced by Lloyds Bank... Known as *Cashpoint, the service is at present available at several branches in Essex. **1977** *Navy News* June 15 (Advt.), All these services, together with our Cashpoint dispenser for instant cash. **1984** *Financial Times* 2 June I. 4 Charges for cashpoint withdrawals and direct debits will remain at 20p. **1781** in *Cal. Virginia St. Papers* I. 438 The articles were furnished at *cash prices. **1879** *U.S. Pat. Off. Gaz.* XVI. 847/1 [Patent No.] 221,360. *Cash Register and Indicator. **1886** *Cassell's Family Mag.* 123/1 The cash register which is represented in the woodcut is only twelve inches in height. **1938** S. Beckett *Murphy* ix. 178 If his mind had been on the correct cash-register lines. **1866** Crump *Banking* vii. 143 The employment of bills in the discharge of debts, whereby *cash remittances are avoided. **1750** Beawes *Lex Mercat.* (1752) 874 Genoa has.. Cash Weights, for Plate and Coin. **1808** J. Steele *Let.* 28 Aug. in *Papers* (1924) II. 558 A *cash sale at present I found to be totally impracticable. **1816** U. Brown *Jrnl.* in *Maryland Hist. Mag.* XI. 350 [He] advises me to sell the whole of Clement Brooks property for cash, or at a Cash Sale. **1838** H. Colman *Rep. Agric. Mass.* 90 At the same time we are always sure of a cash sale. **1879** Tourgée *Fool's Err.* viii. 36 The plantation would never have brought that price at a cash sale. **1811** *Raleigh* (N.C.) *Star* 7 Mar. 1/2 *Cash Store. S. Bond having taken in a partner, the business in future will be conducted under the firm of *Bond & Jones*. **1830** Paulding *Chron. Gotham* 156 The Honourable Peleg Peshell, cash-store keeper at Peshellville. *Ibid.* 159 Passing a unanimous resolution, not to buy anything at his cash-store. **1849** N. P. Willis *Rural Lett.* xviii. 156 You do injustice to the 'cash stores' of Oswego. **1898** W. James *Coll. Ess. & Rev.* (1920) 434 The great English way of investigating a conception is to ask yourself right off, '.. What is its **cash-value*, in terms of particular experience?' **1902** —— *Var. Relig. Exper.* xviii. 443 So Berkeley with his 'matter'. The cash-value of matter is our physical sensations. **1911** A. E. Sprague *Treat. Insurance Companies' Accounts* iii. 26 The cash value of bonuses surrendered when the policy itself remains in force. **1915** S. S. Huebner *Life Insurance* xviii. 234 Some companies allow cash values equal to the full reserve at the end of the second or third year. **1929** C. I. Lewis *Mind & World-Order* i. 32 These empirical criteria.. are the 'cash-value' of the category. **1930** *Pitman's Dict. Life Assurance* 506/1 Every policy-holder who fails to pay his premiums.. when they fall due renders his policy liable to lapse... However, the life office allows him a cash surrender value if he discontinues. This cash value is based on the reserve held against his policy... The minimum cash surrender allowed is one-third of the total payments the policy-holder has made, plus the cash value of any bonuses which have been allotted to the policy. **1935** *Mind* XLIV. 143 But what is the cash-value of this slogan 'Essence involves existence'? **1966** *Performing Right* Oct. 9/1 Twice a year, the total number of points logged is divided into the total distributable revenue to establish the cash value of each point.

b. Applied adjectively to (*a*) commodities purchasable for cash, (*b*) tradesmen or commercial houses doing business for ready money only. Cf. *cash-sale*, etc., above.

1875 *Chicago Tribune* 13 Sept. 6/1 A large Premium on Cash Pork, Wheat and Corn. **1898** *Daily News* 15 June 6/2 Mr. Armour to-day bought all Mr. Leiter's cash wheat in the north-west. **1903** *Daily Chron.* 7 Apr. 5/2 Cash Dispensing Chemists. **1929** D. H. Lawrence *Pansies* 80 Turned my modest penny Over on Boot's Cash Chemist's counter. **1958** *Economist* 18 Oct. 265/1 The continued recovery in copper has now brought cash metal in London to £241 a ton.

cash (kæʃ), *sb.*^{2} [ad. (ultimately) Tamil *kāsu* ('or perhaps some Konkani form of it'), name of a small coin, or weight of money:—Skr. *karsha* 'a weight of silver or gold equal to $\frac{1}{400}$ of a tulā' (Williams); Singhalese *kāsi* coin. The early Portuguese writers represented the native word by *cas*, *casse*, *caxa*, the Fr. by *cas*, the Eng. by *cass*: the existing Pg. *caixa* and Eng. *cash* are due to a natural confusion with cash *sb.*^{1} From an early date the Portuguese applied *caixa* (probably on the same analogy) to the small money of other foreign nations, such as that of the Malay Islands, and especially the Chinese, which was also naturally made into *cash* in English. (Yule.)]

A name applied by Europeans to various coins of low value in the East Indies and China: esp.

a. The basis of the monetary system which prevailed in Southern India up to 1818; in this system 80 cash = 1 fanam, 42 fanams = 1 star pagoda (about 7*s.* 8*d.*).

b. The Chinese *le* and *tsien*, coins made of an alloy of copper and lead, with a square hole in the centre whereby they are strung on cords; of these 1000 made a tael or liang.

1598 tr. *Linschoten's Voy.* 34 (Y.) Certaine copper mynt called Caixa.. in the middle whereof is a hole to hang it on a string. **1699** Dampier *Voy.* II. I. iv. 72 A fine Coat, or about 1000 Cash, as 'tis called, which is a summ about the value of a Dollar. *Ibid.* vii. 131 The Money-changers.. here [Achin], as at Tonquin.. sit in the markets.. with leaden Money called Cash, which is a name that is generally given to small money in all these Countreys: but the Cash here is .. Lead, or Block Tin. **1727** A. Hamilton *New Acc. E. Ind.* II. xli. 109 At Atcheen they have a small Coin of Leaden Money called Cash.

a. **1711** Lockyer *Trade in India* 8 (Y.) Doodos and Cash are Copper Coins. **1718** *Propag. Gospel in East* II. 52 (Y.) *Cass*, a very small coin; eighty whereof make one Fano. **1766** J. H. Grose *Voy. E. Ind.* I. 282 (Y.) 80 casches make a fanam or 3*d.* sterling. **1790** Cornwallis *Let. to E. J. Holland* (Y.), I think that every Cash.. of that ill-judged saving may cost the Company a crore of rupees. **1871** Mateer *Travancore* 109 The smallest coin in use is the copper Kasu, called by Europeans 'cash', equal in value to one nineteenth of a penny.

b. **1750** Beawes *Lex Mercat.* (1752) 793 The Caches (a Copper Money of Hainam and Canton. **1771** J. R. Forster tr. *Osbeck's Voy.* I. 262 Kas, which the Chinese call Lai, is the only current coin which is struck in China. **1779** Forrest *Voy. N. Guinea* 280 The China cash at Magindano .. have holes as in China. **1875** Jevons *Money* (1878) 58 The Chinese cash are well known to be round disks of a kind of brass, with a square hole in the centre.

†**cash**, *sb.*^{3} *Obs. rare*$^{-1}$. [f. cash *v.*^{1}] A dismissal or disbanding of troops.

1617 Moryson *Itin.* II. III. i. 241 His Company of foote, reduced lately in a general cash to 150.

†**cash**, *v.*^{1} *Obs.* [var. of cass *v.*] *trans.* To disband, dismiss, etc.; = cashier 1.

1564 Golding *Justine* (1570) 63 He cashed the old souldiers, and supplied their roumes with yong beginners. **1598** Barret *Theor. Warres* II. i. 20 If the Companie be dissolued or casht. **1601** R. Johnson *Kingd. & Commw.* (1603) 177 The cashed soldier is ever ready to follow any faction. **1632** Le Grys *Velleius* 202 That both Cæsar and Pompey should cast [*corrected in Errata to* 'cash'] of their armies. **1829** *Lond. Encycl.* V. 214 *Cash* or *Cashier*.. is now mostly used to express the breaking of an officer.

cash (kæʃ), *v.*^{2} [f. cash *sb.*^{1}] **1. a.** *trans.* To give or obtain the cash for (a note, cheque, draft, money order, etc.); to convert into cash.

1811 Moore *Let. J. Corry* 4 Nov., Get two bills upon Power in Dublin cashed for me. **1833** Ht. Martineau *Berkeley the B.* I. i. 14 Anybody in London whom she could ask to get it cashed for her. **1863** Fawcett *Pol. Econ.* III. ix. (1876) 415 D. gets his bill cashed by taking it to a discount-house in France. *Mod.* Will you cash me a cheque for a few pounds?

b. *Bridge.* To lead (a winning card); to win (a trick) by leading a winning card.

1934 E. Culbertson in *Amer. Speech* IX. 11/1 *To cash* a card is simply to take it while the taking is good. **1936** —— *Contract Bridge Complete* xlii. 479 Cash all idle top cards in trump or plain suits. **1959** *Times* 14 Jan. 10/4 Suppose that he cashes four spades and two hearts and can safely assume that East.. has nothing left but clubs. **1963** *Listener* 14 Feb. 314/1 The best line of play is to cash the top winners.

2. a. *cash in*, to settle accounts in the game of poker; hence in general use, to clear accounts; to close up a matter. (Sometimes *trans.* with *checks* as object.) *U.S. colloq.*

1888 [see below]. **1889** *Kansas Times & Star* 20 Mar., The market value now is about $1,700 a front foot, and many members favor 'cashing in' at such a fancy price, and building elsewhere. **1896** G. Ade *Artie* v. 46 If you're struck on him I'll cash in right here and drop out of the game. **1899** —— *Doc Horne* xxi. 232, I lost back the $2,500 and cashed in. **1904** S. E. White *Blazed Trail Stories* xii. 224 By all the rules of the game, Peter should have failed long since, should have 'cashed in and quit' some five years back.

b. *fig.* To die. (Also without *in.*) Also with *checks* as object.

1884 H. Dougherty *Oratorical Stump Speaker* 14 When Bob cashes in his checks and is toasted like a sirloin steak.. on the top of Old Nick's pitchfork. **1888** *Amer. Humorist* 11 Aug. (F.), Till death calls upon you to cash in your earthly checks. **1908** Mulford *Orphan* xix. 250 The Orphan not only saved me but also some of them, for I'd a gotten some of them before I cashed. **1920** —— *J. Nelson* xx. 220 He's been follerin' me around steady since Wolf cashed in. **1948** *Sat. Even. Post* 10 July 88/2 Cashing in or shipping out, it made no difference as long as you didn't watch them die. **1966** D. Varaday *Gara-Yaka's Domain* vii. 75 Because of the size of the dead animal, at first I thought it to be buffalo. 'Poor Bill or Phyl, cashed in?'

c. To 'get in' *with*; now usu., to make a profit *on*, (fig.) to take advantage of (an opportunity, etc.). orig. *U.S.*

1904 S. E. White *Blazed Trail Stories* viii. 146, I don't stack very high in the blue chips when it comes to cashin' in with th' gentle sex. **1927** *Daily Express* 12 Sept. 11 An enterprising American company.. 'cashed in' on Mr. Arlen by acquiring the screen-rights of one of his earliest stories. **1928** *Sunday Express* 16 Dec. 4/3 She is appearing in too many films, even for a star who would be justified in 'cashing in' on her popularity while the popularity is good. **1930** *Publishers' Weekly* 1 Mar. 1040 Cash in on this tremendous wave of interest and enthusiasm! A large national advertising campaign will start the novel toward a big sale! **1934** Wodehouse *Right Ho, Jeeves* ii. 26 With a thing like that to give you a send-off, why didn't you cash in immediately? **1935** *Economist* 8 June 1295/1 Japan's diplomats are now trying to 'cash in on' the opportunities which its soldiers have created. **1955** A. L. Rowse *Expansion of Eliz. Engl.* ix. 368 That rather unattractive journalist, Barnabe Rich, cashes in on the rising interest in military matters with a series of tracts. **1958** *Spectator* 1 Aug. 156/2 A possible autumn election, designed to cash in on what the Conservatives hope will be the flood tide of their popularity. **1966** *Listener* 2 June 794/2 Are not some of them.. cashing in quite shamelessly on the current debased fascination with evil?

d. *trans.* To pay *in* to a bank; to earn, gain.

1904 'Mark Twain' *$30,000 Bequest* (1906) 10 I'm going to cash-in a whole three hundred on the missionaries. *a* **1910** 'O. Henry' *Trimmed Lamp* (1916) 229 With his gold dust cashed in to the merry air of a hundred thousand.. the Man from Nome sighed to set foot again in Chilkoot. **1910** W. M. Raine *B. O'Connor* 21, I know your kind—hell-bent to spend what you cash in. **1933** D. L. Sayers *Murder must Advertise* xvi. 278 If all these vouchers were cashed in at once, it would send up the cost per packet.

3. a. To pay *over* or *up*. Now chiefly *U.S.*

1818 Keats *Let.* 10 Jan. (1958) I. 203, I will.. ask Kingston and Co to cash up. **1825** *New Monthly Mag.* XIV. 193 When it came to 'cashing-up', affairs assumed a soberer complexion. **1831** *Examiner* 296/2 A certain Alderman.. did not cash up to his supporters on the former election. **1842** Barham *Ingol. Leg.* II. 54 He could not cash up, spite of all he could do. **1854** M. J. Holmes *Tempest & Sunshine* xxi. 227 Tempest is in a desput hurry to know whether I'm goin to cash over and send her to market in New Orleans. **1924** Wodehouse *Leave it to Psmith* i. 26 I'm game to spill it and leave it to your honesty to cash up if the thing looks good to you.

b. In *pass.*: to be supplied with money. *Austral.* and *N.Z. colloq.*

1940 F. D. Davison *Woman at Mill* 151, I.. went to Sydney well cashed up. **1961** B. Crump *Hang on a Minute* (1963) 191, I couldn't even go on the bash when we were cashed-up.

c. *trans.* and *intr.* With *up*. To count and reconcile (the takings) at a cash register, etc., after a period of trading.

1960 *National Cash Register Factory Post* Nov. 6 The register-printed sales bill.. can be used as a Paid Out voucher, retained in the cash drawer to be taken into account when cashing up. **1962** E. Godfrey *Retail Selling & Organ.* ix. 84 Other selling system forms which the assistant must know.. are.. cashing-up forms for totalling the money in a cash register drawer. **1969** D. Clark *Death after Evensong* ii. 37 Don't parsons cash up the takings after the service with the church wardens? **1985** J. Winterson *Oranges are not only Fruit* 14 We went past the shop... Mrs Arkwright was there cashing up.

Hence **cash-in** *sb.*, an instance of 'cashing in'.

1940 Harrisson & Madge *War begins at Home* iv. 95 Apart from this commercial cash-in, all the comments.. were satirical. **1950** 'G. Orwell' in *World Rev.* June 35 Margesson's entry into the Cabinet is.. a deliberate cash-in on Wavell's victory.

cashable ('kæʃəb(ə)l), *a.* [f. cash *v.*^{2} + -able.] Capable of being cashed. Also *fig.* (cf. *cash-value*).

1891 *Pall Mall Gaz.* 21 Sept. 2/1 The money card would not be cashable. **1928** *Daily Express* 2 July 10/2 Cashable orders on retail or manufacturing firms. **1953** H. H. Price *Thinking & Exper.* ii. 36 It is part of the nature of a concept to be 'cashable' by instances, whether or not it is actually cashed. *Ibid.* vii. 229 There can be no symbols unless *some* symbols are empirically cashable.

cashaw, var. cushaw.

cashee: see cassia^2.

‖**cashel** ('kæshəl). *Irish Antiq.* [= Irish *caiseal* bulwark, wall, prob. ad. L. *castell-um* fortlet.] (See quots.)

1845 Petrie *Eccl. Archit. Irel.* 421 All separate edifices, surrounded by a cashel, or circular wall. **1885** Stokes in *Contemp. Rev.* May 742 In Ireland alone does he find in the West cashels such as he finds in Egypt. A cashel is a strong fence or ring-wall enclosing a group of churches with their annexed monastic buildings, e.g. at Glendalough.

casher, var. of cosher (*Irish Hist.*).

†**cashet.** *Sc. Obs.* Also casset. [a. F. *cachet* seal.] A seal; = CACHET.

1609 *Sc. Acts 20 Jas. VI*, xiv, Past his Heighnes Cashet, Register and ordinare seales. *a* **1662** R. BAILLIE *Lett.* (1775) I. 364 (Jam.) Lanerk had sent letters under the cashet to many noblemen. **1706** *Act 6 Anne* xi. Art. xxiv, The privy seal signet, casset signet of the Justiciary Court, etc.

cashew (kə'ʃuː). Also 8 **casheu**, 9 **cashoe**, **caju**; also ACAJOU, q.v. [ad. F. *acajou*, ad. Brazilian *acajoba* (Littré).]

1. *cashew-tree*, a large tree (*Anacardium occidentale*) cultivated in the West Indies and other tropical countries, bearing a kidney-shaped fruit (*cashew-nut*) placed on the end of a thickened fleshy pear-shaped receptacle (*cashew-apple*), popularly taken for the 'fruit'.

The shell of the nut consists of three layers, of which the middle one contains an extremely acrid black oil, which is rendered harmless by roasting the nuts before eating. The oil is sometimes used in India to protect floors from the attacks of white ants. The receptacle has an acid flavour.

1703 DAMPIER *Voy.* III. *New Holland* 68 The Cashew is a Fruit as big as a Pippin, pretty long, and bigger near the Stemb than at the other end.. The Seed of this Fruit grows at the end of it; 'tis of an Olive Colour shaped like a Bean. **1756** P. BROWNE *Jamaica* 226 The Cashew Tree.. The almond or kernel is of a delicate taste. **1796** STEDMAN *Surinam* II. xxii 139 The real acajow or cashew nuts. **1852** F. A. NEALE *Resid. Siam* xii. 194 The cashoe-nut and apple. *c* **1865** LETHEBY in *Circ. Sc.* I. 106/1 Caju apple oil.

2. cashew-bird, the name given in the West Indies to an insessorial bird, *Tanagra zena*.

1852 TH. ROSS tr. *Humboldt's Trav.* II. xviii. 172 The curassaos and cashew-birds.. going down several times a-day to the river to allay their thirst.

cashiclaws, misreading of CASCHIELAWIS.

cashier (kæ'ʃɪə(r)), *sb.* Also 7 **cassier**, **casheer**, **-ire**. [ad. F. *caissier* treasurer (Cotgr.); in Du. *cassier*: see CASH and -IER.] One who has charge of the cash of a bank or mercantile firm, paying and receiving money, and keeping the cash account.

1596 NASHE *Saffron Walden* 97 The Cashiers or Prouiditores for lame Souldiours. **1598** B. JONSON *Ev. Man in Hum.* II. i, I haue made him my Cashier, And giu'n him, who had none, a surname, Cash. **1617** MORYSON *Itin.* III. II. iv. 95 They tooke young youths of that Nation [the Dutch] to be their Cassiers. **1705** VANBRUGH *Confed* I. ii, Go to my Cashier, let him give you six and fifty pound. **1848** MACAULAY *Hist. Eng.* xxiii. (L.) To accept the place of cashier of the excise.

†**b.** A money-dealer. *Obs.*

1643 T. VIOLET *Declar. Bullion* 9 Many Gold-smiths and Casheers of London. *a* **1687** PETTY *Pol. Arith.* ix. (1691) 110 It was observed by the general consent of Cashiers.

Hence **ca'shiership**.

1884 *Graphic* 25 Oct. 422/2.

cashier (kə'ʃɪə(r)), *v.* Forms: 6 **casseir**, 6–7 **casseer(e**, **casheer(e**, **cashiere**, 7 **cassir**, **-ier(e**, **-ere**, **caszier**, **casier**, **cachier**, **cashieere**, **casher(e**, 7–8 **cashire**, **casheir(e**, 6– **cashier**. [16th c. a. Flem. or Du. *casser-en*, in same sense: Kilian has *kasseren de krieghslieden*, exauctorare milites, to disband soldiers, and *kasseren een testament*, rescindere testamentum, to rescind a will; cf. Ger. *kassiren*; and, for the sense, CASS *v.*, CASH *v.*^{1}

Fr. verbs adopted in Du. and Ger. frequently retain the inf. *-er*, *-ir*, as part of the stem, but few of these have been adopted in Eng. *Cashier* probably dates to the campaign in the Netherlands of 1585. The instance quoted by Richardson from Strype *Eccl. Mem.* II. *App.* EE. of 1549 has no existence: see CASS *a.*]

1. *trans.* To dismiss from service or fellowship. †**a.** *Mil.* To discharge, break up, disband (troops).

1598 HAKLUYT *Voy.* I. 63 Our men must not.. depart and casseir their bandes, or separate themselues asunder. **1580** NORTH *Plutarch* 923 He could not abide very fat men, but cashiered a whole band of them for that cause onely. **1604** E. GRIMSTONE *Hist. Siege Ostend* 188 He hath casziered and dismissed about 600 men. **1625** CHAS. I. in Ellis *Orig. Lett.* I. 319 III. 211 To casier my Monsers. **1697** POTTER *Antiq. Greece* III. v. (1715) 53 Power to cashire any of the Common Soldiers. **1734** tr. *Rollin's Anc. Hist.* (1827) VI. xv. §17. 291 He returns suddenly into his tent, cashiers his old gard.

b. *generally.* *Obs.* (exc. as in 2 b).

1592 GREENE *Groatsw. Wit* 28 Hee was casseerde by Lamilia that had coosened him of all. **1610** *Histrio-m.* iii. 85 All the Lords have now cashierd their traines. **1640** G. WATTS tr. *Bacon's Adv. Learn.* 472 Those points.. which.. quite casseere them from the communion and fellowship of the faithfull. **1649** MILTON *Eikon.* iv. (Bohn) 351 By him nicknamed and cashiered for a mongrel parliament. **1716** ADDISON *Freeholder* No. 11 (1751) 65 The Ladies.. have already cashiered several of their Followers. **1791** COWPER *Odyss.* XIX. 405 That man shall be cashiered Hence instant.

2. To dismiss from a position of command or authority; to depose. (In the army and navy involving disgrace and permanent exclusion from the service.) **a.** *Mil.*

1599 SANDYS *Europæ Spec.* (1632) 131 The Pope.. it is thought will cashiere some worthy authours who.. holde ranke among them. **1604** SHAKS. *Oth.* II. iii. 381. **1624** HEYWOOD *Gunaik.* IX. 442 The King.. not onely cashiered them from their commaunds, but banished them his kingdome. **1763** *Act 4 Geo. III*, ii. §22 Such Military Officer shall.. be deemed and taken to be ipso facto cashired. **1830** E. CAMPBELL *Dict. Mil. Sc.*, *Cashiered*, when an Officer is ordered by His Majesty, or sentenced by a Court-Martial, to be dismissed the Service, he is said to be cashiered. **1879** SEGUIN *Black For.* xiii. 225 All the officers who took part in the capitulation, were cashiered or otherwise punished.

b. *transf.* and *fig.*

1609 C. BUTLER *Fem. Mon.* (1634) 3 But if they [bees] have many Princes, as when two fly away with one swarm.. they will not be quiet till one of them be cassiered. *a* **1639** W. WHATELEY *Prototypes* I. xix. (1640) 227 When pride is thus cashiered by the entering in of true humiliation, there it no longer raigneth. *c* **1640** in *Sc. Pasquils* (1868) 126 That Lad who late rewl'd all, Now cashier'd goes, most like to catch a fall. **1650** A. A[SCHAM] *Reply Sanderson* 13 If he had a King to day, he would go neer to cachier him to morrow. **1789** BELSHAM *Ess.* II. xl. 503 The people have a right to cashier their Governors for misconduct. **1793** LD. SHEFFIELD in *Corr. Ld. Auckland* (1861) II. 496 When a majority of the people thought another kind of Government preferable they undoubtedly had a right to cashier the King. **1839** SYD. SMITH *Let. Singleton* Wks. 1859 II. 267/2 You are cashiered and confiscated before you can look about you.

3. To discard, get rid of, cast off, put away, lay aside, dismiss, banish (a thing).

1603 HARSNET *Pop. Impost.* 28 Let them cassier those old Monuments of Ethnick prophane learning. **1628** PRYNNE *Love Lockes* 16 To casheere their Ruffianly Haire. **1641** MILTON *Ch. Discip.* II. (1851) 56 To cashier, and cut away from the publick body the noysum, and diseased tumor of Prelacie. **1656** TRAPP *Comm. Hebr.* x. 26 Others.. have.. cashiered this Epistle out of the canon. **1775** SHERIDAN *Rivals* II. i, I shall.. cashier the hunting-frock. **1848** H. ROGERS *Ess.* (1878) I. vi. 282 All reject.. some dialogues (though.. they are not quite agreed.. which they are to cashier).

†**4.** To make void, annul, do away with. *Obs.*

1596 H. CLAPHAM *Briefe Bible* I. 58 They see the very ground of all their hope, cashierde, & quasht. **1601** F. GODWIN *Bps. Eng.* 174 As for the election.. he caused the same to be cassired and made void. **1650** BAXTER *Saints' R.* IV. xii. (1662) 772 This Argument would certainly cashier all Spiritual obedience.

5. To deprive *of*. (*rare.*)

1668 CHILD *Disc. Trade* (1694) Pref. 26 How it comes to pass that the Dutch low interest has not cashiered us of these trades. **1835** I. TAYLOR *Spir. Despot.* IV. 156 To cashier the ministers of religion of all dignity and power.

¶ 'In the slang of Bardolph it seems to mean: to ease a person of his cash' (Schmidt).

1598 SHAKS. *Merry W.* I. i. 184, I say the Gentleman.. being fap, sir, was (as they say) casheerd.

Hence **ca'shiered** *ppl. a.*, **ca'shiering** *vbl. sb.*

c **1605** ROWLEY *Birth Merl.* III. v. 325 Hath re-united all his cashier'd troops. **1628** EARLE *Microcosm.*, *Flatterer* 68 Makes him doubt his casheering. **1633** T. STAFFORD *Pac. Hib.* xxi. (1821) 214 The cashiering of fiue hundred Foot. **1634** HEYWOOD *Mayden-head lost* I. i. Wks. 1874 IV. 105 He return'd me home A Cashierd Captaine. **1826** MISS MITFORD *Village* Ser. II. (1863) 326 From the first cashiering of my blue ribands. **1844** DISRAELI *Coningsby* VI. viii. 248 The cause of fallen dynasties and a cashiered nobility.

cashierer (kə'ʃɪərə(r)). [f. prec. vb. + -ER^1.] One who cashiers or dismisses from office.

1790 BURKE *Fr. Rev.* 98 The heroic band of cashierers of monarchs. **1807** *Ann. Rev.* V. 186 The cashierers of their dynasties.

cashierment (kə'ʃɪəmənt). [f. CASHIER *v.* + -MENT.] The action of cashiering; dismissal.

1656 DUGARD *Gate Lat. Unl.* §766 By the cashierment of the son. **1865** CARLYLE *Fredk.* X. xxi. vii. 145 Friedrich.. continued his salutary cashierment of the wigged Gentlemen.

cashless ('kæʃlɪs), *a.* [f. CASH *sb.*^{1} + -LESS.] Without cash, penniless, impecunious.

1833 *Niles' Register* 20 July XLIV. 347 They with rich land, and staple productions.. are becoming poor and cashless. **1858** CARLYLE *Fredk. Gt.* II. IX. iv. 432 Friedrich .. being totally cashless. **1874** MASSON *Chatterton* I. ii. 28 Drawn up by Chatterton in a cashless moment.

†**cash'marie.** *Sc. Obs.* [ad. F. *chasse-marée* a rippier (Cotgr.), f. *chasser* to drive in haste (in ONF. *cacher*) + *marée* tide, fresh fish.]

A rippier; one who brings fish from the sea-coast to market in the inland country. (Jamieson.)

a **1600** *Leg. Bp. St. Andrews* in *Sc. Poems 16th C.* (1801) 328 (Jam.) Lyk a court of auld cashmaries Or cadyers coming to ane fair.

cashmere ('kæʃmɪə(r), kæʃ'mɪə(r)). Also **cashmeer**, **cachemire**, **-mere**, and with capital initial. [*Cashmere* or *Kashmīr*, name of a kingdom in the Western Himalayas, used attrib.]

a. More fully ***cashmere shawl***: A costly shawl made of fine soft wool obtained from the Cashmere goat and the wild goat of Tibet. **b.** The material of which cashmere shawls are made. **c.** Also applied to a woollen fabric made in France and England in imitation of the true cashmere.

1822 J. W. CROKER *Diary* 11 Jan., She.. and Lady Eliz. were dressed in rich cashmeres.. the wide borders of the shawls making the flounce of the gown. **1827** LYTTON *Pelham* (L.) If you can bring me a Cachemire shawl.. Perhaps you could get my old friend Madame de —— to choose the Cachemire. *a* **1845** HOOD *Desert-Born* ii, In yellow folds voluminous she wore her long cachemere. **1860** EMERSON *Cond. Life* i. *Fate* Wks. (Bohn) II. 311 You may as well ask a loom which weaves huckaback, why it does not make cashmere. **1884** *Health Exhib. Catal.* 35/1 Kashmir (a substitute for flannel).

cashmerette (ˌkæʃmɪ'rɛt). [f. prec. + -ETTE.] A fabric made in imitation of cashmere, with a soft and glossy surface, for ladies' dresses.

1886 *York Herald* 10 Aug. 3/1 All-Wool French Cashmerettes.

cashou, cashu, obs. ff. CACHOU.

1683 *Lond. Gaz.* No. 1800/4 The best Spanish Lozenges and Cashu, to be eaten. **1710** STEELE *Tatler* No. 245 ¶2 Cashu and Carraway Comfits.

casible, casica, obs. ff. CASEABLE, CACIQUE.

casimire, -inet, var. CASSIMERE, CASSINETTE.

Casinese, var. CASSINESE.

'casing, *sb. north. dial.* Usually in pl.; also 6 **casen**, 9 **cazzan**, **cassons**, **cazzons**. (See quots.)

1516 *Promp. Parv.* (W. de W.), Casen [**1499** casard, netes donge], *bozetum*. **1669** WORLIDGE *Syst. Agric.* (1681) 323 *Casings* or *Cowblakes*, Cow-dung dryed and used for fewel as it is in many places where other fewel is scarce. **1734** D. WATERLAND *Scripture Vind.* iii. 94 (T.) Dried casings, to bake his bread with. **1870** E. PEACOCK *Ralf Skirl.* II. 105 Stackin' peats and cassons aback o' th' laithe. **1875** ROBINSON *Whitby Gloss.*, *Cazzons*, cattle-dung. **1877** *Holderness Gloss.*, *Cazzan*, a dried cow's dung, formerly used for fuel.

casing ('keɪsɪŋ), *vbl. sb.* [f. CASE *v.*^{2} + -ING^1.]

1. a. The action of the verb to CASE.

1575 TURBERV. *Venerie* 239 Turne his skinne over his eares all alongst the bodie.. this is called casing. **1868** FREEMAN *Norm. Conq.* (1876) II. viii. 249 By skilful reproduction of earlier forms or by no less skilful casing of an earlier shell.

b. The action of CASE *v.*^{2} 5; inspection, planning, etc., esp. in preparation for a robbery (see quots.). *slang* (orig. *U.S.*).

1928 *Amer. Mercury* May 80/2 Laying out the route of escape before consummating a robbery comes under *casing*. **1942** *Amer. Speech* XVII. 91/1 *Casing*, looking over the prospective customers [by street vendors], so that they will be able to judge to some extent the amount of business they will be able to do. **1946** *Ibid.* XXI. 70/1 *Casing* and 'planning a crime' can.. hardly be synonymous, for the casing of an individual, a place of business, the movements of payrolls or registered mail, etc., only supplies certain information which enables the mob to plan the crime. **1960** *Argosy* May 53 The casing will be done by the Thomases. They can go anywhere.

2. *concr.* **a.** Something that encases.

1839 R. S. ROBINSON *Naut. Steam Eng.* 49 The valve is enclosed in a valve casing of cast iron. **1856** KANE *Arct. Expl.* II. vi. 70 Allow the winds to break up its iron casing [of ice]. **1867** F. FRANCIS *Angling* vi. (1880) 195 The fly throws off yet another complete casing.

b. *Building.* (cf. CASE *v.*^{2} 2 a.)

1791 SMEATON *Edystone L.* §47 We must suppose that the outside casing had been then begun from the rock. *c* **1854** STANLEY *Sinai & Pal.* i. (1858) 99 Wells.. deeply built with marble casings round their mouths.

c. in various technical uses (see quots.).

1869 J. R. BROWNE *Adv. Apache Country* 525 They are all true fissure veins, with well-defined casings. **1874** KNIGHT *Dict. Mech.*, *Casing* (*Metal-working*), the middle wall of a blast-furnace.. (*Shipbuilding.*) The cylindrical curb around a steamboat funnel, protecting the deck from the heat ..(*Blasting*) A wooden tunnel for powder hose in blasting. **1881** RAYMOND *Mining Gloss.*, *Casing* (Cornwall) 1. A partition or brattice, made of casing-plank, in a shaft. 2. (Pacific slope) Casings are zones of material altered by vein-action, and lying between the unaltered country rock and the vein.

d. The framing round a door or window. orig. *U.S.*

1873 J. H. BEADLE *Undevel. West* xxii. 449 Grasping the casing I got in at the door. **1913** MRS. STRATTON-PORTER *Laddie* ii. 65 All the casings were oiled wood, and the walls had just a little yellow. *Ibid.* xviii. 584 He carefully loaded his gun, and leaned it against the front casing. **1940** *Chambers's Techn. Dict.* 140/2 *Casing*, the frame enclosing the sash-weights... The frame within which a door hangs.

'casing, *ppl. a.* [f. as prec. + -ING^2.] That encases or incloses.

1605 SHAKS. *Macb.* III. iv. 23 As broad, and generall as the casing ayre. **1812** S. ROGERS *Columbus* VI. 44 High-hung in forests to the casing snows.

casino (kə'siːnəʊ). [a. It. *casino* small house, dim of *casa* house:—L. *casa* cottage.]

‖**1.** A pleasure-house, a summer-house (in Italy).

1831 B'NESS BUNSEN in Hare *Life* I. ix. 375 An old acquaintance of many years' standing, who possesses a casino in a delightful situation out of the town. **1832** G. DOWNES *Lett. Cont. Countries* I. 372 It is separated from the sea only by a casino of the king's.

2. A public room used for social meetings; a club-house; *esp.* a public music or dancing saloon.

1789 MRS. PIOZZI *Journ. France* I. 160 The nightly rendezvous, the coffee-house, and casino. **1838** *Murray's Handbk. N. Germany* 205 In all the principal German towns, Societies corresponding nearly with a London club, and known by such names as the Casino, Museum, Harmonie, or the like, are to be found. **1848** THACKERAY *Van. Fair* (L.) That kind of company.. which nightly fills casinos and dancing rooms. **1870** SWINBURNE *Ess. & Stud.* (1875) 94 This poor hireling of the streets and casinos.

3. A game of cards: see CASSINO.

4. A building for gambling, often with other amenities. (Now the usual sense.)

1851 E. Ruskin *Let.* 15 Aug. in M. Lutyens *Effie in Venice* (1965) II. 180 He lost in gambling at Chamouni to the Master of the Casino 25,000 francs. **1950** *Oxf. Jun. Encycl.* IX. 115/1 *Casinos*..were originally public buildings with music and dancing rooms... Gambling games..were soon introduced, and gradually the word began to be accepted as meaning a gambling house. **1966** *Oxford Mail* 23 Sept. 1/7 A conspiracy to defraud a Plymouth casino by using illegal dice in a game of craps, and obtaining gaming chips by false pretences.

† **ˈcasitive**, *a. Obs. rare*$^{-1}$. Having cases.

1652 Urquhart *Jewel* Wks. (1834) 201 Each casitive or personal part of speech is endued with all the numbers.

cask (kɑːsk, -æ-), *sb.* Also 6–7 **caske**. [app. a. F. *casque* masc. 'the head-peece tearmed a caske' (Cotgr.), ad. Sp. *casco* 'a caske or burganet, also a head, a pate, a skonce, an earthen pot, sheard or galley cup' (Minsheu), which Diez thinks derived from *cascar* to break into pieces, with the original sense of 'something broken, sherd'. The meaning 'head-piece, burgonet' coincides with sense 4 (in later times also spelt *casque*, as in French); but sense 1 appears only in Eng., and its origin is not clear. Cf. also casket.]

1. a. The general term for a wooden vessel of a cylindrical form, usually bulging in the middle, and of greater length than breadth, formed of curved staves bound together by hoops, with flat ends or 'heads'; a barrel. Cf. barrel *sb.* 1.

[**1526–56** cited in Rogers *Agric. & Prices* III. 167/1. 574/4. **1548** cited from Procl. Edw. VI, in Strype *Eccl. Mem.* II. 193.] **1557** *Tottell's Misc.* (Arb.) 153 New wine will search to finde a vent, Although the caske be neuer so strong. **1633** T. James *Voy.* 80 With our Caske to Buoy her off. **1660** S. Fisher *Rusticks Alarm* Wks. (1697) 583 Empty Casks, that ever sound the loudest among their shallow Waters. **1708** J. Philips *Cider* II. (R.) Entertained With foreign vintage from his cider cask. **1816** J. Smith *Panorama Sc. & Art* II. 824 This cask must have a bung about an inch and a half from the bottom. **1853** Sir H. Douglas *Mil. Bridges* 246 Let the bung diameter of a cask be 34 inches, its head diameter 27 inches, and its length 50 inches.

†**b.** *collect.* Casks collectively; 'the commodity or provision of casks' (J.). *Obs.*

1598 Hakluyt *Voy.* I. 300 (R.) Because we be not sure what timber they shall find there to make caske, we have laden in these ships 140 tunnes emptie caske, that is 94 tunnes shaken caske, and 46 tunnes whole. **1695** *Lond. Gaz.* No. 3109/3 Having thrown over-board her Boat, Guns, and several Cask. **1745** P. Thomas *Jrnl. Anson's Voy.* 28 We righted her by shifting some of our full Cask and Iron Ballast.

c. A cask and its contents; hence as a measure of capacity, varying according to place, time, and commodity.

1727–51 Chambers *Cycl.* s.v., A cask of almonds is about three hundred weight. **1740** Somerville *Hobbinol* I. (1749) 117 To broach his mellow Cask. **1752** Hume *Ess. & Treat.* (1777) I. 228 Negroes..sell..their wives and mistresses, for a cask of brandy. **1863** Morton *Cycl. Agric.* (E.D.S.) Cask of cider, usually 110 gallons. **1887** *Whitaker's Almanack* 408 In 1885 British Guiana exported of molasses 10,349 casks.

2. *fig.*

1598 E. Gilpin *Skial.* (1878) 45 Philosophy Hauing so well fore-season'd thy minds caske. ? *c* **1600** *Distracted Emp.* IV. iii. in Bullen *O. Pl.* (1884) III. 237 A verye windye caske of emptynes. **1857** Heavysege *Saul* (1869) 216 Ye binding hoops that bind the cask o' the soul.

†**3. a.** = casket. **b.** Case, shell. *Obs.*

1593 Shaks. *2 Hen. VI*, III. ii. 409 A Jewell lockt into the wofullst Caske That euer did containe a thing of worth. **1646** R. Baillie *Anabapt.* (1647) 150 Not denying the shell and the cask to them who enjoy the kirnell and the pearl. **1647** Ward *Simp. Cobler* 28 Continually putting up English-women into Out-landish caskes [= garments]. **1650** Fuller *Pisgah* I. iv. 10 Wax, the cask of honey. **1727** A. Hamilton *New Acc. E. Ind.* I. xxiv. 296 The Fibres of the Cask that environs the Nut.

†**4. a.** A head-piece or helmet; = casque. *Obs.*

1580 Sidney *Arcadia* II. 325 A strong caske..with which he covered his head. **1598** Barret *Theor. Warres* V. ii. 142 A strong cask with his open visier. **1606** Shaks. *Tr. & Cr.* V. ii. 169. *a* **1649** Drumm. of Hawth. *Hist. Jas. V.* Wks. (1711) 105 Their casks, corslets, and vantbraces. **1696** [see casque]. **1776** *Pall Mall G.* 26 Aug. (1870) 4 The infantry should have casks and cuirasses made of strong leather.

†**b.** as a type of military life or authority.

1607 Shaks. *Cor.* IV. vii. 43 Nature..not mouing From th' Caske to th' Cushion.

5. *attrib.* and *Comb.*, as ***cask-body***, ***-head***, ***maker***, ***-steamer***, ***-washer***; ***cask-like*** adj.; **cask-conditioned** *a.*, of beer: that has been aged by traditional methods in the wood: see *real ale* s.v. real *a.*^{2} 4b.

1886 *Pall Mall G.* 21 Sept. 2/1 The ordinary cask butter from Cork market. **1874** *Spons' Dict. Engin.* VIII. 2919 Having thus far followed the shaping of the staves, and the conversion of the same into cask bodies, it will be necessary to direct our attention to the formation of cask-heads. **1975** *Guardian* 12 Sept. 14/4 Some companies use the words 'draught beer' to cover both cask-conditioned beer and keg. **1985** *Financial Times* 19 Nov. 18/7 A completely modern brewhouse capable of using the latest technology..to produce traditional cask conditioned beer. **1874** [see *cask body* above]. **1905** *Daily Chron.* 10 Oct. 2/5 The old-fashioned cask-heads with the familiar legend of 'Fine old Port'. **1598** E. Gilpin *Skial.* (1878) 64 Empty caske like minds. **1856** Kane *Arct. Expl.* I. xvii. 209 Old cask-staves. **1881** *Instr. Census Clerks* (1885) 61 Cask Washer, Steamer. **1891** *Daily News* 12 Feb. 2/8 A cask-washer, employed at the Berkshire Brewery. **1921** *Dict. Occup. Terms* (1927) §459 *Washer, barrel*; *cask washer*..(i) *cask steamer*; rolls barrels to feed end of washing machine..(ii) cleans barrels by pouring water and stone into them.

cask (kɑːsk, -æ-), *v.*^{1} *trans.* [f. prec.] To put into a cask (or *obs.* a casket, box).

1562 *Act 5 Eliz.* v. §6 Any Herring, being not sufficiently salted, packed and casked. **1596** Nashe *Saffron Walden* Wks. (Grosart) III. 204 Doctor Perne is caskt vp in lead, and cannot arise to plead for himselfe. **1749** *Wealth Gt. Britain* 55 They are..casking..the fish. **1879** Baring-Gould *Germany* II. 86 Casking this costly drink for men.

Hence **casked** *ppl. a.*; **casking** *vbl. sb.* (also casks collectively; in *pl.* wines in casks).

1624 Capt. Smith *Virginia* III. xi. 86 Searching our casked corne. **1791** Smeaton *Edystone L.* §206 What quantity of casking would hold a given quantity of burnt lime was a matter untried.

†**cask**, *v.*^{2} *Obs. rare*$^{-1}$. [? ad. Sp. *cascar*.] ? To crack, break in pieces.

1600 *Weakest to the Wall* (1618) (N.) This hand Now shaking with the palsie, caske the bever Of my proud foe.

caskable, obs. form of cascabel.

caskade, obs. form of cascade.

†**caskanet.** *Obs.* Also cascanet, -kenet, -kinet, casknet. [Made up by some confusion of *casket* and *carkanet*, *carcanet*: perh. orig. a misprint for the latter, mistaken for a genuine word.]

A word common in the 17th c., which some appear to have identified with carcanet, others to have used in the sense casket.

1607 *Lingua* in Hazl. *Dodsley* IX. 426 Such stir with sticks and combs, cascanets, dressings..necklaces, carcanets, rebatoes. **1621** Burton *Anat. Mel.* III. ii. IV. i. (1651) 520 A chain of Pearl, a cascanet of Jewels. **1623** Webster *Devils Law Case* I. ii, Reach me the caskanet. **1638** *Lanc. Wills* (1861) III. 200 A caskenett wth red stones in it. **1641** W. Cartwright *Siege* II. vi, The sea yields pearls unto thy Caskinet. *c* **1645** Howell *Lett.* (1650) II. 108 Wheras you please to call it the cabinet that holds the jewell of our times, you may rather term it a wicker casknet that keeps a jet ring. **1651** —— *Venice* 134 Onely women might weare a small Casknet about their necks. **1693** W. Freke *Sel. Ess.* xxxii. 198 The Diamond that is true Brilliant..needs nothing of the Golden Caskanett, to set it off, or adorn it.

casket (ˈkɑːskɪt, -æ-), *sb.*^{1} Also 6 **caskytt**, 7 **cascate**, 9 **casquet**. [Of uncertain etymology: the form suggests a dim. of cask; but *casket* in fact occurs earlier than *cask*, and is without precedent as to meaning in Fr. or other lang.

F. *casquet* is quoted by Littré only of 16th c. in sense 'light helmet', which is also the sense of Sp. *casquete*. Skeat conjectures that *casket* may have been corrupted from Fr. *cassette* 'small casket, chest, cabinet', etc, dim of *casse* box, chest, case; this would give the sense, but evidence of, or analogy for, the corruption is wanting. Moreover Littré has F. *cassette* only from 16th c., when it may have been adopted from It. *cassetta*: there is no trace of it in Eng. in 15th or 16th c.]

1. a. A small box or chest for jewels, letters, or other things of value, itself often of valuable material and richly ornamented.

1467 in *Eng. Gilds* (1870) 379 The same quayer to be put in a boxe called a Casket. **1471** J. Paston *Lett.* 670 III. 7 Syche othyr wryghtynges and stuff as was in my kasket. **1530** Palsgr. 203/1 Casket or hamper, *escrayn*. **1570** in Arnot *Hist. Edinburgh* 30 The confident of the Earl of Bothwell..delivered to the Earls servant his Casket of letters. **1596** Shaks. *Merch. V.* II. vii. 18. **1712** Pope *Rape Lock* I. 133 This casket India's glowing gems unlocks. **1876** Humphrey *Coin Coll. Man.* i. 6 A richly carved casket of ivory.

†**b.** Money-box or 'chest' (? pseudo-*arch*).

1832 L. Hunt *Sir R. Esher* (1850) 357 An order on the King's casket for a thousand pounds.

2. *fig.* **a.** In general uses.

1595 Shaks. *John* V. i. 40 They found him dead..An empty Casket, where the Iewell of life..was rob'd and tane away. **1669** Sturmy *Mariner's Mag.* A iij b, Ransack this Cascate (therefore) where you'll find Plenty of Jewels to adorn the Mind. **1805** Wordsw. *Prelude* v. (1850) 113 A volume..Poor earthly Casket of immortal verse. **1822** Hazlitt *Table-t.* II. x. 223, I unlock the casket of memory.

b. Sometimes used as the title of a selection of musical or literary 'gems'.

1850 (*title*) Casket of Modern and Popular Songs. **1871** (*title*) Casquet of Gems for the Pianoforte. **1877** (*title*) Casquet of Literature.

3. A coffin. *U.S.*

1849 C. Spencer *Let.* 20 Mar. in N. E. Eliason *Tarheel Talk* (1956) 264 The casket, which held this jewel [*sc.* her dead friend], was worthy of it. **1863** Hawthorne *Our Old Home* 102 'Caskets'! a vile modern phrase, which compels a person..to shrink..from the idea of being buried at all. **1870** *Corresp. in New York*, In America a coffin is called a casket. **1881** *Times* 24 Sept. 6 (*New York Corresp.*) Here the casket will be placed on the train for Cleveland. **1885** —— 6 Aug. 5 Members..mounted guard and stood around the casket in the funeral coach. **1895** *Daily News* 29 June 2/1 The strange-looking mahogany coffin (it is called a casket in the United States). **1948** *Atlantic Monthly* Sept. 87/2 Shrouds have long since become slumber robes, and coffins caskets. **1963** J. Mitford *Amer. Way Death* v. 180 The only difference between an English 'casket' and a 'coffin' is in the shape, the former being rectangular, and the latter, tapered or 'kite-shaped'.

casket, *sb.*^{2}, obs. form of casquet, a helmet.

casket, *sb.*^{3}, another form of gasket.

ˈcasket, *v.* [f. casket *sb.*^{1}] *trans.* To enclose or put up in a casket. Hence **ˈcasketed** *ppl. a.*

1601 Shaks. *All's Well* II. v. 26, I have writ my letters, casketted my treasure. **1603** Harsnet *Pop. Impost.* 82 The Priests themselves doe full devoutly Casket up as homelie & brayed wares as these. **1636** Heywood *Challenge* v. i. Wks. 1874 V. 77 This Mirrour, which Ile casket, As my best jewell. **1822** W. Irving *Braceb. Hall* (1845) 32 The beauties casketed like gems within these walls.

casle, var. of casule *Obs.*, chasuble.

Caslon (ˈkæzlən). *Typography.* The name of William *Caslon*, father (1692–1766) and son (1720–1778), applied to the type foundry established by the father, and to the old-face type cut there, or (later) one cut in imitation of this. Also *Comb.*, as ***Caslon-shaped*** adj.

1825 T. C. Hansard *Typographia* 353 The Caslon foundry is still upheld. **1836** *Gentl. Mag.* May 557/2 The printers, whose offices were generally stored with the Caslon founts. *Ibid.* 558/1 The true Caslon-shaped Elzevir types. **1898** J. Southward *Mod. Printing* I. xxii. 136 The Elzevir types prevailed for a long time all over Europe; and the first William Caslon adopted them as his models—hence his types are known as Caslon Elzevirs. **1922** Updike *Printing Types* II. 106 Caslon types are..beautiful in mass, and above all..legible. **1927** McKerrow *Introd. Bibliogr.* 300 It may perhaps be well to warn the reader that 'Caslon' as applied to type has not an absolutely precise connotation. Though, for example, the founts of different sizes cut by Caslon himself are in the same general style, the forms of the letters do not correspond with mathematical exactness... When it is added that 'Caslon' founts have been repeatedly cut in modern times, it will be evident that we must be prepared for a certain range of variety. *Ibid.* 301 The Caslon italic retained something of the angularity of the current script. *Ibid.* 305 The thick strokes of 'old style' are on the whole thinner than in Caslon.

Caspian (ˈkæspɪən), *a.* and *sb.* [f. L. *Caspius* (Gr. Κάσπιος): see -an.] **A.** *adj.* Of or pertaining to the ***Caspian Sea***, an inland sea of central Asia. **B.** *sb.* **a.** The Caspian Sea. **b.** *Anthropol.* (A member of) the easternmost branch of the Mediterranean race.

1586 Marlowe *1st Pt. Tamburl.* I. i, Fled to the Caspean or the Ocean maine. **1590** Spenser *F.Q.* II. vii. xiv. 3 Who swelling sayles in Caspian sea doth crosse. **1607** Topsell *Four-f. Beasts* 96 The haire of the caspian camels is so softe. *Ibid.* 221 Amongst the Caspians they [*sc.* foxes] abound. **1757** J. Dyer *Fleece* IV, And borderers of the Caspian, who renew That ancient path to India's climes. *Ibid.* 174 On the right The Caspian lake. **1759** A. Butler *Lives Saints* IV. II. 982 The coming of the numerous swarm of the Turci from the coasts of the Caspian sea. **1785** Pennant *Arctic Zool.* II. 526 *Caspian Tern*..*Terna Caspia*, inhabits the Caspian Sea. **1788** [see Albanian *a.*^{2} and *sb.*^{2}]. **1854** J. H. Newman *Hist. Turks* i. 9 This is the country, forming the two basins of the Aral and the Caspian. **1876** *Encycl. Brit.* V. 179/1 The temperature of the Caspian area is remarkable for its wide range, both geographical and seasonal. **1923** R. B. Dixon *Racial Hist. Man* 21 Names have been given to the eight fundamental types as follows..Caspian. *Ibid.* v. i. 409 It is impossible to say whether the dolichocephalic element in the Micmac is the Caspian, which would ally them with the Eskimo, or the Mediterranean. **1954** R. Peterson et al. *Birds Brit. & Eur.* 153 Caspian tern, *Hydroprogne caspia*... Almost as big as Herring Gull.

casque (kɑːsk, -æ-). [a. F. *casque*, ad. Sp. *casco* in same sense: see cask *sb.*]

1. A piece of armour to cover the head; a helmet. A term applied very loosely to all kinds of military head-pieces, and now only historical, poetical, or foreign. Formerly written cask.

1580–1649 [see cask *sb.* 4]. **1696** Phillips, *Casque*, a helmet. **1714** Gay *Trivia* III. 363 The fireman sweats beneath his crooked arms, A leathern casque his vent'rous head defends. **1791** Cowper *Iliad* III. 375 They shook them in a brazen casque. **1842** Tennyson *Galahad* 1 My good blade carves the casques of men. **1877** *Daily News* 24 Dec. 5/4 The mitre-like casques of the Pauloff Guard regiment.

2. *transf.* **a.** *Bot.* The upper lip of the corolla of certain *Labiatæ*; also the upper division of the perigone of orchids. **b.** *Zool.* A helmet-like structure, as in the cassowary, the toucans.

1790 R. Bland in *Med. Commun.* II. 456 A very small part of the bony casque. **1794** Martyn *Rousseau's Bot.* iv. 43 The casque or upper lip arched in order to cover the rest of the flower. **1871** Darwin *Desc. Man* II. xiii. 72 In *Buceros corrugatus*, the whole beak and immense casque are coloured more conspicuously in the male.

†**3.** (See quot.)

1753 Chambers *Cycl. Supp.*, *Casque*, in natural history, a name given to a kind of murex, called the helmet-shell.

casqued, *ppl. a.* [f. prec. + -ed^2.] Having a casque on.

1816 Scott *Antiq.* vi, Clothed in a dragoon's dress, belted and casqued.

casquet (ˈkɑːskɪt, -æ-; ‖kaske). Also 7 **casket**. [a. F. *casquet*, dim. of *casque*: see casque, cask *sb.*] A light and open helmet or casque.

1611 Cotgr., *Casque*, the head-peece tearmed a caske, or casket. *Casquet*, the same; or, a little one. **1649** Lovelace *Poems* (1659) 89 He tooke A Sword and Casket. **1864** Burton *Scot Abr.* I. ii. 85 A spread eagle argent, membered and beaked, poised on a casquet of the same.

casquet, var. of CASKET, a box.

casquetel (kɑːskəˈtɛl, kæs-). [f. CASQUET + dim. suff. -EL. App. not in Fr.] 'A small open helmet of a light kind, without beaver or visor, having a projecting umbril, and flexible plates to cover the neck behind' (Fairholt).

1795 SOUTHEY *Joan of Arc* IX. 230 With a light and unplumed casquetel She helm'd her head. **1834** PLANCHÉ *Brit. Costume* 195 Casquetels or steel caps.. are seen in the illuminations of this reign [Hen. VI].

‖**casquette** (kaskɛt). [Fr.; fem. of *casquet*, dim. of *casque* CASQUE.] A head dress resembling a casque.

1840 L. S. COSTELLO *Summ. amongst Bocages* II. 206 His long tresses were confined by an eastern-looking casquette.

cass *sb.*, short for CASSINO, q.v.

†**cass**, *a. Obs.* [ad. L. *cassus* empty, void, vain. Cf. CASS *v.* The word in quot. 1549 may be meant for F. *cassés*.] **a.** Dismissed, cashiered. **b.** Void, null.

1549 LD. PROT. SOMERSET to *Sir P. Hoby* 24 Aug. (cf. Strype *Eccl. Mem.* II. App. EE), The Ruffens among them and Souldyeres Cases wh. be the chefe doeres. *a* **1651** CALDERWOOD *Hist. Kirk* (1843) II. 228 The sentence pronounced by the said Bishop of Rosse against the said James, in pœna contumaciæ, to be casse and null.

†**cass**, *v. Obs.* exc. *Sc.* [a. F. *casser* to break, annul, cashier, the form of which can be derived only from L. *quassāre* to dash or break in pieces, which appears also to have in later times annexed the senses of L. *cassāre* to bring to nought, annul, f. *cassus* empty, void, vain. The latter would have given, in F., *chasser*. Also in form CASH; see QUASH, and cf. CASHIER, also CAST *v.*]

1. To make void, annul, quash. (Now chiefly in *Sc. Law.*)

1460 CAPGRAVE *Chron.* 153 Whan this eleccion came to the Pope, he cassed it. **1509–10** *Act 1 Hen. VIII*, xix. Preamb., His lettres patentes.. cassed and made voyde. **1559–66** *Hist. Estate Scot.* in *Misc. Wodrow Soc.* (1844) 57 That court wes cast. **1609** SKENE *Reg. Maj.* 57 That brieve is nulle, and may be cassen. **1687** *Royal Proclam.* 12 Feb. in *Lond. Gaz.* No. 2221/4 We.. Do therefore, with Advice and Consent aforesaid, Cass. Annul and Discharge all Oaths whatsoever. *c* **1700** in *Sc. Pasquils* (1868) 185 Young Stairs.. the King entic'd To cass the laws. **1851** *Orig. Paroch. Scot.* I. 333 Pope Benedict XIII.. had cassed and annulled all annexations of churches.

2. To discharge, dismiss; disband, cashier.

(In this sense the pa. pple. *cassed* was completely confused with *cast* from CAST *v.* 27.)

1550 [see CASSING below]. **1601** R. JOHNSON *Kingd. & Commw.* 200 When he casseth any gouernor of his prouince. *a* **1616** BEAUM. & FL. *Valentin.* II. iii, Pontius, you are cast. **1622–62** HEYLIN *Cosmogr.* III. (1673) 136/1 Constantine the Great had cassed the Prætorian Souldiers. **1709** STRYPE *A.R.* Introd. §2. 20 To discharge and casse many others.

Hence **cassed** *ppl. a.*, **cassing** *vbl. sb.* and *ppl. a.*

1550 *Prol. 4 Edw. VI* in *N. & Q.* 11 Oct. (1856) 287 Vntill the daie of their cassyng and dismission. **1611** COTGR., *Malandrin*, a cassed souldior. **1638** in *Sc. Pasquils* (1868) 32 Cassing acts of Parlament. **1844** OUTRAM *Lyrics* (1874) 14 An evendown cassin' o' the bargain.

cass, obs. form of CASE *sb.*

cassab (kəˈsɑːb). Also cussab. [Hind., a. Arab. *ḳaṣṣāb* butcher.] A seaman of Asian origin employed in the merchant service.

1881 *Instr. Census Clerks* (1885) 35 Cussab or Cassab.. in P. and O. Service. **1921** *Dict. Occup. Terms* (1927) §735 *Cassub, cussab*; a member of Asiatic crew employed, either as lamp trimmer (on deck) or as storekeeper in steward's department. **1924** *Glasgow Herald* 17 May 4 There is usually an elder, not necessarily a Haji, who carries a copy of the Quran. On board ship he is, as a rule, the cassab. **1960** *Times* 16 Mar. p. xiv/4 There will be the specialist posts of cook, store-keeper and lampman (bhandary, cassab and battiwallah).

cassada. Also 7 **cassawder.** A variant of CASSAVA.

a **1642** SIR W. MONSON *Naval Tracts* iv. (1704) 450/2 We shall not want a sufficient quantity of Maiz and Cassado. **1661** HICKERINGILL *Jamaica* 74 His Bread and drink both made of one root are, *Cassawder* call'd, cook'd by the womens care. **1756** P. BROWNE *Jamaica* 349 Cassava, Cassada, or Cassadar. **1771** ROBERTSON *Hist. Amer.* 1778 I. II. 125 The insipid bread made of the cassada-root. **1802** *Naval Chron.* VIII. 149 A kind of bread.. called cassada, or cassavi. **1826** KIRBY & SP. *Entomol.* x. (1828) I. 337 The larvæ.. feed on the indigo and cassada. **1873** *Act 36 & 37 Vic.* lxxxviii. Sched. i, An extraordinary quantity of.. manioc, or cassada, commonly called farinha.

attrib. **1750** G. HUGHES *Barbados* 249 The poisonous Cassado juice. **1713** DERHAM *Phys.-Theol.* 59 The Cassada-Plant unprepared poisoneth.

†**cassade.** *Obs. rare*$^{-1}$.

1430 LYDG. *Chron. Troy* III. xxii, Some wolde haue.. An hawberion of late wrought cassade That with weight he be not ouer lade.

cassadone: see CASSIDOINE.

†**cassakin.** *Obs.* Also casakene. [a. F. *casaquin* (in It. *casacchino* 'a jerkin, a mandillion', Florio) dim. of *casaque* (or according to Lagarde, its source): see CASSOCK.] = CASSOCK 1, 2.

1560 *Aberdeen Regist.* V. 24 (Jam.) Ane casakene of dammass with pesmentis of siluir & lang buttownis of the samen. **1579** FENTON *Guicciard.* XIV. (1599) 674 He caused his people to put vpon their cassakins the red crosse. **1615** SYLVESTER *St. Lewis* 544 (D.) To turn the skins to Cassakins of Gold.

†**cassall.** *Obs. rare.* [Derivation uncertain: cf. Cat. *caxal*, Pr. dials. *caissal*, *caysal* tooth, grinder.] ? A wisdom-tooth.

1541 R. COPLAND *Guydon's Quest. Chirurg.* (1579) 18 Howe many tethe ought euery persone to haue?.. two douales, two quadruples .viij. molares, and two cassalles [L. *caysales*]. **1548** VICARY *Anat. Man.* (1577) Fiij b, Two Cannines, eyght Morales, and two Cansales [? causales].

cas(s)alty, -elty, dial. ff. CASUALTY.

1886 *Cornhill Mag.* June 582 A Cas'alty Corner is a feature of every district of outcast London, is to be found wherever the poor of the great city most do congregate. *Ibid.*, Cas'alty labourers. **1892** TENNYSON *Church-w. & Curate* i, Nasty, casselty weather!

cassamate, obs. form of CASEMATE.

†**cassan.** *Obs. Thieves' cant.* [cf. L. *caseus*, Du. *kaas*, MDu. *kâse*.] Cheese.

1567 HARMAN *Caveat* 83 Cassan, cheese. **1641** BROME *Jov. Crew* II. Wks. 1873 III. 388 Here's Ruffpeck and Casson, and all of the best.

Cassandra (kæˈsændrə). [L. *Cassandra*, Gr. Κασ(σ)άνδρα.] The name of a daughter of Priam, sought in love by Apollo, who gave her the gift of prophecy; when she deceived him he ordained that no one should believe her prophecies, though true; used allusively, *attrib.*, and *Comb.*

a **1668** LASSELS *Voy. Italy* (1670) Pref. a x, Other Governours (Cassandra like) telling their Pupils many excellent truths, are not believed by them. **1711** ADDISON *Spect.* No. 130 ⁋2 A Cassandra of the [Gypsy] Crew.. told me, That I loved a pretty Maid in a Corner. **1837** CARLYLE *Fr. Rev.* II. I. ii, A Cassandra-Marat cannot do it. **1863** LONGFELLOW *Tales of Wayside Inn* 191 The cawing of the crow,.. Cassandra-like, prognosticating woe. **1901** *N. Amer. Rev.* Feb. 236 Far be from me the Cassandra task of attempting to persuade my countrymen that an army of any given size is a necessity for the Republic. **1926** CHESTERTON *Incredulity of Fr. Brown* v. 177 Lady Diana had recovered a little from her trance of Cassandra. **1941** KOESTLER *Scum of Earth* 155 The censorship continued to suppress Kerillis's Cassandra-cries against the traitors in the Ministries. **1959** *Times* 18 June 13/3 Dr. Bertram gets off to a slow start because he is a very zestful Cassandra.

Hence **Caˈssandrian** *a.*

a **1876** EADIE *Comm. Thess.* (1877) 347 Baxter.. accused Grotius of a design to reconcile Papists and Protestants in a Cassandrian Popery. **1903** H. BEGBIE in *Daily Chron.* 28 May 3/7 Remembering the Cassandrian comparison which has been made between the Transvaal and Ireland.

‖**cassant**, *a. Obs. rare.* [F. *cassant* breaking: Littré has *poires cassantes*.] Brittle; friable.

1725 BRADLEY *Fam. Dict.* s.v. *Pear*, the Pulp is Sugary and Juicy, has a vinous Taste, and is cassant.

‖**cassareep** (ˈkæsəriːp). Also casserepo, cassaripa, -ripe, -reb. [Of Carib origin: Martius *Gloss. Brésil* 391, gives Galibi (Island Carib) *cassiripó*, 'radix Manihot raspata', *cassirí*, *caxirí*, *cachirí*, 'potus e radice fermentata Manihot Aypi' (the sweet manihot).] 'The inspissated juice of the cassava, which is highly antiseptic, and forms the basis of the West Indian pepper-pot' (*Treas. Bot.*).

1832 *Veg. Subst. Food* 155 The juice of bitter cassava.. boiled with meat and seasoned.. forms a favourite soup, called by the Brazilians casserepo. **1853** WHATELEY in *Life* (1866) II. 290 The inspissated juice of the Cassava is called Cassaripa. **1859** *All Y. Round* No. 32. 125 Cassareep.. being also a powerful antiseptic. **1882** *Standard* 14 Dec. 5/3 The cassareb.. the chief ingredient in the famous 'pepper pot'.

cassata (kæˈsɑːtə). [It.] Ice-gâteau; Neapolitan ice-cream containing candied fruit and nuts.

1927 *Harper's Mag.* Feb. 319, I was sitting in front of Gilli's one May afternoon eating *cassata*. **1953** tr. *Bonhoeffer's Lett. fr. Prison* (1963) 114 We.. consumed vast quantities of *granitos* and *cassatas* on the way. **1958** *New Scientist* 2 Jan. 9/1 More exotic concoctions like cassata. **1959** C. MACINNES *Absolute Beginners* 16, I ordered my striped *cassata*.

†**cassate,** *pa. pple.* and *a. Obs.* [ad. L. *cassāt-us*, pa. pple. of *cassāre*: see next.] = CASSED.

1519 HORMAN *Vulg.* 204 b, This testament is cassat and annulled. **1654** HAMMOND *Answ. Animadv. Ignat.* ii. § 1. 27 A voyd or cassate hope. **1659** —— *On Ps.* lxxvii. 10 God's mercies were forgotten, and his promises cassate.

†ˈ**cassate**, *v. Obs.* Also 6–7 **cassat.** [f. L. *cassāt-* ppl. stem of *cassā-re*; see CASS *v.* and -ATE[3].] = CASS *v.*

1512 *Act 4 Hen. VIII*, xiv. Preamb., The said late noble Kyng.. reversed adnulled repelled cassated and made voyde, etc. **1611** SPEED *Hist. Gt. Brit.* IX. viii. (1632) 584 The Pope.. did cassate his Election. *a* **1619** DANIEL *Coll. Hist. Eng.* (1626) 142 Why should he not cassat those Charters? **1686** GOAD *Celest. Bodies* I. xii. 64 This I hope doth not cassate what we have said, but rather corroborate. **1744** J. LEWIS *Pecocke* 254 That he would cassate his bull of restitution.

Hence **cassating** *vbl. sb.*

1656 TRAPP *Comm. Hebr.* vii. 18 For there is verily a disannulling.. an outing, cassating, expunging.

cassation[1] (kæˈseɪʃən). [ad. late L. *cassātiōn-em*, n. of action f. *cassāre*; see CASS *v.* So in F.]

1. The action of making null or void; cancellation, abrogation.

Court of Cassation [Fr. *Cour de cassation*], in France, the appellation of the supreme court of appeal, as having the power in the last resort to alter, or cancel, or quash (*casser*) decisions of the other courts which are wrong in form or law.

c **1425** WYNTOUN *Cron.* IX. xxiii. 70 Quhen of þir Electiownys Twa fell sic Cassatiownys. **1611** COTGR., *Cassation*, a cassation, a quashing, cassing, breaking. *a* **1619** DANIEL *Coll. Hist. Eng.* (1626) 112 There was no cassation of the first [election]. **1750** BEAWES *Lex Mercat.* (1752) 369 Under penalty of Cassation and being mulct. **1850** ALISON *Hist. Europe* II. vi. §29. 28 A new Tribunal, entitled the Court of Cassation, was established at Paris to revise the sentences of inferior tribunals. **1855** MOTLEY *Dutch Rep.* I. ii. (1866) 81 By a general cassation of all their constitutions.

†**2.** Dismissal of a soldier; cashiering. *Obs.*

1602 SEGAR *Hon. Mil. & Civ.* XXV. 32 Cassation causary or reasonable, in consideration of sicknesse or disability, etc... Cassation ignominious, was for some offence, etc.

cassation[2] (kæˈseɪʃən). *Mus.* [a. G. *kassation* serenade, ad. It. *cassazione.*] A piece of instrumental music of the eighteenth century similar to the serenade, and often performed out of doors.

1879 GROVE *Dict. Mus.* I. 319/1 *Cassation*.. designates a piece of music of the last century, for the open air.. much like the *Serenade*. **1911** *Encycl. Brit.* XXIV. 663/1 The *cassation* is a smaller composition [than the serenade], beginning (like Beethoven's serenade op. 8) with a march. **1983** *New Oxf. Compan. Mus.* I. 680/2 *Finalmusik*... A type of piece related to the divertismento, serenade, or cassation which ended an outdoor concert.

cassava (kæˈsɑːvə). Forms: α. 6–7 **casavi**, 7–9 **cassavi, cassavy, -vie, -via,** (**cacavi**); β. 7 **cazava,** 7–9 **cassava,** 8–9 **casava;** γ. 8–9 **cassave**; see also CASSADA. [In F. *cassave*, Pg. *cassave*, Sp. *casabe, cazabe*, all from the Taino language of Hayti, where it is variously given as *caçábi, casávi, cazábbi, cassáve* (see Peter Martyr). Several of these forms have been at times used in English.]

1. A plant, called also by its Brazilian name Manioc, *Manihot utilissima* (N.O. *Euphorbiaceæ*), two varieties (or species) of which are extensively cultivated in the West Indies and tropical America, as also in Africa, for their fleshy tuberous roots, which 'yield the greatest portion of the daily food of the natives of tropical America'.

The root of the Sweet Cassava (*M. Aipi*) is wholesome and is commonly prepared as a vegetable, the root of the Bitter Cassava contains a most virulent poisonous juice, which is however highly volatile, and is expelled by heat.

1555 EDEN *Decades W. Ind.* I. VII. (Arb.) 93 They had only *Cazibi*, that is suche rootes whereof they make theyr breade. **1624** CAPT. SMITH *Virginia* I. 10 Cassavia growes in Marishes. **1657** R. LIGON *Barbadoes* (1673) 31 [Bread] made of the flower of Mayes and Cassavie mixed together. **1711** in A. Duncan *Mariner's Chron.* (1803) III. 315 Sweet cassave and green plantain roasted. **1796** STEDMAN *Surinam* II. xviii, Plantains and sweet cassavas roasted. *a* **1818** M. G. LEWIS *Jrnl. W. Ind.* (1834) 212 The bitter cassava, unless the juice is carefully pressed out of it, is a deadly poison.

2. The nutritious starch or flour obtained from the roots of the Manioc by grating them, and pressing out the juice; the bread made from this.

A prepared form of cassava flour is Tapioca.

1577 FRAMPTON *Joyfull Newes* 103 The Casaui is the bread.. made of an Hearbe that the Indians dooe call Yuca. **1600** HAKLUYT *Voy.* (1810) III. 462 Cassaui, a kinde of breade made of roots. **1613** PURCHAS *Pilgr.* I. VIII. ii. 616 Bread of a great roote called Yuca, which they name Cacavi. **1633** *Gerard's Herbal* 1543 (L.) The Indian bread called Cazava. **1750** BEAWES *Lex Mercat.* (1752) 754 Manioc of whose Roots Cassave is made. **1828** W. IRVING *Columbus* (1848) I. 160 A kind of bread called cassava.

3. *attrib.* and *Comb.*

1777 ROBERTSON *Hist. Amer.* (1783) II. 430 The inhabitants.. had none but Cassava bread. **1884** *Health Exhib. Catal.* 159/1 Cassave Bread. **1796** STEDMAN *Surinam* II. xx. 96 We passed through two old cassava fields. **1836** MACGILLIVRAY tr. *Humboldt's Trav.* xviii. 257 Occupied in preparing cassava-flour. **1837** M. DONOVAN *Dom. Econ.* II. 325 The sweet cassava plant is free from any noxious property. **1719** DE FOE *Crusoe* (1840) I. vii. 116, I searched for the cassave root.

cassaware, etc. obs. ff. CASSOWARY.

cassaydown, cassedon(ne, var. CASSIDOINE.

†**casse**[1]. *Obs. rare.* [cf. OF. *casse* oak.]

1523 FITZHERB. *Husb.* §130 Dyuers apple trees that haue knottes in the bowes as casses or wydes.

‖**casse**[2] (kæs, kas). [Fr., vbl. n. f. *casser* to break.] Incipient souring of certain wines, accompanied by loss of colour and a deposit of sediment.

1883 J. GARDNER *Brewer, Distiller* 226 If the breakage, or *casse*, as it is termed, has not exceeded 7 or 8 per cent. by the time August is reached, he.. lets the wine remain. **1911** *Encycl. Brit.* XXVIII. 720/1 The disease known as *tourne* or *casse* is generally caused by the wine having been made.. from grapes affected by mildew. **1959** W. JAMES *Word-Bk.*

Wine 43 *Casse*, a common disease of wines in which an excess of metallic salts causes cloudiness and an off-taste.

casse, obs. form of CASE *sb.*

casseer(e, casseir, obs. ff. CASHIER.

Cassegrainian (kæsɪˈgreɪnɪən), *a.* Applied to a modification of the Gregorian reflecting telescope suggested in 1672 by M. Cassegrain. Also **Cassegrain**, used *attrib.* and *absol.*

1813 KATER in *Phil. Trans.* No. 206 (*title*) On the light of the Cassegrainian Telescope, compared with that of the Gregorian. **1831** BREWSTER *Optics* xlii. 352 The Cassegrainian telescope .. differs from the Gregorian only in having its small speculum .. convex instead of concave. **1888** *Encycl. Brit.* XXIII. 145/1 The Cassegrain telescope... In comparatively recent years the Cassegrain has acquired importance from the fact of its adoption for the great Melbourne telescope. **1961** *Listener* 7 Sept. 353/3 The Cassegrain mirror is swung down into a compartment let into the telescope tube.

Casseiver (kæˈsiːvə(r)). [f. CASS(ETTE + REC)EIVER[1].] A proprietary term for a combined cassette recorder and radio.

1976 *Gramophone* Jan. 1284/3 Rank Radio International have coined the term 'Casseiver' to describe the new Bush BS3504, which incorporates a stereo cassette deck. **1979** *Comet Discount Price List* 28 Oct.–10 Nov. (*heading*) Casseivers: tuner/amplifier/cassette combinations. **1983** *Trade Marks Jrnl.* 11 May 904/2 *Casseiver*... Electrical and electronic apparatus and instruments; apparatus and instruments, all for recording, reproducing, amplifying and transmitting sound or video... Binatone International Limited.

Cassel (ˈkæsəl). The name of Cassel (now Kassel), a town in Germany, used *attrib.* to designate various pigments, as **Cassel brown, Cassel earth**, a brown prepared from impure lignite, Vandyke brown; **Cassel green**, a green consisting chiefly of barium manganese, Manganese green; **Cassel yellow**, a patent yellow pigment, Chinese yellow, mineral yellow.

1860 URE *Dict. Arts* (ed. 5) I. 805 Vandyke, Cappab, Rubens, Cassel, and Cologne Browns. **1875** T. SEATON *Fret-Cutting* viii. 105 The brown pigment is well known to artist's colourmen as Cassel earth. **1882** *Encycl. Brit.* XIV. 379/1 Another oxychloride, $PbCl_2.7PbO$, known as 'Cassel yellow'. **1885** *Ibid.* XIX. 88/1 Cassel Green, called also Rosenstiehl's Green, is a fine innocuous pigment made by melting together sulphate of baryta and oxide of manganese. .. Vandyke brown and Cologne or Cassel brown, peaty ochres... Real Vandyke Brown .. ought to be a kind of bituminous peaty earth .. allied to which are Cologne and Cassel Earth.

casse paper, cassie-. [perh. repr. a Fr. *papier cassé* broken paper.] The paper of the two outside quires of a ream.

1688 R. HOLME *Armoury* III. iii. 120/1 Cassie Quires, are the two out side Quires in a Ream, called also Cording Quires. Cassie Paper, are Quires made up by Paper-makers of Torn, Wrinkled, Stained or otherwise naughty Sheets. **1825** HONE *Every-day Bk.* I. 1139. **1858** SIMMONDS *Dict. Trade, Casse-paper*, broken or damaged paper.

†**casser.** *Obs.*$^{-0}$ [f. CASS *v.* + -ER[1].] One who 'casses'.

1611 COTGR., *Quasseur*, squasher, casser, canceller.

Casserian (kæˈsɪərɪən), *a.* [According to *Syd. Soc. Lex.* from Giulio Casserio of Piacenza, 1545–1616.] ***Casserian*** (or ***Gasserian***) ***ganglion***: the ganglion of the larger root of the fifth nerve.

1842 E. WILSON *Anat. Vade Mec.* 407 It arises from the upper angle of the Casserian ganglion.

casserole (ˈkæsərəʊl, formerly kæsəˈrəʊl). [Fr. = It. *casserola*, Sp. *cacerola*; the radical form is app. seen in Sp. *cazo*, F. *casse* 'an open-mouthed pan fit to boil things in' (Cotgr.); but its actual history is obscure; cf. F. *cassole*, It. *cazzuola*, Sp. *cazuela*, mentioned under CASSOLETTE.]

1. A kind of stew-pan. Now, a dish cooked and served in a casserole. Also ***à la casserole***, now usually ***en casserole***. Also *attrib.*, as ***casserole cookery, dish, pan***.

1725 BRADLEY *Fam. Dict.* s.v. *Roach*, Roaches may .. be dress'd in a Casserole. **1849** CURZON *Visits Monast.* 342 Not a scrap of furniture, not even a pipkin or a Casserole. **1870** U. DUBOIS *Cosmopol. Cookery* §727 Capon of Caux, roasted 'à la casserole'... Braised or roasted in a stewpan. **1904** C. H. SENN (*title*) Chafing Dish and Casserole Cookery. **1905** A. KENNEY-HERBERT *Common-sense Cookery* 292 A *poulet*, or pheasant *à la casserole*. **1906** FILIPPINI *Internat. Cook Bk.* 378 Heat one tablespoon butter in an earthen casserole pan. *Ibid.* 565 Sweetbreads en Casserole. Blanch and trim six heart sweetbreads. Place in an earthen casserole dish [etc.]. **1928** A. CHRISTIE *Myst. Blue Train* xxxii. 264 The waiter deftly served them with chicken *en casserole*. **1958** A. WHITE tr. *Colette's Claudine in Paris* i. 9 The yellow chanterelles that go so well with creamy sauces and casserole of veal. **1960** *Observer* 17 Jan. 14/4 A casserole, once upon a time, was a pan with a handle, made in tinned copper, earthenware, enamelled iron or some other heat-resistant material... In Britain to-day the casserole has become a portmanteau word for any receptacle in a fire-resistant material, with or without a lid, that goes both into the oven and on to the dinner-table.

2. The edging or outer portion of certain dressed dishes.

1706 PHILLIPS, *Casserole* .. a Loaf stuff'd with a Hash of roasted Pullets, Chickens, etc., and dress'd in a Stew-Pan of the same Bigness with the Loaf; also a kind of Soop or Potage of Rice, etc. with a Ragoo. **1730–6** in BAILEY. **1852** *New Syst. Cookery* 126 Casserol or Rice Edging for a Currie or Fricassee. **1858** SIMMONDS *Dict. Trade, Casserolle* .. a bordering of rice to a dish. *Mod. Dicts.* A mould (in the shape of a hollow vessel) of boiled rice, or of mashed potato, baked, in which meats are served at table. Such meats are said to be served '*en casserole*'.

3. *fig.*

1930 W. J. LOCKE *Town of Tombarel* iv. 127 The affairs of women .. are equally important in this stew, this vast casserole of male and female existence. **1962** *Economist* 17 Nov. 653/1 The .. Bill is one of those casserole measures into which bits and pieces .. from various reports are dropped.

So **ˈcasserole** *v. trans.*, to cook in a casserole.

1930 D. L. SAYERS *Strong Poison* ix. 114 A casseroled chicken with turnips and carrots done in the gravy. *Ibid.* 115 It seemed a shame to casserole it [*sc.* a chicken], for it would 'ave roasted beautiful. **1960** *News Chron.* 11 Oct. 8/6 Instructions for casseroling pigeons in home-made wine.

cassette (kəˈsɛt, ‖ka-). [Fr., dim. of *casse* or *caisse* (cf. CASE), ad. It. *cassetta*.] **1. a.** A casket.

1793 SOUTHEY *Life & Corr.* (1849) I. 196 In very bad weather, take out my casette and write to you. **1807** —— *Espriella's Lett.* (1814) I. 83 One purchase I ventured to make, that of a travelling caissette. **1881** *Contemp. Rev.* June 926 The robbery of Baroness Von Meyerdorff's Cassette.

b. *Photogr.* (See quot. 1875). Also, a light-proof (cylindrical) container for a spool of film; a container for an X-ray plate or film.

1875 tr. *Vogel's Chem. Light* v. 42 For the purpose of transporting the plate .. the photographer employs a little flat box called the cassette. **1934** ST. JOHN & ISENBURGER *Industr. Radiogr.* xi. 81 To secure the proper contact it is customary in medical practice to mount two intensifying screens permanently in a metal 'cassette'. This consists of a cast-aluminium frame to which is attached a sheet of Bakelite or aluminium, forming a window or front transparent to x-rays. **1934** WEBSTER, *Cassette*, a film or plate holder, esp. one for the intensifying screen in X-ray photography. **1940** SOWERBY *Dict. Photogr.* (ed. 15) 111 *Cassette*, container in which 35-mm. film, which has no backing paper, is put up for daylight loading into the camera... The name 'cassette' is also applied to special containers designed for X-ray duplitised film technique... They ensure even pressure over the whole area of the film when intensifying screens are used. **1962** A. GÜNTHER *Microphotogr.* 18 A copying cassette taking 10 metres (30 ft.) or 30 metres (100 ft.) of 35 mm. film. **1964** 'E. PETERS' *Flight of Witch* iii. 44 Miles Mallindine and Dominic Felse were devotedly disentangling finished cassettes from cameras, and securing them in their little yellow bags ready for the post. **1970** *Amat. Photogr.* 11 Mar. 61/3 This is another 'first' for 9·5 mm, the gauge which first introduced the amateur to the joys of cassette-loading cameras and projectors.

c. *Ceramics.* = SAGGAR *sb.* 1.

1909 in WEBSTER.

d. A closed container of magnetic tape with both supply and take-up spools, so designed that it needs merely to be inserted into a suitable tape recorder, computer, or video recorder to be ready for use. Cf. *videocassette* s.v. VIDEO-.

1960 *Tape Recording & Hi-Fi Yearbk. 1959–60* 5 One of the new decks .. is the first British product designed to operate with cassettes (or magazines), with the tape enclosed so that there is no need to thread it in front of the magnetic heads on the deck, nor to anchor it in the spools. **1967** J. GARDNER *Madrigal* viii. 199 Mostyn had his briefcase open and a cassette tape-recorder ready to run. **1969** *Tape Recording Yearbk.* (ed. 9) 6 Insertion of a cassette automatically brings the tape transport system into operation. **1970** O. DOPPING *Computers & Data Processing* iii. 64 The inscribers provided by IBM .. record on special tape in cassettes. The cassettes are read into the computer by means of a special tape reader. **1983** D. H. SANDARS *Computers Today* vi. 159 Magnetic tape cassettes are used in microcomputers and data entry stations. **1984** *Which Micro?* Dec. 1 (Advt.), Cassettes are just one form of program storage and playback.

2. Special Comb.: **cassette player** = *tape player* s.v. TAPE *sb.*[1] 4; **cassette recorder**, a tape recorder designed to accept cassettes.

[**1967** *Punch* 23 Aug. 261/1 You know there's no telly in those rooms? Just radio and a cassette tape-player.] **1968** *Audio* May 25/3 Four-track and 8-track cartridge units do not offer recording facilities in a compact package yet, so they take a back seat to *cassette players in this respect. **1984** A. DESAI *In Custody* vi. 100 Perhaps your department will buy a cassette player one day. **1968** *Mod. Photogr.* Mar. 52/3,I have unhesitatingly recommended the Philips *cassette recorders to many friends. **1975** *Language for Life* (Dept. Educ. & Sci.) xxii. 316 Many schools will have purchased their spool recorders before cassette recorders were fully developed. **1984** *Choosing & using Your Home Computer* 11/1 You will also require a means of saving programs for future use. A cassette recorder or disk system are typical methods.

cassey. Pavement: see CAUSEY.

c **1711** BLACKWELL in Burton *Hist. Scot.* II. 42, I shall be free of the cassey stones of London.

†**casshe.** *Obs.* Also caxes. [See KEX.] The wild chervil, *Anthriscus sylvestris*; also vaguely applied to other Umbelliferous plants.

1548 TURNER *Names of Herbes* 54 *Myrrhis*, is called in Cambrygeshyre casshes, in other places mockecheruel. **1578** LYTE *Dodoens* v. liii. 616 Of Myrrhis Casshes or Caxes. This herbe is called .. in Englishe, as Turner sayth, Casshes, or Caxes, bycause Spinsters use the stemmes .. for quilles and Caxes, to winde yarne upon. **1640** PARKINSON *Theatr. Bot.* (Br. & Holl.), Caxes or Kicsies is hemlock.

casshe, obs. form of CACHE.

cassia[1] (ˈkæsɪə). Also (4 chasee), 4–7 casia. [a. L. *casia* (*cassia*), a. Gr. κασία, ad. Heb. *q'tsīʻāh* 'a bark resembling cinnamon, but less aromatic, so called from being stripped off (f. *qātsaʻ* to cut off, strip off bark)', Gesenius. Wyclif's word points to an OF. form with *ch.*]

1. An inferior kind of cinnamon, esp. the bark obtained from *Cinnamomum Cassia*; thicker, coarser, less delicate in flavour, and cheaper than the true cinnamon. More fully ***cassia-bark***.

c **1000** *Ags. Ps.* xliv. 10 [xlv. 8] Myrre, and gutta, and cassia dropiað of þinum claðum. **1382** WYCLIF *Ex.* xxx. 24 Tak to thee swete smellynge thingis .. of chasee [**1388** casia] fyve hundryd sicles. **1398** TREVISA *Barth. De P.R.* XVII. xxviii. (1495) 621 Though men vse to wryte and to sowne Cassia wyth dowble S yet it sholde be wryten and sowned wyth oo syngle S.—Casia and not Cassia. **1553** EDEN *Treat. New Ind.* (Arb.) 15 Spyces .. as ginger, pepper, mirabolanes, Cardamome, Cassia. **1611** BIBLE *Ps.* xlv. 8 All thy garments smell of myrrhe, and aloes, and cassia. **1626** BACON *Sylva* §620 Cassia, which is now the substitute of Cinnamon. **1693** SIR T. BLOUNT *Nat. Hist.* 41 You may call the thicker Bark Cassia, and the thinner Cinnamon. **1871** tr. *Schellen's Spectr. Anal.* §41. 162 The spectrum .. obtained from oil of cassia.

b. Also distinguished from 4, as ***cassia lignea***.

1398 TREVISA *Barth. De P.R.* XVII. xxvii. (1495) 620 That one manere Cassia is callyd Cassia fistula and the other Cassia lignea .. Cassia lignea is the rynde of a lytyll tree. **1705** *Lond. Gaz.* No. 4146/4 Fine Cinnamon 12 Bales, Ordinary Cinnamon or Cassia Ligna 153 Bales. **1883** *Daily News* 11 Oct. 2/7 Of 1,600 boxes Cassia Lignea offered.

2. The tree itself, *Cinnamomum Cassia.*

1553 EDEN *Treat. New Ind.* (Arb.) 8 A great wood of Precious trees, some of Cinomome & Cassia. **1601** HOLLAND *Pliny* I. 373 Casia or Canell, a plant it is, which groweth neer to the plains from whence the Cinamon comes. **1832** *Veg. Subst. Food* 347 Cassia .. is a native of .. the south of Asia .. The bark and buds are known in commerce as cassia lignea and cassia buds.

3. *poet.* A fragrant shrub or plant. This is partly a rhetorical use of the word from the Bible (*Ps.* xlv. 8), partly a reference to the *casia* of Vergil and Ovid, explained by Lewis and Short as 'a fragrant, shrub-like plant, mezereon', thought by some to be *Osyris alba* Linn., by Prof. Daubeny to be *Daphne Gnidium*.

1594 GREENE *Look. Glasse* (1861) 135 This offering of .. myrrh and cassia, freely I do yield. **1616** BULLOKAR, s.v. *Casia*, Poets understand often by it some sweet-smelling herbe. **1667** MILTON *P.L.* v. 293 Through Groves of Myrrhe, And flouring Odours, Cassia, Nard, and Balme, A Wilderness of sweets. **1697** DRYDEN *Virg. Georg.* IV. 430 Beneath his Body, broken Boughs and Thyme, And pleasing Casia just renew'd in prime. *a* **1821** KEATS *Epist.* 271 And intertwined the cassia's arms unite, With its own drooping buds.

4. *Bot.* A genus of trees, shrubs, or herbs (N.O. *Leguminosæ*) distributed in numerous species over the warmer regions of the earth. The leaflets of several species constitute what are known in medicine as *Senna leaves*. The name ***cassia fistula*** was given already in the Middle Ages, to one species, the Pudding Pipe tree, a native of India, but cultivated in Northern Africa, the West Indies, etc., which produces the ***cassia pods*** containing a pulp used as a laxative. Thence botanists have extended the name to the genus.

1398 TREVISA *Barth. De P.R.* XVII. xxviii. (1495) 621 Cassia fistula is the fruyte of a certen tree that beryth longe sede .. the mery within is blacke and moyst and swete and is medlyd wyth certen whyte greynes. **1585** LLOYD *Treas. Health* H v, Lentyl, roses, Licorise & a lytle of Cassia-fistula. **1688** R. HOLME *Armoury* II. 97/1 Cassia .. the Flowers are yellow, many growing together on a long stalk. **1703** *Lond. Gaz.* No. 3940/3 Their Cargo's, consisting of .. Lignum Vitæ, Molosses, Cashia Fistula, Shruff, etc. **1789** W. BUCHAN *Dom. Med.* (1790) 545 Some manna and pulp of cassia may be dissolved in boiling water. **1866** LIVINGSTONE *Jrnl.* ix. I. 235 Cassias and another tree .. are now in flower.

b. Any medicinal product obtained from this.

1543 TRAHERON *Vigo's Chirurg.* IX. 256 Purge the norice with cassia or manna. **1671** SALMON *Syn. Med.* III. lxxxiii. 726 Gently purge with Cassia mixed with turpentine. **1727–51** CHAMBERS *Cycl.* s.v., Cassia of the islands .. is sent from the Antilles; where it is produced in such abundance, that the vessels, in their home voyages, use it as ballast. **1796** STEDMAN *Surinam* II. xxv. 225 The cassia, a shining hard yellow seed inclosed in a woody shell near sixteen inches long .. with a black soft pulp as sweet as honey: this is considered as a very safe laxative.

5. *attrib.* and *Comb.*, as **cassia-bark, lignea** (see above, 1); **cassia fistula** (see 4); **cassia-buds**, the unexpanded buds of several species of cinnamon, esp. *Cinnamomum aromaticum*, used like cinnamon or cloves; **cassia-oil**, common oil of cinnamon; **cassia-pods, -pulp**, the fruit of *Cassia fistula* (see 4); **cassia-stick tree**, a name of *C. fistula*; **cassia-tree** (see 2).

1851–9 HOOKER in *Manual Sc. Enq.* 426 An inferior kind of *Cassia Buds known as Lovengoopor is found at Madras. **1756** P. BROWNE *Jamaica* 222 The *Cassia-stick Tree .. The pulp that surrounds the seeds .. is an easy gentle laxative. **1779** FORREST *Voy. N. Guinea* 266 On the hills we saw a

great many *cassia trees. **1811** A. T. THOMSON *Lond. Disp.* (1818) 225 The *cassia tree is a native of Malabar, Ceylon, Sumatra, and Java.

†**cassia**[2]. *Obs.* Also cashee. (See quots.)

1692 LUTTRELL *Brief Rel.* (1857) II. 572 Mr. Wightman.. has cast 2 cassia brass guns of 7 foot long, to throw bombs of 10 inches diameter. *Ibid.* III. 28 A tryall of some Cassia guns to shoot granadoes.. before his majestie in Hyde park. *Ibid.* III. 93, 6 brass cashee pieces.. to shoot granado's thro' the side of a ship, then breaks and setts fire to the same.

cassideous (kæˈsɪdiːəs), *a. Bot.* [f. L. *cassidem* helmet + -EOUS.] Helmet-shaped, helmet-like.

1835 LINDLEY *Introd. Bot.* (1848) I. 335 If the corolla is very irregular with one petal very large and helmet-shaped it is sometimes called cassideous. **1880** GRAY *Bot. Text-bk.*

cassidiform (kæˈsɪdɪfɔːm), *a.* [on L. type *cassidiform-is*: see prec.] Helmet-shaped.

1866 *Intell. Observ.* 134 The large cassidiform Thymalus.

†**cassidoine, -done, -dony**[1]. *Obs.* Forms: α. 4 cassidoin, casydoyn, 7 cassidoin(e; β. 5 cassedon(ne, 5–6 cassidon, 6 cassaydown, cassa-, cassidone, -en; γ. 7 cassidonie, 8 cassidony; δ. 6 casyldon, cassilden. [a. OF. *cassidoine*, a semi-popular form of *calcidoine*, *calcedoine*, ad. L. *chalcedōnius* (*lapis*) a stone of Chalcedon: see CHALCEDONY.] = CHALCEDONY.

a **1300** *Floriz & Bl.* 286 Suþþe riche cassidoines, And Jacinctes and topaces. *c* **1325** *E.E. Allit. P.* B. 1471 Casydoynes, & crysolytes, & clere rubies. **1488** *Inv. Jas. III*, in Tytler *Hist. Scot.* (1864) II. 392 A collar of cassedonis. **1500** *Inv.* in *Ann. Reg.* (1768) 135 A pair of beads ten stones, cassidens. **1503** *Will of Both* (Somerset Ho.), A peyre of bedes of Casyldon. *c* **1530** in Gutch *Coll. Cur.* II. 297 A garnysshing for a Salte for a Cassadone. **1534** in *Eng. Ch. Furniture* (1866) 195 Item x bedes of lambre & ij cassildens with a stryng of silk. **1548** *Will of Dame M. Kingston* (Somerset Ho.), A paire of beades of Cassaydown. **1601** HOLLAND *Pliny* II. 454 We digged into the same earth for Cassidonie and Crystall. *Ibid.* 605 In these crystals as well as in Cassidoins. **1611** COTGR., *Cassidoine*, a cassidonie; a base, and brittle stone, of small value, though it shine like fire. **1753** CHAMBERS *Cycl. Supp.*, *Cassidony*, a name given by the Italians and Germans to a sort of beads made of the yellow and red chalcedony.

attrib. **1601** HOLLAND *Pliny* II. 603 These rich Cassidoine vessels [called in Latine Murrhina] from out of the Leuant.

cassidony[2] (ˈkæsɪdənɪ). *Bot.* [Of uncertain etymology: suggestions are that it is the same word as prec., or of the same derivation.

(Skinner's guess that it might be a corruption of *Stœchas sidonius* labours under the fatal objection that no such name is known.)]

1. The plant *Lavandula Stœchas*, French lavender.

1578 LYTE *Dodoens* II. lxxxvii. 266 It is called.. in English French Lauender, Cassidonie, and of some Lauender gentle. **1597** GERARD *Herbal* (1633) 586 (L.) In English.. Cassidonie; and some simple people, imitating the same name do call it 'Cast me down'. **1629** PARKINSON *Kitchen Gard.* I. vii. 471 Cassidonie is a small kinde of Lauender, but differing both in forme & qualitie. **1713** J. PETIVER in *Phil. Trans.* XXVIII. 43 Cassidony or French Lavander. **1753** in CHAMBERS *Cycl. Supp.* App., and in mod. Dicts.

2. '***Mountain*** or ***Golden Cassidony***: names used for the Gnaphalium of authors', Chambers *Cycl. Supp.* App. (*Gnaphalium Stœchas* Treas. Bot.)

cassie[1], **-y** (ˈkæsɪ). *dial.* Also cazzie, cosie. [= Icel. '*kass.* mod. *kassi* a case, large box, creel'.] A kind of basket made of straw, used in Orkney and Caithness.

1693 WALLACE *Orkney* 34 A sort of Vessel made of Straw, called Cassies, in which they keep and transport their Corn. **1793** *Statist. Acc. Scot.* VII. 524 Straw cazzies which were used as sacks for carrying Victual. *Ibid.* X. 23 (Jam.) Straw creels called cassies, made very compactly of long oat straw. **1880** *Times* 30 Sept., A peculiar basket made of plaited straw and called a 'cassy'. The 'cassy' is strapped to the shoulders in such a way as to leave the hands free.

cassie[2] (ˈkæsiː). = CASSE PAPER; also see quots.

1688 [see CASSE PAPER]. **1770** LUCKOMBE *Concise Hist. Printing* 496 *Cassie paper*, broken paper. **1889** BARRÈRE & LELAND *Dict. Slang* I. 218/2 *Cassie* (printers), wrinkled, or outside sheets of paper. **1940** *Chambers's Techn. Dict.* 140/2 *Cassie*, the damaged tops and bottoms of a ream of paper.

cassie[3] (ˈkæsiː). *U.S.* [Fr., ad. Pr. *cacio* acacia.] A leguminous shrub with yellow flowers, *Acacia farnesiana*.

1876 C. E. HOBBS *Bot. Hand-bk.* 20 Cassie, the flowers yield a perfume, Acacia Farnesiana. **1905** *Yng. Woman* Apr. 230/1 Mignonette, and cassie. **1952** A. G. L. HELLYER *Sanders' Encycl. Gardening* (ed. 22) 3 *A[cacia]*.. *Farnesiana*, 'Popinac', 'Cassie'.. Tropics.

cassier(e, cassir, obs. ff. CASHIER *v.*

cassilden: see CASSIDOINE.

cassimere (ˈkæsɪmɪə(r)). Also 8 **kassimere**, 9 **casimire**. [in F. *casimir* ('mot récent'), Sp. *casimiro*, Ger. *kasimir*. Another form of CASHMERE; the country was called *Keshimur* by Marco Polo, *Queximir* by Barros, *Kachemire* by Bernier, *Cassimer* by Herbert 1665.]

A thin fine twilled woollen cloth used for men's clothes. Cf. KERSEYMERE.

[**1704** DRYDEN *Aurungz.* III. i. (Y.) The Queen of Cassimere. **1784** in Seton-Karr *Sel. Calcutta Gaz.* I. 47 (Y.) For sale—superfine cambrics and edgings.. scarlet and blue Kassimeres. **1814** J. FORBES *Orient. Mem.* III. 177 (Y.) The shawls of Cassimer and the silks of Iran.]

1774 *Westm. Mag.* II. 259 The favourite Riding-Dress is a light-coloured Cassimere, lined with different coloured silks. **1807–8** W. IRVING *Salmag.* (1826) 77 His white cassimere small clothes. **1822** BYRON *Juan* IX. xliii, Brilliant breeches.. Of yellow casimire. **1842** BISCHOFF *Woollen Manuf.* II. 421 Coatings, cassimeres, hosiery. **1843** CARLYLE *Past & Pres.* (1858) 203 Of fustian, of cassimere, of Scotch-plaid.

cassin, obs. Sc. f. CASTEN *pa. pple.* of CAST *v.*

‖**cassine.** *Obs.* [F. *cassine* (16th c. in Littré), repr. late L. *cassīna* hut, farm-house (dim. of *cassa*, *casa* cottage); cf. It. *casino*.]

'In the military language, a farm-house, where a number of soldiers have posted themselves, in order to make a stand against the approaches of an enemy' (Chambers *Cycl. Supp.* 1753).

1708 KERSEY, *Cassine*, a Country Farm-House in Italy, such as are occasionally fortify'd to maintain a particular Post, etc. **1720** *Lond. Gaz.* No. 5915/1 The Moors entring the Cassine set up their Colours there.. a Cassine before a Half-Moon that covered our Centre.

Cassinese (kæsɪˈniːz), *a.* and *sb.* Also **Casinese**. [a. It. *Cassinese*, f. Monte *Cassino*, on which the earliest Benedictine monastery was founded *c* 529: see -ESE.] **A.** *adj.* Of or pertaining to the Benedictine monks of Monte Cassino, or to a congregation of Benedictine abbeys. **B.** *sb.* A monk of the monastery of Monte Cassino, or of the Cassinese congregation; an inhabitant of the town of Cassino below Monte Cassino.

[*c* **1643** in *Cath. Rec. Soc. Publ.* (1933) XXXIII. 82 Some Bennedictine fathers, who were of the Italian Congregation, otherwise called the Cassine or the Congregation of S. Justina.] **1878** J. L. PATTERSON *Maguire's Pius the Ninth* xviii. 357 Supposing.. the libraries were not open to the public, what right had the State to confiscate them... The Cassinese, the Roman College, and the Angelica libraries.. have been massed together. **1881** *Weldon's Chronol. Notes* Pref. p. x, The reigning Pope Julius II gave the name of the Cassinese Congregation to the whole body of the reformed Benedictines of Italy. *Ibid.* Index p. iv, Cassinese Monks on English Mission. **1893** ADDIS & ARNOLD *Cath. Dict.* 82/2 There is a monastery at Ramsgate belonging to the Cassinese branch of the order. **1910** M. HAILE *Life R. Pole* 127 The Benedictines of St. Giustina at Padua—who were beginning to call themselves Casinese to denote their union with Monte Casino. **1954** *Biogr. Studies* II. 225 Preston was the Mission Superior of the Cassinese in England. **1957** F. MAJDALANY *Cassino* I. viii. 53 The few thousand Cassinese who, citizens of Cassino, had stubbornly insisted on their right to stay there. *Ibid.* III. iii. 117 The bitterness and bewilderment of the Cassinese monks.

cassinette (kæsɪˈnɛt). Also **casinet**. [? A factitious name suggested by *cassimere*.] A light mixed cloth, a modification of cassimere, with the warp of cotton, and the weft of very fine wool, or wool and silk.

1846 in WORCESTER. **1863** DICEY *Federal St.* I. 255 Casinet pants, and yellow gauntlet gloves. **1881** *Echo* 2 Feb. 1/5 Scarlet woollen blankets pay 51 per cent. on their value.. cassinetts, 135 per cent.

cassing: see CASS *v.*

Cassinian (kæˈsɪnɪən), *a.* [f. proper name *Cassini* + -IAN.] Of or pertaining to G. D. Cassini (1625–1712), or his descendants, a celebrated family of French astronomers, or to their scientific researches. ***Cassinian oval***: = CASSINOID.

1726 tr. *Gregory's Astron.* I. 394 This Cassinian Hypothesis.. has this Physical Disadvantage. **1886** *Academy* 10 July 29/2 The curve of sines, the cassinian oval, the catenary, and such like curves. **1882** MINCHIN *Unipl. Kinemat.* 204 One of the Cassinian ellipses.

cassinite. *Min.* A variety of orthoclase containing barium.

1875 *Min. of Pa.* 93 The more laminate.. bluish green feldspar, the cassinite, is found at Blue Hill, Delaware Co. (Pa.)

cassino (kəˈsiːnəʊ). Also **casino**. [Another form of CASINO.] A game at cards in which the ten of diamonds, called ***great cassino*** (or ***great cass***) counts two points, and the two of spades, called ***little cassino*** (or ***little cass***) counts one; eleven points constituting the game. Also *attrib.*, as ***cassino table***.

1792 W. ROBERTS *Looker-on* (1794) I. 250 A large party at Faro and Cassino was made.. at a great house in Piccadilly. **1800** JANE AUSTEN *Lett.* (1884) I. 245 A whist and a casino table. **1811** —— *Sense & Sens.* II. i. 122 Lady Middleton proposed a rubber of Cassino to the others. **1811** E. NARES *Thinks I to myself* (1816) II. 132 (D.) Two whist, cassino, or quadrille tables will dispose of four couple.. Great cass, little cass, and the spades, Ma'am.

cassinoid (ˈkæsɪnɔɪd). *Geom.* [a. F. *cassinoide*: see CASSINIAN and -OID.] A curve which Cassini wished to substitute for the ellipse, in explanation of the planetary movements: an oval having two foci, such that the product of the focal radii of any point on the curve is constant (instead of their sum being constant as in the ellipse).

cassioberry (ˈkæsɪəʊˌbɛrɪ). The fruit of *Viburnum lævigatum*, the ***cassioberry-bush***.

1753 CHAMBERS *Cycl. Supp.* App., *Cassioberry-tree*, in botany, the name of a genus of plants called by Linnæus *Cassine.* **1864** in WEBSTER. **1884** in MILLER *Plant-n.*

Cassio'peian, *a.* Of Cassiopeia, one of the northern constellations. (In this constellation a brilliant new star appeared in 1572, which subsequently disappeared again.)

c **1630** DRUMM. OF HAWTH. *Poems* Wks. (1711) 55 And if perhaps no Cassiopeian spark (Which in the north did thy first rising mark) Shine o're thy hearse.

cassiopeium (ˌkæsɪəˈpiːəm). [mod.L. (C. A. von Welsbach in *Sitzungsberichte d. Akad. d. Wissenschaften Wien, Math.-naturw. Klasse*, sect. 2b, CXVI. 1435), f. *Cassiopeia* (see CASSIOPEIAN *a.*).] An alternative name (now *disused*) for a rare-earth element now known as lutetium or lutecium.

1908 *Chem. Abstr.* IV. 1393 Following the publication of the first article by the author [*sc.* G. Urbain] on this subject, Auer von Welsbach.. described two substances obtained from ytterbium... He gave them the names aldebaranium and cassiopeium... The author claims priority in this work. **1966** *McGraw-Hill Encycl. Sci. & Technol.* VII. 623 C. F. Auer von Welsbach.. named the element cassiopeium, but lutetium is the accepted form at present.

cassique, obs. form of CACIQUE. Also, a name of the Mocking Bird of Guiana.

1825 WATERTON *Wand. S. Amer.* II. (1887) 167 The Cassique is gregarious.. he goes by no other name than that of mocking-bird amongst the colonists. **1826** SYD. SMITH Wks. (1859) II. 78 The cassique, in size, is larger than the starling; he courts the society of man.

cassiri (kæˈsɪərɪ). Also **casserie, cassiree, kasiri**. [a. Carib *cassirí*: see CASSAREEP.] An intoxicating liquor made in Guyana from fermented sweet potatoes.

1796 STEDMAN *Surinam* I. 392 Another drink called *cassiree* is also much used by these Indians. **1851** W. H. BRETT *Indian Missions Guiana* 103 There is another drink made in a more cleanly manner from potatoes, called Kasiri. **1854** H. G. DALTON *Hist. Brit. Guiana* I. 82 They have also another intoxicating beverage, called cassiri. **1879** BODDAM-WHETHAM *Roraima* 248 The favourite beverage among the inhabitants was a disagreeable-looking compound called cassiree. **1904** W. H. HUDSON *Green Mansions* i. 26 More cups of casserie followed this outburst. **1934** E. WAUGH *Handful of Dust* v. 272 Cassiri.. the local drink made of fermented cassava.

cassis (kæˈsiːs). [Fr., black currant; black-currant liquor, app. f. L. *cassia* (see CASSIA[1]).] A syrupy liquor made from black currants and used chiefly to flavour vermouth, spirits, etc. Hence ***vermouth cassis***.

[**1877** E. S. DALLAS *Kettner's Bk. Table* 106 *Cassis*, the French name for black currants and for the syrup made from them. The cassis of Dijon has a great reputation.. as a cooling drink.] **1907** *Yesterday's Shopping* (1969) 100/2 Cassis, made from Black Currants grown in Burgundy. **1911** M. BEERBOHM *Z. Dobson* xxiv. 346 Vermouths secs, vermouths cassis. **1913** C. MACKENZIE *Sinister St.* I. II. x. 312 We always play billiards in the evening, and drink cassis. **1948** A. WAUGH *Unclouded Summer* iii. 25 A *vermouth cassis* and a cigarette. **1954** W. FAULKNER *Fable* (1955) 47 The bottle of wine.. and one of *cassis.*

cassit: see CHASED.

cassiterite (kəˈsɪtəraɪt). *Min.* [f. Gr. κασσίτερος tin + -ITE.] Native stannic dioxide, the most common ore of tin, occurring in various forms, as tin stone, wood tin, toad's-eye tin, stream tin.

1858 SHEPARD *Min.* 264 Wood-tin of the Cornish miners is only a variety of cassiterite. **1873** WATTS *Fownes' Chem.* 445 Dioxide, or Stannic Oxide, occurs native as tin-stone or cassiterite. **1879** RUTLEY *Stud. Rocks* x. 148.

caˌssitero'tantalite. *Min.* [f. as prec. + TANTALITE.] A variety of tantalite in which part of the tantalic acid is replaced by stannic acid.

1850 DANA *Min.* 403 The tantalite from Finbo.. (cassitero-tantalite) contains much oxide of tin.

Cassius (ˈkæsɪəs). Name of a German physician of 17th c.; whence ***purple of Cassius***, a splendid purple pigment: see quot.

c **1865** J. WYLDE in *Circ. Sc.* I. 373/2 The purple powder, produced by precipitating a solution of chloride of gold by means of the chloride of tin, is employed for the purpose of colouring China ware. It is termed in the arts, the 'purple powder of Cassius'. **1869** ROSCOE *Elem. Chem.* 252 A splendid purple colour called purple of cassius.

cassock (ˈkæsək), *sb.* Forms: α. 6–7 cassacke, 7 cassack, (cass-, casaque); β. 6 cassoke, cassocke, (8–9 cassoc), 6– cassock. [a. F. *casaque* 'a cassocke, mandilion, long coat', 16th c. in Littré, (corresp. to Sp. and Pg. *casaca* 'a souldiers cassocke, a frock, a horsemans coat', Minsheu, It. *casacca* 'a frocke, a horse-mans cote, a long cote; also a habitation or dwelling' Florio). The military use is the original; the

ecclesiastical use appears to have arisen in English, in the 17th century.

If the It. is the original, and *casacca* 'cassock' the same word as *casacca* ' dwelling' (see above), then it is a deriv. of *casa* house (as if 'a garment that covers like a house': cf. CASULE, CHASUBLE); but the identification is doubtful. The *Dict. de Trevoux* suggests that *casaque* is a variant of *Cosaque* Cossack, from whom the military cassock might take its name. Lagarde (*Götting. Gelehrte Anzeiger*, 15 Apr. 1887, 238) maintains that F. *casaque* is a back-formation from *casaquin* (by incorrectly viewing the latter as a dimin. form), and that *casaquin*, It. *casacchino*, was a corruption of Arab. *kazāyand*, ad. Pers. *kazhāyand*, a padded jerkin, or acton, f. *kazh* = *kaj* raw silk, silk floss + *āyand* stuffed. The word *kasagân* actually occurs in MHG. as 'riding-cloak' ('reitrock' Schade), and *gasygan* in OF. as padded jerkin or vest' (Godef.), but the relation of these to *casaquin* and *casaque* has yet to be settled.]

†**1.** A cloak or long coat worn by some soldiers in 16–17th c.; also that of a horseman or rider in the 17th c. ('A name given to the cloaks worn by musketeers and gardes du corps', Littré.) *Obs.*

1574 *Lanc. Lieutenancy* II. (1859) 137 Also a Cassocke of the same motley. **1580** BARET *Alv.* C 164 A cassocke: also a souldiours cloke, *sagum.* **1598** B. JONSON *Ev. Man in Hum.* II. v, He will neuer come within.. the sight of a cassock, or a musket-rest againe. [Cf. F. *rendre le casaque.*] **1601** SHAKS. *All's Well* IV. iii. 191. **1609** TOURNEUR *Fun. Poeme* Wks. 1878 I. 199 Brave Vere was by his scarlet cassock known. **1638** SHIRLEY *Mart. Soldier* II. i in Bullen *O. Pl.* I. 190 A Soldado Cassacke of Scarlet. **1667** E. CHAMBERLAYNE *St. Gt. Brit.* I. III. iv. (1743) 173 Upon a Cloak, Coat, or Riding Cassock. **1699** LUDLOW *Mem.* (1771) 384 Monk's army was.. thought to deserve the fool's coat rather than the soldier's casaque. [**1826** SCOTT *Woodst.* III. xi. 318 The coarse frieze-cassock of the private soldier.]

†**2.** A kind of long loose coat or gown. (Fairholt.) Originally applied to garments worn by both sexes.

a. as worn by women. (App. not after 1600.)

c **1550** C. BARNSLEY *Pride & Abuse of Women* 119 A caped cassock much like a players gown. *a* **1553** UDALL *Royster D.* (Arb.) 35 We shall go in our frenche hoodes euery day, In our silke cassocks fresh and gay. **1589** PUTTENHAM *Eng. Poesie* (Arb.) 290 A ridiculous thing to see a Lady in her milke-house with a veluet gowne, and at a bridall in her cassock of mockado. **1590** GREENE *Poems* (1600) 112 Her taffata cassock might you see Tuckèd up aboue her knee.

b. as worn by men: mentioned as worn by rustics, shepherds, sailors; also by usurers, poor scholars, etc.

1590 GREENE *Neuer too late* (1600) 93 Corydon in his gray cassocke and Manalcas.. in his sheepheardes cloake. **1598** BARNFIELD *Conscience & Covet.* 12 Clad in a Cassock, lyke a Vsurer. **1601** HOLLAND *Pliny* XXXIV. vi. II. 491 [The statue] of Romulus is without any coat or cassocke at all [est sine tunica]. **1603** —— *Const. & Canons Eccl.* §74 Persons ecclesiastical may use any comely and scholar-like apparel, provided that it be not cut or pinkt; and that in publick they go not in their doublet and hose, without coats or cassocks. **1612** DEKKER *If not good Pl.* Wks. 1873 III. 276 Greater Schollers languish in beggery: And in thin thred-bare cassacks weare out their age. **1624** CAPT. SMITH *Virginia* VI. 231 Two or three old Iron things.. bound vp in a Sailers canuase Cassocke. **1628** WITHER *Brit. Rememb.* IV. 1765 Those many silken-Doctors, who did here In shining satten Cassocks late appeare. [**1825** SCOTT *Talism.* xxiii, The cassock of chamois which he wore under his armour.]

3. A garment worn by clergymen.

a. A long close-fitting frock or tunic worn by Anglican clergymen, originally along with and under the gown; but, in recent times, also under the shortened surplice, and sometimes by 'High-Church' clergymen, like the *soutane* of Roman Catholic priests, apart from these vestments, as a kind of ecclesiastical garb. Also, sometimes worn by vergers, choristers, and others engaged in ecclesiastical functions. See quots.

In this sense, which appears to date from the Restoration, it seems to be the continuation of the scholar's cassock, in sense 2; it had probably some reference to the canon of 60 years before, requiring clergymen not to appear in public 'without coats or cassocks' (see sense 2).

1663 KILLIGREW *Parson's Wedding* (Fairh.) He was so poor and despicable, he could not avow his calling for want of a cassock. **1666** PEPYS *Diary* 27 Sept., I.. to speak for a cloak and cassock for my brother.. and I will have him in a canonical dress. **1708** SWIFT *Baucis & Phil.* 121 His waistcoat to a cassoc grew And both assum'd a sable hue. **1710–20** C. WHEATLEY *On Bk. Com. Prayer* (1720) 110 Made fit and close to the Body like a Cassock. **1727** DE FOE *Hist. Appar.* iii. (1840) 24 If the Devil should put on the gown and Cassock, or the black cloak, or the Coat and the Cord. **1728** POPE *Dunc.* II. 326 Gave him the cassock, surcingle, and vest. **1755** JOHNSON, *Cassock*, a close garment; now, generally, that which clergymen wear under their gowns. **1807** CRABBE *Par. Reg.* III. 862 He knew no better than his cassock which. **1849** ROCK *Ch. of Fathers* II. vi. §9 The old English cassock differed in its shape very little, if anything, from the same kind of robe still worn by the Catholic priesthood. **1854** HOOK *Church Direct.*, *Cassock*.. the under dress of all orders of the clergy: it resembles a long coat, with a single upright collar. **1866** *Direct. Angl.* (ed. 3) 352 *Cassock*, the garment worn by ecclesiastics under their official vestments: usually black, and for Bishops purple. **1866** C. WALKER *Ritual, Reason Why* 35 The Cassock is a long coat buttoning over the breast, and reaching to the feet. It is confined at the waist by a broad sash called the cincture. The collar is made to fasten right round the throat. **1870** DISRAELI *Lothair* v. 13 One or two curates in cassocks.

b. Used to render F. *soutane*, L. *subtaneum*, the 'frock' of a Roman Catholic ecclesiastic.

1796 H. HUNTER tr. *St. Pierre's Stud. Nat.* (1799) III. 136 A tall man dressed in a blue cassock.. an ecclesiastical missionary of the island. **1824** HEBER *Jrnl.* (1828) I. iii. 76 A tall stout ecclesiastic, with.. a long black cassoc. **1859** JEPHSON *Brittany* vi. 69 A short stout man.. dressed in cassock, bands, and cocked hat.

c. A short, light, double-breasted coat or jacket, usually of black silk, varying in length, but generally reaching down to the thighs, worn under the Geneva gown by presbyterian and other ministers.

a **1888** *Scotch Newspaper.* He has been presented by the ladies of his congregation with a pulpit gown and cassock.

4. a. As a mark of the clerical office, esp. that of a clergyman of the Church of England.

1687 DRYDEN *Hind & P.* III. 232 And quit the cassock for the canting coat. **1769** ROBERTSON *Chas. V*, VI. VI. 124 During the war, he laid aside the cassoc. **1848** MACAULAY *Hist. Eng.* II. 217 The scarf and cassock could hardly appear there without calling forth sneers.

b. A wearer of a cassock; *esp.* a clergyman.

1628 BP. EARLE *Microcosm.* (Fairholt) A vulgar-spirited man.. one that thinks the gravest cassock the best scholar. **1649** G. DANIEL *Trinarch., Rich. II*, cccxliii, But the Gray Cassock makes a double noyse. **1859** THACKERAY *Virgin.* v, [He] had a suspicion of all cassocks, and said he would never have any controversy with a clergyman but upon backgammon.

5. *attrib.*

1587 FLEMING *Cont. Holinshed* III. 317/1 Yeomen.. apparelled in cassocke coats, and venetian hose of crimson veluet.

'cassock, *v.* [f. prec. 3.] To dress in a cassock. Hence **cassocked** ('kæsəkt), *ppl. a.*

1780 COWPER *Progr. Err.* 111 A cassocked huntsman, and a fiddling priest. **1853** M. ARNOLD *Neckan* xii, A cassock'd priest rode by. **1883** *Ch. Times* 855/3 The occasion was taken advantage of to cassock and surplice the choir.

†**cassole.** *Obs. rare*$^{-1}$. [a. 16th c. F. *cassole* 'coffin, box', Cotgr., prob. ad. Prov. *cassolo*, dim. of *cassa* case. (Not the same as mod.F. *cassolle* 'little pan': see next.)] A box or case.

1590 A. M. tr. *Gabelhouer's Bk. Physicke* 343/2 We must applye thereon a freshe playster, and must sett the Legge in a Cassole, or case.. and let it rest therin.

cassolette (kæsəʊ'lɛt). Also 7 casolette, 7–9 cassolet. [a. F. *cassolette* dim. of *cassole*, *-olle*, 'little pan', dim. of *casse* 'pan.' Cat. *cassa*, It. *cazza*, fire pan (Florio). Cp. Sp. *cazo*, *cazuela*, *cazoleta*; med.L. *caza*, *cazia*, *cazola*, *cazeola*. See Diez, Littré, and Du Cange.]

1. A vessel in which perfumes are burned.

1657 TOMLINSON *Renou's Disp.* 213 Put in a brasen or silver pot which the Vulgar call a cassolet. **1726** *Dict. Rust.* (ed. 3) s.v. *Cassolet*, a small Vessel us'd in the Burning of Pastils or other odours. **1834** BECKFORD *Italy* II. 43 Silver braziers and cassolettes diffusing a very pleasant perfume. *a* **1847** MRS. SHERWOOD *Lady of Manor* IV. xxiii. 45 Cassolettes, which, being now lighted up, exhaled all the perfumes of the East.

2. A box for perfumes with a perforated cover to allow of their diffusion.

1851 SIR F. PALGRAVE *Norm. & Eng.*, Boudoir essences and cassolette perfumes. **1884** *Health Exhib. Catal.* 94/1 Aromatic Ozonized Pocket Cassolette.

3. A small casserole; a dish cooked in such a receptacle.

1813 L. E. UDE *French Cook* 418 Mind that the *cassolettes* are to be made quite cold before you take them out of the mould. **1898** MRS. ROUNDELL *Pract. Cookery Bk.* 195 Scoop out the insides and fill them with mince and sauce, after heating the Cassolettes in the oven. **1905** A. KENNEY-HERBERT *Common-sense Cookery* 177 Potato cassolettes. **1951** *Good Housek. Home Encycl.* 393/1 The cassolettes may be served as a hot hors d'œuvre, an entrée or an after-dinner savoury.

†**casson.** *Obs.* [a. 16th c. F. *casson*, now *caisson* chest: see CAISSON.] A chest.

1613 PURCHAS *Pilgr.* I. 607 Twelve Cassons or Chests.

casson, var. of CASING.

†**cassonade.** *Obs.* [a. F. *cassonade*, f. *casson* chest, case: cf. CASSONS.] Unrefined cane-sugar imported in boxes or casks; brown or moist sugar.

1657 TOMLINSON *Renou's Disp.* 224 Another kind of Sugar.. which the vulgar call Cassonade or Castonade. **1725** BRADLEY *Fam. Dict.* s.v. *Sugar*, The Cassonade is nothing but Muscovadoe that has been purify'd with the Whites of Eggs and Lime-Water. **1810** *Encycl. Brit.* (ed. 4) V. 239 *Cassonade*, in commerce, cask-sugar, or sugar put into casks or chests, after the first purification, but which has not yet been refined.

‖**cassone** (kas'sone). Pl. -ni (ni), -es. [It., augmentative of *cassa* chest.] A large Italian coffer, esp. one made to hold the trousseau of a bride, often elaborately carved and decorated. Also *attrib.*

1882 J. W. MOLLETT *Illustr. Dict. Art & Archæol.* 60 *Cassone*, an Italian chest, richly carved and gilt, and often decorated with paintings, which frequently held the *trousseau* of a bride. **1886** *Athenæum* 22 May 687/2 The first and second [pictures] are decorative panels from *cassoni*, and represent scenes at tournaments. **1904** *Studio* Sept. 303/2 The collecting of wedding-coffers, or 'cassones' as they are sometimes called. **1922** *19th Cent.* May 803 The fourteenth century round-backed chair and the *cassone* attributed to Ammannati, which are shown in the same room. **1932** *Times Lit. Suppl.* 21 Apr. 285/2 The cassone panels representing Satyrs hunting. **1949** E. POUND *Pisan Cantos* lxxvi. 47 And the gilded cassoni.

†**cassons, cassyns.** *Obs.* [perh. a. F. *casson* 'shapeless loaf of fine sugar' (Littré), f. *casson* case, chest: cf. CASSONADE] ? Sugar in some form.

[**1443** in Rogers *Agric. & Prices* 526/3 Cassons 6 lb. at /8.] **1469** *Ord. Dk. Clarence* in *Househ. Ord.* (1790) 103 Item, Cassyns 300 lb. at ii *d.*

cassoon (kə'su:n). [ad. It. *casone*, or OF. *casson* large chest, mod.F. *caisson.*] An occasional variant of CAISSON: **a.** an ammunition chest; **b.** *Arch.* a sunken panel. (= CAISSON 1 a, 3.)

1799 *Chron.* in *Ann. Reg.* 3/1 Twelve brass field pieces three pounders with their cassoons. **1850** LEITCH *Müller's Anc. Art* §53. 27 The ornamental forms of the cassoons (φατνώματα, lacunaria).

‖**cassoulet** (kasulɛ). [Fr. (19th c.), dim. of dial. *cassolo* tureen, stew-pan.] A stew-pan; hence, a ragout, orig. a regional speciality of Languedoc, consisting of meat (esp. duck, goose, or pork) and haricot beans.

[**1939** M. MOSSER *Good Maine Food* 93 The only satisfactory way to cook an old wild goose is to.. place the strips in a bean pot, cover them with a quart of pea beans and a pound of salt pork, and bake 8 hours in a slow oven. This dish, in the south of France, would be called a *cassoulet.*] **1940** G. WESCOTT *Pilgrim Hawk* 65 They always telephoned a certain small unsuccessful restaurant to prepare a supreme *cassoulet* which took two days. **1942** B. BREUER in *55 Short Stories from 'New Yorker'* (1949) 328 A casserole, the veritable French *cassoulet*, and inside.. squabs and tiny vegetables. **1959** *Times* 16 Feb. 11/3 *Cassoulet* is one of the great dishes of rural French cooking. **1963** N. FREELING *Because of Cats* xi. 168 Good lunch... Cassoulet. Beans with goose.

cassowary ('kæsəwəri). Forms: α. 7 casso-, cassaware, 9 cassowar; β. 7 cassawarway, -waraway, cassa-, cassiowary, 8 cassuary, (casuari), 7– cassowary. [a. Malay *kasuārī* or *kasavārī* (Yule). In F. *casoar*, It. *casuario*, mod.L. *casuārius.* The earliest Eng. form was app. through Du. or F.]

1. A genus of large cursorial birds, related to the Ostrich, inhabiting the islands in the Indian Archipelago as far as New Guinea. They stand about five feet high; the wings are of no use for flight, but are furnished with stiff featherless quills, like spines, which serve for combat or defence.

'Named *Emeu* by the early Portuguese navigators. It is the *Emeu* vulgo *Casoaris* (the latter appearing to be the Malay appellation) of Bontius.' *Penny Cycl.* XXIII. 142/2. (See EMU.)

1611 CORYAT *Crudities* Pref. Verses, Saint James his Ginney-hens the Cassawarway moreover.. (*Margin.* An East Indian bird at St. James in the keeping of Mr. Walker). **1630** J. TAYLOR (Water P.) *Gt. Eater Kent* 11 From the tit-mouse to the estrich or cassawaraway. **1656** MORE *Antid. Ath.* II. xi. (1712) 74 In the Cassoware or Emeu. **1690** LOCKE (J.), The relation between dam and chick, between the two cassiowaries in St. James's Park. **1729** *Dampier's Voy.* IV. I. 266 The Cassawaris is about the bigness of a large Virginia Turkey. **1772** *Weekly Mag.* 25 June 386/1 The casuari is black, and in size equal to an ostrich. **1774** GOLDSM. *Nat. Hist.* III. 39 The Cassowary is a bird which was first brought.. into Europe by the Dutch from Java. **1801** SOUTHEY *Thalaba* VII. xviii, Large as the hairy Cassowar was that o'ershadowing Bird. **1880** HAUGHTON *Phys. Geog.* vi. 263 Papua is the proper centre of the Cassowaries.

2. ***New Holland cassowary***: the EMU.

1842 *Penny Cycl.* XXIII. 142 British naturalists.. now apply the term Emeu to the New Holland Cassowary.

‖**cassu'munar.** *Med.* Also **casumunar, -muniar, casmunar.** [app. a corruption of some eastern name.] The tuberous root of an East Indian plant (apparently *Curcuma aromatica* Salisb., *C. Zedoaria* Roxb.); it is warm, bitter and aromatic, smells like ginger, and is used in hysterical, epileptic and paralytic affections. (Cf. ZEDOARY.)

1693 PECHEY (*title*) Some Observations made upon the Root Casmunar, brought from the East Indies. **1700** SLOANE in *Phil. Trans.* XXII. 580 A root.. made great use of .. in Epileptic, Convulsive and Head diseases.. called Cassumuniar. **1718** QUINCY *Compl. Disp.* 92 Casamunar is lately come into use. **1753** CHAMBERS *Cycl. Supp.* App., *Cassumniar*.. a root approaching to the nature of zeodary. **1885** DYMOCK *Veg. Mat. Med. of Ind.* 770 Identical with the Cassumunar described by Pereira.

cass-weed: see CASE-WEED.

cast (kɑ:st, -æ-), *sb.* [f. the vb.]

I. The act of casting or throwing (simply).

1. a. A throw of a missile, a bowl, or other object.

1382 WYCLIF *Numb.* xxxv. 17 If a stoon he throwe, and with the cast [**1388** strook] sleeth. *c* **1425** WYNTOUN *Cron.* VIII. xxxii. 140 The fyrst kast that it [the engyne] kest, bot ane, It hyt the towre a mery strak. **1565–78** COOPER *Thesaur.*, *Iactus*, a throwe.. or cast. **1609** C. BUTLER *Fem. Mon.* I. (1623) C ij, One or other spying him.. will haue a cast at him. **1756** *Connoisseur* No. 129 At bowls, if any one is near winning the game, he never fails, in the next cast, to mistake his bias. **1860** EMERSON *Cond. Life, Power* Wks.

(Bohn) II. 332 The opponent has the sun and wind, and, in every cast, the choice of weapon and mark. **1868** *Daily Tel.* 7 Sept., Counting a cast with the right hand and another with left as one throw.

b. Considered, as a performance, with reference to its quality. ***measuring cast***: a competitive throw at a mark in which the results are so close as to require measurement.

c **1400** *Sowdone Bab.* 2603 The shotte, the caste was so stronge Syr Bryer was slayn there. **1567** HARMAN *Caveat* 46 They coulde not agree vpon a caste. **1647** FULLER *Good Th. in Worse T.* (1841) 96 Is it a measuring cast whether it be lawful or no? **1655** —— *Ch. Hist.* VII. 407 Yet was their precedencie no measuring cast, but clear in the view of any unpartiall eye. **1676** WYCHERLEY *Pl.-Dealer* I. i. 4 My Brother and I were quarrelling about a Cast. **1816** SCOTT *Antiq.* (1879) II. 110 The disputed cast was a drawn one. *fig.* **1660** INGELO *Bentivolio & Urania* II. (1682) 20 It is a cast beyond Laughter to see..how proud they grow.

c. The distance which anything can be thrown.

1387 TREVISA *Higden* (1865) I. 215 Pilers as hiȝ as a stones cast. *c* **1400** MAUNDEV. viii. 92 A Stones cast fro that Chapelle, is another Chapelle. **1611** BIBLE *Luke* xxii. 41 He was withdrawen from them about a stones cast. **1671** *Phil. Trans.* VI. 2102 Sinking from cast to cast, (*i.e.* as high as a man can conveniently throw up the Ore with a shovel). **1870** BRYANT *Homer* II. XXIII. 344 He fell as far behind As a quoit's cast.

d. Manner or way of throwing (e.g. seed).

1677 PLOT *Nat. Hist. Oxfordsh.* 246 In Sowing they have their several methods, viz., the single Cast, the double Cast. **1707** J. MORTIMER *Husb.* (J.) Some..sow wheat or rye.. with a broad cast, some only with a single cast.

†**2.** The delivery of a blow, a stroke. *Obs.*

[Cf. **1382** in 1.] *c* **1420** *Anturs of Arth.* xlviii, With a cast of the car-honde. **1530** PALSGR. 563/1 He had thought to gyue me a caste with a horse combe.

3. a. *spec.* A throw of dice; the achievement of the throw. Phrase, ***to set, stake upon a cast.***

1509 BARCLAY *Ship of Fooles* (1570) 109 That playeth for money..And on his felowes caste taketh onely heede. **1594** SHAKS. *Rich. III*, v. iv. 9. **1611** SPEED *Hist. Gt. Brit.* IX. xviii. (1632) 916 Here is a gay goodly cast, foule cast away for hast. **1641** MILTON *Ch. Discip.* I. (1851) 32 'Tis no winning cast. **1648** —— *Observ. Art. Peace* (1851) 579. **1777** ROBERTSON *Hist. Amer.* (1783) II. 187 Their clothes, their arms, are staked..upon a single cast. **1820** *Hoyle's Games Impr.* 303 To hit the one, that cast [of dice] must be eight.

b. *fig.*

a **1300** *Cursor M.* 25480 On domesdai be-for iustise, þar all es casten on a cast. **1692** BENTLEY *Boyle Lect.* v. 164 It would be absurd to ascribe the formation of Human Bodies to a Cast of this Chance. **1761** STERNE *Tr. Shandy* III. 59, I was my father's last stake..he had been unfortunate in his three first great casts for me. **1855** MACAULAY *Hist. Eng.* III. 423 Neither Rosen nor Schomberg wished to put every thing on a cast. **1879** FROUDE *Cæsar* xxv. 430 It was the last cast of the dice for the old party of the aristocracy.

4. a. A throw or stroke of fortune; *hence*, fortune, chance, opportunity; lot, fate. *Obs.* or *dial.*

a **1300** *Cursor M.* 6205 Him suld þan reu his cast þat þis folk was fra him past. *c* **1450** *Erle Tolous* 452 To reste hym there he toke hys caste. **1513** DOUGLAS *Æneis* IX. v. 14 Glaid of this cast, seand thair tyme maste gane. *a* **1605** MONTGOMERIE *Flyting* 340 Cauld be her cast. **1722** W. HAMILTON *Wallace* 323 (Jam.) Black be their cast! great rogues. **1820** SCOTT *Monast.* iv, Before the death of Walter Avenel, haly be his cast! **1871** BROWNING *Balaust.* 2038 Now that one cast of fortune changes all!

†**b.** Hence (or from 3), ***at the last cast***: at the last shift, in extremities, near to death or ruin.

c **1449** PECOCK *Repr.* 338 Into tyme he be at his last Caste. **1549–62** STERNHOLD & H. *Ps.* cxix (1583) 93 Thou hast my lyfe restor'd When I was at last cast. **1615** BP. M. SMYTH *Pref. Babington's Wks.*, Having the plague about him, and being at the last cast. **1617** COLLINS *Def. Bp. Ely* 540, I returne to him, who is now at his last casts. **1700** J. WELLWOOD *Mem.* 251 As the last Cast for their Liberty they applied to the Prince of Orange.

5. a. A throw of the sounding-lead, of a fishing-line, net, dredge, etc.

1616 B. JONSON *Forest* Poems 92 And Pikes (run into thy net) As loth the second draught or cast to stay. **1662** FULLER *Worthies* (1840) I. 442 The next cast shall be no less than fourteen or fifteen fathom water. **1805** A. DUNCAN *Mariner's Chron.* III. 290 We had less water every cast of the lead. **1824** SCOTT *Red-gauntlet* Let. vi, He couldna help taking a cast [with the fishing rod]. **1848** *Life Normandy* (1863) II. 205 He had not made above half a dozen casts before he called out 'I have one!' **1864** BURTON *Scot. Abr.* I. ii. 99 The right to a cast of a net was a feudal privilege. **1868** CARPENTER in *Sci. Opin.* (1869) 6 Jan. 175/1 A cast of the dredge was therefore taken at this point.

b. That which is so cast, or used in casting; now *spec.* in *Angling*.

1556 J. HEYWOOD *Spider & Fl.* (N.) In eche weake place is woven a weaving cast. **1883** *Century Mag.* 378 Very killing flies, and a cast admirably suited to the state of the water. **1887** *Illust. Lond. News* 2 July 27/1 It is a mistake to coil up the fly casts in the tackle book.

c. *Angling.* A spot suited for casting the line.

1823 SCOTT *Peveril* xi, He chose..with an angler's eye, the most promising casts. **1867** F. FRANCIS *Angling* i. (1880) 41 It is so easy to pass good casts.

6. A throwing or turning of the eye in any direction; a glance, a look, expression. ? *Obs.*

c **1325** *E.E. Allit. P.* B. 768 He conueyen hym con with cast of his yȝe. **1631** GOUGE *God's Arrows* I. §41. 66 Passion will soone manifest itselfe..by a fierce cast of his eyes. **1632** MILTON *Penseroso* 43 With a sad, leaden, downward cast. **1661** *Origen's Opin.* in *Phœnix* (1721) I. 5 A direct View of him without so oblique a Cast upon his Opinions. **1768** STERNE *Sent. Journ.* (1778) I. 161, I had given a cast with my eye into half a dozen shops.

7. A 'lift' in a conveyance, given to one to put him forward on his way. Also *fig.*

1630 J. TAYLOR (Water P.) *Wks.* (N.), I o'r the water will give thee a cast. **1741** RICHARDSON *Pamela* II. 88 If..you are for the Village, I'll give you a Cast. **1787** *Gentl. Mag.* Sept. 819/2 They met with some good-natured waggoners, who gave them a cast. **1822** *New Monthly Mag.* IV. 103, I should get a cast to Newbury by one of the mails. **1885** L. B. WALFORD *Nan & other St.* II. 26 So you can't give a cast to this lassie? Well, I must take her on myself.

†**8.** ***cast of the hand***: a helping turn. *Sc. Obs.*

1637 S. RUTHERFORD *Lett.* cxxix. (1881) 238 A right cast of his holy and gracious hand. **1775** *Guthrie's Trial* 82 To delay their soul-business, hoping for such a cast of Christ's hand in the end.

9. *fig.* 'A stroke, a touch' (J.), specimen, 'taste'. esp. ***a cast of one's office.***

a **1553** UDALL *Royster D.* (Arb.) 19 Shall I go call your folkes, that ye may shewe a cast? **1575** LANEHAM in Nichols *Progr. Q. Eliz.* I. 418 Bringing with them a cast of their office, by courtly mean. **1589** GREENE *Arcadia* (1616) 32 Shew vs a cast of your cunning. **1625** SANDERSON *Serm. Ps.* cvi. 30 Do not show a cast of thy office for the promise or hope of a reward. **1673** *Answ. Season. Disc.* 4 This Dutchman has scribled and thrown amongst us (as a cast of his office) this bone of Division. **1676** WYCHERLEY *Pl. Dealer* IV. i. (1678) 53 If you hate Verses, I'll give you a cast of my Politics in Prose. **1699** BENTLEY *Phal.* 360 To receive this as a Cast of his Rhetoric. **1749** WESLEY *Wks.* (1872) IX. 12 Now, Sir, give us a cast of your office. **1832** SIR W. HAMILTON *Discuss.* (1852) 248 Whose only cast of surgery is blood-letting.

†**10.** Said of a bow: ?Casting power, ?elasticity, ?flexibility. *Obs.* Cf. CASTING *ppl. a.* 1 a.

1545 ASCHAM *Toxoph.* I. (Arb.) 28 Two bowes that I haue, wherof the one is quicke of cast, tricke, and trimme both for pleasure and profyte; the other is a lugge slowe of cast, folowing the string. *Ibid.* II. 116 A faste and harde woode.. stronge and myghtye of cast.

II. The act of throwing down, off, etc.

11. A throw in wrestling; a fall; an overthrow or defeat. *arch.*

1375 BARBOUR *Bruce* XIV. 321 He thoucht ȝeit to cowir his cast. *c* **1400** *Gamelyn* 248 Shal it be holde for a cast? **1530** PALSGR. 179 *Sombresault*, a tumblyng caste. *a* **1607** *Descr. Cleveland* in *Topog. & Geneal.* (1853) II. 410 Not without hazard of a breaknecke tumblinge caste.

†**12.** Bringing forth young, laying of eggs. ?*Obs.*

1646 SIR T. BROWNE *Pseud. Ep.* 149 After the first cast, there remaine successive conceptions.

III. What is thrown; the quantity thrown.

13. A throwing (*of* anything); the quantity thrown.

c **1450** *Bk. Curtasye* in *Babees Bk.* (1868) 305 þay schyn haue two cast of hay. **1481** CAXTON *Reynard* viii. (Arb.) 16 Bruyn receyued of hem many a caste of stones. **1523** FITZHERB. *Husb.* §11 How many castes of corne euery lande ought to haue. **1697** DRYDEN *Virg. Georg.* IV. 86 A cast of scatter'd dust. **1753** CHAMBERS *Cycl. Supp.*, *Cast*, among wax-chandlers, denotes a laddleful of melted wax, poured on the wicks of candles made by the laddle. **1797** W. MACRO in A. Young *Agric. Suffolk* 46 Drawing the land over with a heavy harrow when only one cast, or half the seed is sown.

14. *Hawking.* The number of hawks cast off at a time; a couple; also of other birds.

c **1470** *Hors, Shepe, & G.* (1822) 31 A caste of hawkes of the tour. **1530** PALSGR. 203/3 Caste of haukes, *niee doiseaux*. **1562** PILKINGTON *Exp. Obadiah* v. Wks. (1842) 255 A kennel of hounds or a cast of hawks. *c* **1611** CHAPMAN *Iliad* XVI. 406 As, on some far-looking rock, a cast of vultures fight. **1615** —— *Odyss.* XXII. 390 A cast Of hill-bred eagles, cast off at some game. **1826** SIR J. SEBRIGHT *Observ. Hawking* (1828) 41 A cast of falcons is always flown at a rook. **1852** R. F. BURTON *Falconry in V. Indus* v. 60 The sport is better with single birds than with 'casts'. **1881** E. B. MICHELL in *Macm. Mag.* Nov. 41 An exceptionally good cast of female merlins.

15. The quantity of bread or ale made at one time (*obs.*); a certain quantity of clay made into flower-pots.

1470–85 MALORY *Arthur* VII. xiv, Two cast of bread, with fat venison baked, and dainty fowls. **1538** BALE *Comedie of Nat.* (N.) If the bruar please me nat, The cast shall fall down flat And never haue any strength. **1587** HARRISON *England* II. vi. (1877) I. 154 Of the flower of one bushell..they make fortie cast of manchet. **1636** B. JONSON *Discov.* ix. 163 An elephant, in 1630..was every day allowed twelve cast of bread, twenty quarts of Canary sack, besides nuts and almonds. **1802** W. FORSYTH *Fruit Trees* viii. (1824) 210 [Flower] pots are denominated by the number contained in what the potters call a cast.

16. So many (herrings, etc.) as are thrown into a vessel at once, a 'warp'; a set of three or four.

1577 HOLINSHED *Chron.* III. 914/2 A cast of red herrings. **1808** JAMIESON s.v., A cast of herrings, haddocks, oysters, etc.; four in number. S. **1884** F. POLLOCK in *Eng. Illustr. Mag.* 159/1 Three fish = one cast (as much as can be held in one hand).

†**17. a.** A set or suit of other things. *Obs.* (exc. as in 5 b).

1535 STEWART *Cron. Scot.* I. 140 With courtlie cast of cotarmour abufe. **1591** PERCIVALL *Sp. Dict.*, *Sartal de cuentos*, a cast of counters. *a* **1659** CLEVELAND *Surv. World* vi, A cast of Lackeys, and a Lady-bird.

†**b.** (?) A standard size or quantity of wood in a billet. *Obs.*

1542–3 *Act 34 & 35 Hen. VIII*, iii, Euerie byllette to be onely of one cast and not aboue. **1553** *Act 7 Edw. VI*, vii. §2 Every Billet named to be a Cast, to contain ten Inches about, and every billet named of two cast, to containe fourteene inches about.

IV. That which is thrown off or out.

18. A second swarm of bees thrown off by a hive in one season.

1662 FULLER *Worthies* I. 22 Though only old Stocks of Bees were kept, without either Casts or Swarmes. **1664** EVELYN *Kal. Hort.* (1729) 207 Look to your Bees for Swarms and Casts. **1675** J. SMITH *Chr. Relig. Appeal* I. 36 The Swarm, that hived in Plato's mouth..was a Cast of the School of the Prophets. **1777** *Terrier* in Briscoe *Old Nottinghamsh.* I. 37 Every swarm of Bees sixpence, and every Cast..threepence. **1825** in Hone *Every-day Bk.* I. 647. **1875** J. HUNTER *Man. Bee-keeping* (ed. 2) 92 If lighter ..they would probably be casts or second swarms.

19. What is thrown up from the crop by a hawk or other bird of prey. Also, the convoluted earth thrown out by an earthworm; or sand on the sea-shore by the lug-worm.

1793 WHITE *Selborne* (1853) 382 Earth-worms make their casts most in mild weather. **1864** TENNYSON *Aylmer's F.* 849 Where the two contrived their daughter's good Lies the hawk's cast. **1880** HUXLEY *Cray-Fish* ii. 67 As a hawk or an owl rejects his casts.

20. a. The number of lambs produced in a season. **b.** The yield of corn (? *obs.*).

1787 MARSHALL *E. Norfolk* (E.D.S.) *Cast*, yield; applied to corn crops. **1887** *Scott. Leader* 10 Aug. 4 To estimate what the result of the year's cast [of lambs] will amount to.

V. †**21.** A burden cast or laid upon people; an impost, a charge. *Obs.*

1597 *Cartmel Ch. Acc.* in Stockdale *Ann. Cartmel* 36 A caste or laye should bee forthwith had throughout all the parish to the value of twenty marks. **1619** in *N. Riding Rec.* (1884) II. 209 Paying castes imposed on him by the parishe for..the poore. **1696** *Let. W. Cunningham* in *Diary* (1887) Introd. 36 Not putting you to the pains of a Cast or Act of Imposition.

VI. 22. a. Calculation, reckoning; an act of calculation; *techn.* the addition of the columns of an account.

1575 LANEHAM *Let.* (1871) 56 By great cast & cost. *Mod.* If the account does not balance now, there must be an error in the cast.

b. Conjecture, forecast.

1519 *St. Papers Hen. VIII*, I. 4 Lettres devised by the prudent caste of Your Grace. **1877** *Fraser's Mag* XVI. 221 That..must be taken into account in any casts a-head.

VII. Mental revolving, contrivance, device.

†**23.** Device, purpose, design, aim. *Obs.*

c **1325** *E.E. Allit. P.* A. 1162 Out of þat caste I watz bycalt. *c* **1440** *Bone Flor.* 1406 Thus then ys my caste. **1513** DOUGLAS *Æneis* VIII. Prol. 20 Thair is na sege for na schame that schrinkis at short, May he cum to his cast. *a* **1529** SKELTON *Dk. Albany* 101 Such trechery..Is all your cast. **1532** HERVET *Xenophon's Househ.* (1768) 61 Teche me the very point and cast of husbandry.

†**24. a.** A contrivance, device, artifice, trick. *Obs.*

c **1340** HAMPOLE *Psalter* lxxxix. 10 Ydell & swykil kastes about erthly thynge. *c* **1386** CHAUCER *Knts. T.* 1610 The derke tresoun, and the castes olde. **1398** TREVISA *Barth. De P.R.* II. xx. (1495) 48 The preuy werkes and false castes of Sathanas. *c* **1470** HENRY *Wallace* v. 740 He was full sle, and ek had mony cast. **1513** DOUGLAS *Æneis* I. Prol. 255 Quent and curious castis poeticall, Perfyte similitudes and examplis all. **1530** PALSGR. 658, I playe a caste of legyer demayne. **1609** HOLLAND *Amm. Marcell.* XIV. xi. 26 Subtile sleights and juggling casts [*præstigiis*].

†**b.** Skill, art. *Obs.*

c **1320** *Seuyn Sag.* 2105 (W.) We beth mazouns queinte of cast.

VIII. Form into which a thing is thrown; disposition, arrangement.

†**25.** Plan, design; shape, conformation, of a building, etc. *Obs.*

a **1300** *Floriz & Bl.* 338 To makie a tur after þis cast. *c* **1330** R. BRUNNE *Chron. Wace* (Rolls) 8735 He dide masons diuise a cast What werk myghte lengest last. *c* **1384** CHAUCER *H. Fame* 1178 The caste, crafte, and curiositie Ne can I not to you devise. **1509** FISHER *Wks.* (1876) 270 His buyldynges ..after the newest cast. **1579** GOSSON *Sch. Abuse* (Arb.) 24 My onely endeuour shalbe to show you that in a rough cast.

26. a. *Theat.* The assignment of the parts in a play to the several actors; the part assigned to any actor (*obs.*); the set of actors to whom the parts of a particular play are assigned.

1631 BRATHWAIT (*title*), Whimzies: or a new Cast of Characters. **1732** T. FULLER *Gnomol.* 115 If thy Cast be bad, mend it with good Play. **1795** T. WILKINSON *Wand. Patentee* I. 61 Played several characters..but did not please in the lovers, in which cast I wanted Mr. Kniveton. **1798** *Epitaph* in Hone *Every-day Bk.* II. 390 To play a comic cast of characters in this great theatre—the World. **1876** *World* V. No. 116. 3 The best representatives for the complete cast of a comedy. **1880** *Dramatic List* 219 The cast included the following admirable players. **1880** *Manch. Guard.* 20 Dec., He had brought together 'an unusually powerful cast'.

†**b.** Hence, ***to speak in a man's cast***: to speak during his part; to interrupt. *Obs.*

1580 LYLY *Euphues* (Arb.) 274 If I may speak in your cast, quoth Issida. *Ibid.* 412 The Lady Flauia speaking in his cast, proceeded in this manner. **1611** COTGR., *Entreparlement*, an interruption, a speaking in a mans cast. **1642** ROGERS *Naaman* 46 As when the minde is filled with businesse, all that is spoken is, as it were, spoken in a mans cast.

27. *Painting.* The adjustment of draperies in art.

1784 J. BARRY *Lect. Art* v. (1848) 187 The several textures ..afford an extensive variety in the cast and manner of their several foldings. **1859** GULLICK & TIMBS *Paint.* 201 The 'cast' or adjustment of draperies is made the object of a special course of study.

28. The form into which any work is thrown.

1775 T. WARTON *Hist. Eng. Poetry* I. ii. 34 Some of Aldhelm's verses are exactly in this cast. **1865** M. ARNOLD *Ess. Crit.* iv. (1875) 152 The turn of the phrase.. the happy cast and flow of the sentence. **1875** WHITNEY *Life Lang.* Pref. 7 The compendious cast of the work.

IX. Casting metal, etc; mould; model.

†**29.** Casting or founding (of cannon, etc.). *Obs.*

1602 SHAKS. *Ham.* I. i. 73 And why such dayly Cast of Brazon Cannon.

30. a. A model made by running some liquid or forcing some soft substance into a mould or shape. Sometimes applied to the negative impression taken from the original; more usually to the copy of the original moulded in this.

1502 ARNOLDE *Chron.* (1811) 240 Plouer roosted, un caste de gely florisshyd, creues deudose. **1645** EVELYN *Diary* (Chandos) 175 My purchases of books, pictures, castes. *a* **1763** SHENSTONE *Lett.* cvii, A most excellent figure, and I shall wish much to get a good cast of it. **1777** JOHNSON in Boswell (1831) IV. 63 Direction to send you a cast of my head. **1869** PHILLIPS *Vesuv.* ii. 38 A cast in plaster of Paris. **1872** ELLACOMBE *Bells of Ch.* i. 9 *note*, Taking therefrom a cast to constitute the outer mould for the bell. **1875** FORTNUM *Maiolica* ix. 77 The Alhambra vase was copied.. after a cast and photographs.

b. A model of a fossil organism formed by mineral matter which has filled up the cavity originally occupied by the organism itself.

1873 DAWSON *Earth & Man* iii. 38 Casts of sponges or fucoids. **1881** LUBBOCK in *Nature* No. 618. 408 The green sands of the geologist are largely made up of casts of foraminifera. **1881** HUXLEY *ibid.* No. 619. 453 Their solid substance may be dissolved away entirely, or replaced by mineral matter, until nothing is left of the original but a cast, an impression.

c. *Path.* 'A mould of an interior, specially applied to casts of the urinary tubules in kidney disease, or of the respiratory tubes in croup,' etc. (*Syd. Soc. Lex.*).

1867 J. HOGG *Microsc.* I. iii. 223 Urinary deposits (as casts, epithelium, crystals). **1880** WEBSTER *Suppl.* s.v., *Renal casts* (Med.), microscopic bodies found in the urine of persons affected with disease of the kidneys.

†**31.** (See quots.)

1726 R. NEVE *Builder's Dict.*, These casts are Pipes of Wax .. proportion'd to the Bigness of the Work. **1753** CHAMBERS *Cycl. Supp.*, *Cast*, among plumbers, denotes a little brazen funnel, at one end of a mould, for casting pipes without soldering, by means of which the melted metal is poured into the mould. *Ibid.*, Cast also denotes a cylindrical piece of brass or copper, slit in two lengthwise, used by the founders in sand to form a canal or conduit in their moulds, whereby the metal may be conveyed to the different pieces intended to be cast.

32. *fig.* Mould.

1709 *Tatler* No. 28 ⁋3 The true Cast or Mould in which you may be sure to know him. **1761** CHURCHILL *Rosciad* Poems (1769) I. 47 In whate'er cast his character was laid, Self still, like oil, upon the surface play'd.

X. A twist, or turn.

33. A permanent twist or turn, esp. to one side; a warp. ***cast of the eye***: a slight squint.

1505 F. MARSIN, etc. *Mem. Hen. VII* (1858) 278 He hathe a litell caste with his lefte eye. **1635** GLAPTHORNE *Lady Mother* II. i. My lady has got a cast of her eye. **1677** *Lond. Gaz.* No. 1251/4 Trots all, and hath a Cast in her Gallop with her Off leg before. *Ibid.* No. 1183/4 Very small Eyes, with a squint or cast with one of them. **1710** STEELE *Tatler* No. 120 ⁋4 Her eyes.. had odd Casts in them. **1725** RAMSEY *Gentle Sheph.* III. iv, Which gi'es their sauls a cast, That turns them downright beggars at the last. **1816** SCOTT *Old Mort.* iv, A cast of eye which, without being actually oblique, approached nearly to a squint. **1825** WATERTON *Wand. S. Amer.* I. (1887) 100 Seldom placing it [the blowpipe] in an oblique position, lest it should receive a cast.

34. A bearing in some direction; inclination of one's route.

1768 ROSS *Helenore* 79 (Jam.) Gang east, but ay some northward hald your cast.

XI. Dash or shade of colour.

[It is difficult to say whether the original notion was that of dashing in an admixture or 'eye' of some colour, or associated with casting a shade.]

35. a. A 'dash' of some colour, thrown into or over, or interspersed with another; tinge, hue; shade.

1602 SHAKS. *Ham.* III. i. 85 Thus the natiue hew of Resolution Is sicklied o're with the pale Cast of Thought. **1712** *Spect.* No. 425 ⁋5 A Robe.. of a yellowish Cast. **1772** *Hist. Rochester* 66 Of a gray colour with a cast of green. **1791** HAMILTON *Berthollet's Dyeing* II. II. iv. i. 264 The effect.. is to give the colour a gold cast. **1822** WORDSW. *Scen. Lakes* iii. (1823) 70 The colour of the house ought.. to have a cast or shade of the colour of the soil. **1841** CATLIN *N. Amer. Ind.* II. lviii. (1844) 227 The teeth of the Indians.. are not white, having a yellowish cast.

b. *fig.* Hue, tinge, shade, of guilt, conduct, etc.

1655 FELLOWES tr. *Milton's 2nd Def.* 245 What follows is of a more shocking and atrocious cast. **1762** *New Dial. of Dead* 30 The crime was of such a deep and malignant cast. **1791** BOSWELL *Johnson* (1816) I. Introd. 4 Of a dark uncharitable cast. **1815** *Scribbleomania* 118b, His thoughts were of the sombre cast. **1820** W. IRVING *Sketch Bk.* I. 341 His countenance assumed a deeper cast of dejection.

36. A 'dash' of some ingredient or quality.

1662 FULLER *Worthies* (1840) III. 499 This mungrel name seemeth to have in it an eye or cast of Greek and Latin. **1768** STERNE *Sent. Journ.* (1778) I. 102 La Fleur had a small cast of the coxcomb. **1816** SCOTT *Antiq.* i, A countenance in which habitual gravity was enlightened by a cast of ironical humour. **1823** —— *Peveril* xiii, Julian, who had in his disposition some cast of the romantic. **1855** MILMAN *Lat. Chr.* (1864) II. IV. iv. 270 The wild cast of religious adventure in his life.

XII. Sort, kind, style, quality, stamp, type, as determined by characteristics.

This section, which is of modern use, and chiefly since 1700, appears to blend figurative uses of many of the foregoing senses, VIII.–XI., one or more of these being prominent, according to the feeling of the moment. Thus the notions of *conformation, mould, turn, inclination, colouring, complexion, quality*, appear all to contribute vaguely to the result.

37. in reference to outward form, configuration, *tournure*, esp. in phrase ***cast of features***, which sometimes chiefly refers to facial expression.

1653 WALTON *Angler* xi. 198 This fish is of a fine cast and handsome shape. **1727** POPE, &c., *Art Sinking* 93 The figures must be so turned, as to manifest that intricate and wonderful cast of head, which distinguishes all writers of this kind. **1816** SCOTT *Antiq.* i, His countenance was of the true Scottish cast. **1816** J. SCOTT *Vis. Paris* 36 The general cast of feature is the same. **1833** MARRYAT *P. Simple* (1863) 139 An officer, with a very sinister cast of countenance. **1837** DISRAELI *Venetia* III. i. 160 A cast of features delicately moulded. **1879** HARLAN *Eyesight* ii. 27 The pictures of Mephistopheles owe much of their devilish cast to the twitching upwards of the external angles of the lid.

38. a. in reference to the mind or character.

1711 ADDISON *Spect.* No. 106 ⁋6 This Cast of Mind.. renders his Conversation highly agreeable. **1764** REID *Inquiry* vi. §1 He must have a very strange cast of understanding who can seriously doubt, etc. **1798** FERRIAR *Illustr. Sterne* iii. 62 Nothing is more seductive.. to minds of this cast. **1805** FOSTER *Ess.* I. ii. 21 A strongly individual cast of character. **1865** MERIVALE *Rom. Emp.* VIII. lxiii. 2 His character was not of the severe and antique cast. **1836** I. TAYLOR *Phys. The. Another Life* 6 Minds of philosophic cast. **1879** M. ARNOLD *Mixed Ess.* 148 The professions so naturally share.. the cast of ideas of the aristocracy.

b. with the notion of 'bent' or 'turn' emphasized.

1711 BUDGELL *Spect.* No. 197 ⁋2 The business men are chiefly conversant in, does not only give a certain cast or turn to their minds. **1711** ADDISON *ibid.* No. 163 ⁋10 The Mind that hath any Cast towards Devotion. **1745** J. MASON *Self-Knowl.* I. vii. (1853) 51 Every Man hath something peculiar in the Turn or Cast of his Mind. **1782** PAINE *Let. Abbé Raynel* (1791) 44 The present condition of the world.. has given a new cast to the mind of man.

c. with the notion of 'tinge' or 'colouring' emphasized.

1779 COWPER *Lett.* 14 Nov., My mind has always a melancholy cast, and is like some pools.. which though filled with a black and putrid water, will nevertheless on a bright day reflect the sunbeams.

39. in reference to actions.

1750 JOHNSON *Rambl.* No. 99 ⁋16 A cast of talk, peculiar to their own fraternity. *Ibid.* No. 181 ⁋10, I had now wholly changed the cast of my behaviour. **1789** BELSHAM *Ess.* I. ii. 23 His language has acquired a certain obsolete cast. **1817** *Monthly Rev.* LXXXIII. 499 Certainly a loose cast prevailed in the literature of the times. **1838–9** HALLAM *Hist. Lit.* II. II. vii. §36. 311 The reflections are usually of a moral cast.

40. Kind, sort, style; 'stamp, type': **a.** of persons. App. there has often been vague association with CASTE (formerly spelt *cast*).

1673 MARVELL *Reh. Transp.* II. 361 The design of you and those of your cast has been.. against all the forraign Churches. **1713** BERKELEY *Hylas & P.* iii, I am of a vulgar cast, simple enough to believe my senses. **1728** YOUNG *Love Fame* iii. (1757) 101 As if men now were of another cast, They meanly live on alms of ages past. **1742** RICHARDSON *Pamela* III. 216 Better than twenty humble Servants of Mr. Murray's Cast. **1776** GIBBON *Decline & F.* I. ix. 180 Heroines of such a cast may claim our admiration. **1829** SCOTT in *Croker P.* (1884) II. xiv. 30 Strict Presbyterian and Whig of the old Scottish cast. **1842** J. H. NEWMAN *Ess.* (1871) II. 376 Here is a man of the cast of Hooker and Butler.

b. of animals, or things.

1772–84 COOK *Voy.* (1790) IV. 1290 Farther up the hills, it [the soil] is of a grey tough cast. **1785** BURKE *Nab. Arcot's debts* Wks. 1842 I. 318 Crimes of the same blood, family, and cast. **1802** HUNTINGTON *Bank of Faith* 73 A dapple-grey, very spotted, and of the tabby cast.

XIII. 41. a. *Hunting.* The spreading out of the hounds in different directions in search of a lost scent.

c **1830** C. WICKSTED in R. Eg.-Warburton *Hunt. Songs* (1883) 226 Those sons of old Bedford.. So quick at a cast, and so ready to turn. **1846** R. EG.-WARBURTON *Hunt. Songs* (1883) 4 Friends, gentlemen, foxhunters, pray now, Hold hard, let 'em make their own cast. **1861** G. BERKELEY *Sportsm. W. Prairies* xviii. 311 No cast that I could make, or the hound in his sagacity imagine, could recover her line again. **1885** DK. BEAUFORT & M. MORRIS *Hunting* (Badm. Libr.) ii. 87 Always allow your hounds to make their own cast before you make yours.

b. *fig.*

1846 R. EG.-WARBURTON *Hunt. Songs* (1883) No. xx. v. 53 How his Muse o'er the field made each season a cast.

c. *Austral.* and *N.Z.* The sweep a trained dog makes when mustering sheep. Cf. CAST *v.* 60 c.

1933 L. G. D. ACLAND in *Press* (Christchurch) 30 Sept. 15/7 A heading dog.. goes wide round sheep so as not to disturb them and make them go faster. This curve or sweep is called a cast. **1946** F. D. DAVISON *Dusty* (1947) 115 The trial had four phases; the cast, when the owner sent the dog forward by himself to find the sheep. **1947** P. NEWTON *Wayleggo* (1949) ii. 28 [The dog] had a tremendous cast, and I used to marvel at the unerring way he would land out at the head of sheep in country where his cast took him far out of sight of them.

XIV. 42. *Comb.* (in some cases perh. the verb stem): as ***cast-maker***; **cast-fly**, a fly for angling; **cast-hole** (see quot.); **cast-house** (see quot.); **cast-net**, a net which is cast and drawn immediately, as distinguished from a net which is set and left.

1647 HEXHAM *Dutch Dict.* s.v. *Net*, A cast-net, *een werpnet.* **1681** CHETHAM *Angler's Vade-m.* ii. §11 (1689) 12 Your line for Dub-fly, Cast-fly or Artificial fly. **1747** HOOSON *Miner's Dict.* E ij, Cutting a Square Hole, about a Yard every way, throwing out the Earth as far as he can with his Spade, which will be.. about three Yards Deep, and this is called a *Cast-hole.* **1767** FAWKES *Theocritus* XXI. 13 The seine, the cast-net, and the wicker maze. **1877** SYMONDS in *Academy* 3 Nov. 419/2 As a cast-maker uses plaster of Paris. **1880** *Times* 10 Sept. 9/4 The hops when.. swept from the floors of the cast-houses are packed in sacks by the pressure of machinery. **1881** RAYMOND *Mining Gloss.*, *Cast-house*, the building in which pigs or ingots are cast. **1883** DAY *Indian Fish* 46 In some places several cast-nets are joined together, to stop up all passage of fish along a stream. **1952** HEMINGWAY *Old Man & Sea* 13 I'll get the cast net and go for sardines. **1963** *Times* 8 Feb. 12/6 Most of his days are spent plying his cast-net in the shallow waters of the south Arabian coast.

cast (kɑːst, -æ-), *v.* Pa. t. and pa. pple. **cast.** Forms: *Infinitive* 3–5 **casten**, (5 **castin, -yn**), **kaste(n, keste(n**, 6 **caste**, 3– **cast.** *Pa. t.* 3–5 **caste, kast(e**, 3–7 **kest(e**, (5, 6 **cest, kiste, keist, kyste**), 7 *Sc.* **cuist**, 8 *Sc.* **coost**, 3– **cast**; also 4–7 **casted**, 4–5 **-id(e.** *Pa. pple.* 3–8 *north.* **casten, -in, -yn**, 4–6 **caste, kast(e, kest(e**, (4 **icast**), 6 *Sc.* **cassin, -yn, caissen**, 4– **cast**; also 4–6 **castid.** [ME. *cast-en*, a. ON. *kasta* wk. vb. to cast, throw (Icel. and Sw. *kasta*, Da. *kaste*, North Fris. *kastin*): cf. *kös* (*kasu*), *köstr* (:—*kastuz*), pile, heap thrown up, which has been compared with L. *gerĕre* (*ges-*) *gestus.* It took in ME. the place of OE. *weorþan* (see WARP), and has now in turn been largely superseded in ordinary language and in the simple literal sense by THROW, q.v. '*Cast* it into the pond' has an archaic effect in comparison with '*throw* it into the pond'. But it is in ordinary use in various figurative and specific senses, and in many adverbial combinations, as *cast about.*]

General arrangement: I. To throw. II. To throw down, overthrow, defeat, convict, condemn. III. To throw off so as to get quit of, to shed, vomit, discard. IV. To throw up (earth) with a spade, dig (peats, a ditch, etc.). V. To put or place with haste or force, throw into prison, into a state of rage, sleep, etc. VI. To reckon, calculate, forecast. VII. To revolve in the mind, devise, contrive, purpose. VIII. To dispose, arrange, allot the parts in a play. IX. To cast metal, etc. X. To turn, twist, warp, veer, incline. XI. To plaster, daub. XII. *Hunting* and *Hawking* senses, those of doubtful position, and phrases. XIII. Adverbial combinations.

I. The simple action: To throw.

1. a. *trans.* To project (anything) with a force of the nature of a jerk, from the hand, the arms, a vessel, or the like; to THROW (which is now the ordinary equivalent); to fling, hurl, pitch, toss.

c **1230** *Hali Meid.* 41 Ha [pride] cast hire fader sone se ha iboren wes fram þe hehste heuene in to helle grunde. *c* **1275** LAY. 1919 Corineus.. caste hine adun mid þe cleue. *a* **1300** *Cursor M.* 20962 His hand.. he schok and in þe fir hir [þe neder] kest. *c* **1340** *Ibid.* 19461 (Fairf.) þe witnes sulde be-gyn þe first stane for to caste. *c* **1450** *Merlin* iii. 42 Pendragon caste in fier, and brente vp Vortiger. **1477** EARL RIVERS (Caxton) *Dictes* 101 Certayn men beyng at a wyndow keste water vpon him. **1595** SHAKS. *John* v. i. 39 They found him dead, and cast into the streets. **1611** BIBLE *John* viii. 7 Hee that is without sinne among you, let him first cast a stone at her. **1664** EVELYN *Kal. Hort.* (1729) 195 Never cast Water on things newly planted. **1678** N. WANLEY *Wond. Lit. World* v. ii. §86. 473/1 He would cast a Horse-man's Mace .. farther than any other of his Court. **1704** J. HARRIS *Lex. Techn.* s.v. *Baile*, Casting the water by hand out of a Boat. **1829** HOOD *Eug. Aram* xxi, I took the dreary body up And cast it in a stream. **1870** MORRIS *Earthly Par.* I. I. 300 Men fell to play at casting of the stone; And strong men cast it mighty of their hands. **1887** *Cornh. Mag.*, *Gaverocks* I. 7 'Take my rein' said the girl.. casting the reins towards him.

†**b.** *absol.* Also, To aim, deliver a blow. *Obs.* or *arch.*

c **1340** *Gaw. & Gr. Knt.* 1901 þe wyȝe.. braydez out þe bryȝt bronde, & at þe best castez.

c. *fig.*

a **1340** HAMPOLE *Psalter* 498 þan kest behynd þi bake all my synnys. *a* **1541** WYATT *Poet. Wks.* (1861) 83 From my heart I cest That, I had first determin'd for the best. **1642** T. TAYLOR *God's Judg.* I. I. xv. 49 Hee.. doth.. cast behind his backe the grace of God's spirit. **1704** POPE *Windsor For.* 173 Lodona's fate, in long oblivion cast.

d. † *to cast seed.* Now chiefly *fig.*

1577 B. GOOGE *Heresbach's Husb.* I. (1586) 24b, Neither can it be certaynely appoynted, howe muche seede is generally to be cast uppon an acre. **1611** BIBLE *Eccles.* xi. 1 Cast thy bread vpon the waters. **1861** T. TROLLOPE *La Beata* II. 73 (Hoppe) These hints had not been cast on barren ground. **1864** TENNYSON *Flower*, Once in a golden hour I cast to earth a seed.

e. To throw (dice) from the box. Also *absol.* Hence † *to cast a chance* (*obs.*).

1458 *MS. Christ's Hosp. Abingd.* in *Dom. Archit.* III. 42 They cockid for cartes, & cast for her chisyng. **1565–78** COOPER *Thesaur.*, *Fritillus*, a little boxe to cast dice on the table. **1595** SOUTHWELL *Tri. Death* 22 God casteth the dice, and giueth vs our chaunce. *a* **1628** F. GREVILLE *Sidney* (1652) 58 He might.. cast a chance for all our goodes, lives, and liberties. **1820** *Hoyle's Games Impr.* 362 Any throw which the caster may be going to cast.

f. To deposit (a voting paper or ticket); to give (a vote).

1871 SMILES *Charac.* x. (1876) 273 The immense majority of votes would be cast in favour of Plutarch. **1885** *Contemp. Rev.* June 886 Inability..to read the ballot they are expected to cast.

†**g.** *to cast cross and pile*: to toss up a coin as a way of casting lots. *Obs.*

1637 T. BRIAN *Pisse-proph.* (1679) 164 He should notwithstanding cast cross and pile which of these [remedies] he should appoint. *c* **1645** *Vox Turturis* 23 They had a Custome, when buyer and seller could not agree, to draw Cutts (as we do) or cast crosse and pile.

h. *to cast lots*: see LOT.

i. *fig.* To cause to fall or happen.

1633 BP. HALL *Hard Texts* 46 Pray ye that this flight of yours..be not cast upon such a time.

†**2.** Formerly said also of military engines, bows, and the like, which throw or shoot projectiles; often *absol.* (like *to shoot*). Also of the general or soldiers. *Obs.*

a **1300** *Cursor M.* 9890 þis castel..it es hei sett a-pon þe crag..þan na maner engine o were Mai cast þar-til it for to dere. *c* **1325** *Coer de L.* 4116 The engyne was bente..A gret ston into the toun was keste. **1330** R. BRUNNE *Chron.* (1810) 165 Bothe day & nyght unto þe toure he kast. **1382** WYCLIF *2 Kings* xiii. 17 Helise seyde, kast an arowe; and he kest. **1544** ASCHAM *Toxoph.* (Arb.) 117 So that he be..spedye ynough for far casting. **1599** THYNNE *Animadv.* (1865) 41 The trepeget must nedes also be one instrumente to cast stones. **1609** BIBLE (Douay) 1 *Macc.* vi. 51 Arbalists and engins, and instruments to cast fyre.

3. Said of the sea, waves, wind, or the like: esp. in *cast ashore*. Cf. *cast away*, 72 e.

1611 BIBLE *Acts* xxvii. 26 Howbeit we must be cast vpon a certaine Iland. **1618** M. BARET *Horsemanship* I. 4 Aristippus trauailing to Rhodes by Sea, was cast a-land by shipwracke. **1634** HERBERT *Trav.* 21 The wind blowing strongly, we were cast upon the shoales..of Mozambique.

4. Said of any similar motion however produced. *arch.* (In quot. used *absol.*)

1340 *Ayenb.* 66 Ase þe wyȝte þet ualþ ine hot weter þet kest hyer and þer, and scoldeþ alle þo þet byeþ þer aboute.

5. a. *refl.* To throw oneself. (not colloq.)

1330 R. BRUNNE (1810) 274 þam to kest smertly to þe assaute. **1579** TOMSON *Calvin's Serm. Tim.* 203/2 Not shewing themselues too muche, nor casting themselues at randome. **1611** BIBLE *Pref.* 2 He casteth himselfe headlong vpon pikes. **1653** H. COGAN tr. *Pinto's Trav.*, viii. §2. 23, I cast myself at the feet of the Elephant whereupon the King rode. **1693** *Mem. Ct. Teckely* II. 121 To cast themselves on any other side upon the Emperor's Lands. **1714** ELLWOOD *Autobiog.* 14 At length I found Means to cast my self into the Company of the Daughter. **1783** AINSWORTH *Lat. Dict.* (Morell) IV. s.v. *Alcyone*, Alcyone..hearing of her husband's death, cast herself into the sea. **1832** TENNYSON *Mariana in S.* 27 Low on her knees herself she cast.

†**b.** *intr.* (for *refl.*) *Obs.*

c **1300** *St. Brandan* 517 Ther-over [A..rock] the see caste i-lome.

6. a. To throw forth (a net, fishing line, hook, or the like, also the sounding lead, an anchor).

a **1300** *K. Horn* 1014 Hi strike seil, And ankere gunne caste. **1526** *Pilgr. Perf.* (W. de W. 1531) 133 b, He casteth his nettes in vayne before them yᵗ be as byrdes full flygge. **1535** COVERDALE *Acts* xxvii. 28 They cast out the leade & founde it twentye feddoms. **1610** B. JONSON *Alch.* II. i, The Temple Church, there I have cast my angle. **1651–7** T. BARKER *Art of Angling* (1820) 6 You can cast your flye. Be sure you be casting alwayes down the stream. **1674** EVELYN *Navig. & Comm.* §54. 101 Those of Flanders, who never presum'd to cast a Net without Permission. **1798** CAPT. BERRY in Nicolas *Disp. Nelson* (1845) III. 51 Hauling the braces, etc., preparatory to our casting anchor. **1855** MACAULAY *Hist. Eng.* III. 353 Some angler casting his fly on the foam of the river. **1860** PUSEY *Min. Proph.* 413 Shall he ..cast his emptied net, unceasingly.

b. *Hawking. to cast a lure.*

1682 DRYDEN *Epilogue King & Queen* (Globe) 457 Methinks some vizard mask I see Cast out her lure from the mid gallery. **1704** WORLIDGE *Dict. Rust. et Urb.* s.v. *Faulcon*, Cast the Lure so near her, that she may catch it within the length of her lease.

c. *intr.* (for *refl.*) of an anchor.

1646 H. LAWRENCE *Comm. Angels* 171 Our anchor casts deepe in heaven.

d. *trans.* To throw the line over (a piece of water). Hence ˈ**castable** *a.*

1892 *Field* 16 July 104/2 A fairly strong stream of only about 2 ft. in depth, and just a nice 'castable' width. *Ibid.* 1 Oct. 522/2, I therefore began to cast the lower portion of the pool. **1953** J. MASTERS *Lotus & Wind* xviii. 229 She..took her rod and..began listlessly to cast the pool.

7. a. *to cast an eye, glance, look*, etc. Still in common use.

a **1225** *Ancr. R.* 56 To kesten kang eien upon ȝunge wummen. *a* **1300** *Cursor M.* 15952 [Jesus] þan turnd him a-bute on petre his hei he kest. *c* **1385** CHAUCER *L.G.W.* 1852 As she felle adoun she kaste hir loke. *a* **1450** *Knt. de la Tour* 57 For a leude loke that he kiste on Barsaba. **1577** B. GOOGE *Heresbach's Husb.* III. (1586) 124 Horses..if they cast their looke upon their belly. **1605** SHAKS. *Lear* IV. vi. 13 How fearefull And dizie 'tis to cast ones eyes so low. **1662** STILLINGFL. *Orig. Sacr.* Ded. 2 Cast your eye on the matter contained in it. **1697** DRYDEN *Virg. Georg.* IV. 708 Th' unwary Lover cast his Eyes behind. **1732** LEDIARD *Sethos* II. IX. 302 My family have cast their eyes on an excellent person. **1812** J. WILSON *Isle of Palms* III. 866 They cast their eyes around the isle. **1816** SCOTT *Antiq.* xliv, I have sometimes thought that you have cast your eyes upon Miss Wardour. **1863** G. ELIOT *Romola* I. vi. (1880) I. 97 He cast a keen glance of surprise at the group before him.

†**b.** Formerly, also, *to cast a thought, a reflection upon*; *to cast one's heart, affections*, etc. (now, *to set*); also, *to cast love, favour, a fancy unto. Obs.*

1297 R. GLOUC. (1810) 151 þe kyng in hys syde ys herte al up hym caste. *c* **1385** CHAUCER *L.G.W.* 1878 Ther as they kaste hir hert, there it dwelleth. **1470–85** MALORY *Arthur* (1816) I. 36 The king cast great love unto her. **1540** HYRDE tr. *Vives' Instr. Chr. Wom.* (1592) M iv, Men never cast any favor to a woman but for some good profite. **1601** HOLLAND *Pliny* I. 64 An harlot that Anniball cast a fancie vnto. *c* **1665** MRS. HUTCHINSON *Mem. Col. H.* 9 A rich widow..cast her affections on him. **1736** BUTLER *Anal.* I. iii. 64 Who casts a transient reflection upon the Subject.

†**8.** To emit, give out, send forth (light, darkness, fire, heat, cold, an odour). *Obs.* (exc. as in 9).

a **1300** *Cursor M.* 23218 Euer it brennes dai and night, bot neuermare it castes light. *c* **1340** *Gaw. & Gr. Knt.* 2001 Clowdes kesten kenly þe colde to þe erthe. **1513** DOUGLAS *Æneis* XIII. Prol. 68 Hornyt Lucyne castand bot dym lycht. **1637** RUTHERFORD *Lett.* clxxxi. (1862) I. 436 How soon can he with his flint cast fire. **1667** MILTON *P.L.* I. 183 Voyd of light Save what the glimmering of these livid flames Casts pale and dreadful. **1695** WOODWARD *Nat. Hist. Earth* (J.) This..casts a sulphureous smell. **1704** WORLIDGE *Dict. Rust. et Urb.* s.v. *England*, Coal..casts a greater heat, and is more lasting. **1742** POPE *Dunc.* IV. 539 Turned to the sun, she casts a thousand dyes.

9. a. To throw or cause to fall (light, etc.) *on* or *over* any object, or in some particular direction. Now chiefly in *cast a shadow (on)*.

a **1300** *Cursor M.* 9925 It castes lem ouer al sa bright, þat reches to þe dunjon light. *Ibid.* 10060 þe grace þat of hir brestis Ouer all þis world þat grace it kestis. **1535** COVERDALE *Judith* ix. 8 Castinge a thick darcknes before them. **1634** BP. HALL *Occas. Medit.* Wks. (1808) 109 The sun darkens the full moon, in casting the shadow of the earth upon her opposed face. *Ibid.* xxxii. 134 On the sight of a dark lantern ..he can discern another man, by that light, which is cast before him. **1738** POPE *Epil. Sat.* II. 97 Or round a quaker's beaver cast a glory. **1752** J. GILL *Trinity* iii. 72 Though they do not prove the doctrine of the Trinity, yet they cast some light upon it. **1801** CAMPBELL *Lochiel* 56 Coming events cast their shadows before. **1830** TENNYSON *Poems* 79 There is no bright form Doth not cast a shade. **1860** RUSKIN *Mod. Paint.* V. VI. iv. 33 Every shadow which one casts on the next. **1860** TYNDALL *Glac.* I. §16. 106 A pine-fire was..casting its red light upon the surrounding objects.

†**b.** *intr.* (for *refl.*) *Obs.*

1692 in *Capt. Smith's Seaman's Gram.* II. 154, I..find.. the Shadow of the top of the Tower to cast at D. **1704** WORLIDGE *Dict. Rust. et Urb.* s.v. *Low Bell*, The light will cast a great distance before you very broad.

c. *to cast (a thing) into the shade*: usually *fig.*

1884 *Manch. Exam.* 2 May 4/7 Internal taxation..is so excessive..as to cast even an illiberal tariff into the shade.

†**10.** To toss (the head), to shrug (the shoulders).

a **1225** *Leg. Kath.* 1351 þe keiser kaste his heaued, as wod mon, of wreðδe. *c* **1430** *How Gd. Wijf* 61 in *Babees Bk.* (1869) 39 Braundische not with þin heed, þi schuldris þou ne caste. *c* **1500** *Cocke Lorell's B.* (1843) 8 Than Cocke cast a syde his hede. **1792** BURNS *Duncan Gray* Maggie coost her heed fu' heigh.

II. To throw down, overthrow, defeat.

11. To throw down, throw on the ground.

1481 CAXTON *Reynard* (Arb.) 3 The wulf caste his glove to fight with the foxe. **1755** JOHNSON *Dict.* s. v., The king was cast from his throne. **1861** THACKERAY *Four Georges* iii. 176 Low he lies..who was cast lower than the poorest.

12. To throw (a beast) on its back or side. The pa. pple. is used of a sheep or other beast that has got upon its back, and is unable to rise.

1577 B. GOOGE *Heresbach's Husb.* III. (1586) 133 For kibed heeles, take and cast him, and binde his legges fast together. **1607** TOPSELL *Four-f. Beasts* 313 Cast the Horse..and with that Oyl rub the Splent. **1810** *Treat. Choice, Buying, &c., Live Stock* 63 The animal is first cast, or thrown, and his legs bound. **1882** ROMANES *Anim. Intell.* 448 A collie which.. would run off to seek any sheep that might be cast, and.. assist it to rise. **1886** *Sat. Rev.* 6 Mar. 327 Granted..that it is a triumph of ingenuity [for a horse] to get cast in a loose box half as big as a barn.

13. To throw to the ground, *esp.* in wrestling; *fig.* to overthrow (an antagonist). *arch.* or *dial.*

a **1300** *Cursor M.* 25671 þe feindes fraistes me ful fast, wele i hope i sal þaim cast. *c* **1400** *Gamelyn* 245 And kaste him on the lefte syde that thre ribbes tobrak. *c* **1489** CAXTON *S. Aymon* i. 55 Guenes..casted hym ded to the erth. **1580** LYLY *Euphues* (Arb.) 158 Either she should sit fast, or else I should cast her. **1605** SHAKS. *Macb.* II. iii. 46 Though he tooke vp my Legges sometime, yet I made a shift to cast him. *a* **1615** *Brieue Cron. Erlis of Ross* (1850) 1 He had sic craft in wrasling, that he cuist all men that assilȝeit him. **1887** *Cornh. Mag., Gaverocks* i. 6 His father..tripped up his heels, and cast him sprawling on his back.

14. To defeat in an action at law.

1542 BRINKLOW *Compl.* viii. (1874) 22 The promoter payth no charges though he be cast. **1655** FULLER *Ch. Hist.* III. 20 Their cause thereby was cast by their own confession. **1659** HAMMOND *On Ps.* li. 4 What ever suite thou wagest against me, thou art sure to cast me. **1730** FIELDING *Temple Beau* Wks. 1755 I. 119, I have resolved never to go to law with a beggar or a lord: the one will never be cast, and the other you will get nothing by casting. **1818** JAS. MILL *Brit. India* I. II. iv. 144 A punishment seems to be inflicted on the defendant in all actions for debt wherein he is cast. **1854** H. MILLER *Sch. & Schm.* xxii. (1857) 495 The magistrates were cast in damages.

†**15.** To defeat in competition. Chiefly in *passive. Obs.* or *dial.*

1610 HEALEY *St. Aug. City of God* 6 Shee [*i.e.* Juno] was cast, in the contention of beauty, by the judgement of Paris. **1628** FELTHAM *Resolves* I. lxxii. Wks. (1677) 111 Juno was content with her beauty, till the Trojan Youth cast her, by advancing Venus. **1686** BURNET *Trav.* i. (1750) 56 A Man may have more than two thirds sure, and yet be cast in a Competition.

†**16.** To find or declare guilty; to convict. *Obs.*

1536 SIR J. RUSSELL *Let.* 12 May in *Lisle Papers* VII. 35 This day, Mr. Norris and such other as you know are cast; and the Queen shall go to her judgment on Monday next. **1649** MILTON *Eikon.* 15 The Commons by farr the greater number cast him: the Lords agreed to the Sentence. **1660** STANLEY *Hist. Philos.* (1701) 90/2 Socrates was cast by 281 voices. *a* **1714** BURNET *Own Time* (1766) I. 33 When it went to the vote seven acquitted but eight cast him. **1849** GROTE *Greece* II. lxvii. VIII. 463 There was no man..who might not be cast or condemned, or fail in his own suit, even with right on his side.

†**17. a.** To condemn. Const. *for* (the penalty).

1567 JEWEL *Def. Apol.* (1611) 107 Thinke you, he would determine matters, before he knew them: So might he cast Christ, and quit Barabbas. **1649** LOVELACE *Poems* (1659) 155 As a prisoner new cast Who sleeps in chaines that night his last. **1709** STRYPE *Ann. Ref.* I. xv. 192 Strangways and his crew..were..all cast to suffer death. *a* **1714** BURNET *Own Time* (1766) II. 49 He was cast; and he prepared himself very seriously for death. **1772** MACKENZIE *Man World* II. xxii. (1823) 495, I was tried for the crime, & was cast for transportation. **1816** J. H. VAUX in Knapp & Baldw. *Newgate Cal.*, *Cast for death* for privately stealing.

b. *fig.* and *transf.* To condemn.

a **1375** *Joseph Arim.* 117 'What, mon?' quaþ þe kyng 'þou castest þiseluen.' **1567** HARMAN *Caveat* 88 The learned lawes do quite or do cast, Such suttile searchers. **1606** DEKKER *Sev. Sins* I. (Arb.) 15 Thy last will, at the last day, will be an Inditement to cast thee. **1669** PENN *No Cross* i. §10 (1682) 17 That..thy unsutable & un-Christ-like life may not cast thee at that great assize of the world.

III. To throw off, out, away: with stress on the notion of getting quit of or losing.

18. a. To throw off. Of a horse: *to cast his rider* (arch. or dial.), *to cast a shoe* (the ordinary phrase).

a **1300** *Cursor M.* 27067 Quen man has casten his birthing o sin þat on him forwit lai. **1477** EARL RIVERS (Caxton) *Dictes* 64 Like the hors that castethe his maistre. **1596** SPENSER *F.Q.* IV. iv. 30 To stumble, that his rider nigh he cast. **1649** SELDEN *Laws Eng.* II. xxiii. (1739) 108 Having once won the Saddle, he is loth to be cast. *a* **1700** *Trooper's Proph.* in *Sc. Pasquils* (1868) 271 Sir Presbyter, ye spur Your speavie mear too fast..Your covenant she'll cast. **1816** SCOTT *Antiq.* i, One of the horses had cast a fore-foot shoe. **1822** BEWICK *Mem.* 24 One may soon get what one will never cast. **1840** THACKERAY *Catherine* vii, The horse had cast a shoe.

†**b.** Of a pen, etc.: To shed (ink, colour).

1639 FULLER *Holy War* II. xxvi. (1647) 76 His penne will seldom cast ink when he meeteth with the corruption of the Romish court. **1716** HORNECK *Crucif. Jesus* 597 If the Pencil in his Hand should..cast no Colour.

19. To throw off (clothes). Now chiefly *dial.* (esp. *Sc.*), except where it has the sense of 'discard', = throw off for good or for the season, cease to wear. Cf. *cast off* (79 b).

a **1300** *Cursor M.* 21527 Of he kest al to his serk. **16..** DRYDEN (J.), When I begin, In virtue clothed, to cast the rags of sin. **1711** ADDISON *Spect.* No. 98 ⁋1 They have cast their Head-dresses in order to surprise us. **1787** BURNS *Amer. War*, Till Suthrons raise, an' coost their claise Behind him in a raw, man. **1845** HOOD *Mermaid of Marg.* i, The widow comes..to cast her weeds. *a* **1889** *Old maxim.* Cast not a clout till May be out.

20. a. To throw off in process of growth (*esp.* the skin, as reptiles, caterpillars); also (somewhat *arch.* or *dial.*) to shed (hair, horns, teeth, leaves).

1486 *Bk. St. Albans* E iv b, At saynt andrew day his hornys he will cast. **1577–87** HOLINSHED *Chron. Irel.* (1808) VI. 331 As the woolfe which often casteth his haires but neuer changeth his conditions. **1626** BACON *Sylva* §732 The Creatures that cast their Skin are, the Snake, the Viper, the Grashopper, the Lizard, the Silk-worm, etc. **1649** SELDEN *Laws Eng.* I. xlvii. (1739) 77 The Eagle had cast its Feathers, and could towre no more. **1676** *Walton's Angler* iv. (1864) 62 Some hollies or oaks are longer before they cast their leaves. **1678** BUTLER *Hud.* III. II. 649. **1704** WORLIDGE *Dict. Rust. et Urb.* s.v. *Oxen*, He will cast his two foremost Teeth in ten Months of his first Year. **1789** WHITE *Selborne* II. xlvi, A skin or coat, which must be cast before the insect can arrive at its perfect state. **1801** STRUTT *Sports & P.* I. ii. 33 At the moulting time, when they cast their feathers.

†**b.** To give birth to, bear (young); to lay (eggs), deposit (spawn). *Obs.* or *dial.*

1587 TURBERV. *Trag. T.* (1837) 161 Shee was the fairest hewde..that ever kinde Had cast. **1653** WALTON *Angler* i. 26 There be divers fishes that cast their spawne on flags and stones. **1711** ADDISON *Spect.* No. 120 ⁋5 Some Creatures cast their Eggs as Chance directs them. **1769** HERD *Coll. Sc. Songs* II. 7 Four-and-twenty gude milk kye..a' cast in ae year. **1774** GOLDSM. *Anim. Nat.* (1776) IV. 174 They make a second departure in March to cast their young.

†**c.** To void (excrements). *Obs.*

1704 WORLIDGE *Dict. Rust. et Urb.* s.v. *Badger*, One [sort] casteth his Fiants long like a Fox. *Ibid.* s.v. *Wolf-Hunting*, The Bitch casteth her Fiaunts commonly in the midst of the High-way.

d. To 'yield' (as corn). *dial.*

1879 MISS JACKSON *Shropshire Word-bk*, 'Ow did that w'eät cast as yo' wun thrashin'? Middlin' like..it dunna cast like it did last 'ear.

21. *esp.* To throw off, or shed, or drop, out of due season; to give birth to or bear prematurely. (In common use of animals, fruit-trees.)

1477 NORTON *Ord. Alch.* v. in Ashm. *Theat. Chem.* (1652) 71 A Mare woll cast her Foale. **1523** FITZHERB. *Husb.* §69 Lesse hurte..to haue his cowe caste her calfe, thanne an ewe to caste her lambe. **1549** COVERDALE, etc. *Erasm. Par. 1 Cor.* xv. 8 An vnseasonable borne apostle..lyke an vnperfite chyld, rather caste, than wel borne. **1587** HARRISON *England* II. xxi, The spring maketh him that drinketh it to cast all his teeth. **1602** *Return fr. Parnass.* III. v. (Arb.) 46 It was a

terrible feare that made vs cast our haire. **1611** Bible *Rev.* vi. 13 As a figge tree casteth her vntimely figs when she is shaken of a mighty winde. **1617** J. Moore *Mappe Mans Mortal.* iii. iii. 199 The Elephant (being coursed) casteth her precious tooth and so escapeth. **1658** Ussher *Ann.* vi. 220 Darius his wife..cast the child of which she went, and died. **1882** *Garden* 168/3 Nature may..relieve herself by casting the whole of the crop.

22. Of bees: To throw off (a swarm); generally *absol.* to swarm. (The ordinary term in Sc.)

1523 Fitzherb. *Husb.* §122 At the tyme that they shall cast the swarme. *Ibid.* In June and July they do moost comynly cast. **1577** B. Googe *Heresbach's Husb.* iii. (1586) 188 b, From the fifth Ides of May, till the tenth, or the twelfth of June, they use to cast theyr swarmes. **1609** C. Butler *Fem. Mon.* v. (1623) I iv, A good stocke doth..vsually cast twise, a prime swarme, and an after swarme. **1747** Maxwell *Bee Master* 34 (Jam.) A hive, which to appearance was ready to cast.

23. †**a.** Of plants: To throw out (branches or shoots). *Obs.*

1340 *Ayenb.* 31 Þis zenne his a to kuead rote þet kest uele kueade boȝes. **1631** Markham *Weald of Kent* ii. i. (1668) 11 The former Marle..is but a dead Clod..nor casteth any profitable grass at all.

b. Of crops: to yield, bear fruit, produce. *dial.*

1890 Gissing *Village Hampden* vii, They tell me as the Lammas wheat be a-casting badly. **1893** *Field* 8 Apr. 530/1 A dry March..is of universally good omen for the coming corn crops. These never 'cast' so well as they do when a warm soil causes the under ground progress to be earlier and quicker than is that above the surface.

24. *to cast colour*: to lose colour, become pale, fade, esp. by the action of light. Also *absol.* in mod. dial. use.

c **1350** *Will. Palerne* 881 He cast al his colour and bi-com pale. ? *a* **1400** *Morte Arth.* 118 The kynge keste colours.. with crouelle lates. *Mod.Sc.* A very good colour, if it do not cast.

25. a. To throw up from within; to vomit. *to cast the gorge*: to vomit violently, or make violent attempts to vomit. Now, only of hawks or other birds (exc. *dial.*).

a **1300** *Cursor M.* 26783 Þai þaim to þair filthes fest als hund to þat he forwit kest. **1398** Trevisa *Barth. De P.R.* xvii. xciii. (1495) 661 The sede of clete helpith theym whyche castyth blood. **1486** *Bk. St. Albans* C vij, Ye se yowre hawke nesyng and Castyng wat thorogh her Nostrellis. **1535** Lyndesay *Satyre* 4355 Till scho had castin ane cuppill of quarts. **1607** Shaks. *Timon* iv. iii. 40. **1614** Raleigh *Hist. World* II. v. iii. §18. 483 Somewhat that shall make him cast his gorge. **1768** Ross *Helenore* 56 (Jam.) Gut and ga' she keest wi' braking strange. **1835-6** Todd *Cycl. Anat.* I. 324/2 The undigestible parts of the prey of the Owl ..are regularly cast or regurgitated from the stomach.

b. *absol.* Also *fig.*

c **1440** *Promp. Parv.* 63 Castyn or brakyn [*K.* as man owt the stomack]. **1493** *Festivall* (W. de W. 1515) 52 He might not receyue ye sacrament for castynge. **1607** Topsell *Four-f. Beasts* 278 These feathers will make him to cast immediately at the nose. **1623** Hart *Arraignm. Ur.* v. 110. **1735** Pope *Donne's Sat.* iv. 157 Like a big wife, at sight of loathsome meat Ready to cast. **1850** *Fraser's Mag.* 557 The swallow casts after the fashion of a hawk or owl.

fig. **1632** Rutherford *Lett.* xxiii. (1862) I. 91 Let your soul..cast at all things and disdain them, except one only. *a* **1665** W. Guthrie *Serm. Mark* viii. (1709) 25 (Jam.) They have broken the covenant, casten at his ordinances.

c. Said also of the sea, a volcano, etc.

1592 *No-body & Some-b.* (1878) 296 All the chimneyes shall cast smoake at once. **1601** Holland *Pliny* I. 106 The hill Chimæra, which casteth flames of fire euery night. **1610** Shaks. *Temp.* ii. i. 251 We all were sea-swallow'd, though some cast againe.

†**26.** To ejaculate, utter (words), heave (a sigh).

a **1300** *Cursor M.* 10464 Wit the bolnning of hir hert, Sco kest sum wordes son ouerthuert. **1330** R. Brunne *Chron.* (1810) 295 Þe kest all suilk a crie, þat men mot here a myle. *c* **1450** *Sir Beues* (MS. M.) 2740 The dragon had of ham a smell And he keste vp a gret yell. *c* **1489** Caxton *Sonnes of Aymon* (1885) 485 Whan the byshop turpyn sawe this, he casted a grete sighe. **1712-4** Pope *Rape Lock* iii. 157 Not louder shouts to pitying Heav'n are cast.

27. To throw or set aside, reject, discard; *esp.* to set aside as disqualified; to reject (horses) as unfit; to dismiss (soldiers, etc.).

[In this sense the pa. pple. ran together with that of cass *v.* (sense 2), so that about 1600 *cast* may be either.]

a **1375** *Joseph Arim.* 703 Forte cristene þe folk, and casten þe false. **1587** Turberv. *Trag. T.* (1837) 52 No more must all Cupidos knyghtes be cast because of some. [**1604** E. Grimston *Siege of Ostend* 80 He hath cast and dismist so many olde experimented Captaines.] **1604** Shaks. *Oth.* i. i. 150 The State..Cannot with safetie cast him. [**1614** Raleigh *Hist. World* II. v. iv. §5. 523 Many Companies.. of forrein Auxiliaries are presently cast.] **1690** Locke *Hum. Und.* iii. vi. §26 This Child..was..near being excluded.. and 'tis certain a Figure a little more oddly turn'd had cast him. **1715** in *Wodrow Corr.* (1843) II. 78 If that [Revelation] be once casten, we shall fall upon no other. **1817** Keatinge *Trav.* II. 103 The number of horses cast from the cavalry. **1854** H. Miller *Sch. & Schm.* vi. (1857) 114 He determined that Cousin George should be cast in the examination. **1872** *Anteros* ii. 9 No more thought of rejecting him as a suitor, than a trainer would of casting a colt for showing temper.

¶ Improperly for cass, to make void.

1717 Wodrow *Corr.* (1843) II. 331 It is nothing..less.. than a total casting and making void the patrons' power in all time coming.

IV. To throw up with a spade or shovel.

28. a. To throw up (earth, etc.) whence the current northern use in *to cast sods, turf, peat*: to dig them up. Also in ploughing.

1497 in *Ld. Treas. Acc. Scotl.* I. 364 To the monk that castis the gardin. **1523** Fitzherb. *Husb.* §13 Let him caste his barley-erthe, and shortly after rygge it agayne. **1616** Surfl. & Markh. *Countr. Farm* 307 It being vsed to be cast and tilled with thicker raisings of the earth. **1663** Spalding *Troub. Chas. I* (1792) I. 166 (Jam.) Peats and fire was very scarce, through want of servants to cast and win them. *Ibid.* 216 The servants, who should have casten the peats. **1799** J. Robertson *Agric. Perth* 131 To be preserved always in the same form, by casting, that is, by ploughing two ridges together, beginning at the furrow that separates them, and ploughing round and round, till the two ridges be finished. **1860** J. F. Campbell *Tales W. Highl.* II. 36 The Laird was getting his peats cast. *Mod. Sc.* Casting divots on the edge of the common.

b. To shovel coal from the keels into the collier (vessels); see caster 2 b.

1882 J. Green *Tales & Ballads Wearside* (1885) 223 He had commenced to cast at two o'clock in the morning.

†**29.** To dig or clear out (a ditch or the like), throwing the soil up on the edges. *Obs.*

1481-90 *Howard Househ. Bks.* (1841) 21 For casting the poondes at Wysnowe vj.*s.* viij.*d.* **1522** *MS. Acc. St. John's Hosp., Canterb.*, Paied for castyng of xxj roddis of dykyng. **1576** *Act 18 Eliz.* x. §7 No Person..shall cast or scour any Ditch and throw or lay the Soil thereof into the Highway. **1579** Twyne *Phis. agst. Fort.* i. xc. 111 b, Thou hast planted trees, thou hast cast ryuers, thou hast plashed hedges. **1617** Collins *Def. Bp. Ely* A iij a, I will not draine the fenne, or stand casting the ponde. **1614** Raleigh *Hist. World* v. vi. §7 A newe ditch lately cast by Perseus.

†**30.** To form by throwing up, to raise (a mound, bank, earthwork, or the like). *Obs.* See *cast up* (83 e).

1593 *Althorp MS.* in Simpkinson *Washingtons* Introd. 36 Payde for casting the causey iijs. *jd.* **1603** Knolles *Hist. Turks* (1621) 526 He commanded..the broken passages to be cast even. **1608** Shaks. *Per.* i. i. 100 The blind Mole cast Copt hills toward heauen. **1611** Bible *2 Kings* xix. 32 The king of Assyria shall not come into this city..nor cast [Coverdale dygge] a bank against it. **1667** Milton *P.L.* i. 675 Pioneers..to trench a field Or cast a rampart.

V. To put, or place, with haste, violence, force, or power, so that the effect resembles throwing.

31. a. To lay, place, put, with an action of force, decisiveness, or haste. (Now usually *throw*.)

a **1300** *Cursor M.* 3152 Þe child he kest a-pon an ass. *Ibid.* 5441 He kest a-boute þam aiþer arm. *a* **1300** *Havelok* 2448 [They] keste him on a scabbed mere. **1526** Tindale *Matt.* xxvi. 12 She casted this oyntment on my body. **1535** Coverdale *Acts* xii. 8 Cast thy mantle aboute the, and folowe me. **1652** Needham tr. *Selden's Mare Cl.* 87 Against that man who hath cast a Dam or Pile into the Sea an Interdict is allowed him who..may be endamaged thereby. **1667** Milton *P.L.* i. 286 His ponderous shield behind him cast. **1837** J. H. Newman *Par. Serm.* III. v. 117 To be cast on the world, and to see life..is a variety. **1859** Tennyson *Enid* 1609 She cast her Arms about him. **1861** S. Wilberforce *Agathos, Tent in Pl.* (1865) 151 My guide cast on my shoulders a beautiful mantle.

b. *fig.* Of care, blame, or the like.

c **1400** *Apol. Loll.* 82 Who..þat in þe last our of his deþ kastiþ not al his bisines & his affeccoun in to God. **1483** Caxton *G. de la Tour* F vij, Sentence of dethe was cast on her. **1577** B. Googe *Heresbach's Husb.* i. (1586) 7 b, Businesse..which they would be lothe to beare themselves, they cast all uppon his backe. **1614** Raleigh *Hist. World* ii. 253 Casting ungratefully on Moses all their misadventures. **1751** Jortin *Serm.* (1771) II. ii. 34 Let us cast our cares upon him. **1842** Miss Mitford in L'Estrange *Life* III. ix. 137 Do not fancy..that I cast the slightest blame on my.. father. **1883** *Law Rep. 11 Queen's B.* 593 The imputation cast upon Mr. M. was altogether unfounded.

32. To throw or put *into prison*.

a **1225** *St. Marher.* 4 Ant het hire casten into cwarterne. *a* **1300** *Havelok* 1784 Þe oþre shal ich kesten In feteres. *a* **1300** *Cursor M.* 13072 In prisoun heroude dud him cast. **1566** Knox *Hist. Ref.* Wks. 1846 I. 383 The ane was escaipit, and the uthir in vyle preassoun cassin. **1608** Golding *Epit. Frossard's Chron.* i. 34 The Pope..cast this fryer in prison. **1611** Bible *John* iii. 24 John was not yet cast into prison. **1875** Jowett *Plato* (ed. 2) III. 513 They were being taken away to be cast into hell.

†**33. a.** To put, or cause to fall, *into* (a state or condition, *e.g.* sleep, rage). *Obs.* or *arch.*

a **1300** *Cursor M.* 10100 Þis caitif casten in care. *Ibid.* 12941 In glotoni he wend him cast. *c* **1400** *Destr. Troy* 11311 The kyng at his karping cast was in ire. *c* **1440** *York Myst.* xvi. 36 Be they kyngis or knyghtis, in care ȝe þaim cast. *c* **1555** Harpsfield *Divorce Hen. VIII* (1878) 289 Being cast in love with a wanton maid. **1611** Bible *Ps.* lxxvi. 6 Both the chariot and horse are cast into a dead sleepe. **1650** T. Vaughan *Anthrop. Theom.* 37 His Fall..did cast asleep his Intellectuall Faculties. **1697** Dampier *Voy.* I. xix. 500 Our continuing wet for the last two days, cast us all into Fevers. **1709** Steele *Tatler* No. 79 ⁋1 This cast him into such a rage, that he threw down the table.

†**b.** To deliver, set free, bring out *of* (a state).

a **1300** *Cursor M.* 5289 He has me cast of al mi care. *Ibid.* 25705 Has kyd þi merci mare To man-kind for to cast o care.

†**34.** To set (a person) *to* (*upon*) some action. Also *refl.* To set oneself with resolution. *Obs.*

c **1386** Chaucer *Melibeus* ⁋624 He that..casteth hym to no bisynesse..shal falle in-to pouerte. *c* **1430** Lydg. *Chichev. & Bycorne*, Bycorne castith hym to devoure Alle humble men. **1470-85** Malory *Arthur* (1816) II. 371, I cast me never to be married. **1533** Bellenden *Livy* i. (1822) 48 In time of pece, he kest him to find occasioun of weir. *c* **1565** Lindesay (Pitscottie) *Chron. Scot., Jas. II*, The Earl of Douglas cast himself for to be stark against the King. **1579** Spenser *Sheph. Cal.* Feb. 189 To this this Oake cast him to replie Well as he could. **1662** More *Antid. Atheism* ii. vi. (1712) 57 It cast them with more courage upon attempting the virtue of those (plants).

†**35.** To add, throw in, as an addition *to*. *Obs.*

c **1380** Wyclif *Serm.* Sel. Wks. II. 274 Þis childhede is betere ȝif vertues be castid þerto. *c* **1449** Pecock *Repr.* v. viii. 528 A religion caste to the lawe of kinde. **1528** More *Heresyes* ii. Wks. 197/2 All other thinges..shal be cast vnto vs. **1554** Philpot *Exam. & Writ.* (1842) 365 Not so bold that he would cast anything to the institution of Christ.

36. To bestow, confer, allot. *arch.* or *obs.*

1612 Brinsley *Lud. Lit.* 285 God..wil cast learning vpon them so far as shall be good. *a* **1626** Bacon *Use Com. Law* (1635) 25 Leaving it to goe (as the law casteth it) upon the heire. **1809** Tomlins *Law Dict.* s.v. *Descent*, An heir is he upon whom the law casts the estate immediately on the death of his ancestor.

VI. To reckon, calculate.

37. To count or reckon, so as to ascertain the sum of various numbers, orig. by means of counters, to the manipulation of which the word probably refers.

a. *intr.* Formerly in the phrases *to cast in* or *at accounts*. Now, to add a column of figures.

1330 R. Brunne *Chron.* (1810) 135 If any man in dede wille keste in a countes. *c* **1340** *Cursor M.* App. (Edinb. MS.) 20834 Qua wel can caste sal finde it euin. *a* **1360** *Song Yesterday* 66 in *E.E.P.* (1862) 135 And in vr hertes acountes cast Day bi day. **138.** *Antecrist* in Todd *3 Treat. Wyclif* 138 To cast at þe countes. **1842** Tennyson *Audley Crt.* 43 Who would cast and balance at a desk? **1884** *Law Times* 25 Oct. 419/2 A resort to the court in order that..a mistake in casting be corrected.

b. *trans.* To reckon up, sum up; now technically, to add up (a column of figures or amounts).

c **1305** *St. Edmund* 223 in *E.E.P.* (1862) 77 His figours drouȝ aldai & his numbre caste. **1330** R. Brunne *Chron.* (1810) 248 Þei..Examend þam & cast ilk amountment. *c* **1340** *Cursor M.* 22062 (Fairf.) To be laused atte þe laste quen þa þousande ȝere ware caste. **1496** *Dives & Paup.* (W. de W.) i. xxv. 62/1 They that calculen & casten yeres dayes & monethes. **1526** *Pilgr. Perf.* (W. de W. 1531) 133 The marchaunt..vseth euery nyght to cast his boke. *c* **1590** Marlowe *Jew Malta* i. ii, This ten years tribute..we have cast, but cannot compass it. **1624** Bedell *Lett.* xii. 161 Review it, and cast it ouer againe. **1742** Young *Nt. Th.* iv. 240 Archangels fail'd to cast the mighty sum. **1805** *Naval Chron.* XIV. 341 The books were cast and..adjusted. **1886** *Law Times* LXXX. 165/2 Every column cast before the bill is left for taxation.

c. esp. in *to cast accounts*, originally to sum up or reckon accounts (so *to cast reckonings*); now, to perform the ordinary operations of arithmetic.

1399 Langl. *Rich. Redeles* iii. 279 Caste all þe countis þat þe kyng holdith. **1529** More *Supplic. Soules* Wks. 294/1 Folke that will learn to cast accompt. **1530** Palsgr. 477/1, I caste an accomptes, after the comen maner, with counters, *je compte par ject.* **1565-78** Cooper *Thesaur.*, *Abaculus*..a counter or other like thing, that men doe use to cast reckenings with. **1574** Hellowes *Gueuara's Ep.* (1584) 85 The count being wel cast, the wood costes as deare as the dressing. **1581** J. Bell *Haddon's Answ. Osor.* 44 b, You cast your accomptes amisse in your numbryng. **1655-60** Stanley *Hist. Philos.* 26/1 Counters used in casting accounts..sometimes stand for a great number, sometimes for a lesser. **1766** Goldsm. *Vic. W.* xi. (1857) 66 They can read, write, and cast accounts. **1871** Ruskin *Fors Clav.* iv. 3 To be taught to read, and write, and cast accounts.

†**38. a.** To reckon, calculate, estimate. *Obs.*

a **1300** *Cursor M.* 8775 Þe king did cast wit scantliun, And did mak al þe timber bun. **1475** *Bk. Noblesse* 39 After as it may be cast it was .cc.iiij^{xx}xj. yere. **1542-75** Recorde *Gr. Artes* 78 Then will I caste the whole charge of one monethes commons at Oxforde. **1606** G. W[oodcocke] tr. *Ivstine* 2 a, Wisely casting the inconuenience that might redound hereby vpon himself. *a* **1642** Sir W. Monson *Naval Tracts* iii. (1704) 341/2 He must be..perfect in Casting the Tides. **1660** Pepys *Diary* 29 Oct.

†**b.** *absol.* *Obs.*

c **1386** Chaucer *Knts. T.* 1313 Of fiue and twenty yeer his age I caste. **1575** Laneham *Let.* (1871) 48 Yoor iewellers by their Carrets let them cast. **1602** Shaks. *Ham.* ii. i. 115 It is as proper to our Age To cast beyond our selves in our Opinions. **1633** Ford *'Tis pity* i. ii, You need not cast upon the dearth of flesh.

39. a. To calculate astrologically, as *to cast a figure, horoscope, nativity*, etc.; also *absol.*

c **1374** Chaucer *Troylus* ii. 25 [He] cast, and knew in good plyte was the Mone To do viage. **1430** Lydg. *Chron. Troy* i. vi, She gan anone to casten and deuyse When that the moone on heauen would aryse. **1591** Spenser *M. Hubberd* 511 Or cast a figure for a bishoprick. **1621** Burton *Anat. Mel.* Democr. (1676) 36/1 For casting a Nativity. **1667** Dryden *Sir M. Mar-all* Epil., We by tomorrow will our Fortune cast. **1823** *New Monthly Mag.* VIII. 257 Casting figures and preventing the butter from coming when they churn. **1841** Brewster *Mart. Sc.* iii. ii. (1856) 181 Drawing an income from casting nativities. **1855** E. Smedley *Occult Sc.* 312 Cardan..has cast the horoscope of our Saviour.

†**b.** To interpret (a dream). *Obs.*

1382 Wyclif *Gen.* xli. 15, I sawȝ sweuens, ne there is that opnith, the which I haue herd the most wiseli to caste.

†**40.** *to cast water*: to diagnose disease by the inspection of (urine). Also *fig. Obs.* or *dial.*

1580 Lyly *Eupheus* (Arb.) 296 An Italian [physician].. casting my water..commaunded the chamber to be voyded. **1589** Greene *Menaphon* (Arb.) 35 Able to cast his disease without his water. **1599** W. Goddard *Mastiff-Whelp* xlvi. D ij b, Your vrine..I'le truly cast, and tell you your disease. **1605** Shaks. *Macb.* v. iii. 50 If thou could'st Doctor, cast The Water of my Land, finde her Disease. **1632** B. Jonson *Magn. Lady* (T.), I had it of a Jew, and a great rabbi, Who every morning cast his cup of white-wine With sugar. **1647** Cleveland *Char. Lond.-Diurn.* 2 It casts the water of the State, ever since it staled blood. **1706** Hearne *Collect.* (1883) I. 189, I don't cast Water now, but Accounts. **1877** E. Peacock *N.-W. Linc. Gloss.* (E.D.S.) s.v., A person is said to

cast another's water who pretends to discover diseases by the inspection of urine.

†**41.** To calculate or conjecture as to the future; to anticipate, FORECAST: **a.** *intr.* (sometimes with *subord. cl.*) ***to cast beyond the moon***: to conjecture wildly; to indulge in wild conjectures.

c **1384** CHAUCER *H. Fame* 1148 Thoo gan I in myn hert cast That they were molte awey with hete. **1387** TREVISA *Higden* (Rolls) VI. 137 As fer forþ as we conne caste. **1530** in W. H. Turner *Select. Rec. Oxford* 92 As far as may be cast or imagiened. **1559** *Mirr. Mag.* 529 Beyond the moone when I began to cast..what place might be procur'd. **1562** J. HEYWOOD *Prov. & Epigr.* (1867) 158 He casth beyonde the moone . great diuersitie Betweene far castyng and wise castyng, may be. **1588** GREENE *Pandosto* (1843) 8 [She] began to cast beeyond the moone..which way she should offend her husband. **1599** MONTGOMERIE *Cherry & Sl.* 524 He sall nevir schaip to sayle the se, That for all perrils castis. **1607** HEYWOOD *Woman kild* Wks. 1874 II. 138 But oh, I talke of things impossible, And cast beyond the moone. **1658** USSHER *Ann.* 309 Every man cast in his mind, that Eumenes would be all in all.

†**b.** *trans.*, as in ***to cast danger, peril, the worst.***

c **1400** *Destr. Troy* 259 He..the kynges couetous cast not before. *c* **1449** PECOCK *Repr.* I. xi. 53 Thanne perel is castid. **1494** FABYAN VI. clxxxii. 181 The kynge, castyng no parell, thanked hym of his kynde request. **1530** PALSGR. 476/2 It is wysdome to cast afore what may come after. **1532** HERVET *Xenophon's Househ.* (1768) 22 Man can not caste theym afore hande. **1553** EDEN *Treat. New Ind.* (Arb.) 9 To caste the worste, yf they should perishe in this viage. **1627** E. F. *Hist. Edw. II*, 126 With a world of melancholy thought he casts the danger.

VII. To resolve in the mind, devise, contrive, purpose, plan.

†**42.** To revolve in one's mind, debate with oneself, consider, ponder, deliberate. *Obs.* or *dial.*

a. *intr.* often with subordinate clause.

a **1340** HAMPOLE *Psalter* xiii. 2 Þai kast & studis how þai moght doe in dede þat þai haf wickedly thoght. **1393** GOWER *Conf.* III. 161 He caste and hath compassed ofte, How he his prince might plese. *c* **1449** PECOCK *Repr.* v. vi. 518 Thei schulen desire and caste and..be constreyned to abide. **1480** CAXTON *Chron. Eng.* ccxiii. 199 They caste..how they myght breng hym out of prison. **1549** COVERDALE *Erasm. Par. Phil.* i. 23, I haue cast what is best for me. **1600** HOLLAND *Livy* x. xlv. 385 Men began to cast in their minds ..how they should do. *a* **1634** CHAPMAN *Alphons.* Wks. 1873 III. 202 They ward, they watch, they cast, and they conspire. **1678** WANLEY *Wond. Lit. World* VI. xxvii. §4. 611/2, I lay still..casting and discoursing with my self, whether I waked or was in a dream.

†**b.** *trans. Obs.* or *dial.*

1530 PALSGR. 477/2, I have caste many thynges in my mynde, sythe the mater began. **1577** HANMER *Anc. Eccl. Hist.* (1619) 168 The Judge, casting doubts with himselfe. *c* **1590** MARLOWE *Faust.* v. 26 Cast no more doubts. *a* **1719** ADDISON (J.), I have lately been casting in my thoughts the several unhappinesses of life.

43. To machinate, contrive, devise, scheme.

†**a.** *intr.* Const. with *inf.* (or *clause*). *Obs.*

c **1325** *E.E. Allit. P.* B. 1455 To compas and kest to haf hem clene wroȝt. *c* **1380** WYCLIF *Sel. Wks.* III. 439 Antecrist hab cast to be knyttid wiþ kyngis. **1393** LANGL. *P. Pl.* C. I. 143 [Thei] Caste þat þe comune sholde hure comunes fynde. *c* **1450** LONELICH *Grail* lvi. 150 Oure londis they casten to wasten ful pleyn. **1590** MARLOWE *Edw. II*, v. ii, Edmund casts to work his liberty. **1597** MORLEY *Introd. Mus.* 77, I thought I should haue gone madde, with casting and deuising. **1611** BEAUM. & FL. *King & No K.* III. 48 A strange Land, where mothers cast to poyson Their only Sons. **1612–5** HALL *Contempl. O.T.* xx. *Athaliah & J.* 16 She straight casts for the kingdom of Judah. **1653** WALTON *Angler* iv. 109 Before you begin to angle, cast to have the wind on your back.

b. *trans.* To contrive or devise (an action, etc.).

1382 WYCLIF *Gen.* xlii. 11 Ne thi seruauntis eny thing casten [**1388** ymaginen] of evil. *c* **1420** —— *Esther* Prol. (MS. M.) He [Aman] castide the deeth of Mardochee. *c* **1440** *Bone Flor.* 2181 Be hyt nevyr so slylye caste. *c* **1590** MARLOWE *Jew Malta* v. ii, I'll set Malta free; And thus we cast it. **1613** BEAUM. & FL. *Captain* II. ii, To cast A cheape way how they may be all destroyed. **1833** MRS. BROWNING *Prometh. Bd.* Poems (1850) I. 184 Do not cast Ambiguous paths, Prometheus, for my feet.

†**c.** Phrase. ***to cast counsel.***

c **1460** *Play Sacram.* 224 After ward more counselle among vs shall [be] caste. **1596** SPENSER *State Irel.* 1 Good plottes devised, & wise Councels cast already.

†**44. a.** To design, purpose, intend, determine (*to do* a thing). *Obs.*

138. WYCLIF *Serm.* Sel. Wks. II. 104 No man doiþ ouȝt in hiddis and ȝit he castiþ to be in apert. **1398** TREVISA *Barth. De P.R.* xv. xii. (Tollemache MS.), I wonder þat þou castes [**1535** purposeste] to fyȝte with women. *c* **1430** *Hymn Virg.* (1867) 106 He þat casteþ, wiþ conscience clere, To kepe, wel Cristes Comaundement. *c* **1430** *Syr Gener.* (Roxb.) 1444 When I am more of elde I cast my armes forto welde. **1567** DRANT *Horace's Epist.* I. ii. C v, That owner..hauing riches competent, doth cast to vse theim well. **1653** WALTON *Angler* iii. 70 That has made me and my friend cast to lodge here too. **1660** LASSELS *Voy. Italy* I. 67 We cast to be there at the solemne entry, which this Duke made for his new Spouse. **1808** SCOTT *Marm.* IV. xvii, The marshall and myself had cast To stop him.

†**b.** ***to cast oneself, one's advice***: to form a design, purpose. *Obs.*

1470–85 MALORY *Arthur* (1817) II. 61 As yet I caste me not to marye in this countrey. **1523** LD. BERNERS *Froiss.* I. ccccxlvii. 789 This lorde of Destornay dyde cast his aduyce to get agayne Andwarpe.

VIII. To put 'into shape' or into order; to dispose, arrange.

(Some senses originally belonging here, have prob. been subsequently influenced by IX since that became a leading sense of the vb.)

†**45.** To put into shape, dispose, arrange, or order; to lay out in order, plan, devise: **a.** a piece of ground, piece of work, or other thing material.

a **1300** *Cursor M.* 9947 A tron of iuor graid, Craftili casten wit compass. *c* **1320** *Sir Beues* 4610 A faire chapel of marbel fin, þat was ikast wiþ queint engin. *c* **1320** *Cast. Love* 807 Þreo bayles.. i-cast wᵗ cumpas and walled abouten. *c* **1384** CHAUCER *H. Fame* 1170 Ne coude casten no compace Swich another for to make. *c* **1440** *Promp. Parv.* 63 Caste warke or dysposyn, *dispono.* **1563** SHUTE *Archit.* B iij b, Ye must furst haue knowlaige how to cast your ground plotte. **1577** B. GOOGE *Heresbach's Husb.* III. (1586) 162 b, Let your nestes and lodginges, both for laiyng and brooding, be orderly cast. **1596–7** S. FINCHE in *Hist. Croydon* App. (1783) 153 The measure of the ground..that the plotte might be caste square. **1611** BIBLE *Pref.* 8 They did not cast the streets, nor proportion the houses in such comely fashion. **1762–71** H. WALPOLE *Vertue's Anecd. Paint.* (1786) IV. 276.

†**b.** things not material. (Cf. 52.) *Obs.*

1340 HAMPOLE *Pr. Consc.* 1976 Þan byhoved us our lyf swa cast Als ilk day of our lif war þe last. *c* **1430** *Syr Gener.* (Roxb.) 2310 So thei can here iournes cast. **1589** *Pappe w. Hatchet* (1844) 18 The sermon is not yet cast. **1597** MORLEY *Introd. Mus.* 151 Yᵉ musicke is so to be cast as the point bee not offensiue.

46. a. To dispose or arrange in divisions; to divide or 'throw' *into* divisions.

1340 HAMPOLE *Pr. Consc.* 432 Alle mans lyfe casten may be..in þis partes thre. **1622–52** HEYLIN *Cosmogr.* III. (1673) 62/1 Constantine cast it into three provinces. **1689** BURNET *Tracts* I. 69 They were cast into little States, according to the different Valleys which they inhabited. **1710** STEELE & ADD. *Tatler* No. 253 ¶4, I shall cast what I have to say under Two principal Heads. **1835** T. WALKER *Original* ii. (1887) 21 By casting them into other distinctions to abolish the first and great distinction.

b. To 'throw' *into* a (particular) form.

1711 ADDISON *Spect.* No. 5 ¶6 Casting into an Opera the Story of Whittington and his Cat. **1854** H. MILLER *Sch. & Schm.* xx. (1857) 437 Casting my facts..into a series of letters.

47. *Painting.* †**a.** To arrange or dispose (colours). *Obs.*

1567 JEWEL *Def. Apol.* (1611) 274 M. Harding casteth his colours to shadow that thing, that will not bee hidde. **1579** LYLY *Euphues* (Arb.) 37 Cunning Painters who for the whitest worke, cast the blackest ground. **1596** SPENSER *F.Q.* I. VII. 1 Cast her colours To seeme like Truth. **1633** T. ADAMS *Comm. 2 Peter* i. 5 Some painters are so skilful in casting their colours, and can paint a fire so lively, that at the first blush you would think it to be a fire indeed.

b. To dispose (the draperies in a painting).

1706 *Art of Painting* (1744) 30 To set or cast a Drapery. **1813** *Examiner* 8 Feb. 90/2 The draperies are cast with much ease.

48. a. *Theat.* To allot (the parts of a play) *to* the actors; to appoint (actors) *for* the parts.

1711 ADDISON *Spect.* No. 219 ¶12 Our parts in the other world will be new cast. **1737** FIELDING *Hist. Reg.* III, *Apollo.* Is there anything to be done? *Prompter.* Yes, Sir, this play to be cast. **1809** MALKIN *Gil. Bl.* (Rtldg.) 372 They ..wanting a boy..to personate the young King of Leon, cast me for the part. **1864** *Realm* 30 Mar. 8 The piece is very strongly cast, and..was most creditably performed. **1866** MARK LEMON *Wait for End* xxviii. 365 She had been cast (as it is called in the language of the stage) a most interesting mother. **1875** MACREADY *Remin.* 125 The part of Hermione was cast to Mrs. Egerton.

b. ? *transf.*

1763 CHESTERFIELD *Lett.* ccclxxii. IV. 192 You will have known..from the office, that the departments are not cast as you wished.

IX. To cast (molten) metal; to found. Now one of the most used literal senses.

†**49.** To throw (anything plastic or fluid) into a particular shape. *Obs.* in general sense.

a **1300** *Cursor M.* 22941 Þe potter..whenne he fordoþ his new vessel he casteþ soone al in a bal a bettre for to make. **1693** J. BEAUMONT *On Burnet's The. Earth* I. 23 A fluid mass always casts it self into a smooth and spherical Surface.

50. To form (metal, or the like) *into* a shape, by pouring it when melted or soft into a mould, where it is allowed to cool or harden.

1512 *Act 4 Hen. VIII*, viii. §7 Untrue or deceivable Metal ..of Tin or Pewter..wheresoever it be cast..or wrought. **1546** in W. H. Turner *Select Rec. Oxford* 182 For takyng doune the leade..and castyng hit into sowes. **1553** EDEN *Treat. New Ind.* (Arb.) 29 They..melte it & caste it fyrste into masses or wedges. **1581** *Act 23 Eliz.* viii. § 2 Every Piece of Wax..so melted and cast. **1728** WOODWARD *Fossils* (J.), It ..will not run thin, so as to cast and mould. **1750** BEAWES *Lex Mercat.* (1752) 694 The several Species of Metals, cast and wrought here. **1814** *Lett. fr. England* III. lxxv. 341 A large collection..have..been cast into candlesticks and warming pans.

51. To form (an object) by running molten metal, etc. into a mould; to found.

1496 in *Ld. Treas. Acc. Scot.* I. 285 To the man that castis the chameris to the brassin gun. **1535** COVERDALE *Ex.* xxv. 12 Cast foure rynges of golde. **15..** LINDESAY (Pitscottie) *Chron. Scot.* 112 Seven Canons, called the Seven Sisters, casten by Robert Borthwick, the Master-Gunner. **1668–9** PEPYS *Diary* 1 Mar., Did bring home a piece of my face cast in plaister. **1677** MOXON *Mech. Exerc.* (1703) 35 You must Cast a Nut of Brass upon the Spindle. **1753** HOGARTH *Anal. Beauty* 10 A figure cast in soft wax. **1834** LYTTON *Pompeii* I. ii, Buckets of bronze, cast in the most graceful shapes. **1851** D. WILSON *Preh. Ann.* (1863) I. II. ii. 345 A mould of serpentine..and another of granite intended to cast ornamented celts of two sizes.

52. *fig.*

1593 HOOKER *Eccl. Pol.* Pref. ii. §8 All cast according to that mould which Calvin had made. **1606** DAY *Isle of Gulls* III. i. 24 Let's cast our inventions in a new mould. **1671** EVELYN *Mem.* (1857) III. 230 Hereafter to cast it into other languages. **1711** ADDISON *Spect.* No. 40 ¶1 Several of the celebrated Tragedies of Antiquity, are cast in the same Form. **1844** EMERSON *Ess. Self-Reliance* Wks. (Bohn) I. 28 Is the parent better than the child into whom he has cast his ripened being? **1876** —— *Lett. & Soc. Aims, Poet. & Imag.* III. 158 Our habit of casting our facts into rhyme to remember them the better.

X. To turn, twist. [Parallel to *warp*:—OE. *weorpan* to throw, and *throw*:—OE. *þrāwan* to twist, turn.]

53. Of timber, etc.: To warp. **a.** *intr.*

1544 ASCHAM *Toxoph.* (Arb.) 28 My goode bowe clene cast on the one side. **1641** BEST *Farm. Bks.* (1856) 112 When oake cometh to dry, it will shrink, cast, drawe a nayle. **1669** WORLIDGE *Syst. Agric.* (1681) 239 If you lay them in the Sun or Wind, they chap, or shrink, or cast. **1677** MOXON *Mech. Exerc.* (1703) 110 Stuff is said to Cast, or Warp, when by its own Droughth or Moisture..or other Accident, it alters its flatness and straightness. **1881** *Eng. Mechanic* 23 Dec. 368 In consequence of the liability of this wood to cast.

b. ? *trans.* (only in *pa. pple.*)

1641 BEST *Farm. Bks.* (1856) 122 To prevent them [theire pikes] from beinge casten. **1717** TABOR in *Phil. Trans.* XXX. 551 They [bricks] were very firm, and not in the least Warp'd or Cast in Burning. **1726** R. NEVE *Builder's Dict.* (ed. 3) s.v., A Piece of Timber..is said to Cast or to be Cast when..it alters its Flatness. **1824** CARLYLE in Froude *Life* (1882) I. 237 The old tile roof is cast by age, and twisted into all varieties of curvature. **1874** KNIGHT *Dict. Mech.* I. 497 *Cast*, warped—said of sprung timber.

†**54. a.** *intr.* To turn in one's course. *Obs.*

c **1450** *Bk. Curtasye* 336 in *Babees Bk.* (1868) 309 Noþer to harme chylde ne best, With castyng, turnyng west ne est. **1600** *Roxb. Ball.* (1887) VI. 404 The birds of Heauen the nearest way haue flowne, And under earth the moules doe cast aright.

b. *Naut.* To veer, turn.

1671 *Lond. Gaz.* No. 580/2 Which causing a mistake at Helm, the ship cast a contrary way. **1798** CAPT. MILLER in *Nicolas Disp. Nelson* (1846) VII. Introd. 159 We cast so as to open the view of our broadside to her. **1882** NARES *Seamanship* (ed. 6) 199 Prepare for casting to port. **1885** W. C. RUSSELL *Strange Voy.* I. xiv. 208 The wind has so got hold of her that she won't cast one way or the other.

c. *trans.* To bring (a ship) round.

1769 FALCONER *Dict. Marine* (1789) *Jib*.. It's effort in casting the ship, or turning her head to leeward is very powerful. **1836** MARRYAT *Three Cutt.* i, Her foresail is loose, all ready to cast her.

55. To turn (the scale or balance). *Obs.* or *arch.* Cf. *casting-vote.*

1597–8 BACON *Faction, Ess.* (Arb.) 83 When matters have stuck long in ballancinge, the Wynning of some one man casteth them. **1637** RUTHERFORD *Lett.* ccliii. (1862) I. 355 One grain-weight less would have casten the balance. **1667** *Naphtali* (1761) 139 Such advantages do preponderate and cast the scales. **1676** MARVELL *Mr. Smirke* sig. I, He cast the Scales against Arrius. **1837** J. H. NEWMAN *Proph. Office Ch.* 112 Nor can we cast the balance between the outward advantages and disadvantages.

†**56.** *intr.* To have an inclination; to incline, slope, slant; to lie away. *Obs.*

1599 SANDYS *Europæ Spec.* (1632) 193 Their Countries casting so much as they doe towards the North are out of his way. **1787** BEST *Angling* (ed. 2) 66 After some sudden rain, or breaking up of a great snow in winter, you will plainly see which way the ground casts.

XI. †**57.** To cover by casting (mortar, or the like) on; to plaster, daub. *Obs.* Cf. ROUGH-CAST.

1577 HARRISON *England* II. xii. (1877) I. 233 They..cast it all ouer with [thicke] claie to keepe out the wind. **1663** SPALDING *Troub. Chas. I*, II. 63 (Jam.) Our minister..kest with lime that part where the back of the altar stood, that it should not be kent.

XII. Senses of doubtful position, and phrases.

†**58.** To tie or make (a knot): also to catch (in a cord, etc.), to entangle. *Obs.*

1591 DRAYTON in Farr's *S.P.* (1845) I. 133 The bar'd steed with his rider..Whose foot in his caparison is cast. *a* **1605** MONTGOMERIE *Sonn.* xxxvii, I can not chuse; my kinsh is not to cast. **1607** TOPSELL *Four-f. Beasts* 320 Of hurts in the legs, that cometh by casting in the halter or collar. **1637** RUTHERFORD *Lett.* cxxii. (1862) I. 304 When Christ casteth a knot, all the world cannot loose it. **1691** RAY *Creation* II. (1704) 316 Cast a strait Ligature upon that part of the Artery. **1825** JAMIESON *Dict.* s.v. *Kinsch, To cast a kinsch*, to cast a single knot on the end of a rope, or of a web; a term commonly used by weavers.

59. *Hawking.* ***to cast a hawk***: in various senses: cf. V, III, and see quots.

c **1430** *Bk. Hawkyng* in *Rel. Ant.* I. 296 Ye shull say cast your hawke thereto [to her game], and say not lete flee. **1486** *Bk. St. Albans* A ij b, Bere thi hawke home on thi fiste and cast hir on a perch. *Ibid.* A vj b, Ye shall say cast yowre hawke to the perch, and not set youre hawke vppon the perch. *Ibid.* B vj, Whan she is cast to a fowle, she fleith a waywarde as thogh she knewe nott the fowle. **1615** LATHAM *Falconry* Gloss., To *cast* a Hawke, is to take her in your hands before the pinions of her wings, and to hold her from bating or striuing, when you administer any thing vnto her. **1623** FLETCHER *Maid in Mill* III. ii, If you had..handled her as men do unman'd hawks, Cast her, and mail'd her up in good clean linen. **1704** WORLIDGE *Dict. Rust. et Urb.* s.v. *Eyess*, It will be proper to shew how to Seel a Hawk.. Casting your Hawk, take her by the Beak, and put the needle through her Eye-lid.

60. a. *Hunting. intr.* Of dogs (or huntsmen): To spread out and search in different directions for a lost scent. Cf. *cast about.*

1704 WORLIDGE *Dict. Rust. et Urb.* s.v. *Hare-hunting*, So will they [Greyhounds] soon learn to cast for it at a doubling or default. **1846** R. EG.-WARBURTON *Hunt. Songs* xiii. (1883)

36 Whenever check'd, whenever crost, Still never deem the quarry lost; Cast forward first.. Cast far and near, cast all around, Leave not untried one inch of ground. *Ibid.* xliv. 129, I can only backwards cast, or Blow my horn and take 'em home. **1863** WHYTE-MELVILLE *Gladiators* I. 233 Like a hound.. casting forward upon a vague speculation. **1885** DK. BEAUFORT & M. MORRIS *Hunting* (Badm. Libr.) ii. 80 When they [harriers] come to a check.. let them swing and cast;.. only when they are utterly non-plussed should the huntsman go to their assistance. *Ibid.* 87 In casting, do not be afraid to cast forward in the first instance.

b. *transf.* and *fig.* ***to cast about one***: to look about (mentally).

1823 SCOTT *Peveril* vii, I cast round the thicket. **1825** in Hone *Every-day Bk.* I. 292, I remember the old squire and his sporting chaplain casting home on spent horses. **1867** HOWELLS *Ital. Journ.* 277 Spinabello cast about him to find a suitable husband for her. **1879** BROWNING *Pheidipp.* 28 Gravely they turned to take counsel, to cast for excuses. **1885** *Law Times* LXXIX. 190/1 He casts about him for the wherewithal to meet the.. expenditure.

c. *N.Z.* Of a trained dog: to make a wide sweep when mustering sheep. Also, to direct a dog to make such a sweep. Cf. CAST *sb.* 41 c.

1911 W. H. KOEBEL *In Maoriland Bush* v. 77 He must acquire the art of 'casting' a sheep-dog. **1947** P. NEWTON *Wayleggo* (1949) 153 It is instinctive for a heading dog to cast when running out i.e. to make a wide detour so as to get round his sheep without disturbing them. **1966** *Weekly News* (N.Z.) 6 Apr. 45/5 She cast out very wide and then she spotted the sheep on the huntaway course.

61. *trans.* ***to cast hounds***: to 'throw off', put on the scent.

1781 P. BECKFORD *Hunting* (1802) 163 When he casts his hounds, let him begin by making a small circle.

62. *intr.* (*Sc.*) Of the sky: To clear of clouds. Cf. *overcast*.

1768 ROSS *Helenore* 58 (Jam.) The sky now casts an' syne wi' thrapples clear, The birds about begin to mak their cheer.

63. *trans.* ***to cast loose***: to unfasten or let loose with force or decisiveness, set adrift; said esp. of a boat, or the like; also ***to cast adrift***. Also *fig.*

1582–8 *Hist. Jas. VI* (1804) 85 All the people were cassin sa louse, and were become of sic dissoluit myndis. **1660** J. GUTHRIE in *Life* (1846) 249 The Lords Day disregarded and casten loose. **1751** ADM. HAWKE in *Naval Chron.* VII. 464 Instead of daring to cast the squadron loose. **1805** A. DUNCAN *Mariner's Chron.* III. 353 The captain ordered the boat to be cast loose. *Ibid.* 354 The boat.. turned bottom upwards, her lashings being cast loose. *Ibid.* IV. 27 The boat was veered astern, and soon after cast adrift. **1856** DOVE *Logic Ch. Faith* v. i. ii. 284 The smallest possibility of error on the part of God would cast the universe loose from its moral obligation. **1884** *Mehalah* ii. 27 She.. cast loose, and began to row.

†**64.** ***to cast clean***: to cleanse. ***to cast open***: to open suddenly, 'throw open'; also to open a way through. *Obs.*

1522 *World & Child* in Hazl. *Dodsley* I. 256 From sloth clean you cast. **1633** BP. HALL *Hard Texts* 474 Therefore will I cast open the frontiers of Moab. **1663** SPALDING *Troub. Chas. I* (1792) I. 126 (Jam.) The watchword.. being heard, the gates are casten open.

65. † ***to cast*** (***any one***) ***in the teeth***: to reproach or upbraid him (*with*, *that*) *obs.*; later construction ***to cast*** (***a thing***) ***in one's teeth***.

1526 TINDALE *James* i. 5 Which geveth to all men.. without doublenes, and casteth no man in the teth [**1611** upbraideth not]. **1530** PALSGR. 764/2, I caste him in the tethe or in the nose. **1563** *Homilies* II. *Repentance* III. (1859) 346 That we shall never be cast in the teeth with them. **1578** TIMME *Calvin on Gen.* 254 He casteth the Jews in the teeth that their fathers served strange Gods. **1642** ROGERS *Naaman* 30 He cast them in the teeth with their former injurious casting him out.

b. 1562 J. HEYWOOD *Prov. & Epigr.* (1867) 36 Deuiseth to cast in my teeth Checks. **1579** LYLY *Euphues* (Arb.) 125 The trecheries of his parents.. will be cast in his teeth. **1611** BIBLE *Matt.* xxvii. 44. **1675** BROOKS *Golden Key* Wks. 1867 V. 328 God.. will never hit him in the teeth with his former enormities, nor never cast in his dish his old wickednesses. **1716** HORNECK *Crucif. Jesus* 33 Strangers cast it in his Teeth so often, Where is now thy God? **1875** JOWETT *Plato* (ed. 2) I. 101, I would not have you cast in my teeth that I am a haughty Aexonian.

†**66.** ***to cast one's wits***: to exercise or apply one's wits. *Obs.*

c **1400** *Destr. Troy* 11428 Þan þai comynd in the cas, castyn hor wittes. **15..** LINDESAY (Pitscottie) *Chron. Scot.*, Cast his ingine to set a remedy thereto. **1579** TOMSON *Calvin's Serm. Tim.* 236/2 If the enterprise bee great, he must cast all his wit y^t way.

†**67.** ***to cast their heads*** (***together***): to unite in consultation. *Obs.*; now *put, lay heads together*.

1535 COVERDALE *Prol. Bible*, Occasion to cast their heads together, and to make provision for the poor. **1577** PATERICKE *Agst. Machiavell* 318 They of the nobilitie all casting their heads, and employing their abilities for their gentleman.

68. ***to cast eggs***: **a.** to beat them up; **b.** 'to drop them for the purpose of divination' (Jam.).

a **1825** *MS. Poem* (Jam.) By.. casting eggs, They think for to divine their lot. *a* **1825** *Receipts Cookery* 7 (Jam.) Mix with it ten eggs well cast. *Ibid.* 8 Cast nine eggs and mix them with a chopin of sweet milk.

69. ***to cast a clod between*** (Sc.); to widen the breach between. † ***to cast galmoundis*** (Sc.): to cut capers. ***to cast a*** (***point of***) ***traverse***: (see quots.). † ***to cast stones against the wind***: to labour in vain. Also ***to cast ambs-ace, anchor, a bone, cantraips, cavel, a damp, damper, an essoin*** (excuse), ***lots, a spell***; for which see those words.

1529 LYNDESAY *Compl. King* 181 Castand galmoundis with bendis and beckis. **1657** R. LIGON *Barbadoes* (1673) 43, I grew weary of casting stones against the wind. **1704** J. HARRIS *Lex. Techn.*, *Cast a Point of Traverse*, in Navigation, signifies, to prick down on a chart the Point of a Compass any Land bears from you, or to find on what Point the Ship bears at any instant, or what way the Ship has made. **1768** ROSS *Helenore* 105 (Jam.) Betweesh them sae by casting of a clod. **1867** SMYTH *Sailor's Word-bk.*, *To cast a traverse*, to calculate and lay off the courses and distances run over upon a chart.

XIII. In combination with adverbs.

70. cast about.

a. *trans.* See simple senses and ABOUT *adv.*

1648 HERRICK *Hesper.* (1885) 36 Sighs numberless he cast about. **1697** DRYDEN *Virg. Past.* iv. 73 Begin.. to cast about Thy Infant Eyes. **1789** WOLCOTT (P. Pindar) *Subj. for Paint.* 69 She cast about her eyes in thought profound.

b. *intr.* To turn about. *Naut.* To change the course, to go on the other tack. Cf. 54.

1591 RALEIGH *Last Fight Rev.* (Arb.) 19 Perswaded.. to cut his maine saile, and cast about. **1611** BIBLE *Jer.* xli. 14 The people.. cast about and returned, and went into Johanan. **1635** LD. LINDSEY in Sir W. Monson *Naval Tracts* III. (1704) 335/1 If I cast about in the night, I will shoot a Piece of Ordnance. *a* **1716** *Sc. Pasquils* (1868) 277 Prone to cast about to th' other shore.

c. To go this way and that in search for game, a lost scent, etc., *orig.* a hunting locution. Cf. 60.

1575 TURBERV. *Venerie* xl. 120 Huntesmen may caste about in the moste conuenient moyst places, and.. vnder some bushe or shade. **1607** TOPSELL *Four-f. Beasts* 111 Dogs.. will cast about for the game, as a disputant doth for the truth. **1857** HUGHES *Tom Brown* I. vii, There is nothing for it but to cast about for the scent. **1879** STEVENSON *Trav. Cevennes* 166, I began to cast about for a place to camp in.

d. *fig.*

1677 HALES *Prim. Orig. Man.* I. i. 22, I cast about for all circumstances that may revive my Memory. **1732** BERKELEY *Alciphr.* vi. §32 They who cast about for difficulties will be sure to find or make them. **1875** E. WHITE *Life in Christ* III. xix. (1878) 252 Casting about for some explanation of the Atonement.

e. To consider, contrive, devise means, lay plans. Const. with *inf.* or *clause*. Cf. 42, 43.

c **1590** MARLOWE *Jew Malta* II. ii, Like a cunning Jew so cast about, That ye be both made sure. **1603** KNOLLES *Hist. Turks* (1621) 428 The Turkes being mo in number, cast about to han encloased them. **1677** YARRANTON *Engl. Improv.* 18 Now he casts about how to preserve himself from the Storm. **1704** SWIFT *Batt. Bks.* (1711) 248 She cast about to change her Shape. **1712** *Spect.* No. 524 ¶9, I was casting about within myself what I should do. **1861** S. WILBERFORCE *Agathos, Tent in Pl.* (1865) 141, I cast about in my mind how I should speak to him.

71. cast aside.

a. *trans.* See simple senses and ASIDE.

1864 TENNYSON *Aylmer's F.* 803 For on entering He had cast the curtains of their seat aside.

b. To throw aside from use, discard.

a **1420** OCCLEVE *De Reg. Princ.* 319 He.. cast our holy cristen feithe aside. **1605** SHAKS. *Macb.* I. vii. 35 Worne now in their newest glosse Not cast aside so soone. **1697** DRYDEN *Virg. Georg.* III. 664 A Snake.. has cast his Slough aside. **1885** *Manch. Exam.* 11 Nov. 3/3 Purchased for railway reading and then carelessly cast aside.

72. cast away.

a. *trans.* See simple senses and AWAY.

a **1300** *Cursor M.* 1954 Lok þai cast a way þe blod. **1388** WYCLIF *Gen.* xxi. 15 Sche castide awei the child vndur a tre. **1549** *Compl. Scot.* iii. 28 The file.. is vorne ande cassin auaye. **1885** STEVENSON *Dynamiter* 125 To cast the bag away from him.

b. esp. *fig.* To put from one, part with forcibly, dismiss, reject.

a **1300** *Cursor M.* 25675 (Gött.) Mi soru i cast away. **1382** WYCLIF *Ezek.* xvi. 45 Thi modir, which castide a wei hir husbonde and hir sones. **1535** COVERDALE *Jer.* xxxiii. 24 Two kynreddes had the Lorde chosen and those same two hath he cast awaye. **1613** *Answ. Uncasing of Machiav.* F b, All Cards and Dice.. discard and cast away. **1758** JOHNSON *Idler* No. 1 ¶10 Hope is not wholly to be cast away. **1812** LANDOR *Ct. Julian* II. iv. 27 Egilona.. casts away, Indifferent or estranged the marriage-bond.

†**c.** To thrust, push, turn or drive away. *Obs.*

a **1300** *Cursor M.* 5688 Come hirdes and awai þam kest. *c* **1340** *Ibid.* 14332 (Trin.) Þe graue lid awey þei kist. **1483** CAXTON *G. de la Tour* vi. 9 Her husbonde kiste away his herte from his wyff.

d. To throw away, i.e. in waste or loss; to spend uselessly, waste wantonly, squander, ruin.

1530 PALSGR. 477/1 Thou wylte caste away thyselfe and need nat. **1595** SHAKS. *John* II. 334 France, hast thou yet more blood to cast away? **1629** SHIRLEY *Wedding* v. ii, What d' ye mean To cast yourself away? **1713** ADDISON *Cato* v. ii, Our father will not cast away a life So needful to us all. **1885** WINGFIELD *B. Philpot* I. iii. 43 Never with my consent shall you thus be cast away.

e. To wreck (a ship); to throw upon the shore, to strand. Also *transf.* and *fig.*

1596 SHAKS. *Merch. V.* III. i. 105 Anthonio.. Hath an Argosie cast away comming from Tripolis. **16..** SACKVILLE (J.) Our fears tempestuous grow, And cast our hopes away. **1667** E. CHAMBERLAYNE *St. Gt. Brit.* (1684) 141 Goods floating on the Sea, and Goods cast away by the Sea on the Shore. **1684** *Lond. Gaz.* No. 1988/1 The Capitana of the Gallies of Naples.. was in a great storm cast away. **1717** *Act 4 Geo. I*, xii, If any owner.. shall.. wilfully cast away burn or otherwise destroy the ship. **1779** ARNOT *Hist. Edinb.* 98 The very next day, the vessel was cast away in the Forth. **1810** *Naval Chron.* XXIV. 474 Our fatigue has been very great, being cast away on a barren place. **1840** R. DANA *Bef. Mast* xvii. 47 The small Mexican brig which had been cast away in a south-easter, and which now lay up, high and dry. **1864** TENNYSON *En. Arden* 714 Enoch, poor man, was cast away and lost.

73. cast back.

a. *trans.* See simple senses and BACK. †**b.** ? To put or thrust back, repulse, defeat (*obs.*); ? to leave behind. †**c.** To throw behind, hold or drag back, impede (*obs.*). **d.** *intr.* To go back over the same course, revert.

c **1450** *Boctus, Laud MS.* 559 fol. 9, ij, That in here lawe were holden wys For to despute with Sidrak, But he caste hem all a bakke And ouercome all here reasoun. **1622** R. PRESTON *Godly Man's Inquis.* II. 47 Crooked wayes, and crooked feete will cast backward. **1671** MILTON *Samson* 337 Mine [feet], cast back with age, Came lagging after. **1862** MRS. RIDDLE *City & Suburb* 197 (Hoppe) You cast back for hundreds of years, and rake up every bit of pleasure I ever had in my life. *Ibid.* 202, I think there must have been a dreadful misalliance somewhere in our genealogy, and that you have cast back to it.

74. cast behind.

a. *trans.* See simple senses and BEHIND. **b.** 'To leave behind in a race' (J.).

16.. DRYDEN (J.) You cast our fleetest wits a mile behind. **1714** ELLWOOD *Autobiog.* (1765) 85 We were so far cast behind the Trooper that we had lost both sight and hearing of him. **1735** SOMERVILLE *Chase* III. 464 Tho' far he cast the ling'ring Pack behind. **1850** BROWNING *Easter Day* xxvii, The mind So miserably cast behind To gain what had been wisely lost.

†**75. cast by.** To throw aside from use. *Obs.*

1592 SHAKS. *Rom. & Jul.* I. i. 100 Verona's ancient Citizens Cast by their Graue beseeming Ornament. **1647** W. BROWNE *Polex.* II. 319 That great heart.. cast by the scepter of Gheneoa. **1690** LOCKE (J.) Men.. cast by the votes and opinions of the rest of mankind as not worthy of reckoning.

76. cast down.

a. See senses 11–13 and DOWN.

a **1300** *Cursor M.* 23720 Dame fortune turnes þan hir quele And castes vs dun. *a* **1340** HAMPOLE *Psalter* cxx. 3 Pride kastes men down. **1530** PALSGR. 477/1 Who wolde have thought that so lytell a felowe coulde have caste him downe. **1535** COVERDALE *Lament.* ii. 1 As for the honoure of Israel, he hath casten it downe from heauen. **1565–78** COOPER *Thesaur* s.v. *Abjiceo*, He.. cast himselfe downe a long in the grasse. **1860** TYNDALL *Glac.* I. §15. 101 The blocks which had been cast down from the summit. **1885** CREIGHTON *Age of Eliz.* 22 Henry VIII delighted to show that he could cast down and could raise up.

b. *trans.* To overthrow, demolish (a building).

c **1230** *Hali Meid.* 5 And warpeð eauer toward tis tur for to kasten hit adun. *c* **1300** *Cursor M.* 16705 Þou said þat þou suld cast it [þe temple] dun and ras it þe thrid dai. *c* **1425** WYNTOUN *Cron.* VII. viii. 90 The castelle than on Twedmouth made.. Wes tretyd to be castyn down. **1572** *Lament. Lady Scotl.* in *Sc. Poems 16th C.* II. 247, I se ȝour tempills cassin downe. **1637** S. RUTHERFORD *Lett.* cxlv. (1881) 267 Bulwarks are often Casten down.

c. To bend and turn downward (the head, face, the gaze of the eyes).

c **1374** CHAUCER *Boeth.* I. i. 7 Þus þis compaygnie of muses I-blamed casten wroþely þe chere adounward to þe erþe. *a* **1533** LD. BERNERS *Huon* li. 172 Huon.. spake no worde but cast downe his hede. **1752** JOHNSON *Rambl.* No. 190 ¶1 Every eye was cast down before him. **1873** BLACK *Pr. Thule* iv. 60 Sheila cast down her eyes, and said nothing.

d. To deject in spirits, disappoint, dispirit. Chiefly in *pa. pple.* = downcast.

1382 WYCLIF *Job* xl. 28 And alle men seende he shal ben kast down. **1605** SHAKS. *Lear* v. iii. 6 For the oppressed king I am cast downe. **1711** ADDISON *Spect.* No. 256 ¶8 How often is the Ambitious Man cast down and disappointed, if he receives no Praise where he expected it? **1775** SHERIDAN *Rivals* v. iii, Come, Mrs. Malaprop, don't be cast down. **1853** G. RAWSON *Hymn 'In the dark & cloudy Day'*, Comfort me, I am cast down.

77. cast forth.

a. *trans.* See simple senses and FORTH.

1667 MILTON *P.L.* II. 889 The gates.. like a Furnace mouth cast forth redounding smoak and ruddy flame. **1694** *Acc. Sev. Late Voy.* i. (1711) 114, I caused the Lead to be cast forth, but could not get ground at eighty Fathom. **1704** WORLIDGE *Dict. Rust.* s.v. *Withering*, This will not only cause her to cast forth her latter Burden, but dead Calf.

b. To throw or put out of doors, company, etc., expel, eject.

1382 WYCLIF *Jer.* xxxvi. 30 His careyn shal be cast forth at the hete bi the dai. **1593** SHAKS. *Rich. II*, I. iii. 157 To be cast forth in the common ayre. **1596** SPENSER *F.Q.* VI. xii. 15 That litle Infant.. which forth she kest. **1611** BIBLE *Nehem.* xiii. 8, I cast foorth all the houshold stuffe of Tobiah out of the chamber.

†**c.** To throw out (roots, branches). *Obs.*

1611 BIBLE *Hosea* xiv. 5 Hee shall grow as the lillie, and cast foorth his rootes as Lebanon.

78. cast in.

a. *trans.* See simple senses and IN. **b.** *fig.* To throw in (as an addition, or something extra).

1688 CULPEPPER & COLE *Barthol. Anat.* II. i. 86 We shall treat of the Dugs of Women, casting in between while, wherein those of Men differ therefrom. **1682** DRYDEN *Relig. Laici* 283 'Twere worth both Testaments, and cast in the creed.

c. ***to cast in one's lot among*** or ***with***: to become a partner with, to share the fortunes of.

1535 COVERDALE *Prov.* i. 14 Cast in thy lott amonge us. **1816** SCOTT *Old Mort.* xx, Numbers of these men.. prepared to cast in their lot with the victors of Loudon-hill. **1848** MACAULAY *Hist. Eng.* iv. (L.) Baxter cast in his lot with his proscribed friends, refused the mitre of Hereford, quitted the parsonage of Kidderminster.

†**d.** To choose partners at cards. *Obs.*

1741 RICHARDSON *Pamela* II. 259 We cast in, and Miss Boroughs and my master were together.

79. cast off.

a. *trans.* See simple senses and OFF. **b.** To throw off (clothes or anything worn).

c **1400** *Destr. Troy* 12661 Palomydon..cast of his clothis cantly & wele. *c* **1400** MAUNDEV. v. 41 A woman myghte wel passe there, withouten castynge of of hire Clothes. **1609** BP. BARLOW *Answ. Nameless Cath.* 274 Them hee casteth off as the fellow..did his spectacles. **1697** DAMPIER *Voy.* I. vii. 165 In a weeks time the Tree casts off her old Robes.

c. *fig.* To throw off as clothes, a yoke, etc.

1597 HOOKER *Eccl. Pol.* v. lxviii. §6 The Christian religion they had not utterly cast off. **1667** MILTON *P.L.* v. 786 To cast off this Yoke. **1690** LOCKE (J.) Disown and cast off a rule. **1751** JORTIN *Serm.* (1771) V. i. 11 Casting of the belief of the true God. *a* **1876** J. H. NEWMAN *Hist. Sk.* I. I. iv. 179 National habits and opinions cannot be cast off at will without miracle.

d. *fig.* To put from one, discard, abandon, disown.

1535 COVERDALE *Ezek.* xvi. 45 Thy mother..that hath cast of hir houszbonde and hir children. **1611** BIBLE *Ps.* lxxi. 9 Cast me not off in the time of old age. **16..** DRYDEN (J.) To cast off my father when I am great. **1713** ADDISON *Cato* III. vii, When I have gone thus far, I'd cast her off. **1850** HT. MARTINEAU *Hist. Eng. Peace* II. v. xvii. 455 [The Prince] did make the other [Brummell] the fashion, and then cast him off. **1875** E. WHITE *Life in Christ* I. viii. (1878) 72 To be cast off by God may be to perish.

e. *Hawking* and *Hunting*. To throw off (the couplings of hounds); to slip (dogs); to let fly (hawks).

1602 *2nd Pt. Return fr. Parnass.* II. v. (Arb.) 32 Another company of houndes..had their couples cast off. **1611** COTGR., *Ajetter un oiseau*, to cast, or whistle, off a hawke; to ..let her flie. **1677** N. COX *Gentl. Recreat.* I. (1706) 42 You may then cast off your young Hounds. **1725** DE FOE *Voy. round W.* (1840) 274 Just as a huntsman casts off his hounds. **1774** GOLDSM. *Retal.* 107 He cast off his friends, as a huntsman his pack, For he knew when he pleas'd he could whistle them back. **1826** SIR J. SEBRIGHT *Observ. Hawking* (1828) 26 When a magpie is seen at a distance, a hawk is immediately to be cast off.

†**f.** To throw off, as vapour, or the like; to run off melted metal. *Obs.*

1674 RAY *Smelt. Silver* 115 The Lead..is cast off by the blowing of the bellows. **1692** —— *Discourses* XI. (1732) 80 The ocean doth evaporate and cast off to the dry Land. **1704** WORLIDGE *Dict. Rust. et Urb.* s.v. *Calaminaris*, They cast not off above twice in 24 hours.

g. *Naut.* To loosen and throw off (a rope, sail, etc.), to let go, let loose; to loosen (a vessel) from a mooring. Also *intr.* for *refl.*

1669 STURMY *Mariner's Mag.* I. ii. 17 It is like to over-blow..cast off the Top-sail Sheets. **1745** P. THOMAS *Jrnl. Anson's Voy.* 146 On the 2[d] there being little Wind and variable, we cast off the Gloucester, and the next Day took her again in Tow. **1779** FORREST *Voy. N. Guinea* 252 Cast off, and rowed down the river. **1805** A. DUNCAN *Mariner's Chron.* IV. 29 One of the crew..jumped on shore and cast off the stern-fast of the boat. **1806** —— *Nelson* 30 La Minerve..cast off the prize. **1853** KANE *Grinnell Exp.* xvi. (1856) 124 We cast off again about 7 A.M. **1855** RUSSELL *War* 47 The gaskets cast off the fore topsail.

h. *Dancing.*

1760 GOLDSM. *Cit. World* xxviii, She..makes one in a country dance, with..one of the chairs for a partner, casts-off round a joint stool, and sets to a corner-cupboard.

i. *Knitting.* To take the work off the wires, closing the loops and forming a selvedge. Cf. 58.

1880 *Plain knitting, &c.* 11 To cast off which is done by knitting two loops and pulling the first made loop over the last. **1887** *Fancy Work-basket* No. 4. 62 Cast off 5 stitches in the usual way.

j. *Printing.* To estimate how much printed matter will correspond to (a piece of MS. copy). Also *absol.* (Cf. CAST-OFF *sb.*[1] 2.)

1683 MOXON *Mech. Exerc., Printing* xxii. ¶9 Casting off Copy..is to examine..how much..of Printed Copy will Come-in into any intended number of Sheets..; or how much Written Copy will make an intended number of Sheets..: Therefore if I shew you how the Compositer Casts off Written Copy, I do at the same time inform you how to Count off Printed Copy. **1784** B. FRANKLIN in *Ann. Reg.* (1817) *Chron.* 389 The compositors in your chapel do not cast off their copy well. **1808** STOWER *Printer's Gramm.* 135 To cast off manuscript with accuracy and precision, is an essential object. **1824** J. JOHNSON *Typogr.* II. 89 To cast off manuscript..is a task of a disagreeable nature. **1892** OLDFIELD *Man. Typogr.* xii. 97 Sometimes copy is so badly arranged that it is almost impossible to cast-off accurately... In casting-up allowance must be made for chapter-heads, &c.

80. cast on.

a. *trans.* To throw on (a plaid, or shawl); to put on (clothes).

1813 W. BEATTIE *Fruits of Time* (1871) 25 The young man now cast on his plaid.

b. To make the initial loops or stitches on the wires in knitting. Cf. 58.

1840 in *Westmrld. Gloss.* **1887** *Fancy Work-basket* No. 4. 62 Cast on 83 stitches. *Mod.* Will you cast on a stocking for me?

81. cast out.

a. *trans.* See simple senses and OUT.

c **1200** *Trin. Coll. Hom.* 177 þe se flouweð þe hi casteð ut þat water of hire stede into þat lond. **1535** COVERDALE *Lament.* i. 17 Sion casteth out hir hondes, and there is no man to comforte her. **1674** RAY *Allom Work Whitby* 139 After the second water is drawn off they cast out the Mine. **1697** DAMPIER *Voy.* I. iii. 64 When we see them we cast out a Line and Hook. *a* **1719** ADDISON (J.) Why dost thou cast out such ungenerous terms against the lords.

b. To drive out forcibly, to expel, make an outcast. *lit.* and *fig.*

1297 R. GLOUC. 375 He caste oute of hom & hous of hys men gret route. *c* **1340** HAMPOLE *Prose Tr.* 17 When all vayne lufe and drede, vayne joy and sorowe es casten owte of þe herte. **138.** WYCLIF *Serm.* Sel. Wks. II. 67 þei token Crist and kesten him out of Jerusalem. **1382** —— *Mark* ix. 37 Maistir, we sy3en sum oon for to caste out fendis in thi name. **1488** CAXTON *Chast. Goddes Chyld.* 42 Yf thou cast us out sende us in to a herde of hogges. **1637** RUTHERFORD *Lett.* lxxxv. (1862) I. 217 Christ now casten out of His inheritance. **1667** MILTON *P.L.* I. 37 His Pride Had cast him out from Heav'n. **1884** *Chr. World* 9 Oct. 766/3 Fear casts out love, just as constantly as love casts out fear.

c. To throw out of one's house, one's keeping or preservation; to fling away; to thrust out of doors, society, etc.

1388 WYCLIF *Matt.* v. 13 To no thing it is worth ouere, no but that it be cast out. **1535** COVERDALE *Jer.* xxxvi. 30 His deed corse shalbe cast out. **1597** HOOKER *Eccl. Pol.* v. lxiv. §5 Whom the cruelty of unnatural parents casteth out. **1730** THOMSON *Autumn* 47 Raiser of human kind! by Nature cast Naked, and helpless out amid the Woods. **1887** *Academy* 4 June 391 A sorceress..cast out by her own father for her infamous conduct.

†**d.** To set forth by power, set free, deliver. *Obs.*

a **1300** *Fall & Pass.* 96 in *E.E.P.* (1862) 15 Of þe pit vte he ham cast an bro3t ham to heuen ly3t. *c* **1400** MANDEV. *Voy.* xxi. 225 God..wolde casten hem out of servage. *c* **1489** CAXTON *Sonnes of Aymon* ix. 226 Good lorde..that dydest cast danyell out fro the lyons.

e. To eject from the mouth, to vomit. Also *transf.* and *absol.* Cf. 25. *arch.*

1388 WYCLIF *Job* xx. 15 He schal cast [*v.r.* spue] out the richessis, which he deuouride. **1483** CAXTON *Gold. Leg.* 306/3 What he ete or dranke alweye he vomyted and casted oute. **1561** HOLLYBUSH *Hom. Apoth.* 15 a, He that hath a drye cough and doth not caste out. **1611** BIBLE *Isa.* xxvi. 19 The earth shall cast out the dead. **1751** CHAMBERS *Cycl.* s.v. *Casting*, In the morning she [the hawk] will have cast them [pellets of cotton] out.

f. *intr.* To disagree, quarrel, fall out. *Sc.* and *north. dial.*

1730 A. RAMSAY *Mercury in Q. Peace*, The gods coost out, as story gaes. **1851** MRS. OLIPHANT *Marg. Maitland* 180 To be together but one week..and to cast out in the time. **1861** RAMSAY *Remin.* vi. (ed. 18) 213 He's gane to mak four men agree Wha ne'er cast out. **1877** E. PEACOCK *N.-W. Linc. Gloss.* (E.D.S.) They cast out wi' one another six year sin'.

82. cast over. See simple senses and OVER.

a. *trans.* To turn over in one's thought. *dial.*

1877 E. PEACOCK *N.-W. Linc. Gloss.* (E.D.S.) I've been castin' ower i' my heäd what you said.

83. cast up.

a. *trans.* See simple senses and UP.

c **1340** *Gaw. & Gr. Knt.* 1192 Ho..stel to his bedde Kest vp þe cortyn & creped with-inne. **1535** COVERDALE *Ps.* lix. [lx.] 4 A token..y[t] they maye cast it vp in the treuth. *Ibid. Ruth* iii. 2 Boos oure kynsman..casteth up barly now this night in his barne. **1577** B. GOOGE *Heresbach's Husb.* III. (1586) 181 b, A little dust cast up on hie.

†**b.** To vomit. Cf. 25. *Obs.* or *dial.* (*to cast up one's accounts* is used humorously in this sense.)

1484 CAXTON *Curial* 6 We ete so gredyly..that otherwhyle we caste it vp agayn. **1597** SHAKS. *2 Hen. IV*, I. iii. 96. **1629** EARLE *Microcosm.* (Arb.) 80 As in a nauseeating stomacke, where there is nothing to cast vp. **1633** ROGERS *Treat. Sacraments* ii. 12 A penitentiall triall, by which a beleever..searches himselfe and casts up his gorge that he might..return to God. **1704** WORLIDGE *Dict.* s.v. *Bear*, Which she eats and casts up again to her young ones, and so feeds them. **1735** M. POOLE *Dial.* 128 The very Body of Christ..may be cast up by Vomit. **1808** R. ANDERSON *Cumbrld. Ball.* 26 The breyde she kest up her accounts In Rachel's lap.

c. Said of the action of the sea.

1398 TREVISA *Barth. De P.R.* xvi. xlvii. (1495) 569 Some precyous stones ben cast vp out of the grete see. **1556** *Chron. Gr. Friars* (1852) 46 Grete men and women of Spanyarddes ..ware drownyd and lost and gast up. **1611** BIBLE *Isa.* lvii. 20 The troubled sea, when it cannot rest, whose waters cast vp myre and dirt. **1883** *Manch. Guard.* 18 Oct. 4/7 Yesterday the body of a man..was cast up at Southport.

d. To throw, turn up or raise suddenly (the eyes, the head; formerly also, the nose, arms, etc.).

c **1384** CHAUCER *H. Fame* 935 Now quod he thoo cast vp thyn ye. **1535** COVERDALE *Ezek.* viij. 17 Purposely to cast vp their noses vpon me. **1590** LODGE *Euphues Gold. Leg.* (1887) 21 Casting up his hand he felt hair on his face. **1704** WORLIDGE *Dict. Rust.* s.v. *Bridle*, To make him Rein well and not cast up his Head. **1859** SALA *Tw. round Clock* 39 His eyes..cast up to count the peaches on the wall.

e. To throw up (with a shovel), to form by this means, to raise (a ridge, mound, rampart, etc.).

1603 KNOLLES *Hist. Turkes* (1621) 737 To cast up new fortifications within. **1611** BIBLE *Isa.* lvii. 14 Cast yee vp, cast yee vp; prepare the way. **1618** BUNYAN *Pilgr.* I. 17 The way..was cast up by the Patriarchs. **1721** DE FOE *Mem. Cavalier* (1840) 99 Two hundred [men] had orders to cast up a large ravelin. **1783** WATSON *Philip III* (1839) 67 Casting up entrenchments to secure his troops. **1881** RUSSELL *Haigs* ii. 35 To cast up a barrier between them and the aggressive inhabitants.

†**f.** To dig up, to dig. *Obs.*

1660 SHARROCK *Vegetables* 100 This he onely did by casting up their nests.

†**g.** To shake or toss up. *Obs.*

1557 F. SEAGER *Sch. Vertue* 62 in *Babees Bk.* (1868) 338 To cast vp thy bed It shalbe thy parte, Els may they say that beastly thou art. **1563** HYLL *Art Garden.* (1593) 75 The hearb sodden with oyle, and after cast vp in glister forme, doth put away the paines.

†**h.** To 'throw up'; give up, abandon. *Obs.*

1530 PALSGR. 478/2 She hath ben his soverayne lady, this tenne yeres, and nowe he casteth her up. **1540** HYRDE tr. *Vives' Instr. Chr. Wom.* (1592) N j, Men have dispised & cast them [mistresses] up. **1663** SPALDING *Troub. Chas. I* (1792) II. 115 (Jam.) His wife cast up all labouring.

i. To rake up and utter as a reproach; to cast in one's teeth. *Sc.* and *north. dial.* (or in lit. Eng. by northern writers).

1604 *Glasgow Kirk Sess. Rec.* in *Hist. Glasgow* xvii. (1881) 149 To speak ill of the dead or to cast up their demerits. **1609** BP. BARLOW *Answ. Nameless Cath.* 12 To cast vp such a disastrous example in his Maiesties teeth. **1725** RAMSAY *Gentl. Sheph.* III. ii, Unless ye may cast up that she's but poor. **1823** *Ann. Reg.* 21 Mar., No one shall cast up to me, that I killed my father. **1848** MRS. GASKELL *M. Barton* xxv, But we shall ne'er cast it up against you. **1864** TENNYSON *North. Farmer* (*Old Style*), But a cost oop, thot a did, 'boot Bessy Marris's barne. **1876** GEO. ELIOT *Dan. Der.* II. xxxi. 274 It was to be hoped that he would never cast it up to her that she had been going out as a governess.

j. To add up, reckon up, calculate.

1539 *Househ. Ord.* in *Thynne's Animadv.* (1865) Introd. 33 The Clerke of the Greencloth shall..cast up all the particular Breifments of the House. **1600** HOLLAND *Livy* XXXIII. xlvii. 850 After he had cast up the bookes. **1660** PEPYS *Diary* 10 Dec., Did go to cast up how my cash stands. **1704** J. HARRIS *Lex. Techn.* s.v. *Abacus*, sometimes signifies ..a Table of Numbers for casting up Accounts. **1849** GROTE *Greece* II. lxviii. (1862) VI. 149 An arithmetician, may.. cast-up incorrectly, by design. **1873** *Act 36 & 37 Vic.* lxxi. §30 The returning officer..shall..cast up and ascertain the number of valid votes given to each person.

k. *intr.* To 'turn up'; emerge into view; to come up as it were accidentally. *Sc.* and *north.*

1723 WODROW *Corr.* (1843) III. 16 It will be strengthening to our brethren to have our sentiments on what casts up among them. **1753** *Stewarts' Trial* App. 128 If Allan Breck did not soon cast up in the country. **1824** SCOTT *Redgauntlet* Let. xi, If the money cast up. **1864** BURTON *Scot Abr.* II. ii. 183 Another countryman, and Jesuit priest now casts up.

l. Of the weather, the day: to clear up (cf. 62); also, of clouds: to gather for a storm, etc. *Sc.*

1825 JAMIESON s.v., *It's castin' up*, the sky is beginning to clear, after rain. *Mod.* It's casting up for a storm.

cast (kɑːst, -æ-), *ppl. a.* [See CAST *v.*]

1. a. Thrown, that has been thrown. (See the vb.) ***cast shadow***, in painting, a shadow cast by an object within the picture, and serving to bring it out against the objects behind it.

1621 QUARLES *Argalus & P.* (1678) 24 Her liveless hands did, by degrees, Raise her cast body. **1849** J. D. HARDING *Less. Art* liii, In shading this Lesson care must be taken to make the cast shadow GHF darker at the points G and F, and also sharp on the edge. **1859** GULLICK & TIMBS *Paint.* 196 An eclipse is a vast cast shadow. **1890** *Adeline's Art Dict.* 362/1 The cast shadow is always darker than the shadow, properly so called, if the body casting the shadow and the surface receiving it are of the same tonality.

b. Cf. CAST *v.* 12.

1877 *Trans. N.Z. Institute* 310 Sheep that were 'cast' were soon attacked by the blow fly. **1947** R. B. KELLEY *Sheep Dogs* v. 69 She [*sc.* a ewe]..was 'cast', that is, lying on her back in a depression, unable to rise. **1953** BANNERMAN *Birds Brit. Isles* I. 15 A 'cast' sheep, whether healthy or sick, is always in danger, the eyes being torn from the sockets [by crows].

c. *Austral* and *N.Z.* ***cast-for-age***, see quot. 1965.

1933 L. G. D. ACLAND in *Press* (Christchurch) 30 Sept. 15/7 *Cast for age*, etc., means 'culled' for etc. This term is used for stud sheep rather than flock sheep. **1950** *N.Z. Jrnl. Agric.* Sept. 217/3 Cast-for-age ewes..are sold in late summer or autumn. **1965** J. S. GUNN *Terminol. Shearing Indust.* I. 13 *Cast for age*, a term to describe sheep that are got rid of..because they are too old.

†**2.** Condemned; beaten in a law suit. *Obs.*

1577 HOLINSHED *Chron.* III. 865/2 About foure of the clocke he was brought as a cast man to the Tower. **1642** MILTON *Apol. Smect.* (1851) 258 Sitting..upon his poore cast adversaries both as a Judge and Party.

3. Cashiered, dismissed from office (*obs.*); discarded, cast off. (***cast captain*** was app. orig. *cassed captain*; this led to other uses.)

1607 DEKKER *Northw. Hoe* v. Wks. 1873 III. 74 A new trade come up for cast gentlewomen. **1622** FLETCHER *Span. Cur.* I. i. 25 The Sonne Of a poore cast-Captain. **1636** HEALEY *Theophrast.* 33 Some cast Captaine, or cassierd Souldier. **1672** DRYDEN *Secret Love* I. ii, If thou should'st prove one of my cast mistresses. **1755** WALPOLE *Corr.* (1837) I. 258 It is sung by some cast singers.

4. Of horses, etc.: Rejected, as unfit for service, broken down.

1580 NORTH *Plutarch* 291 To keep cast Horses. **1653** H. COGAN *Pinto's Trav.* x. § I. 30 Put a grasing like a cast horse. **1844** *Regul. & Ord. Army* 376 The sale of Cast Horses.

5. Of garments: Thrown aside, discarded, no longer worn. Now usually CAST-OFF.

1597 *1st Pt. Return fr. Parnass.* III. i. 967 A moste lousie caste sute of his. **1611** *Jer.* xxxviii. 11 Old cast cloutes. *a* **1719** ADDISON *Drummer* I. i, A wardrobe for my Lady's cast cloaths. **1828** SCOTT *F.M. Perth* xxx, It is not for Rothsay to wear your cast garments, Sir John.

6. *gen.* Thrown off, disused, worn out, abandoned, forsaken. Now usually CAST-OFF.

1597 BP. HALL *Sat.* VI. i, In Margent of some old cast bill. **1599** SHAKS. *Hen. V*, IV. i. 23 With casted slough, and fresh legeritie. **1600** —— *A.Y.L.* III. iv. 17 A pair of cast lips of Diana.

7. Thrown up with the spade.

1487 *Newminster Cartul.* (1878) 263 An olde casten dike. **1593** *Tell-trothe's N.Y. Gift* 42 Fortified with deepe cast-rauelinges.

8. a. Of metal, etc.: Made by melting, and leaving to harden in a mould. See also CAST-IRON.

1535 COVERDALE *Isa.* xlviii. 5 My carued or cast ymage. **1544** *Ludlow Churchw. Acc.* (Camd.) 19 Item, for xx li. of cast lede . . xx *d.* **1692** in Capt. Smith *Seaman's Gram.* II. xiv. 111 A Cast-Bullet of Iron. **1765** *Univ. Mag.* XXXVII. 84/1 Cast copper or brass. **1794** *Rigging & Seamansh.* I. 154 Sheaves are made of cast metal. **1831** CARLYLE *Sart. Res.* (1858) 20 Proposal for a Cast-metal King. **1851** MAYHEW *Lond. Labour* II. 18 (Hoppe) Before cast glass was so common.

b. ***cast stone***: a manufactured substance resembling stone.

1925 *Pop. Mechanics Mag.* May 743 (*title*) Making cast stone; a new building material from marble. **1938** *Archit. Rev.* LXXXIII. 223 The photograph shows the rough texture of the facing bricks which contrasts with the smooth white cast-stone trim of the fenestration. **1956** *Gloss. Terms Concrete* (*B.S.I.*) 9 *Cast stone*, a building material manufactured from cement and natural aggregate, for use in a manner similar to and for the same purpose as natural building stone.

9. *Cookery.* 'Whipped', curded.

1597 *Bk. Cookerie* 46 How to make caste creame.

†**10.** Calculated, planned. *Obs.*

c **1400** *Destr. Troy* 10448 He . . Neuer kyld no kyng . . but with cast treson.

11. Like the verb, it may be used with many adverbs. See also CASTAWAY, CAST-BY, CAST-OFF.

1580 SIDNEY *Arcadia* (1622) 321 With smiling and cast-vp looke. **1645** RUTHERFORD *Tryal & Tri. Faith* (1845) 183 A cast-down mourner. **1653** H. COGAN *Pinto's Trav.* li. § 1. 201 With cast down looks, and tears in their eyes. **1834** MARRYAT *Jac. Faithf.* iii, Cast up wrecks.

†**cast**, *a. Obs.* [ad. L. *cast-us*.]. Chaste.

c **1430** LYDG. *Lyfe St. Albon* (1534) C ij, To serue Diana that was the cast goddesse That Venus had with them non intraunce.

castable ('kɑːstəb(ə)l, 'kæst-), *sb. rare.* [f. CAST *v.*] The projection of waste metal on cast articles.

1821 *Trans. Soc. Arts* XXXIX. 101 (Of an improved bullet mould and nipper for bullets) . . When the castable is removed by means of the common cutter . . a portion of the castable will be left behind.

castagnet, obs. form of CASTANET.

†**ca'staldick, ca'staldy.** *Obs.*—⁰. [ad. med.L. *castaldic-um*, *castaldia*, variants of *gastaldicum*, *gastaldia*, office of the *gastaldus* or *castaldus* (It. *castaldo*) manager, bailiff, steward, ad. Goth. *gastald-s* (found in comp.) occupying, administering. Common in the Laws of the Longobards, etc., but never in English use.]

1623 COCKERAM, *Castaldy*, Stewardship. **1678–96** PHILLIPS, *Castaldy*, or *Castaldick*, a Stewardship; from *Castaldius*, a word received for Latin. **1721–1800** BAILEY, *Castaldick*, *Castaldy*, a Stewardship. *Old Word.*

Castalia (kæ'steɪlɪə), **Castalie, -ly** ('kæstəlɪ). [L. *Castalia*, Gr. Κασταλία, pr. name.] Proper name of a spring on Mount Parnassus, sacred to the Muses; often used allusively.

1591 SPENSER *Virg. Gnat.* 23 The . . waues of . . Castaly. **1600** TOURNEUR *Transf. Metamorph.* lxxxvii. (1878) 172 Conuert each riuer to pure Castalie. **1748** THOMSON *Cast. Indol.* II. xxi, And brought them to another Castalie. **1847** TENNYSON *Princ.* IV. 275, I led you then to all the Castalies.

Ca'stalian, *a.* [f. L. *Castali-us* + -AN] Of Castalia or the Muses. Also *absol.* Hence †**Ca'stalianist**.

1602 *Metamorph. Tobacco* (Collier) 44 The Castalian Muses. **1667** MILTON *P.L.* IV. 274 Th' inspir'd Castalian Spring. **1783** COWPER *Task* III. 251 Lips wet with Castalian dews. **1607** WALKINGTON *Opt. Glass* 53 This made the Castalianist or poet of yore, to be esteemed. **1863** C. READE *Hard Cash* III. ii. 41 He had better have the courage to plunge into the Castalian stream, like Virgil and Lucan. **1882** G. M. HOPKINS *Let.* 4 Nov. in *Lett. to R. Bridges* (1955) 159 What I call Castalian or Parnassian, that is the language of poetry draping prose thought.

†**castane, -anie, -ayne.** *Obs.* Also 4 **casteyn(e, kasteyne,** 5 **castany,** 6 **kastainy.** [a. ONF. *castanie*, *castaine* (mod.F. *châtaigne*):—L. *castanea* chestnut.] A chestnut.

1398 TREVISA *Barth. De P.R.* XVII. lxxxviii. (Tollemache MS.) Kasteynes [**1535** Casteyns] bredeþ swellynge yf men eteþ to many þerof. *Ibid.* XVII. lxxxviii. (1495) 656 The casteyne tree is a grete tree and an highe . . Suche trees ben callyd Castanie. *Ibid.* cxxii. 684 The colour of a castane. *c* **1440** *Promp. Parv.* 73, Castany [**1499** chesteyne], frute or tre. **1480** CAXTON *Ovid's Met.* XIII. xv, Thou shalt have also castaynes grete plente. **1567** MAPLET *Gr. Forest* 48 The Kastainy is a tree of good high growth.

ca'stanean, *a.* In 8 -ian. [f. as next + -AN.] Of or pertaining to the chestnut.

1728 YOUNG *Love of Fame* (1741) 65 Since apes can roast the choice castanian nut.

castaneous (kæ'steɪnɪəs), *a.* [f. L. *castane-us* (f. *castanea*) + -OUS.] Chestnut-coloured.

1688 R. HOLME *Armoury* II. 311/2. **1848** *Proc. Berw. Nat. Club* II. No. 6. 336 Legs . . dirty castaneous white.

castanet ('kɑːstənɪt, 'kæst-, -ə'nɛt). Also (7 **castannetta, castanieta, castinetta),** 7–8 **castagnet,** 9 **castinet, (castagnette).** [ad. Sp. *castañeta* (or its Fr. adaptation *castagnette*), dim. of *castaña*:—L. *castanea* chestnut. See quot. 1647.]

An instrument consisting of a small concave shell of ivory or hard wood, used by the Spaniards, Moors, and others, to produce a rattling sound as an accompaniment to dancing; a pair of them, fastened to the thumb, are held in the palm of the hand, and struck with the middle finger.

1647 STAPYLTON *Juvenal* 240, *Castinettas*, knackers, of the form of chestnuts used . . by the Spaniards in their dances. **1648** GAGE *West Ind.* xi. (1655) 37 Dancing with their Castannettas, or knockers on their fingers. **1665** DRYDEN *Indian Emp.* IV. iii, Two Spaniards . . dance a saraband with castanietas. **1697** *C'tess D'Aunoy's Trav.* (1706) 21 They play admirable well on the Castagnets. **1700** CONGREVE *Way of World* IV. i, They had gone together by the ears like a pair of castanets. *a* **1754** FIELDING *Pleas. of Town* Wks. 1775 I. 214 A Blackamore lady, who comes to present you with a Saraband and castanets. **1783** AINSWORTH *Lat. Dict.* (Morell) II. s.v. *Testa*, Like the Spanish castagnets. **1828** MOORE *Maltese Air* i, Gaily sounds the castanet, Beating time to bounding feet. **1832** W. IRVING *Alhambra* I. 181 The tinkling of innumerable guitars, and the clicking of castañets. **1843** LEVER *J. Hinton* liii, The chink of the castanet and the proud step of the fandago echoed around us. **1850** LEITCH *Müller's Anc. Art* §425 *note*, A young maiden dancing in light dress with castagnettes.

castanite ('kæstənaɪt). *Min.* [ad. G. *castanit* (L. Darapsky 1890, in *Neues Jahrb. Min.* II. 267), f. Gr. κάσταν-α chestnut, in allusion to its colour: see -ITE¹.] = HOHMANNITE.

1892 DANA *Syst. Min.* (ed. 6) 964 Castanite . . Monoclinic, with a prismatic angle of 82°. **1951** PALACHE et al. *Dana's Syst. Min.* (ed. 7) II. 614 Castanite has been considered to be identical with amarantite but was later shown to be in all probability the same as hohmannite.

†**castar.** *Obs.* [? for CASTER in some sense.]

1570 *Wills & Inv. N.C.* (1835) 341, X mylke skelues *vs.* a castar for lyinge cheases of ijs.

castaway ('kɑːstəweɪ, 'kæst-), *a.* and *sb.* [f. CAST *v.* + AWAY.]

A. *adj.* Thrown away, cast off, rejected; reprobate; 'useless, of no value' (J.).

1542 BRINKLOW *Compl.* xvi. 41 Masterles and castaway courtyers. **1580** SIDNEY *Arcadia* (1622) 57 Certaine castaway vowes, how much he would doe for her sake. **1614** RALEIGH *Hist. World* (J.) We . . only remember, at our castaway leisure, the imprisoned immortal soul. **1818** SCOTT *Hrt. Midl.* xxxi, If I had minded . . I had never been the cast-away creature that I am. **1876** PAGE *Adv. Text-bk. Geol.* xx. 413 Castaway bones of the deer, bear, and wild-ox.

b. Cast adrift, stranded.

1769 FALCONER *Dict. Marine* (1789), *Cast away*, the state of a ship which is lost . . on a lee-shore, bank, or shallow. **1885** STEVENSON *Dynamiter* 75 A young lady and a mass of baggage standing castaway at midnight on the streets of London.

B. *sb.* One who or that which is cast away or rejected; a reprobate.

1526 TINDALE *2 Cor* xiii. 5 Knowe ye not . . how that Jesus Christ is in you excepte ye be castawayes [CRANMER cast a wayes, COVERD. cast awayes, *Rhem.* & **1611** reprobates]. **1563** *Homilies* II. *Passion* II. (1859) 419 Plaine reprobates and castawaies, being perpetually damned to the everlasting paines of hell-fire. **1594** SHAKS. *Rich. III*, II. ii. 6 Why do you . . call vs Orphans, Wretches, Castawayes. **1611** BIBLE *I Cor.* ix. 27. **1829** SOUTHEY *All for Love* ii, 'Dost thou . . For ever pledge thyself to me?' . . 'I do; so help me, Satan!' said The wilful castaway. **1871** E. BURR *Ad Fidem* xi. 220 Castaways from God.

b. *esp.* One cast adrift at sea; a shipwrecked man. Also *fig.* (from both senses) One cast adrift upon the world, or by society, an outcast.

1799 COWPER (*title*), The Castaway. **1816** J. WILSON *City of Plague* I. iii. 92 A lone castaway upon the sea. **1835** MARRYAT *Jac. Faithf.* xviii, Those who . . leave it [youth] to drift about the world, have to answer for the cast-away. **1865** SWINBURNE *Felise* 80 [Such things] As the sea feeds on, wreck and stray and castaway. **1869** LECKY *Europ. Mor.* II. i. 36 The moral wellbeing of the castaways of Society. **1870** *Times* 27 Aug. 4/4 The visit of Her Majesty's ship Blanche to the Auckland Islands in search of the castaways of the Motoaka.

castayne, var. of CASTANE *Obs.*, chestnut.

'cast-by, *sb.* A person or thing cast aside and neglected.

1818 SCOTT *Hrt. Midl.* xx, Wha could tak interest in sic a cast-bye as I am now. **1877** E. PEACOCK *N.-W. Linc. Gloss.* (E.D.S.), These ritualists are bringing in all sorts of old things which I thought had been cast-bys ever since Popery was done away with.

caste (kɑːst, -æ-). Forms: 6–9 **cast,** 6, 8– **caste.** [ad. Sp. and Pg. *casta* 'race, lineage, breed' (Minsheu); orig. according to Diez 'pure or unmixed (stock or breed)', f. *casta* fem. of *casto*:—L. *castus* *-a* pure, unpolluted (see CHASTE). App. at first from Sp.; but in its Indian application from the Portuguese, who had so applied it about the middle of the 16th c. (Garcia 1563). The current spelling (after F. *caste*, which appears in the Academie's Dict. of 1740), is hardly found before 1800; it was previously written *cast*, and app. often assumed to be merely a particular application of CAST *sb.*]

†**1. a.** A race, stock, or breed (of men). *Obs.* in general sense.

1555 *Fardle Facions* II. i. 118 The Nabatheens . . Their caste is wittye in winning of substaunce. **1596** RALEIGH *Disc. Guiana* (1887) 134 One sort of people called Tinitiuas, but of two casts as they term them. **1615** BEDWELL *Arab. Trudg.*, *Beni*, A family, nation, kinred, or *cast* as they call it. **1704** *Collect. Voy.* (Churchill) III. 5/1 Who are a cast of Men that are their Doctors. **1732** BERKELEY *Alciphr.* vi. §2 All the various casts or sects of the sons of men have each their faith and their religious system. **1774** J. BRYANT *Mythol.* II. 328 There is a cast of Indians, who are disciples of Bontas.

b. For Spanish *casta*, applied in South America, to the several mixed breeds between Europeans, Indians, and Negroes.

1760 tr. *Juan & Ulloa's Voy. S. Amer.* (1772) I. I. iv. 29 The inhabitants may be divided into different casts or tribes, who derive their origin from a coalition of Whites, Negroes, and Indians. *Ibid.* II. VII. v. 53 The inhabitants of Lima are composed of whites or Spaniards, Negroes, Indians, Mestizos, and other casts, proceeding from the mixture of all three. *Ibid.* II. VIII. viii. 266 Between fifty and sixty families, most of them Mestizos, though their cast is not at all perceivable by their complexion.

c. Breed of animals.

1799 CORSE in *Phil. Trans.* 205 (*Elephants*) Both males and females are divided into two casts, by the natives of Bengal, viz. the *koomareah* and the *merghee*.

2. a. *spec.* One of the several hereditary classes into which society in India has from time immemorial been divided; the members of each caste being socially equal, having the same religious rites, and generally following the same occupation or profession; those of one caste have no social intercourse with those of another.

The original casts were four: 1st, *Brahmans* or priestly caste; 2nd, the *Kshatriyas* or military caste; 3rd, the *Vaisyas* or merchants; 4th, the *Sudras*, or artisans and labourers. These have in the course of ages been sub-divided into an immense multitude, almost every occupation or variety of occupation having now its special caste.

This is now the leading sense, which influences all others.

1613 PURCHAS *Pilgr.* I. 485 (Y.) The Banians kill nothing: There are thirtie and odd severall casts of these. **1630** LORD *Banians* 72 (Y.) The common Bramane hath eighty-two Casts or Tribes. **1766** J. H. GROSE *Voy. E. Ind.* I. 201 (Y.) The distinction of the Gentoos into their tribes or casts. **1782** BURKE *Corr.* (1844) III. 7 The illustrious and sacred *caste* to which you belong. **1796** HUNTER tr. *St. Pierre's Stud. Nat.* (1799) III. 792 Her mother . . had lately been burnt alive with the body of her father, conformably to the practice of her caste. **1800** WELLINGTON *Let.* in Gurw. *Disp.* I. 125 They are of the cast of the old Rajahs. *c* **1813** MRS. SHERWOOD *Ayah & Lady* Gloss. s.v., The natives of India are divided into various ranks, called casts. **1818** JAS. MILL *British India* I. II. ii. 182 The Hindus were thus divided into four orders or castes. **1875** MAINE *Hist. Inst.* viii. 244 The problem of the origin of castes.

b. *transf.* A hereditary class resembling those of India. *fig.* A class who keep themselves socially distinct, or inherit exclusive privileges.

1807 VANCOUVER *Agric. Devon* (1813) 468 The peasant's mind should never be inspired with a desire to amend his circumstances by the quitting of his cast. **1816** J. GILCHRIST *Philos. Etym.* Introd. 18 Likely to unite the learned casts against him and provoke classic hostility. **1833** TENNYSON *Lady Clara* v, Her manners had not that repose Which stamps the caste of Vere de Vere. **1839** THIRLWALL *Greece* I. 119 An ancient priestly caste. **1852** DISRAELI *Ld. G. Bentinck* xxiv. 497 The peculiar and chosen race touch the hands of all the scum and low castes of Europe. **1856** EMERSON *Eng. Traits* Wks. (Bohn) II. 136 The feudal system survives in . . the social barriers which confine patronage and promotion to a caste.

c. *transf.* Applied to the different classes in a community of social insects, as ants.

1859 DARWIN *Orig. Spec.* ii. (1873) 36 The castes are connected together by finely graduated varieties. *Ibid.* viii. (1873) 230 The castes, moreover, do not commonly graduate into each other.

3. a. The system or basis of this division among the Hindoos; also the position it confers, as in ***to lose***, or ***renounce caste***.

[**1796** in *Ann. Rev.* (1803) I. 212/1 (Low as it was) he should lose his cast.] **1811** MRS. SHERWOOD *Henry & Bearer* 63 He has lost caste for becoming a Christian. **1858** MAX MÜLLER *Chips* (1880) II. xxvii. 302 In India caste, in one form or other, has existed from the earliest times. **1858** J. B. NORTON *Topics* 181 The stationary institutions of India, especially that of caste.

b. *gen.* and *fig.* A system of rigid social distinctions in a community; ***to lose caste***: to lose social rank, to descend in the social scale.

1816 *Times* in Hone *Every-day Bk.* I. 918 Loss of cast in society. **1828** MISS MITFORD *Village* Ser. III. (1863) 65 A natural fear of losing *caste* among her neighbours. **1841** MYERS *Cath. Th.* IV. 423 [Christianity] exercises the spirit of caste. **1870** EMERSON *Soc. & Solit. Civiliz.* Wks. (Bohn) III. 9 The diffusion of knowledge, overrunning all the old barriers of caste. **1882** HINSDALE *Garfield & Educ.* II. 240 In this country there are no classes in the British sense of that word,—no impassable barriers of caste.

4. *attrib.* and in *comb.*, as ***caste feeling***, ***-mark***, ***system***; ***caste-bound***, ***caste-ridden*** adj. See also HALF-CASTE.

1840 ARNOLD *Let.* in *Life & Corr.* (1844) II. ix. 200 The caste system is an insuperable difficulty. **1868** M. PATTISON *Academ. Org.* §4. 73 By the abolition of the rank of 'nobleman' . . the last remnant of the caste system will be swept away. **1875** HAMERTON *Intell. Life* VIII. i. 279 The caste-feeling in one class or another. **1901** KIPLING *Kim* xi. 290 Kim splashed in a noble caste-mark on the ash-smeared

brow. **1941** C. KIRKUS *Let's go Climbing* xiv. 177 At the temple at Gangotri red caste-marks were put on our foreheads. **1955** T. H. PEAR *Eng. Social Diff.* 133 The mass of Americans.. took it for granted that the typical Briton is essentially a caste-bound snob.

Hence **castehood**, the condition of belonging to a caste; **castism**, a system resembling caste.

1862 R. PATTERSON *Ess. Hist. & Art* 464 Even the out-casts—those who had fallen or been expelled from castehood—band themselves together in castes of their own. **1881** J. KERR *(title)*, Essays on Castism and Sectism.

†**caste**, *v. Obs. rare.* [A doublet of CHASTE *v.*; a. ONF. *castier* (mod.F. *châtier*:—L. *castigāre*.] To chasten, chastise.

c **1200** *Trin. Coll. Hom.* 137 Mid softnesse he castede þe sinfulle.

†**'casted**, *ppl. a. Obs.* [see CAST *v.*] An earlier form of CAST.

1599 SHAKS. *Hen. V*, iv. i. 23 With casted slough, and fresh legeritie.

casteel, -el, -ell(e, obs. ff. CASTLE.

Castelan, var. CASTILIAN² *Obs.*, a coin.

Castel Durante (ˌkæstɛl duːˈræntei). The name of a small Italian town, now called Urbania, used to designate a kind of tin-glazed ware of which the finest examples were produced in the 16th cent.

1857 MARRYAT *Hist. Pott. & Porc.* (ed. 2) iv. 58 The manufacture of Castel Durante.. flourished under Duke Francesco Maria II (1574 to 1631). *Ibid.*, The characteristics of the Castel Durante majolica are very uniform. **1951** 'M. INNES' *Operation Pax* III. iii. 91 The Castel Durante dishes that were a relic of her childhood in Rome. **1962** *Vict. & Albert Mus. Internat. Art Treasures Exhib.* 76/1 A Castel Durante plate by Giovanni Maria, with sunk centre, painted with a seated putto within a narrow white border.

casteless (ˈkɑːstlɪs), *a.* [f. CASTE *sb.* + -LESS.] Having no caste or castes.

1886 *Fortn. Rev.* Feb. 103 The dominion of a busy, roving, casteless nation. **1898** *Daily News* 15 Aug. 6/2 Reformed casteless Hindoos. **1906** *Macm. Mag.* July 714 While he [*sc.* the Maharajah of Travancore] journeyed over the black water to distant, and to them casteless and almost godless, Britain. **1949** G. BATESON in M. Fortes *Social Struct.* 46 It is wrong for a casteless person to address a prince in other than the 'polished language'.

castelet, variant of CASTELLET.

castellan (ˈkɑːstələn, ˈkæst-). Forms: 4–5 **castellin, -elleyn**, 4–7 **castellaine**, 5–7 **castelane**, 7, 9 **castellane, castelyn, castelain, castelan**, 7– **castellan**. See also CHATELAIN. [ME. *castelain* a. ONF. *castelain* (mod.F. *châtelain* = Pr. and Sp. *castellan*, It. *castellano*):—L. *castellan-us*, f. *castellum* castle, the current form is refashioned after L. or Sp.] The governor or constable of a castle.

1393 GOWER *Conf.* I. 184 Of this castell was castellaine Elda the kinges chamberlaine. *c* **1430** *Syr Gener.* (Roxb.) 2735 The Castelleyn That of the prison was wardeyn. **1591** GARRARD *Art Warre* 48 It is not lawful for the *Castellane* to leave his Castle. **1641** *Termes de la Ley* 47. **1678** *Lond. Gaz.* No. 1286/2 The Comptroller and Castelyn of the Princes Hof to continue. **1684** *Scanderberg Rediv.* i. 5 His Father being James Sobiesky Castellan of Cracovia. **1827** F. COOPER *Prairie* I. xii. 178 Obliged to constitute the girl herself castellain. **1844** H. H. WILSON *Brit. India* (1845) I. 173 The castellans of the forts of Kalinjar and Ajaygerh. **1876** GREEN *Short Hist.* iii. §1 (1882) 129 The piety of the Norman Castellans rebuilt almost all the parish churches of the city [Oxford].

Hence **castellanship**.

1885 J. H. ROUND in *Dict. Nat. Biog.* IV. 33/1 He was.. restored to his shrievalty and castellanship.

castellany (ˈkɑːstələnɪ, ˈkæst-). [ad. med.L. (Pr., It., Sp.) *castellania*, f. *castellān-us*: see above. (In mod.F. *châtellenie*.)] The office or jurisdiction of a castellan; the lordship of a castle, or the district belonging to a castle.

[**1357** in Sir T. D. Hardy *Syllab. Rymer's Fœdera* I. 392 The castelanny of Reule shall be committed only to Englishmen.] **1696** PHILLIPS, *Castellany*, the Lordship of a Castle, and the extent of his Land and Jurisdiction. **1756** NUGENT *Gr. Tour, Netherl.* I. 292 The country round about Ipres, called the castellany, or castleward, and containing about thirty villages, depends upon the government of the town. **1788** KELHAM *Domesday Bk.* 147 (T.) Earl Allan has within his castellany.. 200 manors. **1849** tr. *V. Hugo's Hunchback* 162 The seven castellanies of the viscounty of Paris.

castellar (kæˈstɛlə(r)), *a.* [f. L. *castell-um* castle + -AR. (L. had *castellāri-us*.)] Pertaining to, or of the nature of, a castle.

1789 H. WALPOLE *Lett.* IV. 480 (D.) Ancient castellar dungeons. **1881** PALGRAVE *Vis. of Eng.* 153 The entire disappearance of the castellar element from our country-houses.

castellate (ˈkæstəleɪt), *v.* [f. med.L. *castellāre* to build or fortify as a castle, f. *castellum* CASTLE: see -ATE³.] **a.** *trans.* To build in the manner of a castle; to build with battlements. **b.** *intr.* (*nonce-use.*) To grow into a castle.

1831 J. WILSON *Unimore* i. 77 Clouds slowly castellating in a calm. **1840** H. TAYLOR *Autobiog.* (1885) I. xx. 321 The citizen who castellates a Villa at Richmond.

†**'castellate**, *sb. Obs. rare*⁻¹. [ad. med.L. *castellāt-us* 'castellaniæ districtus' (Du Cange).] The district belonging to a castle.

1809 BAWDWEN tr. *Domesday Bk.* 230 In the Castellate of Roger of Poictou.

'castellate, *a. rare.* [ad. med.L. *castellāt-us*, fortified as a castle: see next.] = CASTELLATED.

1830 W. PHILLIPS *Sinai* I. 212 The living porphyry, in towers around Grotesquely castellate. **1834** DISRAELI *Rev. Epick* II. xix, Heights castellate.

castellated (ˈkæstəleɪtɪd), *ppl. a.* [f. med.L. *castellāt-us* (see above) + -ED. (Earlier than the vb.)]

1. a. Built like a castle; having battlements.

1679 PLOT *Staffordsh.* (1686) 448 A Castellated mansion. **1829** J. HODGSON in J. Raine *Mem.* (1858) II. 165 Large additions.. in the castellated style. **1844** DISRAELI *Coningsby* IV. v. (L.) It was a castellated building, immense and magnificent. **1860** HAWTHORNE *Marb. Faun* (1878) II. xv. 173 On the top of Hadrian's castellated tomb.

b. *transf.* Formed like a castle, castle-like.

1762–71 H. WALPOLE *Vertue's Anecd. Paint.* (1786) IV. 140 Rocks and precipices and castellated mountains. **1839–40** W. IRVING *Wolfert's R.* (1855) 271 Stately dames, with castellated locks and towering plumes. **1865** LIVINGSTONE *Zambesi* vii. 171 The somewhat conical shape of Zakavuma.. and the more castellated form of Morumbwa.

c. *transf.* Of a nut or disc: having grooves or recesses on its upper face.

1904 A. B. F. YOUNG *Complete Motorist* iv. 74 Castellated nuts are used throughout, with split pins. **1922** *Times* 20 June 8/5 The wheel and consequently the castellated shaft will be rotated.

†**2.** 'Inclosed within a building, as a fountain or cistern.' *Obs.* [cf. L. *castellum* reservoir for water.]

1720 *Stow's Surv.* (ed. Strype 1754) I. I. v. 26/1 The first cistern of Lead castellated with stone in the city of London was called the great conduit in West cheap. *Ibid.* II. viii. 459/2 A fair Conduit of sweet water Castellated in the midst of that Ward and street. **1766** ENTICK *London* IV. 66 It [a conduit] was castellated with stone and cisterned with lead.

3. Furnished or dotted with castles, 'castled'.

1808 R. PORTER *Trav. Sk. Russ. & Swed.* (1813) I. iv. 30 This castellated island. **1823** BYRON *Juan* X. lxi, The castellated Rhine. **1862** S. LUCAS *Secularia* 78 History, like the Rhine, passes through a castellated region.

4. Lodged or ensconced in a castle. *rare.*

1837 LANDOR *Wks.* (1846) II. 317 His unbiassed justice.. struck horror into the heart of every castellated felon.

castellation (kæstəˈleɪʃən). [ad. med.L. *castellātiōn-em*, n. of action f. *castellā-re*: see above and -ATION.] The building of castles; the furnishing of a house with battlements; *concr.* a fortified or castellated structure; a battlement.

1818 in TODD. **1853** H. JENKINS *Colchest. Castle*, The whole system of Norman castellation. **1858** *Lond. Rev.* Oct. 123 We are treading, as it were, upon the battlements of this immense natural castellation [Snowdon]. **1861** MISS BEAUFORT *Egypt. Sepulchres* II. xx. 176 The castellations and battlements of this [the Damascus Gate of Jerusalem] are so quaint as to be quite ludicrous.

'castellet, -elet. [a. ONF. *castelet* (mod.F. *châtelet*), dim. of *castel* (*château*) castle. See also CHATELET.] A small castle.

c **1320** *Seuyn Sag.* (W.) 2754 With seuen Soudans biset, Wal and gate and castelet. *c* **1325** *Coer de L.* 7010 Ryghte off Jaffa castellette. **1538** LELAND *Itin.* II. 35 A strong Pile or Castelet. **1772** PENNANT *Tours Scotl.* (1774) 68 The battlemented top of their castelet. **1841** *Archæol.* XXIX. 30 (D.) The erection of a castelet at this point would then become desirable. **1846** D. W. PUGHE *Harlech Castle* 29 Tradition notes the spot as the site of a castelet.

Castelli (kæˈstɛlɪ). The name of an Italian town used to designate a kind of majolica formerly made there.

1868 MARRYAT *Hist. Pott. & Porc.* (ed. 3) 540/2 Castelli (Abruzzo) majolica. **1877** LADY C. SCHREIBER *Jrnl.* (1911) II. 34 Only rewarded by one Castelli plate. **1960** H. HAYWARD *Antique Coll.* 60/1 Castelli wares of late 17th cent. date are often decorated with mythological or historical scenes in a subdued range of colours, dominated by a pale, greyish blue.

†**castellion**, obs. form of CASTELLAN.

c **1430** *Syr Gener.* (Roxb.) 3128 Tho the castellion he cleped ner And bad haue him to the tour ageyn.

'castellite. *Min.* A silicate containing titanic acid and near to titanite and sphene. (Dana.)

castelry: see CASTLERY.

†**casten**, *ppl. a. Obs.* exc. *dial.* Also *dial.* **cassen.** A by-form of CAST pa. pple. after strong pples. like *washen.*

1493 *Will of Franke* (Somerset Ho.) A casten kercher. **1535** COVERDALE *Nahum* i. 14 The carued and casten ymages. *a* **1560** ROLLAND *Crt. Venus* II. 307 They will me call ane cassin Courticiane. **1825** BROCKETT *N. Country Gloss.* 38, *Cassen*, cast off; as 'cassen clothes'.

caster (ˈkɑːstə(r), -æ-). [f. CAST *v.* + -ER¹.]

1. a. One who casts, in various senses of the verb.

1382 WYCLIF *Prov.* xxiii. 7 In licnesse of a deuynour and of a fals castere. **1552** HULOET, Brayder or caster in teeth. **1553** *Act 1 Mary* Sess. 3 viii. §1 Forcers of Wools, Casters of Wools, and Sorters of Wools. **1580** BARET *Alv.* C 171 A caster of lottes, *sortitor*. **1598** FLORIO, *Abbachiere*, caster of accountes. **1611** COTGR., *Mathematicien*, a caster of Natiuities. **1623** BINGHAM *Xenophon* 117 The caster of the first stone. **1669** ETHEREDGE *Love in Tub* II. iii, The Caster wins if he fling above Ten with Doublets upon three dice. *a* **1719** ADDISON (J.), Set up for a caster of fortunate figures. **1840** THACKERAY *Catherine* iii, Three to two against the caster [of dice]. **1856** R. VAUGHAN *Mystics* (1860) II. VIII. iii. 49 Casters of horoscopes and makers of cunning toys. **1885** *Harper's Mag.* 776/1 The caster stands on a platform. **1887** *Athenæum* 414 Artificial casters of the evil eye.

b. also with adverb following.

c **1340** *Cursor M.* 16703 (Trin.) Heil þou temple caster doun. **1601** DEACON & WALKER *Spirits and Dev.* To Rdr. 16 A coniurour or caster foorth of spirits and diuels. **1617** S. COLLINS *Def. Bp. Ely* 304 They are made to be casters on of the perfume. **1836** E. HOWARD *R. Reefer* xxvi, The caster-up of sums.

2. *spec.* **a.** One who casts metal; a founder.

1535 COVERDALE *Jer.* x. 14 Confunded be all casters of ymages. **1662** GERBIER *Princ.* 31 Architect, Sculptor, and Caster in Brass. **1865** MR. COWPER in *Parlt.* 12 May, The model of the first lion is completed, and now in the hands of the casters. **1884** W. M. FENN *Sweet Mace* III. vi. 84 Woe to the caster of cannon.

b. One employed in shovelling or 'casting' coals from the keels into the ships (on the Wear).

1793 *Ship Owner's Manual* (1795) 141 Many seamen, keelmen, casters. **1815** J. SYKES *Local Records* (1832–57) A number of misguided persons, principally keelmen and casters on the River Wear. **1846** MᶜCULLOCH *Acc. Brit. Emp.* (1854) I. 601 Keel-men, coal-boatmen, casters, and trimmers. **1861** *Act 24 & 25 Vict.* c. §40 Whosoever shall.. prevent any seaman, keelman, or caster from working at his lawful trade. **1882** J. GREEN *Tales & Ballads of Wearside* (1885) 229 The first coal staiths.. erected at Sunderland.. 1815; but the keelmen and casters.. pulled them to the ground. **1888** *Sunderland Daily Echo* 22 Mar. 2/5 Casters and trimmers.. their work was to cast the coals from the keels into the ships.

c. One who takes or makes a model by running some liquid or forcing a plastic substance into a mould.

1921 *Dict. Occup. Terms* (1927) §105 Potters; ware-makers, casters and finishers. *Ibid.* §414 *Caster*, takes plaster cast of foot where any special form of boot is required, as in case of malformation, etc.

d. (See quot.)

1921 *Dict. Occup. Terms* (1927) §049 *Caster*, examines coals sent from screens, and removes splints, *i.e.* slaty coal, in readiness for sale as house coal.

e. *Typogr.* = *casting-machine* (b) s.v. CASTING *vbl. sb.* 4.

1902 *Census Bull.* (U.S.) No. 216 59/2 The caster and setter resembles a sewing machine, being but little larger. **1921** Caster attendant [see *casting-machine* s.v. CASTING *vbl. sb.* 4]. **1973** S. JENNETT *Making of Bks.* (ed. 5) iv. 77 The formative parts of the caster are the matrix case, the mould, and the wedges controlling the mould blade, and thus the width of the mould opening.

3. *Cant.* 'A cloke' (Harman). ? *Obs.*

1567 HARMAN *Caveat* 77 For want of their Casters and Togemans. **1609** DEKKER *Lanthorne & Candle-L.* Wks. 1885 III. 199. **1640** W. M. *Wandering Jew* (1857) 22 A poore Alehouse is your Inne.. a Plimouth cloake your Caster. **1690** in B. E. *Dict. Cant. Crew.* **1725** in *New Cant. Dict.*

4. *colloq.* [f. CAST *ppl. a.* + -ER¹, as in *deader.*] = cast one.

1859 LANG *Wand. India* 144 The horse which drew the buggy had been a caster.. a horse considered no longer fit for the cavalry or horse artillery, and sold by public auction, after being branded with the letter R on the near shoulder.

5. See CASTOR.

casteyn(e, var. of CASTANE *Obs.*, chestnut.

†**castical.** *Obs.* [? for *castifical.*] 'Making chaste, pure or continent' (Blount *Glossogr.* 1656).

†**castifi'cation.** *Obs. rare*⁻¹. [as if ad. L. **castificātiōn-em*, f. L. *castificāre* to purify, f. *castus* chaste.] A making chaste, purification; chastity.

1653 JER. TAYLOR *Serm. at Gold. Grove* (1678) 226 Let no impure spirit defile the virgin purities and castifications of the soul.

†**'castigable**, *a. Obs. rare.* [see next and -ABLE.] To be chastised, deserving of chastisement.

1716 M. DAVIES *Athen. Brit.* II. 144 How censurable and castigable soever.

castigate (ˈkæstɪgeɪt), *v.* [f. L. *castīgāt-* ppl. stem of *castīgā-re* to chastise, correct, reprove (f. *castus* pure, chaste) + -ATE³. See CHASTISE.]

1. *trans.* To chastise, correct, inflict corrective punishment on; to subdue by punishment or discipline, to chasten; now usually, to punish or rebuke severely.

1607 SHAKS. *Timon* IV. iii. 240 If thou didst put this soure cold habit on To castigate thy pride, 'twere well. **1665** GLANVILL *Sceps. Sci.* 167 He.. that cannot castigate his passions. **1865** MOZLEY *Mirac.* vii. 291 It has only.. castigated and educated the belief, and not destroyed it. **1873** H. SPENCER *Stud. Sociol.* vii. 170 Daily we castigate the political idol with a hundred pens. **1878** S. COX *Salv. Mundi* vi. (ed. 3) 142 Discipline by which they should be castigated for their sins.

2. To correct, revise, and emend (a literary work).

1666 EVELYN *Mem.* (1857) III. 190 Seneca's tragedies.. have..been castigated abroad by several learned hands. **a 1742** BENTLEY *Lett.* 237 He had adjusted and castigated the then Latin Vulgate to the best Greek exemplars.

†**3.** *transf.* To chasten or subdue (in intensity).

1653 H. MORE *Conject. Cabbal.* (1713) 174 Morning is.. a parcel of that full Day which was first created, and is castigated and mitigated by its conjunction with the dark Matter into a moderate Matutine Splendour. **1662** GLANVILL *Lux Orient.* xiv. (T.) Being so castigated, they are duly attempered to the more easy body of air again. **1669** W. SIMPSON *Hydrol. Chym.* 112 If the narcotick Sulphur was castigated.

Hence ˈ**castigated** *ppl. a.*, chastened.

1728 YOUNG *Love Fame* v. (1757) 136 The modest look, the castigated grace. **1784** J. BARRY *Lect. Art* vi. (1848) 228 This happily castigated style of design. **1787** BURNS *Unco Guid* iv, When your castigated pulse Gies now and then a wallop.

†**castigate**, *a. Obs.* [ad. L. *castīgāt-us*, pa. pple. of *castīgāre*: see prec. vb. and -ATE².] Subdued, chastened, moderated; revised and emended.

1640 H. MORE *Antipsychop.* Pref., Being suppresst or very much castigate and kept under. **1678** CUDWORTH *Intell. Syst.* I. v. 673 Seeming more cautious and castigate. **1837** HALLAM *Hist. Lit.* III. iv. §14 The later editions..are castigate.

Hence †**castigately** *adv.*

1707 HUMFREY *Justif. Baxter.* 8 They have spoken many times..not castigately as they ought.

castigation (kæstɪˈgeɪʃən). [ad. L. *castīgātiōn-em* correction, chastisement, n. of action f. *castīgā-re*; see CASTIGATE *v.*]

†**1.** Chastisement, corrective punishment or discipline, correction, chastening. *Obs.*

c **1397** CHAUCER *Lack Stedf.* 26 Shewe forþe þy swerde of castigacioune. **1509** HAWES *Conv. Swearers* 35 Blessyd be ye of my castycacyon. **1594** HOOKER *Eccl. Pol.* v. (1632) 413 He also inuested them..with the power of the holy Ghost for castigation and relaxation of sin. **1634** SIR T. HERBERT *Trav.* 35 Carroon is not yet sensible of those castigations. **1677** GALE *Crt. Gentiles* II. IV. 143 Castigation is defined the curation of the soul from sin.

b. In modern use: Severe punishment or rebuke, chastisement, 'flagellation'.

1640 BP. HALL *Episc.* II. §20. 201 It is enough for me to leave him to the castigation of Bellarmine. **1759** DILWORTH *Pope* 77 The most complete piece of poetical castigation in our language. **1831** MRQ. LONDONDERRY *Sp. Ho. Lords* 21 May, He has given a well-merited castigation to the Noble Lords on that side of the House. **1844** H. H. WILSON *Brit. India* (1845) I. 71 Holkar then occupied himself in the castigation of the Raja of Bundi. **1876** GRANT *Burgh Sch. Scot.* II. v. 207 Smart castigation is in our opinion much preferable to fool's cap, imprisonment, etc.

2. Correction, emendation (of a book, etc.).

c **1611** CHAPMAN *Iliad* I. (R.) To oppose his arrogant and ignorant castigations. **1641** *Vind. Smectymnuus* 32 A castigation of the Liturgie. **1673** J. HOWELL (*title*), French and English Dictionary, with another English and French.. with accurate castigations throughout the whole work. **1756** JOHNSON in *Boswell* (1831) I. 307 He submitted that work to my castigation; and I remember I blotted a great many lines. **1882** J. H. BLUNT *Ref. Ch. Eng.* II. 76 The Breviary of the old Sarum use underwent a considerable castigation.

†**3.** Purification. *Obs. rare.*

1615 CROOKE *Body of Man* 325 [The air in the lungs] vndergoeth a peculiar Castigation before it bee admitted to the heart.

†**4.** Correction, subduing, moderating. *Obs. rare.*

1677 HALE *Prim. Orig. Man.* II. ix. 222 Floods and Conflagrations..either for the Castigation of the Excesses of Generation..or to the total Dissolution thereof.

ˈ**castiˌgative**, *a. rare.* [f. L. *castīgāt-*; see above, and -ATIVE.] = CASTIGATORY.

1641 SIR F. WORTLEY *Truth Asserted* 11 A coercive and castigative power.

castigator (ˈkæstɪgeɪtə(r)). [a. L. *castīgātor*, agent-noun f. *castīgāre*; see CASTIGATE.]

One who castigates; see the verb.

1618 R. HOULDER *Barnevelt's Apol.* F ij b (T.) The Latin castigator hath observed that the Dutch copy is corrupted and faulty here. **1873** SYMONDS *Grk. Poets* iv. 108 A sincere castigator of crime, extravagance, and folly. **1878** J. H. GRAY *China* II. xviii. 60 The beggar received his punishment without a murmur, his castigator being..the head of his clan. **1885** H. MORLEY *Introd. Montaigne's Ess.* (Rtldg.) 20 The Pope's castigator of books.

castigatory (ˈkæstɪgətərɪ), *a.* (*sb.*) [f. L. *castīgātōrius*, f. *castīgātor*: see prec. and -ORY.]

A. *adj.* Pertaining to a castigator or to castigation; chastising, corrective, punitive.

1613 T. GODWIN *Rom. Antiq.* (1625) 187 The corporall punishments are either..Capitall..or Castigatory, such corrections as serued for the humbling and reforming of the offender. **1675** BAXTER *Cath. Theol.* I. I. 108 The sin itself is castigatory, and hath such like effects. **1866** *Pall Mall G.* 3 Mar. 11 The castigatory measures in which our soldiers and sailors..were subsequently employed.

†**B.** *sb.* An instrument of chastisement. *Obs.*

c **1640** J. SMYTH *Lives Berkeleys* (1883) I. 201 Stocks, cage, tumbrell, pillory, Cuckingstoole, and other Juditialls and castigatories. **1769** BLACKSTONE *Comm.* IV. xiii. (R.) A certain engine of correction called the trebucket, castigatory, or cucking stool.

Castile soap (kəˈstiːl ˈsəʊp). Formerly castle-soap. [from *Castile*, a province of Spain, in which the soap was originally made.]

A fine hard soap made with olive-oil and soda. There are two kinds, the white and the mottled. Called also *Spanish soap*.

1616 B. JONSON *Devil an Ass* v. iii, Foam at the mouth. A little castle-soap Will do't to rub your lips. **1641** FRENCH *Distill.* (1651) v. 153 You may make candles of Castle-sope. **1710** *Lond. Gaz.* No. 4674/7 Castile marbled Soap. **1712** ADDISON *Spect.* No. 458 ¶1 A word or two upon the present Duties on Castle-soap. **1766** ENTICK *London* IV. 86 White soap in hard cakes, called Castile soap. **1866** MRS. RIDDELL *Race for W.* xxix, Like Castile soap..generally mottled.

†**caˈstilian**, *sb.*¹ *Obs.* Also -illian. [A variant or doublet of CASTELLAN: cf. next; also med.L. '*castellanus*, castelli incola' (Du Cange).] One living in or belonging to a castle; one of the garrison of a castle. Applied *e.g.* to those who held the Castle of St. Andrews in 1547, and frequent during the civil war of the 17th c.

1570-87 HOLINSHED *Scot. Chron.* (1806) II. 389 In which action also the adverse part forgot not to requite the castillians. **1828-41** TYTLER *Hist. Scot.* (1864) III. 51 The Castilians sent an envoy to Henry the Eighth..declaring that their only object was to gain time to revictual the castle. **1649** *Jrnl. Siege of Pontefract Cast.* 106 We were upon treaty with the castillians. *c* **1665** MRS. HUTCHINSON *Mem.* (1838) 79/1 Now the name of cavalier was no more remembered, Castilian being the term of reproach with which they branded all the governor's friends.

Castilian (kæˈstɪlɪən), *a.* and *sb.*² [in sense 1, ad. Sp. *Castellano* pertaining to the Spanish province of Castile (*Castella*, so called from the numerous forts erected by Alfonso I for its defence)].

1. Of or pertaining to Castile; a native of Castile; the language of that province, *hence*, standard Spanish, as distinct from any provincial dialect.

1796 MORSE *Amer. Geog.* II. 393 The old Castilians are laborious. **1822** K. DIGBY *Broadst. Hon.* I. 219 Willing to adopt the Castilian maxim, that 'every man is the son of his own works'. **1860** *All Y. Round* No. 68. 419 The Castilian is driving all the provincial idioms of Spain from the field. **1867** LADY HERBERT *Impress. Spain* 122 Whose pure Castilian accent made his Spanish perfectly intelligible.

†**2.** A Spanish gold coin worth about 5*s.* sterling. *Obs.*

1526 EDEN *Decades W. Ind.* (Arb.) 238 Barres of golde.. of suche byggenesse that sum of them way more then two hundreth Castilians [*ed.* **1577** Castelan] or ducades of golde. [**1846** PRESCOTT *Ferd.* II. ix. 463 Two hundred thousand castellanos of gold went down in the ships with Bobadilla.]

3. Castilian furnace: a lead-smelting furnace first used in Spain (but invented by an Englishman named Goundry), which is specially adapted for the treatment of ores of low produce. It is arranged so as to run off a constant stream of slag into cast-iron wagons which succeed each other as they are filled.

1875 URE *Dict. Arts* III. 62. *Ibid.* 74 The slag-hearth.. might in many cases be advantageously exchanged for the Castilian furnace.

ˈ**castillite.** *Min.* [from proper name *Castillo.*] A sulphide of copper, zinc, and lead from Mexico. Dana *Min.* 1868.

†ˈ**castimony.** *Obs. rare*⁻¹. [ad. L. *castimōnia* purity, chastity; ceremonial purity, f. *cast-us* chaste; see -MONY.] Chastity, purity.

1490 CAXTON *Eneydos* ix. 37 To make foul the holy purpose of thy castymonye by thuntrue note of lykryke and slypper luxurye.

casting (ˈkɑːstɪŋ, -æ-), *vbl. sb.* [f. CAST *v.* + -ING¹.] The action of the verb CAST in various senses.

1. a. *trans.* Throwing, throwing up; ejection, vomiting; calculation; swarming (of bees); arranging, etc. *esp.* the action or process of founding (metal or glass).

1398 TREVISA *Barth. De P.R.* XVII. cxxxiii. (1495) 690 Juys of leke to drynke ayenst castynge of blood. **1428-1474-5** in *M.E.D.* **1493** [see CAST *v.* 25 b]. **1540** *Mem. Ripon* (Surtees) III. 289 Pamenntt of viij *li.*..for castynge and makyng of yᵉ thyrd bell. **1542** *Ludlow Churchw. Acc.* (Camden Soc.) 11 The castynge of a new peise for the clocke. **1557** RECORDE *Whetst.* R iv b, Trust not to my castynge. **1615** LATHAM *Falconry* (1633) 23 So great casting and long fasting maketh her to dye. **1626** BACON *Sylva* (J.) Every casting of the skin. **1657** W. COLES *Adam in Eden* cxvi. 167[Whortle-berries].. do somewhat bind the belly, and stay castings and loathings. **1668** MARKHAM *Way to Wealth* 77 In the time of casting [of bees]. **1783** AINSWORTH *Lat. Dict.* (Morell) I, The casting of a deer's head. **1801** STRUTT *Sports & Past.* II. ii. 68 Casting of the bar is..one part of an hero's education. **1825** HONE *Every-day Bk.* I. 172 A scheme to teach the casting of nativities. **1832** G. R. PORTER *Porc. & Glass* II. i. 139 The first English establishment of magnitude for the casting of plate glass was undertaken in 1773. **1865** M. ARNOLD *Ess. Crit.* (1875) 36 A new casting of that story. **1872** YOUATT *Horse* (ed. W. Watson) xxii. 456 We are no friends to the casting of horses, if it can possibly be prevented. **1962** *Gloss. Terms Glass Ind.* (*B.S.I.*) 21 *Casting*, a process of shaping glass by pouring it into a mould or on to a table or passing it between rollers.

b. with adverbs.

1340 *Ayenb.* 15 Þe zixte kestinge out of the ilke boȝe is wyþstondinge. **1382** WYCLIF *Heb.* ii. 16 Casting up of yuel fame vpon thi glorie. **1549** LATIMER *Serm.* v. (Arb.) 157 A casting away of God. **1580** HOLLYBAND *Treas. Fr. Tong, Delaissement*, a forsaking, a casting off. **1742** R. BLAIR *Grave* 550 Nor anxious casting-up of what might be. **1769** *Wilkes' Corr.* (1805) I. 265 The casting up of the books..by the sheriffs. **1845-6** TRENCH *Huls. Lect.* Ser. II. v. 220 A casting off of its old and wrinkled skin. **1871** WALFORD *Insurance Cycl.* I. 460 Casting away of ships—an offence of very frequent occurrence.

c. *Theatr.* and *Cinemat.* The assigning of parts to suitable actors and actresses.

1814 JANE AUSTEN *Mansf. Park* I. xiii. 253 From the first casting of the parts, to the epilogue, it was all bewitching. **1926** *Contemp. Rev.* June 757 The initial failure of Ivanov in a private theatre..was accidental and due mainly to wrong casting. **1952** ELIOT & HOELLERING *Film of Murder in Cathedral* 8 In the theatre, the first problem to present itself is likely to be that of casting.

d. In ploughing, the method and operation of turning all the furrow-slices of a ridge in one direction, and those of the adjoining ridge in the opposite direction.

1825 LOUDON *Encycl. Agric.* II. v. 471 The form of the old ridges, and the situation of the inter-furrows, are preserved by what is called *casting*, that is, the furrows of each ridge are all laid in one direction, while those of the next adjoining ridges are turned the contrary way. **1837** J. F. BURKE *Brit. Husb.* II. 46 It is sometimes desirable to throw two ridges into one... This operation is called casting. **1855** MORTON *Cycl. Agric.* II. 646/1 The mysteries of 'gathering up', 'rown and furrow' ploughing, 'casting', 'yoking or coupling' ridges [etc.].

2. *intr.* Also with adv.

1575 TURBERV. *Venerie* xl. 120 If they cannot make it out at the first casting about. **1690** LOCKE *Hum. Und.* I. ii, All Reasoning is search, and casting about. **1794** *Rigging & Seamanship* II. 247 *Casting*, the motion of falling off, so as to bring the direction of the wind on either side of the ship. **1823** P. NICHOLSON *Pract. Build.* 221 *Casting or Warping*, the bending of the surfaces of a piece of wood. **1856** RUSKIN *Mod. Paint.* III. IV. v. §13 The casting about for sources of interest in senseless fiction.

3. *concr.* **a.** Any product of casting in a mould; an object in cast metal. **b.** The convoluted earth cast up by worms. **c.** Vomit; *esp.* the excrementitious substances cast up by hawks and the like; also in *Falconry*, 'anything given to a hawk to cleanse and purge her gorge, whether it be flannel, thrummes, feathers, or such like' (Latham *Falconry* 1615).

1388 WYCLIF *2 Pet.* ii. 22 The hound turnede aȝen to his castyng. *c* **1430** *Bk. Hawkyng* in *Rel. Ant.* I. 297 An hawke that hath casting, and may not cast. **1486** *Bk. St. Albans* A iij b, Looke that hir castyng be plumage. **1558** BP. WATSON *Seven Sacram.* x. 58 A dogge turneth backe to eate agayne his castynge. **1565-78** COOPER *Thesaur.* s.v. *Crusta*, Covered with..the playster of a wall or rough casting. **1618** BEAUM. & FL. *Loyal Subj.* III. v, The onely casting for a crazie conscience. **1657** RUMSEY *Org. Salutis* iv. (1659) 24 All manner of Hawks cast their castings every morning. **1704** WORLIDGE *Dict. Rust. et Urb.* s.v. *Gerfaulcon*, Since they are crafty Birds..instead of cotton, give 'em a Casting of Tow. **1788** J. FITCH *Original Steam-boat Supported* 10 His application..for castings for a steam-engine. **1851** *Crystal Palace & Great Exhib.* xi. 156 In the castings, for which Germany is deservedly famous, there is much to admire. **1869** *Eng. Mech.* 3 Dec. 274/2 The best castings are seldom or never made in an open mould. **1874** WOOD *Nat. Hist.* 282 In the 'castings' of this species have been found the remains of mice. **1881** DARWIN *Veg. Mould* 9 Earth-worms abound..Their castings may be seen in extraordinary numbers on commons. **1884** *Law Times Rep.* LI. 536/2 Means by which the owners of the foundry can remove their castings.

4. *attrib.* and in *Comb.*, as ***casting-darts***, ***-house***, ***-line***, ***-net***, ***-shovel***, ***-time***, etc.; also **casting-box**, †(*a*) a dice-box (*obs.*); (*b*) a box used in taking a cast for stereotyping; **casting-couch** *colloq.* (orig. *U.S.*), see quots.; †**casting-counters** *pl.*, counters used in calculation or reckoning; **casting director**, one responsible for casting (sense 1 c); **casting-ladle**, an iron ladle used for conveying the molten metal into the mould in casting; **casting-machine**, (*a*) in a blast furnace a machine used in casting metal; (*b*) a machine for founding type; **casting-pit**, that part of a foundry where the moulds are placed and the castings made; **casting-plate** = *casting-table*; **casting-pot**, (*a*) a box in which a stereotype plate is cast; (*b*) a crucible; **casting-press**, an apparatus for subjecting metal to pressure during the process of casting; **casting-reel**, the reel of a casting-line; **casting sand**, black moulding sand that has been used for castings; †**casting-sheet** (see quot.); **casting-shop**, the place where the operation of casting metal, etc., is carried out; **casting-slab**, **-table**, a table of polished metal with raised edges which serves as a mould for plate-glass; †**casting-top**, a peg-top.

1616 HOLYDAY *Persius* 311 Cogging forth a die Out of the small-neck'd *casting-box. **1880** *Print. Times* 15 Mar. 61/1 The matrix must be allowed to dry without the application of heat, or the blocks will split. The casting-box, slightly heated, is generally used in such cases. **1948** MENCKEN *Amer. Lang.* Suppl. II. XI. ii. 704 Terms emanating from Hollywood wits..**casting-couch* for the divan in a casting-director's office. **1963** *Sunday Express* 27 Jan. 22/6 In the old days..the only way anyone got anywhere in this

business was by way of the casting couch. **1966** C. FENN *Pyramid of Night* ix. 183 Get a load of that casting couch. What girl wouldn't want to be laid on velvet? *a* **1529** SKELTON *Vox populi*, Thes are the vpstart gentylmen With *castinge cownteres and ther pen. **1612** T. JAMES *Corrupt. Script.* IV. 1 Vsing them, as Merchants doe their casting counters, sometimes they stand for pounds, sometimes for shillings, sometimes for pence. **1622** BACON *Hen. VII*, 199 They would not bring him in amongst the Kings Casting-Counters. **1924** G. S. DOUGHERTY *Criminal as Human Being* ii. 48 You have all heard of the *casting director who selects actors of suitable type for the movies. **1950** T. S. ELIOT *Cocktail Party* III. 150 We've got the casting director: He's looking for some typical English faces. **1883** *Pall Mall G.* 30 June 3/2 Morice's bronze statue of the Republic..was transported last night..from the *casting-house. **1861** FAIRBAIRN *Iron* 157 No sooner is the mixture of the metals effected than the *casting-ladle is brought under the mouth of the vessel. **1880** *Encycl. Brit.* XIII. 345/1 The casting ladle into which the contents of the converters are emptied. **1872** *Echo* 30 Sept., Busy..renovating *casting lines, assorting hooks. **1899** *Chambers's Jrnl.* 25 Nov. 829/2 Pig-iron *casting-machines. **1902** *Census Bulletin 216*, 28 June 58 (Cent. Dict. Suppl.), The monotype..consists of two machines—a perforating device operated by a keyboard, and a casting-machine. **1921** *Dict. Occup. Terms* (1927) §524 *Monotype caster attendant*..operates and adjusts casting machine. *a* **1680** BUTLER *Rem.* (1759) I. 52 Threw *Casting-nets, with equal Cunning at her [the moon] To catch her with, and pull her out o' th' Water. **1859** LANG *Wand. Ind.* 310 A clear stream called the Ram Gunga, in which we caught a quantity of fish with a casting-net. **1884** W. H. GREENWOOD *Steel & Iron* xxi. 469 In the centre of the [Bessemer] *casting-pit is fixed a hydraulic crane. **1921** *Dict. Occup. Terms* (1927) §279 *Moulder, casting pit*..shapes moulds in sand, in casting pit. **1881** *Spons' Encycl. Industr. Arts* III. 1061 The impressions are given by projections on the *casting-plate, which acts as a mould. **1846** DODD *Brit. Manuf.* VI. 60 The *casting-pot, with the mould,..is gradually forced down into the molten mass. **1858** SIMMONDS *Dict. Trade* 75/1 *Casting-pot*, a pot adapted for melting metals. *Casting-pot and Crucible maker*, a special trade in the iron districts. *a* **1877** KNIGHT *Dict. Mech.*, *Casting-press*, one in which metal is cast under pressure, as in the car-wheel press. **1892** NIVEN *Brit. Angler's Lexicon* 192 The 'Malloch' *casting reel is used for spinning only. **1849** N. KINGSLEY *Diary* (1914) 30 Our sugar is black enough for *casting sand. **1644** *Bury Wills* (1850) 186, I doe give with my owne hands vnto Alice my wife, my *castinge sheet. **1871** *Daily News* 2 Jan. 3/5 He was carrying some lead from one part of the yard to the *casting shop. **1805** R. W. DICKSON *Pract. Agric.* (1807) II. 299 To have the grain cleaned by means of the *casting-shovel. *a* **1877** KNIGHT *Dict. Mech.*, *Casting-slab. **1728** CHAMBERS *Cycl.* s.v. *Glass*, When the first Annealing Furnace is full, the Casting-table is to be carried to another. **1838** *Penny Cycl.* XI. 256/1 The cuvette is withdrawn from the furnace and taken to the casting-table. **1668** MARKHAM *Way to Wealth* 77 Too little hives procure bees, in *casting time..to cast before they be ripe. **1657** W. COLES *Adam in Eden* 169 The fruit is in forme like a *casting-Top.

5. **casting-bottle**, a bottle for sprinkling perfumed waters; a vinaigrette. So †**casting-glass**.

c **1530** in Gutch *Coll. Cur.* II. 342 A Cheyne and Howke for twoo casting Bottellis. **1544** *Privy Purse Exp. P'cess Mary* (1830) 144 Item my lady Buttler a Casting-glasse and a Smoke. **1602** B. JONSON *Ev. Man out Hum.* IV. (N.) His civet and his casting-glass Have helpt him to a place among the rest. **1638** FORD *Fancies* I. ii. 127 Enter Secco, sprinkling his hat and face with a casting bottle. **1883** J. PAYNE *1001 Nts.* VI. 211 A casting-bottle full of rose water.

casting ('kɑːstɪŋ, -æ-), *ppl. a.* [f. CAST *v.* + -ING².]

1. That casts, in various senses of the vb.

a. *trans.* Of a bow, etc.: Throwing, shooting (see also quot. 1483). **b.** *intr.* Of bees: Swarming.

a **1300** *Cursor M.* 26020 Þis reuth es like a castand gin. **1483** *Cath. Angl.* 55 Castynge as a bowe, *flexibilis*. **1485** CAXTON *Higden* v. xiv. (1527) 201 A wonder fell man and ferre casting. **1545** ASCHAM *Toxoph.* I. (Arb.) 29 Except they be..vnbent like a good casting bowe. **1565–78** COOPER *Thesaur.* *Acer arcus*, a strong or quicke casting bowe. **1627** DRAYTON *Agincourt* 28 Like casting Bees that they arise in swarmes.

2. That turns the scale, deciding, decisive (see CAST *v.* 55), as in ***casting voice, vote, weight***.

1622 in Heath *Grocers' Comp.* (1869) 101 There can be in a Court but one casting voyce or ball. **1646** SIR T. BROWNE *Pseud. Ep.* 231 Which..containe within themselves the casting act, and a power to command the conclusion. **1692** BENTLEY *Boyle Lect.* iv. 141 Even the Herbs of the Field give a casting vote against Atheism. **1711** STEELE *Spect.* No. 17 ¶3 The President to have the casting Voice. **1735** POPE *Prol. Sat.* 177 That casting-weight pride adds to emptiness. **1828** D'ISRAELI *Chas. I*, I. vi. 160 The alliance of England was a casting weight in the government of the world. **1855** MACAULAY *Hist. Eng.* IV. 783 The question was decided by the casting vote of the Chancellor.

cast iron, cast-'iron. [see CAST *ppl. a.*]

1. Iron run in a molten state into moulds where it has cooled and hardened.

1664 EVELYN *Kal. Hort.* (1729) 232 The..Pipes..should they be of the best Cast Iron. **1665** D. DUDLEY *Metallum Martis* 31 Give me leave to mention that there be three sorts of cast iron. **1679** PLOT *Staffordsh.* (1686) 164 For the back of chimneys..they use a sort of cast-iron. **1788** ALDERSON *Ess. Fevers* 49 If the ingenious workers of Cast Iron would turn their thoughts to this Article, Iron Bedsteads might be supplied. **1812** SIR H. DAVY *Chem. Philos.* 392 The process for reducing cast iron into malleable iron called blooming. **1869** ROSCOE *Elem. Chem.* 240 Cast iron is manufactured..chiefly from clay ironstone.

2. *attrib.* (*commonly hyphened.*)

1692 in *Capt. Smith's Seaman's Gram.* II. xiv. 110 A Cast Iron-Bullet of 4 Inches Diameter. **1756** C. LUCAS *Ess. Waters* III. 104, I took a..shallow cast iron pot. **1816** *Gentl. Mag.* LXXXVI. II. 424 We have Cast-Iron Bridges, Cast-Iron Boats, Cast-Iron Roads. **1881** *Metal World* 21 May 28/2 Cast iron fences of much elaboration of pattern.

b. *fig.* Hard, insensible to fatigue; rigid, stern, unbending; 'hard-and-fast', unyielding, wanting in pliancy or adaptiveness. (*hyphened.*)

1830 A. FONBLANQUE *Eng. under 7 Admin.* II. 27 He [Wellington] was esteemed a cast-iron Statesman. **1831** CARLYLE *Sart. Res.* (1858) 19 His look..of that cast-iron gravity frequent enough among our own Chancery suitors. **1856** EMERSON *Eng. Traits* xii, Those eupeptic studying mills, the cast-iron men. **1870** LOWELL *Study Wind.* 159 He laid down..no cast-iron theorem, to which circumstances must be fitted as they rose. **1876** LUBBOCK in *Contemp. Rev.* June 80 It is very undesirable to lay down cast-iron rules of this kind. **1886** C. D. WARNER *Summer in Garden* 51 What a man needs in gardening is a cast-iron back, with a hinge in it.

castle ('kɑːs(ə)l, -æ-), *sb.* Forms: 1–6 **castel**, (4 **castill, caastel, kastell, castele**, 4–5 **castelle**), 4–7 **castell**, (5 **castylle, -ille, caystelle**), 6– **castle**. [Taken into Eng. at two different times: (1) bef. 1000, *castel* neut. (pl. *castel(l, castelu*), ad. L. *castell-um* in the Vulgate, rendering κώμη 'village' of the Greek; (2) *c* 1050–1070 *castel* masc. (pl. *castelas*) a. ONF. *castel* (mod.F. *château*) 'castle':—L. *castellum* in sense 'fort, fortress'. (Under the influence of this, *castel* village also became masc. by 12th c.) L. *castellum* was dim. of *castrum* fort; for the later sense 'village' Du Cange quotes an ancient glossary '*Castellum, municipium*, κώμη'; compare the later use of *castrum, castra* for 'town': cf. CHESTER.]

I. From Latin.

†**1.** Used to render L. *castellum* of the Vulgate (Gr. κώμη), village. *Obs.*

This continued in Bible translations and quotations till the 16th c., but was probably often understood in sense 3. Thus the author of *Cursor Mundi* evidently thought that Bethany 'the *castel* of Mary and her sister Martha, was like the castle of an English feudal lord.

c **1000** *Ags. Gosp.* Matt. xxi. 2 Farað on þæt castel [*Hatton* to þam castelle]. —— Mark vi. 6 He þa castel be-ferde. —— Luke ix. 12 þæt hiȝ farun on þas castelu & on þas tunas [*Hatton* on þas castelles]. *c* **1175** *Lamb. Hom.* 3 Goð in þane castel. *a* **1300** *Cursor M.* 14132 Þis lazarus..Had sisters..A castel was bath his and þairs. **138.** WYCLIF *Serm.* Sel. Wks. I. 197 Jesus wente aboute..boþ to more places and lesse, as citees and castellis..Castels ben undirstonden litil touns. **1382** —— *Luke* xix. 30 Go ȝe in to the castel, which is aȝens ȝou. **1515** W. DE WORDE *Inform. Pylgrymes* E vij, Fro Kames is xij myles to the castell of Emaus. *a* **1564** BECON *Christ's Chron.* (1844) 547 He entered into a certain castle, where a certain woman called Martha made him a dinner.

†**2.** *pl.* Used to render L. *castra* camp. *Obs.*

a **1300** *E.E. Psalter* lxxvii. 28 In mid þar kastelles fellen þai. *a* **1340** HAMPOLE *Psalter* xxvi. 5 If castels be set agaynes me..Kastels are conspiracyons of oure foes. **1388** WYCLIF *Lev.* xxiv. 14 Lede out the blasfemere without the castels [**1382** tentis]. **1483** CAXTON *Gold. Leg.* 58/2 The Angel of god wente to fore the castellis of Israhel.

II. From French.

3. a. A large building or set of buildings fortified for defence against an enemy; a fortress, stronghold. Retained as a name for large mansions or country houses, which were formerly feudal castles, but not, like F. *château*, transferred to this sense.

a **1075** *O.E. Chron.* (Laud MS.) an. 1048 Þa hæfdon þa welisce men ȝewroht ænne castel on Herefordscire. *Ibid.* an. 1069 Se eorl Walðeof..and Eadgar æðeling..þa castelas ȝewunnan. *a* **1154** *Ibid.* an. 1140 He beset heom til hi aiauen up here castles. *a* **1225** *Ancr. R.* 62 Þeo hwile þæt me..wiðuten asaileð þene castel. **1297** R. GLOUC (1810) 540 Tho the barons adde the toun, and the castel the king. *c* **1386** CHAUCER *Frankl. T.* 477 A castel al of lime and ston. **1393** GOWER *Conf.* I. 184 Of this castell was castellaine Elda the kinges chamberlaine. **1424** *Paston Lett.* I. 15 At the comyng of..the Duc of Norfolk fro his Castell of Framyngham. **1584** POWEL *Lloyd's Cambria* 3 The cities, townes, Castels and villages. **1597** SHAKS. *Rich. II*, III. iii. 52 This castles tatter'd battlements. **1611** BIBLE *1 Chron.* xi. 7 Dauid dwelt in the castell. **1638** DK. HAMILTON in *H. Papers* (1880) 12 Itt is imposabill to put ani of itt in to Ed[in]bur[gh] Castell. **1756–7** tr. *Keysler's Trav.* (1760) I. 496 The old castle of Pisa. **1856** EMERSON *Eng. Traits, Wealth* Wks. (Bohn) II. 72 New men prove an overmatch for the landowner, and the mill buys out the castle. *Mod.* The Round Tower of Windsor Castle. Dover Castle is still a fortress.

b. A model or similitude of a castle, made in any material; a castle-like pile of anything. (Applied by boys to four cherry-stones placed like a pyramid.)

1627 MASSINGER *Gt. Duke Flor.* IV. ii, Sit down and eat some sugar-plums. Here's a castle Of march-pane too. **1641** *G. Cavendish's Life Wolsey* in *Select. Harl. Misc.* (1793) 103 The officers brought into the house a casteel of fine manchet. *Mod.* The whole collapsed like a castle of cards.

c. Loosely applied to a large building.

1886 *Pall Mall G.* 10 Aug. 10/2 The Duchess of Teck..opened a 'Babies' Castle' at Hawkhurst yesterday, in connection with Dr. Barnardo's homes.

d. *the Castle*, in reference to Ireland, means specifically *Dublin Castle*, as the seat of the vice-regal court and administration; hence, in politics, the authority centred at Dublin Castle, the officials who administer the government of Ireland. Also *attrib.* as in ***Castle influence***, ***Castle government***, etc. So also ***Castleism***, the officialism of Dublin Castle.

1735 MRS. SICAN in *Swift's Lett.* (1768) IV. 129 Our Irish ladies made a fine appearance the birth-day at the castle. *c* **1795** BURKE *Corr.* (1844) IV. 321 The constant meddling of the bishops and the clergy with the Castle, and of the Castle with them, will infallibly set them ill with their own body. **1800** GRATTAN *Speech* in Irish Ho. Comm. 5 Feb., Whether you will go, with the Castle at your head, to the tomb of Charlemont..and erase his epitaph. **1813** O'CONNELL *Speech* 24 Dec., A newspaper in the pay of the Castle. **1843** MADDEN *United Irishm.* II. xvii. 367 Hired spies, informers, and witnesses kept in the pay of the Castle. **1880** A. M. SULLIVAN *New Irel.* xxii. 267 The Castle raised a petty squabble with the prison board as to the expense. **1887** *Pall Mall G.* 22 Sept. 4/1 So long as the whole machinery of Castle government is..anti-popular..such elements of popular government as exist will be anti-Castle. **1887** R. WALLACE *Sp. Ho. Comm.* 7 June, The unauthorised tyranny which was the animating spirit of Dublin Castleism.

e. Phrase. ***an (English)man's house his castle.***

[**1567** STAUNFORDE *Plees del Coron* 14 b, Ma meason est a moy come mon castel hors de quel le ley ne moy arta a fuer.] **1588** LAMBARD *Eiren.* II. vii. 257 Our law calleth a man's house, his castle, meaning that he may defend himselfe therein. **1600–16** COKE 5 *Rep.* 91 b, The house of every man is to him as his Castle and Fortresse, as well for his defence against injury and violence, as for his repose. **1856** EMERSON *Eng. Traits, Wealth* Wks. (Bohn) II. 73 The house is a castle which the King cannot enter. **1868** FREEMAN *Norm. Conq.* (1876) II. vii. 128 An Englishman's house is his castle.

f. A heap of brushwood or sticks under which rabbits hide when being hunted.

1898 *Encycl. Sport* Mar. 175/1 The whole space is laid out in lines of some 20 to 30 yards in breadth, marked out by heaps of sticks or brushwood euphemistically termed 'castles'. *Ibid.* 175/2 When three or more residents turn out together from the same 'castle', and perchance bolt backwards, then complications ensue.

g. *Cricket.* The wicket a batsman defends.

1959 I. PEEBLES in *Sunday Times* 31 May 38/3 In support came..Alfie Hall..with a low action which ensured his hitting the castle. **1960** —— *Bowler's Turn* 59, I..knocked ..Robinson's castle down first ball.

4. *fig.* (or *allegorical*). 'Stronghold, fortress'.

c **1300** *Cursor M.* 9881 Þis castel es o luue and grace. *c* **1320** (*title*), Her byginet a tretys þat is yclept Castel off loue. **1477** EARL RIVERS (Caxton) *Dictes* 64 Suffisaunce is a castell that kepeth wyse men from euyl werkis. **1533** ELYOT (*title*), The Castel of Helth. **1551** RECORDE (*title*), The Castle of Knowledge. **1783** COWPER *Task* v. 525 Seeing the old castle of the state so assail'd. **1823** LAMB *Elia* Ser. I. xxvi. (1865) 211 Shake not the castles of his pride.

5. *poet.* or *rhetorical* for: A large ship (esp. of war); usually with some attribute.

1642 HOWELL *For. Trav.* (Arb.) 46 Great Britaine..having so many invincible castles in motion (I meane Her Ships). **1695** BLACKMORE *Pr. Arth.* v. 224 The floating Castles dance upon the Tide. **1821** SHELLEY *Hellas* 24 Our winged-castles [fly] from their merchant ships. **1856** EMERSON *Eng. Traits* viii. Wks. (Bohn) II. 63 These sea-kings may take once again to their floating castles.

6. a. A small wooden tower used for defence in warfare; a tower borne on the back of an elephant.

c **1380** *Sir Ferumb.* 3252 To þe castel þat was ymad of treo al þat host he broȝte. *c* **1400** MAUNDEV. xviii. 191 The Castelles of Tree..that craftily ben sett up on the Olifantes Bakkes, for to fyghten aȝen hire Enemyes. **1489** CAXTON *Faytes of A.* I. xxiv. 77 The girdell that helde vp the castell vpon theyre backes. **1503** HAWES *Examp. Virt.* ix. 167 Syttynge in a castell..On an olyphauntes backe. **1843** MACAULAY *Proph. of Capys* xxiv, The beast on whom the Castle With all its guards doth stand. **1868** FREEMAN *Norm. Conq.* (1876) II. 624 The temporary towers..used in the military art of the time..sometimes called castles.

b. A tower in general.

1642 HOWELL *For. Trav.* (Arb.) 77 There is a Castle in the grand Caire in Egypt called the Niloscope, where there stands a Pillar.

7. *Naut.* A tower or elevated structure on the deck of a ship. Cf. FORECASTLE. *Obs.*

? *a* **1400** *Morte Arth.* 3617 The toppe-castelles he stuffede with toyelys. *c* **1460** *Towneley Myst.* 27 The helme and the castelle also wille I [Noah] take. **1521** EDEN *Decades W. Ind.* I. III. (Arb.) 76 The watche men lokinge owte of the toppe castell of the shyppe. **1611** COTGR., *Gaillard*, the round house, or hinder castle, of a ship.

8. Applied (in proper names) to ancient British or Roman earthworks, as *Abbotsbury Castle* between Weymouth and Bridport, *Maiden Castle* at Dorchester, *Round Castle* near Oxford, *Yarnbury Castle*, etc.

9. *Chess.* One of the pieces, made to represent a castle; also called a ROOK.

[**1610** GUILLIM *Heraldrie* IV. xiii. (1611) 222 They [the Rooks] stand in the vttermost corners of the Chesbord, as frontier Castles.] *a* **1649** DRUMM. OF HAWTH. *Fam. Ep.* Wks. (1711) 146 Here is a king defended by a lady, two bishops, two knights, at the end of the lists, with two rooks, fortresses, or castles. **1847** STAUNTON *Chess-pl. Handbk.* 5 The Rook, or Castle is next in power to the Queen.

†**10.** 'A kind of close helmet' (Nares): but perh. only a *fig.* use. *Obs.*

1577 HOLINSHED *Chron.* II. 815 Then..entred Sir Thomas Kneuet, in a castell of cole black, and ouer the castell was written The dolorous castell. **1606** SHAKS. *Tr. & Cr.* v. ii. 187 Stand fast, and weare a Castle on thy head.

11. ***castle in the air***, visionary project or scheme, day-dream, idle fancy. Common since 1575, varied occasionally with ***castle in the skies***, and the like; ***castle in Spain*** [= F. *château en Espagne*] is found 1400–1600, and

occasionally as a Gallicism in modern writers. *Castle* alone is also used where the allusion is obvious: cf. CASTLE-BUILDER, -BUILDING.

[As to the Fr. *faire des châteaux en Espagne* (found in 13th c.) see Littré; since it varied with *châteaux en Asie*, *en Albanie*, it appears that the phrase at bottom meant only to build castles in a foreign country where one had no standing-ground, Spain being finally taken as the nearest Moorish country to Christendom, or perhaps with some reference to the arms of Castile.]

c **1400** *Rom. Rose* 2573 Thou shalt make castels thanne in Spayne, And dreme of joye, alle but in vayne. **1475** CAXTON *Jason* 19 He began to make castellis in Spaygne as louers doo. **1575** GASCOIGNE *Steel Gl.* 55 (Arb.) Things are thought, which neuer yet were wrought, And castels buylt aboue in lofty skies. **1580** NORTH *Plutarch* (1676) 171 They built Castles in the air, and thought to do great wonders. **1586** T. B. *La Primaud. Fr. Acad.* II. (1594) 182 Some.. have their wittes a wool-gathering, and as wee use commonly to say, are building of castles in Spaine. **1590** GREENE *Orl. Fur.* (1599) 16 In conceite builde castles in the skie. **1611** COTGR., *Faire des chasteaux en Espaigne*, to build castles in the aire (say we). **1621** BURTON *Anat. Mel.* I. iii. I. ii. (1651) 187 That castle in the ayr, that crochet, that whimsie. *c* **1630** DRUMM. OF HAWTH. *Poems* 42. 2 Strange castles builded in the skies. **1738** KEILL *Anim. Oecon.* Pref. 27 To explain Nature by Theories.. is only building Castles in the Air. *a* **1763** SHENSTONE *Odes* (1765) 237 To plan frail castles in the skies. **1829** MARRYAT *F. Mildmay* xvi, I built castles till bed-time. **1860** MOTLEY *Netherl.* IV. 282 The explosion of the Gunpowder Plot blowing the castles in Spain into the air. **1867** MAURICE *Patriarchs & Lawg.* vi. (ed. 4) 120 In looking back to the castles of earliest boyhood. **1871** M. COLLINS *Mrq. & Merch.* II. vii. 203 We have all had our castles in Spain.

12. *Comb.*, as ***castle-battlement, -court, -ditch, -gate, -guardian, -wall***; ***castle-born, -buttressed, -crowned*** adjs.: also † **castle-boon**, an unpaid service due to a castle from neighbouring owners or tenants; see BOON *sb.*[1] 6; † **castle-bote**, the keeping of a castle in repair, a contribution levied for this purpose; **Castle-chamber** (Court of), the Irish analogue of the Court of Star-chamber, under the Tudors and Stuarts; † **castle-cloud**, a castle-like cloud, a cumulus: † **castle-come-down**, used by Foxe for ruin, total destruction; **castle-garth**, ? a yard or enclosure belonging to a castle; † **castle-gilliflower**, the plant *Matthiola incana*; † **castle-hunter**, one who builds castles in the air; † **castle-monger**, one who builds or owns castles; **castle-nut**, a castellated nut (see CASTELLATED *ppl. a.*); **castle pudding**, a pudding steamed or baked in a dariole mould; † **castle-soap**, see CASTILE SOAP; † **castle-stead** (see quot.); **castle-top**, a tall humming top (still in *north. dial.*); **castle-town**, a town defended by a castle; also (*Sc.*) a collection of houses lying near or under a castle; **castlewards** *adv.*, towards the castle; **castle-wick** = CASTLESHIP; **castle-work** (see quot.). See also CASTLE-BUILDER, -GUARD, -WARD, -WISE.

[**15..** *Plumpton Corr.* Introd. 20 They and their tenants were to be quit of *Castell-boone and of drink-money for the foresters, upon payment of a rent of four shillings a year.] **1848** KINGSLEY *Saint's Trag.* II. iii, The *castle-born brat is a senator born, Or a saint, if religion's in vogue. **1628** COKE *On Litt.* 127 a, Bote signifieth amerciament or compensation, or sometimes freedom from the same, as *castle-bote. **1648** *Art. of Peace betw. Ormond & Irish* xxi, Persons.. authoriz'd by Commission under the Great Seal to regulate the Court of *Castle-chamber. **1686** GOAD *Celest. Bodies* II. ii. 160 Hot and dry, misty air, *castle clouds. **1563-87** FOXE *A. & M.* (1596) 1902/1 Her high buildinges of such ioyes and felicities, came all to a Castle Comedowne. **1815** SCOTT *Ld. of Isles* v. xxvii, Man and guard the *castle-court. **1610** *Mirr. Mag.* 776 That ancient *castle-crowned hill. *c* **1475** *Voc.* in Wr.-Wülcker 784. 19 *Hec listia*, a *castylledyche. **1598** SHAKS. *Merry W.* v. ii. 1 Wee'll couch i'th Castle-ditch. **1596** SPENSER *F.Q.* II. xi. 6 Seuen of the name against the *castle-gate.. he did closely place. **1851** SIR F. PALGRAVE *Norm. & Eng.* I. 567 Isembard's *castlegarth now constitutes a suburb of Saint Valory. **1578** LYTE *Dodoens* II. iv. 152 The great *Castell or stocke Gillofer. **1597** GERARDE *Herbal* cxiv. 373 Castle Gilloflower. **1752** BERKELEY *Lett.* in *Wks.* IV. 334 We have not the transports of your *castle-hunters; but our lives are calm and serene. **1655** FULLER *Ch. Hist.* III. ii. 53 (D.) The Bishops (being the greatest *castle-mongers in that age), very stubborn, and not easily to be ordered. **1902** *Automobile Rev.* July 1, **Castle nut*, a nut having three grooves cut across its top face to receive a split pin. **1940** *Chambers's Techn. Dict.* 141/2 *Castle nut*, a six-sided nut in the top of which six radial slots are cut. Two of these line up with a hole drilled in the bolt or screw, a split pin being inserted to prevent loosening. **1845** E. ACTON *Mod. Cookery* xviii. 472 *Sutherland or *Castle Puddings*.. equal weight of eggs.. butter.. flour.. sugar... Pour the mixture.. into well-buttered cups, and bake. **1965** E. J. HOWARD *After Julius* xv. 250 Hanwell was having some castle puddings in the kitchen. **1965** A. CHRISTIE *At Bertram's Hotel* xi. 107 Veal cutlets.. succeeded by some small castle puddings with a blackberry sauce. **1829** CARLYLE *Misc.* (1857) I. 274 A deep tragedy of the *Castle-Spectre sort. **1678-1706** PHILLIPS, **Castlesteed*.. anciently used for any Fortress or Bulwark. [Also in KERSEY, and BAILEY 1721-1800]. **1768-74** TUCKER *Lt. Nat.* (1852) II. 633 The kites, and marbles, and *castle tops he was fond of then. **1665** *Select. fr. Harl. Misc.* (1793) 169 This was a *castle-town, and of great strength. **1864** *Glasgow Her.* 16 May, These cothouses were often called the Castletoun, because they belonged to or lay near the castle. *c* **1175** *Lamb. Hom.* 141 Alse an *castel wal. **1815** SCOTT *Ld. of Isles* IV. viii, That lovely lady sate and wept Upon the castle-wall. **1831** J. WILSON *Unimore* vi. 313 He moves *Castle-wards. **1611** COTGR., *Chastellenie*, a *Castle-wicke, a castleship. **1448** R. GLOUC. (1810) 450 (*MS. College of Arms*) That suche *castellwerk was nat semyng to Religion. **1846** WRIGHT *Ess. Mid. Ages* I. v. 195 Grievously they oppressed the miserable people of the land with their castle-works.

castle ('kɑːs(ə)l, -æ-), *v.* [f. prec. sb.]

1. a. *trans.* To inclose or place in, or as in, a castle; also *fig.* † **b.** To inclose (a cistern, etc.) within a building (*obs.*; cf. CASTELLATED 2). Also ***castle up***, etc.

1587 FLEMING *Cont. Holinshed* III. 1354/1 The conducting of Thames water, cesterning the same in lead, and castelling with stone. **1611** FLORIO, *Castellare*, to encastle, to Castle. **1655** GURNALL *Chr. in Arm.* Introd. iv. §1 (1669) 13/2 Castle me in the arms of thy everlasting strength. **1704** HEARNE *Duct. Hist.* (1714) I. 449 The first Cistern Castled with Stone was the great Conduit in West-Cheap. **1792** W. ROBERTS *Looker-on* No. 30 After having castled himself up, as it were, in his own exclusive spirit. **1871** BROWNING *Pr. Hohenst.* 116 Some fierce tribe, castled on the mountain peak.

† **2.** To ornament with battlements or in imitation of a castle. *Obs.*

c **1386** CHAUCER *Pers. T.* ¶ 371 Bake metes and dish metes.. peynted and castelled with papir.

3. *Chess.* **a.** *intr.* To bring the castle or rook up to the square next the king, and move the king to the other side of the castle. Also said of the king.

1656 BEALE *Chess* 8 He [the king] may change (or Castle) with this Rooke, that is, he may goe two draughts at once towards this Rooke.. causing the Rooke to stand next to him on either side. **1820** *Hoyle's Games Impr.* 210 If you have your choice on which side to castle. **1847** STAUNTON *Chess-pl. handbk.* 19 If he castle on the Queen's side, he plays his King to Q.B.'s square, and Q.'s rook to Q.'s sq. The object of this compound move is generally to place the royal Piece in safety, and at the same time bring the Rook.. into better play. **1870** HARDY & WARE *Mod. Hoyle, Chess* 38 He can move only one square at a time except when he castles, which he may do once during each game.

b. *trans.*

1764 R. LAMBE *Hist. Chess* 97 After you have opened your Game a little, and castled your King, bring out your Pieces. **1820** *Hoyle's Games Impr.* 202 Castle your king as soon as convenient. **1868** C. R. MARKHAM in *Macm. Mag.* No. 103. 87/2 The Abyssinian is allowed time to castle his king and take the pieces.

Hence **'castling** *vbl. sb.*

1813 *Monthly Rev.* LXXII. 355 His games are drawn up as if Castling was not in use. **1880** *Boy's own Bk.* 586 Castling is a compound move of king and castle.

'castle-ˌbuilder. One who builds castles; commonly, one who builds castles in the air (see CASTLE *sb.* 11), a day-dreamer, a visionary schemer.

1711 STEELE *Spect.* No. 167 ¶ 3 One of that Species of Men.. denominated Castle-Builders, who scorn to be beholden to the Earth for a Foundation. **1822** IRVING *Braceb. Hall* II. 36, I have been always something of a castle-builder. **1873** SYMONDS *Grk. Poets* xi. 376 All day-dreamers and castle-builders.

So **'castle-ˌbuilding** *vbl. sb.* and *ppl. a.*; **'castle-built** *ppl. a.*

1740 CHEYNE *Regim.* Pref. 7 Enthusiasm, Romanceing, and Castle-building. **1750** *Student* I. 223 (T.) Castle-building, or the science of aerial architecture. **1833** HT. MARTINEAU *Berkeley the B.* I. i. 11 The castle-building father bestowed almost all his thoughts for the next half-hour on the new rector. **1836-7** SIR W. HAMILTON *Metaph.* xxxiii. (1859) II. 272 Reverie or Castle-building, is a kind of waking dream. **1841** ORDERSON *Creol.* xx. 242 Castle-built schemes. **1850** KINGSLEY *Alt. Locke* xxvi. 191 As I lay castle-building.

castled ('kɑːs(ə)ld, -æ-), *ppl. a.* [f. CASTLE + -ED.]

1. Furnished with a castle or castles.

1662 FULLER *Worthies* (1840) III. 282 John of Killingworth, born in that castelled village. **1676** DRYDEN *Aureng-z.* I. i. 119 Castl'd Elephants o'erlook the town. **1808** SCOTT *Marm.* I. i, Day set on Norham's castled steep. **1839** LONGF. *Flowers* i, One who dwelleth by the castled Rhine.

2. Built in the style of a castle, castellated.

1789 MACNEILL *Poet. Wks.* (1812) I. 82 [Thou] view'st sublime her castled towers. **1877** M. ARNOLD *Youth of Man* Poems II. 160 In the castled house.. Which sheltered their childhood.

3. Inclosed or placed in a castle.

1821 JOANNA BAILLIE *Met. Leg.*, *Wallace* xlviii, Rush'd Stirling's castled warriors to the plain.

Castleford ('kɑːs(ə)lfəd, 'kæs-). The name of a town in the West Riding of Yorkshire used to designate a type of pottery made there at the beginning of the 19th century.

1863 W. CHAFFERS *Marks & Monogr.* 133 *Castleford Pottery.* Castleford, in the West Riding of Yorkshire, a pottery about 1800. **1871** LADY C. SCHREIBER *Jrnl.* (1911) I. 114 Found a small piece of Castleford pottery. **1961** *Connoisseur New Guide to Antique Eng. Pott.* 74 The comparatively shallow relief of Castleford and other earlier analogous wares.

castle-guard. Also 6-7 -gard(e.

1. The guard of a castle.

2. *Feudal Syst.* A kind of knight-service, whereby a feudal tenant was bound, when required, to defend the lord's castle; the tenure of such service.

1576 LAMBARDE *Peramb. Kent* (1826) 140 The service of Castlegarde [at Dover].. was with the assent of King Henrie the third converted into a paiment of money. **1610** HOLLAND *Camden's Brit.* I. 345 Lands in Kent.. to be held in Castle-gard. **1628** COKE *On Litt.* 87 a, The tenant ought by himselfe or by another to doe Castle-gard. **1700** TYRRELL *Hist. Eng.* II. 815 No Constable shall distrein any Knight to give Money for Castle-Guard, if he will perform it in his own Person. *a* **1779** LD. LYTTELTON (T.) One species of knight-service was castle-guard.

3. A tax originally in commutation of this service; also the territory chargeable therewith.

1576 LAMBARDE *Peramb. Kent* (1826) 140. **1641** *Termes de la Ley* 48 Castlegard is an imposition layd upon such.. as dwell within a certain compasse of any Castle, to the maintenance of such as watch and ward the Castle. It is sometimes vsed for the circuit itselfe, which is inhabited by such as are subject to this seruice. **1888** *Archæol. Rev.* I. 57 In Pevensey Rape much of the land round the Castle was wardable, i.e. paid Castle-guard or Castle-ward.

attrib. **1704** WORLIDGE *Dict. Rust. et Urb.*, *Castle-guard-rents*; are Rents paid by those that dwell within the Precincts of any Castle, towards the Maintenance of such as Watch and Ward the same. **1888** *Archæol. Rev.* I. 57 A large number of manors in Hastings Rape were held by *Castle-guard* tenure. The Earl of Chichester, as owner of Hastings Castle, still receives Castle-guard rents in the Hundreds of Baldslow, etc.

'castle-like, *a.* and *adv.*

A. *adj.* **1.** Like a castle. **2.** Of or pertaining to a castle, castellar.

1611 COTGR., *Chastelain*, the Lord.. of a territorie, vnto which Castle-like Jurisdiction and Royalties belong.

B. *adv.* After the manner of a castle.

1610 HOLLAND *Camden's Brit.* I. 769 A stately house built Castlelike.

† **'castlery, castelry.** *Obs.* [f. *castel*, CASTLE *sb.* + -ERY; or ad. OF. *castelerie*, *chastelerie* territory belonging to a castle, med.L. *castellaria* in same sense.] The government or jurisdiction of a castle; the territory subject to it.

1679 BLOUNT *Anc. Tenures* 116 The Castelry which he and his ancestors have of Baynards Castle. **1877** G. T. CLARK in *Archæol. Cambr.* 121 Both are mentioned.. as the seats of a Castelry, a sort of honour or superior lordship attached to the castle.

† **'castleship.** *Obs.* = prec.

1598 FLORIO, *Castellania*, a castleship, the privileges or territories of a castle. **1611** COTGR., *Chastellenie*, a Castle-wicke, a Castleship, the Tenure or Honour of a Castleship.

castle-soap, obs. f. CASTILE SOAP.

'castlet. [A var. of CASTELLET, assimilated to CASTLE: see -ET[1].] A small castle.

1538 LELAND *Itin.* (T.) There was in it a castlet of stone and brick. **1610** HOLLAND *Camden's Brit.* I. 587 It hath in this Moreland Carswell a Castlet situate upon it. **1813** 'ÆDITUUS' *Metrical Remarks* 22 These walls so thick,.. With castlets by their sides, squat shapeless things. **1907** E. H. COLERIDGE in S. T. Coleridge *Christabel* 24 Triermain Castle must have been but a 'castlet' compared with Naworth.

'castleward.

† **1.** The warden of a castle. *Obs.*

c **1425** WYNTOUN *Cron.* VIII. xxxviii. 129 (Jam.) The Castelwartis on the Marche herde say, etc.

2. *Feudal Syst.* = CASTLE-GUARD 2, 3.

1576 LAMBARDE *Peramb. Kent* (1826) 140 The lande beeing charged with tenne shillings (called Castlewards) for every Warder that it was bound to finde. **1611** COTGR. s.v. *Chastelain*, Castlewicke, or castleward. **1616** BULLOKAR, *Castleward*, a payment made by some dwelling within a certaine compasse of a Castle for the maintenance of those that do watch and ward the Castle. Also the Circuite of land which oweth this Seruice. **1704** in WORLIDGE *Dict. Rust.* **1756** [see CASTELLANY]. **1888** [see CASTLE-GUARD 3].

† **3.** *fig.* ? Defence. *Obs.*

1674 N. FAIRFAX *Bulk & Selv.* 40 The main Castleward to shrowd these weaklings from blows and qualmes.

'castlewise, *adv.* In the manner of a castle.

c **1600** NORDEN *Spec. Brit.*, *Cornw.* (1728) 55 An auntient howse castlewise buylded. **1831** *Blackw. Mag.* XXX. 478 Clouds.. piled.. about him castlewise.

† **castling** ('kɑːstlɪŋ, -æ-), *sb. Obs.* [f. CAST *ppl. a.* or *sb.* + dim. suffix -LING.]

1. The offspring of an untimely birth, an abortion.

1580 HOLLYBAND *Treas. Fr. Tong*, *Avorton*, that which is brought forth before the tyme, a castling. **1611** COTGR., *Cadel*, a castling, a staruelíng. **1646** SIR T. BROWNE *Pseud. Ep.* 84 We should rather relie upon the urine in a Castlings bladder. **1664** BUTLER *Hud.* II. II. 539 Castling Foles of Bal'am's Ass. **1704** WORLIDGE *Dict. Rust. et Urb.* s.v. *Wet-Glover*, Castling skins.. are slender, thin, and gentle.

2. The second (or third) swarm which leaves a hive in the season; = CAST *sb.* 18. Also *transf.*

1609 C. BUTLER *Fem. Mon.* (1634) 5, 17 [queen bees], whereof one went forth with the prime swarm, 5 were brought out dead fowr days before the Castling rose, other five came forth with the Castling. **1622-62** HEYLIN *Cosmogr.* (1674) Introd. 6/1 Those Countries were of an elder Plantation, than to be a second or third Castling of some other Swarm. **1630** J. LEVETT *Order. Bees* (1634) 27 When you have a second swarme or castling (as some call it). **1662** STILLINGFL. *Orig. Sacr.* III. iv. §11. 562 Not to have been that ancient people but rather some latter Castlings.

castling ('kɑːslɪŋ, -æ-), *vbl. sb.*: see CASTLE *v.*

† **cast-me-down.** *Obs.* A popular corruption of CASSIDONY (*Lavandula stœchas*).

1597 GERARD *Herbal* II. clxxx. 470 Some simple people imitating the said name doe call it Castte me downe. **1678** LITTLETON *Lat. Dict.*, Cassidony, vulg. cast-me-down, or French lavender, *Stœchas.*

castock ('kɑːstɒk, -æ-). *Sc.* and *north. dial.* Also 4 caule stok, 5 cale stok, caustocke, 5–6 calstok, 6 calstock(e. [f. *cal*, KALE + STOCK: the vowel being shortened and the *l* at length lost before the consonant group: in mod.Sc. further reduced to *casto*', *casta*. Uncombined, it remains *kale-stock*, *kail-stock*.] The stalk or stem of a cabbage.

1398 TREVISA *Barth. De P.R.* XVII. xxii. (MS.), Men may graffe on a bete stok, as men dop on a caule stok [**1495** caustocke]. *c* **1425** *Voc.* in Wr.-Wülcker 644 *Hoc magudere*, calstok. **1483** *Cath. Angl.* 51 A cale stok, *magudaris*, **1522** SKELTON *Why Nat to Court* 350 Nat worth a shyttel-cocke, Nat worth a sowre calstocke. *c* **1620** Z. BOYD *Zion's Flowers* (1855) 72 The Killings, Herrings, Castocks. **1785** *Jrnl. Lond. to Portsmouth* in *Poems Buchan Dial.* 5 (Jam.) As freugh as kaill-castacks. **1808–79** JAMIESON, *Castock, castack, custoc*; often *kail-castock*.

'**cast-off,** *ppl. a.* and *sb.*[1] [f. CAST *ppl. a.*]

A. *ppl. a.* Thrown off, rejected from use, discarded: as clothes, a favourite, a lover, etc.

1746 W. THOMPSON *R.N. Advoc.* (1757) 40 Cast-off Hunters, turn'd upon the Road for Post Chaise Service. **1755** *Connoisseur* No. 80 A cast-off suit of my wife's. **1809** W. IRVING *Knickerb.* (1861) 139 To strut at his heels, wear his cast-off clothes. **1840** MILL *Diss. & Disc.* (1859) I. 235 The cast-off extravagances of Goethe and Schiller. **1844** STANLEY *Arnold* (1858) I. iv. 169 The worn and cast-off skin. **1853** ROGERS *Ecl. Faith* 44 To array your thoughts in the tatters of the cast-off Bible.

B. *sb.* **1.** A person or thing that is cast-off or abandoned as worthless or useless. (For the plural *cast-offs* is more according to analogy.)

1741 RICHARDSON *Pamela* I. 49 And how.. must they have look'd, like old Cast-offs. **1850** BLACKIE *Æschylus* I. 82 Thou shalt be From the city of the free Thyself a cast-off. **1867** SMYTH *Sailor's Word-bk.*, *Cast-offs*, landsmen's clothes. **1872** SPURGEON *Treas. Dav.* Ps. lxxvii. 7 The objects of his contemptuous reprobation, his everlasting cast-offs. **1884** *Longm. Mag.* Apr. 607 Our horses, casts-off from the flat.

2. *Printing.* A calculation of the amount of space which will be required by a given amount of copy. (Cf. CAST *v.* 79j.)

1898 J. SOUTHWARD *Mod. Printing* I. xlii. 263 These two lines must be reckoned for in the cast off. **1917** F. S. HENRY *Printing for School & Shop* iii. 32 If the cast-off leaves but two or three lines on the last page, it is better to have the few previous pages each a line long. **1934** *Proc. Brit. Acad.* XIX. 388 In February 1903 fifty Letters of Erasmus were dispatched to the Press for a 'cast-off'.

cast-off, *sb.*[2] *Gunnery.* [f. CAST *sb.* + OFF.] The 'twist' of a gun-stock, the extent to which the stock is thrown laterally out of the line of the longitudinal axis of the barrel.

1881 GREENER *Gun* 249 He adjusts the bend or crook of the gun, and the amount of cast-off. *Ibid.* 432 The object of the cast-off is to bring the centre of the barrels in a line with the shooter's eye.

castor[1] ('kɑːstə(r), -æ-). Also 6 castour, 7 -er. [a. F. *castor* (16th c.) and L. *castor*, a. Gr. κάστωρ beaver, prob. a foreign word. Cf. Skr. *kastūrī* musk.]

1. The beaver. (Now rarely used).

[**1398** TREVISA *Barth. De P.R.* XVIII. xxix. (1495) 789 The Castor hyght Fyber also.] **1547** BOORDE *Introd. Knowl.* vi. 141 Ther [in Norway] be many castours and whyte beares. **1612** DRAYTON *Poly-olb.* vi. 87 Cleere Tivy.. Which of thy Castors once, but now canst onlie boast The Salmons. **1666** DRYDEN *Ann. Mirab.* xxv, Like hunted castors conscious of their store. **1750** BEAWES *Lex Mercat.* (1752) 822 Skins, especially Castor. **1875** URE *Dict. Arts* s.v., The sacs are cut off from the castors when they are killed.

2. A reddish-brown unctuous substance, having a strong smell and nauseous bitter taste, obtained from two sacs in the inguinal region of the beaver; used in medicine and in perfumery; castoreum.

1601 HOLLAND *Pliny* II. 430 Two drams.. is thought to be a sufficient dose of Castor. **1646** SIR T. BROWNE *Pseud. Ep.* 150. **1693** *Phil. Trans.* XVII. 935 Castor he proves to be the Scent-bags adjoyning to the Intestinum Rectum, and not the Testicles of the Beaver, as some assert. **1750** MRS. DELANY *Autobiog. & Corr.* (1861) II. 550 Your letters.. have been my castor, pearl cordial, and sal volatile. **1768–74** TUCKER *Lt. Nat.* (1852) II. 91 Bezoar, civet, and castor, are the diseases of animals. **1834** J. FORBES *Laennec's Dis. Chest* 385 Musk and castor.. give more speedy relief. **1875** URE *Dict. Arts* s.v., Chemists.. have examined castor, and found it to be composed of a resin, a fatty substance, a volatile oil, an extractive matter, benzoic acid, and some salts.

3. A hat, orig. either of beaver's fur, or intended to be taken as such; in the end of the 17th and beginning of 18th c. distinguished from 'beaver', and said to be of rabbit's fur; at that time also usually spelt *caster*. Now mostly *colloq.* or *slang*. Cf. BEAVER 3. (So in Fr.)

1640 in Entick *London* II. 175 Bever hats, Demi-casters. **1656** BLOUNT *Glossogr.* To Rdr. A iij a, In London many of the Tradesmen have new Dialects.. The Haberdasher is ready to furnish you with a Vigone, Codevec, or Castor. **1675** *Lond. Gaz.* No. 1031/4 A parcel of Hats, being Mens, Womens, and Boyes, Castors. **1680** *Ibid.* No. 1513/4 A thick short boy.. with a.. gray caster hat. **1688** *Ibid.* No. 2363/4, 2 black Hats, one a Beaver, the other a new Caster. **1688** R. HOLME *Armoury* III. 129/1 Of Hats.. the Caster.. is made of Coney Wooll mixt with Polony Wooll. **1709** STEELE *Tatler* No. 46 ¶1 His Imperial Castor, which he always wears cock'd in Front. **1750** BEAWES *Lex Mercat.* (1752) 578 The Manufactures of this Shire [Derby] are.. some Felt, Castor, and Beaver Hats. **1768** STERNE *Sent. Journ.* (1774) I. 133. **1827** SCOTT *Chron. Can.* Ser. I. Introd. iii, A white castor on my head. **1838** DICKENS *O. Twist* xxv. **1849** C. BRONTË *Shirley* xiii. 193 His coat and castor having been detained at the public-house in pledge.

4. 'A heavy quality of broadcloth used for overcoats' (Webster).

5. *oil of castor.* (Littré has *huile de castor* in sense of *castoreum* from Paré *c* 1550.)

1727–51 CHAMBERS *Cycl.* s.v. *Castoreum*, They draw an oil from it called *Oil of Castor.*

6. Glove leather made from goat-skins; it is given a very soft finish of a grey colour.

1897 C. T. DAVIS *Manuf. Leather* xxxviii. 519 When finished, [they] bear a close resemblance in texture and quality, to deer-skin or castor. **1910** FLEMMING *Tanning* (ed. 2) 292 The tanner who wants to make mocha castor glove leather from kid and goat skins. **1923** *Daily Mail* 14 Feb. 11 Ladies' good quality Washable Castor Gloves.

7. A light drab colour.

1904 *Daily Chron.* 24 Oct. 8/4 Castor-coloured cloth (a soft beaver shade). **1923** *Daily Mail* 5 June 1 Colours: Nude, Fawn,.. Mouse, Castor, Dark Tan.

castor[2] ('kɑːstə(r), -æ-). Also **caster.** [A variant of CASTER, f. CAST *v.* (in sense 1 'to throw', and 54 'to turn or veer') + -ER. The spelling in *-or* prob. arose primarily from confusion, and from missing the actual derivation; but it is now predominant, though one might write *pepper-caster.*]

1. A small vessel with a perforated top, from which to cast or sprinkle pepper, sugar, or the like, in the form of powder; extended to other vessels used to contain condiments at table, as in 'a set of castors', *i.e.* the castors and cruets usual in a cruet-stand.

1676 *Lond. Gaz.* No. 1079/4 Stole.. Six Salts. A Sugar Castar. A Pepper Caster. A Mustard Pot. **1681** *Ibid.* No. 1591/4 One Sett of Casters. **1801** JEKYLL *Tears of Cruets*, The Sugar Castor Wilberforce supplied. **1809** R. LANGFORD *Introd. Trade* 84 A Silver Set of Castors. **1836** MARRYAT *Midsh. Easy* ix, Put before our hero a tin bread-basket.. and the pepper-castor. **1861** DICKENS in *All Y. Round* IV. 461 The table-cloth and spoons and castors.

2. A small solid wheel and swivel attached to the foot of each leg of a piece of furniture, so that it may be turned in any direction without lifting.

1748 MRS. MONTAGU in Doran *Lady of last Cent.* (1873) Like a slate-bed running on castors. **1800** SIR W. HERSCHEL in *Phil. Trans.* XC. 491 An arrangement of twelve bricks, placed on a stand, with casters. **1833** BREWSTER *Nat. Magic* xi. 269 The machine runs on casters. **1872** BLACK *Adv. Phaeton* xxv. 345 You can't have castors on old oak chairs. **1873** J. RICHARDS *Wood-working Factories* 42 Trucks with casters.

3. *attrib.* and *Comb.*, as **castor-stand**; **castor action** (see quot. 1940); **castor angle**, the angle at which the steering-head of the front wheels of a motor vehicle is set; **castor-sugar**, powdered sugar, so called from its suitability for use in a castor; **castor-wheel**, a small wheel which turns on its own and a vertical axis, used to support or steer an agricultural machine, or enable it to be turned short round.

1926 *Motor Man.* (ed. 26) xix. 193 *Caster action*, an action tending to maintain the front wheels in the course they are following, obtained by tilting the steering pivots as viewed from the side. **1936** Castor action [see CAMBER *sb.* 1 d]. **1940** *Chambers's Techn. Dict.* 141/1 *Caster action*, the use of inclined king-pins by which the steerable front wheels of a motor vehicle are given fore-and-aft stability.. on the principle of the domestic caster. **1936** Castor angle [see CAMBER *sb.* 1 d]. **1959** *Motor* 2 Sept. 92/1 Caster angle (the fore-and-aft inclination of the swivel axis). **1963** BIRD & HUTTON-STOTT *Veteran Motor Car* 151 There was no rake or castor-angle to the steering-heads. **1867** F. S. COZZENS *Sayings* iii. 13 The reflected sunshine from those cut bottles in the castor-stand. **1855** E. ACTON *Mod. Cookery* xx. 405 Morella cherries.. simmered.. with three quarters of a pound of castor-sugar. **1894** T. F. GARRETT *Encycl. Pract. Cookery* II. 533/1 White [sugar].. being sometimes sold in the form of a powder as 'caster Sugar'. **1901** *Daily Chron.* 30 Nov. 8/4, 1½ oz. of castor sugar. **1951** MRS. BEETON *Househ. Managem.* xxxiv. 870 *Sago snow*.. 2 ozs. of sago, 2 pints of milk, 2 ozs. of castor sugar, 2 or 3 eggs, vanilla. **1805** DICKSON *Pract. Agric.* I. Plate ix. to face p. 40 The profile of a six-shared horse-hoe on the principle of the pentagraph, improved by Mr. Amos by the addition of two castor-wheels to regulate depth. *a* **1877** KNIGHT *Dict. Mech.* s.v., The caster-wheel is used as a support to the front parts of machines, such as harvesters.. and plowing machines, to enable them to be steered or to turn short around at the end of the row.

Hence '**castorless** *a.*, and comb. ***castor-maker***, etc.

1690 *Lond. Gaz.* No. 2539/4 Charles Mansell, a Caster-maker. **1883** J. PAYN *Thicker than Water* II. xx. 29 Chairs rickety and castorless.

'**Castor**[3]. In Greek mythology, name of one of the twin sons (Castor and Pollux) of Tyndarus and Leda, brothers of Helena; represented in the constellation Gemini or the Twins, of which Castor is the first, and Pollux the second star.

1526 TINDALE *Acts* xxviii. 11 A ship of Alexandry, which had wyntred in the Yle, whose badge was Castor and Pollux. **1647** WARD *Simp. Cobler* 38 Truth and Peace are the Castor and Pollux of the Gospell. **1868** LOCKYER *Heavens* (ed. 3) 350 *note*, Castor is a binary system to which.. doubtless belongs a third star, which participates in the proper movement of the two others.

2. A name given to the phenomenon called also CORPOSANT or St. Elmo's Fire. On the appearance of two at once they were called Castor and Pollux, and were thought to portend the cessation of a storm.

1708 MOTTEUX *Rabelais* v. xviii. (1737) 77 He had seen Castor at the Main-yard-arm. **1769** FALCONER *Dict. Marine* (1789), *Feu Saint-Elme*, a corposant, sometimes called Castor and Pollux.

castor[4] ('kɑːstə(r), -æ-). [perh. some corruption of CASTANE, or L. *castanea* chestnut, in F. *chataigne*.] (See quot. and cf. CHESTNUT *sb.*)

1888 *Brit. Med. Jrnl.* 25 Feb., The singular patch of hard integument known as the castor on the inside of the foreleg of the horse. **1888** *Veterinarian* May 304 Another organ in process of disappearance is that piece of horn inside the fore-arm, where it is termed the chestnut, and that inside the hock, where it is termed the castor; it corresponds to the finger-nail of the thumb of our hand, and of the foot of the five-toed ancestor of the horse.

castor[5]. *Min.* See CASTORITE.

Castor[6] ('kɑːstɔː(r), -æ-). Applied to ancient Romano-British pottery made in the neighbourhood of Castor in Northamptonshire.

[**1828** E. T. ARTIS *Durobrivae of Antoninus* Pl. 48 Fine red Ware in relief, collected in excavating the remains of a Roman Pottery in the parish of Castor.] **1857** C. R. SMITH *Coll. Antiqua* IV. 81 Ancient pottery discovered in this country.. a particular kind.. belongs to a class.. termed Castor or Northamptonshire ware, on account of its having occurred frequently in immediate connection with potters' kilns discovered near Castor, by the late Mr. E. T. Artis. **1923** COLLINGWOOD *Roman Britain* 73 The imported Samian ware.. provoked the British manufacturer to.. put on the market a style of pottery which resembled it in having ornament in relief and a highly glazed surface. Thus was produced what is known as Castor ware. **1945** S. E. WINBOLT *Britain under Romans* ix. 123 Somewhat more fragile, but more interesting in their designs, were the slate-coloured vessels of 'Castor' ware, decorated in raised creamy slip with hunting-scenes. **1963** *Times* 12 Mar. 5/2 A Roman beaker of about A.D. 200 decorated with a hound chasing a hare, possibly Castor ware.

'**castor-bean.** *U.S.* [See CASTOR OIL.] The castor-oil bean. Cf. CASTOR OIL b.

1819 *Baltimore Morn. Chron.* 23 Apr. 4/5 Physical herb seed.. palma christi or castor bean. **1835** J. MARTIN *Gaz. Virginia* 250 There is here [*sc.* Northampton, Va.] an article of culture which is not much met with in other parts of the state—it is the palma christi, called castor bean. **1865** *Trans. Ill. Agric. Soc.* 1862 V. 508 The cotton plant in its habits of growth is similar to the castor bean. **1901** C. MOHR *Plant Life Alabama* 56.

‖**castoreum** (kæ'stɔəriːəm). [L. *castoreum*, f. *castor* beaver. Also Fr. *castoréum*.] = CASTOR[1] 2.

1398 TREVISA *Barth. De P.R.* XVIII. xxix. (1495) 791 Castorium helpyth ayenst many syknesses. **1585** LLOYD *Treas. Health* C iv, Anoynte the eares, eyes and nodle with myrth, storax, Castoreum. **1626** BACON *Sylva* §692 The parts of Beasts putrified (as Castoreum and Musk). **1673** *Phil. Trans.* VIII. 6136 The art of driving away and sinking Whales by Castoreum. **1869** ROSCOE *Elem. Chem.* 404 The castoreum contained in a gland of the beaver.

Hence ***castoreum oil***, ***resin***, chemical products of castoreum.

1863–72 WATTS *Dict. Chem.* I. 815.

ca'storial, *a. nonce-wd.* [f. CASTOR[1] 3.] Pertaining to a hat (*jocose*).

1864 LOWELL *Fireside Trav.* 1 A graduated arc.. by which he meted out to each his rightful share of castorial consideration.

'**castorin.** *Chem.* [f. CASTOR[1] + -IN.] A crystalline substance obtained from castoreum.

1831 J. DAVIES *Manual Mat. Med.* 292 Castorine is, according to M. Bizio, the active principle of castor. **1861** HULME tr. *Moquin-Tandon* II. III. ii. 121. **1872** WATTS *Dict. Chem.* I. 815 The mother liquor deposits crystals of castorin.

castoring ('kɑːstərɪŋ, -æ-), *ppl. a.* [f. CASTOR *sb.*[2] + -ING[2].] Acting as a castor (cf. CASTOR *sb.*[2] 2).

1948 *Jrnl. R. Aeronaut. Soc.* LII. 32/1 The castoring undercarriage makes possible the general construction at low cost of many single strip private landing grounds. **1950** *Engineering* 29 Sept. 280/2 The triangular base is mounted on three rubber tyred castoring wheels.

'**castorite.** *Min.* [This mineral and another closely associated with it were at first fancifully named *Castor* and *Pollux*.] A variety of Petalite occurring in distinct transparent crystals.

1868 DANA *Min.* 230 Petalite occurs.. on Elba (castorite) in detached crystals.

castor oil ('kɑːstə, -æ-, 'ɔɪl). [Origin of name uncertain: it has been suggested that this oil actually took the place of the drug *castor*, or perh. of *oil of castor* (see CASTOR[1] 5), in use in midwifery, etc., and thus popularly assumed its

name. So 'castor oil pills' is now a popular name for certain pills which have the same laxative effect but contain no castor oil.]

a. A pale yellow oil obtained from the seeds of *Ricinus communis* or Palma Christi (N.O. *Euphorbiaceæ*), having a nauseous slightly acrid taste; used in medicine as a purgative, and in some parts of the world in lamps.

1746 P. CANVANE (*title*), Dissertation on the Oleum Palmæ Christi..commonly called Castor Oil. **1799** *Med. Jrnl.* I. 468 A very useful medicine, where the stomach will bear it, is castor oil. **1803** *Ibid.* X. 492 His bowels to be kept open by castor oil. **1870** YEATS *Nat. Hist. Comm.* 205 Castor-oil is obtained by expression from the seeds without heat, hence it is called 'cold-drawn castor oil'. *fig.* **1873** TRISTRAM *Moab* xv. 281 The canebrake tops.. are 'castor-oil to camels' stomachs'.

b. *attrib.*, as in ***castor-oil plant*** or ***tree***; **castor-oil bean**, the bean or seed from which the oil is obtained; also, the castor-oil plant; cf. CASTOR-BEAN.

1814 F. PURSH *Flora Amer. Septentr.* II. 603 Ricinus communis... Frequent in old plantations in Virginia and Carolina... Known by the name of Castor-oil Bean. **1845** DARWIN *Voy. Nat.* xxi. (1852) 492 An occasional green castor-oil plant..may be met with. **1845** A. WOOD *Class-bk. Bot.* II. 336 *R[icinus] communis*... From its seeds is expressed the well known castor-oil of the shops..Castor-oil Bean. **1857** LIVINGSTONE *Trav.* xv. 272 The Palma-Christi, or castor-oil-plant. **1901** C. MOHR *Plant Life Alabama* 594 *Ricinus communis*. Castor Oil Bean.

castor pomace: see POMACE 2 b.

†**'castory.** *Obs.* [ad. L. *castoreum*; in OF. *castoire, castore.*] = CASTOREUM. Also 'a colour extracted from castoreum'. (Godef.)

1398 TREVISA *Barth. De P.R.* VII. xiv. (1495) 233 The pacyent shall vse sage and castory..to helpe the palsey. **1586** COGAN *Haven Health* xxxix. (1636) 56 Castory (that is, the stones of the beast Castoreum). **1596** SPENSER *F.Q.* II. ix. 41 Overlayd with fayre vermillion or pure castory. **1634** HARINGTON *Salerne Regim.* 132 Castorie hath many Vertues. **1657** W. COLES *Adam in Eden* ix, Sage, Castory, Lavender..cure members infected with the Palsie.

castral ('kæstrəl), *a.* [f. L. *castra* camp (pl. of *castrum* fort) + -AL[1].] Belonging to the camp.

1844 KINGLAKE *Eöthen* xxiii. (1878) 308 The castral life of the Arabs.

castrametation (ˌkæstrəmɪ'teɪʃən). [a. F. *castramétation* (16th c.), f. L. *castra mētā-ri* to measure or lay out a camp.]

a. The art or science of laying out a camp. **b.** *concr.* The outline of a camp traced out (*obs.*).

1679 PLOT *Staffordsh.* (1686) 404 Choul's discourse of the Castrametation of the Romans. *Ibid.* 406 That entrenchment..has been one of these Roman Castrametations. **1816** SCOTT *Antiq.* i, Discussion concerning urns, votive altars, Roman camps and the rules of castrametation. **1842** W. RAMSAY in *Smith's Gr. & Rom. Antiq.* (1848) 244/2 A technical memoir on the art of castrametation.

castrate ('kæstreɪt), *a.* (*sb.*) [ad. L. *castrāt-us* pa. pple. of *castrāre*; see the vb.]

A. *adj.* Castrated. *Obs.* exc. in *Bot.*

1704 J. HARRIS *Lex. Techn.*, *Androgynus*, an Hermaphrodite, or one who is Castrate or Effeminate. **1754** WATSON in *Phil. Trans.* XLVIII. 873 But the castrate fish.. were always in season. **1880** GRAY *Bot. Text-bk.* 401 *Castrate*, said of a stamen which wants the anther.

B. *sb.* A castrated man, a eunuch. *arch.* (= F. *castrat*, It. *castrato.*)

1639 G. DANIEL *Ecclus.* xxx. 61 The Imperfect Castrate. **1691** T. HEYRICK *Misc. Poems* 31 The Castrate's sneaking looks. **1782** ELPHINSTON *Martial* I. iii. 3 No castrate or suborner shall there be: Erewhile the castrate was the debauchee. **1905** W. G. HOLMES *Justinian & Theod.* I. 134 *note*, The emperor cannot even uncover his head without the castrates closing round him to intercept the gaze of rude mankind.

castrate ('kæstreɪt), *v.* [f. L. *castrāt-* ppl. stem of *castrāre* to castrate, prune, expurgate, deprive of vigour, etc.: see -ATE[3].]

1. *trans.* To remove the testicles of; to geld, emasculate.

1613 [see CASTRATED]. **1633** BP. MORTON *Discharge Imput. Romish Party* 138 (T.) Origen—having read that scripture, 'There be some that castrate themselves for the kingdom of God'..he did castrate himself. **1646** SIR T. BROWNE *Pseud. Ep.* 113 To eunuchate or castrate themselves. **1781** GIBBON *Decl. & Fall* II. 90. **1831** YOUATT *Horse* ii. (1847) 19 The Barb.—They are never castrated, for a Mussulman would not mutilate..the beast of the Prophet.

b. *Bot.* To remove the anthers (or the pistil) of (a flower) before fecundation. (*Syd. Soc. Lex.*)

1859 DARWIN *Orig. Spec.* ix. (1873) 236 A plant, to be hybridised, must be castrated.

†**2.** *Gardening.* To prune, remove superfluous suckers from. *Obs.*

1658 EVELYN *Fr. Gard.* (1675) 255 When your strawberries shoot their strings, you must castrate them. **1753** CHAMBERS *Cycl. Supp.*, *Castrating*..in speaking of melons and cucumbers..signifies the same with pruning or pinching.

3. *transf.* and *fig.* To deprive of vigour, force, or vitality; to mortify.

1554 T. MARTIN *Marriage of Priestes* Y i b (T.) Ye castrate the desires of the flesh. *a* **1670** HACKET *Abp. Williams* II. (1692) 181 Every subsequent action of that Parliament did castrate their hope. **1670** W. SIMPSON *Hydrol. Ess.* 123 Whether they [mineral waters] do not..sooner precipitate an Ocre to the bottom, nor sooner become castrated thereby. *a* **1930** D. H. LAWRENCE *Last Poems* (1932) 163 The Victorians..Successfully castrating the body politic.

†**b.** To mutilate, 'cut down'. *Obs.*

1728 MORGAN *Algiers* I. iii. 56 The noble kingdom of Numidia was so castrated, that it dwindled away to the Eastern Province of the Algerines.

4. To mutilate (a book, etc.) by removing a sheet or portion of it; *esp.* to remove obscene or objectionable passages from; to expurgate.

1627 *Let.* in *Crt. & Times Chas. I.* (1848) I. 295 An Oxford man..had his sermon perused and castrated before he came there. **1711** ADDISON *Spect.* No. 179 ¶5 The following letter, which I have castrated in some places. **1753** CHAMBERS *Cycl. Supp.*, *Castrating a book.* **1753** WARBURTON *Lett. Late Prelate* (1809) 136 The letter..is castrated of one of its most curious anecdotes. **1791** BOSWELL *Johnson* (1816) III. 210 Talking of Rochester's Poems, he said, he had given them to Mr. Steevens to castrate for the edition of the poets. **1816** SOUTHEY *Lett.* (1856) III. 33 Gifford is at his old work of castrating my reviews. **1873** SYMONDS *Grk. Poets* xi. 344 The monk Planudes amended, castrated..and remodelled ..the Greek Anthology of Cephalas.

Hence **'castrated** *ppl. a.* (in *lit.* and *fig.* senses).

1613 R. C. *Table Alph.* (ed. 3), *Castrated*, gelded, diminished. **1646** SIR T. BROWNE *Pseud. Ep.* 124 Castrated animals..are longer lived. **1791-1824** D'ISRAELI *Cur. Lit.*, *Bible prohib.*, This castrated copy of the Bible. **1828** SOUTHEY *Ess.* (1832) II. 417. **1871** DARWIN *Desc. Man* II. xvii. 247 The horns are not developed..in the castrated male.

castration (kæ'streɪʃən). [a. F. *castration*, or ad. L. *castrātiōn-em*, n. of action f. *castrāre* to castrate.] The action of castrating, in various senses.

1. a. The removing of the testicles; gelding.

c **1420** *Pallad. on Husb.* VI. 92 Now..is goode castracion Of litel boles. **1607** TOPSELL *Four-f. Beasts* 37. **1714** MANDEVILLE *Fab. Bees* (1733) II. 102 That castration preserves and strengthens the voice. **1875** BLAKE *Zool.* 30 Castration produces diminution in size of the horns.

b. **castration-complex** *Psycho-analysis*, a group of repressed ideas based on a feared potential loss of the genitals in childhood, and resulting in anxiety.

1914 tr. *Freud's Psychopath. Everyday Life* ix. 223 A 'castration-complex'—namely, a childhood fear, often continued in a disguised form into adult life. **1922** J. RIVIERE tr. *Freud's Introd. Lect. Psycho-anal.* xiii. 175 The *castration complex*, the reaction to that intimidation in the field of sex or to that restraint of early infantile sexual activity which is ascribed to the father. **1929** P. MAIRET *Adler's Problems of Neurosis* v. 67 The Freudians have interpreted this fact as the so-called 'castration complex', because girls frequently have the fantasy that the male organs have been surgically removed from them. **1962** T. KAYE *David, from where he was Lying* xvii. 147 No doubt, I've suffered from a castration complex like everyone else.

†**2.** The act of taking away a portion of the honey from the hive. *Obs.* [Cf. L. *castrāre alveāria* (Palladius); Fr. *châtrer une ruche.*]

c **1420** *Pallad. on Husb.* XI. 267 Castracion the been have efte this moone. **1623** BUTLER *Fem. Mon.* x. (1623) Vj, Exsection or castration..is the cutting out of part of the Combes, part being left for the Bees prouision.

†**3.** Mutilation, 'cutting down'. *Obs.*

1728 MORGAN *Algiers* I. *List Subscribers*, Near 100..have desired to be excused, and accordingly they are erased... I almost repent my consenting to so great a Castration.

4. The removal of objectionable parts from a literary work; expurgation. Also *concr.*

1791-1824 D'ISRAELI *Cur. Lit.* (1859) II. 448 A partial suppression, or castration of passages..fatal to the cause of truth. **1806** in *Holinshed's Scot. Chron.* I. 7 In this second edition, several sheets..were castrated for containing some passages disagreeable to Queen Elizabeth..but the castrations have since been printed apart.

castrative (kæ'streɪtɪv), *a.* [f. L. *castrāt-* ppl. stem of *castrāre* (see CASTRATE *v.*) + -IVE.] Of, or relating to, or tending to produce the same effect as, castration.

1943 T. M. FRENCH in S. S. Tomkins *Contemp. Psychopath.* xiii. 208 A little girl will ward off the dangerous temptation to father incest by castrative impulses toward the father. **1949** M. MEAD *Male & Female* iv. 85 Societies in which..the initiatory rites are not accompanied by any such overwhelming castrative feelings. **1960** J. B. BROADBENT *Some Graver Subject* i. 33 It seems likely that, powerful, widowed, son-ambitious, a jealous god, he had a 'castrative' effect on Milton.

‖**castrato** (ka'strato). Pl. **castrati.** [Ital.; pa. pple. of *castrare* used substantively:—L. *castrāre* to castrate.] A male singer castrated in boyhood so as to retain a soprano or alto voice.

1763 J. BROWN *Poetry & Mus.* v. 63 An Italian Castrato (who hath laboured at this Refinement through his whole Life). **1879** E. GOSSE *Lit. N. Europe* 147 The Italian Opera ..with its gang of castrati.

castrator (kæ'streɪtə(r)). [a. L. *castrātor*, f. *castrāre.*] One who castrates; see the vb.

1818 SOUTHEY *Lett.* (1856) III. 93 The reviewal of 'Evelyn's Memoirs' (part of which goes to the grand castrator with this letter).

castrel, another form of KESTREL, a hawk.

†**ca'strensial**, *a. Obs. rare*[—1]. [f. L. *castrensi-s* belonging to a camp (f. *castra* camp) + -AL[1].] = next.

1658 SIR T. BROWNE *Gard. Cyrus* ii. 44 According unto military marches, or castrensiall mansions.

castrensian (kæ'strɛnsɪən), *a.* [f. as prec. + -AN.] Of or pertaining to a camp: camp-.

1657 G. STARKEY *Helmont's Vind.* 261 Castrensian or Camp Feavers. **1776** *Kentish Trav. Compan.* 144 The castrensian amphitheatre. **1807** G. CHALMERS *Caledonia* I. I. iv. 125 No castrensian remains. **1832-4** DE QUINCEY *Caesars* Wks. IX. 102 A mere military title..purely castrensian.

castrensic (kæ'strɛnzɪk), *a.* [f. L. *castrensis* (f. *castra* camp) + -IC.] Of or pertaining to a camp; military; = CASTRENSIAN *a.*

1840 KEIGHTLEY *Rom. Emp.* III. iv. 348 The emperor distributed civic, naval, and castrensic crowns to those who had most distinguished themselves.

Castroism ('kæstrəʊɪz(ə)m). [See -ISM.] The political principles or actions of Fidel *Castro* Ruz (1927-), Cuban statesman, or of his adherents or imitators. So **'Castroist**, an adherent of Castroism; also **'Castroite** *a.* and *sb.* Cf. FIDELISM.

1960 *U.S. News & World Rep.* 14 Nov. 60/3 Three members of the International Staff of 'U.S. News and World Report' have just completed an on-the-spot survey of Castroism in the Caribbean. **1961** W. BENTON *Voice Latin Amer.* iv. 132 More than 400 members of the..faculty have been fired, many of them..because they lacked sufficient enthusiasm for Castroism. **1961** *Daily Tel.* 28 Aug. 10/2 They must be, it seems, either Castroist and pro-Communist, or reactionary and fostered by Washington. **1962** *Times* 12 Jan. 11/6 The bugbear..of Mexican Castroism. **1963** *Economist* 4 May 425/2 Some form of Castroite uprising. **1964** *New Statesman* 17 Apr. 587/3 The [Mexican] left came to regard him [*sc.* de Gaulle] almost as a Castroite.

ca'strometer. *nonce-wd.* [f. L. *castra* camp + Gr. -μέτρης, in L. *-metra*, measurer.] A surveyor of (ancient) camps.

1857 J. RAINE *Mem. J. Hodgson* I. 138 Not merely as an archæologist or castrometer, but as an agriculturist.

castrum ('kæstrəm). Pl. **castra.** [L.] A Roman encampment or fortress.

1836 *Penny Cycl.* VI. 353/2 Roman Castra were probably sometimes formed on the sites of British works. **1850** C. R. SMITH *Antiq. Richborough* 31 The remains of the castrum at Richborough. **1886** *Athenæum* 13 Mar. 365/2 Another characteristic of a Roman castrum,..a huge wine cellar filled with thousands of amphoræ.

cast-steel. [CAST *ppl. a.* 8.] A hard steel made from broken-up blistered steel melted in a crucible and run into ingot-moulds; crucible-steel. Also *attrib.*

1778 P. THICKNESSE *Year's Journey* (ed. 2) I. xvi. 149 An English cast steel razor. **1792** *Brit. Pat. 1869* 2 The greatest part of the metal will be found to be steel, and sufficiently converted for making into cast steel. **1800** *Repertory of Arts* XIV. 177 The general principles of my process or processes are the fusion of malleable iron or of iron ore in such manner and by such means as immediately to convert them into cast-steel. **1812, 1858** [see STEEL *sb.*[1] 1 c]. **1824** W. IRVING *Salmag.* 203 His learned distinctions between wrought scissors and those of cast-steel. **1848** W. H. EMORY *Notes Mil. Reconn.* 132 The wooden plough, the harrow, and the cast-steel axe. **1868** *Jrnl. Chem. Soc.* XXI. 281 Cast-steel containing less than 0·3 per cent. of carbon is no longer capable of being hardened. **1880** *Encycl. Brit.* XIII. 356/2 Cast steel products. **1923** *Man. Seamanship* (*H.M.S.O.*) II. 257 Cast Steel is employed [in ship-building] in several qualities.

casual ('kæʒ(j)uːəl, 'kæzjuːəl), *a.* (*sb.*) Also 4-5 casuel, 5-7 -all. [a. F. *casuel*, ad. L. *cāsuāl-is* depending on chance, f. *cāsu-s*: see CASE *sb.*[1]]

A. *adj.* **1. a.** Subject to, depending on, or produced by chance; accidental, fortuitous.

c **1374** CHAUCER *Troylus* IV. 391 It is but casuel plesaunce. *c* **1440** *Gesta Rom.* 40 (Harl. MS.) By a casuel happe or by chaunce I was ny dreynt. **1590** SWINBURN *Testaments* 132 Of conditions..Some be casuall, such as are not in the power of that man to whome they are imposed, but either in the power of some other thing, or person, so that the euent thereof is to vs vncertaine. **1614** RALEIGH *Hist. World* (J.) That which seemeth most casual and subject to fortune, is yet disposed by the ordinance of God. **1670** DRYDEN *Tyran. Love* III. i, Him who thought A casual World was from wild Atoms wrought. **1672** *Covent Gard. Drollery* 231* His words like casual Atoms made a thought. **1705** STANHOPE *Paraphr.* II. 497 How casual soever things..may appear, yet there is One who ruleth over all. **1763** J. BROWN *Poetry & Mus.* vi. 113 The Improvement..was not casual, but the Result of a natural Progression. **1879** LUBBOCK *Sci. Lect.* ii. 52 Are these differences merely casual and accidental, or have they a meaning and a purpose?

†**b.** Non-essential; = ACCIDENTAL 3. *Obs.*

1398 TREVISA *Barth. De P.R.* IV. iv. (1495) 84 Some proprytees..ben secundary and casuall. **1655-60** STANLEY *Hist. Philos.* (1701) 196/1 It is Principle of the Platonists, that every created thing hath a three-fold being; Casual, Formal, participated.

†**c.** Used, like *accidental*, of untoward events.

c **1386** [cf. CASUALLY 1 b]. **1577** HOLINSHED *Chron.* I. 130/1 In Ethelberts time the citie of Canturburie was burned by casuall fire. **1586** COGAN *Haven Health* ccxiii. (1636) 222 Naturall death, which few attaine unto, but are prevented by death casuall. **1667** MILTON *P.L.* XI. 566 Where casual fire

Had wasted woods. **1758** JOHNSON *Idler* No. 4 ¶9 Who, by a casual hurt..lie pining in want and anguish.

d. Golf. ***casual water***: see quot. 1899.

1899 *Rules of Golf, St. Andrews* 3 'Casual water' shall mean any temporary accumulation of water (whether caused by rainfall or otherwise) which is not one of the ordinary and recognised hazards of the course. **1957** *Encycl. Brit.* X. 506A/1 Paths, bare patches of ground and temporary accumulations of water (called casual water) are not hazards.

2. Occurring or coming at uncertain times; not to be calculated on, uncertain, unsettled.

c **1460** FORTESCUE *Abs. & Lim. Mon.* (1714) 47 The Kyngs Extraordynary chargys ar so casuel, that no Man may knowe them in certeynte. *c* **1525–30** MORE *De Quat. Noviss.* Wks. 80/2 We call no sicknes by that name, but such as be casual and come and goe. **1647** CLARENDON *Hist. Reb.* I. i. 5 Both the known and casual Revenue. **1788** PRIESTLEY *Lect. Hist.* IV. xxi. 231 The accounts of the royal revenue, whether certain or casual. **1818** CRUISE *Digest* III. 437 An escheat is a casual profit, *quod accidit domino ex eventu et ex insperato.* **1876** GROTE *Eth. Fragm.* v. 174 Not for a casual period but for a complete lifetime.

3. Occurring or brought about without design or premeditation; coming up or presenting itself 'as it chances'.

1667 MILTON *P.L.* IX. 223 What wonder if..object new Casual discourse draw on. *a* **1674** CLARENDON *Hist. Reb.* (J.) The commissioners entertained themselves..in general and casual discourses. **1722** DE FOE *Col. Jack* (1840) 245 They talked of casual things. **1794** SULLIVAN *View Nat.* I. 97 Anaxagoras..would seem to have had more than a casual glimpse of truth. **1863** BURTON *Bk. Hunter* 17 A mere casual spectator. **1864** D. MITCHELL *Sev. Stor.* 70, I made some casual remark about the weather. **1865** DICKENS *Mut. Fr.* xii. 263 I'll mix with 'em in a casual way.

†**4.** Liable to happen; incidental *to*. *Obs.*

c **1440** *Gesta Rom.* 275 (Harl. MS.) Of such men it is to dred, for casuall vengeaunce. *c* **1565** LINDESAY (Pitscottie) *Chron. Scot.* (1728) 46 It is but casual to a man to fall in an offence. **1593** BILSON *Govt. Christ's Ch.* 284 When they dissent, which in all persons is casuall. **1610** HEALEY *St. Aug. City of God* I. viii. 14 Tell me whether any thing be casuall vnto the good, that tendeth not to their good. *c* **1645** HOWELL *Lett.* (1650) II. 121.

†**5. a.** Subject to chance or accident; frail, uncertain, precarious. *Obs.* †**b.** Liable *to*. *Obs.*

(Cf. mod.F. use of *casuel* for *fragile*, censured by Littré.)

1529 MORE *Comf. agst. Trib.* III. Wks. 1219/1 Landes seme not so casual as money is or plate. **1568** ABP. PARKER *Corr.* (1853) 325, I carry about me such a casual body. **15..** VAUX *Content. Mind* in *Parad. Dainty Devices* (1576) The body..to a million of mishaps Is casual every hour. **1611** SHAKS. *Cymb.* I. iv. 100 Your brace of vnprizeable Estimations, the one is but fraile, and the other Casuall. **1620** MARKHAM *Farew. Husb.* (1625) 127 Of all Graine it [Oats] is least casuall. **1669** WORLIDGE *Syst. Agric.* (1681) 200 In case..the weather prove casual. **1727** SWIFT *State Irel.* Wks. 1755 V. II. 166 A trade casual, corrupted and at mercy. **1729** FRANKLIN *Ess.* Wks. 1840 II. 272 If the security is casual.

6. a. Of persons or their actions: Not to be depended on, uncertain, unmethodical, haphazard, 'happy-go-lucky'. *colloq.* or *slang.*

[**1624** FLETCHER *Rule a Wife, &c.* III. Wks. 1778 III. 457 *Sanc.* Wilt thou lend me any? *Cac.* Not a farthing, captain; Captains are casual things.] **1883** *Durham Univ. Jrnl.* 24 Mar., A 'casual' man is one whose manner of life is altogether the sport of chance. **1886** W. HOOPER *Sk. Academic Life* 10 He takes his meals in a casual sort of way, without any attempt at regulation.

b. Showing (real or assumed) unconcern or lack of interest.

1916 'BOYD CABLE' *Action Front* 105 'Don't feel particularly hungry,' answered Toffee, with an attempt to appear as off-handed and casual and at ease as his questioner. **1924** R. MACAULAY *Orphan Island* xvi. 230 She was casual and indifferent, but Rosamond..stood up and said 'Yes'.

†**7.** Casuistic. *Obs. rare.*

1672 MARVELL *Reh. Transp.* I. 114 The Casual Divinity of the Jesuites. **1753** CHAMBERS *Cycl. Supp.* s.v., Osiander.. has published a system of *casual theology*, containing the solution of dubious questions, and cases of conscience.

¶**8.** Confused with CAUSAL. *Obs.*

1578 TIMME *Calvin on Gen.* 314 We must put in the casuall word Fear not Abram: *bycause* I am thy buckler. **1668** HOWE *Bless. Righteous* (1825) 28 It is not at all casual of this blessedness, but is that which the..Lawgiver thought meet..to make requisite thereto.

9. In such phrases as ***casual labourer***, one who does casual or occasional jobs, but has no fixed employment; also ***casual hand***; ***casual labour***: see quot. 1923; ***casual poor***, those occasionally in a state of poverty; those not receiving regular or systematic relief, *esp.* those not permanently inmates of workhouses, etc., but admitted for occasional relief (cf. B. 3 b); ***casual ward***, a ward reserved for such occasional relief.

1593 NASHE *Christ's T.* 85 a, If wee cannot keepe and cherrish the casuall poore amongst vs. **1849** BRIGHT *Irel., Sp.* (1876) 164 For the support of the Irish casual poor. *a* **1852** MAYHEW *Lond. Labour* (1861) II. 220/2 This mixture of constant and casual hands is..a necessary consequence of all trades which depend upon the seasons... Those who have paid attention to the subject of dock labour and the subject of casual labour in general. *Ibid.* 336/1 Greenwich may be looked upon as the first stage or halt for casual labourers, on their way to London. **1860** *Ibid.* III. 382 (Hoppe) He considered a casual ward necessary in every union. **1876** GREEN *Stray Stud.* 17, The bulk of its population consisted of casual labourers. **1887** *Pall Mall G.* 24 Oct. 1/2 The casual wards in the central parts of the metropolis. **1905** *Daily Chron.* 25 July 5/4 He would not admit that the policy of the guardians had increased the casual labour system. **1908** H. W. CASLON *Letterpress Printing* 64 Casual labour is, and must be, a disturbing element in the costing of work. **1923** J. D. HACKETT *Labor Terms* in *Management Engineering* May, *Casual Labor.* 'Unskilled help, employed and discharged at frequent intervals, and dependent upon the varying demand of the labor market from day to day, without any prospect of continuous employment.' (*What's What in Labour Movement*, Waldo R. Brown, p. 59.)

10. *Law.* ***casual ejector***, the defendant in the fictitious action formerly allowed for the purpose of determining a title to land.

The casual ejector, a fictitious person, was stated to have ejected the plaintiff from the land, which (as was stated) he held on lease of the person actually claiming the land. The action involved the proving of the lessor's right to grant the lease, and so incidentally determined his title to the land.

1768 BLACKSTONE *Comm.* III. 202 The lessee is entitled to his action of ejectment against the tenant, or this casual ejector, whichever it was that ousted him.

11. Of clothes: suitable for informal wear. (Cf. B. 4.)

1939 M. B. PICKEN *Lang. of Fashion* 23/3 Casual, designed for easy, informal wear; of sports or semi-sports type; as, a casual coat. **1952** *Evening News* 5 Jan. (Advt.), 560 Prs. casual shoes. **1958** *Times* 20 Jan. 11/1 It is sport and casual clothes that visitors come especially to see.

B. *sb.*

†**1.** A casual event, a chance. (Chiefly in *pl.*)

1566 DRANT *Horace's Sat.* v. C iv, To sterte up in astrologie the casuals of men. **1652** GAULE *Magastrom.* 162 Providence is in the ordering of casuals as well as fatals.

2. A casual revenue or income; see sense 2 above.

1825 T. JEFFERSON *Autobiog.* Wks. 1859 I. 103 The tithes and casuals of the Clergy.

3. a. A casual workman; a casual visitor, etc. *colloq.*

a **1852** MAYHEW *Lond. Labour* (1861) II. 218/1 The 'casuals' being mostly paid by the day. *Ibid.* 220/2 Of the scavagers proper there are..two distinct orders of workmen, 'the regulars and casuals' to adopt the trade terms. **1878** *Hallberger's Ill. Mag.* 32 (Hoppe) The family, tradespeople, visitors and casuals [not to mention run-away knocks]. **1880** BLACKMORE *Erema* li. (Hoppe), Not a farthing did his lordship ever pay..to support his casual [bastard]. **1887** *19th Cent.* Oct. 488 The true casual is seldom employed. **1889** C. BOOTH *Life & Labour* I. 202 The work of the casuals was a dead loss to the contractor. **1930** L. G. D. ACLAND *Early Canterbury Runs* v. 94 He did not of course pay the casuals very big wages.

b. A casual pauper; a casual ward. See sense 9 above. *colloq.*

1865 *Pall Mall G.* 24 Oct. 11 The guardians of Marylebone had to admit 800 or 900 casuals a week into their workhouse. **1865** DICKENS *Mut. Fr.* II. 69. **1866** J. GREENWOOD in *Pall Mall G.* Feb., A night in a workhouse, by an amateur casual. **1887** *Pall Mall G.* 24 Oct. 1/2 The accommodation in casuals and workhouses. *Ibid.* This ward ..holds ninety—about the usual number for a London casual.

c. *Bot.* and *Zool.* A plant, animal, etc., found away from its normal area or habitat; an alien, casual immigrant.

1899 *Westm. Gaz.* 24 Aug. 3/1 The wanton slaughter of our rarer-winged 'casuals' is positively exasperating. **1926** TANSLEY & CHIPP *Study of Veget.* ii. 11 A species which is a mere alien intruder into the association..may be called a *casual.* **1959** A. R. CLAPHAM et al. *Excursion Flora Brit. Isles* 550 *Casual*, an introduced plant which has not become established though it occurs in places where it is not cultivated. **1959** E. F. LINSSEN *Beetles* I. 12 'Casuals', i.e. casual immigrants, accidental introductions, etc.

4. *Mil.* Cf. CASUALTY 2 b.

1853 STOCQUELER *Milit. Encycl.* 53 *Casuals*, or *Casualties*, a term..signifying men that are dead (since first enlisted), or have been discharged, or have deserted.

5. Esp. in *pl.* Casual clothes (cf. A. 11); *spec.*, a style of shoe with a low heel and shallow vamp.

1941 *Amer. Speech* XVI. 96 They are all right for *casuals* or *spectator* wear, but I'd get that formal. **1958** *Woman's Jrnl.* Mar. 3 (Advt.), Classic casual in pebbleweave. **1958** *Observer* 20 Apr. 11/4 Into the series of fashion shows will go ..casuals from Italy and France. **1959** *Vogue* June 71 Lastly, casuals—not all necessarily flat but on rounded cotton-reel and thimble-heels.

C. *Comb.* †**casual-wise** *adv.*, casually.

1601 CHESTER *Love's Mart.* cxlviii, If any happen casuall-wise to dye.

'casualism. [f. CASUAL + -ISM.] **a.** A state of things in which chance reigns. **b.** The doctrine that all things exist or happen by chance.

1873 *Contemp. Rev.* XXI. 187 The most arbitrary casualism in place of the orderliness of law. **1882–3** SCHAFF *Relig. Encycl.* III. 1949 From infidelity and scepticism sprung materialism..sensualism, and casualism.

'casualist. [f. as prec. + -IST.]

†**1.** = CASUIST. *Obs.*

1633 AMES *Agst. Cerem.* App. 39 Divers interpretations out of the Casualists.

2. One who holds the doctrine of casualism.

†**casu'ality.** *Obs.* [a. F. *casualité*:—med.L. *cāsuālitas*, f. *cāsuālis*; see CASUAL. The form now used is CASUALTY.]

1. Chance; the state of being 'casual'; a chance or casual occurrence, contingency; *esp.* an unfortunate occurrence, accident, casualty.

1540 RAYNALD *Birth Man.* I. ii. (1634) 19 By cutting or apostumation, or by other casuality. **1574** tr. *Marlorat's Apocalips* 5/4 Nothing happeneth by casualitie. *a* **1618** RALEIGH *Royal Navy* 19 More subject to casualitie and danger. **1679** HOBBES *Behemoth* Wks. (1840) VI. 246 Mere contingency, casuality, and fortune. **1792** W. ROBERTS *Looker-on* No. 7 (1794) I. 86 Superior to common casualities.

2. A casual or incidental charge or source of income; = CASUALTY 4.

c **1568** MURRAY in *Love-lett. Mary Q. Scots* App. (1824) 211 The intromissioun or disponyng upoun hir propertie, casualities, or quhatsumever thing pertening, or that ony wayis might pertene, to hir. **1607** DAVIES *1st Let. Earl Salisbury* (1787) 242 An allowance out of the fines and casualities of that county. *a* **1649** DRUMM. OF HAWTH. *Hist. Jas. V* Wks. (1711) 96 His partner and fellow-governour in distribution of casualities and ruling the country.

,casuali'zation. [f. CASUAL + -IZATION.] Conversion to a system of employing casual labour; the system itself. Hence (as back-formation) **'casualize** *v. trans.*, to convert (regular employees) into casual labourers. Cf. DECASUALIZATION s.v. DE- II. 1.

1920 *Rep. Ld. Shaw's Ct. of Inquiry on Dock Lab.* (*H.M.S.O.*) 9 The system of casualisation must..be torn up by the roots. **1934** *Times* 20 July 12/5 The employment of those engaged in theatres..would be reduced to such a state of casualization that they would have to go back to the state of casual employment among the dockers in the eighties for a parallel. **1950** *Hansard Commons* CDLXXVII. 825 The major reason..is the decision..to refrain from casualising the waiters and waitresses.

'casually, *adv.* Also 4–5 **casuelly**, 5 **caswelly**. [f. CASUAL + -LY².]

1. By chance; accidentally.

c **1384** CHAUCER *H. Fame* 679 And moo loves casuelly That betyde no man wote why. **1447** BOKENHAM *Seyntys* (1835) 174 He homward ayen..Hys journe took, and caswelly To the hyl he neyhyd. **1539** *Act 31 Hen. VIII*, xii, By chance negligently or casually. **1658** SIR T. BROWNE *Hydriot.* ii. 9 The Monument of Childerick..casually discovered three years past. **1667** BOYLE *Orig. Formes & Qual.* 4 That Matter barely put into Motion, and then left to itself should Casually constitute this beautiful and orderly world. **1691** RAY *Creation* I. (1704) 102 If the Clouds moved casually.

†**b.** Accidentally (= by a mischance). *Obs.*

c **1386** CHAUCER *Nonne Pr. T.* 281 Casuelly the schippes bothom rent. **1576** LAMBARDE *Peramb. Kent* (1826) 151 In a fire that casuallie consumed the Popes owne chamber. **1678** WANLEY *Wond. Lit. World* v. ii. §38 Basilius..was.. casually killed by a Stag.

2. Without design or previous intention; as it happens or happened; by mere chance.

1547 BOORDE *Introd. Knowl.* 205 Casually going over the bredge..I dyd mete with ix Englyshe..parsons. **1627** *Lisander & Cal.* II. 24 With whom Lisander casually being. **1647** CLARENDON *Hist. Reb.* (1702) I. IV. 294 All men, who ..had been casually present in the Hall. **1823** LAMB *Elia* Ser. II. (1865) 246 He casually looketh in about dinner-time.

3. Incidentally, by the way, in a chance way.

1697 *Snake in Grass* (ed. 2) 366 The Joint Answers of the Quakes..is not only Casually mention'd, but particularly insisted upon. **1794** PALEY *Evid.* I. iii. (1817) 53 Grounds of argument..casually and undesignedly disclosed. **1855** BAIN *Senses & Int.* III. ii. §14 A word casually spoken..will often revive a stream of recollections. **1862** STANLEY *Jew. Ch.* (1877) I. xvii. 328 Shiloh is casually mentioned.

¶? Causally.

1661 BRAMHALL *Just Vind.* i. 5 The Papacy..is become.. in a great part actually, and altogether casually, guilty..of.. all the greater schismes in Christendome.

'casualness. [f. CASUAL + -NESS.] Casual state or quality. (See CASUAL 5, 6.)

1882 *Sat. Rev.* No. 1393. 45 Stacks of umbrellas and bales of neglected great coats which in Scotland Yard await their owners, and mutely reproach the casualness of man. **1924** R. MACAULAY *Orphan Island* xvi. 222 There's a prodigious deal too much casualness about the business... I'm all for marriage or nothing. **1958** *Times* 20 Jan. 11/2 These three models are typical of spring styles... The casualness is both disciplined and chic.

casualty ('kæʒ(j)uːəltɪ, 'kæzjuːəltɪ). Also 5 **caswelte**. [ad. L. *casūālitas*, on model of forms like *royalty*, *fealty*, *penalty*; the fuller form was CASUALITY: cf. *speciality*, *special-ty*; see -TY.]

1. Chance, accident (as a state of things). ? *Obs.*

1423 JAS. I. *Kingis Q.* xxii, Were it causit throu hevinly Influence Off goddis will, or othir casualtee. *c* **1500** *Merch. & Son* in Halliw. *Nugæ P.* 23, I have seyn men bothe ryse and falle, hyt ys but caswelte! **1548** WRIOTHESLEY *Chron.* (1877) II. 6 Sainct Annes church..brente by casualtie of fire. **1639** W. WHATELEY *Prototypes* III. xxxix. (1640) 34 Sometimes by meere casualty almost they light upon a very good servant. **1779** JOHNSON *Pope* Wks. IV. 17 Combinations of skilful genius with happy casualty. **1856** KANE *Arct. Expl.* I. 398 Of too much worth to be left to casualty.

2. a. A chance occurrence, an accident; *esp.* an unfortunate occurrence, a mishap; now, generally, a fatal or serious accident or event, a disaster. **b.** *Mil.* Used of the losses sustained by a body of men in the field or on service, by death, desertion, etc.

1494 FABYAN VII. 336 By syknesse and other casueltyes, he loste moche of his people. **1530** WOLSEY in Ellis *Orig. Lett.* II. II. 30 If any casueltie of deth..chaunced unto hym. **1539** TAVERNER *Erasm. Prov.* (1552) 16 Betwene the cuppe and the lyppes maye come many casualties. **1608** SHAKS. *Per.* v. i. 94. **1612** ROWLANDS *Knaue Harts* 29 Losses on Land, and casualties at Seas. **1655** FULLER *Hist. Camb.* (1840) 20 Many sad casualties were caused by these meetings..Arms and legs were often broken, as well as spears. **1727** SWIFT *Country Post* Wks. 1755 III. I. 178 Several casualties have

happened this week, and the bill of mortality is very much increased. **1779** JOHNSON *L.P.* Wks. 1816 XI. 73 He that runs against Time has an antagonist not subject to casualties. **1810** WELLINGTON *Let.* in *Gurw. Disp.* VI. 480 Not enough to provide for the casualties of the service. **1861** *Lond. Rev.* 16 Feb. 168 The annual loss of property from casualties on our coast.

c. Used of an individual killed, wounded, or injured. Also *fig.*

1844 A. W. KINGLAKE *Eothen* xvi. 226 Although there may have been some 'casualties' in the way of eyes black.. and women 'missing', there was no return of 'killed'. **1900** W. S. CHURCHILL *London to Ladysmith* 393 In spite of more than a hundred casualties, the advance never checked for an instant. **1916** 'BOYD CABLE' *Action Front* 144 Such casualties as could walk back walked. **1925** E. F. NORTON *Fight for Everest, 1924* 87 With half a dozen porters to wait for our return in case there should be casualties to carry down the glacier. **1956** A. H. COMPTON *Atomic Quest* 198 The education of students at the university of Chicago was a war casualty.

†**3. a.** State of subjection to chance (see CASUAL 5); liability to accident; precariousness, uncertainty.

1503–4 *Act 19 Hen. VII*, xxv. Preamb., The casueltie of this worlde is suche & lyfe as uncertayne, etc. **1558** BP. WATSON *Sev. Sacram.* xvi. 104 The casualtie of oure frayle life. **1668** MARVELL *Corr.* civ. Wks. 1872–5 II. 260 Because of the distance of our lodgings and the casualty of finding one another. **1812** *Monthly Rev.* LXVII. 529 The casualty of public office, its distribution by accidental allotment.. tended to form a gambling spirit.

†**b.** *concr.* A thing subject to chance. *Obs.*

1667 PRIMATT *City & C. Build.* 6 Mines.. in England, are for the most part very great casualties.

4. A casual or incidental charge or payment; *spec.* in *Sc. Law*, a payment due from a tenant or vassal on the occurrence of certain casual events. ***casualty of wards***: feudal incidents accruing to superiors in ward holdings.

1529 W. FRANKELEYN in Fiddes *Wolsey* (1726) II. 166 Worthe the two hundrethe markes a yere of standyng rents bysids casualties. **1643** PRYNNE *Sov. Power Parl.* II. 57 The Chauncellor.. alleaging that the King was much endebted, and that he had neede retaine such casualties to himselfe. **1725** *Lond. Gaz.* No. 6378/3 His Majesty's Land Rents and Casualties in Scotland. **1759** ROBERTSON *Hist. Scot.* (1817) 225 The King received the feudal casualties of the ward. **1887** *Pall Mall G.* 4 Aug. 2/1 This right.. the casualty of composition on the estate passing to a singular successor, was so irregular in its incidence, and so arbitrary, that it has been so constantly evaded, whether rightly or wrongly, as never to constitute an appreciable addition to the value of the feudal superior's income.

5. *Mining.* (See quot.)

1753 CHAMBERS *Cycl. Supp.*, *Casualty*, in the tin-mines, a word used to denote the earth and stony matter which is, by washing in the stamping-mills, etc., separated from the tin ore, before it is dried and goes to the crazing mill. [In *Phil. Trans.* (1678) XII. 952, and Bradley *Fam. Dict.* (1725) called *causalty*.]

6. *attrib.*, as in ***casualty ward***, the ward in a hospital in which accidents are treated; similarly ***casualty nurse***, ***sister***; **casualty insurance** (chiefly *U.S.*) = *accident insurance* (ACCIDENT *sb.* 10); **casualty list**, a list of the dead, wounded, etc. in an engagement or campaign; so ***casualty returns***; **casualty man** = CASUAL *sb.* 3.

1836–7 DICKENS *Sk. Boz* (1850) 147/1 We were conducted to the casualty ward in which she was lying. **1846** *Colburn's United Service Mag.* May 127 Casualty Return. **1864** *Standing Orders, Dress Regul. Artillery* 73 The casualty returns being the documents on which the correctness of Brigade Records mainly depends. *Ibid.* 173 (in List of Periodical Returns) Casualty list. **1885** *Barthol. Hosp. Rep.* XXI. 89 The casualty department of St. Bartholomew's. **1887** BEATRICE POTTER in *19th Cent.* Oct. 489 A considerable number of men, possessing a preferred right to employment, act as an intermediate class between the permanent staff and the 'casualty' men. **1896** *Daily News* 17 June 8/3 The casualty nurse. **1902** *Encycl. Brit.* XXIX. 509/2 Another large class of casualty insurance applies to various forms of damage to property. **1919** G. B. SHAW *Heartbreak House* p. xxii, The emotional strain, complicated by the offended economic sense, produced by the casualty lists. **1925** W. DEEPING *Sorrell & Son* xxix. 294 He performed three minor operations, with the.. casualty-sister assisting him with critical and voiceless composure. **1958** L. VAN DER POST *Lost World of Kalahari* i. 22, I have forgotten the precise extent of the casualty list but I remember there were.. several horses among the dead.

¶ Erroneous for CAUSALITY; cf. CASUAL 8.

1635 SWAN *Spec. M.* (1670) 296 The same thing may be both a sign and a cause.. And therefore when the stars are called signs, their casualty is not excluded. **1668** HOWE *Bless. Righteous* (1825) 51 Its casualty is that of an objective cause.. that operates only as it is apprehended.

‖**casuarina** (ˌkæsjuːəˈraɪnə). *Bot.* [f. mod.L. *casuarius* cassowary, from fancied resemblance of the branches to the feathers of the bird.]

A genus of curious trees, with jointed leafless branches, having the appearance of gigantic horse-tails (*Equiseta*), natives of Australia and the Indian Archipelago. The Australian species is known as *Beef-wood*, and 'Oak'.

1806 *Naval Chron.* XV. 460 Clubs made of the wood of the *casuarina*. **1866** *Treas. Bot.* 237 The Fiji Islanders eat human flesh with forks made of the hard wood of a casuarina. **1883** *Sunday Mag.* Sept. 547/1 Splendid date-palms.. lofty Australian acacias, casuarinas, and eucalypti.

casuist (ˈkæzjuːɪst, ˈkæʒ(j)uːɪst). [a. F. *casuiste* (Sp. *casuista*, It. *casista*), f. L. *cāsu-s* case: see -IST.] A theologian (or other person) who studies and resolves cases of conscience or doubtful questions regarding duty and conduct. (Often with a sinister application: see CASUISTRY.)

1609 B. JONSON *Sil. Wom.* IV. v. (1616) 576 To talke with a Casuist about his diuorce. *a* **1661** HOLYDAY *Juvenal* Pref., Like an exact casuist does he not make conscience man's keeper and judge? **1663** COWLEY *Cutter Colem. St.* III. v, Like cunning Casuists as all Lovers are. *a* **1668** DENHAM *Progr. Learning* 118 Casuists, like cocks, struck out each other's eyes. **1732** POPE *Ep. Bathurst* 2 Who shall decide, when Doctors disagree And soundest Casuists doubt, like you and me? **1836** *Penny Cycl.* VI. 359. **1836** H. ROGERS *J. Howe* iii. (1863) 71 Provided we state a real reason.. it is agreed by all casuists, that we are not bound to state every reason. **1855** MACAULAY *Hist. Eng.* IV. 566 Casuists willing and competent to soothe his conscience with sophisms.

Hence †ˈ**casuist** *v.*, to play the casuist; ˈ**casuistess**, a female casuist; †ˈ**casuistly** *adv.*, according to the principles of casuists.

1643 MILTON *Divorce* II. xx. (1851) 119 We never leave subtilizing and casuisting. **1650** B. *Discolliminium* 7 Uncasuistly or unconscientiously asserted. **1865** M. ARNOLD *Ess. Crit.* v. (1875) 219 No casuistess in the gay Science.

casuistic (kæzjuːˈɪstɪk), *a.* [f. prec. + -IC.] = next. (Often with a sinister application: see CASUISTRY.)

1660 GAUDEN *Brownrig* 208 All points and parts of Religion, Dogmatick, Polemick, Practick, Casuistick. **1816** *Monthly Mag.* XLII. 36 Diving into the weedy pool of casuistic argument. **1872** TULLOCH *Ration. Theol.* I. vi. 353 Those casuistic tendencies which.. gave complexion to his [Jeremy Taylor's] theological culture. **1875** I. G. SMITH *Dict. Chr. Antiq.* s.v. *Celibacy*, The great casuistic Epistle [1 Corinthians].

casuistical (kæzjuːˈɪstɪkəl), *a.* [f. as prec. + -AL^1.] Pertaining to casuists or casuistry; relating to the solving of cases of conscience.

1649 ROBERTS *Clavis Bibl.* 617 His Casuisticall Sermon, wherein the Prophet at large resolves the Jews in a case of conscience touching Fasting. **1748** HARTLEY *Observ. Man* II. iii. 293 The endless Subtleties and Intricacies of Casuistical Divinity. **1791** BOSWELL *Johnson* (1831) V. 201 We talked of the casuistical question, 'Whether it was allowable at any time to depart from truth?' **1876** FREEMAN *Norm. Conq.* V. xxiii. 143 We also see in Anselm himself the beginning of those casuistical distinctions.

casuˈistically, *adv.* [f. prec. + -LY^2.] In a casuistical manner; sophistically.

1678 CUDWORTH *Intell. Syst.* I. v. 898 Themselves are necessitated.. Casuistically to allow, etc. **1691** WOOD *Ath. Oxon.* II. 282 [Jeremy Taylor] obtained in that house much of that learning wherewith he was enabled to write casuistically. **1856** DOVE *Logic Chr. Faith* Introd. 6 A similar method may be casuistically brought to bear against theology.

casuistry (ˈkæzjuːɪstrɪ, ˈkæʒ(j)uː-). [f. CASUIST + -RY. App. at first contemptuous = 'the casuist's trade'; cf. *sophistry*, *Jesuitry*, *foolery*. A term of more respectful application would prob. have been *casuism*: Fr. has *la casuistique*, as if 'casuistics'.]

The science, art, or reasoning of the casuist; that part of Ethics which resolves cases of conscience, applying the general rules of religion and morality to particular instances in which 'circumstances alter cases', or in which there appears to be a conflict of duties. Often (and perhaps originally) applied to a quibbling or evasive way of dealing with difficult cases of duty; sophistry.

1725 POPE *Rape Lock* v. 122 Cages for gnats.. and tomes of casuistry. **1736** BOLINGBROKE *Patriot.* (1749) 170 Casuistry.. destroys, by distinctions and exceptions, all morality, and effaces the essential difference between right and wrong. **1836** *Penny Cycl.* VI. 359 The science of casuistry.. has been termed not inaptly the 'art of quibbling with God'. **1841** EMERSON *Lect. the Times* Wks. (Bohn) II. 254 The Temperance-question.. is a gymnastic training to the casuistry and conscience of the time. **1862** MILL *Utilit.* 37 Self-deception and dishonest casuistry. **1887** FOWLER *Princ. Morals* II. vi. 247 Granted that duties may clash, or that general rules may be modified by special circumstances, it is surely most important to determine beforehand, as far as we can, what those circumstances are, and, in the case of clashing duties, which should yield to the other. Now this, and this alone, is the task which 'Casuistry' or the attempt to 'resolve cases of conscience' proposes to itself.

2. A register or record of (medical) cases.

1883 J. W. LEGG in *Barthol. Hosp. Rep.* XIX. 202 Nor can I find any similar case in the casuistry of pemphigus as recorded in the year-books.

†ˈ**casule.** *Obs.* exc. *Hist.* Also in 6 casle. [OE. *casul*, also OF. *casule*, ad. L. *casula* (dim. of *casa* cottage), used in late L. for 'a vestment covering the whole person' ('casula est vestis cucullata, dicta per diminutionem a casa, quod totum hominem tegat, quasi minor casa', Isidore XIX. xxiv. 17).] = CHASUBLE.

a **1000** *Voc.* in Wr.-Wülcker 196 *Byrrum*, casul. **1557** *Wills & Inv. N.C.* (1835) 159 Item more a casle of geld price viij *l.* **1563–87** FOXE *A. & M.* (1596) 207/1 His [the archbishop of York's] casule, chimer, and rochet. **1656** BLOUNT *Glossogr.*, *Casule*, or Planet, one of those attires wherewith the Priest is vested, when he says Mass. **1824** SOUTHEY *Bk. of Ch.* (1841) 211 Plucked the priestly casule from his back.

†ˈ**casure.** *Obs. rare.* [f. L. *cās-* ppl. stem of *cadĕre* to fall + -URE (as if ad. L. **cāsūra*).] Cadence, rhythm.

1565 CALFHILL *Answ. Treat. Crosse* (1846) 298 (D.) Allured with the pleasant casure of the metre.

‖ˈ**casus.** *Obs.* [L. *cāsus* fall, falling.] Each of the segments of the base of a triangle cut off by a perpendicular falling thereon from the vertex.

1571 DIGGES *Pantom.* II. xxiv. Piijb, Diuide both the Casus, that is to say, BD, and DC the distance of eyther Angle from the perpendicular.

‖**casus belli** (ˈkeɪsəs ˈbɛlaɪ). [f. L. *casus* CASE *sb.*^{1} + *belli*, gen. of *bellum* war.] An act justifying, or regarded as a reason for, war. Also *transf.*

1849 J. S. MILL in *Westm. Rev.* LI. 28 To assist a people struggling for liberty.. is not a *casus belli* set down in Vattel. **1853** H. GREVILLE *Diary* 22 June (1884) 60 He thought the Russians would soon occupy the principalities, which, however, the other Powers would not pronounce to be a *casus belli*. **1868** TROLLOPE *He knew*, etc. I. xlviii. 374 The Juno from the Close had come quite prepared to declare her casus belli.. and to fling down her gauntlet. **1878** *Times* 2 Feb. 6/3 He did not say what was to be the *casus belli* or the *casus armandi*. **1920** D. H. LAWRENCE *Touch & Go* 11 Some men might acknowledge the bone to be merely a pretext, another hollow *casus belli*.

‖**casus fœderis** (ˈkeɪsəs ˈfiːdərɪs). [f. L. *casus* CASE *sb.*^{1} + *fœderis*, gen. of *fœdus* treaty.] A situation or occurence covered by the provisions of a treaty or compact, and so requiring the action of the parties thereto. Also *attrib.* and *fig.*

1780 J. ADAMS *Let.* 31 Dec. in *Wks.* (1852) VII. 348 These powers will not be duped by the artifice of the British Court, and adjudge this war not a *casus fœderis*. **1834** H. GREVILLE *Diary* 30 July (1883) 16 A quadripartite treaty, of which your person is the *casus fœderis*. **1882** *Standard* 20 Dec. 5/7 The Treaty of Alliance with the Austrian Empire, including those paragraphs.. which define the special obligations of each contracting party under a casus fœderis. **1941** AUDEN *New Year Let.* III. 51 Which of these calls to conscience is For mine the casus foederis. **1962** *Times* 4 Jan. 9/3 Dr. Salazar admits the *casus foederis* argument.

caswellite (ˈkæzwəlaɪt). *Min.* [Named after John H. *Caswell*, 19th-c. Amer. mineralogist: see -ITE^1.] A micaceous aluminosilicate of manganese of a copper-red colour, probably an altered form of biotite.

1894 A. H. CHESTER in *Trans. N.Y. Acad. Sci.* XIII. 183 Inasmuch as these results seem to justify the view that it is a new mineral species, I propose for it the name Caswellite. **1896** *Jrnl. Chem. Soc.* LXX. II. 309 It is supposed that the caswellite has been derived by the local action of water containing manganese and calcium on this biotite. **1966** *Amer. Min.* LI. 1120 The name caswellite has since been applied more specifically.. to the garnet pseudomorphs themselves... The name caswellite lacks species or varietal significance and should be abandoned.

caswelly, -elte, obs. ff. CASUALLY, CASUALTY.

casydoyn, casyldon: see CASSIDOINE, obs. var. of CHALCEDONY.

cat (kæt), *sb.*^{1} Forms: 1 catte, catt, 2–7 catt, 4–6 catte, (3–7 kat, 6 katte), 1– cat. [The ME. and mod. *cat* corresponds at once to OE. *cat* and ONF. *cat*. The name is common European of unknown origin: found in Lat. and Gr. in 1–4th c., and in the modern langs. generally, as far back as their records go. Byzantine Gr. had *κάττα* (in Cæsarius *c* 350) and later *κάττος*, as familiar terms = *αἴλουρος*; mod.Gr. has *γάτα* from Ital. Latin had *catta* in Martial *a* 100, and in the Old Latin Bible version ('*Itala*'), where it renders *αἴλουρος*. Palladius, ? *c* 350, has *catus*, elsewhere scanned *cātus* (Lewis and Short), and prob. in both cases properly *cattus*. From *cattus*, *catta*, came all the Romanic forms, It. *gatto*, Sp., Pg. *gato*, Cat. *gat*, Pr. *cat*, ONF. *cat*, F. *chat*, with corresponding feminines *gatta*, *gata*, *cata*, *cate*, *chate*, *chatte*. The Teutonic forms recorded are OE. *cat*, *catt*, ON. *kött-r* (:—*kattuz*) masc., genit. *kattar* (Sw. *katt*, Da. *kat*); also OE. *catte* ? fem., WGer. **katta* (MLG. *katte*, MDu. *katte*, *kat*, Du. *kat*, also Sw. *katta*), OHG. *chazzâ* (MHG., mod.G. *katze*) fem.; OHG. had also *chataro*, MHG. *katero*, *kater*, mod.G. and Du. *kater*, he-cat. The OTeut. types of these would be **kattuz* masc., **kattôn-* fem., **kat(a)zon-* masc.; but as no form of the word is preserved in Gothic, it is not certain that it goes back to the OTeut. period. It was at least WGer. *c* 400–450. It is also in Celtic: OIr. *cat* masc., Gael. *cat* com., Welsh and Cornish *cath* f., Breton *kaz*, Vannes *kac'h* m. Also in Slavonic, with type *kot-*: OSlav. *kot'ka* f., Bulg. *kotka*, Slovenish *kot* m., Russ. *kot* m., *kotchka*, *koshka* f., Pol. *kot* (*koczur* m.), Boh. *kot* m.,

kotka f., Sorabian *kotka*; also Lith. *kate*; Finnish *katti*.

(These forms indicate extensive communication of the word, but do not fix the original source. History points to Egypt as the earliest home of the domestic cat, and the name is generally sought in the same quarter; Martial's attribute might incline us to a Slavonic or Teutonic origin: *c* **75** MARTIAL xiii. 69 Pannonicas nobis nunquam dedit Umbria cattas. *a* **250** *Baruch* vi. 21 ('Itala') Noctuæ et hirundines et aves, similiter et cattæ [LXX. καὶ οἱ αἴλουροι].)

I. The animal.

1. a. A well-known carnivorous quadruped (*Felis domesticus*) which has long been domesticated, being kept to destroy mice, and as a house pet.

a **800** *Corpus Gloss.* 863 *Fellus* (*felis*), catte. *a* **1000** ÆLFRIC *Voc.* in Wr.-Wülcker 120 *Muriceps, uel musio, murilegus*, catt. *c* **1050** *Gloss.* ibid. 445 *Muriceps*, cat. *a* **1225** *Ancr. R.* 416 Ne schulen habben no best, bute kat one. *c* **1300** *K. Alis.* 5275 By nighth als a cat hy seeth. *c* **1386** CHAUCER *Wife's Prol.* 348 Who so wolde senge the cattes skin, Than wol the cat wel dwellen in hire in. *c* **1520** ANDREWE *Noble Lyfe* in *Babees Bk.* (1868) 224 The mouse hounter or catte is an onclene beste, & a poyson ennemy to all myse. **1556** *Chron. Grey Fr.* (1852) 88 Item..was a katte hongyd on the gallos in Cheppe clothed lyke a preste. **1602** SHAKS. *Ham.* v. i. 315 The Cat will mew, and Dogge will haue his day. **1699** B. E. *Dict. Cant. Crew* s.v. *Mouse*, He watcht me as a Cat does a Mouse. **1752** JOHNSON *Rambl.* No. 188 ¶12 Purring like a cat. **1832** A. FONBLANQUE *Engl. under 7 Admin.* (1837) II. 272 The ruffians who threw dead dogs and dead cats at the Duke.

b. The male or *he-cat* (formerly also *boar-cat*, *ram-cat*) is now colloquially called *tom-cat* (see TOM); formerly and still in north Engl. and Sc. *gib-cat* (see GIB); the female or *she-cat* was formerly also *doe-cat*.

c **1400** *Rom. Rose* 6207 Gibbe our cat That awaiteth mice and rattes to killen. *a* **1529** SKELTON *P. Sparowe* 22 To call Phylyp agayne, Whom Gyb our cat hath slayne. **1596** SHAKS. *1 Hen. IV*, I. ii. 83, I am as Melancholy as a Gyb-Cat. **1607–1797** [See BOAR-CAT]. **1611** COTGR., *Chate*, a she-cat or doe-cat. **1667** PEPYS *Diary* 29 Nov., Our young gibb-cat did leap down our stairs..at two leaps. **1749** COLES *Eng. Lat. Dict.*, A gib-cat, *felis mas*. **1760** *Life & Adv. of a Cat* iv, Tom the Cat is born of poor but honest parents. **1785** GROSE *Dict. Vulgar T.*, *Gib cat*, a northern name for a he cat, there commonly called Gilbert. **1791** HUDDESFORD *Salmagundi* (1793) 141 Cats..of titles obsolete or yet in use, Tom, Tybert, Roger, Rutterkin, or Puss. **1795** WOLCOTT (P. Pindar), *Peter's Pension*, Clapping their dead ram-cats in holy ground. **1839** [see 13 c] Tom-cat.

c. wild cat, *Felis Catus*, the only representative of the feline genus found native in Great Britain; it is larger and stronger than the domestic cat, and is by some considered a distinct species.

c **1400** in *Cod. Dipl.* IV. 236 For hare, and foxe, and wild cattes. **1577** NORTHBROOKE *Dicing* (1843) 23 The church is no wylde cat: it will stande still. **1847** CARPENTER *Zool.* §190 The Wild Cat..is now confined to Scotland, some of the woods in the North of England, the woody mountains of Wales, and some parts of Ireland.

2. *fig.* **a.** As a term of contempt for a human being; *esp.* one who scratches like a cat; a spiteful or backbiting woman. *spec.* an itinerant worker (*U.S. slang*).

a **1225** *Ancr. R.* 102 Hweðer þe cat of helle claurede euer toward hire. **1601** SHAKS. *All's Well* IV. iii. 295 A pox upon him for me, he's more and more a Cat. **1607** —— *Cor.* IV. ii. 34 'Twas you incenst the rable-Cats. **1763** MRS. BROOKE *Lady J. Mandeville* (1782) II. 72 An old cat..who is a famous proficient in scandal. **1778** JOHNSON in *Boswell* (1887) III. 246 She was a speaking cat. **1840** MARRYAT *Poor Jack* xii, His mother called me an old cat. **1926** J. BLACK *You can't Win* vi. 67 Buy nothin'... It's you kind of cats that make it tough on us, buyin' chuck. *Ibid.* xvi. 220 Harvest workers were called blanket stiffs or gay cats. *Ibid.* 221 They stuck up the cats, took their money, [etc.].

†**b.** *slang.* A prostitute. *Obs.*

[**1401** *Pol. Poems* II. 113 Be ware of Cristis curse, and of cattis tailis.] **1535** LYNDESAY *Satyre* 468 *Wantonnes.* Hay! as ane brydlit cat, I brank. **1670** B. E. *Dict. Cant. Crew*, *Cat*, a common Whore. **1708** MOTTEUX *Rabelais* (1737) V. 217 Wrigglers, Misses, Cats, Rigs.

c. An expert in, or one expertly appreciative of, jazz. *slang* (orig. *U.S.*). Cf. HEP-CAT.

[**1922** J. A. CARPENTER (*title of ballet*) Krazy Kat.] **1932** *Melody Maker* Oct. 836/1 [citing L. Armstrong] All the cats were there. **1935** *Down Beat* 1 Nov. 8. The slanguage of swing-terms that 'cats' use. **1936** *Delineator* Nov. 49/2 *Cats*, the musicians of a swing orchestra. **1937** *Amer. Speech* XII. 183/1 *Cats*, those members of the audience who are receptive to jazz music or who understand it. **1937** L. ARMSTRONG *Swing that Music* xiii. 111, I wanted to give 'em a load of how we swing that music at home. My 'cats' understood it the same way and began lickin' their chops, as we say it. **1955** SHAPIRO & HENTOFF *Hear Me talkin' to Ya* xix. 299 Minton's was just a place for cats to jam... When you went in you'd see cats half-stewed who weren't paying much mind to what was happening on stage. **1958** *Woman's Own* 19 Feb. 22/1 'It's got beat and a lot of excitement,' said one teenage 'cat' I talked to.

d. *slang.* A 'regular guy', fellow, man.

1957 MEZZROW & WOLFE *Really the Blues* 372 *Cat*, regular fellow, guy. **1959** A. ANDERSON *Lover Man* 116 'At-*dam*, man, youre the selfishest kat I seen yet. **1959** C. MACINNES in *Encounter* Aug. 35/2 The coloured cats saw I had an ally, and melted.

3. *Zool.* Extended (usually in *pl.*) to the members of the genus *Felis*, including the lion, tiger, panther, leopard, etc.; the feline animals or *cat-kind, cat tribe*. It enters into the name of some of these, as the *tiger-cat* of South America.

1607 TOPSELL *Four-f. Beasts* 383 Panthers, Pardals, Linxes, or Tygers, had been all of the kinde of Cats. **1796** STEDMAN *Surinam* II. xviii. 51 The tyger cat is a very lively animal, with its eyes emitting flashes like lightning. **1834** MCMURTRIE *Curier's Anim. Kingd.* 68 Of all the Carnaria the Cats are the most completely and powerfully armed. **1839** *Penny Cycl.* XIII. 430/2 Leopards, the name by which the greater spotted cats are known.

4. a. With qualifications (or contextually) applied to some animals of similar appearance, as *civet-cat*, *musk-cat*, *pole-cat*, etc.; and in further extension to other animals, as **flying-cat** (*Cant*), an owl (cf. Fr. *chat-huant*); **sea-cat**, the Wolf-fish.

1553 EDEN *Treat. New Ind.* (Arb.) 25 In this region are founde many muske cattes. **1600** SHAKS. *A. Y. L.* III. ii. 70 Ciuet is..the verie vncleanly fluxe of a cat. **1605** —— *Lear* III. iv. 109 Thou ow'st..the Cat, no perfume. **1699** B. E. *Dict. Cant. Crew* s.v. *Flutter*, An Owl is a Flying-Cat. **1859** YARRELL *Brit. Fishes* (ed. 3) II. 384 The wolf-fish, sea-wolf, sea-cat, Scotland. *Ibid.* 385 The savage Sea-cat is speedily rendered incapable of doing further harm. **1870** *Every Boy's Ann.* (Rtldg.) 628 The polecat had pounced upon the bait.. Between the two [dogs] the cat was killed.

b. Short for CATFISH 1 b.

1705 R. BEVERLY *Hist. Virginia* (1722) 129 Conger-Eels, Perch, and Cats. **1796** STEDMAN *Surinam* II. xviii. 60 The spotted-cat..this fish is formed not unlike a pike. **1848–60** BARTLETT *Dict. Amer.* s.v. *Catfish*..is also called by the name of Horned-pout, Bull-head, Mud-pout, Minister, or simply Cat.

†**5.** Short for CAT-SKIN, cat's fur. *Obs.*

1656 *Sheph. Kalendar* xxvii, Cats, Conies, Lambs, and diverse other thicke furres that be good and wholesome. **1677** HOBBES *Homer* 148 And from him then they took his cap of cat.

II. Transferred senses.

6. a. A movable pent-house used in early times by besiegers to protect themselves in approaching fortifications, also called *cat-house*: cf. BELFRY, SOW. In OF. *chat-chastel* (Cotgr.), med.L. *cattus*.

(Caxton has *barbed cat*: otherwise little evidence appears of its use in Eng., except by modern historians translating Lat. *cattus* or Fr. *chat*.)

1489 [see BARBED-CAT]. **1605** [see *cat-house* in 18]. **1833** SOUTHEY *Naval Hist. Eng.* I. 85 Machines which, under the names of 'Cats' and 'Sows', were used in sieges. **1860** READE *Cloister & H.* xliii. (D.) A strong pent-house, which they called a cat. **1885** C. W. OMAN *Art of War* 58 If the moat could be filled, and the cat brought close to the foot of the fortifications.

†**b.** A lofty work used in fortifications and sieges; a CAVALIER. *Obs.*

1628 WITHER *Brit. Rememb.* IV. 1304 A warlike Fort; A new rais'd Mount, or some fire-spitting Cat. **1647–8** COTTERELL *Davila's Hist. Fr.* (1678) 524 *Cavalier*, a Mount raised on purpose to plant cannon on. Some call it a Cat. **1652** SHIRLEY *Honoria & Mam.* I. ii, Of turnpikes, flankers, cats, and counter-scarps.

7. *Naut.* Applied to different parts of the contrivance by which an anchor is raised out of the water to the deck of the ship, or suspended outside clear of the bow; chiefly = CAT-HEAD *sb.*, but also used for the *cat-purchase* and the *cat-fall* (see 18).

1626 CAPT. SMITH *Accid. Yng. Seamen* 12 The forecastle ..the Cat, Catshead and Cates holes. **1627** —— *Seaman's Gram.* ii. 11 The Cat is also a short peece of timber aloft right ouer the Hawse. **1670** DRYDEN *Tempest* I. i, Haul Catt, haul Catt. **1769** FALCONER *Dict. Marine* (1789), *Cat*, is..a.. strong tackle, or complication of pullies, to hook and draw the anchor..up to the cat-head. **1825** H. GASCOIGNE *Nav. Fame* 50 The Cat is hook'd 'Haultaught!' their weight they ply By Sticking-out more Cable they supply. **1860** H. STUART *Seaman's Catech.* 56 The cat, for lifting the whole weight of the anchor, is rove through the foremost sheave of the cat-head, through the inner sheave of the cat-block. **1864** S. FERGUSON *Forging Anchor* vi, A shapely one he is, and strong, as e'er from cat was cast. **1867** SMYTH *Sailor's Wd.-bk.* 173 When the cat is hooked and 'cable enough' veered and stoppered, the anchor hangs below the cat-head. **1880** *Boy's Own Bk.* 315 *Cat*, a projecting piece of wood or iron to which sheets or halyards are made fast.

8. Short for CAT-O'-NINE-TAILS.

1788 FALCONBRIDGE *Afr. Slave Tr.* 40 A cat (an instrument of correction, which consists of a handle or stem, made of a rope three inches and a half in circumference, and about eighteen inches in length, at one end of which are fastened nine branches, or tails, composed of log line, with three or more knots upon each branch). **1789** WOLCOTT (P. Pindar) *Subj. for Paint.* Wks. 1812 II. 149 This Cat's a cousin-german to the Knout. **1824** *Order in Council* in *Ann. Reg.* (1824) 64*/2 Any whip, cat, stick, or other such like instrument. **1846** A. FONBLANQUE *Life & Labours* ii. (1874) 210 The Duke's professional prejudice makes him cling to the cat.

9. A double tripod with six legs, formed by three bars joined in the middle and so placed that it always rests on three legs, as a cat is said always to land on its feet.

1806 *Ann. Reg.* 960 A new toast-stand, or an improvement on the articles called cats or dogs, upon which things are placed before the fire. **1826** SCOTT in S. Gibson *Remin.* (1871) 17 A mahogany thing, which is called a cat, with a number of legs, so that turning which way it will it stands upright. **1847** MRS. SHERWOOD in *Life* vi. 88 There was an ebony cat standing before the fire, supporting a huge plate of toast and butter. **1884** *Pall Mall G.* 24 July 9/1 There are also at least a couple of 'cats', stands for open fireplaces.

10. A term used in various games.

a. A small piece of wood tapering at each end, used in the game of tip-cat, etc.; it is hit at one end by the *cat-stick*, and made to spring from the ground, and then driven away by a side stroke.

1598 FLORIO, *Lippo*, a trap or cat, such as children play at. *a* **1627** MIDDLETON *Wom. beware Wom.* I. ii, Prithee, lay up my cat and cat-stick safe. *a* **1652** BROME *New Acad.* IV. i. Wks. 1873 II. 66 All my storehouse of tops, gigs, balls, cat and catsticks. **1801** STRUTT *Sports and Past.* 101 (N.) The cat is about six inches in length, and an inch and a half or two inches in diameter, and diminished from the middle to both ends, in the manner of a double cone.

b. The game itself; tip-cat.

1626 in *Windsor & Eton Gaz.* (1886) 6 Mar. 4/5 Playing at Catt in the Parke medow. **1653** J. TAYLOR (Water P.) *Journ. Wales* (1859) 26 The lawful and laudable games of trapp, catt, stool-ball, racket, etc. **1801** STRUTT *Sports & Past.* II. iii. 101. **1885** J. BROWN *Bunyan* 61 He was one Sunday in the midst of a game of cat.

†**c.** The cat-stick. *Obs.*

1636 *Divine Trag. lately Acted* 23 Sundry youths playing at Catt on the Lords day, two of them fell out, and the one hitting the other under the eare with his catt, he therwith fell downe for dead.

d. The stick in the game of Cat-in-the-hole. (Jamieson.)

1721 KELLY *Sc. Prov.* 325 (Jam.) *Tine Cat, tine Game*, an allusion to a play called Cat i' the Hole, and the English Kit-Cat. Spoken when men at law have lost their principal evidence.

e. In names of games: † ***Cat and trap, Cat i' the hole*** (Sc.). Also CAT AND DOG 3.

1598 FLORIO, *Gatta orba*, a kinde of Christmas game called *blinde is the cat*. **1611** COTGR., *Martinet*..the game called Cat and Trap. **1837–40** HALIBURTON *Clockm.* (1862) 442 What do you say to a game at..odd and even, wild cat and 'coon, or somethin' or another? **1825–79** JAMIESON *Dict.*, *Cat in the Hole*, a game played by boys.

11. a. 'A mess of coarse meal, clay, etc., placed in dove-cotes, to allure strangers' (Halliwell). More fully *salt-cat*.

1669 WORLIDGE *Syst. Agric.* ix. §2 (1681) 177 A Salt-Cat ..which makes the Pigeons mostly affect the place: and such that casually come there, usually remain where they find such good entertainment.

b. *pl.* The salt which crystallizes round the edge of the pan or beneath the holes in the bottom of the trough in which salt is put to drain. Cf. CAT *v.* 5.

1886 R. HOLLAND *Gloss. Chester*, *Cats*, salt-making term. Masses of salt formed under a pan when it leaks. **1892** *Cornhill Mag.* Sept. 265 The 'cats', or salt that has become encrusted round the edges of the pan, is sent to the pottery works for glazing pipes and pitchers.

III. Phrases.

12. ***to turn the cat in the pan***: †**a.** to reverse the order of things so dexterously as to make them appear the very opposite of what they really are; to turn a thing right about. *Obs.*

[Origin unknown: the suggestion that cat was originally CATE does not agree with the history of that word.]

1532 *Use Dice Play* (1850) 18 These vile cheaters turned the cat in the pan, giving to divers vile, patching thefts, an honest & goodly title, calling it by the name of a law. *c* **1536–40** *Pilgr. T.* 692 in Thynne *Animadv.*, Ther was a prouerbe I knew wan, callyd 'turnyng the cate in the pane'. **1543** BECON *Invect. agst. Swearing* Wks. (1843) 353 God saith, 'Cry, cease not', but they turn cat in the pan, and say, 'Cease, cry not'. **1572** HULOET (L.) A subtile turning the catte in the panne, or wresting of a false thing to some purpose. **1576** NEWTON tr. *Lemnie's Complex.* (1633) 208 Turning the Cat in the Pan, full of Leiger-du-maine. **1619** H. HUTTON *Follie's Anat.* 31 I'l, with the proverbe, Turne the cat i' th' band.

b. To change one's position, change sides, from motives of interest, etc.

1622 T. STOUGHTON *Chr. Sacrif.* vii. 91 How do they shrinke? yea, how fouly do they..turne cat in pan, and become themselves persecuters of other? **1675** CROWNE *City Polit.* II. i, Come, Sirrah, you are a Villain, have turn'd Cat-in-pan, and are a Tory. *a* **1720** *Song, Vicar of Bray*, I turned the cat in pan once more, And so became a Whig, sir. **1816** SCOTT *Old Mort.* xxxv, 'O, this precious Basil will turn cat in pan with any man'.

13. a. ***a cat may look at a king***: there are certain things which an inferior may do in presence of a superior. **b.** ***care killed the cat***: care will kill any one even though he had, like the proverbial cat, *nine lives*. **c.** ***enough to make a cat speak***: said of something very extraordinary (frequently of good drink). **d.** ***to jerk, shoot, whip the cat***: to vomit, especially from too much drink. **e.** ***to see*** (***watch***) ***which way the cat jumps***: i.e. what direction events are taking. **f.** ***to fight like Kilkenny cats***: to engage in a mutually destructive struggle. ***to bell the cat, to hang the bell about the cat's neck***: see BELL *v.* and *sb.* ***to let the cat out of the bag***: to disclose a guarded secret: see BAG. ***to grin like a Cheshire cat*** (see N. & Q. 1852 V. 402). **g.** ***cat and monkey trick*** (cf. CAT'S-PAW). **h.** ***like a cat on hot bricks***: see HOT *a.* 12 c. **i.** ***not a cat*** (***in hell***)***'s chance***: no chance whatever. **j.** ***to make a cat laugh***: said of something excruciatingly funny. **k.** ***that cat won't jump*** (orig. *U.S.*): that suggestion is implausible or impracticable. **l.** ***the cat's pyjamas, whiskers*** (*slang*, orig. *U.S.*): the acme of excellence. **m.** ***to look*** (***feel***) ***like something the***

cat has brought in: to appear, or to feel, exhausted or bedraggled.

a. 1562 J. Heywood *Prov. & Epigr.* (1867) 57 A cat maie looke on a king, ye know. 1590 Greene *Never too late* (1600) 94 A Cat may looke at a King, and a swaines eye hath as high a reach as a Lords looke. 1730–6 Bailey s.v., A Cat may look at a King. This is a saucy Proverb, generally made use of by pragmatical Persons.

b. 1562 J. Heywood *Prov. & Epigr.* (1867) 162 A woman hath nyne lyues like a cat. 1592 Shaks. *Rom. & Jul.* III. i. 81 Good King of Cats, nothing but one of your nine liues. 1599 —— *Much Ado* v. i. 133 Though care kil'd a cat, thou hast mettle enough in thee to kill care. 1682 N. O. *Boileau's Lutrin* IV. 332 Exiling fretting Care, that kills a Cat! 1684 Bunyan *Pilgr.* II. (1862) 331 He had, as they say, as many Lives as a Cat. 1886 *Sat. Rev.* 6 Mar. 322/2 That Arab cat-o'-nine-lives, Osman Digna.

c. [1600 Shaks. *Temp.* II. ii. 86 Here is that which will giue language to you cat.] 1719 D'Urfey *Pills* III. 272 Old Liquor able to make a Cat speak. 1839 Dickens *Nich. Nick.* xii, It's enough to make a Tom cat speak French grammar, only to see how she tosses her head.

d. 1609 Armin *Maids of More-cl.* (1880) 70 Ile baste their bellies and their lippes till we haue ierk't the cat with our three whippes. 1630 J. Taylor (Water P.) *Brood Cormor.* Wks. III. 5/1 You may not say hee's drunke.. For though he be as drunke as any rat He hath but catcht a fox, or *whipt the Cat.* 1830 Marryat *King's Own* xxxii, I'm cursedly inclined to *shoot the cat*.

e. 1827 Scott in *Croker Pap.* (1884) I. xi. 319 Had I time, I believe I would come to London merely to see how the cat jumped. 1863 Kingsley *Water Bab.* 289 He.. understood so well which side his bread was buttered, and which way the cat jumped. 1885 *Pall Mall G.* 19 Mar. 1/2 The Opposition is as much devoted to the cult of the jumping cat as are the Liberals.

f. 1770–1819 Wolcott (P. Pindar) 91 (D.) Lo! like a Cheshire cat our court will grin. 1855 Thackeray *Newcomes* xxiv. (D.), Mr. Newcome says..'That woman grins like a Cheshire cat'.

g. 1856 Olmsted *Slave States* 494 So successfully was this cat-and-monkey trick performed.

i. 1796 Grose *Dict. Vulg. Tongue* (ed. 3), No more chance than a cat in hell without claws; said of one who enters into a dispute or quarrel with one greatly above his match. 1902 C. Hyne *Mr. Horrocks, Purser* 100 Crutches by themselves wouldn't have stood a cat's chance. 1927 *Daily Express* 13 Dec. 16/6 There did not seem a cat's chance for Oxford on comparative form. 1958 M. Procter *Man in Ambush* ii. 19 He hasn't a cat-in-hell chance. 1962 'H. Howard' *Double Finesse* xvi. 168 You haven't a cat-in-hell's chance of getting away. 1966 *Guardian* 22 June 3/6 One seaman said the union had not 'a cat in hell's chance' of beating the Government as well as the shipowners.

j. [*c* 1598 Haughton *Englishm. for my Money* (1616) E 4, Oh maister Mouse,..it would make any Mouse, Ratte, Catte, or Dogge, laugh to thinke, what sport we shall have.] 1838 J. R. Planché *Puss in Boots* 24 Allow us just applause to win Enough to make a cat laugh. 1907 W. W. Jacobs *Short Cruises* 230 It would ha' made a cat laugh. 1929 J. B. Priestley *Good Compan.* III. iv. 551 Make a cat laugh, the way she takes people off.

k. 1838 Haliburton *Clockmaker* xvi. 242 Them Yankee villains would break up our laws, language, and customs; that cat wouldn't jump at all, would it? 1906 Galsworthy *Man of Property* III. ix. 372 'They talk of suicide here,' he said at last. '*That* cat won't jump.' 1934 F. W. Crofts *12.30 from Croydon* xiii. 178 They know I was hard up...No, Charles, that cat won't jump. 1965 'S. Troy' *No More a-Roving* ii. 57 If you're telling me she fell in, just like that—oh no! That cat won't jump.

l. 1923 W. A. Roberts in *Saucy Stories* 1 Mar. 121/1 It would have landed us in jail, if we had published it... But as literature, it was the cat's whiskers. 1924 Wodehouse *Leave it to Psmith* ix. 181 'Well, if this ain't the cat's whiskers!' said Miss Peavey. 1925 S. Lewis *M. Arrowsmith* xxxix. 460 This kid used to think Pa Gottlieb was the cat's pyjamas. 1930 *Times Lit. Suppl.* 4 Sept. 693/2 We were the absolute and utter cat's pyjamas. 1958 *Times* 15 Aug. 9/4 Lord Montgomery..holds that to label anything the 'cat's whiskers' is to confer on it the highest honour.

m. 1928 R. Knox *Footsteps at Lock* viii. 79 Bredon felt, in an expressive modern phrase, like something the cat had brought in. 1940 R. Postgate *Verdict of Twelve* II. ii. 112 Rosalie realized that for the family she was something the cat brought in. 1967 A. Wilson *No Laughing Matter* III. 170 The sweet toothy smile froze to a 'what's that the cat's brought in' disdain.

14. ***to draw through the water with a cat***, also ***to whip the cat***: to practise a practical joke, thus described by Grose:

'A trick often practised on ignorant country fellows, by laying a wager with them that they may be pulled through a pond by a cat; the bet being made, a rope is fastened round the waist of the person to be catted, and the end thrown across the pond, to which the cat is also fastened by a pack-thread, and three or four sturdy fellows are appointed to lead and whip the cat; these on a signal given, seize the end of the cord, and pretending to whip the cat, haul the astonished booby through the water.'

1614 B. Jonson *Barthol. Fair* I. iv. (N.), I'll be drawn with a good gib cat through the great pond at home. 1682 in *Lond. Gaz.* No. 1725/3 We hope, sir, that this Nation will be too Wise, to be drawn twice through the same Water by the very same Cat. 1690 B. E. *Dict. Canting Crew, Catting*, drawing a Fellow through a Pond with a Cat. 1785 Grose *Dict. Vulgar T.* s.v. *Cat-whipping*. 1847 Halliwell s.v. *Whip-the-Cat*. 1876 *Times* 13 Aug., Drawing a cat through the Lea [Trial for manslaughter at Central Criminal Court 10 Aug. 1876]. 1888 *N. & Q.* Ser. VII. V. 310.

15. In many other proverbs and phrases.

c 1450 Henryson *Mor. Fab.* 65 It is ane olde Dog..that thou begyles, Thou weines to draw the stra before the Cat. *c* 1530 Ld. Berners *Arth. Lyt. Bryt.* (1814) 66 Wysdome is greate if the cat neuer touched mylke. *a* 1535 More *Wks.* 241 (R.) It was alway that yᵉ cat winked whan her eye was oute. 1539 Taverner *Erasm. Prov.* 47 The catte wyll fyshe eate, but she wyl not her feete wette. 1562 J. Heywood *Prov. & Epigr.* (1867) 10 When all candels be out, all cats be grey. 1577 Holinshed *Chron.* II. 731 The Englishmen in those daies were cats not to be caught without mittens. 1600 Shaks. *A.Y.L.* III. ii. 109 If the Cat will after kinde, so be sure will Rosalinde. 1651 Culpepper *Astrol. Judgem. Dis.* (1658) 114 The disease will stay in one state as long as a Cat is tyed to a Pudding. 1665 Pepys *Diary* 14 Aug., The king shall not be able to whip a cat but I mean to be at the tayle of it. 1708 Motteux *Rabelais* v. vii, As analogous as Chalk and Cheese, or a Cat and a Cartwheel! 1771 Smollett *Humph. Cl.* II. 8 June, At London, I am pent up in frowzy lodgings, where there is not room enough to swing a cat. 1887 *Pall Mall G.* 17 Oct. 2/2 They play a cat-and-mouse game with him for some time.

IV. *Attrib.* and *Comb.*

16. *attrib.* Of or pertaining to cats; cat-like. (Often hyphened, as in next.)

1500–20 Dunbar *Of Ane Blake-moir* 8 Quhon hir schort catt nois vp skippis. 1720 *Stow's Surv.* (ed. Strype 1754) I. I. xvi. 84/1 One lion, one lioness, one leopard, and two cat Lions in the said Tower. 1774 Goldsm. *Nat. Hist.* (1776) III. 249 Animals of the cat kind. 1839–47 Todd *Cycl. Anat. & Phys.* III. 302/1 In the..cat-tribe, there is a cæcum, though it is simple and short. 1865 Dickens *Mut. Fr.* I. viii, Mouldy little plantation or cat-preserve. 1881 Mivart *Cat* 366 We cannot of course, without becoming cats, perfectly understand the cat-mind.

17. General comb.: **a.** attributive, as ***cat-bolt, -food, -land, -scratch, -show, -speech***; **b.** objective, as ***cat-catcher, -killer***; **c.** parasynthetic, as ***cat-eyed, -faced, -headed*** adjs.; also ***cat-wise*** adv.

1592 G. Harvey *Pierce's Super.* 8 Instead of thunderboltes shooteth nothing but dogboltes or *catboltes. 1799 Southey *Nondescr.* v, Rare music! I would rather hear *cat-courtship Under my bed-room window in the night. 1613 Rowlands *Four Knaves* (1843) 42 Night-Raven, and such *Cat-eyed Fowle. *a* 1700 Dryden *Lucretius* IV. (R.) If cat-ey'd, then a Pallas is their love. 1816 'Quiz' *Grand Master* VIII. 212 Some *cat-fac'd General. 1907 *Yesterday's shopping* (1969) 58 **Cat food*, doz. packets, 0/9. 1966 A. Prior *Operators* vii. 87 The food cupboard..contained at least three dozen tins of cat food. 1905 E. F. Benson *Image in Sand* i, Close to them stood the great *cat-headed statue. 1905 *Daily Chron.* 4 Sept. 3/1 The power was divinised in the cat-headed Pasht. 1880 *Atlantic Monthly* June 737 It is merely a *cat-scratch. 1883 E. M. Bacon *Dict. Boston, Mass.* 304 *Cat-shows, dog-shows. 1789 Wolcott (P. Pindar) *Subj. for Paint.* Wks. 1812 II. 187 As if with knowledge of *Cat-speech endued. *a* 1845 Hood *Irish Schoolm.* xvi. (1871) 191 Climbeth, *catwise, on some London roof.

18. Special comb.: **cat-and-clay** (*Sc.*), straw and clay worked together into pretty large rolls and laid between the wooden posts in constructing mud-walls; **Cat-and-mouse Act**, nickname for the Prisoners (Temporary Discharge for Ill-health) Act of 1913 to enable hunger-strikers to be released temporarily; used chiefly *attrib.* (now without capital initials) of (*esp.* official) action taken (repeatedly or for a prolonged period) against a weaker party; **cat-back** *Naut.* (see *cat-rope*); **cat-beam** (*Naut.*), the beak-head beam, the broadest beam in a ship (see beak-head 3 and cat-head *sb.* 1); **cat-bear**, the red bear-cat or lesser panda; **cat-blash** (*dial.*) = cat-lap; **cat-block** (*Naut.*), a two- or three-fold block forming part of the cat-tackle; **cat-brain** (*dial.*), a soil consisting of rough clay mixed with stones; **cat-brier**, an American name for *Smilax* (*Treas. Bot.*); **cat-burglar**, a burglar who enters by extraordinarily skilful feats of climbing; hence **cat-burgling** *vbl. sb.*; **cat's-carriage** (*Sc.*), the game of king's-cushion; **cat-castle** (see cat *sb.*[1] 6 and quot. 1907); **cat chain** (see quot.); **cat-chop**, a plant, *Mesembryanthemum felinum*; **cat-collops** (*dial.*), cat's-meat; **cat-dirt**, a kind of clay; **cat-door**, a small door, usually swinging, which can be opened by a cat for its own ingress and egress; **cat-face** (*U.S.*), a mark in lumber-wood (see quot.); **cat-fall** (*Naut.*), in the cat-tackle, the rope between the cat-block and the sheaves in the cat-head; **cat-footed** *a.*, (*a*) stealthy in movement; (*b*) (see quot. 1883); hence **cat-footedness**, surefootedness; **cat-, cat's-gold** (Ger. *katzengold*, Sw. *kattguld*), a yellowish variety of mica (cf. cat-silver); †**cat-harrow** (*Sc.*), a nursery game, played by pulling crossing loops of thread, *cat-saw*; **cat-haw** (*dial.*), the fruit of the hawthorn; **cat-heather**, the name given to various kinds of heather in Scotland (Jamieson, 1825); see *Sc. Nat. Dict.* s.v. *Cat.* n.[1] I. 2; **cat-hook** (*Naut.*), the hook on the cat-block by which it is connected with the anchor when the latter is to be catted; **cat-house** (*a*) (see 6 above); (*b*) a house for cats; (*c*) *slang*, a brothel; **cat-ice, cat's ice**, thin ice of a milky white appearance in shallow places, from under which the water has receded; **cat-in-clover**, Bird's-foot Trefoil, *Lotus corniculatus*; **cat-keys, cat's-keys, cats and keys** (*dial.*), the fruit of the ash-tree, culver-keys; **cat-ladder**, a kind of ladder used on the sloping roofs of houses; †**cat-leap** (see quot.); also the distance a cat leaps; **cat-lick**, colloq. expression for a perfunctory manner of washing; also as vb.; **cat-mallison** (see quots.); **cat('s)-nap**, a short nap while sitting; hence as *v. intr.*, to take a cat-nap; **cat-owl**, a North American species of owl; †**cat-pipe**, a cat-call (see cat-call 1); **cat-purchase** (*Naut.*) = *cat-tackle*; **cat-rope** (*Naut.*), †(*a*) = *cat-fall*; (*b*) 'a line for hauling the cat-hook about; also ***cat-back-rope***' (Smyth *Sailor's Word-bk.*); **cat-salt**, 'a beautifully granulated kind of common salt..formed out of the bittern or leach brine' (Chambers *Cycl. Supp.*); **cat-saw** = *cat-harrow*; **cat-scaup, -scalp** (*dial.*), an ironstone nodule (see cat-head *sb.* 2); **cat-sleep** = *cat-nap*; †**cat-sloe**, the Wild Sloe; **cat-squirrel**, (*a*) the common squirrel (*dial.*); (*b*) the grey American squirrel; **cat-steps**, (*a*) 'the projections of the stones in the slanting part of a gable' (Jamieson), crow-steps; (*b*) *U.S. Geol.* (see quot.); **cat-stopper** (*Naut.*), the cat-head stopper (see cat-head *sb.* 1); †**cat-succory**, the Wild Succory; **cat-suit**, an all-in-one garment reaching from neck to feet, generally tight-fitting, and with trouser legs; **cat-tackle** (*Naut.*), the tackle to raise the anchor to the cat-head (see cat-head *sb.* 1); **cat-thyme**, a species of *Teucrium*, which causes sneezing; **cat-trail** (*dial.*), the Great Valerian, or its root, used to attract cats; **cat-tree, -wood**, the Spindle-tree; **cat-whin** (*dial.*), a name of various plants as Dog-rose, Burnet-rose, etc.; **cat('s) whisker**, a fine adjustable copper or gold wire in a crystal wireless receiver or in certain types of electronic circuit (see also sense 13 l); †**cat-wort** = catmint; †**cat-wralling**: see caterwauling. Also cat and dog, cat-call, etc.

1756 Mrs. Calderwood *Jrnl.* (1884) 18 [The cottage] was built of timber stoops, and what we call *cat and clay walls. 1833 *Fraser's Mag.* VIII. 410 The cat-and-clay hovels..have given place to neat..cottages. 1913 *Punch* 23 July 81/1 Plural Residence, which will still be permitted after abolition of Plural Voting, is being encouraged by the *Cat-and-Mouse Act. 1926 G. B. Shaw *Transl. & Tomfooleries* 225 The Cat and Mouse principle..is a part of the law of England. 1937 F. P. Crozier *Men I Killed* viii. 156 The Absolutists [conscientious objectors] went to jail, again and again and again, as men 'deemed to have been enlisted'... During this cat-and-mouse performance every conceivable kind of inducement, temptation, and privation were used by the Government..in order to make the objectors surrender. 1949 Koestler *Promise & Fulf.* ii. 18 The Administration played a curious cat-and-mouse game with the Jewish self-defence organization. 1965 G. McInnes *Road to Gundagai* ii. 28 He was..prepared to enjoy a game of cat-and-mouse with the superior little English boy. 1882 Nares *Seamanship* (ed. 6) 91 *Cat-backs..are led through leading blocks. *c* 1850 *Rudim. Navig.* (Weale) 95 *Cat-Beam, or Beak-Head Beam. 1888 W. T. Blanford *Mammalia* 190 *Aelurus fulgens*. The red *Cat-bear..South-eastern Himalayas.. lives in holes of trees, or perhaps amongst rocks. 1931 H. L. Myers *Prince Jali* vi. 61 His parents had given him a pair of cat-bears, charming creatures that were exceedingly tame. 1877 E. Peacock *N-W. Linc. Gloss.* (E.D.S.) s.v., You call this tea maybe, I call it sore *cat-blash. 1769 Falconer *Dict. Marine* (1789) F iij, The *Cat-block is employed to draw the anchor up to the cat-head. 1840 R. Dana *Bef. Mast* xxiii. 68 The cat-block being as much as a man could lift. 1679 Plot *Staffordsh.* (1686) 345 The *Cat-brain, i.e. a sort of barren clay and stone mixt. 1879 Miss Jackson *Shropsh. Word-bk., Cat-brain*, a rough clayey kind of soil full of stone. 1875 Emerson *Lett. & Soc. Aims* iv. 117 A clump of alders, with *cat-briers. 1907 *Daily Chron.* 18 Apr. 1/7 Owing to his skill in climbing he was known as 'the *cat burglar'. 1927 *Daily Express* 24 Mar. 2/6 A 'cat' burglar broke into the house.. by climbing a stackpipe. 1958 D. Emmet *Function, Purpose & Powers* ix. 253 What about a man seized with an irresistible urge for cat-burgling. 1861 *Chambers's Encycl.* II. 668/1 *Cat*, or **cat-castle*, in the military engineering of the middle ages, was a kind of movable tower to cover the sappers as they advanced to a besieged place. 1907 Collingwood in *Trans. Cumbld. & Westmld. Archæol. Soc.* (1908) VIII. 100 'Catcastle' in local [Kendal] dialect is the second figure in the game of Cat's-cradle. 1883 *Man. Seamanship Boys' Training Ships* 195 Q. What is a *cat chain? A. A chain which is rove through the cat block, and shackled on to the upper end of ground chain to bring the anchor to cat head. 1855 *Whitby Gloss.*, **Catcollop*, cat's meat, more particularly the inmeats of animals. 1747 Hooson *Miner's Dict.* E ij, *Catdirt-Clay [is] a kind of Clay that is short in cutting, and mixed with joynts that are whiter than the Clay itself. 1794 Sullivan *View Nat.* II. 153 Cat-dirt, channel, &c. found in Derbyshire, are all lava. 1959 M. Summerton *Small Wilderness* i. 16 Bella jumped down, and went through her private *cat-door. 1879 *Lumberman's Gaz.* 3 Dec., Logs that have *cat faces or burnt places..the cat face or knots. 1769 Falconer *Dict. Marine* (1789) L iv, A rope called the *cat-fall..communicates with the cat block. 1849 R. Dana *Bef. Mast* xxviii. 97 All hands tallied on to the cat-fall. 1882 Nares *Seamanship* (ed. 6) 175 The cat-fall..is rove through a sheave in the cathead. 1598 E. Gilpin *Skial.* (1878) 52 *Cat-footed for slie pace, and without sound. 1847 Tennyson *Princ.* I. 103, I stole..Cat-footed thro' the town. 1883 G. Stables *Our Friend the Dog* vii. 59 *Cat-footed*—Having the toes well knuckled up, making the foot short and round. 1929 W. J. Locke *Jorico* 94 He had the peculiar, sure cat-footedness of those who follow the sea. 1762 tr. *Busching's Syst. Geog.* I. 42 *Cats-gold, which is semi-transparent. 1776 Seiferth *Gellert's Metal. Chym.* 10 Cat-gold..So the glimmer is called by the Germans, when it has the colour of gold. 1529 Lyndesay *Complaynt* 308 Thay gan to draw at the *cat harrow. 1721 Kelly *Sc. Prov.* 329 (Jam.) They draw the Cat Harrow; that is, they thwart one another. 1864 T. Guthrie *Let.* 9 July in *Autobiogr.* (1877) xii. 645 The hum of bees who are all on the *qui vive*, as the heather (the '*cat-heather' as it is called) is

now coming out. **1886** BRITTEN & HOLLAND *Dict. Eng. Plant-Names* 92 Cat-heather, more than one kind of heath seems to be so called in Scotland..(*Calluna vulgaris*),.. *Erica cinerea*,..or possibly *E. Tetralix*. **1922** D. H. LAWRENCE *England, my England* 33 Bits of cat-heather were coming pink in tufts. **1605** CAMDEN *Rem.* (1657) 206 This *cat-house answerable to the cattus mentioned by Vegetius, was used in the siege of Bedford castle in the time of King Henry the third. **1840** L. RITCHIE *Windsor Cast.* 215 The gattus or cat house, the belfry and sow..were covered machines, used to protect soldiers in their attacks upon the gates or walls. **1895** C. J. CORNISH *Life at Zoo* 236 It is obvious that so active and beautiful an animal could not be seen with advantage..in the cramped little cages of the present Cat House. **1931** 'D. STIFF' *Milk & Honey Route* 202 *Cat house*, a brothel. **1934** THORNTON WILDER *Heaven's My Destination* vi. 113 On Sunday you raped a whole cat-house. **1935** 'G. ORWELL' *Clergyman's Daughter* ii. 113 He's took her abroad an' sold her to one o'dem flash cat-houses in Parrus. **1968** D. FRANCIS *Forfeit* x. 120 He walked straight out of the Cat House. **1884** *Daily News* 10 Nov. 5/7 The worst that would happen to him would be to break through the *cat ice in shallows. **1695** WESTMACOT *Script. Herb.* 189 The Sycomore with us..leaves an imperfect Fruit, called Pods, or *Cat-keys. **1883** *Standard* 23 Feb. 3/6 A *cat ladder, twelve feet in length [was] placed on the roof. **1611** COTGR. s.v. *Chat, Sault du chat*, the *cat-leape; a certaine tricke done by Tumblers, and vaulters upon a table set aslope against a wall. [*c* **1450** *Jacob's Well* 187/25 þe feend seyde: 'come hedyr, freend, þou art catlycked & qwyt of þi synnes in þi schryfte.'] **1859** GEO. ELIOT *A. Bede* xi, Th' men ne'er know whether that floor's cleaned or *cat-licked. **1892** *Leeds Merc.* Suppl. 12 Mar. (E.D.D.), That's nobbut gien thisen a cat-lick asteead ov a reight wesh. **1898** *Eng. Dial. Dict.* s.v. *Cat* sb.[1], Yer may ev catlicked the flooer; yer hevn't weshed it. **1906** W. DE MORGAN *Joseph Vance* vii. 65 Anne..soaped me with a vigour far beyond any experience of washing I had had up to that date. My method had been Cat-licking, she said. **1915** D. H. LAWRENCE *Rainbow* 11. 61 Let's finish wiping your face—it'll pass wi' a cat-lick. *a* **1953** DYLAN THOMAS *Quite early one Morning* (1954) 30 They catlicked their hands and faces, but never forgot to run the water loud and long as though they washed like colliers. **1583** *Will of Isab. Walker, Kendal* (Somerset Ho.) One doughe trough with one thinge to putt chease in, alijs *Cattmaddeson. **1781** J. HUTTON *Tour to Caves* Gloss. (E.D.S.) Catmallisons, the cupboards round the chimneys in the north, where they preserve their dried beef and provisions. **1823** J. F. COOPER *Pioneers* xxxii, I just closed my eyes in order to think the better with myself... It was only some such matter as a *cat's nap. **1856** KANE *Arct. Expl.* II. iv. 54 Catching cat-naps as I could in the day..but carefully waking every hour. **1885** *N.Y. Weekly Sun* 13 May 2/7 Catnaps were caught in the chairs as the players sat. **1938** *Amer. Speech* XIII. 182/2 To cat-nap. **1958** *Times* 19 May 3/7 Mr. Hugh Bentley, who cat-naps every afternoon between 3 and 3.30. **1854** THOREAU *Walden* xv. (1886) 271 An unmistakable *cat-owl..with the most harsh and tremendous voice..responded. **1694** R. L'ESTRANGE *Fables* clxxvi. (1714) 190 Put them [*i.e.* Songsters] out of their Road once, and they are Meer *Cat-Pipes and Dunces. **1627** CAPT. SMITH *Seaman's Gram.* vi. 28 The *Cat rope is to hale vp the Cat. **1630** J. TAYLOR (Water P.) *Navy of Landsh.* Wks. I. 81/1. **1723** BROWN in *Phil. Trans.* XXXII. 354 The Liquor..will crystalize to the Sticks, something like Sugar-candy, but in much larger Shoots; and this they call *Cat-Salt, or Salt-Cats. **1875** URE *Dict. Arts* III. 748 Lymington cat-salt. **1728** WOODWARD *Fossils* (J.) The nodules..found in the rocks near Whitehaven in Cumberland, where they call them *catscaups. **1837** MISS SEDGWICK *Live & let L.* (1876) 63 Roused from her *cat-sleep by the unwonted noise. **1578** LYTE *Dodoens* VI. xlvii. 721 The fruite..growing upon the blacke thorne, is called *Catte Slose, and Snagges. **1587** M. GROVE *Pelops & Hipp.* (1878) 124 Change..For grapes most pure his cat sloes sower frute. **1826** J. GODMAN *Amer. Nat. Hist.* II. 129 The *Cat-Squirrel, *Sciurus Cinereus*. **1834** MCMURTRIE tr. *Cuvier's Anim. Kingd.* 80 The Cat Squirrel (*Sciurus cinereus*, Lin.) of America is cinerous above, white beneath. **1882** *Sc. Gossip* July 161 The following is a list of names now or lately in use in the vicinity of Whitby..'Catswerril' squirrel. **1943** W. J. HAMILTON *Mammals East. U.S.* 225 Gray Squirrel. Cat Squirrel. *Sciurus carolinensis*. **1833** *Fraser's Mag.* VIII. 399 He sought refuge on the top of his master's house, and, sidling up the *cat-steps, disappeared with his prize. **1939** A. K. LOBECK *Geomorphol.* iii. 93 Small, backward-tilted terraces due to slumping, features which are sometimes called *catsteps*. **1715** PETIVER in *Phil. Trans.* XXIX. 231 Blew *Cat-Succory. **1960** *Guardian* 16 Nov. 5/3 Miss Odell wears a '*cat-suit' which is sleeveless, low-cut, tight round the shanks and everywhere else. **1970** *Oxf. Mail* 27 Jan. 1/9 Courreges' best inspiration for ready-to-wear were his flare-legged cat suits in P.V.C. or cotton. **1840** R. DANA *Bef. Mast* xv. 40 The *cat-tackle-fall was strung along. **1915** A. F. COLLINS *Bk. of Wireless* 205 Adjust the wire until the pointed end presses on the crystal and you will have what is called a *cat-whisker detector. **1923** *Daily Mail* 28 June 13 A crystal called 'Radiocite'..used with a 'cats-whisker' contact, and the pressure necessary is extremely light. **1948** *Electronic Engin.* XX. 354 The catswhiskers can be mounted in slots at the top of the copper base pins, using a dummy crystal..to align the tips of the wires. **1949** *Ibid.* XXI. 448 Two 1N34's will be required to provide the two cats-whiskers, leaving a spare crystal. *a* **1450** *Alphita* (Anecd. Oxon.) 27 *Calamentum magis*, *catwort. *Ibid.* 125 *Nepta*, catwort.

19. Comb. with *cat's*: **a.** † **cat's-pellet**, † **cat's-play**, ? tip-cat or some other game with a cat (see 10 above); **cat's-purr**, a thrill felt over the region of the heart in certain heart-diseases; **cat's-tooth** (see quot.). Also CAT'S-CRADLE, -EYE, -HAIR, -MEAT, -PAW, etc.

1609 *Manchester Crt. Leet Rec.* (1886) I. 248 A game or games vsed in the towne of Manchest[r] called giddye guddye or *catts pallett. **1648** *Brit. Bellman* in *Harl. Misc.* VII. 625 (D.) Who beats the boys from cat's-pellet and stool-ball? **1668** R. L'ESTRANGE *Vis. Quev.* (1708) 179 They had been either at *Cats-play, or Cuffs. **1776** WOULFE in *Phil. Trans.* LXVI. 620 *Cat's tooth, white lead ore, from Ireland.

b. *esp.* in plant-names: **cat's-claw**, (*a*) Common Kidney-Vetch, *Anthyllis vulneraria*; (*b*) = *cat-in-clover* (18); **cat's-ear**, (*a*) the book-name of the genus *Hypochæris*; (*b*) Mountain Everlasting, *Antennaria dioica*; † **cat's-grass**; **cat's-milk**, a species of spurge, Sun-spurge, *Euphorbia helioscopia*: † **cat's-spear**, Reed-mace, *Typha latifolia*. Also CAT'S-EYE, -FOOT, -TAIL, etc.

1756 P. BROWNE *Jamaica* 294 *Cat's claws. This little plant is frequent about Old Harbour. **1848** C. A. JOHNS *Week Lizard* 310 *Hippochæris maculata*, Spotted *Cat's-ear. *c* **1450** *Alphita* (Anecd. Oxon.) 38 *Centinodium*, swyne-grece *uel* *cattesgres. **1861** MISS PRATT *Flower. Pl.* V. 5 Sun Spurge..Country people call it..*Cat's milk..it is a troublesome weed.

† **cat**, *sb.*[2] *Obs.* exc. in *Comb.* Also **catt.** [Originally, the same word as prec.; Du Cange has *catta* 'navis species', also *gatus* of date *c* 1175; OF. *chaz, chat, catz* (see Jal. and Godef.); but the relation between these and the Eng. word, and the reason of the name, do not appear.]

A name given to a vessel formerly used in the coal and timber trade on the north-east coast of England; see Falconer's description (quot. 1769).

(The name is unknown to the oldest of the Elder Brethren of Trinity House, Newcastle (aged 82), and to the oldest North Sea pilots there. One of the latter, however, remembers to have heard as a boy the joke 'Do you know when the mouse caught the cat?' (the *Mouse* being a sand-bank in the Thames); and several remember the expression *cat-built* in the early part of the century. The last 'cat-built' ship is said to have been lost more than 30 years ago. *N.E.D.*)

1699 in *Dict. Nat. Biogr.* VIII. 305/1, I was made a lieutenant by the lords of the admiralty for boarding a cat that was laden with masts. **1747** (Dec. 4) J. GAMBIER to *Secretary Adm'lty* (MS.) Drove a new cat of near 500 tons on the Barrough Sand. **1759** ADM. SAUNDERS in *Naval Chron.* XIII. 439 Two Cats, armed and loaded with provisions. **1769** FALCONER *Dict. Marine* (1789) *Cat*, a ship employed in the Coal trade, formed from the Norwegian model. It is distinguished by a narrow stern, projecting quarters, a deep waist, and by having no..figure[head]. These vessels are generally built remarkably strong, and carry from four to six hundred tons. *Chatte*, a small two-masted vessel, formed like a cat or Norwegian pink. **1794** *Rigging & Seamanship* I. 236 *Cat*, a vessel, used by the Northern Nations of Europe, with three masts and a bow-sprit, rigged similar to an English ship; having, however, pole-masts and no top-gallant sails. *c* **1825** J. DUGDALE *New Brit. Trav.* iv. 303 Certain vessels, called Ipswich Cats of large tonnage..formerly employed in the coal-trade here.

Hence (perh.) **cat-boat**, a kind of sailing-boat having the mast placed very forward and rigged with one sail; **cat-rig**, a rig of one fore-and-aft mainsail, used for pleasure-boats in smooth water; so ***cat-rigged*** adj.; ***cat-built*** (see above).

1867 F. LUDLOW *Little Bro.* 96 The cat-rig boat..carries a main-sail only and is a favourite on the Shrewsbury river. **1883** *Harper's Mag.* Aug. 444/2 Victories of which cat-boats might be ashamed. **1885** *Sat. Rev.* 3 Jan. 11/1 Open boats of one jib and mainsail and cat varieties. **1887** *Daily Tel.* 10 Sept. 2/5 A couple of trim-looking catboats..were dropped astern at a great rate..The catboatman is ambitious.

cat, *sb.*[3], var. KAT.

1877 *Encycl. Brit.* VI. 110/2 In Arabia the beverage [*sc.* coffee]..only supplanted a preparation from the leaves of the cat, *Celastrus edulis*. **1904** *U.S. Consular Rep.* No. 285. 549 The cat is a plant containing a medicinal principle which acts as a tonic upon the muscles of the heart. **1934** DYLAN THOMAS *Let.* 15 Apr. (1966) 103 If I..could see them as a Yucatan people, call them to a cat-drinking ceremony.

cat, *sb.*[4] Colloq. abbrev. of CATALYTIC *a.*, in ***cat cracker, cracking***, etc. (cf. CATALYTIC *a.*).

1943 *Fortune* Sept. 50/1 'Cat cracker' is the oil industry's nickname for the new catalytic cracking processes now producing high-octane gas. **1952** *Economist* 6 Sept. 581/1 (*heading*) Premium Petrol and Cat Crackers. **1957** *New Scientist* 18 July 36/2 'Cat-cracking'..show[s] the power of catalysis in large-scale chemical industry.

CAT (kæt), *sb.*[5] *Med.* Abbrev. of *comput(eriz)ed axial* (or *computer-assisted*) *tomography*, a form of tomography in which a computer controls the motion of the X-ray source and detectors, processes the data, and produces the image. Cf. *CT* s.v. C 3a. Used *attrib.* in ***CAT scanning***, etc.

1975 *Wall Street Jrnl.* 10 Dec. 1 The machine, known as a CAT scanner, produces in minutes an X-ray picture revealing the deadly tumor that had escaped her physicians' notice. **1976** A. RICHARDSON in R. W. P. Russell *Cerebral Arterial Dis.* xi. 225/1 In the routine elective radiology pride of place must now be taken by the use of computerised transverse axial tomography (CAT scan) by the apparatus devised by EMI. **1976** *Americana Ann.* 1977 322/2 CAT scanning came of age in 1976. **1979** L. SHAINBERG *Brain Surgeon* (1980) i. 20 He had an X-ray of his cerebral tissue called a CAT-scan. **1983** *Listener* 28 Apr. 2/3 Voluntary groups have raised the money..to buy CAT scanners for their local hospitals.

cat (kæt), *v.* [f. CAT *sb.*[1]]

1. *Naut.* **a.** *trans.* To raise (the anchor) from the surface of the water to the cat-head. Also *absol.*

1769 FALCONER *Dict. Marine* (1789) To cat the Anchor, is to hook a tackle called the cat to it's ring, and thereby pull it up close to the cat-head. **1833** M. SCOTT *Tom Cringle* ii. (1859) 80 Lend a hand to cat the anchor. **1882** NARES *Seamanship* (ed. 6) 203 The cable..will..clear itself in catting. **1890** W. CLARK RUSSELL *Ocean Trag.* iii, They had catted, and were fishing the anchor forwards.

b. ***to cat and fish***: to raise the anchor to the cat-head and secure it to the ship's side.

1808 *Regul. Service at Sea* v. iv. §25 Never..to give her head-way untill the anchors are catted and fished. **1881** W. C. RUSSELL *Sailor's Sweeth.* I. iii. 59 Everything was now snug forward, the anchor catted and fished, and the decks clear.

2. To 'draw through a water with a cat': see CAT 14.

3. To flog with the cat-o'-nine-tails.

1865 *Spectator* 18 Nov. 1271/1 Thirty of them were lashed to a gun, and catted with fifty lashes each.

4. *dial.* and *colloq.* To vomit. See *to shoot the cat* (CAT *sb.*[1] 13 d).

5. *intr.* To be deposited in the manner of salt, etc., round objects, in crevices, or the like. (Cf. CAT *sb.*[1] 11 b.)

a **1909** *Buck's Handbk. Med. Sci.* VII. 901 (Cent. Dict. Suppl.), The material which cats here is in a state not capable of ready absorption, and must act locally.

Hence **'catted** *ppl. a.*; **'catting** *vbl. sb.*

cata-, cat-, cath-. Gr. κατα-, κατ-, καθ-, a preposition used in comp. with the senses **a.** down (locally); **b.** down (of diminution, reduction, consumption, waste), away, entirely, 'up'; **c.** implying disparagement or abuse (= *mis-*); **d.** inferior, subsidiary; **e.** down upon, against (as blows fall); **f.** against and reflected back, *hence*, answering to, according to, alongside of, each to each; **g.** intensive, downright, thoroughly, completely; **h.** *hence*, like Eng. *be-*, making a verb transitive. All these senses occur in Eng. words into which *cata-* enters; most of these are adapted or formed from compounds already made in Greek, others follow or extend Greek analogies. See also KATA-.

cata'ballitive, *a. nonce-wd.* [f. Gr. καταβάλλειν to cast down.] Tending to throw down.

1815 T. PEACOCK *Headlong Hall* 79 A machine containing a peculiar cataballitive quality.

† **Cata'baptist.** *Obs.* [ad. Gr. καταβαπτιστής 'coined by Gregory Nazianzen as opp. to βαπτιστής' (L. and S.); f. κατά down + βαπτιστής one who dips, baptizer.]

'One that abuseth or depraveth, or is an adversary to the sacrament of Baptism' (Blount *Glossogr.* 1656). A nickname of 16–17th c. for any one who rejected the orthodox doctrine of baptism.

1561 T. NORTON *Calvin's Inst.* IV. xv. (1634) 648 Catabaptists, which denie that we be rightly baptised, because we were baptised by wicked men and idolaters in the Popish Kingdome. **1640** BP. HALL *Episc.* II. vii. 128 The receiving of Infants to holy Baptisme is a matter of so high consequence, that we justly Brand our Catabaptists with heresie, for denying it. **1642** FEATLY *Dippers Dipt* 23 (R.) They [Anabaptists] are called also Catabaptists, from the preposition κατὰ and βαπτίζω, signifying an abuser or prophaner of baptism. **1725** tr. *Dupin's Eccl. Hist.* I. VI. ii. 227 The Anabaptists, whom he calls Catabaptists. **1864** *Mem. W. Bull* ii. (1865) 27 He was a Catabaptist, holding that the ordinance of baptism was to be administered only to Jews and Pagans.

So † **Cata'baptism**; † **Catabap'tistical** *a.*; † **Cata'baptistry** [cf. ANABAPTISTRY], the doctrine of Catabaptists.

1574 WHITGIFT *Def. Answ.* III. Wks. 1851 I. 368 Neither is this any title of 'catabaptistry'. **1655** J. GOODWIN (*title*), Cata-Baptism; or new Baptism waxing old, and ready to vanish away. **1661** GAUDEN *Consid.* 12 The Liturgy.. vindicates the..Catholick use of Infant Baptiam against the Anabaptistical novelty and Catabaptistical perverseness.

‖ **catabasion** (-'bæzɪən). [Gr. καταβάσιον.] A place for relics under the altar of a Greek church.

1753 in CHAMBERS *Cycl. Supp.* (Also in mod. Dicts.)

catabatic (-'bætɪk), *a. Med.* [ad. Gr. καταβατικός affording an easy descent, f. καταβαίνειν to go down.] 'Descending or declining by degrees. Applied to a fever which gradually abates in severity till its termination' (*Syd. Soc. Lex.* 1881).

‖ **catabi'bazon.** *Astrol. Obs.* [Gr. καταβιβαζόν bringing down, lowering.] (See quot.)

1696 in PHILLIPS. **1721–1800** in BAILEY. **1751** CHAMBERS *Cycl.*, *Catabibazon*, in Astronomy, the moon's descending node; called also Dragon's Tail.

catabolic (kætə'bɒlɪk), *a. Biol.* Also 9 **katabolic.** [f. as next + -IC.]Of, pertaining to, or exhibiting catabolism.

1876 FOSTER *Phys.* §30 (1888) 43 To distinguish the products..into waste products proper, the direct results of katabolic changes, and into bye products..which cannot.. be considered as necessarily either anabolic or katabolic. **1894** H. DRUMMOND *Ascent Man* 290 The act of fertilization is the anabolic restoration, renewal, and rejuvenescence of a

katabolic cell. **1957** *Encycl. Brit.* XV. 303/1 The manifold chemical transformations involved in the building up (anabolism) of more complex materials and the breaking down (catabolism) of these and other substances... exchange and storage of energy occur—storage of energy in anabolic and release of energy in catabolic change.

catabolism (kəˈtæbəlɪz(ə)m). *Biol.* Also 9 katabolism. [f. Gr. καταβολ-ή a throwing down (f. καταβάλλειν to throw down) + -ISM.] That phase of the metabolism of living bodies which consists in the breaking down of complex organic compounds into simpler ones; destructive metabolism.

1876 FOSTER *Phys.* §530 (1888) 807 Wherever destructive metabolism, katabolism, is going on, heat is being set free. **1889** GEDDES & THOMSON *Evol. Sex* ii. 27 The male reproduction is associated with preponderating katabolism. **1889** *Nature* 26 Sept. 525/1 The words in question, 'anabolism', which being interpreted means winding up, and 'catabolism', running down, are the creation of Dr. Gaskell. Prof. Hering's equivalents for these are 'assimilation', which, of course, means storage of oxygen and oxidizable material, and 'disassimilation', discharge of these in the altered form of carbon dioxide and water. **1894** KIDD *Soc. Evolut.* ix. 287 The tendency—by itself disintegrating and destructive—known as katabolism. **1957** [see CATABOLIC].

catabothron: see KATAVOTHRON.

catacathartic: see CATOCATHARTIC.

†**Cataˈcatholic,** *a. Obs. nonce-wd.* [f. CATA- in sense of perversion.] Catholic by a perversion of the name.

1608 BP. KING *Serm.* 25 Let..Catholique, Catacatholique cruelty be a prouerbe.

catacaustic (kætəˈkɔːstɪk), *a.* and *sb.* [mod. f. Gr. κατα- back, again (as in *catoptrics*) + καυστικ-ός CAUSTIC. So F. *catacaustique.*] *catacaustic* (*curve*); a CAUSTIC curve formed by reflexion.

1708 KERSEY, *Catacaustick Curve.* **1721** BAILEY, *Catacausticks*, causticks by Reflection. **1751** CHAMBERS *Cycl.* s.v. *Caustic*, Every curve has its twofold caustic: accordingly, caustics are divided into catacaustics and diacaustics. **1807** in G. GREGORY *Dict. Arts.*

catachese, -ise, var. of CATECHESE, -IZE.

‖**catachresis** (kætəˈkriːsɪs). Also 7 kata-, cate-. [a. L. *catachrēsis*, a. Gr. κατάχρησις misuse (of a word), f. καταχρῆσθαι to misuse, f. κατά with sense of perversion + χρῆσθαι to use.]

Improper use of words; application of a term to a thing which it does not properly denote; abuse or perversion of a trope or metaphor.

1589 PUTTENHAM *Eng. Poesie* (Arb.) 190 *marg.*, Catachresis or the Figure of abuse. **1605** J. DOVE *Confut. Atheism* 81 The three famous Lakes..which are commonly by the figure catachresis called seas. **1662** FULLER *Worthies* III. 185 The general Katachresis of Good for Great (a good blow, good piece, etc.). **1810** COLERIDGE *Friend* (ed. 3) III. 221 The proverb is current by a misuse, or a catachresis at least, of both the words, fortune and fools.

catachrestic (kætəˈkrɛstɪk, -ˈiːstɪk), *a.* [ad. Gr. καταχρηστικός misused, misapplied: see prec.] Of the nature of catachresis; wrongly used, misapplied, wrested from its proper meaning.

1656 BLOUNT *Glossogr.*, *Catachrestical*, *Catachrestique*, abusive, as when one word is improperly put for another. **1725** J. REYNOLDS *View of Death* x, Go Doating, fond Philosophy, With all thy Catachrestic Names. **1818** HALLAM *Mid. Ages* (1872) III. 238 The phrase is, so to say, catachrestic, not used in a proper sense.

cataˈchrestical, *a.* [f. as prec. + -AL[1].] Having to do with catachresis; also = prec.

1609 BP. BARLOW *Answ. Nameless Cath.* 156 This.. Misbegotten Catachresticall companion. **1651** BAXTER *Inf. Bapt.* 88 An abusive Catechresticall sence. **1695** HUMFREY *Mediocria* 35 Justification *from* a law, and not *by* it, is a Catechrestical speech. **1884** C. A. BRIGGS *Bibl. Study* 355 Hyperboles, analogies, and loose catachrestical expressions.

cataˈchrestically, *adv.* [f. prec. + -LY[2].] In a catachrestic manner; by improper use of language or terms.

c **1600** *Timon* IV. iii. (1842) 67. **1603** SIR C. HEYDON *Jud. Astrol.* xviii. 375 He would catachrestically, or improperly, apply them to the partes of the Zodiacke. **1702** C. MATHER *Magn. Chr.* IV. ii. (1852) 49 The churches (as they were catechrestically called). **1864** J. H. NEWMAN *Apol.* 274 And (to speak catachrestically) they are most likely to die in the Church, who are..most prepared to leave it.

catachthonian (kætəkˈθəʊnɪən), *a.* [f. Gr. καταχθόνιος subterranean, f. κατά down, under + χθόνιος of the ground, f. χθών ground + -IAN.] Subterranean.

1888 RHYS *Hibbert Lect.* 131 Pluto..was always..a chthonian or catachthonian Zeus.

So **catachˈthonic** *a.*

1884 *Athenæum* 8 Mar. 314/3 In the Takashima coal-mine ..an underground, or, as he prefers to call it, a catachthonic observatory.

cataclasm (ˈkætəklæz(ə)m). [ad. Gr. κατάκλασμα breakage, f. κατα-κλᾶν to break down, break off.] A break or disruption.

1829 SOUTHEY *Sir T. More* II. 201 The cataclasms of the moral and social world. **1834** —— *Doctor* cxxiii. (1862) 304 The history of the human race is but a parenthesis between two cataclasms of the globe which it inhabits. **1870** BOWEN *Logic* ix. 301 To suppose that there was any Cataclasm, any violent disruption of what is the usual course of nature.

Hence **cataˈclasmic** *a.*

1888 H. S. HOLLAND *Christ or Eccles.* 37 Something abrupt, violent, cataclasmic.

cataclastic (kætəˈklæstɪk), *a. Geol.* [ad. Norw. *kataklas(-struktur)* (T. Kjerulf 1885, in *Nyt Mag. Naturvidensk.* XXIX. 268), f. Gr. κατά down + κλαστός broken (κλᾶν to break).] Designating a structural character due to intense crushing.

1887 J. J. H. TEALL in *Geol. Mag.* IV. 493 The structures are of the kind for which Prof. Kjerulf has proposed the term cataclastic. I venture to suggest..that we should distinguish between the three types of clastic rocks at present recognized by using the terms epiclastic, cataclastic and pyroclastic... *Cataclastic*—Rocks largely composed of fragments produced during the deformation of older rocks by the earth stresses. **1896** J. W. JUDD *Student's Lyell* 560 Many metamorphic rocks exhibit a similar 'cataclastic' structure. **1903** GEIKIE *Text-bk. Geol.* (ed. 4) 421 When the temperature is 300° C. or 400° C. no cataclastic structure is observable. **1958** *Van Nostrand's Sci. Encycl.* (ed. 3) 287/1 *Cataclastic*..has the same meaning as crush breccias. This term is also applied to the deformation and granulation of minerals such as may take place during dynamic metamorphism.

cataclinal (kætəˈklaɪnəl), *a. Geol.* Now *rare.* [f. Gr. κατακλινής sloping, f. κατά down + κλίνειν to bend + -AL. Cf. MONOCLINAL *a.* and *sb.*] (See quot. 1875.) Cf. ANACLINAL *a.*

1875 J. W. POWELL *Expl. Colorado River* II. xi. 160, I have ..classified these valleys..in the following manner.. *cataclinal*, valleys that run in the direction of the dip. **1960** B. W. SPARKS *Geomorphol.* vi. 104 Terms originally proposed by Powell, such as cataclinal..have found no wide usage, as they are unnecessarily obscure.

cataclysm (ˈkætəklɪz(ə)m). Also 7 -clisme. [a. F. *cataclysme* (16th c. in Littré), ad. Gr. κατακλυσμός deluge (also *fig.*), f. κατα-κλύζειν to deluge, f. κατά down + κλύζ-ειν to wash, dash as a wave.]

A great and general flood of water, a deluge; *esp.* the Noachian deluge, the Flood.

In *Geology* resorted to by some as a hypothesis to account for various phenomena; hence used vaguely for a sudden convulsion or alteration of physical conditions.

1637 HEYWOOD *Roy. Ship* 3 More soules..then perisht in the first Vniversall Cataclisme. **1660** R. COKE *Power & Subj.* 91 Mankind sinned Malitiously, before God brought the general cataclysme upon them. **1833** LYELL *Princ. Geol.* III. 101 For the proofs of these general cataclysms we have searched in vain. **1878** H. M. STANLEY *Dark Cont.* II. ii. 52 The accumulated waters..will sweep through the ancient gap with the force of a cataclysm. **1879** tr. *Haeckel's Evol. Man* I. iv. 77 The hypothesis usually called the Theory of Cataclysms or Catastrophes.

2. *fig.*; esp. a political or social upheaval which sweeps away the old order of things.

1633 *True Trojans* II. i in Hazl. *Dodsley* XII. 468 Ready to pour down cataclysms of blood. **1633** T. ADAMS *Exp. 2 Peter* ii. 6 Heaven rained on them great cataclysms of flames. **1861** *Sat. Rev.* 20 July 67 That the Indian army surgeons will be swept away in the general cataclysm. **1882** J. H. BLUNT *Ref. Ch. Eng.* II. 108 In the general upheaval of doctrine..during the Reformation cataclysm.

cataclysmal (kætəˈklɪzməl), *a.* [f. prec. + -AL[1]: cf. *abysmal.*] = CATACLYSMIC.

1857 PAGE *Adv. Text-bk. Geol.* xviii. (1876) 337 It is never cataclysmal save over the most partial and isolated tracts. **1862** D. WILSON *Preh. Man* (1864) I. iii. 50, I could detect nothing..indicating cataclysmal action.

fig. **1882** *Q. Rev.* July 275 We now know what it is the Radical party are waiting for..It is a cataclysmal catastrophe. **1885** *Spectator* 19 Dec. 1693 [He] is too old to stand the shock of such a cataclysmal enlightenment.

cataclysmatist (kætəˈklɪzmətɪst). *rare*$^{-1}$. [f. Gr. κατάκλυσμα, -ματος (taken as = κατακλυσμός CATACLYSM) + -IST.] = CATACLYSMIST.

1855 MAURY *Phys. Geog. Sea* xv. §645 It is nominated, say the cataclysmatists, that though the two hemispheres do receive annually the same amount of solar heat, etc.

So **catacly'smatic** *a.* = CATACLYSMAL.

1883 MERIVALE *White Pilgr.*, *Häckel*, Fast dying out are man's later appearances, Cataclysmatic geologies gone.

cataclysmic (kætəˈklɪzmɪk), *a.* [f. CATACLYSM + -IC. Cf. F. *cataclysmique.*] Of, pertaining to, or of the nature of, a cataclysm.

1851 KINGSLEY *Yeast* Epil., What if the method whereon things have proceeded since the Creation were..a cataclysmic method? **1879** LE CONTE *Elem. Geol.* 551 The old geologists regarded these changes..as sudden and cataclysmic.

cataclysmically (kætəˈklɪzmɪkəlɪ), *adv.* [f. CATACLYSMIC: see -ICALLY.] By a cataclysm.

1889 I. TAYLOR *Aryans* iii. 132 The civilization..was not introduced cataclysmically, by the immigration of a new race.

cataclysmist (kætəˈklɪzmɪst). [f. CATACLYSM + -IST.] One who adopts the hypothesis of cataclysms in Geology; a 'catastrophist'.

1887 *Athenæum* 24 Sept. 410/3 In 1865 the battle of the 'Uniformitarians' and 'Cataclysmists', 'Sub-aërialists' and 'Marinists', was still raging.

cataˈclystic, *a.* *rare*$^{-1}$. [f. Gr. type *κατακλυστικ-ός, f. κατακλύζειν (see above).] Cataclysmic.

1864 *Reader* No. 88. 298/2 The cataclystic geology.

catacomb (ˈkætəkəʊm, -kuːm). [a. F. *catacombe*, ad. It. *catacomba* (= Pr. *cathacumba*, Sp. *catacumba*):—late L. *Catacumbas*, a name of which even the original application is uncertain: see below.]

1. A subterranean place for the burial of the dead, consisting of galleries or passages with recesses excavated in their sides for tombs.

a. Representing the Latin *catacumbas* (*catecumpas*), or (?) *ad catacumbas*, used as early as the 5th c. in connexion with the subterranean cemetery under the Basilica of St. Sebastian, on the Appian Way, near Rome, in or near which the bodies of the apostles Peter and Paul were said to have been deposited: this is the only sense in which the word occurs in English before the 17th c.

971 *Blickl. Hom.* 193 Eal folc Romwara befeng þa lichoman on þære stowe Catacumbe þy weʒe þe hate Appia. **1483** CAXTON *Gold. Leg.* 119/1 Whan thou hast wasshed it [my body] thou shalt burye it at Cathacombes by the appostlis. *Ibid.* 205/2 The grekes..threwe the bodyes [of the two apostles] in a pitte at catacumbas. **1636** ABP. WILLIAMS *Holy Table* (1637) 220 The famous place called Catacombe (a word of mongrell composition, half Greek, half Latin, and signifying as much as near the Tombs), a kind of vaulted Church under the earth. **1756–7** tr. *Keysler's Trav.* (1760) II. 207 From this church a pair of stairs leads down into the Roman catacombs. **1854** CDL. WISEMAN *Fabiola* II. ii, The cemetery of St. Sebastian [among] other names had that of *Ad Catacumbas*: the meaning of this word is completely unknown. **1870** W. B. MARRIOTT *Test. Catacombs* 1 Catacombs—this name properly applies only to one particular cemetery beneath the church of St. Sebastian.

b. In later times applied (in the plural) to all the subterranean cemeteries lying around Rome (which, after having been long covered up and forgotten, were fortuitously discovered in 1578). In the singular applied to a single crypt or gallery.

1662 J. BARGRAVE *Pope Alex. VII* (1867) 121 Ten miles, almost, round about Rome, under the vineyards and cornfields, are hollow caves, streets, rooms, chappells, finely painted, etc., which is called Rome underground, or the Catacombs. **1683–4** ROBINSON in *Phil. Trans.* XXIX. 479 Those Quarries became Catacombes. **1709** STEELE *Tatler* No. 129 ⁋7 There has lately been found an Humane Tooth in a Catecomb [at Rome]. **1782** PRIESTLEY *Corrupt. Chr.* I. IV. 395 It was..after the discovery of the Catacombs. **1841** W. SPALDING *Italy & It. Isl.* II. 35 Sextus, bishop of Rome, had been slain in the catacombs. **1870** W. B. MARRIOTT (*title*), Testimony of the Catacombs, and of other Monuments of Christian Art. **1876** E. VENABLES in *Dict. Chr. Antiq.* 313/2 The catacombs became places of refuge in times of persecution (..though not to the extent popularly credited). *Ibid.* 314/1 At the entrance of the Jewish Catacomb on the Via Appia.

c. Extended to similar works elsewhere, as at Naples, at Syracuse, in Egypt, etc.

1705 BERKELEY *Cave of Dunmore* Wks. 1871 IV. 508 Those artificial caves of Rome and Naples called catacombs. **1717** LADY M. W. MONTAGUE *Lett.* II. xlvii. 39 During his wonderful stay in the Egyptian catacombs. **1732** LEDIARD *Sethos* II. IX. 327 Bury the king's corpse in the catacombs of Utica. **1796** MORSE *Amer. Geog.* II. 271 Under the mountains adjoining the Kiow are several catacombs. **1858** R. VAUGHAN *Ess. & Rem.* I. 5 The Necropolis, with its Catacombs. **1862** STANLEY *Jew. Ch.* (1877) I. xv. 290.

2. In a wider sense, applied to any subterranean receptacle of dead bodies, as the catacombs of Paris, which are worked-out stone-quarries (see quot.); also *fig.* place of entombment of former races of animals, etc.

1836 *Penny Cycl.* VI. 359/2 The catacombs of Paris could not be called catacombs with any propriety until very recent times, when, by a decree of the French government, all the churchyards were emptied of their contents, and the skulls and bones sent to the spacious subterranean quarries, where they are now arranged in a manner that is grotesquely horrible. **1845** DARWIN *Voy. Nat.* iv. (1879) 80 This point being a perfect catacomb for monsters of extinct races.

3. *transf.* A place arranged with crypts and recesses, like the catacombs.

1884 *Harper's Mag.* Nov. 828/1 These are, indeed, catacombs of books, with lettered avenues.

b. *spec.* A compartment in a cellar with recesses for storing wine.

1795 *Edin. Advert.* 2 Jan. 2/1 One half of the sunk flat or cellars, neatly laid out and furnished with catacombs. **1816** SCOTT *Old Mort.* ix, He ran down to the cellar at the risk of breaking his neck, to ransack some private catacomb.

[NOTE.—The name regularly applied to the Roman catacombs during the first four centuries, when they were in use, as well as during the succeeding four or five centuries, while they were still objects of attention and care, was *cœmētērium. Catacumbas, catecumbas*, appears in the 4th (?), 5th, and following centuries only in connexion with the name of the cemetery of St. Sebastian on the Appian Way, which is distinguished as *Cœmeterium Catacumbas*, or

shortly *Catacumbas*. In other cases *Catacumbas* appears to be used as name of the locality, or perhaps of the part of the Appian Way, in which this cemetery lay. The earliest instances are:

? **a 400** *Inscr.* in *Orelli* 4575 Comparaui..uiuus in catacum[b]as a[d] lumenarem a [f]lossore.. **411** [or ? **354**] *Martyrology* (Bucher *ad Canon. Pasch.* 237) *Depositio martyrum*..Decimo tertio Kalendas Februarij, Fabiani in Callisti et Sebastiani in Catacumbas... Tertio Kalendas Iulij, Petri in Catacumbas et Pauli Ostiense. **a 600** (*List of Cemeteries*) Cimeterium catecumbas ad St. Sebastianum Via Appia. **a 600** GREG. MAGN. *Epist.* iv. Ind. xii. Ep. 30 In loco qui dicitur catacumbas collocata sunt. **a 700** *Imperia Cesarum* (Eccard *Corp. Hist. Med. Æv.* I. 31) Maxentius [A.D. 311] Termas in Palatio fecit et Circum in Catecumpas. **c 705** BÆDA *De Sex Æt. Mund.* ad ann. 4327 Damasus..fecit basilicam..aliam in catacumbas ubi jacuerunt corpora sancta apostolorum Petri et Pauli. **a 900** ANASTASIUS *Hadrian* I. §343 In loco qui appellatur catacumbas ubi corpus beati Sebastiani martyris cum aliis quiescit. **a 1300** *De Mirabil. Romæ*, Cœmeteria Calisti juxta Catacumbas.

The evidence does not settle the disputed question whether the name originally belonged to the cemetery, or (as the majority of investigators now appear to think) to the locality. Some of the other cemeteries were named from their locality, e.g. *Ostiense, Ad Septem Columbas, Ad Duas Lauros* (names of taverns), but most from a personal name as *Calisti, Domitillæ, Cyriacæ*. The word *catacumbas* was in later times treated as an acc. pl., with nom. sing. *catacumba*; but in earlier use it appears to be invariable. To account for this, some have surmised that the full name was *Ad Catacumbas*, others that it was itself a Greek phrase κατὰ κύμβας. The recorded meanings of Gr. κύμβη are 'the hollow of a vessel, a drinking vessel, cup, or bowl (whence a possibility that κατὰ κύμβας was the name of a tavern); a boat, L. *cymba*; a knapsack, wallet'. But the question how a Greek phrase was likely to become the name of something near Rome, when it is not known what that thing was, is manifestly futile; still more profitless are conjectures that the word might contain the Greek preposition combined with a Latin, Sabine, or Celtic word or root, which may be seen in works or articles treating of the Catacombs. There appear to be no examples of the application of the word to the other Roman subterranean cemeteries in ancient times, though *catacumba* is apparently used by Joannes Diaconus (9th c.) of those of Naples: see Du Cange. But the actual extension of the name belongs to modern times, since the discovery of 'Subterranean Rome'.]

catacombish (ˈkætəkəʊmɪʃ), *a.* *nonce-wd.* Savouring of the catacombs.

1826 *Blackw. Mag.* XIX. 242 The smell..is dull, dead, almost catacombish.

catacornered: see CATER, -CORNERED *adv.* and *a.*

catacorolla (ˌkætəkəʊˈrɒlə). *Bot.* [f. CATA- + COROLLA.] 'An additional corolla, either inside or outside the natural one' (*Syd. Soc. Lex.*).

catacoustics (kætəˈkaʊstɪks). [mod. f. CATA- in sense 'against and back from' + ACOUSTICS. In F. *catacoustique*. Cf. CATOPTRICS.]

1. A name for the science of reflected sounds.

1683 *Phil. Trans.* XIV. 473 Hearing may be divided into Direct, Refracted, and Reflex'd, which are yet nameless, unless we call them Acousticks, Diacousticks, and Catacousticks. **1721** in BAILEY. **1751** in CHAMBERS *Cycl.* In all mod. Dicts.

2. (See quot.)

1803 REES *Cycl.*, *Catacoustics* are *écoutes* or small galleries from distance to distance in front of the glacis of a fortified place.

catacumbal (kætəˈkʌmbəl), *a.* *rare.* [f. late L. *catacumba* (see CATACOMB) + -AL¹.] Of or resembling a catacomb.

1865 LITTLEDALE *North Side Altar* 8 Two distinct types of churches..(*a*) the Catacumbal form, (*b*) the Basilican.

catadioptric (ˌkætədaɪˈɒptrɪk), *a.* [f. CATA- in CATOPTRIC + DIOPTRIC. Cf. F. *catadioptrique*.] Pertaining to or involving both the reflexion and the refraction of light.

1723 HADLEY in *Phil. Trans.* (*title*), An Account of the Catadioptric or Reflecting Telescope, made by him. **1759** *Gentl. Mag.* 72 Mr. Dollond's new catadioptric Micrometer. **1866** *Reader* 3 Nov. 913 A catadioptric apparatus, in which lenses are combined with totally reflecting prisms.

So **catadiˈoptrics**, the science of catadioptric phenomena.

1755 *Gentl. Mag.* XXV. 30 A..work on Catadioptrics, which he began about the year 1723.

catadiˈoptrical, *a.* = prec.

1672 *Phil. Trans.* VII. 4004 An Accompt of a New Catadioptrical Telescope invented by Mr. Newton. **1696** *Ibid.* XIX. 215 Catoptrical or Dioptrical or Cata-dioptrical Machines. **1831** BREWSTER *Nat. Magic* iv. 86 The apparatus ..may be called the catadioptrical phantasmagoria, as it operates both by reflexion and refraction.

catadrome (ˈkætədrəʊm). [ad. Gr. καταδρομος (L. *catadromus*) a course for exercise, lists, a rope for rope-dancers, f. δρόμος race, course.]

†**1.** A course or lists for tilting. *Obs.*⁻⁰

1623 COCKERAM, *Catadrome*, a tilt-yard. **1656** BLOUNT *Glossogr.*, *Catadrome*, a place where they run with horses, for prize; a Tilt-yard.

2. (See quot.)

1656 BLOUNT *Glossogr.*, *Catadrome*, an engine which builders use like a Crane, in lifting up or putting down any great weight. **1874** KNIGHT *Dict. Mech.*, *Catadrome.*

catadromous (kəˈtædrəməs), *a.* [f. Gr. κατάδρομος (f. κατά down + -δρομος running) + -OUS. Cf. ANADROMOUS.]

1. *Zool.* Of fishes: Descending periodically from the upper to the lower reaches of the river, or to the sea, in order to spawn; as the Eel.

1883 *Fisheries Exhib. Catal.* (ed. 4) 97 Fresh-water fishes may be..catadromous or such as reside in fresh waters.

2. *Bot.* (See quot.)

1881 J. G. BAKER in *Nature* XXIII. 480 Milde's classification of ferns into a catadromous and anadromous series according as to whether their lowest secondary branches originate on the posterior or anterior side of the pinnæ.

†**ˈcatadupe.** *Obs.* Also 7 -doup, -dupa. [a. F. *catadoupe, catadupe*, ad. L. *catadūpa* (pl.), ad. Gr. κατάδουποι (pl.) the cataracts of the Nile, f. κατά down + δοῦπος thud, heavy sound of falling, δουπέ-ειν to sound heavy, fall with a thud. (But see Liddell and Scott.)]

1. A cataract or waterfall, *orig.* those of the Nile.

1596 LODGE *Wit's Miserie* (N.) Sien of my science in the catadupe of my knowledge, I nourish the crocodile of thy conceit. **1662** FULLER *Worthies* III. 142 In the River Caun in this County, there be two Catadupæ or Waterfalls. **1681** CHETHAM *Angler's Vade-m.* ii. §1 (1689) 111 At Kilgarran upon the Tivy..is a Catadoup, or very high Cataract. **1708** MOTTEUX *Rabelais* IV. xxxiv, The Catadupes of the Nile in Ethiopia. **1755** J. ISMAY in *Yorksh. N. & Q.* I. 206 The dams across the river are in the nature of Cataracts, and are a sort of catadupes.

2. *pl.* [L. *Catadūpi.*] The dwellers by the cataracts of the Nile.

1607 BREWER *Lingua* III. vii. (R.) The Egyptian Catadupes never heard the roaring of the fall of Nilus because the noise was so familiar unto them.

catafalque (ˈkætəfælk), **cataˈfalco.** Also 8 -falch, 9 -falc, -falk. [a. mod.F. *catafalque*, ad. It. *catafalco* (which also occurs in English); in Pr. *cadafalcs, cadafaus*, OCat. *cadafal*, Sp. *cadafalso, cadahalso, cadalso*, ONF. *caafaus* (in rég. -*faut*), OF. *chaafaus* (-*faut*), *chafaut, chafauld*, whence OF. *escafaut, eschafaut*, mod.F. *échafaud*, Eng. SCAFFOLD; in med.L. variously found as *catafaltus, cadafaldus, cadaffale, cadapallus, cadaphallus, chafallus*. Of unknown derivation; even the orig. form is uncertain; F. pointing to -*fald-* or -*falt-*, It. to -*falc-*, Sp. to -*fals* (see SCAFFOLD).

The derivation proposed by Diez is entirely discarded (see *Romania* I. 490). M. Paul Meyer thinks the first element may be the Gr. κατα- which was sometimes used in med.L. in sense 'beside', 'alongside' (*Romania* II. 80). 'The *cadafals* or *chaafaus* in OF. was a wooden erection crowning walls, and projecting from them on both sides. Thence the besieged commanded assailants beneath'.]

1. 'A stage or platform, erected by way of honour in a church to receive the coffin or effigy of a deceased personage' (Littré); 'a temporary structure of carpentry, decorated with painting and sculpture, representing a tomb or cenotaph, and used in funeral ceremonies' (Gwilt).

1641 EVELYN *Diary* (1871) 36 In the middle of it was the hearse or catafalco of the late Arch-Dutchesse. **1643** —— *Mem.* (1857) I. 46 In the nave of the church lies the catafalque, or hearse, of Louis XIII. **1766** *Ann. Register* 58 The supposed corpse was deposited upon a magnificent catafalco, or scaffold, erected from the bottom to the top of the church and illuminated all over with wax candles. **1760** POCOCK *Tour Scotl.* (1881) 242 A sort of small wooden Catafalch placed over the tomb. **1831** LANDOR *Fra Rupert* Wks. 1846 II. 579 Never drops one but catafalc and canopy Are ready for him. **1834** *Gentl. Mag.* CIV. I. 104 A rich catafalque was erected in the centre, in which the remains of the Marshal were deposited during the service.

2. A movable structure of this kind; a kind of open hearse or funeral car.

1855 BROWNING *Statue & Bust* 57 The door she had passed was shut on her Till the final catafalk repassed. **1864** *Daily Tel.* 16 Sept., The open hearse—one of the most extraordinary catafalcoes ever seen upon wheels.

3. *transf.* (*humorous.*)

1876 GEO. ELIOT *Dan. Der.* I. iii, The black and yellow catafalque known as 'the best bed'.

catagenesis (kætəˈdʒenɪsɪs). [See CATA- and GENESIS.] Retrogressive evolution. Cf. ANAGENESIS.

1884 E. D. COPE in *Amer. Assoc. Advancem. Sci.* XXXIII. 468 The process of creation by the retrograde metamorphosis of energy, or, what is the same thing, by the specialization of energy, may be called *catagenesis.* **1893** [see ANAGENESIS]. **1900** B. D. JACKSON *Gloss. Bot. Terms.*

Hence **catagenetic** (ˌkætədʒɪˈnɛtɪk) *a.*, of the nature of retrogressive evolution.

1896 E. D. COPE *Org. Evol.* 482 If the tendency of the catagenetic energies is away from vital phenomena.

cataˈglottism. *rare.* [a. F. *cataglottisme* 'a kisse or kissing with the tongue' (Cotgr.), ad. Gr. καταγλώττισμα, -ισμός 'a lascivious kiss'.]

1656 BLOUNT *Glossogr.*, *Cataglottism*, a kissing with the tongue. *Cotgr.* **1678** PHILLIPS, *Cataglottism*, a thrusting out the tongue in kissing. **1905** H. ELLIS *Stud. Psychol. Sex* IV. 5 The kiss is not only an expression of feeling; it is a means of provoking it. Cataglottism is by no means confined to pigeons.

†**cataˈglyphic.** *a.* *Obs. rare*⁻¹. [f. Gr. type *καταγλυφικ-ός, f. κατα-γλύφειν to carve out, groove.] Of carving out or incising.

1708 MOTTEUX *Rabelais* v. xli, Carv'd in Cataglyphick Work [*à ouvrage cataglyphe*].

catagˈmatic, *a.* and *sb.* *Med.* [a. F. *catagmatique* (Cotgr.), f. Gr. κάταγμα, -ατος breakage, fracture, f. κατ-αγνύναι to break, shatter.]

A. *adj.* Of or belonging to fractures or their medical treatment.

1684 tr. *Bonet's Merc. Compit.* VII. 250 [The stump after amputation] being every day covered with dry thread and a catagmatic Powder. **16..** WISEMAN *Surg.* (J.), I put on a catagmatick emplaster. **1704** J. HARRIS *Lex. Techn.*, *Catagmatick Medicines*, are such as are used to help to consolidate Broken Bones. **1881** in *Syd. Soc. Lex.*

B. quasi-*sb.* A medicine having the property of healing fractures.

1657 *Phys. Dict.*, *Catagmaticks*, medicines to consolidate, or knit together broken bones. **1751** in CHAMBERS *Cycl.*; and in mod. Dicts.

So †**catagˈmatical**, *a.* *Obs.*

1657 TOMLINSON *Renou's Disp.* 123 Of them that apply Catagmatical Plaisters to all diseases.

†**ˈcatagraph.** *Obs.*⁻⁰ [ad. Gr. κατάγραφ-ος drawn in outline, f. κατα-γράφειν to delineate.]

1656 BLOUNT *Glossogr.*, *Catagraph*, the first draught or delineation of a picture. **1721** in BAILEY, etc.

†**Caˈtaian**, *a.* *Obs.* A variant of *Cathaian*, a man of Cathay or China; 'used also to signify a sharper, from the dexterous thieving of those people' (Nares); ? a thief, scoundrel, blackguard.

[**1577** EDEN & WILLES *Hist. Trav.* 237 The Cathaian kyng is woont to graunt free accesse vnto..forreiners.] **1598** SHAKS. *Merry W.* II. i. 148, I will not beleeue such a Cataian, though the Priest o' th' Towne commended him for a true man. **1601** —— *Twel. N.* II. iii. 80 My Lady's a Catayan. **1630** DEKKER *2nd Pt. Honest Wh.* Wks. 1873 II. 143 Ile make a wild Cataine of forty such: hang him, he's an Asse. **1649** DAVENANT *Love & Hon.* (N.) Hang him, bold Cataian, he indites finely.

catal(le, obs. f. CATTLE.

Catalan (ˈkætəlæn), *a.* and *sb.* **A.** *adj.* Of or belonging to Catalonia, the most northeasterly province of Spain, once an independent principality. **Catalan forge**, a blast-furnace for reducing iron ores, extensively used in Catalonia and the neighbouring districts: so ***Catalan furnace, hearth***, etc. **B.** *sb.* **1.** A native of Catalonia; the language of Catalonia, a dialect of Provençal or Langue d'Oc, with affinities towards Spanish. **2.** The language of Catalonia.

1480 CAXTON *Chron. Eng.* cclvi. (1482) 334 Pope Calyxte the iij was a Catalane. **1792** A. YOUNG *Travels* 25 Region of the Pyrenees..the language of the country is a mixture of Catalan, Provençal, and French. **1807** SOUTHEY *Lett. fr. England* III. lxxiii. 335 Scotch..differs far more from English than Portugueze from Castilian, nearly as much as the Catalan. **1839** URE *Dict. Arts* 709 The Catalan forge can be profitably employed only where wood is exceedingly cheap and abundant. **a 1859** MACAULAY *Hist. Eng.* (1861) V. 97 The Catalans had risen in rebellion. **1861** FAIRBAIRN *Iron* 42 The disposition of the Catalan hearth during the process of reduction. **1867** BLOXAM *Chem.* 321 In the Pyrenees, where the Catalan process is employed. **a 1877** KNIGHT *Dict. Mech.*, *Catalan-furnace*, a blast-furnace for reducing iron ores, extensively used in the North of Spain. **1881** RAYMOND *Mining Gloss.*, *Catalan forge*, a forge with a tuyere for reducing iron ore, with charcoal, to a loup of wrought iron; a bloomary. **1906** BELLOC *Hills & Sea* 261 Hundreds of men had spoken to me in Catalan. **1933** H. J. CHAYTOR *Hist. Aragon* iv. 62 Catalan presents a different problem; the question whether it belongs to the Hispanic or to the Gallo-Roman branches of the Romance languages is even yet in dispute. **1960** W. D. ELCOCK *Romance Lang.* v. 435 The question whether Catalan should be considered as a language has at times given rise to debate, much of it ill-formed and coloured by political partisanship... During the later medieval period it came to rank as one of the 'great languages' of western Europe.

Catalanist (ˈkætəlænɪst), *sb.* (and *a.*). [f. CATALAN + -IST.] One who favours the independence of Catalonia; usually *attrib.* or as *adj.* So **ˈCatalanism**, the favouring of independence for Catalonia; also, an idiom or

mode of expression belonging to the Catalan language.

1905 *Daily Chron.* 23 Sept. 5/3 The Catalanist Agitation. **1907** *Westm. Gaz.* 25 May 2/1 The 'Catalanist' Home Rulers. **1923** *Glasgow Herald* 8 Oct. 9 The suspension of.. more or less seditious Catalanist journals. **1930** S. DE MADARIAGA *Spain* xviii. 304 Catalanism is, above all, a Barcelona affair. **1949** —— *C. Columbus* 433 Ulloa.. led by his strong Catalanist bias, paints this struggle as an effort of the Catalans to liberate themselves. **1958** *Archivum Linguisticum* X. 31 Gallicisms (including Provençalisms and Catalanisms).

catalase (ˈkætəleɪs, -z). *Chem.* Also **katalase**. [f. CATAL(YSIS + -ASE.] Any of the hæm-containing enzymes that catalyse the reduction of hydrogen peroxide.

1901 O. LOEW in *Rep. U.S. Dept. Agric.* LXVIII. 12 Since it is clear that the power of catalyzing hydrogen peroxid is not due to any of the known enzyms, it appears justifiable to ascribe this power to a special enzym. The writer proposes to call this catalase. **1904** *Brit. Med. Jrnl.* 20 Aug. 28 Yeast contains.. nuclein, zymase, endotrypsin, and katalase. **1911** *Encycl. Brit.* XIX. 921/1 Certain oxydases, catalases and de-amidizing enzymes.. play an important part in the various metabolic processes. **1958** *New Biol.* XXVII. 118 Hydrogen peroxide, a powerful poison against which most organisms—but not *Ascaris*—are protected by an enzyme, catalase, which destroys it.

catalectic (kætəˈlɛktɪk), *a. Pros.* [ad. late L. *catalēctic-us*, a. Gr. καταληκτικός leaving off, incomplete, f. κατα-λήγειν to leave off, stop. Cf. F. *catalectique*.] **A.** *adj.* Of a verse: Incomplete in its syllables; wanting a syllable in the last foot. Often in postposition in imitation of Latin. **B.** *sb.* A catalectic line or verse.

1589 PUTTENHAM *Eng. Poesie* (Arb.) 142 The Greekes and Latines vsed verses in the odde sillable of two sortes, which they called Catalecticke and Acatalecticke.. the catalectik or maymed verse. **1631** B. JONSON *Staple of News* IV. iv, Pentameters, Hexameters, Catalecticks. **1842** *Penny Cycl.* XXIV. 228/1 The Iambic Tetrameter Catalectic. **1883** tr. *Ten Brink's E.E. Lit.* 155 The catalectic tetrameter, well known to antique poetry. **1903** SAINTSBURY *Short Hist. Eng. Lit.* (ed. 3) II. ii. 52 A strict iambic form of tetrameter catalectic, or alternate dimeters acatalectic and catalectic.

catalecticant (kætəˈlɛktɪkənt). *Math.* (See quots. 1852, 1860.) So **cataˈlectic** *a.*, **cataˈlectically** *adv.*

1851 J. J. SYLVESTER *Canonical Forms* in *Coll. Math. Papers* (1904) I. 211 The theory of the catalectic forms of functions of the higher degrees of two variables. *Ibid.*, If, however, certain further relations obtain between the coefficients of *F*, the canonical form reappears catalectically, the function becoming in fact representable as a single cube. **1852** *Ibid.* 293, I shall hereafter refer to a determinant formed in this manner from the coefficients of *f* as its catalecticant. **1860** CAYLEY *Coll. Math. Papers* (1891) IV. 606 The name catalecticant denotes a certain invariant of a binary quantic of an even order.

† **ˈcatalects**, *sb. pl. Obs. rare.* [ad. L. *catalecta* (see below), a. Gr. *κατάλεκτα, f. καταλέγειν to reckon in the list of, reckon among. Cf. F. *catalectes*, and ANALECTS.] In sense of L. *catalecta*, name of a collection of short poems ascribed to Vergil; also, fragments or detached pieces.

1610 HOLLAND *Camden's Brit.* (1637) 10 That grammarian whom Virgil in his catalects so taunteth. *Ibid.* 46 Joseph Scaliger, in his Catalects, hath saved.. certain verses of a most learned poet.

catalency, corrupt. of *catalempsy*, CATALEPSY.

catalepsy (ˈkætəlɛpsɪ). Also 4–6 **-lempsie, -lencie**. [ad. med.L. *catalēpsia*, f. Gr. κατάληψις a seizing upon (see next); the L. form *catalēpsis* was formerly in common use. In F. *catalepsie*.]

1. *Med.* A disease characterized by a seizure or trance, lasting for hours or days, with suspension of sensation and consciousness.

1398 TREVISA *Barth. De P.R.* VII. x. (1495) 229 There ben thre manere of Epilency.. Epilencia.. Analempsia.. Cathalempsia. **1547** BOORDE *Brev. Health* lxiv. 27 b, The Catalency which is one of the kyndes of the fallynge sickenes. **1646** SIR T. BROWNE *Pseud. Ep.* 200 Apoplexies, Catalepsies, and Coma's. **1732** ARBUTHNOT *Rules of Diet* 366 There is a Disease of the same kind call'd a Catalepsis. **1866** A. FLINT *Princ. Med.* (1880) 839 Catalepsy.. is evidently allied to one of the forms of hysteria.

2. *Philos.* Comprehension, apprehension.

[**1580** NORTH *Plutarch* (1676) 446 The old Academicks.. hold, that a man may certainly know and comprehend something, and called that Catalepsin.] **1656** BLOUNT *Glossogr.*, *Catalepsie*, occupation, deprehension, knowledge. **1847** LEWES *Hist. Philos.* (1867) I. 365 The doctrine of Acatalepsy recalls to us the Stoical doctrine of Catalepsy, or Apprehension.

cataleptic (kætəˈlɛptɪk), *a.* (and *sb.*) [ad. late L. *catalēptic-us*, a. Gr. καταληπτικός cataleptic, f. καταληπτ-ός seized, f. καταλαμβάνειν to seize upon.]

A. *adj.* **1.** *Med.* **a.** Affected by catalepsy.

1684 tr. *Bonet's Merc. Compit.* III. 86 Galen.. allows Malmsey-wine to Cataleptick persons. **1862** LYTTON *Str. Story* II. 224 A cataleptic or ecstatic patient. **1866** *Cornh. Mag.* Sept. 379 A soulless body, a cataleptic subject mesmerized by a stronger will.

b. Of or pertaining to catalepsy.

1794–6 E. DARWIN *Zoon.* (1801) I. 325 Reverie is a disease of the epileptic or cataleptic kind. **1817** MAR. EDGEWORTH *Love & L.* III. xliv. 171 The cataleptic rigidity of his figure relaxed. **1861** GEO. ELIOT *Silas M.* i. 7 Silas's cataleptic fit occurred during the prayer-meeting.

2. *Philos.* Pertaining to apprehension.

1847 LEWES *Hist. Philos.* (1867) I. 356 Of true phantasms, some are cataleptic (apprehensive) and others non-cataleptic... The cataleptic phantasm is that which is impressed by an object that exists.

B. *sb.* One affected by catalepsy.

1851 H. MAYO *Pop. Superst.* (ed. 2) 118 The cataleptic apprehends or perceives directly the objects around her. **1862** J. CUNNINGHAM in *Macm. Mag.* Apr. 514 There have been cataleptics.. who had two distinct currents of existence.

Hence (in *Med.*) **cataˈleptiform**, **cataˈleptoid** *adjs.*, resembling catalepsy.

1847–9 TODD *Cycl. Anat. & Phys.* IV. 695/1 This contraction.. may keep it [the limb] fixed in a cataleptiform manner. **1881** *Syd. Soc. Lex.*, *Cataleptoid*.

catalexis (kætəˈlɛksɪs). [f. Gr. κατάληξις termination, f. καταλήγειν to leave off.]

1. Absence of a syllable in the last foot of a verse.

1830 SEAGER tr. *Hermann's Metres* II. xix. 46 Cretic verses are for the most part terminated by that same foot, and have no other catalexis. **1898** SAINTSBURY *Short Hist. Eng. Lit.* II. iii. 77 Halidon is told [by Minot] in octave eights admitting catalexis. **1957** W. BEARE *Latin Verse* vii. 82 From iambic trimeters we pass freely to dimeters, monometers, iambics with catalexis and syncopation.

2. A catalectic verse or line.

1850 MURE *Lit. Greece* III. 55 The combination of a single short verse or 'catalexis' with one or more longer verses.

catallactic (kætəˈlæktɪk), *a.* [ad. Gr. καταλλακτικός (not recorded in this sense), f. καταλλάσσειν to change, exchange.]

A. *adj.* Pertaining to exchange (see B.).

1862 RUSKIN *Unto this Last* 133 The perfect operation of catallactic science.. Do away with these, and catallactic advantage becomes impossible.

B. *sb. pl.* A proposed name for Political Economy as the 'science of exchanges'.

1831 WHATELY *Lect. Pol. Econ.* i. (1855) 4 The name of Political Economy.. The name I should have preferred as the most descriptive, and on the whole least objectionable, is that of Catallactics, or the 'Science of Exchanges'. **1862** RUSKIN *Unto this Last* 132 The Science of Exchange, or, as I hear it has been proposed to call it, of 'Catallactics', considered as one of gain, is.. simply nugatory.

Hence **cataˈllactically** *adv.*, by way of exchange.

1862 RUSKIN *Unto this Last* 155 You may grow for your neighbour.. grapes or grapeshot; he will also catallactically grow grapes or grapeshot for you, and you will each reap what you have sown.

catalo (ˈkætələʊ). *U.S.* Also **cattalo, cattelo.** [f. CAT(TLE + BUFF)ALO.] A cross between the male buffalo and the domesticated cow.

1889 *Kansas Times & Star* 20 May, Colonel [Charles] Goodnight was the first man to experiment with crossing buffalo and cattle. A big herd of the hybrids, called 'cattalo', is now on his Texas ranch. **1894** *San Francisco Midwinter Appeal* 10 Feb. 3/3 Grand Exhibit of Buffaloes and Cattleos. **1899** C. J. JONES in H. Inman *Buffalo Jones' Forty Years of Adv.* 243 To these cross-breeds I have given the name 'Catalo', from the first syllable of *cattle* and the last three letters of *buffalo*. **1906** *Harper's Mag.* Apr. 798 [The buffaloes] sad captives sinking to slow extinction in the hybrid cattelo with his mongrel name. **1923** *Chambers's Jrnl.* July 454/1 The crossing of buffalo with domestic cattle. From the mating.. has been evolved the 'cattalo'. **1958** *Irish Times* 23 Aug., The Cattalo, which was bred in Alberta, is an animal with fine beef qualities.

catalogic (kætəˈlɒdʒɪk, -ˈlɒgɪk), *a.* [f. CATALOGUE + -IC.] Of the nature of, or pertaining to, a catalogue. So **cataˈlogical** *a.*

1882 *Athenæum* 9 Sept. 331/1 The former [article] is 'pre-scientific', the latter too catalogic.

catalogist, variant of CATALOGUIST.

catalogistic (ˌkætələʊˈdʒɪstɪk), *a. rare.* Of or pertaining to cataloguing.

1840 W. H. MILL *Applic. Panth. Princ.* (1861) 29 In the Sankhya or Catalogistic school of philosophy.

† **catalogize** (ˈkætəlɒˌdʒaɪz, -ˌgaɪz). *Obs.* [f. Gr. καταλογίζ-εσθαι to count up, recount, reckon among; with the meaning partly from this, and partly from CATALOGUE + -IZE. Cf. CATALOGUIZE.]

1. To reckon up.

1602 CAREW *Cornwall* 54 b, As the Welshmen catalogize Ap Rice, etc... vntill they end in the highest of the stock.

2. To enumerate or insert in a catalogue.

1632 W. LITHGOW *Totall Disc.* 320 He deserueth to be Catalogized as founder of this kingdome. **1660** S. FISHER *Rusticks Alarm* Wks. (1679) 505 Sure enough the man Catalogized all these together out of his Concordance. **1665** MOXON *Tutor to Astron.* I. (1686) 19 Which.. may be Catalogised either for the memory of the Observer, or the knowledge of Posterity.

catalogue (ˈkætəlɒg), *sb.* Forms: 5 **cateloge, cathaloge, catholog, cattologue,** 7 **cathalogue,** 6, 9 **catalog,** 6– **catalogue.** [a. F. *catalogue*, and ad. late L. *catalogus*, a. Gr. κατάλογος register, list, catalogue, f. καταλέγειν to choose, pick out, enlist, enroll, reckon in a list, etc., f. κατά down + λέγ-ειν to pick, choose, reckon up, etc.]

1. a. A list, register, or complete enumeration; in this simple sense now *Obs. or arch.*

1460 CAPGRAVE *Chron.* 71 And than was Cyriacus Pope, but.. he is not put in the Cateloge of Popes. **1483** CAXTON *Gold. Leg.* 295/4 He was.. set to the Cathaloge of martirs. *c* **1535** DEWES *Introd. Fr.* in *Palsgr.* 936 They be noted.. among the Catalogue of verbes. **1587** in Ellis *Orig. Lett.* II. 229 III. 133 That leaving a Catalog of all our names we may depart. **1630** WADSWORTH *Sp. Pilgr.* vii. 72 A Catalogue of the Monasteries, Seminaries, and Nunneries in Flanders. **1660** (*title*), Englands Glory, Or, an Exact Catalogue of the Lords of His Maiesties most Honourable Privy Councel. **1711** ADDISON *Spect.* No. 74 ¶10 In the Catalogue of the Slain the Author has followed the Example of the greatest ancient Poets. **1839** YEOWELL *Anc. Brit. Ch.* xi. (1847) 127 In some of the catalogues of the bishops, St. Petrock is mentioned as the first.

b. *fig.* List, roll, series, etc.

1590 BARROW & GREENWOOD in *Conferences* 41 Your cattologue of lyes wherof you accuse vs. **1611** SHAKS. *Cymb.* I. iv. 5 Though the Catalogue of his endowments had bin tabled by his side. **1719** YOUNG *Revenge* II. i, I have turn'd o'er the catalogue of woes. **1792** BURGESS in *Corr. Ld. Auckland* (1861) II. 438 To fill up the catalogue of their calamities. **1824** TRAVERS *Disc. Eye* 325 The frightful catalogue of disasters which the spirit of controversy promulgates.

2. Now usually distinguished from a mere list or enumeration, by systematic or methodical arrangement, alphabetical or other order, and often by the addition of brief particulars, descriptive, or aiding identification, indicative of locality, position, date, price, or the like.

1667 PEPYS *Diary* (1879) IV. 227 Home, and to my chamber, and there finished my Catalogue of books. **1676** LISTER in *Ray's Corr.* (1848) 124, I am well pleased your Catalogue of Plants is again to be printed. **1727** SWIFT *Gulliver* III. iii. 196 They have made a catalogue of ten thousand fixed stars. **1834** MRS. SOMERVILLE *Connex. Phys. Sc.* xxxvii. (1849) 416 The first catalogue of double stars, in which their places and relative positions are given. **1870** L'ESTRANGE *Miss Mitford* I. v. 154 [It] may apply almost as well to the Booksellers' Catalogue as to the Parish Register. *Mod.* (*title*), The London Catalogue of British Plants. The British Museum Catalogue.

3. a. A list of college or university graduates, alumni, or teachers. **b.** A university or college calendar. *U.S.*

1682 J. BISHOP in *Mass. Hist. Coll.* (1868) 4th Ser. VIII. 311, I lately received.. a Catalogue of Harvard's sons. **1786** in J. Maclean *Hist. Coll. N.J.* (1877) I. 344 Ordered, That a complete catalogue of the graduates of this College be prepared and published at the expense of the present Senior class. **1812** (*title*) Catalogue of the Officers and Students [of Harvard]. **1823** (*title*) Catalogue of officers and students in Yale College November 1823. **1842** Z. THOMPSON *Hist. Vermont* II. 155 Middlebury College.. Catalogue of Alumni and Honorary Graduates. **1873** J. H. BEADLE *Undevel. West* xxxi. 686 The 'University of Deseret' puts forth a pretentious catalogue, with a lengthy list of professors. **1945** G. SANTAYANA *Middle Span* viii. 159 My name had figured in the Harvard Catalogue.. for 30 years.

4. Miscellaneous attrib. uses.

1892 *Photogr. Ann.* II. 127 Each of the catalogue plates will have two exposures. **1899** *Daily News* 29 Apr. 7/3 A Piccadilly firm have offered to buy at catalogue price the picture by Policeman Jones, of Leeds, accepted for the Royal Academy. **1908** *Amer. Libr. Assoc. Catalog Rules* p. v, The size and quality of catalog cards. **1961** *Oxf. Mail* 6 Oct. 2/3 (Advt.), Catalogue paster required.

catalogue (ˈkætəlɒg), *v.* [f. the sb. Cf. F. *cataloguer*.]

1. *trans.* To make a catalogue or list of; to enumerate in catalogue form.

1598 CHAPMAN *Iliad* II. Argt., Beta.. catalogues the navall knights. *a* **1612** HARINGTON *Brief View Ch.* 80 (T.) He so cancelled, or catalogued, and scattered our books. **1705** PROWSE in Hearne *Collect.* (1885) I. 10, I am.. busie in Catalogueing his Books. **1863** MISS BRADDON *Eleanor's Vict.* I. i. 3, I would rather not catalogue her other features too minutely. **1884** *Law Times* 3 May 11/1 [He] had begun to lot and catalogue the furniture. **1886** *Pall Mall G.* 15 Jan. 6/2 While engaged in cataloguing a library.

2. To inscribe or insert in a catalogue. Also *fig.*

1635 HEYWOOD *Lond. Sinus Sal.* Wks. 1874 IV. 298 Amongst Schollars (In which number I may Catalogue your Lordship). **1762–71** H. WALPOLE *Anecd. Paint.* III. i. (R.) If religion is thrown into the quarrel, the most innocent acts are catalogued with sins. **1870** MISS BRIDGMAN *R. Lynne* II. iii. 64 He had catalogued Dicky Blake as a fool. **1886** *Law Times* LXXX. 165/1 The book.. was catalogued under the author's name only.

3. *absol.*

1602 WARNER *Alb. Eng.* IX. xliv. (1612) 212 And here occasion apteth that we catalogue a while.

Hence **ˈcatalogued** *ppl. a.*, **ˈcataloguing** *vbl. sb.*

1795 BURKE *Regic. Peace* iv. Wks. IX. 102 Their studied, deliberated, catalogued files of murders. **1830** HERSCHEL *Stud. Nat. Phil.* 79 Mineralogy ceased to be.. a mere laborious cataloguing of stones and rubbish.

cataloguer (ˈkætəˌlɒgə(r)). [f. prec. + -ER. Cf. F. *catalogueur*.] One who catalogues.

1841 D'ISRAELI *Amen. Lit.* (1867) 120 The pen of a slumbering cataloguer. **1849** E. WARWICK *Poet's Pleas.* (1853) 42 An accurate cataloguer of his flowers. **1884** *Harper's Mag.* Nov. 828/1 Girls.. trained as cataloguers and library assistants.

‖ **catalogue raisonné** (katalɔg rɛzɔne). Also erron. **raisonnée** [Fr., = carefully studied or methodical catalogue.] A descriptive catalogue

arranged according to subjects, or branches of subjects; hence *gen.* or loosely, a classified or methodical list.

1784 H. WALPOLE *Descr. Strawberry-Hill* p. i, Catalogues raisonnés of collections are very frequent in France and Holland. **1792** C. SMITH *Desmond* III. 169 He had glided away on a descriptive tour to his own seat near Bath; and was giving a *catalogue raisonnée* of its conveniences. **1803** *Edin. Rev.* Oct. 79 A *catalogue raisonnée*, if executed with judgment and impartiality, would be a very useful appendage to every work. **1818** HAZLITT *Eng. Poets* viii. 324 There is no Gay in the present time to give a *Catalogue Raisonné* of the performances of the living undertaker of epics. **1835** *Penny Cycl.* IV. 380/2 The best specimen of a *Catalogue Raisonné* that we know of any of the more considerable collections of this country, is that of the library of the writers to the Signet in Edinburgh, published in one volume quarto in 1805. **1903** F. L. GARDNER (*title*) A Catalogue raisonné of works on the occult sciences. **1948** *Ann. Reg.* *1947* 227 An expenditure of £37,528 million. It was a huge figure, but the *catalogue raisonné* of its component items challenged its critics at their weakest point. **1960** *Guardian* 16 June 8/5 The erudition embodied in the catalogue raisonné is quite exceptional.

ˈcataˌloguish, *a.* *nonce-wd.* [see -ISH.] Savouring of a catalogue.

1791 T. TWINING *Country Clergym.* (1882) 148 Dry, prosaic and cataloguish [verses].

ˈcataˌloguist. [f. CATALOGUE + -IST.] = CATALOGUER.

1860 *All Y. Round* II. 252 Our old friend the cataloguist .. when he gets into the Chamber of Horrors. **1883** M. & F. COLLINS *You play me false* xii. 85 She did all her work, whether as amanuensis or cataloguist, at the famous table.

cataloguize (ˈkætəlɒˌgaɪz). [f. CATALOGUE + -IZE; cf. CATALOGIZE.] *trans.* To CATALOGUE.

1609 BP. BARLOW *Answ. Nameless Cath.* 22 He shall be denounced an Heretike, and so Cataloguised on Holy-Thursday. **1634** SIR T. HERBERT *Trav.* 94 Amongst which rabble may be cataloguized, the swarmes of Gnats, Flies and Snakes. **1820** SHELLEY *Ess. & Lett.* (1852) 522 More .. than I am able To cataloguize in this verse of mine.

Catalonian (kætəˈləʊnɪən), *a.* and *sb.* [f. *Catalonia*, the Spanish province (*Cataluña*, Cat. *Catalunya*): see -IAN.] = CATALAN.

1707 MORTIMER *Husb.* xviii. 496 The Catalonian or Spanish jessamine .. is not so high as the former. **1781** DILLON *Lett. Eng. Trav. Spain 1778* v. 63 The Aragonians and Catalonians adopted the Castilian dialect. **1823** T. ROSS tr. *Bouterwek's Hist. Span. & Pg. Lit.* I. 6 In the kingdom of Arragon, the language in general use was the Catalonian. **1829** K. H. DIGBY *Broad Stone, Orlandus* xxi. 531 He spoke Greek, Hebrew, Latin, Catalonian, and Italian. **1836** *Penny Cycl.* VI. 361/2 During the war of the Spanish succession, the Catalonians .. took the part of the Archduke Charles of Austria against Philip of France. **1875** *Encycl. Brit.* II. 433/2 This Catalonian work of the 14th and 15th centuries. **1876** *Ibid.* V. 217/2 The Catalonians are a frugal, sharp-witted and industrious people. **1958** A. R. RADCLIFFE-BROWN *Method in Social Anthropol.* II. v. 185 From the many Latin dialects there came into existence the present Romance languages—French, Provençal, Italian, Catalonian, Castilian, Portugese. **1963** *Times* 25 Feb. 9/2 The accused, all Catalonians, included six lawyers.

‖**catalpa** (kəˈtælpə). *Bot.* [From the language of the Indians of Carolina, where Catesby discovered *C. bignonioides* in 1726.]

A genus of trees (N.O. *Bignoniaceæ*), natives of N. America, W. Indies, Japan and China, having large simple leaves, and terminal panicles of trumpet-shaped flowers. Two species, known also as Indian Bean, and St. Domingo or French Oak, are cultivated in England. Also *attrib.*

1731–48 CATESBY *Nat. Hist. Florida* (1754) I. 49 The Catalpa Tree. **1794** MARTYN *Rousseau's Bot.* xxii. 317 The Catalpa is a large tree with leaves remarkably simple and heart shaped. **1856** BRYANT *Winds* i, Before you the catalpa's blossoms flew. **1860** GOSSE *Rom. Nat. Hist.* 174 The large white blossoms of a catalpa tree .. just under my window.

catalyse (ˈkætəlaɪz), *v.* Also †kata-, -lyze. [f. CATALYSIS after *analyse*, *analysis*.] *trans.* To increase the rate of (a reaction or process) by catalytic action; to produce by means of catalysis. Also *fig.* Hence **ˈcatalyser, -or,** (*rare*) **ˈcatalysator**, a catalyst; **ˈcatalysing** *vbl. sb.* and *ppl. a.*

1890 *Nature* 13 Nov. 25/1 Every micro-organism produces, from the substances which it katalyzes .. a material or materials, which, on accumulation, inhibit its growth. **1893** *Ann. Rep. Smithsonian Inst.* 237 Numberless specific catalysators exist which act only upon certain phenomena. **1901** *Jrnl. Amer. Chem. Soc.* Apr. 236 The ratio of the velocity of the reaction to the concentration of the catalysor is nearly constant in dilute solutions of strong acids. **1904** *Jrnl. Phys. Chem.* May 373 Measurements were made of the effect of catalyzers on the formation of C_6H_5Cl and $C_6H_6Cl_6$ from benzene and chlorine. **1904** J. MCCABE tr. *Haeckel's Wonders of Life* ii. 47 Many recent chemists and physiologists are of opinion that plasm is a colloid catalysator. **1917** *Chambers's Jrnl.* Nov. 726/2 Some of these natural catalysers can be manufactured. **1926** *Spectator* 21 Aug. 280/1 [Advertising] is .. the great mover of merchandise, the catalyser of commerce. **1937** *Discovery* June 181/1 Traces of impurities that catalyse reactions may lead to erroneous inferences. **1943** KOESTLER in *Horizon* Apr. 242 But tradition might act on a man in two ways: either as a sterilizing, or as a catalysing agent. **1944** J. S. HUXLEY *Living in Rev.* xi. 115 They do not impose their own plans, but they catalyse planning jointly with others. **1955** *Sci. News Let.* 29 Oct. 274/1 Peroxidase .. catalyzes, or sparks, the transfer of oxygen from hydrogen peroxide .. to another substance. **1966** *McGraw-Hill Encycl. Sci. & Technol.* V. 19/2 Most of the chemical reactions that take place in living organisms are catalyzed by specific enzymes, without which such reactions would proceed at a negligible rate, if at all. **1969** *Nature* 27 Dec. 1250/1 The technology bred of science has catalysed stupendous economic growth.

catalysis (kəˈtælɪsɪs). [a. Gr. κατάλυσις dissolution (e.g. of a government), f. καταλύειν to dissolve, f. κατά down + λύ-ειν to loosen.]

†**1.** Dissolution, destruction, ruin. *Obs. rare.*

1655 EVELYN *Mem.* (1857) III. 67 In this sad catalysis and declension of piety to which we are reduced. **1660** JER. TAYLOR *Duct. Dubit.* I. iv, The sad catalysis did come, and swept away eleven hundred thousand of the nation.

2. *Chem.* The name given by Berzelius to the effect produced in facilitating a chemical reaction, by the presence of a substance, which itself undergoes no permanent change. Also called *contact action.*

1836 BERZELIUS in *Edin. New Phil. Jrnl.* XXI. 223 Many bodies .. have the property of exerting on other bodies an action which is very different from chemical affinity. By means of this action they produce decomposition in bodies, and form new compounds into the composition of which they do not enter. This new power, hitherto unknown, is common both in organic and inorganic nature .. I shall .. call it catalytic power. I shall also call Catalysis the decomposition of bodies by this force. **1842** W. GROVE *Corr. Phys. Forces* Pref. 12, I am strongly disposed to consider that the facts of Catalysis depend upon voltaic action. *c* **1865** in *Circ. Sc.* I. 83/1 By means of what has been termed catalysis, alcohol is .. converted into acetic acid.

catalysotype (kætəˈlɪsətaɪp). *Photogr.* [f. prec. + Gr. τύπος TYPE.] A picture produced by a calotype process using iodide of iron: see quot.

1853 R. HUNT *Man. Photogr.* 80 It would seem as if the salt of silver, being slightly affected by the light, sets up a catalytic action, which is extended to the salts of iron .. The catalysis which then takes place has induced me to name this process .. the Catalysotype. **1854** SCOFFERN in *Orr's Circ. Sc.* Chem. 85.

catalyst (ˈkætəlɪst). *Chem.* [f. CATALYSIS, on the analogy of *analyst.*] A substance which when present in small amounts increases the rate of a chemical reaction or process but which is chemically unchanged by the reaction; a catalytic agent. (A substance which similarly slows down a reaction is occas. called a *negative catalyst.*) Also *fig.*

1902 *Nature* 3 Apr. 523/1 No reactions are possible under the influence of catalysts that could not take place in their absence without a breach of one of the laws of energy. **1920** *Chambers's Jrnl.* 284/1 Nickel is used as a 'catalyst', or a carrier of hydrogen in the hydrogenation .. of oils for use in the manufacture of margarine. **1927** HALDANE & HUXLEY *Anim. Biol.* viii. 169 We have begun to isolate many of the intermediate products of metabolism and the catalysts that govern the course of the reactions by which they are formed. **1943** H. READ *Politics of Unpolitical* xiv. 160 Shelley called poets the *unacknowledged* legislators of the world, and the epithet was well chosen. The catalyst is unchanged, unabsorbed; its activity therefore not acknowledged. **1948** GLASSTONE *Physical Chem.* (ed. 2) xiii. 1126 If the reaction is hindered by the added substance it is said to be a negative catalyst, and the word catalyst, when used alone, is almost invariably taken to imply acceleration of the chemical process. **1953** *Sci. News* XXVIII. 117 There is no reason why a catalyst .. should be rendered totally inactive by a change in the geometry of the substance acted upon. **1954** J. I. M. STEWART *Mark Lambert's Supper* 139 In the intricate chemistry that gives motive-power to the machine he has himself acted as an obscure catalyst. **1968** A. WHITE et al. *Princ. Biochem.* (ed. 4) x. 209 Enzymes are catalysts peculiar to living matter.

catalytic (kætəˈlɪtɪk), *a.* [ad. Gr. καταλυτικός able to dissolve, f. κατάλυσις CATALYSIS.] Of the nature of, or pertaining to, catalysis; having the power of acting by catalysis. Also *fig.* ***catalytic cracker***: the device in which catalytic cracking is carried out; ***catalytic cracking*** [CRACK *v.* 23]: the cracking of petroleum oils by a process using a catalyst.

1836 [see CATALYSIS 2]. **1839–47** TODD *Cycl. Anat.* III. 153/2. **1842** W. GROVE *Corr. Phys. Forces* 86 That the increased electrolytic power of water .. depends upon a catalytic effect. **1861** *Times* 26 Oct. 6/5 Bodies known as catalytic agents. **1876** tr. *Schutzenberger's Ferment.* 43 The theory of catalytic forces .. maintained by Berzelius. **1927** *Chem. Abstr.* 644 (*title*) Catalytic cracking of heavy fractions of petroleum... A special exptl. app. for catalytic cracking, in which a continuous influx of oil and recovery of the gas, oil and volatile products is carried out, is described. **1943** in *Amer. Speech* (1944) XIX. 150/1 Supersonics .. may usher in a new age of chemistry with radio being used as a catalytic agent. **1945** KOESTLER *Yogi & Commissar* 32 It has to act as a catalytic agent, as the saliva in the process of creative assimilation. **1951** *Economist* 11 Aug. 358 The modern catalytic cracker .. may use as many as 350 instruments measuring and controlling such variables as flow, pressure and temperature.

Hence **cataˈlytically** *adv.*, in a catalytic manner, by catalytic action.

1845 G. DAY *Simon's Anim. Chem.* I. 19 Fibrin is stated to have the power of decomposing binoxide of hydrogen catalytically.

catalytical (kætəˈlɪtɪkəl), *a.* = CATALYTIC *a.*

1889 in *Cent. Dict.* **1923** *Glasgow Herald* 30 May 8 Catalitical salts.

catamaran (ˌkætəməˈræn, kəˈtæmərən). Also 7 cattamaran, 8 catamoran, kattamaran, 9 catamarran. [ad. Tamil *kaṭṭa-maram* tied tree or wood (*kaṭṭa* tie, bond; *maram* wood).]

1. a. A kind of raft or float, consisting of two, three or more logs tied together side by side, the middle one being longer than the others; used in the East Indies, especially on the Coromandel coast, for communication with the shore. Also applied to similar craft used in the West Indies for short voyages, and to others of much larger size used off the coast of South America; as well as to a kind of raft made of two boats fastened together side by side, used on the St. Lawrence and its tributaries. In recent use, a sailing boat with twin hulls placed side by side, widely used as pleasure craft and in sailing contests.

1697 DAMPIER *Voy.* I. vi. 143 The smaller sort of Bark-logs .. are more governable than the other .. This sort of Floats are used in many places both in the East and West Indies. On the Coast of Coromandel .. they call them Catamarans. These are but one Log, or two, sometimes of a sort of light Wood .. so small, that they carry but one Man, whose legs and breech are always in the Water. **1698** FRYER *Acc. E. India & P.* 24 (Y.) Coasting along some Cattamarans made after us. **1779** FORREST *Voy. N. Guinea* 263 Rafts of bamboo, like the catamarans on the coast of Coromandel. **1794** *Rigging & Seamanship* I. 242 *Balsas*, or *Catamaran*, a raft made of the trunks of the balsa .. lashed together, and used by the Indians .. in South America. The largest have 9 trunks of 70 or 80 feet in length, are from 20 to 24 feet wide, and from 20 to 25 tons burthen. **1804** A. DUNCAN *Mariner's Chron.* III. 112 We saw two of the catamarans .. coming towards us, with three black men on each. **1834** CAUNTER *Orient. Ann.* i. 4 The catamaran .. is generally about ten feet long by eighteen inches broad. **1876** *Times* 25 Oct. (D.) The fan of her screw propeller came in contact with a floating catamaran. **1957** *Times* 13 Dec. 15/2 The catamaran has strongly caught the fancy of those to whom speed is the prime satisfaction to be had from sailing. There were races for catamarans at Cowes last summer.

b. *attrib.*

1883 *Fisheries Exhib. Catal.* 47 Tumble overboard Life-raft. Reversible Catamaran principle.

†**2.** Applied to a kind of fire-ship or instrument of naval warfare resembling the modern torpedo; *esp.* to those prepared in 1804 to resist Napoleon's intended invasion of England. *Obs.*

1804 *Chron.* in *Ann. Reg.* 419/2 This undertaking commonly known by the appellation of the Catamaran expedition. **1809** *Naval Chron.* XXII. 453 The explosion of a catamaran. **1882** ALLARDYCE in *Athenæum* 26 Aug. 268/2 He experimented with Fulton's 'catamarans'—the prototypes of the modern fish torpedoes—against the Boulogne flotilla.

fig. **1822** BYRON in Moore *Life* V. 319 If you have any political catamarans to explode, this is your place. **1832** *Blackw. Mag.* XXXI. 480 He is .. the very catamaran of oratory, and when he explodes, etc.

3. Applied to a cross-grained or quarrelsome person, *esp.* a woman. *colloq.* [? Associated with *cat.*]

1833 MARRYAT *P. Simple* vi, The cursed drunken old catamaran. **1848** LYTTON *Harold* iv. 168 To dress that catamaran in mail. **1868** M. COLLINS *Anne Page* II. 223 That old catamaran of a maiden aunt of his.

ˌcatamaˈran, *v.* *nonce-wd.* [f. prec. sb.] To blow up with a catamaran. Also *fig.*

1820 H. MATTHEWS *Diary Invalid* (1835) 288 In fact, Napoleon has so catamaranned the foundations, that more than one *écroulement* has already taken place.

‖**catamenia** (kætəˈmiːnɪə), *sb. pl.* *Phys.* [Gr. καταμήνια menses, properly neut. pl. of καταμήνιος monthly, f. μήν month.] The menstrual discharge.

1754–64 SMELLIE *Midwif.* I. 107 If the Catamenia do not flow at the stated time the patient is soon after seized with the Chlorosis. **1845** G. DAY *Simon's Anim. Chem.* I. 271 A woman labouring under suppression of the catamenia.

catamenial (kætəˈmiːnɪəl), *a.* [f. prec. + -AL[1].] Pertaining to the catamenia; menstrual.

1851 CARPENTER *Man. Phys.* (ed. 2) 314 The Catamenial discharge. **1859** TODD *Cycl. Anat.* V. 662/2 The catamenial period and interval together occupy a space of one lunar month.

†**cataˈmidiate**, *v.* *Obs.* [f. Gr. καταμειδιά-ειν to despise.] 'To put one to open shame and punishment for some notorious offence, to scorn, to defame' (Blount *Glossogr.* 1656).

catamite (ˈkætəmaɪt). [ad. L. *Catamītus* corrupt form of *Ganymēdes* name of Jupiter's cup-bearer; also, a catamite.] A boy kept for unnatural purposes.

1593 DRAYTON *Moon-Calf* Wks. 1753 II. 484 His smooth-chin'd .. catamite. **1601** HOLLAND *Pliny* I. 111 Called Cinedopolis, by reason of certain Catamites and shamefull baggages that king Alexander the Great left there. **1699** BENTLEY *Phal.* 417 Agatho himself .. was a Catamite. **1795** T. TAYLOR *Apuleius* VIII. (1822) 185 A certain young man .. a common catamite.

Hence **ˈcatamited, ˈcatamiting** *ppl. adjs.* (as if from a vb. *catamite*).

1624 HEYWOOD *Captives* II. ii, That ould catamiting cankerworme. **1697** POTTER *Antiq. Greece* I. I. xxvi, The catamited Boy shall have no Action issued out against him.

catamount ('kætəmaʊnt). [Shortened from CATAMOUNTAIN.]

† **1.** = CATAMOUNTAIN; a pard or panther. *Obs.*

1664 POWER *Exp. Philos.* I. 5 With clea's or tallons (like a Catamount). **1730-6** BAILEY *(folio) Cat-a-mount*, a Mongrel, or wild Cat.

2. A common name in U.S. of the puma or cougar (*Felis concolor*), also called Panther, Painter, and Mountain (or American) Lion.

1794 S. WILLIAMS *Vermont* 86 The catamount seems to be the same animal which the ancients called Lynx. **1825** *Bro. Jonathan* I. 109 A wild beast.. I say! twarn't a cattermount tho', was it? **1855** O. W. HOLMES *Poems* 193 The woods were full of Catamounts, And Indians red as deer. **1870** EMERSON *Soc. & Solit., Courage* Wks. (Bohn) III. 108 The hunter is not alarmed by bears, catamounts, or wolves. **1884** *Echo* 24 Nov. 4/3 In Pennsylvania, bears and catamounts are so numerous.. in Pike county as to be a perfect nuisance to the farmers.

catamountain, cat o' mountain (kætə'maʊntɪn, -əʊ'maʊntɪn). Forms: 5-7 **cat of the mountain**, 6-7 **cat of mountain**, 7-8 **catamountain(e**, (8 **cat-amountant**), 6- **cat o mountain**, 7- **cat-a-mountain**. [app. of English formation: it does not appear that the ME. 'cat of the mountain' was a translation from another language.]

1. A name applied originally to the leopard or panther; by Goldsmith to the Ocelot (*Felis pardalis*), and by others to species of Tiger-cat.

1432-50 tr. *Higden* (Rolls) I. 159 [In Ethiopia] cattes of the mownteyne [*pardi*]. **1526** TINDALE *Rev.* xiii. 2 And the beast which I sawe was lyke a Catt off the Mountayne. **1598** G. GIFFORD *Disc. Relig.* 134 The black Moore cannot change his hew, nor the cat of the mountaine her spots. **1701** *Lond. Gaz.* No. 3708/4 On the Third is a Cat-amountant. **1774** GOLDSM. *Nat. Hist.* III. 262 The Catamountain, or Ocelot, is one of the fiercest.. animals in the world. **1840** AINSWORTH *Tower of Lond.* (1864) 163 Moustaches, bristling like the whiskers of a cat-a-mountain. **1865** CARLYLE *Fredk. Gt.* VI. XVI. vii. 211 He springs upon the throat of Hirsch like a cat-o'-mountain.

2. *transf.* A wild man from the mountains.

1616 BEAUM. & FL. *Cust. Country* I. i. 400 To a wild fellow that would worry her.. To the rude claws of such a cat-o'-mountain. **1650** A. B. *Mutat. Polemo* 14 To bragg (meerly on the dependance o' these crafty Catamountaines). **1842** LYTTON *Zanoni* IV. vi, These wild cats-a-mountain!

3. *attrib.*

1598 SHAKS. *Merry W.* II. ii. 27 Your Cat-a-Mountaine-lookes, your red-lattice phrases. *a* **1857** CARLYLE *Misc.* I. 29 Boisterous outlaws with huge whiskers, and the most cat-o'-mountain aspect. **1878** H. M. STANLEY *Dark Cont.* II. vii. 220 Animated with a ferocious cat-o-mountain spirit.

† **cata'nadromous**, *a. Obs. Zool.* [f. mod.L. *catanadromi* (Gesner), f. Gr. κατά down + ἀνά up + -δρομος running.] An epithet preferred by some early naturalists to ANADROMOUS.

[**1753** CHAMBERS *Cycl. Supp.*, *Anadromous*.. Some use the word *Catanadromi* in the same sense.] Hence in some mod. Dicts.

catananche (kætə'næŋkiː). *Bot.* [mod.L. (Linnæus 1735), f. L. *catanancē* plant used in love potions, Gr. καταναγκη, f. κατά down + ἀνάγκη compulsion.] The name of a genus (*Catananche*) of herbs of the family Compositæ with blue or yellow flowers; a plant of this genus.

1798 tr. *J. F. Gmelin's Linnæus' Syst. Nat.* XIV. 291 Compositae... The genera are.. Catananche, Candia lion's-foot. **1836** LOUDON *Encycl. Plants* 678 *Catananche*... The modern genus, which contains two or three species of ornamental border annuals, can have no reference to that of the ancients. **1868** S. HEREMAN *Paxton's Bot. Dict.* 116/2 *Catananche*.. a pretty genus, that succeeds well in common soil. **1961** *Times* 25 Nov. 11/4 The artemisias, catananches, [etc.]. **1962** *Amat. Gardening* 19 May 21 A packet of seed of catananche which gave me a lovely group of lavender-blue daisy-like flowers in August.

cat and dog, cat-and-dog.

1. Referring to the proverbial enmity between the two animals: *attrib.* Full of strife; inharmonious; quarrelsome.

1579 GOSSON *Sch. Abuse* (Arb.) 27 He.. shall see them agree like Dogges and Cattes. *a* **1745** SWIFT *Phyllis* (D.) They keep at Staines the old Blue Boar, Are cat and dog, and rogue and whore. **1821** SCOTT *Kenilw.* ii, Married he was.. and a cat-and-dog life she led with Tony. **1822** in Cobbett *Rur. Rides* (1885) I. 96 The fast-sinking Old Times newspaper, its cat-and-dog opponent the New Times. **1867** TROLLOPE *Chron. Barset* I. xliii. 384 They.. were gracious.. and abstained from all cat-and-dog absurdities.

2. *to rain cats and dogs*: to rain very heavily. Also *attrib.*, raining heavily.

[*a* **1652** R. BROME *City Wit* (1653) IV. i, It shall raine.. Dogs and Polecats.] **1738** SWIFT *Polite Conv.* II. (D.), I know Sir John will go, though he was sure it would rain cats and dogs. **1819** SHELLEY *Let. to Peacock* 25 Feb., It began raining cats and dogs. **1849** THACKERAY in *Scribner's Mag.* I. 551/1 Pouring with rain.. and the most dismal.. cat and dog day. **1949** A. WILSON *Wrong Set* 188 It always 'rained cats and dogs'.

3. A game played with a piece of wood called a cat (cf. CAT *sb.*[1] 10 a.) and a club called a dog.

1808 in JAMIESON. **1884** *Public Opinion* 5 Sept. 301/2 Cat and dog is in one sense a classical game. Bunyan tells us that he was playing at it.

Hence **cat-and-doggish** *a.*

1878 *Cornh. Mag.* XXXVIII. 648 To live under the same roof, a cat-and-doggish life.

† **ca,tanti'phrastical**, *a. Obs. rare*$^{-1}$. [f. Gr. κατ' ἀντίφρασιν by antiphrais: cf. ANTIPHRASTICAL.] = ANTIPHRASTIC.

1645 J. GOODWIN *Innocency & Tr. Triumph.* 51 It may be that this argument is figurative and cat-antiphrastical: And so, by confusions, disorders, etc. he means peace, unitie and concord amongst men.

catapan ('kætəpæn). [ad. med.L. *catapan-us, cate-, cati-*; in F. *catapan*; according to Littré, f. Gr. κατεπάνω τῶν ἀξιωμάτων (he who is) placed over the dignities.] The officer who governed Calabria and Apulia under the Byzantine emperors.

1727-51 CHAMBERS *Cycl.*, *Catapan* or *Catipan*, a name the later Greeks, about the twelfth century, gave the governor of their dominions in Italy. **1832** tr. *Sismondi's Ital. Rep.* i. 24 From time to time.. a catapan, or other magistrate, was sent. **1855** MILMAN *Lat. Chr.* (1864) III. VI. ii. 428 The Greek Argyrous the last catapan, the ally of Leo IX. had retired in despair.

† **'catapasm.** *Obs. Med.* [ad. Gr. κατάπασμα ('Paulus Ægineta vii. 13', *Syd. Soc. Lex.*), f. καταπάσσ-ειν to besprinkle, strew over.] 'A former term.. for any dry medicine in powder, which was sprinkled on ulcers' (*Syd. Soc. Lex.*).

1657 TOMLINSON *Renou's Disp.* 201 Odoriferous Powders.. strewed upon cloaths are properly called Catapasms. **1678-96** in PHILLIPS. **1818** in TODD. **1849** in SMART.

catapeltic, *a.* (*sb.*) *rare*$^{-0}$. [a. Gr. καταπελτικ-ός pertaining to a CATAPULT *sb.*] **A.** *adj.* Pertaining to a catapult. **B.** *sb.* A catapult.

1849 in SMART (*adj.*). **1864** in WEBSTER (*adj.* and *sb.*).

catapetalous (kætə'pɛtələs), *a. Bot.* [f. Gr. κατά each to each + πέταλον PETAL *sb.* + -OUS.] Having the petals 'united only by cohesion with united stamens, as in Mallow' (Gray *Bot. Text-bk.* 401).

1847 in CRAIG.

‖ **catapetasma** (kætəpɪ'tæzmə). [Gr. καταπέτασμα curtain, veil, the veil of the temple, f. καταπεταννύ-ναι to spread out over.] The curtain at the chancel-screen, veiling the altar from the congregation, in the Greek Church.

1798 W. TOOKE *Catherine II* (ed. 2) II. v. 85 On the roof, over the catapetasma and holy doors, is a representation of the supreme being.

cataphatic (kætə'fætɪk), *a. Theol.* [ad. Gr. καταφατικ-ός affirmative (καταφῆναι to assent).] Defining God positively or by positive statements, opp. APOPHATIC *a.*

1869 [see APOPHATIC *a.*]. **1937** WALL & ADAMSON tr. *Maritain's Degrees Knowl.* iv. 291 It is clear.. that *apophatic* theology, which knows God by the mode of negation or ignorance, knows him better than *cataphatic* theology, which proceeds by that of affirmation and science. **1951** *Theology* LIV. 29 In an end age he [*sc.* Berdyaev] turned.. from a cataphatic to an apophatic theology.

Hence **cata'phatically** *adv.*

1937 WALL & ADAMSON tr. *Maritain's Degrees Knowl.* iv. 297 Theological faith.. must first advance cataphatically, making known the mysteries of the Godhead to us in communicable enunciations.

cata'phonic, *a.* [f. Gr. κατά + φωνή voice, sound + -IC. Cf. CATACOUSTICS.] Pertaining to cataphonics.

In mod. Dicts.

cataphonics (kætə'fɒnɪks), *sb. pl.* The science of reflected sounds; = CATACOUSTICS.

1683 *Phil. Trans.* XIV. 473 Unless we call them Cataphonicks. **1819** REES *Cycl.*, *Cataphonics*, in Music, synonymous with catacaustics.

† **'cataphor.** *Obs.* [medical L. *cataphora*, coma, a. Gr. καταφορ-ά, a bringing down, a lethargic attack.] 'A deep or dead sleep' (Blount 1656).

cataphoresis (,kætəfə'riːsɪs). Also **kata-**. [f. Gr. κατά down + φόρησις being carried.] **a.** *Med.* The action of causing medicinal substances to pass through the skin into living tissue by the use of an electric current. **b.** = ELECTROPHORESIS. Hence **,catapho'retic** *a.*

1889 *N.Y. Med. Jrnl.* 27 Apr. 449/1 (*heading*) Electric cataphoresis as a therapeutic measure. *Ibid.*, The cataphoretic action of electricity has often been made use of experimentally to introduce drugs into the system through the skin. **1895** *Buck's Handbk. Med. Sci.* Suppl. 267/1 The use of iodine by cataphoresis has been attempted in cases of goître. **1908** *Times* 9 Oct. 10/1 The possibility of using cataphoresis as a means of conveying foods and drugs to the system. **1944** *Electronic Engin.* XVI. 341 When a solid particle becomes suspended in a liquid medium of higher dielectric constant it becomes, in general, negatively charged relative to the dispersion medium and will therefore be attracted to the anode of an electrode system placed in the solution. This phenomenon is known as cataphoresis. *Ibid.*, It is logical to regard electrolytic conduction as the limiting case of cataphoretic conduction. **1944** S. FIELD *Princ. Electrodeposition* xx. 279 Since colloidal suspensions are electrically charged they migrate to one electrode or the other under the influence of an applied P.D. This motion is known as cataphoresis or electrophoresis. **1949** *Electronic Engin.* XXI. 405 One application of these aspect ratio resistors is to coat a sheet of insulating material by a capillary process, by spraying or by cataphoresis with a uniform resistance film of constant value of ohms per square. **1954** *Ibid.* XXVI. 404 It has been found that the cataphoretic coating process has some advantages.

cataphoric (kætə'fɒrɪk), *a.* Also 9 **kataphoric.** [ad. Gr. καταφορικ-ός, f. καταφορά a bringing down, f. κατά down + φέρειν to carry.] **1.** Of the action of an electric current: Carrying a fluid along with it, producing electric osmose.

1887 in *Syd. Soc. Lex.* **1890** M. A. STARR in *Electricity in Daily Life* (1891) 271 The second action of a continuous galvanic current is to move along with it the fluids which lie in its path. This is called its cataphoric action. **1891** M. A. STARR in *Electr. Daily Life* 271 The second action of a continuous galvanic current is to move along with it the fluids which lie in its path. This is called its cataphoric action. **1895** *Buck's Handbk. Med. Sci.* Suppl. 267/1 The cataphoric transfer of molecules of protoplasm and fluid from one cell to another. **1903** *Med. Record* 7 Mar. 363/1 The cataphoric electrode.. is connected with the positive pole of the battery.

2. *Gram.* Of, pertaining to, or designating reference to a succeeding word or group of words; contrasted with ANAPHORIC *a.*

1976 HALLIDAY & HASAN *Cohesion in English* i. 17 So far we have considered cohesion purely as an anaphoric relation... But the presupposition may go in the opposite direction, with the presupposed element following. This we shall refer to as cataphora... The presupposed element may.. consist of more than one sentence. Where it does not, the cataphoric reference is often signalled in writing with a colon. **1983** BROWN & YULE *Discourse Analysis* vi. 192 Endophoric relations are of two kinds: those which look back in the text for their interpretation, which Halliday & Hasan call anaphoric relations, and those which look forward in the text for their interpretation, which are called cataphoric relations. **1985** R. QUIRK et al. *Comprehensive Gram. Eng.* 185 When the adverbial follows the past tense, this may be called the cataphoric use of the definite past..:We *went* to the theatre.

cataphract ('kætəfrækt). [In sense 1, ad. L. *cataphractes*, a. Gr. καταφράκτης coat of mail; in 2, ad. L. *cataphractus*, Gr. κατάφρακτος clad in full armour; f. καταφράσσειν to clothe in mail.]

† **1.** An ancient coat of mail. *Obs.*

1581 SAVILE *Tacitus Hist.* I. lxxix. (1591) 44 *Cataphracts*, a kind of harnish.. composed of iron plates or stiffe bend-lether. **1855** tr. *Labarte's Arts Mid. Ages* iv. 117 The ancient cataphract, the military habit of the patricians.

fig. **1627** FELTHAM *Resolves* II. viii, Virtue is a Cataphract: for in vain we arm one Limb, while the other is without a defence.

b. *Zool.* 'The armor of plate covering some fishes.' Webster cites Dana.

2. A soldier in full armour.

1671 MILTON *Samson* 1619 Before him and behind, Archers and slingers, cataphracts and spears. **1814** H. BUSK *Fugit. Pieces* 173 Around, in panoply complete, Grim cataphracts await.

¶ Catachrestically for CATARACT.

1581 SIDNEY *Apol. Poetrie* (Arb.) 72 Borne so neere the dull making Cataphract of Nilus, that you cannot heare the Plannet-like Murick of Poetrie. **1603** SIR C. HEYDON *Jud. Astrol.* To Rdr. 7 As he were borne neere the dull making cataphract of Nilus.

Hence **'cataphracted** *a.*, *Zool.* covered with a scaly or horny armour; **cata'phractic** *a.*, 'pertaining to or resembling a cataphract' (Webster); covered with or as with armour.

1881 *Syd. Soc. Lex.*, *Cataphracted*, covered with a horny skin, as with a scaly cuirass. **1890** MEREDITH *One of our Conq.* (1891) I. v. 67 Not even the flower.. would hold constant, as they, to the constantly unseen—a trebly cataphractic Invisible.

† **'cataphragm.** *Obs. rare.* [ad. Gr. type *κατάφραγμα, f. as CATAPHRACT] Defensive covering or coating.

1656 J. SERJEANT tr. *White's Peripatet. Inst.* 380 The left side.. necessarily participates more of the Vegetative Vertue then any other member of the exteriour Cataphragm.

Cataphrygian (kætə'frɪdʒ(ɪ)ən), *a.* and *sb. Ch. Hist.* One of a heretical sect in the 2nd century who followed the errors of Montanus; a Montanist; so called because they originated in Phrygia.

1585-7 ROGERS *39 Art.* 65 The.. Cataphrygians.. who held how Christ not in body but in soul ascended into heaven. **1750** LARDNER *Wks.* (1838) III. 90.

cataphyllary (kætə'fɪlərɪ), *a. Bot.* [f. Gr. κατά down, degraded + φύλλον leaf + -ARY.] *cataphyllary leaves*: the colourless or brownish scales found on various parts of plants, esp. underground, regarded as modifications of foliage-leaves.

1875 BENNETT & DYER *Sachs' Bot.* I. iii. 193 Scale- or 'Cataphyllary-Leaves' are usually produced on underground shoots.. although they also frequently occur above ground, especially as an envelope to the winter-buds of woody plants (as the horse-chestnut, oak, etc.).

† **cata'physic**, *a. Obs.* [f. Gr. κατά down, against, etc. + φύσις nature + -IC.] Contrary to

nature. So **cataphysics** *sb. pl.* (*nonce-wd.*); see quot.

1654 JER. TAYLOR *Real Pres.* A ij, The wildnesse..of their Cataphysicks (for Metaphysicks it is not) their affirmatives and negatives are neither natural, nor above, nor besides nature, but against it. 1656 BLOUNT *Glossogr.*, *Cataphysick*, against nature.

cata'physical, *a. nonce-wd.* [f. as prec. + -AL¹.] Against nature, unnatural; infra-natural.

1839 DE QUINCEY *Autobiog. Sk.* Wks. I. 337 (D.) A visual object, falling under hyper-physical or cata-physical laws. *Ibid.* II. v. 251 Some artists..have given to Sir Walter Scott a pile of forehead which is unpleasing and cataphysical, in fact a caricature of anything..seen in nature.

cataplasm ('kætəplæz(ə)m). *Med.* [a. F. *cataplasme*, ad. L. *cataplasma*, a Gr. κατάπλασμα poultice, f. κατα-πλάσσειν to plaster over, apply a plaster.] A poultice: formerly also a plaster.

1563 T. GALE *Antidot.* I. i. 2 Cataplasmes made with the iuse of these herbes, and with floure. 1602 SHAKS. *Ham.* IV. vii. 144. 1612 WOODALL *Surg. Mate* Wks. (1653) 90 A Cataplasme made of bread crums, milk, and a little Saffron. 1626 COCKERAM *Cataplasme*, a plaister, compounded of certaine oyntments to cure sores. c1720 GIBSON *Farriers Disp.* xiii. (1734) 261 Some make a distinction between Poultise and Cataplasm. 1866 S. THOMSON *Dict. Dom. Med.* 356 The well known mustard plaster or cataplasm.

b. *fig.*

1622 FLETCHER *Spanish Cur.* IV. v, This Cataplasm of a well-cozened Lawyer. 1796 BURKE *Regic. Peace* Wks. VIII. 135 The emollient cataplasms of robbery and confiscation. 1831 GEN. P. THOMPSON *Exerc.* (1842) I. 462 Endeavour has been made to provide a cataplasm.

cata'plasmic, *a.* [f. prec. + -IC.] Of the nature of a cataplasm. So **cata'plasmical** *a.*

1630 J. TAYLOR (Water P.) *Wks.* II. 259/2 A Cataplasmicall Satyre..very profitable to cure the impostumes of vice. 1689 MOYLE *Sea Chyrurg.* II. xxviii. 84 To make it into a Cataplasmick consistence.

cata'plectic, *a.* [mod. ad. Gr. καταπληκτικ-ός fitted to strike or be stricken down: see CATAPLEXY.] Of or pertaining to cataplexy.

1883 ROMANES *Ment. Evol. Anim.* xviii. 309 Such an animal as a wood-louse or death-watch, which fall into a kataplectic state immediately on being alarmed.

catapleiite (kætə'pliːaɪt). *Min.* [Named 1850, f. Gr. κατά together with + πλεῖον more + -ITE, because it occurs along with several other minerals.] A hydrous silicate of zirconium and sodium; a hexagonal opaque mineral of light yellowish-brown colour.

1854 DANA *Min.* (1868) 401.

cataplexy ('kætəplɛksɪ). [In Ger. *kataplexie*, mod. f. Gr. κατάπληξις (Hippocrates) stupefaction, f. καταπλήσσ-ειν to strike down with terror or the like.] The temporary paralysis or hypnotic state in animals when ' shamming death'.

1883 ROMANES *Ment. Evol. Anim.* xviii. 308 The researches of Professor Preyer on the hypnotism of animals ..showed that fright is a strong predisposing cause of 'Kataplexy', or mesmeric sleep in animals..He ascribes the shamming dead of insects to the exclusive influence of kataplexy.

†**cata'podially.** *Obs. nonce-wd.* [? f. Gr. κατὰ πόδα(ς close behind, immediately after.]

c1600 *Timon* IV. iii. (1842) 66 The moone may bee taken 4 manner of waies; either specificatiuely, or quidditatiuely, or superficially, or catapodially.

†**cata'presbyter.** *Obs. nonce-wd.* [f. Gr. κατά against + PRESBYTER.] A presbyter catachrestically so called; or an opposition-presbyter.

1659 GAUDEN *Tears of Ch.* 429 (D.) Various factions.. have each their Anti-Ministers, their Cata-Presbyters, or counter-preachers bandying one against the other.

†**catapuce.** *Obs. Herb.* [a. F. *catapuce*; in It. *catapuzza*, med.L. *cataputia*: cf. L. *catapotium*, Gr. καταπότιον that which can be gulped down, pill, bolus (whence It. *catapotio*, Florio).] Lesser Spurge *Euphorbia Lathyris*.

c1386 CHAUCER *Nonne Pr. T.* 145 Of catapus or of gaytre beriis. [1791 HUDDESFORD *Salmag.* (1793) 140 Without purge or catapotium. 1794 MARTYN *Rousseau's Bot.* xx. 284 Called Broad leaved Spurge or Cataputia.]

catapult ('kætəpʌlt), *sb.* Forms: 6 catapelt, -pulte, 6- catapulta (only in sense 1), 7- catapult. [a. F. *catapulte* or L. *catapulta*, a. Gr. καταπέλτης catapult, prob. f. κατά against + πάλλειν to hurl, cast, poise (a missile).]

1. An ancient military engine for discharging darts, stones, or other missiles; the motive power being obtained by a strong lever working on an axis, which was tightly strained with twisted ropes and suddenly released.

The *ballista* and *catapulta* were originally distinct, the former being used for throwing stones, etc., and the latter for darts; but afterwards the names were used synonymously.

1577 HANMER *Anc. Eccl. Hist.* (1619) 495 The great hollow Catapelts which shoote the darts from aloft. 1599 THYNNE *Animadv.* (1875) 41 The Ramme..farr different in forme from the magonell or catapulte. 1605 CAMDEN *Rem.* (1657) 206 When a catapult was first seen at Lacedemon, Archimedes exclaimed: O Hercules, now manhood is come to an end. 1732 LEDIARD *Sethos* II. IX. 277 Catapulta's and battering rams. 1761 STERNE *Tr. Shandy* III. xxiv, May my brains be knock'd out by a..catapulta. 1795 SOUTHEY *Joan of Arc* VIII. 533 The catapults Drove there their dreadful darts. 1829 W. IRVING *Granada* (1850) 338 The mangled body of the Moor was..thrown into the City from a catapult. 1850 'BAT' *Cricket-Man.* 49 By the application of the Catapulta to peaceful purposes, the batting has been.. improved. 1878 B. SMITH *Carthage* 392 The Matrons cut off their long hair and twisted it into ropes for the catapults.

2. An instrument consisting of a forked stick with an elastic band fastened to the two prongs, used to shoot small stones, bullets, peas, etc.

1871 A. R. HOPE *Schoolboy Fr.* (1875) 227 The holes seem to have been made by a catapult. 1887 *Manch. Guard.* 7 May 9 He..shot the bird with a catapult. *Mod.* The police have orders to seize all catapults.

3. A mechanical contrivance by which aircraft are launched at a high speed; also *attrib.* So *catapult launching*, etc.

1927 *Daily Express* 12 Dec. 11/4 Béarn, new aircraft carrier, will carry forty airplanes to be launched by a compressed air catapult at forty-seven miles per hour after a run of sixty-five feet along the deck. 1928 *Times* 28 Aug. 12/6 Catapult Air Mail. 1929 *Air Ann. Brit. Empire* 56 Catapult launching which has been successfully developed and can be used from ships. 1934 *Flight* 15 Feb. 148/1 For use as a catapult ship on the South Atlantic route. 1940 E. C. SHEPHERD *Britain's Air Power* 11 The aeroplane is set on the catapult carriage while its engine is started and run up. 1941 W. S. CHURCHILL *Secret Session Speeches* (1946) 39 A number of special vessels carrying catapult Hurricane aircraft are employed on patrolling duties. 1959 *Times* 28 Apr. 11/7 Eagle..equipped to take the new generation of aircraft, made possible by the installation of steam catapults.

Hence **cata'pultic** *a.*, **catapul'tier**, one who works a catapult (cf. *fusilier*, etc.).

1831 J. WILSON in *Blackw. Mag.* XXIX. 306 Balls are showered upon them..from a hundred catapultic arms. 1859 HELPS *Friends in C.* Ser. II. I. ii. 146 Flinging the ball with catapultic force. 1860 READE *Cloister & H.* xliii. (D.) The besiegers..sent forward their sappers, pioneers, catapultiers, and crossbowmen.

'catapult, *v.* [f. prec. sb.] **a.** *trans.* To hurl as from a catapult. Also *fig.* **b.** To shoot or shoot at with a catapult. **c.** *intr.* To discharge a catapult.

1848 *Blackw. Mag.* LXIII. 499 The throne itself was catapulted into the square. 1880 *Daily Tel.* 17 Feb., Lovely creatures are catapulted into the air and fall down into a net. 1883 D. PRYDE *Highways of Lit.* ii. 30 He [a boy] catapults sparrows. 1929 C. C. MARTINDALE *Risen Sun* 202 Like a fresh breeze, thus to get the pure truth catapulted at you! 1944 BLUNDEN *Cricket Country* iv. 56 The second ball which T. catapulted down, swung out. 1959 *Times* 13 Jan. 9/6 Modern technology is catapulting some aspects of Asian life into the twentieth century.

d. To discharge by means of a catapult contrivance. Cf. prec. 3.

1912 *Sci. Amer.* 14 Dec. 512 (*heading*) Catapulting a Hydro-aeroplane from a Fighting Ship. 1928 *Daily Express* 29 Aug. 8/2 The Post Office has just announced that for a special fee it will accept British letters and postcards for the United States on the understanding that before arriving in New York they are to be catapulted from the ship by seaplane. 1928 *Scotsman* 30 Aug. 9/6 The aeroplane will be catapulted into the air on approaching the American coast. 1931 *Air Ann. Brit. Empire* 318 The machine is a tractor biplane..capable of being catapulted from the deck. 1959 *Daily Tel.* 23 Feb. 11/6 The rocket-powered North American X-15..will be catapulted from a B-36 bomber at 35-40,000 ft. and..may reach a height of 300 miles and a speed of 4,000 m.p.h.

e. *intr.* To fling oneself as though hurled by a catapult.

1928 *Daily Express* 10 Apr. 5/2 Langley catapulted into the room and drove his axe through the window. 1962 K. ORVIS *Damned & Destroyed* xx. 148, I catapulted to my feet.

Hence **'catapulting** *vbl. sb.*

1881 *Chequered Career* 5 The lead..we saved for catapulting, an amusement only indulged in by lower boys. 1938 *Jrnl. R. Aeronaut. Soc.* XLII. 864 The German catapulting ships stationed in mid-ocean and forming seaplane stations.

†**cataput.** *Obs.* [in med.L. and It. (Florio) *cataputia*.] (See quot.)

1688 R. HOLME *Armoury* II. 420/2 The Catheter of some termed a Cataput, and Cataputia; it is an Instrument long, narrow and round..it is to search a deep wound, and also.. to pour or squirt in liquid Oyntments and Salves.

cataract ('kætərækt), *sb.* Forms: 5 cataracte, (cateracte, catterak, 6 catracte, catharact, catarrhacte, 6-7 catarract(e, 7 cattaract, chateract, 8 catarect, 6- catarack), 7- cataract. [a. F. *cataracte* (in senses 1-4, 6), ad. L. *cataracta* waterfall, portcullis, floodgate, a. Gr. καταρ(ρ)άκτης down-rushing, a down rushing bird, a portcullis, waterfall, ? (in LXX) floodgate; f. καταράσσ-ειν to dash down, dash headlong, rush or fall headlong, as rain or a river, f. κατ' or κατά down + ἀράσσ- or ῥάσσ-ειν to dash. (But some think it a deriv. of καταρρηγνύ-ναι to break down.) The sense-development in Gr., L., and Fr.-Eng., is not in all respects clear.]

†**1.** *pl.* The 'flood-gates' of heaven, viewed as keeping back the rain (with reference to *Gen.* vii. 11, viii. 2, where Heb. has *'rbt* lattices, windows, LXX καταρράκται, Vulg. *cataractæ*, the former prob., the latter certainly, = flood-gates, sluices; hence also Fr. *cataractes du ciel*). This, the earliest use in Eng., is now *Obs.*

1430 LYDG. *Chron. Troy* III. xxiv, It seemed in the high heauen The Cataractes hadden be vndo. c1460 *Towneley Myst.* 32 (Mätz.) Now ar the weders cest, and cateractes knyt. 1612 BREREWOOD *Lang. & Relig.* xiii. 137 To open the Cataracts of Heaven, and pour down water continually. 1656 EARL MONM. *Adv. fr. Parnass.* 93 That he would open the Chateracts of Heaven. 1667 MILTON *P.L.* XI. 824. 1684 BURNET *Th. Earth* I. 13 The rain descended for forty days, the cataracts or floodgates of heaven being open'd.

†**b.** applied to waterspouts; also *transf.*

1555 EDEN *Decades W. Ind.* (Arb.) 386 They say..that in certeyne places of the sea, they sawe certeyne stremes of water which they caule spoutes faulynge owt of the ayer into the sea..Sum phantasie that these shulde bee the cataractes of heauen whiche were all opened at Noes fludde. 1605 SHAKS. *Lear* III. ii. 2 Blow windes, and crack your cheeks; Rage, blow You Cataracts, and Hyrricano's spout. 1634 HERBERT *Trav.* 7 A long spout of stinking raine Pyramide wise, dissolved itselfe very neere us. This hidious Cataract. 1667 MILTON *P.L.* II. 176 What if all..this Firmament Of Hell should spout her Cataracts of Fire.

2. A waterfall; properly one of considerable size, and falling headlong over a precipice; thus distinguished from a CASCADE.

[A rare sense in Gr., but common in L., where applied to the Cataracts of the Nile.]

1594 BP. KING *Jonas* (1618) 346 We see what catarrhactes and downe-falls there are by the rage of the water. 1601 HOLLAND *Pliny* I. 98 The lowest cataract or fal of water [of the Nile]. 1612 DRAYTON *Poly-olb.* vi. 88 Where Tivy falling down doth make a Cataract. 1725 DE FOE *Voy. round W.* (1840) 343 A terrible noise..as of a mighty cataract, or waterfall. 1834 MRS. SOMERVILLE *Connex. Phys. Sc.* §16 (1849) 151 The great cataracts of the Oronoco. 1839 THIRLWALL *Greece* II. 185 From the steppes of Scythia to the cataracts of the Nile.

b. *transf.* A violent downpour or rush of water.

1634 HERBERT *Trav.* 54 A violent storme of raine..caused such a sudden Deluge and Cattaract, that a Carravan of two thousand Camels perisht. 1762 FALCONER *Shipwr.* III. 290 From on high huge Cataracts descend. 1842 TENNYSON *Locksley Hall* iii, The hollow ocean-ridges roaring into cataracts. 1860 FROUDE *Hist. Eng.* VI. 1 Cataracts of water flooded the houses in the city, and turned the streets into rivers.

c. *transf.* and *fig.* (cf. *flood*).

c1630 DRUMM. OF HAWTH. *Poems* 61 And Tongues ..(Could ye amidst Worlds Cataracts them heare). 1784 COWPER *Task* IV. 73 Cataracts of declamation thunder here. 1864 CARLYLE *Fredk. Gt.* I. III. v. 164 His cataract of black beard. *Ibid.* V. XIII. iv. 44 Never came such a cataract of evil news on an Aulic Council before.

†**3.** A portcullis; also the grating of a window. *Obs.* [Prob. in Gr. earlier than sense 1; common in med.L. but rare in Eng.]

[1360-1 *MS. Vicars' Roll York*, In j cateracta facta ante hostium Will. de Preston, 6d.] 1656 BLOUNT *Glossogr.*, *Cataract*, a Portcullis. a1693 URQUHART *Rabelais* III. Prol., Others..assured the Port-culleys, fastned the Herses, Sarasinasks and Cataracts. 1853 STOCQUELER *Milit. Encycl.*, *Cataract*, a portcullis.

4. *Pathol.* An opacity of the crystalline lens of the eye, or of the capsule of the lens, or of both, 'producing more or less impairment of sight, but never complete blindness' (*Syd. Soc. Lex.*).

[App. a fig. use of the sense portcullis. In Fr., the physician A. Paré (c 1550) has 'cataracte ou coulisse'; and Cotgr. (1611) has *coulisse* 'a portcullis.. also a web in the eye', the notion being that even when the eye is open, the cataract obstructs vision, as the portcullis does a gateway. (But if originally in med.L., it might arise from the sense 'window-grating' *fenestra clathrata*, Du Cange.)]

1547 BOORDE *Brev. Health* lxvi. 28b, A Catharact, the which doth let a man to se perfytly. 1575 TURBERV. *Falconrie* 235 Ther is a Cataract, which doth light upon the eyes of a Hawke. 1599 A. M. tr. *Gabelhouer's Bk. Physicke* 54/2 For Catarracts or Pearles of the Eyes. 1611 FLORIO, *Catarátta*.. called a Cataract or a pin and web. 1782 W. HEBERDEN *Comm.* lxvi. (1806) 329 A cataract is always preceded by a dimness, or blue cloudiness of objects. 1791 BOSWELL *Johnson* (1831) I. 221 To understand that he would couch her gratis, if the cataract was ripe. 1822 GOOD *Study of Med.* (1844) III. 168 Simple cataract comes on without pain. 1876 tr. *Wagner's Gen. Pathol.* 40 Cataract is especially transmissible in the female line.

fig. 1630 BRATHWAIT *Eng. Gentlew.* (1641) 319 Those thicke Cataracts of earthly vanities are dispersed. a1711 KEN *Hymnotheo* Poet. Wks. 1721 III. 41 Your eyes thus dimly will Things Heav'nly see, Till they from sensual Cataracts are free.

†**5.** A brake for flax. *Obs. rare.*

a1693 URQUHART *Rabelais* III. l. 401 Athwart those Cataracts they break and bruise to very Trash the woody parcels.

6. *Mech.* A form of governor for single-acting steam-engines, in which the stroke is regulated by the flow of water through an opening.

1832 BABBAGE *Econ. Manuf.* iii. (ed. 3) 27 Another very beautiful contrivance for regulating the number of strokes made by a steam-engine..is called the Cataract. 1861 RANKINE *Steam Eng.* 58 A pump brake of a simple kind is exemplified in the apparatus called the cataract.

†**7.** (See quot.) *Obs.*

?a1400 *Rel. Ant.* I. 9 *Cataracta*, a catarac of the ethere, i. *via subterranea*.

8. *attrib.* and *Comb.*, as *cataract patient, curls, wig*, etc.; *cataract-like* adj.; *cataract-wise* adv.; **cataract-bird**, an Australian bird (see quot.); **cataract-knife**, **cataract-needle**, a knife and

needle used in the extraction of cataract, or in couching.

1868 WOOD *Homes without H.* xii. 215 The bird..is called ..the *Cataract Bird (*Origma rubricata*) because it is always found where water-courses rush through rocky ground [in Australia]. **1864** SALA in *Daily Tel.* 21 Nov., That beaming belle..with the *Cataract curls. **1860** TYNDALL *Glac.* I. ii. 12 An avalanche pours *cataract-like over a ledge. **1688** R. HOLME *Armoury* III. 399/2 A *Cataract-needle..is used to draw up the Cataract off the sight of the eye while it is cuting away. **1882** GOOD *Study of Med.* (1844) III. 165 A *cataract patient sees a lighted candle as if it were involved in a cloud. **1870** *Athenæum* 31 Dec. 881 Boileau Despréaux himself, in his court suit and his *cataract wig. **1879** J. HAWTHORNE *Laugh. Mill* 39 The stream fell *cataract-wise into a deep pool below.

cataract, *v.* [f. prec. sb.]

a. *trans.* To pour like a cataract, to pour copiously (*nonce-use*). **b.** *intr.* To fall in a cataract.

1796 COLERIDGE *Let.* in *Biogr. Lit.* App. (1847) II. 370 The Monthly has cataracted panegyric on me. **1832** J. WILSON in *Blackw. Mag.* XXXII. 125 No river should cataract larger than the Clyde. **1844** E. WARBURTON *Crescent & Cross* (1845) I. 285 The whole body of the Nile precipitates itself..cataracting very respectably.

cataractal (ˈkætəræktəl), *a.* [f. CATARACT + -AL[1].] Of the nature of a cataract (*lit.* and *fig.*).

1888 W. CLARK RUSSELL *Death Ship* xxxviii, A cataractal roaring of water. **1891** *Illustr. Lond. News* 17 Jan. 74/2 The sea swept..with a cataractal fury. **1926** C. L. WARR *Principal Caird* 237 The outburst of popular indignation.. was simply terrific in its power of cataractal denunciation.

ˈcataracted, *ppl. a.* [f. CATARACT *sb.* or *v.* + -ED.] Having cataracts: poured in cataracts.

1830 *Blackw. Mag.* XXVIII. 146 With rivers cataracted among the mountains. **1832** WILSON *ibid.* XXXI. 866 They look down into the cataracted abysses.

†**cataˈractic**, *a. Obs.* [f. CATARACT + -IC.] Of the nature of a cataract (see senses 2 and 5 of the sb.). So **cataˈractical** *a.*

1693 J. BEAUMONT *On Burnet's Th. Earth.* I. 56 Cataractical Falls, and Serpentine Courses of Rivers. *a* **1693** URQUHART *Rabelais* III. I. 401 Certain Catarractick Instruments.

cataˈractine, *a.* [f. as prec. + -INE.] = prec.

1856 KANE *Arct. Expl.* I. 335 These cataractine glaciers.

†**cataractist.** *Obs.* [f. as prec. + -IST.] A surgeon or practitioner who treats cataracts.

1660 tr. *Paracelsus Archid.* II. 140 According to the prescription of the Catarractists, or blind Doctors.

cataractous (kætəˈræktəs), *a. Pathol.* [f. CATARACT + -OUS.] Affected with cataract.

1824 TRAVERS *Dis. Eye* (ed. 3) 319 The cataractous eye is not unfrequently amaurotic. **1875** H. WALTON *Dis. Eye* 743 In ordinary cataractous capsular opacity.

catarie, var. of CATERY.

catarrh (kəˈtɑː(r)), *sb.* Forms: 6 cattar, cattarue, catarh, catterhe, *Sc.* caterr, catter, 6–7 catar, catarre, catarrhe, 7 catarr, cathar, catharre, cather, 7– catarrh. [a. F. *catarrhe*, in 15th c. *caterre*, 16th c. *catarre* (= Pr. *catar*, Sp., It. *catarro*), ad. L. *catarrh-us*, ad. Gr. καταρρους running down, rheum, f. καταρρεῖν to flow down.]

†**1.** The profuse discharge from nose and eyes which generally accompanies a cold, and which was formerly supposed to run down from the brain; a 'running at the nose'. *Obs.*

[**1398** TREVISA *Barth. De. P.R.* VII. iv. (1495) 224 Dissoluynge and shedynge thumours of the heed highte Catarrus.] **1533** ELYOT *Cast. Helth* (1541) 23 b, Egges be good ageinst Catars, or stilling out of the hed into the stomake. *Ibid.* 69 b, Catarres or reumes. **1536** BELLENDEN *Cron.* 46 a (Jam.) In the nixt winter Julius Frontynus fell in gret infirmite be imoderat flux of catter. **1586** T. B. *La Primaud. Fr. Acad.* II. (1594) 364 Sodainely choked by catarrhes, which like to floods of waters, runne downewards. **1607** TOPSELL *Four-f. Beasts* 272 The catar or rhume, which, in a horse, is called the glaunders. **1656** in BLOUNT *Glossogr.* **1794–6** E. DARWIN *Zoon.* (1801) I. 425 When the secretion of these capillary glands is increased, it is termed simple catarrh.

†**2.** Formerly also applied to: Cerebral effusion or hæmorrhage; apoplexy. *Obs.*

1552 LYNDESAY *Monarche* 5117 Sum ar dissoluit suddantlye Be Cattarue or be Poplesye. **1579** FENTON *Guicciard*, III. (1599) 142 King Charles dyed..of a catterhe which the Phisitians call apoplexie. **1708** KERSEY, Catarrh of the Spinal Marrow, a Falling-out of the Marrow of the Back-bone. **1721–1800** in BAILEY.

3. Inflammation of a mucous membrane; usually restricted to that of the nose, throat, and bronchial tubes, causing increased flow of mucus, and often attended with sneezing, cough, and fever; constituting a common 'cold'.

Often with qualifying word, as ***alcoholic, bronchial, chronic, gastric, uterine catarrh***; ***epidemic catarrh***, influenza; ***summer catarrh***, hay-asthma.

1588 R. PARKE tr. *Mendoza's Hist. China* 132 A generall sicknesse..called the Cattarre or murre. **1675** GASCOIGNE in Rigaud *Corr. Sc. Men* (1841) I. 221 The great epidemical catarrh, which hath ranged through so many countries. **1771** SMOLLETT *Humphr. Cl.* (1815) 107 Rheumatisms, catarrhs, and consumptions, are caught in these nocturnal pastimes. **1782** E. GRAY in *Med. Commun.* I. 47 At Venice ..the common name of the disease, Russian catarrh [influenza]. **1797** M. BAILLIE *Morb. Anat.* (1807) 117 The Symptoms which attend catarrh are too generally known to require being mentioned. **1818** MOORE *Fudge Fam. Paris* vi. 171 Your cold, of course, is a *catarrh*. **1831** YOUATT *Horse* xii. (1847) 258 Various names..influenza, distemper, catarrhal fever, and epidemic catarrh. **1868** DICKENS *Lett.* (1880) II. 338 So oppressed am I with this American catarrh, as they call it.

catarrh, *v. nonce-wd.* [f. prec.] To remove or take by catarrh.

1822 LAMB in *Life & Lett.* xii. (1837) 111 As many clerks have been coughed and catarrhed out of it [the War-Office] into their freer graves.

catarrhacte, obs. form of CATARACT.

†**catarrhaˈgogal**, *a. Obs. rare.* [Implies a sb. *catarrhagogue*, f. CATARRH *sb.* + -αγωγος leading.] Carrying off catarrh.

1651 BIGGS *New Disp.* ¶240 A catarragogall Remedy.

catarrhal (kəˈtɑːrəl), *a.* [f. CATARRH *sb.* + -AL[1]: in mod.F. *catarrhal.*] Of the nature of, or pertaining to, catarrh.

1651 BIGGS *New Disp.* ¶258 Catarrhall defects. **1787** *Gentl. Mag.* Nov. 1020/2 Catarrhal fevers have now become more frequent. **1824** J. McCULLOCH *Highl. Scotl.* III. 193 The catarrhal phenomenon of St. Kilda. **1848** KINGSLEY in *Fraser's Mag.* 104 A soulless, skyless, catarrhal day. **1870** ROLLESTON *Anim. Life* Introd. 17 *note*, A spasmodic and catarrhal affection, not unlike hay fever.

catarrhine, catarhine (ˈkætəraɪn), *a.*, and *sb. Zool.* [f. Gr. κατά alongside of + ῥίς, ῥῖν-α nose, nostril.]

A. *adj.* Designating one of the two divisions of the order *Quadrumana*, including those apes or monkeys, which have the nostrils close together, oblique, and directed downwards, and opposable thumbs on all the limbs. It includes all the apes of the old world. **B.** as *sb.* A catarrhine monkey.

1862 DANA *Man. Geol.* 422 *note*, The Catarrhines, confined to Africa and Asia, excepting one at Gibraltar. **1863** HUXLEY *Man's Place Nat.* i. 23 The man-like apes.. are what are called 'Catarrhine apes'; that is, their nostrils have a narrow partition, and look downwards. **1881** *Spectator* 25 Dec., Our common ancestor the catarrhine ape.

†**caˈtarrhish**, *a. Obs.* [f. CATARRH *sb.* + -ISH[1].] Of the nature of catarrh.

1689 MOYLE *Sea Chyrurg.* III. x. 114 To purge the Brain, and all the Body of that Catarrish humour.

†**caˈtarrhopous**, *a. Obs.* [f. Gr. κατάρροπ-ος (f. κατά down + ῥοπή downward inclination) + -OUS.] Tending or moving downwards.

1666 G. HARVEY *Morb. Angl.* x. 92 Why the same corrosive humour should sometimes prove Anarrhopous.. and otherwhiles Catarrhopous (flowing downwards).

caˈtarrhous, *a.* ? *Obs.* [f. CATARRH + -OUS: app. after 16th c. F. *catarreux, catarrheux.*] Pertaining to, subject to, or of the nature of, catarrh; = CATARRHAL.

1651 BIGGS *New Disp.* ¶250 To excrete the catarrhous matter. **1782** JOHNSON in *Boswell* (1831) V. 29, I am now harassed by a catarrhous cough. **1819** REES *Cycl.* s.v., Cure for a catarrhous cough..the inhalation of the vapour of warm water.

†**cataˈrumpant**, (?)**-rampant**, *a. nonce-wd.* (humorous): cf. Gr. κατά, *cat* and *rampant.*

1689 T. PLUNKET *Char. Gd. Commander* 49, I hope.. Their Cat-like Cause, that lusty Puss is nigh To hanging; notwithstanding that she is So Catarumpant now.

catasetum (kætəˈsiːtəm). *Bot.* [mod.L. (L. C. Richard 1822, in K. S. Kunth *Synopsis Plantarum* I. 330) f. Gr. κατά down + L. *seta* bristle.] A plant of the genus *Catasetum*, a genus of epiphytic orchids native to tropical America, in which the rostellum of the male flower is developed into two slender horns or bristles.

1829 LOUDON *Encycl. Plants* I. xx. 756. **1843** *Florist's Jrnl.* IV. 184 A beautiful dwarf orchideous plant, resembling a catasetum in habit. **1914** *Chambers's Jrnl.* Oct. 631/1 Catasetums have established themselves, some with huge pseudo-bulbs. **1956** *Dict. Gardening* (*R. Hort. Soc.*) (ed. 2) I. 412/2 When growing, all Catasetums benefit by a tropical atmosphere. **1962** *Amat. Gardening* 7 Apr. 6/3 In most of the catasetums and mormodes the male and female flowers are carried on separate spikes or separate plants.

†**catаskeuˈastic**, *a. Obs. rare*[−1]. [ad. Gr. κατασκευαστικός constructive (in Aristotle *Rhet.* 2. 26, 3, opposed to λυτικός destructive), f. κατασκευάζειν to equip, prepare, construct, f. κατασκευή preparation.] Constructive.

1645 J. G[OODWIN] *Innoc. & Truth Tri.* 41 No occasion to argue any thing..in a cataskeuastique or positive Way.

†**catasophistry.** *Obs. rare*[−1]. [f. SOPHISTRY, after Gr. κατασοφίζεσθαι to outwit, to evade by quibbling, f. κατά down, etc. + σοφίζ-εσθαι to quibble, etc.] Quibbling, deceit.

1609 J. MELVILL *Let.* in *Diary* (1842) 782 Greater craft.. and catasophistrie wer nevir usit.

cataspilite (kəˈtæspɪlaɪt). *Min.* [Named in 1867 f. Gr. κατάσπιλος spotted, defiled + -ITE.] A hydrous silicate of alumina, with some iron, manganese, etc.; an ash-grey pearly mineral found in Sweden.

1868 DANA *Min.* 403.

‖**catasta.** [a. L. *catasta* scaffold, stage for selling slaves, etc., also an engine of torture. According to Lewis and Short, f. Gr. κατάστασις settling, putting down, fixed state, etc. (? Thence It. *catasta* funeral-pile, Pg. *catasta* stall in which slaves are set for sale).]

a. *Hist.* A block on which slaves were exposed for sale. **b.** *Hist.* A stage or bed of torture used in early Christian times. †**c.** Humorously or affectedly used for the stocks (*obs.*).

1650 A. B. *Mutat. Polemo* 12 What will not money do with a Scot (now their Catasta is in readiness). **1664** BUTLER *Hud.* II. I. 238 In close Catasta shut [*ed.* **1694** 401 *note*, Catasta is but a pair of Stocks in English]. **1685** J. SCOTT *Chr. Life* (1747) III. 91 How could they have sung in the midst of Flames, smiled upon Racks, triumphed upon Wheels and Catastaes. **1853** KINGSLEY *Hypatia* xiii. (Hoppe) Standing an hour on the catasta to be handled from head to foot in the minimum of clothing.

catastaltic, *a. Med.* [ad. L. *catastaltic-us*, a. Gr. κατασταλτικός, f. καταστέλλειν to repress, check.] Restraining, checking: formerly applied to astringent and styptic substances.

1851 in MAYNE.

‖**catastasis** (kəˈtæstəsɪs). [Gr. κατάστασις settling, appointment; settled condition; f. καθιστάναι to set down, appoint, establish, settle; f. κατά down + στα- stand. In mod.F. *catastase.*]

1. (See quots.) [This sense not in Gr. or L.]

1656 BLOUNT *Glossogr.*, *Catastasis*, the third part of a Comedy, and signifies the state and full vigour of it. Tragedies and Comedies have four principal parts in respect of the matter treated of. 1. *Protasis.* 2. *Epitasis.* 3. *Catastasis.* 4. *Catastrophe.* **1668** DRYDEN *Dram. Poesy* in Arb. *Garner* III. 520 Thirdly. The Catastasis or Counter-turn, which destroys that expectation. **1751** CHAMBERS *Cycl.*, *Catastasis*..the third part of the antient drama; being that wherein the intrigue is supported, carried on, and heightened till it be ripe for the unravelling in the catastrophe. **1761** STERNE *Trist. Shandy* IV. *Slawkenb. Tale*, The epitasis, wherein the action is more fully entered upon and heightened, till it arrives at its state or height, called the catastasis. **1837** CARLYLE *Fr. Rev.* (1872) II. VI. i. 223 No catastrophe, rather a catastasis or heightening.

2. *Rhet.* The narrative part of a speech, usually the beginning of it, in which the orator sets forth the subject to be discussed. (In mod. Dicts.)

3. *Med.* 'The state or condition of anything; constitution; habit of body'. (In mod. Dicts.)

†**catastematic**, *a. Obs. rare*[−1]. [ad. Gr. καταστηματικός established, sedate, moderate, tranquil (in ἡδονὴ καταστηματική moderate pleasure, a term of the Epicurean philosophy), f. κατάστημα settlement, constitution, f. καθιστάναι; see prec.]

1655–60 STANLEY *Hist. Philos.* (1701) 134/2 Catastematick, permanent pleasure, which consisteth in privation of Grief and a quiet void of all disturbance, which Epicurus held [to be our ultimate end].

cataster. [ad. It. Sp., *catastro.*] = CADASTRE.

1855 MILMAN *Lat. Christianity* IX. XIV. i. 18 The valuation of Pope Nicholas, the established cataster which had been acted on for above a century.

catasterism (kəˈtæstərɪz(ə)m). [ad. Gr. καταστερισμός a 'placing among the stars; Καταστερισμοί was the name of a treatise attributed to Eratosthenes giving the legends of the different constellations' (Liddell and Scott); (ult.) f. κατά + ἀστήρ star. Cf. ASTERISM.]

a. *pl.* The treatise mentioned above. **b.** A constellation.

1803 G. S. FABER *Cabiri* II. 251 The remarkable assemblage of catasterisms..in the neighbourhood of the supposed ship of Jason. **1837** WHEWELL *Hist. Induct. Sc.* I. iv. §1 (L.) The 'Catasterisms' of Eratosthenes..were an enumeration of 475 of the principal stars according to the constellations in which they are. **1852** TH. ROSS *Humboldt's Trav.* Introd. 17 The catasterisms of their zodiac.

catastrophal (kəˈtæstrəfəl), *a.* [f. CATASTROPHE + -AL[1].] Of the nature of a catastrophe; disastrous.

1842 P. SCROPE *Volcanos* 6 The great catastrophal earthquake of Riobamba. **1882** *Daily News* 6 Feb., Mr. Proctor, after his catastrophal forebodings.

catastrophe (kəˈtæstrəfɪ). Also 7 catastrophy. [a. Gr. καταστροφή overturning, sudden turn, conclusion, f. κατα-στρέφειν to overturn, etc., f. κατά down + στρέφειν to turn.]

1. 'The change or revolution which produces the conclusion or final event of a dramatic piece' (J.); the dénouement.

1579 E. K. in *Spenser's Sheph. Cal.* May, Gloss., This tale is much like to that in Aesops fables, but the catastrophe and ende is farre different. **1584** R. SCOT *Discov. Witchcr.* III. x.

44 *marg.*, A comicall catastrophe. **1602** *2nd Pt. Return fr. Parnass.* II. i. (Arb.) 21 Sad is the plot, sad the Catastrophe. **1616** R. C. *Times' Whis.* (1871) 111 Thou shalt be the protasis and catastrophe of my epistle. **1684** T. BURNET *Th. Earth* II. 157 That happy catastrophe and last scene which is to crown the work. **1714** GAY *What d'ye call it* Pref., They deny it to be Tragical, because its Catastrophe is a Wedding. *a* **1876** J. H. NEWMAN *Hist. Sk.* I. I. iii. 158 Such was the catastrophe of this long and anxious drama.

2. 'A final event; a conclusion generally unhappy' (J.); a disastrous end, finish-up, conclusion, upshot; overthrow, ruin, calamitous fate.

1601 SHAKS. *All's Well* I. ii. 57 On the Catastrophe and heele of pastime When it was out. **1609** ARMIN *Ital. Taylor* (1880) 194 Thinking to deuower And worke my liues Catastrophy. **1628** MEAD in Ellis *Orig. Lett.* I. 343 III. 265 This was the obscure catastrophe of that great man. **1672** MARVELL *Reh. Transp.* I. 251 The late war, and its horrid catastrophe. **1678** LITTLETON *Lat. Dict.*, A *Catastrophe* or upshot of a business, *catastrophe exitus.* **1728** MORGAN *Algiers* II. iii. 256 This catastrophe had the brave Barbarossa and all his vast Designs. **1783** LD. HAILES *Antiq. Chr. Ch.* iv. 128 The catastrophe of that siege is well known. **1850** W. IRVING *Mahomet* II. 290 This miserable catastrophe to a miserable career.

†**b.** *humorously.* The posteriors. *Obs.*

1597 SHAKS. *2 Hen. IV*, II. i. 66 Away you Scullion.. Ile tickle your catastrophe.

3. An event producing a subversion of the order or system of things.

1696 *Month. Mercury* VII. 91 The Consternation and Confusion.. upon such a sudden Catastrophy. **1717** DE FOE *Hist. Ch. Scot.* (1844) 5 Her many Revolutions, Convulsions, and Catastrophes. **1871** FARRAR *Witn. Hist.* iii. 92 God reveals His will not by sudden catastrophes and violent revolutions.

b. *esp.* in *Geol.* A sudden and violent change in the physical order of things, such as a sudden upheaval, depression, or convulsion affecting the earth's surface, and the living beings upon it, by which some have supposed that the successive geological periods were suddenly brought to an end. (Cf. CATACLYSM, CATASTROPHISM.)

1832 LYELL *Princ. Geol.* I. 89, II. 160. **1858** WHEWELL *Novum Org. Renov.* 25 (L.) There are, in the palætiological sciences, two antagonist doctrines: catastrophes and uniformity. **1887** *Spectator* 7 May 626/1 No geologist of repute now believes that mountain-ranges originated in catastrophes.

4. A sudden disaster, wide-spread, very fatal, or signal. (In the application of exaggerated language to misfortunes it is used very loosely.)

1748 ANSON *Voy.* III. ii. (ed. 4) 429 Thus were we all.. reduced to the utmost despair by this catastrophe. **1795** BURKE *Corr.* (1844) IV. 289 The public catastrophe was actually completed by the actual recall of Lord F. **1855** MOTLEY *Dutch Rep.* (1861) II. 270 An inundation, more tremendous than any.. recorded in those annals so prolific in such catastrophes. **1856** KANE *Arct. Expl.* II. xiii. 131 This fishery is fearfully hazardous; scarcely a year passes without a catastrophe. *Mod.* Our hostess was immensely relieved that dinner had gone off without any catastrophe. My luggage has not arrived: what a catastrophe!

catastrophic (kætə'strɒfɪk), *a.* [ad. Gr. καταστροφικ-ός, f. καταστροφή CATASTROPHE.] Of the nature of, or belonging to, a catastrophe: *esp.* in the history of the earth or the universe.

1837 WHEWELL *Hist. Induct. Sc.* (1857) III. 512 The supposed proofs of catastrophic transition. **1849** MURCHISON *Siluria* xx. 491 A catastrophic destruction of such animals. **1871** E. H. PLUMPTRE *Spirits in Pris.* (1884) 348 Events which are not continuous, but catastrophic.. such as the Resurrection and the Last Judgment.

cata'strophical, *a.* [f. as prec. + -AL[1].]

Referring to, dealing with, catastrophes; also = prec.

1826 *Blackw. Mag.* XIX. Pref. 24 Paragraphs circuitously approaching.. to a catastrophical climax. **1876** *Contemp. Rev.* XXVIII. 740 A.. disturbance of the laws and direction of matter and force,—sudden, and catastrophical.

Hence **cata'strophically** *adv.*

1872 BAGEHOT *Physics & Pol.* (1876) 155 As soon as that repression was catastrophically removed.

catastrophism (kə'tæstrəfɪz(ə)m). [f. CATASTROPHE 3 + -ISM.] The theory that certain geological and biological phenomena were caused by catastrophes, or sudden and violent disturbances of nature, rather than by continuous and uniform processes.

1869 HUXLEY in *Sci. Opinion* 21 Apr. 464/1 By Catastrophism I mean any form of geological speculation which.. supposes the operation of forces different in their nature.. from those which we at present see in action. **1883** H. DRUMMOND *Nat. Law in Spir. W.* 19 It was the Geology of Catastrophism.

fig. **1885** *Century Mag.* XXXI. 68 The Craig household.. was conducted on the theory of 'catastrophism' rather than that of 'uniform law'.

catastrophist (kə'tæstrəfɪst). *Geol.* [f. as prec. + -IST.] One who holds the theory of catastrophism; opposed to *uniformitarian.* Also *attrib.*

1837 WHEWELL *Hist. Induct. Sc.* (1857) III. 509 Geologists who had been bred up in the catastrophist creed. **1879** SPENCER *Data of Ethics* iv. §17 For a generation after geologists had become uniformitarians in Geology, they remained catastrophists in Biology. **1879** *Lit. World* 161/1 We are still catastrophists in judging of history.

†**ca'tastrophize.** *Obs.*[−0] 'To end a Comedy or the like' (Cockeram 1623).

†**catastrophonical**, *a.* (A nonsense word.)

1605 MARSTON *Dutch Court.* II. i, A signe of good shaving, my catastrophonicall fine boy.

†**catastrum.** *Obs.*[−0] [ad. Gr. κατάστρωμα deck.] 'The decke or hatch of a ship' (Cockeram).

†**Catath'leba.** *Obs. rare*[−1]. [? f. Gr. καταθλιβ- to press down.] Some fabulous monster.

c **1300** *K. Alis.* 6564 Another best ther is, of eovel kynde.. Catathleba is hire name.

catathymia (kætə'θaɪmɪə). *Psychiatry.* [mod.L., ad. G. *katathymie* (H. W. Maier 1912, in *Zeitschr. f. Neurol. & Psychiat.* XIII. 555), f. Gr. κατά according to + θυμός spirit, temper.] A condition in which the mind falls under the control of the emotions. Hence **cata'thymic** *a.*, **cata'thymically** *adv.*

1934 E. B. STRAUSS tr. *Kretschmer's Text-bk. Med. Psychol.* II. vi. 71 By *catathymia*.. we mean the transformation of the psychic content by affective influences. The primitive world-picture is much more catathymic than our own... This is sufficient to bring about the catathymically determined conviction. *Ibid.* vii. 101 In such cases of schizophrenia the type of thought is again almost entirely catathymic, even to the extent of the loss of all contact with the realities. **1949** *Brit. Jrnl. Psychol.* XL. 13 In catathymia we are dealing with changes to which the psychic content is subjected, and transformed, by affective influences.

catatonia (kætə'təʊnɪə). *Path.* Also 9 **katatonia**. [f. Gr. κατά down + -τονία, from τόνος TONE.]

A form of insanity, characterized by epilepsy and catalepsy.

1889 in *Cent. Dict.* **1917** C. R. PAYNE tr. *Pfister's Psychoanal. Method* I. vi. 132 Probably there was catatonia; her brother suffered from a severe form of this disease and was cared for in an insane asylum. **1937** 'C. CAUDWELL' *Illusion & Reality* 258 In catatonia the affects are repressed. **1956** A. HUXLEY *Heaven & Hell* App. 84 In psychological terms.. from catatonia and feelings of unreality to a sense of heightened reality in vision and, finally, in mystical experience. **1963** *New Scientist* 18 July 146 The inert state called catatonia which is characteristic of some kinds of schizophrenia.

Hence **cata'toniac**, one who is affected with catatonia.

1888 *Alien. & Neurol.* July 458 Kiernan found four head injuries among 30 katatoniacs.

catatonic (kætə'tɒnɪk), *a.* [f. as prec.: see -IC 1.] Characterized by CATATONIA. Hence as *sb.*, one affected by catatonia.

1908 *Practitioner* Jan. 12 There may be catatonic stupor, automatic obedience, and occasionally impulsive automatism. **1917** C. R. PAYNE tr. *Pfister's Psychoanal. Method* II. xix. 499 The overcoming of the resistance is impossible in catatonics of an advanced stage. **1948** *Brit. Jrnl. Psychol.* Dec. 89 Catatonic schizophrenia is characterized by negativism, catalepsy, suggestibility, stupor, excitement, mannerisms, stereotypy. **1957** P. LAFITTE *Person in Psychol.* 7 The scale or scope of activity may vary, down to the limit of the catatonic schizophrenic, whose endless wars and reconciliations are conducted in strict privacy.

catavothron: see KATABOTHRON.

catawampous (kætə'wɒmpəs), *a. slang* (chiefly *U.S.*). Also **cata'wamptious** (-ʃəs). [A humorous formation, the origin of which is lost: the first part of the word was perhaps suggested by *catamount*, or ? by words in Gr. κατα-.] Fierce, unsparing, destructive. Also, askew, awry. (A high-sounding word with no very definite meaning.)

1840 *Spirit of Times* 25 Jan. 561/2 Him is done up—used up catawampous—kicked up into eberlasting hoki! **1844** [see CHAW *v.* 3]. **1856** *Househ. Words* XIII. 148 It had fallen a victim to the jaws of deadly alligator, or catawampous panther. **1885** 'C. E. CRADDOCK' *Prophet Gt. Smoky Mts.* ix. 153 She got me plumb catawampus. **1889** —— *Broomsedge Cove* iii. 44 But it's a powerful differ ter please this man an' not git that one set catawampus. **1917** L. M. MONTGOMERY *Anne's House of Dreams* xxxvi. 308 Dear me, everything has gone catawampus with me this week.

Hence **cata'wampus** *sb.*, a bogy, a fierce imaginary animal; **cata'wampously**, **cata'wamptiously** *adv.*, 'fiercely, eagerly. To be ***catawamptiously chawed up*** is to be completely demolished, utterly defeated' (Bartlett *Dict. Amer.*).

1843 'R. CARLTON' *New Purchase* I. xxviii. 265 The tother one what got most sker'd is a sort of catawampus (spiteful). **1852** LYTTON *My Novel* in *Blackw. Mag.* LXXI. 434 To be catawampously champed up [*ed.* **1853** chawed up] by a mercenary selfish cormorant of a capitalist. **1857** F. DOUGLASS *Speech* (Bartlett) To take to our heels before three hundred thousand slaveholders, for fear of being catawampiously chawed up? **1874** M. COLLINS *Frances* I. 162 The catawampuses you see about harvest time—they fly quite pretty in the air, but, O my gracious, don't they sting! **1893** YONGE & COLERIDGE *Strolling Players* xvii. 145 Classes had better.. swallow each other, like the crocodile and the catawampus.

Catawba (kə'tɔːbə). [From the river *Catawba* in S. Carolina, U.S. (named from the *Katahba* Indians), where the grape was first discovered.

1775 ADAIR *Amer. Ind.* 223, I begin with the Katahba, because their country is the most contiguous to Charles-Town.]

a. An American species of grape (*Vitis Labrusca*), which is largely cultivated in the central States of the American Union. **b.** The light sparkling rich-flavoured wine made from this grape (first made *c.* 1830). More fully ***Catawba grape, wine.***

1857 *Rep. Commiss. Patents Washington* 433 The Catawba is the grape generally planted in vineyards for the production of wine. *c* **1857** LONGF. *Birds of Passage*, '*Catawba Wine*', For Catawba wine Has need of no sign, No tavern-bush to proclaim it. **1864** BROWNING *Sludge*, It was your own wine, sir, the good Champagne (I took it for Catawba, you're so kind). **1867** *Atlantic Monthly* Aug. 241 Five thousand gallons of the still unvexed Catawba.

catayl(e, catayll(e, obs. ff. CATTLE.

†**cata'zaner.** *Obs. rare*[−1].

1632 SHIRLEY *Ball* v. I O the Catazaners, we turned there!

†**cat-band.** *Sc. Obs.* 'A bar or iron for securing a door; a chain drawn across a street for defence' (Jam.). The exact sense is doubtful.

1650 ROW *Hist. Kirk* (1842) 507 Also the toun.. made catbands of yron to hold off horses, brought the canons.. within the toune, &c. *a* **1670** SPALDING *Troub. Chas. I* (1829) 80 To make preparations for defence.. to big up their own back gates, closes, and ports, have their catbands in readiness. **1671** *Acts of Sederunt* 11 Feb. (Jam.) In case they have not sufficient catbands upon the doors of their prisons.

catbird ('kætbɜːd). [See quot. 1885.] **1. a.** An American thrush (*Mimus Carolinensis*).

1731 MORTIMER in *Phil. Trans.* XXXVII. 175 *Muscicapa vertice nigro.* The Cat-Bird. **1858** O. W. HOLMES *Aut. Breakf.-t.* 230, I hear the whispering voice of Spring, The thrush's trill, the cat-bird's cry. *a* **1879** LOWELL *Poet. Wks.* (1879) 38 The cat-bird croons in the lilac-bush. **1885** *Pall Mall G.* 21 May 4/2 The 'cat-bird'.. derives its name from its ordinary cry of alarm, which somewhat resembles the mew of a cat.

b. The name given to several species of Australian birds whose cry resembles the mewing of a cat.

1848 J. GOULD *Birds Australia* IV. pl. 11 Ptilonorhynchus Smithii... Cat Bird. *Ibid.*, Situations suitable to the Regent and Satin Birds are equally adapted to the habits of the Cat Bird. **1887** D. MACDONALD *Gum Boughs* 36 One of the most peculiar of birds' eggs found about the Murray is that of the locally-termed 'cat-bird', the shell of which is veined thickly with dark thin threads as though covered with a spider's web. **1889** R. B. ANDERSON tr. *Lumholtz's Among Cannibals* vii. 96 The cat-bird (*Ælurædus maculosus*), which makes its appearance towards evening, and has a voice strikingly like the mewing of a cat. **1957** *Encycl. Brit.* V. 24/2 *Catbird*... In Australia, a name given to any of several bowerbirds, especially to *Ailuroedus crassirostris*, which builds no bower.

2. Phr. ***the catbird seat***: a superior or advantageous position. *U.S. slang.*

1942 J. THURBER in *55 Short Stories from New Yorker* (1949) 61 'Sitting in the catbird seat' meant sitting pretty, like a batter with three balls and no strikes on him. **1958** WODEHOUSE *Cocktail Time* xiii. 114 'I get you. If we swing it, we'll be sitting pretty,' 'In the catbird seat.'

cat-boat: see CAT *sb.*[2]

catcall ('kætkɔːl), *sb.* Also 8 **catcal**. [From the nocturnal cry or 'waul' of the cat.]

1. A squeaking instrument, or kind of whistle, used esp. in play-houses to express impatience or disapprobation. (See *Spectator* No. 361.)

1659-60 PEPYS *Diary* (1879) I. 67, I.. called on Adam Chard, and bought a cat-call there, it cost me two groats. **1712** ADDISON *Spect.* No. 361 ¶2, I was very much surprised with the great Consort of Cat-calls.. to see so many Persons of Quality of both Sexes assembled together at a kind of Catterwawling. **1732** FIELDING *Covent Gard. Trag.* I. i, I heard a tailor sitting by my side, Play on his catcal, and cry out, 'Sad stuff!' **1753** *Gray's Inn Jrnl.* No. 61 A shrill toned Catcall, very proper to be used at the next new Tragedy. **1865** *Lond. Rev.* 30 Dec. 687/1 That vilest of all the inventions of Jubal, the catcall.

2. The sound made by this instrument or an imitation with the voice; a shrill screaming whistle.

1749 JOHNSON *Irene* Prol., Should partial cat-calls all his hopes confound He bids no trumpet quell the fatal sound. *a* **1764** LLOYD *Author's Apol.* Wks. 1774 I. 1 Powerful cat-call from the pit. **1817** MAR. EDGEWORTH *Harrington* (1833) 82. **1881** *Daily Tel.* 27 Dec., In the face of catcalls and other occasional demonstrations from the 'gods'.

3. One who uses the instrument.

1714 BUDGELL *Spect.* No. 602 A notorious Rake that headed a Party of Cat-cals.

catcall ('kætkɔːl), *v.* [f. prec.]

1. *intr.* To sound a catcall, *esp.* at a theatre or similar place of amusement.

1734 FIELDING *Univ. Gallant* Prol., 'Tis not the poet's wit affords the jest, But who can catcall, hiss, or whistle best? **1762** CANNING in *Poet. Register* (1807) 455 Let them cat-call and hiss as they will. **1820** *Blackw. Mag.* VIII. 5 Some catcalled, and some roared 'go on'.

2. *trans.* To receive or assail with catcalls.

a **1700** DRYDEN *Prologue Pilgrim* (R.) His cant, like merry Andrew's noble vein, Cat-calls the sects to draw them in again. **1843** MACAULAY *Mad. D'Arblay, Ess.* (1854) 711/2

Better to be hissed and catcalled by her Daddy than by a whole sea of heads in the pit of Drury Lane Theatre.

Hence **'catcalling** *vbl. sb.* and *ppl. a.*

c **1781** MAD. D'ARBLAY in Macaulay *Ess.* (1887) 748 That hissing, groaning, catcalling epistle. **1864** *Daily Tel.* 9 Dec., The gods indulged in their usual habit of whistling and cat-calling. **1881** LD. W. PITT LENNOX *Plays, Players, &c.* I. 77 A sound of hissing and cat-calling was now heard.

catch (kætʃ), *sb.*[1] Also 5 cacche, kache, *Sc.* cach, 5–6 *Sc.* caich(e. 6 catche, cache, 6–7 katch, 7 *Sc.* caitche, 7–9 (chiefly in sense 14) ketch. [f. the vb. (The senses are taken from different uses of the verb, and form no regular series among themselves.)]

1. a. The act or fact of catching in various senses; see the vb.

1580 SIDNEY *Arcadia* I. (1613) 91 She would faine the catch of Strephon flie. **1649** G. DANIEL *Trinarch., Rich. II*, lxviii, Demands To Princes made in Catch of Rebel Hands. **1722** DE FOE *Col. Jack* (1840) 203 She intended to have me, if she could catch, and it was indeed a kind of a catch. **1870** *Daily News* 20 Sept., The French captured a German schooner.. and this wretched little catch called forth an uncommon deal of enthusiasm and cheering. **1884** J. PAYN *Thicker than W.* vi. 42 There was a 'catch' in her breath. **1887** *Blackw. Mag.* Nov. 692 The young people.. play at catch with coloured balls.

†**b.** *to lie* (or *be*) *at* (*the*) *catch, to lie* (or *be*) *upon the catch*: to lie in wait; to be on the watch for an opportunity of catching or seizing something, *esp.* of catching a person's words, finding fault, making objections, etc. *Obs.*

1630 SIBBES *Bruised Reed* xv. Wks. 1862 I. 68 As one sitting at a catch for all advantages against them. **1642** ROGERS *Naaman* 528 As a prisoner.. always lies at the catch and opportunity to seeke his escape. **1656** H. MORE *Antid. Ath.* II. xi. §7. 75 Scaliger lay at catch with him [Cardan] to take him tripping wherever he could. **1742** RICHARDSON *Pamela* IV. 170, I saw he was upon the Catch, and look'd stedfastly upon me whenever I mov'd my Lips. **1814** JANE AUSTEN *Lady Susan* xiv. (1879) 230 Miss M. is absolutely on the catch for a husband.

c. In Rugby football and baseball (see quots.).

1867 [see FAIR *a.* 10 d]. **1868** H. CHADWICK *Base Ball* 45 A running catch is made when the ball is caught on the fly while the fielder is on the run. **1896** R. G. KNOWLES & MORTON *Baseball* 14 He.. must be as proficient in making running catches as in bringing off standing ones. **1897** *Encycl. Sport* I. 431/1 If a player makes a fair catch he shall be awarded a free kick. **1960** E. S. & W. J. HIGHAM *High Speed Rugby* xiii. 183 The method of making a fair-catch is to make a mark on the ground with the heel as the ball is caught, and to call: 'Mark!'

d. *Rowing.* The grip of the water taken with the oar at the beginning of a stroke.

1881 *Standard* 30 Mar. 3/7 The shallow waters of the Cam .. make it very difficult for a crew to imitate the catch at the beginning of the stroke. **1898** *Encycl. Sport* II. 296/2 *Catch*, the instant application of the weight and muscles of legs and body to the oar at the moment it enters the water.

e. In full *glottal catch* (see GLOTTAL *a.*). Often used as a synonym of the more frequent *glottal stop*.

1925 P. RADIN tr. *J. Vendryès's Lang.* I. i. 30 It is directly after the vowels, when the emission of air is complete, that this catch or 'stop' occurs. **1964** CRYSTAL & QUIRK *Prosodic Features in Eng.* iii. 43 One flap of tremulousness.. is equivalent to a 'catch' in the voice (i.e. one flap or brief roll of glottal trill).

2. a. The catching of fish. **b.** The number of fish caught at one time, or during one season.

1465 *Mann. & Househ. Exp.* 473 To axe of my lord of Duram in yifte the kache of Hangeford. **1799** J. ROBERTSON *Agric. Perth* 377 The expence of fishing must be paid.. after which the benefit of the catch is supposed to accrue to the proprietors. **1875** BUCKLAND *Log-bk.* 12 The catch depends very much upon the weather. **1884** *Stubbs' Merc. Circular* 27 Feb. 194/1 The total catch of mackerel by the New England fleet was 236,685 barrels.

c. A crop, esp. one sufficient to render further sowing unnecessary. *U.S. colloq.*

1868 G. BRACKETT *Farm Talk* 128 That's one reason why I sowed the field to barley—so as to get a good catch. **1941** *Harper's Mag.* Aug. 329/1 My newly laid down field, where I didn't get a very good catch of grass.

3. *Cricket.* **a.** The act of catching the ball, when struck by the batsman, before it reaches the ground, and so putting him 'out'. Also, a ball so hit that a fielder may catch it. *catch-and-bowl*, a catch made by the bowler.

1770 J. LOVE *Cricket* 17 Weymark unhappily misses a Catch. **1816** W. LAMBERT *Instr. & Rules Cricket* 15 Strikers are generally cautious at first, which will frequently cause a catch. **1837** DICKENS *Pickw.* vii, At every bad attempt at a catch.. he launched his personal displeasure at the head of the devoted individual in such denunciations as.. 'now butter-fingers'. **1886** GURNEY *Phantasms of Living* I. 561 His mental condition after just missing a catch. **1888** STEEL & LYTTELTON *Cricket* iii. 110 A catch in the slips or at point, or a catch and bowl, is not infrequently the result. **1906** A. E. KNIGHT *Compl. Cricketer* iv. 146 Rightly judged by the eye, a catch should drop into the hands. **1907** *Westm. Gaz.* 20 July 15/1 Hence the number of catches-and-bowls he used to bring off.

b. *transf.* A player who catches well.

1854 F. LILLYWHITE *Guide to Cricketers* 58 [He is a] beautiful field at long-leg, being a sure catch. **1884** *Lillywhite's Cricket Ann.* 102 H. J. Ford; a safe catch in the long-field.

†**4.** *Sc.* A chase, pursuit. *Obs.*

c **1450** HENRYSON *Mor. Fab.* 83 Yee shall rew this race. What was the cause yee gaue mee sic a katch?

†**5.** *Sc.* Tennis. (Cf. CACHESPELL.) *Obs.*

c **1475** *Ratis Raving* I. 1245 Ryne at baris, and at the ball, And at the caich play with all. **1496** *Treasurer's Acc.* in Tytler *Hist. Scot.* (1864) II. 261 *note*, To the king in Strivelin, to play at the cach. **1535** STEWART *Cron. Scot.* III. 509 James Stewart.. playand.. wes with his peiris all Than at the catche. **1535** LYNDESAY *Satyre* 3411 Thocht I preich not, I can play at the caiche. **1599** JAMES I *Basil. Doron* III. (1603) 121 Playing at the caitche or tennise.

†**6.** A trick. *Obs.*

c **1430** *Lerne or be Lewd* in *Babees Bk.* (1868) 9 Warre Knavis cacches.

7. †**a.** A catching or entangling question. *Obs.*

1674 N. FAIRFAX *Bulk & Selv.* 86 The catch is so unphilosophical, that that which gainsays it most, is most true. **1693** W. FREKE *Sel. Ess.* xii. 62 Most of their arguments.. are nothing but a few empty Catches in mere words.

b. A hidden element (in a proposal, etc.) designed to take advantage of another person; something concealed with the intention of catching or tripping one up; hence, an unforeseen difficulty or awkwardness, a 'snag'.

1855 BARNUM *Life* 120 The old farmer, who was pretty 'cute, was sure that there was some 'catch' in this offer. **1913** *Punch* 18 June 474/1, I say, I'm a burglar. There is no catch in it. **1914** *Daily Express* 22 Dec. 2 It is not a toy or a 'catch', but a genuine game. **1919** WODEHOUSE *Damsel in Distress* x, There's nobody I think a more corking sportsman than Maud, if you know what I mean, but—this is where the catch comes in—I'm most frightfully in love with somebody else. **1951** C. V. WEDGWOOD *Last of Radicals* iv. 83 I've just been reading your Henry George.. and I.. can't see the catch in it.

c. ***Catch 22***: a supposed law or regulation containing provisions which are mutually frustrating (see quot. 1961); a set of circumstances in which one requirement, etc., is dependent upon another, which is in turn dependent upon the first. Freq. *attrib.*, esp. as ***Catch-22 situation.*** [f. a paradoxical rule postulated in the novel *Catch-22* (1961, released as a film in 1970), by Joseph Heller (b. 1923), U.S. author.

The first chapter of Heller's novel was published in 1955 (*New World Writing* No. 7 54ff) under the title 'Catch-18'. For Heller's explanation of why this was changed to *Catch-22*, see Kiley and MacDonald '*Catch-22*' *Casebook* (1973) 294–95.]

1961 J. HELLER *Catch-22* v. There was only one catch, and that was Catch-22... If he flew them [more missions] he was crazy and didn't have to; but if he didn't want to he was sane and had to. **1971** *Atlantic Monthly* Mar. 47/2 In the opinion of many sociologists, the 'combination of diagnosis, evaluation, treatment and classification' so highly rated by Dr. Karl Menninger is in fact the Catch-22 of modern prison life. **1972** *Observer* (Colour Suppl.) 30 July 15/1 The rest.. have to work for one year before they can send for their families, and then only if they can prove they have housing. But, catch 22, they cannot apply for the Government-subsidised housing.. unless they have their families with them. **1974** *Sumter* (S. Carolina) *Daily Item* 22 Apr. 8A/5 His Public Interest Group now finds itself in a Catch 22 situation. It cannot prove the device works without EPA funds, but EPA won't grant the funds unless they prove the device works. **1978** *Encounter* July 74/2 Caught in the Victorian equivalent of *Catch 22* he [*sc.* Tennyson] is made to collude in an ethic which he knows to be repressive. **1980** *Brit. Med. Jrnl.* 29 Mar. 951/1 How best can the profession inject medical advice into the NHS at local level? For the BMA it is a classic Catch 22 dilemma. **1985** C. RYCROFT *Psychoanalysis & Beyond* x. 125 A peculiar kind of impossible Catch-22 situation in which children can be caught.

8. Something intended to catch the attention, the popular fancy or demand, etc.

1781 COWPER *Lett.* 5 Mar. Wks. (1876) 66 The passage you objected to I inserted merely by way of catch. **1871** S. S. JORDAN in *Ess. & Lyrics* (1878) 204 This is a ha'penny catch.

†**9.** A catching sight; a glimpse, view. *Obs.*

1775 JOHNSON in *Boswell* (1831) III. 258 Such houses as had any catch of the river. **1796** MORSE *Amer. Geog.* I. 610 [It] presents to the eye, through the cleft, a small catch of smooth blue horizon.

10. *concr.* That by which anything is caught and held; any contrivance for checking the motion of a piece of mechanism, a door, etc.

1520 *MS. Acc. St. John's Hosp. Canterb.*, Payd for a lache and a cache and a stapylle ijd. **1647** *Ibid.* 86 For a katch for my gate jd. **1644** NYE *Gunnery* (1670) 31 These catches, being either of steel or brass. **1686** *Lond. Gaz.* No. 2132/4 A pair of plain Pistols with.. one of the Catches broke off from the Lock. **1829** *Nat. Philos.* I. *Mechanics* II. vi. 25 (Libr. Usef. Knowl.), The ratchet-wheel and catch. **1851** *Illust. Lond. News* 42 The derrick being supported by a catch or pall. **1882** MALLOCK *Soc. Equality* viii. 203 A catch attached to the beam of the engine.

11. a. That which is caught or is worth catching; something gained; an acquisition.

1596 SHAKS. *Tam. Shr.* II. i. 333 No doubt but he hath got a quiet catch. **1606** —— *Tr. & Cr.* II. i. 109 Hector shall haue a great catch, if he knocke out either of your braines; he were as good cracke a fustie nut with no kernell. **1662** DRYDEN *Wild Gall.* III. i, The Gentleman had got a great Catch of her, as they say. **1830** GALT *Lawrie T.* IV. ix. (1849) 174 He would be a great catch to the settlement. **1840** MARRYAT *Poor Jack* li, She.. was considered quite a catch at card-parties.

b. *colloq.* A person matrimonially desirable on account of wealth or position.

[**1722** DEFOE *Col. Jack* (1723) 240 She intended to have me, if she could catch, and it was indeed a kind of catch.] **1749** CLELAND *Mem. Woman Pleasure* II. 215 Your surprize that one of my blood and relish of life, should count a gallant of threescore such a catch. **1835** T. MOORE *Fudge Fam. in Eng.* i. 2 Sole encumbrance, Miss Fudge to be taken therewith. Think, my boy, for a Curate how glorious a catch! **1837** MARRYAT *Snarleyyow* xx, She.. fully proved to his satisfaction that, independent of her beauty, she would be a much greater catch than Frau Vandersloosh. **1917** H. A. VACHELL *Fishpingle* x, Matrimonially he was no great 'catch' for an heiress of quality.

c. *Austral.* and *N.Z.* (See quot. 1933.)

1933 L. G. D. ACLAND in *Press* (Christchurch) 23 Sept. 13/7 *Catch.* Just before stopping time in a wool shed, a shearer tries to finish the sheep he is on and catch another which he can finish at ease after knock-off. This is called *getting a catch*. E.g., 'How many more can you do this run?'—'Two and a catch.' **1956** G. BOWEN *Wool Away!* (ed. 2) 155 *Catch*, the last sheep of a mob. Very often this sheep produces one extra for the tally of the shearer who shears well enough to catch it first. **1965** D. S. GUNN *Terminol. Shearing Ind.* I. 7 The 'bell sheep', or 'the catch' as it is often called, may be an easy one.

†**12.** The point to be caught or seized. *Obs.*

1600 HOLLAND *Livy* XXXIV. xxxii. 873 a, I will not use many words.. but come to the very catch and point of the matter.

†**13.** A fragment or scrap of anything caught up; 'a snatch; a short interval of action' (J.).

a **1626** BACON (J.) All which notions are but ignorant catches of a few things, which are most obvious to mens observations. **16..** LOCKE (J.) It has been writ by catches, with many intervals. **1665** GLANVILL *Sceps. Sci.* i. 10 We retain a catch of these pretty stories. **1742** RICHARDSON *Pamela* III. 362 Down she sat, and sung a little Catch, and cry'd Hem! twice. **1830** T. HAMILTON *Cyril Thornton* (1845) 78, I made speeches, and roared catches of songs.

14. *Music.* Originally, a short composition for three or more voices, which sing the same melody, the second singer beginning the first line as the first goes on to the second line, and so with each successive singer; a ROUND. 'The catch was for each succeeding singer to take up or catch his part in time' (Grove). Subsequently specially applied to rounds in which the words are so arranged as to produce ludicrous effects, one singer catching at the words of another. Also *attrib.* and in *comb.*, as ***catch-club, catch-maker.***

1601 CORNWALLYES *Ess.* II. xliii. (1631) 207 Like a singing catch, some are beginning when others are ending. *a* **1613** OVERBURY *A Wife* (1638) 217 The wakefull ketches on Christmas Eve. [**1625** BACON *Masques & Tri., Ess.* (Arb.) 539 Seuerall Quires.. taking the Voice by Catches, Antheme wise.] **1636** FEATLY *Clavis Myst.* xxvii. 343 Singing as it were a catch, and taking the word one from another. **1721** ADDISON *Spect.* No. 72 ⁋9 Several old Catches, which they sing at all Hours. **1802** MAR. EDGEWORTH *Moral T.* (1816) I. viii. 56. *a* **1859** MACAULAY *Biog.* (1867) 5 Dean Aldrich, a divine now chiefly remembered by his catches. **1787** WOLCOTT (P. Pindar) *Ode upon Ode* Wks. 1794 I. 385 *note*, Though not a Purcell.. a very pretty catch-maker. **1807** W. IRVING *Salmag.* (1824) 197 Straddle was.. a member of a catch-club.

¶ Sense obscure.

1596 SHAKS. *1 Hen. IV*, II. iv. 252 Thou Horson obscene greasie Tallow Catch.

†**catch**, *sb.*[2] *Obs.* Forms: 5–7 cache, 6–7 catch, 7 katch, 7– KETCH, q v. [ME. *cache*; prob. f. CATCH *v.* or *sb.*[1] The later *ketch* is analogous to *keg* for *cag*, *kennel* for *cannel*, etc.

It may be the sb. CATCH[1] (in ME. *cach(e)* in sense 4 'chase, pursuit', as YACHT is Du. *jagt, jacht* 'chase, pursuit', for *jachtschip, jageschip*, in reference to its swiftness.]

A strongly-built vessel of the galiot order, usually two-masted, and of from 100 to 250 tons burden; = KETCH.

1481–90 *Howard Househ. Bks.* (1841) 397 Rede oker to send be watyr with the sayd hoppes, in Ferdes cache of Brekemlynsey. **1561** EDEN *Art Navig.* Pref., Fyshermen that go a trawlyng for fyshe in Catches or mongers. **1580** SIR R. BINGHAM in *Spenser's Wks.* (Grosart) I. 468 A small catch or craer of Sir William Wynters. **1624** CAPT. SMITH *Virginia* II. 23 The river.. is navigable.. with Catches and small Barkes 30 or 40 myles farther. **1625** J. GLANVILLE *Voy. Cadiz* (1883) 116 Catches, being short and round built, bee verie apt to turne up and downe, and usefull to goe to and fro, and to carry messages betweeen shipp and shipp almost with anie wind. **1642** NICHOLAS *Let.* in Carte's *Coll.* (1735) 89 Sir John Hotham hath lately apprehended.. one of the King's caches. *a* **1693** URQUHART *Rabelais* III. lii. 429 Catches, Capers, and other Vessels.

†**catch**, *sb.*[3], obs. f. KEDGE, small anchor.

1791 SMEATON *Edystone L.* §143 We immediately let go another small anchor or Catch.. paying out the hawser of the catch-anchor.

†**Catch**, *sb.*[4] *Obs.* = KETCH, 'Jack Ketch'.

a **1672** WOOD *Life* (1848) 234 When he had hanged about half an hour [he] was cut down by Catch or Ketch, and quartered under the gallows.

catch (kætʃ), *v.* Pa. t. and pple. caught (kɔːt). Forms: 2–4 cache(n, 3 *Orm.* kæchenn, kecchen, 3–4 cacchen, 4 kachen, 4–5 kache, cacche, kacche, 4–6 cach, catche, 5 kach, katche, cachche, cahch, 5–6 cache, 6 *Sc.* caucht; (also 3–4 keche, 5 kecche, ceche, 6 ketch(e), 6– catch, (9 *dial.* cotch). *Pa. t. a.* 4 cached, katched, 5 cacchid, -it, cacht, 6– catched, 7–8 catch'd, catcht. *β.* 3 *Orm.* cahhte, 3–4 cahte, cauhte, 3–5 caȝte, kaȝte, 4–5 cauȝte, kauȝte, (kaufte), caȝt, kaȝt, cauȝt, kauȝt, cawght, 5 caghte, kaghte, caute,

caght, kaght, kaught, coght, cought, 4–6 caughte, 5– caught; (also 3 (bi) -kehte, keihte, 5 keȝte, 6 keight.) *Pa. pple.* α. 3 *Orm.* (bi)- cæchedd, 4–5 cached, -id, cacchit, katched, 5 cacchid, cachet, 5–6 cachit, kachit, 6 cacchide, catchte), 6–9 catcht, catched, (7 catch't), 7–8 catch'd, (9 *dial.* cotcht, cotch'd). β. 3 (bi)- kahht, icaht, 4 caht, cauht, ycauȝt, ikauȝt, kawht, cawght, (kight), 4–5 caȝt, cauȝt, cought, 5 caght, kaght, (caut, keghet), (6 caughte, y-, i-caught, caucht), 5– caught. [ME. *cache-n, cacche-n*, a. ONF. *cachier* (3rd sing. pr. *cache*), = central OF. *chacier*, later *chassier*, mod.F. *chasser* (Picard *cacher*) = Pr. *cassar*, Sp. *cazar* (OSp. *cabzar*), Pg. *caçar*, It. *cacciare*:—late L. **captiāre*, f. *capt-us* 'taken captive', which took in Romanic the place of L. *captāre* 'to strive to seize, seek to catch, lie in wait for', and in late use = *venāri* 'to hunt, chase', which is the sense in all the Romanic langs. This sense was also original in Eng.; and continued in Scotch to 16th c. (see sense 1); but for this the central OF. *chacier, chace* was adopted in form *chace-n* by 1300, and *catch* was gradually confined to its present sense, which is unknown to French and the other langs., but is that of OE. *læcc(e)an*, ME. *lacchen, lachen*. With the latter, *cachen* seems to have been very early treated as synonymous, and at length entirely took its place. Hence, app. the pa. t. *cahte, cauhte, cauȝte, caught*, like *lahte, lauhte, lauȝte, laught*, which was used along with the regular *cacched, catchte, catched*, and during the present century has superseded it in literary use (though *catched, cotched* is still widely prevalent in dial. or vulgar speech).]

I. †**1.** *trans.* To chase, to drive. *Obs.*

c **1250** *Gen. & Ex.* 949 Gredi foueles fellen ðor-on.. abram..kaȝte is [= them] wei. *c* **1305** *Disp. Mary & Cross* 102 in *Leg. Rood* 134 þe Jewes from þe cros me keiȝt. **1330** R. BRUNNE *Chron.* (1810) 120 Mald þorgh þe Lundreis fro London is katched. **138.** WYCLIF *Serm.* Sel. Wks. II. 364 þis is vois made of þe fend bi which he cacchiþ on his carte. **1440** *York Myst.* xlviii. 326 Caytiffis ȝe cacched [*Towneley Myst.* chaste] me feo youre ȝate. **1499** *Promp. Parv.* 58 (Pynson) Catchyn [**1440** chasyn] or dryue forth bestis, *mino*. **1513** DOUGLAS *Æneis* I. i. 4 Our land and see cachit [*jactatus*] with mekle pyne.

†**2.** *intr.* To chase, run, hasten; to press *on*.

c **1325** *E.E. Allit. P.* B. 629 He cached to his cob-hous & a calf bryngez. *c* **1340** *Gaw. & Gr. Knt.* 1794 Kysse me now comly, & I schal cach heþen. *c* **1400** *Destr. Troy* 2014 þai.. kachyn on kyndly, & þaire course held. **1526** SKELTON *Magnyf.* 1513 Hercules..with hys stubborne mace That made Cerberus to cache.

II. To capture, *esp.* that which tries to escape; hence, to ensnare, surprise, overtake, reach, get at.

†**3.** *trans.* To take forcible possession of, capture (a town, castle, ship, country, etc.). *Obs.*

c **1205** LAY. 4547 Monie scipen he þer cahte. **1382** WYCLIF *2 Kings* xiv. 7 And he cauȝte [**1388** took] the place, that hatte Petra, in bateyl. *c* **1400** *Destr. Troy* 1467 To cache a castell þat was kene holdyn. *Ibid.* 9766 Carles þaire cuntre cacht as þaire aune. **1535** COVERDALE *Judg.* v. 12 Catch him yt catched the, thou sonne of Abinoam.

4. *esp.* To capture or lay hold of (that which tries or would try to escape, as a man or animal). This may be done by superior speed and force, by surprise, by any snare or engine of capture. (The proper word for this action, which is also its main sense, and lies at the base of most of the others.)

c **1205** LAY. 31501 ȝif he me mihte cacchen [**1275** cache] he me wolde quellen. *a* **1225** *Ancr. R.* 294 Capite nobis uulpes paruulas..kecched us..þe ȝunge uoxes. *c* **1325** *Pol. Songs* 152 He may scape ant we aren ever caht. *c* **1386** CHAUCER *Reeve's T.* 185 They cowde nat..Here capil cacche, it ran away so fast. —— *Melibeus* ¶212 He..setteth a nette byfore his feet to cacchen him. **1393** GOWER *Conf.* III. 258 As the tigre his time awaiteth In hope for to cacche his pray. *c* **1400** *Destr. Troy* 12993 He purpost hym priuely..at his comyng to kacche hym olyue. **1486** *Bk. St. Albans* E viij a, Theys houndes all Bayen and cryen when thay hym ceche shall. **1593** *Tell-trothe's N.Y. Gift* 35 The siliest creatures are seldome catcht in ordinary trappes. **1601** SHAKS. *Twel. N.* II. iii. 65 Some dogs will catch well. **1607** —— *Cor.* I. iii. 66, I saw him run after a gilded Butterfly, & when he caught it, he let it go againe, and after it againe..& catcht it again. **1642** ROGERS *Naaman* 375 He had fished all night and catcht nothing. **1672–5** COMBER *Comp. Temple* (1702) 91 Some silly Bird..suddenly catcht in the Fowler's snare. **1713** C'TESS WINCHELSEA *Misc. Poems* 96 Till thinking Thee to've catched, Himself by thee was caught. **1716** *Let.* in *Wodrow Corr.* (1843) II. 143 He catched four or five of the rebels that were lurking in Angus. **1797** BEWICK *Brit. Birds* (1847) I. 14 Small birds..caught in a singular manner. **1815** *Monthly Mag.* XXXVIII. 435 One might almost say they would come to be catched. **1847** TENNYSON *Princ.* v. 105 Like tender things that being caught feign death. **1866** *N. & Q.* Ser. III. IX. 498/1 True amphibians, catching their prey in the water.

fig. **1715** BURNET *Own Time* II. 43 He was early catched by the Jesuits and bred many years among them.

5. *fig.* To ensnare, entrap; to deceive, 'take in'.

1382 WYCLIF *1 Cor.* iii. 19, I schal catche wyse men in her fell wysdom. **1460** CAPGRAVE *Chron.* 189 Othir lordis he cacchid, or caute, with fayre wordes. **1611** BIBLE *Mark* xii. 13 To catch him in his words. **1654** CROMWELL *Sp.* 4 Sept. (Carlyle) For few have been catched by the former mistakes. **1699** BENTLEY *Phal.* 283 To see how Error is propagated, even Petavius too was caught here. **1887** *Manch. Guard.* 8 Mar. 8 With a dollar only minted in London..someone would be 'caught'.

†**6.** *fig.* To obtain by exertion (viewed as a race or chase); to attain, get possession of. *Obs.*

1382 WYCLIF *1 Tim.* vi. 12 Catche euerlastyng lyf [TINDALE, COVERD. laye honde on; *Rhem.* apprehend; **1611** lay hold on]. *c* **1420** *Metr. Life St. Kath.* (Halliw.) 19 Many have there kaght ther heele. **1561** DAUS tr. *Bullinger on Apoc.* (1573) 61 A feruent zeale to follow and catch thy saluation. **1593** SHAKS. *3 Hen. VI*, III. ii. 179, I..Torment my selfe, to catch the English Crowne. **1605** —— *Macb.* I. vii. 3 If th' Assassination Could..catch With his surcease, Successe.

†**b.** in a weaker sense: To gain or obtain (e.g. money) by one's own action. *Obs.* (Cf. 29, 38.)

1377 LANGL. *P. Pl.* B. XI. 168 For no cause to cacche siluer þere-by. **1393** GOWER *Conf.* II. 202 Where they the profit mighten cacche. *c* **1550** BALE *K. Johan* (1838) 17 Besydes what ye cacche for halowed belles & purgatorye.

7. To overtake, come up with (an agent in motion). Now more usually ***to catch up***.

1610 SHAKS. *Temp.* v. i. 315 Saile, so expeditious, that shall catch Your Royall fleete farre off. **1678** LITTLETON *Lat. Dict.*, To catch or overtake one, *assequor, apprehendo*. **1791** 'G. GAMBADO' *Ann. Horsem.* xii. (1809) 115 He made a loose ..and catch'd them, within twenty yards of the ending post. **1848** MRS. GASKELL *M. Barton* xxvii, You'll be down the river in no time, and catch Will, I'll be bound.

b. To reach, get to (a person or thing before it moves away); as in 'to catch a train, a boat, the post, etc.', where the idea of *being in time* enters in. (The opposite is *to miss, lose*.)

1826 DISRAELI *Viv. Grey* IV. iii. 146, I was afraid my note might not have caught you. **1870** MISS BRIDGMAN *R. Lynne* I. xiii. 220, I shall be able to catch the Sandgate train. **1872** JENKINSON *Guide Eng. Lakes* (1879) 232 The tourist may.. walk..to the Bassenthwaite station, and there catch the train. **1879** *Daily News* 12 Dec. 5/3 The popular pastime known as 'catching a train'..The number of disappointed train-catchers..reached a daily total of ten. *Mod.* I must finish my letter in time to catch the post.

8. Said of rain, a storm, etc., which overtakes one before reaching one's destination. Most frequently in the *passive*; const. usually *in*.

1712 ADDISON *Spect.* No. 317 ¶9 Caught in a Shower.. Returned home and dryed my self. **1758** JOHNSON *Idler* No. 33 ¶19 Catched in a shower coming back. **1791** SMEATON *Edystone L.* §111 The stone vessels, if catched by a storm.. retreat into Weymouth Harbour. *Mod.* We were caught in the rain. The rain caught us just as we had reached the shoulder of the hill.

9. a. To come upon suddenly or unexpectedly; to surprise, detect (a person *in* or *at* some action, or *doing* something).

1610 B. JONSON *Alch.* v. iii, What shall I doe? I am catch'd. **1650** BAXTER *Saints' Rest* II. (1662) Pref. 175 His Adversaries would soon have catched him in it. **1712** STEELE *Spect.* No. 466 ¶3, I catched her once..at Chuck-Farthing among the Boys. *a* **1734** NORTH *Exam.* III. viii. ¶13. 591 They will be caught napping. **1772** JOHNSON in *Boswell* (1816) II. 162, I never catched Mallet in a Scotch accent. **1861** DICKENS *Gt. Expect.* vii, My sister catching him in the act. **1883** LLOYD *Ebb & Flow* II. 94, I used to catch myself saying 'Where's Frank?'

b. *pass.* (Always in pa. t. or as pa. pple.) To become pregnant. Also ***caught out***. *colloq.*

1858 QUEEN VICTORIA *Let.* 15 June in *Dearest Child* (1964) 115 The pride of giving life to an immortal soul is very fine ..perfectly furious as I was to be caught. **1919** M. STOPES *Let. to Working Mothers* 4 Very often it happens that you get 'caught', and you know that the baby that you feared might come has really begun. **1935** E. BOWEN *House in Paris* II. ix. 202 Being caught is the word for having a child, sometimes. **1955** 'C. BROWN' *Lost Girls* xiii. 142 She's been caught.. she's about five months gone. **1957** J. OSBORNE *Look Back in Anger* I. 29 I'm pregnant. After three years of married life, I have to get caught out now.

†**10.** To reach, attain, arrive at (a goal). *Obs.*

1393 GOWER *Conf.* II. 387 Till they the haven of Troie caught.

11. To reach or get at (any one) with a blow. Said also of the missile, etc. To hit (as opposed to *miss*). (The part reached is introduced by some prep.)

1583 GOLDING *Calvin on Deut.* clvi. 965 Wee must not thinke to escape the scourges of God..wee shall euer bee caught by the backe if God bee against vs. **1834** *Gentl. Mag.* Dec. II. 587/2 In the act of catching the Saint with the hot iron under the right ear. **1885** *Manch. Exam.* 10 Jan. 5/1 [The missile] caught him on the side of the head. *Mod.* She caught him a sounding box on the ear.

III. To seize and keep hold of.

12. a. To take hold of suddenly or forcibly; to grasp, seize.

a **1225** *Ancr. R.* 102 Hweðer þe cat of helle..cauhte, mid his cleafres, hire heorte heaued? *c* **1340** *Cursor M.* 18379 Oure lord by the hond Adam cawght. *c* **1400** *Destr. Troy* 13508 Wele his cosyn he knew, & kaght hym in armys. **1530** PALSGR. 723/2, I snappe at a thyng to catche it with my tethe. **1596** SPENSER *F.Q.* III. ii. 30 Betwixt her feeble armes her quickly keight. **1611** BIBLE *Matt.* xiv. 31 Iesus stretched foorth his hand, and caught him. **1676** HOBBES *Iliad* II. 284 The Serpent catched her by the wing. **1766** GOLDSM. *Vic. W.* xxi, I caught the dear forlorn wretch in my arms. **1842** TENNYSON *Day-Dream* 49 The page has caught her hand in his. **1857** HUGHES *Tom Brown* II. iv, He may throw him, if he catches him fairly above the waist.

b. *Rowing.* To grip the water with the oar at (the beginning of a stroke).

1886 *Encycl. Brit.* XXI. 32/1 The oar should be struck down firmly and decisively into the water.., and the weight of the body be thrown entirely upon it, by which the beginning of the stroke is caught. **1898** *Encycl. Sport* II. 273/2 The beginning must be caught with full power. **1902** *Encycl. Brit.* XXXII. 307/2 Swivel rowlocks..are considered unsuitable to eight-oared rowing, where the beginning of the stroke has to be firmly and smartly caught.

c. Of a crop: to germinate and grow. *U.S.* (Cf. CATCH *sb.*[1] 2 c.)

1843 W. OLIVER *Eight Months in Illinois* 95 Putting in hayseed without ploughing the ground... The seed catches quick and grows well.

13. *fig.* To seize, seize on, lay hold on, affect violently. *Obs.* exc. as in 14.

1382 WYCLIF *Micah* iv. 9 Sorewe hath cachid thee. **1426** AUDELAY *Poems* 13 Thai be caȝt with covetyse. **1539** TAVERNER *Erasm. Prov.* 10 Whan..the disease catcheth ones strength. **1601** HOLLAND *Pliny* I. 127 Beyond the riuer Ganges..the people are caught with the Sun, and begin to be blackish. **1604** SHAKS. *Oth.* III. iii. 90 Perdition catch my Soule, But I do loue thee. *c* **1630** RISDON *Surv. Devon* §216 (1810) 225 You have taken the cold, or the cold hath caught you. **1789** WOLCOTT (P. Pindar) *Expost. Odes* iii, Perdition catch the money-grasping wretch!

†**b.** intr. *to catch to*: to seize on. *Obs. rare*⁻¹.

c **1325** *E.E. Allit. P.* A. 50 Fore careful colde þat to me caȝt.

14. Of fire: To seize on, lay hold of, attack. Also in wider application.

1734 tr. *Rollin's Anc. Hist.* (1827) I. II. 392 The fire catched all the engines. **1766** GOLDSM. *Vic. W.* xxi, The flames were just catching the bed. **1865** CARLYLE *Fredk. Gt.* IV. XII. vi. 167 The fire caught many houses. **1925** G. L. MALLORY in E. F. Norton *Fight for Everest, 1924* 213 The wind and sun between them have fairly caught us all these last three days.

b. *intr.* To seize on anything; to be communicated, spread; also *fig.*

1560 BIBLE (Genev.) *Ex.* xxii. 6 If fire breake out, and catch in the thornes. **1634** BP. HALL *Occas. Medit.* xxvi, Let but some spark of heretical opinion be let fall upon some.. busy spirit, it catcheth instantly. **1713** ADDISON *Cato* II. vi. 37 Does the sedition catch from man to man, And run among their ranks? **1715** DESAGULIERS *Fires Impr.* 136 The Fire that may chance to catch in the Chimney. **1814** SOUTHEY *Carmen Triumph.* xv, The flame hath caught, the flame is spread!

†**15.** *intr.* To set in fairly, begin. *Obs. rare.*

1686 GOAD *Celest. Bodies* II. ii. 168 Rains when they once Catch, are apt to last.

16. *trans.* †**a.** To fasten, attach. *Obs. rare*⁻¹.

c **1400** *Destr. Troy* 1077 Cogges with cablis [they] cachyn to londe.

b. To fasten, attach (some object) *back* or *up*.

1893 *Funk's Stand. Dict.*, To *catch up*, to raise by attaching something; festoon; loop up; as, her dress was caught up with ribbons. **1898** *Daily News* 11 May 4/4 [Her] rose-tinted brocaded train was caught back at one side.

17. To lay hold of and detain; to grip, entangle; said of merely physical action.

1611 BIBLE *Gen.* xxii. 13 A Ramme caught in a thicket by his hornes. **1644** EVELYN *Diary* (Chandos) 99 A chayre which catches any who sitts doune in it so as not to be able to stirr out. **1694** *Acc. Sev. Late Voy.* (1711) II. 43 The Ships..are often catcht between [the Ice-fields], and broken by them. **1734** tr. *Rollin's Rom. Hist.* III. 402 His arms were catched in the trunk of the trees.

b. To fasten or hold with a catch.

1881 GREENER *Gun* 160 The Vernier is..catched under the sliding bar.

18. *intr.* (for *refl.*) To be laid hold of and detained; to become entangled or fixed.

1787 'G. GAMBADO' *Acad. Horsem.* (1809) 12 His foot catching and hanging in the stirrup. **1875** JOWETT *Plato* (ed. 2) I. 84 The scythe end caught in the rigging. *Mod.* The bolt would not catch.

¶ *to catch hold*: see 45.

IV. Less forcibly: To take.

†**19.** *trans.* To take hold of, to take. Often with *off, forth*, etc. *Obs.*

c **1325** *E.E. Allit. P.* A. 237 [She] caȝte of her coroun of grete tresore. **1382** WYCLIF *Prov.* xxxi. 19 Hir fingris caȝten the spindle. *c* **1385** CHAUCER *L.G.W.* 1850 Pryvely she kaught forthe a knyfe. **1393** GOWER *Conf.* I. 291 He tho cought A yerde, which he bare on honde..and smote hem. **1605** CAMDEN *Rem.* 18 So they called parchment which wee have catcht from the Latine *Pergamentum*. **1626** DONNE *Serm.* 37 And so the Roman Church hath catched a *Trans* and others a *Con* and a *Sub* and an *In*, and varied their poetry into a *Transubstantiation* and a *Consubstantiation* and the rest. **1667** MARVELL *Corr.* xxxvi. Wks. 1872–5 II. 82 Strange reasons..which must be catched or waived.

†**b.** In several *fig.* uses (chiefly *poetical*): ***to catch leave, courage, council, the field; to catch haste***. *Obs.*

c **1340** *Gaw. & Gr. Knt.* 1118 þay..Kysten ful comlyly, & kaȝten her leue. *c* **1350** *Will. Palerne* 1053. *c* **1386** CHAUCER *Pers. T.* ¶615 Agayns this..synne of accidie..schulden men..manly and vertuously cacchin corrage wel to doo. *c* **1400** *Destr. Troy* 3192 Counsell was kaght of knightes & oþer. *Ibid.* 8285 Thre thousand full þro þrang into batell.. kaghten the fild. **1513** DOUGLAS *Æneis* III. x. 51 The scherp dreide maide ws so to cache haist.

20. *fig.* To take, get (rest, sleep, breath, etc.). *Obs.* in simple sense; in mod. use implying something momentary or sudden, and passing into next branch.

c **1325** *Poem temp. Edw. II* (Percy) xxviii, For to cache his rest. *c* **1330** *Pol. Songs* 331 Anon therafter he fondeth to kacche reste. **1393** GOWER *Conf.* II. 111 That I may cacche slepe. **1513** DOUGLAS *Æneis* IX. v. 3 The othir bestis..Ful sownd on sleip dyd cawcht thair rest. **1684** *Gt. Frost* 10 The prentices starv'd at home for want of coals To catch them a heat do flock thither in shoals. **1733** POPE *Ess. Man* III. 18 By turns we catch the vital breath, and die. **1821** CLARE *Vill. Minstr.* I. 24 Old women, overpowered by heat..Seeking..

the mole-hill seat, To tell their tales and catch their breath awhile. **1848** MRS. GASKELL *M. Barton* vii, Before she could catch a wink of sleep. **1856** KANE *Arct. Expl.* II. 54 Catching cat-naps as I could in the day.

V. To snatch.

21. To lay hold of forcibly and take away; to snatch, esp. in ***catch away***, ***catch up***, q.v.

c **1525** *Vox populi* 91 in Hazl. *E.E.P.* III. 271 All men.. Which can ketche any lande Out of the poore mans hande. **1553** GRIMALDE *Cicero's Offices* III. (1558) 122 If euery one of us catche to himselfe the commodities of other. **1667** MILTON *P.L.* XII. 88 Upstart Passions catch the Government From Reason. **1864** TENNYSON *En. Ard.* 236 He.. hastily caught His bundle.. and went his way.

†**22.** *intr.* To make a sudden motion in order to lay hold; to make a snatch. *Obs.* exc. as in 23.

1597 J. KING *Jonas* (1618) 188 It is not for vs to catch after death. **1607** TOPSELL *Four-f. Beasts* 83 How she [a cat] beggeth, playeth, leapeth, looketh, catcheth. **1642** R. CARPENTER *Experience* v. xviii. 315 Catching and scraping for mony. **1642** FULLER *Holy and Prof. St.* II. x. 92 Mercy is a Grace which they hold the fastest, that most catch after it.

b. *fig.* To carp, criticize. (Cf. also 5.)

1628 EARLE *Microcosm.* (Arb.) 43 He comes.. not to learne, but to catch.

23. ***to catch at***: to snatch at; to make a quick or eager attempt to lay hold of; often *fig.* (Also with *indirect passive.*) Cf. 25 b.

1601 CORNWALLYES *Ess.* II. xxvii. (1631) 20 Fearing they would be catcht at. **1606** SHAKS. *Ant. & Cl.* v. ii. 215 Sawcie Lictors Will catch at vs like Strumpets. **1721–33** STRYPE *Eccl. Mem.* III. App. xx. 57 We hunted for praise from impiety, and catched at commendation from al kind of wickednes. **1782** COWPER *Gilpin* 198 Catching at his rein.

VI. To intercept and lay hold of a thing in its course.

24. *trans.* To seize or intercept (anything) in its passing through the air, or in falling.

1589 PUTTENHAM *Eng. Poesie* (Arb.) 239 We do.. catch the ball.. before it come to the ground. **1684** T. BURNET *Th. Earth* I. 59 They might be catcht and stopt.. in their descent. **1711** ADDISON *Spect.* No. 160 ¶11 Tossing up Eggs, and catching them again without breaking them. **1734** SALE *Koran* Prelim. Disc. §1 (Chandos) 3 To use rain-water which they catch in cisterns. **1849** *Laws Cricket* in 'Bat' *Cricket Man.* (1850) 56 A ball being caught, no run shall be reckoned. **1857** HUGHES *Tom Brown* II. i. (1882) 37/3. **1866** G. MACDONALD *Ann. Quiet Neighb.* xxx. (1878) 523 Find a basin or plate.. and put it to catch the drop here.

b. *fig.*

1611 BIBLE *1 Kings* xx. 33 The men did diligently obserue whether any thing would come from him, and did hastily catch it.

c. *Cricket.* ***to catch*** (a person) ***out***, also simply ***to catch***: to put (a batsman) 'out' by catching the ball when struck by his bat. Also *absol.*, to make a catch. ***to catch and bowl***: usu. in pa. t. ***caught and bowled***, caught by the bowler; also as *ppl. a.* and *sb.*

1712 *Devil & Peers* (Broadside) in W. J. Lewis *Lang. Cr.* (1934) 44 I'll catch them both out in three or four stroaks. **1744** *Laws* [of Cricket] in *New Dict. Arts & Sci.* (1755) IV. 3459/2 So as to hinder the bowler from catching her. **1746** in 'Bat' *Cricket Man.* (1850) 80 Newland.. 15 c[aught by] Ld. J. Sackville. **1850** *Ibid.* 46 If a striker is caught out, state the fieldsman's name. **1873** R. A. FITZGERALD *Wickets in West* 287 Gilbert.. was also caught and bowled by Eastwood. **1883** in *Daily Tel.* 15 May 2/7 Peate.. caught and bowled Hearn. **1897** *Encycl. Sport* I. 245/2 *Caught and Bowled*, caught by the bowler who delivered the ball. **1904** P. F. WARNER *Recov. Ashes* v. 78 Rhodes missed catching and bowling Gregory. **1924** J. B. HOBBS *Cricket Mem.* 169 Then Mr. Simms got rid of Woolley with a magnificent 'caught and bowled'. **1950** W. HAMMOND *Cricketers' School* v. 52, I have seen Larwood take some of the speediest single-handed caught-and-bowled catches ever put up on any cricket field. **1956** R. ALSTON *Test Commentary* xvi. 136 A 'caught-and-bowled' off a hard hit from May.

d. Similarly in ***Baseball***, ***to catch*** (a person) ***out***.

1858 F. PIGEON in A. G. Spalding *Amer. Nat. Game* (1911) iv. 61 Next man got scared; caught out. **1874** CHADWICK *Base Ball Man.* 88 There he was when Mills was caught out on the fly. **1902** *Encycl. Brit.* XXVI. 160/2 In base-ball if the ball is knocked in a certain direction it is called a foul, and the player who knocked it has not the privilege of making a run, but may be caught out.

e. *Baseball. trans.* To catch the pitcher's deliveries. *intr.* To act as catcher.

1865 *Wilkes' Spirit of Times* (N.Y.) 8 July 301/1 Wansley caught behind in a handsome manner. **1887** *Courier-Jrnl.* (Louisville, Ky.) 26 May 2/6 Young Love Cross caught Ramsey in fine style, and Greer also handled Porter's delivery as well as could be desired. **1890** WILL CARLETON *City Legends* 39 'An' will you pitch or catch?' Says I, 'I'll catch, if so desired'.

25. To lay hold of (an opportunity) as it occurs.

1548 UDALL, etc. *Erasm. Par. Matt.* xix. 3 Thinking that they hadde caughte nowe an occasion. **1658** SIR T. BROWNE *Hydriot.* Ep. Ded., We.. catched the Opportunity to write of old Things. **1734** FIELDING *Quix. in Eng.* II. iv, His design is to rob the house, if he could catch an opportunity. *a* **1764** LLOYD *Voltaire's Henriade* Wks. 1774 II. 224 The Guises.. Catch'd the fair moment which his weakness gave. **1791** SMEATON *Edystone L.* §278 The first opportunity he could catch after the violent storm.

b. *intr.* with *at*. Cf. 23.

c **1680** BEVERIDGE *Serm.* (1729) I. 202 You catch at all opportunities. **1833** HT. MARTINEAU *Berkeley the B.* I. iii. 49 Martin caught at the idea.

26. ***to catch one's breath***: to check the breath suddenly; see BREATH 5 b.

1593 SHAKS. *2 Hen. VI*, III. ii. 371 A greeuous sicknesse.. That makes him gaspe, and stare, and catch the aire, Blaspheming. **1833**, **1864** [see BREATH 5 b]. **1855** TENNYSON *Maud* I. xiv. iv, I.. Felt a horror.. Prickle my skin and catch my breath. **1859** —— *Elaine* 620 She caught her breath.

27. To check, interrupt in speaking. (Now only with *up* (54 d); *colloq.*; cf. *take up*.)

1670 COTTON *Espernon* III. xii. 623 Not that I do (he presently caught himself) in the least confess, etc. *a* **1726** PENN *Wks.* I. App. 233 Saying one Day thus.. he immediately catch'd himself, and fell into this Reflection.

28. A nail, hook, projecting corner, or the like, is said to catch anything which comes against it in passing, and is stopped or retarded by it.

1734 tr. *Rollin's Anc. Hist.* (1827) V. XIV. 380 His robe being catched by a bramble. **1791** SMEATON *Edystone L.* §250 Our stone vessels were liable to be catched by the keel in going out. **1880** BLACK *White Wings* II. i. 15 The back sweep of the oars sometimes caught the waves.

VII. To get or take a thing passively, through being in its way.

†**29.** To receive, get, obtain, derive (from or by another's action). *Obs.* exc. as in next.

c **1205** LAY. 10843 Hu he hauede þene nome icaht. *a* **1225** *Ancr. R.* 154 Neuer ȝet i monne floc ne keihte he swuche biȝete. *c* **1350** *Will. Palerne* 5267 Sone þei cauȝt cumfort. **1393** LANGL. *P. Pl.* C. I. 134 Þe cardinales at court þat cauȝt han such a name. *c* **1400** *Destr. Troy* 2155 Myche comforth he caght or þaire kynd speche.

30. *esp.* To get, receive, incur (something injurious or unpleasant). Now chiefly in colloquial language, esp. in phr. ***to catch one's death*** (***of cold***) (cf. 42), ***catch a mischief***, and ***catch it*** (see 41).

a **1225** *Ancr. R.* 66 Heo hunteð efter pris, & keccheð lastunge. *Ibid.* 88 Wo is me þet he, oðer heo, habbeð swuch word ikeiht. **1297** R. GLOUC. (1724) 375 Rychard caȝte þer hys deþ. *c* **1330** *Amis & Amil.* 2455 All that thei there lafte, Grete strokes there thei caufte. *c* **1420** *Avow. Arth.* xvi, As he hade keghet scathe. **1480** CAXTON *Chron. Eng.* ccxliii. 290 Ther he caught deths wounde. **1537** W. T. *Expos. St. John* 79 They be taken tardy and ketch a fall. *a* **1593** H. SMITH *Wks.* (1867) II. 148 Always climbing till we catch a fall. **1593** SHAKS. *3 Hen. VI*, III. ii. 23 Fight closer, or.. you'le catch a Blow. **1678** BUNYAN *Pilgr.* I. 84 He.. went by, and catcht no hurt. **1712** ADDISON *Spect.* No. 517 ¶2, I am afraid he caught his Death the last County Sessions. **1872** BLACK *Adv. Phaeton* IV. 40, I will not allow Bell to catch her death of cold. **1904** 'G. B. LANCASTER' *Sons o' Men* xvi. 204 Don't you dare take him till I get some more clothes on him! He'd catch his death! **1951** G. GREENE *End of Affair* v. vii. 215 She had walked in the rain seeking a refuge and 'catching her death' instead.

31. To receive, incur, or contract, through exposure; as †***to catch heat*** (obs.), ***to catch the breeze***. (Cf. also *to catch cold*, 42.)

1297 R. GLOUC. (1724) 28 Þer it cacheþ hete. *c* **1369** CHAUCER *Dethe Blaunche* 781 As a white walle or a table.. ys redy to cachche and take Al that men wil theryn make. **1535** COVERDALE *Matt.* xiii. 6 Whan the Sonne arose it caught heate. **1700** ADDISON *Lett. Italy* Wks. (1721) 133 To catch the breeze of breathing air. **1704** WORLIDGE *Dict. Rust. et Urb.* s.v. *October*, Least the Carnations catch too much wet. **1764** GOLDSM. *Trav.* 47 Ye lakes, whose vessels catch the busy gale. **1848** MRS. GASKELL *M. Barton* xxxiv, His face had caught.. the ghastly foreshadowing of Death. **1878** BOSW. SMITH *Carthage* 231 [The] tops [of the hills] were catching the first rays of the rising sun.

b. *ellipt.* To catch the wind (*Naut.*); to catch fire; to catch frost, begin to freeze.

1794 *Rigging & Seamansh.* II. 292 Her sails begin to catch a-back. **1825** in Hone *Every-day Bk.* II. 1378 The powder soon may catch. **1879** JEFFERIES *Wild Life S.C.* 382 Causing the water to catch—that is, the slender, thread-like spicules form on the surface, and, joining together, finally cover it. **1886** F. C. PHILIPS *Jack & Three Jills* I. vii. 96 We arrived at the lake to find it was caught over, scantily, but with promise of skating to come.

†**32.** To conceive, become affected by or inspired with (a desire or emotion). *Obs.* exc. as in 34.

c **1385** CHAUCER *L.G.W.* 1746 [He] caughte to this lady swich desyr. *c* **1430** LYDG. *Bochas* I. xiv. (1554) 27 a, She caught an indignation. *c* **1570** THYNNE *Pride & Lowl.* (1841) 5 Love, or feare, Which any wight.. hath icaught. **1715–20** POPE *Iliad* xv. 439 Presumptuous Troy.. catch'd new fury at the voice divine.

33. To take or contract (a disease); to take by infection (*of* or *from*). (See also *to catch cold* 42.)

1547 BOORDE *Introd. Knowl.* 126 If I do go barlegged, I do cach the coffe. **1601** SHAKS. *Twel. N.* I. v. 314 Euen so quickly may one catch the plague? **1611** —— *Wint. T.* I. ii. 386, I cannot name the Disease, and it is caught Of you. **1667** MILTON *P.L.* x. 544 They.. the dire form Catcht by Contagion. **1747** BERKELEY *Tar-water in Plague* Wks. III. 480 Useful to prevent catching the small-pox. **1806** *Med. Jrnl.* XV. 219 The small-pox raging here, he caught the infection from some neighbouring children.

34. *fig.* To take up as by infection; to acquire by sympathy or imitation; to become imbued or infected with (accent, tone, spirit, etc.).

1590 SHAKS. *Mids. N.* I. i. 189 My tongue should catch your tongues sweet melodie. **1709** POPE *Ess. Crit.* 409 Some ne'er advance a judgment of their own, But catch the spreading notion of the town. **1747** HERVEY *Medit. & Contempl.* (1818) 103 Who can forbear catching the general joy? **1778** ROBERTSON *Hist. Amer.* I. II. 112 He seemed to have catched the same spirit with his subjects. **1848** MRS. GASKELL *M. Barton* ix, She 'caught the trick of grief, and sighed'. **1857** MAURICE *Ep. St. John* i. 3.

VIII. To seize by the senses or intellect.

35. a. To apprehend by the senses or intellect; to hear, see, etc., by an effort; to succeed in hearing, seeing, understanding, etc.

1588 SHAKS. *L.L.L.* II. i. 70 Euery obiect that [his eye] doth catch. **1606** —— *Ant. & Cl.* I. ii. 144 Cleopatra catching but the least noise of this, dies instantly. **1766** GOLDSM. *Vic. W.* xx, Listening to catch the glorious sounds. **1822** HAZLITT *Table-t.* II. iv. 78 You cannot from the rapidity and carelessness of his utterance catch what he says. **1837** WHEWELL *Hist. Induct. Sc.* (1857) I. 24 It does not appear.. easy to catch his exact meaning. **1848** MRS. GASKELL *M. Barton* x. (1882) 26/2 Catching the state of the case with her quick.. eyes. **1875** JOWETT *Plato* (ed. 2) III. 58, I only caught the words, 'Shall we let him off?'

b. To watch (a theatrical performance or television programme); to listen to (a concert, etc.).

1906 H. GREEN *At Actors' Boarding House* 150 Where are you on the bill at Moctor's this week? I must come in an' ketch you guys. **1937** *Amer. Speech* XII. 45/2, I caught Wright's band last night and are they tough. **1965** *Listener* 7 Oct. 551/2 This modest programme.. was the kind of late-evening music item that is so often well worth catching. **1969** *Oxf. Times* 15 Aug. 13/1 You can have a cigarette or a drink, read the newspaper or catch the television news.

36. To apprehend so as to adopt or appropriate; as, *e.g.* a musician 'catches' a melody, or an artist the expression of a face.

1560 SHAKS. *Macb.* I. v. 19 Thy nature.. is too full o' th' Milke of humane kindnesse, To catch the neerest way. **1753** H. WALPOLE *Corr.* (1837) I. 210 Sir Christopher Wren who built the tower of the great gate-way at Christ Church has catched the graces of it as happily as you could do. **1805** SCOTT *Last Minstr.* Introd. 87 When he caught the measure wild. **1883** LLOYD *Ebb & Fl.* II. 256 The attitude had evidently been caught from life.

IX. To arrest the attention, mind, fancy, etc.

37. To arrest the attention of (a person); to captivate, charm. Cf. *take*, *fetch*.

c **1386** CHAUCER *Doctor's T.* 127 So was he caught wiþ beaute of þis mayde. **1613** SHAKS. *Hen. VIII*, II. iii. 77 Beauty and Honour in her are so mingled, That they haue caught the King. *a* **1700** DRYDEN (J.) The soothing arts that catch the fair. **1771** *Junius Lett.* lxi. 319 A concession merely to catch the people. **1850** BROWNING *Easter-Day* xxxiii, She still each method tries To catch me.

b. To arrest (a faculty or organ of sense—*attention*, *affection*, *sight*; *eye*, *ear*, etc.).

1606 SHAKS. *Tr. & Cr.* III. iii. 183 Things in motion sooner catch the eye. **1712** HUGHES *Spect.* No. 467 ¶5 It is below him to catch the Sight with any Care of Dress. **1736** BUTLER *Anal.* I. v. 131 Any one of a thousand objects, catching his eye. **1777** SIR W. JONES *Seven Fount.* 44 Melodious notes.. caught with sweet extasy his ravish'd heart. **1806** *Med. Jrnl.* XV. 228, I hope this paper may catch his eye. **1820** W. IRVING *Sketch Bk.* I. 46 The figurative style of my language caught the excited imagination of Leslie. **1832** HT. MARTINEAU *Homes Abr.* vii. 100 A rustle outside the door.. caught her excited ear. **1874** BLACKIE *Self-Cult.* 24 A card, with a few leading words to catch the eye.

38. *fig.* To obtain, get (money, etc.) by attracting the popular fancy or by similar means; with a mixture of senses 5, 6 b, 24 and 37.

1377 [see 6 b]. **1662** GERBIER *Princ.* 17 The various devices of Smiths, to catch Money out of the Builders Purses. **1833** *Chamb. Jrnl.* No. 72. 156 Every lure is set, every trap is baited, to catch the contents of the Cockney's purse. **1886** MORLEY *Voltaire* 160 He sought to catch some crumb of praise.

X. Phrases.

39. a. ***catch that catch may***, ***catch as catch can***, etc.: phrases expressing laying hold of in any way, each as he can. Also as *sb.* and *attrib.*

1393 GOWER *Conf.* III. 240 Was none in sight But cacche who that cacche might. **1562** J. HEYWOOD *Prov. & Epigr.* (1867) 171 Catch that catch may. **1611** COTGR., *Griffe, graffe*, by hooke or by crooke.. catch that catch may. **1616** BEAUM. & FL. *Scornf. Lady* I. i. Men, women, and all woo: catch that catch may. **1752** JOHNSON *Rambl.* No. 197 ¶3 In a world where all must catch that catch can. **1764** K. O'HARA *Midas* III. 62 There's catch as catch can, hit or miss Luck is all, And Luck's the best tune of life's Toll lol de roll. *a* **1777** S. FOOTE in M. Edgeworth *Harry & Lucy Concluded* (1825) II. 153 They all fell to playing the game of catch as catch can, till the gun powder ran out at the heels of their boots. **1936** *World Film News* Sept. 4/1 The present catch-as-catch-can method of entry. **1949** R. HARVEY *Curtain Time* 130 The production was usually a hurried, catch-as-catch-can affair. **1958** G. BARKER *Two Plays* 23 Davy Jones and his daughter at catch-as-catch-can. **1959** *Manchester Guardian* 14 July 7/1 Tonight's papers are full of catch-as-catch-can interviews with the.. survivors.

b. ***catch-as-catch-can***, the Lancashire style of wrestling. Also *attrib.* and *transf.*

[**1617** MIDDLETON & ROWLEY *Fair Quarrel* II, I'le wrestle with any man for a good supper... I'le take your part there, catch that catch may.] **1889** W. ARMSTRONG *Wrestling* Introd. p. xiv, In 1871, the late Mr. J. G. Chambers.. endeavoured to introduce and promote a new system of wrestling at the Lillie Bridge Grounds, West Brompton, which he denominated, 'The Catch-as-catch-can Style; first down to lose'. **1898** *Encycl. Sport* II. 548/2 The principal chips associated with catch as catch can wrestling are the double Nelson, the half Nelson, the heave [etc.]. *Ibid.* 549/2 Turkish wrestling is principally carried out in catch as catch can style. **1905** *Daily Chron.* 21 Dec. 9/5 A catch-as-catch-can wrestler needs to be wonderfully active. **1913**, **1934** [see ALL-IN 2]. **1935** C. ISHERWOOD *Mr. Norris changes Trains* xv. 243 Arthur's orientally sensitive spirit shrank from the rough, healthy, modern catch-as-catch-can of home-truths and confessions. **1957** *Encycl. Brit.* XXIII. 806/2 The Lancashire style, generally known as 'catch-as-catch-can', is practised in Lancashire, throughout Great Britain generally, and is the most popular style in the United States, Canada, Australia, Switzerland. **1958** *Times* 13 Aug. 9/4 A

bull..decided that here was a catch-as-catch-can event in which he was free to join.

40. ***catch me!*** or ***catch me at it!*** (sense 9): a phrase expressing emphatically that one will never be found doing a thing. Also with pronouns other than *me*. *colloq.*

1830 GALT *Lawrie T.* v. iv. (1849) 207 Catch me again at such costly daffin. **1879** MISS BRADDON *Vixen* I. i. 15 Catch me going to London! exclaimed Vixen. **1886** MALLOCK *Old Ord. Changes* II. 58 He never did a stroke [of work]..Catch him! **1890** G. B. SHAW in *Time* Feb. 201 'Does Christine ever lecture them?'..'Catch her at it!' said Krogstad... 'They would soon show her the door.' **1936** N. COWARD *Fumed Oak* 41 *Mrs. Rockett*: I can always go to a boarding-house or a private hotel. *Doris*: Catch you!

41. ***to catch it***: to get a thrashing or a scolding. *colloq.*

1835 MARRYAT *Jac. Faithf.* xxxviii, We all thought Tom was about to catch it. **1848** MRS. GASKELL *M. Barton* xxxi, I shall catch it down stairs, I know. **1872** BLACK *Adv. Phaeton* xvi. 218 He catches it if he does not bring home a fair proportion to his wife.

42. ***to catch cold***: *formerly*, to become chilled by exposure to cold; *now*, to contract the ailment called a 'cold' or catarrh, to 'take cold'. Also, in this sense, ***to catch a cold***.

1591 SHAKS. *Two Gent.* I. ii. 136 Here they shall not lye, for catching cold. **1670** LASSELS *Voy. Italy* II. 98 It was my fortune to find her [an Echo] when she had catched a cold. **1712** ADDISON *Spect.* No. 517 ¶1 The old man caught a cold at the county-sessions. **1734** BERKELEY *Wks.* (1871) IV. 217, I can hardly stir abroad without catching cold. **1776** JOHNSON *Lett. Mrs. Thrale* (1788) I. 321 Mrs. Williams says that I have caught a cold this afternoon. **1861** FLOR. NIGHTINGALE *Nursing* 7 Never be afraid of open windows.. People don't catch cold in bed.

43. A person is said ***to catch the eye of*** another when their eyes meet, either fortuitously, or (more usually) when the one is purposely looking and thus arrests the glance of the other.

1813 JANE AUSTEN *Pride & Prej.* iii. 9 He looked for a moment at Elizabeth, till, catching her eye, etc. **1865** TROLLOPE *Belton Est.* v. 48 Clara caught her cousin's eye and smiled. **1883** LLOYD *Ebb & Fl.* I. 11 Here he caught Pauline's eye and stopped. *Mod.* Mr. A. and Mr. B. rose together, but the latter managed to catch the Speaker's eye.

44. ***to catch fire*** (formerly also ***to catch a fire***): to become ignited, 'take fire'; *fig.* to become inflamed or inspired (with passion, zeal, etc.).

1377 LANGL. *P. Pl.* B. xvii. 219 A candel þat cauȝte hath fyre & blaseth. **1601** HOLLAND *Pliny* I. 45 In Illyricum there is a cold spring, ouer which, if ye spread any clothes, they catch a fire and burne. **1734** WATTS *Relig. Juv.* (1789) 160 His soul catched fire. **1796** H. HUNTER tr. *St. Pierre's Stud. Nat.* (1799) I. 480 But how comes it, that air and water, though agitated ever so much, never catch fire? **1872** GEO. ELIOT *Middlem.* I. 338, I have a hyperbolical tongue: it catches fire as it goes.

45. ***to catch hold of*** (obs. *at, on*): to lay hold of, take hold of, seize, apprehend. Also *fig.*

1537 W. T. *Expos. St. John* 80 The deuel can ketch no hold on them. **1602** CAREW *Cornwall* 2 a, They will still gripe fast, what they haue once caught hold on. **1606** G. W[OODCOCKE] *Ivstine* 103 b, Which..caught hold at the least occasion [that] might intrap him. **1611** BIBLE *2 Sam.* xviii. 9 His head caught hold of the Oke. **1692** WASHINGTON tr. *Milton's Def. Pop.* ii. (1851) 44 This saying you catch'd hold of, thinking it would make for your purpose. **1719** DE FOE *Crusoe* (1840) I. xv. 251, I catched hold of Friday. **1848** MRS. GASKELL *M. Barton* xxxii, Catching hold of some rails.

46. ***to catch a glimpse, a sight of***: to get a momentary or sudden view of. ***to catch sight of***: to come abruptly in view of, to see all at once.

1825 KNAPP & BALDW. *Newgate Cal.* IV. 378/1 My daughter caught a sight of me. **1837** DICKENS *Pickw.* xxxvi, She..caught sight of what was going forward. **1848** MRS. GASKELL *M. Barton* vii, He turned to catch a look at her sweet face. **1848** MACAULAY *Hist. Eng.* I. 580 If once the train-bands had caught sight of his well known face. **1851** DIXON *W. Penn* i. (1872) 2 He caught some glimpses of the pirate holds. **1872** BLACK *Adv. Phaeton* xxx. 406 You catch a glimmer of the blue peaks of Westmoreland. **1875** JOWETT *Plato* (ed. 2) I. 193, I caught a sight of him over their heads.

47. ***to catch*** (someone) ***bending***: see BEND *v.* 9 d.

¶ *to catch a* CRAB, *a* TARTAR: see these words.

XI. Combined with adverbs.

48. catch away.

†**a.** *trans.* To chase away. *Obs.* See 1.

c **1325** *Metr. Hom.* 151 Alle thar kache me away. *c* **1440** *Promp. Parv.* 57 Cachyn away, *abigo*.

b. To seize and take away, snatch away.

c **1325** *E.E. Allit. P.* B. 1275 þay [Nebuchadnezzar's army] caȝt away þat condelestik. **1611** BIBLE *Matt.* xiii. 19 Then commeth the wicked one, and catcheth away that which was sowen. **1711** *Spect.* No. 524 ¶8 These would sometimes very narrowly miss being catched away.

†**49. catch forth.** *trans.* To drive out. *Obs.*

c **1400** *Destr. Troy* 2710 Caches furthe his cold wirdis.

†**50. catch off.** *trans.* To snatch or take off. *Obs.* See 19.

c **1420** *Anturs of Arth.* xlix, Wilfulle Waynour Keȝte of hur curonalle.

51. catch on. a. See 1 and 2.

b. *intr.* To attach or fix oneself to, join on, catch hold of. *colloq.*

1884 *Lisbon* (Dakota) *Star* 27 June, Now is the time to catch on in order to keep up with the procession. **1885** *Milnor* (Dakota) *Free Press* 28 Mar. 1/5 His sagacious mind immediately recognized and caught on to the only plan of salvation in sight.

c. *U.S.* To apprehend; = 35 a. *colloq.*

1884 *Cambridge* (Mass.) *Tribune* 18 July, He Didn't Catch-On to the Pronunciation. **1885** J. HAWTHORNE *Love or Name* 97, I dont think I catch on.

d. To 'take', make its way. Hence ***catch-on*** sb., a success (*rare*). *colloq.*

1887 *Pall Mall G.* 9 Mar. 1/2 A publisher never knows whether a new book will 'catch on'. **1895** G. B. SHAW *Our Theatres in Nineties* (1932) I. 274 The ordinary commercial west end theatre, with its ignoble gambling for 'a catch-on'. **1897** *Ibid.* III. 28 Commercial enterprise, always dreaming of 'catches-on', long runs, and 'silver mines', attempted to exploit the occasion in the usual way.

52. catch out. a. See 1 and 2. **b.** *Cricket*: see 24 c.

1330 R. BRUNNE *Chron.* (1810) 331 þe Inglis þe katched out. **1340** *Ayenb.* 171 Ase þet hote weter cacheþ þane hond out of þe kechene.

c. *fig.* To catch in a mistake, catch napping or in the act.

1816 JANE AUSTEN *Emma* II. xiv. 275 Ah! there I am—thinking of him directly. Always the first person to be thought of! How I catch myself out! **1881** MRS. LYNN LINTON *My Love* xvii, Randolph caught himself out in the vileness of wishing that she was just a trifle less superior. **1956** A. L. ROWSE *Early Churchills* xii. 230 His methods were distinctly unorthodox: that was what alarmed the Dutch text-book generals and caught out the French.

53. catch over. To freeze over: see 31 b.

54. catch up.

a. *trans.* To raise or carry suddenly aloft.

c **1325** *E.E. Allit. P.* C. 102 Cachen vp þe crossayl, cables þay fasten. **1611** BIBLE *2 Cor.* xii. 2 Caught vp to the third heauen. **1678** BUNYAN *Pilgr.* I. 33, I saw many catch'd up and carried away into the Clouds. **1873** BROWNING *Red Cott. Nt.-Cap* 234 An angel caught you up and clapped you down.

b. To take up or lift suddenly.

c **1400** *Destr. Troy* 13027 He comaund the corse cacche vp onone. **1602** SHAKS. *Ham.* II. ii. 532 A blanket in th' Alarum of feare caught vp. **1815** *Hist. Decastro & Bat* I. 112 She catched her feet up as if the floor burned her toes.

c. To take up or adopt quickly or eagerly.

1644 MILTON *Areop.* (Arb.) 35 This project..was catcht up by our Prelates. **1868** J. H. BLUNT *Ref. Ch. Eng.* I. 428 The tone of irreverence..which his followers too often caught up. **1887** *Atlantic Monthly* LX. 281 Catching up a popular neologism from the newspapers.

d. To interrupt, stop, 'pull up'.

1840 DICKENS *Barn. R.* xl, You catch me up so very short.

e. To overtake. Also in non-physical senses, and *intr.* esp. in ***to catch up on, to, with***. So **catching-up** *vbl. sb.*

1855 KINGSLEY *Westw. Ho* xiv. (1871) 244 If they catch us up—as they are sure to do, knowing the country better than we. **1857** TROLLOPE *3 Clerks* v. (1874) 55 We shall catch them up..before they leave the park. **1883** LLOYD *Ebb & Fl.* II. 242 Come along or we shall never catch them up. **1886** *Calcutta Englishman* in J. M. DIXON *Dict. Idiomatic Eng. Phrases* (1891) 58 He has not caught up (overtaken) his rival by the time earlier educational honours are distributed. **1923** H. CRANE *Let.* 5 Dec. (1965) 159 Getting things straightened around again and catching up on our supply of wood. **1925** E. F. NORTON *Fight for Everest, 1924* 114, I had to wait quite half an hour for him to catch up. **1925** *Times* (weekly ed.) 26 Nov., The police caught up on the men just as they entered a dark archway. **1926** *Ibid.* 5 Aug., Its sanitation can never catch up to its needs. **1927** JESPERSEN *Mod. Eng. Gram.* (1928) III. 271 Where an Englishman says 'I shall *catch you up*', or 'I'll *catch up with* you', Americans know only the latter phrase. **1941** A. L. ROWSE *Tudor Cornwall* xv. 412 Killigrew found himself in prison; his own misdemeanours..had at last..caught up with him. **1942** *19th Cent.* Feb. 90 This rapid catching-up on Western ideas. **1967** 'LA MERI' *Sp. Dancing* (ed. 2) vii. 89 Toward the middle of the [nineteenth] century the *Seguidillas Manchegas* caught up the waning popularity of the Bolero.

f. *U.S.* 'Among travellers across the great prairies, the phrase means, to prepare the horses and mules for the march' (Bartlett *Dict. Amer.*). *trans.* and *absol.*

18.. *N.Y. Spirit of Times, Frontier Tale* (Bartlett), They ..stayed till about noon, catched up their fresh horses, etc. **18..** *Prairie Scenes* (Bartlett), We've a long march before us; so catch up, and we'll be off.

catch-, in *comb.* and *attrib.* [Mainly the vb. used in phraseological combination, as *catch-all*, 'that can or will catch all'; or *attrib.*, as in *catch phrase*, catching phrase, 'phrase to catch'; but in sense 4 it may be the sb.]

I. With sbs., etc., in objective relation. (The resulting combination is a *sb.*, but capable also of being used *attrib.* or as *adj.*)

1. In sense 'one who or that which catches (what is expressed by the object)', as † ***catch-bit***, †***-cloak***, †***-coin***, †***-credit***, †***-fish***, †***-fool***, †***-plume***, ***-shilling*** (cf. CATCHPENNY); † **catch-dolt**, some form of cheating or swindling; † **catch-dotterel**, ? a cheat, sharper; **catch-'em-alive-o**, slang name for a 'fly-paper' for catching flies; **catch-water**, (*a*) (see quots. 1887, 1879); (*b*) a vessel designed to catch water. (Primarily *sbs.* but sometimes also used *attrib.* or as *adjs.*: see *catch-all*, *-shilling*, *-water*.) See also CATCHFLY, CATCHPENNY, CATCHPOLL.

Few of these are found before 1600.

1611 COTGR., *Tirelupin*, a *catch-bit or captious companion; a scuruie fellow. **1679** HOBBES *Dial. Com. Laws* (1840) 81 Cheaters, cutpurses, picklocks, *catchcloaks, coiners of false money. **1611** COTGR., *Gripp argent*, a *Catch-coyne; a greedie or couetous Judge. **1629** GAULE *Holy Madn.* 86 Hath made him a new kinde of *Catch-credit, of his old couer-shame. **1592** GREENE *Def. Conny-catch.* (1859) 4 At Dequoy, Mumchaunce, *Catch-dolt, Ourelebourse..none durst euer make compare with me for excellence. **1671** GLANVILL *Disc. M. Stubbe* 2 Impostors, *Catch-Dotterels, Fops, Tories. **1855** DICKENS *L. Dorrit* (Hoppe) Sticky old Saints, with..such coats of varnish that every holy personage served for a fly-trap, and became what is now called in the vulgar tongue a *'catch-'em-alive-o'. **1859** SALA *Tw. round Clock* (1861) 163 Itinerant vendors of catch-'em-alive-o's. *a* **1661** HOLYDAY *Juvenal* 53 Sons of some *catch-fish, or chief fencer. **1598** E. GILPIN *Skial.* (1878) 8 For pleasant *catch-fooles..he spares not To sweare hee's carelesse. *a* **1661** HOLYDAY *Juvenal*, The retiarius wore a feather in his crest: and so it might be render'd a *catch-plume. **1815** SOUTHEY *Lett.* (1856) II. 402 (D.) The other article is upon a catch penny or rather *catch shilling 'Life of Wellington'. **1799** A. YOUNG *Agric. Lincoln* xii. 275 The *catch-water drain runs all winter. **1838** *Civil Engin. & Archit. Jrnl.* I. 256/2, I shall now proceed to describe the mode of discharging, by catch-water courses or drains, all the brooks and rivers which flow into it. **1842** G. FRANCIS *Dict. Arts, Catch-water drains*, drains, or channels, cut in a slanting direction across and down embankments, therefore catching and carrying off the water which falls upon them. **1861** SMILES *Engineers* II. 160 Intercepting or catchwater drains. *a* **1877** KNIGHT *Dict. Mech.* I. 503/2 *Catch-water Drain*, a drain to intercept waters from high lands, to prevent their accumulation upon lower levels. **1877** LD. HATHERLEY in *Law Rep.* App. Cases II. 844 The weirs or catchwaters are used to divert the water to the lades. **1879** *Cassell's Techn. Educ.* VII. 23 In catch-water meadows the water is allowed to flow on to the most elevated portion..by means of a 'feeder'. **1869** *Echo* 9 Oct., *Catch-work, or running men, when with the threshing machines, received as much as 3*s.* a day. **1888** *Lockwood's Dict. Terms Mech. Engin., Interceptor*, a **T**-shaped cylindrical vessel employed in connection with marine engines to prevent particles of water from being carried over with the steam into the cylinders... Called also catch water. **1901** M. W. TRAVERS *Exper. Study Gases* 33 The water runs into a catch-water below the bulb, and is conducted away. **1963** *Times* 7 Mar. 10/6 Fourteen miles of catchwaters have been built around the valley, and it is hoped they will catch about 90 per cent of the rain that falls.

2. In sense 'to catch, the catching of (the object)', as ***catch-ball***, ***-cold*** (also *attrib.*); hence ***catch-coldy*** adj.

1631 J. BURGES *Answ. Rejoined* Pref. 70 You are as good at *catch-ball..but you strike not so well. **1881** MRS. HOLMAN HUNT *Childr. Jerus.* 30 Children..playing catch-ball. **1824** J. MCCULLOCH *Highl. Scotl.* III. 192 Sufficient warranty for this *catch cold. **1825** SCOTT *Diary* in *Lockhart* (1839) VIII. 148 No man..has less dread than I of the catch cold. **1884** *Daily News* 14 Nov. 5/4 Catch-cold weather. **1884** *Blackw. Mag.* Mar. 332/1, I am not a catch-coldy person.

II. In attributive relation to a sb.

3. In sense 'that catches or for catching'; **a.** *lit.*, as ***catch-bar***, ***-bolt***, ***-boom***, †***-hook***, ***-lock***, ***-pot***, ***ratline*** (see RATLIN(E 2), ***-tank***; **catch-basin**, (*a*) the receptacle placed beneath the grating of a sewer or other opening, to catch the dirt that is washed in; (*b*) a reservoir for catching and retaining surface-drainage over large areas; **catch-box**, a box-like clutch of a spinning machine; **catch-drain**, a drain or ditch, *esp.* on a hillside, to catch the surface water; also a drain by the side of a canal or conduit to catch the surplus water; **catch-fake** (see quot.); **catch-meadow**, ? a meadow irrigated by means of catch-drains; **catch-pit**, a pit to catch drainage sediment in water, etc.; also = *catch-basin*; **catch plate** (*Colliery*), an iron plate for catching the safety hook of the winding rope, and preventing the load from falling back, in case of overwinding; **catch-point**, a switch or point intended to derail a train, wagon, etc. (e.g. to prevent it from running on to a main line); **catch reservoir** (cf. *catch pit*); **catch siding**, a railway siding placed on steep inclines so as to catch and stop a carriage, etc. accidentally running back down the slope; **catch-stitch**, (*a*) *Bookbinding* = KETTLE-STITCH; (*b*) (see quot. 1968); also as vb.; **catch-wheel**, a wheel capable of motion in one direction only, a ratchet-wheel; **catch-work**, the method of irrigating a sloping meadow by means of catch-drains (see quot.); also *attrib.* See also CATCHWEED.

1850 *Rep. U.S. Comm. Patents 1849* 170 The second crank to slide the *catch bar. *a* **1877** KNIGHT *Dict. Mech.* 503/1 *Catch-bar* (Knitting-machine), a bar employed to depress the jacks. *Ibid.*, **Catch-basin*, a cistern at the point of discharge into a sewer. **1884** *Science* III. 372/1 Whether any ..system of catch-basins or reservoirs, could..mitigate.. such..floods. **1859** *U.S. Patent Off., Ann. Rep. 1858* I. 537 The levers or arms are designed to force back the *catch-bolt and lock-bolt. *a* **1877** KNIGHT *Dict. Mech.* 503/1 *Catch-bolt*, a cupboard or door-bolt which yields to the pressure in closing and then springs into the keeper in the jamb. Usually retracted by a small knob. **1905** *Terms Forestry & Logging* 33 **Catch boom*, a boom fastened across stream to catch and hold floating logs. **1825** J. NICHOLSON *Oper. Mech.* 426 When the *catch-box 14 is in contact with the sheeve *s*. **1892** NASMITH *Students' Cotton Spinning* 320 The wheel..is provided with a catch box..and by its means drives the shaft. **1834** *Brit. Husb.* I. 528 Where..the plane of the surface..presents a considerable descent, the *catch-drains instead of being carried straight across it, are cut in an angular direction across the line of descent. **1867** SMYTH *Sailor's Word-bk.*, **Catch-fake*, an unseemly doubling in a badly coiled rope. **1751** S. WHATLEY *Eng. Gazeteer, Higham* (*Leic.*), Great *catch-hooks and keepers of silver, with links

of a great gold chain. **1863** READE in *All Y. Round* 3 Oct. 126/2 His door..closed with a *catch-lock. **1843** PUSEY in *Jrnl. R. Agric. Soc.* IV. II. 314 The worthless slope would be converted into *catch-meadow. **1870** *Echo* 6 May 1/4 Forming a number of large *catch pits, and passing the water on its way to the river through them. **1882** *Gard. Chron.* No. 420. 45 A slight slope to one corner, to a small catch-pit, for the purpose of collecting the drainage. **1887** *Daily News* 11 Jan. 2/7 The force with which the cage was hurled into the head gear was so great that the bolts which fasten the *catch-plate to the girders were torn away. **1883** *Peel City Guardian* 27 Jan. 6/1 The mineral train came on at considerable speed, passed the signals, and through the *catch-points. **1895** *Daily News* 7 Dec. 7/7 That catch points should be more clearly indicated. **1902** *Encycl. Brit.* XXXII. 144/2 A throw-off or derailing switch ('catch-points'). **1936** *Gloss. Terms Rly. Signalling* (*B.S.I.*) 12 *Catch points*, trailing points provided on a rising gradient for the purpose of derailing a vehicle running back after breaking away. **1909** *Westm. Gaz.* 26 Oct. 11/4 Tin..runs through a channel..into a *catch-pot, whence it is ladled by small gourds..and poured. **1962** *New Scientist* 12 July 82/3 The catchpot was designed to hold the cathode in the event of its failure by fracture or melting. **1887** *Daily News* 4 July 3/4 To construct a *catch reservoir and pump into it water from the springs. **1846** DODD *Brit. Manuf.* VI. iv. 87 'Kettle-stitch'..is supposed by some to be a corruption of '*catch' or 'ketch' stitch, while others refer it to 'chain' stitch. **1906** D. COCKERELL in E. Johnston *Writing & Illum.* xvi. 347 At about ½ inch from either end make an additional line across the back for the 'kettle' or catch stitch. **1932** D. C. MINTER *Mod. Needlecraft* 123/1 Herring-bone Stitch..used for the same purposes as catch-stitch. *Ibid.* 208/2 Catch-stitch..all round on to the linen—no stitches showing through. **1964** *McCall's Sewing* xiv. 259/1 Lap front shoulder darts to stitching line and catch-stitch halfway down from the top. **1968** J. IRONSIDE *Fashion Alphabet* iii. 83 *Catch-stitch*, large cross-stitch used to hold heavy hems, invisible on right side. **1920** *Blackw. Mag.* May 706/2 The glen stream was never again diverted from its course, nor the *catch-tank drained. **1845** *Encycl. Metrop.* VIII. 619/1 This cylinder carries a *catch wheel..the teeth of which engage the click.. attached to the wheel C by a screw. **1799** T. WRIGHT *Art Floating Land* 82, I have seen the common plan of *catch-work watering resorted to. **1844** H. STEPHENS *Bk. Farm* III. 1022 Catch-work irrigation.

b. *fig.* in sense 'that catches or is meant to catch the eye, ear, fancy, etc.'; as ***catch-cry***, ***idea***, ***phrase***, ***sound***, CATCHWORD. **catch-line**, a short line of type that catches the eye; *spec.* in *Typogr.* (see quot. 1938); **catch title**, an abbreviated title sufficiently expressive of the full title to identify the book. (In this use, it is often treated as an independent adj. and written without hyphen.)

1901 *Daily Chron.* 20 Nov. 4/5 Some very sound remarks ..on certain *catch-cries of the day. **1916** W. B. YEATS *Eight Poems*, The clever man who cries The catch cries of the clown. **1884** *Chr. World* 19 June 454/1 He has..got hold of a few *catch-ideas. **1866** DICKENS *Repr. Pieces* 146 What you wanted was two or three good *catch-lines for the eye to rest on. **1909** WEBSTER, *Catch line*,..(*a*) A line containing the catchword at the foot of a page. (*b*) A short line in displayed matter. **1938** L. M. HARROD *Librarians' Gloss.* 35 *Catch line*, a line [of type] inserted at the top of matter by the compositor in order to identify it. **1958** T. LANDAU *Encycl. Librarianship* 66/1 *Catchline*, a temporary descriptive headline on galley proofs. Also a short line of type in between two large displayed lines. *a* **1850** CALHOUN *Wks.* (1874) IV. 206 The whole scheme, with all its plausible *catch-phrases. **1856** DOVE *Logic Chr. Faith* I. ii. 73 Catch phrases of this kind are sufficient to satisfy the simple. **1878** PAGE ROBERTS *Law & God* 127 It is not the *catch-sound of a verse which has authority, but the divine spirit of God's revelation. **1909** WEBSTER, **Catch title*, a short expressive title used for abbreviated book lists, etc. **1959** L. M. HARROD *Librarians' Gloss.* (ed. 2) 62 *Catchword title*... Also called 'Catch title'.

c. catch question, a question that catches one out or has a catch in it; also as vb.

a **1860** ALB. SMITH *Med. Student* (1861) 14 Legendary 'catch questions'. *Ibid.* 116 The inquisitors..are willing to help a student out of a scrape, rather than 'catch question' him into one. **1905** *Westm. Gaz.* 22 Apr. 3/1 The critics and commentators for centuries have been, like the philosophers, fooled by the catch-question of the Stuart King concerning the weight of a live fish in a bucket full of water.

d. That is or may be taken or 'caught' to one's advantage.

1895 *Westm. Gaz.* 4 Dec. 7/1 Until the end of President Cleveland's term Great Britain has a statesman, and not a catch-vote politician, to deal with. **1905** *Spectator* 7 Jan. 5/2 To put the policy of development at the mercy of a catch vote. **1907** *Daily Chron.* 15 Aug. 7/5 There was a strong catch tide in favour of the swimmers.

4. More loosely; as **catch-crop**, a crop got by catching or seizing an opportunity when the ground would otherwise lie fallow between two regular or main crops; hence **catch-cropping**, the raising of catch-crops; † **catch-land** (see quot.); **catch-match**, a match which is 'a catch' or great advantage to one of the parties; **catch-weight** (*Horse-racing*); also in Boxing and *Wrestling* (see quot. 1897).

1884 SIR T. ACLAND in *Pall Mall G.* 25 Feb. 2/1 *Catch crops rarely pay on a farm. **1887** *Daily News* 16 July 3/8 'Catch-cropping'..is now coming to be looked upon as a mark of skilful and thrifty farming. **1674** RAY *S. & E. Countr. Wds.* Coll. 61 **Catch-land*, land which is not certainly known to what Parish it belongeth; and the Minister that first gets the tithes of it enjoys it for that year. **1824** SCOTT *St. Ronan's* vi, She made out her *catch-match, and she was miserable. **1820** *Hoyle's Games Impr.* 477 General rules concerning Horse-racing. *Catch Weights are, each party to appoint any person to ride without weighing. **1863** *Punch* XLV. 86 The Archimandrite Nilos has offered to fight the Bishop of London for 20 pound a side, catch-weight. **1872** *Pall Mall G.* 1 Aug. 11 The 'catch' in 'catch weight'—which is almost synonymous with 'chance weight'—originally applied only to the weight which was 'caught' as best it might be. **1887** G. B. SHAW *Let.* 8 Feb. (1965) 164 The Socialist League have been challenged by C. Bradlaugh to pick a man to fight him at catch weight. **1897** *Encycl. Sport* I. 139/1 *Catchweight* (*To box at*)—Boxing without restrictions as to weight. **1907** *Daily Chron.* 18 Oct. 9/3 To wrestle the best of three falls for £50 a side at catch-weight. **1971** *Wrestling Rev.* XVI. v. 4/1 A catchweight contest.

catchable ('kætʃəb(ə)l), *a.* [f. CATCH *v.* + -ABLE.] That can be caught.

a **1695** LD. HALIFAX (T.) The eagerness of a knave maketh him often as catchable as the ignorance of a fool. **1866** CARLYLE *Remin.* (1881) II. 189 Both catchable and eligible. **1870** *Law Rep.*, *Com. Pleas* V. 670 A migratory fish..in a catchable and marketable state.

'catch-all, *sb.* orig. *U.S.* [CATCH- I.] A general receptacle. Also *fig.* and *attrib.*

1838 *Congress. Globe* 16 Apr. App. 275/1 [The party includes] old Federalists,..Antimasons, and Abolitionists. They have, sir, been a kind of catch-all, or *omnium gatherum*. **1866** MRS. STOWE *Lit. Foxes* ii. 27 The general catch-all and menagerie..for all the family litter. **1875** HOWELLS *Foregone Concl.* xviii. 296 A catch-all closet in the studio. **1892** *Harper's Mag.* June 29/1 A shrewd spider..had spread his gossamer catch-all beneath the bramble. **1897** 'MARK TWAIN' *Following Equator* xli. 383 It seemed to have been designed as a catch-all for every thing that can damage it. **1923** L. J. VANCE *Baroque* xiv. 86 The tenement yard was a simple black hole, for generations a common catch-all. **1945** 'L. LEWIS' *Birthday Murder* (1951) vi. 88 That cupboard.. has been a catchall for odds and ends for a long time. **1957** N. FRYE *Anat. Criticism* 304 The word novel..has since expanded into a catchall term which can be applied to practically any prose book that is not 'on' something. **1961** *Times* 10 Feb. 17/4 At Cambridge..history had become a 'catch-all' for students who found classics too difficult and science too serious. **1963** *Lancet* 19 Jan. 125/2 There is danger that it may become a catch-all term for maladies with puzzling clinical and anatomical features.

catchee. *nonce-wd.* [f. CATCH *v.* + -EE.] One who is caught: the correlative of *catcher*.

1839 *Fraser's Mag.* XX. 339 An uncomfortable 'catch'; the old god being the catchee, instead of the catcher.

catcher ('kætʃə(r)). [f. CATCH *v.* + -ER[1].]

† **1.** One who chases or drives; huntsman, driver. (Cf. CATCH *v.* I.) *Obs. rare.*

c **1340** *Gaw. & Gr. Knt.* 1139 Þenne þise cacheres þat couþe, cowpled her houndez. *c* **1440** *Promp. Parv.* 57 Cahchare or dryvare, *minator, abactor.*

2. One who or that which catches, in various current senses of the verb.

c **1400** *Test. Love* Prol., This booke..is..so drawe togider to maken the catchers [**1560** calthers] therof ben the more ready to hent sentence. **1541** PAYNELL *Catiline* iii. 4 A waster of his owne goodes, and a catcher of other mennes. **1553** BALE *Vocacyon* in *Harl. Misc.* (Malh.) I. 329 Deliuered from the snare of the catcher. **1562** J. HEYWOOD *Prov. & Epigr.* (1867) 18 The rough net is not the best catcher of burdis. **1580** SIDNEY *Arcadia* (1622) 219 The catcher now is caught. **1587** *Mirr. Mag.*, *Rudacke* v. 6 Watchers thereon..And catchers thereat. **1635** N. R. tr. *Camden's Hist. Eliz.* II. an. 14. 143 What jests lewd catchers of words made. **1779** FORREST *Voy. N. Guinea* 137 The natives catch them with bird-lime..the catchers kill them immediately. **1872** *Daily News* 13 July, The name of a new bowler or catcher. **1886** F. H. BURNETT *Little Ld. Fauntleroy* 122 The attitudes of pitcher and catcher and batter in the real game.

b. *techn.*

1832 HT. MARTINEAU *Hill & Vall.* iv. 61 The roller and his catcher who stand on each side of the rolling machine. **1861** SMILES *Workmen's Earn.* 27 Rate of wages..Rollers £5 10*s.* 0*d.*.. Catchers to ditto £1 10*s.* 0*d.*

† **3.** One who sings in a catch. *Obs. rare*$^{-1}$.

1641 BROME *Jov. Crew* IV. i. Wks. 1873 III. 419 Where be my Catchers? Come a Round.

4. *Comb.* **catcher-warp**, part of a loom.

1879 *Cassell's Techn. Educ.* IV. 390/2 The catcher-warps ..put in to hold down the chenille by its 'back-bone'.

catchfly ('kætʃflaɪ). [f. CATCH *v.* + FLY *sb.*] A name originally given by Gerard to *Silene Armeria* (see quot.); now used for *Lychnis Viscaria* and the various species of *Silene*.

1597 GERARD *Herbal* clxxvi. §1. 482, I have called it Catchflie, or Lime woort, The whole plant, as wel leaues as stalkes, and also the flowers, are couered ouer with a most thicke and clammie matter like vnto Birde lime. **1656** COLES *Art of Simpling* ix. 29 Some have a viscous matter adhering to it, as Catchfly. **1741** *Compl. Fam.-Piece* II. iii. 362 Hardy annual Flowers, as..sweet-scented Peas, Lobel's Catch-fly. *Ibid.* 373 Double Catchfly. **1776** WITHERING *Bot. Arrangem.* (1796) II. 413 *Silene anglica*, English Catchfly. **1863** BARING GOULD *Iceland* 192 Among the pebbles grows the red alpine catchfly.

catch-hold. *Wrestling.* [f. phr. *to catch hold*: see CATCH *v.* 45.] (See quot. 1889.)

1883 *Encycl. Brit.* XXIV. 690/2 The 'catch hold, first down to lose' style of wrestling. **1889** W. ARMSTRONG *Wrestling* 34 The catch-hold fashion is a most rational style of wrestling, as the competitors are..at liberty to catch each other as they please..provided they do not hold by the legs or clothes. **1898** *Encycl. Sport* II. 546/1 A style on the 'catch hold' principle.

'catchiness. [f. CATCHY *a.*] The quality of being catchy.

1898 *Century Mag.* Mar. 773 In spite of its dangerously instantaneous catchiness, it [*sc.* an étude] expresses just the sentiment of flattery in all its shades.

catching ('kætʃɪŋ), *vbl. sb.* [f. CATCH *v.* + -ING[1].]

a. The action of the verb CATCH, in various senses.

1297 R. GLOUC. (1724) 265 So muche vyss hii ssolde hym brynge, þat ech man wondry ssal of so gret cacchynge. *c* **1400** *Destr. Troy* 2281 Why couet we combraunse, or cachyng of harme? **1571** GOLDING *Calvin on Ps.* xxxvii. 7 Craftines and hurtfull catchinges. **1653** WALTON *Angler* ii. 48 The catching of a Trout. **1767** R. COTTON in F. S. Ashley-Cooper *Hambledon Cricket Chron. 1772–96* (1924) 183 Here's guarding, and catching, and throwing, and tossing. **1873** BLACK *Pr. Thule* xiv. 219 A quick catching of her breath. **1904** P. F. WARNER *Recov. Ashes* viii. 160 Rhodes bowled splendidly, as did Hirst, but our catching was wretched.

b. *spec.* Twitching.

1744 WALL in *Phil. Trans.* XLIII. 218, I found him delirious, with convulsive Catchings in the Tendons. **1758** J. S. *Le Dran's Observ. Surg.* (1771) 302 Catchings and Cramps. **1771** SMOLLETT *Humph. Cl.* (1815) 199 Profound sleep, uninterrupted by any catching or convulsion. **1870** BENNETT *Baby May* 13 Catchings up of legs and arms.

c. *attrib.*, as ***catching-hook***, ***-pen***, ***-season***.

a **1877** KNIGHT *Dict. Mech.*, *Catching-hook*, a crochet-hook. A crook or animal-catching hook. **1874** HARDY *Madding Crowd* xxii, In one angle a catching-pen was formed, in which three or four sheep were continously kept ready for the shearers to seize without loss of time. **1894** A. ROBERTSON *Nuggets* 4 He dashed into the catching pen, and seized the smaller of two sheep that remained. **1904** H. BUCKLAND in M. Cradock *Sport in N.Z.* II. vi. 172 The 'wool shed' where all shearing is done has a row of pens ('catching pens', they are called) in it..each pen holding some twenty-five to thirty sheep. **1914** H. B. SMITH *Sheep & Wool Ind. Australasia* vi. 34 Two shearers generally have one pen to catch their sheep from. They are called catching pens. **1891** *Scribner's Mag.* X. 470 During the planting-time [for oysters] as well as in the catching-season.

'catching, *ppl. a.* [f. as prec. + -ING[2].]

1. *gen.* That catches, in various senses; see the vb.

1413 LYDG. *Pylgr. Sowle* II. xlv. (1859) 51 Nayles hoked, and catchyng. *c* **1450** *Merlin* 106 Couetouse and cacchynge. **1597** J. KING *Jonas* (1618) 473 Busie and catching natures. **1684** T. BURNET *Th. Earth* II. 66 Still more catching and more combustible. **1806–7** J. BERESFORD *Miseries Hum. Life* vi. (1826) 35 A charming morsel of the picturesque.. delicious catching lights on the principal objects.

2. *spec.* Of diseases: Liable to be communicated from one person to another, infectious. Also *fig.*

1590 SHAKS. *Mids. N.* I. i. 186 Sicknesse is catching. **1662** FULLER *Worthies, Warwicksh.*, Bad Latin was a catching disease in that age. **1713** STEELE *Guardian* No. 24 ¶25 The virtues of men are catching as well as their vices. **1837** CARLYLE *Fr. Rev.* III. VI. iii. (L.) The assassin mood proves catching. **1885** *Law Times* LXXIX. 161/2 The mare was suffering from no catching disease.

3. In an uncertain or precarious state.

c **1611** CHAPMAN *Iliad* XXI, Fields that haue been long time cloide With catching weather. *a* **1670** HACKET *Abp. Williams* I. (1692) 114 Peace between the two kingdoms was but in a doubtful and catching condition. **1768–74** TUCKER *Lt. Nat.* (1852) II. 93 When..frequent showers double his charges, his labour, his care..in a catching harvest. **1832** MISS MITFORD *Village* Ser. v. (1863) 473 The weather..was, on the contrary, of that description which is termed 'catching'. **1876** *Rep. Vermont Board Agric.* III. 481 The 'catching' rains of harvest time..will always fetch a lugubrious wail from any farmer.

4. *fig.* Entrapping; deceptive, 'catchy'.

1603 KNOLLES *Hist. Turks* (1638) 175 What to answer him vnto this his catching question. **1658–9** *Burton's Diary* (1828) III. 334 This is an exceeding catching question. **1880** MACALPIN *Money-lenders* 289 Catching bargains with 'expectant heirs' are set aside.

5. That catches the eye, the fancy, etc.; attractive, captivating, 'taking'.

1654 *Burton's Diary* (1828) I. Introd. 26 These words were extremely catching to the generality of the House. **1816** KEATINGE *Trav.* II. 126 The objects most catching to the eye of the navigator.

Hence **'catchingness**, catching quality.

1655 FULLER *Hist. Camb.* 37 Carelesness of coals and candles, catchingness of Papers. **1884** *Spectator* No. 2903. 221 The irresistible catchingness of Gay's ballads.

catchment ('kætʃmənt). [f. CATCH *v.* + -MENT.]

= CATCHING; appropriated to the catching and collection of the rainfall over a natural drainage area, in ***catchment basin***, ***area*** (also *transf.* and *fig.*, as the region from which a hospital's patients, a school's pupils, etc., are drawn).

1847 J. DWYER *Hydr. Engineer.* 19 A great portion of the catchment basin is very little raised above the level of the lake. **1878** HUXLEY *Physiogr.* 34 The catchment-basin is a term applied to all that part of a river-basin from which rain is collected, and from which therefore the river is fed. **1881** *Times* 2 Feb., We have..eleven [rivers] with catchment basins exceeding a thousand square miles. **1885** *Blackw. Mag.* Jan. 109/1 A vast catchment-area of encircling rock. **1959** *Times* 28 May 13/7 The catchment area for Leeds [prison] is dense—reputedly four and a half million people. **1960** *Library Assoc. Record* Aug. 261/2 *Catchment Area*, in library planning denotes the area from which readers may be expected to be drawn to a given library service point. **1961** *Lancet* 12 Aug. 357/2 It [*sc.* the hospital] has been used for patients of good prognosis from all parts of the Metropolitan area, instead of being more strictly attached to a catchment area. **1962** A. NISBETT *Technique Sound Studio* 248 It [*sc.* the diaphragm of a microphone] should be..big enough to present a sufficiently large catchment area to the pressure of the sound wave. **1970** *Daily Tel.* (Colour Suppl.) 3 Apr. 21/1

For the children's sake, they are going to buy a house in the catchment area of a modern primary school which has a nursery class.

catchoo, variant of CACHOU, CATECHU.
c **1760** J. H. GROSE *Voy. E. Ind.* I. 238 (Y.) What they call Catchoo, of a blackish granulated perfumed composition.

catchpenny ('kætʃpɛnɪ), *sb.* (*a.*) [f. CATCH- I + PENNY.]
1. Something (esp. a publication) of little value, designed to attract purchasers.
1760 *Lond. Mag.* XXIX. 36 The general run of catch penny's upon the subject. **1785** WESLEY *Wks.* (1872) IV. 321 The late pretty tale of her being the Emperor's daughter is doubtless a mere catch-penny. **1850** W. IRVING *Goldsmith* x. 133 You know already by the title that it is no more than a catch-penny.
2. *attrib.* or *adj.* Designed to attract purchasers; got up merely to sell.
1759 GOLDSM. *Butler's Rem.* Wks. 1837 IV. 467 One of those catchpenny subscription works. **1850** L. HUNT *Autobiog.* vi. (1860) 113 The catchpenny lyrics of Tom Dibdin. **1879** GEO. ELIOT *Theo. Such* xiv. 257 Full of catchpenny devices and stagey attitudinising.

catchpole, -poll ('kætʃpəʊl). Forms: ? 1 kæcepol, cæccepol, 2–4 cachepol, 4 cacchepol, 4–5 kachepol(l, 4–6 cachepoll, 5 cachepoll, cahchpolle, 6 catchepolle, -pole, catchipolle, catchpoule, catchepoll, 6–7 catchpol, 4– catchpoll, 6– catchpole. [a. med.L. *cacepollus*, ONF. **cachepol* = central OF. *chacepol, chacipol, chassipol*, in med.L. also *cachepolus, chacepollus, chacipollus, chassipullus* (Du Cange), lit. 'chase-fowl', one who hunts or chases fowls. The form of the word appears to indicate that it arose in Provençal, where it would be *cassapol*, or It., where it would be *cacciapollo*. The OF. was apparently adapted from Pr. or med.L.
A charter of 1107 (St. Hugues, Grenoble) has the word as a surname, 'ego Franco *cassat pullum*', 'ego Franco de Biveu quem vocant *cassa pullum*', where the first element is the Provençal, (and thence med.L.) verb *cassare* (:—L. *captiāre*) in 3rd pers. sing. Of similar names, Geraldus *Cazaporcs* 'swine driver' witnesses a charter of 1097 (St. Victor of Marseilles); Petrus *Chaceporc*, clericus regis Henrici III, witnesses a charter of 1246 (Bordeaux); *Cacheleu* appears as the older form of *Chasseloup* 'wolf-hunter'; *Cachepouil*, in 15th c. *Cachapeolls*, f. *pediculus* louse, is the name of a mill near Perigueux. (P. Meyer).)]
†**1.** A tax-gatherer, an exactor of taxes or imposts; a (Roman) publican. *Obs.*
a **1050** ÆLFRIC *Voc.* in Wr.-Wülcker 111 *Exactor*, kæcepol [*printed* hæce wol]. *c* **1175** *Lamb. Hom.* 97 Matheus þet wes cachepol þene he iwende to god-spellere. *c* **1500** *Cocke Lorelles B.* (1843) 4 Crystofer catchepoll a crystes course gaderer. *a* **1563** BECON *Fasting* in *Catechism. &c.* (1844) 536 What usurer leaveth his usury?..what catchpole his extortion? **1612–15** [see CATCHPOLESHIP]. **1652** C. STAPYLTON *Herodian* xx. 167 Then all the Catchpole Officers were slain.
2. A petty officer of justice; a sheriff's officer or sergeant, *esp.* a warrant officer who arrests for debt, a bum-bailiff. (Used in early times to render L. *lictor*; since 16th c., at least, a word of contempt.)
1377 LANGL. *P. Pl.* B. XVIII. 46 *Crucifige*, quod a cacchepolle I warante hym a wicche. **1382** WYCLIF *1 Sam.* xix. 20 Saul sente catchpollis [Vulg. *lictores*] for to take David. **1393** LANGL. *P. Pl.* C. XXI. 76 Quikliche cam a cacchepol and craked a-two here legges. *c* **1440** *Promp. Parv.* 58 Cahchpolle or pety-seriawnte, *angarius, exceptor.* *c* **1440** *Gesta Rom.* 21 (Harl. MS.) The Cachepollys And the mynistris of the Emperour mette with hem. **1596** NASHE *Saffron Walden* 9 As ready as any catchpoule..to torment him. **1607–72** COWELL *Interpr.*, *Catchpole*, though now it be used as a word of contempt, yet, in ancient times, it seems to have been used without reproach. **1668** R. L'ESTRANGE *Vis. Quev.* (1708) 3 Your Algouazils (or Catch poles) and your Devils are both of an order. **1760** GOLDSM. *Cit. W.* xcviii, The catchpole watches the man in debt. **1809** W. IRVING *Knickerb.* (1861) 81, I have a mortal antipathy to catchpolls, bumbailiffs, and little great men. **1841** MACAULAY *Ess., Hastings* (1854) II. 623 Miserable catchpoles..with Impey's writs in their hands.
b. *attrib.* and in *comb.*
a **1643** BOYS in Spurgeon *Treas. Dav.* Ps. xlv. 2 The very catch-poll officers..gave this testimony. **1601** *Downf. Earl Huntington* I. iii. in Hazl. *Dodsley* VIII. 118 Follow him, ye catchpole-bribed grooms. **1784** COWPER *Task* II. 684 As fast as catchpole claws Can seize the slipp'ry prey.
Hence **'catchpolery, catchpollery** [OF. *chassipollerie*, med.L. *chacipollaria*]; **'catchpoleship; 'catchpoll** *v.*, (*a*) *intr.* to exercise the function of a catchpole; (*b*) *trans.* only in *passive*, to be seized or arrested by a catchpole; **'catchpolling** *vbl. sb.*
1576 NEWTON tr. *Lemnie's Complex.* (1633) 93 The fourth part of the goods, for their catchpolling, falleth to them, for their lot and share. **1604** DEKKER *Honest Wh.* xii. Wks. 1873 II. 66 A rescue (prentises) my masters catchpol'd. **1612–15** BP. HALL *Contempl. N.T.* IV. iii. (1833) 175 This catchpoleship of Zaccheus carried extortion in the face. **1668** R. L'ESTRANGE *Vis. Quev.* (1708) 2 A Devil catchpol'd, and not a Catchpole bedevil'd. **1835** *Fraser's Mag.* XII. 171 All the duns, bums..and the other accursed components of that diabolical system called 'Catchpollery'.

†**catchpole, -ule**, var. CACHESPELL, tennis.
1663 BLAIR *Autobiog.* i. (1848) 8 The exercise of my body by archery and the catchpole.

catchup ('kætʃʌp), **catsup** ('kætsʌp). [see KETCHUP.] A liquor extracted from mushrooms, tomatoes, walnuts, etc., used as a sauce. (Common in N. Amer., but in the U.K. now only KETCHUP.)
1690 B. E. *Dict. Cant. Crew, Catchup*, a high East-India Sauce. **1730** SWIFT *Paneg. on Dean* Wks. 1755 IV. I. 142 And, for our home-bred british cheer, Botargo, catsup, and caveer. **1751** MRS. GLASSE *Cookery Bk.* 309 It will taste like foreign Catchup. **1832** *Veg. Subst. Food* 333 One..application of mushrooms is..converting them into the sauce called Catsup. **1845** ELIZA ACTON *Mod. Cookery* v. (1850) 136 (L.) Walnut catsup. **1862** *Macm. Mag.* Oct. 466 He found in mothery catsup a number of yellowish globular bodies.

catchweed ('kætʃwiːd). *Herb.* [f. CATCH *v.* + WEED.] Goose-grass or Cleavers (*Galium Aparine*).
1776 WITHERING *Bot. Arrangem.* (1796) II. 193 Catchweed, Goosegrass, Cleavers, Clivers. **1861** MISS PRATT *Flower. Pl.* III. 154 Leaves, stems, and globular fruits are all bristly, and the latter often cling to the clothing..thus it is called..Catchweed.

catchword ('kætʃwɜːd). [f. CATCH- 3 b + WORD.]
1. *Printing.* The first word of the following page inserted at the right-hand lower corner of each page of a book, below the last line. (Now rarely used.) Also in *Manuscripts.*
1730–6 in BAILEY. **1755** JOHNSON, *Catchword*, with printers, the word at the corner of the page under the last line, which is repeated at the top of the next page. **1817** MAR. EDGEWORTH *Love & L.* III. xxxvi. 22 In the last page..the catch-words at the bottom were Countess Christina. **1824** J. JOHNSON *Typogr.* I. 68 Catch-words, now generally abolished, were first used at Venice, by Vindeline de Spire. **1882** GROSART in *Spenser's Wks.* IV. 3/2 Catch-word is misprinted. **1885** E. M. THOMPSON in *Encycl. Brit.* XVIII. 144/2 Catch-words to connect the quires date back to the 12th century. **1957** N. R. KER *Catal. MSS. Anglo-Saxon* p. xl, Some quires of..f. 245ᵛ have catchwords.
2. A word so placed as to catch the eye or attention; *spec.* **a.** the word standing at the head of each article in a dictionary or the like; **b.** the rime word in verse; **c.** the last word in an actor's speech, serving as a guide to the next speaker; a cue.
c **1780** C. LLOYD *Rhyme* (R.) More demands the critic ear Than the two catchwords in the rear Which stand like watchmen in the close To keep the verse from being prose. **1814** JANE AUSTEN *Mansf. Park* I. xviii. 346 The others aspired at nothing beyond his remembering the catchword, and the first line of his speech. **1863** *Reader* 28 Nov. 638 A tick at the beginning and end of [the passage] and a line under the word show of what extent the passage is to be, and what the catchword is. **1868** C. WORDSWORTH in Spurgeon *Treas. Dav.* Ps. xxxiii. 1 This Psalm is coupled with the foregoing one by the catchword with which it opens. **1879** *Directions to Readers for Dict.*, Put the word as a catchword at the upper corner of the slip. **1884** *Athenæum* 26 Jan. 124/2 The arranging of the slips collected..and the development of the various senses of every Catchword. **1885** *Law Q. Rev.* 297 The Digester should..revise every catch-word in the Reports.
3. A word caught up and repeated, *esp.* in connexion with a political or other party. (Cf. *catch-phrase* under CATCH- 3 b.)
1795 WINDHAM *Speeches Parl.* (1812) I. 259 The Influence and dangerous tendency of these party catchwords. **1812** *Examiner* 25 May 332/1 Public virtue is only the catch-word of knaves to delude fools. **1870** LOWELL *Study Wind.* 106 Many of his phrases have become the catchwords of party politics. **1886** W. S. LILLY *Europ. Hist.* II. 229 His [the Abbé Fauchet's] catch-word [Fraternity]..has survived him..as the third article of the Revolutionary symbol.
4. catchword entry (see quots.).
1893 in *Funk's Stand. Dict.* **1938** L. M. HARROD *Librarians' Gloss.* 35 *Catchword entry*, entry by some striking word in a book's title, other than the first, and likely to be remembered by an enquirer. **1956** F. C. AVIS *Bookman's Concise Dict.* 54/1 *Catchword Entry*, an entry of the name of a book in a catalogue under its most important word, as Pickwick Papers.

catchy ('kætʃɪ), *a. colloq.* [f. CATCH *v.* + -Y¹.]
1. Adapted to catch the attention or fancy; attractive, 'taking'.
1831 *Fraser's Mag.* III. 679 A catchy, stage-like effect. **1885** *Athenæum* 9 May 593 Catchy titles. **1887** *Ayrshire Post* 4 June 5 The building is..by no means, unduly striking or 'catchy' to the eye.
2. That catches or entraps; deceptive. Also, liable to 'trip one up', difficult to manage or execute.
1877 *Coursing Calendar* 285 Mr. Hedley, for the second time, pleased everyone with his judging; whilst Johnston, who slipped for the first time on such catchy ground, performed his duties well. **1882** R. HUNTER et al. *Encycl. Dict.* II. 1, *Catchy*,..difficult, not easy to learn or to execute. (*Colloquial.*) **1885** SIR N. LINDLEY in *Law Times Rep.* 482/1 The condition imposed was a catchy and not a fair condition.
3. Readily caught up.
1881 *Pall Mall Budget* 29 April 12/2 A smaller number of catchy tunes. **1885** *Pall Mall G.* 2 Sept. 4/1 The music is not particularly original, but it is tuneful, smooth, and 'catchy'.
4. Occurring in snatches, fitful, spasmodic.
1872 MARK TWAIN *Innoc. Abr.* 137 Catchy ejaculations of rapture. **1883** *Blackw. Mag.* Aug. 214 The wind..was very catchy.
5. *Sc.* 'Merry, jocund' (Jam.).
1804 TARRAS *Poems* 2 (Jam.) He..langs To crack wi' San', and hear his catchie glees.

†**'catcluke.** *Sc. Obs.* [f. CAT *sb.*¹ + CLUKE claw.] The plant Bird's-foot Trefoil.
1513 DOUGLAS *Æneis* XII. Prol. 116 The clavyr, catcluke, and the cammamyld. *a* **1568** in Sibbald *Chron. Sc. Poetry* (1802) III. 203 (Jam.) Ane hat..With catclukes strynklit in that steid, And fynkill grein.

catdom ('kætdəm). [f. CAT *sb.*¹ + -DOM.] The condition or quality of cats; the world of cats.
1888 *Pall Mall Gaz.* 25 Oct. 3/1 A charming specimen of catdom in one 'Jimmy'. **1890** *Illustr. Lond. News* 10 May 599/3 The winning ways of 'catdom' and 'kittenhood'.

cate, usually in *pl.* **cates** (keɪts), *sb.*¹ Also 6 caittes. [aphetized form of ACATE: the original sense being 'purchase'.]
†**1.** *pl.* Provisions or victuals bought (as distinguished from, and usually more delicate or dainty than, those of home production); in later use, sometimes merely = victuals, food. *Obs.* See ACATE 2.
1461–83 *Ord. R. Househ.* 38 Upon frydaye is made paymente for all manner of freshe cates. **1530** *Test. Ebor.* (Surtees) V. 293 The vetulers howse..wher I bought my caittes. **1548** UDALL, etc. *Erasm. Par. Mark* vi. 48 To by them cates to eate. **1579** LYLY *Euphues* (Arb.) 132 Purvayour for his cates at home. **1590** GREENE *Fr. Bacon* ix. 237 Bid them fall unto their frugal cates. **1658** USSHER *Ann.* VI. 300 Provision enough of corn, and salt, and water, but there was no store of fresh Cates to be had. **1782** HAN. MORE *David* II. 32 Such plain cates and rural viands as suit his frugal fortune. **1816** SCOTT *Old Mort.* xii, The cates which she had provided. **1866** FELTON *Anc. & Mod. Gr.* I. II. iii. 321 Sprinkling with flour the boiling cates.
b. Its frequent use with *delicate, dainty*, and the like, led to sense 2.
1579 LYLY *Euphues* (Arb.) 152 For the desire of delicate cates. **1594** BARNFIELD *Aff. Sheph.* I. vi, Where daintie Cates upon the Board were set. **1637** NABBE *Microcosm.* in *Dodsley* IX. 146 All the ambrosian cates Art can devise for wanton appetite. **1729** SAVAGE *Wanderer* I. 241 Sav'ry cates, upon clean embers cast. **1735** SOMERVILLE *Chase* III. 126 Well fed with every nicer Cate.
2. Choice viands; dainties, delicacies.
1578 TIMME *Calvin on Gen.* 92 The best fruits, what and how many cates and delights had he in one kind. **1594** GREENE *Look. Glass* Wks. 1831 I. 122 These curious cates are gracious in mine eye. **1596** SHAKS. *Tam. Shr.* II. i. 190 Kate, the prettiest Kate in Christendome, Kate of Kate-hall, my super-daintie Kate, for dainties are all Kates, and therefore Kate Take this of me, Kate of my consolation. **1652** C. STAPYLTON *Herodian* xv. 126 While he in Silks and Cates did much abound. **1742** SHENSTONE *Schoolmistr.* 206 Whence oft with sugar'd cates she doth 'em greet. **1870** DISRAELI *Lothair* xxviii. 130 He fed her with cates as delicate as her lips.
b. occas. in *sing.*: A viand, dainty.
1634 HEYWOOD *Witches Lanc.* III. i. Wks. 1874 IV. 204 Taste of every cate. **1710** ADDISON *Tatler* No. 255 ¶3 The Christmas Pye, which in its very Nature is a kind of consecrated Cate. **1864** SIR F. PALGRAVE *Norm. & Eng.* III. 23 The finest wheat-corn; then a cate or luxury. **1875** F. I. SCUDAMORE *Day Dreams* 22 Though it is a toothsome cate.
3. *fig.*
1615 T. ADAMS *Blacke Devill* 22. **1624** MASSINGER *Bondman*, The pleasant taste these cates of comfort yield me. **1633** BENLOWES *Pref. Verses* in *P. Fletcher's Purple Isl.*, Let Readers judge thy book: Such Cates, should rather please the Guest, than Cook.

†**cate**, *sb.*² *Obs.* [Pg. *cate*, prob. ad. Hindī. *kaṭh* catechu.] The same as CATECHU or CUTCH.
[**1554** in Nunes; **1578** in D'ACOSTA (Yule).] **1698** *Phil. Trans.* XX. 465 The preparation of Cate (which he takes to be the same with Catechu).

†**cate**, *v. Obs.* [f. CATE *sb.*¹] To dress (food).
1617 HIERON *Wks.* II. 51 The same meate cated one way content the stomake, which in some other fashion would not please.

cate, obs. f. CAT and CATTY *sb.*

†**catechese.** *Obs. rare.* In 7 catachese. [a. F. *catéchèse*, ad. L. *catēchēsis*.] = next.
1617 COLLINS *Def. Bp. Ely* II. x. 419 Which words were the conclusion of his last Catachese.

‖**catechesis** (kætɪ'kiːsɪs). [L., a. Gr. κατήχησις instruction by word of mouth, n. of action f. κατηχεῖν to instruct orally, orig. to resound, sound amiss, 'din one's ears', f. κατά down, thoroughly, etc. + ἠχεῖν to sound, ring.]
1. Oral instruction given to catechumens; catechizing.
1753 CHAMBERS *Cycl. Supp.* s.v., In the antient church catechesis was an instruction given, viva voce, either to children, or adult Heathens, preparatory to their receiving of baptism. **1845** R. HAMILTON *Pop. Educ.* vi. (ed. 2) 135 The little community shall become the Bible class and be addicted to a Bible catechesis.
2. A book for catechetical instruction, *spec.* the name of a work of St. Cyril of Jerusalem.
1753 CHAMBERS *Cycl. Supp.* s.v., The catecheses of St. Cyril, are the principal work of that father. **1849** W. FITZGERALD tr. *Whitaker's Disput.* 597 How far he is from approving unwritten traditions, he shews plainly in the fourth Catechesis.

catechetic (kætɪˈkɛtɪk), *a.* and *sb.* Also 7–8 **-tick.** [ad. L. *catēchētic-us*, a. Gr. κατηχητικ-ός, f. κατηχητ-ής oral instructor: deriv. as prec.]

A. *adj.* Of or pertaining to catechesis; according to the manner of a catechism. See CATECHETICAL 1 and 2.

1661 FELL *Dr. Hammond* (R.) In the catechetick institution of the youth of his parish. *a* **1672** WOOD *Life* (1848) 243 *note*, Of such sort a Catechetic Lecture must be. **1702** ADDISON *Evid. Chr. Relig.* (1727) 302 In the year 202 the great Origen was appointed Regent of the Catechetick School in Alexandria. **1718** HICKES & NELSON *J. Kettlewell* II. i. 65 Catechetick Lectures upon the Creed. **1858** BUSHNELL *Serm. New Life* 181 Catechetic orthodoxy.

B. *sb.* mostly *pl.* **catechetics.** That part of Christian theology which treats of catechesis.

1849 J. BROWN *J. Fisher* ii. 16 He answered his catechetics and chronological questions on the last half of the 10th century. **1882** W. BLAIKIE *Minist. of Word* 296 Ample treatises on Homiletics, Liturgics, Catechetics and Poimenics. **1882–3** SCHAFF *Relig. Encycl.* 417 Catechetics.. corresponds to catechesis, as theory to practice.

b. Catechetic writings or treatises. (Gr. κατηχητικά.)

1849 W. FITZGERALD tr. *Whitaker's Disput.* 596 Cyril of Jerusalem..in his Catechetics.

catechetical (kætɪˈkɛtɪkəl), *a.* Also 7 **-call.** [f. as prec. + -AL[1].]

1. Of, pertaining to, or connected with catechetics or catechesis; pertaining to instruction in the elementary principles of Christianity.

1624 GATAKER *Transubst.* 43 To omit Cyril of Jerusalem his Catecheticall Sermons. **1702** ECHARD *Eccl. Hist.* (1710) 515 In this city was a famous catechetical school for training persons up in divine knowledge. **1882** FARRAR *Early Chr.* I. 279 The great catechetical school of Alexandria, which claimed as its founder the Evangelist St. Mark.

2. Of, pertaining to, or in accordance with the catechism of a church.

1618 HALES *Let.* in *Golden Rem.* (1688) 386 There should be observed a three-fold Catechizing..A third in the Church by Catechetical Sermons. **1726** AMHERST *Terræ Fil.* xlix. 266 A considerable sum to buy advowsons of livings, and to maintain a catechetical lecture. **1849** J. BROWN *J. Fisher* ii. 17 *note*, To show that he preached catechetical doctrine.

3. Resembling the method of instruction by questions and answers, as in the catechism; 'consisting of questions and answers' (J.).

1691 BP. WORCESTER *Charge* 18 The true Grounds of Religion; which are easiest learn'd, and understood, and remembered in the short Catechetical Way. **1704** NELSON *Fest. & Fasts* (1739) Pref. 17 To throw the whole Subject.. into a catechetical Form. **1711** ADDISON *Spect.* No. 239 ¶3 Socrates introduced a catechetical Method of Arguing. He would ask his Adversary Question upon Question, till he had convinced him out of his own Mouth that his Opinions were wrong. **1845** R. HAMILTON *Pop. Educ.* iv. (ed. 2) 65 Stout advocates of catechetical methods and forms.

Hence **cateˈchetically** *adv.*, in a catechetical manner; in the authoritative manner of a catechism.

1730–6 in BAILEY. *a* **1834** LAMB *Misc. Wks.* (1871) 451 To pronounce, dogmatically and catechetically, who was the richest..man that ever lived. **1842** G. S. FABER *Provincial Lett.* (1844) II. 28 All those who had been catechetically instructed and duly baptised.

ˈcatechin. *Chem.* A substance obtained from catechu, etc., after the removal of the tannin; a white powder composed of very small silky needles.

1853 *Pharm. Jrnl.* XIII. 79 He has detected catechine in kino. **1876** HARLEY *Mat. Med.* 641 The insoluble portion is a mass of acicular crystals, catechin or catechuic acid.

†**catechise** (ˈkætɪkɪz). *Obs.* exc. *dial.* In 6 catechis. [app. ad. F. *catéchèse* CATECHESE, confounded with the vb. CATECHIZE, in F. *catechise-r*. The Sc. corruption *carritches* rests upon a pronunciation (ˈkatətʃɪs); cf. F. (kateʃɛz).] = CATECHESIS, CATECHISM.

1552 ABP. HAMILTON *Catech.* (1884) 7 In the foure partis of this present Catechis. *Ibid.* 122 In the thrid part of this Catechis, quhilk intraittis of the sevin sacramentis. **1637** GILLESPIE *Eng. Pop. Cerem.* II. ii. 13 For every particular head of Catechise. **1659** GAUDEN *Tears of Ch.* 619 No Sermons, no Prayers, no Catechises. **1707** E. WARD *Hud. Rediv.* I. VIII, And open all thy Peoples Eyes, To read th' Assembly's Catechise. **1715** DE FOE *Fam. Instruct.* I. i. (1841) I. 13 You know your catechise. **1825** *Bro. Jonathan* III. 150 After the fashion of your..Yankee, when he is.. teaching the 'catechise'. [In mod.Eng. dialects, where generally treated as a corruption of *catechism.*]

b. in *comb.*, as *catechise-point.*

1655 GURNALL *Chr. in Arm.* (1669) 125/1 Fundamental Truths, or, as we call them, Catechise-points.

catechism (ˈkætɪkɪzm). Forms: 6 (?) **catechyzon, cathecysme, chatechisme,** 6–7 **catechisme,** 6– **catechism.** [ad. L. *catēchismus* (in med.L. also *cathecismus*), on Gr. type *κατηχισμός (n. of action f. κατηχίζ-ειν) taken as = κατήχησις; see CATECHESIS. Cf. F. *catéchisme.*]

†**1.** Catechetical instruction; catechesis. *Obs.*

1502 *Ord. Crysten Men* I. ii. (W. de W. 1506) 14 And that suffyseth as now of the exorcysme and cathecysme. **1579** FULKE *Heskins' Parl.* 407 The learners of Catechisme were dismissed after the Lessons that were read. **1600** SHAKS. *A.Y.L.* III. ii. 241 To say I and no, to these particulars, is more then to answer in a Catechisme.

2. An elementary treatise for instruction in the principles of the Christian religion, in the form of question and answer; such a book accepted and issued by a church as an authoritative exposition of its teaching, as the *(Church) Catechism*, that of the Church of England in the Book of Common Prayer, the ***Longer*** and ***Shorter Catechisms***, of the Westminster Assembly of Divines, used by the Presbyterian churches, etc.

1509 J. COLLET *Foundat. Stat. St. Paul's Sch.* in *Lib. Cantab.* (1855) 452/3 The maister shall..first se, that they can saye the catechyzon [? -yzm]. I will the children learne first above all the catechyzon in Englishe. [**1540** CRANMER (*title*), Catechismus; that is to say, a Shorte Instruction into Christian Religion, for the synguler commoditie and profyte of Children and yong people.] **1549** *Bk. Com. Prayer*, A Catechism, that is to say, an Instruction to be learned of every child before he be brought to be confirmed of the Bishop. **1552** ABP. HAMILTON *Catech.* 26 Ane Catechisme, that is ane common instruction contenand schortly and plainly thai thingis quhilk ar necessary to tham to ken and keip, to the plesour of God and thair eternal salvation. **1597** *Pilgr. Parnass.* III. 354 Twoo or three hundreth of chatechismes of Jeneva's printe. **1648** (*title*) The Shorter Catechism, agreed upon by the Assembly of Divines at Westminster. **1653** WALTON *Angler* i. 31 That good, plain, unperplext Catechism, that is printed with the old Service Book. *a* **1711** KEN *Direct. Prayer* Wks. (1838) 339 The doctrine delivered in the Catechism. **1752** A. MAIR (*title*), Brief Explication of the Assemblie's Shorter Catechism. **1841–4** EMERSON *Ess. Circles* Wks. (Bohn) I. 130 We can never see Christianity from the catechism.

3. *transf.* A book of instruction in other subjects by question and answer. (In 17th c. chiefly applied to works which parodied the preceding; its serious use and general extension came later.)

a **1637** B. JONSON *Verses on Drayton's Muse* (R.) This book! is a catechism to fight And will be bought of every lord and knight, That can but read. **1643** HEYLIN (*title*), The Rebels Catechism. **1754** (*title*), The Freethinker's Catechism; that is to say an Instructor, to be learned by every Young Fellow, before he can know the world. **1795** J. ROSE (*title*), A Constitutional Catechism, adapted to all ranks and capacities. **1806** DALBIAC (*title*), A Military Catechism for the use of young Officers. **1844** *Regul. & Ord. Army* 127 These examinations are to be..arranged in the order laid down in a 'Military Catechism' which is appended to the 'Regulations'. **18..** W. PINNOCK, Catechisms of the Arts, Sciences, History, Religion, etc.

4. *fig.* A course of question and answer; a series or form of interrogatories put to candidates, etc.

1596 SHAKS. *1 Hen. IV*, v. i. 144 Honour is a meere Scutcheon, and so ends my Catechisme. **1848–55** MACAULAY *Hist. Eng.* III. 327 The catechism by which the lords lieutenants had been directed to test the sentiments of the country gentlemen consisted of three questions. *Mod.* The candidate met the electors and was put through his catechism.

5. *attrib.*

1637 HEYLIN *Answ. Burton* 167 A Catechisme Lecture of some two houres long.

catechismal (kætɪˈkɪzməl), *a.* [f. prec. + -AL[1]: there may have been a med.L. *catēchismālis.*] Of the nature of, or pertaining to, a catechism.

1819 COLERIDGE *Lit. Rem.* (1838) III. 64, I believe that the so-called Apostles' Creed was..the catechismal rather than the baptismal creed. **1860** DORA GREENWELL *Ess.* 215 [She] puts her little niece through her catechismal paces.

†**catechismy.** *Obs.* A variant of CATECHISM.

1578 *Richmond. Wills* (1853) 279 Absis [A. B. C.'s] and Catechismies, viijd. **1579** FULKE *Heskins' Parl.* 360 Let our catechismies..beare witnesse of the same.

catechist (ˈkætɪkɪst). [ad. L. *catēchista*, ad. Gr. κατηχιστ-ής he who catechizes, f. κατηχίζ-ειν to CATECHIZE. In F. *catéchiste.*] One whose duty is to catechize; a teacher of catechumens or in a catechetical school; a teacher appointed to give oral instruction in the elements of Christianity according to a catechism, or by question and answer; a native teacher in a mission church.

a **1563** BECON *New Catech.* (1844) 9 The office of the catechist was not only to instruct and teach, but also to examine. **1597** HOOKER *Eccl. Pol.* v. lxxviii. §10 Catechists, Exorcists, Readers, and Singers. **1673** *Lady's Call.* II. 82, I do not say that the mistress should set up for a catechist or preacher. **1725** BERRIMAN *Hist. Acc. Trinity* 77 Clemens was the celebrated Schoolmaster and Catechist of Alexandria. **1876** DAVIS *Polaris Exp.* ii. 54 In the absence of the regular clergyman the catechist conducts the worship. **1886** *Pall Mall G.* 27 Nov. 5/2 The native catechist who accompanied the Bishop on that final mission.

catechistic (kætɪˈkɪstɪk), *a.* [f. on Gr. type *κατηχιστικ-ός; see prec. and -IC.] = next.

1683 CAVE *Ecclesiastici* 339 His [Cyril's] Catechistick Lectures. **1884** CRADDOCK in *Academy* 19 July 40/1 The catechistic terrors of the Last Day.

catechistical (kætɪˈkɪstɪkəl), *a.* [f. as prec. + -AL[1].] Of or pertaining to the office, teaching, or method of instruction of a catechist, or of the catechism he expounds; consisting of question and answer. Cf. CATECHETICAL.

1618 HALES *Let.* in *Gold. Rem.* (1688) 386 The custom is in Catechistical Sermons..to take..a portion of the Catechism for their Text and Theme. **1662** FULLER *Worthies* (1840) III. 432 His flock was..well bottomed on catechistical divinity. **1702** C. MATHER *Magn. Chr.* III. I. i. (1852) 259 He thrice went over the body of divinity in a catechistical way. **1835** *Blackw. Mag.* XXXVIII. 641 The catechistical method.

Hence **cateˈchistically** *adv.*

1645 USSHER (*title*), A Body of Divinity, or The summe and substance of Christian Religion: Catechistically propounded and explained, by way of Question and Answer. **1692** SOUTH *Serm.* VII. v. (R.) The principles of Christianity briefly and catechistically taught.

catechizable (ˈkætɪˌkaɪzəb(ə)l), *a.* [see -ABLE.] That may be catechized.

1772 PENNANT *Tours Scotl.* (1774) 352 Four thousand catechisable persons. **1867** H. SCOTT *Fasti Eccles. Scot.* II. 459 The parish contained 6 hundred and 20 catechisable persons.

catechization (ˌkætɪkaɪˈzeɪʃən). Also 7– **sation.** [ad. med.L. *catēchizātiōn-em*, n. of action f. *catēchizāre* to catechize; cf. F. *catéchisation.*] The action of catechizing.

16.. BURNET *Records* II. I. No. 53 (R.) The catechization of young chaplains in the rudiments of our faith. *a* **1734** NORTH *Lives* II. 355 That they might be prepared for his future catechisations. **1869** *Daily News* 17 Mar., The usual catechisation of Ministers [in Parlt.].

catechize (ˈkætɪkaɪz), *v.* Forms: 5 **cathezize,** (6 **cathecyse,** 7 **catachise),** 6– **catechise,** 7– **chize.** [ad. L. *catēchizā-re*, Tertullian (in med.L. also *catecizare, catezizare, cathezizare*, in F. *catéchiser* (16th c. in Littré), Pr. *cathezizar*, Sp. *catequizar*, It. *catechizzare*), f. Gr. κατηχίζ-ειν to instruct orally, a derivative of factitive form from κατηχέ-ειν to resound, to sound amiss, to din in, instill, teach or instruct orally, f. κατά down, thoroughly + ἠχεῖν to sound, ring. The primary vb. is in N.T.; the derivative, of later introduction, had only the technical ecclesiastical application.]

1. *trans.* To give systematic oral instruction; to instruct (the young or ignorant) in the elements of religion by repeating the instruction until it is learnt by heart, or (as always implied in modern times) by the method of formal questions and answers; to instruct by means of a catechism; in the Church of England, to teach the catechism, *esp.* in preparation for confirmation.

1449 [see CATECHIZED]. **14..** in *Anglia* VIII. 164 A chile shulde be catecized, þat is to seye enformed in þe feith atte chirchedore. [**1502** *Ord. Crysten Men* I. ii. (W. de W. 1506) 13 Cathecyser is as moche to saye as to instruct or teche the fundacyons and artycles necessary of our holy fayth.] **1577** tr. *Bullinger's Decades* (1592) 907 Pastour..catechiseth, that is to say, instructeth them that be yonglings in religion. **1609** HOLLAND *Amm. Marcell., Chronol.* E j a, Constantine, being confirmed by a signe from heaven, becommeth catechized in the Faith. **1611** BIBLE *Prov.* xxii. 6 Train up [*marg.* Catechise] a child in the way he should go. *a* **1639** SPOTTISWOOD *Hist. Ch. Scotl.* an. 1616 (R.) That children should be carefully catechised, and confirmed by the bishops. *a* **1711** KEN *Direct. Prayer* Wks. (1838) 341. **1732** BERKELEY *Alciphr.* iv. §3, I..was once upon a time catechised and tutored into the belief of a God. **1836** HOOK in *Life* I. 292 To become a good catechist you must catechise.

b. *fig.* (*ironical.*)

1639 FULLER *Holy War* III. xx. (D.) Reclaimed with gentle means, not catechised with fire and fagot.

†**2.** To teach orally, instill (religious instruction).

a **1625** BOYS in Spurgeon *Treas. Dav.* I. 312 Their voices are well understood, catechising the first elements of religion.

†**3.** To instruct orally (in any subject). *Obs.*

1621 BURTON *Anat. Mel.* To Rdr. (1676) 35/2 Such Visitor..might..root out atheism..catechise gross ignorance, purge Italy of luxury and riot. **1623** COCKERAM, *Catechize*, to instruct by mouth. **1678** CUDWORTH *Intell. Syst.* 313 Whether Herodotus were rightly Catechized and instructed in the Egyptian Doctrine..may very well be questioned.

4. To examine with a catechism or in the manner of a theological catechism; to question as to belief.

1684 BUNYAN *Pilgr.* II. 78 And because Prudence would see how Christiana had brought up her children, she asked leave of her to Catechise them. *Ibid.* 81 Come Matthew, shall I also Catechise you? **1869** *Daily News* 22 Dec., These gentlemen wanted Dr. Temple..to admit their right to catechise him. **1873** MORLEY *Rousseau* I. 228 He was closely catechized by a commission of members of the consistory.

5. To question or interrogate systematically or at length; *esp.* to question or examine with a view to reproof or condemnation; to take to task.

1604 SHAKS. *Oth.* II. iv. 16, I will Catechize the world for him, that is, make Questions, and by them answer. *a* **1649** DRUMM. OF HAWTH. *Prophecy* Wks. (1711) 181 Armed vagabonds catechising every man by the purse. **1659** PEARSON *Creed* (1839) 62 God..catechised the prophet Jeremy in a potter's house, saying, O house of Israel, cannot I do with you as this potter? **1727** SWIFT *To very yng. Lady*, Catechising him where he has been. **1784** COWPER *Task* III. 203 Pierce my vein, Take of the crimson stream meandring there, And catechise it well. **1847** MRS. SHERWOOD *Lady of Manor* I. viii. 309 She was catechised without end; perhaps she suffered corporeal chastisement. **1863** EMERSON *Thoreau* Wks. (Bohn) III. 334 Asking questions of Indians is like catechizing beavers and rabbits.

Hence **ˈcatechized** *ppl. a.*

c **1449** PECOCK *Repr.* IV. ii. 426 No man baptisid or Cathezized. **1640** YORKE *Union Hon.* Pref. Verses, Their catechised Childe. **1858** F. PAGET *Parish & Priest* 70 He may be as heretical as he will, but he will do no mischief if he preaches to a catechized congregation.

catechizer (ˈkætɪkaɪzə(r)). One who catechizes, or teaches by a catechism; a catechist; one who interrogates systematically.

c **1449** PECOCK *Repr.* IV. ii. 427 The Baptiser and Cathezizer is a mynystre oonli undir God forto sette water on the persoon. **1613** R. C. *Table Alph. Catechiser*, that teacheth the principles of Christian religion. **1691** WOOD *Ath. Oxon.* I. 169 (R.) In 1550 he [Jewell]..became a preacher and catechiser at Sunningwell. **1884** *Manch. Exam.* 6 Dec. 5/4 If the Tuesdays and Fridays..were given over to the catechisers, the public loss would be less.

catechizing (ˈkætɪˈkaɪzɪŋ), *vbl. sb.* The action of the vb. CATECHIZE: **a.** in religion.

1561 T. NORTON *Calvin's Inst.* IV. xix. (1634) 720 A Catechising, whereby children or they that were neere to the age of discretion did declare an account of their faith before the Church. *a* **1623** W. PEMBLE *Wks.* (1633) 7. **1642** FEATLY *Dippers Dipt* 36 (L.) Originally and properly catechizing [is] such a kind of teaching wherein the principles of religion, or of any art or science, are often inculcated, and by sounding and resounding beat into the ears of children or novices. *a* **1694** TILLOTSON *Serm.* I. lii. (R.) That particular way of instruction..called catechising. **1782** PRIESTLEY *Nat. & Rev. Relig.* I. Pref. 24. **1858** F. PAGET *Parish & Priest* 74 The mere propounding a string of questions is not catechizing. Any fool can ask questions.

b. generally, Examination by questioning.

1599 SHAKS. *Much Ado* IV. i. 79 What kinde of catechizing call you this? To make you answer truly to your name. **1825** *Blackw. Mag.* in *Byron's Wks.* (1846) 582/2 We should like to have the catechising of the..man. **1880** FOWLER *Locke* i. 8 The professorial lecture, however learned, or the tutorial catechizing, however searching.

c. *attrib.* or ? *ppl. a.*

1581 J. FIELDE (*title*), Exposition of the Symbols.. gathered out of the catechising Sermons of G. O. Treuir. *c* **1590** MARLOWE *Jew Malta* II. ii, As it were in catechising sort, To make me mindful of my mortal sins. **1615** J. WRIGHT *Acc. Lady J. Gray* in *Phenix* (1708) II. 39 This catechising Argument between the Lady Jane and Mr. Feckenham.

catechol (ˈkætɪtʃɒl). *Chem.* [f. CATECH(U + -OL.] = *pyro-catechin* (s.v. PYRO- 2 b); = CATECHIN.

1880 *Jrnl. Chem. Soc.* XXXVIII. 417 The author denies the presence of catechol in the leaves of *Ampelopsis hederacea.* **1892** *Photogr. Ann.* II. 87 Catechol in dilute solution develops slowly, but gives excellent detail and opacity. **1964** N. G. CLARK *Mod. Org. Chem.* xxi. 439 The three dihydroxybenzenes are called catechol, resorcinol and hydroquinone (quinol). **1964** D. NICHOLS in *Oceanogr. & Marine Biol.* II. 408 The coelomic fluid will slowly oxidize catechol and 'dopa' *in vitro* at pH7·4 and 30°C.

catechu (ˈkætɪʃuː, -tʃuː). [In mod.L. *catechu* (also Ger. *katechu, kateschu*), app. ad. Malay *kachu*, (Tamil, Telugu, Canarese *kācchu, kaycchu, kāshu*) catechu (of acacia). The direct representatives of the latter are Pg. *cacho*, F. *cachou*; the exact history of the form *catechu* is obscure. See also the other names CACHOU, CASHOU, CATE², CUTCH.]

a. A name given to several astringent substances, containing from 40 to 55 per cent. of tannin, which are obtained from the bark, wood, or fruits of various Eastern trees and shrubs. They are used in medicine, and in tanning, calico printing, and dyeing. Also *attrib.* or *Comb.*: **catechu brown**, a brown colour produced by the use of catechu as a dye.

The name was apparently first applied (in Europe) to the pale sort called also GAMBIER, obtained from the leaves and young shoots of *Uncaria* or *Nauclea Gambir*; this is the *Catechu* of Pharmacy (*Syd. Soc. Lex.*): when first brought to Europe in the 17th c. it was from its appearance believed to be an earth, and called *Terra Japonica.* The dark sort obtained from the wood of *Acacia Catechu*, is more commonly called CUTCH; of this *Pegu Catechu* is a good variety. (There is doubt whether the connexion with Japan assumed in the name *terra japonici* is not purely imaginary, and owing to the Burmese name for *Acacia Catechu, sha-pin, shabin*, or *shaben.*)

[**1654** SCHRÖDER *Pharmacop. Medico-chym.* (Lyons), *Catechu..Terra Japonica*..genus terræ exoticæ (Y.) **1679** HAGENDORNIUS (*title*), Tractatus Physico-Medicus de Catechu, seu Terra Japonica.] **1683** *Weekly Mem. Ingen.* 157 A history of Catechu, or Terra Japonica. **1741** *Compl. Fam.-Piece* I. i 64, 2 Drams of choice Catechu or Japan Earth. **1805** C. HATCHETT in *Phil. Trans.* XCV. 288 Twenty grains of the common cutch or catechu being dissolved in nitric acid. **1860** URE *Dict. Arts* (ed. 5) I. 805 Catechu Brown, rich and transparent. **1875** *Ibid.* (ed. 7) I. 749 Gambir Catechu..imported under the name of Gambir, from Singapore and some of the neighbouring islands..In the trade it is distinguished from the black catechu and cutch by the name of *Terra Japonica.* **1880** J. DUNBAR *Pract. Papermaker* 41 Catechu dyed papers. **1902** *Encycl. Brit.* XXVII. 564/1 Catechu browns are fast to a variety of influences.

b. catechu acacia, -tree; the *Acacia Catechu.*

1831 J. DAVIES *Manual Mat. Med.* 450 Catechu tree. **1876** HARLEY *Mat. Med.* 640 Catechu Acacia is a small tree, with straggling thorny branches, and hard, heavy, dark-red wood.

Hence ˌ**catechuˈtannic acid**, the tannic acid of catechu.

1863–75 WATTS *Dict. Chem.*, Catechutannic acid softens when heated, and yields by distillation a yellow empyreumatic oil.

catechuic (kætɪˈ(t)ʃuːɪk), *a.* Of or pertaining to catechu. *catechuic acid* = CATECHIN.

1838 T. THOMSON *Chem. Org. Bodies* 112 Of catechuic acid. **1875** H. WOOD *Therap.* (1879) 29 It contains kino-tannic and catechuic acid.

catechumen (kætɪˈkjuːmən). Also in 7 catechumene, -eumen; in L. form 6 cathecuminus; *pl.* 6–7 **catechumeni, -ini,** 7 **-any;** also 5 **cathecumynys,** 7 **catechumenies.** [ad. F. *catechumène*, ad. L. *catēchūmen-us*, a. Gr. κατηχούμενος 'one being instructed (in the rudiments of religion)', pr. pple. passive of κατηχεῖν: see CATECHESIS. The Latin word was long retained: the modern form, first found after 1600, was not universal till about 1700; the irregular pl. in *-ys, -ies* occurs in 15th and 17th c.]

1. A new convert under instruction before baptism. Used in reference to the ancient church and in modern missionary churches. Sometimes applied to young Christians generally, and especially to those preparing for the rite of confirmation.

14.. LANGL. *P. Pl.* B. XI. 77 (MS. O.) Rather þan to baptise barnes þat ben cathecumynys [*v.r.* catekumeling]. **1502** *Ord. Crysten Men* I. i. (W. de W. 1506) 9 And they that duely were cathecuminus, yᵗ is to saye instructe of the artycles of yᵉ fayth. **1581** MARBECK *Bk. of Notes* 246 Theie sate amonge the Cathecumeni. *c* **1615** *Lives Women-Saints* (1886) 31 A Catechumene, or learner of the faith. *c* **1630** JACKSON *Creed* IV. II. vii, One of their catechumenies. **1642** J. BALL *Answ. to Can.* I. 133 Thus they make their catechumine. **1651** *Life of Colet* in *Fuller's Abel Rediv.* 100 One is for your Catechumany. **1662** GUNNING *Lent Fast* 106 Catechumens or Competentes. **1667** *Decay Chr. Piety* ix. 303 What brief and plain instructions S. Peter gives his catechumeni. *a* **1711** KEN *Hymnotheo* Wks. 1721 III. 384 He faithful care of Catechumens took. **1837** J. H. NEWMAN *Par. Serm.* (1842) VI. xii. 186 Thousands..who are not baptized, yet are virtually catechumens. **1878** LADY HERBERT tr. *Hübner's Ramble* II. vi. 348 He boldly presented himself, with two catechumens, at the court of the Mikado.

attrib. **1887** *Contemp. Rev.* May 727 Driblets of religious teaching in catechumen classes and Sunday-schools.

2. *transf.* One who is being initiated in any set of opinions, science, art, etc.

a **1751** BOLINGBROKE *Let. Windham* (T.) The same language is still held to the catechumens in Jacobitism.

catechumenal (kætɪˈkjuːmənəl), *a.* [f. CATECHUMEN + -AL.] = CATECHUMENICAL *a.*

1883 C. C. PERKINS *Italian Sculpture* Introd. p. liv, He had laid aside his white catechumenal robes.

catechumenate (kætɪˈkjuːməneɪt). [f. CATECHUMEN + -ATE¹; cf. F. *catéchuménat.*]

a. Condition or position of a catechumen. **b.** A house for catechumens.

1673 CAVE *Prim. Chr.* I. viii. 218 Having passed through the state of the Catechumenate. **1865** W. STRICKLAND *Cath. Missions S. India* 204 Those who enter the catechuminates must be fed and supported for several days. **1878** *Q. Rev.* Jan. 426 The catechumenate of Scripture is that of adults. **1885–6** *Centr. Afr. Mission Rep.* 40 Confirmation, Baptism, and admission to the catechumenate.

catechumenical (ˌkætɪkjuːˈmɛnɪkəl), *a.* [f. as prec. + -ICAL.] Of or pertaining to catechumens.

1790 J. COURTENAY *Philos. Reflect.* 19 Have not these catechumenical lectures been translated into all languages? **1836** G. S. FABER *Prim. Doct. Elect.* (1842) 155 The whole of his catechumenical and post-catechumenical instruction.

Hence **catechuˈmenically** *adv.*

1840 G. S. FABER *Prim. Doct. Regen.* 198 The Living Word of Truth delivered to him catechumenically.

cateˈchumenism. [f. as prec. + -ISM] The condition of a catechumen.

1840 G. S. FABER *Prim. Doct. Regen.* 196 The preparatory stage of Catechumenism.

†**cateˈchumenist.** *Obs.* [f. as CATECHUMEN + -IST.] = CATECHUMEN.

1629 LYNDE *Via tuta* 155 Holy bread giuen to the Catechumenists. **1650** S. CLARKE *Eccl. Hist.* (1654) I. 113 They took Ambrose, who was but a Catechumenist. **1651** H. L'ESTRANGE *Smect.-mastix* 13 Let us pray earnestly for the catechymenists.

†**cateˈchumenize,** *v. Obs.* [f. as prec. + -IZE.] *trans.* To instruct as a catechumen.

1676 MARVELL *Mr. Smirke* 24 Suppose..that the [Ethiopian] Treasurer were..in so short a time.. catechumenized.

cateˈchumenship. The position of a catechumen.

1855 CDL. WISEMAN *Fabiola* 361 To pass through the three stages of catechumenship.

catechyzon, obs. f. CATECHISM.

catecomb, obs. f. CATACOMB.

categorem (ˈkætɪgəˌrɛm, kəˈtɛgərɛm). *Logic.* [ad. Gr. κατηγόρημα accusation, (in logic) predicate, f. κατηγορεῖν to speak against, accuse, allege, assert, predicate; cf. κατήγορ-ος accuser, etc., f. κατά against + ἀγορά assembly, place of public speaking; cf. ἀγορεύ-ειν to speak in public, harangue.]

†**a.** = PREDICATE (*obs.*). **b.** A categorematic word.

1588 FRAUNCE *Lawiers Logike* I. ii. 10 b, These generall heades of argumentes..sometimes they are called Categoremes. **1655–60** STANLEY *Hist. Philos.* (1701) VIII. *Zeno* xx. 43 Universally negative axioms are those, which consist of an universall negative particle, and a Categorem; as, No man walketh. **1864** SHEDDEN *Elem. Logic* ii, Names are called categorematic words, or categorems.

categorematic (ˈkætɪgɒrɪˈmætɪk), *a. Logic.* [f. on Gr. type *κατηγορηματικός, f. κατηγόρημα; see prec. Cf. F. *catégorématique.*] Of a word: Capable of being used by itself as a term.

1827 WHATELEY *Logic* 63 It is not every word that is categorematic, that is, capable of being employed by itself as a term. **1846** MILL *Logic* I. ii. §2. **1863** BURTON *Bk. Hunter* 2 If it be a question whether a term is categorematic, or is of a quite opposite description..one may take up a very absolute positive position, without finding many people prepared to assail it.

†**categoreˈmatical,** *a. Obs.* [f. as prec. + -AL¹.] = CATEGORICAL. Hence **categoreˈmatically** *adv.*

1654 JER. TAYLOR *Real Pres.* xi. §14 Can there possibly be two categorematical, that is, positive substantial infinites? *Ibid.* xi. §29 That some quantitative bodies should not be in a place, or else that quantitative bodies were Categorematically infinite.

categorial (kætɪˈgɔərɪəl), *a.* Also **categoreal.** [ad. G. *kategorial* (W. Wundt *Logik* (1880) I. 107), f. CATEGORY + -AL.] Relating to, or involving, categories, *spec.* in Logic and Linguistics. Hence **cateˈgorially** *adv.*

1912 S. ALEXANDER in *Mind* XXI. 18 In material things we contemplate their categorial characters. **1920** —— *Space, Time & Deity* I. II. i. 185 The pervasive characters of existents are what are known from Kant's usage as the categories of experience, and I shall call them, in distinction from the empirical ones or qualities, categorial characters. **1925** C. D. BROAD *Mind & its Place* iv. 216 (*title*) The Categorial Factor in Sense-Perception. **1929** A. N. WHITEHEAD *Process & Reality* 10 The gradual elaboration of categoreal schemes. **1959** P. F. STRAWSON *Individuals* v. 172 The categorial criterion. *Ibid.* 175 The categorially predicable. **1965** N. CHOMSKY *Theory of Syntax* ii. 68 Functional notions like 'Subject'..are to be..distinguished from categorial notions such as 'Noun Phrase'. **1965** *Language* XLI. 490 Categorial and phrase-structure grammars.

categoric (kætɪˈgɒrɪk), *a.* (*sb.*) ? *Obs.* [ad. L. *catēgoricus*, a. Gr. κατηγορικός accusatory, affirmative, (later) categorical, f. κατήγορ-ος accuser; see CATEGOREM and -IC.]

A. *adj.* = CATEGORICAL.

1678 GALE *Crt. Gentiles* III. 162 None is more categoric and positive in this than judicious Davenant. *a* **1693** URQUHART *Rabelais* III. xxxviii. 317 Predicamental and Catagorick fool. *a* **1797** H. WALPOLE *Mem. Geo. II* (1847) II. vii. 240 She gave him an evasive answer. He demanded a categoric one.

B. *sb.* A categorical proposition or statement.

1677 GALE *Crt. Gentiles* II. IV. Proem 12 A Dilemma.. consistes of a disjunctive syllogisme..and two Categorics. *a* **1734** NORTH *Exam.* II. v. ¶ 146. 407 He..comes up to the Categoric very roundly, saying And so it was really and in Effect. **1839** *New Monthly Mag.* LV. 548.

categorical (kætɪˈgɒrɪkəl), *a.* (*sb.*) [f. as prec. + -AL¹.]

A. *adj.* **1.** *Logic.* Of a proposition: Asserting absolutely or positively; not involving a condition or hypothesis; unqualified. *categorical syllogism*: one consisting of categorical propositions.

1598 FLORIO *Categorico*, categoricall, predicable. **1616** BULLOKAR, *Categoricall Axiome.* **1638** FEATLY *Transub.* 88 Of our simple categoricall proposition, there can be but one true sense. **1724** WATTS *Logic* (1736) 301 Most [conjunctive Syllogisms] may be transformed into categorical Syllogisms. **1827** WHATELEY *Logic* in *Encycl. Metrop.* (1845) 206/1 The division of Propositions according to their substance; viz. into categorical and hypothetical. **1837–8** SIR W. HAMILTON *Logic* xvi. (1866) I. 294 As used originally by Aristotle, the term *categorical* meant merely affirmative, and was opposed to negative. By Theophrastus it was employed in the sense of absolute,..opposed to conditional; and in this signification it has continued to be employed by all subsequent logicians.

b. *gen.* Of a statement (or him who makes it): Direct, explicit, express, unconditional.

a **1619** FOTHERBY *Atheom.* I. ix. §1 (1622) 59 A simple and categoricall denying of it. **1657** CROMWELL *Sp.* 3 Apr., You do necessitate my answer to be categorical. **1696** LUTTRELL *Brief Rel.* (1857) IV. 83 On condition he give his categorical answer by the 18th instant. **1778** MAD. D'ARBLAY *Diary*, etc. (1842) I. 116, I could never persuade her to be categorical. **1866** MOTLEY *Dutch Rep.* v. i. 668 The ratification of the Ghent treaty..was in no wise distinct and categorical, but was made dependent on a crowd of deceitful subterfuges.

c. *categorical imperative*: in the ethics of Kant, the absolute unconditional command of the moral law, a law given by the pure reason, and binding universally on every rational will.

1827 HARE *Guesses* Ser. II. (1873) 337 [Kant] spun a new [system of ethics]..out of his categorical imperative. **1856** DOVE *Logic Chr. Faith* II. §2. 117 The categorical imperative of conscience. **1871** FARRAR *Witn. Hist.* iv. 161 'The Categorical imperative' (Duty, Conscience, Thou must).

2. *Logic.* Of or belonging to the categories.

1817 COLERIDGE *Biog. Lit.* 66 [It] will apply..to all the other eleven categorical forms.

B. *sb.* A categorical proposition or syllogism.

1619 W. SCLATER *Expos. 1 Thess.* (1630) 439 Reduce thy Hypothesis to a Categoricall; thus lies thy Proposition. **1827** WHATELEY *Logic* II. iv. §2 (L.) A hypothetical proposition is defined to be two or more categoricals united by a copula. **1837-8** SIR W. HAMILTON *Logic* xvi. (1866) I. 303 The proximate canons by which Deductive Categoricals are regulated.

Hence **cate'goricalness.**

1672 MARVELL *Reh. Transp.* I. 58 To find out the reason of his own Categoricalness. *Ibid.* I. 192 The word of Mr. Bayes's that he has made notorious is categoricalness.

categorically (kætɪ'gɒrɪkəlɪ), *adv.* [f. prec. + -LY².] In a categorical manner; with absolute assertion, absolutely, positively, unconditionally.

1603 HOLLAND *Plutarch's Mor.* 1355 Of this particle or Conjunction Εἰ, that is to say, If..nothing can be made nor categorically affirmed. **1635** PAGITT *Christianogr.* 53 Not one word Categorically, plainly, and distinctly set downe, by which Purgatory is taught. *a* **1676** HALE *Let. from Dort* (R.) Warn them to lay by all other answers, and at the next sessions categorically answer, whether they would..or no. **1874** SIDGWICK *Meth. Ethics*, The categorically imperative function. **1875** GLADSTONE *Glean.* VI. lxxxi. 184 That every cause be resolved categorically by an Aye or a No.

categorist ('kætɪgərɪst). *rare.* [f. CATEGORIZE: see -IST.] **a.** One who categorizes or classifies. **b.** One who deals with the 'categories'.

1847 EMERSON *Repres. Men, Swedenborg* Wks. (Bohn) I. 332 Swedenborg's revelation is a confounding of planes,—a capital offence in so learned a categorist. **1857** *Chamb. Jrnl.* VIII. 294 Fencing cleverly..with a categorist.

categorize ('kætɪgəraɪz), *v.* [f. CATEGORY + -IZE; cf. F. *catégoriser.*] *trans.* To place in a category or categories; to classify.

1705 HICKERINGILL *Priest-cr.* I. (1721) 41 Priest-craft has Categorized Sacrilege as the greatest Sin, next to the Sin against the Holy Ghost. **1883** *Westm. Rev.* July 99 Propertius categorizes the penalties endured by the wicked.

Hence ˌ**categori'zation,** the action of categorizing; classification.

1886 *Spectator* 6 Nov., Lit. Supp. 1506 A generation ago, botany was mainly a categorisation of plant-forms under so called natural systems.

category ('kætɪgərɪ). [ad. L. *catēgoria*, a. Gr. κατηγορία accusation, assertion, predication, abst. sb. from κατήγορ-ος accuser, etc.: see CATEGOREM.]

1. *Logic* and *Metaph.* A term (meaning literally 'predication' or 'assertion') given to certain general classes of terms, things, or notions; the use being very different with different authors.

a. Originally used by Aristotle, the nature and meaning of whose ten categories, or predicaments (as, after the Latin translation, they are also called) has been disputed almost from his own day till the present; some holding that they were 'a classification of all the manners in which assertions may be made of the subject', others that they were 'an enumeration of all things capable of being named, the most extensive classes into which things could be distributed', or again, that they were 'the different kinds of notions corresponding to the definite forms of existence'. Hence many criticisms of Aristotle's classification, with modifications of it, or the substitution of new 'categories,' proposed by the Stoics, and later philosophers, according as they viewed them logically or metaphysically.

The ten 'categories' or 'predicaments' of Aristotle were: 1 Substance or being (οὐσία), 2 Quantity, 3 Quality, 4 Relation (πρός τι), 5 Place, 6 Time, 7 Posture (κεῖσθαι), 8 Having or possession (ἔχειν), 9 Action, 10 Passion.

1588 FRAUNCE *Lawiers Logike* I. ii. 10b, These generall heades of argumentes..sometimes..are called Categoremes, and the handling or discoursing of the same Categories. **1677** GALE *Crt. Gentiles* II. IV. Proem 4 Objective Ideas or real Beings, considered in Logic, are reduced by the Aristoteleans..to Ten Categories or Predicaments. **1724** WATTS *Logic* (1736) 25 The famous ten Ranks of Being, called the ten Predicaments or Categories of Aristotle, on which there are endless Volumes of Discourses formed by several of his Followers. **1849** ABP. THOMSON *Laws Th.* §97 Logicians in almost every age have endeavoured to frame schemes of classification in which things should be arranged according to their real nature. To these the name of Categories..has been given. **1858** MANSEL *Bampton Lect.* iii. (ed. 4) 49 Existence itself, that so-called highest category of thought. *c* **1866** GROTE *Aristotle* I. 144 We may illustrate the ten Categories of Aristotle by comparing them with the four Categories of the Stoics. *Ibid.* 149 Galen also recognizes five Categories; but not the same five as Plotinus. **1882** E. WALLACE tr. *Aristotle's Psychol.* 5 The first point..is to determine in which of the higher classes soul is included, and what is its generic character—whether, in other words, it is an individual thing and real substance, or a quality, or a quantity, or any other of the categories, as they have been distinguished. **1883** LIDDELL & SCOTT *Grk. Lex.* s.v., The categories are a classification of all the manners in which assertions may be made of the subject.

b. Kant applied the term to: The pure *a priori* conceptions of the understanding, which the mind applies (as forms or frames) to the matter of knowledge received from *sense*, in order to raise it into an *intelligible* notion or object of knowledge.

1829 SIR W. HAMILTON *Disc.* (1853) 26 The Predicaments of Aristotle are..objective, of things as understood; those of Kant subjective, of the mind as understanding..In reality, the whole Kantian Categories would be generally excluded from those of Aristotle..as determinations of thought, and not genera of real things. **1856** MEIKLEJOHN tr. *Kant's Crit. Pure Reason* 64 In this manner there arise exactly so many pure conceptions of the understanding, applying *a priori* to objects of intuition in general, as there are logical functions in all possible judgments..These conceptions we shall, with Aristotle, call categories, our purpose being originally identical with his, notwithstanding the great difference in the execution. Table of the Categories. 1. *Of Quantity*: Unity, Plurality, Totality. 2. *Of Quality*: Reality, Negation, Limitation. 3. *Of Relation*: Of Inherence and Subsistence (*substantia et accidens*), of Causality and Dependence (cause and effect), of Community (reciprocity between the agent and patient). 4. *Of Modality*: Possibility—Impossibility, Existence—Non-existence, Necessity— Contingence. **1877** E. CAIRD *Philos. Kant* II. viii. 342 Certain general conceptions which are principles of relation for all the manifold of sense..these are the categories.

c. Hence in more general use (see quot. 1901). Also *attrib.*

1901 BALDWIN *Dict. Philos.* I. 161/2 The term category, in post-Kantian philosophy, comes to mean any relatively fundamental philosophical conception. **1938** G. RYLE in *Proc. Arist. Soc.* XXXVIII. 206 'Quality', 'state', 'substance', [etc.]..we could call..'category-words'. **1949** —— *Concept of Mind* i. 16 A category-mistake..represents the facts..as if they belonged to one logical type or category ..when they actually belong to another. **1960** J. O. URMSON *Encycl. Western Philos.* 79/2 Today the word 'category' is used by philosophers, if at all, for any supposedly ultimate type, without any settled convention about what it is a type of.

2. a. A predicament; a class to which a certain predication or assertion applies.

1678 R. BARCLAY *Apol. Quakers* v. xxvi. 187 He that cannot hear a thing, as being necessarily absent, and he that cannot hear it, as being naturally deaf, are to be placed in the same Category. **1855** MACAULAY *Hist. Eng.* IV. 228 Any offender who was not in any of the categories of proscription. **1856** MISS MULOCK *J. Halifax* (ed. 17) 382 Lord Ravenel's case would hardly come under this category. **1880** *Nat. Responsib. Opium Trade* 24 To place opium in the same category as alcohol and tobacco.

b. A class, or division, in any general scheme of classification. *spec.* in *Linguistics* (see quots.).

1660 JER. TAYLOR *Duct. Dubit.* I. v, Doubts..must be derived from their several heads and categories. **1818** HAZLITT *Eng. Poets* v. (1870) 129 With him there are but two moral categories, riches and poverty. **1856** EMERSON *Eng. Traits, Race* Wks. (Bohn) II. 24 We must use the popular category..for convenience, and not as exact and final. **1871** TYNDALL *Fragm. Sc.* II. xiv. (1879) 349 The body..falls into the category of machines. **1883** LD. GRANVILLE *Circular* in *Pall Mall G.* 9 July 7/2 The following specimens of bad English..have been taken from despatches recently received at the Foreign Office..'category' for class. **1933** BLOOMFIELD *Language* xvi. 270 Large form-classes which completely subdivide either the whole lexicon or some important form-class into form-classes of approximately equal size, are called *categories.* Thus, the English parts of speech (substantive, verb, adjective, and so on) are categories of our language. **1964** HALLIDAY et al. *Ling. Sciences* ii. 23 Grammar deals with closed system choices, which may be between items ('this/that'..) or between categories (singular/plural, past/present/future). *Ibid.* 24 The four theoretical categories that are required if we want to account fully for the kind of patterning in language that we recognize as the level of grammar..class and system.. unit and structure. **1965** N. CHOMSKY *Theory of Syntax* ii. 68 The notion 'Subject'..designates a grammatical function rather than a grammatical category.

¶ 'An accusation.' *Obs.*

1613 in R. C. *Table Alph.*, and other 17th c. Dicts.

†**catekumeling.** *Obs. rare*⁻¹. [see -LING.] A (young) catechumen.

1377 LANGL. *P. Pl.* B. XI. 77 To baptise barnes þat ben catekumelynges.

catel, obs. form of CATTLE.

catelectrode (kætɪ'lɛktrəʊd). [f. Gr. κατά down + ELECTRODE; cf. ANELECTRODE.] The negative pole of a galvanic battery.

‖**catelectrotonus** (ˌkætɪlɛk'trɒtənəs). *Phys.* [mod. f. Gr. κατά down + ἤλεκτρον amber (see ELECTRIC) + τόνος strain, tension; cf. ANELECTROTONUS.] A state of increased irritability produced in a nerve near the negative pole of an electric current which traverses it.

1866 A. FLINT *Nerv. Syst.* iii. 116 Near the cathode, the excitability is increased, and this condition has been called catelectrotonus.

Hence ˌ**catelectro'tonic** *a.*, pertaining to catelectrotonus.

1881 in *Syd. Soc. Lex.*

catell, obs. form of CATTLE, KETTLE.

†'**catelles**, *a. Obs.* [f. *catel*, CATTLE + -LESS.] Without property.

1362 LANGL. *P. Pl.* A. x. 68 ʒif..þei ben pore or Catelles.

cateloge, obs. form of CATALOGUE.

‖**catena** (kə'tiːnə). [L. *catēna* chain.] A chain, a connected series:

a. (More fully ***catena patrum***): A string or series of extracts from the writings of the fathers, forming a commentary on some portion of Scripture; also, a chronological series of extracts to prove the existence of a continuous tradition on some point of doctrine. Also *transf.*

1644 MILTON *Areop.* (Arb.) 64 For a parochiall Minister ..to finish his circuit in..a Harmony and a Catena. **1684** T. BURNET *Th. Earth* I. 261 The ancient glosses and catenæ upon scripture. **1858** R. VAUGHAN *Ess. & Rev.* I. 29 The authorship of many, though assigned in the catenæ to Origen, is..open to question. **1862** MAURICE *Mor. & Met. Philos.* IV. 192 A catena of opinions in favour of an ecclesiastical system. **1882-3** SCHAFF *Relig. Encycl.* I. 419 The true catena consists merely of extracts from a..number of exegetes.

b. *generally.* 'Chain, string.'

1862 *Sat. Rev.* 15 Mar. 303 The Mausoleum is mentioned as existing by a catena of writers reaching down to the 12th century of the Christian era. **1868** *Pall Mall G.* 23 July 4 Carried down in an unbroken catena of conscious observance. **1883** *Spectator* 6 Oct. 1274 His speech is but a catena of Tory platitudes writ large. **1884** F. HARRISON in *19th. Cent.* Mar. 494 One long catena of difficulty.

c. In full *soil catena* (see quots.).

1935 G. MILNE in *Soil Research* IV. 194, I propose the word catena (Latin, = a chain). This term will help to indicate that the soils so grouped are linked by their topographic relationship. *Ibid.*, The Uganda soils might be spoken of as the Bukalasa catena. **1954** W. D. THORNBURY *Princ. Geomorphology* iv. 78 A soil catena consists of a group of soils within a particular soil region which developed from similar parent material but differ in the characteristics of their profiles because of the varying topographic and drainage conditions under which they formed.

catenarian (kætɪ'nɛərɪən), *a.* (*sb.*) [f. L. *catēnāri-us* CATENARY (f. *catēna* chain) + -AN.]

1. Math. ***catenarian curve*** = CATENARY. So ***catenarian arch***, an arch of this shape; ***catenarian principle***, the principle of constructing a suspension bridge with a chain of this shape.

1751 JOHNSON *Rambl.* No. 179 ¶8 The properties of the catenarian curve. **1788** T. JEFFERSON *Writ.* (1859) II. 547 The catenarian arch..its nature proves it to be in equilibrio in every point. **1831** J. HOLLAND *Manuf. Metals* I. 107 The new bridge constructed upon the catenarian principle.

b. as *sb.* = CATENARY.

1872 *Contemp. Rev.* XX. 477 It may be a catenarian, a cycloid, a spiral.

2. Of the nature of a chain, chainlike.

1863 *Lepsius' Stand. Alphabet* 24 The Indians, Persians, Greeks, Romans, Slavonians, and Germans form a catenarian series.

catenary (kə'tiːnərɪ), *sb.* and *a.* [ad. L. *catēnāri-us* relating to a chain, f. *catēna* chain.]

A. *sb. Math.* [mod.L. *catenaria.*] The curve formed by a chain or rope of uniform density hanging freely from two fixed points not in the same vertical line. The ***common catenary*** is the curve so formed by a chain of uniform thickness.

1788 T. JEFFERSON *Writ.* (1859) II. 546 Every part of a catenary is in perfect equilibrium. **1798** HUTTON *Course Math.* (1828) II. 175 A heavy flexible cord or chain, left to adjust itself into a hanging catenary. **1856** RUSKIN *Mod. Paint.* IV. v. xvii. §12 One of the most beautifully gradated natural curves—called the catenary.

B. *adj.* **1.** Math. ***catenary curve*** = CATENARY; see A.

1872 RUSKIN *Eagle's N.* §139 The parabolas of .. waterfalls and fountains..the catenary curves of their falling festoons. **1887** HARDY *Woodlanders* I. i. 6 A hook to which the reins were hitched..forming a catenary curve.

2. Relating to a catena or series.

1855 I. TAYLOR *Restor. Belief* 221 By processes of catenary deduction.

catenate ('kætɪneɪt), *v.* [f. L. *catēnāt-* ppl. stem of *catēnāre* (f. *catēna* chain); see -ATE³.]

1. *trans.* To connect like the links of a chain, to link, to string together; to form into a catena or series. Hence '**catenated** *ppl. a.*

1623 COCKERAM, *Catennate*, to chaine. **1656** BLOUNT *Glossogr.*, *Catenate*, to link, chain or tie. **1794-6** E. DARWIN *Zoon.* (1801) I. 112 If this activity be catenated with the diurnal circle of actions. *a* **1876** J. H. NEWMAN *Hist. Sk.* II. v. v. 477 He fused those catenated passages into one homogeneous comment. **1876** MAUDSLEY *Phys. Mind* v. 308 A transference of energy from one to another of the catenated cells.

2. *fig.* (*humorously.*) To bind as with a chain.

178. *Mock Ode* in Boswell *Johnson* (1816) IV. 428 This gigantic frame..*catenated* by thy charms, A captive in thy *ambient* arms.

catenation (kætɪ'neɪʃən). [ad. L. *catēnātiōn-em*, f. *catēnāre*; see prec.]

1. A linking into a chain; connexion like that between the links of a chain; arrangement in a connected series; connected succession.

1641 R. BROOKE *Eng. Episc.* I. v. 21 A perfect and universall catenation of all essentials and circumstantials. **1646** SIR T. BROWNE *Pseud. Ep.* 240. **1654** 'PALÆMON' *Friendship* 24 So by this Catenation of Vices some one link

of the chain would be found confessedly too heavy. **1838** *Blackw. Mag.* XLIV. 234 In the catenation of the objects.. constituting that universe. **1876** MAUDSLEY *Phys. Mind* iii. 164 An association or catenation of movements.

catenist (kəˈtiːnɪst). [f. CATENA + -IST.] A maker of a catena of authorities or evidence.
1880 SWETE *Theodore of Mopsuestia on St. Paul's Ep.* I. 240 Theodoret followed his master, without, however, condescending to the level of the mere catenist.

catenoid (ˈkætɪnɔɪd), *a.* and *sb.* [f. CATENA + -OID.] **A.** *adj.* Catenary, chain-like. **B.** *sb. Math.* The surface formed by the revolution of a catenary about its axis.
1876 *Encycl. Brit.* V. 68/2 This catenoid..is in stable equilibrium only when the portion considered is such that the tangents to the catenary at its extremities intersect before they reach the directrix. **1901** CALKINS *Protozoa* 156 Such pseudoconjugation frequently leads to the formation of catenoid colonies.

catenulate (kəˈtiːnjʊlət), *a.* [f. L. *catēnula*, dim. of *catēna* chain + -ATE² 2.] **a.** *Bot.* Formed of parts united end to end like the links of a chain. **b.** *Zool.* Having on the surface a series of oblong tubercles resembling a chain.
1880 GRAY *Bot. Text-bk.* 401.

†**ˈcater**, *sb.*¹ *Obs.* Forms: 5–7 catour, -tor, -ter, (5 -tore, -tur(e, kator, -tour, 6 kater). [ME. *catour*, aphetic form of *acatour*, ACATER, q.v. Superseded before 1700 by CATERER.]
A buyer of provisions or 'cates'; in large households the officer who made the necessary purchases of provisions; a CATERER.
c **1400** *Gamelyn* 321, I am oure Catour [*v.r.* Catur] and bere oure Alther purse. **1481** *Howard Househ. Bks.* (1841) 17 My lorde toke to the Kator, for Hossolde, xxvj. *s.* iiij. *d.* **1512** *MS. Acc. St. John's Hosp. Canterb.*, Rec. for iij calvys off þᵉ cater of Crystis Cherche. **1567** MAPLET *Gr. Forest* 89 He is as good a meates man and Catour for him selfe as any thing living is. **1587** J. HARMAR tr. *Beza's Serm.* 377 (T.) Their katers, butlers, and cooks. **1598** BARCKLEY *Felic. Man* III. (1603) 203 To eate of such a Caters provision. **1613** BP. HALL *Holy Panegyr.* 29 The glutton makes God his cator, and himselfe the guest. **1621** QUARLES *Argalus & P.* (1678) 43 Th'impatient fist Of the false Cater.
b. *transf.* and *fig.* = 'Purveyor'.
c **1430** LYDGATE *Bochas* VII. x. 19 (1558) 161 b, Of his diete catour was scarsite. **1590** GREENE *Mourn. Garm.* (1616) 31 The eye is loues Cator. **1612** R. CARPENTER *Soules Sent.* 27. **1665** BOYLE *Occas. Refl.* (1675) 49 Many of the Beasts, and Birds, and Fishes, are but our Caters for one another.

cater (ˈkeɪtə(r), ˈkætə(r)), *sb.*² [ad. F. *quatre* four. See also QUATRE.]
†**1.** Four. *Obs. rare*⁻¹.
1553 T. WILSON *Rhet.* 86 b, The auditour..cometh in with sise sould, and cater denere, for vi.*s.* and iiii.*d.*
†**2.** Four at dice or cards; also ***cater-point.*** *Obs.*
1519 HORMAN *Vulg.* 280 b, Cater is a very good caste. **1708** KERSEY, *Caterpoint*, the Number Four, at Dice. **1721–1800** BAILEY, *Cater-point.* **1730–6** —— *Cater*, four at cards or Dice. In JOHNSON; and in mod. Dicts.
b. ***cater-trey***: the four and the three; hence, apparently, a cant term for dice (or ? falsified dice).
?*a* **1500** *Chester Pl.* II. (1847) 56 Here is catter traye, Therfore goe thou thy waye. **1532** *Dice Play* (1850) 23 A well favoured die, that seemeth good and square, yet is the forehead longer on the cater and tray than any other way. *Ibid.* 24 Such be also called bard cater tres, because, commonly, the longer end will, of his own sway, draw downwards, and turn up to the eye sice, sinke, deuis or ace. **1589** *Pappe w. Hatchet* (1844) 15 The quarrel was about cater-tray, and euer since he hath quarrelled about cater-caps. **1608** DEKKER *Belman Lond.* Wks. 1884–5 III. 118 A Bale of bard Cater-Treas. *c* **1620** FLETCHER & MASS. *Trag. Barnavelt* v. ii. in Bullen *O. Pl.* II. 304. *a* **1700** *Songs Lond. Prentices* 152 If any gallant haue with cater-tray, Play'd the wise-acre, and made all way.
3. *Change-ringing.* (See quot. 1878.)
1872 ELLACOMBE *Bells of Ch.* ii. 29 The very terms of the art are enough to frighten an amateur. Hunting, dodging.. caters, cinques, etc. **1878** GROVE *Dict. Music* s.v., The name given by change ringers to changes of nine bells. The word should probably be written quaters, as it is meant to denote the fact that four couples of bells change their places in the order of ringing.

cater (ˈkeɪtə(r)), *v.*¹ [f. CATER *sb.*¹]
1. *intr.* To act as 'cater', caterer, or purveyor of provisions; to provide a supply of food *for*.
1600 SHAKS. *A.Y.L.* II. iii. 44 He that doth the Rauens feede, Yea prouidently caters for the Sparrow. **1713** ADDISON *Guardian* No. 139 §2 Androcles.. lived many days in this frightful solitude, the lion catering for him with great assiduity. **1828** SCOTT *F.M. Perth* xxxii, You were wont to love delicate fare—behold how I have catered for you. **1853** KINGSLEY *Hypatia* xiv. 169 In order to cater for both.
b. *absol.* To buy or provide food.
1822 MAIR *Lat. Dict.*, *Obsōno*, to cater or buy in victuals. **1849** C. BRONTË *Shirley* III. i. 29 See if I don't cater judiciously.
c. *trans.*
a **1634** RANDOLPH *Poems* (1638) 4 Noe widdowes curse caters a dish of mine. *a* **1643** W. CARTWRIGHT *Siege* II. ii, And cater spiders for the queasie creature When it refuseth comfits. **1866** NEALE *Seq. & Hymns* 190 He..Catered the poorest of food.
2. *transf.* and *fig.* To occupy oneself in procuring or providing (requisites, things desired, etc.) *for*.
1650 W. FENNER *Christ's Alarm* 10 To cater for heaven, to bring in custome for the Kingdome of God. **1700** CONGREVE *Way of World* III. v, What! you are..catering (says he) or ferreting for some disbanded officer. **1789** BURNS *Let. R. Ainslie* 6 Jan., I am still catering for Johnson's publication. **1838–9** HALLAM *Hist. Lit.* IV. vi. §50 He rarely caters for the populace of the theatre by such indecencies as they must understand. **1872** MINTO *Eng. Lit.* Introd. 25 He does not cater for the pleasure of his jurors.
b. occasionally const. *to.* [Cf. *pander to.*]
1840 THACKERAY *Paris Sk. Bk.* (1872) 134 Catering to the national taste and vanity. **1860** KINGSLEY *Misc.* II. 102 Nine years afterwards we find him..catering to the low tastes of James I. **1864** *Sat. Rev.* 10 Dec. 711/1 Machinery for catering to the wants of the profane and the dissolute.

cater (ˈkeɪtə(r)), *v.*² *dial.* [f. CATER *sb.*² or F. *quatre* four.] To place or set rhomboidally; to cut, move, go, etc., diagonally. Hence **ˈcatering, ˈcatered,** *ppl. a.*
1577 B. GOOGE *Heresbach's Husb.* (1586) 69 b, The trees are set checkerwise and so catred [partim in quincuncem directis], as looke which way ye will, they lye level. *Ibid.* 71 Two sortes of this catred order [quincuncialis ordinis duplicem rationem], one wherin my trees stand foure square like the chequer or Chessebord. **1873** *Silverland* 129 (Hoppe) 'Cater' across the rails [at a level crossing] ever so cleverly, you cannot escape jolt and jar. **1875** PARISH *Sussex Dial.*, *Catering*, slanting, from corner to corner.

ˈcater, *adv. U.S.* and *dial.* [Related to prec.] Diagonally. So **ˈcatercross, caterways, ˈcaterwise,** *adv.* See also CATER-CORNERED *adv.* and *a.*
1874 in *N. & Q.* Ser. v. I. 361 (Surrey words) *Caterways*, catering, to cross diagonally. **1875** PARISH *Sussex Dial.* s.v. *Catercross*, If you goos caterwise across the field you'll find the stile. **1881** *Leicester Gloss.* (E.D.S.), *Cater* and *Cater-cornered*, diagonal; diagonally. To 'cut cater' in the case of velvet, cloth, etc., is..'cut on the cross'. *Cater-snozzle*, to make an angle; to 'mitre'.

cater, obs. form of CATARRH.

cateran (ˈkætərən). Forms: 6 **ketheri(n)ck, ketharin, catherein,** 8 **kettrin, (kaitrine),** 9 **catheran, katheran, cateran.** [Lowland Sc. *catherein, kettrin*, appears to represent Gael. *ceathairne* collective 'peasantry', whence *ceathairneach* 'sturdy fellow, freebooter' (McAlpine); Cormac has Ir. *ceithern*, which O'Donovan renders 'band of soldiers', thence *ceithernach* 'one of a band'.
The *th* has long been mute in Celtic, and the Ir. *ceithern* (ˈkeərn) is phonetically represented by Eng. KERN. It is not easy to account for the preservation of the dental in Lowland Sc., unless perh. through the intermediation of med.L. as in Bower's *cateranos.* (Stokes refers *ceithern* to OIr. **keitern*, OCelt. *keterna*, a fem. *ā*-stem.)]
1. †**a.** *prop.* a collective sb. Common people of the Highlands in a troop or band, fighting men (*obs.*). Hence, **b.** One of a Highland band; a Highland irregular fighting man, reiver, or marauder.
1371–90 *Stat. 12 Robt. II* (Jam.), Of Ketharines or Sorneris. They quha travells as ketharans..etand the cuntrie and..takand their gudis be force and violence. [*c* **1430** BOWER *Contn. Fordun* an. 1396 (Jam.) Per duos pestiferos cateranos et eorum sequaces.] *c* **1505** DUNBAR *Sir T. Norray* 13 Full many catherein hes he cheist..Amang thai dully glennis. **15..** *Scot. Field* in Furniv. *Percy Folio* I. 219 There came at his commandement: ketherinckes full many from Orkney that Ile. **1768** ROSS *Helenore* 120 (Jam.) Ask yon highland kettrin what they mean. **1816** SCOTT *Old Mort.* vi, Grahame of Montrose, and his Highland caterans. **1832** *Blackw. Mag.* 65/2 These overgrown proprietors with their armies of catherans. **1887** DK. ARGYLL *Scotl. as it Was* II. 6 Plundering Caterans always ready to flock to those who promised booty.
2. *gen.* Brigand, freebooter, marauder.
1870 LOWELL *Study Wind.* 216 The statecraft of an Ithacan cateran. **1880** MRQ. SALISBURY in *Manch. Guard.* 27 Oct., They [the Montenegrins] are caterans, cattle-lifters.

†**ˈcaterbrawl.** *Obs.* [f. CATER *sb.*² four + BRAWL *sb.*³ a dance.] A kind of dance; a particular kind of 'brawl'.
1565–6 *Reg. Stationers' Co.*, Thomas Colwell for his lycense for prynting of a ballett intituled the Cater bralles, bothe wytty and mery. **1581** J. BELL *Haddon's Answ. Osor.* 303 b, You may pype uppe this kynde of caterbrawle. **1584** *Handf. Pleasant Delights* (*title*), Historie of Diana and Acteon, to the Quarter Braules. **1611** J. DAVIES *Pref. Verses* in *Coryat's Crudities*, And lookes as if he danced a Caterbrall. *a* **1618** —— *Extasie* Wks. (1876) 94 And foote fine horne-pipes, jigges, and caterbralls.

†**ˈcatercap.** *Obs.* [f. CATER *sb.*² four, referring to the four-cornered top + CAP.] The square cap worn by academics. Cf. CAP *sb.*¹ 4 e. Hence *transf.* A wearer of a catercap, a university man.
1588 *Marprel. Epist.* (Arb.) 44 You presbyter Iohn Cater-cap are some man in the land. **1589** NASHE *Almond for P.* 5 a, They [Sir Peter and Sir Paul] were none of these Cartercaps, Graduates, nor Doctors. **1691** WOOD *Ath. Oxon.* I. 228 He feareth neither proud Priest, Antichristian Pope, Tyrannous Prelate, nor godless Catercap.
Hence †**ˈcater-capt**, *a.*, wearing a catercap, academic. *Obs.*
a **1669** BP. H. KING *Poems & Ps.* (1843) Pref. 50 A proud prelate..and a most pragmaticall malignant against the parliament, as all his cater-capt companions also are.

cater-cornered (ˈkætəˌkɔːnəd), *adv.* and *adj. U.S.* and *dial.* Also **catacornered, catercorner, catty-cornered,** etc. [f. CATER *adv.* + CORNERED *ppl. a.*] Diagonally; diagonal. So **cater-cornering, catty-cornering** *a.* and *sb.*
1878 MISS JACKSON *Shropsh. Wd.-bk.*, *Cater-cornered*, diagonal. A house standing diagonally to the street would be cater-cornered. **1881** [See CATER *adv.*]. **1838** J. C. NEAL *Charcoal Sk.* 196 One of that class..who, when compelled to share their bed with another, lie in that engrossing posture called 'catty-cornered'. **1843** 'R. CARLTON' *New Purchase* xxvii. 261 With directions how..to secure by two strings diagonally fastened, or as he better understood it—'katterkorner'd-like'. **1841** 'DOW, JR.' *Short Patent Sermons* xxi. 52 Unless you..took too many catty-cornered tracks, Making but little headway with the tacks, While calling on the ladies. **1885** *Century Mag.* Nov. 64/1 He just takes them records..and brings his side line down catercornerin'—that way. **1888** J. KIRKLAND *McVeys* 59 Now, suppose the railroad runs diagonally across a field, 'cater-cornering', as he says. **1893** *Harper's Mag.* June 112/1 He leaned against the wall, eying me catacornered, but innocent. **1902** S. F. WHITE *Blazed Trail* vii. 53 When the log had been cat-a-cornered from its bed, the chain was fastened [etc.]. **1906** *Harper's Mag.* July 252 'You do leave things so catacornered,' Martha observed. **1919** F. HURST *Humoresque* 86 The optical department, cater-corner from the children's shoes. **1945** J. STEINBECK *Cannery Row* i. 4 If you walk catty-cornered across the grass-grown lot. *Ibid.* v. 16 Lee Chong's grocery was on its catty-corner right and Dora's Bear Flag Restaurant was on its catty-corner left. **1957** *New Yorker* 29 June 22/1 There was a girl sitting down one row, catty-corner from me. **1959** *Listener* 22 Jan. 174/2 A square cat, going cater-cornered among the leeks. **1962** R. DEMING *Careful Man* ii. 21 She took a catty-corner shortcut. **1964** *New Yorker* 21 Nov. 222/2 Temple Square..is catercorner to the site of the Kennecott Copper Corporation's new eighteen-story building.

cater-cousin (ˈkeɪtəˌkʌz(ə)n). [derivation and original literal meaning doubtful.
The ordinary conjecture (since Skinner) has been that *cater* is F. *quatre* four, used in the sense of *quatrième* fourth, 'from the ridiculousness of calling cousin or relation to so remote a degree' (Johnson); but etymologically this receives no support from French (where *quatre-cousin* would be absurdly impossible), nor from the Eng. use of *cater* in CATER *sb.*², CATER *adv.*, or CATERCAP, nor is there any trace of the word having ever been *quater*, *quatre*, or *quarter*; moreover Johnson's explanation seems hardly to suit early usage, however it may have influenced later use.
Fewer difficulties appear in supposing *cater* to be the Eng. CATER *sb.*¹ or *v.*¹, and taking *cater-cousins* as originally those who were 'cousins' by being catered for or boarded together, or by catering for each other: cf. *companion* lit. 'fellow bread-eater'. It would be easiest perhaps to account for such a formation from the verb, but as there is not at present evidence that this was in use so early as 1547, we must consider the possibility that the derivation was *cater sb.* + *cousin*, perh. as = 'catering cousin': cf. esp. *foster-father*, *-mother*, *-brother*, *-sister*, etc.]
A term formerly applied to persons on terms of 'cousinship', intimate friendship, or familiarity with each other, who, though not cousins by blood, were 'next cousins' in some respect, or perhaps called each other 'cousin' from some community of life, interests, or employments (cf. COUSIN, to CALL *cousins* 17 b.). ***to be*** (or ***be made***) ***cater cousins***: to be good friends, to be on the best of terms. It still survives as a traditional expression (chiefly from Shakspere), but without any distinct notion of its intrinsic meaning.
1547 LATIMER *Serm. & Rem.* (1845) 425 Corrupt nature [is] against the will of God; and so to be natural may seem to be cater-cousin, or cousin-germain with to be diabolical. **1583** STUBBES *Anat. Abus.* II. 24 Of Drapers I haue little to say, sauing that I thinke them cater cosins, or cosin germans to merchants. **1596** SHAKS. *Merch. V.* II. ii. 139 His Maister and he (sauing your worships reuerence) are scarce catercosins. **1598** R. BERNARD tr. *Terence's Andria* v. ii, They are not now cater cousins [*inimicitia est inter eos*]. **1599** NASHE *Lent. Stuffe* (1871) 24 Not that it is sib, or cater-cousin to any mongrel Democratia. **1600** J. DARRELL *Detection S. Harsnet* 202 One falling out with her as she was at Meate had lyke to have been choaked..untill Alice and shee were made Cater-cousins, and then loe she was as well as might be. **1622** MABBE tr. *Aleman's Guzman d'Alf.* I. (1630) 62, I was not halfe Cater-cousins with him, because by his Meanes I had lost my Cloake. **1650** A. B. *Mutat. Polemo* 8 Cats and Dogs will sooner be cater-cosins. **1680** DRYDEN *Kind Keeper* III. i. **1702** S. PARKER tr. *Tully's De Finibus* 247 The Stoicks are so far Cater-Cousins to these Philosophers, that they confine the Summum Bonum to Vertue. **1857** SIR F. PALGRAVE *Norm. & Eng.* II. 57 A Lay Rector,—a lay Abbot's cater-cousin, at the present day. **1876** BROWNING *Pacchiarotto* 52 Proving you were cater-cousins, kith and kindred, king and you!
Hence **cater-cousinship.**
1870 LOWELL *Study Wind.* 102 There is something nearer than cater-cousinship in a certain impetuous audacity of temper common to them both.

caterect, obs. form of CATARACT.

caterer (ˈkeɪtərə(r)). [f. CATER *sb.*¹ or *v.*¹ + -ER¹; supplanting the earlier CATER *sb.*¹ (Some words in *-erer* seem to have been formed, not on verbs, but on the earlier sbs. in *-er*, or perh. from the

nouns of state in *-ery*; cf. *fruiterer*, *poulterer*, *sorcerer*.)]

1. One who caters or purveys provisions for a household, club, etc.; one who supplies the viands at an entertainment, fête, etc.

[**1469** *Catourer* is printed in *Househ. Ord.* (1790) 97. But the ed. is untrustworthy, and this portion of the MS. is now lost.]

1592 NASHE *P. Penilesse* (ed. 2) 21 a, They drawe out a dinner with sallets..and make Madona Nature their best Caterer. **1599** —— *Lent. Stuffe* (1871) 83 The Popes caterer ..asked what it was he had to sell. **1630** WADSWORTH *Sp. Pilgr.* iii. 30 Sr. Gerard Kemps brother, who is a Caterer to the Colledge. **1752** JOHNSON *Rambl.* No. 206 ¶4 The succession of dishes with which their cooks and caterers supply them. **1833** MARRYAT *P. Simple* xxviii, The marine officer..was the gun-room caterer. **1872** *City Press* 20 Jan., The Tallow-chandlers' Company dined at the hall.. Messrs. —— were the caterers.

b. *fig.*

1618 BRATHWAIT *Descr. Death*, Death is worm's caterer. *a* **1716** SOUTH *12 Serm.* II. 40 Nature is their Cook, and Necessity their Caterer. **1746-7** HERVEY *Medit. & Contempl.* (1818) 143 All nature is our caterer. **1784** COWPER *Task* II. 371 Grand caterer and dry-nurse of the church.

2. *gen.* One who caters in any way for the requirements of others.

1709 STEELE *Tatler* No. 46 ¶2 A Prince is no more to be his own Caterer in his Love, than in his Food. *a* **1723** MRS. CENTLIVRE *Love at Vent.* I. i, I like no caterer in Love's market. **1877** *Manch. Guard.* 26 Feb. 7 Caterers for public amusement. **1884** *Cassell's Fam. Mag.* Mar. 243/1 The dress caterers have all their plans laid for the summer.

Hence **'caterership**, purveyorship.

1830 MARRYAT *King's Own* xl, Why don't you give up the caterership?

cateress ('keɪtərɪs). [f. CATER *sb.*[1] + -ESS.] A female caterer; a woman who caters for others.

1634 MILTON *Comus* 764 She, good cateress, Means her provision only to the good. *a* **1683** OLDHAM *Wks. & Rem.* (1686) 52 As if whole Nature were your Cateress. *a* **1800** COWPER *Odyss.* (ed. 2, 1802) II. 115 Food of all kinds..The cat'ress of the royal house supplied. **1885** R. BURTON *1001 Nts.* I. 104 This dame, the cateress, hired me to carry a load.

caterfoile, -foyle, obs. ff. QUATREFOIL.

catering ('keɪtərɪŋ), *vbl. sb.* [f. CATER *v.*[1] + -ING[1].] Purveying of food or other requisites.

1820 KEATS *Eve St. Agnes* xx, I scarce dare On such a catering trust my dizzy head. **1828** J. T. RUTT in *Burton's Diary* (1828) III. 163 *note*, Diligent..catering for the intellectual palates of his readers.

catering ('keɪtərɪŋ), *ppl. a.* [f. CATER *v.*[1] + -ING[2].] That caters; concerned with catering.

1923 *Glasgow Herald* 21 Mar. 11 A large London catering firm. **1951** *Oxf. Jun. Encycl.* VII. 88/1 The catering industry in this country is specially interesting, for the way in which it reflects social and economic changes.

caterpillar ('kætəpɪlə(r)), *sb.* Forms: 5 **catyrpel**, 6 **-pyllar**, **catirpiller**, 7 **catterpiller**, 7–8 **-pillar**, 6– **caterpiller**, **-pillar**. [*Catyrpel*, in Promp. Parv., may be merely an error of the scribe for *catyrpelour* (or *-er*); Palsgr. has the full form. Generally compared with the synonymous OF. *chatepelose*, lit. 'hairy or downy cat' (cf. the Sc. name *hairy woubit* 'woolly bear'), of which the ONF. would be *catepelose*. This is a possible source, though no connexion is historically established: the final sibilant might be treated in Eng. as a pl. formative, and the supposed sing. *catepelo* would be readily associated with the well-known word *piller*, *pilour*, pillager, plunderer, spoiler. This is illustrated by the fact that in the fig. sense, *piller* and *caterpiller* are used synonymously in a large number of parallel passages (see sense 2). The regular earlier spelling was with *-er*; the corruption *caterpillar* (? after *pillar*), occasional in 17th c., was adopted by Johnson, and has since prevailed.

(Some think the word a direct compound of *piller*. The giving to hairy caterpillars a name derived from the cat, is seen not only in the French word cited, but also in Lombard. *gatta*, *gattola* (cat, kitten), Swiss *teufelskatz* (devil's cat); cf. also F. *chenille* (:—*canicula* little dog), Milan. *can*, *cagnon* (dog, pup) a silk-worm (Wedgwood). Cf. also *catkin*, F. *chaton*, applied to things resembling hairy caterpillars.)]

1. a. The larva of a butterfly or moth; sometimes extended to those of other insects, especially those of saw-flies, which are also hairy.

c **1440** *Promp. Parv.* 63 Catyrpel, wyrm among frute, *erugo*. **1530** PALSGR. 203/2 Catyrpyllar worme, *chatte pellevse*. **1535** COVERDALE *Ps.* lxxvii[i]. 46 He gaue their frutes vnto the catirpiller. **1597** SHAKS. *Rich. II*, III. iv. 47 Her wholesome Hearbes Swarming with Caterpillers. **1611** BIBLE *Joel* ii. 25 The canker worme, and the caterpiller, and the palmer worme. **1661** LOVELL *Hist. Anim. & Min.* Introd., Catter-pillers, which turne into butter-flies. **1664** EVELYN *Kal. Hort.* (1729) 193 Cut off the Webs of Caterpillars. **1859** TENNYSON *Guinevere* 33 The gardener's hand Picks from the colewort a green caterpillar. **1880** EARLE *Philol. Eng. Tongue* (ed. 3) 434 We know that the caterpiller and the butterfly are the same individual.

b. In full ***caterpillar tractor*** [*Caterpillar*, proprietary term]: a type of tractor which travels upon two endless steel bands, one on each side of the machine, to facilitate travel over very rough ground. Also ***caterpillar lorry***, ***tank***, ***wheel***, etc.; ***caterpillar-wheeled*** adj.

1908 *Sci. Amer.* 16 May 348/1 The 'Caterpillar' Tractor. For some months past the British military authorities have been experimenting with a new type of tractor for the haulage of heavy vehicles over rough and unstable ground. .. The soldiers at the Aldershot military center, where it is in operation, promptly christened it the 'caterpillar'. **1911** *Official Gaz. U.S. Pat. Off.* 28 Nov. 1079/2 The Holt Manufacturing Company, Stockton, Cal. *Caterpillar*. Gasolene, Steam, and Traction Engines, Harvesters, and Road-Working Machines. **1914** *Illustr. London News.* 5 Sept. 369 A 21-centimetre siege-mortar—with 'caterpillar' wheels. **1915** W. S. CHURCHILL *Let.* 5 Jan. in *World Crisis* (1923) II. 74 The caterpillar system would enable trenches to be crossed quite easily. —— *Memo.* 3 Dec. *Ibid.* 87 The Caterpillars will be so close to the enemy's line that they will be immune from his artillery. **1915** *Lit. Digest* 4 Sept. 467/1 Government road-building throughout the interior has paved the way for automobiles, caterpillars and traction-engines. **1915** *Trade Marks Jrnl.* 8 Dec. 1224 Class 6. *Caterpillar*. Tractors and Traction Engines, being Machinery included in Class 6. Caterpillar Tractors, Limited,..Queen Victoria Street, London, E.C. **1922** *Westm. Gaz.* 28 Dec., From In-Salah the caterpillar-wheeled cars will cross the plateau of Tidikelt. **1923** *Contemp. Rev.* Oct. 487 The arrangement of 'caterpillar' traction, with which they were fitted. **1925** FRASER & GIBBONS *Soldier & Sailor Words* 50 *Caterpillar*, a familiar name for the tractor fitted with 'girdles', or flat slabs of metal, round their wheels, employed to haul heavy guns and large vehicles on soft ground. **1935** H. G. WELLS *Things to Come* v. 33 Long lines of tanks and caterpillar lorries. **1935** *Times* 21 Dec. 9/3 The main body of the Italian troops, with light caterpillar tanks, advanced southwards. **1940** *War Illustr.* 16 Feb. 108 Caterpillar tractors built in the U.S.A. are awaiting shipment to France. **1958** *Listener* 19 June 1004/1 We were shown a huge iron machine on caterpillar tracks.

c. Also applied to the undercarriage of an aeroplane equipped with a similar device.

1931 *Jrnl. R. Aeronaut. Soc.* XXXV. 492 (*heading*) Safety in flying and caterpillar undercarriages. *Ibid.*, The caterpillar landing wheel has an equivalent wheel diameter ..with small resistance in flight. **1943** in *Jrnl. R. Aeronaut. Soc.* (1944) XLVIII. (Abstr.) 73 (*title*) Caterpillar track landing gear.

2. *fig.* A rapacious person; an extortioner; one who preys upon society. In early times distinctly transferred, and used synonymously with the earlier *piller*, but afterwards only *fig.* with conscious reference to the literal sense.

[**1475** *Bk. Noblesse* (1860) 31 Pilleris, robberis, extorcioneris. **1539** BIBLE (Great) *1 Cor.* vi. 10 Nether theues, nether couetouse..nether pyllers. **1545** JOYE *On Daniel* xi, Extortioner and pieller of the people. *a* **1570** BECON *Jewel of Joye* Wks. 1564 II. 16 b, Pollers and pyllers of the contrey.] **1541** BARNES *Wks.* (1573) AAa iij, The Augustine friers in London..those Caterpillers and blouddy beastes. **1552** LATIMER *Serm. Lord's Prayer* v. 40 The children of this worlde, as couetous persons, extorcioners, oppressours, catirpillers, userers. **1579** GOSSON (*title*), The Schoole of Abuse, Conteining a plesaunt inuectiue against Poets, Pipers, Plaiers, Iesters, and such like Caterpillers of a Commonwelth. **1631** WEEVER *Anc. Fun. Mon* 417 Empson and Dudley (cater-pillers of the common-wealth, hatefull to all good people). **1631** *High Commission Cases* (1886) 259 For his saying against the officers that they are caterpillers I let that passe. **1696** PHILLIPS s.v., When we see a company of Lacqueys at the tail of a coach, we say, There goes a Bunch of Caterpillers. **1726** AMHERST *Terræ Fil.* xl. 211 Such nurseries of drones and caterpillars, to prey upon it. **1826** SCOTT *Lett. Mal. Malagr.* ii. 66 We have become the caterpillars of the island, instead of its pillars.

3. ***black caterpillar***: **a.** The larva of the Turnip Saw-fly. **b.** A fly or an imitation of it used as a bait in angling.

1787 BEST *Angling* (ed. 2) 113 The black Caterpillar comes on about the beginning of May..if winds and clouds appear, they then grow weak for want of the sun, and fall upon the waters in great quantities. The wings are made from a feather out of a jay's wing, the body of an ostrich's feather. **1799** G. SMITH *Laborat.* II. 303 Black-caterpillar-fly. **1848** *Proc. Berw. Nat. Club* II. No. 6. 329 The larva of *Athalia centifolæ*..named the nigger or black caterpillar, is an enemy..much dreaded by the agriculturist..In 1780 it was abundant in Northumberland.

4. *Herb.* **a.** A name given to the leguminous plants of the genus *Scorpiurus* from the shape of their pods. **b.** By Gerard *Myosotis palustris*, the true Forget-me-not or Scorpion-grass, 'is included in the same chapter and under the same name' (Britten and Holland *Plant-n.*).

1597 GERARD *Herbal* i. §10. 267 Our English gentle-women and others do call it Caterpillers, of the similitude it hath with the shape of that canker worme called a caterpiller. **1672** W. HUGHES *Flower Gard.* (1683) 8 Snails and Caterpillers..raised from Seed sowed in April..cannot properly be called Flowers, but they have very pretty heads. **1713** PETIVER *Rare Plants* in *Phil. Trans.* XXVIII. 212 Prickley Caterpillars. **1750** G. HUGHES *Barbados* 170. **1866** *Treas. Bot.*, *Caterpillar*, a name for *Scorpiurus*.

5. *attrib.* and *Comb.*: **a.** *simple attrib.* Of, pertaining to, or resembling a caterpillar. **b.** **caterpillar-catcher**, a sub-family of shrikes which feed on caterpillars; **caterpillar-eater**, (*a*) the larva of an ichneumon fly; (*b*) = *caterpillar catcher*; **caterpillar-fly** = 3 above; **caterpillar-plant** = 4 above; **caterpillar-like** *a.*

a. 1859 DARWIN *Orig. Spec.* iv. (1878) 67 The caterpillar and cocoon stages. **1864** LOWELL *Fireside Trav.* 95 The caterpillar wooden bridges crawling with innumerable legs across the flats of Charles.

b. 1880 A. R. WALLACE *Isl. Life* 407 *Caterpillar-catchers ..abundant in the old-world tropics. **1753** CHAMBERS *Cycl. Supp.* s.v., One of the species of these *caterpillar eaters. **1611** COTGR., *Chenillé*, *Caterpiller-like. **1862** ANSTED *Channel Isl.* II. ix. (ed. 2) 237 A fleshy, caterpillar-like body. **1841** *Penny Cycl.* XXI. 415/1 The Ceblepyrinæ, or *Caterpillar Shrikes. **1847** EMERSON *Woodnotes* i. Wks. (Bohn) I. 220 Pondering clouds, Grass-buds, and *caterpillar-shrouds.

6. A member of the *Caterpillar Club* founded by Leslie Leroy Irvin in 1922 (see quots. 1930).

1925 *Literary Digest* 26 Sept. 50 (*title*) Are you eligible for the Caterpillar club? **1930** C. DIXON *Parachuting* vii. 61 Each caterpillar has saved his life with a parachute. **1930** *Engineering* 26 Dec. 811/3 The Caterpillar Club (this being the name given to persons who have saved their lives by the agency of a parachute).

Hence **'caterpillared** *a.*, (*a*) fitted with a caterpillar; (*b*) fitted with caterpillar tracks.

1608 TOPSELL *Serpents* 671 The trout..deceived with a caterpillered hook. **1917** *Blackw. Mag.* Mar. 379/2 New armoured cars, caterpillared and powerfully armed, would make their bow to Brother Boche.

'caterpillar, *v.* [f. the sb.] To move like a caterpillar or on caterpillar tracks (see prec. 1 b).

1916 *Daily Sketch* 23 Nov. 3/1 Three tanks started... One of the machines moved..caterpillaring its laborious way up the slope. **1928** *Daily Express* 2 July 3 These 'tank' drivers have developed enormous calf muscles, due to caterpillaring over rough country.

† **caterquibble.** *Obs. rare*[−1].

1691 *Long Vacation* Ded. 2 Thou..hadst such Magnificent Puns, such Exalted Clinches, such Caterquibbles and Cunundrums.

† **ca'terve.** *Obs. rare*[−1]. [a. OF. *caterve* (Cotgr.), ad. L. *caterva*.] A band, a company.

1491 CAXTON *Vitas Patr.* (W. de W.) III. xlv. 329 b/2 He sawe tweyne caterues & companyes of deuylles.

caterwaul ('kætəwɔːl), *sb.* [see next: the sb. is app. from the vb.] The cry of the cat at rutting time. Also *transf.* Any similar sound.

1708 *Brit. Apollo* No. 73. 2/2 His softest Courtship's like his Midnight Call, You'd swear it was not Talk, but Caterwaul. **1855** O. W. HOLMES *Poems* 125 The lovely caterwaul, Tart solo, sour duet, and general squall,—These are our hymn. **1880** MARK TWAIN *Tramp Abr.* I. 215 That variegated and enormous unanimous caterwaul.

caterwaul ('kætəwɔːl), *v.* Forms: 4–5 **caterwrawe**, 4–6 **-wawe**, 6 **katerwaue**, 6–8 **catterwawl**, **-wall**, 8 **-wowl**, 7–9 **-waul**, 7 **-waule**, **caterwaule**, **-wawl**, **catterwrall**, (**catwrall**), 8 **catterwaw**, 6– **caterwaul**. [This occurs in the various forms *caterwrawe*, *-wawe*, *-wrawl(e*, *-wawle*, *-waul*. The second element appears separately in the vb. *wrawen* used (of a cat) by Caxton, *wrawlen*, *wraule* of cats, squalling children, etc., frequent in Googe, Tusser, Holland, and others from *c* 1570 to 1625 or later; *waul* is of doubtful occurrence before 1600. The precise relation between these is not clear; all are prob. imitative of the sound, but whether the forms in *-l* are formed on the others (cf. *mew*, *mewl*, Ger. *miauen*, *miaulen*, and F. *miauler*) is doubtful.

Forms akin to *wrawe*, *wrawl* in other langs. are Da. *vraale*, Sw. *vråla*, to roar, bellow, bawl, Norw. dial. *råla*, in the north of Norway 'to cry as a cat', LG. *wralen* (Bremen Wbch.) said of a stallion in heat, also of an ill-behaved man, 'to be noisy and unruly'; cf. also Bavarian *rauen*, *rauelen* 'to howl, whine', said esp. of the cat, also Swiss *rauen*, *räulen*, the latter esp. of the cry of the cat when in heat. (*Wr-* becomes *r-* in HG.: an OE. **wreawlian*, ME. *wrawlen* would answer exactly to Bav. *rauelen*.) The sense of the Ger. words also comes near the Eng., since both in Chaucer and in the transf. use of the 16–17th c., the word was spec. applied to the cry and behaviour of the cat when 'after kind'. As to the *-waul* form, an exact LG. counterpart *katterwaulen* '(von Kindern) schreien und heulen wie streitende Katzen' is given by Schambach, *Göttingisches Grubenhagen'sches Idiotiken* 1858, but its history is uncertain; cf. also Icel. *vála* to wail.

Cater is, of course, connected with CAT, but the form is not certainly explained: some would see in it a parallel to Du. and Ger. *kater* male cat, which may once have existed in OE.; but the word appears too late to prove this. Others would take *-er* as some kind of suffix or connective merely.]

1. *intr.* Of cats: To make the noise proper to them at rutting time.

Prof. Skeat explains *Caterw(r)awet*, in Chaucer, as a verbal sb., on the type of OE. *on huntað*, a-hunting.

c **1386** CHAUCER *Wife's Prol.* (Harl.) 354 If the cattes skyn be slyk and gay, forth she wil, er eny day be dawet, To schewe hir skyn, and goon a caterwrawet [so *Corpus*: 5 texts have *-wawed*]. [**1481** CAXTON *Reynard* x. (Arb.) 22 Thenne began he [Tybert the Cat] to wrawen..and made a shrewde noyse.] **1530** [see CATERWAULING]. [**1596** SPENSER *F.Q.* VI. xii. 47 Cats, that wrawling still do cry.] **1610** *Chester's Tri., Envy & L.* 51 Oh it grates my gall To hear an apish kitling caterwall. **1630** J. TAYLOR (Water P.) *Garret's Ghost* Wks. II. 177/1 Dead midnight came, the Cats 'gan catterwaule. **1749** FIELDING *Tom Jones* II. viii, A noise, not unlike..in shrillness, to cats, when cater-wauling. **1876** SMILES *Sc. Natur.* vi. (ed. 4) 100 Two cats..caterwauling in the grave-yard.

2. *transf.* To utter a similar cry; to make a discordant, hideous noise; to quarrel like cats.

1621 BURTON *Anat. Mel.* I. ii. III. x. (1676) 66/2 They will let them [children] caterwaule, sterue, begge and hang. **1651** CLEVELAND *Smectym.* 87 Thus might Religions Catterwaul

and spight Which uses to Divorce, might once unite. *a* **1680** BUTLER *Rem.* (1759) II. 311 Those that are concerned in one another's Love and Honour, are never quiet, but always catterwalling. **1721** MRS. DELANY *Autobiog.* (1861) I. 276 They agreed to sing a duetto.. such catterwauling was never heard and we all laughed.

3. To be in heat; to be lecherous; to behave amorously or lasciviously; to woo (*contemptuous*).

1599 NASHE *Lent. Stuffe* (1871) 89 The friars and monks caterwauled, from the abbots and priors to the novices. **1621** BURTON *Anat. Mel.* III. ii. I. ii. (1651) 445 She catter-wauls, and must have a stallion.. she must and will marry again. **1713** ROWE *Jane Shore* Prol. 1 They caterwaul'd in no Romantick Ditty, Sighing for Phillis's, or Chloe's Pity. **1730** FIELDING *Author's Farce* Wks. 1775 I. 206 So, so, very fine: always together, always caterwauling. **1870** [see CATERWAULING *vbl. sb.* 2].

'caterwauler. [f. prec. + -ER[1].] One that caterwauls (*transf.* in quot.).

a **1774** GOLDSM. tr. *Scarron's Com. Romance* (1775) I. 185 These two catter-wallers were accompanied by the organ.

'caterwauling, *vbl. sb.* Forms: see prec., also 6–7 **catterwaling, -wralling,** (7 **cat-wralling**). [f. as prec. + -ING[1].]

1. The cry of cats at rutting time; their rutting or heat.

1530 PALSGR. 175 *Larre des chatz*, the caterwawyng of cattes. *Ibid.* 235/2 Katerwayng. **1607** TOPSELL *Four-f. Beasts* 82 In the time of their lust (commonly called cat-wralling) they are wilde and fierce. **1820** SCOTT *Ivanhoe* xvii, His serenade.. as little regarded as the caterwauling of a cat in the gutter. **1834** MUDIE *Brit. Birds* (1841) I. 150 Thus, if owls were established at every farm, the caterwauling of cats .. would be less necessary.

b. *to go a caterwauling*: to go 'after kind'.

1562 J. HEYWOOD *Prov. & Epigr.* (1867) 57 My cat gothe a catterwawyng. **1577** B. GOOGE *Heresbach's Husb.* (1586) 156b, They goe a catterwalling about Februarie. **1582** HESTER *Secr. Phiorav.* III. lxxxviii. 113 The Catte.. is neuer in loue or goeth a catterwallyng, but in the coldest weather. **1616** SURFL. & MARKH. *Countr. Farm* 194. **1737** MILLER *Gard. Dict.* s.v. *Cataria*, When they go a Catter-wauling.

2. Going after the opposite sex; lecherous motions or pursuits.

1530 PALSGR. 829 A katerwavyng, *agars.* **1532** MORE *Confut. Tindale* Wks. 342/1 Priestes, freres, monkes and nunnes.. may runne out a caterwawing. *c* **1555** HARPSFIELD *Divorce Hen. VIII* (1878) 275 To see old doting.. priests.. run a catterwawling. **1611** COTGR., *Aller à gars*, (a wench) to goe a caterwawling. [See also *garouage, iar*, etc.] **1672** WYCHERLEY *Love in Wood* II. i, This new-fashioned caterwauling, this midnight coursing in the Park! **1708** MOTTEUX *Rabelais* V. xxix.

3. *transf.* Any hideous, discordant howling noise.

1588 SHAKS. *Tit. A.* IV. ii. 37. **1598** B. JONSON *Ev. Man in Hum.* IV. ii, Why, you Munkies you, what a Catter-waling do you keep? **1612** DEKKER *If not Good* Plays 1873 III. 289 Welsh harpes, Irish bag-pipes, Jewes trompes, and french kitts.. their dambd catter-wralling, frighted me away. **1712** ADDISON *Spect.* No. 361 ¶1 A kind of catter-wawling.. whatever the musicians themselves might think of it. **1853** KINGSLEY *Hypatia* xviii. 212 There they are at it now, with their catterwauling, squealing, all together.

4. *fig.* Whining.

1850 CLOUGH *Dipsychus* II. iv. 152 These pitiful rebellions of the flesh, These caterwaulings of the effeminate heart. **1870** HUXLEY *Lay Serm.* iv. 69 Sensual caterwauling.

'caterwauling, *ppl. a.* That caterwauls.

a **1652** BROME *Covent Gard.* IV. i. Wks. 1873 II. 60 This may warne you out of such caterwaling company. **1663** BUTLER *Hud.* I. II. 702 Was no dispute a-foot between The Caterwauling Brethren? **1791** G. HUDDESFORD *Salmag.* 145 Of Cats that grace a Caterwauling age. *c* **1834** tr. *Uniomachia* (1875) 23 Each caterwauling Tom consoles his spouse.

† **'catery.** *Obs.* Also 5 **catarie.** [Aphetic form of ACATERY, a. OF. *acaterie*; see CATER *sb.*[1] and -Y[3].] The office concerned with the supply of the provisions of the royal household.

1455 in *Househ. Ord.* (1790) 21 Th' office of the Catery. **1531** *Dial. Laws of Eng.* II. xlii. (1638) 136 The Serjeant of the Catery shall satisfie all the debt. **1779** KELHAM *Dict. Norman* (T.) *Serjeaunt de l'acaterie*, serjeant of the catery.

catery, obs. form of CATTERY.

cates, provisions, dainties: see CATE *sb.*[1]

† **catesnd** (kə'teɪnd), *pa. pple. Obs.* [of implied vb. *catesne* = *catene*, ad. L. *catēnāre.*] Enchained.

1566 DRANT *Horace's Sat.* iv. B viij, Sum lyve catesnd in cupids chaines.

catexochen. Variant of KAT' EXOCHEN *adv. phr.*

cat-eyed: see CAT *sb.*[1] in *comb.*

'cat-fish.

1. A name given to various fishes; particularly to: **a.** The *Anarrhicas* or Wolf-fish. **b.** Several species of *Pimelodus*, North American fresh-water fish, esp. *P. catus*, the common cat-fish; †**c.** The *Lophius* or Fishing Frog. **d.** Also applied to various species of fish in Australia, New Zealand, and Africa.

1620 J. MASON *Newfoundland* (1887) 152 What should I speake of.. crabbes, catfish, etc.? **1697** DAMPIER *Voy.* I. 148 The Catfish is much like a Whiting.. It hath a great wide Mouth, and certain small strings pointing out from each side of it, like Cats Whiskers. **1769** PENNANT *Brit. Zool.* III. 88 [Given as a synonym for the greater dogfish]. **1773** WILLIAMSON in *Phil. Trans.* LXV. 96 Its head was flat and its mouth wide, like that of a cat-fish. **1803** SIBBALD *Hist. Fife* 121 (Jam.) *Lupus marinus*.. our fishers call it the sea-cat, or cat-fish. **1817–8** COBBETT *Resid. U.S.* (1822) 286 Saw a cat-fish in the market, just caught out of the river by a hook and line, 4 feet long and eighty pounds weight. **1834** G. BENNETT *Wanderings N.S.W.* I. 343 The '*Cat-fish*', (*Silurus*,) said to have the power of stinging with the tentaculae or feelers, which pend from about the external part of the mouth,.. and several species of bream, were caught in.. the splendid harbour of Port Jackson. **1851** J. HENDERSON *Excurs. N.S.W.* II. 207 The Cat-fish, which I have frequently caught in the McLeay, is a large and very ugly animal. **1864** J. T. BAINES *Explor. S.W. Africa* i. 3 Beyond was a broad flat, covered with cat, dog and other mud-frequenting fish. **1871** *Cape Monthly Mag.* II. 135 A most horrible creature called a 'catfish', but which ought more properly to have been named 'a sea devil',.. as it was all arms and legs, and huge goggle-eyed head. **1878** *Daily News* 16 Sept. 3/7 A large catfish.. was placed in the tank, whereupon the bass immediately combined their forces and commenced an attack on the intruder. **1897** PARKER & HASWELL *Text-bk. Zool.* II. 212 The Cat-fishes (*Siluridæ*). **1900** H. A. BRYDEN *Anim. Africa* 196 When.. African rivers dry up, there is nothing left for the Cat-fish but to burrow in the mud. **1947** K. H. BARNARD *Pict. Guide S. Afr. Fishes* iii. 59 The best known South African river Cat-fish is the Mud-Barbel or Platkop Barger (*Clarias mossambicus*). **1963** P. H. GREENWOOD *Norman's Hist. Fishes* (ed. 2) xvi. 284 The only fishes of the order Ostariophysi in the Australian region are certain freshwater genera and species of Cat-fishes. These belong to two families (Ariidae; Plotosidae)... The characteristic African families of.. Cat-fishes (Clariidae, Mochocidae, Amphiliidae, etc.).

2. The cuttle-fish or other cephalopod.

1678 PHILLIPS, *Catfish*, a sort of Fish in some parts of the West Indies, so called from the Round-head, and large glaring Eyes, by which they are discovered in the Concavities of the Rocks. **1758** BAKER in *Phil. Trans.* L. 785 Sea Polypi are frequent in the Mediterranean.. A different species.. came from the West Indies, where it is called a Cat-fish. **1880** *Antrim & Down Gloss.* (E.D.S.) Cat-fish, a cuttle fish, *Sepia officinalis.*

'cat-foot, *v.* Chiefly *U.S.* [CAT *sb.*[1] + FOOT *sb.*] *intr.* To walk stealthily or noiselessly. Also with *it.*

1916 H. L. WILSON *Somewhere in Red Gap* iii. 119 Mebbe it's a Blackhander's camp, I think; so I didn't yell any more. I cat-footed. And in a minute I was up close. **1928** *Collier's Mag.* 10 Nov. 42/2 Tichenor arose and nonchalantly cat-footed down the field for a deceitful touchdown. **1960** 'R. SIMONS' *Frame for Murder* viii. 103 Crow began to cat-foot it up the stairs.

catgut ('kætgʌt). Forms: 7 **cat's-guts,** 8 **cat's-gut,** 8– **catgut.** [So in Du. *kattedarm.* So far as the *name* can be traced back, it distinctly means guts or intestines of the cat, though it is not known that these were ever used for the purpose. Cf. also CATLING.

(Some have conjectured a humorous reference to the resemblance of the sound to caterwauling.)]

1. The dried and twisted intestines of sheep, also of the horse and ass; used for the strings of musical instruments; also as bands in lathes, clocks, etc.

1599 *Warn. Faire Wom.* I. 9 What, yet more cats guts? oh, this filthy sound Stifles mine ears.. I'll cut your fiddle strings If you stand scraping thus to anger me! [**1607** MARSTON *What you will* III. i. in *N. & Q.* (1886) 10 Apr., The musitions Hover with nimble sticks ore squeaking crowds [fiddles] Tickling the dryed gutts of a mewing cat.] **1680** COTTON in Singer *Hist. Cards* (1816) 334 Strung, or run upon cat's guts. **1688** R. HOLME *Armoury* III. 357/1 Made of the Guts of Beasts as sheep, etc., though the generall name of it is Cats-Guts. **1780** COWPER *Progr. Err.* 126 With wire and catgut he concludes the day, Quavering and semiquavering care away. **1807–8** W. IRVING *Salmag.* (1824) 27 Sympathise at every twang of the cat-gut, as if he heard at that moment the wailings of the helpless animal that had been sacrificed to harmony. **1878** HUXLEY *Physiogr.* 71 The effect of moisture upon catgut.

2. A violin; stringed instruments collectively.

1709 *Brit. Apollo* II. No. 19. 2/2 Great Patron of Cat-guts. **1740** SOMERVILLE *Hobbinol* I. 142 Hark, from aloft his tortur'd Cat-gut squeals. **1867** *Cornh. Mag.* Jan. 30 Drowned in a roar of brass and catgut.

3. 'A coarse cloth formed of thick cord, woven widely and used in the last century for lining and stiffening dress, particularly the skirts and sleeves of a coat' (Fairholt).

1731 MRS. DELANY *Autobiog.* (1861) I. 282, I have not sent you any catgut for working handkerchiefs. **1823** GALT *Entail* I. i. 7 The vast head-dress of catgut and millinery.

4. *sea catgut*: a slender cord-like sea-weed; sea-lace, *Chorda filum.*

5. *attrib.* and *Comb.* as **catgut-scraper,** a contemptuous designation of a violinist.

1633 MASSINGER *Guardian* IV. ii, Wire-string and catgut men, and strong-breathed heautbois. **1711** *Lond. Gaz.* No. 4890/4 A Cats-gut string. **1723** *Ibid.* No. 6222/8 William Burridge, Catgut-spinner. **1806** WOLCOTT (P. Pindar) *Tristia* Wks. 1812 V. 267 Behold! the Cat-gut-scraper with his croud Commands at will the house of hospitality. **1832** W. STEPHENSON *Gateshead Poems* 23 Two nightly cat gut scrapers. **1833** *Manuf. Metal* II. 137 (Cabinet Cycl.) Transferring the catgut band from one groove to the other. **1881** *Syd. Soc. Lex.* s.v. *Catheter, railway*, It is introduced over a catgut bougie or guide.

catha-, a former var. of CATA-, e.g. *cathacomb, cathalogue.*

cathæretic: see CATHERETIC.

cat-hammed ('kæt'hæmd), *a.* [see HAM.] Having hams like those of the cat.

1695 *Lond. Gaz.* No. 3120/4 Lost or stolen.. a brown bay Nag.. a little Cat-ham'd. **1697** *Ibid.* No. 3303/4 Lost.. one white Nag.. cut Tail'd, cat Hamm'd, fallen at the Crest with the Harness. **1831** YOUATT *Horse* ii. (1847) 30. **1880** H. ST. JOHN *Wild Coasts Nipon* viii. 169 The Japanese pony is.. cat-hammed as a rule, big-headed.

Cathar ('kæθə(r)). Also **-are.** Pl. **Cathars,** ‖**Cathari.** [ad. med.L. *Cathari*: see CATHARAN.] = CATHARAN. Also used *attrib.* or as *adj.*

1637 GILLESPIE *Eng. Pop. Cerem.* II. v. 24 The old Waldenses before us, were also named by their adversaries, Cathares or Puritanes. **1806** M. PEMBRIDGE *Roman Cath. Ch. Vind.* III. 560 There was another sect, of *Cathari*, or Catharists, so named from a Greek word, signifying a cleansing or purging, from a certain execrable manner of cleansing from their execrable uncleanness, that they made use of. **1907** *Cath. Encycl.* I. 557/1 The Cathares and the Patarines. **1910** *Encycl. Brit.* V. 515/2 Cathars (Cathari or Catharists). **1920** H. G. WELLS *Outl. Hist.* II. xxxiii. 465/2 In the south of France the people.. were called the Cathars or Albigenses. **1927** F. J. E. RABY *Hist. Chr.-Lat. Poetry* xiii. 416 Based like the Cathar and Waldensian [religions], on poverty and renunciation. **1947** S. RUNCIMAN *Med. Manichee* vi. 125 The Dualism of the Cathars. *Ibid.* 126 In England Cathar heretics were found as late as 1210.

† **'Catharan.** *Obs.* Also **Ca'tharian.** [f. Gr. Καθαροί, med.L. *Cathari*, 'the pure', the name assumed by the Novatian heretics, and by other sects later. Cf. F. *Cathare.*]

One who professes superior purity; a puritan; a name applied to various sects, as the Novatians, Paulicians, Waldenses; also, like CATHARIST, to the English Puritans. So **Catha'rinian.**

1574 WHITGIFT *Def. Answ.* I. Wks. 1851 I. 172 Puritans or Catharans. **1585–7** T. ROGERS *39 Art.* (1607) 138 The Catharans.. which think Gods people be regenerate into a pure and angelical state. **1656** BLOUNT *Glossogr.*, *Catharians*, were a branch of the Novatian Hereticks. **1657** GAULE *Sap. Just.* 10 So [maintain] the Pighians and Catharinians.

Catharism ('kæθərɪz(ə)m). [ad. N.-T. Gr. καθαρισμός purification, f. καθαρίζειν to make clean.]

1. The doctrine of the Catharists.

1574 WHITGIFT *Def. Answ.* I. Wks. 1851 I. 174 That very perfection.. which you challenge unto yourselves.. well deserveth the name of Catharism. **1575** T. CARTWRIGHT *2nd Replie*, in *Whitgift's Wks.* 1852 II. 61 Uncharitable suspicions of papism, anabaptism, Catharism, Donatism, etc. **1832** S. MAITLAND *Facts & Documents* 362 It was reported that he had imbibed your Catharism. **1838** G. S. FABER *An Inquiry* 153 The mode wherein the Canons of Orleans were converted to Catharism.

2. *Chem.* The process of making a surface chemically clean.

1869 *Sci. Opin.* 17 Mar. 380/2 Mr. Tomlinson explained the sense in which he applied the new term Catharism.. distinguishing between 'clean' in its ordinary and its chemical sense.

'Catharist. [ad. med.L. *Catharist-æ* (= Gr. καθαρισταί, f. καθαρίζειν to purify). Cf. F. *Cathariste.*] A Paulician or Manichæan; also applied to similar sects; cf. CATHARAN.

1600 O. E. *Repl. Libel* II. iii. 52 The Catharistes do boast much of their merits. **1616** DONNE *Serm.* Wks. 1839 VI. 103 The Catharists thought no creature of God pure, and therefore they brought in strange ceremonial purifications of those creatures. **1630** PRYNNE *Lame Giles* 12 The Novatian Catherist. **1645** MILTON *Tetrach.* (1851) 148 Like the vermin of an Indian Catharist, which his fond religion forbids him to molest. **1832** S. MAITLAND *Facts & Documents* 431 Any Catharist.. of whatever sect.

Hence **Catharistic** *a.*

1838 G. S. FABER *An Inquiry* 103 From the Paulicians of the East to their Catharistic Successors in the West.

† **'Catharite.** *Obs.* [see CATHARAN.] A puritan.

1555 BALE in Strype *Eccl. Mem.* III. App. xxxix. 108 Our holy Communion hath not the face of a popish mas, as our new Catharites have most wickedly.. reported.

catharize ('kæθəraɪz), *v.* [ad. Gr. καθαρίζ-ειν to make clean, purify, f. καθαρός clean.]

1. *trans.* To purify (by some ceremony).

1832 S. MAITLAND *Facts & Documents* 359 The unhappy person who is to be baptized or Catharized.

2. To make chemically clean (see CATHARISM 2). Hence **,cathari'zation.**

1881 in *Syd. Soc. Lex.*

† **catharm.** *Obs. rare*[−1]. [ad. Gr. καθαρμός purification, purging, f. καθαίρειν to cleanse, purge, f. καθαρός clean.] A purging or purgation.

1678 CUDWORTH *Intell. Syst.* 787 Those Ancients made use of Catharms, or Purgations to the same end and purpose.

cat-harpings: see HARPINGS.

‖**catharsis** (kə'θɑːsɪs). *Med.* Also **katharsis.** [mod.L., a. Gr. κάθαρσις cleansing, purging, f. καθαίρειν to cleanse, purge, f. καθαρός clean.]

a. Purgation of the excrements of the body; *esp.* evacuation of the bowels.

1803 *Med. Jrnl.* IX. 418 Causing vomiting, catharsis, or diabetes. **1875** H. WOOD *Therap.* (1879) 449 The production of catharsis is the surest mode of relief in general dropsy.

b. The purification of the emotions by vicarious experience, esp. through the drama (in reference to Aristotle's *Poetics* 6). Also more widely.

[**1867** J. A. SYMONDS *Let.* 22 Aug. (1967) I. 751 The world desiderates now..a trilogy, whereof the whole third part shall exhibit 'the height, the space, the gloom, the glory', of ultimate final and perfect *κάθαρσις*.] **1872** G. S. MORRIS tr. *Ueberweg's Hist. Phil.* I. I. 179 Aristotle can not have meant ..to exclude from among the effect of the Tragedy, its effect as..ethical discipline. With the 'Catharsis'..are..joined.. the other effects of the same,—the latter effects flow from the 'Catharsis'. **1897** COSTELLOE & MUIR tr. *Zeller's Philos. Greeks* II. xv. 311/2 According to Aristotle there is a kind of music which produces a catharsis, although it possesses no ethical value..—namely, exciting music. **1904** DOWDEN *Browning* 289 Balaustion, stricken at heart, yet feels that this tragedy of Athens brings the tragic katharsis. **1920** D. H. LAWRENCE *Touch & Go* III. i. 72 It's a cleansing process—like Aristotle's Katharsis. We shall hate ourselves clean at last, I suppose. **1924** L. COOPER *Aristotelian Theory Com.* 180 Aristotle..would recognize some sort of catharsis, and the resultant pleasure, to be the proper end of comedy. **1924** SELBIE *Psychol. Relig.* 159 There may..be cases where experiences of this kind produce a moral catharsis which has good results. **1959** *Chamber's Encycl.* I. 592/1 The word *catharsis* (purgation), in which he [*sc.* Aristotle] summed up the emotional effect of tragedy, has also received much fanciful interpretation; in reality it is a medical term, with no directly moral or spiritual implications.

c. *Psychotherapy.* The process of relieving an abnormal excitement by re-establishing the association of the emotion with the memory or idea of the event which was the first cause of it, and of eliminating it by abreaction.

1909 A. A. BRILL in *Freud's Sel. Papers Hysteria* 6 The German abreagiren..has different shades of meaning, from defense reaction to emotional catharsis. **1951** J. C. FLUGEL *Hundred Years Psychol.* (ed. 2) viii. 280 The mere bringing back and discussing of memories..which Freud and Breuer called subsequently 'abreaction' or 'catharsis'.

cathartic (kəˈθɑːtɪk), *a.* and *sb.* [ad. L. *cathartic-us*, a. Gr. *καθαρτικός* fit for cleansing, purgative; see prec. Cf. F. *cathartique*.]

A. *adj.*

1. *Med.* Cleansing (the bowels), promoting evacuation, purgative.

1612 WOODALL *Surg. Mate* Wks. (1653) 351 Cartharticke or purging Medicines. **1667** BOYLE *Orig. Formes & Qual.*, The purgative faculty of Rhubarb, Senna, and other Cathartick Vegetables. **1801** *Med. Jrnl.* V. 220 An ounce of the common cathartic salts. **1868** GEO. ELIOT *Sp. Gipsy* 239 Honey's not sweet, commended as cathartic.

2. *gen.* (and *fig.*) Cleansing, purifying, purging.

1678 CUDWORTH *Intell. Syst.* 787 As this Earthy Body is washed by Water, so is that Spirituous Body Cleansed by Cathartick Vapours. **1795** T. TAYLOR *Apuleius* (1822) 364 This philosophic death..is effected by the cathartic or purifying virtues. **1841-4.** EMERSON *Ess. Heroism* Wks. (Bohn) I. 104 We need books of this tart cathartic virtue.

B. *sb.* A medicine which has the power of purging or evacuating; a purgative. More strictly: 'a medicine which is capable of producing the second grade of purgation, of which laxative is the first and drastic the third' (*Syd. Soc. Lex.*).

1651 WITTIE tr. *Primrose's Pop. Err.* IV. 265 Aloes, which is such a gentle cathartick. **1768-74** TUCKER *Lt. Nat.* (1852) II. 147, It may be proper for jockeys and running footmen to keep themselves spare and light by cathartics. **1830** LINDLEY *Nat. Syst. Bot.* 208 A mild cathartic.

b. *fig.*

1667 *Decay Chr. Piety* v. 230 Lustrations and catharticks of the mind were sought for. **1712** ADDISON *Spect.* No. 507 ¶1 Plato has called mathematical demonstrations the cathartics or purgatives of the soul. **1860** ABP. THOMSON *Laws Th.* §35 Logic..is called the Cathartic of the Mind.

caˈthartical, *a.* [f. as prec. + -AL¹.] = prec.

1656 H. MORE *Antid. Ath.* (1712) Gen. Pref. 8 Not only to a Political degree of vertue, but Cathartical. **1680** BOYLE *Scept. Chem.* v. 336 Scarce any Elementary Salt is in small quantity Cathartical. **1822** *Blackw. Mag.* XI. 117 A leading article..To Tories and to Whigs alike cathartical.

Hence **caˈthartically** *adv.*, **caˈtharticalness**.

1816 T. TAYLOR in *Pamphleteer* VIII. 48 Or it [the soul] lives cathartically, the exemplar of which is the Saturnian kingdom. **1730-6** BAILEY, *Catharticalness*..purging Quality. Hence in JOHNSON and in mod. Dicts.

caˈthartin. [see -IN.] A bitter substance extracted from senna, and acting as a purgative.

1830 LINDLEY *Nat. Syst. Bot.* 91 The active principle of Senna is called Cathartine. **1840** HENRY *Elem. Chem.* II. 333 In examining the leaves of Senna, Lassaigne and Fenuelle obtained a peculiar substance, to which they gave the name of cathartine. **1879** WATTS *Dict. Chem.* VII. 270 Cathartin.

ˈcat-haul, *sb. U.S.* [CAT *sb.*¹ 17.] (See quot.) Also **ˈcat-haul** *v. trans.*, to subject to this punishment; *fig.* to examine stringently; hence **cat-hauling** *vbl. sb.*

1824 'A. SINGLETON' *Lett. fr. South & West* 79 The cat-haul; that is, to fasten a slave down flatwise..and then to take a huge fierce tom-cat by the tail backward, and haul him down along the..bare back, with his claws clinging into the quick all the way. **1840** *Congress. Globe* 12 Jan., App. 99/2 White people of the South..hunting slaves with dogs and guns,—cat-hauling slaves, &c. **1844-7** *Chambers' Misc. Useful Tracts* cxlix. 17, I saw a slave punished by cat-hauling. The cat was placed on the bare shoulders, and forcibly dragged by the tail down the back..of the prostrate slave. **1881** *Congress. Rec.* 28 Feb. 2202/2 You begin to ransack and examine and cat-haul the whole navy, big and little. **1950** R. STARNES *And when she was Bad* xvii. 109 Brafferton's cathauling by the Harford Committee commanded a banner headline.

Cathay (kæˈθeɪ). *arch.* or *poet.* Also formerly **Cathaye**, ‖**Cataya, Cathaia.** [ad. med. and Renaissance L. *Cat(h)aya*, ad. Turkic *Khitāy*: cf. Kazan Tartar *Kytai*, Russ. *Kitay* China.] = CHINA *sb.*¹ 1.

1565 A. JENCKYNSON in *S.P. Dom. Eliz.* XXXVI. LX. f. 134 This Region of Cathaye. **1576** (*title*) A trve discovrse of the late voyages of discouerie, for the finding of a passage to Cathaya, by the Northvveast, vnder the conduct of Martin Frobisher. **1576** (*title*) A discovrse of a discouerie for a new passage to Cataia. Written by Sir Hvmfrey Gilbert. *a* **1625** FLETCHER *Woman's Prize* IV. v. (1647) 118/2 I'le wish you in the Indies, or Cataya. **1823** BYRON *Don Juan* XII. ix. 9 The ship From Ceylon, Inde, or far Cathay, unloads. **1842** TENNYSON *Locksley Hall* 184 Thro' the shadow of the globe we sweep into the younger day: Better fifty years of Europe than a cycle of Cathay. **1954** W. FAULKNER *Fable* 348 A world such as caesar nor sultan nor khan ever saw, Tiberius nor Kubla nor all the emperors of the East ever dreamed of —no Rome and Baiae:..no Cathay.

Cathayan (kæˈθeɪən), *a.* and *sb.* Also **-aian.** [f. med.L. *Cat(h)aya* + -AN. Cf. CATAIAN.] Chinese.

1667 MILTON *P.L.* x. 293 Mountains of Ice, that stop th'imagin'd way Beyond Petsora Eastward, to the rich Cathaian Coast. *Ibid.* XI. 388 Cambalu, seat of Cathaian Can. **1757** J. DYER *Fleece* in *Poems* (1761) III. 140 A double wealth; more rich than Belgium's boast, Or the Cathayan's, whose ignobler care Nurses the silkworm. **1876** *Encycl. Brit.* V. 628/1 The identity of these Cathayans with the Seres of classic fame. **1928** *Blackw. Mag.* Jan. 1/1 To push back a Cathayan encroachment. **1928** H. LAMB *Genghis Khan* xiii. 126 The Cathayans must have suffered that winter.

cat-head (ˈkæthɛd), *sb.* Also 7 **cat's-head.** **1.** *Naut.* A beam projecting almost horizontally at each side of the bows of a ship, for raising the anchor from the surface of the water to the deck without touching the bows, and for carrying the anchor on its stock-end when suspended outside the ship's side; it is furnished with sheaves at the outer end, and the inner end, which is called the cat's-tail, fays down upon the cat-beam.

The anchor is catted or raised to the cat-head by means of the ***cat-tackle*** or ***cat-purchase***, which consists of the ***cat-block***, ***cat-fall***, and the sheaves in the cat-head; the cat-block is furnished with a strong hook, the ***cat-hook***, which is hooked to the ring of the anchor by means of the ***cat-rope***, or ***cat-back-rope***; when raised, the anchor is fastened by its ring to the cat-head with the ***cat-head-stopper*** or ***cat-stopper***. See also CAT *sb.* 7 and 18.

1626 CAPT. SMITH *Accid. Yng. Seamen* 12 The Cat, Cats head and Cats holes. **1679** *Exec. Bury* 3 The Prisoner was.. shooting at the Cat-head of his own ship as a mark. **1769** FALCONER *Dict. Marine* (1789) The cat-head serves to suspend the anchor clear of the bow. **1805** in Nicolas *Disp. Nelson* (1846) VII. 156 *note*, She ceased firing and waved a Union Jack at her cat-head. **1840** R. DANA *Bef. Mast* xv. 40 The anchor came to the cat-head pretty slowly. **1869** SIR E. REED *Ship Build.* xv. 292 In order to reduce both the weight and the cost of the catheads..box catheads have been introduced instead of solid forgings.

2. *dial.* A nodule of ironstone, containing fossil remains.

1670 W. SIMPSON *Hydrol. Ess.* 63 Usually called by them Doggers, or Catsheads. **1719** STRACHEY in *Phil. Trans.* XXX. 970 Certain Lumps of Stone..like a Caput mortuum not inflammable, called Cats-head. **1728** WOODWARD *Fossils* (J.) The nodules with leaves in them, called catheads, seem to consist of a sort of iron stone.

3. *Mining.* **a.** A small capstan (Simmonds *Dict. Trade* 1858). **b.** A broad-bully hammer (Raymond *Mining Gloss.*).

c. 'An attachment to a lathe to assist in supporting long bars when they are being turned' (*Cent. Dict.* Suppl. 1909).

1940 *Chambers's Techn. Dict.* 141/2 *Cathead* or *spider*, a lathe accessory consisting of a turned sleeve.

4. *attrib.*, as ***cat-head stopper*** (see small-type note at sense 1 above).

1829 *Patents* in *Ann. Reg.* 551/2 Improvements in the construction of cat-head stoppers. **1883** *Man. Seamanship for Boys' Training Ships* 10 For lifting the anchor from the water's edge to the cat head in order to pass the cat head stopper.

Hence **cat-head** *v.*, to cat the anchor.

1840 R. H. DANA *Bef. Mast* xxv, Everything was sheeted home and hoisted up, the anchor tripped and cat-headed. **1874** *Chamb. Jrnl.* 10 Oct. 651/1 (Hoppe) Let us cat-head our anchor.

cathect (kəˈθɛkt), *v. Psycho-analysis.* [Back-formation f. CATHECTIC *a.*] To charge with mental energy; to give (ideas, etc.) an emotional loading.

1936 A. STRACHEY tr. *Freud's Inhibitions* xi. 145 A repressed instinctual impulse can be activated (newly cathected) from two directions. **1951** C. KLUCKHOHN et al. in Parsons & Shils *Toward Gen. Theory of Action* IV. ii. 399 Disvalued activities are cathected.

cathectic (kəˈθɛktɪk), *a. Psychol.* [ad. Gr. *καθεκτικός* capable of holding.] Of or relating to cathexis.

1927 J. RIVIERE tr. *Freud's Ego & Id* iv. 63 We know this trait; it is characteristic of the cathectic processes in the id. **1936** A. STRACHEY tr. *Freud's Inhibitions* v. 58 The commonest symptoms of conversion hysteria..are cathectic processes. **1951** C. KLUCKHOHN et al. in Parsons & Shils *Toward Gen. Theory of Action* IV. ii. 394 Values synthesize cognitive and cathectic elements in orientations to an object world.

cathecyser, -ysme, obs. f. CATECHISER, -ISM.

†**cathed**, *ppl. a. rare*⁻¹.

1677 N. COX *Gentl. Recreat.* I. (1706) 93 Give them [Coneys] not too much green juicy meat, unless you intermix therwith what is dry..otherwise they will be Cathed, or tun-belly'd.

‖**cathedra** (kəˈθiːdrə, ˈkæθɪdrə). [L. *cathedra*, a. Gr. *καθέδρα* chair; *esp.* seat of a bishop, teacher's or professor's chair: f. *κατά* down + *ἑδ-* sit.]

1. The chair or seat of a bishop in his church; hence, the episcopal see or dignity.

1829 *Trial J. Martin* (York) 35 The curtains of the cathedra were up on Sunday. **1863** J. R. WALLRAN *Mem. Fountains Abbey* 20 When Archbishop Turstin ascended the cathedra of York in 1114. **1866** J. H. NEWMAN *Let. to Pusey* (ed. 2) 144 Chrysostom..was in close relations with the once Semi-arian Cathedra of Antioch.

2. Latin phr. ***ex cathedrâ***, 'from the chair', *i.e.* in the manner of one speaking from the seat of office or professorial chair, with authority; also used attrib. = officially uttered. So † ***in cathedrâ***.

1635 PAGITT *Christianogr.* I. i. (1636) 23 And that he in cathedra cannot erre. **1674** HICKMAN *Hist. Quinquart.* Ep. A iv b, When they can neither say, that the Pope was misinformed, or that he was not *in Cathedra.* **1818** SCOTT *Rob Roy* xxii, He was a great lover of form, more especially when he could dictate it ex cathedra. **1820** BYRON *Blues* I. 150 Old Botherby's spouting ex-cathedrâ tone. **1875** JOWETT *Plato* (ed. 2) I. 128 He, *ex cathedrâ*, was determining their several questions to them. **1885** *Manch. Exam.* 4 May 5/2 The President's *ex cathedrâ* judgment.

†**catheˈdraical**, *a. Obs. rare.* [irreg. f. prec.: cf. *algebraical*.] = CATHEDRAL I.

1676 DEGGE *Parson's Counsellor* 284 (L.) To prove them one and the same with the cathedraical duty.

cathedral (kəˈθiːdrəl), *a.* [a. F. *cathédral*, or ad. (its source) med.L. *cathedrālis* of or belonging to the (bishop's) seat, f. *cathedra*: see prec. (But some adj. uses have arisen anew from the sb.)]

1. Of or pertaining to the bishop's throne or see.

a. *esp.* in ***cathedral church*** (formerly also *church cathedral*), the church which contains the bishop's throne, the principal church of a diocese; = CATHEDRAL *sb.* [F. *église cathédrale*.] (It has been applied loosely to a collegiate or abbey church.)

1297 R. GLOUC. (1724) 282 Atte heye chyrche of Wynchester, þer ys se was ydo, þat me clupede chyrche cathedral. *a* **1384** WYCLIF *Wks.* (1880) 73 þei maken men to ȝeue here nedi liflode to here cathedral chirches þat han no nede. *a* **1420** OCCLEVE *De Reg. Princ.* 2906 The chapitre of a chirche cathedralle. **1480** CAXTON *Descr. Brit.* 25 Boniface ..songe in euery Cathedrall chirche of Wales a mas. **1577** tr. *Bullinger's Decades* (1592) 344 To make sacrifices in the high places, in their Cathedral Churches at Bethel and at Dan. **1593** SHAKS. *2 Hen. VI*, I. ii. 37 Me thought I sate in Seate of Maiesty, In the Cathedrall Church of Westminster. **1597** HOOKER *Eccl. Pol.* v. lxxx. §11 Bishops and churches cathedral being sufficiently endowed with lands. **1845** MᶜCULLOCH *Acc. Brit.* (1854) II. 277 The several cathedral and collegiate churches in England and Wales.

b. *generally.*

1570 LEVINS *Manip.* 13 Cathedral, *cathedralis.* **1613** R. C. *Table Alph.* (ed. 3), *Cathedrall*, chiefe in the Diocesse. *a* **1640** JACKSON *Creed* XII. xv, If in this cathedral constitution he did not err. **1641** MILTON *Animadv.* (1851) 207 More savoury knowledge in one Lay-man, than in a dozen of Cathedrall Prelates. **1688** R. HOLME *Armoury* II. 391/1 The Broad, or Cathedral Beard..because Bishops and Grave Men of the Church antiently did wear such Beards. **1882-3** SCHAFF *Relig. Encycl.* III. 2305 He found his cathedral chair full of thorns.

2. Of or pertaining to the chair of office or authority; *ex cathedrâ*: **a.** ecclesiastically.

1638 HEYWOOD *Lucrece* I. Wks. 1874 V. 170 Heere we enthrone our selves, Cathedrall state Long since detaind us, justly we resume. **1647** JER. TAYLOR *Lib. Proph.* vii. 125 To dissent from any of his [the Pope's] Cathedrall determinations is absolute heresy. **1886** *Sat. Rev.* 10 July 47/1 The cathedral utterances of Leo XIII.

b. professorially.

1603 FLORIO *Montaigne* II. iii. (1632) 193 To resolve belongs to a cathedrall master [F. *cathedrant*] . **1605** B. JONSON *Volpone* I. ii. (1616) 455 Hood an asse with reuerend purple..And he shall passe for a cathedrall Doctor. **1618** HALES *Let.* in *Gold. Rem.* (1688) 423 The Schoolmens Conclusions and Cathedral Decisions had been received as Oracles and Articles of Faith. **1849** T. B. SHAW *Outlines Eng. Lit.* 299 The style is too uniformly didactic, cathedral, and declamatory.

†**3.** (See quots.)

1690 B. E. *Dict. Cant. Crew*, *Cathedral*, old-fashioned, out of Date, Ancient. **1755** JOHNSON, *Cathedral*, in low phrase, antique, venerable, old.

¶ In some cases, e.g. *cathedral town*, it is difficult to distinguish between the original adjective, and the sb. used attributively: see next 3.

cathedral (kəˈθiːdrəl), *sb.* [originally *cathedral church*: see prec. F. *cathédrale*.]

1. a. The principal church of a diocese, containing the bishop's cathedra or throne; usually remarkable for size and architectural beauty. (It has been applied to the Abbey Church of Westminster.)

1587 HARRISON *England* II. i. (1877) I. 16 As the number of churches increased, so the repaire of the faithfull vnto the cathedrals did diminish. **1663** GERBIER *Counsel* D vij a, The great Cathedralls of St. Paul, and St. Peter, in this Metropolitan City. **1718** LADY M. W. MONTAGUE *Let. to Pope* 28 Sept., The great Cathedral of St. John [in Lyons] is a good Gothic building. **1848** MACAULAY *Hist. Eng.* I. 339 Cathedrals decorated by all the art and magnificence of the middle ages. **1852** TENNYSON *Ode Wellington* ix, Lay your earthly fancies down, And in the vast cathedral leave him. **1861** A. B. HOPE (*title*), The English Cathedral.

b. Taken as a type of the Episcopal system.

1679 *Establ. Test* 11 They had..ruin'd the Monarchy, and pull'd down the old Cathedral, without Establishing.. any Church at all.

2. *fig.* Chief centre of authority and teaching.

1643 MILTON *Divorce* To Parlt., Our ancient Druides, by whom this Iland was the Cathedral of Philosophy to France. **1651** BIGGS *New Disp.* Pref. 5 Let England then keep that honour..to be the Cathedral to other Nations.

3. *attrib.* and *Comb.*, as ***cathedral air, chime, city, close, dome, family, front, man, music, service, spire, tower, town, walk*** (= resembling an aisle in a cathedral); ***cathedral-like, -wise*** advbs.; **cathedral glass**, coloured glass leaded after the fashion of the stained windows of churches, used (e.g.) in the panels of the vestibule doors of houses.

1644 T. HILL *Right Separation* (1645) 34 This made *Cathedrall aire (for the most part) so impure. **1902** W. S. WALKER *Zealandia's Guerdon* i. 16 A pretty cottage in the North Belt of Christchurch, the *Cathedral City of New Zealand. **1983** *Time* 25 July 44/2 The castle is 60 miles from the great cathedral city of York. **1841** *Penny Cycl.* s.v. *Salisbury*, There is in the *cathedral close a college or almshouse for ten clergymen's widows. **1877** BRYANT *Lit. People of Snow* 155 Like some vast *cathedral-dome. **1740** in *Swift's Lett.* (1766) II. 264 When there is a place vacant in your family..I mean your *cathedral family. **1864** TENNYSON *Sea Dreams* 211 Huge *cathedral fronts of every age. **1850** *Archaeol. Inst. Gt. Brit.: Mem. Lincoln 1848* 122 Many modern windows in which stain is used, especially those composed of the yellow tinted '*Cathedral glass', appear at a little distance as if they were wholly yellow. **1885** *Spon's Mechanic's Own Bk.* 630 'Roundels' and 'bullions' are small discs of glass..used in fretwork with cathedral glass. **1905** H. A. EVANS *Highways & Byways Oxf. & Cotswolds* 329 The exquisite pale green transparent glass of the windows,..displaced to make room for the vulgar abomination known as 'cathedral glass'. **1960** WILLMOTT & YOUNG *Family & Class* i. 11 Stained 'Cathedral' glass..is used for the top halves of doors. **1631** WEEVER *Anc. Fun. Mon.* 628 This Church is spatious, beautifull, and built *Cathedrall-like. **1694** *Providence of God* 67 As ready and perfect in their Responses, as any *Cathedral-man whatever. **1880** GROVE *Dict. Mus.*, **Cathedral Music*, music composed for use in English Cathedral Service since the Reformation. *a* **1704** LOCKE (J.) His constant and regular assisting at the *cathedral service. **1842** TENNYSON *Gardener's Dau.* 213 The gray *cathedral towers Reveal'd their shining windows. *a* **1859** MACAULAY *Hist. Eng.* (1861) V. 157 Visions of..closes in old *cathedral towns. **17..** POPE *Imitat. Cowley* 13 Here aged trees *Cathedral walks compose. *a* **1780** BLACKSTONE *Farewell Muse* 22 Aged elms ..In long cathedral walks extend. **1713** STEELE *Guardian* No. 80 (1756) I. 354 The service was performed *cathedral-wise.

Hence **caˌthedraˈlesque**, **catheˈdralic**, **caˈthedralish**, *adjs.*, like a cathedral; **caˈthedralized** *a.*, converted into a cathedral; **caˈthedralism**, the cathedral system.

1884 *Pall Mall G.* 7 Jan. 2/2 Such magnificent minsters and cathedralesque churches as Tewkesbury, Malvern, Wimborne. **1870** HAWTHORNE *Eng. Note-bks.* (1879) II. 206 Almost cathedralic in its dimensions. **1840** TUPPER *Let.* in *My life as Author* (1886) 43 A large cathedralish church. **1885** G. N. BOARDMAN in *Advance* (Chicago) 3 Dec. 777 One large element of English religious character..is, if I may coin a word, Cathedralism. **1861** A. B. HOPE *Eng. Cathedr. 19th C.* 178 The cathedralised abbey churches.

cathedraled (kəˈθiːdrəld), *a.* [f. CATHEDRAL *sb.* + -ED².] In various nonce-uses, as †**a.** Seated on a cathedra or throne; **b.** Vaulted like a cathedral; **c.** Adorned with or having a cathedral.

1611 HEYWOOD *Gold. Age* III. i. Wks. 1874 III. 37 The cittadell Where the Cathedral'd Saturne is enthron'd. **1830** TENNYSON *Poems* 125 Cathedralled caverns of thick ribbed gold. **1840** *Fraser's Mag.* XXI. 126 Cathedraled Bristol, castled Nottingham. **1850** L. HUNT *Autobiog.* III. xxi. 106 Florence lay clear and cathedralled before us.

†**caˈthedralist.** *Obs.* [see -IST.] A supporter of the cathedral or episcopal system; one of the clergy of a cathedral.

1644 *Jus Populi* 12 We need not doubt this promissor was some Cathedralist within orders, he does so shuffle Priests and Princes together. **1644** JESSOP *Angel of Eph.* 30 Our Cathedralists pretend the Church but meane the Bishops and themselves. **1661** PRYNNE *Exub. in Com. Prayer* 23 Sober, judicious Protestants, Prelates and Cathedralists.

catheˈdrarian, *a. nonce-wd.* [f. L. *cathedrāri-us* (f. *cathedra*) + -AN.] Of or belonging to a cathedra or chair (*pedantic*).

1830 LYTTON *Eugene A.* i. 5 The traveller taking advantage of Peter's hasty abandonment of his cathedrarian accommodation, seized the vacant chair.

†**cathedrate,** *a. Obs. rare*⁻¹. [f. CATHEDRA + -ATE².] Containing a cathedra or bishop's seat.

1536 in Atterbury *Addit. 1st ed. Rights Convoc.* (1701) App. 43 You our said Bishops..in your Cathedrate Churches.

So †**cathedrated** *ppl. a.*, enthroned on the bishop's seat; installed in the professorial chair.

1626 W. SCLATER *Expos. 2 Thess.* (1629) 128 At length wee finde him [Antichrist] a Bishop Cathedrated in the Church. **1654** R. WHITLOCK *Observ. Manners Eng.* 385 (T.) With the cathedrated authority of a prælector or publick reader.

catheˈdratic, *a.* and *sb.* [ad. med.L *cathedrāticus*, f. *cathedra*. Cf. F. *cathédratique*.]

1. *Law.* Pertaining to the bishop's seat; belonging to the episcopal see; in ***cathedratic payment, imposition, right.***

1661 J. STEPHENS *Procurations* 85 This Cathedratick payment to the Bishop from the beneficed Clergie within his Diœcess. *Ibid.* 97 This Cathedratick imposition. **1725** tr. *Dupin's Eccl. Hist.* I. II. iii. 41 They gave the Bishop the Third Part of these Oblations, which was called the Right Cathedratick [*droit cathédratique*].

2. Pronounced *ex cathedrâ*, or from the chair, authoritative.

18.. *Fraser's Mag.* (O.) There is the prestige of antiquity which adds the authority of venerability to cathedratic precepts. **1871** T. A. TROLLOPE *Durnton Abb.* II. xvii. 281 'Nothing is a matter of course!' said Mr. Burrows, in a very cathedratic manner.

B. quasi-*sb.* = *cathedratic payment* in 1. Also in the L. form *cathedrāticum* (see Du Cange).

1670 BLOUNT *Law Dict.*, *Cathedratick* (*Cathedraticum*) is a Sum of 2*s.* paid to the Bishop by the Inferior Clergy, in Argumentum subjectionis and ob honorem Cathedræ. **1721** in BAILEY. **1774** T. WEST *Antiq. Furness* (1805) 203 The cathedreticum, synodales, and the procurations of the apostolic see. **1846** MCCULLOCH *Acc. Brit. Empire* (1854) II. 305 The emoluments of a [Roman Catholic] bishop arise from his parish, from licenses, and from the cathedraticum.

catheˈdratical, *a.* and *sb.* = prec.

a **1670** HACKET *Abp. Williams* II. (1692) 54 When you do not pay your procurations only, but your cathedraticals and synodals also.

Hence **catheˈdratically** *adv.*, authoritatively.

1828 *Edin. Rev.* XLVIII. 505 The wisdom of this world cannot tolerate the idea that so little is left for it cathedratically to perform, with dogmatic certainty.

cathepsin (kəˈθɛpsɪn). *Biochem.* [ad. G. *kathepsin* (Willstätter & Bamann 1929, in *Zeitschr. f. physiol. Chem.* CLXXX. 130), f. Gr. καθέψ-ειν to boil down (ἕψειν to boil) + -IN.¹] Any of various proteolytic enzymes, present in most animal tissues, which aid in autolysis of cells after death or in diseased cells.

1929 *Chem. Abstr.* 1653 The enzymes of leucocytes... For the proteinase which is active at slightly acid reaction the name cathepsin is proposed. **1963** *Lancet* 19 Jan. 153/1 In.. the concentration of enzymes within the diseased muscle-cell..the acid phosphatases and cathepsins, both acid and alkaline, were increased.

†**cather, cayther.** *Obs.* exc. *dial.* [? a. Welsh *cader* chair, cradle, wooden frame.] A cradle; a scaffolding.

1568 *Ludlow Churchw. Acc.* (Camden) 129 Paid for poles and bordes to make the cather for the steple. [Cf. 130 For makinge of a cradelle to goe about the steple.] **1750** J. COLLIER *Wks.* 66 (*Lanc. Gloss.*) Th' barn ot wur i' th' keather. **1859** E. WAUGH (*ibid.*) Keep th' keyther stirrin' gently.

catheran, catherein: see CATERAN.

catheretic (kæθəˈrɛtɪk), *a.* and *sb. Med.* Sometimes written **cathæretic.** [ad. Gr. καθαιρετικός (in Galen) destructive, consuming, f. καθαιρεῖν to take down, reduce, destroy (f. κατά down + αἱρεῖν to take). Cf. F. *cathérétique*.] Having power to destroy, reduce or consume; corrosive. As *sb.*: An agent for consuming superfluous flesh: a name given to the milder caustics.

1634 T. JOHNSON *Parey's Chirurg.* XXVI. xviii. (1678) 640 Some [Pyroticks] are termed Cathereticks or corroding, for that they waste the proud flesh of an ulcerated..part. **1713** *Lond. & Country Brew.* IV. (1743) 299 A hot pungent, acrid Matter, of a catheretic Nature, insomuch that, if applied Plaister-wise to the Skin, it will raise a Blister. **1887** HOBLYN *Med. Dict.*, *Cathæretics*, the milder caustics, as iodine, creasote, etc., also remedies which reduce superfluous flesh.

So †**catheˈretical** *a.* = prec.

1638 A. READ *Chirurg.* ix. 66 Cathereticall medicaments.

Catherine (ˈkæθərɪn). Also **Catharine, Kath-.** [F. *Catherine*, mod.L. *Catharīna*, earlier *Katerina*, repr. Gr. Αἰκατερίνα name of the saint, subseq. assimilated in spelling to καθαρός pure.] The name of a legendary Saint and Martyr of Alexandria; whence a female Christian name.

1. The name of a kind of carriage.

1861 AINSLIE *Remin. Sc. Gentleman* 172, I accompanied Miss Baillie to the review in her catherine, a carriage nearly similar to a gig, but with a roof raised on rods, to give protection from the sun. [This was in Jamaica.]

2. Catherine pear. A small and early variety of pear. Also a variety of plum.

1641 SUCKLING *Ballad on Wedding* Wks. (1709) 31 Streaks of red were mingled there, Such as are on a Katherine Pear, The Side that's next the Sun. **1664** EVELYN *Kal. Hort.* (1729) 233 Catalogue of..excellent Fruit Trees, Plums.. Damasq, Violet, Date, Catherine. **1720** GAY *Pastorals* iii, Catherine pears adorn my ruddy cheek. **1819** CRABBE *T. of Hall* x. 599 'Twas not the lighter red, that partly streaks The Catherine pear, that brighten'd o'er her cheeks.

Catherine wheel.

1. The figure of a wheel with spikes projecting from its circumference (in reference to the legend of St. Catherine's martyrdom). *esp.* in Heraldry.

[*a* **1225** *Leg. Kath.* 1942 Hat ȝarkin fowr hweoles, ant let þurhdriuen þrefter þe spaken ant te felien mid irnene gadien.] **1584** R. SCOT *Discov. Witchcr.* XII. xv. 206 Others likewise have (as they brag) a Katharine wheel upon their bodies. **1650** B. *Discolliminium* 17 Though they turn their Rowels into Katherine-wheeles till they have over-taken their Ends. **1703** *Lond. Gaz.* No. 3906/4 The Coat 2 Spread Eagles quarter'd with Catharine Wheels. **1864** BOUTELL *Heraldry Hist. & Pop.* xxi. (ed. 3) 360 A Catherine wheel or. *attrib.* **1607** WEBSTER *Northw. Hoe* III. i, A short Dutch waist, with a round Catherine-Wheel Fardingale.

2. *Arch.* (Also ***Catherine-wheel window.***) 'A window or compartment of a window of a circular form with radiating divisions or spokes' (Gwilt).

1848 RICKMAN *Goth. Archit.* xxxviii, A circular window filled with fine flowing tracery, of the character often called a 'Catherine wheel'.

3. A kind of firework which rotates, while burning, in the manner of a wheel. (Also called *pin-wheel.*)

1760 WILSON in *Phil. Trans.* LI. 906 In the same manner that a Catherine-wheel is made to turn round in a direction contrary to that in which the small rockets affixed to its periphery discharge themselves. **1836** E. HOWARD *R. Reefer* xvi, A noble Catherine wheel had just begun to fizz. **1836-7** DICKENS *Sk. Boz* (1850) 188/2 A noise like the first indication a catherine-wheel gives of..its going off.

4. *transf.* and *fig.* (chiefly from 3). Also *attrib.* ***to turn Catherine-wheels***: to turn lateral summersaults (= CART-WHEEL *sb.* 3).

1861 *Times* 29 July, The Catherine wheel is busy throwing out sparks and fiery flashes all round the world. **1870** LOWELL *Study Wind.* (1886) 79 Catharine-wheel republics, always in revolution while the powder lasts. **1881** E. J. WORBOISE *Sissie* xxiv, I have seen that boy put down his basket of medicine and turn 'Catherine wheels' in the street. **1887** *Sat. Rev.* 16 July 100/1 [Mr. Gale] admits that the 'Catherine Wheel' style of bowling has enabled bowlers to acquire a double break.

†**cathering.** *Obs.* = CATHETER.

1541 R. COPLAND *Galyen's Therap.* 2 H iij, Ye can nat wel vse a syring of bras yᵗ the grekes call Cathering, but yf ye knowe parfytely the posycyon..of all the bladder.

ˈCathern. [Corruption of CATHERINE. Cf.:

1669 DRYDEN *Epil. Tyrannic Love* 30 Here Nelly lies, who, though she lived a slattern, Yet died a princess, acting in St. Catherine.]

A festival or merry-making on St. Catherine's day (Nov. 25). So **Catherning** *vbl. sb.*

1596 FORMAN *Diary* 27 §3 At 4 I went first to see the garden catherne. **1730** LAMOTTE *Ess. Poetry & Paint.* 126 (Brand) Young women meeting on the 25th of November, and making merry together, which they call Catherning. *attrib.* [**1476** *Will of Scotton* (Somerset Ho.) A flatte pece of siluur called a Kateryn cupp.] **1849** HALLIWELL *Pop. Rhymes* (Brand), The Dean of Worcester informs me that the Chapter have a practice of preparing a rich bowl of wine and spices, called 'The Cathern Bowl', for the inhabitants of the college precincts upon that day [Nov. 25].

cathern, obs. form of CAULDRON *sb.*

cathetal (ˈkæθɪtəl), *a.* Also **k-.** [f. CATHETUS + -AL¹.] Pertaining to a cathetus; perpendicular.

1874 tr. *Lommel's Light* 64 The rays which fall perpendicularly upon the kathetal surface pass without deflection through the glass. **1880** WEBSTER *Supp.*

catheter (ˈkæθɪtə(r)). *Med.* [a. L. *cathetēr*, a. Gr. καθετήρ anything let down into, a catheter, f. καθιέναι to send or let down.] A long tubular instrument, of metal or caoutchouc, more or less curved at the end, for passing into the bladder in order to draw off urine, etc.; a similar tube for use with other canals (*e.g.* the Eustachian catheter).

1601 MANNINGHAM *Diary* Feb. 23 A crooked instrument concaued at the one ende called a catheter. **1684** R. JOHNSON *Enchirid. Med.* III. xxiv. 275 Draw away the Urine with a Catheter. **1844** DUFTON *Deafness* 43 Warm water..may be injected, by means of a catheter introduced into the Eustachian tube, into the meatus. **1876** GROSS *Dis. Bladder* 35.

ˈcatheterism. *Med.* [ad. L. *catheterism-us* (in Kersey 1708 21), a. Gr. καθετηρισμός, f. καθετήρ (see prec.).] The employment of a catheter.

1721 BAILEY *Catheterism*, the Operation of injecting any thing into the Bladder by a Catheter. **1839-47** TODD *Cycl. Anat.* III. 924/1. **1844** DUFTON *Deafness* 71 The application of catheterism to the Eustachian tube.

So ˈcatheterize *v.* [cf. F. *cathétériser*], *intr.* to employ a catheter; also *trans.*, to employ a catheter on (a patient); to introduce a catheter into; ˌ**catheteriˈzation**.

1849–52 TODD *Cycl. Anat.* IV. 1260/1 The patient..had been frequently the subject of catheterization. **1874** ROOSA *Dis. Ear* 38 Restoration of hearing by means of catheterization of the tube through the nose. **1881** *Syd. Soc. Lex. Catheterise*, to introduce a catheter. **1887** R. HARRISON *Surg. Disorders Urinary Organs* (ed. 3) v. 60 If you are only accustomed to catheterise patients standing with their backs against a wall how can you expect to be dexterous with the lithotrite. **1908** *Practitioner* Jan. 44 A true stricture,..forming an irregular channel, through which urine passes with difficulty, and which it is almost impossible to catheterise. **1954** M. CAMPBELL *Urology* II. XIII. 1472 Having catheterized the ureters, the specimens are collected. **1967** S. BECKETT *No's Knife* 83, I catheterize myself, unaided, with trembling hand.

cathetometer (kæθɪˈtɒmɪtə(r)). [f Gr. κάθετο-ς CATHETUS + -METER. Cf. F. *cathétomètre*.] An instrument for measuring vertical distances, *esp.* small differences of level of liquid columns in tubes.

1864 in WEBSTER. **1871** B. STEWART *Heat* §63 The difference of level between the surface of mercury in the two tubes was read by means of a cathetometer. **1879** THOMSON & TAIT *Nat. Phil.* I. I. §429 The Cathetometer is used for the accurate determination of differences of level.

‖**cathetus** (ˈkæθɪtəs). Also **kath-**. [a. L. *cathetus*, a. Gr. κάθετος (sc. γραμμή) a perpendicular line, κάθετος adj. 'let down, perpendicular', f. καθιέναι to let down.] A straight line falling perpendicularly on another straight line or surface.

1571 DIGGES *Pantom.* IV. Def. 20 It shal be named the Axis or Kathetus of that body. **1622** PEACHAM *Gentl. Exerc.* I. xi. (1634) 38. **1676** BAKER in Rigaud *Corr. Sc. Men* (1841) II. 13 Having the cathetus of the first and the common hypotenuse given, to find the cathetus of the simple angle. **1751** CHAMBERS *Cycl.* s.v., *Cathetus of Incidence*..a right line drawn from a radiant point, perpendicular to the reflecting line, or the plane of the speculum, or mirror. *Cathetus of Reflexion*, etc. **1817** COLEBROOKE *Algebra* 59 The cóti or upright is the cathetus. **1875** GWILT *Archit.* Gloss. *Cathetus*, a perpendicular line passing through the centre of a cylindrical body as a baluster or a column. It is also a line falling perpendicularly, and passing through the centre or eye of the volute of the Ionic capital.

cathexis (kəˈθɛksɪs). *Psychol.* [a. Gr. κάθεξις holding, retention; intended as a rendering of G. (*libido*)*besetzung* (Freud).] The concentration or accumulation of mental energy in a particular channel.

1922 J. STRACHEY *Freud's Group Psychol.* iii. 48 Dread in an individual is provoked either by the greatness of a danger or by the cessation of emotional ties (libidinal cathexes [orig. *Libidobesetzungen*]). **1923** E. JONES in *Internat. Jrnl. Psycho-Analysis* IV. 299 In hetero-suggestion..a hypercathexis of the idea of the operator is correlated with a hypo-cathexis of all ideas in conflict with his. **1948** *Brit. Jrnl. Psychol.* XXXVIII. 172 There are a number of very specific factors responsible for any particular process of 'cathexis'. **1951** C. KLUCKHOHN et al. in Parsons & Shils *Toward Gen. Theory of Action* IV. ii. 398 Since value always involves affect, cathexis and value are inevitably somehow interrelated.

‖**cathisma** (kəˈθɪzmə). Pl. **cathismata**. [a. Gr. κάθισμα seat, f. κατά down + ἵζειν to sit.] In the Greek Church: a portion of the psalter, containing from three to eleven psalms. Also, a short hymn used as a response.

1850 J. M. NEALE *Holy Eastern Ch.* I. II. 844 The Greeks rarely sit in church: the cathismata are therefore pauses for rest; and are longer than the usual troparia. **1880** *Encycl. Brit.* XII. 580/1 In various parts of the services solitary troparia are sung, under various names, 'contacion', 'œcos', 'cathisma', &c.

cathodal (ˈkæθəʊdəl), *a.* Also **kath-**. [f. Gr. κάθοδος way down (see next) + -AL¹.]

1. *Electr.* Belonging to the cathode.

1882 *Athenæum* 8 July 50/3 The character (anodal or kathodal) of the electric charge.

2. *Bot.* = CATHODIC 2.

1882 VINES *Sachs' Bot.* 366 In Fontinalis the branch arises beneath the median line of the leaf; but in Sphagnum beneath its cathodal half.

cathode (ˈkæθəʊd). *Electr.* Also **kath-**. [ad. Gr. κάθοδος a going down, way down, f. κατά down + ὁδός way.] **a.** The path by which an electric current leaves the electrolyte and passes into the negative pole; the point or surface in contact with the negative pole; in electro-metallurgy the object to be electro-plated. **b.** The negative pole. Opposed to *anode*: see ELECTRODE.

1834 FARADAY *Res. Electr.* (1839) §663 The cathode is that surface at which the current leaves the decomposing body, and is its positive extremity. **1839** *Proc. Amer. Phil. Soc.* I. 100 The lower electrode formed the cathode. **1870** R. FERGUSON *Electr.* 161 The poles..are called electrodes..the – pole being called the cathode. **1875** URE *Dict. Arts* II. 219 The deposit was formed in twenty-four hours upon the whole of the cathode. **1881** *Metal World* No. 9. 131 The object to be coppered is to be..attached as a cathode..when it will become rapidly coated with an adherent film of metallic copper. **1883** E. H. GORDON *Electr. & Magn.* (ed. 2) II. 1 The electrode attached to the zinc of the battery is called the cathode, and the other, the anode.

c. *attrib.* and *Comb.* **cathode dark space** = *Crookes* (*dark*) *space*; **cathode follower**, a type of electric circuit (see quots.); also *attrib.*; **cathode ray**, a beam of electrons issuing from the cathode of a high-vacuum tube under the action of an electric field; hence **cathode-ray oscillograph**: see OSCILLOGRAPH and quot. 1922; **cathode-ray oscilloscope** (see quot.); **cathode-ray tube**, a vacuum tube in which cathode rays are projected upon a fluorescent screen.

1914 *R. Soc. Catal. Sci. Papers 1800–1900, Subject Index* III. II. 685/2 Cathode dark space, origin. **1920** *Discovery* July 217/1 The dark space around the negative pole, which has since been referred to as the Crookes or Cathode Dark Space. **1939** *Electronics* Mar. 35 Connections of the cathode-coupled ('cathode-follower') stage, used for low-impedance output applications. **1941** *Wireless World* July 176/1 In essence, the cathode-follower stage is a device to avoid mismatching. *Ibid.* 177/1 The cathode-follower gives an output voltage equal to its input voltage (the cathode potential *follows* the grid potential—hence the name 'cathode-follower'). **1942** *Electronic Engin.* XV. 287 The 'cathode follower' type of circuit has the distinction of being one of the most versatile circuits used by the Radio Engineer ..and derives its name from the fact that an input signal that makes the grid go positive with respect to HT. negative will also make the cathode go positive with respect to HT. negative. **1905** *Jrnl. Chem. Soc.* LXXXVIII. II. 224 With copper, nickel, gold, and bright platinum, the cathode potential for a given current density goes on increasing for hours. *Ibid.*, Cathode process and anode liquid are opposed to each other. [**1879** *Phil. Trans. R. Soc.* CLXX. 144 It excludes such rays of the cathode as impinge upon it from reaching the side.] **1880** *Phil. Mag.* X. 411 It was further examined whether the negative discharges which excite the green light, the so-called kathode-rays, do really propagate themselves only in straight lines. **1898** [see CORPUSCLE 2 c]. **1900** *Jrnl. Chem. Soc.* LXXVIII. II. 587 Electrical Conductivity in Gases traversed by Cathode Rays. **1912** J. W. MELLOR *Mod. Inorg. Chem.* xliii. 825 The cathode rays is [*sic*] a stream of negatively charged electrons sent from the cathode with a high velocity. **1951** J. R. PARTINGTON *Gen. & Inorg. Chem.* (ed. 2) viii. 184 These cathode rays were discovered in 1859 by Plücker, who showed that they are easily deflected by a magnet. **1957** *Encycl. Brit.* V. 41/1 Cathode rays have many applications, one of the chief being the excitation of X-rays by the impinging of swift electrons against a hard anticathode. **1922** GLAZEBROOK *Dict. Appl. Physics* II. 146/2 *Cathode ray oscillograph*, an apparatus for delineating the instantaneous values of the current or voltage in a circuit by the deflection of a fine cathode stream. **1937** *Discovery* Jan. 4/1 A cathode ray oscillograph..is an instrument in which a fast beam of electrons passes between deflecting plates and impinges on a screen, where it produces a spot of light. **1951** UVAROV & CHAPMAN *Dict. Science* (ed. 2) 44 *Cathode ray oscilloscope*, apparatus consisting essentially of an 'electron gun' producing a beam of electrons which passes through horizontal and vertical deflecting plates, to fall upon a fluorescent screen. **1905** VARLEY & MURDOCH in *Electrician* 16 June 335/1 (*title*) Some Applications of the Braun Cathode-Ray Tube. **1934** *Discovery* Apr. 106/1 The advances made in the use of short waves and the introduction of cathode-ray tubes have enabled us to transmit images on screens 3 or 4 feet square. **1957** AMOS & BIRKINSHAW *Television Engin.* I. ix. 210 In the majority of television receivers the picture is produced on the face of a cathode-ray tube which is viewed directly or by reflection at a plane mirror.

cathodic (kəˈθɒdɪk), *a.* Also **kath-**. [f. as prec. + -IC.]

1. *Phys.* Of nerve force: Proceeding from a nerve-centre; efferent.

1852 M. HALL *Diastaltic Nervous Syst.* (Mayne).

2. *Bot.* (Of leaves arranged on the axis spirally.) See quots.

1882 VINES *Sachs' Bot.* 190 If the spiral winds from right to left, the right edge of the leaves (as you ascend) is called the Kathodic, the left edge the anodic. *Ibid.* 199 So that.. all the segments are broader on the anodic than on the kathodic side. **1884** BOWER & SCOTT *De Bary's Phaner. & Ferns* 238 Between the median and descending, or kathodic lateral bundle.

3. *Electr.* **a.** Of or pertaining to a cathode.

1837 [see ANODIC *a.* 1 a]. **1896** *Daily News* 18 Jan. 5/4 Taking photographs with cathodic rays. **1951** *Engineering* 13 Apr. 443/1 [In corrosion] If the water contains a salt..the products formed..at the cathodic (unattacked) part.. are freely soluble.

b. *cathodic protection*: protection of an underground or underwater structure from corrosion by a technique that causes the structure to act as the cathode of an electrolytic cell.

1931 *U.S. Bur. Standards Techn. News Bull.* May 52/1 A number of soils..are severely corrosive with respect to the commonly used pipe materials. Four methods of preventing corrosion in these soils have been considered: (1) the surrounding of the pipes by noncorrosive soils transported from other regions; (2) electrical or cathodic protection; [etc.]. **1964** *Electronics Weekly* 18 Nov. 24/3 The cathodic protection equipment..has been installed in a number of naval vessels. Designed to protect the ship's hull against corrosion..the system..sets up a current flow between a set of anodes and the ship's hull, which acts as the cathode.

cathodo- (ˈkæθədəʊ), used as combining form of CATHODE.

1909 *Physical Rev.* XXVIII. 349 With regard to the dependence of kathodo-luminescence upon discharge potential and current strength. **1914** *Ibid.* 2nd Ser. IV. 21 The brightness of the crests of the red and blue bands of the white and pink kunzite under kathodo-excitation. **1923** *Amer. Jrnl. Sci.* Oct. 373 The minimum energy required to excite cathodo-luminescence.

cathodograph (kəˈθɒdəʊgrɑːf, -æ-). Also **cathodegraph, kathodograph**. [f. CATHODO- + -GRAPH.] A photograph of normally invisible objects taken by means of cathode rays, an X-ray photograph. (*Disused.*) Hence **caˈthodograph** *v. trans.*, to take an X-ray photograph of; **cathodography** (kæθəʊˈdɒgrəfɪ), photography by cathode rays.

1896 *Century Mag.* May 120/1 No school or college has considered the day well spent in which..it has not taken 'cathodographs' of hands and coins. *Ibid.* 121/1 Key cathodographed through a book of 526 pages. *Ibid.* 126/2 A cathodograph picture. *Ibid.*, Cathodography of corked bottles would uncork them. **1897** *Daily News* 2 Feb. 5/2 Its transparent honesty was recognised by the 'cathodegraph' showing only the setting, the diamond being represented by a white space.

cat-hole, *sb.* Forms: 1 **catthola**, 7 **cat's-hole**, 7– **cat-hole**.

†**1.** The hole or den of the wild cat. *Obs.*

854 *Chart. Æthelwolf* in *Cod. Dipl.* V. 105 Of ðam wogan hlince on ða catthola; of ðan cattholan on Wenbeorhȝe.

2. A hole in a wall, door, etc., large enough to let a cat through.

a **1625** FLETCHER *Mad Lover* III. ii, Is there ne'er a cat-hole Where I may creep through? **1721** KELLY *Sc. Prov.* 145 (Jam.) 'He has left the key in the cat hole' to signify that a man has run away from his creditors. **1808** *Med. Jrnl.* XIX. 120 A large round ball..which rolled along the floor of the room until it came to a cat-hole in the door.

3. *Naut.* One of the two holes at the stern of the ship, through which a cable or hawser can be passed for steadying or heaving the ship astern, etc.

a **1642** SIR W. MONSON *Naval Tracts* III. (1704) 346/1 Cat-holes are over the Ports in the Gun-Room, right with the Capstain, to heave the Ship a stern by a Cable, or Hause.

4. A deep pool in a river.

1883 *Century Mag.* 378 He seated himself at the edge of a deep pool, or 'cat-hole'.

catholic (ˈkæθəlɪk), *a.* and *sb.* With capital initial exc. in senses 1 to 3. [a. F. *catholique* (13th c. in Littré) ad. late L. *catholic-us*, a. Gr. καθολικός general, universal, f. καθόλου (i.e. καθ' ὅλου) on the whole, in general, as a whole, generally, universally, f. κατά concerning, in respect of, according to + ὅλος whole. (If immed. derived from L. or Gr., the Eng. word would, according to the regular analogy of words in -IC, have been accented *caˈtholic*).]

A. *adj.* **I.** In non-ecclesiastical use.

1. *gen.* Universal.

1551 T. WILSON *Logike* 1 b, Catholike being a greeke word signifieth nothing in English but universall or common. **1613** R. C. *Table Alph.* (ed. 3) *Catholicke*, vniuersall or generall. **1660** INGELO *Bentiv. & Ur.* (1682) 11, The Indisputable Commands of a Catholick Dictator in knowledge. **1885** *Times* (weekly ed.) 11 Sept. 7/1 Science is truly catholic, and is bounded only by the universe.

†**2.** In specific uses: **a.** Universally prevalent: said *e.g.* of substances, actions, laws, principles, customs, conditions, etc. *Obs.*

1561 T. NORTON *Calvin's Inst.* III. 248 This is to be holden for a catholike principle. **1615** CROOKE *Body of Man* 418 It is a Catholicke principle, Euery thing is preserued and refreshed with his like. **1657** S. PURCHAS *Pol. Flying-Ins.* 95 This is a common, but no catholique custome [among bees] for I have often observed the contrary. **1660** SHARROCK *Vegetables* 79 The universal and catholick order of all bulbous plants, is..that about St. James' tyde they be taken out of the ground. **1662** STILLINGFL. *Orig. Sacr.* III. ii. §14 The Catholick Laws of nature which appear in the world. **1665–6** *Phil. Trans.* I. 192 All Bodies are made of one Catholick matter common to them all. **1675** EVELYN *Terra* (1729) 10 There is but one Catholic homogeneous, fluid matter. **1692** BENTLEY *Boyle Lect.* 112 This Catholick Principle of Gravitation. **1696** EDWARDS *Exist. & Provid. God* I. 3 A great proof of the catholick degeneracy of this present age.

†**b.** Universally applicable or efficient; *spec.* of medicines, remedies. *Obs.*

1612 WOODALL *Surg. Mate* Wks. (1653) 43 It hath the prime place, for a Catholick medicine in exulcerations. **1621** BURTON *Anat. Mel.* II. v. I. v. (1651) 393 There is no Catholike medicine to be had: that which helps one is pernitious to another. **1658** A. FOX *Wurtz' Surg.* IV. ii. 309 A Catholick Plaister, used for all wounds and stabs. **1671** SALMON *Syn. Med.* III. xlix. 559 A noble Extract, and a catholick purge. **1691** RAY *Creation* I. (1704) 115 Fire.. which is the only Catholick Dissolvent. **1693** SLARE in *Phil. Trans.* XVII. 906 Tho' Spirit of Wine be a very Catholic Menstruum. **1713** *Lond. & Country Brew.* IV. (1743) 261 [Water] is the only Catholick Nourishment of all Vegetables, Animals, and Minerals. **1752** HUME *Ess.* (1777) II. 11 Accurate and just reasoning is the only Catholic remedy.

†**c.** More loosely: Common, prevalent. *Obs.*

1607 DEKKER *Northw. Hoe* V. Wks. 1873 III. 74 What is more catholick i' the city than for husbands daily for to forgive the nightly sins of their bedfellows? **1631** MASSINGER *Emper. of East* IV. iv, The pox, sir.. Is the more catholic sickness. **1660** SHARROCK *Vegetables* 130 Hot beds are the most general and catholick help.

†**d.** Entire, without exception. *Obs.*

1664 EVELYN *Sylva* 19 Deep interring of Roots is amongst the Catholick Mistakes. **1671** DRYDEN *Even. Love* IV. i, *Alon.* And, how fares my Son-in-law that lives there? *Mel.* In Catholick Health, Sir.

3. In current use: **a.** Of universal human interest or use; touching the needs, interests, or sympathies of all men.

a1631 DONNE *Serm.* lxvi. (1640) So are there some.. Catholique, universal Psalmes, that apply themselves to all necessities. 1704 SWIFT *Mech. Operat. Spirit* (1711) 279 All my Writings..for universal Nature, and Mankind in general. And of such Catholick Use I esteem this present Disquisition. 1838–9 HALLAM *Hist. Lit.* III. v. §4 Catholic poetry, by which I mean that which is good in all ages and countries. 1844 EMERSON *Lect. New Eng. Ref.* Wks. (Bohn) I. 264 A grand phalanx of the best of the human race, banded for some catholic object. 1867 FROUDE *Short Stud.* 363 What was of catholic rather than national interest.

b. Having sympathies with, or embracing, all: said of men, their feelings, tastes, etc.; also *fig.* of things. (Closely connected with 8.)

1586 BRIGHT *Melanch.* iv. 16 The stomach becommeth the most Catholicke part in all the bodie, carying a more indifferent affection to what soever is receiued then anie part beside. 1817 COLERIDGE *Biog. Lit.* I. iv. 73 Others more catholic in their taste. 1620 J. PARKINSON *Paradisus* xxvi. 215 Such as are Catholicke obseruers of all natures store. 1833 LAMB *Elia, Books & Read.*, I bless my stars for a taste so catholic, so unexcluding. 1851 CARLYLE *Sterling* I. iv. (1872) 31 Of these two Universities, Cambridge is decidedly the more catholic (not Roman catholic, but Human catholic). 1878 STEVENSON *Inland Voy.*, On these different manifestations, the sun poured its clear and catholic looks. 1879 TOURGEE *Fool's Err.* xxxviii. 271 A man of unusually broad and catholic feeling.

4. ***Catholic Epistle***: a name originally given to the 'general' epistles of James, Peter, and Jude, and the first of John, as not being addressed to particular churches or persons. The second and third epistles of John are now conventionally included among the number.

It is not certain that this was the original sense of ἐπιστολὴ καθολική, since some early writers appear to use it in the sense 'genuine and accepted' (see CANONICAL): but the attribute has been understood in the sense 'encyclical' or 'general' since the 10th or 11th c.

1582 N. T. (*Rhem.*) *James* (*heading*) The Catholic Epistle of St. James the apostle. 1725 tr. *Dupin's Eccl. Hist.* I. v. 69 The Encyclick, Circular, or Catholick Letters, were address'd to all Churches, or to all the Faithful. 1855 WESTCOTT *Canon N.T.* (1881) 395 It may be inferred that the seven Catholic Epistles were formed into a collection at the close of the third century.

II. In ecclesiastical use.

The earlier history of this lies outside English, and may be found in such works as Smith's *Dict. Christian Antiq.* or in Lightfoot's *Ignatius* I. 398–400, 605–607; II. 310–312. 'Ἡ καθολικὴ ἐκκλησία 'the catholic church' or 'church universal', was first applied to the whole body of believers as distinguished from an individual congregation or 'particular body of Christians'. But to the primary idea of extension 'the ideas of doctrine and unity' were super-added; and so the term came to connote the Church first as orthodox, in opposition to heretics, next as one historically, in opposition to schismatics. Out of this widest qualitative sense arose a variety of subordinate senses; it was applied to the faith the Church held, to particular communities or even individual members belonging to it, and especially in the East, to cathedrals as distinguished from parish churches, then later to parish churches as opposed to oratories or monastic chapels. After the separation of East and West 'Catholic' was assumed as its descriptive epithet by the Western or Latin Church, as 'Orthodox' was by the Eastern or Greek. At the Reformation the term 'Catholic' was claimed as its exclusive right by the body remaining under the Roman obedience, in opposition to the 'Protestant' or 'Reformed' National Churches. These, however, also retained the term, giving it, for the most part, a wider and more ideal or absolute sense, as the attribute of no single community, but only of the whole communion of the saved and saintly in all churches and ages. In England, it was claimed that the Church, even as Reformed, was the national branch of the 'Catholic Church' in its proper historical sense. As a consequence, in order to distinguish the unreformed Latin Church, its chosen epithet of 'Catholic' was further qualified by 'Roman'; but see sense 7. On this analogy ANGLO-CATHOLIC has been used by some, since about 1835, of the Anglican Church.

5. ***Catholic Church, Church Catholic***: the Church universal, the whole body of Christians.

1559 *Injunctions by Queens Majestie* D iv, Ye shall praye for Christes holy Catholique church, that is, for the whole congregation of Christian people, dispearsed throughout the whole worlde, and specially for the Church of England and Irelande. 1560–61 *Scotch Conf. Faith* xvi, Whiche Kirk is Catholik, that is universall, becaus it conteanes the Elect of all aiges, all realmes, nationis, and tounges, be thai of the Jewis or be thai of the Gentiles, who have communioun and societie with God the Father, and with his Sone Christ Jesus. 1630 PRYNNE *Anti-Armin.* 129 There is a holy Catholicke Church, to wit, the whole company of Gods Elect. 1645 USSHER *Body Div.* (1647) 187 The Catholick Church, that is, God's whole or universall Assembly. 1651 BAXTER *Inf. Bapt.* 304, I hope this learned man doth not take the particular Romane Church, for the Catholick Church. 1685 KEN *Ch. Catech.*, '*Holy Cath. Ch.*' 1839 YEOWELL *Anc. Brit. Ch.* xi. (1847) 110 As members of the church catholic. *Mod.* In this sense many accept the article of the Creed, 'I believe in the holy catholic church'.

b. Of or belonging to the church universal, universal Christian.

1579 FULKE *Heskins' Parl.* 94 He can neuer prooue his reseruation to be catholike or vniversally allowed and practised of the Church. 1651 C. CARTWRIGHT *Cert. Relig.* I. 10 That Church whose Doctrine is most Catholick and universall must be the Catholick Church. 1657 CROMWELL *Sp.* 3 Apr., Such a Catholic interest of the people of God. 1777 FLETCHER *Reconcil.* Wks. 1795 IV. 211 A great friend to a catholic gospel. 1807 KNOX & JEBB *Corr.* I. 370 A catholic liturgy must be formed on a catholic plan; that is, from a harmony of those dispersed and vital truths, which in different ages, different countries, and different churches, were popularly, and effectually embodied, in established liturgies. 1882 FARRAR *Early Chr.* I. 250 Christianity in all Churches was, and ever must be, in its essence Catholic—one and indivisible.

6. a. As an epithet, applied to the Ancient Church, as it existed undivided, prior to the separation of East and West, and of a church or churches standing in historical continuity therewith, and claiming to be identical with it in doctrine, discipline, orders, and sacraments. (*a*) After the separation, assumed by the Western or Latin Church, and so commonly applied historically. (*b*) After the Reformation in the 16th c. claimed as its exclusive title by that part of the Western Church which remained under the Roman obedience (see 7); but (*c*) held by Anglicans not to be so limited, but to include the Church of England, as the proper continuation in England, alike of the Ancient and the Western Church.

(Whatever the application, the implied sense is 'the Church or Churches which now truly represent the ancient undivided Church of Christendom'.)

1532 MORE *Confut. Tindale* Wks. 690/1 The very name he sayth of catholike, yt is to sai vniuersal, gaue to ward ye getting of hys credence ye catholike church gret autoritye. c1534 ABP. LEE in Lingard *Hist. Eng.* (1855) V. i. 18/1 *note*, So that..the unitie of the faiethe and of the Catholique Chyrche [be] saved. 1552 ABP. HAMILTON *Catech.* (1884) 47 Quhilk catholike kirk is trewly represented in all general counsellis. 1651 HOBBES *Leviath.* Wks. 1839 III. 517 The Christians of that time [before Constantine], except a few, in respect of whose paucity the rest were called the Catholic Church and others heretics. c1670 JER. TAYLOR *Duty of Clergy* ii. 4 The Catholic Church hath been too much and too soon divided..but in things simply necessary, God hath preserved us still unbroken: all nations and all ages recite the Creed..and all Churches have been governed by Bishops. 1704 NELSON *Fest. & Fasts* vii. (1739) 538 The ancientest Fathers of the Catholick Church. 1834 *Tracts for Times* No. 61, We [English Church] are a branch of the Church Catholic. 1854 HOOK *Ch. Dict.* s.v. *Creed*, There are three creeds recognized by the catholic church. *Ibid.* s.v. *Tradition*, The great deference paid by the Church of England as a branch of the Catholic Church to tradition. 1866 LD. ROMILLY in *Law Rep.* 3 Eq. 29 The Catholic Church of Christ, of which the Church of England is a branch. 1872 FREEMAN *Gen. Sketch* vi. 111 The people of the Oriental provinces..putting forth or adopting doctrines which the Catholic Church, both of the Old and of the New Rome, looked on as heretical.

b. *Hence*, Of or belonging to this Church; of the true apostolic Church, orthodox:

(*a*) Of belief, doctrine, etc.

c1500 *Melusine* (1888) 31 My byleue is as a Catholique byleue oughte for to be. a1556 CRANMER *Wks.* (1844) I. 9 An explication and assertion of the true catholic faith in the matter of the sacrament. 1549 *Bk. Com. Prayer, Athan. Crede*, And the Catholike faithe is this: That we worship one God in trinitie, and trinitie in unitie. 1634 HABINGTON *Castara* (Arb.) 112 The Catholique faith is the foundation on which he erects Religion. 1840 *Tracts for Times* No. 85 vi, The Catholic or Church system of doctrine and worship. 1854 HOOK *Ch. Dict.* s.v. *Image worship*, Protesting against Roman corruptions of the Catholic Faith.

(*b*) Of persons: Holding the faith of this Church; rightly believing, orthodox. (This and sense a appear to be the earliest uses in English. The sb. is in 1425.)

c1500 *Melusine* (1888) 32 A man very catholoque & of good feith. 1531 ELYOT *Govt.* III. xxiii, Wherein no good catholyke man wyll any thynge doute, though they be meruaylous. 1552 HULOET, Catholyke or perfect Christian, *orthodoxus*. 1854 HOOK *Ch. Dict.* s.v., In ecclesiastical history..a *catholic* Christian denotes an *orthodox* Christian. 1881 FREEMAN *Hist. Geog. Eur.* I. iv. 101 The lands ruled either by the Catholic Frank or by the Arian Goth.

(*c*) Of the writers, fathers, or antiquity, of the ancient undivided church, or accepted by the orthodox historical church.

1548 UDALL, etc. *Erasm. Par.* Pref. 14 Whatsoeuer in any catholike wryter is conteyned. 1593 BILSON *Govt. Christ's Ch.* xi, What Presbytery the primitiue Churches and Catholike fathers did acknowledge. 1842 *Tracts for Times* No. 86 v. §3 What is popularity when it is opposed to Catholic Antiquity?

(*d*) Of a particular body: Forming part of, or in communion with, this church. (Cf. ANGLO-CATHOLIC.)

1833 CRUSE *Eusebius* VI. xliii. 265 One bishop in a catholic church. 1854 HOOK *Ch. Dict.* s.v. *Lights*, We of the Anglo-Catholic Church. *Ibid.* s.v. *Catholic*, A Catholic Church means a branch of this one great society, as the Church of England is said to be *a* Catholic Church: *the* Catholic Church includes all the Churches in the world under their legitimate Bishops.

7. As applied (since the Reformation) to the Church of Rome (*Ecclesia apostolica catholica Romana*) = ROMAN CATHOLIC, q.v. (Opposed to *Protestant, Reformed, Evangelical, Lutheran, Calvinistic*, etc.)

ROMAN CATHOLIC is the designation known to English law; but 'Catholic' is that in ordinary use on the continent of Europe, especially in the Latin countries; hence historians frequently contrast 'Catholic' and 'Protestant', especially in reference to the continent; and, in familiar non-controversial use, 'Catholic' is often said instead of Roman Catholic.

1554 (March) *Q. Mary's Injunct.* in Wilkins *Concilia* (1737) IV. 90 To remove them, and place catholic men in their rooms. a1555 J. BRADFORD in Foxe *A. & M.* (1583) 1647 This Latine seruice is a playne marke of anti-christs Catholike Synagoge. 1563 *Ibid.* 1844 The Catholike prelates of the Popes band. 1588 ALLEN *Admon.* in Lingard *Hist. Eng.* (1855) VI. 358 She [Q. Eliz.] hath abolished the Catholic religion. 1602 CAREW *Cornwall* 71 a, A matter practised..as well by the reformed as Catholike Switzers. 1620 FR. HUNT (*title*), Appeal to the King, proving that our Saviour was Author of the Catholic Roman Faith. 1622 RUSHW. *Hist. Coll.* (1659) I. 287 His Majesties *Roman* Catholick-Subjects. 1660 R. COKE *Power & Subj.* 215 If the Pope would be Head of the Catholique Church, the King would be Head of the Church of England. 1790 BURKE *Fr. Rev.* Wks. V. 60 Whether..the catholick heir [gave way] when the protestant was preferred. 1845 S. AUSTIN *Ranke's Hist. Ref.* II. 513 What was begun by the evangelical governments, was carried on in an analogous manner by the catholic. 1845 BRIGHT *Sp. Maynooth Grant* 16 Apr., A Protestant soldiery, who, at the beck and command of a Protestant priest, have butchered and killed a Catholic peasant. 1872 FREEMAN *Gen. Sketch* xiii. 252 That the government of each German state might set up which religion it pleased, Catholic or Protestant. 1873 MORLEY *Rousseau* I. 229 A Catholic country like France.

†**b.** ***Catholic Seat***: = APOSTOLIC *See*. *Obs.*

In ancient times the καθολικοὶ θρόνοι or catholic sees, were those of Rome, Alexandria, Antioch, and Jerusalem.

1563 FOXE *A. & M.* (1583) 798 The proud, cruell, and bloudy rage of the Catholique Seat.

c. ***Catholic King, his Catholic Majesty***: a title given to the kings of Spain.

(In much earlier times the title belonged to the kings of France, Pipin being so called A.D. 767.)

1555 EDEN *Decades W. Ind.* To Rdr. (Arb.) 50 By the moste catholyke & puissaunt kynge Ferdinando. *Ibid.* 288 Wheruppon I wente into Spayne to the Catholyke kynge. 1588 ALLEN (*title*), Admonition to the Nobility and People of England..by the high and mightie kinge Catholike of Spaine. 1627 SANDERSON *Serm.* I. 281 He that..hath better title to the stile of most catholick king than any that ever yet bare it..I mean the devil, the prince of this world. 1636 MASSINGER *Bashf. Lover* IV. i. 1704 *Lond. Gaz.* No. 3987/3 To wait upon his Catholick Majesty. 1725 DE FOE *Voy. round W.* (1840) 280 Does not his Catholic majesty claim a title to the possession of it?

d. See also B.

8. Recognizing, or having sympathies with, all Christians; broadly charitable in religious matters. (Cf. 3 b. which differs only in not being restricted to things ecclesiastical or religious.)

1658 BAXTER in H. Rogers *J. Howe* iii. (1863) 59 The Lord Protector is noted as a man of a catholic spirit, desirous of the unity and peace of all the servants of Christ. 1719 DE FOE *Crusoe* (1840) II. vii. 158 If such a temper was universal, we might be all Catholic Christians, whatever church or particular profession we joined to, or joined in. 1734 WATTS *Reliq. Juv.* (1789) 155 To see all the disciples of Christ grown up into such a catholic spirit, as to be ready to worship God their common Father..in the same assembly. 1874 BLACKIE *Self-Cult.* 80 A spirit of deep and catholic piety.

†**9.** *transf.* Orthodox (applied *e.g.* to orthodox Mohammedans). *Obs.*

1613 PURCHAS *Pilgr.* VII. vii. 575 They are not all Catholike Mahumetans. 1625 —— *Pilgrimes* VI. i. §3 By some they are accounted Catholique or true Mahumetans, and by others they are holden for heretiks.

10. ***Catholic (and) Apostolic Church***: the religious body otherwise called Irvingites. (See quots. 1861, 1867.)

[1837 *Testimony to Bps., etc.* 32 That no section of the baptized bears the character of the one Holy Catholic Apostolic Church.] 1861 NORTON *Restor. Apostles and Proph. in Cath. Apostolic Ch.* 159 In assuming, as our only title and name, that of 'the Catholic and Apostolic Church'—we arrogate to ourselves nothing, for we do not appropriate it in any exclusive sense. 1867 *Address* in Miller *Irvingism* i. 5 Catholic and Apostolic Churches, a name which we have not assumed, and to which we have no exclusive right..But it is the only name by which we can, without protest, suffer ourselves to be called. 1888 *Whitaker's Almanac, Relig. Sects*, Places..certified to the Registrar-General on behalf of persons described as.. Catholic Apostolic Church.

11. *Comb.*, as ***Catholic-minded*** adj.

1879 *Dublin Rev.* Jan. 95 The learned, irresolute, yet pious and Catholic-minded men at the head of whom was Fisher's friend, Cuthbert Tunstal. 1964 P. F. ANSON *Bishops at Large* xi. 534 An alternative to Roman Catholicism to a catholic-minded people.

B. *sb.*

1. A member of a church recognized or claiming to be 'Catholic' in sense A. 6; *e.g.* an orthodox member of the Church before the disruption of East and West, as opposed to an Arian or other 'heretic'; of the Latin Church as opposed to the Greek or any separating sect or community (*e.g.* the Lollards); of a church or churches now taken to represent the primitive Church.

c1425 WYNTOUN *Cron.* IX. xxvi. 63 He was a constant Catholike All Lollard he hatyt and Heretike. 1594 HOOKER *Eccl. Pol.* IV. §5 Let the Church of Rome be what it will,.. hold them for Catholics, or hold them for Heretics, it is not a thing..in this present question greatly material. 1597 J. JONES *Preserv. Bodie & Soule* Ded., It is..of the faithfull, Christian, and Catholike certainly beleeued. 1609 BIBLE (Douay) *Proemial Annot.*, Some of these bookes..were sometimes doubted of by some Catholiques, and called Apochryphal. 1702 tr. *Le Clerc's Prim. Fathers* 241 An Edict bearing date the 27th of February (380)..That those who would profess it should be called Catholics, and the others Hereticks. 1854 HOOK *Ch. Dict.* s.v., Let the member of the Church of England assert his right to the name of Catholic, since he is the only person in England who has a right to that name. The English Romanist is a Roman Schismatic, and not a Catholic. 1860 FROUDE *Hist. Eng.* VI. 39, I must again remind my readers of the distinction between Catholic and Papist. Three quarters of the English

people were Catholics; that is, they were attached to the hereditary and traditionary doctrines of the Church. **1872** FREEMAN *Gen. Sketch* v. 102 He [Chlodwig] became..not only a Christian but a Catholic..all the other Teutonic Kings were Arians.

2. a. *spec.* A member of the Roman Church. ***English Catholic*** = English Roman Catholic.

1570 B. GOOGE *Pop. Kingd.* IV. (1880) 60 Accounting here for Catholickes, themselves & all their traine. **1581** (*title*) A Checke or Reproofe of M. Howlet..with an answere to the Reasons why Catholikes (as they are called) refuse to goe to Church. **1584** in Foley *Rec. Eng. Prov. S.J.* (1880) VI. 740 He said..that all English Catholics were bound to pray for the King of Spain. **1588** ALLEN *Admon.* in Lingard *Hist. Eng.* (1855) VI. 358/1 Not tolerable to the masters of her [Q. Eliz.] own sect, and to all Catholics in the world most ridiculous. **1602** BP. J. RIDER (*title*), A caveat to Irish Catholicks. **1602** WARNER *Alb. Eng.* IX. xlix. (1612) 226 Euen Catholiques (that erred name doth please the Papists). **1611** BIBLE *Pref.* The Catholicks (meaning Popish Romanists). **1636** FEATLY *Clavis Myst.* xxxiv. 483 Other of the Pope his stoutest champions..[say] we are sirnamed catholikes, therefore we are so. **1641** J. LOUTH in A. H. Mathew *Convers. Sir T. Matthew* (1904) 176 The innocency and loyalty of English Catholics towards others. **1650** SIR E. NICHOLAS in *N. Papers* (1886) I. 180 That which has been proposed concerninge the Catholics. **1715** in Estcourt & Payne *Eng. Cath. Nonjurors of 1715* (1885) 8, I, Henry Englefield, do declare that I am, by the grace of God, an English Catholic. **1719** DE FOE *Crusoe* (1840) II. vi. 155, I am a Catholic of the Roman Church. **1800** C. BUTLER *Life Alban Butler* xvi, A person would deserve well of the English Catholics who should translate it into English. **1845** BRIGHT *Sp.* 16 Apr., The Irish Catholics would thank you infinitely more if you were to wipe out that foul blot. **1872** FREEMAN *Gen. Sketch* xiii. 254 The religious wars between the Catholics and Protestants within the country [France]. **1876** GREEN *Short Hist.* vii. §4 The last hopes of the English Catholics were dispelled by the Queen's refusal to take part in the Council of Trent. **1889** J. O. PAYNE (*title*) Records of the English Catholics of 1715.

b. ***Old Catholic***, a term introduced after the secession of John Henry Newman and others to distinguish members of Catholic families in England since the Reformation from Catholic immigrants and converts.

1846 J. H. NEWMAN *Let.* 14 July in Gasquet *Ld. Acton* (1906) p. xiii, It will be one of your collisions with old Catholics. **1909** *Dublin Rev.* Jan. 56 The friction between converts and old Catholics..was inevitable. **1918** L. STRACHEY *Emin. Victorians* I. v. 56 It seemed as if the harvest was to be gathered in by a crowd of converts, who were proclaiming on every side as something new and wonderful the truths which the Old Catholics..had not only known, but for which they had suffered, for generations. **1962** V. A. MCCLELLAND *Cardinal Manning* i. 3 If one is to understand the opposition to Cardinal Manning and to the Oxford converts, one has to appreciate the feelings and position of the 'Old Catholics'.

3. Defined or limited by a word prefixed, as †*English Catholic*, †*Popish Catholic*, ANGLO-CATHOLIC, ROMAN CATHOLIC, q.v.

(See a different use of *English Catholics*, in sense 2 quot. 1876.)

1577 FULKE (*title*), Two Treatises..Answere of the Christian Protestant to the proud challenge of a Popish Catholicke. **1585** SIR W. HARBERT (*title*), Letter to a Roman pretended Catholike. **1598** HAKLUYT *Voy.* I. 597 Many rebels against her maiestie and popish catholiques. **1837** J. H. NEWMAN *Par. Serm.* (1840) III. xiv, The Holy Church throughout all the world is broken into many fragments.. we are the English Catholics, abroad are the Roman Catholics..elsewhere are the Greek Catholics, and so on. **1854** HOOK *Ch. Dict.* s.v. *Protestant*, We tell the Papist that with respect to him we are Protestant; we tell the Protestant Dissenter that in respect to him we are Catholics; and we may be called Protestant or Protesting Catholics, or as some of our writers describe us, Anglo-Catholics.

b. ***German Catholic***, ***Old Catholic***: names taken by religious parties who separated from the Roman Catholic communion in Germany, the former under Ronge in 1845 (reunited 1848), the latter after the Vatican Council in 1870–71. *Old Catholic* is also applied to members of other churches separated from Rome, and united by acceptance of the Declaration of Utrecht of 1889.

1871 *Sunday Mag.* Nov. 84/1 The Old Catholics have great hopes of support from the High Church party in England. **1871** *Union Rev.* 273 For German Catholics to succumb to the Vatican decrees, would be an act of moral suicide. **1931** W. TEMPLE *Thoughts on Probl. of Day* iv. 92 The Conference..was concerned with advances towards union in two directions—on the one hand towards union with the Orthodox and the Old Catholic Churches, and on the other hand with the non-episcopal Churches. **1948** C. B. Moss *Old Catholic Movement* i. 1 The Old Catholic Churches are a group of self-governing national churches, united by their acceptance of the Declaration of Utrecht (1889) as their dogmatic basis. *Ibid.* xxviii. 348 Eight Dutch Old Catholic priests came to England to see the English Church for themselves. **1969** D. W. D. SHAW tr. *Heyer's Catholic Church* vi. 149 Political factors had produced an initial wave of interest in the 'German Catholic' movement.

†**4.** = CATHOLICOS. *Obs.*

1612 BREREWOOD *Lang. & Relig.* xxiv. 213 The Catholick of Armenia. *Ibid.* 210 They acknowledge obedience..to two Patriarchs of their own: whom they term Catholicks. **1735** JOHNSON tr. *Lobo's Abyssinia* 307 Catholick like Patriarch is no more than an empty Title without the Power.

C. *attrib.* Of, relating to, affecting, or on the side of (Roman) Catholics. In ***Catholic Emancipation***, etc. [In construction not distinct from the adj.]

1791 J. MILNER (*title*), A short Pamphlet on the Catholic Question. **1795** DUIGENAN (*title*), Speech on the Catholic Bill in the Irish House of Commons. **1805** LD. HAWKESBURY (*title*), Speech in the House of Lords, 10th of May on the Catholic Petition. **1809** SOUTHEY *Ess.* (1832) II. 301 For these people Catholic Emancipation can do nothing. **1878** SPENCER WALPOLE *Hist. Eng.* II. vii. 145 The anti-Catholic members of the Cabinet [in 1826] were as much opposed to their Catholic colleagues as to their regular opponents. *Ibid.* note, Persons in favour of emancipation were classed as Catholic statesmen.

†**ca'tholical**, *a. Obs.* [f. CATHOLIC *a.* + -AL[1].] Of or belonging to all, general, universal; *esp.* belonging to the universal faith = CATHOLIC *a.* 5 b, 6 a, etc.

1526 *Pilgr. Perf.* (W. de W. 1531) 186 Ye catholicall or generall fayth of ye chirche. **1556** LAUDER *Tractate* 540 The Potent Kyng of kyngis all Preserue all Prencis Catholycall. **1642** J. EATON *Honey-c. Free Justif.* 5 The Church Apostolicall and Catholicall. **1674** HORTON *Serm. Rom.* viii. 277 The comforts of Religion and Christianity..are Catholical and Universall.

b. of medicines: = CATHOLIC *a.* 2.

1626 W. FENNER *Hidden Manna* Wks. II. 377 But, like an Apothecaries drug, Catholical. **1644** N. JOCELINE (*title*), Parliament Physick for a Sin-Sick Nation..containing a Catholicall Medicine for all Natures and Nations.

catholically (kəˈθɒlɪkəlɪ), *adv.* [f. prec. + -LY.] In a catholic manner.

1526 *Pilgr. Perf.* (W. de W. 1531) 197 They..that in a true herte catholycally byleueth the same. **1829** *Blackw. Mag.* XXV. 153 He did catholically dread the very name of what they called reform. **1855** MOTLEY *Dutch Rep.* I. 304 To consent that his niece should live Catholically after the marriage. **1887** *Times* 7 Apr. 3/5 The Conservatives..were more catholically minded.

So **ca'tholicalness**.

1731 BAILEY II, *Catholicalness*..being of a catholick spirit, universalness.

†**Ca'tholican**, *a. Obs. rare*[−1]. = CATHOLIC 7 c.

1518 *Dispatch* in Ld. Berners *Froiss.* Pref. 15 Whiche the king Catholicans Cownsell goothe faste abowte to lette.

ca'tholicate. *rare.* [ad. med.L. *catholicāt-us.*] The jurisdiction of an Armenian *catholicus*.

1878 STUBBS *Lect. Study of Hist.* (1886) 159 The Armenian Catholicos..took refuge at Sis and founded there an independent or national Catholicate.

Catholicism (kəˈθɒlɪsɪz(ə)m, ˈkæθəlɪsɪz(ə)m). [f. CATHOLIC + -ISM. Cf. F. *catholicisme.*]

1. The system, faith, and practice of the Catholic Church; adherence to the Catholic Church.

1656 BLOUNT *Glossogr.*, *Catholicisme*..the orthodox Faith of the Catholick Church. **1685** BAXTER *Paraphr.* Rom. xi. Annot., Much less will God ever confine the Church and Covenant of peculiarity to the Jewish Nation, and take it from the Gentiles, and cease Catholicism.

b. usually of the Roman Catholic Church.

1613–7 PURCHAS *Pilgr., Descr. India* (1864) 131 Thomæan Christians. These Thomæans are now, as the Iesuites report, reduced to their Catholicisme. **1779** SWINBURNE *Trav. Spain* xxix. (T.) All the gipsies that I have conversed with assured me of their sound catholicism. **1871** MORLEY *Voltaire* (1886) 1 We may think of Voltairism..as we think of Catholicism or the Renaissance or Calvinism.

c. so ***Roman Catholicism***.

1870 *Daily News* 5 Dec., Mrs. Craik can do justice to the earnest and beautiful side of Roman Catholicism. **1876** GRANT *Burgh Sch. Scot.* II. xiii. 412 The object..being no doubt to ridicule Roman Catholicism.

d. A trait, note, or act of a good Catholic.

1609 T. MORTON *Answ. Higgons* 2 Who hold it a Catholicisme to brand me with only an imaginarie imputation. **1842** G. S. FABER *Provinc. Lett.* (1844) II. 286 Censure of what..we have been led to deem genuine Catholicisms.

†**2.** = CATHOLICITY 4. *Obs.*

1647 JER. TAYLOR *Dissuas. Popery* II. ii. Introd. (R.) This broken consent is not an infallible testimony of the catholicism of the Doctrine.

3. = CATHOLICITY 1. *rare.*

1796 MORSE *Amer. Geog.* I. 454 All religions..are tolerated and a spirit of liberality and catholicism is increasing.

catholicist (kəˈθɒlɪsɪst). *rare.* [f. as prec. + -IST.] An adherent or partisan of catholicism.

1812 *Monthly Mag.* XXXIII. 133 We reproach a man by terming him a Deist, Methodist, Catholicist.

catholicity (kæθəˈlɪsɪtɪ). [f. as prec. + -ITY; cf. F. *catholicité.*] Catholic quality or character.

1. The quality of being comprehensive in feeling, taste, sympathy, etc.; freedom from sectarian exclusiveness or narrowness.

1843 *Edin. Rev.* Dec. 274 One of the greatest and most attractive characteristics of his mind—its catholicity. **1855** H. REED *Lect. Eng. Lit.* ii. (1878) 55 It is important to cultivate a true catholicity of taste. **1882** J. HAWTHORNE *Fort. Fool* I. xxxi, Royalty itself could not compete with Lady Mayfair in the brilliant catholicity of her entertainments.

b. of religious feeling.

1841 MYERS *Cath. Th.* IV. 435 This great principle of Christian Brotherhood..a stronger feeling of the true Catholicity of Christianity. **1868** MRS. BALFOUR *Wrkg. Women* (ed. 3) 173 True Christian catholicity of spirit. **1882** FARRAR in *Contemp. Rev.* XLII. 813 The lessons of catholicity and toleration.

2. Universal prevalence; universality.

1868 HUXLEY *Phys. Basis Life* 137, I share this catholicity of assimilation with other animals.

3. Of a church or doctrine: The character of being universally recognized or diffused.

1843 tr. *Mariotti's Italy Past & Pr.* (1848) I. 113 Universality of dominion was now to be cemented by catholicity of faith and worship. **1845** J. H. NEWMAN *Ess. Developm.* Introd. (L.) An appeal to the catholicity of the church, in proof that its doctrines are true, is an appeal to the voice of the multitude upon a dispute as to truth. **1887** *Times* (weekly ed.) 7 Oct. 3/1 Thus will the catholicity of our Church be at length realized.

4. The character of belonging to, or in accordance with, the Catholic Church.

1830 COLERIDGE *Table Talk* 6 June, In the first century, catholicity was the test of a book or epistle..being canonical. **1842** PUSEY *Crisis Eng. Ch.* 139 They wish to claim for the English Church the character of Catholicity. **1868** G. HARDY in *Guardian* 29 Apr. 494 A sincere and faithful trust in the Catholicity of the Church of England.

b. *spec.* of the Church of Rome: The doctrine or faith of that Church, catholicism.

1847 DICKENS *Lett.* (1880) I. 175 The Swiss radicals.. know what Catholicity is. **1849** SOUTHEY *Comm.-Pl. Bk.* Ser. II. 80 When the professors of Catholicity arrogate to themselves political command.

catholicization (kəˌθɒlɪsaɪˈzeɪʃən). [f. CATHOLICIZE *v.* + -ATION.] The action of making Catholic.

1905 *Nation* (U.S.) 28 Dec. 522 The catholicization of France by Clovis. **1945** R. HARGREAVES *Enemy at Gate* 309 Italy's conquest of Abyssinia was the occasion of the peremptory Catholicisation of the old Coptic Church of Ethiopia.

catholicize (kəˈθɒlɪsaɪz, ˈkæθəlɪsaɪz), *v.* In 7 -ickise, -ikize. [f. as CATHOLICITY + -IZE: in its earlier form f. *Catholick.*]

1. *trans.* To make catholic or Catholic (in various senses of the adjective).

1629 H. BURTON *Babel no Bethel* 126 Doth not the Pope monopolize and Catholickise (as I may so say) the Church of Rome..as the onely Catholick Church over the earth? **1799** *Monthly Rev.* XXVIII. 570 To catholicise the phraseology of natural history. **1809** KNOX & JEBB *Corr.* I. 535 They will yet by their writings, serve to catholicise the romanists. **1865** PUSEY *Truth Eng. Ch.* 281 It seemed..before these secessions that..nothing but time was needed to Catholicize England. **1878** DOWDEN *Stud. Lit.* 333 To liberalise the [Papal] Church, to catholicise Liberalism.

2. *intr.* To become, or behave as, a Catholic.

1611 COTGR., *Catholizer*, to catholikize it..become a Catholicke. **1853** W. HAZLITT tr. *Monston's Israel of Alps* xxvii. 194 All protestant foreigners settled in Piedmont are ordered to catholicize or to quit the country.

Hence **catholicized** *ppl. a.*, **catholicizing** *vbl. sb.* and *ppl. a.*

1826 C. BUTLER *Life Grotius* App. 256 He is said to have had in view the catholicising, as it was termed, the Northern Part of Germany. **1868** M. PATTISON *Academ. Org.* §5. 299 The collision which is impending between the Catholic, or catholicising party, and the liberal party in Oxford. **1870** *Daily News* 3 Oct., The forcible abduction and catholicizing of the little Mortara boy. **1878** DOWDEN *Stud. Lit.* 337 A catholicised liberalism.

catholicly (ˈkæθəlɪklɪ), *adv.* [f. as prec. + -LY.]

1. Universally, with universal application. ? *Obs.*

1631 SIR L. CARY *Elegy on Donne* (T.) No druggist of the soul bestow'd on all So catholicly a curing cordial. **1645** MILTON *Tetrach.* (1851) 170 That Mariage is indissoluble, is not Catholickly true; wee know it dissoluble for Adultery and for desertion.

2. In accordance with the faith or teaching of the Catholic Church.

1542 BOORDE *Dyetary* xl. (1870) 302 That the sycke person may fynysshe his lyfe Catholyckely in the fayth of Iesu Cryste. **1583** W. FULKE *Defence* 63 The late new English Testament catholicly translated and printed at Rheims. **1679** EVERARD *Popish Plot* 1, I was one of her privatest Friends, and Catholickly affected. **1853** CDL. WISEMAN *Ess.* II. 377 We own we do not see it, if viewed Catholicly.

b. so ***Roman Catholicly***.

1793 H. WALPOLE *Lett. H. Mann* (1834) I. lxviii. 250 You are either run Roman Catholicly devout or take me to be so.

†**'catholicness.** ? *Obs.* [f. as prec. + -NESS.] Catholic quality, catholicity.

1605 A. WOTTON *Answ. Pop. Articles* 34 Neither can you reasonably thinke, that the catholicknesse of the Church requires a continuall being in all places at once. **1633** T. ADAMS *Exp. 2 Peter* ii. 6 The catholicness of their doctrine. **1664** MORE *Myst. Iniq.* 284 Their..pretence to Catholicness of Universality. **1674** BREVINT *Saul at Endor* 10 (R.) Thus one may judg of the catholikness, which Romanists brag of.

Ca'tholico-. Combining form of CATHOLIC.

1864 BURTON *Scot. Abr.* II. i. 69 To advance the Catholico-Pontifical interest in Great Britain.

catholicon (kəˈθɒlɪkən). [a. 16th c. F. *catholicon*, *-cum*, a. L. *catholicum*, or Gr. *καθολικόν* adj., neut. sing., universal.]

1. An electuary supposed to be capable of evacuating all humours; a universal remedy or prophylactic; panacea. *arch.* [Used in Fr., in 16th c. by Ambrose Paré; its earlier history does not appear.]

1611 BIBLE *Pref.* 3 Men talke much..of Catholicon the drugge, that it is in stead of all purges. **1642** SIR T. BROWNE *Relig. Med.* II. §9 Death is the cure of all diseases. There is no Catholicon or universal remedy I know but this. **1732–69**

De Foe, etc. *Tour Gt. Brit.* (ed. 7) II. 364 A Catholicon, and good for every thing. **1808** *Med. Jrnl.* XIX. 338 Nor do I mean to assert, that it is such a catholicon as to exclude other adjuvants. **1833** *Chamb. Jrnl.* No. 62. 73 A little plaister is his catholicon for all evils.

b. *fig.*

1631 Gouge *God's Arrows* I. §66. 109 The spiritual Catholicon, that generall remedy which is fit for any malady, prayer. **1638** Baker tr. *Balzac's Lett.* (1654) II. 29 A good wife is a Catholicon, or universal remedy for all the evils that happen in life. *a* **1734** North *Life Ld. Kpr. Guildford* (1742) I. 224 He..so made his Wit a Catholicon, or Shield, to cover all his weak Places and Infirmities. **1832** Southey *Lett.* (1856) IV. 274 The panacea for all moral and political evils—the true and only catholicon. **1859** Jowett *Ep. Romans, Atonement & Satisf.* §3 To assume revelation or inspiration, as a sort of shield or Catholicon, under which the weak points of theology may receive protection.

†**2. a.** A universal formula. *Obs.* **b.** A comprehensive treatise.

In the latter sense applied by Johannes de Balbis de Janua, as the title of his celebrated Latin Grammar and Dictionary, the *Catholicon* or *Summa*, made in 1286; whence in later times given to various vocabularies of Latin and some vernacular, e.g. the *Catholicon Anglicum*, an English-Latin Vocabulary dated 1483.

1647 Jer. Taylor *Lib. Proph.* vii. 131 Neither one sense nor other can be obtruded for an Article of Faith, much lesse as a Catholicon instead of all. **1837–9** Hallam *Hist. Lit.* (1847) I. i. §90. 79 The Catholicon of John Balbi, a Genoese monk..consists of a Latin grammar, followed by a dictionary. **1865** Way *Promp. Parv.* Pref. 23 The student of mediaeval antiquities will find in the *Catholicon* an auxiliary rarely to be consulted without advantage and instruction. *Ibid.* 64 The valuable English-Latin Dictionary, frequently cited as the 'Catholicon Anglicum'.

‖**Catholicos** (kəˈθɒlɪkɒs). [a. Gr. καθολικός: see catholic *sb.* 4.] The Patriarch of Armenia.

1625 Purchas *Pilgrims* II. 1269 The Armenians..hauing a Primate of their owne whom they calle a Catholicon. **1878** Stubbs 17 *Lect. Study of Hist.* (1886) 159 The Armenian Catholicos..took refuge at Sis. **1883** *Daily News* 20 July 5/3 Certain rights affecting the election of the Catholicos.

†ˈ**catholicship.** *Obs.* [f. catholic + -ship.] = catholicity.

1653 Chisenhale *Cath. Hist.* 10 The Doctors Arguments ..concerning Romes Catholiqueship. **1674** Staveley *Rom. Horseleach* Ep. Ded., The true marks and signs of the Catholicship thereof.

catholog, obs. form of catalogue.

catholyte (ˈkæθəlaɪt). [f. cath(ode + electr)olyte.] That part of the electrolyte which adjoins the cathode.

1890–1949 [see anolyte].

cathood (ˈkæthʊd). [f. cat + -hood, after *manhood*, etc.] The state of a (full grown) cat.

1791 Huddesford *Salmag.* 140 Sent..In prime of Cathood to the Catacomb. **1834–43** Southey *Doctor* xxv. (D.) My kitten should never attain to cathood.

ca'-thro'. *Sc.* [f. *ca'*, call, in sense 'drive' + through *prep.*] 'A great disturbance' (Jamieson).

1816 Scott *Antiq.* xxiv, There was siccan a ca'-thro', as the like was never seen. **1818** —— *Hrt. Mid.* xvi, Ye never saw sic a ca'throw.

catif, caitiffe, obs. ff. caitiff.

Catiline, *a.* [ad. L. *Catilīna.*] The name of a Roman who conspired against his country B.C. 63: sometimes taken as the type of a profligate conspirator. Hence **Catiliˈnarian,** †**Catiˈlinary** *sb.* and *a.*, †ˈ**Catilinism.**

1592 G. Harvey in Nashe *Strange News* Wks. 1883 II. 263. **1594** Bp. King *Jonas* (1618) 190 The.. vncompassionate style of these Catilinary dispositions. **1611** Cotgr., *Catilinisme*, Catilinisme, conspiracie. **1774** *Hist. Europe* in *Ann. Reg.* (1775) 71/1 Catalines at home who ought to be dragged forth to public disgrace and punishment. **1798** G. Ellis in *Anti-Jacobin* 12 Feb. 65 The Catiline of modern times [Fox]. **1824** J. H. Newman *Cicero* in *Hist. Sketches* (1872) II. 291 The eloquence of his Catilinarians and Philippics. *Ibid.* 292 The Catilinarian conspirators. **1875** Symonds *Renaiss. in Italy* I. vi. 319 The Catilinarian riots of Tiburzio. **1889** Skrine *Mem. Thring* 155 The senate which quelled the Catilinarians met in the Temple of Concord. **1925** *Glasgow Herald* 16 Apr. 9 He is still a sort of Catilinarian doomed to reckless experiments.

†**catillate,** *v. Obs.*$^{-0}$ [f. L. *catillāt-* ppl. stem of *catillā-re* to lick a plate, f. *catillus* dish, plate.] 'To licke dishes' (Cockeram 1623).

cation (ˈkætaɪən, formerly ˈkætɪən). *Electr.* [a. Gr. κατιόν (a thing) going down, neut. of pr. pple. of κατ-ιέναι to go down, f. κατά down + ἰ- go.] **a.** An ion carrying a positive charge which moves towards the cathode (negative electrode) during electrolysis. Opp. *anion.*

1834 Faraday *Res. Electr.* (1839) §655, I require a term to express those bodies which can pass to the electrodes, or, as they are usually called, the poles..I propose to distinguish such bodies by calling those *anions* which go to the anode of the decomposing body; and those passing to the cathode, *cations.* **1839** Grove in *Corr. Phys. Forces* 238 The cations of the electrolytes. **1885** Watson & Burbury *Math. Th. Elect. & Magnt.* I. 231.

b. cation exchange, ion exchange involving cations; also *attrib.*; so **cation exchanger,** a substance capable of cation exchange. **cation-active** *a.*, having an active cation.

1834, 1931 [see anion]. **1946** *Nature* 26 Oct. 585/2 The addition of divalent metallic ions greatly enhances the surface-active properties of anion-active detergents, and it was suggested..that a similar effect should occur on adding divalent anions to cation-active substances. **1931** *Soil Science* XXXI. 320 If the cation exchange capacity depends upon the number of free silicate or other acidoid valences, [etc.]. **1950** *Amer. Jrnl. Med. Sci.* CCXX. 547 (*title*) Treatment of Potassium Retention in Anuria with Cation Exchange Resins. **1957** *Encycl. Brit.* XII. 573/2 In water softening..calcium and magnesium ions..are removed by a granular bed of cation exchanger and replaced by sodium ions from the cation exchanger. **1963** [see anion].

cationic (kætaɪˈɒnɪk), *a.* [f. cation + -ic.] **a.** Of, relating to, or consisting of cations. **b.** Characterized by an active cation.

1928 *Jrnl. Chem. Soc.* I. 905 The former may repel electrons..but it cannot without disruption provide a seat for the cationic charge. **1946** *Nature* 3 Aug. 155/1 Following the relatively rapid achievement of cationic equilibrium between perfusate and soil, manganese usually disappears from the perfusate. **1957** *Textile Terms & Defs.* (ed. 3) 23 *Cationic Dye*, a dye which dissociates in aqueous solution to give a coloured ion which is positively charged. **1964** M. Hynes *Med. Bacteriol.* (ed. 8) ii. 22 Cationic detergents are more bactericidal than the anionic types used for domestic cleaning.

cationoid (ˈkætaɪənɔɪd, kæˈtaɪənɔɪd), *a.* Also **kationoid.** [f. cation + -oid.] Resembling a cation.

1925–1953 [see anionoid *a.*].

catkin (ˈkætkɪn). *Bot.* Also 6 **catteken, catken,** 8–9 **katkin.** [Taken by Lyte from Du. *katteken* 'kitten' and 'catkin' of hazel, willow, etc. (in Dodoens), dim. of *katte* cat. The 16th c. L. *catulus*, F. *chaton* (f. *chat*), and Ger. *kätzchen*, have the same two senses; the *catkin* being named from its soft downy appearance: cf. catling 4.]

A unisexual inflorescence, consisting of rows of apetalous flowers ranged in circles along a slender stalk; the whole forming a cylindrical, downy-looking, and generally pendant part, which falls off in a single piece after flowering or ripening; as in the willow, birch, poplar, pine, hazel, etc.; a deciduous spike; an amentum. (Called by Turner 1568 *tagge*, and by various 16–17th c. writers *aglet.*)

1578 Lyte *Dodoens* VI. lviii. 733 Leaues spring foorth after the Catkins, agglettes, or blowinges. *Ibid.* lxvii. 743 Withy ..his flower or blossom is lyke a fine throm or thicke set veluet heaped vp togither about a little stemme, the which when it openeth is soft in handling, and lyke downe or Cotton, and therefore the whole flower is called a Chatton, Kitekin or Catteken. **1611** Cotgr., *Chattons*, the Catkins, Cattails, aglet-like blowings, or bloomings, of nut-trees, etc. **1731–7** Miller *Gard. Dict.* (J.) The pine tree hath amentaceous flowers or katkins. **1821** Clare *Vill. Minstr.* II. 131 Golden catkins deck the sallow tree. **1860** Gosse *Rom. Nat. Hist.* 6 The willows..are gay with their pendant catkins.

Hence **catkined** *ppl. a.*

1866 Geo. Eliot *F. Holt* 2 The bushy hedgerows.. shrouded the grassy borders..with catkined hazels. **1869** Ruskin *Q. of Air* §78 Catkined trees, whose blossoms are only tufts and dust.

cat-lap (ˈkætlæp). *slang.* or *dial.* [Cf. Shaks. *Temp.* II. i. 288 'They'll take suggestion as the cat laps milk'.] Stuff fit for a cat to lap: contemptuously applied to tea or other weak drink.

1785 Capt. Grose *Dict. Vulg. Tongue, Cat-Lap*, tea, called also scandal broth. **1824** Scott *Redgauntlet* ch. xiii, We have tea and coffee aboard..You are at the age to like such catlap. **1865** Miss Braddon *Sir Jasper* xxvii. 282 The clerk only muttered, 'Oh, d——n! nobody wants your catlap!'

catless (ˈkætlɪs), *a.* [f. cat *sb.* + -less.] Having no cat. (*playful.*)

1758 Mrs. Delany *Autobiog. & Corr.* (1861) III. 503, I, alas! am catless! **1858** *Chamb. Jrnl.* IX. 338 We returned to a catless fireside.

ˈ**cat-like,** *a.* (*adv.*) Like a cat, or that of a cat; *esp.* stealthy, noiseless of tread.

1600 Shaks. *A.Y.L.* IV. iii. 116 A Lyonnesse..Lay cowching head on ground, with catlike watch. **1789** Wolcott (P. Pindar) *Subj. for Painters* 18 Hugging her husband in her cat-like clutches. **1836** Yarrell *Brit. Fishes* (1859) II. 384 A ferocious-looking, cat-like head. **1866** *Cornh. Mag.* Aug. 222 With stealthy, cat-like steps.

catling (ˈkætlɪŋ). Also 7 **catlin.** [f. cat *sb.* + -ling, dim. suffix. The connexion of sense 3 does not appear: perh. it is a distinct word.]

1. A little cat; a kitten.

c **1630** Drumm. of Hawth. *Poems* Wks. (1711) 50 Never cat nor catling I shall find. **1791** Huddesford *Salmag.* 134 Cats and Catlings of ignoble line. **1866** Ld. Osborne *Educ. Children* 23 The fate of the brother and sister catlings.

2. Catgut for a violin, lute, or the like; 'the smallest-sized lute-strings' (Stainer & Barrett).

[**1592** Shaks. *Rom. & Jul.* IV. v. 132 (*To Musician*) What say you Simon Catling?] **1606** —— *Tr. & Cr.* III. iii. 306 Vnlesse the Fidler Apollo get his sinewes to make catlings on. **1708** Kersey, *Catlings* or *Catlins*, a sort of small Cat-gut Strings for Musical Instruments. **1721** C. King *Brit. Merch.* I. 284 Lutestrings, Catlings, Minikings. **1812** J. Smyth *Pract. Customs* 53 Catlings are small strings for fiddles and other musical instruments. **1833** *Act 3 & 4 Will. IV*, lvi, Catlings, the Gross, containing 12 Dozen Knots.

b. *transf.* (*pl.*) Stringed instruments.

1652 Benlowes *Theoph.* III. li, Still Tort'ring the deep mouth'd Catlins, till Hoarse-thundring Diapasons should the whole room fill.

3. *Surg.* 'A long, narrow, double-edged, sharp-pointed, straight knife for performing amputations' (*Syd. Soc. Lex.*).

1612 Woodall *Surg. Mate* Wks. (1653) 2 Of the dismembring knife, and of the Catling..Whatsoever the Catling or dismembring knife cannot come at by reason of their greatnesse, etc. **1689** Moyle *Sea Chyrurg.* II. i. 25 With your Catling divide the Vessels between the bones. **1824** *Ann. Reg. Chron.* 16 Jan. 9/1 Sir Astley [Cooper].. with the limb in one hand, and the catling in the other, commenced the operation.

†**4.** = catkin. (But possibly a misprint.) *Obs.*

1665–76 Ray *Flora* 221 The flowers [of mulberry] are downy Catlins, which turn into berries. **1704** Harris (J.), *Catling*, The down or moss growing about walnut-trees, resembling the hair of a cat. Hence in Kersey, Bailey, Johnson, and mod. Dicts.

catlinite. *Min.* [Named by C. T. Jackson, 1839, after Geo. Catlin, the famous delineator of the American Indians.] The sacred pipe-stone of the American Indians, a kind of indurated red clay occurring in a bed of considerable extent in the region of the Upper Missouri, referred by Hayden to the Cretaceous formation. (Dana.)

1858 Dana *Min.* 252. **1883** Barter in *Amer. Naturalist* July, Catlinite: its antiquity as a material for Tobacco pipes.

catmint (ˈkætmɪnt). Also **cats-mint,** 7 **catamint.** [f. cat + mint; cf. med.L. *herba catti, cataria*, F. *herbe du chat*, G. *katzenmünze*, Du. *kattekruid.* See quot. 1776.] A labiate plant, *Nepeta Cataria*, a native of Britain and the continent of Europe, naturalized in North America. Also taken as the English name of the genus.

c **1265** *Voc.* in Wr.-Wülcker 557 *Nepta*, kattesminte. **1578** Lyte *Dodoens* II. lxvi. 248 The third kinde [of Calamynte] is now called in English Neppe, and Cat mynte. **1597** Gerard *Herbal* ccxvi. §1. 553 Cat Mint or Nep groweth high. **1774** Goldsm. *Nat. Hist.* (1776) III. 206 The cat..is excessively fond of some plants, such as valerian, marum, and cat-mint; against these it rubs, smells them at a distance, and at last.. wears them out. **1834** J. Forbes *Laennec's Dis. Chest* 645 Aromatics are also exceedingly useful, and particularly the infusion of cat-mint. **1882** Gr. Allen *Colours Flowers* ii. 55 Ground-ivy..is bright blue; catmint..pale blue.

catnache. *rare.* Apparently a corruption of *catananche* (*C. cærulea*), the Blue Succory, a perennial herbaceous plant, of the south of Europe.

1803 *Wheat & Weeds* in *Poet. Monitor* 113 With star-like rays, and sky-like blue..The catnache blue may serve to name The proud, conceited, flirting dame.

cat-nip. [f. cat + nep.] **a.** The common name in U.S. of catmint.

1796 Morse *Amer. Geog.* I. 189 (Medicinal plants in New England) Catmint or catnip. **1807** W. Irving *Salmag.* (1824) 144 The healing qualities of hoarhound, catnip and penny-royal. **1852** Hawthorne *Blithedale Rom.* I. iv. 66 A decoction of catnip. **1861** Mrs. Stowe *Pearl Orr's Isl.* 20 A ..tea-pot, which fumed strongly of catnip-tea.

b. *fig.*

1934 A. Woollcott *While Rome Burns* 183 It was so much catnip to 'that ill-looking, squinting man'. **1962** *Observer* 25 Mar. 24/3 She is catnip to failures.

‖**catoblepas.** *Zool.* [L. *catōblepas*, Gr. κατῶβλεψ, f. κάτω downwards + βλέπ-ειν to look; see quots.] In ancient authors, some African animal, 'perhaps a species of buffalo, or the gnu, a species of antelope' (Lewis & Short, s.v.). Now made the name of a genus including the gnu.

1398 Trevisa *Barth. De P.R.* XVIII. xvi. (1495) 776 A wylde beest that hyghte Catoblefas and hath a lytyll body and nyce in all membres and a grete heed hangynge alway to-warde the erth. **1587** Golding *De Mornay* xvi. 299 Yᵉ eye of the beast of Ægipt which killeth those whom it looketh vpon. *Marg.* The catopleb and also the cockatryce. **1601** Holland *Pliny* VIII. xxi, A wild beast, called Catoblepes. **1613** Purchas *Pilgr.* I. VI. i. 467 The Catoblepas is said to bee of like venemous nature. **1616** Bullokar, *Catoblepa*, a strange beast..some thinke it to bee the Basiliske, or Cockatrice. **1725** Pope *Odyss.* XI. 777, *note* (ed. 1753), In the same region the Catoblepon is found, a creature like a bull, whose eyes are so fixed as chiefly to look downward.

catocalid (kætəˈkeɪlɪd), *a.* and *sb.* *Ent.* [f. mod.L. *Catocala*, f. Gr. κάτω below + καλός beautiful: see -id³.] **A.** *adj.* Belonging to the genus *Catocala* of noctuid moths. **B.** *sb.* A moth of this genus.

1896 J. W. Tutt *Brit. Moths* x. 224 It is possible that the Geometers..went a short way with the Catocalids. *Ibid.* 225 We have only four species of Catocalid Moths inhabiting Britain, one of which has blue-banded hindwings, the others red. **1913** *Oxf. Univ. Gaz.* 4 June 960/2 A fine set of 28 Catocalid moths. **1963** V. Nabokov *Gift* ii. 95 Your blue stripe, Catocalid, shows from under its grey lid.

catocathartic (ˌkætəʊkəˈθɑːtɪk), *a.* and *sb.* [mod. f. Gr. κάτω downwards + καθαρτικός CATHARTIC; cf. ANOCATHARTIC. Also formerly *cata-*.]

A. *adj.* Causing evacuation of the bowels, purgative. **B.** *sb.* A purgative medicine.

1704 J. HARRIS *Lex. Techn.*, Catacatharticks, are Medicines that purge downwards.. *Cato-cathartick Medicines*, are such as work downwards. **1721** BAILEY, *Catacathartic*.

‖**catoche** (ˈkætəkiː). *Med. Obs.* [Gr. κατοχή catalepsy (Galen), f. κατέχειν to hold down, take possession of, seize.] = next.

1656 RIDGLEY *Pract. Physic* 53 It differs.. from a Catoche, because in Carus the eyes are shut. **1707** FLOYER *Physic. Pulse-Watch* 129 The Pulse in the Catoche remain'd entire.

‖**catochus** (ˈkætəkəs). *Med.* [Gr. κάτοχος (Galen) = κατοχή; see prec.] 'An old term for catalepsy. Also, for an affection similar to catalepsy, but with rigidity of the limbs; also, for coma-vigil' (*Syd. Soc. Lex.*).

1656 H. MORE *Antid. Ath.* I. xi. (1712) 35 The Nerves.. have no sense, as is demonstrable from a Catalepsis or Catochus. **1851** H. MAYO *Pop. Superst.* (ed. 2) 81 A second [kind of spasm] is catochus.

‖**catogan.** [F.] = CADOGAN.

1885 *N.Y. Weekly Sun* 29 Apr. 3/5 To dress the hair on the top of the head and form it into a catogan loop in the nape of the neck, as ultra-fashionable women are arranging their coiffure at this moment.

catogenic (kætəˈdʒɛnɪk), *a.* [mod. f. Gr. κάτω downwards + γένος race, kind, sort + -IC.] Pertaining to decomposition.

1878 LAWRENCE tr. *Cotta's Rocks Class.* 336 Regarding the red hematites as products of catogenic transmutation from brown hematite.

cat o'mountain: see CATAMOUNTAIN.

†**caton.** *Obs.* Also **cathon.** [a F. *Caton*, ad. L. *Catōn-em*, *Cato*.] The *Disticha de moribus* attributed to Dionysius Cato, a book of ethics in Latin verse, of the 3rd or 4th c., much esteemed in the middle ages as a manual of instruction.

c **1460** *Towneley Myst.* 94 It semys by youre Laton Ye have lerd youre Caton. **1481–3** CAXTON *Bk. for Trav.* in *Promp. Parv.* 63 George the booke sellar hath doctrinals, catons, etc. oures of our Lady, Donettis, partis, accidents. **1484** —— *Cato* (ad fin.) Here fynyssheth this present book whiche is sayd or called Cathon.

Catonian (kəˈtəʊnɪən), *a.* and *sb.* [ad. L. *Catōniān-us*, f. *Cato* name of several celebrated Romans, *esp.* Cato the Censor, and his descendant Cato of Utica, both remarkable for the severity of their manners.]

A. *adj.* Pertaining to or resembling Cato; severe, stern, austere. **B.** *sb.* A follower of Cato.

1534 LD BERNERS *Gold. Bk. M. Aurel.* (1546) Bij, Catoniens, Peripateciens, Academiens. **1676** R. DIXON *Two Test.* 246 Be not.. morose, sullen.. nor of Catonian or lyrical Spirits. **1851** S. JUDD *Margaret* ii. (1871) 9 Her brother had a more catonian look.

So **Caˈtonic** *a.*, **Caˈtonically** *adv.*, **ˈCatonism**; also **ˈCatoism**.

1792 BURKE *Corr.* (1844) IV. 21 'I am weary of conjectures'—but I do not mean to end them Catonically [*i.e.* by suicide]. **1837** SYD. SMITH *Ballot* Wks. 1859 II. 309/2 All the penalties of austerity and Catonism. **1850** JAMES *Old Oak Chest* I. 119 The age of Catoism is passed away. **1883** AUSTIN DOBSON *Fielding* v. 131 The Catonic Thwackum drinks considerably more.

cat-o'-ˈnine-tails, *sb.* Also 8 **catanine-tails, cat-and-nine-tails,** 8–9 **cat-of-nine-tails,** (9 **cat with nine tails**). [see CAT 8: prob. the name was originally one of grim humour, in reference to its 'scratching' the back.]

1. A whip with nine knotted lashes; till 1881 an authorized instrument of punishment in the British navy and army.

1695 CONGREVE *Love for L.* (L.) If you should give such language at sea, you'd have a cat-o'-nine-tails laid cross your shoulders. **1707** J. STEVENS tr. *Quevedo's Com. Wks.* (1709) 208 He hung up the Catanine-tails. **1748** SMOLLETT *Rod. Rand.* xxvii, To whip him up with the Cat-and-nine-tails. **1763** *Chron.* in *Ann. Reg.* 90/2 The plaintiff received 300 lashes with a cat o' nine tails. **1806–7** J. BERESFORD *Miseries Hum. Life* (1826) XII. xxv, You would joyfully submit to the cat-and-nine-tails by way of a flapper to your dormant excitability. **1866** R. CHAMBERS *Ess.* Ser. I. 97 The disgusting operation of flaying a man alive with a cat-o'-nine-tails. **1879** *Daily News* 14 Aug. 5/2 A fac-simile of a cat-o'-nine-tails.. was exhibited.

fig. *a* **1726** VANBRUGH *False Friend* Prol. (T.) You awful cat-o'-nine-tails to the stage.

attrib. **1834** GEN. P. THOMPSON *Exerc.* (1842) III. 99 What is your cat-of-nine-tails man, in a battle or a storm?

2. A bulrush. (U.S.).

1858 O. W. HOLMES *Aut. Breakf. T.* (1883) 246 It swayed back and forward like a cat-o'-nine-tails (bulrush) with a bobolink on it. **1883** *Harper's Mag.* Dec. 100/1 A mossy bank with overhanging ferns and cat-o'-nine-tails.

Hence **cat-o'-nine-tail,** *v.* (*humorous*).

1796 SOUTHEY in *Life* (1849) I. 272 Must man be cat-a-ninetailed by care, until he shields himself in a shroud?

catopleb: see CATOBLEPAS.

†**catoptic.** *Obs. rare.* [? f. Gr. κάτοπτος to be seen, visible + -IC.] ? One skilled in optics.

1605 Z. JONES *Loyer's Spectres* 27 This do the Catoptikes themselves teach. **1656** BLOUNT *Glossogr. Catopticks*, professors of the Opticks or art speculative.

catoptric (kæˈtɒptrɪk), *a.* (*sb.*) [ad. Gr. κατοπτρικός of or in a mirror, f. κάτοπτρον mirror, f. κατά against + ὀπ- see + -τρον suffix of instrument.]

A. *adj.* Relating to a mirror or reflector, or to optical reflexion.

a **1774** GOLDSM. *Exper. Phil.* (1776) II. 340 There have been catoptric instruments formed for the amusement of philosophers. **1779** *Phil. Trans.* LXIX. 425 The telescope to which the catoptric micrometer is applied. **1831** BREWSTER *Optics* xli. 338 This catoptric lens, as it may be called. **1838** *Proc. Amer. Phil. Soc.* I. 97 The catoptric examination of the eye. **1862** ANSTED *Channel Isl.* I. ii. 33 The light-houses each having a catoptric light of the first order. **1867–77** G. CHAMBERS *Astron.* VII. i. 606.

B. *sb.* **1.** *pl.* **catoptrics** (formerly in *sing.*): That part of Optics which treats of reflexion.

1570 DEE *Math. Præf.* 20 That part hereof, which dealeth with Glasses.. is called Catoptrike. **1587** GOLDING *De Mornay* xxv. 447 He must gather together the Beames of the Skie in a mirrour, which they call Alchemusie, according to the rules of Catoptrik. **1667** *Phil. Trans.* II. 626 The Catoptricks, that have for their object, Rays Reflected. **1700** GREGORY in *Collect.* (Oxf. Hist. Soc.) I. 321 Catoptricks and Dioptricks. Where the effects of Mirrors and glasses are shewed. **1864** BURTON *Scot Abr.* II. i. 126.

†**2.** An instrument or apparatus for producing effects by reflexion. *Obs.*

1621 BURTON *Anat. Mel.* I. iii. III. (1651) 211 'Tis ordinarie to see strange uncouth figures by Catoptricks. **1644** EVELYN *Diary* 8 Nov., With Dutch patience, he shew'd us his perpetual motions, catoptrics, magnetical experiments.

catoptrical (kæˈtɒptrɪkəl), *a.* [f. as prec. + -AL[1].] Relating to a mirror or to reflexion; = prec. Hence **catoptrically** *adv.*

1696 *Phil. Trans.* XIX. 215 The Power of Catoptrical or Dioptrical or Cata-dioptrical Machines. **1754** *Ibid.* XLVIII. 622 Philosophers began to increase their catoptrical experiments. **1819** H. BUSK *Tea* 63 By catoptrical devise survey Stars. **1870** *Eng. Mech.* 501/3 It may be used catoptrically.

catoptromancy (kæˈtɒptrəˌmænsɪ). [f. Gr. κάτοπτρον mirror + μαντεία divination; see -MANCY.] Divination by means of a mirror.

1613 PURCHAS *Pilgr.* I. IV. v. 310 Catoptromancie received those resemblances in cleare glasses. *a* **1693** URQUHART *Rabelais* III. xxv. 207 Catoptromancy.. held in such account by the Emperor Didius Julianus. **1758** *Ann. Reg.*, *Charac.* 275/2 He.. understands all the mysteries of.. catoptromanchy, he having a magical glass to be consulted upon some extraordinary occasions. **1855** SMEDLEY *Occult. Sci.* 321 *Catoptromancy*, a species of divination by the mirror.

Hence **catoptroˈmantic** *a.*

†**cator(e, -tour,** var. of CATER, *Obs.*

catostomid (kəˈtɒstəmɪd), *sb.* and *a.* [ad. mod.L. *Catostomidæ*, f. *Catostomus*, the typical genus, f. Gr. κάτω down + στόμα mouth.] **A.** *sb.* A freshwater fish of the family Catostomidæ, found chiefly in North America, and including the suckers and buffalo fishes. **B.** *adj.* Of or pertaining to this family.

1889 in *Cent. Dict.* **1908** *Smithsonian Misc. Coll.* V. 97 This character suggests a cyprinid or a Catostomid. **1957** P. J. DARLINGTON *Zoogeography* i. 32 This is consistent with its [sc. *Myxocyprinus*] being a relict of an earlier Chinese catostomid fauna... The closest relatives of the catostomids are the cyprinids, the carps and their allies.

catpiece (ˈkætpiːs). *U.S.* [f. CAT *sb.*[1] + PIECE *sb.*] In logging, a perforated bar of wood fitting on the tops of uprights in floating booms, so that the space between the booms may be narrowed when necessary.

1905 in *Terms Forestry & Logging* 33.

cat's-cradle. Also **cat-cradle.** [Origin probably fanciful: the guess that it 'may have been' *cratch-cradle* is not founded on facts.]

A children's game in which two players alternately take from each other's fingers an intertwined cord so as always to produce a symmetrical figure.

1768 TUCKER *Lt. Nat.* (1852) I. 388 An ingenious play they call cat's cradle; one ties the two ends of a packthread together, and then winds it about his fingers, another with both hands takes it off perhaps in the shape of a gridiron, the first takes it from him again in another form, and so on alternately changing the packthread into a multitude of figures whose names I forget, it being so many years since I played at it myself. **1823** LAMB *Elia*, *Christ's Hosp.* 326 Weaving those ingenious parentheses called cat-cradles. **1867** TROLLOPE *Chron. Barset* II. lxvii. 246 Old Mr. Harding.. was in bed playing cat's-cradle with Posy.

attrib. **1824** *Edin. Rev.* XL. 84 One of those cats-cradle reasoners who never see a decided advantage in any thing but indecision. **1887** *Pall Mall G.* 29 Sept. 3/2 The senseless accidents, and cat's-cradle plots of old romance.

ˈcat's-eye. [In sense 2, prob. a translation: cf. F. *œil de chat*, It. *occhi de gatti*, Pg. *olhos de gatos*, Ger. *katzenauge*, etc.]

1. The eye of a cat; a cat-like eye.

1555 EDEN *Decades W. Ind.* (Arb.) 266 Stones lyke vnto cattes eyes. **1611** COTGR. s.v. *Chat*, *Oeil de chat*.. a cat-eye, or sight that is as good by night as in the day.

2. A precious stone, a variety of chalcedonic quartz, very hard and transparent, which, when cut *en cabochon*, displays, on being held to the light, a peculiar floating lustre, resembling the contracted pupil of a cat's eye, supposed to be caused by small parallel fibres of asbestos. The finest come from Ceylon and Malabar. Also *attrib.*

[**1555** EDEN *Decades W. Ind.* (Arb.) 265 They bore a fine hole in these [diamonds] throughe the myddest, wherby they appere lyke the eyes of a catte.] *a* **1599** HAKLUYT *Voy.* II. I. 226 It [Ceylon] bringeth foorth great store of Christall Cats eyes, or Ochi de Gati. **1704** *Collect. Voy.* (Churchill) III. 657/1 Called Olhos de Gatos, i.e. Cats-eyes, by the Portugueses. **1798** GREVILLE in *Phil. Trans.* LXXXVIII. 414 Reflection of light, which, in a polished state, gives varieties to the cat's eye, star-stone, sun-stone, etc. **1859** LANG *Wand. India* 70 Confined his purchases to a large cat's-eye ring. **1859** TENNENT *Ceylon* I. I. i. 37 The Cat's-eye is one of the jewels of which the Singhalese are especially proud. **1874** *Jrnl. Chem. Soc.* XXVII. 555 The so-called Cat's-eye and Fibrous Quartz. **1899** T. M. ELLIS (*title*) The three Cat's-eye Rings. **1903** *Daily Mail* 8 Sept. 7/4 A.. narrow edging of cat's-eye green.

3. A rural name of the Germander Speedwell, *Veronica Chamædrys*; also of the Forget-me-not, and various other small bright flowers.

1817 KEATS *Calidore*, The glow Of the wild cat's eyes. **1861** MISS PRATT *Flower. Pl.* IV. 96.

4. The calcareous operculum of turban shells, esp. the south Pacific *Turbo petholatus*.

1898 MORRIS *Austral Eng.* 83/1 *Cat's Eyes*.. the name given in Australia to the opercula of *Turbo smaragdus*. **1949** E. DE MAUNY *Huntsman in Career* ii. 70 He collected a pocketful of cats' eyes, and sat on a shelf of rock to watch the sea. **1962** ABBOTT & ZIM *Sea Shells of World* 32 Its [sc. *Turbo petholatus*] operculum is the famous blue-green 'cat's eye'.

5. One of the chain of light-reflecting studs used to demarcate traffic lanes on roads at night. Also *attrib.*

1940 *New Statesman* 20 Jan. 63/1 Few motorists.. in Oxfordshire will deny that the 'cats-eyes', with which the County Council has studded its main roads, are an improvement for night driving on the old white line. **1948** *Times* 4 Dec. 3/2 Drivers of vehicles.. had reason to challenge the decision of the Ministry of Transport.. to dispense with 'cat's eye' reflector studs in roads provided with street lighting. **1958** E. HYAMS *Taking it Easy* iv. 200 The endless chaplet of cat's eye reflectors.. was conjured out of the road's long darkness.

cat's-foot.

1. The foot of a cat; †used *lit.* in reference to the fable or tale of a monkey (or a fox) using the foot or paw of a cat to rake roasted chestnuts out of the burning coals.

(The story is told by some of a monkey belonging to Pope Julius II., 1503–13; see *N. & Q.* Ser. VI. VII. 286.)

[**1623** MABBE tr. *Aleman's Guzman d'Alf.* II. 167 To take the Cat by the foote, and therewith to rake the coales out of the Ouen.] *c* **1661** *Argyle's Last Will* in *Harl. Misc.* (1746) VIII. 30/1 Like the Monkey, that took the Cat's Foot to pull the Chesnut out of the Fire. **1666** PEPYS *Diary* 6 June, My Lord Brouncker, which I make use of as a monkey do the cat's foot. *c* **1680** *Humane Prudence* (1717) 214 The polite man makes use of others as the Fox did of the Cat's Foot, to pull the Apple out of the Fire.

†**2.** Hence *fig.* = CAT'S-PAW 2. *Obs.*

1675 PENN *Eng. Pres. Interest Disc.* 40 It is the Interest of Governours.. not to be the Cat's Foot. **1693** T. PITTS *West. Martyrol.* (1705) 7. **1699** B. E. *Dict. Cant. Crew*, *Tool*.. the Creature of any Cause.. or Cat's Foot.

3. A plant: **a.** Ground-ivy, *Nepeta Glechoma*. **b.** Mountain Cudweed, *Antennaria dioica*.

1597 GERARD *Herbal* I. ccc. 705 In English ground Iuie.. Tunehoofe, and Cats foote. **1758** J. S. *Le Dran's Observ. Surg.* (1771) 122 An Infusion made with the Head of white Poppies, Cat's-foot, Colt's-foot, and Maiden-hair. **1775** LIGHTFOOT *Flora Scot.* (1777) I. 470 Mountain Cudweed or Cats-Foot. **1878** in BRITTEN & HOLL. *Plant-n.* [Still used in both senses.]

cat's hair, cat-hair. [f. CAT + HAIR, in Fr. *poil de chat* (Cotgr.).]

†**1.** A kind of tumour or sore. *Obs.*

1552 HULOET, Cattes heere.. *furunculus*. **1562** TURNER *Herbal* II. (1568) 64 b, Cresses.. driueth furth.. sores such as one is called Cattis hare. **1585** LLOYD *Treas. Health* T iv, The sore y[t] is called a cattes heare & brekinge out in the fingers. **1611** COTGR., *Poil de chat*, a Cats haire. **1616** SURFL. & MARKH. *Countr. Farm* 116 Hard swellings, whether they be called cat-haires or cornes.

2. *Sc.* **a.** 'The down on the face of boys, before the beard grows'. **b.** 'The thin hair that often grows on the bodies of persons in bad health' (Jamieson).

cat's-head. **1.** 'A kind of apple' (J.).

1617 RIDER, A Cats head, *Pomum decumanum*. **1676** WORLIDGE *Cyder* (1691) 207 The Cats head, by some called the Go-no-further, is a very large Apple. **1767** ABERCROMBIE *Ev. Man own Gard.* (1803) 671/2 List of Fruit Trees. Apples.. French rennet, Cat's head, Leather-coat russet.

2. An ornament in Norman architecture.

1848 RICKMAN *Goth. Archit.* (ed. 5) xxiii, The doorway.. combines the zigzag, and cat's-head with the tooth ornament. **1853** *A.P.S. Dict. of Arch.* I, *Bird's Head ornament*, sometimes called *Bird's beak head*, and *Cat's head*

molding..decoration consisting of conventional heads of monsters generally terminating in a beard formed of one or more other heads, of foliage, or of beaks.

3. See CAT-HEAD *sb.*

†**cat-silver.** *Obs.* [In Ger. *Katzensilber*, Sw. *kattsilfver.* Mod.L. *argentum felium*; perh. with reference to its shining when it is nearly dark.] Mica with a silvery appearance.

1583 J. HIGINS tr. *Junius' Nomenclator* (N.) Hujus species est et..mica..Cat silver. **1677** PLOT *Oxfordsh.* 72 Whence I rather concluded it to be *argentum felium*, or Cat-silver, but that it would not shine in the dark. **1729** WOODWARD *Fossils* (J.) Catsilver..is of three sorts, the yellow or golden, the white or silvery, and the black. **1776** SEIFERTH *Gellert's Metal. Chym.* 10 Cat-silver, so the glimmer is called by the Germans, when it has the colour of..silver.

catskin, cat-skin (ˈkætskɪn).

1. a. The skin of the cat (wild or tame), used for fur, etc. Chiefly *attrib.*

1692 *Lond. Gaz.* No. 2805/4, 2 Purses, one a Catskin, and the other a colour'd Purse. **1805** SCOTT *Let.* in *Lockhart Life* (1839) II. 249 If Mrs. Ellis takes a fancy for cat-skin fur, now is the time. **1830** GEN. P. THOMPSON *Exerc.* (1842) I. 228 We want no more wars for cat-skins.

b. *catskin earl*, each of the three senior earls in the House of Lords, viz. the Earls of Shrewsbury, Derby, and Huntingdon.

1869 W. HOOK *Lives Abps.* 2nd Ser. III. iv. 264 The Earl of Huntingdon is one of the three catskin earls of the present day,—one of the first three earls in the House of Lords. **1926** G. E. COKAYNE *Complete Peerage* VI. 655 The robes of an Earl consist now of three rows of ermine, but in some early representations an Earl is depicted with four rows... It seems..probable that the four rows..may have given the name of *Catskin* (or Quatreskin) to the Earl of ancient creation whose robes were thus described.

2. †**a.** Short for a catskin bag (*obs.*). **b.** *slang.* An inferior kind of silk-hat.

1600 HEYWOOD *2 Edw. IV*, III. iii, (Enter Jockie, loden.) Heres her cat-skin till she come. **1857** HUGHES *Tom Brown* I. v, Tom is arrayed..in a regulation cat-skin at seven-and-sixpence.

cat's-meat (ˈkætsmiːt). The flesh of horses, etc., prepared and sold by street dealers as food for domestic cats. Also *attrib.*, as in *cat's-meat-man.*

1593 NASHE *Strange News* Ep. Ded. Wks. 1883–4 II. 180 We haue cattes meate and dogges meate inough for these mungrels. **1632** MASSINGER *Maid of Hon.* III. i, I will cry broom, or cat's-meat, in Palermo. **1826** in Hone *Every-day Bk.* II. 861, I saw her pass with her cats-meat barrow. **1836** DICKENS *Pickw.* xxxiii, Purveyor of cat's-meat to the Lord Mayor and Sheriffs. **1836** E. HOWARD *R. Reefer* lvi, A parcel of..dogs..following the catsmeat-man's barrow.

†ˈ**catso.** *slang. Obs.* Also catzo. [a. It. *cazzo*, membrum virile, also word of exclamation: Florio says 'also as *Cazzica*, interjection, 'what! gods me! god forbid! tush!'] Frequent in 17th c. in the Italian senses; also = Rogue, scamp. Cf. the later GADSO.

1602 B. JONSON *Ev. Man out Hum.* II. i, Nimble-spirited Catso's, that ha' their euasions at pleasure. **1606** *Wily beguiled* in Hazl. *Dodsley* IX. 285 Cunningly temporise with this cunning Catso. **1650** WELDON *Crt. Jas. I*, 99 Catzo. **1653** URQUHART *Rabelais* I. 39 Catso. **1671** *Haymarket Hectors* in *Roxb. Ballads* (1883) IV. 521 Catzo. **1708** MOTTEUX *Rabelais* v. viii. Cat-so! let us..drink.

cat's ˈpaw, ˈcat's-paw.

1. The paw of a cat; *fig.* that which comes down like the paw of a cat upon its victim.

1821 KEATS *Isabel* xvii, These Florentines..In hungry pride and gainful cowardice..Quick cat's-paws on the generous stray-away.

2. A person used as a tool by another to accomplish a purpose; see the earlier CAT'S-FOOT.

[**1657** M. HAWKE *Killing is Murder*, These he useth as the Monkey did the Cat's paw to scrape the nuts out of the fire.] **1785** GROSE *Dict. Vulgar T.*, *Tool*, cat's paw. **1817** in *Churchyard's Chippes* 165 *note*, Bothwell was merely the cat's-paw of Murray, Morton, and Maitland. **1837** RICHARDSON s.v. *Cat*, *Cat's-paw*, common in vulgar speech, but not in writing. **1877** MRS. FORRESTER *Mignon* I. 105, I am not going to be made a cat's paw of. **1883** *American* VI. 245 Making themselves mere catspaws to secure chestnuts for those publishers.

3. *Naut.* A slight and local breeze, which shows itself by rippling the surface of the sea.

1769 FALCONER *Dict. Marine* (1789), *Cats-paw*, a light air of wind perceived..by the impression made on the surface of the sea, which it sweeps very lightly, and then decays. **1835** MARRYAT *Jac. Faithf.* xxxix, Cat's-paws of wind, as they call them, flew across the water here and there, ruffling its smooth surface. **1851** LONGF. *Gol. Leg.* v. *At Sea*, Sudden flaws Struck the sea with their cat's-paws.

4. *Naut.* 'A twisting hitch, made in the bight of a rope, so as to induce two small bights, in order to hook a tackle on them both' (Smyth).

1794 [implied in vb., q.v.]. **1840** R. DANA *Bef. Mast* xxxiii. 125 When the mate came to shake the catspaw out of the down-haul. *c* **1860** H. STUART *Seaman's Catech.* 34 Make a cat's-paw in the fall of the luff.

ˈ**cat's-paw,** *v.* [f. prec. sb.]

Naut. **a.** Of the wind: To ruffle slightly and in part the surface of water. **b.** To make a catspaw in the bight of a rope; to join by a cat's-paw.

1794 *Rigging & Seamansh.* I. 217 A luff-tackle is cats-pawed to the other end of the sheet. **1853** KANE *Grinnell Exp.* ix. (1856) 69 The surface of the sea at this time was cat's-pawed as far as could be seen.

cat's tail, ˈcat's-tail. Also cat-tail.

1. The tail of a cat; a fur for the neck, so called.

1550 LEVER *Serm.* (Arb.) 131 Bryngynge home sylkes and sables, cat-tayls, and folyshe fethers to fil the realm full of such baggage. **1578** LYTE *Dodoens* VI. lvi. 730 Yellowe ragged things compact of certayne scales, hanging vpon the tree, like smal Cattes tayles. **1731–7** MILLER *Gard. Dict.*, *Catkins*..join'd together in Form of a Rope or Cat's-tail.

2. A name given to several plants from the resemblance of parts to the tail of a cat.

†**a.** ? The Great Mullein, *Verbascum Thapsus.*

c **1450** *Alphita* (Anecd. Oxon.) 68 Flosmus..tapsus barbatus..angl. feltwort uel cattestayl. **1483** *Cath. Angl.* 55 A Cattyle [*v.r.* Catalle], *lanugo, herba est.*

b. The Reed-Mace, *Typha latifolia*; from the long cylindrical furry spikes which form its fruit.

1548 TURNER *Names of Herbes* 79 It is called in englishe cattes tayle or reed-mace. **1578** LYTE *Dodoens* IV. liii. 512 Typha palustris, Reede Mace, Cattes tayle, or Water torche. *Ibid.* 513 This plant yeeldeth his cattes tayles. **1597** GERARD *Herbal* (1633) 46 (L.). **1612** DRAYTON *Poly-olb.* xx, Cat-tails ..which from the sedge doth grow. **1794** MARTYN *Rousseau's Bot.* xxviii. 430 The greater, or broad-leaved Cat's-tail, otherwise called Reed-Mace. **1873** MISS BROUGHTON *Nancy* II. 109 The tall cat's tails, and all the flags, stand absolutely motionless.

c. The Horse-tail, *Equisetum.*

1552 HULOET, Cattes tayle, herbe, which some cal horse taile, *cauda equina, equisetum.* **1649** BLITHE *Eng. Improv. Impr.* (1652) 26 So bad and boggy it was that..it bore nothing but Cattayles. **1880** JEFFERIES *Gt. Estate* 25 She pulled the 'cat's-tails', as she learned to call the horse-tails, to see the stem part at the joints.

†**d.** Viper's Bugloss, *Echium vulgare.* **e.** Monk's-hood, *Aconitum Napellus.* **f.** Horse-tail Rush, *Eriophorum vaginatum.* **g.** = Cat's-tail grass (see 3).

1538 TURNER *Libellus*, Cattes tayle, *cirsion.* **1551** —— *Herbal* I. (1568) 29 Thys herbe is called in some places of Englande cattys tayles, in other places wylde buglose. **1789** D. DAVIDSON *Poems* 10 (Jam.) The cat-tails whiten through the verdant bog: All vivifying Nature does her work. **1789** MRS. PIOZZI *Journ. France* II. 229 Slopes all flourishing with cat's-tail and poppy. **1837** W. IRVING *Capt. Bonneville* (1849) 329. **1861** MISS PRATT *Flower. Pl.* VI. 63 Alpine Cat's-tail.

3. *cat's-tail grass*: the name of the genus *Phleum*; esp. *P. pratense*, one of the earliest and most productive of British grasses, Timothy Grass.

1597 GERARD *Herbal* I. viii. 11 Great Cats-taile Grasse hath very small roots. **1794** MARTYN *Rousseau's Bot.* xiii. 133 [Of] Cat's-tail grass..the spike..seems rough. **1863** BARING-GOULD *Iceland* 242 Among the marshes I found the alpine catstail grass.

4. A catkin.

[Cf. **1578** in 1.] **1611** COTGR., *Minons*, Cat-tailes, or Catkins: the long aglet-like buds of nut-trees. **1656** DUGARD *Gate Lat. Unl.* §119 In the Hazel the Cats-tail [breaketh out] before the budding. **1721** BAILEY, *Cats-tail*, a Substance, growing upon Nut-trees, Pines, etc. **1875** PARISH *Sussex Dial.*, *Cats Tails*, the male blossom of hazel or willow.

5. *Naut.* The inner end of the CAT-HEAD *sb.* (sense 1).

cat-stairs. *dial.* and *U.S.* Also cat's-. [CAT *sb.*[1] 19.] (See quots.)

1825 JAMIESON *Suppl.*, *Cat's-stairs*, a plaything for children, made of thread, small cord, or tape, which is so disposed by the hands as to fall down like steps of a stair, Dumfr., Gall. **1828** CARR *Dial. Craven* (ed. 2) 64 *Cat-stairs*, Tape, &c. so twisted, that by its alternate hollows and projections, it resembles stairs. **1886** *Leslie's Pop. Monthly* XXI. 150/1 'Twere vain to tell what sylvan treasures accumulated in our back yard that summer. The flights of catstairs [etc.].

ˈ**cat-stick.** A stick or bat used in the games of tip-cat and trap-ball.

a **1626** MASSINGER *Women beware W.* I. ii, Prithee, lay up my cat and cat-stick safe. *a* **1652** BROME *New Acad.* III. ii. Wks. 1873 II. 61 That gall their hands with stool-balls, or their Cat-sticks. **1690** B. E. *Dict. Cant. Crew*, *Catstick*, used by Boies at Trap-ball. **1721** MRS. CENTLIVRE *Perpl. Lovers* III, E'gad my legs are fall'n away to catsticks! **1748** RICHARDSON *Clarissa* (1811) IV. iv. 16 Armed with prongs, pitchforks, clubs, and catsticks.

catsup = CATCHUP and KETCHUP.

cat-tail: see CAT'S TAIL.

cattalo, var. CATALO.

catted (ˈkætɪd), *ppl. a.* See CAT *v.* 1. So ˈ**catting** *vbl. sb.*

1867 SMYTH *Sailor's Word-bk.*, *Catting*, the act of heaving the anchor by the cat-tackle. **1883** *Man. Seamanship for Boys' Training Ships* 210 When stowing the anchor for sea after the second catting. **1901** *Daily Chron.* 12 June 7/2 The 'catted' port anchor of the schooner.

†**cattelmute.** *Sc. Law. Obs.* See CAPILMUTE.

catter, catterhe, obs. Sc. forms of CATARRH.

catterpillar, -wall, -waul, etc.: see CATER-.

ˈ**cattery** (ˈkætərɪ). Also 8 catery. [f. CAT + -ERY.] An establishment of cats.

1791 HUDDESFORD *Salmag., Death Dick* 133 Enshrin'd celestial Cateries among, the sable Matron. **1830** SOUTHEY *Lett.* (1856) IV. 171 All the royal Cattery of Cats' Eden. **1834–43** —— *Doctor* 684 (D.) An evil fortune attended all our attempts at re-establishing a cattery.

cattily (ˈkætɪlɪ), *adv.* [f. CATTY *a.* + -LY[2].] In a catty manner.

1924 N. COWARD *Rat Trap* III. 59 *Naomi*: I'm sure her Cockney humour is inimitable (cattily). **1946** R. MACAULAY *They went to Portugal* 307 Shaw..added, rather cattily, that though the Lancers were in very good order and looked smart, they were seldom in contact with the enemy.

cattimandoo (kætɪˈmænduː). Also **cattemundoo, kattimundoo, callemundoo.** [Telugu *kattimandu*, the name of the plant.] A resinous substance obtained from the milky juice of *Euphorbia cattimandoo* or other species of *Euphorbia*; used as a cement and as a medicine for rheumatism. **b.** The plant from which the gum is obtained.

1851 *Catal. Gt. Exhib.* IV. i. 877/2 Cutteemundoo, or Kattimundoo gum. **1858** SIMMONDS *Dict. Trade*, Cattemundoo, Callemundoo. **1880** *Encycl. Brit.* XI. 339/2 Many of the euphorbias yield milky juices... The chief among these are the cattimandoo..and the Indian spurge tree.

ˈ**cattiness.** [f. CATTY *a.* + -NESS.] = CATTISHNESS.

1920 *19th Cent.* Nov. 752 Her antagonism to her own sex —known colloquially as 'cattiness'. **1928** *Sunday Express* 6 May 4 Manx folk are wonderfully good-natured,..and cattiness..is practically non-existent. **1951** R. KNOX *Stimuli* III. v. 98 It is not an impossible Lenten resolution to give up..the delights of saying 'I told you so': to cut from our conversation..the spirit which I think St. Paul..would probably have labelled 'cattiness'.

†ˈ**catting,** *vbl. sb. Obs.* Also 7 **cating, cateing.** [as if f. vb. *cat.*] Caterwauling; going after the opposite sex (*contemptuously*).

1681 COLVIL *Whig's Suppl.* (1695) 116 The language us'd by Catts, When in the Night they go a Cating. *c* **1684** *Elegy Lady Stair* in Law *Mem.* (1818) 228 (Jam.) A strange unluckie fate..Which sent her [a cat] thus a cateing into hell. **1725** *New Cant. Dict.*, *Catting*, Whoring.

¶ Also in other senses of CAT *v.*, q.v.

cattish (ˈkætɪʃ), *a.* [f. CAT *sb.*[1] + -ISH[1].]

a. Belonging to or resembling a cat; feline.

1598 FLORIO, *Gattino*, of a cat kinde, cattish. *c* **1630** DRUMM. OF HAWTH. *Phillis on Death of Sparrow* Wks. (1711) 50 Vengeance falling on the cattish race. **1818** LAMB *Prince Dorus* 5 All her cattish gestures plainly spoke. **1877** BLACKIE *Wise Men* 95 Flaring cattish eyes.

b. Of a sly or spiteful character. (Cf. CAT *sb.*[1] 2.)

1883 W. BLACK *Yolande* III. vii. 127 The cattish temper of an old woman. **1893** E. E. SALTUS *Madam Sapphira* 15 The stealthy air and cattish smile of the mother.

Hence ˈ**cattishly** *adv.*, in a cattish manner or spirit; ˈ**cattishness**, the quality of being 'cattish', spitefulness.

1894 MEREDITH *Ld. Ormont* III. iv. 69 Thither he walked ..prepared for cattishness. **1907** *Daily Chron.* 8 July 3/2 Thus..was Mrs. Steel's cattishness brought home to her. **1909** *Westm. Gaz.* 8 June 3/2 Elizabeth, we are afraid, is developing into a little 'cat', as her female friends would probably say... That is where the 'cattishness' of Elizabeth shows itself. **1913** W. OWEN *Let.* 7 Nov. (1967) 207, I drank milk so doggedly, (or cattishly) even with raw egg in it, that strength has returned. **1923** M. ARLEN *These Charming People* 180 'Society Hostess Robbed.' It's almost worth it for her, he thought cattishly, to be called a Society Hostess. **1938** R. G. COLLINGWOOD *Princ. Art* v. 87 The biographies of cattishness, whose aim is to release the reader from the irksome reverence..for persons who were important in their day. **1967** J. GARDNER *Madrigal* iii. 58 The sergeant turned out to be cattishly agile.

cattle (ˈkæt(ə)l), *sb.* Forms: 3–5 (occas. 6) catel, (4 cadel, catil, catele, cathel, katel, -ell, ketele, 4–5 (occas. 6–7) catell, catelle, 4–6 catayl, 5 catail, catayll(e, catal, -ale, 5–8 -all); 6–8 cattel, cattell, (6–7 cattal, -all, cattaile, 6 cattayle); 7– cattle. See also CHATTEL. [ME. *catel*, a. ONF. *catel* (= central OF. *chatel*, Pr. *captal*, *capdal*):—late L. *captāle*, L. *capitāle*, neuter of the adj. *capitālis* head-, principal, CAPITAL, used subst. in mediæval times in the sense 'principal sum of money, capital, wealth, property'; cf. mod. Eng. CAPITAL = stock in trade. Thus Papias has '*capitale*, caput pecuniæ, capitis summa', the Catholicon '*capitale*, pecunia'. Under the feudal system the application was confined to movable property or wealth, as being the only 'personal' property, and in English it was more and more identified with 'beast held in possession, live stock', which was almost the only use after 1500, exc. in the technical phrase 'goods and catells (cattals)' which survived till the 17th c. In legal Anglo-French, the Norman *catel* was superseded at an early period by the Parisian *chatel*; this continued to be used in the earlier and wider sense (subject however to legal

definition), and has in modern times passed into a certain current use as CHATTEL, so that the phrase just cited is now also since 16th c. 'goods and chattels'. Down to 1500 the typical spelling was *catel*; in the 16th c. this became *cattel*, *cattell*; only since 1600, and chiefly since 1700, spelt *cattle*. As this spelling is never found in earlier use, and, hence, never in the earlier sense, it would be possible to treat this sense as a separate word *Catel*, property; but on the other hand the modern sense has all the forms *catel*, *cattel(l*, *cattle*, according to date, and the history is better elucidated by treating the word as a historical whole. CHATTEL, however, as a distinct modern form and sense, is dealt with in its own place.

OF. (besides the *ch-* forms, for which see CHATTEL) had, according to dialect and date, the forms *catel*, *katel*, *cathel*, *cateul*, *cateil*. Hence the ME. variants *cathel*, *catail*, *-ayl*. The Norman word was again latinized as *catellum*, *catallum*, the latter esp. current in English law-Latin, whence the forms *catal(l*, *cattal(l*, so frequent in 15–16th c., esp. in the legal phrase 'goods and cattals'.]

†**I.** Property, article of property, chattel. *Obs.* (Forms *catel*, *cattel(l*.)

†**1. a.** Property, substance; strictly personal property or estate, wealth, goods. *Obs.*

c **1275** LAY. 30673 He nam tonnes [gode] and þat catel [**1205** æhte] dude [þer] ine. *a* **1300** *Sarmun* 46 in *E.E.P.* (1862) 6 Siþ þat þe world nis noȝt and catel nis bot vanite. *c* **1300** *Cursor M.* 27934 It wastes bodi and als catel [*v.r.* ketele]. *c* **1325** *Metr. Hom.* (1862) 131 An unseli knafe That wald gladli katel have. **1387** TREVISA *Higden* VI. ix, Clerkes .. spende the catayle of holy chyrche in other places at theyr owne wille. ? *a* **1400** *Manuale Sarisb.*, *Sponsalia* in Maskell *Mon. Rit.* (1882) I. 58 With all my worldely cathel I the endowe. *a* **1400** *Relig. Pieces fr. Thornton MS.* (1867) 6 Robes or reches or oþer catell. *c* **1440** *Promp. Parv.* 63 Catelle [*K.* catal], *catalum*, *census*. **1495** W. DE WORDE ed. *Barth. De P.R.* III. iii. 57 By loue of worldly catall.

†**b.** Money; *esp.* capital, as distinct from interest.

c **1330** *Amis & Amil.* 1855 Al her catel than was spent Saue tvelf pans. *a* **1340** HAMPOLE *Psalter* xiv. 6 He þat gaf noght his katel til okyre. **1340** *Ayenb.* 36 Þet hi habbe huet cas yualle: hire catel sauf. **1483** CAXTON *Gold. Leg.* 267/1 Fader I haue wonne nothyng but haue lost your catayll.

†**c.** *fig. Obs.*

1388 WYCLIF *Ecclus.* xxx. 15 No catel is aboue the catel [**1382** monee] of helthe of bodi. *c* **1400** MAUNDEV. Prol. 2 More precious Catelle, ne gretter Ransoum ne myghte he put for us then his blessede body.

†**d.** Sometimes used in conjunction with other terms for 'property': see 3.

1387 TREVISA *Higden* (Rolls) I. 229 Þey þat .. gadereþ money and corn and catel of oþer men. **1393** GOWER *Conf.* II. 128 Of golde, of catel, or of londe. *c* **1394** *P. Pl. Crede* 116 Oþer catell oþer cloþ to coveren wiþ our bones.

e. *fig.* Rubbish, trash. (But cf. *1 Cor.* ix. 9.)

1643 MILTON *Divorce* iv. (1851) 28 Certainly not the meere motion of carnall lust, not the meer goad of a sensitive desire; God does not principally take care for such cattell.

†**2. a.** As an *individual sing.* = CHATTEL, with *collective pl.* originally in association with 'goods' or other pl. noun. *Obs.*

This use was evidently derived from law-Latin, in which *catallum*, *catalla* were so used. Cf. *cum suis catallis omnibus mobilibus*, cited by Du Cange, from *Leg. Edw. Conf.* p. 894, and the phrase *melius catallum* the best chattel, *droit de meilleur catel*, the heriot, *ibid.*

1477 EARL RIVERS (Caxton) *Dictes* 68 Sapience .. can not be lost as other catalles and wordely goodes may. **1502** ARNOLDE *Chron.* (1811) 245 The residew of alle my goodis, catellis, and dettis. **1641** *Termes de la Ley* 49 Catals comprehend in it selfe all goods mooveable & immooveable, except such as are in nature of freehold .. Catals are either reall or personall. **1644** *Jus Populi* 37 The condition of a slave is worse than of a beast or any inanimate Cattels. **1720** *Stow's Surv.* (ed. Strype 1754) II. v. xxvi. 457/1 That they ought not to be taxed of their rents and Catalls.

†**b.** *fig.* (see 1 c.) *Obs.*

1489 CAXTON *Faytes of A.* III. xv. 203 They setten in aduenture so dere a catell as is .. the lyffe. **1567** *Wills & Inv. N.C.* (1835) I. 273 Superstitions and feyned cattells onlye deuised to illud the symple and vnlerned.

3. Often used in the phrase ***goods and cattel***; later more frequently ***goods and cattels***, of which the extant form is *goods and chattels*: see CHATTEL.

As in this sense the form *cattals* is specially prevalent, it looks like a translation of a legal Anglo-Lat. *bona et catalla*. Du Cange quotes from *Leg. Edw. Conf.* c. 35 Cum decimis omnium terrarum, ac bonorum aliorum sive catallorum.

c **1430** *Freemasonry* 468 Take here goodes and here cattelle Unto the kynges hond, everydelle. **1436** *Test. Ebor.* (1855) II. 76 Y^e residewe of all my godes and my catell. **1464** in *Paston Lett.* 493 II. 167 The administracion of the goods and catell. **1495** *Act 11 Hen. VII*, xlv, Londes, tenementes, godes, catail, and all other the premysses.

1418 *E.E. Wills* (1882) 35 The Residue of alle my Godes and my Catallys mebles. **1450** in *Paston Lett.* 107 I. 144 Whiche riotous peple .. bare awey alle the goodes and catalx. **1454** in Ellis *Orig. Lett.* II. 38 I. 121 And toke godes and catals. **1528** in W. H. Turner *Select. Rec. Oxford* 61 Y^e goods or catells of ye said schollers. **1597** *1st Pt. Return fr. Parnass.* I. i. 185 It's all the goods and cattels thy father lefte thee. **1660** R. COKE *Power & Subj.* 211 All contributions to the see of Rome .. were forbidden upon pain of forfeiture of all the goods and cattals for ever.

¶ The transition to sense 4 is seen in the following:

1529 FRITH *Pistle to Chr. Reader* 10 Commaunded to destroye the Kynge of Amelech and all his goodes, howbeit he spared the kinges liffe & ye fayrest goodes & catelles, makinge sacrifice with them. **1547** *Homilies* I. *Falling from God* I, Y^t he should kyl al the amalechites, and destroye them clerely with their goodes and cattals: yet he .. saued .. all the chief of their cattall [*ed.* **1574** *has* cattel, cattell], therwith to make sacrifice.

II. Live stock. (Forms *catel*, *cattel(l*, *cattle*.)

4. a. A collective name for live animals held as property, or reared to serve as food, or for the sake of their milk, skin, wool, etc.

The application of the term has varied greatly, according to the circumstances of time and place, and has included camels, horses, asses, mules, oxen, cows, calves, sheep, lambs, goats swine, etc. The tendency in recent times has been to restrict the term to the bovine genus, but the wider meaning is still found locally, and in many combinations. As this sense was originally comprised under 1, distinct instances before 1500 are scarce.

a **1300** *Cursor M.* 6002 Hors, asse, mule, ox, camell, Dun þan deid all þair catell. **1375** BARBOUR *Bruce* XVIII. 274 Bot cattell haf thai fundyn nane, Outane a kow that wes haltand. *c* **1425** WYNTOUN *Cron.* I. xiii. 8 And tyl all catale pasture gwde. **1523** FITZHERB. *Husb.* §37 Shepe in myne opynyon is the mooste profytablest cattell that any man can haue. **1535** FISHER *Wks.* I. (1876) 391 When hee goeth to hys pastures to see hys Cattayle. **1577** B. GOOGE *Heresbach's Husb.* (1586) 125 b, The Camel is cheefly used in ye east parts, which some suppose to be the serviceablest cattell for man that is. *Ibid.* 153 b, The Dogge (though the Lawyer alloweth him not in the number of cattel) and though he yeeldes of himselfe no profite, yet is he .. to be esteemed. **1580** SIDNEY *Arcadia* III. 400 Blithe were the common cattell of the field. **1604** E. G[RIMSTON] *D'Acosta's Hist. Indies* III. xvi. 170 There are great numbers of cattell, especially swine. **1607** TOPSELL *Four-f. Beasts* 183 The goatherds of the countrey do give thereof to their cattel. **1650** FULLER *Pisgah.* II. ii. 80 How came the Gadarens, being undoubtedly Jews .. to keep such a company of useless cattell [= swine]? **1697** DRYDEN *Virg. Georg.* III. 590 Is Wool thy Care? Let not thy Cattle go .. where Burs and Thistles grow. **1741–2** *Act 15 & 16 Geo. II*, xxxiv, By cattle, in this act, is to be understood any bull, cow, ox, steer, bullock, heifer, calf, sheep, and lamb, and no other cattle whatever. **1767** A. YOUNG *Farmer's Lett. People* 297 Cattle of no kind will thrive but in the master's eye. *a* **1856** LONGF. *Psalm of Life*, Be not like dumb driven cattle, Be a hero in the strife. **1875** JEVONS *Money* (1878) 89 The former use of cattle as a medium of exchange.

†**b.** Extended to fowls, bees, etc. *Obs.* or *arch.*

c **1420** *Pallad. on Husb.* I. 1057 So made that lysardes may not ascende, Ne wicked worme this catell [bees] for to offende. **1577** B. GOOGE *Heresbach's Husb.* (1586) 163 I wilnot refuse to shew you somwhat also of my feathered cattel. **1589** R. HARVEY *Pl. Perc.* 17 Take heed, thine owne Cattaile sting thee not. **1622** MABBE tr. *Aleman's Guzman D'Alf.* I. 139 In breeding of Cattell, as Pigs, Hens, and Chickens, and the like. **1830** CARLYLE *Misc.* (1857) II. 129 Among all manner of bovine, swinish and feathered cattle.

c. Now usually confined to, or understood of, bovine animals.

1555 EDEN *Decades W. Ind.* I. x. (Arb.) 104 Neat or cattall becoome of bygger stature. **1570** LEVINS *Manip.* 55 Cattel, *boves, jumenta.* **1605** CAMDEN *Rem.* 1 Replenished with cattell both tame and wilde. **1673** RAY *Journ. Low C.* 57 Their Horse and Cattel. **1756** *Gentl. Mag.* XXVI. 73 Fair for the sale of black cattle once a fortnight .. There is belonging to Chillingham Castle a large park where there is a kind of wild cattle which are all white. **1836** *Penny Cycl.* VI. 378/2 In the usual acceptation of the word [cattle] it is confined to the ox. **1887** *Daily News* 11 Jan. 2/4 A fair demand for both cattle and sheep.

d. In the language of the stable, applied to horses.

a **1680** BUTLER *Rem.* (1759) I. 224 Such as a Carrier makes his Cattle wear, And hangs for Pendents in a Horse's Ear. **1733** FIELDING *Quix. in Eng.* I. iii, Your worship's cattle are saddled. **1750** COVENTRY *Pompey Litt.* II. iv. (1785) 58/1 He kept a phaeton chaise, and four 'bay cattle'. **1826** SCOTT *Woodst.* xxxii. **1835** SIR G. STEPHEN *Search of Horse* ii. 34 All the disabled cattle of the summer stages to Brighton, Southampton, and so forth. **1886** J. S. WINTER *In Quarters*, To cast reflections unfavorable to .. the color of their uniform, the class of their cattle.

e. Applied by slaveholders to their slaves.

1850 MRS. STOWE *Uncle Tom's C.* xxxiii, What have any of you cussed cattle to do with thinking what's right?

5. a. Used also as an ordinary plural of number. †**b.** *rarely* as a singular = beast, ox, etc.

1624 CAPT. SMITH *Virginia* IV. 123 We found there in all one hundred twentie eight cattell. **1725** *Minute Bk. Soc. Antiq.* (Brand s.v. *Funerals*), A hundred black cattle are killed. **1796** W. MARSHALL *Yorksh.* (ed. 2) I. 158 A cattle, when it goes into a drinking pit .. throws the chief part of its weight upon its fore feet.

6. With attributes; ***neat cattle***, ***horned cattle***: oxen, bovine animals. ***black cattle***: 'oxen, bulls, and cows' (J.); prob. at first properly applied to the black breeds found in the highlands of Scotland, Wales, and other districts, to which it is still by some restricted, but as other colours appear in the progeny of these, the name has come to have a general application.

1535 COVERDALE *1 Kings* iv. 23 Ten fat oxen, and twenty small catell, and an hundreth shepe. **1701** *Col. Rec. Penn.* II. 27 That there shall be no neat Cattle kill'd. **1725** *Min. Book Soc. Antiq.* 21 July (Brand), After the body [of a Highland chief] is interred, a hundred black cattle and two or three hundred sheep are killed for the entertainment of the company. **1753** CHAMBERS *Cycl. Supp.* s.v. *Cattle*, Black Cattle more particularly denotes the cow kind. These are also denominated neat cattle. **1781** GIBBON *Decl. & F.* II. xlii. 555 Their sheep and horned cattle were large and numerous. **1803** J. BRISTED *Pedest. Tour* II. 450 We now turned due west over the mountains, and .. met some black-cattle drovers. **1815** SCOTT *Guy M.* iv, Green pastures, tenanted chiefly by herds of black cattle, then the staple commodity of the country. **1836** *Penny Cycl.* VI. 378/2 [Cattle] In the usual acceptation .. is confined to the ox, or what is called black cattle or horned cattle. But as many varieties are not black, and several have no horns, the name neat cattle is more appropriate. **1864** D. MITCHELL *Wet Days at Edgew.* 257 Known for his stock of neat cattle. **1868** G. DUFF *Pol. Surv.* 209 The horned cattle, horses, and sheep are remarkably fine.

7. In various extended uses; mostly contemptuous: **a.** of vermin, insects, and the like. ? *Obs.*

1616 SURFL. & MARKH. *Countr. Farm* 170 In the holes of this wicked cattell [Rats]. *Ibid.* 318 Lizards and serpents, and other noysome cattell. *a* **1656** BP. HALL *Invis. World* III. iii, Doth he fetch frogs out of Nilus? .. they can store Egypt with loathsome cattle as well as he. **1639** T. DE GRAY *Compl. Horsem.* 100 It hath caused the Horse to voyd many of these bad Cattle [worms]. **1673** CAVE *Prim. Chr.* II. vii. 169 Flies, Wasps, and such little Cattel. **1685** R. BURTON *Eng. Emp. Amer.* iv. 86 Tame Cattel they have none except lice.

b. of men and women, with reference to various preceding senses. *arch.*

1579 GOSSON *Sch. Abuse* (Arb.) 27 We haue infinite Poets, and Pipers, and suche peeuishe cattel among vs in Englande, that liue by merrie begging. **1600** SHAKS. *A.Y.L.* III. ii. 435 Boyes and women are .. cattle of this colour. **1682** EVELYN *Diary* 24 Jan., The Dutchess of Portsmouth, Nelly, .. concubines, and cattell of that sort, as splendid as jewells .. could make them. **1690** B. E. *Dict. Cant. Crew*, *Sad Cattle*, Impudent Lewd Women. **1768** H. WALPOLE *Hist. Doubts* 11 To have consulted astrologers and such like cattle. **1823** SCOTT *Peveril* xx, To sweep this north country of such like cattle [priests].

III. *Attrib.* and *Comb.* (all belonging to branch II, and referring mainly to bovine animals).

8. General relations: **a.** objective or obj. gen. with verbal sb. or agent noun, as ***cattle-breeder***, ***-breeding***, ***-dealer***, ***-driving***, ***-drover***, ***-farming***, ***-hougher***, ***-houghing***, ***-killing***, ***-maiming***, ***-raiding***, ***-raiser***, ***-raising***, ***-rearing***, ***-rustler***, ***-rustling***, ***-stealing***, ***-thief***.

1827 WHATELY *Logic* in *Encycl. Metrop.* (1845) 234/1 Bakewell, the celebrated *cattle-breeder. **1877** tr. *Tiele's Hist. Relig.* 17 Without neglecting *cattle-breeding and agriculture. **1824** MISS MITFORD *Village* Ser. I. (1863) 103 A rich and liberal *cattle-dealer in the neighbourhood. **1878** SIMPSON *Sch. Shaks.* I. 60 If *cattle-driving was to be interpreted as levying war. **1806** FORSYTH *Beauties Scotl.* IV. 260 The object of *cattle-farming is chiefly breeding. **1886** *Pall Mall G.* 8 May 1/1 Executing the just judgment of offended Heaven upon *cattle-houghers, traitors, and assassins. **1831** SOUTHEY *Lett.* (1856) IV. 217 B —— .. is literally a *cattlejobber. **1907** *Westm. Gaz.* 6 Sept. 5/1 The renewed outbreak of *cattle-maiming in this parish [*sc.* Great Wyrley]. **1965** K. H. CONNELL in *Pop. in Hist.* xvii. 433 Arson and murder, the boycott and cattle-maiming were some of their weapons. **1899** *Daily News* 13 Nov. 7/4 The real object of this *cattle-raiding expedition. **1853** 'P. PAXTON' *Yankee in Texas* 122 He lived on the frontier amid the Ingens, and *cattle-raisers. **1896** *Daily News* 16 Jan. 5/6 All the victims were well-known cattle-raisers. **1878** I. L. BIRD *Lady's Life in Rocky Mts.* (1879) x. 170 Perry's Park is one of the great *cattle-raising ranches in Colorado. **1883** *Athenæum* 2 June 693 In Galicia cattle-raising is rapidly superseding tillage. **1923** *Daily Mail* 15 Feb. 8 A great crisis has fallen upon the cattle-raising industry of this Republic. **1953** E. SMITH *Guide to Eng. Trad.* 3 Some livestock farmers .. specialize in sheep-rearing rather than in cattle-raising. **1872** YEATS *Techn. Hist. Comm.* 37 *Cattle-rearing formed an important branch of Egyptian agriculture. **1903** A. ADAMS *Log Cowboy* vii. 86 The stampede .. was the work of *cattle rustlers. **1907** S. E. WHITE *Arizona Nights* I. iii. 60 We .. saw the beginning of the cattle rustling. **1960** *Farmer & Stockbreeder* 15 Mar. 75/1 The alleged case of cattle-rustling. **1803** *Edin. Rev.* I. 404 The renown of *cattle-stealers. **1862** T. E. DEVOE *Market Bk.* I. 172 A foraging party, under .. the city's former governor .. extensively known as a '*Cattle Thief'. **1903** A. ADAMS *Log Cowboy* vii. 101 The biggest cattle-thief ever born in Medinah County.

b. attrib., as ***cattle-cabbage***, ***-camp*** (CAMP *sb.*^{2} 4 c), ***-close***, ***-country***, ***-culture***, ***-dropping***, ***-farm***, ***-feed***, ***-food***, ***-herd***, ***-kraal***, ***-market***, ***-park***, ***-path***, ***-pen***, ***-show***, ***-track***, ***-trade***, ***-trough***, ***-yard***, etc.; (connected with the transport of cattle), as ***cattle-boat***, ***-car***, ***-ship***, ***siding***, ***-steamer***, ***-train***, ***-truck***, ***-wagon***, etc. **c.** instrumental and parasynthetic, as ***cattle-specked***, ***-sprent***, etc.; ***cattle-proof*** adj. **d.** ***cattle-farm*** vb. (*rare*).

1860 SALA *Make your Game* 14 Not a *cattle-boat luckily, though, in some pens forward, there were a few sheep. **1889** C. EDWARDES *Sardinia* 375 This Black Hole of a cattle-boat. **1945** WYNDHAM LEWIS *Let.* 13 Mar. (1963) 381 There still is no alternative: a cattle-boat .. or stop here. **1900** H. LAWSON *Verses Pop. & Humorous* 219 The old bark-school .. Is a *cattle-camp in winter. **1931** V. PALMER *Separate Lives* 122 Its wild horns and glossy red coat had become a familiar figure on the cattle-camp when he mustered to cut out the half-yearly mob of fats. **1864** C. H. COOKE *Let.* 4 May in *Wisconsin Mag. Hist.* (1921) V. 65 We took the train for Chattanooga. Our cars were *cattle cars. **1951** M. MCLUHAN *Mech. Bride* 23/1 Why doesn't somebody write of a last-minute gamble for happiness in a cattle car headed for Buchenwald? **1865** MISS CARY *Ball. & Lyrics* 5 She .. found him In the dusty *cattle-close. **1886** T. ROOSEVELT in *Cent. Mag.* July 340/1 The *cattle country of western Dakota. **1943** *Collier's* 28 Aug. 11/1 This stirring tale of the cattle country. **1886** *Bazaar* 18 Oct. 415 We devote the greatest attention to oyster-culture, bee-culture, *cattle-culture. **1810** F. CLATER (*title*), Every Man his own *Cattle Doctor. **1883** G. C. DAVIES *Norfolk Broads* xxxiv. (1884) 267 In a place where *cattle-droppings were abundant. **1881** MRS. PRAED *Policy & P.* I. 51 He *cattle-farms a few thousand acres. **1832** HT. MARTINEAU *Demerara* iii. 34 We have the *cattle-feed to gather. **1821** in Cobbett *Rur. Rides* (1885) I. 29 My .. system of *cattle-food husbandry. **1844**

MARG. FULLER *Woman 19th C.* (1862) 45 Penelope is no more meant for a baker or a weaver solely than Ulysses for a *cattle-herd. **1897** J. BRYCE *Impressions S. Afr.* ix. 86 All round on the lower ground are large inclosures rudely built of rough stones, and probably intended for *cattle-kraals. **1932** C. FULLER *L. Trigardt's Trek* xi. 142 When this area was first settled by Europeans, old cattle-kraal sites.. were found in the fly country. **1838** DICKENS *O. Twist* xvi, Pens for beasts: and other indications of a *cattle-market. **1813** WELLINGTON *Let.* in Gurw. *Disp.* X. 428 If.. our *Cattle parks are to be plundered with impunity. **1838** HAWTHORNE *Amer. Note-Bks.* 9 Sept. (1868) I. 257 Followed a *cattle-path till I came to a cottage. **1887** *Outing* (U.S.) May 117/2 The bank was worn away on the other side by a cattle-path just wide enough for one. **1837** CARLYLE *Fr. Rev.* III. I. ii, Hurled in thither as into *cattle-pens. **1882** ARMSTRONG & CAMPBELL *Austral. Sheep Husbandry* xvii. 187 This fence possesses the advantage over the ordinary wire fence of being *cattle-proof, or nearly so. **1908** *Daily Chron.* 17 Sept. 7/2 A twelve-foot barrier of cattle-proof wire. **1915** *N.Z. Jrnl. Agric.* 20 Feb. 190 Can you advise me as to the best hedge to grow.. to make a good cattle-proof fence? **1630** J. WINTHROP *Hist. New Eng.* (1908) I. 29 Mr. Weatherell, whose father was master of one of the *cattle ships. **1891** *Scribner's Mag.* X. 610 The loading of cattle-ships. **1815** *N. Amer. Rev.* II. 136 The *Cattle show.. at Pittsfield. **1844** *Ainsworth's Mag.* VI. 534 Farmers,.. who had been in town enjoying the spectacle of the 'cattle-show'. **1877** C. M. YONGE *Womankind* i. 2 African chieftainesses are fattened on milk like pigs for a cattle-show. **1870** *Daily News* 23 Apr., The *cattle sidings have been lately set apart for goods waggons. **1876** GEO. ELIOT *Dan. Der.* VIII. lxiv. 574 She saw the *cattle-specked fields. **1800** HURDIS *Favourite Vill.* 195 Its *cattle-sprent enclosures. **1858** T. VIELE *Following the Drum* 150 It was a beaten *cattle-track cut thru the chapparal. **1905** HUBBARD *Neolithic Dew-Ponds & Cattle-Ways* iii. 55 A quarry has been formed cutting through the lines of the cattle-tracks. **1883** *Fortn. Rev.* 1 Aug. 188 If the *cattle-truck and *cattle-steamer had not brought some inveterate plague. **1887** *Whitaker's Almanack* 98 On 1st June 1886 there were in London 633 *cattle-troughs and 594 drinking-fountains. **1860** W. G. CLARK in *Vacat. Tour.* 62, I found a train of empty trucks and *cattle-waggons just starting. **1825** J. LORAIN *Pract. Husb.* 357 The back of them forms the *cattle yard fence. **1840** *Kyle Farm Rep.* in *Libr. Usef. Knowl., Husb.* III. 36 A farm dependent on the cattle-yard for manure. **1960** *Farmer & Stockbreeder* 9 Feb. 98/1 The three small cattle-yards which house the remaining 300 hogs.

9. Special combs.: **cattle-bell**, a bell borne by the leader of a herd of cattle; **cattle-bird** *U.S.* (see quot. 1837); also *gen.* (quot. 1932); **cattle-bush**, any of various Australian shrubs or trees used as fodder for cattle during periods of drought; **cattle chips** *U.S.*, dried cattle-dung used for fuel; **cattle creep** = CREEP *sb.* 4; **cattle-dog** *Austral.* and *N.Z.*, a dog bred and trained for 'working' cattle; **cattle-duffer** *Austral.*, a cattle-rustler; hence (as back-formation) **cattle-duff** *v. intr.*; **cattle-duffing** *vbl. sb.* and *ppl. a.*; **cattle-egret**, a small Egyptian heron belonging to the genus *Bubulcus*; **cattle-feeder**, a mechanical arrangement for regulating the supply of food to cattle; **cattle-fever** = TEXAS *fever*; **cattle-gate**, a 'walk' or pasture for one's cattle, beast-gate; **cattle-grid** (see quot.); **cattle king** *U.S.*, an owner or rearer of cattle on a large scale; **cattle-leader**, a nose-ring to lead dangerous cattle; **cattle lick** *U.S.*, a salt-lick for cattle; **cattle-lifter**, a marauder or robber who practises the stealing of cattle; so ***cattle-lifting***; **cattle-pad** *Austral.*, a cattle-path, cattle-track; **cattle-piece**, a painting representing cattle; **cattle-pit** (see quot.); **cattle-post**, **-ranch** (so **cattle-ranching** *vbl. sb.*), **-range**, **-run**, **station**, a district, tract of country, etc., occupied for the pasturing of cattle; **cattle-pump**, a contrivance by which cattle coming to drink, are made to raise the water out of the well; **cattle-puncher**, a 'cow-puncher'; also **cattle-punching** *vbl. sb.*; **cattle-racket** (see quot.); **cattle-raik** (*Sc.*), 'a common, or extensive pasture, where cattle feed at large' (Jam.); **cattle-road**, a road made for the use of cattle; **cattle-sickness**, sickness of cattle; *spec.* = *bush-sickness*; **cattle-stop** *N.Z.*, = *cattle-grid*; **cattle-tick**, any of several ticks (esp. of the genus *Boöphilus*) attacking cattle in the Americas, Australia, and New Zealand; **cattle-trail**, a trail or path made by cattle; **cattle-way**, = *cattle-road*. Also CATTLE-GUARD, -MAN, -PLAGUE.

1872 ELLACOMBE *Bells of Ch.* vii. 154 Judging from.. its size, may it not be considered to have been a *cattle bell? **1837** C. F. PARTINGTON *Brit. Cycl. Nat. Hist.* II. 158 Cow-bunting or *Cattle-bird (*Molothrus pecoris* Swainson)... The American cattle-bird.. is a small bird about the size of the European sky-lark. **1932** W. B. YEATS *Words for Music* 12 The heron-billed pale Cattle-birds. **1889** J. H. MAIDEN *Useful Native Plants* 116 *Cattle Bush... The leaves of this tree are eaten by stock, the tree being frequently felled for their use during seasons of drought. **1933** *Bulletin* (Sydney) 7 June 25/2 A tall shrub with dense foliage and long leaves is cattle bush. Sheep as well as cattle eat it with avidity and thrive on it. **1903** A. ADAMS *Log Cowboy* xiii. 210 We were frequently forced to resort to the old bed grounds.. for *cattle chips. **1893** *N. & Q.* 8th Ser. III. 151 **Cattle-creep*.., a low arch, just high enough to enable cattle to pass under a railway. **1922** JOYCE *Ulysses* 486 What did you do in the cattlecreep behind Kilbarrack? **1940** *Gloss. Terms Highway Engin.* (*B.S.I.*) 26 *Cattle Creep*, a shallow subway constructed to permit the passage of cattle underneath a road or railway. **1955** *Times* 6 July 10/1 Big motorways like this were not going to be popular with farmers, but the authorities would.. arrange for 'cattle creeps' under roads which divided farms. **1878** E. S. ELWELL *Boy Colonists* 48 Fricker.. [was] delighted to shew the ' new chum' how to work a *cattle dog. **1920** *N.Z. Jrnl. Agric.* 20 July 55 A cattle-dog which has gone lame. **1930** K. HANCOCK *Australia* xiii. 289 In the evolution of an Australian cattle-dog, the native dingo strain has been decisive. **1963** A. LUBBOCK *Austral. Roundabout* 40 A blue-heeler cattle-dog. **1886** *Melbourne Punch* 15 July (Morris), *Cattle-duffers on a jury may be honest men enough, But they're bound to visit lightly sins in those who cattle duff. **1963** A. LUBBOCK *Austral. Roundabout* 161 Horse- and cattle-duffers. **1888** 'R. BOLDREWOOD' *Robbery under Arms* I. xiii. 165 My word, this is a smart bit of *cattle-duffing. **1928** 'BRENT OF BIN BIN' *Up Country* xiii. 212 I'll take no second place for any bastard of a cattle-duffing lag. **1930** *Bulletin* (Sydney) 19 Mar. 23/2 Cattle-duffing is as far removed from sheep-stealing as expert forgery is from snow-dropping among suburban clotheslines. **1905** *Spectator* 14 Jan. 47/1 In Egypt the *cattle-egret, a small white heron, is pointed out by the dragoman, and accepted.. as the true sacred ibis. **1963** *Times* 27 Feb. 11/6 Little egrets predominate, followed by cattle egrets and night herons. **1893** *U.S. Dept. Agric. Bureau Anim. Ind., Bull.* No. 1, Investigation into the nature, causation, and prevention of Texas or Southern *cattle fever. **1909** *Westm. Gaz.* 6 Sept. 7/3 The cattle-fever epidemic. **1817** W. SELWYN *Law Nisi Prius* II. 663 Ejectment for 10 acres of pasture and *cattlegates, with their appurtenances, in a close, called, etc. in Yorkshire. **1880** J. WILLIAMS *Rights Common* 83 The phrase cattle gate or beast gate was a popular mode of expressing the ownership of an undivided share in the soil.. by putting thereon so many cattle in common with the cattle of the other owners. **1940** *Gloss. Terms Highway Engin.* (*B.S.I.*) 26 **Cattle Grid*, a system of bars so laid at road level upon the carriageway, or adjacent thereto, as to prevent cattle straying, while permitting the passage of other traffic. **1874** *Chicago Times* 2 Jan. 5/4 They are.. 'the *cattle kings' of the United States. **1888** T. ROOSEVELT in *Century Mag.* Feb. 500 Anything more foolish than the demagogic outcry against 'cattle-kings' it would be difficult to imagine. **1921** MULFORD *Bar-20 Three* ix. 106 Soon a bundle of handbills was on its way to the office of the cattle king. **1887** *Harper's Mag.* Feb. 349/1 Large blocks of it [*sc.* salt] are sent to the Western Plains for '*cattle licks'. **1860** FROUDE *Hist. Eng.* V. 195 The services of the mountain *cattle-lifter were made valuable to Exeter. **1860** G. H. K. in *Vacat. Tour.* 158 His every tradition pointed to *cattle-lifting as an honourable pursuit. **1931** F. D. DAVISON *Man-Shy* (1934) ii. 25 The cattle-pad.. had been worn deep and narrow by the upward and downward passing of many generations of station cattle. **1954** B. MILES *Stars my Blanket* xvii. 122 The one [*sc.* track] we were on now was nothing but a wandering cattle-pad, honeycombed with steep creeks. **1860** RUSKIN *Mod. Paint.* V. IX. vi. 264 From that time *cattle-pieces become frequent.. Cuyp's are the best. **1883** J. B. PASH *Report on N.Z.* 5/1 Cattle, sheep, horses, &c., are prevented straying on the [railway] line by what is termed a '*cattle pit' or 'catcher'. This is a pit sunk between the rails and fences, about 2 feet 6 inches deep and 10 feet wide, covered by bars of wood placed parallel with the lines, and about 5 inches apart. **1865** LIVINGSTONE *Zambesi* xi. 223 Mosele-katse's principal *cattle-posts. **1887** *Pall Mall G.* 22 Feb. 11/2 The cattle ranche business has been almost destroyed. **1928** *Collier's Mag.* 18 Aug. 19/1 We wasn't horse breakers; we was *cattle punchers. **1907** W. H. KOEBEL *Return of Joe* 282 During no time of.. that first eventful day of '*cattle punching'.. did the Gunner put in an appearance. **1847** 'A. HARRIS' *Settlers & Convicts* 294 A *Cattle-racket. The term at the head of this chapter was originally applied in New South Wales to the agitation of society which took place when some wholesale system of plunder in cattle was brought to light. It is now commonly applied to any circumstance of this sort, whether greater or less, and whether really springing from a felonious intent or accidental. **1857** OLMSTED *Journ. Texas* 160 Some live upon the produce of farms and *cattle-ranches owned in the neighborhood. **1879** BODDAM-WHETHAM *Roraima* 114 Two boatmen who once rowed us over.. to visit a cattle ranch, were both generals. **1946** *Illinois State Arch. Soc. Jrnl.* July 32/1 She owns and operates a large cattle ranch. **1866** 'MARK TWAIN' *Lett. fr. Hawaii* (1967) 289 The whole country is given up to *cattle ranching. **1888** T. ROOSEVELT in *Century Mag.* Feb. 500 Cattle-ranching can only be carried on in its present form while the population is scanty. **1640** in *Essex Inst. Hist. Coll.* V. 170 Ordered that none of the land within the *cattle range shall be granted.. to any man. **1835** C. F. HOFFMAN *Winter West* II. 130 We entered at once upon a large and beautiful park or chase (*Note*, called a cattle-range, if I mistake not, in Kentucky). **1948** *Southwestern Rev.* Summer 272 They.. had passed across a forbidden cattle range. **1905** *Spectator* 18 Feb. 248/1 The important feature which the *cattle-roads make even to-day in modern embankments. **1853** C. B. HALL *Let.* 6 Sept. in T. F. Bride *Lett. Vict. Pioneers* (1898) 218 Various cows and bullocks, on a *cattle run. **1887** *Spectator* 10 Sept. 1220 Going West to hold cattle-runs. **1944** W. E. HARNEY *Taboo* (ed. 3) 86 Roy Johnstone was boss of a cattle-run. **1903** *Pall Mall Gaz.* 7 July 7/1 *Cattle-sickness is alarmingly on the increase in Rhodesia. **1950** *N.Z. Jrnl. Agric.* July 74/1 It was in this period that cobalt was introduced as a cure for cattle sickness. **1851** *Lyttleton Times* (N.Z.) 1 Mar. 8/3 A Canterbury colonist.. would undertake the entire management of a *cattle Station or Farm. **1857** LIVINGSTONE *Trav.* xii. 220 Numbers of cattle-stations.. are dotted over the landscape. **1949** D. M. DAVIN *Roads fr. Home* 250 John worked his way round the cattlestops by the.. glare of the engine's fire-box. **1953** M. C. SCOTT *Breakfast at Six* i. 12 Presently we came to a cattle-stop... Paul bumped noisily across. **1869** *Amer. Naturalist* III. 51 *The Cattle Tick[s].. drop from the cattle.. along the cattle paths. **1950** *N.Z. Jrnl. Agric.* Sept. 196/1 Where cattle ticks are plentiful spraying or dipping should be carried out. **1878** BLACK *Green Past.* xiii. 100 Riding along a *cattle-trail on the high-lying and golden-yellow plains of Colorado. **1905** HUBBARD *Neolithic Dew-Ponds & Cattle-Ways* 38 The length of the ascending cattle-way is a quarter of a mile or more.

cattle-guard. A wide and deep trench cut across a railway (under the rails), on each side of a level crossing, to prevent cattle from straying along the line; a 'cow-pit'. (In *U.S.*)

1843 in Edwards' *Chancery Cases* III. 489 The first cattle guards he saw were in one thousand eight hundred and thirty six. **1881** *Chicago Times* 14 May, The night was.. dark, and in groping along the track the negro fell into a cattle-guard.

ˈcattleist. A cattle-painter.

1834 J. WILSON in *Blackw. Mag.* XXXVI. 11 In company with Hills the celebrated cattleist.

ˈcattleless, *a.* Devoid of cattle. Cf. CATTELLES.

1851 MECHI *2nd Paper on Brit. Agric.* 40 Poverty-stricken and cattleless districts.

ˈcattleman. A man who attends to cattle; a rearer of cattle on a ranche or run.

1878 E. C. G. MURRAY *Round about France* 298 You promised me one, answered the cattleman. **1885** *Boston* (Mass.) *Jrnl.* 26 July 2/3 His proclamation ordering the removal of the cattlemen. **1887** *Pall Mall G.* 22 Feb. 11/2 The cattle men cannot legally keep the sheep men off their ranges. Under these circumstances, the cattle ranche business has been almost destroyed in many parts of the United States.

ˈcattle-ˌplague. A highly contagious disease affecting cattle, characterized by running from the eyes, nose, and mouth, fever, cessation of rumination, constipation, then diarrhœa, and emphysema before death; rinderpest.

1866 *Times* 1 Jan. *Summary 1865* The appearance of the cattle plague in Great Britain.. Down to the middle of December 50,000 reported cases of cattle disease had in the great majority of cases ended fatally. **1866** BRIGHT *Sp. Reform* 13 March, [He] said that I, even in the matter of the cattle plague, set class against class.

cattleya (ˈkætlɪə). *Bot.* [mod.L., f. name of William *Cattley*, an English patron of botany: see -IA.] An epiphytal plant belonging to the orchidaceous genus *Cattleya*, native to Central America and Brazil, bearing handsome violet, rose-coloured, or yellow flowers.

1828 *Bot. Reg.* XIV. 1172 Curled-petaled Cattleya. **1838** *Paxton's Mag. Bot.* V. 6 Cattleyas thrive best in a degree of heat below that required for the major part of orchidæous plants. **1927** *Times* (weekly ed.) 2 June 603/1 An absolutely clear yellow cattleya. **1938** S. BECKETT *Murphy* iv. 50 Neary arrived with a superb bunch of cattleyas.

ˈcattlish, *a.* Pertaining to cattle.

1877 *Tinsley's Mag.* XXI. 503 Fresh hay, clover, or some other cattlish delicacy.

cattologue, obs. var. of CATALOGUE.

catty (ˈkætɪ), *sb.* Also 7 **catte, cate,** 8 **katty.** [Malay-Javanese *kātī*, *katī*: see CADDY.] A weight used in China and the Eastern Archipelago, equal to 16 taels, i.e. $1\frac{1}{3}$ lb. avoird., or 625 grammes.

[**1555** EDEN *Decades W. Ind.* (Arb.) 259 They receaued in Cambie.. For xvii. Cathyls of quicke syluer, one Bahar.] **1598** W. PHILLIPS tr. *Linschoten's Trav. Ind.* 34 (Y.) Everie Catte is as much as 20 Portingall ounces. **1604** CAPT. J. DAVIS in *Purchas* I. 123 (Y.) Their pound they call a Cate. **1609** KEELING *ibid.* I. 199 (Y.) One cattie of spice. **1653** H. COGAN tr. *Pinto's Trav.* viii. §1 He gave me two Cates of Gold. **1699** DAMPIER *Voy.* II. I. vii. 132, 100 Catty make a Pecul, which is 132 *l.* English weight. **1771** J. R. FORSTER *P. Osbeck's Voy.* I. 262 A Katty or Chinese Kann is 1 lb. $12\frac{11}{16}$ of half ounce. **1813** W. MILBURN *Orient. Comm.* II. 496 Bringals 3 candareen per catty. **1857** R. TOMES *Amer. in Japan* 399 Water at the rate of six-hundred copper cash.. for 1000 Catties.

catty (ˈkætɪ), *a.* [f. CAT *sb.*[1] + -Y[1].] Of or pertaining to cats; concerned with the breeding or exhibiting of cats.

1903 F. SIMPSON *Bk. Cat* v. 84 The question of open judging at cat shows has frequently been discussed in catty circles.

b. = CATTISH b.

1886 MRS. ARGLES *Lady Branksmere* ix, There is a sly, *catty* look about her. **1909** *Westm. Gaz.* 11 Dec. 16/2 A noted prelate.. said recently in addressing a community composed of the fair sex that all such communities had the temptation to be 'catty'. **1936** A. CHRISTIE *ABC Murders* xxiii. 173 Women.. are a bit catty about other women.

catty-corner(ed), -cornering: see CATER-CORNERED *adj.* and *adv.*

‖**catur.** *Obs.* [Original language unknown: Portuguese writers call them *catures*: Capt. Burton has suggested identity with Arab. *ˈkaṭīreh*, a small craft,' but this seems phonetically unlikely; moreover Jal identifies the *catur* of Calicut with the Arab. ALMADIA. Some would see in *catur* the source of CUTTER.]

'A light rowing vessel used on the coast of Malabar in the early days of the Portuguese' (Yule); according to Jal, a vessel 60 to 65 feet long, sharp at both ends and curving back, having both sails and oars.

1653 H. COGAN tr. *Pinto's Trav.* vi. §1. Meanwhile a Catur arrived from the Town of Din with a Letter. **1686** DRYDEN *Life Xavier* IV. (1821) 200 They found a good bark of those they call catur, besides seven old foysts.

cature, var. of CATER.

catvall, var. COTWAL, police officer (in India).

catwalk ('kætwɔːk). [f. CAT *sb.*[1] + WALK *sb.*[1]] A narrow footway or platform.

[**1885** B. POTTER *Jrnl.* 20–22 Mar. (1966) 136 Fine rooms and such a slip of a garden at the back, a cat-walk.] **1917** H. J. STEPHENS *Gloss. Aeronaut. Words* 4 *Cat walk*, narrow passage in the interior of an airship. **1925** FRASER & GIBBONS *Soldier & Sailor Words* 50 *Cat walk*, a Western Front name for the brick-paved pathway, usually one brick (nine inches) wide, laid down across farm fields in Flanders. **1952** W. GRANVILLE *Dict. Theatr. Terms* 39 *Cat-walk*, a narrow bridge communicating with the two fly-galleries above and below the proscenium arch. **1959** C. S. FORESTER *Hunting the Bismarck* 63 On the cat-walk two dark figures of Fleet Air Arm officers watched them circle. **1961** F. H. BURGESS *Dict. Sailing* 47 *Cat walk*, any long narrow gangway, especially when erected high over anything or above a deck that is awash in heavy weather. **1970** J. YARDLEY *Kiss the Boys* ii. 38 Halfway up the catwalk she stopped and the cape fell clear of her body. *Ibid.* 39 Lucie began..her..mannequin perambulations...the spotlight followed her down the catwalk and back again.

'cat-witted, *a.* Small-minded, obstinate, and spiteful.

1673 O. WALKER *Educ.* 76 Catwitted, dissolute, foolish. **1804** R. ANDERSON *Cumbrld. Ball.* 84 A silly proud cat-witted fuil. **1862** *Leis. Hours in Town* 18 Multitudes of men are what in Scotland is called catwitted..It implies a combination of littleness of nature, small self-conceit, readiness to take offence, determination in little things to have one's own way, and general impracticability. **1864** CARLYLE *Fredk. Gt.* IV. 260 Very cat-witted woman.

catydid, var. KATYDID.

†**catzerie**. *Obs. rare.* [? f. CATSO + -ERY.]

1592 MARLOWE *Jew Malta* IV. v, Who..looks Like one that is imploy'd in Catzerie and crosbiting.

‖**cau'been.** [Ir. *caipín* dim. of *cap*; or ? dim. of Ir. *cába* cap, head-covering.] An Irish hat.

1831–4 LOVER *Leg. & Stories* 306 Pull off your caubeen and sit down. **1859** F. MAHONEY *Rel. Father Prout* 73 A huge black crape round his 'caubeen'. **1877** A. M. SULLIVAN *New Irel.* xi. 128 English men and women who think all Irishmen wear 'Caubeens' with pipes stuck in the rim.

Caucasian (kɔː'keɪʃ(ɪ)ən, -zɪən), *a.* and *sb.* [f. *Caucasus*, name of a mountain range between the Black Sea and the Caspian + -IAN.]

A. *adj.* Of or belonging to the region of the Caucasus: a name given by Blumenbach (*a* 1800) to the 'white' race of mankind, which he derived from the region of the Caucasus.

1807 W. LAWRENCE *Short Syst. Compar. Anat.* **1847** CARPENTER *Zool.* §141 Those nations (commonly termed Caucasian) which in the form of their skulls and other physical characters resemble Europeans. **1861** HULME *Moquin-Tandon* I. vi. 36 Three varieties or principal races —Caucasian, Mongolian, and Ethiopian. **1937** C. W. FERGUSON *Fifty Million Brothers* v. 76 At first it was said that the candidates must be 'Caucasian' but this evidently was aimed at Negroes, for Jews were later admitted. **1939** A. HUXLEY *After many a Summer* I. i. 5 The first thing to present itself was a slum of Africans and Filipinos, Japanese and Mexicans... The population took on a more Caucasian tinge. **1967** *Economist* 9 Sept. 892/3 The top business jobs in Hawaii tend to be reserved for 'Caucasians'... Poorly-paid labour is not 'Caucasian' almost by definition.

B. *sb.* **a.** A native or inhabitant of the Caucasus.

1843 J. C. PRICHARD *Nat. Hist. Man* xxiv. 253 The proper or aboriginal inhabitants of the Caucasian region are known ..to consist of four distinct races... They are distinguished ..as the western, middle, eastern, and southern Caucasians; the latter division including the Georgians. **1955** J. THOMAS *No Banners* xxx. 302 A hefty Caucasian orderly asked Henry: 'What's wrong with your comrade?' The Caucasian pulled a thermometer out of the mouth of another sufferer. **1961** S. V. UTECHIN *Everyman's Conc. Encycl. Russia* 88 *Caucasians*,..in the wider sense it is applied to all the native peoples of the Caucasus, including both North Caucasus and Transcaucasia. In the narrower sense it denotes only those peoples of the Caucasus whose languages belong to the Caucasian or Japhetic..family.

b. A member of the 'Caucasian' family, an Indo-European; spec. a member of the 'white race', opp. one of other ethnic descent.

1958 LEDERER & BURDICK *Ugly American* (1959) xv. 177 Colonel Edwin Hillandale of the U.S. Air Force..is the only living Caucasian who is a graduate of the Chungking School of Occult Sciences. **1964** J. H. ROBERTS '*Q' Document* (1965) vi. 152 She was quite obviously the only Caucasian in the crowd of formally dressed Japanese. **1967** [see sense A above].

Caucasic (kɔː'kæsɪk), *a.* [f. *Caucasus* + -IC.] Caucasian.

1890 D. G. BRINTON *Races & Peoples* v. 142 The North Mediterranean Branch includes..the Euskaric, the Aryac, and the Caucasic stocks. **1898** *Q. Rev.* Apr. 418 That particular offset of the Caucasic stock. **1899** A. H. KEANE *Man* xii. 449 Fresh accessions to the original and later (historical) Caucasic domains. **1920** *Q. Rev.* July 176 The Kayans and their congeners of South Eastern Asia may be partly of Caucasic stock.

Caucasoid ('kɔːkəsɔɪd), *a.* [See prec. and -OID.] Of, pertaining to, or resembling the Caucasian race. Also as *sb.*

1902 *Encycl. Brit.* XXV. 372/2 There is lacking any biological evidence of Caucasoid or Negroid blood flowing in the veins of Americans before the invasions of historic times. **1956** *Nature* 7 Jan. 40/2 The thousand caucasoids of the United States. **1959** J. D. CLARK *Prehist. S. Afr.* iv. 89 There is..evidence to suggest that, as a result of population movement, a proto-Caucasoid or 'Erythriote' type was introduced into southern Africa.

‖**cauchero** (kau'tʃero). [f. next + *-ero*.] A rubber-gatherer.

1898 *Board of Trade Jrnl.* June 674 Many of the 'caucheros' (or rubber collectors) are working on Brazilian rivers. **1921** *Glasgow Herald* 3 May 3 The cauchero would laugh immoderately were it claimed for him that he is a civilising agent.

‖**caucho** ('kautʃo). [S. Amer. Sp., a. Quechua *cauchu*, *caucho*, *cauchuc*, the base of CAOUTCHOUC.] Any of several varieties of rubber produced in the Amazon basin and Central America, esp. from species of *Castilloa*. Also *attrib.*

1899 *Board of Trade Jrnl.* June 673 The tree which produces the quality of india-rubber exported from Peru through Pará under the name of *caucho*, has recently been determined by M. Huber... The total shipments of *caucho* from Amazonian ports amount to about 2,000 tons annually. *Ibid.* 674 It would now..appear that the *caucho* tree of Peru is a *castilloa*. **1921** *Glasgow Herald* 3 May 10 The caucho trees are smaller than the shiringas. **1957** *Encycl. Brit.* XIX. 602/2 Caucho rubber from *Castilloa elastica*, a large tree found in Central America and portions of Brazil.

caucht, obs. Sc. f. CATCH, CAUGHT.

caucion, -cioun, -cyon, obs. ff. CAUTION.

caucus ('kɔːkəs). [Arose in New England: origin obscure.

Alleged to have been used in Boston U.S. before 1724; quotations go back to 1763. Already in 1774 Gordon (*Hist. Amer. Rev.*) could obtain no 'satisfactory account of the origin of the name'. Mr. Pickering, in 1816, as a mere guess, thought it 'not improbable that *caucus* might be a corruption of *caulkers*', the word "meetings" being understood'. For this, and the more detailed statement quoted in Webster, there is absolutely no evidence beyond the similarity of sound; and the word was actually in use before the date (1770) of the event mentioned in Webster. Dr. J. H. Trumbull (*Proc. Amer. Philol. Assoc.* 1872) has suggested possible derivation from an Algonkin word *cau'-cau-as'u*, which occurs in Capt. Smith's *Virginia* 23, as *Caw-cawaassough* 'one who advises, urges, encourages', from a vb. meaning primarily 'to talk to', hence 'to give counsel, advise, encourage', and 'to urge, promote, incite to action'. For such a derivation there is claimed the general suitability of the form and sense, and it is stated that Indian names were commonly taken by clubs and secret associations in New England; but there appears to be no direct evidence.]

1. In *U.S.* A private meeting of the leaders or representatives of a political party, previous to an election or to a general meeting of the party, to select candidates for office, or to concert other measures for the furthering of party interests; opprobriously, a meeting of 'wire-pullers'.

1763 J. ADAMS *Diary* Feb. Wks. II. 144 (Bartlett) This day learned that the caucus club meets, at certain times, in the garret of Tom Dawes. **1788** W. GORDON *Hist. Amer. Rev.* I. 240 (Bartlett) More than fifty years ago, Mr. Samuel Adams's father, and twenty others..used to meet, make a caucus, and lay their plan for introducing certain persons into places of trust and power. **1809** KENDALL *Trav.* I. xv. 174 A caucus is a political, and what is in practice the same thing, a party meeting; but it is not a popular meeting..It is in caucuses that it is decided, for whom the people shall be instructed to vote, and by what course of politics the party may be secured. **1818** SYD. SMITH *Wks.* (1869) 271 Caucus, the cant word of the Americans. **1847** in CRAIG. *a* **1850** CALHOUN *Wks.* I. 41 Party organization, and party caucuses. **1853** LYTTON *My Novel* XII. xii. (D.), I think of taking a hint from..America, and establishing secret caucuses: nothing like 'em. **1855** MOTLEY *Dutch Rep.* I. 360 The meeting was, in fact, what we should call a caucus, rather than a general gathering. **1870** LOWELL *Among my Bks.* Ser. II. (1873) 98 In the Greek epic, the gods are partisans, they hold caucuses, they lobby and log-roll for their candidates.

b. in reference to other countries.

1886 *New Zealand Her.* 1 June 4/5 The Auckland members are to have a caucus this morning, to consider what action should be taken in connection with the appropriation.

2. In English newspapers since 1878, generally misused, and applied opprobriously to a committee or organization charged with seeking to manage the elections and dictate to the constituencies, but which is, in fact, usually a representative committee popularly elected for the purpose of securing concerted political action in a constituency.

It was first applied in 1878, by Lord Beaconsfield and the *Times* newspaper, to the organization of the Birmingham Liberal 'Six Hundred', and thence to those which were speedily formed on its model elsewhere; the implication being that this was an introduction of 'the American system' into English politics, which deserved to be branded with an American name. But the name was grotesquely misapplied: in American use, *a caucus* is a meeting; English newspapers apply *the caucus* to an organization or system. Such organizations have since been, in one form or another, adopted by all parties; and *caucus* is now a term which partizans fling at the organizations of their opponents, and disclaim for their own.

1878 *Times* 31 July 10/4 The policy of the politicians of the Midland capital will bring upon us the 'caucus' with all its evils..The introduction and progress of the 'caucus' system among us. J. CHAMBERLAIN *Let. ibid.* 1 Aug. 8/1 The 'Birmingham system'..I observe that you, in common with the Prime Minister [Ld. Beaconsfield] have adopted the word 'caucus' to designate our organization. *Ibid.*, *Correspondent*, To secure their election as members of a 'caucus'. **1879** *Times* 30 Jan. 9/2 The Southwark Caucus. **1882** *Sat. Rev.* 29 Apr., When he has made it impossible for any man to obtain a seat in Parliament except by dint of the Caucus. *Ibid.* 27 May, 'Government by Caucus.' The English Liberal Associations with their ruling committees.. *Ibid.* 21 Oct., Mr. Davitt represents Communism and the Caucus. **1883** *Birmingh. Weekly Post* 14 Apr. 4/7 A history of the Tory Caucus..would go a long way back. **1884** *Fortn. Rev.* June 831 The Caucus, as it is now adopted by the Tories, is a species of organization fundamentally different from that..employed by the Liberals.

3. *attrib.* and *comb.*

1763 [see 1]. **1879** CAMPBELL *White & Bl. in U.S.* 63 The caucus system which prevails in America in regard to elections. **1878** BLACK *Green Past.* xvi. 128 He was accustomed to much recondite diplomacy, caucus meetings, private influence. **1882** *Q. Rev.* Oct. 56 The Caucus-mongers have not given any reflection to this point. **1884** *Sat. Rev.* 5 July 9/1 Whatever the real feeling..it is.. obvious that the Caucus-mongers are going the precise way to obscure it.

'caucus, *v.* [f. the sb.] **a.** *intr.* To hold a caucus; **b.** *trans.* To control or 'work' by caucuses.

1850 CARLYLE *Latter-d. Pamph.* I. 24 Men that sit idly caucusing and ballotboxing on the graves of their heroic ancestors. **1883** *Philada. Times* No. 2894. 2 They, too, had conferred or caucused. **1885** *St. James's Gaz.* 27 Nov. 3 They were to be caucussed, gerrymandered and bullied into silence by a pack of provincial wirepullers.

Hence **'caucusing**, *vbl. sb.*

1788 W. GORDON *Hist. Amer. Rev.* 216 *note*, Caucusing means electioneering. **1840** R. DANA *Bef. Mast* xxi. 64 Instead of caucusing, paragraphing..promising, and lying, as with us. **1868** *Daily News* 2 Dec., They [Conservatives] have recently been wheedled by caucusing into household suffrage. **1885** *Sat. Rev.* 28 Mar. 410/2 To take to class-baiting and to Caucussing.

Also (in the abusive vocabulary of English party politics), **'caucusable** *a.*, **'caucusdom**, **caucu'seer**, **'caucuser**, **cau'cusian**, **'caucusified**.

1885 *Sat. Rev.* 14 Mar. 329/1 Counties, now hardly by any means caucusable, are to be brought under the operation of the Caucus. *Ibid.* 24 Jan. 101/2 Gnashing of teeth in Caucusdom. **1884** *Ibid.* No. 1476. 169/1 Their own place-men and Caucuseers. **1888** *Ibid.* 18 Feb. 203 A thorough-going Caucuser, a machine politician. **1886** *Ibid.* No. 1597. 773/2 Peace and good-will even among Caucussians. **1888** *Ibid.* 21 Mar. 375/2 Nothing Caucusian is alien from Mr. Chamberlain. **1885** EARL WEMYSS *Sp. Ho. Lords* 18 May, They [the Peers] did not inhale the mephitic and caucusified atmosphere which elsewhere numbed the senses and paralyzed independent action.

cauda ('kɔːdə). *Anat.* and *Zool.* [L.] A tail-like appendage, as **cauda equina**, the bundle of nerves at the base of the spinal cord (= MARE'S TAIL 3).

1696 *Phil. Trans. R. Soc.* XIX. 325 Dr. Balflour found Eggs in the *Cauda* of it [*sc.* a Barnacle]. **1848** *Quain's Anat.* (ed. 5) II. 820 The nerves of the cauda equina are vertical. **1889** *Buck's Handbk. Med. Sci.* VIII. 135/1 The *caudatum*.. in man, and some other mammals the form is such as to suggest the application of..*cauda* to the tapering continuation along the medicornu. **1892** OSLER *Princ. Med.* 855 Cases of injury of the cauda equina. **1962** *Lancet* 29 Dec. 1367/1 A remarkable tribute to the relative tolerance of the cauda equina.

Hence **'caudad** *adv.* [-AD], towards the tail, in the direction of the tail.

1889 *Buck's Handbk. Med. Sci.* VIII. 135/2 At the meson it is seen as a raised transverse band, but laterad, on account of its deflection caudad, it is divided obliquely. **1898** *Proc. Zool. Soc.* 973 At the level of the posterior border of the palatine instead of a little caudad of this.

caudal ('kɔːdəl), *a. Zool.* [ad. mod.L. *caudāl-is*, f. *cauda* tail.] Of or belonging to the tail; situated in or near the tail; of the nature of a tail.

1661 LOVELL *Hist. Anim. & Min.* 30 Three drops of the bloud out of the caudale veine of a boor Cat. **1769** PENNANT *Zool.* III. 126 It wanted the pectoral, ventral, and caudal fins. **1841–71** T. R. JONES *Anim. Kingd.* 445 Its body is round, having as yet no appearance of caudal appendages. **1849** MURCHISON *Siluria* xii. 303 The superior and inferior spines of the caudal vertebræ. **1871** DARWIN *Desc. Man* I. viii. 269 The male..bird, remarkable for his caudal plumes. **1872** NICHOLSON *Palæont.* 312 The caudal fin or tail.

b. quasi-*sb.* (= *caudal fin*, *vertebra*, etc.)

1834 MCMURTRIE *Cuvier's Anim. Kingd.* 202 The ventrals and caudal are wanting. **1854** OWEN in *Circ. Sc.* (1865) II. 63/1 It continues marking off the anterior third of the centrum in all the other caudals.

caudally ('kɔːdəlɪ), *adv.* [f. prec. + -LY[2].] In caudal fashion; in the manner of a tail.

1881 *Athenæum* 10 Dec. 782/3 The centres whence are derived and caudally continued the homologues of the vertebrate myelon.

caudate ('kɔːdeɪt), *a.* [ad. L. *caudāt-us*, f. *cauda* tail; see -ATE.]

1. Having a tail, tailed.

1600 FAIRFAX *Tasso* XIV. xliv. 259 How comate, crinite, caudate starres are fram'd. **1661** LOVELL *Hist. Anim. & Min.* Introd., Birds..black, ceruleous, caudate, cristate. **1837** SIR F. PALGRAVE *Merch. & Friar* iv. (1844) 180 A caudate variety of the human species.

2. Furnished with a structure or appendage resembling a tail: **a.** *Zool.*

1839–47 TODD *Cycl. Anat.* III. 647/2 Caudate nerve-vesicles. **1847–9** *Ibid.* IV. 120 The caudate cell is held to arise from the prolongation of opposite points of the wall of a spherical cell. **1854** WOODWARD *Mollusca* II. 283 The caudate species of Trigonia.

b. *Bot.*

1830 in LINDLEY *Nat. Syst. Bot.* **1851** T. MOORE *Brit. Ferns* (1864) 66 The very much attenuated apices of the fronds and their pinnæ, which are..what is called caudate. **1880** GRAY *Bot. Text-bk.* 401 *Caudate*, furnished with..a slender tip or appendage resembling a tail.

'caudated, *a.* [f. as prec. + -ED.] **a.** = prec.
1829 E. JESSE *Jrnl. Nat.* 114 Its caudated seeds.
b. caudated rime = *tailed rime* (see TAILED[1] 1 d); **caudated sonnet**, a sonnet with an additional couplet.
1886 W. SHARP *Sonn. Century* 308 For all their structural drawbacks they [*sc.* stanzas in G. Meredith's 'Modern Love'] are in other things essentially 'caudated sonnets'. **1898** G. WYNDHAM *Poems Shakes.* 248 A caudated sonnet with two couplets instead of one after the third quatrain. **1907** CHAMBERS & SIDGWICK *Early Eng. Lyrics* 286 A habit of translating the couplets of a caudated poem.

cau'dation. *nonce-wd.* [f. L. *cauda* tail + -ATION.] The furnishing of a tail; tailed condition.
1857 READE *Never too late* lxxvi. (D.) For a single moment he really suspected premature caudation had been inflicted on him for his crimes.

†**caude.** *Obs. rare*$^{-1}$. [ad. L. *cauda.*] A tail.
1572 BOSSEWELL *Armorie* II. 41 b, The Caude, or Taile of this Prelate his Lyon, is..of a bright blewe colour.

[**caude** in Peele's *Eclogue* 1589 (Nares): Dyce reads *laudes.*]

†**caudebeck.** *Obs.* In 7 cawdebink. [a. F. *caudebec*, a kind of woollen *chapeau*, so called from Caudebec in Normandy (Littré).] (See quots.)
1680 W. CUNNINGHAM *Diary* 30 July (1887) 116 For a black Cawdebink hat £06 0 0 [Scots]. **1708** KERSEY *Caudebec* (F.), a sort of light Hat, first made at Caudebec, a Town of Normandy in France. **1730–6** BAILEY, *Caudebeck.* **1755** JOHNSON, *Caudebeck* (cites Phillips). **1847–78** HALLIWELL *Dict.*, *Caudebec*, a French hat, worn in England about 1700.

cauderoun, etc. obs. ff. CAULDRON.

‖**caudex** ('kɔːdɛks). *Bot.* Pl. caudices ('kɔːdɪsiːz). [L. *caudex, codex* trunk or stem of a tree.] 'The axis of a plant, consisting of stem and root' (*Treas. Bot.* 1866): esp. applied to the stem of palms, ferns, and the like.
1830 LINDLEY *Nat. Syst. Bot.* 280 Some [Palms] have a low caudex..others exhibit a towering stem. **1851** T. MOORE *Brit. Ferns* (1864) 7 The stem of a Fern forms either an upright stock, called a caudex,..or it extends horizontally..and forms what is called a rhizome.

caudicle ('kɔːdɪk(ə)l). *Bot.* [ad. L. **caudiculus*, dim. of *caudex*; see prec. Also in the erroneous L. form.] The small stalk-like appendage to the *pollinia* or pollen-masses of orchids.
1830 LINDLEY *Nat. Syst. Bot.* 265 Pollen masses with a caudicula. **1842** GRAY *Struct. Bot.* vi. iv. (1880) 234 Caudicle or stalk. **1859** DARWIN *Orig. Spec.* vii. (1878) 195 A mass of pollen-grains attached to an elastic foot-stalk or caudicle.

†**'caudie.** *Obs. rare*$^{-1}$.
1596 SHAKS. *1 Hen. IV*, I. iii. 251 Why what a caudie deale of curtesie, This fawning Grey-hound then did proffer me [*Mod. edd. read* candy].

caudie, variant of CADDIE.

caudiform ('kɔːdɪfɔːm), *a. Zool.* [ad. mod.L. *caudiformis*, f. *cauda* tail; see -FORM.] Tail-shaped, resembling a tail.
1839–47 TODD *Cycl. Anat.* III. 699/1 A caudiform prolongation of the upper portion. **1856–8** W. CLARKE *Van der Hoeven's Zool.* I. 642 *Branchipus*, abdomen caudiform.

‖**caudillo** (kau'diʎo). [Sp., leader, chief: late L. (Rom.) *capitellum*, dim. of *caput* head.] The head or chief of state of a Spanish-speaking country; *spec.* the title (*El Caudillo*) assumed by General Francisco Franco in 1938 as head of the Spanish state, in imitation of DUCE and FÜHRER. So **caudi'llismo**, a political system organized under the rule of a caudillo.
1852 F. WHITE *Diary* 182 in *Publ. Archives Canada* The era of the caudillos has passed away [in Argentina]. **1918** W. H. HUDSON *Far away & Long Ago* viii. 130 The greatest and most interesting of all the South American Caudillos or leaders. **1939** *Ann. Reg. 1938* 264 The *Caudillo* took unto himself yet another imposing title, Captain-General of Spain. **1955** *Ann. Reg. 1954* 323 It was apparent that *caudillismo* was generally accepted as the normal method of government. **1958** *Times Lit. Suppl.* 28 Mar. 163/1 The Franco régime has already survived longer than most European dictatorships... The Caudillo seems as firmly in the saddle as ever. **1969** J. MANDER *Static Soc.* i. 69 It was this crisis of legitimacy that gave rise to the Latin American *caudillo. Ibid.* viii. 274 *Caudillismo* of the old type was no longer tolerable.

caudle ('kɔːd(ə)l), *sb.* Forms: 3–6 caudel, 4–7 cawdel(l, 5 cawdelle, cawdille, 5–6 caudelle, 5–7 caudell, (6 cadle, cawdale), 7–8 cawdle, (8 *Sc.* caddel), 6– caudle. [a. ONF. *caudel* (= central OF. *chaudel*, mod.F. *chaudeau*):—med.L. *caldellum*, dim. of *caldum, calidum* (neut. of *caldus, calidus* warm) 'a hot drink'.]
1. A warm drink consisting of thin gruel, mixed with wine or ale, sweetened and spiced, given chiefly to sick people, esp. women in childbed; also to their visitors.
1297 R. GLOUC. (1824) 561 As me seiþ, wan ich am ded, make me a caudel. **1362** LANGL. *P. Pl.* A. v. 205 Glotoun was a gret cherl..and cowhede vp a cawdel in clementes lappe. *c* **1400** *Beryn* 431 Sit and ete þe cawdell..þat was made With sugir and with swete wyne. ? **1483** CAXTON *Bk. for Trav.*, Potages, caudell for the seke, *chaudel.* **1540** RAYNALD *Byrth Man* II. x. (1634) 152 It is a common vsage to give often to women in theyr childbed, caudels of Ote-meale. **1570** LEVINS *Manip.* 9 A cadle, *potiuncula ouacea.* **1612** WOODALL *Surg. Mate* Wks. (1653) 164 A comfortable Caudle made with some Wine, Spices, Sugar, and the yolk of an egge. **1642** FULLER *Holy & Prof. St.* II. xxi. 137 They cast out of their ship..much suger, and packs of spices, making a caudle of the sea round about. **1659–60** PEPYS *Diary* (1879) I. 85 Went to bed and got a caudle made me, and sleep upon it very well. **1765** *London Chron.* 29 Aug. 202 The resort of different ranks of people at St. James's to receive the Queen's Caudle is now very great. **1855** THACKERAY *Newcomes* I. 90 She went to see the grocer's wife on an interesting occasion, and won the heart of the family by tasting their caudle.
†**b.** *caudle of hemp-seed, hempen caudle* (ironically): = hanging. *Obs.*
1588 *Marprel. Epist.* (1845) 22 He hath prooued you to haue deserued a cawdell of Hempseed, and a playster of neckweed. **1593** SHAKS. *2 Hen. VI*, IV. vii. 95 Ye shall haue a hempen Caudle then, and the help of hatchet.
2. *Comb.* **caudle-cup.**
1657 in Picton *L'pool Munic. Rec.* (1883) I. 153 One Cawdell Cupp with a top. **1672** DAVENANT *News fr. Plymouth* (1673) 14. **1743** FIELDING *Jon. Wild* III. vii, A pint silver caudle-cup, the gift of her grandmother. **1820** D. TURNER *Tour Normandy* II. 150 The odd mixture of caudle-cup, compliment and courtly flattery.

caudle ('kɔːd(ə)l), *v.* [f. prec. sb.]
1. *trans.* To administer a caudle to.
1607 SHAKS. *Timon* IV. iii. 226 Will the cold brooke Candied with Ice, cawdle thy Morning taste. **1672** DAVENANT *Love & Hon.* (1673) 256 Cawdled like a Haberdashers Wife That lies in of her first Child. **1832** *Blackw. Mag.* XXXII. 458 [They] have caudled and beflannelled themselves.
2. To mix, as in a caudle.
1790 H. BOYD in *Poet. Register* (1808) 133 Blessings unsophisticate and pure; Not caudled for our taste with dregs terrene. **1845** CARLYLE *Cromwell* (1871) V. 44 His Highness has inextricably caudled the two together.
3. To talk over, lecture (a husband). [A nonce-use from '*Mrs. Caudle's Curtain Lectures*'.]
1845 *Tait's Mag.* XII. 482 The mother is easily convinced ..she must Caudle her husband into the same conviction.

caudo- ('kɔːdəʊ), combining form from L. *cauda* tail, as in **caudo-'femoral** *a.* pertaining to the tail and the thigh (of a bat; see quot.).
1854 OWEN in *Circ. Sc.* (1865) II. 86/1 An..appendage.. which helps to sustain the caudo-femoral membrane.

caudren, -dron, etc., obs. ff. CAULDRON *sb.*

cauel(l)acion, -tion: obs. ff. CAVILLATION.

†**cauf.** *Obs.* [Prob. illiterate form of CORF, basket.] (See quot.)
? **1662** BLOUNT *Glossogr.* (1670) *Cauf*, a little trunk or chest with holes in it, wherein Fishermen keep Fish alive in the water, ready for use. (Hence in COLES, PHILLIPS, KERSEY, BAILEY, JOHNSON, and mod. Dicts.)

cauf, Sc. f. CALF[1], CHAFF; dial. f. CORF.
1862 in Hislop *Prov. Scot.* 28 A wamefu's a wamefu' wer't but o' bare cauf.

caufee, obs. form of COFFEE *sb.*

caufle, variant of COFFLE.

caufte, cauȝt, cauht, obs. ff. CAUGHT.

Caughley. The name of a village in Shropshire, used in ***Caughley porcelain***, a soft-paste porcelain of Caughley, made by Thomas Turner (1749–1809), resembling Worcester porcelain.
[**1829** S. SHAW *Hist. Staffs. Potteries* ix. 212 The late Mr. John Turner, of Caughley, Salop..commenced the manufacture of Porcelain at a place named Caughley, near Broseley, Salop... In 1780, he completed the first Blue Printed Table Service made in England. **1863** W. CHAFFERS *Marks & Monogr.* 148 Caughley. The letter S, in blue, is sometimes placed alone.] **1868** MARRYAT *Hist. Pott. & Porc.* (ed. 3, index) Caughley porcelain. **1878** L. JEWITT *Ceramic Art* I. ix. 268 An excellent example of dated Caughley ware is the puzzle-jug..here engraved. **1960** H. HAYWARD *Antique Coll.* 61/1 *Caughley porcelain*... Turner manufactured at Caughley a soapstone similar to that of Worcester but slightly different in colour and less well potted.

caught (kɔːt), pa. t. and pa. pple. of CATCH *v.*

caught (kɔːt), ppl. adj. of CATCH *v.* (For the sense 'pregnant' see CATCH *v.* 9 b.)
1883 R. W. DIXON *Mano* I. xiii. 44 But she, like a caught adder, stood aghast. **1934** H. G. WELLS *Exper. Autobiogr.* I. iv. 114 A considerable number..get that caught feeling rather later.

cauilero: see CAVALIER.

cauk (kɔːk), *sb. Obs.* and *dial.* Also 5–6 calk(e, 7–8 cauke, (8 calk, 9 caulk, cawk). [Cf. Du. *kalk*, MDu. *calc*; OHG. *chalch*, MHG. *calch, calc*, mod.G. *kalk*; also OE. *cealc* (:—**cælc*, **calc*); see CHALK. It is not clear whether *calk, cauk* is simply the northern form of CHALK, or adopted independently from Du. or Low German.]
1. = CHALK (*dial.*). †**2.** Lime. *Obs.* **3.** ? Calc spar. **4.** Barytes, or heavy spar: see CAWK.
(The quotations cannot easily be separated, but 1653–1729 are app. in sense 4.)
c **1440** *Promp. Parv.* 58 Calke or chalke, erye, *calx, creta.* *c* **1475** *Voc.* in Wr-Wülcker 769 *Hec cals*, a calkestone. **1483** *Cath. Angl.* 51 Calke, *creta, calx.* **1536** BELLENDEN *Cron. Scot.* (1821) I. Introd. 19 This Ile wes callit Albion..fra the quhit montanis thairof, full of calk. **1641** FRENCH *Distill.* v. (1651) 154 Take very strong lime, such as the dyers use, and call cauke. **1653** MANLOVE *Lead-mines* 265 (E.D.S.) Cauke, Sparr, Lid-Stones, Twitches, Daulings and Pees. **1684–5** BOYLE *Min. Waters* 21 Other Ingredient as Spar, Cauke, Sulphur, Orpiment, Arsenick. **1699** DE LA PRYME *Diary* (Surtees) 212 Four-squair bitts of brick, slate and cauk, set in curious figueres. **1724** RAMSAY *Tea-t. Misc.* (1733) I. 87 Wi' cauk and keel I'll win your bread. **1729** MARTYN in *Phil. Trans.* XXXVI. 31 Cauk..Dr. Woodward says is a coarse talky Spar. **1816** W. SMITH *Strata Ident.* 10 A singular variety..is there called red caulk. **1851** TAPPING *Gloss. Manlove's Chron.* (E.D.S.) *Calk, calc, cauke*, or calcareous spar, is the base mineral constituting with brownhen, etc. the deads or rubbish of a quick vein.

†**cauk,** *v.*[1] *Obs.* Also 5 kauke, 6–7 cawk. [a ONF. *caukier, cauquer* (mod.Picard *coker*, F. *côcher*):—L. *calcāre* to tread.] *intr.* To tread, to copulate as birds. Hence **'cauking** *vbl. sb.*
(Quots. 1486–1575 are difficult: cf. CAWK *v.* to call as some birds.)
1377 LANGL. *P. Pl.* B. XI. 350 Some bryddes at þe bille þorwgh brethynge conceyued; And some kauked. **1393** *Ibid.* C. xv. 162 He [kynde] tauhte þe tortle to trede, þe pokok to cauke. **1486** *Bk. St. Albans* A ij a, Hawkis..in the tyme of their loue call and not kauke. **1575** TURBERV. *Falconrie* 21 When the Eagle beginneth to growe to lyking neare cawking or calling time. **1675** *Phil. Trans.* X. 466 Her natural male dares not sit by her [the Peregrine falcon]..but only in cawking time. **1704** WORLIDGE *Dict. Rust. et Urb. Cawking-time*, by this in the Art of Faulconry is meant Hawk's treading-time.

cauk, cawk, *v.*[2] *Sc.* To CHALK.
1725 RAMSAY *Gentle Sheph.* IV. i, I'll cawk my face..and shake my head. **1862** in Hislop *Prov. Scot.* 223 Ye're cawking the claith, ere the wab be in the loom.

cauk, variant of CALK *v.*[2], to rough-shoe.

caukin, -en, obs. forms of CALKIN.
1572 MASCAL *Govt. Cattle* (1627) 157 Make the outside of the shooe alwayes with a caukin. **1617** MARKHAM *Caval.* VI. 61 If he be for the..draught, chiefly in paued streets, then, instead of thick spunges, deep caukens are more commodious. **1688** R. HOLME *Armoury* III. 324/2 A Patten Shooe..hath both Caukins to secure sore Heels.

cauking, caulking ('kɔːkɪŋ), *vbl. sb. Archit.* and *Carp.* Also cocking. [Cf. COCK *v.*[2], COCKET.]
1721–42 BAILEY, *Cauking*, in Architecture, signifies Dovetailing a Cross [**1782–90** a-cross]. **1753** CHAMBERS *Cycl. Supp.* s.v. **1874** KNIGHT *Dict. Mech.* I. 506 *Cauking* (Joinery), a dovetail, tenon, and mortise-joint by which cross-timbers are secured together. Used for fitting down tie-beams or other timbers upon wall-plates. **1876** GWILT *Archit.* Gloss., *Caulking* or *Cocking*, the mode of fixing the tie-beams of a roof or the binding joists of a floor down to the wall-plates.

cauky, var. of CAWKY *a.*

caul (kɔːl), *sb.*[1] Forms: 4–6 calle, 6 caull(e, 6–7 call, cal, kall, caule, cawle, 7 kal, kaull, kawle, 7–9 cawl, 7– caul. See also KELL. [a. F. *cale* a kind of small cap or head-dress.]
1. A kind of close-fitting cap, worn by women: a net for the hair; a netted cap or head-dress, often richly ornamented. *Obs.* exc. *Hist.*
a **1327** *Pol. Songs* (1839) 158 Heo..scrynketh for shome, ant shometh for men, Un-comely under calle. *c* **1374** CHAUCER *Troylus* III. 725 And makyn hym a howe [hood] above a calle. *c* **1391** —— *Astrol.* I. §19 A maner krokede strikes..like to the werk of a womanes calle. *c* **1450** *Voc.* in Wr.-Wülcker 607 *Reticulum*, a calle. **1530** PALSGR. 202/2 Call for Maydens, *retz de soye.* **1557** *Tottell's Misc.* (Arb.) 201 On her head a caule of gold she ware. **1600** HAKLUYT *Voy.* (1810) III. 524 Feathers, and cals of net worke. **1697** DE LA PRYME *diary* (Surtees) 125 Having opend a coffin they found a skelliton, and, about the skull, an antient caul, which was a sort of cap or cornet that women wore formerly on their heads. **1729** T. COOKE *Tales, Prop. etc.* 92 With paralytic Hands she pulls the Caul From Head as naked as the Billiard-ball. **1834** PLANCHÉ *Brit. Costume* 114 The hair ..gathered up behind into a caul of golden network.
†**b.** The netted substructure of a wig. *Obs.*
1693 *Lond. Gaz.* No. 2897/4 A..Perriwig..with a Seal on the Caul almost worn of. **1761** STERNE *Tr. Shandy* III. xxxiii, He..inserted his hand..between his head and the cawl of his wig. **1786** WOLCOTT (P. Pindar) *Bozzy & P.* Wks. 1812 I. 363 To the foretop of his Wig..Down to the very net-work, named the Caul.
c. The hinder portion of a woman's cap.
1740–61 MRS. DELANY *Life & Corr.* (1861) III. 400 Her cap..had a very good effect with a pompon; and behind, where you may suppose the bottom of the caul, a knot of diamonds. **1798** JANE AUSTEN *Lett.* I. 177, I took the liberty a few days ago of asking your black velvet bonnet to lend me its cawl. **1851** MAYHEW *Lond. Lab.* I. 387 Net for making caps and 'cauls', which are the plain portion at the back, to

be trimmed or edged according to the purchaser's taste. **1862** Mrs. H. Wood *Mrs. Hallib. Troub.* I. xii. 61 The peculiar net cap, with its high caul and neat little border.

2. *gen.* A net for wrapping something in; any ornamental network. *Obs.*

1481–90 *Howard Househ. Bks.* (1841) 339 Item for iij. callis iiijd. ob. **1552** *Inv. Churches of Surrey* 73 A calle for the pyx. **1578** Lyte *Dodoens* vi. lvii. 732 A greene thicke huske .. under the same .. certayne thinne skinnes, lyke to cawles or nettes. **1634** Herbert *Trav.* 199 The women .. weare a large long cawle or sack, lik net-worke, which as a garment hides them wholy. **1681** Grew *Museum* (J.) An Indian Mantle of Feathers, and the Feathers wrought into a caul of pack-thread.

†**3.** A spider's web. *Obs.*

1548 Hall *Chron.* (1809) 462 Like a Spyder that daily weaveth when hys Calle is torne. **1598** Sylvester *Du Bartas* II. i. iv. (1641) 104/1 The low-rooft broken wals (Instead of Arras) hung with Spiders cauls. **1631** Brathwait *Whimzies, Almanack-maker*, His shelves .. are subtilly inter-woven with spiders caules.

fig. **1594** W. Percy *Cœlia* iv. in Arb. *Garner* VI. 141 What be mens sighs but cauls of guilefulness?

†**4.** *Anat.* Any investing membrane or structure, as the membranes of the brain. ***caul of the heart***: app. the pericardium; also *fig.* (from *Hosea* xiii. 8; cf. *Joel* ii. 13). *Obs.* in general sense.

1398 Trevisa *Barth. De P.R.* v. iii. (1495) 107 A merueyllous calle in whiche calle the brayne is wounded and by-clypped. **1533** Elyot *Cast. Helth* (1541) 12 Calles betwixt the uttermoste skinne and the fleshe. **1610** Barrough *Meth. Physick* iv. i. (1639) 216 The plure or kall that girdeth in the ribbes. **1611** Bible *Hosea* xiii. 8, I .. will rent the kall of their heart. **1684** tr. *Bonet's Merc. Compit.* iii. 112 Worms are bred in the heart and in its Caul.

fig. **1579** Lyly *Euphues* (Arb.) 63 Who so is blinded with the caule of beautie. **1636** Featly *Clavis Myst.* ii. 26 Custome in sinne hath drawne a kall over my conscience. **1643** S. Marshall *Let.* 15 Their long conversing with *God-dam-mee's* hath .. drawn such a kawl over their hearts, that to them damnation is ridiculous.

5. *spec.* **a.** The fatty membrane investing the intestines; the epiploön or omentum.

1382 Wyclif *Ex.* xxix. 13 The calle of the mawe, and the two kydneers. *c* **1440** *Anc. Cookery* in *Househ. Ord.* (1790) 442 Wynde hom in the calle of the swyne. **1611** Cotgr., *Alzatin*, the fat cawle, or kell, wherein the bowels are lapt. **1713** Cheselden *Anat.* iii. iv. (1726) 159 Omentum, or Cawl, is a fine membrane larded with fat, somewhat like network. **1802** Paley *Nat. Theol.* xi. The omentum, epiploon, or cawl, is an apron, tucked up, or doubling upon itself, at its lowest part.

b. The amnion or inner membrane inclosing the fœtus before birth; *esp.* this or a portion of it sometimes enveloping the head of the child at birth, superstitiously regarded as of good omen, and supposed to be a preservative against drowning.

1547 Boorde *Brev. Health* cccxix. 103 b, A skyn or a call in the whiche a chylde doth lye in the mothers bely. **1610** B. Jonson *Alch.* i. ii. (1616) 613 Yo' were borne with a caule o' your head. **1798** Morton *Secr. worth know.* i. 9 (L.) Was he not born with a cawl? **1826** Hood *Sea-Spell*, In his pouch confidingly He wore a baby's caul. **1849** Dickens *Dav. Copp.* i, I was born with a caul, which was advertised for sale, in the newspapers, at the low price of fifteen guineas.

6. *attrib.* and *Comb.*, as (senses 1 and 2) ***caul fringe, silk, work***; †***caul-visarded*** adj.; (sense 5 a) ***caul fat***.

1882 *Daily Tel.* 29 Aug. 5/1 When oleomargarine is made from *caul fat. **1653** H. Cogan *Pinto's Trav.* xxxii. (1663) 129 A cloth of state of white damask .. with a deep *cawl frenge of green silk and gold. **1483** *Act 1 Rich. III*, x. §1 Laces, *calle sylk or coleyn silk throwen or wrought. **1593** Nashe *Christ's T.* (1613) 146 Masker-like *cawle-visarded. **1577** Harrison *England* ii. xv. (1877) i. 272 Some ladies exercise their fingers .. in *caulworke. **1830** James *Darnley* xxv. 114/1 Here stood a frame for caul work.

†**caul**, *sb.*[2] *Obs.* [ad. L. *caulis*, in Gr. καυλός stem, stalk, esp. cabbage-stalk, cabbage. Already in OE. in sense 1, in forms *caul, cawl, cawel*: see also cawel, cole, kale.]

1. A cabbage. Also in comb. ***caul-stock***, a cabbage-stalk, castock.

c **1000** *Sax. Leechd.* I. 240 Genim þysse wyrte croppas þe man brassicam siluaticam, & oðrum naman caul nemneþ. *a* **1100** *Voc.* in Wr.-Wülcker 323 (Plant Names) *Caula, vel magudaris*, caul. *c* **1265** *Voc.* ibid. 559 *Caulus*, cholet, kaul. **1398** [see castock]. **1590** R. Payne *Descr. Irel.* (1841) 9 The profite of the swine, winter milke, caules. **1727** Bradley *Fam. Dict.* s.v. *Cabbage*, Cauls and Sprouts.

2. Stem, stalk.

c **1420** *Pallad. on Husb.* xi. 381 Take leef, or roote, or caule of malowe agrest.

†**caul**, *sb.*[3] *Obs.*⁻⁰ [ad. L. *caulæ* opening, sheepfold.] A sheepfold.

1483 *Cath. Angl.* 56 A Caule, *caula.* **1570** Levins *Manip.* 43 A caule, pen, *caula.* **1691** Ray *N.C. Wds.* (E.D.S.) Cawel, *chors* [*cohors*].

caul, *sb.*[4] [? a. F. *cale*, thin piece of wood, stone, or the like, inserted under an object to level it or steady it: of uncertain origin; cf. L. *cāla* piece or billet of wood, and see Littré.] (See quot.)

1874 Knight *Dict. Mech.* I. 506 *Caul*, a heated board used in laying down large veneers. Its heat keeps up the fluidity of the glue until all that is superfluous has been pressed out at the edges. **1881** *Mechanic* §596. 277 An instrument the shape of the curve .. called a 'caul'.

caul(e, obs. form of call.

cauld (kɔːld), *sb. Sc.* Also **caul.** A weir on a river to divert the water into a mill-lead.

1805 Scott *Last Minstr.* ii. xiii. *note*, He commanded him to build a cauld or dam-head across the Tweed at Kelso. **1818** *Law-case* (Jam.), Right to fish from the head of the Black Pool, down to the caul or dam-dyke of Milnbie. **1839** *Proc. Berw. Nat. Club* I. 104 The whole of the water was .. diverted into the mill-lead by means of a cauld or weir.

cauld, *v. Sc.* [f. prec.] *trans.* To provide with a cauld; to dam.

1886 J. Russell *Remin. Yarrow* ix. 294 The stones were handy for caulding the river.

cauld, Sc. form of cold, *a.* and *sb.*

cauldrife ('kɔːldrɪf), *a. Sc.* [f. *cauld* cold + -rife, q.v.]

1. Having a tendency to cold, chilly. **a.** Of things: Causing the sensation of cold. **b.** Of persons: Susceptible to cold.

1768 Ross *Helenore* 142 (Jam.) 'T has been a cauldriffe day. *a* **1774** Fergusson *Poems* (1845) 5 Auld Reekie .. bield for mony a cauldrife soul. **1837** R. Nicoll *Poems* (1842) 108 Through it the blast sae cauldrife does gae.

2. *fig.* Cold or chilling in feeling or manner.

a **1774** Fergusson *Poems* (1789) II. 75 (Jam.) She tholes .. the taunt o' cauldrife joes. **1825** Ld. Cockburn *Mem.* 238 [Church patronage] gave us cauldrife preachers.

Hence '**cauldrifeness.**

a **1662** R. Baillie *Lett.* (1775) I. 442 (Jam.) We were looked upon for our coldrifeness, with a strange eye.

cauldron, caldron ('kɔːldrən), *sb.* Forms: 3 **caudroun**, 4 **cauderoun, cawdroun, caudren,** (**gaudroun**), 4–5 **cawdrone, -run**, 4–7 **caudron**, 5 **cawdren, -derowne, -durne, -tron, caudryn, calderon**, 5–6 **caldrone**, 5–7 **cawdron**, 6 **caud-, cauld-, cautherne**, 5– **caldron**, 6 **cauldron.** See also chaldron. [ME. *caud(e)ron, -oun*, a. AF. and ONF. *caud(e)ron, -oun*, corresp. to central OF. *chaud(e)ron*, Sp. *calderon*, It. *calderone*, augmentative of **caldario*, **calderio*:—L. *caldārium* hot-bath, of which the pl. *caldāria* exists in It. *caldaja*, Pg. *caldeira*, Sp. *caldera*, Pr. *caudiera*, NF. *caudiere*, F. *chaudière* kettle. The *l* is a later insertion of the Renascence, in imitation of Latin, which has gradually been recognised in pronunciation: Sc. has still *caudron, cauðron.* The spelling *cauldron* decidedly preponderates in modern use, though the dictionaries from Johnson downward have favoured *caldron.*]

1. A large kettle or boiler.

c **1300** *St. Brandan* 158 Hi .. soden hem fisch in a caudroun. *c* **1320** *Seuyn Sag.* (W.) 2460 A gret boiland cauderoun. **1382** Wyclif *Ecclus.* xiii. 3 What shal comune the caudron to the pot? **1387** *E.E. Wills* (1882) 2 þe gaudroun in þe kechyn. **1398** Trevisa *Barth. De. P.R.* xix. cxxviii. (1495) 933 A caudren is a vessel of kechen. *c* **1425** *Voc.* in Wr.-Wülcker 662, *Hoc caldarium*, caldron. *c* **1440** *Anc. Cookery* in *Househ. Ord.* (1790) 433 Sethe it in a pot .. or in a cawdron. *c* **1440** *Gesta Rom.* 381 (Add. MS.) A Cawderowne full of wellyng piche and brymstone. **1535** Coverdale *1 Sam.* ii. 14 The Cauldron, or ketell, or panne, or pot. **1556** *Inv.* in French *Shaks. Geneal.* (1869) 471 In the kitchen .. ij. catthernes. **1556** *Chron. Gr. Friars* (1852) 30 Thys yere [1521] was a man soddyne in a cautherne in Smythfelde .. because he wold a poyssynd dyvers persons. **1605** Shaks. *Macb.* iv. i. 11 Double, double, toile and trouble, Fire burne, and Cauldron bubble. **1611** Speed *Hist. Gt. Brit.* ix. xii. (1632) 686 Fiue hundred Cawdrons made of beasts skins. **1697** Dryden *Virg. Georg.* i. 280 Some steep their Seed, and some in Cauldrons boil. **1725** Pope *Odyss.* xv. 151 These will the caldron, these the tripod give. **1856** Froude *Hist. Eng.* I. 289 For the poisoners of the soul there was the stake, for the poisoners of the body, the boiling cauldron. **1875** B. Taylor *Faust* I. vi. 100 A great caldron, under which a fire is burning.

fig. **1844** Dickens *Mart. Chuz.* (C.D. ed.) 173 Chance contributions that fell into the slow cauldron of their talk. **1864** Lowell *Fireside Trav.* 193 When the great caldron of war is seething.

2. *transf.* **a.** A natural formation suggesting a cauldron, in shape, or by the agitation of a contained fluid.

[**1413** Lydg. *Pylgr. Sowle* iii. x. (1483) 56 This is cleped the Caudron and the pytte of helle.] *a* **1763** Shenstone *Wks.* (1764) I. 23 Vesuvio's horrid cauldrons roar. **1787** Burns *Fall of Fyers*, Still thro' the gap the struggling river toils, And still, below, the horrid caldron boils. **1845** Darwin *Voy. Nat.* xvii. (1852) 375 Deluges of .. lava which have flowed .. over the ruins of the great caldrons. **1872** Blackie *Lays Highl.* 9 The cauldron of the sea.

b. ***cauldron subsidence***, in *Geol.* (see quot. 1961).

1909 *Q. Jrnl. Geol. Soc.* LXV. 611 A cauldron-subsidence which affected an area roughly oval in shape, and measuring not less than 5 miles from side to side. **1961** J. Challinor *Dict. Geol.* 32/2 *Cauldron-subsidence*, the subsidence of a cylindrical or conical mass of rock into underlying magma so that displaced magma flows upwards round and over the subsiding mass... The classic examples are those of Ben Nevis and Glen Coe.

'**cauldron**, *v. rare.* [f. prec. sb.] *trans.* To put or enclose in (or as in) a cauldron.

1791 E. Darwin *Bot. Gard.* i. 129 Where .. Cauldron'd in rock, innocuous Lava burns. **1808** J. Barlow *Columb.* iii. 252 Dark fiend that .. cauldrons in his cave that fiery flood.

†**cauled**, *pa. pple. Obs. rare*⁻¹. [f. caul *sb.*[1] + -ed[2].] Having or adorned with a caul.

1393 Langl. *P. Pl.* C. xvii. 351 In riche robes raþest he walketh, Y-called and ycrymyled.

cauler, obs. Sc. var. of caller *a.*

caulescent (kɔːˈlɛsənt), *a.* [f. L. *caul-is* stalk, after *arborescent*, etc.] Acquiring or growing to a stem or stalk; *spec.* in *Bot.* having an obvious stem growing above the ground.

1794 Martyn *Rousseau's Bot.* xxvi. 405 Dog Violet is one of the caulescent or stalky kind. **1830** Lindley *Nat. Syst. Bot.* 154 Half-shrubby caulescent plants. **1846** Dana *Zooph.* (1848) 494 Caulescent ramose, subdichotomous and lobate. **1881** Baker in *Jrnl. Linn. Soc.* XVIII. 280 A bulbous caulescent herb.

caulf, -ed, obs. forms of calf[1], calved.

caulgarthe, var. of calgarth.

1570 Levins *Manip.* 34 The caulgarthe, *herbarium*.

caulicle ('kɔːlɪk(ə)l). *Bot.* [ad. L. *cauliculus*, dim. of *caulis* stalk.] A little stalk or stem; *spec.* **a.** 'the initial stalk or stem in an embryo, the radicle' (Gray); **b.** a small stem proceeding from a bud formed at the neck of a root, without the previous production of a leaf; **c.** the stipe of certain fungals.

1657 *Phys. Dict.*, *Caulicles*, little stalks. **1880** Gray *Struct. Bot.* ii. 10 Caulicle or Radicle. *Ibid.* iii. 40 The initial stem, the caulicle. **1882** Vines *Sach's Bot.* 448 The foot (caulicle) of the young plant [Salvinia].

caulicole ('kɔːlɪkəʊl). *Arch.* [a. F. *caulicole*, ad. It. *caulícolo*, ad. L. *cauliculus*, all in same sense; see next.] *pl.* 'The eight lesser branches or stalks in the Corinthian capital springing out from the four greater or principal caules or stalks' (Gwilt).

1816 J. Smith *Panorama Sc. & Art* I. 179 These volutes spring out of small twisted husks placed between the leaves of the second row, called caulicoles. **1848** Rickman *Archit.* 39 The small space left of the bell is filled by caulicoles.

caulicolous (kɔːˈlɪkələs), *a. Bot.* [f. L. *caul-is* stem + *-cola* inhabitant + -ous.] 'Applied to parasitical phanerogamous plants that draw their nourishment by means of lateral suckers on their stems', as the Dodder (*Syd. Soc. Lex.* 1881).

caulicule ('kɔːlɪkjuːl). *Bot.* [a. F. *caulicule*, ad. L. *cauliculus*; see next.] (See quot.)

1835 Lindley *Introd. Bot.* (1848) II. 61 The imaginary line of division between the radicle and the cotyledons is the caulicule. **1870** Bentley *Bot.* 335 The point of union of the base of the plumule with the radicle and cotyledons, is called the caulicule or tigelle.

‖**cauliculus** (kɔːˈlɪkjʊləs). [L. dim of *caulis* stem.] in *Bot.* = caulicle, caulicule; in *Archit.* = caulicole.

1830 Lindley *Nat. Syst. Bot.* 116 Embryo very large .. with a long 2-edged cauliculus, having two small cotyledons at the top. **1879** Sir G. Scott *Lect. Archit.* I. 84 Points of resemblance to the Corinthian capital, as the cauliculi.

cauliferous (kɔːˈlɪfərəs), *a. Bot.* [f. L. *cauli-s* stem + *-fer* bearing + -ous.] Producing or having a stem or stalk.

1708–21 Kersey, *Cauliferous Plants* are such as have a true Stalk, which a great many have not. **1753** Chambers *Cycl. Supp.* s.v., Perfectly cauliferous, as cabbage. **1755** in Johnson; and in subseq. Dicts.

cauliflorous (kɔːlɪˈflɔərəs), *a. Bot.* [f. L. *caul-is* stem + *flōr-us* flowering + -ous.] Having flowers on the stem.

1881 in *Syd. Soc. Lex.*

cauliflory ('kɔːlɪflɔərɪ). *Bot.* [f. L. *caulis* stem + *flōs, flōris* flower.] The production of flowers directly from the trunk or branches.

1903 W. R. Fisher tr. *A. F. W. Schimper's Plant-Geogr.* iv. 336 In cauliflory the flowers appear sometimes only on main stems, sometimes only on branches, sometimes, and this is most usual, on both main stems and branches alike. *Ibid.*, In constantly humid tropic forests cauliflory, that is to say, the formation of flowers on old wood, is not rare. **1908** W. H. Lang tr. *Strasburger's Text-bk. Bot.* (ed. 3) 625 The flowers are borne on the main stem or the older branches, and arise from dormant axillary buds (cauliflory). **1952** P. W. Richards *Tropical Rain Forest* iv. 54 Many rain-forest trees .. bear their flowers directly on the trunk or larger branches... This unusual habit, known as cauliflory, is highly characteristic of the Tropical Rain Forest.

cauliflower ('kɒlɪflaʊə(r)), *sb.* Forms: α. 6 **colieflorie**, 6–7 **cole-flory, -florie**, 7 **coly-flory, coley-florey, colliflory.** β. 7 **coleflower, colly-flowre, coly-, cauly-, caully-, cawly-flower**, 7–8 **collyflower, colliflower**, 8– **cauliflower.** [The 16th c. *cole-florye, colie-florie*, was app. corrupted from the mod.L. *cauli-flōra* or F. *chou-flori, chou-fleuri*, assimilated to Eng. cole. (The L. and F. both mean 'flowered cole or cabbage': cf. Ger. *blumenkohl*, Du. *bloemkool* 'flower-cole'. Cf. also It. *cavolfiore*, pl. *cavoli* (*caoli*) *fiori*, Sp. *coliflor.* The later *colly-flower*

and *cauliflower* are assimilated to *flower*, and to the L. *cauliflora*. So mod.F. has made *chou-fleuri* into *chou-fleur* ' cole-flower'.]

1. a. One of the cultivated varieties of the cabbage (*Brassica oleracea botrytis cauliflora*), the young inflorescence of which forms a close fleshy white edible head.

α. **1597** GERARD *Herbal* xxxvi. 246 Cole Florie, or after some Colieflorie. *Ibid.* 316 Cole-flory is called in Latin Cauliflora. **1601** HOLLAND *Pliny* II. 26 There grow out of the same coleworte other fine colliflories (if I may so say). **1610** W. FOLKINGHAM *Art of Survey* I. xi. 37 The Coley-florey, Rape-cole, Muske-melon. **1620** VENNER *Via Recta* (1650) 186 Cole-florie exceedeth all the other kinds of Cole-worts. **1621-6** BACON *Sylva* § 484 Lettuce, or Coleflory, or Artichoake. **1659** R. LOVELL *Herbal* 104 Cole-florie.

β. **1621** G. SANDYS *Ovid's Met.* VIII. (1626) 167 Her husband gathers coleflowrs, with their leaues. **1634** *Althorp MS.* in Simpkinson *Washingtons* Introd. 24 For 20 collyflowres 00 13 00. **1647** R. STAPYLTON *Juvenal* 70 What smells oth' lampe dawbes thy pale colyflowers. **1664** EVELYN *Kal. Hort.* (1729) 190 Early Cauly-flower. *Ibid.* 212 Sow.. Cawly-flowers for Winter Plants. **1688** R. HOLME *Armoury* II. 64/2 The Cole-flower or Colliflower. **1734** MRS. PENDARVES in *Mrs. Delany's Corr.* (1861) I. 478 For dinner ..boiled leg of lamb and loin fried, collyflowers and carrots. **1771** SMOLLETT *Humph. Cl.* (L.) They scarce know a crab from a cauliflower. **1769** MRS. RAFFALD *Eng. Housekpr.* (1778) 353 Take the closest and whitest colly-flowers you can get. **1832** *Veg. Subst. Food* 265 The Cauliflower.. brought into England from the island of Cyprus.

b. Pottery made in the form of a cauliflower. Also *attrib.*

1757 *Pub. Advert.* 12 Apr. 4/1 To be Sold by Auction.. Melons, Colliflowers [*i.e.*, made in porcelain]. **1879** LADY C. SCHREIBER *Jrnl.* (1911) II. 217 The charming teapot of cauliflower ware, all embossed with pastoral objects. **1961** *Connoisseur New Guide to Antique Eng. Pott., Porc. & Glass* 37 [Wedgwood's] famous 'cauliflower' and 'pineapple' wares (teapots and so forth made in these forms).

c. *transf.* A thing which resembles a cauliflower in shape.

1803 R. COUPER *Tourifications* II. xiv. 101 The cheering cauliflower [of froth] of her tight home-brewed ale. **1819** KEATS *Party of Lovers* 15 Romeo! Arise, take snuffers by the handle, There's a large cauliflower in each candle. **1864** C. M. YONGE *Trial* II. xiii. 241 Marvellous adornments of their woolly locks, wigged out sometimes into huge cauliflowers whitened with coral lime. **1892** *Daily News* 31 May 2/3 A tiny fan of black lace with a 'cauliflower' of yellow baby ribbon. **1904** *Amer. Jrnl. Sci.* Jan. 34 The reddish dust 'cauliflowers' accumulated about every half-hour and rolled down the gorge of the Rivière Blanche from the cone.

2. *attrib.* and *Comb.*, as ***cauliflower-like*** adj.; **cauliflower cheese**, a savoury of which the principal ingredients are cauliflower and cheese; **cauliflower ear**, an ear (as of a boxer) thickened and distorted by blows; cf. CAULIFLOWER *v.* 2; **cauliflower excrescence, growth** (*Pathol.*), terms applied to natural or morbid growths that are developed in the form of a stem with branches and branchlets all closely applied to each other or crowded, *e.g.* acinous glands, villous tumours, etc.; **cauliflower wig**, a wig supposed to resemble a cauliflower.

1940 M. DICKENS *Mariana* v. 142 Mary..bought..a cauliflower, which she made into a *cauliflower cheese for supper. **1953** E. TAYLOR *Sleeping Beauty* i. 6 Some dreary woman's meal—cauliflower-cheese, he thought. [**1907** WODEHOUSE *White Feather* v. 56 My right ear feels like a cauliflower. Does it look rum?] **1909** *Sat. Even. Post* 1 May 31/2 It was the '*cauliflower ear' of pugilism. **1923** WODEHOUSE *Good Morning, Bill!* 111, Tell me, doc..have you ever seen a cauliflower ear? **1965** G. MELLY *Owning-up* v. 47 Bouncers with cauliflower ears circling the dance-floor in evening dress. **1882** *Daily Tel.* 10 Oct. 5/4 This gave the porter a fine frothy or *cauliflower head. **1873** RALFE *Physiol. Chem.* 8 The crystals..are arranged in *cauliflower-like groups consisting of oblique prisms. **1936** E. SITWELL *Victoria* xxii. 269 Bunched cauliflower-like dresses. **1832** *Veg. Subst. Food* 266 *Cauliflower seed obtained from England is the most esteemed in Holland. **1753** *London Mag.* (Fairholt), [Names of wigs] The pigeon's wing, the comet, the *cauliflower, etc. **1833** A. FONBLANQUE *Eng. under 7 Admin.* (1837) II. 382 He [a Bishop] had cauliflower wig, apron, shovel hat. **1882** *Daily Tel.* 6 Sept. 5/4 Under the good Queen Anne the 'cauliflower' wig came into clerical fashion.

'cauliflower, *v.* [f. prec. sb.] **1.** *trans.* ? To powder (a wig). *rare*

1799 SOUTHEY *Nondescr.* vi, Some Barber's leathern powder-bag Wherewith he feathers, frosts, or cauliflowers Spruce Beau, or Lady fair, or Doctor grave. **1845** LD. CAMPBELL *Chancellors* (1857) III. lii. 249 To trim the whole Chapter and to cauliflower their wigs.

2. To disfigure (an ear), esp. in boxing. Usu. in pass. or as ppl. adj. **cauliflowered**.

1947 *Time* 27 Jan. 60/2 His dress was sharp..his ears cauliflowered. **1959** *Times* 6 May 4/7 We may get [by substitution]..a heavy-weight boxer being pulled out in the sixth round for some cauliflowered brother. **1961** *Guardian* 26 Jan. 9/2 Mr. Condon's cauliflowered features identified him as a retired boxer.

cauliform ('kɔːlɪfɔːm), *a.* [f. L. *caul-is* stem + -FORM.] Stem-shaped, stem-like.

1847 in CRAIG.

caulin ('kɔːlɪn). *Chem.* [f. L. *caul-is* cabbage + -IN.] The colouring principle of red cabbage.

1881 in *Syd. Soc. Lex.*

'caulinar, -ary, *a.* [Bad formations.] = next.

1851 RICHARDSON *Geol.* vii. 203 They are caulinar, borne on the stem. **1870** BENTLEY *Bot.* 171 When they remain as little leaflets on each side of the base of the petiole, but quite distinct from it, they are called caulinary.

cauline ('kɔːlaɪn), *a. Bot.* [ad. mod.L. *caulīnus*, f. *caulis* stalk.] Of or belonging to the stem.

1756 *Phil. Trans.* XLIX. 835 Cauline leaves. **1807** J. E. SMITH *Phys. Bot.* 130 The Flower-stalk is..cauline, when it grows immediately out of the main stem. **1842** GRAY *Struct. Bot.* iii. (1880) 86 Whatever is produced in the axil of a leaf is cauline. **1870** HOOKER *Stud. Fiora* 21 Cauline leaves sessile auricled. **1884** BOWER & SCOTT *De Bary's Phaner. & Ferns* 340 The vascular elements running into the leaf here abut on the cauline vessels.

‖**caulis** ('kɔːlɪs). Pl. caules ('kɔːliːz). [Lat., stem, stalk; in Gr. καυλός.]

1. *Arch.* Each of the four principal stalks which support the volutes and helices in a Corinthian capital.

1563 SHUTE *Archit.* D iij b, Voluta..which goeth out of Caulis. **1876** GWILT *Archit.* Gloss., *Caulicolæ*, the eight lesser branches or stalks in the Corinthian capital springing out from the four greater or principal caules or stalks.

2. *Bot.* The stalk or stem of a plant, *esp.* of a herbaceous plant in its natural state.

1870 BENTLEY *Bot.* 101 It is called a caulis in plants which are herbaceous, or die down annually.

caulk (kɔːk), *sb. Naut. slang.* [? f. CAULK *v.*]

a. A dram, a 'drop' of liquor; = CAULKER 3.

1833 MARRYAT *P. Simple* (1863) 265, I had no time to take a caulk if I was inclined. **1880** MRS. PARR *Adam & E.* xxxii. 443 I've a had a bit o' a caulk, but not a drap more.

b. A short sleep or 'nap'.

1917 *Chambers's Jrnl.* 14 July 514/2 During the afternoon at sea the tables and stools on the mess-decks will be covered with figures enjoying their afternoon caulk. **1932** NORDHOFF & HALL *Mutiny on Bounty* vii. 100 Hayward was mate of the watch and was fool enough to take a caulk. **1942** H. C. BAILEY *Dead Man's Shoes* vii. 26 'Having a caulk' where he sat and..he woke at eight.

caulk, var. of CAUK chalk, CAWK barytes.

caulk (kɔːk), *v.* Forms: 5 **caulke, kalke,** 5–7 **calke,** 7 **calck(e, kauk, (chalk),** 8 **cawke,** 7– **caulk, calk.** [In 15th c. *calke, caulke* (the same word as CAUK *v.*), a. OF. *cauquer* to tread, to press or squeeze in with force, to tent a wound:—L. *calcāre* to tread, stamp, press close together, press in. The prevailing spelling for a century back has been *caulk*, though dictionaries retain *calk* from Johnson.]

1. *trans.* To stop up the seams of (a ship, etc.) by driving in oakum, or the like, melted pitch or resin being afterwards poured on, so as to prevent leaking.

? *a* **1500** *Chester Plays* I. (1843) 47, I will goe gaither slyche The shippe for to caulke and pyche. **1552** HULOET, Botes or shyppes calked with towgh. **1555** EDEN *Decades W. Ind.* IV. viii. (Arb.) 174 To calke shyppes. **1578** T. N. tr. *Conq. W. India* 313 The Vergantines were calked with Towe and Cotten Wooll. **1611** BEAUM. & FL. *Scornf. Lady* III. i, You smell as if you were new calk'd. *a* **1618** RALEIGH *Royal Navy* 27 Ocum wherewith they Calke the seams of the Ships. **1638-48** G. DANIEL *Eclog.* v. 334 How kauk'd & trim'd yᵉ Ship may be. **1697** DAMPIER *Voy.* (1698) I. x. 295 In the South Seas the Spaniards do make Oakam to chalk their Ships, with the husk of the Coco-nut. **1708** J. C. *Compl. Collier* (1845) 24 Like as a Ship or Vessel is Cawked on the Ocean. **1718** STEELE *Fish-pool* 181 Were her hold..well caulked down. **1779** FORREST *Voy. N. Guinea* 283 The vessel wanting to be fresh calked. **1801** in Nicolas *Disp. Nelson* (1845) IV. 417 They have been caulked and fitted for service. **1840** R. DANA *Bef. Mast* xxvi. 87. **1856** KANE *Arct. Expl.* II. xxv. 247 They were to be calked and swelled. **1869** SIR E. REED *Ship-build.* ii. 45 The butts of the plates can be efficiently caulked before the angle-iron is secured to the bottom.

2. To stop up the crevices of (windows, etc.).

1609 B. JONSON *Sil. Wom.* I. i, The windores close shut, and calk'd. **1725** BRADLEY *Fam. Dict.* s.v. *Fruitery*, Windows..ought to have very good double Sashes made of Paper and well caulk'd. **1796** MORSE *Amer. Geog.* II. 73 The windows are caulked up against winter. **1884** GILMOUR *Mongols* iv. 41 These houses..are log-built, the seams being caulked with moss.

fig. **1777** SHERIDAN *Sch. Scand.* II. ii, The widow Ochre caulks her wrinkles.

3. *Naut. slang.* **a.** *trans.* To stop, 'shut up'. **b.** *intr.* To sleep.

1818 'A. BURTON' *Adv. J. Newcome* 69 When he took a snoose on deck They poured salt water down his neck; Nay once, when *caulking*, for a freak They triced him half way to the Peak. **1836** E. HOWARD *R. Reefer* lxx, I can't sleep, Rattlin, and tarnation glad am I to see that you can't caulk either. **1867** SMYTH *Sailor's Word-bk.* 173 *Caulk*, to lie down on deck and sleep, with clothes on. **1881** W. C. RUSSELL *Ocean Free L.* II. 131 To caulk his banter, I asked him, etc.

caulkage ('kɔːkɪdʒ). *rare*⁻¹. [f. CAULK *v.* + -AGE; cf. *cordage*.] Material for caulking a ship.

1745 P. THOMAS *Jrnl. Anson's Voy.* 171 From the Husk covering the Shell of the Nut..they make Caulkage.

caulken, var. of CALKIN.

1883 CRANE *Smithy & Forge* 47 Caulkens..general on the hind shoes in London, and many parts, for heavy work.

caulker ('kɔːkə(r)). Forms: 5– **calker,** 6 **cawker,** 7– **caulker.** [f. CAULK *v.* + -ER¹.]

1. One whose work it is to caulk ships.

1495 *Act. 11 Hen. VII*, xxii. §1 A maister Calker by the day iiijd. **1552** HULOET, Calkers betle, or malle to dryue in towe. **1611** BIBLE *Ezek.* xxvii. 9, 27. **1653** H. COGAN tr. *Pinto's Trav.* xvi. 55 One was a ship wright, and the other a Caulker. **1780** COXE *Russ. Disc.* 107 Old cordage fit for caulker's use. **1802** *Naval Chron.* VII. 370 The..caulkers continued at their work.

2. A tool for caulking, ? a caulking-iron.

1543 *Richmond. Wills* (1853) 43 Iij payre of pynsowrs, vid. ..ij cawkers, ijd. **1779** *Naval Chron.* (1799) I. 203 It.. shivered two caulkers to pieces. **1899** *Daily News* 10 June 8/7 The pneumatic caulkers.

3. *slang.* A dram, a 'drop' of liquor. [? something 'to keep out the wet'.]

1808 J. MAYNE *Siller Gun* 89 (Jam.) The magistrates wi' loyal din, Tak aff their cau'kers. **1832-53** *Whistle-binkie* (Sc. Songs) Ser. III. 89 Wi' here tak' a caulker, and there tak' a horn. *a* **1854** J. WILSON *Trees*, Neither you nor I..can be much the worse..of a caulker of whiskey.

4. *slang.* Anything surprising or incredible; cf. *crammer*.

caulker, var. of CALKER².

caulking ('kɔːkɪŋ), *vbl. sb.* [f. CAULK *v.*]

1. The action of the verb CAULK. Also *fig.*

1481-90 *Howard Househ. Bks.* (1841) 70 To the Spanyard for kalkyng iijd. **1577** EDEN & WILLES *Hist. Trav.* 224 b, Lycour..lyke vnto pytche..very commodious for the calkyng of shyppes. **1692** in *Capt. Smith's Seaman's Gram.* I. xvi. 76 *Caulking*, is driving of Ockham, Span-hair, and the like into all the seams of the Ship, to keep out Water. **1884** *Law Times* 10 May 26/2 Repairs of caulking.

2. *attrib.* and in *comb.*, as **caulking-chisel**, a chisel for closing the seams between iron plates; **caulking-iron**, an instrument resembling a chisel used for driving the oakum into the seams of ships; **caulking-mallet**, a mallet for driving this.

1627 CAPT. SMITH *Seaman's Gram.* ii. 13 A calking Iron and a Mallet. **1666** DRYDEN *Ann. Mirab.* cxlvi, Their left-hand does the calking-iron guide. *a* **1859** MACAULAY *Hist. Eng.* (1861) V. 75 [Peter the Great] wielded with his own hand the caulking iron and the mallet. **1879** *Cornh. Mag.* Jan. 41 Docks, timber yards, calking basins, and ship-builders' yards.

caulking: see also CAUKING.

caully-flower, obs. var. of CAULIFLOWER.

caulm, var. of CALM *sb.*² mould.

caulme, obs. form of CALM *sb.*¹ ? Heat of the day or weather.

1570 LEVINS *Manip.* 44 The Caulme, *sudum, cauma*.

caulo- ('kɔːləʊ), combining form of Gr. καυλός (or L. *caulis*) stem of a plant, forming first element in various technical terms of Botany, as **'caulobulb**, a leaf-bearing or floriferous stem swollen at the base, as in *Ranunculus bulbosus*, and many orchids. **caulo'carpic, caulo'carpous** *a.* [Gr. καρπός fruit], producing flowers and fruit on its stem and branches many years without perishing, as ordinary shrubs and trees. **caulo'rhizous** *a.* [Gr. ῥίζα root], sending forth roots from the stem. **'caulosarc** = *caulobulb*. **caulo'taxis** [Gr. τάξις arrangement (after *phyllotaxis*)], (see quot.).

1880 GRAY *Bot. Text-bk.* 401 Caulocarpic, applied to plants which live to flower and fructify more than once or indefinitely. **1835-61** HENSLOW (cited by Webster for *caulocarpous*.) **1882** T. HICK in *Jrnl. Bot.* 297 The arrangement and relation of the central and lateral axes of a plant..for these the term caulotaxis will be found convenient.

caulome ('kɔːləʊm). *Bot.* [f. Gr. καυλός stem, after *rhizome*, Gr. ῥίζωμα (f. ῥιζό-ειν to strike root); see -OME. Also in Græco-Latin form *cauloma*.] The general name for the leaf-bearing axis of a plant; a stem or branch, or any member morphologically corresponding to these.

1875 BENNETT & DYER *Sachs' Bot.* I. iii. 129 Applying a common name to all those parts which bear leaves; they may be termed Stem-structures (Caulomes) or simply Axes. **1883** G. ALLEN in *Nature* 492 A central axis or caulome.

Hence **cau'lomic** *a.*, belonging to a caulome.

1880 *Nature* XXIII. 159 The bundles..belonging to the roots spring partly out of the caulomic vascular ring.

caulp, var. of CAUP *sb. Obs.*

†**'cauly,** *a. Obs. rare.* [f. CAUL *sb.*¹ + -Y¹.] Of the nature of a caul.

1615 CROOKE *Body of Man* 94 Immediately vnder these Cipresse wings..or Cauly cobwebs, appeareth the Maze or labyrinth of the guts.

cauly flower, obs. var. of CAULIFLOWER.

caum, var. of CALM and CAME *sb.*

caum, *v. Sc.* 'To whiten with CAMSTONE' (Jamieson).

‖**cauma** ('kɔːmə). *Med.* [L., a. Gr. καῦμα burning heat.] The burning heat of a fever.

1811 HOOPER *Med. Dict.* **1880** in *Syd. Soc. Lex.*

caumatic (kɔːˈmætɪk). *Med.* [f. Gr. καῦμα, καυματ- burning heat + -IC.] Relating to the burning heat of a fever.
1880 in *Syd. Soc. Lex.*

caumbre, obs. form of CHAMBER.

caum stane, var. of CAMSTONE.
1831 in Hone *Year Bk.* 1127 A multifarious variety of articles, such as..sand, caum stane, herrings.

caun-: see CAN-; CAUNGED, see CHANGED.

caunter. *dial.* and *Mining.* [app. a deriv. of CANT *sb.*[1] or *v.*[2]; but the value of the -ER is doubtful. App. diffused in Mining use from Cornwall.]
A. as *sb.* (or ? *absol.* use of *adj.*): **a.** (also **caunter-lode**), a lode crossing the general direction of the veins in a mine, a cross-vein.
1810 J. T. in *Risdon's Surv. Devon* p. xiii, Besides the east and west veins, others are found which run either north or south, or on points of the compass between these; they are called by the miner cross lodes, cross courses, or caunters. **1858** SIMMONDS *Dict. Trade, Caunter-lode*, a lode which inclines at a considerable angle to the other contiguous veins. **1881** RAYMOND *Mining Gloss.*
b. (See quot.)
1880 *W. Cornwall Gloss., Caunter*, a cross-handed blow.
B. *adj.* (or ? *attrib.*) Crossing, cross, transverse.
1880 *Prospectus of W. Frontino & Bolivia Gold Mining Co.* 3 The several lodes..have a strike..crossed by a great number of caunter branches, or feeders.

†**cauntercotte.** *Obs.* [Cf. CANTEL-COPE, CANTORCOPE.] A kind of ecclesiastical vestment.
1552-3 *Inv. Ch. Goods, Staffs.* in *Ann. Lichfield* IV. 26 Itm. v. albes, ij cauntercottes, iiij alterclothes.

†**caup, caulp.** *Sc. Obs.* [Of doubtful derivation: ON. *kaup* stipulation, wages, pay, suits the form, and perhaps the sense; but a Celtic origin would *a priori* be expected.] (See quot. 1597.)
1489 *Act Jas. IV* (1597) § 18 Certaine Gentlemen..heads of kin in Galloway hes vsed to take Caupes. **1597** SKENE *De verb. signif., Caupes, Calpes*, in Galloway and Carrict, signifies ane gift, sik as horse, or vther thing, quhilk ane man in his awin life-time, & liege poustie giues to his Maister, or to onie vther man, that is greatest in power and authoritie, and speciallie to the head & chiefe of the clan, for his maintenance & protection, like as for the samin effect and cause, sindrie persons payis Black-maill to thieues, or mainteiners of thieues, contrair the laws of this realme. Bot in the Iles and Hie-lande of this Realme, the Calpes are presentlie payed be him, quha oblishis him theirfore, after his decease. Swa the Hereȝelde is payed be provision of the Law: and Calpe is given be speciall paction and obligation, baith the ane and the vther, after the decease of the debtor. Ane notable oppression is vsed in taking vp of the Caupe. **1609** —— *Reg. Maj.* xxiii. 137 Caupes sould not be taken be gentlemen, and heads of the kin in Galloway, and Carrick, vnder the paine of oppression. **1617** *Act Jas VI*, xxi, The Vnlawfull taking from them, after their deceisse, vnder the name of Caulpes, of their best aucht, whether it be Oxe, Meare, Horse, or Cowe. **1885** *Edin. Rev.* Apr. 326 Caulpes which were fines on the death of a Vassal or a tenant.

caup, var. of CAP *sb.*[3], a bowl.

cauphe, cauph-house: see COFFEE *sb.*, -HOUSE.

cauple, variant of CAPLE, *Obs.*, a horse.

†ˈ**cauponate,** *v. Obs.* [f. L. *caupōnāt-* ppl. stem of *caupōnāri* to traffic or trade in, f. *caupōnem* retail tradesman, huckster, innkeeper.]
1. *intr.* To sell liquor or victuals, keep a victualling-house.
1656 in BLOUNT *Glossogr.*; **1721** in BAILEY; **1755** in JOHNSON; and in mod. Dicts.
2. *trans.* To deal like a huckster with; to traffic in for the sake of gain. *fig.* [so L. *caupōnāri.*]
1653 GAUDEN *Hierasp.* 195 By cauponating Religion, and handling the Scriptures deceitfully. **1656** BLOUNT *Glossogr.* s.v., To cauponate a war, to make war for money. **1715** BENTLEY *Serm.* x. 360 All the Privileges of the gospel truck'd and cauponated by Popery.

†**caupoˈnation.** *Obs.* [f. as prec.: see -ATION.] Petty dealing or trafficking; tricky or unfair dealing; mixing of liquors, adulteration.
a **1555** LATIMER *Serm. & Rem.* (1845) 348 Some would preach the truth of God..without cauponation, and adulteration of the Word. **1582** N. T. (Rhem.) Pref. 9 Falsification or (to vse the Apostles Wordes) cauponation and adulteration of Gods word. **1675** R. VAUGHAN *Coinage* 2 A second use of Cauponation. **1715** BENTLEY *Serm.* x. 346 Expose their corruptions and cauponations of the Gospel.

†ˈ**cauponize,** *v. Obs.* [f. L. *caupōn-em* (see CAUPONATE) + -IZE.]
1. *intr.* To act as victualler, huckster, or sutler.
1765 WARBURTON *Lett. late Prelate* (1808) No. 171 The wealth of our rich rogues, who cauponised to the Armies in Germany in this last war.
2. *trans.* To traffic in like a retail dealer or tavern-keeper; to mix and adulterate for gain.
1652 GAULE *Magastrom.* To Rdr., To the great dishonouring of God..despising of the Spirit, cauponizing of the Word. **1771** WESLEY *Wks.* (1872) V. 459 We do not cauponize, mix, adulterate, or soften it [the word of God].

caure. *Sc.* Bad spelling of *ca'er*, for *cauver, calver*, calves: see CALF.
1806 R. JAMIESON *Pop. Ballads* I. 286 (Jam.) The caure did haig, the queis low. **1868** G. MACDONALD *R. Falconer* I. 41 Wha ever heard o' caure at this time o' the year?

caurie, caury, obs. forms of COWRIE.

Caursin, -yn, var. of CAORSIN.

Caurus (ˈkɔːrəs). *arch.* [L., also *Corus.*] The stormy north-west wind, often personified.
c **1374** CHAUCER *Boethius* I. met. iii. (1868) 9 A swifte wynde þat hyȝt chorus. **1696** PHILIPS *World of Words* (ed. 5), *Caurus*, a Western or Northwest Wind blowing commonly out of the British Sea. **1748** THOMSON *Cast. Indol.* II. lxxviii, The ground, by piercing Caurus seared.

†**caury-maury.** *Obs.* Also **cawry-mawry, cauri-mauri.** ? A kind of coarse, rough material.
1287 in Rogers *Hist. Agric. & Prices* II. 536/4 [Linen and Clothing] T[? C]aursmaurs. **1362** LANGL. *P. Pl.* A. v. 62, I-cloþed in A Caurimauri [*v.r.* caury maury, cawrymawry, kaurymaury] I couþe him not discreue. *a* **1529** SKELTON *Elynour Rum.* 149 Some loke strawry, Some cawry-mawry.

‖ˈ**causa.** The L. word for CAUSE, occas. used in Eng., *esp.* in the phrases ***causa causans*** a causing cause, i.e. a primary or original cause; ***causa causata*** a caused cause, a secondary or intermediate cause; ***vera causa*** a true or real cause.
c **1420** *Chron. Vilod.* 428 For he was causa of his brotheris deythe. **1659** RUSHW. *Hist. Coll.* I. 461 Among the Logicians there are two causes; there is Causa causans, and Causa Causata. The Causa causans..is not the Warrant from the Lords of the Council, for that is Causa causata.

causable (ˈkɔːzəb(ə)l), *a. rare.* [f. CAUSE *v.* + -ABLE.] That may be caused.
1646 SIR T. BROWNE *Pseud. Ep.* III. xxi, That..which is naturally causable. *Ibid.* VII. vi, The Deluge..being not possibly causable from naturall showres above, or watery eruptions below. **1794-6** E. DARWIN *Zoon.* (1801) I. 43 The fibrous contractions became causable by volition.
Hence **causaˈbility.**
1881 *Nature* No. 616. 372 The causability of tubercle.

causal (ˈkɔːzəl), *a.* (*sb.*) [ad. L. *causālis* relating to a cause, f. *causa* cause: cf. F. *causal.*]
1. Of or relating to a cause or causes.
1570 BILLINGSLEY *Euclid* XI. def. xii. 316 A causall definition geuen by the Cause efficient. **1677** GALE *Crt. Gentiles* II. IV. 268 The independence of the Divine Essence as to al causes and causal limitation. **1858** WHEWELL *Novum Org. Renov.* 121 (L.) Aiming at the formation of a causal section in each science of phenomena.
2. Of the nature of a cause: acting as a cause.
1642 *View of Print. Book int. Observat.* 12 This peoples election..hath no causall influx..into the Regall power conveyed. **1672** H. MORE *Brief Reply* 262 As being a means to this end, and, therefore, Causal thereto. **1699** BURNET *39 Art.* xvii. (1700) 162 The Certainty of the Prescience is not antecedent or causal, but subsequent and eventual. **1858** MANSEL *Bampton Lect.* ii. (ed. 4) 34 The condition of causal activity. **1881** P. BROOKS *Candle of Lord* 101 One supreme causal God.
3. Of the nature of cause and effect.
1656 H. MORE *Antid. Ath.* III. iii. (1712) 91 Any causal connexion betwixt those ceremonies and the ensuing Tempests. **1712** BLACKMORE *Creation* 225 The links of all the causal chain. **1855** H. SPENCER *Princ. Psychol.* (1872) I. IV. vii. 463 The causal connexions among those traits were obscured by other connexions. **1856** EMERSON *Eng. Traits, Lit.* Wks. (Bohn) II. 109 That..the term cause and effect was loosely or gratuitously applied to what we know only as consecutive, not at all as causal.
4. *Gram.* and *Logic.* Expressing a cause. ***causal proposition*** : see quot. 1724.
c **1530** MORE *Answ. Frith* Wks. 840/2 Thoughe I woulde graunt this causale proposicion. *a* **1638** MEDE *Wks.* I. xix. (1672) 70 A causal or conditional Conjunction. **1655** GURNALL *Chr. in Arm.* i. § 2 (1669) 59/1 The words are coupled to the precedent with that causal particle *For.* **1724** WATTS *Logic* 167 Causal propositions are, where two propositions are joined by causal particles; as, houses were not built, that they might be destroyed. **1870** JEBB *Sophocles' Electra* (ed. 2) 8/2 Τήρῳ and χρόνῳ..are causal datives.
B. as *sb.* **a.** A causal conjunction or particle.
1530 PALSGR., 148 Some [conjunctions] be causales & serve to bring in a sentence whereby the cause of a mater spoken of before is expressed. **1750** HARRIS *Hermes* ii. (1786) 245 Causals subjoin causes to effects.
b. A thing implying a cause.
1652 W. SCLATER *Civil Magist.* (1653) 25 Causalls they are ..casual they are not.

causalgia (kɔːˈzældʒɪə). *Path.* [mod.L., f. Gr. καῦσος heat, fever (καίειν to burn) + ἄλγος pain, after NEURALGIA.] A severe burning pain in the extremities resulting from injury to peripheral nerves.
1872 S. W. MITCHELL *Injuries of Nerves* x. 272 Causalgia or burning pain. A vast number of means were tried to ease or cure causalgia, but the one essential for comfort was the use of water-dressings. **1949** R. L. SUTTON *Handbk. Dis. Skin* 467 Causalgia is a neuralgia featuring burning pain of a sort that is tolerable until the patient is touched.

causality (kɔːˈzælɪtɪ). [mod. f. on L. type *causālitās, f. *causāl-is* CAUSAL + -ITY.]
1. Causal quality, character, efficiency, or agency; fact or state of being or acting as a cause.
1603 SIR C. HEYDON *Jud. Astrol.* ii. 69 When they are called signes, their causalitie is not excluded. **1649** JER. TAYLOR *Life Christ* II. x. vii. ⁋6 Faith is the beginning grace, and hath influence and causality in the production of the other. **1678** CUDWORTH *Intell. Syst.* 750 A Power or Causality, whereby that which was Not before, was afterwards Made to Be. **1748** HARTLEY *Observ. Man* II. i. ⁋16. 67 To ascribe a real Causality to Free-will. **1875** GRINDON *Life* ii. 14 Nature has no independent activity, no causality of its own.
2. The operation or relation of cause and effect; 'the law of mind which makes it necessary to recognise power adequate to account for every occurrence' (*Fleming's Vocab. Philos.* 1887).
1642 O. SEDGWICKE *England's Preserv.* 10 By way of order only, and not by causality. **1817** COLERIDGE *Biog. Lit.* 62 The law of causality holds only between homogeneous things. **1836-7** SIR W. HAMILTON *Metaph.* xxxix (1859) II. 376 The nature and genealogy of the notion of Causality. **1860** EMERSON *Cond. Life* ii. (1861) 34 A belief in causality, or strict connection between every trifle and the principle of being..characterizes all valuable minds. **1870** BOWEN *Logic* x. 333 The necessary laws of Causality and Time.
3. *Phrenology.* The mental faculty of tracing effects to causes.
1874 BLACKIE *Self-Cult.* 6 The quality of mind, which.. phrenologists call causality.
¶**4.** An excuse. (? Not Eng.)
1656 BLOUNT *Glossogr., Causality, Causation*, an excuse, essoyning or pretence.

causally (ˈkɔːzəlɪ), *adv.* [f. CAUSAL + -LY[2].] In a causal way, with causal force; in the manner of, or as being the cause; by way of cause and effect.
a **1638** MEDE *Wks.* I. xxiv. (1672) 91 *Καὶ* is..to be taken here [Luke ii. 14] for a conjunction causal..Or both causally and gratulatorily. **1634** RAINBOW *Labour* (1635) 22 It cannot be said to be causally perishing. **1640-4** SIR S. D'EWES in Rushw. *Hist. Coll.* III. (1692) I. 314 The Elector of Saxony is causally guilty..of those Calamities and Slaughters. **1845** *Blackw. Mag.* LVII. 523 From the death of Patroclus to the death of Hector is an entirely new movement, though causally bound..to that antecedent. *a* **1847** CHALMERS *Posth. Wks.* (1847) I. 22 He was appeased causally and efficiently by God, yet proximately and intermediately by the presents..laid before him.

†ˈ**causant,** *a. Obs.* [ad. L. *causans*, pr. pple. of *causāre* to cause.] Causing, acting as a cause.
1677 GALE *Crt. Gentiles* II. IV. 464 Every second cause, whether causant or conservant.

†ˈ**causarily,** *adv. Obs.* [f. CAUSARY + -LY[2].] By reason of a legally recognized cause.
1651 W. G. tr. *Cowel's Inst.* 38 There is also a Guardian simply and originally so called, and a Guardian by accident, from the cause of custody..Causarily, is he who for that he hath the custody of his own Tenant being yet an Infant hath upon that score the custody of another who is Tenant to his Ward.

†ˈ**causary,** *a. Obs.* [ad. L. *causāri-us* discharged because of ill-health, invalid, f. *causa* cause, reason. In med.L. used more widely.] Having good and sufficient cause. ***causary dismission*** (L. *causaria missio*): orig. a dismissal from military service on account of ill-health.
1602 SEGAR *Hon. Mil. & Civ.* I. viii. 11 Dioclesianus and Maximianus ordained, That vnto euery Veteran hauing honestly serued..twentie yeeres, an honourable or causarie dismission [*causaria missio*] should be granted.

†ˈ**causate,** *a.* (*sb.*) *Obs.* Also **caussate.** [ad. med.L. *causāt-us*, pa. pple. of *causāre* to CAUSE.]
A. *adj.* Caused, due to a cause. **B.** *sb.* A thing caused, an effect.
1652 GAULE *Magastrom.* 103 A conscientionall, accidentall event..but no appropriate, causate, and observate experiment. **1657** J. SMITH *Myst. Rhet.* A vij b, The Caussate,..depends upon the Cause, as having its being thence.

cauˈsate, *v. rare.* [f. med.L. *causāt-* ppl. stem of *causāre*; see -ATE[3].] **a.** *trans.* To cause, originate. **b.** *intr.* To originate.
1839 BAILEY *Festus* (1854) 535 That Divinity..Wherein all things authentic do causate. **1855** —— *Mystic* 135 When ..unnumbered times..Have passed, shall God..another world causate.

causation (kɔːˈzeɪʃən). [ad. L. *causātiōn-em* excuse, pretext, used in med.L. in sense 'action of causing', f. med.L. *causāre.* Cf. F. *causation.*]
1. The action of causing; production of an effect.
1646 SIR T. BROWNE *Pseud. Ep.* I. xi, Ascribing effects thereunto [to the stars] of independent causations. **1695** CONGREVE *Love for L.* III. xi. 59 Albertus Magnus..says it [Astrology] teaches us to consider the Causation of Causes, in the Causes of things. *c* **1790** REID *Let.* in Wks. I. 76/1 The thing most essential to causation in its proper meaning—to wit, efficiency—is wanting. **1817** COLERIDGE *Biog. Lit.* 293 It sometimes happens that we are punished for our faults by incidents, in the causation of which these faults had no share. **1875** STUBBS *Const. Hist.* I. i. 1 The causation of any particular movement or the origin of any particular measure.
b. The operation of causal energy; the relation of cause and effect.
1739 HUME *Human Nat.* I. iv, Cousins in the fourth degree are connected by causation. **1809** W. IRVING *Knickerb.* (1861) 13 To detect..some latent chain of causation. **1831** BLAKEY *Free Will* 198 All that we know of physical causation is, that one thing precedes another in a regular order of sequence. **1860** EMERSON *Cond. Life, Fates* (1861) 29 A man

. . looks like a piece of luck, but is a piece of causation. **1883** A. BARRATT *Phys. Metempiric* 85 The broad relation . . between noumena and their phenomena, seems most reasonably conceived as one of Efficient Causation, not the mere sequence of phenomena which we call physical causation.

¶ **2.** An excuse. (L. *causatio*; ? not Eng.)

1656 BLOUNT *Glossogr.*, *Causation*, an excuse, essoyning or pretence. **1662** PHILLIPS, *Causation* (Lat.), an excusing, or alleadging of a cause.

Hence **cau'sationism**, the theory or principle of universal causation; **cau'sationist**, one who believes in this theory or principle.

1847 EMERSON *Repr. Men, Montaigne* Wks. (Bohn) I. 345 We are natural conservers and causationists, and reject a sour dumpish unbelief. **1860** —— *Cond. Life* ii. All successful men have agreed in one thing—they were causationists. They believed that things went not by luck but by law.

causational (kɔːˈzeɪʃənəl), *a.* [f. CAUSATION + -AL.] Belonging to the law or doctrine of causation.

1909 in WEBSTER. **1925** J. E. TURNER *Theory of Direct Realism* 9 The causational aspects of perception. **1930** G. R. DE BEER *Embryology & Evolution* i. 7 The causational idea that the succession of palingenetic stages in ontogeny is due to these stages having succeeded one another in phylogeny.

causative (ˈkɔːzətɪv), *a.* Also 5 **-ife.** [a. F. *causatif*, ad. L. *causātīvus*; see CAUSE *v.* and -IVE.]

1. Effective as a cause, productive *of* (an effect).

a **1420** OCCLEVE *De Reg. Princ.* 3848 It of his dethe was verray causatife. *c* **1425** WYNTOUN *Cron.* IX. xxvii. 255 The Proces Causative That eftyr folowit effective. **1605** BACON *Adv. Learn.* II. viii. §1 That, that is causative in nature of a number of effects. **1830** COLERIDGE *Rem.* (1836) III. 1 That which is essentially causative of all being must be causative of its own. **1877** MORLEY *Crit. Misc.* Ser. II. 321 A superhuman causative agency.

b. *ellipt.* Of causation, of the existence of a causative agency.

1842 W. GROVE *Corr. Phys. Forces* (ed. 6) 9 Hypothetical currents were supposed, for the purpose of carrying out the causative view.

2. *Gram.* Expressing a cause or causation; = CAUSAL 4. Also as *sb.*, a causative word.

c **1600** SWINBURN *Spousals* (1686) 149 These words . . are to be understood causative. **1750–1** *Student* II. 308 (T.) Let any Hebrew reader judge whether *hiphel* . . can properly be said, in general . . to be causative. **1824** J. GILCHRIST *Etymol. Interp.* 150 Lay is manifestly the causative of Lie. **1879** WHITNEY *Skr. Gram.* §540 The secondary or derivative conjugations are . . the passive, the intensive, the desiderative, the causative. *Ibid.* 607 This stem . . has to a great extent a causative value.

Hence **'causativeness, causa'tivity,** the fact of being causative, causative quality.

1846 O. BROWNSON *Wks.* VI. 107 He is the causativeness of all and of each. **1856** J. H. NEWMAN *Callista* 67 The egg comes first in relation to the causativity of the chick, and the chick comes first in relation to the causativity of the egg. **1862** F. HALL *Hindu Philos. Syst.* 208 Its causativity is accounted for by erroneous imputation.

causatively (ˈkɔːzətɪvlɪ), *adv.* [f. prec. + -LY².] In a causative manner; by way of causation, by acting as a cause. **b.** *Gram.* In a causative sense, as expressing cause.

1654 WARREN *Unbelievers* 45 Christ hath causatively removed by his death the guilt of sin. **1750–1** *Student* II. 308 (T.) Several conjugations . . whether they are to be taken actively, passively, causatively, or absolutely. **1824** DE QUINCEY *Pol. Econ. Dial.* v. (1860) 553 Gravitation has causatively impressed that direction on its course.

‖**cau'sator.** *Obs.* [med.L. *causātor*, f. *causāre* to CAUSE.] One who causes, a causer.

1646 SIR T. BROWNE *Pseud. Ep.* I. x, The indivisible condition of the first causator.

‖**cau'satrix.** *Obs.* [fem. of prec.; see -TRIX.] A female causer.

1650 CHARLETON *Paradoxes* Prol. 14 Nature . . the prime and proxime Causatrix of all Sanation.

‖**cau'satum.** [med.L.] That which is caused; the product of causation.

1879 LEWES *Study Psychol.* 24 An effect is the causatum, the incorporation of the causes or co-operant conditions.

cause (kɔːz), *sb.* Also 4–6 **cawse,** 4–7 *Sc.* **causs,** 5–6 *Sc.* **caus,** 5 *Sc.* **caws,** 6 **causse,** 6–7 **caus.** [a. F. *cause* (= Pr., Sp., It. *causa*), ad. L. *causa*, *caussa*. The latter came down in living use as It., Sp., Pr. *cosa*, ONF. *cose*, F. *chose* matter, thing (a sense which *causa* has in the Salic Law, in Gregory of Tours, and the Capitularies). At a later period the med.L. *causa*, of philosophy and the law-courts, was taken into the living languages, in the form *causa, cause*; in Fr. from the 13th c.]

I. General senses.

1. That which produces an effect; that which gives rise to any action, phenomenon, or condition. *Cause* and *effect* are correlative terms.

c **1315** SHOREHAM 117 Cause of alle thyse dignyte . . Was Godes owene grace. **1398** TREVISA *Barth. De P.R.* IX. xxv. (1495) 362 The cause of nyghte is shadowe of the erthe that is bytwene vs and the sonne. *c* **1400** *Test. Love* II. (1560) 285/2 Every cause of a cause is cause of thing caused. **1549** *Compl. Scot.* (1801) 234 The philosophour sais that the cause of ane thing is of mair efficacite nor is the thyng that procedis fra the cause. **1639** ROUSE *Heav. Univ.* x. (1702) 143 To produce effects beyond the cause; which is indeed to make something out of nothing. **1697** DRYDEN *Virg. Georg.* IV. 570 Proteus only knows The secret Cause, and Cure of all thy Woes. **1751** JOHNSON *Rambl.* No. 141 ¶1 The greatest events may be often traced back to slender causes. **1827** POLLOK *Course of T.* v, These were the occasion, not the cause, of joy. **1879** LOCKYER *Elem. Astron.* iii. 83 The Sun's heat and the Earth's rotation are, in the main, the causes of all atmospheric disturbances.

b. as philosophically defined.

1656 tr. *Hobbes' Elem. Philos.* II. ix. (1839) 121 A cause simply, or an entire cause, is the aggregate of all the accidents both of the agents how many soever they be, and of the patient, put together; which when they are all supposed to be present, it cannot be understood but that the effect is produced at the same instant. *c* **1790** REID *Wks.* I. 76/1 We have no ground to ascribe efficiency to natural causes, or even necessary connection with the effect. But we still call them causes, including nothing under the name but priority and constant conjunction. *Ibid.* 77/1 In the strict philosophical sense, I take a cause to be that which has the relation to the effect which I have to my voluntary and deliberate actions. **1846** MILL *Logic* (1856) III. v. §5 We may define . . the cause of a phenomenon, to be the antecedent or the concurrence of antecedents, on which it is invariably and unconditionally consequent. **1870** JEVONS *Elem. Logic* xxviii. 239 By the Cause of an event we mean the circumstances which must have preceded in order that the event should happen.

2. A person or other agent who brings about or occasions something, with or without intention. (Often in bad sense: one who occasions, or is to blame for mischief, misfortune, etc.)

c **1374** CHAUCER *Anel. & Arc.* 257 Þaughe þat yee þus Causelesse þe Cause be Of my dedely aduersitee. **1509** FISHER *Fun. Serm. C'tess Richmond* (1708) 28, I am, sayth he, the veray cause of raysynge of the Body, and I am also the veray Cause of lyfe unto the Soule. **1540** HYRDE tr. *Vives' Instr. Chr. Wom.* (1592) G v, Howe much mischiefe such women bee cause of. **1611** BIBLE *1 Chron.* xxi. 3 Why will hee be a cause of trespasse to Israel? **1660** STANLEY *Hist. Philos.* (1701) 73 The Mind is the disposer and cause of all things. **1697** DRYDEN *Virg. Georg.* I. 92 The Laws Imposed by Nature, and by Nature's Cause. **1713** BERKELEY *Hylas & P.* ii, God is the supreme and universal Cause of all things. **1830** TENNYSON *Dream Fair Wom.* 104 'My youth', she said, 'was blasted with a curse: This woman was the cause.' **1859** —— *Enid* 87 Am I the cause, I the poor cause that men Reproach you?

3. A fact, condition of matters, or consideration, moving a person to action; ground of action; reason for action, motive.

a **1225** *Ancr. R.* 320 Cause is hwi þu hit dudest, oðer hulpe þerto, oðer þuruh hwon hit bigon. **1340** *Ayenb.* 42 Huanne þe seruises byeþ y-do uor onclenliche cause. *c* **1460** FORTESCUE *Abs. & Lim. Mon.* (1714) 67 Movyd therto by non other Cause, save only drede of his Rebellion. **1526** *Pilgr. Perf.* (W. de W. 1531) 1 The cause why we name this treatyse yᵉ pilgrymage of perfeccion. **1575** LANEHAM *Let.* (1871) 3 Az I haue good cauz to think. **1592** WEST *Symbol.* I. §55 (1632) The consideration of instruments is the motiue cause, for which the Instruments are made. **1655** *Comp. Clark* 310 The said F.R. as well for the considerations aforesaid as also . . for divers other good causes and considerations . . doth for himself and his Heirs covenant. **1678** CUDWORTH *Intell. Syst.* (1837) I. 77 To give just cause of suspicion. **1785** REID *Let.* in *Wks.* I. 65/2 A reason . . is often called a cause **1876** GREEN *Short Hist.* iii. §4 (1882) 129 The causes which drew students and teachers within the walls of Oxford.

b. In a pregnant sense: Good, proper, or adequate ground of action; esp. in ***to have cause, have no cause, with cause, without cause***; so ***to show cause***, esp. in Eng. Law, to argue against the confirmation of a 'rule nisi' or other provisionally granted order or judgement.

1375 BARBOUR *Bruce* IX. 25, I had gret causs hym for to slay. **1413** LYDG. *Pylgr. Sowle* III. vii, They . . kepen hit withouten ony cause. *c* **1440** *York Myst.* xvi. 49 For fadir, vnkyndnes ȝe kythe þem no cause. **1520** in W. H. Turner *Select Rec. Oxford* 26 To . . shew a cause why he ought not to be . . disfranchised. **1549** *Bk. Com. Prayer, Matrimony*, If any of you know cause, or just impediment, why these two persons should not be joined together. **1561** T. NORTON *Calvin's Inst.* I. xvii. §1 Modesty, that wee draw not God to yeeld cause of his doings. **1611** BIBLE *Pref.* 9 To amend it where he saw cause. **1747** in *Col. Rec. Penn.* V. 88 The Government of Pennsylvania had not seen cause yet to contribute something towards it. **1768** BLACKSTONE *Comm.* III. 265 Upon good cause shewn to the court. **1865** CARLYLE *Fredk. Gt.* I. II. vi. 84 The Order got into its wider troubles . . with Christian neighbours . . who did not love it, and for cause. **1867** *Law Rep. 2* Q.B. 360 A rule was obtained . . to enter the verdict for the plaintiff . . Hayes, Serjt., and Beasley, shewed cause. **1875** JOWETT *Plato* (ed. 2) III. 347 If a man has cause of offence against another. **1883** *Law Rep. 11 Queen's B.* 597 The plaintiff has been defamed, and has primâ facie a cause of action.

c. ***cause why***: 'reason why', reason. Sometimes used interrogatively, or conjunctively: Why, for the reason that, for this reason. *Obs.* exc. *dial.*

1340 HAMPOLE *Pr. Consc.* 3526 God wate wele þe cause why. *c* **1386** CHAUCER *Sqrs. T.* 177 And cause why? for they kan nat the craft. *c* **1440** *Gesta Rom.* viii. 21 (Harl. MS.) He is gilty of my dethe, and I shalle telle you cause why. *c* **1449** PECOCK *Repr.* II. XIII. 222 Cause whi God wole ȝeue his gracis . . is this. **1548** UDALL, etc. *Erasm. Par. Matt.* v. 42 There is no cause why to cut off these membres. **1581** CAMPION in *Confer.* I. (1584) C b, You must consider . . the cause why. **1856** KINGSLEY *Let.* in *Life* xiv. (1879) II. 21 Such a view . . as tourist never saw, nor will see, 'case why, he can't find it. [Cf. CAUSE *conj.*]

†**4.** The object of action; purpose, end. *Obs.* exc. in **b.** ***final cause***: a term introduced into philosophical language by the schoolmen as a transl. of Aristotle's fourth cause, τὸ οὗ ἕνεκα or τέλος, the end or purpose for which a thing is done, viewed as the cause of the act; *esp.* applied in Natural Theology to the design, purpose, or end of the arrangements of the universe.

c **1386** CHAUCER *Clerkes T.* 386 This Markys hath hire spoused with a ryng Broght for the same cause. **1514** BARCLAY *Cyt. & Uplondyshm* (1847) p. xlix, Then all be fooles . . Which with glad mindes use courting for such cause. **1595** HUNNIS *Joseph* 59 For to sojourne in the land, is cause we come to thee.

b. 1587 GOLDING *De Mornay* x. 149 Let us consequently see the final cause: that is to wit, how and to what ende he guydeth it. *c* **1660** BOYLE *Disquis. Final Causes* §1 Those that would exclude final causes from the consideration of the naturalist . . either that, with Epicurus, they think . . it is improper and vain to seek for final causes in the effects of chance: or . . with Descartes, that . . it is rash for men to think, that they know, or can investigate, what ends [God] proposed to Himself in His actings about His creatures. **1691** RAY *Creation* I. (1701) 49 The Continuation of these two Motions of the Earth . . upon Axes not parallel, is resolvable into nothing but a final and mental Cause, or the τὸ βέλτιστον, because it was best it should be so. **1768** STERNE *Sent. Journ.* (1778) I. 24 The efficient as well as the final causes of travelling. **1857** BUCKLE *Civilis.* I. viii. 541 Descartes . . was, of course, led to abandon the study of final causes. **1881** B. SANDERSON in *Nature* No. 619. 439 The final cause of an animal . . is muscular action, because it is by means of its muscles that it maintains its external relations.

5. In the preceding senses, with various defining attributes.

The *four causes* of Aristotle were the ***efficient cause***, the force, instrument, or agency by which a thing is produced; the ***formal*** (see quot. 1678); the ***material***, the elements or matter from which it is produced; the ***final***, the purpose or end for which it is produced (see 4 b). The ***First Cause***, the original cause or Creator of the Universe; ***secondary causes***, those derived from a primary or first cause. ***occasional causes*** in Cartesian philosophy: see OCCASIONAL, -ISM.

1393 GOWER *Conf.* III. 87 He clepeth god the firste cause. **1398** TREVISA *Barth. De P.R.* III. xvii. (1495) 61 The cause efficient of the syghte is the vertue of the soule that hyghte animalis. **1447** BOKENHAM *Seyntys* Introd. (1835) 1 The fyrste is what, the secunde is why, In wych two wurdys, . . The foure causys comprehended be. **1586** T. B. *La Primaud. Fr. Acad.* (1589) 667 The Philosophers propound fower causes of everie thing, The efficient, the materiall, the formall, and the finall cause. **1646** H. LAWRENCE *Commun. Angels* 31 His [God's] essence (which is the efficient, finall, and exemplary cause of all things). **1656** BEN ISRAEL *Vind. Jud.* in *Phenix* (1708) II. 409 The Knowledg of the one first Cause. **1678** HOBBES *Decameron* ii. 15 Another they call the Formal Cause, or simply the form or essence of the thing caused: as when they say, Four equal Angles and four equal Sides are the Cause of a Square Figure. **1726** AYLIFFE *Parerg.* 147 There are seven Causes consider'd in Judgment, viz. the Material, Efficient, and Formal Cause; and likewise a Natural, Substantial, and Accidental Cause; and lastly a Final Cause. **1733** POPE *Ess. Man* III. 1 The Universal Cause Acts to one end, but acts by various laws. **1742** —— *Dunciad* IV. 644 Philosophy, that lean'd on heaven before, Shrinks to her second cause, and is no more. **1845** CORRIE *Theol.* in *Encycl. Metrop.* 858/1 The main object of Theology is to ascertain the attributes and perfections of this First Great Cause. **1858** MANSEL *Bampton Lect.* ii. (ed. 4) 30 By the First Cause is meant that which produces all things, and is itself produced of none. **1862** H. SPENCER *First Princ.* I. ii. §12 (1875) 37 We are not only obliged to suppose some Cause, but also a first Cause.

6. From the general senses arise various phrases:

†**a.** ***by the cause that***: for the reason that; with the purpose that, to the end that, in order that; ***by the cause of***: by reason of, on account of. *Obs.* Hence *bi-cause*, BECAUSE, q.v.

c **1386** CHAUCER *Knts. T.* 2488 Be þe cause þat þei scholde rise Erly . . Vnto her reste went þei att nihte. *a* **1450** *Knt. de la Tour* 2 Thei had in hem no shame nor drede by the cause thei were so used. *c* **1460** FORTESCUE *Abs. & Lim. Mon.* (1714) 138 Which by the Cause therof lyvyn in the gretter penurye.

†**b.** ***for cause that***: for the reason that (= BECAUSE A. 1, B. 1). ***for cause of***: by reason of, on account of (= BECAUSE A. 2 a); for the sake of (= BECAUSE A. 2 b). *Obs.*

c **1425** WYNTOUN *Cron.* VII. vii. 205 For caws þat he past til Twlows. **1475** CAXTON *Jason* 67 Callid god of bataill for cause of many batailles that he had. **1480** —— *Chron. Eng.* ccxxii. 214 And al he did for cause of spences and for to gadre tresour. **1535** STEWART *Chron. Scot.* II. 334 For caus that tha no wald Resist the wrang. **1578** *Sc. Poems 16th C.* II. 154 For cause his faith was constantly In Christes blude.

†**c.** ***for my*** (***his***, etc.) ***cause***: on my (his, etc.) account, for my (his, etc.) sake. *Obs.*

c **1450** *Merlin* 15 Ye shull neuer be Juged to deth for my cause. *c* **1500** *Lancelot* 3395, I wald not . . for my causs, that such o knycht suld dee. **1607** TOPSELL *Four-f. Beasts* 134 I have described and set him out in this manner . . which I did for use and customs cause. **1611** BIBLE *2 Cor.* vii. 12 I did it not for his cause that had done the wrong.

¶ See also CAUSE *conj.*

II. In legal, and related senses.

(In the *Digest*, 'causa' sometimes means 'the facts of the case.')

7. *Law.* The matter about which a person goes to law; the case of one party in a suit. Hence *to plead a cause.* (Cf. 1883 in 3 b.)

1297 R. GLOUC. (Rolls) 9362þe riȝte of is cause. *c* **1300** *Beket* 1043 To bringe this cause of holi churche tofore the

Pope. *c* **1400** MAUNDEV. xvi. 172 Bothe partyes writen here Causes in 2 Billes. **1474** CAXTON *Chesse* 27 Pletyng of a cause for his client. **1553** T. WILSON *Rhet.* 6 The judges before whom..the determinacion of his cause resteth. **1611** BIBLE *Ex.* xxii. 9 The cause of both parties shall come before the Iudges. **1760** GOLDSMITH *Cit. W.* xcviii, He that has most opinions is most likely to carry his cause. **1802** MAR. EDGEWORTH *Moral T.* (1816) I. 218 Would to heaven my son could have..such a trial! And..that I might plead his cause!

b. *fig.*

c **1489** CAXTON *Sonnes of Aymon* xxvi. 545 Ye can speke shrewdly wythoute a cause lawfull. **1568** BIBLE (Bishops') *Ps.* xxxv. 1 Pleade thou my cause O Lord. **1611** BIBLE *Pref.* 6 This seemeth to argue a bad cause.

8. *Law.* A subject of litigation; a matter before a court for decision; an action, process, suit; = CASE *sb.*^{1} 6.

c **1325** *E.E. Allit. P.* A. 701 To corte..þer alle oure causez schal be tryed. *c* **1330** R. BRUNNE *Chron.* (1810) 128 In alle manere cause he sought þe right in skille. **1399** LANGL. *Rich Redeles* III. 318 To ben of conceill for causis that in the court hangit. **1495** *Act 11 Hen. VII*, xxiv. §1 In any accion or cause personell. **1529** RASTELL *Pastyme Hist. Fr.* (1811) 73 He was in all cawsis so indyfferent. **1652** NEEDHAM tr. *Selden's Mare Cl.* 5 This caus could not by any pretens bee brought into judgment. **1752** JOHNSON *Rambl.* No. 201 ¶11 He was summoned as an evidence in a cause of great importance. **1790** BURKE *Fr. Rev.* 302 The governing power, which, in the midst of a cause, or on the prospect of it, may wholly change the rule of decision. **1879** CARPENTER *Ment. Phys.* II. x. 436 Further proceedings having been taken in a cause which he had heard some years previously.

b. Hence (Sc.) *day* or *hour of cause*: i.e. of trial; also *fig.* and *transf.*

1818 SCOTT *Hrt. Midl.* xxiv, Whispering to Plumdamas that he would meet him at Mac Croskie's..in the hour of cause. **1822** —— *Nigel* xxxvii, I will be with you in the hour of cause.

c. *fig.* Matter in dispute, an affair to be decided.

c **1500** *Lancelot* 1495 Ther god hyme-self hath ton the causs on hond. **1593** SHAKS. *2 Hen. VI*, III. i. 289 What counsaile giue you in this weightie cause? **1665** MANLEY *Grotius' Low-C. Warrs* 283 Ready to decide the cause by Battel.

†**9.** Contextually, and in translating L. *causa* or Gr. *αἰτία*, it sometimes has or approaches the sense 'charge, accusation, blame'. *Obs.*

c **1340** *Cursor M.* 16681 (Laud) The cawse of his deth they wroght Abovyn his hed. **1382** WYCLIF *Acts* xxv. 27 For to sende a boundun man, and not to signifie the cause of him. **1494** FABYAN VII. 494 Many..whiche laye there [in the prisons] for great causes and crymes. *c* **1550** CHEKE *Matt.* xxiii. 37 þei set his caus in writing over his hed. **1605** SHAKS. *Lear* IV. vi. 111, I pardon that mans life. What was thy cause? Adultery?

†**b.** *to be in cause*: to be to blame. *Obs.*

c **1400** *Apol. Loll.* 25 Prelats mai sore drede, þat her vniust & iuilwilly cursing be in cause whi þe puple dredeþ not cursing. *c* **1400** *Rom. Rose* 4525 Who was in cause..But hir silfe? **1635** R. N. tr. *Camden's Hist. Eliz.* I. iv. 38 Shee herselfe is in cause that I cannot satisfie her.

†**10.** *gen.* A matter of concern, an affair, business; the case as it concerns any one (cf. CASE *sb.*^{1} 1). *Obs.* (exc. *dial.*)

1375 BARBOUR *Bruce* III. 302 His causs ȝeid fra ill to wer. **1393** GOWER *Conf.* III. 85 Wisdom is..Above all other thing to knowe In loves cause and elles where. **14..** *Tundale's Vis.* 100 His frendys by sybbe Herd of that cause that hym bytydde. **1477** EARL RIVERS (Caxton) *Dictes* 65 Committe alle thy causes to god. **1593** SHAKS. *Lucr.* 1295 The cause craves haste. **1655–60** STANLEY *Hist. Philos.* (1701) 65 Pericles..could easily reduce the exercise of his mind from secret abstrusive things to publick popular causes. **1880** *W. Cornw. Gloss.* (E.D.S.), *Cause*, case. 'If that's the cause I must work later.'

b. Phrases. *if cause were*, *in cause*. *Obs.* exc. *dial.* (Cf. CASE *sb.*^{1} 3, 10, 11.)

c **1400** *Rom. Rose* 5295 He..shulde it fulfille..Except oonly in cause twoo. **1523** FITZHERB. *Surv.* 10b, In that cause the lorde of the honer or manere may take a distresse for his rentes homages. **1523** LD. BERNERS *Froiss.* (1812) I. 314 We are bounde to ayde him, in cause that he requyre..vs so to do. **1634** *Malory's Arthur* II. lxiv. 402 If cause were that they had to do with Sir Launcelot. **1696** STILLINGFL. *12 Serm.* i. 7, I may say..as our Saviour doth in another cause.

c. *seal of cause*: charter of incorporation.

1806 FORSYTH *Beauties Scotl.* III. 260 The incorporation of Fleshers [of Glasgow] obtained their charter or seal of cause in 1580.

11. That side of a question or controversy which is espoused, advocated, and upheld by a person or party; a movement which calls forth the efforts of its supporters. (Spec. applied in Commonwealth times to the Puritan 'cause'.)

1581 SAVILE *Tacitus' Hist.* III. xxv. (1591) 129 It was the ..publicke act of the cause. **1588** *Marprel. Epist.* (Arb.) 36 Terming the cause by the name of Anabaptisterie. **1595** SHAKS. *John* III. iv. 12 Such temperate order in so fierce a cause. **1660** *Bibl. Fanatica* in *Harl. Misc.* (1746) VIII. 71/1 A pious Brother, and a real Assertor of the good old Cause. **1678** BUTLER *Hud.* III. II. 545 Zeal..made the Church and State and Laws Submit t' old Iron and the Cause. **1705** ADDISON *Italy* Ded., Their Hopes or Fears for the Common Cause rose or fell with Your Lordship's Interest and Authority. **1749** FIELDING *Tom Jones* XIII. iii, I shall ever esteem it the cause of my sex to rescue any woman, etc. **1792** BURKE *Corr.* (1844) III. 472 No cause in the world can..be more clear in my eyes..than that of the Poles. **1827** HALLAM *Const. Hist.* (1876) II. x. 275 The good old cause, as the commonwealth's men affected to style the interests of their little faction. **1842** TENNYSON *Two Voices* 148 In some good cause..To perish. **1884** GLADSTONE in *Standard* 29 Feb. 2/7 We should be traitors to the cause we profess to have taken in hand.

b. Hence *to make common cause* (*with*): to join in behalf of a common object.

1844 H. H. WILSON *Brit. India* (1845) I. 209 Before they made common cause with either French or English. **1848** MACAULAY *Hist. Eng.* I. 101 The two parties..united their strength in a common cause. **1863** MARY HOWITT tr. *F. Bremer's Greece* II. xiv. 114 Epirus will make common cause with Thessaly.

c. Hence applied colloquially in some religious bodies, to their 'cause' as embodied in a particular local organization, enterprise, mission, or church.

Mod. Several new causes have been started in the county during the year. The Baptists have a flourishing cause in the village.

†**12.** Disease, sickness. *Obs.* [A sense, simply transferred from late L., as to the origin of which see the Latin Dicts. In Eng. often vaguely associated with other senses, and used accordingly.]

[**1490** CAXTON *How to Die* 2 What some euer mater or cause be layd to him.. he oughte to suffre and receyue it pacyently. **1509** HAWES *Past. Pleas.* xviii. xvii, I your cause can nothing remedy.] **1578** LYTE *Dodoens* III. xxvi. 353 Hellebor may not be ministred except in desperate causes. **1585** LLOYD *Treas. Health* F iij, In a hote cause, lettis made in a playster is much worth. **1601** SHAKS. *All's Well* II. i. 114 Toucht With that malignant cause. **1607** —— *Cor.* III. i. 235 Leaue vs to cure this Cause.

III. *Comb.*, as *cause-monger*, *-renderer*, *-seeking* adj., *causewise* adv.; **cause-book**, a book in which legal causes are entered; **cause-list**, a list of causes to be tried.

1885 *Law Times' Rep.* LII. 574/2 The cause was re-entered in the *cause-book. **1837** *Edin. Rev.* LXIV. 491 These *cause-mongers go also to the storehouse of their fancy. *a* **1637** B. JONSON *Eng. Gram.*, *For*, a *cause-renderer, hath sometime the force of a severing one. **1877** TYNDALL in *Daily News* 2 Oct. 2/4 He has been described by the German Lichtenberg as 'das rastlose Ursachenthier'—the restless *cause-seeking animal. **1869** *Act 32 & 33 Vict.* c. 91 Sched. i. 1./2 Accounts of various suitors kept *cause-wise.

cause (kɔːz), *v.*^{1} Also 5 cawse, cawes, 6 causse. [ad. med.L. *causāre*, as used, by the Schoolmen, in sense 'efficere'. (Classical L. had only *causārī* (later *causāre*) to plead causes, give reasons or excuses. Hence also It. *causare*, Sp. *cauzar*, F. *causer*, all in same sense as Eng.)]

1. *trans.* To be the cause of; to effect, bring about, produce, induce, make.

c **1340** HAMPOLE *Prose Tr.* viii. 17 A fantasye caused of trubblyng of þe brayne. **1393** GOWER *Conf.* III. 107 They [the stars] causen many a wonder To the climats, that stond hem under. *c* **1430** *Chev. Assigne* 39 His moder..þat cawsed moche sorowe. **1526** *Pilgr. Perf.* (W. de W. 1531). 4 b, That ..oftentymes causeth heresyes & errours. **1697** DRYDEN *Virg. Georg.* III. 763 A Drench of Wine..the Patient's Death did cause. **1764** GOLDSM. *Trav.* 430 How small of all that human hearts endure, That part which laws or kings can cause or cure. **1875** JOWETT *Plato* (ed. 2) V. 55 The ruin of their empire..was caused by the loss of freedom and the growth of despotism.

b. Const. *object* and *inf.* with (formerly also without) *to*.

1393 GOWER *Conf.* III. 114 It causeth..A man to be subtil of wit. *c* **1485** *Digby Myst.* (1882) IV. 543 How durst thou.. to be so bold To cawse hym dy? **1552** ABP. HAMILTON *Catech.* (1884) 34 It sall cause the cum in great dangeir. **1610** B. JONSON *Alch.* II. iii, Take heed, you doe not cause the blessing leaue you. **1611** BIBLE *Amos* viii. 9, I will cause the Sunne to go downe at noone. **1625** HART *Anat. Ur.* II. iv. 73, I caused him bleed oftner then once. **1667** MILTON *P.L.* IV. 216 Out of the fertil ground he caus'd to grow All trees. **1842** W. GROVE *Corr. Phys. Forces* 10 It is the gravitation of the water which causes it to flow.

c. with *obj.* and *inf. pass.*

1494 FABYAN I. iii. 10 They..caused great fyres to be made. **1535** COVERDALE *Ps.* civ. [cv.] 20 Then sent the kinge and caused him be delyuered. **1596** SPENSER *F.Q.* III. i. 42 She caused them be led..Into a bowre. **1678** WANLEY *Wond. Lit. World* v. ii. §84. 472/2 He..caused his five Brethren to be all strangled in his presence. **1821** J. Q. ADAMS in C. Davies *Metr. Syst.* III. 127 To cause a statement in writing..to be hung up in some conspicuous place.

†**d.** with *inf.* simply, as *to cause make*, to have or get (something) made, cause (it) to be made. (Cf. F. *faire faire*, etc.) *Obs.* ? exc. *Sc.*

1535 COVERDALE *1 Kings* ii. 36 The kynge sent, and caused for to call Semei. **1649** DRUMM. OF HAWTH. *Hist. Jas. I*, Wks. (1711) 5 The king..caused abolish the indictment. *a* **1693** URQUHART *Rabelais* III. xliv. 358 She caused kill them. **1753** *Scots Mag.* Feb. 91/2 The directors had caused prepare the draught. **1820** MAIR *Tyro's Dict.* (ed. 10) 5 Numa caused make eleven more [shields] of the same form.

e. with *obj. sentence*. *arch.*

1393 GOWER *Conf.* III. 108 That causeth why that some passe Her due cours to-fore another. *c* **1510** *Virgilius* in Thoms *Prose Rom.* 23 She caused workemen shulde make the walles ageyne. **1611** BIBLE *John* xi. 37 Could not this man..haue caused that euen this man should not haue died? **1722** DE FOE *Plague* (1756) 93 This caus'd, that many died frequently..in the Streets suddenly.

†**2.** To actuate, move, force, drive (an agent) *to* (some action or emotion). *Obs.*

c **1400** *Destr. Troy* 13402 What causet the kyng to his cleane yre. *c* **1430** *Syr Tryam.* 641 Grete nede cawsyth hur therto.

†**3.** As vb. of incomplete predication: To make or render (a thing something). (Cf. L. *efficere*.)

1576 BAKER *Jewell of Health* 90 a, If oftener it shall be dystilled, it is then caused the effectuouser. *Ibid.* 113 a, It causeth them also most white. **1579** LYLY *Euphues* (Arb.) 188 An honest life will cause it a pleasaunt lyuing.

†**4.** To give reasons or excuses [= L. *causārī*].

1596 SPENSER *F.Q.* III. ix. 26 He, to shifte their curious request, Gan causen why she could not come in place.

cause, *v.*^{2} *rare*$^{-1}$. [a. F. *cause-r* to talk, chat.] To speak familiarly, converse, talk, chat.

1839 BAILEY *Festus* xxvii. (1848) 321, I have caused face to face with elements.

†**cause**, *v.*^{3} *Obs. rare.* ? To cast or shed.

c **1420** *Pallad. on Husb.* IV. 862 Thaire myddel teeth aboue at two yere age Thai cause, at yeres IIII an other gage. Ere yeres six gothe the gomes stronge, The caused first at yeres VI are even.

cause, 'cause, *conj. Obs.* exc. *dial.* [An elliptic use of prec. sb. for *because* (dial. *a-cause*).]

†**1.** (with *of*) = BECAUSE of, on account of.

1513 BRADSHAW *St. Werburge* (1848) 184 Churches..were gyuen To god and saynt Werburge cause of deuocion.

2. = BECAUSE. Since *c* 1600 often written *'cause*; now only *dial.*, or *vulgar*; also spelt *cos*, *coz*, *cuz*, *case*, etc.

1556 LAUDER *Tractate* 295 Ȝe suld not chuse thame cause ȝe lufe thame. **1592** MARLOWE *Jew Malta* IV. ii. 1535 Do you mean to strangle me? Yes, cause you use to confess. **1634** SIR T. HERBERT *Trav.* 169 It was the more terrible, cause hee had seene Mecha, and never after lied. **1653** in Walton *Angler* xi. 218, I cannot hate thee [Musick], 'cause the Angels love thee. **1682** N. O. *Boileau's Lutrin* II. Argt., 'Cause he had left her in the Lurch. **1711** E. WARD *Vulgus Brit.* XI. 121 'Cause none will credit what they say. **18..** PROUT in Burrowes *Rem.* 267 All for what? 'Kase his courage was good. **1884** *Harper's Mag.* Feb. 411/2 Jason pitied her 'cause she was lonesome.

‖**cause célèbre** (koz selɛbr). [Fr.] A celebrated legal case; a law-suit that excites much interest.

1763 H. WALPOLE *Let.* 11 Aug. (1960) XXII. 155 An extraordinary law-suit..curious enough for the *Causes célèbres*. **1765** D. GARRICK *Let.* 27 Jan. in R. B. Peake *Mem. Colman Fam.* (1841) I. 136, I have taken a slice at the law-oratory here [Paris]... It was a *cause célebre*. **1857** TROLLOPE *Three Clerks* xli, Of course a *cause célèbre* such as this was not going to decide itself in one day. **1860** *Once a Week* 22 Sept. 363/2 Well-nigh all the great murders—the *causes célèbres* of blood in our day—have been most deliberately planned. **1882** *Standard* 16 Dec. 5/6 In the Criminal Court of Innsprück to-day proceedings were opened in a *cause célèbre* of a..most painful character. **1955** *Times* 27 May 11/1 The defence of the Dutch and Indonesian accused in the *cause célèbre* which recommences today.

'caused, *ppl. a.* Affected by causes.

1875 HOLYOAKE *Co-oper. Eng.* I. 333 No mad, devil-born will, but a caused will, obedient to the laws of evidence.

causedness ('kɔːzɪdnɪs). *rare.* [f. prec. + -NESS.] (See quot.)

1829 JAS. MILL *Hum. Mind* II. xiv. (1869) 43 In abstract discourse effect [means] the same as would be meant by causedness.

causeful ('kɔːzfʊl), *a. rare.* [f. CAUSE *sb.* + -FUL.] †**a.** Showing or yielding a cause or reason. *Obs.* **b.** Having (good) cause or reason, well founded, well-grounded. **c.** That is a cause *of*, productive, fruitful *of*.

c **1400** *Test. Love* III. (1560) 298/2 Withouten causefull evidence, mistrust in jealousie should not be weued. **1586** SIDNEY *Astr. & Stella* (1622) 575 Yet waile thy selfe, and waile with causefull teares. **1613** SHERLEY *Trav. Persia* 7 His causefull indignation. **1849** D. JERROLD *Man of Money* Wks. 1864 IV. 95 More causeful of blood and tears than the hammer of Thor.

†**'causefully**, *adv. Obs. rare.* [f. prec. + -LY^2.] With (good) cause, with reason.

1615 T. ADAMS *Black Devil* 68 If we thrive not in.. Godlines, wee may causefully call our sanctity into question.

causeless ('kɔːzlɪs), *a.* [f. CAUSE *sb.* + -LESS.]

1. Having no antecedent cause: **a.** fortuitous; **b.** not to be explained by any natural cause; **c.** antecedent to all causes.

c **1386** CHAUCER *Merch. T.* 731 Grete God above That knoweth that none act is causeles. **1601** SHAKS. *All's Well* II. iii. 3 They say miracles are past, and we haue our Philosophicall persons, to make moderne and familiar things supernaturall and causelesse. **1712** BLACKMORE *Creation* I. 18 His causeless power, the cause of all things known.

2. Of persons: That has no cause or excuse for his action (*obs.*); that has no cause at law.

c **1374** CHAUCER *Anel. & Arc.* 229 Nowe is he Fals, ellas! and Causelesse, And of my woo he is so rewthelesse. **1598** DRAYTON *Heroic. Epist.* vii. 161 Love causelesse still, doth aggravate his cause. **1607** BP. HALL *Ps.* vii, If I..Doe good unto my causeless foe That thirsted for my overthrow.

3. Of acts, etc.: Without cause; for which there is no justifying cause or reason; groundless.

1535 STEWART *Cron. Scot.* 27472 Condampnit for ane causles cryme, But ony falt. **1587** TURBERV. *Trag. T.* (1837) 29 The causelesse rigour of the cruell Dame. **1597** HOOKER *Eccl. Pol.* v. lxv. §16 And so delivered them from causeless blame. **1649** MILTON *Eikon.* Wks. 1738 I. 387 A causeless and most unjust Civil War. *a* **1711** KEN *Hymns Festiv.* Poet. Wks. 1721 I. 348 He ne're inflicts a causeless Pain. **1852** HAWTHORNE *Tanglewood T.*, *Dragon's Teeth*, The strangest spectacle of causeless wrath.

B. As *adv.* or in quasi-adverbial construction. (Often capable of being explained as an adj. in sense 2, qualifying the subject or object of the vb.)

c **1374** CHAUCER *Troylus* I. 779 What may this be, That thou dispaired art, thus causelesse? *a* **1400–50** *Alexander* 3190 Than kest þam twa of his kniȝtis him causeles to spill. *c* **1440** *Partonope* 4923 He hath betrayed me Causeles. **1533** MORE *Debell. Salem* i. Wks. 934/2 My selfe was not causelesse there moued to fynde fawte. *a* **1555** LYNDESAY *Trag.* 11 Murdreist at Rome, causles and creuellie. **1606** G. W[OODCOCKE] tr. *Ivstine's Hist.* 93 b, The causles banished men. **1611** BIBLE *1 Sam.* xxv. 31 Either that thou hast shed blood causelesse. **1671** MILTON *Samson* 701 [They] causeless suffering The punishment of dissolute days.

ˈcauselessly, *adv.* [f. prec. + -LY².] In a causeless way; without cause or reason.

1561 T. NORTON *Calvin's Inst.* I. xviii. §1 Who dare say that men are caried causelessely with blinde motion while God .. sitteth stil? *Ibid.* IV. vi. §16 Our aduersaries doe no lesse causelesly & falsly boast of the consent. **1622** MALYNES *Anc. Law-Merch.* 433 If an honest man .. become insolvent .. casually and causelesly in himselfe. **1875** WHITNEY *Life Lang.* v. 97 Words .. which as causelessly come to be looked askance at and avoided. **1880** MUIRHEAD *Gaius* I. §53 Any one causelessly killing his slave.

ˈcauselessness. Causeless quality or nature.

a **1660** HAMMOND *Wks.* (1674) I. 196 By your discerning and acknowledging the causelessness of your exceptions.

†**ˈcausely**, *adv. Obs. rare*⁻¹. ? Causally.

c **1449** PECOCK *Repr.* IV. ix. 474 Ther of cometh causeli nedis ful myche yuel.

causer¹ (ˈkɔːzə(r)). Also 5–6 **cawser.** [f. CAUSE *v.*¹ + -ER¹.] He who or that which causes; the agent by whom or which an effect is produced. † *First Causer*: God. *Obs.*

c **1386** CHAUCER *Mother of God* 12 Causer of pees, stynter of wo & stryf. *c* **1420** OCCLEVE *To Dk. York* 62 Out upon pryde, causer of my wo! **1526** *Pilgr. Perf.* (1531) 2 b, Who was þe fyrst causer of all thynges. **1538** LELAND *Itin.* VIII. 30 Olde Erle Thomas .. was Cawser that new Quier of the Collegiate Churche .. was newly reedified. **1577** B. GOOGE *Heresbach's Husb.* (1586) 190 b, It is a causer of sweete and pleasant sleepes. **1662** J. CHANDLER *Van Helmont's Oriat.* 1 Neither are Tartarous humours the causers or Patrons of infirmities. **1748** RICHARDSON *Clarissa* (1811) VII. lxxxix. 383 Thou the causer of all these shocking scenes! **1821** BYRON *Sardan.* II. i. 309 Bel. I trust there is no cause. *Sar.* No cause, perhaps, But many causers. **1866** J. MURPHY *Comm. Ex.* xv. 2 Jehovah is .. the constant Causer of all effects.

†**causer**², **cawser.** *Obs.* [Can this be f. *cause*, CAUSEY, as if a paviour's hammer or mall?

The W. Cornwall Gloss. has '*cos'send, cos'sened*, hammered into shape'; but it is difficult to see any connexion.]

c **1450** *Voc.* in Wr.-Wülcker 589, *Incussorium*, a causer, quidam malleolus est. *c* **1450** *Metr. Voc.* ibid. 627, *Incussoria*, cawser.

†**ˈcauseress.** *Obs.* A female causer.

1631 *Celestina* IV. 54 Thou false Witch, thou Causeresse of secret errors.

‖**causerie** (kozəri, kozri). [Fr., f. *causer* to talk, ad. L. *causārī* to plead, dispute, f. *causa* CAUSE *sb.*] Informal talk or discussion, esp. on literary topics; also, a chatty article or paragraph.

1827 *Edin. Rev.* Oct. 386 The volume which has been the innocent cause of all this *causerie*. **1841** C'TESS BLESSINGTON *Idler in France* I. 269 The lively *causerie* of the *habitués de maison* supersedes the constraint of ceremony. **1892** ZANGWILL *Childr. Ghetto* I. xvi. 154 He was specially polite. .. There was an intimate, tender tone about these causeries. **1903** A. BENNETT *Truth about Author* v. 65 Men who can come fresh to a pile of new books .. and write a fifteen-hundred-word *causerie* on them. **1957** *Times* 31 Oct. 13/4 The very word *causerie* is like a bell whose sound may grate harshly upon the ear of the Higher Critic.

‖**causeuse** (kozøz). [F., fem. of *causeur* fond of talking or conversation.] A small sofa on which two persons can sit.

1844 *Illustr. London News* 12 Oct. 228/2 Luxurious *causeuses* and sofas lined with yellow satin. **1848** M. SAVAGE *Bachelor of Albany* xiii. 139 Mrs. Martin, having made Elizabeth sit down beside her, on the *causeuse* in her dressing room, proceeded [etc.]. **1883** A. G. HARDY *But yet a Wom.* 165 She sat down on the low causeuse in the window. **1967** M. M. PEGLER *Dict. Interior Design* 95 The causeuse is similar to a marquise, love seat, or settee.

causeway (ˈkɔːzweɪ), *sb.* Forms: 5 **cawce wey, cawcy wey**, 6–8 **causey-way**; 6– **cause-way, causeway**; also 6–7 **causway**, 7 **cawsway, cowsway, (caused-, cawsedway), casseway, caseway,** *Sc.* **caulsway.** [In 15th c. *caucé-wey, caucy-wey*, f. *caucé, caucy* CAUSEY + WAY. The compound has to a great extent taken the place of the simple *causey*, which, where it survives in local use, is apt to be treated as a corruption of this. On the other hand, etymologists have erroneously guessed that *causeway* was merely a corruption of *causey*.]

1. A road formed on a 'causey' or mound; a raised road across a low or wet place, or piece of water; formerly also applied to a mole or landing-pier running into the sea or a river; = CAUSEY 2.

the Giant's Causeway (or *Causey*): a natural formation in county Antrim, Ireland, consisting of a collection of basaltic columns extending like a mole or pier into the sea.

c **1440** *Promp. Parv.* 64 Cawcewey [*K.H.* cavuce, **1499** cawcy wey], *calcetum.* **1571** CAMPION *Hist. Irel.* XI. v. (1633) 81 Edified sundry Castles, cawswayes, and bridges. *a* **1619** DANIEL *Coll. Hist. Eng.* (1621) 28 Finding the case-way long and the bridge narrow. **1643** EVELYN *Diary* 12 Nov., To crosse a vally by a causeway and a bridge built over a small river. **1651** JER. TAYLOR *Course Serm.* I. viii. 95 Dig down the Causeywayes. **1662** FULLER *Worthies* I. 34 Builders of Bridges .. and makers of Caused-waies, or Causways (which are Bridges over dirt). **1666** PEPYS *Diary* 5 Jan., The .. running out of causeways into the river. **1796** MORSE *Amer. Geog.* II. 425 Narrow cause-ways are raised a foot and a half on each side, for .. foot passengers. **1855** MACAULAY *Hist. Eng.* III. 244 A narrow paved causeway which ran across the bog. **1853** PHILLIPS *Rivers Yorksh.* ix. 244 Roman roads .. traversing the .. marshy ground by causeways.

fig. **1642** S. ASH *Refuge most Oppressed* 25 The Lord our Saviour hath cast up such a caus-way to Heaven.

2. A highway; usually a paved way, such as existed before the introduction of macadamization. Now historical, or forming part of the name of ancient ways, *esp.* the Roman roads, the military roads of the 17th c., etc.: = CAUSEY 3, 4.

1611 CORYAT *Crudities* 53 Betwixt Nevers and Moulins was a goodly faire pitched casse-way. **1611** SPEED *Theat. Gt. Brit.* xxii. (1614) 43/2 That ancient causey-way, which is called Watling Street. **1708** LUTTRELL *Brief Rel.* 30 Sept., To encamp on the causey ways of Dovay and Arras. **1709** STEELE *Tatler* No. 36 ¶6 The Confederate Army extends .. on the Causeway between Tournay and Lisle, to Epain. **1726** SWIFT *Corr.* Wks. 1841 II. 596 Gallop a foundered horse ten miles upon a causeway and get home safe. **1851** D. WILSON *Preh. Ann.* (1863) II. III. ii. 55 The Roman road popularly styled the Fishwives' causeway. **1860** FROUDE *H.E.* VI. 177 The road or causeway on which Wyatt was expected to advance, ran nearly on the site of Piccadilly.

b. *fig.*

1597 BP. HALL *Sat.* III. v. 22 Much I mervailed, To see so large a caus-way in his head. **1646** J. HALL *Horæ Vac.* 56 These are Cause-wayes of ambition as well as fame. **1649** J. H. *Motion to Parl.* 14 What directer caus-way could you finde to the aggrandization of your owne glory? **1672** MARVELL *Reh. Transp.* I. 76 Who hath paved a broad Causway with Mortal Virtue thorow his kingdom.

3. Put for CAUSEY in other senses.

1828 SCOTT *F.M. Perth* ii, I .. care not which side of the causeway my daughter and I walk upon, so we may keep our road in peace and quietness. **1853** READE *Chr. Johnstone* 175 She drew near enough to the wall to allow room for another on the causeway. **1878** HUXLEY *Physiogr.* 170 A causeway has been erected on the beach to arrest the progress of the sea. **1830** GALT *Lawrie T.* IX. viii. (1849) 433 A woful thing to have heard as causeway talk.

causeway (ˈkɔːzweɪ), *v.* [f. prec. sb.]

1. *trans.* To pave with cobbles or pebbles. Chiefly as a (supposed) anglicizing of CAUSEY *v.*

1740 WILLIAMS in *Phil. Trans.* XLI. 468 A Circle of Two Feet Diameter .. causwayed with small stones laid edgeways. **1814** SCOTT in *Lockhart* (1839) IV. 191 The streets flagged instead of being causewayed. **1848** H. MILLER *First Impr.* xi. (1857) 175 Quartz pebbles, used in causewaying footways. **1854** —— *Sch. & Schm.* xii. (1858) 267 A few loads of water-rolled pebbles for causewaying a floor.

2. To fill up, or cross, with a raised causeway.

1702 in *Register Bk. Cambridge, Mass.* (1896) 230 Those Barrs yt lead into ye sd Meadow on ye easterly Side where it is Caswayed with Gravel & timber. **1870** *Daily News* 24 Sept., They were causewaying the approaches to the timber platform with grassy sods. **1887** E. D. MORGAN in *Proc. R. Geog. Soc.* IX. 237 The worst parts had been roughly bridged or causewayed.

Hence **ˈcausewayed** *ppl. a.* also applied *spec.* to a type of enclosure built by neolithic settlers in southern Britain, **ˈcausewaying** *vbl. sb.* (Mostly for *causeyed, -ing.*)

1865 *Daily Tel.* 28 Nov. 7/3 Ten miles along the causewayed track. **1876** PAGE *Advd. Text-bk. Geol.* vii. 136 Their extensive use in causewaying and macadamising. **1882** R. MUNRO *Sc. Lake Dwellings* 22 What may be called a rough, loose causewaying of stones. **1934** E. C. CURWEN in *Antiquaries Jrnl.* XIV. 99 Whitehawk Camp .. is one of the eight proved neolithic camps of 'causewayed' type in Britain. **1960** N. THOMAS *Guide Prehist. Eng.* 11 The earliest earthworks to survive, the causewayed camps of southern England, were the first to be built by these so-called primary neolithic peasants. Their banks and interrupted ditches afforded protection against wild animals.

causey (ˈkɔːzeɪ, -zɪ, ˈkɔːseɪ), *sb.* Forms: 4 **cauce, kauce, cause, cauci**, 4–6 **causei**, 4–7 **cawse**, 5 **caulce, calse**, 5–7 **causy**, 5–8 **cawsey**, 6 **caucey, caucie, causie, cawsey, causay, calsey, causeie**, 6–7 **cawsy, calcey, calceis,** *Sc.* **calsay**, 7 **caussey, cawsie,** *Sc.* **casey**, 6– **causey.** Also 5 **cauchie, cawchie; chaucie.** [ME. *caucé*, a. ONF. (Norman) *caucie*, earlier *caucíée* (Picard *cauchie* from *cauchíée*, Parisian *chaucíée* occas. *chaucie*, now *chaussée* = Pr. *caussada*, Sp. *calzada*:—late L. *calceāta, calciāta*, in Du Cange (who has also *via calciata, littus calciatum, cheminus calciatus*; prob. f. a late L. *calciāre* 'to stamp with the heels, to tread', recorded by Du Cange. The meaning would then be a mound or dam made firm by stamping or treading down.

This is strengthened by the fact that *calciāre* in med.L. interchanges with *calcāre* to 'tread, stamp', and that *calcāta, calcātum* are actually found instead of *calciāta, calciātum*; also *calcāgium* for the *droit de chaussée* or road-toll. The Romanic forms are (necessarily) identical with those derived from L. *calceāre* to shoe (It. *calzare*, Sp. *calzar*, Cat. *calsar*, Pr. *caussar*, OF. *cauchier, caucier, chaucier*, F. *chausser*), whence some have suggested the meaning 'shod way', whatever this might be. Diez and others have conjectured a vb. of type **calceāre*, or **calciāre*, from *calx, calcem* 'lime', and taken *calceāta* as something built or formed with lime; but there is no trace of such a sense in any language. Other med.L. forms were *calcea* mound, high way, paved way, also *calceia, calcetum, calceta*, all app. formed on the French. The OF. forms in *-ie* (from end of 12th c.), represent earlier ones in *-íée*; the Anglo-F. would be *caucée, caucé.*]

†**1.** A mound, embankment or dam, to retain the water of a river or pond. *Obs.*

[*c* **1170** *Charter Hen. II*, in Dugdale *Monast.* (1683) I. 914 Terra quam vivaria sua et calciæ suæ occupabunt.] *c* **1330** *Arth. & Merl.* 7756 Opon a cauci bi a broke. **1509–10** *Act 1 Hen. VIII*, ix. Preamb., A Cawsey extendyng a Myle .. ynclosyth the Water of themys from the Kinges hygh Waye. **1601** HOLLAND *Pliny* VI. xxvii. I. 139 Spasines .. opposed mightie dams and causies [*oppositis molibus*] against those riuers. **1611** COTGR., *Chaussée*, the causey, banke, or damme of a pond or of a riuer. **1745** P. THOMAS *Jrnl. Anson's Voy.* 187 These Causeys .. are of no little Use, both to keep in the Waters of these Canals, and for those to walk on who drag the Boats along. **1774** GOLDSM. *Nat. Hist.* (1862) I. VI. 480 This dike, or causey, is sometimes ten .. feet thick, at the foundation.

2. A raised way formed on a mound, across a hollow, *esp.* low wet ground, a bog, marsh, lake, arm of the sea, etc.; a raised footway by the side of a carriage road liable to be submerged in wet weather. More fully called *causeyway*, now CAUSEWAY; *causey* being now less used.

c **1300** R. BRUNNE *Chron. Wace* (Rolls) 3088 þorow myres, hylles & vales He made brugges and causes. —— *Chron. Langt.* (1810) 183 Was þer non entre .. Bot a streite kauce, at þe end a drauht brigge. *c* **1450** *Merlin* 380 At the foote of the castell was a maras .. and thereto was noon entre saf a litill cawchie that was narrowe and straite. *Ibid.* 604 Aboue this marasse was a chaucie .. of the brede of a spere lengthe made of chalke and sand. **1577** HOLINSHED *Chron.* III. 830 He .. made a continuall causie of timber ouer the marshes from Walthamstow to Locke bridge. **1598** GRENEWEY *Tacitus' Ann.* I. xiii. (1622) 25 Hauing .. cast bridges and causeyes [*pontesque et aggeres*] ouer the moist and deceitfull passages of the bogs. **1604** E. G[RIMSTON] *D'Acosta's Hist. Indies* V. xiii. 362 There was in the midst of the Lake where the Cittie of Mexico is built, foure large cawseies in crosse. **1611** BIBLE *Prov.* xv. 19 The way of the righteous is made plaine. *Marg.* Hebr. is raised vp as a causey. **1622** CALLIS *Stat. Sewers* (1647) 66 A Calcey or Calsway is a passage made by art of Earth, Gravel, Stones and such like .. through surrounded grounds. **1643** in Rushw. *Hist. Coll.* III. II. 509 A Stone-Causey thorow a Bogg. **1673** RAY *Journ. Low C.* Pisa 268 Castel d'Ovo, built on a rock in the Sea, having an artificial Caussey or Mole leading to it from the shore. *c* **1710** HEARNE *Gloss. Langtoft's Chron.*, *Kauce*, causey .. commonly taken with us for a High way, or Bank, raised in Marshy Ground for Foot passage, tho' even sometimes the Ways for Horse Passage are also known by this name, such as that beyond Friar Bacon's Study in Oxford [Abingdon Road]. **1853** BRYANT *Let.* 16 June, A noble causey, with parapets and a pavement of hewn stone, has been lately made over the low grounds .. as the new Appian way. **1860** J. P. KENNEDY *Horse Shoe R.* xii. 139 A swamp .. rendered passable by a causey of timber. **1877** E. PEACOCK *N.-W. Linc. Gloss.*

†**b.** The solid mounding at the ends of a bridge.

1523 LD. BERNERS *Froiss.* I. ccccxiii. 721 He and his men were by the bridge on the causey, raynging on bothe sydes.

†**c.** Sometimes applied to an arched viaduct.

1615 G. SANDYS *Trav.* II. 127 Athwart the plaine there extendeth a caussey supported with arches.

†**d.** Sometimes app. a row of stepping stones.

1598 YONG *Diana* III. 71 Vpon a fine causey of stones most artificiallie laide in order, they passed all ouer into the iland [*vnas piedras .. puestas in orden*].

†**e.** *the Giant's Causey*: see CAUSEWAY. *Obs.*

1811 PINKERTON *Petral.* II. 301 That kind of earthy limestone, which appears under the Giant's causey in Ireland.

†**3.** Hence, A highway (as originally raised and paved). Applied esp. to the Roman roads, and still given as a proper name to some considered Roman, as the *Devil's Causey* (or *Causeway*) in Northumberland. Otherwise *Obs.*

1495 *Will of Bp. of Llandaff* (Somerset Ho.), Vie Regvulgariter Cawsey. **1540** *Act 32 Hen. VIII*, xvii, The causey or hygh way leading from Algate to White chapel church. **1577** EDEN & WILLES *Hist. Trav.* 254 They determined also to make three causeys or hygh wayes by land. **1606** HOLLAND *Sueton.* 19 To make a cawsie or highway, form the Adriatick Sea, by the ridge or side of the Apennine hill. **1670** MILTON *P.L.* x. 416 Satan went down The causey to Hell-gate. **1704** HEARNE *Duct. Hist.* (1714) I. 372 The Cawsey, called Via Appia. **1708** J. CHAMBERLAYNE *St. Gt. Brit.* II. i. ii. (1743) 305 Evident footsteps of a Roman Causey, or Military Way. **1713** STEELE *Englishman* No. 31. 202 A new Causey from Lisle to Dunkirk.

b. *fig.*

1574 WHITGIFT *Def. Aunsw.* III. Wks. 1851 I. 322 To walk in the broad and beaten way, as it were the common causey of the commandment, rather than an outpath of the example.

4. *esp.* A paved way; the paved part of a way. Still *dial.*

1430 *E.E. Wills* (1882) 85 To the causy atte Wyke, iiij*d.* **1527** *Test. Ebor* (Surtees) V. 228 To the amendyng of Friston his waye and caucey. **1530** PALSGR. 203/2 Caussey in a hye way, *chavsee.* **1572** HULOET, A caucie or a waye paued, *agger solidus, chemin paue de pieres, chaucee.* **1577** HELLOWES *Gueuara's Chron.* 29 He made a paued Calsey, being a broad high waye that lasted two leagues and halfe. **1581** SAVILE *Tacitus' Hist.* III. xxi. (1591) 12 b, He commanded the third Legion to make stand vpon the cawsey of the Posthumian way [*in ipso aggere viæ Postumianæ*]. **1659** *Louth Ch. Acc.* iv. 286 (Peacock *N.-W. Linc. Gloss.*) For paving the causey in the church-yard. **1768** TUCKER *Lt. Nat.* (1852) I. 634 To turn her upon the flowery turf of reward, rather than the rocky-pointed causey of punishment. **1877** *Holderness Gloss.*

(E.D.S.), *Cawsey*..a raised and paved side-walk, or one across a fold-yard, but often any foot path. **1877** E. PEACOCK *N.-W. Linc. Gloss.* (E.D.S.), *Causey*, a footpath, especially when made of flagstones or paved with cobbles.

5. *esp.* A street, or part of a street, paved with cobbles or small boulders (or blocks of trap or granite), as distinguished from flag-stones; a street pavement. Chiefly *Sc.*

The whole street may be a causey; or the road-way may be causey, while the side walks are flagged, or the side walks causey and the centre macadamized.

crown of the causey: the centre or highest part of the pavement, as most public, conspicuous, or honourable.

1535 STEWART *Cron. Scot.* III. 561 Throw all the toun, Quhair on the stairis and all the calsay wnder, Rycht mony stude that tyme on him to wunder. *c* **1538** LYNDESAY *Agst. Syde Tailis* 30 Quhare euer thay go it may be sene How kirk and calsay thay soup clene. **1577** HANMER *Anc. Eccl. Hist.* (1619) 423 The streete commonly called the great Cawsy. **1584** J. CARMICHAEL *Lett.* in *Misc. Wodr. Soc.* (1844) 435 A great bragging between them in the calsay of Edinburgh. **1587** in *Northern N. & Q.* I. 83 Fraynch Calsay Makers to repair Calsayes in the Kowgaitt. **1611** BIBLE *1 Chron.* xxvi. 16 By the causey of the going vp [**1568** The paved streate that goeth vpwarde]. **1635** RUTHERFORD *Lett.* (1862) I. 149 Truth will yet keep the crown of the causey in Scotland. **1650** ROW *Hist. Kirk* 511 The croun, scepter, and sword of honour..which..the Noblemen themselves carried up the casey of Edinburgh. *a* **1774** FERGUSSON *Election* Poems (1845) 42 Glower round the cawsey, up and down. **1820** SCOTT *Abbot* xvii. **1823** GALT *Entail* III. x. 95 It could ne'er be expected that I would let them be married on the crown-o'-the-causey. **1840** BROWNING *Sordello* v. Wks. II. 398 This companion slips On the smooth causey. **1848** S. BAMFORD *Early Days* ix. (1859) 98 A neatly paved footpath and a causey for carts.

6. A piece of pavement (of cobbles, as distinguished from flags), a paved area. Chiefly *Sc.*

1481–90 *Howard Househ. Bks.* (1841) 505 To Robt. Bukton for the makyng of the causey at the stabill dore. **1633** T. JAMES *Voy.* 60 We made a Hearth or Causie in the middle of the house. **1663** GERBIER *Counsel* 98 Rogues have taken up the causey or pavement before a doore. **1880** *Antrim & Down Gloss.* (E.D.S.), *Cawsey, cassy*, the paved or hard-beaten place in front of or round about a farmhouse.

7. *attrib.* and *Comb.*, as ***causey-cleaner, -crown*** (see 5), ***-lamp, -maker, -making, -saint, -side***; † **calsay-paiker** (*Sc.*), a street-walker.

1786 BURNS *Brigs of Ayr* 157 To whom our moderns are but *causey-cleaners. **1837** R. NICOLL *Poems* (1843) 105 He keeps the *causey-crown. **1578** *Glasgow Town Council Proc.* in *Hist. Glasgow* (1881) 133 The expense of the *calsay-making. *a* **1555** LYNDESAY *Trag.* 378 Off *calsay-paikaris, nor of publycanis. **1862** in Hislop's *Prov. Scot.* 83 He's a *causey saint and a house deil. **1652** CULPEPPER *Eng. Physic.* 41 By a *Causey side in the middle of a field by Paddington.

ˈcausey, *v.* Chiefly *Sc.* and *dial.* [f. the sb.] To pave with small stones. Hence **ˈcauseying** *vbl. sb.*

1538 LELAND *Itin.* IV. 126 Martin Bridge..well causied with Stone at both Endes. **1596** *Wills & Inv. N.C.* (1860) II. 341 To the mendinge and cawsiinge with stonnes, of heighewayes. **1658** SIR T. BROWNE *Wks.* (1852) III. 496 By clearing the fennes..and soe comprehending cawsing, paving, drayning, etc. **1758** *Monthly Rev.* 631 Where the bottom is clay, or where it is causeyed. **1822** SCOTT *Nigel* iii, These London kirkyards are causeyed with through stanes. **1877** PEACOCK *N.-W. Linc. Gloss.* (E.D.S.), *Causey*, to pave. 'We mun hev our court-yard causied'.

† **causidic.** *Obs.* [see next.] 'A lawyer, atturney, aduocate, or procter' (Cockeram 1623).

1656 BLOUNT *Glossogr.*, *Causidick*, a lawyer, a pleader, an advocate or counsellor.

Hence **Causidicade** (as title of a poem).

1743 (*title*) Causidicade. A Panegyri-Satiré-.. Poem.

causidical (kɔːˈzɪdɪkəl), *a.* [f. L. *causidic-us* pleader, counsel, (f. *causa* cause + *-dicus* saying, telling) + -AL¹.] Of or pertaining to a pleader of legal causes.

a **1797** H. WALPOLE *Mem. Geo. III* (1845) I. xvi. 241 His foul tongue and causidical boldness..offered him as a proper tool to [the] Court. **1796** J. ANSTEY *Pleader's Guide* (1803) 86 A bold Causidical appearance. **1840** G. S. FABER *Christ's Disc. Capernaum* Introd. 29 Causidical dexterity..employed..to make..the worse appear the better cause.

causing (ˈkɔːzɪŋ), *vbl. sb.* The action of the vb. CAUSE. (Now chiefly gerundial.)

1651 HOBBES *Leviath* I. xii. 53 Things that have no part at all in the causing of it.

ˈcausing, *ppl. a.* That causes.

1829 JAS. MILL *Hum. Mind* xiv. §2 (1869) 43 'Cause' in these cases is a short name for 'causing object'. **1883** *Harper's Mag.* Nov. 878 The causing cause of the building.

Hence **ˈcausingness.**

1829 JAS. MILL *Hum. Mind* xiv. §2 (1869) 43 Cause and Effect are often used in the abstract sense, in which case Cause means the same thing as would be expressed by Causingness.

causion, obs. form of CAUTION.

† **ˈcauson.** *Obs.* [a. med.L. *causōn* burning fever (Du Cange), a. Gr. καύσων burning heat, f. και-: see CAUSTIC.] ? Inflammation, ? heartburn.

1398 TREVISA *Barth. De P.R.* (W. de W.) VII. xli. 254 Somtyme Colera hyghte Causon, for it brennyth and kyndlyth the spyrytuall membres. **1661** LOVELL *Hist. Anim. & Min.* 202 Some apply it against the heart, to help causons, and heate.

causse (kos). Usu. in *pl.*[Fr.] A limestone plateau (in southern France).

1827 G. P. SCROPE *Mem. Geol. Central France* i. 11 These plateaux are called '*Causses*' in the vernacular dialect. **1883** *Encycl. Brit.* XV. 8/2 By the Dordogne and Lot the surface is divided into a number of limestone plateaux known by the name of 'causses'. **1922** *Glasgow Herald* 5 Aug. 4 The weirdly sombre causses of the Cevennes. **1963** *Times* 9 Feb. 11/1 Thus much of the country is wooded and prosperous, though it is interspersed here and there with those more barren strips called *causses*.

caustic (ˈkɔːstɪk, ˈkɒstɪk), *a.* and *sb.* [ad. L. *caustic-us* a. Gr. καυστικός capable of burning, caustic, f. καυστ-ός burnt, burnable, f. και- (future καυσ-) to burn. Cf. F. *caustique.*]

A. *adj.* **1. a.** Burning, corrosive, destructive of organic tissue.

1555 EDEN *Decades W. Ind.* (Arb.) 229 Albeit the water of the sea haue a certeyne caustike qualitie ageynst poyson. **1563** T. GALE *Antidot.* I. vii. 5 Causticke medicynes which doe remoue, and take away fylthines in vlcers. **1605** TIMME *Quersit.* I. vi. 25 Causticke and burning simples. **1727** BRADLEY *Fam. Dict.* I. s.v. *Gourdy legs*, This Stone..from its..caustick or burning Quality, alone destroys Warts. **1863–72** WATTS *Chem. Dict.* I. 818 In the old language of surgery, caustics were divided into the actual, such as red-hot iron and *moxa*, and the potential, such as strong alkalis, acids, nitrate of silver.

b. ***caustic bougie***: a bougie armed with a piece of caustic.

1800 *Med. Jrnl.* III. 480 Caustic bougies, applied to the urethra under pretence of removing strictures. **1805** *Ibid.* XIV. 474 The superiority of the caustic over the common bougie.

c. *Chem.* ***caustic alkali***: a name given to the hydrates of potassium and sodium, called ***caustic potash*** (KHO) and ***caustic soda*** (NaHO) respectively; ***caustic volatile alkali*** or ***caustic ammonia***, ammonia as a gas or in solution; ***caustic lime***, quick lime (CaO).

1774 GOLDSM. *Nat. Hist.* (1776) VIII. 143 These flies, thus dried..yield a great deal of volatile caustic-salt. **1791** HAMILTON *Berthollet's Dyeing* I. I. v. 80 Caustic alkali tinges the infusion of galls of a dark red. **1811** A. T. THOMSON *Lond. Disp.* (1818) 564 Take..water of caustic kali, nine fluid ounces. **1813** SIR H. DAVY *Agric. Chem.* (1814) 21 Lime applied in its Caustic state acquires its hardness and durability, by absorbing the aerial acid. **1845** TODD & BOWMAN *Phys. Anat.* I. 102 Add solution of caustic ammonia. **1869** ROSCOE *Elem. Chem.* 200 Potassium hydroxide or Caustic potash..is a white substance soluble in half its weight of water, and acts as a powerful cautery, destroying the skin. **1876** HARLEY *Mat. Med.* 147 Caustic Soda.

d. *gen.* Burning. (*rare.*)

1863 *Possibil. Creation* 148 At the tops of mountains..the sun's rays are capable of producing very caustic results.

e. caustic bush, plant, vine, Australian names for *Sarcostemma australe*, a plant poisonous to cattle and sheep; **caustic creeper, weed,** Australian names for *Euphorbia drummondii*, the milky juice of which is used by the natives as a remedy for various diseases, but which is poisonous to sheep.

1887 BAILEY & GORDON *Plants reputed Poisonous* 43 *Sarcostemma Australe.* Known as 'Caustic plant' or 'Caustic vine' in Queensland. *Ibid.* 79 *Euphorbia Drummondii*, Caustic Creeper... This weed is unquestionably poisonous to sheep. **1889** J. H. MAIDEN *Useful Native Plants* 127 Euphorbia Drummondii... Called 'Caustic Creeper' in Queensland. Called 'Milk Plant' and 'Pox Plant' about Bourke. This weed is unquestionably poisonous to sheep. **1922** *Jrnl. Proc. R. Soc. N.S.W.* LVI. 183 This plant [sc. *Sarcostemma australe*], which occurs in all the Australian States except Victoria and Tasmania, is known as 'Caustic Vine', or 'Caustic Plant'. **1926** J. M. BLACK *Flora S. Austral.* III. 463 *S*[*arcostemma*] *australe*, R. Br. Milk Bush; Tableland Caustic Bush. **1954** W. E. BLACKALL *W. Austral. Wildflowers* 263 *E*[*uphorbia*] *Drummondii.* Caustic-weed.

2. *fig.* That makes the mind to smart: said of language, wit, humour, and, by extension, of persons; sharp, bitter, cutting, biting, sarcastic.

[Not in JOHNSON 1755.] **1771** SMOLLETT *Humph. Cl.* (L.) And mirth he has a particular knack in extracting from his guests, let their humour be never so caustic or refractory. **1818** SCOTT *Rob Roy* iv, His shrewd, caustic, and somewhat satirical remarks. **1842** MACAULAY *Fredk. Gt.*, *Ess.* (1877) 677 Those who smarted under his caustic jokes. **1876** GEO. ELIOT *Dan. Der.* II. xviii. 147 Well, ma, I think you are more caustic than Amy.

3. *Math.* Epithet of a curved surface formed by the ultimate intersection of luminous rays proceeding from a single point and reflected or refracted from a curved surface; also of the curve formed by a plane section of a caustic surface. A caustic by reflexion is called a *catacaustic*, that by refraction a *diacaustic*. So *caustic line, surface*,

[So called because the intensity of the light, and consequently of the heat, is in general greater at a point on this surface than at neighbouring points not on it, and at special points may become sufficiently intense to initiate combustion in a body there placed. The *focus* of a concave mirror is the cusp of its caustic for incident parallel rays.]

1727–51 CHAMBERS *Cycl.*, *Caustic curve*, in the higher geometry, a curve formed by the concourse or coincidence of the rays of light reflected or refracted from some other curve. **1869** TYNDALL *Notes on Light* §101 The interior surface of a common drinking-glass is a curved reflector. Let the glass be nearly filled with milk, and a lighted candle placed beside it, a caustic curve will be drawn on the surface of the milk. *Ibid.* §166 Spherical lenses have their caustic curves and surfaces formed by the intersection of the refracted rays.

B. *sb.*

1. a. *Med.* A substance which burns and destroys living tissue when brought in contact with it. ***common*** or ***lunar caustic***: nitrate of silver prepared in sticks for surgical use.

1582 HESTER *Secr. Phiorav.* I. vii. 8 Costicke..beeyng laid on the sore doeth mortefie it. *c* **1600** B. JONSON *Elegy Lady Pawlet* (R.) Put Your hottest causticks to, burne, lance, or cut. **1722** DE FOE *Plague* (1884) 111 They burnt them with Causticks. **1771** SMOLLETT *Humph. Cl.* (L.) He applied caustic to the wart. **1800** *Med. Jrnl.* III. 290 The application of lunar caustic to strictures. **1879** HARLAN *Eyesight* v. 52 Quick-lime acts as a powerful caustic.

b. *fig.*

1635 AUSTIN *Medit.* 197 With his Causticks of Repentance, he charitably burnt out, and purged the corruptions of Mens consciences. **1817** SCOTT *Wav.* xx, Pride..applies its caustic as an useful though severe remedy. **1832** L. HUNT *Bacchus in Tusc.* 221, I should like to see a snake..fasten with all his teeth and caustic upon that sordid villain.

2. *Math.* = ***caustic curve*** or ***surface***: cf. A. 3.

1727–51 CHAMBERS *Cycl.* s.v., Every curve has its twofold caustic. **1743** *Phil. Trans.* XLII. 343 In the next place, the Caustics, by Reflexion and Refraction, are determined. **1869** TYNDALL *Notes on Light* §100 When a large fraction of the spherical surface is employed as a mirror, the rays are not all collected to a point; their intersections..form a luminous surface..called a caustic (German, Brennfläche).

caustic (ˈkɔːstɪk), *v.* [f. CAUSTIC *sb.*] *trans.* To treat with a caustic.

1852 MRS. GASKELL *Let.* 1 Oct. (1966) 852 My right arm is very bad & Mr. Mellor comes to see it & caustics it. **1870** LADY AMBERLEY *Diary* 22 Nov. in *Amberley Papers* (1937) II. xiii. 382 My throat was very bad to-day, Mr. Audland causticed it & made me stay in bed. **1888** MRS. H. WARD *R. Elsmere* xii, I causticked all the diphtheritic throats..with my own hand.

† **ˈcaustical,** *a.* *Obs.* [f. CAUSTIC *a.* and *sb.* + -AL¹.] Of caustic nature or operation.

c **1660** WISEMAN *Surg.* (J.) If extirpation be safe, the best way will be by caustical medicines or escaroticks. **1702** E. BAYNARD *Cold Baths* II. (1709) 237 The Caustical Salts.

caustically (ˈkɔːstɪkəlɪ), *adv.* [f. prec. + -LY².] In a caustic manner.

1850 'BAT' *Cricket Man.* 100 A writer..caustically remarked. **1876** E. MELLOR *Priesth.* v. 201 Their divergences of opinion have been caustically likened..to the foxes which Samson bound, which, though united at their tails, were wide apart in their bodies, and widest of all at their heads.

ˈcausticate, *v.* *rare*⁻¹. [f. CAUSTIC + -ATE³.] *trans.* To render caustic; = CAUSTICIZE. Hence **ˈcausticated** *ppl. a.*

1790 WEDGWOOD in *Phil. Trans.* LXXX. 313 Salt of tartar causticated by quicklime.

So **ˈcausticator,** one who applies, or advocates the application of, caustic.

1800 *Med. Jrnl.* III. 480 When radical cures have been confidently promised by the causticators.

causticity (kɔːˈstɪsɪtɪ). [f. CAUSTIC + -ITY. Cf. F. *causticité.*]

1. Caustic quality; burning pungent taste; the property of destroying or corroding organic tissue.

1772 PRIESTLEY in *Phil. Trans.* LXII. 254 Free from causticity. **1791** MACIE *ibid.* LXXXI. 375 This solution had an alkaline taste, but seemingly with little, if any, causticity. **1802** PLAYFAIR *Illustr. Hutton. The.* 523 The causticity produced in limestone by exposure to fire. **1830** LINDLEY *Nat. Syst. Bot.* 7 Acridity, causticity, and poison, are the general characters of this suspicious order.

2. *fig.* of speech or humour.

1785 H. WALPOLE *Lett. C'tess Ossory* II. 220, I..endeavoured to repair my causticity. **1816** SCOTT *Antiq.* xiii, With his usual dry causticity of humour. **1866** FREER *Regency Anne of A.* I. i. 20 The duke was witty, and famous for the causticity of his tongue.

causticize (ˈkɔːstɪsaɪz), *v.* *rare.* [f. as prec. + -IZE.] *trans.* To render caustic.

1881 *Nature* XXIII. 236 On causticising sodium carbonate solutions with lime.

causticly (ˈkɔːstɪklɪ), *adv.* *rare.* [f. CAUSTIC *a.* + -LY².] In a caustic manner.

1870 *Athenæum* 31 Dec. 878 He touched causticly the immoralities, excesses, and crimes of the dwellers in Antioch.

ˈcausticness. *rare.* = CAUSTICITY.

1731 in BAILEY; and in mod. Dicts.

caustive, caustok, obs. ff. COSTIVE, CASTOCK.

causy, variant form of CAUSEY.

† **caut,** *v.* *Obs.* See quot.

1688 R. HOLME *Armoury* II. 134/2 A Panther Cauteth, which word is taken from the sound of his voice.

caut(e, obs. f. *caught*: see CATCH *v.*

† **ˈcautel,** *sb.* *Obs.* or *arch.* Forms: 4 cautell, (*north.* cawteile), 4–7 cautil(e, 5 cauteel, cawtele, 5–6 cawtel(le, 5–7 cautell(e, 6 cautill, (*Sc.* cauteil), 4–7 cautele, 4–7 (9) cautel. [a. F. *cautèle* (13th c. in Littré), ad. L. *cautēla* of Roman Law

(whence also Pr., Sp., It. *cautela*) precaution, f. *caut-* ppl. stem of *cavēre* to take heed.]

1. A crafty device, artifice, stratagem; a trick, sleight, deceit.

138. WYCLIF *Serm.* Sel. Wks. I. 6 Make knowe to þe peple the cautelis of Anticrist. **1413** LYDG. *Pylgr. Sowle* II. lx. (1859) 57 Techinge me for to caste sleyghtes and cauteles. **1549** *Compl. Scot.* xiv. 118 Be ane subtile cauteil thai gart pausanias seruitur pas to the tempil. **1605** BACON *Adv. Learn.* II. xxi. §9 The fraudes, cautels, impostures, and vices of euery profession. **1611** COTGR., *Cautelle*, a wile, cautell, sleight.

b. Applied to things material.

c **1440** *Gesta Rom.* 123 (Harl. MS.) What dude he but yede, and purveyde him of iij cautils; scil. of an honest Garlonde of Rede Rosys. **1533-4** *Act 25 Hen. VIII*, vii, No .. person .. with any deuise or engine made of heare, canuas, or with any other cautele shall .. take any frie, spawne, or broode of yeles.

2. Cunning, craftiness, wiliness, trickery.

c **1375** BARBOUR *Troy-bk.* II. 114 A, what to þe wys mane rytht wele It geynes to haue þe cawteile That he be not the forspekere. *c* **1394** *P. Pl. Crede* 303 But knewen men her cautel & her queynt wordes, þei wolde worchypen hem nouȝt but a litel. **1548** *Act 2 & 3 Edw. VI*, xxiv. §1 Thieves, which .. by Craft and Cautele do escape from the same without Punishment. *c* **1580** HATTON in Ld. Campbell *Chancellors* (1857) II. xlv. 289 Be free from cawtell.

3. Caution, wariness, heedfulness.

1511 ELYOT *Gov.* I. iv, There is required to be therein [in their hearts] moche cautele and sobrenesse. **1555** EDEN *Decades W. Ind.* (Arb.) 186 With great cautele least any parte of their legges or feete bee seene. **1613** SHERLEY *Trav. Persia* 78 As I would preserue my selfe with more cautel heereafter. **1664** MARVELL *Corr.* Wks. 1872-5 II. 170 To entertain them in mutual cautele and suspicion.

4. A precaution; in *Law*, etc., an exception, restriction, or reservation made for precaution's sake.

1541 ELYOT *Image Gov.* 37 One meruailouse cautell he vsed, that is to saie, one man was not oftentymes in that truste of espial. **1563** FOXE *A. & M.* (1596) 202/2 Without cautels & exceptions. **1585** JAS. I *Ess. Poesie* (Arb.) 53 Revlis and cautelis to be obseruit and eschewit in Scottis Poesie. **1586** FULKE *Agst. Allen* 418 (T.) For cautele and provision against the like sins. **1637** GILLESPIE *Eng. Pop. Cerem.* III. viii. 191 Which negative Excommunication, is .. either a bare punishment, or a cautell and animadversion. **1861** C. W. GOODWIN *Mosaic Cosmog.* in *Ess. & Rev.* 209 With such limitations, cautels and equivocations.

b. *Eccl.* A caution or direction for the proper administration of the sacraments; *esp.* in ***cautels of the Mass***.

1541 BARNES *Wks.* (1573) 308/2 Why doe not by this reason your owne priestes abstayne from the wine, seeing that this perill may also chaunce to them, as your cautelles of yᵉ Masse doe graunt. **1638** FEATLY *Strict. Lyndom.* I. 61 The cautels of the Masse appoint what is to bee done in case the Priest, being drunk before, cast up the host. **1641** R. B. K. *Parallel Liturgy w. Mass-bk.* 59 As we may see in these two cautels of the Masse. **1880** *Edin. Rev.* Apr. 286 The reception on the part of certain Ritualists of the Roman 'Cautels' for the celebration of the Mass.

¶ As *adj.* = CAUTELOUS.

1606 G. W[OODCOCKE] tr. *Ivstine's Hist.* 108 Mistrusting himselfe to be deceiued by some cautel treason. **1616** BULLOKAR, *Cautele*, warie, circumspect. **1639** G. DANIEL *Ecclus.* xii. 31 Be circumspect and Cautele to thy foe.

† **'cautel**, *v.* *Obs. rare*⁻¹. [f. prec. sb.; cf. OF. *cauteler*, *cauteller* 'to deceiue, beguile, cousen' (Cotgr.).] *trans.* To devise cunningly or craftily.

1603 HARSNET *Pop. Impost.* 62 It was wisely cauteled by the penner of these savoury Miracles .. why Sara .. should be more Devil-haunted then any of the possessed Men.

† **cautelayre.** *Obs.* [Formation obscure: cf. CAUTER and CULTELER.] A knife-shaped instrument for cautery.

1541 R. COPLAND *Guydon's Quest. Chirurg.* (1579) 49 They be applyed to the lachrymalls to consume the superfluous flesh, and [it] is done with a small actuall cautelayre. Lyke-wise to the temples with a cautelayre to close the veynes.

† **'cautelous**, *a.* *Obs.* or *arch.* Also 6-7 **cautilous**, 7 **-ulous**. [a. F. *cauteleux* (Pr. *cautelos*, Sp. *cauteloso*), on L. type **cautēlōsus*, f. *cautēla*; see prec. and -OUS.]

1. Full of cautels; deceitful, crafty, artful, wily.

138. WYCLIF *Serm.* Sel. Wks. I. 223 Ypocritis ben cautellous for to take men in wordis. *c* **1430** HENRYSON *Mor. Fab.* 16 The Foxe seemes craftie and cautelous. **1509** BARCLAY *Ship of Fooles* (1570) 13 By falshood liuing, and by wayes cautelous. **1607** SHAKS. *Cor.* IV. i. 33 Your Sonne .. caught With cautelous baits and practice. **1661** MORGAN *Sph. Gentry* II. iii. 36 An Adder or Snake .. signifying his cautulous devises and deceivable policies. **1840** BROWNING *Sordello* IV. 364 Cautelous Old Redbeard.

2. Cautious, wary, heedful, circumspect.

1574 HELLOWES *Gueuara's Ep.* (1584) 308, I doe .. approve, that men with their wives be cautelous. **1612** WOODALL *Surg. Mate* Wks. (1653) 239 That they be exceeding cautelous and warie in the inward use of all Mineral medicines. *a* **1734** NORTH *Lives* III. 52 This makes all dealing with them very nice and cautelous. **1829** SCOTT *Hrt. Midl.* Proleg., I have been cautelous in quoting mine authorities.

b. Const. *of*, *inf.*, or *clause*.

1625 *King's Instr. E. Drummond* in Rushw. *Hist. Coll.* (1659) I. 162 You must be cautelous not to proceed any further in this business. **1628** FELTHAM *Resolves* I. xxiii. Wks. (1677) 48 To be more cautelous of him. **1639** R. VERNEY in *V. Papers* (1853) 225 They are very cautelous how they let any thinge of this nature passe. **1670** BAXTER *Cure Ch.-Div.* 343 To be cautelous what wife we choose. *a* **1677** BARROW *Serm.* Wks. 1716 I. 283 We are to be cautelous of meddling with controversies.

† **'cautelously**, *adv.* *Obs.* [f. prec. + -LY².] In a cautelous manner.

1. Craftily, deceitfully, artfully.

1475 CAXTON *Jason* 87 Your uncle hath sent you hether cautelously .. to thende that he might obteyne your royame. **1509** *Act 1 Hen. VIII*, v. §5 As much Money as the Goods .. (so cautelously customed) amounted unto. **1610** DONNE *Pseudo-Mart.* x. 264 Falsely and cautelously insinuated.

2. Cautiously, warily, circumspectly.

1610 HOLLAND *Camden's Brit.* Pref., I have beene so sparing and cautelously forecasting in my coniectures. **1685** BAXTER *Paraphr. N.T.* Matt. x. 16 Be wise to carry your selves inoffensively and cautelously. **1692** *Covt. Grace Conditional* 49 He expresseth himself very cautelously.

† **'cautelousness.** *Obs.* [f. as prec. + -NESS.] Cautelous quality: **a.** craftiness; **b.** wariness.

1584 R. SCOT *Discov. Witchcr.* XV. xlii. 395 Be they with never so much cautelousnesse and subtill circumspection clouded. *a* **1624** BP. M. SMITH *Serm.* (1632) 156 For cautelousnesse to looke ere we leape. **1657** BAXTER *Present Th.* 39 A very great cautelousness .. would be necessary.

† **'cautelty, cau'tility.** *Obs. rare.* [ad. OF. *cautilité*, f. *cautèle*: see CAUTEL and -ITY. For the contracted form cf. *subtility*, *subtlety*.] = CAUTELOUSNESS.

1554 BALE *Declar. Bonner's Articles* in Strype *Eccl. Mem.* III. I. xvi. 139 Such covered cautelty. **1567** *Trial. Treas.* (1850) 22 Circes, the witche, with her craftie cautilitie.

cauter ('kɔːtə(r)). Also 6-7 **cautere**. [a. F. *cautère* (Pr. *cauteri*, Sp. and It. *cauterio*), ad. L. *cautērium*, a. Gr. καυτήριον branding iron; or a. Gr. καυτήρ branding iron, f. καί-ειν to burn.] = CAUTERY 1 (to which 1534 may really belong).

1534 LD. BERNERS *Gold. Bk. M. Aurel.* (1546) S vj, The fistula, where against thou hast giuen cautere. **1541** R. COPLAND *Guydon's Quest. Chirurg.* (1579) 50 How many be there of actual cauters ..? **1677** GALE *Crt. Gentiles* II. IV. 140 Having their conscience cauterised or marqued with a cauter. **1864** *Daily Tel.* 3 Aug., The liberal appliance of the actual cauter, i.e. the red-hot iron. **1881** *Syd. Soc. Lex.*, *Cauter*, an instrument for applying the actual cautery. Also, a liniment or application of a caustic character.

cauterant ('kɔːtərənt), *sb.* and *a.* [as if f. a Fr. **cautérer* to cauter: cf. CAUTERING.]

A. *sb.* A cauterizing substance.

1846 WORCESTER cites LOUDON.

B. *adj.* 'Relating to a cautery or to caustic, or having the properties of either' (*Syd. Soc. Lex.*).

† **cauterification.** *Obs.* = CAUTERIZATION.

1541 R. COPLAND *Guydon's Quest. Chirurg.* (1579) 48 What is cauterification? .. It is an operation made with fire artificially.

† **'cautering**, *vbl. sb.* *Obs.* [f. as CAUTERANT + -ING.] = CAUTERIZING. (Also *attrib.* or *ppl. a.*)

1580 HOLLYBAND *Treas. Fr. Tong.*, *Cauterisation*, the searing vp of a wounde, called by the Surgions Cautering. **1688** R. HOLME *Armoury* III. 324/2 The second is termed a Cauting Iron, or a Cautering Iron, or Searing Iron.

† **'cauterism.** *Obs.* [f. after CAUTERIZE: see -ISM.] The application of cautery.

1640 CHILMEAD tr. *Ferrand's Love Melanch.* 262 (T.) Some use the cauterisms on the legs. **1688** H. WHARTON *Enthus. Ch. of Rome* 91 Necessitated to admit a Cauterism.

† **'cauterizate**, *v.* *Obs. rare*⁻¹. [f. late L. *cautērizāre*: see -ATE³.] = CAUTERIZE.

1576 BAKER *Jewell of Health* 104 a, If it toucheth the fleshe, it doth cauterizate or burne.

cauterization (ˌkɔːtəraɪ'zeɪʃən). In 6 **cauterysacyon**. [n. of action f. CAUTERIZE *v.*: see -ATION. Cf. F. *cautérisation*.] The action of cauterizing, the application of cautery.

1541 R. COPLAND *Guydon's Quest. Chirurg.*, Cauterysacyon .. is an operacyon made wᵗ fyre artyfycyally in yᵉ body of man for certayne vtylytees. **1607** TOPSELL *Four-f. Beasts* 333 Of Cauterization, or giving the fire, as well actual as potential. **1876** GROSS *Dis. Bladder* 53 Cauterization with the solid nitrate of silver.

cauterize ('kɔːtəraɪz), *v.* Also **-ise**. [= F. *cautériser*, ad. late L. *cautērizāre* to burn or brand with a hot iron, f. *cautērium*, ad. Gr. καυτήριον branding-iron.]

1. *Med. trans.* To burn or sear with a hot iron or a caustic.

1541 R. COPLAND *Guydon's Quest. Chirurg.*, After that they be cauterised ye must apply on the sayd places oyle of Roses. **1623** MASSINGER *Bondman* I. iii, Old festered sores Must be lanced to the quick, and cauterized. **1735** SOMERVILLE *Chase* IV. 283. **1800** tr. *Lagrange's Chem.* II. 340 The acetic acid .. is .. so caustic, that it corrodes and cauterizes the skin. **1865** *Public Opinion* 28 Jan. 96 The boy's wound was cauterized and he is doing well.

fig. **1824-9** LANDOR *Imag. Conv.* (1846) II. 222 The unsoundness of doctrine is not cut off or cauterised. **1856** FROUDE *Hist. Eng.* II. 39 To suppose that he could cauterize out heresy.

b. *absol.*

1563 T. GALE *Antidot.* II. 77 Thys water .. wyl cauterise like an whote yron. *a* **1631** DONNE *Serm.* xxvi. 263 Whether he cauterize or foment, he is the same Physitian.

† **2.** To brand with a hot iron. *Obs.*

1591 PERCIVALL *Sp. Dict.*, *Cauterizado*, marked with a hot yron, or cauterised. **1684** *Contempl. State of Man* II. vi. (1699) 191 Fugitive Slaves are Marked and Cauterized with Burning Irons.

fig. **1609** DANIEL *Civ. Warres* VIII. lxxxiii, Now he must Bring home his Reputation Cauteris'd With th' idle Mark of serving Others Lust. **1619** J. TAYLOR (Water P.) *Sco. Baseness* Wks. II. 36, I will Satyrize, cauterize, and stigmatize all the whole kennell of curres.

3. *fig.* To 'sear', deaden, render insensible (the conscience, feelings, etc.). In allusion to 1 Tim. iv. 2 κεκαυτηριασμένων τὴν ἰδίαν συνείδησιν 'having their conscience seared with a hot iron'.

1586 J. HOOKER *Girald. Irel.* in *Holinshed* II. 117/1 His conscience was so cauterised. **1625** BACON *Ess. Atheism*, Hypocrites; which are euer Handling Holy Things, but without Feeling. So as they must needs be cauterized in the End. **1677** GALE *Crt. Gentiles* II. IV. 141 When once conscience is by frequent repetition of sins, cauterised, dispirited, and made senselesse. **1807** SOUTHEY *Espriella's Lett.* (1814) II. 103 Custom soon cauterizes human sympathy. **1874** PUSEY *Lent. Serm.* 139 The true conscience, untill it is cauterised, will .. rebel against the false.

cauterized ('kɔːtəraɪzd), *ppl. a.* [f. prec. + -ED.] Burnt by cautery; seared.

1603 FLORIO *Montaigne* II. v. (1632) 203 A guiltie-cauterized conscience. **1651** BIGGS *New Disp.* ¶243 The cauterized or wounded part. **1655** R. YOUNGE *Agst. Drunkards* 6 An habituated, infatuated, incorrigible, cauterized Drunkard.

cauterizing ('kɔːtəraɪzɪŋ), *vbl. sb.* [f. as prec. + -ING¹.] Burning with a hot iron or a caustic. (Now chiefly gerundial.)

1541 R. COPLAND *Guydon's Quest. Chirurg.* (Baker 1579) 50 To be kept open after the cauterising. **1555** EDEN *Decades W. Ind.* II. IV. (Arb.) 119 By cauterising with hotte Irens. **1607** SHAKS. *Timon* v. i. 136. *c* **1720** W. GIBSON *Farrier's Guide* II. lvi. (1738) 212 Cauterizing is performed by an Instrument made hot, or by corrosive or burning Medicines. **1835-6** TODD *Cycl. Anat.* I. 435/2 No pain is excited by .. cauterizing a bone.

b. *attrib.*, as in ***cauterizing iron***.

1575 TURBERV. *Falconrie* 261 With a cauterizing yron. **1727** BRADLEY *Fam. Dict.* I. s.v. *Cauterizing instr.*, A cauterizing Button, to burn and sear the Head. **1850** W. IRVING *Mahomed's Success.* xlii. (1853) 193 The sight of the fire and cauterising irons again deterred him.

'cauterizing, *ppl. a.* That cauterizes.

1626 BACON *Sylva* §729 No marvel though Cantharides have such a Corrosive and Cauterizing quality.

cautery ('kɔːtərɪ). [ad. L. *cautērium* branding-iron, cautery, ad. Gr. καυτήριον branding-iron: see CAUTER.]

1. A heated metallic instrument used for burning or searing organic tissue; also a caustic drug or medicine for the same purpose. The former is called an *actual*, the latter a *potential*, cautery.

1543 TRAHERON *Vigo's Chirurg.*, *Ulcers* 141 Let the bone be bored through, with a quadrate pointed cauterie. **1599** A. M. tr. *Gabelhouer's Bk. Physicke* 312/1 A little knobbe or tumor, which then with a glowing siluer Cauterye we must Cauterise. **1656** RIDGLEY *Pract. Physic* 326 Let the Chirurgion hold a great actual Cautery in his hand. **1689** MOYLE *Sea Chyrurg.* II. i. 26 Apply Buttons armed with .. your Potential Cautry. **1748** SMOLLETT *Rod. Rand.* xlvi, Bramwell prescribed the actual cautery, and put the poker in the fire. **1878** TENNYSON *Q. Mary* III. iv. 123 The mad bite Must have the cautery. **1881** *Syd. Soc. Lex.* s.v., Practically the term cautery is confined to the actual; a heated metallic instrument.

2. The operation of cauterizing, the application of a cauterizing agent. [cf. abst. sbs. in -ERY.]

1575 TURBERV. *Falconrie* 282 Cawterie to be bestowed upon hawkes. **1607** TOPSELL *Four-f. Beasts* 333 The potential cautery is done by applying unto the grieved place some medicine corrosive, putrifactive, or caustick. **1621** BURTON *Anat. Mel.* II. iv. III. (1676) 238/1 Cauteries or searings with hot yrons. **1758** J. S. *Le Dran's Observ. Surg.* (1771) 19 To consume the Excrescence .. both by Potential and Actual Cautery. **1861** READE *Cloister & H.* I. 343 To lay out blood and money, in flebotomy and cautery.

fig. *a* **1834** COLERIDGE, Who .. With actual cautery staunch'd the Church's wounds. **1853** CDL. WISEMAN *Ess.* III. 5 To apply this actual cautery to the body of the Spanish Church.

† **3.** An eschar made by cauterizing. [So Gr.]

1651 N. BIGGS *New Disp.* ¶239 Cauteries or permanent wounds are thought to be .. related to it.

‖ **cauth, caut.** [Hind. *kāth* catechu.] One of the Indian names of CUTCH or CATECHU, occasionally used in commerce.

1858 SIMMONDS *Dict. Trade*, *Cauth*, a name in Canara for the Terra Japonica of commerce.

cautherne, obs. form of CAULDRON *sb.*

cautie, var. of CAUTY. *Obs.*

cautil(e, cautility, cautilous, variants of CAUTEL, -TY, -OUS.

'cauting-iron. Shortened form of *cautering-iron* (see CAUTERING). = *cauterizing-iron*.

1688 R. HOLME *Armoury* III. 324/2 A Cauting Iron, or a Cautering Iron. **1708** KERSEY, *Cauting-Iron*, a Farrier's Iron to Cauterize. **1721-1800** in BAILEY. **1847** in CRAIG.

caution ('kɔːʃən), *sb.* Forms: 3 **kaucyon**, 3-6 **caucion**, 4 **caucioun**, 5 **cawcion**, 5-6 **caucyon**, 6

cawcyon, causion, *Sc.* cautioun, 7 cawtion, 6– caution. [a. F. *caution* security, surety:—L. *cautiōn-em* taking heed, heedfulness, caution; bond, security, f. *caut-* ppl. stem of *cavēre* to beware, take heed. The earlier uses were as in French; it was only in 16–17th c. that the original L. sense, as a quality, was introduced.]

1. Security given for the performance of some engagement; bail; a guarantee, a pledge. Still in Sc. Law, in U.S., and in *caution-money*; see 6.

bond of caution (Sc. Law): a security given by one person for another that he shall pay a certain sum or perform a certain act.

1297 R. GLOUC. *Chron.* (1810) 506 The kyng suor vpe the boc, and caucion vond god, That he al clanliche to the popes loking stod. *c* **1300** *K. Alis.* 2811 Kaucyon they nolde geve, no bidde. **1413** LYDG. *Pylgr. Sowle* I. xvii. (1859) 18 He ne may..oblyge hym self, ne ley caucyon to pursue forth his accyon. **1531** in Turner *Select. Rec. Oxford* 99 To put yn cawcyon or gage that he schall not sewe the scoller. **1603** KNOLLES *Hist. Turkes* (1621) 1284 Sufficient recognizance or caution sealed with his owne hand. **1651** HOBBES *Liberty* i. Wks. (1841) II. 13 The conqueror may..compel the conquered..to give caution of his future obedience. *a* **1718** PENN *Wks.* (1726) I. 668 Our Caution is as large as the Man that Swears. **1726** AYLIFFE *Parerg.* 25 He..ought to give Caution by the Means of Sureties, that he will persevere in the Prosecution. **1798** in Dallas *Amer. Law Rep.* I. 107 These views are answered here..with as good caution as in England. **1876** GRANT *Burgh Sch. Scotl.* II. iii. 132 To remain in ward until he find caution not to contravene the act of council.

b. The person who becomes security, a surety. *Obs.* exc. *Sc.*

1586 *Let. Earle Leycester* 23 By Othe, Bonds, or Hostages, as cautions for her good and loyal demeanour. **1587** FLEMING *Contn. Holinshed* III. 1584/2 Release of the bonds & hostages that should be giuen for cautions in that behalfe. **1627** RUTHERFORD *Lett.* i. (1862) I. 35 [Christ] becomes caution to His Father for all such as resolve and promise to serve Him. **1656** COWLEY *Pind. Odes* (1687) 3 What God (alas) will Caution be, For living Man's Securitie. **1685** COTTON *Montaigne* vi. 154 Any for whose intentions they would become absolute caution. **1826** J. WILSON *Noct. Ambr.* Wks. 1855 I. 214 For whom you had been caution.

†**c.** An obligation, a bond. *Obs.*

138. WYCLIF *Serm.* Sel. Wks. I. 22 Take þi caucioun and sette soone and wryte fifty barellis. [So **1388** WYCLIF *Luke* xvi. 6; **1382** *has* obligacioun.]

d. = Caution-money: see 6.

1830 BP. MONK *Life Bentley* (1833) II. 107 For some time after his degradation the disputations in theology were entirely dispensed with, on the payment of caution.

†**2.** A saving clause; a proviso. *Obs.*

a **1593** H. SMITH *Wks.* (1867) II. 5 We pray for health, and wealth, and honour..and life, with a caution, If it be Gods will. **1597** HOOKER *Eccl. Pol.* v. lxxvi. §6 It standeth therefore with these cautions firm and true. **1616** SIR H. DOCWRA in *Fortesc. Papers* (1871) 18 The office shold be divided in twoe, but with this speciall cawtion, that our charges shold be kepte aparte. **1667** MILTON *P.L.* v. 513. **1695** WOODWARD *Nat. Hist. Earth* I. (1723) 8, I advance nothing from any Observation that was not made with this Caution.

3. A word of warning; a caveat, monition; a hint or advice to anyone to take heed.

1605 SHAKS. *Macb.* IV. i. 73 What ere thou art, for thy good caution thanks. **1623** COCKERAM, *Caution* = *Caueat*, a warning. **1661** BRAMHALL *Just Vind.* ii. 13 Not by way of censure, but of caution. **1791** (*title*) A Caution to Gentlemen who use Sheridan's Dictionary. **1855** MACAULAY *Hist. Eng.* IV. 659 Measures for conveying to his rival a caution which perhaps might still arrive in time.

b. *Mil.* An explanation previous to the word of command; a preliminary word of command.

1796 *Instr. & Reg. Cavalry* (1813) 103 The squadron leader will give a loud caution that the doubling is to be made either successively, or by the whole squadron at once. **1859** F. GRIFFITHS *Artil. Man.* (1862) 30 The commanding officer will give the caution, *form company squares*.

c. An occurrence, act, or fact, which conveys a warning. (Somewhat *colloq.*: cf. '*warning*'.)

1878 FR. KEMBLE *Rec. Girlhood* I. i. 14 The totally different character imparted by a helmet, or a garland of roses, to the same set of features, is a 'caution' to irregular beauties.

d. *slang.* (Of U.S. origin.) Anything that staggers, or excites alarm or astonishment; an extraordinary thing or person.

1835 C. F. HOFFMAN *Winter West* 234 (Bartlett) The way the icy blast would come down the bleak shore was a caution. **1859** *All Y. Round* No. 22. 520 One man..whose performance was what the Americans call 'a caution'. **1868** H. C. JOHNSON *Argent. Alps* 93 The first fifteen leagues we got over cheerily enough, but the last five were a caution. **1870** M. COLLINS *Vivian* III. ii. 26 His wife was what the Yankees call a 'caution'.

4. The taking of heed; 'provident care, wariness against evil' (J.), as a kind or quality of conduct; cautiousness, heedfulness, circumspectness, prudence in regard to danger.

1651 *Reliq. Wotton.* 11 Solicitudes..which kept the Earle in extream and continuall caution. **1664** EVELYN *Kal. Hort.* (1729) 197 Uncover..your choicest Plants, but with Caution. **1697** DRYDEN *Virg. Georg.* IV. 703 By little Caution, and much Love betray'd. **1719** YOUNG *Revenge* v. ii, A rage In which the wise with caution will engage. **1729** BUTLER *Serm.* Wks. 1874 II. Pref. 7 Caution to avoid being mistaken. **1855** MILMAN *Lat. Chr.* III. vi. iii. 453 Godfrey ..had learned caution by his eventful life; it had degenerated into craft. **1863** W. PHILLIPS *Speeches* vi. 139 Caution is not always good policy. **1876** GREEN *Short Hist.* vii. §6 (1882) 405 The caution and hesitation of Philip.

†**5.** (with *pl.*). A taking of heed, a cautious action or mode of proceeding; a precaution. *Obs.*

1605 SHAKS. *Macb.* III. vi. 44 That..might Aduise him to a Caution t' hold what distance His wisedome can prouide. **1669** BOYLE *Contn. New Exp.* I. xlvii. (1682) 161. **1691** T. H[ALE] *Acc. New Invent.* 26 The neglect of ordinary Cautions. **1768** H. WALPOLE *Hist. Doubts* 21 [Something] which, whether a prudent caution or not, was the first overt act of the new reign. **1801** *Med. Jrnl.* V. 157 By due attention to those cautions in the practice, which have been so fully pointed out.

6. *attrib.*, as **caution money**, money deposited as a security for good conduct, *esp.* by a student on entering a college, or an Inn of Court; †**caution town** = CAUTIONARY town.

1665 *Surv. Aff. Netherl.* 140 They delivered us the Caution-Towns we had taken. **1842** ARNOLD in *Life & Corr.* (1844) II. x. 305 The Colleges take care to secure themselves by requiring caution money. **1848** tr. *L. Blanc's Hist. Ten Y.* II. 631 No freedom of the press, except in favour of those who can deposit an exorbitant sum of caution money.

caution ('kɔːʃən), *v.* [f. prec. sb.; cf. F. *cautionner*, med.L. *cautiōnāre.*]

†**1.** *intr.* To give a caution or warning. *Obs.*

1641 J. JACKSON *True Evang. T.* III. 166 It was cautioned in the Law not to yoake an Oxe, and an Asse together. **1678** CUDWORTH *Intell. Syst.* Pref., We have Caution'd concerning it, in the Book it self.

†**2.** To provide with a 'caution' or saving clause; to guard. *Obs.*

1655 FULLER *Ch. Hist.* IX. iv. §4 Such Prophesyings.. might be..discreetly cautioned and moderated. **1681** BURNET *Hist. Ref.* II. 7 It was added, to caution this, that the person..should do nothing..without the advice and consent of the greater part of the rest.

3. To advise or charge (a person) to take heed; to warn. ***to caution oneself***: to take heed, take precautions. Usual const. *against*, or *to* with *inf.*

1683 LORRAIN *Muret's Rites Fun.* To Rdr. 4 In.. cautioning us against a too late expectation of finding it. *a* **1694** TILLOTSON *Wks.* I. v. (R.) Cautioning us to take heed least we be overcharged with surfeiting and drunkenness. **1702** *Eng. Theophrast.* 113 If a Man..do not caution himself against the Snares, etc. **1845** FORD *Handbk. Spain* i. 28 Don Quixote cautions Sancho to be moderate in his food. **1857** BUCKLE *Civiliz.* I. xiv. 535 He cautions his readers against the common error of looking to antiquity for knowledge.

Hence **'cautioned, 'cautioning,** *ppl. adjs.*

c **1720** PRIOR (J.) To our caution'd soul. **1748** RICHARDSON *Clarissa* (1811) I. xxxviii. 284 More of the cautioning friend, than of the satirizing observer. **1863** GEO. ELIOT *Romola* III. xxi, Romola's belief in him had submerged all cautioning doubts.

†**'cautional,** *a. Obs.* [f. CAUTION *sb.* + -AL.] Of the nature of a caution; warning, cautionary.

1656 BLOUNT *Glossogr.*, *Cautional, Cautionary*, pertaining to caution, pledge or wariness. **1660** WITHER (*title*), Speculum Speculativum..with Cautional Expressions made thereupon. **1692** SOUTH *Serm.* IX. v. (R.) With this cautional observation.

†**'cautionarily,** *adv. Obs.* [f. next + -LY².] In a cautionary manner; as a caution.

1665 WITHER *Lord's Prayer* 44 This is cautionarily intended, without purposing ought in opposition to what is believed by others. **1758** *Herald* II. 173 We surely should be cautionarily guarded against the practices.

cautionary ('kɔːʃənərɪ), *a.* (*sb.*) [f. L. type **cautiōnāri-us*: see CAUTION *sb.* and -ARY¹; cf. F. *cautionnaire.*]

A. *adj.* **1.** Of, pertaining to, of the nature of a pledge or security; held in pledge, or as a security or hostage. Now chiefly *Hist.* or *Sc.*

1597 SIR F. VERE *Comm.* (1657) 70 The ordinary Garrison of the cautionary towns. **1611** SPEED *Hist. Gt. Brit.* IX. viii. (1632) 556 That..all his cautionary Lords should be released. **1659** RUSHW. *Hist. Coll.* I. 3 The Town of Flushing, the Castle of Ramakins in Zealand, and Brill in Holland, which were held by way of caution from the United Provinces, to insure their dependency upon England, the King resolved to render up, as being meerly cautionary. **1696** SOUTHERNE *Oroonoko* IV. ii, And I am made the cautionary pledge, The gage and hostage of your keeping it. **1829** SOUTHEY *More* (1831) II. 95 As a nation withdraws its cautionary troops from fortresses..in a friendly territory. **1844** *Blackw. Mag.* LVI. 140 To bring Affghanistan within the general system of cautionary ties. **1860** MOTLEY *Netherl.* (1868) I. iv. 131 The cautionary towns were to be restored. **1883** *Scotsman* 9 May 6/7 Cautionary obligations undertaken.

†**2.** Marked by caution, cautious. *Obs.*

1605 BACON *Adv. Learn.* (1873) II. xxi. §5 Doctrines.. more fearful and cautionary than the nature of things requireth. **1649** SELDEN *Laws Eng.* II. vi. (1739) 34 The Prelates cautionary way of proceeding. **1806–31** A. KNOX *Rem.* (1844) I. 79 This cautionary conduct.

3. Of the nature of, or conveying, a caution or admonition; warning, admonitory. Freq. in phr. ***cautionary tale.***

1638 ROUSE *Heav. Univ.* x. (1702) 137 An Applicatory and Cautionary Chapter. **1711** STEELE *Tatler* No. 273 Many cautionary precepts for my future conduct. **1806** KNOX & JEBB *Corr.* I. 255 A long cautionary letter against the pernicious influence of philosophy and poetry. **1850** L. HUNT *Autobiog.* v. (1860) 107 It had a cautionary effect. **1884** *Cyclists' Tour. Club Gaz.* Dec. 362/1 Cautionary as well as danger-boards should be prepared. **1907** H. BELLOC (*title*) Cautionary tales for children. **1930** R. MACAULAY *Staying with Relations* xx. 304 Julia rejected Mr. Phipps as a protagonist of a cautionary tale. **1959** *Observer* 15 Mar. 22/7 Professor Bowers's first chapter is full of cautionary tales for practising reviewers and critics of this sort.

†**4. a.** Of the nature of a provision against evil or danger; precautionary. *Obs.*

1678 CUDWORTH *Intell. Syst.* I. iv. §33. 520 Cicero.. makes a Law for them..but with a cautionary provision, that, etc. **1772–84** COOK *Voy.* (1790) VI. 1980 Cautionary severity is ever invidious. **1826** R. PETERS in *Pa. Hist. Soc. Mem.* I. 88 He pursued such cautionary measures.

†**b.** Furnished with precautions. *Obs.*

1684 BUNYAN *Pilgr.* II. 65 These ways are made cautionary enough..by these Posts and Ditch and Chain.

†**B.** *sb.* **a.** A security. **b.** A personal security, a surety. *Obs.*

1655 L'ESTRANGE *Chas. I*, 121 Two his Head Towns should be left to the King as Cautionaries for performing the Covenants. **1655** DIGGES *Compl. Ambass.* 370 The Duke.. would become cautionary for the due observation of the same.

cautionary, var. of CAUTIONRY.

†**'cautionate,** *a. Obs.* [ad. med.L. *cautiōnāt-us* (see next).] Cautious, cautionary.

1616 W. SCLATER *Serm.* 28 To make you cautionate how yee fall by example of like iniustice. *a* **1626** —— *Three Serm.* (1629) 32 With cautionate distinction affirmed.

Hence †**'cautionately** *a.*, †**'cautionateness.**

1619 W. SCLATER *Expos. 1 Thess.* (1630) 33 No sinnes should be more cautionately watched against. **1619** —— *Ibid.* 569 This cautionatenes in God's children. **1626** —— *Expos. 2 Thess.* (1629) 81 Adiuring them to cautionatenesse. **1653** W. SCLATER (Son) *Fun. Serm.* (1654) 23 Though it be (cautionately understood) thus possible.

†**'cautionate,** *v. Obs.* [f. med.L. *cautiōnāt-* ppl. stem of *cautiōnāre*, F. *cautionner*: see -ATE³.] To take or apply precautions; to furnish or guard with 'cautions' or provisos. Hence **'cautionated, 'cautionating** *ppl. adjs.*

1621 W. SCLATER *Tythes* (1623) 176 Practising freely, yea teaching lawfulnesse of cautionated vsurie. **1654** TRAPP *Comm. Ps.* xxxiii. 1 That cautionating counsel of Bernard. **1655** —— *Marrow Gd. Auth.* (1868) 842/2 It is cautionated by the duke of Russia, that there be no schools. **1658–9** in *Burton's Diary* (1828) III. 143 To cautionate any prejudice that can be upon our rights and liberties, by a general question. *Ibid.* 200 If you cautionate it so that the previous vote shall be upon what is debated.

cautioner ('kɔːʃənə(r)). Also 7 *Sc.* catiounar ('keʃənər). [f. CAUTION *sb.* and *v.* + -ER¹.]

1. *Sc. Law.* One who gives or becomes security for another; a surety; = CAUTION *sb.*¹ b.

c **1565** LINDESAY (Pitscottie) *Chron. Scot.* (1728) 8 He became cautioner that such enormities..should not be committed in time coming. **1631** RUTHERFORD *Lett.* xix. (1862) I. 79 Jesus, as the Cautioner, is bound for us. *a* **1662** HEYLIN *Laud* (1671) 299 (D.) That no Presbyter should hereafter become surety or cautioner for any person whatsoever. **1846** LAING in *Knox's Wks.* I. 345 *note*, Patrick Murray..became cautioner for William Harlaw, and was amerciated for his non-appearance to underly the law. **1846** T. CHALMERS *On Romans* xxi, Should an able Cautioner liquidate the whole. **1884** SIR E. E. KAY in *Law Times Rep.* LI. 21/1 The case of a cautioner to the bank for one of their agents.

2. One who cautions or warns.

In mod. Dicts.

†**'cautionist.** *Obs. rare*⁻¹. [f. CAUTION + -IST.] One who affects caution.

a **1657** R. LOVEDAY *Lett.* (1659) 33 Like some over-provident Cautionists.

†**cautionize,** *v. Obs.* ? 'To promote caution in anything' (Latham); ? to take 'caution' or security of, to render cautionary (cf. CAUTIONARY 1).

But it may be a misprint for *cantonize*, the reading in ed. 1638: ed. 1631 (the first ed. of the *Continuation*), and ed. 1687, II. 974, however, have *cautionize*.

1631 *Contn. Knolles' Hist. Turks* 1414 The captain of the Ianizaries rose and slew the Bassa, burnt the Mufti and all his kin, and gave his daughter in mariage to one Aslan Begh, a pretender to the antient inheritance of a bordering prouince, to cautionize that part.

'cautionless, *a.* [f. CAUTION *sb.* + -LESS.] Without caution.

1792–7 GEDDES *Judges* xviii. 7 (R.) The people..dwelled careless, quiet and cautionless. **1859** *Chamb. Jrnl.* XI. 315 Playing a wild game, in a reckless, cautionless way.

cautionment ('kɔːʃənmənt). [a. F. *cautionnement*: see -MENT.] = CAUTION 1.

1815 *Ann. Reg., Chron.* 415 French subjects..who have paid sums under the head of cautionments, deposits, or consignments, into their respective treasuries.

cautionry ('kɔːʃənrɪ). *Sc. Law.* Also -ary, erie. [f. CAUTIONER + -Y: see -ERY, -RY.] The position of a cautioner, suretyship. ***bond of cautionry***: = *bond of caution*; see CAUTION *sb.* 1.

1636 RUTHERFORD *Lett.* lix. (1862) I. 159 Christ's act of cautionary. **1640–1** *Kirkcudbr. War-Comm. Min. Bk.* (1855) 74 Johne Makmollan..cautioner for David Makmollan.. presentit the said David and protests to be liberatit of his cautionerie. **1630** *Acts Chas. I* (1814) VI. 167 (Jam.) Their just and true ingagements, and cautionries. **1754** ERSKINE *Princ. Sc. Law* (1809) 297 Bonds of cautionary.

cautious ('kɔːʃəs), *a.* [f. CAUTION (as if from L. **cautiōs-us*, not used): see -TIOUS.]

Distinguished or marked by caution; heedful, wary, careful, circumspect: said of persons, their conduct, and acts. (In quot. 1640 perh. 'Fearful, over-prudent, timorous'.)

a **1640** MASSINGER (W.) You shall be received at a postern door, if you be not cautious, by one whose touch would make old Nestor young. **1665** GLANVILL *Sceps. Sci.* 52 Where deep and enquiring spirits differ, I judge I have reason to be cautious. **1671** MILTON *Samson* 757 With more cautious and instructed skill. **1718** *Free-thinker* No. 20. 137 Our old cautious English Proverb allows us to Trust every Man so far as we can see Him. **1795** SOUTHEY *Joan of Arc* III. 18 Urging on their way with cautious speed. **1833–48** H. COLERIDGE *N. Worthies* (1852) I. 9 He seems to have been a much more cautious man. **1842** H. ROGERS *Introd. Burke's Works* 1842 I. 22 Further than a cautious policy would warrant. **1872** MORLEY *Voltaire* (1886) 67 Patient and cautious interrogation of experience.

b. Const. *of* (obs.), *how*, *lest*, *to* with *inf.* (*Cautious to* was formerly used where *cautious not to* is now in use: cf. CAREFUL.)

1667 MILTON *P.L.* IX. 59 By Night he fled, and at Midnight return'd.. cautious of day. **1709** HEARNE *Collect.* (1886) II. 241 The late Opposition.. has made me cautious how I enter upon new Experiments. **1725** POPE *Odyss.* IV. 207 Cautious to let the gushing grief appear, His purple garment veil'd the falling tear. **1752** JOHNSON *Rambl.* No. 208 ⁋9 Cautious lest this offence should be.. committed. **1772** *Hist. Rochester* 28 Cautious not to exceed it. **1779** FORREST *Voy. N. Guinea* 71, I was very cautious of touching upon what had happened that morning. **1820** *Hoyle's Games Impr.* 5 Be cautious how you trump out. **1821** J. Q. ADAMS in C. Davies *Metr. Syst.* III. (1871) 119 The act.. is cautious not to tie them down to too close a measure.

cautiously ('kɔːʃəslɪ), *adv.* [f. prec. + -LY².] In a cautious manner, with caution; warily, heedfully, carefully, circumspectly.

1664 EVELYN *Kal. Hort.* (1729) 196 Uncover also Artichoaks cautiously, and by degrees. **1699** BENTLEY *Phal.* 131 He cautiously says, that he *often* uses the *Excerpta*. **1781** GIBBON *Decl. & F.* II. 137 He cautiously suppressed his grief and resentment. **1876** GREEN *Short Hist.* viii. §3 (1882) 488 Cautiously and tentatively they were introducing Roman doctrine. **1877** LADY BRASSEY *Voy. Sunbeam* xiv. (1878) 243 Opening the curtains cautiously.

cautiousness ('kɔːʃəsnɪs). [f. as prec. + -NESS.] The quality or state of being cautious; wariness, heedfulness, caution.

1648 *Eikon Bas.* (1824) 64, I could not but approve their generous constancy and cautiousnesse. **1712** ADDISON *Spect.* No. 399 ⁋7 We should always act with great Cautiousness and Circumspection. **1887** *Law Times* LXXXII. 205/2 A cautiousness which is hardly distinguishable from timidity.

‖**cautor.** *Obs.*$^{-0}$. [Lat.] 'He that foreseeth or bewareth' (Blount *Glossogr.* 1656).

cautulous, obs. form of CAUTELOUS.

†'**cauty,** *a. Obs. rare.* Also **cautie.** [app. f. F. *caut*, *caute* (= It. Sp. *cauto*), or L. *caut-us* cautious, heedful, wary, prop. pa. pple. of *cavēre* to beware; with Eng. ending -Y.] Cautious, wary.

1579 E. HAKE *Newes Powles Churchy.* Hj, O cawty cutthroate. *Ibid.* E vij b, Our cawtie countrey Gentlemen. **1610** *Mirr. Mag.* 754 (R.) With cautie observation.

cauve, dial. form of CALVE, CALF.

cauyll, obs. form of CAVIL.

cauzee, cauzy, var. f. KAZI, Mohammedan judge in India, Indian CADI.

cava, var. of KAVA, an intoxicating drink used in Polynesia.

‖**cava.** *Phys.* Short for *vena cava.*

[**1681** tr. *Willis' Rem. Med. Wks.* Voc., *Cava vena*, the great liver-vein going thorow the body.] **1809** *Med. Jrnl.* XXI. 270 The ascending and descending cava gorged with blood. **1866** HUXLEY *Phys.* ii. (1869) 57 Will reach the right auricle by the superior cava.

cavajar, obs. form of CAVIARE.

cavalcade (kævəl'keɪd), *sb.* Also 6 **cavalgada,** 7 **cavalcado, cavalcata, cavelcade,** (8 *erron.* **calvacade**). [a. F. *cavalcade* (16th c. in Littré), ad. Pr. *cavalcada* or It. *cavalcata* (= Sp. *cabalgada*, Pg. *cavalgata*), f. *cavalcar*:—late L. *caballicāre* to ride on horseback, f. *caballus* horse: see -ADE. The native F. form of the word was *chevauchée*, whence also ME. CHEVACHEE.]

†**1.** A ride, a march or raid on horseback. *Obs.*

1591 UNTON *Corr.* (1847) 257, I am nowe attendinge uppon the Kinge in this cavalcade he maketh towards the Duke of Parma. **1598** BARRET *Theor. Warres* v. i. 141 To make Caualgadas, or great marches, for any sudden surprisall. **1604** JAS. I *Counterbl.* (Arb.) 110 To make some sudden Caualcado vpon your enemies. **1647** CLARENDON *Hist. Reb.* VII. II. 215 He had with some Troops, made a Cavalcade or two into the West.

fig. **1697** *Snake in Grass* (ed. 2) 289 Being thrown into Gaol for that his Blasphemous Cavelcade.

2. A procession on horseback, *esp.* on a festive or solemn occasion. Also loosely used for a procession of carriages. *arch.* or ? *Obs.*

1644 EVELYN *Mem.* (1857) I. 102 Desirous of being present at the cavalcade of the new Pope. **1683** *Brit. Spec.* 260 His Majesty.. made a Glorious and Splendid Cavalcade from the Tower to Westminster. **1687** *Lond. Gaz.* No. 2250/3 Cardinal Medici made a Cavalcata.. wherein he was Accompanied by 14 of the Sacred Colledge on Mules. **1762–71** H. WALPOLE *Vertue's Anecd. Paint.* (1786) III. 97 The king's cavalcade through the gates of the city the day before his coronation.

3. *concr.* A company of riders on the march or in procession.

a **1700** DRYDEN *Pal. & Arc.* III. 540 The following cavalcade.. Proceed by titles marshal'd in degree. **1703–14** *Sc. Pasquils* (1868) 347 He and his noble Cavalcade design To right their native Country. **1786** tr. *Beckford's Vathek* (1868) 25 The cavalcade set forward. **1852** MISS YONGE *Cameos* (1871) II. xix. 206 From Chester the Cavalcade set out for London. **1869** HOOK *Lives Abps.* II. ii. 93 He evidently expected to meet a large cavalcade.

4. *transf.* and *fig.* 'Procession'.

1670 *Caveat Conventiclers* 9, I desired him to raise this Devil before me; which he courteously did, together with the whole procession of the Cavalcade. **1708** MOTTEUX *Rabelais* IV. xiii, He made a Cavalcade of his Devils.. through the Town. **1855** J. FORBES *Tour Mont Blanc* 117 The cows were taken to the valley.. and I regretted extremely that I missed the opportunity of witnessing so singular a cavalcade. **1932** N. COWARD (*title*) Cavalcade. **1937** *Daily Herald* 28 Jan. 15/3 Here is a veritable cavalcade of eighteenth and nineteenth century agricultural history. **1941** N. COWARD *Australia Visited* iv. 25, I was fortunate to be able to administer a little artificial respiration to the word:—'Cavalcade'. Before I wrote the play of that name the word had fallen into disuse... Now.. there are.. Cavalcades of fashion, Hollywood Cavalcades,.. Cavalcades of practically anything that can be cavalcaded.

caval'cade, *v.* [f. prec. sb.; in F. *cavalcader.*] *intr.* To ride in a cavalcade, *esp.* in procession or in company with others. Hence **caval'cading** *vbl. sb.* and *ppl. a.*

1710 *Map of Trav. High Ch. Apostle* 6 His mighty great Cavalcading. **1771** P. PARSONS *Newmarket* I. 113 The hero.. cavalcaded it through a large breach made in the walls, in an open chariot. **1816** KEATINGE *Trav.* II. 1 A large party of horse men was cavalcading.. in celebration of a wedding. **1837** CARLYLE *Fr. Rev.* I. I. III. vi. 71 Tumult of charioteering and cavalcading. **1849** *Fraser's Mag.* 175 The host.. homeward with his nobles cavalcaded.

†**cavalet.** *Obs.* [ad. It. *cavalletto* 'a stay, a prop, a tressell' (Florio), dim. of *cavallo* horse. *Cavalet* was also in 16–17th c. French in sense of 'a long hollow sticke, through which they vse in some places, to blow the fire, in stead of bellowes' (Cotgr.). The native Fr. form of the word is *chevalet.*] (See quot.)

1662 MERRET tr. *Neri's Art of Glass* 243 [In an annealing furnace] there's a round hole through which the flame and heat passeth into the tower; this hole is call'd *Occhio* or *Lumella*, having an Iron ring encircling it call'd the Cavalet or Crown. *Ibid.* xvi, Neer the occhio or the cavalet.

cavalier (kævə'lɪə(r)), *sb.* and *a.* Forms: 6 **cauallere, (cabbaleer, caueelere), 6–7 cavallier,** 7 **cavaliere, -leer(e, cavaglier,** (by perversion) **caviler,** *Sc.* **cavaleire, cavelleir,** 6– **cavalier.** Also (from Spanish) 6 **cavallero, cauilero, caualeiro,** 6–7 **cavaliero,** 7 **cavalero,** 8 **cavalliero.** [Originally adopted in the form *cavallero*, *cavaliero*, etc. from Sp., with occasional use of the It. and Pg. forms. The actual form *cavalier* is a. F. *cavalier* (16th c. in Littré), ad. It. *cavaliere*, f. *cavallo* horse + *-iere*, a termination often occurring in Italian for L. *-ārius*. The late L. *caballārius* (-'*erius*) 'horseman' gave Sp. *caballero* (OSp. *cav-*), Pg. *cavalleiro*, Pr. *cavallier*, ONF. *cavailler*, *cavaler*, OF. and F. *chevalier*, whence also Eng. CHEVALIER.]

A. *sb.*

1. A horseman, *esp.* a horse-soldier; a knight.

[*c* **1470** *Hors, Shepe, & G.* (1822) 3 In duche a rider is called a Knyght, Aragon tonge doth also specyfye Caualero, which in that partie Is named of worship & toke begynnyng Of spores of gold and chiefly of rydyng. **1598** BARRET *Theor. Warres* Gloss. 249 *Cauaglere*, an Italian word.. signifieth a Gentleman seruing on horsebacke.] **1600** HAKLUYT *Voy.* III. 691 That so many cavalleros should all faile in this one attempt. **1640–1** *Kirkcudbr. War-Comm. Min. Bk.* (1855) 51 That all brave cavaleires will tak the business to hart. **1656** BLOUNT *Glossogr.*, *Cavalier*, *Cavalero*, a knight or gentleman, serving on horseback, a man of arms. **1796** H. HUNTER tr. *St. Pierre's Stud. Nat.* (1799) II. 526 Of our cavaliers, or of our foot-soldiers. **1807** SIR R. WILSON *Jrnl.* 2 July, I returned.. decked with mud; but as my horse was seen to fall I did not appear as a dishonoured cavalier. **1870** BRYANT *Iliad* I. III. 97 A mute wonder held The Trojan cavaliers.

2. a. A gentleman trained to arms, 'a gay sprightly military man' (J.); *gen.* a courtly gentleman, a gallant. (Like *gallant*, also applied about 1600, to a roistering swaggering fellow.)

1589 *Pasquil's Ret.* A iij, How now Caualiero, are you come to Scripture? **1593** *Prodigal Son* III. 103 Our guest is a free-handed Cavalier. **1597** SHAKS. *2 Hen. IV*, v. iii. 62 Ile drinke to M. Bardolfe, and to all the Cauileroes about London. **1599** *Warn. Faire Wom.* II. 589 Some swaggering, swearing, drunken, desperate Dicke. Call we them Cabbaleers? masse, they be Canniballes. **1600** ROWLANDS *Lett. Humours Blood* 3 Humours is late crown'd king of Caueeleres. **1641** J. JACKSON *True Evang. T.* III. 175 The tidings.. brought not to cavalliers, but to quiet and simple Shepherds. **1651** *Life Father Sarpi* (1676) 25 Signor Alphonso Antomini a Cavaglier of the most sublime vertues. **1670** COTTON *Espernon* I. iv. 170 Some little dispute.. which had oblig'd him to seek the satisfaction of a Cavalier. **1777** GARRICK *Prol. Sheridan's Sch. Scand.*, He'll fight—that's write—a cavalliero true. **1867** EMERSON *May-day* Wks. (Bohn) III. 413 To greet staid ancient cavaliers.

b. A gentleman attending upon or escorting a lady, a 'gallant', a 'squire' (cf. 5); a lady's partner in a dance.

1752 MRS. LENNOX *Fem. Quix.* II. IX. ii. 213 The rest of the cavaliers and ladies. **1765** STERNE *Tristr. Shandy* VII. xliii, I'll take a dance, said I.. we want a cavalier, said she, holding out both her hands, as if to offer them. **1825** LYTTON *Zicci* 34 He wants to be your cavalier, not your husband. **1829** —— *Disowned* 99 Do come, Mr. Linden will be our cavalier. [**1847** THACKERAY *Mrs. Perkins's Ball*, *Cavalier seul*, This is my friend Bob Hely, performing the Cavalier seul in a quadrille.]

c. As a title or term of address.

1589 NASHE (*title*), The Return of the Renowned Caualiero Pasquill, etc. **1598** SHAKS. *Merry W.* II. iii. 77 Caualeiro Slender, goe you through the Towne to Frogmore.

3. A name given to those who fought on the side of Charles I in the war between him and the Parliament; a 17th c. Royalist.

Originally reproachful, and applied to the swash-bucklers on the king's side, who hailed the prospect of war; cf. CAVALIERISH, -ISM.

1641–2 [see quot. 1651]. **1642** D'EWES *MS. Journ.* 10 Jan. 1641 (*Harl. MS.* 162 lf. 312b) Certain Hamletters.. informed vs of some of the Ingeneers in the Tower to be dangerous men and that some caualiers had gone in thither. **1642** *Ld. Kimbolton's Sp. in Parl.* 4 (not authentic) Ill affected cavaleers and commanders about the Court. **1642** (June 10) *Propositions of Parlt.* in Clarendon v. (1702) I. 504 Several sorts of malignant Men, who were about the King; some whereof, under the name of Cavaliers, without having respect to the Laws of the Land, or any fear either of God or Man, were ready to commit all manner of Outrage and Violence. **1642** *Petition Lords & Com.* 17 June in Rushw. *Coll.* III. (1721) I. 631 That your Majesty.. would please to dismiss your extraordinary Guards, and the Cavaliers and others of that Quality, who seem to have little Interest or Affection to the publick Good, their Language and Behaviour speaking nothing but Division and War. **1642** CHAS. I *Answ. Petition* 17 June 13 The language and behaviour of the *Cavaliers* (a word by what mistake soever it seemes much in disfavour). **1642** *Catal. Pamphlets Harl. Libr.* xxiii. 101/1 No. 325 A Perfect Declaration of the barbarous and cruel Practices committed by Prince Robert, the Cavalliers, and others in his Majesty's Army. **1651** LILLY *Monarchy* 107 [Speaking of what he witnessed during Christmas of 1641–2] The Courtiers againe, wearing long Haire and locks, and alwayes Sworded, at last were called by these men [the Puritans] Cavaliers; and so after this broken language had been used a while, all that adhered unto the Parlament were termed Round-heads; all that tooke part or appeared for his Majestie, Cavaliers, few of the vulgar knowing the sence of the word *Cavalier*. **1656** CROMWELL *Sp.* 17 Sept., Your old enemies, the Papists and Cavaliers. **1656** R. LANE in *Hatton Corr.* (1878) 14 The poore cavilers are by proclamation banishd the towne. **1711** ADDISON *Spect.* No. 125 ⁋1 When the Feuds ran high between the Round-heads and the Cavaliers. **1864** H. SPENCER *Illustr. Univ. Progr.* 62 The Puritans, disapproving of the long curls of the Cavaliers, as of their principles.

4. *Fortification.* 'A work generally raised within the body of the place, ten or twelve feet higher than the rest of the works... to command all the adjacent works and country round' (Stocqueler).

1560 WHITEHORNE *Ord. Souldours* (1573) 18b, Cavaliers or platformes. **1590** MARLOWE *2nd Pt. Tamburl.* II. iv. 102 Raise cavalieros higher than the clouds, And with the cannon break the frame of heaven. **1598** BARRET *Theor. Warres* v. i. 126 These Caualleres ought in no wise to be made within the bulwarkes. **1670** COTTON *Espernon* I. I. 23 He rais'd by the industry of an Italian Engineer, a Cavalier. **1799** BAIRD in Owen *Disp. Wellesley* 127 The whole of the ramparts, and every cavalier in the fort, were.. in the possession of our troops. **1860** *Times* 3 Nov. 7/6 In the centre of the front face.. is a high cavalier mounting two large brass guns.

‖**5.** ***cavalier-servant***, or in It. form ***cavaliere-servente*** (F. *cavalier-servant*): a man who devotes himself wholly to attendance on a lady as her professed slave, either from love or from gratitude. Hence ***cavalier servitude***, ***cavaliere-serventism*** (nonce-formations).

1817 BYRON *Beppo* xl. **1820** —— *Let.* Wks. (1846) 153/1 The conventual education, the cavalier servitude. **1823** —— *Juan* IX. li, Which hovers oft about some married beauties, Called 'Cavalier Servente'. **1878** *Fraser's Mag.* XVIII. 38 Neither married life nor conventional cavaliere-serventism was prolific of inspiration.

B. *attrib.* or *adj.* †**1. a.** Gallant. *Obs.*

a **1641** SUCKLING *Fragm. Aurea* (1648) 94 The people are naturally not valiant, and not much cavalier.

†**b.** Of things: Fine, 'brave', 'gallant'. *Obs.*

1670 LASSELS *Voy. Italy* I. 130 One of the most cavalier curiosityes a man can see in Italy.

2. a. Careless in manner, off-hand, free and easy. **b.** Haughty, disdainful, supercilious.

1657 HAWKE *Killing is M.* To Rdr., Cavalier and nimble wits. **1751** SMOLLETT *Per. Pic.* (1779) II. xxxvii. 25 This cavalier declaration of the young man. **1817** MAR. EDGEWORTH *Ormond* xiv. (1832) 149 Very cavalier, indeed, to go out to walk, without waiting to see us. **1865** CARLYLE *Fredk. Gt.* VI. XVI. xv. 314 This cavalier tone from an unknown person.. did not please me.

3. In reference to the 17th c.: Royalist.

1844 DISRAELI *Coningsby* III. iii. (L.) An old Cavalier family. **1868** *Q. Rev.* 259 Robert South was the very type of a Cavalier preacher in the proper sense of the term.

4. *attrib.* and *Comb.*, as ***cavalier riding habit***; **cavalier cuff**, a cuff of gauntlet shape; **cavalier-hat**, a hat with a feather worn by ladies in imitation of those worn by the Royalists in the time of Charles I; **cavalier-poet** (applied to Lovelace).

1666 EVELYN *Dairy* 13 Sept., The Queene was now in her cavalier riding habite, hat and feather, and horseman's coate. **1860** SALA *Make Your Game* 151 (Hoppe) Ladies with ravishing bonnets and cavalier-hats. **1879** McCARTHY *Own Times* (Hoppe) The fine lines of the cavalier-poet, which remind his mistress that he could not love her so much, loved he not honour more. **1902** *Daily Chron.* 17 Aug. 8/3 The cavalier cuff of stiffened velvet. **1923** *Daily Mail* 1 Mar. 6 Sleeves that end in a flounce..—gowns with no sleeves at all—Cavalier cuffs—there is infinite variety.

Hence **cava'lieress** (*nonce-wd.*); **cava'liership**.

1872 MARK TWAIN *Innoc. at Home* xxi. (Hoppe) Every street was..packed with charging cavaliers and cavalieresses. **1594** NASHE *Unfort. Trav.* Wks. 1883–4 V. 60 Did I cashier the new vocation of my cauailiership? **1596** —— *Saffron-Walden* Wks. 1883–4 III. 153 His Caualiership ..is lewder by nine score times than his Poetry.

cava'lier, *v.* [f. prec. sb.] **a.** *intr.* To play the cavalier. **b.** *trans.* To act as cavalier or escort to (a lady). Hence **cava'liering** *vbl. sb.*

1594 NASHE *Terrors Night* Wks. 1883–4 III. 279 Bridewell or Newgate prooue the ende of your caueleering.
1693 SHADWELL *Volunteers* I. i, I must fly from the University forsooth to run a cavaliering. **1748–61** RICHARDSON *Clarissa* (1811) VII. 171 Cavaliering it here over half a dozen persons of distinction. **1863** MRS. C. CLARKE *Shaks. Char.* xvi. 427 From his cavaliering the ladies Percy and Mortimer.

cava'liering, *ppl. a.* [f. prec. + -ING^2.]
Playing the cavalier; haughty, domineering.

1642 J. GOODWIN (*title*), Anti-Cavalierism..for the suppressing of that butcherly brood of Cavaliering incendiaries. **1647** J. HARE *St. Edw. Ghost* in *Harl. Misc.* (1746) VIII. 91/2 An haughty and cavaliering Nation. **1680** *Hon. Cavalier* 11 A bold Cavaliering Gentleman. **1816** SCOTT *Old Mort.* xxvii, Some old cavaliering Baron.

cava'lierish, *a.* [f. CAVALIER *sb.* + -ISH^1.] **a.** Like a cavalier. **b.** *spec.* Of the cavaliers of Charles I. Hence **cava'lierishness**.

1647 *Myst. Two Juntos* 15 The Countrey..fearing these Cavaliers are kept on free-quarter by a Cavaleerish party for some Cavaleerish Designe. **1657–8** SCOTT in Burton's *Diary* (1828) II. 383, I hope I shall never be suspected to be Cavalierish. **1698** LUDLOW *Mem.* II. 168 (R.) The cavalierish party, who were very numerous. **1860** *All Y. Round* 438 The rollicking cavalierishness of that highwayman.

cava'lierism. [f. CAVALIER *sb.* + -ISM.] The practice or principles of cavaliers, *esp.* of the adherents of Charles I; an expression characteristic of the Cavalier party.

1642 BRIDGE *Serm. Norfolk Volunteers* 6 There is a vaunting, bragging, boasting Cavalierisme, which hath no true courage; such a Cavalier was Rabshakeh. **1643** HERLE *Answ. Ferne* 4 Both Houses of Parliament are cal'd..Rebels and Traytors (the ordinary cavaleerismes of the times). **1818** SCOTT *Hrt. Midl.* viii, When wine and cavalierism predominated in his upper story. **1791–1824** D'ISRAELI *Cur. Lit.* (1866) 287/2 Various kinds of ranting cavalierism.

cavalierly (kævə'lɪəlɪ), *a.* [f. as prec. + -LY^1.] Characteristic of a cavalier; knightly; haughty.

1876 G. MEREDITH *Beauch. Career* II. vi. 88 With a cavalierly charm in the sullen brows she lifted. *Ibid.* III. xi. 196 Tuckham's figure was..neither cavalierly nor kingly. **1879** —— *Egoist* I. ix. 154 He had a cavalierly style.

cava'lierly, *adv.* [f. CAVALIER *a.* + -LY^2.]
†**1.** Finely, magnificently, 'bravely'. *Obs.*

1670 LASSELS *Italy* (1698) I. 24 A stately room, than which nothing can be more cavalierly furnished.

2. With haughty carelessness, disdainfully.

1718 *Free-thinker* No. 76. 147 Pamphilus..engages in Friendships, and in Enmities, very Cavalierly. **1768** GOLDSM. *Good-n. Man* IV. i, You treat me very cavalierly. **1826** DISRAELI *Viv. Grey* I. v. 10 He bowed cavalierly to Mr. Dallas. **1864** H. SPENCER *Illustr. Univ. Progr.* 377 Those who cavalierly reject the Theory of Evolution.

cavaliero, -ship: see CAVALIER.

cavallada, var. CABALLADA. (Cf. next.)

cavallard (kɑːvə'lɑːd, kæ-). *U.S. dial.* Also caviarde, cavalyard. [corruption of *cavallade*, ad. Sp. *caballada* (kaba'ʎaða) CABALLADA, in Texas and New Mexico.] 'A term used, in Louisiana and Texas, by the caravans which cross the prairies, to denote a band of horses or mules' (Bartlett).

1836 W. B. DEWEES *Lett. fr. Texas* (1852) xx. 208 They.. soon obtained a fine cavalyard of horses, which they drove into Arkansas for sale. **1846** SAGE *Scenes in Rocky Mts.* 80 Stealing our whole cavallard, consisting of ten head of horses and mules. **1878** J. H. BEADLE *Western Wilds* iv. 69 All hands sprang up only to witness our noble *cavallard* under full headway before a body of Mexican horsemen.

cavallarie, -erie, -ery, obs. ff. CAVALRY.

†**cavallerice.** *Obs.* [ad. It. *cavallerizza*, (Sp. *caballeriza*) riding-school, f. *cavallo* horse. (Du Cange has med.L. *caballeritia* service with a horse.)] Horsemanship.

1607 MARKHAM (*title*), Cavelarice or the English Horseman. *Ibid.* I. (1617) 41 Least..some other man might come and deny my Cavallarice.

†**ca'vallerize.** *Obs. rare*$^{-1}$. [ad. It. *cavallerizzo* (Sp. *caballerizo*) riding-master.] A riding-master, professor of horsemanship.

1653 URQUHART *Rabelais* I. xxiii, The cavallerize [Fr. *voltigeur*] of Ferrara was but as an Ape compared to him.

cavally (kə'vælɪ). Also 7–9 cavallo, 8 cavalle, cavaly. [ad. Sp. and Pg. *cavalla*, It. *cavallo* mackerel; also applied to the horse-mackerel of various tropical seas. Cf. the specific names *Caranx caballus*, *Cybium caballa* given to species of horse-mackerel.]

A name given by the 17th c. navigators to various species of tropical fish, known also as horse-mackerel.

1634 SIR T. HERBERT *Trav.* 213 The rest are Breame, Tench, Trowte..Cavalloes. **1657** R. LIGON *Barbadoes* (1673) 12 Fish..of various kinds..Snappers, grey and red; Cavallos, Carpians, etc. **1697** DAMPIER *Voy.* I, The chiefest Fish are Bonetas, Snooks, Cavally's. **1772–84** COOK *Voy.* (1790) V. 1695 We also caught..a great quantity of fish, principally consisting of cavallies. **1803** T. WINTERBOTTOM *Sierra Leone* I. iv. 69 They have..snappers, mullets, cavallies. **1847** SIR J. ROSS *Voy. Antarctic Reg.* II. 117 A kind of mackarel, called yellow tail, and sometimes cavallo. **1887** *Nat. Hist. Notes* (fr. *Leisure Ho.*) No. 15, 131 The Kukukina, or young cavally, when caught on the hook.. utters an imperfect guttural sound like 'Ak, ak'.

cavalry ('kævəlrɪ). Forms: 6–7 cavallerie, -arie, 7 cavallery, cavalary, chavallery, cavellerie, cavelrie, 7– cavalry. [In 16–17th c. *cavallery*, a. F. *cavallerie* (16th c. in Littré), ad. It. *cavalleria* (= Pr. *cavalaria* Sp. *caballeria*):—Romanic type *caballa'ria*, f. L. *caballārius* horseman. See -ERY. (The native Fr. form of the word was *chevalerie*, whence Eng. *chivalry*.) Massinger (1632) accented *ca'vallery*, but other spellings appear to indicate '*cavallery*, whence also '*cavalry* in the middle of the 17th c. (See also CHAVALLERY, CHIVALRY.)]

†**1.** Horsemanship; chivalry. *Obs.*

1591 HARINGTON *Orl. Fur.* 266 *note*, The likest to him for armes and cavallarie (as we terme it). **1625** MARKHAM *Souldier's Accid.* i, The Cavallarie or Formes of Trayning of Horse-Troopes. **1644** MILTON *Educ.* Wks. (1847) 101 All the Art of Cavalry. **1670** LASSELS *Voy. Italy* (1698) II. 265 They tilt and use other sports of cavalry.

†**2.** Knighthood; an order of chivalry. *Obs.*

1601 HOLLAND *Pliny* II. 460 Cicero..re-established the Knighthood and Cauallerie of Rome in their former estate and place. **1616** SIR N. BRENT tr. *Sarpi's Hist. Counc. Trent* (1676) 366 To institute a Religion of an hundred persons, like unto a Cavalary. **1625** FLETCHER *Fair Maid* III. i. 37 To keep off the Cavelrie and Gentry. **1632** BROME *Court Begg.* II. i. Wks. 1873 I. 207 All The cavalry of Court.

3. a. The collective name for horse-soldiers; that part of a military force which consists of mounted troops. Opposed to *infantry*.

(Usually construed with plural vb., exc. *a cavalry*, which has pl. *cavalries*.)

1591 GARRARD *Art Warre* 225 The companies of the couragious Cavallerie. **1598** BARRET *Theor. Warres* v. i. 141. **1603** HOLLAND *Plutarch's Mor.* 1245 The cavallery of the Thebanes. **1622** BACON *Hen. VII*, 74 You may haue a good Cauallerie, but neuer good stable Bands of Foot. **1632** MASSINGER *Maid of Hon.* II. iii, I, in mine own person, With part of the cavallery. **1644** MILTON *Educ.* (1738) 137 Two Troops of Cavalry. **1665** MANLEY *Grotius' Low-C. Warrs* 355 The Cavallery belonging to the United States. *a* **1714** BURNET *Own Times* an. 1694 (R.) They sent away their cavalry with so much haste. **1834** GEN. P. THOMPSON *Exerc.* (1842) III. 127 A struggle between the opposing cavalries, which shall keep itself in condition for action longest. **1848** MACAULAY *Hist. Eng.* I. 592 The cavalry were about a thousand in number.

b. *transf.* Horses, horsemen, etc., collectively.

1684 *Dk. Beaufort's Progr. Wales* (1864) 17 Leading horses to supply accidents and defects in the coach-cavalry. **1792** A. YOUNG *Trav. France* 11 A traveller so weak in cavalry as myself. **1870** DISRAELI *Lothair*, Troops of social cavalry cantered..in morning rides. **1881** DUFFIELD *Don Quix.* II. 550 Donkeys..the ordinary Cavalry of Country Maids.

c. (See quot.)

1820 *Hoyle's Games Impr.* 347 A variation of Draughts entitled Constitutional Checkers. *Ibid.* 348 The pieces with the turrets to be considered as Cavalry, and the flat pieces as Infantry. *Ibid.*, A king may not be taken backwards by Cavalry or Infantry unless they have been to king.

4. *attrib.* and *Comb.* ***cavalry charge, day, jacket, man, officer, soldier***, etc.; **cavalry curate**, a curate who rode on horseback to perform his duties in an extensive and scattered parish; **cavalry twill** (see quot. 1957).

1872 MORLEY *Voltaire* (1886) 163 A daring *cavalry-charge. **1894** G. H. HAMILTON *Charge* 8 Mission Chapels —where the '*Cavalry Curates' ought to reside. **1898** *Westm. Gaz.* 14 Jan. 1/3 The immense extent of many parishes, into some of which 'Cavalry curates' have been introduced with advantage. **1837** HT. MARTINEAU *Soc. Amer.* III. 144 On *cavalry days, when guests are invited to dine with the regiment. **1799** *Instr. & Reg. Cavalry* (1813) 266 The principles of all *cavalry evolutions. **1861** *Times* 22 Oct., A blue *cavalry jacket. **1860** GEN. P. THOMPSON *Audi Alt.* III. cxix. 61 *Cavalry-men on both sides. **1838** *Annual Scrap-Book* 19 The amount of a tailor's bill, for fitting out his son as a *cavalry officer. **1854** THACKERAY *Newcomes* vi, This distinguished cavalry officer swore very freely. **1903** *Westm. Gaz.* 5 Oct. 1/3, I bought him on the advice of two cavalry-officer friends who knew him. **1852** GROTE *Greece* II. lxxvi. X. 77 A *cavalry-soldier..was reckoned as equivalent to four hoplites. **1942** J. HOYE *Staple Cotton Fabrics* 146 The name *cavalry twill is used..for a steep double-twill-line whipcord made with colored yarns on 9 harnesses and in a tricotine weave. **1944** G. S. BRADY *Materials Handbk.* (ed. 5) 188 Cavalry twill is not a cotton cloth, but is of worsted or rayon twill woven with a diagonal raised cord. **1953** S. D. BARNEY *Clothes & Horse* ix. 63 Cavalry Twill..was first made..during the early part of the First World War in khaki for Cavalry Regiments, hence the name. **1957** *Textile Terms & Defs.* (ed. 3) 24 *Cavalry twill*, a firm warp-faced cloth in which the weave gives steep double twill lines separated by pronounced grooves formed by the weft. **1959** J. BRAINE *Vodi* iv. 57 A cream silk shirt, fawn cavalry twill slacks and light brown suède shoes.

cavash, -ass = KAVASS, Turkish police officer.

†**cavated**, *a.* *Obs. rare*$^{-1}$. [f. L. *cavāt-us* hollowed + -ED: cf. *excavated*.] Hollowed.

1731–7 MILLER *Gard. Dict.* s.v. *Cotyledon*, The Leaves.. are cavated.

‖**cavatina** (kævə'tiːnə). *Mus.* [Ital.] A short song of simple character, properly one without a second strain and repeat; 'frequently applied to a smooth melodious air, forming part of a grand scena or movement' (Grove).

1836 DICKENS *Sk. Boz* (C.D. ed.) 205 The popular cavatina 'Bid me discourse'. **1845** E. HOLMES *Mozart* 26 An Italian Cavatina which she knew by heart.

†**ca'vation.** *Obs.*$^{-0}$ [ad. L. *cavātiōn-em*, f. *cavāre* to hollow.] (See quot.)

1721 BAILEY, *Cavation*, a hollowing the Ground for Cellarage. [**1731–1800** *Cavation*, a making hollow.]

cavayado, var. CABALLADA.

cavayard, cavy-yard ('kævə-, 'kævɪjɑːd). *U.S.* Also cavvi-, cavvie-yard, caviarde; cavvieyeh, caviya. [Var. of CAVALLARD, with *y* for Sp. *ll*.]

A drove of horses.

α. **1847** W. B. DEWEES *Lett. fr. Texas* (1852) 3 Mar. 301 Two hundred dollars would be sufficient to purchase a cavayard of twenty [mares]. **1851** MAYNE REID *Scalp-Hunters* xxvi, How are 'ee gwine to get at it with this cavayard 'ithout makin' sign?

β. **1821** S. F. AUSTIN in *Texas Hist. Quart.* VII. 288 Erasmo had captured a Caviard of mules & horses. **1824** W. B. DEWEES *Lett. fr. Texas* (1852) viii. 53 Corasco..was driving a large cavyyard of horses and mules to Louisiana. **1836** EDWARD *Hist. Texas* 107 When this powerful tribe wishes to raise the wind as the saying is, they will cavy back a Mexican cavy-yard. **1853** 'P. PAXTON' *Stray Yankee in Texas* 97 Two or three more [men] were mounted, and sent into the prairie in search of the 'caviarde' of horses—and we went in to dinner. **1874** J. C. McCOY *Hist. Sk. Cattle Trade* 11 The extra horses not under the saddle are called the cavvie-yard, and are driven behind the camp wagon. **1901** *Munsey's Mag.* XXV. 404/2 Each man roped a fresh horse from the cavviyard. **1942** E. E. DALE *Cow Country* 47 The band of horses..known as..the *caballado*, sometimes corrupted into 'cavvy yard', 'cavalry yard', or 'cavvy'.

γ. **1908** C. E. MULFORD *Orphan* ii. 24 He was soon able to count seven warriors who were driving another 'cavvieyeh' of horses. **1920** —— *J. Nelson* xxiv. 267 The caviya of a hundred and thirty saddle horses. **1940** E. FERGUSSON *Our Southwest* 32 Unskilled boys wrangled the horse herd, called the 'caviya'.

cavayer, obs. form of CAVIARE.

†**ca'vazion.** *Arch. Obs.*$^{-0}$ [ad. It. *cavazione* (= *cavamento*, *il cavare*) hollowing. Phillips' entry is derived from a passage in Palladio *Quattro Lib. d. Architett.* I. vii. (where, however, ed. 1601 has *cauatione*). Bailey, 1721, has both *cavation* and *cavazion*; in 1731–42 the latter is also entered as *cavation*, but in 1761 and later edd. it is again made *cavazion*. The folios 1730 and 1736 have only *cavazion*, in which they are followed by Johnson.] (See quot.)

1658 PHILLIPS, *Cavazion*, a Term in Art Architecture, being the hollowing, or underdigging of the earth for cellarage, allowed to be the sixth part of the highth of the whole Fabrick. **1721–1800** BAILEY, *Cavazion*, in Architecture, is the digging away the Earth for the Foundation of a Building. [Hence in JOHNSON and mod. Dicts.; not in GWILT.]

cave (keɪv), *sb.*^{1} Also 4 kaave, 4–5 kave. [a. F. *cave*:—L. *cava*, pl. of *cavum* a hollow (place), neuter of *cavus* hollow.]

1. a. A hollow place opening more or less horizontally under the ground; a cavern, den, habitation in the earth.

c **1220** *Bestiary* 251 Caue ȝe [the ant] haueð to crepen in. *a* **1300** *Cursor M.* 2915 In a caue he [Lot] hid him þare And his dohutris. *c* **1340** *Ibid.* 12341 (Trin.) To þe leones caue [*Cott., Gött.* coue] he ȝode. *c* **1350** *Will. Palerne* 25 Þat litel child listely lorked out of his caue. *c* **1385** CHAUCER *L.G.W.* 2307 And to a kaave pryvyly hym spedde. **1494** FABYAN IV. lxxv. 52 The Picts and Scottes beganne to breke out of theyr Dennes and Caues. **1535** COVERDALE *1 Sam.* xxii. 1 Dauid.. fled vnto the caue of Adullam. **1560** JEWELL *Serm. Paul's Cross* A iv, The Temple..was become a caue of theues. **1667** MILTON *P.L.* IV. 454 A murmuring sound Of waters issu'd from a Cave. **1823** W. BUCKLAND *Relig. Diluv.* 5 Caves in limestone are usually connected with fissures of the rock.

b. ***idols of the cave*** (*idola specus*): see IDOL.

†**2.** *gen.* A hollow place of any kind, a cavity.
1605 BACON *Adv. Learn.* II. v. §3 Are not the Organs of the sences of one kinde with the Organs of Reflexion..the Eare with a Caue or Straight determined and bounded? **1607** TOPSELL *Four-f. Beasts* 172 Some creep into the caves of hollow trees. **1626** BACON *Sylva* §272 The Caue of the Eare doth hold off the Sound a little from the Organ. *Ibid.* §282 So is the Eare a sinuous Caue.

3. *Glass-making.* The ash-pit of a glass-furnace.
1875 URE *Dict. Arts* II. 656 The furnace is thrown over an ash-pit, or cave as it is called.

4. *Political slang.* The secession of a small body of politicians from their party on some special question; the malcontent body so seceding: suggested by Mr. Bright's use of 'cave of Adullam' in reference to the secession from the Liberal party in 1866; see ADULLAMITE.
1866 BRIGHT *Sp.* (1876) 349 The right hon. gentleman..has retired into what may be called his political Cave of Adullam, and he has called about him 'every one that was in distress and every one that was discontented'. **1884** *Daily News* 19 Feb., There is no expectation of what Mr. Bright has taught all English politicians to call a 'Cave'. **1887** *Standard* 30 Mar. 5/7 There are rumours of an Anti-coercion Cave in the Conservative ranks. **1887** SIR W. HARCOURT in *Daily News* 21 Oct. 6/1 They [the Dissentient Liberals] are a cave, as it used to be called, and the danger of a cave was long ago pointed out that all the footsteps led into the cave, and none out of it.

5. *attrib.* and *Comb.*, as ***cave-keeper, -mouth, -phantom, -pool***; ***cave-guarded, -keeping, -like, -lodged, -loving*** adjs.; **cave-art**, depiction of animals and figures, etc., on the interiors of caves by prehistoric or primitive peoples; hence ***cave-artist***; **cave-breccia** (*Geol.*), breccia deposited in caves; **cave-deposit** (*Geol.*), any geological formation deposited in caves; **cave-dweller**, one who dwells in a cave, a troglodyte; *spec.* applied to (*a*) those races of prehistoric men who dwelt in natural caves; (*b*) the Bohemian Brethren, a religious sect formed from the remains of the Hussites in the 15th c., so called because they hid in caves to escape persecution; (*c*) *fig.*, one who is uncivilized in behaviour like a prehistoric cave-man; **cave-earth** (*Geol.*), a layer of earth forming the old floor of a cave before the deposition of stalagmite; **cave-fish**, a (blind) fish inhabiting subterraneous streams or lakes in caves; **cave-man**, (*a*) = *cave-dweller*; (*b*) = CAVER 2; **cave-painting** = *cave-art*; also, such a painting or drawing; hence ***cave-painter***; **cave-rat**, a kind of rat that lives underground; **cave-spider**, the spider *Segestria cellaris* Latr.; **cave-swallow**, a West-Indian species of swallow (*Hirundo pocciloma*) which suspends its nest from the roofs of caves; **cave-woman**, a woman who behaves in an uncivilized manner. Also in names of extinct animals whose remains are found in caves, as ***cave-bear, -hyena, -lion, -tiger***.
1921 M. C. BURKITT *Prehistory* xv. 193 The authenticity of the *cave art. **1930** *Times Lit. Suppl.* 3 July 547/1 The meaning of Pleistocene cave-art. **1923** H. H. WILDER *Man's Prehist. Past* 187 In modern art and in imaginative literature the early *cave artists are commonly represented as working upon, or admiring their work. **1865** LUBBOCK *Preh. Times* 237 The remains of the *cave-bear are abundant in Central Europe. **1866** LAING *Preh. Rem. Caithn.* 64 Men..contemporaries of the cave-bear and tiger. **1863** LYELL *Antiq. Man* 1 The occasional occurrence..of the bones of man..in *cave-breccias and stalactites. **1865** LUBBOCK *Preh. Times* 243 The animal was essentially a *cave-dweller. **1906** B'NESS VON HUTTEN *What became of Pam* II. xiii, You will always be a cave-dweller,..for you always were a little savage. **1873** GEIKIE *Gt. Ice Age* xxix. 411 This ancient deposit rests upon a second *cave-earth or breccia. **1865** LUBBOCK *Preh. Times* 244 To question..the value of what may be called *cave-evidence. **1871** BROWNING *Pr. Hohenst.* 145 Found like those famed *cave-fish to lack eye And organ for the upper magnitudes. **1884** *Longm. Mag.* Mar. 527 The blind cave-fish being..probably the descendants of species which once lived above ground. **1874** DAWKINS (*title*), *Cave Hunting. *c* **1611** SHAKS. *Cymb.* IV. ii. 298, I thought I was a *Caue-keeper. **1593** —— *Lucr.* 1250 *Caue-keeping euils that obscurely sleepe. **1856** KANE *Arct. Expl.* I. xxix. 380 This *cave-like abode. *c* **1630** DRUMM. OF HAWTH. *Poems* Wks. (1711) 33 *Cave-loving Eccho, daughter of the air. **1865** LUBBOCK *Preh. Times* x. 255 These ancient *Cave-men. **1897** MARY KINGSLEY *W. Africa* x. 208 These pots have a cave-man look about them; they are unglazed unlidded bowls. **1924** W. M. RAINE *Troubled Waters* xxviii. 280 He was a throw-back to the cave man. **1926** *Westm. Gaz.* 7 Aug., The devotion of the modern girl to the 'cave man' of fiction. **1928** A. HUXLEY *Point Counter Point* xxi. 405 'That passionateness of his, that violence ——.' Philip laughed. 'Quite the irresistible cave-man.' **1932** E. A. BAKER *Caving* i. 3 The caveman must be prepared physically and mentally for any emergency. *Ibid.* 4 The caveman will stuff his pockets with all sorts of gadgets. **1949** A. CHRISTIE *Crooked House* ix. 67 Why do men always think that a caveman must ..be..attractive to the opposite sex? **1906** *Westm. Gaz.* 11 Apr. 2/3 High rocks above my *cavemouth stand. **1937** H. READ *Art & Society* i. 31 The *cave-painter at Altamira. **1882** *Mag. of Art* V. 249 The *cave paintings of the Australians and the bushmen in South Africa. **1942** *Burlington Mag.* June 140/2 The old cave paintings of India. **1930** S. BECKETT *Whoroscope* 3 Shall I swallow *cave-phantoms? **1939** DYLAN THOMAS *Map of Love* 16 Curl-locked and animal *cavepools of spells and bone. **1859** DARWIN *Orig. Spec.* v. (1878) 110 One of the blind animals, namely, the *cave-rat. **1865** LUBBOCK *Preh. Times* 257 These *cave-researches appear to have been conducted with care. **1865** TYLOR *Early Hist. Man.* 196 The Drift series of stone implements passes into the *Cave series. **1861** HULME tr. *Moquin-Tandon* II. v. ii. 260 The *Cave-Spider..is very common in France and Italy. **1865** LUBBOCK *Preh. Times* 238 The cave-hyæna, and *cave-tiger, are found associated with the *Ursus spelæus* in the caverns. **1903** E. T. FOWLER *Place & Power* v, Miss St. Just..belonged to the *cave-woman species. **1951** M. MCLUHAN *Mech. Bride* 23/2 The reader is treated as the sluggish male is treated by the sex-hungry cave woman in the shirt ads.

†**cave**, *sb.*[2] *Obs.* [? for *cavie, cavey*, CAVY.] Colloquial abbreviation of CAVALIER.
1661 A. BROME *Songs* 139 Then the Roundheads and Caves agree.

†**cave**, *sb.*[3] *Obs.* or *dial.* [f. CAVE *v.*[2]] An unwieldy toss of the head, or of a limb.
1808 JAMIESON, *Cave*, 'a stroke, a push; a toss—as signifying to throw up the head. It is applied to the action of an ox or cow. *Ibid.*, *Kaive*, a tossing of the fore legs, rearing; when followed by prep. *up*, it denotes climbing.

cave, *sb.*[4] [f. CAVE *v.*[3]] A fall of earth, a cave-in.
1876 B. HARTE *G. Conroy* VI. viii, Gabriel was amazed to find that during the earthquake a 'cave' had taken place in the drift. **1877** RAYMOND *Statist. Mines & Mining* 319 A very serious cave occurred about 170 feet from the entrance of the drift. **1887** FARRELL *How He Died* 164 A 'cave' had happened in a mine.

†**cave**, *a. Obs.* [a. F. *cave* hollow, ad. L. *cavus.*] Hollow, concave. Of the moon: Waning (L. *luna cava* Plin.). Of a month: Having less than the usual number of days (late L. *mensis cavus*).
1540–64 RAYNALD *Byrth Mank.* 61 Stooles..made..caue or holowe in the middes. **1594** T. B. *La Primaud. Fr. Acad.* II. 356 The..great veine called the caue or hollow veine. **1657** TOMLINSON *Renou's Disp.* 264 Its flowers are albid and cave like a scale. **1670** FLAMSTEED in Rigaud *Corr. Sci. Men* (1841) II. 97 As if the parallax caused the moon to be really cave. **1677** R. CARY *Chronol.* I. I. vii. 19 If the Month were Cave or Lame of 29 Days only.

cave (keɪv), *v.*[1] [f. CAVE *sb.*[1] in various casual applications.] Hence **caved** *ppl. a.*
1. *trans.* To hollow, hollow out, excavate, make into a cave. Cf. CAVE (*in*) *v.*[3]
1541 R. COPLAND *Galyen's Terap.* 2 Dj, Is it possyble..that an vlcere caued my growe togyther..To cure caued vlceres. **1596** SPENSER *F.Q.* IV. v. 33 Vnder a steepe hilles side..where the mouldred earth had cav'd the banke. **1861** HOLME LEE *Tuflongo* 35 As if the ground were caved full of hollow galleries.
2. *intr.* To lodge or lurk in a cave.
1611 SHAKS. *Cymb.* IV. ii. 138 Such as wee Caue heere, hunt heere. **1828** D. MOIR in *Blackw. Mag.* 368 In the same lair the tame beast and the wild Together caved.
3. *trans.* To place or inclose as in a cave.
1816 BYRON *Ch. Har.* III. lxxxiii, They Who in oppression's darkness caved had dwelt.
4. *intr.* To form a political 'cave' or cabal.
1881 *L'pool Mercury* 13 Jan. 5/4 The feeling that (to use a new verb, now heard constantly in the lobby) to 'cave' would be ungenerous.

cave (keɪv), *v.*[2] Also 6 *Sc.* **caue, cawe**, 9 *dial.* **keave, keve, kaive, kayve.** [This includes several senses of uncertain origin, the connexion of some of which is perhaps only apparent. They are taken here chronologically.]
1. *intr.* To fall as a thing does when overturned; to fall clumsily or helplessly. Usually with *over, back over. Sc.* (Cf. CAVE *v.*[3])
1513 DOUGLAS *Æneis* XI. xiii. 43 He cawis our [*ed.* **1553** cauis ouer], furth bokand stremys of blude. *a* **1614** J. MELVILL *Diary* 32 (Jam.) Stitting down on a bedside, he caves back over so that his feet stack out stiff and dead.
2. *trans.* To tilt and overturn; to upset.
1854 BAMPTON *Lanc. Gloss.* (ed. 2), *Kayve*, to upset, to turn over. 'He's keyvt his cart.' **1879** MISS JACKSON *Shropsh. Word-bk.*, *Cave*, to turn over; to tilt up, so as to empty. 'Now then, look afore yo', or yo'n cave that bouk o'er an' sheed all the milk.' **1882** *Lanc. Gloss.* 171 *Kayve*, to overturn, to upset. *Kayvt*, upset, turned over.
3. To stick up in a tilted position.
1641 BEST *Farm. Bks.* (1856) 45 To sette nine of the sheaues with..theire toppes cauen vp soe that they stande just fower square, hauinge three sheaues on euery side, and one in the midst.
4. To toss or push (any part of the body) in a ponderous awkward way.
1808 JAMIESON, *Cave, keve*, to push, to drive backward and forward. *To cave the head*, to toss it in a haughty or awkward way (like a horse or cow). *Ibid.*, *Kaive*, to toss the fore leg, to rear (as a horse, a goat). *Banffsh.*
5. *intr.* (in same sense.)
1697 W. CLELAND *Poems* 66 (Jam.) Up starts a priest..And did not ceese to cave and paut While clyred back was prickt and gald. **1802** R. ANDERSON *Cumbrld. Ball.* 25 Sawney..A whornpeype danc'd, and keav'd and pranc'd. —— 81 The laird's daft son..keaves as he wad wurry me. **1847–78** HALLIWELL, *Keave*, to plunge, to struggle. *Cumbld.*

cave (keɪv), *v.*[3] [Usually *cave in*: in meaning identical with the dial. CALVE *in* (q.v.), and perh. phonetically descended from it (cf. *hā'penny* from *half-penny*); but even if so, it has certainly been associated with other senses of *cave*; cf. esp. CAVE *v.*[1] 'to hollow', CAVE *v.*[2] 'to fall all of a heap'.
(All the earliest instances of *cave in*, in print, are from America, and its literary use appears to have arisen there: but, as the word is given as East Anglian by Forby, 1830, and is widely used in Eng. dialects, it is generally conjectured to have reached the U.S. from East Anglia. Its history requires further investigation.)]
1. a. ***to cave in***: to fall in over a hollow, as the earth on the side of a pit or cutting; to fall in in a concave form, as when the front of a vertical section of earth or soil becomes concave in falling forward, from the greater weight or momentum of the higher part. Chiefly *colloq.*
1707 S. SEWALL *Diary* (1879) II. 186 Grave was caved in. **1728** J. COMER *Diary* 5 Nov. (1893) 57 This day a man..digging a well, after he had dug 20 feet deep, it cav'd in upon him. **1796** MORSE *Amer. Geog.* I. 398 The cellars are walled with brick..to prevent the loose sand from caving in. **1820** W. IRVING *Sketch Bk.* (1859) 196 As some labourers were digging to make an adjoining vault, the earth caved in, so as to leave a vacant space almost like an arch. **1848** BARTLETT *Dict. Amer.* (1860), *To cave in*, said of the earth which falls down when digging into a bank. **1863** KINGSLEY *Water Bab.* viii. 312 The roof caved in bodily. **1883** *Manch. Guard.* 18 Oct. 4/7 Two brothers..were at work..dismantling an old pit shaft, when a portion of the sides caved in and one of the men was partially buried.
b. Without *in.*
1848 THOREAU in *Atlantic Monthly* (1892) LXIX. 744 His cellar..has caved and let one end of the house down. **1873** J. H. BEADLE *Undevel. West* iii. 69 He had dug two wells,..but struck sand which 'caved so he could not curb'. **1882** *U.S. Rep. Prec. Met.* 639 Wherever the rock in the tunnel has a tendency to cave.
c. *transf.* To yield to outward pressure.
1898 HAMBLEN *Gen. Manager's Story* 32, I was caught between the corners of the cars..and heard my ribs cave in.
2. *fig. colloq.* **a.** To yield to pressure from above, or from being morally or physically undermined; to break down, give way, give in, submit, collapse.
1837–40 HALLIBURTON *Sam Slick, Hum. Nat.* 55 (Bartlett) He was a plucky fellow, and warn't a goin' to cave in that way. **1848** *New York Tribune* 4 Mar. (Bartl.), [They] will cave in..though they talk loud against it now. **1851** T. PARKER *Wks.* (1863–71) VII. 372 Politician after politician 'caved in' and collapsed. **1856** KANE *Arct. Expl.* II. ix. 94 He felt so much better that he got up at six: but he caved in soon after. **1859** H. KINGSLEY *G. Hamlyn* xxviii. (D.), A puppy, three weeks old, joins the chase with heart and soul, but caves in at about fifty yards. **1880** J. MARTINEAU *Hours Th.* II. 268 The Romans..found their empire cave in for want of inward moral tension. **1887** *Punch* 12 Mar. 132/1 In the end Government caved in, and unconditionally agreed to inquiry.
b. without *in. slang* (chiefly *U.S.*).
1844 *Spirit of Times* 23 Mar. 42/2 List 'till I tell you, and if you do not agree with me, why, I'll *cave.* **1855** 'P. PAXTON' *Capt. Priest* 64 The one who 'caves' first shall pay the shot. **1860** HOLLAND *Miss Gilbert's Career* xxii. 390, I tell you when a man gets in front of him Sunday, he catches it—no use dodging—might as well cave. **1863** READE *Hard Cash* I. 287 'Now I cave.' **1961** 'A. A. FAIR' *Stop at Red Light* (1962) xi. 169 The guy caved... The guy broke down and admitted the whole damned business.
¶ **3. a.** *trans.* (*causal.*) To smash or 'bash' in.
1857 *Knickerbocker* Mar. XLIX. 278 He would feel like caving my head in, if he knew. **1870** MISS BRIDGMAN *R. Lynne* II. v. 115, I should like to cave his head in. **1873** B. HARTE *Mrs. Skagg's Husbands* 61 Reckons she's caved in his head the first lick! **1916** 'BOYD CABLE' *Action Front* 56 'If we can plant a bomb or two in the right spot, it will bottle up any Germans working inside?' 'Sure to!' said Ainsley. 'It will cave in the entrance completely.' **1957** E. EAGER *Magic by Lake* 96 The ship turned in craven flight and hurried away, fearful of being rammed and caved in.
b. ***to cave down***: to bring down by an excavation caving in. *U.S.*
a **1762** S. NILES *Wars* in *Mass. Hist. Soc. Coll.* (1861) V. 340 Providence prevented them by sending a great rain, and caved down the sides of their trench. **1851** C. CIST *Cincinnati* 244, I obtained permission to open a sand-pit, which had long been closed for fear of caving down a house, by further excavation.
Hence **caved** *ppl. a.* (freq. with *in*), **cave-in** *sb.*
1862 C. F. BROWNE *Artemus Ward, his Book* 92 A old kaved in hat. **1882** 'MARK TWAIN' *Innoc. at Home* vii. 309 An Hour in the Caved Mines. **1884** *Boston* (Mass.) *Jrnl.* 6 Sept., The most extensive cave-in that has occurred in this region for years, nearly one hundred acres of ground settling from four to six feet. ['Common in Suffolk.' F. Hall.] **1953** R. GRAVES *Poems* 19 A caved-in chest, hairy black mandibles.

†**cave** (keɪv), *v.*[4] Also *dial.* **keave, keeave.** Obs. and dial. form of CHAVE, to separate chaff and empty ears from the corn.
c **1420** *Pallad. on Husb.* I. 996 A place high, plain and pure When nede is therto cave upon thi corne. **1530** PALSGR. 479, I cave corne, *Jescoux le grain.* **1669** WORLIDGE *Syst. Agric.* (1681) 323 *To Cave*, or *Chave*, is with a large Rake, or such like Instrument, to divide the greater from the lesser; as the larger Chaff from the Corn or smaller Chaff. Also larger coals from the lesser. **1855** *Whitby Gloss.*, *To Keave*, to rake the short straws and ears from wheat on the barn floor.
Hence **caving** *vbl. sb.*, the action of separating the chaff, etc., from corn; *cavings*, the chaff or ears thus separated. Comb. ***caving-rake, -riddle.***
1641 BEST *Farm. Bks.* 121 They [young trees] will serve for flayle-hande-staffes, cavinge-rake-shaftes..and such other like uses. **1807** R. W. DICKSON *Pract. Agric.* II. 298 The short chaffy substance thus separated, is in some districts termed cavings. **1865** *Cornh. Mag.* July 33 In the

Midland districts, ears of corn when thrashed are ..'cavvins'. **1877** PEACOCK *N.-W. Linc. Gloss.* (E.D.S.), *Cavings*, refuse bits of straw and dirt mixed with small corn, after threshing. *Caving-rake*, a rake used for separating the long bits of straw from corn before dressing. *Caving-riddle*, a riddle used after threshing for separating the corn from the bits of short straw which have come down the machine with it.

cave ('keɪviː), *int. School slang.* [L., imper. of *cavēre* to take care, beware.] Beware! A signal of warning, e.g. of the approach of a master. Also used subst. in phr. ***to keep cave***.

[**1584** R. GREENE *Carde of Fancie* 7 Nowe thou wilte crye Caue when thy coyne is consumed, and beware when thy wealth is wracked.] **1868** *Cassell's Mag.* 17 Oct. 390/1 [Title of Poem] Cave! **1873** 'A. R. HOPE' *Night before Holidays* 110 There was a heavy footstep sounding along the passage... '*Cave!*' '*Canem*,' responded Lessing, burying himself under the bedclothes again. **1906** E. NESBIT *Railway Children* xiv. 295 He won't keep *cave*, shirks his turn And says he came to school to learn! **1922** *Blackw. Mag.* May 557/2 One of their number doing sentry-go gives the native equivalent for the schoolboy's 'Cave' on the reappearance of their employer. **1959** I. & P. OPIE *Lore & Lang. Schoolchildren* xvii. 373 The term 'keeping cave'.. only rarely extends to boys who do not possess any Latin... The look-out in a grammar school.. may call just 'Cave!' (pronounced *kave* or *kay-ve*).

cavea ('keɪvɪə). *Rom. Antiq.* Pl. **-æ**. [L., = a hollow.] The auditorium of an ancient theatre, so called from its concave shape; also the whole theatre.

1611 CORYAT *Crudities* 314 The seats or benches.. incompassing the Cavea. **1842** L. SCHMITZ in W. Smith *Dict. Gr. & Rom. Antiquities* 959/1 The whole of the cavea in the Attic theatre must have contained about 50,000 spectators. **1886** *Athenæum* 4 Dec. 751/2 The peculiarity of this theatre [at Laurium] is the strange form of the cavea, which sweeps inward in a loop to the right as viewed from the proscenium. **1955** *Times* 19 Aug. 2/5 Extending 263 ft. in diameter, the hollow of the cavea is divided into five blocks of white marble seats, separated by narrow stairways.

caveach (kə'viːtʃ), *sb.* [a. Sp. *escabeche* (Minsheu *escaveche*) pickle for fish.] Mackerel pickled in a certain way; so called in the West Indies.

1822 *Female Instructor* 422 *Caveach*, mackarel, cut up, seasoned with spices and salt inserted in the pieces, fried brown in oil, and when cold covered up in a jar.

ca'veach, *v.* [f. prec. sb.] To pickle mackerel or other fish according to a West Indian method.

1750 E. SMITH *Compl. Housewife* 96 Mackrel to caveache. **1778** MRS. RAFFALD *Eng. Housekpr.* 50 To caveach Soles.

cavear, -re, -ree, -ri, -ry, obs. ff. CAVIARE.

caveat ('keɪviːæt), *sb.* Also 6 **caviate**, 6-7 **caveate**. [L. *caveat* let him beware, 3rd sing. pres. subj. of *cavēre* to beware.]

1. *Law.* **a.** A process in court (originally in ecclesiastical courts) to suspend proceedings; a notice given by some party to the proper officer not to take a certain step until the party giving the notice has been heard in opposition. Phrase, ***to enter*** or ***put in a caveat***: also *fig.* see 2 b.

1654 GATAKER *Disc. Apol.* 45 A Caveat they found entred in the Bishops Office, by a Gentleman, one of the Petti-Bag, who pretended a Title. **1656** BLOUNT *Glossogr.*, *Caveat*, used among the Proctors, when a person is dead, and a competition ariseth for the Executorship, or Administratorship, the party concerned enters a Caveat, to prevent or admonish others from intermedling. **1667** MARVELL *Corr.* cxiv. Wks. 1872-5 II. 273, I entered caveats both at Mr. Atturny's and Mr. Sollicitor's. **1726** AYLIFFE *Parerg.* 145 A Caveat in Law.. is an Intimation given to some Ordinary or Ecclesiastical Judge.. notifying to him that he ought to beware how he acts in such or such an Affair. **1818** CRUISE *Digest* V. 95 **1884** *Law Rep.* 9 *Probate Div.* 23 The.. defendant, one of the next of kin, entered a caveat.

b. ***caveat emptor*** [lit., let the purchaser beware], let the purchaser examine the article he is buying before the bargain is completed, so that in case of disappointment after purchase he may not blame the seller.

1523 FITZHERBERT *Husb.* f. xxxvi, He [*sc.* the horse] is no chapmans ware yf he be wylde: but and he be tame and haue ben rydden vpon than caueat emptor be ware thou byer. **1629** T. ADAMS *Pol. Hunting* in *Wks.* 118 We compell none to buy our Ware; *Caueat emptor*. **1809** H. MORE *Let.* 14 Aug. (1925) 139 Mr. C. in his last Review.. feels it is his duty to say, '*Caveat Emptor*'. **1902** *Economic Jrnl.* XII. 12 *Caveat emptor.* It is the employer on whom the responsibility rests of testing the quality of the article he buys. **1950** T. H. MARSHALL *Citizenship & Social Class* iv. 133 The principle of *caveat emptor* is at least plausible when you are buying a horse.

2. *transf.* **a.** A warning, admonition, caution.

1557 RECORDE *Whetst.* Y iij b, A caueat, to be ware of to moche confidence. **1583** STANYHURST *Æneis* III. (Arb.) 85 Such od caueats, as I to the frendlye can vtter. **1646** S. BOLTON *Arraignm. Err.* 50 A Caveat to you how you live. **1651** WITTIE tr. *Primrose's Pop. Err.* IV. 248 Those Caveats, whereof Astrologers do every year warn the people. **1712** BUDGELL *Spect.* No. 365 ¶1, I design this Paper as a Caveat to the Fair Sex. **1791** BOSWELL *Johnson* (1816) IV. 448 A caveat against ostentatious bounty and favour to negroes. **1855** H. SPENCER *Princ. Psychol.* (1872) I. v. iii. 531 With this caveat let us now pass.. to more complex cases.

b. ***to put in*** or ***enter a caveat*** (in senses 2& 3).

1577 tr. *Bullinger's Decades* (1592) 405 It pleased the goodnesse of God by giuing the law to put in a caueat.. for the tranquilitie of mankinde. **1600** HOLLAND *Livy* XXVI. xxiv. 602 They should put in a caveat, that he might have no libertie to warre upon the Ætolians. **1642** FULLER *Holy & Prof. St.* I. xii. 37 She enters a silent caveat by a blush. **1755** YOUNG *Centaur* I. Wks. 1757 IV. 116 Putting in a caveat against the ridicule of infidels. **1875** E. WHITE *Life in Christ* II. x. (1878) 108 To enter a caveat against a misconception.

†**3.** A condition previously laid down; a proviso, reservation; = CAUTION *sb.* 2. *Obs.*

1579 FULKE *Heskins' Parl.* 370 M. Heskins fombleth out the matter with a foolish caueat, that.. he suffreth not violence. **1648** GAGE *West Ind.* xxi. (1655) 196 Some were offered me for nothing, with this caveat, that.. I must, etc.

†**4.** A precaution; = CAUTION *sb.* 5. *Obs.*

1596 SPENSER *State Irel.* Wks. (1862) 539/1 The chiefest caveat and provision in the reformation of the North must be to keep out those Scottes. **1612** BRINSLEY *Lud. Lit.* 54 Let them vse this caueat especially; that they take but little at a time. **1643** BURROUGHES *Exp. Hosea* ix. (1652) 310 God laid in a caveat and provision for the encouragement of them.

5. *U.S. Patent Laws.* 'A description of some invention, designed to be patented, lodged in the office before the patent right is taken out, operating as a bar to applications respecting the same invention, from any other quarter' (Webster).

1879 G. PRESCOTT *Sp. Telephone* 256 A caveat, describing this invention, was filed by Gray.

caveat ('keɪviːæt), *v.* [f. prec. sb.]

†**1.** *trans.* **a.** To enter a caveat or caution against. **b.** To serve with a caveat. *Obs.*

1661 MRQ. ARGYLE *Last Sp.* 27 May in *Naphtali* 288, I would caveat this. **1707** *Col. Rec. Penn.* II. 347 Charged or Caveated the Mr. of the Rolls that he should make out no Exemplification or Coppy thereof.

2. *intr.* To enter a caveat.

In mod. Dicts.

3. *Fencing.* (*intr.*) To shift one's sword from one side to the other of one's adversary's sword, to 'disengage'. Hence **caveating** *vbl. sb.*

1652 URQUHART *Jewel* Wks. (1834) 274 In case the adversary after a *finda*, going to the *parade*, discover his breast to *caveat*. **1690** B. E. *Dict. Cant. Crew*, *Caveating*, or *Disengaging*, slipping the Adversary's Sword, when 'tis going to bind or secure one's own. **1707** HOPE *New Method Fencing* 82 This Contre-Caveating.. is a Circular Parade, that is, a Man in performing it, forms with his Sword not only one, but sometimes (according as his Adversary shall Caveat or shun it) two or three Circles. **1753** CHAMBERS *Cycl. Supp.*, *Caveating* is so necessary a motion in fencing, that without it, there could be scarce any offensive part.

caveator ('keɪviːˌeɪtə(r)). [f. CAVEAT + -OR.] One who enters a caveat; see CAVEAT *sb.* 1, 5.

1881 *Sci. American* Circular, After a Caveat has been filed the Patent Office will not issue a patent for the same invention to any other person without giving notice to the Caveator. **1885** *Law Times* LXXIX. 331/1 Fourteen days' notice is given to the caveator.

caveer, obs. form of CAVIARE.

'cavel, *sb.*[1] *north. dial.* Forms: 4-8 **cavil**, **cavel**, 5 **kevelle**, *Sc. pl.* **caflis**, 6 *Sc.* **cauill, -yll, -eill**, 7 **cavell**, *Sc.* **kavil**, ? 8 *Sc.* **kevel, kevil**, 8 *Sc.* **kavel**, 9 *north. dial.* **kyeval, -el**, etc. [Identical with Du. *kavel* lot, parcel (*kavelen* to cast lots, parcel out by lot), MDu. *cāvele* lot, MLG. and MG. *kavele* 'little stick (inscribed with runes) for casting lots' Franck. Usually identified with ON. *kafli* piece cut off, piece, bit, *kefli* cylinder, stick, piece of wood; but the connexion is not fully traced.]

1. A lot (that is cast). Now applied in the Northumberland collieries to the lots which are cast from time to time to determine in which 'bord' each miner shall hew till the next cavelling.

a **1300** *Cursor M.* 18907, Þan kest þai cauel [*Gött.* caueles; *Fairf.* lottis; *Trin.* lottes] þam emell. *Ibid.* 21157 Als þe cauel on him fell. *a* **1400** *Sir Perc.* 142 Sone kevelles did thay caste. **1513** DOUGLAS *Æneis* I. viii. 27 Be cut or cavil that pleid sone partid was. **1533** GAU *Richt Way* (1887) 41 And thay suld cast cauels apone his kot [= coat]. *a* **1783** *Gil Brenton* xlviii. in Child *Ballads* I. 69/1 The cavil it did on me fa. **1852** *Mining Gloss.* 123, *Kavels*, lots cast by the men at stated periods for the different working places.

b. The response of an oracle [transl. Lat. *sors*].

1513 DOUGLAS *Æneis* IV. vii. 31 The kavillis of Licia.

c. *fig.* One's lot in life or in marriage. *dial.*

1768 ROSS *Helenore* 128 (Jam.), I should be right content For the kind cavel that to me was lent. **1826** T. WILSON *Pitman's Pay.* I. xlviii, To please ma dowly cavel. *Ibid.* III. lxvi, When Sall was for ma kyeval drawn.

†**2.** Lot or share, in any joint privilege, liability, or the like. *Obs.* or ? *Sc.*

c **1400** tr. *Leges Quatuor Burgorum* xiii, He sall not have lot nor cavill equallie with burgessis dwelland within the burgh. **1609** SKENE *Reg. Maj.* Table 82 Lot, cut, and cavill, hes place in ane half dacker of hides.

3. A division or share of property made by lot; an allotment of land.

1652 in Stonehouse *Axholme* (1839) 93 Part of the cavells of 91 acres under Epworth. *a* **1670** SPALDING *Troub. Chas. I* (1792) I. 230/1 (Jam.) 40 chalders of victual and silver rent out of the bishops kavil. **1700** DE LA PRYME *Diary* (1869) 316 A larg map having every field, ing, close, mested, croft, cavel, intack, etc., in the whole parish in it. **1799** J. ROBERTSON *Agric. Perth* 62 The first deviation from run-rig was by dividing the farms into kavels or kenches, by which every field.. was split down into as many lots as there were tenants. **1805** *State, Leslie of Powis, etc.* 17 (Jam.) The Town and Bishop feued out this fishing in shares, six of them called the King's cavil, and the other six the Bishop's cavil. **1856** *Best's Farm. Bks.* 128 *note*.

†**'cavel**, *sb.*[2] *Obs.* Chiefly *Sc.* Also 5 **kevell**. [Of uncertain derivation: Jamieson suggests that it is the ON. *kefli* (the same word as in prec.) used first in the literal sense of 'stick, piece of wood', and then applied contemptuously to a man, 'as the vulgar call a raw-boned fellow *a lang rung*, a stiff old man *an auld stock*'.]

1. Perhaps, a stick or stout staff.

(But it may be in sense 2.)

a **1550** *Christis Kirke Gr.* vii, The kensy cleikit to the cavell, But, lord, than how thay luggit.

2. 'A low fellow' (Jamieson).

c **1430** LYDG. *Min. Poems* (1840) 152 A kevell, corpulent of stature. **1526** SKELTON *Magnyf.* 2217 Ye, wilte thou, hangman? I say, thou cavell. **1535** LYNDESAY *Satyre* 2863 Ane cavell quhilk was never at the scule. **1706-11** in Watson's *Coll. Sc. Poems* iii. 50 (Jam.) The Bride about the Ring she skipped, Till out starts Carle and Cavel.

†**'cavel**, *v. Obs.* exc. *dial.* [f. CAVEL *sb.*[1]]

a. *intr.* To cast lots. **b.** *trans.* To allot, apportion. Hence **'cavelling** *vbl. sb.*

c **1375** BARBOUR *St. Georgis* 101 Quhene þe maste party Of þe folk distroyt war vtrely Be sic cuttis and cawelynge. **1652** in Stonehouse *Axholme* (1839) 91 Lands lying in the Isle of Axholme.. which.. were cavelled out, and allotted to every Participant. **1805** *State, Leslie of Powis, etc.* 123 (Jam.) After the cavelling of the water in April. **1850** *N. & Q.* Ser. I. I. 473/2. **1887** R. O. HESLOP in *letter* 2 Aug., Each collier draws his cavel, and the number on his ticket is the number of the 'bord' at which he must hew for a stated period, till another cavelling, takes place.

cavel, -ell, obs. forms of CAVIL.

cavel, cavil, var. of KEVEL (in a ship).

cavelet ('keɪvlɪt). *rare.* A miniature cave.

1864 *Linnet's Trial* II. III. iii. 4 The aperture of one of those supplemental cavelets. **1885** *Chamb. Jrnl.* 314 Openings in the rocks to tiny cavelets.

caveling, obs. f. CAVILLING.

cavelleir, obs. f. CAVALIER.

cavellerie, cavelry, obs. ff. CAVALRY.

†**cavenard.** *Obs.* Perhaps the same as CAYNARD (? error for *cayenard*).

c **1300** *Havelok* 2389 Hede cauenard! Wat dos thu here at this pathe?

cavendish ('kævəndɪʃ). [see quot. 1844.]

1. Tobacco softened and pressed into solid cakes.

1839 (in a file of prices of Messrs. Grant, Chambers, & Co., London, of this date. It is not in their circular of 1824). **1843** *Hints to Freshmen* (Oxford) 8 He has smoked Cavendish tobacco under the steadfast impression that it was the mildest Turkey. **1844** ANSTIE in *Rep. Comm.* (Ho. of Commons) *Tobacco Trade Q.* 33 'Cavendish' is a species of tobacco reckoned by the Excise under the general denomination of Roll.. I suppose the name is taken from the name of the maker in America. I know of no other reason for the name. **1879** F. HARRISON *Choice Bks.* (1886) 70 Men ..read it.. daily, just as they smoke cavendish. **1886** *Pall Mall G.* 19 June 6/1 The cakes are.. submitted to hydraulic pressure, and in the end a substance is obtained of great solidity, and which cuts like black marble. This is the cavendish which army men, artists, and others affect.

2. Assumed name of the author (H. Jones) of a treatise on Whist (1862); often used allusively.

1878 H. H. GIBBS in B. Price *Pract. Pol. Econ.*, Like a man having his Cavendish at his fingers' ends, who sits down to play a rubber without seeing his cards.

caver ('keɪvə(r)). [App. f. CAVE.]

1. *Mining.* One who goes 'about the mines to beg or steal ore from the miners' coes, or to steal their stowes' (Tapping *Gloss. Manlove's Chron.*). ?*Obs.*

1653 MANLOVE *Lead Mines* 117 To keep in awe Such as be cavers, or do rob men's Coes. **1678-96** PHILLIPS, *Cavers* (a word used by Miners), thieves that steal Oar out of the Mines. **1721-1800** in BAILEY. **1747** HOOSON *Miner's Dict.*, S j, Sauntle [is] the first pee or bit of Ore that the Cavers find in a Morning by Purchassing.

2. An explorer of caves.

1932 *Times Lit. Suppl.* 17 Mar. 191/3 The reader is expected to be something of a caver. **1958** *Spectator* 1 Aug. 172/3 A number of local archæologists and speleologists.. declared the discoveries to be false, and the paintings and engravings to be forgeries done by the *Maquisards* and by cavers in the post-war years.

cavere, obs. form of CAVIARE.

cavern ('kævən), *sb.* Also 4-7 **cauerne**, 5-6 **kauerne**. [a. F. *caverne* cave, ad. L. *caverna* cave, den, cavity, f. *cav-us* hollow: see -ERN.]

1. A hollow place under ground; a subterranean (or submarine) cavity; a cave.

The Fr. *caverne* is the exact equivalent of Eng. *cave*; F. *cave* is a subterranean hollow generally, a cellar, etc. In Eng., *cave* is the ordinary commonplace term, *cavern* is vaguer and more rhetorical, usually with associations of vastness, or indefiniteness of extent or limits.

c **1374** CHAUCER *Boeth.* III. ix. 82 Þe crikes and þe cauernes of þe see yhidd in þe floodes. **1398** TREVISA *Barth. De P.R.*

XIV. lvi. (1495) 487 In cauernes myes and crepynge wormes make theyr dennes and nestes. **1430** LYDG. *Chron. Troy* IV. xxxi, In rochys harde, and in kauernes lowe. **1601** SHAKS. *Jul. C.* II. i. 80 Where wilt thou [conspiracie] finde a Cauerne darke enough To maske thy monstrous Visage? **1697** DRYDEN *Virg. Georg.* I. 268 In hollow Caverns Vermine make abode. **1752** JOHNSON *Rambl.* No. 33 ¶5, I will teach you to.. bring out from the caverns of the mountains metals. **1794** SULLIVAN *View Nat.* I. 23 Mountains of the earth, the caverns of the ocean. **1795** SOUTHEY *Joan of Arc* I. 293 A spacious cavern, hewn amid The entrails of the earth. **1815** MOORE *Lalla R.* viii, Terrific caverns gave Dark welcome to each stormy wave. **1862** STANLEY *Jew. Ch.* I. xv. 300 Vast caverns open in the mountain side.

†**2.** Applied to the cavity of the ear, the frontal sinus, etc.; also to interstices between particles. *Obs.*

1626 BACON *Sylva* §263 The cauerne and structure of the Eare. **1729** SHELVOCKE *Artillery* II. 108 Being reduced to a fine Meal, it [Gunpowder] loses all its little Caverns or Pores. **1789** W. BUCHAN *Dom. Med.* (1790) 463 The small spungy bones of the upper jaw, the caverns of the forehead.

3. *attrib.* and *Comb.*, as ***cavern-door***, ***-house***, ***-pagoda***, ***-temple***, ***well***; **cavernhold**, *nonce-wd.* after *household*; **cavern-limestone**, 'the carboniferous limestone of Kentucky, so called from the innumerable caves which its hard strata contain' (Bartlett); **cavern-like** *a.*

1832 DE LA BECHE *Geol. Man.* 181 The theoretical conclusions that have been deduced from *cavern bones. **1725** POPE *Odyss.* IX. 22 [They] croud the *cavern-door. **1791** COWPER *Odyss.* IX. 434 Like whelps against his *cavern-floor he dashed them. **1873** M. COLLINS *Miranda* I. 185 The various rude household or *cavernhold implements which the Troglodyte had used. **1858** HAWTHORNE *Fr. & It. Jrnls.* (1872) I. 30 A *cavern-like gloom. **1856** EMERSON *Eng. Traits* xvi. Wks. (Bohn) II. 123 The gates of the old *cavern temples.

cavern (ˈkævən), *v.* [f. prec. sb.]

1. *trans.* To enclose or ensconce as in a cavern.

*c*1630 RISDON *Surv. Devon* §215 (1810) 225 The river is gathered into such a streight.. that it seemeth to cavern itself. **1805** SOUTHEY *Madoc in Azt.* xiii, Now the child From light and life is cavern'd. **1822** BYRON *Werner* II. ii. 351 Sickness sits cavern'd in his hollow eye.

2. To hollow out, so as to form a cavern.

1853 KANE *Grinnell Exp.* xlvii. (1856) 438 The sharpness and boldness of the lines where they were caverned and cloven down. **1860** EMERSON *Cond. Life* vii. Wks. (Bohn) II. 421 The dungeons.. dug and caverned out by grumbling.. people. **1887** *Scribner's Mag.* II. 452 Places of exit of the caverning streams.

3. *intr.* To lurk in a cavern; to den.

1860 S. DOBELL in *Macm. Mag.* Aug. 326 Where the last deadliest rout Of furies cavern, to cast out those Dæmons.

ca'vernal, *a. rare.* [f. L. *caverna* cavern + -AL[1].] Pertaining to, or of the nature of, a cavern.

1803 G. S. FABER *Cabiri* II. 266 Hades may be the cavernal space immediately beneath the shell of the earth. **1816** —— *Orig. Pagan Idol.* I. p. lxx, The two-peaked mountain and sacred cavernal door.

caverned (ˈkævənd), *ppl. a.* [f. CAVERN.]

1. Having caverns; hollowed out into caverns.

1715–20 POPE *Iliad* II. 852 Antron's watry dens, and cavern'd ground. **1814** WORDSW. *Excurs.* IV. 1161 Blind recesses of the caverned rocks.

2. Formed as or like a cavern.

1847 DISRAELI *Tancred* VI. vii, Stealing into the caverned chamber.

3. Enclosed or ensconced in a cavern.

1734 POPE *Ess. Man* IV. 42 No cavern'd Hermit rests self-satisfied. **1853** ROBERTSON *Serm.* Ser. III. xi. 140 There is rest on the surface of the caverned lake.

cavernicolous (kævəˈnɪkələs), *a.* [f. L. *caverna* CAVERN + *-colus* inhabiting.] Cave-dwelling.

1889 in *Cent. Dict.* **1924** *Glasgow Herald* 13 Dec. 4 Another feature of many cavernicolous animals is the delicacy of their integument. **1947** *Sci. News* V. 51 The 'Proteus', that extraordinary amphibious newt belonging to the Cave of Istria, which became the most celebrated cavernicolous animal. **1966** C. SWEENEY *Scurrying Bush* iv. 61, I hoped that it might lead to a further system of caves, perhaps to water, for, if so, I anticipated finding some truly cavernicolous animals.

cavernous (ˈkævənəs), *a.* [ad. L. *cavernōsus* (in It. *cavernoso*, Pr. *cavernos*, F. *caverneux*), in same sense, f. *caverna*: see CAVERN and -OUS.]

1. Abounding in caverns.

1447 BOKENHAM *Seyntys* (1835) 108 This hyl is craggy and eke cavernous. **1695** WOODWARD *Nat. Hist. Earth* III. i. (1723) 158 These Countryes being all Mountainous and Cavernous. **1750** WARBURTON *Julian* II. vi. (R.) The town and temple of Delphi were seated on a bare and cavernous rock. **1853** PHILLIPS *Rivers Yorksh.* iii. 111 The mountains are thoroughly cavernous.

2. Full of, or characterized by, cavities or interstices; having a porous texture; hollow in the middle. (Cf. CAVERN *sb.* 2.)

1597 LOWE *Chirurg.* (1634) 116 It [cancer] is hard, unequall, and cavernous, or hollow. **1731** BAILEY, *Cavernous Ulcer* is an Ulcer whose Entrance is straight, and the Bottom broad, wherein are many Holes filled with malignant Matter. **1811** PINKERTON *Petral.* II. 403 The cavernous pumice-stone of Lipari. **1851** CARPENTER *Man. Phys.* 302 The Human Spleen has no true cavernous structure. **1876** T. HARDY *Hand of Ethelberta* I. 118 Till the fire had grown haggard and cavernous.

3. a. Of the nature of or resembling a cavern; hollow.

1830 LYELL *Princ. Geol.* I. 261 Some huge cavernous apertures into which the sea flows. **1865** E. C. CLAYTON *Cruel Fort.* III. 75 His thick eyebrows casting deep shadows on his cavernous eyes. **1853** KANE *Grinnell Exp.* xxiv. (1856) 193 The cavernous recess of its cliffs.

b. *Med.* Applied to respiration marked by a prolonged hollow resonance. (Cf. *broncho-cavernous* adj.)

1853 W. O. MARKHAM tr. *Skoda's Auscult.* 94 'By the term cavernous respiration,' says Laennec, 'I understand the murmur which occurs during inspiration and expiration in a cavity formed in pulmonary tissue.' **1890** F. TAYLOR *Man. Pract. Med.* 341 Breath-sounds which deserve the name of cavernous are often heard over solid lung. **1944** R. COOPE *Dis. Chest* v. 71 All cavities will not necessarily act in this way as resonating chambers, and.. cavities may be present without cavernous breathing.

4. Of or pertaining to a cavern.

1833 I. TAYLOR *Fanat.* iv. 84 This cavernous inspiration. **1839** BAILEY *Festus* (1852) 142 Cavernous darkness.

Hence **ˈcavernously** *adv.*, in a cavernous way.

1849 *Blackw. Mag.* LXVI. 420 A rock that was cavernously hollow at the base. **1885** G. MEREDITH *Diana* II. xii. 277 The Fates.. were then beginning cavernously their performance of the part of the villain.

cavernulated (kəˈvɜːnjʊleɪtɪd), *a.* [f. as next + -ATE[3] + -ED[1].] Formed into a minute cavity; also = next.

1875 QUAIN *Anat.* II. 102 The newly formed bone and.. its cavernulated structure.

cavernulous (kəˈvɜːnjʊləs), *a.* [f. L. *cavernula*, dim. of *caverna* cavern, cavity + -OUS.] Characterized by minute cavities, porous.

1757 LEWIS in *Phil. Trans.* L. 154 The mass.. turned out cavernulous and brittle. **1803** J. BLACK *Lect. Chem.* III. 326 (L.) Copper will not cast either solid or tenacious, but is cavernulous and weak.

cavery, obs. form of CAVIARE.

cavesson (ˈkævɪsən). Forms: 6 cauetzan, 7 cavezan; cavechin; 7–9 caveson, 8 cavezon, (cavesion, 9 cavason), 7– cavesson. [a. F. *caveçon*, ad. It. *cavezzone*, augmentative of *cavezza* halter (cf. Sp. *cabezon* shirt-collar). Ital. had another derivative form, *cavezzana*, whence the earlier Eng. form *cavezan*. Diez associates It. *cavezza*, OF. *chevece*, with Sp. *cabeza*, Pr. *cabeissa* head, repr. L. *capitia*, from *capitium* 'head-covering', later 'the opening in a tunic for the head'.]

A kind of nose-band of iron, leather, or wood, 'fixed to the nostrils of a horse, to curb or render him manageable through the pain it occasions' (Stocqueler *Mil. Encycl.*).

1598 FLORIO, *Cauezzana*, a cauetzan or headstraine. **1611** COTGR., *Camorre*, a sharpe and double-edged Cavesson of yron, for an vnruly horses nose. *Ibid.*, *Caveçon*, a cauechin, or caueson, for a horses nose. **1618** M. BARET *Horsemanship* Cures 38 Extreame commanding bits and tormenting cauezans. **1649** G. DANIEL *Trinarch.* Author 17 That Pegasus.. which others rather chuse to ride rather in a Caveson. **1725** BRADLEY *Fam. Dict.* I. s.v. *Colt*, The Cavesion being placed upon the tender Gristle of his Nose. **1840** BLAIN *Encycl. Rur. Sports* 287 The cavesson is the first active restraint applied to all saddle horses. **1863** *Gambler's Dream* III. 201 No more chance with them than a colt in a cavason. **1875** 'STONEHENGE' *Brit. Sports* II. I. viii. 451.

‖**cavetto** (kaˈvɛtto). *Arch.* [It. *cavetto*, dim. of *cavo*, f. L. *cav-us* hollow: see CAVE.] 'A hollowed moulding, whose profile is the quadrant of a circle. It is principally used in cornices' (Gwilt *Encycl. Archit.*).

1677 MOXON *Mech. Exerc.* (1703) 268 We will describe a Cavetto. **1816** J. SMITH *Panorama Sc. & Art* I. 174 The bedmould should consist of an ovolo, fillet, and cavetto. **1876** GWILT *Encycl. Archit.* 805 The *cavetto, mouth*, or *hollow* is chiefly used as a crowning moulding.. By workmen it is frequently called a *casement*.

cavey, cavialy, var. of CAVIE, CAVIARE.

cavezan, -zon, obs. ff. CAVESSON.

caviare, caviar (see below). Forms: 6 **chauiale**, 7 **cavialy**; 6 **cavery**, 7 **caveari**, **caveary**, (**cauearee**), **cauiarie**, 7–8 **caviary**; **cavear(e**, **caveer**, (7 **gaueare**, **cavere**, **cavajar**, **cavayer**, 8 **cavier**, **kavia**); 7– **caviare**, **caviar**. [Of uncertain origin, found in Turkish as *khāvyār*; in Italian in 16th c. as *caviale* (whence 16th c. F. *cavial*, Sp. *cavial*, 16th c. Eng. *cavialy*), also as *caviaro*, whence F. and Pg. *caviar*.

(It has no root in Turkish, and has not the look of a Turkish word. Redhouse in his MS. Thesaurus marks it as Italian-Turkish, looking upon it as borrowed from Italian.' Prof. Ch. Rieu.)

In English occurring with great variety of spelling and pronunciation, after Italian and French, with various native modifications. Originally, *caviˈāly*, *-ˈāle*, *-ˈārie*, *-ˈāre* was of 4 syllables, with accent on the penult, as in Italian, but was sometimes reduced to 3 syllables, by slurring *-iā-*, as *-yā-*, and later with the accent shifted to the first syllable. As early as 1625, the final *-e*, in *caviare*, *caveare*, was often dropped in speech, and later also in writing, giving *caviar*, *cavear* (cf. F. *caviar*), pronounced (kævɪˈɑː(r), -ˈɛə(r)), sometimes (kævˈjɑː(r), -ˈjɛə(r)), and perh. also with accent shifted (ˈkævɪɑː(r), -ɪə(r), -jə(r)). About 1700, prevalent forms were *caˈvear*, *caˈveer*, riming with *prepare*, and *cheer*; the latter pronunciation appears to have been the only one in common use in the end of the 18th c., for Walker, 1797, who spells *caviare* and pronounces (kəˈvɪə(r)), says,

'Either the spelling or the pronunciation of this word should be altered.. the ancient spelling seems to have been *Caviare*; though Buchanan and Bailey, in compliance with pronunciation, spell it *Caveer*, W. Johnston *Cavear*, and Ash, as a less usual spelling, *Cavier*.'

Smart (1846) pronounces (kævˈjɛə(r)), Webster has the accent on first syllable (ˈkævɪɑː(r)); prevalent pronunciations in England *c* 1890 were (kævɪˈɑː(r), kævˈjɑː(r)), 'etymologically the best' (*N.E.D.*), also (kævɪˈɛə(r)), and as in Smart. The prevalent pronunciation in the late 20th century is as in Webster. Shakspere's *caviˈarie*, and Swift's *caˈveer*, are recognized archaic forms.]

1. The roe of the sturgeon and other large fish obtained from lakes and rivers of the east of Europe, pressed and salted, and eaten as a relish.

α. *cavialy*, *caviarie*, and allied forms:

1591 G. FLETCHER *Russe Commw.* (1857) 12 Of Ickary or cavery, a great quantitie is made upon the river of Volgha. **1598** *Epulario* H ij, To dresse a kind of meat of the spawne of Sturgions, called Chauiale. *a* **1612** HARINGTON *Epigr.* III. (1633) 33 Yet eatst thou Ringoes and potato Rootes And Gaueare, but it litle bootes. *a* **1616** BEAUM. & FL. *Passion. Madm.* v. 353 (N.) Laugh—wide—loud—and vary—.. One that ne'er tasted caveare. **1616** BULLOKAR, *Cauearee*, strange meate like blacke sope. **1620** SKELTON *Quix.* IV. xiii. 103 Black Meat called Caviary, made of Fishes Eggs. **1626** BACON *Sylva* §835 Red-Herrings, Caueary, Parmizan, &c. **1639** NABBES *Spring's Glory*, Anchoves & Caveary. **1655** MOUFET & BENNET *Health's Improv.* (1746) 264 As for Cavialy.. the Italian Proverb will euer be true.. He that eateth of Cavialies, Eateth Salt, Dung, and Flies. **1702** W. J. tr. *Bruyn's Voy. Levant* xlii. 170 They eat it.. like Caviary. **1721–1800** BAILEY, *Caˈviary* [**1731–61** also *Caveˑr*].

β. *caviare*, *caviar*, etc., of 3 or 2 syllables.

1620 E. BLOUNT *Observ. & Disc.* (N.), That the only delicacies be mushrooms, caveare, or snails. **1624** CAPT. SMITH *Virginia* VI. 211 Cauiare and Puttargo. **1628** WITHER *Brit. Rememb.* I. 345 Caveär, and twenty such like bables. **1663** R. HEAD *Hic et Ubique* 24 Potargo, Cavere, Olives and such like. **1673** RAY *Journ. Low-C.* II. 353 The red Cavear .. made of the eggs or roe.. of the Cyprinus. **1680** MORDEN *Geog. Rect.* (1685) 62 Oyl and Cavayer about Volga. *Ibid.* 77 Three or 400 weight of Caveer. **1698** J. CRULL *Muscovy* 163 (N.) Caviare, or cavajar (by the Russians called ikary). **1708** MOTTEUX *Rabelais* IV. xviii, Pots of Cavier. **1708** W. KING *Cookery* (1807) 73 What lord of old, would bid his cook prepare Mangoes, potargo, champignons, caveare? **1730** SWIFT *Panegyr. Dean*, And, for our home-bred British Cheer, Botargo, Catsup, and Caveer. **1740** R. BROOKES *Art of Angling* I. xxxii. 74 A sort of Edible which they call Cavear, or Kavia. **1774** GOLDSM. *Nat. Hist.* (1862) II. I. vi. 267 A kind of cavier. **1782** P. H. BRUCE *Mem.* VII. 236 What the Russians call Ikari, and we caviar. **1837** M. DONOVAN *Dom. Econ.* II. 189 The roe is made into a caviare. **1853** SOYER *Pantroph.* 217 Caviar of an inferior quality. **1870** YEATS *Nat. Hist. Comm.* 325 Russian caviare.

b. The circumstance that *caviare* is generally unpalatable to those who have not acquired a taste for it, is referred to by Shakspere in a phrase which has become one of the commonplaces of literary quotation and allusion.

1602 SHAKS. *Ham.* II. ii. 457 For the Play I remember pleas'd not the Million, 'twas Cauiarie to the Generall: but it was.. an excellent Play. **1822** HAZLITT *Men & Mann.* Ser. II. iii. (1869) 77 Nothing goes down with them but what is caviare to the multitude. **1827** SCOTT *Two Drovers* i, His own legends of clanfights and creaghs.. would have been caviare to his companion. **1847** BARHAM *Ingold. Leg.*, *St. Dunstan*, The fare to which I allude, With as good table-beer as ever was brewed, Was all 'caviare to the multitude'. **1880** *Literary World* 13 Feb. 100/2 They.. will be considered caviare to the general public.

2. *slang.* A passage blacked out by a censor (orig. a Russian censor) by the use of a stamp which when inked and applied to the paper leaves a close network of white lines and black diamonds, resembling to some extent the appearance of caviare spread upon bread and butter. So **caviare** *v. trans.*, to block out or censor in this way.

1890 *St. James's Gaz.* 25 Apr. 7/1 Every one of Mr. Kennan's articles in the *Century* has been 'caviared'. **1894** *Westm. Gaz.* 2 Nov. 1/2 The Czar.. had.. to seem as if he had blotted the assassin's menace out from his mind as completely as his own censors 'caviared' it out of the newspapers. **1899** GISSING *Crown of Life* xix, We call caviare the bits blacked out in our newspapers and periodicals. **1920** *Times* 5 Nov. 13/4 Surely there would have been ample time to prevent its appearance in the book itself.. either by cancelling the leaf on which it was printed.. or by the process called 'caviare'.

cavicorn (ˈkævɪkɔːn). *Zool.* [f. L. *cavus* hollow + *cornu* horn.] A quadruped having hollow horns: one of a family (*Cavicornia*) of Ruminants.

cavie ('keɪvɪ). *Sc.* Also **cavey, cavy.** [app. a. MDu. *kēvie*, Du. or Flem. *kevie*, 16th c. Flem. also *kavie* (Plantin 1573), cage, coop, corresp. to OHG. *chevia*, MHG. *kevje*, Ger. *käfig*, *käfich* cage:—WGer. *kavia* str. fem., a. late L. **cavia*, for *cavea* cage, coop, den, etc., f. *cavus* hollow.] A hen-coop; a house for fowls.

1756 MRS. CALDERWOOD *Jrnl.* v. (1884) 142 It is just like a cavy full of men, instead of hens. **1805** J. NICOL *Poems* II. 90 (Jam.) Nor duck, nor turkie-cavie enter'd. **1808** MAYNE *Siller Gun* 56 (Jam.) Croose as a cock in his ain cavie. **1828** SCOTT *F.M. Perth* xxv, Cooped up in a convent, like a kain-hen in a cavey.

cavier, obs. form of CAVIARE.

cavil ('kævɪl), *sb.* [f. the verb.]

1. A captious, quibbling, or frivolous objection.

1570 LEVINS *Manip.* 124 A cauill, *calumnia.* **1581** J. BELL *Haddon's Answ. Osor.* 336/2, I come now to the other part of your cavill, which is in all respectes as untrue and frivolous. **1596** SHAKS. *Tam. Shr.* II. i. 392 That's but a cauill. **1656** HOBBES *Six Less.* Wks. 1845 VII. 227 The ninth objection is an egregious cavil. **1735** BERKELEY *Free-thinking in Math.* §50 Whether there may not be fair objections as well as cavils. **1850** GLADSTONE *Glean.* V. xliv. 200 To meet this technical cavil on the wording of the Statutes.

2. The raising of frivolous objections; cavilling.

a **1600** HOOKER (J.), Wiser men consider how subject the best things have been unto cavil. **1611** BIBLE *Pref.* init., If there be any hole left for cauill to enter (and cauill, if it doe not finde a hole, will make one). **1729** BUTLER *Serm.* Wks. 1874 II. Pref. 9 The first seems.. the least liable to cavil and dispute. **1860** MOTLEY *Netherl.* (1868) I. v. 144 His measures were sure to be the subject of perpetual cavil. **1868** FREEMAN *Norm. Conq.* (1876) II. viii. 183 There was no candidate whose claims were altogether without cavil.

†**3.** [cf. L. *cavilla.*] A flout, gibe, jeer. *Obs.*

1615 CHAPMAN *Odyss.* XXII. 235 Eumæus on his just infliction pass'd This pleasureable cavil.

4. *Comb.*, as *cavil-proof* adj.

1655 FULLER *Ch. Hist.* III. viii. § 11 James.. granted them a new Corporation Cavill-proof against all exceptions.

cavil ('kævɪl), *v.* Also 6–7 **cavel(l.** [a. OF. *cavill-er* (14th c. in Godef.) to mock, jest, rail, 'to cauill, wrangle, reason crossely, speake ouer thwartly' (Cotgr.), ad. L. *cavillāri* (whence also It. *cavillare*, Sp. *cavilar*, Pg. *cavillar*), to practise jeering or mocking, satirize, jest, reason captiously, f. *cavilla* a jeering, scoffing, raillery.]

1. *intr.* 'To raise captious and frivolous objections' (J.); to object, dispute, or find fault unfairly or without good reason. Const. *at*, *about* (formerly also *against*, *with*, *on*).

1548 UDALL, etc. *Erasm. Par. Mark* ii. 19 b, Wheras ye can not thwarte and cauyll in the thynges you see doen before your iyes. **1564** *Brief Exam.* ***** iij b, Men dyd not cauill agaynst theyr whyte vestures. **1596** SHAKS. *1 Hen. IV*, III. i. 140 But in the way of Bargaine.. Ile cauill on the ninth part of a hayre. **1597** MORLEY *Introd. Mus.* 28 Let no man cauil at my doing in that I have chaunged my opinion. **1635** SWAN *Spec. M.* i. §3 (1643) 14 After this manner, such mockers reasoned and cavilled with S. Peter. **1642** ROGERS *Naaman* 8 He.. who cavelled against the Prophet. **1750** WARBURTON *Lett. late Prelate* (1809) 61 Without finding anything considerable to cavil with you upon. **1798** MALTHUS *Popul.* (1878) 88 When the harvest is over they cavil about losses. *a* **1852** WEBSTER *Wks.* (1877) VI. 163 Those who do not value Christianity.. cavil about sects and schisms. **1871** ROSSETTI *Dante at Ver.* liii, To cavil in the weight of bread And to see purse-thieves gibbeted. **1884** SIR W. BRETT in *Law Times Rep.* LI. 530/1 The rule exists, and I have not the smallest intention of cavilling at it.

†**b.** with object-clause. *Obs.*

1570 BILLINGSLEY *Euclid* I. ix. 19 He may cauill that the hed of the equilater triangle shall not fall betwene the two right lines. **1714** GAY *What d' ye call it* Pref., They cavil at it as a Comedy, that I had partly a View to Pastoral.

2. *trans.* To object to or find fault with captiously.

1581 J. BELL *Haddon's Answ. Osor.* 232/2 This were perhappes not altogether from the purpose, that is cavilled. **1621** BP. MOUNTAGU *Diatribæ* 422 Nor can you cauill him for leauing out the word. **1667** MILTON *P.L.* x. 759 Wilt thou enjoy the good, Then cavil the conditions? **1750** WARBURTON *Wks.* (1811) VIII. 96 The testimony of Amm. Marcellinus, decisive as it is, hath been cavilled. **1875** H. E. MANNING *Mission H. Ghost* ix. 256 There are men whose intellectual pride cavils and perverts.. every truth of the revelation of God.

b. with *away*, *out*: To do away with, bring out, by cavilling.

1642 MILTON *Apol. Smect.* (1851) 294 His seventh section labours to cavill out the flawes which were found in the Remonstrants logick. **1645** W. JENKYN *Serm.* 28 'Tis this which doth cavill away our peace and holinesse. **1863** LYTTON *Caxtoniana* I. 91 Nurse, cherish, never cavil away, the wholesome horror of Debt.

†**3.** in sense of L. *cavillāri*. *Obs.*—⁰

1570 LEVINS *Manip.* 126 Cauil, *calumniari*, *cauillari.* **1613** R. C. *Table Alph.* (ed. 3), *Cauill*, to iest, scoffe, or reason subtilly. **1616** in BULLOKAR.

cavil, variant of KEVEL *sb.*²

cavil, var. KEVEL *sb.*³

1842 GWILT *Archit.* Gloss. s.v. *Nidged Ashlar*, It is brought to the square by means of a cavil or hammer with a sharp point.

cavil(l, var. of CAVEL, lot.

cavillation (kævɪ'leɪʃən). Forms: 4 **kauelacion**, 4–6 **cauel(l)acion**, (**-acyoun**, etc.), 4–7 **cau-**, **cavil(l)-**, **cavyl(l)acion**, 6 **cauel(l)ation**, 7 **cavilation**, 5– **cavillation**. [a. F. *cavillation* (13th c. *cavillacion* in Littré), ad. L. *cavillātiōn-em* a jeering, scoffing, in med.L. a legal subterfuge, chicane, f. *cavillāri* (see CAVIL *v.*).] Cavilling.

1. †**a.** In early use, *esp.* The making of captious, frivolous, quibbling, or unfair objections, arguments, or charges, in legal proceedings; the use of legal quibbles, or taking advantage of technical flaws, so as to overreach or defraud; hence, chicanery, trickery, overreaching sophistry. *Obs.*

c **1340** *Gaw. & Gr. Knt.* 2275 Nawþer fyked I, ne flaȝe, freke, quen þou myntest, Ne kest no kauelacion. **138.** WYCLIF *Sel. Wks.* III. 198 Ne cavyllacion ne procuratour schal be þere. **1413** LYDG. *Pylgr. Sowle* IV. xxix. (1859) 62 Yf lawes be keped stably withoute ony cauyllacions, or fals fauoure of persones. *a* **1500** *Songs & Carols* (Wright) 66 (Mätz.) Was not Adam.. Arystotyll, Vergyll, by a womans cavylacion Browt to iniquyte and to mych woo? **1549** *Compl. Scot.* 167 Aye inuentand cauillatione and vrang titilis to hef ther nychtbours heretagis. **1631** BP. WEBBE *Quietn.* (1657) 190 If these accusations.. are mere surmises or forged cavilations. **1636** FEATLY *Clavis Myst.* xxix. 373 Bribery and forged cavillations [haunt] the courts of justice.

b. = CAVILLING.

c **1540** *Life of Fisher* Wks. II. (1887) Introd. 41 Lest some cavillacion might in time arise about this matter. **1671** *True Non-Conf.* 120 Those who have cleared this point above cavillation. *a* **1734** NORTH *Exam.* II. v. ¶132 We have instead of a Narration, a World of Cavillation. **1838–9** HALLAM *Hist. Lit.* II. II. iii. §16. 112 A good deal more follows in the same sophistical style of cavillation.

c. = CAVIL *sb.* 1. *arch.*

1532 MORE *Answ. Frith* Wks. 835/2 To trifle out the trouth of Goddes wordes; with cauillacions grounded vpon goddes other wordes. **1540** RAYNALD *Byrth Man* (1634) Prol. 9 With diuers other such like cauillations and reasons. *c* **1645** HOWELL *Lett.* (1688) IV. 468 Left-handed Arguments, approaching the nature of cavillations. **1866** MOTLEY *Dutch Rep.* VI. ij. 797 Provided it were interpreted healthily, and not dislocated by cavillations and sinister interpolations.

†**2.** = L. *cavillatio*, a jeering, scoffing. *Obs.*—⁰

1623 COCKERAM II, Merry Taunts, *Cauillations.* **1656** BLOUNT *Glossogr.*, *Cavillation*, a mock or jest.

†'**cavilla,tory**, *a.* *Obs. rare.* [ad. L. type **cavillātōri-us* of a *cavillātor* CAVILLER (agent sb. f. *cavillāri*): see -ORY.] Of the nature of cavilling.

1641 *Answ. to Vind. Smectymnuus* Pref. 10 The contradiction they would raise.. is meerly cavillatory. **1643** PRYNNE *Sov. Power Parl.* IV. 14 These Cavillatory Objections against the Parliaments proceedings.

caviller ('kævɪlə(r)). [f. CAVIL *v.* + -ER.] One who cavils; a captious or frivolous objector, a quibbling disputant.

1574 WHITGIFT *Def. Aunsw.* 429 (R.) You are but a shifting cauiller. **1667** *Phil. Trans.* II. 505 Of greater moment than perhaps Detractors and Cavillers imagine. **1759** JOHNSON *Rasselas* xxx, That it is doubted by single cavillers, can very little weaken the general evidence. **1869** SPURGEON *J. Ploughm. Talk* 17 Cavillers.. find fault for the sake of showing off their deep knowledge.

cavilling ('kævɪlɪŋ), *vbl. sb.* [f. as prec. + -ING¹.] The action of the verb to CAVIL; captious objection or frivolous fault-finding.

1565–78 COOPER *Thesaur.*, *Captio in verbis*, captious cavilling in wordes. **1656** *Artif. Handsomeness* 66 These.. fall to cavillings and menacings. **1840** CARLYLE *Heroes* (1858) 361 Bottomless cavillings and questionings about written laws. **1857** BUCKLE *Civiliz.* I. 751 It is not such petty cavilling which can destroy an European reputation.

'**cavilling**, *ppl. a.* [f. as prec. + -ING².] That cavils, captious; *also*, fraudulent, sophistical (*obs.*).

1578 BANISTER *Hist. Man* IV. 63 To shunne.. the cauelyng tauntes of straungers. **1582** BENTLEY *Mon. Matrones* II. 204 The caueling aduersarie, the enimie of mankind. **1633** T. STAFFORD *Pac. Hib.* iii. (1821) 258 They did use to buy old caveling titles. **1691** HARTCLIFFE *Virtues* 239 An Ignorant Grammarian or a Cavelling Logician. **1692** BENTLEY *Boyle Lect.* iv. 116. **1835** WILLIS *Pencillings* II. xxxix. 18 The most cavilling mind must applaud their devoted sense of duty.

Hence **cavillingly** *adv.*, in a cavilling manner; **cavillingness**, the disposition to cavil.

1563 FOXE *A. & M.* (1596) 46/1 Nero and Domitian.. cauillinglie obiected against our doctrine. **1642** J. EATON *Free Justif.* 273 As they likewise cavillingly object. **1818** TODD *Cavillingness.*

†'**cavillous**, *a.* *Obs.* [ad. L. *cavillōs-us* (f. *cavilla*: see CAVIL and -OUS; or ad. OF. *cavilleus*, *-eux* in same sense.] Full of cavils or cavilling; (of persons) apt to cavil.

1572 BUCHANAN *Detect. Mary* in H. Campbell *Love-lett. Mary Q. Scots* 140 Though we would shift it off by cavillous expounding. **1577** HELLOWES *Gueuara's Chron.* 330 Bassian was.. also more cauillous and troublesome. **1645** DIGBY *Man's Soul* viii. (1657) 78 Cavillous scruples, and wild doubts. **1726** AYLIFFE *Parerg.* 56 Cavillous and unfaithful Advocates, by whose Fraud and Iniquity, Justice is destroy'd. **1851** GALLENGA tr. *Marriotti's Italy* 354 The war-ministry were lukewarm, cavillous, impracticable.

Hence †'**cavillously** *adv.*; **cavillousness**.

1561 T. NORTON *Calvin's Inst.* I. xiii. (1634) 59 Falsly and cavillously they ascribe unto us a device of their owne braine. **1648** MILTON *Observ. Art. Peace* (1851) 559 By the Covenant it self, since that so cavillously is urg'd against us.

[**cavilon**, mistake for *cavison* = CAVESSON.

a **1641** SUCKLING *Brennoralt* III. i, Rid with Cavilons, and with harsh curbs.]

†'**cavilsome**, *a.* *Obs. rare.* [f. CAVIL + -SOME.] Of the nature of cavil, cavilling.

1611 W. SCLATER *Key* (1629) 270 In despight of all cauilsome premisses. **1621** —— *Tythes* (1623) 1 None except cauilsome contradiction.

cavin ('kævɪn). *Mil.* [a. F. *cavin*:—OF. *cavain*, f. L. *cavus* hollow.] A hollow way or natural hollow, sufficiently capacious to hold a body of troops, and facilitate their approach to a fortress.

1708 in KERSEY; in BAILEY, JOHNSON, and mod. Dicts.

caving ('keɪvɪŋ), *vbl. sb.*¹ [f. CAVE *v.*¹ + -ING¹.]

1. The action of CAVE *v.*¹

1867 JEAN INGELOW *Story of Doom* VI. 23 The moon hath grown again in heaven, After her caving.

2. The exploring of caves; spelæology.

1932 E. A. BAKER (*title*) Caving. Episodes of Underground Exploration. *Ibid.* i. 2 How far caving is a scientific affair and how far a mere pastime is a question which calls for an answer. **1952** GEMMELL & MYERS *Underground Adv.* 2 It is by no means easy to put into words the real attractions of caving.

'**caving**, *vbl. sb.*² orig. *U. S.*. [f. CAVE *v.*³ + -ING¹.] The action of CAVE *v.*³, *lit.* and *fig.*; usually ***caving in***.

1809 *Massachusetts Spy* 25 Oct. (Th.), Mr. Benanuel Bucklin was killed by the caving in of a fountain which he was stoning. **1852** *Congress. Globe* 17 May 1385/3 A universal 'caving in' upon the part of Southern Whigs. **1857** R. TOMES *Amer. in Japan* xiv. 330, Stakes or palisades are driven in along the cuttings, to prevent the earth from caving. **1865** *Daily Tel.* 18 Oct. 7/4 There will be such a caving-in and bulging-out of worthless party walls. **1870** *Echo* 11 Nov., The public regard it suspiciously. They seem to think it the prelude to 'caving in'.

caving, -ings, caving-rake: see CAVE *v.*⁴

'**caving**, *ppl. a.* [f. CAVE *v.* + -ING².] Forming caves, overhanging. Also, Falling in, through being hollowed out beneath. Also ***caving-in***.

1850 LYELL *2nd Visit U.S.* II. 214 A caving bank on one side, and an advancing sand-bar.. on the other. **1857** T. B. GUNN *N.Y. Boarding Houses* xi. 98 An especially uncomfortable chair with a caving-in seat. *a* **1877** OUIDA *Tricotrin* I. 350 The deep slopes of caving cliffs.

cavish: see under CAVY *sb.*¹

cavitary ('kævɪtərɪ), *a.* and *sb.* [f. L. *cavitas* hollow, cavity + -ARY; cf. *voluntas*, *voluntary*.]

†**1.** Having a cavity: used as an epithet of those intestinal worms which have a distinct mouth and anus. (Adaptation of Cuvier's term, *vers cavitaires*, in his division of intestinal worms.) Also as *sb. Obs.*

1835 KIRBY *Hab. & Inst. Anim.* I. xi. 319 The Infusories and Polypes, and the Cavitaries of that author (Cuvier). **1836–9** TODD *Cycl. Anat.* II. 117/1 A third order of Cavitary Entozoa. **1847** *Nat. Encycl.* I. 751/2 The cavitary intestinal worms (*cœlelmintha*).

2. Of the nature of, or belonging to, a cavity.

1861 HULME tr. *Moquin-Tandon* II. VII. xiii. 397 A small cavitary vesicle. **1878** BELL *Gegenbauer's Comp. Anat.* 51 The hollow cavitary system which forms the hæmal passages.

cavitate ('kævɪteɪt), *v.* [Back-formation from CAVITATION.] *intr.* To form cavities or spaces in a fluid by the rapid whirling motion of a propeller.

1909 *Westm. Gaz.* 7 Jan. 4/2 The.. difficulty.. of obtaining a suitable screw-propeller that will not cavitate at such speeds as one wishes to attain. **1970** *New Scientist* 29 Jan. 198/1 The propellers of submarines.. can still cavitate.

cavitation (kævɪ'teɪʃən). [f. CAVITY: see -ATION.] **1.** The formation of bubbles or cavities in a fluid, esp. by the rapid motion of a propeller. Also *attrib.*

1895 *Min. Proc. Inst. Civ. Engineers* CXXII. 67 'Cavitation', as Mr. Froude has suggested to the Authors that the phenomenon should be called, appears to manifest itself when the mean negative pressure exceeds about 6¾ lbs. per square inch. **1902** *Nature* 6 Nov. 24/1 The name cavitation is given to the phenomenon met with when a screw is driven in water at speeds above a certain limiting value. **1930** *Engineering* 21 Feb. 268/1 Much attention has also been given to discovering the causes of erosion, which is generally attributable to cavitation. **1934** *Jrnl. R. Aeronaut. Soc.* XXXVIII. 238 Measurements of free running screws in the cavitation tank. **1945** *Ibid.* XLIX. 378/1 Cavitation due to reduction in barometric pressure affects pump efficiency giving rise to reduced and erratic delivery with considerable noise and vibration. **1947** CROWTHER & WHIDDINGTON *Science at War* iv. 156 It was not effective at speeds above twelve knots owing to cavitation noise. **1957** *Spaceflight* I. 51/1 *Cavitation*, a phenomenon occurring in pumps and other hydraulic machinery when the fluid pressure falls locally to a certain critical value.. The formation of bubbles can limit the performance of a pump. **1966** *New Scientist* 12 May 365/1 Cavitation is the formation of microscopic bubbles,

dispersed throughout the liquid, when it is subjected to intense mechanical agitation.

2. *Path.* The formation of cavities in the lungs as a result of disease.

1909 *Practitioner* Dec. 862 'Post-tussive suction'..is a very distinctive feature in advanced cavitation. **1952** J. W. CLEGG in Sellors & Livingstone *Mod. Pract. Tuberculosis* I. v. 83 Acute tuberculous cavitation results from the liquefaction of a mass of caseous tissue and the expectoration of the debris through the bronchial tree.

cavitied ('kævɪtɪd), *ppl. a.* [f. next + -ED.] Having cavities.

a **1864** OWEN is cited by WEBSTER.

cavity ('kævɪtɪ). Also 6 **cauyte, cauitie.** [a. F. *cavité*, in 13th c. *caveté*, (= It. *cavità*, Sp. *cavidad*), on L. type **cavitāt-em* (prob. in late L. or Romanic), f. *cav-us* hollow: see -ITY.]

†**1.** Hollowness. *Obs. rare.*

a **1679** T. GOODWIN *Wks.* III. 565 (R.) The fire of an oven ..into which fire is put to heat it, and the heat made more intense by the cavity or hollowness of the place.

2. A hollow place; a void or empty space within a solid body.

1541 R. COPLAND *Galyen's Terap.* 2 Dj, Before that the cauyte be replete with flesshe. **1603** HOLLAND *Plutarch's Mor.* 1022 The cavities as well of the mouth as of the stomacke. **1695** WOODWARD *Nat. Hist. Earth* (1723) I. 24 Within or without the Shell, in its Cavity or upon its Convexity. **1841–71** T. R. JONES *Anim. Kingd.* 3 Creatures whose hearts are divided into four cavities—Mammalia and Birds. **1862** STANLEY *Jew. Ch.* (1877) I. viii. 159 'The well', the deep cavity sunk in the earth by the art of man. **1878** HUXLEY *Physiogr.* 192 Little cavities, or vesicles, in this scoria, or cellular lava.

3. 'In naval architecture, the displacement formed in the water by the immersed bottom and sides of the vessel' (Smyth *Sailor's Word-bk.*).

c **1850** *Rudim. Navig.* (Weale) 104 *Centre of Cavity*, or of *Displacement*, the centre of that part of the ship's body which is immersed, and which is also the centre of the vertical force that the water exerts to support the vessel.

4. cavity wall, a double wall with an internal hollow space.

1910 *Encycl. Brit.* IV. 522/1 Buildings in exposed situations are frequently built with cavity-walls. **1958** *House & Garden* Feb. 69/1 The cavity walls have an outer leaf of yellow-buff bricks.

cavolinite (kævəʊ'liːnaɪt). *Min.* [Named 1826, after *Cavolini*, an Italian naturalist: see -ITE.] A variety of nephelite, found on Vesuvius, characterized by a silky lustre.

1826 *Amer. Jrnl. Sc.* XI. 260.

‖**cavo-ri'lievo.** [It. ('kavo ri'ljɛvo) = hollow relief.] A style of relief in which the highest portions of the figures are on a level with the general surface; much used in Egyptian sculpture.

cavort (kə'vɔːt), *v.* orig. *U.S.* [Etymology uncertain. Bartlett says, a corruption of *curvet*. The *Slang Dict.* 1874 has '*Cavaulting*, in vulgar phrase equivalent to "horsing"'; Lingua Franca *cavolta*. From this comes the Americanism "cavorting" running or riding around in a heedless or purposeless manner'. But these statements require verification. Webster (Suppl.) conjectures Sp. *cavar* to dig, excavate, paw as a horse; which has nothing to recommend it.]

intr. To curvet, prance, caper about, frisk, bound: said of a horse, or rider, and hence *transf.*

1794 W. B. GROVE *Let.* 2 Apr. in *Papers of J. Steele* (1924) I. 106 The Hon. J–e '*cauvauted*', don't laugh at the expression, it suits the idea I meant to convey. **1829** *Virginia Lit. Museum* 16 Dec. 419 *Cavault* or *Cavort*, ranting, highflying.—West. **1830** *Illinois Monthly Mag.* 71 The most amusing individuals..were cavorting... Cavorting..expresses the conduct of an individual who fancies himself the smartest and best man in the world. **1834** W. G. SIMMS *Guy Rivers* 283 You were then cavorting about her in great style. *a* **1848** *Major Jones's Courtsh.* 41 (Bartlett) A whole gang..came ridin' up, and reinin' in, and prancin' and cavortin'. —— *Georgia Scenes* ibid., On horseback..he cavorted most magnanimously. **1843–4** HALIBURTON *Sam Slick Eng.* xv. (Hoppe) Old Clay in a pastur'..snortin', cavortin', attitudinizin' of himself. **1873** BAILEY *Life in Danbury* 58 For one whole hour you have been cavorting around on that bed. *Ibid.* 110 A snapping and cracking, and general cavorting of hemlock timber, new shingles, window glass. **1883** B. HARTE *Carq. Woods* i. 9 Cavorting round this yer spot for the last half-hour. **1895** *Punch* 30 Mar. 147/3 Yet 'twere no lark, To see the trees cavorting round the Park. **1933** *Catholic Truth* July 149/2 Learned dons and scientists..cavorting about like cows in clover.

†'**cavous,** *a. Obs.* [ad. L. *cavōs-us*, f. *cav-us*, *-um*, hollow: see -OUS.] Hollow, concave.

1698 MOLYNEUX in *Phil. Trans.* XX. 217 One of the joints of the Causway..is Cavous, both at Top and Bottom. **1717** J. FOX *Wanderer* No. 14 What Snout was ever so cavous.. unless that of a Death's Head? **1750** G. HUGHES *Barbados* 58 Large cavous Icicles, which hung down.

†'**cavy, -ey,** *sb.*[1] *Obs.* A familiar or contemptuous abbreviation of CAVALIER. (Cf. CAB, *sb.*[2], CAVE *sb.*[2].) Hence '**cavish** *a.*

1645 *Relat. Defeat to Skellum Greenvile* 4 (D.) In the meane while..were at least sixty great gunnes shot off, which beat up the dirt bravely about the Cavies eares. **1650** A. B. *Mutat. Polemo* 15 The Cavies being at that time ready to turn anything, except Roundhead, for some money to be chirpingly drunk. **1664** A. BROME *Poems* 124 The Roundheads and Caveys no more shall be named. **1650** A. B. *Mutat. Polemo* 29 The Cavish Remora's of this Nation shall have their bellies full of rebelling and jarres.

cavy ('keɪvɪ), *sb.*[2] [modification of CABIAI, the Galibi name in French Guiana. (Perh. through Sp. or Pg.) Also Fr. *cavié*, mod.L. *cavia.*]

A rodent of the genus *Cavia* or family *Cavidæ*, all natives of America, of which the Guinea-pig and the Capybara are the chief species.

1796 STEDMAN *Surinam* II. xxii. 153 The long-nosed Cavy..or Indian Coney, is also very common in Surinam. **1813** BINGLEY *Anim. Biog.* I. 356 Of the Cavy tribe. The Cavies have, in each jaw, two wedge-shaped front teeth, and eight grinders. **1837** M. DONOVAN *Dom. Econ.* II. 95 The Javan Cavy..is not found in Java, but inhabits Surinam. **1838** *Penny Cycl.* XI. 480/2 Guinea Pig, Restless Cavy.

'**cavy,** *sb.*[3] *dial.* Corruption of PECCAVI.

1863 MRS. TOOGOOD *Yorksh. Dial.*, She begged cavy, and he forgave her.

†'**cavy,** *a. Obs.* [f. CAVE *sb.*[1] + -Y[1].] Of the nature of a cave.

1614 CHAPMAN *Odyss.* IX. 57 Divine Calypso, in her cavy house.

cavy, variant of CAVIE, hen-coop.

caw (kɔː), *int.* and *sb.* Also 7 **kaw.** [Imitative.]

1. A representation of the cry of a rook or crow.

1676 ETHEREDGE *Man of Mode* v. ii. (1684) 80 Methinks I hear the hateful noise Of Rooks already—Kaw—Kaw—Kaw. *c* **1780** COWPER *Jackdaw* v, Church, army, physic, law ..Is no concern at all of his, And says—what says he?—caw. **1797** G. COLMAN *Br. Grins, Maid of Moor* ii, The hoarse crow croaked caw! caw! caw!

attrib. **1874** PUSEY *Lent. Serm.* 138 A monotonous, caw-caw repetition of the same lie.

2. *sb.* The cry or call of a rook, crow, raven, etc.

1666 DRYDEN *Ann. Mirab.* 87 The dastard crow..With her loud kaws her craven kind does bring. **1820** KEATS *Fancy* 45 Rooks, with busy caw, Foraging for sticks and straw. **1878** J. BULLER *New Zeal.* I. Introd. 17 The song of the lark, the caw of the rook.

caw (kɔː), *v.* Also 7 **kaw.**

1. *intr.* Of rooks, crows, ravens, etc.: To utter their natural cry.

1590 SHAKS. *Mids. N.* III. ii. 22 Russed-pated choughes ..(Rising and cawing at the guns report). **16..** LOCKE (J.), Jackdaws kawing and fluttering about the nests. *a* **1800** COLERIDGE *Raven*, Round and round flew the Raven, and cawed to the blast. **1820** W. IRVING *Sketch Bk.* II. 195 The rooks cawed from the..tree tops.

2. *transf.* Of persons: To make a similar sound, or one contemptuously likened to it.

1589 *Pappe w. Hatchet* Eij b, Like dawes, you will be cawing a bout Churches. **1756** WESLEY *Wks.* (1872) II. 381 He cawed and cawed, but could utter nothing, hardly three words together.

3. trans. *to caw out*: to utter with cawing.

1616 HOLYDAY *Persius* 323 [Thou] Hoarsly crow-like caw'st out some idle thing.

Hence '**cawing** *vbl. sb.* and *ppl. a.*

1613 W. BROWNE *Brit. Past.* I. v, The early rising Crow with clam'rous kawing. **1670** J. CLARIDGE *Sheph. of Banbury's Rules* iii, The cawing of ravens. **1784** COWPER *Task* I. 203 Cawing rooks, and kites that swim sublime. *a* **1861** CLOUGH *Lond. Idyll* 19 The cawing birds above.

caw, var. of COE, the rot in sheep.

caw, var. of *ca'*, Sc. form of CALL *v.*

cawation, humorous for *cawing*: see -ATION.

cawcion, cawdel, etc.: see CAU-.

cawdie, -dy, obs. ff. of CADDIE.

cawed, var. of COED, affected with sheep-rot.

†**cawel.** *Obs.* [OE. *cawel, cawl, caul*, ad. L. *caul-is* cabbage: see CAUL, COLE, KALE.] Cabbage, cole, kale. Also in *comb.*, †**cawel-hert**, a name applied to the hare; †**cawel-wurm**, a caterpillar, kaleworm.

a **1000** *Voc.* in Wr.-Wülcker 202 *Caulus*, cawel. *c* **1000** ÆLFRIC *Voc.* ibid. 121 *Gurgulio*, cawelwurm. *c* **1000** *Sax. Leechd.* II. 336 Sele him etan ȝesodenne cawel. *Ibid.* II. 240 Wild cawel. *Ibid.* I. 106 On cawles [*v.r.* caules] leaf. *a* **1325** *Names Hare* in *Rel. Ant.* I. 134 In the worshipe of the hare ..The cawel-hert, the worttroppere.

cawel: see also CAWL, fish-creel.

cawepys: see CHAVEPYS, *Obs.*

cawes, obs. form of CAUSE.

cawf, Sc. form of CALF[1], CHAFF.

cawght, etc.: see CAU-.

cawk, *sb.*[1] Also **cawke,** (8 **calk,** 9 **cauk, caulk**). [A variant spelling of CAUK.]

1. 'A miner's term for native sulphate of barium' (Watts *Dict. Chem.*), or heavy spar.

1653 [see CAUK]. **1676** J. BEAUMONT in *Phil. Trans.* XI. 731 The Stones..move in Vinegar..sending forth bubbles, as I find Cawk will very freely. **1722** *Phil. Trans. Abr.* II. 553 Cawk is a ponderous white Stone found in the Lead Mines. **1783** WITHERING in *Phil. Trans.* LXXIV. 307 *Terra ponderosa Vitriolata*, Calk or Cauk. **1806** *Gazetteer Scotl.* 398 In a matrix of sulphate of barytes or cawk. **1811** PINKERTON *Petral.* II. 574 The..cauk-spar, since called barytes. **1813** BAKEWELL *Introd. Geol.* (1815) 289 The matrix..is caulk or the sulphat of barytes. **1877** OUIDA *Puck* III. 25, I picked him out an atom of cawke and a morsel or two of Blue-John.

2. = CAUK, chalk.

cawk (kɔːk), *sb.*[2] [Imitative.] The cry of some birds, rooks, divers, etc.

1856 KANE *Arct. Expl.* I. xxi. 269 These last flew very high, emitting at regular intervals their reed-like 'kawk'. **1879** JEFFERIES *Wild Life in S.C.* 276 Those [rooks] that are diving utter a gurgling sound like the usual cawk prolonged —'caw-wouk'.

Hence **cawk** *v.*

1761 *Life J. Churchman* (1780) 297, I thought I saw also the raven fly, cawking, to and fro, but he did not return.

cawk, var. of CAUK, CAULK.

cawker, variant of CAULKER; also of CALKER[2].

1820 SCOTT *Monast.* xxxiv, The shoe was made by old Eckie..I would swear to the curve of the cawker.

cawkin, obs. f. CALKIN.

cawky ('kɔːkɪ), *a.* Also **cauky, caukey.** [f. CAWK *sb.*[1] + -Y.] Containing cawk, barytous. (Perhaps also = CHALKY.)

1676 J. BEAUMONT in *Phil. Trans.* XI. 730 A white Cawky stone. **1729** WOODWARD *Fossils* (J.), A white opaque cauky spar, shot or pointed. **1747** HOOSON *Miner's Dict.* Sj, Caukey ore. *Ibid.* s.v. *Brassil*, Veins that are Caukey.

†**cawl** (kɔːl). *Obs.* exc. *dial.* In 1 **cawel,** (**couel, ceawl**), 6–9 **cawell,** (9 **cowel(l, -all**), 1–9 **cawl.** [OE. *cawl, ceawl*, basket.] A basket; in modern Cornish dialect, a fish-basket or creel.

a **700** *Epinal Gloss.* 305 *Corvis* (*corbis*), couel. *a* **800** *Corpus Gloss.* 513 *Corbus* (*-is*), cauuel. *c* **893** K. ÆLFRED *Oros.* IV. viii. §4 þæt folc..heora cawlas afylled hæfdon. *c* **950** *Lindisf. Gosp.* Matt. xiv. 20 Tuoelf ceawlas ðæra screadunga fullo [Mark vi. 43 ceaulas]. *c* **1050** *Voc.* in Wr.-Wülcker 365 *Coruis*, cawel. **1568** *Wills & Inv. N.C.* (1835) 285 One almerye and a cawell wth a cownter [Here the meaning is doubtful]. **1865** ESQUIROS *Cornwall* 136 Women, with bent backs, loaded with a dorser called a cowel..bear the enormous loads of fish from the boats to the beach. **1880** MISS COURTNEY *W. Cornw. Gloss.* (E.D.S.), *Cowall, Cawell*, a basket to hold fish, carried by the fish-wives. **1883** *Fisheries Exhib. Catal.* 293 A Lamprey Cawl. A Lamprey Basket.

cawl(e, obs. form of CAUL[1] and [2], CAWEL.

cawlewort: perh. var. of COLEWORT, q.v.

1541 R. COPLAND *Guydon's Formul.* Yiij, Plasters of mountpyller of red cawleworts soden wt lye of asshes.

cawm(e, obs. form of CALM.

caw me, caw thee: see KA *v.*; cf. CLAW *v.*

‖**cawney, cawny** ('kɔːnɪ). [a. Tamil *kāni* property, land (Yule).] A measure of land used in the Madras Presidency: about $1\frac{1}{3}$ acre. The systematic spelling is *káni.*

1807 E. BUCHANAN *Mysore*, etc. I. 6(Y.) The proper canay would only contain 43,778 feet. **1858** J. B. NORTON *Topics* 224, 17,673 cawnies consisted of irrigated land.

‖**cawquaw** ('kɔːkwɔː). [Native name in Cree.] The Urson or Canadian Porcupine *Erethizon dorsatum*, whose spines are used by the Indians as ornaments.

1840 *Penny Cycl.* XVIII. 415/2 The..Canada Porcupine of Forster..Cawquaw of the Cree Indians; and Ooketook of the Esquimaux.

cawr-, caws-, cawt-: see CAU-.

‖**caxa, caxee,** obs. ff. CASH *sb.*[2]; cf. Pg. *caixa.*

1727–51 CHAMBERS *Cycl.* s.v., Old caxas..nearly the same with the caches of China, and the cassies of Japan. **1796** MORSE *Amer. Geog.* II. 503 The caxee..is made of a white metal of about the size of our farthing, with a small square hole driven through the middle.

†**caxon**[1] ('kæksən). [? from the personal surname Caxon.] A kind of wig, now obsolete.

1756 CAWTHORN *Poems* (1771) 77 Though that trim artist, barber Jackson, Spent a whole hour about your caxon. **1762** *Gentl. Mag.* 233 I've let my hair grow, and have thrown off my caxon. **1791** HUDDESFORD *Salmag.* 111 The worthies at Rag Fair old caxons who barter. **1828** MISS MITFORD *Village* Ser. III. (1863) 34 The caxon worn by the then Archbishop of Canterbury. **1834** SOUTHEY *Doctor* cxii. (1862) 270 A wig which, with all proper respect,..I cannot but honestly denominate a caxon.

‖**caxon**[2]. ? *Obs.* [OSp. *caxon*, now *cajon* (ka'xon), augm. of *caxa*, now *caja* CASE, chest; cf. Fr. *caisson* CAISSON, It. *casone* CASSOON.] A case or chest of ores prepared to be refined.

1669 EARL SANDWICH tr. *Barba's Art Mettals* II. xii. 37 He shall certainly know what Silver the Caxon contains. *Ibid.* 40 How much materials they are to put into a Caxon or Chest. **1674** *Phil. Trans.* IX. 212 What he is to do before he incorporates the Caxon for refining. **1775** in ASH; and in mod. technical Dicts.

¶ A misprint of this as *caxou* in Chambers *Cycl. Supp.* 1753, is copied by Todd and later Dicts.

Caxton ('kækstən). [f. the proper name.]

1. *ellipt.* A book printed by William Caxton (died 1492), the first English printer.

1811 DIBDIN *Bibliom.* (ed. 2) 502 From so many Caxtons ..it would be difficult to select a few, which, etc. **1870** W. BLADES (*title*) How to tell a Caxton.

2. A variety of printing-type, imitating that first used in England by Caxton, introduced by Vincent Figgins in 1855 (for his reprint of the Chess book).

Hence **Cax'tonian** *a.*, of or pertaining to Caxton.

1811 DIBDIN *Bibliom.* (ed. 2) 499 The love of black-letter lore and Caxtonian typography.

† **'caxy.** *Obs. rare*⁻¹. (?) A dim. of CAXON[1].

1729 *Dulcinead* 8 His Caxy's powder'd ev'ry Day.

cay (keɪ, kiː). Also KEY[2], q.v. [ad. Sp. *cayo* shoal, rock, barrier-reef, OF. *cay*, *caye* sand bank or bar, in med.L. *caium*. Diez cites from the pseudo-Isidore Gl. *kai* 'cancellæ', *kaij* 'cancelli', bars, barriers; and refers it to Celtic *cae*, pl. *caiou* 'munimenta' in Oxf. glosses. Cf. Welsh *cae* hedge, Breton *kaé* embankment. The sense with which it was applied to the reefs, was thus that of 'bars, barriers'. Orig. the same word as QUAY, q.v. In 17th c. Eng., *key* was pronounced *kay* (keɪ), whence, by assimilation, *cay* was also written *key*, spelling now usual in the West Indies.]

A low insular bank of sand, mud, rock, coral, etc.; a sandbank; a range of low-lying reefs or rocks; orig. applied to such islets around the coast and islands of Spanish America.

1707 SLOANE *Jamaica* I. Introd. 86 Called by the Spaniards Cayos, whence by corruption comes the English word Keys. **1769** FALCONER *Dict Marine* (1789), *Caies*, a ridge of rocks, or sand-banks; called in the West Indies, keys. **1790** BEATSON *Nav. & Mil. Mem.* I. 134 The misfortune to lose the Tyger on a cayo near the island of Tortuga. **1858** in *Merc. Mar. Mag.* V. 159 The Light on Bush Cay [Florida]. **1860** *Ibid.* VII. 71 A beacon..has been erected on this Cay [in Australia]. **1873** *Act 36 & 37 Vict.* c. 6 Preamb., The islands and cays commonly known and designated as the 'Caicos Islands'. **1884** *Littell's Living Age* 674 The entrance..is protected by cays or coral reefs.

cayak, var. of KAYAK[1], Esquimaux canoe.

cayenne (keɪ'ɛn, kaɪ'ɛn). Forms: 8 **cayan, kayan, kian, kyan**; also **chian, chyan**. [In its actual form, referred to Cayenne, the chief town of French Guiana (founded 1634); but this is app. only popular etymology, as the name in Tupi (Brazilian) is given by Martini, p. 419, as *kyýnha*, *quiýnha*, also *quiya*. Gul. Piso, *De Indiæ utriusque Re Nat. et Med.* (1658) has '*qviya* sive *Piper Brasiliensis*. The name *Cayenne Pepper* is unknown to French, and the Ger. *Cayenne-pfeffer* is prob. from Eng. (The somewhat archaic pronunc. (ˌkaɪ'ɑːn) survives from the earlier form.)]

a. (Also called ***Cayenne pepper***). A very pungent powder obtained from the dried and ground pods and seeds of various species of *Capsicum*, esp. *C. annuum* and *C. frutescens*, of South America; used as a condiment in cookery and as a stimulant in medicine; formerly called Guinea pepper.

1756 P. BROWNE *Jamaica* 177 The Cayan pepper or butter of the West Indies. **1774** *Westm. Mag.* II. 447 Her mouth had been so heated with Chian. **1782** *European Mag.* II. 68 His temper hot as Kayan, taste uncouth. **1782** SCHOTTE in *Phil. Trans.* LXXIII. 93 Seasoned with Cayenne pepper. **1796** MRS. GLASSE *Cookery* iii. 28 Put to it..chyan, salt.. and a little lemon juice. **1809** W. IRVING *Knickerb.* (1861) 87 Hideous crimes, which, like cayenne in cookery, do give a pungency and flavour to the dull detail of history. **1823** BYRON *Don Juan* x. lxxii, Leavening his blood as cayenne doth a curry.

b. *fig.*

1784 *New Spect.* VII. 4/2 If you season it with a little Kyan of Scandal. **1836** HOR. SMITH *Tin Trump.* (1876) 216 Jokes —the cayenne of conversation and the salt of life. **1886** *Sat. Rev.* 6 Mar. 328/2 The cayenne pepper of incendiary speeches.

c. ***cayenne whist***, a variety of whist in which the dealer's side names the trumps and in which the suits have different values.

1887 BEATTY-KINGSTON *Music & Manners* II. 253 As much 'cayenne' whist as their means will permit of their indulging in. **1897** *Sears, Roebuck Catal.* 343/1 All the games with cards at present in vogue, including..whist, Cayenne whist, Hearts.

cay'enned, *ppl. a.* [f. prec. + -ED.] Seasoned with cayenne; *fig.* spiced, hot.

1803 LAMB in *Final Mem.* Wks. (1865) 225, I have left off cayenned eggs. **1837** *New Monthly Mag.* L. 290 The panegyric is very handsomely cayenned. **1872** E. YATES *Castaway* (Hoppe), There were devilled biscuits and cayenned legs of poultry.

cayer, obs. form of QUIRE (of a book).

cayeute, cayote, varr. COYOTE.

cayle, obs. form of KALE, cabbage.

cayles, obs. form of KAYLES, ninepins.

caylewey, var. form of CALEWEY, *Obs.*, a pear.

Cayleyan ('keɪlɪən), *a.* and *sb. Math.* [Named after Prof. Cayley of Cambridge.] Name of a certain curve of the third or higher order.

1852 SALMON *Higher Pl. Curves* v. (1879) 151 The Cayleyan may also be considered as the envelope of lines which are cut in involution by the polar conics of a cubic.

Caym, obs. form of CAIN.

cayman, caiman ('keɪmən). Forms: 7 **caimain**, 9 **kay-, kaiman**. [In Sp. and Pg. *caiman*, F. *caïman*, app. from Carib. Martini, *Galibi* (Mainland Carib) *Dict.* has '*cayman* crocodilus'; Rochefort (*c* 1660) *Iles Antilles* 225 'le crocodile que les insulaires nomment *cayeman*. Littré cites Carib *Acayoúman* 'crocodile', from *Dict. Fr. Caraïbe* of P. Raymond Breton, 1661.

Very positive statements, however, assert the word to be African, from Congo; Pigafetta 1598 (*trans.* in Yule) says In this river (Zaire or Congo)..mighty great crocodiles, which the country people there call *caiman*.' And Cuvier *Règne Animal, Sauri* (transl.) IX. 196 says 'The slaves on their arrival from Africa, at sight of a crocodile, gave it immediately the name of *cayman*. It would appear from this that it was the negroes who spread the name throughout America'. But as Bontius 1631 (cited by Yule) says Cayman is the name 'per totam Indiam' (i.e. the East Indies), the name appears to be one of those like *anaconda* and *bom*, *boma*, which the Portuguese or Spaniards very early caught up in one part of the world, and naturalized in another.]

A name applied to some large saurians of the crocodile family. **a.** The genus of these confined to America, and distinguished from the true crocodiles mainly by the shortness and roundness of the muzzle, and the inferior development of the webs between the toes; also called ALLIGATOR. **b.** *esp.* The species of this genus found in the tropics of South America, chiefly *A. palpebrosus* and *trigonatus*, as distinguished from *A. Lucius*, the North American species, to which the term *alligator* is more particularly applied. **c.** Loosely applied to all large American saurians, some of which are true crocodiles; and sometimes extended even to those of Africa or Asia.

1577 FRAMPTON *Joyfull Newes* II. (1596) 73 b, Caimanes, that are called Lagartos [in New Granada]. **1648** GAGE *West Ind.* xii. (1655) 45 The great Lisarts, or Caimains [*on same page*, Caymanes]. **1668** *Phil. Trans.* III. 703 The Stone in the Stomach of a Cayman or Crocodile. **1699** DAMPIER *Voy.* II. II. ii. 75 At the Isle Grand Caymanes, there are Crocodiles, but no Alligators. At Pines by Cuba, there are abundance of Crocodiles, but I cannot say there are no Alligators..Both kinds are called Caymanes by the Spaniards. **1774** GOLDSM. *Nat. Hist.* IV. 67 The crocodile, properly so called, and the cayman or alligator. **1796** STEDMAN *Surinam* I. vii. 145 The alligator or cayman (as called by the natives and negroes). *Ibid.* 146 That [name] which the Indians called them by, viz. the cayman. **1831** TYERMAN & BENNET *Voy.* II. liii. 523 They [native fishermen in Madagascar] frequently have to dispute with a kayman (the alligator) for their property. **1836** MACGILLIVRAY tr. *Humboldt's Trav.* xxiii. 324 He cannot bathe on account of the caymans. **1885** STEVENSON *Dynamiter* 159 See, where the caiman lies ready to devour us.

† **'caynard.** *Obs.* [a. F. *cagnard* sluggard (according to Littré, f. It. *cagna* bitch, fem. of *cane* dog): see -ARD.] A lazy fellow, a sluggard: a term of reproach.

1303 R. BRUNNE *Handl. Synne* 8300 A kaynarde ande a olde folle. *a* **1310** in Wright *Lyric P.* xxxix. (1842) 110 This croked caynard sore he is a-dred. *c* **1386** CHAUCER *Wyf's Prol.* 235 See, olde caynard, is this thin array?

† **cayolac, cayelac, cayolaque.** *Obs.* [Malay *kayu* wood, *laka* the wood of *Myristica iners* (or ? *Tanarius major*) used as incense (Crawford).] (See quots.)

1588 PARKE tr. *Mendoza's China* 41 Euerie morning and euening they do offer vnto their Idolles frankensence, beniamin, wood of aguila, and cayolaque. **1625** PURCHAS *Pilgrims* III. 177 (Y.) A sweet wood which they call Cayolaque. **1750** BEAWES *Lex Mercat.* (1752) 794 [Cargoes on return from Siam to Canton carry] Caye-lac..for burning before their Pagods. **1858** SIMMONDS *Dict. Trade*, *Cayelac*, an aromatic wood obtained in Siam.

cayr(e, var. CAIR *v. Obs.* to turn, go.

cayro: see COIR.

† **caysel.** *Obs.* Some plant.

a **1387** *Sinon. Barthol.* (Anecd. Oxon.) 13 *Brasica*, caysel secundum quosdam. *Ibid.* 26 *Kannus*, caysel.

cayser, obs. var. of KAISER.

caytef, -tif, etc., obs. ff. CAITIFF.

Cayuga ('keɪjuːgə, 'kaɪjuːgə). [Iroquoian place-name.] One of the five (later six) tribes of the Iroquoian confederation of North American Indians; a member of this tribe; their language. Also *attrib.*

1744 *Colon. Rec. Pennsylvania* IV. 722 The several Nations had drawn for the performance of the Ceremony and the *Lot* falling on the Cayogo Nation. **1792** *Affecting Hist. F. Manheim* 34 A number of..Cayugas will commence hostilities. **1823** J. F. COOPER *Pioneers* I. vii. 143 They [*sc.* the Iroquois] consisted of the tribes..of the Mohawks, the Oneidas, the Onondagas, Cayugas and Senecas; who ranked, in the confederation, in the order with which they are named. **1933** BLOOMFIELD *Lang.* iv. 72 The languages of the Iroquois type (Mohawk, Oneida, Onondaga, Cayuga, [etc.]). **1969** *Observer* (Colour Suppl.) 25 May 53/3 Farther west were the Cayuga, a small group.

cayuse (kaɪ'juːs). *U.S. local.* Also †**kiyuse**, †**skyuse.** [Said to be from the language of the Chinook Indians of Oregon.] 'A common Indian pony' (*Scribner's Mag.* II. 510). Also, any horse (*N. Amer. colloq.*).

1841 T. J. FARNHAM *Trav. Gt. West. Prairies* 157 Skyuse horses never make such disagreeable mistakes. **1857** *Oregon Weekly Times* Jan. (Th.), All manner of wrought and cast work,..down to Shoeing a 'Cultus' Cayuse Horse. **1867** *Territorial Enterprise* (Virginia, Nev.) 31 Jan. 2/4 Jane..was mounted behind her lover and away, nor bated they the noble cayuse till many a league was passed. **1869** A. K. MCCLURE *Rocky Mts.* 302 Twice our kiyuse broke nearly out of the harness... The kiyuse is never perfectly tamed. **1873** J. H. BEADLE *Undevel. West* xxxv. 750, I mounted a *cayuse* and rode seven miles over the hills. **1882** *Blackw. Mag.* Dec. 768, I stopped to let the old cayuse rest. **1885** *Century Mag.* Nov. 33 As firm a seat..as any cowboy that ever put leg over a cayuse. **1948** *Chicago Tribune* 27 May II. 2/6 Life atop a cayuse in the professional arenas..is no easier than one astride a bronco on the college rodeo field. **1962** *Field, Horse & Rodeo* (Calgary) Nov. 30/1 Well, chances are Mr. Dude, you've been getting a silent horse laugh yourself from your own trusty cayuse.

caz. *Thieves' cant.* [cf. Du. *kaas*, MDu. *kâse*, L. *caseus*.] Cheese. Cf. CASSAN.

1812 J. H. VAUX *Flash Dict.*, *Caz*, cheeze; *As good as caz*, is a phrase signifying that any projected fraud or robbery may be easily and certainly accomplished.

caza, var. KAZA.

cazee, cazy, var. KAZI, Indian CADI or judge.

cazern, var. of CASERN.

cazibi, obs. form of CASSAVA.

cazimate, obs. form of CASEMATE.

‖ **'cazimi.** *Astrol. Obs.* 'Among the Arabian astronomers the center or middle of the sun' (Chambers *Cycl. Supp.*). ***in cazimi***: said of a planet when distant not more than 17 minutes, or half its apparent diameter, from the sun.

1614 TOMKIS *Albumazar* in *Dodsley* VII. 171 (N.) I'll find the cuspe and Alfridaria, And know what planet is in Cazimi. **1632** MASSINGER *City Mad.* II. ii, Saturn out of all dignities..and Venus in the south angle elevated above him, in cazini of the sun, declare rule, preëminence, and absolute sovereignty, in women. **1647** LILLY *Chr. Astrol.* xix. 113 A Planet is..in the heart of the Sunne, or in Cazimi, when he is not removed from him 17 min. [Hence in PHILLIPS, KERSEY, BAILEY, etc.]

cazique, var. of CACIQUE.

cazzan, cazzons: see CASING.

CB (siː'biː). orig. *U.S.* [The initial letters of *Citizens(') Band.*] = *Citizen('s) Band* s.v. CITIZEN 5; a Citizens' Band radio. Freq. *attrib.*, esp. as ***CB radio***.

1959 *Pop. Electronics* Aug. 130/2 Manufacturers eager to get their CB equipment on the market. **1964** *Electronics World* Jan. 51/1 CB was intended to serve the needs of small business. **1969** *Yachting* Feb. 60/2 The value of CB on a boat hangs on a framework of questions. *Ibid.* 61/1 To use CB, you must have other CB stations..on your waters or shores. **1975** *Courier-Mail* (Brisbane) 26 Oct. 36/4 CBs work on 23 radio channels open to the public. **1976** *National Observer* (U.S.) 24 Apr. 10/2 At least one automobile insurance company in Alabama has made theft coverage of CB radios available only for an additional premium. **1980** *Amer. Speech 1976* LI. 208 It sometimes seems as if each day brings another handbook for CB operators. **1985** *Church Times* 8 Feb. 8/2 The parish raised £2,000 to buy its first twenty-eight portable CB radio sets and batteries; and the CB villagers take them everywhere around the house and garden.

Hence **CBer** (siː'biːə(r)), one who operates a CB radio transmitter or receiver.

1959 *Pop. Electronics* Aug. 130/2 The prospective CB'er ..has many sets to choose from. **1975** *Courier-Mail* (Brisbane) 26 Oct. 36/11 Here in New York 'Cbers' gather ..to meet the people they have been bantering with over the air. **1981** *Daily Tel.* 20 July 3/1 In every city where there have been riots local CB'ers have offered their local police monitoring facilities.

Cd., see *command paper* s.v. COMMAND *sb.* 10.

ce- in OE. words, has become CH- or K-, q.v. No modern word in *ce-* is of Old English origin.

ce (siː), name of the letter C. Cf. CEE.

ce, obs. spelling of SEA, SEE, and in many words for SE- q.v.

ceace, obs. form of CEASE *v.*

ceal, obs. form of SEAL, CEIL.

‖**ceanothus** (siːəˈnəʊθʊs). [mod.L., ad. Gr. κεάνωθος 'a kind of thistle' (Liddell and Scott).] Red-root; a genus of flowering shrubs, belonging to the order *Rhamnaceæ*. The species *C. americanus*, cultivated in English gardens, is known in America as 'New Jersey Tea'.

1882 *Garden* 25 Feb. 129/2 The plant..grew against a south wall mingled with the dense growth of a Ceanothus.

cear, ceare, cearment, obs. ff. SEAR, CERE, CEREMENT.

cearge, var. of CIERGE, *Obs.*, wax candle.

cearse, var. of SEARCE, *Obs.*, sieve.

†ˈ**ceasable.** *Obs. rare.* In 6 -yble. [f. CEASE *v.* + -ABLE.] Liable to ceasing. ***never ceasable***: unceasing.

1510–20 *Compl. too late maryed* (1862) 7 Agenst the ryght canon of the holy byble Offens [have I] done to God never ceasyble.

cease (siːs), *v.* Forms: 4–5 cess-en, cese, 4–6 cesse, 6– cease. Also 4 sesse, ceesse, cece, sees, sesce, 4–5 cees(e, sesse, 4–6 ses(e, 5 sece, cecyn, ceysse, seace, seasse, seece, sees(e, seysse, secyn, sesyn, *Sc.* ceiss, seiss, 5–6 ceasse, 6 ceace, seas(e, seyse. [ME. *cesse-n*, a. F. *cesse-r* (= Pr. *cessar, sessar*, Sp. *cesar*, Pg. *cessar*, It. *cessare*): —L. *cēssāre* to give over, stop, freq. of *cēdĕre, cēss-um* to yield. Some of the obs. senses and constructions appear to be after L. *cēssāre*.]

I. Intransitive.

1. a. Of persons and other agents: To stop, give over, discontinue, desist (*from*, formerly *of*, an action); to come to the end or to an intermission of a state or condition of 'being, doing, or suffering'. Formerly, *cease off* was used, like *leave off*.

1330 R. BRUNNE *Chron.* (1810) 316 Þe kyng..teld his barons how, þat nede behoued him ses. *c* **1340** HAMPOLE *Prose Tr.* 10 Þat we sesse of all vyces. **138.** WYCLIF *Sel. Wks.* III. 302 Bi þis amortysyng þei wolen nevere cesse. *c* **1440** *York Myst.* xxii. 155 Sees of thy sawes, þou Sathanas. **1509** FISHER *Wks.* I. (1876) 59 He..neuer seaseth tyll it comes vnto the hyest parte of the soule. **1509** BARCLAY *Ship of Fooles* (1874) I. 97 Cease of your Foly. **1611** BIBLE *Jonah* i. 15 The sea ceased from her raging. **1651** HOBBES *Leviath.* II. xxviii. 165 Are either Enemies, or else they have ceased from being so. **1761** GRAY *Fatal Sisters* 52 Sisters, cease; the work is done. **1832** TENNYSON *Lotos-eaters* 65 Fold our wings, And cease from wanderings.

b. Const. *inf.* with *to*.

138. WYCLIF *Serm.* Sel Wks. I. 139 Þei wolen not..ceesse to anoye hem silf in bilding of hye housis. **1485** CAXTON *Chas. Gt.* 232 They seaced not to fyght. **1584** GREENE *Arbasto* i, Cease off to inquire farther in the cease. **1702** POPE *Sapho* 259 I'll..either cease to live, or cease to love! **1876** GREEN *Short Hist.* iii. §2. (1882) 120 An excommunicate king had ceased to be a Christian.

c. with pr. pple. expressing the action, after late L. *cessare agens*, used in the Vulgate in imitation of the construction of Gr. παύομαι. This construction coincides in form with 6 b, which see.

†**2.** = *Cease from action*: to rest, take rest, be or remain at rest. *Obs.* Cf. CEASING *vbl. sb.*

1382 WYCLIF *Joshua* xiv. 15 The loond cessside fro bataylis. **1483** *Vulg. abs Terentio* 13 b, Thow sesyste no tyme nor takist no hede to thy selfe. **1513** DOUGLAS *Æneis* VIII. i. 59 The nycht come, and all thing levand seisst. **1535** COVERDALE *2 Esdr.* xv. 22 My swerde shal not ceasse ouer them, that shed the innocent bloude. **1655–60** STANLEY *Hist. Philos.* (1701) 326/2 Matter..will cease if none move it.

3. Of actions, feelings, phenomena, etc.: To come to an end, be at an end. Formerly often conjugated with the auxiliary *be*; but some of the examples may be rather *passive* of 5, 6, or 7.

a **1300** *Cursor M.* 6032 Prai for me now, moyses þi lauerd to do þis thoner ses. *c* **1374** CHAUCER *Troylus* II. 434 But cesyd cause, aie cecith malady. **1413** LYDG. *Pylgr. Sowle* II. xli. (1859) 46 Now is al theyr noious labour secyd. **1535** COVERDALE *Ps.* lxxxiv[v]. 3 O God oure Sauioure..let thine anger ceasse from vs. **1541** ELYOT *Image Gov.* 91. **1599** SHAKS. *Hen. V*, I. i. 67 It must be so; for Miracles are ceast. **1620** tr. *Boccaccio's Decameron* 77 The modest murmure of the Assistants was ceased. **1796** H. HUNTER tr. *St. Pierre's Stud. Nat.* (1799) II. 418 The tomb of his adversary will cease to be honoured. **1819** *Monthly Mag.* XLVIII. 30 The noise was ceas'd Of all the angelic ring. **1879** FROUDE *Cæsar* xiv. 211 The influx of Germans on the Rhine must cease.

†**4.** = *Cease to exist*: to come to an end, fail, become extinct, pass away. *Obs.*

1382 WYCLIF *Ezek.* xxxiv. 25, I shal make for to ceese the werst beestis fro the erthe. **1393** GOWER *Conf.* II. 189 All moral vertu ceseth. **1586** THYNNE in *Animadv.* (1865) Introd. 74 Concerning the high constables of England, which office ceassed and tooke end at the duke of Buckingham. **1611** BIBLE *Deut.* xv. 11 The poore shall neuer cease out of the land. **1710** PRIDEAUX *Orig. Tithes* i. 20 When this Priesthood ceased, the Law..must cease also.

II. Transitive.

†**5.** To put a stop to (the action of others, a state or condition of things), to stop. *Obs.*

1393 GOWER *Conf.* II. 9 Thus was cessed the debate Of love. *c* **1399** *Pol. Poems* (1859) II. 6 He myghte oure dedly werre cesse. *c* **1450** LONELICH *Grail* xlv. 265 Sese this tempest and this torment That we ben nowe inne, Lord. **1534** MORE *On the Passion* Wks. 1300/2 The Pharisies woulde haue had hym ceace yᵉ voice of the people hymself. **1610** BARROUGH *Meth. Physick* I. xxxix. (1639) 62 Sapa..doth cease paine much more then sweet wine. **1629** MILTON *Ode Nativity* 45 He, her fears to cease, Sent down the meek-eyed Peace. **1691** E. TAYLOR tr. *Behmen's Threefold Life* xviii. 313 A dead man's sence is ceased.

6. a. To leave off, discontinue (one's own action; formerly also, one's anger or other passions).

c **1410** *Sir Cleges* 297 Sese your angrye mode! **1528** *Impeach. Wolsey* 178 in Furniv. *Ballads fr. MSS.* I. 357 Seas thyne insaciat covetous mynde. **1548** UDALL *Erasm. Par.* Pref. 4 a, God of his mercie was willing to ceasse his wrath and vengeaunce. **1604** E. GRIMSTON *Siege of Ostend* 199 Whereby he might be constrayned..to cease the dayly alarmes which hee gaue. **1728** GAY *Begg. Op.* II, Cease your funning. *a* **1744** POPE *Dying Chr. to Soul* v. 5 Cease, fond Nature, cease thy strife. **1751** JOHNSON *Rambl.* No. 127 ¶6 Others have ceased their curiosity. **1849** RUSKIN *Sev. Lamps* 3 To cease, for a little while, our endeavours. **1894** *Westm. Gaz.* 3 May 5/1 He appealed to those present who had ceased their connexion with their Union to again join it. **1899** *Ibid.* 24 Apr. 3/2 This plan of ceasing the edition, after a certain number. **1907** *Ibid.* 24 Aug. 2/1 In the United States, where players begin and cease the game years earlier than they do here.

b. with *vbl. sb.* as obj.

The vbl. sb. represents an earlier pr. pple.: see 1 c.

1382 WYCLIF *Ephes.* i. 16, I..ceesse not doynge thankyngis [Vulg. *non cesso gratias agens*] for you. *c* **1440** *Gesta Rom.* 34 (Harl. MS.), þei cessid neuer drinking by þe space of iij. days or iiij. *a* **1533** LD. BERNERS *Huon* xciii. 301 Desyre of hym in my name to sease fyghtynge. **1611** BIBLE *Numb.* viii. 25 From the age of fiftie yeeres they shall cease waiting vpon the service thereof. **1860** TYNDALL *Glac.* 215 Throughout the entire measurement the snow never ceased falling.

c. *Mil. cease fire*: see as main entry.

d. *Campanology.* To bring (a peal) to an end; to let (a bell) down.

1684 R. HOWLETT *School Recreation* 142 For Ceasing a Peal of Bells; Let them fall gradually from a set Peal. **1702** J. D. & C. M. *Campanalogia Impr.* 13 The learning to Raise and Cease a Bell in Peal. **1852** B. THACKRAH *Art of Change Ringing* 8 The raising and ceasing (or settling) a bell in peal. **1901** H. E. BULWER *Gloss. Techn. Terms Bells* 33 *Ceasing in order*, letting the bells down together, but in regular order of striking, as in ringing 'rounds' or some other sequence.

†**7.** To cause (an agent) to leave off (*of* an action); to appease, bring to rest, quiet. *Obs.*

c **1320** *Seuyn Sag.* 781 (W.) The grehound wolde nowt sessed be. *c* **1325** *E.E. Allit. P.* C. 391 Sesez childer of her sok, soghe hem so neuer. **1475** CAXTON *Jason* 66 b, Ysiphile ..cessed herself of her lamentacions. **1480** —— *Chron. Eng.* ccxlii. 282 They wold haue done moche harme..nadde the maire..seced hem with fayre wordes. **1526** TINDALE *Acts* xix. 35 When the toune clarcke had ceased the people. *a* **1560** ROLLAND *Crt. Venus* I. 5 Eolus..ceissit swyith the small foulis of their sang. **1575–85** ABP. SANDYS *Serm.* (1841) 61 The..Lord of our tranquillity hath ceased the waves of the sea.

cease (siːs), *sb.* Also 4 ses, 5 ceasse. [a. OF. *ces*, f. *cesser*: see prec.] = CEASING, CESSATION. *Obs.* exc. in the still occasional ***without cease***, without end, incessantly. (Cf. F. *sans cesse*.)

c **1330** *Arth. & Merl.* 3188 Of swiche bataile nas no ses To the night fram arnemorwe. **1490** CAXTON *Eneydos* xvi. 64 The other he made to watche without ceasse. **1583** STUBBES *Anat. Abus.* II. 57 They brought the world into a woonderfull perplexitie and cease. **1602** SHAKS. *Ham.* III. iii. 15 The cease of Maiestie dies not alone. **1662** R. MATHEW *Unl. Alch.* §99. 163 Which instantly hath caused cease of pain. **1798** *Log Vanguard* 2 Aug. in Nicolas *Disp. Nelson* (1845) III. 54, 55 minutes past 2, a total cease of firing. **1877** E. CONDER *Bas. Faith* ii. 65 We..think of space as..extending without cease in all directions. **1880** A. MITCHELL *What is Civilis.* 183 It is without cease and everywhere undergoing change.

cease, obs. f. of CESS, SEIZE.

ceased, *ppl. a.* [f. CEASE *v.* + -ED.] That has come to an end.

1553 GRIMALDE *Cicero's Offices* II. (1558) 81 The stinges of ceased libertie bee sharper than of libertie continued. **1633** P. FLETCHER *Purple Isl.* III. xv, With never ceas'd dissension. **1927** *Observer* 10 July 11/1 New stations..numbered 22,100, and ceased stations 13,044.

cease fire, cease-fire. Also 9 cease firing. [CEASE *v.* 6.] **a.** *Mil.* A command (by word of mouth, bugle, etc.) to cease firing guns.

1847 *Infantry Man.* (1854) 87 The fire is continued until the bugle sounds the *Cease*. *Ibid.* 89 The *Cease firing* has sounded. **1859** *Musketry Instr.* 56 At the conclusion of the practice..the bugler is to sound the 'cease fire'. **1884** *Daily News* 14 Mar. 6/3 'Cease-fire' presently sounded. **1916** 'IAN HAY' *First Hundred Thousand* xiii. 169 Both sides then proceed to discharge blank ammunition into one another's faces..until the 'cease fire' sounds. **1944** J. S. HUXLEY *On Living in Rev.* 139 The vast stores we shall need to rush into Europe as soon as the 'cease fire' sounds.

b. A cessation of shooting or fighting; an armistice.

1918 *Times* 12 Nov. 9/2 The 'Cease fire' of yesterday must be final and universal. **1926** T. E. LAWRENCE *Seven Pillars* cxiii. 597 Nuri put, as the condition of cease-fire, their instant ejectment of the Turks from the houses. **1949** KOESTLER *Promise & Fulf.* 188 The Jews accepted the Security Council's call for a cease-fire, the Arabs rejected it. **1965** *Spectator* 15 Jan. 64/3 The Indonesians are willing to call a ceasefire.

ceaseless (ˈsiːslɪs), *a.* [f. CEASE *sb.* + -LESS.] Without ceasing, unceasing, uninterrupted.

1586 MARLOWE *1st Pt. Tamburl.* v. j, Make our Souls resolve in ceaseless tears. **1593** SHAKS. *Lucr.* 967 Thou ceaseless lackey to eternity. **1764** GOLDSM. *Trav.* 9 With ceaseless pain. **1843** ARNOLD *Hist. Rome* III. 145 We..listen to their deep and ceaseless roar. **1873** SYMONDS *Grk. Poets* x. 314 Ceaseless beating of the spray.

Hence ˈ**ceaselessly** *adv.*, without ceasing, incessantly; ˈ**ceaselessness**, ceaseless quality.

1593 DRAYTON *Eclog.* x. 16 And me with hate, yet ceaslesly pursue. **1869** FREEMAN *Norm. Conq.* (1876) III. xii. 125 Every sort of damage was ceaselessly inflicted on the country around. **1877** LEGGE *Confucius* 309 To entire sincerity there belongs ceaselessness.

†ˈ**ceaser.** *Obs.* In 6 seaser, -our. [f. CEASE *v.* + -ER[1].] One who stops or puts a stop to.

1509 HAWES *Examp. Virt.* xi. 195 O kynge of loue, and seaser of debate. *Ibid.* xiii. 249 O amyable kynge, seasour of debate.

ceasing (ˈsiːsɪŋ), *vbl. sb.* [f. CEASE *v.* + -ING[1].]

1. The action of the verb CEASE, in its various senses; cessation. ***without ceasing***: incessantly.

a **1340** HAMPOLE *Psalter* cxliv. [cxlv.] 2 Ilk day wiþouten cessynge..i sall loue þe. **1490** CAXTON *Eneydos* xxxvi. 126 Thenne gaffe the kynge seassyng to hys wordes. **1592** GREENE *Art Conny-catch.* III. 19 The time of ceissing betweene the seuerall toyes and fancies hee plaied. **1611** BIBLE *1 Thess.* v. 17 Pray without ceasing. **1745** WARBURTON *Remarks Occas. Refl.* II. (R.) Spencer..did not mean by abrogation a ceasing, but an alteration. **1862** TRENCH *Poems, Justin Mart.* 11 The ceasing of this painful breath.

2. *Comb.* †**ceasing-day**, day of rest, sabbath.

1382 WYCLIF *Lev.* xxiii. 4 Thes ben the holy cesyng daies of the Lord.

ceasyble: see CEASABLE.

cebacic, cebal, obs. ff. SEBACIC, SABLE.

cebadilla: see CEVADILLA.

†**ceˈbell.** *Music. Obs.* or *Hist.* See quot.

1776 SIR J. HAWKINS *Hist. Music* (1853) II. 706 We meet also among the compositions of the English masters of the violin who lived in the time of Charles II, with an air called the Cebell..it appears to have been an air in duple time of four bars or measures, only repeated in division at the will of the composer..the several strains are alternately in the grave and the acute series of notes in the musical scale.

cebine (ˈsiːbaɪn), *a.* [f. CEB-US + -INE: in mod.L. *cebīnus*: see below.] Of, or pertaining to, the family of monkeys of which the Cebus is the type.

1863 HUXLEY *Man's Pl. Nat.* ii. 80 Some of the Cebine apes.

cebocephalic (ˌsiːbəʊsɪˈfælɪk), *a.* [f. Gr. κῆβο-ς monkey + κεφαλή head + -IC.] Monkey-headed.

1881 *Nature* XXIII. 235 A cebocephalic caprine monster.

†**cebratane.** *Obs.* [ad. Sp. *cebratana, cerbatana* of same meaning, app. ad. Arab. (and Pers.) *zabaṭāna, sabaṭāna* blowing tube for shooting birds (for which Piedro de Alcala has *zarbatāna*, Dozy); also found in Pg. *sarabatana*, It. *cerbottana*, Fr. *sarbatane, sarbacane*.]

A blow-pipe for shooting with.

1671 in SKINNER II. [who says it occurs only in a Dict.]. **1708–20** KERSEY, *Cebratan*, a Trunk to shoot at Birds with Clay-pellets. **1775** in ASH.

‖**Cebus** (ˈsiːbəs). [mod.L. a. Gr. κῆβος.] A genus of long-tailed monkeys, inhabiting the forests of S. America, including the Sapajous.

1863 BATES *Nat. Amazons* ix. (1864) 253, The White Cebus..inhabited the forests on the opposite side of the river. **1871** DARWIN *Desc. Man* (1885) 70 Thus Renegger observed an American Monkey (a Cebus) carefully driving away the flies which plagued her infant.

cec, cecchin, obs. forms of SICK, SEQUIN.

cece, obs. form of CEASE.

†ˈ**ceceril.** *Obs.* [? f. CE = C + *ceril* = CERILLA, CEDILLA.] The letter C with a cedilla (ç).

1753 CHAMBERS *Cycl. Supp.* s.v. *Cedilla*, The cedilla is called by some of our printers ceceril.

ceche, cechelle, obs. ff. CATCH *v.*, SATCHEL.

cecias, var. of CÆCIAS, north-east wind.

cecidium (sɪˈsɪdɪəm). Pl. cecidia. [mod.L., f. Gr. κηκίδιον ink, f. κηκίς a gall.] = GALL *sb.*[3] 1; (see also quot. 1902).

1902 *Encycl. Brit.* XXIX. 499/1 A great variety of deformations and growths produced by insects and mites as well as fungi has been described... The whole are now included under the term Cecidia; a prefix gives the name of the organism to which the attacks are due, *e.g.*, Phytoptocecidia are the galls formed by Phytoptid mites. **1946** *Nature* 14 Dec. 852/1 Plant-feeders which induce in their hosts the malformations termed galls or cecidia.

Cecils (ˈsɛsɪlz). 'A name for hashed beef' (Simmonds *Dict. Trade*). Minced meat, crumbs of bread, onions, chopped parsley, etc., with

seasoning, made up into balls, sprinkled with bread-crumbs, and fried.

1819 *New Syst. Dom. Cookery* (Murray) 39 To dress.. Cecils, Mince any kind of meat, crumbs of bread, a good deal of onion, some anchovies, etc... make them into balls of the size and shape of a turkey's egg, with an egg; sprinkle them with fine crumbs, and fry them of a yellow brown. **1831** *New Syst. Cookery* 51 To dress the same [cold beef] called Cecils.

cecily, obs. form of CICELY.

cecions, obs. form of SESSIONS.

cecity ('si:sɪtɪ). *arch.* Also 6 cecite, -tie, 6–9 cæcity. [ad. L. *cæcitās*, f. *cæcus* blind; cf. F. *cécité*. See -ITY.] Blindness. (Usually *fig.*)

1528 ROY *Sat.* (1845), To leade men in blynde cecite. *a* **1600** HOOKER *Serm.* iii. Wks 1845 III. 749 Unreasonable cecity and blindness. **1841** D'ISRAELI *Amen. Lit.* (1867) 355 The cecity of superstition. **1848** *Blackw. Mag.* LXIII. 64 His cecity was perhaps no absolute impediment to the discharge of his pastoral duties. **1882** M. ARNOLD *Ode Westm. Abbey*, After light's term, a term of cecity.

cecograph ('si:kəgrɑ:f, -æ-). [f. L. *cæcus* blind + Gr. γράφειν to write.] A writing apparatus for the blind.

1851 *Catalogue of Exhib.* III. 1187 Two pieces of apparatus called 'cecographo' for writing in black characters and small hand. **1874** KNIGHT *Dict. Mech.*, *Cecograph*, the French writing-apparatus for the blind; a chiragon.

cecropia (sɪ'krəʊpɪə). [mod.L. (C. Linnæus in P. Löfling *Iter Hispanicum* (1758) 272), f. *Cecrops*, an early king of Attica.]

1. Any tree of the genus so called of moraceous trees of tropical America, including some species whose milky sap yields rubber.

1824 H. E. LLOYD tr. *Spix & Martius's Trav. in Brazil* I. II. ii. 209 An impenetrable thicket, amidst which grow immense stems.. of silver-leaved cecropia. **1833** *Penny Cycl.* I. 447/1 Among the airy foliage of the mimosa, the cecropia elevates its giant leaves and heavy candelabra-shaped branches. **1875** *Encycl. Brit.* II. 98/1 The *Cecropia*, or trumpet tree of Central America, is tenanted by ants. **1930** P. C. STANDLEY *Flora of Yucatan* 244 The Cecropias are among the most conspicuous and characteristic trees of the Central American lowlands. **1969** T. H. EVERETT *Living Trees of World* 134/1 Natives use the bark of cecropias for making cordage.

2. A large silk moth, *Hyalophora cecropia*, belonging to the family *Saturniidæ* and found in the eastern United States.

1868 *Amer. Naturalist* II. 313 It is not a soft, flossy cocoon, like that of *Cecropia*. **1884** *Ibid.* XVIII. 1046 Poison Glands in the skin of the Cecropia caterpillar. **1885** *Ibid.* XIX. 1142 The anatomy of the Cecropia moth. **1909** MRS. STRATTON-PORTER *Girl of Limberlost* viii. 157 Big gray Cecropias come from this kind, brown Polyphemus from that. **1947** L. DUBKIN *Enchanted Streets* 152 The Cecropia is predominantly purple and orange, with two white crescents on the hind wings.

cecum, var. of CÆCUM, the blind-gut.

cecutiency (si:'kju:ʃɪənsɪ). [f. L. *cæcūtient-* pr. ppl. stem of *cæcūtīre* to be blind, f. *cæcus* blind. See -ENCY.] A tendency to blindness; partial blindness.

1646 SIR T. BROWNE *Pseud. Ep.* III. xviii. 152 There is in them [moles] no cecity, yet more then a cecutiency. **1656** in BLOUNT *Glossogr.* **1755** in JOHNSON. **1881** *Syd. Soc. Lex.*, *Cecutiency*, dimness of vision.

† **ce'cutient**, *a. Obs.*$^{-0}$ [f. as prec.] Partially blind, dim-sighted.

1721–1800 in BAILEY.

ced, obs. form of SEED.

cedar ('si:də(r)). Forms: 1 ceder, -or, 3–6 cedre, (4 cedri), 4–5 cedir, -ur, -yr, (cyder, -yr, sydyr), 6 ceder, 6– cedar. [ME. *cedre*, a. OF. *cedre*, ad. L. *cedrus*, ad. Gr. κέδρος; (the OF. repr. of *cedrus* would have been *cierre*). OE. *ceder* was directly ad. Lat.]

1. a. A well-known evergreen conifer, the *Pinus Cedrus* of Linnæus, *Abies Cedrus*, *Cedrus Libani* of other botanists, called Cedar of Lebanon from its most famous early locality.

c **1000** *Ags. Ps.* xxviii[ix]. 5 Se God bryсð þa hean ceder on Libano. *a* **1300** *Cursor M.* 1379 þe fader in cedre þou sal take, A tre of heght, þat has no make. *a* **1300** *E.E. Ps.* ciii. 16 þe cedres of Yban Whilk he planted with his hand. **1398** TREVISA *Barth. De P.R.* XVII. xxiii. (Tollem. MS.) The cedre is moste hyȝe tre, lady and quene of all tren. *a* **1520** *Myrr. Our Ladye* 282 Cedre, is a tree.. so durable that yt rotteth neuer. **1560** BIBLE (Genev.) *Song of Solomon* i. 17 The beames of our house are cedars and our rafters of firre. **1588** SHAKS. *Tit. A.* IV. iii. 45 Marcus we are but shrubs, no Cedars we. **1725** BERKELEY *Prop.* Wks. III. 222 Tall cedars that sheltered their orange trees from the north wind. *c* **1854** STANLEY *Sinai & Pal.* ii. (1858) 140 To them the cedar was a portent, a grand and awful work of God.

b. The wood of this tree.

a **1300** *Cursor M.* 8007 Wandis.. Of cydyr, pyne, and of cypress. *c* **1400** MAUNDEV. ii. 10 Cedre may not, in Erthe ne in Watre, rote. **1430** LYDG. *Chron. Troy* II. xi, The tymbre .. Was halfe of Cedre as I reherse can. **1697** DRYDEN *Virg. Georg.* III. 626 With Smoak of burning Cedar scent thy Walls. **1751** CHAMBERS *Cycl.*, *Cedar* is of so dry a nature, that it will not endure to be fastened with iron nails. **1847** TENNYSON *Princ.* II. 331 In halls Of Lebanonian cedar.

2. Applied to the genus *Cedrus*, or subgenus of *Abies*, which contains beside the Cedar of Lebanon, the Mount Atlas or Silvery Cedar (*A.* or *C. atlantica*) and the Deodara or Indian Cedar (*A.* or *C. Deodara*). The distinguishing character of cedars consists in the evergreen leaves disposed, many together, in fascicles, and the erect cones with their carpels separating from the axis.

3. Applied, with or without distinguishing epithet, to various trees more or less resembling the true cedar: including species of *Cedrela, Juniperus, Thuja, Cupressus, Pinus, etc.*: e.g. ***Barbadoes, Bermuda, Canary, pencil-wood, prickly, Virginia red, white cedar***, which are species of Juniper; ***Barbadoes bastard, Brazilian, Chinese, East Indian, falsa, Honduras, Jamaica, red Australian, Singapore, West Indian cedar***, which are species of Cedrela; ***British Columbian, Californian, white cedar***, which are Thujas; ***Bussaco, Goa, Oregon white, Port Orford white cedar***, which are Cypresses. **bastard cedar**, in different countries, applied to species of *Cedrela, Dysoxylon, Guazuma, Icica*. The 'cedar' used for black lead pencils is the wood of *Juniperus bermudiana* and *virginiana*, which also yield *oil of cedar*. Also **Cape cedar**, *Widdringtonia juniperoides*; **Dominica c.**, *Bignonia Leucoxylon*; **incense c.**, *Libocedrus*; **Japan c.**, *Cryptomeria japonica*; **Queensland c.**, *Pentaceras australis*; **red Californian c.**, *Libocedrus decurrens*; **Russian c.**, *Pinus Cembra*; **water c.**, *Chamæcy-paris*.

1703 *Art's Improv.* I. 26 Above all, is commended, the Oil of Cedar, or that of Juniper. **1725** SLOANE *Jamaica* II. 128 Cedar Tree [*Juniperus Barbadensis*].. It has a reddish, not close but lax, odoriferous wood. **1753** CHAMBERS *Cycl. Supp.* s.v., The cedar brought from Barbadoes and Jamaica is a spurious sort. Cedar cups.. are made out of the wood of the bastard cedar. **1756** P. BROWNE *Jamaica* 13 The cedar [*Cedrela odorata*] and mahogany.. may be raised with little care in all the waste hilly lands. **1794** MARTYN *Rousseau's Bot.* xxix. 459 Bermuda Cedar is.. imported for encasing black lead in pencils. **1856** OLMSTED *Slave States* 151 The main production [of the Great Dismal Swamp] has been of cypress and juniper, the latter commonly known as white cedar, at the North. **1872** OLIVER *Elem. Bot.* II. 247 The wood of *Juniperus virginiana* is commonly used for 'lead pencils', under the name of Red Cedar. **1880** 'SILVER & Co.' *S. Africa* (ed. 3) 125 They are patches of Cape Cedar.. and this is the only locality in which the tree is found.

4. *attrib.* and *Comb.*, as **cedar beam** (OE. = *tree*), ***forest, -nut, parlour, -pencil, pillar, -rail, shade, top, -tree, -wood***; ***cedar-coloured, -like*** adjs.; also **cedar apple, cedar ball**, a hard brown excrescence formed on cedar trees by various rusts; **cedar-bird**, the American Wax-wing, *Ampelis carolinensis*, a species of Chatterer haunting cedar-trees; **cedar chest** *U.S.*, a chest made of cedar-wood for the protection of clothing, etc., from moths and other insects; **cedar-nut**, the seed of *Pinus Cembra*; **cedar-swamp** *N. Amer.*, a swamp in which the cedar is the prevailing tree.

1849 C. LYELL *Second Visit to U.S.* II. 244 The cedar.. is often covered at this season with what is termed here the *cedar apple. **1882** WHITMAN *Specimen Days* 87 These cedar-apples last only a little while.. and soon crumble and fade. **1889** *Cent. Dict.*, Cedar-apple.. [is] also called *cedar-ball. *c* **1000** *Ags. Ps.* ciii[iv]. 16 Cwice *ceder-beamas, þa ðu cuðlice sylfa ȝesettest. **1611** BIBLE *1 Kings* vii. 2 With Cedar beames upon the pillars. **1791** W. BARTRAM *Trav. Carolina* (1792) 288 Ampelis garrulus; crown bird or *cedar bird. **1871** LOWELL *Study Wind.* (1886) 7 A flock of cedar-birds comes. **1883** *Century Mag.* Sept. 686/2 Three nests of the cedar-bird.. in a single orchard. **1836** W. IRVING *Astoria* I. 154 A *cedar canoe. **1775** in *Essex Inst. Hist. Coll.* XIII. 178 A Pane of Looking Glass in the same Trunk or the *Cedar Chest. **1895** *Century Mag.* July 323/2 Cedar-chest and camphor-trunk and flowered band-box have been called upon to disgorge their treasures. **1910** J. HART *Vigilante Girl* 219 A cedar chest full of finery made for a carnival dance. **1807** VANCOUVER *Agric. Devon* (1813) 36 A *cedar-coloured soil equally well-stapled. **1802** SOUTHEY *Thalaba* I. xxii, The woodman's face Open'd the *cedar-forest to the sun. **1631** B. JONSON *New Inn* III. i. (R.) His tall And growing gravity so *Cedar-like. **1863** MRS. ATKINSON *Tartar Steppes* 57 Each lady having a plate in her hand filled with *cedar nuts, which she was occupied in cracking and eating. **1878** MORLEY *Diderot* II. 48 The atmosphere of the *cedar-parlour. **1869** 'MARK TWAIN' *Innoc. Abr.* 398 Your friend's *cedar-pencil in your pocket. **1879** *Boy's Own Paper* 18 Jan. 14/3, I generally carry a great many cedar pencils. **1611** BIBLE *1 Kings* vii. 2 Foure rowes of *Cedar pillars. **1856** OLMSTED *Slave States* 151 Rough poles of the juniper, under the name of '*cedar-rails', are sent to New York. *a* **1835** MRS. HEMANS *Graves of Househ.*, The Indian knows his place of rest, Far in the *cedar shade. **1637** in *New Plymouth Col. Rec.* (1855) I. 51 A parcell of land.. betweene the two *cedar swamps at Iland Creeke Pond. **1793** J. MACDONELL *Diary* 18 June in C. M. Gates *Five Fur Traders* (1933) 81 A ditch.. which nature seems to have made through the centre of a *cedar Swamp*. **1876** PAGE *Adv. Text-bk. Geol.* xiv. 267 The pine-barrens and cedar-swamps of America. **1904** S. E. WHITE *Blazed Trail Stories* vi. 87 The high beech-ridge.. ended in a narrow cedar-swamp. **1592** SHAKS. *Ven. & Ad.* 858 *Cedar tops and hills seem burnished gold. *c* **1000** *Ags. Ps.* xxviii[ix]. 5 þæs Godes word brycþ *cedor-treowu. **1611** BIBLE *Numb.* xxiv. 6 As Cedar trees beside the waters. —— *Ezra* iii. 7 Cedar trees from Lebanon. **1719** DE FOE *Crusoe* (1840) I. xvi. 272, I pitched upon a.. cedar-tree. **1611** BIBLE *1 Chron.* xxii. 4 They of Tyre, brought much *Cedar wood to Dauid. **1887** *Whitaker's Almanack* 442 Among the chief exports of Costa Rica are tortoise-shell and cedar-wood.

cedared ('si:dəd), *ppl. a. rare.* [f. CEDAR + -ED².] Furnished with cedars.

1820 KEATS *St. Agnes* xxx, Cedar'd Lebanon. **1864** LOWELL *Fireside Trav.* 146 Cedared solitudes.

† **'cedarly**, *a. Obs. rare*$^{-1}$. Cedar-like.

1633 T. ADAMS *Exp. 2 Peter* iii. 18 Cedarly tallness.

cedarn ('si:dən), *a. poet.* [f. CEDAR + -EN.] Of or pertaining to cedar-trees; made of cedar.

1634 MILTON *Comus* 988 West winds.. About the cedarn alleys fling.. cassia's balmy smells. **1816** COLERIDGE *Kubla Khan*, Down the green hill athwart a cedarn cover. **1856** MRS. BROWNING *Aur. Leigh* v. 510 He cut his cedarn poems, fine As sketchers do their pencils. **1859** TENNYSON *Enid* 136 Moving toward a cedarn cabinet.

† **'cedary**, *a.* In 7 cedry. [f. CEDAR + -Y¹: cf. *sugary*, *watery*.] Having the colour or properties of cedar.

1664 EVELYN *Sylva* II. iii. §2 (T.) That which comes from Bergen being.. of a yellow or more cedry colour, is esteemed much before the white. **1847** in CRAIG, *Cedry*.

cede (si:d), *v.* Also 7 ced. [a. F. *céde-r* (16th c. in Littré), ad. L. *cēdĕre* to give way, yield, retreat. (? or directly from L.)]

† **1.** *intr.* To give way, give place, yield *to*.

1633 W. STRUTHER *True Happiness* 42 It is a great gift of God to seek God: It is second to no gift, because it is the first; It succeedeth no grace, which hath no precedent, and cedeth to none that hath the perfection of all. **1673** O. WALKER *Education* 266 In controversies let the master sometimes cede to his servant. *c* **1675** *Sc. Pasquils* (1868) 184 He only ceds to him [his father] in pedantrie. **1756** C. LUCAS *Ess. Waters* III. 264 [Let] private concerns always cede to the common good.

† **2.** Of possessions: To pass over *to*. *Obs.*

1756 SHENSTONE *Ruin'd Abbey* Wks. 1764 I. 317 This fair domain Had well nigh ceded to the slothful hands Of monks libidinous.

3. *trans.* To give up, grant; to yield, surrender: *esp.* to give up a portion of territory.

1754 A. DRUMMOND *Trav.* 256 (T.) That honour was entirely ceded to the Parthian royal race. **1787** T. JEFFERSON *Writ.* (1859) II. 316 This copy has been ceded to me as a favor. **1798** WELLINGTON in Gurw. *Disp.* I. 8 The provinces which Ld. Cornwallis had compelled him to cede to the Company. **1823** J. MARSHALL *Const. Opin.* (1839) 269 His most Christian Majesty ceded to the Queen of Great Britain, all Nova Scotia, etc.

Hence **'ceded** *ppl. a.*

1844 WILSON *Brit. India* II. II. xii. 545 The Ceded and Conquered provinces. **1886** YULE *Anglo-Ind. Gloss.*, *Ceded Districts*, a name applied familiarly at the beginning of this century to the territory south of the Tungabhadra river, which was ceded to the Company by the Nizam in 1800, after the defeat and death of Tippoo Sultan.

cedent ('si:dənt), *a.* and *sb.* [ad. L. *cēdent-em*, pr. pple. of *cēdĕre* to CEDE.]

† **A.** as *adj.* 'Giving place, departing, yielding'. *Obs. rare*$^{-0}$.

1656 in BLOUNT *Glossogr.*

B. *sb. Rom. & Sc. Law.* One who assigns property to another.

1592 *Sc. Acts Jas. VI* (1597) §145 The cedent remainis Rebelle and at the Horne. **1754** ERSKINE *Princ. Sc. Law* (1809) 345 Letters of diligence, which have been issued in the name of the cedent, cannot be executed by the messenger in the assignee's name. **1818** COLEBROOKE *Oblig. & Contracts* I. 210 The right passes.. from the cedent to the cessionary. [**1880** MUIRHEAD *Ulpian* xix. §9 Cession in court .. is accomplished by cooperation of three persons,—the cedent, the vindicant, and the addicent.]

ceder ('si:də(r)). *rare.* [f. CEDE *v.* + -ER¹.] One who cedes (territory or possession).

1887 *Daily News* 11 May 5/3 Ceder of the infinitely more important position at Zulficar.

cedi ('si:di:). [ad. Fante *sedi* a small shell.] The basic monetary unit of Ghana, equivalent to 100 pesewas.

1965 *Times* 14 July 11/7 All banks in Ghana will be closed from Thursday while the country switches over from pounds, shillings and pence to a decimal currency—cedis and pesewas. **1970** *Daily Tel.* (Colour Suppl.) 17 Apr. 59 (Advt.), When he started school in Accra, one of the first things he learned was that 1 cedi equals 100 pesewa.

cedilla (sɪ'dɪlə). [a. Sp. *cedilla* = It. *zediglia*, on L. type **zēticula*, dim. of *zēta* the letter *z*; see quot. 1878.] **a.** A mark (¸) derived from the letter *z*, written, especially in French and Portuguese (formerly also in Spanish) words, under *c*, to show that it has the 'soft' sound of the letter in positions in which the 'hard' sound would be normal, as before *a*, *o*, *u*. An earlier form was CERILLA.

CHAMBERS 1753 takes *cedilla* as the letter *c* with the subscript mark; printers still sometimes use it in this sense.

1599 MINSHEU *Span. Gram.* 6 Marked with a dash vnder it thus, ç, called ç Cerilla, or ç Cedilla, is proper to the Arabique tongue, from whence it was first taken. **1753** CHAMBERS *Cycl. Supp.*, *Cedilla*.. denotes a sort of small *c*, to the bottom of which is affixed a kind of virgula, as ç... The cedilla is called by some of our printers a ceceril. **1878**

KITCHIN tr. *Brachet's Fr. Dict.* s.v., The cedilla was a *z*, placed first by the side of, afterwards underneath the letter affected.

b. Used in modern Turkish to indicate that a *c* is sounded (tʃ) and an *s* (ʃ).

1929 *Nat. Geogr. Mag.* Jan. 102/1 On the street cars the old bilingual signs in Arabic-script Turkish and Latin-lettered French have given way to clearer signs in New Turkish, which is equally easy for the foreigner to read, even if the 'd' and 't' and the 'b' and 'p' seem to be juggled somewhat and cedilla and umlaut markings added. **1933** *Slavonic & E. European Rev.* XII. 712 *C* with the cedilla.. is in common use in French (also in Portuguese and Turkish). **1978** *Hart's Rules for Compositors* (ed. 38) 134 *Turkish*. Note the accented letters *Ç ç Ş ş* (with cedilla) *Ğ ğ* (with *round* accent).

‖**'cedmata**, *sb. pl.* [mod.L., a. Gr. κέδματα sb. pl.] (See quots.) Hence †**'cedmatous** *a. Obs.*

1715 KERSEY, *Cedmata* (G.), humours falling down upon the joynts, especially about the Hips. **1736** in BAILEY. **1775** in ASH. **1881** *Syd. Soc. Lex.*, *Cedmata*, old name for chronic pains of the joints, particularly the hip-joint.

cedr-, repr. L. *cedr-us* cedar, forming terms of chemistry, etc. **'cedrene**, a liquid hydrocarbon ($C_{32}H_{21}$) found in the resin of the cedar of Lebanon. †**'cedria**, a name applied sometimes to the oil of cedar, sometimes to the pitch or resin, but properly to the crude tears of the cedar. (*Syd. Soc. Lex.*) **cedriret**, a product obtained by Reichenbach from the tar of beechwood, said to crystallize in fine needles. **'cedrium** = *cedria*.

c **1420** *Pallad. on Husb.* I. 926 Thai thurle a nutte, & stuffe it so withinne With brymstoon, chaf, & cedria. **1579** LANGHAM *Gard. Health* (1633) 127 Cedria, the liquor of Cedar swageth toothach being put therein. **1847** CRAIG, *Cedriret* crystallises into a kind of net-work, composed of red crystals. **1708–15** KERSEY, *Cedrium*.

cedrat, -ate ('siːdrɪt). [a. F. *cédrat*, ad. It. *cedrato*, f. *cedro* (:—L. *citrus*) citron.] A variety of the citron or lemon.

1781 J. T. DILLON *Trav. Spain* 399 The cedrats are so large as sometimes to weigh more than six pounds. **1783** HAMILTON in *Phil. Trans.* LXXIII. 195 The agrume (the general name of all kind of orange, lemon, cedrate, and bergamot-trees). **1847** CRAIG, *Cedrate Lemon*, a variety.. with round smooth fruit, having a long acute point.

†**cedrated**, *ppl. a. Obs.*—⁰ [f. mod.L. *cedrātus* + -ED.] 'Anointed with juice or oil of cedar-trees' (Bailey 1736).

1775 in ASH.

‖**'cedre.** *Obs.* [Fr., ad. It. *cedro* citron.] = CEDRAT.

1712 tr. *Pomet's Hist. Drugs* I. 150 That which bears the Name of the Cedre or Bourgamot. **1708–15** KERSEY, *Cedre* (F.), a kind of Citron, or Lemon.

‖**Cedrela** (sɪ'driːlə). [mod.L., a. Sp. *cedrela*, dim. of *cedro*, *cedra* CEDAR. In F. *cédrel*.] A genus of large trees, common in the West Indies, Hindostan, and Australia, species of which are called *Cedar* or *Bastard Cedar*.

1836 MACGILLIVRAY tr. *Humboldt's Trav.* xiv. 169 The thick forest abounding in Cedrelas. **1871** MATEER *Travancore* 98 Febrifuges, such as the bark..of Cedrela.

cedrelaceous (siːdrɪ'leɪʃəs), *a. Bot.* [f. mod.L. *cedrela* + -ACEOUS.] Of, or pertaining to, the *Cedrelaceæ*, or Cedrela order, which includes the cedar of Australia, and the mahogany-tree of the Spanish Main.

‖**cedrelate.** *Obs. rare.* [L. *cedrelatē*, Gr. κεδρελάτη, f. κέδρ-ος cedar + ἐλάτη pine-tree.] (See quots.)

1601 HOLLAND *Pliny* I. 388 Of the greater Cedar there bee two kindes... Some cal this Cedar, Cedrelate: whereof cometh the best Rosin. **1736** BAILEY, *Cedrelate*, the large sort of cedar, which grows as big as a fir-tree, and yields rosin or pitch as that does. **1775** in ASH.

'cedrin. *Chem.* The crystalline active principle of cedron seeds.

1863 WATTS *Dict. Chem.* s.v., The fruit [of Cedron] after exhaustion with ether, yields to alcohol a crystallisable substance cedrin.

cedrine ('siːdrɪn, -aɪn), *a.* [ad. L. *cedrin-us* of cedar.] Of or pertaining to cedar.

1736 BAILEY, *Cedrine*. *a* **1794** SIR W. JONES *Tales* (1807) 179 Iv'ry roofs, and cedrine floors.

'cedron. **a.** A small tree of New Granada (*Simaba Cedron*, N.O. *Simarubaceæ*). **b.** The fruit of this tree. Also *attrib.*

1859 MARCY *Prairie Trav.* iv. 131 Cedron..is a nut that grows on the Isthmus of Panama..said to be an infallible antidote to serpent-bites. **1866** *Treas. Bot.* 1059 The Cedron of commerce which looks like a blanched almond, but is larger, is the kernel of this fruit. **1882** *Syd. Soc. Lex.*, Cedron seeds..are employed as a remedy for the bites of serpents, for hydrophobia, and for intermittent fevers.

cedry, obs. f. CEDARY.

‖**'cedula.** [Sp. *cédula* ('θedula), SCHEDULE, q.v.] A permit or order issued by the Spanish government; also applied to securities issued by some of the S. American governments.

1724 *Lond. Gaz.* No. 6323/2 The King of Spain's Cedula for the South Sea Company's annual Ship. **1739** *King's Declar. War agst. Spain* in Beatson *Nav. & Mil. Mem.* (1790) I. App. 10 Notwithstanding the many promises made, and cedulas issued, signed by the said King [of Spain]. **1919** J. M. KEYNES *Econ. Conseq. Peace* v. 164 Germany has also sold certain overseas securities, such as Argentine cedulas. **1951** J. C. FENNESSY *Sonnet in Bottle* III. i. 56 Passports and cedulas and customs formalities.

cedule, early spelling of SCHEDULE.

†**'ceduous**, *a. Obs. rare*⁻¹. [f. L. *cæduus*, f. *cæd-ĕre* to fell: SEE -UOUS.] Suitable for felling.

1664 EVELYN *Sylva* (1679) 2 These [trees] we shall divide into the greater and more ceduous, fruticant, and shrubby. **1736** BAILEY, *Ceduous*, as ceduous trees, such as are us'd to be cut or lopp'd. **1847** in CRAIG, etc.

cedyr, obs. form of CIDER.

cee (siː). Name of the letter C. **a.** See quot. 1542. **b.** A term formerly current in the Universities for a certain quantity of beer.

1542 RECORDE *Gr. Artes* A vj b, C, a cee, the xvj. part of a penny. q, a kewe, the viij. [part]. **1628** EARLE *Microcosm.* (Arb.) 38 Hee [old College Butler] domineers ouer Freshmen..and puzzles them with strange language of Cues, and Cees, and some broken Latine. **1635** *1st Pt. Jeronimo* in Hazl. *Dodsley* IV. 367 Hast thou..suck'd Philosophy, ate cues, drank cees?

cee, obs. form of SEA, SEE.

ceede, obs. form of CEDE, SEED.

Ceefax ('siːfæks). [Repr. pronunc. of *see*ing + *fac*simile.] The proprietary name for a teletext system operated by the B.B.C. Cf. ORACLE *sb.*¹ 10.

1972 *Guardian* 24 Oct. 24/3 BBC engineers have invented a system which would give television viewers thirty television 'pages' of news at the push of a button. The system [is] patented under the name of Ceefax. **1973** *Trade Marks Jrnl.* 13 June 1139/1 *Ceefax*... Telecommunications apparatus for use with television transmitters and receivers and for the transmission and display of data. The British Broadcasting Corporation. **1975, 1976** [see ORACLE *sb.*¹ 10]. **1983** *Listener* 16 June 38/1 Telesoftware is carried by teletext—in other words, it is part of the BBC's Ceefax service.

ceekenesse, obs. form of SICKNESS.

ceel(e, obs. ff. CEIL *v.*, CELL, SEAL, SELE, time.

ceeldam, celdom, obs. ff. SELDOM.

ceeler, var. of CELURE, *Obs.*

ceem, obs. f. SEAM, SEEM.

ceene, var. of SENE², *Obs.*, synod.

ceerche, ceercle, obs. ff. SEARCH, CIRCLE.

ceere, obs. form of CERE *v.*

ceese, ceesse, obs. ff. CEASE, SEIZE.

cee spring, c-spring. *Coach-building.* A spring, shaped like the letter C, used to support the body of a carriage.

1794 W. FELTON *Carriages* (1801) I. 72 Named according to their shape..the S, the C, the..grasshopper spring. **1825** HONE *Every-day Bk.* I. 1525 The springs..differ not from the present fashionable C spring. **1878** MRS. EDWARDES *Jet* xiii. 568 Her ambition is bounded by a brougham on C springs. **1884** *Times* 30 Oct. (Advt.) 13/5 An elegant light patent landau, brougham, patent cee-spring Princess Victoria and mail phaeton.

cege, cegge, obs. ff. SIEGE, SEDGE.

‖**ceiba** ('saɪbə). [Sp. (θe'iba); possibly of native West Indian origin.] The God-tree, Silk Cotton-tree of the W. Indies, *Eriodendron anfractuosum* (*Bombax Ceiba*). (Miller.)

1812 S. ROGERS *Columbus* x. 157 Ceiba, and Indian fig, and plane sublime. **1843** PRESCOTT *Mexico* II. iv. (1864) 92 He gave three cuts with his sword on a large ceiba tree which grew in the place. **1852** TH. ROSS tr. *Humboldt's Trav.* II. xvi. 3 The ceiba with its large yellow flowers. **1879** BODDAM-WHETTHAM *Roraima* 63 One who..kneels before an oak as the wild Indian does before his ceiba.

ceil (siːl), *sb. poet. rare.* [f. next.] = CEILING. (Cf. the earlier CYLL.)

1840 GALT *Demon Dest.* VII. 48 The awning clouds were as a cavern's ceil. **1861** *Bentley Ballads* 47 As the figures we see in an arabesque..In Gothic vaulted ceils.

ceil, ciel (siːl), *v.* Forms: 5 ceel-yn, selyn, 6 seele, sele, cele, cyle, syle, (*Sc.* syill), 6–7 seel(e, 7 seil(e, siel, ceal, seal, 7– ciel, ceil. [Of *ceil* v. (recorded of date 1428) and the derived *ceiling* (1380), *ceiled*, with the cognate sb. found as CYLL in sense of 'canopy' *c* 1500, *celure*, found as *sylLure*, *sylure* ? *a* 1400, the derivation is doubtful. The group is not very old in Eng., and traces of it in French are scanty.

Three sources have been suggested: (1) L. *cēlāre*, F. *celer* (11th c. in Littré) to hide, conceal, cover up; (2) L. *cælāre* to carve, engrave in relief; (3) L. *cælum* sky, vault of heaven. If L. *cēlāre* could be shown to have acquired in late L. or Romanic the simple sense of 'cover', it would suitably explain the Eng. words in all their uses; but such is not the case, and in particular, F. *celer* does not appear to approach the required sense. In favour of L. *cælāre* (cf. *cieler* Godef.) there are certainly early quotations (see sense 1, and CEILING 1) in which 'carve', 'carving', is a possible sense; but nothing of the kind occurs under CELURE, and if *ceil* ever meant 'carve' this sense evidently soon entirely gave way to one congruous with that of CELURE. On the other hand we have the known fact that med.L. *cælum*, It. *cielo*, F. *ciel*, acquired the sense of 'canopy, vault, roof, tester of a bed, etc.'; and there are traces of a derived vb. *cælāre* to canopy or vault, whence *cælātum*, *cœlātūra*, in senses identical with or derived from *cælum*. Difficulties are that while *ceil* v. and *celure* were so common in 15–16th c. English, and can hardly be connected with L. exc. through Fr., their occurrence in OF. itself is extremely rare: a single instance of *cielee* pa. pple. (with variants *celee*, *chelee*, *couverte*) has been noted in Chrestien de Troyes, Ywain (ed. Förster 964). It is possible that **celeüre*, **celure*:—L. *cælātūra* was common in Anglo-French, and thence passed into English, but the whole subject remains for the present beset with conflicting difficulties; the apparently certain point being that we cannot separate the Eng. words from *cælum*, *ciel*, canopy. See CELURE.]

†**1.** *trans.* ? To furnish with a canopy, hangings, or a screen. *Obs.* Cf. CELURE.

c **1440** *Promp. Parv.* 65 Ceelyn wythe syllure, *celo*. *Ibid.* 452 Selyn wythe sylure, *celo*.

†**2.** To cover with a lining of woodwork, sometimes of plaster, etc. (the interior roof or walls of a house or apartment); to wainscot. *Obs.*

1428 in Heath *Grocers' Comp.* (1869) 6 The seide parlore ..lattizid, glazid and selyd. **1519** HORMAN *Vulg.* in *Promp. Parv.* 65 These wallys shal be celyd with cypruese. The rofe shall be celed vautwyse and with cheker work. **1535** COVERDALE *2 Chron.* iii. 5 The greate house syled he with Pyne tre, and ouerlayed it with the best golde. [WYCLIF covered; **1611** sieled; Vulg. *texit*; Heb. has same word *hpph* for both *syled* and *ouerlayed*.] **1538** LELAND *Itin.* VII. 87 Fine greynyd Okes, apte to sele Howses. **1599** MINSHEU *Sp. Dict.*, *Enyessar*, to seele or plaister houses. ? *a* **1600** *Aberd. Reg.* (Jam. s.v. *Sile*), To syill the kirk. **1611** COTGR., *Plancher*, to seele or close, with boards.

fig. **1598** SYLVESTER *Du Bartas* I. ii. (1641) 18/2 This proud Palace where we rule and dwel..had fall'n long since, Had't not been siel'd-round with moist Elements. **1615** WITHER *Sheph. Hunt.*, *Juvenil.* (1633) 419 A Bower..Seil'd so close, with boughes all greene Tytan cannot pry betweene.

b. To overlay (with gold, marble, etc.).

1601 HOLLAND *Pliny* II. 571 Slitting marble into thin plates, therewith to couer and seel as it were the outsides of walls. **1628** WITHER *Brit. Rememb.* 181 Their Palaces they seele and trim with gold.

3. *esp.* To line the roof of, provide or construct an inner roof for (a building or apartment); *usually*, to plaster the roof. Cf. CEILING 5.

1519 [see 2]. **1696** *Phil. Trans.* XIX. 536 The Church is very Lofty, and Cealed with Irish Oak. **1756** NUGENT *Gr. Tour, Germany* II. 333 The rooms are wainscoted and cieled with ash of Poland. **1799** *Monthly Rev.* XXVIII. 517 Every apartment is floored with sandal, and ceiled with nacre. **1859** JEPHSON *Brittany* iii. 27 The nave has just been ceiled in wood.

fig. **1876** MRS. WHITNEY *Sights & Ins.* xxxiv. 317 Enormous precipices wall it in; the clear blue ceils it over.

4. *Naut.* To line (a ship, or a compartment in a ship). Cf. CEILING 4 b.

1691 T. H[ALE] *Acc. New Invent.* 85 The Bread-room.. being seeled with Lead [on p. 84 the words used are 'lined with lead'].

ceile, var. of SELE, *Obs.*, time, happiness.

ceiled, cieled (siːld), *ppl. a.* [f. prec. + -ED.]

†**1.** Having the interior (roof or walls) overlaid or lined with wood, etc.; wainscoted. *Obs.* exc. *Naut.*; see CEIL *v.* 4.

1539 BIBLE (Taverner) *Haggai* i. 4 Ye your selues can fynd tyme to dwell in syled houses. **1562** J. HEYWOOD *Prov. & Epigr* (1867) 179 Walles, Som seeld, some hangd. *a* **1617** HIERON *Wks.* I. 640 The..large chambers, sieled with ceder, and painted with vermilion. **1611** BIBLE *Haggai* i. 4 Is it time for you, O yee, to dwell in your sieled [**1633** cieled] houses? **1853** KANE *Grinnell Exp.* ii. (1856) 20 The entire interior was lined, ceiled, with cork.

2. Having the roof covered or plastered internally, so as to conceal the rafters, etc.; provided with a ceiling.

1872 BRET HARTE *Prose & P.* I. 159 The dark platform, which led to another low-ceiled room. **1872** *Daily News* 3 Oct. 5 The kitchen is a ceiled, papered, and carpeted room.

3. *transf.* and *fig.* Covered, overlaid; studded.

c **1430** LYDG. *Bochas* VII. v. (1554) 169 a, With plate of gold cyled, yᵗ shone full shene. **1598** SYLVESTER *Du Bartas* (1608) 232 The arches starry seeld, Where th' all-creator hath disposed well The Sun and Moon.

ceiler, variant of CELURE, *Obs.*

ceilidh ('keɪlɪ). Also ceilidhe. [Irish *céilidhe*, Sc. Gael. *cèilidh*, f. OIr. *céile* companion.] In Scotland and Ireland: **a.** An evening visit, a friendly social call. **b.** A session of traditional music, storytelling, or dancing. Also *attrib.* and *fig.*

1875 *Celtic Mag.* I. 40 The Highland Ceilidh. *Ibid.*, The fire in the centre of the room was almost a necessity in the good old *Ceilidh* days. **1904** *Daily Chron.* 17 Mar. 3/1 Participants..narrated their incidents at the 'ceilidh', round the cottage fire. **1935** L. A. G. STRONG *Seven Arms* 76 He was a great man at a ceilidh, a good guest, and a good host. **1959** *Times* 10 Jan. 7/6 All over the British Isles today at ceilidhes, hootenannys and similar gatherings in pubs, clubs

and private houses, folk music is flourishing as it has not done for over a century. **1959** *Times* 7 Aug. 13/6 The informal *ceilidhe* atmosphere. **1965** *Listener* 24 June 925/1 Broadcasting House, London, was a small circle of loved, fond faces, and its programmes a perpetual ceilidh of safe and familiar songs and stories.

ceiling, cieling ('siːlɪŋ), *vbl. sb.* Forms: 4 celyng, (6 sel-, sil-, syling), 6–7 **seeling**, 7 **ceeling**, 7–8 **siel(e)ing**, 6– **cieling**, 7– **ceiling**. [f. CEIL *v.* + -ING[1].]

I. The action of the verb CEIL.

†**1.** The action of lining (the roof or walls of) an apartment with boards, or (more rarely) with plaster, etc. *Obs.* exc. *Naut.*

(The sense 'carving' is possible in the two earliest quots.)
1497 *Acc. Ld. Treas.* I. 357 (Jam. s.v. *Siling*) Item, to the kervour that tuk in task the siling of the chapel, in part of payment, ij *lib.* xiiijs. **1519** HORMAN *Vulg.* 243 Vautynge, and celynge, with cunnyng caruynge and peyntynge.. ornatteth wondersly lordys howsis. **1627** CAPT. SMITH *Seaman's Gram.* ii. 13 There remaines nothing..but onely seeling the Cabins. **1688** R. HOLME *Armoury* III. 149/2 Seileing is House Painting where Plaister Walls are made to look like Wainscate or outlandish Timber.

2. *esp.* The lining of the roof of a room with woodwork, plaster, or the like; now, usually, with lath and plaster.

1764 HARMER *Observ.* iii. 90 Their cieling their rooms with wood and neatly painting, and sometimes gilding them. **1801** HUTTON *Course Math.* (1828) II. 88 Plasterers' work.. namely, ceiling, which is plastering on laths.

II. *concretely.*

†**3.** A screen of tapestry, a curtain. *Obs.*

c **1450** *Voc.* in Wr.-Wülcker 626 Celynge, *velamen.* **1548** HALL *Chron.* (*14 Edw. IV*) I. 232 b, The Frenche kyng.. caused the lord of Countay..with the lord of Argenton.. to stande secretly behynd a selyng or a hangyng in his chamber ..so that what soever were purposed to hym, they standing behind the clothe, might easely se, and facile heare the same. **1577** tr. *Bullinger's Decades* (1592) 342 He is the curtaine and seeling, the rafter and ornament of his church. **1632** SANDERSON *12 Serm.* 343 Creepeth in betweene the walls and seelings.

†**4. a.** The wooden lining of the roof or walls of a room: panelling; wainscoting. *Obs.* Cf. CEIL *v.* 2.

c **1380** *Sir Ferumb.* 1231 þe celynge with-inne was siluer plat & with red gold ful wel yguld. **1555** *Fardle Facions* II. i. 117 They haue—cielinges, voultinges, dores and gates couered with siluer. **1598** FLORIO. *Cielo*, the seeling, vpper-face or rooffe of a house. **1612** BACON *Ess. Vain-glory* (Arb.) 464 Varnish, that makes Seelings not onely Shine, but Last. **1632** *Vestry Bks.* (Surtees) 187 Five yeards and a halfe of square sealing to the orgaine frame. **1634** BRERETON *Trav.* (1844) 67 They go out into the room about three-quarters of a yard, and are faced with some neat sieleing.

b. *Naut.* The inside planking of a ship's bottom carried up to the lowest deck; = FOOT-WALING.

1633 T. JAMES *Voyage* 50 In the runne of her..he cut away the sealing. **1662** FULLER *Worthies* (1840) II. 117 Their cieling was dammed up with a certain kind of mortar to dead the shot. **1688** CLAYTON in *Phil. Trans.* XVII. 783 Cutting..the Seeling of the Ship, they immediately stopt the Leak. **1749** WADDELL *ibid.* XLVI. 112 Another Part of it went through the Starboard Side, without any Hurt to the Ceiling (or inside Plank). **1772–84** COOK *Voy.* (1790) I. 203 Between the inside lining of the ship's bottom, which is called the cieling, and the outside planking, there is a space of about seventeen or eighteen inches. **1869** SIR E. REED *Ship Build.* xix. 424 The Liverpool rule..states that the ceiling in the flat of hold is to be laid in hatches.

5. a. *esp.* The undercovering of a roof or floor, concealing the timbers; the plaster of the top of a room.

1535 COVERDALE *Song of Sol.* i. 17 Y[e] sylinges of oure house are of Cedre tre, & oure balkes of Cypresse. **1598** GRENEWEY *Tacitus' Ann.* IV. xv. (1622) 133 Betweene the roofe and the seeling, the three Senators..hid themselues. **1610** G. FLETCHER *Christ's Vict.*, It [my cottage] doth adore thee with the seeling low. **1667** PRIMATT *City & C. Builder* 67 Every hundred of Laths cover six yards of Ceeling or Partitioning. **1716–8** LADY M. W. MONTAGUE *Lett.* I. xxxvi. 136 The ceiling is always of wood..inlaid or painted with flowers. **1731** FIELDING *Grub St. Op.* I. xi, Do'st thou not expect the cieling to fall down on thy head for so notorious a lie? **1874** PARKER *Illust. Gothic Archit.* I. iii. 53 At Canterbury..the choir itself had a flat boarded ceiling. **1878** GROVE *Dict. Mus.* I. 172 The water had found its way through the ceiling into the room beneath.

b. *to hit the ceiling* : to become very angry, to lose one's temper. *colloq.*

1914 *Living Age* (U.S.) Aug. 374 He will..'get warm round the collar', and may even 'hit the ceiling'. **1930** WODEHOUSE *Very Good, Jeeves!* xi. 287, I haven't breathed a word to Angela. She'd hit the ceiling. **1958** E. DUNDY *Dud Avocado* II. i. 193 Larry hit the ceiling and said he *had* to come along, that he'd spoil everything if he didn't.

6. a. *transf.* and *fig.*

1596 DRAYTON *Leg.* I. 344 The Brow of Heav'n..The gorgeous Seeling of th' immortall Frame. **1614** T. ADAMS *Devil's Banq.* 315 You that haue neglected heauen, which God hath made your more glorious seeling. *c* **1630** DRUMM. OF HAWTH. *Poems* Wks. (1711) 322 Those boundless bounds where stars do move, The cieling of the christal round above. **1821** CLARE *Vill. Minstr.* I. 205 The rose's blushing bloom, Loveliest cieling of the bower.

b. *Aeronaut.* The maximum altitude at which a particular aircraft can maintain horizontal flight (in full *absolute ceiling*, see ABSOLUTE *a.* 16); also, the altitude beyond which the rate of climbing falls below 100 feet per minute (in full *service ceiling*, see SERVICE *sb.*[1]).

1917 *Jane's All the World's Aircraft* 9a/4 The extreme height to which an aircraft will rise,..familiarly known as the 'ceiling' or 'roof' of that particular machine. **1919** *Parlt. Papers* X. 49 In a long flight it is most economical to climb an aeroplane in the attitude corresponding to the maximum value of the lift-drag ratio until it approaches its ceiling. **1919** TRENCHARD in *Lond. Gaz.* 1 Jan. 136/2 Ceiling was of more importance than speed for long-distance day bombing work. **1928** *Fortn. Rev.* Dec. 764 Its ceiling when fully loaded was sometimes far under 10,000 feet.

c. *Meteorol.* (See quots.) See also *cloud-ceiling*. Also *attrib.*

1930 *Monthly Weather Rev.* LVIII. 202/1 Ceilings are seldom low enough to measure by means of a ceiling light, or ceiling balloons. **1931** C. J. MAGUIRE *Aerology* ii. 31 Cloud height or 'ceiling' may be obtained..by releasing a balloon inflated to a known ascensional rate and noting the time elapsing before disappearance in the clouds (special balloons for this purpose are called ceiling balloons). **1939** G. F. TAYLOR *Aeronaut. Meteorol.* ii. 30 The term ceiling as employed in aviation is defined as the distance between the surface of the ground and the base of the lowest cloud layer. **1941** S. PETTERSSEN *Introd. Meteorol.* ii. 40 In the United States the ceiling is defined as the height in feet of the lowest level below 10,000 ft. above the ground at which the total cloudiness covers more than one-half of the sky. **1968** R. M. PATTERSON *Finlay's River* 115 Coming down through a low ceiling of cloud to find, unexpectedly, the river littered with running ice.

d. An upper limit (to quantity, prices, expenditure, etc.); a maximum. Also *attrib.* Cf. FLOOR *sb.*[1] 1 c.

1934 *Sun* (Baltimore) 18 Oct. 19/1 A blanket acreage-reduction contract between farmers and the Government would have approximately the same ultimate effect in keeping the 'calory ceiling' down. *Ibid.* 13 Dec. 1/8 A 'ceiling' or fixed limit..upon all commodity prices. **1936** *Brit. Jrnl. Psychol.* Jan. 270 Towards the 'ceiling' of the test —the highest possible score—it seems reasonable to suppose that the curve will become more horizontal. **1937** *Times* 13 Apr. p. xv/1 Six months' intensive development work..has now made it possible for a car to be driven all out.. indefinitely with a ceiling oil temperature of 180 deg. F. **1938** [see FLOOR *sb.*[1] 1 c]. **1955** L. D. LANDAU in W. Pauli *N. Bohr* 60 The theory considered..seems to have a 'ceiling', in that it cannot in principle be used to discuss an energy greater than $Λ_κ$. **1956** *Jrnl. Educ.* July 290 It is helpful to have a ceiling figure for the purchase of furniture in new buildings. **1958** *Spectator* 15 Aug. 233/1 The national debt ceiling.

7. *Comb.*, mostly *attrib.*, as ***ceiling-board, -joist, -lamp, -light, -relievo, -sky, -work***; also ***ceiling-wards*** adv. **ceiling rose, rosette** (see quot. 1910).

c **1520** *Mem. Ripon* (Surtees) III. 202 Johanni Henryson ..sawyng seylyng bordes per iij dies et di., 21*d.* **1535** COVERDALE *Ps.* lxxiii. [lxxiv.] 6 They cutt downe all the sylinge worke of y[e] Sanctuary with bylles & axes. **1663** GERBIER *Counsel* 68 Seeling Joyses on Cellaring. **1751** CHAMBERS *Cycl.* s.v., A covering of plaster over laths nailed, where there is no upper room, on joists for the purpose: hence called ceiling joists. **1840** HOOD *Kilmansegg* li. 4 Nothing but gold!.. On the walls..the ceiling-sky. **1848** THACKERAY *Van. Fair* vii. 59 The ceiling lamp is muffled up in a dismal sack of brown holland. **1850** LEITCH tr. *Müller's Anc. Art* §402. 537 A Nereid..in a ceiling-relievo at Palmyra. **1879** *Daily News* 21 Aug. 3/1 These princesses who piously fold their hands and look ceiling-wards. **1889** *Brit. Patent* 5955 1 Improved ceiling rose for electrical circuits. **1901** L. M. WATERHOUSE *Conduit Wiring* 36 The ceiling rose boxes would generally be in the run of the conduit. **1910** N. HAWKINS *Electr. Dict.*, *Ceiling rose*, or *rosette*, an ornamental ceiling block for suspending an incandescent lamp. **1915** *Pearson's Mag.* XXXIX. 130 A big room, whose ceiling-lights were veiled with vivid red. **1936** M. BENTINCK tr. *Colette's Saha the Cat* i. 20 Camille switched off the ceiling lights as if in play.

ceilinged ('siːlɪŋd), *ppl. a.* [f. prec. + -ED.] Having a ceiling; also **ceilinged-off**, cut off by a ceiling.

18.. WORDSW. *Miscell. Sonn.* I. xv, Cell..with purpureal shell Ceilinged and roofed. **1862** *Owen* I. 80 A low, black, ceilinged room. **1884** W. URWICK *Nonconf. in Herts* 190 The massive roof of solid oak beams, ceilinged off.

†**ceinte.** *Obs.* Also 4 **seynt**, 5 **ceynte**; also SAINT, SAIN, q.v. [a. OF *ceint, ceinct*:—L. *cinctus* in same sense f. *cingĕre* to gird.] A girdle; the woven portion of a girdle.

c **1340** *Cursor M.* 793 (Add. MS.) Abowte hure myddel a seynt sche souȝt. *c* **1386** CHAUCER *Prol.* 329 Girt with a ceint of silk with barres smale. **1413** LYDG. *Pilgr. Sowle* v. v. (1859) 76 These Aungels ledden thre spirites whiche were.. gyrd with ceyntes of gold. **1530** PALSGR. 268/2 Seynt of a gyrdell, *tissu.*

‖**cein'ture.** *rare.* [F. *ceinture* (sɛ̃tyr):—L. *cinctūra*, f. *cingĕre* to gird.] = CINCTURE.

1856 THACKERAY *Christm. Bks.* (1872) 8 A simple white muslin dress and blue ceinture.

ceiss, ceize, obs. forms of CEASE, SEIZE.

cek, obs. form of SACK, SICK.

cekyn, obs. form of SEEK.

cekyr, obs. form of SICKER, sure.

cel, var. CELL *sb.*[3]

†**ce'lade, ce'late**, obs. ff. SALADE, helmet.

1611 FLORIO, *Bacinetto*, a skull or celate [**1598** sallet] or such head-piece. *Celata*, a morion, a celade [**1598** sallat].

celadine, obs. and dial. var. of CELANDINE.

celadon ('sɛlədɒn). [a. F. *céladon*; according to Littré the colour was named after Céladon, a character in D'Urfé's romance of *Astrée*.]

1. The name of a pale shade of green resembling that of the willow.

1768 E. BUYS *Dict. Terms of Art*, *Celadon*, a Sea-green Colour. **1857** LOCKER *Lond. Lyrics*, *My Neighb. Rose* iii, I doat upon Frail jars, turquoise and celadon. **1876** R. BURTON *Gorilla L.* I. 125 A cool green-blue, a celadon tint that reposed the eye and the brain. **1877** LONGF. in *Harper's Mag.* Dec., A sky Just washed by gentle April rains, And beautiful with céladon.

2. (Chinese) pottery or porcelain with a pale greyish-green glaze.

1850 J. MARRYAT *Coll. Hist. Pott. & Porcelain* vi. 111 King-te-tching is also stated to be the site of the manufactory of the old sea-green and crackle porcelain, generally known by the name of Celadon. This term, however, has been since applied to all porcelain of this description, whatever the colour may be. **1885** *Encycl. Brit.* XIX. 622/1 Céladon, very like that made in China, but greyer in tint, is common earthenware covered with a green enamel. *Ibid.* 634/2 A specimen of this céladon ware. **1954** M. WHEELER *Archaeol. from Earth* xi. 141 Chinese celadon ware penetrated far and wide over Asia and Africa in the ninth and following centuries A.D.

'celadonite. *Min.* [Named 1847, f. prec. and -ITE.] Green earth of Verona (Dana); a hydrous silicate of iron and potassium.

1868 DANA *Min.* (1880) 463 Celadonite, colour deep-olive-green, celandine-green, apple-green.

celandine ('sɛləndaɪn). Forms: 4 **celydoine, -oyne**, 5 **celydon, -oun, celidoyne**, 6 **celidone, celandyne, selandine**, 5–7 **celondine, sellondine, salandine, sal-, sall-, selendyne, -ine, solydyne**, 6–7 **celendine**, 8, 9 *dial.* **celadine**, 6– **celandine**. See also CELIDONY[1]. [ME. *celydoine*, a. OF. *celidoine*:—late L. *celidonia*, Lat. *chelidonia* (*-onium*), ad. Gr. *χελιδόνιον*, f. *χελιδών* swallow.

In reference to the name, ancient writers stated that the flower appeared at the time of the arrival of the swallows, and withered at their departure. The story of the use made of the juice by swallows (see quot. 1601 in 1 a) was probably suggested by the name. For the intrusive *n* cf. *messenger*, *passenger*.]

1. The name of two distinct plants, bearing yellow flowers; by the old herbalists regarded as species of the same plant, and identified (probably correctly) with the 'greater and lesser *chelidonia*' of ancient writers.

a. Common or Greater Celandine, *Chelidonium majus* (N.O. *Papaveraceæ*); called by Lyte *swallow-wort*. Its thick yellow juice was formerly supposed to be a powerful remedy for weak sight.

a **1310** in Wright's *Lyric P.* 26 With celydoyne ant sauge. **1393** GOWER *Conf.* III. 131 His [*i.e.* Ariel's] herbe also..Is celidoine freshe and grene. *c* **1430** *Bk. Hawkyng* in *Rel. Ant.* I. 297 Take the jus of salendyne. *c* **1450** *Nominale* in Wr.-Wülcker 712, *Hec celidonia*, celydoun. **1486** *Bk. St. Albans* B iv b, Take the Juce of Salandyne and wete a morcell of flesh therin. **1538** TURNER *Libellus*, Celendyne. **1549** *Compl. Scot.* vi. 67, I sau celidone, that is gude to help the sycht of the ene. **1562** TURNER *Herbal* II. 15 b, The iuice of Selendine..maketh the eysight clere. **1601** HOLLAND *Pliny* II. 224 The great Celendine, called in Greek Chelidonia, for that the old Swallows with the helpe of this hearb helpe their young ones to see again. **1651** BIGGS *New Disp.* ¶79 Celandin weepeth a golden juice. **1872** OLIVER *Elem. Bot.* II. 135 The juice of Common Celandine is of a bright orange colour.

b. Small or Lesser Celandine, the Pilewort or Figwort, *Ranunculus Ficaria*.

1578 LYTE *Dodoens* I. xx. 32 The small Celandyne was so called, bycause that it beginneth to spring and to floure, at the comming of the Swallowes. **1616** SURFL. & MARKH. *Countr. Farm* 197 The small Celandine, otherwise called Pilewort. **1775** ASH, *Celadine*, the name of a plant, pilewort, chelidonium. **1803** WORDSW. *To Small Celandine*, There's a flower that shall be mine, 'Tis the little Celandine. **1859** LEWES *Sea-side Stud.* 189 The dog-violet and the celandine are gay with colour.

†**2. brave celandine**: applied by Lyte to the Marsh Marigold, *Caltha palustris*. *Obs.*

1578 LYTE *Dodoens* I. xx. 31 There is another herbe much like to small Celandyne in leaues and floures, the which we may call Marsh Marygolde, or Brave Celandyne.

3. tree-celandine: *Bocconia frutescens* of the W. Indies. (*Treas. Bot.*)

Celanese (sɛlə'niːz). [Arbitrarily f. CELLULOSE.] A proprietary name for artificial silk twist and for a woven fabric of artificial silk made by British Celanese Ltd. (formerly British Cellulose and Chemical Manufacturing Company). (See also quot. 1921.)

1921 *Trade Marks Jrnl.* 27 Apr. 886 *Celanese*, filaments, fibres, threads, and fabrics (being goods..made wholly or principally from cellulose derivatives); celluloid-like substances in sheets, bands, films, rods, tubes,..electric insulating materials..; waterproofing compositions. **1923** *Daily Mail* 20 Feb. 1 Celanese Artificial Silk. *Ibid.* 27 Feb. 16 Like silk, 'Celanese' is lustrous, with an even more beautiful sheen. **1931** W. HOLTBY *Poor Caroline* iv. 112 Lady's fur-trimmed coats..Celanese silk underwear.

celarent (siː'lɛərənt). *Logic.* [A Latin word (='they might hide') taken as a mnemonic.] A term designating the second mood of the first

figure of syllogisms, in which the major premiss and the conclusion are universal negatives, and the minor premiss a universal affirmative.

1551 T. WILSON *Logique* G vij b, In Celarent we se twise E, whereby we are taught that the argument..must haue two vniuersall negatives, and one vniuersall affirmative. **1589** *Marprel. Epit.* E iiij b, The moode answereth unto Celarent, elder daughter to Barbara. **1589** *Pappe w. Hatchet* E b, You shall not finde such reasons, they bee all in celarent, and dare not shewe their heads. **1882** MALLOCK *Soc. Equality* vi. 138 We cannot prove it in Barbara, Celarent, or Bocardo.

celate: see CELADE.

celation (sɪˈleɪʃən). Also 6 *Sc.* -ioune. [f. L. *celāre* to conceal: see -ATION.] Concealment; esp. in *Law*, concealment of birth or pregnancy.

1567 *Sc. Acts* (1814) 573 (Jam.) In occultatioun and celatioune of the premissis. **1881** *Syd. Soc. Lex.*, *Celation*, the concealment of pregnancy or parturition.

celature (ˈsiːlətjʊə(r)). Also 7 cælature. [ad. L. *cælatūra*, f. *cælā-re* to emboss, engrave.] **a.** Embossing. **b.** *concr.* Embossed work, an embossed figure.

1430 LYDG. *Chron. Troy* III. xxviii, With craftye archys reysed wonder clene..So merueylous was the celature. **1627** HAKEWILL *Apol.* (1630) 372 These celatures in their drinking cups were so fram'd, that they might put them on or take them off at pleasure. **1649** JER. TAYLOR *Gt. Exemp.* x. §17 They admitted even in the utensils of the Church some celatures and engravings. **1650** FULLER *Pisgah* III. v. 367 Nor was all this flouretry, and other celature of the cedar, lost labour. [In BAILEY, JOHNSON, and mod. Dicts.]

celbenin (ˈsɛlbənɪn). *Med.* An antibiotic substance; methicillin sodium.

1960 *Times* 2 Sept. 6/4 This [new penicillin] has been given the name of 'celbenin'. **1961** *New Scientist* 19 Jan. 135/3 Celbenin (BRL 1241), or dimethoxyphenecillin.

celde, obs. pa. t. of SELL.

celder, -re, celdom, obs. ff. CHALDER, SELDOM.

†**cele**, *sb. Med. Obs.* [mod.L., a. Gr. κήλη; cf. BUBONOCELE, ENTEROCELE, etc.] (See quots.)

1708-15 KERSEY, *Cele*, a swelling in any part of the Body, especially the Groin. **1753** CHAMBERS *Cycl. Supp.*, *Cele*, in a general sense, denotes any tumour, but more particularly that proceeding from a rupture or hernia. **1775** in ASH. **1811** HOOPER *Med. Dict.*, *Cele*, a tumour caused by the protrusion of any soft part. **1881** in *Syd. Soc. Lex.*

†**cele**, *v. Obs.* [a. F. *celer*:—L. *celāre*.] *trans.* To hide, conceal, keep secret.

1483 CAXTON *G. de la Tour* H v b, None ought to cele or hyde nothynge fro his frend yf it be his prouffyte and honour. *a* **1550** *Form. Jurament* in Balfour *Practicks* (1754) 23 (Jam.) Your counsall celand that ye schaw me.

cele, var. of CEIL, SEAL, SELE, *Obs.*, happiness.

cele, obs. form of CHILL *sb.*

celeb (sɪˈlɛb). Colloq. (chiefly U.S.) abbrev. of CELEBRITY 4.

1913 *Lincoln* (Nebraska) *Daily News* 27 Feb. 6/2 Dear Woodrow, you can have your job, You're welcome to it, too; I'm glad I'm just a common lob An' no celeb, like you. **1922** *Dialect Notes* V. 144 *Celeb* (*seleb*), n., a college celebrity. 'She gets a crush on every celeb she meets at tea.' **1952** *N.Y. Daily News* 11 Aug. 27c/5 Each a certified celeb from the realms of cafe, style or theatrical society. **1962** J. P. CARSTAIRS *Pardon my Gun* i. 12, I..asked her to lunch at the *White Elephant*. There were usually more than a sprinkling of Celebs..from the Entertainment World. **1973** *Welcomat* (Philadelphia) 10 Oct. 8 Horseshoe Harry..popped up the other day to tell us about the groups of celebs who were also gifted with one of his Good Luck symbols. **1984** *Spectator* 12 May 8/3 Minor celebs who don't rate a cookbook of their own wind up in recipe anthologies.

†**celeˈberrimous**, *a.* *Obs.* *rare*$^{-1}$. [Humorously f. L. *celeberrim-us*, superl. of *celeber* celebrated.] Very or most celebrated.

1768 TUCKER *Lt. Nat.* (1852) I. 475 The celeberrimous doctor has made the thing as clear as the sun.

†ˈ**celebrable**, *a. Obs. rare.* [a. F. *célébrable*, ad. L. *celebrābilis*, f. *celebrāre* to celebrate.] Worthy to be made famous.

c **1374** CHAUCER *Boeth.* III. ix. 84, I mot graunten..þat þis þing be ryȝt celebrable by clernesse of renoun and noblesse. IV. vii. 147 Hercules is celebrable for hys hard trauaile.

celebrant (ˈsɛlɪbrənt). [a. F. *célébrant*, or L. *celebrant-em*, pr. pple. of *celebrāre*.] One who celebrates, or who performs a solemn rite; *esp.* the priest who officiates at the eucharist.

1839 STONEHOUSE *Axholme* 226 The piscina should be situated near the celebrant. **1863** J. C. MORISON *St. Bernard* II. v. 255 They..answered the prayers recited by the celebrant. **1883** *Ch. Times* 9 Nov. 807/1 There cannot be more than one celebrant or one chief consecrator.

†ˈ**celebrate**, *ppl. a. Obs.* Also 5 -at. [ad. L. *celebrāt-us*, pa. pple. of *celebrā-re* to CELEBRATE, f. L. *celebr-em* honoured by a great assembly, etc., renowned.]

1. Performed with due rites; observed with due formality; solemnly held. (Chiefly as pa. pple.; cf. CELEBRATE *v.*)

1471 RIPLEY *Comp. Alch.* v. in. Ashm. (1652) 148 Nor thy Conjunccion of them [be] perfytly celebrat. **1520** SIR R. ELYOT *Will* in *Elyot's Gov.* (1883) App. A, After hir marriage celebrate. **1523** LD. BERNERS *Froiss.* I. cliii. 183 The same day that the fraternyte of Saynt Owen was celebrate, thenglysshmen toke the towne of Guynes. **1564** *Brief Exam.* ***** iij, Who brought in mariages to be celebrate in Churches?

2. Extolled, celebrated.

1538 STARKEY *England* 212 Whose vertuese are celebrate in our..tempullys. **1574-7** HELLOWES *Gueuara's Fam. Ep.* (1577) 28 Numantia and Sagunto were..muche renoumed and celebrate in Spaine. **1680** HICKES *Spirit of Popery* 35 Vicar was a most Zealous, and Celebrate Professor.

3. Consecrated, dedicated. (Cf. CELEBRATE *v.* 2.)

1632 W. LITHGOW *Totall Disc.* 57 Mount Pindus, celebrate to Apollo and the Muses.

Hence †ˈ**celebrateness**.

1731-6 in BAILEY. **1775** in ASH.

celebrate (ˈsɛlɪbreɪt), *v.* [f. prec., or on analogy of vbs. so formed. See -ATE^3.]

(**1656** BLOUNT *Glossogr.*, *Celebrate*, to frequent, to solemnize with an Assembly of men, to make famous, also to keep a festival day or other time with great solemnity.)

1. a. *trans.* To perform publicly and in due form (any religious ceremony, a marriage, a funeral, etc.); to hold (a church council); to solemnize.

1564 (*title*), A godly and necessary admonition of the decrees and canons of the Council of Trent, celebrated under Pius IV. **1570** T. NORTON tr. *Nowel's Catech.* (1853) 115 What form is to be kept in celebrating the divine mysteries. **1574** *Life 70th Abp. Canterbury* B j b, The Archbisshopp himselfe..celebratinge the holy communion. **1662** *Office Holy Commun., 2nd Exhort.* (1844) §345, I intend, by God's grace, to celebrate the Lord's Supper. **1772** PENNANT *Tours Scotl.* (1774) 300 A couple were in pursuit of him, in order to have their nuptials celebrated. **1840** ARNOLD *Hist. Rome* II. 346 Fabius celebrated his funeral, and pronounced his funeral oration.

b. *absol.* (with the eucharist as implied object).

1534 in Picton *L'pool. Munic. Rec.* (1883) I. 26 The foundation of John, Duke of Lancaster, to celebrate there for the soules of him and his ancestors. **1628** P. SMART *Vanitie Popish Cerem.* 33 No side at which any Minister can stand to celebrate. **1862** KINGTON *Fredk. II*, II. xvi. 349 Had forced priests to celebrate in his presence.

†**c.** *transf.* To execute, enter into (a contract; cf. Sp. *celebrar un contrato*); to perform (an operation; cf. quot. 1471 s.v. CELEBRATE *ppl. a.*). *Obs.*

1592 WEST *Symbol.* I. I. §13 The thing..may be in one place, and the contract celebrated and perfected in another. **1684** tr. *Bonet's Merc. Compit.* XVIII. 646 Bleeding must..be celebrated in an Inflammation of the parts.

†**2.** To consecrate by religious rites. *Obs.*

1584 R. SCOT *Discov. Witchcr.* IV. viii. 65 Virgine parchment, celebrated and holied by a popish priest.

3. To observe with solemn rites (a day, festival, season); to honour with religious ceremonies, festivities, or other observances (an event, occasion). Also *absol.* (see quot. 1937).

1560 BIBLE (Genev.) *Lev.* xxiii. 32 From euen to euen shall ye celebrate [WYCL. halowe, COVERD. kepe] your Sabbath. **1591** SHAKS. *1 Hen. VI.* I. vi. 14 Feast and banquet in the open streets, To celebrate the ioy that God hath giuen vs. **1672** DRYDEN *Conq. Granada* I. i, With Pomp and Sports my Love I celebrate. **1697** —— *Virg. Georg.* I. 466 Celebrate the mighty Mother's Day. **1737** L. CLARKE *Hist. Bible* IX. (1840) I. 376 The Feast of Tabernacles being then celebrating. **1841** LANE *Arab. Nts.* I. 71 The Minor Festival ..is celebrated with more rejoicing than the other. **1929** *Randolph Enterprise* (Elkins, W. Va.) 26 Sept. 3/2 [He] came over..Sunday night to celebrate a little. **1937** PARTRIDGE *Dict. Slang* 136/1 *Celebrate*, v.i., to drink in honour of an event or a person; hence, to drink joyously. **1963** J. T. STORY *Something for Nothing* i. 40 It's Treasure's wedding day. Somebody's got to celebrate.

4. To make publicly known, proclaim, publish abroad.

1597 HOOKER *Eccl. Pol.* v. lxviii. §8 Whose name..we celebrate with due honour. **1660** BARROW *Euclid* (1714) Pref. 2 As it is commonly cited and celebrated by all men. **1738** WESLEY *Hymn, When to the Temple* ii, The stones themselves would find a Voice, To celebrate his Praise. **1795** SOUTHEY *Joan of Arc* IX. 360 His praise the song had ceased to celebrate. **1856** BRYANT *Hymn to Death* 72 And celebrates his shame in open day.

5. To speak the praises of, extol, publish the fame of.

1611 BIBLE *Isa.* xxxviii. 18 Death cannot celebrate thee. **1667** MILTON *P.L.* II. 241 Could we Stand in his presence.. to celebrate his Throne With warbl'd Hymns? **1692** R. L'ESTRANGE *Josephus' Antiq.* VI. vi. (1733) 139 Neither did the People forget to celebrate themselves all this while. **1712** ADDISON *Spec.* No. 513 ¶6 There is a noble Hymn in French, which Monsieur Bayle has celebrated for a very fine one. **1875** JOWETT *Plato* III. 699 He celebrated the surrounding mountains for their number and size and beauty.

celebrated (ˈsɛlɪbreɪtɪd), *ppl. a.* [f. prec + -ED.]

1. Performed with customary rites.

1586 MARLOWE *1st Pt. Tamburl.* v. i. ad. fin., Our celebrated rites of marriage.

2. Much talked about, famed, renowned.

1665-9 BOYLE *Occas. Refl.* (1675) Ded., Those Celebrated Ladies..taught their Children to Sway those Rulers of the World. **1717** LADY M. W. MONTAGUE *Lett.* II. xlvi. 33 This is a dull imperfect description of this celebrated building. **1827** SOUTHEY *Inscript.* xliii, In many a celebrated fight With Rodney [he] had his part. **1855** MAURY *Phys. Geog. Sea* xviii. (1860) §768 Neither India, nor the East coasts of Africa..are celebrated for their fish. **1870** EMERSON *Soc. & Solit.*, *Eloquence* Wks. (Bohn) III. 30 Who prosper, like the celebrated schoolmaster, by being only one lesson ahead of the pupil.

Hence †ˈ**celebrated,ness**.

1731-6 in BAILEY. **1775** in ASH.

ˈ**celebrating**, *vbl. sb.* [f. CELEBRATE *v.* + -ING^1.] **a.** Observing with due ceremony, solemn observance. **b.** Praising or extolling.

1591 PERCIVALL *Sp. Dict.*, *Celebracion*, celebrating. **1611** BIBLE *2 Macc.* v. 26 Hee slewe all them that were gone to the celebrating of the Sabbath. **1667** PEPYS *Diary* VI. 108. **1671** L. ADDISON *West Barbary* in Southey *Com.-pl. Bk.* Ser. II. (1849) 96 They divine of the success of their tillage from.. the due celebrating of their Easter.

celebration (sɛlɪˈbreɪʃən). [ad. L. *celebrātiōn-em*, noun of action f. *celebrā-re* to CELEBRATE.]

1. The performance of a solemn ceremony; *spec.* the action of celebrating the eucharist.

1580 SIDNEY *Arcadia* (J.), He laboured..to hasten the celebration of their marriage. **1662** *Office Holy Commun. Rubric 3rd Exhort.* (1844) §346 The Celebration of the Communion. **1678** WANLEY *Wond. Lit. World* v. iii. §9. 474/1 Telesphorus..instituted..the celebration of three Masses the night of our Saviour's birth. **1756-7** tr. *Keysler's Trav.* (1760) III. 393 Epitaph on a lady who dropt down dead, during the celebration of her nuptials. **1829** SOUTHEY *All for Love* iv, The Church hath been prepared For spousal celebration. *Mod.* She has gone to early celebration.

2. The observing of a feast, day, or special season; the honouring or recognizing of an event by religious ceremonies, festivities, etc.

1529 MORE *Supplic. Souls* Wks. 318/2 Our sauiour hymself went to the celebracion of that same feast. *c* **1613** SHAKS. *Hen. VIII*, IV. i. 10 They are euer forward In Celebration of this day. **1659** PEARSON *Creed* (1839) 377 The Jews do still retain the celebration of the seventh day of the week. **1841-4** EMERSON *Ess. Art* Wks. (Bohn) I. 151 Picture and sculpture are the celebrations and festivities of form. **1844** LINGARD *Anglo-Saxon Ch.* (1858) I. i. 46 Celebration of Easter.

3. Making famous, publicly praising, extolling; in *pl.* laudatory speeches.

a **1674** CLARENDON (J.) His memory deserving a particular celebration. **1751** JOHNSON *Rambl.* No. 104 ¶10 Have never been denied any celebrations which they were willing to purchase. **1779** —— *L.P.*, *Prior* Wks. III. 132 The Carmen Seculare, in which he exhausts all his powers of celebration.

†**4.** = CELEBRITY; renown. *Obs.*

1710 PALMER *Proverbs* viii, The vulgar have a title..to convey the honour of celebration to a saying. **1779** JOHNSON *L.P.*, *Pope* Wks. IV. 44 That house at Twickenham to which his residence afterwards procured so much celebration.

celebrational (sɛlɪˈbreɪʃən(ə)l), *a.* [f. CELEBRATION + -AL.] = CELEBRATIVE *a.*

1925 P. B. BALLARD *Changing School* xiii. 201 New methods, of a ceremonial or celebrational kind, which will supply this stronger appeal. **1937** F. SWINNERTON *Autobiogr.* xi, He was going to give a celebrational dinner to his fifty best friends.

ceˈlebrative (ˈsɛlɪbreɪtɪv), *a.* [f. CELEBRATE *v.* + -IVE.] Pertaining to celebration.

1834 J. WILSON in *Blackw. Mag.* XXXV. 707 Walking in ..procession on the day celebrative of Reform. **1959** *Listener* 8 Jan. 80/1 There is little twentieth-century art in any medium that is celebrative in this sense. **1961** D. HOLBROOK *Eng. for Maturity* 45 Our essential cultural experiences are not celebrative, they are, rather, onanistic.

celebrator (ˈsɛlɪbreɪtə(r)). In 7-8 -ter. [a. L. *celebrā-tor*, agent-n. f. *celebrā-re*; formerly in -ER, as an English agent-n. f. CELEBRATE *v.*]

One who celebrates (see senses of CELEBRATE *v.*).

1609 B. JONSON *Masq. Queens*, ad fin., I know no worthier way of epilogue, than the celebration of who were the celebraters. **1617** HIERON *Wks.* (1619-20) II. 340 He will set himselfe to bee a publisher and a celebrater of his righteousnesse. **1624** A. DARCIE *Birth Heresies* iii. 12 To demand of the Celebrater some flesh. **17..** POPE *Let. Mrs. Fermor*, I am really more a well-wisher to your felicity than a celebrater of your beauty. **1850** L. HUNT *Autobiog.* ii. (1860) 30 The birthplace of Marlowe..and of my friend Horne, his congenial celebrator.

celebratory (ˈsɛlɪbreɪtərɪ), *a.* [f. CELEBRATE *v.* + -ORY^2.] Serving to celebrate; used in or designed for the celebration of an event, etc.

1926 *Glasgow Herald* 1 June 7 Without a celebratory or consolatory bite and sup. **1955** *Times* 23 May 9/3 Celebratory parades at home and oversea.

†ˈ**celebre**, *a. Obs. rare*$^{-1}$. [a. F. *célèbre*, or ad. L. *celeber, -brem.*] Well-known, public.

1539 HEN. VIII. *Let. to Wyatt* (R.) Barking preachers so slaunderously defaming us in so celebre a place.

†ˈ**celebre, -er**, *v. Obs.* [a. F. *célébrer*, ad. L. *celebrāre*.] To CELEBRATE.

1475 CAXTON *Jason* 76 The mystery of the flees of golde shal hyely be celebrerd. **1483** —— *Gold. Leg.* 422/2 The solempnyte of thys glorious Saynt is celebred the xvii day of the kalendys of auguste. *Ibid.* 432/4 Whan he was preest he celebred as dayly.

‖**celebret** (ˈsɛlɪbrɛt). [L., = 'let him celebrate', 3rd pers. sing. pres. subj. of *celebrāre* to CELEBRATE.] A document, signed and sealed by

a bishop, giving a priest permission to say mass in a certain parish.

1844 IGNATIUS SPENCER in Fr. Pius *Life Fr. Ignatius* (1866) xiii. 282, I had forgotten to get credentials from Dr. Wiseman, and so he hesitated, but gave the *celebret*. **1907** *Daily Chron.* 25 Sept. 4/6, I am told that the Pope will give me a celebret. **1908** *Cath. Encycl.* III. 477/1 The absence of the celebret does not suffice for the refusal of permission to say Mass, if persons worthy of belief bear positive testimony to the good standing of the priest. **1918** M. D. PETRE *Modernism* 237 The subsequent refusal, on the part of his bishop, to grant him a *celebret*.

celebrious (sɪˈlɛbrɪəs), *a.* [f. L. *celebri-s* + -OUS; cf. *alacrious*. (Accounted *obs.* by Johnson.)]

†**1.** Of a place or assembly: Thronged, frequented; hence, of a ceremony, festival, etc.: Attended or observed by throngs; festive. *Obs.*

1555 CRANMER in Strype *Eccl. Mem.* III. I. xxx. 236, I have defrauded the souls of the dead of this daily and most celebrious sacrifice. **1627** J. CARTER *Exp. Serm. on Mount* 54 The most celebrious places of the Citie, as the Synagogues, or streets. *a* **1638** MEDE *To Twiss* Wks. IV. lxvi. 841, I see no reason why the Lord's-day should not be a celebrious Day when the Lord reigneth. *a* **1680** BUTLER *Rem.* (1759) I. 407 A grave and weighty Oration pronounced..before this celebrious and renowned Assembly.

2. Well-known, famous, renowned. *arch.* or *dial.*

1608 BP. J. KING *Serm. St. Maries, Oxf.* 15 Make his death..renowned and celebrious to the world. **1674** EVELYN *Navig. & Comm.* Misc. Writ. 638 The most celebrious expeditions that have been made. *a* **1734** NORTH *Exam.* I. ii. ¶1. 31 Men, celebrious in public Affairs. *c* **1860** *Imp. Gazetteer Scotl.* I. 341 The manufacture of wooden snuff boxes..rendered Cumnock not a little celebrious.

Hence †**ceˈlebriously** *adv.*, in a celebrious or famous manner; with great celebration. †**ceˈlebriousness**, renown, fame (J.).

1611 SPEED *Hist. Gt. Brit.* x. i. §10 The day for the Coronation..was celebriously kept. **1755** JOHNSON, *Celebriously, -ness*; and in later Dicts.

celebrity (sɪˈlɛbrɪtɪ). [ad. L. *celebritāt-em*, f. *celebr-em* famous, thronged; cf. F. *célébrité*.]

†**1.** Due observance of rites and ceremonies; pomp, solemnity. *Obs.*

1612 BREREWOOD *Lang. & Relig.* Pref. 6 Their general synods.. they have frequently held with great celebrity. **1631** WEEVER *Anc. Fun. Mon.* 585 Whose body..was remoued with all celebritie, and enshrined.

†**2.** A solemn rite or ceremony, a celebration.

1609 HOLLAND *Amm. Marcell. Chronol.* Civa, As touching this celebrity of Sports, see Capitolinus. **1640** BP. HALL *Chr. Moder.* 9/2 Small cheer in comparison of that which he prepared for the celebrity of his son Isaac's weaning. **1655** L'ESTRANGE *Chas. I*, 6 The celebrities of his Fathers Funerall would be over. **1661** S. STONE (*title*) Sermon at St. Paul's, 20 Oct... At the first Celebrity of Divine Service with the Organ and Choristers. **1774** J. BRYANT *Mythol.* I. 61 It generally shewed itself at times, when a celebrity was held.

3. The condition of being much extolled or talked about; famousness, notoriety.

1600 HOOKER *Eccl. Pol.* VII. viii. §8 The dignity and celebrity of mother cities should be respected. **1751** JOHNSON *Rambl.* No. 165 ¶6, I did not find myself yet enriched in proportion to my celebrity. **1838** ARNOLD *Hist. Rome* I. 332 Recommended to public notice by the celebrity of their family. **1863** M. ARNOLD in *Macm. Mag.* 7 Jan. 255 They [Spinoza's successors] had celebrity, Spinoza has fame.

4. *concr.* A person of celebrity; a celebrated person: a public character.

1849 MISS MULOCK *Ogilvies* ii, Did you see any of those 'celebrities,' as you call them? **1856** EMERSON *Eng. Traits* xi. Wks. (Bohn) II. 86 One of the celebrities of wealth and fashion confessed..that, etc. **1876** M. DAVIES *Unorth. Lond.* 99 Thronged with the spiritual celebrities of London.

†ˈ**celebrous**, *a. Obs.* [f. L. *celebr-em* + -OUS. Cf. CELEBRIOUS.] Famous, well-known.

1624 DARCIE *Birth of Heresies* To Rdr., A people at this day celebrous and famous for their Gouernement. **1657** TOMLINSON *Renou's Disp.* 317 The vulgar [Balm] is most celebrous. **1678** *Pref. Rob. Hood* in Thoms *Prose Rom.* (1858) II. Celebrous for the yielding of excellent whetstones.

celection, obs. form of SELECTION.

celendyne, obs. form of CELANDINE.

celer, var. CELURE, and SOLER, upper room.

celerer, obs. form of CELLARER.

celeriac (sɪˈlɛrɪæk). [Derivative of CELERY; the last syllable has not been explained; the word does not appear to be known outside of English.] A turnip-rooted variety of the garden celery.

1743 *Lond. & Country Brew.* II. Advt., Italian Brocoli, Spanish Cardoon, Celeriac, Finochi, and other foreign Kitchen Vegetables. **1796** C. MARSHALL *Garden.* xv. (1813) 232 Celeriac requires a rich soil. **1861** DELAMER *Kitch. Gard.* 82 Celeriac is easier and less expensive of culture than celery. **1883** *St. James's Gaz.* 20 Dec. 5/2 There is likewise, though far too little known, the celeriac.

†**ceˈlerious**, *a. Obs. rare*⁻¹. [f. L. *celeri-s*, swift + -OUS. Cf. *celebrious*.] Swift, fleet.

1632 W. LITHGOW *Totall Disc.* 357 The most celerious in flying or following, of all the cursares in Turkey.

†**celeripedean**, *sb.* and *a. Obs.*⁻⁰ [f. L. *celeriped-em* swift-footed (f. *celer* swift + *ped-em* foot) + -EAN.] 'A swift footman' (Cockeram).

1623 in COCKERAM. **1656** BLOUNT *Glossogr.*, *Celeripedean*, swift footed, nimble heel'd.

celerity (sɪˈlɛrɪtɪ). Also 5-6 cel-, selerite, 6 celeryte, cel-, seleritie. [ME. *celerite*, a. F. *célérité*, ad. L. *celeritāt-em*, f. *celer* swift.]

1. Swiftness, speed. Now chiefly (as distinguished from *velocity*) with reference to the movements or actions of living beings.

1483 RICH. III in Ellis *Orig. Lett.* II. 39 I. 123 The same with all celerite entendeth for to ordeigne and provide..for his sayd cousyn. **1531** ELYOT *Gov.* I. xxii, The mean.. between sloth and celeritie, commonly called speediness. **1591** HORSEY *Trav.* (1857) 229, I speed my bussynes with as much seleritie as I can. **1607** TOPSELL *Four-f. Beasts* 82 The cats followed with the same celerity and agility. **1691** RAY *Creation* I. (1704) 72 Whirl'd round about the Earth daily with incredible celerity. **1751** JOHNSON *Rambl.* No. 177 ¶3 My quickness of apprehension, and celerity of reply. **1834** MRS. SOMERVILLE *Connex. Phys. Sc.* xxviii. (1849) 323 A wheel revolving with celerity sufficient to render its spokes invisible. *Mod.* The celerity of the squirrel's movements.

†**2.** A particular rate of speed. (In physical science the word now used is *velocity*.) *Obs.*

1734 BERKELEY *Analyst* §4 The fluxions are celerities, not proportional to the finite increments. **1794** SULLIVAN *View Nat.* II. 383 To that center..there is supposed a descent, in various celerities.

celery (ˈsɛlərɪ). Also 7 cellery, 7-8 selleri, -y, 8 sallary, -ery, celeri. [a. F. *céleri* (not in Cotgr.), according to Littré a. dial. It. *sellari*, pl. of *sellaro* (Brescian *ˈseleno*, literary It. *ˈsedano*), repr. Gr. σέλινον parsley.]

1. An umbelliferous plant (*Apium graveolens*) cultivated for the use of its blanched stalks as a salad and vegetable; in its wild form (SMALLAGE) indigenous in some parts of England.

1664 EVELYN *Kal. Hort.* (1669) 34 February, Sow in the beginning..Sellery. **1673** RAY *Journ. Low C.* 406 (*Italian food*) Selleri..the young shoots whereof they eat raw with oyl and pepper. **1732** ARBUTHNOT *Rules of Diet* 256 Parsley and Celery both contain a pungent Salt and Oil. **1753** HANWAY *Trav.* (1762) I. IV. lvii. 263 Poor devotees, who.. subsist upon wild sallary. **1832** *Veg. Subst. Food* 190 Celery ..in its wild state..known by the name of smallage. **1872** OLIVER *Elem. Bot.* II. 183 Celery..is only wholesome when blanched.

attrib.

1719 LONDON & WISE *Compl. Gard.* 203 We earth our Cellery Plants quite up, with Earth taken from the high-rais'd Path-ways. **1858** WOOD *Homes without H.* xiv. 299 Of the Diptera the Celery Fly (*Tephritis onopordinis*) is a good example. **1882** *Garden* 14 Jan. 23/3 For beauty of barring the Celery fly may compare with most.

2. *Comb.* **celery pine**, (also **celery-leaved, -topped**, or **-top pine**), any Australasian tree of the genus *Phyllocladus*, in which the upper part of the branchlets resembles the foliage of the celery; **celery salt**, a mixture of ground celery seed and salt used for seasoning; **celery seed** (see quot. 1964).

1827, etc. [see PINE *sb.*² 2 a]. **1851** *Illustr. Catal. Gt. Exhib.* IV. i. 944 Celery-topped pine (*Phyllocladus asplenifolia*) of Tasmania. *Ibid.*, Celery pine slab (*Phyllocladus aspleniifolia*), squared. **1861** MRS. BEETON *Househ. Managem.* 189 *Celery Vinegar*..½ oz. of celery seed, 1 pint of vinegar. **1883** [see TANEKAHA]. **1889** T. KIRK *Forest Flora N.Z.* 9 The tanekaha is one of the remarkable 'celery-topped pines'. **1897** *Sears, Roebuck Catal.* 13/2 Celery Salt..4 oz. sifting top bottles. **1927** *Blackw. Mag.* Oct. 464/1 Graceful featherwoods and celery-top pines. **1964** R. HEMPHILL *Spice & Savour* (1965) 99 Celery seed is the dried fruit of the celery plant. **1964** R. HEMPHILL *Spice & Savour* (1965) 99 Commercial celery salt is flavoured with ground celery seed, or with ground dried celery stems.

†**ceˈlest**, *a. Obs.* [a. F. *céleste*, or ad. L. *cælestis*, f. *cælum* heaven.] Heavenly, celestial.

1. Of or pertaining to the sky; = CELESTIAL 1. †*blue celest*: sky-blue [Fr. *bleu céleste*] (*obs.*).

1535 STEWART *Cron. Scot.* I. 89 The circulatioun of the sone celes[t]. **1549** *Compl. Scot.* 47 Considir the circlis of the spere celest. **1584** T. HUDSON *Judith*, Her utmost robe was colour blew celest.

2. Of or pertaining to heaven; = CELESTIAL 2, 3.

c **1420** *Pallad. on Husb.* I. 455 Licoure of grace above, a thyng celest. **1549** *Compl. Scot.* 65 Eftir this sueit celest armonye, tha began to dance. **1677** GALE *Crt. Gentiles* II. III. 145 Augustin observed in Paul..a celeste Eloquence.

celesta (sɪˈlɛstə). [app. pseudo-latinization of F. *céleste* (cf. CELESTE).] A keyboard instrument with piano-like action, having hammers that strike upon steel plates placed over wooden resonators, invented by Auguste Mustel of Paris in 1886.

1899 E. PROUT *Orchestra* II. vi. 158 Only a few of the strings are employed to accompanying the *celesta*. **1927** *Grove's Dict. Mus.* I. 591 The tone of the celesta itself is of exquisite purity. **1966** *Listener* 10 Mar. 364 The celesta player on both occasions was Richard Rodney Bennett.

celeste (sɪˈlɛst). [mod. a. F. *céleste*: see CELEST *a.*]

1. The name of a colour, sky-blue: see CELEST *a.*

1881 *Porcelain Wks. Worcester* 35 The..mauve, Celeste, and other enamels present an interesting series.

2. a. (short for *voix celeste*): The name of a stop on the organ or harmonium. **b.** A name for a certain form of the soft pedal on a piano.

1880 in Grove *Dict. Mus.* II. 683/1 The use of the celeste pedal was indicated by Hummel with a special sign. **1886** *Daily News* 14 Dec. 7/2 All of the following are reed stops.. Diapason, melodia, viola, celeste.

c. = CELESTA.

1934 S. R. NELSON *All about Jazz* v. 93 A couple of bars by solo violin, which is taken the second time by celeste. **1958** B. ULANOV *Hist. Jazz* xiv. 164 He tried out every sort of scoring,..celeste interludes, [etc.].

celestial (sɪˈlɛstɪəl), *a.* and *sb.* Also 5-7 -tiall(e, -tyal(le, 6-8 cœl-, cælestial(l, (7 celestall, selestiall). [a. OF. *celestial*, *-el* (= It. *celestiale*, Sp. *celestial*), f. L. *cælesti-s* of same meaning, f. *cælum* sky, heaven; see -AL¹.]

A. *adj.*

1. Of or pertaining to the sky or material heavens. ***celestial equator*** = EQUATOR 1 (cf. EQUINOCTIAL *sb.* 1); ***celestial globe, map***: one representing the heavens; ***celestial mechanics***, gravitational astronomy: see quot. 1959; ***celestial pole***: see POLE *sb.*² 1; ***celestial triangle*** = ASTRONOMICAL *triangle*; †***celestial water***: solution of copper sulphate, used in opthalmia (see quot. 1758).

c **1391** CHAUCER *Astrol.* II. §2 To know the altitude of the sonne or of othre celestial bodies. **1481** CAXTON *Myrr.* III. xxiii. 184 This heuene Celestyall, whyche is aboue alle the other. **1597** HOOKER *Eccl. Pol.* v. lxix. §2 Years, days, hours, minutes..all grow from celestial motion. **1664** MARVELL *Corr.* Wks. 1872-5 II. 120 The influence of the cælestial luminaries..is suspended. *a* **1721** KEILL tr. *Maupertuis' Diss.* (1734) 61 The Cœlestial Bodies that turn about an Axis. **1758** J. S. *Le Dran's Observ. Surg.* (1771) A a iv, Sky-coloured, or celestial Water..For Distempers in the Eyes it must be well diluted. **1821** *New Monthly Mag.* III. 184/2 A simple lunar theory, and a rigorous system of celestial mechanics. **1875** *Encycl. Brit.* II. 764/2 The celestial equator..is the great circle having for its poles..the poles of the heavens. **1879** LOCKYER *Elem. Astron.* IV. xxvi. 145 The celestial sphere—the name given to the apparent vault of the sky. **1936** *Discovery* Jan. 31/1 Important residual effects like the advance of the perihelion of Mercury in celestial mechanics. **1950** *Chambers's Encycl.* V. 379/1 The celestial equator is the great circle in the sky corresponding to the extension of the equator of the earth. **1956** W. A. HEFLIN *U.S.A.F. Dict.* 106/2 Celestial triangle. **1959** *Encycl. Brit.* V. 93/1 Celestial Mechanics is the branch of astronomy that deals with the mathematical theory of the motions of celestial bodies.

2. a. Of or pertaining to heaven, as the abode of God (or of the heathen gods), of angels, and of glorified spirits.

c **1384** CHAUCER *H. Fame* I. 460 Of the goddys celestials. *c* **1386** —— *Prioresse's T.* 129 Folwyng ever in oon The white lomb celestial. **1494** FABYAN 6 To the lorde that is Celestyall, I wyll nowe crye. **1526** TINDALE *Luke* xi. 13 Howe moche more shall youre Father celestiall. **1651** C. CARTWRIGHT *Cert. Relig.* I. 252 Some by Angell there understand not a cælestiall spirit, but a messenger. **1751** JOHNSON *Rambl.* No. 168 ¶10 His celestial protectress thought him not sufficiently secured. **1862** STANLEY *Jew. Ch.* (1877) I. v. 93 Not in any outward form, human or celestial.

b. In *comb.* (nonce-wds.)

a **1743** SAVAGE *Wks.* II. 100 (Jod.) Celestial-hinted thoughts gay hopes inspir'd. **1843** CARLYLE *Past & Pr.* (1858) 92 Alive and miraculous, celestial-infernal.

3. a. Of a divine or heavenly nature.

1483 CAXTON *G. de la Tour* I ij, To whome he gaf celestyals and erthely goodes. **1538** STARKEY *England* 207 He [Christ] cam to make perfayt man..by Hys celestyal and dyvyne doctryne. **1681** DRYDEN *Abs. & Achit.* 306 Desire of Pow'r..is of Cœlestial Seed. **1794** SULLIVAN *View Nat.* II. 449 The celestial dew of knowledge. **1866** NEALE *Sequences & H.* 127 To fortify the parting soul with that celestial Food.

b. Divinely excellent or beautiful, divine, heavenly; also in *comb.*, as quasi-*adv.*

1430 LYDG. *Chron. Troy* II. xiii, So heauenly fayre and so celestyall. **1613** R. C. *Table Alph.* (ed. 3) *Celestiall*, heauenly, diuine, passing excellent. *a* **1704** T. BROWN *Sat. Antients* Wks. 1730 I. 24 The celestial beauties, which we find in the writings of these incomparable men. **1713** *Guardian* No. 4 ¶5 A new sort of Stile..which is above the sublime, and may be called the Celestial. **1725** POPE *Odyss.* I. 149 His bloomy face Glowing cœlestial-sweet.

4. ***the Celestial Empire***: a translation of one of the native names for China. So ***Celestial Emperor***; and humorously ***celestial*** = Chinese.

1824-9 LANDOR *Wks.* (1868) II. 117 England was devising schemes..to the detriment of the Celestial Empire. **1840** *Knickerbocker* XVI. 447 We have seen a Chinese map of the world, in which the celestial country occupies the entire space, with the exception of a few island-like circles. **1872** 'M. TWAIN' *Roughing It* 396 We ate chow-chow with chop-sticks in the celestial restaurants. **1878** H. JAMES *Europeans* I. vi. 246 He possessed the most delightful *chinoiseries*—trophies of his sojourn in the Celestial Empire.

5. Jocularly applied to a 'pug' nose, which turns up at the tip.

6. quasi-*sb.* (in *pl.*) Heavenly objects, bodies, attributes.

1582 N. T. (Rhem.) *Hebr.* ix. 23 It is necessarie therfore that the examplers of the cælestials be cleansed with these. **1652** GAULE *Magastrom.* 122 Inferior things doe obey their celestials. **1748** RICHARDSON *Clarissa* (1811) VIII. 399 Never was..goddess so easily stript of her celestials!

B. *sb.*

1. a. An inhabitant of heaven.

1573 TWYNE *Æneid* x. (R.) King Ioue from golden throne vprose, Whom home to heauenly court celestials garding al did close. **1713** *Guardian* No. 7 ¶1 Diana..or any other Celestial who owes her being to poetry. **1750** JOHNSON *Rambl.* No. 22 ¶1 Of age to be received into the apartments of the other celestials. **1869** SPURGEON *Treas. Dav.* Ps. xix. 3.

b. *fig.* A heavenly being.

1874 BLACKIE *Self-Cult.* 27 You will require steps to mount up to shake hands with these Celestials. **1885** *19th Cent.* July 48 From the parson's daughter up to the celestials behind Spiers and Pond's counters.

2. A subject of the Celestial Empire; a Chinese.

1842 W. DYOTT *Diary* 24 Nov. (1907) II. 365 Accounts arrived with glorious news of peace with China... The terms of peace with the celestials highly favourable. **1863** RUSSELL *Diary India* II. 171 (Hoppe) The China-patterned lands which connect India with the country of the Celestials. **1884** *Christm. Graphic* 7/2 The Celestial inclined his head in grave courtesy.

ce'lestialite. *Min.* [f. CELESTIAL + -ITE.] 'A sulph-hydrocarbon found in certain meteorites' (Dana *Min.* (1884) App. iii).

celestiality (sɪˌlɛstɪ'ælɪtɪ). [f. as prec. + -ITY.]

1. Heavenly quality; heavenliness.

1875 BROWNING *Aristoph. Apol.* 96 But, throw off hate's celestiality. **1884** F. A. PALEY *Ch. Restorer* 56 The celestiality of countenance has never been equalled.

2. A Celestial (Chinese) dignitary. *humorous.*

1824-9 LANDOR *Imag. Conv.* Wks. (1846) II. 118 His celestiality then waved his hand. [So often in L.]

celestialize (sɪ'lɛstɪəlaɪz), *v.* [f. CELESTIAL + -IZE.] *trans.* To make celestial. Hence **ce'lestialized** *ppl. a.*

1826 SOUTHEY in *Q. Rev.* XXXIII. 390 Celestialized humanity. **1830** *Blackw. Mag.* XXVIII. 863 Was there ever a face in this world so celestialized by smiles?

celestially (sɪ'lɛstɪəlɪ), *adv.* [-LY².] **a.** In a heavenly manner. **b.** As from a heavenly source. **c.** After the manner of celestial beings.

1494 FABYAN IV. lxxv. 54 Thou [Quene celestyall] Art to the hyghest Ioyned celestyally. **1529** MORE *Comf. agst. Trib.* II. 1171/2 A certain holy father in makyng of a sermon, spake of heauen..so celestially, that muche of his audyence with the swete sounde therof, beganne to..fal a slepe. **1594** HOOKER *Eccl. Pol.* II. (1617) 62 That supernaturall and celestially reuealed Truth. **1658** FLECKNOE *Epigr.* (1670) 71 They seem to be celestially inspir'd. **1848** THACKERAY *Let.* 1 Nov., These pretty brats..sing..celestially. **1860** LD. LYTTON *Lucile* II. I. §1. 5 Celestially naked,—new queen of the world..Summer stands.

ce'lestialness. [see -NESS.] Heavenliness.

1731 in BAILEY. **1775** in ASH; and in mod. Dicts.

†Ce'lestian. *Obs.* = CELESTINE *sb.*² a.

1532 MORE *Confut. Barnes* VIII. Wks. 798/2 Austine spake ..against..heretikes called Pelagianes, and Celestianes.

†ce'lestical, *a. Obs.* [f. L. *cælesti-s* + -ICAL; cf. *agrestical.*] Celestial, heavenly.

c **1530** LD. BERNERS *Arth. Lyt. Bryt.* (1814) 197 Hie and mighty King of Paradise celestical! **1609** BIBLE (Douay) 204 The celestical God, maker of the whole world. **1695** TRYON *Dreams* x. 194 All celestical vertues.

†celestien, *a. Obs. rare.* [a. OF. *celestien*:—L. type *cælesti-ānus*, f. *cælest-is*: see CELEST.] = CELESTIAL.

c **1330** *Owain Miles* 146 That is paradis celestien; Ther-in com bot Cristen men.

†ce'lestify, *v. Obs. rare.* [f. L. *cælesti-s* + -FY; cf. OF. *celestifier.*] *trans.* To make heavenly.

1646 SIR T. BROWNE *Pseud. Ep.* 231 That heaven were but earth celestified. **1656** BLOUNT *Glossogr.*, *Celestify*, to make celestial, heavenly or excellent. **1768** E. BUYS *Dict. Terms of Art*, *Celestify*, to communicate or endue with the Properties of Heaven.

†'celestine, *a.* and *sb.*¹ *Obs.* [a. OF. *celestin*, ad. L. *cælestīn-us*, f. *cælest-is* heavenly: see -INE.] = CELESTIAL *a.* and *sb.*

c **1430** LYDG. *Min. Poems* (1840) 62 A bright hevenly sterre, Monge celestynes reigneng. **1509** HAWES *Past. Pleas.* xxvi. xi, Lyke Dyane clere in her spere celestyne. **1509** —— *Conv. Swearers* 41 Both god and man in Ioy celestyne.

Celestine ('sɛləstaɪn, -tɪn, sɪ'lɛstɪn), *sb.*² [ad. L. *Cælestīnus*, f. the proper names *Cœlestius* and *Cælestīnus.*]

a. One of a sect (called also *Celestians*) named after Cælestius, an associate of Pelagius, in the 5th c. **b.** One of a reformed branch of the Benedictines, founded by Celestine V. in the 13th c.

1530 PALSGR. 203/2 Celestyn a man of religion, *celestin.* **1577** VAUTROULLIER *Luther on Ep. Gal.* 165 No Monke, no Carthusian, no Celestine bruseth the head of the Serpent. **1686** SERJEANT *Hist. Monast. Conventions* 27 The Celestines [wear] Skie Colour or Blew. **1836** *Penny Cycl.* VI. 21/1 Buonafede..entered the order of the Celestines..was elected general..in 1777.

celestine ('sɛləstɪn), *sb.*³ *Min.* Also cælestine, -in. [named 1798: ? ad. It. *celestino* sky-blue; cf. CELESTE.] A mineral: the same as CELESTITE. Also, formerly applied to a blue alabaster.

1804 R. JAMESON *Syst. Min.* I. 606 Celestine has also been found crystallized. **1811** PINKERTON *Petral.* I. 502 The alabaster called *anydrous* is of several colours, white, rose, grey, and even blue, which is called celestine, a name now strictly belonging to a kind of strontian. **1815** W. PHILLIPS *Outl. Min. & Geol.* (1818) 25 Strontian combined with sulphuric acid..has obtained the name of cœlestine from its delicate tint of light blue colour.

†ceˌlesti'net(te. *Obs. rare.* (See quot.)

1774 H. WALPOLE *Let. Sir W. Hamilton* 19 June, I heard a new instrument yesterday..It is a copulation of a harpsicord and a violin; one hand strikes the keys and the other draws the bow..The instrument is so small it stands on a table, and is called a Celestinette.

†ce'lestious, *a. Obs.* [f. L. *cælesti-s* + -OUS.] = CELESTIAL.

1542 *Primer Hen. VIII*, In the heart ravishment celestious. *a* **1691** BOYLE *Wks.* II. 257 (R.) A book, ennobled by its author with many celestious lights.

celestite ('sɛləstaɪt, sɪ'lɛstaɪt). *Min.* [Altered by Dana from CELESTINE: see -ITE.] A mineral; native-sulphate of strontia, Sr O. SO_3, so called from the sky-blue colour it sometimes presents.

Baryto-celestite, *Calcio-celestite*, are varieties containing baryta and lime respectively.

1854 DANA *Min.* (1880) 620 Wittstein finds that the blue colour of the celestite of Jena is due to a trace of phosphate of iron..Celestite is usually associated with limestone.

ce'lestitude. [f. CÆLESTIS + -TUDE, after *altitude*, etc.] = CELESTIALITY 2. *humorous.*

1824-9 LANDOR *Wks.* (1868) I. 492 Would your Celestitude [King of Ava] believe it! the whole company wept.

†ce'lestly, *a. Obs.* = CELEST *a.* 2.

1400 *Cov. Myst.* (1841) 103 Thou..makyst hym desyre thyngys celestly.

ceˌlesto'barite. *Min.* [see CELESTITE and BARITE.] A variety of BARITE containing much sulphate of strontia.

1868 DANA *Min.* (1880) 617.

†'celestrine, celstine. *Obs.* [app. ad. It. *cilestrino*, *celestino* a garment of sky-blue cloth (Tommaseo).] A kind of blue cloth.

1435-6 *Warden's Acc.* in Heath *Grocers' Comp.* (1869) 419 The clothing murrey and plunket celstyne. **1483** *Act 1 Rich. III*, c. 8 §18 Cloth called *Vervise*, otherwise called *Plonkets, Turkins*, or *Celestrines.*

†ce'letomy, bad form of CELOTOMY.

‖ce'leusma. *Obs. rare.* [late L. *celeusma*, a. Gr. κέλευσμα, f. κελεύ-ειν to order.] A watchword, battle-cry; the call of the signalman who gives the time to rowers.

1680 *Hon. Cavalier* 17 Curse ye Meroz, or such like *Celeusma's.* **1684** *Def. Case of Consc. conc. Symbol. with Rome* 11, I cannot but wonder, at your adventuring into the World this other Celeusma. **1753** CHAMBERS *Cycl. Supp.* s.v., Hymns and psalms were sung in vessels by way of celeusma, in which the words *amen* and *hallelujah* were frequently repeated.

celiac, var. of CŒLIAC.

celibacy ('sɛlɪbəsɪ). Also 7 cœlebacy. [f. L. *cælibātus* in same sense, f. *cælebs*, *cælib-em* unmarried, single: see -ACY 3. (*Cælebs*, and its noun of state *cælibātus*, are the only cognate words found in Latin).] The state of living unmarried.

1663 *Aron-bimn.* 54 St. Paul's advice for cœlebacy, or single life. **1754** HUME *Hist. Eng.* ii, The celibacy of priests was introduced into the English System by Dunstan. **1791** BOSWELL *Johnson* (1831) I. xxiv. 387 Even ill assorted marriages were preferable to cheerless celibacy. **1796** H. HUNTER tr. *St. Pierre's Stud. Nat.* (1799) III. 681 Celibacy may suit an individual, but never a corps. **1855** MILMAN *Lat. Chr.* (1864) II. III. vii. 149 With Gregory celibacy was the perfection of human nature.

celibatair(e (ˌsɛlɪbə'tɛə(r)). *rare.* [a. F. *célibataire*, f. *célibat* = CELIBATE *sb.*¹ + *-aire*, repr. L. *-ārius*: see -ARY.] A bachelor; one who is vowed to celibacy.

1817 W. GODWIN *Mandeville* II. 268 (D.) While the despairing celibataire descanted on his 'whole course of love.' **1839** J. ROGERS *Antipapopr.* xv. §3. 317 If the priesthood individually incline to celibate, let them be celibatairs.

celibatarian (ˌsɛlɪbə'tɛərɪən), *a.* and *sb.* [f. CELIBATE *sb.*¹ + *-arian*; cf. F. *célibataire.*]

A. *adj.* Characterized by, or characteristic of, celibacy; inclined to, or favouring celibacy.

1839 DARLEY *Introd. Beaum. & Fl. Wks.* I 10 An act so little in accord with the Queen's celibatarian prejudices. **1849** *Fraser's Mag.* XL. 137 He had vegetated twenty years in the celibatarian dignities of his fellowship. **1848** CLOUGH *Amours de Voy.* III. 183 Let me offer a single and celibatarian phrase.

B. *sb.* One who lives in or advocates celibacy.

1863 SALA in *Temple Bar* VII. 546 Her chin, like a wavering celibatarian, seemed scarcely to have made up its mind. **1867** H. C. LEA *Sacerd. Celibacy* 168 So ardent a celibatarian as Aldhelm.

celibate ('sɛlɪbeɪt), *sb.*¹ *arch.* Also 7 cælibate, cælibat. [ad. F. *célibat*, ad. L. *cælibātus*: see above.] State of celibacy; order of celibates.

1614 J. KING *Vitis Palat.* 21 Solitude and celibate, a single monasticke life agreeath not to it. **1673** RAY *Journ. Low C.*, *Malta* 319 Hildebrand..the great introducer of the Celibate of Priests. *a* **1711** KEN *Edmund* Poet. Wks. 1721 II. 238 Despairing, I in Celibate would live. **1869** J. ROGERS *Antipapopr.* xv. §1 Has taken care of the celibate of the clergy. **1874** H. REYNOLDS *John Bapt.* iii. §2. 183.

fig. **1862** MERIVALE *Rom. Emp.* (1865) V. xlii. 173 The long celibate of German intelligence may seem designed by a superior Wisdom to crown it with inexhaustible fertility.

Hence **celi'batic** *a.*, of or pertaining to celibacy; **'celibatist**, a professed supporter of celibacy; **'celibatory** (*rare*) = CELIBATARIAN.

1881 *Echo* 11 Apr. 1/6 The remnant of 'celibatic superstition' which even now hangs around some of our academical establishments. **1885** JEAFFRESON *Real Shelley* I. 20 Compensation for the loss of celibatic freedom. **1829** *Blackw. Mag.* XXVI. 758 Elizabeth..was herself a celibatist. **1841** L. HUNT *Seer* II. (1864) 5 A lone lodger, a celibatory.

celibate ('sɛlɪbət), *a.* and *sb.*² [f. L. *cælib-em* unmarried + -ATE (not on L. analogy): see -ATE² 2.]

A. *adj.* Unmarried, single; bound not to marry.

1829 SOUTHEY *Lett.* (1856) IV. 148 If celibate, to lay by sufficient for his old age. **1863** J. M. LUDLOW *Sisterhood* in *Gd. Words* 493 The celibate girls..would scarcely fail to become..a community. **1868** M. PATTISON *Academ. Org.* §5. 205 The present anomalous position of the celibate tutor-fellow. **1882** FARRAR *Early Chr.* I. 505 He [Jesus] never breathed one word to exalt the celibate over the wedded life.

B. *sb.* One who leads a single life, a confirmed bachelor or spinster; one bound not to marry.

1869 J. MARTINEAU *Ess.* II. 26 The proof may be very convincing to celibates. **1879** FARRAR *St. Paul* II. 619 App., An order of female celibates or youthful nuns.

Hence **'celibateness, 'celibateship,** = CELIBACY.

1775 in ASH.

'celibate, *v. nonce-wd.* [f. prec.] *trans.* To restrain from marriage, compel to celibacy.

1659 EVELYN *Gold. Bk. St. Chrysostom* Misc. Writ. 114 That thou shouldst cœlibat him..and make him a monk.

†'celic, *a. Obs.* In 6 cælick. [ad. late L. *cælic-us*, f. *cælum* heaven.] = next.

1652 SPARKE *Prim. Devot.* (1663) 341 Yet all their cælick strains would fall too low.

†'celical, *a. Obs.* Also 6 -icall, -ycalle. [f. as prec. + -AL¹.] Heavenly, celestial.

1513 DOUGLAS *Æneis* XII. Prol. 42 Phebus..defundand from hys sege etheriall Glaid influent aspectis celicall. **1513** BRADSHAW *St. Werburge* (1848) 213 Euer contynuynge in doctrine celicall. **1583** STANYHURST *Æneis* III. (Arb.) 89 By stars..by the ayre, by the celical houshold.

celidography (sɛlɪ'dɒgrəfɪ). [f. Gr. κηλίς κηλῖδο-ς spot + -γραφία writing. In F. *célidographie.*] A description of the spots in the sun or planets.

[**1753** CHAMBERS *Cycl. Supp.* has *Celidographia* from Bianchini 1729.] **1775** in ASH; and in mod. Dicts.

†'celidony¹. *Obs.* Forms: 1 celeþonie, cyleþenie, 5 cely-, seladony, celidoyne, celydoine, -doun, 6 celedonie. [ad. med.L. *celedonia* (in Pliny *chelīdonia*) and OF. *celidoine*: cf. CELANDINE.] = CELANDINE.

c **1000** *Sax. Leechd.* III. 41 Nim..celeþonian moran. **1398** TREVISA *Barth. De P.R.* XVII. xlvi. (Tollem. MS.) By þe iuce of celidony swalowes ȝȝen turneþ aȝen to þe firste state, yf þey ben hurte or put oute. *c* **1440** *Promp. Parv.* 65/2 Celydony, herbe, *celidonia.* *a* **1450** *Alphita* (Anecd. Oxon.) 36 *Celidonia*..gall. et angl. celidoyne. *c* **1450** *Nominale* in Wr.-Wülcker 712 *Hec celidonia*, celydoun. *c* **1475** *Voc.* ibid. 786 *Hec seladonia*, a seladony. **1567** MAPLET *Gr. Forest* 37 Celedonie..beareth a Saffron coloured flower. **1607** TOPSELL *Four-f. Beasts* 278 To bloud-shotten eyes it is good ..to wash them with the juyce of celidony.

†'Celidony². *Obs.* [ad. late L. *celidonius* (in Pliny *chelīdonius*), ad. Gr. χελιδόνιος (λίθος), f. χελιδών swallow: see quot. 1621.] A stone fabled to be found in the belly of a swallow: see quots. Cf. Fr. *chélidoine* 'pierre precieuse: petits cailloux appartenant aux agates: on dit aussi pierres d'hirondelle' (Littré).

[**1621** BURTON *Anat. Mel.* II. iv. I. iv. 232/2 In the belly of a swallow, there is a stone found called Celidonius, which if it be lapped in a faire cloath, and tied to the right arme, will cure lunaticks and mad men.] **1661** *Sir H. Vane's Politicks* 9 The Celedonie Stone, whose property it is to lose all its power and vertue, unless it be rub'd with gold.

celine, *a.* [irregularly f. Gr. κοιλία belly: cf. CŒLIAC.] 'Belonging to the belly.'

In mod. Dicts.

†ce'livagous, *a. Obs. rare*⁻¹. [f. after F. *celivage* (Rabelais), on L. type **cælivag-us*, f. *cæl-um* sky + *vag-us* wandering + -OUS.] Straying heavenwards.

a **1693** URQUHART *Rabelais* III. xxii, By two celivagous Filopendulums.

cell (sɛl), *sb.*[1] Forms: 2 cell (*pl.* -as), 3-6 celle, (4-6 sell(e, 7 cel), 5- cell. [ME. *celle*, a. OF. *celle*:—L. *cella* a small apartment, *esp.* one of several such in the same building, used *e.g.* for a store-closet, slave's room, prison cell; also cell of a honeycomb; in late L. also a monk's or hermit's cell. The late OE. *cell* pl. *cellas* may have been directly ad. L. *cella*.

The adoption of old and development of new senses in English, have proceeded along many lines, and the logical and chronological orders do not agree. Sense 2 appears to be the earliest, while 7 and 8, already used in Latin, appear comparatively late.

(Some would connect L. *cella* with *cera* wax, regarding 'cell of a honeycomb' as the original sense.)]

I. A small apartment, room, or dwelling.

†**1.** A store-closet. (In early quots. after *cella* of the Vulg.). *Obs.*

a **1225** *Ancr. R.* 152 He scheawede þe celles of his aromaz. **1382** Wyclif *Isa.* xxxix. 2 He shewed to them the selle of spices. **1583** Stubbes *Anat. Abus.* II. 45 [They] .. carieng it into their celles, and garners at home, keep it.

2. A monastery or nunnery, generally of small size, dependent on some larger house. [A frequent med.L. sense of *cella* (see Du Cange).]

In the first quot. app. = 'monastery' in general.

a **1131** *O.E. Chron.* an. 1129 þa priores, muneces and canonias þa wæron on ealle þa cellas on Engla land. **1297** R. Glouc. (1724) 233 In þe cyty of Bangor a gret hous þer was, þat were vnder seue cellen [*v.r.* vii celles]. *c* **1330** R. Brunne *Chron.* (1810) 267 A monke of a celle bare him wele þat tide. *c* **1394** *P. Pl. Crede* 314 We maden oure celles To ben in cyties y-set to styȝtle þe people. **1534** *Act 26 Hen. VIII*, c. 3 §8 There be diuers celles apperteining to monasteries and priories. **1651** N. Bacon *Contn. Hist. Disc.* xvii. 147 The Norman and French Cells were in his Predecessor's time seised under this color. **1772** Pennant *Tours Scotl.* (1774) 61 The house was once a cell to the Abby. **1868** Freeman *Norm. Conq.* (1876) II. App. 680 There was a priory of Lapley, which was a cell to Saint Remigius.

3. a. A dwelling consisting of a single chamber inhabited by a hermit or other solitary.

c **1305** *Life St. Dunstan* 60 in *E.E.P.* (1862) 36 A priuei smyþþe bi his celle he gan him biseo. **1362** Langl. *P. Pl.* A. Prol. 28 Ancres and Hermytes þat holdeþ hem in heore Celles. **1393** *Ibid.* C. xviii. 7 Suche eremites .. in here selles lyueden Wiþ-oute borwynge oþer beggynge bote of god one. *c* **1440** *Promp. Parv.* 65 Celle or stodyynge howse [**1499** cell or stody hows], *cella*. **1592** Shaks. *Rom. & Jul.* ii. iv. 193 She shall at Frier Lawrence Cell Be shriu'd and married. *a* **1764** R. Lloyd *Ode Oblivion*, Thou who delightest still to dwell By some hoar and moss-grown cell. **1875** H. E. Manning *Mission H. Ghost* vii. 186 Whose homes are more bare and empty than the cell of an anchorite.

†**b.** *fig.*

1450–1530 *Myrr. Our Ladye* 275 Aue christi cella, Hayle celle of cryste. **1593** Shaks. *Lucr.* 881 In thy shady cell, where none may spy him, Sits sin. **1645** Waller *Div. Love* vi. (R.) The soul contending to that light to fly From her dark cell. **1667** Milton *P.L.* v. 109 [Reason] retires Into her private Cell when Nature rests. **1757** Gray *Epitaph Mrs. Clarke*, A Heart, within whose sacred cell The peaceful Virtues lov'd to dwell.

c. *poet.* A small and humble dwelling, a cottage. Also, a lonely nook: the den of a wild beast.

1577 B. Googe *Heresbach's Husb.* (1586) 11 What meaneth this Cell .. at the entrance? This is syr, my Bayliffes lodging, I lay him by the Gate, that he may see who goeth in and out. **1624** Quarles *Sion's Sonn.*, See how kings' courts surmount poore shepheards' cels. **1647** Herrick *Thanksgiving to God*, Lord, thou hast given me a cell Wherein to dwell. **1735** Somerville *Chase* iii. 222 All the Race Carnivorous .. retire Into their darksome Cells. **1810** Scott *Lady of L.* ii. xxxvii, Like hunted stag, in mountain cell.

d. Applied in poetry to the grave (often with some notion of sense 4).

1750 Gray *Elegy* iv, Each in his narrow cell for ever laid The rude forefathers of the hamlet sleep. **1843** Neale *Hymns for Sick* 49 Nor dreaming of the narrow cell. **1877** Bryant *Among Trees* 49 Their last rest, Their little cells within the burial-place.

4. One of a number of small apartments in a building, serving as the dwelling of a single person:

a. in a monastery, nunnery, or the like. Formerly, also in an almshouse.

1340 *Ayenb.* 267 þer byeþ Monekes uor claustres and uor strayte cellen. *c* **1394** *P. Pl. Crede* 60 þei .. [lurken] in her selles, [And] wynnen werldliche god. **1462** *Hull Trinity House Rec*, Paide for xliii sawne board boght for th' makyng of the Celles of th' said Trenyte House .. iiijs. ijd. **1483** *Cath. Angl.* 56 A Celle, *cella, cellula, conclaue*. **1522** *Hull Trinity House Rec.*, Ye praisels In Agnes Brekhan's Sel prassyd by John Wyssby, etc. .. iiijs. **1526** *Pilgr. Perf.* (W. de W. 1531) 179 b, Some aduysed her to brenne incence in her cell. **1644** *Hull Corporation Bks.* 13 Apr., All such goodes and household stuffe as they should .. use in their seuerall cells or rooms. **1663** Cowley *Verses & Ess.* (1669) 70 The Chartreux wants the warning of a Bell To call him to the duties of his Cell. **1859** Jephson *Brittany* xiii. 220 In passing along .. I saw the cells of the sisterhood.

b. in a prison; formerly, also in a madhouse. ***condemned cell***: a cell occupied by one who is condemned to death. In *pl.*: a *colloq.* term for imprisonment, esp. in solitary confinement as a punishment for offences against military law.

1722 De Foe *Col. Jack* (1840) 166 The cells in Newgate. **1777** J. Howard *State of Pris.* (1792) 213 The rooms and cells [of Old Newgate] were so close, as to be almost constant seats of disease. **1810** Crabbe *Borough* xxiii, Here separate cells awhile in misery keep Two doom'd to suffer. **1828** Carlyle *Misc.* (1857) I. 234 Tasso pines in the cell of a madhouse. **1884** Griffiths *Chron. Newgate* 360 Hence there was a terrible accumulation of prisoners in the condemned cells. **1891** Kipling *Life's Handicap* 23 You 'ave been absent without leave an' you'll go into cells for that. **1910** Galsworthy *Justice* iii. ii, Now I'll get cells, I suppose, or seven days' bread and water. **1918** W. J. Locke *Rough Road* xvii, At the worst they might give him cells when he recovered. **1929** Galsworthy *Exiled* iii. i, In the Court yesterday, you give me a night cells for sleepin' out.

†**5.** A small private room. *Obs. rare.*

1340–70 *Alisaunder* 525 Nectanabus .. passed in his Paleis too a priuie sell. *c* **1460** J. Russell *Bk. Nurture* in *Babees Bk.* (1868) 128 Serue hit [ypocras] forth with wafurs bothe in chambur & celle.

6. *Archit.* = cella (see also 9 a).

1842–75 Gwilt *Archit.*, Gloss. *Cell*, in ancient architecture the part of a temple within the walls.

II. One of the compartments into which anything is divided.

7. *generally.* e.g. a compartment of a dove-cot or the like (so in Lat.), of a drawer or cabinet, a pigeon-hole. *arch.*

1577 B. Googe *Heresbach's Husb.* (1586) 169 For the tame Pigions .. they make .. certaine hollowe roomes, and celles for them. **1727** Pope *Art Sinking* 115 Cells resembling those of cabinets for rarities.

8. One of the compartments in the comb of wax made by bees. [So L. *cella*.]

1577 B. Googe *Heresbach's Husb.* (1586) 175 b, Their Coames that they make are wrought full of holes, which holes .. are their Celles .. these Celles they doe all fill with Honie. **1609** C. Butler *Fem. Mon.* (1634) 57 Ðis Com conteineth about six Cels of ðe bignes and fashion of ðe Bees Cels. **1720** Watts *Hymn, How doth the little busy bee*, How skilfully she builds her cell, How neat she spreads the wax. **1774** Goldsm. *Nat. Hist.* (1776) VIII. 70 The cells of the bees are perfect hexagons. **1816** Kirby & Sp. *Entomol.* (1843) I. 368. **1875** Jowett *Plato* (ed. 2) III. 106 A bee-keeper would cut out the cells of drones.

9. One of a number of spaces into which a surface is divided by linear partitions: *spec.*

a. in *Archit.* (see quot.)

1850 Parker *Gloss. Archit.* (ed. 5) I. 116 The term vaulting cell is applied by Mr. Whewell to the hollow space between the principal ribs of a vaulted roof.

b. *Entom.* 'The space between the nerves of the wings of insects.'

1881 in *Syd. Soc. Lex.*

c. *Math.* See Peaucellier cell.

10. *Electr.* Originally, one of the compartments of the wooden trough of Cruickshank's voltaic battery; afterwards applied to the vessel (in Daniell's or similar batteries) containing one pair of plates of divers metals immersed in fluid. Now, usually, a simple voltaic apparatus, containing only one pair of metallic elements; when several *cells* are united they constitute a *battery*.

1828 *Oxf. Cycl.* III. 521 The plates [in Children's battery] are .. immersed in the cells of a trough. **1848** Walker *Man. Electr.* 329 A single cell of this battery is represented in fig. 142. It consists essentially of a copper cell A, etc. **1882** Watts *Dict. Chem.* II. 425 In Daniell's battery, each cell consists of a copper cylinder. *Ibid.* 428 The two liquids in each cell being separated by a porous diaphragm.

III. An enclosed space, cavity, or sac, in organized bodies, or (*transf.*) in mineral products.

11. *generally.* **a.** Applied to various larger cavities having functions, as the ventricles of the heart, the loculi of the ovary in plants, etc. (In modern scientific language seldom used.)

1398 Trevisa *Barth. De P.R.* xvii. xcix. (1495) 665 The greynes of pomegarnades ben ordenyd in theyr owne selles. **1578** Lyte *Dodoens* ii. xxiii. 174 After them certayne hollow little huskes or Celles. **1607** Topsell *Four-f. Beasts* 110 They [bitches] bring forth many at a time—sometime five, seven, nine, or twelve; for so many cels hath the female in her womb. **1688** R. Holme *Armoury* ii. 85/1 The Cell is the hollow places in puds, husks, or coars .. in the Fruit. **1704** J. Harris *Lex. Techn.* s.v. *Coniferous*, In which Cone are many Seeds, and when they are ripe the several Cells or Partitions in the Cone gape or open, and the Seed drops out. **1751** Chambers *Cycl.*, The name is also given, by botanists, to the partitions in the husks or pods, where the seeds of plants lie. **1776** Withering *Bot. Arrangem.* (1796) I. 320 Capsule roundish, with as many cells as there are styles. **1845** Lindley *Sch. Bot.* i. (1858) 16 The interior of the ovary is called the *cell*.

b. Applied to minute cavities or interstices in the structure of any tissue, mineral substance, etc.

1819 *Pantologia* s.v., *Cellular membrane* .. by means of the communication of the cells of this membrane .. the butchers blow up their veal. **1845** Darwin *Voy. Nat.* xxi. (1852) 493 The central part is coarsely cellular, the cells decreasing in size towards the exterior .. the outside crust of finely cellular lava. **1856** Woodward *Fossil Shells* 39 Horizontal sections exhibit a cellular net-work, with here and there a dark cell, which is empty. **1861** Hulme tr. *Moquin-Tandon* ii. i. 41 Cellular or areolar tissue is composed of numerous lamellæ, which by their interlacement intercept a number of open spaces termed cells.

c. ***cells of the brain***: the imaginary cavities or compartments in that organ, formerly supposed to be the seats of particular mental faculties, or to serve as 'pigeon-holes' for the reception of knowledge. (More scientifically, the ventricles of the brain were called *cells*.) *Obs.* exc. *fig.*

1393 Gower *Conf.* II. 176 Of a man The wit .. Is in the celles of the brain. **1430** Lydg. *Chron. Troy* i. ii, So feble was his celle retentif. **1541** R. Copland *Guydon's Quest. Chirurg.*, Howe many celles hath the brayne after his length. **1605** Bacon *Adv. Learn.* ii. iii. §5 History .. answereth to one of the cells, domiciles, or offices of the mind of man; which is that of the memory. *c* **1720** Prior (J.) The brain contains ten thousand cells, In each some active fancy dwells. **1784** Cowper *Task* vi. 11 It [the sound] opens all the cells Where Mem'ry slept. **1834** H. Miller *Scenes & Leg.* vii. (1857) 88 The corresponding cells of understanding and memory.

12. a. In modern *Biology*: The ultimate element in organic structures; a minute portion of protoplasm, enclosed usually in a membranous investment. Often with a defining word prefixed, as *blood-cell*.

The history of this sense appears to begin with Grew, who observed and described the cells of plants. (See the 17–18th c. quots. that follow.) But the determination of the relation of these cells to the living organism belongs to the present century.

1672–3 Grew *Anat. Plants* (1682) 64 The Microscope .. shews that these Pores are all, in a manner, Spherical, in most Plants; and this Part an infinite Mass of little Cells or Bladders. **1751** Chambers *Cycl.*, *Cells*, in anatomy, are little bags, or bladders, where fluids, or other matters, are lodged; called also *loculi, cellulæ*, etc. **1770** Sir J. Hill *Constr. Timber* 68 We see that cell in its true nature: it is an oval Bladder or Bleb.

1845 Day tr. *Simon's Anim. Chem.* I. 212 The general action of the hepatic cells. **1851** Carpenter *Man. Phys.* (ed. 2) 7 We shall hereafter see that a cell, or closed vesicle, formed of a membranous wall, and containing fluid, may be regarded as the simplest form of a living body. **1855** Bain *Senses & Int.* i. ii. §4 The countless millions of nerve cells. **1861** Hulme tr. *Moquin-Tandon* ii. i. 40 They are accordingly true vesicles; and on that account .. the name of 'blood cells' is to be preferred. **1866** A. Flint *Princ. Med.* (1880) 39 The modern conception of a cell is based, not upon its etymological significance, but upon the presence in it of living matter or protoplasm. Even formless clumps of protoplasm are sometimes called cells. **1871** Tyndall *Fragm. Sc.* (ed. 6) II. xii. 264 The yeast-plant .. is an assemblage of living cells. **1880** Gray *Struct. Bot.* §45 These component parts .. take one common name, that of Cells.

b. *fig.* A small group of people (occas. a single person) working within a larger organization as a nucleus of political, esp. revolutionary, activity; also, the headquarters of such a group.

1925 *Glasgow Herald* 25 Apr. 10 They were Communists and were carrying membership cards of Communist cells. **1931** *Morning Post* 6 Aug. 12/4 The Viennese police have discovered a Communist 'cell' in .. a district of the city. **1937** A. Huxley *Ends & Means* viii. 73 Ten is the number of individuals constituting a Communist cell. **1939** G. B. Shaw *Geneva* i. 20 My butler .. tells me that my footman .. is a cell... A communist cell. Like a bee in a hive. Planted on me by the Communists to make their dreadful propaganda in my household! **1958** L. A. G. Strong *Treason in Egg* v. 93 What if the thing was organised like an underground cell in war-time, when each member of the resistance knew only his own little bit of the chain of activity.

13. The cup-like cavity occupied by an individual polype in a compound polypidom, in the Zoophytes and Polyzoa. Also, a simple shell of one of the Foraminifera.

1847 Carpenter *Zool.* §1053 This horny tube is enlarged at certain points into sheaths or cells for the protection of the Polypes; within these the individuals can retract themselves. *Ibid.* 1054 The cells are arranged upon the sides of these [branched stems] like the minute leaflets of mosses. **1855** Kingsley *Glaucus* (1878) 73 Each polype cell is edged with whip-like spines. **1855** Gosse *Man. Marine Zool.* I. 11 *Lagena*: Cell calcareous, single, globular, with a long external tubular neck. *Ibid.* 21 *Sertularia*: Corallum plant-like .. cells vase-like .. alternate, or in pairs.

IV. Applied to various hollow receptacles or containing cavities.

14. a. *generally.*

1727 A. Hamilton *New Acc. E. Ind.* II. liv. 287 Wells of Fire, that continually burn in their own Cells.

†**b.** The brass socket in which the lenses of a microscope, etc. are mounted. *Obs.*

1704 J. Harris *Lex. Techn.* s.v. *Microscope*, Object-Glasses .. fix'd in Brass Cells ready to screw on. **1784** Herschel in *Phil. Trans.* LXXV. 44 Unscrewing the object-glass or speculum a little in its cell.

c. *Microscopy.* A cavity hollowed out of, or built up upon, a glass slide, for the purpose of receiving an object for microscopical observation.

1881 in *Syd. Soc. Lex.* **1881** Carpenter *Microscope* v. (ed. 6) 216 Where large shallow cells with flat bottoms are required (as for mounting Zoophytes, small Medusæ, etc.).

V. 15. *attrib.* and *Comb.* **a.** (in senses 3, 4) as ***cell-gallery, -grating***; ***cell-bred*** adj.; **b.** (in sense 12), as ***cell-action, -aggregate, -body, -cavity, -cleavage, -division, -evolution, -fibre, -form, -formation, -fusion, -genesis, -germ, -growth, -life, -mass, -membrane, -multiplication, -nucleus, -pigment, -plate, -proliferation, -sap, -stage, -substance, -wall***; ***cell-free*** adj.; **cell-count**, a count or estimate of the number of cells in a given amount of blood, etc.; **cell-layer** = germinal *layer*; **cell line**, a population of cells *in vitro* which are descended through one or more sub-cultures from a single primary culture; also, a group of cells *in vivo* which share a common characteristic because of a common descent; **cell-lineage**, the stages in the development of a

cell or blastomere; **cell-spot**, a spot of colour occurring in the spaces between the nerves in the wings of certain lepidopterous insects; **cell strain**, a population of cells sharing some common characteristic that persists to a greater or lesser extent when they are propagated in cultures.

1847-9 TODD *Cycl. Anat.* IV. 101/2 *Cell-action then must have some influence as the cause of the chemical changes. **1878** BELL tr. *Gegenbauer's Comp. Anat.* 16 A subordinate part of the *cell-body. **1728** POPE *Dunciad* II. 356 A low-born, *cell-bred, selfish, servile band. **1847-9** TODD *Cycl. Anat.* IV. 442/1 Between the cell-wall and the *cell-cavity. **1910** J. TURNER in *Jrnl. Mental Sci.* LVI. 487 The value of a *cell-count for diagnostic purposes. **1962** *Lancet* 5 May 929/1 The cell-count reached 2000 cocci per ml. **1882** VINES *Sachs' Bot.* 762 The fresh formation of parts connected with *cell-division is in general independent of light. *Ibid.* 16 This mode of *cell-formation consists almost invariably in the bipartition of a mother-cell. **1872** AITKEN *Sc. & Pract. Med.* (ed. 6) II. 1054 Other *cell-forms occur in the urine. **1946** *Cell-free [see ANTIBIOTIC *a.* 2]. **1967** *Listener* 3 Aug. 142/3 The solution of the genetic code has come mainly from biochemical studies of protein synthesis in cell-free extracts. **1791** BENTHAM *Panopt.* I. 17 Postsc., The *Cell-Galleries are..perfectly commanded by every station in the Inspection-part. *Ibid.* 55 Postsc., The other [party] immediately within the *Cell-grating. **1859** TODD *Cycl. Anat.* V. 9/1 Minute cells are formed..which may be called reproductive *cell-germs. **1893** TUCKEY *Hatschek's Amphioxus* 55 All changes from the blastula onwards can be traced to these primitive *cell-layers. **1951** *Trans. N.Y. Acad. Sci.* XIII. 324/2 A study of the virus of equine encephalomyelitis on different normal and tumor *cell lines. **1961** M. HYNES *Med. Bacteriol.* (ed. 7) xxv. 379 Cell lines such as the HeLa strain are generally used for routine culture and antibody titration. **1961** *Lancet* 19 Aug. 435/2 If these cells are XXY then the presence of such abnormal cell lines is presumably restricted to a few tissues. **1892** E. B. WILSON in *Jrnl. Morphology* VI. 361 The *cell-lineage of Nereis. **1911** J. A. THOMSON *Biol. of Seasons* ii. 182 The primordium..is continuous through unspecialised cell-lineage with the fertilised egg from which the parent arose. **1946** *Nature* 5 Oct. 461/2 Tissue culture made it possible to prove that the cell-lineages of the ordinary somatic cells of the body are indefinite or indeterminate. **1870** BENTLEY *Bot.* 19 The *cell-membrane of young cells is very thin. **1835** LINDLEY *Introd. Bot.* (1848) I. 34 *Cell-nuclei occur in all classes and orders of plants. **1847-9** TODD *Cycl. Anat.* IV. 117/1 The only true black *cell-pigment. **1882** VINES *Sachs' Bot.* 18 A row of granules now makes its appearance..this is the *cell-plate. **1877** ROBERTS *Handbk. Med.* (ed. 3) I. 45 The first tendency is to the active production of cells,—*cell-proliferation or germination as it is termed. **1902** *Proc. Zool. Soc.* I. 49 The black *cell-spots on the primaries. **1936** *Amer. Jrnl. Cancer* XXVII. 69 Although the diagnoses were different, the *cell strains established from D.Au., H.Da. and A.Ha. I and II were strikingly similar in cytological appearance and cultural behavior. **1958** *Jrnl. Immunol.* LXXXI. 426/1 Advances in tissue culture techniques have made available numerous stable cell strains..which have contributed to recent developments in virology. **1847-9** TODD *Cycl. Anat.* IV. 102/1 The *cell-wall must be the seat of endosmosis and exosmosis. **1882** VINES *Sachs' Bot.* 3 Older wood and cork thus consist of a mere framework of cell-walls.

†**cell**, *sb.*² *Obs. rare*⁻¹. Erroneous f. CAUL.

1607 TOPSELL *Four-f. Beasts* 498 The fat of sheep which is gathered from the caul or cell.

cell, *sb.*³ *Cinemat.* Also cel. [Abbrev. of CELLULOID.] A transparent sheet of celluloid or similar film material; esp. such a sheet bearing opaque matter (e.g. a drawing), used in combination with other sheets to produce a composite picture. Also *attrib.*

1933 G. H. SEWELL *Commercial Cinemat.* x. 160 The two drawings are..replaced on the desk, a cell placed on top of them, and the drawing of the ram in its first position is made on the cell. The subsequent cells receive images of the successive positions of the ram. **1938** S. W. BOWLER in S. G. B. Stubbs *Mod. Encycl. Photogr.* I. 253/2 The next stage is the substitution of a transparent celluloid 'overlay' for the papers on which the figures are drawn. With these celluloid overlays, or 'cels' as they are called, there are almost unlimited possibilities of action available, since at least two or three may be used..over the same background. *Ibid.* 253/2 The drawings are usually made on these 'cels' in non-waterproof ink. **1959** HALAS & MANVELL *Technique Film Anim.* xix. 223 The head of the colouring department..is responsible for handing out the traced cells to the individual colourists. **1959** *Listener* 23 July 126/2 A new pencil called the cell-graph, invented by the London film cartoonist John Halas, enables the key artist to draw his own work directly on to the celluloid sheets. **1966** *New Scientist* 10 Feb. 346/1 The cels have to be individually photographed.

cell, *v.* [f. CELL *sb.*¹] †**a.** *trans.* To shut up in a cell. *Obs. rare.* **b.** *intr.* To dwell in a cell; *spec.* to share a prison cell *with* another person. *slang.*

1592 WARNER *Alb. Eng.* VII. (R.) A recluse from the world, And celled under ground. **1592** WYRLEY *Armorie* 96 An Abbey strong..Wherein there celd a Monke of enuious moode. **1903** J. FLYNT *Rise of Ruderick Clowd* iii. 108, I celled for a couple o' years with old Darbsey—he was doin' life. **1965** T. CAPOTE *In Cold Blood* iii. 130 He was the first fellow I celled with. We celled together I guess a month.

c. *trans.* To store in cells.

1819 WIFFEN *Aonian Hours* 75 Honey, which the bee Cells beneath briery boughs. **1927** *Chambers's Jrnl.* Feb. 90/1 Last autumn one of my stocks celled twelve pounds in twelve hours.

cell, obs. form of SELL, SILL.

‖**cella** ('sɛlə). [Lat.] The body of the temple, as distinct from the portico and other external structures; = CELL 6.

1676 F. VERNON in *Phil. Trans.* XI. 578 The length of its cella is but 73 feet, the breadth, 26. **1846** ELLIS *Elgin Marb.* I. 24 It consisted of a cella, flanked by a double row of pillars. **1878** B. TAYLOR in *N. Amer. Rev.* CXXVI. 118 The cella of the temple was nearly seventy feet wide.

cellæform, erron. form of CELLIFORM.

cellar ('sɛlə(r)), *sb.* Forms: 3-5 celer(e, 4-6 seler, 4-7 celler, (5 celar), 5-7 seller, 6-7 sellar, (7 sellor), 7- **cellar.** [ME. *celer*, a. Anglo-F. *celer*, OF. *celier* (mod.F. *cellier*):—L. *cellārium* set of cells, receptacle for food, f. *cella* CELL.]

†**1. a.** A store-house or store-room, whether above or below ground, for provisions; a granary, buttery, or pantry. *Obs.* exc. *dial.* in *fish-cellar*; see quot. 1848; cf. also *coal-cellar*, *wine-cellar*.

a **1225** *Ancr. R.* 214 He stikeð euer iðe celere, oðer iðe kuchene. *a* **1300** *Cursor M.* 4676 Siþen commanded [ioseph] him-selue Depe selers for to delue. *a* **1340** HAMPOLE *Psalter* cxliii. 15 þaire celers ful riftand. *c* **1375** *O.E. Prayers* in *Rel. Ant.* I. 40 The kyng hath led me in to a wyn-celer. **1382** WYCLIF *Luke* xii. 24 Biholde ȝe crowis..to whiche is no celer, nether beerne, and God fedith hem. *c* **1420** *Liber Cocorum* (1862) 33 Kepe hit fro ayre..In cofer, or huche or seler merke. **1483** *Cath. Angl.* 56 A Celler, *cellarium*..etc. *vbi* a butry. **1483** CAXTON *Esope* 2 b, He fonde the celer open .. and hath eten al the fygges. *c* **1535** DEWES *Introd. Fr.* in *Palsgr.* 1031 Brynge this gentilman to the seller & make him good chere. **1598** FLORIO, *Cella*..a seller or butterie. **1663** COWLEY *Verses & Ess.* (1669) 131 Sellars and Granaries in vain we fill, With all the bounteous Summers store. **1848** C. A. JOHNS *Week at Lizard* 41 Here is a fish-cellar..a place for salting, keeping, and storing away pilchards.

†**b.** *fig. Obs.*

a **1340** HAMPOLE *Psalter* lv. 12 Of þe awtere of my hert and þe celere of my consyens cumes all þat i kyndel in þi luf. **1387** TREVISA *Higden* (Rolls) I. 77 Paradys..was þe celer and place of all fairenesse. **1480** *Cambriæ Epit.* 64 in *Map's Poems* (1841) App., God..Made that lond..To be selere of all hele. **1565** JEWEL *Repl. Harding* (1611) 393 A man.. being brought by God into his inward cellers, may from thence obtaine the true vnderstanding, and interpretation of the Holy Scriptures.

2. a. An underground room or vault.

This sense occurs contextually in some of the earlier quots.; it is impossible to determine at what period the notion of 'store-room' began to give place to that of 'underground chamber'. Cotgr. 1611 has it as the transl. of Fr. *cave*, and Minsheu 1617 gives as its equivalents Fr. *cave* and Lat. *hypogæum*.

[**1331** *Literæ Cantuar.* (Rolls) I. 400 Nostre celer de nostre novele meson de piere en Chepe.] *c* **1330** R. BRUNNE *Chron. Wace* (Rolls.) 2068 In Londone he dide hure kepe Vnder erthe in a seler depe. *c* **1450** *Merlin* 125 In roches or in seleres under erthe. **1583** STUBBES *Anat. Abus.* II. 29 In a moyst seller, vnderneath the grounde. **1633** T. STAFFORD *Pac. Hib.* viii. (1821) 572 They were constrayned to retyre into the Sellors. **1787** T. JEFFERSON *Corr.* (1830) 123 A fine piece of mosaic, still on its bed, forms the floor of a cellar. **1873** MORLEY *Rousseau* I. 41 After..six weeks..passed in the garret or cellar of his rude patroness. **1877** BRYANT *Song of Tower* vii, In..the damp cellar's stifling air.

†**b.** *transf.* Applied to the grave. *Obs.*

c **1550** LACY *Wyl Bucke's Test.*, I bequeth mi body to the colde seler.

c. With defining words prefixed, as *beer-*, *coal-*, *wine-cellar*, which see under their initial element.

3. Often for *wine-cellar*; hence *transf.* the contents of the wine-cellar, a person's stock of wines.

1541 *Act 33 Hen. VIII*, c. 12. §10 The sergeant of the sellar..shall also be than and there redy with a pot of redde wine. **1610** SHAKS. *Temp.* II. ii. 137 My Cellar is in a rocke by th' sea-side. **1706-7** FARQUHAR *Beaux' Strat.* I. i, I have now in my Cellar Ten Tun of the best Ale in Staffordshire. **1841** EMERSON *Lect. Conserv.* Wks. (Bohn) II. 274 O conservatism! your pantry is full of meats and your cellar of wines. *Mod.* He gives very good dinners, but I don't think much of his cellar.

†**4.** A box, a case; *esp.* for holding bottles; a case of bottles. (For SALT-CELLAR cf. SALER, of which *-cellar* is a corruption.) *Obs.*

1632 B. JONSON *Magn. Lady* III. i. (D.) Run for the cellar of strong waters quickly. **1627** CAPT. SMITH *Seaman's Gram.* xiii. 61 Boy fetch my cellar of bottles. **1667** PEPYS *Diary* 1 Apr., His wife afterwards did..give me a cellar of waters of her own distilling.

¶**5.** for SOLER, upper-room.

a **1300** *Cursor M.* 15208 He þam lent..A celer in at ete. **1432-50** tr. *Higden* (Rolls) III. 285 Goenge to a hie parte of the seller [*solarii*] or chamber.

6. *attrib.* and *Comb.*, as *cellar-bin*, *-door*, *-keeper*, etc.; *cellarless* adj.; also **cellar-book**, a book containing an account of the stock of wines, etc. in a cellar; **cellar-flap**, a flap on hinges, level with the surface of the ground, opening into a cellar; **cellar-kitchen**, a kitchen below the ground-floor, a basement kitchen; **cellar-physic**, wine; **cellar-plate**, an iron plate in the pavement covering the entrance-hole of a coal-cellar; **cellar-slug**, a large striped slug found in cellars; **cellar-way**, a passage through, or as if through, cellars.

1883 LLOYD *Ebb & Fl.* I. 2 Its *cellar-bins—some one else's patent. **1769** G. SELWYN *Let.* 4 July in *Hist. MSS. Comm.* (1897) 15th Rep., App. VI. 248 According to my *cellar book you will have had in all ten dozen. **1848** THACKERAY *Van. Fair* xxiv. 202 He..overhauled the butler's cellar-book. **1920** G. SAINTSBURY (*title*) Notes on a cellar-book. **1684** *Gt. Frost* (1844) 14 Their carelessly leaving open *sellar door. **1697** *C'tess D'Aunoy's Trav.* (1706) 193 It is as big as a Cellar-door key. **1884** T. W. HIME *Public Health* 57 Prohibition of occupying of *Cellar Dwellings. **1883** *Daily News* 10 Jan. 6/7 Injuries received.. in falling over the *cellar-flap. **1591** PERCIVALL *Sp. Dict.*, *Cillero*, a *celler-keeper. **1793** J. BERESFORD in *Looker-on* No. 54 Cow-heel and such *cellar-messes. **1697** DAMPIER *Voy.* (1729) I. 542 Fine Air..good Kitchin and *Cellar Physick. **1881** *Daily News* 22 Apr. 2/6 The defendant was legally liable in having his *cellar plate unfastened. **1882** *Garden* 30 Dec. 579/2 A fine example of the *cellar slug. *a* **1762** S. NILES in *Mass. Hist. Soc. Coll.* (1861) V. 512 Two or three were found lying..in the *cellar-way. **1867** HOWELLS *Ital. Journ.* 47 The effect of the buildings vaulted above the sidewalks is that of a continuous cellarway.

cellar ('sɛlə(r)), *v.* [f. prec. sb.] *trans.* To put into a cellar; to store up as in a cellar. Also, *to cellar in*, and *fig.*

16.. COTTON, There underground a magazine Of sovereign juice is cellared in. **1677** R. CARY *Chronol.* I. I. I vii. 23 They had ended their Vintage..and were ready to Seller their Wine. **1873** W. S. MAYO *Never Again* ii. 17 His sympathies..cellared in the depths of his own mind. **1885** *Law Times* LXXX. 191/1 A pipe of port wine, which was cellared for the plaintiffs. **1886** *Athenæum* 3 July 18/2.

cellar, var. of CELURE, *Obs.*

cellarage ('sɛlərɪdʒ). Also 6-7 **-idge, selerage,** 7 **selleredge, -idge.** [f. CELLAR *sb.* + -AGE.]

1. Provision of cellars; cellar accommodation; cellars collectively.

1602 SHAKS. *Ham.* I. v. 151 Come one, you here this fellow in the selleredge Consent to sweare. **1662** GERBIER *Princ.* (1665) 36 Nor ought the Kitchin or other Offices and Selleridge..to be so placed as they may prove prejudiciall to the Court. **1727** BRADLEY *Fam. Dict.* I. s.v. *Building*, A good Ascent..makes a House wholesome, and yields Conveniency for good Cellarage. **1855** DICKENS *Dorrit* 407/2 The old house had had famous cellerage.

b. *transf.* and *fig.*

1865 E. BURRITT *Walk Land's E.* 349 Cornwall..has almost everything in its cellarage except coal. **1878** BAYNE *Purit. Rev.* v. 165 Counting in its ranks Coke and Selden, each with extensive cellarage of brain. [Cf. CELL 11 c.]

2. †**a.** A feudal or seignorial duty upon wine when placed in the cellar (*obs.*). **b.** Charge for the use of a cellar or storehouse. †**c.** Money collected from banqueters at a Lord Mayor's Feast: see quot. 1825.

1512 *Act 4 Hen. VIII*, c. 10 The Bailifwike of Toppsam with the Selerage and Cranage and the Warren of Cones within the same. **1526** *Ord. R. Househ.* (1790) 195 Cellaridge, Cranage, Sponage, Romage, and Carriage of Wine. **1762** tr. *Busching's Syst. Geog.* V. 666 The excise and toll is collected by the King's officers, but the cellerage there by the magistrate to whom it belongs. **1809** R. LANGFORD *Introd. Trade* 122 Paid cellerage £3 5*s.* **1825** in Hone *Every-day Bk.* I. 1335 This was termed cellarage, and was divided between the yeoman of the cellar and the butler.

cellared ('sɛləd), *ppl. a.* [f. CELLAR *sb.* and *v.* + -ED.] That is stored or housed in a cellar. ***cellared fish***: fish prepared in a fish-cellar; cf. quot. 1848 in CELLAR *sb.*¹.

1848 C. A. JOHNS *Week at Lizard* 54 The greater part of the cellared fish are exported. **1855** I. TAYLOR *Restor. Belief* (1856) 298 Cellared wretchedness, and disease.

cellarer ('sɛlərə(r)). *Hist.* Forms: 4-6 cell-, celerer(e, 6 selerer, 7 cellerar, 6- **cellarer.** [ME. *celerer*, *cellerer*, a. Anglo-Fr. *celerer*, for OF. *celerier*, f. *celier* CELLAR.]

The officer in a monastery, or similar establishment, who had charge of the cellar and provisions.

a **1300** *Vox & Wolf* 59 Ac weste hit houre cellerer, He wolde rone after the ȝonge. *c* **1386** CHAUCER *Monkes Prol.* 48 Thou art..Som worthy sexteyn, or som Celerer. **1483** CAXTON *Gold. Leg.* 149/1 He comanded yet to the celerer to gyue it [the oil] to a poure man. **1521** *Test. Ebor.* (Surtees) V. 131 Laurence Clerke, maister sellerar of th'abbay of Whalley. **1662** FULLER *Worthies* (1840) I. 236 Bred a monk in Bury Abbey, and the Cellerar thereof. **1820** SCOTT *Monast.* x, The cellarer will bestow on each a grace-cup and a morsel as ye pass the buttery. **1866** ROGERS *Agric. & Prices* I. xxv. 627.

cellaress ('sɛlərɪs). *Hist.* [f. prec.: see -ESS.] A woman (*e.g.* nun) who had charge of the cellar.

1802 FOSBROKE *Brit. Monach.* x. (1843) 118 The Cellaress of the Gilbertine Nuns. **1825** SCOTT *Betrothed* xvii, The Venerable Mother might be seen..now giving orders to her gardener, now to her cellaress.

cellaret (sɛlə'rɛt). [f. CELLAR *sb.* + -ET¹.]

a. A case of cabinet-work made to hold winebottles, etc. **b.** A sideboard with compartments for the same purpose.

1806-7 J. BERESFORD *Miseries Hum. Life* xx. (1826) 243 With venturous hands At the cellaret stands, Where she picks out so handy Rum, Hollands, and Brandy. **1825** T. COSNETT *Footman's Direct.* 67 Keep proper corks in the cellaret. **1837** THACKERAY *Ravenswing* vii, Under the sideboard stands a cellaret. **1870** DISRAELI *Lothair* xxxii.

'cellarhood. *nonce-wd.* [see -HOOD.] The condition of being a cellar.

1859 SALA *Tw. round Clock* (1861) 361 How it [Evans's supper-room] emerged from a state of brawling night cellarhood, to the dignity of a harmonic meeting.

cellaring ('sɛlərɪŋ), *sb.* [f. CELLAR *sb.* and *v.* + -ING[1].] **1.** = CELLARAGE 1.

1632 SPELMAN *Hist. Sacrilege* (1846) 200 Sir Roger having digged the cellaring of his new house. **1792** A. YOUNG *Trav. France* 158 A wine press and ample cellaring. **1798** T. MORTON *Secr. worth Know.* iii. 4 (L.) Roomy cellaring and commodious attics.

2. *vbl. sb.* Placing in a cellar.

1885 *Law Times* LXXX. 191/1 In the careless cellaring of a pipe of port wine.

†**'cellarist.** *Obs.*—[0] [f. CELLAR *sb.* + -IST.] He who keeps the cellar or buttery; the butler in a religious house or monastery.

1721–1800 in BAILEY. Hence in JOHNSON, WEBSTER, etc.

cellarity. *nonce-wd.* The condition of living in a cellar.

1847 LEWES *Hist. Philos.* (1867) II. 618 Cellarity, when long pent up, is inimical to Life.

cellarless ('sɛləlɪs), *a.* [f. CELLAR *sb.* + -LESS.] Having no cellar.

1853 R. S. SURTEES *Sponge's Sp. Tour* ii. 7 Little cellarless wine-merchants. **1864** E. BURRITT *Walk John O'Gr.* 310 All the damp low cellarless cottages. **1900** *Westm. Gaz.* 9 May 2/2 All this legislation is passed by the cellared population and not by the cellarless population.

cellarman ('sɛləmən). A man who has charge of a cellar; *spec.* the keeper of the Cellar-tavern in old Newgate. Also *transf.*

1658 ROWLAND *Moufet's Theat. Ins.* 920 The Greek Poets make them [drones] to be the Bees cellarmen, or water-bearers. **1772** JACKSON in *Phil. Trans.* LXIII. 11 Through the inattention of the cellarman. **1857** STANLEY *Mem. Canterb.* ii. 58 One of the cellarmen of the Priory. **1870** *Daily News* 27 Dec., The wine in bottle, I was told by the cellarman, is not for sale. **1884** GRIFFITHS *Chron. Newgate* 5 The 'cellarmen' were selected prisoners who could sell candles at their own prices, and got a percentage upon the liquors consumed.

'cellarous, *a. humorous.* Of or pertaining to a cellar.

1860 DICKENS *Uncomm. Trav.* ix. (1861) 133 A little side door..stood open, and disclosed certain cellarous steps. **1867** —— *All Y. Round, Christm. No., No Thoroughf.* 15 Vendale..went down for a cellarous stroll.

†**'cellat,** obs. form of SALADE, sort of helmet.

1598 BARRET *Theor. Warres* III. i. 32 Armed with a skull or close Cellat for the head. (See also CELADE.)

cellate ('sɛleɪt), *a.* [f. on L. type *cellāt-us*, f. *cella*: cf. *caudāt-us* tailed, f. *cauda*.] Celled, having cells. Chiefly in comb., as *unicellate* one-celled, *multicellate* many-celled.

cellated ('sɛleɪtɪd), *ppl. a.* [f. prec. + -ED; cf. *crenated*, *serrated*, etc.] Made in the form of cells; furnished with or divided into cells; celled.

1847 TODD *Cycl. Anat.* IV. 451/1 The cellated cavities of the placenta. **1884** *Health Exhib. Catal.* 71/2 The ovens for these kitcheners are cellated.

celled (sɛld), *ppl. a.* [f. CELL + -ED.]

1. Furnished with cells; arranged or constructed in the form of cells. Often with some defining word prefixed, as ***single-***, ***one-***, ***two-celled***. Also *fig.*

1776 WITHERING *Bot. Arrangem.* (1796) II. 397 Lychnis Caps[ule] 1-3, or 5-celled. **1843–6** OWEN *Lect. Comp. Anat.* iv. (L.) The single-celled plant. **1854** S. THOMSON *Wild Fl.* I. (ed. 4) 65 Anthers..one-celled. **1855** BAILEY *Mystic* 8 Heaven's azure world-hive, celled with stars.

2. Enclosed or ensconced in a cell.

1650 tr. *Bacon's Life & Death* 58 The spirits..seem scattered over their whole bodie, rather than Celled. **1820** KEATS *Fancy*, Thou shalt see the field-mouse peep Meagre from its celled sleep. **1850** D. MOIR *Hour of Thought* v, The monk in hood, With book and rood, And nun in cell'd contrition.

cellendre: see CORIANDER.

cellepore ('sɛlɪpɔə(r)). [ad. mod.L. *cellepora* (Linnæus), f. *cella* CELL, after *madrepora* MADREPORE.] A genus of *Polyzoa* consisting of a group of vase-like chambers with a beak on one or both sides. Also *attrib.*

Hence †**celleporite** (see quot.).

1811 PINKERTON *Petral.* I. 435 Zoophytes..abound in common limestone..Among them may also be classed the milleporite, the celleporite. **1852** TH. ROSS tr. *Humboldt's Trav.* I. v. 184 Their interior is filled with fossil madrepores and cellepores. **1855** KINGSLEY *Glaucus* (1878) 123 There are a few other true cellepore corals round the coast.

celler, cellery, var. CELLAR, CELURE, CELERY.

celli, obs. var. of SELLY, SILLY.

ce'llicolous, *a.* [f. *celli-* comb. form of L. *cella* + *-cola* inhabitant + -OUS.] 'Living in cells or cavities' (*Syd. Soc. Lex.* 1881).

celliferous (sɛ'lɪfərəs), *a. rare.* [f. as prec. + -FEROUS.] Bearing or producing cells.

1754 ELLIS in *Phil. Trans.* XLVIII. 633 Those..corallines, which I call celliferous, from their having rows of cells dispos'd in plant-like ramifications.

celliform ('sɛlɪfɔːm), *a.* Erroneously cellæ-. [f. as prec. + -FORM.] Cell-shaped.

1859 TODD *Cycl. Anat.* V. 503/2 Cellæform termination of a nervous twig. **1877** HUXLEY *Anat. Inv. An.* ii. 90 Cellæform bodies of a bright yellow colour.

cellifugal (sɛ'lɪfjʊgəl), *a.* Also cellulifugal. [f. *celli-*, comb. f. L. *cella* CELL *sb.*[1] + *fugere* to flee: see -AL.] Of the nerve-impulses in a ganglion-cell: passing from the body of a cell. Also **cellipetal** (sɛ'lɪpiːtəl) *a.* [L. *petere* to seek], moving towards the body of a cell.

1900 W. S. HALL *Text-bk. Physiol.* xiii. 538 In monaxons the impulse passes always away from the cell-body, hence is cellulifugal. **1904** TITCHENER tr. *Wundt's Physiol. Psychol.* I. 42 The dendrites are devoted exclusively to cellipetal, the neurites to cellifugal conduction.

'cellist, cellist ('tʃɛlɪst). Shortened form of VIOLONCELLIST, after 'CELLO. Also **'celloist, celloist** ('tʃɛləʊɪst).

1888 MRS. H. WARD *R. Elsmere* v. xxxi, The 'cellist with the hair. **1897** *Daily News* 25 Mar. 9/2 The pianist came, but the 'celloist did not turn up at all. **1954** *Grove's Dict. Mus.* VIII. 823/1 The many fine performances by women cellists.

'Cellite. [a. F. *cellite*, ad. med.L. *cellīta*, f. *cella* (from the cells which they inhabited).] In *pl.* An order of lay brothers hospitallers, called also Bongaris or Alexandrins, founded *c* 1300; they took a special care of madmen. They are now united to the order of Servites. (Littré.)

1882 *Athenæum* 26 Aug. 273/1 A 'Missale Parvum' from the convent of the Cellites of Ghent.

†**'cell-keeper.** *Obs.* [f. CELL *sb.*[1] 1.] A cellar-keeper or cellarer.

1598 FLORIO, *Cellaro*, a butler, or cell keeper.

cello ('tʃɛləʊ). [shortened f. VIOLONCELLO.]

1876 STAINER & BARRETT *Dict. Mus. Terms* 82/1. **1881** *Macm. Mag.* XLIII. 435 In less than a quarter of an hour two 'cellos made their appearance. **1882** *Athenæum* 9 Dec. 782/3 Handel's Concerto Grosso..in seven parts (four violins, viola, cello, and harpsichord) published in 1739. **1954** *Grove's Dict. Mus.* II. 138/2 *Cello*..may be considered as having become an English word by adoption, and there is thus no necessity to spell it with an apostrophe ('cello), as is still frequently done, nor is the Italian plural (*celli*) desirable.

cellobiose (sɛləʊ'baɪəʊs). *Chem.* [f. CELL(ULOSE + -O + BIOSE.] A disaccharide, $C_{12}H_{22}O_{11}$, that is obtained by the partial hydrolysis of cellulose.

1902 *Jrnl. Chem. Soc.* LXXXII. 135 The name cellobiose is now used for the substance previously termed cellose. **1929** *Birm. Post* 22 Feb. 5/4 Over 50% of starch can be converted into maltose, and..cellulose can be transformed into the related disaccharide cellobiose.

celloid ('sɛlɔɪd), *a.* [f. CELL + -OID.] Having the appearance of a cell, cell-like.

1849–52 TODD *Cycl. Anat.* IV. 1108/1 The epithelium consisted of small imperfect celloid particles. **1861** *N. Syd. Soc. Year-bk.* 136 There are certain nuclean or celloid bodies.

celloidin (sɛ'lɔɪdɪn). [a. G. *celloidin*, f. CELL(ULOSE + -OID + -IN[1].] A pure form of pyroxylin, soluble in ether, used chiefly in microscopy for embedding specimens of tissues so that sections may be prepared.

1883 *Jrnl. R. Microsc. Soc.* III. 305 Very elegant results may also be obtained by an imbedding mass originally invented by Duval, and recently much improved by Merkel and Schiefferdecker. This is collodion, or, preferably a solution of so-called celloidin. **1892** *Photogr. Ann.* II. 107 Making an enlarged transparency..on a rapid celloidin film. **1908** *Practitioner* Feb. 201 Three healthy foetuses..were hardened in formol, two of them being cut in celloidin. **1932** *Discovery* May 158/1 The methods of fixing, section-cutting, embedding in paraffin wax or celloidin, [etc.]. **1969** *Jrnl. Anat.* CIV. 212 A large central block, containing the sphenoid bone, pituitary and brain, was then cut out, embedded in celloidin, and cut serially in either the sagittal or the coronal plane.

Cellon ('sɛlɒn). [f. CELL(ULOSE *sb.*] Proprietary name of a composition of cellulose acetate, used as an insulating material, etc. Also *attrib.*

1913 *Chem. Abstr.* VII. 2113 'Cellon' is non-combustible celluloid. **1934** *Archit. Rev.* LXXV. 12/2 As a constructivist painter Moholy-Nagy was the first to use new synthetic materials like galalith, trolith and cellon. **1944** 'N. SHUTE' *Pastoral* iv. 95 Gunnar..scrambled back down the fuselage to the wireless position, where there was a cellon window.

Cellophane, cellophane ('sɛləfeɪn). [f. CELL(ULOSE + -O + *-phane* as in DIAPHANE *a.* and *sb.*] Proprietary name of a glossy transparent material made from regenerated cellulose, used chiefly for wrapping goods, food, etc. Also *fig.* and *attrib.*

1912 CROSS & BEVAN *Res. Cellulose 1905–10* III. v. 162 The 'viscose film' (cellulose) under the powerful auspices of the Société Industrielle de Thaon is at length a *fait accompli*, and is an article of commerce under the descriptive term 'Cellophane'. *Ibid.*, Specimens of 'Cellophane' film. **1921** *Spectator* 23 Apr. 522/2 Ciré, raffia,..tinsels, cellophane, and other ornaments. **1933** R. E. SHERWOOD *Reunion in Vienna* p. xii, To hell with them..and their neuroses, all tidily encased in cellophane. **1935** *Times* 24 Oct. 11/4 A frock in a mixture of cellophane and wool. **1957** *Listener* 26 Sept. 484/1 English itself comes to him as something sparkling Cellophane-fresh instead of the shopworn, finger-soiled article it inevitably seems to ourselves.

Hence **'cellophaned** *a.*, wrapped in cellophane; also *fig.*

1952 *Landfall* VI. 185 The galaxy of cellophaned packets. **1953** C. DAY LEWIS *Italian Visit* i. 14 The white-faced addicts of a patent, cellophaned future.

cellose. An earlier name for CELLOBIOSE.

1901 *Jrnl. Chem. Soc.* LXX. 370 Cellose, a Biose from Cellulose.

cellotape, var. SELLOTAPE, SELLOTAPE.

cellular ('sɛljʊlə(r)), *a.* (and *sb.*). [ad. mod.L. *cellulāris*, f. *cellula* little cell (dim. of *cella*); or perh. ad. F. *cellulaire*: in F. *cellule* has entirely taken the place of *celle*, and its derivatives take the place of those of *cella* both in Fr. and Eng.]

A. *adj.* **1.** Of, pertaining to, or characterized by cells or small apartments for single occupants.

1823 LAMB *Elia* Ser. II. xi. (1865) 308 A poor Carthusian, from strict cellular discipline. **1853** *Fraser's Mag.* XLVII. 139 The cellular vans employed for the transport of criminals. **1868** BROWNING *Ring & Bk.* IX. 1200 Leave these [gauds] for cellular seclusion. **1872** *Daily News* 13 July, The cellular system [of convict discipline] as it is established in Belgium.

2. a. Containing a number of cells, small compartments, or cavities; porous. ***cellular pyrites***: a variety of Marcasite; ***cellular quartz***, etc.

1816 ACCUM *Chem. Tests* (1818) 166 Calcareous cellular stones. **1834** SIR C. BELL *Hand* 292 The skull of the giraffe..is cellular and thin and light as a paper case. **1845** DARWIN *Voy. Nat.* ix. (1879) 180, I had noticed the presence of a few small pebbles of a very cellular basalt. **1868** DANA *Min.* 75 Marcasite..in cellular specimens.

b. Of open texture, as ***cellular linen***; also *sb.*, a material of open texture.

1888 *Cassell's Fam. Mag.* Dec. 60/1 Cellular Clothing. Under-clothing of every kind is now being made of a cellular cloth. **1889** *Pall Mall Gaz.* 5 Jan. 7/1 Cellular linen... Gentlemen have tennis-shirts of real silk cellular now. **1964** *Which?* Apr. 123/1 Cellular, mesh or eyelet fabrics have a regular pattern of small holes over the surface.

3. *Phys.* **a.** Characterized by or consisting of cells (see CELL *sb.*[1], 11–13). As an epithet of vegetable tissues, opposed to *vascular*. See also B.

cellular tissue, in Animal Physiology, a synonym of *areolar* or *connective tissue*; also formerly called ***cellular membrane***; hence ***cellular-membranous*** adj. ***cellular pathology***: a term introduced by Virchow in 1858; 'the doctrine of the origin of disease in a perturbation of action, or an alteration of structure, of some or other of the ultimate cells of which the body is composed' (*Syd. Soc. Lex.*); the study of morbid changes in the cells or ultimate elements of organic tissues.

1753 CHAMBERS *Cycl. Supp.*, *Cellular*, or *Cellulose*, an appellation given by Ruysch, to the second coat of the intestines; in which fat is often found. **1773** *Gentl. Mag.* XLIII. 345 A twisted worm, sometimes six feet long, which introduces itself into the skin, and lodges in the cellular membrane. **1799** SOUTHEY *Nondescr.* iii, My very cellular membrane will be changed, I shall be negrofied. **1830** LINDLEY *Nat. Syst. Bot.* Introd. 15 Vegetables which have no flowers..are..Cellular. **1861** *N. Syd. Soc. Year-bk.* 134 Virchow—Cellular Pathology and Physiological Therapeutics. **1875** DAWSON *Dawn of Life* ii. 33 Cellular plants, as, for example, mosses and lichens. **1876** QUAIN *Anat.* (ed. 8) II. 53 If we make a cut through the skin and proceed to raise it from the subjacent parts, we observe that it is loosely connected to them by a soft filamentous substance of considerable tenacity and elasticity..This is the substance known by the names of 'cellular', 'areolar', 'filamentous', 'connective', and 'reticular' tissue; it used formerly to be commonly called 'cellular membrane'. **1876** BRYANT *Pract. Surgery* (ed. 2) I. 33 The deep cellular-membranous syphilitic sore.

b. Of or pertaining to cells.

1805 W. SAUNDERS *Min. Waters*, This cellular effusion soon disappears. **1836** TODD *Cycl. Anat.* I. 510/1 A very thin albuminous fluid..often termed the cellular serosity.

4. Of, pertaining to, or designating a mobile radio-telephone system in which the area served is divided into sections or 'cells' a few miles across, each with its own short-range transmitter/receiver linked to an automatic switching centre, so that the same frequency can be used in different parts of the area simultaneously and the capacity is thereby increased.

1977 *Wireless World* June 40/1 (*heading*) Cellular mobile radio going ahead. **1982** *New Scientist* 23 Dec. 800/2 Cellular radio is basically automated citizen's band radio with the added extra that you can dial a correspondent, rather than having to set up a conversation by broadcasting a call sign. **1984** *Sunday Times* (Colour Suppl.) 4 Nov. 103/3 (Advt.), So much has been written about developments in cellular car telephones..that the prospective buyer is almost bound to be confused. **1985** *New Scientist* 31 Jan. 5/1 Although owners of cellular radios pay nothing to receive calls in their cars, their callers will pay 43p per minute. **1985** *Times* 15 Feb. 37/7 It will soon be possible to use either of the two cellular networks started this year off almost the entire south coast.

B. *sb. pl.* Cellular plants (in Lat. form *Cellulares*); those having no distinct stem or leaves, but consisting of a cellular expansion of various kinds, which bears the reproductive organs. Applied to Cryptogams, in reference to their markedly cellular structure; but only the humblest orders of these are entirely cellular.

[**1830** LINDLEY *Nat. Syst. Bot.* 1 The presence of flowers, of spiral-vessels, and of cuticular stomata, will at all times distinguish these [*Vasculares*] from *Cellulares*, or flowerless plants.] **1879** *Cassell's Techn. Educ.* I. 54 The least organised plants are termed cellulars.

cellularity (sɛljuːˈlærɪtɪ). [f. CELLULAR + -ITY.] Cellular quality or condition.

1835 LINDLEY *Introd. Bot.* (1848) I. 358 Mirbel however disputes the cellularity of the extine. **1851–9** DARWIN in *Adm. Man. Sc. Eng.* 291 The composition, thickness, and degree of cellularity of any lava-stream.

†**ˈcellulary**, ? *a. Obs. rare*⁻¹. [f. L. *cellula* (cf. CELLULE) + -ARY.] ? Of the nature of a cell.

1597 DANIEL *Civ. Wars* VIII. cii, The good father, with an humble thought, Bred in a cellulary, low retire.

cellulase (ˈsɛljʊleɪs, -eɪz). *Chem.* [f. CELLUL(OSE + -ASE.] An enzyme which brings about the decomposition of cellulose.

1903 *Jrnl. Chem. Soc.* LXXXIV. II. 503 Most moulds attack cellulose, and the action is due to a specific enzyme for which the author [*sc.* G. van Iterson, jun.] supports the name *cellulase*. **1950** *New Biol.* VIII. 99 All enzymes which break down cellulose are called cellulases.

cellulate (ˈsɛljʊleɪt), *a.* [f. L. *cellula*, CELLULE + -ATE² 2.] Composed of or containing cells. Hence **ˈcellulate** *v. trans.*, to furnish with cells; to render cellular. **ˈcellulated** *ppl. a.* = CELLULATE; **celluˈlation**, development of cells.

a **1693** URQUHART *Rabelais* III. i, Matrixes.. Architectonically cellulated. **1836** TODD *Cycl. Anat.* I. 761/1 A vertical section..exhibited a mass..cellulated or porous. **1839–47** *Ibid.* III. 568/1 A section of it, as it thus cellulates the neck. **1854** J. HOGG *Microsc.* II. ii. (1867) 382 *Melosira cribosa*, marine, orbicular, cellulate. **1859** *Ibid.* V. 474/2 A process of..cellulation takes place.

cellule (ˈsɛljuːl). Also 7 cellul. [ad. L. *cellula*, dim. of *cella* CELL *sb.*¹]

1. †**a.** A small compartment; a pigeon-hole. Also *fig.*; cf. CELL *sb.*¹ 11 c. *Obs.*

1652 URQUHART *Jewel* Wks. (1834) 293, I could have firreted out of topick celluls such variety of arguments. *a* **1693** —— *Rabelais* III. xxxiii. 240 The Celluls of his Brain. **1764** FOOTE *Patron* II. i, A kind of bureau; where, in separate cellules, my different knowledge..is stor'd. **1818** J. BROWN *Psyche* 212 So liquor aids myself—like rain, It opes the cellules of the brain. **1819** H. BUSK *Banquet* III. 209 Unlock the cellules, closets of the brain.

b. A small room or cell.

1894 A. MORRISON *Tales Mean Streets* 222 The family should take a whole house..instead of the two rooms and a cellule upstairs now rented. **1908** *Westm. Gaz.* 12 June 8/1 'Each go into a cell and shut the door!' ordered a warderess, indicating a row of tiny cellules.

2. *Phys.* A minute cell (CELL *sb.*¹ 11) or cavity. (In Fr. the dim. *cellule* is used in sense of CELL *sb.*¹ 12.)

1830 LINDLEY *Nat. Syst. Bot.* 237 Cellular tissue, which ..offers an instance of reticulated cellules. **1857** H. MILLER *Test. Rocks* xi. 493 Both possess discs on the side of their cellules. **1869** GILLMORE *Rept. & Birds* Introd. 2 In birds, the lungs are spongy, the cavity of the air-bags becoming obliterated by the multiplication of vascular cellules.

3. *Zool.* (See quot.)

1848 DANA *Zooph.* ii. 16 *note*, By cellule, as hereafter used, the minute pores of the corallum will be referred to.

cellulic (sɛˈljuːlɪk), *a.* [f. CELLULE + -IC.] Of or pertaining to cellules or cells. ***cellulic acid***: a name given by Fremy to an acid supposed to be produced by the action of acids or alkalis on cell walls of vegetables. (*Syd. Soc. Lex.*)

celluliferous (sɛljuːˈlɪfərəs), *a.* [f. L. *cellula* + -FEROUS.] Bearing or producing cellules.

1828 STARK *Elem. Nat. Hist.* II. 436 Expansions flattened ..celluliferous on the external surface. **1849** MURCHISON *Siluria* ix. 187 Two or four very broad celluliferous plants.

cellulin (ˈsɛljʊlɪn). *Chem.* [f. CELLULE + -IN.] **a.** = CELLULOSE. **b.** *esp.* The form of cellulose found in animal bodies.

1854 J. HOGG *Microsc.* II. i. (1867) 257 Composed of cellulin, a material allied to the cellulose of vegetable tissues. **1870** BENTLEY *Bot.* 18 The membrane..consists of the substance called cellulose or cellulin. **1876** HARLEY *Mat. Med.* 712 Cotton is almost pure cellulin.

cellulite (ˈsɛljʊlaɪt, -iːt). [a. F. *cellulite* (also CELLULITIS: see CELLULE, -ITIS.] A special lumpy form of fat supposed to occur in some women, esp. on the hips and thighs, sometimes producing a yellowish puckering of the skin.

1968 *Vogue* 15 Apr. 110/1 Like a swift migrating fish the word *cellulite* has suddenly crossed the Atlantic. *Ibid.* 110/2 In Europe treatments for cellulite vary from acupuncture.. to sea baths. **1969** *Daily Mail* 28 Oct. 19/1 You scrub, either with a hard-core sponge from Switzerland..or a rather alarming double-action massage glove from France. This is said to combat that ugly, dimpled fat called cellulite. **1970** L. AVEDON *Beautiful People's Beauty Bk.* (1971) 71 Cellulite is that most unattractive fat that looks like orange rind when squeezed... Doctors object to the term as inaccurate. **1981** I. FURSTENBERG *Young at any Age* 13 My thighs..(like many women's) accumulate cellulite easily. **1982** S. CONRAN *Lace* xxxvii. 388 Joujou lay back on the bed, having her cellulite massaged away. **1983** *Belle* (Austral.) July–Aug. 6/4 She proceeded to do her leg exercises. She has become obsessed by cellulite.

cellulitic (sɛljuːˈlɪtɪk), *a.* [f. CELLULITIS + -IC.] Pertaining to cellulitis.

1906 FERGUSON in *Trans. Edinb. Obstet. Soc.* XXXI. 127 Where there is no cellulitic abscess which can be evacuated.

‖**cellulitis** (sɛljuːˈlaɪtɪs). *Med.* [mod.L. f. L. *cellula* = CELLULE + -ITIS.] Inflammation of the cellular or areolar tissue. (*Syd. Soc. Lex.*)

1861 BUMSTEAD *Ven. Dis.* (1879) 690 Orbital cellulitis. **1878** T. BRYANT *Pract. Surg.* I. 50 No attempt is made to distinguish between it [erysipelas] and cellulitis.

ˈcellulo-, used as a comb. form of CELLULE, L. *cellula* (for the form cf. BULBO-) forming principally adjs. used in physiology, which in sense are practically compounds of CELLULAR: e.g. ***cellulo-adipose***, (tissue) partly cellular partly adipose; similarly ***cellulo-fibrous***, ***-muscular***, ***-tendinous***, ***-vascular***; ***cellulo-cutaneous***, pertaining jointly to the skin and subcutaneous connective tissue; ***cellulo-membranous***, pertaining to the 'cellular membrane'; ***cellulo-serous***, pertaining jointly to the 'cellular' and 'serous' membranes.

1835 LINDLEY *Introd. Bot.* (1848) I. 140 The disorganised cellulo-vascular structure. **1836** TODD *Cycl. Anat.* I. 12/2 A fibrous or cellulo-fibrous expansion. **1836** *Ibid.* I. 178/2 A middle cellulo-tendinous raphé before and behind that intestine. **1847–9** *Ibid.* IV. 126/1 The cellulo-muscular structures of the limbs. **1857** BULLOCK tr. *Cazeaux' Midwif.* 40 A very thick layer of cellulo-adipose tissue. **1878** T. BRYANT *Pract. Surg* I. 27 Sores or ulcers..of a cellulo-membranous kind. *Ibid.* I. 51 Cellulo-cutaneous forms of the disease.

celluloid (ˈsɛljʊlɔɪd), *a.*¹ [f. L. *cellula* (see above) + -OID.] Having the form or appearance of cells.

celluloid (ˈsɛljʊlɔɪd), *sb.* (and *a.*²). [loosely f. CELLUL-OSE *sb.* + -OID.]

1. a. A solid inflammable material consisting essentially of soluble cellulose nitrate and camphor, used in the manufacture of many articles, esp. photographic film. orig. *U.S.*, as a trade-name.

Invented in America, and first patented in Gt. Britain in April 1871, as a material for dental plates. In its manufacture the cellulose is first reduced by acids to pyroxyline (gun-cotton), camphor is then added, and the mixture subjected to immense hydraulic pressure. It may then be moulded by heat and pressure to any shape, and it becomes hard, elastic, and capable of taking on a fine finish. (The Specification of Hyatt's first British patent (1871, No. 1025) does not contain the name.)

1871 *Amer. Dental Assoc. Trans.* XI. 152 We have many so-called cheap materials..rubber, celluloid, pyroxyline, [etc.]. **1872** *Specif. Hyatt's Patent* No. 3101 The.. manufacture of pyroxyline or soluble cotton into a solid (which is herein denominated 'celluloid'). **1881** *Chamb. Jrnl.* No 909. 349 Celluloid..is an imitation ivory composed of collodion and camphor. **1882** *Whitaker's Almanack* 375/2 One of the most recent uses of the celluloid is for making type and engravers' blocks for printing from. **1892** W. E. WOODBURY *Encyl. Photogr.* 110 *Celluloid Films.* Films of celluloid..may be coated with a gelatine sensitive emulsion, the celluloid taking the place of the glass of the photographic dry plate, the advantage being in the reduction of bulk and weight. **1951** YARSLEY & KITCHEN in H. M. Langton *Synthetic Resins* (ed. 3) ii. 116 The bulk of the..cine film used throughout the world to-day is still celluloid.

b. A piece or sheet of celluloid; *spec.* = CELL *sb.*³

1936 A. JENKINSON *America came my Way* xvii, When each picture comes to be photographed it may actually consist of five different pictures—the background and four celluloids placed one on top of the other. **1959** HALAS & MANVELL *Technique Film Anim.* xix. 223 He is also responsible for seeing that the dye of the celluloids is correct.

c. *transf.* Films; the cinema.

1934 A. G. MACDONELL *How like Angel* II. viii. 147 The British Board of Film Censors..who draw the tenuous line between the decorous and libidinous in the world of celluloid. **1937** A. CALDER-MARSHALL in C. Day Lewis *Mind in Chains* 65 Celluloid now gives them..relief from present trouble. **1938** C. MORGAN *Flashing Stream* 32 There are no heroes but in celluloid.

2. *attrib.* or as *adj.* **a.** Made of celluloid.

1871 *Brit. Jrnl. Dental Sc.* XIV. 364 The material is named the celluloid base, so called from the material of which it is composed. **1882** SWEET & KNOX *Texas Siftings* 9 He is usually swung to a satchel containing a comb and brush,..a clean celluloid collar, and a newspaper. **1892** [see above]. **1923** *Manual of Seamanship* II. 21 Celluloid films should not be allowed on board unless stowed in well-fitting iron boxes. **1962** *Unesco Bull. for Libraries* XVI. 1 In 1887 H. Goodwin produced the first photographic film on celluloid base.

b. Of or pertaining to films; appearing in a film; photographed. Also *fig.*, synthetic; lifeless, unreal.

1922 *Frontier* Nov. 18 The celluloid hero flashed his impartial smile across the screen. **1926** E. WALLACE *More Educ. Evans* (1928) ii. 50 Harold Lloyd favoured them with a celluloid smile as they slipped into the dark interior. **1928** D. H. LAWRENCE *Lady Chatt.* 141 Something that has gone out of the celluloid women of today. **1948** WODEHOUSE *Spring Fever* i. 12 His offspring was contemplating marrying into celluloid circles. **1958** *Times Lit. Suppl.* 15 Aug. p. xxviii/2 A confected thriller plot, complete with flat celluloid characters. **1959** I. & P. OPIE *Lore & Lang. Schoolch.* vii. 118 The celluloid dream-world really begins to have an effect on their thought.

cellulose (ˌsɛljʊˈləʊs; ˈsɛljʊləʊs, -əʊz), *a.* and *sb.* [ad. mod.L. *cellulōs-us*, f. *cellula*, CELLULE.]

A. *adj.* Consisting of an aggregate of 'cells' or small cavities: full of minute cavities.

1753 [see CELLULAR 3.] **1755** MANDUIT in *Phil. Trans.* XLIX. 206 The base is of a stiffer and more cellulose texture. **1854** WOODWARD *Mollusca* II. 241 One small modiola makes its hole in the cellulose tunic of Ascidians.

B. *sb.* **a.** [a. F. *cellulose.*] One of the AMYLOSES. A substance, also called *lignin*, which constitutes the essential part of the solid framework of plants, and occurs to some extent in the animal body. It is amorphous, tasteless, inodorous, absolutely innutritious, insoluble in water, alcohol, ether, dilute acids, and alkalis. The name, introduced by Payen, has become the type of the other chemical terms in -OSE. Also *attrib.*, as in ***cellulose wall***, or *Comb.*, as ***cellulose-digesting*** adj.

1835 LINDLEY *Introd. Bot.* (1848) I. 6 The organic basis of the elementary organs is called cellulose. **1869** ROSCOE *Elem. Chem.* (1874) 403 Gun Cotton..is a substitution product, being cellulose in which three atoms of hydrogen are replaced by NO_2, and is called *trinitro-cellulose*. **1875** DARWIN *Insectiv. Pl.* vi. 125 The gastric juice of animals does not attack cellulose. **1877** WATTS *Fownes' Chem.* II. 207 Cellulose..in fine linen and cotton, which are almost entirely composed of it. **1882** VINES *Sachs' Bot.* 13 In the cell-plates cellulose walls are now formed. **1924** J. A. THOMSON *Science Old & New* xxix. 161 Sheep and cattle live very largely on grass, and yet they are also without cellulose-digesting ferments.

b. Now *esp.* as the basis of important commercial products. In popular use the word commonly designates compounds of cellulose, particularly cellulose acetate and cellulose nitrate, solutions of which form the 'cellulose' finishes used in varnishing metal, woodwork, etc. Also *attrib.*, as ***cellulose lacquer***, ***paint***.

1876 *Jrnl. Chem. Soc.* XXX. 231 (*title*) Cellulose manufacture. **1898** *Daily News* 9 Nov. 4/6 A sawmill and a cellulose factory have just been set up at Mitrovitza. **1902** *Westm. Gaz.* 6 Jan. 2/1 The sulphite cellulose process is due to the labours in the laboratory of Al. Mitscherlich and Tilghmann. **1927** *Observer* 16 Oct. 27 Bodies finished in cellulose. **1930** *Motor Body Building* LI. 105/2 *Cellulose Lacquer*, a finishing material containing nitro-cellulose. **1935** *Discovery* Nov. 326/2 Cellulose lacquers, paints, distempers, etc. **1951** *Good Housek. Home Encycl.* 321/1 Cellulose paint is not very suitable for outdoor work.

c. cellulose acetate, any of several compounds formed by acetylating (usu. with acetic anhydride) some form of cellulose, esp. cotton; used in the manufacture of synthetic fibres, plastics, etc.; **cellulose nitrate**, a compound formed by the action of nitric acid on a cellulose; nitrocellulose.

1880 *Jrnl. Chem. Soc.* XXXVIII. 372 The author describes the properties of five cellulose nitrates. **1895** C. F. CROSS et al. *Cellulose* 35 The cellulose acetates about to be described are of undetermined molecular weight. *Ibid.* 39 Although gun cottons, or pyroxylines, are generally spoken of as nitro-celluloses, they are perhaps more correctly described as cellulose nitrates. **1909** KEANE *Mod. Org. Chem.* 199 Conditions..favourable to explosibility are present in gun-cotton, a mixture of cellulose nitrates, and in blasting gelatine. **1927** T. WOODHOUSE *Artificial Silk* 27 Cellulose Acetate artificial silk, also known as 'Celanese' artificial silk. **1958** *Economist* 20 Dec. 1051/1 Cellulose Acetate makes tough, water-resistant wire and cable coatings. Cellulose Acetate Butyrate produces lacquers, adhesives, airplane dopes and melt and peelable coatings possessing high strength, flexibility and excellent weathering properties.

Hence as *v. trans.*, to treat or coat with a compound of cellulose, esp. with a cellulose lacquer or paint; **ˈcellulosed** *ppl. a.*

1934 *Punch* 29 Aug. 248/2 Dingy Skipper may need re-cellulosing but is fine defensive navigator. **1935** *Times* 23 Oct. 4/5 This last is cellulosed in two shades of metallic blue. **1937** *Times* 23 Dec. 4/7 A less elaborate affair is a cellulosed bed-table. **1958** W. SANSOM *Cautious Heart* 6 Small refectory tables, carved and terribly cellulosed.

cellulosic (ˌsɛljʊˈləʊzɪk), *a.* and *sb.* [f. CELLULOSE *sb.* + -IC.] **A.** *adj.* **a.** Of the nature of cellulose. **b.** Made from (a compound of) cellulose.

1881 *Nature* XXV. 168 Cellulosic substances in their different isomeric states. **1928** *U.S. Pat. 1,817,963* 3 A film sheet for natural color photography comprising a light transmitting support of a cellulosic compound. **1932** *Kodak Abstr. Bull.* XVIII. 508 Process of making cellulosic films. **1949** H. R. SIMONDS et al. *Handbk. Plastics* (ed. 2) i. 14 Synthetic resins..account for about 90% of all the plastics materials now produced. The cellulosic plastics are the second most important group. **1968** J. IRONSIDE *Fashion Alphabet* 248 A cellulosic rayon fibre.

B. *sb.* A substance made from (a compound of) cellulose.

1946 J. M. DEBELL et al. *Germ. Plastics Practice* ix. 203 (*heading*) Water-Soluble Cellulosics and Cellophane. **1949** H. R. SIMONDS et al. *Handbk. Plastics* (ed. 2) xii. 683 Cellulosics are used for bonding paper, thermoplastics, and leather.

cellu'losity. [f. as prec. + -ITY.] The quality or condition of being cellulose; also *concr.* a cellulose structure.

1839–47 TODD *Cycl. Anat.* III. 1002/1 The eye is simply supported on the orbit by a quantity of loose cellulosity. **1854** OWEN in *Circ. Sc.* (1865) II. 72/1 The cut surfaces will demonstrate the..cellulosity of the divided bones.

cellulous ('sɛljʊləs), *a.* [f. CELLULE + -OUS. Cf. Fr. *celluleux.*] = CELLULOSE *a.*; consisting of a single cell or an aggregate of cells.

1800 *Med. Jrnl.* IV. 276 To know whether the most solid, compact..stony part of a bone were cellulous. **1839–47** TODD *Cycl. Anat.* III. 253/1 Cellulous hydatids are simple bags containing fluid. **1852** DANA *Crust.* I. 164 Hand and carpus with a cellulous surface.

ce'lology (siː'lɒlədʒɪ). [f. Gr. κήλη tumour + -(O)LOGY.] That part of medical science which treats of hernia.

1881 in *Syd. Soc. Lex.*

celondine, obs. form of CELANDINE.

celosia (sɪ'ləʊsɪə, -ʃ(ɪ)ə). *Bot.* [mod.L., f. Gr. κήλεος burning, κηλός dry, so called from the burnt appearance of the flowers of some species.] A plant of the amaranthaceous genus so named, esp. the cockscomb, *Celosia cristata.*

1807 T. MARTYN *Miller's Gard. & Bot. Dict.* I. 7 D/8 Celosias or Cock's-combs, are all herbaceous plants. **1899** *Westm. Gaz.* 16 Aug. 4/2 A very fine collection of celosias, a handsome feathery flower, in shades of gold and dark crimson. **1962** *Amateur Gardening* 17 Feb. 4 For an unusually showy plant..nothing can be more effective than celosia or cockscomb.

† **ce'lostomy.** *Obs.* [ad. Gr. κοιλοστομία, f. κοῖλος hollow + στόμα mouth.] Hollowness of voice; speaking with the mouth hollow.

1656 BLOUNT *Glossogr.*, *Celostomy*, when one speaks hollow in the mouth.

ce'lotomy. *Surg.* Also ke-. [ad. Gr. κηλοτομία, f. κήλη rupture + -τομία cutting.] The operation for strangulated hernia by cutting down and dividing the stricture. So **'celotome**, 'the knife or instrument for performing celotomy'.

1847 in CRAIG. **1878** BRYANT *Surgery*, Kelotomy.

celour, var. of CELURE, *Obs.*

† **celse**, *a. Obs. rare*⁻¹. [ad. L. *cels-us* lofty.] Lofty, exalted.

1708 MOTTEUX *Rabelais* (1737) V. 233 Ample Munificence, and Office celse.

† **celsitude** ('sɛlsɪtjuːd). *Obs.* (exc. *humorous*). Also 6 selcitud, 7 celc-, celsitud. [a. F. *celsitude*, ad. L. *celsitūdo* lofty carriage, also in late L. a title of honour, f. *celsus* lofty.]

1. Lofty position, high rank; dignity, eminence.

c **1450** *Crt. of Love* lxxxviii, Honour to thee..Goddess of love, and to thy celsitude. **1500–20** DUNBAR *Gladethe thoue Queyne* 7 Joy be and grace onto thi Selcitud! **1563** FOXE *A. & M.* (1596) 16/2 This celsitude and regalitie of the pope. **1605** BACON *Adv. Learn.* II. xxii. §15 See what Celsitud of honor Plinius secundus attributeth to Traiane. **1680** tr. *Buchanan's De Jure Regni* (1689) 63 It doth over-shadow them all with the Top of its Celsitude.

b. As a title or form of address; = HIGHNESS.

1535 STEWART *Cron. Scot.* I. 177, I beseik, he said, thi celsitude, Exerce thi strenth. **1685** F. SPENCE *Ho. Medici* 265 His Celsitude gave him men to guard him.

2. Loftiness, exaltation; exalted character.

1563–87 FOXE *A. & M.* (1684) II. 294 Whose..celsitude of mind no man may sufficiently express. **1607** *Schol. Disc. agst. Antichr.* 185 Such a celsitude of spirit. *a* **1761** W. LAW *Behmen's Wks.* (1765) 14 Sensibility, Finding, and Celsitude.

3. Height, tallness. (Now *humorous.*)

1678 PHILLIPS, *Celsitude*, tallness, heighth. **1721–1800** BAILEY, *Celsitude*, Highness, Height, Talness. **1824** SCOTT *Redgauntlet* ch. i, Peter Peebles, in his usual plenitude of wig and celsitude of hat.

† **'celsity.** *Obs.*⁻⁰ [f. L. *cels-us* + -ITY.] = prec.

1656 in BLOUNT *Glossogr.*

Celsius ('sɛlsɪəs). The name of a Swedish astronomer, Anders *Celsius* (1701–44), used to designate the centigrade type of thermometer and temperature-scale invented by him in 1742 (see CENTIGRADE *a.*).

1797 *Encycl. Brit.* XVIII. 497/2 Celsius's thermometer. **1850** WEALE *Dict. Terms Archit.* 451/2 The Celsius, or Centigrade thermometer. **1863** E. ATKINSON tr. *Ganot's Physics* §235 On the continent..this division [into 100 parts] is called the centigrade or Celsius scale. *a* **1928** in Gamble *Story North Sea Air Station* 410 My altitude was..about 5,800 metres, the temperature 28° Celsius. **1961** *Times* 23 Dec. 7/4 The Meteorological Office proposal to use the centigrade (Celsius) scale for temperature reports and forecasts to the public.

Celt¹ (sɛlt, kɛlt). Also **Kelt** (kɛlt). [a. F. *Celte*, ad. L. *Celta*, sing. of *Celtæ*, in Gr. Κελτοί. (A later Gr. Κέλται, in Strabo, etc., was probably from L. *Celtæ*.) For conjectures as to a possible derivation, see Rhŷs, *Celtic Britain* (1884) 2.]

1. *Hist.* Applied to the ancient peoples of Western Europe, called by the Greeks Κελτοί, Κέλται, and by the Romans *Celtæ*.

The Κελτοί of the Greeks, also called Γαλάται, *Galatæ*, appear to have been the Gauls and their (continental) kin as a whole; by Cæsar the name *Celtæ* was restricted to the people of middle Gaul (*Gallia Celtica*), but most other Roman writers used it of all the Galli or Gauls, including the peoples in Spain and Upper Italy believed to be of the same language and race; the ancients apparently never extended the name to the Britons.

1607 TOPSELL *Four-f. Beasts* 251 The Indians were wont to use no bridles, like the Græcians and Celts. **1656** BLOUNT *Glossogr.*, *Celt*, one born in Gaul. **1782** WARTON *Hist. Kiddington* 67 (T.) This obstinate war between the insular Britons and the continental Celts. **1839** THIRLWALL *Greece* VIII. 411 The Celts advanced within five or six days' march of his camp.

2. A general name applied in modern times to peoples speaking languages akin to those of the ancient Galli, including the Bretons in France, the Cornish, Welsh, Irish, Manx, and Gaelic of the British Isles.

This modern use began in French, and in reference to the language and people of Brittany, as the presumed representatives of the ancient Gauls: with the recognition of linguistic affinities it was extended to the Cornish and Welsh, and so to the Irish, Manx, and Scottish Gaelic. CELTIC has thus become a name for one of the great branches of the Aryan family of languages (see CELTIC); and the name Celt has come to be applied to any one who speaks (or is descended from those who spoke) any Celtic language. But it is not certain that these constitute one race ethnologically; it is generally held that they represent at least two 'races', markedly differing in physical characteristics. Popular notions, however, associate 'race' with language, and it is common to speak of the 'Celts' and 'Celtic race' as an ethnological unity having certain supposed physical and moral characteristics, especially as distinguished from 'Saxon' or 'Teuton'.

[**1703** PEZRON (*title*), Antiquité de la Nation et de la langue des Celtes. **1706** JONES (*tr. of Pezron*), Antiquities of Nations, more particularly of the Celtæ or Gauls, taken to be originally the same people as our ancient Britains. **1757** TINDAL tr. *Rapin's Hist. Eng.* Introd. 7 Great Britain was peopled by the Celtæ or Gauls.] **1773** MᶜQUEEN in Boswell *Johnson* Sept. 18, As they [Scythians] were the ancestors of the Celts, the same religion might be in Asia Minor and Skye. **1842** PRICHARD *Nat. Hist. Man* 185 This race, who had probably been expelled by the Italian nations and the Celts from Italy and Gaul. **1851** D. WILSON *Preh. Ann.* (1863) II. IV. i. 182 The Celts of Britain are apparently the oldest among the Aryan races. **1856** EMERSON *Eng. Traits, Race* Wks. (Bohn) II. 21 If that be true..that Celts love unity of power, and Saxons the representative principle.

Hence **'Celtified** *ppl. a.* (*nonce-wd.*), made Celtic in fashion or garb. **'Celtism**, the distinctive character of the Celt. **'Celtist**, one who studies the Celtic languages. **Celti'zation**, a making Celtic; conversion to being Celtic.

1837 LOCKHART *Scott* xx. 459 Sir Walter's Celtified pageantry. **1866** M. ARNOLD in *Cornh. Mag.* Mar. 289 A more attentive and impartial study of Celtism than it has yet ever received from us. *Ibid.* May 547 Celtism is.. everywhere manifest still in the French nation. *Ibid.* Mar. 289 This is a very different matter from the political and social Celtization of which certain enthusiasts dream. **1885** *Athenæum* 17 Jan. 86/1 The name of a French Celtist.

celt² (sɛlt). [ad. (reputed) Lat. *celt-es* (or ? *celte*, ? *celtis*) 'stone-chisel, sculptor's chisel'.

The received or Clementine text of the Vulgate has in *Job* xix. 24 *Stylo ferreo, et plumbi lamina, vel celte sculpantur in silice*; but, though this is the reading of some MSS., the Codex Amiatinus and others read *certe* 'surely'. Some hold *certe* to be the original reading (representing *l*ˇ*d* of the Heb., 'for ever' of the Eng., which is not expressed by the LXX), and take *celte* as an erroneous alteration of some kind; others think *celte* a genuine word, and suppose that it was originally a marginal gloss on *stylo*, which was erroneously taken into the text, and subsequently altered to *certe* by some one to whom it was perhaps unfamiliar. But the independent evidence for a word *celtes* or *celte* is slender. The 'vetus inscriptio Romæ', cited by Du Cange, is a late forgery, and *celte* in it is app. from the Vulgate. One of the miscellaneous undated glosses in the Glossarium C. Labbæi (Stephens' *Thesaurus*) is 'Γλυφεῖον *Celte*', but this is prob. later than the Vulgate variant reading, and may be founded on it. Later also than the Vulgate is the gloss on Sidonius *Epist.* vii. 3 (*Anecd. Oxon.*, *Class Ser.* I. v. p. xi. and 50) '*Hoc caelum*, ut *hoc celte*, *celtis*, instrumentum est quo caelatur,' which shows the ordinary explanation of the word in the Middle Ages. *Celtes* occurs however in two charters given in Lacomblet *Urkundenbuch für die Geschichte des Niederrheins*, II. 331 (anno 1267) 'meatum seu transitum..ex fovea capituli Coloniensis, ad educendum celtes seu fracmina lapidum per viam eandem', and II. 382 (anno 1319) 'quod nulli frangentes lapides seu alii quicumque proicient seu mittent celtes seu alia fragmenta in ipsam foveam'. Here the meaning is 'pieces or fragments, ? chips', of stone; the relation of this to the Vulgate word is uncertain. In Welsh, *maen cellt*, with the assumed meaning 'flint stone', occurs in the *Triads of Wisdom* (16–17th c.), in *Myv. Arch.* III. 246; and *cellt* is also said to be (or to have been) known in Breconshire, in the sense of 'shell' of a nut, etc.; but the status of the word is altogether obscure, and its alleged senses help the question little. In any case, *celtes*, whatever its orgin and character, was assumed, on the authority of the Vulgate, to be a genuine word; and, as such, the term was admitted into the technical vocabulary of Archæology, about 1700. 'In Beger's *Thesaurus Brandenburgicus* 1696 a bronze celt adapted for insertion in its haft is described under the name of *celtes*' (Ll. Jewitt *Half-hours among Eng. Antiq.* 1877, p. 32). Apparently the general adoption of the word by antiquaries was influenced by a fancied etymological connexion with CELT¹: thus the *Grand Dict.* of Larousse explains it as 'sorte de hache *gauloise* en bronze'.]

An implement with chisel-shaped edge, of bronze or stone (but sometimes of iron), found among the remains of prehistoric man. It appears to have served for a variety of purposes, as a hoe, chisel, or axe, and perhaps as a weapon of war. Some specimens in bronze are flat, others flanged, others winged, others have sockets to receive a handle, and one, or two, ear-like *ansæ* or loops.

1715 A. PENNECUIK *Descr. Tweeddale* 203 *note* (Jam.), Supposed to be the ancient weapon called the stone celt. **1732–69** DE FOE *Tour Gt. Brit.* I. 309 In the great long Barrow, farthest North from Stone-henge..was found one of those Brass Instruments called Celts. **1796** PEARSON in *Phil. Trans.* LXXXVI. 428 Most probably celts were originally chopping tools. **1830** LYELL *Princ. Geol.* (1875) I. I. i. 3 The..stone hatchets, called Celts, found in our peat bogs. **1851** D. WILSON *Preh. Ann.* (1863) I. II. iv. 383 The Bronze celt..is found in various sizes and degrees of ornament. **1866** LAING *Preh. Rem. Caithn.* 40 The hammers or celts are almost all natural stones from the beach. **1878** W. H. DALL *Later Preh. Man* 8 A skeleton interred in the earth, together with the remains of a small iron celt.

b. *Comb.*, as ***celt-maker.***

1865 LUBBOCK *Preh. Times* 17 The celt-makers never cast their axes as we do ours, with a transverse hole, through which the handle might pass.

Celtdom ('kɛltdəm, s-). [f. CELT¹ + -DOM.] Celtic peoples collectively; the Celtic spirit or genius.

1895 A. NUTT *Voyage Bran* I. 206 That natural magic which we seek in vain outside Celtdom. **1920** *Glasgow Herald* 25 Sept. 6 An Comunn Gaidhealach has done much to unveil the heart of Celtdom.

† **'celter.** *Obs.* A woollen fabric.

1597 in Jeaffreson *Middlesex County Rec.* I. 240.

Celtiberian (sɛltɪ'bɪərɪən), *a.* and *sb.* [f. L. *Celtiberia*: see CELT¹ and IBERIAN.] **A.** *adj.* Of or pertaining to Celtiberia, an ancient province of Spain lying between the Tagus and the Ebro, or to its inhabitants the Celtiberi, a union of Celts with Iberians. **B.** *sb.* An inhabitant of Celtiberia.

1607 TOPSELL *Four-f. Beasts* 288 The Horsses of the Celtiberans [are] somewhat a dusty colour. **1622** PEACHAM *Compl. Gent.* 48 How Titus Sempronius Gracchus subdued the Celtiberian Spaniards. **1797** *Encycl. Brit.* IV. 284/1 The Celtiberians were very cruel towards their enemies. **1845** *Encycl. Metrop.* XXV. 1345/1 The Celtiberian alphabet, of which there are several specimens in inscriptions and on coins, has not as yet been fully deciphered. **1924** *Glasgow Herald* 28 July 5 Numantia, the capital of the powerful Celtiberian tribe, the Arevaci. **1936** *Antiquity* X. 274 The Celtiberians had a two-piece plough.

Celtic ('sɛltɪk, 'kɛltɪk), *a.* Also **Keltic** ('kɛltɪk). [a. F. *celtique* or ad. L. *celtic-us* of the Celts.]

1. *Hist.* & *Archæol.* Of or belonging to the ancient Celtæ and their presumed congeners.

1656 BLOUNT *Glossogr.*, *Celtique*, pertaining to the people of Gaul. **1667** MILTON *P.L.* I. 521 Who..ore the Celtic [Fields] roam'd the utmost Isles. **1756–7** tr. *Keysler's Trav.* (1760) I. Introd. 10 Fragments of Celtic idols lately discovered in the cathedral at Paris. **1839** THIRLWALL *Greece* VI. 3 Drawing a Celtic sword from beneath his garments. **1880** BOYD DAWKINS *Early Man in Britain* xii. 344 Various carvings in spirals, concentric circles, flamboyants and zigzags, forming part of the prehistoric series defined by Mr. Franks as the late Celtic. **1884** RHYS *Celtic Brit.* 2 Britain was considered to be outside the Celtic world.

2. Epithet of the languages and peoples akin to the ancient Celtic; particularly, of the great branch of the Aryan family of languages which includes Breton, Welsh, Irish, Manx, Scotch Gaelic, the extinct Cornish, and the ancient languages which they represent. Also absol. = *Celtic tongue*. ***Celtic cross***: a Latin cross, the centre of which is surrounded by a circle; ***Celtic fringe*** (or *edge*): (the land of) the Scots, Welsh, Irish and Cornish, regarded as occupying the fringe or outlying edge of the British Isles (freq. *derogatory*); ***Celtic twilight***: W. B. Yeats's name for his collection of stories, etc., based on Irish folk-tales; hence *gen.*, (sometimes disparagingly) the atmosphere of, or artistic tendencies associated with, the folklore and legends of Celtic Britain, esp. of Ireland.

1707 E. LLUYD *Archaeol. Brit.* Pref. C, The Latin-Celtic or Comparative Vocabulary [cf. p. 290]. **1739** D. MALCOLM (*title*), Collection of Letters..in which the usefulness of the Celtic is instanced in illustrating the antiquities of the British Isles. **1764** ROWL. JONES (*title*), An English, Celtic, Greek, and Latin-English Lexicon. **1839** KEIGHTLEY *Hist. Eng.* I. 78 Beneath them [Norsemen] were the Celtic princes. **1844** STANLEY *Arnold's Life & Corr.* I. v. 245 *note*, Feudality is especially Keltic and barbarian. **1846** MᶜCULLOCH *Acc. Brit. Empire* (1854) I. 317 The people.. being of Scandinavian, and not Celtic origin. **1851** D. WILSON *Preh. Ann.* (1863) II. II. iii. 366 Bronze weapons.. of a bright yellow colour, like brass or gilded metal—to these the term celtic brass is often applied. **1859** JEPHSON *Brittany* i. 1 [The peasant-girl] relates the Celtic fairy-tale, or the mediæval legend. **1871** TYLOR *Prim. Cult.* I. 40 The keeping up of an old Keltic art. **1873** QUEEN VICTORIA *Jrnl.* 9 Sept. (1968) 281 We..saw the Celtic cross at Logierait put up to

the late Duke of Athole. **1876** BANCROFT *Hist. U.S.* III. iv. 351 The Norman-Irish and Celtic-Irish were drawn nearer to one another by common sorrows. **1886** W. STOKES in *Trans. Philol. Soc.* 202 The Neo-Celtic verb substantive. *Ibid.* 218 In Old-Celtic *bató*. 219 The forms must in proto-celtic have ended in vowels. 242 Both forms in Celtic are toneless proclitics. **1890** MARQUIS OF SALISBURY *Mr. Parnell & Irish Question* 9 The great defect of our present representation is that the Celtic edges of the country on both islands are represented enormously out of proportion to the rest of the Anglo-Saxon population. **1893** W. B. YEATS (*title*) The Celtic twilight. **1894** G. ALLEN *Post-Prandial Philos.* xviii. 155 If Lord Salisbury thinks we are a Celtic fringe he is vastly mistaken. **1899** A. H. KEANE *Man Past & Present* xiv. 523 The 'Keltic fringe', that is, the strips of territory on the skirts of the Teutonic and Neo-Latin domains in the extreme west. **1907** A. S. T. GRIFFITH-BOSCAWEN *Fourteen Yrs. in Parlt.* ii. 11 Their majority [in 1892]..came entirely from Scotland, Wales, and Ireland, or, as Mr. Balfour aptly said, 'the Celtic fringe'. **1908** *Westm. Gaz.* 2 June 2/2 Apparently he has now got tired of his Celtic-fringe seat. **1923** A. HUXLEY *On Margin* 30 If Mr. Yeats understood the Einstein theory..he too could give us, out of the Celtic twilight, his lyrics of relativity. **1936** R. LEHMANN *Weather in Streets* IV. ii. 398 The mixture of Celtic twilight and Aubrey Beardsley decor which..enshrouded her. **1938** L. MACNEICE *I crossed Minch* I. i. 3 That natural..culture which..is only found on the Celtic or backward fringes. **1969** C. CARFAX *Silence with Voices* x. 67 All the tombstones had their backs to the water except one. This, a lichened Celtic cross, faced the others.

Hence **'Celtically** *adv.*, in Celtic fashion; †**'Celtican** *a.* = CELTIC; *spec.* of Gallia Celtica; **'Celticism,** (*a*) a Celtic custom or expression; (*b*) devotion to Celtic customs; **Cel'ticity,** Celtic quality or character; **'Celticize** *v.*, (*a*) *trans.* to put into a Celtic form; to adapt to Celtic use; (*b*) *intr.* to adopt Celtic fashions or usages.

1607 TOPSELL *Four-f. Beasts* 162, I wrote these things, and dedicated the Celtican spoils. **1837** *Fraser's Mag.* XV. 556 Fin Mac Cowl, or, to spell him more Celtically, Fioun Mac Cumhail. **1855** MILMAN *Lat. Chr.* (1864) IX. XIV. vii. 225 *note*, His Celticism appears from his obstinate adherence to the ancient British usage about Easter. **1882** G. ALLEN in *Nature Studies* 175 This element [Euskarian] was Celticized, but not exterminated, by the Aryan Celts. **1885-6** WHITLEY STOKES *Celtic Decl.* 43 The Novara inscription, the celticity of which cannot possibly be doubted.

Celticist ('sɛltɪsɪst, k-). [f. CELTIC *a.*] = CELTIST.

1912 *Irish World* 12 June 7/2 The celebrated philologist and Celticist. **1964** *Punch* 15 July 87/2 A Belgian Celticist.

Celtified, etc.: see CELT *sb.*[1]

celtiform ('sɛltɪfɔːm), *a. Archæol.* [f. CELT[2] + -FORM.] Shaped like a celt.

1932 J. G. D. CLARK *Mesolithic Age* iv. 65 An almost celtiform shape. **1937** *Proc. Prehist. Soc.* III. 283 Celtiform axes or adzes of Large type have been reported from the Solway.

Celtish ('sɛltɪʃ, k-), *a.* [f. CELT[1].] Celt-like, somewhat Celtic; = CELTIC *a.*

1889 in *Cent. Dict.* **1906** *Daily Chron.* 6 Jan. 6/5 The Celtish melancholy and the Celtish gleam in his eyes. **1915** R. BROOKE *Let.* 24 Jan. in Marsh *Mem.* (1918) 136 Where our huts are was an Iberian fort against the Celts—and Celtish against Romans—and Roman against Saxons.

celtium ('sɛltɪəm). *Chem.* [a. F. *celtium* (Urbain 1911, in *Compt. Rend.* CLII. 142), f. L. *Celtæ* (see CELT[1]) + -IUM.] An element now generally known as HAFNIUM.

1911 *Jrnl. Chem. Soc.* C. II. 115 The name celtium is given to the corresponding element, and the symbol Ct assigned to it. **1922** *Nature* 17 June 781/1 Very different conclusions have been reached as to the identity of celtium with the missing element of number 72 on the Moseley classification.

Celto-, combining form of CELT[1] [after Greek analogies], as in **Cel'tologist, 'Celtologue,** a student of the Celtic languages or of Celtic ethnology and antiquities; **Celto'maniac,** one who is crazy on Celtic matters; *esp.* one who pretends to derive all languages from Celtic; **'Celtophil,** a friend of the Celts and Celtic studies; **Celto-Roman,** relating to a mixture of Celtic and Roman; etc.

1887 *Athenæum* 3 Sept. 305/2 The issue of these facsimiles [of Irish MSS.] has vastly lightened the labours of Celtologists. **1886** *Academy* 27 Mar. 223/2 The most rising of the French Celtologues. **1883** *American* VII. 6 The Celtomaniac..wanted to identify some American language with the Welsh. **1886** *Life Sir R. Christison* II. xvii. 453 A Celtophil whom no born Gaul surpasses for Celtic lore and zeal.

†**'celure.** *Obs.* Forms: 4 celure, selure, cylour, 4–5 sylure, 5 celour, -ar, seler, selowyr, silour, sylour, syllure, sillour, siller, 5–6 selour, 6 celler, cellar, seller, ceiler. [The derivation presents many points of obscurity, some of which are touched on under the related CEIL *v.*, while others attach to the history of this particular derivative. *Celure* presuppposes an OF. or AF. *celeüre, *celure, answering to L. *cæ-, cēlātūra*; *celour*, if a genuine form, might answer to an OF. *celeoir, *celoir = L. *cēlātōrium*; both these L. forms occur in med.L., chiefly in sense 'canopy', and both are in ME. Vocabularies glossed by *celure*; but of the required OF. words no examples have yet been found. The L. words were of course derivatives of *cælāre* or *cēlāre*: see CEIL.]

A canopy covering a bed, dais, altar, etc., or carried above the Host during a procession. Also the hangings of a bed, the tapestry of a wall, a screen of drapery. ***rood celure***: a canopy over the rood.

c **1340** *Gaw. & Gr. Knt.* 76 Guenore..Dressed on þe dere des..a selure hir ouer. **1418** *E.E. Wills* 36 A bed of Lyn wit a hool silour and Couerlet..also a bed of red and grene dimi Selour. *a* **1440** *Sir Degrev.* 1474 Hur bede was off aszure With testur and celure. *c* **1440** *Promp. Parv.* 456 Sylure, of valle [*v.r.* of a walle] or a nother thynge, *celatura, celamen.* *c* **1450** *Voc.* in Wr.-Wülcker 571 *Celatorium*, a celour or a coverlet. *c* **1450** *Bk. Curtasye* 445 in *Babees Bk.* (1868) 313 Two beddys..þat henget shalle be with hole sylour. *c* **1475** *Voc.* in Wr.-Wülcker 776 *Hoc supralectum*, a selowyr. **1483** *Cath. Angl.* 340 A Sylour, *anabatrum* ['anabatrum, *cortina*' (curtain) Gloss. in Du Cange, ed. 1883]. **1494** *Will of Sclatter* (Somerset Ho.), Two celars of ooke oon of them to be sette ouer the aulter. *c* **1494** *Art. Hen. VII.* in *Househ. Ord.* (1790) 126 The font to bee hanged with a riche siller over. **1520** *Lanc. Wills* I. 38, I bequethe unto the roode seller off Manchester xls. **1525** LD. BERNERS *Froiss.* II. clvii. [cliii.] 434 The lytter had a celler of a thynne fyne clothe of sylke. **1527** *Ibid.* I. 33 My body to be buryed in the Churche off Croston under the rode celer afore the chancel. **1530** PALSGR. 203/2 Cellar for a bedde, *ciel de lit.* **1553** *Lanc. Wills* I. 105 One seller & tester of reede and greene seye wth curtens of the same.

¶ ? = CEILING 4, 5.

c **1394** *P. Pl. Crede* 201 As a greet chirche..wiþ semlich selure y-set on lofte. *c* **1400** MAUNDEV. xxii. 239 Of gold & Sylver..he maketh cylours, Pyleres, & Paumentes, in his Palays.

Hence †**'celured** *ppl. a.*, canopied; overarched. †**'celuring,** (*sillering*) = CELURE I.

c **1430** LYDG. *Compl. Bl. Knt.* viii, Celured eke alofte With bowys grene. **1558** *Wills & Inv. N.C.* (1835) I. 184 Another pressoure with a portall and ye sillering in the parler.

celwylly, var. of SELWYLLY. *Obs.*

cely, var. of SELY *a. Obs.* blessed.

celycalle, var. of CELICAL *a. Obs.*

celydoine, -don, -doun, var. ff. CELIDONY.

cembalist ('sɛmbəlɪst). *Mus. rare.* [f. It. *cembalo*, properly cymbal or dulcimer, but used in musical scores (abbreviated from *clavicembalo*) for the harpsichord or pianoforte part: see -IST.] One who plays the pianoforte in an orchestra.

1871 E. GRAEME *Beethoven* ii. (1876) 21 Ludwig was appointed cembalist at the orchestra, i.e. to preside at the pianoforte. **1878** GROVE *Dict. Mus.* I. 37 Organist to the cathedral and cembalist to the court at Salzburg.

‖**cembalo** ('tʃembalo). *Mus.* [It.; see CEMBALIST.] Shortened form of CLAVICEMBALO; the harpsichord.

[**1801** BUSBY *Dict. Mus.*, *Cembalo*, the Italian name for a harpsichord.] **1865** WEBSTER, *Cembalo*, the harpsichord. [*Rare.*] **1928** *Radio Times* 23 Nov. 520/1 A cembalo, the delicate-toned ancestor of the pianoforte. **1947** C. GRAY *Contingencies* xi. 161 Scipione Dentice, a writer on music and player of the *cembalo*.

b. = CYMBALO.

1879 [see CYMBALO].

cembra ('sɛmbrə). Also -o. [mod.L., f. G. dial. *zember, zimber*, var. of *zimmer* TIMBER *sb.*[1]] In full ***cembra pine***: the Swiss stone-pine, *Pinus cembra*. Also *attrib.*, as ***cembra nut***.

1785 W. MARSHALL *Planting* 283 *Pinus Cembra*: the Cembro, or Cembro-Pine. **1807** T. MARTYN *Miller's Gard. & Bot. Dict.* II. 8 G/1 The Cembra Pine grows higher up the Alps than any other Pine. **1848** DUNGLISON *Med. Lex.* (ed. 7) s.v. *Pinus Cembra*, The nuts, Cembro nuts, have an eatable kernel. **1909** *Westm. Gaz.* 9 Oct. 14/2 Two bent and stunted cembras. **1920** C. COLTMAN-ROGERS *Conifers* i. 19 The cone of the Cembra is a little round football-shaped specimen.

ceme, obs. form of SEAM, measure of corn.

ceme, -yn, cemely, -nesse, obs. ff. SEEM-.

cemelyn, obs. var. of SEMBLE *v. Obs.*

cemenary, obs. var. of SEMINARY.

cement (sɪ'mɛnt, 'sɛmənt), *sb.* Forms: 3–5 syment, 4 siment, 5–7 cy-, sement, 5 scyment, symonde, 6 sciment, symunt, 6–7 ciment, 7 seiment, symond, cemente, cœment, 8 scement, 6– cement. [ME. *cyment*, a. OF. *ciment* (= Pr. *cimen*, Sp., Pg. *cimento*):—L. *cæment-um* (in late L. *cimentum*), contr. for *cædimentum* rough unhewn stone, chip, lit. 'cutting', 'produce of cutting or chipping', f. *cædĕre* to cut. In 16th c. altered to *cement* after the L. form. The pronunciation '*cement* is found from 14th c., but is now almost superseded by *ce'ment*, after the vb.

The name appears to have been given to broken or pounded stone, tiles, etc. mixed with lime to form a setting mortar, and at length to the mortar or plaster so formed, whence it passed into the modern sense of strong setting mortar, or of mortar generally, however made.]

1. A substance used to bind the stones or bricks of a building firmly together, to cover floors, to form walls, terraces, etc., which being applied in a soft and pasty state, afterwards hardens into a stony consistency; *esp.* a strong mortar, produced by the calcination of a natural or artificial mixture of calcareous and argillaceous matter.

hydraulic cements harden under water, and are used for piers, dock-walls, etc. ***Roman cement***, like all the hydraulic cements, is an argillaceous lime. ***Portland cement*** is so called because it resembles in colour the Portland stone. It is prepared by calcining a mixture of the clayey mud of the Thames with a proper proportion of chalk (Ure).

c **1300** *K. Alis.* 6177 A clay..Strong so yren, ston, or syment. *c* **1320** *Seuyn Sag.* (W.) 2125 The fir..falsed the siment, and the ston. **1398** TREVISA *Barth. De P.R.* XVI. xxiv. (Tollem. MS.), Lyme..is a ston brente; by medlynge þerof with sonde and water sement is made. *c* **1420** *Pallad. on Husb.* VI. 190 This scyment, bryk, stoon, cley togeðer drie. *c* **1440** *York Myst.* viii. 102 Sadly sette it with symonde fyne. **1534** LD. BERNERS *Gold Bk. M. Aurel.* (1546) Hvj, With diuers stones and one ciment. **1662** GERBIER *Princ.* 20 Their Lime..composed a Seiment, which joyned with Stone (or Brick) made an inseparable union. **1712** BLACKMORE *Creation* I. 230 For want of cement strong enough to bind The structure fast. **1791** SMEATON *Edystone L.* §172 Nothing in the way of Cement would answer our end, but what would adhere to a moist surface, and become hard. **1823** P. NICHOLSON *Pract. Build.* 329 Cement, or mortar, is a preparation of lime and sand, mixed with water. **1851** RICHARDSON *Geol.* 361 Ovate nodules of argillaceous limestone..named *septaria*..extensively used for cement. **1862** DARWIN *Fertil. Orchids* i. 15 Setting like a cement hard and dry in a few minutes' time.

2. *gen.* **a.** Any substance applied in a soft or glutinous state to the surfaces of solid bodies to make them cohere firmly.

1562 BULLEYN *Bk. Simples* 85 a, Whan stone pottes be broken, what is better to glew them againe..like the Symunt made of Cheese. **1641** *Vestry Bks.* (Surtees) 191 Wax, rossel, and stone pitch to make symond for mending the fount stone broken by the Scotts. **1664** POWER *Exp. Philos.* II. 97 No Air could pierce the Cœment, that luted the Glass and Lead-Pipe together. **1774** GOLDSM. *Nat. Hist.* (1776) VII. 3 The fluids of the animal itself furnish the cement. **1839-60** URE *Dict. Arts* s.v. (L.), The diamond cement..which is sold as a secret at an absurdly dear price, is composed of isinglass soaked in water..to which a little gum resin, ammoniac, or galbanum, and resin mastic are added. **1884** F. BRITTEN *Watch & Clockm.* 48 The cement generally used by engravers..to fit their work is composed of four parts of pitch, two of plaster of Paris, and one of resin.

b. Any uniting medium or substance. *rare.*

1604 E. G[RIMSTON] *D'Acosta's Hist. Indies* I. iii. 11 Any other ciment or uniting to the earth then the Element of water. **1794** SULLIVAN *View Nat.* I. 466 The quantity of air discharged from metals, is supposed to be the cement or principle, which unites all the parts together.

c. *fig.* A principle of union.

1606 SHAKS. *Ant. & Cl.* III. ii. 29 The peece of Vertue which is set Betwixt vs, as the Cyment of our loue To keepe it builded. **1607** CHAPMAN *Bussy D'Amb.* (1613) Kiij b, But Friendship is the Sement of two mindes. **1742** R. BLAIR *Grave* 88 Friendship! mysterious cement of the soul! **1826** E. IRVING *Babylon* I. III. 246 Faith is the cement of all domestic and social union. **1872** BAGEHOT *Physics & Pol.* (1876) 184 Custom was in early days the cement of society.

3. *transf.* A substance resembling cement, used for some other purpose; *e.g.* for stopping teeth.

1489 CAXTON *Faytes of A.* II. xxxv. 152 Staues of drye wode all holowe withinne and full of fyre of cyment of oyle and of towe. **1625** *W. Beale's Patent* in *Abridgm. Specif.* (1862) 1 Certen compounded stuffes and waters called..cement or dressing for shippes. **1881** *Syd. Soc. Lex.*, *Cement*, a term applied to certain soft compounds used for stopping of carious teeth.

4. *Phys.* The bony tissue forming the outer crust of the fang of the tooth.

1849-52 TODD *Cycl. Anat.* IV. 865/1 'Cement' always closely corresponds in texture with the osseous tissue. **1855** OWEN *Skel. & Teeth* 104. **1872** MIVART *Elem. Anat.* 250 The cement invests the fang.

5. a. *Mining.* (See quot.)

1881 RAYMOND *Mining Gloss.*, *Cement* (Australia and Pacific), gravel firmly held in a silicious matrix, or the matrix itself.

b. (See quots.) Cf. *cement-gold.*

a **1877** KNIGHT *Dict. Mech.*, *Cement*,..3... *a.* The brown deposit in the precipitation tank, wherein the soluble chloride of gold, obtained by the chlorination process, is deposited by the addition of sulphate of iron to the solution. *b.* The material in which the metal is imbedded in the cementing-furnace. **1889** [see CEMENTATION 2 c].

6. *attrib.* and *Comb.*, as ***cement-covered, -forming*** adjs.; **cement-cell,** a CELL (14 c) formed of a ring of cement: **cement-copper** (see quot.); **cement-duct** (*Zool.*), a duct in Cirripeds which conveys through the antenna the 'cement' by which the animal attaches itself; **cement-gland,** the gland at the base of each antenna which secretes this cement; **cement-gold, -silver, -steel** (see quots.); **cement-stone,** a nodule of argillaceous limestone occurring embedded in clay, from which cement is made; **cement wall, cement-water** (see quots.).

1881 CARPENTER *Microscope* 214 A '*cement-cell' answers this purpose very well. **1881** RAYMOND *Mining Gloss.*, **Cement-copper*, copper precipitated from solution. **1849-52** TODD *Cycl. Anat.* IV. 896/2 The *cement-covered

cylindrical base of the tooth. **1855** OWEN *Skel. & Teeth* 292 The enamel organ and *cement-forming capsule. **1871** T. R. JONES *Anim. Kingd.* 498 In each of the antennæ there is situated a duct, derived from a large glandular body (the *cement-gland). **1881** RAYMOND *Mining Gloss.*, **Cement-gold*, gold precipitated in fine particles from solution. *Ibid.* **Cement-silver*, silver precipitated from solution, usually by copper. *Ibid.* s.v. *Steel*, Blister or *cement-steel is made by carburizing wrought iron bars by packing them in charcoal powder and heating without access of air. **1863** A. RAMSAY *Phys. Geog.* xxxv. (1878) 611 *Cement stones are also found ..in the Eocene strata. **1875** URE *Dict. Arts* II. 824 The Blue Lias cement-stones are considered the strongest water-limes of this country. **1688** R. HOLME *Armoury* III. 457/1 A *Cement Wall..is a wall made of River Pebbles, or Marble Stones split in the middle. **1762** tr. *Busching's Syst. Geog.* I. 50 *Cement-Waters, that contain the vitriolic copper; and on laying clean iron in them they corrode its particles, and substitute others of copper.

Hence **ce'mentless** *a.*, devoid of cement.

1856 RUSKIN *Mod. Paint.* IV. v. xix. §12 Rough with cementless and jagged brick.

cement (sɪ'mɛnt), *v.* Forms: 4 **syment**, 4–7 **cyment**, 7 **ciment**, **simment**, 7– **cement**. [f. prec. sb. Cf. F. *cimenter*.]

1. *trans.* To unite (solid bodies) with cement.

1340 HAMPOLE *Pr. Consc.* 9068 Alle manere of precyouse stanes sere, Cymented with gold. *c* **1400** MAUNDEV. xxvi. 268 Of grete Stones and passynge huge, wel symented. **1624** HEYWOOD *Gunaik.* II. 92 The pallace of Cyrus..the stones of which were simmented together with gold. **1781** GIBBON *Decl. & F.* III. 80 Large stones..firmly cemented with lead and iron. **1872** YEATS *Growth Comm.* 24 Bricks..cemented with bitumen.

b. *transf.* To unite as with cement; to cause to cohere firmly.

1660 SHARROCK *Vegetables* 71 That the buds..may be fast cemented before frosts return. **1727** SWIFT *City Shower*, Dust cemented by the rain. **1878** HUXLEY *Physiogr.* 190 The molten matter..cements the loose ashes and cinders into a compact mass.

c. *Alchemy.* (See CEMENTING *vbl. sb.*)

2. *fig.*

1606 SHAKS. *Ant. & Cl.* II. i. 48 How the feare of vs May Ciment their diuisions. **1665** MANLEY *Grotius' Low-C. Warrs* 677 The Common-wealth, which had been built and cemented with the blood of their Fathers and Kinred. **1761** HUME *Hist. Eng.* I. ii. 39 The kingdoms of the Heptarchy.. seemed to be firmly cemented into one state under Egbert. **1867** FREEMAN *Norm. Conq.* (1876) I. vi. 455 The alliance was cemented by a treaty of marriage.

3. To apply cement to (a surface); to coat or line with cement, so as to make water-tight.

1886 *Law Times* LXXXI. 60/1 To cleanse, level, and cement the bottom of the pool.

4. *intr.* (for *refl.*). To cohere firmly by the application of cement; to stick.

1677 MOXON *Mech. Exerc.* (1703) 259 Morter doth not Cement so strongly to the Bricks when it dries hastily. *a* **1709** ATKINS *Parl. & Pol. Tracts* (1734) 191 Iron mixed with Clay, that can never cleave one to another, nor cement. **1739** SHARP *Surg.* (J.), [The parts of a wound] will..cement like one branch of a tree ingrafted on another.

fig. **1660** BONDE *Scut. Reg.* 368 So these knaves cemented together again, like a Snakes tail. **1761–2** HUME *Hist. Eng.* (1806) V. lxvi. 47 The allies..were not likely to cement soon in any new confederacy. **1801** T. JEFFERSON *Writ.* (1830) III. 465 They will..cement and form one mass with us.

cemental (sɪ'mɛntəl), *a. Phys.* [f. CEMENT *sb.* + -AL[1].] Relating to the cement of the teeth.

1849–52 TODD *Cycl. Anat.* IV. 927/2 The cemental tubuli.

†**cementary.** *Obs.* [f. L. *cæmentāri-us* stone-mason: see CEMENT and -ARY.] (See quot.)

1586 FERNE *Blaz. Gentrie* 72 Architecture..deuideth it selfe..into two kindes: the first, called Cementarie, or masonrie (conuersant in the working of stone): the other Carpentarie. **1688** R. HOLME *Armoury* III. 68/1.

cementation (siːmən'teɪʃən). [f. CEMENT *v.* + -ATION.]

1. The action or process of cementing or producing cohesion; the state of cohesion thus produced. Also *fig.*

1660 SHARROCK *Vegetables* 69 Strengthen those that are weak with a stick tyed above and below the grafted place.. till the cementation be made and confirmed. **1799** KIRWAN *Geol. Ess.* 109 Earthy substances acquire a stony hardness.. from..concretion, cementation. **1818** SCORESBY in *Ann. Reg., Chron.* 543 The cementation..of the pieces of a closely aggregated pack [of ice]. **1836** MARRYAT *Midsh. Easy* xxxvii, To this inequality..society owes its firmest cementation.

2. a. 'The process by which one solid is made to penetrate and combine with another at a high temperature so as to change the properties of one of them, without liquefaction taking place' (Watts *Dict. Chem.*).

1594 PLAT *Jewell-ho.* III. 86 Cementations, Blaunchers, and Citrinations. **1605** TIMME *Quersit.* I. xiii. 61 Their colours may be taken away by cementation and reuerberation. **1662** R. MATHEW *Unl. Alch.* §101. 165 Make a good fire of Charcole about it, which is called a Wheel-fire of cementation. **1696** PHILLIPS, *Cementation*, in Chymistry it is used for the purifying of Gold, by laying plates of Gold in the midst of Pouders made of Brick and Vitriol, enclos'd in a close stop'd Vessel, and set in a Fire of Reverberation. **1750** *Phil. Trans.* XLVI. 593 Gold..could not be separated from the Platina..either by Cementation, or by the more ordinary Operations with Lead and Antimony. **1818** FARADAY *Exp. Res.* xvi. (1820) 65 An attempt..to procure the alloy of steel with silver by cementation: a small piece of steel wrapped in silver leaf..was put into a crucible.

b. *spec.* 'The conversion of iron into steel by absorption of carbon...from a mass of ground charcoal in which it lies embedded while exposed to strong ignition' (Watts *Dict. Chem.*).

1780 J. T. DILLON *Trav. Spain* (1781) 142 Steel is made by fusion or cementation. **1816** J. SMITH *Panorama Sc. & Art* I. 4 If the cementation be continued too long, the steel becomes porous..and incapable of being welded. **1862** TIMBS *Year-bk. Facts* 189 The theory of Cementation, or conversion of iron into steel, has undergone a thorough investigation.

c. *attrib.*

1884 W. H. GREENWOOD *Steel & Iron* xviii. 406 The Cementation process for the conversion of bar-iron into cementation or blister steel... The process is conducted in a converting or cementation furnace. **1887** D. A. LOW *Introd. Machine Draw.* xvii. 79 In the cementation process, bars of wrought iron are imbedded in powdered charcoal in a fireclay trough. **1889** *Q. Rev.* July 137 This is known as the 'converting' or 'cementation' process, and the charcoal employed as the recarbonizing agent is termed 'cement'. **1967** *Gloss. Mining Terms* (*B.S.I.*) IX. 7 *Cementation process*, a method of sealing off water-bearing strata by the injection of cement grout through boreholes.

3. The process of encasing or lining with cement.

1886 *Pall Mall G.* 20 Sept. 3/2 Cementation as a substitute for cremation..Encase the body in cement..and you remove sanitary objections, and observe the formalities of the ritual.

ce'mentatory, *a.* [f. on analogy of prec. as if from a L. vb. **cæmentāre*: see -ORY.] Of cementing quality; pertaining to cementation.

1828–32 WEBSTER, *Cementatory*, cementing; having the quality of uniting firmly.

cemented (sɪ'mɛntɪd), *ppl. a.* [f. CEMENT *sb.* or *v.* + -ED.] Treated with cement; united with or as with cement; ***cemented carbide***, powdered carbide of one or more heavy metals compressed into a solid mass and used in cutting-tools, etc.

a **1877** KNIGHT *Dict. Mech.* 509/1 Cemented-back carpet. **1903** *Daily Chron.* 16 June 7/4 To realise the fair dream of a cemented Empire. **1909** *Ibid.* 10 Apr. 3/4 Dry cemented roads. **1909** *Westm. Gaz.* 20 Sept. 4/1 Krupp cemented armour. **1932** *Jrnl. Iron & Steel Inst.* CXXVI. 581 The steels are arranged under the following types: Carbon, high-speed, special alloy, non-deforming, cemented carbides and unclassified.

cementer (sɪ'mɛntə(r)). [f. CEMENT *v.* + -ER[1].] One who or that which cements.

a **1755** LOCKE (J.) Language which was to be the great instrument and cementer of society [but the accepted reading in *Hum. Und.* III. i. *init.* is 'common tie']. **1816** J. LAWRENCE in *Monthly Mag.* XLII. 296 Salts, the.. cementers of all elementary bodies. **1831** J. HOLLAND *Manuf. Metals* I. 242 The cementers and melters affect more or less mystery in their methods. **1903** *Daily Chron.* 24 Feb. 8/5 Envelope Cementers..wanted. *Ibid.* 9 Dec. 9/6 Tortoiseshell Worker.—Good cementer, used to repairs. **1921** *Dict. Occup. Terms* (1927) §429 *Solutioner* (boots); *cementer*; uses a rubber solution or cement, on lining of upper.

ce'menting, *vbl. sb.* [f. CEMENT *v.* + -ING[1].]

1. The action of uniting with or as with cement.

1677 MOXON *Mech. Exerc.* (1703) 241 The Cementing or joining of Tiles, as well as Bricks together. **1868** E. EDWARDS *Raleigh* I. viii. 122 The cementing of an old friendship.

2. *Alchemy.* = CEMENTATION 2.

c **1386** CHAUCER *Chan. Yem. Prol. & T.* 264 Oure cementynge and fermentacioun. **1584** R. SCOT *Discov. Witchcr.* XIV. i, Mysticall termes of art; as (for a tast) their subliming, amalgaming..cementing. **1684** BOYLE *Porousn. Bod.* vii. 108 [Copper] put into a Crucible or Cementing Pot.

ce'menting, *ppl. a.* [f. as prec. + -ING[2].] That cements or unites firmly; *lit.* and *fig.*

1802 PLAYFAIR *Illustr. Hutton. The.* 27 Without the help of any cementing substances. **1858** ROBERTSON *Lectures* ii. 50 The cementing principle of society.

cementite (sɪ'mɛntaɪt). [f. CEMENT *sb.* + -ITE[1].] A hard and brittle carbide of iron, Fe_3C.

1888 H. M. HOWE in *Engin. & Mining Jrnl.* 18 Aug. 132 Minerals which compose iron. Name suggested here.. Cementite. Iron with cement carbon. *Ibid.* 25 Aug. 154/1 Cementite..appears to be intensely hard, brilliant, homogeneous, structureless carbide of iron, containing the whole of the cement carbon. **1889** [see PEARLITE 2]. **1922** C. H. DESCH *Metallography* (ed. 3) xvii. 373 The carbide, cementite, Fe_3C, is the only compound of carbon and iron which has yet been recognized by microscopical means.

cementitious (siːmɛn'tɪʃəs), *a. rare.* [Answering in form to L. *cæmentīcius* of the nature of unhewn stones; but referred in sense to the modern CEMENT.] Of the nature of cement.

1828–32 in WEBSTER. **1883** *Times* 24 Oct. 3 With its cementitious matter.

cementoma (sɪmɛn'təʊmə). Pl. **-omata.** Also **ce'mentome.** [f. L. *cementum* CEMENT *sb.* + -OMA.] (See quot. 1893.)

1893 J. B. SUTTON *Tumours* 35 When the capsule of a tooth becomes enlarged,..and these thick capsules ossify, the tooth will become embedded in a mass of Cementum. To this form of odontome the name cementoma may be applied. *Ibid.*, The largest cementome from a horse known to me..weighs seventy ounces. **1910** *Practitioner* Jan. 124 The curious odontomata known as cementomata.

‖**cementum.** Lat. form of CEMENT; occas. used in some senses, esp. 4.

1612 WOODALL *Surg. Mate* Wks. (1653) 268 Cementum is a mineral matter like lute..wherewith metals spred over are reverberated to cement. **1842** E. WILSON *Anat. Vade M.* 53 The cortical substance, or cementum..of the tooth. **1859** J. TOMES *Dental Surg.* (1873) 40 The cementum or the enamel forming the common investment.

cemeterial (sɛmɪ'tɪərɪəl), *a.* Also 7 **cemiterial(l, cœmeterial.** [f. on L. type **cœmētēriālis*, f. *cœmētēri-um* CEMETERY: see -AL[1].] Belonging or relating to a cemetery.

1606 W. BIRNIE (*title*), The Blame of Kirk-Buriall, tending to perswade Cemiteriall Civilitie. **1658** SIR T. BROWNE *Hydriot.* iii. 40 The Cemiteriall Cels of ancient Christians. **1833** D. ROCK *Hierurg.* (1851) 555 The cemeterial chapels in the catacombs. **1851** D. WILSON *Preh. Ann.* (1863) I. iii. 67 Cemeterial tumuli.

cemetery ('sɛmɪtərɪ). Forms: 5 **cymytery, -torye, cymitory, cymetorye, cimiteri,** 6 **cimitorie, -tory, cemitorie, cœmiteri,** 6–7 **cemiterie,** 7 **cemitory, cyme-, cimitery, sœmeterie, cyme-, cymitier,** 7–8 **cœme-, cœmitery,** 8 **cemitery, ceme-, cœmitary,** 8– **cemetery.** [ad. L. *cœmētērium*, ad. Gr. κοιμητήριον dormitory, (in Christian writers) burial-ground.]

A place, usually a ground, set apart for the burial of the dead.

a. Originally applied to the Roman underground cemeteries or CATACOMBS.

[**1387** TREVISA *Higden* (Rolls) V. 65 A chirche hawe at Rome.. hatte cimitorium calixty.] **1460** CAPGRAVE *Chron.* 67 Anicetus..was biried in the cymytery of Kalixt. **1480** CAXTON *Chron. Eng.* IV. (1520) 37/2 He ordeyned the Cimiteri where many a thousande martyrs is buryed. *a* **1638** MEDE *Wks.* III. (1672) 679 Had the Christians long before used to keep their Assemblies at the Cœmiteries and Monuments of their Martyrs. **1841** W. SPALDING *Italy & It. Isl.* II. 37 Beyond which there extend, in every one of the cemeteries, galleries choked up. **1855** CDL. WISEMAN *Fabiola* II. ii, The very name of cemetery suggests that it is only a place where many lie, as in a dormitory, slumbering for a while.

†**b.** The consecrated enclosure round a church; a churchyard. *Obs.*

1485 CAXTON *Chas. Gt.* 243 Two cymytoyres or chirche-yerdes. **1530–1** *Act 22 Hen. VIII*, c. 14 Any parishe churche, Cimitorie, or other lyke halowed place. **1601** F. GODWIN *Bps. of Eng.* 321 [He] was buried in the Cemitory or church-yard of his owne church. **1644** EVELYN *Mem.* (1857) I. 73 About this cathedral is a very spacious cemetery. **1771** *Antiq. Sarisb.* 74. **1806** *Gazetteer Scotl.* 172 The place on which the buildings of the Parliament Square stand was formerly the cemetery of St. Giles.

c. A burial-ground generally; now esp. a large public park or ground laid out expressly for the interment of the dead, and not being the 'yard' of any church.

1613 PURCHAS *Pilgr.* I. v. vii. 411, I saw a certaine Cœmiterium or burying-place, then which I had never seene a fairer sight. **1711** ADDISON *Spect.* No. 90 ¶2 It is for this Reason (says Plato) that the Souls of the Dead appear frequently in Cœmiteries. **1753** *Phil. Trans.* XLVIII. 337 A public coemetery..was highly requisite. **1841** LANE *Arab. Nts.* I. 71 The women often stay all the days of the festival in the cemeteries. **1883** LLOYD *Ebb & Fl.* II. 119, I should have been in the Protestant Cemetery at Puerto Blanco. *Mod.* He was buried in Abney Park Cemetery.

d. *fig.*

1704 SWIFT *Batt. Bks.*, It is with libraries as with other cœmeteries. **1872** O. W. HOLMES *Poet. Breakf. T.* ii. 70 The old folios that fill the shelves all round the great cemetery of past transactions of which he is the sexton. **1886** SPURGEON *Treas. Dav.* Ps. cxlv. 7 That the goodness of the living God should be buried in the cemetery of silence.

cemiterie, obs. form of SCIMITAR.

cemmed, ME. form of *kembed*, combed.

cemster, var. of KEMPSTER, *Obs.*

cemy, var. of SEMY, *Obs.*

cenacle ('sɛnək(ə)l). [a. F. *cénacle*, ad. L. *cēnāculum* dining-room, f. *cēna* the mid-day or afternoon meal, 'dinner', 'supper'; in the Vulgate used of the 'upper room' in which the Last Supper was eaten, whence its chief use in the modern langs. Also used in Latin form.]

a. A supping room; an upper chamber; *esp.* the upper room in which the Last Supper was held, and in which the apostles met after the Ascension.

a **1400** *Cov. Myst.* (1841) 17 In Hierusalem were gaderyd xij opynly To the Cenacle. **1483** CAXTON *Gold. Leg.* 328/3 A fayr Cenacle honestly arayed with al maner of deyntes. **1491** —— *Vitas Patr.* (W. de W.) III. xix. (1495) 322 b/2 Danyell the prophete..was thre tymes in the cenacle and prayed god deuoutly. **1858** FABER *Xavier* 220 A new tongue..added to the many ancient ones which..had first found expression in the Cenacle of Judea.

b. A place in which a group of people meet for the discussion of common interests; also, the group of people so meeting, *spec.* a literary clique. Also in Fr. form *cénacle* (senakl).

[**1879** *Encycl. Brit.* IX. 676/1 The famous *cénacle* or clique in which Hugo was chief poet, Sainte-Beuve chief critic.] **1889** H. F. WOOD *Englishman Rue Caïn* xiii, The pundit of some cenacle in Garrick Street. **1899** A. C. LYALL *Asiatic*

Studies 2nd Ser. 61 Within the philosophic cenacle I should entirely concur. **1926** *Contemp. Rev.* Jan. 85 In England and France schools and 'cénacles' of literature sprang up round the great writer of the moment.

cenanthy (sɪˈnænθɪ). *Bot.* [as if ad. Gr. *κενανθία, f. κενός empty + ἄνθος flower.] The absence of stamens and pistils in a flower.

1881 in *Syd. Soc. Lex.*

† **ceˈnation.** *Obs.* [ad. L. *cēnātiōn-em* dining-room (etymologically, noun of action from *cēnāre* to dine, sup.)] Dining, supping.

1599 A. M. tr. *Gabelhouer's Bk. Physicke* 42/2 Your cenatione must be moderate and sober, and your sleepe sufficiente. **1646** SIR T. BROWNE *Pseud. Ep.* VI. vii. 309 The roomes of cœnation in the Summer.

† **ˈcenatory,** *a. Obs. rare*⁻¹. [ad. L. *cēnātōrius* pertaining to dinner.] Relating or pertaining to dinner or supper.

1650 SIR T. BROWNE *Pseud. Ep.* V. vi. 206 The Romans washed, were annointed and wore a cenatory garment.

cence, var. of CENSE *sb.*² *Obs.*, census, tribute.

† **ˈcenchrine, cenchris.** *Obs.* [ad. Gr. κεγχρίνης, κεγχρίς, L. *cenchris*, f. κέγχρος millet.] A kind of snake mentioned by the ancients: 'a serpent with millet-like protuberances on the skin' (Liddell & Scott). (Hence, in mod. Zool., *Cenchrina*, a genus of the Rattlesnake family.)

1608 TOPSELL *Serpents* 743 Of the Millet or Cenchrine. **1627** MAY *Lucan* IX. 819 The Cenchris.. Whose speckled belly with nine spots is dect.

cend, obs. form of SEND.

cendal, -el, var. of SENDAL, a silken stuff.

† **cendiary.** *Obs. rare.* Short for INCENDIARY.

1624 T. SCOTT *2nd Pt. Vox Pop.* 16 The onely Boutefeu and Cendiarie of the world.

cendleing, obs. form of KINDLING.

a **1547** EARL SURREY *Æneid* II. 919 (Virg. II. 697), Which full bright cendleing a furrow, shone, By a long tract appointing us the way.

‖ **cendre.** [F. *cendre* cinder, ash, *cendré* ash-coloured, as in *bleu-cendré*.] Ash-.

1805 *Med. Jrnl.* XIV. 383 Produces a fine cendre blue.

cendyn, -ynge, obs. form of SEND, -ING.

† **Cene.** *Obs.* [a. F. *cène* the Last Supper, the Communion:—L. *cēna* mid-day or afternoon meal, dinner, supper.]

The Last Supper; also = *Cene Thursday*, the day on which the Last Supper was eaten, Maundy Thursday.

c **1320** R. BRUNNE *Medit.* 1111 Certys, sayd petyr, þys nyȝt at þe cene. **1382** WYCLIF *Rev.* Prol., That in the cene on his brest he shulde lyn. **1398** TREVISA *Barth. De P.R.* IX. xxx. (1495) 364 Lente lastyth to the Cene of our lord that is Shere thursdaye. **1483** CAXTON *Gold. Leg.* 329/4 He had be wasshen of the kynges honde on Cenethursdaye. **1491** —— *Vitas Patr.* (W. de W. 1495) I. xlii. 70 b/1 The daye of the Cene comen.. Zozimas.. tooke a chalys.

cene, obs. f. of SEEN, and var. SENE *Obs.*, synod.

† **ceneˈfectory,** *a. Obs. rare*⁻¹. [corrupt ad. L. *scēnofactōrius* (Vulg.) pertaining to tent-making, f. Gr. σκηνή tent: see FACTORY.] Tent-making; also app. as *sb.* tent-maker.

1382 WYCLIF *Acts* xviii. 3 Thei weren of cenefectorie [*v.r.* cenefectoryes] craft [**1388** of roopmakeris craft; Vulg. *scenofactoriæ artis*] that is, to make hilingis to trauelinge men.

cenereous, -itious, erron. ff. of CIN-.

ceneth, obs. form of ZENITH.

† **cengle.** *Obs. rare*⁻¹. [a. OF. *cengle*:—L. *cingulum* girdle, f. *cing-ĕre* to gird.] A girdle.

1491 CAXTON *Vitas Patr.* (W. de W. 1495) 19 Gyrde with a cengle.. He made cengles and coverynges of leves of palme woven after the custome of the countree.

cengylle, obs. form of SINGLE.

† **cenkanter,** *a. Obs.*

c **1540** *Pilgrim's T.* 708 in *Thynne's Animadv.* App. (1865) 97 And leuis the slechy podell, full of frogis, to the old cenkanter phariziecall dogis.

cenobite, -itic, cenobium: see CŒ-.

cenogamy, community of wives; see CŒNO-.

Cenomanian (siːnəʊˈmeɪnɪən, sɛn-), *a. Geol.* [ad. F. *cénomanien*, f. med.L. *Cenomania*, now Le Mans, France, f. L. *Cenomani*, an ancient Gallic tribe of northern Italy: see -IAN.] Designating a subdivision of the Upper Cretaceous period, corresponding to the Lower Chalk and Upper Greensand of British geologists; of flora, etc., belonging to or found in these strata.

1882 GEIKIE *Text-bk. Geol.* 829 The Cenomanian formation consists in Hanover of earthy limestones and marls. **1902** *Encycl. Brit.* XXXI. 434/2 The Cenomanian flora of central Europe. **1914** *Brit. Mus. Return* 206 The Cenomanian Chalk Marl of Cambridge. **1960** L. D. STAMP *Britain's Struct. & Scenery* (ed. 5) xii. 138 A great marine transgression.. referred to as the 'Cenomanian Transgression'.

† **Cenophe** (-əʊfeɪ). *Obs.* Corrupt ad. late L. *scēnopēgia*, a. Gr. σκηνοπηγία pitching of tents, (in LXX.) the Feast of Tabernacles.

a **1300** *Cursor M.* 14563 þan heild þe Juus. A fest man clepes cenophe. [**1398** TREVISA *Barth. De P.R.* IX. xxxiii. (1495) 369 Cenophegia is a feest amonge the Ebrewes.. callyd Pytchynge of tentes.]

cenosite (ˈsɛnəʊsaɪt). *Min.* Also **kainosite, cainosite.** [ad. *kainosit* (A. E. Nordenskiöld 1886, in *Geol. Föreningens Förhandl.* VIII. 143), f. Gr. καινός novel, in reference to its unusual composition, + -ITE¹.] A hydrous silicate and carbonate of yttrium, erbium, and calcium, occurring in Norway and Sweden in the form of greasy, yellowish-brown, prismatic crystals.

1888 *Jrnl. Chem. Soc.* LIV. 234 Kainosite. **1892** E. S. DANA *Dana's Syst. Min.* (ed. 6) 698 Cenosite. **1930** *Amer. Min.* XV. 207 The Nordmark cenosite occurs in druses, which have apparently originated through the solution of calcite.

cenotaph (ˈsɛnətɑːf, -æ-), *sb.* In 7- **aphe.** [a. F. *cenotaphe* (16th c.) ad. L. *cenotaphium*, or its original, Gr. κενοτάφιον, f. κενός empty + τάφος tomb. The L. & Gr. pl. *cenotaphia* has also been used in Eng.] **a.** An empty tomb; a sepulchral monument erected in honour of a deceased person whose body is elsewhere.

1603 HOLLAND *Plutarch's Mor.* 1244 Their Cenotaphe or imaginary tombe which was erected in Isthmus. *c* **1630** RISDON *Surv. Devon* §254 (1810) 262 Sir John Sully.. hath here a cenotaphe. **1725** POPE *Odyss.* IV. 794 To Agamemnon's name A Cenotaph I raise of deathless fame. *a* **1859** MACAULAY *Biog.* (1867) 74 Some of Goldsmith's friends.. honoured him with a cenotaph in Westminster Abbey.

b. In etymological sense of 'empty sepulchre' (whence one has risen). Also *fig.*

1642 SIR T. BROWNE *Relig. Med.* 19 To see him [Christ] in his glory, rather than to contemplate him in his Cœnotaphe, or Sepulchre. **1820** SHELLEY *Cloud* 81, I silently laugh at my own cenotaph. **1878** G. MACDONALD *St. George & St. M.* 5 Turning her back on the cenotaph of their former greatness.

cenotaph, *v.* [f. the sb.] *trans.* To honour or commemorate with a cenotaph. So **ˈcenotaphed** *ppl. a.*

1845 PLANCHE *Golden Fleece* II. 29 Lying, dying, Cenotaphed, and paragraphed. **1891** KIPLING *Light that Failed* iv, The oblivion that is preceded by toleration and cenotaphed with contempt. *a* **1893** J. H. BONER *Poe's Cottage* vii. (Funk), And fate that then denied him, And envy that decried him, And malice that belied him, Have cenotaphed his fame.

cenotaphic (sɛnəʊˈtæfɪk), *a.* [f. CENOTAPH *sb.* + -IC.] Of, pertaining to, or of the nature of a cenotaph.

1872 J. FERGUSSON *Rude Stone Mon.* ii. 49 The larger circles were cenotaphic.

cenote (sɛˈnəʊteɪ). [Yucatan Sp., f. Maya *conot.*] A natural underground reservoir of water, such as occurs in the limestone of Yucatan.

1841 J. L. STEPHENS *Incidents Travel Cent. Amer.* II. xxiii. 408 The servant urged us to go immediately and see a cenote... It was a large cavern or grotto, with a roof of broken, overhanging rock.. and at the bottom water pure as crystal.. resting upon a bed of white limestone rock. **1902** *Encycl. Brit.* XXV. 379/2 The cenotes or underground reservoirs were the important factors in locating the ruins of Northern Yucatan. **1902** *Amer. Anthropologist* IV. 128 Offerings.. were cast into.. the deep *cenotes*, or natural wells, to appease the gods believed to dwell therein. **1940** *Geogr. Jrnl.* XCV. 123 All of the ancient cities were located close to sink holes or cenotes. **1963** D. W. & E. E. HUMPHRIES tr. *Termier's Erosion & Sedimentation* xiv. 308 The forms most typical of karst are the *cenotes*.

cenozoic, var. spelling of CÆNO-, CAINOZOIC.

censar(e, obs. form of CENSER.

† **cense,** *sb.*¹ *Obs.* Also 4 **cens,** 4–5 **sense,** 4–6 **sence.** [Shortened form of ME. *encens*, INCENSE.] Incense.

a **1375** *Joseph Arim.* 290 With sencers.. and a viole of sence. **1382** WYCLIF *Song of Sol.* iv. 6 The hil of cens [**1388** encense]. **14..** *Masse* (*Tundale's Vis.* 150), iij. kyngis.. There offorde golde, sense, and myrrre. *c* **1440** *Promp. Parv.* 66 Cense or incense or rychelle. **1513** DOUGLAS *Æneis* IV. viii. 95 On the altaris birnand full of sence The sacrifice scho offerit. **1540** *Inv. Worcester Priory* in Greene *Hist. Worcester* II. App. 5 A navett to putt cense yn.

† **cense,** *sb.*² *Obs.* Also 6–8 **cens,** 7 **cence.** [a. OF. *cense* (mod.F. *cens*):—L. *census* registration of citizens, property, etc., census, f. *censēre* to estimate, rate, assess, etc.]

1. A tax or tribute; = CENSUS 2.

1524 *St. Papers Hen. VIII*, VI. 374 The pention and cense, which the Frenche King payd before the warris. **1582** N. T. (Rhem.) *Matt.* xvii. 25 The kings of the earth of whom receive they tribute or cense? **1661** J. STEPHENS *Procurations* 76 A Cense, or Tribute in money payd to the Bishop.. from the inferiour Clergie. **1741** T. ROBINSON *Gavelkind* i. 3 Which.. yielded no Cens, Rent, or Service in Money. **1763** BURN *Eccl. Law* (1797) III. 120.

2. = CENSUS I, 3.

1533 BELLENDEN *Livy* IV. (1822) 316 Mony yeris eftir thare wes na cens, that is to say, estimacioun of men, be thare gudis. **1600** HOLLAND *Livy* I. xlii. 30 He [Servius Tullius] devised and ordained the Cense. **1720** *Stow's Surv.* (ed. Strype 1754) I. I. i. 3/1 In the year 1636.. Sir Edward Bromfield then Mayor took occasion.. to make a Cense or Computation of the people who were.. found to be 700,000.

b. An enumeration or list (of things).

1615 CROOKE *Body of Man* 279 In all the Cense of Hereditary diseases.

3. Rating, taken as determining position or rank; 'rate'; income.

1627 FELTHAM *Resolves* II. lii. (1677) 264 More resplendent in their robes, than others of a larger cense. **1636** B. JONSON *Discov.* (1692) 713/1 A man whose estate and cense.. you are familiar with. **1650** ELDERFIELD *Tythes* 298 A person of cense and possession.

cense (sɛns), *v.*¹ Forms: 4–6 **sense,** 5 **scence,** 5–6 **sence,** 5- **cense.** [f. CENSE *sb.*¹ (OF. *cense*), or shortened (in Eng. or Fr.) from ENCENSE, F. *encenser.*]

1. a. *trans.* To perfume with odours from burning incense; to burn incense before, offer incense to; *esp.* by way of worship or honour.

c **1386** CHAUCER *Milleres T.* 155 This Absolon.. Goth with a senser on the haly day, Sensing the wyves of the parisch fast. **1447** BOKENHAM *Seyntys* (1835) 49 In the temple.. hem to scence bothe clene and pure. **1536** WRIOTHESLEY *Chron.* (1875) I. 59 With.. sensers to sense the Kinge and Queene as they rode by them. **1581** J. BELL *Haddon's Answ. Osor.* 309 b, To cense them with Frankencense. **1675** J. SMITH *Chr. Relig. Appeal* I. 17 He was censed in his Cratch by the Wise-men of the East. **1700** DRYDEN *Ovid's Met.* XII. 362 The Salii sing, and cense his altars round With Saban smoke. **1716–8** LADY M. W. MONTAGUE *Lett.* I. xxxvii. 141 Two Slaves kneeling censed my hair, clothes, and handkerchief. **1811** H. MARTYN in Sargent *Life* (1881) 289 The priest.. at the time of incense censed me four times. **1852** MISS YONGE *Cameos* (1877) IV. xvii. 189.

fig. **1881** E. PURCELL in *Academy* 22 Jan. 56 The reverent adulation with which the authoress censes her she-Ritualist.

b. *transf.* To fill as with the smoke of incense.

1886 *Pall Mall G.* 7 Sept. 4/2 Clouds waving, dreamily cense the air continually.

2. *intr.* To burn or offer incense. Cf. CENSING *vbl. sb.*¹, CENSING *ppl. a.*

c **1440** *Promp. Parv.* 66 Censyn or caste þe sensere, *thurifico.* *c* **1449** PECOCK *Repr.* 169 It is not leeful and expedient that men.. cense bifore hem. **1483** CAXTON *Gold. Leg.* 171/2 That they shold sacrefyse and sence tofore the goddes. **1563–87** FOXE *A. & M.* (1596) 279/1. **1670** COTTON *Espernon* III. XII. 617 The man that cens'd at Vespers. **1732** NEAL *Hist. Purit.* I. 34 Censing and kneeling before them [images] is allowed.

† **cense,** *v.*² *Obs.* [ad. L. *censēre* to estimate, rate, assess, be of opinion, etc. Cf. CENSE *sb.*²]

1. *trans.* To judge, estimate, reckon.

1606 WARNER *Alb. Eng.* XIV. To Rdr., And most—what but for Nods doe cense Saints, senselesse of more Recompence. **1697** EVELYN *Numism.* ii. 21 The Saracens who likewise are to be censed among the Barbarous.

2. To take a census of, assess.

a **1719** ADDISON *Evid. Chr. Relig.* II. ii, Augustus Caesar had ordered the whole Empire to be censed or taxed.

censer (ˈsɛnsə(r)), *sb.*¹ Forms: 4–5 **censere,** 4–6 **senser, sencer,** 5 **censour, censare, senscer, sensure,** 5–6 **censure,** 6 **censar, senssour,** 6–7 **sensor,** 7–8 **censor,** 4- **censer.** [In sense 1, a. OF. *censier* (*senser*), shortened from *encensier* ENCENSER:—L. type *incensārium*, f. *incens-um* INCENSE. (Mod.F. has *encensoir*:—L. type *incensōrium*.) In Eng. the word would coincide with an agent-noun from CENSE *v.* = F. *encenseur.*]

1. A vessel in which incense is burnt; a thurible.

a **1250** *Meid Maregrete* lxxv, Cherubim ant serafin.. Mid tapres ant mid sensers. **1382** WYCLIF *Rev.* viii. 3 Another aungel.. hauynge a golden censer. *c* **1386** [see CENSE *v.*¹ 1]. **1449** *Churchw. Acc. St. George, Stamford* (Nichols 1797) 132 To the said chirch I bequethe a peyre of censours of sylver.. for frankincense. **1483** *Cath. Angl.* 330 A Sensure, *batillus, thuribulum.* **1552–3** *Inv. Ch. Goods Staffs.* in *Ann. Lichfield* IV. 5 A sensor of brasse. **1553** EDEN *Treat. New Ind.* (Arb.) 17 The Prieste taketh his senser with burning coles. **1584** FENNER *Def. Ministers* (1587) 97 Though he haue no censure, no odours. *a* **1619** FOTHERBY *Atheom.* I. xi. §4 (1662) 116 Who maketh.. his Caldron, his Sensor. **1667** MILTON *P.L.* XI. 24 Prayers.. in this Golden Censer, mixt With Incense. **1716–8** LADY M. W. MONTAGUE *Lett.* I. xxxvii. 146 Four fair slaves.. with Silver Censers in their hands. **1842** TENNYSON *Sir Galahad* iii, The shrill bell rings, the censer swings, And solemn chaunts resound between. **1888** *Church Times* 8 June 507 Then let the priest receive the Censer from the Gospeller.

fig. **1871** MACDUFF *Mem. Patmos* xviii. 242 The flower.. was swinging its tiny censers with their fragrant perfumes.

b. app. = CASSOLETTE. (The commentators are not agreed as to what exactly is referred to.)

1596 SHAKS. *Tam. Shr.* IV. iii. 91 Heers snip, and nip, and cut, and slish and slash, Like to a Censor in a barbers shoppe. **1597** —— *2 Hen. IV*, V. iv. 20.

2. One who perfumes with incense.

1670 COTTON *Espernon* III. XII. 617 The Censor was soon aware of the accident.

3. *Comb.*, as ***censer-box, -pot; censerless*** adj.
1611 CORYAT *Crudities* 229 The Priest's Clarke.. perfumeth the people with his Censor-boxe. **1827** W. G. S. *Excurs. Village Curate* 142 No incense now breathed over its censerless altar. **1870** DISRAELI *Lothair* xlvi. 246 If Popery were only just the sign of the cross, and music, and censer-pots.. I'd be free to leave them alone.

†**censer** *sb.*² *Obs.* [f. CENSE *sb.*² + -ER: cf. CENSURE 7 b; and *Censarii*, villeins paying cense, in Domesday, and in Du Cange from various sources.] One who pays cense or 'censure'.
1691–1713 BLOUNT *Law Dict.* s.v. *Censure*, in divers Manors in Cornwall and Devon, the calling of all Resiants therein above the Age of sixteen, to swear Fealty to the Lord, to pay iid per Poll, and id per. An. ever after, as Cert-money or Common Fine: and these thus sworn are called Censers. [**1729**- See CENSURE *sb.* 7 b.]

†**censer,** *v. Obs. rare*⁻¹. In 7 censor. [f. prec. sb.] = CENSE *v.*¹ 2.
1625 PURCHAS *Pilgrimes* II. 1416 The Priest went round about the Altar three times. The first time hee censored.

censer, obs. form of CENSURE.

[**censerie,** incorrect reading for TENSERIE, q.v. (tallage or tax exacted by lords from their tenants) in *O.E. Chron.* (Laud MS.) an. 1137: see C. Plummer *Saxon Chronicles* (1889) II. 309–310.]

censery ('sɛnsərɪ). *rare*⁻¹. [f. CENSER; see -ERY.] Incense.
1823 BEDDOES *Rom. Lily* (1851) 147 Echo.. Soft spreading her wild harmony, Like a tress of smoking censery.

censing ('sɛnsɪŋ), *vbl. sb.*¹ [f. CENSE *v.*¹ + -ING¹.] The burning or offering of incense.
1499 *Promp. Parv.* (Pynson) Censinge, *thurificatio.* **1556** *Chron. Gr. Friars* (1852) 56 Item this same yere [1548] was put downe.. the sensyng at Powlles at Wytsontyde. **1608** BP. HALL *Epist.* I. i. 14 Your vncleanly vnctions, your crossings, creepings, censings, sprinklings. **1706** tr. *Dupin's Eccl. Hist. 16th C.* II. IV. xx. 333 There were no Censings, nor any Peace given at the Mass. **1873** J. B. DYKES in Fowler *Life* (1897) 306 The prevalence of the practice of censing in the diocese.
comb. **1881** BESANT & RICE *Chapl. of Fl.* II. x. (1883) 188 Posterity will continue to wave the censing-pot and send up wreaths of spicy smoke.

†'**censing,** *vbl. sb.*² *Obs.* [f. CENSE *v.*² + -ING¹.] Estimating, rating, assessing.
1692 O. WALKER *Hist. Illust.* 149 Servius Tullius.. was the first that ordain'd the censing or valuing of the People.

'**censing,** *ppl. a.* [f. CENSE *v.*¹ + -ING².] That censes or offers incense.
1893 *Athenæum* 26 Aug. 296/2 A censing adult angel.

†**cension.** *Obs.* [ad. L. *censiōn-em* taxing, f. *censēre*; see CENSE *v.*²] Assessment, rating.
1612 BP. HALL *Contempl. N.T.* I. iii, God intended this cension.. that Christ might be born where he should.

censive ('sɛnsɪv), *a.* [ad. med.L. *censīvus* subject to taxation, (Du Cange gives *censiva terra*), f. *census* assessed, rated, f. *censēre*.] (See quot.)
1878 G. R. MARRIOTT tr. *Laveleye's Prim. Property* 227 In the feudal system, there were.. military tenure and censive tenure.. 'censive' tenure was that of the cultivator, who owed his superior payments in kind or in labour.

censor ('sɛnsə(r), -ə(r)), *sb.* Forms: 5–6 sensour, 6 sensor, 6–7 censour, 6– censor. [a. L. *censor*, f. *censēre*: see CENSE *v.*²]
1. The title of two magistrates in ancient Rome, who drew up the register or census of the citizens, etc., and had the supervision of public morals.
1533 BELLENDEN *Livy* IV. (1822) 323 In this yere began the office of censouris. **1607** SHAKS. *Cor.* II. iii. 252 Twice being Censor. **1742** MIDDLETON *Cicero* I. 117 These Censors were the guardians of the discipline and manners of the City. **1838–43** ARNOLD *Hist. Rome* III. xliv. 172 Censors, to whom the duty of making out the roll of the senate.. belonged.
2. a. *transf.* One who exercises official or officious supervision over morals and conduct.
1592 GREENE *Upst. Courtier* in *Harl. Misc.* (Malh.) II. 224 A severe sensor to such as offend the law. **1622** MASSINGER, etc. *Old Law* v. i, Cleanthes.. for his manifest virtues, we make such judge and censor of youth. **1776** GIBBON *Decl. & F.* I. xx. 564 The bishop was the perpetual censor of the morals of his people. **1818** SCOTT *Hrt. Midl.* xxxiv, Regarding his father as a rigid censor. **1871** J. DUNCAN *Colloquia Perip.* 118 Punch is a censor, but not censorious.
b. *spec.* An official in some countries whose duty it is to inspect all books, journals, dramatic pieces, etc., before publication, to secure that they shall contain nothing immoral, heretical, or offensive to the government. More explicitly ***dramatic censor, film censor.***
1644 MILTON *Areop.* (Arb.) 56 He.. must appear in print like a punie with his guardian, and his censors hand on the back of his title, to be his bayl and suretye that he is no idiot or seducer. **1732** FIELDING *Covent Gard. Jrnl.* No. 3 A record in the censor's office. **1796** H. HUNTER tr. *St. Pierre's Stud. Nat.* (1799) III. 607, I prevailed so far as to have it submitted to the inspection of a Censor. **1820** W. IRVING *Sketch Bk.* I. 103 Information.. received with caution by the censors of the press. **1839** E. BULWER *Let.* 20 Dec. in C. H. Shattuck *Bulwer & Macready* (1958) 148 Wd the office of censor (Dramatic) be one.. agreeable to yourself? **1872** MORLEY *Voltaire* (1886) 140 A man of letters whose life was tormented by censors of the press. **1888** *Encycl. Brit.* XXIII. 227/2 The master of the revels appears to have been the dramatic censor from 1545 to 1624. **1912** *Times* 30 Nov. 4/6 Mr. G. A. Redford.. now Censor of Cinematograph Films, is engaged in organizing the British Board of Film Censors, of which he is the director. **1930** G. B. SHAW in *Times* 17 Feb. 15/5 Mr. Edward Shortt, who lately succeeded the late T. P. O'Connor as Film Censor.
c. In Universities and Colleges, the title of various officials.
At Oxford and Cambridge it is the title of the official Head of the Non-collegiate or 'Unattached' Students; in the Royal College of Physicians, the officers who grant licenses.
1691 WOOD *Ath. Oxon.* II. 359 Intolerably impudent, saucy and refractory to the Censor. **1876** GRANT *Burgh Sch. Scotl.* II. iv. 146 The providing of Censors and examiners. **1885** *Oxf. Univ. Calendar* 281 The [Non-collegiate] Students are under the supervision of the Censor, who is charged with the care of their conduct and studies. **1885** *Med. Directory* s.v. *Coll. of Physicians*, All other candidates for Membership shall be examined on the subjects of General Education by the President and Censors of the College.
d. *U.S.* (See quot.)
[**1635** N. CARPENTER *Geog. Del.* II. xv. 257 The Censors and moderators to decide controuersies in matters of state.] **1794** S. WILLIAMS *Vermont* 349 A council of censors, to consist of thirteen persons to be elected by the people every seventh year. The duty assigned to them is to inquire whether the constitution has been preserved inviolate. **1876** BANCROFT *Hist. U.S.* V. xxii. 577 Once in seven years an elective council of censors was to take care that freedom and the constitution were preserved in purity.
e. An official whose duty it is to censor private correspondence (as in time of war: cf. CENSOR *v.*).
1914 (*Stamped on envelope of soldier's letter from the Front*) Passed by Censor. **1915** 'IAN HAY' *First Hundred Thou.* xix. 290 These [letters].. are stamped with the familiar red triangle and forwarded to the Base, where they are supposed to be scrutinised by the real Censor. **1918** B. MIALL tr. *A. Hamon's Lessons of World-war* 146 In a letter written from England to a French non-commissioned officer, the censor cut out all that concerned the miners' strike in Wales! *Ibid.* 147 Correspondence from neutrals was examined and bore the paper band now well known in the United Kingdom: 'Opened by the censor'.
3. †**a.** One who judges or criticizes (*obs.*). **b.** *esp.* One who censures or blames; an adverse critic; one given to fault-finding.
1599 MARSTON *Sco. Villanie* II. vi. 199 Hence, thou misiudging Censor. **1615** CROOKE *Body of Man* 502 Referred or brought hereunto as vnto their Iudge and Censor. **1631** GOUGE *God's Arrows* v. Ded. 406 Baited by the differing censures of diverse censors. **1751** JOHNSON *Rambl.* No. 172 ⁋5 Nor can the most.. steady rectitude escape blame from censors, who have no inclination to approve. **1848** MACAULAY *Hist. Eng.* II. 661 Not.. understood either by eulogists or by censors. **1868** M. PATTISON *Academ. Org.* 4 A defence of the Universities against their censors.
4. *Psychol.* [Mistranslation of G. *zensur* censorship.] A mental power or force which represses certain elements in the unconscious and prevents them from emerging into the conscious mind. Also *attrib.* Cf. CENSORSHIP 3.
1912 *Maclean's Mag.* Nov. 152/1 But the 'censor', to use the Freudian terminology, is easily deceived. **1913** BRILL tr. *Freud's Interpr. Dreams* vi. 287 We may state, as a second condition which the elements must satisfy in order to get into the dream, that they must be withdrawn from the censor of resistance. **1920** B. LOW *Psycho-Analysis* 63 This force of the Unconscious.. at times so powerful that the Censor-barrier.. is swept aside. **1926** G. COSTER *Psycho-Analysis* 200 The endopsychic censor, the judge within the soul.

'**censor,** *v.* [f. prec. sb.] *trans.* To act as censor to; see CENSOR *sb.* 2 b; *spec.* with reference to the control of news and the departmental supervision of naval and military private correspondence (as in time of war) or to the censorship of dramatic or cinematographic productions. Often in *ppl. a.*
1882 H. FOLEY *Rec. Eng. Society of Jesus* VII. Introd. 35 The Fathers were constantly engaged by the Inquisitors in censoring books infected with heresy. **1895** *Blackw. Mag.* Feb. 320/1 The severely censored columns of the Russian daily press. **1897** *Daily News* 13 Sept. 5/2 All news is being rigorously censored. **1899** *Westm. Gaz.* 9 Mar. 5/3 Everything read to him is carefully censored. *Ibid.* 22 Nov. 2/1 Finally the correspondent is handed back his censored despatch, probably reduced to a mere sequence of words conveying little intelligence. **1904** *Daily Chron.* 13 May 4/4 Censoring is very strict during the war. No news is allowed to be published which has anything to do with the movements of the army. **1907** *Westm. Gaz.* 21 Oct. 9/2 Ibsen's censored play entitled 'Ghosts'. **1915** R. BROOKE *Let.* Apr. (1968) 681, I must go & censor my platoon's letters.

censor, obs. form of CENSER.

censorable ('sɛnsərəb(ə)l), *a.* [f. CENSOR *v.* + -ABLE.] Subject to censoring; in need of censoring.
1906 *Westm. Gaz.* 27 Jan. 2/2 To avoid Censorable references to prominent politicians. **1926** *Spectator* 30 Oct. 767/2 Mr. Gilhooley is not more censorable, and not less suitable for what used to be called family reading, than psycho-analytic text-books. **1966** D. VARADAY *Gara-Yaka's Domain* xvii. 184 My remarks to, and concerning Freddie in particular and the masonja in general.. were highly censorable.

censorate ('sɛnsərət). [f. CENSOR *sb.* + -ATE¹.] The institution of censors.
1863 ALCOCK *Capit. Tycoon* I. 66 The justly lauded censorate of China.

censorer, obs. form of CENSURER.

censoress ('sɛnsərɪs). A female censor.
1779 MAD. D'ARBLAY *Diary* (1842) I. 157, I am to pass for a censoress now.

censorial (sɛn'sɔərɪəl), *a.* [f. L. *censōri-us* of or pertaining to the CENSOR + -AL¹: so in F.]
1. Of, pertaining to, or characteristic of a censor (see CENSOR 1, 2).
1772 *Junius Lett.* Pref., While this censorial power is maintained. **1791** BURKE *App. Whigs* Wks. 1842 I. 525 The censorial inspection of the publick eye. **1810** BENTHAM *Packing* (1821) 265. **1865** MERIVALE *Rom. Emp.* VIII. lxvii. 301 The father listened with censorial gravity. **1880** MUIRHEAD *Gaius* II. §226 *note*, A citizen, whose fortune was estimated in the censorial register at 100,000 *asses*.
2. Of persons: Like a censor; censorious.
1592 NASHE *Str. Newes* C iij, If in his Epistle he had not been so arrogantly censoriall. **1596** —— *Saffron Walden* Ep. Ded., The.. censoriall animaduertiser of vagrant moustachios. **1866** BP. GOTT *Lett.* (1918) 145 The very nature of a creed is personal, never censorial of others.

censorian (sɛn'sɔərɪən), *a.* Also 7–9 **-ean.** [f. as prec. + -AN.] = prec.
1598 MARSTON *Pygmal.* ii. 142, I dull-sprighted fat Boetian Boore, Doe farre off honour that Censorian seate. **1618** BOLTON *Florus* (1636) 59 Fabricius, using Censorian severity. **1742** MIDDLETON *Cicero* I. 118 This Censorian animadversion. **1852** LD. COCKBURN *Jeffrey* I. 180 It exercises.. a censorian and corrective authority over all the evils, and all affairs, of the church.
†**b.** as *sb.* = CENSOR. *Obs.*
1598 MARSTON *Pygmal.* iv. 154 When pitty Priscians Will needs step vp to be Censorians.

†**cen'sorical,** *a. Obs. rare*⁻¹. [f. as prec. + -ICAL, after Greek derivatives like *historical, rhetorical*: cf. *oratorical*.] = prec.
1589 *Pasquil's Ret.* B iiij b, They think.. to carrie all away with censoricall lookes, with gogling the eye.

censorious (sɛn'sɔərɪəs), *a.* [f. L. *censōri-us* pertaining to a censor (f. *censor*; see CENSOR) + -OUS: cf. OF. *censorieux*.]
1. Addicted to censure; severely critical; faultfinding. Const. *of*; †*on, upon* (obs.).
1536 *St. Trials, Anne Boleyn* (Harl. MS.) (R.), I intreate him to judge favourably.. and not rashly to admit any censorious conceit. **1605** CAMDEN *Rem.* 5 Which you must not reade with a censorious eye. **1646** FULLER *Wounded Consc.* (1841) 288 Those who are most indulgent to their own, are most censorious of others' sins. **1672** MARVELL *Reh. Transp.* I. 199 'Tis possible that the Nonconformists.. may be too censorious of others. **1711** STEELE *Spect.* No. 53 ⁋5 At a Loss to acquit themselves to a Censorious World. *a* **1720** SHEFFIELD (Dk. Buckhm.) *Wks.* (1753) I. 133 Such is the mode of these censorious days, The art is lost of knowing how to praise. **1766** ANSTEY *Bath Guide* xii. 6 Bath is a very censorious Place. **1875** JOWETT *Plato* (ed. 2) I. 161 He is not censorious and does not censure him.
†**2.** Befitting a censor; grave, severe. *Obs.*
1636 B. JONSON *Discov.* ix. (1692) 183 His [Bacon's] language (where he could spare or pass by a jest) was nobly censorious. *a* **1660** HAMMOND *Wks.* IV. 614 (R.) To take upon them.. a solemn censorious majestick garb.

cen'soriously, *adv.* [f. prec. + -LY².] In a censorious manner.
1679 L. ADDISON *Mahomet* 128 (T.) To animadvert too censoriously upon their carriage. *a* **1691** BOYLE *Wks.* II. 304 (R.) Vain pretenders, who speak arrogantly and censoriously both of God and men.

censoriousness (sɛn'sɔərɪəsnɪs). [f. prec. + -NESS.] The quality of being censorious or severely critical; disposition to censure or find fault.
1651 BAXTER *Inf. Bapt.* 281. **1653** —— *Chr. Concord* 103 God will cause men to abhorre that censoriousness of their Brethren. **1709** ADDISON *Tatler* No. 102 ⁋5 All Females addicted to Censoriousness and Detraction. **1750** JOHNSON *Rambl.* No. 50 ⁋12 Another vice of age.. is severity and censoriousness. **1818** HALLAM *Mid. Ages* (1841) I. iii. 300 The bold censoriousness of republican historians.

censorium, obs. erroneous form of SENSORIUM.

'**censorize,** *v. rare.* [f. CENSOR + -IZE.] *trans.* To act as censor over.
1860 *Sat. Rev.* IX. 144/2 Thinks that God's cause is helped by insulting women.. and censorizing clergymen.

censorship ('sɛnsəʃɪp). [see -SHIP.]
1. The office of a Roman censor (or its period).
1600 HOLLAND *Livy* 264 (R.) To stand for a censorship. **1869** RAWLINSON *Anc. Hist.* 361 The dignity of the censorship was.. lessened by the Æmilian law.
2. a. *gen.* The office or function of a censor (see CENSOR *sb.* 2); official supervision. *spec.* control of dramatic production and films (see CENSOR *sb.* 2 b, e).
1591 PERCIVALL *Sp. Dict.*, *Censura*, the censorship or iudgement. **1641** MILTON *Ch. Govt.* II. iii. (1851) 157 Other thing then a Christian censorship. **1856** FROUDE *Hist. Eng.* I. 292 There was no censorship upon speech. **1875** JOWETT *Plato* (ed. 2) V. 42 If I were a lawgiver, I would exercise a

censorship over the poets. **1879** *Encycl. Brit.* IX. 143/1 A notable incident in the history of the stage, inasmuch as it led to the institution of the dramatic censorship. **1912** *Times* 4 July 6/2 (*heading*) Cinematograph film censorship. **1918** B. Miall tr. *A. Hamon's Lessons of World-War* 146 The censorship of all correspondence was a stupendous task. **1930** *Times* 17 Feb. 15/5 Mr. Shaw on Film Censorship.

b. *spec.* of the press: see CENSOR *sb.* 2 b.

1827 Hallam *Const. Hist.* (1876) III. xv. 166 Even during the existence of a censorship, a host of unlicensed publications..bore witness to the inefficacy of its restrictions. **1841** W. Spalding *Italy & It. Isl.* III. 80 In the middle of 1806, a decree of the viceroy declared, that no literary censorship should be instituted. **1855** Macaulay *Hist. Eng.* IV. 540 The law which subjected the press to a censorship. **1876** Green *Short Hist.* viii. §5 (1882) 514 The censorship struck fiercer blows at the Puritan press.

c. as a university or college office.

1880 T. Fowler *Locke* ii. 12 The Censorship of Natural Philosophy..he appears never to have held.

3. *Psychol.* = CENSOR *sb.* 4; the function of a mental censor.

1924 W. B. Selbie *Psych. Relig.* 80 Unpleasant experiences..driven out of consciousness, and kept there by means of what Freud calls a censorship. *Ibid.* 90 The repressions and censorships of which Freud and others make so much are connected with changes in the nervous system. **1925** tr. *Freud's Coll. Papers* IV. iii. 54 Dream-formation takes place under the sway of a censorship which compels distortion of the dream-thoughts.

censour, obs. f. CENSER, CENSOR, CENSURE.

censual ('sɛnsjuːəl), *a.* [ad. late L. *censuālis*, f. *census*: see CENSUS.]

1. Of or relating to a census.

1613 in *Harl. Misc.* (Malh.) III. 153 He caused the whole realm to be described in a censual roll [Domesday]. **1711** J. Gale *Refl. Wall's Inf. Baptism* 470 The censual rolls of Augustus. **1845** Stocqueler *Handbk. Brit. India* (1854) 135 The..systematic investigator into censual truth.

†**2.** ? Subject to tax or tribute; see CENSE *sb.*[2]

1741 T. Robinson *Gavelkind* i. 3 Censual or Rent-Service Land.

†**censur.** *Obs.* [app. corruption of F. *sangsure*, Picard form of *sangsue*.] A leech.

1597 Lowe *Chirurg.* (1634) 155 Applying of censurs or bloud-suckers.

censurable ('sɛnsjʊəræb(ə)l, -ʃ(j)ʊərəb(ə)l), *a.* [f. CENSURE *v.* + -ABLE.] Subject to formal censure; worthy of censure; blamable, culpable; to be found fault with.

1635 Wentworth in Ellis *Orig. Lett.* ii. 276 III. 286, I doubte he will lose his place, and be found deeply censurable in the Castle-Chamber. **1644** Bp. Maxwell *Prerog. Chr. Kings* i. 12 The Pope was deposable (not onely censurable) by a Councell. **1693** *Apol. Clergy Scot.* 35 Ready to censure what is not justly censureable. **1751** Johnson *Rambl.* No. 173 ¶13 There is no kind of impertinence more justly censurable. **1810** Bentham *Packing* (1821) 264 On the declared ground of censurable misconduct.

Hence **'censurable,ness**, **,censura'bility**, the quality of being censurable; **'censurably** *adv.*, in a censurable manner.

1654 R. Whitlock *Mann. of English* 493 (T.) This and divers other are alike in their censurableness by the unskilfull. **1819** *Abeillard & Hel.* 321 Its uncharitableness Is full of censurableness. **1884** *Philadelphia Public Ledger* 17 Apr., The fact..adds to their censurability. **1828** D'Israeli *Chas. I*, I. vi. 186 That Charles I. was censurably remiss in not hanging all these priests. **1885** *Manch. Exam.* 10 July 5/1 No one was..censurably responsible.

'censural, *a. rare.* [f. CENSURE 7 + -AL[1].]

1708 Kersey, *Censural*, belonging to Valuations, or Assessments. **1721-1800** in Bailey; **1731** vol. II. *Censural Book*, a register of taxations.

'censurate. [f. CENSURE 5 + ATE[1].] A censorial body.

1803 *Ann. Reg.* 643 The Censurate is a committee of twenty-one members, nominated by the colleges..It shall reside at Cremona.

censure ('sɛnsjʊə(r), 'sɛnʃ(j)ʊə(r)), *sb.* Also 4-7 sensure, 5 sensour, 6 censoure, censer. [a. F. *censure*, ad. L. *censūra* (so in It., Pr., Sp., Pg.) censorship, judgement, f. *cens-* ppl. stem of *censē-re*.]

†**1.** A judicial sentence; *esp.* a condemnatory judgement. *Obs.*

c **1470** Harding *Chron.* clxiii. iii, He should it haue by execucion due, By sensours of theyr churche and hole sentence. **1547-64** Bauldwin *Mor. Philos.* iii. (Palfr.) 6 According to the infallible censure of God. **1637** Laud (*title*), Speech in the Starr-Chamber at the Censure of Bastwick, Burton and Prinn. **1647** May *Hist. Parl.* ii. vi. 115 He was brought to..the House of Lords to receive his Censure. **1712** Bp. T. Wilson in Keble *Life* ix. (1863) 295 A person..is ordered to be dragged after a boat at Douglas ..and the Governor is desired to give his order for soldiers and a boat to execute this censure. **1727** Swift *Gulliver* i. vii. 82 The council thought the loss of your eyes too easy a censure.

b. *spec.* 'A spiritual punishment inflicted by some ecclesiastical judge.' Ayliffe. (The earliest recorded sense.)

138. Wyclif *Sel. Wks.* III. 361 Censures þat þe fend blowiþ, as been suspendingis, enterditingis, cursingis, and reisingis of croiserie. **1494** Fabyan vi. clxvi. 161 He purchasyd agayne hym the censures of holy churche, & accursed the sayde Bawdewyn. *a* **1694** Tillotson *Serm.* I. xxv. (R.) The publick censures of the church. **1726** Ayliffe *Parerg.* 155. **1845** Graves in *Encycl. Metrop.* 784/1 The deprivation of spiritual advantages, and the censures of the Church.

†**2.** A formal judgement or opinion (of an expert, referee, etc.). *Obs.*

c **1555** Harpsfield *Divorce Hen. VIII* (1878) 81 Reasons ..to underprop.. the Censures..of the said universities. **1625** Ussher *Answ. Jesuit* 305 The Interlinearie Bible approued by the Censure of the Vniversitie of Louain.

†**3.** *gen.* Judgement; opinion, *esp.* expressed opinion; criticism. *Obs.* or *arch.*

1576 Raleigh *Pref. Verses Gascoigne's Steel Gl.*, To write my censure of this booke. **1594** Shaks. *Rich. III*, ii. ii. 144. *c* **1611** Chapman *Iliad* xiii. 655 But, for me, I'll relate Only my censure what's our best. **1624** Heywood *Gunaik.* v. 251 Give me thy free and true censure. **1649** Bp. Hall *Cases Consc.* Pref., Though unworthy to pass my censure on such a subject. **1715-20** Pope *Iliad* iii. 288 Our ears refute the censure of our eyes. **1805** Foster *Ess.* ii. iv. 164 The collective censure of mankind.

4. *spec.* An adverse judgement, unfavourable opinion, hostile criticism; blaming, finding fault with, or condemning as wrong; expression of disapproval or condemnation. (The usual sense.)

1603 Shaks. *Meas. for M.* iii. ii. 197 No might nor greatnesse in mortality can censure scape. **1606-33** Bp. Hall *Occas. Medit.* (1851) 15 They, that, upon the hearing of one part, rashly pass their sentence, whether of acquittal or censure. **1702** *Eng. Theophrast.* 23 An author ought to receive with an equal modesty both the Praise and censure of other People. **1713** Swift *On Himself*, Vices of the graver sort, Tobacco, censure..pride and port. **1748** Anson *Voy.* ii. x. (ed. 4) 334 The whole conduct of this navigation seems liable to very great censure. **1844** Emerson *Lect. Yng. Amer.* Wks. (Bohn) II. 306 Our sensitiveness to foreign and especially English censure.

5. Censorship; the office or action of a censor. **a.** Of the ancient Roman censors (= L. *censūra*): also *concr.* (*obs.*).

1534 Ld. Berners *Gold. Bk. M. Aurel.* (1546) C iij, The Censure, whoe gouerned Rome. **1598** Barckley *Felic. Man* (1631) 609 Plinie said to his master Trajan—the life of a Prince is a censure, that is to say, the rule, the square, the line and the forme of an honest life. **1862** Merivale *Rom. Emp.* (1865) IV. xxxiii. 86 The censure of Camillus..was celebrated. *Ibid.* xxxv. 200 The censure or prefecture of manners.

b. Of any official supervisor, *e.g.* of the censor of the press.

1663 Gerbier *Counsel* 48 The Clarke of the works, ought to be subject to the censure of the Surveyor. **1887** *Pall Mall G.* 15 Nov. 14/1 It is..not easy to get one's papers sent on without censure.

6. Correction; *esp.* critical recension or revision of a literary work. *rare.*

1613 R. C. *Table Alph.* (ed. 3), *Censure*, correction, or reformation. **1837-8** Hallam *Hist. Lit.* (1855) I. 386 So arduous a task as the thorough censure of the Vulgate text.

†**7.** An assessment, a tax. *Obs.* (Cf. CENSE *sb.*[2])

1641 *Sched. Grievances* in Rushw. *Hist. Coll.* iii. (1692) I. 221 By reason..of extream Usage and Censures, Merchants are beggar'd.

b. (See quot.) ? *Obs.*

a **1547** *Cust. Manors Braunton* (MS. penes R. Dymond, Esq.), Tenants having ther chyldern in howshold with theym under their governaunce and charge not to be presented for a Censur tyll tyme that they do be of full age by statute and put owte in huys from theem for wagys or otherwise to be maried then after that they be presented for censur. **1691-1713** Blount *Law Dict.* **1729-62** G. Jacob *Law Dict.*, *Censure*, a custom called by this name, observed in divers manors in Cornwall and Devon, where all persons residing therein above the age of sixteen are cited to swear fealty to the lord, and to pay iid. per poll, and id. per ann. ever after; and these thus sworn are called censers. **1768** E. Buys *Dict. Terms of Art.* **1797-** Tomlins *Law Dict.*

censure ('sɛnsjʊə(r), 'sɛnʃ(j)ʊə(r)), *v.* [a. F. *censure-r* (16th c. in Littré), f. *censure* sb.]

†**1.** *trans.* To form or give a 'censure' or opinion of; to estimate, judge of, pass judgement on, criticize, judge. *Obs.*

1590 Greene *Never too late* (1600) 32 No further euidence came to censure the allegation. **1592** *No-body & Some-b.* (1878) 280 Peruse our evidence and censure it According to your wisdome. **1601** Shaks. *Jul. C.* iii. ii. 16. **1642** R. Carpenter *Experience* i. xiii. 56 The mouth..censuring all that passes, by the taste. **1729** Franklin *Ess.* Wks. 1840 II. 276 As this essay is wrote and published with haste..I hope I shall be censured with candor.

†**2.** With complemental adj. or phrase: To judge (an object) to be (*of such a kind*). *Obs.*

1597 Sir R. Cecil in Ellis *Orig. Lett.* i. 234, I am contented in this to be censured idle. **1610** *Histriom.* vi. 137 We censure thy advice as oracles. **1619** *Let.* in *Eng. & Germ.* (1865), I..censure this for no more then a wild imagination. **1628** Wither *Brit. Rememb.* v. 704 They censure me unkinde or impudent. **1646** Fuller *Wounded Consc.* (1841) 288 Eli..censured Hannah..to be drunk with wine. **1710** Prideaux *Orig. Tithes* v. 283 Censuring it to be done by the Instinct of the Devil.

†**3.** To form or give an opinion; to judge, estimate. *Obs.* **a.** *intr.* with *of* or (rarely) *on.*

1589 Warner *Alb. Eng.* vii. xxxiv. (1612) 167 Too yong were ye to censure of your vncles tyranie. **1591** Shaks. *Two Gent.* i. ii. 19. **1607** Heywood *Wom. Kilde w. Kindn.* Wks. 1874 II. 104 Most severely censur'd on. **1618** Latham *2nd Bk. Falconry* (1633) 148 Censure better of me. **1682** Otway *Venice Pres.* iii. i, Oh thou too rashly censur'st of my loue!

†**b.** with *subord. cl.* (or pron.) as object.

1598 Sylvester *Du Bartas* ii. i. ii. (1641) 90/2 To censure how this change befell Our wits come short. **1609** Heywood *Brit. Troy* iii. xii, Hard it were to censure which were fairer. **1623** Webster *Duch. Malfey* iii. i, Your graver heads..what censure they? **1652** H. Bell tr. *Luther's Colloq.* 208 We ought to censure and hold that we are justified by faith.

†**c.** *absol. Obs.*

1613 Heywood *Silver Age* iii. Wks. 1874 III. 162 Come we hither To trifle or to censure? **1709** Pope *Ess. Crit.* 6 Ten censure wrong, for one who writes amiss.

†**4.** To pronounce judicial sentence on; to sentence *to*. *Obs.*

1603 Shaks. *Meas. for M.* ii. i. 29 When I, that censure him, do so offend, Let mine owne Iudgement patterne out my death. **1618** Bolton *Florus* (1636) 261 Cato censured them to death for their treason. **1621** Slingsby *Diary* (1836) 316 My lord chancellor [Bacon] was this daie censured to go to the tower duringe the Kinges pleasure. **1624** Capt. Smith *Virginia* v. 193 Some were censured to the whipping post. **1682** *Enq. Elect. Sheriffs* 27 He was censured..to be degraded of all Honours and Titles.

†**b.** To adjudge *to be*. *Obs.*

1640 Yorke *Union Hon.* an. 1215 King Johns covenant was censured to be void.

5. To pronounce an adverse judgement on, express disapproval of, criticize unfavourably; to find fault with, blame, condemn. (The current sense.)

1596 Drayton *Legends* i. 409 Duke Robert iustly censured stood, For Disobedience and unnaturall Pride. **1625** Bacon *Ess. Followers & Fr.* (Arb.) 39 Would not Censure, or Speake ill of a Man. *c* **1710** Swift *Wks.* (1841) II. 24 Discourses..which instead of being censured, were universally approved. **1779** Johnson *L.P.* Wks. 1816 X. 138 He was censured as covetous. **1828** Whately *Rhet.* in *Encycl. Metrop.* 296/1 Their ill-success will probably lead them to censure the proposed method.

†**b.** With *of*: To charge (a person) with (some fault). *Obs.*

1634 Jackson *Creed* vii. xxvii, This..writer sometimes censures the seventy interpreters of ignorance in the Hebrew tongue. **1653** Ashwell *Fides Apost.* 58 [He] might be not undeservedly censured of Arrogancy.

c. With *subord. clause. rare.*

1853 F. W. Newman *Odes Horace* 18 We rather lament than censure that he had no inward strength to combat circumstances so unfavourable.

d. *absol.*

1702 J. Chamberlayne *St. Gr. Brit.* ii. ii. iii. (1743) 356 They..proceed accordingly to censure or commend, as they find cause. *a* **1763** Shenstone *Wks.* (1764) I. 54 The souls.. That never flatter'd, injur'd, censur'd, strove.

†**6.** *trans.* To exercise censorship over. *Obs. rare.* (Cf. CENSURE *sb.* 5.)

1605 Bacon *Adv. Learn* ii. xxiii. §49 How the practice, profession, and erudition of law is to be censured and governed.

censure, obs. form of CENSER.

'censureless, *a. rare.* [f. CENSURE *sb.* + -LESS.] Without censure.

1683 Pordage *Myst. Div.* To Rdr. 6 Let me therefore beseech you to be censureless, till the Day of the Lord cometh.

censurer ('sɛnsjʊərə(r), -ʃ(j)ʊərə(r)). Also 6 censorer. [f. CENSURE *v.* + -ER[1].] One who censures.

†**1.** = CENSOR *sb.* 1, 2. *Obs.*

1586 T. B. *La Primaud. Fr. Acad.* (1589) 206 Cato, being the Censurer of the election. **1621** *Bk. Discip. Ch. Scot.* 89 Some to be censurers of the manners of the people.

†**2.** A judge, a critic. *Obs.*

1575-85 Abp. Sandys *Serm.* (1841) 106 To be favourable censurers of our brethren. **1624** Heywood *Gunaik.* ix. 454 How can I..bee a just and equall censurer of such divine beauties? **1661** *Origen's Opin.* in *Phœnix* (1721) I. 81 As candid and equal a Censurer as you are.

3. One who finds fault, blames, or condemns.

1586 T. B. *La Primaud. Fr. Acad.* To Rdr., Like to malicious censorers. *a* **1674** Clarendon *Hist. Reb.* (1720) III. xi. 184 A free Speaker and Censurer of their affected behaviour. **1724** Swift *Riddle*, I'm too profuse, some cens'rers cry. **1751** Johnson *Rambl.* No. 165 ¶7 My opponents and censurers tacitly confessing their despair. **1882** A. W. Ward *Dickens* vii. 205 That Dickens had such a manner his most supercilious censurer will readily allow.

'censureship. = CENSORSHIP.

1606 Holland *Sueton.* 50 Hee had not the honourable title of Censureship. **1611** Speed *Hist. Gr. Brit.* ix. xvi. §54 To begin his vsurped censureship and dictature. **1835** Reeve tr. *De Tocqueville's Democr. in Amer.* I. vi. 138 The censureship of the laws.

'censuring, *vbl. sb.* [f. CENSURE *v.* + -ING[1].] The action of the verb CENSURE.

1599 Marston *Sco. Villanie* 166 Each quaint fashionmonger..Tainting thy lines with his lewd censuring. **1656** *Artif. Handsom.* (1662) 2 The secret censurings or backbiting whispers of some. **1685** J. Scott *Chr. Life* vii. (1747) III. 443 The Power of censuring.

'censuring, *ppl. a.* [f. as prec. + -ING[2].] That censures.

1606 Shaks. *Ant. & Cl.* v. ii. 57 The showting Varlotarie Of censuring Rome. **1638** Brome *Antipodes* Introd. Verses, To censuring Criticks. **1728** R. Morris *Ess. Anc. Archit.* p. xiii, The censuring Part of Mankind.

†**cen'surious**, *a. Obs.* = CENSORIOUS.

1604 T. Wright *Passions* iv. ii. §8. 143 Araigned at the tribunall of euery..censurious Aristarchs vnderstanding. **1684** Baxter *Answ. Theol. Dial.* 22 Censurious disputes.

†**'censurist.** *Obs.* [f. CENSURE + -IST.] A professed or systematic censurer.

1627-8 Feltham *Resolves*, The captious and critical censurist. **1641** I. H. *Petit. agst. Pocklington* 5 He censures

the Censurist for bold and impious. **1670** G. H. tr. *Hist. Cardinals* 29.

† ˈ**censury.** *Obs.* [irreg. f. L. *censūra*, or F. *censure*, with the ending of *injury*, *perjury*, etc.] = CENSURE *sb.* 1 b.

1494 FABYAN VII. 363 He thretened hym with the censuries of the Churche. **1523** LD. BERNERS *Froiss.* I. ccxlii. 358 That he shulde constreyne by censuries of the Churche.

census (ˈsɛnsəs), *sb.* [L. *census* registering of Roman citizens and their property, registered property, wealth, f. *censēre* to rate, assess, estimate.]

1. The registration of citizens and their property in ancient Rome for purposes of taxation.

1634 PRESTON *New Covt.* 337 If there should be a Census of men, as one may so say.. as there was wont to be among the Romans. **1646** J. BENBRIGGE *Vsura Acc.* 28 The first worke of the Census was to value every mans estate. **1781** GIBBON *Decl. & F.* II. 63 An accurate census, or survey, was the only equitable mode of ascertaining the proportion which every citizen should be obliged to contribute for the public service. **1880** MUIRHEAD *Gaius* 469 Entry of the name of a slave, by his owner's authority, in the census.. was one of the Civil modes of freeing him.

†**2.** Applied to certain taxes, *esp.* a capitation or poll-tax. *Obs.*

1613 PURCHAS *Pilgr.* I. IV. xvi. 373 What is properly called Census, the poll-money of his subjects. **1756** NUGENT *Montesquieu's Spir. Laws* (1758) II. xxx. xv. 370 What they called census at that time was a tax raised upon the bondmen. **1818** HALLAM *Mid. Ages* (1872) I. 326 He paid a capitation tax or census to the state. **1828–64** TYTLER *Hist. Scot.* I. 270 Pensions from the census of their burgesses.

3. a. An official enumeration of the population of a country or district, with various statistics relating to them. Also *attrib.*

A census of the population has been taken every tenth year since 1790 in the United States of America, since 1791 in France, and since 1801 in Great Britain. In Ireland the earliest census was in 1813, since which it has been taken simultaneously with that of Great Britain.

1769 GOLDSM. *Rom. Hist.* (1786) II. 115 The census, or numbering the people. **1789** *Constit. U.S.* i. §9 No capitation or other direct tax shall be laid unless in proportion to the census or enumeration [of inhabitants] hereinbefore directed to be taken. **1820** J. MARSHALL *Const. Opin.* (1839) 213 A census exhibiting the numbers of the respective states. **1846** MCCULLOCH *Acc. Brit. Empire* (1854) I. 448 Summary Account of the Population.. at the periods at which Censuses have been taken. **1856** FROUDE *Hist. Eng.* (1858) I. i. 3 A rough census was taken at the time of the Armada.

b. *attrib.*, as in ***census return***, ***-table***, ***-taker***; **census-paper**, a paper left at each house, to be filled up with the names, ages, etc., of the inmates, and returned to the enumerators on the day of taking the census.

1831 J. M. PECK *Guide for Emigrants* 199 The census table of last autumn. **1840** *Picayune* (New Orleans) 25 Aug. 2/2 The following took place between a census taker and a married lady. **1846** MCCULLOCH *Acc. Brit. Empire* (1854) I. 611 The number given in the census returns. **1936** *British Birds* XXIX. 264 To guide future census-takers through some of the difficulties.

ˈ**census,** *v. rare.* [f. prec. sb.] *trans.* To take a census of, enumerate in a census.

1881 *Times* 11 Apr., The visitors were called to be censused.

cent[1] (sɛnt). [a. F. *cent* hundred, or ad. L. *centum* or It. *cento.* (The etymology does not justify senses 3, 4, exc. as *cent* may be a contraction of *centime*, *centesimum*, or other equivalent of 'hundredth'.)]

†**1.** ? A hundred. [a. F. *cent.*] *Obs.*

a **1400** *Octouian* 1463 Hy[s] massengers.. broght with hem many stout cent Of greet lordynges.

2. a. ***per cent***: for (in, to) every hundred; used in stating a proportion; *esp.* of the rate of interest.

[Perh. at first in the It. form *per cento* 'for a hundred'; then pseudo-latinized as *per centum* (which could not have been used in Latin). Whether *per cent.* is merely an abbreviation of this, or is more or less due to the French *pour cent*, 'for a hundred', is not clear.]

1568 GRESHAM in Ellis *Orig. Lett.* II. 182 II. 314 Th' interest of xij. per cent by the yeare. **1583** J. NEWBERY *Let.* in Purchas *Pilgr.* II. (1625) 1643 The exchange.. is sixtie per cento. **1635** AUSTIN *Medit.* 240 Not as heere ten or fifteene per Centum. **1663** GERBIER *Counsel* 65 These Deales are.. sold from foure pound per. Cent. to six pound per. Cent. **1667** PEPYS *Diary* 30 Aug., By that means my 10 per cent will continue to me the longer. *a* **1687** PETTY *Pol. Arith.* vi. (1691) 99 The Interest thereof was within this fifty years, at 10*l.* per Cent. forty years ago, at 8*l.* and now at 6*l.* **1720** *Lond. Gaz.* No. 5825/3 The Interest of one Penny per Centum per Diem. **1843** J. A. SMITH *Product. Farming* 153 The ash of the turnip bulb contains 16½ per cent. of soda. **1846** MCCULLOCH *Acc. Brit. Empire* (1854) I. 403 During the 10 years ending with 1850, the entire population increased at the rate of 13 per cent. **1878** JEVONS *Prim. Pol. Econ.* 54 People fancy that, if they get 25 per cent. more money wages, they must be 25 per cent. more wealthy. **1888** *Resol. Ho. Comm.* 6 July, That the Consolidated Three Pounds per Centum Annuities and the Reduced Three Pounds per Centum Annuities shall be redeemable, etc.

b. ***three*** (***four, five,*** etc.) ***per cents*** = three (etc.) per cent stocks, *i.e.* public securities bearing that rate of interest. Also *attrib.*

1822 BYRON *Juan* XI. lxxvii, Where are those martyred saints the five per cents? **1828** SOUTHEY *Ep. A. Cunningham*, Of loans, of omnium, and of three per cents. **1844** W. H. MAXWELL *Sports & Adv. Scotl.* xiv. (1855) 128 Her four-per-cents. were conveyed to her nephew. **1888** J. MORLEY *Burke* 291 A charge on the four and a half per cent. fund.

c. ***cent per cent***: a hundred for every hundred; interest equal in amount to the principal; loosely, a proportion which approaches this.

1576 GASCOIGNE *Steele Gl.* (Arb.) 71 To gaine no more, but Cento por cento. *c* **1677** MARVELL *Growth Popery* 38 Pay Cent. per Cent. more than the things are worth. **1705** MRS. CENTLIVRE *Gamester* 1, O, impudence, she calls Cent per Cent fair dealing. **1709** E. W. *Life Donna Rosina* 36 The Cargo he had brought home at Cent per Cent profit. **17..** BURNS *Cure for all Care* iii, There centum per centum, the cit with his purse. **1822** T. MITCHELL *Aristoph.* II. 127 Hence with your registers, your cents-per-cent. **1884** *Times* (weekly ed.) 29 Aug. 15/2 A score or so of sheep, which he had sold for nearly cent. per cent. in Scotland.

3. A hundredth. ? *Obs.*

1685 J. WARNER in Boyle *Hist. Air* xvii. (1692) 134 The Mercury subsided 9 Cents of an Inch.

4. In various monetary systems the term used for the hundredth part of a standard unit.

a. In United States of America (also in Canada, British Guiana, and many other British colonies): The hundredth part of a dollar; a copper (or nickel) coin of this value, nearly equal (*c* 1890) to a half-penny of Great Britain. (Often taken as the type of the smallest current coin; whence such expressions as 'I don't care a cent for'.) See also RED *a.* 3 c.

Apparently the first mention of *cent* occurs in the letter of Robert Morris to the U.S. Congress in 1782, suggesting that the American monetary unit should be the $\frac{1}{1440}$ of a dollar, and that a coin equal to 100 of these or $\frac{5}{72}$ of a dollar (about 3¾*d.* Eng.) should be made, and called a *cent.* This proposal was not taken up; but it may have suggested the name 'cent' for the coin = $\frac{1}{100}$ of a dollar, ordained by the Continental Congress on 8 August 1786 (see quot.). There exists, however, an American copper token, commonly called the *Washington cent*, bearing on one side a head in a wreath with the legend 'Washington and Independence', and date '1783'; on the other the words, 'One Cent', and the exergue $\frac{1}{100}$. But it is not certain that 1783 represents the date of issue; this token was probably struck as late as 1789, the date 1783 being merely that of the conclusion of the War of Independence. Previously to the coining of the cent, or $\frac{1}{100}$ of a dollar, and down to 1789, accounts were kept in dollars and ninetieths, a relic of the time when the Spanish piastre or piece of eight reals, called by the colonists 'dollar', was worth 7*s.* 6*d.* (90 pence) of the money of account of Maryland and Pennsylvania. (From notes communicated by the late Prof. J. W. Andrews of Marietta Coll., Ohio.)

1782 MORRIS in Sparks *Life & Writ.* (1832) I. 275 One hundred [units] would be the lowest silver coin, and might be called a Cent. **1786** *Ord. Continent. Congress. U.S.* 8 Aug., Mills, Cents, Dimes, Dollars. **1803** J. DAVIS *Trav. in U.S.A.* 389 But I never wronged Master of a cent. **1804** MITCHELL in *Naval Chron.* XIII. 160 Seamen pay twenty Cents. **1830** 'MAJOR J. DOWNING' *Let.* 17 Feb. in *Life & Writings* (ed. 2, 1834) 68 They don't seem to rip up worth a cent since the first night they begun. **1837** W. IRVING *Capt. Bonneville* II. 45 To pause at any paltry consideration of dollars and cents. **1863** FR. KEMBLE *Resid. Georgia* 40, I will give a cent to every little boy or girl. **1872** RAYMOND *Statist. Mines & Mining* 335 Potatoes, 6 cents. per pound; sugar, 20 to 30 cents. **1872** E. EGGLESTON *End of World* 11, I don't believe that you'd care a cent if she did marry a Dutchman! **1902** HARBEN *Abner Daniel* 59 He'd cut her off without a cent. **1947** K. TENNANT *Lost Haven* (1968) 12 If you marry that Alec, you don't get a cent. *Ibid.* i. 23 He left with my schnapper boat that he promised to pay for and never paid a damn cent. **1968** *Globe & Mail* (Toronto) 17 Feb. 23/6 If Vancouver just had to pay for an orchestra it wouldn't make a cent.

b. The hundredth part of the florin of the Netherlands.

c. A (French) centime.

1810 *Naval Chron.* XXIV. 302, 47 francs 20 cents. **1851** J. H. NEWMAN *Cath. in Eng.* 111 A chair without cushion, two cents; a chair with cushion, four cents.

†**cent**[2]. *Obs.* Forms: 6–7 **saunt, saint, cente,** 7 **sent,** 6– **cent.** ['Called *cent*, because 100 was the game' (Nares). If so, the word is, originally, the same as prec., but prob. taken independently from some Romanic lang. *juego de los ciento*, i.e. 'hundred-game', is the Spanish name of piquet. Cf. CIENTO.]

1. An old game at cards, said to have been of Spanish origin, and to have resembled piquet, with one hundred as the point that won the game. (See Nares, and Singer *Hist. Playing Cards* 267.)

1532 *Dice Play* (1850) 12 Because I alleged ignorance [of dice].. we fell to saunt, five games a crown. **1576** *Househ. Bk. Ld. North* in Nichols *Progr. Q. Eliz.* II. 244 Lost at Saint.. 15*s.* **1577** NORTHBROOKE *Dicing* (1843) 9 To play —post, cente, glebe, or such other games. **1594** CAREW *Huarte's Exam. Wits* (1616) 112 Playing at Cent, and at Triumph, though not so far forth as the Primero of Almaigne. **1600** ROWLANDS *Lett. Humours Blood* iii. 58 He hath Cardes for any kind of game, Primero, Saunt; or whatsoeuer name. **1608** MACHIN & MARKH. *Dumb Knight* in *Dodsley* IV. 483 (N.) It is not saint, but cent, taken from hundreds. **1611** COTGR., *Mariage*.. a game at cards resembling (somewhat) our Saint. **1636** DAVENANT *Wits* in *Dodsley* (1780) VIII. 419 Whilst their glad sons are left seven for their chance At hazard, hundred, and all made at sent. **1636** W. DENNY in *Ann. Dubrensia* (1877) 16 Cent for those Gentry, who their states have marr'd, That Game befitts them, for they must discard.

2. A particular counter used in playing Ombre.

1768 BELLECOUR *Acad. of Play* 90 You are first to distribute twenty Counters and nine Fish to each Player; and remember that each Fish is worth twenty Counters, and is called a Cent. You will then agree on the value of the Fish whether it shall be five, ten, twenty or thirty pence. **1878** H. H. GIBBS *Ombre* 8 The larger round counters which used to be called Cents count as twenty points.

3. *Comb.* †**cent-foot**, a game at cards.

[**1579** GOSSON *Sch. Abuse* (Arb.) 35 Suche playing at foote Saunt without Cardes.] **1640** BRATHWAIT *Boulster Lect.* 163 Playes at Cent-foot purposely to discouer the pregnancy of her conceit. *c* **1650** —— *Barnabees Jrnl.* (1818) 53 At Cent-foot I often moved her to love me whom I loved.

centage (ˈsɛntɪdʒ). [f. CENT[1] + -AGE.] Rate by the hundred; = PER-CENTAGE (which is now the usual term).

1799 J. ROBERTSON *Agric. Perth* 271 It is proper to add this centage to the aggregate sum of the rent. **1807** SOUTHEY *Espriella's Lett.* (1814) II. 69 He stipulated for a centage upon the clear increase of revenue above a certain sum. **1809** R. LANGFORD *Introd. Trade* 130 Brokerage, centage or sum paid to a broker. **1832** CHALMERS *Pol. Econ.* viii. 245 There is scarcely any centage of taxation, however great, that would discourage cultivation.

†**centaine, -ayne.** *Obs. rare.* [a. F. *centaine*, OF. *centeine* (Pr. & Sp. *centena*):—L. *centēna* neut. pl., a hundred things each.] A company of a hundred.

1560 DAUS tr. *Sleidane's Comm.* 281 b, He should ayde hym.. with certen centaynes of horsemen.

cental (ˈsɛntəl). [f. L. *cent-um* a hundred, ? after *quintal*, or perh. *dual*, *plural.*] A weight of one hundred pounds avoirdupois, first introduced into the Liverpool cornmarket of 1 Feb. 1859 and legalized by an Order in Council issued 4 Feb. 1879.

(The name was proposed by Mr. Danson, a barrister.)

1870 *Athenæum* 8 Oct. 470/1 Some years ago the corn trade of Liverpool became convinced that a great improvement would be effected by the adoption of one common measure. The result was that the cental of 100 lb. avoirdupois was unanimously agreed to in that town. **1883** *Times* 9 Mar., A short Bill which has been introduced this session.. to render the use of the cental compulsory in all dealings in corn and the dry products thereof. **1887** *Pall Mall G.* 5 Aug. 7/1 The price having reached the abnormal figure of 2 dols. 17 c. per cental.

centapee, -pie, obs. var. of CENTIPEDE.

centaur (ˈsɛntɔː(r)). Forms: (4–5 *pl.* **centauros, -rus,** 4 **centaury**), 4–5 **sentawre,** 5–7 **centaure,** 6 **centure,** 5– **centaur.** [ad. L. *centaurus*, a. Gr. κένταυρος in same sense; of unsettled origin: see Liddell & Scott.]

1. *Mythol.* A fabulous creature, with the head, trunk, and arms of a man, joined to the body and legs of a horse. In early Greek literature the name appears as that of a savage race of Thessaly, supposed by some to have been the first expert riders the Greeks were acquainted with, and hence to have given rise to the subsequent fables.

c **1386** CHAUCER *Monk's T.* 109 Off Hercules.. He of Centauros leyde the boost adoun. **1475** CAXTON *Jason* 8 These Centaurs were an C men that alway helde hem in armes for to kepe the countreye of thessaylle. **1475** *Bk. Noblesse* (1860) 21 He made tame the proude beestis clepid Centaurus, that be halfe man and halfe best. **1578** T. N. tr. *Conq. W. India* 44 Thinking that he hadde bin a Centaure and that the Horse and man was all one incorporate. **1601** HOLLAND *Pliny* I. 189 The Thessalians called Centaures, inhabiting neere to the mountain Pelius, were the first that fought on horseback. **1616** BULLOKAR, *Centaures*, People of Thessalie. **1680** H. MORE *Apocal. Apoc.* 88 Such monsters as are usually called Centaures. **1794** SULLIVAN *View Nat.* II. 177 Many.. have held the mammouth to be as fabulous as the centaur. **1885** *Mag. of Art* Sept. 443/1 The shaggy centaur, all beast in mood and well-nigh all beast in form.

2. *fig.* **a.** An unnatural hybrid creation. **b.** An intimate union of two diverse natures.

1606 DEKKER *Sev. Sins* VII. (Arb.) 49 Sixe of these Centuares (that are halfe man, halfe beast, and halfe diuell). **1641** MILTON *Animadv.* (1851) 243 Make our selves rather the Bastards, or the Centaurs of their spirituall fornications. **1820** BYRON *Juan* V. clviii, Why don't they knead two virtuous souls for life, Into that moral centaur, man and wife? **1883** W. J. STILLMAN in *Century Mag.* Oct. 826 Master and servant.. a kind of social Centaur, a single brain and a double body.

3. One of the southern constellations.

[**1551** RECORDE *Cast. Knowl.* (1556) 270 There standeth the centaure Chiron.. he hath in him 37 starres.] **1667** MILTON *P.L.* x. 328 Satan in likeness of an Angel bright Betwixt the Centaure and the Scorpion stearing. **1836** *Penny Cycl.* VI. 414/2 From Ptolemy's catalogue, it is evident that he considered the Centaur as holding the wolf .. in one hand, and a thyrsus in the other.

†**4.** A kind of ship. *Obs.*

1622 MALYNES *Anc. Law-Merch.* 173 To describe the diuersitie of ships, as Carracks, Galleons, Galeasses, Galleys, Centaureis, ships of Warre, Flyboats, Busses, and all other kind of ships and vessells.

5. *attrib.* and *Comb.*, as ***centaur-power***; ***centaur-like*** adj.

1580 SIDNEY *Arcadia* (1622) 115 As if Centaur-like he had beene one peece with the horse. **1759** STERNE *Tr. Shandy* I. x, The horse was as good as the rider deserved.. they were

—centaur-like—both of a piece. **1876** GEO. ELIOT *Dan. Der.* I. vii. 123 The thrill of social vanities and centaur-power which belong to human kind.

Hence (chiefly *nonce-words*) **'centaurdom**, the estate of centaurs (cf. quot. 1883 in 2 b). **centau'resque** *a.*, in the style of a centaur. **'centauress**, a female centaur. **cen'taurial** *a.*, pertaining to centaurs. **cen'taurian** *a.*, **cen'tauric** *a.*, of the nature of a centaur. **'centaurize** *v.*, to behave brutally like a centaur.

1883 W. J. STILLMAN in *Century Mag.* Oct. 826 Refusing to recognize Centaurdom as the highest human good. **1842** MRS. BROWNING *Grk. Chr. Poets* 160 Something centauresque and of twofold nature. **1754** YOUNG *Centaur* Ded., All but Centauresses are prudes with you. **1841-4** ANTHON *Classic. Dict.* s.v. *Centauri*, [Buttmann] supposes Hippodamia to have been a Centauress, married to the prince of the Lapithæ. **1883** W. J. STILLMAN in *Century Mag.* Oct. 826 The bluest blood being that of him whose remote forefathers did but follow the original centaurial proposition of taking all they wanted wherever they found it. *Ibid.* 827 This very class which I have in no disparaging sense termed Centauric, the aristocracy, where social independence has reached its highest. **1846** MOZLEY *Ess.* (1878) I. 246 Common sense rejects his.. centaurian image of an evangelising sceptic. **1816** G. S. FABER *Orig. Pag. Idol.* II. 491 The centauric form of Chivan. **1755** YOUNG *Centaur* ii, Time was, when to centaurize was less ridiculous.

centaurea (sɛntɔː'riːə, sɛn'tɔːrɪə). [med.L. *centaurea*: see CENTAURY. Adopted by Linnæus in his *Species Plantarum* (1753) II. 909 as the name of a genus.] A plant of a large genus of herbs, belonging to the family Compositæ, and including the cornflower.

1829 J. C. LOUDON *Encycl. Plants* 735 *Centaurea.* It is said, that with this plant, the *Centaur* Chiron cured the wound in his foot made by the arrow of Hercules. **1835-6** MAUND *Botanic Garden* VI. No. 506 Chiron, the wise centaur, having been represented as using the original Centaurea in the cure of a wound. **1864** OLIVER *Elem. Bot.* 190 Corn Centaurea, or Bluebottle. **1900** *Daily News* 5 May 4/5 The centaurea has for long been regarded as only half-hardy. **1907** *Westm. Gaz.* 18 July 6/3 An exceedingly fine show of roses and centaureas. **1955** A. G. L. HELLYER *Flowers* 30 The centaureas may be considered in three distinct groups.

centaury ('sɛntɔːrɪ, -ərɪ). Forms: (1 centaurie, 4-5 centauria), 4-5 centaure, -ture, sentaurye, 5 centary(e, -torye, 6 sentorye, centuary, 6-7 centorie, centaurie, (7 centry), 6-9 centory, 6- centaury. [ad. med.L. *centaurēa, -ia, for L. centaurēum*, or *centaurion*, a. Gr. κενταύρειον, or κενταύριον, f. κένταυρος CENTAUR.]

1. A plant, of which the medicinal properties were said to have been discovered by Chiron the centaur; two species were distinguished, *Centaurion majus*, and *C. minus* (also *lepton*). The herbalists identified these (probably correctly) with two Gentianaceous plants, More or Yellow Centaury (*Chlora perfoliata*), and Common or Lesser Centaury (*Erythræa Centaureum*). Hence *Centaury* is sometimes used as the book-name for all the species of *Erythræa*.

[*c* **1000** *Sax. Leechd.* II. 186 Nim centaurian þæt is felterre sume hatað..eorð geallan.] *c* **1386** CHAUCER *Nonne Pr. T.* 143 Take youre laxatyues Of lawriol Centaure [*v.r.* sentaurye, Centure] and ffumetere. **1483** *Cath. Angl.* 56 Centary, *centauria, felterre.* **1542** LINACRE *Macer's Herbal* in Prior *Plant-n.* s.v., More Centory or Earthgall hath.. yelowe flowers. **1551** TURNER *Herbal* I. Ij a, Centaurium minus, that is the les centaury.. our common centory in england, is an herbe lyke vnto organe, or wyld marierum, or saynt Johnes worte. **1599** A. M. tr. *Gabelhouer's Bk. Physicke* 138/1 Boyle Sentorye in wine, & drinck therof warme. **1601** HOLLAND *Pliny* XXV. vi, The greater Centaury is that famous herbe wherewith Chiron the Centaure (as the report goeth) was cured. **1688** R. HOLME *Armoury* II. 97/2 Yellow Centory hath the leaves seven or eight on a side. **1784** TWAMLEY *Dairying* 114 Centaury, lesser centaury or gentian, is an extream bitter plant. **1861** MISS PRATT *Flower. Pl.* IV. 8 Common Centaury.. a pretty and frequent plant on heaths.

attrib. **1647** SIR R. FANSHAWE tr. *Guarini's Pastor Fido* (1676) 190 Squeesing out The juice, and mingling it with Centry root.

2. By 16th c. herbalists, ***great centaury*** was (by some confusion) applied to a composite plant or plants; and to the genus containing these the name *Centaurea* was appropriated by Linnæus. *Great Centaury* of Turner was *C. Rhapontica*, of Lyte and his successors, *C. Scabiosa*, and 'Centaury' has since been extended as a book-name to all the species, as ***Australian, black, corn, erect, mealy, mountain centaury***.

1551 TURNER *Herbal* I. Ij a, Great centaury other wyse called ruponticum.. the seed is like wyld safforne wrapped in certayn flockes. **1578** LYTE *Dodoens* II. ix. 325 The great Centorie.. The flowers be of small hearie threddes or thrommes, of a lyght blewe purple colour, and they growe out of the scalye knoppes at the toppes of the braunches. **1741** *Compl. Fam. Piece* II. iii. 386. **1794** MARTYN *Rousseau's Bot.* xxvi. 401 The Great or Officinal Centaury.. the scales of the calyx are ovate.

3. ***American centaury***: a name for *Sabbatia*, a genus of North American herbs of the Gentian family, esp. *S. angularis*.

1831 J. DAVIES *Manual Mat. Med.* 116 American Centaury.. This plant is a pure bitter, justly held in estimation as a valuable tonic and febrifuge.

Hence **'centaurin**, **'centaurite**, names proposed for the bitter substance existing in the leaves of *Erythræa Centaureum*; formerly also for the CNICIN or bitter principle of many *Compositæ*.

1838 T. THOMSON *Chem. Org. Bodies* 707 Centaurite may be given to the bitter substance which exists in the leaves of the centaurea benedicta.

centavo (sɛn'tɑːvəʊ, ‖θen'tavo). [Sp., f. L. *centum* a hundred.] A small coin of Spain and Portugal, and of Central and South America.

1883 *Encycl. Brit.* XVI. 733/1 Chili—100 Centavos = 1 Peso. **1896** *Westm. Gaz.* 18 Mar. 8/1 The 1-centavo stamp is orange-yellow,.. the 20-centavos black. **1920** *Chambers's Jrnl.* 465/2 Two centavos to the escudo is the 'assistance' tax in hotels and restaurants.

cente'narial, *a. rare.* [f. as next + AL.] Of or pertaining to a centenary.

1847 *Illust. Lond. News* 18 Dec. 408/3 In 1788, the centennarial day was kept up with great pomp.

centenarian (sɛntɪ'nɛərɪən), *a.* and *sb.* [f. L. *centēnāri-us* containing a hundred, of a hundred years old (f. *centēnī* a hundred each, f. *centum* a hundred) + -AN.]

A. *adj.* **1.** Of the age of a hundred years.

1849 MISS MULOCK *Ogilvies* xii. (1875) 90 The shroud of its centenarian fabricator. **1868** J. H. BLUNT *Ref. Ch. Eng.* I. 276 The almost centenarian Bishop of Chichester. **1871** *Echo* 15 Aug., Tales of centenarian longevity.

2. Of or belonging to a centenary celebration.

1864 *Realm* 13 Apr. 7 One of Burns' centenarian bards.

B. *sb.* A person a hundred years old.

1846 in WORCESTER. **1856** *Sat. Rev.* II. 210/1 Two-thirds of these centenarians being women. **1877** WALLACE *Russia* viii. 123 From the new born babe to the centenarian.

Hence **cente'narianism**, the condition or fact of being a centenarian.

1872 *Around Oxford* 104 Several cases of centenarianism have been known at Woodstock. **1881** *Pop. Science Monthly* XX. 100 Facts concerning centenarianism are.. abundant.

† **cente'narious**, *a. Obs.*—⁰ [f. as CENTENARIAN + -OUS.] = CENTENARY *adj.*

1730-6 BAILEY *Centenarious*, belonging to 100 years. **1775** in ASH.

cen'tenarize, *v.* To honour with a centenary celebration. Hence **cen'tenarized** *ppl. a.*

1866 *Pall Mall G.* 25 July 9 We shall soon have as many centenarized heroes as.. canonized saints.

centenary (see below), *a.* and *sb.* Also 6 centenaire, 7 centinary. [ad. L. *centēnāri-us* 'consisting of' or 'containing a hundred', hence 'of a hundred years old' (a sense not actually recorded in ancient Lat., though the corresp. sense occurs with the other words of the same class, from *vicēnārius* of twenty years, to *nōnāgēnārius* of ninety years old); f. *centēnī* a hundred each, f. *centum* hundred. In F. *centenaire*.

The regularly analogous pronunciation is ('sɛntɪnərɪ); cf. *millenary, culinary, promontory*; but some say (sɛn'tiːnərɪ); cf. *catenary*; others, with less reason, (sɛn'tɛnərɪ), as if the word were *centennary*, and connected with *centennium*.]

A. *adj.*

1. Of or pertaining to the space of a hundred years.

1647 FULLER *Good Th. in Worse T.* (1841) 92 Centenary years returned but seldom. **1688** *Answ. Talon's Plea* 30 The Centinary possession, as they call it, or the enjoyment for many Ages can make no prescription against Sovereignty. *c* **1811** FUSELI *Lect. Art* iv. (1848) 452 During the course of nearly a centenary practice. **1830** BP. MONK *Life Bentley* (1833) I. 190 The University of Frankfort.. having resolved to celebrate the centenary anniversary of its foundation. **1857** H. MILLER *Test. Rocks* x. 410 Dividing the total thickness of the bed by the centenary elevation.

2. *gen.* Of or belonging to a hundred.

1768 E. BUYS *Dict. Terms of Art, Centenary*, belonging to an Hundred. **1824** HEBER *Jrnl.* ix. (ed. 2) I. 267 The centenary and millesimal way in which the Hindoos express themselves.

3. Relating to the division of a county called a 'hundred'.

1837 SIR F. PALGRAVE *Merch. & Friar* ii. (1844) 53 Marco ascertained that they were the 'sworn centenary deputies', a phrase by which I suppose he means the jurors who answered for and represented the several Hundreds. **1879** GREEN *Read. Eng. Hist.* xxiii. 115.

B. *sb.*

† **1.** A weight of a hundred pounds. *Obs.* [= late L. *centēnārium*].

[*c* **636** ISIDORE *Orig.* xvi. xxv. 23 Centenarium numeri nomen est, eo quod centum librarum ponderis sit. **1398** TREVISA *Barth. De P.R.* XIX. cxxx. (1495) 939 Centenarium is the name of a nombre for it conteyneth an hundryd pounde.] **1598** BARRET *Theor. Warres* V. iii. 134, 300 Centenaires of lead. **1656** DUGARD *Gate Lat. Unl.* §536 A hundred pound make a Centenary, or hundred-pound waight. **1712** *Perquisite-Monger* 7 The Loan of only ten Gold Centenaries. **1788** GIBBON *Decl. & F.* (1846) V. liii. 256 Their pay.. computed at thirty-four centenaries of gold.

2. A space, duration, or age of one hundred years; a centennium or century.

1607 R. C. tr. *H. Estienne's World Wonders* 229 We haue seene sundry strange things in this last centenary of the world. **1627** HAKEWILL *Apol.* iv. 49 If we should allow but one inch of decrease in the growth of men for every Centenary. **1865** DE MORGAN *Paradoxes* (1872) 11 [The editorial system] has grown up in the last *centenary*—a word I may use to signify the hundred years now ending, and to avoid the ambiguity of *century*. **1884** *Birmingh. Weekly Post* 6 Dec. 3/4 Mr. John Hogben.. on Sunday completed his centenary.

3. A centennial anniversary; the celebration of the accomplishment of a centennium.

1788 *Ann. Reg.* 220 Among the clubs of London who celebrated the centenary of the glorious revolution. **1839** T. JACKSON (*title*), The Centenary of Wesleyan Methodism. **1859** *Times* Jan. 26 The Burns centenary was celebrated last night. **1885** *Pall Mall G.* 20 June 3/2 The [Handel] festival is one full year before its time, owing to the present rage for centenaries. This is the second centenary of Handel's birth.

4. A centenarian. *rare.* [= L. **centēnārius*, F. *centenaire.*]

1834-43 SOUTHEY *Doctor* cxxxii, Centenaries, he thought, must have been ravens and tortoises.

5. (See quot.)

1700 SIR H. CHAUNCY *Hist. Antiq. Herts.* (1826) I. 52 Every Hundred was govern'd by a particular officer, called a Centenary or a Hundredary.

Hence **centenary** *v.*

1888 *Scottish Leader* 9 Apr. 4 Those who had already monuments enough might be centenaried, while one whose centenary was not available might have a new monument.

centence, obs. form of SENTENCE.

centenier ('sɛntənɪə(r)). Forms: 4 centener, 6 centenyer, sentener, 6-7 centiner, -ere, 7 centinier, 6- centenier. [a. F. *centenier*:—L. *centēnārius* (see CENTENARY), in 4th c. used for 'a centurion'.]

† **1.** A centurion. *Obs.*

a **1300** *Cursor M.* 19907 A centener, Cornelius. **1523** LD. BERNERS *Froiss.* I. cccxlix. 559 He.. ordayned and made secretely capitayns of the whyte hattes, as Senteners, and Muquateners. **1577** HELLOWES *Gueuara's Gold. Ep.* 178 Pilate.. sent.. a Centenier to discouer a truth. **1580** NORTH *Plutarch* 961 Cornelius the Centiner, chief of this Legation. **1603** FLORIO *Montaigne* II. xxxiv. (1632) 415 His [Cæsar's] Centeniers offered him.. to find him a man at Armes.

† **2.** = CENTURIAN. *Obs.*

1619 T. MILLES *Times Store-House* I. vi. 19/2 They are an hundred, chosen out of euerie Towne or Village, and thereon were tearmed Centeniers, or Centurions.

3. A police-officer in Jersey.

1862 ANSTED *Channel Isl.* IV. xxiii. (ed. 2) 521 Each parish has also two centeniers, except St. Helier's, where there are six. **1880** *Jersey Weekly Express* 13 Nov. 3/2 Charged by Centenier George C. Godfray with having been picked up dead drunk in the Royal Hall, Peter-street.

centennial (sɛn'tɛnɪəl), *a.* (*sb.*) [f. (after *biennial*, etc.) on L. type **centennium* (f. *centum* a hundred + *annus* year) + -AL[1].]

A. *adj.* Of or relating to a space of one hundred years, or to its completion; of a hundred years' standing; a hundred years old; completing a hundred years; of or relating to the hundredth anniversary. ***Centennial State*** (U.S.): appellation of Colorado, admitted as a state in the centennial year of the existence of the United States (1876).

a **1797** MASON *Palinodia* x. (R.) To her alone I rais'd my strain, On her centennial day. **1816** *Monthly Rev.* LXXX. 304 The deciduous willow, and the centennial oak. **1837** CARLYLE *Fr. Rev.* I. I. ii, The blossom is so brief; as of some centennial cactus-flower, which after a century of waiting shines out for hours. **1872** LONGF. *Div. Trag.* III. iv, This ancient olive-tree, that spreads its broad centennial branches. **1874** MOTLEY *Barneveld* II. xiii. 104 With a centennial hatred of Spain. **1881** GEIKIE in *Macm. Mag.* XLIV. 233 (Wyoming) But for the protrusion of this wedge the 'Centennial State' would have been a quiet pastoral or agricultural territory. **1882** HINSDALE *Garfield & Educ.* II. 411 That I would meet her in the Centennial summer. **1940** E. H. MCCORMICK *Lett. & Art in N.Z.* p. viii, Some readers will have seen.. the Centennial Exhibition of New Zealand Art. *Ibid.* vii. 194 Government patronage of artists has more recently marked the celebration of New Zealand's Centennial. **1961** *Spectator* 17 Mar. 382/1 Many English newspapers.. are now referring to the Civil War 'centennial'.

B. as *sb.* A hundredth anniversary or its celebration; a centenary.

1876 HOWELLS, The Centennial is what every one calls the great fair now open at Philadelphia. **1876** *Daily News* 9 Nov. 5/2 America has been of late very much centennialised—that is the word in use now since the great celebration of this year. Centennials have been got up all over the States.

Hence **cen'tennialize** *v. nonce-wd.*: see quot. 1876 above.

cen'tennium. [f. (on L. analogy) L. *cent-um* hundred + *annus* year: cf. *biennium, millennium.*] A space of a hundred years, a century.

center: see CENTRE.

center, var. of CENTURE, CINCTURE.

centerie, obs. form of SANCTUARY.
1600 C. SUTTON *Disce Mori* xiii. (1846) 104 *note*, In time of need no surer centerie.

centering, variant of CENTRING *vbl. sb.* and *ppl. a.*

centesimal (sɛnˈtɛsɪməl), *a.* and *sb.* [f. L. *centēsimus* hundredth, *centēsima* (*pars*) hundredth (part), f. *centum* hundred + -AL[1]. Cf. *decimal.*]

A. *adj.* † **1.** Hundred-fold. *Obs.*
a **1682** SIR T. BROWNE *Tracts* (1684) 40 This centessimal increase [*Matt.* xiii. 23]..this centessimal fructification.

2. Relating to division into hundredths. *centesimal thermometer* = CENTIGRADE thermometer.
1809 TROUGHTON in *Phil. Trans.* XCIX. 135 The centesimal division of the quadrant. **1812–6** PLAYFAIR *Nat. Phil.* (1819) I. 247 When the centesimal thermometer is used. **1852** TH. ROSS tr. *Humboldt's Trav.* I. i. 23 At great depths the thermometer marks 7 or 8 centesimal degrees.

3. Relating to fractions of a hundred; calculated according to percentage.
1829 C. WELCH *Wesl. Polity* 234 The centesimal ratio of increase.

B. *sb.* A hundredth part; the second figure after the decimal point. ? *Obs.*
1698 DERHAM in *Phil. Trans.* XX. 47 The Height of the Mercury in the Barometer, in Inches and Centesimals. **1727** ARBUTHNOT *Anc. Coins, &c.* (J.) The neglect of a few centesimals in the side of the cube.

centesimally (sɛnˈtɛsɪməlɪ), *adv.* [f. prec. + -LY[2].]
Into hundredths, in fractions of a hundred.
1832 *Nat. Philos.* II. *Thermom. & Pyrom.* i. 9 (Usef. Knowl. Soc.) Celsius..divided centesimally the thermometer known..by his name. **1869** *Daily News* 13 Sept., I have..given the result of my examination in ounces and also centesimally.

centesimate (sɛnˈtɛsɪmeɪt), *v.* [f. L. *centēsimāre* (f. *centēsimus* hundredth): see -ATE[3]. Cf. *decimate.*] To select every hundredth person for punishment. So **cenˈtesimation**.
1660 JER. TAYLOR *Duct. Dubit.* ii. 122 (L.) Sometimes the criminals were decimated by lot, as appears in..Julius Capitolinus, who also mentions a centesimation. **1753** CHAMBERS *Cycl. Supp.* s.v., Macrinus sometimes decimated and sometimes centesimated the soldiers. **1768** E. BUYS *Dict. Terms of Art, Centesimation*, a milder Kind of military Punishment..when only every hundredth Man is executed. **1839** DE QUINCEY *Wks.* (1862) VII. 270 Elsewhere, we decimate, or even centesimate.

‖**centesimo** (tʃenˈtezimo). Pl. **centesimi**. [It.] An Italian coin of the value of one hundredth of a lira.
1851 E. RUSKIN *Let.* 2 Nov. in M. Lutyens *Effie in Venice* (1965) II. 210 Gondoliers carrying people across..for which they were paid a centesimo. **1922** D. H. LAWRENCE et al. tr. *Bunin's Gent. from San Francisco* 33 He gambled away to the last farthing all those copper coins.., in all..forty centesimi. **1959** E. POUND *Thrones* civ. 90 And a $ to look like a franc, the franc worth a centesimo.

† **ˈcentesm.** *Obs.* Also 5 centysme, 7 centesme; also 8 in Lat. form **centesima**. [a. OF. *centiesme* (prob. in Anglo-F. *centesme*, *centisme*), mod.F. *centième*, *centime*:—L. *centēsim-um* hundredth.] A hundredth part.
1483 CAXTON *Gold. Leg.* 427/3 The centysme of the goodes of the forsayd bysshop. **1635** GELLIBRAND *Variation Magn. Needle* 2 The Horizon..divided into 360 parts, and each part subdivided into Centesmes or Millesmes. **1827** HUTTON *Course Math.* I. 150 Mr. Briggs also computed the Logarithms of the sines, tangents, and secants, to every degree, and centesm, or 100th part of a degree.

centessence. *nonce-wd.* [f. L. *centum* hundred + ESSENCE, after *quintessence* (the proper analogue of which would be *centesimessence*).]
The hundredth essence, the essence a hundred times distilled.
1871 M. COLLINS *Mrq. & Merch.* II. vi. 161 The—quintessence, shall I say?—no, the centessence of nightmare.

† **ˈcentgrave.** *Obs.* [ad. Ger. *centgraf*, *zentgraf*, f. MHG. *zente*, a district originally of 100 hamlets, ad. late L. *centa*, It. *cinta*, in same sense: see Du Cange. The Centgraf was the president of the Centgerichte, which administered the criminal law in these districts.] Used by Selden as translation of OE. *hundredes ealdor* the presiding officer of the court of the hundred; also, to render Ger. *Centgraf*, *Zentgraf*.
1649 SELDEN *Laws Eng.* I. xxv, He was (per eminentiam), called the Centgrave or Lord of the Hundred. **1762** tr. *Busching's Syst. Geog.* V. 474 Over which is..a Centgrave whose business it is to look to the criminal jurisdiction.

centi-, combining form of L. *centum* hundred, used in the French Metric system of weights and measures to denote the hundredth part of the unit, as *centiare*, $\frac{1}{100}$ of an are, etc.
1810 *Naval Chron.* XXIV. 301 Centiar, square meter. *Ibid.*, Centistere = 0·2920 cubic feet.

centibar (ˈsɛntɪbɑː(r)). *Meteorol.* One hundredth of a bar (see BAR *sb.*[6] 2).

cenˈticipitous, *a. rare*—[0]. [f. L. *centicipit-* (f. *centum* + *caput* head) + -OUS.] Hundred-headed.
1730–6 in BAILEY; **1775** in ASH; and in mod. Dicts.

cenˈtifidous, *a. rare*—[0]. [f. L. *centifid-us* (f. *centum* + *findĕre* to split, divide) + -OUS.] ‘Divided into an hundred parts or ways.’
1730–6 in BAILEY; **1775** in ASH; and in mod. Dicts.

centiˈfolious, *a. rare*—[0]. [f. L. *centifoli-us* (as in *Rosa centifolia* the hundred-leaved or cabbage rose) + -OUS.] Hundred-leaved.
1730–6 in BAILEY; **1755** in JOHNSON; and in mod. Dicts.

centigrade (ˈsɛntɪgreɪd), *a.* [a. F. *centigrade*, f. L. *centum* + *gradus* step, degree.] Having a hundred degrees; usually applied to Celsius's thermometer, in which the space between the freezing and boiling points of water is divided into 100 degrees. (Symbolized by C., as 40° C.)
1812 *Edin. Rev.* XX. 196 This thermometer is exactly the same with what has been since called in France the Centigrade. **1860** *All Y. Round* No. 43. 391 A temperature of 120°..centigrade. **1878** HUXLEY *Physiogr.* 151 The centigrade scale is now frequently used in scientific investigations in this country. **1881** *Nature* XXIII. 476 The Centigrade Photometer, a new optical instrument for determining the intensity of any source of light.

centigramme (ˈsɛntɪgræm, Fr. sɑ̃tigram). [F. *centigramme*: see CENTI- and GRAN[2].] In the Metric system, a weight equal to $\frac{1}{100}$ of a gramme, or ·1543248 of a grain troy.
1801 DUPRÉ *Neolog. Fr. Dict.* 73 *Décigramme*..equal to ten centigrammes. **1833** *Manuf. Metal* II. 123 (Cab. Cycl.) One centigramme of bruised gunpowder.

centile (ˈsɛntaɪl). [f. PER)CENTILE *a.* and *sb.*] = PERCENTILE *sb.*
1902 F. GALTON in *Biometrika* I. 386 Following a nomenclature already adopted, in which the words ‘centile’ and ‘decile’ occur. **1907** G. P. WATKINS *Growth of Large Fortunes* ii. 18 Convenient relative numbers are the ratio of the upper decile, or the upper centile, to the median. **1964** *Punch* 4 Mar. 342/2 A centile rank of 96 would mean..that only 4 per cent..would be liked more..than this one. **1979** *Brit. Med. Jrnl.* 15 Dec. 1560/2 Among our under-5s some 30% had a weight under the third centile for European children.

ˈcentilingued, *a. nonce-wd.* [f. L. *centum* + *lingua* tongue + -ED.] Hundred-tongued.
1859 SALA *Gaslight & D.* ix. 105 Centilingued Rumour.

centilitre (ˈsɛntɪliːtə(r), Fr. sɑ̃tilitr). [F. *centilitre*: see CENTI- and LITRE.] In the Metric system, a measure of capacity equal to $\frac{1}{100}$ of a litre, or ·61028 of a cubic inch.
1801 DUPRÉ *Neolog. Fr. Dict.* 42 *Centilitre*..is the hundredth part of the litre. **1883** *Pall Mall G.* 31 Oct. 4/1 How many bottles of 70 centilitres capacity can be filled out of 4 hectolitres and 34 litres of wine?

centillion (sɛnˈtɪljən). [f. L. *centum* hundred + the termination of *million*: cf. BILLION.] The hundredth power of a million; a number which would be denoted by 1 followed by 600 ciphers. Hence **cenˈtillionth**.
1852 *Tait's Mag.* XIX. 473 There existed not a centillionth of the blessing.

cenˈtiloquy. [ad. L. *centiloquium, f. *centum* + *loqui* to speak.] Name of a work attributed to Ptolemy, consisting of a hundred aphorisms of astrology.
1588 J[OHN] H[ARVEY] *Disc. Probleme* 113 This is the true ..doctrine of Ptolomey as may appear..by his Aphoristicall Centiloquie. **1621** BURTON *Anat. Mel.* I. iii. I. iii. **1635** PERSON *Varieties* II. 69 Hali the Jew his commentary, upon the centiloquy of Ptolomee.

‖**centime** (sɑ̃tim). [Fr.:—OF. *centisme*, *centiesme*:—L. *centēsimus* hundredth: see CENTESM.] A French coin of the value of $\frac{1}{100}$ of a franc.
1801 DUPRÉ *Neolog. Fr. Dict.* 42 A piece of five centimes is equal to a sou. **1816** J. SCOTT *Vis. Paris* 99 A centime, or the tenth part of a halfpenny. **1868** MISS MULOCK in *Macm. Mag.* No. 103. 44/2 Champagne at four francs fifty centimes the bottle.

b. *transf.* Any coin whose value is $\frac{1}{100}$ of that of the standard.
1866 HOWELLS *Venet. Life* vi. 79 The soldo being the centime of the florin.

centimetre (ˈsɛntɪmiːtə(r), Fr. sɑ̃timɛtr). [F. *centimètre*: see CENTI- and METRE.] **a.** In the Metric system, a measure of length equal to $\frac{1}{100}$ of a metre, or ·3937 (nearly $\frac{2}{5}$) of an inch.
1801 DUPRÉ *Neolog. Fr. Dict.* 43 *Centimètre*..is the hundredth part of the mètre. **1809** *Naval Chron.* XXII. 363 Its..diameter did not exceed a centimetre. **1865** *Reader* 11 Feb. 162/3 It amounts to about eighty cubic centimetres.

b. *attrib.* and *Comb.*, as **centimetre-gramme-second**, used attrib. to designate a system of measurement introduced in 1874 in which the unit of length is the centimetre, the unit of mass the gramme, and the unit of time the second; commonly abbreviated *C.G.S.*; **centimetre wave**, an electromagnetic wave of wavelength between 1 and 10 centimetres.
1875 J. D. EVERETT (*title*) Illustrations of the Centimetre-Gramme-Second System of Units. **1883** *Encycl. Brit.* XV. 699/1 In the Centimetre-Gramme-Second system of units, the absolute unit of force produces in one second, in a mass of one gramme, a velocity of one centimetre per second. **1884** F. KROHN tr. *Glaser de Cew's Magn. & Dyn.-Electr. Mach.* p. xiii, The absolute or C.G.S. (centimetre-gramme-second) units. **1940** *Chambers's Techn. Dict.* 147/1 Centimetre waves. **1947** CROWTHER & WHIDDINGTON *Sci. at War* Pl. xxiii, The aerial of a centimetre-wave radar.

centimetric (ˌsɛntɪˈmɛtrɪk), *a.* [f. CENTIMETRE + -IC.] A centimetre in length; *spec.* designating or employing centimetre waves (see prec.).
1941 S. R. ROGET *Dict. Electr. Terms* (ed. 4) 54/1 *Centimetric waves*, electro-magnetic waves of a wave-length between 0·1 and 0·01 metre. **1945** *Times* 15 Aug. 2/1 The result was a centimetric ground Radar set. **1946** *Nature* 6 July 33/1 The numerous war-time applications of centimetric waves.

centimo (s-, ‖ˈθentimo). [Sp.] A Spanish coin of the value of one hundredth of a peseta.
1899 R. ST. BARBE *Mod. Spain* 64 Countless five-centimo cigars. **1926** *British Weekly* 20 May 125/3 Dr. Irwin exhibited an indulgence which he bought for 70 centimos (7*d.*) in Madrid.

centinary, obs. form of CENTENARY.

centinel, -er, obs. ff. SENTINEL, CENTENIER.

† **centinody.** *Obs.* [ad. L. *centinōdia* (*herba*) some unknown plant, f. *centum* hundred + *nodus* knot. Cf. F. *centinode.*] The plant Knotgrass (*Polygonum aviculare*).
[**1578** LYTE *Dodoens* I. lxvii. 98 Knot grasse..The first kinde is called..in Shoppes Centumnodia.] **1611** COTGR., *Herbe nouée*, Centinodie, Knotgrasse.

centipedal (sɛnˈtɪpɪdəl), *a.* [f. L. *centum* + *ped-* foot + -AL[1].] Of one hundred (metrical) feet.
1879 G. MEREDITH *Egoist* II. vi. 136 Your uncertainty.. would only be extended were the line centipedal. **1882** WASHBURN *Early Eng. Lit.* vii. 153 Conversation made up of all the largest centipedal words in Webster.

centipede (ˈsɛntɪpiːd). Also 7 **centapee**, 8 **centapie**, **centipes**, 8–9 **centipee**, 9 (in Dicts.) **centiped**. [ad. L. *centipeda* centipede, f. *centum* + *pes* (*ped-*) foot. The actual form is perhaps a. F. *centipède*; *centipie*, *centapee*, in W.Indies and early navigators was prob. from Sp.]

a. A name given to wingless vermiform articulated animals having many feet, constituting the order *Cheilopoda* of the class *Myriapoda*. Those of tropical countries are very venomous.
1601 HOLLAND *Pliny* II. 381 There be Latine writers who call this worme Centipeda, as if it had an hundred feet. **1646** SIR T. BROWNE *Pseud. Ep.* 141 Some..with many legs, even to the number of an hundred, as Juli Scolopendræ, or such as are termed centipedes. **1697** DAMPIER *Voy.* (1729) I. 320 Centapees, call'd by the English 40 Legs..Their Sting or Bite is more raging than a Scorpion. **1727** A. HAMILTON *New Acc. E. Ind.* II. xxxix. 89 [He] was bit in the Calf of the Leg by a Centipee. **1756** P. BROWNE *Jamaica* 426 The Centapie is reckoned very venomous. **1794–6** E. DARWIN *Zoon.* (1801) I. 261, I once saw a worm..and observed a centipes hanging at its tail. **1799** G. HAMILTON in *Asiatic Res.* II. 339 Stung by a scorpion, or centipee. **1835** KIRBY *Hab. & Inst. Anim.* II. xvi. 67 A specimen of the giant centipede..more than a foot long. **1847** CARPENTER *Zool.* §823 The Centipede and other carnivorous Myriapods, possessing strong and active limbs, varying in number from fifteen to twenty-one pairs.
attrib. **1875** tr. *Ziemssen's Cycl. of Med.* III. 539 In the case of Centipede bites.

b. *transf.* and *fig.*
1866 THOREAU *Yankee in Canada* i. 16 They made on me the impression, not of many individuals, but of one vast centipede of a man. **1867** F. FRANCIS *Angling* vii. (1880) 262 The line will make ‘centipedes’ on the water.

c. *Naut.* A device consisting of a long piece of wood pierced with holes through which ropes are rove, used for suspending an awning. Also, a strong piece of rope running the length of the boom, with short cross-pieces used in stowing jibs.
1883 *Man. Seamanship for Boys' Training Ships* 138 A Centipede, or, as it is sometimes called, a Euphroe..is used as a crowfoot, fitted with a number of legs, for ridge ropes of awnings.

centiplume (ˈsɛntɪpluːm), *a. nonce-wd.* [f. L. *centum* + *plūma* feather.] Having a hundred feathers; applied to a moth whose wings are cut up into many narrow plume-like segments.
1875 BLACKMORE *Alice Lorr.* I. xviii. 196 Like a centiplume moth in a spider's web.

centipoise (ˈsɛntɪpɔɪz). *Physics.* [f. CENTI- + POISE *sb.*²] A unit of dynamic viscosity, one hundredth of a POISE.

1916 P. C. McIlhiney in *Jrnl. Ind. & Engin. Chem.* VIII. 434/1 It would therefore seem to be a rational procedure to use the name 'poise' in the way suggested by Deeley and Parr, to use the 'centipoise' which is one-hundredth the size of this as a unit for practical measurements. **1935** *Jrnl. R. Aeronaut. Soc.* XXXIX. 916 Gasoline viscosities range from about 0·40 centipoises to 0·50 centipoises at 30° C. **1962** J. T. Marsh *Self-Smoothing Fabrics* xi. 160 The final value of the viscosity is expressed in centipoises, against the value of unity for water.

† **ˌcentireˈligious**, *a. Obs. nonce-wd.* [f. as CENTIPLUME *a.* + RELIGIOUS.] Of a hundred religions.

1650 B. *Discollim.* 28, I could demonstrate it to be Heterogeneous.. Pluranimous, Versipellous, Centireligious.

centisecond (ˈsɛntɪsɛkənd). [f. CENTI- + SECOND *sb.*¹] One hundredth of a second.

1950 J. R. Firth *Papers in Linguistics 1934–51* (1957) xiii. 174 When we measure any features of a kymogram in centiseconds, we must realize what the machine itself abstracts from the single instance and what is abstracted by the employment of the kymogram. **1964** *Amer. Speech* XXXIX. 230 Eight Swedish vowels spoken between three voiced plosives /b/, /d/, /g/ at five syllabic rates produced vowels of approximately 5, 10, 15, 20, and 25 centiseconds. **1969** *English Studies* L. 327 As regards [bdg], the average duration of this element turned out to be 3 centi-seconds.

centistoke(s (ˈsɛntɪstəʊk, -əʊks). *Physics.* [f. CENTI- + STOKE(S *sb.*⁴] A unit of kinematic viscosity, one hundredth of a STOKE(S.

1934 *Proc. World Petroleum Congress 1933* II. 508/2 As the unit of kinematic viscosity..the stokes and the derived centistokes have been adopted. **1937** *Jrnl. R. Aeronaut. Soc.* XLI. 735 The two oils had nearly the same viscosity at 50° C., viz., 78 and 76 centistokes respectively. **1956** *Electronic Engin.* XXVIII. 59 Except for the very low viscosity members (0·65 centistokes to about 50 centistokes) the dielectric properties vary very little with viscosity.

centner (ˈsɛntnə(r)). [a. Ger. *centner*, ad. L. *centēnārius* relating to a hundred.]

1. A measure of weight used in Germany.

1683 *Phil. Trans.* XIII. 190 A centner or hundred weight. **1753** Hanway *Trav.* (1762) I. VII. lxxxviii. 408, 120 [Pounds] 1 centner. **1861** *Leeds Mercury* 2 Nov., The Furstenberg works use about 10,000 centners of cast iron.. and produce yearly from 80,000 to 100,000 centners of raw iron. **1875** Ure *Dict. Arts* I. 756 The Zollverein Centner contains 110·231 English lbs. avoirdupois.

† **2.** Proposed as a name for what was at length called the CENTAL. *Obs.*

1862 *Rep. Sel. Parl. Comm. Weights & Meas.* (Evidence of Prof. Leone Levi) §37.

3. *Metallurgy.* (See quot.)

1753 Chambers *Cycl. Supp.* s.v. *Hundred*, Centner in metallurgy and assaying is a weight divisible first into an hundred and thence into a great number of other smaller parts..The centner of the metallurgists contains an hundred pounds, the centner of the assayers is really no more than one dram, to which the other parts are proportioned.

cento (ˈsɛntəʊ). Also 7 centon. [a. L. *cento*, *centōn-em*, pl. *centōnes*, garment of patchwork, also the title of a poem (as the *cento nuptialis* of Ausonius) made up of various verses. In It. *centone*, F. *centon*. Orig. with L. pl. *centones*; afterwards *centoes*, now usually *centos*; the F. and It. forms of the sing. have also been used.]

† **1.** A piece of patchwork; a patched garment.

1610 Healey *St. Aug. City of God* (1620) 605 Centones are peeces of cloath of diuerse colours; vsed anyway, on the back, or on the bed. **1628** Shirley *Witty Fair* II. ii, His apparel is a cento. **1643** Sir T. Browne *Relig. Med.* ii. §13 There is under these Centoes and miserable outsides..a soule of the same alloy with our owne.

2. 'A composition formed by joining scraps from other authors' (J.).

1605 Camden *Rem.* (1614) 14 Quilted..out of shreds of diuers Poets, such as Schollers do call a Cento. **1646** Jer. Taylor *Apol. Liturgy* Pref. §16 A very Cento composed out of the Massbook, Pontifical, Breviaries, Manuals, and Portuises of the Roman Church. **1730** A. Gordon *Maffei's Amphith.* 95 They affected a kind of Medley or Cento. **1882** Farrar *Early Chr.* I. 554 A cento of Scripture phrases.

b. *more loosely*: cf. 'string', 'rigmarole'.

1780 T. Jefferson *Corr.* Wks. 1859 I. 264 Henry's map of Virginia.. is a mere cento of blunders. **1822** Hazlitt *Table-t.* II. viii. 194 A cento of sounding common-places.

3. *transf.* (of persons, etc.) *Obs.*

1626 W. Sclater *Expos. 2 Thess.* (1629) 158 Amongst the many Centones of reuolters of Poperie. **1647** Sanderson *Serm.* II. 217 The Moabites and the Agarens, Gebal and Ammon..a cento and a rhapsody of uncircumcised nations.

Hence **ˈcentoism** (also **ˈcentonism**); **cenˈtonical** *a.*, of the nature of a cento; **ˈcentoize** *v.*, to make into a cento.

c **1618** E. Bolton *Hypercr.* in Haslewood *Anc. Crit. Ess.* (1811) II. 237 The vast vulgar Tomes procured for the most part by the husbandry of Printers..in their tumultuary and centonical writings, do seem to resemble some huge disproportionable Temple. **1838–9** Hallam *Hist. Lit.* I. I. iii. §80 Not too ambitiously chosen, nor in the manner called centonism. *Ibid.* viii. §2 Tassoni has ridiculed its centonism, or studious incorporation of lines from Petrarch. **1842** Mrs. Browning *Gr. Chr. Poets* 24 The tragedy is..a specimen of centoism, which is the adaptation of the phraseology of one work to the construction of another. *Ibid.* 54 Eudocia.. thought good to extend her sceptre..over Homer's poems, and cento-ize them into an epic on the Saviour's life. **1859** *Sat. Rev.* VIII. 257/1 Warton seems to have imagined the text of Comus, Lycidas, etc., to have been little more than a centonism of borrowed thoughts.

† **cenˈtoculated**, *a. Obs. rare.* [f. late L. *centocul-us* (f. *centum* + *oculus* eye) + -ATE³ + -ED¹.] Hundred-eyed.

1627 Feltham *Resolves* I. i, The Centoculated Argus. **1660** *Charac. Italy* 3 His Bastards that closed the Eyelids of centoculated Argus.

† **ˈcentoner.** *Obs.* [A variant of *centener*, CENTENIER.]

1610 Holland tr. *Camden's Brit.* I. 275 Every of them hath their severall Centoner, as one would say Centurion. **1659** E. Leigh *Eng. Descr.* 85 The whole country [Isle of Wight] is divided into eleven parts, and every of them hath their several Centoner or Centurion.

centorie, -tory, obs. ff. CENTAURY.

ˈcentrad, *adv. Phys.* [as if ad. Gr. *κέντραδε to the centre, f. κέντρον centre, after οἴκαδε homewards, f. οἶκος home.] To or towards the centre.

1803 J. Barclay *New Anat. Nomencl.* **1839–47** Todd *Cycl. Anat.* III. 720/2 The change travels no further centrad than the same point.

central (ˈsɛntrəl), *a.* [ad. L. *centrāl-is* central, f. *centrum* CENTRE: cf. F. *central.*]

1. a. Of or pertaining to the centre or middle; situated in, proceeding from, containing or constituting the centre.

1647 H. More *Song of Soul* I. II. iii, Or else his inward life And Centrall rains do fairly him compell Within himself. **1658** Sir T. Browne *Hydriot.* (1736) Introd. 1 Even such as hope to rise again, would not be content with central Interment. **1664** Power *Exp. Philos.* I. 2 Leaving that central spot in the middle of the flea-biting, where the probe entred. *a* **1720** J. Hughes *Ecstasy* (R.) Around the central sun in circling eddies roll'd. **1837** Emerson *Addr. Amer. Schol.* Wks. (Bohn) II. 186 One central fire..flaming now out of the lips of Etna. **1860** Tyndall *Glac.* II. §15. 310 The quicker central flow [of a glacier].

b. Applied to a city, quarter, building, etc., situated in the heart of its district, where population is densest or trade busiest.

1675 Ogilby *Brit.* Pref. 2 Roads to the less central Cities. **1814** Wordsw. *Excurs.* VIII. 221 Palmyra, central in the desert. **1861** Swinhoe *N. China Camp.* 7 The island..from its central position would form a good depôt for troops. *Mod.* The point of departure was the Central Station, Manchester. To let, convenient business premises in a good central position.

c. Belonging to the party that holds a position midway between the two extremes (cf. CENTRE 15).

1860 Froude *Hist. Eng.* VI. 75 The ultra-faction among the Protestants became now powerless. The central multitude, whose belief was undefined, etc.

d. *Phonetics.* Of a vowel: formed with the tongue in a middle position between front and back. Cf. BACK *a.* 1 c; FRONT *sb.* 13 b; MIXED *ppl. a.* 6 b.

1932 D. Jones *Outl. Eng. Phonetics* (ed. 3) xiv. 86, *a*: is a central vowel; in other words the central part of the tongue is raised in order to make it. **1933** Jespersen *Ess. Eng. Gram.* 24 The vowels..are either front, central, or back, according to the part of the tongue that is highest. **1965** W. S. Allen *Vox Latina* 4 Vowels intermediate between front and back are referred to as central.

2. *fig.* **a.** Belonging to the centre as the chief and most significant point or part, which lies at the heart, or dominates the rest; *hence*, chief, principal, leading, dominant. Also const. *to.*

1647 H. More *Song of Soul* IV. xlvi, The most profound and centrall energie, The very selfnesse of the soul. **1776** Adam Smith *W.N.* I. I. vii. 60 The natural price..is, as it were, the central price, to which the prices of all commodities are continually gravitating. **1856** Mrs. Browning *Aur. Leigh* I. 800 Every turn still brought me nearer to the central truth. **1875** Jowett *Plato* (ed. 2) II. 423 Odysseus is the central figure of the one poem. **1882** Farrar *Early Chr.* II. 438 Love is the very central command of Christianity. **1902** *Daily Chron.* 10 June 3/2 The older views of the authority and inspiration of Scripture are central to his whole system. **1937** *Tablet* 23 Oct. 541/1 The Christian religion..is in no sense central to their conception of the African's future. **1957** N. Frye *Anat. Crit.* 243 Literature seems in a way to be central to the arts.

b. Of a governing body, association, etc.: Controlling all branches of the organization from one common centre; opposed to *local.*

1809 Wellington *Let.* in Gurw. *Disp.* V. 3, I am very sensible of the value of the approbation of the Central Junta. **1846** McCulloch *Acc. Brit. Empire* (1854) II. 313 In 1811 the different district societies were incorporated as members of a central association. **1863** Bright *Sp. Amer.* 30 June, The continent would still be united under one central Government. **1888** Gladstone in *Spect.* 562/1 To commence not with local but with central institutions.

3. *Phys.* Of or pertaining to a nerve-centre; in *Pathol.* applied to affections of parts of the body caused by lesions or diseases of the brain or spinal cord, as distinguished from affections of the same parts produced by local disease or lesion.

1865 *New Syd. Soc. Year-bk.* 88 (*title*) On Central Paralysis. **1872** W. Aitken *Sci. & Pr. Med.* (ed. 6) II. 360 Reflex symptoms may be present in central anæsthesia, but they are entirely absent in peripheral anæsthesia. **1875** Gamgee tr. *Hermann's Physiol.* xi. 467 The central end-organs of nerve-fibres are contained in certain structures, which are called 'the central organs of the nervous system'. **1877** Foster *Physiol.* iii. 75 A sensitive cell on the surface of the body connected by means of a sensory nerve with the internal automatic central nervous cell.

4. In various phrases:

Central American adj. and sb., (an inhabitant or native) of Central America, a region extending roughly from Mexico to Colombia; ***central curve*** (***conic***) *Math.*, a curve having a centre; ***central eclipse***, an eclipse in which the centres of the sun and moon are in a line with the spectator; ***Central European*** adj. and sb., (an inhabitant or native) of Central Europe; cf. *middle-European*; ***central force***, a force attracting to or repelling from a centre; so ***central orbit*** (see quot.); ***central heating***, a system of heating a building by hot water, steam, or air conveyed through pipes or ducts from a central source; also applied to any form of heating which simultaneously warms several rooms in a building; so ***central-heated*** adj., supplied with central heating; ***central processing unit***, the part of a computer that performs processing and controls and co-ordinates the activity of other parts, itself comprising the arithmetic and logic unit, the control unit, and usu. the main memory; abbrev. *CPU* s.v. C III. 3; ***central reservation***: see RESERVATION 3 e; ***central reserve***: see RESERVE *sb.* 5 e; † ***central rule*** (see quot.); ***central school***, a secondary school of a type which by the Education Act of 1944 usually became 'secondary modern' schools (see quot. 1919); ***central section***, a section passing through the centre.

1857 Ld. Napier *Let.* 12 Mar. in *Parl. Pap. 1860* LXVIII. 695 A settlement of the *Central American question in conformity with the spirit of the Treaty. **1934** A. Huxley *Beyond Mexique Bay* 46, I have seen a fair amount of Central American art. *Ibid.*, The art of the Central Americans. **1959** T. S. Eliot *Elder Statesman* III. 86 He's Federico Gomez, the Central American. **1860** Salmon *Conic Sect.* x. (1879) 143 The ellipse and hyperbola are hence often classed together as *central curves, while the parabola is called a non-central curve. **1846** J. Joyce *Sci. Dialog.* xv, A *central eclipse. **1931** P. Macdonald *Crime Conductor* II. iv. 176 Donna Sigsbee..has tired of the *central European charms of Mr. Vanesco. **1940** N. Marsh *Surfeit Lampreys* (1941) ii. 34 Aunt V. is..all Central-European. **1941** A. Huxley *Grey Eminence* viii. 187 Large numbers of Central Europeans were in process of being starved and slaughtered. **1967** J. B. Priestley *It's Old Country* iii. 26 Oldish women with Central European accents. **1801** Hutton *Course Math.* (1828) II. 224 The subject of *central forces. **1922** D. H. Lawrence *Aaron's Rod* xiii. 160 The fresh morning air comes startling after a *central-heated house. **1906** *Internat. Libr. Technol.* LXXIV. §38. 5 For use in connection with *central heating plants, such as are frequently installed for heating the various buildings of a university or state institution, the vacuum system of heating is well adapted. **1913** F. W. Raynes *Heating Systems* i. 14 A good method of reducing the production of smoke is by district and large central heating systems in which either water or steam is circulated through the pipes. **1921** R. Hichens *Spirit of Time* iii, There was no central heating on. **1951** *Good Housek. Home Encycl.* 35/2 The efficiency of a central-heating system naturally depends on that of the boiler. **1882** Minchin *Unipl. Kinemat.* 63 *Central Orbit..an orbit described by a moving point whose resultant acceleration is in every position directed to a fixed point or centre. **1961** Leeds & Weinberg *Computer Programming Fund.* iv. 100 The first type [of input-output instruction]—that executed by the control section of the main computer or *central processing unit—will be referred to simply as 'instructions'. **1970** O. Dopping *Computers & Data Processing* v. 77 Control unit, arithmetic unit, and primary storage together form the Central Processing Unit (CPU). Some manufacturers, however, do not consider primary storage as belonging to the CPU. **1985** *Pract. Computing* July 97/2 The traditional multi-user system involves one central processing unit (CPU) being shared between a number of users. **1684** T. Barker *Geometr. Key* 6 The *central rule. **1704** J. Harris *Lex. Techn.*, *Central-Rule*, is a rule found out ..by..Mr. Tho. Baker..whereby he finds the Center of a Circle designed to cut the Parabola in as many Points as an Equation to be constructed hath real Roots. **1919** A. W. Newton *Eng. Elementary School* ix. 167 *Central schools.. are intended to attract the best scholars from the upper classes of neighbouring [elementary] schools, and to provide a higher course than the ordinary school can offer. **1956** J. E. Floud *Social Class* 15 The central schools..are officially designated 'secondary modern schools'. **1865** P. T. Main *Introd. Plane Astron.* i. (1879) 5 Every *central section of a sphere is called a great circle.

5. ***central fire***: applied *attrib.* to a cap or cartridge in which the fulminate occupies a central position, instead of being disposed around the periphery of the flanged capsule.

1881 Greener *Gun* 202 The employment of a central-fire cap. *Ibid.* 204 The central-fire cartridge. **1884** *St. James's Gaz.* 18 Jan. 5/1 Exploded by central-fire action.

central, *sb. U.S.* [f. the adj.] A central telephone exchange; hence, any telephone exchange.

1889 'Mark Twain' *Conn. Yankee* xv. 184, I used to wake ..and say 'Hello, Central!' just to hear her dear voice. **1908** *Busy Man's Mag.* Mar. 113/1 You may establish a direct, permanent connection with the doctor, the fire department,

or the police and call them immediately without the services of 'central'. **1948** *Chicago Sun-Times* 7 Sept. 47/3 He thought all those other rings were somebody calling 'central'.

‖**centrale** (sɛn'treɪliː). *Anat.* [Latin.] Short for *os centrale*, one of the bones of the carpus.

1872 MIVART *Elem. Anat.* 169 The centrale may form a very large and conspicuous part of the carpus. **1878** BELL tr. *Gegenbauer's Comp. Anat.* 482 A centrale, also, is not unfrequently present.

Centralia (sɛn'treɪlɪə). [f. CENTR(AL *a.* + AUSTR)ALIA.] A name orig. proposed for what was then South Australia, but now used to designate the remote central area of Australia. Hence **Cen'tralian** *a.* and *sb.*

1896 J. S. LAURIE *Story of Australasia* xxxiii. 299 The name 'South' Australia, embracing as it does both the central and the northern territory, is anomalous... For telegraphic, postal, and general purposes *one* word is desirable for a name—*e.g.* why not *Centralia*; for West Australia, *Westralia*; for New South Wales, *Eastralia*? **1931** I. L. IDRIESS *Lasseter's Last Ride* i. 3 Through Centralia runs a continuation of the famous Kalgoorlie ore belt. **1936** —— *Cattle King* xix. 179 The utter stillness of a Centralian night. **1944** F. CLUNE *Red Heart* 1 Although his title [*sc.* 'Dead Heart'] applied more particularly to the sunken Lake Eyre region, it was gradually extended to the whole Centralian Area. *Ibid.* 15 Many a camp-fire in Centralia. **1964** *Panorama* (Brisbane) Sept. 7/3 As far as Centralians are concerned, manana is good enough for them!

centralism ('sɛntrəlɪz(ə)m). [f. CENTRAL + -ISM.] A centralizing system, centralization. Also, ***democratic centralism*** (see quot. 1951).

1831 *Deb. Congress* 2 Feb. 51 A system of centralism, hostile to the federative principle of our Union. **1837** CALHOUN *Wks.* II. 638 The tendency of our system to centralism, with its ruinous consequences. *Ibid.* 650. **1886** *Athenæum* 2 Jan. 16 The power of the provinces..destined to put an end to the centralism of the capital. **1870** *Daily News* 3 Nov., Under the influence of Imperial centralism. **1951** *Britannica Bk. of Yr.* 686/1 *Democratic centralism*, a Communist system of government in which recommendations are passed upwards through successive stages of popular assemblies. **1963** *Ann. Reg. 1962* 22 Mr Michael Foot..charged the Gaitskellites with Soviet-style 'democratic centralism' in running the party.

centralist ('sɛntrəlɪst). [f. as prec. + -IST.] An upholder of centralization. Also *attrib.*

1826 E. CRAVEN *Mem. Margravine of Anspach* II. i. 15 Masons of every denomination,—Rosicrucians, Centralists, Illuminati,—had all, under his reign, the liberty of establishing lodges. **1836** D. B. EDWARD *Hist. Texas* 125 The second faction of this party, called the Centralists, wish to..form a central government. **1849** *Tait's Mag.* XVI. 241/2 A federalist must in Texas be a welcome man, simply because General Santa Anna was a centralist. **1864** *Realm* 13 July 4 The Austrian centralists. **1870** *Observer* 9 Oct., The Constitutional, centralist party. **1871** *Daily News* 21 Sept., The Emperor..would gladly..content both the Centralists and the Separatists.

Hence **centra'listic** *a. rare.*

1864 *Realm* 15 June 3 The strangely-centralistic speech of the Hungarian magnate.

centrality (sɛn'trælɪtɪ). [f. CENTRAL + -ITY; in mod.F. *centralité.*]

1. The quality or fact of being central; central nature or position; situation in or at the centre or middle. ***line of centrality***: line (on the earth's surface) along which an eclipse is central.

1647 H. MORE *Song of Soul* IV. xv, If there be but one centrality Of th' Universall soul which doth invade All humane shapes. **1794** SULLIVAN *View Nat.* II. 213 The centrality of the sun. **1879** FARRAR *St. Paul* I. 364 The centrality of its position..made it a great commercial emporium. **1882** *Athenæum* 2 Dec. 789 The line of centrality is confined to the South Pacific Ocean.

b. *fig.*

1691-8 NORRIS *Pract. Disc.* (1711) III. 129 That Centrality of the Divine Nature, whereby he is fully satisfied in himself. **1844** EMERSON *Ess.* Ser. II. iii. 85 Character is centrality, the impossibility of being displaced or overset. **1862** W. M. ROSSETTI in *Fraser's Mag.* Aug. 195 Clear grasp of ideas, centrality of purpose.

2. *Phys.* [so F. *centralité.*] 'A term applied to describe the inherent action of the nervous centres as distinct from those of the peripheric nerves; it is used in contradistinction to conductivity' (*Syd. Soc. Lex.*).

centralization (ˌsɛntrəlaɪ'zeɪʃən, -ɪ'zeɪʃən). [f. CENTRALIZE + -ATION, or ad. F. *centralisation.*]

1. The action of centralizing or fact of being centralized; gathering to a centre.

1801 DUPRÉ *Neolog. Fr. Dict.* 44 Such is the effect of the centralization of government. **1835-6** TODD *Cycl. Anat.* I. 763/2 This tendency to centralization is still more conspicuous in the Phyllosoma. **1849** RUSKIN *Sev. Lamps* vi. §2. 164 It is as the centralisation and protectress of this sacred influence that Architecture is to be regarded. **1869** MILL *Liberty* 204 The greatest possible centralization of information, and diffusion of it from the centre.

2. *esp.* The concentration of administrative power in the hands of a central authority, to which all inferior departments, local branches, etc. are directly responsible.

[See **1801** in 1.] **1822** *Ann. Reg.* II. 793 Centralization—that ferocious hydra which has preyed upon..Europe for a century. **1836** BP. OF EXETER *Charge* 33 The vice of modern legislation..'centralization' as it is called; a word not more strange to our language, than the practice..is foreign to our ancient habits and feelings. **1863** BATES *Nat. Amazon* I. 38 To combine happily the principles of local self-government and centralisation.

3. *Phonetics.* The pronunciation of a vowel in the central (CENTRAL *a.* 1 d) position.

1962 *Amer. Speech* XXXVII. 169 A third distinctive characteristic of Ocracoke pronunciation..is the centralization of the onsets of the diphthongal allophones of /i/ and /e/. **1964** A. C. GIMSON in D. Abercrombie et al. *Daniel Jones* 134 The current complete centralization of the first element in all situations.

centralize ('sɛntrəlaɪz), *v.* Also -ise. [f. CENTRAL + -IZE, or ad. F. *centraliser.*]

1. *intr.* To come together at a centre; to form a centre; to concentrate.

1800 *Monthly Mag.* VIII. 598 A new Popery, or Catholic Patriarchate..which is now to centralise at Mohilow, or Petersburg. **1859** *Sat. Rev.* VIII. 72/1 Art has a tendency to centralize. **1888** *Harper's Mag.* Apr. 764 The eyes..flamed as if the life of the man had centralized and focussed within them.

2. *trans.* To bring to a centre, locate in a centre, make central; *esp.* to concentrate (administrative powers) in a single head or centre, instead of distributing them among local departments; to subject to centralization.

1801 DUPRÉ *Neolog. Fr. Dict.* 44 To centralize the welfare by depurating the committees of false patriots. **1834** ARNOLD *Let.* in *Life & Corr.* (1844) I. vii. 381 If ever the question of National education comes definitely before the government, I am very desirous of their not 'centralizing' too much, but availing themselves of the existing machinery. **1839-48** BAILEY *Festus* 30/1 Draw to thy soul, And centralize the rays which are around Of the Divinity. **1874** HELPS *Soc. Press.* iv. 59 Business always tends to centralize itself. **1884** F. HARRISON *Choice Bks.* (1886) 238 England was centralised earlier than any other European nation. **1885** *Manch. Exam.* 6 July 5/1 The functions that are now centralised in the Government departments in London.

3. To give or assign a centre to.

1851 RUSKIN *Stones Ven.* I. i. 22 The transitional style of the Venetian work is centralised by the date 1180.

centralized ('sɛntrəlaɪzd), *ppl. a.* [f. prec. + -ED¹.] **1.** Made central, referred to a centre.

1842 *Penny Cycl.* XXIV. 270/1 A centralised system of government. **1875** MAINE *Hist. Inst.* i. 11 The formation of strong centralised governments concentrating in themselves the public force of the community. **1885** *Athenæum* 18 Apr. 503/3 In these days of centralized administration.

2. *Phonetics.* Of a vowel: made central (see CENTRAL *a.* 1 d).

1964 J. C. CATFORD in D. Abercrombie et al. *Daniel Jones* 35 A 'muffled' or 'centralized' vowel-quality. **1965** W. S. ALLEN *Vox Latina* ii. 57 The sound in question must..have been a more centralized, i.e. fronted, variety of *u* than the inherited short *u*.

centralizer ('sɛntrəlaɪzə(r)). [f. as prec. + -ER.] One who centralizes or promotes centralization.

1857 TOULM. SMITH *Parish* 421 The centralizers 'only wait the word' to establish such a system. **1876** *N. Amer. Rev.* 360 As strong a centralizer as Jefferson.

centralizing ('sɛntrəlaɪzɪŋ), *vbl. sb.* The action of the verb CENTRALIZE. Also *attrib.*

1845 J. H. NEWMAN *Ess. Developm.* 171 The centralising process by which the See of St. Peter became the Head of Christendom. **1883** J. SIME *All-Israel* 544 The centralizing shadowed out in these new arrangements.

'centralizing, *ppl. a.* [f. as prec. + -ING².] That centralizes.

1846 GROTE *Greece* II. iii. II. 399 Destitute of any centralising city. **1865** BUSHNELL *Vicar. Sacr.* III. v. 280 The will is the grand centralizing element.

centrallassite (sɛntrə'læsaɪt). *Min.* [Named 1859; f. Gr. κέντρον centre + ἀλλάσσ-ειν to change + -ITE, because the change of colour to white begins at the centre.] A hydrous silicate of lime, in composition near Okenite.

1861 H. W. BRISTOW *Gloss. Min.* 68.

centrally ('sɛntrəlɪ), *adv.* [f. CENTRAL + -LY².] In a central manner or position; in or with regard to the centre.

1647 H. MORE *Song of Soul* III. II. xxxiii, Sith all forms in our soul be counite And centrally lie there. **1753** *Scots Mag.* Sept. 457/2 The sun will be centrally and totally eclipsed. **1862** M. HOPKINS *Hawaii* 3 Situated somewhat centrally. **1869** PHILLIPS *Vesuv.* x. 274 An octahedron or double pyramid, whose solid angles meet the inner faces of the prism centrally.

centralness ('sɛntrəlnɪs). [f. as prec. + -NESS.] Central position, centrality.

1881 P. BROOKS *Candle of Lord* 5 Certain philosophies.. would depreciate the importance of man in the world, and rob him of his centralness. **1886** *Manch. Exam.* 22 Feb. 6/1 Sites..mainly determined by centralness of situation.

†**cen'tration.** *Obs. rare.* [ad. med.L. *centrātio.*] Centering; placing in the centre.

1647 H. MORE *Song of Soul* II. III. II. viii, What needs that numerous clos'd centration, Like wastefull sand ytost with boisterous inundation? **1730-6** BAILEY, *Centration* (with Paracelsians) the principal root or foundation of any Thing; as God is the Centre of the Universe.

centre, center ('sɛntə(r)), *sb.* and *a.* Forms: 4-5 sentre, 6 centur, (centure, centrie, centry), 6- center, 4- centre. [a. F. *centre* (It., Sp. *centro*), ad. L. *centr-um*: see CENTRUM below.

The prevalent spelling from 16th to 18th c. was *center*, in Shakspere, Milton, Boyle, Pope, Addison, etc; so the early dictionaries, Cotgr. (*'centre*, F., a center'), Cockeram, Phillips, Kersey, and all the thirty editions of Bailey 1721-1802; but the technical volume of Bailey (Vol. II.) 1727-31 and the folio 1730-36, have *centre*; 'an interleaved copy of the folio of 1730 was the foundation of Johnson's Dictionary', which followed it in spelling *centre*; this has been generally adopted in Great Britain, while *center* is the prevalent spelling in the United States.]

I. The centre of a circle, of revolution, of centripetal attraction; and connected uses.

1. a. The point round which a circle is described; the middle point of a circle or sphere, equally distant from all points on the circumference.

c **1374** CHAUCER *Boeth.* IV. v. 132 þe sterres of arctour yturned neye to þe souereyne centre or point. *c* **1391** —— *Astrol.* I. §4. *c* **1400** MAUNDEV. xvii. 185 Aboute the poynt of the gret Compas, that is clept the Centre..Alle the Lynes meeten at the Centre. **1413** LYDG. *Pylgr. Sowle* I. iii. (1483) 4 The Centre of the erthe was wonder derck. **1570** BILLINGSLEY *Euclid* XI. xiv. 316 The centre of a Sphere is that poynt which is also the centre of the semicircle. **1591** MORLEY *Introd. Mus.* 18 His signe is a whole cirkle with a prick or point in the center or middle, thus ⊙. **1613** R. C. *Table Alph.* (ed. 3), *Centre*, middest of any round thing or circle. **1651** HOBBES *Leviath.* IV. xlvi. 375 The center of the Earth is the place of Rest. **1683** SALMON *Doron Med.* I. 91 From the Center to the Circumference. **1774** M. MACKENZIE *Maritime Surv.* 23 The Lines..will intersect each other in..the Center of the Circle. **1822** IMISON *Sc. & Art* I. 15 They are all drawn towards the center of the earth. **1879** LOCKYER *Elem. Astron.* vii. xli. 239 A circle is a figure bounded by a curved line, all the points in which are the same distance from a point within the circle called the centre.

b. *fig.*

1600 SHAKS. *Sonn.* cxlvi, Poore soule the center of my sinfull earth. *a* **1631** DONNE *Poems* (1650) 7 This bed thy center is, these wals thy spheare. **1836** EMERSON *Nature* v. Wks. (Bohn) II. 157 The moral law lies at the centre of nature, and radiates to the circumference.

2. *ellipt.* **a.** The centre of the earth.

138. WYCLIF *Serm.* Sel. Wks. I. 356 As þe sentre is lowest of alle þingis. **1602** SHAKS. *Ham.* II. ii. 159, I will finde Where truth is hid, though it were hid indeede Within the Center. **1611** TOURNEUR *Ath. Trag.* IV. iii, I will search the Center but Ile find out the murderer. **1823** LAMB *Elia* Ser. I. xvi, With the feeling of an English freeholder, that all betwixt sky and centre was my own.

b. The earth itself, as the supposed centre of the universe.

1606 SHAKS. *Tr. & Cr.* I. iii. 85 The Heauens themselues, the Planets, and this Center, Obserue degree, priority, and place. **1667** MILTON *P.L.* I. 74 As far remov'd from God and light of Heav'n As from the Center thrice to th' utmost Pole.

†**3. a.** The prick or dot in the middle of a circle; the hole pricked by the stationary point of a pair of compasses. [cf. Gr. κέντρον.] *Obs.*

c **1391** CHAUCER *Astrol.* I. §18 The centre þat standith a-Middes the narwest cercle is cleped the senyth. **1551** RECORDE *Pathw. Knowl.* I. Def., When a pricke standeth in the middell of a circle (as no circle can be made by compasse without it) then is it called a centre. —— *Cast. Knowl.* (1556) 10 Although the earthe in it selfe haue a greate and notable quantity, yet in comparison to the firmament, it is to bee esteemed but as a centre or little pricke.

†**b.** *Astrol.* The sharp point or extremity of the metal tongue representing a star in the 'rete' of an astrolabe. *Obs.*

c **1386** CHAUCER *Frankl. T.* 549 Ne hise rootes ne hise othere geeris As been his centris and hise Argumentz. *c* **1391** —— *Astrol.* I. §21 Of whiche sterres the smale poynt is cleped the Centre. *Ibid.* II. §19 Set the Sentre of the sterre vp-on the est Orisonte.

4. The point, pivot, axis, or line round which a body turns or revolves; the fixed or unmoving centre of rotation or revolution.

c **1386** CHAUCER *Squieres T.* 14 Of his corage as any Centre stable. **1671** MILTON *P.R.* IV. 534 As a rock Of adamant, and as a centre, firm. **1677** MOXON *Mech. Exer.* (1703) 177 The Pole may move upon that Nail, or Pin, as on a Center. **1717** S. CLARKE *Leibnitz's 3rd Paper* §17 If God would cause a Body to move free in the Æther round about a certain fixed Centre. **1825** J. NICHOLSON *Operat. Mech.* 777 Gudgeon, the centres or pivots of a water-wheel. **1837** CARLYLE *Fr. Rev.* (1872) III. v. v. 197 Not even an Anarchy but must have a centre to revolve round.

5. A particular form of bearing adjustable in the direction of its length and having a conical point entering into a corresponding depression in the end of the revolving object which it supports. In the lathe, long works are supported either at one or both ends upon 'centres'.

[**1680** MOXON *Mech. Exerc.* No. x. 180 Upon the points of this Screw [*i.e.* the 'centre'] and Pike the centers of the Work are pitcht.] **1797** *Trans. Soc. Arts* XV. 273 The treadle moveable at the end of the platform..between two centers. **1879** HOLTZAPFFEL *Turning* IV. 47 The crank [shaft] has been made to run in bearings, on centers. *Ibid.* IV. 91 The distance at which the axis of the lathe mandrel stands above the surface of the bed or bearers..called the height of center is used as the term to designate the dimensions of all lathes. *Ibid.* IV. 99 The five-inch centre lathe.

6. *fig.* **a.** The point round which things group themselves or revolve, or that forms a nucleus or point of concentration for its surroundings. *spec.* (orig. *U.S.*) a place or a collection of buildings forming a central point in a town, district, etc., or the main area for a particular

activity, interest, or the like; freq. with defining word, as ***city centre, civic centre, shopping centre, training centre*** (see CITY, CIVIC *a.*, etc.).

1685 PRIDEAUX *Lett.* (1875) 146 We live here remote from yᵉ center of affairs. **1712** STEELE *Spect.* No. 474 §1 The Center of Business and Pleasure. **1796** H. HUNTER tr. *St. Pierre's Stud. Nat.* (1799) II. 492 The centre of all the powers of the kingdom. **1843** J. HAYWARD *Gaz. U.S.* 48 Buxton Centre. *Ibid.* 49 Cumberland Centre. **1855** E. A. CHARLTON *New Hampshire* 295 At Meredith Centre are a meeting house..and three stores. **1877** MRS. OLIPHANT *Makers Flor.* i. 1 The great centres of old Italian life, Rome and Venice and Florence. **1883** GILMOUR *Mongols* xxxii. 366 The officers at the nearest military centres. **1896** *Punch* LXI. 143 But here we are at Market Street... This is the spot our parsons call 'The city's pulsing centre'. **1898** E. HOWARD *To-morrow* vii. 75 The Arcade is..designed to be ..the great shopping centre of the town. **1928** [see TRAINING *vbl. sb.* 5]. **1959** *Cambridge Rev.* 9 May 493/1 The planners of Plymouth have..built a 'centre' which is tolerable only to a man in a hot tin box who has already become a part of the box. **1961** *Deb. Senate Canada* 25 Sept. 1170/2, I am delighted to know that the Prime Minister is interested in having a centre in Ottawa for the performing arts. **1970** *Sunday Times* 19 Apr. 27/5 The new arts centre would operate all year round with summer schools and special courses.

b. A point towards which things tend, move, or are attracted.

[**1606** SHAKS. *Tr. & Cr.* IV. ii. 110 The strong base and building of my loue Is as the very Center of the earth, Drawing all things to it.] **1626** DONNE *Serm.* iv. 31 A center of Reverence..to which all reverence flowed. **1653** WALTON *Angler* ii. 63 Viewing the Silver streams glide silently towards their center, the tempestuous Sea. **1827** POLLOK *Course T.* v, Centre to which all being gravitates. **1850** TENNYSON *In Mem.* lxiv, The centre of a world's desire.

c. A point from which things, influences, etc. emanate, proceed, or originate. *Esp.* in biology, etc. (see also 7).

1738 GLOVER *Leonidas* VI. 250 The center of corruption. **1812** SIR H. DAVY *Chem. Philos.* 195 The light..proceeds in right lines or rays from the luminous body as a center. **1859** DARWIN *Orig. Spec.* xii. (1885) 322 The question of single or multiple centres of creation. **1865** TYLOR *Early Hist. Man.* i. 10 Diffused from a single geographical centre. **1872** W. AITKEN *Sci. & Pr. Med.* (ed. 6) II. 60 All new cells proceed from 'centres of nutrition', from other cells, or from the nuclei of them. **1876** MOZLEY *Univ. Serm.* ix. 188 Sick lives are centres of improving and refining influence.

7. a. Short for ***nerve-centre***.

1847 CARPENTER *Zool.* §998 A number of ganglia or distinct centres of nervous action. From these diverging filaments are sent off, which are distributed to the various organs. **1869** HUXLEY *Phys.* xi. 297 The grey matter of the upper part of the cord is..a vaso-motor centre for the head and face. **1881** *Syd. Soc. Lex.* s.v. *Centre, visual,* Destruction of this centre on one side causes complete, but temporary, blindness of the opposite eye.

b. Short for *centre of ossification* (see 16).

1876 QUAIN *Anat.* (ed. 8) I. 19 The lateral centres [for each vertebra] appear about the 7th week.

8. The name given to a leader of the Fenian organization, the chief being called ***head-centre***.

1865 *Ann. Reg.* 178 In the language of the party he was termed the 'Head Centre' of the Fenians in Ireland.

9. a. The part of a target between the 'bull's-eye' and the 'outer'. **b.** *ellipt.* The hitting of this.

1887 *Whitaker's Almanack* 540 In this case a bull's-eye counts four points, a centre three, and an outer two.

II. Of other things, the middle point.

10. *Geom.* The point at equal distances from the extremities of a line, of any regular surface or solid, or at a mean distance from all points in the periphery of an irregular surface or body (centre of magnitude); the central or middle point.

So the centre of a regular polygon, quadrilateral figure, triangle, cube, cylinder, etc. ***centre of a conic section***: the point which bisects any diameter, or in which all diameters intersect each other; the ***centre of an ellipse*** or ***hyperbola***, is the point midway between the two foci; that of a ***parabola*** is at infinity; ***centre of a higher curve***, the point in which two diameters meet; ***centre of a dial***, the part in which the gnomon intersects the plane of the dial.

1796 HUTTON *Math. Dict.* I. 262 Centre or center, a point equally remote from the extremes of a line, plane, or solid; or a middle point dividing them so that some certain effects are equal on all sides of it. **1840** LARDNER *Geom.* 91 Lines drawn from the centre to the angles of the polygon.

11. a. *gen.* The middle point or part, the middle or midst of anything.

1591 SHAKS. *1 Hen. VI,* II. ii. 6 The Market-Place, The middle Centure of this cursed Towne. *c* **1645** HOWELL *Lett.* VI. 86 Though they dwelt in the center of Spain not far from Toledo. **1706** ADDISON *Rosamond* I. vi, Full in the center of the grove. **1776** WITHERING *Bot. Arrangem.* (1796) I. 205 Florets all fertile, those of the center smaller. **1781** COWPER *Verses A. Selkirk* 3 From the centre all round to the sea. **1816** SCOTT *Antiq.* vii, Near the centre of a deep but narrow bay. **1878** MORLEY *Carlyle* 175 The puniness of man in the centre of a cruel and frowning universe. **1880** *Scribner's Mag.* June 221 The centers of the great gummy logs.

b. *fig.* (or of things not material).

1628 T. SPENCER *Logick* 169 Predication is the very Center, and life of Logicke. **1683** TRYON *Way to Health* 317 If the Disorder happen near the Center of Life. **1835** BROWNING *Paracelsus* Wks. I. 71 There is an inmost centre in us all, Where truth abides in fulness. **1846** PRESCOTT *Ferd. & Is.* I. Introd. 27 Those dismal scenes of faction which convulsed the little commonwealths to their centre.

c. ***centre of a bastion***: 'a point in the middle of the gorge of the bastion, from whence the capital line commences, and which is generally at the inner polygon of the figure' (C. James).

d. In various games, a player on each side whose position is the middle of a line or field of players; esp. in rugby football = centre-threequarter; in other games, the player in the middle of the field.

1866 *Spirit of Times* (N.Y.) 23 June 262/3 Edwards, as centre, is decidedly the best fielder in the nine. **1868** *Chambers's Encycl.* X. 597/1 La Crosse... In the arrangement of the men on each side..centre is in the centre of the field. **1892** *Young England* Sept. 442/1 The big 'centre', taking in the situation at a glance, slips round. **1897** *Encycl. Sport* I. 411/2 [Rugby football.] Three Three-quarters.—The Centre—A centre is the correlative of the half-back. *Ibid.*, The centre will, of course, be on the look out for a drop at goal. **1922** *Daily Mail* 8 Dec. 12 M.A. Ap-Rhys Price, Marlborough's best centre, was unable to play.

e. Of chocolates and other sweets: the central portion which is enclosed in chocolate or other covering.

1877 [see PAN-DROP]. **1929** *Sears, Roebuck Catal., Spring & Summer* 1929 469 Extra fine..filled and hard candies. A tempting assortment with fruit and nut centers. **1935** *Discovery* Nov. 322/1 The centres [of the chocolates] are passed by an automatic feeding attachment through a curtain of temperature-controlled chocolate. **1959** *Economist* 13 June 1015/2 A hard covered chocolate with a soft centre.

f. *Cricket.* A guard (GUARD *sb.* 3 b) covering the middle stump.

1887 *Cricket* 24 Nov. 460/1 Miss Rogers..fell when taking 'centre'. **1923** E. W. HORNUNG *Old Offenders* 250 He waited by the umpire while Chrystal took centre.

g. *Football* and *Hockey*. A kick or pass from either of the wings towards the centre of the pitch. Cf. CENTRE *v.* 4 b.

1900 *Westm. Gaz.* 23 Apr. 8/3 The forwards..were never where they should have been when centres..were put across. **1927** *Daily Express* 20 Apr. 13/2 Hill met with his head a glorious centre by Williams. **1967** J. POTTER *Foul Play* vi. 79 Bob enjoyed two dramatic races down the right wing, but they came to nothing when Julian wasn't fast enough to pick up the centres.

h. ***the Centre***, the remote interior of Australia, Central Australia. See also ***Red Centre***.

1912 SPENCER & GILLEN *Across Austral.* I. i. 5 Central Australia and the Northern Territory..consists of four distinct parts... Of these four areas the second and the third, which together occupy a large part of the Centre, may be known as the Australian Steppe lands. **1934** A. RUSSELL *Tramp-Royal in Wild Austral.* ix. 71 For years he had spent his time drifting about 'the Centre', which he probably knew as well as any man living. **1954** B. MILES *Stars my Blanket* xxiii. 198, I asked him if he had much trouble with scrub bulls as they do in The Centre.

12. The point or position of equilibrium of a body. Also *fig.* See also *centre of gravity, of inertia* in 16.

c **1391** CHAUCER *Astrol.* I. §2 Hit [the ring] disturbeth nat the instrument to hangen aftur his rihte centre. **1668** TEMPLE in *Four C. Eng. Lett.* 127 Things drawn out of their center are not to be moved without much force, or skill, or time; but, to make their return to their center again, there is required but little of either. **1704** SWIFT *Batt. Bks.* (1711) 230 By his own unhappy Weight and Tendency towards his Center. **1860** EMERSON *Cond. Life* Wks. (Bohn) II. 384 If the man is off his centre, the eyes show it.

13. *Archit.* A temporary framework supporting any superstructure; now *spec.* the wooden support and 'mould' upon which an arch or dome is supported while building.

1611 SHAKS. *Wint. T.* II. i. 102 In those Foundations which I build vpon, The Centre is not bigge enough to beare A Schoole-Boyes Top. **1630** PRYNNE *Anti-Armin.* 113 This ..is the onely center vpon which the whole fabricke is erected. **1823** P. NICHOLSON *Pract. Build.* 338 Centres, the frame of timber-work for supporting arches during their erection. **1861** SMILES *Engineers* II. 182 The centres spanning the..width of the arch were composed of eight ribs.

14. *Mil.* **a.** The main body of troops occupying the space between the two wings. **b.** 'The division of a fleet between the van and the rear of the line of battle, and between the weather and lee divisions in the order of sailing' (Adm. Smyth).

1598 BARRET *Theor. Warres* Gloss. 250 *Centre*, a French word, is the middle of a battell, or other things. **1710** STEELE *Tatler* No. 210 ¶8 One [body] to be commanded by himself in the Center. **1769** ROBERTSON *Chas. V,* III. XII. 386 Brought some pieces of cannon to bear upon their center. **1871** SMILES *Charac.* i. (1876) 17 At the combat of Vera, when the Spanish centre was broken.

c. The middle man of any rank of soldiers, or an imaginary point in the middle of any body of soldiers. '*Centre of a battalion on parade*: the middle, where an interval is left for the colours; of an encampment, it is the main street; and on a march, is an interval for the baggage; when it is so placed' (C. James).

1672 VENN *Mil. & Mar. Discipline* I. 127 Secondly, wheelings on the midst (or Center). I shall not use the word Center, for it is more proper to a circular body than to a square. **1796** *Instr. Cavalry* (1813) 226 The squadron will receive the word Center Dress. **1832** *Prop. Reg. Instr. Cavalry* II. 33 Their Centres and Lefts move up.

15. *Politics.* In the French Chamber (which is arranged in the form of an amphitheatre), the deputies of moderate opinions who occupy the central benches in front of the president, between the extreme parties who sit to the right and left. ***right centre, left centre***: divisions of this party inclining towards the opinions of the right and left respectively, and sitting adjacent to them. Also transferred to the political opinions so indicated; and to the politics of other countries. In Germany the *Centre* is the Catholic or Ultramontane party.

(This use originated in the French National Assembly of 1789, in which the nobles as a body took the position of honour on the President's right, and the Third Estate sat on his left. The significance of these positions, which was at first merely ceremonial, soon became political.)

1837 CARLYLE *Fr. Rev.* VI. ii, Answered, from Right side, from Centre and Left, by inextinguishable laughter. **1874** *Times Summ. of Year*, The Left Centre has withdrawn in some degree from its alliance with the Left, and overtures are from day to day on both sides tendered and rejected by the two divisions which form the Centre. *Ibid.* The party which is known in [the German] Parliament as the Catholic Centre. **1884** BERTHA M. GARDINER *Fr. Rev.* iii. 52. **1907** [see HISTORY *sb.* 4 c]. **1962** *Listener* 3 May 774/2 Those socialists and others orientated left (or right) of centre who are automatically biased against the United States. **1962** *Ibid.* 19 July 87/2 All three parties in Bonn are now parties of the centre, and there is virtually no opposition.

III. 16. Phrases.

centre of attack (*Mil.*): 'when a considerable front is taken before a besieged place, and the lines of attack are carried upon three capitals, the capital in the middle, which usually leads to the half-moon, is styled the center of attack' (C. James).

centre of attraction (*Physics*): the point to which bodies tend by gravity, or by the action of centripetal force; (*fig.*) the object or point which attracts attention, interest, or curiosity.

centre of buoyancy, of cavity, of displacement, of immersion: the mean centre of that part of a ship or floating body, which is immersed in the water.

centre of conversion: the point in a body about which it turns or tends to turn when force is applied at a given point.

centre of curvature: see CURVATURE.

centre of excellence: an institution acknowledged for the outstanding quality of its research or other work.

centre of friction: that point in the base of a body on which it revolves when put in rapid rotation, *e.g.* the point of the peg of a top.

centre of gravity orig. = *centre of attraction*; afterwards, and still popularly (see quot. 1879) = *centre of mass*: in the case of a single body or a system of bodies rigidly connected, the point about which all the parts exactly balance each other, and which being supported, the body or system will remain at rest in any position; also *fig.*, the point or object of greatest importance or interest.

centre of gyration: the point at which if the whole mass of a revolving body were collected, the rotatory motion would remain the same.

centre of inertia: = *centre of gravity* or *mass*.

centre of magnitude: = sense 10.

centre of mass: that point in relation to a body or system of bodies so situated that any plane whatever that passes through it divides the body or system into two parts of which the masses or weights are exactly equal.

centre of motion: the point which remains at rest while all the other parts move round it.

centre of oscillation: the point of a body suspended by an axis at which, if all the matter were concentrated, the oscillations would be performed in the time actually taken.

centre of ossification: the point (or points) in the cartilage or fibrous membrane of an immature bone in which the bone salts are first deposited, and from which they extend until the whole bone is ossified.

centre of percussion: in a moving body, that point where the percussion or stroke is greatest, in which the whole percutient force of the body is supposed to be collected.

centre of pressure: the point at which the whole amount of pressure may be applied with the same effect as when distributed.

1727–51 CHAMBERS *Cycl.*, *Center of Gravitation* or **Attraction.* **1796** HUTTON *Math. Dict.*, *Centre of *Conversion*, a term first used by M. Parent. **1968** J. M. ZIMAN *Public Knowledge* v. 92 The enormous expansion of graduate studies and scientific research..has been too rapid for this spirit to percolate from the few centres of *excellence to all the institutions now engaged in the training of scientists. **1971** R. COCKBURN in *Minutes of Evidence Sel. Comm. Sci. & Technol.* 1/2 in *Parl. Papers 1970–71* XLVIII. 71 Originally, I think, there was the concept that the National Computing Centre might provide a kind of centre of excellence. **1976** *Physics Bull.* Feb. 57/2 Designated 'centres of excellence' are in general undesirable and impracticable. **1985** *British Med. Jrnl.* 2 Nov. 1274/2

To be awarded the accolade 'centre of excellence' a hospital must offer much more than a bright array of scanners. **1659** LEAK *Water-wks.* 4 They fall towards their centre of *gravity in the Water. **1704** J. HARRIS *Lex Techn.* s.v. *Earth*, The Earth doth not describe an Orbit round the Sun properly by her own Centre, but by the Common Centre of Gravity of the Earth and the Moon. **1822** IMISON *Sc. & Art* I. 449 The centre of gravity is that point in which the weight of a body may be supposed to be collected. **1831** CARLYLE *Sart. Res.* (1858) 150 The casting of this pebble from my hand alters the centre-of-gravity of the Universe. **1903** 'VIGILANS SED AEQUUS' *German Ambitions* 48 Loss of millions of Germans ..has moved the world's centre of gravity in a sense unfavourable to them [*sc.* the German people]. **1937** *Discovery* Sept. 266/2 The wage-earner is now the centre of political gravity. **1963** *Higher Educ.* (Cmnd. 2154) x. §384 The centre of gravity should be in science and technology. **1796** HUTTON *Math. Dict.* I. 269 The distance of the centre of *gyration, from the point of suspension, is a mean proportional between those of gravity and oscillation. **1829** *Nat. Philos.* I. *Hydraulics* iii. 28 (Usef. Knowl. Soc.), The point of percussion, or of greatest effect, (which, in revolving bodies, is called the centre of gyration). **1879** THOMSON & TAIT *Nat. Phil.* I. I. §230 The Centre of *Inertia or Mass is thus a perfectly definite point in every body, or group of bodies. The term Centre of Gravity is often very inconveniently used for it. **1796** HUTTON *Math. Dict.* I. 267 *Centre of *magnitude* is..the same as the centre of gravity in homogeneal bodies, as in a cylinder or any other prism. **1727–51** CHAMBERS *Cycl.* s.v., If the weights P and Q revolve about the point N, so that when P descends, Q ascends, N is said to be the *Center of *Motion. Ibid.* He found, in this case, the distance of the centre of *oscillation, from the axis in a circle, to be ¾ of the diameter. **1796** HUTTON *Math. Dict.* I. 267 *Centre of oscillation*..in a compound pendulum, its distance from the point of suspension is equal to the length of a simple pendulum whose oscillations are isochronal with those of the compound ones. **1867** J. MARSHALL *Physiol.* II. 651 The cranial bones begin by one or more flat radiating centres of *ossification. **1869** HUXLEY *Physiol.* xii. 321 A long bone has usually, at fewest, three centres of ossification. **1727–51** CHAMBERS *Cycl.* s.v., The *center of *percussion* is the same with the center of gravity, if all the parts of the percutient body be carried with a parallel motion. **1796** HUTTON *Math. Dict.* I. 269 When the percutient body revolves about a fixed point, the centre of percussion is the same with the centre of oscillation. *Ibid.* The *centre of *pressure* of a fluid against a plane, is that point against which a force being applied equal and contrary to the whole pressure, it will just sustain it.

IV. *attrib.* and in *comb.*

17. *attrib.* or quasi-*adj.* Of or pertaining to the centre, central. Hence CENTREMOST.

1791 BENTHAM *Panopt.* I. *Postcr.* 99 The center one of the 5 uppermost Cells. **1796** *Instr. & Regul. Cavalry* (1813) 233 Trumpeters and music are behind the center interval. **1829** I. TAYLOR *Enthus.* ix. 219 The centre illusion of the system. **1860** J. KENNEDY *Horse Shoe R.* lvii. 586 The centre division of the assailing army. **1879** R. K. DOUGLAS *Confucianism* iv. 92 The centre figures of his philosophy.

18. Obvious combinations: as ***centre-arbor***, ***-line***, ***-pin***, ***-pinion***, ***-point***, ***-truth***, etc. Also ***centre-ward***, ***centre-wise*** advs.

1884 F. BRITTEN *Watch & Clockm.* 266 The *centre arbor ..turns once in an hour. **1804** *Med. Jrnl.* XII. 202 The distance between the *centre-pin and blade. **1807–26** S. COOPER *First Lines Surg.* 303 In order to fix the centre-pin of the trephine. **1884** F. BRITTEN *Watch & Clockm.* 266 The teeth round the barrel drive the *centre-pinion. **1648** BP. HALL *Sel. Th.* §22 What a mere *centrepoint the earth is in comparison of the vast circumference of heaven. **1866** LIDDON *Bampton Lect.* v. (1875) 253 Christ is the centre-point of the history and hopes of man. **1858** SEARS *Athan.* II. xi. 245 The *centre-truth in his system of doctrines. **1843** CARLYLE *Past & Pr.* I. ii, At all moments it is moving *centreward. **1853** KANE *Grinnell Exp.* xvii. (1856) 126 It contracts itself *centrewise, and rounds itself endwise.

19. Special combs.: **centre-bully**, a bully taken in the middle of the field at the start or re-start of play (see BULLY *sb.*[2] 2); **centre-chisel**, a pointed cold-chisel; **centre-chuck**, a kind of chuck for a lathe; **centre-drill**, 'a small drill used for making a short hole in the ends of a shaft about to be turned, for the entrance of the lathe-centres' (Weale); **centre field** *Baseball*, the part of the outfield beyond second base and between right field and left field; also, a fielder in this position; **centre-fire** = *central fire* (see CENTRAL 4); also *attrib.*, as in *centre-fire cartridge*; †**centre-fish**, a mollusc allied to the limpet; **centrefold** chiefly *U.S.*, the centre spread of a newspaper or magazine, esp. one depicting a nude model; hence, one whose picture appears on a centrefold; **centre-forward**, (*a*) a player in association football, hockey, and other games, who plays from a central position in the forward line; (*b*) the position occupied by that player; **centre-half**, **centre half-back**, (*a*) a player who plays from a central position among the half-backs; (*b*) the position of that player; **centre-lathe**, a turning-lathe in which the work is supported or held by centres (sense 5); **centre light**, a lamp suspended from the centre of a ceiling; **centre-line**, any line passing through a centre; *spec.*, in drawing, a line from which measurements are made, and in ship-building, a line passing lengthways through the hull and dividing it into two sections; in various games, a line of centres (sense 11 d); **centre-piece**, (*a*) a piece in the centre of anything; *spec.* an ornamental piece of plate or glass for the centre of a table, etc., an épergne; (*b*) *fig.* the most conspicuous or important item in a collection, exhibition, etc.; **centre-plate**, (*a*) each of the metal plates composing the bearing for a railway carriage or engine on the centre of the truck; (*b*) each of the metal plates used to hold a dowelled pattern while it is being turned in the lathe; (*c*) a metal centre-board; **centre-punch**, a punch with a conical point for marking the centre of work to be turned in the lathe, or the centre of a hole to be drilled; **centre-rail**, a third or middle rail, sometimes used on railway lines, in connexion with a cogged wheel or other device on the engine, for the ascent or descent of steep inclines; also *attrib.*; **centre-saw**, a kind of circular saw which cuts round timber in sections meeting in the centre, for spokes, pick-handles, etc.; **centre-second(s**, applied to a seconds hand on a clock or watch mounted on the centre arbor, and completing its revolution in one minute; also to a clock, etc. having such a seconds hand; **centre section** *Aeronaut.* (see quot. 1950); **centre-split** (see quot.); **centre spread**, printed matter occupying the two facing middle pages of a newspaper, periodical, etc.; **centre-square**, an instrument for finding the centre and radius of a circle; **centre-table**, a table intended for the centre of a room, formerly often used for the display of books, albums, etc.; **centre-valve**, in gas-works, a rotating valve by which the gas is distributed to several sets of purifiers; **centre-velic**, see VELIC; **centre-wheel**, the third wheel of a watch in some kinds of movements; **centre-zero** *a.*, designating a meter which has zero at the centre of the scale and can therefore indicate both positive and negative values of the quantity registered.

1910 *Westm. Gaz.* 1 Mar. 16/2 From the *centre-bully Cambridge again pressed. **1863** SMILES *Indust. Biog.* 247 His self-adjusting double driving *centre-chuck, for which the Society of Arts awarded him their silver medal in 1828. **1857** *Spirit of Times* 29 Aug. 404/3 Enterprise Club. Maxfield, catcher;..England, third base; Bleecker, *centre field. **1865** *Sunday Mercury* (Philadelphia) 3 Sept. 3/5 Dick McBride struck a ball over to centre field. **1948** *Miami* (Oklahoma) *Daily News-Rec.* 4 July 4/4 For sensational catches in centerfield you can't beat him. **1985** *N.Y. Times* 10 Aug. 45/4 Baylor kept the hit parade going, tagging one of Stanley's offerings into centerfield. **1668** WILKINS *Real Char.* II. v. §2. 130 Univalvs; having but one Shell..being unmoved..1 Limpet, *Center fish. **1966** *McCall's Mag.* Oct. 195/1 The reader is treated to an illustrated biography of the young..maiden, replete with details of her wholesome family life..before stumbling on her stretched over the *center fold in full bloom and triple exposure. **1970** *Washington Post* 30 Sept. B2/1, I don't mind telling you, every time I pick up a copy of Playboy...I'm afraid to turn to the centerfold! **1986** 'A. BURGESS' *Homage to QWERTYUIOP* p. xii, The rest of the household knows you are at work, as a blacksmith is, and does not suspect you of covertly devouring a *Playboy* centrefold. **1891** *Peel City Guardian* IX. 7/3 The teams were as follows:..*centre forward [etc.]. **1897** *Encycl. Sport* I. 421/1 The centre-forward is in the middle of the other four; the two on each side of him form the wings. **1891** *Peel City Guardian* IX. 2/4 Our friend John at *centre-half. **1908** *Westm. Gaz.* 30 Nov. 14/4 If he were to stick to centre-half always. **1920** E. GREEN *Hockey* iv. 38 More work falls on the centre half than to the other two put together. **1890** C. W. ALCOCK *Football* vii. 46 An inside man can give him a pass when he is clear from the *centre half-back. **1969** *Melbourne Truth* 12 July 23/2, I prefer Peter Steward at centre half-back. **1819** REES *Cycl.* s.v. *Turning*, Lathes are..called *centre lathes where the work is supported at both ends. **1879** HOLTZAPFFEL *Turning* IV. 99. **1878** LADY C. SCHREIBER *Jrnl.* (1911) II. 128 Excellent *centre light, or chandelier, of hammered iron. **1966** G. GREENE *Comedians* I. iii. 94, I found Marcel hanging from his own belt from the centre light. **1777** *Monthly Review* LV. 306 Section through the *center line of the Register Office, from North to South. **1807** *Monthly Mag.* 1 Feb. 66/1 Placed in the centre line of the vessel. *Ibid.*, Its relative distance from the centre line of the vessel's progress. **1887** D. A. LOW *Machine Draw.* 2 After drawing the centre line of any part the dimensions of that part must be marked off from the centre line. **1920** E. GREEN *Hockey* i. 24 *Centre Line.*—A line across the centre of the ground with a small circle in the centre from which the initial bully takes place. **1967** *Jane's Surface Skimmer Systems 1967–68* 90/2 A companion ladder at the centreline leads to the main deck foyer. **1969** *Australian* 24 May 39/3 There is not likely to be a great deal in the centreline duels. **1803** *Deb. Congress* 10 Jan. (1851) 345 An appropriate and characteristic equestrian statue..as a beautiful *centre piece for the entire plan. **1836** DISRAELI *H. Temple* VI. vi. (Hoppe) A bouquet which might have served for the centre-piece of a dinner table. **1854** *Illust. Lond. News* 18 Mar. 259/1 The..testimonial is a silver centre-piece consisting of a column encircled by two gracefully-formed figures representing Peace, etc. **1858** HAWTHORNE *Fr. & It. Jrnls.* II. 100 With screws..and a silver centre-piece. **1937** *Discovery* Dec. 361/2 The centre-piece of the exhibition is C. T. R. Wilson's original expansion-chamber apparatus. **1965** *Economist* 16 Jan. 214/2 President Johnson's proposals on education..are the centrepiece of his efforts to raise the quality of American life. **1875** M. N. FORNEY *Catech. Locomotive* XII. 316 The weight of the front end of the engine rests on a cast iron *centre-place. *a* **1884** KNIGHT *Dict. Mech.* Suppl. 185/1 *Center-plate. **1894** *Outing* (U.S.) XXIV. 194/2 The movable center-plate will always let you know when you get on a shoal. **1879** HOLTZAPFFEL *Turning* IV. 192 A steel *center punch is driven into the flat end. **1874** KNIGHT *Dict. Mech.* s.v., Another form of *center-rail railway. *Ibid.* s.v., The largest *centre-second clock..is the turret-clock for the Bombay Harbour Board [with] a dial 8½ feet in diameter. **1884** F. BRITTEN *Watch & Clockm.* 49 [A] Centre Seconds ..[is] a long seconds hand moving from the centre of a watch dial. **1917** 'CONTACT' *Airman's Outings* 9 The sloping half-strut of his top *centre section. **1921** *Flight* XIII. 147/1 The wings are of wood construction, fabric covered, and are attached, high up on the *fuselage*, to a 'centre section' which forms the roof of the cabin. **1950** *Gloss. Aeronaut. Terms* (*B.S.I.*) I. 36 *Centre section*, the portion of the fuselage or hull forming a continuous structure with the main planes. In a biplane or a parasol monoplane, the central structure to which the main planes are connected. **1886** *Daily News* 15 Oct. 5/6 They are made of '*centre splits'. Good, honest hides..are skilfully split into three skins, and the centre one, having no grain, and being of a soft, flimsy substance, is nevertheless capable of being made to assume the guise of serviceable leather. **1940** G. BUTLER *Kiss Blood* xi. 201, I turned the paper open at the *centre spread, where they put the next most important news. *a* **1877** KNIGHT *Dict. Mech.* III. 2294/1 The *center-square, for finding the center of a circle. **1886** Centre square [see RADIUS *sb.* 5]. **1833** *Knickerbocker* I. 158 The whole family are collected around the *centre table. *c* **1845** C. BRONTË *Professor* (1857) I. iv. 59 He removed from the centre-table to the side-board a few pamphlets. **1868** HOLME LEE *B. Godfrey* xxxvi. 195 He.. remained standing by the centre-table. **1902** W. JAMES *Var. Relig. Exper.* xix. 460 A 'home' upon a veldt or prairie with one sitting-room and a Bible on its centre-table. **1929** *Star* 21 Aug. 13/3 Polished walnut centre table, overmantel to match. **1884** F. BRITTEN *Watch & Clockm.* 266 The *centre wheel drives the third wheel pinion. **1940** *Chambers's Techn. Dict.* 148/2 *Centre-zero instrument. **1963** B. FOZARD *Instrumentation Nucl. Reactors* viii. 90 The indication is provided by a centre-zero moving coil instrument.

centre, center (ˈsɛntə(r)), *v.* [f. CENTRE *sb.* or a. F. *centre-r.* In 17th and 18th c. often spelt *center*, still prevalent in U.S. Cf. CENTRING.]

I. *intr.*

†**1. a.** To rest as on a fixed centre or pivot; to repose. *Obs.* (as a distinct sense, though it often colours 2).

1622 BACON *Cæsar* Wks. (Bohn) 503 He..admitted none to his intimacies, but such whose whole expectations centered upon him. **1664** *Decay Chr. Piety* (J.) Where there is no visible truth wherein to centre. **1669** BUNYAN *Holy Citie* 97 Here centreth Luke the Evangelist, here centreth Jude. **1708** PENN in *Pa. Hist. Soc. Mem.* X. 268 He assures me he intends to centre with us, and end his days in that country. **1719** W. WOOD *Surv. Trade* 144 We have a Balance..to the value of 1,750,000*l.* which centers and remains among us.

†**b.** To unite, agree. *Obs.*

1622–62 HEYLIN *Cosmogr.* To Rdr., I wondred how they could all center upon the same Proposal. **1657** REEVE *God's Plea* 5 Let us both center together in this qualification.

2. a. To find or have their (or its) centre; to be concentrated as at a centre; 'to be collected to a point' (J.), to gather or collect as round a centre; to be placed as at a centre; to move or turn round as a centre. Often with a mixture of notions, including that of sense 1.

1691–8 NORRIS *Pract. Disc.* IV. 186 He that makes himself his End, that Centers and Terminates in himself. **1736** BUTLER *Anal.* II. vii. 365 Whom all the prophecies referred to, and in whom they should center. **1764** GOLDSM. *Trav.* 424 That bliss which only centres in the mind. **1765** BLACKSTONE *Comm.* I. 208 In his person also centered the right of the Saxon monarchs. **1777** ROBERTSON *Hist. Amer.* (1778) II. VII. 272 The supreme authority centered at last in a single person. **1781** COWPER *Convers.* 134 His sole opinion ..Centering at last in having none at all. **1796** MORSE *Amer. Geog.* I. 173 The trade, wealth and power of America, may, at some future period, depend, and perhaps centre upon the Missisippi. **1818** CRUISE *Digest* VI. 550 If the whole property should center in one person. **1823** J. BADCOCK *Dom. Amusem.* 20 All three tubes afterwards centre in one. **1867** HALES in *Percy Folio* I. 143 The rare adventure on which the tale centres. **1876** GREEN *Short Hist.* v. §4 (1882) 246 The hopes of the peasants centred in the young sovereign.

b. ***to centre*** (or ***be centred***) ***about, around*** or ***round***: to have (something) as one's or its centre or focus; to move or revolve round (something) as a centre; to be concentrated on, to turn on (see TURN *v.* 3); to be mainly concerned with.

1868 FREEMAN *Norm. Conq.* (1876) II. viii. 262 It is around the King..that the main storm of battle is made to centre. **1870** *Chambers's Jrnl.* 12 Nov. 731/1 The only man she had ever loved—around whom centred her most precious memories. **1878** *Harper's Mag.* 308/2 The real interest of the story centres about the lives of four personages. **1886** *Chambers's Jrnl.* 17 July 449/2 The assistant's chief hardships centre round the abnormal length of his working-day. **1893** H. B. CLARKE *Spanish Lit.* 163 The plot invariably centres round the love intrigue of persons in the middle or upper classes of life. **1893** KIPLING *Day's Work* (1898) 7 The little cluster of huts where he and his gang lived centred round the tattered dwelling of a sea-priest. **1909** *Daily Chron.* 27 July 4/6 Its most enduring traditions centre round the ancient cathedral. **1929** *Times Lit. Suppl.* 3 Oct. 753/2 The group of gifted men and women who centred round Henry Adams. **1931** A. L. ROWSE *Politics & Younger Generation* 271 The foremost problems in European politics..will centre round the revision of the Treaty of Versailles.

†**3.** To converge (*on*) as a centre. *Obs.*

1789 H. WALPOLE *Remin.* viii. 65 All those mortifications centering on a constitution evidently tending to dissolution.

II. *trans.*

4. a. To place or fix in the centre; to provide or mark with a centre. Also, to occupy, distinguish, or mark the centre of; *fig.* to be the central point of.

1610 G. FLETCHER *Christ's Vict.* (R.) Where the sun centres himself by right. **1667** MILTON *P.L.* VII. 228 In his hand He took the golden Compasses.. One foot he center'd, and the other turn'd. **1886** W. J. TUCKER *E. Europe* 260 There is the eternal 'Kugelhupf' (a genuinely Austrian coffee-cake) centring the table. **1887** KNOX LITTLE *Broken Vow* 9 A plot of smooth green grass.. centred by a basin in which there is a continual plash of falling water. **1894** *Daily News* 2 July 3/4 When the scarlet liveries of Royalty are seen centreing the procession across the bridge. **1898** *Ibid.* 27 May 4/6 Centring the Hall was the dais. **1902** C. N. & A. M. WILLIAMSON *Lightning Conductor* 95 This châteaux country of the Loire.. centreing as it did the old court life of France.

b. In football and hockey, to kick or hit (a ball) towards the centre of the line of forwards. Also *absol.* Cf. CENTRE *sb.* 11 g.

1890 C. W. ALCOCK *Football* vii. 47 When.. the ball is centred.. from the left wing. **1891** *Peel Chron.* 14 Mar. 5/4 Radcliffe neatly centred. **1897** *Daily News* 22 Feb. 8/6 The latter, as.. the Cambridge back dashed at him, again centred the ball. **1904** *Daily Chron.* 15 Feb. 8/4 Wright ran smartly down on the left and centred. **1920** E. GREEN *Hockey* v. 50 Centering while travelling at top speed.. is a very difficult stroke to perform with any degree of accuracy.

†**5.** To fix *to*, repose *upon*, as a fixed centre or pivot. *Obs.* (But often colouring 6.)

1623 AILESBURY *Serm.* (1624) 2 Man.. doth center his restlesse motions vpon nothing but the Almighties fruition. **1649** G. DANIEL *Trinarch., Hen. V*, xxxv, Men cent'red to Selfe-Interest and lock't To their wild Causes. **1721** BERKELEY *Prev. Ruin Gt. Brit.* Wks. III. 205 Centering all our cares upon private interest.

6. To place or put as in a centre; to collect, bring, or direct, as to a centre; to concentrate *in*, *on*. *To be centred in* or *on* has often a shade of sense 5.

1702 POPE *Sapho* 50 Once in her arms you center'd all your joy. **1776** GOLDSM. *Haunch of Ven.*, While thus I debated, in reverie centred. **1794** GODWIN *Cal. Williams* 291 Each of these centered in himself a variety of occupations. **1844** THIRLWALL *Greece* VIII. lxii. 179 All his hopes were henceforth centred in Antigonus. **1875** STUBBS *Const. Hist.* I. xiii. 606 The process of centering the administration of justice in the hands of the itinerant justices. **1878** BLACK *Green Past.* xxxvii. 295 As if her whole thoughts had been centred on the Falls.

7. In various technical uses: To place or fix in the (exact) centre; to find the centre of; to grind (a lens) so that the thickest part is in the centre.

1793 SIR G. SHUCKBURGH in *Phil. Trans.* LXXXIII. 109 If this [the object glass] be not correctly centered.. that is, if its axis be not concentric with the axis of the cell, in which it is fixed. **1796** HUTTON *Math. Dict.* I. 289 Cassini the younger has a discourse expressly on the necessity of well centring the object glass of a large telescope. **1831** BREWSTER *Optics* xli. 339 When the aperture was well centered. **1868** LOCKYER *Elem. Astron.* §518 It is of the last importance.. that it should be correctly centred,—that is that the centre of movement should be also the centre of graduation.

'centre-bit. [see BIT *sb.*¹ 6.] An instrument turning on a projecting centre-point, used for making cylindrical holes. (Noted as a burglar's tool.)

1794 *Rigging & Seamansh.* I. 150 *Centre-bit*, a bit, having in the middle of its end a small steel point, with a sharp edge on one side to cut horizontally, and a sharp tooth on the opposite side to cut vertically. **1833** A. FONBLANQUE *Eng. und. 7 Admin.* (1837) II. 315 There are picklocks, files, and centre-bits available for robbery. **1838** DICKENS *O. Twist* xix, 'None,' said Sikes. ''Cept a centre-bit and a boy.' **1845** DARWIN *Voy. Nat.* xviii. (1852) 409 [He] then rapidly turns the curved part, like a carpenter's centre-bit. **1855** TENNYSON *Maud* I. I. xi, And Sleep must lie down arm'd, for the villainous centre-bits Grind on the wakeful ear in the hush of the moonless nights. **1857** READE *Never too late* ii. (D.) His intelligence bored like a centre-bit into the deep heart of his enemy.

centre-board ('sɛntəbɔəd). In a flat-bottomed sailing-boat, a movable board or plate of iron, which can be lowered through the keel in deep water to prevent lee-way and increase the stability under canvas, and in shallow water can be lifted up within the boat; often *attrib.* as in ***centre-board boat, cutter***. **b.** Short for *centre-board boat*.

1867 J. MACGREGOR *Voy. Alone Rob Roy* (1868) 93 All rigs and all sizes there were even to a great centre board cutter. **1881** *Times* 19 Jan. 8/2 Mr. Young went.. to cross the bay in a centre-board boat. **1883** *Harper's Mag.* Aug. 443/2 Two keels are being laid down to every centre-board designed. *Ibid.* 449/1 The centre-board is generally lowered. **1886** *Times* 25 Oct. 13 (*Article*) A week in a Centre-board.

'centre-,boarder. [f. CENTRE-BOARD.] A boat with a centre-board.

1886 *Outing* (U.S.) VIII. 58/1 The boats are necessarily of light draught and center-boarders. **1897** *Ibid.* XXX. 337/1 The slippery bilge of an eggshell centreboarder.

centred, centered ('sɛntəd), *ppl. a.* [f. CENTRE *v.* or *sb.* + -ED.]

1. Placed at the centre or in a central position.

1590 SPENSER *Muiopot.* 19 Betwixt the centred earth, and azure skies. **1683** TEMPLE *Mem.* Wks. 1731 I. 403 They were .. easie of Access from all Parts; center'd between Spain and Sweden. **1829** TENNYSON *Timbuctoo*, A center'd glory-circled memory, Divinest Atalantis.

2. Fixed on a centre as a point of support or equilibrium; furnished with a centre.

1649 G. DANIEL *Trinarch., Rich. II*, ccxcvii, Soe may a Cent'red Rocke Bee made a Tennis-ball. **1847** EMERSON *Repr. Men, Plato* Wks. (Bohn) I. 309 Plato is so centred, that he can well spare all his dogmas. **1850** TENNYSON *In Mem.* lix, My centred passion cannot move, Nor will it lessen from to-day.

3. Brought together to a centre, concentrated.

1805 SOUTHEY *Madoc in Azt.* xxii, There to collect their strength, and thence with centered numbers urge the war.

4. Having a centre: also in *comb.*, as in ***deep-centred***, etc.

centreing, variant of CENTRING *vbl. sb.*.

†**cen'treity.** [app. formed after words like *corporeity*, *spontaneity*, which rest upon L. adjs. in *-eus*; but there was no L. *centreus*.] The fact of being the centre; central quality.

1642-7 MORE *Song of Soul, Psychathan.* III. II. xx, In every thing compost Each part of th' essence its centreity Keeps to it self. *Ibid.* II. App. xiv, So do these Atomes change their energies, Themselves unchanged, into new Centreities. *Ibid.* II. II. iii. xiv. *Ibid.* II. III. II. xx, Trees.. they want their fixed centreities.

'centreless, *a.* [see -LESS.] Without a centre.

1856 FERRIER *Inst. Metaph.* IV. xviii. 138 A centreless circle is absolutely incogitable in itself.

'centrement. *nonce-wd.* [see -MENT.] The action of centring; that in or about which anything is centred.

18.. STEVENSON *Cornh. Mag., Falling in Love*, That state in which another person becomes to us the very gist and centrement of God's creation.

'centremost, *a. rare.* [a superlative form from CENTRE 17; cf. *middlemost*, *topmost*.] Most central; midmost.

1866 NEALE *Sequences & H.* 146 The spice-fields.. that girdle the centremost mountain. **1871** JOAQUIN MILLER *Songs of Italy* (1878) 53 In the centremost star Of all whirling stars.

centress ('sɛntrɪs). [f. CENTRE *sb.* (sense 8) + -ESS.] A female '(head) centre'.

1866 *Morning Star* 6 Mar. 6/1 Head centress of the Fenian Sisterhood.

centric ('sɛntrɪk), *a.* [mod. ad. Gr. *κεντρικ-ός* pertaining to the centre, f. *κέντρον*: see CENTRUM.]

1. That is in or at the centre, central.

c **1590** MARLOWE *Faustus* vi, The substance of this centric earth. **1594** *1st Pt. Contention* iv. 18 To pierce the bowels of this Centricke earth. *a* **1631** DONNE *Poems* (1650) 33 Some that have deeper digg'd Loves Mine than I, Say, where his centrique happinesse doth lie. **1642** H. MORE *Song of Soul* I. II. xvi, Centrick all like one pellucid Sun. **1802** G. COLMAN *Br. Grins, Elder Bro.* i, Centric in London noise.. Proud Covent Garden blooms.

2. Of, pertaining to, or characterized by a centre.

1712 BLACKMORE *Creation* II. (R.) Orbs centric and excentrick he prepares. **1850** MRS. BROWNING *Dead Pan* iv, Stung to life by centric forces. **1884** BOWER & SCOTT *De Bary's Phaner. & Ferns* 406 In the first type, which may be called the centric, the chlorophyll-parenchyma is uniformly distributed around the entire organ.

3. *Phys.* Of or pertaining to a nerve centre.

1871 SIR T. WATSON *Princ. & Pract. Med.* (ed. 5) I. 570 When the irritating cause operates directly on the spinal cord itself, he calls the disease centric tetanus. **1873** F. E. ANSTIE in E. H. Clarke *Sex in Educ.* 110 A non-inflammatory centric atrophy. **1879** CARPENTER *Ment. Phys.* I. ii. §73. 77 Movements.. simply centric, depending upon an excited condition of the ganglionic centres.

B. quasi-*sb.* A circle or circular orbit with the earth in its centre.

1667 MILTON *P.L.* VIII. 83 How gird the Sphear With Centric and Eccentric scribl'd o're, Cycle and Epicycle. *a* **1764** LLOYD *Wks.* (1774) II. 154 Talk of words little understood, Centric, eccentric, epicycle.

-centric (sɛntrɪk), *suffix*, as in CONCENTRIC, ECCENTRIC *adjs.*, forming adjs. with the sense 'having (such) a centre', as POLYCENTRIC *a.*; 'having a specified centre', as ANTHROPO-, ETHNO-, HELIO-, HOMOCENTRIC *adjs.*

2. In *Biol.* [perh. f. CENTR(OMERE], 'having the centromere attached at a specified point', as ACRO-, META-, TELOCENTRIC *adjs.*

centrical ('sɛntrɪkəl), *a.* [f. as CENTRIC *a.* + -AL¹.]

1. Situated at or in the centre or middle; central; = CENTRIC 1.

1741 MONRO *Anat. Nerves* (ed. 3) 42 In the Centrical Part of the optic Nerve. **1768** WHITEFIELD *Let. Gov. Wright* 27 The late addition of the two Floridas renders Georgia more centrical. **1803** WELLINGTON *Let.* in Gurw. *Disp.* II. 208 To leave the infantry in a centrical situation. **1864** GUTHRIE in *Gd. Words* 510 Situated in a centrical part of the town.

fig. *a* **1659** OSBORN *Ess.* iii. (1673) 566 It is not unlikely to have been the Primary and Centrical Sin.

2. Of or pertaining to a centre.

1837 WHEWELL *Hist. Induct. Sc.* II. VI. ii. §2. 30 A certain extension of the centrical medium. **1876** F. BRODIE in G. Chambers *Astron.* 325 The second centrical envelope [of the comet] just embraced both these eccentric envelopes.

centri'cality. *rare.* [f. prec. + -ITY.] Central position; centrality.

1777 H. WALPOLE *Lett. C'tess Ossory* I. 261 Its centricality made it very agreeable.

centrically ('sɛntrɪkəlɪ), *adv.* [f. as prec. + -LY².]

1. In a central position; centrally.

1799 *Med. Jrnl.* II. 445 The bone is seldom fractured, unless the ball strikes centrically. **1810** WELLINGTON *Let.* in Gurw. *Disp.* VI. 297 In the pine wood.. where they will be more centrically situated. **1817** *Edin. Rev.* XXIX. 50 Centrically and commodiously situated.

2. On or with the centre or centres.

1882 GEIKIE *Text-bk. Geol.* IV. II. 507 A pile of balls standing exactly centrically one upon the other, an arrangement which seems hardly possible.

'centricalness. *rare.* [f. as prec. + -NESS.] 'Situation in the centre' (Craig 1847).

centricity (sɛn'trɪsɪtɪ). [mod. f. CENTRIC + -ITY; cf. *eccentricity*.] Centric quality or position; relation to a centre.

1826 KIRBY & SP. *Entom.* (1828) IV. xxxvii. 6 Gives a decided character of centricity to the whole nervous system. **1854** J. HOGG *Microsc.* I. iii. (1867) 164 First, their centricity, and secondly the fittest condensation of the light to be employed. **1879** RUTLEY *Stud. Rocks* vii. 57 In order to get proper centricity in the movement.

centrifugal (sɛn'trɪfjʊgəl, ˌsɛntrɪ'fjuːgəl), *a.* [f. mod.L. *centrifug-us* (Newton, f. *centrum* centre + *-fugus* fleeing, avoiding) + -AL¹. (Cf. CENTRIPETAL). In mod.F. *centrifuge*.]

1. Flying or tending to fly off from the centre as **a.** ***centrifugal force***, also ***centrifugal tendency***: the force with which a body moving round a centre tends to fly off from that centre; the tendency which a revolving body has to do this.

('Centrifugal force' is really Inertia.)

[**1687** NEWTON *Principia* Sect. II. Prop. iv. *Schol.*, Hæc est vis centrifuga, qua corpus urget circulum; et huic æqualis est vis contraria.] *a* **1721** KEILL *Maupertuis' Diss.* (1734) 5 It is under the Equator that the Centrifugal Force is greatest. **1841-4** EMERSON *Ess. Hist.* Wks. (Bohn) I. 2 As the poise of my body depends on the equilibrium of centrifugal and centripetal forces. **1855** MAURY *Phys. Geog. Sea* i. (1860) 3 At the height of 26,000 miles from the earth, the centrifugal force would counteract gravity. **1866** AIRY *Pop. Astron.* 241 The centrifugal tendency is powerfully in operation at the equator, but not at all at the poles. **1876** ROUTLEDGE *Discov.* 7 If.. the velocity of the engine increases, the balls diverge from increased centrifugal force.

b. *fig.* or *transf.*

1817 COLERIDGE *Biog. Lit.* I. xii. 275. **1856** R. VAUGHAN *Mystics* (1860) I. 93 A process of evolution, a centrifugal movement in the Divine Nature. **1868** G. DUFF *Pol. Surv.* 21 So strong are the centrifugal forces in Spain.

c. ***centrifugal current***: 'applied to that arrangement of a battery in galvanizing an animal body, in which the positive pole is the nearer to the centre... of the nervous system' (*Syd. Soc. Lex.*).

2. Applied to machines or parts of mechanism in which centrifugal force is employed: as †**centrifugal bellows**, a fan or blowing machine; **centrifugal casting**, the casting of objects (usu. cylindrical) in a rotating mould; **centrifugal filter**, a sugar-filter in which a porous cylinder rotates rapidly so as to drive off liquid from the sugar; **centrifugal gun**, a kind of machine-cannon with a rotating chambered disk whence balls are driven tangentially; **centrifugal machine**, *gen.* any machine in which centrifugal force is employed; *spec.* a machine, also called a *hydro-extractor*, for drying yarn, cloth, sugar, or other substance, this being placed in a rapidly revolving cage, whence the moisture is thrown off by centrifugal force; **centrifugal mill**, Barker's mill; **centrifugal pump**, a rotary pump in which the fluid is driven outward and upward from a centre; there are many forms of it; ***centrifugal dresser***, etc.

1765 *Gentl. Mag.* 555 This centrifugal machine. **1803** BANKS *Power Machines* 41 Centrifugal machine or Erskine's centrifugal pump. **1807** T. YOUNG *Nat. Philos.* I. 781 The centrifugal bellows. By the revolution of the fly the air is caused to enter at A and is discharged at B. **1874** KNIGHT *Dict. Mech.* 514 Le Demour's centrifugal pump is supposed to have been the first of its kind. *Ibid.* 515 Andrew's centrifugal pump resembles a helix or snail's shell. **1884** *Bath Herald* 27 Dec. 6/5 After being carried through.. detachers, the wheat passes through centrifugal dressers. **1925** *Jrnl. Iron & Steel Inst.* CXII. 38 A method of centrifugal casting seemed to have come into commercial use. **1940** J. D. DEVONS *Metall. Deep Drawing* xvi. 595 Centrifugal casting has always attracted the attention of imaginative foundrymen.

3. *Bot.* **a.** Of inflorescence, in which the terminal flower opens first and the lateral ones successively after; inflorescence terminal or definite. **b.** Of an embryo: Having the radicle turned toward the sides of the fruit. **c.** Said of the order of cell division.

1830 LINDLEY *Nat. Syst. Bot.* 134 Flowers often with a centrifugal inflorescence. **1870** HOOKER *Stud. Flora* 277 Labiatæ.. Flowers solitary or in axillary opposite centrifugal cymes. **1884** BOWER & SCOTT *De Bary's Phaner. & Ferns* 545 In the course of the tangential divisions in an initial cell and the radial row derived from it, two extreme

forms may in the first instance be distinguished .. termed the centripetal and centrifugal forms.

4. *Phys.* Of nerve-fibres: Conveying impulses from a 'centre' (see CENTRE *sb.* 7 a); efferent.

1855 H. SPENCER *Princ. Psychol.* (1872) I. v. vi. 568 The centre .. from which issue through centrifugal nerves motor impulses. **1876** tr. *Wagner's Gen. Pathol.* 20 The properties of centrifugal fibres.

5. Obtained by the use of a centrifuge.

1880 *Army & Navy Co-op. Soc. Price List* 34 Sugars .. Centrifugal, or White Crystals. **1901** *U.S. Dept. Agric. Year-bk 1900* 613 Fresh butter, made from sweet centrifugal cream. **1958** *Catal. County Stores, Taunton* June 28 Sugars .. centrifugal crystals.

Hence as *sb.*, a centrifuge.

1866 'MARK TWAIN' *Lett. fr. Hawaii* (1967) 266 Close to the grinder are six centrifugals—small metallic tubs, whose sides are pierced with a few thousand pinholes to the square inch. **1904** BRANNT tr. *Bersch's Cellulose* ix. 221 The bleached skeins of silk are .. dehydrated in a centrifugal.

cenˌtrifu'gality. [f. CENTRIFUGAL *a.* + -ITY.] The operation of centrifugal force; dispersal or movement away from a centre (esp. *transf.*, in Pol. and Econ. contexts).

1934 V. M. YEATES *Winged Victory* I. iii. 30 He was .. unable to pull himself back into the seat because of centrifugality. **1957** V. W. TURNER *Schism & Continuity in Afr. Society* p. xxiii, Centrifugality is confined within the bounds of the total socio-geographical system of the Ndembu nation. **1968** *Economist* 11 May 49/1 The size, diversity and centrifugality of the United States make it heavily dependent for the functioning of its institutions upon the services of .. middle-men who can introduce and interpret, represent and mediate. **1982** *Nat. Geogr. Jrnl. India* XXVIII. 67/2 Reasons for centrifugality.

centrifugalization (sɛnˌtrɪfjuːgəlaɪ'zeɪʃən). [f. CENTRIFUGALIZE *v.*: see -ATION.] The process of subjecting to centrifugal action.

1900 in DORLAND *Med. Dict.* **1901** *Science* 29 Mar. 513 Juices, blood, etc., taken at various stages of the disease, with and without centrifugalization. **1908** *Practitioner* June 830 Sedimentation and centrifugalisation. **1964** M. HYNES *Med. Bacteriol.* (ed. 8) vii. 85 Antibody, however, combines with bacteria under these circumstances and can be removed with them from the solution by centrifugalization.

cen'trifugalize, *v.* [f. CENTRIFUGAL *a.* + -IZE.] **a.** *trans.* To impart a centrifugal motion to.

1879 *Cassell's Techn. Educ.* IV. 395/2 Would not that ocean .. be also centrifugalised or driven outwards?

b. To subject to a centrifugal process. Also *absol.*

1903 *Science* 6 Mar. 369/2 The blood was .. centrifugalized to get rid of the stroma. **1910** *Practitioner* June 866 Hyaline casts may be found .. if the urine be centrifugalised. **1925** C. H. BROWNING *Bacteriology* vi. 122 By .. re-suspending the sediment in .. sodium chloride solution and again centrifugalising, the corpuscles are freed from .. the serum.

cen'trifugally, *adv.* [f. as prec. + -LY[2].] In a centrifugal manner; from the interior or centre towards the exterior.

1819 H. BUSK *Vestriad* IV. 955 Hemm'd skirts centrifugally through Concentric orbits, glitter'd as they flew. **1833** SIR C. BELL *Hand* Prelim. Disc. (1874) 17 The nervous agency which excites the muscles proceeds outwardly from the brain, or centrifugally. **1871** TYNDALL *Fragm. Sc.* (ed. 6) II. vi. 76 The British Association then .. pushes knowledge centrifugally outwards. **1876** *Daily News* 27 Oct. 5/6 When a shell explodes the splinters fly centrifugally upwards.

cen'trifugate, *v. rare.* [f. as CENTRIFUGAL + -ATE[3]: cf. L. vbs. in *-ficāre* from *-ficus*. Cf. mod.F. *centrifuger* in same sense.] **1.** *intr.* To move away from the centre; to disperse.

1876 MRS. WHITNEY *Sights & Ins.* vii. 88 To meet again at the great focus, before we centrifugated off again upon our diverse tracks.

2. *trans.* To expel from the centre, *spec.* by centrifugal force; to centrifugalize.

1860 A. J. DAVIS *Great Harmonia* V. 196 She centrifugated it in a thousand different forms of expression. *a* **1909** *Buck's Handbk. Med. Sci.* I. 564 (Cent. D. Suppl.), The fluid should be centrifugated, the sediment spread on cover slips.

centrifugate (sɛn'trɪfjʊgət), *sb.* [f. CENTRIFUGAL *a.* + -ATE[2] 3.] Material separated by centrifugation.

1927 *Jrnl. Agric. Res.* XXXV. 825 When centrifugates were used the agreement was better. **1946** *Nature* 7 Sept. 344/1 The emulsions obtained from these pieces of brain or nerve tissue were centrifuged; the centrifugate was placed in a water bath. **1961** *Lancet* 2 Sept. 514/1 On direct microscopy of the centrifugate of this fluid .. we observed gram-positive and gram-negative rods.

centrifugation (ˌsɛntrɪfjʊ'geɪʃən). [f. CENTRIFUG(E *v.* + -ATION.] The action or process of CENTRIFUGE *v.*

1903 *Phil. Med. Jrnl.* 31 Jan. 201 The mixture was expressed, 30 cm. of this quantity taken, the solid particles separated by centrifugation and the amount of the nitrogen in the solid and liquid parts determined. **1946** *Nature* 31 Aug. 313/1 Liquids are usually separated from solids by centrifugation rather than filtration. **1958** *Immunology* I. i. 3 The cells suspended in the filtrate were washed by two or three gentle centrifugations in Ringer-phosphate. **1961** *Lancet* 26 Aug. 459/1 The homogenates were fractioned by differential centrifugation.

'centrifuge, *a.* and *sb.* [a. F. *centrifuge* centrifugal.]

A. *adj.* = CENTRIFUGAL.

1801 FUSELI *Lect. Art* iii. (1848) 408 The projectile and centrifuge qualities of the system.

B. *sb.* A centrifugal machine; *spec.* one for separating cream from milk by rotary motion.

1887 *Pall Mall G.* 27 Sept. 2/2 Two of the Danish centrifuges, which have a rotary motion equal to 4,000 revolutions a minute. They .. effect an instantaneous partition of the cream from the milk. **1887** *Scot. Leader* 29 Sept. 4 His dairymaids are Danish centrifuges. **1902** *Chemist & Druggist* 18 Oct. 660/1 A centrifuge .. exerts a sifting or separating action on such a mixture. **1935** *Nature* 4 May 719/2 The recognition by Ledingham and Gye, by the use of the high-speed centrifuge, of minute particles resembling those of other viruses. **1937** *Ann. Reg. 1936* 54 By use of the Svedberg centrifuge, X-ray and mathematico-physical methods, advance was made towards an understanding of the molecular architecture of the cell. **1947** CROWTHER & WHIDDINGTON *Sci. at War* 143 Yet another method consists of whirling vapours containing isotopes in a powerful centrifuge. **1957** *Observer* 10 Nov. 1/3 The Farnborough Institute has a human centrifuge in which human toleration to acceleration is tested. **1969** *Listener* 5 June 774/1 It might be possible to separate fissile uranium from the non-fissile variety in which it is naturally mixed by the use of centrifuges—rapidly spinning cylinders containing the gas uranium fluoride.

centrifuge ('sɛntrɪfjuːdʒ), *v.* [f. the sb.] *trans.* To subject to centrifugal motion; to separate by means of a centrifuge. So **'centrifuged** *ppl. a.*; **'centrifuging** *vbl. sb.* and *ppl. a.*

1902 *Chemist & Druggist* 18 Oct. 660/1 The creamy layer which collects on the top of the centrifuged liquid is skimmed off. **1903** *Nature* 3 Dec. 111/2 By mixing bacteria with the white cells of the blood obtained by centrifuging and adding blood serum. **1908** *Practitioner* Jan. 12 If the cerebro-spinal fluid withdrawn by this operation is centrifuged, and a deposit found, .. we can certainly exclude neurasthenia. **1910** *Ibid.* Apr. 447 Centrifuged specimens. **1920** L. DONCASTER *Introd. Cytology* iv. 54 Owing to the centrifuging, the polar spindle of an egg is greatly elongated. **1922** F. W. ASTON *Isotopes* 131 If therefore we have a mixture of isotopes in a gaseous or liquid state partial separation should be possible by gravity or centrifuging. **1930** FIELD & WEILL *Electro-Plating* 88 Centrifuging machines are used in dealing with numerous small parts. **1938** R. W. LAWSON tr. *Hevesy & Paneth's Man. Radioactivity* (ed. 2) xviii. 169 The precipitated lead hydroxide is centrifuged off.

cen'trifugence, -'fugience. *rare.* [f. L. **centrifug-us*: cf. *beneficentia* f. *benefic-us*.]

1847 EMERSON *Repr. Men* i. *Uses Gt. Men* Wks. (Bohn) I. 285 The centripetence augments the centrifugence. **1870** —— *Soc. & Solit.* vi. 120 A hoarding to check the spending; a centripetence equal to the centrifugence. **1883** S. WAINWRIGHT *Sci. Sophisms* vii. 114 As congelation is a property of water, or centrifugence of gas.

†cen'trifugous, *a. Obs.* [f. mod.L *centrifug-us* (see above) + -OUS.] = CENTRIFUGAL.

1709 *Brit. Apollo* II. No. 77. 3/1 Their Centripetous Motion .. detracts from their Centrifugous Motion.

†'centrine. *Obs.* [a. F. *centrine*, ad. Gr. *κεντρίνης* in same sense.] The Spiny Shark or Ray.

1661 LOVELL *Hist. Anim. & Min.* 233 Flesh .. like that of a Centrine, the hardest of all fishes, and of evil juyce.

centrinel, -onel, obs. variants of SENTINEL.

a **1593** MARLOWE *Dido* II. i. 323 These milk-white doves shall be his centronels. **1598** YONG *Diana* 120 The gate .. was opened to them out of hand by the Centrinels, who had notice of that was past and what they shuld do.

centring, centering ('sɛnt(ə)rɪŋ), *vbl. sb.* Also centreing. [f. CENTRE *v.* + -ING[1]; the standard spelling (on the analogy of *settle*, etc.) is now *centring*, but as the word is of 3 syllables (in careful pronunciation), *centering* (more rarely *centreing*) has freq. been used, esp. in technical senses.]

1. The action of the verb CENTRE; placing in the centre, convergence to the centre.

1667 MILTON *P.L.* IX. 109 As God in Heav'n Is Center, yet extends to all, so thou [Earth] Centring receav'st from all those Orbs. *a* **1732** ATTERBURY (J.) The visible centring of all the old prophecies in the person of Christ.

2. A placing in the centre or making central; the bringing of two or more centres into coincidence; *spec.* the setting of lenses so that their axes are in the same straight line.

1768 E. BUYS *Dict. Terms of Art*, Centering of an Optick-glass, is the grinding it so that the thickest part is exactly in the Middle. **1831** BREWSTER *Optics* xliii. 358 The .. risk of imperfect centering, or of the axes of the three lenses not being in the same straight line. **1881** *Edin. Rev.* Oct. 537 Mr. Carter recommends that people should look to the centreing of their spectacles for themselves. **1883** *Daily News* 10 Sept. 2/1 When the ring rotates at high speed, any slight error of centring tends to injure the ring.

3. *Arch.* 'The temporary woodwork or framing, whereon any vaulted work is constructed' (Gwilt).

a **1766** *Parentalia* in Entick *London* (1766) IV. 206 Both centering and scaffolding. **1861** SMILES *Engineers* II. 182 The centering upon which the arches of the bridge were built. **1879** SIR G. SCOTT *Lect. Archit.* II. 194 The use of continuous timber centering. **1885** RUSKIN *Præter.* iii, Well-made centreings .. made this model .. attractive.

4. *attrib.* and *Comb.*, as ***centring motion, punch*** (sense 2), ***stone*** (sense 3).

1855 I. TAYLOR *Restor. Belief* 138 A centering-stone of that structure which in the age of the Antonines had arched over the Roman world. **1883** *Knowledge* 27 Apr. i, Secondary stage with centering motion [in a microscope]. **1884** F. BRITTEN *Watch & Clockm.* 148 Another spring .. carrying a fine centreing punch.

'centring, -ering, -reing, *ppl. a.* [f. as prec. + -ING[2].] That centres. *spec.* of a diphthong (see quot. 1952). Cf. CENTRAL *a.* 1 d.

1647 CRASHAW *Poems* 157 All-circling point, all cent'ring sphere, The world's one, round, eternal year. **1917** H. E. PALMER *First Course of Eng. Phonetics* I. 23 English diphthongs (or double-vowels) .. four (in view of the fact that the tongue passes from the sides to the centre of the triangle) may conveniently be termed the *Centring Diphthongs.* **1952** A. COHEN *Phonemes of English* iv. 91 'Centring diphthongs' (i.e. those with [ə] as second element.) *Ibid.* 100 There are three of these 'centring diphthongs' to be considered in English, [ɪə, ʊə, ɛə]. **1964** R. H. ROBINS *Gen. Linguistics* iii. 98 These last three diphthongs are often called centring diphthongs, from the direction of their movement.

centriole ('sɛntrɪəʊl). *Cytology.* [ad. G. *centriol* (T. Boveri 1895, in *Verh. d. Physik.-Med. Ges. Würzburg* XXIX. 1. 66), f. mod.L. *centriolum*, dim. of *centrum* centre.] A minute, apparently self-reproducing particle which is present, usu. as one of a pair, in the centrosome and which is important for its part in forming and organizing the mitotic apparatus during cell-division.

1896 E. B. WILSON *Cell* 334 *Centriole*, a term applied by Boveri to a minute body or bodies .. within the centrosome. In some cases not to be distinguished from the centrosome. **1912, 1925** [see CENTROSOME]. **1960** L. PICKEN *Organiz. Cells* vii. 269 In *Gallus domesticus*, the proximal centriole is a hollow sphere; .. in .. sea-urchins, the centriole appears as a curved disc .. In the toad .. the centriole is a cylindrical structure.

centripetal (sɛn'trɪpɪtəl), *a.* [f. mod.L. *centripet-us* (Newton) centre-seeking + -AL[1]. With mod.L. *centrifugus*, *centripetus*, cf. *Isid.* XII. viii. 9 'musca lucipeta, blatta lucifuga est'; *heredipeta*, *lucripeta* also occur in L. Cf. mod.F. *centripète*.]

1. Tending toward the centre; the opposite of *centrifugal*.

a. ***centripetal force***: a force which draws or impels a body toward some point as a centre, and thus acts as a counterpoise to the centrifugal tendency in circular motion; for this the name ***centripetal tendency*** is substituted by some.

[**1687** NEWTON *Principia* Defin. v, Vim conatui illi contrariam .. Centripetam appello.] **1709** *Tatler* No. 43 ¶7 Thus the Tangential and Centripetal Forces, by their Counter-struggle, make the Celestial Bodies describe an exact Ellipsis. **1764** REID *Inquiry* ii. §9 Centripetal force is put for the cause, which we conceive to be some power or virtue in the centre or central body. **1841-4** [see CENTRIFUGAL 1]. **1868** LOCKYER *Elem. Astron.* 306 Were the centrifugal tendency to cease, the centripetal force would be uncontrolled, and the body would fall upon the attracting mass.

b. *fig.* and *transf.*

a **1711** KEN *Sion* Wks. 1721 IV. 419 They Unwing'd, as swiftly flew the spacious way, By their centripetal connat'ral Force, To their Triune, co-amiable Source. *a* **1763** SHENSTONE *Ess.* 112 Indolence is a kind of centripetal force. **1870** GLADSTONE *Glean.* IV. vi. 202 While centripetal and centrifugal forces are thus engaged in mortal tug.

2. Applied to machines or parts of mechanism which employ centripetal action: as **centripetal press, centripetal pump.**

1874 KNIGHT *Dict. Mech.*, *Centripetal pump* .. in one form it is the exact converse of the Barker Mill.

3. *Bot.* Tending or developing from without toward the centre. ***centripetal inflorescence***, that in which the lowest or outermost flowers blossom first, as in spikes and umbels; also called ***indeterminate*** or ***indefinite***.

1870 HOOKER *Stud. Flora* 184 Compositæ .. Inflorescence a centripetal head of many small flowers. **1880** GRAY *Struct. Bot.* v. 145 The Indefinite or Indeterminate type of inflorescence has been called Centripetal, because .. the evolution is seen to proceed from circumference to centre. **1882** VINES *Sachs' Bot.* 536 The acropetal or centripetal order of succession of the floral leaves.

4. *Biol.* **a.** Proceeding from the exterior to the interior or centre. **b.** Of nerves: Conveying an impulse from the periphery to the 'centre'; afferent.

1836 TODD *Cycl. Anat.* I. 763/1 The law of centripetal development. **1855** OWEN *Skel. & Teeth* 131 As the centripetal calcification proceeds, the caps are converted into horn-shaped cones. **1877** ROBERTS *Handbk. Med.* (ed. 3) I. 52 The centripetal or sensory nerves.

centripetalism (sɛn'trɪpɪtəlɪz(ə)m). [f. CENTRIPETAL *a.* + -ISM.] Movement towards a centre.

1887 *Westm. Rev.* June 409 The plague of centripetalism is a curse which has come to us [*sc.* New Zealand] across the seas from older countries.

cen'tripetally, *adv.* [f. CENTRIPETAL *a.* + -LY².] In a centripetal manner or direction; from the exterior towards the interior or centre.

1854 R. OWEN in *Circ. Sc.* (1865) II. 57/2 Ossification.. proceeds centripetally. **1881** *Pennsylv. Sch. Jrnl.* XXX. 86 While the adult may be educated centrifugally, the child must be educated centripetally. **1884** BOWER & SCOTT *De Bary's Phaner.* 362 The development..begins at the periphery of the ring, and in general proceeds centripetally.

cen'tripetence. [f. on L. type **centripetentia*; cf. *centrifugence*. In mod.F. *centripétence*.] Centripetal motion or action.

1847 [see CENTRIFUGENCE]. **1867** EMERSON *Lett. & Soc. Aims* vii. (1875) 179, I shall never believe that centrifugence and centripetence balance, unless mind heats and meliorates, as well as the surface and soil of the globe.

cen'tripetency. [f. as prec. + -ENCY.] Tendency toward the centre.

1846 WORCESTER cites *Monthly Rev.*

† **centripetous,** *a. Obs.* [f. mod.L. *centripet-us* (see CENTRIPETAL) + -OUS.] = CENTRIPETAL.

1709 [see CENTRIFUGOUS].

centrique, obs. form of CENTRIC.

centrism ('sɛntrɪz(ə)m). [f. CENTRE *sb.* + -ISM.] (The policy of adopting) a middle position between extreme views.

1935 R. B. PERRY *Tht. & Char. W. James* I. 574 A plea for some sort of philosophical centrism that should preserve the British tradition. **1960** *Commentary* June 543/2 Bell's centrism and 'moderationism' lead him rather seriously astray.

centrist ('sɛntrɪst). [a. F. *centriste*, f. *centre* CENTRE: see -IST.] **a.** *Polit.* A member of the Centre Party (in France).

1872 *Daily News* 31 July, That weak-kneed congregation who sit in the middle of the House, and call themselves 'Centrists'. **1882** *Pall Mall G.* 31 Jan., A close game was then being played between the Centrists and M. Gambetta.

b. *transf.* Also *attrib.* or as *adj.*

1923 E. A. ROSS *Russian Soviet Republ.* 22 The 'Berliner Tageblatt' and the 'Vossische Zeitung' demand an understanding with Russia by all means. The Centrists favor an agreement. **1928** F. UTLEY tr. *Illustr. Hist. Russ. Rev.* I. 135 In international Social Democracy 'Centrists' are those who swing to and fro between the Jingoes..and the Left such as:..MacDonald and Co. in England. **1928** *Manch. Guardian Weekly* 21 Sept. 224/1 The 'Temps' shows some uneasiness..at the attacks on Herr Müller in the Centrist and Populist press. **1958** *Economist* 8 Nov. 504/1 A cautiously centrist position on 'welfare state' issues. **1968** *Guardian* 20 Nov. 9/2 The subsequent struggle for supremacy between Mr Gomulka's 'centrists' and Mr Moczar's 'extremists' is in the classical tradition of Communist intrigue.

centro- (sɛntrəʊ). Stem of L. *centrum* and Gr. *κέντρον*, used as a combining form, with senses 'centre, central, centrally': as **centro'acinar** *a.*, of or belonging to the centre of an acinus (of the pancreas); **centro'clinal** *a.* (*Geol.*), see quots; **centro'dorsal** *a.*, of or belonging to the centre of the back; **centro'lecithal** *a. Biol.*, having the food yolk in the centre of the ovum; **centro'linead** (*Geom.*), see quots; **centro'lineal** *a.*, applied to a series of lines converging to a centre; **'centromere** *Cytology* [ad. G. *centromer* (W. Waldeyer 1903, in Hertwig *Handb. d. Entwick. d. Wirbeltiere* (1906) I. 204), f. Gr. *μέρος* part], (*a*) see quot. 1925 (*disused*); (*b*) the part of a chromosome to which the spindle is attached during mitosis; hence **ˌcentro'meric** *a.*; **'centrosphere,** (*a*) *Cytology* [ad. G. *centrosphäre* (E. Strasburger 1893, in *Anat. Anzeiger* VIII. 179)], a region of clear, differentiated cytoplasm from which the asters extend during cell-division and containing the centriole(s) if present; (*b*) *Geol.*, the central or inner part of the earth; **centro'staltic** *a.* (*Med.*), 'applied by Hall to the action of the vis nervosa in the spinal centre' (*Syd. Soc. Lex.*); **centro'stomatous** *a.* (*Zool.*), having the mouth perfectly central, as a star-fish; **centrosy'mmetrical** *a.* (*Crystall.*), having **centro'symmetry,** symmetry to a point or centre; **cen'trotylote** *a.*, of a biradiate sponge-spicule, having a central swelling.

1881 *Jrnl. Microsc. Sc.* Jan. 115 The *centroacinar cells of Langerhaus. **1876** PAGE *Adv. Text-bk. Geol.* iv. 83 When strata dip..to a common centre, they are said to be *centroclinal. **1877** GREEN *Phys. Geol.* ix. §3. 347 They have a centroclinal dip or form a basin. **1878** tr. *Gegenbauer's Comp. Anat.* 218 The *centro-dorsal plate. **1880** CARPENTER in *Jrnl. Linn. Soc.* XV. 193 A specimen with a more regular centrodorsal and pointed muscle-plates. **1880** BALFOUR *Comp. Embryol.* I. iii. 90 The food-yolk is however placed, not at one pole, but at the centre of the ovum. This group of ova I propose to name *centrolecithal. **1888** ROLLESTON & JACKSON *Anim. Life* p. xxvi, Centrolecithal ova are confined to Arthropoda. **1966** *McGraw-Hill Encycl. Sci. & Technol.* IX. 459 Centrolecithal, or centrally located yolk, occurs in eggs of insects and cephalopod mollusks. **1814** P. NICHOLSON in *Trans. Soc. Arts* XXXII. 67 An instrument of my invention called a *centro-linead, for drawing lines to inaccessible vanishing points in perspective. **1878** STANLEY *Drawing Instr.* 169 The centrolinead was invented by Peter Nicholson, a man of great geometrical ingenuity. **1925** E. B. WILSON *Cell* (ed. 3) 1127 **Centromere*, that part of the sperm containing the central bodies; especially the neck-region. **1936** C. D. DARLINGTON in *Jrnl. Genetics* XXXIII. 466 The chromosomes of the Acridinae..have always been described as of two types, with submedian and with terminal centromeres (or spindle attachments). **1949** *New Biol.* VII. 73 The centromere of a fully contracted chromosome is generally recognisable as a non-staining constriction. **1968** *Brit. Med. Bull.* XXIV. 261/1 A chromosome may appear to have two centromeres if the outline alone is taken into consideration. **1960** *Lancet* 14 May 1063/2 The *centromeric index expressed as the ratio of the length of the shorter arm to the whole length of the chromosome. **1896** E. B. WILSON *Cell* 232 The *centrosphere has a radiate structure, being traversed by rays which stretch between the centrosome and the peripheral microsome-circle. **1899** *Geogr. Jrnl.* XIII. 228 The Earth consists of three parts: there is the vast unknown interior, or 'centrosphere' [etc.]. **1960** L. PICKEN *Organization of Cells* vii. 253 In experiments in which removal of the centrosphere alone was attempted, asters always re-formed eventually. **1878** GURNEY *Crystallogr.* 40 In the Anorthic system..a holohedral form can only be *centro-symmetrical. *Ibid.* 36 The crystal can only possess symmetry to a point or *centro-symmetry. **1887** *Encycl. Brit.* XXII. 417/2 A *centrotylote microxea. **1900** *Proc. Zool. Soc.* 131 The microstrongyles..are occasionally centrotylote.

centrobaric (sɛntrəʊ'bærɪk), *a.* [f. CENTRO- + Gr. *βάρ-ος* weight + -IC.]

1. Of or relating to the centre of gravity, or to the process of finding it.

centrobaric method (*Math.*): a method of determining the area of a surface, or the volume of a solid, generated by the revolution of a line or surface respectively about a fixed axis, on the principle that the superficies or solid so formed is equal to the product of the generating line or surface and the length of the path of its centre of gravity; sometimes called the *theorem of Pappus*.

1727-51 in Chambers *Cycl.* s.v. *Centrobaryc Method.* **1796** HUTTON *Math. Dict.*, *Centrobaric method.*

2. See quot.

1867 THOMSON & TAIT *Nat. Philos.* (1883) §534 If the action of..gravity on a rigid body is reducible to a single force in a line passing always through one point fixed relatively to the body..that point is called its centre of gravity, and the body is called a centrobaric body. **1885** WATSON & BURBURY *Math. The. Electr. & Magn.* I. 64 A body, which has the same potential at all points outside of itself, as if its mass were collected at a point *O* within it, is a centrobaric body, and *O* its centre. It follows..that if a body be centrobaric, its centre is its centre of inertia.

So **centro'barical** *a.*

1704 J. HARRIS *Lex. Techn.*, *Centrobarycal*, is what relates to the Center of Gravity. **1768** E. BUYS *Dict. Terms of Art*, *Centrobarical.*

centrode ('sɛntrəʊd). *Math.* [f. Gr. *κέντρον* or L. *centrum* CENTRE + *ὁδός* path. (The earlier proposed name was CENTROID.)] (See quot.)

1878 CLIFFORD *Elements of Dynamic* I. 136. **1882** MINCHIN *Unipl. Kinemat.* 39 A locus traced out by the successive positions of an instantaneous centre of pure rotation has received the special name of a centrode..We shall have therefore, in all cases, both a body centrode and a space centrode. **1884** *Athenæum* 15 Sept. 339/2 Instantaneous centres and centrodes are not introduced till a late stage, link work and teeth of wheels being discussed without their aid.

centro'dontous, *a.* [f. Gr. *κέντρον* sharp point + *ὀδοντ-* tooth + -OUS.] 'Having sharp and subulate teeth' (*Syd. Soc. Lex.*).

centroid ('sɛntrɔɪd). *Math.* [f. CENTRE (or its source) + -OID.]

1. = CENTRODE. [In this sense introduced by Prof. A. B. W. Kennedy, 1876, on the analogy of *cycloid* and other names of curves, but subsequently abandoned for *centrode*.]

1876 A. B. W. KENNEDY tr. *Reuleaux's Theoret. Kinemat.* **1876** *S. Kens. Mus. Catal.* No. 563 Sinoidic cams. Cardioids. With second disc and centroid. **1884** *Athenæum* 13 Sept. 339/2 The author erroneously calls the loci of the instantaneous centre 'centroids', a term which has become appropriated in a very different sense. **1886** A. B. W. KENNEDY *Mech. of Machin.* 49 (*note*).

2. Centre of mass, or of gravity.

1882 MINCHIN *Unipl. Kinemat.* 96 To find..the position of the Centroid ('centre of gravity') of any plane area.

† **'centron,** *sb. Obs.* ? The plant centaury.

1570 LEVINS *Manip.* 163 Centron, *centaurum*.

centronel: see CENTRINEL.

centronote ('sɛntrəʊnəʊt). [a. F. *centronote*, ad. mod.L. *centronōtus*, f. Gr. *κέντρον* sharp point, spine + *νῶτος* back.] A genus of fishes (*Centronotus*) having a spur-like prickle pointing forwards in the back.

1836 *Blackw. Mag.* XXXIX. 306 The thorny lophoderme of a centronote or stickleback.

centrosome ('sɛntrəsəʊm). *Cytology.* Also **centrosoma** (pl. **centrosomata**). [ad. G. *centrosoma* (T. Boveri 1888, in *Jenaische Zeitschr. Naturw.* XXII. 752), f. CENTRO- + Gr. *σῶμα* body.] **a.** = CENTRIOLE. **b.** A small region of cytoplasm present in the cells of many animals and lower plants which during interphase is usu. situated next to the nucleus but is occas. within it and which comprises the centrosphere and the centriole(s). Hence **ˌcentro'somic** *a.*

1889 GEDDES & THOMSON *Evolution of Sex* xi. 146 Both Van Beneden and Boveri have recently agreed on the existence of two 'central corpuscles' (centrosomata) in the protoplasm. **1893** PARKER & RÖNNEFELDT tr. *Weismann's Germ-Plasm* 23 We now know..that even in Phanerogams a small cell-body surrounds the nucleus [of the male cell in fertilization], and that a special structure, the 'centrosome',—which is absolutely essential for the commencement of development,—is contained within it. **1900** [see TELO-¹]. **1912** E. A. MINCHIN *Stud. Protozoa* vi. 81 To the primary centrosome or centriole there may be added adventitious elements of protoplasmic or nuclear origin, thus forming a centrosomic complex. **1925** E. B. WILSON *Cell* (ed. 3) i. 26 In addition to the nucleus, the cytosome often contains a structure known as the *central apparatus* or *microcentrum* of which the most essential component is the central body (*centrosome, centriole*) about which as a center arise the *asters*. *Ibid.* 1127 *Centrosome*, (1) originally, the central body lying at the astral center..(Boveri, 1888); (2) Subsequently, in a more specific sense, the larger central body, composed of *centroplasm*, within which lies the much smaller *centriole* (Boveri, 1895, 1901). **1943** L. W. SHARP *Fund. Cytol.* 28 The aspect of the centrosome varies widely in cells of different kinds and especially in different stages of nuclear division. **1964** BROWN & DANIELLI in G. H. BOURNE *Cytol. & Cell Physiol.* (ed. 3) vi. 292 The second stage [of egg activation] follows engulfment of the spermatozoon and it is the centrosome which plays the active role and organizes the division apparatus.

‖ **centrum** ('sɛntrəm). [L. *centrum* CENTRE of rotation, etc., a. Gr. *κέντρον* sharp point, a goad, a peg, the stationary point of a pair of compasses; f. same root as *κεντέ-ειν* to prick, goad, stab, etc.]

1. The Latin word for centre, used technically in *Animal Phys.*: The body of a vertebra; the solid part to which the arches and processes are attached.

1854 R. OWEN in *Circ. Sc.* (1865) II. 62/2 The centrums coalesce. **1869** GILLMORE *Rept. & Birds* Introd. 5 Free vertebræ, forming a series of separate centrums, deeply cupped at both ends. **1870** ROLLESTON *Anim. Life* 5 The articulate ends of their centra. **1871** DARWIN *Desc. Man* I. i. 29.

2. The place from which an earthquake originates.

1887 *Nature* 31 Oct. 657 The determination of earthquake origins, the depth of 'centrums', [etc.]. **1938** L. D. LEET *Practical Seismol.* viii. 280 With growth of the concept that ordinarily the focus was actually at a finite depth below the surface, the term 'centrum' was modified to *hypocenter*, signifying the deep center, or focus; and *epicenter*, or point on the surface vertically above the focus.

† **centry,** *sb. Obs.* [f. CENTRE; the ending is not explained.]

1. Centre, middle, midst.

1583 STUBBES *Anat. Abus.* II. 5 This country is scituate as it were in the centrie, or midst of others. **1594** SHAKS. *Rich. III*, v. ii. 11 This foule Swine Is now euen in the Centry of this Isle.

2. The centre or centering of a bridge.

1651 JER. TAYLOR *Serm.* (1678) 143 Pleasure is but like centries or wooden Frames, set under Arches, till they be strong by their own weight and consolidation to stand alone. *a* **1834** COLERIDGE *Lit. Rem.* I. 342 Centries..put under the arches of a bridge, to remain no longer than until the latter are consolidated.

† **centry,** *a. Her.* Also **sentry.** [a. F. *centré* centred.]

1486 *Bk. St. Albans, Her.* B iv b, A Cootarmure..sentry of dyuerse colowris.

centry, obs. form of SENTRY, CENTAURY.

centuary, obs. var. CENTAURY.

‖ **centum** ('kɛntəm). Also **kentum.** [L. *centum* hundred.]

1. A hundred: see CENT.

2. *Philol.* [from its pronunc. with (k), as opposed to SATEM.] A name given by philologists to one, chiefly western, group of Indo-European languages, distinguished by their use of velar consonants where the corresponding sounds in cognate words in the eastern group (cf. SATEM) are sibilants.

1901 P. GILES *Short Man. Compar. Philol.* (ed. 2) 24 As the most characteristic sound is found in the word for 'hundred', the two sections are named the *centum* and the *satem* section respectively. **1912** J. WRIGHT *Compar. Gram. Greek Lang.* vi. 95 The former group [Greek, Italic, Keltic, Germanic] is generally called the centum- and the latter [Aryan, Armenian, Albanian, Baltic-Slavonic] the satəm-group of languages, where Latin *centum* and Zend *satəm* represent the original Indg. word **kmtóm*, hundred. **1926** J. R. R. TOLKIEN in *Year's Work in Eng. Stud. 1924* 27 The *centum-satəm* division becomes more, not less, puzzling, as does the whole question of the interrelations of the surviving Indo-European languages. **1932** W. L. GRAFF *Language* x. 365 The languages in which I.-E. *k, g*, etc., are preserved as gutturals are called kentum languages, the others satem languages. **1939** E. PROKOSCH *Compar. Germ. Gram.* 43 *Kentum* and *Satem*..It is customary to distinguish two groups of Indo-European languages according to the treatment of the Indo-European palatals: they became sibilants in the eastern group, but appear as velars in the western group. **1952** O. R. GURNEY *Hittites* vi. 119 The 'centum' group (comprising Latin, Greek, Celtic, and the various Germanic languages).

‖**cen'tumvir.** *Rom. Antiq.* pl. cen'tumviri. [L. *centum* hundred, *viri* men.] (In *pl.*) A body of judges appointed by the prætor to decide common causes among the Roman people. They were elected out of the thirty-five tribes, three from each tribe, which made the number one hundred and five, though for the sake of conciseness called 'the Hundred Men', which name they retained even when increased under the emperors to 180.

1601 B. JONSON *Poetaster* (T.) Thou art one of the centumviri, old boy, art not?

centumviral (sɛn'tʌmvɪrəl), *a.* [f. L. *centumvirāl-is*, f. prec.: see -AL[1].] Of or pertaining to the centumviri.

a **1693** URQUHART *Rabelais* III. xxxix, That Centumviral Court. **1821** LOCKHART *Valerius* I. v. 75 The appearance he had made the day before in the Centumviral Court. **1880** MUIRHEAD tr. *Gaius* IV. §15 *note*.

centumvirate (sɛn'tʌmvɪrət). [f. on L. type **centumvirāt-us* (cf. *triumvirātus*), f. *centumvir*: see above, and -ATE[1].]

1. The office of the Roman centumviri, or the body of these collectively.

1727–51 CHAMBERS *Cycl.*, *Centumvirate*, among the Romans, a court of one hundred magistrates or judges. **1765** C. SMART *Phædrus* III. ix. (Bohn) 503 Th' accusers take the woman straight, And drag to the centumvirate.

2. *gen.* A body of 100 men.

1761 STERNE *Tr. Shandy* III. xx, Finding food and raiment all that term for a centumvirate of the profession.

centu'plation. [n. of action f. CENTUPLE: see -ATION.] Multiplication a hundred-fold.

1641 W. GASCOIGNE in Rigaud *Corr. Sci. Men* (1841) I. 47 The decuplation, or, if need be, centuplation of the bars.

centuple ('sɛntju:p(ə)l), *a.* [a. F. *centuple*, ad. L. *centŭp-lus*, in late use for *centuplex*, f. *centum* hundred + *plic-* fold. Cf. *double*, *treble*, *quadruple*.] A hundred-fold.

1609 B. JONSON *Sil. Wom.* II. i, It were a vengeance centuple. **1639** MASSINGER *Unnat. Combat.* I. i, I wish his strength were centuple. **1674** PETTY *Disc. Royal Soc.* 109 Of Centuple value. **1829** CARLYLE *Misc.* (1857) II. 10 To more than centuple that sum. **1844** EMERSON *Ess.* Ser. II. i. (1876) 12 The quadruple, or the centuple, or much more manifold meaning, of every sensuous fact.

centuple ('sɛntju:p(ə)l), *v.* [a. F. *centuple-r*, or f. on L. type **centuplāre* = *centuplicāre* on analogy of *quadruplāre*, f. *centupl-us*: see prec.] *trans.* To multiply or increase a hundredfold. Hence **centupled** *ppl. a.*

1607 CHAPMAN *Bussy D'Amb.* Plays (1873) II. 27 And shall your royall bountie Centuple. **1614** in Spurgeon *Treas. Dav.* Ps. cxxvi. 5 All that you have lost shall be centupled to you. **1636** G. SANDYS *Paraphr. Ps.* lxix, Behold, and centuple their joyes. *a* **1687** PETTY *Pol. Arith.* (1690) 2 The same Land being built upon may centuple the Rent. **1812** *Examiner* 19 Oct. 666/1 Which..would more than centuple the ministerial majority. **1856** EMERSON *Eng. Traits, Wealth* Wks. (Bohn) II. 72 Every stroke of the steam-piston.. doubles, quadruples, centuples the Duke's capital.

centuplicate (sɛn'tju:plɪkət), *a.* and *sb.* [ad. L. *centuplicāt-us*, *-um* pa. pple.: see next.] Hundred fold. (Cf. *duplicate* a. and sb.)

1835 *Tait's Mag.* II. 579 He received his richly-adorned ass-skin copy, with..a big patent centuplicate lock. **1882** *Sat. Rev.* LIII. 585 Ready for telegraphic transmission in centuplicate.

cen'tuplicate, *v.* [f. L. *centuplicāt-* ppl. stem of *centuplicāre*, f. *centuplic-* (*centuplex*) a hundred fold: see above.] = CENTUPLE *v.* Hence, **cen'tuplicated** *ppl. a.*

c **1645** HOWELL *Lett.* IV. ii, I perform'd the civilities you enjoyn'd me to your frends here, who return you the like centuplicated. **1654** COKAINE *Dianea* II. 135 Their kisses were centuplicated. **1768** E. BUYS *Dict. Terms of Art*, *Centuplicated*, made an Hundredfold.

cen,tupli'cation. [n. of action, f. L. *centuplicāre*.] Multiplication a hundred fold.

1881 BLACKMORE *Christowell* in *Gd. Words* May 291 When a man is in a hurry..every little thing that can converge to a confluence of tangles turns its whole vitality to that centuplication [*printed* centumplication].

†**'centuply,** *v. Obs. rare.* [ad. L. *centuplicā-re*, on analogy of *multiply*, etc.] = CENTUPLICATE.

1622 FLETCHER *Sp. Curate* I. ii, Though my wants Were centuplied upon myself, I could be patient.

cen'tuply, *adv.* [f. CENTUPLE *a.* + -LY[2].] A hundred-fold.

1876 BROWNING *Pacchiarotto* 99 Like the gem Centuply-angled o'er a diadem.

†**'centure, 'center.** *Obs.* [ad. It. *centura*, or F. *ceinture*.] A waist-belt, girdle, or CINCTURE.

1595 SHAKS. *John* IV. iii. 155 Now happy he, whose cloake and center can Hold out this tempest! **1624** A. DARCIE *Birth Heresies* xii. 51 The Stole, Ephod, Zone, or Centure.

centurial (sɛn'tjʊərɪəl), *a.* [ad. L. *centuriāl-is*, f. *centuria*: see CENTURY and -AL[1].]

1. Of or pertaining to a century (senses 1, 2).

1610 HEALEY *St. Aug. City of God* 81 The kings being casheered out of Rome by the great Centuriall Parliament. **1656** J. HARRINGTON *Oceana* (1700) 185 The Suffrage in the Centurial Assemblys. **1851** D. WILSON *Preh. Ann.* (1863) II. III. ii. 42 Legionary or centurial tablets and other Roman inscriptions. **1880** *Athenæum* 11 Dec. 781.

2. Of or pertaining to a century or hundred years.

1864 LOWELL *Fireside Trav.* 71 Quadrangles mossy with centurial associations. **1877** BP. S. BUTCHER *Eccl. Calendar* xxx. 36 In any two consecutive centurial years, the 1st of January in the one year will be 6 week-days apart from January 1 in the other.

†**centurian.** *Obs.* [f. on L. type **centuriān-us*, f. *centuria* century: see -AN.] **a.** An officer appointed over each hundred. **b.** (?) A hundred (a division of a county).

1641 in *Harl. Misc.* (Malh.) V. 47 Those earls..divided them [each county] into centurians or hundreds; and in every hundred was appointed a centurian or constable.

¶ See also CENTURION.

cen'turiate, *a.* [ad. L. *centuriāt-us* pa. pple. of *centuriā-re*: see next.] In ***centuriate assemblies*** (or ***comitia***), translating L. *comitia centuriata*, a meeting in which all the Roman people voted by centuries (see CENTURY 2). Also, of, pertaining to, or divided into centuries.

1600 HOLLAND *Livy* VI. xli. 247 In the Centuriate assemblies holden by degrees, and Curiat-meetings by the wardes and parishes. **1901** F. F. ABBOTT *Hist. & Descr. Rom. Pol. Instit.* 27 The action of the centuriate *comitia* in electing magistrates, in passing laws, and in deciding appeals was of no great immediate value to the plebs. *Ibid.* 76 The reformed centuriate assembly was essentially democratic. **1918** HAVERFIELD in *Eng. Hist. Rev.* XXXIII. 296 The boundaries of Roman centuriate land.

centuriate, *v. rare.* [f. L. *centuriāt-* ppl. stem of *centuriā-re*, to divide into centuries, f. *centuria* CENTURY.] †**1.** 'To divide into bands of hundreds' (Bailey 1721). *Obs.*

2. In Roman colonization, to divide and assign land (see CENTURIATION).

1918 HAVERFIELD in *Eng. Hist. Rev.* XXXIII. 289 It would follow that the *territorium* of..a provincial *colonia*.. would be centuriated when first surveyed and laid out. *Ibid.* 296 The whole of northern Essex..would have been surveyed and centuriated on one general scheme.

centuriation (sɛntjʊərɪ'eɪʃən). *Hist.* [ad. L. *centuriātio*, *-ōnem*, n. of action f. *centuriāre* to CENTURIATE.] (See quots.)

1869 H. C. COOTE in *Archæologia* XLII. 133 The territory having been thus appropriated to the colony, the next step was to divide and assign it..in *centuriæ*, or private estates, to and amongst the colonists. This *centuriation*, as it was called, was the legal and constitutional act which perfected the change from public land into private property. **1918** HAVERFIELD in *Eng. Hist. Rev.* XXXIII. 291 Numerous attempts have been made to detect centuriation, or something like it, in Britain. **1961** L. MUMFORD *City in History* viii. 209 In many regions colonization was accompanied by..dividing fields into long rectangular parcels that are still visible from the air and respected in daily use. This system of 'centuriation' characterizes large parts of lowland Italy, Dalmatia, and Africa.

Centuriator (sɛn'tjʊərɪeɪtə(r)). [a. L. *centuriātor*, n. of action f. *centuriāre* to CENTURIATE.] *pl.* (usually *Centuriators of Magdeburg*): A name given to a number of Protestant divines who in the 16th c. compiled a Church History in thirteen volumes, each volume embracing a century. Formerly called CENTURISTS.

1660 JER. TAYLOR *Duct. Dubit.* II. iii, The innumerable errors in the matter which have been observed by the centuriators of Magdeburg. **1706** tr. *Dupin's Eccl. Hist. 16th C.* II. v. 93 He particularly answers the Objections of the Centuriators. **1883** *Pall Mall G.* 1 Sept. 1/2 The painstaking criticism of the Magdeburg Centuriators.

centurie, obs. f. SANCTUARY, CENTURY.

1655 FULLER *Ch. Hist.* VI. ii. *Prime Officers* §17 Sanctuarium, or the Centurie, wherein Debtours taking refuge from their Creditours..lived..in all security.

centuried ('sɛntjʊərɪd), *a.* [f. CENTURY + -ED[2].] Established for centuries; centuries old.

1820 BYRON *Proph. Dante* III. 62 This centuried eclipse of woe. **1831** *Blackw. Mag.* XXIX. 226 Its centuried roots gave way.

†**'centurine.** *Obs.* [ad. It. *centurino* 'a little girdle or waist band' (Florio), dim. of *centura* belt, girdle:—L. *cinctūra* CINCTURE] A waist-belt formerly worn.

1721 CIBBER *Love's Last Shift* II, The Cravat string, the Garter, the Sword-knot, the Centurine, Bardash..the long Sleeve, the Plume, and full Peruke, were all created..by me.

centurion (sɛn'tjʊərɪən). Also 4 -ioun, -ien, -yone, centorioun, 6 centurian. [a. F. *centurion* (12th c. in Littré) or ad. L. *centurio*, *-ōnem*, f. *centuria* CENTURY. The L. *centurio* is found unchanged in the Wycliffite versions, and other works of 13th–15th c.]

1. The commander of a century in the Roman army.

c **1275** *Passion our Lord* in *O.E. Misc.* 485 þet iseyh centurio þat þer bisydes stod. **1382** WYCLIF *Acts* xxi. 32 Knyȝtis takun to, and centuriouns [**1388** centuriens]. *c* **1400** *Apol. Loll.* 2 Corneli centurio, ȝet vncristund, is clensid wiþ þe Hooli Goost. *c* **1440** *Gesta Rom.* lviii. 241 (Harl. MS.) The Emperoure..seide to his centurio, þat he shulde feche that knyȝt. **1525** TINDALE *Matt.* viii. 5 *marg. note*, Whom I call sometime a centurion, but for the most part a hunder-captain. **1607** SHAKS. *Cor.* IV. iii. 47 The Centurions..to be on foot at an houres warning. **1838–43** ARNOLD *Hist. Rome* I. xiii. 223 To seize and execute every centurion whose century had fled.

2. *transf.* Any officer in command of 100 men.

1382 WYCLIF *Deut.* i. 15, I haue ordeynd hem princes, and tribunes, and centuriouns, and quynquagenaryes, and denes. **1555** EDEN *Decades W. Ind.* I. II. (Arb.) 72 He sent forth dyuers other Centurians with their hundrethes. *c* **1730** BURT *Lett. N. Scotl.* (1818) II. 24 One of the centurions, or captains of a hundred is said to strip his other tenants of their best plaids wherewith to clothe his soldiers.

3. *Sport.* A player who makes a hundred or more runs in an innings at cricket; one who has ridden, etc., a hundred miles in one journey; ***double centurion***, a player who makes a double century (see CENTURY 3b). *colloq.*

1886 *Graphic* 31 July 107/2 Some other 'centurions' have been Chatterton (108) for M.C.C., A. Shuker (103 not out) for Trent. **1897** *Outing* (U.S.) XXX. 346/1 There are long-distance riders, too, galore in the N.Y.A.C. and not a few centurions. **1900** *Westm. Gaz.* 18 July 2/3 This is the third time he has been a double centurion.

†**Centurist.** *Obs.* [ad. L. *centuria* + -IST.] = CENTURIATOR.

1636 *Unbishop. Timothy & Tit.* 15 Making the Succession of Bishops..as questionable as the Centurists orders. **1652** SPARKE *Prim. Devot.* (1663) 81 The centurists acknowledge this gesture the most ancient. **1686** *Catholic Representer* II. 87 These Fathers are rejected by the Centurists.

century ('sɛntjʊərɪ). Also 6–7 -ie. [a. F. *centurie* or ad. L. *centuria*, an assemblage or division of one hundred things, a company of 100 men, one of the 193 orders into which Servius Tullius divided the Roman people.]

1. a. *Rom. Hist.* A division of the Roman army, constituting half of a maniple, and probably consisting originally of 100 men; but in historical times the number appears to have varied according to the size and subdivision of the legion.

1533 BELLENDEN *Livy* I. (1822) 24 The first centurie of thir horsmen war namit Ramnenses. **1600** HOLLAND *Livy* I. xiii. 11 Three centuries of gentlemen or knights. **1607** SHAKS. *Cor.* I. vii. 3 If I do send, dispatch Those Centuries to our ayd. **1613** T. GODWIN *Exp. Rom. Antiq.* (1658) 257 Every cohors containing 3 maniples, every maniple two centuries, every century an hundred soldiers. **1838–43** ARNOLD *Hist. Rome* I. i. 25 The thirty centuries which made up the legion. **1850** MERIVALE *Rom. Emp.* II. xv. 199 The whole body of the legionaries, century by century.

b. *transf.* Any body of 100 men or soldiers.

1612–5 HALL *Contempl. O.T.* XIX. i, As many centuries of Syrians, as Israel had single souldiers. **1839** DE QUINCEY *Casuistry* Wks. VIII. 267 Forty-two centuries of armed men ..firing from windows, must have made prodigious havoc.

2. *Hist.* One of the 193 political divisions of the Roman people instituted by Servius Tullius, by which they voted in the *comitia centuriata*.

1604 EDMONDS *Observ. Cæsar's Comm.* II. 3 The people being deuided first into their Tribes, and then into their classes and centuries. **1631** HEYWOOD *London's Jus. Hon.* Ded., Censors..set a rate vpon euery mans estate, registring their names, and placing them in a fit century. **1850** MERIVALE *Rom. Emp.* (1865) IV. xxxii. 4 Assembled in their centuries, the Roman citizens appointed to all the higher magistracies of the republic.

transf. **1768** TUCKER *Lt. Nat.* (1852) I. 647 None could ever fail in distinguishing the classes [the good and the wicked], however they might mistake in the particular centuries under each.

3. a. A group of a hundred things; a hundred. *arch.*

1598 J. DICKENSON *Greene in Conc.* (1878) 104 A Centurie of sowltyring passions. **1611** SHAKS. *Cymb.* IV. ii. 391 When with wild wood-leaues and weeds I ha' strew'd his graue And on it said a Century of prayers. **1672** MANLEY *Cowel's Interpr.* Pref., Some Centuries of words therein totally omitted. **1737–40** H. CAREY (*title*), The Musical Century in One Hundred English Ballads. **1855** BROWNING *One Word More*, Rafael made a century of sonnets. **1867** BOYD *Oakw. Old* 111, Printing centuries of copies, In the usual pamphlet-form.

b. A hundred 'points' in the score of a game. *spec.* in *Cricket*, a hundred or more runs, esp. made by one player in the same innings; in *Cycling*, etc., a hundred miles in a race or ride; ***double century***, (*a*) *Cricket*, two hundred runs by the same player in one innings; (*b*) *Cycling*, a cycling run of two hundred miles.

1864 *Bell's Life* 11 June 8/4 Another century was piled up before the second wicket fell. **1871** F. GALE *Echoes Cricket Fields* viii. 43 There are slang writers who will tell me that the Lions' or the Nonpareils' [batting] average will be over a quarter of a century. *Ibid.* xiv. 90 He went in last, and joined Mr. Attfield, and between them ninety-nine runs were scored; or as a slang penny-a-liner would say, 'the two last gents wrote up a century bar one.' **1884** *York Herald* 23 Aug. 7/6 At 4.15 the third century was reached, Pullen having made exactly half the number. **1884** *St. James's Gaz.* 29 May 5/2 Mr. W. G. Grace and Barnes each scored upwards of a century in the same innings. **1897** *Outing* (U.S.) XXX. 343/1 The probability is that he will place to his credit on the [cycling] club records one or more double

centuries. *Ibid.* 348/1 The more enthusiastic indulge in century runs. **1955** *Times* 25 June 7/5 A boy who..can be relied on to score a century in most school cricket matches.

c. A hundred dollars. *U.S. slang.*

1859 MATSELL *Vocabulum* 18 *Century*, one hundred dollars. **1930** J. DOS PASSOS *42nd Parallel* v. 79 'You must have made big money.'.. 'I saved pretty near a century.' **1964** R. CHANDLER *Killer in Rain* 3 He..arranged five century notes like a tight poker hand.

d. A hundred pounds. *slang.*

1861 [see STOATER]. **1864** *Derby Day* 131 (Farmer), I'll lay you an even century about Nimrod. **1883** *Echo* 1 Nov. 4/2 (ibid.),.Golding..purchased Passaic from F. Archer for a century. **1888** F. W. J. HENNING *Recoll. Prize Ring* 155 Having made up his mind that he was going to pocket the century.

4. A period of 100 years; originally expressed in full a 'century of years'.

1626 W. SCLATER *Expos. 2 Thess.* (1629) 109 In as few centuries of yeeres after the floud. *c* **1645** HOWELL *Lett.* (1650) II. 6 About the latter end of the last century of yeers. **1662** STILLINGFL. *Orig. Sacr.* III. iv. §9 By that proportion ..it would amount to many thousands within a Century. *a* **1691** BOYLE (J.), Though our joys, after some centuries of years, may seem to have grown older. **1727** A. HAMILTON *New Acc. E. Ind.* I. Introd. 19 One intire Century would be too short a Time to learn them all. **1849–50** ALISON *Hist. Europe* I. i. §71. 115 Not years, but centuries must elapse during the apprenticeship to liberty.

5. Each of the successive periods of 100 years, reckoning from a received chronological epoch, *esp.* from the assumed date of the birth of Christ: thus the hundred years from that date to the year A.D. 100 were the *first century* of the Christian Era; those from 1801 to 1900 inclusive were the *nineteenth century*.

a **1638** MEDE *Wks.* II. i. (R.) Through every one of the first three centuries. **1649** S. CLARK *Marrow Eccl. Hist.* Ep. Chr. Rdr., Here [the Learned, etc.] shall see in what Centuries, Ages and Places the famousest Lights of the Church..have flourished. **1771** *Junius' Lett.* liv. 284 The rebellion in the last century. **1780** HARRIS *Philol. Enq.* (1841) 471 Soon after the end of the sixth century, Latin ceased to be spoken at Rome. **1846** KNIGHT *Pass. Working Life* I. §1. 18 The learned had settled, after a vast deal of popular controversy, that the century had its beginning on the 1st of January, 1801, and not on the 1st of January, 1800. **1852** TENNYSON *Ode Wellington* 142 Thro' the centuries let a people's voice ..Attest their great commander's claim. **1872** MORLEY *Voltaire* (1886) 4 Voltaire may stand for the name of the Renaissance of the eighteenth century.

†**6.** A 'hundred', as a division of a county. *rare.*

1611 SPEED *Theat. Gt. Brit.* ii. 3/2 Elfred..ordained Centuries, which they terme Hundreds.

†**7.** A hundred in numeration; one of the figures expressing 'the hundreds'. *Obs.*

1773 HORSLEY in *Phil. Trans.* LXIV. 299 Collect the corrections for the units, decades, and centuries of fathom in the approximate height.

8. *pl.* The Church History of the CENTURIATORS of Magdeburg, divided into centuries.

1606 EARL NORTHAMPTON in *True & Perf. Relation* V viij b, The iudgement of the Centuries in this circumstance concerning Childericke.

9. *Attrib.* and *comb.* as ***century-clock, century-circled*** adj.; (senses 4 and 5) ***century*** (or ***centuries***)***-long*** adj. and adv., ***century*** (or ***centuries***)***-old*** adj.; **century-plant**, the AGAVE or American Aloe; **century-writer** = CENTURIATOR.

18.. WHITTIER *Ship-builders* iii, The *century-circled oak. **1870** EMERSON *Soc. & Sol.* xii. 255 Not know that the *century-clock had struck seventy instead of twenty. **1883** 'MARK TWAIN' *Life on Mississippi* xlii. 386 Even the children know that a dead saint enters upon a *century-long career of assassination the moment the earth closes over his corpse. **1924** R. GRAVES *Mock Beggar Hall* 62 They themselves May century-long be doomed to walk these rooms. **1933** L. BLOOMFIELD *Language* i. 4 A century-long controversy. **1963** *Time* 30 Aug. 11/3 There cannot, in fact, be any real understanding of the Negro revolution of 1963 without some understanding of the Negro's centuries-long struggle in America. **1845** LONGFELLOW *Nuremberg* in *Poems* (1845) 88 Thy castle, time-defying, *centuries old. **1857** WHITTIER *Mabel Martin* 63 The household ruin century-old. **1873** D. M. P. tr. *Wellmer's C'tess zu Stolb.* ii. 23 The century-old motto of the Stolbergs. **1901** *Sketch* 31 July 56/2 Buried in its centuries-old bosom. **1958** B. ABEL-SMITH in N. Mackenzie *Conviction* 63 The eerie, century-old building. **1843** J. L. STEPHENS *Incidents of Travel in Yucatan* II. ii. 44 Growing on the roof are two maguey plants, Agave Americana, in our latitude called the *century plant, but under the hot sun of the tropics blooming every four or five years. **1884** *Harper's Mag.* Jan. 193/2 The great gray-blue swords of the century-plant. **1626** W. SCLATER *Expos. 2 Thess.* (1629) 202 In euery age inclinations of doctrine are wel obserued by the *century-writers. **1637** GILLESPIE *Eng. Pop. Cerem.* III. iv. 79 The Centurie-writers make out of Dionysius..his Epistle..that the Custome of the Church of Alexandria..was, etc. **1684** BAXTER *Cath. Communion* 36 Noted Divines and Century Writers.

Hence **centuryism**, as in *nineteenth-centuryism*, a characteristic of the 19th century.

1882 *Athenæum* No. 2836. 277 The vapid eighteenth centuryisms of Le Bailly.

century, obs. var. of SENTRY.

1649 *Lanc. Tracts Civil Wars* 223 Walk to the Deansgate, and from thence to the other Centuries, using his best encouragements to prop up their hearts. **1759** ROBERTSON *Hist. Scotl.* I. II. 87 Having placed Centuries at door of the Cardinals apartment.

century, obs. form of CENTAURY.

ceny. *Obs.* [ad. F. *signe*, SIGN.] = SIGN.

c **1440** *Promp. Parv.* 66 Ceny, or tokyn, *signum. Ibid.* Ceny, or tokyn of an in or ostrye, *texera.*

cenyth, obs. form of ZENITH.

ceol, the OE. original of KEEL, q.v.

ceorl (cɛəɹl, tʃɛəɹl), the OE. original of CHURL; often retained by historical writers, to avoid the associations of the later form: An Old English freeman of the lowest class, opposed on one side to a *thane* or nobleman, on the other to the servile classes.

a **1000** *Laws of Eth.* vii. 21 (Thorpe I. 334) We witan ðæt þurh Godes ȝyfe, præl wearþ to þeȝene, and ceorl wearþ to eorle. **1611** SPEED *Theat. Gt. Brit.* ii. (1614) 4/1 Ceorle or Churle of their yeomanly condition. **1650** ELDERFIELD *Tythes* 85 Every ceorle or husbandman. **1735–8** BOLINGBROKE *Parties* 193 The Ceorles were Freemen to all Intents and Purposes. **1761** HUME *Hist. Eng.* I. App. i. 95 If the person killed be a clown or ceorle. **1867** FREEMAN *Norm. Conq.* (ed. 3) I. iii. 97 The ceorl was..sinking into the villain. **1875** BRYCE *Holy Rom. Emp.* viii. 132 In England all who did not become thanes were classed as ceorls.

'cep, 'cept, shortened colloq. forms of EXCEPT *prep.* and *conj.*

1851 H. MAYHEW *Lond. Labour* I. 268 One gets reconciled to anything, 'cept, to a man like me, a low lodging-house. **1867** *Goodwife at Home* 6 But never gyangs it o'er my hawse, 'Cep at an antren time. **1898** J. D. BRAYSHAW *Slum Silhouettes* 4 They all gits aht somehow, 'cept me. **1932** W. FAULKNER *Light in August* xiv. 306 You couldn't hear what Brother Bedenberry was saying, cep he never tried to hit back nor nothing. **1967** A. WILSON *No Laughing Matter* III. 305 I don't know anyone who cooks better. Well, cept my Mum did, of course. **1967** L. FORRESTER *Girl called Fathom* xiv. 180 That's all I can tell you for now... Cept..there's one more reason I'm takin' you along.

ce'paceous, cæ-, *a.* ? *Obs.* [f. L. *cæpa*, *cēpa*, onion; see -ACEOUS.] Of the nature of an onion.

1657 TOMLINSON *Renou's Disp.* 305 Scilla is cæpacious.

‖**cèpe** (sɛːp). Also **cep** (sɛp). [a. F. *cèpe* a boletus, f. Gascon *cep* tree-trunk, mushroom, f. L. *cippus* a stake.] An edible fungus of the genus *Boletus*.

1865 M. EYRE *Lady's Walks* xxix. 316 Stew it whole in *vin ordinaire*, together with some ham, a little butter, a *little* garlic, mushrooms or *ceps*, and a little salt. **1898** *U.S. Dept. Agric. Yearbk. 1897* 465 To this genus [*sc.* Boletus] belong the fungi known in France as *cèpes*, under which they are imported into this country. **1924** 'A. D. SEDGWICK' *Little French Girl* I. i. 6 Alix was sometimes allowed to go to the forest with her and find *cèpes*. **1959** *Times Lit. Suppl.* 27 Feb. 113/4 The dark-headed *fungo porcino*, the cep, *Boletus edulis*, was called *suillus* by the Romans.

cephal- ('sɛfəl), combining form of Gr. κεφαλή head, as **'cephalad** *adv. Zool.* [-AD], towards the head; **cepha'letron** (sɛfə'liːtrɒn) *Zool.* [Gr. ἦτρον abdomen], Owen's name for the head or anterior division of the body of some of the crustaceans, as the king-crab; hence ***cephaletral*** adj.; **ˌcephalhæma'toma** *Path.*, a bloody swelling beneath the pericranium; **cephal'hydrocele** *Path.*, a serous or watery swelling outside the cranium; **cepha'lotic** *a. Biol.* [Gr. ὠτ-, οὖς ear], characterized by the presence of the ears on the middle line of the head.

1887 WILDER in *Amer. Nat.* June 545 In Ceratodus alone ..is there a prerima,—that is, a rima extending cephalad from the margin of the porta. **1872** Cephaletral [see *thoracetral* s.v. THORACO-]. **1872** Cephaletron [see *thoracetron* s.v. THORACO-]. **1900** DORLAND *Med. Dict.* 147/1 Cephalhematoma. **1962** *Lancet* 6 Jan. 54/1 There were 2 cases of cephalhaematoma (5·2%), which resolved by the age of 1 month. **1900** DORLAND *Med. Dict.* 147/1 Cephalhydrocele. **1908** *Practitioner* Apr. 466 The conditions necessary for the formation of a cephalhydrocele are a fracture with laceration of the dura. **1894** W. BATESON *Stud. Variation* 458 Dareste also declares that the cephalotic state is similarly first indicated by a premature union of the folds in the region of the medulla.

cephalalgic (sɛfə'lældʒɪk), *a.* (*sb.*) [f. next + -IC.]

A. *adj.* Of, pertaining to, or affected with head-ache. **B.** *sb.* A medicine for head-ache.

1727 SWIFT *Gulliver* III. vi. 216 Administer to each of them..cephalalgics. (In mod. Dicts.)

cephalalgy ('sɛfəlældʒɪ). Forms: 6 **cephalarge**, 7 **-alge**, 7–8 **-algie**, 8–9 **-algy**. Also 7– **cephalalgia.** [ad. L. *cephalalgia*, a. Gr. κεφαλαλγία (found also as *cephalargia*, κεφαλαργία), f. κεφαλή head + -αλγία pain, ache, f. ἄλγος pain; cf. F. *cephalalgie*. Now usually, as a medical term, in L. form.] Head-ache.

1547 BOORDE *Brev. Health* lxviii. 29 Cephalarge or an universal peyne in the head. **1607** TOPSELL *Four-f. Beasts* 61 He is troubled with a Cephalalgie; that is, a pain in his head. **1669** W. SIMPSON *Hydrol. Chym.* 75 Spasms, Convulsions, Cephalalgia's. **1681** tr. *Willis' Rem. Med. Wks.* Voc., Cephalalge, the head-ach. **1822** *New Monthly Mag.* V. 110 Dividing their discourses into heads..which always afflicts me with a Cephalalgy. **1878** HABERSHON *Dis. Abdomen* 5 In indigestion, we find cephalalgia.

‖**cepha'lanthium.** *Bot.* [mod.L., f. Gr. κεφαλή + ἄνθος flower.] 'Name by L. C. Richard for the compound flower of Linnæus, the head or capitulum of modern botanists' (*Syd. Soc. Lex.*).

1880 GRAY *Bot. Text-bk.* 401 Cephalanthium..A synonym of ANTHODIUM.

Hence **cepha'lanthous**, *a. Bot.* having flowers united in heads, as in the *Compositæ*.

cepha'lartic, *a.*, [? shortened from CEPHALOCATHARTIC.] 'Having power to purge or clear the head' (*Syd. Soc. Lex.*).

‖**Cepha'laspis.** *Palæont.* [mod.L., f. Gr. κεφαλή + ἀσπίς shield, buckler.] A genus of fossil ganoid fishes found in the Old Red Sandstone, having a large buckler-shaped plate attached to the head: also called *buckler-heads*.

1842 H. MILLER *O.R. Sandst.* vii. (ed. 2) 161 The Cephalaspis is one of the most curious ichthyolites of the system.

Hence **cepha'laspean, cephala'spidean** *adjs.*

1854 H. MILLER *Sch. & Schm.* xxiv. (1857) 527 The Cephalaspean genera, too..greatly puzzled me. **1872** W. SYMONDS *Rec. Rocks* vi. 202 The little Cephalaspidean fish.

cephalate ('sɛfələt). *Zool.* [f. Gr. κεφαλή + -ATE[2]. Cf. F. *céphalé* adj.] A mollusc having a distinct head, or belonging to the Encephalous division (*Cephalata*).

1862 DANA *Man. Geol.* 155 The ordinary Mollusks are usually divided into..The Cephalates, having a head.

cephaleonomancy, improp. form for **cepha'lonoˌmancy.** [f. CEPHALO- + Gr. ὄνο-ς ass + μαντεία divination.] = *cephalomancy* (in CEPHALO-): see quot.

1652 GAULE *Magastrom.* 165 Cephaleonomancy, [pretending to divine] by broyling of an Asses head. **1807** SOUTHEY *Espriella's Lett.* (1814) III. 28 Cephaleonomancy, or the art of divination by an ass's head, is a species of art magic which still flourishes in England.

cephalic (sɪ'fælɪk), *a.* (*sb.*) [a. F. *céphalique*, ad. L. *cephalicus*, a. Gr. κεφαλικός belonging to the head, f. κεφαλή head.]

1. Of or pertaining to the head, situated in the head; of the nature of a head.

a. *Phys.* and *Biol.*

cephalic artery: the common carotid artery on either side. ***cephalic ganglia***: the anterior ganglia of the nervous chord in Arthropoda and Mollusca, answering to the brain of higher animals. ***cephalic index***: a number indicating the ratio of the transverse to the longitudinal diameter of the skull. ***cephalic-median*** (or ***median cephalic***) ***vein***: 'the outer..division of the median vein which joins with the radial vein to form the cephalic vein' (*Syd. Soc. Lex.*). ***cephalic vein***: the principal vein of the arm, so called because the opening of this vein was anciently supposed to relieve disorders of the head.

1599 A. M. tr. *Gabelhouer's Bk. Physicke* 1/2 The Cephalick vayne on the hande, behinde the thumbe. **1681** tr. *Willis' Rem. Med. Wks.* Voc., Cephalic arterie consists of two branches which, springing out of the great artery, ascend up into the head. **1766** G. CANNING *Anti-Lucretius* v. 401 Order reigns in each cephalick cell. **1836** TODD *Cycl. Anat.* I. 763/1 Each pair is a counterpart of..every other pair, without even excepting the cephalic ganglion. **1852** DANA *Crust.* I. 34 There is sometimes a cephalic segment. **1866** HUXLEY *Preh. Rem. Caithn.* 83 The cephalic index. **1871** DARWIN *Desc. Man* I. x. 370 A single cephalic horn. **1872** W. R. GREG *Enigmas* ii. 85 *note*, Barren marriages..so frequent among persons of preponderatingly cephalic temperaments.

b. in general sense. (Chiefly *humorous.*)

1650 BULWER *Anthropomet.* i. (1653) 2 The first Cephalique Fashion-mongers..so called, because there were found many Macrocephali, that is, such Long Heads, as no other Nation had the like. **1837** SYD. SMITH *Let. Singleton*, The objection of certain cephalic animalcula to the use of small-tooth combs. **1844** G. S. FABER *Eight Dissert.* (1845) II. 382 The Cephalic Teraphim of the Rabbins. *a* **1845** BARHAM *Ingol. Leg.* (1876) 370 Spinning away on his cephalic pivot.

2. Curing or relieving disorders of the head.

1656 RIDGLEY *Pract. Physic* 169 With Cephalick powders. **1707** FARQUHAR *Beaux' Strat.* III. i, Shall I send to your Mother, Child, for a little of her Cephalick Plaister to put to the Soals of your Feet? **1776** WITHERING *Bot. Arrangem.* (1796) I. 270 The plants..are odoriferous, cephalic, and resolvent. **1813** MAR. EDGEWORTH *Patron.* I. xx. 351 He ordered some cephalic snuff to be administered.

B. *sb.* **1.** A cephalic remedy.

1656 RIDGLEY *Pract. Physic* 56 Conserve of Roses.. mingled with hot Cephalicks. **1756** P. BROWNE *Jamaica* 117 It is a gentle cephalic and diaphoretic.

2. Short for *cephalic snuff*.

1828 *Blackw. Mag.* XXIII. 182 Take a pinch of cephalic from the little agate box. **1834** BECKFORD *Italy* II. 165 A pinch of her best cephalic.

†**ce'phalical**, *a. Obs.* [f. as prec. + -AL[1].] = prec., in various senses.

1599 A. M. tr. *Gabelhouer's Bk. Physicke* 54/1 Phlebotomize also the Cephalicalle vayne. **1658** A. FOX *Wurtz' Surg.* III. vi. 234 The medicine must be Cephalical.

Hence **ce'phalically** *adv.*, in relation to the head.

1852 DANA *Crust.* II. 1412 Number of annuli cephalically absorbed. **1874** —— *Text-Bk. Geol.* 342 Improvement in the..organs of the head, that is, cephalically.

cephalin[1] (ˈsɛfəlɪn). *Zool.* [ad. F. *céphalin* (A. Schneider 1875, in *Arch. Zool. Exp. Gen.* IV. 518), f. Gr. κεφαλή head + -IN[1].] = CEPHALONT.
1888 ROLLESTON & JACKSON *Anim. Life* 858 A Polycystid possessing all three segments is known as a Cephalin or Cephalont. **1912** E. A. MINCHIN *Introd. Study Protozoa* xiv. 326 In the earlier phase, in which an epimerite is present, the parasite was termed by Aimé Schneider a cephalont ('cephalin').

cephalin[2] (ˈsɛfəlɪn). *Biochem.* [f. CEPHAL- + -IN[1].] Now the usual spelling of KEPHALIN: a phospholipid similar to lecithin, originally isolated from brain-tissue and capable of accelerating the coagulation of blood.
1900 in DORLAND *Med. Dict.* **1920** J. J. R. MACLEOD *Physiol. & Biochem.* (ed. 2) lxxvii. 689 Other phospholipins present in nervous tissue are cephalin, cuorin and sphingomyelin. **1961** *Lancet* 5 Aug. 286/2 In normal plasma 50–55% of the protein-bound calcium is bound to albumin, and the rest mainly to globulin and cephalins. **1964** *Oceanogr. & Marine Biol.* II. 173 Plasmalogens..are closely related to the classical lecithin (phosphatidyl choline) and cephalin (phosphatidyl ethanolamine).

cephaˈlistic, *a. rare.* [f. Gr. κεφαλή + -IST + -IC.] Pertaining to the head. Improper synonym of CEPHALIC.
18.. I. TAYLOR (in Ogilvie) A cranium, the cephalistic head-quarters of sensation.

‖**cephalitis** (sɛfəˈlaɪtɪs). *Med.* [f. Gr. κεφαλή + -ITIS.] 'Inflammation of the brain and its membranes; all inflammatory conditions of the central nervous system' (*Syd. Soc. Lex.*).
1811 HOOPER *Med. Dict.* **1888** F. VACHET *Infanticide* 4 Deaths..ascribed to convulsions, cephalitis, meningitis.

cephalization (ˌsɛfəlaɪˈzeɪʃən). *Biol.* [f. as if from a vb. **cephalize* (f. Gr. κεφαλή + -IZE) + -ATION: cf. *specialization*.] A term introduced by Dana to express the degree to which the head is developed and dominates over the rest of the body.
1864 *Q. Jrnl. Sc.* I. 523 Mr. James D. Dana has continued the publication of his memoir on the classification of animals, based on the principle of Cephalization. **1880** *Libr. Univ. Knowl.* III. 632 Degrees of cephalization may be illustrated by the subdivisions of the mammalia.
So **ˈcephalized** *a.*, organized with a head, having the head developed.
1862 DANA *Man. Geol.* 596 Cephalized species.

cephalo- (ˈsɛfələʊ), combining form of Gr. κεφαλή head, used as the first element in many technical words:
a. in combinations, such as **ˌcephalo-ˈbranchiate** *a.* [see BRANCHIATE], having gills upon the head; **ˌcephalo-caˈthartic** *a.*, 'purging the head' (*Syd. Soc. Lex.*); **ˌcephalo-exˈtractor**, an instrument for extracting a fœtus by the head; **ˌcephalo-ˈhumeral** *a.* [see HUMERAL], name of a muscle in the horse and other animals, analogous to the cleido-mastoid part of the sterno-cleido-mastoid in man; **ˌcephalo-ˈorbital** *a.* [see ORBITAL], see quot.; **ˌcephalo-phaˈryngeal** *a.* [see PHARYNGEAL], relating to the head and pharynx; **ˌcephalo-rhaˈchidian** *a.* [Gr. ῥάχις spine], belonging to the head and the spine, cerebro-spinal; **ˌcephalo-ˈspinal** *a.*, bad synonym of prec.
b. in derivative formations, as **ˈcephalocele** [see CELE], a tumour in the head. **ˈcephalograph** [Gr. -γραφος writer], an instrument by which the contour of the head may be reproduced on paper. **cephaˈlography** [Gr. -γραφία writing], a description of the head. **ˌcephalohæˈmometer** [Gr. αἷμα blood + μέτρον measure], an instrument for measuring variations of blood-pressure in the head. **cephaˈlology**, 'a treatise on the head' (*Syd. Soc. Lex.*). †**ˈcephaloˌmancy** [Gr. μαντεία divination], divination by means of a head (see quot.). **ˈcephalomant** [Gr. μάντις diviner], a professor of cephalomancy. **cephaˈlometer** [Gr. μέτρον measure], 'an instrument formerly used for ascertaining the size of the fœtal head during parturition; also, an instrument used in the measurement of the different angles of the skull' (*Syd. Soc. Lex.*). **cephaˈlophorous** *a.* [Gr. -φορος bearing], having a distinct head, applied to the Cephalates among molluscs. **cephaˈlopterous** *a.* [Gr. πτέρον wing], having a winged or feathered head. **ˈcephaloˌstat** [Gr. στατός standing], a head-rest; an instrument for fixing the head during an operation. **cephaˈlostegite** [Gr. στέγειν to cover closely + -ITE], 'the anterior division of the large calcified dorsal shield of *Podophthalmia*' (*Syd. Soc. Lex.*). **ˌcephaloˈtaxus** [L. *taxus* yew], *Bot.*, a genus of Conifers, called *Cluster-flowered Yew*, natives of N. China and Japan. **ˈcephaloˌtome** [Gr. -τομος adj., cutting], 'an instrument for cutting or breaking down the head of the fœtus in the operation of embryotomy' (*Syd. Soc. Lex.*). **cephaˈlotomist** [see -IST], one skilled in cephalotomy. **cephaˈlotomy** [Gr. -τομία sb., cutting], the dissection of the head; also, the operation mentioned under *cephalotome*. **ˌcephaloˈtractor**, a term for the midwifery forceps. **ˈcephaloˌtribe** [Gr. τρίβειν to rub, bruise], an instrument used in cephalotripsy. **ˈcephaloˌtripsy** [Gr. τρῖψις rubbing, bruising], the operation of crushing the head of the fœtus with a cephalotribe, in cases of difficult delivery.
1871 W. A. HAMMOND *Dis. Nerv. Syst.* 56 Experiments with the *cephalo-hæmometer. **1881** MIVART *Cat* 137 The origin of the *cephalo-humeral. *a* **1693** URQUHART *Rabelais* III. xxv, *Cephalomancy, often practised amongst the High Germans in their boiling of an Asses Head upon burning Coals. **1860** READE *Eighth Commandm.* 202 The *cephalomant is he who opposes a priori reasoning, or mere assumption, to direct evidence, present or accessible. **1878** BARTLEY tr. *Topinard's Anthrop.* II. iii. 296 A special *cephalometer. *Ibid.* II. ii. 232 The sum of the volume of both orbits thus obtained he compares with the cerebral capacity. This is the *cephalo-orbital index. **1839–47** TODD *Cycl. Anat.* III. 945/2 This aponeurosis, named *cephalo-pharyngeal. *Ibid.* V. 106/1 The *cephalorachidian fluid. **1870** ROLLESTON *Anim. Life* 91 The anterior portion of the cerapace is called the *cephalostegite. **1883** *Harper's Mag.* Apr. 726/2 A *cephalotaxus—a yew-like Japanese plant—with very light foliage. **1869** *Eng. Mech.* 19 Mar. 577/2 A *cephalotomist and neurologist. **1836–9** TODD *Cycl. Anat.* II. 332/2 The necessity of performing *cephalotomy. **1860** CHURCHILL *Midwifery* 366 M. Baudeloque junr. has invented an instrument which he calls a '*cephalotribe'. **1876** LEISHMAN *Midwifery* xxxii, *Cephalotripsy.

cephalodiscus (ˌsɛfələʊˈdɪskəs). [mod.L. (W. C. M'Intosh 1882, in *Ann. & Mag. Nat. Hist.* 5th Ser. X. 337), f. Gr. κεφαλή head (see CEPHALO-) + δίσκος DISC.] A member of the genus so named of primitive deep-sea chordates of the class Pterobranchia.
1882 M'INTOSH in *Ann. & Mag. Nat. Hist.* X. 343 *Cephalodiscus* also diverges in regard to the thin postoral lamella. **1885** *Encycl. Brit.* XIX. 435/1 The dwelling of Cephalodiscus is a gelatinous, irregularly branched, and fimbriated mass. **1915** E. R. LANKESTER *Divers. Naturalist* 8 One of the most interesting deep-sea creatures discovered by the 'Challenger'..received the name Cephalodiscus. **1955** N. J. BERRILL *Orig. Vertebrates* xi. 117 Cephalodiscus, Rhabdopleura, and balanoglossids seem never to have become completely sessile forms.

cephaloid (ˈsɛfəlɔɪd), *a.* [a. Gr. κεφαλοειδής head-shaped: see -OID.] Shaped like a head; 'in *Bot.* having the appearance of a *capitulum*'.
1847 in CRAIG.

cephalon (ˈsɛfələn). *Zool.* [mod.L., f. Gr. κεφαλή head: cf. ENCEPHALON.] The region of the head in certain arthropods.
1875 HUXLEY & MARTIN *Elem. Biol.* xii. 123 An anterior division, which belongs to the head or cephalon. **1945** T. H. SAVORY *Spiders Brit. Isles* (ed. 2) 199 Cephalon short, broader than long, smooth.

cephalont (ˈsɛfələnt). *Zool.* [f. CEPHAL- + Gr. ὀντ-, ὤν, pres. pple. of εἶναι to be, exist.] A protozoan parasite at the stage of development in which an epimerite is attached to the anterior cyst.
1885 *Encycl. Brit.* XIX. 854/1 The epimerite serves to attach the parasite to its host... The phase in which it is present is called a 'cephalont', the phase after it has broken off a 'sporont'. **1888** [see CEPHALIN[1]]. **1961** MACKINNON & HAWES *Introd. Study Protozoa* III. 183 Such fully developed trophozoites are called cephalonts.

cephalopod (ˈsɛfələpɒd). [prob. a. mod.F. *cephalopode, -es*, ad. mod.L. *cephalopoda*: see next.] An animal of the class *Cephalopoda*.
1826 KIRBY & SPENCE *Entomol.* (1828) IV. xlv. 243 The Cephalopods have no smell. **1835–6** TODD *Cycl. Anat.* I. 519/2 Cephalopods resembling the Nautilus. **1881** *Modern Rev.* II. No. 5. 45 The habits of a cephalopod.

‖**cephalopoda** (sɛfəˈlɒpədə), *sb. pl. Zool.* [mod.L., f. Gr. κεφαλή head + πούς (ποδ-) foot. For the sing. *cephalopod* or *cephalopodan* is used.]
The most highly organized class of *Mollusca*, characterized by a distinct head with 'arms' or tentacles attached to it; comprising Cuttle-fishes, the Nautilus, etc., and numerous fossil species.
1802 *Med. Jrnl.* VIII. 372 The cuttlefish, one of the cephalopoda. **1851** RICHARDSON *Geol.* viii. 230 The Cephalopoda have..their locomotive organs arranged round the head, in the form of eight or more arms or tentacula.
Hence **cephaˈlopodal**, **ˌcephaloˈpodic** *adjs.* = next.; **cephaˈlopodan** *a.*, in same sense; *sb.* = CEPHALOPOD.
1885 A. STEWART *Twixt Ben Nevis & Gl.* iii. 25 Arrived at the years of Cephalopodal discretion. **1854** HUXLEY in Woodward *Mollusca* (1856) 447 It takes on the cephalopodic form. **1859** DARWIN *Orig. Spec.* xiv. (1872) 390 The cephalopodic character.

cephalopodous (sɛfəˈlɒpədəs), *a.* [f. prec. + -OUS.] Belonging to the *Cephalopoda*; pertaining to or characteristic of a cephalopod.
1833 *Blackw. Mag.* XXXIV. 392. **1877** HUXLEY *Anat. Inv. An.* viii. 528 The apparent resemblances between the cephalodous and the vertebrate eye.

cephalosporin (ˌsɛfələʊˈspɔərɪn). [f. mod.L. *Cephalosporium* (see below) + -IN[1].] Any of several antibiotic substances, closely related to penicillin, developed from *Cephalosporium*, a genus of fungi.
1951 A. C. RITCHIE et al. in *Brit. Jrnl. Pharmacol.* VI. 430 Cephalosporin P_1 is an antibiotic from a species of *Cephalosporium*... The cephalosporin used was lyophil-dried material that had been prepared by chromatography and countercurrent distribution between solvents. **1961** *Times* 14 Sept. 8/3 Cephalosporin N is stated to be a new form of penicillin. **1964** M. HYNES *Med. Bacteriol.* (ed. 8) x. 136 The cephalosporins can be given to penicillin-sensitive patients.
Hence **cephaloˈsporinase** (see quots.).
1963 *New Scientist* 11 July 94/1 In bacteria that respond to cephalosporin treatment the enzymes, called cephalosporinases, have not been demonstrated. **1964** *Ibid.* 12 Nov. 431/3 Anti-cephalosporin enzymes, cephalosporinases..are found among some types of pathogenic bacteria.

cephalot, -ote (ˈsɛfəlɒt, -əʊt). *Chem.* [in F. *cephalote*, f. Gr. κεφαλή head.] 'A name applied by Couerbe to a yellow elastic fatty substance, insoluble in alcohol, but soluble in ether, which he obtained from the brain' (Watts *Dict. Chem.*).

cephalothorax (ˌsɛfələʊˈθɔəræks). *Zool.* [f. Gr. κεφαλή head + THORAX; see quot. 1835.] The anterior division of the body, consisting of the coalesced head and thorax, in certain *Arachnida* and *Crustacea* (as common spiders and crabs).
1835 KIRBY *Hab. & Inst. Anim.* The head and trunk..forming together what he [Latreille] names a cephalothorax. **1861** J. BLACKWALL *Hist. Spiders* I. Introd. 1 Spiders, with few exceptions, have a cephalo-thorax. **1880** HUXLEY *Cray-Fish* 19 The fore part is termed the Cephalothorax.
Hence **ˌcephalothoˈracic** *a.*
1851 RICHARDSON *Geol.* viii. 260 The King-Crabs..have the body covered with a large cephalo-thoracic shield. **1859** TODD *Cycl. Anat.* V. 299/1 The cephalo-thoracic division.

cephalous (ˈsɛfələs), *a.* [f. Gr. κεφαλ-ή head + -OUS.] = CEPHALATE.
1874 CARPENTER *Ment. Phys.* I. ii. (1879) 49 In the Cephalous Mollusks, we always find a pair of ganglia situated in the head.

Cepheid (ˈsɛfiːɪd, ˈsiːfiːɪd), *a.* and *sb. Astr.* Also **cepheid.** [f. L. *Cēpheus*, Gr. Κηφεύς Cepheus, a mythical king whose name was given to a constellation + -ID[2].] **A.** *adj.* Pertaining to or resembling the variable star δ Cephei. **B.** *sb.* A variable star of the type of δ Cephei.
1904 *Astrophys. Jrnl.* XX. 184 Spectroscopic studies of *Cepheid* variables. **1921** *Discovery* Feb. 38/1 To determine the absolute magnitude..of every Cepheid variable in the heavens. **1927** *Glasgow Herald* 7 Oct. 11/2 When a Cepheid's period was noted its brightness could be stated. **1927** A. S. EDDINGTON *Stars & Atoms* 93 In 1924 Hubble discovered a number of Cepheid variables in the great Andromeda nebula. **1964** *Yearbk. Astr. 1965* 149 It has been found that the longer the period of a Cepheid, the greater its real luminosity. If one knows how bright a star really is and how bright it appears, one can at once deduce its distance. Cepheids therefore act as standard candles among the stars.

†**ˈcephen.** *Obs.* [a. Gr. κηφήν drone-bee.] A drone-bee.
[**1601** HOLLAND *Pliny* I. 318 The Drones at the beginning be termed Sirenes or Cephenes.] **1609** C. BUTLER *Fem. Mon.* I. (1623) C iij, They will..call out the Drones, yea and pull out the Cephens that are shut vp in the cells. **1657** S. PURCHAS *Pol. Flying-Ins.* 21 They lay their Cephen-seeds in a wide comb by themselves.

ceˈpivorous, *a. nonce-wd.* [f. L. *cēpa* onion + *-vor-us* devouring + -OUS.] Feeding on onions.
1864 WEBSTER cites STERLING for *cepevorous.*

cepotaph (ˈsiːpəʊtɑːf, -æ-). *rare.* [ad. Gr. κηποτάφιον, f. κῆπος garden + τάφος tomb.] (See quot.)
1846 C. MAITLAND *Ch. in Catacombs* iii. 67 The word cepotaph is derived from the Greek κηποτάφιον, a tomb in a garden. As the cinerary urns occupied but little space..the ashes of the dead were generally deposited in the garden or courtyard of the house.

†**ˈcepous**, *a. Obs.* [f. L. *cæpa, cēpa*, onion + -OUS.] Like an onion; bulbous.
1657 TOMLINSON *Renou's Disp.* 265 Its root is cepous, crass and white.

‖**ceppo** (ˈtʃeppo). [It.] The cemented glacial gravels of northern Italy.
1881 J. GEIKIE *Prehistoric Europe* 316 Those wide-spread masses of conglomerate, which are called *Ceppo* by the Italian geologists. **1894** —— *Gt. Ice Age* (ed. 3) xxxiv. 562 The highly denuded 'Ceppo' underlying the great terminal moraines of Ivræa, Como, etc.

'cept: see 'CEP.

† **'ceptionable**, *a. Obs. rare*⁻¹. Shortened form of EXCEPTIONABLE.
1702 *Eng. Theophrast.* 23 Judges in their own case, being suspected of Partiality, are therefore ceptionable.

cepture, -tyr, obs. forms of SCEPTRE.

ceraceous (sɪˈreɪʃəs), *a.* [f. L. *cēra* wax + -ACEOUS.] Of the nature of wax, waxy.
1768 TUCKER *Lt. Nat.* (1852) I. 389 Ceraceous injections. **1796** DE SERRA in *Phil. Trans.* LXXXVI. 502 An aggregate of solid parts, of a ceraceous appearance.

ce'raginous, *a.* [? f. next.]
1657 TOMLINSON *Renou's Disp.* 407 Pliny mentions another sort..which he refers to ceraginous honey.

cerago (sɪˈreɪgəʊ). [f. L. *cēra* wax.] Bee-bread.
1839 in CRABB; also in later Dicts.

cerain (ˈsɪəreɪɪn). *Chem.* [f. L. *cēra* wax + -IN.] 'A name applied by Boudet and Boissenot to the portion of beeswax which is sparingly soluble in alcohol, and, according to their statement, is not saponified by potash. It appears to be chiefly impure myricin' (Watts *Dict. Chem.*).

ceral (ˈsɪərəl), *a.* [f. (in sense 1) CERE, or (in sense 2) L. *cēr-a* + -AL¹.]
1. Pertaining to the CERE of a bird's bill.
1874 COUES *Birds N.-W.* 605 Ceral longer than the ungual portion of the bill.
2. Relating to wax.
1883 S. WAINWRIGHT *Sci. Sophisms* ix. 181 Had Mr. Darwin lived two thousand years ago, his ceral experiments might have furnished a target for the shafts of Aristophanes.

ceramal (sɛˈræməl). [f. CERAM(IC *a.* + AL(LOY *sb.*] = CERMET.
1949 *Jrnl. R. Aeronaut. Soc.* July 661/1 Combinations of metals and ceramics, termed 'ceramals' by the N.A.C.A., appear to possess outstanding properties at elevated temperatures. **1950** *Engineering* 29 Dec. 577/1 Ceramics or the new metal-ceramic compacts ('ceramals' or 'cermets'). **1953** *Jrnl. Brit. Interplan. Soc.* XII. 266 The development of metal/ceramic mixtures (ceramals or cermets) promises an improvement in these essential properties.

cera'mean, *a. nonce-wd.* [f. Gr. κεραμεύς a potter + -AN.] Of or pertaining to a potter.
1783 BURNEY in *Parr's Wks.* (1828) VII. 386, I praised Potter's Ode exceedingly, even when I had been stark mad at his pompous, saucy, ceramean criticisms.

ceramet, var. CERMET.

ceramic (sɪˈræmɪk), *a.* (*sb.*) Also **keramic**. [ad. Gr. κεραμικός of or for pottery, κεραμική (τέχνη) the potter's art, pottery, f. κέραμος potter's earth, pottery. Cf. F. *céramique*.]
1. Of or pertaining to pottery, *esp.* as an art.
[Not in CRAIG 1847.] **1850** J. MARRYAT *Pottery & Porc.* Introd., The Plastic or Keramic [*ed.* **1868** Ceramic] Art. **1862** THORNBURY *Turner* I. 245 About 1775 Mr. Wedgwood ..began to introduce high art into ceramic manufacture. **1879** *Academy* 38 Imitations of ancient ceramic work.
2. a. As *sb.* in *pl.* The ceramic art, the art of making pottery.
1859 GULLICK & TIMBS *Paint.* 30 Writers on ceramics. **1879** *Academy* 38 (*Article*) Recent Ceramics.
b. As *sb.* (usu. in *sing.*) Products of the ceramic art; pottery.
1880 'MARK TWAIN' *Tramp Abroad* I. xx. 178 My chief solicitude was about my collection of keramics. **1902** *Jrnl. Anthrop. Inst.* XXXII. 373 As..a considerable body of prehistoric pottery has accumulated in our museums, the time has arrived when some attempt should be made to arrange this early ceramic in approximately chronological order. **1932** *Antiquity* VI. 221 The stratification of the ceramic was accurately noted.

ceramicist (sɪˈræmɪsɪst). [f. CERAMIC + -IST.] = CERAMIST.
1930 *Observer* 25 May 18/3 Many countries have great ceramicists capable of building up a great pottery industry.

ceramidium (sɛrəˈmɪdɪəm). *Bot.* [mod.L., f. Gr. κεραμίδιον, dim. of κεραμίς earthen vessel.] The outer covering of the cystocarp, found in algæ of the family Rhodomelaceæ.
1849 W. H. HARVEY *Man. Brit. Marine Algæ* (ed. 2) 69 In the ceramidium the conceptacular fruit is brought to its highest development. This organ is ovate or urn-shaped, furnished with an apical pore, and containing a tuft of pear-shaped spores, rising from the base of the cavity. **1902** *Encycl. Brit.* XXV. 270/1 In *Rhodomelaceæ* there is a special urn-shaped envelope surrounding the sporogenous filaments. This is a ceramidium.

ceramist (ˈsɛrəmɪst). Also **keramist**. [f. CERAM-IC + -IST.] One skilled in making pottery; a ceramic artist.
1855 tr. *Labarte's Arts Mid. Ages* viii. 287 The Keramists of Pesaro. **1865** E. METEYARD *Wedgwood* I. 63 The Italian ceramists. **1875** FORTNUM *Maiolica* xi. 109 An accomplished ceramist of Urbania.

† **'ceramite.** *Obs.* [a. F. *ceramite* (Cotgr.), in both senses, ad. Gr. κεραμῖτις, f. κέραμος (see above).]
1656 BLOUNT *Glossogr.*, *Ceramite*, a precious stone of the colour of Tyle. *a* **1693** URQUHART *Rabelais* III. v, A kind of Potters Earth, which is called *Ceramite*.

cera'mography. [f. Gr. κέραμος + -γραφία writing: see -GRAPHY.] The historical description of pottery.
1853 C. T. NEWTON *Ess. Archæol.* 53 Ceramography presents to the student of art another and special interest.

cerargyrite (sɪˈrɑːdʒɪraɪt). *Min.* [improperly f. Gr. κέρας (κερατ-) horn + ἄργυρος silver + -ITE.] Native chloride of silver, horn silver.
1868 DANA *Min.* 115 Ceratargyrite, the proper derivative, being contracted to cerargyrite.

cerasin (ˈsɛrəsɪn). *Chem.* [f. L. *cerasus* cherry-tree + -IN.] The insoluble portion of the gum which exudes from the cherry, and other trees.
1838 T. THOMSON *Chem. Org. Bodies* 677 Probably arabin was originally in the same state with cerasin. **1854** BALFOUR *Bot.* 29.

† **'cerasine.** *Min. Obs.*
1852 C. SHEPARD *Min.* 441 An old name for both mendipite and phosgenite, which were formerly not separated.

'cerasite. *Min.* Another form of CERASINE.
1844 DANA *Min.* 275.

† **cerast(e.** *Obs.* [a. F. *céraste* (Cotgr.), ad. L. *cerastēs*, a. Gr. κεράστης.] = next.
1572 BOSSEWELL *Armorie* II. 62 b, O. beareth sable, a ceraste nowey d'Argent. This is an horned Serpente, as Isidore saithe. **1608** TOPSELL *Serpents* 732 Cerasts and lean Hæmorrhs are ever lame.

‖ **cerastes** (sɪˈræstiːz). *Zool.* [L. *cerastēs*, a. Gr. κεράστης horned, a horned serpent, f. κέρας horn.] A genus of venomous serpents found in Africa and some parts of Asia, having a projecting scale or 'horn' above each eye; the horned viper. Early and poetic uses are drawn vaguely from Pliny, and other ancient writers, who probably meant a species of the same genus.
1398 TREVISA *Barth. De P.R.* XVIII. xxxi. 794 Cerastes is an hornid serpent. **1591** SYLVESTER *Du Bartas* I. vi. (1641) 51/1 Th' horned Cerastes, th' Alexandrian Skink. **1625** K. LONG tr. *Barclay's Argenis* I. iii. 10 Like the new-horn'd Cerastes, violent. **1667** MILTON *P.L.* x. 525 Cerastes hornd, Hydrus, and Ellops drear. *a* **1711** KEN *Hymnoth.* Wks. 1721 III. 20 As horn'd Cerastes wont to..watch for Mischief in a beaten Road. **1814** CARY *Dante's Inf.* IX. 42 Adders and cerastes crept Instead of hair, and their fierce temples bound. **1863** WOOD *Nat. Hist.* iii. 107 The true Cerastes or Horned Viper is a native of Northern Africa.

cerastium (sɪˈræstɪəm). *Bot.* [mod.L. (Linnæus *Hortus Cliffortianus* (1737) 173), f. Gr. κεράστης horned, from the horn-shaped capsule of many species.] A plant of the caryophyllaceous genus of that name, including the mouse-ear chickweed and other weeds, as well as species cultivated for their silvery foliage.
1799 SOWERBY & SMITH *Eng. Bot.* VIII. 538 This is certainly rather a *Stellaria* than a *Cerastium*. **1829** LOUDON *Encycl. Plants* 1059 Caryophylleæ... Many are common weeds, as most of the Cerastiums, Spergulas, and others. **1925** *Chambers's Jrnl.* Jan. 35/2 He had observed..what he knew to be a very rare cerastium. **1958** F. STARK *Alexander's Path* 150 Drifts of vetch purple and yellow, grey-leaved cerastium, [etc.].

cerate (ˈsɪərət). *Med.* Also 7 cerat. [ad. L. *cērātum* cerate, neut. pa. pple. of *cērāre* to cover with wax, which seems to have in use varied with *cērōtum*, a. Gr. κηρωτόν cerate, neut. of κηρωτός waxed, covered with wax, f. κηροῦν to cover with wax. Cf. F. *cérat* (in Cotgr.), in 16th c. *cérot*.]
A kind of stiff ointment composed of wax together with lard or oil and other ingredients.
1543 TRAHERON *Vigo's Chirurg.* VIII. 199 The description of Oyntments, Cerates, Playsters, etc. **1658** ROWLAND *Moufet's Theat. Ins.* 916 It [wax] is also the ground of all Cerats and Plaisters. **1810** HENRY *Elem. Chem.* (1840) II. 294 Fixed oils unite with wax, and form..cerates.

'cerated, *a.* [f. L. *cerāt-us* waxed (see prec.) + -ED.] 'Waxed, covered with wax' (J.).
1730-6 in BAILEY; thence in JOHNSON and later Dicts.

† **'ceratine**, *a. Obs.*⁻⁰ [ad. L. *ceratina*, or Gr. κερατίνης 'the fallacy called the HORNS, thus stated in Diog. L. VII. 187, εἴ τι οὐκ ἀπέβαλες, τοῦτο ἔχεις· κέρατα δὲ οὐκ ἀπέβαλες· κέρατα ἄρα ἔχεις', If you have not cast a thing (away), you have it: but you have not cast horns; therefore you have horns.]
1656 BLOUNT *Glossogr.*, *Ceratine*, as ceratine arguments, sophistical and intricate arguments. **1678-96** PHILLIPS, *Ceratine*, Horny, as Ceratine Arguments, Horny and subtile Arguments. **1721-1800** BAILEY (from Blount).

ceratinous (sɪˈrætɪnəs), *a.* [f. Gr. κεράτινος of horn, horny (f. κέρας horn) + -OUS.] Of horny structure or nature.
1881 *Athenæum* 18 June 818/1 The existence of ceratinous material in the skeleton.

ceratioid (sɪˈrætɪɔɪd), *a.* and *sb.* Also **ceratoid**. [f. *Ceratias*, a genus of fishes: see -OID.] **A.** *adj.* Of or pertaining to the family Ceratiidæ of fishes (or the genus *Ceratias*.) **B.** *sb.* A fish of this family.
1889 in *Cent. Dict.* **1925** *Glasgow Herald* 21 Mar. 4 The fishes..belong to the Ceratioid section of the Anglers. **1931** *Discovery* Apr. 106/2 Parasitic pigmy males among the ceratoid angler-fishes.

† **ceration.** *Obs.* [ad. med.L. *cērātion-em* in F. *cération*, noun of action f. L. *cērāre* to smear with wax, to wax.] 'Alchemical term for the action of covering anything with wax, or of softening a hard substance..not capable of being liquefied; also, the fixation of mercury' (*Syd. Soc. Lex.*).
1610 B. JONSON *Alch.* II. v, Name the vexations, and the martyrizations of mettalls in the worke..Putrefaction, Solution, Ablution..Calcination, Ceration, and Fixation. **1678** R. R[USSELL] *Geber* II. I. 4. xviii. 139 Ceration is the mollification of an hard Thing not fusible unto Liquefaction. **1721-1800** BAILEY, *Ceration*, among Chymists, the making of a Substance fit to be dissolved, or melted. **1727-51** CHAMBERS *Cycl.*, *Ceration*, in chymistry, the operation of waxing.

ceratite (ˈsɛrətaɪt). [f. Gr. κέρας, κερατ- horn + -ITE.] A fossil Cephalopod, with a discoidal shell having lobed sutures, with the lobes oviculated.
1847 ANSTED *Anc. World* vii. 119 Among the cuttle fish.. there is a curious example..known as the Ceratite.

‖ **ceratium** (sɪˈreɪʃ(ɪ)əm). *Bot.* [L. *ceratium* = *siliqua*, a. Gr. κεράτιον carob-bean, *lit.* little horn, dim. of κέρας horn: the application is modern.]
A long slender one-celled many-seeded superior fruit, shaped like a *siliqua*, but having placentæ alternate with the lobes of the stigma.
1880 GRAY *Bot. Text-bk.* 402 Ceratium, a siliquiform capsule, such as that of Corydalis, Cleome, etc.

† **cerative**, *a. Obs.* [f. L. *cerāt-* ppl. stem of *cerāre* to wax: see -IVE.] That causes ceration. Also as *sb.* a cerative substance.
1650 ASHMOLE *Chym. Collect.* 51 Oil it self, the cerative of all Elements. **1678** R. R[USSELL] tr. *Geber* IV. xxiii. 269 Our other Philosophical Cerative Water.

cerato- (ˈsɛrətəʊ), combining form of Gr. κέρας, κερατ- horn, used chiefly to denote relation to a cornu or horn, as of the hyoid bone, or to the cornea; as in **cerato-branchial** (-ˈbræŋkɪəl), *a. Anat.* [Gr. βράγχια gills], epithet of one of the main portions of permanent branchial cartilage in fishes and Amphibia; where there are only two segments the lower is the cerato-branchial. **ceratocele** (-siːl), *Pathol.* [Gr. κήλη tumour, rupture], a hernia of the cornea of the eye. **cerato-glossal** (-ˈglɒsəl), *a. Anat.* [Gr. γλῶσσα tongue], pertaining to the cerato-glossus muscle. **cerato-glossus** (-ˈglɒsəs), 'that part of the hyoglossus muscle which arises from the cornu of the hyoid bone' (*Syd. Soc. Lex.*). **cerato-hyal** (-ˈhaɪəl), *a.* [see HYOID], the part of the hyoid arch in mammals below the styloid process. **cerato-hyoid** (-ˈhaɪɔɪd), *a.*, epithet of a bundle of muscular fibres (see quot.). **cerato'phyllous**, *a.* [Gr. φύλλον leaf], horn-leaved; having simple, linear, subulate leaves. **'ceratophyte** (-faɪt), *Zool.* [Gr. φυτόν plant; cf. *zoophyte*], a kind of coral polyp, the internal axis of which has the appearance of wood or horn. **'ceratoplasty** (-ˌplæstɪ), *Med.* [Gr. πλάσσειν to form, mould], 'the artificial restoration of the cornea'. **'ceratostome** (-stəʊm), *Bot.* [Gr. στόμα mouth], 'a perithecium with an elongated and firm-walled neck'. **'ceratotome** (-təʊm), [Gr. -τομος cutting], 'a knife for dividing the cornea' (*Syd. Soc. Lex.*).
1849-52 TODD *Cycl. Anat.* IV. 1144/2 Each arch.. consists of a short inferior piece..surmounted by a long, curved piece, the cerato-branchial. **1880** GUNTHER *Fishes* 58 The next much longer one, the ceratobranchial. **1849-52** TODD *Cycl. Anat.* IV. 1150/2, I would suggest the name of Cerato-glossal for it. *Ibid.* 1133/1 The cerato-glossus arising from the greater cornua. *Ibid.* 1144/1 Two long and stout cylindrical pieces, the cerato-hyals. **1854** R. OWEN in *Circ. Sc.* (*c.* 1165) II. 52/1 The ceratohyal part of the hæmapophysis. **1849-52** TODD *Cycl. Anat.* IV. 1150/2 A cerato-hyoid passing from the posterior cornua to the uro-hyal.

ceratodus (sɪˈrætədəs). *Zool.* [mod.L., f. Gr. κέρας, κερατ- horn + ὀδούς tooth.] A popular name for the Australian lungfish, *Neoceratodus*

forsteri, belonging to the order Dipteriformes; also, a genus of fossil fish related to this lungfish.
1874 DARWIN *Desc. Man* (ed. 2) I. ii. 37 The opinion lately advanced by Dr. Günther on the paddle of Ceratodus. **1897** E. R. LANKESTER in *Times* 8 Feb. 10/6 The larval stages of the remarkable fish ceratodus of Queensland. **1899** *Daily News* 10 Apr. 8/2 The ceratodus, a fish with lungs, which, though its fossil remains are scattered over the world, is now confined to two rivers in the south of Queensland, the Mary and the Burnett.

ceratosaurus (ˌsɛrətəʊˈsɔːrəs). [mod.L., f. Gr. κέρας, κερατ- horn + -o + σαῦρος lizard.] In full *Ceratosaurus nasicornus*, an extinct dinosaurian reptile such as those reconstructed from remains found in the Upper Jurassic rocks of Colorado.
1884 O. C. MARSH in *Amer. Jrnl. Sci.* XXVII. 330 This interesting fossil is quite distinct from any hitherto described, and as it represents a new genus and species, may be called *Ceratosaurus nasicornis*. It also belongs to a new family, which may be named the *Ceratosauridæ*. *Ibid.* 333 The brain in *Ceratosaurus* was of medium size, but comparatively much larger than in the herbivorous Dinosaurs. **1892** H. N. HUTCHINSON *Extinct Monsters* vi. 79 Externally, also, the Ceratosaurus differs from other members of the Carnivorous group. **1930** *Discovery* Nov. 386/2 The bipedal dinosaurs were of two kinds, vegetable feeders and flesh eaters. The ceratosaurus was one of the latter, and derives its name from the short bony horn on its nose.

ˈcerature. ? *Obs.* [ad. L. *cērātūra* a waxing, f. *cērāre* to wax.] The application of a cerate.
1730-6 BAILEY, *Cerature*, a dressing.

ceraunics (sɪˈrɔːnɪks), *sb. pl. rare.* [f. Gr. κεραυνός thunderbolt + -ICS: see -IC.] That branch of physics which treats of heat and electricity.
In mod. Dicts.

†**ceraunite** (sɪˈrɔːnaɪt). *Obs.* [ad. Gr. κεραυνίτης (λίθος), f. κεραυνός thunderbolt.] 'Thunderstone': applied by some early mineralogists to a meteorite or to meteoric iron; by others to belemnites, and to flint arrow-heads of prehistoric times viewed as 'thunder-bolts'.
1814 T. ALLAN *Min. Nomen.* 10 Ceraunite (used as a synonym of meteoric iron or stone). **1822** P. CLEVELAND *Min.* 269 Ceraunite, or thunderstone often belongs to jasper.

ceraunoscope (sɪˈrɔːnəskəʊp). [ad. Gr. κεραυνοσκοπεῖον a machine for producing stage-thunder.] An apparatus used by the ancients in their mysteries to imitate thunder and lightning.
1827 MOORE *Epicurean* (1839) 220 *note*, Imitations of the noise of earthquake and thunder..by means of the Ceraunoscope, and other such contrivances.

‖**cerbas.** *Obs.* A supposed tree of vast circumference, formerly rumoured to grow in the West Indies.
1598 SYLVESTER *Du Bartas* II. i. (1641) 86/1 Yet envying all the massie Cerbas fame, Sith fifty pases can but clasp the same. **1623** COCKERAM III, *Cerbas*, an Indean tree fifteene fathom about.

Cerberean (sɜːˈbɪərɪən), *a.* Improp. -ian. [L. *Cerbere-us*, f. CERBERUS.] Of, pertaining to, or resembling Cerberus. So **Cerberic**.
1628 M. LAYMON *Syon's Plea* 24 Such Cerberean Porters; as shut the gates upon Christs Friends, and intertain his foes. **1667** MILTON *P.L.* II. 655 A cry of Hell Hounds never ceasing bark'd With wide Cerberean mouths. **1731** SWIFT *Cassinus & P.*, But hark, The loud Cerberian triple bark. **1787** MAD. D'ARBLAY *Diary* (1842) III. 410 By no means so much disconcerted as by a similar *Cerberic* detection. **1817** COLERIDGE *Biog. Lit.* x. (1870) 90 Cerberean whelps of feud and slander.

Cerberus (ˈsɜːbərəs). [Lat., a. Gr. Κέρβερος.] In Greek and Latin mythology the proper name of the watch-dog which guarded the entrance of the infernal regions, represented as having three heads. Used allusively, esp. in phrase, ***to give a sop to Cerberus*** (so as to stop his mouths for the moment: cf. *Æneid* VI. 417).
c **1386** CHAUCER *Monkes T.* 112 He drow out Cerberus, the hound of helle. **1513** DOUGLAS *Æneis* VI. vi. 69 Cerberus, the hidduus hund..Quham til the prophetes..A sop stepit intill hunny..gan cast. **1632** MILTON *L'Allegro* 2 Melancholy, of Cerberus and blackest Midnight born. **1640** SIR E. DERING *Sp. on Relig.* 14 Dec. v. 14 A three-fold Chimæra, a monster to our Lawes, a Cerberus to our Religion. **1695** CONGREVE *Love for L.* I. iv. 17 If I can give that Cerberus a sop, I shall be at rest for one Day. **1773** FOOTE *Nabob* I, There is but one way of managing here; I must give the Cerberus a sop, I suppose. **1825** HOR. SMITH *Gaities & Grav.*, I will throw down a napoleon, as a sop to Cerberus.
b. *attrib.*
1807 W. IRVING *Salmag.* (1824) 6 We keep more than a Cerberus Watch over the golden rules of female delicacy.

‖**Cercaria** (səˈkɛərɪə). *Zool.* [mod.L., f. Gr. κέρκος tail.] A kind of trematode worm or fluke in its second larval stage, shaped like a tadpole, found as a parasite in the bodies of molluscs. Formerly supposed to be a genus of Infusoria.
1841-71 T. R. JONES *Anim. Kingd.* 159 In these yellow worms, which are about 2 lines long..the Cercariæ, which are the larvæ of the actual Flukes, are developed. **1877** HUXLEY *Anat. Inv. Ann.* iv. 204 The Cercaria has a long tail with lateral membranous expansions.
Hence **cerˈcarial**, **cerˈcarian**, **cerˈcariform** *adjs.*
1876 BENEDEN *Anim. Parasites* 45 This trematode passes its cercarial life freely in the sea. **1836-9** TODD *Cycl. Anat.* II. 113/2 The Cercarian tribe. **1869** NICOLSON *Zool.* xxiv. (1880) 237 In many cases the larvæ are 'cercariiform' or 'tailed'. **1877** HUXLEY *Anat. Inv. An.* iv. 205 Having undergone no Cercarian metamorphosis. *Ibid.* xii. 675 The Trematoda, with their cercariform larvae.

cerce, obs. f. SEARCE to sift.

†**cerceaus.** *Obs. rare*⁻¹. [a. OF. *cerceau-s*:—L. *circellus*, dim. of *circus*, *circulus* anything bent into a ring or arch, a hoop.] A hoop.
1340 *Ayenb.* 159 Hi went ayen ase deþ þe cerceaus.

‖**cercelle.** *Obs.* [OF. *cerelle* (mod.F. *sarcelle*), med.L. *cercella*:—L. *querquedula*.] The teal duck.
1387 TREVISA *Higden* I. 371 Seynt Colman his briddes.. beeþ i-cleped cercelles [Higden *cercellæ*] and comeþ homeliche to manis honde.

cercle, obs. form of CIRCLE.

cercomonad (sɜːkəʊˈmɒnəd). *Zool.* [ad. mod.L. *cercomonas*, f. Gr. κέρκος tail + μονάς: see MONAD.] An infusorial entozoon of the genus *Cercomonas*.
1861 HULME tr. *Moquin-Tandon* II. vii. 407 The Cercomonads are extremely active.

‖**cercopithecus** (ˌsɜːkəʊpɪˈθiːkəs). *Zool.* [L. *cercopithēcus*, a. Gr. κερκοπίθηκος a long-tailed monkey, f. κέρκος tail + πίθηκος ape.] A genus of long-tailed monkeys found in Africa, having cheek-pouches, and callosities on the buttocks. Hence **cercopiˈthecoid** *a.*, akin to this genus.
1572 BOSSEWELL *Armorie* II. 48 Twoo Apes Cercopetikes combattante. **1883** *New York Nation* 29 Mar. 281/1 A cercopithecoid monkey.

cercus (ˈsɜːkəs). *Zool.* Pl. cerci. [mod.L., f. Gr. κέρκος tail.] One of a pair of small appendages found at the hind end of the abdomen of certain insects and other arthropods.
1826 KIRBY & SPENCE *Introd. Entom.* III. xxxiii. 718 These [appendages] are..the cerci of the Blattidæ and Gryllina. **1937** *Discovery* Mar. 90/2 Hairy tails or cerci which may be jointed. **1951** COLYER & HAMMOND *Flies Brit. Isles* 33 A pair of small appendages, known as 'cerci' may be visible, which are probably tactile in function. **1957** RICHARDS & DAVIES *Imms's Textbook Ent.* (ed. 9) I. 55 The most conspicuous of the persistent appendages are the *cerci* of the 11th segment, which exhibit wide diversity of form and may even be transformed into forceps, as in the Japygidae and the earwigs.

cerd. Cf. CAIRD, L. *cerdo*.
1885 McCRIE *Sketches & Stud.* 30 The family furnished cerds or artificers to the monastery.

cere (sɪə(r)), *sb. Ornith.* Also 5, 7, 9 sere, 9 sear. [a. F. *cire* wax, cere:—L. *cēra* wax; also in med.L. in this sense.]
The naked wax-like membrane at the base of the beak in certain birds, in which the nostrils are pierced. It is supposed to be an organ of touch.
[*c* **1230** FRIDERICUS II, *De Falconibus* II. (DU CANGE), Pars illa corii..ubi sunt nares, quam vocamus ceram.] **1486** *Bk. St. Albans* A viij a, The skynne abowt your hawkys leggis & her fete is callyd the Serys of her leggis & here fete. **1610** GUILLIM *Heraldry* III. xx. (1660) 223 The Yellow between the Beak and the Eys [of a Hawk] is called the Sere. **1767** G. WHITE *Selborne* 9 Sept., With regard to the falco..its cere and feet were yellow. **1852** BURTON *Falconry Indus* viii. 76 A splendid goshawk..with..bright yellow sear. **1875** BLAKE *Zool.* 98 The nostrils are placed at the anterior margin of the cere.

cere (sɪə(r)), *v.* Forms: 5-7 sere, 6 ceare, ceere, (cerre), 6-7 sear, 7 seare, 4- cere. [a. F. *cirer*:—L. *cērāre* to wax, f. *cēra* wax.]
†**1.** *trans.* To smear or cover with wax, to wax.
c **1489** CAXTON *Sonnes of Aymon* vii. 173 Mawgys..toke a threde of sylke and cered it well. **1580** HOLLYBAND *Treas. Fr. Tong, Bougier*, to ceare veluet, or any silk cloth. **1601** HOLLAND *Pliny* II. 425 If the vessells be sered with wax.
2. a. To wrap in a cerecloth. †**b.** To anoint with spices, etc.; also (app.) to embalm (*obs.*).
c **1465** *Eng. Chron.* (1856) 21 He leet close and sere him in lynne cloth alle save the visage. **1494** FABYAN 160 Yᵉ corps ..to be seryd and enoynted with ryche and precyous bawmys. **1555** *Fardle Facions* I. v. 78 Then do thei ceare it [the bodye] ouer with mirrhe and cinamome. **1557** *K. Arthur* (W. COPLAND) v. viii, Ceere them in thre score folde of ceered cloth. *c* **1580** J. HOOKER *Sir P. Carew* in *Archæol.* XXVIII. 144 His body beinge unbowelled and throughtlye seared, he was then chested. **1608** TOURNEUR *Rev. Trag.* I. ii, The bowel'd Corps May be seared in. **1790** PENNANT *Tour Scotl.* III. 284 The body..was embalmed, cered and wrapped in lead.
†**c.** To shut up (a corpse in a coffin); to seal up (in lead, or the like). *Obs.*
1525 LD. BERNERS *Froiss.* II. ccxxxvi[xxii]. 706 His body was enbaumed and seared in lead and couered.
d. *fig.*
1611 SHAKS. *Cymb.* I. i. 116 Seare vp my embracements from a next, With bonds of death. **1818** SHELLEY *Julian & Mad.* 437 Let the silent years Be closed and cered over their memory.

cere, obs. form of SERE.

cereal (ˈsɪəriːəl, -ɪəl), *a.* and *sb.* [ad. L. *Cereālis* pertaining to Ceres, the goddess of agriculture: cf. mod.F. *céréale*.]
A. *adj.* Of or pertaining to corn or edible grain.
1818 COLEBROOKE *Import. Colon. Corn* 20 Wheat..is, of all the cereal seeds, the best adapted to the making of bread. **1853** G. JOHNSTON *Nat. Hist. E. Bord.* I. 19 The sylvan and cereal grounds of Blanerne. **1872** OLIVER *Elem. Bot.* II. 276 Corn-producing or Cereal Grasses, called Cereals.
B. *sb.* **a.** (usually in *pl.*; also in Lat. form *cerealia*.) A name given to those plants of the order *Graminaceæ* or grasses which are cultivated for their seed as human food; commonly comprised under the name *corn* or *grain*. (Sometimes extended to cultivated leguminous plants.)
1832 *Veg. Subst. Food* 10 The chief corn-plants, or cerealia, are wheat, rye, barley, oats, millet, rice, and maize. **1868** DARWIN *Anim. & Pl.* I. ix. 318 The slow and gradual improvement of our cereals. **1872** BAKER *Nile Tribut.* iv. 54 The cultivation of this cereal.
b. An article of food (esp. a breakfast dish) made from a cereal; freq. ***breakfast cereal***. orig. *U.S.*
1899 *Chicago Daily News* 9 May 7 Free with 6 packages of Hazel Cereals, any assortment, a handsomely decorated tea canister. **1907** *Yesterday's Shopping* (1969) 11/2 Breakfast cereals. **1909** H. G. WELLS *Tono-Bungay* II. iii. 196 There's all these patent grain foods,—what Americans call cereals. **1934** A. THIRKELL *Wild Strawberries* iv. 95 Clarissa looked so sweet eating her cereals. **1958** WODEHOUSE *Cocktail Time* xii. 103 when I was a young man..there were no cereals. We ate good wholesome porridge for breakfast and throve on it. **1962** A. CHRISTIE *Mirror Crack'd* i. 9 All these great packets of breakfast cereal instead of cooking a child a proper breakfast of bacon and eggs.
¶ Used to render L. *Cerealia*, ancient Roman games in honour of Ceres.
1600 HOLLAND *Livy* XXX. xxxix. 768 The Dictatour and Generall..exhibited the games called Cereales..to the honour of Ceres.
Hence **cereˈalian**, **cereˈalic** *adjs.*; **ˈcerealism** (after *vegetarianism*).
1849 THOREAU *Week Concord Riv.* 235 These cerealian blossoms expanded. **1881** *Academy* 1 Oct. 252 A vast cerealic and frugiferous region. **1888** G. J. HOLYOAKE in *Co-operative News* 14 Apr. 337 The progress which vegetarianism, or rather cerealism, is making everywhere.

cerealin (ˈsɪəriːəlɪn). *Chem.* [mod. f. prec. + -IN.] A nitrogenous substance found in bran, closely resembling diastase.
1861 *Times* 26 Oct. 6/5 The internal coat of the wheaten grain..is an infinitely more important alimentary substance than its mere bulk would indicate..This substance, which has been named by the discoverer [M. Mège Mouries] 'cerealine', has a most powerful solvent action in the presence of warmth and moisture in gluten and starch. **1883** *Knowledge* 10 Aug. 93/2 Cerealin shares with some of the other albuminoids this peculiar property [sweetness].

†**cerealious**, *a. Obs.* = CEREAL *a.*
a **1682** SIR T. BROWNE *Tracts* (1686) 16 Any edulious or cerealious Grains.

cerealist (ˈsɪəriːəlɪst). [f. CEREAL *sb.* + -IST.]
1. One who advocates a cereal diet.
1905 *Daily Chron.* 7 Aug. 4/5 Cerealists preach absolute abstention from pheasant, turbot, and turtle.
2. One who makes a special study of cereals and the conditions necessary for their cultivation.
1907 L. H. BAILEY *Cycl. Amer. Agric.* II. 663/2 Cerealists as well as practical producers of grains. **1920** *Glasgow Herald* 29 Sept. 9 The present year's wheat yield is nothing of which to boast, but it relieves the apprehensions of cerealists. **1924** *Ibid.* 13 Sept. 6 Dr. Saunders had been the Dominion cerealist.

†**ˈcerebel.** *Obs. Phys.* Also -ell. [ad. L. *cerebellum* (cf. OF. *cervel*, F. *cerveau*).] = CEREBELLUM.
1621 BURTON *Anat. Mel.* I. i. II. iv, The Cerebell or little braine and marrowe of the back-bone. **1713** DERHAM *Phys.-Theol.* (1727) 320 The Base of the Brain and Cerebell. **1819** H. BUSK *Tea* 28 Whose unctuous fumes by sovereign power dispel All other vapours from the cerebel. **1836** A. WALKER *Beauty in Wom.* 158 The thinking organs, namely, the organs of sense, cerebrum and cerebel.

cerebellar (sɛrɪˈbɛlə(r)), *a. Phys.* [f. CEREBELLUM + -AR.] Of or pertaining to the cerebellum.
1831 R. KNOX *Cloquet's Anat.* 752 The inferior cerebellar veins. **1855** BAIN *Senses & Int.* II. iv. §11 The other movements may be cerebellar.
So **cereˈbellic** *a.*
1835-6 TODD *Cycl. Anat.* I. 279/1 The cerebellic prominence.

cerebello- (ˈsɛrɪbɛləʊ), used as combining form of CEREBELLUM = pertaining to the cerebellum (and another part).
1900 DORLAND *Med. Dict.* 148/1 *Cerebellospinal*, pertaining to the cerebellum and spinal cord. **1903** *Ibid.* (ed. 3), *Cerebello-olivary*, connecting the cerebellum and olivary body. **1907** *Practitioner* Apr. 584 The disturbing influence

exerted by the tumour upon the cerebello-vestibular apparatus.

‖**cerebellum** (sɛrɪˈbɛləm). *Phys.* [L. *cerebellum*, dim. of *cerebrum* brain; in ancient Lat. used only in sense ‘small brain’, and in Romanic substituted for the lost primitive *cerebrum*: cf. It. *cervello*, Cat. *cervell*, Pr. *cervel*, OF. *cervel* mod.F. *cerveau*, also (from pl. *cerebella*) OF. *cervele*, mod.F. *cervelle*, brain. But the mediæval translators of Galen and Aristotle used *cerebellum* to render the παρεγκεφαλίς, as distinguished from the ἐγκέφαλον or *cerebrum*. For this sense the Romanic langs. have formed a secondary dim. F. *cervelet*, It. *cervelletto*.

Galen, περὶ ἀνατ. ἐπιγερ. (Kühn 714) has ὀπίσθιον δὲ λέγειν ἐγκέφαλον ἢ ἐγκράνιον ἢ παρεγκεφάλιδα διαφέρει οὐδέν, which the Old Latin transl. renders ‘posterius cerebrum, vocesne cerebellum, Encranium, vel parencephalidem, nihil interest’.]

The little or hinder brain; the mass of nervous matter forming the posterior part of the brain, situated behind and below the cerebrum, and above the medulla oblongata, and divided, like the cerebrum, into two ‘hemispheres’, one on each side.

1565 J. HALL *Anat.* III. i, The fourth [ventricle] is behynde, in an other lyttle brayne called also in Latyne by diminution Cerebellum, and of the Grecians Parencephalis. **1615** CROOKE *Body of Man* 432 The Cerebellum that is, the backeward or after-braine. **1677** PLOT *Oxfordsh.* 302 His placing the Spirits to serve to voluntary actions in the Cerebrum, and those that serve Involuntary in the Cerebellum, is a noble and useful discovery. **1778** *Anatom. Dial.* ii. (1785) 57 Wounds in the Cerebellum.. are mortal. **1855** BAIN *Senses & Int.* I. ii. §18 The cerebellum is looked upon as the centre of the higher order of combined actions.

cerebral (ˈsɛrɪbrəl), *a.* (and *sb.*) [a. F. *cérébral*, f. on L. type **cerebrālis*, f. *cerebrum*: see -AL[1].]

1. a. Pertaining or relating to the brain, or to the cerebrum; of the nature of or analogous to a brain, *e.g.* a ***cerebral ganglion***. ***cerebral hemispheres***: the two great divisions of the cerebrum. ***cerebral nerves***: the twelve pairs of nerve-trunks which arise from the brain. ***cerebral palsy***: see PALSY *sb.*

1816 W. LAWRENCE *Comp. Anat.* 500 (L.) If the nobler attributes of man reside in the cerebral hemispheres. **1858** O. W. HOLMES *Aut. Breakf. T.* xii. 116 Written under cerebral excitement. **1871** W. A. HAMMOND *Dis. Nervous Syst.* 33 Cerebral congestion. *Ibid.* 74 Cerebral hæmorrhage. **1875** LYELL *Princ. Geol.* II. III. xliii. 491 Man's superior cerebral development.

b. Intellectual; appealing to the intellect (rather than to the emotions); clever.

1929 D. H. LAWRENCE *Pansies* 60 Since we have become so cerebral We can't bear to touch or be touched. **1935** T. E. LAWRENCE *Lett.* (1938) 853, I was then trying to write; to be perhaps an artist.. or to be at least cerebral. **1946** *Amer. Speech* XXI. 81 The only congresswoman who may be described plausibly as both cerebral and beautiful. **1951** R. HOGGART *Auden* i. 19 The verse of a young man.. anxious to evolve a hard, cerebral style. **1959** *Camb. Rev.* 25 Apr. 449/2 Everything is suitably cerebral, and the emotional sterility does not obtrude. **1970** *Daily Tel.* 19 May 16/4 A kind of cerebral comedy, pondering the difference between appearance of reality and keeping us on our intellectual toes.

2. ***cerebral letters***: a name given by some to a class of consonants recognized in Sanskrit and other Indian languages, developed from the dentals by retracting the tongue and applying its tip to the palate. Also as *sb.*

1805 COLEBROOK *Gram. Sanskr. Lang.* 24 A dental consonant.. being contiguous to a cerebral, or following (not preceding) ष is changed to the corresponding cerebral. **1857** MONIER WILLIAMS *Sanskr. Gram.* i. 9 The.. cerebrals should be.. produced by turning back the tip of the tongue towards the palate, or top of the head (*cerebrum*). **1879** WHITNEY *Sanskr. Gram.* §45 Lingual series.. They are called by the grammarians *mūrdhanya*, literally ‘head sounds, capitals, cephalics’; which term is in many European grammars rendered by ‘cerebrals’. **1918** D. JONES *Outl. Eng. Phonetics* xvi. 100 Cacuminal sounds (also called ‘inverted’ sounds or ‘cerebral’ sounds) are defined as sounds in which the tip of the tongue is ‘inverted’ or curled upwards towards the hard palate. **1934** *Year's Work in Eng. Stud. 1932* 53 The consonant apparently became a cerebral (inverted) *r* before its disappearance.

Hence **ˈcerebralism**, the theory that mental operations arise from the action of the brain; also, intellectualism; **ˈcerebralist**, one who holds this theory; also, an intellectual, intellectualist; **ˌcerebraˈlistic** *a.*, of or pertaining to cerebralism; **cereˈbrality**, cerebral or intellectual quality, cleverness; **ˌcerebraliˈzation**, a making a consonant ‘cerebral’ (cf. *labialization*, *palatalization*).

1881 N. POTTER in *Trans. Victoria Inst.* XIV. 63 Bain's gross physiological cerebralism. **1892** W. JAMES *Coll. Ess. & Rev.* (1920) 326 A critic of cerebralism in psychology ought to do one of two things. **1931** C. GRAY *Contingencies* (1947) 156 Excessive cerebralism on the one hand and excessive sensationalism on the other. **1890** W. JAMES *Princ. Psychol.* I. 4 The spiritualist and the associationist must both be ‘cerebralists’. **1943** C. WILLIAMS *Figure of Beatrice* 20 So much only to prevent too great an ‘elevation’ of Dante's thought; we are not to suppose him a mere cerebralist. **1892** W. JAMES *Coll. Ess. & Rev.* (1920) 316 The cerebralistic point of view which is becoming so popular in psychology today. **1901** *Scribner's Mag.* XXIX. 505/2 There is one trait that belongs in common to every artistic effort of Americans, and that is the *cerebrality*.. of such effort. **1903** *Daily Chron.* 9 May 4/5 The adventures of Sherlock Holmes are cerebrality raised to the power of *n*. **1869** W. H. FERRAR *Compar. Gram. Skr.* I. 340 Cerebralisation is a phenomenon that has arisen within the limits of the Sanskrit language.

cerebrally (ˈsɛrɪbrəlɪ), *adv.* [f. CEREBRAL *a.* + -LY[2].] In a cerebral manner; in or with the brain.

1893 in *Funk's Standard Dict.* **1901** G. GISSING *Our Friend the Charlatan* xxi, If I am not cerebrally oxidised,.. it's all over with my hopes of leading a moral life. **1929** D. H. LAWRENCE *Pansies* 60 For if, cerebrally, we force ourselves into touch, into contact Physical and fleshly, We violate ourselves. **1962** H. C. WESTON *Sight, Light & Work* (ed. 2) fig. 17 (*caption*), The half images.. are ‘superimposed’ and united cerebrally.

†**cerebrand.** *Obs.* Corruption of SARABAND.

1677 E. RAVENSCROFT *Wrangling Lov.* (N.) The song ended, a cerebrand is danc'd.

cerebrate (ˈsɛrɪbreɪt), *sb.* *Chem.* A salt of cerebric acid.

1872 J. H. BENNETT *Text-bk. Physiol.* III. 494 We have now Cerebrate of Soda mixed with phosphate of lime, etc.

ˈcerebrate, *v.* *rare.* [app. f. next.] **1.** *trans.* To perform by ‘cerebration;’ to subject to brain-action (esp. unconscious or mechanical).

1874 *Contemp. Rev.* XXIV. 205 To say that a man cerebrates a thing more quickly than he could calculate it. **1917** *Chambers's Jrnl.* Oct. 699/1 Up, up, they came, cerebrating agonised thoughts.

2. *intr.* To cogitate.

1928 A. BENNETT *Strange Vanguard* xliv. 303 The baron who was still most actively cerebrating, rang the bell. **1940** H. G. WELLS *New World Order* §7. 106 Many among them will cease to cerebrate further and fall by the wayside, but many will go on thinking. **1953** ‘S. RANSOME’ *Drag the Dark* (1954) ii. 20 He.. just sat there cerebrating.

cerebration (sɛrɪˈbreɪʃən). [f. L. *cerebrum* brain + -ATION.] Brain-action. First used by Dr. W. B. Carpenter in the phrase ***unconscious cerebration***, to express that action of the brain which, though unaccompanied by consciousness, produces results which might have been produced by thought.

1853 CARPENTER *Phys.* (ed. 4) §819 It is difficult to find an appropriate term for this class of operations.. The designation unconscious cerebration is perhaps less objectionable than any other. **1866** ARGYLL *Reign Law* vi. (1871) 282 There are philosophers who appear to think.. that thought is in some measure explained when it is called Cerebration. **1869** *Daily News* 15 July, An example of what physiologists call reflex cerebration.

Hence **cereˈbrational** *a.*

1874 *Contemp. Rev.* 206 The cerebrational assumption.

cerebric (səˈrɛbrɪk), *a.* [f. L. *cerebrum* + -IC.] Pertaining to the brain; esp. in *Cerebric acid* (*Chem.*), a fatty acid obtained from the brain.

1839–47 TODD *Cycl. Anat.* III. 587/2 Cerebric acid, when purified, is white, and is in the form of crystalline grains. **1883** *American* VI. 410 The English naturalists defined identity as a cerebric habit.

cerebricity (sɛrɪˈbrɪsɪtɪ). *rare.* [f. CEREBRUM brain, after *electricity*.] Brain-cell power.

1890 O. W. HOLMES *Over Teacups* i. 15 Your incident is a typical example of cerebral induction from a source containing stored cerebricity. I use this word, not to be found in my dictionaries, as expressing the brain-cell power corresponding to electricity. **1894** *Arena* IX. 336 Mere manifestations of psychic power, referable to the dark field of cerebricity and clairvoyance.

cerebriform (səˈrɛbrɪfɔːm), *a.* [f. L. *cerebrum* + -FORM: cf. F. *cérébriforme*.] Resembling the brain in form or texture; encephaloid.

1834 J. FORBES *Laennec's Dis. Chest* 365 Their penetration of the cerebriform matter. **1846** DANA *Zooph.* (1848) 616 The cerebriform hemispherical surface.

cereˈbrifugal, *a.* [f. as prec. + L. *-fug-us* fleeing + -AL[1].] An epithet of nerve-fibres which run from the brain to the spinal cord, and convey cerebral impulses outward.

So **cereˈbripetal** *a.*, epithet of the nerve fibres which run in the opposite direction, and convey sensations from the outer parts to the brain.

1879 *Syd. Soc. Lex.*

cerebrin (ˈsɛrɪbrɪn). *Chem.* Also **-ine**. [f. as prec. + -IN.] A name that has been applied to several substances obtained from brain; *esp.* a light white hygroscopic powder, obtained by the action of baryta and heat on brain-tissue. (See Watts *Chem. Dict.*, and *Syd. Soc. Lex.*)

1830 R. KNOX *Béclard's Anat.* 332 M. Chevreul has found in the blood a characteristic ingredient of the nervous substance, which is named cerebrine. **1878** KINGZETT *Anim. Chem.* 267 Kuhn gave to one of the principles of the brain the name of cerebrine.

‖**cerebritis** (sɛrɪˈbraɪtɪs). *Path.* [f. L. *cerebrum* + -ITIS.] Inflammation of the substance of the brain.

1866 A. FLINT *Princ. Med.* (1880) 717. **1878** A. HAMILTON *Nerv. Dis.* 105 During a cerebritis.. a number of serious muscular distortions of a permanent character may ensue.

cerebro- (ˈsɛrɪbrəʊ), combining form of L. *cerebrum* brain; as in **cerebro-ˈcardiac** *a.*, relating to the brain and the heart; **cerebro-ocular**, relating to the brain and the eye; **cerebro-thoracic**, relating to the brain and thorax; **cerebro-visceral**, relating to the brain and viscera. Also CEREBROSPINAL. **b.** Also used to form several hybrid derivatives, of which the second element is Greek; as **cerebrology** (-ˈɒlədʒɪ), [see -LOGY], *nonce-wd.*, the science or discussion of brains. **cerebrometer** (-ˈɒmɪtə(r)), [see -METER], an instrument for recording cerebral pulsations. **cerebropathy** (-ˈɒpəθɪ), [Gr. -πάθεια suffering], ‘the series of hypochrondriacal and other symptoms of like nature accompanying overwork of the brain’ (*Syd. Soc. Lex.*). **ceˈrebroscope** (-skəʊp), *nonce-wd.*, after *horoscope* (see quot). **cereˈbroscopy** (-ˈɒskəʊpɪ), [Gr. -σκοπια examination, f. σκοπεῖν to look, examine], the use of the ophthalmoscope to determine the state of the retina and deduce the condition of the brain. (*Syd. Soc. Lex.*)

1881 *Sci. American* XLV. No. 3. 36 Cerebrology of criminals. **1875** H. WOOD *Therap.* (1879) 278 By means of a cerebrometer set into the skull of the dog. **1849–52** TODD *Cycl. Anat.* IV. 1459/2 The cerebro-ocular congestion. **1838** *Blackw. Mag.* XLIII. 658 A material ingredient in casting the cerebroscope. **1836** TODD *Cycl. Anat.* I. 206/2 The [first] ganglion.. may be termed cerebro-thoracic. **1831** YOUATT *Horse* xiii. (1847) 287 The cerebro-visceral nerve.

cerebroˈcentric, *a.* [f. CEREBRO- + -CENTRIC.] Centring on the brain.

1930 J. LAIRD *Knowl., Belief & Opinion* iii. 64 Arguments based upon the so-called egocentric predicament in cogitation, or upon the cerebrocentric, anthropocentric, or sociocentric predicaments. **1949** *Mind* LVIII. 390 The ‘cerebrocentric’ conception (either Epiphenomenalist or Behaviourist).. is accepted nowadays by the majority of scientifically educated persons. **1956** J. B. RHINE in A. Pryce-Jones *New Outl. Mod. Knowl.* 205 This brain-centred approach to man, this *cerebro-centric* psychology.

cerebroid (ˈsɛrɪbrɔɪd), *a.* [f. L. *cerebr-um* + -OID.] Resembling or akin to brain; brainlike.

1854 WOODWARD *Mollusca* II. 182 The labial nerve, which comes from the front margin of the cerebroid. **1870** ROLLESTON *Anim. Life* 53 A.. Cord is seen to connect the cerebroid mass with the.. ganglion.

cerebrol (ˈsɛrɪbrɒl). *Chem.* [a. mod.F. *cérébrol*, f. L. *cerebrum* brain.] ‘An oily reddish substance.. obtained by Couerbe from brain’ (Watts *Dict. Chem.*).

1872 [see CEREBROT].

cereˈbrose, *a.* *rare.* [ad. L. *cerebrōsus* headstrong, passionate, f. *cerebrum* brain.] ‘Brainsick, mad-brained, wilful, stubborn’ (Bailey 1727).

Hence †**cereˈbrosity**.

a **1586** SIDNEY *Wanst. Play* Wks. (1674) 622 (D.) Till I have endoctrinated your plumbeous cerebrosities. **1647–8** WOOD *Life* (1848) 36 To admit.. a meer frog of Helicon to croak the cataracts of his plumbeous cerebrosity before your sagacious ingenuities. **1656** HEYLIN *Extraneus Vap.* 38.

cerebroside (ˈsɛrɪbrəʊˌsaɪd). *Biochem.* [f. CEREBR(O- + -OSE[2] + -IDE.] Any of a group of nitrogenous fatty substances found in the brain and other nerve tissue, that by hydrolysis yield galactose, sphingosine, etc.

1883 J. L. W. THUDICHUM in *Brit. Med. Jrnl.* 15 Sept. 525/1 Let us cast a glance at a class of immediate principles of the brain, which I have termed *cerebrosides*. The principal one is *phrenoid*; the second in order of quantity is *kerain*; together they form about 5 per cent. of the weight of the brain. **1956** *Nature* 7 Jan. 21/2 Dr. H. E. Carter.. gave further information regarding cerebrosides and cerebroside sulphuric ester. **1957** *Sci. News* XV. 93 The cerebrosides are found chiefly in the human brain... When hydrolysed they give one molecule each of D-galactose or D-glucose, a fatty acid, and a nitrogenous base, sphingosine.

cerebro-spinal (ˌsɛrɪbrəʊˈspaɪnəl), *a.* [f. CEREBRO- (see above) + SPINAL.] Relating to the brain and spinal cord.

cerebro-spinal axis the brain and spinal cord as together constituting the central or main part of the ***cerebro-spinal system***, the chief of the two great nerve-systems of vertebrates. ***cerebro-spinal fluid***: a serous fluid occupying the space between the arachnoid membrane and *pia mater*. ***cerebro-spinal fever*** or ***meningitis***, inflammation of the meninges of the brain and the spinal cord, otherwise called *spotted fever*.

1826 KIRBY & SP. *Entomol.* (1828) IV. xxxvii. 4 In the cerebro-spinal the nervous tree may be said to be double. **1836** TODD *Cycl. Anat.* I. 723/2 The cerebro-spinal axis. **1866** HUXLEY *Phys.* xi. (1869) 283 The nervous apparatus consists of two sets of nerves and nerve-centres.. These are the cerebro-spinal system and the sympathetic system. **1889** OSLER *Cerebral Palsies* 18 Cerebro-spinal meningitis was stated to be the cause of the trouble. **1897** *Trans. Amer. Pediatric Soc.* IX. 189 Four ounces of turbid cerebrospinal fluid were collected and measured. **1901** OSLER *Princ. & Pract. Med.* (ed. 4) 101 Sporadic cerebro-spinal fever occurs in all the larger cities.. of this continent. **1955** *Sci. News Let.* 19 Mar. 190/2 This kind of meningitis is also called cerebrospinal fever and spotted fever.

cerebrot, -ote (ˈsɛrɪbrɒt, -əʊt). *Chem.* [a. mod.F. *cérébrote*, f. L. *cerebrum* brain, after *céphalote.*] 'Brain-fat': 'a substance containing sulphur and phosphorus, which Couerbe obtained by treating the deposit which separates the alcoholic and ethereal extracts of the brain with ether. According to Frémy it is merely a mixture of cerebric acid with small quantities of cerebrate of potassium and brain-albumin' (Watts). Cf. CEPHALOT.

1839-47 TODD *Cycl. Anat.* III. 643/2 The following constituents [of the brain] are enumerated..3. cholesterim; 4. cerebrote. **1845** G. DAY tr. *Simon's Anim. Chem.* I. 188 The brain-fat, denominated cerebrot by Couerbe. **1872** J. H. BENNETT *Text-bk. Physiol.* III. 495 Other substances have been found in Brain, termed cerebrin, cerebrol, and cerebrote, but it is probable they are one and the same substance.

cerebrotonic (ˌsɛrɪbrəʊˈtɒnɪk), *a.* and *sb.* [f. CEREBRO- + TONIC *a.* 1 a.] **A.** *adj.* Designating or characteristic of a type of personality which is introverted, intellectual, and emotionally restrained, classified by Sheldon as being associated with an ECTOMORPHIC physique. **B.** *sb.* One having this type of personality. So **cerebrotonia** (-ˈtəʊnɪə), cerebrotonic personality or characteristics.

1937 A. HUXLEY *Ends & Means* xi. 165 Dr. William Sheldon, whose classification [of types of human beings] in terms of somatotonic, viscerotonic and cerebrotonic I shall use. *Ibid.* xii. 193 The cerebrotonic is not such a 'good mixer' as the viscerotonic. **1940** W. H. SHELDON *Var. Human Physique* 8 In the economy of the cerebrotonic individual the sensory and central nervous systems appear to play dominant roles. **1945** A. HUXLEY *Let.* 2 Apr. (1969) 517 There was just enough of the somatotonic in his.. cerebrotonic make-up to make him regret his cerebrotonia. **1950** —— *Themes & Var.* i. 121 Too secretively the introvert, too inhibitedly cerebrotonic, to be willing to take the risk of 'giving himself away'. **1951** AUDEN *Nones* (1952) 28 Cerebrotonic Cato may Extol the Ancient Disciplines. **1954** R. FULLER *Fantasy & Fugue* iv. 75 You.. unfortunately incline to the cerebrotonic ectomorph—you worry too much, you're too good looking, and you can't abandon yourself happily to booze.

cerebrovascular (ˌsɛrɪbrəʊˈvæskjʊlə(r)), *a. Physiol.* [f. CEREBRO- + VASCULAR *a.* 2.] Of or pertaining to the brain and the blood-vessels supplying it.

1935 S. WEISS in Blumer & Sullivan *Practitioners Libr. Med. & Surg.* VIII. II. vii. 677 *Cerebrovascular Accidents.* —Rupture or thrombosis of the cerebral vessels with resulting debility..is probably the most frequent of all the diseases of the blood vessels. **1961** *Lancet* 29 July 221/2 The regimen followed in all cases of cerebrovascular accident was [etc.]. **1961** *Ibid.* 5 Aug. 306/1 Diseases of the central nervous system... The commonest disorders in this group resulted from cerebrovascular disease.

‖**cerebrum** (ˈsɛrɪbrəm). *Anat.* [L. *cerebrum* brain] The brain proper; the convoluted mass of nervous matter forming the anterior, and, in the higher vertebrates, largest part of the brain; in man it overlaps all the rest and fills nearly the whole cavity of the skull.

1615 CROOKE *Body of Man* 475 It filleth almost the whole Scull; and this is properly called Cerebrum or the Braine. **1718** PRIOR *Alma* III. 155 Surprise my readers, whilst I tell 'em Of cerebrum and *Cerebellum.* **1855** H. SPENCER *Princ. Psychol.* (1872) I. 62 *note*, The cerebrum is generally recognised as the chief organ of mind. **1879** CALDERWOOD *Mind & Brain* ii. 10 Enveloped within three membranes, is the brain proper, or cerebrum.

†**cere-candle.** *Obs.* [see CERE *sb.*] A wax candle.

1632 T. RANDOLPH *Jealous Lov.* v. vi, Who in thy Temple Will light a Cere-Candle.

cerecloth (ˈsɪəklɒθ, -ɔː-), *sb.* Also 6-8 sear(e-, 7 cear(e-. [App. originally *cered cloth*: see CERED.] Cloth smeared or impregnated with wax or some glutinous matter:

1. used for wrapping a dead body in; a waxed winding-sheet or a winding-sheet in general.

[**1475-1608** see CERED.] **1553** EDEN *Treat. New Ind.* (Arb.) 27 Inuoluinge with cere clothe & pounderinge with spyces the body. **1596** SHAKS. *Merch. V.* II. vii. 51. **1678** WYCHERLEY *Pl.-Dealer* II. i, Thou Bag of Mummy, that wou'dst fall asunder, if 'twere not for thy Cere-cloaths. **1868** STANLEY *Westm. Abb.* iii. 142 The wax of the king's cerecloth renewed.

fig. **1866** MOTLEY *Dutch Rep.* Introd. xiv. 46 The monastic ..spirit which now kept..all learning..wrapped in the ancient cerecloths.

†**2.** used as a plaster in surgery; a CERATE.

1547 BOORDE *Brev. Health* xlvii. 22 b, For aches and peyne in the armes use seare clothes. **1609** C. BUTLER *Fem. Mon.* x. (1623) Z iij, A Cere-cloth to refresh the wearied Sinewes and tired Muscles. **1625** DONNE *Serm.* 663 A Sear-Cloth that Souples all bruises. **1667** PEPYS *Diary* 14 July, I..did sprain my right foot..To bed, & there had a cerecloth laid to my foot. **1755** SMOLLETT *Quix.* (1803) I. 121, I am at present more fit for a searcloth than such conversation. **1818** *Art Preserv. Feet* 148 Fix the cere-cloth close to the surrounding skin.

3. for various other uses, *esp.* as a waterproof or protective material.

1540 WYATT *Let.* Wks. (1816) 371 Out of his bosom he took a bag of a cerecloth with writings therein. **1658** EVELYN *Fr. Gard.* (1675) 106 Cerecloth to cover the clefts of your trees. **1764** HARMER *Observ.* v. v. 213 A thing like an horse litter..covered all over with sear-cloth. **1844** PUGIN *Gloss. Eccl. Ornament* 53 *Cerecloath*, a waxed cloth fixed over a consecrated altar-stone to protect it from desecration.

†**ˈcerecloth,** *v. Obs.* [f. prec. sb.]

trans. **a.** To apply a 'cerecloth' or cerate to. **b.** To wrap in a cerecloth.

1620 SHELTON *Quix.* II. liii, I must seare-cloth myself: for I beleeve all my Ribs are bruised. **1658** SIR T. BROWNE *Hydriot.* ii. 31 The body of the Marquis of Dorset seemed sound and handsomely cereclothed. **1666** DRYDEN *Ann. Mirab.* cxlviii, Some..sear-cloth Masts with strong Tarpawling coats.

cered (sɪəd), *ppl. a.* [f. CERE *v.*] Smeared, anointed, saturated, or rendered waterproof, with wax, *esp.* in ***cered cloth***: = CERECLOTH.

c **1386** CHAUCER *Chan. Yem. Prol. & T.* 255 Ceride poketes, sal peter, and vitriol. **1475** CAXTON *Jason* (1477) 114 b, Her epistle which she rapped in a cered cloth. **1541** *Act 33 Hen. VIII*, c. 12. § 12 Seared clothes, sufficient for the surgeon to occupie about the same execucion. **1608** TOURNEUR *Rev. Trag.* I. ii, The faults of great men through their searde clothes breake. **1634** *Malory's Arthur* (1816) I. 169 He did sew them in threescore folds of seered cloth of Sendale, and then laid them in chests of lead. **1821** JOANNA BAILLIE *Metr. Leg.*, *Colum.* lxii, His cered corse lies here.

cereiore, -owre, obs. forms of SEARCHER.

cereless (ˈsɪəlɪs), *a.* [f. CERE *sb.* + -LESS.] Of birds: Without a cere.

1866 WOOD *Nat. Hist.* (1874) 283 The Passeres, distinguished by their cere-less and pointed beak.

cerement (ˈsɪəmənt). Forms: 7 **cerment,** 9 **cerement, cearment, searment.** [a. F. *cirement* 'a waxing, a searing; a dressing, closing, covering, or mingling with wax' (Cotgr.), f. *cirer* to wax: cf. also CERE *v.* in sense 2, to wrap (a corpse) in a waxed cloth or shroud. Always concretely in Eng.: cf. *covering, wrap, wrapping, shroud,* and similar vbl. sbs. (Sometimes erroneously pronounced ˈsɛrɪ- after *ceremony.*)]

Almost always in *pl.*: Waxed wrappings for the dead; *loosely*, grave-clothes generally. Rarely in *sing.* = cerecloth; winding-sheet, shroud. (App. caught up by modern writers from Shakspere, and used in the same loose rhetorical way as *urn, ashes,* etc.)

1602 SHAKS. *Ham.* I. iv. 48 Tell Why thy Canoniz'd bones Hearsed in death, Haue burst their cerments. **1820** SCOTT *Ivanhoe* xliii, The ghost of Athelstane himself would burst his bloody cerements. **1825** —— *Talism.* iv, Like a voice proceeding from the cearments of a corpse. *a* **1845** HOOD *Bridge Sighs* 10 Look at her garments Clinging like cerements. **1836** MRS. BROWNING *Poet's Vow*, Nor wore the dead a stiller face Beneath the cerement's roll. **1856** CAPERN *Poems* 144 In her cerements enfolded Pale and beautiful she slept.

attrib. **1877** A. B. EDWARDS *Nile* iv. 76 Shreds of cerement cloths.

b. *fig.* (Chiefly in reference to 'bursting cerements' or similar notions.)

1804 W. AUSTIN *Lett. fr. London* 87 Prior..the only one who burst the cearments of servitude and rose to eminence. **1821** BYRON *Two Fosc.* III. i. 81 Just men's groans Will burst all cerement, even a living grave's. **1879** FARRAR *St. Paul* I. 5 The man who loosed Christianity from the cerements of Judaism.

2. The action of 'cering' a dead body or its covering; the wax used. *rare.*

1868 STANLEY *Westm. Abb.* iii. 142 The renewal of the cerement ceased. (Cf. CERECLOTH 1, 1868.)

3. Waxy coating generally. *rare.*

1860 *All Y. Round* No. 47. 493 The very lips seemed stiff with cerement, and the skins that were not hard red, were of a ghastly cosmeticised whiteness.

Hence **cerement** *v.*, to wrap in cerements.

1858 *Sat. Rev.* V. 308/1 Cemented in inodorous fallacies.

ceremonial (sɛrɪˈməʊnɪəl), *a.* and *sb.* Forms: 4 **cerimonial, -yal, cerymonial, (sermonyal),** 5 **ceremonyalle, cerymonyal,** 5-7 **ceremoniall,** 6 **ceremonyall, cerimoniall,** 5- **ceremonial.** [ad. L. *cærimōniāl-is* (3rd c.), f. *cærimōnia*: see -AL[1]. So mod.F. *cérémonial* (16th c. in Littré).]

A. *adj.*

1. Relating to, consisting of, or characterized by ceremonies; of the nature of a ceremony or rite; ritual; formal.

138. WYCLIF *Serm.* Sel. Wks. II. 57 Kepyng of þe Sabot was sumwhat a comandement and sumwhat cerymonial, to figure þat Christ shuld reste in þe tombe al þe satirdai. **1483** CAXTON *Gold. Leg.* 392/1 To accomplysshe the commaundementes ceremonyalles of the feythe. **1545** BRINKLOW *Lament.* (1874) 87 A vayne supersticious cerimoniall Masse. **1596** SHAKS. *Tam. Shr.* III. ii. 6 The ceremoniall rites of marriage. **1634** CANNE *Necess. Separ.* (1849) 288 A curate that will keep the ceremonial law. **1755** ADAIR *Amer. Ind.* 106 Speaking certain old ceremonial words. **1853** ROBERTSON *Serm.* IV. xix. (1876) 248 The ceremonial law, which constrains life by customs. **1883** GILMOUR *Mongols* xxvi. 316 The head lama..in his most imposing ceremonial costume.

b. Relating to or involving the formalities of social intercourse.

1549 *Compl. Scot.* xvii. 145 Ther vas no ceremonial reuerens nor stait, quha suld pas befor or behynd. **1750** JOHNSON *Rambl.* No. 1 ¶2 Such ceremonial modes of entrance. **1851** DIXON *W. Penn* xxiv. (1872) 214 Laying on one side all ceremonial manners.

†**2.** Of persons: Addicted to ceremony or ritual; precise in observance of forms of politeness; formal, ceremonious. *Obs.*

1579 FULKE *Conf. Sanders* 550 A ceremoniall and superstitious man. **1599** SANDYS *Europæ Spec.* (1632) 152 Very magnificall and ceremoniall in his outward comportement. **1653** MILTON *Hirelings* Wks. (1851) 357 They quote Ambrose, Augustin, and some other ceremonial Doctors.

B. *sb.*

†**1.** A ceremonial commandment or ordinance.

1382 WYCLIF *Prol. Bible* ii, The old testament is departid ..in to moral comaundementis, iudicials, and cerimonyals. *c* **1449** PECOCK *Repr.* v. viii. 526 God ordeyned the ceremonialis and the iudicialis..to the Iewis. **1621** R. JOHNSON *Way to Glory* 35 If, then, tythes be neither ceremonials nor judicials, they must needes be morals.

2. A prescribed system of ceremonies; a series of rites or formalities observed on any occasion; a ritual. *rarely*, A rite or ceremony.

1672-9 TEMPLE *Mem.* ii, I remember no other points of the ceremonial, that seem to have been established by the course of this assembly. **1750** JOHNSON *Rambl.* No. 78. ¶6 To adjust the ceremonial of death. **1830** D'ISRAELI *Chas. I,* III. x. 214 The ceremonial prescribed in the Anglican service. **1840** G. S. FABER *Regen.* 150 The use of water is not a mere empty ceremonial. **1880** McCARTHY *Own Times* IV. lix. 308 No ceremonial could be at once more useless and more mischievous.

3. A usage of formal courtesy or politeness; the observance of conventional forms in social intercourse; = CEREMONY 2, 3.

1749 FIELDING *Tom Jones* XVI. viii, The two ladies..after very short previous ceremonials, fell to business. **1771** SMOLLETT *Humph. Cl.* 23 Apr., Maintaining a ceremonial more stiff, formal, and oppressive than the etiquette of a German Elector. **1858** GLADSTONE *Homer* II. II. 69 We do not hear a great deal respecting mere ceremonial among the Olympian divinities.

†**4.** A robe or garment worn on some ceremonial occasion; = CEREMONY 4. *Obs.*

c **1610** SIR J. MELVIL *Mem.* (1827) 122 The ceremony [the installation of Lord Robert Dudley as Earl of Leicester] took place at Westminster, herself [Elizabeth] helping to put on his ceremonial.

5. *R.C. Ch.* The order for rites and ceremonies, or a book containing this.

1612 E. GRIMSTONE tr. *Matthieu's Heroyk Life* I. 31 This is a History, not a Ceremoniall. **1753** CHAMBERS *Cycl. Supp.* s.v., The Roman ceremonial was first published by the bishop of Corcyra in 1516.

ceremonialism (sɛrɪˈməʊnɪəlɪz(ə)m). [f. prec. + -ISM.] Addiction to or fondness for external ceremonies in religion; ritualism.

1854 *Tait's Mag.* XXI. 269 A priesthood, submission to ecclesiastical supremacy, and an imposing ceremonialism. **1859** JOWETT *Ep. St. Paul* (ed. 2) II. 385 The ceremonialism of the age..passed by a sort of contagion from one race to another, from Paganism or Judaism to Christianity. **1879** A. B. HOPE in *Trans. St. Paul's Eccl. Soc.* (1885) I. 1 That newer movement..called Ritualism, but which ought more properly to be called Ceremonialism.

ceremonialist (sɛrɪˈməʊnɪəlɪst). [f. as prec. + -IST.] One addicted to external ceremonies in religion; a ritualist.

1682 *2nd Plea for Nonconf.* 69 The Ceremonialists, that preached Circumcision. **1882** *Contemp. Rev.* XLII. 680 The ceremonialist in his church is the enthusiast in his parish.

†**ceremoniˈality.** *Obs.* [f. as prec. + -ITY.] Ceremonial character or quality.

1621 W. SCLATER *Tythes* (1623) Some accessories of Caeremonialitie and iudicialitie also perhaps annexed thereto. **1660** JER. TAYLOR *Duct. Dubit.* II. ii, The whole ceremoniality of it is confessedly gone.

ceremonialize, *v. rare.* [f. as prec. + -IZE.] **a.** *trans.* To render ceremonial or ritualistic.

1858 MASSON *Milton* I. 346 To ceremonialise the Church to the full extent of his [Laud's] wishes. *a* **1935** T. E. LAWRENCE *Mint* (1955) I. xix. 67 This pretence to ceremonialize a job of scavenging. **1960** KOESTLER *Lotus & Robot* II. x. 229 It is ceremonialized in a series of ablutions, purifications, recitations.

b. *intr.* To carry out a ceremony or ritual.

1948 C. WILLIAMS *Seed of Adam* 32 Must we stand by while the king ceremonializes?

ceremonially (sɛrɪˈməʊnɪəlɪ), *adv.* [f. as prec. + -LY[2].] In a ceremonial manner; in relation to ceremonies or the ceremonial law.

1643 MILTON *Doctr. Divorce* v, David..did eat the Shewbread..which was ceremonially unlawful. *a* **1679** T. GOODWIN *Wks.* IV. IV. 168 (R.) Persons clean or unclean ceremonially. **1872** J. MURPHY *Comm. Lev.* vi. 11 Ceremonially or essentially holy.

†**cereˈmonialness.** *Obs. rare.* [f. as prec. + -NESS.] Ceremonial quality, ceremoniality.

a **1679** T. GOODWIN *Wks.* IV. IV. 166 (R.) The Circumcision and the Passover, had assuredly, besides the ceremonialness annexed to them, the institution of typifying Christ to come.

ceremoniarius (ˌsɛrɪməʊnɪˈɛərɪəs). *Eccl.* Also ceremonarius. [mod.L., sb. use of adj. f. *cærimōnia* CEREMONY: see -ARY[1].] An official who

superintends the ceremonies and assists the ministers in a liturgical service.

1865 F. G. LEE *Direct. Anglicanum* 264 The ceremoniarius should be vested in cassock and cotta. **1898** *Westm. Gaz.* 10 Nov. 5/2 Before the prayer for the Church Militant the ceremonarius..again said the requiem æternam. **1913** C. MACKENZIE *Sinister St.* I. II. v. 216 I'm the Ceremonarius, and I can tell you I have my work cut out.

†**cere'moniary.** *Obs.* [on L. type *cærimōniārium*: see -ARY[1] B. 2, and cf. *antiphonary*, *breviary*, etc.] A directory or rule of ceremony.

1567 JEWELL *Def. Apol.* (1611) 593 Your owne Ceremoniarie of Rome telleth you, that Abbats haue right.. to determine and subscribe in Councell, as well as Bishops.

†**cere'moniate,** *v. Obs.* [f. CEREMONY + -ATE[3]; perh. after L. *cærēmōniāri*, *-ātus*, to treat with ceremony, worship.] *trans.* To celebrate with a ceremony; to observe as a ceremony.

1654 L'ESTRANGE *Chas. I* (1655) 2 To ceremoniate his dismission agreeable to his reception. *Ibid.* 20 Ceremoniated as it [Coronation] is, with such formalities, it representeth itself a serious vanity. **1659** —— *Alliance Div. Off.* 451 The rites wherewith they are ceremoniated.

†**cere'monical,** *a. Obs. rare.* = CEREMONIAL.

a **1626** W. SCLATER *Expos. Rom.* iv. (1650) 3 Abraham obtained not righteousness, by any work Ceremonicall. **1661** K. W. *Conf. Charac.* (1860) 55 Zealous sacrificers in their ceremonicall works.

†**'ceremoniless,** *a. Obs. rare*[−1]. [f. CEREMONY + -LESS.] Devoid of ceremony.

1603 FLORIO *Montaigne* III. xiii. (1632) 619 That.. masculine and ceremonielesse maner of life.

ceremonious (sɛrɪ'məʊnɪəs), *a.* [ad. F. *cérémonieux*, or L. *cærimōniōsus*, f. *cærimōnia* CEREMONY: see -OUS.]

1. Pertaining to, or consisting of, ceremonies or outward forms and rites; = CEREMONIAL, formal.

1555 EDEN *Decades W. Ind.* (Arb.) 57 The ceremonious lawe of Moises. **1602** SEGAR *Hon. Mil. & Civ.* III. xlvii §1. 182 When he should haue been anointed with the holy oile, there was none found in the ceremonious Horne. **1634** SIR T. HERBERT *Trav.* 34 Ceremonious rites due to the Coronation. *a* **1720** SHEFFIELD (Dk. Buckhm.) *Wks.* (1753) I. 53 Ty'd in Hymen's ceremonious chain. **1737** WATERLAND *Eucharist* 443 Ceremonious Observances.

2. Full of ceremony; accompanied with rites, religious or showy.

1611 SHAKS. *Wint. T.* III. i. 7 O, the Sacrifice, How ceremonious, solemne, and vn-earthly It was i' th' offring. **1658** MANTON *Exp. Jude* 3 A ceremonious ritual religion. **1805** SOUTHEY *Madoc in Azt.* v, The pomp of ceremonious woe. **1883** *Manch. Exam.* 14 Dec. 5/2 A statue has been raised to him..and there was a ceremonious unveiling.

3. According to prescribed or customary formalities or punctilios.

1593 SHAKS. *Rich II*, I. iii. 50 Let vs take a ceremonious leaue..of our seuerall friends. ?**1650** *Don Bellianis* 36 Words of ceremonious thanks. **1759** JOHNSON *Idler* No. 50 ⁋10 Either in friendly or ceremonious condolence. **1780** COWPER *Lett.* 12 July, To enter a room..with a most ceremonious bow. **1863** MARY HOWITT tr. *F. Bremer's Greece* II. xi, His..somewhat ceremonious politeness.

†**4.** According to the Ceremonial Law. *Obs.*

1656 S. WINTER *Serm.* 120 The holiness of children, which some say was ceremonious.

5. Of persons: Addicted to ritual observances (*obs.*); given to ceremony; punctilious in observance of formalities, *esp.* those of intercourse between ranks or persons.

1553 BALE *Vocacyon* in *Harl. Misc.* (Malh.) I. 337 [The earlier monks and hermits] were sumwhat ceremonious, but these [later corrupt monks] altogether superstitiouse. **1621** BURTON *Anat. Mel.* I. ii. IV. vii, Wholly ceremonious about titles, degrees, inscriptions. **1667–8** PEPYS *Diary* 1 Jan., To see the different humours of the gamesters to change their luck when it is bad, how ceremonious they are to call for new dice, to shift their places, etc. **1829** K. DIGBY *Broadst. Hon.* I. 223 The ceremonious and ungrateful courtiers of Vienna.

cere'moniously, *adv.* [f. prec. + -LY[2].] In a ceremonious manner; formally, in due form; with strict observance of formalities; †in accordance with the Ceremonial Law (*obs.*).

1596 SHAKS. *Merch. V.* v. i. 37 Ceremoniously let vs prepare Some welcome for the Mistresse of the house. **1621** W. SCLATER *Tythes* (1623) 225 Tithes..caeremoniously, not morally, payable. **1655** FULLER *Hist. Camb.* (1840) 217 It was never ceremoniously consecrated. **1791** BOSWELL *Johnson* (1831) I. 21 Scrupulously and ceremoniously attentive not to offend them.

cere'moniousness. [f. as prec. + -NESS.] Ceremonious quality; addiction to ceremonies; strict observance of formalities.

1583 GOLDING *Calvin on Deut.* xlviii. 286 This consisteth not in bare ceremoniousnesse but it lyeth altogether in the heart. **1666** PEPYS *Diary* 11 July, The Ceremoniousnesse of the King of Spayne. **1783** W. F. MARTYN *Geog. Mag.* II. 177 The general characteristics of the Hamburghers are complaisance, ceremoniousness, and frugality. **1843** BORROW *Bible in Sp.* xlviii. (1872) 278 With much stiffness and ceremoniousness. **1884** *Manch. Exam.* 7 June 4/6 The excessive ceremoniousness and warmth of the reception.

†**'ceremonize,** *v. Obs.* [f. CEREMONY + -IZE.] *intr.* To practise or observe ceremonies.

1633 AMES *Agst. Cerem.* II. 380 We must ceremonize [trans. *ceremoniandum est*] according to God's Word onely. **1663** SPARKE *Prim. Devot.* (ed. 3) 542 Without staying to.. ceremonize with his relations.

ceremony ('sɛrɪmənɪ). Forms: 4 ceri-, cery-, ceremoyn(e, cerymone, *pl.* -nis; 4–5 sermony(e, -ie, serimonie, 4–6 ceri-, cery-, sery-, seri-, seremony(e, -ie, 5 ceri-, cery-, serymonij, 6 cerimonie, 6–7 ceremonye, -ie, 6– ceremony, *pl.* -ies; earlier -yes. (*Sc.* 6 seremons). [ME. *cerymonye*, *sery-*, prob. a. OF. *cerymonie*, *serimonie*, ? *cerimoine*, ad. L. *cærimōnia* sacredness, sanctity; awe, reverence; exhibition of reverence or veneration, religious rite, ceremony: for conjectures as to derivation of which see the Lat. Dicts. and Skeat. The ME. forms in *-moyne* prob. represent Anglo-Fr. variants: cf. the F. ending *-moin* from L. *-mōnium*, and pairs like *glorie*, *gloire*, etc., and see -MONY. In med.L. often spelt *cere-*; since 16th c. this spelling has been established in Fr. and Eng.]

1. An outward rite or observance, religious or held sacred; the performance of some solemn act according to prescribed form; a solemnity.

c **1380** WYCLIF *Sel. Wks.* III. 431 And cerimonyes of yᵉ olde lawe, betere þan þes, ben tauht to be left bi lore of Poul. **1382** BIBLE *Gen.* xxvi. 5 That Abraham..wolde holde my seremonyes and lawis. —— *Deut.* iv. 8 Ceremoyns and ryȝtwis domis. **1447** BOKENHAM *Seyntys* (1835) 11 It was doon in ful solemne wyse And with many a cerymonye. *c* **1535** DEWES *Introd. Fr.* in *Palsgr.* 1067 The ceremonyes of the Masse. **1549** *Compl. Scot.* Ded. 7 Ensens to mak the seremons of his sacrefeis. **1590** SHAKS. *Mids. N.* v. i. 55 Some Satire..Not sorting with a nuptiall ceremonie. **1611** BIBLE *Numb.* ix. 3 According to all the ceremonies thereof shall ye keepe it. **1641** 'SMECTYMNUUS' *Vind. Answ.* §13. 163 It is ordinarily said, No Ceremony, no Bishop. **1710** *Answ. Sacheverell's Serm.* 7 Old antiquated Ceremonies. **1770** LANGHORNE *Plutarch* (1879) I. 161/2 The vestals remained a considerable time at Cære..and hence those rites were called *Ceremonies*. **1856** EMERSON *Eng. Traits* Wks. (Bohn) II. 49 They repeated the ceremonies of the eleventh century in the coronation of the present Queen.

b. *disparagingly.* A rite or observance regarded as merely formal or external; an empty form. †Sometimes regarded as symbolic or typical.

a **1533** FIRTH *Purgatory* II. Wks. (1573) 38 Shal we become Jewes and go backe to the shadow and ceremonie, sith we haue the body and signification whiche is Christ? **1621** BURTON *Anat. Mel.* II. iii. II. (1676) 197/1 It is *non ens*, a meer flash, a ceremony, a toy, a thing of nought. **1631** J. BURGES *Answ. Rejoined* 29 A Ceremony is an outward action designed or purposely observed and done in reference to some other thing to the substance whereof it doth not belong. **1693** *Col. Rec. Penn.* I. 420 There is no obligation to use the seal. It is onlie a Ceremonie. **1841** THIRLWALL *Greece* (1844) VIII. lxii. 141 The custom had probably been long a mere ceremony.

c. *loosely.* Applied to a thing done in a formal or ceremonious way; a stately formality.

1802 MAR. EDGEWORTH *Moral T.* (1816) I. i. 5 Thank God, the ceremony of dinner is over.

2. A formal act or observance, expressive of deference or respect to superiors in rank, or established by custom in social intercourse; a usage of courtesy, politeness, or civility.

c **1386** CHAUCER *Squire's T.* 507 This god of loue..Doeth so hise cerymonyes and obeisances. **1528** MORE *Heresyes* I. Wks. 107/2 Without any strayning of curtesie, whereof the serimonyes in disputacion marreth much of the matter. **1597–8** BACON *Ess. Cerem. & Resp.* (Arb.) 26/1 Ceremonies ..be not to bee omitted to straungers and strange natures. **1778** MISS BURNEY *Evelina* vii, I seldom use the ceremony of waiting for answers.

3. (without *a* or *pl.*) Formal observances or usages collectively, or as an order of things: **a.** in reference to matters of religion or state: Performance of rites, ceremonial observance.

1759 ROBERTSON *Hist. Scot.* I. IV. 266 Intrusted with matters of mere ceremony alone. **1771** *Junius Lett.* lv. 273 A true and hearty christian, in substance, not in ceremony. **1836** HOR. SMITH *Tin Trump.* (1876) 76 Ceremony..all that is considered necessary by many in religion and friendship. **1856** EMERSON *Eng. Traits* xiii. Wks. (Bohn) II. 97 The national temperament deeply enjoys the unbroken order and tradition of its church; the liturgy, ceremony, architecture.

b. Precise observance of conventional forms of deference or respect; formality, ceremoniousness. ***without ceremony***: off-hand, unceremoniously. ***to stand upon ceremony***: to insist upon the punctilious observances of formalities or refuse to go on without them. (Cf. Shakspere's use in 5.)

1603 JAS. I. in Ellis *Orig. Lett.* Ser. I. 243 III. 78 Not with that ceremonie as towardis straingeris. **1605** SHAKS. *Macb.* III. iv. 36 The sawce to meate is Ceremony. **1709** STEELE *Tatler* No. 21 ⁋8 Without further Ceremony, I will go on to relate a singular Adventure. **1798** JANE AUSTEN *Northang. Ab.* viii, I never stand upon ceremony with such people. **1833** HT. MARTINEAU *Loom & Lugg.* II. vi. 113 Without ceremony the two young ladies ran out of the room. **1866** G. MACDONALD *Ann. Q. Neighb.* xxv. (1878) 436, I was shown with much ceremony..into the presence of two ladies.

†**c.** Ceremonious respect or regard.

1607 TOPSELL *Four-f. Beasts* 264 The Romans had the Equestrial Statues in great reverence and ceremony. **1675** tr. *Machiavelli's Wks.* (1675) 255 Oliveretto having paid his ceremony fell in with the rest.

d. Ceremonial display, pomp, state. *arch.*

1599 SHAKS. *Hen. V*, IV. i. 256 What haue Kings, that Priuates haue not too, Saue ceremonie. **1710** *Lond. Gaz.* No. 4742/2 He was brought in Ceremony from the Princess-Royal's Apartment. **1859** TENNYSON *Enid* 297 His dress a suit of fray'd magnificence, Once fit for feasts of ceremony.

†**4.** *concr.* An external accessory or symbolical 'attribute' of worship, state, or pomp. *Obs.*

1581 SIDNEY *Apol. Poetrie* (Arb.) 47 Æneas..carrying away his religious ceremonies. **1601** SHAKS. *Jul. C.* I. i. 70 Disrobe the Images If you do finde them deckt with Ceremonies. **1603** —— *Meas. for M.* II. ii. 59. **1605** *Journ. Earl Nottingh.* in *Harl. Misc.* (Malh.) II. 553 Dukes of especial name bearing divers ceremonies..as the Salera or salt borne by one, the taper of wax by another, the chrism by another. **1709** STRYPE *Ann. Ref.* xliv. 454 The ceremonies of cap and surplice.

†**5.** A portent, omen: (drawn from the performance of some rite). *Obs.*

1601 SHAKS. *Jul. C.* II. i. 197 He is Superstitious growne of late, Quite from the maine Opinion he held once, Of Fantasie, of Dreames, and Ceremonies. *Ibid.* II. ii. 13, I neuer stood on Ceremonies, Yet now they fright me.

6. ***master of the ceremonies***: the person who superintends the ceremonies observed in a place of state or on some public occasion.

1662 GERBIER *Princ.* (1665) Ded., My place of Master of the Ceremonies, which the King confirmed unto me during my life. **1748** SMOLLETT *Rod. Rand.* lv, Mr. Nash.. commonly attends in this place..as master of the ceremonies. **1798** JANE AUSTEN *Northang. Ab.* I. iii, The master of the ceremonies introduced to her a very gentlemanlike young man as a partner. **1888** *Court Guide*, H. M. Household, Master of Ceremonies. General Sir F. Seymour.

7. *Comb.*, as ***ceremony-monger***.

1681 in *Roxb. Bal.* (1886) VI. 3 A Ceremony-Monger, who rails at Dissenters, And damns Non-Conformists in the Pulpit he enters. **1710** *Answ. Sacheverell's Serm.* 6 The rigid Ceremony-mongers did hate the Religious part of the Nation.

†**'ceremony,** *v. Obs. rare.* [f. prec. sb.] *trans.* To sanctify or treat with ceremony.

1635 QUARLES *Embl.* v. viii. (1718) 278 If..Hymen's bands Have ceremonied your unequal hands. **1656** S. H. *Gold. Law* 36 Call'd and ceremony'd like a King.

Cerenkov, Cherenkov (tʃɛ'rɛŋkəf, -'rjɛŋkəf). The name of P. A. Čerenkov (born 1904), Russian physicist, used *attrib.* in ***Cerenkov effect, radiation***, etc. (see quots.).

1940 *Physical Rev.* LVII. 490/2 The Cerenkov radiation ..does not represent a loss of energy to be added to that calculated with the Bohr theory. **1955** *Sci. Amer.* Oct. 22/3 A photograph of the swimming-pool reactor showing its uranium fuel load, bathed in the blue glow known as the Cerenkov effect. **1958** *Chambers's Techn. Dict.* 964/1 *Cerenkov radiation*, visible radiation produced when charged particles traverse a medium which increases their initial velocity to a velocity greater than that of light. **1958** *Times* 29 Oct. 8/6 The Cherenkov effect for which the three Russian physicists have received their award is the emission of light waves by electrons moving at very high speeds. **1959** *Times* 23 Oct. 17/2 The counters used will be of the kind, known as Cerenkov counters, in which incoming high-energy particles are detected by the flashes of light that they produce when they pass through a tank of water. **1969** *Listener* 12 June 823/2 The bow wave's equivalent for light is Cerenkov radiation, and it is emitted, by a particle travelling faster than light, in a certain direction, depending on the actual speed of the particle.

†**'cereole.** *Obs.* [? f. L. *cēra* wax + *oleum* oil; or ? ad. L. *cereol-us* wax-coloured.] A cerate of wax and oil.

1657 TOMLINSON *Renou's Disp.* 123 Whence it is called ceratum or more properly cereole.

cereolite. *Min.* obs. var. of CEROLITE.

1814 ALLAN *Min. Nomen.* 10. **1835** SHEPARD *Min.* 120.

cereous ('sɪərɪəs), *a.* [f. L. *cēre-us* waxen + -OUS.] Of the nature of wax, waxen, waxy.

1601 HOLLAND *Pliny* II. 135 That cereous substance Propolis. **1654** GAYTON *Fest. Notes* II. v. 52 What is worth his observation, goes into his cereous tables. **1679** SIR T. BROWNE *Wks.* (1852) III. 459 The bones of a dead body cereous or somewhat soft like wax. **1803–4** SYD. SMITH in *Athenæum* (1884) 18 Oct. 490/3 The room..is lighted up.. and in this cereous galaxy, etc.

'cerer. [f. CERE *v.*] One who ceres (a corpse).

1587 GOLDING *De Mornay* xxii. 339 The Cearer of dead folks.

cererite, cererium; see CERITE, CERIUM. (The former name is used in the *Brit. Mus. Catal. of Minerals.*)

ceresin, ceresine ('sɛrəsɪn, -iːn). [f. mod.L. *ceres*, irreg. f. L. *cēra* wax + -IN[1], -INE[5].] A whitish wax, hard and brittle, prepared from ozocerite, or a petroleum wax, mixed with, or used as a substitute for, beeswax. Also ***ceresin wax***.

1885 *Encycl. Brit.* XVIII. 113/1 Under the name of ceresin or ozocerotin a large proportion of the high-melting paraffin extracted from the mineral [*sc.* ozocerite] goes into commerce, to be used chiefly for the adulteration of beeswax. **1935** *Nature* 19 Jan. 113/2 Initially, the strong colour of petroleum ceresin was a disadvantage in this

connexion, but this is overcome by incorporation of the ceresin during the manufacture of the paraffin wax and refining the two together. **1951** H. M. Langton et al. *Synthetic Resins* (ed. 3) xvii. 661 Ceresin and paraffin wax are the more waxy constituents and find use in the electrical industry mainly for impregnating condensers and small coils which are not subjected to any temperature rise. **1958** M. L. Wolf *Dict. Painting* 54 Ceresin wax, occasionally used as a surface coating on paintings, sculpture, and other objects of art.

‖**Cereus** (ˈsɪəriːəs). *Bot.* [L. *cēreus* waxen, resembling wax, f. *cēra* wax.] A large genus of cactuses, natives of tropical America, remarkable for their singularity of form and the beauty of their flowers; the Torch-thistle.

1730 Stack in *Phil. Trans.* XXXVI. 462 This Cereus.. exposed in open air all Summer, grew without pushing forth Branches. **1767** J. Abercrombie *Ev. Man own Gard.* (1803) 382 The tenderer sorts of cereuses. **1844** Tupper *Heart* iv. 38 Lustrous to look upon, even as the night-blowing Cereus. **1872** Reade *Put yourself, &c.* II. xi. 173.

cereuse, obs. form of ceruse.

cereˈvisial, *a.* [f. L. *cerevisia* beer + -al[1].] Of or pertaining to beer.

17.., **1862** [see cervisial].

cereˈvisious, *a. nonce-wd.* = prec.

1841 *Fras. Mag.* XXIV. 26 Those flasks of Falernian, and cans cerevicious.

†**ˈcerfoil.** *Obs. rare.* [a. OF. *cerfoil*, F. *cerfeuil*, ad. L. *cærefolium* (Pliny), Latinized form of Gr. χαιρέφυλλον (which Columella has as *chærephyllum*).] = chervil, q.v.

[*c* **1265** *Voc.* in Wr.-Wülcker 557, *Cerfolium* (Anglo-Fr.), cerfoil, villen.] **14..** *Med. Receipts* in *Rel. Ant.* I. 55 Tak confery..cerfoyle, herbe Robert, ambrose, etc. *c* **1420** *Pallad. on Husb.* x. 158 Parsnepe and cerfoile also forth may stande. **1567** Maplet *Gr. Forest* 37 Cerfolie is an herbe in operation and working in a maner fiery.

cerge, variant of cierge, *Obs.*, taper.

cergyn, obs. form of search.

c **1440** *Promp. Parv.* 67/1 Cergyn, *scrutor, rimor.*

ceriatly, var. of seriatly *adv. Obs.* in order.

ceriawnt, obs. form of sergeant, serjeant.

ceric (ˈsɪərɪk), *a.*[1] *Chem.* [f. cer-ium + -ic.] Of or belonging to cerium; applied to compounds in which cerium combines as a tetrad, as in *ceric oxide*, CeO_2, *ceric* (or *cerium*) *salts.*

1863-79 Watts *Dict. Chem.* I. 834 Ceric fluoride..is a yellow precipitate. **1879** *Ibid. 3rd Supp.* 421 Normal and basic ceric salts. **1873** Watts *Fownes' Chem.* 380 The ceric compounds, in which it is apparently trivalent.

ceric (ˈsɪərɪk), *a.*[2] *Chem.* [f. L. *cēra*, Gr. κηρός wax + -ic.] Chemically related to wax; as in *ceric acid*, a brownish diaphanous waxy mass obtained by treating cerin with nitric acid.

1838 T. Thomson *Chem. Org. Bodies* 1045 An acid..to which we may give the name of ceric acid.

ceriferous (sɪˈrɪfərəs), *a.* [f. L. type **cērifer* (f. *cēra* + *-fer* bearing) + -ous; cf. F. *cérifère.*] Producing wax.

cerigerous (sɪˈrɪdʒərəs), *a.* [f. L. *cēr-a* cere + *-ger* bearing + -ous; cf. F. *cérigère.*] Of the beak of a bird: Furnished with a cere.

1856-8 W. Clark *Van der Hoeven's Zool.* II. 423 Bill.. thick, cerigerous at the base.

†**cerigo, -gon.** *Obs. rare.* [see quot. 1753; and cf. F. *sarigue* opossum, from Brazilian *çarigueya* (Littré). Florio has It. *cerigone* (explained as in Kersey), which in form looks like an augmentative of *cerigo* 'clerk, shaveling'.] The opossum.

1708 Kersey, *Cerigon*, an American wild Beast having a Skin under the Belly like a Sack, which serves to carry its Young Ones. **1721-1800** in Bailey. **1753** Chambers *Cycl. Supp.* s.v., The Americans in some places call this animal in their language carigueya; and it is probable that this name cerigo is only a corruption of that word, though it be received generally in the world as a proper name.

†**ceˈrilla.** *Obs.* [Sp. *cerilla*, variant of *cedilla*, due to interchange of *d* and *r*; also in 17th c. F. *cerille* (Cotgr.).] = cedilla.

1591 Percivall *Sp. Dict., Gram.*, C before a o u like k.. if the nature of the word require any other pronunciation, it is noted with a little taile, as ç, and is called Cerilla, sounding almost as the Italian *z.* *a* **1646** J. Gregory *Terrest. Globe* in *Posthuma* (1650) 268 The Açores, or Azores, for so the cerilla will endure to be pronounced. **1708** Kersey, *Cerilla* (in the Art of Printing), a Mark set under the Letter ç in French and Spanish, to shew that it is to be pronounc'd as an *s.* **1863** Miss Sewell *Chr. Names* i. 32 The mark is called a cedilla or cerilla.

ceriman (ˈsɛrɪmən). *Bot.* [ad. Amer. Sp. *cerimán.*] A climbing plant, *Monstera deliciosa*, of the family Araceæ, which is a native of Mexico and yields an edible fruit.

1871 Kingsley *At Last* vii, Up the next [stem] the Ceriman spreads its huge leaves, latticed and forked again and again. **1946** K. & J. Morton *Fifty Tropical Fruits of Nassau* p. x, Trees or plants..cultivated in the Bahamas.. as ornamentals, such as the Jamaica Cherry,..Ceriman, Giant Grenadilla and the Passionfruits.

cerimony, -moyn, -monial, etc., obs. ff. ceremony, ceremonial.

cerin (ˈsɪərɪn). *Chem.* [f. L. *cēra* wax + -in.]

1. 'A waxy substance extracted by alcohol or ether from grated cork. (Cork contains from 1·8 to 2·5 per cent. of waxy matter.) Watts *Dict. Chem.*

†**2.** 'A name applied by John to the portion of beeswax which is readily soluble in alcohol; according to Brodie...merely impure cerotic acid'.

1850 Daubeny *Atom. The.* viii. 258 Pure bees-wax is composed of two vegetable principles, the one..most readily dissolved being called cerin, that less so, myricin. **1861** Hulme tr. *Moquin-Tandon* II. iii. 210 Wax contains three distinct principles—viz. cerine, myricine, and ceroleine. The cerine, or cerotic acid, forms the greatest part. *c* **1865** Letheby in *Circ. Sc.* I. 98/1 About twenty-two per cent. of a peculiar fatty acid (cerotic)..formerly named *cerine.*

cerine (ˈsɪəraɪn). *Min.* [f. cer-ium + -ine; named (in Swedish) by Hisinger in 1815.] A variety of the mineral allanite or cerium-epidote.

1814 Allan *Min. Nomen.* s.v. *Cerium*, Brown Oxide, Allanite, Cerin. **1868** Dana *Min.* (1880) 286 s.v. *Allanite*, *Cerine* is the same thing..subtranslucent in thin splinters. *Ibid.* 289 Cerine occurs at Bastnäs in Sweden.

cering (ˈsɪərɪŋ), *vbl. sb.* [f. cere *v.* + -ing[1].]

1. Waxing, covering with wax.

1480 *Wardr. Acc. Edw. IV* (1830) 125 For rede threde, ceringe, sowing. **1565-78** Cooper *Thesaur., Ceratura*, a dressing with waxe, searing.

2. *attrib.*, as in *cering-candle*, *cering-cloth.*

1480 *Wardr. Acc. Edw. IV* (1830) 121 For ceryng candell' at ii tymes vd. **1502** *Priv. Purse Exp. Eliz. York* (1830) 83 Searing candelles for the awter clothys. **1530** Palsgr. 479/2, I ceare a garment of sylke or velvet, as a taylour doth with a ceryng candell, *Jencire.* **1545** Ascham *Toxoph.* (Arb.) 109 Take a searynge cloth made of fine virgin waxe and Deres sewet, and put nexte your fynger. **1686** tr. *Chardin's Trav.* 154 A little Searing Candle.

cerinin (ˈsɪərɪnɪn). *Chem.* [f. Gr. κήριν-ος waxy + -in.] 'A waxy fat which forms about 18 per cent. of the lignite of Garstewitz near Merseberg' (Watts *Dict. Chem.*).

ˈcerinite. *Min.* [f. as prec. + -ite: named 1859.] An amorphous silicate of alumina, a yellowish white mineral with a waxy lustre.

1861 H. W. Bristow *Gloss. Min.* 69.

Cerinthian (sɪˈrɪnθɪən), *a.* and *sb.* [f. *Cerinthus* + -ian.] **A.** *adj.* Of or pertaining to the teaching of Cerinthus, one of the earliest heresiarchs of the Christian Church (*c* A.D. 88), who attempted to unite Christianity with a mixture of Gnosticism and Judaism, the main peculiarity being the assumption that Jesus was a man and the Christ an æon who entered into Jesus. **B.** *sb.* An adherent of the teaching of Cerinthus.

1576 Hanmer *Aunc. Eccl. Hist.* (1585) 57 Cerinthus, founder of the Cerinthian heresie. **1585-7** T. Rogers *39 Art.* (1607) 48 They..which either deny or impugn the Deity of our Saviour, as did the Cerinthians. **1879** Farrar *St. Paul* (1882) 766 Any Cerinthian attempt to distinguish between Jesus the man of sorrows and Christ the risen Lord.

ceriore, -iowre, obs. ff. of searcher.

ceriph (ˈsɛrɪf). [Deriv. obscure. A writer in *N. & Q.* 8 May '69 suggests Du. and Flem. *schreef* line, stroke (*schreve* 'linea; norma, et terminus' Kilian), which fairly suits sense and form; but historical evidence is wanting, and the quasi-French form of *sans-ceriph* is not accounted for.]

One of the fine lines of a letter, *esp.* the fine 'hair-line' at the top or bottom of capitals, as of I; hence ***sans-ceriph*** a name for the block type that has no hair-lines. See serif.

1830 in Figgins *Spec. Printing Types*, Sans-cerif. **1833** in Blake & Stephenson *Printing Types*, Nonpareil sans-surryphs. **1841** Savage *Dict. Print.* 163. **1876** *Phonetic Jrnl.* 20 Sept. 454/1 The capital C in sans-ceriph type is too much like G.

‖**cerise** (səˈriːz), *a.* and *sb.* [a. F. *cerise* cherry, *rouge-cerise* cherry-red.] Name of a light bright clear red, resembling that of some cherries.

1858 *Times* 30 Nov. 10/2 Well-dressed beauties..in all the glowing grandeur of cerise and blue. **1865** *Pall Mall G.* 25 Oct. 10 Gladiateur's colours are blue and red, and Nu's are cerise (which is very like red) and blue. **1882** *Garden* 3 June 395/1 The colours are..cerise, maroon, orange, rose.

cerite[1] (ˈsɪəraɪt). *Min.* [Named 1804: f. as cerium + -ite.] A very rare mineral, the hydrated silicate of Cerium (of which it is the chief source).

Found as yet only in an abandoned copper mine at Bastnäs near Riddarhyttan in Westmannland, Sweden, in compact fine-grained masses of indistinct blackish-red colour, and also in short six-sided prisms. It contains also the rare metals Lanthanum and Didymium, and generally a small quantity of Yttrium. Called by Klaproth *ochroite.*

1804 W. Nicholson *Jrnl. Nat. Phil.* XII. 105 (*title*) Experiments on a Mineral formerly called false Tungsten, now Cerite, in which a new Metal has been found. **1812** Sir H. Davy *Chem. Philos.* 433 There is a mineral found at Ridderhytta in Sweden, very like tungsten, of a reddish colour, and which has been called cerite. **1837-68** in Dana *Min.* **1885** Erni *Min.* 317 Color of cerite, reddish-gray.

b. *Cerite metals*: cerium, didymium, and lanthanum (Watts *Dict. Chem.* 3rd Supp. 418).

ˈcerite[2]. *Palæont.* [a. F. *cérite*, ad. mod.L. *cerithium*, name of the genus.] A genus of fossil brachiopod molluscs. Also *attrib.*

1811 Pinkerton *Petral.* I. 497 Some of the marl beds contain cardites..cerites or screws. **1852** Th. Ross tr. *Humboldt's Trav.* I. v. 184 The cerite limestone of the banks of the Seine is sometimes mixed with sandstone.

cerium (ˈsɪərɪəm). *Chem.* [Named by Hisinger and Berzelius, along with its source *cerite*, after the planet *Ceres*, whose discovery (in 1801) was then one of the most striking facts in physical science. The ending is as in *potassium* and other names of metals. Klaproth, in 1807, changed the names to *cererium* and *cererite* 'lest they should appear to be derived from *cēra*, κηρός wax', but the change was not accepted (Dana).]

One of the chemical elements: a rare metal, discovered in the mineral called cerite; it has the colour and lustre of iron, and takes a high polish, which it retains in dry air, but in moist air it becomes covered with coloured films like heated steel; it is malleable and ductile, of specific gravity 6·63 to 6·73. Atomic weight 138; symbol Ce.

1804 W. Nicholson *Jrnl. Nat. Phil.* IX. 290 (*title*) Account of Cerium, a New Metal found in a Mineral Substance from Bastnas in Sweden. **1808** Henry *Epit. Chem.* (ed. 5) 266 From the planet Ceres, discovered about the same period, it has been called Cerium; and the mineral that contains it is termed Cerite. **1812** Sir H. Davy *Chem. Philos.* 433 Cerium had not been obtained in the metallic form till I succeeded in reducing some oxide sent me by M. Berzelius, by means of potassium..[forming] a deep gray metallic powder, which became brown by oxidation. **1844-68** Dana *Min.* 414 In 1839 Mosander proved that the oxyd of cerium contained the new metal *lanthanum*, and in 1842 another new metal *didymium.* **1865** A. H. Church in *Chem. News* XII. 121 A new British mineral containing cerium. **1875** Ure *Dict. Arts* I. 757 Cerium has also been detected by Prof. Church in a Cornish mineral.

b. *attrib.*: in ***cerium compounds***, ***group*** (of metals), ***salts***, etc. = ceric[1].

1879 Watts *Dict. Chem.* 2nd Supp. 273 Preparation of pure cerium salts. *Ibid.* 3rd Supp. 420 A piece of cerium wire burns with even greater brilliancy than magnesium. **1886** Roscoe *Elem. Chem.* 166 Class VI, Cerium Group.

cerke, variant of serk, *Obs.*, a shirt.

c **1380** *Sir Ferumb.* 2449 Al naked..saf hir cerke.

cermet (ˈsɜːmɛt). Also **ceramet.** [f. cera(mic *a.* + met(al *sb.*] A ductile, heat-resistant alloy of metal and ceramic substances. Cf. ceramal.

1950, **1953** [see ceramal]. **1953** *Americana Ann.* 436/1 Cermets, which are combinations of ceramic materials with metals,..employ such substances as carbides, borides, nitrides, and oxides, cemented with binders of iron, nickel, or cobalt. **1958** *Engineering* 31 Jan. 141/3 New alloy steels, molybdenum, fused quartz, ceramics, cermets and high-temperature plastics are entering the arena.

cermocination, -trix, etc.: see ser-.

cern (sɜːn), *v.*[1] [ad. L. *cern-ĕre* 'to separate, to decide', in judicial language 'to resolve to enter upon an inheritance', 'to make known this determination', 'to enter upon an inheritance' (Lewis and Short).] Used in translation of Roman law-books for: To declare acceptance of an inheritance. Hence **ˈcerning** *vbl. sb.*

1880 Muirhead *Gaius* II. §166 If the individual so instituted desire to be heir, he must cern within the time for cretion... I enter upon and cern to his inheritance. —— *Ulpian* xxii. §25 A stranger heir, if he be instituted with cretion, becomes heir by cerning.

So **ˈcerniture**, formal declaration of the acceptance of an inheritance. [Not formed on L. analogies: the L. is *crētio.*]

1880 Muirhead *Ulpian* xxii. §28 To cern is to recite the words of cerniture in this way. —— *Gaius* II. §482 Cerniture in compliance with the cretion-clause.

†**cern**, *v.*[2] *Obs. rare*$^{-1}$. Short for concern.

1596 Shaks. *Tam. Shr.* v. i. 77 What cernes it you, if I weare Pearle and gold.

†**cerne**, *sb. Obs. rare.* [a. F. *cerne* circle:—L. *circin-us* circle, deriv. of *circus* circle.] A circle; an enceinte.

1393 Gower *Conf.* III. 46 With Cernes bothe square and rounde He traceth ofte upon the grounde, Makend his invocation. *c* **1450** *Merlin* 309 Merlin..made a cerne with a yerde in myddell of the launde.

cerne (sɜːn), *v. rare.* [a. F. *cerne-r* to encircle, surround:—L. *circināre*, f. *circin-us*: see the sb.] *trans.* To surround, invest.

1857 SIR F. PALGRAVE *Norm. & Eng.* II. 548 The cavalry occupied the undulating valleys..and they cerned the lofty fortress on all sides.

† **ˈcernicle.** *Obs. rare.* [ad. med.L. *cerniculum* sieve, f. *cernĕre* to sift.] A sieve.

1657 TOMLINSON *Renou's Disp.* 559 Dates..must be brayed..then trajected through a cernicle.

cernuous (ˈsɜːnjuːəs), *a.* [f. L. *cernu-us* inclined forwards + -OUS.] Bowing downwards; in *Bot.* of a flower: Having the top bent downwards; drooping, nodding.

1653 J. HALL *Paradoxes* 48 That very weight which sinks us downe from our erect constitution, into the cernuous lownesse of beasts. **1836** *Penny Cycl.* V. 252 (*Bot. Terms*) *Cernuous*, drooping. **1853** G. JOHNSTON *Nat. Hist. E. Bord.* I. 42 The flowers are cernuous after their blow.

cero (ˈsɪərəʊ). [Altered f. Sp. *sierra* saw, sawfish.] A fish of the mackerel family, *Scomberomorus regalis*, found in warm parts of the western Atlantic.

1884 GOODE *Nat. Hist. Aquat. Anim.* 307 The Spotted Cero, or King Cero, *Scomberomorus regalis*. **1965** A. J. MCCLANE *Standard Fishing Encycl.* 174/2 Cero are found from Cape Cod to Brazil and are abundant around southern Florida and the West Indies.

cero- comb. form of L. *cera* or Gr. κηρός wax; as in **cero-mastic, cero-mimene, cero-resin.** Also the first element in many derivatives.

1804 HATCHETT in *Phil. Trans.* XCIV. 215 Lac may be denominated a cero-resin. **1828** S. F. GRAY *Operat. Chem.* 805 Ceromimene, or prepared stearine, is brilliant, white, and semi-transparent. **1884** A. J. BUTLER *Coptic Ch. Egypt* II. i. 28 Mixed with ceromastic.

ˈcerofer. *rare.* [repr. Gr. κηροφόρος wax-taper-bearer, and med.L. *cēriforus* and *cēroferārius* formed on the Gr., with influence of L. *fer-re*, *-fer*: the pure L. form would be *cerifer*.] A wax-taper-bearer; an acolyte.

1884 W. H. R. JONES *Register S. Osmund* ii. Gloss. 197 An engraving of cerofers in rochets holding their tapers.

ceroferary (sɪˈrɒfərərɪ). *rare.* Also **cerophérary.** **a.** = CEROFER [in F. *céroferaire*.] **b.** A candlestick, candelabrum [= L. *cēroferārium*].

[ISIDORE *Orig.* VII. xii. 29 Acolythi Græce, Latine ceroferarii dicuntur, a deportandis cereis, quando legendum est Evangelium, aut sacrificium offerendum.] **1398** TREVISA *Barth. De P.R.* XIX. lxi. (1495) 898 They that serue in chyrches of wexe candyls ben callyd *Ceroferarii*. *c* **1650** FULLER is cited by Webster for sense a; sense b is given without quotation in mod. Dicts.

cerography (sɪˈrɒgrəfɪ). [ad. Gr. κηρογραφία painting with wax, encaustic painting, f. κηρός wax + -γραφία writing.] Writing or painting on or in wax. **a.** Applied to the encaustic painting of the ancients. **b.** 'Engraving on wax spread on a sheet of copper, from which a stereotype plate is taken' (Webster, 1856).

So **ˈcerograph,** a writing or engraving on wax; an encaustic painting. **ceroˈgraphic, -ical,** *a.*, pertaining to cerography. **ceˈrographist,** one skilled in cerography.

1593 B. BARNES *Parthen. & P.* in Arb. *Garner* V. 465 Which Cerography In unknown character of Victory, Nature hath set. **1731** BAILEY Vol. II, *Cerography*, a painting or writing in wax. **1846** S. E. MORSE *Geography* Title, Illustrated with more than fifty cerographic maps. *Ibid.* Pref. 5 The new art of Cerography is applied for the first time to the illustration of a work of this kind.

cerolein (sɪˈrəʊliːɪn). *Chem.* [f. L. *cēra* wax + OLEIN.] A soft substance containing carbon, hydrogen, and oxygen, obtained by treating beeswax with boiling alcohol.

1861 HULME tr. *Moquin-Tandon* II. III. 210. **1876** HARLEY *Mat. Med.* 793 Cerolein forms about 5 per cent. of wax, and gives to it the appropriate colour and odour.

cerolite (ˈsɪərəlaɪt). *Min.* Also **kerolite.** [ad. *kerolith* (Breithaupt 1823), f. Gr. κηρός wax + λίθος stone: see -LITE.] A hydrous silicate of aluminum, having a somewhat waxy lustre and greasy feel.

1868 DANA *Min.* (1880) 470 Breithaupt unites deweylite to cerolite.

‖ **ceroma** (sɪˈrəʊmə). [Lat. *cērōma* ointment for wrestlers, place for wrestling, etc., a. Gr. κήρωμα anything made of wax, ointment for wrestlers, f. κηροῦν to wax.] 'An apartment in the Gymnasia and baths of the ancients, where the bathers and wrestlers were anointed' (Gwilt).

ceromancy (ˈsɪərəmænsɪ). [a. F. *céromancie*, med.L. *cēromantia*, f. Gr. κηρός wax + μαντεία divination.] Divination from the figures produced by dropping melted wax into water.

1652 GAULE *Magastrom.* 165-6. **1656** BLOUNT *Glossogr.*, *Ceromanty*, divination or sooth-saying by wax put into water. *a* **1693** URQUHART *Rabelais* III. xxv, By ceromancy, where, by the means of wax dissolved into water, thou shalt see the..lively representation of thy future wife.

ceromel (ˈsɪərəmɛl). [a. F. *céromel*, f. L. *cēra* wax + *mel* honey.] A mixture of wax and honey, 'used as an application to wounds and ulcers in hot climates, where ointments soon turn rancid' (*Syd. Soc. Lex.*).

† **ceˈroneous,** *a. Obs. rare.* [f. med.L. *ceroneum* an ointment chiefly composed of wax.] Consisting of or containing wax.

1657 TOMLINSON *Renou's Disp.* 123 They admit of wax as many Plaisters which are therefore..called ceroneous.

ceˈroon. 'The American mode of spelling SEROON, a bale or package made of skins' (Simmonds *Dict. Trade* 1858).

1824 *Shipping & Commercial List* 31 July (D.A.), A sale of 30 ceroons of Cuba [tobacco]. *a* **1861** T. WINTHROP *Isthmiana* (1883) 242 A little ragamuffin, who had come into town on a nag between two hide ceroons, full of mami apples.

cerophérary: see CEROFERARY.

ceroplast (ˈsɪərəʊplæst). *rare.* [ad. Gr. κηρόπλαστος moulded in wax; see next.] A mould in wax, etc.; also *attrib.*

1872 DE MORGAN *Budg. Paradoxes* 149 He spread a thick block of putty over a wooden chair and sat in it until it had taken a ceroplast copy of the proper seat.

ceroplastic (sɪərəʊˈplæstɪk), *a.* [a. Gr. κηροπλαστικός relating to modelling in wax, f. κηρός wax + πλάσσειν to form, mould, πλαστός moulded.]

1. Of or relating to modelling in wax.

1801 *Monthly Mag.* XII. 423 The first application of ceroplastic to anatomical science. **1855** tr. *Labarte's Arts Mid. Ages* i. 37 The ceroplastic art. **1882** *Daily Tel.* 27 Mar., A ceroplastic panorama of the Men..of the Time.

2. ceroplastics *sb.*, the art of modelling in wax; *concr.* waxworks.

1882 *Daily Tel.* 27 Mar., A permanent Museum of Ceroplastics, or in plainer English, a waxwork exhibition. **1884** *Ibid.* 14 July 5/4 The unrivalled collection of ceroplastics in Baker street.

So **ˈceroplasty,** 'the making of anatomical models in wax' (*Syd. Soc. Lex.*).

cerosin (ˈsɪərəsɪn). *Chem.* [f. L. **cerōs-us* waxy + -IN.] A wax-like substance obtained by scraping the surface of some kinds of sugar-cane.

c **1865** LETHEBY in *Circ. Sc.* I. 97/2 A wax-like substance, named *cerosine* by Dumas, is..obtained from the surface of many species of sugar-cane.

ceroso-. *Chem.* Combining form of CEROUS *a.*[1]

1863-72 WATTS *Dict. Chem.* I. 834 *Ceroso-ceric Oxide*.. may be regarded as a compound of cerous and ceric oxide. **1873** —— *Fownes' Chem.* 380 The ceroso-ceric compounds, of intermediate composition. **1879** —— *Dict. Chem., 3rd Supp.* 421 The brown-red hexagonal [sulphur] salt remains also a ceroso-ceric salt according to the new atomic weight.

† **cerote.** *Obs.* Also **cerot.** [ad. L. *cērōtum*, a. Gr. κηρωτόν waxed, f. κηρο- to wax.] = CERATE.

1562 TURNER *Herbal* II. 30 b, The roote..is good for brused places and wyth a cerote or treat made of waxe. **1562** BULLEYN *Bk. Simples* 64 b, Sondrie oyntementes and Cerots. **1602** HOLLAND *Pliny* 'Wds. of Art', Cerote is of a middle nature between an ointment and a plastre, not so hard as the one nor so soft as the other. **1669** W. SIMPSON *Hydrol. Chym.* 364 Added to cerots and plaisters.

cerotic (sɪˈrɒtɪk). *Chem.* [f. Gr. κηρωτ-όν (see prec.) + -IC.] In ***cerotic acid***, $C_{27}H_{54}O_2$, 'the essential constituent of that portion of beeswax which is soluble in boiling alcohol' (Watts *Dict. Chem.*). See CERIN. Its salts are called **ˈcerotates.**

1850 DAUBENY *Atom. The.* viii. 258 As cerin forms a soap with potass, Brodie regards it as an acid, which he therefore calls the cerotic. **1873** WATTS *Fownes' Chem.* 695 Cerotic Acid is the essential constituent of cerin.

So **ˈcerotene,** an olefine ($C_{27}H_{54}$) obtained by the dry distillation of Chinese wax; **ˈcerotin,** hydrate of ceryl, $C_{27}H_{56}O$; **ˈcerotyl,** = CERYL.

1850 DAUBENY *Atom. The.* viii. 258 Mr. Brodie..also detected in a species of wax from China a substance..which he calls cerotin. *c* **1865** LETHEBY in *Circ. Sc.* I. 98/1 Chinese wax..is made up of cerotic acid and an alcohol named *oxide of cerotyl*. **1869** ROSCOE *Elem. Chem.* 334 Cerotyl Alcohol, is contained in Chinese wax.

cerous (ˈsɪərəs), *a.*[1] *Chem.* [f. CER-IUM + -OUS.] Of the nature of Cerium; applied to chemical compounds in which cerium combines as a triad, as in *cerous salts*; *cerous chloride*, $CeCl_3$, *cerous oxide*, Ce_2O_3. *cerous silicate*, $Ce_2Si_3O_{12}$.

1863-72 WATTS *Dict. Chem.* I. 834 Cerous fluoride is obtained as a white precipitate by adding an alkaline fluoride to a cerous salt. *Ibid.* 835 Cerous silicate exists in nature as Cerite; the phosphate as Monazite, Edwardsite, Cryptolite, and Phosphocerite; the carbonate in Parisite.

cerous (ˈsɪərəs), *a.*[2] *Ornith.* [f. CERE *sb.*, or L. *cēra* + -OUS.] Of the nature of a cere.

1869 GILLMORE *Rept. & Birds* Introd. 190 In the Goose, we find the bill..covered at the base with a cerous skin.

cerre, obs. form of CERE *v.*

† **cerre-tree.** *Obs. rare*[−1]. [ad. L. *cerrus*, a kind of oak + TREE.] A species of oak: the Turkey Oak (*Quercus Cerris*), or the Holm Oak (*Q. Ilex*).

1577 B. GOOGE *Heresbach's Husb.* (1586) 102 b, An other Mast bearing Oke there is..a kinde whereof some thinke the Cerre tree to be, called in Latine Cerrus.

† **ˈcerrial,** *a. Obs.* Also **cerial, serriale.** [a. OIt. *cereale*, f. *cerro* (*cero*) evergreen oak, L. *cerrus* Turkey or bitter oak; see -AL[1].] Of or pertaining to evergreen oak.

c **1386** CHAUCER *Knts. T.* 1432 A coroune of a grene ook cerial [*v.r.* serial; Boccaccio *Teseide*, Corona di querzia cereale]. *a* **1500** *Flower & Leaf* xxx, Chapelets fresh of okes serrial, Newly sprong. [*a* **1700** DRYDEN *Flower & Leaf* 284 Branches..Of palm, of laurel, or of cerrial-oak.]

† **cerse, cers, cerss,** *v. Sc. Obs.* [cf. OF. *cercer*, dial. var. of *cercher* (SEARCH), *chercher*.] An obsolete variant of SEARCH *v.*

1503 *Acts Jas. IV* (1814) 242 (Jam.), To cerss the salaris and passaris furth of the Realme. **1516** in Pitcairn *Crim. Trials* I. 265* To cerse and seik George Howme. **1533** BELLENDEN *Livy* v. (1822) 414 The two men sall cers the bukis of Sibilla.

cerse, obs. f. SEARCE to sift.

† **cert,** *adv. Obs.* [a. OF. *cert* adj. and adv.:—L. *cert-us* sure, settled, determined, *certē* surely, certainly. The adj. use does not appear in Eng. (exc. as in 2), and prob. the adverbial use is mixed up with that of CERTES.]

1. Certainly, certes, of a truth.

c **1300** *K. Alis.* 5803 So hy ben delited in that art That wery ne ben hy neuere, cert. *c* **1330** *Arth. & Merl.* 3569 Thir while the knightes cert Were y-went into desert.

2. Phrase. ***in cert***: of a certainty, in truth.

c **1440** *Launfal* 297, I dar well say yn sert.

cert (sɜːt), *sb. slang.* Also **cert.** (with full stop). [Abbrev. of CERTAIN *a.*, CERTAINTY.] A certainty (esp. in phr. ***a dead cert***); *spec.* in horse-racing, a horse that is considered certain to win.

1889 *Man of the World* 29 June 3/2 Love-in-Idleness is bound to take the Rous Memorial, and I hear Pioneer is a cert. for the St. James's. **1889** G. & W. GROSSMITH *Diary of Nobody* in *Punch* 2 Mar. 97/1 It is not speculation—it's a dead cert. **1899** T. M. ELLIS *3 Cat's-eye Rings* 32 Tatwood, you know—the trainer—he tips me all the certs. **1904** E. NESBIT *Phoenix & Carpet* vii. 128 Aunt Emma would be out to a dead cert. **1906** E. DYSON *Fact'ry 'Ands* i. 8 This is somethin' er cut above *you*, for er cert. **1927** S. KAYE-SMITH in *Sunday Express* 11 Sept. 9 They had guessed for a cert where he was. **1936** AUDEN & ISHERWOOD *Ascent of F6* II. 73 We'll be able to start tomorrow for a cert.

certain (ˈsɜːtɪn, -t(ə)n), *a.*, *sb.*, and *adv.* Forms: *α.* 3-6 certein, -eyn, (eine, -eyne), 4-7 certen, 4-6 certayn(e, 4-7 certaine, 4- certain; (also 4-5 certan, 4-6 -tane, 5-6 certyn, 7 certaint, certien); *β.* 4-6 serteyn(e, 5-6 serten, 4-5 sertan, -tain, -tayn, 5-6 sertayne, 6 sarteyn, -tayne, 8 *dial.* sartan. [a. OF. *certain* (= Pr. *certan*, Sp. and It. *certano*), repr. late L. or Romanic type *certān-us*, *certān-o*, f. *cert-us* determined, settled, sure, orig. pa. pple. of *cern-ĕre* to decide, determine, etc. The sense-development had taken place already with L. *certus*. The comparative and superlative, *certainer*, *certainest*, are of common occurrence up to the middle of 18th c., but are now seldom used.]

A. *adj.* **I. 1. a.** Determined, fixed, settled; not variable or fluctuating; unfailing. To avoid ambiguity from confusion with sense 7, the adj. is sometimes put after its sb., as *a certain day*, *a day certain*.

certain price: in Foreign Exchanges, the fixed sum in one currency, of which the value is expressed by a varying sum in another.

1297 R. GLOUC. (1724) 378 To a man to bere þeruore a certeyn rente by þe ȝere. **1461-83** *Lib. Niger Edw. IV* in *Ord. R. Househ.* (1790) 18 A formal and convenient custume more certayne than was used byfore his tyme. **1597** MORLEY *Introd. Mus.* 6 Musicke is included in no certaine bounds. **1597** HOOKER *Eccl. Pol.* v. lxvii. §5 That which produceth any certain effect. **1611** BIBLE *1 Cor.* iv. 11 We..haue no certaine dwelling place. **1631** WEEVER *Anc. Fun. Mon.* 384 The number of them hath not beene certaine in our dayes: at this time there are about sixty and eight..in former ages, they were but twelue. **1670** MILTON *Hist. Eng.* II. 500 Wandering up and down without certain seat. **1741** T. ROBINSON *Gavelkind* v. 79 A Fair or Market with Toll certain. **1817** W. SELWYN *Law Nisi Prius* II. 669 Apartments were taken 'for 12 months certain, and six months' notice afterwards'. **1845** STEPHEN *Laws Eng.* II. 111 Payment of money on a day certain. **1866** CRUMP *Banking* vii. 146 Paris is said to give to London the 'uncertain' for the 'certain' price, when a [varying] number of francs and cents are exchanged for the £ sterling.

b. Definite, exact, precise. *arch.*

1393 GOWER *Conf.* III. 143 So that his word be..so certeine, That in him be no double speche. *a* **1541** WYATT *Let.* in *Wks.* (1861) Introd. 22 The certain time how long I tarried after..I remember not. **1676** MARVELL *Gen. Counc.* Wks. 1875 IV. 152 The answer is now much shorter and certainer. **1736** BUTLER *Anal.* I. i. Wks. 1874 I. 21 No means of determining..what is the certain bulk of the living being each man calls himself. **1788** J. POWELL *Devises* (1827) II.

75 It is of more importance that rules of this description should be certain.

2. a. Sure, unerring, not liable to fail; to be depended upon; wholly trustworthy or reliable.

a **1300** *Cursor M.* 12785 To bring fra iohn certan tiþand. *c* **1314** *Guy Warw.* (A.) 900 His stede That certeyne was and gode at nede. *c* **1325** *Coer de L.* 3028 Rychard bad his men seche For some wys clerk and sertayn leche.. For to loke hys uryn. **1561** T. NORTON *Calvin's Inst.* I. 12 The righter and certainer mark to know him by. **1650** R. STAPYLTON *Strada's Low-C. Warres* VII. 40, I have no more, nor no certainer Intelligence then others. **1752** JOHNSON *Rambl.* No. 203 ⁋2 To repose upon real facts, and certain experience. **1834** MRS. SOMERVILLE *Connex. Phys. Sc.* xv. (1849) 141 A certain indication of a coming tempest.

b. Sure to come or follow; inevitable.

a **1300** *Cursor M.* 23732 Es nathing certainur þan dede, Ne vncertainner þan es þe tide. **1596** SPENSER *F.Q.* I. i. 24 Fearfull more of shame Then of the certeine perill he stood in. **1634** SIR T. HERBERT *Trav.* 29 Those certaine tortures, he had doubtlesse received, had he stood upon his Justification. **1669** SHADWELL *Royal Sheph.* v, Such.. Do on themselves the certain'st ruin bring. **1884** GUSTAFSON *Found. Death* Pref. 6 Truth's laborious but certain advance.

c. Sure in its operation or effects; 'unfailing; that always produces the expected effect' (J.).

1636 E. DACRES tr. *Machiavel's Disc. Livy* II. 593 There is no truer nor certainer way, than to make them doe some foule act against him. *a* **1754** R. MEAD (J.), I have often wished that I knew as certain a remedy for any other distemper. **1771** *Lett. Junius* lxi. 317 The abuse of a valuable privilege is the certain means to lose it. **1809** ROLAND *Fencing* 80 To give any certain directions to deceive the adversary would be impossible.

3. Established as a truth or fact to be absolutely received, depended, or relied upon; not to be doubted, disputed, or called in question; indubitable, sure.

c **1400** *Destr. Troy* 2273 Hit semes more sertain, sothely, to me.. Hit may negh vs with noy. **1548** UDALL, etc. *Erasm. Par. Mark* xiii. 29 It is muche certayner that that day shall cum, then it is certayne that summer foloweth after wynter. **1605** SHAKS. *Macb.* II. iv. 15 Duncans Horses, (A thing most strange, and certaine).. Turn'd wilde in nature. **1611** BIBLE *Deut.* xiii. 14 Then shalt thou enquire.. and.. if it be trueth, and the thing certaine, etc. **1690** LOCKE *Hum. Und.* IV. xviii. §4 Whatsoever Truth we come to the clear discovery of from the.. Contemplation of our own Ideas, will always be certainer to us, than those which are convey'd to us by Traditional Revelation. **1705** S. CLARKE *Being & Attrib. of God* (R.), One of the certainest and most evident truths in the world. **1729** BUTLER *Serm.* Wks. 1874 II. 199 It is certain that effects must have a cause. **1761** HUME *Hist. Eng.* III. xlvi. 13 A fact as certain as it appears incredible. **1856** DOVE *Logic Chr. Faith* Introd. §2. 3 We can conceive nothing more absolutely certain than that we exist. **1877** E. CONDER *Bas. Faith* iv. 175 It appears to me not only conceivable, but probable, if not certain.

4. Of persons: Fully confident upon the ground of knowledge, or other evidence believed to be infallible; having no doubt; assured; sure (= 'subjectively certain'). Const. *of* a thing, *that* it is so.

morally certain: so sure that one is morally justified in acting upon the conviction.

1362 LANGL. *P. Pl.* A. III. 77 Þei timbrede not so hye, Ne bouȝte none Borgages, beo ȝe certeyne. **138.** WYCLIF *Sel. Wks.* III. 362 We ben certein þat crist may not axe oþir obedience. **1382** —— *Rom.* xv. 14, I my silf am certeyn of ȝou, for and ȝe ȝou silf ben ful of loue. **1606** SHAKS. *Ant. & Cl.* II. ii. 57, I know you could not lacke, I am certaine on't. **1645** EARL GLAMORGAN *Let.* 28 Nov. in *Carte MSS.*, I am morally certain a total assent from the Nuncio shall be declared to the propositions for peace. **1679** PENN *Addr. Prot.* II. 146 A man can never be Certain of that, about which he has not the Liberty of Examining, Understanding, or Judging: Confident (I confess) he may be; but that's quite another thing than being Certain. **1796** H. HUNTER tr. *St. Pierre's Stud. Nat.* (1799) I. 6 We are certain, at least, of the existence of those beings. **1837** CARLYLE *Fr. Rev.* (1871) II. IV. vii. 148 Besides one is not sure, only morally-certain. **1864** TENNYSON *Grandmother* xxi, I am not always certain if they be alive or dead.

†**5.** Blending senses 1 and 4. *Obs.*

a. Confirmed by experience or practice; well-founded, well-grounded; fully established.

c **1340** *Cursor M.* 19507 (Fairf.), Walcande fra stede to stede in mare certain faiþ þen þai ware are. **1393** GOWER *Conf.* I. 180 Whan they ben of the feith certein, They gone to Barbarie ayein. *Ibid.* III. 303 He taught her till she was certeine Of harpe, citole and of riote. **1483** CAXTON *Gold. Leg.* 159/1 He was certeyn in the doctryne of the gospel.

†**b.** Self-determined, resolved; steadfast. (Cf. L. *certus mori.*) *Obs.*

1667 MILTON *P.L.* IX. 953 However I with thee have fixt my Lot, Certain to undergoe like doom, if Death Consort with thee. **1672** MARVELL *Corr.* ccvii. Wks. 1872–5 II. 408 He doth still continue certain to the former resolutions. **1690** LOCKE *Hum. Und.* II. xxi. §48 The certainer such Determination is, the greater is the Perfection.

6. By a change of construction, a person or agent is said to be *certain to do* a thing, when the fact that he will do it is certain. The use thus attaches itself logically to 1, and in such a sentence as 'the town is certain to be taken', *certain* might be referred to that sense.

1653 WALTON *Angler* ii. 49 I'l be as certain to make him a good dish of meat, as I was to catch him. **1868** E. EDWARDS *Raleigh* I. xxiii. 537 The truth that honest and unselfish labour is just as certain to grow as it is to live. *Mod.* We are certain to meet him in the course of our rambles.

II. 7. a. Used to define things which the mind definitely individualizes or particularizes from the general mass, but which may be left without further indentification in description; thus often used to indicate that the speaker does not choose further to identify or specify them: in *sing.* = a particular, in *pl.* = some particular, some definite.

Different as this seems to be from sense 1, it is hardly separable from it in a large number of examples: thus, in the first which follows, the *hour* was quite 'certain' or 'fixed', but it is not communicated to the reader; to him it remains, so far as his knowledge is concerned, quite indefinite; it may have been, *as far as he knows*, at any hour; though, *as a fact*, it was at a particular hour. (The absolute uses are in B 4–6.)

a **1300** *Cursor M.* 8933 Ilk dai a certain hore! þar lighted dun of heuen ture Angels. **138.** WYCLIF *Wks.* (1880) 220 How religious men should kepe certayne Articles. **1393** GOWER *Conf.* II. 16 A certain ile, which Paphos Men clepe. **1483** CAXTON *G.L.* 242/1 Saynt domynyk spak to the pryour.. of certeyne mater. **1526** TINDALE *John* xi. 1 A certayne man was sicke, named Lazarus. **1536** WRIOTHESLEY *Chron.* (1875) I. 61 In Aprill 1536, certen comyssions were sente into the weste countrye. **1578** LYTE *Dodoens* II. v. 152 The rootes be.. covered with certayne scales. **1600** F. WALKER *Sp. Mandeville* 18 b, Theyr garments are made of a certaine fine wall, like Bombast. **1603** SHAKS. *Meas. for M.* v. i. 129 For certaine words he spake against your Grace. **1651** HOBBES *Leviath.* II. xix. 94 Not every one but Certain men distinguished from the rest. **1710** STEELE *Tatler* No. 173 ⁋3 There are certain faces for certain Painters, as well as certain Subjects for certain Poets. **1711** ADDISON *Spect.* No. 37 ⁋1 A Letter.. directed to a certain Lady whom I shall here call by the Name of Leonora. **1744** BERKELEY *Siris* §1 In certain parts of America, Tarwater is made. **1805** *Med. Jrnl.* XIV. 437 The Reports which certain public associations have circulated. **1856** RUSKIN *Mod. Paint.* III. IV. vi. §1 Everything that is natural is, within certain limits, right. **1875** JEVONS *Money* (1878) 5 If a certain quantity of beef be given for a certain quantity of corn. **1879** M. ARNOLD *Equality, Mixed Ess.* 65 Certain races and nations, are on certain lines pre-eminent and representative. **1887** (Police Notice) 'Whereas certain persons unknown did, on the night of.., feloniously enter', etc.

†**b.** ***some certain***: some particular, some... which might be particularized. *Obs.*

1561 HOBY tr. *Castiglione's Courtyer* (1577) T viij b, In case some certayne Circe should tourne into wilde beastes al the French Kings subiectes. **1591** SHAKS. *Two Gent.* II. v. 6 A man is.. neuer welcome to a place, till some certain shot be paid. **1599** —— *Hen. V*, I. i. 87 His true Titles to some certaine Dukedomes, And generally, to the Crowne and Seat of France. **1732** POPE *Ess. Man* II. 189 Lust, thro' some certain strainers well refin'd, Is gentle love.

†**c.** With *pl. sb.*, often (like *some*) referring to number; usually: Some definitely, some at least, a restricted or limited number of.

c **1400** *Destr. Troy* 10947 There þai fourmyt a fest.. Serten dayes by-dene duly to hold. **1582** G. MARTIN in Fulke *Defence* (1843) 229 You abuse the people for certain years with false translations. **1635** N. R. tr. *Camden's Hist. Eliz.* 1 The death of Queen Mary having been certaine hours concealed. **1670** G. H. *Hist. Cardinals* II. III. 192 In Rome.. he was certain months in the character of Ambassador.

d. Of positive yet restricted (or of positive even *if* restricted) quantity, amount, or degree; of *some* extent at least.

1538 STARKEY *England* 13 Ther ys a certyn equyte and justyce among all natyonys and pepul. **1711** ADDISON *Spect.* No. 106 ⁋6 His Virtues.. are as it were tinged by a certain Extravagance. **1763** FR. BROOKE *Lady Mandeville* in Barbauld *Brit. Novelists* (1820) XXVII. 22 A prodigious passion for people of a certain rank, a phrase of which she is peculiarly fond. *Ibid.* 63, I knew her rage for title, tinsel, and 'people of a certain rank'. **1810** G. ROSE *Diaries* (1860) II. 476 Mr. Perceval.. found a *certain* improvement in him. **1845** S. AUSTIN *Ranke's Hist. Ref.* III. 131 He kept up a certain degree of intercourse.. with the Gonfaloniere Capponi. **1860** TYNDALL *Glac.* I. 123 The ice is disintegrated to a certain depth. **1875** JEVONS *Money* (1878) 117 The bank makes a certain profit out of the business.

e. Sometimes euphemistically: Which it is not polite or necessary further to define. ***a certain age***: an age when one is no longer young, but which politeness forbids to be specified too minutely: usually, referring to some age between forty and sixty (mostly said of women). Also, ***(a woman) of a certain description***, i.e. of the demi-monde; ***in a certain condition***, pregnant; ***a certain disease***, venereal disease.

1748 LADY FEATHERSTONHAUGH in Lady Chatterton *Mem. Ld. Gambier* (1861) I. ii. 25 Some very handsome ladies of a certain sort, who always make part of his suite. **1754** *Connoisseur* 28 Nov. 261, I could not help wishing that some middle term was invented between *Miss* and *Mrs.* to be adopted, at a certain age, by all females not inclined to matrimony. **1803** JANE PORTER *Thaddeus* xxviii, At the epoch, called a certain age, she found herself an old maid. **1803** LEMAISTRE *Rough Sk. Mod. Paris* xiv. 122 Women, too, of a certain description, do not ply for custom. *Ibid.* xxviii. 232 When I first came here, I supposed that these ladies were of a certain description. **1817** BYRON *Beppo* xxii, She was not old, nor young, not at the years Which certain people call a *certain age*, Which yet the most uncertain age appears. **1822** —— *Juan* VI. lxix, A lady of a 'certain age', which means Certainly aged. **1840** DICKENS *Barn. Rudge* i, A very old house, perhaps as old as it claimed to be, and perhaps older, which will sometimes happen with houses of an uncertain, as with ladies of a certain, age. **1882** HOWELLS *Out of Question*, His feet are set rather wide apart in the fashion of gentlemen approaching a certain weight. **1927** *Rev. Eng. Stud.* Oct. 433 As instances may serve *lavatory, illegal operation, social evil, a certain disease.* **1958** B. NICHOLS *Sweet & Twenties* viii. 103 'Syphilis' had always been described as 'a certain disease', just as an attempt at rape had been described as 'a certain suggestion', and the result of the rape on the lady was described as leaving her in 'a certain condition'.

f. With a proper name, it implies that the person so indicated is presumed to be unknown except by name = 'a certain person called' or 'calling himself'; hence often conveying a slight shade of disdain.

1785 COWPER *Let.* 5 Feb., A certain lord Archibald Hamilton has hired the house of Mr. Small.. for a hunting seat. **1833** SOUTHEY *Lett.* (1856) IV. 348 A certain Benjamin Franklin French writes to me from New Orleans. **1870** L'ESTRANGE *Miss Mitford* I. v. 139 Mrs. Raggett brought with her a certain Miss Lucy.

B. quasi-*sb.* or *ellipt.* What is certain.

I. †**1.** Fixed, settled, or appointed condition, order, etc.; certainty. *Obs.*

1377 LANGL. *P. Pl.* B. VI. 153 It is an vnresonable Religioun þat hath riȝte nouȝte of certeyne. **1393** GOWER *Conf.* III. 251 But every time hath his certain. **1631** T. POWELL *Tom All Trades* 146 Having no such pensions in certaine.

†**2. a.** Certain state of matters, fact, or account; that which may be relied on; certainty. *Obs.*

a **1300** *Cursor M.* 27001 Sant paule sais of vr last dai, Es nan mai certain þer-of sai. **1470–85** MALORY *Arthur* (1816) II. 362 That knight that hurt him knew the very certain that he had hurt Sir Launcelot. *a* **1533** LD. BERNERS *Huon* cxliii. 530 He sent out his spyes to knowe the sartayne which waye the emperours nephue shulde come. **1599** SHAKS. *Hen. V*, II. i. 16, That's the certaine of it. **1607** C. LEVER in Farr's *S.P. Jas. I* (1848) 169 Honour, beautie, nor desire of golde, Cannot the certaine of their death withhold.

b. ***for certain, in certain***, etc.: see 7–10 below.

†**3.** The state of mental certainty, certitude. *Obs.*

138. WYCLIF *Sel. Wks.* III. 339 But as God wole of þre þingis, þat we knowun hem not in certein. **1393** GOWER *Conf.* III. 348 I hove In none certein betwene the two. **1470–85** MALORY *Arthur* (1817) II. 290 Than they were at certayne that they were of naturel colours withoute payntynge. **1523** LD. BERNERS *Froiss.* I. ccxxxiii. 326 As than they were nat in certayne yf they shulde passe that way. *Ibid.* (1812) I. 464 It is of certayne that we shall conquere you.

II. †**4. a.** A definite quantity or amount (*of*). *Obs.*

c **1386** CHAUCER *Chan. Yem. Prol. & T.* 471 Biseching him to lene him a certeyn Of gold. *c* **1449** PECOCK *Repr.* III. xiii. 358 He ȝaf a certein of possessioun. **1522** *MS. Acc. St. John's Hosp., Canterb.*, Paied for a certen of bryk by the lumpe. **1598** GRENEWEY *Tacitus' Germanie* iii. (1622) 264 To pay a certaine of corne, or cattell, or apparell.

†**b.** *ellipt.* A fixed or definite sum of money.

1330 R. BRUNNE *Chron.* (1810) 39 For þes he þam bisouht, to gyf þam a certeyn. **1401** *Pol. Poems* (1859) II. 81 Ne non suffragies selle for a certeyn bi ȝere. **1505** *E.E. Wills* (1882) 135 A perpetual serteyn.. to be distribute to xij powre persons on seynt Brices day. **1563–87** FOXE *A. & M.* (1596) 180/2 The preests paieng a certeine to the King.

†**5. a.** A definite (restricted) number (*of* things).

c **1374** CHAUCER *Troylus* III. 547 She to soper come.. With a certeyn of her owne men. **1462** J. DAUBENEY in *Paston Lett.* 452 II. 102 Ye wolle late me have a serteyn of your bulloks for the vetelyng of the Barge. **1547** in Strype *Eccl. Mem.* II. II. App. D 24 A certen of the wysest.. men. **1549** COVERDALE *Erasm. Par. 1 Peter* iii. 20 Put of for a certayn of yeares. **1621** *Bk. Discip. Ch. Scot.* 9 A certaine of the nobilitie were convened.

†**b.** Occasionaly without *of*: cf. A. 7. *Obs.*

1523 LD. BERNERS *Froiss.* I. xiv. 13 A certayne noble knightis.. she kept styl about her. **1548** UDALL, etc. *Erasm. Par. John* 119 b, After I haue taried a certayne dayes among them.

†**c.** *ellipt.* A fixed number of prayers or masses.

[**1431** in *Eng. Gilds* (1870) 278 His certeyntee [**1448** certeyn] of messes.] **1466** *Fun. J. Paston* in *Lett.* II. 271 To the said parson for a certeyn unto Mighelmesse next after the said yere day, viiis. viiid. **1496** *Will of J. Burgh* (Somerset Ho.), I bequeith xxxs. iiijd. for to have a certeyn rehersed in the church. **1849** ROCK *Ch. of Fathers* III. viii. 126.

†**d.** *ellipt.* A restricted number of persons; some. *Obs.*

1532 MORE *Confut. Tindale* Wks. 611/1 God chooseth a certayne whome he lyketh. **1541** PAYNELL *Catiline* xxvii. 47 They chose out a certayne, whiche shulde besyege Pompeys house.

6. Closely related to this is the current (though somewhat archaic) use without *a*, both followed by *of* and absolutely, which may also be treated as a pronominal or absolute use of sense 7 in A.

a. of persons.

c **1400** *Destr. Troy* 1709 Ector.. and certen hym with. **1450** W. SOMNER in *Four C. Eng. Lett.* 3 He sente.. certyn letters to certyn of his trustid men. **1526** TINDALE *Acts* xii. 1 To vexe certayne [WYCLIF sum men] of the congregacion. **1538** STARKEY *England* 54 Polytyke rule.. may be other vnder a prynce, commyn conseyl of certayn, or vnder the hole multytude. **1601** SHAKS. *Jul. C.* I. iii. 122, I haue mou'd already Some certaine of the Noblest minded Romans. **1611** BIBLE *Pref.* 1 Certaine, which would be counted pillars of the State.

b. of things.

1841 MYERS *Cath. Th.* III. §17. 62 Certain of the Psalms. **1855** DICKENS *Dorrit* iii, Mrs. Clennam dipped certain of the rusks and ate them; while the old woman buttered certain other of the rusks.

III. *Phrases.*

7. ***for certain***; formerly (and still *dial.*) also ***for a certain***: as a certainty, assuredly. [= F. *pour certain*, Littré.]

c **1320** *Seuyn Sag.* (W.) 2901 Sir, for sertayn, That wald I here and that ful fayn. **1534** LD. BERNERS *Gold. Bk. M.*

Aurel. (1546) B iij, For certaine al the fruites cometh not togither. **1607** TOPSELL *Serpents* 625 It was reported for a certain, that a Viper entring into a Mans mouth, etc. **1611** BIBLE *Jer.* xxvi. 15 But know ye for certaine, That, etc. **1646** CROMWELL *Let.* 10 Aug., I hear for certain that Ormond has concluded a peace with the Rebels. **1707** E. WARD *Hud. Rediv.* (1715) II. v, He meant the Butcher, for a certain. **1718** HICKES & NELSON *J. Kettlewell* I. §16. 39 He was for certain a most useful Member. **18..** SOUTHEY *Roprecht* iv, Roprecht for certain is not dead!

†**8.** ***in certain***: in truth, certainly, truly. *Obs.* [Cf. OF. *à certain*, Dewes.]

c **1340** *Cursor M.* 11577 (Laud), This was þe somme in certayn Of the childryn þat were slayne. **1483** CAXTON *G. de la Tour* G iij, For in certayne he hath leyd thre egges. *c* **1489** —— *Sonnes of Aymon* i. 52 In certeyn the duke of Aygremounte is ryght myghty. **1493** *Petronilla* 57 (Pynson), And she fulfylled his byddynge in certeyn Withoute grutchinge of virgynall mekenesse.

9. ***of a certain*** (arch.), formerly ***of certain***: as a matter of certainty, certainly, assuredly. [= OF. *de certain*, Dewes.] To this may belong Caxton's *a certain*; but this may be from Fr. (cf. 8).

c **1485** *Digby Myst.* (1882) ii. 229, I know of a certayn. **1488** CAXTON *Chast. Goddes Chyld.* 46 Yf we knew a certen that suche men deyed wythout repentaunce. **1575** *Brieff Disc. Troub. Franckford* 97 It began to be muttred off certeyne that the Magistrate, etc. **1650** FULLER *Pisgah* II. iv. 112 They..who of a certain report, that, etc. **1828** SCOTT *F.M. Perth* iv, Of a certain, those whingers are pretty toys.

C. *adv.* **1.** Certainly, of a truth, assuredly. (Mostly *parenthetic* = CERTAINLY 4.)

1330 R. BRUNNE *Chron.* (1810) 82 My boke sais certayn, þat he gaf neuer þat rede. *c* **1386** CHAUCER *Prol.* 375 And elles certeyn hadde thei ben to blame. ? *a* **1400** *Arthur* 501 Þus worschup god dude certeyn To Englond, þat þo was Bretayn. **1509** HAWES *Examp. Virt.* x. 191 It brenneth hote lyke fyre certeyn. **1596** SHAKS. *Merch. V.* II. vi. 29 Lorenzo certaine, and my loue indeed. **1704** ROWE *Ulyss.* IV. i. 1768 She is lost—most certain—gone irrevocable. **1859** BARTLETT *Dict. Amer.* (ed. 2), *Certain*, for certainly. 'He's dead certain'. 'I'll go to-morrow sure and certain'. Very common. **1872** SCHELE DE VERE *Americanisms* 450 He's done it sure and certain.

2. With certainty, surely.

1382 WYCLIF *Acts* xxiii. 20 As thei ben to sekinge sum thing certeynere [*v.r.* and **1388** more certeynly of him]. *a* **1734** NORTH *Lives* II. 346 There is no place..in which an ingenious person comes sooner and certainer to preferment, than in the Turkish Court.

†**3.** Emphasizing *sooth, true, sure. Obs.* or *dial.*

a **1500** in Hazl. *E.P.P.* I. 205 Certain sothe. *a* **1593** H. SMITH *Wks.* (1867) II. 401 Being most undoubted and certain true. **1804** SOUTHEY in Robberds *Mem. W. Taylor* I. 482 You will, I am certain-sure, be well pleased. **1875** PARISH *Sussex Dial.*, *Certain Sure*, the superlative of certainly.

†**certain**, *v. Obs. rare.* [f. prec.: cf. OF. *certainer*, and ASCERTAIN.] *trans.* To make certain; to certify. Hence **certaining** *vbl. sb.*

a **1300** *Cursor M.* 26973 Bot if þat it be suilk a thing þat þou wat of na certanyng. **1523** LD. BERNERS *Froiss.* I. cclxx. 401 He certeyned them how he wolde ryde forthe.

certainly (ˈsɜːtənlɪ), *adv.* [f. CERTAIN *a.* + -LY².]

1. In a manner that is certain; in a way that may be surely depended on; with certainty.

a **1300** *Cursor M.* 16232 (Gött.), Gode men quat es þan ȝur dome, sais me sertainli [*Cott.* certanli]. **1509** HAWES *Past. Pleas.* XXIV. viii, Nor yet the handes fele nothyng certaynly. **1649** *Bounds Publ. Obed.* 17 Those things are certainlyer knowne to us. **1793** WOLLASTON in *Phil. Trans.* LXXXIII. 150 This was made more certainly steady. **1863** FR. KEMBLE *Resid. Georgia* 37, I can not ascertain very certainly. **1875** JEVONS *Money* (1878) 44 The earliest tin coinage of which any thing is certainly known.

b. With certainty as to quality, amount, etc.; definitely, precisely, exactly. ? *Obs.*

c **1460** FORTESCUE *Abs. & Lim. Mon.* (1714) 44 The Kyngs Werks [fortifications], of which the yerely Expensis may not certeynly be estemyd. **1588** LAMBARDE *Eiren.* II. ii. 110 To take sufficient Suertie, in a summe certainly prescribed. *a* **1626** BACON *Use Com. Law* 12 Except the punishment be certainly appointed by speciall Statutes.

2. Without fail, unfailingly, infallibly.

a **1300** *Cursor M.* 9270 (Gött.), 'Jesse', he said, 'of his rotyng Certaynly a wand suld spring.' *c* **1440** *Gesta Rom.* i. 2 (Harl. MS.), If thou do not, certenly thy ymage shalle be smytene, and thou bothe. **1607** HIERON *Wks.* I. 189 The Lord will..certenly recompence them their sinne into their bosome. **1711** STEELE *Spect.* No. 155 ¶5 Merchants..who call in as certainly as they go to 'Change. **1813** SOUTHEY *March Moscow* 4 Morbleu! Parbleu! And he'll certainly march to Moscow!

b. Fixedly, so as not to be altered.

1591 SHAKS. *1 Hen. VI*, v. i. 37 Therefore are we certainly resolu'd, To draw conditions of a friendly peace. **1704** ROWE *Ulyss.* v. i. 2041 'Tis certainly decreed, Fix'd as that Law by which Imperial Jove Ordains..to Good or Evil.

3. With subjective certitude, with assurance, surely.

a **1300** *Cursor M.* 5834 And certainli þou vnderstand Al that þou draus vte o þat flod It sal be turnd al in-to blod. *c* **1450** LONELICH *Grail* xii. 483 How knowest thou this so certeinly? **1622** SPARROW *Bk. Com. Prayer* (1661) 10 What he Commands he accepts most certainly. *c* **1680** BEVERIDGE *Serm.* (1729) I. 364 There is nothing that we know more certainly in this world, than that we know nothing certainly of the other, but what we are taught by God himself. *Mod.* You ought not to speak so certainly about it.

4. Parenthetically, or as an assurance or admission of the truth of an assertion as a whole: Without doubt; in truth and fact; of a certainty; assuredly, undoubtedly, unquestionably. *Certainly there are drawbacks* = we may say certainly that, (or, it is certain that) there are drawbacks. Sometimes it expresses an admission of an opponent's contention, to be followed by 'but', etc. Often it conveys a strong assent or affirmative reply, as in 'You were present?' 'Certainly.' 'Can you recommend him?' 'Certainly.'

a **1300** *Cursor M.* 17495 3a, sertainli, þat soth it es. *c* **1350** *Will. Palerne* 2653 But sertenli on boþe sides was slayn muche puple. *c* **1450** LONELICH *Grail* xxxi. 152 ȝit was that schipe..Anoured with diuers iowellis certeinle. **1596** SHAKS. *Merch. V.* III. i. 126 Anthonio is certainely vndone. **1644** EVELYN *Kal. Hort.* (1729) 191 Snow..certainly rots, and bursts your early-set Anemonies. **1712** ADDISON *Spect.* No. 405 ¶3 If the Gods were to talk with Men, they would certainly speak in Plato's Stile. **1752** HUME *Ess. & Treat.* (1777) I. 91 Machiavel was certainly a great genius. **1781** *Trial of Ld. G. Gordon* 8 One of Lord George's Counsel applied to the Court..to permit the prisoner to sit down. Lord Mansfield answered, 'Yes! Certainly'! **1801** FOSTER in *Life & Corr.* (1846) I. 129, I have certainly learnt much. **1875** JEVONS *Money* (1878) 16 We might certainly employ one substance as a medium of exchange.

†**ˈcertainness.** *Obs. rare.* [f. CERTAIN + -NESS.] The quality or fact of being certain.

1571 GOLDING *Calvin on Ps.* lxii. 12 He commendeth the certeinnes therof. **1599–1623** MINSHEU, *Certeza*, certainty or certainnesse, assurance, surety.

certainty (ˈsɜːtəntɪ). Forms: 4 **certaynte**, 4–5 **-teynte, -tante**, 5 **certeyntee, -tente, -tainte**, 6 **certaynete, sertente, -tinty, scertayntie, certentie, -teynty, -tie, certeintie, -tayntie, -taynetye, -tainety**, 6–7 **certaintie**, (**certainetie, -ty**), 7 **certenty, teinty**, 6– **certainty**. [a. Anglo-Fr. *certeinté*, OF. *certaineté* (—Pr. *certanetat*, OSp. *certanedad*), on L. or Rom. type *certānitāt-e(m*: see CERTAIN and -TY.]

1. That which is certain; the certain state of matters, the fact, the truth; a certain account. ? *Obs.*

[**1292** BRITTON IV. viii. §2 Et si ele dedie par la affirmative ou la negative, sourd une doute dount la certeinté fet a enquere del ordinarie.] **1330** R. BRUNNE *Chron.* (1810) 25 Right story can me not ken, þe certeynte what spellis. **1489** CAXTON *Faytes of A.* I. xxi. 65 As we may be infourmed and knowe the certeynte therof. **1565** GRAFTON *Chron. Edw. I*, an. 8 (R.), The king..woulde therevnto geue no credite vntill he had sent thether, and receyued the certaintie. **1662** STILLINGFL. *Orig. Sacr.* I. ii. §10 We have then no certainty at all..of any certain Records..unless they be contained in those sacred inscriptions from whence Manetho took his history.

2. A fact or thing certain or sure (with *pl.*)

1611 SHAKS. *Cymb.* I. vi. 96 For Certainties Either are past remedies; or timely knowing, The remedy then borne. **1684** *Comtempl. State Man* I. vii. (1699) 75 It being not then a suspicion, but an apparent certainty that Death will come. **1711** LADY M. W. MONTAGUE *Lett.* lxxxii. 135, I would not advise you to neglect a certainty for an uncertainty. **1775** STRAHAN in Boswell *Johnson* xlviii, Small certainties are the bane of men of talents. *Mod.* To surrender a certainty for a mere prospect.

†**3.** Assurance, surety, pledge. *Obs.*

1303 R. BRUNNE *Handl. Synne* 8218 He hadde seyde hym hys certeynte. **1330** —— *Chron.* (1810) 69 My broþer delyuer þou me, my neuow þou me grante, & hold þi certeynte, and salle hold couenante. **1425** *Sc. Acts Jas. I* (1596) §62 Bot gif that man haue ane letter or certainetie of the Lord of that land..for quhat cause he cummis in this Realme.

4. The quality or fact of being (objectively) certain.

1340 HAMPOLE *Pr. Consc.* 7837 Þare es ay blysfulle certaynté. **1634** SIR T. HERBERT *Trav.* 91 The Starres..without whose ayme there is no certaintie. **1738** KEILL *Anim. Œcon.* Pref. 26 Geometry, which truly boasts the Beauty of Certainty. **1880** E. WHITE *Cert. Relig.* 3 The Evangelist distinguishes between what we now term certitude—or the belief of the mind—and certainty, or the solid reality of the facts or truths believed in.

5. The quality or state of being subjectively certain; assurance, confidence; absence of doubt or hesitation; = CERTITUDE. ***moral certainty***: see CERTAIN 4.

a **1340** HAMPOLE *Psalter* vi. 1 The seven psalmes..bygynnys all in sorrow..and bitternes of forthynkynge, and þai end in certaynte of pardoun. **1393** GOWER *Conf.* I. 43 For love is blinde and may nought se, Forthy may no certeinte Be sette upon his jugement. **1601** SHAKS. *All's Well* II. i. 172 Vpon thy certainty and confidence, What dar'st thou venter? **1646** *Burd. Issach.* in *Phenix* (1708) II. 276 That this is truth, I am as much assur'd of, as moral Certainty can assure any Man of moral Truth. **1711** ADDISON *Spect.* No. 101 ¶7 This is all we can affirm with any Certainty of his Person and Character. **1837** HALLAM *Hist. Lit.* III. iii. §93 The soul's progress from opinion to doubt, and from doubt to certainty. **1838** DE MORGAN *Ess. Probab.* 3 (Cab. Cycl. Nat. Philos.), Our moral certainty of the fact.

b. with *pl.*

1605 BACON *Adv. Learn.* I. v. §8 If a man will begin with certainties, hee shall end in doubts.

†**6.** A certain or definite number or quantity. *Obs.*

1431 in *Eng. Gilds* (1870) 278 The vicarye..schal haue iiijs. and iiijd. for his certeyntee of messes. **1601** F. TATE *Househ. Ord. Edw. II*, §11 (1876) 11 Setting downe the certenti of the price. *Ibid.* §51. 35 By reson of the certenty which is theron assesed. **1603** DANIEL *Def. Rhime* Poems (1717) 14 Nature, that desires a Certainty, and comports not with what is infinite.

7. ***for, (in, at*** obs.), ***of, to (a) certainty***: as a matter of certainty, beyond doubt, assuredly.

c **1400** *Rom. Rose* 5435 They wene to have in certeynte Of hertly freendis so grete noumbre. *c* **1460** FORTESCUE *Abs. & Lim. Mon.* (1714) 47 The Kyngs Extraordynary chargys ar so casuel, that no Man may knowe them in certeynte. **1526** *Pilgr. Perf.* (W. de W. 1531) 4 No persone may knowe for certeynty, whether he haue it or not. **1580** NORTH *Plutarch* (1676) 26 It is of certainty that her proper name was Nicostrata. **1611** BIBLE *Joshua* xxiii. 13 Know for a certainety, that the Lord your God, etc. —— *Dan.* ii. 8, I know of certeinty that ye would gaine the time. *a* **1635** NAUNTON *Fragm. Reg.* (Arb.) 24 This will be of certainty—that, etc. **1665** MARVELL *Corr.* li. Wks. 1872–5 II. 287 But pray tell us once more in certainty whether it must consequently make 600 *li* a Yeare. **1789** *Trifler* No. 33. 420 Since music has become the rage, all our ladies must at a certainty, learn this sweet language. **1820** SCOTT *Abbot* xix, Thou restless boy—Thou hast quicksilver in the veins of thee to a certainty. **1873** MRS. OLIPHANT *Innocent* ix, One or other will fall in love with her to a certainty.

†**cerˈtation.** *Obs.* [ad. L. *certātiōn-em*, f. *certāre* to contend, etc.] Contention, strife.

1572 FORREST *Theoph.* 916 Man..Shall have assiste in that certation. **1623** COCKERAM, *Certation*, strife.

¶In the following it appears to be = Certification.

c **1500** *Blowbol's Test.* in Halliw. *Nugæ P.* 2 He gaf me many a good certacion, With right and holsom predicacion.

[**certelle**, erron. f. CERCELLE, teal.]

certes (ˈsɜːtɪz), *adv. arch.* Forms: 4–5 **sertes, sertis**, 4–7 **certis**, 4–5 **certys**, 5 **certus**, 6 **certeyse, certesse**, (5)–7 **certs**, 3– **certes**. [ME. *certes*, a. OF. *certes*, more fully *a certes*, according to Littré:—L. **a certis* from certain (grounds), certainly. Cf. OSp. *certas*, Cat. *certes*.

In French now pronounced (sɛrt): in Eng. usually dissyllabic, but, from 1300, occasionally found as a monosyllable, spelt *cert* or *certs*, or shown by the rime or rhythm to be so pronounced when written *certes*. See CERT.]

Of a truth, of a certainty, certainly, assuredly. Used to confirm a statement. ('An old word' (J.); used chiefly in poetry or archaic prose.)

a **1250** *Owl & Night.* 1769 Certes cwaþ þe ule þat is soþ. *a* **1300** *Cursor M.* 4907 'Sertes', said þai, 'leue lauerdinges, Haue we noght þan o þe kinges. **138.** WYCLIF *Serm.* Sel. Wks. I. 6 Certis noon but the lord of þis feeste. *c* **1386** CHAUCER *Knts. T.* 64 ffor certes [*v.r.* certus] lord ther is noon of vs alle, That she ne hath been a duchesse or a queene. *c* **1449** PECOCK *Repr.* I. ii. 8 Wherfore certis if eny man can be sikir, etc. *c* **1557** in Hazl. *E.P.P.* III. 121 Many a man certesse. **1597** BP. HALL *Sat.* I. iii. 29 Then certes was the famous Corduban Never but half so high tragedian. **1600** TOURNEUR *Transf. Met.* xxxiii, Yet certis, if the naked truth I say. **1759** STERNE *Tr. Shandy* (1802) II. xix. 240 Then certes the soul does not inhabit there. **1802** WORDSW. *Stanzas* in *Castle Indolence* vi, And certes not in vain; he had inventions rare. **1870** MORRIS *Earthly Par.* I. I. 47 Certes, we might have gathered wealth untold.

†*β. monosyllabic. Obs.*

c **1300** *K. Alis.* 1359 He thonkid alle therof, certes, And starf anon withoute smert. *c* **1400** *Apol. Loll.* 13 Certs to þis I sey þei owe boþe to curse & wari. **1613** SHAKS. *Hen. VIII*, I. i. 48 As you guesse: One certes, that promises no Element. **1640** FULLER *Joseph's Coat, David's Sin* (1867) 213 This, certs, I know. *Ibid. David's Pun.* 237 But certs I know that such mistake their ground.

certie, certy (ˈsɜːtɪ, *Sc.* ˈsɛrtɪ). *Sc.* [In *my certies*, which is in use as well as *my certie*, the word may be identical with *certes*, taken as a plural sb., of which *certie* would be the assumed singular. But the history of the phrase is not clear; and it is difficult to say whether *by my certy* (*certes*) is genuine, or merely a literary 'improvement'.]

Chiefly in phrase, ***my certie***, as an ejaculation: By my faith, in good troth.

[Some have suggested a corruption of the F. *mais certes* 'but certainly'; of this there is no evidence.]

1814 *Saxon & Gael* I. 80 (Jam.) By my certy ye shake your fit wi' the youngest o' them. **1816** SCOTT *Antiq.* xxv, 'My certie! few ever wrought for siccan a day's wage.' **1820** —— *Abbot* xvii, By my certes, I will warrant her a blithe dancer either in reel or revel. **1848** KINGSLEY *Saint's Trag*, IV. ii. 112 Certie, we were in luck. **1870** BLACKMORE *Maid of Sk.* 156 My certy, no low curiosity is this.

certifiable (ˈsɜːtɪˌfaɪəb(ə)l), *a.* [f. CERTIFY + -ABLE.] **a.** Capable of being certified.

1846 GROTE *Greece* I. xviii. I. 646 Ordinary and certifiable history. **1859** MILL *Dissert & Disc.* II. 543 To arrive at so considerable an amount of positive and certifiable results.

b. = NOTIFIABLE *a. U.S.*

1911 STEDMAN *Med. Dict.* 159/2 *Certifiable*, that can and should be certified, noting certain infectious diseases, the occurrence of which must, by law, be reported to the health authorities.

c. Of a person: so deranged as to be certifiably insane; of mental disease: of such a type as to warrant certification.

1912 B. HOLLANDER *First Signs of Insanity* I. i. 33 The difference between this stage and certifiable insanity is a quantitative difference, a difference of degree only. **1931** 'F. ILES' *Malice Aforethought* xiii. 268 'I've always said she was mad,' exulted Dr. Bickleigh. 'Not certifiable, unfortunately; but certainly over the border-line.' **1939** H. G. WELLS *Holy Terror* II. iii. 194 If half this stuff about him is true, he's certifiable.

certifiably (ˈsɜːtɪfaɪəblɪ), *adv.* [f. CERTIFIABLE *a.* + -LY^2.] In a certifiable degree; so as to admit of being certified.

1891 *Daily News* 12 Mar. 2/3 The evidence showed that as soon as Mrs. Stoney became certifiably insane the defendant took measures for her removal. **1970** *Guardian* 18 May 8/4 Even to pose such questions..makes him..certifiably sane.

cerˈtificate, *ppl. a. Obs.* [ad. med.L. *certificāt-us*, pa. pple.: see next.] Certified, assured.

1547 *Homilies* I. *Faith* I. (1859) 38 A certificate and sure looking for them. **1560** in Hazl. *E.P.P.* IV. 175 Chryst.. Which is our brother by proue certyficate.

certificate (səˈtɪfɪkət), *sb.* Also 5-8 **-at,** 5 **cert-, sertyfycate.** [a. F. *certificat*, or ad. med.L. *certificātum* thing certified, a subst. use of pa. pple. of *certificāre* to CERTIFY. In sense 1 it appears to answer to a L. sb. in *-ātus* (4th decl.)]

†**1.** The action or fact of certifying or giving assurance; certification. *Obs.*

c **1480** *St. Ursula* (Roxb.) A j, Wastynge the church with force and cruelte So sayeth the croncyles for our certyfycate. **1555** EDEN *Decades W. Ind.* (Arb.) 259 For the better certificat therof he consyderd the stations of the moone.

†**2.** The action whereby a responsible person or persons attest a fact within their knowledge; certification, attestation. *Obs.*

1472 MARG. PASTON *Lett.* 705 III. 63 Send for the shereffes debute to wete how thei be disposid for certificate of the knyghtes. **1495** *Act 11 Hen. VII*, c. 10 §1 Upon certificat of the delyvere of the seid Writtes. **1560** DAUS tr. *Sleidane's Comm.* 95 a, Before they make certificat home to their cities. **1563** *Homilies* II. *Repentance* I. (1859) 534 For a certificate, and assurance thereof. **1661** J. STEPHENS *Procurations* 30 Since the Certificate of their value into the Exchequer about the 26 of H. 8.

3. a. A document wherein a fact is formally certified or attested.

[**1447** in *Paston Lett.* I. 64 Comme il apparest par le certificat a eulx par nous donné.] **1489-90** *Plumpton Corr.* 91 Send up the sayd wrytts with his sertyfycat. **1592** GREENE *Art Conny-catch.* II. 5 Who buyeth a horse without this certificat or proofe, shalbe within the nature of fellony. **1601** HOLLAND *Pliny* I. 182 Six men brought a certificate that they had liued an hundred yeares apiece. **1642** *Two Ord. Lords & Comm.* 3 Dec. 3 A true and exact Certificate..of the quantity of Gunpowder. **1722** DE FOE *Plague* (1754) 9 To get Passes and Certificates of Health..for, without these, there was no being admitted to pass thro' the Towns. **1763** *Brit. Mag.* IV. 174 No cyder and perry, exceeding six gallons, shall be removed, etc., without a certificate. **1790** J. HUNTINGFORD (*title*), The Forging and counterfeiting of Certificates of Servants' Characters. **1824** SCOTT *St. Ronan's* xxv, My father's contract of marriage, my own certificate of baptism. **1858** SIMMONDS *Dict. Trade* s.v., A certificate of origin is a Custom-House document, testifying to particular articles being the growth of a British colony. **1887** *Whitaker's Almanack* 368 A certificate of birth, marriage, or death costs one penny.

b. *esp.* A document certifying the status or acquirements of the bearer, or his fulfilment of conditions which authorize him to act or practise in a specified way; hence, often equal to *licence.*

1549 *Compl. Scot.* xi. 95 Nane of them sal cum vitht in the mane cuntre of ingland vitht out ane certificat fra the sc[h]eref. **1593** NASHE *Foure Lett. Confut.* 19 A Certificate (such as rogues haue) from the head men of the Parish. **1615** tr. *De Montfart's Surv. E. Indies* 8 [He] must bring back a good certificat from the Captaine of the Carauan. **1816** *Trial Berkeley Poachers* 29 Allen makes no secret of his shooting; he takes out a certificate. **1852** DICKENS *Bleak Ho.* (Hoppe), I am now admitted..on the roll of attornies, and have taken out my certificate. **1863** *Illust. Lond. News* 21 Nov. (Hoppe) The suspension of Captain Stone's certificate for six months. **1874** *Sat. Rev.* Apr. 499 (Hoppe) The vessel was licensed to carry only twenty passengers; but it seems that the restrictions of the certificate did not apply to trade between Mediterranean ports.

c. In a more general sense: Anything which has the force or effect of the preceding; a certification.

1718 *Free-thinker* No. 76. 146 Admit no Opinions but such as come recommended with proper Certificates. **1856** EMERSON *Eng. Traits, Wealth* Wks. (Bohn) II. 68 The Englishman has pure pride in his wealth, and esteems it a final certificate. **1875** JEVONS *Money* (1878) 191 Bills of exchange, which are signs or certificates of debt.

d. *bankrupt's certificate*: (see quot. 1858).

1707 *Lond. Gaz.* No. 4341/4 His Certificate will be confirmed as the Act directs. **1858** SIMMONDS *Dict. Trade* s.v., A bankrupt's certificate is the legal document issued by the Commissioner of the Bankruptcy Court, certifying that he has surrendered his estate, passed the examinations and forms required, and..is permitted to recommence his trading operations.

e. A document committing a person to an institution as insane.

[**1883** T. S. CLOUSTON *Clin. Lect. Mental Dis.* xix. 612 It may..be necessary, before certifying, to get a letter.. protecting the doctor from risk of legal action. That is a risk no medical man in signing a certificate of lunacy should subject himself to.] **1927** HENDERSON & GILLESPIE *Text-Bk. Psychiatry* xvii. 492 The granting of a certificate of this nature carries with it very serious legal obligations; for the person certified may..ask for a trial by jury as to his alleged insanity. **1932** KIPLING *Limits & Renewals* 168 He'd been tried too high—too high. I had to sign his certificate a few weeks later.

f. *Certificate of Secondary Education*, an examination usually set and marked by individual schools for pupils in secondary schools in England and Wales (now replaced by the GCSE: see quot. 1981); the certificate obtained by passing this. Abbrev. *C.S.E.*: see C III. 3.

1961 (*title*) The Certificate of Secondary Education. A proposal for a new School Leaving Certificate other than the G.C.E. Fourth Rep. Secondary School Examinations Council. **1981** D. ROWNTREE *Dict. Educ.* 36 *Certificate of Secondary Education* (*CSE*) (UK), a school-based examination taken by pupils around the age of 15 or 16 years, and aimed at the 40% of the ability-range, in any given subject, who lie below the top 20% at whom GCE (ordinary level) is aimed... During the 1980s, the CSE system is to be combined with that of the General Certificate of Education (GCE).

4. *Law.* A writing made in one court, by which notice of its proceedings is given to another, usually by way of transcript. *trial by certificate*: a form of trial in which the testimony of facts as certified by another court, or by any proper authority, decides the point at issue.

1607-72 COWELL *Interpr.*, A Certificate of the Cause of Attaint is a transcript made briefly, and in few words, by the Clerk of the Crown, etc. to the Court of the King's Bench, containing the tenor and effect of every Indictment. **1768** BLACKSTONE *Comm.* III. 333 When the issue is whether a person was absent in the army, this is tried by the certificate of the proper officer, in writing, under his seal. **1818** CRUISE *Digest* II. 300 The Judges certified that Mr. Bromfield took a vested estate in fee simple..The Master of the Rolls decreed in conformity to this certificate.

5. *attrib.*, as in *certificate goods* (see 3, quot. 1858).

1710 *Lond. Gaz.* No. 4674 An Act..for better preventing Frauds in Drawbacks upon Certificate Goods. **1710** *Act 8 Anne* in *Lond. Gaz.* No. 4701/2 Persons, who..cause..to be re-landed such Tobacco, and other Certificate-Goods.

certificate (səˈtɪfɪkeɪ(ɪ)t), *v.* [f. prec. sb.]

1. *trans.* To attest (a fact) by a certificate.

2. To furnish (a person) with a certificate. (*to certificate out of*: cf. ARGUE *v.* 8, 9.)

1818 TODD, *Certificate*, a word of very recent date, signifying to give a certificate to a person, that he has passed a particular examination, or that he is justly entitled to some claim. **1865** DICKENS *Mut. Fr.* I. 256 The homely stock of love that had never been examined or certificated out of her. **1870** *Daily News* 12 Nov., To register and certificate midwives. **1881** *New Eng. Jrnl. Education* XIV. 345 The teacher..was certificated for one of the lower grades.

3. To license or authorize by certificate.

1884 *Manch. Exam.* 9 Sept. 5/3 Few of the excursionists know how many people the boat is certificated to carry.

Hence **cerˈtificated, cerˈtificating.**

1768 BLACKSTONE *Comm.* I. ix. 365 Apprentice or servant to such certificated person. **1858** SIMMONDS *Dict. Trade*, *Certificated Bankrupt*, one who is freed from his liabilities, and holds a certificate from the Bankruptcy Court. **1864** *Bp. of Lincoln's Charge* 6 A smaller supply of trained and certificated teachers. **1869** *Pall Mall G.* 29 Sept. 12 It does not parade this certificating character upon its title-page.

certification (sɜːtɪfɪˈkeɪʃən). [a. F. *certification*, or ad. med.L. *certificātiōn-em*, n. of action f. *certificāre*: see CERTIFY *v.* and -ATION.] The action of certifying or fact of being certified; the form in which this is embodied.

1. Information making one certain of a fact, etc.; certain notification or notice.

c **1440** *Gesta Rom.* xlv. 174 (Harl. MS.) Of the whiche ridinge that othere kniȝt had certificacione. **1683** E. HOOKER *Pref. Pordage's Mystic Div.* 99 (Style it what you please) Revelation, Manifestation, Inspiration, Communication, Certification, Declaration, or if you wil Information.

2. *Sc. Law.* Notice to a party of what is demanded of him, certifying him of the consequences of his non-compliance.

1634-46 ROW *Hist. Kirk* (1842) 42 That such..be admonished to return to his Majestie's obedience; with certification, if they contemptouslie refuise, the spirituall sword shall be used aganis them. **1679** *Roy. Proclam. Edinb.* 4 May in Hickes *Spir. Popery* (1680) 62 With Certification to such of the said Tenants, Cottars and Servants as shall be absent, they shall be reputed as accessory to the said Crime. **1679-1714** BURNET *Hist. Ref.*, With this certification that if he appeared not, they would proceed.

3. a. The action of certifying or guaranteeing the truth of anything; attestation.

1532 MORE *Confut. Barnes* VIII. Wks. 801/2 The tradicyon of the fathers..is for the certificacion of a trouth a sure vndoubted authoritie. **1865** MOZLEY *Mirac.* iv. 81 That final certification of these great truths which will be given in another world. **1881** J. H. INGRAM in *Poe's Wks.* I. Mem. 20 He obtained a certification of the fact from several companions.

†**b.** = CERTIFICATE 4. *Obs.*

1574 tr. *Littleton's Tenures* 22 a, It shalbee tried by the certificacion of the constable of the kings host.

†**4.** *Law.* A process of obtaining an examination or alteration of a judicial decision, when the omission of important evidence or other oversight is alleged. *Obs.*

[**1292** BRITTON IV. ix. §9 Meutz remedie par certificacioun qe par atteynte.] **1641** *Termes de la Ley* 49 Certification of Assise of Novel disseisin, etc. is a writ awarded to re-examine or review a matter passed by Assise before any Justices.

5. The action of making (a person) certain or sure; assurance.

a **1555** LATIMER *Serm. & Rem.* (1845) 364, I read in scripture of two certifications: one to the Romans, Justificati ex fide, pacem habemus. **1577** tr. *Bullinger's Decades* (1592) 35 They call that πληροφόρημα, which we call a certification, as when a thing by perswasions is so beate into our minds, that after that we neuer doubt anye more. *a* **1638** MEDE *Wks.* I. liii. 309 This Assurance or Certification..comes in the third place, not in the first.

6. The action of providing with a legal certificate, esp. of insanity.

1881 *Philada. Record* No. 3470. 1 $15000 to be expended for the certification of the health of cattle shipments. **1883** T. S. CLOUSTON *Clin. Lect. Mental Dis.* xix. 611 His.. business is to convince the patient's responsible relatives of the necessity for certification. **1885** in *19th Cent.* May 859 Defence of the present system of certification. *a* **1889** *Mod.* The certification of elementary teachers. **1912** B. HOLLANDER *First Signs of Insanity* I. i. 33 The general diagnosis of insanity, when once pronounced so as to necessitate certification. **1959** *New Statesman* 10 Jan. 34/1 Certification, as was expected, is to disappear. The decision to detain an unwilling patient will be a purely medical decision.

†**7.** A certified statement, a certificate. *Obs.*

a **1563** BALE *Sel. Wks.* (1849) 90 This certification..is untruly forged against him. **1630** WADSWORTH *Sp. Pilgr.* iv. 33 Hauing taken a false certification from the gouernor of Callis, that the ship..belonged thereunto. **1772** EARL MALMESBURY *Diaries & Corr.* (1844) I. 79 As soon as the Certifications can be signed and exchanged between the Courts.

certificator (səˈtɪfɪkeɪtə(r)). [Agent-noun, in L. form, f. *certificāre*: see CERTIFY and -TOR. In F. *certificateur* (16th c.).] The giver of a certificate; a CERTIFIER.

1796 *Monthly Rev.* XXI. 480 We hastily copied the name of the certificator for that of the inventor.

†**cerˌtificaˈtorial,** *a. Obs.* = next.

1702 *Hist. Convoc. Canterbury* 30 These Certificatorial Letters from the Bishop.

certificatory (səˈtɪfɪkətərɪ), *a.* and *sb.* [ad. med.L. *certificātōrius*, f. *certificātor*: see -ORY.]

A. *adj.* Having the function of certifying; of the nature of a certificate. *letter certificatory* (transl. of med.L. *certificatoria littera*): a certificate, a written testimonial.

1520 SIR R. WINGFIELD in Ellis *Orig. Lett.* I. 59 I. 167 The manner of the delivery..of the Kyngs Lettres certificatory. **1563-87** FOXE *A. & M.* (1596) 227/2 The king..sent abrode his letters certificatorie. **1627** J. CARTER *Expos. Serm. Mount* 66 He maketh our forgiving of others..the certificatory cause (if I may so speake). **1837** CARLYLE *Fr. Rev.* III. III. v, Every Citizen must produce his certificatory *Carte de Civisme*, signed by Section-President.

†**B.** *sb.* Short for *letter certificatory. Obs.*

1695 KENNETT *Par. Antiq.* ix. 647 To return their Certificatories before they had duely publish'd their Citations. **1702** *Hist. Convoc. Canterbury* 29 The Bishop of London presented his Certificatory or Return, upon Execution of the Archbishop's Mandate.

certified (ˈsɜːtɪfaɪd), *ppl. a.* [f. CERTIFY *v.*]

a. Made certain; assured; certainly informed; attested by certificate; furnished with a certificate.

1611 COTGR., *Certifié*, certified, assured, ascertained. **1865** DICKENS *Mut. Fr.* ii. 9, I must refer you to the Registrar of the District..for the certified cause of death. **1879** MCCARTHY *Own Times* lii. (Hoppe) A minister of religion, a lawyer, a doctor, a certified schoolmaster. **1883** J. RUSSELL *New Educ. Code* 37 An elementary teacher..in.. Certified Industrial Schools or Certified Reformatories.

b. *certified cheque* (N. Amer.), a cheque which is guaranteed by the bank upon which it is drawn. Cf. CERTIFY *v.* 2 b.

1880 WEBSTER *Supp.*, *Certified check*, a bank-check, the validity of which is certified by the bank on which it is drawn. **1883** *Century Mag.* July 334/1 When a producer.. wants to use his oil in store as collateral to borrow upon..he gets what is called an acceptance, which is virtually a certified check. **1970** *Globe & Mail* (Toronto) 25 Sept. 14/2 (Advt.), Send self addressed envelope plus certified cheque or money order to: *Oh! Calcutta!* in trust.

c. *certified public accountant* (U.S.), an accountant who has passed State examinations and has received a certificate of professional competence.

1896 *Laws State N.Y.* I. 263 Any citizen of the United States..who shall have received from the regents of the university a certificate of his qualifications to practice as a public expert accountant..shall be styled and known as a certified public accountant. **1922** *Certified Public Accountant* Mar. 20/2 It would be well for all Certified Public Accountants..to bear in mind that we are passing through a crisis in accountancy. **1979** *Jrnl. Accounting Res.* XVII. 436 A number of recent studies..have dealt with the motivation of Certified Public Accountants (CPAs).

d. *certified milk*, milk guaranteed free from tubercle bacillus.

1899 TAYLOR & WELLS *Man. Dis. Children* v. 115 A movement..has resulted in the production of a very superior milk, known as certified milk. **1905** F. L. DODD *Municipal Milk* 13 *Certified Milk.* The Borough of Sunderland..has started a movement for the improvement of the milk supply by..certificates granted to those producers who fulfil certain definite conditions. **1936** *Milk (Special Designation Order)* xi. §1 A licence to sell milk as 'Certified' or as 'Grade A (Tuberculin Tested)' shall be deemed to be a licence authorising the use of the special designation 'Tuberculin Tested'.

e. *certified mail* (U.S.), mail sent by a system of recorded delivery (see RECORDED *ppl. a.* 1 b); the system itself.

1955 *Federal Register* (U.S.) 19 Feb. 1075/1 Certified mail service provides a receipt to the sender and a record of delivery at the office of address. *Ibid.* Only first-class letter mail having no value will be accepted as certified mail. **1976**

New Yorker 8 Mar. 90/2 Her letter was to be sent certified mail, return receipt requested.

certifier ('sɜːtɪfaɪə(r)). [f. CERTIFY *v.* + -ER[1].] One who certifies; the giver of a certificate.

1598 FLORIO, *Certificatore*, an assurer, a certifier. **1687** A. FARMER in *Magd. Coll. & Jas. II* (Oxf. Hist. Soc.) 73 Mr. Brabourne, the other Certifier. **1885** in *19th Cent.* May 858 Each certificate must set forth the facts, observed by the certifier himself.

certify ('sɜːtɪfaɪ), *v.* Forms: 4–7 certifie, -fye, 4–6 certyfye, 5–6 certefie, -fye, 6 certyfie, 7 certefy, (5 sertefye, 7 sertifie), 6– certify. [a. F. *certifie-r*, in 13th c. *certefier*, ad. med.L. *certificāre*, f. *cert-us* certain + *-ficāre*: see -FY.]

1. *trans.* To make (a thing) certain; to guarantee as certain, attest in an authoritative manner; to give certain information of. (Often with *clause* as object.)

1330 R. BRUNNE *Chron.* (1810) 249 þis was certified & sikere. **1393** GOWER *Conf.* I. 192 Though we such thing.. Upon our trouthe certifie. *c* **1400** *Destr. Troy* 12715 He certifiet sothely in his sad lettur, þat Agamynon had goten to his gay spouse, Of Priam a prise doghter. *c* **1440** *York Myst.* xxx. 46 Nowe saye itt save may ye saffely For I will certefie þe same. *a* **1530** LD. BERNERS *Arth. Lyt. Bryt.* (1814) 32 To certefye this thinge, sende for the damoysell; and than shal ye know, by her owne mouthe. **1603** HOLLAND *Plutarch's Mor.* 282 (R.) [To] certifie that Arion was alive and safe. **1804** ABERNETHY *Surg. Observ.* 29 To certify this remark I may mention the case of a man. **1860** J. KENNEDY *Rob of Bowl* xi. 110 We may certify what we have seen to his Lordship.

2. a. To declare or attest by a formal or legal certificate. (Often with *compl. inf.*, or object *clause*.)

1461 R. CALLE in *Paston Lett.* 420 II. 58 Jenney and Yelverton hathe certified up in to the Kynges Benche inssurrecions [and] congregacions ayenste me. **1483** *Act 1 Rich. III*, c. 7 § 2 The said Justices.. to certify the same Proclamation to the Kings Justices of the Common Pleas. **1651** N. BACON *Cont. Hist. Disc.* xxii. 180 In case of sickness, or other good cause, sertified and allowed by the Captain. **1768** BLACKSTONE *Comm.* III. 214 Unless the judge shall certify under his hand that the freehold or title of the land came chiefly in question. **1788** FRANKLIN *Autobiog.* Wks. 1840 I. 222 The proper officers, comparing every article with its voucher, certified them to be right. **1801** in *Med. Jrnl.* (1804) XII. 444 This is to certify, that Drs. Marshall and Walker attended at the hospital at Malta, etc. **1818** CRUISE *Digest* VI. 120 It was certified by the Court of King's Bench to the Court of Chancery, in a modern case. **1885** *Law Times* 16 May 38/1 The magistrate confidently reversed the previous medical opinion, and certified the man as not insane.

b. *U.S. Banking. to certify a cheque*: see quot.

1864 SALA in *Daily Tel.* 16 July, In lieu of our protective system of 'crossing', there is a process known as 'certifying' a cheque. The teller puts his initials in one corner, thus warranting the genuineness of the instrument and the fact of the drawer having sufficient funds in the hands of the bank to meet it. **1880** [see CERTIFIED *ppl. a.* a].

c. To declare (a person) officially insane. (Cf. quot. 1874 for sense 4.)

1877 J. M. GRANVILLE *Care & Cure of Insane* II. 150 A serious mistake has been made in requiring that a patient shall be certified insane before he is removed to an asylum. **1883** T. S. CLOUSTON *Clin. Lect. Mental Dis.* xix. 612 The question of whether the patient should be certified as a lunatic or not. *Ibid.* 613 It is proper, having determined that he should be certified, to ask what legal risk there is. **1892** H. H. NEWINGTON in D. H. Tuke *Dict. Psychol. Med.* I. 189/2 Asylum officers or medical men officially in charge of certified patients. **1927** HENDERSON & GILLESPIE *Text-Bk. Psychiatry* xvii. 487 It is not justifiable to certify a patient while in an epileptic fit, or while under the influence of alcohol. **1930** SAYERS & EUSTACE *Docum. in Case* 72 The man's as mad as a hatter! I nearly sent round to get him certified. **1958** WODEHOUSE *Cocktail Time* xiv. 120 He had to be certified. He thought he was Stalin's nephew.

3. a. To make (a person) certain or sure (*of* a matter); to assure, inform certainly; to give (a person) legal or formal attestation (*of*).

1340 HAMPOLE *Pr. Consc.* 6846 Pilat sent til Tyberius.. to certifie hym of þis cas. *c* **1440** *Gesta Rom.* xlv. 175 (Harl. MS.) Was certifijd of the dethe of the cockes. **1535** COVERDALE *Job* xii. 8 Speake.. to the fysshes of the see, and they shal certifie the. **1581** B. RICHE *Farew. Militarie Prof.* 58 Certifying his mother the truthe which he had learned. **1675** *Pennsylv. Archives* I. 32 These are to Certifye all whom it may concerne. **1765** H. WALPOLE *Lett.* (1861) IV. 334 The next post will probably certify you of his death. **1797** SOUTHEY in *Life* (1849) I. 317 As to what is the cause of the incalculable wretchedness of society.. I have long felt certified in my own mind.

b. with *clause* as second object.

14.. *Mann. & Househ. Exp.* 564, I.. sertefynge ȝowe I was late.. a monge ryte worschepeful folke. **1526** TINDALE *Rom.* viii. 16 The same sprete certifieth oure sprete that we are the Sonnes of God. **1591** SHAKS. *1 Hen. VI*, II. iii. 32, I goe to certifie her Talbot's here. **1651** W. G. tr. *Cowel's Inst.* 237 The Sheriff is to make his return, and certefy the Justices, whether the party have sufficient Goods and Chattells. **1878** SIMPSON *Sch. Shaks.* I. 56 The following letter certified Cecil that.. White was not to inherit all.

c. *refl.* To make oneself certain, inform oneself certainly; to ascertain.

1600 HAKLUYT *Voy.* (1810) III. 470 After hee had fully certified himselfe of the riches abouesayd. **1858** MAXWELL *Let.* in *Life* x. (1882) 308, I hope to certify myself ere long what sort of 'friend's wife' I am to have.

4. a. *intr.* To make certification; to testify *to*, vouch *for*.

1625 BACON *Plantations, Ess.* (Arb.) 531 They will.. be Lazie.. and spend Victuals, and be quickly weary, and then Certifie ouer to their Country, to the Discredit of the Plantation. **1829** SOUTHEY in *For. Rev. & Cont. Misc.* III. 49 Those for whom the priests would certify might remain. **1874** A. S. TAYLOR *Med. Jurispr.* lxii. (ed. 9) 707 One of the medical men certifying to the insanity of a gentleman.

b. *Law.* To give a certificate for costs on a certain scale.

1867 *Act 30 & 31 Vict.* c. 142 §5 He shall not be entitled to any Costs of Suit unless the Judge certify on the Record that there was sufficient Reason for bringing such Action in such Superior Court. **1889** C. A. WHITE *Archbold's County Crt. Pract.* (ed. 10) 135 A judge has no power to allow costs on a higher scale unless he certify under the above section. **1910** *Encycl. Brit.* VII. 224/2 In every indictable case in which the committing justices or the court of trial certify for legal aid.

Hence **'certifying** *vbl. sb.*, certification.

1387 TREVISA *Higden* (Rolls) I. 43 By.. certefienge of cheueteynes of londes, it was i-founde.

†**certionate**, *v. Obs.* [Du Cange has *certionare* 'securum reddere': but the word looks like a mistake for *certiorate.*] = CERTIORATE.

1558 *Sc. Acts Mary* (1814) 522 The partie defendar aucht and suld be warnit of the said continewatioun, and certionat of the last day affixit be vertew thairof.

certiorari (ˌsɜːʃɪɒːˈrɛəraɪ). *Law.* [L. *certiōrāri* 'to be certified, informed, apprized, shown', which occurs in the original Latin of the words of the writ, 'we, being desirous for certain reasons, that the said record should by you *be certified* to us'.]

A writ, issuing from a superior court, upon the complaint of a party that he has not received justice in an inferior court, or cannot have an impartial trial, by which the records of the cause are called up for trial in the superior court.

1523 in W. H. Turner *Select Rec. Oxford* 38 By no wryt of error of certiorare. **1641** *Jrnls. Ho. Commons* II. 162 Upon what Grounds they issued forth those Certiorаries. **1649** FULLER *Just Man's Fun.* 16 If one conceive himself wronged in the Hundred.. he may by a *certiorari*, or an *accedas ad curiam*, remove it to the King's-Bench or Common-Pleas. **1693** CONGREVE *Doub. Dealer* II. iv, I'll firk him with a certiorari. **1712** ARBUTHNOT *John Bull* (1727) 9 He talks of nothing but.. *replevins, supersedeas's, certiorari's, writs of error*, etc. **1881** *Times* (weekly ed.) 11 June 3/4 The Court granted the rule *nisi* for the removal here by writ of *certiorari*.

certiorate ('sɜːʃɪɒreɪt), *v.* [f. L. *certiōrā-re* to certify (= *certiōrem facĕre*): see -ATE.] *trans.* To certify, inform authoritatively.

1637 GILLESPIE *Eng. Pop. Cerem.* Ep. Biij, We certiorate you.. that.. you have wrapped your selves in a very evill snare. **1820** BYRON in Moore *Life* 442, I.. should like to be certiorated of its safety in leaving Venice. **1853** *Blackw. Mag.* LXXIII. 133 The juveniles.. are wont to certiorate mamma when the footstalks are tall enough for tartlets.

†ˌ**certio'ration.** *Obs.* [noun of action f. L. *certiōrāre*: see prec. and -ATION.] A making certain or sure; certification.

1653 MANTON *Exp. James* ii. 21 Fittest to receive the witness and certioration of the Spirit. **1680** J. C. *Vind. Oaths* (ed. 2) 3 An oath then is for confirmation, and certioration.

certitude ('sɜːtɪtjuːd). [a. F. *certitude* certainty, objective or subjective f. late L. *certitūdinem* (in S. Gregory, Boethius, etc.), f. L. *cert-us* certain.]

1. Subjective certainty; the state of being certain or sure of anything; assured conviction of the mind that the facts are so and so; absence of doubt or hesitation; assurance, confidence. (There has been a growing tendency since the time of Hobbes to restrict the word to this sense; which, though not etymologically founded, is practically useful.)

1432–50 tr. *Higden* (Rolls) I. 183 Whiche childer.. not knowenge their faders in certitude. **1554** KNOX *Godly Let.* A iij, You wolde knowe the tyme, and what certitude I haue here off. **1656** HOBBES *Liberty, Necess. & Ch.* (1841) 247 An infallible certitude of the understanding in that which it knows to be, or that it shall be. **1699** *Phil. Trans.* XXI. 359 Moral Certitude Absolute, is that in which the Mind of Man entirely acquiesces, requiring no further Assurance. **1727** CHAMBERS *Cycl.*, *Certitude*, is properly a quality of the judgment, importing an adhesion of the mind to the proposition we affirm, or the strength wherewith we adhere to it. **1864** J. H. NEWMAN *Apol.* 80 My argument is.. that certitude was a habit of mind, that certainty was a quality of propositions. **1880** E. WHITE *Cert. Relig.* 3 The Evangelist distinguishes between what we now term certitude—or the belief of the mind—and certainty, or the solid reality of the fact or truths believed in. **1883** FROUDE *Short Stud.* IV. II. v. 228 The truths of faith must be held with absolute certitude.

b. A feeling of certainty in a particular case; the opposite of a doubt. With *a* and *pl.*

1611 SPEED *Hist. Gt. Brit.* IX. ix. §89 To sound the truth of the Electors and Peoples affections, which they found entire, and with that certitude returne. **1617** DONNE *Serm.* cxxxviii. V. 476 Delude themselves with imaginary Certitudes of Salvation. *c* **1645** HOWELL *Lett.* (1650) III. 4 Heaven.. wher Desires turn to Fruition, Doubts to Certitudes.

2. Objective certainty. ? *Obs.*

1538 BALE *God's Promises* in *Dodsley* (1780) I. 9 They come that thereof wyll shewe the certytude. *c* **1540** *Pilgr. Tale* 50 in *Thynne's Animadv.* (1865) App. i, For a-mongst an hundreth—this is of certitude. **1655–60** STANLEY *Hist. Philos.* (1701) 180/2 Science.. hath Certitude and Stability as being conversant in things certain and stable. **1790** MORRIS in Sparks *Life & Writ.* (1832) II. 110 It will be very long before political subjects will be reduced to geometric certitude. **1856** P. E. DOVE *Logic Chr. Faith* Introd. 3 We have evidence of the utmost conceivable certitude.

†**b.** Fixedness, permanency; invariableness. *Obs.*

1534 LD. BERNERS *Gold. Bk. M. Aurel.* (1546) Mm vj b, Thou sawest neuer certitude in the loue of a woman. **1605** CAMDEN *Rem.* 37 That there is an Orthotes or certitude of names among all Nations.

c. Sureness of action, execution, or event; unfailing quality.

1597 LOWE *Chirurg.* (1634) 139 The excellency of it [the eye] is knowne in the certitude of the actions. **1601** HOLLAND *Pliny* II. 375 That certitude which it hath in effecting any thing. **1662** EVELYN *Chalcogr.* (1769) 107 A method, how, by a constant and regular certitude, one may express to the eye, etc. **1877** A. B. EDWARDS *Up Nile* iv. 91 Expressed with masterly certitude. **1886** SWINBURNE in *Athenæum* 10 July 49/1 Trust in the certitude of compensatory justice.

†**cert-money.** *Law. Obs.* [Cowel says 'quasi *certa moneta*'; but *cert* appears to be from *certum letæ* or *pro certo letæ*, as in the quotations.]

A common fine, paid yearly by the residents and tenants of a manor to the lord or the hundred, *pro certo Letæ*, for the certain keeping of the Leet.

1607–1672 in COWEL *Interpr.* **1670** BLOUNT *Law Dict.* s.v., The Mannor of Hook, in Dorsetshire, pays Cert-money to the Hundred of Egerdon. This in ancient Records is called *Certum Letæ*. **1708** in KERSEY; in BAILEY, etc.

certs, obs. var. of CERTES.

certy, var. of CERTIE *sb.*

ceruce, obs. form of CERUSE.

cerule ('sɪər(j)uːl), *a.* Also cæ-. [ad. L. *cærul-us* = *cæruleus* blue: see CERULEAN.] A poetical equivalent of CERULEAN.

1591 SPENSER *Virg. Gnat* 164 A foord Whose cærule streame.. Crept under mosse as greene as any goord. **1610** W. FOLKINGHAM *Art of Survey* I. iii. 5 Pellucid Onyx, cerule Tarqueis. **1757** DYER *Fleece* II. 66 The bark That silently adown the cerule stream Glides with white sails. **1852** *Fraser's Mag.* XLVI. 165 Those fir-clad hills, so softly pencilled 'gainst the cerule sky!

b. quasi-*sb.* (in quot. accented *ce'rule*).

1830 W. PHILLIPS *Mt. Sinai* IV. 336 The Eternal.. Dispersed his pillar through the deep cerule Of heaven.

†**ce'ruleal**, *a. Obs. rare*$^{-1}$. [see -AL[1].] = next.

1634 SIR T. HERBERT *Trav.* 196 They paint themselues from top to toe with a cæruleall colour.

cerulean (sɪˈruːlɪən), *a.* Also cæ-. [f. L. *cærule-us* dark blue, dark green, applied to the sky, the sea (Mediterranean), but occas. to leaves, fields: cf. Welsh *glas*. In the mod. langs. always taken as deep blue.]

A. *adj.* **a.** Of the colour of the cloudless sky, pure deep blue, azure. Chiefly poetic.

1667 PRIMATT *City & C. Build.* 71 For Painting the best Cerulian or Blew colour in Oyl is. 6*d.* a yard. **1677** SIR T. HERBERT *Trav.* 129 (T.) Mosques and hummums with their cerulean tiles and gilded vanes. **1695** BLACKMORE *Pr. Arth.* IV. 83 He spread the pure Cerulean Fields on high. **1725** POPE *Odyss.* VIII. 284 We.. through cærulian billows plough the way. **1791** COWPER *Iliad* II. 545 Her eyes cerulean rolled. **1847** EMERSON *Threnody* Wks. (Bohn) I. 487 Within the air's cerulean round.

b. *humorous* = BLUE *a.* 7.

1831 *Cat's Tail* 28 Being cerulean (which so much the *ton* is).

c. ***cerulean blue***, an artist's colour prepared from cobalt, a brilliant light blue pigment.

1889 in *Cent. Dict.* **1962** R. G. HAGGAR *Dict. Art Terms* 71/2 *Cerulean blue*, a lovely, bright,.. turquoise blue made from cobalt and tin oxides, first prepared in about 1860. It is.. of great value for use in rendering atmospheric effects in landscape painting.

B. quasi *sb.* (ellipt.).

1. Cerulean colour or hue.

1756 *Gentl. Mag.* 39 Tinctured with a bright cerulean, then with a fine azure. **1835** *New Monthly Mag.* 299 The sky was clear and of the milky cerulean of chrysoprase.

2. *humorous.* A blue-stocking, a 'blue'.

1821 BYRON *Juan* IV. cviii, O ye, who make the fortunes of all books! Benign Ceruleans of the second sex!

†**ce'ruleated**, *ppl. a. Obs.* [f. L. *cærule-us* + -ATE + -ED.] Made cerulean, coloured blue.

1634 SIR T. HERBERT *Trav.* 119 Azure paint wherewith they are ceruleated. **1680** MORDEN *Geog. Rect., Persia* (1685) 385 Cupoloes curiously cæruleated with a feigned Turquoise.

cerulein (sɪˈruːliːɪn), **cerulin** ('sɪərəlɪn). Also cæ-. [f. L. *cærule-us* blue + -IN.] †**a.** An intensely blue substance obtained from indigo. **b.** A deep blue substance contained in many essential oils, also called azulene.

1810 HENRY *Elem. Chem.* (1840) II. 281 Cerulin appeared to consist of 1 atom of indigo + 4 atoms of water. **1838** T. THOMSON *Chem. Org. Bodies* 200 He gave the name of cerulin, from its blue colour, to the soluble indigo contained in it, and that of ceruleo-sulphates to the salts. **1872** WATTS *Dict. Chem.* IV. 185 An oily compound of a very deep blue

colour called cærulein. **1880** *Syd. Soc. Lex.*, *Cærulein*, same as Azulene.

ce'ruleo-, combining form of L. *cærule-us*, in the names of various chemical compounds, as ***ceruleo-sulphuric acid***; ***ceruleo-lactin***, etc.

1810 Henry *Elem. Chem.* (1840) II. 281 Ceruleo-sulphate of Potassa. **1838** Ceruleo-sulphate [see cerulein]. **1875** Ure *Dict. Arts* II. 906 s.v. *Indigo*, A peculiar acid, to which the names of indigo-sulphuric, sulphindigotic, sulphindylic, or cæruleo-sulphuric acid have been applied [Watts (III. 258) calls this Sulphocærulic acid]. **1879** Watts *Dict. Chem.*, *2nd Supp.* 276 *Ceruleolactin*, a hydrated aluminium phosphate.. found in botryoïdal and reniform masses.

b. ***ceruleo-nasal***: humorous for blue-nose 2.

1858 O. W. Holmes *De Sauty*, Tell me, O Provincial; speak, Ceruleo-nasal.

†**ce'ruleous**, *a. Obs.* Also cæruleous, 8 -ious. [f. L. *cærule-us* cerulean + -ous.] = cerulean.

1575 Laneham *Let.* (1871) 10 A Poet..in a long ceruleoous garment. **1633** T. Adams *Exp. 2 Peter* iii. 7 The heavens are pure, bright, ceruleous. **1680** Boyle *Exper. Chem. Princ.* II. 100. **1717** *Phil. Trans.* XXX. 569 The Pyrmont Waters excell all..in its bright Cærulious Lustre.

cerulescent (sɪər(j)ʊ'lɛsənt), *a.* Also cæ-. [as if ad. L. **cærulēscent-em* pr. pple., becoming blue, f. *cæruleus.*] Tending to cerulean.

1880 *Syd. Soc. Lex.*, *Cærulescent*, sky blue. **1881** *Jrnl. Bot.* X. 113 The gelatina-hymenea is cærulescent, then slightly tawny with iodine.

‖**ceruleum, cæ-** (sɪ'ruːlɪəm). [neut. of L. *cæruleus.*] (See quots.)

1859 *Times* 28 Dec. 2/2 (*Advt.*) *Cæruleum*, a new permanent colour, prepared for the use of artists. **1875** Ure *Dict. Arts.* I. 570 *Cæruleum*..consisting of stannate of protoxide of cobalt, mixed with stannic acid and sulphate of lime.

ce'rulic, *a. Chem.* Also cæ-. [f. L. *cærul-us* blue + -ic.] In ***cerulic acid*** (see quot.).

1880 *Syd. Soc. Lex.*, *Cærulic acid*, an acid of coffee, by some regarded as an oxidation product of caffetannic acid.

†**ceru'lific**, *a. Obs. rare*$^{-1}$. [as if ad. L. **cærulific-us* making blue, f. *cærul-us* blue + *-ficus* making.] 'Having the power to produce a blue colour' (J.).

1701 Grew *Cosm. Sacr.* II. ii. (R.), The several species of rays, as the rubifick, cerulifick, and others.

cerulignol (sɪər(j)uː'lɪgnɒl). *Chem.* Also cœrulignol. [ad. G. *caerulignol* (A. Grätzel 1882, in *Arch. d. Pharm.* CCXX. 606), f. L. *cæruleus* dark blue (cf. quot. 1923) + *lign-um* wood + -ol.] A colourless oily phenolic liquid, $C_{10}H_{14}O_2$, which has astringent properties and an odour like that of creosote and is obtained by the distillation of various wood-oils and fruits.

1883 *Jrnl. Chem. Soc.* XLIV. 393 The rough creasote.. contains another substance, recently isolated by the author and named by him cœrulignol. **1923** *Nature* CXI. 763/1 The presence of cerulignol in these tars, giving a blue coloration in alcoholic solution with lime or baryta. **1955** *Canadian Jrnl. Chem.* XXXIII. 723 The UV absorption maximum of this hydrocarbon, coerulignol, is 281 mμ.

cerulignone (sɪəruː'lɪgnəʊn). *Chem.* Also cœ-, †co-, †-on. [ad. G. *cörulignon* (C. Liebermann 1872, in *Ber. d. Deut. Chem. Ges.* V. 746), f. L. *cæru-leus* (also written *cœruleus*) dark blue + *lign-um* wood + quin)one.] A quinone derivative, $C_{16}H_{16}O_6$, which is obtained when wood-vinegar is treated with potassium dichromate and which crystallizes in small bluish-grey needles.

1873 *Chem. News* 24 Jan. 38/1 As cœrulignon is insoluble in wood-vinegar, and not volatile, it cannot be contained as such in the distilled wood-vinegar, but must be formed after the distillation. **1874** *Jrnl. Chem. Soc.* XXVII. 1028 (*heading*) Use of Corulignone in Calico Printing. **1961** L. F. & M. Fieser *Adv. Org. Chem.* xxii. 767 The deeply colored cerulignone is sparingly soluble in ordinary organic solvents and is best crystallized from phenol.

cerulin: see cerulein.

†**'cerulous**, *a. Obs. rare.* [f. L. *cærul-us* = *cæruleus* blue + -ous.] = ceruleous.

1651 *Raleigh's Ghost* 44 [Flowers] cerulous or blewish. **1717** Slare in *Phil. Trans.* XXX. 565 A Cerulous azure Blue.

cerumen (sɪ'ruːmɪn). [a. mod. (or ? med.) L. *cērūmen*, f. L. *cēra* wax, or ad. Gr. κηρούμενος formed of wax. Also mod.F. *cérumen.*] The yellow wax-like secretion in the external canal of the ear.

1741 Monro *Anat. Nerves* (ed. 3) 25 The *Cerumen* of the Ears is of a watry Consistence. **1844** Dufton *Deafness* 87 A pellet of hardened cerumen.

cerumi'niferous, *a.* [f. mod.L. *cērūmen*, *-inis* (see prec.) + -ferous.] Producing cerumen.

ceruminous (sɪ'ruːmɪnəs), *a.* [f. mod.L. *cērūmin-* stem of *cērūmen* (see prec.) + -ous.] Of, or of the nature of, cerumen; chiefly in ***ceruminous glands***, the glands which secrete the wax of the ear.

1801 Cooper in *Phil. Trans.* XCI. 447 A discharge from the ceruminous glands. **1834** Mason Good *Study Med.* (ed. 4) II. 105 [The discharge] then ceases and is succeeded by a copious ceruminous secretion.

ceruse ('sɪəruːs, sɪ'ruːs). Forms: 4, 7 ceruce, 4, 6 seruse, 6 cereuse, 6–9 cerusse, 7–9 ceruss, (7 cerus), 5– ceruse. [a. F. *céruse* (Pr. *ceruza*, Sp. *cerusa*, It. *cerussa*), or ad. L. *cērussa* ceruse, according to Vossius perh. for a possible Gr. κηροῦσσα (contr. f. κηρόεσσα) waxy, f. κηρός wax.]

1. A name for white lead, a mixture or compound of carbonate and hydrate of lead (usually 2 $PbCO_3 + PbH_2O_2$); largely used as a white paint, formerly also in medicine for ointments, etc.

c **1386** Chaucer *Prol.* 630 Boras, Ceruce [*v.r.* seruse], ne oille of Tartre noon..That hym myghte helpen. *a* **1500** in *E.E. Misc.* (1855) 72 To temper ceruse. **1585** Lloyd *Treas. Health* F j, Cerusse dropped into thyne eyes taketh away the paine and cleareth the eyes. **1621** Burton *Anat. Mel.* II. ii. I. i, Galen hath taken exceptions at such waters, which run through leaden pipes..for that unctuous ceruse, which causeth dysenteries and fluxes. **1748** *Phil. Trans.* XLV. 107 A Phial coated within and without with Ceruse, *i.e.* the Calx of Lead. **1808** Henry *Epit. Chem.* 308 The insolubility of the cerusse in boiling distilled vinegar. **1873** A. W. Williamson *Chem.* §168 Until a thick crust of ceruse is formed over the surface of the lead.

b. *esp.* as a paint or cosmetic for the skin: often used vaguely.

1519 Horman *Vulg.* 169 They whyte theyr face, necke, and pappis with ceruse. **1603** B. Jonson *Sejanus* II. i, 'Tis the sun, Hath given some little taint unto the ceruse: You should have used of the white oil I gave you. **1623** Massinger *Dk. Milan* v. ii, Your ladyship looks pale; But I, your doctor, have a ceruse for you. **1653** Manton *Exp. James* i. 23 The artificial ceruse and varnish of the face. **1664** Butler *Hud.* II. I. 608 Others make Posies of her Cheeks..In which the Lilly, and the Rose, For Indian Lake, and Ceruse goes. **1754** *Connoisseur* No. 5 At Paris the face of every lady you meet is besmeared with unguent, ceruss, and plaister. **1822** Byron *Juan* XI. xlviii, Youth, ceruse, Against his heart preferr'd their usual claims. *a* **1859** Macaulay *Biog. Johnson* 84 Johnson..whose eye-sight was too weak to distinguish ceruse from natural bloom.

2. The native carbonate of lead; = cerussite.

†**3.** ***ceruse of antimony***: 'a preparation of the regulus of that mineral, powdered, mixed with spirit of nitre, and distilled in a retort till no more fumes will rise' (Chambers *Cycl. Supp.* 1753).

1692 Boyle *Hist. Air* xxxviii. 233 A Parcel of his own Ceruss of Antimony. **1754** Huxham in *Phil. Trans.* XLVIII.

†**ceruse**, *v. Obs.* [f. prec. sb.] *trans.* To paint (the face) with ceruse. Hence **cerused** *ppl. a.*

1622 Fletcher *Sp. Curate* v. i, I dare tell you To your new ceruz'd [*1st folio*, cerviz'd] face, what I have spoken Freely behind your back. **1622** —— *Sea Voy.* (T.), What ladies cheek, Though cerus'd over, comes near it. **1667** Denham *Direct. Paint.* IV. viii, Vermilion this mans guilt, ceruse his fears.

†**ce'russal**, *a. Obs. rare*$^{-1}$. [f. L. *cērussa*, ceruse + -al^1.] Of or pertaining to ceruse.

1651 Biggs *New Disp.* 120 The distill'd waters in the leaden stills..partake of a saturnine cerussal quality.

cerussite, cerusite ('sɪərəsaɪt). *Min.* [f. L. *cērussa* ceruse + -ite. (Named 1845.)] Native carbonate of lead, white lead ore.

1850 Dana *Min.* 498 Cerusite isomorph with aragonite. **1885** Erni *Min.* 262 Color of cerussite, white.

ceruyce, ceruyn, etc., obs. ff. service, serve.

cervalet: see cervelat.

cer'vanthropy. *nonce-wd.* [f. L. *cerv-us* stag + Gr. ἄνθρωπ-ος man, after *lycanthropy*.]

1839 *Gentl. Mag.* Nov. 490/1 It shewed itself by cervanthropy, for he [Actæon] fancied himself turned into a stag.

Cervantic (sɜː'væntɪk), *a.* [f. the name of Cervantes, author of Don Quixote.] Characteristic of or resembling the style of Cervantes. So **Cer'vantist**, a student or admirer of Cervantes.

1759 Sterne *Tr. Shandy* (1802) I. xii. 48 It was uttered with something of a Cervantic tone. **1882** Traill *Sterne* iv. 36 Mr. Shandy is of course the Cervantic centre of the whole. **1881** *Athenæum* 19 Nov. 665/2 Lockhart was by no means abreast of the Cervantists of his time.

cervantite (sɜː'væntaɪt). *Min.* [Named 1856, from *Cervantes* (in Galicia, Spain) + -ite.] A native tetroxide of antimony (Sb_2O_4), or combination of antimonious and antimonic oxides, called also *Antimony ochre*, found as a crust or powder, or in pale yellow acicular crystals.

1868 in Dana.

cervawnte, obs. f. servant.

‖**cervelat** (sɛrvəla). Also cervelas, cervalet. [OF. *cervelat* (mod.F. *cervelas*), a kind of short thick sausage, hence applied to the musical instrument, ad. It. *cervellata* sausage.]

1. (See quots.)

1613 J. Chamberlain *Let.* 9 Sept. (1939) I. 477 The duke of Savoyes ambassador..hath brought..a present from his wife of salaccioni, cervellate, mortadelle. **1708** Kersey, *Cervelas* (F.), a large kind of sausage. **1730–6** Bailey, *Cervelas, Cervelat* (in Cookery) a large sort of Sausage, eaten cold, or in Slices. **1877** E. S. Dallas *Kettner's Bk. of Table* 48 Things which..retain names no longer their own—cervelas without brains,..cheesecakes without curds. **1958** *Catal. County Stores, Taunton* June 5 Continental sausages ..Cervelat—a lb. 9/-. **1965** *House & Garden* Jan. 60 *Cervelas.* There are many varieties of this sausage. Some are cured and dried and can be eaten as is. Others should be cooked.

2. (Also *cervalet.*) A short reed musical instrument, resembling the bassoon in tone.

1864 Webster cites Warren.

cervical ('sɜːvɪkəl, sɜː'vaɪkəl), *a. Phys.* [f. L. type **cervīcāl-is* (cf. *cervīcāl* bolster), pertaining to the neck, f. *cervix*, *-īcis*; cf. F. *cervical.*]

1. a. Of or belonging to the cervix or neck.

1681 tr. *Willis' Rem. Med. Wks.* Voc., *Cervical*, belonging to the neck. **1741** Monro *Anat.* (ed. 2) 106 They serve for the Passage of the cervical Veins. **1834** J. Forbes tr. *Laennec's Dis. Chest* 327 The mesenteric or cervical glands. **1866** Huxley *Preh. Rem. Caithn.* 109 A horse's skull with its upper cervical vetebræ.

b. Used in regard to other structures: see cervix. *spec.* of or pertaining to the cervix of the womb.

1860 Tanner *Pregnancy* ii. 54 A plug of viscid cervical mucus. **1884** R. & F. Barnes *Syst. Obstetric Med.* I. vii. 239 The cervical mucous membrane, lined by the connective tissue which sustains it, yields and slides on the muscular layer. **1923** in M. Box *Trial of Marie Stopes* (1967) 99 The small occlusive pessary for the cervix—the cervical cap. **1963** G. F. Kantorowicz et al. *Inlays, Crowns & Bridges* vii. 70 This stage will complete the cutting of a 'cervical collar' of sound tissue. **1966** *New Statesman* 11 Mar. 326/3 Cervical cancer—a disease that kills about 2,500 women a year in England and Wales alone. **1966** *Lancet* 24 Dec. 1423/1 There is a large variety of arrangements throughout Scotland for taking cervical smears. **1967** *Guardian* 17 May 4/5 The pill and the cervical coil gave women protection against..enforced pregnancy.

2. as *sb.* = Cervical nerve, vertebra, etc.

1767 Gooch *Treat. Wounds* I. 369 The phrenic nerve is derived from the cervicals. **1875** Blake *Zool.* 2 The cervicals are 7 in number.

cervice, obs. form of service.

cervicide ('sɜːvɪsaɪd). *rare.* [ad. med.L. *cervicīda*, f. L. *cerv-us* stag: see -cide.] The killing of a deer.

[Cf. *c* **1196** W. Novoburg *Hist. Rer. Anglic.* I. iii. (Rolls) I. 30 [Hen. I]..in publicis animadversionibus cervicidas ab homicidis parum discernebat.] **1864** Webster cites B. Taylor.

cervicitis (sɜːvɪ'saɪtɪs). *Path.* [mod.L., f. L. *cervix, cervic-* neck + -itis.] Inflammation of the neck of the uterus.

1889 L. Tait *Dis. Women* I. 108 Traumatic cervicitis often occurs after operations on the cervix. **1910** *Practitioner* Mar. 395 Every cervical erosion, cervicitis, or irritating leucorrhoeal discharge. **1964** M. Hynes *Med. Bacteriol.* (ed. 8) xi. 173 The infection does not cause urethritis in women, although it may produce cervicitis.

cervico- (sə'vaɪkəʊ). *Phys.* Assumed combining form of L. *cervix*, *-īcis* neck, as in ***cervico-dorsal*** adj.; **cer,vico-'brachial** *a.*, belonging to the neck and arm; **cer,vico-'branchial** *a.*, belonging to the branchiæ and the neck; **cer,vico-'facial** *a.*, belonging to the neck and face; **cer,vico-'scapular** *a.*, belonging to the neck and the shoulder-bone, etc.

1836–9 Todd *Cycl. Anat.* II. 292/1 A branch of the inferior or cervico-facial division. **1842** E. Wilson *Anat. Vade M.* 401 The Cervico-facial divides into a number of branches. **1872** W. Aitken *Sci. & Pr. Med.* (ed. 6) II. 354 Cervico-brachial Neuralgia is located among the sensory twigs of the brachial plexus. **1908** *Practitioner* Sept. 404 The cervico-dorsal spine.

cervicose (,sɜːvɪ'kəʊs), *a. rare*$^{-0}$. [ad. L. *cervicōs-us* obstinate, f. *cervix*, *-īcis* neck; see -ose.] 'Having a hard, strong neck' (*Syd. Soc. Lex.* 1881).

cerviculate (sə'vɪkjʊlət), *a. rare*$^{-0}$. [f. L. *cervīcul-a*, dim. of *cervix* + -ate^2.] 'Having a little or a short neck. Also, having a goitre' (*Syd. Soc. Lex.* 1881).

cervid ('sɜːvɪd). Also cervide. [f. mod.L. *Cervidæ*, a large family of ruminant mammals (order Artiodactyla), including the deer, elk, and moose; cf. L. *cervus* deer, -id^3.] A ruminant mammal of the family Cervidæ, the members of which shed their antlers. Also *attrib.* or as *adj.*

1889 in *Cent. Dict.* **1928** G. B. Brown *Art of Cave Dweller* i. 17 The slender daintiness of the legs of Cervides or of the Reindeer. **1938** *Antiquity* XII. 163 In style the engraving reminds one more of the cervids on the well-known Maglemose antler-haft. **1950** *Proc. Prehist. Soc.* XVI. 128 The general indications from the cervid antler material are consistent.

cervine (ˈsɜːvaɪn), *a.* [ad. L. *cervīn-us*, f. *cervus*, *cerva* deer. In F. *cervin*.] Of or belonging to deer, or the family *Cervidæ*; of the nature of or resembling deer. Also, *absol.* = cervine animal.
1832 *Fraser's Mag.* VI. 149 The solitary exception in favour of the cervines is at the Easter hunt. **1858** BEVERIDGE *Hist. India* I. Introd. 11 The Nepal stag, and many other varieties of the cervine tribe. **1880** DAWKINS *Early Man* iv. 88 The cervine antler..becomes more complex.
b. Of a deep tawny colour (see quot.).
1866 *Treas. Bot.*, *Cervine*, deep tawny, such as the dark part of a lion's hide.

cervise, obs. form of SERVICE.

cerˈvisial, *a. humorous.* [f. L. *cervisia* (*cerevisia*) beer + -AL[1].] Of or pertaining to beer.
17.. *Mock Ode* in Boswell *Johnson* (1816) IV. 428 Cervisial coctor's viduate dame. **1862** *Temple Bar* IV. 472 Differences..anent sundry cervisial shortcomings between her husband and the vexed landlord of the Blue Posts.

‖**cervix** (ˈsɜːvɪks). *Phys.* [L.] The neck, *esp.* the back part of the neck. Hence applied to a similar part in various organs, as the neck of the womb (*cervix uteri*), of the bladder (*cervix vesicæ*), of the thigh-bone (*cervix femoris*), and of a tooth (*cervix dentis*, 'the line of junction between the crown and the fang').
1741 MONRO *Anat.* (ed. 3) 278 The *Cervix* of the *Os Femoris* has a great many large Holes. **1836** TODD *Cycl. Anat.* I. 387/1 The cervix of the bladder is of a compressed conical form. **1860** TANNER *Pregnancy* ii. 78.

cervyce, cervyse, obs. ff. SERVICE.

†**cervylle**, *v. Obs.*[−0] [cf. OF. *escerveler*, f. *cervelle* the brains.] To remove or knock out the brains; hence **cervyller**, one who does this.
1483 *Cath. Angl.* 57 To Ceruylle, *excerebrare*. *Ibid.* A Ceruyller, *excerebrator*.

ceryl (ˈsɪərɪl). *Chem.* [f. Gr. κηρός wax + -YL.] The hypothetic radical ($C_{27}H_{55}$)' of *ceryl* or *cerotyl alcohol* or cerotin, $C_{27}H_{56}O$, a white solid waxy substance, melting at 79° C., obtained from ceryl cerotate or Chinese wax. Hence **ˈcerylene** [see -ENE], the same as CEROTENE ($C_{27}H_{54}$); **ceˈrylic** *a.*, of ceryl.
1873 WATTS *Fownes' Chem.* 610 Ceryl Alcohol is obtained from Chinese wax..This wax consists mainly of ceryl cerotate. *Ibid.* (1877) II. 303 Ceryl cerotate..yields cerotic acid and cerylene by dry distillation. **1879** —— *Dict. Chem.* I. 838 A solution of cerotate of potassium is obtained holding cerylic alcohol in suspension..The hydrate of ceryl ..forms a waxy substance melting at 79°C.

cerymony, -moyn, etc., obs. ff. CEREMONY.

ceryn, ceryows, obs. ff. SEAR, SERIOUS.

Cesar, -ean, etc.: See CÆ-.

cesare (ˈsiːzəriː). *Logic.* [med.L.] A mnemonic term for the first mood of the second figure of syllogisms, in which the major premiss and the conclusion are universal negatives, and the minor a universal affirmative.
1588 FRAUNCE *Lawiers Log.* 105 b. **1838** SIR W. HAMILTON *Logic* xxii. I. 434 In the Second Figure the first mood is Cesare, of which the formula is:—No P is M; But all S are M; Therefore, no S is P.

cesare, obs. f. SICER, strong drink.

Cesarewitch (sɪˈzærɪvɪtʃ, -zɑːr-). [ad. Russ. *tsesarévich*, title as heir to the imperial Russian throne of the prince who became Alexander II.] A long-distance handicap horse-race run at Newmarket, instituted in 1839.
1839 *Sporting Mag.* 2nd. Ser. XIX. 263 *Newmarket.*—His Imperial Highness the Grand Duke of Russia having presented the Jockey Club with the sum of £300, to be run for annually, the first race for it will take place in the Second October Meeting, and is thus officially announced:—'The Cesarewitch Stakes—a free Handicap Sweepstakes.' **1856** 'STONEHENGE' *Brit. Sports* 373/1 Cesarewitch Course..2 miles, 2 furlongs, 28 yards. **1883** [see WEIGHT *sb.*[1] 12 a]. **1891** G. CHETWYND *Racing Remin.* I. 29 It was at Warwick, too, that the big Cesarewitch commissions usually made their first appearance in the market. *Ibid.* 31 At the next Newmarket meeting Cardinal York won the Cesarewitch by six lengths. **1934** [see ADD *v.* 1 a].

cesarowitz, var. of CZAREVITCH.

cese, cesse, obs. ff. of CEASE.

ceserera, var. of SISERARY, a hard blow.

†**cesil.** *Obs.* Some kind of fur.
1492 *Will of Borne* (Somerset Ho.) Gowne..furrid wt Cesill wombes.

cesium, var. CÆSIUM.

cesment, var. of CESSMENT, *Obs.*

†**cesolfa.** *Obs.* [f. *C*, *sol*, *fa*, names of musical notes: cf. *Effaut*.] The name of a musical note, the treble C, which was *sol* of the 6th hexachord and *fa* of the 7th. Cf. A RE.
a **1325** *Old Eng. Song* in *Rel. Ant.* I. 291 The song of the cesolfa dos me syken sare.

cesone, obs. form of SEASON, SEISIN.

†**ˈcespitate.** *Obs. rare*[−0]. [ad. med.L. *cespitāre* to stumble, 'said esp. of a horse' (Du Cange); f. L. *cæspit-em* turf.] (See quots.)
1623 COCKERAM, *Cespitate*, to stumble. **1678** PHILLIPS, *Cespitate*, to stumble, as it were to hit ones foot against a Turf.

†**cespiˈtation.** *Obs.* [f. as prec.; see -ATION.] Stumbling; sudden stoppage in a course.
1653 R. BAILLIE *Dissuasive Vind.* (1655) 1 Mr. Cottons clear cespitation on the threshold. **1654** TRAPP *Comm. Ps.* xxiii. 3 Wherein I may walk..without cessation or cespitation. **1669** W. SIMPSON *Hydrol. Chym.* 128 An instantaneous Asthma, together with a cespitation of the animal Spirits.

cespititious (sɛspɪˈtɪʃəs), *a.* [f. L. *cæspitīci-us* made of turf + -OUS.] Made of turf, turfen.
17.. GOUGH (T.) Height and breadth of the cespititious ramparts. **1867** BURTON *Hist. Scot.* (1873) I. i. 33 It is called a cespititious wall. **1880** —— *Reign Q. Anne* III. xiv, 50 Redoubts or bastions, called 'cæspititious', as made out of the materials available on the spot.

cespitose (ˌsɛspɪˈtəʊs), *a.* Also CÆSPITOSE, q.v. Turfy, growing in dense tufts or clumps.
1793 T. MARTYN *Lang. Botany* s.v. *Cespitosa planta*, A cespitose or turfy plant has many stems from the same root, usually forming a close thick carpet. **1828** STARK *Elem. Nat. Hist.* II. 432 Cespitose; branches short, erect, thick. **1846** DANA *Zooph.* iv. (1848) 71 Crowded cespitose clumps. **1882** VINES *Sachs' Bot.* 380 Small cespitose Mosses which are very leafy and much branched.

cespiˈtoso-, cæspiˈtoso-, combining f. of prec. = in a cespitose manner, cespitose and ——.
1846 DANA *Zooph.* (1848) 470 Arborescent or cespitoso-arborescent. *Ibid.* 452 Between the proper cespitose Madrepores, and the cespitoso-arboriform. *Ibid.* 325 Cespitoso-hemispherical. *Ibid.* 504 Cespitoso-ramose.

cespitous (ˈsɛspɪtəs), *a.* [f. L. *cæspit-em* turf + -OUS: cf. mod.F. *cespiteux*, *-euse* in same sense.] Turfy, cæspitose.
1832 in WEBSTER; and in later Dicts.

cess (sɛs), *sb.*[1] Also SESS(E. [The etymological spelling is SESS, aphetic f. ASSESS *sb.* in same sense: the spelling *cess*, due app. to mistaken notion of the etymology, has been more or less established in some senses.]
1. An assessment, tax, or levy: in various *spec.* applications.
a. A rate levied by local authority and for local purposes. Now superseded in general English use by *rate*, but frequent *dial.*; in Ireland it is still the official term. ***church cess***: see quot. 1868.
1531 *Act 22 Hen. VIII*, c. 3 § 1 Diuers and sundry Cesses, Scots, and Taxes. **1580** NORTH *Plutarch* (1676) 73 To appoint..what time the Sess should continue. **1642** *Vestry Bks.* (Surtees) 104 Received more for a cease of 2d. pound, 19s. 1d. ob. *a* **1745** SWIFT *Wks.* (1841) II. 49 Unless when the parish cess was gathered. **1827** HALLAM *Const. Hist.* (1876) III. xviii. 374 A cess or permanent composition for every plough-land. **1847** BARHAM *Ingol. Leg.* (1877) 206 There's the rent and the rates and the sesses. **1851** HT. MARTINEAU *Hist. Peace* (1877) III. iv. ix. 35 The Tories were disposed to uphold the dues of the Church, even to the last penny of Church-cess. **1863** *Possibil. Creation* 93 We have our world lit up regularly without any lamp cess being levied. **1868** *Pall Mall G.* 29 June 3/1 The Act of the 3 and 4 Will. IV, c. 37..abolished..the church vestry cess, as church rates in Ireland were then called. **1877** *Holderness Gloss.* (E.D.S.) *Cess*, a parochial or municipal rate.
b. *Scotland.* The land tax.
1662 *Sc. Acts* (1820) VII. 409 Act in favour of [the Earls of Queensberry and Annandale] for payment of a moneths Cesse advanced by them for the Shire of Dumfreis. **1678** *Ibid.* VIII. 221 **1701** J. LAW *Counc. Trade* 133 All extraordinary taxes as cess, pole, hearth-money, and such like grievous and unequal dutys. **1702** *Lond. Gaz.* No. 3824/2 An Act [Scotland] for a Supply of Ten Months and half's Cess upon Land-Rents, received the Royal Assent. *c* **1706** in *Sc. Pasquils* (1868) 388 From paying us our Darien Costs, By laying on cess, and new imposts. **1746–7** *Act 20 Geo. II*, c. 50 §2 Their respective proportions of His Majesty's cess or land tax.
c. *India.* A tax levied for a specific object; often with prefixed word defining the object.
1818 JAS. MILL *Brit. India* II. v. i. 309 With regard to the cesses or arbitrary taxes. **1841** ELPHINSTONE *Hist. Ind.* 133 Various taxes and cesses, some falling directly on the land, and others more or less circuitously affecting the cultivator. **1883** *Contemp. Rev.* Oct. 584 Imposing additional taxes.. such as the road cess, the irrigation cess, the public works cess, and the education cess.
†**2.** *Ireland.* The obligation to supply the soldiers and the household of the lord deputy with provisions at prices 'assessed' or fixed by government; hence loosely used for military exactions generally. *Obs.* exc. *Hist.*
1571 CAMPION *Hist. Ireland* II. x. (1633) 126 With sesse and souldiours. **1586** J. HOOKER *Girald. Irel.* in *Holinshed* II. 144/2 Cesse is..a prerogatiue of the prince, to impose vpon the countrie a certeine proportion of all kind of vittels for men and horsse, to be deliuered at a reasonable price called the queen's price, to all and euerie such souldiors as she is contented to be at charge withall, and so much as is thought competent for the lord deputies house. **1596** SPENSER *State Irel.* 56. **1612** DAVIES *Why Ireland, &c.* (1787) 20 By their continual cess and extortion [p. 159 sess of soldiers]. **1628** tr. *Camden's Hist. Eliz.* II. (1688) 219 Ceass..is an Exaction of Victuals at a certain Rate or Price ..for the Maintenance of the Lord Deputie's Houshold and Garrison-souldiers. **1809** TOMLINS *Law Dict.*, *Cesse* or *cease* in Ireland..for soldiers in garrison.
†**3.** Assessment, valuation, estimation. In phrase ***out of all cesse***. *Obs.*
1588 *Marprel. Epit.* 49 This..ouerthroweth the puritans out of all cesse. **1596** SHAKS. *1 Hen. IV*, II. i. 8 The poore Iade is wrung in the withers, out of all cesse.
4. *Comb.*, as ***cess-gatherer***, ***-payer***; **cess-tax** = 2.
1877 E. PEACOCK *N.-W. Linc. Gloss.* (E.D.S.) *Cess-getherer*, one who gathers a local tax. 'John Lockwood, th' cess-getherer's been for th' Court o' Sewers rate.' **1880** *Edin. Rev.* Jan. 135 (*Ireland*) The associated cess-payers are not chosen by election. **1882** J. TAYLOR *Sc. Covenanters* 180 Renwick was brought to trial for teaching that it was unlawful to pay the cess-tax.

†**cess**, *sb.*[2] *Obs.* = DECEASE, q.v.
1419 *Will of Thomas* (Somerset Ho.) After þe cesse of her.

†**cess**, *sb.*[3] *Obs.* [var. of CEASE: cf. CESS *v.*[2]]
1. Cessation, interruption.
1703 DE FOE *Orig. Power People* Misc. 135 If Power at any time meets with a Cess, if Government and Thrones become Vacant, to this Original all Power..returns.
2. = CESSER 3.
1689 *Proposals* in *7th Coll. Papers Pres. Juncture of Affairs* 1 This is a Cess of that nature that requires a Judgment to be made upon it.

†**cess**, *sb.*[4] *Obs.* exc. *dial.* [Etymology uncertain.]
1. A peat-bog; also a piece of peat, a turf.
1636 R. JAMES *Iter Lanc.* 308 Ye deepe Lowe spongie mosses yet remembrance keepe Of Noah's flood: on numbers infinite Of firre trees swaines doe in their cesses light. **1847** *Jrnl. Agric. Soc.* VIII. I. 100 This substance..is dug and dried into small sods called 'turfs' or 'cesses' for fuel.
2. 'A space of ground lying between a drain or river and the foot of its bank' (E. Peacock *N.-W. Linc. Gloss.*, E.D.S.); a haugh. **b.** 'The foreshore of a drain or river' (*Ibid.*).
1874 *Ancholme Navigation Notice* in E. Peacock *N.-W. Linc. Gloss.* s.v., The occupiers of the land adjoining the cesses of the Navigation..are authorized to discharge all persons trespassing thereon.

cess (sɛs), *sb.*[5] *Anglo-Irish.* [? for *success*, or from CESS[1] sense 2.] In phrase ***bad cess to*** = 'bad luck to, evil befall'.
1859 *Punch* 17 Dec. Carlisle and Russell—bad cess to their clan! **1860** LOVER *Leg. & Stories* (ed. 10) 313 Bad cess to you, can't you say what you're bid.

†**cess** (sɛs), *v.*[1] *Obs.* exc. *Hist.* Also 5–8 SESS, 6 **cease, ceasse.** [Etymologically spelt SESS, aphetic f. ASSESS; see CESS *sb.*[1].]
1. *trans.* To determine the amount of (a tax, fine, or contribution; also of rent, and the prices at which articles are to be sold); = ASSESS *v.* 1.
1523 LD. BERNERS *Froiss.* I. cccIxxxvii. 663 As soone as the kyng was departed fro Paris, the commons rose in harnesse, and slewe all those that had ceassed the aydes. **1531–2** *Act 23 Hen. VIII*, c. 4 § 5 The same rates and prices to be named and cessed by them and euery of them by their discrecions. *c* **1590** in *Secr. Mem. Earl Leicester* (1706) 74 Compelling the tenant to pay him new rent & what he ceaseth. *c* **1613** *Social Condit. People Anglesey* (1860) 21 In some parts of the countrey, this mite was never cessed; in other parts it was cessed, but never leavied. **1764** R. BURN *Hist. Poor Laws* 73 To sess, tax, and limit upon every such obstinate person, what sum the said person shall pay weekly.
2. To impose (taxation, a fine, etc.) *upon* (a person or community); = ASSESS *v.* 2.
1495 *Act 11 Hen. VII*, iv, Suche fynes and amerciamentis as upon them shalbe cessid. **1612** in Picton *L'pool Munic. Rec.* (1883) I. 171 Diverse fynes and Amerciaments cessed upon him in Mr. Maior's Court.
3. *Ireland.* To impose (soldiers) upon a community who are to support them at a fixed rate.
1612 DAVIES *Why Ireland, &c.* (1787) 142 There was no means to maintain the army but by cessing the soldiers upon the subject, as the Irish were wont to impose their bonaught. **1880** BURTON *Reign Q. Anne* II. xvii. 178 None..shall cosher, lodge, or cess themselves upon the inhabitants.
4. To subject (a person, community, or property) to a contribution, tax, or fine; to rate, to tax; = ASSESS *v.* 3. Also (*Ireland*) To subject to military exactions or requisitions; cf. CESS *sb.*[1] 2.
1494 FABYAN VII. 344 He prysonyd theym, and after sessyd theym at greuouse fynys. **1523** LD. BERNERS *Froiss.* I. ci. 121 Yf I wolde sore cease you, ye shulde pay me xxx. or xl. M. scutes. *Ibid.* I. cccIxxxvii. 664 With their owne good wylles they ceased theymselfe to paye weekly a tenne thousande florence. **1609** B. JONSON *Sil. Wom.* IV. ii, A man of two thousand a-year is not cess'd at so many weapons as he has on. **1652** T. MAY *Old Couple* in *Dodsley* (1780) X. 504, I shall be..sess'd More to the poor. **1738** *Hist. View Crt. Excheq.* ii. 21 If he did not come at all, then he was cessed for all the Lands he held. **1856** FROUDE *Hist. Eng.* II. vii. (L.) The English garrisons cessed and pillaged the farmers of Meath and Dublin.
5. To estimate officially the taxable value of (property, land, etc.); to rate; = ASSESS *v.* 4.

1598 Stow *Surv.* xv. (1603) 130 To the fifteene it is cessed at foure pound ten shillings.

†**cess**, *v.*² *Obs.* Also 6 sese. [Variant of CEASE *v.*; after special senses of OF. *cesser*.]

1. *intr.* To cease to perform a legal duty: cf. CESSAVIT.

1555 Perkins *Prof. Bk.* v. §374 (1642) 162 If there bee Lord Mesne and Tenant and the Tenant doth cesse. *Ibid.* §389. 168 If..the Tenant take a wife and afterwards cesseth. **1670** Blount *Law Dict.* s.v. *Cessor*, Where it is said the Tenant cesseth..the Tenant ceaseth to do what he ought. **1741** T. Robinson *Gavelkind* II. vi. 253 If a Tenant cessed to pay his Rent for two Years.

2. *trans.* To cede, give up, surrender.

1523 Ld. Berners *Froiss.* I. ccxii. 259 They [are] to transport, cesse, and leaue eche kyng to other perpetuelly, al the right that they ought to haue in all these sayd thynges. *Ibid.* 258 We transport and sese all the right that we might have in any of these thynges.

†**'cessant**, *a. Obs. rare.* [ad. L. *cessānt-em*, pr. pple. of *cessāre* to CEASE.] That ceases to act; characterized by cessation or intermission. Hence **'cessantly** *adv.*, intermittently, at intervals.

1648 W. Mountague *Devout Ess.* Ep. Ded., Such a way as renders even this cessant state in some sort active. **1701** Howe *Occas. Conformity* Wks. (1834) 183/1 As the cessant or diminished weight of such reasons shall allow. **1746** Parsons in *Phil. Trans.* XLIV. 44, I personally knew a Gentleman..who cessantly winked with one Eye.

†**'cessate**, *v. Obs. rare.* [f. L. *cessāt-*, ppl. stem of *cessāre* to CEASE.] *trans.* To make to cease; to put an end to.

1701 Beverley *Apoc. Quest.* 33 That Variety of Barbarous Nations, their taking Rome, Cessating the Western Empire.

cessation (sɛ'seɪʃən). [ad. L. *cessātiōn-em*, n. of action f. *cessāre* to CEASE. Practically treated as n. of action from Eng. *cease*; see -ATION.]

1. Ceasing, discontinuance, stoppage; either permanent or temporary.

a **1400** *Cov. Myst.* 107 Withowte cessacion They crye. **1580** North *Plutarch* (1676) 985 The Cessation of the Oracles. **1615** G. Sandys *Trav.* 7 The cessation of trafficke with the Mahometans. **1628** Le Grys tr. *Barclay's Argenis* 128 These are, as it were cessations from Armes, with which sometimes wee doe beguile our common griefs. **1641** Baker *Chron. Hen. VI* an. 1450 (R.) Jack Cade affirming no cessation of arms, unless the King in person would hear the grievances of the subject. **1725** Pope *Odyss.* xx. 387 A long cessation of discourse ensu'd. **1748** Anson *Voyage* III. i. 301 The cessation of the storm. **1876** Grant *Burgh Sch. Scotl.* II. v. 182 Cessation from work in all the schools.

†**b.** ellipt. = *Cessation of* or *from arms* (see in prec.): suspension of hostilities; armistice, truce: also in *comb.* as ***cessation-breaker***. *Obs.*

1645 *King's Cab. Opened* in *Select. Harleian Misc.* (1793) 353 The eminent inevitable necessity, which caused me to make the Irish cessation. **1653** Holcroft *Procopius* II. 46 They gave Hostages for observing the Cessation. **1736** Carte *Ormonde* II. 285 To join with general Preston for suppressing and reducing the cessation-breakers. **1755** —— *Hist. Eng.* IV. 479 After the cessation for that county [Cheshire] and Lancashire had been annulled.

†**2.** A ceasing to hold office. *Obs.*

1460 Capgrave *Chron.* 272 On Mihelmesse day, the Kyng..red the Act of his Cessacion before these lordis. **1640** Bp. Hall *Episc.* II. §12 If any Bishop..shall there keep him against this decreed Cessation, Let him..be barred from Communion.

†**3.** Desistence from action; inactivity, idleness.

1603 Florio *Montaigne* III. x. (1632) 576 They accuse my cessation, when as all the world was convicted of too much doing. **1613** R. C. *Table Alph.*, *Cessation*, rest, idleness. **1697** Dryden *Virg. Georg.* I. 109 The spent Earth may gather heart again; And, better'd by Cessation, bear the Grain.

‖**cessavit** (sɛ'seɪvɪt). [Lat. 3rd sing. perf. of *cessāre* = CEASE *v.*, CESS *v.*² 1.] A writ so called, originating in Stat. 6 Edw. I. and abolished by 3 and 4 Wm. IV. (See quot. and cf. CESS *v.*², CESSER.)

1555 Perkins *Prof. Bk.* v. §389 The Lord bringeth a Cessavit and doth recover. **1641** *Termes de la Ley* 50. **1768** Blackstone *Comm.* III. 232 The writ of cessavit: which lies, by the statutes of Glocester..and of Westm. 2..when a man who holds lands of a lord by rent or other services, neglects or ceases to perform his services for two years together. **1809** Tomlins *Law Dict.* s.v., If the lord distrains pending the writ of cessavit against his tenant, the writ shall abate.

cesse, obs. form of CEASE, SEISE.

cessement, var. of CESSMENT. *Obs.*

cesser ('sɛsə(r)). Also 6 ceasser, 6, 9 (incorrectly) cessor. [a. F. *cesser* to cease; the infin. being used subst. as in *trover*, *misnomer*.]

1. *Law.* Ceasing (of a tenant) to pay rent, or perform legal duties, for the space of two years.

1531 *Dial. Laws of Eng.* II. xxxiv. (1638) 122 The sufferance of the Abbot onely may disherit the house, as by his ceasser. **1555** Perkins *Prof. Bk.* v. §389 (1642) 168 The cessor doth not lye in any act done by the husband. **1741** T. Robinson *Gavelkind* iv. 42 The Lord may enter for the Cesser of his Tenant. **1755** Carte *Hist. Eng.* IV. 21 Upon a Cesser in the king's case, no receipt for 100 years together would make it good or hinder the estate from being avoided.

2. A coming to an end; cessation, termination.

1809 Tomlins *Law Dict.*, *Cessure*, or *cesser*, ceasing, giving over; or departing from. **1844** Williams *Real Prop.* (1877) 412 If a proviso for cesser of the term should not be inserted in the deed by which it is created. **1883** J. Payne *1001 Nts.* III. 172 Wherefore it is God's gift to thee, for the cesser of thine ill fortune. **1884** Ld. Coleridge in *Law Times Rep.* 8 Mar. 48/1 There is a condition in the charter-party providing for a cesser of the liability of the charterers as soon as the cargo is on board.

†**3.** Vacation of office, abdication; = CESSION 2.

1689 *Proposals* in *7th Coll. Papers Pres. Junct. Aff.* 1 This seems to be a Cesser of this Government, and may amount to as much as if he had died. **1689** *Consid. Succession & Alleg.* 6 To comprehend all kinds of Cesser from the Government, whether by Death or otherwise.

cesser, var. of CESSOR, SESSOR.

[**cesshery**, error for COSHERY.

c **1580** J. Hooker *Sir P. Carew* in *Archæol.* XXVIII. 134 Cessheries and cesses, and suche other Ireshe customes.]

†**cessi'bility.** *Obs.* [f. next: see -ITY.] The quality of being cessible; yieldingness.

1645 Digby *Nat. Bodies* ix. (1658) 92 If the subject strucken be of a proportionate cessibility, it seemeth to dull and deaden the stroke. **1658** R. White tr. *Digby's Powd. Symp.* (1660) 27 The density, and figure, of the descending body acting upon the cessibility of the medium.

†**'cessible**, *a. Obs. rare.* [as if ad. L. **cessibilis*, f. *cess-us*, pa. pple. of *cēdĕre* to yield; see -IBLE. Cf. 16th c. F. *cessible* 'that may be given up'.] Yielding; ready to yield or give way.

1645 Digby *Nat. Bodies* ix. (1658) 93 If the parts of the strucken body be so easily cessible, as without difficulty the stroke can divide them, then it enters into such a body.

cessile ('sɛsaɪl), *a. rare.* Also 6 cessil. [as if ad. L. **cessilis*, f. *cessus* (see CESSIBLE *a.*) + -ILE.] Yielding (applied only to the air, in imitation of the first quot.).

a **1599** A. Hume *Poems* (1902) 28 Sa silent is the cessile air. *Ibid.* 49 The massiue earth reposis still, Suspended in the cessil eire. **1911** Quiller-Couch *Brother Copas* xxiii. 319 A faint tapping sound reached them, borne on 'the cessile air'. **1922** Joyce *Ulysses* 416 Scintillant circumambient cessile air.

cessing ('sɛsɪŋ), *vbl. sb.*¹ *Obs.* exc. *Hist.* [f. CESS *v.*¹ + -ING¹.] The levying of a cess; rating.

1882 J. Taylor *Sc. Covenanters* 50 Finings and cessings for causes for which there are no warrants.

†**'cessing**, *vbl. sb.*² *Obs.* [f. CESS *v.*² + -ING¹.]

1. The ceasing to perform legal duties; = CESSER 1.

1570-6 Lambarde *Peramb. Kent* (1826) 498 The Lord, after such a Cessing, ought..to seeke..whether any distresse may be found upon the Tenement, or No. **1641** *Termes de la Ley* 175 By this word Gavelet the Lord shall have the land for the cessing of the Tenant.

2. Cession, surrender, abdication.

1480 Caxton *Chron. Eng.* ccliii. 328 The peple woundred of the cesyng and resygnyng of pope felix to nycholas.

3. Stopping, stoppage.

1512 *Act 4 Hen. VIII*, c. 19 Preamb., Oure seid holye Fader..for the cessyng of the seid Scisme and errours hath ..sent for ayde..into oure seid Sovereign Lorde.

‖**cessio bonorum** (L. 'cession of goods') = CESSION 3 b: in *Sc. Law*, a legal proceeding by which a debtor is entitled to be free from imprisonment, if innocent of fraud, on surrendering his whole means and estate to his creditors.

Mod. Sc. Newspr. (*heading*) Bankruptcies and Cessio Bonorum.

cession ('sɛʃən). [a. F. *cession*, ad. L. *cessiōn-em*, f. *cessus*, pa. pple. of *cēdĕre* to yield.]

†**1.** The action of giving way or yielding: **a.** to physical force or pressure. *Obs.*

1626 Bacon *Sylva* §354 They both [Flame and Air] have quickness of Motion, and facility of Cession, much alike. **1660** Boyle *New Exp. Phys.-Mech.* i. 36 It is the equal pressure of the Air on all sides upon the Bodies that are in it, which causes the easie Cession of its parts. **1693** Tyrrell *Law of Nat.* 52 That Cession or giving place to each other, which is so necessary for the performance of their motions.

†**b.** to moral force, persuasion, or temptation.

1607 *Schol. Disc. agst. Antichr.* II. vi. 50 Certaine cessions of the godly, who yelded even to the very doing of certaine things imposed on them. **1612** Bacon *Vain-glory, Ess.* (Arb.) 464 Excusations, cessions, modesty it selfe well gouerned, are but arts of ostentation.

†**2.** The vacating of an office either by retirement or death; a ceasing to hold office. *Obs.*

1608 Bp. J. King *Serm. S. Mary's Oxf.* 5 There are two persons, Dauid and Salomon, and accordingly two partes, first the cession or decease of the one, secondly the succession and supply of the other. **1683** *Brit. Spec.* 65 By the Cession of many little Princes, these Petty Kingdoms were united, and greater Monarchies created. **1718** Hickes & Nelson *J. Kettlewell* I. ix. 31 The Fellowship..vacant by the Cession of Mr. John Radcliffe. **1738** Warburton *Div. Legat.* (1741) II. 408 The cession was in consequence of his [God's] own declaration to Samuel.

b. *Eccl. Law.* 'One manner of vacating or voiding an ecclesiastical benefice'; see quots.

1641 *Termes de la Ley* 50 When an Ecclesiasticall person is created Bishop, or when a Parson of a Parsonage taketh another Benefice without dispensation or otherwise not qualified..their first Benefices are..said to become void by cession. **1809** Tomlins *Law Dict.*, *Cession*, in the case of bishops does not take place till consecration.

3. The action of ceding, or surrendering to another, rights, property or anything to which one has a title or claim; also giving up anything in compliance with a demand; concession.

c **1440** *Promp. Parv.* 67 Cessyone, *cessio.* *c* **1600** Swinburn *Spousals* (1686) 179 Who..hath no direct action ..without Cession, or grant first made by the Proctor. **1775** Johnson in *Boswell* (1831) III. 106 Not..that you had personally made any cession of the rights of your house. **1788** T. Jefferson *Writ.* (1859) II. 458 They will make great cessions to the people, rather than small ones to the parliament. **1848** Arnould *Mar. Insur.* III. vi. (1866) II. 858 If notice of abandonment have been duly given, a deed of cession, or formal transfer, is unncessary. **1867** Freeman *Norm. Conq.* (1876) I. iv. 238 Notwithstanding his former cession of his rights.

b. *Civil Law.* The voluntary surrender by a debtor of all his effects to his creditors. (L. *cessio bonorum.*)

1622 Malynes *Anc. Law-Merch.* 429 The manner of Cedere bonis, or to make cession of goods, is verie hainous, and of wonderfull disgrace. **1751** Chambers *Cycl.* s.v., The Cession originally carried with it a mark of infamy, and obliged the person to wear a green cap or bonnet. **1768** Blackstone *Comm.* II. 473, I mean the law of cession, introduced by the christian emperors; whereby if a debtor ceded, or yielded up, all his fortune to his creditors, he was secured from being dragged to a gaol.

c. The ceding, giving up, or 'handing over' of a portion of territory to another ruler or state. Sometimes *concr.* a portion of territory surrendered.

1678 Temple *Let. Ld. Treasurer*, Sept. (R.) To write.. about the..cession of Maestricht. **1772** Pennant *Tours Scotl.* (1774) 207 Content to make a cession of the islands to Alexander III. **1803** Wellington *Let.* in Gurw. *Disp.* I. 624 The troops which are hereafter to occupy the Marhatta cessions to the southward. **1862** Ld. Brougham *Brit. Const.* App. iii. 432 All treaties for any cession or exchange of territory must be ratified by the Legislature. **1879** Lubbock *Addr. Pol. & Educ.* i. 9 We reluctantly consented to accept the cession of the Fiji Islands.

¶ Misused for CESSATION.

c **1800** K. White *Rem.* (1837) 407 A golden age and its cession.

‖**cessio'naire.** [F., f. *cession* = prec.] = next 2.

1881 *Daily Tel.* 1 Feb., The party interested, his successors, cessionaires, or legal representatives.

cessionary ('sɛʃənərɪ). [ad. med.L. *cessionāri-us*, f. L. *cessio* (*bonorum*) yielding up of goods: see -ARY.]

†**1.** A bankrupt who makes *cessio bonorum. Obs.*

1611 Cotgr., *Cessionnaire*, a cessionarie; one that abandons, or giues vp his goods..who though hee looseth his credit thereby, yet is hee not held so base as a bankrupt. **1632** Sherwood, A cessionarie Bankerout, which renounceth his goods in open court, *cessionaire*. [Similarly in Bailey, Johnson, and mod. Dicts. as *adj.*] **1694** Falle *Jersey* iv. 111 The last Creditor is asked whether he will substitute, or put himself in the place of the Cessionary.

2. One to whom an assignment has been legally made; an assignee.

1754 Erskine *Princ. Sc. Law* (1809) 342 He who grants the assignation is called the cedent, and he who receives it, the assignee or cessionary. **1818** Colebrooke *Oblig. & Contracts* I. 210 The right passes..from the cedent to the cessionary. **1880** Muirhead *Gaius* II. §35 The cessionary becomes heir just as if the inheritance had devolved upon him by operation of law.

†**'cessioner.** *Sc. Obs.* Also 6-7 -ar, -are. [f. as prec.] The person to whom a cession of property is legally made; an assignee; = CESSIONARY.

1491 *Acta Domin. Audit.* 158 (Jam.) As Cessionare and assignay to Schir Andrew Purves. **1565** *Aberdeen Reg.* V. 26 (Jam.) His assignay, cessionar & donatour. **1652** Z. Boyd in *Zion's Flowers* (1855) App. 24/1 My lawful cessioners and assigneyes.

†**'cessive**, *a. Obs. rare.* [f. L. *cess-* ppl. stem of *cēdĕre* to yield + -IVE.] Of a yielding quality.

1678 R. Russell *Geber* III. II. I. x. 168 Softness by Sulphur is Cessive, but Softness by Argentrive is Extensive.

†**'cessment.** *Obs.* Also 6 cesm-, 7 ceas-, ceassement. [var. spelling of SESSMENT, aphetic f. ASSESSMENT.] = ASSESSMENT.

c **1540-1660** [see SESSMENT]. **1584** *Vestry Bks.* (Surtees) 16 Item receaved a cesment for mending the leades, xiijs. vjd. **1613** R. C. *Table Alph.* (ed. 3) *Cessement*, tribute. **1621** Molle *Camerar. Liv. Libr.* II. xii. 113 The Tholousans.. made a great ceassement of money, which was gathered and leuied, but with great difficultie. **1635** *Vestry Bks.* (Surtees) 97 A ceasment of sex penns a pound. **1645** *Martin's Echo* in Prynne *Discov. New Blazing-Stars* 44 Is it not you that pay all the Taxes, Cessements, and oppressions whatsoever. **1721-33** Strype *Eccl. Mem.* II. I. II. ii. 261 To put their said order and cessement in writing.

†**'cessor**¹. *Obs.* Also 6 -ar, -er. [f. CESS *v.*¹ + -ER, -OR.] One who determines the amount of a cess; = ASSESSOR 3 a.

1565-78 Cooper *Thesaur.*, *Censor*, a cessar; one that valueth or mustreth. **1580** Hollyband *Treas. Fr. Tong Censeur*, a Cesser. **1580** North *Plutarch* (1676) 221 The Sessors of the People. **1596** Spenser *State Irel.* 505 The corruption of victuallers, cessors and purveyors.

cessor[2] (ˈsɛsɔː(r), -ə(r)). *Law.* [f. CESS *v.*[2] + -OR.]
1727–51 CHAMBERS *Cycl.*, *Cessor*, in law, one dilatory, and delinquent in his duty or service, and is liable to have the writ *Cessavit* brought against him. **1809** TOMLINS *Law Dict.*

cessor, erron. f. CESSER.

cesspipe (ˈsɛspaɪp). [f. *cess* in CESSPOOL + PIPE.] A pipe for carrying off the overflow from cesspools, sinks, or drains.

cesspit (ˈsɛspɪt). [f. as prec. + PIT.] = A pit for the reception of night-soil and refuse; a midden.
1864 R. A. ARNOLD *Cotton Fam.* 440 The deep cesspool system is bad enough, but the middens or cesspits of the cotton districts are a very great deal worse. **1884** *Law Times Reports* 19 Apr. 230/2 The defendant, owning one well, began to use it as a cesspit. **1887** *Melbourne Daily Telegraph*, A sum..flung yearly into the cesspit of this single vice!

cesspool (ˈsɛspuːl). Forms: 7 cest-, 9 sus-, sess-, 8– cesspool. [Of uncertain derivation.
The form *cesperalle* has suggested connexion or popular confusion, with SUSPIRAL breathing hole, air-hole, ventilator, q.v. The form *cestpool*, if genuine (compared with the dial. '*cist*, a cesspool' in Halliwell) has suggested that the initial element may be a contraction of *cestern*, CISTERN, or at least that it has at some time been associated by popular etymology with that word. Prof. Skeat compares the form *suspool* with the dial. words *suss* 'hogwash', *soss* 'anything dirty or muddy' (Halliwell); others have proposed derivation from CESS *sb.*[1] bog. More suitable is that from It. *cesso* privy (:—L. *secessus* place of retirement, privy, drain), esp. as this is also commonly used for *cessino* the solid contents of the *cesso*, 'materie grosse che si cavano dalle cloache delle case, che servano per ingrasso dei terreni' (La Crusca). The spelling *sess-pool* taken with the essential meaning of a 'pool for the retention of sediment', might indicate connexion with L. *sedēre*, *sess-um* in sense 'to sink, settle down'. But all these are merely suggestions, calling for further evidence.]

1. A small well or excavation made in the bottom of a drain, under a grating, to collect and retain the sand or gravel carried by the stream.
[**1583** in BACON *Annalls of Ipswiche* (1884) Cesperalle to be made for stopping of filthe by the brooke.]
1671 *Act Common Council Lond.* 27 Oct. ¶5. 18 A Fall or Cestpool of convenient bigness shall be made..to every Grate of the Common Sewer..to receive the Sand or Gravel coming to the same, so to prevent the choaking thereof. **1823** P. NICHOLSON *Pract. Build.* 592/2 Sesspool, or *Cesspool*, a deep hole or well, under the mouth of a drain, for the reception of sediment, etc., by which the drain might be choked.

2. A well sunk to receive the soil from a water-closet, kitchen sink, etc.: properly one which retains the solid matter, and allows the liquid to escape.
It is sometimes built dry, so that the water escapes by percolation through the joints of the stone or brickwork into the surrounding soil, or it is built in mortar, and a drain formed to carry off the surplus water from near the top of it. (Gwilt.)
1782 *Phil. Trans.* LXXII. 364 We estimated the fall of the drain, from the eastern sink..to its termination in the cess-pool..at two feet. **1815** T. FORSTER *Atmospheric Phenom.* (ed. 2) 150 The smell of drains and suspools. **1850** KINGSLEY *Alt. Locke* (1876) 11 The horrible stench of the cesspools. **1860** PIESSE *Lab. Chem. Wonders* 98 [It will] render harmless the most offensive cesspool or drain.

b. (See quot.)
1871 *Daily News* 16 Dec., In Yorkshire effluvium-traps are frequently called cess-pools. **1883** PARKES *Pract. Hygiene* (ed. 6) x. 367 The common Mason's or dip-trap and the notorious D trap both of which are simply cess-pools.

3. *fig.* (Cf. *sink*, *common sewer*, etc.)
1837 CARLYLE *Fr. Rev.* III. v. i. (L.) The cesspool of agio, now in a time of paper money, works with a vivacity unexampled. **1864** *Soc. Sci. Rev.* 52 Australia refuses again to be made a moral cesspool for England. **1879** FARRAR *St. Paul* (1883) 235 Seneca..speaks of Rome as a cesspool of iniquity.

Hence **cesspoolage** [cf. *drainage*, *sewerage*]. *rare.*
1851 MAYHEW *Lond. Lab.* (ed. 2) II. 491 (Hoppe) Two modes of removing the wet refuse of the Metropolis..sewerage and..cesspoolage. By the system of cesspoolage the wet refuse of a household is collected in an adjacent tank, and, when the reservoir is full, the contents are removed to some other part.

†**ˈcessure.** *Obs. rare.* [f. CESS *v.*[2] + -URE.] **a.** Cessation, end. **b.** = CESSER.
1607 W. S. *Puritan* I. (L.) Since the cessure of the wars, I have spent a hundred crowns out of purse. **1809** TOMLINS *Law Dict.* s.v. *Cessavit*, In other cases the heir may not bring this writ for cessure in the time of his ancestor.

cessyone, obs. form of SESSION.

cest, ceste. [a. F. *ceste*, ad. L. *cestus*.] = CESTUS[1].
1577 HANMER *Anc. Eccl. Hist.* (1619) 110 Of Cestes or Wedding Girdles. **1606** SYLVESTER *Du Bartas, Magnif.* 949 And thy brest Gird'st with a rich and odoriferous cest. **1675** COTTON *Poet. Wks.* (1765) 203 Mercury..Whips me away her am'rous cest. **1678** PHILLIPS, *Cest*, a Marriage Girdle. **1746** COLLINS *Ode Poet. Character*, To whom prepar'd and bath'd in heaven, The cest of amplest power is given. **1842** *Fraser's Mag.* XXVI. 80 The Graces' charm-conferring cest Seems bound around her flower-tipp'd breast.

†**ceste.** *Obs.* [a. F. *ceste*.] = CESTUS[2].
1616 HOLYDAY *Persius* 321 They did array their arms and hands with the cestes, which were made of the hide of the buffle..fill'd with lead within.

cestern(e, obs. form of CISTERN.

†**cestes.** *Obs. rare*[−1]. The game of chess.
1578 FLORIO *First Fruites* 8, I can play at Cardes, at Dyse, at Tables, at Cestes [It. *cacchi*].

cestoid (ˈsɛstɔɪd), *a.* and *sb.* Also cestode. [mod. f. L. *cest-us* (see CESTUS[1]) + -OID. Cf. F. *cestoïde*, and mod.L. *Cestoidea*, given to an order of Entozoa by Zeder in 1808.]
A. *adj.* Ribbon-like: a term applied to certain intestinal worms, as the tape-worm.
1836–9 TODD *Cycl. Anat.* II. 137/1 The ovaries in the most simple of the Cestoid worms..are situated in the centre of each joint. **1864** *Intell. Observ.* No. 33. 196 Cestoid parasites are not common amongst reptiles. **1870** ROLLESTON *Anim. Life* 137 The cestode many-jointed tapeworms.
B. *sb.* A worm of this kind. Also *attrib.* The mod.L. **cestoidea** is sometimes used as plural.
1837 *Penny Cycl.* IX. 461/2 The Cestoid order of Entozoa. **1859** TODD *Cycl. Anat.* V. 27/2 All these cestoids are complete animals. **1870** ROLLESTON *Anim. Life* 252 Not being developed except in the cestoid stage. **1876** BENEDEN *Anim. Parasites* 90 Different Cestoidea, or tape-worms.

†**ˈceston.** *Obs.* [= F. *ceston* in same sense; deriv. of *ceste*, CESTUS[1].] = CESTUS[1].
1583 T. WATSON *Poems* (Arb.) 119 Venus..Posthaste to haue God Vulcan's ayde, Solde him her Gemmes, and Ceston therewithall. **1584** PEELE *Arraignm. Paris* III. vi, *Mercury*. Venus, give me your pledge. *Venus*. My ceston, or my fan, or both? *c* **1611** CHAPMAN *Iliad* XIV. 181. **1648** HERRICK *Hesper.*, *Oberon's Palace*, Citherea's ceston, which All with temptation doth bewitch.

‖**Cestracion** (sɛˈstreɪsɪɒn). *Zool.* [mod.L., invented by Cuvier; cf. Gr. κέστρα name of a kind of fish, also κέστρος sharpness, and ἀκή point.] A kind of shark now peculiar to Australia; the Port Jackson shark. It has sharp teeth in front, and flat pavement-like teeth behind, and has a spine in front of each dorsal fin.
1876 PAGE *Adv. Text-bk. Geol.* xvii. 320 Shark-like genera resembling the cestracion of Australian seas.

cestraciont (sɛˈstreɪsɪɒnt), *sb.* and *a. Zool.* [f. prec.: cf. *anodon*, *-ont*, etc.] Belonging to the family of fishes of which the Cestracion is the representative. Used also as sb.
1847 CARPENTER *Zool.* §589 The teeth..not so much flattened as those of the Cestracionts. **1862** DANA *Man. Geol.* 276 The Cestraciont family of sharks. **1863** A. RAMSAY *Phys. Geog.* xiv. 230 Many of the Placoids are Cestraciont fish.

†**ˈcestred, ˈsestred,** *ppl. a. Obs. rare.* [Cf. OE. *þeostrod*, ME. *þestred* darkened: see THISTER.] Obscured, made dark.
a **1300** *E.E. Psalter* lxxiii[iv]. 20 Ful-filled er þai þa þat sestrede er [Vulg. *obscurati sunt*] in mirkenes Of erthe. *Ibid.* cxxxviii[ix]. 12 For mirkenesses, alle þat be, Noght cestred sal be [*non obscurabuntur*] fra þe.

cestren, -on, obs. ff. CISTERN.

Cestrian (ˈsɛstrɪən), *a.* [f. *Cester*, *Ceaster*, OE. forms of *Chester* + -IAN] Of or pertaining to the city of Chester or to Cheshire.
1703 J. PHILIPS *Splendid Shilling*, A Cargo of famed Cestrian Cheese. **1805** SOUTHEY *Madoc in Azt.* xviii, Holy Dee Through Cestrian pastures rolls his tamer stream.

‖**ˈcestrin.** *Obs.* [F. *cestrin* 'a kind of yellow stone whereof beads are made' (Cotgr. 1611).
The original of the passage in Rabelais does not speak of it as a stone, and French writers have suggested that it may have been the resin of the Socotrine aloe, med.L. *aloes cicatrina*.]
1653 URQUHART *Rabelais* II. xxi, Her Patenotres..made of a kind of yellow stone called Cestrin.

†**ˈcestuan,** *a. Obs.* [f. CESTU-S[2] + -AN.] Of or pertaining to a boxer's cestus.
1711 *Brit. Apollo* III. No. 144. 2/1 To prevent Cestuan Knocks and Bruises.

‖**cestui** (ˈsɛstwi). Also 6–8 cestuy, pl. cestuis. [AF., OF. *cestui* (demonstr. pron.) that person, orig. only accusative (nom. *cest*):—late L. *ecce istum*, with analogical final after *cui*, *lui*: cf. *celui*.] A person, or the person (who), he (who). Only in phrases:
cestui que (qui) trust, ***cestui que use***, more fully ***cestui a que use*** (= ***al use de qui***) ***le trust est créé***: the person for whose benefit or use anything is given in trust to another.
cestui (a) que vie: he on whose life land is held, or the person for whose life lands, tenements or hereditaments are granted.
cestui que is also used *attrib.* as *sb.*, and ***cestui que use*** as the name of a procedure.
1555 PERKINS *Prof. Bk.* viii. §579 When freehold or inheritance of Lands, tenements, etc...are devised by cestuy que use. **1670** BLOUNT *Law Dict.*, *Cestui qui vie* (in true French, *Cestui a vie de qui*), is he for whose life any Land or Tenement is granted. **1714** *Act 13 Anne* c. 13 §4 in *Oxf. & Camb. Enactm.* 61 Such person or persons as they have reason to believe to be the cestuyque trust of the advowson. **1789** BENTHAM *Princ. Legisl.* xviii. §25 *note*, The phrase in full length would run in some such manner as this, cestuy al use de qui le trust est créé: he to whose use the trust or benefit is created. In a particular case a cestuy que trust is called by the Roman Law fidei-commissarius. **1809** TOMLINS *Law Dict.*, *Cestui que use*, he to whose use any other man is enfeoffed of lands or tenements. **1844** WILLIAMS *Real Prop.* (1877) 20 The person for whose life the land is holden is called the *cestui que vie*. **1853** WHARTON *Pennsylv. Digest* II. 781 If a trustee invest trust money in land, the *cestui qui trust* may at his option accept the land or refuse it. **1858** LD. ST. LEONARDS *Handy Bk. Prop. Law* xxi. 159 There are few social questions of more importance than ..the relation between trustees and their cestuis que trust.. or the persons for whom they are trustees. **1859** HELPS *Friends in C.* Ser. II. II. iii. 79 A great many *cestuique* trusts.

‖**cestus**[1] (ˈsɛstəs). Also cestos. [L. *cestus*, ad. Gr. κεστός; properly vbl. adj., 'stitched'.]
A belt or girdle for the waist; particularly that worn by a bride in ancient times.
1577 tr. *Bullinger's Decades* (1592) 236 For Cestus signifieth the Marriage girdle which the Bride did weare. **1736** BAILEY (*Folio*), *Cestus*, a Marriage-girdle, that of old Times the Bride used to wear, and the Bridegroom unloosed on the Wedding-night. **1778** SIR N. WRAXALL *North. Courts* (*Warsaw*) The princess wore round her waist a girdle or cestus of silk, nine inches broad: it is the zone of the Greeks and is still worn in Wallachia. **1870** L'ESTRANGE *Miss Mitford* I. ii. 40 To complete the set of amethysts by a bandeau and tiara, a cestus for the waist.
b. *spec.* That of Aphrodite or Venus.
a **1661** HOLYDAY *Juvenal* 130 Like the outragious love of Jupiter to Juno, effected by the cæstus, or girdle of Venus, as it is in Homer, Iliad 18. **1709** STEELE & ADDISON *Tatler* No. 147 ¶3. **1712** ADDISON *Spect.* No. 425 ¶4 Venus, without any ornament but her own beauties, not so much as her own cestus. **1850** LEITCH tr. *Müller's Anc. Art* §376. 474 She also appears half-draped, girding herself with the cestus, on coins of Domitian.
c. *fig.*
1651 JER. TAYLOR *Holy Dying* iii. §6 (L.) As soon as that cestus [of lust and wanton appetite], that lascivious girdle, is thrown away, then the reins chasten us. **1865** CARLYLE *Fredk. Gt.* IX. XXI. iii. 295 The brightest jewel in the cestus of Polish Liberty is this right of confederating.

‖**cestus**[2] (ˈsɛstəs). [a. L. *cæstus*, commonly regarded as anomalously f. *cædĕre* to strike; perh. it was an incorrect spelling of *cestus* girdle, band, ligature: see prec.]
A contrivance consisting of thongs of bull-hide, loaded with strips of iron and lead, and wound round the hands. Used by Roman boxers as a protection and to give greater weight to the blows.
1734 tr. *Rollin's Anc. Hist.* (1827) I. 76 The Cestus was a kind of gauntlet, or glove, made of straps of leather, and plated with brass, lead, or iron. **1791** COWPER *Iliad* XXIII. 774 For thou shalt wield The cæstus..never again. **1807** ROBINSON *Archæol. Græca* III. xx. 323 The hands and arms of the combatants were..surrounded with thongs of leather called cestus. **1870** BRYANT *Iliad* II. XXIII. 369 Since thou wilt wield No more the cestus.

cestvaen, var. of CISTVAEN.

cesun, obs. form of SEASON, SEISIN.

cesure: see CÆSURA.

cet-, f. L. *cētus*, Gr. κῆτος whale, is used to form names of a series of chemical substances derived from spermaceti, i.e. *sperma ceti* whale's sperm. The chief are **cetane** (ˈsiːˌteɪn), the paraffin of the hexdecyl or cetyl series, $C_{16}H_{34}$, a colourless liquid; so ***cetane number***, a measure of the ignition value of a diesel fuel oil. **cetene** (ˈsiːˌtiːn), the olefine of the same series ($C_{16}H_{32}$), formerly called *Cetylene*, a colourless oily liquid. **ˈcetic** *a.*, of the whale, or of spermaceti: applied to what was supposed to be a peculiar acid resulting from the saponification of cetin, but which has been ascertained to be only a mixture of margaric acid and cetin. **cetin** (ˈsiːˌtɪn), improperly *cetine*, a white crystalline fatty substance ($C_{32}H_{64}O$) forming the essential part of spermaceti, and used in the manufacture of candles. **cetine** (ˈsiːtaɪn), the ethine or acetylene member of the cetyl series ($C_{16}H_{30}$) also called *hexdecine*, and formerly *cetenylene*, a colourless liquid lighter than water. **cetyl** (ˈsiːtɪl), the hydrocarbon radical ($C_{16}H_{33}$), assumed to exist in cetic acid, and the other members of the *cetyl*, or *cetylic* series: among these are ***cetyl*** or ***cetylic alcohol***, a white crystalline substance ($C_{16}H_{33}{\cdot}OH$), also called *ethal*; ***cetyl hydride*** = *cetane*; ***cetyl-salt*** any salt of cetyl, as ***cetyl-acetate***, ***cetyl-palmitate***. **ˈcetylaˌmine** (see quot.). **ˈcetylate**, a compound of cetyl with a base, as potassium cetylate. **ˈcetylene** = *cetene*. **ceˈtylic** *a.*, of cetyl, as in *cetylic alcohol*, *cetylic acid* = *cetic acid*.
1871 WATTS *Dict. Chem.* 1st Supp. 421 *Cetane or Cetyl hydride is one of the constituents of American petroleum. **1884** *Athenæum* 699/1 Cetane (boiling at 278°). **1935** *Proc. Amer. Soc. Test. Mat.* XXXV. 342 More reliable results may be possible when using cetane rather than cetene. For this reason, this classification substitutes the cetane number, which is determined and expressed in the same manner as the cetene number, namely, as the percentage of cetane in a

blend of cetane and alphamethylnaphthalene. **1959** *Chambers's Encycl.* VII. 640/2 Ignition quality is defined by 'cetane number', i.e. the percentage of cetane in a blend with α-methylnaphthalene which gives the same delay period, under standardized test conditions, as that given by the fuel in question. **1838** T. THOMSON *Chem. Org. Bodies* 322 This new substance has been distinguished by Dumas and Peligot by the name of *cetene. It is a colourless oily liquid, which stains paper. **1826** HENRY *Elem. Chem.* (1840) II. 405 Chevreul separated a substance, which he terms *cetic acid. It is a white solid, fusible at nearly the same point as spermaceti. **1836** *Blackw. Mag.* XXXIX. 310 One of three acids, either the oleïc, margaritic, or cetic; the first being contained in oils, the second in animal fats, the third in spermaceti. **1836–9** TODD *Cycl. Anat.* II. 234/1 It deposits the purified spermaceti in white crystalline scales, and in this state, Chevreul terms it *Cetine. **1838** T. THOMSON *Chem. Org. Bodies* 724 It has nearly the feel of cetin. **1876** HARLEY *Mat. Med.* 794 Nearly pure cetin obtained, mixed with oil, from the head of the sperm whale. **1868** ROYLE & HEADLAND *Mat. Med.* (ed. 5) 750 Ethal is also called Cetylic Alcohol, for it seems to be the hydrated oxide of a radical called *cetyle. **1873** WATTS *Fownes' Chem.* 610 Cetyl alcohol, or Ethal, is a white crystalline mass, which melts at about 50°. **1850** DAUBENY *Atom. The.* vii. (ed. 2) 229 Spermaceti is a compound of cetylic acid with the oxide of cetyle. **1863–79** WATTS *Dict. Chem.* I. 840 *Cetylamines.. bases formed by the substitution of cetyl in place of hydrogen in a molecule of ammonia. **1880** *Athenæum* 27 Nov. 713/1 The authors..have thus prepared aluminic methylate..*cetylate, etc. **1864** H. SPENCER *Biol.* I. 6 *Cetylene is a liquid which boils at 527°. *c* **1865** LETHEBY in *Circ. Sc.* I. 97/2 A fatty acid (*cetylic), which fuses at 131°.

‖**cetacea** (sɪˈteɪʃ(ɪ)ə), *sb. pl. Zool.* [mod.L., f. *cētus*, a. Gr. κῆτος whale; see -ACEA.]
The order of marine Mammalia containing the whales and their congeners.

1830 LYELL *Princ. Geol.* I. 151 The bones of whales and other cetacea. **1833** SIR C. BELL *Hand* (ed. 3) 110 In the Cetacea..we have mammalia unprovided with hind feet. **1865** GOSSE *Land & Sea* (1874) 168 [Foraminifers and Diatoms] constitute the principal sustenance of the giant Cetacea.

cetacean (sɪˈteɪʃ(ɪ)ən), *a.* and *sb. Zool.* [f. prec. + -AN (see -ACEAN), forming a sing. to prec.]
A. *adj.* Of or pertaining to the *Cetacea*.

1850 DANA *Geol.* App. i. 722 Fragments of other cetacean bones. **1851** D. WILSON *Preh. Ann.* (1863) I. ii. 49 The cetacean remains lay above the highest tide level.

B. *sb.* An animal belonging to the *Cetacea* (to which word this supplies a singular).

1836 TODD *Cycl. Anat.* I. 562/2 The horizontal position of the tail-fin at once distinguishes the cetacean from the fish.

cetaceous (sɪˈteɪʃəs), *a. Zool.* Also 7 cetacious, (erron.) setaceous. [f. as prec.; see -ACEOUS.] Belonging to the order *Cetacea*; of the whale kind, of the nature of the whale.

1646 SIR T. BROWNE *Pseud. Ep.* 203 Cetacious and cartilagineous fishes. **1660** BOYLE *New Exp. Phys.-Mech.* Digress. 370 Such [fishes] as are not Setaceous..have not Respiration, properly so call'd. **1759** B. STILLINGFLEET *Misc. Tracts* (1762) 84 The cetaceous fish have warm blood, and they bring forth their young alive, and suckle them. **1802** BINGLEY *Anim. Biog.* (1813) I. 19 The Cetaceous Animals..Linnæus's seventh Order of Mammalia.
transf. **1862** B. TAYLOR *Home & Abr.* Ser. II. 418, I suspected a huge cetaceous mirthfulness behind this repose.

cetare, *Chem.*: see CET-.

†**ˈcetaries**, *sb. pl. Obs.* [app. ad. L. *cētārius* pertaining to fish, *sb.* a fishmonger, f. *cētus* sea-monster, whale.] Provisions of the nature of fish.

1661 LOVELL *Anim. & Min.* 196 Cows, Asses, Doggs, Dog-fishes, and all cetaries salted have made many Idiots.

cete[1] (siːt). [a. OF. *cete*, fem., ad. L. *cētus* whale, in pl. *cētē* neut. a. Gr. κήτη, κήτεα whales: see quot. 1802.] A whale, a sea-monster.

c **1220** *Bestiary* 513 in *O.E. Misc.* 16 Ðis cete ðanne hise chaueles lukeð. **1398** TREVISA *Barth. De P.R.* XIII. xxvi. (1495) 463 The whale is callyd Cete. **1802** BINGLEY *Anim. Biog.* (1813) I. 22 Cete or Whales. **1854** BADHAM *Halieut.* 205 This real cete of a scomber measured thirty-two feet lengthways, and had..a girth of sixteen feet.

†**cete.**[2] *Obs.* [possibly ad. L. *cœtus* (in med. spelling *cetus*) meeting, assembly, company.] A 'company' of badgers.

1486 *Bk. St. Albans* F vj a, A Cete of Graies. **1801** STRUTT *Sports & Past.* I. i. 19. [**1886** *Standard* 13 Oct., Keeping what the old writers used to call a 'cete of badgers'.]

cetene, *Chem.*: see CET-.

ceteosaur, -us (ˈsiːtiːəʊsɔːə(r), -ˈsɔːrəs). *Palæont.* [ad. mod.L. *cēteosaurus*, f. Gr. κῆτος (gen. κήτεο-ς) whale + σαῦρος lizard.] A gigantic fossil saurian, whose remains are found in the oolite and chalk.

1872 CARPENTER in *Gd. Words* 700 In..[the great Oolitic formation] we have remains of gigantic Reptiles (such as the Cetiosaurus). **1877** LE CONTE *Elem. Geol.* (1879) 433 The Ceteosaur (Whale-lizard) was probably the largest reptile..which has ever existed.

ceterach (ˈsɛtəræk). *Bot.* Also 6 cetrac, 6–7 citterach(e, 7 ceteratche, cetrache. [a. med.L. *ceterach*, *ceterah* (Du Cange), in F. *cétérac*, It. *cetracca*, *citracca*, med.Gr. κιταράκ; the origin has been variously sought in Arabic and in Celtic.]
A genus of ferns, having the back of the fronds thickly covered with scales among which the sori are hidden. One small species with simply pinnate fronds, *C. officinarum*, Scale-fern or Miltwaste (formerly *Grammitis*) is a native of Britain.

1551 TURNER *Herbal* I. E v a, The leues of Ceterach.. made hote in vynegre, and dronken of..waste vp the mylt. **1565–78** COOPER *Thesaur.* s.v. *Scolopendrium*, That the Apothecaries call Cetrac. **1578** LYTE *Dodoens* III. lxvii. 408 This herbe is called..in English Scaleferne..Ceterach, and Myltewaste. **1621** BURTON *Anat. Mel.* II. iv. I. iii, Ceteratche, Mugwort, Liuerwort. **1884** *Harper's Mag.* Jan. 209/1 We searched for ferns, finding the rusty ceterach.

‖**ceteris paribus** (ˈsiːtərɪs (or ˈsɛt-, ˈkeɪt-) ˈpærɪbəs). Also **cæteris paribus**. [mod.L.] Other things being equal, other conditions corresponding.

1601 T. WRIGHT *Passions* Pref. A 4 b, Yet my meaning is alwayes *cæteris paribus*, because [etc.]. **1690** LOCKE *Govt.* II. § 105. 325 *Cæteris paribus*, they commonly prefer the Heir of their deceased King. **1751** CHESTERFIELD *Lett.* (1774) II. 124 And *cæteris paribus*, a French minister will get the better of an English one, at any third court in Europe. **1887** W. J. HARRIS in *Nat. Rev.* Dec. 454 The wonder is that France is not in a far worse state than ourselves. *Cæteris paribus*, she ought to be, with her unsettled government [etc.]. **1964** *Economist* 29 Aug. 828/2 That comfortable hold-all, *ceteris paribus*.

cetewale, obs. form of SETWALL.

†**cethegrande**. *Obs.* [OF. *cete grande* great whale.] A whale.

c **1220** *Bestiary* 499 in *O.E. Misc.* 16 *Natura cetegrandie.* Cethegrande is a fis ðe moste ðat in water is.

cethyn, obs. form of SEETHE.

cetic, cetin, cetine: see CET-.

ceticide (ˈsiːtɪsaɪd). *nonce-wd.* [f. L. *cētus* + -CIDE, slayer, as in *homicide*.] A whale-killer.

1836 SOUTHEY in *Life & Corr.* (1849–50) VI. 317 At Killerton we met Scoresby the Ceticide.

cetology (siːˈtɒlədʒɪ). *rare.* [f. L. *cētus* or Gr. κῆτος + -λογία: see -LOGY.] That part of zoology which treats of the whales. Hence **cetoˈlogical** *a.*, of or pertaining to cetology; **ceˈtologist**, one versed in cetology.

1851 H. MELVILLE *Moby Dick* xxxi. 147 To project the draught of a systematization of cetology. **1851** *Ibid.* 179 But I now leave my cetological system standing thus unfinished. **1955** *Sci. Amer.* Jan. 67/1 Some cetologists believe that the gray whale survived along our Atlantic seaboard until historic times.

ceton, obs. form of SETON.

cetotolite (sɪˈtɒtəlaɪt). *Palæont.* [f. Gr. κῆτος whale + οὖς(ωτ-) ear + λίθος stone (see -LITE).] A name given to fossil ear-bones, found with associated cetaceous remains, in the Red Crag of Suffolk, where they are extensively used for the manufacture of superphosphate of potash.

cetrac, obs. form of CETERACH, scale-fern.

cetrarin (ˈsɛtrərɪn, ˈsiː-). *Chem.* [f. mod.L. *cetraria*, generic name of Iceland moss, f. L. *cetra* targe, small shield of leather, so called from the shape of the apothecia.] A white crystalline substance ($C_{18}H_{16}O_8$) forming the bitter principle of Iceland moss (*Cetraria islandica*). Also called **cetraric acid** (sɪˈtrærɪk).

1861 H. MACMILLAN *Footn. Page Nat.* 98 A peculiar astringent principle in it called cetrarin. **1876** HARLEY *Mat. Med.* 362 Cetraric acid is a bitter, colourless, crystalline substance. **1886** *Lancet* 15 May 938/2 Large doses of extract of cetrarin slightly increase it [the secretion of bile].

cetrimide (ˈsɛtrɪmaɪd). *Med.* [f. *cetyltrimethylammonium bromide*.] A preparation of cetyltrimethylammonium bromide, used as an antiseptic and sterilizing detergent.

1948 A. D. GARDNER in *Lancet* 13 Nov. 762/1 (*heading*) Cetrimide (C.T.A.B. or Cetavlon). *Ibid.*, 10% cetrimide in 70% alcohol, as a rapid disinfectant, nearly equals the performance of alcoholic iodine. **1962** *Which?* May 158/2 Cetrimide solution may be used to clean the area round the burn. **1966** *Lancet* 24 Sept. 678/2 (*title*) Experimental use of cetrimide in the prevention of wound implantation with cancer cells.

cette, cettyn, -ynge, obs. ff. SET, SETTING.

cetyl, cetylene, cetylic, etc.: see CET-.

cevadic (sɪˈvædɪk), *a. Chem.* [f. next + -IC: cf. F. *cévadique*.] In *cevadic acid*, a volatile fatty acid found in cevadilla. Also called *sabadillic acid*.

1868 ROYLE & HEADLAND *Mat. Med.* (ed. 5) 680.

‖**cevaˈdilla, cebaˈdilla.** Also SABADILLA. [a. Sp. *cebadilla*, dim. of *cebada* barley.] The seeds of *Asagræa officinalis*, a Mexican plant of N.O. *Melanthaceæ*.

1753 CHAMBERS *Cycl. Supp.*, *Cevadilla*, in botany, a name used by some authors for..Indian caustic barley. **1866** *Treas. Bot.* 98 Cebadilla seeds were formerly used to destroy vermin. **1876** HARLEY *Mat. Med.* 391 Cevadilla was known to Monardes in 1573.

cevene, -yn, etc., obs. ff. SEVEN, etc.

cevy, var. of CIVY, *Obs.*, a kind of black sauce.

cewe, ceware, obs. ff. SEW, SEWER.

cex(e, cextene, cexty, obs. ff. SIX, -TEEN, -TY.

cexteyne, cextrye, obs. ff. SEXTON, SACRISTY.

ceyl(e, obs. f. SAIL.

ceylle, var. of SELE, *Obs.*, bliss.

Ceylon (sɪˈlɒn). The name of an island in the Indian Ocean, used attrib. in **Ceylon moss** (see MOSS *sb.*[1] 4); **Ceylon pumpkin**, a large pumpkin found originally in Ceylon; **Ceylon rose**, the common oleander or rose-bay, *Nerium oleander*, a poisonous flowering shrub of the Mediterranean region; **Ceylon tea**, a Pekoe tea produced in Ceylon; also *ellipt.*, as *Ceylon*.

1861 BENTLEY *Man. Bot.* 721 *Gracilaria lichenoides* or *Plocaria candida*, is our commercial Ceylon Moss. **1875** *Encycl. Brit.* V. 508/2 *Gracilaria lichenoides*, under the name of Ceylon moss, is used for soups and jellies. **1913** PETTMAN *Africanderisms* 118 *Ceylon pumpkin*, a large, oval-shaped pumpkin with orange-coloured flesh. **1842** *Sketches East. Dist. Cape of Gd. Hope* 67 Lemon trees, interspersed with the acacia and Ceylon rose. **1868** J. CHAPMAN *Trav. S. Africa* II. 15, I find that the Ceylon rose..is..the other poison with which the Damaras tip their arrows in war. **1886** in *Ceylon Mercantile & Planting Directory* (1891) 50 The reply to your question as to whether Ceylon tea can be laid down in London at 6d per pound, depends a good deal on rates of freight. **1907** *Moore Brothers' Delicious Teas* 16 Pure Ceylon...2/- per lb. **1962** J. BRAINE *Life at Top* xxiii. 253 London water and the cheapest brand of Ceylon didn't make a very enlivening brew. **1966** P. V. PRICE *France* 33 China tea, with lemon, may be had as well as Ceylon or Indian tea.

Ceylonese (siːləˈniːz), *a.* and *sb.* [f. prec. + -ESE.] **A.** *adj.* Of or pertaining to the island of Ceylon or its inhabitants; Cingalese. **B.** *sb.* A native or inhabitant of Ceylon.

1797 *Encycl. Brit.* IV. 310/2 The Ceylonese make use of boats hollowed out of the trunks of trees. *Ibid.* 311/1 The Ceylonese monarch was driven from his capital. **1836** *Penny Cycl.* VI. 457/2 The sailing of vessels at the Ceylonese ports. **1948** *Amer. Speech* XXIII. 171 The English cling to.. *Sinhalese* or *Singhalese* for one [*sc.* an inhabitant] of Ceylon. But in the last case there seems to be a movement toward *Ceylonese.* **1960** G. DURRELL *Zoo in Luggage* (1965) ii. 55 Some weird devil-masks from a Ceylonese dance.

ceylonite, ceylanite (ˈsiːlənaɪt). *Min.* [a. F. *ceylanite*, f. *Ceylan*, Fr. form of *Ceylon*; see -ITE.] A ferruginous variety of spinel from Ceylon; Iron-Magnesia Spinel.

1802 BOURNON in *Phil. Trans.* XCII. 318 The stone called Ceylanite, by Mr. La Metherie..is also sometimes found in the sand of Ceylon. **1804** R. JAMESON *Syst. Min.* 79 The ceylanite which is here mentioned. **1884** DANA *Min.* 174 Ceylonite, or iron-magnesia spinel.

ch, a consonantal digraph, which in various languages (e.g. Welsh, Spanish, Czech) is treated as a distinct letter, placed in the Alphabet after *c*. In English it is not so treated formally, but in its characteristic and proper sound (tʃ) which it has in all native words, it practically adds an additional symbol to the alphabet. It has, however, in English other values; viz. those in *chyle*, and *champagne*, which might be expressed otherwise by *k* and *sh*; and that in *loch*, which occurs only in Scotch, Welsh, or foreign words.
The combination *ch* was foreign to native Roman spelling; it was introduced to represent the Greek aspirate or affricate *X* (as *Θ*, *Φ*, were similarly represented by *th*, *ph*). In Latin practice, however, simple *c* was often substituted, e.g. χάρτης, *charta*, *carta*, χαιρέφυλλον, *chærephyllum*, *cærefolium*, and this represented the actual pronunciation, for in the development of the Romanic languages, *ch* in popularized words was treated precisely as *c*. But in these languages, the symbol *ch* has been laid hold of for various purposes. In Italian it is a supplemental symbol used to indicate the hard or (k) sound of *c* before the vowels *i* and *e*, where *c* itself stands for (tʃ), as in *archi* (ˈarki) pl. of *arco*, *chi* (ki):—L. *qui*. In very early French, it also occurs in the writing of some dialects, or some scribes, with the value of (k); but its typical OF. use was to represent the palatalized sound which Central Old French developed from original *c* (k) before *a*, as in L. *carrus*, *cārus*, *causa*, OF. *char*, *chier*, *chose*, but which

Northern Old French, on the other hand, developed from *c* before *e* and *i*, as in *chertain*, *cachier*, *cherise*, where Central Old French had *c* (= ts), *certain*, *chacier*, *cerise*. The symbol *ch* was not used (or only accidentally) in OE.; for, although the sound (tʃ) was already developed in English before the 10th c., it was still written *c(e)*, as in *ceosan*, *ceaster*, *fecc(e)an*. But at the Norman Conquest, the symbol *ch* was introduced from France, and used not only for the new French words as *charite*, *richesse*, but also in the OE. words as in *cheosen*, *chester*, *fecche*, etc. This value of the digraph has ever since been retained in English, while in French the sound was at length worn down from (tʃ) to (ʃ), as in *chief*, *chef*, OF. (tʃ(i)ɛf) now (ʃɛf), Eng. *chief* (tʃiːf). Where the *c* was originally double, and after a short vowel, the early writing was *cch*, but subsequently *tch*, as in OE. *wrecc(e)a*, ME. *wrecche*, now *wretch*. After a long vowel, simple *ch* is used, as in *coach*, *teach*, *brooch*; but sometimes (from various historical causes) simple *ch* occurs after a short vowel, as in *rich*, *much*, and *tch* (rarely) after a long vowel, as in *aitch*. After a consonant (preserved or lost) simple *ch* is used, as in *perch*, *which*, *such*.

The sound (tʃ) also occurs in Slavonic and many non-European languages, and is usually spelt *ch* in words thence taken into English, as in *chabouk*, *chark*, *cheetah*, *chintz*, *chouse*.

ch has the sound of (k) in words taken from Greek (or Hebrew through Greek) directly, or through Latin, Italian, or French, as in *chasm*, *chimera*, *chirography*, *chyle*, *Rechabite*. Only in a few of these, which were popular words in Romanic, e.g. *cherub*, *archbishop*, does the (tʃ) sound occur.

ch has the sound of *sh* (ʃ) in words from modern French; occasionally in words really from Old French, which are now erroneously treated as if from modern French, as *chivalry*, *champaign*.

ch has also the value of a guttural spirant (x); but this is not a native English sound, and is only used in English in an accurate pronunciation of Scotch, Celtic, Dutch, German, Slavonic, or Oriental words, in which the sound occurs. This sound existed in OE., but was there written *h* (and *ȝ*) as in *burh*, *riht*; for this the Norman scribes substituted the digraph *gh* (*burgh*, *right*), which is still retained, though the sound was lost in the 16–17th century. The same digraph is used to represent the Irish guttural spirant in *lough*, *Monaghan*, *curragh*; but the Celtic languages themselves use *ch* (as in Welsh *Machynlleth* and Gaelic *clachan*), and this is followed in Lowland Scotch, as in *loch*, *pibroch*, *broch*, *tocher*. The Old Teutonic languages generally used *h* or *hh* for this sound, as in Goth. *mahts*, OS. and OHG. *maht*, OE. *meaht*; but *ch* (rarely *kh*) was introduced initially, in Upper German, for the affricated sound of *c* (k) as *chamara* (ˈkxamərа), *chirihha*, *chalch*, whence it was extended to the spirant (x), and gradually substituted for the earlier OHG. spelling *h*, *hh*; so that this is now regularly written *ch* in German and Dutch: cf. Goth. *ahtau*, OS. and OHG. *ahto*, OE. *eahta*, mod.G. and Du. *acht* eight. The same symbol is used for this sound in most Slavonic languages which use the Roman alphabet, and thus sometimes in the Romanization of Russian *X* (*Cherson*, *Astrachan*), and also of the kindred sounds in some Eastern languages (where however *kh* is more general); and from all these sources it enters to some extent into English spelling, though the mere English reader usually pronounces it as (k).

As OE. *c(e)*-, *c(i)*-, has regularly become *ch*-, these constitute one important section of the *ch*- words in modern English; another consists of the Old French words in *ch*- from L. *ca*-. Of the rest, the chief are those derived from Gr. words in *χ*-, directly, or through L. (Italian, French) *ch*-. The remainder consist of a few words from Slavonic or non-European languages, or of onomatopœic origin.

ch initial interchanges with *c*, *k*, *sh*. Since Old Northern French retained the *ca*-, which Central French changed to *cha*-, *che*-, French words were often adopted in English in both forms, usually first from Northern (Norman) French, and afterwards from Central French. Sometimes one, sometimes the other, sometimes both, of these have survived, see e.g. CAITIFF, CAMEL , CAMPION, CHAMPION, CANNEL, CHANNEL, CANAL, CHALICE, CHAMP, CATCH, CHASE, CHACCHE, CATTLE, CHATTEL. The Northern English also in certain cases resisted the palatalization of OE. *c*, or took the parallel *k* form of Norse or Low German: hence northern *caf*, CAUK, KIRK, CARL, KEESLIP, beside southern CHAFF, CHALK, CHURCH, CHURL, CHEESLEP. Cf. on the other hand Kentish *chalf* = CALF. Confusion between *ch*, *sch*, *sh*, was not infrequent in ME., e.g. *schin* = CHIN, *chever* = SHIVER. This was sometimes graphical, but partly also dialectal; there are varieties of northern dialect which still use initial (ʃ) for (tʃ). Variant forms like CHACO, SHAKO, CHAGRIN, SHAGREEN, *champoo*, SHAMPOO, are of more recent, and chiefly of phonetic origin.

b. abbreviation of *chapter*, *church*. **Ch. B.** = L. *Chirurgiæ Baccalaureus*, Bachelor of Surgery. **Ch. Ch.** = Christ Church (Oxford). **Ch. D.** = L. *Chirurgiæ Doctor*, Doctor of Surgery.

†**ch, 'ch,** *pron. dial. Obs.* Aphetic form of *ich*, *utch*, southern form of the first personal pronoun I, occurring before verbal forms beginning with a vowel, *h*, or *w*; chiefly with auxiliary verbs, but also with others; as in *cham* (tʃam), (earlier *icham*) I am, *cha*, *chave* (earlier *ichabbe*) I have, *chad* I had, *chard* I heard, *chill* I will, *chold*, *chud* I would, *chote* I wot, etc.

Found in remains of s.e. (Kentish) dial. in 16th and early 17th c., in s.w. dialect 16–18th c., and often introduced in specimens of dialect speech in the dramatists. Now obsolete; though *utchill* = I will, and *utchy* = I, were still heard in 1875, in remote parts of Somersetshire. (See Prince L. L. Bonaparte in *Phil. Soc. Trans.* 1875–6 p. 580.) *Utchy* corresponds to the 16th c. CHE; see further under ICH.

[*c* **1420** *Chron. Vilod.* 136, I cham þe pylgrym. *Ibid.*, Do as ychave þe rede.] **1528** MORE *Heresyes* IV. Wks. 278/1 An olde sage father fole in Kente..said, ye masters, say euery man what he wil; cha marked this matter wel as som other. *Ibid.*, By my fayth maysters quod he..by the masse cholde twere a faire fish pole. *Ibid.*, Nay byr Ladye maisters, quod he, yche cannot tell you why, but chote well it hath. *c* **1530** REDFORDE *Play Wit & Sc.* (1848) 29 Oh! cham a-cold. *Ibid.*, 31 Chyll go tell my moother. **1538** BALE *Thre Lawes* 397 Cha caute a corage of slouth. *a* **1553** UDALL *Royster D.* I. iii, Chad not so much, i chotte not whan: Nere since chwas born. **1575** J. STILL *Gamm. Gurton* I. iii, Chwere but a noddy to venter where cha no neede. **1599** PEELE *Sir Clyom.* Wks. III. 85 Jesu! how cham berayed. **1605** SHAKS. *Lear* IV. vi. 239 Chill not let go Zir..and 'chud ha' bin zwaggerd out of my life. **1633** B. JONSON *Tale of Tub* I. i, 'Cham no man's wife, But resolute Hilts. **1635** BROME *Sparagus Gard.* IV. v. Wks. 1873 III. 185 Then zay cha bewrai'd the house I coame on. *c* **1645** T. DAVIES *Somersetsh. Man's Compl.* 2 (Elworthy *Exmoor Scolding*.) 'Chill sell my cart. *Ibid.*, 'C ham sure that made vs slaues to be. **1668** WILKINS *Real Char.* 4 A Western man [would speak it] thus, Chud eat more cheese an chad it. **1746** *Exmoor Courtship* (E.D.S.) 104 Now chave a-zeed ye, tes zo good as chad a-eat ye.

cha, chah. Also tcha, chau, chaw. [Chinese (Mandarin) *ch'a* tea. Also in earlier It. *cia* (Florio), Russ. *tchaĭ* tea.] Properly, the name of TEA in the Mandarin dialect of Chinese, which was occasionally used in English at the first introduction of the beverage. (Some subsequently applied it as a name to the special form of rolled tea used in Central Asia.) Now used *slang* for 'tea'; cf. CHAI, CHAR *sb.*[6].

1616 COCKS *Diary* I. 215 (Y.), I sent..a silver chaw pot and a fan to Capt. China wife. **1655** tr. *Semedo's China* 19 Chá is a leaf of a tree in China, about the bigness of Mirtle. **1656** BLOUNT *Glossogr.*, *Cha.* [Hence in PHILLIPS, KERSEY, BAILEY.] **1658** *Mercurius Polit.* 30 Sept. (*Advt.*) That excellent..drink called by the Chineans Tcha, by other nations Tay alias Tee. **1742** BAILEY, *Cha*, Tea, which the Chinese steeping in Water, use as their common Drink. **1885** OGILVIE, *Cha* (Hind.), a kind of tea, rolled up like tobacco, which goes to the interior of Asia. **1919** DOWNING *Digger Dial.* 15 *Chai* (Arab.) or *cha* (Hind.), tea. **1930** *N. & Q.* 22 Mar. 206/2 The army slang 'Cha' in the sense of tea. **1935** E. WEEKLEY *Something about Words* x. 183 A bus-driver, who would probably..describe tea as *chah.* **1940** *Manch. Guardian Weekly* 6 Sept. 165/4 Untrammelled canteen helpers are sometimes mystified by requests for 'chah' from thirsty soldiers.

cha, *Obs.*, I have: see CH *pron.*

chaack. [Imitative.] The cry of the jackdaw.

1906 *Westm. Gaz.* 9 June 13/2 With a little flutter of the wing and a cheery 'Chaack!' he hopped off one head on to another. **1907** *Ibid.* 19 Oct. 16/1 The cheering 'cha-ack' of the jackdaw is everywhere in the air.

chaafe, obs. form of CHAFE.

chaalamy, var. of CALAMY[1], *Obs.*

chaan, chaapt, obs. ff. KHAN[1], CHAPED.

chaar, chaarmer, obs. ff. CHAIR, CHARMER.

†**chaas.** *Obs.* Variant of CAS, ? overthrow, fallen mass.

c **1386** CHAUCER *Knts. T.* 162 (Harl. MS.) Out of the chaas the pilours han hem torn [3 *MSS.* taas, 3 caas].

chaas, obs. f. CHASE; obs. pa. t. of CHOOSE.

chaast, obs. form of CHASTE.

chabazite, chabasite (ˈkæbəzaɪt). *Min.* Also chabasie, -zie. [A blundered name, which ought to be *Chalazite*; cited by Dana as first used, in form *chabazie*, by Bosc d'Antic, *Journ. d'Hist. N.* 1780, II. 181; formed on *χαβάζιε, an erroneous spelling which stood in the text of the Greek treatise *Λιθικά* or *Περὶ λίθων* (of the pseudo-Orpheus *a* 400), up to the publication of the ed. of Tyrwhitt in 1781. The actual Gr. word is χαλάζιε, vocative of χαλάζιος, which also occurs elsewhere in the forms χαλαζίας, χαλαζίτης λίθος, in Latin *chalāzius lapis*, and *chalāzias* (Pliny); the meaning being 'hail-stone', f. Gr. χάλαζα hail; so called from its form and colour (Pliny). The erroneous form disappeared a hundred years ago from Gr. lexicons and editions, but has been retained in the vocabulary of the mineralogists.]

A colourless, or flesh-coloured, mineral occurring, widely distributed, in glassy rhombohedral, almost cubic crystals, composed chiefly of silica, alumina and lime.

1804 *Edin. Rev.* III. 311 The chabasie [corresponds] to the Zeolytes called cubic. **1814** ALLAN *Min. Nomen.* Chabasie. Cubic zeolite. **1822** CLEAVELAND *Min.* 392 Crystals of chabazie are sometimes attached to the interior of geodes of agate. **1843** PORTLOCK *Geol.* 219 Chabazite.. extending throughout all the basaltic area. **1850** DANA *Geol.* ix. 513 Chabazite occurs in the hills..in small unmodified rhombohedrons. **1869** PHILLIPS *Vesuv.* xi. 305 The beautiful natrolites and chabasites, which occupy cavities in basalt at the Giant's Causeway.

chabbe: *I chabbe* is sometimes written in ME. southern dial. for *ichabbe* = *ich habbe*, I have.

‖**Chablis** (ʃabliː). Also 8 **chablee.** [Fr., f. the name of the small town *Chablis* (Yonne), near which it is made.] A celebrated white French wine.

1668 SHADWELL *Sullen Lov.* v, Have your cellar full of Champaign, Chablee, Burgundy. *c* **1678** OLDHAM *Paraphr. Horace's Odes* I. xxxi, Their Manto, Champagnes, Chablis, Frontiniacs tell. **1844** BROWNING *Gard. Fancies* II. iv, A loaf, Half a cheese, and a bottle of Chablis.

'chabot. *Her.* Also chalbot. [a. F. *chabot* (the Miller's Thumb, also *Her.*), earlier F. *cabot* (see CABOT).] The fish called Miller's Thumb.

1610 GUILLIM *Heraldrie* III. xxiii. 170 He beareth Or, three Chalbots Gules..A Chalbot fish seemeth to haue the shape of a Gournard. **1688** R. HOLME *Acad. Arm.* II. xv. No. 32 He beareth Azure, a Bul-Head Fish, proper..with us it is most known by the term..Millers Thumb; Gull, and a Chabot. **1708** KERSEY, *Chalbot* or *Chabot* (in Heraldry), a Fish having a great Head, commonly call'd a Bull-head, or Miller's-Thumb. So **1721–1800** in BAILEY.

‖**chabouk, -buk** (ˈtʃɑːbʊk). [Pers. and Urdū *chābuk*.] A (Persian) horse-whip. Formerly commonly anglicized as CHAWBUCK, q.v.

1815 MOORE *Lalla R.*, *Lt. of Harem*, Concerning..the chabuk, as connected therewith. **1827** SCOTT *Surg. Dau.* xiv, Said Tippoo 'Drag forward that Fakir, and cut his robe into tatters on his back with your chabouks'.

chabutra (tʃəˈbuːtrа). *India.* Also **chabootah, chaboot(e)ra, chapudra, chebootura.** [Hind. *chabūtrā*, *chabūtara*.] 'A paved or plastered terrace or platform, often attached to a house, or in a garden' (Yule).

1827 SCOTT *Surg. Dau.* xiv. This splendid procession having entered the royal gardens, approached..a chabootra, or platform of white marble..which occupied the centre. **1848** 'J. KIRKLAND' *Eerie Laird* x. 111 The..*chabooteras* of Delhi. **1882** F. M. CRAWFORD *Mr. Isaacs* x. 227 Some ryots had been called in to..raise a rough *chapudra* or terrace. **1895** MRS. B. M. CROKER *Village Tales* 154 He sat on his chaboota stolidly smoking his huka. **1963** *Times* 30 Jan. 12/6 The temple buildings clustered round a stone 'chabutra', a central meeting-point common to many villages.

chacal, obs. form of JACKAL *sb.*

chac-chac. [From the sound.] An instrument of noise used by negroes in the West Indies.

1870 KINGSLEY in *Gd. Words* May 317 The Indian shot.. which the Negro grows..because its hard seed put into a bladder furnishes him with that detestable musical instrument the chac-chac wherewith he accompanies nightly that equally detestable instrument the tom-tom.

†**chacche,** *v. Obs.* [a. south-Norman F. *chachier* (3rd sing. *chache*) = north-Norm. and Pic. *cachier*, and central OF. *chacier*; thus, a doublet of CATCH and CHASE.] **a.** = CHASE; **b.** = CATCH.

1362 LANGL. *P. Pl.* A. II. 180 And ȝif ȝe chacche lyȝere let him not a-skape. **138.** WYCLIF *Wks.* (1880) 293 Charite chacchiþ men to þis iust jugement. *Ibid.* 431 Lawe & skile chacchiþ men to ȝyue to trewe prestis þes dymes. *a* **1400–50** *Alexander* 748 Cure, for þi kene carpe chache nowe a schame. *Ibid.* 4227 We miȝt sum connynge per cas chach of ȝoure wordis.

chace, obs. f. CHASE; obs. pa. t. of CHOOSE.

chacen, obs. form of CHASTEN.

cha-cha ('tʃɑːtʃɑː), **cha-cha-cha** (ˌtʃatʃaˈtʃɑː). [Amer. Sp. *cha-cha-cha.*] A type of ballroom dance to Latin-American rhythm; also, the music for this dance. Hence as *v. intr.*

1954 *Melody Maker* 11 Dec. 15/2 What Touzet means by 'cha-cha', as far as I can make out, is simply a mambo with a pronounced güiro rhythm. **1955** *Ibid.* 16 July 5/3 'Cha-cha-cha' is danced very much more delicately over here than in England. **1959** *Camb. Rev.* 31 Jan. 279/1 We called on an old boy, to find him cha-cha-cha-ing with a young lady. **1959** *Economist* 4 Apr. 46/1 Cha-cha dance music. **1962** *Times* 11 June 3/1 Brazilian claques..cheered, cha cha-ed.

chachem, var. HAHAM.

chack (tʃæk), *v.*[1] In 6 chak. [In sense 1 imitative of the sound and action; cf. *clack*; senses 2 and 3 may be distinct words.]

1. Chiefly *Sc.* To snap with the teeth; to squeeze or crush with a snap of the jaws or by the sudden shutting of a window, door, drawer, or the like; also to make a noise like that of snapping teeth, to click, clatter, click. Also *gen.*, of the cry of a bird. Hence **'chacking** *ppl. a.*

1513 DOUGLAS *Æneis* XII. xii. 152 With hys wyd chaftis at hym makis a snak The byt oft falȝeis for ocht he do mycht And chakkis waist togiddir his wapynnis wycht. **1536** BELLENDEN *Cron. Scot.* (1821) II. 390 The cais chakkit to suddanlie, but ony motion or werk of mortall creaturis. **1697** CLELAND *Poems* 35 (Jam.) Some's teeth for cold did chack and chatter. **1801** HOGG *Scot. Pastoral* 23 (Jam.) For.. chackin' mice, and houkin' moudies, His match was never made. **1919** MASEFIELD *Reynard the Fox* 56 A blue uneasy jay was chacking. **1924** J. A. THOMSON *Science Old & New* iv. 22 Numerous 'chacking' wheatears with brilliantly white rump feathers. **1929** MASEFIELD *Hawbucks* 316 An owl came down..and tore something, with chacking cries between the tears.

2. 'Used of a horse that beats upon the hand when his head is not steady; but he tosses up his nose, and shakes it all of a sudden, to avoid the subjection of the bridle' (Bailey Vol. II. 1731; and repeated in mod. Dicts.). ? *Obs.*

chack (tʃæk), *sb. Sc.* [f. prec., or of parallel formation.]

1. The act of chacking (in sense 1).

2. A 'bite' (of food); a snack.

1818 SCOTT *Rob Roy* xxiv, '[An] invitation to come back and take part o' his family-chack, at ane preceesely.' **1824** —— *Redgauntlet* Let. ix, He..gives a bit chack of dinner to his friends. **1830** GALT *Lawrie T.* IV. x. (1849) 181 Take a chack of supper. **1852** CARLYLE *Let.* 20 Sept., Glad to get to the inn..and there procure some chack of dinner.

3. A local name of the Wheat-ear, also called (from its note) **chack-bird, chacker**, STONE-CHACKER and CHECK.

1804 TARRAS *Poems* 10 (Jam.) Death—trailt him aff i' his dank car, As dead's a chackart. **1805** BARRY *Orkney* 308 (Jam.) The White Ear—here denominated the chack.

chack, Sc. f. CHECK *v.*

chack-chack. [Imitative.] The cry of the fieldfare and wheatear. Also as *vb.* Cf. CHACK *v.*[1] and CHACK *sb.* 3.

1906 *Westm. Gaz.* 29 Dec. 16/3 The hoarse 'chack-chack' of the fieldfare. **1908** *Ibid.* 21 Mar. 14/1 Even if you only hear his [*sc.* the wheatear's] sharp note 'Chack-chack'. **1930** E. W. HENDY *Wild Exmoor* 236 Stonechats 'chack-chack' from the top of a spray.

†**'chackstone.** *Obs.* (See quot.) Cf. mod. Sc. CHUCKIESTANE.

1611 COTGR., *Cailleteau*, a chackestone, or little flintstone.

‖**chacma** ('tʃækmə). A kind of baboon (*Cynocephalus porcarius*) found in S. Africa.

1835 *Penny Cycl.* III. 229/2 The Chacma, so called from the Hottentot word T'Chackamma, the aboriginal name of this baboon in South Africa..when full grown, is equal in size, and much superior in strength, to a common English mastiff. *Ibid.* 230/1 A full-grown chacma is more than a match for two good dogs. **1855** MAYNE REID *Bush Boys* 447 Totty dispersing the Chacmas.

chaco ('ʃækəʊ). Also **chako**, and more usually SHAKO, q.v. [a. Magyar *csákó* ('tʃaːkoː); in Ger. *tschako*, Fr. *schako* (Littré).] A military cap of cloth and leather, formerly worn by the infantry in the British army, having the form of a truncated cone with a peak in front.

1826 *Soldier's Album* 11 Snatching up my chaco, I flew to the street. **1840** *Times* 1 Sept., The cumbersome bear-skin cap..is to be discontinued, and replaced by a smart chaco. **1851** *Ord. & Regul. R. Engineers* §24. 119 The Scales of the Chaco are to be worn under the chin on all Parades and Duties under Arms. **1866** *Army & Navy G.* 29 Sept., The chaco is reported as quite unsuited to the climate and hot sun.

‖**chaconne** (ʃakɔn, tʃəˈkɒn). *Mus.* Also 7-8 chacon, 8 chacoon, 9 chacona. [Fr. *chaconne*, ad. Sp. *chacona*, according to Spanish etymologists, ad. Basque *chucun* pretty.]

An obsolete dance, or the music to which it was danced, moderately slow, and usually in 3-4 time. 'The chaconne served as finale to a ballet or an opera: it is no longer in use' (Littré).

1685 DRYDEN *Albion & A.* II, Chacon, Two Nymphs and Triton sing. **1692** SOUTHERNE *Wives Excuse* I. i, The Sonatas and the Chacons which I know. **1721-1800** BAILEY, *Chaconne, chacoon*, a sort of Saraband Dance, the Measure of which is always Triple Time. **1774** *Westm. Mag.* II. 316 A chaconne, executed by eight principal dancers with great ease and agility. **1878** *Saturday Pop. Concert Programme Bk.* 23 Feb. 1003 A pianoforte accompaniment was added to the Chaconne by Mendelssohn.

‖**chacun à son goût** (ʃakœ̃ a sõ gu), *phr.* [Fr.] Each to his own taste.

1784 W. COWPER *Let.* 4 Dec. (1904) II. 280, I envy those happy voyagers [*sc.* balloonists],..but..as I say, *chacun à son goût*; and mine is rather to creep than fly. **1879** C. M. YONGE *Magnum Bonum* III. xxxii. 680 'What are your plans?' '*Rotifer*, as before.' '*Chacun à son gout*,' said Bobus, shrugging his shoulders. **1961** A. WILSON *Old Men at Zoo* viii. 350 'I'm afraid,' I said, 'I can't see it as simply as that. You see, I knew them all.' Hales laughed. '*Chacun à son goût*.'

chad, I had: see CH *pron.*

chad, var. of SHAD, a fish.

Chad, chad (tʃæd). [Origin obscure.] In full *Mr. Chad.* The figure of a human head appearing above a wall, etc., with the caption 'Wot, no——?', as a protest against a shortage or the like.

1945 *Sunday Express* 2 Dec. 2/3 What is the origin of that peculiarly laughable figure called Chad we see so often scribbled across our walls? **1946** *Times* 1 Apr. 5/4 Mr. Chad probably went through a number of evolutions at the hands of a vast number of people before reaching the present state and can claim no one man as creator. 'Wot! No father,' it might well complain. **1950** M. KENNEDY *Feast* 220 She drew a picture of Mr. Chad on the terrace wall saying: 'Wot? No black amber?' **1965** *Oxford Mail* 28 Sept. 6 The person.. staring chad-like in indolence across the desk-tops.

chadar, chaddar, varr. CHUDDAR.

Chadband ('tʃædbænd). [Name of a character, 'the Rev. Mr. *Chadband*', in Dickens's *Bleak House.*] A canting unctuous hypocrite. So **Chad'bandian** *a.*; **'Chadbandism**; **'Chadbandize** *v. intr.*

[**1852** DICKENS *Bleak Ho.* xix. 187 The Chadband style of oratory is widely received and much admired.] **1908** *Daily Chron.* 4 Nov. 5/3 There is no Chadbandian caricaturing of the parson. **1913** G. B. SHAW *Quint. Ibsenism* 189 Any attempt to Chadbandize on the wickedness of such crimes is at once resented as..'moral babble'. **1920** *Punch* 14 Jan. 33/2 His caustic dispraise Of President Wilson's Chadbandian ways. **1923** A. G. GARDINER *Cadbury* 259 His dislike of narrowness of view and Chadbandism kept him free from censoriousness.

chaddar, see CHADAR.

†**Chad-farthing.** *Obs.* [app. from name of St. Chad, patron saint of Lichfield.] (See quot.)

c **1588** *Comm.-pl. bk. R. Columbell, Darley Hall, Derbysh.* [Diocese of Lichfield] in *Rel. Ant.* I. 255 A dewtye belonging of oulde tyme to the churches. Every house payd at Easter..j farthynge called a waxfarthinge, and another called a chaddfarthinge..the chaddfarthinge to hallow the fonte for christining of children and for oyle and creame to anoyle sicke folkes wyth. **1806** HARWOOD *Hist. Lichfield* 109 Called Whitsun-farthings or Pentecostals, because it was usually given on Midlent or Whitsunday; and at Lichfield it was called *Chad-pennies* or *Chad-farthings*, in allusion to the founder of the cathedral.

Chad-pennies, 'pennies paid at the cathedral of Lichfield, dedicated to St. Chad, on Whit-Sunday, in aid of the repairs' (Brewer *Dict. Phr. & Fable*).

1806 [see above].

Chadian ('tʃædɪən), *sb.* and *a.* Also **Tchadian.** [f. the name of the North Central African state of *Chad* (F. *Tchad*) + -IAN.] **A.** *sb.* A native or inhabitant of Chad. **B.** *adj.* Of, pertaining to, or characteristic of Chad or its people.

1960 THOMPSON & ADLOFF *Emerging States Fr. Equatorial Afr.* xxiv. 426 All Tchadians have an awareness of their territory's weaknesses. *Ibid.* 427 No reliable basis has yet been found for classifying the Tchadian populations. **1968** in WEBSTER Add. s.v., Chadian. **1970** *Sunday Times* (Colour Suppl.) 5 Apr. 39/2 The Chadian army have lost 250 men. **1971** *Standard* (Tanzania) 7 Apr. 3/4 In his closing speech the President called on Chadians who had not yet found the road of reconciliation to join those who had returned to the ranks of the party. **1983** *Daily Tel.* 31 Jan. 1/2 Its government believes there may be as many as 700,000 Chadians returning home from Nigeria. **1983** *Times* 24 June 6/4 The garrison town of Faya-Largeau in northern Chad was attacked yesterday..the Chadian embassy announced here.

chadlock, var. f. CHARLOCK.

chæfle, early ME. f. CHAVEL, now JOWL.

chaer, chaere, obs. ff. CHAR, CHAIR.

chæta ('kiːtə). Pl. **chætæ** ('kiːtiː). [mod.L., ad. Gr. χαίτη long flowing hair.] = SETA.

1866 LINDLEY & MOORE *Treas. Bot.*, *Chæta*, a bristle, the slender stalk of the spore-case of mosses; also called Seta. **1896** W. B. BENHAM in Harmer & Shipley *Cambr. Nat. Hist.* II. 266 The chaetae or bristles are mainly used in locomotion. **1902** *Encycl. Brit.* XXV. 689/2 The Chætopoda are characterized by the possession of horny epidermic chætæ embedded in the integument and moved by muscles. **1963** [see next].

chætigerous (kiːˈtɪdʒərəs), *a. Zool.* [f. Gr. χαίτη: see prec. and -GEROUS.] Setigerous.

1896 W. B. BENHAM in Harmer & Shipley *Cambr. Nat. Hist.* II. 263 Chaetigerous segments. *Ibid.* 312 The peristomium is chaetigerous. **1963** R. P. DALES *Annelids* viii. 171 In other larvae the first chaetigerous segment may have hypertrophied chaetae.

‖**Chætodon** ('kiːtəʊdɒn). *Zool.* Also **chætodont.** [mod.L. f. Gr. χαίτη hair + ὀδούς (ὀδοντ-) tooth.] A Linnæan genus of spiny-finned fishes (modern family *Chætodontidæ*), remarkable for their bristle-like teeth and bright colours.

c **1750** HILL *Hist. Anim.* 275 (Jod.) The chætodon variegated with longitudinal lines and a forked tail. This is a native of the American ocean. **1774** GOLDSM. *Nat. Hist.* (1790) VI. i. 302 (Jod.) The chætodon or catfish. **1854** OWEN in *Circ. Sc.* (1865) II. 95/1 Setiform teeth are common in the fishes thence called Chætodonts. **1887** T. MARTIN in *Blackw. Mag.* Sept. 402 The prickly roach, the chaetodon with him And the hammer fish.

chætognath ('kiːtɒgnæθ). [f. mod.L. *Chætognatha*, neut. pl. of *chætognathus*, f. Gr. χαίτη (see CHÆTA) + γνάθος jaw.] A member of the Chætognatha, a phylum of small enterocœlous marine planktonic animals having two rows of stout spines on the head and a single row of sickle-shaped setæ or jaws; an arrow-worm.

1889 in *Cent. Dict.* **1896** A. E. SHIPLEY in Harmer & Shipley *Cambr. Nat. Hist.* II. 191 *S[agitta] hexaptera* is the largest Chaetognath known. **1962** D. NICHOLS *Echinoderms* x. 131 Other lesser phyla of the coelomates with three pairs of coelomic sacs, such as the chaetognaths.

chætophorous (kiːˈtɒfərəs), *a. Zool.* [f. Gr. χαίτη hair, mane + -φορ-ος bearing + -OUS: after mod.L. *chætophora.*] Bristle-bearing; applied to 'the Annelids which have bristle-bearing foot-tubercles, such as tube-worms and sand-worms; and also those which have locomotive bristles, such as earth-worms' (*Syd. Soc. Lex.*).

1877 HUXLEY *Anat. Inv. An.* v. 218 Such segmented Invertebrates as the chætophorous Annelida.

chætopod ('kiːtəʊpɒd). *Zool.* [f. mod.L. *chætopoda* neut. pl., f. as prec. + πούς (ποδ-) foot.] Belonging to the order *Chætopoda* of Annelids, marine worms, with bristle-bearing feet.

1864 WEBSTER s.v. *Lug-worm* cites BAIRD, A chætopod worm.

chætotaxy ('kiːtəʊtæksɪ). [f. Gr. χαίτη + τάξις: see CHÆTA and -TAXY.] The arrangement or plan of distribution of the bristles on the bodies of insects.

1893 E. A. BUTLER *Our Household Insects* 188 The plan of their distribution has been called by Osten-Sacken chætotaxy, i.e., bristle arrangement. **1903** *Entomol. News* 247 A careful exposition of the chaetotaxy of the Muscidæ. **1925** A. D. IMMS *Gen. Textbk. Ent.* I. 8 In recent years chætotaxy, or the study of the arrangement of the more important setæ, has assumed a good deal of significance from the taxonomic point of view, particularly with reference to the Cyclorrhapha and larval Lepidoptera.

chaf, obs. form of CHAFF *sb.*[1]

'chafant, *a. Her.* [f. CHAFE *v.* + -ANT[1].] Applied to a boar when represented as enraged or furious.

1847 *Gloss. Brit. Heraldry* (Parker), *Chafant*, enraged, applied to the wild boar.

chafar(e, -ayre, obs. ff. CHAFFER.

chafe (tʃeɪf), *v.* Forms: 4 **chaufe-n, chawffe, chafen,** 4-6 **chauffe,** 5 **chawfe,** 4-6 **chauf, chaffe,** 5-7 **chaufe,** 6 **chaafe, caff(e, chafen,** 6-9 **chaff,** 5- **chafe.** *Pa. t.* and *pple.* 4 **chauffede, chaufid, chefede, chauffit,** 4-6 **chaufed, chauffed,** 5 **chaufet, chauffid, chaffyd,** 6 **caffed, chafde, chafte, chauft, chafid,** 7 **chaft,** 5-9 **chaffed,** 5- **chafed.** [ME. *chaufe-n*, a. OF. *chaufe-r*, mod. *chauffer* to warm = Pr. *calfar*, It. *calefare*:—late L. or Rom. **calefāre*, contr. from L. *calefacĕre* to heat, make warm, f. *calēre* to be warm + *facĕre* to make. In Eng. the diphthong *au* was, as in other AF. words, reduced to long (aː), and this in regular phonetic course to (eɪ): cf. *gauge, safe, Ralph, chamber.*]

I. Transitive senses.

†**1.** To warm, heat. *Obs.*

1382 WYCLIF *Isa.* xliv. 15 He toc of hem, and is chaufed [**1388** warmed]. *c* **1420** *Anturs of Arth.* xxxv, A schimnay of charcole, to chaufen the knyȝte. *c* **1440** *Anc. Cookery* in *Househ. Ord.* (1790) 455 Chauf hit over the fyre. **1525** LORD BERNERS *Froissart* cxvi[xii]. 333 His bedde was wont to be chafed with a bason with hote coles. *c* **1535** DEWES *Introd. Fr.* in *Palsgr.* 940 To caffe or warme, *chauffer.* *a* **1577** GASCOIGNE *Dulce Bellum inexp.* Wks. (1587) 123 Whose grease hath molt all caffed as it was. **1601** HOLLAND *Pliny* II. 108 To heat and chaufe any part of the bodie. **1657** S. PURCHAS *Pol. Flying-Ins.* 331 Waxe when it is chafed will take an impression. **1672** MARVELL *Reh. Transp.* I. 86 It cannot be any vulgar furnace that hath chafed so cool a Salamander.

†2. *fig.* To inflame (the feelings), excite, warm, heat. *Obs.*

c **1325** *E.E. Allit. P.* B. 128 þat he wolde..cherisch hem alle with his cher, & chaufen her Ioye. **1393** LANGL. *P. Pl.* C. xv. 68 Leste cheste chaufe ous so and choppe ech man oþere. **1483** *Knt. de la Tour* (1868) 174 The goddesse of loue whiche kyndeleth and chauffeth the amerous hertes. *c* **1500** *Melusine* (1888) 22 Raymondyn, whiche was chaffed, doubted not of hys lyf. **1553** BRENDE *Q. Curtius* U vij, When he was chafed with drinking. **1682** BUNYAN *Holy War* 81 Their continuing in rebellion did but chafe and heat the spirit of the Captains. **1691** HARTCLIFFE *Virtues* 79 The use now made of it [Dancing]..serves only to chaff the Blood. **1716** HORNECK *Crucif. Jesus* 9 The Heart must be prepared, the Soul chafed, the Affections warmed.

3. To rub with the hand; *esp.* to rub (a person's limbs, etc.) in order to restore warmth or sensation.

c **1440** *Promp. Parv.* 68 Chafyn or rubbyn, *frico.* **1551** T. WILSON *Logike* 10 Waxe chaufed with the handes is made softer. **1581** MULCASTER *Positions* xxxiv. (1887) 122 The vse of chafing, and rubbing the body. **1719** DE FOE *Crusoe* (1840) I. xvi. 284 He took his arms..and chafed and rubbed them with his hands. **1842** TENNYSON *Morte d'Arth.* 211 She..laid his head upon her lap..and chafed his hands. **1877** BRYANT *Lit. People of Snow* 290 They..bore her home, and chafed her tender limbs.

absol. **1742** FIELDING *J. Andrews* II. v, She fell to chafing more violently. **1879** BROWNING *Ivan Iv.* 54 Chafe away, keep chafing, for she moans: She's coming to!

4. To rub so as to abrade or injure the surface; to fret, gall.

1526 *Pilgr. Perf.* (W. de W. 1531) 256 All his ioyntes were ..losed..his body so chafed. *a* **1547** SURREY *Æneid* IV. 535 With their [ants'] travaile chafed is eche pathe. **1602** *Vestry Bks.* (Surtees) 136 Wiche old book was frett and chafed. **1704** J. HARRIS *Lex. Techn.* s.v., Seamen say..The Cable is chafed in the Hawse, when it is fretted or begun to be worn out there. **1787** 'G. GAMBADO' *Acad. Horsem.* (1809) 31 The flap of your saddle..chafing you between the confines of the boot and breeches. **1856** KANE *Arct. Expl.* II. xxvi. 264 All the boats were badly chafed. **1861** FLO. NIGHTINGALE *Nursing* 92 How easily its tender skin gets chafed.

b. With some mixture of sense 10 (to rage, fume).

1813 SCOTT *Rokeby* II. vii, He..May view [the torrent] chafe her waves to spray, O'er every rock.

5. *fig.* To heat or ruffle in temper; to vex, irritate.

? *a* **1400** *Arthur* 95 Arthour was chafed & wexed wrothe. **1489** CAXTON *Faytes of A.* I. xxiv. 75 To theym that be fyrst chaffed and angry. **1490** —— *Eneydos* xxvii. 97 Whan the see was well chaffed and..ayenst them sore moeued. **1596** SHAKS. *Tam. Shr.* II. i. 243, I chafe you if I tarrie. Let me go. **1611** BIBLE *2 Sam.* xvii. 8. **1635** N. R. tr. *Camden's Hist. Eliz.* I. 73 Being frustrate of his hope, and sore chafed in minde. **1813** HOGG *Queen's Wake* 313 The youth was chaffed, and with disdain Refused to touch his harp again. **1840** DICKENS *Old C. Shop* lix. 267 To chafe and vex me is a part of her nature.

†6. To scold. *Obs.*

c **1485** *E.E. Misc.* (1855) 11 For his hyre he doth me chawfe. **1549** LATIMER *Serm. bef. Edw. VI*, vii. (Arb.) 197 We wyll..chyde, braule, fume, chaufe, and backbite them. **1637** GILLESPIE *Eng. Pop. Cerem.* III. vi. 104 The Parret.. being beaten and chaffed, returneth to its owne naturall voice. *c* **1677** TEMPLE in Courtenay *Mem.* (1836) I. 499 The King..chafing us for spending him so much money, and doing nothing.

b. *slang.* (See quot.; an ironical use of 1 or 3 or other prec. sense: cf. ANOINT.)

1673 R. HEAD *Canting Acad.* 36. **1690** B. E. *Dict. Cant. Crew*, Chaft, well beaten or bang'd.

II. Intransitive senses.

†7. To become warm or hot. *Obs.*

1393 LANGL. *P. Pl.* C. XVIII. 49 Then grace sholde growe ..And charite, þat child is now sholde chaufen of him-self. *c* **1450** *Merlin* 283 The day be-gan to chauffe, and the sonne was risen right high. **1525** LD. BERNERS *Froiss.* II. ciii. [xcix.] 301 The dayes chafed meruaylously, for it was aboute mydsomer. **1581** J. BELL *Haddon's Answ. Osor.* 407 He so chaufeth and moyleth in sturryng the coales.

†8. ?To spoil by heating, to undergo decomposition (? by heating or rubbing). *Obs.*

? *a* **1400** *Morte Arth.* 2301 They bussche[d] and bawmede þaire honourliche kynges, Sewed theme in sendelle sexti faulde aftire, Lappede them in lede, lesse that they schulde Chawnge or chawffe. **1470–85** MALORY *Arthur* I. xcv. (1634) 169 Then laid them in chests of lead, because they should not chafe nor savour.

9. To rub; to press or strike with friction (*on, upon, against*). (Often with mixture of other notions: cf. 10 c.)

1605 SHAKS. *Lear* IV. vi. 21 The murmuring Surge, That on th' vnnumbred idle Pebble chafes. **1704** J. HARRIS *Lex. Techn.* s.v., Seamen say, a Rope chafes, when it galls or frets, by rubbing against any rough and hard thing. **1805** SCOTT *Last Minstr.* I. xii, Is it the roar of Teviot's tide, That chafes against the scaur's red side? **1855** MAURY *Phys. Geog. Sea* xiv. §599 If the currents chafe upon it. **1861** HOLLAND *Less. Life* xiii. 178 As a caged bear chafes..against the walls of his cell.

10. *fig.* To wax warm (in temper); to be angry, to rage; now usually, to display irritation of temper and impatience of restraint or obstacles, by fuming, fretting, and worrying oneself or others.

1525 LD. BERNERS *Froiss.* II. cxxiii. [cxix.] 348 If ye fynde hym harde and highe of wordes, chafe not with hym, treate hym swetely. **1535** JOYE *Apol. Tindale* 32 The man began to fume and chaafe. **1581** J. BELL *Haddon's Answ. Osor.* 26 b, Though you..chaufe and fume never so much agaynst him. **1633** G. HERBERT *Temple, Church-Porch* liii, Calmnesse is great advantage: he that lets Another chafe, may warm him at his fire: Mark all his wandrings, and enjoy his frets. **1760** STERNE *Tr. Shandy* II. 93, I never chaff, but take the good and the bad as they fall in my road. **1791** COWPER *Iliad* I. 172 Let the loser chafe. **1837** HT. MARTINEAU *Soc. Amer.* II. 78 The wilder adventurers..had chafed at his advice. **1843** PRESCOTT *Mexico* VII. i. (1864) 416 While the exasperated prelate was chafing under this affront. **1864** ATKINSON *Whitby Gloss., Chaff*, to chafe or chaffer, to quarrel. 'They chaff'd at teean t'other varry sairly.' **1879** FROUDE *Cæsar* xv. 246 The aristocratic party could but chafe in impotent rage.

b. with *complement.*

a **1561** G. CAVENDISH *Wolsey* (1825) I. 220 He had an occasion greatly to chafe or fret the heart out of his belly.

c. Of the sea, etc: To fret, rage, or fume. (Sometimes with a tinge of sense 9.)

1611 SHAKS. *Wint. T.* III. iii. 89, I would you did but see how it chafes, how it rages, how it takes vp the shore. **1822** PROCTER (B. Cornwall) *Flood of Thess.* I. 477 The great sea chafes And the wild horses of the Atlantic shake Their sounding manes. **1840** THIRLWALL *Greece* VII. liv. 35 Their conflicting waters roared and chafed in eddies and waves. **1840** DICKENS *Barn. Rudge* lxiii, Chafing like an angry sea, the crowd pressed after them.

chafe (tʃeɪf), *sb.* Also 6 chaufe, chauff, 7 chaff. [f. prec. vb.]

1. Heat of mind or temper; rage, passion, fury; state of vexation, pet, 'temper'. *arch.*

1551 ASCHAM *Lett.* Wks. 1865 I. II. 312 The pope is in a wonderful chafe. **1566** T. STAPLETON *Ret. Untr. Jewell* iv. 105 The Emperour answered in a great chafe. *a* **1593** H. SMITH *Wks.* (1866–7) I. 176 He went away like Naaman in a chafe. *a* **1693** URQUHART *Rabelais* III. xxviii. 238 A March-Hare was never in such a Chaff as I am. *a* **1703** BURKITT *On N.T.* Rom. xi. 15 That..I might see them at last believe for anger, or for very shame, and go to heaven in a holy chafe. **1823** SCOTT *Peveril* xxi, Into what an unprofitable chafe you have put yourself! **1825** *Bull-baiting* II. in *Houlston Tracts* I. xxviii, To take bulls by the nose, and put them in a bit of a chafe.

2. Rubbing, fretting, friction.

1848 KINGSLEY *Saint's Trag.* I. i. 84 The chafe Comes not by wearing chains, but feeling them. **1876** R. BURTON *Gorilla L.* I. 71 Causing painful chafes and sores. **1882** NARES *Seamanship* (ed. 6) 66 They catch the chafe of the sail.

3. A chafing against restraints.

1869 *Pall Mall G.* 9 Aug. 11 His utterances are..marked already with a restlessness of spirit, and move with a chafe and impetuosity of rhythm, that seem to bode revolt.

4. *Comb.* †**chafe-gall** (see quot.); †**chafe-, chaff-halter**, cf. CHASE-. Also CHAFE-WAX, etc.

1678 A. LITTLETON *Lat. Dict., Intertrigo*..a galling in a man or beast by going, riding, or rubbing of one thing against another; a chafegall. **1704** WORLIDGE *Dict. Rust.* s.v. *Bridle*, Chaff-Halter, a Woman's Bridle is the same, only it's double Rained.

chafed (tʃeɪft), *ppl. a.* Also **chauf(f)ed, chauft, chaf'd, chaft**, etc. [f. CHAFE *v.* + -ED[1].] Heated; rubbed, fretted; angered, irritated, vexed.

c **1330** *Arth. & Merl.* 7145 Vp he lepe with chaufed blod. **1583** STANYHURST *Æneis* I. (1880) 20 On coast thee chauft flud is hurled. **1590** SPENSER *F.Q.* I. iii. 33 When his [the horse's] hot rider spurd his chauffed side. **1593** SHAKS. *3 Hen. VI*, II. v. 126 Warwicke rages like a chafed Bull. **1642** H. MORE *Song of Soul* I. I. li, His chafed feet, and the long way to town. **1764** CHURCHILL *The Author* Wks. 1774 II. 180 The chaf'd blood flies mounting to his cheeks. **1791** COWPER *Iliad* III. 265 Some chafed and angry idiot. **1816** SHELLEY *Alastor* 322 The white ridges of the chafèd sea.

chafer[1], **chaffer** ('tʃeɪfə(r), 'tʃæfə(r)). Forms: 1 ceafor, cefer, 5 cheaffer, chauer, 7– chafer, chaffer. [OE. *cefer* corresponds to OS. (MDu. and mod.Du.) *kever*, OHG. *chevar (chevaro)*, MHG. *kever, kefere*, Ger. *käfer* beetle:—OTeut. type *kefro-z*; OE. *ceafor*, if from earlier **cafr*, points to OTeut. ablaut-variant **kafroz, -uz*. Possible derivations are from a stem *kaf-* to gnaw (see CHAVEL), or from that of CHAFF, an animal enclosed in scales or husks. Mod. German use applies the name to all *Coleoptera*, from the ladybird to the stag-beetle.]

A name given to certain beetles, now chiefly the COCK-CHAFER and ROSE-CHAFER; used alone, it generally means the former of these. Apparently, originally applied to species destructive to plants.

α. form *chafer.*

c **1000** ÆLFRIC *Gloss.* in Wr.-Wülcker 121 *Bruchus*, ceafor. *c* **1000** *Ags. Ps.* civ. 30 [cv. 34] Sona cwoman gangan gærshoppan, and grame ceaferas [*bruchus*]. *c* **1400** *Trevisa's Higden* (Rolls) II. 211 (MS. α) Of hors i-roted comeþ cheaffers [**1387** harnettes, CAXTON chauers]. **1609** C. BUTLER *Fem. Mon.* (1634) 59 These [dors]..do openly engender with their Females, as the chafers do. **1816** KIRBY & SP. *Entomol.* (1828) II. xxi. 254 Take one of the common chafers or dung-beetles into your hand.

β. form *chaffer.*

1669 WORLIDGE *Syst. Agric.* (1681) 314 The great appearances of Chaffers, or other Insects. **1770–4** A. HUNTER *Georg. Ess.* (1803) III. 99 Cock-Chaffer..called.. the Chaffer..the Jeffry-Cock, the May-bug and (in Norfolk) the Dor. **1829** E. JESSE *Jrnl. Nat.* 324 Every sparrow that flies by has a chaffer in its mouth.

chafer[2] ('tʃeɪfə(r)). ? *Obs.* Forms: 4–5 **chaufour(e, 5 chafor, -ur, -ir, -our(e, -owre, chaufur, -yr, chawfer, chaffire, -our, chalfer, 5–7 chaufer, chaffer, 6 chaver, chauffer, 6– chafer.** [f. CHAFE *v.* + -ER[1]; or (in sense 1) a. F. *chauffoir*:—late L. type **calefātōrium* for *calefactōrium*. See CHAUFFER.]

†**1.** A vessel for heating something: **a.** A vessel for heating water, a saucepan. **b.** A portable grate, a chafing-dish. *Obs.*

α. form *chauf(f)our, -er.*

1395 *E.E. Wills* (1882) 5 A chaufour of siluer. **1427** *Mem. Rip.* (1882) I. 329, j chawfer. **1434** *E.E. Wills* (1882) 101 A chaufur of bras. **1558** *Wills & Inv. N.C.* (1835) II. 162, ij fyer chauffers. **1603** HOLLAND *Plutarch's Mor.* 215 Faire chaufers and goodly pots.

β. form *chafour, -er.*

1420 *E.E. Wills* (1882) 46 þe best of yren broches, & a chafur. *c* **1440** *Promp. Parv.* 68 Chafowre to make whote a thynge as watur, *calefactorium.* **1488** *Inv. Jewels Jas. III* in Tytler *Hist. Scot.* (1864) II. 392 A chalfer, of silver ouregilt. *c* **1590** MARLOWE *Faust* v. (*stage direction*) Re-enter Mephistophilis with a chafer of coals. **1688** R. HOLME *Armoury* III. 398/1 Barbers..carry about with them..a small Chafer. **1721–33** STRYPE *Eccl. Mem.* II. I. i. 2 Basin and chavers of silver and gilt..to wash the Prince. **1825** HONE *Every-day Bk.* I. 1257 These [barbers'] chafers are no longer made in London.

γ. form *chaffer.*

c **1460** J. RUSSELL *Bk. Nurture* in *Babees Bk.* (1868) 161 Lay þem vppon youre galantyne stondynge on a chaffire hoote. **1505** *Will of Horwood* (Somerset Ho.) A large chaffer of laton. **1629** *Inv. Hatfield Priory* in *Trans. Essex Archæol. Soc.* New Ser. III. II. 160, j great brasse chaffer to heat water in.

†**2.** = CHAFE-WAX. *Obs.*

1577 HOLINSHED *Chron.* III. 920/2 A clearke of the hamper; and a chafer of the wax. **1647** HAWARD *Crown Rev.* 2 Chafer of Wax. Fee.—7*l.* 6*s.* 7*d.* **1805** *Lett. Patent* in *Law Times* LXXXI. 442/2 The office or place of chaffer of the wax.

3. One who chafes or fumes. ? *Obs.*

1598 FLORIO, *Bronfatore*..a snorter, a huff snuff, a chafer. **1604** T. WRIGHT *Passions* IV. ii. §1. 127 Chafers in play are couetous, great gamesters are foolish.

chafer, *v.* [? mispr. for *chafe.*]

a **1625** FLETCHER & MASS. *Elder Bro.* IV. ii. (1679) 117 *M.* Do they chafer roundly? *A.* As they were rubb'd with Soap, Sir..*M.* Long may they chafe, and long may we laugh at 'em.

chafer, obs. form of CHAFFER.

†'**chafern**, '**chaffern**. *Obs.* [app. altered from CHAFER[2], after words like *cistern, lantern.*] = CHAFER[2] 1 a.

1613 *Inv.* in *Stratford-on-Avon MSS.* (N.) Five brasse pottes..and one chaferne. **1688** R. HOLME *Armoury* III. 426/2 In our refined speech some call a Barbers Chaffer..a Chaffern, and a Caldafer. **1693** W. ROBERTSON *Phraseol. Gen.* 277 A brass-pot, chafern, or kettle. **1721–1800** BAILEY, *Chaffern*, a Vessel to heat Water in.

chafery ('tʃeɪfərɪ). *Metallurgy.* [prob. coming down from an earlier **chauferie*, a. F. *chaufferie* in same sense, f. *chauffer* to heat; see CHAFE *v.* and -ERY.] (See quots.)

1663 in *Jrnl. Derbysh. Archæol. Soc.* X. 35 Anvil, chafery bellows and wheels. **1679** PLOT *Staffordsh.* (1686) 163 The Forges..are of two sorts, one whereof they call the Finery, the other the Chafery. **1731** BAILEY, *Chafery*, one of the Forges in an Iron-Work. **1825** J. NICHOLSON *Operat. Mechanic* Gloss. 774. **1881** RAYMOND *Mining Gloss.*, *Chafery*, a forge fire for reheating.

†'**chafe-wax**. *Obs.* Also **chaff-wax**. [f. CHAFE *v.* (sense 1) + WAX *sb.*] An officer attending on the Lord Chancellor, whose duty it was to prepare the wax for sealing documents. The office was abolished in 1852.

1607 COWELL *Interpr.*, Chafewax is an officer in chauncery, that fitteth the waxe for the sealing of the writs. **1614** ELLESMERE in Ld. Campbell *Chancellors* (1857) II. l. 358 The poore Sealer and Chaffewax and ther dependantes. **1703** *Lond. Gaz.* No. 750/4 The Chafe wax to the Great Seal. **1886** *Law Times* LXXXI. 442/2 The now obsolete office of chaffwax to the Lord Chancellor.

'**chafeweed**, '**chaffweed**. *Herb.* [According to Turner and other early writers, f. CHAFE + WEED; see quot. 1551: otherwise it might be plausibly explained from CHAFF *sb.*[1] and WEED, in reference to the chaffy receptacle of *Filago.*]

A name given by Turner to the plant *Gnaphalium sylvaticum*; extended by Gerard to other species of *Gnaphalium* and the allied *Filago*; applied by some especially to *F. germanica*, the CHAFEWORT of Turner. (By Lyte erroneously applied to *Diotis maritima*, the Sea Daisy.)

1548 TURNER *Names of Herbes* s.v. *Centunculus*, Centunculus named in greke Gnaphalion..It maye be called in englishe Chafweede, it is called in Yorke shyre cudweede. **1551** —— *Herbal* I. I ij, Centunculus is called.. in Northumberlande Chafweede, because it is thought to be good for chafynge of any mans fleshe wyth goynge or rydynge. **1578** LYTE *Dodoens* I. lxii. 90 This herbe [Gnaphalion] is called..in English of Turner Cudweed, Chafeweed. **1598** FLORIO, *Herba impia*..we call it chaffweede or cudweede. **1853** in G. JOHNSTON *Bot. E. Bord.* (= *Filago germanica*). **1879** PRIOR *Plant-n.*, *Chafeweed*..as Ray expresses it in Cat. Plant. Cant., 'quoniam ad intertrigines valet'.

†'**chafewort.** *Obs.* [f. CHAFE + WORT.] A name given by Turner to *Filago germanica.*

1548 TURNER *Names of Herbes* 83 *Cartafilago* otherwise Ceratophilax, is called in english Cudwurt, or Chafewurte.

chaff (tʃɑːf, -æ-), *sb.*[1] Forms: 1 ceaf, cef, 2 chæf, 2–4 chef, (2, 4 cheue, 4 chaue), 4 cheff, 3–5, 7 chaf, 4–7 chaffe, 3–4, 6- chaff; *north.* 4 caf, 5 kaf, kaff, kafe, 6 caiff, 4–7 caffe, 5–9 caff. (Occasional 4 schaf, 5 shaffe.) [OE. *ceaf*, corresp. to MDu. *caf* (Du. *kaf*), MHG., MLG., dial. Ger. *kaf* neut., related to OHG. *cheva* husk, pod, and possibly to a Teut. root *kef-* gnaw: cf. CHAVEL, JOWL. The southern form in ME. was *chef*, the midland *chaff*; the northern *caf*, *caff*, still extant; in Scotl. also *cauve*. Commonly collective.]

1. a. A collective term for the husks of corn or other grain separated by threshing or winnowing.

α. form *chef.*

c **1000** ÆLFRIC *Voc.* in Wr.-Wülcker 148 *Palea*, ceaf. *c* **1000** *Ags. Gosp.* Luke iii. 17 þæt ceaf he forbærnþ. *c* **1160** *Hatton G.* ibid., þæt chæf he forbernð. *c* **1175** *Lamb. Hom.* 85 þet smal chef þet flid ford mid þe winde. *Ibid.* Of þe smal cheue. *a* **1225** *Juliana* 79 þat dusti chef. *c* **1340** *Ayenb.* 210 Be-tuene þe cheue and þe corn [nom. *passim* chef].

β. form *chaff.*

c **1200** ORMIN 1483 And siþþenn winndwesst tu þin corn, And fra þe chaff itt shædesst. *c* **1205** LAY. 29256 þer biforen he gon ȝeoten draf and chaf and aten. *c* **1340** *Cursor M.* 4791 (Trin.) To fynde þe chaue Corn þere shul we fynde to haue. *Ibid.* 21113 (Fairf.) Quik þai haue his bodi flaine & waltered him in barli chaf. *c* **1394** *P. Pl. Crede* 663 And so þei chewen charitie as chewen schaf houndes. *c* **1400** *Ywaine & Gaw.* 1684 Barly brede with al the chaf. **1526** *Pilgr. Perf.* (W. de W. 1531) 134 b, As the flayle tryeth ye corne from the chaffe. **1667** MILTON *P.L.* IV. 985 Least on the threshing floore his hopeful sheaves Prove chaff. **1715–20** POPE *Iliad* v. 613 The light chaff, before the breezes borne. *a* **1811** J. LEYDEN *Ld. Soulis* lxii, The barley chaff to the sifted sand They added still by handfuls nine.

γ. form *caf*, *caff.*

a **1300** *Cursor M.* 4751 (Cott.) Þe caf he cast o corn sumquile In the flum þat hait þe nile. *a* **1340** HAMPOLE *Psalter* xxxiv. 21 Caf þat is light to fle wiþ þe wynd. **1483** *Cath. Angl.* 51 Caffe, *acus*, *palea*. **15..** *Scot. Poems 16th C.* (1801) 98 (Jam.) As.. caffe before the wind. **1670** RAY *Proverbs* 285 Kings caff is worth other mens corn. **1826** J. WILSON *Noct. Ambr.* Wks. 1855 I. 334 To sleep on caff. **1875** *Lanc. Gloss.* (E.D.S.) *Caff* (N. Lanc.), chaff, refuse. **1877** *Holderness Gloss.* (E.D.S.) *Caff*, chaff.

†**b.** A plural occurs in OE. and ME., *e.g.* to translate *paleæ* of the Vulgate. *Obs.*

c **1000** *Ags. Gosp.* Matt. iii. 12 þa ceafu [*Lindisf.* halmas; *c* **1160** *Hatton G.* chefu] he forbærnð on unadwæscendlicum fyre. **1382** WYCLIF *Matt.* iii. 12 But chaffis he shal brenne with fyr unquenchable. —— *Ezek.* xiii. 10 With outen chaffis [Vulg. *absque paleis*].

†**2.** *transf.* The husks of pease and beans. *Obs.*

c **1420** *Pallad. on Husb.* IV. 110 Two basketfull of bene chaf. **1611** COTGR., *Faval*, the chaffe, shalings, hullings, offals, or cleansing of Beanes.

3. Cut hay and straw used for feeding cattle. (It is doubtful whether the early instances of 'chaff' used in brick-making, etc., belong here. A chaff-cutting machine is described in Lewis *Hist. Thanet* 1736 Plate IV. p. 16, but not by this name, being called 'a cutting box to cut horse's meat in'.)

[*c* **1000** ÆLFRIC *Exod.* v. 7 Ne sylle ȝe leng nan cef ðis Ebreiscan folc to tiȝel ȝeweorce. *c* **1250** *Gen. & Ex.* 2889 Hem-seluen he fetchden ðe chaf ðe men ðor hem to gode gaf. **1382** WYCLIF *Isa.* lxv. 25 The leoun and the oxe shuln ete chaf [**1388** stree]. **1483** CAXTON *Gold. Leg.* 44/1 In my faders hows is place ynough to lodge the & thy camels & plente of chaf & heye for them. *c* **1535** DEWES *Introd. Fr.* in *Palsgr.* 915 Litter or chaff, *paille.*] **1772** W. BAILEY *Advancem. Arts* (1783) I. 42 Mr. Edgill's Machine for cutting chaff. **1834** *Brit. Husb.* viii. 212 If fed.. upon indifferent hay and straw, it then becomes necessary to cut it into chaff.

4. *Bot.* **a.** The thin dry leaves or bracts of the flower of grasses, *esp.* the inner pair now usually called *pales* or *glumelles*, distinct from the outer pair called *glumes.* **b.** The bracts at the base of the florets in Compositæ. (The plural is *obs.*)

1776 WITHERING *Bot. Arrangem.* (1796) I. 195 *Eryngium* .. florets sitting, separated by chaff. *Ibid.* III. 669 *Hyoseris*, Receptacle naked: Down hair-like; encompassed by awned chaff. **1794** MARTYN *Rousseau's Bot.* xiii. 133 [Canary-grass] the chaffs being turgid and hairy. *Ibid.* 134 The keel of the chaffs is ciliate. **1846** J. BAXTER *Libr. Pract. Agric.* II. 406 In the blooming season, for wheat, there are three stamens, or male portions, thrown out beyond the chaff or calyx. **1880** GRAY *Struct. Bot.* v. 142 Palets, also called Chaff, are diminutive or chaff-like bracts or bractlets on the axis (or receptacle) and among the flowers of a dense inflorescence, such as a head of Compositæ.. the name is also given to an inner series of the glumes of grasses.

5. a. In various fig. or allusive contexts, from sense 1. (Cf. *Matt.* iii. 12, etc.)

c **1386** CHAUCER *Man Lawes T.* 603 Me lust not of the caf ne of the stree Make so long a tale, as of the corn. **1393** GOWER *Conf.* II. 59 It were a short beyete To winne chaffe and lese whete. **1535** LYNDESAY *Satyre* 3531 Thy words war nather corne nor caiff. **1579** GOSSON *Sch. Abuse* (Arb.) 18 You may wel thinke that I sell my corne and eate Chaffe. **1596** SHAKS. *Merch. V.* I. i. 117 His reasons are two graines of wheate hid in two bushels of chaffe: you shall seeke all day ere you finde them, & when you haue them they are not worth the search. **1732** BERKELEY *Alciphr.* vi. §9 You may see here [*Jer.* xxiii. 28] a distinction made between wheat and chaff, true and spurious. **1850** TENNYSON *In Mem.* vi, Vacant chaff well meant for grain. **1882** *Athenæum* 5 Aug. 171/3 Though there is a little chaff there is also a good deal of wheat.

b. Proverb. ***an old bird is not caught with chaff***; and allusions to it.

1481 CAXTON *Reynard* 110, I am no byrde to be locked ne take by chaf, I know wel ynowh good corn. *c* **1600** SHAKS. *Timon* IV. ii, An olde birde is not caught with chaffe. **1665–9** BOYLE *Occas. Refl.* v. x. (1675) 336 The empty and Trifling Chaff, Youth is wont to be caught with. **1771** SMOLLETT *Humph. Cl.* (L.) The doctor, being a shy cock, would not be caught with chaff. **1856** J. H. NEWMAN *Callista* (1885) 249, I am too old for chaff. **1873** HALE *In His Name* vi. 50 That's old chaff for such as we.

6. *transf.* and *fig.* **a.** Refuse, worthless matter.

? *a* **1400** *Morte Arth.* 1064 Caffe of creatours alle, thow cursede wriche! **1555** EDEN *Decades W. Ind.* I. VIII. (Arb.) 96 (*marg.*) Perles as common as chaffe. **1596** SHAKS. *Merch. V.* II. ix. 48 How much honor Pickt from the chaffe and ruine of the times. **1606** —— *Tr. & Cr.* I. ii. 262 Asses, fooles, dolts, chaffe and bran. **1621** BURTON *Anat. Mel.* I. ii. III. xv, Some poor scholler, some parson chaff. **1670** DRYDEN *Prol. Conq. Granada* 42 Wheel-broad hats, dull humour, all that chaff, Which makes you mourn, and makes the vulgar laugh. **1799** WORDSW. *Poet's Epit.* iv, A soldier, and no man of chaff. **1842** TENNYSON *Epic* 40 Twelve books of mine.. Mere chaff and draff, much better burnt.

b. Strips of metal foil or similar material released in the atmosphere to interfere with radar detection. orig. *U.S.*

1945 *Sun* (Baltimore) 29 Nov. 8/4 Under the disguise provided by aluminum 'chaff'—a few ounces of which gives a radar reflection comparable to that of three heavy bombers. **1947** SIEGERT & PURCELL in L. N. Ridenour *Radar System Engin.* iii. 82 'Window' is the British and most commonly used code name for conducting foil or sheet cut into pieces of such a size that each piece resonates as a dipole at enemy radar frequency... The strong signals it returns so effectively mask the radar signals from aircraft that are in the midst of a cloud of window that several tons of aluminum used to be dispersed.. on each.. bomber raid. The U.S. Army referred to this material as 'chaff'. **1962** *Observer* 11 Mar. 1/4 Metallic objects called 'chaff' were used by the Russians yesterday.. in a new attempt to interfere with air traffic... The objects are about four inches long and about the width of a flat knitting needle. **1968** *New Scientist* 4 Apr. 9/1 As for the chaff itself, the move away from strips of aluminium foil to coated glass fibres has meant that twice as much deception can be stuffed into the same package.

7. a. *attrib.* Of or resembling chaff.

1636 JAMES *Iter Lanc.* 112 Those chaffe sands which doe in mountains rize.

b. *Comb.*, as ***chaff-bait, -biscuit, -bread, -heap, -house, -knife, -net, -room***; **chaff-bed**, a 'bed' or mattress stuffed with chaff instead of feathers, etc.; **chaff-box**, a chaff-cutter to be worked by hand; **chaff-cutter**, one who cuts chaff; a machine for cutting hay and straw for fodder, also called **chaff-engine**; **chaff-flower**, a name for *Alternanthera achyrantha*; **chaff-scale** *Bot.* (see quots.); **chaff-seed**, a name for *Schwalbea americana.* Also CHAFF-WEED.

1649 G. DANIEL *Trinarch.*, *Hen. IV*, xxxii, The Birds come in To his *Chaffe-baite. **1582** *Inv. of R. Hodgson, Kendal* (Somerset Ho.), A *Caffe bed. **1663** *Inv. Ld. Gordon's Furniture*, Thair is in the bed, a caffe bed, a fethir bed, a pair blankets, and a red worset rug. **1683** TRYON *Way to Health* 592 Straw, or rather Chaff-Beds, with Ticks of Canvas. **1839** DICKENS *Nich. Nick.* xxii, Salt meat and new rum, pease-pudding and *chaff-biscuits. **1840** *Flemish Husb.* 89 in *Libr. Usef. Knowl.*, *Husb.* III, The chaff-cutter is exactly like our common *chaff-box, where the work is done by the hand. **1908** *Essex Rev.* XVII. 24 A century or so ago, a handworked chaff-box was in almost daily use on every large farm. **1611** COTGR., *Pain de bale*, *chaffe bread.. the coursest kind of bread. **1772** W. BAILEY *Advancem. Arts* (1783) I. 192 A new invented *chaff cutter invented by Mr. Wm. Bailey. **1807** VANCOUVER *Agric. Devon* (1813) 124 Chaff-cutters are used by Mr. Fellows and other gentlemen in the county. **1854** *Illust. Lond. News* 5 Aug. 118/3 Occupations of the People. Chaffcutter. **1633** BP. HALL *Hard Texts* 323 Since the house of Jacob is now as a little corne left in a *chaffe-heape. *c* **1425** *Voc.* in Wr.-Wülcker 670 *Hoc palare*, *chaf-house. **1483** *Cath. Angl.* 51 A Caffe hows, *paliare*, *paliarium.* **1833** *Manuf. Metal* iii. II. 55 (Cab. Cycl.) *Chaff-knife backs, and hay-knife backs. *c* **1440** *Promp. Parv.* 68 *Chaffenette to take byrdys, *retiaculum.* **1801** STRUTT *Sports & Past.* I. ii. 34. **1834** *Brit. Husb.* I. 99 Along the opposite side of the yard are the *chaff-room, various domestic offices, etc. **1856** W. B. CARPENTER *Microsc.* 447 The hairs with which the *paleæ* (*chaff-scales) of most Grasses are furnished, are strengthened by the like siliceous deposit. **1888** *Encycl. Brit.* XXIV. 531 At the base of each spikelet [of wheat] are two empty boat-shaped glumes or 'chaff-scales'.

chaff (tʃɑːf, -æ-), *sb.*[2] *colloq.* [Of this and the related CHAFF *v.*[2], the origin is not quite certain: if the sb. is earlier, it may be a fig. use of prec. (cf. senses 5, 6 there); if the vb. is the starting point, it may be a playful or light use of *chaff*, CHAFE *v.*, senses 5 and 6 of which come very near to it.]

Banter, light and good-humoured raillery, or ridicule, calculated to try the temper of the person to whom it is addressed; badinage (App. of slang origin, and still somewhat vulgar.)

(The first quot. is uncertainly placed: it may mean 'scolding': cf. CHAFE *v.* 6.)

[**1648** JENKYN *Blind Guide* iv. 76 You pretend to nothing but chaffe and scoffes.] **1840** DICKENS *Barn. Rudge* (C.D. ed.) 42, 'I do', said the 'prentice. 'Honour bright. No chaff, you know.' **1855** THACKERAY *Newcomes* I. 286 There's enough of this chaff. I have been called names and blackguarded enough. **1858** *Sat. Rev.* 7 Aug. 127/2 Chaff, as the vulgar call it, when it is real good chaff, is an element in statecraft. **1885** *Manch. Even. News* 6 July 2/2 They got through a few overs.. amidst the chaff of a good-natured crowd.

chaff (tʃɑːf, -æ-), *v.*[1] [f. CHAFF *sb.*[1]] Hence **chaffed** *ppl. a.*, '**chaffing** *vbl. sb.*

1. *trans.* To mix with chaff; = CHAVE *v.*[1]

1552 HULOET, Chaffed or myxt with chaffe, *paleatus.*

2. To cut (hay, straw, etc.) for fodder.

1883 *Hertfordsh. Mercury* 6 Dec. 4/4 In most other cases the grass has been chaffed when put into the silo. **1887** *Times* 7 Sept. 3/3 Mr. Henry Simmonds fed.. the young stock on chaffed hay and straw. *Ibid.* [He] was in the habit of supplying winter food.. by chaffing up the straw.

chaff (tʃɑːf, -æ-), *v.*[2] *colloq.* [see CHAFF *sb.*[2]: the relative priority of vb. and sb. is unsettled.] *trans.* To banter, rail at, or rally, in a light and non-serious manner, or without anger, but so as to try the good nature or temper of the person 'chaffed'.

(A word or sense which probably arose as cadgers' slang, and is still considered slangy, and usually apologized for by inverted commas.)

1827 [see CHAFFING]. **1850** H. GREVILLE *Leaves fr. Diary* (1883) 375 Charles was very amusing in chaffing Lady C. for her violent anti-Catholic feeings. **1857** KINGSLEY *Two Y. Ago* xv. (D.) A dozen honest fellows grinned when their own visages appeared, and chaffed each other about the sweethearts who were to keep them while they were out at sea. **1879** MCCARTHY *Own Times* II. 264 Palmerston is in the Home office, pleasantly 'chaffing' militia colonels. **1885** DICEY *Introd. Lect. Law of Const.* 174 The Regent treated the affair as a sort of joke, and, so to speak, 'chaffed' the supposed author of the satire.

b. *absol.* or *intr.*

a **1845** BARHAM *Ingold. Leg.* (1877) 319 Not pausing to chaff or to parley.

Hence '**chaffing** *vbl. sb.* and *ppl. a.*, '**chaffingly** *adv.*

[Cf. **1575** in CHAFING *vbl. sb.* 1.]

1827 HONE *Every-day Bk.* II. 1009 Much 'chaffing' passed between them. **1861** N. A. WOODS *Pr. Wales in Canada* 426 There were 'chaffing' signals too, going on between the vessels. **1876** BURNABY *Ride Khiva* vi, Being a little annoyed at the chaffing remarks of the grinning peasants. **1871** *Daily News* 24 Jan., The men took to criticising each other's performances, not chaffingly, but quite seriously. **1883** PROCTOR in *Knowledge* 13 July 28/1 A habit chaffingly attributed to the Missourian belles.

chaff (tʃɑːf, -æ-), *v.*[3] *Bread-making. trans.* To roll up (dough) into a rounded form in the moulding of a round loaf. Hence '**chaffing** *vbl. sb.*

1892 R. WELLS *Pract. Bread Baker* 44 How to mould a round loaf... Divide the dough into parts, having the right hand piece smaller than the left. Now chaff this into two round pieces. **1925** *Glasgow Herald* 9 Oct. 6 The loaf is shaped on the chaffing table.

chaff, var. CHAFT, jaw, and obs. form of CHAFE.

chaffaire, -are, obs. forms of CHAFFER.

chaffed (tʃɑːft, -æ-), *ppl. a.*

1. See CHAFF *v.*[1] **2.** See CHAFF *v.*[2]

†**3.** ? Spoiled by heating, that has begun to decompose: see CHAFE *v.* 8. *Obs.*

1734 T. SHERIDAN *Let.* in *Swift's Wks.* (1841) II. 724 You live upon chaffed mutton, I live upon venison.

chaffer ('tʃæfə(r)), *sb.*[1] Forms: 3 chaffere, 4 cheapfare, chapfare, -vare, 3–5 cheffare, 3–6 chaffare (chaffere, chafare, chefare), 4–7 chaffar, 4- chaffer. (Also 5 chafar, -ir, -yr, -ayre, chaffour, chaffur, chafre, caffer, 5–6 chaffre, 5–7 chafer, 6 chaffayre, 7 chaffaire.) [In the *Ayenbite* (1340) *cheapfare*, *chapfare*:—OE. type **céapfaru*, f. *céap* bargain, sale + *faru* faring, going; not recorded, but the cognate ON. *kaupfǫr* is extant in sense 'trading journey'. Assimilation of *pf* to *ff* gave the general ME. types *cheffare*, *chaffare*; with the *a* in the latter, cf. OE. *céapmǫnn*, ME. *chepmon* and *chapman*, now CHAPMAN. Apparently the original sb. became obs. in the 17th c., but has been formed anew from the vb., in sense 1 b.]

†**1.** Traffic, trade; buying and selling, dealing. *Obs.* exc. as in b.

a **1225** *Ancr. R.* 418 None cheffare ne driue ȝe. *c* **1230** *Hali Meid.* 9 Weilaweil!.. hwuch unwurðe chaffere. *c* **1320** *Sir Beues* 2062 God ȝeue it.. We hadde driue þat chefare. **1340** *Ayenb.* 36 Þe vifte manere [*sc.* of gauelinge] is ine cheapfare. *Ibid.* 45 Þe eȝtende boȝ of auarice is chapfare.. Ine uele oþre maneres me may zeneȝi ine chapfares. **138.** WYCLIF *Serm.* Sel. Wks. I. 50 Sum [wenten] after chaffare of þis worldely richesse. *c* **1450** MYRC 1299 Hast thow by-gylet in chafare? **1551–6** ROBINSON tr. *More's Utop.* 63 Money, wherewith to mayneteyne their dayly occupieng and chaffayre. **1613** R. C. *Table Alph.* (ed. 3), *Chaffar*, buying and selling. **1662** FULLER *Worthies* III. 150 By sad chaffer, they were fain to give money for water.

b. In modern use, chiefly from the vb.: Chaffering, bargaining, haggling as to price.

1851 LONGF. *Gold. Leg.* VI. *Sch. Salerno*, What do I care for the Doctor Seraphic, With all his wordy chaffer and traffic? **1870** MORRIS *Earthly Par.* I. II. 589 The dark-eyed merchants of the southern seas In chaffer with the base Propœtides. **1878** H. M. STANLEY *Dark Cont.* II. xvi. 431, I was unable to purchase anything more than a few ground-

nuts, because it involved such serious controversy and chaffer as sickened the hungry stomach.

†**2.** That which is bought and sold; wares, merchandise, goods for barter or sale. *Obs.*

c **1250** *Gen. & Ex.* 1951 Fro galaad men wið chafare sa3 he ðor kumen wid spices ware. **1297** R. GLOUC. 539 To late in tueie wolmongers, hor chaffare in to lede. **1362** LANGL. *P. Pl.* A. v. 174 þer weore chapmen I-chose þe chaffare to preise. *c* **1440** *Gesta Rom.* 285 (Add. MS.), X. asses chargede with dyuerse chaffare. **1441** *Plumpton Corr.* Introd. 54 None of the Kings said tenants might, ne durst come att the towne of Ripon..to utter their caffer, wherewith to pay his farme. **1526** *Pilgr. Perf.* (1531) 25 As a marchaunt sheweth his marchaundyse or chafer. *c* **1612** ROWLANDS *Four Knaves* (1843) 96 His good daies are when 's chaffer is well sold. *a* **1693** URQUHART *Rabelais* III. iv, Gold, silver..chains, rings, with other ware and chaffer of that nature.

†**b.** *good chaffer*: a good commodity in the market. *Obs.*

1340 *Ayenb.* 191 Merci is guod chapuare, uor hi deþ wexe þe timliche guodes. **1581** J. BELL *Haddon's Answ. Osor.* 271/2 The old Proverbe (Gold is good chaffer howsoever it come). **1601** HOLLAND *Pliny* I. 134 Another Island..wherein pearles are good chaffer, and yeeld gainfull trafficke. *Ibid.* 377 Those cuttings are good chaffer, and sold very well to the merchant. **1610** —— *Camden's Brit.* I. 186 They be very good chaffer and right welcome merchandise.

†**3.** *fig.* cf. *ware, stuff.*

c **1449** PECOCK *Repr.* I. xvii. 100 As thou3 Cristis seid lawe were so feble chaffare. **1567** DRANT *Horace's De Arte Poet.* B vij, He will..ornaments superfluous from better chaffer scum. **1607** WALKINGTON *Opt. Glass* Ep. Ded. 3 Whoe have inriched whole reames of paper with the Indian mine, and golden chaffaire of their invention.

4. *Comb.* **chaffer-whale**, 'the round-lipped whale' (Jam.).

1809 EDMONSTON *Zetland* II. 300 (Jam.) *Delphinus Orca* (Linn.), Chaffer-whale, Grampus. **1822** SCOTT *Pirate* x, He is like the greedy chaffer-whale, that will change his course and dive for the most petty coin which a fisher can cast at him. [Merely taken from Edmonston, l.c.]

chaffer ('tʃɑːfə(r), -æ-), *sb.*^{2} *colloq.* [f. CHAFF *v.*^{2} + -ER^1.] One who chaffs or indulges in banter.

1851 MAYHEW *Lond. Labour* 327 She was considered to be the best 'chaffer' on the road; not one of them could stand against her tongue.

chaffer, *sb.*^{3}: see CHAFER.

chaffer ('tʃæfə(r)), *v.* Forms: 4 chapfari, 4-5 **cheffare(n**, **chaffare(n**, 5-6 **chaffare**, **chaffere**, 5- **chaffer.** (See also the sb.) [In the *Ayenbite* (1340) *chapfar-i*, f. *chapfare*, CHAFFER *sb.*^{1}: cf. the vbs. *to trade, traffic*, also f. the sbs.]

†**1.** *intr.* To trade, buy and sell, deal in merchandise; to traffic. *Obs.* exc. as in b.

1340 *Ayenb.* 162 þe borgeys wylneþ to chapfari an to wynne. **1340-70** *Alisaunder* 1210 It [Byzaunce] was chosen for cheefe to cheffaren in. **1388** WYCLIF *Luke* xix. 13 Chaffare 3e, til Y come. *c* **1440** *Gesta Rom.* 389 (Add. MS.) He wente, ande Chaffared faste, and wanne mekille. **1601** HOLLAND *Pliny* I. 94 With whom they chaffer and traffick only for a certaine precious stone..which we call a Carbuncle. **1640** H. GRIMSTON in Rushw. *Hist. Coll.* III. (1692) I. 122 This great Arch-bishop of Canterbury..hath most unworthily trucked and chaffered in the meanest of them.

b. passing into the sense of 2.

1692 DRYDEN *Epil. Hen. II*, 24 The play-house is a kind of market-place; One chaffers for a voice, another for a face. *a* **1700** —— *Fables, Gd. Parson* 70 To chaffer for preferment with his gold, Where bishoprics and sinecures are sold. **1858** LONGF. *M. Standish* VII. 37 The traders Touching at times on the coast, to barter and chaffer for peltries.

†**c.** Const. *to.* (*Obs. rare.*)

1649 G. DANIEL *Trinarch., Rich. II*, clxiii, But Hee, who knew the valew of his blood, Chaffers to his Ambition.

2. Now chiefly in the sense: To treat about a bargain; to bargain, haggle about terms or price.

1725 DE FOE *Voy. round W.* (1840) 86 They were longer than ordinary in making their market. While they were thus chaffering on board, etc. **1759** STERNE *Tr. Shandy* (1802) I. ix. 21, I hate chaffering and higgling for a few guineas in a dark entry. **1828** MISS MITFORD *Village* Ser. III. (1863) 78 They were chaffering about the price. **1851** D. JERROLD *St. Giles* vi. 54 Titled gentlemen, coming about me and chaffering with me for that little jewel. **1856** MRS. BROWNING *Aur. Leigh* v. 1264 Having chaffered for my book's price with the publisher. **1865** W. PALGRAVE *Arabia* I. 155 They will chaffer half a day about a penny. **1871** *Athenæum* 30 Sept. 423 The merchants go in, not to dally and chaffer, but to buy.

3. *transf.* and *fig.* (from 1 and 2). To deal, bargain, haggle, discuss terms, bandy words.

1377 LANGL. *P. Pl.* B. xv. 160 Charite..ne chaffareth nou3te, ne chalengeth, ne craueth. *a* **1617** HIERON *Wks.* I. 60 The best course..is..not so much as to vse any speeches of chafering with him [the atheist]. **1827** SCOTT *Highl. Widow* v, Thinkest thou to chaffer with Him, who formed the earth, and spread out the heavens? **1828** CARLYLE *Misc.* (1857) I. 227 And so stand chaffering with Fate. **1860** MOTLEY *Netherl.* (1868) I. ii. 59 That each Province should chaffer as little as possible about details.

4. *trans.* †**a.** To buy and sell; to traffic in; to exchange, barter. *Obs.*

c **1400** *Plowman's T.* xii. in *Chaucer's Wks.* (1562),[That] with pride punished the poore..With money filled many a male And chaffren churches when thei fall. **1591** SPENSER *M. Hubberd* 1159 He chaffred Chayres in which Churchmen were set. **1650** FULLER *Pisgah* II. v. 127 Horsemen as well as horses were chaffered in their markets. **1680** H. MORE *Apocal. Apoc.* 182 Great Dignities and Preferments, which she chaffered for the maintaining..her own interest.

†**b.** *fig.* (*to chaffer words*: to exchange or bandy words.) *Obs.*

1596 SPENSER *F.Q.* II. v. 3 He never staid to greete, Ne chaffar words, prowd corage to provoke. **1600** FAIRFAX *Tasso* XVI. xliii. 289 Sworne foes sometime will talke, and chaffer words. **1624** BP. MOUNTAGU *Gagg* 89 Merchants..that chaffer Heaven and Happinesse for the reward of iniquity. **1652** BENLOWES *Theoph.* I. xxix, Go chaffer blisse for pleasure.

c. modified by *away, down,* †*forth.*

1530 LATIMER *Serm. & Rem.* (1845) 307 Not to hide..but to chaffer it forth to others. **1649** BP. REYNOLDS *Hosea* ii. 77 Wicked men..chaffer and grant away their time, and strength. **1813** SCOTT *Trierm.* II. xxi, 'Reserve thy boon, my liege,' she said, 'Thus chaffered down and limited.' **1827** HALLAM *Const. Hist.* (1876) II. xi. 353 They saw with indignation that Dunkirk..had been chaffered away by Charles.

¶**5.** '*To chaffer* is now to talk much and idly' (Trench *Select Gl.* (1859-73) 32).

Hence in WEBSTER, OGILVIE, etc.; but the statement seems doubtful; cf. however CHAFFERING *ppl. a.* 1856.

¶**6.** ? To mingle, interchange, exchange.

1720 W. GIBSON *Diet. Horses* i. (ed. 3) 5 Horses..which have too much White on any Part of their Body, which is not mixed or chaffered with Hairs of the Horse's Colour.

chaffer, obs. form of CHAFER.

†'**chaffered**, *ppl. a. Obs.* [f. CHAFFER *v.* 4 + -ED^1.] Trafficked or dealt in, bartered.

1377 LANGL. *P. Pl.* B. xv. 105 Tythes of vntrewe þinge ytilied or chaffared. **1597** *2nd Pt. Return Pernass.* II. iii. 646 With the reuenewes of my chafred church. *Ibid.* III. ii. 1265 And make Indentures of their chaffred skins.

chafferer ('tʃæfərə(r)). [f. CHAFFER *v.* + -ER^1.] One who chaffers; a dealer, bargainer.

1382 WYCLIF *Ecclus.* xxvi. 28 Hard is delyuered the chaffarere [**1388** marchaunt] fro his necgligence. **1552** HULOET, Chafferer of wares, *negotiator.* **1631** SANDERSON *Serm. ad Aulam* i. (1681) II. 5 Bribing and Simoniacal Chafferers have climbed up the highest rounds of Civil and Ecclesiastical Preferments. **1870** LOWELL *Study Wind.* 258 The tongue..learned of nurses and chafferers in the market.

chaffering ('tʃæfərɪŋ), *vbl. sb.* The action of the vb. CHAFFER: †**a.** buying and selling, dealing, trading; **b.** bargaining, haggling; **c.** *fig.*

1382 WYCLIF *Prov.* iii. 14 Betere is the purchasing of it than the chaffering [**1388** marchaundie] of gold and siluer. *c* **1440** *Promp. Parv.* 68 Chafferynge, *mercacio.* *c* **1449** PECOCK *Repr.* I. iii. 16 In mennis bargenyngis and cheffaringis to gidere. **1583** GOLDING *Calvin on Deut.* lxxv. 463 If we fall to such Chaffering with him [God]. **1597-8** BP. HALL *Sat.* II. v. 14 A thousand patrons..bring Their new-falne churches to the chaffering. **1794** GODWIN *Cal. Williams* 250 After some chaffering, they agreed to accept eleven guineas. **1860** MOTLEY *Netherl.* (1868) I. vi. 299 Now began a series of sharp chafferings on both sides.

'**chaffering**, *ppl. a.* [f. as prec. + -ING^2.] That chaffers.

1483 *General Sentence* in *Festival* (1532), Al maner of marchaundyse of chaffryng men and of men of craft. **1592** WYRLEY *Armorie* 114 Chaffering townsmen. **1856** MRS. BROWNING *Aur. Leigh* I. 954 Near all the birds Will sing at dawn, and yet we do not take The chaffering swallow for the holy lark. **1870** MORRIS *Earthly Par.* I. I. 117 In the market-place He stood and saw the chaffering folk go by.

chaffern, variant of CHAFERN.

†'**chaffery.** *Obs. rare.* Also 6 *Sc.* **chafery.** [f. CHAFFER *sb.*^{1} + -Y^3: see -ERY.] **a.** Merchandise, wares. **b.** Buying and selling, traffic.

1535 LYNDESAY *Satyre* 4495 Heir I haue bocht gude chafery. **1596** SPENSER *State Irel.* Wks. (1862) 552/2 Merchandize and chafferie, that is, buying and selling.

chaffinch ('tʃɑːfɪnʃ, -æ-). Forms: 5 **caffynche**, **chaffynche**, 6 **cafinche**, **chofinch**, 7 **chawfinch**, **chaffe-finch**, (8 **chaffinge**, 9 *dial.* **chaffy**), 6- **chaffinch.** [f. CHAFF *sb.*^{1} + FINCH; as the species of finch which haunts the barndoor and homestead, where it may be seen picking grains of corn out of the chaff and barn-sweepings: cf. the late L. name *furfurio* (in Isidore), f. *furfur* bran.]

A very common British bird, *Fringilla cælebs*, with pretty plumage and pleasant short song.

c **1440** *Promp. Parv.* 68 Caffynche, byrde, *furfurio.* **1570** LEVINS *Manip.* 134 A cafinche, bird, *frugella.* **1580** BARET *Alv.* C 288 A Chaffinch, a birde singing in colde weather: a spinke, *frigilla.* **1661** MORGAN *Sph. Gentry* III. v. 50 The Chawfinch. **1678** PHILLIPS, *Chaffinch*..so called because it delighteth in Chaff. **1711** STEELE *Spect.* No. 14 ¶13 The Sparrows and Chaffinches at the Hay-Market fly as yet very irregularly. *a* **1793** G. WHITE *Selborne* xii. (1853) 55 Vast flocks of chaffinches have appeared in the fields. **1845** DARWIN *Voy. Nat.* xvii. (1852) 379 Beaks..from one as large as that of a hawfinch to that of a chaffinch.

chaffing: see CHAFF *v.*^{1}, ^{2}, and ^{3}.

chaffire, obs. form of CHAFER.

chaffless ('tʃɑːflɪs, -æ-), *a. rare.* [f. CHAFF *sb.*^{1} + -LESS.] Without or free from chaff.

1611 SHAKS. *Cymb.* I. vi. 178 The loue I beare him, Made me to fan you thus, but the Gods made you (Vnlike all others) chaffelesse. **18..** WHITTIER *What of the Day*, The threshing-floor..heaped with chaffless grain!

chaffour, obs. form of CHAFFER.

'**chaffron.** Also 6-7 **shaffron**, 7 **shafron(e**, **shaferne**, 9 **chafron.** Another form of CHAMFRON.

1547-8 *Order Hen. VIII's Funeral* in Strype *Eccl. Mem.* II. II. App. A. 11 Seven great horses..on their fronts shaffrons of armes. **1610** GUILLIM *Heraldry* IV. (1660) Table 266 Ordained for Defence and Ornament; as the Shafrone, Cranet, Barde. **1617** MARKHAM *Caval.* II. 119 Then putting a Shaferne vppon the horses head, you shall softly..rappe him with the sworde vppon the Shaferne. **1811** MRS. GRANT *Highl. Superst.* II. 260 With a chafron of steel on each horse's head. **1835** SWAINSON *Quadrupeds* 297 A coarse dark patch of hair, like a mask or chaffron, which covers the forehead.

chaffur, obs. form of CHAFFER.

chaff-wax, var. of CHAFE-WAX.

chaff-weed ('tʃɑːfwiːd, -æ-). [app. orig. the same as CHAFEWEED (written *chafweed* by Turner), but in later times referred to CHAFF.

Turner applied *chafweed* to his '*Centunculus*', which was *Gnaphalium sylvaticum*, and to this or the allied *Filago* the name continued to be applied. But later botanists applied *Centunculus* to an entirely different plant, to which chaffweed is now attached as an English book-name.]

†**1.** = CHAFEWEED. *Obs.*

2. *Centunculus* or Bastard Pimpernel.

1776 WITHERING *Bot. Arrangem.* (1796) II. 199 Bastard Pimpernel. Pimpernel Chaffweed. **1848** C. A. JOHNS *Week Lizard* 290 Small Chaff-weed, frequents the gravelly banks. **1878** BRITTEN & HOLL. *Plant-n.* s.v., *Chaffweed, Centunculus minimus*, L.—With. Generally applied to this plant by authors subsequent to Withering.

chaffy ('tʃɑːfɪ, -æ-), *a.*^{1} [f. CHAFF *sb.*^{1} + -Y^1.]

1. Full of or covered with chaff.

1552 HULOET, Chaffye or full of chaffe, *acerosus.* **1601** HOLLAND *Pliny* XIX. i, To lie and sleep upon straw-beds and chaffy couches. **1797** COLERIDGE *Kubla Khan*, Like..chaffy grain beneath the thresher's flail. **1865** *Lisabee's Love Story* I. 80 Looking dubiously at his chaffy trowsers.

2. Consisting of, or of the nature of, chaff; *spec.* in *Bot.* paleaceous.

1597 GERARD *Herbal* I. ii. 4 Whereupon do grow small scaly or chaffie huskes. **1683** TRYON *Way to Health* 201 From the Straw and Chaffy part mixed with their Oates. **1791** E. DARWIN *Bot. Gard.* II. 9 *note*, The chaffy scales of the calyx. **1851** GLENNY *Handbk. Fl. Gard.* 19 The flowers..are..of the chaffy texture known as 'everlasting'.

3. Resembling chaff.

1583 STANYHURST *Poems* Ps. i. (Arb.) 126 Lyke the sand, or chaffye dust. **1791** J. ARMSTRONG *Imit. Shaks.* (R.), Winnow the chaffy snow.

4. *fig.* Light, empty, and worthless as chaff. (Said of things and persons.)

1594 WILLOBIE *Avisa* 39 b, Chaffye thoughtes. **1603** CHETTLE *Eng. Mourn. Garm.* in *Harl. Misc.* (Malh.) II. 485 Stir up the chaffy multitude. **1612** SHAKS. & FL. *Two Noble K.* III. i. 41 Thou liest, and art..a chaffy lord, Not worth the name of villain! **1642** R. CARPENTER *Experience* v. xix. 331 That swelling and wordy, but chaffie, senselesse, and empty Pamphlet. **1819** J. MILNER *End Relig. Controv.* II. (ed. 2) 57 A dry and chaffy Epistle.

5. *Comb.*, as ***chaffy-textured.***

1877 F. HEATH *Fern W.* 21 Covered with various-coloured, chaffy-textured scales.

chaffy ('tʃɑːfɪ, -æ-), *a.*^{2} Now *rare.* [f. CHAFF *sb.*^{2} + -Y^1.] Given to chaff or chaffing.

1855 A. MACMILLAN in C. L. Graves *Life* (1910) 78 The comic 'chaffy' vein is very monstrous. **1876** E. C. STEDMAN *Vict. Poets* i. 24 The time is off-hand, chaffy, and must be taken in its mood. **1889** MRS. H. L. CAMERON *Lost Wife* I. v. 94 He answered in the most 'chaffy' tone.

chafing ('tʃeɪfɪŋ), *vbl. sb.* Also **chaffing.** [f. CHAFE *v.* + -ING^1.]

1. The action of the verb CHAFE, q.v., in its various senses.

1398 TREVISA *Barth. De P.R.* XVII. liv. (1495) 635 The juys of Elitropium..helpyth moche ayenst chauffyng and stoppynge of the lyuour. *c* **1440** *Promp. Parv.* 68 Chafynge, *confricacio.* **1483** CAXTON *Gold. Leg.* 100/3 Wythout felyng of ony hete or chauffyng. **1555** EDEN *Decades W. Ind.* (Arb.) 227 Vncessant rubbynge & chafynge. **1575** LANEHAM *Let.* (1871) 17 With spitefull obrayds and vncharitabl chaffings alweiz they freat. **1577** NORTHBROOKE *Dicing* (1843) 128 There is no harm if they play..without swearing, chafing, or couetousnesse. **1580** HOLLYBAND *Treas. Fr. Tong.*, *Eschauffement*, chafing, warming, heating. *c* **1590** MARLOWE *Faust.* viii. 6 He keeps such a chafing with my mistress about it. **1600** HOLLAND *Livy* II. xxix. 62 k, There was more clamour, brawling and chafing than any hurt done. **1656** RIDGLEY *Pract. Physic* 265 Until the part be first heated by Chafing. **1826** E. IRVING *Babylon* I. II. 151 The chaffing of its [the sea's] rocky and pebbled bed. **1845** R. HAMILTON *Pop. Educ.* x. (ed. 2) 314 The chafings of party strife. **1873** G. C. DAVIES *Mount. & Mere* xvi. 142 The chafing of the sheets, the rattling of the blocks, and the whistling of the gale in the shrouds.

2. *Comb.*, as **chafing-cheeks** *sb. pl.* (*Naut.*), 'a name given by old sailors to the sheaves instead of blocks on the yards in light-rigged vessels'; **chafing-gear** (*Naut.*), 'the stuff put upon the rigging and spars to prevent their being chafed' (Smyth *Sailor's Word-bk.*); **chafing-mat** (see quot.); **chafing-pan** = CHAFING-DISH.

1840 R. DANA *Bef. Mast* iii. 5 Wherever any of the..ropes..are chafing or wearing upon it, there 'chafing gear', as it is called, must be put on. **1867** *Chamb. Jrnl.* 30 Nov. 767/2 An improved chafing-pan..which instead of fuel, has a small lamp. **1882** *Daily Tel.* 12 Sept. 2/1 Dead-eyes to turn in, chafing gear to look after, reef-knots to point. **1883** *Century Mag.* Oct. 941/1 Putting on chafing-mats to protect those parts of the rigging most exposed to wear.

ˈchafing, *ppl. a.* [f. as prec. + -ING².] That chafes; in various senses of the vb.

1539 *St. Papers* in Froude *Hist. Eng.* (1880) III. 433 He is so hawte & chafing that men be afeared to speak to him. **1561** HOLLYBUSH *Hom. Apoth.* 27 b, Let hym eate no..chafynge or inflamynge meate. **1762** CHURCHILL *Ghost* III. Wks. 1774 II. 55 Not quite so fast as Terror rides When He the chafing winds bestrides. **1843** J. MARTINEAU *Chr. Life* (1867) 239 The miseries of a blank and chafing mind. **1865** LIVINGSTONE *Zambesi* xii. 251 To spill us all into the chafing river.

ˈchafing-dish. Also 6 chaffyndyche, 6–8 chafindish, 7 chaffendish, chafen-dish, 5–9 chaffing-dish. [f. CHAFING *vbl. sb.* + DISH *sb.*] A vessel to hold burning charcoal or other fuel, for heating anything placed upon it; a portable grate.

1483 *Act 1 Rich. III*, c. 12 §2 Holy-water Stopps, Chaffing-dishes, Hanging Lavers. **1538** *Bury Wills* (1850) 134, I beqwethe Allso to my syster Mason a chaffyndyche. **1580** NORTH *Plutarch* (1676) 473 A Chafindish with Coals. **1612** WOODALL *Surg. Mate* Wks. (1653) 203 Have ever ready a Chaffen-dish with fire..to warm clouts. **1653** WALTON *Angler* ii. 58 Let him [a Chub] then be boiled gently over a Chafing-dish with wood coles. **1693** BOYLE *Med. Exp.* iii. 27 A Chafen-dish with Embers. **1825** SCOTT *Talism.* vii, A chaffing-dish filled with charcoal. **1843** PRESCOTT *Mexico* (1850) I. 131 The meats were kept warm by chafing-dishes.

chafir, -or, -our, -yr, etc., obs. ff. CHAFER, CHAFFER.

†**chaflet.** *Obs. rare.* [Cf. OF. *chafault*, SCAFFOLD.] ? A scaffold, platform, elevated stage. (Cf. CHASELETTE.)

1470–85 MALORY *Arthur* (1817) II. 436 Kynge Arthur dremed a wonderful dreme, & that was this, that hym semed he satte vpon a chaflet in a chayer, and the chayer was fast to a whele.

chafron, var. of CHAFFRON.

chaft (tʃɑːft, -æ-). *Obs.* exc. *north. dial.* In 5 schaft, 9 dial. chaff. [a. ON. **kjǫft-* (in Icel. *kjǫptr, kjaptr*, Sw. *käft* (pronounced *chäft*) jaw, Da. *kieft* (chops), answering to a Gothic type **kiftus*, OTeut. **keftu-z*, possibly from a stem **kef-* **kaf-* 'to make a chewing movement with the under jaw', whence also OE. *ceafl*, ME. *chavel* JOWL, and various cognate words in Ger. and Du.]

1. The jaw, chap; usually in *pl.* (Chiefly *north.*, and since 17th c. only *dial.*)

a **1300** *Cursor M.* 7510 (Cott.) A bere, a leon, bath i mete ..And scok þam be þe berdes sua þat i þair chafftes [*other MSS.* chauelis, chaulis, chaules] raue in tua. *c* **1420** *Anturs Arth.* xi, Off the schaft & the shol shaturt to the shin. **1483** *Cath. Angl.* 57 A Chafte, *maxilla.* **1535** COVERDALE *Job* xxix. 17, I brake the chaftes of yᵉ vnrighteous. *Ibid.* xl. 12 Canst thou..bore his chaftes thorow with an aule? **1558** Q. KENNEDY *Compend. Tract.* in *Misc. Wodr. Soc.* (1844) 160 To cry out with oppin chaftes. **1597** LOWE *Chirurg.* (1634) 195 Debility of the nerves which moveth the chaftes. **1686** G. STUART *Joco-Ser. Disc.* 64 As slyly as thy fause chafts waggs. **1818** SCOTT *Hrt. Midl.* x, 'Like to gaunt our chafts aff.' **1864** ATKINSON *Whitby Gloss.*, *Chafts* or *Chaffs*, the jaws. 'Chaffs tied up', dead. **1875** *Lanc. Gloss.* (E.D.S.), *Chaffs* (N. Lanc.), *Chuffs* (S. Lanc.), jaw bones.

2. *Comb.*, as *chaft-blade, -bone*; *chaft-fallen* adj.

a **1300** *Cursor M.* 1073 Wit þe chafte ban of a ded has.. slan he was. **1535** COVERDALE *Ps.* lvii[i]. 6 Smyte the chaft bones of the lyons whelpes. **1597** LOWE *Chirurg.* (1634) 140 Underneath the chaftbone. **1863** ATKINSON *Danby Provinc.*, *N. Riding Yorksh.*, *Chaff-bone*, the jaw-bone.

chaft(e, obs. form of SHAFT: obs. pa. t. & pple. of CHAFE *v.*

[**chafter** (in Levins), mispr. for CHASTER.]

chagal (ˈtʃɑːgəl). Also **chaghal, chagul.** [a. Hindi *chāgal*, ad. Skr. *chāgala-* coming from a goat.] A water-bottle usually of canvas or leather.

1909 WEBSTER, Chagul. **1920** *Blackw. Mag.* Oct. 461/2 Laughing men carrying canvas chagals for water. **1923** *Ibid.* Sept. 398/2 Our chaguls or canvas water-bottles..are always ice-cold from the joggling about and evaporation. **1925** E. O. SHEBBEARE in E. F. Norton *Fight for Everest 1924* 367 It is suggested that a future expedition take a couple of pakhals or collapsible chaghals. **1959** M. PUGH *Chancer* 101 Both of my hands were at holding the chagal straps off my weary shoulders.

‖**chagan** (kaˈgɑːn). *Hist.* [ad. late L. *chagānus, cagānus*, in Byz. Gr. χαγᾶνος, ad. Old Turkish *khāqān* king, sovereign; see CHAM and KHAN.] An ancient form of the word KHAN; applied (after the mediæval Latin and Greek chroniclers) to the sovereign of the Avars in the 6th and 7th centuries.

1776–81 GIBBON *Decl. & F.* xlii. (1875) 719 The Avars.. the chagan, the peculiar title of their king. *Ibid.* xlvi. (1875) 800 When the Roman envoys approached the presence of the chagan. **1842** *Penny Cycl.* XXIV. 73/2 The Khazars.. their kings were called Chagan or more correctly Khaghan, which was the name of the old Mongol kings a thousand years before the appearance of the Khazars. *Ibid.* 74/2 The Russians in 1016..made their khaghan Georges Tzula a prisoner.

Chagas'(s) disease (ˈtʃɑːgəs). [f. the name of Carlos *Chagas*, Sr. (1879–1934), Brazilian physician.] A progressive trypanosomiasis, often fatal in young children, which is endemic in South and Central America and in Africa and is due to *Trypanosoma cruzi*, a parasite carried by armadillos and certain other mammals and transmitted by various blood-sucking bugs of the family Reduviidæ.

1912 *Jrnl. Amer. Med. Assoc.* 27 July 318/1 Chagas' Disease... The trypanosomiasis or parasitic thyroiditis caused by the *Schizotrypanum cruzi*, the parasite first described by Chagas. **1922** *Encycl. Brit.* XXXI. 896/2 Other Reduviid bugs have been shown to transmit the trypanosome of Chagas's disease in South America. **1959** SOUTHWOOD & LESTON *Land & Water Bugs* 152 The members of the subfamily Triatominae are blood suckers... In South America they carry Chagas' disease, a human trypanosomiasis.

Chagigah (həˈgiːgə). [Heb. *ḥᵃgīgāh.*] The voluntary sacrifices offered at the three great feasts, Passover, Pentecost, and Tabernacles.

1846 GEO. ELIOT tr. *D. F. Strauss's Life Jesus* III. 144 It [*sc.* the entering of a Gentile house in the morning] would have been such [*sc.* a disqualification] for the partaking of the Chagiga, which was eaten in the afternoon. **1891** A. W. STREANE (*title*) A translation of the treatise Chagigah from the Babylonian Talmud. **1933** H. DANBY tr. *Mishnah* II. 211 *Hagigah* ('The Festal-*Offering*')... The principal subject is the manner of fulfilment of Deut. 16¹⁶. **1966** WERBLOWSKY & WIGODER *Encycl. Jewish Relig.* (1967) 167/2 *Ḥagigah*,.. last tractate in the Mishnah order MOED. It deals with the festival duties, pilgrimage to Jerusalem, rejoicing, and the ḥ-offering.

chagrin (ʃəˈgriːn, -ˈgrɪn, ˈʃæ-), *sb.* Also 7 **shagrin,** 8 **chagreen.** [a. F. *chagrin* (1) rough skin, shagreen, (2) displeasure, ill-humour, etc. The sense-development took place in French, where the word meaning 'rough and granular skin employed to rub, polish, file', became by metaphor the expression for gnawing trouble (Littré). In English the word in the original material sense is now written SHAGREEN, q.v.

In the sense *shagreen* It. has *zigrino*, Venetian *sagrin* (Diez); ad. Turkish *çāghrī, çaghrī, saghrī*, rump of a horse, hence the prepared skin of this part, shagreen.]

†**I.** = SHAGREEN.

†**1.** A species of skin or leather with a rough surface: now commonly spelt SHAGREEN, q.v.

1678 PHILLIPS, *Chagrin*,..also the rough skin of a Fish, of which Watch Cases and handles of Knives are made. **1697** tr. *C'tess D'Aunoy's Trav.* (1706) 151 It is cover'd with Chagrin, and nail'd with Gold Nails. **1766** *Phil. Trans.* LVI. 190 The skin, which is black, is full of small scales, resembling chagrin. **1842** PRICHARD *Nat. Hist. Man* 92 It is of the tuberculated skin of the wild ass that the Levantines make the grained leather termed chagrin.

†**2.** *fig.* A shagreen-like surface. *Obs.*

a **1734** NORTH *Exam.* II. v. ¶129. 394 Thoughts which.. had made their skin run into a Chagrin.

II. Of the mind or feelings. (Often referred to, *c* 1700, as an affected and frenchified term.)

[COTGR. (1611) explains F. *chagrin*, carke, melancholie, care, thought; perplexitie, heauinesse, anxietie, pensiuenesse, vexation, or anguish of mind; also a disease or maladie: especially, such a one as comes by melancholie.]

†**3.** That which frets or worries the mind; fretting trouble, carking care, worry, anxiety; melancholy. *Obs.*

1656 BLOUNT *Glossogr.*, *Chagrin*, cark, melancholy, heaviness, anxiety, anguish of mind; also a disease coming by melancholy. **1656** COWLEY *Pind. Odes* Wks. 1710 I. 236 There are who all their Patients chagrin have, As if they took each morn worse Potions than they gave. **1677** TEMPLE *Let.* Wks. 1731 II. 426 His illness..derived, perhaps, from the Fatigue and Chagrin of his Business. *a* **1680** BUTLER *Rem.* (1759) I. 121 For, if he feel no Shagrin, or Remorse, His Forehead's shot-free, and he's ne'er the worse. **1712** POPE *Rape Lock* IV. 77 Hear me, and touch Belinda with chagrin; —That single act gives half the world the spleen. **1751** JOHNSON *Rambl.* No. 181 ¶7, I hid myself..in the country, that my chagrin might fume away without observation. **1840–7** BARHAM *Ingol. Leg.* (1877) 259 Each Saturday night when, devour'd by chagrin, he sits listening to singers.

4. *esp.* Acute vexation, annoyance, or mortification, arising from disappointment, thwarting, or failure.

1716–8 POPE in *Lady M. W. Montague's Lett.* II. xli. 4 If there be any circumstance of chagrin in the occasion..I must..feel a part of it. **1770** LANGHORNE *Plutarch* (1879) I. 474/1 Marius died, with the chagrin of an unfortunate wretch, who had not obtained what he wanted. **1807–8** W. IRVING *Salmag.* (1824) 152 Think of my chagrin at being obliged to decline the host of invitations that daily overwhelm me, merely for want of a pair of breeches! **1876** E. JENKINS *Blot on Queen's H.* 4 They managed..to.. conceal their chagrin if they felt any.

b. in *plural.* Troubles; vexations.

a **1744** POPE *Letters* (L.), I grieve with the old, for so many additional inconveniences and chagrins, more than their small remain of life seemed destined to undergo. **1771** NICHOLLS in *Corr. w. Gray* (1843) 148 If I met with any chagrins, I comforted myself that I had a treasure at home. **1824** MISS FERRIER *Inher.* xlvi, Mrs. Major had her own petty chagrins. **1887** MORLEY *Crit. Misc.* III. 154 Whom no vexations, chagrins, nor perversities of fate could daunt from fighting the battle out.

†**chagrin,** *a. Obs.* Also **chagreen, shaggarin.** [a. F. *chagrin* (15th c. in Littré) f. the sb.: see prec.]

†**1.** Grieved, disquieted, troubled; melancholy.

1666 PEPYS *Diary* 6 Aug., My wife in a chagrin humour, she not being pleased with my kindnesse to either of them. **1678** EARL QUEENSBURY *Let.* in M. Napier *Life Dundee* II. 58, I know he is very high, and often shaggarin, and angry. **1691** *Islington Wells* 9 To say they've Melancholly been, Is Bar'brous; no, they are Chagrin. **1721** RAMSAY *Wks.* (1848) II. 312 Weak, frantic, clownish and chagreen. **1722** DE FOE *Relig. Courtsh.* I. ii. (1840) 38, I grew chagrin and dull.

2. Chagrined; acutely vexed, mortified.

1706 DE FOE *Jure Div.* VII. 149 Hell's bauk'd; the shagrin Fiends the Conquest own. **1708** J. DOWNES *Hist. Rev. Eng. Stage* 29 At which the French look'd very Shaggrin. **1711** P. H. *View late Parl.* 127 He is not a little chagrin about the Habeas Corpus Act being suspended.

chagrin (ʃəˈgriːn, -ˈgrɪn, ˈʃæ-), *v.* [a. F. *chagrine-r* (16th c. in Littré), f. the sb.: see above.]

1. *trans.* To trouble, vex, worry, grieve. *arch.*

1733 FIELDING *Int. Chamberm.* II. iii, Pray remember the condition she is in, and don't do anything to chagrin her. **1755** *Mem. Capt. P. Drake* i. 5 Which so chagrined me, that ..I waited only an Opportunity of quitting them. **1792** ABP. MOORE in *Ld. Auckland's Corr.* (1861) II. 475 Those west winds chagrin me exceedingly, as they keep me in the dark about George. **1841–4** EMERSON *Ess. Self-Reliance* Wks. (Bohn) I. 23 Every word they say chagrins us, and we know not where to begin to set them right.

2. *esp.* To vex acutely by disappointing or thwarting; to mortify. (Chiefly *passive.*)

1748 *Anson's Voy.* I. i. 4 Mr. Anson was extremely chagrined at the losing the command of..so desirable an enterprize. **1796** MORSE *Amer. Geog.* I. 139 The captain.. was so chagrined at his disappointment, that he died of grief. **1826** C. BUTLER *Grotius* xii. 200 The contradictions which he met with chagrined him. **1878** BLACK *Green Past.* v. 37 Surprised and chagrined by the coldness of her manner.

3. ? *intr.* To feel trouble or vexation; to 'trouble'. [= F. *se chagriner.*] *rare.*

(In quot. it may be the adj.)

1727 FIELDING *Love in sev. Masques*, I would not have your ladyship chagrin at my bride's expression.

chagrined (ʃəˈgriːnd), *ppl. a.* [f. CHAGRIN *v.* + -ED¹.] Vexed, mortified; disappointed; formerly, afflicted, troubled, melancholy.

1665 PEPYS *Diary* 15 Jan., How chagrined the Prince was the other day, when he thought he should die. **1724** DE FOE *Mem. Cavalier* (1840) 10 The queen-mother and her party were chagrined at the cardinal, therefore the queen was under dissatisfaction. **1733** FIELDING *Int. Chamberm.* II. i, Be not chagrined, enjoy your friends, and take no notice of it. **1792** ABP. MOORE in *Ld. Auckland's Corr.* (1861) II. 477 Mr. Pitt was in the House, evidently chagrined. **1844** DISRAELI *Coningsby* VIII. ii. 293 Mourning over his chagrined fortunes.

chagul, var. CHAGAL.

chai (tʃaɪ) *Mil. slang.* [See CHA; perh. borrowed afresh from Russian or Arabic.] Tea. Cf. CHA.

1919 [see CHA]. **1946** *Penguin New Writing* XXVIII. 172 Here's a drop o' chai. **1959** G. SLATTER *Gun in Hand* vi. 141 Faces you'd meet..brewing up the chai in *casas* along the front.

chailles, obs. form of CHALICE.

chain (tʃeɪn), *sb.* Forms: (4 keigne), 4–6 **cheyne, chayn(e,** 5–7 **chaine,** 6– **chain,** (occas. 4 **cheine, cheingne,** 4–5 **cheigne,** 6 **cheynne**); *north.* and *Sc.* 4–5 **chenye,** 4–6 **cheny,** 4–7 **chenyie,** 5–6 **chenȝei,** 7 **cheinȝie,** 9 *dial.* **chain-, chenzie;** 4–5 and 9 *dial.* **chyne, chine,** 5 **schene,** 6 **schyne, chene, cheane, chane.** [ME. *chayne, cheyne*, a. OF. *chaeine, chaaine, chaene, chaane*, in ONF. *caeine, caenne* (= Pr. & Sp. *cadena*, It. *catena*):—L. *catēna* chain. With the ME. types in *-gne*, Sc. *-nȝe, -nȝie*, cf. mod.Picard *cagne*; mod.Sc. is *cheen* (tʃin).]

I. General sense.

1. a. A connected series of links (of metal or other material) passing through each other, or otherwise jointed together, so as to move on each other more or less freely, and thus form a strong but flexible ligament or string.

Chains differ in structure according to the shape of their links and the mode in which these are united; also in material and size, in accordance with their purpose of fastening, restraint, traction, ornament, etc. Hence such qualifying attributes as *gold, iron, cable, draught, watch*, etc.

c **1300** *K. Alis.* 683 His men him brought, by a chayn..a ragged colt. **1330** R. BRUNNE *Chron.* (1810) 174 þe chyne in tuo he hew. *c* **1340** *Cursor M.* App. i. 22054 (Edin.) An angel ..wiþ a mikil keigne [*other MSS.* cheigne, cheingne, cheny, cheyne] in hande. **1375** BARBOUR *Bruce* XVII. 623 And with ane stark cheyne [*v.r.* chenyie, stark chenȝeis] hald thame thar. **1480** *Wardr. Acc. Edw. IV* (1830) 123 A spering cheyne with staples and hookes. **1483** *Cath. Angl.* 63 Chine, *cathena.* **1530–50** GREGORY *Chron.* 192 Made ij stronge schynys of yryn, unto the draught brygge of London. **1552–3** *Inv. Ch. Goods Staff.* in *Ann. Lichfield* IV. 24 Itm. ij sensors of masten, on of them hath chanes of silver. **1598** BARRET *Theor. Warres* v. iii. 135 Many chaines of iron to draw the artillery. **1667** MILTON *P.L.* II. 1051 Hanging in a golden Chain This pendent World. **1680** *Lond. Gaz.* No. 1538/4 A Silver Watch..without String or Chain. **1712** STEELE *Spect.* No. 504 ¶5, I am to be hang'd in chains. **1712** *Lond. Gaz.* No. 4972/4 Abraham Deseser,..Watch-chain-

maker. **1859** F. GRIFFITHS *Artil. Man.* (1862) 126 No. 8 keys and unkeys the draught chain. **1884** F. BRITTEN *Watch & Clockm.* 50 When the timekeeper is going, the chain is drawn off the fusee on to the barrel. *Mod.* Children making daisy chains.

b. as a substance. (No plural.)

16.. in *Reliques Anc. Poetry* (1823) III. 15 He put in chaine full nine yards long, And he let goe his great gunnes shott. **1637** *MS. Abst.* in Maclaurin *Crim. Cases* xl. (Jam.), He was sentenced to be hanged in chenyie on the gallowlee till his corpse rot.

2. a. As employed to restrain or fetter; hence a bond or fetter generally; esp. in *pl.* fetters, bonds; *abstr.* confinement, imprisonment, captivity. ***chain and ball***: see BALL *sb.*[1] 1 b; also *attrib.* and *fig.* (*U.S.*).

1393 GOWER *Conf.* II. 132 They bounden him with cheines faste. **1611** BIBLE *Ps.* lxviii. 6 Hee bringeth out those that are bound with chaines.

1382 WYCLIF *Jer.* xxvii. 2 Mac to thee bondis and cheynus [COVERD. chaynes, **1611** yokes] and thou shalt putte them in thi necke. **1526** TINDALE *Acts* xii. 7 The cheynes fell of from his hondes. **1555** in Strype *Eccl. Mem.* III. App. xliv. 125 Jeremie..made a chain of wood..and [Hananiah] took the chain from his neck and brake it. **1667** MILTON *P.L.* I. 48 To bottomless perdition, there to dwell In Adamantine Chains and penal Fire. **1712** BERKELEY *Pass. Obed.* Wks. III. 129 The natural dread of slavery, chains, and fetters. **1734** POPE *Ess. Man* IV. 234 Who noble ends by noble means obtains, Or failing, smiles in exile or in chains. **1866** 'F. KIRKLAND' *Pict. Bk. Anecdotes* 154/1 One year's hard labor with chain and ball. **1879** FROUDE *Cæsar* iv. 40 Brought in chains to Rome. **1887** F. FRANCIS Jr. *Saddle & Mocassin* 62 A chain-and-ball gang of convicts slowly advanced, sweeping the dusty road. **1904** H. E. RIVES *Castaway* 213 Dragging the chain and ball of a life sentence of desperation.

b. *fig.* A binding or restraining force which prevents freedom of action. (Cf. *fetters, bonds.*)

c **1374** CHAUCER *Anel. & Arc.* 284 For either mot I haue yow in my cheyn Or with the dethe ye mot departe vs tweyn. **1526** *Pilgr. Perf.* (W. de W. 1531) 57 Excepte the chaynes & bondes of synne be vtterly broken. **1792** S. ROGERS *Pleas. Mem.* II. 142 Dusky forms in chains of slumber cast. **1787** BURNS *Streams that glide*, Streams..Never bound by winter's chains. **1822** HAZLITT *Table-t.* I. iii. 62 The chain of habit. **1871** MORLEY *Voltaire* (1886) 36 The first band of men who had shaken off their chains.

†**c.** A constraining force; a bond of union or sympathy; a tie. *Obs*

1377 LANGL. *P. Pl.* B. v. 616 þow shalt see in þi-selue treuthe sitte in þine herte, In a cheyne of charyte as þow a childe were. *c* **1400** *Rom. Rose* 4815 Love..is a sykenesse of the thought Annexed and kned bitwixe tweyne, With male and female, with oo cheyne. **1655–60** STANLEY *Hist. Philos.* (1701) 186/1 There is a Divine Chain, which..maketh one of it self, and those things which are united to it.

3. A personal ornament in the form of a chain worn round the neck; sometimes an ensign of office (***chain of office***).

(The chain of a locket, a watch chain, and the like, combine senses 1 and 3.)

1397 *Will* in Fairholt *Hist. Costume* Gloss. s.v., A chain of gold of the old manner, with the name of God in each part. **1429** *Sc. Acts* in Tytler *Hist. Scot.* (1864) II. 77 Serpis, beltis, uches, and chenȝies. **1463** *Mann. & Househ. Exp.* 154 My mastyr sold to my lord off Norfolke a schene of gold. **1535** COVERDALE *Prov.* i. 9 That shal brynge grace vnto thy heade, and shal be a cheyne aboute thy necke. **1580** LYLY *Euphues* (Arb.) 433 The new found Glasse Cheynes that you weare about your neckes. **1599** SHAKS. *Much Ado* II. i. 197 What fashion will you weare the Garland off? About your necke, like an Vsurers chaine? **1725** N. ROBINSON *Th. Physick* Introd. 4 Physicians at Milan..wear Chains of Gold, as a Mark of Distinction. *Mod.* The mayor was present wearing his chain of office.

4. *fig.* A connected course, train, or series; a sequence: **a.** of action or condition. ***chain of being(s)***, (a conception of the universe as) a continuous series or gradation of types of being in order of perfection, stretching from God as the infinite down through a hierarchy of finite beings to nothingness; the scale of being or nature (see SCALE *sb.*[3] 5); ***chain of command***, a series of positions of military or civil authority such that each holder is directly responsible to, and takes his orders from, the next above.

[*a* **1593** H. SMITH *Serm.* (1866) II. 186 Draws sin upon sin, till there be a chain of many links. **1605** BACON *Adv. Learn.* I. I. 3 The highest link of nature's chain must needs be tied to the foot of Jupiter's chair.] **1651** HOBBES *Leviath.* I. vii. 30 In the chain of Discourse, wheresoever it be interrupted, there is an End for that time. **1655** FULLER *Ch. Hist.* III. ii. §31 Here no chain of succession could be pleaded, where no two links followed in order. **1711** STEELE *Spect.* No. 109 ¶1 Without..Care to preserve the Appearance of Chain of Thought. **1712** ADDISON *Spect.* No. 519, The Chain of Beings, which has been often termed the *nexus utriusque mundi*. **1732** POPE *Ess. Man* I. 237 Vast chain of being, which from God began, Natures aethereal, human, angel, man, Beast, bird, fish, insect! **1742** [see CONNEXION 4 a]. **1794** MARTYN *Rousseau's Bot.* Introd. 1 This false idea ..reduced the vegetable chain to a small number of interrupted links. **1809–10** COLERIDGE *Friend* (1865) 31 The simplest chain of reasoning. **1875** DAWSON *Dawn of Life* i. 3 Link in a reproductive chain of being. *a* **1889** *Mod.* The chain of proof is complete. **1915** *Sphere* 23 Jan. 96/1 The general headquarters with the chain of command branching out into three corps headquarters. **1936** A. O. LOVEJOY (*title*) The Great Chain of Being. **1951** AUDEN & KALLMAN *Rake's Progr.* II. 35 In secular abundant bliss He shall ascend the chain Of Being to its top. **1957** *Times* 23 Aug. 3/1 Whether the traffic branch was directly responsible to the Chief Constable or whether the chain of command led through the Superintendent. **1959** *Listener* 23 Apr. 700/1 President Eisenhower has cherished the General's devotion to the chain of command: the habit of delegating total responsibility. **1970** *Daily Tel.* 11 May 9/5 The 15 companies of Independent Television have managed to avoid bureaucracy: their chains of command have been kept short.

b. of individual facts, acts, events, or the like.

1696 WHISTON *The. Earth* II. (1722) 184 Purely Mathematical Propositions are demonstrated by a chain of deductions. **1719** YOUNG *Revenge* IV. i, Day buries day; month, month; and year the year; Our life is but a chain of many deaths. **1789** BENTHAM *Princ. Legisl.* i. §11 A chain of proofs must have their commencement somewhere. **1871** FREEMAN *Norm. Conq.* (1876) IV. xx. 571 A strange chain of events. **1885** SIR R. BAGGALLAY in *Law Times Rep.* LII. 672/1 The Act provides for a complete chain of trustees.

c. A number of cigarettes or cigars smoked in continuous succession. Cf. *chain-smoker* in 19.

1908 *Field* 19 Sept. 544/3 Mr. Travis smoked a chain of long black cigars during all his matches... Mr. Hilton used to smoke a chain of cigarettes. **1930** AUDEN *Poems* 67 Smoking cigarettes in chains until their heads are in a whirl.

5. A continuous linear series of material objects:

a. of objects purposely connected, or connecting points in a line.

1791 SMEATON *Edystone L.* (1793) 197 The Chain of triangles from the Edystone to..Plymouth, for ascertaining their distance trigonometrically. **1810** HENRY *Elem. Chem.* (1826) I. 168 Another modification of the apparatus, which may be called the Chain of Cups, was proposed by Volta. **1838** *Murray's Handbk. N. Germ.* 464 By means of the chain of steamers now navigating the Rhine. **1870** ROLLESTON *Anim. Life* 132 The chain of nerve ganglia.

b. of objects naturally disposed in a linear series (with connexion actual or imagined).

1695 WOODWARD *Nat. Hist. Earth* III. i. (1723) 172 The Andes, that prodigious Chain of Mountains. **1748** *Anson's Voy.* III. v. 458 The Ladrones..an extensive chain of Islands. **1808** *Med. Jrnl.* XIX. 411 The vibrations will pass ..by the chain of bones, to the Membrana Fenestræ Ovalis. **1813** BAKEWELL *Introd. Geol.* 57 The most extensive mountain chains have a northern and southern direction. **1867** W. W. SMYTH *Coal & Coal-mining* 87 South of the St. Lawrence and the great chain of lakes. **1883** LLOYD *Ebb & Fl.* II. 218 A chain of undulating hills.

c. Short for *mountain-chain* (as in b.).

1830 LYELL *Princ. Geol.* I. 277 A submarine chain extending from Boulogne to Folkestone. **1846** GROTE *Greece* (1862) II. i. 1 The chain called Olympus. **1872** RAYMOND *Statist. Mines & Mining* 152 A southerly continuation of the Humboldt chain.

d. ***ladies' chain*** [Fr. *chaine des dames*]: a part of the second figure in a quadrille.

1825 *Analysis of London Ball-Room* 102 *Quadrilles*... Ladies chain. **1869** *Eng. Mech.* 3 Dec. 271/3 Performing with his partner a 'ladies' chain' in their fantastic quadrille.

e. A series of branch businesses, stores, etc., controlled by one owner or firm. Also *attrib.* (Cf. *chain store* in 19.) orig. *U.S.*

1846 W. L. MACKENZIE *Van Buren* 208 A convenient instrument for regulating future state elections through a chain of banks. **1895** *N.Y. Dramatic News* 14 Dec. 6/2 A chain of eleven theatres. **1906** S. E. SPARLING *Introd. Business Org.* 205 A better illustration of the chain of stores operated by the manufacturer is the Douglas chain of shoe stores and the Lipton tea stores. **1928** *Sat. Even. Post* 12 May 59/2 Managing director of a big chain-grocery concern. **1930** *Economist* 15 Feb. 367/2 Numerous concerns owning extensive 'chain' shops. **1931** *Ibid.* 14 Nov. 897/2 In Britain, taking chains and co-operatives together, some 3,500 groups controlling 45,000 retail outlets..occupy much the same position as do chain stores alone in the United States. **1933** P. GODFREY *Back-Stage* xiv. 181 Mr. J. J. Shubert..whose syndicate..owns a chain of 800 theatres in America. **1964** *Daily Tel.* 18 Jan. 8/2 The cuts that have already been announced by some retail chains in the past few days.

f. A line of people formed for a particular purpose, *spec.* a bucket chain (see BUCKET *sb.*[1] 6); ***grand chain***: a dance-figure in which each person dances with a line of people one after another (cf. sense 5 d).

1864 DICKENS *Mut. Fr.* I. xi. 104 Sixteen disciples of Podsnappery went through the figures of..the grand chain. **1876** C. M. YONGE *Three Brides* v. 72, I tried to get them to form a chain and drench the warehouses. **1932** [see *bucket chain*, BUCKET *sb.*[1] 6]. **1941** J. CARY *House of Children* 61 We went through a lancers together where all the girls.. shouted: 'Grand chain—do think what you're doing.' **1963** *Guardian* 17 Jan. 16/4 The staff..formed a human chain to rescue Chinese ceramics..from the firm's main showroom after a water main burst.

g. *Chem.* A number of similar atoms (usu. of carbon) joined in series in a molecule. ***closed chain***, a ring of similar linked atoms; ***open chain***, one the ends of which are not joined together.

1881 ROSCOE & SCHORLEMMER *Chem.* III. I. 113 The atoms may thus be represented as forming a chain, one atom being linked on to the other, so that when one of them is removed without altering the position of the others, the chain is broken. **1904** GOODCHILD & TWENEY *Technol. & Sci. Dict.* 111/1 When a number of atoms are joined together in a ring as distinct from a chain, the system is called a closed chain, and its derivatives closed chain compounds. **1928** KINGZETT *Chem. Encycl.* (ed. 4) 131 Open chains are regarded as having terminal atoms not mutually in combination, by which, for example, aliphatic combinations, such as the olefines and paraffins, are characterized. *Ibid.* 132 In closed chains, the terminal atoms are regarded as mutually combined, forming a ring, as in benzene. **1946** *Nature* 14 Dec. 864/1 The total chain-length of the alkyl substituents ranges from 13 to 15 carbon atoms. **1964** N. G. CLARK *Mod. Org. Chem.* ii. 11 The skeleton of carbon atoms forming a paraffin molecule is usually referred to as a 'chain'.

h. *Bacteriology.* A series of cells joined end to end.

1910 *Encycl. Brit.* III. 160/2 (*caption*) A chain of motile rodlets still growing and dividing. **1917** *Jrnl. Bacteriol.* II. 155 Though chains of cells may be developed. **1928** W. GILTNER *Gen. Microbiology* iii. 33 The spherical forms may divide in one plane and, if they cohere, form chains usually called *streptococcus*. *Ibid.* 34 The rods separate after fission, or form chains (the *streptobacillus*). **1930** R. ST. JOHN-BROOKS in *Syst. Bacteriol.* (*Med. Res. Council*) I. ii. 104 Division occurs either in one direction, whereby chain-formation takes place (streptococci) or in two directions... Among the staphylococci, however, short chains of organisms may be demonstrated, which show their relationship to the streptococci. **1951** MCLEAN & IVIMEY-COOK *Theoret. Bot.* I. 346 Bacteria were classified in the past chiefly on their microscopical appearance... The simplest form is..known as coccus. When these occur separately they are put in the genus *Micrococcus*,..if in chains, the genus *Streptococcus*.

i. *Computing.* A set of data, records, etc., related by chaining (CHAINING *vbl. sb.* 2); a linear list in which each item except the last contains the address of one successor.

1959 *Loading & maintaining Chained File for RAMAC 305* (IBM) 7 If the record is a link of the chain, but not the first link (home address), the record is deleted and the overflow address field of the deleted record is placed in the previous link. **1963** *Communications Assoc. Computing Machinery* VI. 273/2 The tree representation of this serial search reduces to the trivial case of a chain. **1967** H. HELLERMAN *Digital Computer Syst. Princ.* iii. 154 Loading can also be done in one stage instead of two by proper maintenance of chains already established when it becomes necessary to start a new chain at an address already used by a chained item. **1969** D. LEFKOVITZ *File Structures for On-Line Syst.* iii. 48 The system must..be able to extend the length of any chain indefinitely by adding more records to a given subfile. **1983** *Dict. Computing* 90/2 A block of data can be a member of more than one chain. The personnel file of a company may for instance be chained by factory number, by alphabetical order.., by age.

II. Specific uses.

6. A chain or similar construction used as a barrier to obstruct the passage of a bridge, street, river, the entrance into a harbour, etc.; a boom.

c **1374** CHAUCER *Troylus* II. 569 For other wey is fro the gatis none, Of Dardanus, there opyn is the cheyne. **1523** LD. BERNERS *Froiss.* I. ccccxxvi. 748 The chenesse of euery strete taken downe and brought into the palayes. **1556** *Chron. Gr. Friars* (1852) 19 Malpas of London drewe the cheynne of London brygge. **1697** DAMPIER *Voy.* (1729) I. 223 There was a Chain of great Trees placed cross the Creek ..we were afterwards near half an hour cutting the Boom or Chain. **1720** BURCHETT *Naval Trans.* III. xix. 400 The Dutch..broke their way through, and burnt the three ships which lay to defend the Chain.

7. A chain fixed to a door-post, which serves to secure a house door within when slightly opened.

1839 DICKENS *Nich. Nick.* liii, 'Top bolt' muttered Arthur, fastening as he spoke, 'bottom bolt—chain—bar—double-lock—and key.' **1862** THACKERAY *Philip* II. xix, Mary came down stairs, and opened the hall-door, keeping the chain fastened, and asked him what he wanted.

8. Part of a curb or bridle.

1617 MARKHAM *Caval.* II. 14 The Cavezan..in fashion of a Chaine, & in our English phrase commonly called the Chaine.

9. a. A measuring line, used in land-surveying, formed of one hundred iron rods called links jointed together by eyes at their ends.

At first chains of varying length were used or proposed; but that described by Gunter in 1624 is the one now adopted; it measures 66 feet or 4 poles, divided into 100 links.

1610 W. FOLKINGHAM *Art of Survey* To Rdr. 1 The Beame and Chaine balke no Truthes, nor blaunch Vntruthes. **1624** GUNTER *Descr. Sector, &c.* in *Penny Cycl.* VI. 462/2 We may measure the length and breadth by chains, each chain being four perches in length, and divided into 100 links. **1669** STURMY *Mariners Mag.* II. v. i. 3 The Chains now used and in most esteem among Surveyors are Three. The first I will name is Mr. Rathborn's..and that of Mr. Gunter's..this year Mr. Wing hath described a chain of 20 Links in a Perch. **1790** BURKE *Fr. Rev.* Wks. V. 312 An accurate land-surveyor, with his chain, sight, and theodolite. **1801** HUTTON *Course Math.* (1828) II. 54 Land is measured with a chain, called Gunter's Chain..of 100 equal links; and the length of each link is therefore..7·92 inches.

b. A chain's length, as a lineal measure, equal to 66 feet, or 4 poles.

An area of ten chains in length by one in breadth, or 100,000 square links = an acre.

1661 S. PARTRIDGE *Doub. Scale Prop.* 40 Let a piece of land be 36 poles broad, and the length 23 chains and an half. **1725** BRADLEY *Fam. Dict.* s.v. *Surveying*, It contains 12 Chains, 5 Links. **1850** MAYHEW *Lond. Labour* (ed. 2) III. 333 (Hoppe) The London and North-Western..in its long and branching extent of 477 miles 35½ chains.

10. *Arch.* A bar of iron, etc. built into walls to increase their cohesion; see also *chain-bond, -timber* in 19, CHAIN-PLATE 2.

1764 WATSON in *Phil. Trans.* LIV. 217 In edifices of this kind, for additional strength, the builders employ bars of iron, connected together in such a manner as their exigencies require; and these, though they have no links, are denominated chains. **1842** GWILT *Archit.* (1876) §1495 There are other means [for uniting the voussoirs]..such as dowels and cramps..these are far better than the chains and ties of iron introduced by the moderns.

11. *Mil.* Short for CHAIN-SHOT.

1804 MONSON in *Wellesley's Disp.* 544 A most tremendous discharge of round, grape, and chain, from their guns.

†**12.** Short for CHAIN-PUMP. *Obs.*

1682 *Lond. Gaz.* No. 1750/4 An Engine that delivers.. more Water than the Chain, and with greater Ease.

13. *Weaving.* The longitudinal threads in a woven fabric; the warp. (So in F. and Ger. App. sometimes misused for woof; cf. Cotgr. '*chaine de drap*, the woofe of cloth; the thread which in weauing runs ouercrosse it'.)

1721 C. KING *Brit. Merch.* II. 17 All worsted Chains, and only the Shute of Woollen-Yarns. **1774** *Act 14 Geo. III*, c. 25 Taking the Biers out of the Chains and withholding Part of the Woof or Abb Yarn delivered to them. **1810** J. T. in *Risdon's Surv. Devon* Introd. 25 The one [yarn]..forms the chain or woof. **1875** URE *Dict. Arts* III. 1110 The longitudinal threads, which are to form the chain of the web. *Ibid.* 1113 The European loom..[has] a warp-beam, round which the chain has been wound.

14. *Naut.* A contrivance used to carry the lower shrouds of a mast outside the ship's side, and by thus widening the basis of support to increase the firmness of the mast.

a. The part which secures the shroud to the ship's side, now commonly called CHAIN-PLATE.

1627 CAPT. SMITH *Seaman's Gram.* v. 20 The Chaines are strong plates of iron fast bolted into the Ships side by the Chaine-waile. **1769** in FALCONER *Dict. Marine.* *c* **1850** *Rudim. Navig.* (Weale) 105 *Chain* or *chains*, the links of iron which are connected to the bindings that surround the dead-eyes of the channels. They are secured to the ship's side by a bolt through the toe-link, called the *chain-bolt*.

b. *pl.* The assemblage of chain-wale, chain-plates, dead-eyes, etc., which form the contrivance to extend the basis of the shrouds; usually qualified, as *fore-*, *main-*, *mizen-chains*, according to the mast. *in the chains*: standing upon the chain-wale between two shrouds (whence the leadsman heaves the hand-lead).

1720 DE FOE *Capt. Singleton* xi. (1840) 193 To board her [a ship]..at her fore-chains on one side. **1825** H. GASCOIGNE *Nav. Fame* 52 In each Main-chains an able seaman stands, With well coil'd line and plummet in his hands. **1836** MARRYAT *Midsh. Easy* xiii. 45 Climbed up the fore chains, and found the deck empty.

15. The connexion in a galvanic battery.

1802 *Med. Jrn.* VIII. 318 These phenomena, however, only take place the moment the Galvanic chain is shut, or when it is suffered to remain shut..If the opposite action, occasioned at the moment the chain is separated, had entirely supplanted..the former.

16. The series of bubbles on the surface of the water marking the course of an otter.

1865 G. BERKELEY *Life & Recoll.* II. 317, I at once observed the 'Chain' or bubbles of an otter.

III. *Attrib.* and *Comb.*

17. *attrib.* Of chains; chain-like; of the nature of chain-mail (cf. 19).

c **1425** in *Hampole's Psalter* 1 This same sauter in all degre is the self in sothnes That ly3t at hampole in surte..þar it ly3t in cheyn bondes. **1886** RIDER HAGGARD *K. Solomon's Mines* xv. 240 We managed to get off the chain shirts.

18. General combs., as ***chain-link***, ***-maker***, ***-making***, ***-retailing***, ***-shop***, ***-verse***, ***-way***; ***chain-drooped***, ***-swung***, adjs.

1820 KEATS *Eve St. Agnes* xl, A *chain-droop'd lamp was flickering by each door. **1896** A. SHARP *Bicycles & Tricycles* xxvi. 400 The rivet..bears along the whole width of the inner *chain-link [of a bicycle chain]. **1920** MASEFIELD *Enslaved* 30 A stirring sleeper struck the bell Of chain-links upon stones. **1958** *Archit. Rev.* CXXIII. 310 The subtopian effect of chainlink fencing. **1960** *Farmer & Stockbreeder* 2 Feb. 121/1 The bottom half of the 6ft-high front is composed of galvanized sheeting, above this being chain-link netting because of the danger from foxes. **1860** *Offic. Report* in *Merc. Mar. Mag.* VII. 141 *Chain-makers, shipowners. **1886** *Pall Mall G.* 27 Aug. 11/1 The 2,500 chainmakers of both sexes who went out on strike on the 7th inst. *Ibid.* *Chainmaking is only possible by skilful hand-labour. **1887** *Daily News* 18 June 3/2 Mr. Matthews..said the wages in the chainmaking trade..were probably not more on the average than 7*s.* per week. **1935** *Economist* 14 Dec. 1215/1 The report of this '*chain retailing' organisation..does not lend itself to comparison with previous results. **1886** *Pall Mall G.* 27 Aug. 11/2 Working for some hours in the *chain-shops. **1820** KEATS *Ode Psyche* 33 No incense sweet From *chain-swung censer teeming. **1597–8** BP. HALL *Sat.* Postscr., Ariosto..whose *chaine-verse, to which he fettereth himselfe. **1690** *Lond. Gaz.* No. 2573/4 A plain Silver *Chain Watch.

19. Special combs.: **chain-argument** (*Logic*), a sorites; **chain-armour** = *chain-mail*; **chain-bag**, a woman's hand-bag made of fine metal chain-work; **chain-bearer** = *chain-man*; **chain-belt**, (*a*) see quot.; (*b*) a chain adapted as a belt for transmitting power; **chain-boat** (see quot.); **chain-bolt**, (*a*) *Naut.* one of the bolts by which chain-plates are fastened to the ship's side; (*b*) the bolt or knob at the end of a door-chain (see 7); **chain-bond** (*Arch.*), a chain or tier of timber built in a brick-wall to increase its stability and cohesion (see 10); †**chain-bridle**, a bridle with a chain (see 8); **chain-brow way** *Coal-mining* (see quot.); †**chain-bullet** = CHAIN-SHOT; **chain-carrier** = *chain-man*; so *chain-carrying* vbl. sb.; **chain case**, the protective covering of the chain gear of a bicycle, motor vehicle, etc.; **chain chest** *Naut.*, a locker in the channels for storage of wash-deck gear; **chain coral**, a kind of fossil coral, *Catenipora escharoides*; **chain-coupling**, a secondary coupling, consisting of chains and hooks, between railway carriages or trucks, which acts in case of any accident to the primary coupling; **chain dog**, (*a*) a dog restrained by a chain; (*b*) a chain having at each end a 'dog' or hook, which is driven into logs to fasten them together into a raft (*Funk's Stand. Dict.* 1893); **chain-dotted** *a.*, (of a line) marked with alternate dot and dash; **chain drive, driving**, a method of transmitting power by means of a chain gear, esp. from the engine to the driving wheels of a bicycle, motor vehicle, etc.; **chain-driven** *a.*, driven by means of chain gear; hence **chain driver**, a vehicle driven by this method; **chain gammoning** *Naut.*, gammoning consisting of a chain; **chain-gang**, a gang or number of convicts chained together while at work, etc., to prevent escape; **chain gear, gearing**, a gear for transmitting motion by means of an endless chain; esp. one in which the chain transmits motion from one sprocket-wheel to another; **chain gemma** *Bot.* (see quot. 1900); **chain-grate (stoker)** (see quot. 1889); **chain-guard**, a mechanism in watches to prevent over-winding; **chain-harrow**, a harrow composed of chain-work; hence ***chain-harrow*** v. trans. and intr., ***chain-harrowing*** vbl. sb.; **chain-hook**, (*a*) a hook fixed to a chain; (*b*) *Naut.* 'an iron rod with a handling-eye at one end, and a hook at the other, for hauling the chain-cables about' (Smyth); **chain horse**, a horse harnessed with chain traces, employed as an additional horse in drawing heavy loads, esp. up a hill; **chain inclinometer**, an instrument for indicating the inclination of a surveyor's chain; **chain-instinct** *Psychol.* (see quot.); **chain knot** (see quot.); †**chain-lace**, ? lace made with chain-stitch; **chain letter**, a letter written with an invitation to the recipient to pass it on to another (or copies of it to others), the process being repeated in a continuous chain until a certain total is reached; **chain-lightning**, lightning which appears to form a long zig-zag or broken line; see also quot. 1885; **chain-line** *Papermaking*, the mark of a chain-wire; = *wire line*, *-mark* (*a*) (see WIRE *sb.* 16); **chain-locker** (*Naut.*), the receptacle for storing the chain-cable; **chain-mail**, mail or body-armour made of interlaced links or rings; **chain-man**, the bearer of the measuring chain in surveying; **chain-mark** = *chain-line*; **chain messenger** *Naut.*, a messenger consisting of an endless chain; **chain-moulding**, an ornamental moulding imitating chains; **chain-pier**, a promenade pier, supported by chains like a chain-bridge; **chain-pin**, an iron pin or 'arrow' used in marking distances in measuring with the chain; **chain pipe** *Naut.* (see quot.); **chain printer**, a line printer in which the printing types are carried on a moving endless chain spanning the width of the printed line, a type being activated when it reaches the right position in the line; **chain-pull** [PULL *sb.*[2] 7], a chain used as the device for operating an electric switch; also *attrib.*; **chain-pulley**, a pulley having depressions in its periphery to fit the links of a chain with which it is worked; **chain reaction**, a chemical or nuclear reaction forming intermediate products which react with the original substance and are repeatedly renewed; also *fig.*, any such self-maintaining process; hence ***chain-reacting*** adj.; **chain-reflex** *Psychol.*, a series of reflexes in which each sets off the next; **chain riveting** (see quots.); **chain road** (see quot.); **chain-rule**, a rule of arithmetic, by which is found the relation of equivalence between two numbers for which a chain of intervening equivalents is given, as in Arbitration of Exchanges; **chain-saw**, (*a*) *Surg.*, a vertebrated saw forming a chain, having hook and handle at either extremity; (*b*) see quots.; **chain-sling** (*Naut.*), a chain fitted to encircle a large article, for hoisting or lowering; **chain-smith**, a mechanic whose trade is to make chains; **chain-smoker** [tr. G. *kettenraucher*] (see quot. 1890 and sense 4c); hence ***chain-smoke*** v. trans. and intr., ***chain-smoking*** vbl. sb. and ppl. a.; **chain-snake**, a species of lizard, allied to the Slow-worm; **chain store** orig. *U.S.*, one of a series of stores belonging to one firm and dealing in the same class of goods; **chain-syllogism** = *chain-argument*; **chain-timber** = *chain-bond*; **chain-towing**, a system of towing vessels in rivers, etc., by means of a chain or cable lying along the bed of the river which is wound over a drum on board the vessel; **chain-well** = *chain-locker*; **chain-wheel**, (*a*) a wheel used with a chain for the transmission of power; (*b*) a machine for utilizing water-power, which is an inversion of the chain-pump, the descending water pressing upon the plates or buckets and so driving the machinery; **chain wire** *Paper-making* (see quot.). Also in the names of various appliances of which a chain is an important part. Also CHAINBRIDGE, -CABLE, -PUMP, etc.

1860 ABP. THOMSON *Laws Th.* 200 The German title [for Sorites] *chain-argument (*Kettenschluss*). *a* **1797** *Walpoliana* xv. 9 The *chain, or ring armour was that used in the Middle Ages. **1851** H. MELVILLE *Whale* xlv. 293 The dolphin was drawn in chain-armor like Saladin's. **1902** *Westm. Gaz.* 29 Dec. 3/3 These glasses..can easily be carried in the modish silver or gold *chain-bag along with the handkerchief. **1736** in *Cal. Virginia St. Papers* (1875) I. 226 We do..appoint you James Thomas jun^r, Surveyor,.. To take three *Chain-bearers. **1798** *Let.* in *Deb. Congress 1808* (1852) 2741 You will see I have omitted taking those [depositions] of Mr. Gillespie and the chain-bearers. **1869** *Overland Monthly* III. 248 The chain-bearers signaling to those holding the ropes. **1794** W. FELTON *Carriages* (1801) I. 217 The *chain-belt is a contrivance to fix round the trunk, which it locks to the platform. **1794** *Rigging & Sea.* I. 164 **Chain-boat*, a large boat fitted with a davit over its stem, and two windlasses, one forward, and the other aft, in the inside. It is used for getting up mooring-chains, anchors, etc. *c* **1850** *Rudim. Navig.* (Weale) 105 **Chain-bolt*, a large bolt to secure the chains of the dead-eyes, for the purpose of securing the mast by the shrouds. **1880** BLACKMORE *Erema* xxii. (Hoppe) He..politely put the chain-bolt on the door when he retired to take advice. **1876** GWILT *Archit.* Gloss. s.v. *Bond*, The term *chain bond is sometimes applied to the bond timbers formerly placed in one or more tiers in the walls of each story of a building, and serving not only to tie the walls together during their settlement, but afterwards for nailing the finishings thereto. **1690** J. MACKENZIE *Siege Londonderry* 2/2 Some of their Clergy also..procured several *Chain-bridles to be made. **1883** GRESLEY *Gloss. Coal-m.*, **Chain-brow Way*, an underground inclined plane worked by an endless chain. **1636** HEYWOOD *Challenge Beautie* II. Wks. 1874 V. 26 My friend and I Like two *chaine-bullets, side by side, will fly Thorow the jawes of death. **1649** G. DANIEL *Trinarch., Hen. IV*, cccv, Chaine-Bulletts of his will Run through all Streets, and in the Waft, they kill. **1702–3** J. LOGAN *Let. to Penn* 3 Jan. in *Corr.* (1870) I. 174 Neither surveyors nor *chain-carriers will go thither. **1798** *U.S. Statutes* I. 543 For compensation to the assistant surveyors, chain carriers, axe men and other persons. **1816** U. BROWN in *Maryland Hist. Mag.* XI. 220 This afternoon hunts up Chain Carriers and an Axman or marksman. **1838** *S. Lit. Messenger* IV. 307 The surveyor and two of his chain-carriers were killed. **1798** *Let.* in *Deb. Congress 1808* (1852) 2739 The surveying at present is done by Mr. Gillespie, the *chain-carrying by Mr. Ellicott and Mr. Walker. **1909** 'O. HENRY' *Roads of Destiny* vi. 93 I'll..go back to chain-carrying for the county surveyor. **1907** *Westm. Gaz.* 9 Nov. 14/2 The Daimler Company..have designed their *chain-cases to act at the same time as radius-rods. **1909** *Ibid.* 17 Nov. 5/2 Detachable oil-bath chain-cases. **1884** S. B. LUCE *Seamanship* 4 *Chain chests. **1808** J. PARKINSON *Org. Rem. Former World* II. 20 The *chain coral (*Tubipora catenulata*, Linn.) composed of parallel tubes. **1871** LYELL *Student's Elem. Geol.* 449 The 'chain-coral', *Halysites catenularius*. **1895** K. MEYER tr. *Voy. Bran* I. 81 [She had] a large *chain-dog with her. **1878** ABNEY *Photogr.* 260 *Chain-dotted straight lines. **1931** *Engineering* 16 Jan. 91/3 One of the ropes is indicated by chain-dotted lines in Fig. 1. **1967** A. BATTERSBY *Network Analysis* (ed. 2) iii. 40 Ladder activities can be strung together as shown in Fig. 3.15 to form a ladder diagram. The chain-dotted lines which connect them represent lead and lag times. **1903** *Daily Chron.* 20 Apr. 7/2 The *chain-drive is infinitely superior to the belt. **1907** *Ibid.* 17 Oct. 8/2 A 5 h.-p. twin-cylinder Roc, fitted with a Peugeot engine and chain drive. **1969** *Sears Catal.* Spring/Summer 12 This automatic garage door opener... Boasts permanently lubricated ½-HP motor with center-mounted T-rail chain drive. **1887** LD. BURY & HILLIER *Cycling* xiii. 353 *Chain-driven geared-up Safety bicycles. **1898** *Cycling* 59 We do not anticipate that for serious riding it will oust the chain-driven safety. **1900** *Engineering Mag.* XIX. 740 Chain-driven heavy freight vehicles. **1909** *Daily Chron.* 22 Nov. 9/1 The new light Phelon and Moore is chain-driven. **1910** *Westm. Gaz.* 17 Feb. 5/1 The 65-h.p. and 75-h.p. six-cylinder *chain-drivers. **1887** LD. BURY & HILLIER *Cycling* xiii. 348 The successful use of the chain in tricycles opened the eyes of inventors to the possibilities which *chain-driving possessed for Safety machines. **1883** *Man. Seamanship for Boys' Training Ships* 22 Gammoning Fish..are..nailed on the upper part of the bowsprit, in the wake of the *chain gammoning. **1834** *Westm. Rev.* July 47 *Chain gang... They are to wear chains and the yellow dress, with the word 'felon' stamped upon it in several places. **1858** GEN. P. THOMPSON *Audi Alt.* II. lxxx. 37 How nearly the felon and the chain-gang are allied. **1882** *Harper's Mag.* Dec. 49/1 Chain-gangs of convicts are brought out from the prison. *a* **1877** KNIGHT *Dict. Mech.*, *Chain-gear. **1902** *Daily Chron.* 5 Sept. 7/5 Another car stopped near Hickstead with a chain-gear mishap. **1896** A. SHARP *Bicycles & Tricycles* xxvi. 422 The *average* speeds of two shafts connected by *chain gearing are inversely proportional to the numbers of teeth in the chain wheels. **1897** *Daily News* 30 Oct. 5/2 A boy..got drawn into the chain-gearing of the wheels. **1893** *Funk's Stand. Dict.*, *Chain-gemma. **1900** B. D. JACKSON *Gloss. Bot. Terms*, *Chain-gemma*, in Fungi, having the form of a septate confervoid filament, the segments of which are capable of growth; termed also sprout-gemma. **1889** *Cent. Dict.*, **Chain-grate*, a feeding-device for furnaces. The fuel..is slowly carried forward by an endless apron formed of cross-bars attached at each end to moving chains. These bars form the grate. **1930** *Engineering* 7 Feb. 178/2 It would..be simpler to burn it on chain-grate stokers. *Ibid.* 21 Mar. 391/2 In chain grates..a zone of reducing gas..is apt to form immediately behind the bed of coal. **1870** *Rep. Comm. Agric. 1869* 322 Only one patent was taken out during the year of the class known as '*chain' harrows, *i.e.* composed entirely of iron chains, no

beams whatever being employed. 1931 *Times* 16 Mar. 17/2 The desirability of chain-harrowing the land. 1931 *Times Educ. Suppl.* 28 Mar. 113/2 On stale pastures it is better to use chain harrows. *Ibid.*, Each hour one can do three acres of zigzag harrowing or chain-harrowing. 1950 *N.Z. Jrnl. Agric.* Feb. 116/2 Then..chain harrow to level the surface. 1884 F. Britten *Watch & Clockm.* 50 [The] *Chain Hook ..[is] the hook fixed at each end of the chain to attach it to the fusee and the barrel. 1876 *Porcupine* 22 Apr. 58/3, I have seen (when they have been carthorses) a chain put round their neck, and a *chain-horse hooked to it. 1906 *Westm. Gaz.* 7 May 8/1 Now we have a request to establish a chain-horse on Surbiton-hill. 1955 *Times* 11 May 14/4 He has been a navvy, chain horse boy and..a professional boxer and wrestler. *a* 1877 Knight *Dict. Mech.*, **Chain-inclinometer*, a form of level in which the inclination of the surveyor's chain is indicated on a scale by the pointer on the end of the level. 1914 W. McDougall *Introd. Soc. Psychol.* (ed. 8) 392 '*Chain instincts', instincts each of which manifests itself in a chain of activities. *a* 1877 Knight *Dict. Mech.*, **Chain-knot*. 1. A succession of loops on a cord, each loop in succession locking the one above it... 2. A kind of knot used in splicing. 3. The loop-stitch in some sewing-machines. 1578 *Richmond. Wills* (1853) 279, Vij own. of *chean lace, viijs. vjd. 1598 Florio, *Cadenelle*, little chaines, chaine-lace or chaine-stitch. 1906 *Daily Chron.* 27 July 6/2 In 1896 Miss Audrey Griffin, of Hurstville, New South Wales initiated a '*chain letter' with the object of obtaining 1,000,000 used postage stamps. 1940 C. McCullers *Heart is Lonely Hunter* (1943) II. xiii. 259 Think about chain letters. If one person sends a letter to ten people and then each of the ten people send letters to ten more—you get it? 1966 S. Marcus *Other Victorians* ii. 35 Half the legends.. can be traced, like the links of some bizarre chain letter, to their original source in these volumes. 1843 Haliburton *Attaché* I. xv. 262 They hante no variety in them [*sc.* drinks] nother; no white-nose, apple-jack, stone-wall, *chain-lightning, [etc.]. 1882 J. Parker *Apost. Life* I. 148 No man can report chain lightning. 1885 *Daily Tel.* 28 Dec. 7/2 'Chain lightning' [is] a strong foreign spirit. 1880 *Athenæum* 10 Jan. 56 The position of the water-mark and the direction of the *chain-lines, which are uniformly the same in every sheet of laid paper. 1960 Glaister *Gloss. Bk.* 63/2 *Chain lines*, the vertical lines on laid paper. 1883 *Chain locker [see *chain pipe*]. 1822 Scott *Nigel* iii, 'It's not made of iron, I wot, nor my claithes of *chenzie-mail.' 1855 Kingsley *Heroes* iv. 137 Clothed from head to foot in steel chain-mail. 1714 W. Winthrop in *Mass. Hist. Soc. Coll.* (1892) V. 299 The survayer and *chainmen being under oath. 1862 Smiles *Engineers* III. 157 Accompanied by an assistant and a chainman. 1923 *Handbk. Quality-Standard Papers (Amer. Writing Paper Co.)* 370 **Chain mark*, one of the wider parallel lines of a laid watermark. 1961 T. Landau *Encycl. Librarianship* (ed. 2) 189/2 Chain marks due to its manufacture on a mould in which the wires are laid side by side rather than woven. 1883 *Man. Seamanship for Boys' Training Ships* 14 An iron band fitted with teeth.., which enters the long links of the *chain messenger in weighing anchor. *a* 1863 Thackeray *Misc.* V. 359 (Hoppe) On the *chain-pier of Brighton. 1883 *Man. Seamanship for Boys' Training Ships* 12 Q. What are *chain pipes? A. Apertures through which chain cables pass from the chain lockers to the deck above. 1962 *Control Engin.* Jan. 91/1 *Chain printers have their print characters molded on a continuous steel chain and a magnet-driven hammer presses the form being printed against the chain. 1970 O. Dopping *Computers & Data Processing* xi. 166 In some variations of the chain printer, the chain is replaced by another device, for example, a reciprocating type bar. 1979 *Sci. Amer.* Jan. 105/1 (Advt.), Vertical and horizontal alignment is maintained to a precision usually found only in much more costly chain printers—within 0.005 inch in graphics mode. 1911 *Chambers's Jrnl.* 17 June 475/1 Users of electric light.. will be interested in a *chain-pull switch. 1945 H. D. Smyth *Gen. Acct. Devel. Atomic Energy Mil. Purposes* ii. 22 To run a *chain-reacting system at a high temperature and to convert the heat generated to useful work is very much more difficult than to run a chain-reacting system at a low temperature. 1956 A. H. Compton *Atomic Quest* 52 The idea of the plutonium bomb..gave military significance to the chain-reacting pile. 1926 *Chem. Abstr.* XX. 2122 Photochemical equivalence and *chain reactions. 1938 *Ann. Reg. 1937* 348 A chain reaction theory of excitation was put forward. 1938 R. W. Lawson tr. *Hevesy & Paneth's Man. Radio-activity* (ed. 2) xxiv. 254 An elementary process may be immediately succeeded by a 'chain reaction', and then the amount of chemical change may be enormous. 1945 *Statements relating to Atomic Bomb (H.M.S.O.)* 14 It was generally accepted that a chain reaction might be obtained in uranium which would yield enormous amounts of energy. 1947 *Sat. Even. Post* 22 Mar. 140/3 If you publish a candid article about any community, giving actual names of people ..you are..braving a chain reaction of lawsuits, riots and civil commotion. 1949 *Mind* LVIII. 270 The 'chain-reactions' let loose by the breakdown of belief in absolutes. 1954 *Sci. News* XXXII. 48 Polymerizations proceed as chain reactions, growth being propagated by activated molecules (free radicals). 1900 J. Loeb *Compar. Physiol. & Psychol.* (1901) ix. 144, I am inclined to recommend using the word *chain-reflexes, whereby the performance of one reflex acts at the same time as the stimulus for setting free a second reflex. 1959 *Encycl. Brit.* IV. 3/2 In a 'chain-reflex' the result of a foregoing reflex's execution is to evoke execution of the next succeeding one. 1888 *Lockwood's Dict. Terms Mech. Engin.*, **Chain Riveting*, rows of rivets placed in parallel lines, both in the longitudinal and transverse directions. 1895 G. J. Burns *Gloss. Techn. Terms Archit.*, *Chain riveting*, in this kind of riveting the rivets are placed in parallel rows in the direction of the stress, the rivets in adjacent rows being opposite each other. 1883 Gresley *Gloss. Coal-m.*, **Chain Road*, an underground wagon-way worked upon the endless chain system of haulage. 1846 Brittan tr. *Malgaigne's Surg.* x. 184 You may use the ordinary or *chain-saw. 1862 *Med. Times* II. 264 Plate of T. Matthew's chain-saw. 1909 Webster, *Chain saw*, ..a large saw for cutting coal, as one set with chisel points. 1957 *Gloss. Terms Stone in Build. (B.S.I.)* 13 *Chain saw*, a power-driven saw consisting of a chain which has cutting tips attached to the links. 1958 *Times* 18 Oct. 9/1 With a chain saw we can cut a cord of wood into logs in two Saturday afternoons. 1856 Kane *Arct. Expl.* I. xxix. 402 Away went one of our *chain-slings, and she fell back. 1934 Dylan Thomas *Let.* 25 Apr. (1966) 110 I've *chain-smoked for nearly five years. 1937 Koestler *Sp. Testament* 303 Got into a rage and chain-smoked all seven cigarettes. 1957 C. MacInnes *City of Spades* II. xv. 203 Have a fag..I chain-smoke myself. 1890 *Review of Reviews* I. 279/2 Bismarck is, or used to be, what the Germans call a *chain-smoker, that is to say, that he would smoke on and on an endless chain of cigars, lighting each from the ashes of its forerunner. 1930 V. M. Sackville-West *Edwardians* i. 17 These parties..were like chain-smoking: each cigarette was lighted in the hope that it might be more satisfactory than the last. 1953 *Encounter* Nov. 69/1 Only their very young, chain-smoking officer stared across the border. 1736 Mortimer in *Phil. Trans.* XXXIX. 256 *Anguis annulatus*, the *Chain-Snake. 1789 Morse *Amer. Geogr.* 61 Of the Snakes which infest the United States, are the following, viz... Chain [snake]. 1875 *Field & Forest* I. 30, I observed..a reptile which proved to be the Chain, or Thunder snake (*Ophibolus getulus*). 1910 *Sat. Even. Post* 10 Sept. 76/2 There were loud declarations of war from the manager of the association that buys goods for retail grocers fighting the *chain stores. 1922 S. Lewis *Babbitt* iv. §5 One of these cash-and-carry chain-stores.. cutting prices below cost. 1930 *Economist* 4 Jan. 18/1 The company's expansion into the chain store business has been carried on at too rapid a rate. 1957 J. I. M Stewart *Use of Riches* i. 11 And what about the chain stores—the poor man's Army and Navy, the suburban housewife's Harrods? 1870 Bowen *Logic* vii. 222 The complex abbreviated reasoning thus formed is called a *Chain-Syllogism, or Sorites. 1823 P. Nicholson *Pract. Build.* 582 **Chain-timber*, in brick building, a timber of large dimensions placed in the middle of the height of a story, for imparting strength. 1874 Knight *Dict. Mech.* I. 521/2 The *chain-towing system was first tried in France in 1732. 1845 *Athenæum* 1 Feb. 118 The enormous chain and *chain-wheel for driving the screw. 1889 *Ibid.* 30 Mar. 409 There are stout wires, about an inch apart, called '*chain wires',.. which run from top to bottom [of the mould].

chain (tʃeɪn), *v.* Forms: 4–5 **cheyne, chyne,** 4–7 **chayne,** 5 **cheyn-yn,** 6 **cheine,** 6–7 **chaine,** 6– **chain.** [f. prec. sb. in various senses. French has *chaîner* only with the meaning 'to measure with a chain', but *enchaîner* is cited in Littré from the 11th c.; *enchain* barely appears in late ME.]

1. a. *trans.* To bind, fasten, secure, with a chain.

1393 Langl. *P. Pl.* C. xxi. 287 Barre we þe ȝates. Cheke we and cheyne we. 1593 Shaks. *2 Hen. VI*, v. i. 203 The rampant Beare chain'd to the ragged staffe. 1667 Milton *P.L.* i. 210 The Arch-fiend lay Chain'd on the burning Lake. 1856 Emerson *Eng. Traits* xii. Wks. (Bohn) II. 90 The books in Merton Library are still chained to the wall. 1882 J. H. Blunt *Ref. Ch. Eng.* II. 305 He was chained to the stake.

b. *transf.* and *fig.*

138. Wyclif *Serm.* Sel. Wks. II. 367 Whanne that riȝtwisnesse is cheyned to God and al his creaturis. 1398 Trevisa *Barth. De P.R.* v. xxvi. (1495) 135 The sholders ben nedefull to bynde and cheyne togyders the bones of the breste. 1591 Shaks. *Two Gent.* i. i. 3 Wer't not affection chaines thy tender dayes To the sweet glaunces of thy honour'd Loue. 1795 Southey *Joan of Arc* i. 215 A hair that chains to wretchedness The slave who dares not burst it. 1858 J. Martineau *Stud. Chr.* 143 The mind given up to passion, or chained to self..dwells..in the dark and terrible abyss. 1876 Trevelyan *Macaulay* II. ix. 131.

2. a. To fetter or confine with a chain or chains; to put in chains.

c 1440 *York Myst.* xxx. 212 We charge you þat chorle be wele chyned. *c* 1440 *Promp. Parv.* 72 Cheynyn or put yn cheynys, *catheno*. 1591 Shaks. *1 Hen. VI*, ii. iii. 39, I will chayne these Legges and Armes of thine. *c* 1850 *Arab. Nights* (Rtldg.) 499 They chained him, and put handcuffs and fetters on him. 1850 Mrs. Stowe *Uncle Tom's C.* x. 86 Buying men and women, and chaining them, like cattle!

b. *fig.* To fetter, confine, bind; to restrain.

1377 Langl. *P. Pl.* B. i. 192 Chastite wiþ-outen charite worth cheyned in helle. *c* 1393 Chaucer *Mariage* 14 But thilke doted foole..hath levere Y-cheyned [*v.r.* ychyned, ychayned] be, than out of prison crepe. *c* 1440 *York Myst.* xxxii. 278 The payment chenys þe with-all, The thar no nodir comenaunte craue. 1593 Shaks. *Lucr.* 900 Or free that soul which wretchedness hath chain'd. 1634 Milton *Comus* 660 If I but wave this wand, Your nerves are all chained up in alabaster. 1870 L. Morris *Epic Hades* i. (1883) 53 Horror chained My parting footsteps. 1879 Stainer *Music of Bible* 167 Until such a system came into existence music was chained up within the narrowest limits.

3. To obstruct or close with a chain.

1603 Knolles *Hist. Turks* (J.), The admiral seeing the mouth of the haven chained..durst not attempt to enter. *c* 1630 Risdon *Surv. Devon* §192 (1810) 203 The haven is.. chained over when need requireth. 1674 in Picton *L'pool Munic. Rec.* (1883) I. 286 His new intended street..shall not be chained or obstructed against any of the towne.

†**4.** To surround like a chain; to embrace. *Obs.*

1606 Shaks. *Ant. & Cl.* iv. viii. 14 Oh thou day o' th' world, Chaine mine arm'd necke.

5. To measure with a (surveyor's) chain. Also with *out*.

1610 W. Folkingham *Art Survey* ii. v. 55 Extende lines from each station..(chayning the stationall line onely). 1816 U. Brown in *Maryland Hist. Mag.* XI. 224 [But for the rain] I should Certainly have Caused this line on the river to have been Correctly run and Chain'd. 1845 J. F. Cooper *Chainbearer* xxv, You're welcome to chain out just as much of this part of the patent as you see fit.

6. To secure (a door) with the chain; *absol.* to 'put on the chain'.

1839 Dickens *Nich. Nick.* lvi, Ralph..chained the door to prevent the possibility of his returning secretly by means of his latch key. 1886 Baring-Gould *Crt. Royal* I. v. 59 'Joanna..lock and chain after the gentleman.'

7. *Arch.* To bind (masonry) with a chain: cf. chain *sb.* 10.

1842–75 Gwilt *Archit.* ii. iii. §18. 962 A large number of steeples would..be found to have been well chained with timber or with metal.

8. *Computing.* **a.** *trans.* To relate (a data item, record, etc.) to a successor by means of chaining (chaining *vbl. sb.* 2); to order (a file, etc.) by means of chaining.

1962 W. Buchholz *Planning Computer Syst.* iii. 29 The control word also contains a refill address which can specify the address of another control word. Control words can thus be chained together to define memory areas that are not adjacent. 1967 G. H. Mealy in S. Rosen *Programming Syst. & Lang.* v. 556 Since entries in DICT do not usually appear in the order in which labels and principal pseudo-operations appear in the text, we need to chain these entries in the right order. 1969 C. W. Gear *Computer Organiz. & Programming* viii. 338 If the entries are chained together in memory, the speed is not improved, but it is possible to remove entries from the chain without leaving blank entries in the table. 1983 [see chain *sb.* 5 i]. 1985 *Personal Computer World* Feb. 150/1 Files held on the RAM file can be deleted, merged and chained.

b. *intr.* To lead or to be related *to* a successor in a chain (chain *sb.* 5 i).

1969 D. Lefkovitz *File Structures for On-Line Syst.* vii. 150 If this key in turn did not match, then it would chain to another list, and so forth. 1983 *Your Computer* (Austral.) July 21/1 The pointer for the first customer's record is the number of his first order record in the order file. Its pointer, in turn, is set to the number of his second order, which in this case is the record in the order file. It, in turn, chains to the fifth record of the file.

†ˈ**chainage.** *Obs.* [f. chain *sb.* + -age; cf. F. *chaînage*.] **a.** A fastening with a chain; chaining. **b.** ? A fee due for the use of mooring-chains, etc., in a harbour.

1611 Cotgr., *Enchainure*, a chayning..chaynage. 1691 T. H[ale] *Acc. New Invent.* p. 95 The Chainage of Ships belongs to the Admiral.

ˈ**chain-ˌbridge.** A suspension-bridge supported by chains or jointed rods of wrought iron, which hang in a curve between two elevated points of support.

1818 J. Anderson (*title*), A Design for a Chain bridge to be thrown over the Firth of Forth at Queensferry. 1836 *Penny Cycl.* V. 413/1 The Menai or Beaumaris Chain Bridge. 1846 G. N. Wright *Cream Sci. Knowl.* 60 Suspension or chain-bridges are employed, supported by tension-rods hung from continuous suspension chains fastened into highly elevated piers built on either bank.

ˈ**chain-ˌcable.** A ship's cable formed of a chain. Also *attrib.*

So called on coming into more general use in the early part of this century, to distinguish it from the ordinary (hemp) cable; now that it has almost entirely superseded the latter, 'cable' alone generally means chain-cable.

1830 Marryat *King's Own* xix, His nerves were like a chain-cable. 1839 Thirlwall *Greece* VI. l. 200. 1848 Dickens *Dombey* ix, Chain-cable forges.

‖**chaîné** (ʃɛne). *Ballet.* [Fr.] A quick step or turn from one foot to another, or a series of these, performed in a line.

1946 G. Robert *Borzoi Bk. Ballets* 354 *Chaîné*, a traveling step in which the feet are held in a firm first position, on point or demi-point, for a series of small regular turns. 1949 A. Chujoy *Dance Encycl.* 90 *Chaîné*, in ballet, a series of short, generally fast, turns, done in a chain, or straight line, across the stage.

chained (tʃeɪnd), *ppl. a.* [f. chain + -ed.]

1. From the vb.: **a.** Made fast, bound, closed, connected, united, with (or as with) a chain; fettered.

1613 Chapman *Rev. Bussy d'Amb.* iv, Chained shot. 1637 Rutherford *Lett.* cciv. (1881) 345 He hath left me a chained man. 1660 Ingelo *Bentiv. & Urania* (1682) ii. 181 [The assailants] set upon the chain'd-bridge. 1684 *Lond. Gaz.* No. 1979/1 Chained Bullets made at Brescia. 1816 Byron *Parisina* xiii, While Hugo raised his chained hands. 1860 Tyndall *Glac.* ii. §3. 244.

b. Of a book: secured to a shelf, desk, table, etc., by a chain in order to prevent its removal; also applied to a library of such books.

1846 *Wesleyan-Meth. Mag.* (Abr. ed.) II. 155/2 What a hold he has of that great chained Bible! 1890 W. Blades *Books in Chains* (1892) 4 The chained library at Wimborne Minster. 1908 *Daily Chron.* 10 Jan. 6/7 The old chained-Bible table previously in the church of St. Mary Bourne.. has been restored. 1931 B. H. Streeter *Chained Library* i. 48 The chained library in the mediaeval system was not the equivalent of what we mean by a library, it corresponded rather to a 'reference library'. 1963 *Times* 2 Feb. 10/4, I direct my trustees to hand over my said chained library to Sir Robert Hall.

2. From the sb.: Fitted, provided, or adorned with a chain or chains.

1552 Huloet, Chayned, *torquatus*. 1627 Capt. Smith *Seaman's Gram.* ii. 8 In great ships they use chained pumps. *a* 1796 Burns *Meg o' the Mill*, A fine pacing horse wi' a clear chained bridle. 18.. Sala *Mrs. Mellor's Diam.*, [He] was highly curled..chained, pinned, and locketed.

3. Of lightning: Having the form of a chain or jointed line. ***chained-lightning.*** Also *transf.*

1859 *All Y. Round* No. 17. 400 Lightning..now and then 'chained' or 'forked' was visible. 1872 Schele de Vere *Americanisms* 217 Chain-lightning..is generally..changed into *chained-lightning*. In both forms it is constantly applied to inferior whiskey.

chainer (ˈtʃeɪnə(r)). [f. chain + -er[1].] **a.** One of a surveyor's party who carries the chain; a

chain-carrier. **b.** One who twists material into a chain. **c.** One who tends the chain of a haulage system.

1849 C. Sturt *Narr. Exped. C. Australia* I. 323, I had sent Mr. Stuart and Mr. Piesse with a party of chainers, to measure along the line on which I intended to move. **1921** *Dict. Occup. Terms* (1927) §§03, 367, 399.

† **chainet.** *Obs. rare.* [ad. F. *chaînette*, dim. of *chaîne* CHAIN.] A small chain; a chainlet.

1623 Favine *Theat. Hon.* III. xvii. 560 From his tongue were extended forth small chainets of gold.

chaining ('tʃeɪnɪŋ), *vbl. sb.* [f. CHAIN *v.* + -ING¹.] **1.** The action of the vb. CHAIN; putting in chains; enchainment; connexion.

1387 Trevisa *Higden* (Rolls) II. 359 (Mätz.) þe chaynyng and teienge of þe grete hound Cerberus. **1398** —— *Barth. De P.R.* v. xxviii. (1495) 138 The ouer cheynynge of the honde hath thre bones that entre in to the holownes of the armes. **1583** *Grindal's Will* Wks. (1843) 459 Ten pounds towards the clasping, bossing and chaining of the same [books]. **1661** G. Bishope (*title*), New England Judged..a brief relation of the Sufferings of the People called Quakers..wherein the Cruel..Bonds and Imprisonments, Beatings and Chainings ..are shortly touched.

2. *Computing.* A method of organizing or storing data in which each item contains an address by which a successor may be located, so obviating the need to use contiguous storage locations.

1957 *Proc. Western Joint Computer Conf.* Feb. 225/2 We find that the over-all chances of a particular match being successful are 0.3 per cent for substitution, 13.4 per cent for detachment, 13.8 per cent for forward chaining, and 9.4 per cent for backward chaining. **1967** H. Hellerman *Digital Computer Syst. Princ.* iii. 156 The performance of the hashing methods [of organizing a file], especially the chaining method, is quite high; fewer probes are required on average than with the binary search. **1971** R. W. Lott *Basic Data Processing* (ed. 2) vi. 114 Chaining may provide for more efficient programs since such instructions don't require storage space for the address, and the movement and analysis of the address are eliminated. **1979** *Personal Computer World* Nov. 69 (Advt.), Supports full file control, chaining, integer and extended precision variables etc. **1983** *80 Microcomputing* Jan. 24/2 The program has also been updated to include chaining, killing, and merging of files.

chainless ('tʃeɪnlɪs), *a.* [f. CHAIN *sb.* + -LESS.] **1.** Without chain or chains: unchained. *poetic.*

1816 Byron *Sonn. Chillon*, Eternal Spirit of the chainless Mind! **1850** Blackie *Æschylus* I. 213 Free and chainless, Wild and reinless.

2. Of a machine, vehicle, etc.: without chain gear or chain drive as a part of the mechanism. (Usually implying its former use.)

1897 *Queen* 16 Oct. (Advt.), The best Chainless Cycle for Ladies. **1905** *Daily Chron.* 17 June 9/2 Mr. Napier was the first constructor to use this chainless form of transmission for a powerful car.

chainlet ('tʃeɪnlɪt). [f. CHAIN *sb.* + -LET dim. suff.] A little chain.

1805 Scott *Last Minstr.* VI. iv, Spurs, and ringing chainlets, sound. **1881** Miss Braddon *Asph.* III. 135 The handsomest of the chains, a cluster of many slender chainlets.

'chain-plate.

1. *Naut.* [see CHAIN *sb.* 14.] One of the strong links or plates of iron fastened to the ship's side under the chainwale, to which the shrouds are secured.

1692 in *Capt. Smith's Seaman's Gram.* I. xiv. 64 Main Chains and Chain Plaits. **1769** Falconer *Dict. Marine* (1789) *Cadenes de haubans*, the chains of the shrouds, the chain-plates. **1840** R. Dana *Bef. Mast* xxix. 106 We were loaded down to the bolts of our chain-plates.

2. *Arch.* One of a series of connected plates built into the walls of a building to give it greater stability: cf. CHAIN *sb.* 10.

1842 Gwilt *Archit.* (1876) §1882 The best remedy against this inconvenience [settlement of the foundation] is to tie the walls together by the means of chain plates.

'chain-pump. A machine for raising water by means of an endless chain; most commonly the chain passes in its upward course through a tube, and raises the water by means of disks or valves which fit the tube; sometimes the chain has simply a number of buckets or cups, by which the water is lifted to the top and there emptied out.

a **1618** Raleigh *Inv. Shipping* 16 The Chaine pumpe, which takes up twice as much water as the ordinary did. **1781** Archer in *Naval Chron.* XI. 288 The chain pump was choaked. **1830** Marryat *King's Own* xix, He requires the chain-pumps to be manned.

'chain-shot. A kind of shot formed of two balls, or half-balls, connected by a chain, chiefly used in naval warfare to destroy masts, rigging, and sails; a shot or discharge of this. Also *fig.*

1581 Sidney *Apol. Poetrie* (Arb.) 55 Thys argument..is ..indeed, a chaine-shot against all learning. **1591** Horsey *Trav.* (1857) 186 Everie shipe caries cannon and..powder [and] cheyne-shott. **1627** Capt. Smith *Seaman's Gram.* xiv. 67 Chaine shot..contriued round as in a ball, yet will spred in flying their full length in bredth. **1642** Fuller *Holy & Prof. St.* II. vii. 73 Dilemma's, two-edged swords that cut on both sides; Sorites, chain-shot. **1660** Ingelo *Bentiv. & Urania* (1682) II. 184 A chain'd-shot..cut off Atheophilus his main Mast in the middle. **1708** *Lond. Gaz.* No. 3878/4 The Admiral..had his Leg broke by a Chain-Shot. **1850** Prescott *Peru* II. 277 He was hit by a chain-shot from an arquebuse.

'chain-stitch. **1.** In needlework: A kind of ornamental stitch resembling the links of a chain; the work so produced, chain-work.

1598 Florio, *Cadenelle*..chaine-lace or chaine-stitch. **1640** J. Taylor (Water P.) *Praise of Needle* Pref., Fine Ferne-stitch, Finny-stitch, New-stitch, and Chain-stitch. **1820** Hazlitt *Lect. Dram. Lit.* 266 His figures are wrought in chain-stitch. **1876** Rock *Text. Fabr.* 83.

2. In a sewing-machine: A stitch produced by looping the upper thread, when only one is used, into itself on the under side of the article sewn, or by using a second thread to engage the loop of the upper thread; as distinguished from the lock-stitch; also *attrib.*, as in 'a chain-stitch machine'.

1867 *Gd. Words* 419/2 The sewing-machine..There are some which make what is termed the chain-stitch; they are useful for simpler work, such as hemming.

'chain-wale. *Naut.* [f. CHAIN *sb.* 14 + WALE.] A strong piece of timber secured outside the ship's side, almost abreast but somewhat behind the mast, whose lower shrouds it serves to extend and secure; now usually corrupted into CHANNEL *sb.*².

1611 Cotgr., *Port 'aubans*, chaine-wales. **1627** Capt. Smith *Seaman's Gram.* ii. 6 The chaine waile is a broad timber set out amongst them, a little aboue where the chaines and shrouds are fastened together to spread the shrouds the wider the better to succour the masts. **1704** J. Harris *Lex. Techn.* s.v. *Fishes*, The Anchor is haled up to the Ships Bow, or Chainwale. **1867** Smyth *Sailor's Word-bk.*, *Chains*, properly Chain-wales, or Channels.

'chain-work, chain work.

1. Ornamental work, in sculpture, etc., resembling chains.

1551 Bible *1 Kings* vii. 17 And whopes of chayne-worcke for the heed peces. **1611** *ibid.*, Wreathes of chaine worke, for the chapiters. **1720** De Foe *Capt. Singleton* ii. (1840) 35 One of the bracelets [was] of chain-work. **1815** Moore *Lalla R.* (1862) 29 But a light, golden chain-work round her hair. **1851** Ruskin *Stones Ven.* II. iii. §31 The..archivolts enriched with studded chainwork.

2. Work consisting of metal rings or links intertwined so as to form a net-work.

1864 *Times* 5 July (L.) The efficiency of iron chain-work as a defensive armour for ships of war. **1874** Boutell *Arms & Arm.* vii. 107 The body armour is a shirt..formed of interwoven rings, or chain-work. **1886** Rider Haggard *K. Solomon's Mines* xv. 240 We examined the armour..It was the most beautiful chain work we had ever seen.

3. A texture formed by knitting or looping with a single thread, as in the manufacture of hosiery.

1833 Brewster *Nat. Magic* xi. 289 The article Chain-work in the Edinburgh Encyclopædia. **1875** Ure *Dict. Arts* II. 813 Hosiery..is composed of a single thread united or looped together in a peculiar manner, which is called stocking-stitch, and sometimes chain-work.

chaip, obs. Sc. form of CHEAP *sb.*

chaip, var. of CHAPE *v. Obs.* to escape.

chair (tʃɛə(r)), *sb.*¹ Forms: 3 chaere, 4 cheiere, chaȝer, 4-5 chaier(e, chayer(e, 5 chaiare, chare, schayer, cheyer, cheare, chayr, 5-7 chayre, 6 cheyar, 6-7 chaire, 7- chair. [ME. *chaere, chaiere*, a. OF. *chaëre* (western and Anglo-Fr.), *chaiere* (= Pr. *cadera, cadeira*, Cat. *cadira*, OSp. *cadera*, Pg. *cadeira*):—L. *ca'tedra, cathedra* seat, a. Gr. καθέδρα, see CATHEDRA. *Cha-iè-re* was the regular OF. phonetic descendant of *ca-'ted-ra*; it was in Eng. also orig. of three syllables, afterward reduced to two *'cha-yer*, and finally (? under later F. infuence) to one, *chair*. In the dialects it is still commonly of two, as Sc. *cha-yer* ('tʃejər). In mod.Fr. the phonetic variant *chaise* (see CHAISE *sb.*) has taken the popular senses, while *chaire* is restricted to the ecclesiastical or professorial *cathedra*.]

1. a. A seat for one person (always implying more or less of comfort and ease); now the common name for the movable four-legged seat with a rest for the back, which constitutes, in many forms of rudeness or elegance, an ordinary article of household furniture, and is also used in gardens or wherever it is usual to sit. ***to take a chair***: to take a seat, be seated.

a **1300** *Cursor M.* 9954 A tron of iuor graid. Was neuer yeitt king ne kaiser, þat euer sait in sli[c] chaier [*G.* chayer, *T.* chaiere, *F.* cheiere]. **1297** R. Glouc. (1724) 321 Up a chaere he [Cnut] sat adoun, al vp þe see sonde. **1382** Wyclif *Matt.* xxi. 12 He turnyde vpsadoun the bordis of chaungeris, and the chaiers of men sellynge culueris. **1382** —— *Song of Sol.* iii. 9 A chaȝer..of the trees of Liban. *c* **1400** Maundev. xxiii. 253 Men setten him in a Chayere. *c* **1450** *Nominale* in Wr.-Wülcker 723 *Hec cathedra*, a chare. *c* **1450** *Merlin* xxi. 362 He sholde do sette ther a cheyer. **1553** Eden *Treat. New Ind.* (Arb.) 40 Tables, coberdes, cofers & chayres. **1555** —— *Decades W. Ind.* I. v. (Arb.) 85 Thynges necessary to bee vsed, as cheyars. **1564** Haward *Eutropius* IV. 39 In a chaire fast besides him. **1601** Shaks. *All's Well* II. ii. 17 Like a Barbers chaire that fits all buttockes. **1704** Steele *Lying Lover* II. (1747) 36 Set chairs and the Bohea Tea and leave us. **1751** Johnson *Rambl.* No. 141 ⁋10 Mistaking a lady's lap for my own chair. **1753** *Scots Mag.* XV. 36/2 She..desired me to take a chair. **1840** Marryat *Poor Jack* xlvi, Take a chair. **1870** Mrs. Gaskell *Cranford* viii. 116 The chairs were all a-row against the walls.

b. With various substantives or adjs. indicating the nature, material, purpose, etc., as ***bed-, bedroom, camp, cane, compass, folding, garden, hall, kitchen, leather, library, lobby, obstetrical, office, rocking, swinging, Turkey, wheel-chair***; † **great-chair** (dial. *big-chair*), an arm-chair. Also ARM-, BATH- (*sb.*²), CURULE-, EASY-, ELBOW-CHAIR.

1580 Baret *Alv.* C 295 A compasse chaire: halfe a circle, *hemicyclus.* **1711** Steele *Spect.* 52 ⁋3 An easy chair..at the upper End of the Table. **1711** Addison *Spect.* No. 72 ⁋4 The great Elbow-chair which stands at the upper end of the Table. **1737** Ozell *Rabelais* V. 220 Easy Leather-Chairs made..with..Springs. **1790** J. C. Smyth in *Med. Commun.* II. 477, I..found him..sitting in a great chair. **1796** H. Hunter tr. *St. Pierre's Stud. Nat.* (1799) III. 539 Having requested the indulgence of an easy chair at the sittings of the French Academy..the King, instead of one easy chair, sent forty to the Academy. **1830** Galt *Lawrie T.* IV. i. (1849) 145 He sat in the swinging chair. **1841** Thackeray *Sec. Fun. Nap.* iii, A servant passes, pushing through the crowd a shabby wheel-chair.

c. A glass-blower's seat furnished with long arms upon which he rolls the pontil; hence, the gang of men consisting of the glass-blower and his assistants.

1845 G. Dodd *Brit. Manuf.* IV. 51 Another workman receives it and sits down in a chair having two flat parallel arms sloping downwards. **1890** W. J. Gordon *Foundry* 137 Every two crucibles supply one 'chair'. The glassworker's chair is practically his lathe. **1897** *Worc. County Express* 3 Apr., There were ten chairs at the works, each occupied by a glassmaker, servitor, and footmaker. **1902** *B'ham Daily Post* 2 Apr., Eighty is the limit number of strawstem wineglasses to be made in six hours by a 'chair', which consists of three men and a boy. **1962** *Gloss. Terms Glass Ind.* (*B.S.I.*) 23 *Chair*, a special long-armed chair in which the craftsman sits when shaping glass. *Ibid.* 45 *Chair*, a team or gang of workers producing blown or pressed glassware by hand.

d. = *electric chair* (s.v. ELECTRIC *a.* 2). *U.S.*

1900 'Flynt' & Walton *Powers that Prey* 170 He was a copper, and we fly cops have got to send some bloke to the chair for blastin' him. **1917** J. Farnol *Definite Object* xviii. 173 I've left papers—proofs, 'n' it'ud be the chair for yours —savvy? **1926** G. D. H. & M. I. Cole *Blatchington Tangle* xiv. 102 The discovery of the murderer's handkerchief.. was the means of bringing a most notorious criminal to the chair.

2. *fig.* **a.** Seat.

1509 Hawes *Past. Pleas.* XVI. xxxv, Yf ye wyll tell me where your herte is set. In the chayre of sorowe no great doubt it is. **1547-64** Bauldwin *Mor. Philos.* (Palfr.) ix. 4 Our soules sit in a sure chaire of a certaine expectation. **1597** Hooker *Eccl. Pol.* v. lxv. §7 Imagination, the only storehouse of wit and peculiar chair of memory. **1738** Wesley *Psalms* i. 1 The Persecutor's Guilt to share Oppressive in the Scorner's Chair.

b. As an attribute of old age, when rest is the natural condition.

1591 Shaks. *1 Hen. VI*, III. ii. 51. *Ibid.* IV. v. 5 When saplesse Age, and weake vnable limbes Should bring thy Father to his drooping Chaire.

3. a. A seat of authority, state, or dignity; a throne, bench, judgement-seat, etc.

a **1300** [see 1].

c **1325** *E.E. Allit. P.* B. 1218 Nabigo-de-nozar noble in his chayer. **1393** Gower *Conf.* III. iv. 125 Ianus with double face In his chare hath take his place. *c* **1440** *Gesta Rom.* 400 (Add. MS.) Sette hym in the Chayere as domysman. **1602** *2nd Pt. Return fr. Parnass.* II. i. (Arb.) 21 O how it greeues my vexed soule to see, Each painted asse in chayre of dignitie. **1667** Milton *P.L.* I. 764 At the Soldans chair Defi'd the best of Panim chivalry. **1757** Gray *Bard* II. iii, Close by the regal chair Fell Thirst and Famine scowl. **1879** Maclear *Celts* ix. 146 Holdelm..was chosen by him as the seat of his episcopal chair.

b. *fig.* Place or situation of authority, etc.

1382 Wyclif *Matt.* xxiii. 2 Vpon the chaier of Moyses, scribis and Pharisees seeten. *c* **1400** *Rom. Rose* 6891 'Uppon the chaire of Moyses'..That is the olde testament. **1562** J. Heywood *Prov. & Epigr.* (1867) 38 Euery man may not syt in the chayre. **1692** Washington tr. *Milton's Def. Pop.* iii. (1851) 82 He and Tiberius got into the Chair by the Tricks and Artifices of their Mothers. **1859** Tennyson *Enid* 1788 He rooted out the slothful officer..And in their chairs set up a stronger race.

c. A chair occupied by a Welsh bard at an Eisteddfod, esp. one awarded as a trophy; also, a convention, now each of the four conventions, connected with the Welsh Eisteddfod.

1820 *Cambro-Briton* I. 36 He was placed, by the general voice, in the bardic chair, and invested with a blue ribbon. **1874** *Cassell's Mag.* IX. 431/1 The grand event of the whole Eisteddfod..—the giving of the Chair Prize. **1877** *Encycl. Brit.* VII. 791/1 The chair was a kind of convention where disciples were trained, and bardic matters discussed preparatory to the great Gorsedd... There are now existing four chairs in Wales. **1909** T. R. Roberts *The Eisteddfod* 27 The earliest Eisteddfodau, or 'Chairs' as they were then called,..were held under the patronage of the Princes of Wales at the beginning of the sixth century. *Ibid.* 36 The Gwyneddigion offered a silver chair to the bard who could write the best verses.

4. a. The seat of a bishop in his church; hence *fig.* episcopal dignity or authority. *Obs.* or *arch.*

1480 Caxton *Chron. Eng.* xl. 28 Seynt peter preched in antyoche and ther he made a noble chirche in whiche he sate

fyrste in his chaier. **1591** *Troub. Raigne K. John* II. (1611) 109 Treade downe the Strumpets pride, That sits vpon the Chaire of Babylon. **1642** JER. TAYLOR *Episc.* (1647) 337 S. Peter would have advanc'd him to the Honour and power of the Bishops chaire. **1647** BREVINT *Saul at Endor* 15 His first Chair, namely that of Antioch. **1757** BURKE *Abridgm. Eng. Hist.* Wks. X. 465 Henry..took measures, not only to humble Becket, but also to lower that Chair [of Canterbury]. **1867** FREEMAN *Norm. Conq.* (1876) I. vi. 292 Ealdhun now moved his chair to a site nobler than that occupied by any other minster in England.

†**b.** = SEE. *Obs.*

1615 G. SANDYS *Trav.* 3 It is the chaire of an Archbishop; inhabited for the most by Grecians. **1647** [see 4 a].

†**5.** A pulpit. *Obs.*

1648 MILTON *Tenure Kings* (1650) 45 A charge not performed by mounting twise into the chair with a formal preachment. **1873** BROWNING *Red Cott. Nt.-Cap* 1279 Whether he preach in chair, or print in book.

6. a. The seat from which a professor or other authorized teacher delivers his lectures.

c **1449** PECOCK *Repr.* v. vi. 518 To be rad..in the chaier of scolis. **1691** WOOD *Ath. Oxon.* II. 506 His prudent presiding in the Professors chair. **1691–8** NORRIS *Pract. Disc.* (1711) III. 219 Our Saviour..should have taken the chair, and have given the Inquisitive World a clear determination concerning the Question. *a* **1711** KEN *Hymnoth.* Poet. Wks. 1721 III. 14 Give that small Insect you contemn, The Chair in Porch or Academ. **1876** GREEN *Short Hist.* iii. §4. 129 English scholars gathered in thousands round the chairs of William of Champeaux or Abelard.

b. Hence: The office or position of a professor.

1816 SCOTT *Antiq.* xxxi, Fighting his way to a chair of rhetoric. **1856** EMERSON *Eng. Traits* xii. Wks. (Bohn) II. 93 Many chairs and many fellowships are made beds of ease. **1875** M. ARNOLD *Ess. Crit.* Pref. 10 *note*, The author had still the Chair of Poetry at Oxford.

7. A seat of judicial inquiry; a tribunal.

1629 CHAS. I. in H. Cox *Instit.* I. ix. (1863) 158 Now there are so many chairs erected, to make inquiry upon all sorts of men. **1645** MILTON *Colast.* Wks. (1851) 348 For a Licenser is not contented now to give his single Imprimatur, but brings his chair into the Title leaf; there sits and judges up or judges down what book hee pleases.

8. The seat, and hence the office, of the chief magistrate of a corporate town; mayorship. ***past, above,*** or ***below the chair*** (of aldermen of the City of London): having served or not served as Lord Mayor.

1682 *Eng. Elect. Sheriffs* 26 Some people..did so industriously stickle for Sir John Moor's Election to the Chair. **1714** *Lond. Gaz.* No. 5261/4 The Aldermen below the Chair on Horseback in Scarlet Gowns. **1751** CHAMBERS *Cycl.* s.v. *Chain*, A gold chain..remains to the person after his being divested of that magistrature, as a mark that he has passed the Chair. **1766** ENTICK *London* IV. 263 The judges are the lord-mayor, the aldermen past the chair, and the recorder. **1885** *Whitaker's Almanack* 251 All the above have passed the Civic Chair.

9. a. The seat occupied by the person presiding at a meeting, from whence he directs its business; hence, the office or dignity of chairman of a meeting, or of the Speaker of the House of Commons.

In various phrases, as ***to take the chair***, to assume the position of chairman, which in most cases formally opens a meeting; ***to put in the chair***, to elect as chairman; ***in the chair***, acting as chairman; ***to leave*** or ***vacate the chair***, to cease acting as chairman, which marks the close of a meeting.

1647 CLARENDON *Hist. Reb.* IV. (1843) 118/1 The committee of the Commons appointed Mr. Pym to sit in their chair. **1659** in Burton *Diary* (1828) IV. 462, I move that your Speaker forbear the Chair. **1806** *Med. Jrnl.* XV. 536 That the thanks of this meeting be given to Dr. Brandreth, for his cool and patient attention and conduct in the Chair. **1807** CRABBE *Newspaper* 163 Pleased to guide His little club, and in the chair preside. **1848** MACAULAY *Hist. Eng.* i, John Hampden..was put into the chair.

b. Often put for the occupant of the chair, the chairman, as invested with its dignity (as *the throne* is for the sovereign), *e.g.* in the cry *Chair! Chair!* when the authority of the chairman is appealed to, or not duly regarded; ***to address the chair, support the chair***, etc. Now also used as an alternative for 'chairman' or 'chairwoman', esp. deliberately so as not to imply a particular sex.

1658–9 in Burton *Diary* 23 Mar. (1828) 243 The Chair behaves himself like a Busby amongst so many school-boys ..and takes a little too much on him. **1676–7** GREW *Salts in Water* i. §1 (Read bef. Royal Soc.), It was referred to Me by this Honourable Chair, to examine and produce the Experiment. **1837** DICKENS *Pickw.* i, Cries of 'Order', 'Chair', 'Yes', 'No', 'Go on'. **1860** *All Y. Round* No. 46. 475 An amiable discussion between the 'chair' and an.. obstinate person at the other end of the room. **1887** *Times* 5 Sept. 9/2 It can hardly be conceived that the Chair would fail to gain the support of the House. **1976** MILLER & SWIFT *Words & Women* (1977) v. 76 Seventeen members of the university's Department of Linguistics, including the department's distinguished chair, Calvert Watkins, had written a letter to the *Crimson* on the subject of the students' action. **1982** J. A. SHARWOOD in *Occasional Papers Univ. Sydney Austral. Lang. Res. Centre*) xx. 29 The chairman of directors of each packing company is called the *chair*. **1984** *New Yorker* 13 Aug. 37/1 Martha Layne Collins..is to serve as chair of the Convention. **1986** *Tribune* 12 Sept. 7/1 She has annoyed the Black Sections by refusing to resign as chair of the party black advisory committee.

c. *pl.* The chairman and deputy chairman of the East India Company.

1772 BURKE *Corr.* (1844) I. 344 This seems to be the scheme most approved by the chairs. **1844** H. H. WILSON *Brit. India* I. 499 Letter from the Chairs to the Right Honourable Robert Dundas, 16th December, 1808.

†**10.** An enclosed chair or covered vehicle for one person, carried on poles by two men; a sedan.

1634 *Sir S. Duncombe's Patent for setting up Sedans* in Pegge *Curial. Misc.* 290 In many parts beyond the seas the people there are much carried in the streets in chairs that are covered. **1647** R. STAPYLTON *Juvenal* 12 Using close chayres or sedans. **1688** SHADWELL *Sqr. Alsatia* II. ii, Thy Mask will cover all. There is a chair below in the Entry to carry thee. **1713** SWIFT *Cadenus & V.*, She..lik'd three footmen to her chair. **1722** STEELE *Consc. Lovers* I. ii, Call a Chair! **1752** JOHNSON *Rambl.* No. 195 ¶6 At the proper time a chair was called. **1777** SHERIDAN *Trip Scarb.* II. i, Help the gentleman into a chair, and carry him to my house. **1836** J. MAYNE *Siller Gun*, The belle and beau, In chairs and chariots, stop the way.

11. A light vehicle drawn by one horse; a chaise; also a particular kind of light chaise (see quot. 1795). Also *attrib.*

1753 *Scots Mag.* XV. 31/2 The profits..have enabled me to set up a one-horse chair. **1761** STERNE *Tr. Shandy* III. xxiv. 124 There is not a greater difference between a single-horse chair and madam Pompadour's *vis a vis.* **1795** W. FELTON *Carriages* (1801) II. 184 A chair is a light chaise without pannels for the use of parks and gardens, and is a name commonly applied to all light Chaises. **1821** COMBE (Dr. Syntax) *Wife* I. 614 As I please to take the air, Command the ponies to a chair. **1909** R. W. CHAMBERS *Firing Line* ix, They went together in a double chair, spinning noiselessly over the shell road. *Ibid.* xiv, Their black chair-boy lay asleep under a thicket of Spanish bayonet.

12. *Railways.* †**a.** The support or carriage of a rail (cf. CARRIAGE 32 b). *Obs.* **b.** An iron or steel socket with a deep notch, into which the rail is fixed, and by which it is secured to the sleeper or cross-tie.

1816 *Specif. Losh & Stephenson's Patent* No. 4067. 2 To fix both the ends of the rails..immoveable in or upon the chairs or props by which they are supported. **1836** SIR G. HEAD *Home Tour* 204 Each of these sleepers being a heavy block of stone, having a small cradle of iron, or chair as it is called, rivetted on the top for the purpose of supporting the rails. **1862** SMILES *Engineers* III. 131 The flat base of the chair upon which the rails rested being tilted.

13. *Min.* (See quot.)

1802 MAWE *Mineral. Derbysh.* Gloss., *Chair*, used in drawing up ore or coal.

14. Phrase. ***to put in the chair.*** (*slang.*)

1864 *Soc. Sc. Rev.* I. 408 Some hirers [*i.e.* drivers of cabs] ..boast of the number of owners whom they have 'put in the chair' or in polite English neglected to pay.

15. *Comb.*, as ***chair-attendant, -back, -bearer, -bottoming, -caner, -caning, -cover, -factory, -hire, -leg, -maker, -mare, -mending, -room, -saddle, -slumber; chair-ridden, -shaking,*** adjs.; **chair-back,** (*a*) the back of a chair; (*b*) an anti-macassar; **chair-bard** [Welsh *cadair fardd*], the successful competitor in the bardic competition held on 'chair day' of the Welsh National Eisteddfod; **chair-bed, -bedstead,** a kind of chair which can be unfolded into a bed; **chair binder** (see quot. 1921); †**chair-boll, -bow,** a chair-back; **chair-borne** *a.*, *Mil.*, ironically descriptive of troops whose duties are administrative; cf. AIR-BORNE *a.*; also *absol.*; **chair-car** orig. *U.S.*, a railway carriage furnished with chairs (two on each side of the aisle) instead of the usual seats; also, a parlour car (see PARLOUR 6); **chair-carver** (see quot.); **chair day,** the chief day of the Welsh National Eisteddfod (see quot.); **chair-days,** old age, when rest in a chair is the most natural condition; **chair-door** (see quot.); **chair frame maker, chair-framer** (see quots.); **chairlady** (orig. *U.S.*) = CHAIRWOMAN; **chair-lift** (see LIFT *sb.*²); **chair-marking** *slang* (see quots. and sense 14); so ***chair-mark*** v. and sb., ***chair-marked*** ppl. a.; **chair matter** (see quot.); **chair-organ** (see quots.); **chair-post** *U.S.*, one of the main uprights of a chair; **chair-rail** (see quot.); **chair road,** a railway having the rails fastened by chairs to the sleepers; **chair rusher, seater** = *chair matter*; **chair-side** *attrib.*, of or pertaining to dental work performed while the patient is seated in a dentist's chair; also in other uses (see quots.); **chair-table,** a table convertible into a chair or settle; **chair turner,** a wood turner who specializes in chair legs, rails, etc.; †**chair-volant,** sedan-chair; **chair-warmer** *slang*, orig. *Theatr.* (see quot. 1909); hence *gen.* a 'passenger' in any enterprise or situation. Also CHAIRMAN *sb.*, etc.

a **1953** DYLAN THOMAS *Quite early one Morning* (1954) 33 The clip of the *chair-attendant's puncher. **1747** H. GLASSE *Art of Cookery* xxii. 166 Hang the rest of your Bedding on the *Chair-backs. **1858** TROLLOPE *Dr. Thorne* III. xxxv. 89, I should like to work it into a chair-back instead of floss-silk. **1883** LADY C. SCHREIBER *Jrnl.* (1911) II. 405, I did some work, cutting up some lengths of Turkish embroidery into chair backs. **1874** *Cassell's Mag.* IX. 431/1 The successful competitor will be installed as the *Chair Bard. **1895** *Daily News* 20 May 5/3 The chair-bard for this year of the Welsh National Eisteddfod. **1647** R. STAPYLTON *Juvenal* 110 *Chair-bearers or Sedan-men. **1805** *Times* 7 Nov. 1/2 (Advt.), Sofa Beds, *Chair Beds, and Tables. **1912** COMPTON MACKENZIE *Carnival* xxiii. 235 Mr. Dale was generally comatose on a flock-exuding chair-bed in what was known as 'dad's room'. **1881** *Instr. Census Clerks* (1885) 53 *Chair..Binder. **1921** *Dict. Occup. Terms* (1927) §504 *Chair binder*, tacks hessian or other stuffing cover over padding of back and seat of chair and over webbing under seat. **1556** J. HEYWOOD *Spider & F.* lxxxiv. 20 Vpon the *cheyreboll hard beating his fist. **1943** C. H. WARD-JACKSON *Piece of Cake* 21 *Chair-borne division*, manned by uniformed personnel who labour in offices. **1947** N. BALCHIN *Lord, I was Afraid* 166 The old sneer of the airborne at the chair-borne. **1954** J. MASTERS *Bhowani Junction* 171 For Christ's sake, wake up, you chairborne bastard. **1483** *Cath. Angl.* 57 A *chare bowe, *fultrum.* **1887** *Century Mag.* Oct. 858/2 Broom-making, *chair-bottoming, and the cobbling of shoes. **1868** *Times* 27 Feb., Described as a *chair-caner. **1906** *Daily Chron.* 9 Mar. 8/5 Umbrella-mending, *chair-caning..are..genteel occupations to be pursued by the caravan 'smart set'. **1880** G. A. SALA *Amer. Revisited* 166/2 The Pullman Parlor car—commonly termed a '*chair' car. **1901** *Westm. Gaz.* 11 July 6/1 A fire..partially destroyed a dining car and a chair-car. **1909** 'O. HENRY' *Options* (1916) 210 My chair-car was profitably well filled with people of the kind one usually sees on chair-cars. **1969** *National Herald* (New Delhi) 29 July 4/4 The average number of air-conditioned chair car seats occupied per trip was 290. **1858** SIMMONDS *Dict. Trade*, *Chair-carver, one employed in carving the upright posts and other parts of beds, arm-chairs, sofas, &c. **1824** MISS MITFORD *Village* Ser. I. (1863) 227 The ornaments, the reticules, bell-ropes, ottomans, and *chair-covers. **1877** *Encycl. Brit.* VII. 792/1 The great day of the Eisteddfod is the '*chair' day—usually the third or last day—the grand event of the Eisteddfod being the adjudication on the chair subject and the chairing and investiture of the fortunate winner. **1593** SHAKS. *2 Hen. VI*, v. ii. 48 In thy Reuerence, and thy *Chaire-dayes, thus To die in Ruffian battell. **1865** *Cornh. Mag.* July 38 The end of life is the 'sere of life'..In Yorkshire it is 'the chair-day'. **1906** HARDY *Dynasts* II. VI. vi, In addition to the grand entrance..there is a covert little '*chair-door'..for sedans only. **1827** DRAKE & MANSFIELD *Cincinnati* viii. 65 Six *Chair Factories, 38 hands. **1903** *Daily Chron.* 10 Mar. 10/4 Foreman required for large chair factory. **1897** *Daily News* 9 Mar. 2/6 *Chair frame maker. **1921** *Dict. Occup. Terms* (1927) §473 *Chair frame maker, chair framer*, assembles parts of chair frames, prepared by woodworking machinist. **1762** GOLDSM. *Nash* 10 Who spend more in *chair hire than housekeeping. **1925** *New Republic* 16 Sept. 92 In the clothing trades there are union shop chairmen and *chairladies who exercise a workers' control that [etc.]. **1931** *Atlantic City News* 7 Aug. 10/4 Mrs. Joseph Foy is chairlady of the card party. **1959** P. BULL *I know the Face* i. 15 A lovely play..which..was written by Miss Bertha Graham, the chairlady of The 1930 Players. **1813** *Examiner* 15 Feb. 102/1 J. Finlayson,..*chair-maker. **1799** JANE AUSTEN *Lett.* (1884) I. 221 Price sixty guineas, of which the *chair mare was taken as fifteen. **1890** *Pall Mall Gaz.* 18 Sept. 7/3 Unless these particulars are filled in no cabman can get employment; and it is almost as difficult for him if the licence is '*chair-marked'. This is done in several ways: one is by writing big; another by writing out the date..a third by using red..ink. 'Chair-marking' is generally the result of spite... At Marylebone..a cab proprietor was fined £5 and costs for 'chair-marking'. **1894** *Daily News* 23 Oct. 2/6 This he contended was a 'chair mark', conveying to other proprietors the information that he had not paid his cab hire up. **1939** H. HODGE *Cab, Sir?* 218 Certain employers attempted to pass comments about drivers..by writing the date in code... It was called: 'chairmarking'. **1921** *Dict. Occup. Terms* (1927) §472 **Chair matter*; *chair rusher*; *chair seater*; weaves rushes, by hand, into chair seats or frames. **1694** *Lond. Gaz.* No. 2955/4 Following the Trade of *Chairmending in the Streets. **1636–7** *Royal Warrant* in *N. & Q.* Ser. III. (1867) XI. 11/2 Our Chapell at Hampton Court, and for the making of a newe *Chaire Organ there, Conformable to those alreadie made in our Royal Chapells at Whitehall and Greenwiche. **1880** GROVE *Dict. Mus.*, *Chair organ*, a corruption of Choir organ, in use in the last century, not impossibly arising from the fact that in cathedrals the choir organ often formed the back of the organist's seat. **1788** *Amer. Museum* IV. 519 The snake was ..about the thickness of a common *chair-post. **1872** *Congress. Globe* App. 578/2 They went out and got great big long brushes, as big as these chair posts. **1911** *Roxboro* (N.C.) *Courier* Nov., The snake was as large around as a chair post. **1842–75** GWILT *Archit.* Gloss., **Chair Rail*, a piece of wood fastened to the wall, to prevent the backs of the chairs injuring the plastering when placed against it. **1885** *Pall Mall G.* 28 May 4 [There] sat the mother..*chair-ridden by sciatica. **1895** *Westm. Gaz.* 12 July 2/1 In America the authorities assert that our *chair roads are not strong enough to stand their traffic. **1664** PEPYS *Diary* (1879) III. 14 There comes out of the *chayre-room Mrs. Stewart. **1865** *Pall Mall G.* 11 Apr. 11 A lady on a donkey in one of those *chair-saddles which supply the place of side-saddles in the south of Spain. **1819** L. HUNT *Indicator* No. 1 *Chair-shaking merriment. **1950** M. PALYI *Compulsory Medical Care* 77 [Dentist's] actual *chairside work. **1958** *Times* 12 Sept. 2/7 (Advt.), Young assistant required for old-established busy dental practice... Chairside assistance. **1963** J. OSBORNE *Dent. Mech.* (ed. 5) viii. 100 Both methods ..require somewhat more chair-side and laboratory time. **1966** *Listener* 18 Aug. 238/3 New kinds of trains are being planned..with standards of..service borrowed from the airlines—chairside meals and so forth. **1966** 'S. RANSOME' *Hidden Hour* iii. 38 He reached for the extension telephone on the chairside table. **1558** A. CRANEWISE in *Wills & Inventories Bury St. Edmund's* (Camden Soc., 1850) 150, I giue to my sonne Thomas..my round *chaire table in the parlour. **1891** I. W. LYON *Colonial Furniture* 197 A chair table is mentioned in the inventory of John Copse, of Watertown, Mass., made in 1644. **1909** *Cent. Dict.* Suppl., *Table-chair*... Also chair-table. **1904** *Daily Chron.* 5 Jan. 2/7 He was a *chair turner by trade. **1667** DENHAM *Direct. Painter* I. viii. 18 Rupert, that knew no fear, but health did want, Kept state suspended in a *Chair volant. **1909** WARE *Passing Eng.* 69/1 A '*chair-warmer' is a lady whose talent is comprised in her physical charms, and who can neither sing, dance, nor act. **1926** J. BLACK *You can't Win* viii. 101 The judge frowned at me. The courtroom chair warmers craned necks in my direction. **1957** K. A. WITTFOGEL *Oriental*

Despotism 306 Bureaucratic chair-warmers can be annoying and harmful.

†**chair**. *sb.*[2] *Obs.* or *arch.* [Variant of CHAR, assimilated in spelling to prec.; perhaps associated with it also in meaning.] A chariot or car.

c **1374** CHAUCER *Anel. & Arc.* 39 Emelye..Faire in a chare [*Shirley MS.* chaier] of golde he with him lad. **1480** CAXTON *Chron. Eng.* II. (1520) 14/1 Helyas..was lyfted up into paradye..in a chayre. **1494** FABYAN *Chron.* VII. 617 Wᵗ great apparayll of chayris and other costious ordenaunce for to conueye the forenamed lady Margarete into Englande. **1559** T. BRYCE in Farr's *S.P. Eliz.* (1845) I. 164 When worthy Web and George Roper In Elyes' chayre to heauen were sent. *c* **1630** DRUMM. OF HAWTH. *Poems* Wks. (1711) 6 Phœbus in his chair, Ensaffroning sea and air. **1697** DRYDEN *Virg.* x. 807 Niphæus, whom four coursers drew..They threw their master headlong from the chair. **1814** SCOTT *Ld. of Isles* v. xiv, Like a prophet's fiery chair..travelling the realms of air.

chair (tʃɛə(r)), *v.* [f. CHAIR *sb.*[1]]

1. a. *trans.* To place or seat in a chair; *esp.* to install in a chair of authority.

1552, 1796 [see CHAIRED *ppl. a.*]. **1761** *Brit. Mag.* II. 179 Chairing your speaker for the commons, when he is chosen by the house. **1850** P. CROOK *War of Hats* 52 A Guy Fawkes figure toiletted and chaired. **1877** TENNYSON *Harold* I. ii. (D.) And thou Chair'd in his place.

b. To place in a chair or on a seat, and carry aloft in triumph, as an honour to a favourite, a successful competitor, and formerly often to the successful candidate at a parliamentary election.

1761 *Brit. Mag.* II. 179 The practice of chairing the candidate.. still, I find, obtains among you. **1812** *Examiner* 19 Oct. 670/2 Were declared duly elected, and were chaired through the principal streets. **1812** AMYOT *Windham* I. 86 *note.* **1844** DISRAELI *Coningsby* v. ii. 192 The day the member was chaired. **1857** HUGHES *Tom Brown* II. viii, Tom ..was chaired round the quadrangle, on one of the hall benches borne aloft by the eleven.

c. To award the chair to (the successful competitor at the Welsh Eisteddfod). Chiefly as *ppl. a.* and *vbl. sb.*

1876, etc. [see CHAIRED *ppl. a.*]. **1877** [see *chair day* s.v. CHAIR *sb.* 15].

d. To direct (a meeting, etc.) as chairman; to preside over. Cf. CHAIRMAN *v.*

1921 L. S. HUNTER *J. Hunter* vii. 142 He was rarely quite happy and spontaneous at business..meetings. The prospect of having to 'chair' one would sometimes distract him from his work throughout the day. **1952** *Landfall* Mar. 50 He was chairing the first meeting of the congress. **1957** *BBC Handbk.* 167 Discussions chaired by Edgar Lustgarten.

2. To carry or wheel in a chair.

1886 J. PENDLETON *Hist. Derbysh.* 99 The bride, owing to her infirmities, had to be chaired to the altar.

3. To provide with a chair or chairs.

1844 DICKENS *Mart. Chuz.* xxvii, The offices were newly chaired. **1885** [see CHAIRING below].

Hence **chaired** *ppl. a.*, **'chairing** *vbl. sb.*

1552 HULOET, Chayred or stalled, *cathedratus.* **1796** COLERIDGE *Ode Depart. Year*, From the chaired gods advancing, The Spirit of the Earth made reverence meet. **1797** HOLCROFT tr. *Stolberg's Trav.* (ed. 2) II. lxii. 418 *note*, The chairing of a Westminster election. **1876** *Encycl. Brit.* V. 318 The chief of song was also called a chaired bard, because he was one of the fourteen entitled to a chair at court. **1880** *Daily News* 18 Sept. 6/4 It was resolved..that all chaired bards be appointed honorary members. **1885** *Leisure Hour* Jan. 48/2 Seldom is a large building erected.. without a visit to Wycombe..with a view to the chairing of it. **1890** *Pall Mall Gaz.* 11 Sept. 6/3 Tudno, the chaired bard at Bangor.

chair, obs. form of CHARE.

chair-: see CHAR-.

†**'chairie**, *a. Obs. rare.* [app. f. F. *chair* flesh + -Y[1].] ? Fleshy.

1633 W. STRUTHER *True Happines* 62 Like a pulpous or chairie root.

chairman ('tʃɛəmən), *sb.*

1. a. The occupier of a chair of authority; *spec.* the person who is chosen to preside over a meeting, to conduct its proceedings, and who occupies the chair or seat provided for this function.

1654 TRAPP *Comm. Job* xxix. 25, I sate chief, and was Chair-man. **1660–1** PEPYS *Diary* 22 Jan., To come..to this place..where Sir G. Downing (my late master) was chaireman. **1697** LUTTRELL *Brief Rel.* (1857) IV. 254 This day the parliament mett here, the earl of Oxford chairman. **1857** TOULM. SMITH *Parish* 58 It is the duty of the chairman, immediately on taking the chair, to cause the minutes of the preceding meeting to be read.

b. The member of a corporate body appointed or elected to preside at its meetings, and in general to exercise the chief authority in the conduct of its affairs; the president.

Chairman of Committees: in either House of Parliament the member appointed to preside over it whenever it resolves itself into Committee.

1727–51 CHAMBERS *Cycl.* s.v. *Companies*, East India, The directors are twenty-four in number, including the chairman and deputy-chairman. **1835** URE *Philos. Manuf.* 291 The committee..on factory employment, of which Mr. Sadler was the mover and chairman. **1887** MORLEY *Crit. Misc.* III. 306 The chairman of the Hudson's Bay Company. *Mod.* Chairman of the Metropolitan Board of Works.

c. A master of ceremonies (see quot. 1951).

1836 DICKENS *Astley's* in *Sk. Boz* I. 312 It requires no great exercise of imagination to identify..the comic singer with the public-house chairman. **1951** *Oxf. Compan. Theatre* 119/2 *Chairman*, an important feature of the early music-hall... He sat at the head of a table in front of the footlights, with his back to the stage... He announced the 'turns' and kept the somewhat unruly audience in order. **1970** *Radio Times* 16 Apr. 39/1 *The Good Old Days* Old-Time Music-Hall..Chairman Leonard Sachs.

2. a. One whose occupation it is to carry persons in chairs or chair-like conveyances; *spec.* the two men who carried a sedan-chair.

1682 *Lond. Gaz.* No. 1683/4 A tall Blackamore..in a Green Doublet and Breeches, with a large Chairmans Coat of the same colour. **1703** *Ibid.* 3942/3 Twenty Chairmen, with Sedans. **1721** CIBBER *Lady's Last St.* v, Chair, Chair! (Enter a Chairman) Here: Who calls Chair? **1750** JOHNSON *Rambl.* No. 113 ⁋6 Disputing for sixpence with a chairman. **1833** *Act 3 & 4 Will. IV*, c. 46 §113 The misbehaviour of coachmen, drivers, chairmen, carters, and porters. **1855** THACKERAY *Newcomes* I. 161 When ladies' chairmen jostled each other on the pavement.

b. One who wheels a Bath-chair.

1766 ANSTEY *Bath Guide* i. 115 But soft—my Chairman's at the Door. **1829** MARRYAT *F. Mildmay* xvi, A Bath chairman. **1869** *Daily Tel.* 18 Aug., The invalids..in their Bath chairs..The chairmen..are an honest, genial, hard-working set of fellows.

chairman ('tʃɛəmən), *v.* [f. the sb.] *trans.* To preside over (a meeting) as chairman; = CHAIR *v.* 1 d.

1888 *Pall Mall Gaz.* 11 Oct. 4/1 We refused to attend the meeting to be chairmanned by Sir William. **1897** *Westm. Gaz.* 29 Jan. 2/3 The firm Which is chairman'd by Masham at Manningham! **1904** F. LYNDE *Grafters* xxiii. 293 It was late in the afternoon..that the Federative Council sent its committee, chairmaned by Engineer Scott, to interview the ex-general manager.

'chairmanship. [f. CHAIRMAN *sb.* + -SHIP.]

1. The office of chairman or president of a meeting, a company, corporate body, etc.

1847 *Fraser's Mag.* XXXVI. 224 Elevation to the chairmanship of the Great Western. **1878** *N. Amer. Rev.* 72 The retirement of Mr. Sumner from the chairmanship.

2. The action of presiding as chairman; performance of a chairman's duty.

1859 SALA *Tw. round Clock* (1861) 142 A philanthropic peer, always..to the fore with his chairmanship. **1864** *Realm* 1 June 1 A body of gentlemen sat down to dinner, under the sympathetic chairmanship of Lord Houghton.

chairoplane ('tʃɛərəpleɪn). Also **char-a-plane, chairplane.** [f. CHAIR *sb.*[1], after *aeroplane, airplane.*] A roundabout with seats suspended by chains, the riders being swung round in a wide circle by the revolution of the machinery.

1922 *Westm. Gaz.* 3 Nov., 'Char-a-plane' victim. **1926** *Daily Express* 6 Aug. 3/2 'Chairplane' Tragedy. **1927** *Bulletin* 5 Dec. 7/2 A chairoplane erected on a fairground. *a* **1953** DYLAN THOMAS *Quite early one Morning* (1954) 29 He whirled in his chairoplane giddily above the upturned laughing faces of the town girls.

'chairperson. [f. CHAIR *sb.*[1] + PERSON *sb.*, after *chairman*, etc.: see PERSON *sb.* 2 f.] A chairman or chairwoman: usu. intended as an alternative that avoids sexual definition. Cf. CHAIR *sb.* 9 b.

1971, etc. [see PERSON *sb.* 2 f]. **1977** *Maledicta* I. 39 Send a flyer to appropriate chairpersons for departmental announcements. **1980** *Amer. Speech* LV. 129 In Great Britain..any revision of gender has stopped with the half-hearted use of *chairperson*. **1984** S. TOWNSEND *Growing Pains A. Mole* 80 Dear Chairperson, Arthur, it is with the deepest regret that I offer my resignation as vice-chairperson of the Elm Ward Labour Party.

Hence **'chairpersonship** = CHAIRMANSHIP.

1982 *Nature* 9 Dec. 550/1 On the more general aspects of the *arriviste's* upward trajectory, however, such as the craft of..chairpersonship, he has much less to say. **1983** *Listener* 14 Apr. 43/1 The panel consisted of the distinguished authors Nina Bawden, Elizabeth Jane Howard, under the 'chairpersonship' of the equally distinguished Maureen Duffy.

†**'chairship.** *Obs. rare*[−1]. [see -SHIP.] The occupancy of the (papal) chair.

1660 *Charac. Italy* 13 Alexander the Sixth, who during his Chairship scrap'd together so much wealth.

'chair-woman. A woman who occupies the chair of presidency at a meeting, in a committee, etc. (Hardly a recognized name until 19th c.)

1699 T. BROWN in R. L'Estrange *Erasm. Colloq.* (1711) 404 We ought to have..four chairwomen of our four committees. **1734** FIELDING *Univ. Gallant* 11, She sits.. chairwoman of a committee of fools, to criticize on fashions. **1869** *Pall Mall G.* 9 Sept. 8 The Duchess rose and said.. then I think the arduous duties of chairman—or shall I say chairwoman?—will cease.

chairwoman, obs. form of CHARWOMAN.

chaise (ʃeɪz), *sb.* Also 8 chaiz, (shazess). [a. mod.F. *chaise* (*chaize* Cotgr.), a phonetic alteration of *chaire* (so *Pazis* for *Paris*, etc.), established in the ordinary sense 'chair', whence by extension 'sedan-chair', and by transference a wheeled vehicle for travelling in. In this later sense alone *chaise* passed into English, notwithstanding that *chair* had itself here received the same development (see CHAIR *sb.*[1] 11, which however was not always an exact synonym of this word, but often used as the name of a particular sort of chaise). (*Cathedra, chair, chaise*, are thus all forms of the same word.) The vulgar take (ʃeɪz) for a plural sb., and form on it a singular (ʃeɪ) CHAY, SHAY.

(The change of lingual *r* to *z* in French is a phenomenon widely exemplified. It appears fully established at Orleans in 15th c., but did not come down beyond 1620.)]

1. A term applied to various pleasure or travelling carriages, the exact application having varied from time to time:

a. A light open carriage for one or two persons, often having a top or calash; those with four wheels resembling the phaeton, those with two the curricle; also loosely used for pleasure carts and light carriages generally.

Kersey, Bailey, Ash and Johnson explain *chaise* as 'a carriage for pleasure drawn by one horse'; Todd says this was the case formerly, before post-chaises were in request, and defines it as 'A chaise and pair; a chaise and four: the term of later days for a light vehicle, with four wheels, drawn by two or four horses'.

1701 *Lond. Gaz.* No. 3700/1 The Empress..and the Arch-Dutchesses [were] in open Chaises. **1703** *Ibid.* No. 3945/4 A Leather Body-Coach..and several sorts of Shazesses. **1707** *Ibid.* No. 4390/4 Two Geldings, one a dark-brown..used to a Chaiz. **1708** *Ibid.* No. 4439/4, 2 four wheel'd Chaises. *a* **1719** ADDISON (J.) Instead of the chariot he might have said the chaise of government; for a chaise is driven by the person that sits in it. **1786** *Trials John Shepherd* 40 He was in a one-horse chaise. **1794** FELTON *Carriages* (1801) II. 117 The Grasshopper, or three-quarter pannel Chaise, or Whiskey..by some called Quakers' Chaises. *Ibid.* 121 The Rib chair, or Yarmouth Cart. For lawns or parks these sort of chaises have been mostly used. **1825** HONE *Every-Day Bk.* I. 436 Public pony-chaises. **1858** O. W. HOLMES *Poems* (1886) 291 The wonderful one-hoss shay. *Mod. vulgarism.* The pony-shay (also *po' shay* = post chaise).

b. A carriage for travelling, having a closed body and seated for one to three persons, the driver sitting on one of the horses; more distinctively called a POST-CHAISE, q.v.

1709 LUTTRELL *Brief Rel.* (1857) VI. 474 The chaise he made use of (being wounded in the foot) was found broke to peices. **1716–8** LADY M. W. MONTAGUE *Lett.* I. xvi. 52, I never went out of my chaise from Prague to this place. **1749** MRS. MONTAGU *Lett.* III. 125 We went out together in a post-chaise. **1773** GOLDSM. *Stoops to conq.* II. i, I'll clap a pair of horses to your chaise. **1837** LYTTON *E. Maltravers* 27 In little more than twenty minutes, the chaise was at the door. **1873** MORLEY *Rousseau* II. 66 He was thrust into a chaise and despatched on the first stage of eight melancholy years of wandering.

c. *to take chaise*: to use a chaise as a means of conveyance. ***a chaise and pair, four, six***: a chaise drawn by a pair, four, six horses.

1704 ADDISON *Italy* (1766) 23 From Genoa we took chaise for Milan. **1713** STEELE *Englishman* No. 21. 139 That gay thing that flies along the Road in a Chaise and Six. **1737** POPE *Hor. Epist.* I. i. 158 The poor..run They know not whither, in a chaise and one. **1782** COWPER *Gilpin* 9 To-morrow is our wedding-day, And we will then repair Unto the Bell at Islington, All in a chaise and pair.

2. *attrib.* and *Comb.*, as ***chaise-box, -umbrella***; **chaise-cart**, a light cart suitable for driving in (cf. CART *sb.* 3); **chaise-house**, a coach-house; **chaise-undertaker, -vamper**, one who undertakes to renovate chaises, a dealer in second-hand chaises. Also **'chaiseless** *a.*

1768 STERNE *Sent. Journ.* (1778) II. 185 The hammer in the *chaise-box being of no great use. **1821** COBBETT *Rur. Rides* (1855) I. 29 Riding in a little sort of *chaise-cart. **1794** FELTON (1801) I. 129 The *chaise coach-box..This kind.. may be made to fix on a one-horse *chaise carriage. *Ibid.* 202 *Chaise Heads..Heads to phaetons or chaises, etc., are found great conveniences for sheltering from the sun, wind or rain. **1812** *Examiner* 24 Aug. 533/1 It..entered the *chaise-house. **1850** THACKERAY *Pendennis* xxxiv, Mrs. Bacon..as yet a *chaiseless woman. **1765** STERNE *Tr. Shandy* VII. xxix, A pert vamping *chaise-undertaker. *Ibid.* VIII. xxxvii, In selling my chaise, I had sold my remarks along with it, to the *chaise-vamper.

chaise, *v. Obs. rare.* [f. the sb.] *to chaise it*: to go by chaise.

1792 W. B. STEVENS *Jrnl.* 28 Sept. (1965) I. 47 Chais'd it to Wirksworth, dined and slept at Winster. **1822** SOUTHEY *Lett.* (1856) III. 306, I shall follow your course to Skipton, and chaise it, solo, from thence.

chaise, obs. form of CHASE.

†**chaisel, cheisil.** *Obs.* [a. OF. *cheisīl, chesil*, var. of *cheincil, chensil, chansilh, cainsil*:—late L. *camisīle, -is* (8th c. in Du Cange), f. *camisia*: see CHEMISE.]

1. A fine linen (sometimes identified with BYSS or BYSSUS). Often used *attrib.*

c **1205** LAY. 23761 Warp he an his rugge ænne cheisil scurte [*c* **1275** ane cheiselne seorte] & ænne pallene curtel. *c* **1275** *Passion* 509 in *O.E. Misc.* 51 Ioseph nom vre Louerd a-dun of þe rode And wond him on o cheysil cloþ. *c* **1300** *K. Alis.* 279 Theo lady lyght on hire bedde..Yn a chaisel smok scheo lay. *c* **1300–20** *Joachim & Anne* in *Leg. Cathol.* (1840) 152 Of flex, of silk, of cheisel, Of porpre & of palle.

2. Applied to various things made of this fabric, as a chemise, smock, shirt, veil, etc.

c **1320** *Seuyn Sag.* (W.) 1814 Sche hadde on a pilche of pris, And a chaisel theron, I wis.

‖**chaise-longue** (ʃɛːzlɔ̃g). [F. *chaise longue* 'long chair'. In Ogilvie's Dict. called *chaise-lounge*.] A kind of sofa with a rest for the back at one end only; a 'couch', a 'lounge'. Also *ellipt.* as *chaise*.

1800 Mrs. Hervey *Mourtray Family* III. 76 She only begged they would permit her to lie down on her *chaise longue*. **1825** T. Lister *Granby* vii. (1836) 45 Lady Elizabeth lay on a chaise-longue by them. **1826** Disraeli *Viv. Grey* (1868) 338 Stiff or stretching, lounging on a chaise-longue. **1837** Marryat *Dog-fiend* 194 What are now termed chaise longues, were drawn to the sides of the table. **1852** Miss Sewell *Exper. Life* xxxviii. (1858) 278 The addition of a chaise longue and an ottoman. **1953** R. Chandler *Long Good-Bye* xxiv. 154, I stretched out on a padded aluminium chaise. **1965** E. O'Brien *August is Wicked Month* xvii. 215 He was on the edge of the chaise, totally ill at ease.

‖**chaise-marine** (ʃɛzmarin). *Obs.* [F. *chaise-marine* 'a sort of seat on board a ship so supported as to be free from the effects of rolling and pitching', but Littré has not the Eng. sense.]

? A kind of chaise, the body of which rests on suspension-straps between cee-springs.

1739 Cibber *Apol.* (1756) II. 79 A chaise-marine to carry our moving wardrobe to every different play. **1763** C. Talbot in *Lett.* I. 538, I could not help telling her of the overthrow of the Chaise marine. **1823** *Act 4 Geo. IV*, c. 95 §19 Nothing in..this Act..shall extend..to any chaise marine, coach, landau, berlin.

‖**chaise percée** (ʃɛz pɛrse). [Fr., lit. 'pierced chair'.] A chair incorporating a chamber-pot; a commode.

1939 A. Huxley *After many a Summer* II. vi. 233 What Consistency, pray, do you find..between your appearances at Court and your *chaise percée*. **1958** *Listener* 27 Nov. 889/1 A world in which the *chaise percée* was the real, semi-confidential throne where all might sit supreme.

chaist-: see chast-.

chaitif, a ME. variant form of caitiff.

chaitya (ˈtʃaɪtjə). [Skr., relating to a funeral pile or mound (*citā*); as *sb.*, funeral monument, sacred tree, etc.] A Buddhist place or object of reverence or worship. Cf. chorten.

1875 *Encycl. Brit.* II. 394 Of the next two classes of Buddhist architecture, the temples (Chaityas) and monasteries (Viharas), no built examples exist in India. **1882** *Ibid.* XIV. 500 The peculiar Buddhist objects of adoration which we know as *dagobas* or *chaityas*. **1920** *Blackw. Mag.* May 622/1 Rows of pyramidical chaityas. **1927** A. Huxley *Proper Studies* 181 The old Chaitya or meeting-hall of the Buddhists. **1945** S. Piggott *Some Anc. Cities India* 51 The rock-cut structures fall into two classes—*chaityas* or halls of worship and *viharas* or monasteries.

chak, obs. form of chack, check.

chaker, obs. form of checker, chequer.

chakil, chako, obs. ff. of shackle, chaco.

chakra (ˈtʃʌkrə). Also chakr, chakrah. [Skr. (cogn. w. wheel *sb.*).] **1.** A circular weapon used by the Sikhs (see quots.).

1883 *Encycl. Brit.* XX. 111/2 The chakr or chakra is a thin knife-edged ring of flat steel, a severe missile in skilled hands. **1959** *Chambers's Encycl.* I. 616/2 A sharp-edged metal quoit known as the *chakra* of the Sikhs.

2. A discus or mystic circle placed in the hands of pictured Hindu gods, etc.

1891 *Murray's Hand-Bk. India & Ceylon* 384/1 A small temple dedicated to the Chakrah, or discus, of Vishnu. **1903** E. Thurston in *Madras Govt. Mus. Bull.* IV. 199 A few men are branded on both shoulders with chank and chakra.

3. *Yoga.* One of the centres of spiritual or ethereal power in the human body.

1888 B. D. Basu in *Theosophist* Mar. 373 These *Chakras* are the vital and important sympathetic plexuses and preside over all the functions of organic life. **1921** D. H. Lawrence *Psychoanalysis* v. 86 Having begun to explore the unconscious, we find we must go from center to center, chakra to chakra. **1956** R. M. Lester *Towards Hereafter* iv. 54 These spiritual centres are known by the name of 'chakras'—a word derived from Yoga.

4. The emblem on the flag of the Indian Union.

1947 *Constituent Assembly of India, Resolution* 22 July 761 The design of the Wheel shall be that of the Wheel (*Chakra*) which appears on the abacus of the Sarnath lion Capital of Asoka. **1964** V. S. Agrawala *Wheel Flag of India* p. i, The *Chakra* has a two-fold aspect, viz., the centre and the circumference. There is rest at the centre and movement in the circumference.

‖**chal.** The Gipsy word for 'person, man, fellow': sometimes (with the corresponding feminine *chai*) used in speaking of gipsies, by way of displaying familiarity with them and their language.

1865 *Dubl. Univ. Mag.* II. 25 Romany chals with their nomad tents upon wheels. **1871** M. Collins *Mrq. & Merch.* I. i. 47 He..delighted the chals with tobacco. **1876** Whyte-Melville *Katerfelto* xii. 134 The Romany chal marries with the Romany chi.

chalamine, obs. form of calamine.

chalan (ˈtʃʌlən). *India.* [Hind. *chalān*.] (See quot. 1858.)

1858 Simmonds *Dict. Trade*, *Chalan, Chillaum, Chulan*, a common Indian name for an invoice, pass, voucher, or way-bill. **1906** *Advice Note, Off. Supt. Govt. Printing, India* Voucher No. 5656 Payments should be made either by remittance transfer receipt or treasury chalan.

†**chaˈlandre.** *Obs.* Also 4 chal-, chelaundre. [perh. repr. OF. **chalandre*, var. of *calandre*, in Pr. *calandri*, app. (with Romanic insertion of *n*, and dissimilation of *r-r* to *l-r*):—L. *caradrius*, ad. Gr. χαραδριός a species of bird. (See P. Meyer *Contes moralisés de Bozon* Notes 248.)]

ME. form of calander, a Mediterranean species of lark, *Alauda calandra*. (To ME. writers probably only a name, known from French romances.)

c **1305** *Land Cokaygne* 97 in *E.E.P.* (1862) 159 Chalandre and wodwale, And oþer briddes wiþout tale. *c* **1400** *Rom. Rose* 81 Than is blisful many sithe The chelaundre and the papyngay. *Ibid.* 663 Chalaundres fele sawe I there.

†**chalandrie**, (?). [Jamieson suggested some connexion with prec.]

1596 Burell *Entry Quene* in Watson *Coll. Sc. Poems* II. 2 (Jam.) In tapestries ye micht persaue Young ramel, wrocht like lawrell treis; With syndrie sorts of chalandrie In curious forms of carpentrie.

chalang(e, -ans (*Sc.*), obs. ff. challenge, etc.

chalastic (kəˈlæstɪk), *a.* (and *sb.*) *Med.* [ad. mod.L. *chalastic-us*, a. Gr. χαλαστικός laxative, from χαλᾶν to relax. Cf. F. *chalastique*.] Having power to remove rigidity or stiffness; relaxing; laxative. Also *sb.* a chalastic medicine.

1621-78 [see calastic]. **1704** J. Harris *Lex. Techn.*, *Chalastick Medicines*, are such as by their temperate and moderate Heat, do comfort and strengthen the Parts to which they are applied. **1708** Kersey, *Chalasticks* or *Chalastick Medicines*, such as are of a loosening or soft'ning Quality. **1721-1800** Bailey, *Chalasticks*. In mod. Dicts.

chalaunge, obs. form of challenge.

chalays, obs. form of chalice.

‖**chalaza** (kəˈleɪzə). *Pl.* **chalazæ**. [mod.L., a. Gr. χαλαζα hail, any small lump or knot like a hail-stone. Cf. F. *chalaze*.]

1. *Zool.* Each of the two membranous twisted strings by which the yolk-bag of an egg is bound to the lining membrane at the ends of the shell, and kept near the middle of the albumen, with the germinating point uppermost; the tread or treadle.

1704 J. Harris *Lex. Techn.*, *Chalaza*, the Treadle of an Egg; every Egg has two of them..each Chalaza consists, as it were, of so many Hailstones separated from each other by that White. **1774** Goldsm. *Nat. Hist.* (1776) II. 29. **1841-71** T. R. Jones *Anim. Kingd.* 786 An almost invisible membrane, the chalazæ, which, being twisted by the revolutions of the yelk, as it is pushed forward in the oviduct, is gathered into two delicate and spiral cords, whereby the yelk is retained *in situ*.

2. *Bot.* A spot on the seed where the nucleus joins the integuments.

1830 Lindley *Nat. Syst. Bot.* 123 Raphe and chalaza usually very distinctly marked. —— *Introd. Bot.* (1848) I. 398 This raphe..expands into a vascular dish or plate, which is called the chalaza. **1880** Gray *Struct. Bot.* vi. §8. 277 The proper base of the ovule..is the Chalaza..In the simplest form of ovule, hilum and chalaza are one.

chalazal (kəˈleɪzəl), *a.* [f. prec. + -al[1].] Pertaining to the chalaza.

1835 Lindley *Introd. Bot.* (1848) I. 398 The amphitropal ovule, whose foraminal and chalazal ends are traverse with respect to the hilum. **1882** Vines *Sachs' Bot.* 580 The cells at its lower (chalazal) end.

chalaziferous (kæləˈzɪfərəs), *a.* [f. as prec. + -ferous; cf. F. *chalazifère*.] Bearing the chalaza or chalazæ: ***chalaziferous membrane***, 'the layer of albumen round the yolk of a bird's egg, to which the chalazæ are attached' (*Syd. Soc. Lex.*).

1859 Todd *Cycl. Anat. & Phys.* V. 65/1 The membrane which proceeds from the Chalazæ over the surface of the yolk has been called Chalaziferous.

‖**chalazion** (kəˈleɪzɪən). Sometimes in latinized form *chalazium*. [a. Gr. χαλάζιον, dim. of χάλαζα chalaza.] A small pimple or tubercule; *esp.* one on the eyelid, a stye.

1708 Kersey *Chalazion*, a Stithe, a small Pimple, or Wart on the Eye-lid. **1731** Bailey II, *Chalaza, Chalazion*. **1878** T. Bryant *Pract. Surg.* I. 343 A tarsal cyst sometimes degenerates into a hard fibrous little mass, feeling somewhat like a large shot beneath the skin, known as a chalazion.

chalazogamic (ˌkæləzəʊˈgæmɪk), *a. Bot.* [ad. F. *chalazogame* (M. Treub 1891, in *Ann. Jardin Bot. de Buitenzorg* X. 219), f. Gr. χάλαζα chalaza + γάμος marriage + -ic.] Defining fertilization in which the pollen-tube penetrates the ovule by the chalaza. Hence **ˈchalazogam**, a plant characterized by this mode of fertilization; **chalaˈzogamy**, chalazogamic fertilization.

1894 *Times* 11 Aug. 11/3 Miss Benson read a paper upon 'Chalazogamic Amentiferæ'..showing that..the pollen-tube forces its way through the chalaza in order to effect fertilization, and hence must be included among the group of chalazogams... Professor Vines..was inclined to regard chalazogamy as an adaptation. **1895** [see porogamic *a.*]. **1898** H. C. Porter tr. *Strasburger's Text-bk. Bot.* II. ii. 492 According to recent investigations some undoubted *Amentaceae* are also chalazogamic. **1902** *Encycl. Brit.* XXV. 436 The pollen-tube..may pierce the embryo-sac at the chalazal end or at the side (basigamy or chalazogamy).

chalbot, *Her.*: see chabot.

†ˈ**chalcanth, chalˈcanthum.** *Obs.* Also c(h)alcanthus, calcanth. [a. F. *calcante* (Cotgr.), and L. *c(h)alcanthum, -us*, a. Gr. χάλκανθον, χάλκανθος 'a solution of blue vitriol used for ink and blacking', f. χαλκός copper + ἄνθος a flower.]

An old name for blue vitriol (sulphate of copper), and for a kind of ink made therefrom; sometimes also applied to green vitriol (sulphate of iron).

1678 Phillips, *Calcanth*, a Chymical word, being the same as Vitriol. **1730-6** Bailey (folio), *Calcanthum*, vitriol rubified. *Chalcanthum*, vitriol or copperas. **1717** Berkeley in Fraser *Life & Lett.* 586 A vapour sulphurous with some tincture of nitre, calcanthus, and bitumen. **1718** Quincy *Compl. Disp.* 14/1 Vitriol, when all its Moisture is dry'd away, becomes Chalcanthum.

chalcanthite (kælˈkænθaɪt). *Min.* [named 1853; f. chalcanth-um + -ite.] Native blue vitriol or sulphate of copper.

1857 Shepard *Mineral.* 441.

†**chalˈcanthous**, *a. Obs. rare*[−1]. In 7 cal-. [f. as prec. + -ous.] Of the nature of ink or blacking.

1646 Sir T. Browne *Pseud. Ep.* vi. xii. 337 A Calcanthous or Atramentous quality. **1656** Blount *Glossogr.*, *Calcanthous*, pertaining to Shoomakers black or Vitriol.

†**chalcedon.** *Herb. Obs.* One of the various plants which have the specific name *chalcedonicus*, as *Lychnis chalcedonica*, *Lilium chalcedonicum*, etc.

1664 Evelyn *Kal. Hort.* (1729) 205 Stock Gilly-Flowers, Spanish Nut, Star-flowers, Chalcedons.

†**chalceˈdonian.** *sb.*[1] *Obs.* Also cal-. [f. L. *chalcedoni-us* chalcedony + -an.] = chalcedony.

1622-62 Heylin *Cosmogr.* ii. (1682) 54 Chalcedonians also of such bigness, that whole Drinking-cups are made of them. **1750** tr. *Leonardus' Mirr. Stones* 801 The Calcedonian pale white, and also the hardest dun.

Chalcedonian (kælsɪˈdəʊnɪən), *sb.*[2] and *a.* [f. *Chalcedon*, city of ancient Bithynia + -ian.] **A.** *sb.* One who upholds the canons, etc., of the council of Chalcedon (a.d. 451). **B.** *adj.* Of or pertaining to the council of Chalcedon or its canons, etc.

1758 A. Maclaine tr. *Mosheim's Eccl. Hist.* I. 421 The controversy between the Monophysites and Chalcedonians is not merely a dispute about words. **1788** Gibbon *Decl. & F.* IV. xlvii. 616 A parrot might be taught to repeat the *words* of the Chalcedonian or Monophysite creed. **1880** *Encycl. Brit.* XIII. 796/1 Then the Chalcedonian party would be purged from any appearance of sympathy with the errors of Nestorius. **1892** W. Bright *Canons of First Four Gen. Councils* 143 While..he [*sc.* Justellus] followed the older Latin version called the Prisca by omitting the Ephesine canons so called, he inserted the Laodicene which the Prisca omitted, and did not place the Constantinopolitan, as the Prisca did, after the Chalcedonian. **1946** E. L. Mascall *Christ, Christian & Church* iii. 54 No amount of discussion of our Lord's psychology can have any *direct* bearing on the Catholic creeds and the Chalcedonian definition.

chalcedonic (kælsɪˈdɒnɪk), *a.* [f. chalcedon-y + -ic.] Of or belonging to chalcedony.

1828 in Webster. **1861** *Temple Bar* III. 388 Chalcedonic varieties of quartz. **1876** Page *Adv. Text-bk. Geol.* xviii. 353 Successive crops of chalcedonic crystals proceed.

chalcedony, calcedony (kælˈsɛdənɪ, ˈkælsɪdənɪ). Forms: α. 4 calsydoyne, calcidoine; β. 4 chalcedun, 6-8 calcedon, 7-8 chalcedon; γ. (4-5 calcedonius), 5 calsydony, calcideny, (6 chalcedonium), 7 calchedonie, calsidonie, chalcidonye, 5- calcedony, 6- chalcedony. See also cassidoine, -dony. [The current form *c(h)alcedony* is directly adapted from L. *c(h)alcedonius*, used in the Vulgate to render Gr. χαλκηδών, in *Rev.* xxi. 19, the name of the precious stone forming the third foundation of the New Jerusalem, but found nowhere else. Adapted forms of the same word in OF. were *calce-, calcidoine*, whence the ME. *calcidoine, calcedun*; also *cassidoine*, whence ME. cassidoine and its varieties, which are separately treated. The 16th c. *chalcedon* was perh. directly from N.T. Greek.

The word is of very complicated history. The L. is commonly assumed to be the same as the adj. *chalcēdonius* of Chalcedon in Asia Minor, as if it were 'Chalcedonian stone', but this is very doubtful. In interpreting the name in the Vulgate, which has the variant form *carcedonius*, the early writers identified it with a stone mentioned by Pliny xxvii. §§103, 104, where MSS. have the variants *carchedonia, charcedonia, calcedonia, calchedonia, carchedonius*, said to be found in North Africa, and to be brought by way of Carthage (Καρχηδών), which, from the description, could

have nothing to do with the chalcedony of the moderns. Isidore has *carchedonia*; Epiphanius *de Gemmis* iv, says it is produced ἐν Καρχηδόνι τῆς Λιβύης. The *carchedonius* or *chalcedonius* is mentioned and moralized upon by a whole catena of writers, including esp. Bæda; but to none of them was it more than a traditional name, about which there clustered notions originally derived from Pliny with an accretion of later fables. The first to try to identify it with any known stone was apparently Albertus Magnus (1205–1282), who may have had in view some form of the stone to which the name is now given. (See the exhaustive article of Schade *Altdeutsches Wbuch.* 1363.)]

A precious (or semi-precious) stone, which in its various tints is largely used in lapidary work: a cryptocrystalline sub-species of quartz (a true quartz, with some disseminated opal-quartz), having the lustre nearly of wax, and being either transparent or translucent.

It is not safe to carry the modern application back before the 16th or at earliest the 15th c.; and references to earlier notions come down to the 17th. In modern lapidary work, chalcedony receives different names according to its varieties of colour and structure, as *agate, cornelian, cat's eye, chrysoprase, onyx, sard*, etc. Most of the varieties were included by Pliny under his *jaspis*. (Westropp.)

α. *c* **1325** *E.E. Allit. P.* A. 1002 þe calsydoyne..withouten wemme. **1393** Gower *Conf.* III. 133 The calcidoine..for his stone he underfongeth.

β. *c* **1305** *Land Cokaygne* 94 in *E.E.P.* (1862) 158 Ametist and crisolite, Chalcedun and epetite. **1555** Eden *Decades W. Ind.* iii. v. (Arb.) 158 Precious stones cauled smaragdes, calcedones & Iaspers. **1586** Ferne *Blaz. Gentrie* 142 A Calcedon is the fifth stone, being most strong and hard by nature, instructing the Soueraigne that he exercise the cardinall vertue Fortitude. **1648** Gage *West Ind.* xii. (1655) 53 Adorned with Emeralds, Turquies, Chalcedons. **1686** *Lond. Gaz.* No. 2116/4 A great Calcedon truly Oriental of a Foot long, and half a Foot broad. **1747** Dingley in *Phil. Trans.* XLVI. 503 Of the Beryl there are three species, the Red..the Yellow..and the White, commonly called the Chalcedon, of the Colour of sheer Milk.

attrib. **1644** Evelyn *Mem.* (1857) I. 98 In another [cabinet] with calcedon pillars, was a series of golden medals.

γ. **1382** Wyclif *Rev.* xxi. 19 The thridde, calcedonyus [**1526** Tindale, calcedony; **1557** *Genev.* chalcedony]. **1398** Trevisa *Barth. De P.R.* xvi. xxvii. (1495) 561 Calcidonius is a pale stone and sheweth dymme colour meane bytwene Berell and Iacynct and comyth and is gendred of the reyne of our lorde. *c* **1460** *Play Sacram.* 171 Crepawdis & calcedonyes semely to se. **1463** *Bury Wills* (1850) 41 My bedys of calsydony. **1482** Marg. Paston *Lett.* 861 III. 287 My peir bedys of calcidenys gaudied with silver and gilt. **1621** Burton *Anat. Mel.* ii. iv. i. iv, There is a kind of Onyx called the Chalcidonye. **1688** R. Holme *Armoury* ii. 40/1 The Calcedon or Calchedonie..being well chafed & warmed, will draw a Straw or a Rush to it. [From Pliny.] **1756–7** tr. *Keysler's Trav.* (1760) II. 47 Pieces of agate, jasper, oriental chalcedony. **1833** Lyell *Princ. Geol.* III. 222 Opal calcedony, resinous silex. **1855** Longf. *Hiaw.* iv. 262 Arrow-heads of chalcedony, Arrow-heads of flint and jasper. **1861** C. King *Ant. Gems* (1866) 7 Calcedony..is a semi-transparent white quartz, slightly tinted with yellow or blue. **1876** Page *Adv. Text-bk. Geol.* vii. 146 Many of the older lavas yield agates, chalcedony, leucite.

chalce'donyx. *Min.* [f. prec. + onyx.] A variety of agate: see quot.

1822 Cleaveland *Min.* 270 When white and grey layers alternate, it is called Chalcedonyx.

† **'chalcelet.** *Her. Obs.*

1572 Bossewell *Armorie* ii. 119 b, A Chalcelet on the first quarter, Diamonde. **1688** R. Holme *Armoury* ii. 256/2 The Chalcelet..is a long & black Bird.

chalcenterous (kæl'sɛntərəs), *a.* [ad. Gr. χαλκέντερος of brazen bowels, applied by Suidas to the grammarian Didymus, f. χαλκ-ός copper + ἔντερ-ον intestine + -ous.] With bowels of bronze, tough. Also **chal'centeric** *a.*

1946 *Times Lit. Suppl.* 12 Oct. 492/2 The most chalcenterous Scotsman who may hereafter seek the shelter of Oxford. **1948** R. W. Chapman *Lexicography* 15 Sir James Murray added to his linguistic acumen and his tireless industry (which did not scruple to tire less chalcenterous workers) a Scotsman's hard, keen sense of the practical. **1964** R. M. Ogilvie *Latin & Greek* 95 For less chalcenteric readers there were the historical novelists.

chalchuite ('tʃæltʃuːaɪt). *Min.* [f. the Mexican name of the stone, *chalchihuitl* + -ite.] A green variety of turquoise from Mexico.

1843 Prescott *Mexico* (1850) I. 274 Four precious stones of considerable size, resembling emeralds, called by the natives chalchuites. **1883** *Amer. Jrnl. Sc.* Ser. iii. XXV. 197 The Green Turquois known as Chalchuite.

chalcid ('kælsɪd), *a.* and *sb. Ent.* [f. mod.L. *Chalcididæ*: see chalcididan.] **A.** *adj.* Of, pertaining to, or characteristic of the superfamily Chalcidoidea of the order Hymenoptera. **B.** *sb.* A member of this superfamily. So **chal'cidian** *a.*², **'chalcidid** *a.* and *sb.*

1882 *Encycl. Brit.* XIV. 49 Parasitic hymenoptera of the chalcidian group. **1891** *Proc. U.S. Nat. Museum* XIV. 570, I know no case in which a chalcidid is a parasite of a proctotrypid. *Ibid.* 571 Chalcidid parasites of the Hemiptera-Heteroptera are very rare. **1893** Ormerod *Injur. Insects* 16th Rep. 66 The little Chalcids were a species of Entedon. *Ibid.*, We should get no good by endeavouring to rear these Chalcid flies. **1895** *Cambr. Nat. Hist.* V. 545 In the cells of the same bee Newport discovered another curious parasitic Chalcid, *Anthophorabia retusa*. **1957** E. B. Ford *Butterflies* (ed. 3) vi. 111 Chalcids are stouter insects than are Ichneumons. **1959** J. Clegg *Freshwater Life* (ed. 2) 227 Two genera of Chalcid Wasps are also aquatic.

chalcidian (kæl'sɪdɪən), *a.*¹ *Zool.* [f. mod.L. *chalcid-æ* (f. L. *chalcis* = Gr. χαλκίς a kind of lizard) + -ian.] Of or pertaining to the family Chalcidæ or Snake Lizards.

Chalcidian (kæl'sɪdɪən), *sb.* and *a.*³ [f. L. *Chalcis, Chalcid-* (Gr. Χαλκίς, Χαλκιδ-) + -ian.] **A.** *sb.* A native or inhabitant of Chalcis, the chief city of Eubœa. **B.** *adj.* Of or pertaining to Chalcis. So **Chal'cidic** *a.* [L. *Chalcidicus*].

1654 Ogilby *Virg., Bucol.* x. 57 The Verses of Euphorion the Chalcidean. **1838** *Penny Cycl.* X. 60 While Alexander was absent in his Persian wars, the Chalcidians increased and improved their fortifications. **1876** F. Tozer *Classical Geogr.* x. 118 All these were Chalcidic cities, and the rivalry between these and the other colonies, which were mostly of Doric origin, materially affected their subsequent history. **1880** *Encycl. Brit.* XI. 95 Naxos, founded by the Chalcidians of Eubœa (735 b.c.). *Ibid.*, The sharp distinction between Dorian and Ionian (or 'Chalcidic'). *Ibid.* XIII. 125 The alphabet used by the Romans is identical with that of the Chalcidian colonies in southern Italy and Sicily..except the three aspirates θ, φ, χ. **1934** A. Toynbee *Study Hist.* III. 68 The Chalcidian and Megarian lines of overseas colonization. **1956** A. Lane *Gk. Pottery* (ed. 2) iv. 42 The distribution of finds, and certain resemblances to native Italian wares, indicate that the 'Chalkidian' vases were made by Eubœan settlers in South Italy.

chal'cidic. *Arch.* [ad. L. *chalcidicum* 'chamber at the corner of a basilica, on each side of the tribunal'. More usually in the L. form.]

1730–6 Bailey, *Chalcidick* [with ancient Architects], a large stately Hall belonging to a court of Justice. **1775** Ash, *Chalcidica, Chalcidicum.* **1832** Gell *Pompeiana* I. ii. 14 It has been thought..to justify the application of the term Chalcidicum to the edifice in question. **1849** Freeman *Archit.* 155 A kind of transept, called chalcidica. **1876** Gwilt *Archit.* Gloss. '*Chalcidicum.*

chalcididan (kæl'sɪdɪdən). *Entom.* [f. mod.L. *Chalcidid-æ*, f. the generic name *Chalcides*, f. Gr. χαλκός brass.] A member of a family of small hymenopterous insects, ornamented with brilliant metallic colours.

1835 Kirby *Hab. & Inst. Anim.* II. xx. 334 A minute species..belonging to the family of Chalcididans.

chalcidony, obs. form of chalcedony.

‖ **chal'cites.** [L. *chalcītes*, ad. Gr. *χαλκῖτις copper-ore.] Green vitriol (sulphate of copper).

1626 Bacon *Sylva* §696 In Furnaces of Copper and Brass, where Chalcites is often cast in, to mend the working.

chalco- ('kælkəʊ). *Min.* Occas. **chalko-**. Stem and combining form of Gr. χαλκός copper, brass, used in the names of many minerals, as **'chalcocite** [Dana's alteration of the older name *chalcosine* (see below)], native sulphide of copper, copper glance. **'chalcodite** [named 1851; f. Gr. χαλκώδ-ης like copper + -ite], a hydrous silicate of iron, found in velvety coatings, having a brass-like lustre, a variety of stilpnomelane. **'chalcolite** [see -lite], a synonym for torbernite, which was erroneously supposed to be an ore of copper. **chalco'menite** [Gr. μήνη the moon; named with reference to *selenite*, f. σελήνη moon], a copper selenite from S. America. **chal'cophacite** [Gr. φακός lentil], a synonym for Liroconite, a native arseniate of copper, occurring in small lentil-shaped crystals. **chal'cophanite** [Gr. φαν- appearing, showing], a hydrous oxide of zinc and manganese, having sometimes a bronze-like lustre. **chalco'phyllite** [Gr. φύλλον leaf: named 1847], a green, foliated arseniate of copper. **chalco'pyrrhotite** [named 1870], a variety of pyrrhotite, a sulphide of iron and copper, resembling chalcopyrite. **chalco'siderite** [Gr. σίδηρος iron], a hydrous phosphate of copper and iron, a variety of Dufrenite. **'chalcosine** [badly formed on Gr. χαλκός + -ine], earlier name of *chalcocite* (see above). **chalco'stibite** [Gr. στίβι (στίμμι), sulphuret of antimony: named 1847], a rare sulphantimonide of copper. **chal'cotrichite** [Gr. (θρίξ), τριχ- hair], a variety of cuprite occurring in acicular or capillary crystals, known as *plush copper-ore*.

1868 Dana *Min.* (1884) 53 Specimens referred to chalcocite. **1857** Shepard *Min.*, Chalcodite. **1868** Dana *Min.* (1880) 460 Brush ascertained the identity of chalcodite and stilpnomelane. **1801** tr. *Klaproth's Ess. Min.*, Werner has given it the name Chalcolite. **1868** Dana *Min.* (1884) 586 Chalcolite has since crept back again, but is no more appropriate now than it was sixty years ago. **1881** *Nature* XXIV. 41 A new selenite of copper..*Chalcomenite*..occurs in the Argentine Republic. **1850** Dana *Min.* 529 Chalcophacite. **1875** *Amer. Chemist* July 1 On chalcophanite, a new mineral species. **1850** Dana *Min.* 529 Chalcophyllite. **1875** *Ibid.* App. ii. 11 Chalcopyrrhotite. **1884** *Ibid.* App. iii. 24 Chalcosiderite. **1835** Shepard *Min.* 123 Chalkosine. **1868** Dana *Min.* 85 Chalcostibite. **1832** Shepard *Min.* 123 Chalkotrichite, the capillary variety of red copper ore. **1868** Dana *Min.* 133 Capillary cuprite, chalcotrichite.

chalcograph ('kælkəʊgrɑːf, -æ-). [cf. next and *photograph*.] A copper-engraving.

In mod. Dicts.

chalcographer (kæl'kɒgrəfə(r)). [f. mod.Gr. χαλκογράφος (f. χαλκός copper, brass + γράφειν to scratch, write, draw, design) + -er. Cf. F. *chalcographe*.] One who engraves on copper.

1662 Evelyn *Chalcogr.* 9 Our Burnisher (another tool us'd by Chalcographers). **1677** Plot *Oxfordsh.* 268 Mr. David Loggan, Chalcographer to the University. **1865** Sala *Diary in Amer.* II. 127 A monstrous map of the island of Cuba. It had been graven by a Spanish chalcographer.

chalcographic (kælkəʊ'græfɪk), *a.* [f. as prec. + -ic; cf. F. *chalcographique*.] Of, pertaining to, or of the nature of chalcography.

1815 *European Mag.* LXVIII. 111 The noblest aims of the calcographic art. **1816** Singer *Hist. Cards* 201 Not only the infancy of xylography, but also that of the chalcographic art.

So **chalco'graphical** = prec.

18.. (*title*) Calcographical Memorials of Literary Personages..a collection of 234 Engravings. **1884** *Athenæum* 1 Nov. 568/2 In order to promote the study of engraving in its earlier stages, it is proposed to form an International Chalcographical Society.

chalcographist (kæl'kɒgrəfɪst). [f. as chalcographer + -ist.] = chalcographer.

1730–6, Bailey, *Calcographist*, an Engraver in Brass. **1864** Webster, *Chalcographist.*

chalcography (kæl'kɒgrəfɪ). [f. Gr. type *χαλκογραφία, f. χαλκογράφος: see above. In F. *chalcographie*.] The art of engraving on copper.

1661 Evelyn *Mem.* (1857) I. 364, I..had recommended to me the publishing what I had written of Chalcography. **1662** —— (*title*) Sculptura; or, the History and Art of Chalcography and Engraving in Copper. **1816** Singer *Hist. Cards* 93 *note*, The curious in Chalcography. **1882** Sala in *Illust. Lond. News* 15 July 55/2 The masterpiece of Mr. Hablot Browne's great capacity in chalcography.

chalcolithic (kælkəʊ'lɪθɪk), *a. Archæol.* [f. chalco- + Gr. λίθος stone + -ic.] Of or pertaining to a period of culture characterized by the concurrent use of stone and bronze implements. (Cf. aeneolithic *a.*)

1902 *Nature* 6 Nov. Suppl. p. iii, The Neolithic vase-types..merge insensibly into those of the earliest dynastic period, which was 'Chalcolithic' in character. **1911** J. L. Myres *Dawn Hist.* x. 224 A long chalcolithic..phase, in which good cheap stone and bad expensive bronze were in use concurrently. **1928** V. G. Childe *Most Anc. East* iv. 98 All the elements that distinguish neolithic and chalcolithic culture..had been created in Egypt out of the common palæolithic heritage of south and north. **1959** *Chambers's Encycl.* XIII. 404/2 The chalcolithic age passes imperceptibly into the early bronze, which covers approximately the 3rd millennium b.c.

chalcologue ('kælkəʊlɒg). *nonce-wd.* [f. Gr. χαλκός brass + -logue: cf. *astrologue, theologue*, etc.] A student of brasses.

1861 *Sat. Rev.* 22 June 647 A zealous and, at the same time, rational student of brasses—the fashion of the day might almost tempt us to say a chalcologue, or perhaps more accurately still, a chalcotribe.

chalco'morphite. *Min.* [app. a bad spelling of *calcomorphite*, named 1873, f. L. *calc-* lime (see calco-) + Gr. μορφή form.] A hydrous silicate of calcium.

1875 Dana *Min.* App. ii. 11.

chalcopyrite (ˌkælkəʊ'paɪraɪt). *Min.* [ad. mod.L. *chalcopyrites* (in Henckel 1725), f. chalco- + pyrite: probably the χαλκῖτις of Aristotle, and included under the πυρῖτις of Dioscorides, *chalcitis* and *pyrites* (in part) of Pliny, *pyrites ærosus, aureo colore, flavus*, of early mineralogists.]

An important ore of copper, called yellow or copper pyrites, native sulphide of copper and iron.

1835 Shepard *Min.* 123 Chalkopyrite. **1862** Dana *Man. Geol.* §30. 64 Chalcopyrite resembles iron pyrites, but is of a deeper yellow color, much softer, being scratched with a knife. **1869** Phillips *Vesuv.* x. 278 Chalcopyrite..found in ejected blocks.

chalcotribe ('kælkəʊtraɪb). *nonce-wd.* [as if ad. Gr. *χαλκοτρίβης, f. χαλκός brass + τρίβειν to rub.] One who takes rubbings of brasses.

1861 [see chalcologue].

chalcotript ('kælkəʊtrɪpt). *nonce-wd.* [f. as prec. + τρίπτ-ης one who rubs, f. τρίβειν.] = prec.

1882 *Ch. Times* 7 July 462 Chalcotripts might with advantage hunt Leicestershire and Derbyshire for this purpose.

chald: see cheald *a. Obs.*, cold.

Chaldaic (kæl'deɪɪk). [ad. L. *Chaldaic-us.*]

A. *adj.* Of or pertaining to Chaldea. **B.** *sb.* The language of the Chaldeans.

So **Chal'daical** *a.* **'Chaldaism**, a Chaldaic idiom or mode of speech, esp. occurring in the Old Testament. **'Chaldaize** *v.* [cf. Gr.

χαλδαΐζειν], to imitate or follow the Chaldeans. †'**Chalday** *a.*, †'**Chaldic** *a.* = CHALDEE.

1662 STILLINGFL. *Orig. Sacr.* II. vii. §10 This..Chaldaick superstition. **1832** W. IRVING *Alhambra* II. 77 It was of fine green silk, covered with Hebrew and Chaldaic characters. **1678** CUDWORTH *Intell. Syst.* 292 The Oracles, called by some Magical..but by others Chaldaical. **1812** *Monthly Mag.* XXXIV. 520 All those Graecisms, Syriaisms, or Chaldaisms, which deform the Hebrew text. **1652** GAULE *Magastrom.* 120 To take heed of Chaldaizing, Judaizing, etc. **1678** CUDWORTH *Intell. Syst.* 293 Those Chalday or Magick Oracles. **1623** LISLE *Ælfric on O. & N.T.* (1638) Pref. 11 They wrote some Caldick, some Syriack.

Chaldean (kæl'di:ən), *a.* and *sb.* [f. L. *Chaldæus* = Gr. *Χαλδαῖος* Chaldean + -AN.]

A. *adj.* Of or pertaining to Chaldea or its inhabitants; hence, to occult science or magic.

1732 BERKELEY *Alciphr.* vi. §20 Whether in Daniel's prophecy of the Messiah we should compute by the Chaldean or the Julian year. **1845** MAURICE *Mor. & Met. Philos.* in *Encycl. Metrop.* II. 566/1 This Chaldean imposture, the substitution of grand notions of nature for a belief in God.

B. *sb.* A native of Chaldea, *esp.* (as at Babylon) one skilled in occult learning, astrology, etc.; hence *gen.* a seer, soothsayer, astrologer. (So Gr. *Χαλδαῖος*, L. *Chaldæus.*) Also, = CHALDEE *sb.* b.

1581 MARBECK *Bk. of Notes* 77 The Chaldeans wer most renowmed in Astrologie that euer were anie. **1611** BIBLE *Dan.* ii. 2. **1642** MILTON *Apol. Smect.* (1851) 305 The feind therefore that told our Chaldean the contrary was a lying feind. *a* **1649** DRUMM. OF HAWTH. *Fam. Ep.* Wks. (1711) 148 How can a Chaldean, by that short minute..in which a man is born, set down the diverse changes..of his life. **1690** *Le Clerk's Five Lett. Insp. Holy Scriptures* ii. 89 The Greek Language then was spoken in Judea, together with the antient Language which the Jews brought from Babylon, that is to say the Chaldean. **1859** RAWLINSON *Bampton Lect.* v. 23 In Daniel the Chaldæans are a special set of persons at Babylon, having a 'learning' and a 'tongue' of their own, and classed with the magicians, astrologers, etc. **1897** J. H. BRIDGES *Opus Majus R. Bacon* iv. lxviii, With Hebrew went Chaldaean, and, in more distant relationship, Arabic. **1944** H. VAN ZELLER *Ezekiel* ii. 22 If only Chaldean could be picked up quickly.

Hence †**Chal'deanizing** *ppl. a.*

1652 GAULE *Magastrom.* 278 Why might not the Chaldæanizing oracle be drawn to confesse so much?

Chaldee ('kældi:, kæl'di:), *a.* and *sb.* Also 4 **Caldey**, 6 **Chalde**, 7 **Caldie**, **Chaldy**.

A. *adj.* = CHALDEAN, CHALDAIC. **B.** *sb.* **a.** A native of Chaldea. **b.** The language of the Chaldeans: also the biblical 'Syriac' or Aramaic.

1382 WYCLIF *Dan.* ii. 10 Eche dyuynour, and witche, and Caldey. **1588** R. PARKE tr. *Mandoza's Hist. China* 304 Martin Simion..is a Chalde borne. **1602** T. FITZHERBERT *Defence* 49 As wel in the Greeke text, as in the Siriac & Caldie. **1668** WILKINS *Real Char.* 5 A Language..which is sometimes called Syriac, and sometimes Chaldee.

So †**Chaldeish**, **Chaldæism** (= CHALDAISM).

c **1511** *1st Eng. Bk. Amer.* (Arb.) Introd. 30/2 Some of them speketh Caldesche some Arabier. **1535** COVERDALE *Dan.* i. 4 To lerne for to speake Caldeish. **1684** N. S. *Crit. Enq. Edit. Bible* viii. 48 There are so many Chaldæisms in the Hebrew Text.

chalder[1] ('tʃɔ:ldə(r)). *Sc.* Also 6 **chawlder**, **chaudder**, 7 **chauder**. [app. a. OF. *chaudière* (also *chaudere*, *chaldere*, *caldere*) = Pr. *caudiera*, Sp. *caldera*, Pg. *caldeira*:—L. *caldāria*, f. *cald-us*, *calid-us* hot; but possibly a shortened form of CHALDRON, q.v. In sense 1, a med.L. *celdra* occurs in early Scottish statutes, and a corresponding vernacular form *celdre* is found.]

1. An obsolete dry measure of capacity: in Scotland 16 bolls or 64 firlots of corn, making nearly 12 quarters Winchester measure: used in the computation of the stipends of the parish ministers. For lime and coal it varied from 32 to 64 imperial bushels. (Formerly, also †*celdre.*)

[*a* **1300** *Leg. 4 Burg.* lxvii, Pistor habeat ad lucrum de qualibet celdra.]

a. **15..** *Chart. Aberd.* 140 (Jam.) Alsmekill land as a celdr of aits will schawe. *Ibid.*, George of Gordoun..occupeis a celdre of atis sawyne pertenand to Dunmetht.

β. *a* **1500** *Act Will.* in Skene *Reg. Maj.* (1609) 3 Ane husband man and ane fermer, sall gif the thritten veschell of their lands of service: and maireour of ane chalder, ane firlot (for knawship). *c* **1540** *Rev. Coldingham Priory* in *Proc. Berw. Nat. Club* II. No. 11. 62 *note*, Wheat, 6 chalders, 7 bolls, 3 firlots, 2 pecks. *c* **1610** SIR J. MELVIL *Mem.* (1735) 408 His Part..was thirteen Chalders of Victual. **1730–69** DE FOE, etc. *Tour Gt. Brit.* II. 151 The Quantity of Coals..supposed to be about 500,000 Chalders, every Chalder containing 36 Bushels. **1799** J. ROBERTSON *Agric. Perth* 286 The [lime] shells are sold at two shillings and twopence the boll, and the raw stones at seven shillings the chalder. **1730** T. BOSTON *Mem.* vi. 63 The stipend..was five chalders of victual and 8 merks. **1813** N. CARLISLE *Topog. Dict. Scotl.* II. *Halkirk*, The stipend..was 2 chalders of meal, and 2 chalders of bear, £600 Scotch, and £30 Scotch for Communion Elements. **1812** CHALMERS *Let.* in *Life* (1851) I. 274, I had only got three chalders of augmentation where I asked and had reason to look for six.

†**2.** In England = CHALDRON, but for coal and lime varying in quantity from 32 to 40 bushels, according as the measure was stroked or heaped. (Apparently a northern word, introduced into the London market with coal.) *Obs.*

1570 *Wills & Inv. N.C.* (1860) II. 324, XV Chalders of Coales. **1582** *Ibid.* 88 A chaudder of corne. **1581** *MS. Acc. Hull Charterhouse*, For sleckinge & siftinge of half a chawlder of lyme, iiij*d.* **1641** BEST *Farm. Bks.* (1856) 126 Of barley..they..carry but a chalder, i.e. fower quarter, or nine seckes in a waine. **1722** DE FOE *Plague* (1756) 255 The publick Fires..cost the City about 200 Chalders of Coals a Week. **1778** *Chron.* in *Ann. Reg.* 161/1 Last year there was imported into London from Newcastle and Sunderland 692093¼ chalders of coals.

3. As a liquid measure. (*humorous.*)

1630 *Tincker of Turvey* 11 Whole chauders of strong ale.

chalder[2] ('tʃɔ:ldə(r)). *Naut.* A rudder-brace or gudgeon.

1867 SMYTH *Sailor's Word-bk.*, *Chalders*, synonymous with gudgeons of the rudder.

chaldern(e, obs. form of CHAWDRON.

chalderon, obs. form of CHALDRON.

†**chal'dese**, *v. Obs.* Also **caldese**. [Presumed to be f. *Chaldee* or *Chaldees*, with the notion of 'cheat as an astrologer'; but evidence is lacking.] *trans.* To cheat, trick, 'take in'.

1664 BUTLER *Hud.* II. III. 1010 He stole your cloak and pick'd your pocket, Chows'd and Caldes'd you like a block-head. *a* **1680** —— *Rem.* (1759) I. 24 Asham'd, that Men so grave and wise Should be chaldes'd by Gnats and Flies. **1697** DENNIS *Plot & no Plot* 1, I caldes'd a Judge while he was taking my Depositions.

chaldron ('tʃɔ:ldrən, 'tʃɑ:drən). Forms: 6 **chauderne**, 7 **chaudron**, **chawdron**, **chauldron**, **chalderon**, 7– **chaldron**. [Another form of CAULDRON *sb.*; a. OF. *chauderon*, mod.F. *chaudron* (= Sp. *calderon*, It. *calderone*), augm. of *chaudère*, *chaudière* (= Sp. *caldera*) kettle:—L. *caldāria*, pl. of *caldārium* hot-bath, f. *cald-us*, *calid-us* hot. The etymological form is *chaudron*; as in *cauldron*, an *l* has been inserted in recognition of the remoter derivation, and *u* subsequently dropped.]

†**1.** An obsolete form of CAULDRON *sb. Obs.*

1555 EDEN *Decades W. Ind.* (Arb.) 223 A chauderne of water. **1601** HOLLAND *Pliny* I. 259 The tunnel or mouth of the furnace must be a good way off from the lead and chawdron. **1639** T. DE GREY *Compl. Horsem.* 137 Fill up the Chalderon with faire water. **1750** G. HUGHES *Barbados* 248 The juice..is boiled first in a very large copper or chaldron.

2. A dry measure of 4 quarters or 32 bushels; in recent times only used for coals (36 bushels).

1615 *Trade's Incr.* in *Harl. Misc.* (Malh.) III. 295 Chauldron of coals. **1664** PEPYS *Diary* (1879) III. 21 This afternoon came my great store of Coles in, being 10 Chaldron. **1710** STEELE *Tatler* No. 73 ¶ 16 All such that shall Poll for Sir Arthur..shall have one Chaldron of good Coals ..And half a Chaldron to every one that shall not Poll against him. **1801** HUTTON *Course Math.* (1827) I. 28. **1834** *Brit. Husb.* I. xii. 296 Lime..from 6*s.* to 18*s.* per chaldron of 36 bushels. **1844** DICKENS *Mart. Chuz.* (C.D. ed.) 515 She had laid in several chaldrons of live coals and was prepared to heap them on the heads of her enemies. **1851** *Coal Tr. Terms Northumbld. & Durh.* 13 The Newcastle chaldron is a measure containing 53 cwt. of coals..It has been found, by repeated trials, that 15 London Pool chaldrons are equal to 8 Newcastle chaldrons.

b. *Comb.*, as ***chaldron-wagon***.

1851 *Coal Tr. Terms Northumbld. & Durh.* s.v. *Chaldron*, The content of the chaldron waggon..is 217,989 cubic inches. **1881** RAYMOND *Mining Gloss.*, *Chaldron-wagons*, containing this quantity, convey the coal from the pit to the place of shipment.

†**3.** In sense of CHALDER[1] 1. *Obs.*

1617 MORYSON *Itin.* III. III. iv. 155 The Gentlemen reckon their reuenewes, not by rents of monie, but by chauldrons of victuals. **1628** HOBBES *Thucyd.* (1822) 138 Valued at three hundred chaldrons.

chaldron, obs. form of CHAWDRON, entrails.

Chaldy, obs. form of CHALDEE.

chaleis, -es(se, obs. forms of CHALICE.

chalenge, obs. form of CHALLENGE.

chalet ('ʃæleɪ, ʃale). [F. *chalet* (not *châlet*, as often in English books) a Swiss word (in la Gruyère pronounced *tsalet*), supposed to have been introduced into Fr. by Rousseau (Littré *suppl.*). Perh. a dim. of *casella*, *cassella*, a little cottage, cot (Du Cange), itself dim. of *casa* house (or of its Romanic representative); less probably, as concerns the sense, = It. *cataletto*, F. *châlit* wooden bedstead. (Littré's suggestion of identity with *castelletum*, *châtelet* is phonetically untenable, because *st* becomes in la Gruyère ç, as *chastel*, *tsaçi*.)]

1. A hut or cabin on the Swiss mountains, where cattle are lodged in the summer, and where cheese is made; hence, the small wooden house or cottage of the Swiss peasant; *gen.* a house or villa built in the style of a Swiss cottage. Also, a small, usually wooden, dwelling for holiday-makers.

1817 BYRON *Manfred* I. ii. 121 The Chalet will be gain'd within an hour. **1818** *Blackw. Mag.* IV. 88 There are many chalets in very lofty situations. **1860** TYNDALL *Glac.* I. §2. 12 On the slopes were innumerable châlets. **1861** *Times* 18 May 5/2 Among all watering places, none can be put in comparison with the fine and large Establishment at Fécamp... There is found the invaluable advantage of having in the same establishment lodging house, chalets, taverns. **1878** LADY HERBERT tr. *Hübner's Ramble* I. xi. 171 A poor little hut or châlet inhabited by a planter and his family. **1910** *Lancet* 5 Nov. 1380/1 Chalets for consumptives at Swansea. **1953** E. HYAMS *Gentian Violet* 19 [A holiday camp] consisted of orderly rows of hideous concrete huts known as châlets.

2. = F. *chalet de nécessité*, a street lavatory, urinal, etc. (In Paris these are elegant structures.)

1882 *Pall Mall G.* 5 Oct. 3 A protest against the proposed erection of the chalets at Ludgate-Circus. **1886** *Daily News* 17 Dec. 2/3 (*Commissioners of Sewers, London*) A large deputation of ratepayers from Ludgate-circus..the petitioners suggesting that the chalets should be placed underground, as..at the Royal Exchange.

chaleys, obs. form of CHALICE.

chalf, **chalfer**, obs. ff. CALF[1], CHAFER.

chali, obs. form of KALI.

chalibeat(e, **-biate**, obs. ff. CHALYBEATE.

chalice ('tʃælɪs). Forms: *α.* 1 cel(i)c, cælc, cælic, 1–3 calic, 2 calc, 3 calch; *β.* 3 caliz, calis, 4 calice; *γ.* 4–6 chalis, -ys, -yce, 4– chalice, (5 **chaleys**, 5–6 **chales**, 6 **challes**, **-is**, **-ece**, **-yce**, **chalesse**, **chalays**, **-eis**, **chaliche**, **chailles**, **calles**, 7 **challice**). [L. *calix*, *calic-em* cup, has appeared in Eng. in various forms. (1) Early OE. *cęlic*, genitive *cęlces*, corresp. to OS. *kelik* (MDu. *kelec*, *kelc*, Du. *kelk*), OHG. *kelihh*, *chelih* (MHG. and mod.G. *kelch*):—WGer. ***kalik**, an early (pre-Christian) adoption of L. *calic-em.* (2) The Latin word was re-adopted in later OE., in Christian use, as *calic*, *cælic*, *cælc*, whence early ME. *calc*, *calch* (cf. ON. *kalk-r*). (3) These were ousted in 12th c. by the OF. *caliz*, *calice.* (4) Before 1350 this was in turn ousted by a central OF. form *chalice*, which gave Eng. *chalis*, *chalice*. While this was the case in English, in France itself *calice* was the form which came down to modern French. (OF. *caliz*, *calice* was of learned origin, but early enough to undergo the phonetic change to *chalice* in central F.; in the struggle between the two forms, the influence of L. *calix*, familiar in ecclesiastical use, was effective in making *calice* the ultimate victor.) Strictly, *cel(i)c*, *calch*, *calice*, *chalice*, are separate words; but their relations are best seen by treating them together.]

1. A drinking-cup or goblet. (Now only in poetic or elevated language.)

α. *c* **825** *Vesp. Ps.* xv. 5 Dryhten dael erfewordnisse minre and celces mines [*elsewhere* calices[1], calic[2].] *c* **950** *Lindisf. Gosp.* Matt. x. 42 Cælc *vel* scenc wætres caldes [*c* **975** *Rushw.* ibid., Cælc fulne wættres galdes]. *c* **1000** *Ags. Ps.* (Thorpe) cxv. 4 Ic her hælu calic hæbbe befangen. *c* **1000** *Ags. Gosp.* Matt. xxiii. 26 þæt wiðinnan ys calicys [*v.r.* -es] and discys [*Hatton G.* calices and discas]. *c* **1000** *Sax. Leechd.* II. 268 Sele þonne cælic fulne to drincanne.

β. *a* **1225** *Ancr. R.* 284 þe caliz þet was imelt iðe fure.

γ. **1382** WYCLIF *Gen.* xl. 13 Thow shalt ȝyue to hym a chalice, after thin office. *c* **1440** *Promp. Parv.* 68 Chalys, *calix.* **1605** SHAKS. *Macb.* I. vii. 11 This euen-handed Iustice Commends th' Ingredience of our poyson'd Challice To our owne lips. **1648** HERRICK *Hesper.*, *Welcome to Sack* 63 Had Cassius..but tasted one Small chalice of thy frantick liquor. **1794** COLERIDGE *Chatterton* 74 Ah! dash the poisoned chalice from thy hand! **1870** BRYANT *Iliad* I. III. 94 With mingled wine they filled a chalice.

b. *fig.* (mostly with reference to certain scriptural passages: see the quotations.)

a. *c* **1000** *Ags. Gosp.* Luke xxii. 42 Fæder, ȝif þu wylt, afyr þysne calic [Vulg. *calicem*] fram me. *c* **1275** *Passion* 158 in *O.E. Misc.* 41 Of þis ilche calche nv forber þu me.

β. *a* **1300** *Cursor M.* 15633 Quer i sal þis calice drinc, or i sal pass þar-bi.

γ. *a* **1340** HAMPOLE *Psalter* xv[i]. 5 Lord is part of myn heritage & of my chalice [Vulg. *calicis mei*]. **1382** WYCLIF *Isa.* li. 17 That thou drunke of the hond of the Lord the chalis of his wrathe. **1483** CAXTON *Gold. Leg.* 16/4 This chalys is the passyon whiche lightly may approþre our lord to the. *c* **1800** K. WHITE *Nelsoni Mors* 18 Tho' from the Muse's chalice I may pour No precious dews of Aganippe's well. **1882** W. B. SCOTT *Poet's Harv. Home* 83 Life is God's chalice filled with tears.

2. *spec.* The cup in which the wine is administered in the celebration of the eucharist.

a. *c* **1000** *Ags. Gosp.* Matt. xxvi. 27 And he ȝenam þone calic þanciende [*Lindisf.*, *Hatton* calic, *Rushw.* cælic]. *a* **1123** *O.E. Chron.* an. 1102 Roden and calicen and candel sticcan. *c* **1200** *Trin. Coll. Hom.* 93 þenne understonde he þat husel and drinke of þe calice. *Ibid.* 215 Boc oðer belle calch oðer messe-ref.

β. *c* **1200** *Trin. Coll. Hom.* 163 Ðe caliz of tin..and hire nap of mazere. *a* **1225** *Ancr. R.* 418 þe chirche uestimenz, ne þene caliz. **1297** R. GLOUC. (1724) 489 The calis of the weued me ssolde ther to. *c* **1300** *Havelok* 187 The caliz, and the pateyn ok. *c* **1340** *Ayenb.* 41 þe crouchen, þe calices, þe creyme.

γ. *a* **1300** *Cursor M.* 15237 Siþen þe chalice [*Gött.* chalis] vp he laght, And blisced als þe win. *c* **1386** CHAUCER *Pers. T.* ¶805 This is a fouler thefte than for to breke a chirche and stele the chalice. **1529** RASTELL *Pastyme*, *Hist. Pap.* (1811) 54 He was impoysoned by venym put in his chales. **1528** MORE *Heresyes* I. Wks. 114/2 That proper comparison betwene treen chalices and golden priestes of olde, and nowe golden chalices & treen priestes. **1654** JER. TAYLOR *Real*

Pres. 31 It is.. as necessary to drink the chalice as to eat the bread, and we perish if we omit either. **1789** Mrs. Piozzi *Journ. France* I. 368 The lightning melted one of the chalices completely. **1875** *Dict. Chr. Antiq.* I. 339/2 Pope Leo IV (847–855) lays down the rule that no one should celebrate mass in a chalice of wood, lead, or glass. **1881** Goldw. Smith *Lect. & Ess.* 47 Bearing the Hussite emblems of the chalice and sword.

3. *transf.* A flower-cup (cf. chaliced).

1650 R. Stapylton *Strada's Low-C. Warres* I. 8 The Lilly suddenly breaking her Challice.. began to blow. **1810** Scott *Lady of L.* III. ii, The water-lily to the light Her chalice reared of silver bright.

4. *Comb.*, as ***chalice-cover***, ***-cup***, †***-piece***, ***-veil***; **chalice-flower**, said to be an old name for the Daffodil; **chalice-moss**, *Cenomyce pyxidata.*

1420 *E.E. Wills* (1882) 46 A stondyng cuppe of seluer y-clepyd a *chales cuppe. *a* **1849** Mangan *Poems* (1859) 54 Sacred Chalice-cup. **1824** H. Phillips *Fl. Historica* I. 99 They were also called *Chalice flowers, from the nectary being shaped like the chalice. **1610** W. Folkingham *Art of Survey* I. ii. 38 The *Chalice or Chin-cough Mosse creeps along the barren.. ditch banckes. **1679** Plot *Staffordsh.* (1686) 199 Scarlet-headed Cup or Chalice-Moss. **1443** *Test. Ebor.* (1836) I. 132 A *chalespece of silver round covered.

chaliced ('tʃælɪst), *a.* [f. prec. + -ed².]

1. Of flowers: Having a cup-like blossom.

1611 Shaks. *Cymb.* II. iii. 24 His Steeds to water at those Springs on chalic'd Flowres that lyes. **1858** O. W. Holmes *Aut. Breakf.-t.* (1865) 78 The golden-chaliced crocus burns. **1872** Swinburne *Ess. & Stud.* (1875) 26 The opening in heaven of the chaliced flower of dawn.

2. Contained in a chalice or cup. Also *fig.*

1836 W. Freshney *Rime of Nun* 4 To sip again The bitter dregs of chalic'd pain. **1850** Mrs. Browning *Poems* I. 284 Better loveth he Thy chaliced wine.

‖**chalicosis** (kælɪ'kəʊsɪs). *Med.* [mod. f. Gr. χαλίξ small stone + -osis.] Disease of the lungs produced by the inhalation of fine siliceous particles, by stone-masons and like workers.

1878 tr. *Ziemssen's Cycl. Med.* VIII. 75 The trouble originated from chalicosis. **1886** Fagge *Princ. & Pract. Med.* I. 984 Miekel has recently proposed to term the resulting lung affection Chalicosis.

chalicothere ('kælɪkəʊθɪə(r)). *Palæont.* [f. mod.L. *chalicotherium*, f. Gr. χάλιξ, χάλικ- gravel + θηρίον beast.] A perissodactyl mammal of the extinct genus *Chalicotherium* (fam. Chalicotheriidæ), with a horse-like head and clawed toes.

[**1833** J.-J. Kaup *Descript. d'Ossements Fossiles de Mammifères* II. ii. 4 Chalicotherium, *Kaup.* Nouveau genre de Pachydermes... J'ai donné ce nom à deux fort grands Pachydermes.] **1907** *Amer. Naturalist* XLI. 733 (*title*) Preliminary notes on some American chalicotheres... Little is known of the American forms of the Chalicotherioidea,—an extinct family of mammals. **1910** H. F. Osborn *Age of Mammals* ii. 143 *Bartonian Stage*... The supposed chalicothere *Pernatherium*, a very aberrant perissodactyl, is first known at this stage. **1937** *Discovery* Dec. 372/2 a Chalicothere, that remarkable beast of the late Miocene period, with a horse-like head, and toed, clawed 'hoofs', a horse-cum-sloth creature in appearance. **1958** Zeuner *Dating the Past* (ed. 4) 430 The average period of existence of a genus was 5·6 million years in the line of the horses (*Hyracotherium-Equus*), 5·9 million years in the chalicotheres.

chalifah, var. khalifa.

chalilite ('kælɪlaɪt). *Min.* [named 1836; f. Gr. χαλίξ pebble, flint + -lite.] A variety of Thomsonite of a reddish-brown colour.

1836 T. Thomson *Min.* I. 324 Chalilite.. occurs in the Donegore mountains. **1843** Portlock *Geol.* 218 Chalilite, common, in.. the Sandy Braes district in County Antrim.

chaling(e, obs. form of challenge.

chalis, obs. form of chalice.

†**chalishing.** *Obs. rare*⁻¹.

a **1500** *Eger & Gr.* 1116 in Furniv. *Percy Folio* I. 390 It was euer Sir Gray-steeles desiring that for his death shold be made noe chalishing.

chalk (tʃɔːk), *sb.* Forms: 1 calc, cealc, 4–7 **chalke**, (5 **chaalke**, **shalke**), 6 **chauke**, **chawke**, 6–7 **chaulk(e**, 6– **chalk**. See also cauk *sb.* [Common WGer.; OE. *cealc* (:—**ceælc*, **cælc*, **calc*) = OS. *calc* (MDu. *calk*, Du. *kalk*), OHG. *chalch* (MHG. *kalc*, mod.G. *kalk*, *kalch*); also Da., Sw., mod.Icel. *kalk*); a. L. *calc-em*, *calx* lime; this sense is retained in the Teutonic languages generally, but in English the word passed at an early period into the sense of L. *crēta*, OHG. *krîde*, F. *craie*. Cf. the quotations in which L. *calx* is translated *cealcstan* limestone, and the fact that chalk is the chief 'limestone' of the S.E. of England.]

¶ It occurs in the oldest Eng. Glossaries, as rendering L. *calculus* (? = later *cealcstan*.)

c **700** *Epinal Gl.* (also Erf. & Cott.) 165 *Calculus*, cealc. *c* **1050** *Gloss.* in Wr.-Wülcker 362/1 *Calculus*, cealc, numestan (? *read* pumestan).

†**1.** ? Lime. (Traces of this sense after the OE. period are very uncertain; quot. 1572 is doubtful.)

c **893** K. Ælfred *Oros.* VI. xxxii. §2 Sume niht on anum niwcilctan huse [*nuper calce illitorum*].. þa ongon se cealc mid unȝemete stincan. *c* **1050** *O.E. Voc.* in Wr.-Wülcker 334 *Calx*, cealcstan [= limestone]. *a* **1200** *Ibid.* 551 *Calcx*, chalcston. **1572** J. Jones *Bathes of Bath* II. 17 b, Snow is very cold, and chalke is very hot, yet eyther of them is most whyte.

2. An opaque white soft earthy limestone, which exists in deposits of vast extent and thickness in the south-east of England, and forms high cliffs along the sea-shore.

Chemically, chalk consists of carbonate of lime with some impurities. Geologically, it is a deep-sea formation composed of fragments of shells of Foraminifera, abounding in certain important animal fossils, and interspersed with nodules of flint. It is burned for lime, and prepared for writing or marking on blackboards or other dark surfaces. In 17–18th c. it is often mentioned as eaten by young women suffering from chlorosis: cf. quot. 1811.

956 [see *Cealcpytt*, chalkpit in 7]. *c* **1400** *Destr. Troy* 3047 Hir chekes.. as the chalke white. *c* **1440** *Promp. Parv.* 68 Calke or chalke, erþe, *calx, creta.* *c* **1450** *Voc.* in Wr.-Wülcker 576 *Creta*, chaalke. *c* **1500** *Cocke Lorell's B.* (1843) 3 Shele floure and put chauke therin. **1587** *Mirr. Mag.*, *Elstride* xxxiv. 7 Shee lookt as pale as chalke with wrathfull ire. **1694** *Reply Ladies' & Bachelor's Petit.* in *Harl. Misc.* IV. 438 (D.) How can any man.. believe that ten thousand green-sickness maidens.. would rather die martyrs to oatmeal, loam, and chalk than accept.. matrimony? **1700** Farquhar *Const. Couple* v. iii. (D.) You might have had me once; but now, Madam, if you should by chance fall to eating chalk or gnawing the sheets, 'tis none of my fault. **1787** Winter *Syst. Husb.* 51 Chalk is an absorbent earth. **1811** Hooper *New Med. Dict.*, *Chlorosis*.. a preternatural appetite for chalk, lime, and other absorbents.. usually attend on this disease. *c* **1850** *Arab. Nts.* (Rtldg.) 640 The robber quickly made a mark on the door with some chalk. **1857** Kingsley *Misc.* II. 372 It [chalk] was deposited as white lime mud, at a vast sea-depth. **1859** *Musketry Instr.* 21 A black board and a piece of chalk.. to describe the figures. **1880** Geikie *Phys. Geog.* iv. 191 Chalk.. is formed of the broken remains of minute forms of marine animal life.

3. a. Applied to other earths resembling chalk. ***fuller's chalk***: ? fuller's earth. In quot. 1658 probably = calx. ***brown chalk***: a name for umber. ***French chalk***: a kind of steatite. ***red chalk***: a bed of chalk of a deep red colour in Norfolk; also applied to 'ruddle, a red argillaceous ore of iron' (*Syd. Soc. Lex.*). ***black chalk*** (see quots.).

1601 Holland *Pliny* II. 560 Sundry sorts of chaulkes for to scoure clothes, and namely the Tuckers earth. **1607** Topsell *Four-f. Beasts* 200 Mingled with Fullers chaulke. **1658** Rowland *Moufet's Theat. Ins.* 911 The chaulk or salt of it.. is.. commended by Chymicks, and Chirurgeons, for to cure that kernell or tumour of flesh. **1854** *Encycl. Brit.* VI. 402/1 *Black Chalk*, a mineral used by artists for drawing. It is a variety of bituminous shale, the *schiste-graphique* of Haüy. **1886** J. W. Anderson *Prospector's Handbk.* 115 Black Chalk—a variety of clay containing carbon. *Mod.* The section of the Red Chalk at Hunstanton.

b. *spec.* Applied to various coloured preparations resembling chalk in texture, and used like it in the form of crayons for drawing. With *pl.* Also *attrib.* drawn with chalk, executed in chalk.

1481–90 *Howard Househ. Bks.* (1841) 202 Item, in yelu okyr.. Item, in blak chalke. *c* **1790** Imison *Sch. Art* II. 55 Sketching chalk.. a composition made of whiting and tobacco-pipe clay rolled like crayons. **1816** J. Smith *Panorama Sc. & Art* 702 Chalks are.. held in a steel or brass case, called a portcrayon. **1832** G. Downes *Lett. Cont. Countries* I. 161 Two heads in chalks by.. Rahn. **1883** Lloyd *Ebb & Fl.* I. 30 A beautiful chalk head of a dog. **1884** *Cassell's F.M.* 216/1 Shading in chalk from the flat.

4. In reference to the old custom at alehouses, etc., of 'ticking' or writing up with chalk a 'score' or account of credit given: transferred from the chalk used to the chalk marks or ticks on the door, etc., the 'score' entered in chalk, the reckoning or account; credit, 'tick'.

a **1529** Skelton *El. Rummyng* 613 We're fayne with a chalke To score on the balke. *c* **1570** Thynne *Pride & Lowl.* (1841) 58 Your cheker man for it doth keepe no chalke. **1590** Tarleton *Newes Purgat.* (1844) 82 His score growing very great, and much chalk upon the post. **1592** Nashe *P. Penilesse* B j b, Hee that hath no money must goe and dine with sir John best betrust, at the signe of the chalke and the Post. **1634** S. R. *Noble Soldier* v. iii. in Bullen *O. Pl.* I. 333 There's lesse chalke upon you[r] score of sinnes. **16..** *Songs Lond. Prentices* (1841) 157 When we have no mony, Wher shall we find chalk? *a* **1704** T. Brown *Sat. on Fr. King* Wks. 1730 I. 60, I trespassed most enormously in chalk. **1719** D'Urfey *Pills* (1872) I. 270 This wheedling talk You fancy will rub out my Chalk.

5. a. A mark, line, or 'score' made with chalk; *spec.* in various games (formerly scored with chalk).

1680 Cotton *Compl. Gamester* in Singer *Hist. Cards* (1816) 341 The eldest must show how many chalks he hath in his hand to set up. **1801** Strutt *Sports & Past.* III. vii. 242 Thirty-one chalks complete the game. **1861** Gen. P. Thompson *Audi Alt.* III. cxlvi. 135 Draw a chalk, and let those who are disposed, step over it. **1887** *Sporting Life* 24 June 1/4 Skittles.. Curry went out with 4 chalks.

b. *fig.* A scratch or scar. *slang.*

1840 Marryat *Poor Jack* vi, I got this chalk.

6. Phrases. **a.** *Chalk* and *cheese* are opposed in various proverbial expressions as things differing greatly in their qualities or value, though their appearance is not unlike, and their names alliterate.

1393 Gower *Conf.* I. 17 Lo, how they feignen chalk for chese. **1541** Barnes *Wks.* (1573) 258 This deffinition agreeth as well with your key, as Chalke and Cheese. *a* **1555** Latimer in Foxe *A. & M.* (1684) III. 413 As though I could not discern cheese from chalk. **1579** Gosson *Sch. Abuse* To Rdr., Making black of white, Chalke of Cheese. **1600** Rowlands *Lett. Humours Blood* vi. 75 Tom is no more like thee, then Chalks like Cheese. **1708** Motteux *Rabelais* v. xvi, Words.. as analogous as Chalk and Cheese! **1826** Scott *Woodst.* xxiv, This Scotch scare-crow was no more to be compared to him than chalk was to cheese.

b. (*by*) ***a long chalk***, also ***by long chalks***, ***by chalks*** (colloq.): in a great degree, by far (in allusion to the use of chalk in scoring 'points', etc.; see 4, 5). ***to walk one's chalks*** (slang): to go away, be off.

1835 A. B. Longstreet *Georgia Scenes* 6 Oh, wake snakes, and walk your chalks. **1837–40** Haliburton *Clockm.* (1862) 26 Your factories down east.. go ahead on the English a long chalk. **1840–5** Barham *Ingol. Leg.*, *St. Romwold* (D.), Sir Alured's steed was by long chalks the best. *a* **1849** Mangan *Poems* (1859) 459, I could once beat all of them by chalks. *a* **1859** De Quincey *Syst. Heavens* Wks. III. 171 *note*, As regards the body of water.. the Indus ranks foremost by a long chalk. **1857** Kingsley *Two Years Ago* i. (D.) The prisoner has.. cut his stick, and walked his chalks, and is off to London.

7. a. *attrib.* and *Comb.*, as ***chalk-bank***, ***-cliff***, ***-country***, ***-down***, ***-dust***, ***-formation***, ***-hill***, ***-land***, ***-licker***, ***-lime***, ***-ridge***, ***-score*** (see 4), ***-stripe***; ***chalk-eating***, ***-faced***, ***-like***, adjs.; **chalk-back day** (see quots.); **chalk-bed**, a stratum of chalk; **chalk-cutter**, one who digs chalk; **chalk-drawing**, a drawing executed in chalk (see 3 b); **chalk-flint**, a flint found in the chalk: so **chalk-fossil**, etc.; **chalk-head** (*humorous*), a good head for chalking scores (see 4); **chalk-lime**, lime made from chalk; **chalk-mark** *sb.*, a mark, esp. a distinctive mark, made with chalk; *v. trans.*, to mark with chalk, esp. with a distinctive mark; to draw (a line) with chalk; hence ***chalk-marked*** adj.; **chalk-marl**, an argillaceous stratum situated just beneath the Lower White Chalk; **chalk period**, the cretaceous period (see cretaceous *a.* 2); **chalk-pit**, **chalk-quarry**, a pit or quarry from which chalk is dug; **chalk stream**, a stream flowing over chalk; **chalk talk** *U.S.*, a lecture or speech illustrated by chalk sketches made by the speaker; hence ***chalk-talker***.

1851 *N. & Q.* IV. 501/2 At Diss, Norfolk, it is customary for the juvenile populace, on the Thursday before the third Friday in September.. to mark.. each other's dress with white chalk, pleading a prescriptive right to be mischievous on '*chalk-back day'. **1906** *Westm. Gaz.* 27 Feb. 2/3 In Norfolk there used to be an annual 'Chalk-back Day', the servants hired at the September fair at Diss being marked with chalk on either jacket or dress to indicate that they were settled. **1823** Cobbett *Rur. Rides* (1885) I. 309 You actually have a *chalk-bank to your right and a sand-bank to your left. **1802** Playfair *Illustr. Hutton. The.* 177 In the *Chalk-beds of England.. a great proportion of the petrifactions belong to the tropical seas. **1773** G. White *Selborne* xxxviii, The next church, ruin, *chalk-cliff.. may become their *hybernaculum.* **1830** Cobbett *Rur. Rides* (1885) II. 321 The houses white and thatched, as they are in all *chalk-countries. **1876** Green *Short Hist.* i. §3 (1882) 17 Sitting.. on the *chalk-down above Minster. *a* **1723** D'Urfey *Plague of Impert.* (D.), Discouler'd, pale, as.. *chalk-eating girl That oatmeal with it chew'd. **1896** *Daily News* 6 Apr. 6/5 A not very distant *chalk-faced hill. **1935** C. Day Lewis *Time to Dance* 47 Not for long will your chalk-faced bravado Stand the erosion of eternity. **1823** W. Buckland *Reliq. Diluv.* 193 The diluvium contains.. fragments of chalk and *chalk-flints. **1881** Carpenter *Microsc.* (ed. 6) xxi. 826 The Ventriculites which are well known as *chalk-fossils. **1863** Mark Lemon *Wait for End* (Hoppe), 'Haven't got a *chalk-head, and can't keep score,' replied Tom [the waiter]. **1823** Cobbett *Rur. Rides* (1885) I. 315 A great *chalk-hill. **1832** Tennyson *Miller's D.* xxxi, On the chalk-hill the bearded grass Is dry and dewless. **1941** *Proc. Prehist. Soc.* VII. 149 The cultural succession observed on the south English *chalk-lands. **1712** Steele *Spect.* No. 431 §3 These craving Damsels, whether.. Pipe-champers, *Chalk-lickers, Wax-nibblers, etc. **1842** E. Turner *Elem. Chem.* (ed. 7) 759 The white *chalk-like excrement of Serpents. **1754** Hales in *Phil. Trans.* XLVIII. 827 *Chalk-lime.. will not preserve water from putrefaction: though stone-lime.. does preserve water in a great measure. **1862** Thackeray *Round. Papers* 166 On the doorpost.. is a little *chalk-mark. **1878** *Chambers's Jrnl.* 14 Dec. 791/2 The white chalk-mark on his [*sc.* a Brahmin's] forehead, which signifies his rank to the world. **1927** *Scots Observer*, 11 June 2/2 A happy-go-lucky Customs officer chalk-marked my suit case. **1928** *Daily Tel.* 9 Oct. 8/1 He has to toe the line which I chalk-mark, otherwise out he goes. **1880** R. Rowe *Picked up in Streets* 221 Rows of broken, dusty, *chalk-marked shutters. **1876** Page *Adv. Text-bk. Geol.* xviii. 344 Bones of birds.. obtained from the *chalk-marl of England. **1811** A. T. Thomson *Lond. Disp.* (1818) 653 An elegant and useful adjunct to the *chalk mixture. **1904** J. R. A. Davis *Nat. Hist. Animals* III. lii. 309 The toothless Pterosaurs (species of *Pteranodon*), which flourished during the *Chalk period. **956** *Chart. Eadwiȝ* in *Cod. Dipl.* V. 346 Of Deohholes hylæ on ðonæ *cealcpyt; swa forð.. oððа ðа dunæ ufewearde. **1884** *Contemp. Rev.* Aug. 331 The chalk-pits.. are usually unfenced. **1832** Tennyson *Miller's D.* xv, The white *chalk-quarry from the hill Gleam'd to the flying moon. **1866** Carlyle *Remin.* I. 239 Now have a *chalk-score and no money. **1829** T. Arnold *Jrnl.* 7 Aug. in Stanley *Life & Corr.* (1846) App. D. 658 As gentle and as limpid as one of the clear rapid *chalk streams of the south of Hampshire. **1858** Kingsley in *Fraser's Mag.* Dec. 330/1 In chalk streams the largest fish are found oftener in the mill-heads

than in the mill-tails. **1904** E. F. Benson *Challoners* xiv, The chalk-stream..was brimful from bank to bank of hurrying translucent water. **1906** *Macm. Mag.* Apr. 453 The chalk stream regions to-day are not fishing countries in the sense that Devon, Hereford, or Wales are. **1943** R. Chandler *Lady in Lake* (1944) i. 7 Smooth grey flannel with a narrow *chalk stripe. **1953** 'S. Ransome' *Drag the Dark* (1954) ii. 24 A double-breasted blue chalk-stripe suit. **1881** *Christian Miscell.* V. 40 His inimitable '*chalk-talk'. **1969** *New Yorker* 31 May 78/2 We are treated to a vicious and numbing chalk-talk from the writings of the founder. **1888** *St. Paul & Minneapolis Pioneer Press* 22 July (Farmer), The celebrated *chalk-talker.

b. In the names of butterflies and moths, as ***chalk carpet, chalk hill blue, chalk pit*** (see quots.).

1832 J. Rennie *Butterfl. & Moths* 18 The Chalk Hill Blue (*Polyommatus Corydon*, Stephens). *Ibid.* 117 The Chalk Carpet (*Larentia bipunctaria*, Ochsenheimer). *Ibid.* 125 The Chalk Carpet (*Xerene procellata*, Ochsenheimer). *Ibid.* 230 The Chalk-pit Plume (*Pterophorus migadactylus*, Fabricius) 'frequents chalky districts'. **1892** Kipling *Lett. Travel* (1920) 36 A lordly swallow-tailed butterfly,..very like the flitting 'chalk-blue' of the English downs. **1927** *Daily Express* 14 July 5/5 The chalkhill and holly blues would make beauty spots among the yellow iris.

chalk (tʃɔːk), *v.* Also 6–7 chalke, chaulk(e, chauk(e, 7 chawke. See also cauk *v.*² [f. prec. sb.]

1. *trans.* To mix or treat with chalk.

1575 Laneham *Let.* (1871) 39 Mylk for theyr flawnez, not pild nor chalked. **1649** Blithe *Eng. Improv. Impr.* (1653) 183 Land..Dunged, Limed, Marled, or Chalked, or otherwise made fat and warm. **1759** tr. *Duhamel's Husb.* I. viii. (1762) 35 It was the custom of the Britons to chalk their lands. **1875** [see chalking *vbl. sb.*].

2. a. To rub, mark, or inscribe with chalk.

1592 Greene *Disput.* 11 The boyes..shall chalke him on the backe for a Crosbite. **1677** Moxon *Mech. Exerc.* (1703) 207 They chalk the Flat side of it. **1679** R. Mansell *Narr. Popish Plot* Addr. c, Wisest Counsels, which by ill success have been chalkt o' th' back for Follies. **1813** Moore *Post Bag* viii. 36 Thou know'st the time..It takes to chalk a ball-room floor. **1839** Dickens *Nich. Nick.* xiv, Morleena..had the soles of her shoes chalked.

b. *fig.* To make white or pale as by rubbing with chalk; to blanch.

1633 G. Herbert *Temple, Forerunners* vi, Let a bleak palenesse chalk the doore. **1847** Tennyson *Princ.* iv. 358 Fear Stared in her eyes, and chalk'd her face.

c. ***to chalk*** **(a person's)** ***hat, to have one's hat chalked***: to allow, be allowed, free travel (as on a railway). *U.S. colloq. Obs.* exc. *Hist.*

1823 Quitman *Let.* in J. F. H. Claiborne *Life & Corr.* (1860) 78, I will 'chalk your hat' for the journey. **1880** A. A. Hayes *New Colorado* (1881) xi. 149 Twenty-five seedy, second-class ruffians, who proposed to travel, as they say in the West, 'with their hats chalked', or free. **1887** *Nation* (N.Y.) 21 Apr. 329/1 It would seem that all railway officers and most railway employees have their 'hats chalked' all over the U.S. **1928** J. W. Starr *100 Yrs. Amer. Railroading* 76 The practice out there was called 'chalking the hat', from the custom of the conductor in placing a white mark or ticket on the..headgear of the passenger.

d. To mark (an object) with chalk as an indication that it has been officially admitted, e.g. by a customs officer, or directed. *U.S.*

1867 Mrs. Whitney *L. Goldthwaite* iii, Stooping to examine the trunk..[he said,] 'These things is chalked all right for Littleton.' **1893** 'Mark Twain' *£1,000,000 Banknote* 258 In his first agitation he was going to try to bribe the postman to chalk it through.

3. a. To write with chalk; to draw, mark, line with chalk.

1580 G. Harvey *3 Wittie Lett.* 38 Whom..I recount and chaulke uppe in the Catalogue. **1589** R. Harvey *Pl. Perc.* 25 So I will chalke thy praises vp. **1709** Steele & Add. *Tatler* No. 93 ¶4, I have chalked out in every Figure my own Dimensions. *a* **1720** Sheffield (Dk. Buckhm.) *Wks.* (1753) I. 96 As painters first chalk out the future face. **1823** J. Badcock *Dom. Amusem.* 156 One chalks down nine figures. **1849** F. B. Head *Stokers & Pok.* vi. (1851) 58 Large letters were chalked on consecutive compartments.

b. *spec.* To write up in chalk (a record, *esp.* of credits given); to score. Hence ***to chalk it***: to run up a score, take 'tick'. Now esp. common in phr. ***to chalk it up (to)***, to charge it (to) (a person, an account, experience, etc.). Also, to write *down*; to set down as a sum or estimate.

1597 *1st Pt. Return Parnass.* I. i. 451 All my debts stande chaukt upon the poste for liquor. *a* **1704** T. Brown *Wks.* (1760) I. 182 (D.) A country parliament man that chalk'd it plentifully last winter session. **1826** T. Wilson *Pitman's Pay* (1843) 11 She chalks up 'scores' at a' the shops. **1835** R. M. Bird *Hawks of Hawkhollow* II. viii. 78 He chalked me down like a fool, me and Tom Staples; being old friends, or sort of. **1845** *Whitehall* xliv. 306 May I never chalk another pint. **1845** Disraeli *Sybil* (1863) 282 Every man I chalked up was of the same opinion as the landlord of the Cat and Fiddle. **1877** E. Peacock *Gloss. Manley & Corringham* 53/1 *Chalk*, to mark on a board with chalk the number of pints of beer a person is in debt to a publican. 'Benny Mason's been to th' Gouden Cup an' had two quarts o' ale *chalk'd* down to you.' **1886** Elworthy *W. Somerset Word-Bk.* 122 Publicans are accustomed to keep the score by *chalk* marks behind the door, hence to be (*chau·kd* aup) is to be entered as a debtor. **1895** in *N. & Q.* (1941) CLXXXI. 117/1 We want a drink. .. So, Miss, do chalk it up. **1939** N. Monsarrat *This is Schoolroom* ii. vii. 176 One of those superb nights when everything is so perfectly in tune..that one unconsciously chalks it up, to have something to aim at in the future. **1953** W. P. McGivern *Big Heat* vi. 82 Well, we can chalk it up to experience.

4. chalk out. *fig.* †**a.** To mark *out*, as with chalk (*obs.*). **b.** To delineate, *esp.* by the main features; to outline, sketch *out*, adumbrate.

1571 Golding *Calvin on Ps.* xviii. 44 God did but (as it were under a dark shadowe) chalk out the..kingdome of his sonne. **1579** Tomson *Calvin's Serm. Tim.* 309/2 They are chalked out as enimies. **1634** W. Wood *New Eng. Prosp.* I. viii, The Princely Eagle, and the soaring Hawke, Whom in their unknowne wayes there's none can chawke. **1678** Bunyan *Pilgr.* I. Apol., This Book it chaulketh out before thine eyes The man that seeks the everlasting Prize. **1765–93** Blackstone *Comm.* (ed. 12) 412 We have now chalked out all the principal outlines of this vast title of the law.

c. *fig.* To trace *out*, mark out, as a course to be followed. Also occas. ***chalk forth*** (obs.).

1579 Gosson *Sch. Abuse* (Arb.) 25 Chaulk out the way to do the like. **1610** Shaks. *Temp.* v. i. 203 It is you, that haue chalk'd forth the way Which brought vs hither. **1613** —— *Hen. VIII*, I. i. 60. **1643** Digges *Unlawf. Taking Arms* §2 (1647) 14 That way to eternall glory, which our Saviour hath chalked out. **1670** Cotton *Espernon* I. II. 77 His Majesty being pleas'd..to chalk him out what he would have him do. **1707** *Vulpone* 25 They have a much shorter way chalked out by this Article. **1754** Richardson *Grandison* VII. li. 259 Lay down your own plan: Chalk out your future steps. **1807** Byron *Childish Recoll.* 68 When now the boy is ripen'd into man, His careful sire chalks forth some wary plan. **1872** J. Grant *Newsp. Press* III. xi. 253 [He] pursued the course which he had from the first chalked out for himself.

chalked (tʃɔːkt), *ppl. a.* Also 6 chaukt, 7 chalkt, chalkd. [f. prec. + -ed¹.] Marked, rubbed, mixed, etc., with chalk; see the vb.

1599 Marston *Sco. Villanie* I. iii. 182 Thy chalked score. **1616** Holyday *Juvenal* (1618) 15 With his chalked feet. **1677** Plot *Oxfordsh.* 243 'Tis Proverbial here..That chalkt Land makes a rich Father but a poor Son. **1823** J. Badcock *Dom. Amusem.* 157 To draw a chalked line.

So **'chalker**. One who chalks, marks, mixes, etc., with chalk.

1865 *Daily Tel.* 7 Sept., London milkmen are known in the vocabulary of slang as 'chalkers'.

chalkiness ('tʃɔːkɪnɪs). [f. chalky + -ness.] Chalky quality.

1805 Lucock *Nat. Wool*, The chalkiness of the land. **1866** Miss Braddon *Lady's Mile* (Hoppe), Pictures were accepted, and 'skyed': critics talked about coldness, and blackness, and chalkiness.

chalking ('tʃɔːkɪŋ), *vbl. sb.* [f. chalk *v.* + -ing¹.] The action of the verb chalk.

1. The manuring of land with chalk.

1626 Bacon *Sylva* §596 After the chalking of the Ground. **1875** *Act 38 & 39 Vict.* c. 92. §5 An improvement comprised in either of the three classes following: chalking of land, clay-burning, claying of land.

2. Marking, drawing, writing, etc., with chalk; running up an account (at an alehouse, etc.); tracing out or designing.

1613 W. Browne *Brit. Past.* I. iv, Let your steps be stitcht to wisdome's chalking. **1638** Brathwait *Barnabees Jrnl.* I, Till long chalking broke my credit. **1764** (*title*) Handmaid to the Arts, teaching..means of delineation by off-tracing, chalking, etc. **1851** *Coal-tr. Terms Northumbld. & Durh.* 13 Chalking Deal, a flat board, upon which the craneman.. keeps account of the work.

†**'chalkish**, *a. Obs. rare.* [f. chalk *sb.* + -ish¹.] Somewhat chalky.

1658 W. Burton *Itin. Anton.* 218 A whitish or chalkish soil.

chalk-line. a. (Of uncertain meaning.) **b.** 'A cord rubbed with chalk or similar material, used by artificers for laying down straight lines on the material as a guide for a cutting instrument' (Knight *Dict. Mech.*). **c.** A line drawn with chalk; a straight line; also *transf.* and *fig.* So, in allusive use, ***to walk a chalk-line***: to behave with propriety; to keep undeviatingly to a course of action (*U.S. colloq.*).

a **1450** *Fysshynge wyth an Angle* (1883) 15 A good fyne lyne of þak thryde made yn maner of a chalke lyne. **1631** Winthrop *Let.* 28 Mar. in *Hist. New Eng.* (1853) I. 458 Store of shoe-maker's thread and hobnails; chalk and chalk-line. **1771** *Carroll Papers in Maryland Hist. Mag.* XIII. 173 Pray desier Mr Deards to send me by him two Drumlines. .. The Chalk lines are too weak & small. **1825** *Bro. Jonathan* I. 55 Eight or ten young women at work; not one..stayed her needle or chalk-line for a single moment. **1855** T. C. Haliburton *Nature & Human Nature* II. viii. 324 He returns as straight as a chalk-line or as we say the crow flies. **1859** H. E. Taliaferro *Fisher's River* xxii. 246 You can't swindle this boy; he's walked too many chalk-lines fur that. **1887** in *Amer. Speech* (1950) XXV. 31/2 The owners of those dives also knew they would have to close up shop and walk the chalk-line once the police took the matter in hand. **1904** C. Martyn *Fables of Hotel Profession* 26 Everybody had to walk a Chalk Line or Get Out. **1948** *Time* 2 Aug. 12/2 Many of whom deny that they are Communists but all of whom walk the Communist chalk line.

chalk-stone ('tʃɔːkstəʊn).

†**1.** Lime, limestone: see chalk *sb.* 1. *Obs.*

†**2.** ? A piece of chalk. *Obs.*

c **1386** Chaucer *Chan. Yem. Prol. & T.* 654 Goth, walkith forth, and brynge a chalk-stoon. **1611** Bible *Isa.* xxvii. 9 When he maketh all the stones of the Altar as chalke stones.

3. A concretion chiefly of sodium urate, resembling chalk, occurring in the tissues and joints, *esp.* of the feet and hands, in severe gout. Hence **'chalkstony** *a.*

1738 Birch *Milton* Milton's Wks. 1738 I. 38 His Hands and Fingers gouty, and with Chalk-Stones. **1782** W. Heberden *Comm.* ix. (1806) 35. **1836–9** Todd *Cycl. Anat.* II. 152/1 Lithic acid..is deposited in cases of chalk-stone in the textures..surrounding the joints of the fingers and toes. **1862** Sala *Seven Sons* II. ii. 51 His hands [were] much afflicted with chalkstones. *Ibid.* v. 116 Some whose hands were stiff or chalkstony.

'chalk-white, *a.* White like chalk.

? *a* **1400** *Morte Arth.* 1026 A chargour of chalke whytt sylver. *a* **1400–50** *Alexander* 1584 Bathe chambirlayn & chaplayne in chalk-quite wedis. *a* **1440** *Sir Degrev.* 1490 ffayre schetus of sylk Chalk-whyȝth as the mylk. **1865** *Dublin Univ. Mag.* I. 18 Treeless chalk-white roads across the downs.

chalky ('tʃɔːkɪ), *a.* [f. chalk *sb.* + -y¹.]

1. Consisting of or characterized by chalk; abounding in chalk.

c **1400** *Test. Love* Prol. (1560) 271 b, Some men there been, that painten..with coles and chalke; and yet is there good matter to the leude people of thicke chalkie purtreyture. **1580** Baret *Alv.* C 304 Chalkie or full of chalke. **1593** Shaks. *2 Hen. VI*, III. ii. 101. **1598** Yong *Diana* 485 Chalkie cliffes are steept in Brittish seas. **1610** W. Folkingham *Art of Survey* I. ii. 3 Chaulkie, Clayie, Sandie Earth. **1662** J. Bargrave *Pope Alex. VII* (1867) 125 Of a chauchy or brimstony matter. **1762–9** Falconer *Shipwr.* I. 38 The chalky cliffs salute their longing eyes. **1785** Cowper *Tiroc.* 307 To kneel and draw The chalky ring and knuckle down at taw. **1812** Byron *Waltz* xiii, Round the chalky floor how well they trip. **1846** J. Baxter *Libr. Pract. Agric.* I. 98 The beech-tree is..in high, chalky, and gravelly soils.

2. Resembling chalk in colour or consistence, chalk-white.

1611 Bible *Song 3 Child.* i. 22 *marg.*, Naphtha, which is a certaine kind of fat and chalkie clay. **1616** Holyday *Persius* 329 Whom candidate chaulky ambition Draws gaping to her lure. **1762–71** H. Walpole *Vertue's Anecd. Paint.* (1786) I. 268 The colouring is flat and chalky. **1802** *Med. Jrnl.* VIII. 290 A very white, chalky appearance of the fæces. **1882** *Garden* 1 Apr. 223/3 Chalky white flowers.

3. *Pathol.* Of the nature of chalk, or of a chalk-stone (sense 3), or containing chalk-stones.

1782 A. Monro *Anat.* 43 It may be..chalky from the gout. **1834** J. Forbes *Laennec's Dis. Chest* 351 Bony and chalky concretions. **1876** tr. *Wagner's Gen. Pathol.* 320 Chalky calculi consist chiefly of carbonate and phosphate of lime.

4. *Comb.*, as ***chalky-faced*** adj.

1807 W. Irving *Salmag.* (1824) 293 Such a little chalky-faced puppet.

challance, -anss, obs. Sc. ff. challenge.

challece, obs. f. chalice.

challenge ('tʃælɪndʒ), *sb.* Forms: α. 4–6 calenge, (4 caleng, 6 callenge). β. 4 *Sc.* challanss, 4–5 chalange, chalaunge, 4–7 chalenge, (4 chaleng, 5 challeng), 5 *Sc.* chalans, (6 chaling), 6– challenge. [ME. *calenge*, *chalange*, a. OF. *ca-*, *chalenge*, *-lange*, orig. *-longe* (with many other forms) = Pr. *calonja*, OSp. *caloña*:—L. *calumnia*, trickery, artifice, misrepresentation, false accusation, malicious action at law; prob. f. *calvi*, *calvere* to devise tricks. With the phonetic development in OF. cf. that of *somnium*, *songe*. OE. had both the Northern F. *calenge*, and the central F. *chalenge*; the latter has (as in many other words) survived. *Challenge* is thus originally the same word as *calumny*. Some of the senses still in use go back to the ME. and OF. sb., but others are taken immediately from the vb., as in *blame*, etc., so that the sequence is not simple.]

†**1.** An accusation, charge, reproach, objection.

a **1300** *Cursor M.* 6714 Þe bestis lauerd sal ga quite Of al-kines chalange and wite. *c* **1315** Shoreham 131 Thou hast y-broȝt ous out of cry Of calenge of the fende. **1388** Wyclif *Jer.* vii. 6 If ȝe maken not fals caleng to a comelyng, & to a fadirless child, & to a widewe. **1483** *Cath. Angl.* 58 A chalange, *calumpnia*. **1610** Guillim *Heraldry* III. xv. (1660) 197 Sufficient difference to prevent all causes of Challenge. *a* **1626** Bacon *Max. Com. Law* Pref. 2 The incertainty of law ..is the principall and most just challenge that is made to the lawes of our nation. **1692** W. Robertson *Phraseol. Gen.* 1057 He refuses the challenge of the crime, or denies he did commit it.

2. a. The act of calling to account; *esp.* the act of a sentry in demanding the countersign.

1375 Barbour *Bruce* VIII. 82 But challanss eschapit [he] had, Ne war ane hynt hym by the brand. **1526** *Pilgr. Perf.* (W. de W. 1531) 300 b, Peter at the chalenge of a poore handmayde, for feare dyd deny the [= thee] his lorde. **1754** Richardson *Grandison* V. xlii, The creature..had subjected herself to your challenges. *Mod.* Startled by the challenge of a sentinel.

b. *Hunting.* The opening and crying of hounds at finding the scent; see challenge *v.*

In mod. Dicts.

3. *Law.* **a.** 'An Exception taken, against either persons or things' (Blount); *spec.* an objection made to one or more of the jurymen in a trial, as in ***principal challenge, peremptory challenge, challenge to the array, to the polls, to the favour***. Also, an exception taken to a vote, etc.

[**1292** Britton I. ii. §11 Et si defendoms a touz Corouners qe nul remue jurour par chaleng de nule partie.] **1530** *1 Act 22 Hen. VIII*, c. 14 §8 No person arrained for any pety

treason, murder, or felony be . . admitted to any peremytorie chalenge aboue the nombre of xx. **1607–72** *Cowell's Interpr.*, *Challenge* principal, otherwise called peremptory, is that which the Law alloweth without cause alledged, or farther examination . . peremptory being used onely in matters Criminal, and alledged without other cause than barely the Prisoners fancy; but principal in civil Actions for the most part, and with naming some such cause of exception, as being found true, the Law alloweth without farther scanning. **1660** *Trial Regic.* 32 If you will not agree in your Challenges, we must be forced to Try you severally. **1768** Blackstone *Comm.* III. 359 As the jurors appear . . they shall be sworn, unless challenged by either party. Challenges are of two sorts; challenges to the array and challenges to the polls . . Challenges to the array are at once an exception to the whole panel, in which the jury are arrayed. *Ibid.* 361 Challenges to the polls, in capita, are exceptions to particular jurors. *Ibid.* 363 Challenges to the favour, are where the party hath no principal challenge; but objects only some probable circumstances of suspicion, as acquaintance, and the like. **1853** Wharton *Pa. Digest* II. 115 Interest in a juror is a principal cause of challenge.

b. *East Indies.* (See quot.)

1858 J. B. Norton *Topics* 198 Another check . . is the right of 'challenge' . . long . . recognised in this district . . Any ryot who imagines that his wealthier neighbour's field is more lightly assessed than his own, offers to take it at a higher rate, claiming a corresponding reduction for his poorer holding.

4. A calling in question or disputing; the state of being called in question.

1820 Scott *Monast.* xvi, Whatever schemes may be pursued for bringing her title into challenge.

†**5.** A claim; the act of demanding as a right. In early use, often, a false claim. *Obs.*

c **1314** *Guy Warw.* A. 5466 Swithe thai priked . . Chalaunge on Herhaud to legge. **1340** *Ayenb.* 34 Of þe rote of auarice guoþ out manye smale roten . . þe þridde roberye. Þe uerþe chalenge. *c* **1440** *Promp. Parv.* 68 Chalaunge or cleyme, *vendicacio.* **1570–6** Lambarde *Peramb. Kent* (1862) 295 To Maude so soone as ever she made her chalenge to the Crowne. **1613** Purchas *Pilgr.* I. vii. ii. 556 They lay challenge to Jerusalem for their inheritance. **1750** Johnson *Rambl.* No. 1 ¶10 A publick challenge of honours and rewards.

6. a. An invitation or summons to a trial or contest of any kind; a defiance.

c **1325** *Coer de L.* 525 When none wolde . . With schafft to him make chalenge, etc. **1551** Edw. VI. *Jrnl.* in *Lit. Rem.* (1858) II. 312, I lost the chaling of shoting at roundes, and wane at rovers. **1649** Bp. Reynolds *Hosea* vii. 157 The pride and wrath of man to give a chalenge to the justice and power of God. **1722** Sewel *Hist. Quakers* (1795) I. iv. 314 The Baptists sent him a letter by way of challenge, that they would discourse with him. **1847** L. Hunt *Men, Women, & B.* II. xi. 275 His whole countenance is a challenge to scrutiny. **1856** Emerson *Eng. Traits* xi. Wks. (Bohn) II. 80 A challenge to duty and honour. **1879** McCarthy *Own Times* II. xxix. 387 It was a challenge to established beliefs and prejudices.

b. In weakened use: a difficult or demanding task, esp. one seen as a test of one's abilities or character.

1954 W. Faulkner *Fable* 23 It was not that his trained professional judgment told him that the affair . . would be touch-and-go and hence more than doubtful . . that would have been a challenge, as if the old destiny had not abandoned him at all. **1957** A. E. Stevenson *New Amer.* iii. iv. 147 One of tomorrow's great challenges will be to make good use of what will very possibly be a greatly increased leisure. **1966** *Hockey Coaching* (Hockey Association) 5 The game of hockey in this country is facing a real challenge. **1972** E. Longford *Wellington* xxii. 340 Today the Martyrs' Memorial stands like a rock of tranquillity in the roaring currents of the twentieth century, an occasional challenge to the climbing skills of students, pot in hand. **1979** D. Halberstam *Powers that Be* (1980) i. ii. 71 He almost seemed to welcome the challenge of the war, it would test America's worthiness.

7. *spec.* A summons to fight, *esp.* to single combat or duel.

1530 Palsgr. 202/2 Calenge or provokyng to do armes, *chalenge.* **1581** Mulcaster *Positions* xxxvii. (1887) 151 He must abyde both chalenge and combate with all the rest. **1601** Shaks. *Twel. N.* iii. iv. 157 Heere's the Challenge, reade it. **1660–1** Marvell *Corr.* xvi. Wks. 1872–5 II. 48 Upon some words Gen. Mountagu sent a chalenge to the Duke of Buckingham. **1769** Blackstone *Comm.* IV. 167 Challenges to fight, either by word or letter . . are punishable by fine and imprisonment. **1838** Marryat *Midsh. Easy* xxii, It was not in Captain Tartar's nature to refuse a challenge.

8. *attrib.*

1813 Scott *Trierm.* iii. x, The valiant Knight of Triermain Rung forth his challenge-blast again.

9. A dose of an antigen given, by injection or other means, to an animal or person that has been sensitized to it by a previous dose. Also *attrib.*

1950 *Yale Jrnl. Biol. & Med.* XXIII. 29 Thephorin was injected intra-abdominally 15 minutes before the challenge with histamine. **1952** *Proc. Soc. Exper. Biol. & Med.* LXXXI. 110/1 Even after 10 days a high mortality rate results following antigenic challenge of a series of mice sensitized with a mixture of horse serum and vaccine. **1964** W. G. Smith *Allergy & Tissue Metabolism* i. 5 The second injection of antigen, which brings about anaphylactic shock, is termed the challenge dose.

challenge (ˈtʃælɪndʒ), *v.* Forms: α. 3 **kalange-n, kalenge-n,** 3–5 **calange(n,** 3–6 **calenge(n.** β. 3–6 **chalange,** 3–7 **chalenge,** 4 **chalaunge, -unge, -inge, -ynge, -ang, schalange,** ? **chalain,** (4–5 *Sc.* **challanss,** 6 **chaleng, chalynch, challynge,** *Sc.* **challance,** 6–7 **challeng),** 7 **challendge,** 5– **challenge.** [ME. *kalange-n, chalange-n*, a. OF. *ca-, chalonger, -langer, -lenger* (with numerous variant forms) = Pr. *calonjar*, OSp. *caloñar*:—late L. *calumniāre*, for *calumniārī* to accuse falsely, f. *calumnia*: see prec. Cf. F. *songer* from L. *somniāre*.]

†**1. a.** *trans.* To accuse, bring a charge against, arraign, impeach. Also *absol.* *Obs.* (or ? *dial.*)

a **1225** *Ancr. R.* 54 Hwarof kalenges tu me? **1340** *Ayenb.* 43 Þe zenne . . of sergons þet accuseþ and calengeþ þet poure uolc. **1375** Barbour *Bruce* xix. 60 Gud schir dauid the brechyne Thai gert challanss richt stratly syne. *c* **1449** Pecock *Repr.* v. xiv. 558 If eny man wolde chalenge a frere. **1580** Sidney *Arcadia* ii. 169 To be challenged of unkindness. **1593** Q. Eliz. *Sp.* in *Harl. Misc.* (1809) II. 261 The king of Spain doth challenge me to be the quarreller, and the beginner of all these wars. **1649** Bp. Guthrie *Mem.* (1702) 75 The E. of Stafford was Challeng'd and made Prisoner. **1655** Fuller *Waltham Abb.* 6 Let none challenge the words of impropriety. **1693** W. Robertson *Phraseol. Gen.* 321 To challenge, or accuse one.

†**b.** To lay (an offence) to one's charge, accuse one of. *Obs.*

1297 R. Glouc. (1724) 279 Seyn Dunston . . kalangede her mys-dede. *a* **1340** Hampole *Psalter* lv[i]. 6 If þai myght chalange oght in vs. **1485** Caxton *Trevisa's Higden* iv. xxxiii. (1527) 180 b, Unwyse handelynge is chalenged of the.

2. a. To find fault with, reprove, reprehend; to call upon to answer for something, or to give account of oneself; to call to account. Now only *dial.* exc. as in b.

a **1300** *Cursor M.* 19148 Es it . . resun þat we Calanged [*v.r.* chalaunged, schalanged, chalanged] for ur gode dede be? **1377** Langl. *P. Pl.* B. v. 174 [I] am chalanged in þe chapitel hous, as I a childe were. *c* **1440** *Promp. Parv.* 68 Chalengyn or vndyrtakyn, *reprehendo.* **1597** Hooker *Eccl. Pol.* v. lxiv. §6 Why were they dumb, being thus challenged? **1642** R. Harris *Serm.* 20 If God fill not every vessell, challenge him upon that his word, Open thy mouth wide, and I will fill it. *a* **1714** Burnet *Own Time* II. 411 He was warned of it, and challenged him on it. **1855** *Scotticisms corrected* 10 His father never challenged him for lying. *Mod. Sc.* I have never been challenged for crossing these fields.

b. Said of a sentinel; and in derived *fig.* uses.

1796 Southey *Joan of Arc* vi. 50 The sentinel . . with uplifted lance Challenged the darkling travellers. **1833** *Reg. Instr. Cavalry* i. 28 On any one approaching his post, he must challenge them by the words '*Who comes there*'? **1856** Froude *Hist. Eng.* (1858) I. i. 44 In the country every unknown face was challenged and examined. **1878** Browning *La Saisiaz* 6 No blue space in its outspread . . challenged my emerging head.

c. Also said of the hounds giving mouth on finding a scent.

1677 N. Cox *Gentl. Recreat.* i. (1706) 17 When Hounds or Beagles at first finding the Scent of their Game presently open and cry, we then say, they Challenge. **1751** in Chambers *Cycl.* s.v. *Hunting.* **1781** P. Beckford *Hunting* (1802) 238 It is a great pleasure, when a hound challenges, to be certain that he is right.

3. *Law.* To object or take exception to (a juryman, evidence, etc.); to take an initial exception to (any proceeding). Also *absol.*

[**1292** Britton i. v. §8 Et cum . . les jurours soint venuz en court, si porunt il estre chalengez: Sire, il n' i deit estre, car mei endita, etc.] *c* **1570** Thynne *Pride & Lowl.* (1841) 17 Ye may him chalenge from your jury. **1572** Fulke *Heskins' Parl.* 389 We may lawfully chalenge the aray, being enpanelled by . . a partial shirif. **1772** *Chron.* in *Ann. Reg.* 104/2 The corporation objected to the whole jury, which in law language is called challenging the array. *c* **1781** *Trial George Gordon* 8 When the panel was called over a second time, the prisoner by his counsel, peremptorily challenged nineteen, and the Attorney-General for the Crown, challenged seven. **1875** Jowett *Plato* (ed. 2) V. 87 Anybody may challenge on the ground that so and so is unfit. **1883** *Law Rep.* XI. *Queen's B. Div.* 598 The evidence of the women was accepted and not challenged.

4. To call in question, dispute.

c **1386** Chaucer *Wyf's T.* 344 Povert is . . Possessioun that no wight wil chalenge. **1489** Caxton *Faytes of A.* iii. xi. 189 Whether the lordes by whos landes a kynge . . muste passe may challenge hym the passage. **1625** Bp. Mountagu *App. Cæsar* 1 Whatsoever they have challenged and articled against in their accusation. **1825** Scott *Talism.* ii, I were wrong to challenge . . the privilege of thy speech, since boasting is more natural to thee than truth. **1869** Huxley in *Sci. Opinion* 5 May 486/2 As a temporary measure, I do not presume to challenge its wisdom.

5. To assert one's title to, lay claim to, demand as a right, claim *for*, arrogate (*to* obs.) oneself. *arch.* or *Obs.* **a.** with simple object. *arch.*

a **1240** *Wohunge* in *Cott. Hom.* 275 Þi derue deað o rode . . calenges al mi heorte. *c* **1300** *K. Alis.* 7512 Heo is my qwene; Y hire chalenge. *c* **1386** Chaucer *Frankl. T.* 596 Nat that I chalenge eny thing of right Of yow, my soverayn lady, but youre grace. **1480** Caxton *Chron. Eng.* iv. (1520) 31/1 To calenge the trybute whiche they did denye. **1513** More *Edw. V*, 3 [He] began not by warre, but by Law to challenge the crown. **1549** Coverdale *Erasm. Par. 1 Peter* i. 21 That we should therby chalenge no prayse vnto our selues. **1568** Grafton *Chron.* II. 298 It is for the French King, who is here taken prisoner, and there are mo then .x. knights and squires that challenge the taking of him and of his sonne. **1634** Sir T. Herbert *Trav.* 1, I challenge no thankes for what I publish. **1658** Sir T. Browne *Hydriot.* i. (1736) 13 These Urns will challenge above 1300 Years. **1699** Bentley *Phal.* 329 A Gentleman that challenges the Title of Honourable. **1746** Smollett *Reproof* 7 An injured friend!—who challenges the name? If you, what Title justifies the claim? **1867** Freeman *Norm. Conq.* (1876) I. iii. 140 Causes which led them to challenge Imperial rank.

†**b.** with inf. as object. *Obs.*

c **1300** *K. Alis.* 7303 Ye chalangith al to habbe. **138.** Wyclif *Serm.* Sel. Wks. I. 220 Men that calengen here to be evene wiþ Crist. **1579** Lyly *Euphues* (Arb.) 190 As thou challengest to be noble in bloud, etc. **1633** Bp. Hall *Hard Texts* 483 Can yee challenge to possesse the land? **1683** *Pennsylv. Archives* I. 70 Where he challenged . . to have spoak so.

†**c.** with object clause. *Obs.*

c **1400** *Apol. Loll.* 76 Nowe clerkis . . chalungen to hem þat only it pertenіþ to hem to punisch symony, etc. **1660** Fuller *Mixt Contempl.* i. (1841) 197 If fifth monarchy men challenge to themselves that they must be exempted from their obedience.

†**d.** with object and complement. *Obs.*

c **1450** Lonelich *Grail* xxxvii. 717 For his love that ye calangen youre lord, I schal yow socowren. **1493** *Festivall* (W. de W. 1515) 4 b, Fendes chalengynge hym theyres as by ryght. **1559** Bp. Scot in Strype *Ann. Ref.* I. ii. App. vii. 15 Challynging Christe to be ther foundation. **1655** Fuller *Ch. Hist.* i. iv. §9 The Chronicle of Westminster challengeth the same to be done in their Convent.

†**e.** *absol.*

1605 Shaks. *Lear* i. i. 54.

6. a. *fig.* To have a natural right or claim to; to demand, to call for. *arch.*

1577 B. Googe *Heresbach's Husb.* ii. (1586) 89 b, The Peare . . chalengeth the nexte place, and is one of the cheefest beauties of the Orcharde. **1622** Fletcher *Sp. Curate* iii. iii, Whose honest cause . . Will challenge Iustice. **1648** Evelyn *Corr.* (1857) III. 10 Yours of the 6th and 9th of May received, challenges this account from me. **1673** Ray *Journ. Low C.* 4 Bruges . . may well challenge place among the Cities of the second rate in Europe. *a* **1704** T. Brown *Eng. Sat.* Wks. 1730 I. 26 Horace and Juvenal . . challenge a superiority above all the rest.

b. Now *esp.* To claim (some responsive action or recognition on the part of others, *e.g.* attention, regard, respect, approbation, admiration).

1615 G. Sandys *Trav.* 33 The Aquæduct made by the Emperour Valentinian . . doth principally challeng remembrance. **1691** Ray *Creation* ii. (1704) 455 Our better part challenges our greatest care and diligence. **1766** Anstey *Bath Guide* viii. 42 Men . . That challenge Respect from all Persons of Birth. **1787** Bonnycastle *Astron.* i. 3 Astronomy . . has challenged the admiration of all ages. **1818** Hallam *Mid. Ages* (1872) II. 71 Unless his merit should challenge the popular approbation. **1841** Myers *Cath. Th.* iv. §32. 330 A strange thing—one sufficiently anomalous to challenge attention.

7. a. To summon or invite defiantly to a contest or any trial of daring or skill; to defy, dare. (Often *to do* something, or *to* an *action.*) Freq. in fig. contexts, esp. in weakened sense 'to present a challenge to'.

1513 Douglas *Æneis* v. xiii. 7 South pipand windis . . Challancis to pas on burd. **1529** More *Comf. agst. Trib.* ii. Wks. 1178/2 Euery man that feeleth him selfe challenged and prouoked by temptacion. **1633** P. Fletcher *Pisc. Ecl.* i. vii, I durst to challenge all my fisher-peers. **1671** Milton *Samson* 1151, I . . challenge Dagon to the test. **1769** *Lett. Junius* xix. 85 We . . are challenged to produce a precedent. **1796** H. Hunter tr. *St. Pierre's Stud. Nat.* (1799) III. 368 Challenge the son of Tendal to a competition in song with you. **1855** Kingsley *Heroes, Theseus* ii. 211 He challenges all comers to wrestle with him. **1866** —— *Herew.* x. 151 You must not challenge me to find it out. **1927** V. Woolf *To Lighthouse* iii. iv. 245 Form, were it only the shape of a white lamp-shade looming on a wicker table, roused one to perpetual combat, challenged one to a fight in which one was bound to be worsted. **1963** J. Wiesenfarth *Henry James* v. 105 The narrator's theory is challenged by Grace Brissenden's. **1965** A. J. P. Taylor *Eng. Hist. 1914–45* i. 28 Lloyd George spoke publicly in all-out support for the war. From that moment, he challenged Asquith... Unconsciously, perhaps even unwillingly, he was offering himself as the man who could run the war better. **1973** E. F. Schumacher *Small is Beautiful* ii. i. 77, I [*sc.* C. P. Snow] was asking something which is about the scientific equivalent of: 'Have you read a work of Shakespeare's?' Such a statement challenges the entire basis of our civilisation.

b. To invite (emulous, hostile, or critical action of any kind). (Cf. 6 b.)

1614 Bp. Hall *Recoll. Treatises* 770 Wee doe utterly deny it, and challenge your proofe. **1663** Gerbier *Counsel* D iv a, Your Apollo's Oracle-like Arcenall, may challenge the most sublime proffers of men of parts. **1718** *Free-thinker* No. 75. 142 Prudence is a real Perfection, which Challenges the nicest Observation. **1850** Prescott *Peru* II. 205 Such a one as might have challenged comparison with the bravest of his ancestors. **1873** Black *Pr. Thule* xiv. 226 They could challenge criticism with an easy confidence. **1882** J. H. Blunt *Ref. Ch. Eng.* II. 283 Challenging controversy in every possible way.

8. *spec.* **a.** To call upon to answer an imputation by combat; to summon to fight, or to a duel.

1588 Shaks. *L.L.L.* v. ii. 696 Hector will challenge him. **1601** —— *Twel. N.* iii. ii. 36 Challenge me the Counts youth to fight with him. **1655–60** Stanley *Hist. Philos.* (1701) 37/1 Pittacus . . challeng'd Phryno to single Combat. **1839** Thirlwall *Greece* II. 166 With the intention . . of challenging him to a conflict. *Mod.* The officer challenged his rival.

b. *intr.* or *absol.*

c **1380** *Sir Ferumb.* 399 Y chalenge wiþ þe to fiȝt. **1697** Dryden *Virg. Georg.* iv. 125 They challenge, and encounter Breast to Breast. **1762** Churchill *Ghost* i. 297 So he that challenges might write Only to those who would not fight.

†**c.** *to challenge a person the field.* *Obs.*

[**1556** *Chron. G. Friars* (1852) 7 Roberte of Vere chalynched them in the felde and was overcome.] **1601** Shaks. *Twel. N.* ii. iii. 136 To challenge him the field, and then to breake promise with him. **1693** W. Robertson *Phraseol. Gen.* 477 The disagreement grew so high, that they challenged the field one of another. [*Ibid.* 601 To challenge one into the field: *in arenam provocare.*]

9. To give a dose that constitutes a challenge (see prec.) to (an animal or person);

1946 [see CHALLENGING *ppl. a.*] **1962** LUNTZ & WRIGHT in A. Pirie *Lens Metabolism Rel. Cataract* 322 Leucocytes from each group of guinea-pigs were transferred to normal guinea-pigs who were then challenged with lens protein. **1966** W. C. BOYD *Fund. Immunol.* (ed. 4) xvii. 729 If we are testing the immunizing effect of an antigen, we shall challenge our animals, after a suitable interval, with a dose of the infectious micro-organism, or with a toxic product of this organism.

Hence **'challenged** *ppl. a.*, **'challenging** *vbl. sb.* and *ppl. a.*

1330 R. BRUNNE *Chron.* (1810) 173 Isaak a partie had mad a chalangyng. *c* **1440** *Ipomydon* 1280 Sithe I was not at the justynge, I will not be at the chalengynge. **1578** THYNNE *Let.* in *Animadv.* Introd. (1865) 59, I haue thought yt my chalenged dutye..by penne to desplay my inwarde mynde. **1697** [see CHALLENGER b.]. **1825** BENTHAM *Ration. Rew.* 20 The practice..in many schools, called challenging..he who stands at the head of the class begins the exercise: does he make a mistake, the next to him in succession corrects him and takes his place. **1842** H. E. MANNING *Serm.* (1848) I. vii. 94 The whole inmost soul is bent into a challenging array. **1946** *Proc. Soc. Exper. Biol. & Med.* LXIII. 189/2, 210 mice were sensitized..by 4 consecutive intraperitoneal injections of 1 ml each of undiluted horse serum every other day. Twenty-one days later a challenging dose of 1 ml. of undiluted horse serum..was injected intravenously. **1969** *Times* 7 July 5/7 It has been possible to treat challenged lungs with drugs known to have an effect in reducing inflammation. **1975** *Aviation Week & Space Technol.* 27 Jan. 63 Clearly the most challenging problem facing the ECM strategist today is to operate efficiently and effectively in a high-density threat environment. **1985** *Aerospace America* May B54 The innovative techniques evolving in the application of new technology in solving the challenging problems in today's flight test program.

challengeable ('tʃælɪndʒəb(ə)l), *a.* [f. CHALLENGE *v.* + -ABLE.] That may be challenged; open to accusation, criticism, or objection.

1377 LANGL. *P. Pl.* B. XI. 296 A chartre is chalengeable byfor a chief iustice. *c* **1449** PECOCK *Repr.* 538 Noon of hem alle is challengeable and blameable. *a* **1603** T. CARTWRIGHT *Confut. Rhem. N.T.* (1618) 262 They are partiall and for their partiality chalengable. **1671** *True Non-Conf.* 73 A fault no less challengeable in a Minister of the Gospel. **1845** R. CHAMBERS *Vest. Creation, Commenc. Org. Life*, It is a challengeable stranger upon the face of the Earth.

challengee (ˌtʃælən'dʒiː). *rare.* [f. CHALLENGE *v.* + -EE.] One who is challenged.

1616 B. JONSON *Devil an Ass* III. iii, Eyther by Chartell, Sir, or ore-tenus, Wherein the Challenger, and Challengee ..haue their seuerall courses.

challengeful ('tʃælɪndʒfəl), *a.* [f. CHALLENGE *sb.* + -FUL.] Fraught with a challenge; challenging.

1903 HARDY *Dynasts* I. II. v. 52 And I only own—such is my challengeful character—that perhaps He [*sc.* Napoleon] do eat pagan infants when He's in the desert. **1927** *Chamber's Jrnl.* June 381/2 An interrogation..vital and challengeful.

challenger ('tʃælɪndʒə(r)). [f. CHALLENGE *v.* + -ER[1].] One who challenges, in various senses: *spec.* †**a.** An accuser; a plaintiff, claimant. *Obs.*

[**1292** BRITTON I. xvi. §3 Et la chose soit deliveré au chalengeour.] **1382** WYCLIF *Job* xxxv. 9 For the multitude of chalengeres [**1388** fals chalengeris; Vulg. *calumniatorum*] thei shul crie. *c* **1449** PECOCK *Repr.* v. xiv. 559 If the chalenger wole contynue in his chalenging. **1600** HOLLAND *Livy* III. xliv. 117 The plaintife or challenger [*petitor*] declareth against her. **1612** BREREWOOD *Lang. & Relig.* xxv. 217 The other challenger of the same dignity. **1839** STONEHOUSE *Axholme* 144 If the challenger could neither ascertain his property, nor proue his accusation.

b. One who defies; one who calls upon another to fight, or to any trial or contest.

1511 in Ellis *Orig. Lett.* II. lx. I. 181 It shall be lefull for the iiij chalengers to enter the felde the seconde daye. **1600** SHAKS. *A.Y.L.* I. ii. 180 Haue you challeng'd Charles the Wrastler? No faire Princesse: he is the generall challenger. **1622** ROWLANDS *Good Newes & B.* 41, I..challenge thee to meet on Callis sand..This challenge past, the challenger at Douer, Imbarks for Callis. **1697** COLLIER *Ess. Mor. Subj.* I. (1709) 140 The Challenger is punished as well as the Challenged. **1854** EMERSON *Lett. & Soc. Aims, Eloquence* Wks. (Bohn) III. 187 He is the challenger, and must answer all comers.

challenging: see after CHALLENGE *v.*

challengingly ('tʃælɪndʒɪŋlɪ), *adv.* [f. CHALLENGING *ppl. a.* + -LY[2].] In a challenging manner; so as to convey a challenge.

1907 A. BENNETT *Grim Smile Five Towns* i. 165 Toby gazed around, half challengingly and half nervously. **1921** A. S. M. HUTCHINSON *If Winter Comes* II. i. 67 His face seemed to say to the world challengingly, 'I am here!'

challes, -ice, -is, obs. ff. of CHALICE.

challis ('tʃælɪs, ‖ʃali). [In mod.F. *challis, chalys, chaly*: but the name is app. of Eng. origin, and not improbably from the surname Challis.]

A fine silk and worsted fabric, very pliable and without gloss, used for ladies' dresses, 'introduced at Norwich about 1832, where it speedily became fashionable' (Beck *Draper's Dict.*). Also *attrib.*

1849 *Blackw. Mag.* LXVI. 476 Broad cloth and silks, challis and shawls. **1876** MISS BRADDON *J. Haggard's Dau.* I. vi. 174 She wore a flowered-challis gown. **1882** BECK *Draper's Dict.*, *Challis* was made on a similar principle to the Norwich crape, only thinner and softer, composed of much finer materials, and instead of a glossy surface, as in Norwich crapes, the object was to produce it without gloss, and very pliable and clothy.

Hence **challis-printer** (Simmonds, *Comm. Dict.*).

†**challo.** *Obs.* See CHELLO, a fabric.

†**challoir.** *Obs. rare.* [a. OF. *chaloir* caring for, care, subst. use of infinitive *chaloir* to be of importance, to trouble = It. *calere* (e.g. *non mi cale* it does not trouble me):—L. *calēre* to be hot.] In ***to put in no chaloir*** (= It. *mettere in non cale*): to make of no account; not to care about.

1475 CAXTON *Jason* 16 Hast thou put in no recching ner no challoir the promesse that thou madest at that tyme.

challybeat, challys, obs. ff. CHALYBEATE, CHALICE.

chalmer, -lane, obs. ff. CHAMBER, -LAIN.

chalmoogra, var. CHAULMOOGRA.

†**chalon.** *Obs.* Also 4–5 chaloun, 5 -one, -un. [app., as stated by Du Cange, from its place of manufacture, Chalons-sur-Marne, in France. *Chalon* is not in Godefroy, nor in Cotgrave. Littré has it merely as a modern commercial term 'a sort of woollen stuff', and without derivation or historical instances; but he has from Scarron *ras de Chalons* = SHALLOON.]

1. A blanket or coverlet for a bed.

1301 in *Rot. Parl.* II. 228–265 Chalons [are mentioned among the household goods of the tradespeople of Colchester]. **1374** *Will of Brokelesby* (Somerset Ho.), Vnum chalonem. *c* **1386** CHAUCER *Reeves T.* 220 A bed With schetys and with chalouns fair i-spred. *c* **1440** *Promp. Parv.* 68 Chalun [*K.H.* or chalone], bedde clothe, *thorale, chalo.* **1480** CAXTON *Ovid's Met.* XI. xx, Hys bedde was coverd with a chalon. *a* **1500** *Metr. Voc.* in Wr.-Wülcker 626 *Lectus* bedde, *linthiamen* schete, *tapetum* chalon, *culcitra* quylte. **1616** BULLOKAR, *Chalons*, blankets, Couerings. **1868** [see CHALONER].

2. *Comb.*, as ***chalon-maker, -work.***

a **1400** in *Eng. Gilds* (1870) 351 þe chaloun..shal habbe in worke þre ellen to-fore þe chaloun-makyere. **1426–7** *Will of Talworth* (Somerset Ho.), Lectum de chalonwerk.

chalone ('kæləʊn, 'keɪləʊn). *Biochem.* [ad. Gr. χαλῶν, pres. pple. of χαλάω slacken, after HORMONE.] An internal secretion that reduces or inhibits the action of certain organs and tissues, opp. HORMONE. Hence **cha'lonic** *a.*

1914 E. SCHÄFER *Introd. Study Endocrine Glands* i. 11 Effects are either in the direction of excitation, in which case the endocrine substances producing them..would come under the expression 'hormones', or in the direction of restraint and inhibition, in which case they may be termed restraining or inhibiting autacoids and be classed as 'chalones'. And the action of an autacoid may be described as hormonic or chalonic, according to the kind of effect it produces. **1923** *Glasgow Herald* 18 Jan. 12 Hormones and chalones (specific chemical messengers) produced by the ductless or endocrine glands. **1925** J. A. THOMSON *Gosp. Evol.* ii. 59 Hormones, which stimulate organs and tissues to greater activity; others are called chalones, which put on a brake. **1962** *Times* 6 July 6/3 Substances, or active principles, known as chalones.

†**'chaloner.** *Obs.* [f. CHALON + -ER[1].] A maker of 'chalons'; frequently mentioned in 14–15th c.

1372 in *Will Index* (Somerset Ho.), Hugh Alright, Chaloner in arch: London. **1427** *Will of Everard* (Somerset Ho.), Unum coverlite operis de lez chaloners. **1868** *Athenæum* 25 July 104/2 Chaloners, or makers of chalons, the stuff being procured from the French town so called, —a town which has given its name to our modern shalloons.

‖**chaloupe** (ʃalup). Also 8 chaloup. [F.; prob. ad. Du. *sloep* SLOOP.] A kind of French boat; = SHALLOP.

1699 R. L'ESTRANGE *Colloq. Erasm.* (1711) 47 A great many People at Calis that took a Chaloup to put them aboard a great Ship. **1721** *Phil. Trans.* XXXI. 248 The Chaloups that tow, are in close Fight liable to be sunk by the Enemy's Cannon. **1867** SMYTH *Sailor's Word-bk.* s.v., The gun-boats on the French coasts were frequently termed chaloupes, and carried one heavy gun, with a crew of 40 men.

†**'chalter,** *v. Obs. trans.* ? To bind, fetter.

a **1400–50** *Alexander* 746* A store & a styf stede stalworthy bondyn; His choll chaltird & chauelez in chynez of yren. *c* **1400** *Destr. Troy* 894 As stiffe bounden, As þai chaltrede were choisly with chenys of yerne. *Ibid.* 9159 Thus Achilles by chaunse is chaltrid in grym, With loue of this lady, þat ledis to þe dethe.

‖**chalukah** (ha'lʊkə). Also **khalukah, haluka, halukkah, haluqqah.** [Talmudic Heb. *ḥᵃluqqāh* distribution, f. Heb. *ḥālaq* to distribute.] The distribution of contributions or donations sent by the Jews of the diaspora to support the Jews in Palestine. Now *Hist.*

1880 *Encycl. Brit.* XIII. 686/2 Annual contributions (*haluka*) amounting to about £50,000 a year. **1920** *19th Cent.* Oct. 627 Fear has been expressed that Jewry in Palestine..will degenerate into a new form of 'Chalukah'. **1923** W. P. LIVINGSTONE *Galilee Doctor* 48 The Jew who followed his native genius, engaged in commerce, and made a success of it, was independent of the khalukah. **1927** *Scots Observer* 9 Apr. 8/3 This class has not increased owing to the failure of the Haluka by which it was supported. **1941** *Universal Jewish Encycl.* V. 188/2 In..the 1930's and 1940's, the collections dwindled away... The Halukkah had been replaced..by contributions through Zionist organizations. **1944** M. HADAS tr. *Elbogen's Cent. Jewish Life* III. i. 246 A system of distributing alms to the various national groups (*kolelim*)..was elaborated and given the name *Halukkah*. *Ibid.* 250 He also worked for the education of girls and for freeing the Jewish population from the scourge of the *Halukkah*. *Ibid.* 251 The *Halukkah* used its power to penalize parents who sent their children to the modern schools and to hinder any progress in making them productive. **1957** S. W. BARON *Social & Relig. Hist. Jews* (ed. 2) V. xxiii. 37 The..'Babylonian' congregation.. demanded independent control over the distribution of charitable funds..for the poor of the Holy Land. It thus adumbrated the nineteenth-century struggles over the distribution of *ḥaluqqah* funds raised in the various countries of the dispersion. **1962** *New Jewish Encycl.* 185/2 Halukkah..began in olden times and continued until replaced by modern fund-raising. **1970** *New Stand. Jewish Encycl.* 831/1 *Halukkah*, the distribution of collections made abroad for the support of the poor in Palestine. 'H. Jews' were those living on such contributions.

‖**chalumeau** (ʃalymo). [Fr.:—OF. *chalemel* = Pr. *calamel*:—L. *calamell-us*, dim. of *calam-us* reed. Cf. CALUMET.] **a.** A pastoral instrument of music; a reed, pipe. **b.** The lowest register of the clarinet.

1713 *Lond. Gaz.* No. 5106/2 Two hundred of their People riding..with Timbals and Chalumeaux. **1829** SCOTT *Anne of G.* (Black) 658/1 Who listened to the husband's or lover's chalumeau. **1880** GROVE *Dict. Mus.* I. 361.

chalunge, obs. form of CHALLENGE.

Chalybean (kælɪ'biːən), *a.* [f. L. *chalybēi-us* Chalybeian, of steel + -AN; f. Gr. χαλυβηΐς, f. χάλυψ, χάλυβ-ος, 'sing. of Chalybes' also 'steel'.

(It is not certain whether steel was named from the Chalybes or *vice versa*.)]

Pertaining to the Chalybes, an ancient nation of Asia Minor famous for their skill in working iron.

1671 MILTON *Samson* 133 Chalybean tempered steel and frock of mail Adamantean proof.

chalybeate (kə'lɪbiːət), *a.* and *sb.* Also 7 calibeate, chalybiate, chalibiate, 7–8 chalybeat, 7–9 chalibeat(e, 8 challybeat. [app. ad. mod.L. *chalybeāt-us*: but the regular Lat. form. would be *chalybāt-us*: cf. F. *chalybé*; f. L. *chalybs* steel, a. Gr. χάλυψ: see prec. and -ATE.]

A. *adj.* Impregnated or flavoured with iron, *esp.* as a mineral water or spring; relating to such waters or preparations.

1634 T. JOHNSON tr. *Parey's Chirurg.* XXII. xl. (1678) 522 His drink shall be Calibeate-water. **1652** FRENCH *Yorksh. Spa* ix. 82 A chalybiate Course of Physick. **1655** CULPEPPER *Riverius* x. v. 293 Chalybeate Vinegar. **1732** ARBUTHNOT *Rules of Diet* 245 All acidulated and chalybeat Waters. **1753** BOND in *Phil. Trans.* XLVIII. 184, I..found the surface.. cover'd with a thick scum, like that of a chalybeat Spa. **1816** J. SMITH *Panorama Sc. & Art* II. 385 The chalybeate waters form the best tonics. **1878** HUXLEY *Physiogr.* 27 Mineral springs..some..chalybeate, others sulphureous.

B. *sb.* A chalybeate medicine or spring.

1667 N. FAIRFAX in *Phil. Trans.* II. 546 She..took Chalybeats for the Green-sickness. **1753** BOND in *Phil. Trans.* XLVIII. 189 A strong and agreeable chalybeat. **1771** SMOLLETT *Humph. Cl.* II. 4 July, I have received benefit both from the chalybeate and the sea. **1805** W. SAUNDERS *Min. Waters* 223 The saline chalybeate of Cheltenham.

†**cha'lybeate,** *v. Obs.* [f. as prec.: it occurs first in the ppl. adj. *cha'lybeated* = prec.: see -ATE[3].] *trans.* To impregnate with iron.

1599 A. M. tr. *Gabelhouer's Bk. Physicke* 20/2 With Chalybeated water. **1609** *Shuttleworth Acc.* (1856) I. 182 A quarte of ale calibeated. **1710** T. FULLER *Pharm. Extemp.* 10 You may Chalybeate any sort of Ale by this easie process.

chalybeous (kə'lɪbɪəs), *a.* [f. L. *chalybēius* Chalybeian, of steel + -OUS.] Of a steel-blue colour; dark blue with a metallic lustre.

1826 KIRBY & SPENCE *Entomol.* IV. xlvi. 283 Chalybeous. .. The blue splendour of steel case-hardened, or of the mainspring of a watch.

chalybite ('kælɪbaɪt). *Min.* [Named by Glöcker 1847; f. Gr. χάλυβ- steel + -ITE.] A synonym of SIDERITE, or native carbonate of iron.

1858 DANA *Min.* 445 Chalybite occurs in many of the rock strata. **1868** *Ibid.* 691 *Chalybite* should yield to Haidinger's earlier name *Siderite*.

chalyce, -ys, obs. ff. CHALICE.

Chalydony, obs. f. CHELIDONY, CELIDONY[2].

chalynch, obs. form of CHALLENGE.

chalypsography. *nonce-wd.* [Bad formation on Gr. χάλυψ steel + -GRAPHY; the etymological form being *chalybography*.] Steel engraving.

1878 SALA in *Gentl. Mag.* May 565 His [Cruikshank's].. abandonment of chalcography for chalypsography.